R.E.D. CD CATALOGUE edition 17

R.E.D. CD CATALOGUE edition 17

Retail Entertainment Data Publishing Limited
Paulton House, 8 Shepherdess Walk, London N1 7LB, UK
Tel: +44 (0)171 566 8216 Fax: +44 (0)171 566 8259

Editor	Matthew Garbutt
Assistant Editor	Gary Ford
Researcher	Howard Richardson
Editorial Assistants	Alixe Boardman
	Nick Griffiths
	Simon Liss
	Adrian Perkins
Sales Executives	Matthew Rundle
	Sally Thompson
Product Manager	Becca Bailey
Sales & Marketing Assistant	Abigail Clarkson
Circulation Assistant	Michelle Tarrant
Production Manager	Keith Hawkins
Publisher	Brenda Daly

All enquiries:
Retail Entertainment Data Publishing Ltd,
Paulton House, 8 Shepherdess Walk, London N1 7LB, UK
Tel: +44 (0)171 566 8216 Fax: +44 (0)171 566 8259

Database typeset by BPC Whitefriars, Tunbridge Wells, Kent, UK

Front cover image supplied by The Image Bank, London, UK
Photographer Elle Schuster

Printed and bound by BPC Wheatons, Exeter, Devon, UK

ISBN 1 900105 06 3

Recording and distributing companies reserve the right to withdraw products without giving previous notice, and although every effort is made to obtain the latest information for inclusion in this catalogue, no guarantee can be given that all the recordings listed are immediately available. Any difficulties should be referred to the issuing company concerned. The publisher cannot accept responsibility for the consequences of any error. When ordering, purchasers are advised to quote all relevant information in addition to catalogue numbers.

Contents

Introduction vii

How To Use ix

Main Section 1

Compilations 988

Soundtracks: Main Section 1241

Collections 1297

Composer Collections 1312

Introduction

Welcome to the 17th edition of the R.E.D. CD Catalogue, the UK's only completely comprehensive listing of CD albums. Since its launch in this country in 1983, the CD has established itself as the overwhelming leader in music formats.

The data for this edition has been extracted from the world famous R.E.D. pop database and contains details on the 72,000 CDs released and still available in the UK - that is 12,000 more than last year's 16th edition and a staggering 70,000 more than the first edition published in 1986.

The CD Catalogue covers all forms of popular music - Blues, Country, Dance, Folk, Indie, Jazz, Reggae, Rock, Soul and Soundtracks and is therefore the ideal reference source for collectors, enthusiasts and music lovers in general.

How To Use

The R.E.D. CD Catalogue is divided into the following sections:

The ***Main Section*** contains the majority of the recording information. The 'black-strip' artist headings and subsequent recording titles are arranged alphabetically. After the recording title, tracks are listed where we have been advised. The catalogue number is displayed in bold, followed by issuing label, release date and distributor/s. The distributors are arranged in alphabetical order.

Recording title

'Black-strip' artist heading

Spice Girls

SPICE

Wannabe / Say you'll be there / 2 become 1 / Love thing / Last time lover / Mama / Who do you think you are / Something kinda funny / Naked / If U can't dance

CD ________________ **CDV 2812**

Virgin / Oct '96 / EMI

Catalogue number

Release date

The ***Compilations*** section is arranged alphabetically by recording title and thereafter the layout is as the Main Section.

ANTHEMS VOL.2 1988-1992

(Mixed By Slipmatt/2CD Set)

Subheading

Track listing

You got the love: *Source & Candi Staton* / Baby let me love you tonite: *Kariya* / Sueno Latino: *Sueno Latino* / Break 4 love: *Raze* / Rescue me: *Malone, Debbie* / Come get my lovin': *Dionne* / I can dance: *Fast Eddie* / Acid thunder: *Fast Eddie* / Monkey say monkey do: *West Bam* / Airport 89: *Allen, Woody* / Phantom: *Renegade Soundwave* / Humanoid: *Stakker* / Bring forth the guilotine: *Silver Bullet* / 20 to get in: *Shut Up & Dance* / Total confusion: *Homeboy, A Hippy & A Funki-Dred* / Mr. Kirk's nightmare: *4 Hero* / What have you done: *One Tribe & Gem* / Papua New Guinea: *Future Sound Of London* / Dextrous: *Nightmares On Wax* / LFO: *LFO* / Give me the energy: *Pink Noise* / Pure: *GTO* / Kaos: *Dr. Baker* / Sound clash: *Kick Squad* / Go: *Moby* / Cubes: *Modular Expansion* / Just let go: *Petra & Co* / Stratosphere: *Trigger* / Quadrophonia: *Quadrophonia* / Take it easy: *Winkleburger, Cedric* / Bombscare: *2 Bad Mice* / DJ's unite: *Seduction & Fantasy* / Compounded/Edge 1: *Edge* / Hurt you so: *Johnny L* / Hypnosis: *Psychotropic* / Panic: *Rabbit City*

Label

CD Set ________________ **UMCD 04**

United Dance / Jun '97 / Alphamagic / Mo's Music Machine / Pinnacle

Distributor/s

How To Use

The ***Soundtracks*** section is arranged into three separate parts:

1 : Soundtracks – an alphabetical listing by title of film, show and TV soundtrack recordings.

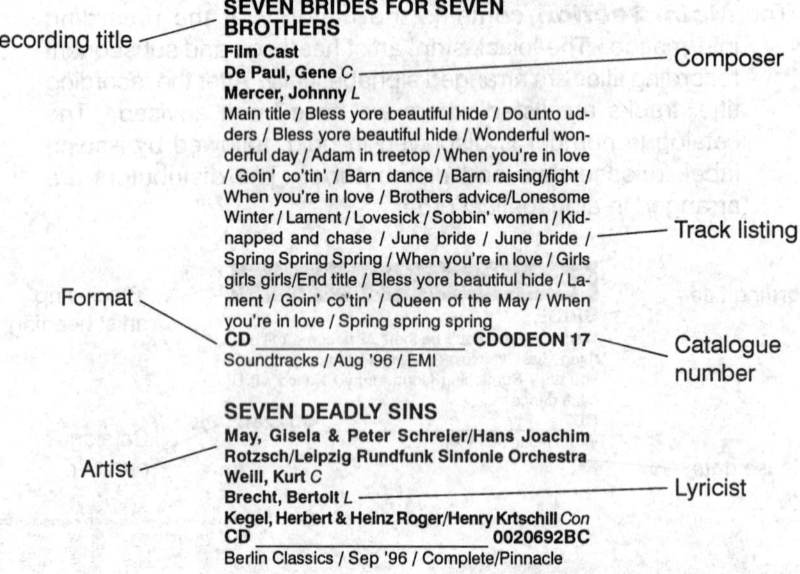

2 : Collections -- soundtrack compilations listed by recording title.

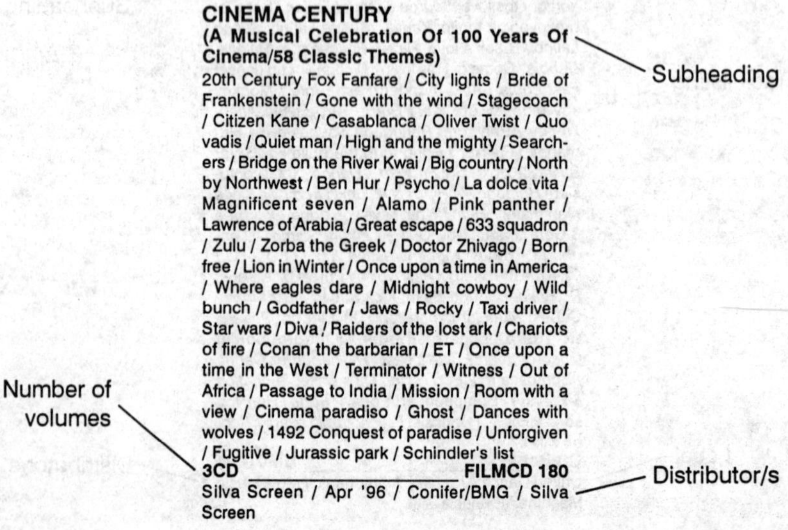

3 : Composer Collections – compilation recordings devoted to the work of specific composers. Listed alphabetically by composer.

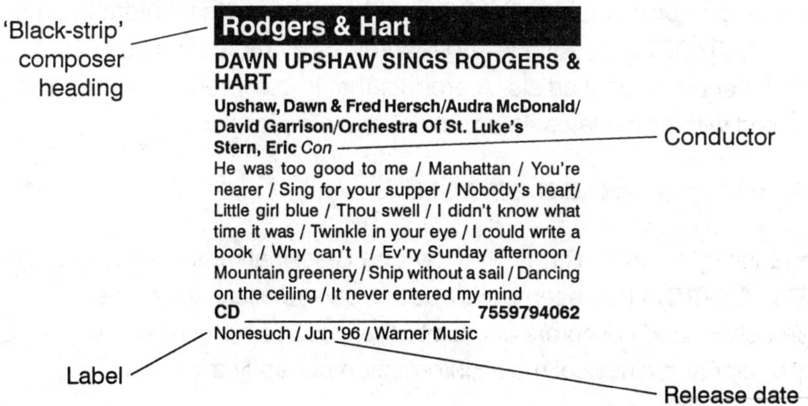
'Black-strip' composer heading

Rodgers & Hart

DAWN UPSHAW SINGS RODGERS & HART

Upshaw, Dawn & Fred Hersch/Audra McDonald/ David Garrison/Orchestra Of St. Luke's

Stern, Eric *Con* — Conductor

He was too good to me / Manhattan / You're nearer / Sing for your supper / Nobody's heart/ Little girl blue / Thou swell / I didn't know what time it was / Twinkle in your eye / I could write a book / Why can't I / Ev'ry Sunday afternoon / Mountain greenery / Ship without a sail / Dancing on the ceiling / It never entered my mind

CD ________________ **7559794062**

Nonesuch / Jun '96 / Warner Music

Label

Release date

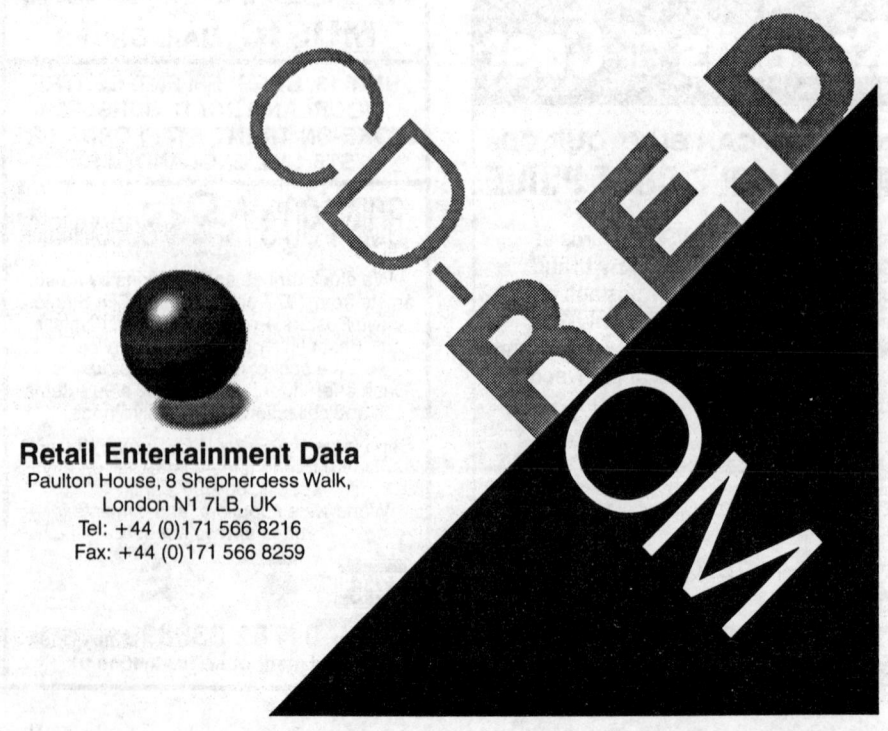

Numerical

1 Love

TIME
CD MGOUTCD 9
Granite / Dec '96 / Pinnacle

2 Bad

ANSWERMACHINE
CD XM 039CD
X-Mist / Jul '93 / Cargo / SRD

2 Bad Card

HUSTLING ABILITY
CD ONUCD 78
On-U Sound / Sep '95 / Jet Star / SRD

2 Foot Flame

2 FOOT FLAME
Lindauer / To the sea / Already walking / MR II / Reinvention / Compass / Arbitrator / Cordoned off / Chisel
CD OLE 1622
Matador / Oct '95 / Vital

ULTRA DROWNING
Sample stars / Lunar intuition / Dance alone / Salt doubt / Ultra drowning / Pipeline to vertigo / Everwilling / I think you're the weird one / Peacock coal / Resin box
CD OLE 2092
Matador / Apr '97 / Vital

2 Rocks

WHEN SANITY IS ACTING KIND OF WILD
CD WKFMXD 174
FM / Jul '91 / Revolver / Sony

2 Unlimited

GET READY
CD HFCD 23
PWL / Feb '92 / Warner Music

LIMITED 2 TECHNO (A Tribute To 2 Unlimited) (Megatek)
Get ready for this / Twilight zone / Real thing / Let the beat control your body / Tribal dance / Maximum overdrive / Faces / Do what's good for me / No one / Jump for joy / Magic friend / Nothing like the rain / Spread your love / Here I go / No limit
CD SUMCD 4064
Summit / Nov '96 / Sound & Media

NO LIMITS
CD HFCD 27
PWL / May '93 / Warner Music

REAL THINGS
CD HFCD 38
PWL / Jun '94 / Warner Music

2nd Communication

2ND COMMUNICATION
CD KK 038CD
KK / '89 / Plastic Head

INTERACTION
CD KK 066CD
KK / Feb '94 / Plastic Head

MY CHROMOSOMAL FRIEND
CD KK 044CD
KK / Aug '90 / Plastic Head

2nd Heat

SHREDDERVISION
CD RTN 41204
Rock The Nation / Nov '94 / Plastic Head

2nd Voice

APPROACHING LUNA
CD HY 39100682
Hyperium / Nov '93 / Cargo / Plastic Head

CELEBRATE OUR DEATH
CD HY 39100433CD
Hyperium / Aug '93 / Cargo / Plastic Head

2Pac

2PACALYPSE NOW
Young black male / Trapped / Soulja's story / I don't give a fuck / Violent / Words of wisdom / Something wicked / Crooked ass nigga / If my homie calls / Brenda's got a baby / Lunatic / Rebel of the underground / Part time mutha
CD IND 91767
Interscope / Feb '97 / BMG

ALL EYEZ ON ME (2CD Set)
Ambitionz az a ridah / All about U / Skandalouz / Got my mind made up / How do U want it / 2 of Amerikaz most wanted / No more pain / Heartz of men / Life goes on / Only God can judge me / Tradin' war stories / California love / I ain't mad at cha / Whatz ya phone number / Can't c me / Shorty wanna be a thug / Holla at me / Wonda why they call u bytch / When they ride / Thug passion / Picture me rollin' / Check out time / Ratha be ya nigga / All eyez on me / Run tha streetz / Ain't hard 2 find / Heaven ain't hard 2 find
CD Set 5242492
Death Row/Island / Mar '96 / PolyGram

DON KILLUMINATI, THE (Makavelli)
Intro / Bomb first (my second reply) / Hail Mary / Toss it up / To live and die in LA / Blasphemy / Life of an outlaw / Just like daddy / Krazy / White man'z world / Me and my girlfriend / Hold ya head / Against all odds
CD IND 90039
Interscope / Feb '97 / BMG

ME AGAINST THE WORLD
Intro / If I die 2nite / Me against the world / So many tears / Temptations / Young niggaz / Heavy in the game / Lord knows / Dear Mama / It ain't easy / Can U get away / Old school / Fuck the world / Death around the corner / Outlaw
CD IND 92399
Interscope / Feb '97 / BMG

STRICTLY 4 MY NIGGAZ
Holler if ya hear me / 2 Pac's theme / Point the finga / Something 2 die 4 / Last wordz / Souljah's revenge / Peep game / Strugglin' / Guess who's back / Representin' / Keep ya head up / Strictly 4 my NIGGAZ / Streetz R deathrow / I get around / Papa'z song / Five deadly venomz
CD IND 92209
Interscope / Feb '97 / BMG

THUG LIFE VOL.1 (Thug Life)
Bury me a G / Don't get it twisted / Shit don't stop: *Thug Life & YNV* / Pour out a little liquor / Stay true / How long will they mourn me: *Thug Life & Nate Dogg* / Under pressure / Street fame / Cradle to the grave / Str8 ballin'
CD IND 92360
Interscope / Feb '97 / BMG

3 Colours Red

PURE
This my Hollywood / Nerve gas / Nuclear holiday / Copper girl / Sixty mile smile / Sunny in England / Alright Ma / Mental blocks / Fit boy & faint girl / Halfway up the downs / Hateslick / Love's cradle / Aniseed
CD CRECD 208
Creation / May '97 / 3mv/Vital

3 Grand

3 BAD BROTHERS
CD GRA 4157CD
Ichiban / May '94 / Direct / Koch

3 Mustaphas 3

BAM - BIG MUSTAPHAS PLAY STEREOLOCALMUSIC
Intro/Lebedik un freylekh / Singe tema / To tilefono tis xenitias / Mehmeteli / Chilling tale / Thalasso p'ola ta nera / Vranjanski ekspres / O memetis / Hora lui marin / Besarabia / Niska banja / Ainy la la/Ah ya ass mar el lawn / Cabra / Svadba / Bam
CD CDFEZ 005
Fez-O-Phone / Apr '97 / Pinnacle

FRIENDS, FIENDS AND FRONDS
Si vous passez par la / Starehe Mustapha I, II and III / Maldita guajira / Linda Linda / Fiz'n / DJ Trouble Fezz meets 3 Mustaphas 3 / Buke e kripe ne vater tone / Kalaxhojne / Anapse to Tsigaro / Shouffi rhirou / Niska banja / Kac kuzulu Ceylan / Selma
CD CDORB 070
Globestyle / May '91 / Pinnacle

HEART OF UNCLE
Awara hoon / Mama O / Anapse to tsigaro / Yeni yol / Kaba mustafa / Taxi driver / Aj zajdi zajdi jasno sonce / Sitna Lisa / Ovcepolsko oro / Kem kem / Trois fois trois (city version) / Vi bist du geveyzn far prohibish'n / Benga taxi / Trois fois trois (country version)
CD CDORB 043
Globestyle / May '89 / Pinnacle

SHOPPING
Ljubav kraj izvora/zvezdanova (skupovo) kolo / Shika shika / Xamenh evtexia/Fiz'n / Musafir / Szegerely farewell / Night off Beirut / Selver / Shouffi rhirou / Valle e pogradecit / Darling don't say no / Voulez vous danser
CD CDORB 022
Globestyle / Aug '87 / Pinnacle

SOUP OF THE CENTURY
Buke e kripe ne vater tone / Kalaxhojne / Zohar no.2 / Soba song / Golden clarinet / Ti citron / Sadilo mome / Tropnalo oro / This city is very exciting / Madre / Ya habibi, ya ghaybine / Mamo, snezhets navalyalo / Yogurt koydum dolaba / Televizyon / Upovacko kolo
CD CDFEZ 004
Fez-O-Phone / Aug '90 / Pinnacle

3 O'Clock Heroes

KERRANGGGG
CD LBT 210
LBT / Jun '97 / Greyhound

3 Phase

SCHLANGEN FARM (2CD Set)
CD Set MONU 23CD
Mute / Nov '93 / RTM/Disc

STRAIGHT ROAD
CD EFA 017552
Tresor / Jun '94 / 3mv/BMG / Prime / SRD

3D's

STRANGE NEWS FROM THE ANGELS
Dust / Seven days of kindness / Fangworld / Animal / Vector 27 / Riding the whale / Fiery angel / Ben / Devil red / Big red heart / I believe in you / Castaway / Carrion / Wish
CD FNCD 351
Flying Nun / Mar '97 / RTM/Disc

VENUS TRAIL
CD FNCD 281
Flying Nun / Apr '94 / RTM/Disc

3rd Bass

DERELICTS OF DIALECT
Merchant of grooves / Derelicts of dialect / Ace in the hole / French toast / Portrait of the artist as a hood / Pop goes the weasel / Sea vessel soliloquy / Daddy rich in the land of 1210 / Word to the third / Herbalz in your mouth / Al's a b cee'z / No master plan no master race / Come in / No static at all / Eye jammie / Microphone techniques / Problem child / Three strikes 5000 / Kick 'em in the grill / Green eggs and swine / Check yourself
CD 5235022
Def Jam / Jan '96 / PolyGram

3T

BROTHERHOOD
Anything / 24/7 / Why: *3T & Michael Jackson* / Gotta be you / With you / Sexual attention / Memories / I need you / Give me all your lovin' / Tease me / Words without meaning / Brotherhood
CD 4816942
MJJ Music / Feb '96 / Sony

4 Hero

PARALLEL UNIVERSE
CD RIVCD 4
Reinforced / Jun '94 / SRD

4 Mat 4

GET DOWN GET BUSY
CD MA 009
M / Apr '97 / Timewarp

4 Non Blondes

BIGGER, BETTER, FASTER, MORE
Train / Superfly / What's up / Pleasantly blue / Morphine and chocolate / Spaceman / Old Mr.Heffer / Calling all the people / Dear Mr. President / Drifting / No place like home
CD IND 92112
Interscope / Aug '96 / BMG

4 Runner

4 RUNNER
CD 5273792
A&M / May '95 / PolyGram

4 Skins

BEST OF THE 4 SKINS, THE
One law for them / Yesterday's heroes / Brave new world / Chaos / Wonderful world / Evil / Sorry / 1984 / ACAB / I don't wanna die / Plastic gangsters / Yeaterday's heroes (single version) / Get out of my life / Justice / Jack the lad / Low life / Bread or blood / Seems to me / Norman / On the streets / Five more years / Betrayed / Saturday / Dambusters
CD DOJOCD 140
Dojo / Jun '93 / Disc

FISTFUL OF...4 SKINS, A
CD AHOYCD 8
Captain Oi / Nov '93 / Plastic Head

GOOD THE BAD AND THE 4 SKINS, THE
Plastic gangsters / Jealousy / Yesterday's heroes / Justice / Jack the lad / Remembrance day / Manifesto / Wonderful world / Sorry / Evil / I don't wanna die / ACAB / Chaos / One law for them
CD AHOYCD 3
Captain Oi / Jul '93 / Plastic Head

4D

PURE IDEAS
CD DBMLABCD 7
Labworks / Feb '96 / RTM/Disc / SRD

4E

BLUE NOTE
CD HE 010
Home Entertainment / Dec '96 / Cargo

5 Day Week Straw People

5 DAY WEEK STRAW PEOPLE
CD MER II
Merlin / Jun '97 / Greyhound

5-6-7-8's

5-6-7-8'S, THE
CD ANDA 179CD
Au-Go-Go / Apr '97 / Cargo / Greyhound / Plastic Head

CAN'T HELP IT
CD ROCK 60962
Rockville / Mar '93 / Plastic Head / SRD

5ive Style

5IVE STYLE
CD SP 309B
Sub Pop / Sep '95 / Cargo / Greyhound / Shellshock/Disc

5th Dimension

BEST OF THE 5TH DIMENSION, THE
Last night I didn't get to sleep at all / One less bell to answer / Aquarius / Let the sunshine in / Wedding bell blues / Save the country / Love's lines, angles and rhymes / Puppet man / Up, up and away / Never my love / Together let's find love / Light sings / If I could reach you / Go where you wanna go / Sweet blindness / Working on a groovy thing / MacArthur park
CD 74321225452
Arista / Oct '94 / BMG

5U4

U-TURN
CD TUMICD 058
Tumi / May '96 / Discovery / Stern's

5UU's

HUNGER'S TEETH
CD RER5UU 1
ReR/Recommended / May '94 / ReR Megacorp / RTM/Disc

6th Sense Approach

RELAX 2000
CD REL 972002
Reload / Jun '97 / Intergroove

007

LANDSCAPES (007 & The Scene)
CD DRCD 005
Detour / Mar '96 / Detour / Greyhound

7 Hills Clash

SIGNALS FROM THE SHEFFIELD UNDERGROUND
CD DON 1
DON / Jan '97 / Kudos

7 Year Bitch

SICK 'EM
CD CZ 048CD
C/Z / Oct '92 / Plastic Head

8 Bold Souls

ANT FARM
Half life / Little encouragement / Antfarm / Corner of walk and don't walk / Furthest from my mind / Big dig
CD AJ 0114
Arabesque / Feb '95 / New Note/Pinnacle

SIDESHOW
CD AJ 0103
Arabesque / Jul '94 / New Note/Pinnacle

8 Eyed Spy

LIVE (8 Eyed Spy & Lydia Lunch)
CD DANCD 087
ROIR / Jun '97 / Plastic Head / Shellshock/Disc

8 Storey Window

8 STOREY WINDOW
CD TOPPCD 006
Ultimate / Apr '94 / Pinnacle

8 Up

LIE DOWN AND STAY CALM
Rubberneckin' / Ya don't quit / Not cometh of goest / Bottom end (buy the big issue) / Bup / Rip's rub / Keep it like that / Stan Gettes / Bright moments
CD SJRCD 021
Soul Jazz / Oct '94 / New Note/Pinnacle / Timewarp / Vital

9 Invisibles

PUREHEADSPACE
King dubby / Dreadnought / Gliding silently / Velvet mind flush / Gandwanaland (water song) / Outback sunset / Social narcotics / Meltdown / Power from the sun / Zero zero / Dolphin / Highway 9 / Earth mother (instruction)
CD DELECCD 053
Delerium / Apr '97 / Cargo / Pinnacle / Vital

9.0

TOO FAR GONE
CD RR 93442
Roadrunner / Dec '90 / PolyGram

9th Dream

RHYTHM AND IRRELEVANCE
Canfield / Play garden / Red of fire / Summer offering / Benediction / Letter in three parts / La lune de miel / Life a stormy point
CD 4509962572
Warner Bros. / May '94 / Warner Music

10 Seconds

10 SECONDS
CD DGM 9603
Discipline / Apr '96 / Pinnacle

10cc

10CC
CD EXP 002
Experience / May '97 / TKO Magnum

ALIVE - GREATEST HITS PERFORMED LIVE
CD CMCD 0010
Creative Man / Mar '94 / Total/Pinnacle

BLOODY TOURISTS
Dreadlock holiday / For you and I / Take these chains / Shock on the tube / Last night / Anonymous alcoholic / Reds in my bed / Life line / Tokyo / Old mister time / From Rochdale to Ocho Rios / Everything you've wanted to know about
CD 8269212
Mercury / Jul '93 / PolyGram

CHANGING FACES (The Very Best Of 10cc/Godley & Creme) (10cc & Godley & Creme)
Dreadlock holiday: *10cc* / Wall Street shuffle: *10cc* / Under your thumb: *Godley & Creme* / Life is a minestrone: *10cc* / Englishman in New York: *Godley & Creme* / Art for art's sake: *10cc* / Donna: *10cc* / Snack attack: *Godley & Creme* / Cry: *Godley & Creme* / Things we do for love: *10cc* / Wedding bells: *Godley & Creme* / I'm Mandy fly me: *10cc* / Good morning judge: *10cc* / Rubber bullets: *10cc* / Save a mountain for me: *Godley & Creme* / I'm not in love: *10cc*
CD 8163552
Polydor / Mar '94 / PolyGram

COLLECTION, THE
CD CCSCD 214
Castle / Apr '89 / BMG

DECEPTIVE BENDS
Good morning judge / Things we do for love / Marriage bureau / Rendezvous / People in love / Modern man blues / Honeymoon with B troop / I bought a flat guitar tutor / You've got a cold / Feel the benefit
CD 5349742
Mercury / Jul '97 / PolyGram

FOOD FOR THOUGHT
Life is a minestrone / Don't hang up / Good morning judge / Last night / 1-2-5 / We've heard it all before / Twenty four hours / Dreadlock holiday / Rock 'n' roll lullaby / Take these chains / Power of love / Survivor / Feel the love / Food for thought
CD 5500042
Spectrum / May '93 / PolyGram

HITS, THE
CD 15193
Laserlight / Aug '91 / Target/BMG

HOW DARE YOU
Art for art's sake / Don't hang up / Head room / How dare you / I wanna rule the world / Iceberg / I'm Mandy fly me / Lazy ways / Rock 'n' roll lullaby
CD 5349752
Mercury / Jul '97 / PolyGram

LIVE AND LET LIVE
Second sitting for the last supper / You've got a cold / Honeymoon with B troop / Art for art's sake / People in love / Wall Street shuffle / Ships don't disappear in the night / I'm Mandy fly me / Good morning judge / Feel the benefit / Things we do for love / Waterfall / I'm not in love / Modern man blues
CD 8388612
Mercury / Feb '94 / PolyGram

LIVE IN CONCERT VOL.1
Wall Street shuffle / I'm Mandy fly me / Good morning Judge / Welcome to paradise / Night the stars didn't show / Dreadlock holiday / Shine a light in the dark / Feel the benefit
CD QED 018
Tring / Nov '96 / Tring
CD 100012
CMC / May '97 / BMG

LIVE IN CONCERT VOL.2
I'm not in love / Things we do for love / Across the universe / Art for art's sake / Paperback writer / Slow down / Bullets medley
CD QED 019
Tring / Nov '96 / Tring
CD 100022
CMC / May '97 / BMG

MEANWHILE
Woman in love / Wonderland / Fill her up / Something special / Welcome to paradise / Stars didn't show / Green eyed monster / Charity begins at home / Shine a light in the dark / Don't break the promise
CD 5132792
Polydor / Jan '92 / PolyGram

MIRROR MIRROR
CD AVEXCD 6
Avex / Nov '96 / TKO Magnum

ORIGINAL SOUNDTRACK, THE
Une nuit a Paris / I'm not in love / Blackmail / Second sitting for the last supper / Brand new day / Flying junk / Life is a minestrone / Film of my love / Channel swimmer / Good news
CD 5329642
Mercury / Sep '96 / PolyGram

SHEET MUSIC
Wall Street shuffle / Worst band in the world / Hotel / Old wild men / Clockwork creep / Silly love / Somewhere in Hollywood / Baron Samedi / Sacro-liac / Of effendi
CD CLACD 186
Castle / Aug '90 / BMG

VERY BEST OF 10CC, THE
Donna / Rubber bullets / Dean and I / Wall Street shuffle / Silly love / Life is a minestrone / Une nuit a Paris / I'm not in love / Art for art's sake / I'm Mandy fly me / Things we do for love / Good morning judge / Dreadlock holiday / People in love / Under your thumb: *Godley & Creme* / Wedding bells: *Godley & Creme* / Cry: *Godley & Creme* / Neanderthal man: *Hotlegs*
CD 5346122
Mercury / Mar '97 / PolyGram

VERY BEST OF THE EARLY YEARS, THE
CD MCCD 107
Music Club / May '93 / Disc / THE

12 Rounds

JITTER JUICE
Spitting in the sunshine / Pleasant smell / Fits nicely / Hesitate / Mug / Strange daze / Dog / Keeling over / Something's burning / Business / Barbed wire hair / Holed / Joyous
CD 5318942
Polydor / Jul '96 / PolyGram

13 Candles

ANGELS OF MOURNING SILENCE
Power of eternal damnation / Join me in death / Hunger within / Woman of dark desires / Siren / Death awaits you (Dracula the undead) / Carmille (addiction) / Bleed my emotion / Ghosts / In the name of darkness / Ultimatum / Carpathian moonrise / Between the dark and the light
CD NIHIL 22CD
Vinyl Solution / Jun '97 / RTM/Disc

COME OUT AND...
CD NIGHTCD 008
Nightbreed / Nov '95 / Plastic Head

13 Ghosts

LEGEND OF THE BLOOD YETI (13 Ghosts & Thurston Moore/Derek Bailey)
CD CHUGCD 5
Infinite Chug / May '97 / Cargo

13th Floor Elevators

BEST OF THE 13TH FLOOR ELEVATORS, THE
You're gonna miss me / I had to tell you / Never another / Thru the rhythm / Slip inside this house / Splash / Dr. Doom / Earthquake / May the circle remain unbroken / Levitation / She lives (in a time of her own) / I'm gonna love you too / Kingdom of heaven / Monkey island / Fire engine / Roller coaster / Reverberation (doubt) / You're gonna miss me (live)
CD 642370
EVA / Jun '94 / ADA / Direct

BEST OF THE 13TH FLOOR ELEVATORS, THE
CD NTMCD 516
Nectar / Jan '96 / Pinnacle

BULL OF THE WOODS
Livin' on / Barnyard blues / Till then / Never another / Rose and the thorn / Down by the river / Scarlet and gold / Street song / Dr. Doom / With you / May the circle remain unbroken
CD CDGR 113
Charly / Feb '97 / Koch
CD 14886
Spalax / Jul '97 / ADA / Cargo / Direct / Discovery / Greyhound

EASTER EVERYWHERE
Slip inside this house / Slide machine / She lives in a time of her own / Nobody to love / It's all over now baby blue / Earthquake / Dust / I had to tell you / Postures (leave your body behind)
CD CDGR 111
Charly / Feb '97 / Koch
CD 14888
Spalax / Jul '97 / ADA / Cargo / Direct / Discovery / Greyhound

ELEVATORS LIVE
Before you accuse me / She lives in a time of her own / Tried to hide / You gotta take that girl / I'm gonna love you too / Everybody needs somebody to love / I've got levitation / You can't hurt me anymore / Rollercoaster / You're gonna miss me
CD CDGR 112
Charly / Feb '97 / Koch

I'VE SEEN YOUR FACE BEFORE
Fire engine / Tried to hide / Levitation / Don't fall down / Kingdom of heaven / You're gonna miss me / Reverberation (doubt) / Monkey Island / Splash / She lives in a time of her own / Rollercoaster
CD CDWIK 82
Big Beat / Oct '88 / Pinnacle

INTERPRETER
Fire in my bones / Don't fall down / Thru' the rhythm / Dust / Monkey island / You don't know / Roller coaster / Levitation blues / Tried to hide / Fire engine / You're gonna miss me / Catch the wind / For Brian Jones / Lay down your weary tune / Right track now / May the circle remain unbroken / Levitation / Radio commercial / Stand for the fire demon / Interpreter / Don't shake me Lucifer / Wind and more / Interview / Bopping bopping back / Sputnik / Bermuda
CD CDTB 508
Thunderbolt / Sep '96 / TKO Magnum

LEVITATION - IN CONCERT
Levitation / Rollercoaster / Fire engine / Reverberation (doubt) / Don't fall down / Tried to hide / Splash 1 / You're gonna miss me / Monkey island / Kingdom of heaven / She lives in a time of her own
CD CDTB 147
Thunderbolt / Mar '94 / TKO Magnum

OUT OF ORDER
Everybody needs somebody / To love / Before you accuse me / You don't know / I'm gonna love you too / You really got me / Splash / Fire engine / Roll over Beethoven / Word / Monkey island / Rollercoaster
CD CDTB 124
Thunderbolt / Jun '93 / TKO Magnum

PSYCHEDELIC SOUNDS OF THE 13TH FLOOR ELEVATORS, THE
You're gonna miss me / Rollercoaster / Splash 1 / Reverberation (doubt) / Don't fall down / Fire engine / Thru the rhythm / You don't know / Kingdom of heaven / Monkey island / Tried to hide
CD CDGR 119
Charly / Jun '96 / Koch
CD SPALAX 14819
Spalax / Nov '96 / ADA / Cargo / Direct / Discovery / Greyhound

REUNION CONCERT, THE
Beast / Splash 1 / Don't slander me / You're gonna miss me / Clear night for love / Don't shake me lucifer / Bloody hammer / Two headed dog
CD CDTB 153
Thunderbolt / Apr '95 / TKO Magnum

13th Sign

DA STORY NEVER ENDS
Take me to a distant bass / Pressures / Have you met the glisses / Happytime / Hysteria / Moonweed / Come of this trip / Someday / Rainbow / Too far gone / 90 Infinity / Dittonia blue / Back in a day
CD KOBICD 003
On Delancey Street / Nov '96 / Vital

16 Horsepower

16 HORSEPOWER
CD 5404362
Paradox / Jun '96 / PolyGram / Vital

LOW ESTATE
Brimstone rock / My narrow mind / Low estate / For Heaven's sake / Sac of religion / Denver grab / Coal black horses / Pure clob road / Phyllis Ruth / Black lung / Dead run / Golden rope / Hang my teeth on your door
CD 5407092
Paradox / Sep '97 / PolyGram / Vital

SACKCLOTH AND ASHES
Seen what I saw / Black soul choir / Haw / Scrawled in sap / Horse head / Ruthie Lingle / Harm's way / Black bush / Heel on the shovel / American wheeze / Red neck reel / Prison show romp / Neck on the new blade / Strong man
CD 5405912
Paradox / Apr '97 / PolyGram / Vital

16 Volt

LETDOWNCRUSH
CD REC 022
Re-Constriction / Oct '96 / Cargo

16-17

GYATSO
CD PATH 12CD
Big Cat / Feb '94 / 3mv/Pinnacle

17 Years

17 YEARS
CD GMM 117
GMM / Jul '97 / Cargo

18 Wheeler

TWIN ACTION
Sweet tooth / Nature girl / Kum back / Golden candles / Revealer / Honey mink / Gram / Prock shake / Hotel 167 / Suncrush / Frosty hands / Life is strange / I won't let you down / Wet dream
CD CRECD 164
Creation / Jul '94 / 3mv/Vital

YEAR ZERO
CD CRECD 192
Creation / Mar '97 / 3mv/Vital

18th Dye

CRAYON
Aug / Sixteen ink / Ray / Mystics 11 / Crank / Nuit N
CD OLE 1182
Matador / Dec '94 / Vital

DONE
CD CHE 12CD
Che / May '94 / SRD

TRIBUTE TO A BUS
CD CHE 26CD
Che / Mar '95 / SRD

22 Jacks

UNCLE BOB
CD SD 1203
Side One / Feb '97 / Cargo

22 Pistepirkko

RUMBLE CITY, LALA LAND
CD 5270752
Bare Bone Business / Mar '96 / RTM/Disc

23 Degrees

ENDLESS SEARCHING FOR SUBSTANCE, AN
CD SR 9467
Silent / Oct '94 / Cargo / Plastic Head

24 Carat Black

GHETTO: MISFORTUNE'S WEALTH
Synopsis One: In the Ghetto/God save the world / Poverty's paradise / Brown-baggin' / Synopsis Two: Mother's Day / Mother's Day / Foodstamps / Ghetto: Misfortune's wealth / 24 Carat Black / God save the world
CD CDSXE 090
Stax / Sep '93 / Pinnacle

25 Ta Life

KEEPIN' IT REAL
CD WB 2137CD
We Bite / Jan '96 / Plastic Head

44 Xes

BANISH SILENCE
CD WENCD 002
When / Jun '95 / Pinnacle

45 Grave

DEBASEMENT TAPES
CD CLEO 2143CD
Cleopatra / Jan '94 / Cargo / Greyhound / Plastic Head / RTM/Disc / SRD

48 Cameras

EASTER, NOVEMBER A YEAR
CD SA 54028
Semantic / Apr '94 / Plastic Head

49th Parallel

49TH PARALLEL
CD FLASH 008
Flashback / Jun '97 / Greyhound

50ft Hose

CAULDRON
And after / If not this time / Opus 777 / Things that concern you / Opus 11 / Red the sign post / For Paula / Rose / Fantasy / God bless the child / Cauldron / Fly free / Desire / Bad trip / Skins
CD ____ CDWIKD 158
Chiswick / Jan '96 / Pinnacle

LIVE AND UNRELEASED
CD ____ CTCD 052
Captain Trip / Jun '97 / Greyhound

54:40

SMILIN' BUDDHA CABARET
Blame your parents / Radio luv song / Assoholic / Daisy / Once a killer / Punk grass / Lucy / Beyond the outsider / Don't listen to that / Ocean pearl / Higher / Friends end / What Buddy was / Save yoruself / Nice to love you / You don't get away (that easy) / She la
CD ____ REVXD 1001
Black / Nov '94 / Revolver / Sony

TRUSTED BY MILLIONS
Lies to me / Cheer up / Stick to Milly / Love you all / Couldn't be sorry / This is my haircut / Desperately seeking anyone / Crossing a canyon / I love candy / Frank's revenge / Nothing ever happens / I wish I knew / Puddle of love
CD ____ REVXD 5440
Revolver / Sep '97 / Revolver / Sony

59 Times The Pain

BLIND ANGER AND HATE
CD ____ BHR 013CD
Burning Heart / Aug '95 / Plastic Head

MORE OUT OF TODAY
CD ____ BHR 029CD
Burning Heart / May '95 / Plastic Head

TWENTY PER CENT OF MY HAND
CD ____ BHR 052CD
Burning Heart / Dec '96 / Plastic Head

60ft Dolls

BIG 3, THE
New loafers / Talk to me / Stay / Hair / Happy shopper / One / Good times / No.1 pure alcohol / Streamlined / Loser / Pig Valentine / Terminal crash fear / Buzz
CD ____ DOLLSCD 004
Indolent / May '96 / 3mv/BMG / Vital

64 Spoons

LANDING ON A RAT COLUMN
It's all overture / Agressive travelling / Fat chance / Ich bin heidi / Nib (Synthesizer party) / Tails in the sky / Ivory ball / Plonder on / Weird Granny / It's only a party / Dear Clare / Lens / Five miles / Julius Caesar / Do's and the dont's of path laying / Landing on a rat column
CD ____ FCR 001CD
Freshly Cut / Sep '94 / Vital

69

SOUND OF MUSIC, THE
My machines / Microlour / Jam the box / Desire / Rushed / Sub seducer / Sound on sound / Poi et pas / Filter king / Highs / Finale / No
CD ____ RS 90578CD
R&S / Jul '95 / Vital

70 Gwen Party

ANTI BLUE NAZI
CD ____ SR 017
Snape / Sep '96 / RTM/Disc / Shellshock/ Disc

PEEL SESSIONS, THE
CD ____ SR 013
Snape / Apr '95 / RTM/Disc / Shellshock/ Disc

78th Fraser Highlander's ...

LIVE IN SCOTLAND (78th Fraser Highlander's Pipe Band)
Slow airs / 4/4 Marches / Waulking songs medley / Solo pipe set / Reels-band, solo pipe, duet / Jigs / Slow air / Piobaireachd / Medley / Drum fanfare / Cape Breton medley / Journey to Skye
CD ____ LCOM 8016
Lismor / Jan '95 / ADA / Direct / Duncans / Lismor

NOO THAT'S WHIT A CA'CEILIDH VOL.1 (78th Fraser Highlander's Pipe Band)
Dashing white sergeant / Dashing white sergeant (Encore) / Polka / Gay Gordons / Gay Gordons (encore) / St. Bernard's waltz / Eightsome reel / Strip the willow / Strip the willow (Encore) / Canadian barn dance / Canadian barn dance encore / Holley ganz jig / Boston two step / Boston two step encore / Virginia reel / Military two step
CD ____ LISMOR 8016
Lismor / Jan '95 / ADA / Direct / Duncans / Lismor

88 Fingers Louie

88 FINGERS UP YOUR ASS
CD ____ HR 6192
Hopeless / Jun '97 / Cargo / Greyhound

BEHIND BARS
CD ____ BTR 011CD
Bad Taste / Oct '96 / Plastic Head

92 Degrees

92 DEGREES
CD ____ BV 192952
Black Vinyl / Nov '96 / Cargo

95 South

QUAD CITY KNOCK
CD ____ WRA 8117CD
Wrap / Feb '94 / Koch

100 Proof (Aged In Soul)

100 PROOF AGED IN SOUL
Somebody's been sleeping in my bed / Love is sweeter / One man's leftovers / I've come to save you / Ain't that lovin' you / Not enough love to satisfy / Age ain't nothing but a number / She's not just another woman / Too many cooks (spoil the soup) / I can't sit and wait / Backtrack / If I could see the light in the window / Driveway / Ninety day freeze / Everything good is bad / I'd rather fight than switch / Don't scratch (where it don't itch) / Nothing sweeter than love / Since you been gone / Never my love
CD ____ HDHCD 504
HDH / Apr '92 / Pinnacle

101 Strings

ARE YOU LONESOME TONIGHT
CD ____ EMPRCD 009
Emporio / Feb '94 / Disc

COUNTRY COLLECTION, THE
CD ____ EMPRCD 017
Emporio / Feb '94 / Disc

GREAT AMERICAN COMPOSERS, THE
CD ____ EMPRCD 016
Emporio / Feb '94 / Disc

GREAT LOVE SONGS, THE
CD ____ EMPRCD 008
Emporio / Feb '94 / Disc

GREAT STRAUSS WALTZES, THE
CD ____ EMPRCD 015
Emporio / Feb '94 / Disc

MAGIC OF HAWAII, THE
CD ____ EMPRCD 014
Emporio / Feb '94 / Disc

MEMORIES ARE MADE OF THIS - THE 50'S
CD ____ EMPRCD 013
Emporio / Feb '94 / Disc

MEMORIES ARE MADE OF THIS - THE 60'S
CD ____ EMPRCD 012
Emporio / Feb '94 / Disc

MEMORIES ARE MADE OF THIS - THE 70'S
CD ____ EMPRCD 011
Emporio / Feb '94 / Disc

MOONLIGHT SERENADES
CD ____ EMPRCD 002
Emporio / Feb '94 / Disc

MUSIC FOR SWINGIN' LOVERS
CD ____ EMPRCD 020
Emporio / Feb '94 / Disc

MUSIC OF THE WORLD
CD ____ EMPRCD 006
Emporio / Feb '94 / Disc

POWER & THE GLORY, THE
CD ____ EMPRCD 005
Emporio / Feb '94 / Disc

RHAPSODY AND BLUES
CD ____ EMPRCD 003
Emporio / Feb '94 / Disc

THAT LATIN SOUND
CD ____ EMPRCD 004
Emporio / Feb '94 / Disc

THEY WRITE THE SONGS
CD ____ EMPRCD 019
Emporio / Feb '94 / Disc

108

CURSE OF INSTINCT
CD ____ LF 251CD
Lost & Found / Dec '96 / Plastic Head

HOLYNAME
CD ____ EVR 005CD
Equal Vision / Apr '97 / Plastic Head

SONGS OF SEPARATION
CD ____ LF 096CD
Lost & Found / Jun '94 / Plastic Head

THREEFOLD MISERY
CD ____ LF 230CD
Lost & Found / May '96 / Plastic Head

108 Grand

ALBUM, THE
CD ____ OMCD 002
OM / Nov '94 / Cargo / SRD

112

112
112 Intro / Now that we're done / Pleasure and pain / Why / Cupid / Call my name / Come see me / Sexy you / Can I touch you / I can't believe: *112 & Faith Evans* / Keep it real / Only you: *112 & Notorious BIG/Mase* / I will be there / In love with you / Just a little while / Why does / This is your day / Throw it all away / Only you: *112 & Notorious BIG*
CD ____ 74321418362
RCA / Sep '96 / BMG

123 Stab Wounds

DEITY OF PERVERSION, THE
CD ____ HNF 023CD
Head Not Found / Jul '96 / Plastic Head

311

311
Down / Random / Jack O'Lantern's weather / All mixed up / Hive / Guns / Misdirected hostility / Purpose / Loco / Brodels / Don't stay home / DLMD / Sweet / T&P combo
CD ____ 5325302
Capricorn / Oct '96 / PolyGram

TRANSISTOR
CD ____ 5362902
Capricorn / Aug '97 / PolyGram

$400 Suits

NEVER GIVE WHAT YOU CAN'T TAKE BACK
CD ____ CMCD 77144
Century Media / Mar '97 / Plastic Head

454 Big Block

YOUR JESUS
CD ____ CMCD 77084
Century Media / Sep '95 / Plastic Head

601

MOTION ARCHAOS
CD ____ JUNK 002
Totem / Apr '96 / Grapevine/PolyGram / THE

RUB-A-DUB
CD ____ JUNK 001
Totem / Mar '96 / Grapevine/PolyGram / THE

702

NO DOUBT
CD ____ 5307382
Motown / Nov '96 / PolyGram

808 State

DON SOLARIS
Intro / Bond / Bird / Azura / Black dartangnon / Joyrider / Lopez / Balboa / Kohoutek / Mooz / Jerusahat / Banacheq
CD ____ 0630143562
ZTT / Feb '97 / Warner Music

EX.EL
San Francisco / Spanish heart / Leo Leo / Qmart / Nephatiti / Lift / Ooops / Empire / In yer face / Cubik / Lambrusco / Techno bell / Olympic
CD ____ 9031737752
ZTT / Dec '96 / Warner Music

GORGEOUS
Plan 9 / Moses / Contrique / Ten times ten / Timebomb / One in ten / Europa / Orbit / Black morpheus / Southern cross / Nimbus / Colony
CD ____ 4509911002
ZTT / Dec '96 / Warner Music

911

JOURNEY, THE
Don't make me wait / Bodyshakin' / Can't stop / Day we find love / Our last goodbye / Night to remember / Take good care / Love sensation / One more try / Swing / Rhythm of the night / Journey
CD ____ CDV 2820
Virgin / Feb '97 / EMI

999

BIGGEST PRIZE IN SPORT, THE
Boys in the gang / Inside out / Trouble / So long / Fun thing / Biggest prize in sport / Hollywood / Stranger / Lie lie lie / Found out too late / Made a fool of you / Boiler / Shake / English wipeout / Stop stop
CD ____ CDPUNK 67
Anagram / Nov '95 / Cargo / Pinnacle

EMERGENCY
Don't know I love you / Crazy / Feeling alright with the crew / Emergency / Pick it up / Indian reservation / Quite disappointing / My street stinks / Rael raen / Subterfuge / Hollywood / Inside out / Biggest prize in sport / Chicane destination / Obsessed / Hit me / Nasty nasty / Tulse Hill nights / Mercy mercy / English wipeout / Fun thing / Titanic reaction / Boys in the gang / Lil red riding hood / Me and my desire / Homicide / Let's face it / I'm alive / Found out too late
CD ____ RRCD 245
Receiver / Aug '97 / Grapevine/PolyGram

FACE TO FACE
CD ____ OBSESSCD 003
Obsession / May '93 / RTM/Disc

INDEPENDENT PUNK SINGLES COLLECTION
CD ____ CDPUNK 78
Anagram / Jun '96 / Cargo / Pinnacle

LIVE AT THE NASHVILLE 1979
Brent Cross / Quite disappointing / Let's face it / Hit me / Biggest prize in sport / Me and my desire / Lie lie lie / Trouble / Crazy / Boys in the gang / Ain't gonna tell / Feelin' alright with the crew / Inside out / Titanic (my over) reaction
CD ____ CDPUNK 93
Anagram / Apr '97 / Cargo / Pinnacle

YOU US IT
Black flowers for the bride / (There is no glory in) Mary's story / Signed dangerous of Hollywood / Bye bye bones / Everybody needs it / It's over now / Bye bye England / All of the days / Big fast car / Absolution / Deep in the shadow / Run for your life / Don't tell me / Crazy crazy crazy / White light
CD ____ CDPUNK 92
Anagram / Apr '97 / Cargo / Pinnacle

1000 Homo DJ's

SUPERNAUT
CD ____ CDDVN 5
Devotion / Feb '92 / Pinnacle

2066 & Then

REFLECTIONS
CD ____ SB 025
Second Battle / Jun '97 / Greyhound

3080 Yen

HUMANOID HA HA
CD ____ EFA 123042
Vince Lombard / Dec '95 / SRD

7669

EAST FROM A BAD BLOCK
Heree ah cumm / Session (interlude) / 69 ways to love a (black) man / Ma, I luv him (interlude) / Joy / Shoot the MF in his kneecap (interlude) / Changes / Conversation fo yo ass (interlude) / RMA (Will you remember me) / Crossover message (interlude) / Last song / Who dez bytches anyway (interlude) / So high / Tic away / By your side / Cabaret (interlude) / Cloud 69 / 1-800 dial f... / King size bed / Shmoken' em up y'all (interlude) / Phillies, 40's and 69
CD ____ 5328422
Motown / Mar '94 / PolyGram

9353

MAKE YOUR LAST DAYS LOUD DAYS
CD ____ AS 6D
Adult Swim / May '93 / SRD

OVERDOSE AT YOUR MOTHER'S HOUSE
CD ____ AS 5D
Adult Swim / May '93 / SRD

10,000 Maniacs

BLIND MAN'S ZOO
Eat for two / Please forgive us / Big parade / Trouble me / You happy puppet / Headstrong / Poison in the well / Dust bowl / Lion's share / Hateful hate / Jubilee
CD ____ 9608152
Elektra / May '89 / Warner Music

HOPE CHEST (The Fredonia Recordings 1982-1983)
Planned obsolescence / Latin one / Katrina's fair / Pour de chirico / Grey victory / National education week / Death of manolete / Orange / Tension / Anthem for doomed youth / Daktari / Groove dub / Pit viper / My mother the war
CD ____ 7559609622
Elektra / Oct '90 / Warner Music

IN MY TRIBE
What's the matter here / Hey Jack Kerouac / Like the weather / Cherry tree / Painted desert / Don't talk / Peace train / Gun shy / My sister Rose / Campfire song / City of angels / Verdi cries
CD ____ 9607382
Elektra / Aug '87 / Warner Music

MTV UNPLUGGED
These are days / Eat for two / Candy everybody wants / I'm not the man / Don't talk / Hey Jack Kerouac / What's the matter here / Gold rush brides / Like the weather / Trouble me / Jezebel / Because the night / Stockton gala days / Noah's dove
CD ____ 7559615692
Elektra / Oct '93 / Warner Music

OUR TIME IN EDEN
Noah's dove / These are days / Eden / Few and far between / Stockton gala days / Gold rush brides / Jezebel / How you've grown / Candy everybody wants / Tolerance / Circle dream / If you intend / I'm not the man
CD _______________ 7559613852
Elektra / Oct '92 / Warner Music

WISHING CHAIR, THE
Can't ignore the train / Just as the tide was flowing / Scorpio rising / Lilydale / Maddox table / Everyone a puzzle lover / Arbor day / Back o' the moon / Tension makes a tangle / Among the Americans / Grey victory / Cotton Alley / My mother the war
CD _______________ 9604282
Elektra / '89 / Warner Music

46,000 Fibres

DIAPHONOUS
CD _______________ MTB 022
MTB / Dec '96 / RTM/Disc

EMANATES
CD _______________ MTB 018
TEQ / May '95 / Cargo / Plastic Head

A

A Certain Ratio

CHANGE THE STATION
CD CDROB 50
Rob's Records / Nov '96 / Pinnacle / RTM/Disc

FORCE
Only together / Bootsy / Fever 103 degrees / Naked and white / Mickey way / And then she smiled / Take me down / Anthem / Si fermi o gredo
CD CREV 027CD
Rev-Ola / Oct '94 / 3mv/Vital

GRAVEYARD AND THE BALLROOM, THE
CD CREV 022CD
Rev-Ola / Oct '94 / 3mv/Vital

I'D LIKE TO SEE YOU AGAIN
CD CREV 025CD
Rev-Ola / Oct '94 / 3mv/Vital

LOOKING FOR A CERTAIN RATIO - REMIX
CD CRECD 159
Creation / Jun '94 / 3mv/Vital

OLD AND THE NEW, THE
CD CREV 026CD
Rev-Ola / Oct '94 / 3mv/Vital

SEXTET
CD CREV 024CD
Rev-Ola / Oct '94 / 3mv/Vital

TO EACH
CD CREV 023CD
Rev-Ola / Oct '94 / 3mv/Vital

A House

NO MORE APOLOGIES
Start / Into the light / Cry easily / No more apologies / My sweet life / Sister's song / Twist and squeeze / Love is... / Without dreams / Just because / I can't change / Clothes horse / My mind / Broken / Happy ending
CD SETCD 028
Setanta / Sep '96 / Vital

A Minor Forest

CONSTITUENT PARTS 1993-1996
CD THRILL 034CD
Thrill Jockey / Oct '96 / Cargo / Greyhound

A One

FREE ASSOCIATION
CD ZEN 004CD
Indochina / Aug '95 / Pinnacle

A Positive Life

SYNAESTHETIC
CD RBADCD 10
Beyond / Oct '94 / Kudos / Pinnacle

A Split Second

VENGEANCE COD
CD HY 210526
Hypertension / Feb '94 / ADA / CM / Direct / Total/BMG

A Subtle Plague

NO REPRISE
Young girl / I seperate / Same story / Microfaction / Weak and deprived / Growing upsidedown / Cheyenne's lullaby / I wanna kill the president / Planting minds / Ship song / Butcher's death parade / Dreaming you dead
CD RTD 15730162
World Service / Jun '95 / Vital

A-Ha

EAST OF THE SUN, WEST OF THE MOON
Crying in the rain / I call your name / East of the sun and west of the moon / Waiting for her / Way we talk / Seemingly nonstop July / Early mornings / Slender frame / Sycamore leaves / Cold river / Rolling thunder
CD 7599263142
WEA / Dec '96 / Warner Music

HEADLINES AND DEADLINES
Take on me / Cry wolf / Touchy / You are the one / Manhattan skyline / Blood that moves the body / Early morning / Hunting high and low / Move to memphis / I've been losing you / Living daylights / Crying in the rain / I call your name / Stay on these roads / Train of thought / Sun always shines on TV
CD 7599267732
WEA / Dec '96 / Warner Music

HUNTING HIGH AND LOW
Take on me / Train of thought / Hunting high and low / Blue sky / Living a boy's adventures tale / Sun always shines on TV / And you tell me / Love is reason / Dream myself alive / Here I stand and face the rain
CD 9253002
WEA / Nov '85 / Warner Music

MEMORIAL BEACH
Dark is the night / Move to Memphis / Cold as stone / Angel in the snow / Locust / Lie down in darkness / How sweet it was / Lamb to the slaughter / Between your mama and yourself / Memorial beach
CD 9362452292
WEA / Jun '93 / Warner Music

SCOUNDREL DAYS
Scoundrel days / Swing of things / I've been losing you / October / Manhattan skyline / Cry wolf / Looking for the whales / Weight of the wind / Maybe maybe / Soft rains of April
CD 9255012
WEA / Feb '95 / Warner Music

STAY ON THESE ROADS
Blood that moves the body / Touchy / This alone is love / Hurry home / Living daylights / There's never a forever thing / Out of blue comes green / You are the one / You'll end up crying / Stay on these roads
CD 9257332
WEA / Feb '95 / Warner Music

A-La-Tex

ROUGH 'N' TUMBLE
Just sit back and laugh / Young dogs / Don't stop at the borderline / Signpost / Set me free / Girl from the west country / Gold of Eldorado / Loving chain / Don't leave me again / In the doghouse / I'll follow you / Parchman farm / I've got my foolhead on
CD ZNCD 1008
Zane / Oct '95 / Pinnacle

Aaberg, Philip

CINEMA
CD 01934111102
Windham Hill / Jan '95 / BMG

Aag

FIRE
CD OZ 002CD
Ozone / Jul '90 / Mo's Music Machine / Pinnacle / SRD

Aaliyah

AGE AIN'T NOTHING BUT A NUMBER
Throw your hands up / Back and forth / Age ain't nothing but a number / Down with the clique / At your best you are love / Me quite like you do / I'm so into you / Street thing / Young nation / Old scool / I'm down / Thing I like
CD CHIP 149
Jive / Mar '97 / Pinnacle

ONE IN A MILLION
Got to give it up / Hot like fire / If your girl only knew / One in a million / Choosey lover (old school new school) / Everything's gonna be alright / Heartbroken / I gotcha' back / Never givin' up / Came to give love / Beats 4 da streets / One I gave my heart to / Ladies in da house / Never comin' back / Giving you more / 4 page letter / Girl like you
CD 7567927152
Blackground / Aug '96 / Warner Music

Aardvark Jazz Orchestra

PSALMS AND ELEGIES
CD LEOLABCD 028
Leo Lab / May '97 / Cadillac

Aardvarks

BARGAIN
Bargain day / Cheyenne woman / Office no.1 / Girl on a bike / Fly my plane / Mr. Inertia / Arthur C Clarke / When the morning comes / Fifty hertz man / You're my loving way / Merry go round / Time to fly
CD DELECCD 029
Delerium / Jun '95 / Cargo / Pinnacle / Vital

Aaron, Lee

EMOTIONAL RAIN
CD 341952
No Bull / Nov '95 / Koch

LEE AARON
Powerline / Hands are tied / Only human / Empty heart / Number one / Don't rain on my parade / Going off the deep end / If this is love / Eye for an eye / Heartbeat of the world / Dream with me
CD ACDM 1231
Attic / May '97 / Greyhound

METAL QUEEN
Metal Queen / Lady of the darkest night / Head above water / Got to be the one / Shake it up / Deceiver / Steal away your love / Hold out / Breakdown / We will be rockin'
CD ACDM 1188
Attic / May '97 / Greyhound

SOME GIRLS DO
CD ACD 1322
Attic / May '97 / Greyhound

Aatabou, Najat

COUNTRY GIRLS AND CITY WOMEN
Wind (Ar-rih) / Spare me (Taqi fia Allah) / No way out (La hila bidi) / God meant it to be that way (Hekda rad Allah) / Ever since that night (Min deek leela) / Burning pain (Baadou Ihih) / Go find another guy (Shoufi Ghirou)
CD ROUCD 5077
Rounder / Feb '97 / ADA / CM / Direct

VOICE OF THE ATLAS, THE
Baghi narjah / Finetriki / Shouffi rhirou / Lila ya shaba / Ouardatte Lajnane / Zourouni lilah / Ditih
CD CDORBD 069
Globestyle / Sep '91 / Pinnacle

AB Skhy

AB SKHY
CD OW 30011
One Way / Jul '94 / ADA / Direct / Greyhound

Aba Shanti

JAH LIGHTNING AND THUNDER
CD ABACD 003
Aba Shanti / Dec '96 / SRD

WRATH OF JAH, THE
CD ABACD 001
Falasha / Mar '96 / SRD

Abacush

LIFE
CD ABACD 01
Abacush / May '94 / Jet Star

Abadzi, Rita

RITA ABADZI 1933-1938
CD HTCD 36
Heritage / May '96 / ADA / Direct / Hot Shot / Jazz Music / Swift / Wellard

Abana Ba Nasery

NURSERY BOYS GO AHEAD
CD CDORBD 076
Globestyle / Feb '92 / Pinnacle

Abate, Greg

BOP CITY - LIVE AT BIRDLAND (Abate, Greg Quartet)
Bop city / Minorism / What is this thing called love / Gypsy / Peaks beaks / Basting the bird / Andromeda / These foolish things / Young 'uns / Opportunity / Gemini / Sax O'Brien
CD CCD 79513
Candid / Feb '97 / Cadillac / Direct / Jazz Music / Koch / Wellard

DR. JEKYLL AND MR. HYDE (Abate, Greg Quintet & Richie Cole)
Fast lane rhythm / From the heart / CCA / Dr. Jekyll and Mr. Hyde / Chan's house of Jazz / My friend from Rio / I'll remember Murph / Tommyhawk / Parallel / For Tony / Vera's song / Bebop baby
CD CCD 79715
Candid / Feb '97 / Cadillac / Direct / Jazz Music / Koch / Wellard

STRAIGHT AHEAD
Straight ahead / Kelly blue / Denise Marie / Nica's dream / Jessica / 2-22 / Con alma / Bossa for Gregory / It's all right with me
CD CCD 79530
Candid / Feb '97 / Cadillac / Direct / Jazz Music / Koch / Wellard

Abba

ABBA
Mamma mia / Hey hey Helen / Tropical loveland / SOS / Man in the middle / Bang a boomerang / I do I do I do I do I do / Rock me / Benny Andersson intermezzo N1 / I've been waiting for you / So long / Waterloo / Hasta manana / Honey honey / Ring ring / Nina, pretty ballerina
CD 8315962
Polydor / Sep '92 / PolyGram

ABBASALUTELY (Various Artists)
CD FNCD 315
Flying Nun / Jan '96 / RTM/Disc

AGNETHA & FRIDA - THE SOUND OF ABBA
Heat is on: *Faltskog, Agnetha* / I know there's something going on: *Frida* / You're there: *Faltskog, Agnetha* / To turn the stone: *Frida* / Just one heart: *Faltskog, Agnetha* / That's tough: *Frida* / Turn the world around: *Faltskog, Agnetha* / I got something: *Frida* / We should be together: *Faltskog, Agnetha* / Shine: *Frida* / I won't let you go: *Faltskog, Agnetha* / Here we'll stay: *Frida* / Wrap your arms around me: *Faltskog, Agnetha* / Heart of the country: *Frida*
CD 5502122
Spectrum / Mar '94 / PolyGram

ALBUM, THE
Eagle / Take a chance on me / One man one woman / Name of the game / Move on / Hole in your soul / Girl with the golden hair / Three scenes from a mini musical
CD 8212172
Polydor / Sep '92 / PolyGram

AND THE MUSIC STILL GOES ON
Does your Mother know / Ring ring / On and on and on / When I kissed the teacher / If it wasn't for the nights / As good as new / Eagle / Dance (while the music still goes on) / Visitors / When all is said and done / So long / Bang a boomerang / Me and I / Move on / Gonna sing you my love song / Arrival
CD 5511092
Spectrum / Mar '96 / PolyGram

ARRIVAL
My love my life / When I kissed the teacher / Dancing queen / Dum dum diddle / Knowing me, knowing you / Money, money, money / That's me / Why did it have to be me / Tiger / Arrival
CD 8213192
Polydor / Sep '92 / PolyGram

FOREVER GOLD (2CD Set)
CD Set 5330832
Polydor / Oct '96 / PolyGram

GOLD (Greatest Hits)
Dancing queen / Knowing me, knowing you / Take a chance on me / Mamma mia / Lay all your love on me / Super trouper / I have a dream / Winner takes it all / Money, money, money / SOS / Chiquitita / Fernando / Voulez vous / Gimme gimme gimme / Does your mother know / One of us / Name of the game / Thank you for the music / Waterloo
CD 5170072
Polydor / Sep '92 / PolyGram

INTERVIEW DISC
CD SAM 7021
Sound & Media / Nov '96 / Sound & Media

MORE ABBA GOLD
CD 5193532
Polydor / May '93 / PolyGram

PLAY ABBA/BEATLES/QUEEN (Royal Philharmonic Orchestra)
CD HRCD 8011
Kenwest / Nov '92 / THE

RING RING
Ring ring / Another town another train / Disillusion / People need love / I saw it in the mirror / Nine, pretty ballerina / Love isn't easy (but it sure is hard enough) / Me and Bobby and Bobby's brother / She's my kind of girl / I am just a girl / Rock 'n' roll band
CD 8436422
Polydor / Sep '92 / PolyGram

ROYAL PHILHARMONIC ORCHESTRA PERFORM CLASSIC ABBA (Royal Philharmonic Orchestra)
Abbature / SOS / Mamma mia / Eagle / I have a dream / Does your mother know / Money, money, money / Knowing me, knowing you / Gimme, gimme, gimme / Summer night city / Chiquitita / Finale
CD QED 037
Tring / Nov '96 / Tring

ROYAL PHILHARMONIC ORCHESTRA PLAY ABBA (Royal Philharmonic Orchestra)
Waterloo/Dancing queen/Fernando / SOS / Mamma mia / Eagle / I have a dream / Does your mother know / Money money money / Knowing me knowing you / Gimme gimme gimme/Summer night city / Chiquitita / Waterloo/Name of the game/Take a chance on me
CD CD 6033
Music / Sep '96 / Target/BMG

RPO PLAYS ABBA (Royal Philharmonic Orchestra)
Abbature / Waterloo / Dancing Queen / Fernando / SOS / Mamma mia / Eagle / I have a dream / Does your mother know / Money money money / Knowing knowing you /

Gimme gimme gimme / Summer night city / Chiquitta / Finale
CD ____ **EMPRCD 585**
Emporio / Oct '95 / Disc

SALUTE TO ABBA (Various Artists)
Money money money / Chiquitita / Waterloo / I have a dream / Mama mia / Super trouper / Gimme gimme gimme (A man after midnight) / Winner takes it all / Knowing me knowing you / I do I do I do I do / Dancing queen / Does your Mother know / Day before you came / Fernando / SOS / Thank you for the music
CD ____ **306772**
Hallmark / May '97 / Carlton

SUPER TROUPER
Super trouper / Winner takes it all / On and on and on / Andante Andante / Me and I / Happy New Year / Our last summer / Piper / Lay all your love on me / Way old friends do
CD ____ **8000232**
Polydor / Sep '92 / PolyGram

THANK YOU FOR THE MUSIC
CD Set ____ **5234722**
Polydor / Nov '94 / PolyGram

VISITORS, THE
Visitors / Head over heels / When all is said and done / Soldiers / I let the music speak / One of us / Two for the price of one / Slipping through my fingers / Like an angel / Passing through my room / Eagle
CD ____ **8000112**
Polydor / Sep '92 / PolyGram

VOULEZ VOUS
As good as new / Voulez vous / I have a dream / Angel eyes / King has lost his crown / Does your mother know / If it wasn't for the night / Chiquitita / Lovers (like a little longer) / Kisses of fire
CD ____ **8213202**
Polydor / Mar '90 / PolyGram

Abbacadabra

ABBACADABRA
CD ____ **ALMYCD 03**
Almighty / Jan '93 / Total/BMG

ABBACADABRA REVIVAL
CD ____ **ALMYCD 18**
Almighty / Oct '96 / Total/BMG

Abbasi, Rez

THIRD EAR
CD ____ **EFA 015042**
Ozone / Jul '95 / Mo's Music Machine / Pinnacle / SRD

Abbfinoosty

STORM
CD ____ **CYCL 034**
Cyclops / Aug '96 / Pinnacle

Abbott, Bobby

WELCOME TO GLENSHARRAGH
CD ____ **LCOM 9046**
Lismor / Jul '91 / ADA / Direct / Duncans / Lismor

Abbud, Malik Ahmel

JAZZ SAHARA
CD ____ **OJCCD 182**
Original Jazz Classics / Jun '95 / Complete/Pinnacle / Jazz Music / Wellard

ABC

ABSOLUTELY ABC (The Greatest Hits)
Poison arrow / Look of love / All of my heart / Tears are not enough / That was then but this is now / SOS / How to be a millionaire / Be near me / When Smokey sings / Night you murdered love / King without a crown / One better world / Look of love (1990 remix) / When Smokey sings (12" mix) / Be near me (12" remix) / One better world (12" remix) / Ocean blue
CD ____ **8429672**
Neutron / Apr '90 / PolyGram

BEAUTY STAB
That was then but this is now / Love's a dangerous language / If I ever thought you'd be lonely / Power of persuasion / Beauty stab / By default, by design / Hey citizen / King money / Bite the hand / Unzip / SOS / United Kingdom
CD ____ **8146612**
Neutron / Nov '83 / PolyGram

COLLECTION, THE
Poison arrow / Look of love / Night you murdered love / Tears are not enough / Be near me / I'm in love with you / Real thing / Love's a dangerous language / Greatest love of all / When smokey sings / One better world / Vanity kills / Bite the hand / Chicago / Minneapolis / Think again / Never more than now / All of my heart
CD ____ **5518312**
Spectrum / Mar '96 / PolyGram

LEXICON OF LOVE (Remastered)
Show me / Poison arrow / Many happy returns / Tears are not enough / Valentine's day / Look of love (part one) / Date stamp / All of my heart / 4 ever 2 gether / Look of love (part four) / Tears are not enough / Poison arrow / Look of love / Alphabet soup / Theme from Mantrap / Look of love
CD ____ **5149422**
Mercury / Mar '96 / PolyGram

LEXICON OF LOVE, THE/BEAUTY STAB (2CD Set)
Show me / Poison arrow / Many happy returns / Tears are not enough / Valentine's day / Look of love / Date stamp / All of my heart / 4 ever 2 gether / Look of love (pt 4) / That was then but this is now / Love's a dangerous language / If ever I thought you'd be lonely / Power of persuasion / Beauty stab / By default, by design / Hey citizen / King money / Bite the hand / Unzip / SOS / United Kingdom
CD Set ____ **5286002**
Neutron / Aug '95 / PolyGram

SKYSCRAPING
Stranger things / Ask a thousand times / Skyscraping / Who can I turn to / Rolling sevens / Only the best will do / Love is its own reward / Light years / Seven day weekend / Heaven knows / Faraway
CD ____ **74321456532**
Blatant / Mar '97 / BMG

TEARS ARE NOT ENOUGH
Poison arrow / Tears are not enough / Be near me / Never more than now / Love's a dangerous language / Bite the hand / Night you murdered love / Greatest love of all / Minneapolis / Vanity kills / Think again / I'm in love with you / Real thing / Chicago
CD ____ **5500002**
Spectrum / May '93 / PolyGram

ABC Diablo

GIVE RISE TO DOUBTS
CD ____ **EFA 124052**
Common Cause / Sep '95 / Plastic Head / SRD

LAST INTOXICATION OF THE SENSES
CD ____ **CC 001CD**
Common Cause / Jun '93 / Plastic Head / SRD

Abcess

URINE JUNKIES
CD ____ **RR 6923CD**
Relapse / Nov '95 / Pinnacle / Plastic Head

Abdel-Al, Aboud

BEST OF MODERN BELLYDANCE FROM ARABIA
CD ____ **EUCD 1244**
ARC / Nov '93 / ADA / ARC Music

Abdelli

NEW MOON
Adarghal introduction / Adarghal / Achaah / Lawan / Walagh / Ayafrouk / Imanza / JSK / Iggantiw / Amegh asinigh
CD ____ **CDRW 54**
Realworld / Jun '95 / EMI

Abdelwahab, Mohamed

KOLINA NEHIB ELQAMAR 1920-1935
CD ____ **829132**
BUDA / Feb '96 / Discovery

Abdul, Paula

FOREVER YOUR GIRL
Way that you love me / Knocked out / Opposites attract: *Abdul, Paula & The Wild Pair* / State of attraction / I need you / Forever your girl / Straight up / Next to you / Cold hearted / One or the other
CD ____ **CDSRN 19**
Siren / Apr '92 / EMI

HEAD OVER HEELS
Crazy cool / My love is for real / Ain't never gonna give you up / Love don't come easy / If I were your girl / Sexy thoughts / Choice is yours / Ho-down / Under the influence / I never knew it / Get your groove on / Missing you / It's all about feeling good / Cry for me
CD ____ **CDVUS 90**
Virgin / Jun '95 / EMI

SHUT UP AND DANCE (Dance Remixes)
Cold hearted / Straight up / One or the other / Forever your girl / Knocked out / Way that you love me / Opposites attract / Medley / State of attraction
CD ____ **CDVUS 28**
Virgin / Apr '92 / EMI

SPELLBOUND
Promise of a new day / Rock house / Rush rush / Spellbound / Vibeology / Will you marry me / U / My foolish heart / Blowing kisses in the wind / To you / Alright tonight / Goodnight my love (pleasant dreams)
CD ____ **CDVUS 33**
Virgin / Jul '91 / EMI

Abdulai, Alhaji Ibrahim

MASTER DRUMMERS OF DAGBON
CD ____ **ROUCD 5016**
Rounder / '88 / ADA / CM / Direct

Abe, Kaoru

JAZZ BED
CD ____ **PSFD 66**
PSF / Dec '95 / Harmonia Mundi

Abee, Steve

JERUSALEM DONUTS
CD ____ **NAR 087CD**
New Alliance / May '93 / Plastic Head

Abeng

UNCONQUEREBEL
CD ____ **LRCD 001**
Lush / Oct '94 / Prime / SRD

Abercrombie, John

ANIMATO
Right now / Single moon / Agitato / First light / Last light / For hope of hope / Bright reign / Ollie Mention
CD ____ **8417792**
ECM / Mar '90 / New Note/Pinnacle

CHARACTERS
Parable / Memoir / Telegram / Backward glance / Ghost dance / Paramour / Afterthoughts / Evensong
CD ____ **8293722**
ECM / '88 / New Note/Pinnacle

CURRENT EVENTS
Clint / Alice in Wonderland / Ralph's piano waltz / Lisa / Hippityville / Killing time / Still
CD ____ **8277702**
ECM / Jun '86 / New Note/Pinnacle

FAREWELL
CD ____ **500462**
Musidisc / Nov '93 / Discovery

GATEWAY
CD ____ **8291922**
ECM / Jun '86 / New Note/Pinnacle

GATEWAY VOL.2
Opening / Sing song / Blue / Reminiscence / Nexus
CD ____ **8473232**
ECM / Dec '95 / New Note/Pinnacle

GETTING THERE
Sidekick / Upon a time / Getting there / Remember hymn / Thalia / Furs on ice / Chance / Labour day
CD ____ **8334942**
ECM / Feb '88 / New Note/Pinnacle

JOHN ABERCROMBIE TRIO (Abercrombie, John & Marc Johnson/ Peter Erskine)
Furs on ice / Alice in Wonderland / Innerplay / Drum solo / Samurai hee-haw / Stella by starlight / Beautiful love / Light beam / Four on one / Haunted heart
CD ____ **8377562**
ECM / Apr '89 / New Note/Pinnacle

NIGHT
Etherreggae / Night / Three East / Look around / Believe you me / Four on one
CD ____ **8232122**
ECM / Nov '84 / New Note/Pinnacle

NOVEMBER
Cat's back / JS / Right brain patrol / Prelude / November / Rise and fall / John's walts / Ogeda / Tuesday afternoon / To be / Come rain or come shine / Big music
CD ____ **5190732**
ECM / Oct '93 / New Note/Pinnacle

SPEAK OF THE DEVIL (Abercrombie, John Trio)
Angel food / Now and again / Mahat / Chorale / Farewell / BT-U / Early to bed / Dreamland / Hell's gare
CD ____ **8496482**
ECM / May '94 / New Note/Pinnacle

TACTICS (Abercrombie, John & Dan Wall/Adam Nussbaum)
Sweet sixteen / Last waltz / Bo Diddley / You and the night and the music / Chumbioh / Dear rain / Mr. Magoo / Long ago and far away
CD ____ **5336802**
ECM / Feb '97 / New Note/Pinnacle

TIMELESS
Lungs / Love song / Ralph's piano waltz / Red and orange / Remembering / Timeless
CD ____ **8291142**
ECM / '87 / New Note/Pinnacle

WHERE WE WERE (Abercrombie, John & Andy Laverne)
End of a love affair / Soulstice / Where we were / Dream team / Dream gypsy / John's waltz / Turn out the stars / Quality of your silence / Softly as in a morning sunrise
CD ____ **DTRCD 110**
Double Time / Nov '96 / Express Jazz

WORKS: JOHN ABERCROMBIE
Red and orange / Night / Ralph's piano waltz / Backward glance / Nightlake / Dreamstalker / Isla / Sing song
CD ____ **8372752**
ECM / Jun '89 / New Note/Pinnacle

Aberdeen FC

COME ON YOU REDS (Aberdeen FC/ Supporters)
Up the Dons: *Shepherd, Robbie* / Northern lights: *Shepherd, Robbie* / European song: *Aberdeen FC* / Northern lights: *Aberdeen FC* / Pride of Aberdeen: *Ames, Paul* / Aberdeen: *Red Brigade* / Wee red devils: *Red Brigade* / Ye canna beat us: *Red Balloon Soccer Crew* / Rap up: *Red Balloon Soccer Crew* / Tae the Dons frae Donside: *Cath & Jean* / Aberdeen vs Queens Park: *Gordon, Harry & Jack Holden* / Aberdeen vs Queens Park: *Gordon, Harry & Jack Holden* / Don't tell me it's over: *Scammels* / Football statistician: *Stephen, Graham* / It's half past four and we're two nil down: *Stephen, Graham* / What a happy day: *Bagsy* / Here we go: *Aberdeen FC*
CD ____ **CDGAFFER 15**
Cherry Red / Apr '97 / Pinnacle

Aberdeen Youth Choir

MY SONG IS LOVE
CD ____ **25004**
Divine Art / Dec '96 / CM / Kingdom

Aberg, Lennart

GREEN PRINTS
CD ____ **12762**
Caprice / Oct '87 / ADA / Cadillac / CM / Complete/Pinnacle

Aberjaber

Y BWCED PERFFAITH
Taith Madoc / Medley / Braint / Medley / Medley / Medley / Rmbling pitchfork / Medley / O Mama / Bread man / Perfect bucket
CD ____ **SCD 2157**
Sain / May '97 / ADA / Direct / Greyhound

Abhinanda

ABHINANDA
CD ____ **DFR 16**
Desperate Flight / May '97 / Cargo

SENSELESS
CD ____ **DFR 4**
Desperate Flight / Jun '97 / Cargo

Abhisheki, Jitendra

HYMNS FROM THE VEDAS AND UPABNISHADS
Salutations to the gurus / Peace chants / Gayatri mantara / Bhhagavad selections / Jayadeva's song to Krishna / Radha's pangs for krishna / Hymn on the greatness of shiva / Bhagavad gita verses chapter 2 / O mind go to kasi (Sung in Hindu)
CD ____ **RMSCD 105**
Ravi Shankar Music Circle / May '94 / Conifer/BMG

Abhorder

ZYGOTICAL SABBATORY ANABAPT
CD ____ **CYBSR 1012CD**
Cyber / Jun '96 / Amato Disco / Arabesque / Plastic Head

Abies Alba

IN PUNTO ALLA MEZZANOTTE
CD ____ **MMSCD 105**
MMS / Aug '96 / ADA

Abigail

FEEL GOOD
CD ____ **GAILCD 1**
Rumour / Oct '94 / 3mv/Sony / Mo's Music Machine / Pinnacle

Abigail

INTERCOURSE AND LUST
CD ____ **MIM 7342CD**
Modern Invasion / Jun '97 / Plastic Head

Abigor

INVOKE THE DARK AGE
CD ____ **SPV 08407962**
Napalm / Apr '95 / RTM/Disc

OPUS 4
CD ____ **NPR 020**
Napalm / Jul '96 / RTM/Disc

ORKBLUT...THE RETALIATION
CD ____ **SPV 08007992**
SPV / May '95 / Koch / Plastic Head

Abisko

SAMHRADH
CD ____ **829012**
Muance / Mar '96 / ADA

Ablaze My Shadows

IF EMOTIONS STILL BURN
CD ____ **NFR 015CD**
No Fashion / Jun '96 / Plastic Head

Able Tasmans

CUPPA TEA AND A LIE DOWN
CD ____ **FNCD 75**
Flying Nun / Jul '96 / RTM/Disc

STORE IN A COOL PLACE
CD ____ FNCD 312
Flying Nun / Mar '96 / RTM/Disc

Abnegate

INSANE SOULS
CD ____ MOLTEN 002CD
Molten Head / Jul '95 / Plastic Head

Abomination

ABOMINATION
CD ____ NB 028CD
Nuclear Blast / '92 / Plastic Head

TRAGEDY STRIKES
CD ____ NB 050CD
Nuclear Blast / Jul '91 / Plastic Head

Abou-Khalil, Rabih

AL-JADIDA
Catania / Nashwa / Evening with Jerry / When the lights go out / Storyteller / Ornette never sleeps / Nadim / Wishing well
CD ____ ENJ 60902
Enja / Oct '91 / New Note/Pinnacle / Vital/ SAM

ARABIAN WALTZ
Arabian waltz / Dreams of a dying city / Ornette never sleeps / Georgina / No visa / Pain after
CD ____ ENJ 90592
Enja / Apr '96 / New Note/Pinnacle / Vital/ SAM

BETWEEN DUSK AND DAWN
CD ____ MMP 170886CD
MMP / Mar '89 / New Note/Pinnacle

BLUE CAMEL
Sahara / Tsarka / Ziriab / Blue camel / On time / Night in the mountains / Rabou Abou Kabou / Beriut
CD ____ ENJ 70532
Enja / Oct '92 / New Note/Pinnacle / Vital/ SAM

BUKRA
CD ____ MMP 170889CD
MMP / Feb '89 / New Note/Pinnacle

NAFAS
CD ____ 8357812
ECM / Sep '88 / New Note/Pinnacle

ROOTS AND SPROUTS
Remembering Machghara / Walking on air / Nida / Revelation / Wordless / Sweet tain / Outlook / Caravan / Dreams of a dying city
CD ____ MMP 170890CD
MMP / Jul '90 / New Note/Pinnacle

SULTAN'S PICNIC, THE
Sunrise in Montreal / Solitude / Dog river / Moments / Lamentation / Nocturne au vilaret / Happy sheik / Snake soup
CD ____ ENJ 80782
Enja / Oct '94 / New Note/Pinnacle / Vital/ SAM

TARAB
Bushman in the desert / After dinner / Awakening / Haneen wa hanaan / Lost centuries / In search of the well / Orange fields / Tooth lost / Arabian waltz
CD ____ ENJ 70832
Enja / Oct '93 / New Note/Pinnacle / Vital/ SAM

Above All

DOMAIN
CD ____ RR 88822
Roadrunner / May '96 / PolyGram

Above The Law

TIME WILL REVEAL
CD ____ TBCD 1154
Tommy Boy / Oct '96 / RTM/Disc

Above The Ruins

SONGS OF THE WOLF
CD ____ ATR 1
Above The Ruins / Oct '96 / World Serpent

Abrahams, Brian

IMGOMA YABANTWANA (Abrahams, Brian District Six)
McGregorian chant / Home in a home / Maras dance / Django's jungle / Opskud (Let's jump) / Imgoma yabantwana (Song for the children) / Out of the question
CD ____ D 6002
District 6 / Jan '90 / Cadillac / Pinnacle

Abrahams, Mick

AT LAST
When I get back / Absent friends / Time now to decide / Whole wide world / Up and down (part 1) / Up and down (part 2) / Maybe because / Good old days / You'll never get it from me
CD ____ EDCD 335
Edsel / Sep '91 / Pinnacle

LIVE - ALL TORE DOWN
CD ____ IGOCD 2011
Indigo / Nov '94 / ADA / Direct

LIVE IN MADRID
Let's get down to business / Wanna know how to love / Let me love you baby / Stay with me / Automobile / Blues / Steel blues / Cat squirrel / Guitar boogie / Rock me
CD ____ IGOCD 2065
Indigo / Jul '97 / ADA / Direct

MICK ABRAHAMS
Greyhound Bus / Awake / Winds of change / Why do you do me this way / Big queen / Not to rearrange / Seasons
CD ____ BGOCD 95
Beat Goes On / Aug '94 / Pinnacle

MICK'S BACK
River's invitation / Bad feeling / Cold women with warm hearts / Time to love / Leaving home blues / Long grey mare / You'd be a millionaire / Send me some lovin' / Yolanda / Little red rooster / Ain't no love in the heart of the city / So much hard luck / Skyline drive
CD ____ IGOXCD 501
Indigo / Aug '96 / ADA / Direct

ONE
CD ____ ANDCD 7
A New Day / Feb '97 / Direct

PIG IN THE MIDDLE (Abrahams, Mick & Blodwyn Pig)
CD ____ ANDCD 10
A New Day / Feb '97 / Direct

Abram, Vic

SERENISSIMA
CD ____ HY 2000104CD
Hypertension / Sep '93 / ADA / CM / Direct / Total/BMG

Abrams, Muhal Richard

1-0 QA + 19
CD ____ 1200172
Black Saint / Oct '90 / Cadillac / Harmonia Mundi

BLU BLU BLU
CD ____ 1201172
Black Saint / Jan '92 / Cadillac / Harmonia Mundi

BLUES FOREVER
CD ____ BSR 0061
Black Saint / Jun '86 / Cadillac / Harmonia Mundi

DUET WITH AMINA CLAUDINE MYERS
CD ____ 1200512
Black Saint / Jan '94 / Cadillac / Harmonia Mundi

FAMILYTALK
CD ____ 1201322
Black Saint / Nov '93 / Cadillac / Harmonia Mundi

LEVELS AND DEGREES OF LIGHT
Levels and degrees of light / Bird song / My thoughts are my future-now and forever
CD ____ DD 413
Delmark / Mar '97 / ADA / Cadillac / CM / Direct / Hot Shot

ONE LINE, TWO VIEWS
CD ____ 804692
New World / Dec '95 / ADA / Cadillac / Harmonia Mundi

OPEN AIR MEETING, THE (Abrams, Muhal Richard & Marty Ehrlich)
Marching with honor / Dark sestina / Crossbeams / Price of the ticket / Bright canto / Blues to you
CD ____ 805122
New World / May '97 / ADA / Cadillac / Harmonia Mundi

SONG FOR ALL
Song for all / Dabadubada / Marching for honor / GMBR / Over the same over / Linetime / Steamin' up the road / Imagine
CD ____ 1201612
Black Saint / May '97 / Cadillac / Harmonia Mundi

THINGS TO COME FROM THOSE NOW GONE
CD ____ DELMARK 430
Delmark / Sep '89 / ADA / Cadillac / CM / Direct / Hot Shot

VIEW FROM WITHIN
CD ____ BSR 0081
Black Saint / Jun '86 / Cadillac / Harmonia Mundi

YOUNG AT HEART/WISE IN TIME
Young at heart / Wise in time
CD ____ DE 423
Delmark / Nov '96 / ADA / Cadillac / CM / Direct / Hot Shot

Abrasive Wheels

VICIOUS CIRCLE
CD ____ AABT 807CD
Abstract / May '92 / Cargo / Pinnacle / Total/BMG

WHEN THE PUNKS GO MARCHING IN
CD ____ AHOY 25
Captain Oi / Nov '94 / Plastic Head

Abraxas

SKIN THRILLS
CD ____ TF 136512
TFI / Jul '95 / Plastic Head

Abraxas Pool

ABRAXAS POOL
Boom ba ya ya / Million miles away / Baila mi cha cha / Waiting for you / Going home / Szabo / Guajirona / Cruzin / Don't give up / Liego / Jingo
CD ____ IRS 993172
IRS / Apr '97 / Cargo

Abruptum

IN UMBRA MALFTJAE
CD ____ ANTIMOSH 009CD
Deathlike Silence / Apr '94 / Plastic Head

Abscess

IN YOUR MIND
CD ____ EFA 112812
Glasnost / May '95 / SRD

SEMINAL VAMPIRES AND MAGGOT MEN
CD ____ RR 69452
Relapse / Feb '97 / Pinnacle / Plastic Head

Abshire, Nathan

FRENCH BLUES (Abshire, Nathan & The Pinegrove Boys)
CD ____ ARHCD 373
Arhoolie / Apr '95 / ADA / Cadillac / Direct

GREAT CAJUN ACCORDIONIST, THE
La valse de meche / La valse de bayou teche / La valse du kaplan / T'en as eu mais t'en n'auras plus / La calse de belezaire / Le two-step de l'acadien / Cher ti-monde / Allons tuer la tortue / La valse des valses / Le blues francais / La valse de grand basile / Le two-step de choupique / Pauvre hobo / J'aimerais connaitre / La valse de la porte ouverte / Blues du tac tac / La valse du reveur / Hip et taiau / Jolie blon / Pine grove blues / La valse de choupique / Les flames d'enfer / Le temps est apres finir
CD ____ CDCHD 401
Ace / Apr '93 / Pinnacle

PINEGROVE BLUES/THE GOOD TIMES ARE KILLING ME
Pine grove blues / La valse de Holly Beach / Games people play / Service blues / Musician's life / Fee-fee pon-cho / Lemonade song / La valse de bayou teche / Sur la courtableau / I don't hurt anymore / Phil's waltz / Shamrock / Choupique two step / Tracks of my buggy / Nathan's lafayette two step / Dying in misery / Tramp sur la rue / Partie a grand basile / J'ai etais au balle / Valse de kaplan / If you don't love me / Off shore blues / Let me hold your hand / La noce a Rosalie
CD ____ CDCHD 329
Ace / Nov '93 / Pinnacle

Abstinence

FRIGID
CD ____ SR 9468
Silent / Jan '95 / Cargo / Plastic Head

REVOLT OF CYBERCHRIST
CD ____ SR 9440
Silent / Sep '94 / Cargo / Plastic Head

Absu

BARATHRUM VITRIOL
CD ____ OPCD 020
Osmose / Apr '94 / Plastic Head

SUN OF TIPERETH, THE
CD ____ OPCD 029
Osmose / May '95 / Plastic Head

THIRD STORM OF...
CD ____ OPCD 045
Osmose / Feb '97 / Plastic Head

Abutilon

TCH
CD ____ DOROBO 004CD
Dorobo / Oct '95 / Plastic Head

Abysmal

PILLORAIN AGE
CD ____ AV 007
Avant Garde / Feb '95 / Plastic Head / RTM/Disc

Abyss

OTHER SIDE, THE
CD ____ NB 1262
Nuclear Blast / Mar '95 / Plastic Head

SUMMON THE BEAST
CD ____ NB 209CD
Nuclear Blast / Nov '96 / Plastic Head

Abyssinians

BEST OF THE ABYSSINIANS, THE
Leggo beast / Let's my days be long / Satta a masagana / Jason Whyte / Reason time / Crashie sweeps / Jerusalem / Satta me born ya / Love comes and goes / Tena yistillin
CD ____ 111922
Musidisc / Mar '94 / Discovery

ORIGINAL ABYSSINIANS
CD ____ 021101
Graylan / Apr '97 / Grapevine/PolyGram / Jet Star

SATTA MASSAGANA
CD ____ HBCD 120
Heartbeat / Mar '93 / ADA / Direct / Greensleeves / Jet Star

AC

40 MORE REASONS TO HATE US
Face it, you're a metal band / Steroids guy / Trapped / Theme from Three's Company / Metamorphosis / I'm sick of you / Tom Arnold / Your family is dumb / Everyone in the underground music scene is stupid / Gloves of metal
CD ____ MOSH 149CD
Earache / Sep '97 / Vital

EVERYONE SHOULD BE KILLED
Some songs / Some more songs / Blur including new HC song / Even more songs / Tim / Judge / Spin cycle / Song 8 / Pavarotti / Unbelievable / Music sucks / Newest HC song / Chiffon and chips / Guy Smiley / Seth / I'm not allowed to like AC anymore / EXA Blur / GMOTR / I'm wicked underground / Blur including G / Shut up Mike / Abomination of unnecessarily augmented... / Radio hit / Loser / When I think of the true punk rock bands / Eddy Grant / MTV is my source for new music / Song titles are fucking stupid / Having to make up song titles sucks / Well you know, mean Gene / Song 5 / Iron funeral / Chapel of gristle / Hellbent for leatherman / Alcoholic / Chump change / Slow song for split 7" / Des Bink's hairstyle / Newest HC song / Greatful dead / Aging disgracefully / Brutally morbid axe of Satan / Surfer / You must be wicked underground if you own this / Choke edge / Otis Sistrunk / Russty knoife / Fred Bash / Guess which 10 of these are actual song titles / Our band is wicked sick (we have flu) / Guy le Fleur / Song 3 / Empire sandwich shop / Morrisey / Selling out by having song titles / Grindcore is very terrifying / Song 6 / Guy Lombardo
CD ____ MOSH 101CD
Earache / Sep '97 / Vital

I LIKE IT WHEN YOU DIE
CD ____ MOSH 169CD
Earache / Mar '97 / Vital

TOP 40 HITS
Some hits / Some more hits / Pepe, the gay waiter / Even more hits / MJC / Flower shop guy / Living colour is my favourite black metal band / Lenny's in my neighbourhood / Stayin' alive (oi version) / Benchpressing the effects on Kevin Sharp's vocal's / Josue / Delicious face style / Nineteen to go / Stealing Seth's idea (The new book by John Chang) / Morbid dead guy / Believe in the King / Don't call Japanese hardcore Jap core / Shut up Mike / Hey, aren't you Gary Spivey / Breastfeeding JMJ Bullocks' toenail collection / Fore play with a tree shredder / Two down five to go / I liked Earache better when Dig answered the phone / Brain dead / Newest HC Song / Sultry ways of Steve Berger / Escape (Pina colada song) / Lives ruined by music / Still a freshman after all these years / I'm still standing / Art fag / John / Newest HC song / Song 9 / Cleft palate / A-Team / Old lady across the hall with no life / Shut up Paul / Lazy eye (once a hank, always a hank) / American woman
CD ____ MOSH 129CD
Earache / Sep '97 / Vital

AC Acoustics

ABLE TREASURY
CD ____ ELM 21MCD
Elemental / Apr '94 / RTM/Disc

VICTORY PARTS
Hand pressed empty / Stunt girl / Ex quartermaster / Admirals all / Hammerhead / Kill Zane / Fast / Continuity freak / High divers / Absent luck liner / I messiah, am jailer / Can't see anything (red not yellow)
CD ____ ELM 31CD
Elemental / Jun '97 / RTM/Disc

Ac Alun, John

OS NA DDAY YFORY
CD ____ SCD 2112
Sain / Dec '95 / ADA / Direct / Greyhound

Ac Dhonncha, Sean

AN SPAILPIN FANACH
CD ____ CICD 006
Clo Iar-Chonnachta / Jan '92 / CM

AC Marias

ONE OF OUR GIRLS HAS GONE MISSING
Trilby's couch / Just talk / There's a scent of rain in the air / Our dust / So soon / Give me / To sleep / Looks like / Sometime / One of our girls has gone missing / Time was

CD CDSTUMM 68
Mute / Aug '89 / RTM/Disc

AC Temple

BLOWTORCH
CD FU 6CD
Furthur / Jul '88 / RTM/Disc

SOURPUSS
Sundown pet corner / Miss Sky / Stymied / Mother tongue / Crayola / Devil you know / Horsetrading / Mouthful / Faith is a wind-sock / Ringpiece / (Dirty) weekend
CD BFFP 45CD
Blast First / Sep '89 / RTM/Disc

AC/DC

74 JAILBREAK
CD 7567924492
Atlantic / Sep '94 / Warner Music

BACK IN BLACK
Back in black / Hell's bells / Shoot to thrill / Given the dog a bone / What do you do for money honey / Rock 'n' roll ain't noise pollution / Let me put my love into you / You shook me all night long / Shake a leg / Have a drink on me
CD 7567924182
Atlantic / Aug '94 / Warner Music

BALLBREAKER
Hard as a rock / Cover you in oil / Honey roll / Burnin' alive / Hail Caesar / Love bomb / Caught with your pants down / Whiskey on the rocks / Ballbreaker
CD 7559617802
Atlantic / Sep '95 / Warner Music

BLOW UP YOUR VIDEO
Heatseeker / That's the way I wanna rock 'n' roll / Meanstreak / Go zone / Kissin' dynamite / Nick of time / Some sin for nuthin' / Ruff stuff / Two's up / This means war
CD 7818282
Atlantic / Feb '88 / Warner Music

COVERED IN BLACK (A Tribute To AC/DC) (Various Artists)
CD CLP 9811
Cleopatra / Oct '96 / Cargo / Greyhound / Plastic Head / RTM/Disc / SRD

DIRTY DEEDS DONE DIRT CHEAP
Dirty deeds done dirt cheap / Love at first feel / Big balls / Rocker / Problem child / There's gonna be some rockin' / Ain't no fun waiting round to be a millionaire / Ride on / Squealer
CD 7567924142
Atlantic / Jul '94 / Warner Music

DIRTY WORDS (Interview)
CD 3D 006
Network / Dec '96 / Total/BMG

FLICK OF THE SWITCH
Rising power / Badlands / Brain shake / Flick of the switch / Deep in the hole / Landslide / Guns for hire / Bedlam in Belgium
CD 7567924482
Atlantic / Sep '94 / Warner Music

FLY ON THE WALL
Fly on the wall / Shake your foundations / First blood / Danger / Sink the pink / Playing with girls / Stand up / Hell or high water / Back in business / Send for the man
CD 7812632
Atlantic / Jul '85 / Warner Music

FOR THOSE ABOUT TO ROCK (WE SALUTE YOU)
For those about to rock (we salute you) / Put the finger on you / Let's get it up / Inject the venom / Snowballed / Evil walk / COD / Breaking the rules / Night of the long knives / Spellbound
CD 7567924122
Atlantic / Jul '94 / Warner Music

HIGH VOLTAGE
It's a long way to the top (if you wanna rock 'n' roll) / Rock 'n' roll singer / Jack / TNT / Can I sit next to you girl / Little lover / She's got balls / High voltage / Live wire
CD 7567924132
Atlantic / Jul '94 / Warner Music

HIGHWAY TO HELL
Highway to Hell / Girl's got rhythm / Touch too much / Beating around the bush / Shot down in flames / Get it hot / If you want blood (you've got it) / Love hungry / Night prowler
CD 7567924192
Atlantic / Aug '94 / Warner Music

IF YOU WANT BLOOD YOU'VE GOT IT
Riff raff / Hell ain't a bad place to be / Bad boy boogie / Jack / Problem child / Whole lotta Rosie / Rock 'n' roll damnation / High voltage / Let there be rock / Rocker
CD 7567924472
Atlantic / Sep '94 / Warner Music

LET THERE BE ROCK
Go down / Dog eat dog / Let there be rock / Bad boy boogie / Overdose / Crapsody in blue / Hell ain't a bad place to be / Whole lotta Rosie
CD 7567924452
Atlantic / Sep '94 / Warner Music

LIVE (2CD Set)
Thunderstruck / Shoot to thrill / Back in black / Sin City / Who made who / Heatseeker / Fire your guns / Jailbreak / Jack / Razor's edge / Dirty deeds done dirt cheap / Moneytalks / Hell's bells / Are you ready / That's the way I wanna rock 'n' roll / High voltage / You shook me all night long / Whole lotta Rosie / Let there be rock / Bonny / Highway to hell / TNT / For those about to rock (we salute you)
CD Set 7567922122
Atlantic / Nov '92 / Warner Music

LIVE (Highlights)
Thunderstruck / Shoot to thrill / Back in black / Who made who / Heatseeker / Jack / Moneytalks / Hell's bells / Dirty deeds done dirt cheap / Whole lotta Rosie / You shook me all night long / Highway to hell / TNT / For those about to rock (we salute you)
CD 7567922152
Atlantic / Nov '92 / Warner Music

POWERAGE
Gimme a bullet / Down payment blues / Gone shootin' / Riff raff / Sin City / Up to my neck in you / What's next to the Moon / Cold hearted man / Kicked in the teeth
CD 7567924462
Atlantic / Sep '94 / Warner Music

RAZOR'S EDGE, THE
Thunderstruck / Fire your guns / Moneytalks / Razor's edge / Mistress for Christmas / Rock your heart out / Are you ready / Got you by the balls / Shot of love / Let's make it / Goodbye and good riddance to bad luck / If you dare
CD 7567914132
Atlantic / Sep '90 / Warner Music

TRIBUTE TO AC/DC, A (Various Artists)
Riff raff: *AB/CD* / Razor's edge: *Belt* / Hell's bells: *Violent Work Of Art* / Hell ain't a bad place to be: *Straitjackets* / You shook me all night long: *Diamond Dogs* / Whole lotta Rosie: *Masquerade* / Jailbreak: *Tornado Babies* / Sin city: *Trilogy* / Back in black: *Fistfunk* / Overdose: *Downstroke* / Let there be rock: *Transport League* / Send for the man: *Feed*
CD TR 005CD
Tribute / Oct '96 / Plastic Head

WHO MADE WHO (Film Soundtrack For Maximum Overdrive)
Who made who / You shook me all night long / DT / Sink the pink / Ride on / Hell's bells / Shake your foundations / Chase the ace / For those about to rock (we salute you)
CD 7816502
Atlantic / May '88 / Warner Music

Acanto

LABIRINTO
CD BRAM 1989022
Brambus / Nov '93 / ADA

VERSO SERA
CD BRAM 1991232
Brambus / Nov '93 / ADA

Acapella

WE HAVE SEEN HIS GLORY
Sing to the glory / We have seen his glory / Glory in his name / We will see Jesus / How can I truly say / Good livin' / Talk to Jah / Angels long to look / I understood / To him who sits on the throne
CD 7019299601
Nelson Word / Mar '92 / Nelson Word

Acceleration

ACCELERATION
CD 8334732
ECM / May '88 / New Note/Pinnacle

Accelerators

DREAM TRAIN
CD FILERCD 404
Profile / Jun '91 / Pinnacle

Accept

ACCEPT
Lady Lou / Tired of me / Seawinds / Take him in my heart / Sounds of war / Free me now / Glad to be alone / That's rock 'n' roll / Hell driver / Street fighter
CD CLACD 404
Castle / Nov '95 / BMG

BREAKER
Starlight / Breaker / Run if you can / Can't stand the night / Son of a bitch / Burning / Feelings / Midnight highway / Breaking up again / Down and out
CD CLACD 245
Castle / Apr '92 / BMG

COLLECTION, THE
Lady Lou / I'm a rebel / Thunder and lightning / Breaker / Burning / Son of a bitch / Fast as a shark / Restless and wild / Princess of the dawn / Ball to the wall / London leather boys / Love child / Metal heart / Up to the limit / Screaming for a love bite / Monster man / TV War / King
CD CCSCD 311
Castle / Oct '91 / BMG

HUNGRY YEARS
Fast as a shark / Burning / Son of a bitch / Princess of the dawn / I'm a rebel / Breaker / Restless and wild / King / Midnight highway
CD CLACD 405
Castle / Oct '95 / BMG

I'M A REBEL
I'm a rebel / Save us / No time to lose / Thunder and lightning / China lady / I wanna be no hero / King / Do it
CD CLACD 244
Castle / '92 / BMG

OBJECTION OVERRULED
Bullet proof / I don't wanna be like you / Slaves to me:l / Objection overruled / This one's for you / Sick, dirty and mean / Projectors of terror / All or nothing / Rich and famous / Anamos la vida / Instrumental
CD 74321124662
RCA / Jun '96 / BMG

RESTLESS AND WILD
Fast as a shark / Restless and wild / Demon's night / Ahead of the pack / Shake your hands / Neon nights / Get ready / Flash rockin' man / Don't go stealing my soul away / Princess of the dawn
CD HMIXD 6
Heavy Metal / Apr '87 / Revolver / Sony

STEEL GLOVE
CD CCSCD 422
Castle / Oct '95 / BMG

Accidents

KISS ME ON THE APOCALYPSE
CD DRCD 004
Detour / Nov '95 / Detour / Greyhound

Accroche Note

LIVE IN BERLIN
CD FMPCD 83
FMP / May '97 / Cadillac

Accused

GRINNING LIKE AN UNDERTAKER
CD CDJUST 17
Rough Justice / Dec '90 / Pinnacle

MARTHA SPLATTERHEAD'S MADDEST STORIES EVER TOLD
CD WB 043CD
We Bite / Feb '89 / Plastic Head

SPLATTER ROCK
CD NMR 7103CD
Nasty Mix / Jun '92 / Pinnacle

Accuser

CONFUSION ROMANCE
CD CC 025052CD
Shark / May '95 / Plastic Head

TAKEN BY THE THROAT
CD 341682
No Bull / Oct '95 / Koch

Ace

BEST OF ACE, THE
How long / I'm a man / Ain't gonna stand for this no more / Rock 'n' roll runaway / Real feeling / Rock 'n' roll singer / You're all that I need / Twenty four hours / Crazy world / No future in your eyes / Tongue tied / Time ain't long / Sail on my brother / I think it's gonna last
CD SEECD 214
See For Miles/C5 / May '93 / Pinnacle

VERY BEST OF ACE
CD MCCD 123
Music Club / Aug '93 / Disc / THE

Ace Of Base

BRIDGE, THE
Beautiful life / Never gonna say I'm sorry / Lucky love / Edge of heaven / Strange ways / Ravine / Perfect world / Angels eyes / Whispers in blindness / My deja vu / Wave wet sand / Que sera / Just 'n' image / Experiemental / Blooming
CD 5296552
London / Nov '95 / PolyGram

HAPPY NATION
CD 5214722
London / Jul '93 / PolyGram

Aceto, Robby

CODE
Equation / Trust / Into indigo / Bells / Being there / Dog it was / Shane heads for the immaculate mountains / Black roses / Archangel
CD ALCD 1006
Alchemy / Aug '97 / Pinnacle

Acetone

CINDY
Come on / Pinch / Sundown / Chills / Endless summer / Intermission / Louise / Don't cry / No need swim / Barefoot on Sunday
CD CDHUT 13
Hut / Oct '93 / EMI

I GUESS I WOULD
Juanita / Late John Garfield blues / I guess I would / Sometimes you just can't win / All for the love of a girl / How sweet I roamed / Border lord
CD HUTMCD 21
Hut / Jan '95 / EMI

IF YOU ONLY KNEW
If you only knew / I don't really care / In the light / I've enjoyed as much of this as I can stand / Final say / When you're gone / Hound dog / 99 / What I see / Nothing at all / Esque / Always late
CD CDHUT 31
Hut / Mar '96 / EMI

Achenza, Paolo

DO IT (Achenza, Paolo Trio)
CD RTCD 401
Right Tempo / Jul '96 / New Note/Pinnacle / Timewarp

Achkar, Elie

MIDDLE EAST QANUN SONGS
CD 925582
BUDA / Jun '93 / Discovery

Acid Brass

ACID BRASS
CD BFFP 137CD
Blast First / Jul '97 / RTM/Disc

Acid Drinkers

DIRTY MONEY - DIRTY TRICKS
CD CDFLAG 59
Under One Flag / Jun '91 / Pinnacle

Acid Farm

SILVER SPIRAL, THE
CD PROPSCD 013
Proper / Jun '96 / Plastic Head

Acid Jesus

ACID JESUS
CD KLANGCD 1
Klang Elektronik / Aug '94 / Plastic Head

Acid Reign

FEAR, THE/MOSHKINSTEIN
CD CDFLAG 31
Under One Flag / Mar '89 / Pinnacle

OBNOXIOUS
CD CDFLAG 39
Under One Flag / Jul '92 / Pinnacle

WORST OF ACID REIGN, THE
CD CDFLAG 60
Under One Flag / Sep '91 / Pinnacle

Acid Scout

MUSIK FOR MILLIONEN
CD EFA 122882
Disko B / Oct '96 / SRD

SAFARI
CD EFA 122672
Disko B / Feb '95 / SRD

Ackerman, Will

OPENING OF DOORS, THE
CD 01934111142
Windham Hill / Sep '95 / BMG

PASSAGE
Remedios / Processional / Impending death of the virgin spirit / Pacific I / Bricklayer's beautiful daughter / Hawk circle / Annie's song / Passage
CD 01934110142
Windham Hill / Jul '93 / BMG

WINDHAM HILL RETROSPECTIVE, A
Bricklayer's beautiful daughter / Processional / Ventana / Santos and the well travelled bear / Slow motion roast beef restaurant seduction / Visiting / Anne's song / Impending death of the virgin spirit / Climbing in geometry / Opening of doors / Brother A teaches 7 / Seattle / Lago de montans (mountain lake) / Hawk circle / Region of clouds
CD 01934111212
Windham Hill / Mar '93 / BMG

Aconcha, Leandro

PIANO BAR (Aconcha, Leandro & Remi Chaudagne)
Entertainer / Don't start now / Seven days blues / Up to my house / All of me / Come in please / Give me a little peace / Don't try this / My baby's town / On the sunny side of the street / Nothing today / So tender for me / My little girl / C'est si bon
CD CDSGP 0161
Prestige / Sep '95 / Else / Total/BMG

Acoustic Alchemy

AGAINST THE GRAIN
Against the grain / Lazeez / Different kind of freedom / Lady Laynda / Road dogs / Shot the loop / Papillion / Silent partner / Nouveau tango

CD ______ GRP 97832
GRP / Oct '94 / New Note/BMG

ARCAN'UM
Columbia / Homecoming / Chance meeting / Lazeez / Mr. Chow / Same road same reason / Casino / Something she said / Jamaica heartbeat / Catalina kiss / Reference point / Hearts in chains
CD ______ GRP 98482
GRP / Jun '96 / New Note/BMG

BACK ON THE CASE
Alchemist / Jamaica heartbeat / Georgia Peach / Playing for time / When lights go out / Clear air for miles / Fire of the heart / Freeze frame / On the case / Break for the border
CD ______ GRP 96482
GRP / Aug '91 / New Note/BMG

BLUE CHIP
Catalina kiss / Blue chip bop / Making waves / With you in mind / Bright tiger / Ariane / Highland / Boulder coaster / Hearts in chains / No more nachos (por favor)
CD ______ GRP 01402
GRP / Mar '94 / New Note/BMG

EARLY ALCHEMY
Santiago / Sarah Victoria / Last Summer song / Slap it down / Sira's song / Moonstone / Wind it up / Casino / Little bercheres / Amanecer / Waiting for you / Return flight / Daybreak / Dream of fair women
CD ______ GRP 96662
GRP / Feb '92 / New Note/BMG

NATURAL ELEMENTS
Drake's dream / Overnight sleeper / Natural elements / Casino / If only / Ballad for Kay / Evil the weasel / Late night duke street
CD ______ GRP 01412
GRP / Mar '94 / New Note/BMG

NEW EDGE
Oceans apart / Notting Hill two-step / Slow ride home / Cool as a rule / Santa cafe / Arc en ciel / London skyline / Liason / Until always / Rive gauche / Act of innocence
CD ______ GRP 97112
GRP / Mar '93 / New Note/BMG

RED DUST & SPANISH LACE
Mr. Chow / Ricochet / Stone circle / Rideout / Girl with a red carnation / Colonel and the ashes / One for the road / Sarah Victoria / Red dust and spanish lace
CD ______ GRP 01392
GRP / Mar '94 / New Note/BMG

REFERENCE POINT
Reference point / Missing your touch / Take five / Same road, same reason / Make my day / Caravan of dreams / Homecoming / Cuban heels / Lullaby for the first born
CD ______ GRP 96142
GRP / Aug '90 / New Note/BMG

Acoustic Art

INTERLUDE
CD ______ BEST 1024CD
Acoustic Music / Nov '93 / ADA

Acoustick

OCTOBER
CD ______ ART 00052
Extreme / Nov '94 / Vital/SAM

Acquaragia Drom

ZINGARI
CD ______ SN 0044CD
Sudnord / Aug '96 / ADA

Acrimony

ACID ELEPHANT, THE
CD ______ GOD 019
Godhead / Oct '95 / Plastic Head

HYMNS TO THE STONE
CD ______ GOD 010
Godhead / May '95 / Plastic Head

TUMULI SHROOMAROOM
CD ______ CDVILE 68
Peaceville / Jul '97 / Pinnacle

Acrylic Tones

ACRYLIC TONES
CD ______ DRCD 002
Detour / Jan '95 / Detour / Greyhound

Act Of Faith

ONE VISION
Whole thing / Lost on a breeze / Doing it with love / Love not love / Soul love / Perfect world / Dream about you / Summer in the city / What'cha gonna do for me / Lite up your life / All for love / Looking at the world
CD ______ BRCD 613
4th & Broadway / Mar '95 / PolyGram

RELEASE YOURSELF
Release yourself / All over now / If u believe / From me to u / Do it right / Find your love / Do u remember / Only a child / Lost in love / Pleasure / Free / Forever sing / If u believe / Only a drum and a bass
CD ______ EXCDP 11
Expansion / Feb '97 / 3mv/Sony

Action

ULTIMATE ACTION, THE
I'll keep holding on / Harlem shuffle / Never ever / Twenty fourth hour / Since I lost my baby / My lonely room / Hey Sha-lo-ney / Shadows and reflections / Something has hit me / Place / Cissy / Baby you got it / I love you (yeah) / Land of 1000 dances
CD ______ EDCD 101
Edsel / Jan '88 / Pinnacle

Action Swingers

DECIMATION BOULEVARD
CD ______ TOAD 6CD
Newt / Jun '94 / Plastic Head

QUIT WHILE YOUR AHEAD
CD ______ TOAD 7CD
Newt / Oct '94 / Plastic Head

Acuff, Roy

KING OF COUNTRY MUSIC (2CD Set)
Tied down / What will I do / Is it love or is it lies / Lonesome Joe / Sweep around your back door / Don't say goodbye / Swamp Lily / Sixteen chickens and a tamborine / Rushing around / Whoa mule / Sunshine special / I closed my heart's door / I'm planting a rose / River of crystal / Please daddy forgive / Streamline heartbreaker / Six more days / Thief upon thee tree / Don't judge your neighbor / Night spots (Of the town) / Great speckled bird / Lonely mound of clay / Pins and needles (In my heart) / Wabash cannonball / Great judgement morning / Wreck on the highway / Precious jewel / Night train to Memphis / That's what makes the jukebox play / Little Moses / What do you think about me / Oh those tombs / Come back little pal / Fireball mail / I'm building a home (In the sky) / Great Titanic / Goodbye Mr. Brown / Mother hold me tight / Crazy worried mind / Along the China coast / It's hard to love / Plant some flowers by my graveside / I wanta to be loved / I like mountain music / Jesus died for me / Thank god / Were you there when they crucified my Lord / How beautiful heaven must be / Unclouded day / Hold to God's unchanging hand / Lord build me a cabin / Where the soul never dies / Shake my mother's hand for me / Take my hand, Precious Lord / This world is not my home / Where could I go but to the Lord
CD Set ______ BCD 15652
Bear Family / Mar '93 / Direct / Rollercoaster / Swift

Acuff's Rose

SON OF THE NORTH WIND
CD ______ 422444
WMD / Jan '97 / Discovery

Acustic

ACUSTIC VOL.1
CD ______ APR 012CD
April / Feb '97 / Plastic Head / Shellshock/ Disc

AD

AD
CD ______ RGE 101
Enemy / Nov '94 / Grapevine/PolyGram

DEAD WILL RISE
Joy for the world / If I could fly / Listen to the worlds / Pop song / Drop heavy / Bloodshed / Speak freely / Resting place / Dead will rise / Something special
CD ______ CDVEST 53
Bulletproof / Aug '95 / Pinnacle

AD.

ART OF THE STATE
CD ______ NUMA 0002
Numavox / Mar '97 / Cargo

Ad Vielle Que Pourra

AD VIELLE QUE POURRA
CD ______ GLCD 1099
Green Linnet / Mar '90 / ADA / CM / Direct / Highlander / Roots

COME WHAT MAY
CD ______ GLCD 1112
Green Linnet / Apr '92 / ADA / CM / Direct / Highlander / Roots

MENAGE A QUATRE
Menage a quatre / Les bois noirs / Ar vestrez kollet / Je ne voulais voir l'oiseau / La turlutte de la dure lutte / Ca manque pas de celtes / Ecoutez les mamans / Kalamatiano / Petite solo du matin / La fille du marechal de france / Cine citta / Le cultiv ateur / Flambee Saint-Marcoise / Un froncas au kebak / Ad va que pour elle / Bransle bas le con bas / Tarondelle / Andromadere
CD ______ XENO 4048CD
Xenophile / Mar '97 / ADA / Direct

MUSAIQUE
CD ______ GLCD 4017
Green Linnet / Apr '94 / ADA / CM / Direct / Highlander / Roots

Adam Ant

ANTICS IN THE FORBIDDEN ZONE
Zerox / Whip in my valise / Car trouble / Kick / Kings of the wild frontier / Ant music / Dog eat dog / Los Rancheros / Killer in the home / Stand and deliver / Beat my guest / Prince Charming / Ant rap / Desperate but not serious / Place in the country / Friend or foe / Goody two shoes / Strip / Puss 'n' boots / Apollo 9 / Vive le rock
CD ______ 4687622
Columbia / Jun '91 / Sony

DIRK WEARS WHITE SOX (Adam & The Ants)
Car trouble / Nine plan failed / Catholic day / Idea / Never trust a man (with egg on his face) / Animals and men / Family of noise / Table talk / Day I met God
CD ______ 4805212
Columbia / Jul '95 / Sony

FRIEND OR FOE
Friend or foe / Something girls / Place in the country / Desperate but not serious / Here comes the grump / Hello I love you / Goody two shoes / Crackpot history and the right to lie / Made of money / Cajun twisters / Try this for sighs / Man called Marco
CD ______ 4844362
Columbia / Jul '96 / Sony

HITS
Kings of the wild frontier / Dog eat dog / Ant music / Stand and deliver / Prince Charming / Ant rap / Goody two shoes / Friend or foe / Desperate but not serious / Puss 'n' boots / Strip / Apollo 9 / Vive le rock
CD ______ 4500742
CBS / Sep '86 / Sony

KINGS OF THE WILD FRONTIER (Adam & The Ants)
Dog eat dog / Ant music / Feed me to the lions / Los rancheros / Ants invasion / Killer in the home / Kings of the wild frontier / Magnificent five / Don't be square / Jolly Roger / Making history / Human beings
CD ______ 4779022
Columbia / Oct '94 / Sony

PRINCE CHARMING (Adam & The Ants)
Prince Charming / Scorpios / Picasso visita el planeta de los Simios / Five guns west / That voodoo / Stand and deliver / Mile high club / Ant rap / Mowhok / SEX
CD ______ 4746062
Columbia / Mar '96 / Sony

STRIP
Baby let me scream at you / Libertine / Spanish games / Vanity / Puss 'n' boots / Playboy / Strip / Montreal / Naval to neck / Amazon
CD ______ 4872392
Columbia / Mar '97 / Sony

VIVE LE ROCK
Vive le rock / Miss thing / Razor keen / Rip down / Scorpio rising / Apollo 9 / Hell's eight acres / Mohair lockeroom pin-up boys / No zap / POE / Human bondage den
CD ______ 4785042
Columbia / Feb '95 / Sony

WONDERFUL
Won't take that talk / Beautiful dream / Wonderful / 1969 again / Yin and yang / Image of yourself / Alien / Gotta be a sin / Vampires / Angel / Very long ride
CD ______ CDEMC 3787
EMI / Sep '97 / EMI

Adam Bomb

PURE SEX
CD ______ WKFMCD 140
FM / Mar '90 / Revolver / Sony

Adamo

LES MEILLEURS
Vous permettez, monsieur / La nuit / Laissons dire / J'aime une fleur / Les files du bord de mer / Car je veux / Une larme aux nuages / Ma tete / Vivre / Amour perdu / Sans toi, ma mie / Le barbu sans barbe / Il n'est pas fou / Les mal aimes / Quand tu reviendras / Femme aux yeux d'amour
CD ______ DCA 864502
Disky / Nov '96 / Disky / THE

Adamo, Salvatore

LA VIE COMME ELLE PASSE
CD ______ 472359
Flarenasch / Jul '96 / Discovery

Adams, Bruce

LET'S FACE THE MUSIC (Adams, Bruce/Alan Barnes Quintet)
Let's face the music and dance / Blowing with Bruce / Cool heights / Come back to bed / Give a little whistle / When it's sleepy time down South / Instep / Rosie B / Cubicle / Thrill is gone / Raincheck / Hollywood stampede
CD ______ ESJCD 547
Essential Jazz / Apr '97 / BMG

ONE FOOT IN THE GUTTER
One foot in the gutter / Blame it on my youth / Oh look at me now / Darn that dream / Scrapple from the apple / Over the rainbow / Someday sweetheart / What is there today / Robbins nest / Portrait of Jenny / Five brothers / (How little it matters) How little we know
CD ______ ESJCD 545
Essential Jazz / Apr '97 / BMG

SIDE-STEPPIN' (Adams, Bruce/Alan Barnes Quintet)
Side-steppin' / Coopers blues / Toot toot tootsie / Jitterbug waltz / Eternal triangle / Touch of your lips / Opus de funk / Soft shoe / Johnny come lately / Tin tin deo / Best thing for you is me / Ticklin / Quicksilver
CD ______ ESJCD 542
Essential Jazz / Apr '97 / BMG

Adams, Bryan

18 'TIL I DIE
Only thing that looks good on me is you / Do to you / Let's make a night to remember / 18 'til I die / Star / (I wanna be your) Underwear / We're gonna win / I think about you / I'll always be right there / It ain't a party...if ya can't come round / Black pearl / You're still beautiful to me / Have you ever really loved a woman
CD ______ 5406752
A&M / Feb '97 / PolyGram

BRYAN ADAMS
Hidin' from love / Win some lose some / Wait and see / Give me your love / Wastin' time / Don't ya say it / Remember / State of mind / Try to see it my way
CD ______ CDMID 100
A&M / Oct '92 / PolyGram

CUTS LIKE A KNIFE
Only one / Take me back / This time / Straight from the heart / Cuts like a knife / I'm ready / What's it gonna be / Don't leave me lonely / Best was yet to come
CD ______ CDMID 102
A&M / Oct '92 / PolyGram

INTERVIEW DISC
CD ______ SAM 7030
Sound & Media / Mar '97 / Sound & Media

INTO THE FIRE
Heat of the night / Into the fire / Victim of love / Another day / Native son / Only the strong survive / Rebel / Remembrance day / Hearts on fire / Home again
CD ______ CDMID 185
A&M / '92 / PolyGram

LIVE LIVE LIVE
She's only happy when she's dancin' / It's only love / Cuts like a knife / Kids wanna rock / Hearts on fire / Take me back / Best was yet to come / Heat of the night / Run to you / One night love affair / Long gone / Summer of '69 / Somebody / Walkin' after midnight / I fought the law / Into the fire
CD ______ 3970942
A&M / Aug '94 / PolyGram

RECKLESS
One night love affair / She's only happy when she's dancin' / Run to you / Heaven / Somebody / Summer of '69 / Kids wanna rock / It's only love: *Adams, Bryan & Tina Turner* / Long gone / Ain't gonna cry
CD ______ CDA 5013
A&M / Feb '85 / PolyGram

SO FAR SO GOOD (Collection Of The Best Of Bryan Adams)
CD ______ 5401572
A&M / Nov '93 / PolyGram

WAKING UP THE NEIGHBOURS
Is your mama gonna miss ya / Hey honey I'm packin' you in / Can't stop this thing we started / Thought I'd died and gone to heaven / Not guilty / Vanishing / House arrest / Do I have to say the words / There will never be another tonight / All I want is you / Depend on me / Everything I do (I do it for you) / If you wanna leave me (can I come too) / Touch the hand / Don't drop that bomb on me
CD ______ 3971642
A&M / Oct '91 / PolyGram

YOU WANT IT, YOU GOT IT
Lonely nights / One good reason / Don't look now / Coming home / Fits ya good / Tonight / Jealousy / You want it, you got it / Last chance / No one makes it right
CD ______ CDMID 101
A&M / Oct '92 / PolyGram

Adams, Cliff

AT YOUR REQUEST
We'll gather lilacs / It had to be you / Barcarolle / Entertainer/Solace / Come rain or come shine / That old black magic / Bewitched, bothered and bewildered / Air on a G string / Dancing in the dark / Lonely Man theme / Ole buttermilk sky / Intermezzo from Cavalleria Rusticana / La vie en rose / Unforgettable/They didn't believe me / They can't take that away from me / Sophisticated lady / Adagio in G minor / Satin doll / East of the sun and west of the moon
CD ______ CDMFP 6135
Music For Pleasure / Oct '94 / EMI

FORTIES ON PARADE, THE (Adams, Cliff Singers)
White cliffs of Dover / You'll never know / If I didn't care / I don't want to walk without you / When they sound the last all clear / I'll be with you in apple blossom time / Bless 'em all / It's a lovely day tomorrow / Hut sut song / Yes, my darling daughter / Don't sit under the apple tree / I'll never smile again / I don't want to set the world on fire / I'll walk alone / It's been a long, long time / Nightingale sang in Berkeley Square / We're gonna hang the washing out on the Siegfried line / This is the army Mr Jones / Ma I miss your apple pie / Kiss me goodnight Sergeant Major / I know why / At last / Elmer's tune / Tuxedo junction / Chattanooga choo choo / Little on the lonely side / Tangerine / Dolores / Who's taking you home tonight / If I should fall in love again / I yi yi yi yi I like you very much / Lili Marlene / Maybe / I'm gonna get lit up when the lights go on in London / You'd be so nice to come home to / You say the sweetest things baby / Yours / More I see you / Coming home / Roll out the barrel / Quarter master's store / Roll me over / Glorious victorious / She'll be coming round the mountain / Underneath the arches / Dreaming / Run rabbit run / London pride / Take me back to dear old blighty / Pack up your troubles (In your old kit bag) / It's a long way to Tipperary / Goodbye-ee / I'll get by / I'll be seeing you / We'll meet again
CD ______ **303600912**
Carlton / Apr '97 / Carlton

GOLDEN YEARS OF SONG, THE (Adams, Cliff Singers)
I hear you calling me / Drink to me only / Mighty like a rose / My old Kentucky home / Deep river / Sylvia / Will ye no come back again / Little yellow bird / Rosary / Can I forget you / Brown bird singing / Parted / Eriskay love lilt / Just a-wearyin' for you / Until / Old rustic bridge / Love's old sweet song / I'll take you home again, Kathleen / Kashmiri song / White wings / Lost chord / Good night ladies / Home sweet home
CD ______ **306252**
Hallmark / Jan '97 / Carlton

SING SOMETHING CHRISTMAS VOL.2 (Adams, Cliff Singers)
Let it snow, let it snow, let it snow / It's gonna be a cold, cold Christmas / Deck the halls with boughs of holly / Angels from the realms of glory / Amazing Grace / I saw three ships / Here we come a-wassailing / Morning has broken / Miner's dream of home / Do they know it's Christmas / Itty bitty baby / My ain folk / Mister Santa / When Santa got stuck up the chimney / Walking in the air / Christians awake / Sleigh ride / Sleep, baby, sleep / God rest ye merry gentlemen / Everything is beautiful / Lift a glass to friendship / It came upon a midnight clear / See amid the Winters snow / Happy Xmas (war is over) / Auld Lang Syne
CD ______ **CDMFP 6244**
Music For Pleasure / Oct '96 / EMI

SING SOMETHING COUNTRY (Adams, Cliff Singers)
Hey won't you play another somebody done somebody wrong song / Sweet dreams / I fall to pieces / He'll have to go / Sing me an old fashioned song / Don't it make my brown eyes blue / Red River Valley / Your cheatin' heart / Gentle on my mind / Don't let the stars get in your eyes / You're the only good thing that's happened / Rose garden / Rhinestone cowboy / I'm just a country boy / Hey good lookin' / Heartaches by the number / Jambalaya / Little bitty tear / Lucille / You're my best friend / Tip of my fingers / Help me make it through the night / It ain't me babe / Crazy / I love you because / Moonlight and roses / Most beautiful girl in the world / Galveston / Tennessee waltz / I recall a gypsy woman / Blanket on the ground / Honey come back / Fallen start / Walk on by / All I have to do is dream / Welcome to my world / King of the road / Story of my life
CD ______ **PWKS 4188**
Carlton / Feb '93 / Carlton

SING SOMETHING SIMPLE AT CHRISTMAS (Adams, Cliff Singers)
Sing something seasonal / Christmas alphabet / Winter wonderland / Have yourself a merry little Christmas / First Noel / Past three o'clock / Mary's boy child / Little donkey / When a child is born / Twelve days of Christmas / Little boy that Santa Claus forgot / I'm going home for Christmas / Jingle bells / Little drummer boy / Ding dong merrily on high / Good Christian men rejoice / Coventry carol / We wish you a Merry Christmas / I saw Mommy kissing Santa Claus / All I want for Christmas (is my two front teeth) / Rudolph the red nosed reindeer / Do you hear what I hear / We three kings / While shepherds watched their flocks by night / Once in Royal David's City / Hark the herald angels sing / Good King Wenceslas / Santa Claus is coming to town / Rockin' around the Christmas tree / Wonderful Christmas time / Silent night / Mistletoe and wine / Saviour's day / Holly and the ivy / In the bleak midwinter / Away in a manger / O come all ye faithful (Adeste Fidelis) / Christmas song / White Christmas
CD ______ **CDPR 104**
Premier/MFP / Dec '94 / EMI

SING SOMETHING SIMPLE FOR LOVERS (Adams, Cliff Singers)
I don't know why / Glory of love / Love in bloom / Melody of love / My wonderful one / Longing for you / Everywhere you go / Red roses for a blue lady / Lover and his lass / May you always / Matrimony / Forgotten dreams / Lover's concerto / I just called to say I love you / Let us be sweethearts / I'll always be in love with you / I love my baby / Honeysuckle and the bee / If I should plant a tiny seed of love / Be my little baby bumble bee / Love's last word / Parlez-moi d'amour / That'a amore / You are my sunshine / Viva l'amour / These foolish things / Peggy Sue / Every day / Moonlight sonata / Softly as I leave you / Stone in love with you / All alone / Because I love you / Speak to me pretty / Very thought of you / Touch of your lips
CD ______ **CDMFP 5997**
Music For Pleasure / Oct '93 / EMI

SING SOMETHING SIMPLE THE SINATRA WAY (Adams, Cliff Singers)
I'm beginning to see the light / You make me feel so young / I thought about you / High hopes / London by night / Foggy day / Girl from Ipanema / All or nothing at all / Fly me to the moon / It's nice to go trav'lling / Come fly with me / Three coins in the fountain / Young at heart / All the way / New York, New York / Chicago / My kind of town (Chicago is) / Gender trap / Love and marriage / Too marvellous for words / Swinging down the lane / Somethin' stupid / Strangers in the night / Lady is a tramp / It's all right with me / Something's gotta give / Nice 'n' easy / Witchcraft / At long last love / In the wee small hours of the morning / I couldn't sleep a wink last night / Nancy with the laughing face
CD ______ **CDMFP 5930**
Music For Pleasure / Nov '91 / EMI

VERY BEST OF SING SOMETHING SIMPLE VOL.1 (Adams, Cliff Singers)
CD ______ **PWKS 4187**
Carlton / Mar '94 / Carlton

VERY BEST OF SING SOMETHING SIMPLE VOL.2 (Adams, Cliff Singers)
CD ______ **PWKS 4189**
Carlton / Mar '94 / Carlton

Adams, Dave

DAVE ADAMS STORY, THE (The Joe Meek Collection)
CD ______ **GEMCD 013**
Diamond / Sep '97 / Pinnacle

Adams, Don

GET SMART
Washington 4 Indians 3 / School days / Satan place / Cone of silence / Too many chiefs/Countersign / Latest devices / All in the mind / Incredible Harry Hoo / I'm only human / Kisses for kaos / Plane sequence / Too many chiefs/Hotel sequence / Weekend vampire / Sorry 'bout that / 99 / Max / Get smart
CD ______ **RVCD 61**
Raven / Dec '96 / ADA / Direct

Adams, Elliott

THAT DEMON RAG
CD ______ **SOSCD 1299**
Stomp Off / Jul '96 / Jazz Music / Wellard

Adams, Gayle

GAYLE ADAMS/LOVE FEVER
Your love is a life saver / Stretchin' out / For the love of my man / You brought it on yourself / I don't wanna hear it / Plain out of luck / Baby I need your loving / Don't blame it on me / You don't owe me nothing / Let's go all the way / Love fever / I can't get enough of you / Don't jump to conclusions / I loved every minute of it
CD ______ **DEEPM 027**
Deep Beats / Apr '97 / BMG

Adams, George

CITY GATES (Adams, George & Don Pullen Quartet)
Mingus metamorphosis / Samba for now / Thank you very much Mr. Monk / Nobody knows the trouble I've seen / City gates
CD ______ **CDSJP 181**
Timeless Jazz / Aug '91 / New Note/ Pinnacle

DECISIONS (Adams, George & Don Pullen Quartet)
Trees and grass and things / His eye is on the sparrow / Message urgent / Decisions / Triple over time / I could really for you
CD ______ **CDSJP 205**
Timeless Jazz / Feb '91 / New Note/ Pinnacle

DON'T LOSE CONTROL (Adams, George & Don Pullen Quartet)
CD ______ **SNCD 1004**
Soul Note / Jan '87 / Cadillac / Harmonia Mundi / Wellard

EARTH BEAMS (Adams, George & Don Pullen Quartet)
Magnetic love / Dionysus / Saturday nite in the cosmos / More flowers / Sophisticated Alice
CD ______ **CDSJP 147**
Timeless Jazz / Mar '90 / New Note/ Pinnacle

HAND TO HAND (Adams, George & Danny Richmond Quartet)
CD ______ **SNCD 1007**
Soul Note / Jun '86 / Cadillac / Harmonia Mundi / Wellard

LIVE AT MONTMARTRE (Adams, George & Don Pullen Quartet)
CD ______ **CDSJP 219**
Timeless Jazz / Jan '88 / New Note/ Pinnacle

LIVE AT THE VILLAGE VANGUARD (Adams, George & Don Pullen Quartet)
Necessary blues / Solitude / Intentions / Diane
CD ______ **SNCD 1094**
Soul Note / May '85 / Cadillac / Harmonia Mundi / Wellard

SOUND SUGGESTIONS
CD ______ **5177552**
ECM / Jul '94 / New Note/Pinnacle

Adams, John

CHAIRMAN DANCES, THE
Chairman dances / Christian zeal and activity / Two fanfares for orchestra / Tromba lontana / Short ride in a fast machine / Common tones in simple time
CD ______ **7559791442**
Nonesuch / Jan '95 / Warner Music

CHAMBER SYMPHONY/GRAND PIANOLA MUSIC
CD ______ **7559792192**
Nonesuch / Jan '95 / Warner Music

DEATH OF KLINGHOFFER, THE
CD ______ **7559792812**
Nonesuch / Jan '95 / Warner Music

FEARFUL SYMMETRIES/THE WOUND DRESSER
CD ______ **7559792182**
Nonesuch / Jan '95 / Warner Music

HARMONIELEHRE
CD ______ **7559791152**
Nonesuch / Dec '95 / Warner Music

HARMONIUM
Negative love (part one) / Because I could not stop for death - Wild nights (part 2) / Negative love / Because I could not stop for death / Wild nights / Why do I / Laughin' and clownin' / If I ever had a good time / Scarred knees / Your love is so doggone good / We don't see eye to eye / Roadblock / Teach me to forget
CD ______ **8214652**
ECM / Apr '87 / New Note/Pinnacle

HOODOO ZEPHYR
CD ______ **7559793112**
Nonesuch / Jan '95 / Warner Music

NIXON IN CHINA (3CD Set)
CD Set ______ **7559791772**
Nonesuch / Jan '95 / Warner Music

Adams, Johnny

AFTER DARK
CD ______ **ROUCD 2049**
Rounder / '88 / ADA / CM / Direct

BEST OF NEW ORLEANS RHYTHM & BLUES VOL.1
CD ______ **MG 9007**
Mardi Gras / Feb '95 / Jazz Music

FROM THE HEART
I feel like breaking up somebody's home / Why do I / Laughin' and clownin' / If I ever had a good thing / Scarred knees / From the heart / Your love is so doggone good / We don't see eye to eye / Roadblock / Teach me to forget
CD ______ **ROUCD 2044**
Rounder / '88 / ADA / CM / Direct
CD ______ **FIENDCD 26**
Demon / Mar '92 / Pinnacle

GOOD MORNING HEARTACHE
CD ______ **ROUCD 2125**
Rounder / Oct '93 / ADA / CM / Direct

ONE FOOT IN THE BLUES
Won't pass me by / One foot in the blues / Baby don't you cry / Ill wind / Road block / Angel eyes / Half awoke / I wonder where our love has gone / Two years of torture / Cookin' in style / I know what I've got
CD ______ **ROUCD 2144**
Rounder / Oct '96 / ADA / CM / Direct

ROOM WITH A VIEW OF THE BLUES
Room with a view / I don't want to do wrong / Not trustworthy / Neither one of us / Body and fender man / I owe you / Wished I'd never loved you at all / Hunt is on / World I never made
CD ______ **ROUCD 2059**
Rounder / '88 / ADA / CM / Direct
CD ______ **FIENDCD 111**
Demon / Sep '91 / Pinnacle

VERDICT, THE
CD ______ **ROUCD 2135**
Rounder / Feb '95 / ADA / CM / Direct

Adams, Oleta

CIRCLE OF ONE
Rhythm of life / Get here / Circle of one / You've got to give me room / I've got to sing my song / I've got a right / Will we ever learn / Everything must change
CD ______ **8487402**
Fontana / Aug '91 / PolyGram

EVOLUTION
CD ______ **5149652**
Fontana / Jun '93 / PolyGram

MOVIN' ON
Never knew love / Once in a lifetime / I knew you when / You need to be loved / Slow motion / We will meet again / This is real / Life keeps moving on / Long distance love / Love begins at home / If this love should ever end / New star / Between hello and goodbye / Don't let the sun go down on me
CD ______ **5289902**
Fontana / Feb '96 / PolyGram

Adams, Pepper

10 TO 4 AT THE 5-SPOT (Adams, Pepper Quintet)
CD ______ **OJCCD 312**
Original Jazz Classics / Sep '93 / Complete/Pinnacle / Jazz Music / Wellard

CONJURATION/FAT TUEDAY'S SESSION
CD ______ **RSRCD 113**
Reservoir Music / Nov '94 / Cadillac

MASTER, THE
Enchilada / Chelsea Bridge / Bossallegro / Rue Serpente / Lovers of their time / My shining hour
CD ______ **MCD 5213**
Muse / Sep '92 / New Note/Pinnacle

MEAN WHAT YOU SAY (Adams, Pepper & Thad Jones)
CD ______ **OJCCD 464**
Original Jazz Classics / Jul '94 / Complete/Pinnacle / Jazz Music / Wellard

OUT OF THIS WORLD
CD ______ **FSRCD 137**
Fresh Sound / Dec '90 / Discovery / Jazz Music

PEPPER
Twelfth & pingree / A child is born / Well you needn't / Bossa nouveau / Osage Autumn / My funny valentine
CD ______ **ENJ 90792**
Enja / Sep '96 / New Note/Pinnacle / Vital/ SAM

STARDUST (The Bethlehem Blues) (Adams, Pepper & Donald Byrd)
CD ______ **BET 6000**
Bethlehem / Jan '95 / ADA / ZYX

Adams, S.A.

REDEMPTION
CD ______ **RTN 41209**
Rock The Nation / Feb '95 / Plastic Head

Adams, Terry

TERRIBLE
CD ______ **804732**
New World / Aug '95 / ADA / Cadillac / Harmonia Mundi

Adams, Tom

RIGHT HAND MAN
Bluegrass breakdown / John Hardy / You are my sunshine / Fiddle and the banjo / I saw the light / Old rugged cross / Old Joe Clark / Fireball mail / Polk country breakdown / Little Maggie / Cumberland gap
CD ______ **ROUCD 0282**
Rounder / '90 / ADA / CM / Direct

Adamson, Barry

DELUSION
CD ______ **CDIONIC 004**
Mute / Aug '91 / RTM/Disc

MOSS-SIDE STORY
Ring's the thing / Real deep cool / Final irony / For your ears only
CD ______ **CDSTUMM 53**
Mute / Feb '89 / RTM/Disc

NEGRO INSIDE ME
CD ______ **CDSTUMM 120**
Mute / Jun '93 / RTM/Disc

OEDIPUS SCHMOEDIPUS
CD ______ **CDSTUMM 134**
Mute / Jul '96 / RTM/Disc

SOUL MURDER
CD ______ **CDSTUMM 105**
Mute / Apr '92 / RTM/Disc

Adamson, Deirdre

COME SCOTTISH COUNTRY DANCING (Adamson, Deirdre Quartet)
CD ______ **DACD 9614**
Dee-Ay / Oct '96 / Duncans / Highlander

Add N To X

VERO ELECTRONICS
CD ____ BLOWUP 4CD
Blow Up / Aug '97 / Arabesque / SRD

Adderley, Cannonball

AFRICAN WALTZ
African waltz / Barefoot Sunday blues / Kelly blue
CD ____ OJCCD 258
Original Jazz Classics / Sep '93 / Complete/ Pinnacle / Jazz Music / Wellard

AUTUMN LEAVES (Adderley, Cannonball & Miles Davis)
CD ____ CD 53125
Giants Of Jazz / Jan '94 / Cadillac / Jazz Music / Target/BMG

CANNONBALL ADDERLEY COLLECTION VOL.3 (Jazz Workshop Revisited)
Pimitiva / Jessica's day / Unit 7 / Jive samba / Marney / Mellow buno / Lillie
CD ____ LCD 13032
Landmark / Jul '88 / New Note/Pinnacle

CANNONBALL ADDERLEY COLLECTION VOL.4 (The Poll Winners)
Chant / Azule serape / Heart alone / Lolita / Au privave / Never will I marry
CD ____ LCD 13042
Landmark / Apr '91 / New Note/Pinnacle

CANNONBALL ADDERLEY COLLECTION VOL.5 (At The Lighthouse)
Sack o' woe / Azule serape / Our delight / Big P / Blue Daniel / Exodus / What is this thing called love
CD ____ LCD 13052
Landmark / Apr '91 / New Note/Pinnacle

CANNONBALL ADDERLEY COLLECTION VOL.6 (Cannonball Takes Charge)
If this isn't love / I guess I'll hang my tears out to dry / Serenata / I've told every little star / Barefoot Sunday blues / Poor butterfly / I remember you
CD ____ LCD 13062
Landmark / Apr '91 / New Note/Pinnacle

CANNONBALL ADDERLEY COLLECTION VOL.7 (Cannonball In Europe)
P Bouk / Gemini / Work song / Trouble in mind / Dizzy's business
CD ____ LCD 13072
Landmark / Apr '91 / New Note/Pinnacle

CANNONBALL ADDERLEY IN CONCERT
CD ____ RTE 10042CD
RTE / Apr '95 / ADA / Koch

CANNONBALL AND COLTRANE (Adderley, Cannonball & John Coltrane)
Limehouse blues / Stars fell on Alabama / Wabash / Grand Central / You're a weaver of dreams / Sleeper
CD ____ 8345882
Mercury / Jul '92 / PolyGram

COUNTRY PREACHER
CD ____ CD 56053
Jazz Roots / Mar '95 / Target/BMG

DEEP GROOVE - BEST OF CANNONBALL ADDERLEY
Walk tall / Shake a lady / Why am I treated so bad / Mercy mercy mercy / Do do do (what now is next) / I'm on my way / Games / Happy people / Up and at it / Aries / Taurus
CD ____ CDP 8307252
Blue Note / Sep '94 / EMI

DIZZY'S BUSINESS
CD ____ MCD 47069
Milestone / Oct '93 / Cadillac / Complete/ Pinnacle / Jazz Music / Wellard

IN NEW YORK (Adderley, Cannonball Quintet)
CD ____ OJCCD 142
Original Jazz Classics / Feb '92 / Complete/Pinnacle / Jazz Music / Wellard

IN SAN FRANCISCO (Adderley, Cannonball Quintet)
CD ____ OJCCD 352
Original Jazz Classics / Feb '92 / Complete/Pinnacle / Jazz Music / Wellard

INSIDE STRAIGHT (Adderley, Cannonball Quintet)
Introduction / Inside straight / Saudade / Inner journey / Snakin' the grass / Five of a kind / Second son / End
CD ____ OJCCD 750
Original Jazz Classics / Oct '93 / Complete/ Pinnacle / Jazz Music / Wellard

JAZZ MASTERS
CD ____ 5226512
Verve / Apr '94 / PolyGram

JAZZ MASTERS
CD ____ CDMFP 6305
Music For Pleasure / Mar '97 / EMI

JAZZ PROFILE
One for Daddy-O / Au privave / Sack o' woe / Gemini / Mercy mercy mercy / Bohemia after dark
CD ____ CDP 85488982
Blue Note / May '97 / EMI

JULIAN 'CANNONBALL' ADDERLEY QUINTET (Adderley, Cannonball Quintet)
CD ____ COD 020
Jazz View / Jun '92 / Harmonia Mundi

KNOW WHAT I MEAN
Arriving soon / Well you needn't / New Delhi / Winetone star eyes / Lisa / Waltz for Debby / Goodbye / Who cares / Elsa / Toy / Nancy / Venice / Know what I mean
CD ____ OJCCD 105
Original Jazz Classics / Feb '92 / Complete/ Pinnacle / Jazz Music / Wellard

LIVE IN PARIS APRIL 1966
CD ____ 087172
Ulysse / Sep '95 / Discovery

LUGANO 1963
Jessica's birthday / Jive samba / Bohemia after dark / Dizzy's business / Trouble in mind / Work song / Unit seven
CD ____ TCB 02032
TCB / Sep '95 / New Note/Pinnacle

MERCY, MERCY, MERCY
Fun / Games / Mercy mercy mercy / Sticks / Hippodelphia / Sack o' woe
CD ____ CDP 8299152
Capitol Jazz / Jul '95 / EMI

NIPPON SOUL
CD ____ OJCCD 435
Original Jazz Classics / Feb '92 / Complete/Pinnacle / Jazz Music / Wellard

PARIS 1960 (Adderley, Cannonball Quintet)
Intro / Jeannine / Dis here / Blue Daniel / Chant / Bohemia after dark / Work song
CD ____ PACD 5303
Pablo / Aug '97 / Cadillac / Complete/ Pinnacle

PORTRAIT OF CANNONBALL (Adderley, Cannonball Quintet)
Minority / Minority (Take 2) / Minority (Take 3) / Straight life / Blue funk / Little taste / People will say we're in love / Nardis (take 5) / Nardis (take 4)
CD ____ OJCCD 361
Original Jazz Classics / Apr '93 / Complete/ Pinnacle / Jazz Music / Wellard

QUINTET PLUS
CD ____ OJCCD 306
Original Jazz Classics / Feb '92 / Complete/Pinnacle / Jazz Music / Wellard

RADIO NIGHTS
Little boy with the sad eyes / Midnight mood / Star fell on Alabama / Fiddler on the roof / Work song / Song my lady sings / Unit seven / Cannonball monologues on / Oh babe / Country preacher
CD ____ VNCD 2
Virgin / Feb '91 / EMI

SOMETHIN' ELSE (Adderley, Cannonball & Miles Davis)
Autumn leaves / Love for sale / Something else / One for Daddy O / Dancing in the dark / Alison's uncle
CD ____ CDP 7463382
Blue Note / Mar '95 / EMI

SPONTANEOUS COMBUSTION
Still talkin' to ya / Little taste / Caribbean cutie / Bohemia after dark / Chasm / Willow weep for me / Late entry / Spontaneous combustion / Flamingo / Hear me talkin' to ya / With apologies to Oscar / We'll be together again
CD ____ VGCD 650104
Vogue / Oct '93 / BMG

THINGS ARE GETTING BETTER (Adderley, Cannonball & Milt Jackson)
CD ____ OJCCD 322
Original Jazz Classics / Feb '92 / Complete/Pinnacle / Jazz Music / Wellard

THIS HERE
CD ____ CD 53121
Giants Of Jazz / Nov '92 / Cadillac / Jazz Music / Target/BMG

Adderley, Nat

BLUE AUTUMN (Adderley, Nat Quintet)
CD ____ ECD 220352
Evidence / Sep '92 / ADA / Cadillac / Harmonia Mundi

GOOD COMPANY (Adderley, Nat Quintet)
CD ____ CHR 70009
Challenge / Jun '95 / ADA / Direct / Jazz Music / Wellard

IN THE BAG (Adderley, Nat Sextet)
CD ____ OJCCD 648
Original Jazz Classics / Nov '95 / Complete/Pinnacle / Jazz Music / Wellard

LIVE AT THE 1994 FLOATING JAZZ FESTIVAL
CD ____ CRD 334
Chiaroscuro / Jun '96 / Jazz Music

MUCH BRASS (Adderley, Nat Sextet)
CD ____ OJCCD 848
Original Jazz Classics / Nov '95 / Complete/Pinnacle / Jazz Music / Wellard

ON THE MOVE (Adderley, Nat Quintet)
Malandro / Boy with the sad eyes / To wisdom, the prize / Naturally / Scene / Come in out of the rain
CD ____ ECD 220642
Evidence / Nov '93 / ADA / Cadillac / Harmonia Mundi

TALKIN' ABOUT YOU (Adderley, Nat Quintet)
Talkin' about you, Cannon / I can't give you anything but love / Arriving soon / Plum street / Azule serape / Ill wind / Mo's theme / Big P
CD ____ LCD 15282
Landmark / May '91 / New Note/Pinnacle

Addrisi Brothers

CHERRYSTONE
CD ____ DFCD 71254
Del-Fi / Apr '97 / Cargo / Koch

Addy, Obo

LET ME PLAY MY DRUMS (Addy, Obo & Kukrudu)
CD ____ BCA 00102
Burnside / Jul '96 / Koch

RHYTHM OF WHICH..., THE
CD ____ 42561
Earthbeat / Aug '96 / ADA / Direct

TRADITIONAL MUSIC OF GHANA
CD ____ CDEB 2500
Earthbeat / May '93 / ADA / Direct

Ade, King Sunny

LIVE JUJU
CD ____ RCD 10047
Rykodisc / Aug '91 / ADA / Vital

Aden

ADEN
CD ____ FOR 42
Fortune 4 / Jun '97 / Cargo

Adeva

ALL THE HITS IN YA FACE
Respect / Musical freedom: *Adeva & Paul Simpson/Carmen Marie* / Warning / I thank you / Beautiful love / Treat me right / Ring my bell: *Adeva & Monie Love* / It should've been me / Don't let it show on your face / I'm the one for you / Until you come back to me / Respect (Mix)
CD ____ MOCD 3005
More Music / Feb '95 / Sound & Media

HITS
Respect / I thank you / Warning / Beautiful love / It should've been me / Independent woman / Musical freedom: *Adeva & Paul Simpson* / I'm the one for you / Don't let it show on your face / Until you come back to me / You've got the best of my love / Ring my bell: *Adeva & Monie Love*
CD ____ CTCD 30
Cooltempo / Oct '92 / EMI

ULTIMATE ADEVA
Respect / I thank you / Warning / Beautiful love / Musical freedom / I'm the one for you / It should've been me / Don't let it show on your face / Until you come back to me / You've got the best of my love / Ring my bell: *Adeva & Monie Love* / Treat me right / It should've been me / I thank you
CD ____ CDGOLD 1035
EMI Gold / May '96 / EMI

Adhesive

SIDEBURNERS
CD ____ ASR 8
Ampersand / Jun '97 / Cargo

YOGURT
CD ____ BROOL 009CD
Adhesive / Mar '96 / Plastic Head

Adicts

27
Angel / Love sucks / Do it / That's happiness / Shangri la / Football fairy story / Rossini / Breakdown / Give me more / Fuck it up / GIRL / What am I to do / Rockers in rags / Let's dance / 7.27 / Bog / Come out to play / Just wanna dance with you
CD ____ CDPUNK 87
Anagram / Feb '97 / Cargo / Pinnacle

BEST OF THE ADICTS, THE
CD ____ DOJOCD 263
Dojo / May '96 / Disc

COMPLETE ADICTS SINGLES COLLECTION, THE
This week / Easy way out / Straight jacket / Organised confusion / Viva la revolution / Steamroller / Numbers / Chinese takeaway / You'll never walk alone / Too young / Bad boy / Joker in the pack / Shake rattle bang your head / Tokyo / Old couple / ADX Medley / Falling in love / It's a laugh / Saturday night / Champ elysees / Sound of music / Who split my beer / Cowboy
CD ____ CDPUNK 33
Anagram / Jun '94 / Cargo / Pinnacle

ROCKERS IN RAGS (Live In Alabama)
CD ____ FALLCD 046
Fallout / Jan '90 / RTM/Disc

SHE'S A ROCKER
CD ____ 15394
Laserlight / Aug '91 / Target/BMG

SONGS OF PRAISE
England / Hurt / Just like me / Tango / Telepathic people / Mary Whitehouse / Distortion / Get addicted / Viva la revolution / Calling calling / In the background / Dynasty / Peculiar music numbers / Sensitive / Songs of praise
CD ____ CLEO 2481CD
Cleopatra / Jan '94 / Cargo / Greyhound / Plastic Head / RTM/Disc / SRD

SOUND OF MUSIC
CD ____ CLEO 3315CD
Cleopatra / Jan '94 / Cargo / Greyhound / Plastic Head / RTM/Disc / SRD

THIS IS YOUR LIFE (1978-1980)
CD ____ FALLCD 021
Fallout / Sep '92 / RTM/Disc

TOTALLY ADICTED
Viva la revolution / Songs of praise / Get adicted / Sensitive / Just like me / Too young / Chinese takeway / Joker in the pack / Steamroller / How sad / Let's go / Easy way out / Smart Alex / Troubadour / Tokyo / Crazy / Bad boy / Runaway / Come along / I wanna be sedated / Falling in love again / It's a laugh / Saturday night / Zimbabwe brothers are go
CD ____ DOJOCD 69
Dojo / Feb '94 / Disc

ULTIMATE ADICTION (The Best Of The Adicts)
CD ____ CLP 9963
Cleopatra / Jul '97 / Cargo / Greyhound / Plastic Head / RTM/Disc / SRD

Adler, Larry

BEST OF LARRY ADLER, THE
CD ____ SWNCD 004
Sound Waves / Oct '95 / Target/BMG

BEST OF LARRY ADLER, THE
Genevieve waltz / Love themes & blues / Caravan / Stormy weather / I've got my love to keep me warm / Slumming on Park Avenue / Night and day / Tiger rag / It ain't necessarily so / Continental (you kiss while you're dancing) / Smoke gets in your eyes / I've got you under my skin / St. Louis blues / Shadow blues / Romance for harmonica & orchestra / Why was s I born / Pam-Poo day / Body and soul / Malaguena / Theme on four notes / Weeping willows (I'm stepping thro' plate glass windows) / Rhapsody in blue
CD ____ CDMFP 6259
Music For Pleasure / Sep '96 / EMI

GOLDEN ERA OF LARRY ADLER VOL.1
Continental / Smoke gets in your eyes / I won't dance / Why was I born / They all laughed / Caravan / Rhapsody in blue / Stormy weather / I've got my love to keep me warm/Slumming on Park Avenue / I've got you under my skin / Night and day / Tiger rag / Body and soul / Love come back to me / My melancholy baby / I got rhythm
CD ____ CDSGP 0119
Prestige / Aug '94 / Else / Total/BMG

GOLDEN ERA OF LARRY ADLER VOL.2
How high the moon / Blues in the night / Girl friend / Love for sale / My funny valentine / Le grisbi / This can't be love / Summertime / There's a boat dat's leaving for New York / Sophisticated lady / Little girl blue / Genevieve / Begin the beguine
CD ____ CDSGP 0120
Prestige / Oct '94 / Else / Total/BMG

GREAT LARRY ADLER
CD ____ PASTCD 7081
Flapper / Feb '96 / Pinnacle

MOUTH ORGAN VIRTUOSO, THE
I won't dance / Foggy day / Smoke gets in your eyes / Genevieve waltz / I got rhythm / Bolero / It ain't necessarily so / Continental / Londonderry air / Bach goes to town / Rifiti / My melancholy baby / Someone to watch over me / Hora staccato / They all laughed / They can't take that away from me / Le grisbi / Lover come back to me / La mer / Ritual fire dance / Bess you is my woman now / Tiger rag / Rhapsody in blue / Gershwin - King of rhythm
CD ____ CDEMS 1543
EMI / Nov '94 / EMI

PIANO ROLL RECORDINGS, THE
Our love is here to stay / My funny valentine / How high the moon / Begin the beguine / I can't get started / Rhapsody in blue / Minuet from L'Arlesienne / Blues in the night / As time goes by / Little girl blue / Mountain greenery / When day is done / Summertime / Man I love / It ain't necessarily so / I got rhythm / Tea for two
CD ____ CDSGP 0143
Prestige / Mar '95 / Else / Total/BMG

RHAPSODY IN BLUE
Continental / Smoke gets in your eyes / Sophisticated lady / Night and day / Tiger rag / Rhapsody in blue / Caravan / September in the rain / Moon at sea / Home town /

Creole love call / Isn't this a lovely day (to be caught in the rain) / Rubenstein's melody in F / Love me forever / Solitude / They all laughed / I've got you under my skin / I know now / Whispers in the dark / It looks like rain in Cherry Blossom Lane / Hungarian dance / They can't take that away from me / With plenty of money and you / Why was I born / Stormy weather / I won't dance
CD ____ RAJCD 835
Empress / Oct '94 / Koch

SUMMERTIME (The Best Of Larry Adler)
CD ____ PLSCD 131
Pulse / Apr '96 / BMG

Admiral Tibet

EXCITEMENT
Call upon Jah Jah / Burn in flames / Set me free / Keep the fire burning / Not a fool for you / Want to talk / Never overcome / Excitement / Since you've been gone / Rude boys
CD ____ 117502
Musidisc UK / Aug '95 / Grapevine/ PolyGram
CD ____ VPCD 1432
VP / Sep '95 / Greensleeves / Jet Star / Total/BMG

REALITY TIME
CD ____ VYDCD 5
Vine Yard / Sep '95 / Grapevine/PolyGram

TIME IS GOING TO COME, THE
CD ____ RNCD 2031
Rhino / Dec '93 / Grapevine/PolyGram / Jet Star

WEEPING AND MOURNING
CD ____ 794022
Melodie / Jul '97 / ADA / Discovery / Grapevine/PolyGram / Greensleeves / Jet Star

Adolescents

ADOLESCENTS, THE
I hate children / Who is who / Wreckin' crew / LA girl / Self destruct / Kids of the black hole / No way / Amoeba / Word attack / Rip it up / Democracy / No friends / Creatures
CD ____ 01022
Epitaph / May '97 / Pinnacle / Plastic Head

BALBAO FUN ZONE
CD ____ RR 94942
Roadrunner / Nov '88 / PolyGram

Adorable

AGAINST PERFECTION
Glorious / Favourite fallen idol / A to fade in / I know you too well / Homeboy / Sistine chapel ceiling / Cut / Crash sight / Still life / Breathless
CD ____ CRECD 138
Creation / Mar '93 / 3mv/Vital

FAKE
Feed me / Vendetta / Man in a suitcase / Submarine / Lettergo / Kangaroo court / Radio days / Go easy on her / Road movie / Have you seen the light
CD ____ CRECD 165
Creation / Sep '94 / 3mv/Vital

Adorjan, Andras

LAS FLAUTAS DE BUENOS AIRES (Adorjan, Andras & Jorge De La Vega)
Sur / Canaro en Paris / Cuando tu no estas / Jalouise / Fuimos / Palomita blanca / El choclo / El dia que me quieras / Taquito militar / Los mareados / A fuego lento
CD ____ 74321428122
Milan / Jul '97 / Conifer/BMG / Silva Screen

Adulescents UK

SOCIETY OWES ME A LIVING
Society owes me a living / No no / Jelly machete / Witch of insanity / No war no more / Deathwish
CD ____ REPCD 001
Rage / Oct '94 / Nervous / TKO Magnum

Advent

ELEMENTZ OF LIFE
There's no danger / Where in heaven / Audio illusion / Spaceism / Mad dog / It one jah / Overseyah / Bad boy / Farencounters / Electric jazz / Heights / Rhythm / Anno domini / Call God / Lie / City limits
CD ____ TRUCD 8
Internal / Sep '96 / Pinnacle / PolyGram

SHADED ELEMENTZ
CD ____ TRCDR 8
Internal / Sep '96 / Pinnacle / PolyGram

Adventures

SEA OF LOVE, THE
Drowning in the sea of love / Broken land / You don't have to cry / Trip to bountiful / Heaven knows which way / Hold me now / Sound of Summer / When your heart was young / One step from heaven
CD ____ 9607722
Elektra / Apr '88 / Warner Music

Adventures In Stereo

ADVENTURES IN STEREO
CD ____ BENT 015
Creeping Bent / Mar '97 / RTM/Disc

Adverse, Anthony

SPIN
Paradise lost / Best friend / Wednesday's child / Cold winds / Centre of your world / Good girl / Night and day / No sweet surrender / Wastelands of your soul / Spin
CD ____ ACME 22CD
El / Sep '89 / Pinnacle

Adverts

CROSSING THE RED SEA WITH THE ADVERTS
One chord wonders / Bored teenagers / New church / On the roof / New boys / Bombsite boys / No time to be 21 / Safety in numbers / Drowning men / On wheels / Great British mistake / Gary Gilmore's eyes / We who wait / New day dawning
CD ____ ESMCD 451
Essential / Mar '97 / BMG

LIVE AT THE ROXY
CD ____ RRCD 136
Receiver / Jul '93 / Grapevine/PolyGram

PUNK SINGLES COLLECTION, THE
One chord wonders / Quick step / Gary Gilmore's eyes / Bored teenagers / Safety in numbers / We who wait / No time to be 21 / New day dawning / Television's over / Back from the dead / My place / New church / Cast of thousands / I will walk you home
CD ____ CDPUNK 95
Anagram / May '97 / Cargo / Pinnacle

RADIO SESSIONS
One chord wonders / Bored teenagers / Gary Gilmore's eyes / New boys / Quickstep / We who wait / New church / Safety in numbers / Great British mistake / Fate of criminals / Television's over / Love songs / Back from the dead / I surrender / Adverts / I looked at the sun / Cast of thousands / I will walk you home
CD ____ PILOT 003
Burning Airlines / Jun '97 / Total/Pinnacle

Adzido

AKWAABA
CD ____ EUCD 1263
ARC / Mar '94 / ADA / ARC Music

SIYE GOLI (Adzido Pan African Dance Ensemble)
CD ____ EUCD 1223
ARC / Sep '93 / ADA / ARC Music

UNDER AFRICAN SKIES
CD ____ EUCD 1127
ARC / '91 / ADA / ARC Music

Aero

MASQUELERO
CD ____ 8357672
ECM / Jul '88 / New Note/Pinnacle

Aerosmith

AEROSMITH
Make it / Somebody / Dream on / One way street / Mama Kin / Write me a letter / Movin' out / Walking the dog
CD ____ CK 64401
Columbia / Nov '94 / Sony
CD ____ 4749622
Columbia / May '97 / Sony

BIG ONES
Walk on water / Love in an elevator / Rag doll / What it takes / Dude (looks like a lady) / Janie's got a gun / Cryin' / Amazing / Blind man / Deuces are wild / Other side / Crazy / Eat the rich / Angel / Livin' on the edge / Dude (looks like a lady) (live)
CD ____ GED 24546
Geffen / Oct '94 / BMG

BOX OF FIRE (13CD Set)
CD Set ____ 4778032
Columbia / May '97 / Sony

CLASSICS LIVE VOL.1
Train kept a rollin' / Kings and Queens / Sweet emotion / Dream on / Mama kin / Three mile smile / Lord of the thighs / Major Barbara
CD ____ 4749712
Columbia / Nov '93 / Sony

CLASSICS LIVE VOL.2
Back in the saddle / Walk this way / Movin' out / Draw the line / Same old song and dance / Last child / Let the music do the talking / Toys in the attic
CD ____ 4749722
Columbia / Nov '93 / Sony

DONE WITH MIRRORS
Let the music do the talking / My fist, your face / Shame on you / Reason a dog / She La / Gypsy boots / She's on fire / Hop / Darkness
CD ____ GFLD 19052
Geffen / May '94 / BMG

DRAW THE LINE
Draw the line / I wanna know why / Critical mass / Get it up / Bright light fright / Kings and Queens / Hand that feeds / Sight for sore eyes / Milk cow blues
CD ____ 4749662
Columbia / May '97 / Sony

GEMS
Rats in the cellar / Lick and a promise / Chip away the stone / No surprize / Mama kin / Adam's apple / Nobody's fault / Round and round / Critical mass / Lord of the Thighs / Jailbait / Train kept a rollin'
CD ____ 4749732
Columbia / Nov '93 / Sony

GET A GRIP
Intro / Eat the rich / Get a grip / Fever / Livin' on the edge / Flesh / Walk on down / Shut up and dance / Cryin' / Gotta love it / Crazy / Line up / Can't stop messin' / Amazing / Boogie man
CD ____ GED 24444
Geffen / Apr '93 / BMG

GET YOUR WINGS
Same old song and dance / Lord of the thighs / Woman of the world / Train kept a rollin' / Spaced / SOS (too bad) / Seasons of wither / Pandora's box
CD ____ 4749632
Columbia / May '97 / Sony

GREATEST HITS
Dream on / Same old song and dance / Sweet emotion / Walk this way / Remember (walkin' in the sand) / Back in the saddle / Draw the line / Kings and Queens / Come together / Last child / Mama Kin / Lightning strikes / Chip away the stone / Sweet emotion / One way street / Big ten inch record / Seasons of wither
CD ____ 4873502
Columbia / May '97 / Sony

LIVE BOOTLEG
Back in the saddle / Sweet emotion / Lord of the thighs / Toys in the attic / Last child / Come together / Walk this way / Sick as a dog / Dream on / Mama kin / SOS / Train kept a rollin' / Sight for sore eyes / Chip away the stone / I ain't got you / Mother popcorn
CD ____ 4749672
Columbia / May '97 / Sony

NIGHT IN THE RUTS
No surprize / Chiquita / Remember (walkin' in the sand) / Cheese cake / Three mile smile / Reefer head woman / Bone to bone (Coney Island white fish boy) / Mia / Think about it
CD ____ 4749682
Columbia / May '97 / Sony

NINE LIVES
Nine lives / Falling in love (is hard on the knees) / Hole in my soul / Taste of India / Full circle / Something's gotta give / Ain't that a bitch / Farm / Crash / Kiss your past good-bye / Pink / Falling off / Attitude adjustment / Fallen angels
CD ____ 4850206
Columbia / Mar '97 / Sony

PANDORA'S BOX
When I needed you / Make it / Movin' out / One way street / On the road again / Mama kin / Same old song and dance / Train kept a rollin' / Seasons of wither / Write me a letter / Dream on / Pandora's box / Rattlesnake shake / Walking the dog / Lord of the Thighs / Toys in the attic / Round and round / Krawhitham / You see me crying/Sweet emotion / No more no more / Walk this way / I wanna know why / Big ten inch record / Rats in the cellar / Last child / All your love / Soul saver / Nobody's fault / Lick and a promise / Adam's apple / Draw the line / Critical mass / Kings and Queens / Milkcow blues / I live in Connecticut / Three mile smile / Let it slide / Cheese cake / Bone to bone (Coney Island white fish boy) / No surprize / Come together / Downtown Charlie / Sharpshooter / Shithouse shuffle / South station blues / Riff and roll / Jailbait / Major Barbara / Chip away the stone / Helter skelter / Back in the saddle
CD Set ____ 4692932
Columbia / Dec '91 / Sony

PANDORA'S TOYS
Sweet emotion / Draw the line / Walk this way / Dream on / Train kept a rollin' / Mama Kin / Seasons of wither / Big ten inch record / All your love / Helter skelter / Chip away the stone / Rattlesnake shake
CD ____ 4769562
Columbia / Jun '94 / Sony

PERMANENT VACATION
Hearts done time / Magic touch / Rag doll / Simoriah / Dude (looks like a lady) / St. John / Hangman jury / Girl keeps comin' apart / Angel / Permanent vacation / I'm down / Movie
CD ____ GFLD 19254
Geffen / May '94 / BMG

PUMP
Young lust / FINE / Love in an elevator / Monkey on my back / Janie's got a gun / Other side / My girl / Don't get mad get even / Voodoo medicine man / What it takes
CD ____ GFLD 19255
Geffen / May '94 / BMG

ROCK IN A HARD PLACE
Jailbait / Bitches brew / Cry me a river / Jig is up / Push comes to shove / Lightning strikes / Bolivian ragamuffin / Prelude to Joanie / Joanie's butterfly / Rock in a hard place
CD ____ 4749702
Columbia / May '97 / Sony

ROCKS
Back in the saddle / Last child / Rats in the cellar / Combination / Sick as a dog / Nobody's fault / Get the lead out / Lick and a promise / Home tonight
CD ____ 4749652
Columbia / May '97 / Sony

TELLTALES (Interview Disc)
CD ____ TELL 12
Network / Jun '97 / Total/BMG

TOYS IN THE ATTIC
Toys in the attic / Uncle Salty / Adam's apple / Walk this way / Big ten inch record / Sweet emotion / No more no more / Round and round / You see me crying
CD ____ 4749642
Columbia / May '97 / Sony

TOYS IN THE ATTIC/DRAW THE LINE/ ROCKS (3CD Set)
Toys in the attic / Uncle salty / Adam's apple / Walk this way / Big ten inch record / Sweet emotion / No more no more / Round and round / You see me crying / Draw the line / I wanna know why / Critical mass / Get it up / Bright light fright / Kings and Queens / Hand that feeds / Sight for sore eyes / Milk cow blues / Back in the saddle / Last child / Rats in the cellar / Combination / Sick as a dog / Nobody's fault / Get the lead out / Lick and a promise / Home tonight
CD Set ____ 4853122
Columbia / Oct '96 / Sony

Affif, Ron

52ND STREET (Affif, Ron Trio)
Bohemia after dark / Stompin' at the Savoy / Moonray / Nightingale sang in Berkeley Square / I'll be seeing you / Yardbird suite / You don't know what love is / Steeplechase / Tadd's delight / Eric's zinc bar blues
CD ____ 23109582
Pablo / Nov '96 / Cadillac / Complete/ Pinnacle

Affinity

THIS IS OUR LUNCH
CD ____ CD 940
Music & Arts / Apr '97 / Cadillac / Harmonia Mundi

TRIBUTE TO ERIC DOLPHY, A
CD ____ CD 939
Music & Arts / Oct '96 / Cadillac / Harmonia Mundi

TRIBUTE TO ORNETTE COLEMAN, A
CD ____ CD 938
Music & Arts / Oct '96 / Cadillac / Harmonia Mundi

Afflicted

DAWN OF GLORY
CD ____ MASSCD 055
Massacre / Mar '95 / Plastic Head

PRODIGAL SUN
CD ____ NB 063CD
Nuclear Blast / Nov '92 / Plastic Head

Afghan Whigs

BLACK LOVE
CD ____ CDSTUMM 143
Mute / Mar '96 / RTM/Disc

GENTLEMEN
CD ____ BFFP 90CD
Blast First / Oct '93 / RTM/Disc

Afi

ANSWER TO THAT AND SAY
CD ____ 158112
Nitro / May '97 / Pinnacle / Plastic Head

VERY PROUD OF YA
CD ____ 158052
Nitro / Oct '96 / Pinnacle / Plastic Head

Africa System Dance

AFRICA SYSTEM DANCE VOL.2
CD ____ CD 77172
Eddy Black/Sonodisc / Jan '97 / Stern's

African Children's Choir

ARMS AROUND THE WORLD
It takes the whole village / Arms around the world / John 3:16 / Not too far from here / Abataka / Spread his love / Lord be magnified / Piletek / Take up your cross / Wanabino / Because he lives / I live
CD ____ ALD 078
Alliance Music / Oct '96 / EMI

WALKING IN THE LIGHT
Walking in the light / Man of the Lord / Be bold, be strong / Ndyahimbisa / Jubulant Africa / Awesome God / Generation song /

Steal away / Seed to sow / Nimoljwe kana / Mpulia Ebiwobe (cries of the Lord) / From a distance / We are the world
CD ALD 030
Alliance Music / Jun '95 / EMI

African Dream

AFRICAN DREAM, THE
CD EBCD 30
Eightball / Jan '95 / Vital

African Headcharge

AKWAABA
Can't waste time / Yes I / Glory dawn / To fari hail / More peace / Power from Zion / World peace / Cheer up / Walking thrill / All of the love / Irie day / Live good / Child's play
CD JAZIDCD 129
Acid Jazz / Nov '95 / Disc

GREAT VINTAGE VOL.1
CD ONUCD 2
On-U Sound / Jul '89 / Jet Star / SRD

GREAT VINTAGE VOL.2
CD ONUCD 3
On-U Sound / Sep '89 / Jet Star / SRD

IN PURSUIT OF SHASAMANE LAND
CD ONUCD 25
On-U Sound / Nov '93 / Jet Star / SRD

OFF THE BEATEN TRACK
CD ONUCD 40
On-U Sound / Mar '88 / Jet Star / SRD

SANKOFA
CD BONJO 2CD
Bonjo I / Jul '97 / Cargo

SONGS OF PRAISE
CD ONUCD 12
On-U Sound / '92 / Jet Star / SRD

Africando

GOMBO SALSA
CD SV 9604
Syllart / Jan '97 / Stern's

Afro Blue Band

IMPRESSIONS
CD MCD 92372
Milestone / Feb '96 / Cadillac / Complete/ Pinnacle / Jazz Music / Wellard

Afro Celt Sound System

VOL.1 (Sound Magic)
Saor/Free / News from nowhere / Whirl y reel 1 / Inion/Daughter / Sure as not / Sure as knot (Jungle segue) / Nil cead againn dul abhaile/We cannot go home / Dark moon, high tide (Including farewell to Eireann) / Whirl y reel 2 / House of the ancestors / Eistigh liomas sealand/Listen to me / Soar reprise
CD CDRW 61
Realworld / Jul '96 / EMI

Afro Cuba

ECLECTICISM
CD JHCD 039
Ronnie Scott's Jazz House / Mar '95 / Cadillac / Jazz Music / New Note/Pinnacle / TKO Magnum

After 7

AFTER 7
Don't cha think / In the heat of the moment / Can't stop / My only woman / Love's been so nice / One night / Ready or not / Sayonara
CD CDVUS 7
Virgin / Sep '89 / EMI

REFLECTIONS
Till you do me right / Cryin' for it / Save it up / Damn thing called love / How did he love you / What U R 2 me / How do you tell the one / Sprung on it / How could you leave / Givin' up this good thing / I like it like that / Honey (oh how I need you)
CD CDVUS 88
Virgin / Jul '95 / EMI

VERY BEST OF AFTER 7, THE
Sara smile / Ready or not / Can't stop / Heat of the moment / One night / Baby I'm for real (natural high) / Not enough hours in the night / Can he love u like this / Takin' my time / Gonna love you right / Nights like this / 'Til you do me right
CD CDVUS 121
Virgin / Mar '97 / EMI

After Dinner

AFTER DINNER
After dinner / Sepia-ture / Accelerating etude, An / Soknya doll / Shovel and little lady / Cymbals at dawn / Glass tube / Dessert / Sepia-ture II / Walnut / Cymbals at dawn II / RE / Kitchen life / Glass tube II / Variation of Would you like some mushrooms / Ironclad mermaid / After dinner II / Room of hair-mobile
CD RERADCD
ReR/Recommended / Apr '91 / ReR Megacorp / RTM/Disc

PARADISE OF REPLICA
CD RECDEC 28
Rec Rec / Oct '95 / Cadillac / Plastic Head / ReR Megacorp / SRD

After Hours

UP TO HERE
CD CMCD 069
Celtic Music / Mar '94 / CM

After Hours

TAKE OFF
Love attack / Better late than never / Stay by my side / Take off / Game / Another lonely night / Paint it black / Without you
CD WKFMXD 89
FM / Aug '88 / Revolver / Sony

After The Fire

DER KOMMISSAR
Der Kommissar / Who's gonna love you / Frozen rivers / Joy / Dancing in the shadows / Billy / 1980-F / Rich boys / Starlight / Laser love / Love wll always make you cry / One rule for you / Sailing ship
CD 4809732
Columbia / Aug '95 / Sony

Afterlife

JUST TRIP
CD VIRUS 192CD
Alternative Tentacles / Jun '97 / Cargo / Greyhound / Pinnacle

Afternoons

HOMAGE
CD CBM 008CD
Cross Border Media / Jan '94 / ADA / Direct / Grapevine/PolyGram

Age

ORION YEARS
CD EFA 006532
Force Inc. / Jul '94 / Amato Disco / Arabesque / SRD

Agent Orange

REAL LIVE SOUND
CD 725292
Restless / Feb '95 / Vital

THIS IS THE VOICE
CD 725402
Restless / Feb '95 / Vital

VIRTUALLY INDESTRUCTIBLE
CD 245T4
Gunka Disc / Jan '97 / Cargo

WHEN YOU LEAST EXPECT IT
CD 722182
Restless / Feb '95 / Vital

Agent Provocateur

WHERE THE WILD THINGS ARE
Where the wild things are / Red tape / Spinning / Agent Dan / Kicks / Sabotage / Elvis economics / Sandpit / Hercules / You're no good / Dumb / Red tape / Agent Dan / Sabotage / Dumb
CD AGENTP 1CD
Wall Of Sound/Epic / Mar '97 / Sony

Agent Steel

UNSTOPPABLE FORCE
CD CDMFN 66
Music For Nations / Aug '89 / Pinnacle

Aghast

HEXERI IM ZWEILICHT
CD CM 1033CD
Cold Meat Industry / Aug '95 / Plastic Head / RTM/Disc

Agincourt

FLY AWAY
CD HBG 123/6
Background / Jun '97 / Background / Greyhound

Agnew, David

CELTIC MOODS (Agnew, David & David Downes)
Mo ghile mear / Katie / Lift the wings / Move on / Into the mist / Death of Richard-In-Irons / Riverdance / Celtic dawn / Winter's end / Airwaves / Bright blue rose / My Lagan love / In this heart / Still haven't found what I'm looking for / My Rathfarnham darlin's
CD KCD 405
Celtic Collections / Jan '97 / Target/BMG

Agnostic Front

CAUSE FOR ALARM
CD CDJUST 3
Rough Justice / May '86 / Pinnacle

RAW UNLEASHED
CD GTA 002R051
Grand Theft Auto / Jul '95 / Cargo / Plastic Head

Agony

FIRST DEFIANCE, THE
Hey Suze / Falling rain / Discipline / Chasing dreams / Ah-ha / Sailors on the sea / Stalk the girls / Dream girl / Strung out on you / Country girl / Goodnight darling
CD CDFLAG 19
Under One Flag / Apr '88 / Pinnacle

Agony Column

BRAVE WORDS AND BLOODY KNUCKLES
CD 341422
No Bull / Oct '95 / Koch

Agothocles

BLACK CLOUDS DETERMINATE
CD CYBERCD 10
Cyber / Aug '94 / Amato Disco / Arabesque / Plastic Head

THEATRICAL SYMBOLIZATION
CD CYBERCD 2
Cyber / Jun '92 / Amato Disco / Arabesque / Plastic Head

Agression

DON'T BE MISTAKEN
CD BYO 003CD
Better Youth Organisation / Jan '97 / Cargo

Agressor

SATAN'S SODOMY
CD BMCD 36
Black Mark / Jun '94 / Plastic Head

SYMPOSIUM OF REBIRTH
CD BMCD 55
Black Mark / Oct '94 / Plastic Head

TOWARDS BEYOND
Intro / Forteress / Positonic showering / Antediluvian / Epileptic aura / Hyaloid / Crypt / Future past/Eldest things / Turkish march
CD BMCD 23
Black Mark / Sep '92 / Plastic Head

Agudo, Luis

DONA FIA
CD 123442
Red / Apr '93 / ADA / Cadillac / Harmonia Mundi

Aguilera, Paco

GUITARRA AND CANTO FLAMENCO
CD KAR 983
IMP / Sep '96 / ADA / Discovery

Agyeman, Eric

HIGH LIFE SAFARI
CD STCD 3002
Stern's / Nov '92 / ADA / CM / Stern's

Ah Club

KISS THE SKY GOODBYE
CD SHR 76CD
Shrimper / Feb '97 / Cargo

Ahlam

LES RIAM
CD BARBARITY 012
Barbarity / Jan '97 / Stern's

Ahmad

AHMAD
Freak / Back in the day / Touch the ceiling / Jones / Can I party / You gotta be / We want the funk / Palladium / Homeboy's first / Ordinary people / Back in the day (remix)
CD 74321199282
Arista / Jul '94 / BMG

Ahmed, Mahmoud

ERE MELA MELA
CD CRAW 9
Crammed Discs / Feb '96 / Grapevine/ PolyGram / New Note/Pinnacle / Prime / RTM/Disc

Ain Soph

KSHATRIYA
CD EEE 21
Musica Maxima Magnetica / Aug '94 / Cargo / Plastic Head

Ainsworth, Alyn

MOTOWN PARTY (30 Blockbuster Hits)
Standing in the shadows of love / It's the same old song / Reach out, I'll be there / Walk away Renee / Supremes medley / Ain't no mountain high enough / I'm still waiting / Sir Duke / Superstition / Living for the city / I'm gonna make you love me / Signed, sealed, delivered (I'm yours) / With you I'm born again / Dancing in the street / What becomes of the broken hearted / I hear a symphony: *City Dread* / My cherie amour / Stop in the name of love / Baby love / Where did our love go / You can't hurry love / Still water (love) / You are the sunshine of my life / Yester-me, yester-you, yesterday / I was made to love her / I just called to say I love you / Reach out and touch / Tears of a clown
CD CDSIV 1127
Horatio Nelson / Jul '95 / Disc

Ain't

SLAP THE JUDGE
CD SEMAPHORE 36162
Subway / Nov '96 / Cargo / Vital

Aints

ASCENSION
It's still nowhere / What's it like out there / Good soundtrack / Like an oil spill / Both worlds / Ascension
CD HOT 1035CD
Hot / May '97 / Hot Records

AUTOCANNIBALISM
You can't please everybody / Other side of the creek / Linda and Abilene / Ill wind / Red aces / Aints go pop camping
CD HOT 1037CD
Hot / May '97 / Hot Records

MOST PRIMITIVE BAND IN THE WORLD, THE (Live From The Twilight Zone, Brisbane 1974)
Wild about you / Do the robot / One way street / Knock on wood / Erotic neurotic / River deep, mountain high / Lies / Misunderstood / Messin' with the kid / Stranded
CD HOT 1053CD
Hot / May '97 / Hot Records

SHELF LIFE UNLIMITED - HOTTER THAN BLAZING PISTOLS
Like an oil spill / Ill wind / River deep, mountain high / It's still nowhere / Erotic neurotic / Aints go pop dancing / What's it like out there / Linda and Abilene
CD HOT 1054CD
Hot / Aug '95 / Hot Records

Air

AIR TIME
CD NCD 12
Nessa / Jun '97 / Harmonia Mundi

Air

AIR
CD RSNCD 10
Rising High / Sep '93 / 3mv/Sony

Air Command Band ...

SILENT SKY (Air Command Band Canadian Forces)
John Gay suite / Gordon Lightfoot medley / Far and Away / Copland portrait / Wind beneath my wings / Music for a tattoo / White cliffs of Dover / Airman's prayer / RCAF march past
CD BNA 5100
Bandleader / Jul '95 / Conifer/BMG

Air Liquide

AIR LIQUIDE
CD 8597082
Harvest / Aug '97 / Cargo / SRD

AIR LIQUIDE LIVE
CD RSNCD 37
Rising High / Jul '95 / 3mv/Sony

NEPHOLOGY
CD RSNCD 15
Rising High / Apr '94 / 3mv/Sony

SONIC WEATHER MACHINE
CD RSNCD 38
Rising High / Jun '96 / 3mv/Sony

Air Supply

MAKING LOVE (The Best Of Air Supply)
Lost in love / Even the nights are better / One that you love / Every woman in the world / Two less lonely people in the world / Chances / Making love out of nothing at all / All out of love / Here I am / Sweet dreams / Keeping the love alive / Now and forever
CD 260757
Arista / May '90 / BMG

VANISHING RACE, THE
CD 74321147972
Giant / Feb '96 / BMG

Airdash

BOTH ENDS OF THE PATH
CD BMCD 14
Black Mark / '92 / Plastic Head

Airstream

RICKY TICK
Bright lights / Stay with me / I'll dream of you / Airstream / Follow through / Statue Queen / Fortuna / Jessica / My eyes / Brush your hair

CD _______________ TPLP 36CD
One Little Indian / Mar '93 / Pinnacle

Aisha

DAUGHTERS OF ZION
CD _______________ NG 538CD
Twinkle / May '93 / Jet Star / Kingdom / SRD

RAISE YOUR VOICE
CD _______________ NGCD 551
Twinkle / Jul '90 / Jet Star / Kingdom / SRD

TRUE ROOTS
CD _______________ ARICD 084
Ariwa Sounds / Mar '94 / Jet Star / SRD

Ait

MODERN BERBER SONGS
CD _______________ AAA 145
Club Du Disque Arabe / Apr '97 / ADA / Harmonia Mundi

Aitken, Laurel

EARLY DAYS OF BLUE BEAT, SKA AND REGGAE (Aitken, Laurel & Friends)
CD _______________ BRMCD 025
Bold Reprive / Oct '88 / Harmonia Mundi

GODFATHER OF SKA
CD _______________ GAZCD 009
Gaz's Rockin' Records / Apr '95 / Shellshock/Disc

LONG HOT SUMMER (Aitken, Laurel & The Skatalites)
CD _______________ PHZCD 59
Unicorn / Nov '93 / Plastic Head

RINGO THE GRINGO
CD _______________ PHZCD 50
Unicorn / Jun '93 / Plastic Head

RISE AND FALL/IT'S TOO LATE
CD _______________ PHZCD 71
Unicorn / Jun '93 / Plastic Head

ROCKSTEADY PARTY
Rocksteady party / That was then / Do the jerk / Burnin' fire / Pancho / Bluebeat suit / Things that I do / Dial m for murder / Reburial / Car chase / Got to go / He man versus
CD _______________ CDBM 115
Blue Moon / Nov '96 / Cadillac / Discovery / Greensleeves / Jazz Music / Jet Star / TKO Magnum

WOPPI KING - REGGAE VOL.1
CD _______________ TRRCD 02
Trybute / Jul '97 / SRD

Akabu

WARRIOR QUEEN
CD _______________ ONUCD 71
On-U Sound / Oct '95 / Jet Star / SRD

Akademia

ANCIENT ECHOES
CD _______________ 09026680552
RCA Victor / May '95 / BMG

Akagi, Kei

MIRROR PUZZLE
CD _______________ AQ 1028
Audioquest / Apr '95 / ADA / New Note/ Pinnacle

Akendague, Pierre

MALADALITE
CD _______________ 669762
Melodie / Jul '96 / ADA / Discovery / Grapevine/PolyGram / Greensleeves / Jet Star

Akers, Karen

JUST IMAGINE
Night, make my day / Nightingale sang in Berkeley Square / Remind me / Just imagine/You're nearer / Ain't misbehavin' / I'd rather be blue / More than you know / Angels, punks and raging queen / Twentieth century blues / I see the world through your eyes / My ship / I am your child / Two for the road
CD _______________ DRGCD 5231
DRG / Sep '94 / Discovery / New Note/ Pinnacle

LIVE FROM THE RAINBOW AND STARS
CD _______________ DRGCD 91450
DRG / Sep '97 / Discovery / New Note/ Pinnacle

UNCHAINED MELODIES
If I sing / Sooner or later / Blame it on the summer night / I fall in love too easily / I never know when to say when / I waltz alone / How sad no one waltzes anymore / Picture in the hall / Life story / Unchained melody / Bewitched, bothered and bewildered / L'Annee ou Piccoli / Isn't it a pity / Every time we say goodbye / Here I'll stay / Falling in love again / What'll I do / Dream a little dream of me
CD _______________ CDSL 5214
DRG / Mar '92 / Discovery / New Note/ Pinnacle

Akhbari, Djalal

ART OF THE PERSIAN SANTUR
CD _______________ ARN 60351
Arion / Sep '96 / ADA / Discovery

Akhenation

DIVINE SYMPHONIES
CD _______________ CDAR 030
Adipocre / Jan '96 / Plastic Head

Akins, Rhett

SOMEBODY NEW
No match (for that old flame) / love you back / Somebody knew / K-i-s-s-i-n-g / Don't get me started / Where angels live / Too much Texas / Every cowboy's dream / Carolina line / I was wrong
CD _______________ MCD 11508
MCA / Sep '96 / BMG

Akipa, Bryan

FLUTE PLAYER, THE
CD _______________ 14941
Spalax / Jun '97 / ADA / Cargo / Direct / Discovery / Greyhound

Akita, Masami

PROSPERITY OF VICE, THE MISFORTUNE OF VIRTUE
CD _______________ IRE 2022
Che / Mar '97 / SRD

Akiyoshi, Toshiko

AKIYOSHI/MARIANO QUARTET (Akiyoshi, Toshiko & Charlie Mariano Quartet)
CD _______________ CCD 9012
Candid / Jun '88 / Cadillac / Direct / Jazz Music / Koch / Wellard

INTERLUDE
Interlude / I know who loves you / Blue and sentimental / I ain't gonna ask no more / Pagliacci / Solitude / So in love / You stepped out of a dream
CD _______________ CCD 4324
Concord Jazz / Sep '87 / New Note/ Pinnacle

LIVE AT MAYBECK RECITAL HALL VOL.36
Village / Come Sunday / Con alma / Polka dots and moonbeams / It was a very good year / Things we did last summer / Old devil moon / Sophisticated lady / Quadrille, anyone / Tempous fugit
CD _______________ CCD 4635
Concord Jazz / Feb '95 / New Note/ Pinnacle

REMEMBERING BUD
CD _______________ ECD 220342
Evidence / Sep '92 / ADA / Cadillac / Harmonia Mundi

TOSHIKO MARIANO QUARTET (Akiyoshi, Toshiko & Charlie Mariano Quartet)
When you meet her / Little T / Toshiko's elegy / Deep river / Long yellow road
CD _______________ CCD 79012
Candid / Feb '97 / Cadillac / Direct / Jazz Music / Koch / Wellard

Akkerman, Jan

CAN'T STAND THE NOISE
Pietons / Everything must change / Back to the factory / Journey (a real elegant gypsy) / Heavy treasure / Just because / Crackers / Burger blues / Prima donna / Sketches of pleasure
CD _______________ INAK 11001CD
In Akustik / Jul '97 / Direct / TKO Magnum

COMPLETE GUITARIST, THE
Old tennis shoes / Come closer / Funkology / It could happen to you / Pietons / Journey (a real elegant gypsy)
CD _______________ CDCHARLY 17
Charly / Jun '86 / Koch

KIEL/STUTTGART LIVE (Akkerman, Jan & Joachim Kuhn)
Santa Barbara / Santa Barbara
CD _______________ INAK 868CD
In Akustik / Jul '97 / Direct / TKO Magnum

LIVE
CD _______________ CDP 1034DD
Pseudonym / Jun '97 / Greyhound

PUCCINI'S CAFE
Burger's eyes / Your eyes in the whisky / Spanish roads / Key to the highway / It comes and goes / Albatross / Blue train / Love is uneven / Puccini's cafe
CD _______________ INAK 9027
In Akustik / May '95 / Direct / TKO Magnum

Al Junayd, Hamud

TRADITIONAL YEMENI SONGS
CD _______________ NI 5481
Nimbus / Apr '96 / Nimbus

Al-Dhil, Nuba Rasd

AL-ALA
CD _______________ W 260029
Inedit / Feb '96 / ADA / Discovery / Harmonia Mundi

Alabama

DANCING ON THE BOULEVARD
Dancin' shaggin' on the boulevard / Sad lookin' moon / Anytime / She's got that look in her eyes / My girl / Of course I'm alright / I just couldn't say no / Is the magic still there / Calling all angels / One more time around
CD _______________ 07863674262
RCA / Apr '97 / BMG

Alan, Josh

WORST, THE
CD _______________ GORSE 6CD
Gorse / Jul '95 / RTM/Disc

Alanski, Jay H.

HONEY ON A RAZOR BLADE
CD _______________ 592204
FNAC / Oct '93 / Discovery

Alarm

DECLARATION
Declaration / Marching on / Where were you when the storm broke / Third light / Sixty eight guns / We are the light / Shout to the devil / Blaze of glory / Tell me / Deceiver / Stand (prophecy) / Howling wind
CD _______________ CDMID 103
A&M / Oct '92 / PolyGram

Alaska

HEART OF THE STORM
Whiteout / Don't say it's over / Voice on the radio / Susie blue / Heart of the storm / Need your love / Can't let go / Other side of midnight / Headlines / Sorcerer
CD _______________ CLACD 423
Castle / Nov '96 / BMG

Alastis

AND DEATH SMILED
CD _______________ CDAR 029
Adipocre / May '95 / Plastic Head

Albanatchie

NATIVE
CD _______________ CDLDL 1242
Lochshore / Aug '96 / ADA / Direct / Duncans

Albania

LIFE AFTER DEATH IS ON THE PHONE
So OK / Albania (are you all mine) / Addicts of the first night / Take it away / French farewell / Cold light of day / Great Zambesi / Kaytie King / Men in a million / Deathwatch / Word is out / Today and tomorrow / I told you so / Little baby / Could this be love / Go go go
CD _______________ CDWIKD 157
Chiswick / Nov '96 / Pinnacle

Albany, Joe

BIRD LIVES
CD _______________ STCD 4164
Storyville / Feb '90 / Cadillac / Jazz Music / Wellard

Albatross

C'EST LA VIE LIVE IN FRANCE
CD _______________ BSCD 4714
Blue Shadow / '92 / Swift

Albert, Christine

UNDERNEATH THE LONE STAR SKY
CD _______________ DOS 7014
Dos / Sep '95 / ADA / CM / Direct

Albertbridge Accordian Band

ONWARD TO THE FIELD
CD _______________ COCD 7002
Outlet / Aug '96 / ADA / CM / Direct / Duncans / Koch / Ross

Alberto Y Los Trios Paranoias

RADIO SWEAT
CD _______________ OVER 56CD
Overground / Feb '97 / Shellshock/Disc / SRD

SNUFF ROCK: THE BEST OF THE ALBERTOS
Old trust / Brrrr / I'll come if you let me / Invocation of the fundamental Orifice of St. Agnes / No change / Peon in the neck / Happy to be on (an island away from) Demis Roussos / Teenager in schtuck / Italians from outer space / Ballad of Colonel Callen / Fistful of spaghetti / Mandrax sunset variations, part VI / Neville / Breakfast / Whole food love / Holiday frog / Teenage promise / Willie Baxter's blues / It never rains in El Paso / Whispering grass / Death of rock and roll / Heads down no nonsense mindless boogie / Jesus wept / Kill / Gobbing on life / Snuffin' like that / Snuffin' in a Babylon / Twenty three / Dead meat / Juan Lopez / Anadin / Pavlov / Anarchy in the UK
CD _______________ MAUCD 604
Mau Mau / '91 / Pinnacle

Alberto, Jose

ON TIME
Fotos y recuerdos / Quien como tu / Estas a tiempo / Como ellas son / A la hora que me llamen voy / Como fue / Con sandra en la cama / Celia / Cuestion
CD _______________ 66058093
RMM / Feb '96 / New Note/Pinnacle

Albesteanu, Ion

DISTRICTS OF YESTERYEAR (Romania)
CD _______________ 926612
BUDA / Feb '97 / Discovery

Albino Slug

ALBINO SLUG
CD _______________ MAD 001CD
Mad / May '94 / Plastic Head

BARRABBAS
CD _______________ MAD 002CD
Mad / Mar '95 / Plastic Head

Albion Band

1990
Yellow dress / Power and the glory / Fairford breakdown / Fossie shuffle / Ramble away / Flood / Nameless kind of hell / Adam and Eve / Lock up your daughters / Party's over
CD _______________ TSCD 457
Topic / Aug '90 / ADA / CM / Direct

ACOUSTICITY
CD _______________ HTDCD 13
HTD / Oct '93 / CM / Pinnacle

ALBION HEART
CD _______________ HTDCD 30
HTD / Mar '95 / CM / Pinnacle

BATTLE OF THE FIELD
CD _______________ BGOCD 354
Beat Goes On / Apr '97 / Pinnacle

BEST OF THE ALBION BAND 1993-1997, THE
Love is an abandoned car / Reels / Man of war / Devil in me / Rainbow over the hill / Dancer to the drum / Ivory tower / Forester's medley / Willow / Along the pilgrim's way / Albion heart / Head-smashed-in / Front porch game / We lie / White water running / Circle round the sun / Oak / Bedtime at Bryn Rhodyn / 36 miles
CD _______________ HTDCD 74
HTD / Jul '97 / CM / Pinnacle

CAPTURED (The Albions Who Nearly Got Away)
Ball, anchor and chain / Yellow dress / Horseshoe hornpipe/Chasing the jack / Party's over / Adam and Eve / Nameless kind of hell / Fossie shuffle / Go north / Chapel keithack/House in the county / Up the crooked spire / Set their mouths to twisting / Hanging tree / Fireman's song
CD _______________ HTDCD 19
HTD / Apr '94 / CM / Pinnacle

DEMI-PARADISE
CD _______________ HTDCD 54
HTD / Mar '96 / CM / Pinnacle

GIVE ME A SADDLE AND I'LL TRADE YOU A CAR
Ash on an old man's sleeve / Geoff Collings / Postman's polka / See their mouth's to twisting / Seven curses / Cardhouse / Striking for another land / Bury my eyeballs on top of Boot Hill / Kitty come down the lane / Think it over / Don't look at me/Trip to Cheltenham / Throw out the lifeline
CD _______________ TSCD 454
Topic / Aug '89 / ADA / CM / Direct

LARK RISE TO CANDLEFORD (A Country Tapestry)
Girl I left behind me / Lemady/arise and pick a posy / All of a row / Tommytoes / John Dory / Witch Elder / Abroad for pleasure / Day thou gavest Lord is ended / Battle of the Somme / Grand circle dance / Speed the plough / Snow falls / Cart music / Holly and the ivy / Postman's knock / Hunt music / Scarlet and the blue / Dare to be a Daniel / Jacob's well
CD _______________ CDSCD 4020
Charisma / Aug '92 / EMI

RISE UP LIKE THE SUN
Ragged heroes / Poor old horse / Afro blues/Danse Royale / Ampleforth/Lay me low / Time to ring some changes / House in the country / Primrose / Gresford disaster / Postman's knock / Pain and paradise / Lay me low / Rainbow over the hill
CD _______________ CDEMS 1460
EMI / Aug '92 / EMI

SONGS FROM THE SHOWS
Here we come a wassailing / While shepherds watched / Rudolph blues / Run rudolph run / Broom dance / In the cross of Christ / Tramp on the street / Lamb of God / Sweet theme run softly / Poor old horse /

Swan upping song / Lemady/Arise and pick a posy / Foxy comes to town / Dominion of the sword / When the fighting is over / Rumour hill / Bells of paradise / Snow falls / Ket to the north / Life on the river / Sheep shearing song / Building of our bridge / Twickenham ferry / Letters / Horse music / Burning the clavie / Speed the plough / All in the morning / Judas / Jesus and shall it ever be / Poor old man / Wastelands of England / Big yellow taxi/New Jerusalem / Wayfaring stranger / Dragonfly / Haxey hood game/estample / 15 Louisiana
CD RGFDCD 006
Road Goes On Forever / May '97 / Direct

SONGS FROM THE SHOWS VOL.1
CD RGFCD 006
Road Goes On Forever / Feb '91 / Direct

SONGS FROM THE SHOWS VOL.2
CD RGFCD 007
Road Goes On Forever / Feb '91 / Direct

STELLA MARIS
CD SPINCD 130
Making Waves / Oct '94 / CM

UNDER THE ROSE
CD SPINCD 110
Making Waves / Aug '96 / CM

Albion Ensemble

MISSISSIPPI FIVE
Mississippi five / Spring moonlight and flowers over the river / Partita for wind quartet / Quintet for wind instruments Op43 (1922) FS 100
CD PROUCD 142
Proudsound / May '96 / Conifer/BMG

Albion Jazz Band

ONE FOR THE GUV'NOR
CD SOSCD 1206
Stomp Off / Oct '92 / Jazz Music / Wellard

THEY'RE ALL NICE TUNES
CD SOSCD 1249
Stomp Off / May '93 / Jazz Music / Wellard

Albita

NO SE PARECE A NADA
Que manera de quererte / No se parece a nada / Que culpa tengo yo / La esperanza / Bolero para nostalgiar / Solo porque vivo / Para que me beses tu / Quien le prohibe / Un solo beso / Mi guaguanco
CD 4809432
Epic / Oct '95 / Sony

Alboth

LIED
CD PPP 118
PDCD / Apr '94 / Plastic Head

Albrigtsen, Steinar

BOUND TO WANDER
CD RTMCD 52
Round Tower / Jan '94 / Avid/BMG

Alcapone, Dennis

FOREVER VERSION
Nanny version / Run run / Riddle I this / Baby version / Sunday version / Version I can feel / Forever version / Baby why version / Dancing version / Midnight version / Sweet talking version / Version you to the ball
CD CD 3505
Heartbeat / Nov '91 / ADA / Direct / Greensleeves / Jet Star

PEACE AND LOVE
CD RB 3014
Reggae Best / Apr '95 / Grapevine/ PolyGram

UNIVERSAL ROCKERS
CD RASCD 3221
Ras / Nov '92 / Direct / Greensleeves / Jet Star / SRD

WAKE UP JAMAICA
CD RNCD 2118
Rhino / Sep '95 / Grapevine/PolyGram / Jet Star

Alcatraz

DC IN THE MIX
CD SUB 20D
Subversive / Sep '96 / 3mv/Sony / Amato Disco / Mo's Music Machine / Prime / Vital

Alcatrazz

LIVE SENTENCE
CD CDMFN 134
Music For Nations / Jun '92 / Pinnacle

NO PAROLE FROM ROCK'N'ROLL
CD CDMFN 133
Music For Nations / Jul '92 / Pinnacle

Alchemy

CELTIC PANPIPES
Ride on / Spinning wheel / Love thee dearest / Spancil Hill / She moved thru' the fair / Flight of the earls / My Lagan love / Steal away / Mountains of Mourne / Sally gardens / Ag criost an siol / Carrickfergus / Derry air / Lonesome boatman / Mise Eire
CD KCD 415
Celtic Collections / Jan '97 / Target/BMG

Alcoholics Unanimous

DR. KEGGER MD
CD TEAR 009CD
Tear It Up / Jan '96 / Plastic Head

Alcorn, Alvin

GAY PARIS STOMPER
CD AMCD 65
American Music / Aug '94 / Jazz Music

SOUNDS OF NEW ORLEANS VOL.5
CD STCD 6012
Storyville / Jul '96 / Cadillac / Jazz Music / Wellard

Alden, Howard

13 STRINGS (Alden, Howard & George Van Eps)
Just you, just me / My ideal / I hadn't anyone till you / Beautiful friendship / Touch of your lips / Ain't misbehavin' / Too marvellous for words / Love walked in / Queerology / How long has this been going on / Mine / Embraceable you / Emaline
CD CCD 4464
Concord Jazz / Jun '91 / New Note/ Pinnacle

CONCORD JAZZ GUITAR COLLECTIVE, THE (Alden, Howard/Jimmy Bruno/ Frank Vignola)
Bittersweet / Strictly confidential / String thing / Mating call / Seven come eleven / Body and soul / Donna Lee / Perdido / Swing 39 / Four brothers / Song d'autumne / Ornithology
CD CCD 4672
Concord Jazz / Dec '95 / New Note/ Pinnacle

ENCORE (Alden, Howard & Ken Peplowski)
It all depends on you / Palo alto / Since we met / I hear a rhapsody / Dolphin / Wabash / Fading star / With every breath I take / You
CD CCD 4654
Concord Jazz / Jul '95 / New Note/Pinnacle

HAND CRAFTED SWING (Alden, Howard & George Van Eps)
CD CCD 4513
Concord Jazz / Jul '92 / New Note/ Pinnacle

MISTERIOSO (Alden, Howard Trio)
Song of the dove / Misterioso / Everything but you / Waltz for Julie / This can't be love / Reflections in D
CD CCD 4487
Concord Jazz / Nov '91 / New Note/ Pinnacle

NO AMPS ALLOWED (Alden, Howard & Jack Lesberg)
CD CRD 303
Chiaroscuro / Mar '96 / Jazz Music

SEVEN AND SEVEN (Alden, Howard & George Van Eps)
Surrender dear / I may be wrong, but I think you're wonderful / Lullaby of Birdland / Stella by starlight / Skylark / My romance / Last night when we were young / Salute to Basie / Night and day / Ja da / Just friends
CD CCD 4584
Concord Jazz / Dec '93 / New Note/ Pinnacle

SNOWY MORNING BLUES (Alden, Howard Trio)
One morning in May / I'm through with love / Bye-ya / Melancholia / Sleepy time gal / Le sucrier velours / Dancers in love / Snowy morning blues / Ask me now / You leave me breathless / Swing '39
CD CCD 4424
Concord Jazz / Aug '90 / New Note/ Pinnacle

TAKE YOUR PICK
I concentrate on you / UMMG (Upper Manhattan Medical Group) / House party starting / Warm valley / Gig / My funny valentine / Sweet and lovely / You're my thrill / How deep is the ocean / After all
CD CCD 47432
Concord Jazz / Feb '97 / New Note/ Pinnacle

YOUR STORY (The Music Of Bill Evans) (Alden, Howard & Frank Wess)
Tune for a lyric / Loose bloose / Displacement / Time remembered / Two lonely people / Funkallero / Only child / Laurie / Maxine / Five / Your story
CD CCD 4621
Concord Jazz / Nov '94 / New Note/ Pinnacle

Aldrich, Ronnie

SEA DREAMS (Aldrich, Ronnie & His Two Pianos)
La mer / Hello / Sailing by / Bermuda triangle / Sound of the sea / Last farewell / Calypso / Stranger on the shore / Sailing / Trading winds / To all the girls I've loved before / How deep is the ocean
CD SEWCD 1003
Seaward / May '92 / Target/BMG

Alemany, Jesus

CUBANISMO
Descarga de hoy meta y guaguanco / Tumbao de coqueta / Aprovecha / Pa que goven / Paca y pa ya / Recordando a arcano / La rumba y el tumbador / Cicuta tibia / Ahora me voy
CD HNCD 1390
Hannibal / Nov '96 / ADA / Vital

Ales, Brian

CREATURE OF HABIT
Your small kindnesses / Older road than this / Happy town / Cinema saga / Waltz fatale / Cinema saga / Aho dze
CD INT 31622
Intuition / Feb '97 / New Note/Pinnacle

Alex Party

ALEX PARTY
CD 8288212
Systematic / Oct '96 / PolyGram

Alexander Brothers

ALEXANDER BROTHERS
CD CDITV 568
Scotdisc / May '93 / Conifer/BMG / Duncans / Ross

BEST OF THE ALEXANDER BROHERS
CD MATCD 248
Castle / May '94 / BMG

BEST OF THE ALEXANDER BROTHERS
Scotland, Scotland / Any dream will do / Mull of Kintyre / Oil rigger / Road to Dundee / Wild side of life / All along Loch Long / Nobody's child / Flying Scotsman / Caledonia / Northern lights of Aberdeen / Medley / Reels / Blackboard of my heart / He bought my soul at Calvary / Come by the hills / Jigs / Cornkisters / Farewell my love / Hiking song
CD TRTCD 135
TrueTrax / Oct '94 / THE

BEST OF THE ALEXANDER BROTHERS, THE
CD PLSCD 226
Pulse / Jul '97 / BMG

FLOWER OF SCOTLAND
Scotland the brave / Skye boat song / Campbeltown loch / Road and the miles to Dundee / Northern lights of old Aberdeen / My ain folk / Marie's wedding / Scottish soldier / Amazing grace / Heilan' lassie / Rowan tree / Wild rover / Cock o' the North / Tunes of glory / How are things in Glocca Morra / Flower of Scotland / These are my mountains / Two highlands lads / When you and I were young Maggie / Ballad of Glencoe
CD CDMFP 5889
Music For Pleasure / Jun '90 / EMI

GLORIOUS NORTH, THE
Glorious North / Caledonia / Hill o'Benachie / Lass of bon accord / Oil rigger / Northern lights of old Aberdeen / Dark island / Lonely scapa flow / Jigs medley / Farewell my love / McGinty's meal and ale
CD CDITV 593
Scotdisc / Nov '94 / Conifer/BMG / Duncans / Ross

NOW
Welcome medley / Nobody's child / Old button box / Pistonette / Gentle Annie / Inverary Inn / Daisy a day / Dark island / Doon in the wee room / When you and I were young Maggie / Sing along medley / Way old friends do / Home from the sea / On the rebound / Goodnight Bobby / Mary mack / Could I have this dance / Glencoe / Flying Scotsman / Bunch of thyme / Catch me if you can / Flower of Scotland
CD LCDM 9023
Lismor / Aug '90 / ADA / Direct / Duncans / Lismor

TOAST TO ABSENT FRIENDS, A
Opening medley / Any dream will do / Midges / After the ball / High level hornpipe / Absent friends / Take me back / Working man / After all these years / Tartan / It is no secret / Jaqueline waltz / Helen of Invergarry / Marching through the heather / Bricklayer's song / Fisherman's son
CD LCOM 6035
Lismor / Sep '92 / ADA / Direct / Duncans / Lismor

Alexander, Arthur

ADIOS AMIGO (A Tribute To Arthur Alexander) (Various Artists)
CD FIENDCD 754
Demon / Aug '94 / Pinnacle

GREATEST, THE
Anna / Soldier of love / You don't care / Call me lonesome / Where have you been / Don't you know / All I need is you / Keep her guessing / In the middle of it all / Without a song / Black night / You're the reason / I hang my head and cry / Dream girl / Are you / Shot of rhythm and blues / You better move on / Detroit city / Go home girl / Whole lot of trouble / I wonder where you are tonight
CD CDCHD 922
Ace / Jun '89 / Pinnacle

LONELY JUST LIKE ME
If it's really got to be this way / Go home girl / Sally Sue Brown / Mr. John / Lonely just like me / Every day I have to cry / In the middle of it all / Genie in the jug / Johnny Heartbreak / All the time / There is a road / I believe in miracles
CD 7559614752
Nonesuch / Jul '93 / Warner Music

WARNER BROS. RECORDINGS, THE
Rainbow road / Down the backroads / I'm coming home in the middle of it all / Call me honey / Lover please / You got me knockin' / It hurts to want it so bad / Love's where life begins / Come along with me / Burning love / Go home girl / They'll do it every time / Mr. John / Thank God he came
CD 9362455812
Warner Bros. / Jul '96 / Warner Music

Alexander, David

BEST OF DAVID ALEXANDER VOL.1 (20 Great Songs)
CD DARCD 4
One Stop / Apr '96 / Koch

BEST OF DAVID ALEXANDER VOL.2 (18 Great Songs)
CD DARCD 6
One Stop / Apr '96 / Koch

CONCERT, THE
CD DARCD 11
One Stop / Apr '96 / Koch

FEED THE FIRE STOKE THE COAL
CD DARCD 7
One Stop / Apr '96 / Koch

IF I NEVER SING ANOTHER SONG
CD DARCD 3
One Stop / Apr '96 / Koch

MORE & MORE
CD DARCD 8
One Stop / Apr '96 / Koch

ONE DAY
CD DARCD 9
One Stop / Apr '96 / Koch

THERE YOU ARE
CD DARCD 10
One Stop / Apr '96 / Koch

Alexander, Eric

NEW YORK CALLING (Alexander, Eric Quintet)
CD CRISS 1077CD
Criss Cross / Nov '93 / Cadillac / Direct / Vital/SAM

STABLEMATES (Alexander, Eric & Lin Halliday)
Eternal triangle / Blue bird / Polka dots and moonbeams/Old folks / Speak low / Like someone in love / Night has a thousand eyes / Stablemates
CD DE 488
Delmark / Jun '97 / ADA / Cadillac / CM / Direct / Hot Shot

STRAIGHT UP
Straight up / What are you doing the rest of your life / Be my love / Blues waltz / Laura / An Oscar for Treadwell / End of a love affair / Love is a many splendored thing
CD DE 461
Delmark / Mar '97 / ADA / Cadillac / CM / Direct / Hot Shot

Alexander, Monty

ECHOES OF JILLY'S
I've got you under my skin / Summer wind / You make me feel so young / I'm a fool to want you / Just one of those things / All the way / Fly me to the moon / In the wee small hours of the morning / Call me irresponsible / Angel eyes / Come fly with me / Here's that rainy day / Strangers in the night
CD CCD 47692
Concord Jazz / Aug '97 / New Note/ Pinnacle

FACETS
When Johnny comes marching home / Lost April / I'm walkin' / Hard times / Hold 'em Joe / Consider / Speak low / Tune up / Blues for Dewey / To the ends of the earth
CD CCD 4108
Concord Jazz / Nov '96 / New Note/ Pinnacle

IVORY AND STEEL
CD CCD 4124
Concord Jazz / Jul '88 / New Note/ Pinnacle

JAMBOREE
CD CCD 4359
Concord Picante / Oct '88 / New Note/ Pinnacle

JUST IN TIME (2CD Set)
Out of many one people / Work song / Bossa nova do marilla / Tricrotism / Angel eyes / Body and soul / That's the way it is

/ Just in time / Soft winds / On Green Dolphin Street / Black orpheus / Blue bossa
CD Set JLR 103605
Live At EJ's / May '96 / Target/BMG

LIVE AT MAYBECK RECITAL HALL VOL.40
When the saints go marching in / When I grow too old to dream / Close enough for love / Serpent / Where is love / Renewal / Island in the sun / Estate / (I love you) for sentimental reasons / Speak low / Smile
CD CCD 4658
Concord Jazz / Aug '95 / New Note/ Pinnacle

LIVE IN HOLLAND
Funji Mama / Betcha by golly wow / You'll never find another love like mine / Where is love / That's the way it is / Bye bye blackbird / Everything must change / Candy man
CD 8356272
Verve / Jul '92 / PolyGram

MONTREUX ALEXANDER LIVE (Alexander, Monty Trio)
Nite mist blues / Feelings / Satin doll / Work song / Drown in my own tears / Battle hymn of the Republic
CD 8174872
MPS Jazz / Mar '93 / PolyGram

OVERSEAS SPECIAL
But not for me / Time for love / Orange in pain / F S R / For all we know / CC rider
CD CCD 4253
Concord Jazz / Nov '96 / New Note/ Pinnacle

REUNION IN EUROPE (Alexander, Monty Quartet)
Two bass hit / Got my mojo working / Smile / Yesterdays / Blues for Stephanie / Love you madly / Ben / Eleuthra / That's why
CD CCD 4231
Concord Jazz / May '97 / New Note/ Pinnacle

RIVER, THE
Stand up, stand up for Jesus / River / Serpent / Ave Maria / David danced before the Lord with all his might / Renewal / Ain't gonna study war no more / Holy Holy Lord God Almighty / What a friend we have in Jesus / How great thou art
CD CCD 4422
Concord Jazz / Aug '90 / New Note/ Pinnacle

SATURDAY NIGHT (Alexander, Monty Quartet)
CD MCD 024
Timeless Jazz / May '89 / New Note/ Pinnacle

SO WHAT
CD 591482
Black & Blue / Jun '91 / Discovery / Koch / Wellard

SOLO
CD BLR 84006
L&R / May '91 / New Note/Pinnacle

STEAMIN'
Pure imagination / Just a little bit / Dear Diz / 3000 Miles / Lively up yourself / Make believe / I'll never stop loving you / Maybe September / Tucker avenue stomp / Theme from Prawnbroker / Honest I do / When you go / Young at heart
CD CCD 4636
Concord Jazz / Apr '95 / New Note/ Pinnacle

TO NAT WITH LOVE
Unforgettable / What is this thing called love / Moonlight in Vermont / Honeysuckle rose / Three little words / Nature boy / Straighten up and fly right / Too marvellous for words / Yes sir that's my baby
CD CHECD 12
Master Mix / Oct '91 / Jazz Music / New Note/Pinnacle / Wellard

TO THE ENDS OF THE EARTH
To the ends of the earth / One love / Old devil moon / Island Ray / When I fall in love / Mangorengue / Reunion blues / Body and soul / Boogsie's bounce / September song / Killer Joe
CD CCD 4721
Concord Picante / Oct '96 / New Note/ Pinnacle

TRIO (Alexander / Brown / Ellis)
CD CCD 4136
Concord Jazz / Dec '90 / New Note/ Pinnacle

TRIPLE TREAT VOL.2 (Alexander, Monty & Ray Brown/Herb Ellis)
Lined with a groove / Straighten up and fly right / It might as well be Spring / Seven come eleven / Smile / I'll remember April / Trip man (tracer and inst. mix) / Lester leaps in
CD CCD 4338
Concord Jazz / May '88 / New Note/ Pinnacle

TRIPLE TREAT VOL.3 (Alexander, Monty & Ray Brown/Herb Ellis)
I told ya I love ya, now get out / In the wee small hours of the morning / Renewal / My one and only love / There will never be another you / Secret love / Hi-heel sneakers / I love you / Corcovado
CD CCD 4394
Concord Jazz / '89 / New Note/Pinnacle

YARD MOVEMENT
Exodus / Regulator / Crying / Moonlight city / Love notes / Sneaky steppers
CD IJCD 4001
Island Jamaica Jazz / May '96 / PolyGram

Alexander, Peter

EBENFALLS ERHALTLICH (4CD Set)
Das machen nur die Beine von Dolores / Bye bye mein Hawaii / Ich lade dich ein in die kleine Taverne / Erzahl mir keine Marchen / Im weissen weissen schnee / Sag es mit Musik Fahr auf dem Zigeunerwagen / Es ist ein abschied nur fur heut / Der alte Liebesbrief / Wenn ich dich seh' / Ich hab' nach dir soviel Heimweh Addio / Donna Grazia / Santa Fe / Wo am weg die apfel reifen ein musikus / Bumms / Weil du schon bist / Ich kusse ihre hand, Madame / Ich weiss es nicht / So ein kleines bisschen liebe / Isabella / Die sussesten fruchte (fressen nur die) / Braucht dein Herz keinen freund / Komm mit nach Palermo / Verliebte music / Ach, Herr Kuhn / Bolero (geheimnis der sudichen nachte) / Die panne panne mit Susanne / Gross kann sie sein, klein kann sie sein / Was versteht denn ein Cowboy von liebe / Margarita / Ich weiss was du dir denkst / Damais in Rom Angelina / Pony serenade / Tabak und Rum / Hannelore / Bella bella Donna / Optimisten boogie / Die alte kuckucksuhr / Es war das letzte mal / Alte lieder traute weisen / Das lied vom sonntag / Ein italiano / Nein nein ich will night bitte lass mich / Bella musica / Der alte stiefel / Ach hatt ich das gefuhl, doch mal / Keine angst vor grossen tieren / Immer wieder du / Jambalaya / Jonathan boogie / Kotettier nicht mit mir / Mein grosser bruder / Ich lieb dich so wie du bist / Die frau kommt direkt aus Spanien / Uno momento Maria / Plim plim, plum plum / Die sussesten frucht (fressen nur die) / Wir wir wir haben ein klavier / Was hat der Bobby mit der Lisa gemacht / Oh Mister Swoboda / Dann ist er furchtbar mude / In sorrent / Nicolo Nicolo Nicolo / Jede frau in bogota / Die treuen augen / Die schonen frauen haben immer recht / Es war in Napoli vor vielen Jahren / Continental / Es liegt was in der luft / Ich finde dich / Ich sing' heut vergnugt vor mich hin / Du bist die Richtige / Ich hap vor'm kussen immer lampenfieber / Der primas / Agustino / Der bunte traum / Schlager revue No. 8 / Weinlied/Sagbiem abschied leise servus
CD Set BCD 15455
Bear Family / Jul '96 / Direct / Rollercoaster / Swift

FILMTREFFER VOL.1
Margarita / Gluck muss man haben / Blauer tango / Die sussesten Fruchte / Bongo boogie / Wenn sie wollen, bringen sie mal Stein in's roll'n / Ich finde dich... / Ich sing 'Heut' vergnugt vor mich hin / Sing, baby sing / Eventuell / Damit haben sie gluck in der Bundesrepublik / Komm' ein bisschen mit nach Italien / Gespensterblues / Ein mann muss nicht immer schon sein / Kleines Haus auf der Sierra Nevada / Ich weiss was dir fehlt / Im hafen uns'rer traume / Mamma-di-mandolin / Schin wieder mal / Weil du mir sympathisch bist / Grosses finale
CD BCD 15992
Bear Family / Jun '97 / Direct / Rollercoaster / Swift

FILMTREFFER VOL.2
Das ist alles langst vorbei / Vergiss mich nicct so schnell / Mamitscka / Das ganze Haus ist schief / Vergiss mich nicht so schnell / O Josefin, die nacht in Napoli / Jassa Bobo / Probier dein gluck mit mir / Das grosse Gluckskarussel / Wenn das die andern wussten / Wehe, wenn sie losgelassen / Das schonste auf der Welt / Du hast mir heut mein Herz gestohlen / Der freundliche Franz / Wir sehen uns wieder / Venga, Venga musica / Fabelhaft / Tun sie's nicht / Er war ein Musikant / Hab'n sie nicht ein schones grosses Fass da / Lass mich nie, nie, nie mehr allein / Wir tanzen Huckepack / Die Reblaus / Mann musste Klavier spielen konnen / Ich wunsch' dir einen schlaflosen Abend / In der Schweiz / See you later alligator
CD BCD 15993
Bear Family / Jun '97 / Direct / Rollercoaster / Swift

ROT-WEISS-ROT AUFNAHMEN
Guten morgen, Frauline Scholz / Ich lad sie ein, faulein / Ich mocht von dir ein foto / Warum sagt dein mund / Jo der kleine Julius / Was die kleinen madchen singen / Eine kleine mansarde / Oh Donna Clara / Nachts sind die strassen so leer / Deine liebe is zuckersuss (Quien sera) / Chef, wir brauchen bitte vorschuss / Komm, wir fahren mit 10ps / Manuela Mambo / Adieu, Mimi / Mule train / Bunny hop
CD BCD 15998
Bear Family / Jul '96 / Direct / Rollercoaster / Swift

STRASSE MEINER LEIDER
CD BCD 15599
Bear Family / Feb '90 / Direct / Rollercoaster / Swift

Alexander, Ray

RAIN IN JUNE (Alexander, Ray Sextet)
Dizzy atmosphere / Nightingale sang in Berkeley Square / Lamp is low / Our love is here to stay / Let's fall in love / Rain in June / Angelique / Easy to love / Twinkletoes / Oh lady be good / Swinging on a star
CD CDSGP 0139
Prestige / Jun '95 / Else / Total/BMG

Alexander, Sara

HAMSIN
CD KAR 985
IMP / Nov '96 / ADA / Discovery

Alexander, Texas

TEXAS ALEXANDER VOL.1 (1927-1928)
Range in my kitchen blues / Long lonesome day blues / Cornbread blues / Section gang blues / Levee camp moan blues / Mama I heard you brought it right back home / Farm hand blues / Evil woman blues / Sabine River blues / Death bed blues / Yellow girl blues / West Texas blues / Bantam rooster blues / Deep blue sea blues / No more woman blues / Don't you wish your baby was built up like mine / Bell cow blues
CD MBCD 2001
Matchbox / Feb '93 / Cadillac / CM / Jazz Music / Roots

TEXAS ALEXANDER VOL.2 (1928-1930)
CD MBCD 2002
Matchbox / Jan '94 / Cadillac / CM / Jazz Music / Roots

TEXAS ALEXANDER VOL.3 (1930-1950)
CD MBCD 2003
Matchbox / Jan '94 / Cadillac / CM / Jazz Music / Roots

Alexander, Willie

PASS THE TABASCO (Alexander, Willie 'Loco' & The Boom Boom Band)
You've lost that lovin' feelin' / Rock 'n' roll '78 / Everybody knows / Look at me / Radio heart / You beat me to it / Looking like a bimbo / Kerouac / Mass Avenue / Modern lovers / You looked so pretty / Pass the tabasco / Melinda / Hitchiking / RA baby / Sky Queen / Bring your friend / For old time's sake
CD MAUCD 646
Mau Mau / Jul '96 / Pinnacle

Alexandria, Lorez

ALEXANDRIA THE GREAT
Show me / I've been in love before / Satin doll / My one and only love / Over the rainbow / Get me to the church on time / Best is yet to come / I've grown accustomed to his face / Give me the simple life / I'm through with love / But beautiful / Little boat / Dancing on the ceiling / It might as well be Spring / Once / Wildest gal in town / Angel eyes / This could be the start of something big / No more / That far away look
CD MCAD 33116
Impulse Jazz / Jan '90 / New Note/BMG

TALK ABOUT COPY
CD HCD 605
Hindsight / Oct '95 / Jazz Music / Target/ BMG

Alford, Clem

MIRROR IMAGE
CD MC 1003CD
Magic Carpet / Oct '96 / Greyhound

Alford, John

JOHN ALFORD
CD LUVITCD 2
Love This / Nov '96 / Pinnacle / Total/ BMG

Alfred, Jerry

ETSI SHON (Grandfather Song) (Alfred, Jerry & The Medicine Beat)
CD RHRCD 93
Red House / Aug '96 / ADA / Koch

NENDAA (Alfred, Jerry & The Medicine Beat)
CD RHRCD 97
Red House / Apr '97 / ADA / Koch

Algaion

OIMES ALGAION
CD FMP 002CDM
Full Moon / Jun '95 / Plastic Head

Alger, Pat

SEEDS
CD SHCD 1041
Sugar Hill / Jan '94 / ADA / CM / Direct / Koch / Roots

TRUE LOVE AND OTHER STORIES
True love / Lone star state of mind / Goin' gone / Like a hurricane / This town / Love can be a dangerous thing / I do / She came from Fort Worth / Forever lovin' you / Small town Saturday night / Once in a very blue moon / Blue highway 29
CD SHCD 1029
Sugar Hill / Aug '96 / ADA / CM / Direct / Koch / Roots

Alhaits, Jean-Michel

FANTAISIE (Alhaits, Jean-Michel & J.P. Rolland)
CD 868CD
Escalibur / May '97 / ADA / Discovery / Roots

Alhambra

ART OF JUDEO-SPANISH SONG
CD GV 127CD
Global Village / Nov '93 / ADA / Direct

Ali, Rajab

FEELINGS
CD DMUT 1051
Multitone / Mar '96 / BMG

UMANG
CD DMUT 1250
Multitone / Mar '96 / BMG

Ali, Salamat

NAZAKAT AND SALAMAT ALI (Ali, Salamat & Nazakat)
CD HNCD 1332
Hannibal / Sep '91 / ADA / Vital

Alias

METAL TO INFINITY
CD RTN 41202
Rock The Nation / Nov '94 / Plastic Head

Alias Ron Kavana

COMING DAYS
Galtee mor / Irish ways / Saddle the pony / Merrily kiss the quaker / Kinnegad slashers / Annie Mulligan's / Thoughts of Abilene / Psycho Mary's voodoo blues / Ain't that peculiar / Fox hunter's reel / Pennies for black babies / Cajun ceili / Freedom crazy / Walk don't walk / Hand me down / Connemara / Handcuffs / Johnny / If I had a rocket launcher
CD CDWIKD 94
Chiswick / Mar '91 / Pinnacle

GALWAY TO GRACELAND
CD CDARK 002
Alias / Oct '95 / Direct

HOME FIRE
CD SPDCD 1043
Special Delivery / Jun '91 / ADA / CM / Direct

ROLLIN' AND COASTIN' (In Search Of America)
CD APCD 042
Appaloosa / Apr '94 / ADA / Direct / TKO Magnum

THINK LIKE A HERO
Waxin' the gaza / Every man is a king (in the US of A) / Gone shopping / Soweto trembles (the Jo'burg jig) / Felice / This is the night (fair dues to "The Man") / Midnight on the water / Caoineadh roisin / Four horsemen / Rap 'n' reel / Tre ceather a hocht / Ochra at Killarney point to points / Reconciliation
CD CDWIK 88
Chiswick / Oct '89 / Pinnacle

Alice

ALICE
CD 280827
Magic / Jul '97 / Greyhound

Alice Donut

BUCKETFULS OF SICKNESS AND HORROR (In An Otherwise Meaningless Life)
CD VIRUS 73CD
Alternative Tentacles / Jul '89 / Cargo / Greyhound / Pinnacle

DONUT COMES ALIVE
CD VIRUS 61CD
Alternative Tentacles / '92 / Cargo / Greyhound / Pinnacle

DRY HUMPING THE CASH COW
CD VIRUS 143CD
Alternative Tentacles / Apr '94 / Cargo / Greyhound / Pinnacle

MULE
CD VIRUS 82CD
Alternative Tentacles / Nov '90 / Cargo / Greyhound / Pinnacle

PURE ACID PARK
Millennium / Dreaming in Cuban / Freaks in love / Big cars and blow jobs / I walked with a zombie / Senator and the cabin boy / Mummenschantz pachinko / Insane / Shining path / Unspeakable pleasure of being me / Lost in space / Cain
CD VIRUS 163CD
Alternative Tentacles / Jul '95 / Cargo / Greyhound / Pinnacle

UNTIDY SUICIDES OF YOUR DEGENERATE CHILDREN
CD VIRUS 115CD
Alternative Tentacles / Sep '92 / Cargo / Greyhound / Pinnacle

Alice In Chains

ALICE IN CHAINS
Grind / Brush away / Sludge factory / Heaven beside you / Head creeps / Again / Shame in you / God am / So close / Nothin' song / Frogs / Over now
CD 4811142
CD 4811149
Columbia / Nov '95 / Sony

DIRT
Them bones / Dam that river / Rain when I die / Down in a hole / Sick man / Rooster / Junkhead / Dirt / God smack / Hate to feel / Angry chair / Would
CD 4723302
Columbia / Oct '92 / Sony

FACELIFT
We die young / Man in the box / Sea of sorrow / Bleed the freak / I can't remember / Love hate love / It ain't like that / Sunshine / Put you down / Confusion / I know somethin' ('bout you) / Real thing
CD 4672012
Columbia / Mar '96 / Sony

JAR OF FLIES/SAP (2CD Set)
Rotten apple / Nutshell / I stay away / No excuses / Whale and wasp / Don't follow / Swing on this / Brother / Got me wrong / Right turn / Am I inside / Love story
CD Set 4757132
Columbia / Jan '94 / Sony

MTV UNPLUGGED
Nutshell / Brother / No excuses / Sludge factory / Down in a hole / Angry chair / Rooster / Got me wrong / Heaven beside you / Would / Frogs / Over now / Killer is me
CD 4843002
Columbia / Jul '96 / Sony

Alien Boys

SEEDS OF DECAY
CD SR 330391CD
Semaphore / '91 / Plastic Head

Alien Mutation

DNA
Dubula technoid / Dreamscape / Exotic ocean / Shimmer / Marijuana / Sea of colours / Water
CD KINXCD 9
Kinetix / Jun '97 / Pinnacle

Alien Nation

MICROCOSM MICROCOSM
CD KINXCD 4
Kinetix / Apr '96 / Pinnacle

Alien Rebels

STRANGE FEELINGS
CD AREB 001
Alien Rebels / Feb '97 / Nervous

Alien Sex Fiend

ACID BATH
In God we trust / Dead and reburied / She's a killer / Hee-haw (here come the bone people) / Smoke my bones / Breakdown and cry (lay down and die goodbye) / EST (trip to the moon) / Attack / Boneshaker baby / I'm a product / Thirty second coma
CD CDMGRAM 18
Anagram / Jun '97 / Cargo / Pinnacle

ALL OUR YESTERDAYS (The Singles Collection 1983-1987)
Ignore the machine / Lips can't go / RIP / Dead and buried / EST (trip to the moon) / Drive my rocket (up Uranus) / I'm doing time in a maximum security twilight home / I walk the line / Smells like... / Hurricane fighter plane
CD CDGRAM 34
Anagram / May '93 / Cargo / Pinnacle

ALTERED STATES OF AMERICA, THE
Wild women / Now I'm feeling zombiefied / Class of '69 / Ignore the machine / Magic / Coma / Eat eat eat / RIP
CD CDGRAM 60
Anagram / Feb '93 / Cargo / Pinnacle

ANOTHER PLANET
Bun ho / Everybody's dream / Radiant city / Spot your lucky warts / Sample my sausage / Outer limits / Instant Karma Sutra / So much to do, so little time / Alien / Wild green fiendy liquid / Nightmare zone / Another planet / Silver machine
CD CDGRAM 38
Anagram / Jun '97 / Cargo / Pinnacle

CURSE
Katch 22 / Now I'm feeling zombiefied / Stress / Blessings / Eat eat eat (an eye for an eye) / Ain't got no time to bleed / Bleeding reprise / Dalisms / Burger bar baby / I think I / Mad daddy drives a UFO / Wuthering wind / Radio Jimi / Hand of the silken / Blessing in disguise
CD CDGRAM 46
Anagram / Sep '90 / Cargo / Pinnacle

DRIVE MY ROCKET
CD CLEO 94122
Cleopatra / Aug '94 / Cargo / Greyhound / Plastic Head / RTM/Disc / SRD

FIRST ALIEN SEX FIEND CD
I'm doing time in a maximum security twilight home / Mine's full of maggots / In and out of my mind / Spies / Fly in the ointment / Seconds to nowhere / Beaver destroys forests / Do you sleep / Depravity lane / EST (Trip to the moon) / Boneshaker baby / Ignore the machine / Attack
CD CDGRAM 25
Anagram / Apr '94 / Cargo / Pinnacle

HERE CUM GERMS
Here cum germs / Camel camel / Impossible mission / Isolation / My brain is in the cupboard above the kitchen sink / You are soul / Death / Boots on / They all call me crazee / Stuff the turkey
CD CDGRAM 31
Anagram / May '92 / Cargo / Pinnacle

I'M HER FRANKENSTEIN
CD CLEO 9508CD
Cleopatra / Jun '95 / Cargo / Greyhound / Plastic Head / RTM/Disc / SRD

INFERNO
Inferno / Human installation / Take off tune / Space 1 / Happy tune / Planet 1 / Human atmosphere / Happy finale / Alien installation / Dramatic tune / Moon tune / Planet 2 / Bad news / Space 2 / Alien atmosphere / Death tune / Sad finale / Moon tune (lunaphases mix) / Planet 2 (together dreamscape mix)
CD CDGRAM 80
Anagram / Oct '94 / Cargo / Pinnacle

IT
Smells like... / Manic depression / Believe it or not / April showers / Wop-bop / Get into it / Lesson one / Do it right / To be continued / Buggin' me / Hurricane fighter plane / It lives again
CD CDGRAM 26
Anagram / Nov '91 / Cargo / Pinnacle

LEGENDARY BATCAVE TAPES, THE
Wardance of the Alien Sex Fiend / In heaven / I walk alone / Outta control / I'm her Frankenstein / Boneshaker baby / RIP / Wild women of Wongo / Funk in hell / Drive my rocket (up Uranus) / School's out
CD CDMGRAM 69
Anagram / Oct '93 / Cargo / Pinnacle

LIQUID HEAD IN TOKYO
RIP (blue crime truck) / EST (trip to the Moon) / Dead and re-buried / In God we trust (in cars we rust) / Back to the egg / Attack / Lips can't go / Wild women
CD SUMCD 4087
Summit / Jan '97 / Sound & Media

NOCTURNAL EMISSIONS
CD FULLCD 1301
13th Moon / Mar '97 / Pinnacle

OPEN HEAD SURGERY
Clockwork banana, banana-moon / Magic / Class of '69 / Alien sex fiend / Coma / Lickin' ma bone / Stressed out / B-B-bone boogie
CD CDGRAM 51
Anagram / Mar '92 / Cargo / Pinnacle

SINGLES 1983-1995, THE (2CD Set)
Ignore the machine / Lips can't go / RIP / New Christian music / Dead and buried / EST (trip to the moon) / I'm doing time in a maximum security twilight home / I walk the line / Smells like... / Hurricane fighter plane / Impossible mission / Here cum germs / Stuff the turkey / Bun ho / Haunted house / Now I'm feeling zombiefied / Magic / Inferno
CD Set CDGRAM 99
Anagram / Oct '95 / Cargo / Pinnacle

TOO MUCH ACID
It lives again / I walk the line / Nightmare zone / Get into it / EST (trip to the moon) / So much to do, so little time / Haunted house / Smells like... / Hurricane fighter plane / Sample my sausage / Boneshaker baby
CD CDGRAM 41
Anagram / May '93 / Cargo / Pinnacle

WHO'S BEEN SLEEPING IN MY BRAIN
Wish I woz a dog / Wild women / I'm not mad / New christian music / Wigwam wipeout / I'm her frankenstein / I am a product / Ignore the machine / Lips can't go / Black rabbit / New christian music (live) / Crazee
CD CDGRAM 10
Anagram / '88 / Cargo / Pinnacle

Alimatov, Turgen

TURGEN ALIMATOV
CD C 560086
Ocora / Jan '96 / ADA / Harmonia Mundi

Alisha's Attic

ALISHA RULES THE WORLD
Irresistable U R / Intense / I am, I feel / Alisha rules the world / White room / Stone in my shoe / Personality lines / Indestructible / I won't miss you / Golden rule / Just the way you like it / Air we breathe / Adore u
CD 5340272
Mercury / Nov '96 / PolyGram

Alke, Bjorn

FOREVER LULU
CD DRCD 217
Dragon / Oct '89 / ADA / Cadillac / CM / Roots / Wellard

JAZZ IN SWEDEN
CD 10722
Caprice / Oct '90 / ADA / Cadillac / CM / Complete/Pinnacle

All

ALLROY FOR PREZ
CD CRZ 004CD
Cruz / Jan '90 / Plastic Head

ALLROY SEZ...
CD CRZ 001CD
Cruz / Jan '90 / Plastic Head

ALLROY'S REVENGE
CD CRZ 006CD
Cruz / Jan '90 / Plastic Head

BREAKING THINGS
CD CRZ 031CD
Cruz / Sep '93 / Plastic Head

DOT
CD CRZ 024CD
Cruz / May '93 / Plastic Head

PERCOLATER
CD CRZ 022CD
Cruz / May '93 / Plastic Head

All 4 One

ALL 4 ONE
So much in love / Oh girl / Better man / I swear / Down to the last drop / Without you (she's got) skillz / Breathless / Something about you / Bomb / Here if you're ready
CD 7567825882
Atlantic / Apr '94 / Warner Music

AND THE MUSIC SPEAKS
CD 7567527462
Atlantic / May '95 / Warner Music

All About Eve

ALL ABOUT EVE
Flowers in our hair / Gypsy dance / In the clouds / Martha's harbour / Every angel / Shelter from the rain / She moved through the fair / Wild hearted woman / Never promise / What kind of fool
CD 8342602
Mercury / Aug '95 / PolyGram

SCARLET AND OTHER STORIES
Road to your soul / Dream now / Gold and silver / Scarlet / December / Blind lemon Sam / More than the blues / Tuesday's child / Empty dancehall / Only one reason / Pearl fishermen
CD 8389652
Mercury / Aug '95 / PolyGram

TOUCHED BY JESUS
Strange way / Farewell Mr. Sorrow / Wishing the hours away / Touched by Jesus / Dreamer / Rhythm of life / Mystery we are / Hide child / Ravens / Are you lonely / Share it with me
CD 5101462
Mercury / Aug '91 / PolyGram

WINTER WORDS, HITS AND RARITIES
CD 5141542
Mercury / Oct '92 / PolyGram

All Day

NOBODY LIKES A QUITTER
Smells like Long Beach / One way ticket / Cry for help / Number 56 / Insane love commandos / Get some / Nobody knows my name / Spain / War on the boulevard / Kim's dead/Michael / Hell no / Daddy / How does it feel / Ain't she sweet / Doreen Shelton / Friends are forever / Thank you
CD KNR 115
Know / Apr '97 / Cargo / Greyhound

All Souls' Orchestra

KENDRICK COLLECTION, THE (All Souls' Orchestra & Choir)
Lord is King: *Wilson, Precious/All Souls' Orchestra/Choir* / Servant King: *Wilson, Precious/All Souls' Orchestra/Choir* / Such love: *Wilson, Precious/All Souls' Orchestra/Choir* / Burn on: *Richard, Cliff/All Souls' Orchestra/Choir* / Fighter: *Richard, Cliff/All Souls' Orchestra/Choir* / May our worship be acceptable: *Kendrick, Graham/All Souls' Orchestra/Choir* / May the fragrance of Jesus fill this place: *Kendrick, Graham/All Souls' Orchestra/Choir* / Meekness and majesty: *Kendrick, Graham/All Souls' Orchestra/Choir*
CD LANGD 003
Myrrh / '89 / Nelson Word

PROM PRAISE FESTIVAL (Recorded Live At The Royal Albert Hall) (All Souls' Orchestra & Choir)
He's got the whole world in his hands / Give me joy / All people that on earth do dwell / Pomp and circumstance march No.4 / Let the bright seraphim / Hevenu Shalom Alechem / O happy day / Festival overture / At the river / Steal away / With loving hands / Death of Jesus / Fanfare for the common man / Easter prelude / He's alive / Come sing the praise of Jesus / Behold the man / Yours be the glory
CD LANGD 010
Myrrh / May '95 / Nelson Word

Alla, Tanakoul

UD AND PERCUSSION
CD ALCD 190
Al Sur / Sep '96 / ADA / Discovery

Allan, Johnnie

PROMISED LAND
Promised land / South to Louisiana / She's gone / Let's do it / Cry foolish heart / What'cha do / Your picture / Somebody else / Please accept my love / You got me whistling / I'll never love again / Secrets of love / Nights of misery / Cajun man / Graduation night (as you pass me by) / Please help me, I'm falling / Somewhere on Skid Row / Isle of Capri / Sweet dreams / I cried / Stranger to you / I can't wait / I'm missing you / Little fat man / Today I started loving you again / Homebound train / Let's go get drunk / Tennessee blues
CD CDCHD 380
Ace / Jun '92 / Pinnacle

Allan, Laura

HOLD ON TO YOUR DREAMS
CD SE 1020CD
Skyline / Apr '96 / ADA / Target/BMG

Allan/Hallberg/Riedel

TRIO CONTROMBA
CD DRCD226
Dragon / May '88 / ADA / Cadillac / CM / Roots / Wellard

Allaway/Antonia Quartet

SAMIZDAT
Crossing the rubicon / Next time round / Groovin' / Coopers calling / Blues for BB / Let this one go / Cogito ergo sum / Trick of the light / Leonard B / Peel me a grape / Samizdat / Seal it
CD CDAA 001
Mapa Music / Jan '95 / New Note/Pinnacle

Alldis, Dominic

TURN OUT THE STARS
Peri's scope / Waltz for Debby / You and the night and the music / Very early / Like someone in love / Two lonely people / Emily / My bells / You must believe in spring / Turn out the stars / My foolish heart / Days of wine and roses / Laurie / For Nenette (In April)
CD CANZCD 1
Canzona / Apr '96 / New Note/Pinnacle

Alldred, Bill

SWING THAT MUSIC (Alldred, Bill Goodtime Jazz Band)
It don't mean a thing / Mooche / Struttin' / With some barbecue / Basin street blues / Swing that music / Limehouse blues / Royal garden blues / Wabash blues / King porter stomp / Beale street blues / Old miss / Running wild
CD ESJCD 539
Essential Jazz / Apr '97 / BMG

Allegiance

BLODORNSOFFER
CD NFR 021CD
No Fashion / Apr '97 / Plastic Head

HYMN TILL HANGAGUD
CD NFR 014CD
No Fashion / May '96 / Plastic Head

Allegro Milano

ALLEGRO MILANO PLAYS RONDO VENEZIANO
Magica melodia / La serenissima / Rondo Veneziano / Scaramucce / Visioni di venezia / Fantasia Venezia / Misteriosa Venezia / Rosso Veneziano / Musica...fantasia / Capriccio venziano / Odissea Veneziana / Carme veneziano / Venezia lunare / Andante Milano / Molto allegro / Alla turca
CD GRF 190
Tring / Jan '93 / Tring

Allen, Carl

PICCADILLY SQUARE (Allen, Carl & Manhattan Projects)
Piccadilly Square / Autumn leaves / 'Round midnight / Lullaby of birdland / Annie's mood / Biscuit man / New joy / What's new / In the still of the night / Afterthoughts
CD SJP 406

Timeless Jazz / Oct '93 / New Note/ Pinnacle

Allen, Daevid

BANANA MOON
Time of your life / Memories / All I want is out of here / Fred the fish / White neck blooze / Stoned innocent Frankenstein / His adventures in the land of Flip / I am a bowl
CD _______ CDCRH 110
Charly / Feb '97 / Koch
CD _______ 14945
Spalax / Jul '97 / ADA / Cargo / Direct / Discovery / Greyhound

DEATH OF ROCK AND OTHER ENTRANCES, THE
Death of rock / Poet for sale / Tally's birthday song / You never existed at all / Afraid / Radio gnome concert intro loop / Switch doctor / Gong ORFT invasion 1971
CD _______ BP 114CD
Blueprint / Aug '96 / Pinnacle

DIVIDED ALIEN CLOCKWORK BAND
Preface / SQ invocation / When / Well / Bell / Boom / Dab / Gay / Poet for sale / I am a freud / Fastfather / Disguise / Gone and wandering waltz / Sex is a careless sea / Death of rock / Tally's birthday party / Pearle / Bodygas / Froghello / Strong woman / Smile
CD _______ BP 269CD
Blueprint / Sep '97 / Pinnacle

DIVIDEDALIENPLAYBAX 8
When / Well / Bell / Boon / Dab / Gay / Rude / Disguise / Pearls / Bodygas / Froghello / Fast-father / Smile
CD _______ 14837
Spalax / Jul '96 / ADA / Cargo / Direct / Discovery / Greyhound

DREAMING A DREAM
CD _______ AGASCD 007
GAS / Oct '96 / Pinnacle

GLISSANDO SPIRIT (Invisible Opera Company Of Tibet)
Landing / Uluwatu / Electric bird / Baliman energy / Cosmic dancer / Inner voice / High mountains dance / Dreaming / Moon in the sky / Mirage / Distant shore / Stars can frighten you / 7 keys / Wizard's garden / Eastside
CD _______ VP 147CD
Voiceprint / Mar '97 / Pinnacle

JEWEL IN THE LOTUS (Invisible Opera Company Of Tibet)
CD _______ AGASCD 006
GAS / Sep '96 / Pinnacle

LIVE 1963 (Allen, Daevid Trio)
Love is a careless sea / My head is a nightclub / Capacity travel (parts 1 - 4) / Song of the jazzman / Dear olde Benny Green is a-turning in his grave / Ya sunny WOT / Frederique la Poissonavec Frite sur le dos
CD _______ VP 122CD
Voiceprint / Mar '94 / Pinnacle

N'EXISTE PAS
CD _______ 542817
Spalax / May '96 / ADA / Cargo / Direct / Discovery / Greyhound

NOW IS THE HAPPIEST TIME OF YOUR LIFE
Flamenco zero / Why do we treat ourselves like we do / Tally and Orlando meet the coconut pixie / See you on the moontower / Poet for sale / Only make love if you want to / I am / Deya Goddess / Crocodile nonsense poem
CD _______ 542825
Spalax / May '96 / ADA / Cargo / Direct / Discovery / Greyhound
CD _______ CDCRH 116
Charly / Feb '97 / Koch

OPIUM FOR THE PEOPLE/ALIEN IN NEW YORK
CD _______ 14844
Spalax / Oct '96 / ADA / Cargo / Direct / Discovery / Greyhound

SHE
CD _______ DMCD 1025
Demi-Monde / Feb '90 / RTM/Disc / TKO Magnum

TWELVE SELVES
Introdrone / Mystico Fanatico / Away away away / Colage/Bellyful of telephone / She/ Isis is calling / Collage patafisico/Divided alien manifesto / I love sex but / Wargasm / Children of the new world / O Wichitio / Sexual blueprint / Gaia / My heart's song
CD _______ VP 111CD
Voiceprint / Nov '93 / Pinnacle

VOICEPRINT RADIO SESSION
CD _______ VPR 012CD
Voiceprint / Oct '94 / Pinnacle

Allen, Eddie

R & B
Frick and frack / As quiet a it's kept / Clairvoyant / Almost you / Schism / Seduction / Quest
CD _______ ENJ 90332
Enja / Aug '95 / New Note/Pinnacle / Vital/ SAM

Allen, Ernestine

LET IT ROLL
Let it roll / I want a little boy / Lullaby of Broadway / Mean and evil / Love for sale / Miss Allen's blues / Baubles, bangles and beads / Man I love / Tea for two
CD _______ OBCCD 539
Original Blues Classics / Nov '92 / Complete/Pinnacle / Wellard

Allen, Geri

EYES IN THE BACK OF YOUR HEAD
Mother wit / New eyes opening / Vertical flowing / MOPE / FMFFMF / Dark eyes / Little waltz / In the back of your head / Windows to the soul / Eyes have it
CD _______ CDP 8382972
Blue Note / Jun '97 / EMI

IN THE YEAR OF THE DRAGON (Allen, Geri & Charlie Haden/Paul Motian)
Oblivion / For John Malachi / Rollano / See you at per tutti's / Last call / No more Mr. Nice Guy / Invisible / First song / In the year of the dragon
CD _______ 8344282
jMT / May '91 / PolyGram

LIVE AT THE VILLAGE VANGUARD (Allen, Geri & Charlie Haden/Paul Motian)
CD _______ DIW 847
DIW / Jul '91 / Cadillac / Harmonia Mundi

SOME ASPECTS OF WATER (Allen, Geri Trio/1996 Jazzpar Nonet)
CD _______ STCD 4212
Storyville / May '97 / Cadillac / Jazz Music / Wellard

Allen, Harry

CELEBRATION OF SAM FAIN (Allen, Harry Trio)
CD _______ ACD 261
Audiophile / Jan '93 / Jazz Music

CELEBRATION OF STRAYHORN (Allen, Harry & Keith Ingham)
CD _______ PCD 7101
Progressive / Apr '94 / Jazz Music

CELEBRATION OF STRAYHORN NO.2 (Allen, Harry & Keith Ingham)
CD _______ PCD 7102
Progressive / Apr '94 / Jazz Music

HOW LONG HAS THIS BEEN GOING ON
CD _______ PCD 7082
Progressive / '92 / Jazz Music

I KNOW THAT YOU KNOW (Allen, Harry Trio)
CD _______ CHECD 00104
Master Mix / Jul '92 / Jazz Music / New Note/Pinnacle / Wellard

I'LL NEVER BE THE SAME (Allen, Harry & Howard Alden)
All through the night / I won't dance / I'll close my eyes
CD _______ CHECD 106
Master Mix / Jun '93 / Jazz Music / New Note/Pinnacle / Wellard

JAZZ IN AMERIKA HAUS VOL.1 (Allen, Harry Quartet)
CD _______ CD 011
Nagel Heyer / May '96 / Jazz Music

LITTLE TOUCH OF HARRY, A (Allen, Harry Quartet)
From this moment on / Luck be a lady tonight / Nobody's heart / Just like another dream / All god's chillun' got rhythm / I wanna be around / This is all I ask / I never knew / It might as well be spring / Spring can really hang up the most / Easy to love / I get along without you very well
CD _______ CHECD 00118
Master Mix / Sep '97 / Jazz Music / New Note/Pinnacle / Wellard

LIVE AT RENOUF'S (Allen, Harry Quartet)
In a mellowtone / Man I love / Nightingale sang in Berkeley Square / Shadow of your smile / Too close for comfort / Ev'ry time we say goodbye / One note samba / Danny boy
CD _______ CHECD 00117
Master Mix / Nov '96 / Jazz Music / New Note/Pinnacle / Wellard

NIGHT AT BIRDLAND VOL.1 (Allen, Harry Quintet)
CD _______ CD 007
Nagel Heyer / May '96 / Jazz Music

NIGHT AT BIRDLAND VOL.2 (Allen, Harry Quintet)
CD _______ CD 010
Nagel Heyer / May '96 / Jazz Music

SOMEONE TO LIGHT UP YOUR LIFE (Allen, Harry Quartet)
CD _______ CHECD 00100
Master Mix / Apr '92 / Jazz Music / New Note/Pinnacle / Wellard

Allen, Henry 'Red'

CLASSICS 1929-1933
CD _______ CLASSICS 540
Classics / Dec '90 / Discovery / Jazz Music

CLASSICS 1933-1935
CD _______ CLASSICS 551
Classics / Dec '90 / Discovery / Jazz Music

CLASSICS 1935-1936
CD _______ CLASSICS 575
Classics / Oct '91 / Discovery / Jazz Music

CLASSICS 1936-1937
CD _______ CLASSICS 590
Classics / Sep '91 / Discovery / Jazz Music

CLASSICS 1937-1941
CD _______ CLASSICS 628
Classics / Oct '92 / Discovery / Jazz Music

COLLECTION VOL.1, THE
CD _______ COCD 01
Collector's Classics / Dec '89 / Cadillac / Complete/Pinnacle / Jazz Music

COLLECTION VOL.2, THE
CD _______ COCD 02
Collector's Classics / Sep '92 / Cadillac / Complete/Pinnacle / Jazz Music

COLLECTION VOL.3, THE
CD _______ COCD 13
Collector's Classics / Oct '89 / Cadillac / Complete/Pinnacle / Jazz Music

DOCTOR JAZZ VOL.9
CD _______ STCD 6049
Storyville / Jul '96 / Cadillac / Jazz Music / Wellard

HENRY 'RED' ALLEN 1936-1937
CD _______ CD 590
Classic Jazz Masters / Sep '91 / Wellard

INTRODUCTION TO HENRY 'RED' ALLEN 1929-1941, AN
CD _______ 4031
Best Of Jazz / Mar '96 / Discovery

ORIGINAL 1933-1941
River's takin' care of me / Believe it, beloved / Rosetta / Body and soul / He ain't got rhythm / KK boogie / Jack the bellboy / When my dreamboat comes home
CD _______ TAXS 32
Tax / Aug '94 / Cadillac / Jazz Music / Wellard

SWING OUT
CD _______ TPZ 1037
Topaz Jazz / Jan '96 / Cadillac / Pinnacle

Allen, Pete

BEAU SEJOUR
Seagull strut / Body and soul / I'm gonna sit right down and write myself a letter / St. Phillip's street breakdown / Elephant stomp / Roses of Picardy
CD _______ PAR 492CD
PAR / Apr '91 / Koch

BIG CHIEF (Allen, Pete Jazz Band)
CD _______ LOTCD 4305
Loose / Nov '96 / BMG / Wellard

JAZZ YOU LIKE IT (Allen, Pete & Clinton Ford)
Royal Garden blues / Melancholy baby / Swanee River / Apple blossom time / Mood indigo / Sailing down the Chesapeake Bay / Georgia / Wreck of ol' 97
CD _______ PAR 491CD
PAR / Apr '91 / Koch

Allen, Peter

PETER ALLEN
CD _______ RVCD 53
Raven / Mar '96 / ADA / Direct

Allen, Red

KITCHEN TAPES, THE (Allen, Red & Frank Wakefield)
CD _______ ACD 11
Acoustic Disc / Jul '97 / ADA / Koch

Allen, Rex

VOICE OF THE WEST
Tyin' knots in the Devil's tail / Moonshine steer / Fireman cowboy / Today I started loving you again / Windy Bill / Little Joe the wrangler / When the work's all done this fall / Droop ears / Streets of Laredo / Braggin' drunk from Wilcox / Gone girl / Catfish John / You never did give up on me / Just call me lonesome / Reflex reaction
CD _______ BCD 15284
Bear Family / Aug '86 / Direct / Rollercoaster / Swift

Allen, Rex

REX ALLEN & HIS SWING EXPRESS
CD _______ CD 016
Nagel Heyer / May '96 / Jazz Music

Allen, Steve

STEVE ALLEN PLAYS JAZZ TONIGHT
Tangerine / One I love (belongs to somebody else) / Body and soul / After you've gone / Don't cry little girl / Steve's blues / Gone with the wind / Sinner kissed an angel / You go to my head / I can't get started (with you) / Everyone can see how much I love you / I should have told you so / Fine and dandy
CD _______ CCD 4548
Concord Jazz / May '93 / New Note/ Pinnacle

Allen, Terry

HUMAN REMAINS
CD _______ SHCD 1050
Sugar Hill / Feb '96 / ADA / CM / Direct / Koch / Roots

LUBBOCK (ON EVERYTHING)
Amarillo highway / Highplains jamboree / Great Joe Bob / Wolfman of del rio / Lubbock woman / Girl who danced Oklahoma / Truckload of art / Collector (and the art mob) / Oui / Rendevous USA / Cocktails for three / Beautiful waitress / Blue asian reds / New Delhi freight rain / FFA / Flatland farmer / My amigo / Pink and black song / Thirty years waltz / I just left myself
CD _______ SHCD 1047
Sugar Hill / Aug '96 / ADA / CM / Direct / Koch / Roots

PEDAL STEAL (Allen, Terry & The Panhandle Mystery Band)
CD _______ FATE 7655266
Fate / Apr '93 / ADA / Direct

SILENT MAJORITY, THE
CD _______ FATE 7453266
Fate / May '93 / ADA / Direct

SMOKIN' THE DUMMY
Heart of California / Cocaine cowboy / Whatever happened to jesus / Helena Montana / Texas tears / Cajun roll / Feelin' easy / Night Cafe / Roll truck roll / Red bird / Lubbock tornado (I don't know)
CD _______ FRCD 02
Fate / '92 / ADA / Direct

SMOKIN' THE DUMMY/BLOODLINES (Allen, Terry & The Panhandle Mystery Band)
CD _______ SHCD 1057
Sugar Hill / May '97 / ADA / CM / Direct / Koch / Roots

Allen, Thomas

IF I LOVED YOU (Allen, Thomas & Valerie Masterson)
CD _______ VIRCD 8317
Shanachie / Nov '93 / ADA / Greensleeves / Koch

Alleyne-Johnson, Ed

FLY BEFORE DAWN
CD _______ WINGCD 001
Backs / Jul '95 / RTM/Disc

PURPLE ELECTRIC VIOLIN CONCERTO
Oxford suite / Inner city music / Improvisation / Concrete eden
CD _______ EQCD 001
Equation / Feb '93 / Pinnacle / RTM/Disc

ULTRAVIOLET
CD _______ EQCD 002
Equation / Jun '94 / Pinnacle / RTM/Disc

Alligators

HISTORY OF ROCK 'N' ROLL, THE
CD _______ POCD 015
Popcorn / Aug '96 / Nervous

Allin, G.G.

HATED IN THE NATION
CD _______ RE 148CD
ROIR / Nov '94 / Plastic Head / Shellshock/Disc

MURDER JUNKIES
CD _______ 422008
New Rose / May '94 / ADA / Direct / Discovery

TERROR IN AMERICA
CD _______ OVER 43CD
Overground / Nov '95 / Shellshock/Disc / SRD

Allin, Ralph

TEA FOR THREE
Nightingale sang in Berkeley square / Hungarian dance no. 5 / Liebesleid / Cheek to cheek / Misty / Ain't misbehavin' / Play gypsy dance / Georgia on my mind / Tango / Czardas / Memory / Entertainer / Salut d'amour / I can't give you anything but love / Way down yonder in New Orleans / Largo from Winter, four seasons / Yesterday / Josika / I know him so well / Tea for two / Summertime / Fiddler on the roof
CD _______ CDGRS 1246
Grosvenor / '91 / Grosvenor

Allison

WAILING
CD _______ NGCD 544
Twinkle / Jul '94 / Jet Star / Kingdom / SRD

Allison, Amy

MAUDLIN YEARS, THE
CD 379112
Koch International / Sep '96 / Koch

Allison, Ben

SEVEN ARROWS
CD 378322
Koch Jazz / Nov '96 / Koch

Allison, Bernard

HANG ON
Mai / Going down / Cadillac assembly line / Voodoo thang / Missing Stevie / Action speaks louder than words / Rockin' Robin / You're hurting me / Hang on / Looking beyond the past / Idols in mind / Voodoo chile medley
CD INAK 9017CD
In Akustik / Jul '97 / Direct / TKO Magnum

Allison, David

GUITAR GI-TAR
CD LDL 1211CD
Lochshore / Mar '94 / ADA / Direct / Duncans

REPORTING
Birnam oak / Dreamdays / Excuse me / Ceuta / Chinese whispers / Ishka / Spiral / Journey / Something more comfortable / Forgive, forget... / Border / Going home
CD DUNCD 007
Dunkeld / Feb '92 / ADA / CM / Direct

Allison, Luther

BAD LOVE
CD RRCD 901295
Ruf / Aug '94 / Pinnacle

BLUE STREAK
CD TRIP 7712
Ruf / Nov '95 / Pinnacle

HAND ME DOWN MY MOONSHINE
Good morning love / One more / Lightning bolt / I need a friend / Castle / She's fine / Stay with me / Farmer's child / Don't burn my bread / You're the one / Hand me down my moonshine / Meet me in my hometown
CD INAK 9015CD
In Akustik / Jul '97 / Direct / TKO Magnum

HERE I COME
CD 493332
Melodie / Mar '96 / ADA / Discovery / Grapevine/PolyGram / Greensleeves / Jet Star

LIFE IS A BITCH
CD 493312
Melodie / Mar '96 / ADA / Discovery / Grapevine/PolyGram / Greensleeves / Jet Star

LIVE 1989
CD RRCD 901309
Ruf / Apr '95 / Pinnacle

LIVE IN MONTREUX 1974-1994
CD RUF 1008
Ruf / Jan '97 / Pinnacle

LOVE ME MAMA
CD DE 625
Delmark / Nov '96 / ADA / Cadillac / CM / Direct / Hot Shot

LOVE ME PAPA
CD ECD 260152
Evidence / Jan '92 / ADA / Cadillac / Harmonia Mundi

RECKLESS
CD RUF 1012
Ruf / Mar '97 / Pinnacle
CD ALCD 4849
Alligator / May '97 / ADA / CM / Direct

RICH MAN
Chicago / Rich man / Love is free / Cold as ice / Freedom / Fight / Big mistake / Get down / Cry (crying for peace)
CD TRIP 8001
Ruf / Apr '96 / Pinnacle

SWEET HOME CHICAGO (Charly Blues Masterworks Vol.37)
Dust my broom / I got worries / You don't love me / Goin' down / I'm gonna leave you alone / Sweet home Chicago
CD CDBM 37
Charly / Jan '93 / Koch

Allison, Mose

AUTUMN SONG
Promenade / Eyesight to the blind / It's crazy / That's alright Mama / Devil in the cane field / Strange / Autumn song / Do nothin' 'til you hear from me / Spires / Groovin' high
CD OJCCD 894
Original Jazz Classics / Nov '96 / Complete/ Pinnacle / Jazz Music / Wellard

BEST OF MOSE ALLISON, THE
CD RSACD 814
Sequel / Oct '94 / BMG

DOWN HOME PIANO
Dinner on the ground / Crepuscular air / Mule / Creek bank / Town / Devil in the cane field / Minstrels / Moon and cypress / Carnival / Mojo woman
CD OJCCD 922
Original Jazz Classics / Jun '97 / Complete/ Pinnacle / Jazz Music / Wellard

EARTH WANTS YOU, THE
Certified senior citizen / This ain't me / You can't push people around / My ideal / Earth wants you / Cabaret cards / Red wagon / Variation on Dixie / What a shame / Nataral born Malcontent / Who's in, who's out / Children of the future / I don't love you
CD CDP 8276402
Blue Note / Dec '95 / EMI

HIGH JINKS (The Mose Allison Trilogy/ 3CD Set)
Transfiguration of Hiram Brown suite / Barefoot, dirt road / City home / Cuttin' out / Gotham day / Gotham night / Ech / River / Finale / How little we know / Baby, please don't go / Make yourself comfortable / Deed I do / Love for sale / Barefoot, dirt road / I love the life I live / News / Fool's paradise / You turned the tables on me / Isobel / You're a sweetheart / Night ride / Path / Mad with you / Hittin' on one / I ain't got nobody / Can't we be friends / Pretty girl is like a melody / Am I blue / V8 Ford blues / Please don't talk about me when I'm gone / Baby, please don't go / Hey, good lookin' / I love the life I live / A ain't got nobody / Back on the corner / Life is suicide / Deed I do / Ask me nice / You're a sweetheart / Mad with you / High jinks / So rare / Hills
CD Set J3K 64275
Sony Jazz / Feb '97 / Sony

JAZZ PROFILE
Ever since the world ended / Top forty / Putting up with me / I looked in the mirror / Getting there / What's your movie / Ever since I stole the blues / Was / Getting paid waltz / My backyard / Certified senior citizen / This ain't me / You can't push people around / Earth wants me
CD CDP 8552302
Blue Note / May '97 / EMI

SINGS AND PLAYS
Seventh son / Eyesight to the blind / Yardbird suite / That's alright Mama / Parchman farm / I hadn't anyone till you / Do nothin' 'til you hear from me / Young man / Bye bye blues
CD CDJZD 007
Fantasy / Sep '91 / Jazz Music / Pinnacle / Wellard

TELL ME SOMETHING (The Songs Of Mose Allison) (Various Artists)
One of these days: *Morrison, Van* / You can count on me (to do my part): *Morrison, Van* / If you live: *Sidran, Ben* / Was: *Fame, Georgie* / Look here: *Sidran, Ben* / City home: *Fame, Georgie* / No trouble living: *Sidran, Ben* / Benediction: *Morrison, Van & Ben Sidran/Georgie Fame* / Back on th corner: *Fame, Georgie* / Tell me something: *Morrison, Van* / I don't want much: *Morrison, Van & Mose Allison* / News nightclub: *Morrison, Van* / Perfect moment: *Morrison, Van & Mose Allison*
CD 5332032
Verve / Sep '96 / PolyGram

Allman Brothers

ALL LIVE
Jessica / Stormy Monday / Statesboro blues / Can't lose what you never had / Ain't wastin' time no more / Done somebody wrong / Ramblin' man / Don't mess up a good thing / Turn on your love light / Will the circle be unbroken / Queen of hearts
CD 5518242
PolyGram / Nov '96 / PolyGram

ALLMAN BROTHERS BAND, THE
Don't want you no more / It's not my cross to bear / Black hearted woman / Trouble no more / Every hungry woman / Dreams / Whipping post
CD 8236532
Polydor / '94 / PolyGram

BROTHERS AND SISTERS
Wasted words / Ramblin' man / Come and go blues / Jelly jelly / Southbound / Jessica / Pony boy
CD 8250922
Polydor / Jan '89 / PolyGram

DECADE OF HITS 1969-1979, A
Whipping post / Dreams / In memory of Elizabeth Reed / One way out / Blue sky / Wasted words / Revival / Crazy love / Little Martha / Ain't wastin' time no more / Jessica / Melissa / Southbound / Midnight rider / Ramblin' man / Statesboro blues
CD 5111562
Polydor / Mar '92 / PolyGram

EAT A PEACH
Ain't wastin' time no more / Le bers in A minor / Melissa / Mountain jam / One way out / Trouble no more / Stand back / Blue sky / Little Martha
CD 8236542
Polydor / Jul '88 / PolyGram

FILLMORE CONCERTS
CD 5172942
Polydor / Apr '96 / PolyGram

HELL & HIGH WATER (Best Of The Arista Years)
Hell and high water / Mystery woman / From the madness of the west / I got a right to be wrong / Angeline / Famous last words / Brothers of the road / Leavin' / Straight from the heart / Judgement / Never knew how much (I needed you)
CD 07822187242
RCA / Sep '94 / BMG

IDLE WIND SOUTH
CD 8333342
Polydor / Mar '89 / PolyGram

LIVE AT FILLMORE EAST (2CD Set)
Statesboro blues / (I) done somebody wrong / They call it stormy Monday / You don't love me / Hot lanta / In memory of Elizabeth Reed / Whipping post
CD Set 8232732
Polydor / Jul '88 / PolyGram

Allman, Duane

ANTHOLOGY
Hey Jude / Road of love / Goin' down slow / Weight / Games people play / Shake for me / Rollin' stone / Mean ol' world / Layla / Stand back / Dreams / Little Martha
CD 8314442
Polydor / Apr '89 / PolyGram

Alloy

ALLOY
CD VROOM 4
Engine / Aug '93 / Vital

Allred, John

IN THE BEGINNING
CD ARCD 19115
Arbors Jazz / Nov '94 / Cadillac

Allure

ALLURE
Introduction / Anything you want / You're gonna love me / Head over heels / No question / All cried out / Story / Come into my house / When you need someone / Give you all I got / I'll give you anything / Wanna get with you / Last chance / Mama said
CD 4875242
Crave / May '97 / Sony

Allyn, David

SOFT AS SPRING
CD ACD 155
Audiophile / Jan '94 / Jazz Music

Allyson, Karrin

AZURE-TE
How high the moon / Ornithology / Gee baby / Bernie's tune / Night and day / Blame it on my youth / Yardbird suite / Good morning heartache / Stompin' at the Savoy / Azure te / Some other time / Samba '88
CD CCD 4641
Concord Jazz / May '95 / New Note/ Pinnacle

COLLAGE
It could happen to you / Fried bananas / Autumn leaves (Les fueilles mortes) / Robert Frost / All of you / And so it goes / Joy Spring / Ask me now / Cherokee / Here, there and everywhere / Give it up or let me go / Faltando um pedaco / Live for life
CD CCD 4709
Concord Crossover / Jul '96 / New Note/ Pinnacle

DAYDREAM
Daydream / Like someone in love / My foolish heart / So danca samba / Corcovado / Show me / Monk medley / Everything must change/Donna Lee/Indiana / I ain't got nothin' but the blues / You can't rush spring
CD CCD 47732
Concord Jazz / Sep '97 / New Note/ Pinnacle

SWEET HOME COOKIN'
One note samba / I cover the waterfront / Can't we be friends / Yeh yeh / Goodbye Pork Pie Hat / No moon at all / Sweet home cookin' man / You are too beautiful / Social call / Dindi / In a sentimental mood / I love Paris
CD CCD 4593
Concord Jazz / Apr '94 / New Note/ Pinnacle

Alma Flamenca

ANDALUCIA VIVA
CD 31064
Divucsa / Oct '96 / Discovery

Almadraba

CANTOS DEL CAMPO Y DE LA MER
CD CDH 008
Sonifolk / Dec '94 / ADA / CM

Almanzor

TRIO DE VEUZE BRETAGNE
CD AVPL 14CD
Diffusion Breizh / Apr '95 / ADA

Almeida, Laurindo

ARTISTRY IN RHYTHM (Almeida, Laurindo Trio)
Chariots of fire / Astronauta / Andante / Te amo / Artistry in rhythm / Always on my mind / Slaughter on 10th Avenue / Up where we belong / Almost a farewell / Liza / Puka shells in a whirl
CD CCD 4238
Concord Jazz / Mar '94 / New Note/ Pinnacle

BRAZILIAN SOUL (Almeida, Laurindo & Charlie Byrd)
CD CCD 4150
Concord Picante / Jul '88 / New Note/ Pinnacle

BRAZILLIANCE VOL.1 (Almeida, Laurindo & Bud Shank)
CD CDP 7963392
Blue Note / Jan '92 / EMI

CHAMBER JAZZ
Dingue li bangue / Unaccustomed Bach / Odeon / Bourree and double / Melissa / You and I / Clair de Lune / Chopin a la breve / Turuna
CD CCD 4084
Concord Jazz / May '91 / New Note/ Pinnacle

DANCE THE BOSSA NOVA
CD CD 62055
Saludos Amigos / May '94 / Target/BMG

LATIN ODYSSEY (Almeida, Laurindo & Charlie Byrd)
Memory / Zum and ressurection / El nino / Gitanerias / Adios / El cavilan / Estrellita / Turbilhao / Intermezzo malinconico
CD CCD 4211
Concord Picante / Jan '90 / New Note/ Pinnacle

MUSIC OF THE BRAZILIAN MASTERS (Almeida, Laurindo & Charlie Byrd)
CD CCD 4389
New Note / Oct '89 / Cadillac / New Note/ Pinnacle

OUTRA VEZ (ONCE AGAIN)
Outra vez / Jolly crow / Danza five / Blue skies / Goin' home / Samba de break / Beethoven and Monk / Esacdo / Um a zero / Carinhoso / Corcovado / Girl from Ipanema / Desafinado
CD CCD 4497
Concord Jazz / Feb '92 / New Note/ Pinnacle

TANGO (Almeida, Laurindo & Charlie Byrd)
Orchids in the moonlight / Blue tango / Jalousie / Los enamorados / La Rosita / Tanog alegre / La cumparsita / Moon was yellow / Hernando's hideaway / Tanguero / Breakin' away: *Laima*
CD CCD 4290
Concord Picante / Jul '88 / New Note/ Pinnacle

Almighty

BLOOD, FIRE AND LIVE
Full force lovin' machine / Lay down the law / Destroyed / Resurrection mutha / You've gone wild / Blood, fire and love / Wild and wonderful / You ain't seen nothin' yet
CD 8471072
Polydor / Oct '89 / PolyGram

BLOOD, FIRE AND LOVE
CD 8413472
Polydor / Sep '89 / PolyGram

CRANK
Ultraviolet / Wrench / Unreal thing / Jonestown mind / Move right in / Crank and deceit / United state of apathy / Welcome to defiance / Way beyond belief / Crackdown / Sorry for nothing / Cheat / Shitzophrenic
CD CDCHR 6086
Chrysalis / Sep '94 / EMI

JUST FOR LIFE
CD RAWCD 118
Raw Power / May '96 / Pinnacle

SOUL DESTRUCTION
Crucify / Free 'n' easy / Joy bang one time / Love religion / Bandaged knees / Praying to the red light / Sin against the light / Little lost sometimes / Devil's toy / What more do you want / Hell to pay / Loaded
CD 8479612
Polydor / Mar '96 / PolyGram

Almond, Marc

FANTASTIC STAR
Caged / Out there / We need jealousy / Idol (parts 1 & 2 All Gods fall) / Baby night eyes / Adored and explored / Child star / Looking for love (in all the wrong places) / Addicted / Edge of heartbreak / Love to die for / Betrayed / On the prowl / Come in sweet assassin / Brilliant creatures / Shining brightly
CD 5286592
Some Bizarre/Mercury / Nov '95 / PolyGram

MOTHER FIST AND HER FIVE DAUGHTERS
Mother fist / There is a bed / St. Judy / Room below / Angel in her kiss / Mr. Sad / Melancholy rose / Sea says / Champ / Ruby red / Hustler
CD CDFTH 2
Some Bizarre/Mercury / Apr '87 / PolyGram

SINGLES 1984-1987
Boy who came back / You have / Tenderness is a weakness / Stories of Johnny / Love letters / House is haunted / Woman's story / Ruby red / Melancholy rose / Mother fist
CD CDFTH 3
Some Bizarre/Mercury / Nov '87 / PolyGram

STORIES OF JOHNNY
Traumas, traumas, traumas / Stories of Johnny / House is haunted / Love letters / Flesh is willing / Always / Contempt / I who never / My candle burns / Love and little white lies
CD CDFTH 1
Some Bizarre/Mercury / Oct '85 / PolyGram

TENEMENT SYMPHONY
Meet me in my dream / Beautiful brutal thing / I've never seen your face / Vaudeville and burlesque / Champagne / Prelude / Jackie / What is love / Trois chansons de bilitis / Days of Pearly Spencer / My hand over my heart
CD 9031755182
Some Bizarre/WEA / Feb '95 / Warner Music

TREASURE BOX
City of nights / Waifs and strays / King of the fools / Libertine's dream / Only the moment / Gambler / Tears run rings / Everything I wanted love to be / Something's gotten hold of my heart / Bittersweet / Frost comes tomorrow / She took my soul in Istanbul / Stars we are / Lover spurned / Real evil / Exotica rose / Desperate hours / Old Jack's charm / These my dreams are yours / Sea still sings / Madame de la luna / Death's diary / Toreador in the rain / Orpheus in red velvet / Sensualist
CD Set CDMATBOX 1
Parlophone / Aug '95 / EMI

TWELVE YEARS OF TEARS
Tears run rings / Champagne / Bedsitter / Mr. Sad / There is a bed / Youth / If you go away / Jackie / Desperate hours / Waifs and strays / Something's gotten hold of my heart / What makes a man / Tainted love / Say hello, wave goodbye
CD 4509920332
Some Bizarre/WEA / Apr '93 / Warner Music

VIRGIN'S TALE VOL.1, A
Stories of Johnny / Love letter / Blond boy / House is Haunted / Broken bracelets / Cara a cara / Heel / Salty dog / Plague / Little white cloud that cried / For one moment / Just good friends
CD CDVIP 163
Virgin VIP / Oct '96 / EMI

VIRGIN'S TALE VOL.2, A
Gyp of the blood / World full of people / Black lullabye / Pirate Jenny / Surabaya Johnny / Two sailors on the beach / Anarcoma / Jackal jackal / Broken hearted and beautiful / I'm sick of you tasting of somebody else
CD CDVM 9011
Virgin / Sep '92 / EMI
CD CDVIP 173
Virgin VIP / Apr '97 / EMI

Almqvist, Thomas

REWIND
Intro / Traces of pangaea / Voice of the moth / No sense / Borders / Hot fingers / Quebec / Sun signs / Michael's butterfly / Conscious dreams / Shadow of a black crow / Changing winds / Sortie
CD RESCD 513
Resource / Jul '97 / ADA / Direct

Alomar, Carlos

DREAM GENERATOR
Hallucination / Siamese dreams / Global alpha / Winkin' blinkin' and nod / Insomniac / Dream generator / REM / Feline lullaby (Sam's song)
CD 259964
Private Music / Nov '89 / BMG

Alonso, Tom

INDIAN SUMMER
Indian summer / Pearl / Mashed potato valley breakdown / Blue hearts / Don't forget to dream / Rain / Cold coffee suite / Screenscape
CD CCD 711
Clean Cuts / Nov '96 / Direct / Jazz Music / Wellard

Alonson, Pachito

UNA SALSA EN PARIS
CD 74321433542
Milan / Feb '97 / Conifer/BMG / Silva Screen

Aloof

COVER THE CRIME
CD 0630102322
East West / May '95 / Warner Music

SINKIN'
CD 0630145842
East West / Jun '96 / Warner Music

SINKING
One night stand / Bittersweet / Stuck on the shelf / Abuse / Wish you were here / Sinking / One night stand / Hot knives at lunchtime / Losing it / Sunk / Last stand
CD 0630177392
East West / Mar '97 / Warner Music

Aloof Proof

INSIDE THE QUIET
CD CDCB 0103
Carbon Base / Jun '95 / Plastic Head

Alpamayo

FOLKLORE DE PERU Y ECUADOR
CD EUCD 1220
ARC / Sep '93 / ADA / ARC Music

MUSIC FROM PERU AND ECUADOR
CD EUCD 1184
ARC / Apr '92 / ADA / ARC Music

Alperin, Mikhail

WAVE OF SORROW (Alperin, Mikhail & Arkady Shilkloper)
Song / Poem / Wave of sorrow / Toccata / Unisons / Introduction and dance / Short storey / Prelude in B minor / Miniature / Epilogue
CD 8396212
ECM / Jan '90 / New Note/Pinnacle

Alperin, Misha

NORTH STORY
Morning / Psalm No.1 / Ironical evening / Alone / Afternoon / Psalm No.2 / North story / Etude / Kristi blodsdraper (Fucsia)
CD 5310222
ECM / May '97 / New Note/Pinnacle

Alpert, Herb

SECOND WIND
CD ALMCD 010
Almo Sounds / Jul '96 / Pinnacle

VERY BEST OF HERB ALPERT
Lonely bull / Taste of honey / Tijuana taxi / Spanish flea / Zorba the Greek / What now my love / Casino Royale / This guy's in love with you / Without her / Jerusalem / Rise / Rotation / Keep your eye on me / Diamonds / Jump Street
CD CDMID 170
A&M / Oct '92 / PolyGram

Alpert, Pauline

KEYBOARD WIZARDS OF THE GERSHWIN ERA VOL.1
CD GEMMCD 9201
Pearl / Dec '95 / Harmonia Mundi

Alpha & Omega

ALMIGHTY JAH (Alpha & Omega & Dub Judah)
CD AOCD 77
Alpha & Omega / Oct '92 / Jet Star / SRD

DANIEL/KING & QUEEN
CD AOCD 1
Alpha & Omega / Nov '93 / Jet Star / SRD

DUB PLATE SELECTION VOL.1
CD AOCD 95
Alpha & Omega / Apr '95 / Jet Star / SRD

DUB PLATE SELECTION VOL.2
Promised land / Dub signs / Shashamani / Ancient wisdom / Jerusalem / Jah is calling / Warrior / King and queen / Stepping up / Firmament / No man's land / Africa Ethiopia
CD AOCD 98
Alpha & Omega / Apr '97 / Jet Star / SRD

EVERYDAY LIFE
CD AOCD 93
Alpha & Omega / Jun '93 / Jet Star / SRD

FAITH IN THE DARK
CD AOCD 94
Alpha & Omega / Mar '94 / Jet Star / SRD

OVERSTANDING/WATCH & PRAY
CD AOCD 27
Alpha & Omega / Sep '93 / Jet Star / SRD

SIGNS, THE
CD BTT 0292
Buback / Aug '94 / SRD

SOUND SYSTEM DUB
CD RUSCD 8216
ROIR / Oct '95 / Plastic Head / Shellshock/Disc

TREE OF LIFE
CD AOCD 96
Alpha & Omega / Nov '95 / Jet Star / SRD

VOICE IN THE WILDERNESS
Words of thy mouth / Rastafari / Firmament / Voice in the wilderness / Seven seas / Rightful ruler / Dub prophet / This judgement / Ancient of days / Shashamani / Break every chain / Words
CD AOCD 97
Alpha & Omega / Oct '96 / Jet Star / SRD

Alpha Band

INTERVIEWS (Alpha Band & T-Bone Burnett)
Interviews / Cheap perfume / Ten figures / Dogs / Last chance to dance / East of East / You angel you / Spark in the dark / Rich man / Mighty man / Back in my baby's arms again
CD EDCD 272
Edsel / Jul '91 / Pinnacle

Alpha Blondy

BEST OF ALPHA BLONDY, THE
CD SHANCD 43075
Shanachie / Oct '90 / ADA / Greensleeves / Koch
CD CDRRS 034
Jayrem / Oct '96 / CM / Jet Star

BEST OF ALPHA BLONDY, THE
Cocody rock / Apartheid is Nazism / Come back Jesus / Jerusalem / Politiqui / Sweet Fanta Diallo / Banana / Cafe Cacao / Masada / Rendezvous / Yeye / Fulgence kassy / Amour papier / Longeur
CD CDEMC 3746
Premier/EMI / Mar '96 / EMI

COCODY ROCK
Cocody rock / Tere / Super powers / Interplanetary revolution / Fangandan kameleba / Bory samory
CD SH 64011
Shanachie / Dec '94 / ADA / Greensleeves / Koch

RASTA POUE
CD 387262
Syllart / Nov '92 / Stem's

Alpha Seven

GREAT LIFT JOURNEYS OF NORWICH & OTHER STORIES
CD AFOS 2
Sofacom / Jan '97 / Cargo

Alphabet Soup

LAYIN' LOW IN THE CUT
Opression / Take a ride / First day, last night / What I am / Meditate / For your conscious / Walkin' roots / Zone / Year 2000 / Streets / Music in my head
CD MR 0822
Mammoth / Feb '95 / Vital

Alphastone

STEREOPHONIC POP ART MUSIC
CD BCD 4054
Bomp / Sep '96 / Cargo / Greyhound / RTM/Disc / Shellshock/Disc

Alphaville

FOREVER YOUNG
Victory of love / Summer in Berlin / Big in Japan / To Germany with love / Fallen angel / Forever young / In the mood / Sounds like a melody / Jet set / Lies
CD 2404812
WEA / Nov '84 / Warner Music

Alquimia

DEAD TONGUES
CD RERALQ 1
ReR/Recommended / Aug '96 / ReR Megacorp / RTM/Disc

Altan

ALTAN
Cat that ate the candle/Over the water to Bessie / An tSeanchaileach Ghallda/Dermot Byrne's / Lass of Glenshee / Tommy Peoples/Loch Altan/Danny Meehan's / Ta mo Chleamhnas a Dheanamh / Come ye by Atholl/Kitty O'Connor / An Feochan-Wedding jig/Huddai Galagher's march / A Bhean Udai Thall / Con Cassidy's Highland/ Neilly O'Boyle's Highland and reel / An Feochan / Moll Dubh a Ghleanna / Tommy Bhetty's waltz / Brenda Stubberts/Breen's/ The red box / Paddy's trip to Scotland/Dinky's/Shetland fiddler
CD KCD 440
Celtic Collections / Jan '97 / Target/BMG

BEST OF ALTAN, THE
Tommy Peoples/Windmill/Finton McManus's / Moll Dubh a' Ghleanna / Jimmy Lyon's/The teelin/The red crow/The broken bridge / Sunset / Glory reel/Heathery Cruach / Flower of Magherally / Mazurka / A Bhean Udai Thall / King of the pipers / 'Si do Mhaimeo I / Jug of punch / Emyvale/Ril gan ainm/Three merry sisters of fate / An Mhaighdean Mhara / Dulaman / Drowsy Maggie/Rakish Paddy/Harvest storm / An Feochan
CD GLCD 1177
Green Linnet / Feb '97 / ADA / CM / Direct / Highlander / Roots

BLACKWATER
Johnny Boyle's / King of the pipers / Dark haired lass / Biddy from Muckross / Sean Maguire's 'stor a stor a ghra / Strathspey / Con McGinley's / Newfoundland reel ta me 'mo shui / An gasur mor / Bunker hill / Among the bushes / Molly na gcuach ni chilleanain / Jenny picking cockles / Farewell to Leitrim / John Doherty's ar bhruach na carraige baine / Dance of the honeybees / Blackwaterside / Tune for Frankie
CD CDV 2796
Virgin / Mar '96 / EMI

FIRST TEN YEARS, THE (1986-1995)
CD GLCD 1153
Green Linnet / May '95 / ADA / CM / Direct / Highlander / Roots

HARVEST STORM
Pretty Peg/New ships a-sailing/Bird's nest/ Man from Bundoran / Donal Agus Morag / King of the pipers / Seamus O'Shanahan's/ Walking in Liffey Street / Mo choill / Snowy path / Drowsy Maggie/Rakish Paddy/Harvest storm / Si do Mhaimeo / Marley's/Mill na maidi / Rosses highlands / Nobleman's wedding / Bog an Lochain/Margaree reel/ Humours of Westport / Dobbin's flowery vale
CD GLCD 1117
Green Linnet / '92 / ADA / CM / Direct / Highlander / Roots

HORSE WITH A HEART
Curlew/McDermott's reel/Three scones of Boxty / Lass of Glenshee / Con Cassidy's and Neil Gow's highlands/Moll and Tiarna / McSweeney's reels / Road to Durham / An t-Oilean Ur / An grianan/Horse with a heart / Bhean udai thall / Welcome home grainne/ Con McGinley's / Tuirse mo chroi / Come ye bey atholl/Kitty O'Connor / An feochan / Paddy's trip to Scotland/Dinky's/Shetland fiddlers
CD GLCD 1095
Green Linnet / Aug '89 / ADA / CM / Direct / Highlander / Roots

ISLAND ANGEL
Tommy Peoples/The windmill/Fintan McManus / Brid og ni Mhaille / Fernanagh highland/Donegal highland/John Doherty's / King George IV / An Mhaighdean Mhara / Andy De Jarlis/Ingonish/Mrs. McGhee / Humours of Andytown/Kylebrack rambler/ Gladstone / Dulaman / Mazurka / Jug of punch / Glory reel/Heathery cruach / An cailin Gaelach / Drumnagarry/Pirrie wirrie/ Big John's / Island angel / Preety Peg/New ships a-sailing/Birds nest/Man from Bundoran
CD GLCD 1137
Green Linnet / Oct '93 / ADA / CM / Direct / Highlander / Roots

RED CROW, THE
CD GLCD 1109
Green Linnet / Mar '92 / ADA / CM / Direct / Highlander / Roots

RUNAWAY SUNDAY
Suil Ghorm / John Doherty's reels / Caide sin don te sin / Germans / Clan Ronald's/ JB's reel / Paddy Mac's reel/Kitty Sheain / I wish my love was a red red rose / Mazurka / Australian waters / Moment in time / Ciaran's capers / Citi ni Eoahra / Flood in the holm/Scots Mary/The dancer's denial / Gleanntain Ghlas Ghaoth Dobhair / Time has past
CD CDV 2836
Virgin / Jul '97 / EMI

Altar

EGO ART
CD D 00046
Displeased / Jul '96 / Plastic Head / RTM/ Disc

YOUTH AGAINST CHRIST
CD D 00033
Displeased / Oct '94 / Plastic Head / RTM/Disc

Altar Of The King

ALTAR OF THE KING
CD RTN 41203
Rock The Nation / Feb '95 / Plastic Head

Altena, Maarten

CITIES AND STREETS
CD ARTCD 6082
Hat Art / Aug '91 / Cadillac / Harmonia Mundi

CODE (Altena, Maarten Ensemble)
CD ARTCD 6094
Hat Art / Jan '92 / Cadillac / Harmonia Mundi

RIF (Altena, Maarten Octet)
CD ARTCD 6056
Hat Art / Nov '90 / Cadillac / Harmonia Mundi

Alter Ego

ALTER EGO
CD HHCD 006
Harthouse / Jun '94 / Mo's Music Machine / Prime / Vital

DECODING THE HACKER MYTH
CD _______ HHCD 016
Harthouse / Feb '96 / Mo's Music Machine / Prime / Vital

LYCRA
CD _______ HHCD 087
Harthouse / Feb '96 / Mo's Music Machine / Prime / Vital

Alter Ego

MEMOIRES D'OUTREMER
CD _______ GL 4035CD
Green Linnet / Nov '95 / ADA / CM / Direct / Highlander / Roots

MEMORIES FROM OVERSEAS
CD _______ XENO 4035CD
Xenophile / Sep '95 / ADA / Direct

Alter, Myriam

SILENT WALK (Alter, Myriam Quintet)
CD _______ CHR 70035
Challenge / Sep '96 / ADA / Direct / Jazz Music / Wellard

Altered Images

HAPPY BIRTHDAY
Happy birthday / Love and kisses / Real toys / Idols / Legionaire / Faithless / Beckoning strings / Midnight / Day's wait / Leave me alone / Insects
CD _______ 4805282
Columbia / May '95 / Sony

REFLECTED IMAGES (The Best Of Altered Images)
Intro - Happy Birthday / Dead pop stars / Happy birthday / Love and kisses / Real toys / I could be happy / See those eyes / Pinky blue / Forgotten / See you later / Don't talk to me about love / Bring me closer / Love to stay / Change of heart / Thinking about you / Happy birthday (12" mix) / Don't talk to me about love (12" mix) / Love to stay (12" mix) / Bring me closer (12" mix) / Last goodbye (don't talk to me about love) / Outro - Happy birthday
CD _______ 4843392
Epic / Jul '96 / Sony

Altered States

CAFE 9.15 (Altered States & Ned Rothenberg)
CD _______ PP 001
Phenotype / Jan '97 / Harmonia Mundi

Alternative Radio

WOOD, WIRE & SKIN
CD _______ PULCD 3
Pulse / Jul '95 / Grapevine/PolyGram

Alternative TV

IMAGE HAS CRACKED, THE (Alternative TV Collection)
Alternatives / Action time vision / Why don't you do me right / Good times / Still life / Viva la rock 'n' roll / Nasty little lonely / Red / Splitting in two / Love lies limp / Life / How much longer / You bastard / Another coke / Life after life / Life after dub / Force is blind / Lost in a room / How much longer / You bastard
CD _______ CDPUNK 24
Anagram / Oct '96 / Cargo / Pinnacle

INDUSTRIAL SESSIONS, THE
CD _______ OVER 49CD
Overground / Apr '96 / Shellshock/Disc / SRD

LIVE AT THE RAT CLUB 1977
CD _______ OBSESSCD 005
Obsession / Sep '93 / RTM/Disc

MY LIFE AS A CHILD STAR
CD _______ OVER 39CD
Overground / Oct '94 / Shellshock/Disc / SRD

PEEP SHOW
Chrissie's dream / Let's sleep now / River / Tumbletime / My baby's laughing / Scandal / White walls / Animal
CD _______ OVER 54CD
Overground / Oct '96 / Shellshock/Disc / SRD

RADIO SESSIONS, THE
CD _______ OVER 44CD
Overground / Sep '95 / Shellshock/Disc / SRD

VIBING UP THE SENILE MAN/WHAT YOU SEE IS WHAT YOU ARE
CD _______ CDMGRAM 102
Anagram / Mar '96 / Cargo / Pinnacle

Alternatives

BUZZ
Pudgy / Sex face / Black hole / Half cheek sneek / Nubbing
CD _______ SST 245CD
SST / Oct '89 / Plastic Head

Altschul, Barry

VIRTUOSI (Altschul, Barry & Paul Bley/ Gary Peacock)
CD _______ 1238442
IAI / May '92 / Cadillac / Harmonia Mundi

Alva

FAIR-HAIRED GUILLOTINE
CD _______ AVANT 72
Avant / May '97 / Cadillac / Harmonia Mundi

Alvarez, Adalberto

A BAILAR EL TOCA TOCA
CD _______ 74321401362
Milan / Sep '96 / Conifer/BMG / Silva Screen

MAGISTRAL
Bailala / Como gozan los Cubanos / A la hora de la telenovela / Soy yo no busques mas / Uno nunca sabe / La vi caminando: *Alvarez, Adalberto & Michel Camilo* / Las puertas del corazon / Por esto te llaman Gil / Mi veneracion / Aun no es tarde
CD _______ 74321491372
Milan / Jul '97 / Conifer/BMG / Silva Screen

Alvarez, Javier

PAPALOTL - TRANSFORMACIONES EXOTICAS
CD _______ CDSDL 390
Saydisc / Nov '92 / ADA / Direct / Harmonia Mundi

Alvin & The Chipmunks

CHIPMUNK CHRISTMAS
It's beginning to look like Christmas / Chipmunk jingle bells / Chipmunk song / Spirit of Christmas / Have yourself a merry little Christmas / Crashup's Christmas / Here comes Santa Claus / Silent night / Sleigh ride / Deck the halls with boughs of holly / We wish you a Merry Christmas
CD _______ 4727402
Columbia / Nov '95 / Sony

Alvin, Dave

BLUE BLVD
CD _______ DFGCD 8424
New Rose / Jun '94 / ADA / Direct / Discovery

EVERY NIGHT ABOUT THIS TIME
Every night about this time / 4th of July / Long white cadillac / Romeo's escape / Brother (on the line) / Jubilee train / Border radio / Fire away / New tattoo / You got me / I wish it were Saturday night
CD _______ FIENDCD 90
Demon / Apr '87 / Pinnacle

INTERSTATE CITY (Alvin, Dave & The Guilty Men)
CD _______ HCD 8074
Hightone / Aug '96 / ADA / Koch

KING OF CALIFORNIA
CD _______ HCD 8054
Hightone / Oct '94 / ADA / Koch

MUSEUM OF HEART
CD _______ HCD 8049
Hightone / Jul '94 / ADA / Koch

ROMEO'S ESCAPE
CD _______ RE 2074
Razor & Tie / Jun '96 / Koch

Alvin, Phil

COUNTRY FAIR 2000
CD _______ HCD 8056
Hightone / Nov '94 / ADA / Koch

Always August

LARGENESS WITH (W)HOLES
CD _______ SST 135CD
SST / May '93 / Plastic Head

Alzir, Bud

BUD ALZIR
CD _______ HANCD 2
Hansome / Oct '95 / Pinnacle

AM 4

AND SHE ANSWERED
CD _______ 8396202
ECM / Nov '89 / New Note/Pinnacle

Ama, Shola

MUCH LOVE
You're the one I love / Much love / You might need somebody / Who's loving my baby / Celebrate / I love your ways / We got a vibe / Summer love / (I don't know) Interlude / I can show you / All mine / One love
CD _______ 3984200202
WEA / Sep '97 / Warner Music

Amalgamation Of Soundz

AMALGAMATION OF SOUNDZ
Tears for Yazd / Maternal blues / Eric / Hut / Fiesta de Castellon / 63rd suite / Cat in the rain / Orchid
CD _______ FILT 020CD
Filter / Jun '97 / Pinnacle / Prime / RTM/ Disc

Amampondo

DRUMS FOR TOMORROW
Cumbele / Tchokola / Nobabheha / Kudo junction / Salawena / Drums for tomorrow / Vukani nobanile / Ingxoxo / Gumboot dance / Collective for changuito / Mpondomse / Tere tere / Skahl' abantwana
CD _______ BW 096
Melt 2000 / Jun '97 / Vital/SAM

Amaro Del

WORLD OF GYPSY MUSIC (Amaro Del & Big String Orchestra)
CD _______ 323055
Koch / Feb '94 / Koch

Amarok

CANCIONES DE LOS MUNDOS PERDIDOS
CD _______ 21066CD
Sonifolk / Nov '95 / ADA / CM

ELS NOSTRES PETITS AMICS
CD _______ BCD 001
SBD / May '96 / ADA

Amayon

PURULENCE SPLIT
CD _______ CDAR 016
Adipocre / Feb '94 / Plastic Head

Amazing Band

ROAR
CD _______ FMRCD 40
Future / Aug '97 / ADA / Harmonia Mundi

Amazing Blondel

AMAZING BLONDEL/A FEW FACES
CD _______ EDCD 421
Edsel / Mar '95 / Pinnacle

BLONDEL
CD _______ EDCD 460
Edsel / Apr '96 / Pinnacle

ENGLAND
Paintings / Seascape / Landscape / Afterglow / Spring air / Cantus firmus to counterpoint / Sinfonia for guitar and strings / Dolor dulcis / Lament to the Earl of Bottesford Beck
CD _______ EDCD 501
Edsel / Nov '96 / Pinnacle

EVENSONG
CD _______ EDCD 458
Edsel / Feb '96 / Pinnacle

FANTASIA LINDUM
CD _______ EDCD 459
Edsel / Apr '96 / Pinnacle

LIVE ABROAD
CD _______ HTDCD 56
HTD / Apr '96 / CM / Pinnacle

RESTORATION
Benedictus / Praeludium in D / Highwayman / Fugue / Cawdor and widdershins / Aubaird / Love lies bleeding / Edagio / Sir John in love again / Interlude / Road to Sedgemoor / Cawdor revisited
CD _______ HTDCD 70
HTD / Mar '97 / CM / Pinnacle

Amazone

DEMONS
CD _______ NZ 019CD
Nova Zembla / Nov '94 / Plastic Head

Amazulu

AMAZULU
Too good to be forgotten / Excitable / After tonight / All over the world / Things the lonely do / Montego bay / Don't you just know it / Cairo / Moonlight romance / Upright, forward
CD _______ 5521062
Spectrum / Mar '96 / PolyGram

Ambassadeurs

AMBASSADEURS FEATURING SALIF KEITA (Ambassadeurs & Salif Keita)
CD _______ ROUCD 5053
Rounder / May '94 / ADA / CM / Direct

Ambassadors Of Funk

MONSTER JAM
CD _______ NOMIS 1CD
Living Beat / Feb '89 / Grapevine/ PolyGram

Ambel, Eric

ROSCOE'S GANG
If you gotta go, go now / Total destruction to your mind / Girl that ain't got / Forever came today / Thirty days in the workhouse / Power lounger theme / Don't wanna be your friend / I waited for you / Next to the last waltz / Loose talk / You must have we confused / Vampire blues
CD _______ FIENDCD 157
Demon / Oct '89 / Pinnacle

Ambelique

AMBELIQUE SINGS THE CLASSICS
CD _______ VPCD 1498
VP / Jun '97 / Greensleeves / Jet Star / Total/BMG

Amber

THIS IS YOUR NIGHT
This is your night / Move your body / Colour of love / You are the one / One more night / Push it to the limit / Being with you / Hold my body tight / Can you feel the love / Losing myself in your love / Let it rain / This is the right time / This is your night / Colour of love
CD _______ TBCD 1170
Tommy Boy / Apr '97 / RTM/Disc

Amber Asylum

FROZEN IN AMBER
CD _______ SAG 001CD
Misanthropy / Nov '96 / Plastic Head

NATURAL PHILOSOPHY OF LOVE, THE
Cupid / Looking glass / Song of the spider war / Jorinda and Joringel / Poppies
CD _______ RR 69552
Relapse / Jun '97 / Pinnacle/Plastic Head

Ambersunshower

WALTER T
CD _______ GEECD 19
Gee Street / Aug '96 / PolyGram

WALTER T. SMITH
CD _______ GEE 1000572
Gee Street / Sep '97 / 3mv/Pinnacle

Ambient Disciples

ENTER THE DREAMZONE
Insomnia / Dreaming in the rain / 7 Days and one week / Dreamscape / Last inferno / Fable / Easy dreams / Exception / Pitfall / Dreamchild / Diablo / Driven by you / Distant dreams / Puke
CD _______ DC 881022
Disky / Jul '97 / Disky / THE

Ambrose

AMBROSE (Ambrose & His Orchestra)
Don't let that moon get away / Says my heart / Love bug will bite you / Two sleepy people / Rhythm's OK in Harlem / Blue skies are round the corner / Goodnight to you all / I've got a pocketful of dreams / Sailor, where art thou / While a cigarette was burning / Lord and Lady Whoozis / Moon or no moon / Lambeth Walk / Chestnut tree / I may be poor but I'm honest / Oh they're tough, mighty tough, in the West / Ten pretty girls / Organ, the monkey and me / In a little French casino / Fifty million robins can't be wrong / Smile when you say goodbye / Sympathy
CD _______ CDAJA 5066
Living Era / Feb '90 / Select

AT THE MAYFAIR HOTEL 1927-1935 (Ambrose & His Orchestra)
Dance little lady / I'm more than satisfied / My heart stood still / My dream memory / Nicolette / Didn't I tell you / Little dream nest / Song of the sea / Somewhere / Then I'll be tired of you / Punch and Judy show / Ambrose's jubilee cavalcade / Humming to myself / For you / Lovable and sweet / 'S wonderful / Me and the man in the moon / Take your finger out of your mouth / Whispering pines of Nevada / Birth of the blues / Adoree' / Chirp chirp / Roll away clouds
CD _______ PASTCD 9713
Flapper / '90 / Pinnacle

CONTINENTAL, THE
Continental / Way you look tonight / Fine romance / You and the night and the music / Easter parade / I travel alone / Beautiful lady in blue / My kid's a crooner / I'll be tired of you / Maracas / Carmba / Snowman / Little boy blue / Night was yellow / Lost my man / I'm all in / Keep me in your dreams / Red sails in the sunset / It looks like rain in Cherry Blossom Lane / Too marvellous for words / Stars fell out of Heaven / Until the real thing comes along / Life begins / Lost in a fog / When day is done
CD _______ CDEA 6002
Vocalion / Aug '97 / Complete/Pinnacle

GLAMOUR OF THE THIRTIES (Ambrose & His Orchestra)
CD _______ PASTCD 7055
Flapper / Nov '94 / Pinnacle

Ambrosetti, Flavio

FLAVIO AMBROSETTI ANNIVERSARY 1949-1976 (2CD Set)
Perdido / Dancing on the ceiling / Just one of those things / Out of bush / Flavio's blues / It don't mean a thing / Anthropology / Junior's idea / Gentilino's serenade / Straight no chaser / Our suite dig / Atisiul / Age of prominence / Darn that dream / Blues for Ursula / Moon dreams / Alpen honky tonk
CD Set _______ ENJ 90272
Enja / Jul '96 / New Note/Pinnacle / Vital/ SAM

Ambush

AMBUSH
CD HHCD 005
Harthouse / Apr '94 / Mo's Music Machine / Prime / Vital

LACH
CD CC 008CD
Common Cause / May '95 / Plastic Head / SRD

PIGS
CD EFA 124062
Common Cause / Dec '95 / Plastic Head / SRD

Amebix

ARISE
CD VIRUS 46CD
Alternative Tentacles / Jul '94 / Cargo / Greyhound / Pinnacle

MONOLITH
Monolith / Nobody's driving / Power remains / Time bomb / Last will and testament / ICBM / Chain reaction / Fallen from grace / Coming home
CD HMRXD 99
Heavy Metal / Aug '87 / Revolver / Sony

Amen Corner

NATIONAL WELSH COAST LIVE EXPLOSION COMPANY
MacArthur Park / Baby, do the Philly dog / You're my girl (I don't want to discuss it) / Shake a tail feather / So fine / (Our love) Is in the pocket / Penny Lane / High in the sky / Gin house / Bend me, shape me / (If paradise is) half as nice
CD CDIMM 016
Charly / Feb '94 / Koch

VERY BEST OF AMEN CORNER
CD 12360
Laserlight / Aug '94 / Target/BMG

America

AMERICA
Riverside / Sandman / Three roses / Children / Here / I need you / Rainy day / Never found the time / Clarice / Donkey jaw / Pigeon song
CD 7599272572
WEA / Jan '93 / Warner Music

AMERICA IN CONCERT
Tin man / I need you / Border / Sister golden hair / Company / You can do magic / Ventura Highway / Daisy Jane / Horse with no name / Survival
CD CDGOLD 1072
EMI Gold / Oct '96 / EMI

BEST OF AMERICA, THE (Centenary Collection)
You can do magic / Border / Last unicorn / All my life / Survival / Tall treasures / One morning / Honey / My dear / One in a million / Right before your eyes / We got all night / Lady with a bluebird / Only game in town / Ventura highway / Daisy Jane / I need you / Tin man / Sister golden hair / Horse with no name
CD CTMCD 307
EMI / Feb '97 / EMI

HEARTS
Daisy Jane / Half a man / Midnight / Bell Tree / Old Virginia / People in the valley / Company / Woman tonight / Story of a teenager / Sister golden hair / Tomorrow / Seasons
CD 9362459862
WEA / Jun '95 / Warner Music

HISTORY (America's Greatest Hits)
Horse with no name / I need you / Ventura highway / Don't cross the river / Only in your heart / Muskrat love / Tin man / Lonely people / Sister golden hair / Daisy Jane / Woman tonight / Sandman
CD 256169
WEA / Jan '87 / Warner Music

VIEW FROM THE GROUND
You can do magic / Never be lonely / You girl / Inspector Mills / Love on the vine / Desperate love / Right before your eyes / Jody / Sometimes lovers / Even the score
CD NSPCD 509
Connoisseur Collection / Mar '95 / Pinnacle

YOU CAN DO MAGIC
CD DC 864352
Disky / Mar '96 / Disky / THE

American Boys' Choir

ON CHRISTMAS DAY
First Noel / Personent hodie / Sussex carol / Once in Royal David's City / Deck the halls with boughs of holly / Jesus Christ the apple tree / Twelve days of Christmas / O come all ye faithful (Adeste Fidelis) / God rest ye merry gentlemen / I sing of a maiden / Hark the herald angels sing / Salvator mundi
CD RCD 30129
Rykodisc / Dec '92 / ADA / Vital

American Breed

BEND ME SHAPE ME (The Best Of American Breed)
CD VSD 5493
Varese Sarabande / Oct '94 / Pinnacle

American Jazz Orchestra

PLAYS THE MUSIC OF JIMMIE LUNCEFORD
CD MM 65072
Music Masters / Oct '94 / Nimbus

American Jazz Quintet

FROM BAD TO BADDER
CD 1201142
Black Saint / Mar '92 / Cadillac / Harmonia Mundi

American Music Club

CALIFORNIA
Firefly / Somewhere / Laughing stock / Lonely / Pale skinny girl / Blue and grey shirt / Bad liquor / Now you're defeated / Jenny / Western sky / Highway 5 / Last harbour
CD FMCD 1
Demon / Apr '93 / Pinnacle

ENGINE, THE
Big night / Outside this bar / At my mercy / Gary's song / Night watchman / Lloyd / Electric light / Mom's TV / Art of love / Asleep / This year
CD ZONGCD 020
Zippo / Oct '87 / CM / Pinnacle / Swift

EVERCLEAR
Why won't you stay / Rise / Miracle on 8th street / Ex-girlfriend / Crabwalk / Confidential agent / Sick of food / Dead part of you / Royal cafe / What the pillars of salt held up
CD A 015D
Alias / Oct '91 / Vital

MERCURY
Gratitude walks / If I had a hammer / Challenger / I've been a mess / Hollywood 4-5-92 / What Godzilla said to God when his name wasn't... / Keep me around / Dallas, airports, bodybags / Apology for an accident / Over and done / Johnny Mathis' feet / Hopes and dreams of heaven's 10,000 whores / More hopes and dreams / Will you find me / Book of life
CD CDV 2708
Virgin / Mar '93 / EMI

SAN FRANCISCO
Fearless / It's your birthday / Can you help me / Love doesn't belong to anyone / Wish the world away / How many six packs does it take to screw in a light / Cape Canaveral / Hello Amsterdam / Revolving door / In the shadow of the valley / What holds the world together / I broke my promise / Thorn in my side is gone / I'll be gone / Fearless reprise / I just took my two sleeping pills and now I'm like a...
CD CDV 2752
Virgin / Sep '94 / EMI

UNITED KINGDOM
Here they roll down / Dreamers of the dream / Never mind / United Kingdom / Dream is gone / Heaven of your hands / Kathleen / Hula maiden / Animal pen / California
CD FMCD 2
Demon / Apr '93 / Pinnacle

American Patrol Orchestra

SOUNDS OF THE BIG BANDS VOL.1
CD PRCDSP 207
Prestige / Jul '95 / Else / Total/BMG

American Poijat

FINISH BRASS IN USA
CD GVCD 810
Global Village / Mar '95 / ADA / Direct

American Standard

WONDERLAND
CD LF 177CD
Lost & Found / Jul '95 / Plastic Head

aMiniature

DEPTH FIVE RATE SIX
Physical climber / No bonds / Featurist / Weepo / Maestro / Ouisghian zodahs in panoply / Towner on the B side / Foreign room / Shadowned / Last night in Sakura's / Zero in trust / Hiker atlas
CD 727402
Restless / Feb '94 / Vital

MURK TIME CRUISER
He, the bad feeler / Peddler's talk / Bores spy / Maximun accident / Secret enemy / Prizefighters / Signer's strut / Murk time cruiser / Flux is flux / Long live soul miner
CD 727882
Restless / Apr '95 / Vital

Amisi, Reddy

PRUDENCE
CD 503802
Declic / Apr '95 / Jet Star

ZIGGY
CD GP 9710
Galaxie / Jan '97 / Stern's

AMM

AMMUSIC 1966
Later during a flaming Riviera sunset / Later during a flaming Riviera sunset / Ailantus glandulosa / In the realm of nothing whatever / After rapidly circling the Plaza / After rapidly circling the Plaza / What is there in uselessness to cause you distress / Silence
CD RERAMMCD
ReR/Recommended / Feb '96 / ReR Megacorp / RTM/Disc

FROM A STRANGE PLACE
CD PSFD 80
PSF / Oct '96 / Harmonia Mundi

GENERATIVE THEMES
CD MRCD 6
Matchless / Oct '95 / Cadillac / ReR Megacorp

INEXHAUSTIBLE DOCUMENT, THE
CD MRCD 13
Matchless / Oct '95 / Cadillac / ReR Megacorp

LAMINAL (3CD Set)
CD Set MRCD 31
Matchless / Jun '97 / Cadillac / ReR Megacorp

LIVE AT THE CRYPT
CD MRCD 5
Matchless / Oct '95 / Cadillac / ReR Megacorp

NAMELESS UNCARVED BLOCK
CD MRCD 20
Matchless / Oct '95 / Cadillac / ReR Megacorp

NEWFOUNDLAND
CD MRCD 23
Matchless / Oct '95 / Cadillac / ReR Megacorp

TO HEAR AND BACK AGAIN
CD MRCD 3
Matchless / Oct '95 / Cadillac / ReR Megacorp

AMM III

IT HAD BEEN AN ORDINARY ENOUGH DAY IN PUEBLO, COLORADO.
Radioactivity / Convergence / Kline / Spitfields' Slide / For A
CD 8432062
ECM / May '91 / New Note/Pinnacle

Ammerians Octet

NOORDERZON
CD BVHAASTCD 9306
Bvhaast / Oct '93 / Cadillac

Ammonia

MINT 400
Ken Carter / Drugs / Sleepwalking / Face down / In a box / Suzie Q / Little death / Mint 400 / Burning plant smell / Z-man / Million dollar man / Lucky no.3
CD 4837902
Epic / Jul '96 / Sony

Ammons, Albert

BACK BEAT VOL.2 (The Rhythm Of The Blues) (Ammons, Albert & His Rhythm Kings)
Ammons stomp / Suitcase blues / Doin' the boogie woogie / Oh lady be good / Why I'm leaving you / Red sails in the sunset / Deep in the heart of Texas boogie / Hiroshima / Roses of Picardy / In a little Spanish town / Margie tuxedo boogie / Rhythm boogie / Baltimore breakdown / Clipper
CD 5102862
Mercury / Jan '95 / PolyGram

BOOGIE WOOGIE MAN
CD TPZ 1067
Topaz Jazz / Aug '97 / Cadillac / Pinnacle

BOOGIE WOOGIE VOL.1 (Ammons, Albert & Pete Johnson/Meade 'Lux' Lewis)
CD STCD 8025
Storyville / Jul '96 / Cadillac / Jazz Music / Wellard

BOOGIE WOOGIE VOL.2 (Ammons, Albert & Pete Johnson/Meade 'Lux' Lewis)
CD STCD 8026
Storyville / May '97 / Cadillac / Jazz Music / Wellard

CLASSICS 1939-1939
CD CLASSICS 715
Classics / Jul '93 / Discovery / Jazz Music

CLASSICS 1939-1946
CD CLASSICS 927
Classics / Apr '97 / Discovery / Jazz Music

Ammons, Gene

BLUE GENE
CD OJCCD 192
Original Jazz Classics / Aug '94 / Complete/Pinnacle / Jazz Music / Wellard

BOSS IS BACK, THE
CD PCD 24129
Prestige / Dec '95 / Cadillac / Complete/ Pinnacle

BOSS TENOR
Hittin' the jug / Close your eyes / My romance / Canadian sunset / Blue Ammons / Confirmation / Savoy
CD OJCCD 297
Original Jazz Classics / Feb '93 / Complete/ Pinnacle / Jazz Music / Wellard

GROOVE BLUES (Ammons, Gene All Stars)
CD OJCCD 723
Original Jazz Classics / Nov '95 / Complete/Pinnacle / Jazz Music / Wellard

JAMMIN' WITH GENE (Ammons, Gene All Stars)
Jammin' with Gene / We'll be together again / Not really the blues
CD OJCCD 211
Original Jazz Classics / Jun '96 / Complete/ Pinnacle / Jazz Music / Wellard

PREACHIN'
CD OJCCD 792
Original Jazz Classics / Nov '95 / Complete/Pinnacle / Jazz Music / Wellard

Amon Duul

AIRS ON A SHOESTRING
Hymn for the hardcore / Pioneer / One moment of anger is two pints of blood / Marcus Lied / Olaf
CD CDTB 043
Thunderbolt / Jul '87 / TKO Magnum
CD 14515
Spalax / Apr '97 / ADA / Cargo / Direct / Discovery / Greyhound

BEST OF AMON DUUL II 1969-1974, THE (Amon Duul II)
CD CLP 9902
Cleopatra / Jan '97 / Cargo / Greyhound / Plastic Head / RTM/Disc / SRD

COLLAPSING
CD 14949
Spalax / Oct '96 / ADA / Cargo / Direct / Discovery / Greyhound

DIE LOSUNG (Amon Duul & Bob Calvert)
Big wheel / Urban Indian / Adrenalin Rush / Visions of fire / Drawn to the flame / They call it home / Die Losung / Drawn to the flame (part 2)
CD CDTB 115
Thunderbolt / '91 / TKO Magnum

DISASTER
CD 14948
Spalax / Oct '96 / ADA / Cargo / Direct / Discovery / Greyhound

EXPERIMENTE
CD 14842
Spalax / Oct '96 / ADA / Cargo / Direct / Discovery / Greyhound

FLAWLESS (Amon Duul II)
Nada Cairo / Surrounded by the stars / Castaneda da dream / Wie der wind am ende einer strasse / Kiss ma eee / Cerberus / Speed inside my shoes / La paloma / Nada moonshine union / Dancing on fire / Jam '71 / What you gonna do / Jim hai jam UK '96
CD MYSCD 113
Mystic / Aug '97 / Pinnacle

FOOL MOON
Who who / Tribe / Tik tok song / Haupmotor / Hymn for the hardcore
CD CDTB 117
Thunderbolt / Mar '95 / TKO Magnum
CD 14516
Spalax / Jun '97 / ADA / Cargo / Direct / Discovery / Greyhound

HAWK MEETS PENGUIN
One moment of anger is two pints of blood / Hawk meets penguin
CD CDTB 102
Thunderbolt / Jun '92 / TKO Magnum
CD 14848
Spalax / Apr '97 / ADA / Cargo / Direct / Discovery / Greyhound

KOBE (RECONSTRUCTIONS) (Amon Duul II)
CD CTCD 039
Captain Trip / Jul '97 / Greyhound

LIVE IN TOKYO (Amon Duul II)
CD MYSCD 107
Mystic / Nov '96 / Pinnacle

MEETINGS WITH MENMACHINES (Unremarkable Heroes Of The Past)
Pioneer / Old one / Marcus lied / Song / Things aren't always what they seem / Burundi drummer's nightmare
CD CDTB 107
Magnum Music / Mar '93 / TKO Magnum
CD 14820
Spalax / Jun '97 / ADA / Cargo / Direct / Discovery / Greyhound

NADA MOONSHINE (Amon Duul II)
Casteneda da dream / Nada moonshine / Speed inside my shoes / Sirens in Germanistan / Ca va / Kiss ma eee / Carpetride in velvet night / Black pearl of wisdom / Lilac lillies / Guadalquivir / Surrounded by stars / Dancing on fire / Casteneda da dream
CD ______ MYS 106CD
Mystic / Aug '96 / Pinnacle

PARA DIES WARTS DUUL
CD ______ 14946
Spalax / Oct '96 / ADA / Cargo / Direct / Discovery / Greyhound

PHALLUS DEI (Amon Duul II)
CD ______ MANTRA 012
Mantra / Feb '97 / Cargo / Direct / Discovery

PSYCHEDELIC UNDERGROUND
CD ______ 14947
Spalax / Oct '96 / ADA / Cargo / Direct / Discovery / Greyhound
CD ______ REP 4616WY
Repertoire / Jun '97 / Greyhound

WOLF CITY (Amon Duul II)
CD ______ MANTRA 013
Mantra / Feb '97 / Cargo / Direct / Discovery

Amon Tobin

BRICOLAGE
Easy muffin / Yasawas / Dream sequence / New York editor / Defocus / Nasty / Bitter and twisted / Mission / Wires and snakes / Creatures / Stoney Street / One small step / One day in my garden / Chomp samba
CD ______ ZENCD 029
Ninja Tune / May '97 / Kudos / Pinnacle / Prime / Vital

Amorphis

BLACK WINTER DAY
CD ______ NB 1172
Nuclear Blast / Mar '95 / Plastic Head

ELEGY
CD ______ NB 141CD
Nuclear Blast / May '96 / Plastic Head

KARELIAN ISTHMUS
Karelia / Gathering / Grail's mysteries / Warrior's trail / Black embrace / Exil of the sons of Uisliu / Lost name of God / Pilgrimage / Misery path / Sign from the north side / Vulgar necrolatry
CD ______ NB 072CD
Nuclear Blast / Oct '95 / Plastic Head
CD ______ RR 60452
Relapse / Jun '97 / Pinnacle / Plastic Head

MY KANTELE
My kantele / Brother slayer / Lost son (the brother slayer part 2) / Leviation / I hear you call
CD ______ RR 69562
Relapse / Jun '97 / Pinnacle / Plastic Head

PRIVILEGE OF EVIL
Pilgrimage from darkness / Black embrace / Privilege of evil / Misery path / Vulgar necroloatry / Excursing from existence
CD ______ RR 60242
Relapse / Jun '97 / Pinnacle / Plastic Head

TALES FROM 1000 LAKES
CD ______ NB 097CD
Nuclear Blast / Jul '96 / Plastic Head

Amos, Tori

BOYS FOR PELE
Beauty queen / Horses / Blood roses / Father Lucifer / Professional widow / Mr. Zebra / Marianne / Caught a lite sneeze / Muhammad my friend / Hey Jupiter / Way down / Little Amsterdam / Talula / Not the Red Baron / Agent Orange / Doughnut song / In the springtime of his voodoo / Putting the damage on / Twinkle
CD ______ 7567828622
East West / Jan '96 / Warner Music
CD ______ 7567806962
East West / Jan '97 / Warner Music

INTERVIEW DISC
CD ______ UFOMWW 12CD
UFO / Nov '96 / Pinnacle

INTERVIEW DISC
CD ______ SAM 7017
Sound & Media / Nov '96 / Sound & Media

LITTLE EARTHQUAKES
Crucify / Girl / Silent all these years / Precious things / Winter / Happy phantom / China / Leather / Mother / Tear in your hand / Me and a gun / Little earthquakes
CD ______ 7567823582
East West / Jan '92 / Warner Music

UNDER THE PINK
Pretty good year / God / Bells for her / Past the mission / Baker baker / Wrong band / Waitress / Cornflake girl / Icicle / Cloud on my tongue / Space dog / Yes, Anastasia
CD ______ 7567825672
East West / Jan '94 / Warner Music

AMP

ASTRALMOONBEAMPROJECTIONS
CD ______ KRANK 17CD
Kranky / May '97 / Cargo / Greyhound

SIRENES
CD ______ WJ 9
Wurlitzer Jukebox / Jun '97 / Cargo

Ampersand

MUG OF MISCHIEF
CD ______ CDHOLE 007
Golf / Jun '96 / Plastic Head

Amps

PACER
Pacer / Tipp city / I am decided / Mom's drunk / Bragging party / Hoverin' / First revival / Full on idle / Breaking the split screen barrier / Empty glasses / She's a girl / Dedicated
CD ______ CAD 5016CD
4AD / Oct '95 / RTM/Disc

Amps For Christ

AMPS FOR CHRIST
CD ______ VMFM 35CD
Vermiform / Jun '97 / Cargo / Greyhound / Plastic Head

BEGGARS GARDEN
CD ______ SHR 87
Shrimper / Jun '97 / Cargo

Amram, David

AT HOME/AROUND THE WORLD
Travelling blues / Birds of Montparnasse / Splendour in the grass / Sioux rabbit song / Home on the range / Kwahare / Pescau / Homenaje a Guatemala / From the Khyber pass / Aya zehn
CD ______ CDFF 094
Flying Fish / Oct '96 / ADA / CM / Direct / Roots

NO MORE WALLS
Waltz from After The Fall / Wind from the Indies / Pull my daisy / Brazilian memories / Sao Paulo / Going North / Tompkins Square Park consciosness expander
CD ______ CDFF 752
Flying Fish / Jun '97 / ADA / CM / Direct / Roots

Amsallem, Franck

IS THAT SO
CD ______ SSC 171D
Sunnyside / Apr '96 / Discovery

REGARDS (Amsallem, Franck & Tim Ries Quartet)
CD ______ FRLCD 020
Freelance / Nov '93 / Cadillac / Koch

Amsterdam Jazz Quintet

PICTURES OF AMSTERDAM
Sailing / Windows / Market / Homecoming / Stress / Traces / Listen to the wind / Omar's bakery
CD ______ AL 73042
A / Nov '96 / Cadillac / Direct

Amuedo, Leonardo

DOLPHIN DANCE
CD ______ CHR 70008
Challenge / Aug '95 / ADA / Direct / Jazz Music / Wellard

Amundson, Monti

I SEE TROUBLE
I see trouble / Oh Johnny why / Looking back / What I was thinking / King bee / You win, I lose / Broke down car / Continental breakfast / Cornbread blues / Lesson or two / I'm good / Worried about my life / I live a good life
CD ______ MMBCD 2
Me & My / Nov '96 / Direct

MEAN 18, THE
CD ______ TRACD 9914
Tramp / Jul '93 / ADA / CM / Direct

MONTI AMUNDSON & THE BLUBINOS (Amundson, Monti & The Blubinos)
Man on the floor / Would I lie / All I wanna do / Sweet talk / Easy way out / Four in the morning / Better to be lonely / Cream in my heart / Hat back blues / Your turn to be the fool / Killing time
CD ______ MMBCD 3
Me & My Blues / May '97 / CM / Direct

An Emotional Fish

JUNKPUPPETS
Rain / Harmony central / Sister change / If God was a girl / Careless child / Star / Hole in my heaven / Innocence / Half moon / Digging this hole / Yeah yeah yeah
CD ______ 4509923572
WEA / May '93 / Warner Music

An Teallach Ceilidh Band

SHIP IN FULL SAIL, A
Reels / Marches / Jigs / Song / Slip jig / Waltz / Slow air and reel / Polkas
CD ______ LCOM 5237
Lismor / Aug '94 / ADA / Direct / Duncans / Lismor

Anacrusis

REASON
Stop me / Not forgotten / Silent crime / Afraid to feel / Vital / Terrified / Wrong / Misshapen intent / Child inside / Quick to doubt
CD ______ CDATV 9
Active / Feb '90 / Pinnacle

SCREAMS & WHISPERS
Sound the alarm / Sense of will / Too many prophets / Release / Division / Tool of seperation / Grateful / Screaming breath / My soul's affliction / Driven / Brotherhood / Release (remix)
CD ______ CDZORRO 59
Metal Blade / May '93 / Pinnacle / Plastic Head

Analogue

AAD
CD ______ GUM 027CD
Sonic Bubblegum / Oct '96 / Cargo

Anam

ANAM
CD ______ CACD 001CD
CACD / Apr '95 / ADA

FIRST FOOTING
Mylie's revenge/Pipers wedding / Take this moment / Siul a ruin / Last pint/Trimthe velvet / Next market day/The market square / Planxty Joe Burke / Lovely Joan / Dan Amhairgin / Shetlag / Sally free and easy / Sweet flowers of Milltown/Paddy's trip to Lake Arthur / Liberty
CD ______ JVC 90112
JVC World Library / May '97 / ADA / CM / Direct

SAOIRSE
CD ______ CACD 002CD
CACD / Apr '95 / ADA

Anao Atao

ESOTERIC STONES (Celtic Music From Cornwall & Beyond)
Esoteric stones / Ros Keltek's favourite / Other side of Carna / Forest cry / International waters / Tinner's puzzle / An Gernyas / Quadrilles / Marvor / Mai Soazig / Dr. Syntax's head / Yntra Deu Dyr
CD ______ KESCD 001
Kesson / Jul '94 / CM

Anastasia Screamed

LAUGHING DOWN THE LIMEHOUSE
CD ______ NECKCD 002
Roughneck / Sep '90 / RTM/Disc

MOONSHINE
CD ______ NECKCD 007
Roughneck / Oct '91 / RTM/Disc

Anathema

ETERNITY
CD ______ CDXVILE 64
Peaceville / Nov '96 / Pinnacle

PENTECOST 3
CD ______ CDMVILE 51
Peaceville / Mar '95 / Pinnacle

SILENT ENIGMA, THE
Restless oblivion / Sunset of age / Silent enigma / Shroud of frost / Nocturnal emission / Dying wish / Alone / Cerulean twilight / Black orchid
CD ______ CDVILE 52
Peaceville / Oct '95 / Pinnacle

Anatomy

WHERE ANGELS LIE
CD ______ DSTK 7662CD
Destruktive Kommndoh / Dec '96 / Plastic Head

Anche Passe

ENTRE TARENTELLE
CD ______ Y 225032CD
Silex / Dec '93 / ADA / Harmonia Mundi

Ancient

CAINIAN CHRONICLE, THE
CD ______ 398414110CD
Metal Blade / Jul '96 / Pinnacle / Plastic Head

SVARTALVHEIM
CD ______ POSH 006CD
Osmose / Jan '95 / Plastic Head

Ancient Beatbox

ANCIENT BEATBOX
Laride / Raining / Wooden box / I'll wait for you / Bouree a pichon / Diamond / Many lives of Diana / All we live for
CD ______ COOKCD 021
Cooking Vinyl / Jul '96 / Vital

Ancient Future

ASIAN FUSION
Prelude / Bookenka (the adventurer) / Trader / Mezgoof / Empress / Ja nam / Sunda straits / Morning sung / Sumbatico / Dusk song of the fisherman / Ladakh / Garuda
CD ______ ND 63023
Narada / Jun '93 / ADA / New Note/ Pinnacle

NATURAL RHYTHMS
CD ______ PH 9006CD
Philo / Feb '94 / ADA / CM / Direct

Ancient Rites

BLASFEMIA ETERNAL
CD ______ M 7017CD
Osmose / Feb '96 / Plastic Head

Ancient Wisdom

CALLING
CD ______ AV 020
Avant Garde / May '97 / Plastic Head / RTM/Disc

And Also The Trees

AND ALSO THE TREES
CD ______ NORMAL 85CD
Normal / Mar '94 / ADA / Direct

ANGELFISH
CD ______ MEZCD 1
China / Aug '96 / Pinnacle

FAREWELL TO THE SHADE
Prince Rupert / Nobody Inn / Lady D'Arbanville / Pear tree / Horse fair / MacBeth's head / Belief in the rose / Misfortunes / Ill omen
CD ______ NORMAL 114CD
Normal / Mar '94 / ADA / Direct

FROM HORIZON TO HORIZON
CD ______ NORMAL 154CD
Normal / Mar '94 / ADA / Direct

GREEN IS THE SEA
CD ______ NORMAL 134CD
Normal / Mar '94 / ADA / Direct

KLAXON, THE
CD ______ NORMAL 164CD
Normal / Mar '94 / ADA / Direct

MILLPOND YEARS, THE
CD ______ NORMAL 100CD
Normal / Mar '94 / ADA / Direct

RETROSPECTIVE 1983-1986, A
Shantell / Talk without words / Shrine / Midnight garden / Impulse of man / Twilights pool / Room lives in Lucy / Scarlet arch / Slow pulse boy / Maps in her wrists and arms / Dwelling place / Vincent Crane / Gone like the swallows / Virus meadow
CD ______ 422010
New Rose / May '94 / ADA / Direct / Discovery

VIRUS MEADOW
Slow pulse boy / Maps in her wrists and arms / Dwelling place / Vincent Crane / Jack / Headless clay woman / Gone like the swallows / Virus meadow
CD ______ NORMAL 90CD
Normal / Mar '94 / ADA / Direct

And Did Those Feet

SPIRIT OF THE AGE
Things in the world (money can't buy) / It's the quiet life / Spirit of the age / Never waste a good bit / Surprisingly most unsurprising / Come the day / Green place / Almost Elizabeth / Element waltz / Who are you / Living fire
CD ______ TERRCD 005
Terra Nova / Feb '97 / Direct

And One

IST
CD ______ MA 612
Machinery / Nov '94 / Koch

SPOT
CD ______ MA 342
Machinery / Nov '93 / Koch

Andarta

ABRED
CD ______ KMCD 61
Keltia Musique / Feb '96 / ADA / Discovery

Anders, Christian

SEINE GROSSEN ERFOLGE
Das Schiff der grossen Illusionen / Wer liebt hat keine Wahl / Das schonste madchen / Am strand von Las Chapas / Verliebt in den lehrer / Wenn die liebe dich vergisst / Denn ich liebe dich so sehr / Ich leb' nur fur dich allein / In den augen der andern / Maria Lorena / In Chicago (In the ghetto) / Nur mit dir will ich leben / Love dreamer / Tu's nicht

Jenny / Der letzte tanz / Einsamkeit hat viele namen
CD DC 875402
Disky / Mar '97 / Disky / THE

SINGLE HITS (1968-1971)
CD 16013
Laserlight / Aug '91 / Target/BMG

Anders, Lezlie

WITH LOVE LEZLIE
Here's to life / Fever / Cry me a river / Guess who I saw today / Our love is here to stay / Lover man / Very thought of you / Miracles / On the Southside of Chicago / Perfect / More than you know / Fine and mellow / At the same time / What a difference a day makes / My buddy
CD CYCD 74801
Celebrity / Feb '97 / Cadillac / Direct / Wellard

Andersen, Arild

HYPERBOREAN
Patch of light / Hyperborean / Patch of light II / Duke Vinaccia / Infinite distance / Vanishing waltz / Island / Invisible sideman / Rambler / Dragon dance / Stillness / Too late for a picture
CD 5373422
ECM / Sep '97 / New Note/Pinnacle

IF YOU LOOK FAR ENOUGH
If you look / Svev / For all we know / Backe / Voice / Woman / Place / Drink / Main man / Song I used to play / Far enough / Jonah
CD 5139022
ECM / '90 / New Note/Pinnacle

SAGN
CD 8496472
ECM / Oct '91 / New Note/Pinnacle

Anderson, Al

PAY BEFORE YOU PUMP
CD CURCD 034
Curb / Feb '97 / Grapevine/PolyGram

Anderson, Alistair

GRAND CHAIN, THE
CD CROCD 216
Black Crow / Jun '88 / CM / Roots

Anderson, Angry

BEATS FROM A SINGLE DRUM
CD CDGRUB 11
Food For Thought / Apr '89 / Pinnacle

Anderson, Bill

MAGIC OF BILL ANDERSON, THE
CD TKOCD 018
TKO / '92 / TKO

Anderson, Carleen

TRUE SPIRIT (Remix Album/2CD Set)
True spirit / Morning loving / Mama said / Ain't givin' up on you / Only one for me / Nervous breakdown / Secrets / Let it last / Feet wet up / Welcome to changes / Ian Green's groove conclusion / Mama said / True spirit / Apparently nothin' / Nervous breakdown / Let it last
CD Set CIRCDD 30
Circa / Feb '95 / EMI

TRUE SPIRIT
True spirit / Morning loving / Mama said / Ain't givin' up on you / Only one for me / Nervous breakdown / Secrets / Let it last / Feet wet up / Welcome to changes / Ian Green's groove conclusion
CD CIRCD 30
Circa / Jan '95 / EMI

Anderson, Cat

PLAYS W.C. HANDY
CD BLE 591632
Black & Blue / Apr '91 / Discovery / Koch / Wellard

Anderson, Clive

BLUES ONE (Anderson, Clive Trio)
CD DIW 607
DIW / Nov '91 / Cadillac / Harmonia Mundi

Anderson, Eric

AVALANCHE
CD 7599267792
WEA / Jan '96 / Warner Music

ERIC ANDERSON
CD 7599267782
WEA / Jan '96 / Warner Music

GHOSTS UPON THE ROAD
Belgian bar / Spanish steps / It starts with a lie / Trouble in Paris / Listen to the rain / Ghosts upon the road / Too many times (I will try) / Carry me away / Six senses of darkness / Irish lace
CD PLUCD 003
Plump / Apr '96 / Grapevine/PolyGram

Anderson, Ernestine

ERNESTINE ANDERSON (The Toast Of The Nation's Critics)
Running wild / Stardust / Heatwave / My ship / Azure te / Welcome to the club / There's a boat that's leavin' soon for New York / Social call / There will never be another you / Sleepin' bee / Interlude
CD 5140762
Mercury / May '93 / PolyGram

GREAT MOMENTS WITH ERNESTINE ANDERSON
I love being here with you / Day by day / Ain't nobody's business if I do / As long as I live / Don't get around much anymore / Please send me someone to love / Skylark / In a mellow tone / Someone else is steppin' in / Time after time / Body and soul / Never make your move too soon
CD CCD 4582
Concord Jazz / Nov '93 / New Note/ Pinnacle

LIVE AT THE 1990 CONCORD JAZZ FESTIVAL
Blues in the closet / I let a song go out of my heart / I should care / There is no greater love / Skylark / On my own / Never make your move too soon
CD CCD 4454
Concord Jazz / May '91 / New Note/ Pinnacle

SUNSHINE
Love / Summertime / Time after time / God bless the child / I've got the world on a string / I'm walkin' / I want a little boy / You are my sunshine / Satin doll / Sunny
CD CCD 4109
Concord Jazz / Jan '92 / New Note/ Pinnacle

WHEN THE SUN GOES DOWN
Someone else is steppin' in / In the evening / I love being here with you / Down home blues / I'm just a lucky so and so / Alone on my own / Mercy mercy mercy / Goin' to Chicago blues
CD CCD 4263
Concord Jazz / '88 / New Note/Pinnacle

Anderson, Fred

MISSING LINK
CD NCD 23
Nessa / Jun '97 / Harmonia Mundi

Anderson, Ian

WALK INTO LIGHT
Fly by night / Made in England / Walk into light / Trains / End game / Black and white television / Toad in the hole / Looking for Eden / User friendly / Different Germany
CD BGOCD 350
Beat Goes On / Jun '97 / Pinnacle

Anderson, Ian A.

UNRULY (English Country Blues Band)
CD CDFMS 27
Rogue / Apr '93 / Stern's

Anderson, Ivie

INTRODUCTION TO IVIE ANDERSON 1932-1942, AN
CD 4020
Best Of Jazz / May '95 / Discovery

IVIE ANDERSON (Anderson, Ivie & Duke Ellington)
CD CD 14561
Jazz Portraits / May '95 / Jazz Music

Anderson, John

I'M IN THE MOOD FOR SWING VOL.1
CD LPCD 1021
Disky / Apr '94 / Disky / THE

I'M IN THE MOOD FOR SWING VOL.2
CD LPCD 1022
Disky / Apr '94 / Disky / THE

SWING THE MOOD
American patrol / Tequila / In the mood / Hawaii 5-0 / Moonlight melody / At the sign of the swinging / String of pearls / Pretty blue eyes / Little brown jug / Tuxedo medley / Chattanooga medley / Midnight in Moscow / Manhattan spiritual / Cherry pink / Stranger on the shore / 12 bar thingy / Stripper / Peanut vendor / March of the mods / Glenn Miller medley
CD MCVD 30005
Emerald Gem / Nov '96 / BMG

Anderson, Jon

CHANGE WE MUST
State of independence / Shaker loops / Hearts / Alive and well / Kiss / Chagall duet / Run on, Jon / Candle song / View from the coppice / Hurry home / Under the sun / Change we must
CD CDC 5550882
EMI / Oct '94 / EMI

DESEO
Amor real / A-de-o / Bridges / Seasons / Floresta / Cafe / This child / Danca do ouro / Midnight dancing / Deseo / Latino / Bless this
CD 01934111402
Windham Hill / May '94 / BMG

DESEO REMIXES, THE
Deep Floresta / Intercity 125 / Speed deep / Master Mute vs The Tone-E / FSOL Deseo reconstruction / Amor real / Master Mute / Bless this
CD 72902103382
High Street / Jul '95 / BMG

OLIAS OF SUNHILLOW
Ocean song / Meeting / Sound out the galleon / Dance of Ranyart Olias / Qoquaq en transic / Solid space / Moon ra chords song of search / To the runner / Naon / Transic to
CD 7567802732
Atlantic / Jan '96 / Warner Music

SONG OF SEVEN
For you, for me / Some are born / Don't forget / Heart of the matter / Hear it / Everybody loves you / Take your time / Days / Song of seven
CD 7567814752
Atlantic / May '96 / Warner Music

TOLTEC
Part 1 / Part 2 / Part 3
CD 72902103462
High Street / Jun '96 / BMG

Anderson, Krister

SKANDIA SKIES
CD LICD 3166
Liphone / Jan '97 / Cadillac / Jazz Music

Anderson, Laurie

BIG SCIENCE
From the air / Big science / Sweaters / Walking and falling / Born never asked / O superman / Example 22 / Let X = X / It tango
CD 257002
WEA / Apr '82 / Warner Music

BRIGHT RED
Speechless / Bright red / Puppet motel / Speak my language / World without end / Freefall / Muddy river / Beautiful pea green boat / Love among the sailors / Poison / In our sleep / Night in Baghdad / Tightrope / Same time tomorrow
CD 9362455342
WEA / Dec '96 / Warner Music

MISTER HEARTBREAK
Sharkey's day / Langue d'armour / Gravity's angel / Blue lagoon / Excellent birds / Sharkey's night
CD 9250772
WEA / Feb '84 / Warner Music

STRANGE ANGELS
Strange angels / Monkey's paw / Coolsville / Ramon / Baby doll / Beautiful red dress / Day the devil comes to getcha / Dream before / My eyes / Hiawatha
CD 9259002
WEA / Mar '94 / Warner Music

UGLY ONE WITH THE JEWELS
CD 9362458472
WEA / Mar '95 / Warner Music

Anderson, Leif

SWING SESSIONS VOL.1 (Anderson, Leif 'Smoke Rings')
CD ANC 9093
Ancha / Sep '94 / Cadillac / Jazz Music / Wellard

Anderson, Little Willie

SWINGING THE BLUES
CD CD 4930
Earwig / Feb '95 / ADA / CM

Anderson, Lynn

COWBOY'S SWEETHEART
CD 12128
Laserlight / Jul '94 / Target/BMG

LEGENDS IN MUSIC
CD LECD 056
Wisepack / Jul '94 / Conifer/BMG / THE

ROSE GARDEN
CD WMCD 5655
Woodford Music / Jun '92 / THE

ROSE GARDEN
Promises promises / Worst is yet to come / No other time / Crying / Love of the common people / Penny for your thoughts / I've been everywhere / Paper Mansions / Two rolls of scotch tape / Sing me a sad song / Hundred times today / Lie a little / Rose garden
CD 100692
CMC / May '97 / BMG

Anderson, Marc

NATURE'S DRUMS (Anderson, Marc & Jai Bunito Aeo)
CD 2666
NorthSound / Aug '96 / Gallant

Anderson, Marian

GREAT VOICES OF THE CENTURY
CD CDMOIR 423
Memoir / Apr '96 / Jazz Music / Target/ BMG

SPIRITUALS (He's Got The Whole World In His Hands)
He's got the whole world in his hands / De-re's no hidin' place / I want Jesus to walk with me / Oh, didn't it rain / I am bound for de kingdom / Oh wasn't dat a wide ribber / My soul's been anchored in de lord / Lord I can't stay away / Sometimes I feel like a Motherless child / Hold on / Scandalise my name / Great gittin' up mornin' / Done foun' my los' sheep / I stood on de ribber ob Jerdon / Behold that star / Heav'n Heav'n / Oh Peter, go ring dem bells / Trampin' / Hard trials / Oh heaven is one beautiful place / I know / Lord how come me here / Prayer is de key / He'll bring it to pass / You go / Jus' keep on singin' / Ain't got time to die / I been in de storm so long / I've been 'buked / Let's have a union / Jus' keep on singin' / Ride on King Jesus
CD 09026619602
RCA Victor / Jun '95 / BMG

SPIRITUALS
CD PASTCD 7073
Flapper / Aug '95 / Pinnacle

Anderson, Mildred

NO MORE IN LIFE
Everybody's got somebody but me / I ain't mad at you / Hard times / No more in life / Roll 'em Pete / What more can a woman do / That ole devil called love / Mistreater / I'm lost
CD OBCCD 579
Original Blues Classics / Jun '96 / Complete/Pinnacle / Wellard

Anderson, Moira

20 SCOTTISH FAVOURITES
Dark island / Farewell my love / Soft lowland tongue o' the borders / Loch Lomond / Always Argyll / John Anderson, my Jo / Rowan tree / O Waly Waly / Isle of Mull / Sleeps the noon / O lovely land of Canada / Eriskay love lilt / Way old friends do / Ye banks and braes o' bonnie Doon / Durisdeer / Glencoe / Ae fond kiss / My ain folk / Calling me home / Amazing grace
CD LCOM 9033
Lismor / Nov '90 / ADA / Direct / Duncans / Lismor

LAND FOR ALL SEASONS, A
Uist tramping song / Mull of Kintyre / Mairi's wedding / D'ye mind lang lang syne / Loch Maree / These are my mountains / Land for all seasons / Come by the hills / Dancing in Kyle / Skye boat song / Wild mountain thyme / Flowers of the forest / Leaving Lismore / Road to the Isles
CD LCOM 6022
Lismor / Aug '96 / ADA / Direct / Duncans / Lismor

MOIRA - IN LOVE
Time after time / Love is the sweetest thing / You light up my life / Shadow of your smile / Here's that rainy day / And I love you so / More I see you / Until it's time for you to go / Nearness of you / I won't last a day without you / I just fall in love again / Sometimes when we touch / If / I'll walk alone / You needed me / Somewhere my love
CD DLCD 104
Dulcima / Oct '87 / Savoy / THE

Anderson, Pink

BALLAD & FOLKSINGER
CD OBCCD 577
Original Blues Classics / Jan '96 / Complete/Pinnacle / Wellard

CAROLINA BLUES MAN
My baby left me this morning / Baby, please don't go / Mama where did you stay last night / Big house blues / Meet me in the bottom / Weeping willow blues / Baby I'm going away / I had my fun / Every day in the week / Thousand woman blues
CD OBCCD 504
Original Blues Classics / Nov '92 / Complete/Pinnacle / Wellard

Anderson, Ray

BIG BAND RECORD
Lips apart / Anabel at one / My wish / Raven-a-ning / Leo's place / Seven monsters / Waltz for Phoebe / Literary lizard / Don't mow your lawn
CD GCD 79497
Gramavision / Sep '95 / Vital/SAM

CHEER UP (Anderson, Ray & Hans Bennink/Christy Doran)
CD ARTCD 6175
Hat Art / Dec '95 / Cadillac / Harmonia Mundi

DON'T MOW YOUR LAWN
Don't mow your lawn / Diddleybop / Damaged but good / Alligatory peccadillo / What'cha gonna do with that / Airwaves / Blow your own horn / Disguise the limit
CD ENJACD 80702
Enja / Aug '94 / New Note/Pinnacle / Vital/ SAM

EVERYONE OF US
Funkalific / Brother can you spare a dime / Kind garnerish / Muddy and Willie / Snoo tune (for Anabel) / Lady day / Dear Lord
CD _____ **GCD 79471**
Gramavision / Sep '95 / Vital/SAM

HEADS AND TALES
Hunting and gathering / Heads and tales / Matters of the heart / Unsung songs / Cheek to cheek / Tapajack / Tough guy / Road song / Drink and blather
CD _____ **ENJ 90552**
Enja / Nov '95 / New Note/Pinnacle / Vital/ SAM

RIGHT DOWN YOUR ALLEY
CD _____ **SNCD 1087**
Soul Note / Dec '86 / Cadillac / Harmonia Mundi / Wellard

SLIDERIDE (Anderson, Ray & Craig Harris/George Lewis/Gary Valente)
CD _____ **ARTCD 6165**
Hat Art / Mar '96 / Cadillac / Harmonia Mundi

WISHBONE
Gahtooze / Ah soca / Duke Ellington's sound of love / Comes love / Cape Horn / Cheek to cheek / Wishbone suite
CD _____ **GV 794542**
Gramavision / Mar '91 / Vital/SAM

Anderson, Roshell

ROLLING OVER
CD _____ **ICH 1142CD**
Ichiban / Feb '94 / Direct / Koch

Anderson, Stuart

ACTS NATURALLY
CD _____ **CDITV 559**
Scotdisc / Oct '92 / Conifer/BMG / Duncans / Ross

SCOTLAND OUR HOME (Anderson, Stuart Jnr. & Snr.)
CD _____ **MMCD 9602**
Mariner Music / Sep '96 / Duncans

STUART ANDERSON'S PARTY
Doon in the wee room / Bonnie Wee Jeannie McCall / Donald, where's yer troosers / Stuart's song / Marriage / Coulter's candy / Ghostie / Catch me if you can / Wee Kirkcudbright centipede / Come to the Ceilidah
CD _____ **CDITV 502**
Scotsdisc / Nov '89 / Conifer/BMG / Duncans / Ross

Anderson, Tom

SILVER BOW: SHETLAND FOLK FIDDLING (Anderson, Tom & Aly Bain)
Jack broke da prison door/Donald Blue/ Sleep soond / Lasses trust in Providence/ Bonnie Isle o'Whalsay / Da day dawn/Da cross reel / Shive her up/Ahint da deakes o'Voe / Da silver bow / Auld Foula reel/Wynadepla / Da slockit light/Smith o'Couster/ Da grocer / Da auld resting chair/Hamnavoe polka/Maggie's reel / Bridal march/Da bride's a bonnie ting / Jack is yet alive/Auld clettenroe / Da mill/Doon da Rooth / Pit hame da borrowed Claes/Wha'll dance wi' Wattie / Bush below da gairden / Soldier's joy / Shetland moods / Dean brig/Banks / Ferrie reel/Lay Dee at Dee/Spencie's reel / Up an'doon the harbour/Lucky can you link ony / Silvery voe/Pottinger's reel / If I get a bonnie lass/Jeannie shoke da bairn / Auld swaara / Faroe rum/Aandowin' at da Bow / Mrs. Jamieson's favourite/Lady Mary Ramsay / All da ships ir sailin'/Sheldor Geo/Mak a kishie needle dye / Freddie's tune/Da blue yow / Full rigged ship/New rigged ship / Naanie an' Betty/A yow cam to wir door yarmin / Maggie O'Ham/Da Foula shaalds / Come agen ye're welcome/Da corbie an' da craw / Ian S Robertson/Madam Vanoni
CD _____ **TSCD 469**
Topic / Sep '93 / ADA / CM / Direct

Anderson, Tony

STRICTLY DANCING: WALTZ (Anderson, Tony String Orchestra)
CD _____ **15341**
Laserlight / May '94 / Target/BMG

Anderson, Wayne

BACK TO THE GROOVE
CD _____ **CPCD 8142**
Charly / Nov '95 / Koch

Andersson, Krister

ABOUT TIME
CD _____ **FLCD 1**
Flash Music / Feb '94 / Cadillac

CONCORD AND TIME (Andersson, Krister Quartet)
CD _____ **FLCD 2**
Flash Music / May '97 / Cadillac

Andes

LES GUARANIS
CD _____ **339353**
Musidisc / Dec '86 / Discovery

Andi Sex Gang

ARCO VALLEY
CD _____ **FREUDCD 24**
Jungle / Jul '89 / RTM/Disc / SRD

Andre, Peter

NATURAL
Flava / Natural / Mysterious girl / I feel you / You are (part 2) / All I ever wanted / Show U somethin' / To the top / Tell me when / Only one / Message to my girl / Turn it up / PS Get down on it
CD _____ **7432145945**
CD _____ **D 2005**
Mushroom / Sep '96 / 3mv/Pinnacle

Andreone, Leah

VEILED
It's alright, it's ok / Happy birthday / Mother tongue / You make me remember / Who are they to say / Problem child / Come sunday morning / Kiss me goodbye / Hell to pay / Will you still love me / Imagining you
CD _____ **07863668972**
RCA / Mar '97 / BMG

Andrews Sisters

36 UNFORGETTABLE MEMORIES (2CD Set)
Bei mir bist du schon / Sing sing sing / Shoo shoo baby / In the mood / Woodpecker song / Beer barrel polka / Chico's love song / Don't sit under the apple tree / House of blue lights / I'll be with you in apple blossom time / Nice work if you can get it / Rhumboogie / Three little sisters / Ti pi tin / Daddy / Hit the road / Oh Johnny oh Johnny oh / South American way / Rum & coca cola / Don't be that way / Hold tight, hold tight (Seafood Mama) / Say Si Si / Beat me Daddy eight to the bar / Boogie woogie bugle boy / Tu-Li tulip time / Straighten up & fly right / Well all right / Strip polka / Corns for my country / Down by the Ohio / Joseph Joseph / Says my heart / Elmer's time / Oh Mama / Jitterbug lullaby / Sonny boy
CD Set _____ **TNC 96208**
Natural Collection / Aug '96 / Target/BMG

ANDREWS SISTERS 1937-1943
CD _____ **394672**
Music Memoria / Mar '94 / ADA / Discovery

ART VOCAL 1937-1944
CD _____ **700172**
Art Vocal / Sep '96 / Discovery

BEAT ME DADDY, EIGHT TO THE BAR (1937-1940)
Beat me Daddy, eight to the bar / Beer barrel polka / Bei mir bist du schon / Ciribiribin: *Andrews Sisters & Bing Crosby* / Cock-eyed mayor of Kaunakakai / Ferryboat serenade / From the land of the sky blue water / Hold tight, hold tight / I love you too much / I want my mama / Let's have another one / Long time no see / Nice work if you can get it / 1-2-3 O'Leary / Oo-oo-oo-oh boom / Pagan love song / Pennsylvania 6-5000 / Rumboogie / Shortnin' bread / Well alright / Why talk about love / You don't know how much you can suffer
CD _____ **CDAJA 5096**
Living Era / Dec '95 / Select

BEST OF THE ANDREWS SISTERS, THE
CD _____ **MATCD 318**
Castle / Dec '94 / BMG

BEST OF THE ANDREWS SISTERS, THE
CD _____ **MCCD 199**
Music Club / May '95 / Disc / THE

BEST OF THE ANDREWS SISTERS, THE
CD _____ **PLSCD 222**
Pulse / Jul '97 / BMG

BOOGIE WOOGIE BUGLE BOY
Bei mir bist du schon / Joseph Joseph / Oh ma-ma / Sha-sha / When a Prince of a fella meets a Cinderella / Begin the beguine / Beer Barrel Polka / Jumpin' jive / Oh Johnny oh Johnny oh / South America Way / Let's have another one / Say si si / Rumboogie / Beat me Daddy, eight to the bar / Pennsylvania 6-5000 / Boogie woogie bugle boy
CD _____ **HADCD 173**
Javelin / May '94 / Henry Hadaway / THE

COLLECTION, THE
CD _____ **COL 052**
Collection / Jan '95 / Target/BMG

CREAM OF THE ANDREWS SISTERS, THE
Beat me Daddy, eight to the bar / Joseph Joseph / Pennsylvania 6-5000 / Oh Johnny oh Johnny, oh / Bei mir bist du schon / Hold tight, hold tight / Rumboogie / Say "si, si" / South American way / Jumpin' jive / Where have we met before / Pagan love song / Oh, ma-ma / Sha-sha / Begin the beguine / Billy boy / When a Prince of a fella meets a Cinderella / Just a simple melody / Love is where you find it / Why talk about love / Let's have another one
CD _____ **PASTCD 9766**
Flapper / Oct '91 / Pinnacle

HOLD TIGHT...IT'S THE ANDREWS SISTERS (20 Greatest Hits)
Don't sit under the apple tree / Sabre dance / Rum and coca cola / Put that ring on my finger / Twenty four hours of sunshine / I can dream, can't I / That lucky old sun / Coca roca / Pussy cat song / Lulaby of Broadway / Is you is or is you ain't my baby / Three caballeros / Accentuate the positive / Hold tight, hold tight / Beer barrel polka / Boogie woogie bugle boy / Pennsylvania polka / Victory polka
CD _____ **DBCD 12**
Dance Band Days / Oct '87 / Prism

MAGIC OF THE ANDREWS SISTERS, THE
Well all right / Beat me Daddy, eight to the bar / Bei mir bist du schon / Pennysylvania 6-5000 / I'll be with you in apple blossom time / Ferryboat serenade / Rhumboogie / Long time, no see / Short'nin bread / Say "Si Si" / Oh, Johnny, oh Johnny, oh / Hold tight hold tight / Sonny boy / Don't sit under the apple tree / Let's have another one / Ti-pi-tin / Yes my darling daughter / Boogie woogie bugle boy / South America way / Nice work if you can get it / Beer barrel polka / Jospeh Joseph / Strip polka / Oh Ma Ma (The Butcher's boy)
CD _____ **PAR 2063**
Parade / Jul '96 / Disc

MAXENE: AN ANDREWS SISTER (Andrews, Maxene)
Bei mir bist du schoen / Don't sit under the apple tree / Remember / Fascinating rhythm / I'll be with you in apple blossom time
CD _____ **CDSL 5218**
DRG / May '92 / Discovery / New Note/ Pinnacle

MISTER FIVE BY FIVE
Mister five by five / Strip polka / What to do / That's the moon my son / One meat ball / Sing a tropical song / Lonesome Mamma / I've got a guy in Kalamazoo / Massachusetts / Straighten up and fly right / Well alright / Begin the beguine / Long time no see / Little jitterbug / I love you too much / Beat me Daddy eight to a bar / Cock-eyed Mayor of Kaunakakai / Pennsylvania 65000 / Say si si / Beer barrel polka / Pross Tchai / Ferryboat serenade / Rhumboogie
CD _____ **RAJCD 869**
Empress / Mar '96 / Koch

PORTRAIT OF THE ANDREWS SISTERS, A
CD _____ **GALE 401**
Gallerie / May '97 / Disc / THE

RUM AND COCA COLA
CD _____ **RMB 75018**
Remember / Nov '93 / Total/BMG

TICO TICO
CD _____ **DAWE 49**
Magic / Apr '97 / Cadillac / Harmonia Mundi / Jazz Music / Swift / Wellard

VERY BEST OF THE ANDREWS SISTERS, THE
Boogie woogie bugle boy / Sonny boy / Hit the road / Beer barrel polka / Rhumboogie / Say si si / Well alright / Lullaby to a jitterbug / I'll be with you in apple blossom time / Beat me Daddy / South American way / Bei mir bist du schoen / Joseph Joseph / Ti-pi-tin / Long time no see / Yes my darling daughter
CD _____ **SUMCD 4047**
Summit / Nov '96 / Sound & Media

Andrews, Chris

DIE SUPERHITS
CD _____ **15144**
Laserlight / Aug '91 / Target/BMG

HIT SINGLE COLLECTABLES
CD _____ **DISK 4508**
Disky / Apr '94 / Disky / THE

SIMPLY THE BEST
CD _____ **WMCD 5707**
Disky / Oct '94 / Disky / THE

Andrews, Ernie

GREAT CITY, THE
Great city / Time after time / Jug and I got up this morning / Skylark / Fire and rain / If I loved you / Come back little girl / If I had your love
CD _____ **MCD 5543**
Muse / Dec '95 / New Note/Pinnacle

NO REGRETS
When they ask about you / Don't you know I care (or don't you care to) / I'll never be free / You call it madness / Hunt is on / Until the real thing comes along / When did you leave Heaven / Sweet Lorraine / Sweet slumber
CD _____ **MCD 5484**
Muse / Nov '93 / New Note/Pinnacle

Andrews, Harvey

25 YEARS ON THE ROAD
CD _____ **HYCD 200105**
Hypertension / Feb '95 / ADA / CM / Direct / Total/BMG

MARGERITA COLLECTION, THE
CD _____ **HASKA 001CD**
Haska / Nov '96 / ADA

SNAPS
CD _____ **HYCD 295159**
Hypertension / Dec '95 / ADA / CM / Direct / Total/BMG

SOMEDAY FANTASY
CD _____ **LBEECD 006**
Beeswing / Jan '95 / ADA / Broadside / CM / Roots

WRITER OF SONGS
CD _____ **LBEE 002CD**
Beeswing / Jan '94 / ADA / Broadside / CM / Roots

Andrews, Inez

TWO SIDES OF INEZ ANDREWS, THE
CD _____ **SH 6019**
Shanachie / Mar '96 / ADA / Greensleeves / Koch

Andreyev Balalaika Ensemble

BALALAIKA
CD _____ **MCD 61713**
Monitor / Jul '94 / CM

Andromeda

ANDROMEDA
CD _____ **SB 042**
Second Battle / Jun '97 / Greyhound

RETURN TO SANITY
CD _____ **HBG 122/5**
Background / Apr '94 / Background / Greyhound

Andromeda

ANTHOLOGY 1966-1969
CD _____ **KSCD 9492**
Kissing Spell / Jun '97 / Greyhound

Andromeda

SEE INTO THE STARS
CD _____ **SARCD 003**
Saraja / Mar '93 / THE

Andwella's Dream

LOVE AND POETRY
CD _____ **SPACD 1961**
Fingerprint / Jun '97 / Greyhound

Andy, Bob

BOB ANDY'S SONG BOOK
CD _____ **SOCD 1121**
Studio One / Feb '96 / Jet Star

FIRE BURNING
CD _____ **CDTRL 343**
Trojan / Feb '95 / Direct / Jet Star

FRIENDS
CD _____ **AV 001CD**
I-Anka / Apr '96 / Jet Star

HANGING TOUGH
CD _____ **VPCD 1484**
VP / Mar '97 / Greensleeves / Jet Star / Total/BMG

SONGS OF BOB ANDY, THE (Various Artists)
CD _____ **JOVECD 1**
Jove Music / Sep '93 / Jet Star / SRD

SWEET MEMORIES (Andy, Bob & Marcia Griffiths)
Learning things about you / Hung up on you / Still the most / Lean on me / Touch me again / I'm ready / Will you come back to me / Let's be friends / We belong / Who can I want but you / You've got a friend / Music inside me / Wife and sweetheart / Hung up dub / Most dub / Touch dub / Belong dub / Wife dub / Sweetheart dub
CD _____ **NTRCD 078**
Nectar / Apr '97 / Pinnacle

YOUNG, GIFTED AND BLACK
CD _____ **CDTRL 343**
Trojan / Nov '94 / Direct / Jet Star

Andy, Horace

ELEMENTARY (Andy, Horace & The Rhythm Queen)
CD _____ **RNCD 2016**
Rhino / Jul '93 / Grapevine/PolyGram / Jet Star

GOOD VIBES 1975-1979 (Originals And Versions)
Reggae rhythm / Serious thing / Skylarking / Youth of today / Problems / Mr. Bassie discomix / Pure ranking discomix / Good vibes / Control youself / Ital vital
CD _____ **BAFCD 019**
Blood & Fire / Jul '97 / Vital

HITS FROM STUDIO ONE AND MORE
CD _____ **RNCD 2116**
Rhino / Sep '95 / Grapevine/PolyGram / Jet Star

IN THE LIGHT (Dub/Vocal)
Do you love my music / Hey there woman / Government land / Leave Rasta / Fever /

In the light / Problems / If I / Collie herb / Rome / Music dub / Dub there / Government dub / Rasta dub / Fever dub / Dub the light / Problems dub / I and I / Collie dub / Dub down Rome
CD ______ BAFCD 6
Blood & Fire / May '95 / Vital

LIFE IS FOR LIVING
CD ______ ARICD 106
Ariwa Sounds / Mar '95 / Jet Star / SRD

PRIME OF HORACE ANDY, THE (20 Classic Cuts From The 1970's)
Skylarking / Love of a woman / Zion gate / Just say who / Something on my mind / You are my angel / Money money / Rain from the sky / My guiding star / Bless you / Don't try to use me / Nice and easy / True love shines bright / Collie weed / Ain't no sunshine / Sea of love / Love you to want me / Natural mystic / Better collie / Riding for a fall
CD ______ MCCD 302
Music Club / Jun '97 / Disc / THE

ROOTS AND BRANCHES
CD ______ ARICD 125
Ariwa Sounds / Mar '97 / Jet Star / SRD

SEEK AND YOU WILL FIND
CD ______ BLKCD 15
Blakamix / Nov '95 / Jet Star / SRD

SKYLARKING (The Best Of Horace Andy)
Spying glass / Natty Dread a weh she want / Rock to sleep / One love / Problems / Fever / Children of Israel / Money money / Girl I love you / Elementary / Every tongue shall tell / Skylarking / Do you love my music / Spying glass
CD ______ CSAD 1
Melankolic / Sep '96 / EMI

SKYLARKING
CD ______ SOCD 1116
Studio One / May '97 / Jet Star

YOU ARE MY ANGEL
Thank you Lord / I'll forgive you / You are my angel / I'm not a know it all / Keep on trying / Ain't no sunshine / Can I change your mind / Don't break your promise / Dream lover / John saw them coming / Riding for a fall / Rain from the skies
CD ______ CDTBL 197
Trojan / Nov '96 / Direct / Jet Star

Andy, Kendrick

ANOTHER NIGHT IN THE GHETTO
CD ______ FBKCD 1
Fence Beater / Mar '95 / Jet Star

Andyboy

ONE MAN, SIX STRINGS AND A WHOLE LOTTA MISERY
CD ______ WB 3117CD
We Bite / Jan '95 / Plastic Head

Anesthesia

PVC
CD ______ BR 043CD
Blue Room Released / Jun '97 / Essential/ BMG / SRD

Anesthesy

EXALTATION OF THE ECLIPSE
CD ______ BMCD 54
Black Mark / May '94 / Plastic Head

Ange

A DIEU
CD ______ 992005
Wotre Music / Jul '96 / Discovery / New Note/Pinnacle

Angel Cage

SOPHIE MAGIC
CD ______ ORGAN 016CD
Org / Jul '95 / Pinnacle

Angel Corpse

HAMMER OF GODS
CD ______ OPCD 047
Osmose / Nov '96 / Plastic Head

Angel Corpus Christi

WHITE COURTESY PHONE
CD ______ ALMOCD 004
Almo Sounds / Nov '95 / Pinnacle

Angel, Dave

CLASSICS
Bounce back / Sighting / Jungle love / Trip to darkness / Free flow / Fallen destiny / Endless motions / Brother from jazz / Down deep / Lust / Dimension of drums / Great Daine
CD ______ RS 96089CD
R&S / May '96 / Vital

GLOBETROTTING
Coming on / Philly bluntz / Funk music / Club hell / Sensor Zurich / K road NZ / This is disco / Tokyo stealth fighter / Liquid rooms / Chicago emerald city
CD ______ 5244402
CD ______ BRCD 625
4th & Broadway / Aug '97 / PolyGram

TALES OF THE EXPECTED
Arabian nights / Big tight flares / Timeless / Scatman / Over here / Bump / It's too hot in here / Be bop / DOB / Rudiments
CD ______ BVMCD 2
Blunted Vinyl / Oct '95 / PolyGram / Vital

TRANCE LUNAR PARADISE
CD Set ______ 3DIMCD 1
Sound Dimension / Dec '94 / Total/BMG

Angel Witch

'82 REVISITED (Live At The East Anglia Rock Festival)
Gorgon / Nowhere to run / They wouldn't dare / Sorceress / Evil games / White witch / Angel of death / Angel witch / Evil games / They wouldn't dare / Nowhere to run
CD ______ CDTB 173
Thunderbolt / May '97 / TKO Magnum

ANGEL WITCH
Angel Witch / Gorgon / Atlantis / White witch / Confused / Sorceress / Sweet danger / Free man / Angel of death / Devil's tower
CD ______ CLACD 239
Castle / May '91 / BMG

SCREAMIN' ASSAULT
She don't lie / Frontal assault / Something wrong / Straight from hell / Reawakening / Screamin' n' bleedin' / Waltz the night / Rendezvous with the blade / Goodbye / Take to the wing / Fatal kiss / Undergods / UXV
CD ______ KILCD 1001
Killerwatt / Dec '88 / Kingdom

Angelic Gospel Singers

BEST OF THE ANGELIC GOSPEL SINGERS, THE
CD ______ NASH 4509
Nashboro / Feb '96 / Pinnacle

Angelic Upstarts

ANGEL DUST (The Collected Highs)
Murder of Liddle Towers / Police oppression / I'm an upstart / Teenage warning / Never 'ad nothin' / Last night another soldier / Two million voices / Kids on the street / England / Hearts lament / Shotgun solution / Never say die / Woman in disguise / Solidarity / Lust for glory / Never give up / Waiting, hating / Reason why / Nobody was saved / Geordie's wife / Loneliness of the long distance runner / 42nd Street / Burglar / Five flew over the cuckoo's nest / As the passion / Young punk / Where we started
CD ______ CDMGRAM 7
Anagram / Aug '93 / Cargo / Pinnacle

BOMBED OUT
CD ______ DOJOCD 198
Dojo / Aug '94 / Disc

GREATEST HITS LIVE
Murder of liddle towers / Teenage warning / Police / Oppression / Young ones / We're gonna take the world / Last night / Another soldier / Guns for the Afghan rebels / Mr. Politician / Shotgun solution / I understand / Kids on the street / Enland / You're nicked / Two million voices / I'm an upstart / White riot / Leave me alone / Never 'ad nutter
CD ______ DOJOCD 127
Dojo / Mar '93 / Disc

INDEPENDENT SINGLES COLLECTION
Murder of the Liddle Towers / Police oppression / Woman in disguise / Lust for glory / Solidarity / 42nd Street / Five flew over the cuckoo's nest / Dollars and pounds / Don't stop / Not just a name / Leech / Leave me alone / White riot / Machine gun Kelly / Young ones / We're gonna take the world / England / Soldier / Thin red line / Brighton bomb / There's a drink in it
CD ______ CDPUNK 59
Anagram / May '95 / Cargo / Pinnacle

REASON WHY
Woman in disguise / Never give up / Waiting, hating / Reason why / Nobody was saved / Geordie's wife / Loneliness of the long distance runner / 42nd Street / Burglar / Solidarity / As the passion / Young punk / Where we started / Lust for glory / Five flew over the cuckoo's nest / Dollars and pounds / Don't stop / Not just a name / Leech / Leave me alone / Murder of Liddle Towers / White riot
CD ______ SUMCD 4086
Summit / Jan '97 / Sound & Media

TWO MILLION VOICES
Two million voices / Ghost town / You're nicked / England / Heath's lament / Guns for the Afghan rebels / I understand / Mensi's marauders / Mr. Politician / Kids on the street / Jimmy / We're gonna take the world / Last night another soldier / I wish
CD ______ DOJOCD 81
Dojo / May '93 / Disc

Angelopoulos, Lycourgos

BYZANTINE MASS - AKATHISTOS HYMN (Angelopoulos, Lycourgos & The Greek Byzantine Choir)
CD ______ PS 65118/9
PlayaSound / Nov '93 / ADA / Harmonia Mundi

Angels

BEST OF THE ANGELS, THE
My boyfriend's back / He's so fine / 'Till / He's the kissing kind / Little Beatle boy / I adore him / Thank you & goodnight / Guy with the black eye / Why don't the boy leave me alone / World without love / Wow wow wee (he's the boy for me) / Dream boy / Boy from Crosstown / Snowflakes & teardrops / Has anybody seen my boyfriend / Guess the boy don't love me anymore / You can't take my boyfriend's Woody / Cry baby cry / (Love me) now / Jamaica Joe / My boyfriend's back
CD ______ 5527602
Spectrum / Feb '97 / PolyGram

Angels Ov Light

PSYCHICK YOUTH RALLY
CD ______ CSR 8CD
Cold Spring / Aug '95 / Plastic Head / RTM/Disc

Angels With Dirty Faces

SOUNDS OF WORLD
CD ______ BFR 43101CD
Rock The Nation / Nov '94 / Plastic Head

Anger

MIAMI, FLORIDA
CD ______ SPV 08436212
SPV / Nov '94 / Koch / Plastic Head

Angina Pectoris

ANGUISH
CD ______ SPV 08445612
SPV / Oct '94 / Koch / Plastic Head

INSOMNIA
CD ______ SPV 08445802
SPV / Apr '96 / Koch / Plastic Head

Angkor Wat

CORPUS CHRISTI
CD ______ CDZORRO 5
Metal Blade / May '90 / Pinnacle / Plastic Head

WHEN OBSCENITY BECOMES THE NORM...AWAKE
CD ______ 398414088CD
Metal Blade / Jun '97 / Pinnacle / Plastic Head

Anglaspel

JAZZ IN SWEDEN 1982
CD ______ 1270
Caprice / Jan '89 / ADA / Cadillac / CM / Complete/Pinnacle

Angra

ANGELS CRY
CD ______ DCD 9412
Dream Circle / Feb '97 / Cargo / Plastic Head

FREEDOM CALL
Freedom call / Queen of the night / Reaching horizons / Stand away / Painkiller / Deep blue
CD ______ 358853
Rising Sun / Nov '96 / Cargo / Plastic Head

HOLY LAND (Collectors Edition - 2CD Set)
CD Set ______ 35741
Rising Sun / Nov '96 / Cargo / Plastic Head

Angry Samoans

RETURN TO SAMOA
CD ______ YUPPY 008CD
Vermiform / Jun '97 / Cargo / Greyhound / Plastic Head

Angst

CRY FOR HAPPY
CD ______ SST 206CD
SST / Nov '88 / Plastic Head

Anibaldi, Leo

VIRTUAL LANGUAGE, THE
CD ______ PWD 7448
Pow Wow / May '94 / Jet Star

VOID
CD ______ CAT 031CD
Rephlex / Sep '96 / Prime / RTM/Disc

Animal New Ones

LAKE SIDE BASH
CD ______ FLIGHT 13013CD
Flight 13 / Nov '92 / Plastic Head

Animals

ANIMALS LIVE IN NEWCASTLE 1963/ YARDBIRDS LIVE AT THE MARQUEE (Animals/Yardbirds)
CD ______ 14550
Spalax / Jun '97 / ADA / Cargo / Direct / Discovery / Greyhound

ANIMALS WITH SONNY BOY WILLIAMSON (Newcastle, December 1963) (Animals & Sonny Boy Williamson)
Sonny's slow walk / Pontiac blues / My babe / I don't care no more / Baby don't you worry / Night time is the right time / I'm gonna put you down / Fattenin' frogs for snakes / Nobody but you / Bye bye Sonny bye bye / Coda
CD ______ CDCHARLY 215
Charly / Jul '90 / Koch

ANIMALS, THE
CD ______ 16137
Laserlight / Jul '95 / Target/BMG

ARK
Loose change / Love is for all time / My favourite enemy / Prisoner of the light / Being there / Hard times / Night / Trying to get to you / Just can't get enough / Melt down / Gotta get back to you / Crystal nights
CD ______ CLACD 412
Castle / Nov '96 / BMG

COMPLETE ANIMALS, THE (The Complete Mickie Most Productions - 2CD Set)
Boom boom / Talking 'bout you / Blue feeling / Dimples / Baby let me take you home / Gonna send you back to Walker / Baby what's wrong / House of the rising sun / F-E-E-L / I'm mad again / Right time / Around and around / I'm in love again / Bury my body / She said yeah / I'm crying / Take it easy / Story of Bo Diddley / Girl can't help it / I've been around / Memphis, Tennessee / Don't let me be misunderstood / Club a gogo / Roadrunner / Hallelujah, I love her so / Don't want much / I believe to my soul / Let the good times roll / Mess around / How you've changed / I ain't got you / Roberts / Bright lights big city / Worried life blues / Bring it on home to me / For Miss Caulker / I can't believe it / We gotta get out of this place / It's my life / I'm gonna change the world
CD Set ______ CDEM 1367
EMI / Jul '90 / EMI

GREATEST HITS LIVE
It's too late / House of the rising sun / It's my life / Don't bring me down / Don't let me be misunderstood / I'm crying / Bring it on home to me / O lucky man / Boom boom / We gotta get out of this place / When I was young
CD ______ CLACD 424
Castle / Nov '96 / BMG

INSIDE LOOKING OUT (1965-1966 Decca Sessions)
Inside looking out / Outcast / Don't bring me down / Cheating / Help me girl / CC rider / One monkey don't stop now show / Maudie / Sweet little sixteen / You're on my mind / Clapping / Gin house blues / Squeeze her, tease her / What am I living for / I put a spell on you / That's all I am to you / She'll return it / Mama told me not to come / I just want to make love to you / Boom boom / Big boss man / Pretty thing
CD ______ NEXCD 153
Sequel / Feb '91 / BMG

INSIDE OUT (Burdon, Eric & The Animals)
San Franciscan nights / Ring of fire / I put a spell on you / Mama told me not to come / Good times / Help me girl / Sky pilot / Inside looking out / River deep, mountain high / When I was young / Monterey / Sweet little sixteen / Gin house blues / Don't bring me down
CD ______ 5501192
Spectrum / Oct '93 / PolyGram

LOVE IS
CD ______ OW 30338
One Way / Sep '94 / ADA / Direct / Greyhound

MOST OF THE ANIMALS
CD ______ RVCD 05
Raven / May '91 / ADA / Direct

RARITIES
CD ______ PRCDSP 500
Prestige / Aug '92 / Else / Total/BMG

ROADRUNNERS (1966-1968 Live)
CD ______ RVCD 11
Raven / Oct '92 / ADA / Direct

SINGLES PLUS
Baby let me take you home / Gonna send you back to Walker / House of the rising sun / Talkin' 'bout you / I'm crying / Take it easy / Don't let me be misunderstood / Club a gogo / Bring it on home to me / For Miss Caulker / We gotta get out of this place / I can't believe it / It's my life / I'm going to change the world / Bury my body / Dimples / She said yeah / Right time / Bright lights big city / Let the good times roll
CD ______ CZ 10
EMI / Aug '88 / EMI

SINGLES PLUS, THE
CD _______ CDP 7466052
Premier / Oct '87 / Mo's Music Machine

Animals That Swim

I WAS THE KING, I REALLY WAS
CD _______ ELM 37CD
Elemental / May '96 / RTM/Disc

WORKSHY
CD _______ ELM 24CD
Elemental / Sep '94 / RTM/Disc

Anitas Livs

WILD WORLD WEB
CD _______ SLACD 014CD
Slask / Nov '95 / ADA

Anka, Paul

BEST OF PAUL ANKA, THE
CD _______ 472106
Flarenasch / Apr '96 / Discovery

DIANA
CD _______ 15191
Laserlight / Aug '91 / Target/BMG

GOLDEN HOUR OF PAUL ANKA
You and me today / My way / She's a lady / Let me be the one / Jubilation / We make it happen / Everything's been changed / Yesterday my life was more of just the same / Les filles de Paris / Do I love you / Something good is coming / Double life / Love is / Some kind of friend / Life song / Pretty good / Kathum
CD _______ 12844
Laserlight / Sep '96 / Target/BMG

GREATEST HITS COLLECTION
CD _______ CDSR 033
Telstar / Nov '93 / BMG

HAVING MY BABY
CD _______ 16122
Laserlight / May '95 / Target/BMG

HIS GERMAN RECORDINGS
CD _______ BCD 15613
Bear Family / Feb '92 / Direct / Rollercoaster / Swift

TOUCH OF CLASS, A
Anytime (I'll be there) / I don't like to sleep alone / Out of my mind in love / It's sad to see the old hometown again / There's nothing stronger than our love / Wake up / Today I became a fool / Girl, you turn me on / Walk away / Water runs deep / Bring the wine / One man woman, one woman man / Something about you / (You're) Having my baby / Let me get to know you / Love is a lonely song / How can anything be beautiful / I gave a little and lost a lot / Papa / It doesn't matter anymore
CD _______ TC 861882
Disky / May '97 / Disky / THE

Ann Can Be

27 ON AND OFF
CD _______ TOODAMNHY 62
Too Damn Hype / Jan '95 / Cargo / SRD

Anna

101-1 SM
CD _______ CDFRE 3
Free / Oct '93 / RTM/Disc

Annabouboula

GREEK FIRE
CD _______ SHCD 64027
Shanachie / Jul '91 / ADA / Greensleeves / Koch

Anne Marie

BE TOUGH
CD _______ EBSC 004
Echo Beach / Oct '96 / Cargo / Shellshock/Disc

Annie Anxiety

JACKAMO (Bandez, Annie Anxiety)
As I lie in your arms / Bastinado / Chasing the dragon down Broadway / Jackamo / One mourning / Jak yo mama / Rise
CD _______ TPCD 4
One Little Indian / Nov '87 / Pinnacle

Annihilator

ALICE IN HELL
Crystal Ann / WTYD / Burns like a buzzsaw blade / Schizos (are never alone) / Human insecticide / Alison Hell / Wicked mystic / Word salad / Ligeia
CD _______ RR 94882
Roadrunner / Sep '96 / PolyGram

BAG OF TRICKS
Alison Hell / Phantasmagoria / Back to the crypt / Gallery / Human insecticide / Fun Palace / WTYD / Word salad / Live wire / Knight jumps Queen / Fantastic things / Bats in the belfry / Evil appetite / Gallery / Alison Hell / Phantasmagoria
CD _______ RR 89972
Roadrunner / Sep '96 / PolyGram

IN COMMAND LIVE 1989
CD _______ RR 88522
Roadrunner / Nov '96 / PolyGram

KING OF THE KILL
Box / King of the kill / Hell is a war / Bliss / Second to none / Annihilator / Twenty one / In the blood / Fiasco (slate) / Fiasco / Catch the wind / Speed / Bad child
CD _______ CDMFN 171
Music For Nations / Oct '94 / Pinnacle

NEVER NEVER LAND
CD _______ RR 93742
Roadrunner / Sep '96 / PolyGram

REFRESH THE DEMON
CD _______ CDMFN 197
CD _______ CDMFNX 197
Music For Nations / Mar '96 / Pinnacle

REMAINS
Murder / Dead wrong / Bastiage / Never / Human remains / I want / No love / Tricks and traps / Wind / Sexecution / REaction
CD _______ CDMFN 228
Music For Nations / Jul '97 / Pinnacle

SET THE WORLD ON FIRE
CD _______ RR 92002
Roadrunner / Mar '96 / PolyGram

Anonymous 4

LOVE'S ILLUSION
CD _______ HMU 907109
Harmonia Mundi / Oct '94 / Cadillac / Harmonia Mundi

Another Fine Day

LIFE BEFORE LAND
CD _______ RBADCD 7
Beyond / Jun '94 / Kudos / Pinnacle

Another Green World

INVISIBLE LANDSCAPE
CD _______ MEYCD 16
Magick Eye / Sep '96 / Cargo / SRD

Another Tale

NIGHTMARE VOICES
CD _______ HY 3910012
Hyperium / Nov '92 / Cargo / Plastic Head

Ansill, Jay

ORIGAMI
CD _______ FF 530CD
Flying Fish / '92 / ADA / CM / Direct / Roots

Ant & Dec

CULT OF ANT & DEC, THE
Cult of Ant & Dec / When I fall in love / Shout / Falling / Crazy / Cloud 9 / Just a little love / Better watch out / Game of love / Bound / Masterplan / Universal sun / Apology
CD _______ TCD 2887
Telstar / May '97 / BMG

Ant Bee

WITH MY FAVOURITE "VEGETABLE" AND OTHER BIZARRE MUZIK
Lunar eggs - clips run amuck / Girl with the stars in her hair / Motorhead snorks - Motorhead speaks / Live jam / Jimmy Carl Black speakin' at ya / In a star / Do you like worms / Bunk speaks / Another gardner variation / Pachuco falsetto laughs / Here we go round the lemon tree / Who slew the beast / Dom Dewild speaks / Dom Dewild transforms (Before your very ears) / Dom Dewild speaks again
CD _______ DIVINE 003CD
Voiceprint / Sep '94 / Pinnacle

Ant Trip Ceremony

24 HOURS
CD _______ ANT 23
Anthology / Jul '97 / Cargo / Greyhound

Antediluvian Rocking Horse

MUSIC FOR THE ODD OCCASION
CD _______ SEELAND 505
Seeland / Mar '97 / Cargo / SRD

Antena, Isabelle

CAMINO DEL SOL
CD _______ TWI 1142
Les Disques Du Crepuscule / Oct '96 / Discovery

EN CAVALE
CD _______ TWI 6102
Les Disques Du Crepuscule / Oct '96 / Discovery

HOPING FOR LOVE
Des Calins, Des Caresses / Laying on the sofa / Naughty, naughty / Sweet boy / La tete contre les murs / Le poisson des mers du sud / Quand le jazz entre en lice melodie / L'ideal / Musique de 4 a 6 / Toutes les etoiles de tunisie / Otra bebera
CD _______ TWI 7592
Les Disques Du Crepuscule / Oct '96 / Discovery

TOUS MES CAPRICES
CD _______ TWI 842CD
Les Disques Du Crepuscule / Oct '96 / Discovery

Antenna

HIDEOUT
Shine / Wallpaper / Stillife / Rust / Dreamy / Don't be late / Fade / Easy listening / Danger buggy / Second skin / Hallelujah / Grey St.
CD _______ MR 00462
Mammoth / Apr '93 / Vital

Anthem

GYPSY WAYS
Gypsy ways (win, lose or draw) / Bad habits die hard / Cryin' heart / Midnight sun / Final risk / Love in vain / Legal killing / Silent child / Shout it out / Night stalker
CD _______ CDMFN 103
Music For Nations / Aug '90 / Pinnacle

HUNTING TIME
Juggler / Evil touch / Sleepless night / Let your heart beat / Hunting time / Tears for the lovers / Jailbreak / Bottle bottom
CD _______ CDMFN 104
Music For Nations / Aug '90 / Pinnacle

NO SMOKE WITHOUT FIRE
Shadow walk / Blinded pain / Love on the edge / Power and blood / Night we stand / Hungry soul / Do you understand / Voice of thunderstorm / Fever eyes
CD _______ CDMFN 101
Music For Nations / Aug '90 / Pinnacle

Anthony B

REAL REVOLUTIONARY
CD _______ GRELCD 230
Greensleeves / Aug '96 / Jet Star / SRD

Anthony, Mike

SHORT MORNING
CD _______ GPCD 005
Gussie P / Dec '92 / Jet Star

Anthony, Ray

22 ORIGINAL BIG BAND RECORDINGS
CD _______ HCD 412
Hindsight / Sep '92 / Jazz Music / Target/ BMG

ALL THAT JAZZ (Anthony, Ray Orchestra)
CD _______ AERO 1030
Aerospace / Jul '96 / Jazz Music / Montpellier

BOOGIE, BLUES AND BALLADS (Anthony, Ray Orchestra)
Boogie blues / Birth of the blues / Swingin' shepherd blues / Beat me Daddy eight to the bar / Lil' darlin' / Our love is here to stay / Kansas City / Girl talk / Fly me to the moon / Memories of you / Cow cow boogie / I left my heart in San Francisco / Bad bad Leroy Brown / Night train
CD _______ RACD 1041
Aerospace / Jun '97 / Jazz Music / Montpellier

DANCE PARTY (Dances From Waltz To Tango) (Anthony, Ray & Arthur Murray)
Swing / Shuffle my boogie / Guantanamera / Bunny hop cha cha / New York, New York / Last cheater's waltz / Don't cry for me Argentina / Coffee song / Riviera rumba / Tango, anyone
CD _______ AERO 1009
Aerospace / Jul '96 / Jazz Music / Montpellier

DANCING IN THE DARK
Dancing in the dark / True blue Lou / Begin the beguine / Cheek to cheek / Dancing on the ceiling / I wonder what's become of Sally / Continental / You and the night and the music / Taking a chance on love / You're the cream in my coffee / It's delovely / I get a kick out of you
CD _______ AERO 995
Aerospace / May '96 / Jazz Music / Montpellier

DIRTY TRUMPET FOR A SWINGIN' PARTY/HAPPY TRUMPETS (Anthony, Ray Orchestra)
Let me entertain you / Some of these days / St. Louis blues / Harlem nocturne / Sugar blues / Booby trap / Walkin' the Sunset Strip / Big stomp / Skoklaan / Candy wrapper / Mr. Anthony's blues / Shoutin' truth / Inka dinka doo / String of pearls / Elmer's tune / Happiness is / Popcorn / Bill Bailey / Tijuana taxi / Taste of honey / What now my love / Spanish flea / Zorba the Greek / Mame
CD _______ RACD 1027
Aerospace / Jun '97 / Jazz Music / Montpellier

DREAM DANCING IN HAWAII/DREAM DANCING MEMORIES (Anthony, Ray Orchestra)
Hawaiian sunset / Beyond the reef / Harbour lights / Hawaiian nights / Tiny bubbles / Now is the hour / Paradise / Hawaiian wedding song / Blue Hawaii / Blue moon / Sweet Leilani / Aloha / Still wind / Evening sun / World belongs to me / Why should we wonder / Misty night / Goodnight ladies / Moonlight madness / Heaven only knows / Reverie / Raindrops and moonbeams / Londonderry air / Summer breezes
CD _______ RACD 1026
Aerospace / Jun '97 / Jazz Music / Montpellier

DREAM GIRL/MOMENTS TOGETHER
Love is here to stay / Careless / Everything I have is yours / Many faces / Goodnight waltz / No other love / Please Mr.Sun / Things I love / With you in mind / Oh what it seems to be / In time / If I ever love again / Dream girl / Bewitched / Nearness of you / When I fall in love / My foolish heart / You'll never know / Pretend / I fell in love / Darn that dream / I didn't know what time it was / My private melody / It's the talk of the town
CD _______ CTMCD 119
EMI / Jun '97 / EMI

HITS OF RAY ANTHONY, THE
Slaughter on 10th Avenue / Man with the horn / Mr. Anthony's boogie / Oh mein papa / Bunny hop / Thunderbird / Dragnet / At last / Harlem nocturne / Stardust / Peter Gunn / Tenderly / When the saints go marching in
CD _______ AERO 999
Aerospace / May '96 / Jazz Music / Montpellier

HOOKED ON BIG BANDS (Live)
CD _______ AERO 1012
Aerospace / Jul '96 / Jazz Music / Montpellier

I REMEMBER GLENN MILLER
Tuxedo Junction / Chattanooga choo choo / Serenade in blue / Elmer's tune / Sunrise serenade / Song of the Volga boatmen / In the mood / I know why / Sweet as apple cider / At last / Little Brown jug / Moonlight serenade
CD _______ AERO 1011
Aerospace / Jul '96 / Jazz Music / Montpellier

MUSIC OF YOUR MEMORIES
What's new / Here's that rainy day / Like someone in love / My funny valentine / To love and be loved / All the way / Misty / I should care / I'm through with love / Guess I'll hang my tears out to dry / Alone together / Party's over
CD _______ AERO 1019
Aerospace / Jul '96 / Jazz Music / Montpellier

SWEET AND SWINGIN' 1949-1953
CD _______ CCD 96
Circle / May '95 / Jazz Music / Swift / Wellard

SWING'S THE THING
Baby but you did / Roll 'em around / South Dakota / This may be the time / Every dog has his day / Why should I worry / Why don't you want to come home / You gotta get lucky sometime / Mr. Moon / Indubitably / You're the one for me / Lavender mood
CD _______ AERO 998
Aerospace / May '96 / Jazz Music / Montpellier

SWINGIN' AT THE TOWER
Flying home / Night train / How high the moon / Perdido / One o'clock jump / Swingin' at the Tower
CD _______ AERO 996
Aerospace / May '96 / Jazz Music / Montpellier

TENDERLY
CD _______ AERO 1029
Aerospace / Jul '96 / Jazz Music / Montpellier

TRIP THROUGH 50 YEARS OF MUSIC, A (Live From The Royal Hawaiian Hotel) (Anthony, Ray Orchestra)
Vehicle / Hold on I'm coming / Get ready / It's impossible / Aquarius/Let the sun shine in / Everything is beautiful / Everybody's talkin' / Sing sing sing / Toot toot tootsie goodbye / I wanna be loved by you / Black bottom / Varsity drag / Charleston / Tuxedo junction / In the mood / Jukebox Saturday night / Flat foot floogie / Bei mir bist du shoen / Opus no.1 / Take the 'A' train / Spanish flea / Tijuana taxi / Spinning wheel / Lucretia MacEvil / Smiling phases / Free / Love story / Oh happy day
CD _______ RACD 1025
Aerospace / Jun '97 / Jazz Music / Montpellier

Anthrax

AMONG THE LIVING
Among the living / Caught in a mosh / I am the law / Efilnikufesin (NFL) / Skeleton in the closet / Indians / One world / ADI Horror of it all / Imitation of life
CD _______ IMCD 186
Island / Mar '94 / PolyGram

ARMED AND DANGEROUS
CD _______ CDMVEST 55
Bulletproof / Aug '95 / Pinnacle

ATTACK OF THE KILLER B'S
Milk (Ode to Billy) / Bring the noise / Keep it in the family / Startin' up a posse / Protest and survive / Chromatic death / I'm the man / Parasite / Pipeline / Sects / Belly of the beast / NFB
CD ____ IMCD 179
Island / Mar '94 / PolyGram

FISTFUL OF METAL
Death rider / Eighteen / Subjagator / Howling furies (US remix) / Death from above / Across the river / Metal thrashing mad / Panic / Soldiers of metal (American remix) / Soldiers of metal / Anthrax / Howling furies
CD ____ CDMVEST 56
Bulletproof / Aug '95 / Pinnacle

PERSISTENCE OF TIME
Time / Blood / Keep it in the family / In my world / Gridlock / Intro to reality / Belly of the beast / Got the time / H8 red / One man stands / Discharge
CD ____ IMCD 178
Island / Mar '94 / PolyGram

SOUND OF WHITE NOISE, THE
Potter's field / Only / Room for one more / Packaged rebellion / Hy pro glo / Invisible / 1000 points of hate / Black lodge / C11 H17... / Burst / This is not an exit
CD ____ 7559614302
Elektra / May '93 / Warner Music

SPREADING THE DISEASE
Gung ho / Armed and dangerous / Afters / Enemy / SSC / Stand or fall / Mad house / Lone justice / AIR
CD ____ IMCD 136
Island / Aug '91 / PolyGram

STATE OF EUPHORIA
Be all, end all / Out of sight out of mind / Make me laugh / Anti-social / Who cares wins / Now it's dark / Schism / Misery loves company / Thirteen / Finale
CD ____ IMCD 187
Island / Mar '94 / PolyGram

STOMP 442
CD ____ 7559618562
Elektra / Dec '95 / Warner Music

Anti Cimex

MADE IN SWEDEN (Live)
CD ____ DISTC 53
Distortion / Sep '93 / Plastic Head

RAPED ASS
CD ____ DISTCD 9
Distortion / Feb '95 / Plastic Head

SCANDINAVIAN JAWBREAKER
CD ____ DISTCD 7
Distortion / Jul '93 / Plastic Head

Anti Flag

DIE FOR THE GOVERNMENT
CD ____ NRA 70CD
New Red Archives / Apr '97 / Cargo / Plastic Head

Anti Nowhere League

ANTI NOWHERE LEAGUE PUNK SINGLES COLLECTION
Streets of London / So what / I hate people / Let's break the law / Woman / Rocker / World War III / For you / Ballard of JJ Decay / Out on the wasteland / We will survive / Queen and country / So what (live) / I hate people (live) / Snowman / Fuck around the clock
CD ____ CDPUNK 44
Anagram / Jan '95 / Cargo / Pinnacle

BEST OF THE ANTI NOWHERE LEAGUE
Streets of London / I hate people / We are the league / Let's break the law / Animal / Woman / Rocker / For you / Ballad of JJ Decay / Out on the wasteland / We will survive / Queen and country / On the waterfront / Let the country feed you / Going down / Snowman / So what
CD ____ CLEO 07279CD
Cleopatra / Jan '94 / Cargo / Greyhound / Plastic Head / RTM/Disc / SRD

HORSE IS DEAD, THE (The Anti Nowhere League Live)
CD ____ RRCD 219
Receiver / May '96 / Grapevine/PolyGram

SO WHAT (A Tribute To The Anti-Nowhere League) (Various Artists)
CD ____ SPV 08453982
SPV / Jul '97 / Koch / Plastic Head

WE ARE THE LEAGUE
We are the league / Animal / Woman / Can't stand rock 'n' roll / (We will not) Rememeber you / Snowman / Streets of London / I hate people / Reck-a-nowhere / World War III / Nowhere man / Let's break the law / Rocker / So what
CD ____ DOJOCD 128
Dojo / Apr '93 / Disc

Anti Pasti

BEST OF ANTI PASTI, THE
CD ____ DOJOCD 230
Dojo / Mar '96 / Disc

CAUTION IN THE WIND
Caution in the wind / One Friday night / X affair / Get out now / Mr. Mystery / East to the West / See how they run / Hate circulation / Agent ABC / Best of us / Guinea pigs / Beyond belief
CD ____ CDPUNK 53
Anagram / May '95 / Cargo / Pinnacle

LAST CALL, THE
No government / Brew your own / Another dead soldier / Call the army (I'm alive) / City below / Twenty four hours / Night of the war cry / Freedom row / St. George (get's his gun) / Last call / Ain't got me / Truth and justice / Hell / I wanna be your dog
CD ____ CDPUNK 48
Anagram / Mar '95 / Cargo / Pinnacle

Anti System

ANTI SYSTEM
CD ____ REB ICD
Rebellious Construction / Nov '92 / Plastic Head

Antidote

TRUTH, THE
CD ____ SHARK 026CD
Shark / Apr '92 / Plastic Head

Antidote NYC

VIVA PENDEJOS
CD ____ CDATV 24
Active / Apr '92 / Pinnacle

Antique Six

CAUGHT AT THE TROUT INN
CD ____ JCD 001
Trout / Nov '96 / ADA

Antisect

IN DARKNESS THERE IS NO CHOICE
CD ____ 18524 2
Southern / Sep '94 / SRD

Antiseen

HELL
CD ____ BSR 011CD
Tear It Up / Nov '95 / Plastic Head

HERE TO RUIN YOUR GROOVE
CD ____ SPV 08545882
SPV / Dec '96 / Koch / Plastic Head

Antoine Rencontre Les ...

1960'S FRENCH EPS COLLECTION, THE (Antoine Rencontre Les Problems)
CD ____ 519372
Magic / Jul '97 / Greyhound

Antoine, Marc

CLASSICAL SOUL
Smart but casual / French dream / P C H (Pacific coast highway) / Unity / Universal language / Timeless line / Follow your bliss / New boundaries / Classical soul
CD ____ NYC 60102
NYC / Dec '94 / New Note/Pinnacle

URBAN GYPSY
Latin quarter / Quand le jazz hip-hop / Sand castle / Steppin' / El matador / First rain / Urban gypsy / Forget-me-not / Brazil 96 / Paris jam / Hollywood viscount / Storytime
CD ____ NYC 60202
NYC / Sep '95 / New Note/Pinnacle

Antolini, Charly

COOKIN' (Antolini, Charly Jazz Power)
After you've gone / My romance / Jumpin' at the woodside / My ship / Yesterdays / Dick blues / Soon / Tickle toe / Like someone in love / Perdido / Oh lady be good
CD ____ CDLR 45024
L&R / Feb '91 / New Note/Pinnacle

CRASH
CD ____ BLR 84 002
L&R / May '91 / New Note/Pinnacle

IN THE GROOVE
CD ____ INAK 806
In Akustik / Sep '95 / Direct / TKO Magnum

Anton, Paul

LIVIN' IT UP
CD ____ SIAMCD 111
Siam / Dec '96 / BMG / Siam

PAUL ANTON
I know a man / Just don't matter / Forgive me / What's a guy supposed to do / I know a man (Smooth vibe) / We had it going on / Just say / Looking at you / In my life
CD ____ SIAMCD 108
Siam / Feb '95 / BMG / Siam

Antones Women

BRINGING THE BEST IN BLUES
Something's got a hold on me / Hurtback / Big town / Playboy / Neighour neighbour / Down South in New Orleans / You'll lose a good thing / I'm a good woman / Queen Bee / But I forgive you / Cuban getaway / Twelve bar blues / Richest one / Wrapping up our love
CD ____ ANTCD 9902
Antones / Jan '93 / ADA / Hot Shot

Antonov, Yuri

MIRROR
CD ____ MK 437052
Mezhdunarodnaya Kniga / Jul '92 / Complete/Pinnacle

Antonym

TONANYSM
CD ____ RM 1
Radiator / Jun '97 / Plastic Head

Anubian Lights

ETERNAL SKY
CD ____ CLEO 96032
Cleopatra / Apr '96 / Cargo / Greyhound / Plastic Head / RTM/Disc / SRD

Anuna

ANUNA
Media vita / Invocation / Pater noster / Suantrai / Cormacus / Jerusalem / Crist and St.Marie / Fionnghuala / Si do mhaimeo / Blue bird / Silent O'Moyle / Bean phaidin an poc ar buile / Sanctus / Raid / First day / Faigh an gleas
CD ____ 7567827332
Atlantic / Apr '95 / Warner Music

DEEP DEAD BLUE
CD ____ DANU 007CD
Danu / Feb '97 / ADA

OMNIS
CD ____ DANU 005
Anuna Teo / Oct '95 / CM / Direct

OMNIS (Rerecorded Version)
CD ____ DANU 008CD
Anuna Teo / Jun '97 / CM / Direct

Anvil

FORGED IN FIRE
CD ____ RR 349927
Roadrunner / '88 / PolyGram

METAL ON METAL
CD ____ RR 349917
Roadrunner / Jun '89 / PolyGram

PLUGGED IN PERMAMENT
CD ____ MASSDP 098
Massacre / Jun '96 / Plastic Head

POUND FOR POUND
CD ____ MASSCD 097
Massacre / Jun '96 / Plastic Head

Any Old Time

PHOENIX (Traditional Music From Cork & Beyond)
CD ____ DARA 025CD
Dara / Jun '96 / ADA / CM / Direct / Else / Grapevine/PolyGram

Any Old Time String Band

I BID YOU GOODNIGHT
CD ____ ARHCD 433
Arhoolie / Apr '96 / ADA / Cadillac / Direct

Any Trouble

WRONG END OF THE RACE
Open fire / Old before your time / Lover's moon / Lucky day / Coming of age / Baby, now that I've found you / All the time in the world / Wheels in motion / Turning up the heat / Yesterday's love / Playing Bogart / Eleventh hour / Cheating kind / Snapshot / Between the black and the grey / Kid gloves / Like a man / Learning the game / Wrong end of the race
CD ____ BGOCD 295
Beat Goes On / Nov '95 / Pinnacle

Anyways

LOVE LIES
CD ____ PAXCD 011
Pax / Apr '92 / Pax Records

AOS 3

DIVERSIONARY TACTICS
CD ____ ANOK 1CD
Inna State / Oct '95 / SRD

GOD'S SECRET AGENT
CD ____ WOWCD 28
Words Of Warning / Mar '94 / SRD / Total/ BMG

Apache Indian

MAKE WAY FOR THE INDIAN
Make way for the Indian / Armagideon time / Boba / Raggamuffin girl / I pray / Born for a purpose / Back up / Right time / Who say / Boom shak-a-lak / Ansa dat
CD ____ CID 8016
Island / Mar '95 / PolyGram

NO RESERVATIONS
Don raja (prelude) / Chok there / Fe real / Fix up / AIDS warning / Guru / Wan' know me / Come follow me / Don't touch / Arranged marriage / Drink problems / Movie over India / Magic carpet / Badd Indian / Don raja
CD ____ IMCD 215
Island / Mar '96 / PolyGram

Aparis

DESPITE THE FIRE-FIGHTERS EFFORTS
Sunrice / Waveterms / Welcome / Fire / Green piece / Orange / Hannibal
CD ____ 5177172
ECM / May '93 / New Note/Pinnacle

Apartment 3-G

SHIT NOBODY WANTS TO LISTEN
CD ____ CDR 021
Cravedog / Feb '97 / Cargo

Apartments

APART
Doll hospital / No hurry / Breakdown in Vera Cruz / To live for / Welcome to Walsh world / Your ambulance rides / Friday rich/Saturday poor / World of liars / Place of bones / Cheerleader / Everything is given to be taken away
CD ____ HOT 1063CD
Hot / Jul '97 / Hot Records

LIFE FULL OF FAREWELLS, A
Things you'll keep / Failure of love is a brick wall / You became my big excuse / End of some fear / Not every clown can be in the circus / Thank you for making me beg / Pain the days white / She sings to forget you / All the time in the world
CD ____ HOT 1050CD
Hot / Mar '95 / Hot Records

Apaza, L.

PERUVIAN HARP & MANDOLIN
CD ____ CDT 105CD
Music Of The World / Nov '95 / ADA / Target/BMG

Apazie, Don

DON APAZIE (Apazie, Don & His Havana Casino Orchestra)
CD ____ HQCD 10
Harlequin / '91 / Hot Shot / Jazz Music / Swift / Wellard

APE

STRIP LIGHT
CD ____ DOR 41CD
Dorado / Jun '95 / Pinnacle

Apemen

APEMEN
CD ____ NITR 004
Demolition Derby / Jan '97 / Greyhound / Nervous

PHANTACITY
Phantacity / Get it right / Someone like me / Love train / Remember Thomas A-Beckett / Mrs. Applegate / Tell the truth / She's a girl / Let the good times surround you / Love in / Creation / Mary Anne / Fire
CD ____ DRCD 011
Detour / Sep '96 / Detour / Greyhound

Aperghis, George

PARCOURS
CD ____ TE 008
BUDA / Jan '97 / Discovery

Apes, Pigs & Spacemen

SNAPSHOT
Unknown territories / Beanman / Monster / Blood simple / Ice cream / Virtual / Hollow / Chair / Mother Courage / Nine lives / Humiliation / Trouble / Suits
CD ____ CDMFNX 219
CD ____ CDMFN 219
Music For Nations / Jun '97 / Pinnacle

TRANSFUSION
Great place / Fragments / Do I need this / Come round the world / Safety net / Twice the man / Regurgitate / PVS / Take our sorrow's swimming / Seep / Open season
CD ____ CDMFN 192
CD ____ CDMFNX 192
Music For Nations / Oct '95 / Pinnacle

Apex

BARRICADE
CD ____ PD 008CD
E-Bon / Apr '97 / Jet Star

Apfelbaum, Peter

JODOJI BRIGHTNESS
CD ____ 5123202
Antilles/New Directions / Apr '92 / PolyGram

LUMINOUS CHARMS
CD GCD 79511
Gramavision / Jun '96 / Vital/SAM

SIGNS OF LIFE
Candles and stones / Walk to the mountain / Grounding / Last door / Word is gifted / Chant 2 / Forwarding / Samantha Smith / Folksong No. 7 / Waiting
CD ANCD 8764
Antilles/New Directions / May '91 / PolyGram

Aphex Twin

CLASSICS
Digeridoo / Flaphead / Phloam / Isoprophlex / Polynomial - C / Tamphex (head fhug mix) / Phlange place / Dodeccaheedron / Analogue bubblebath / En trange to exit / Afx 2 / Metapharstic / We have arrived
CD RS 94035CD
R&S / Jan '95 / Vital

I CARE BECAUSE YOU DO
CD WARPCD 30
Warp / Apr '95 / Prime / RTM/Disc

RICHARD D. JAMES
CD WARPCD 43
Warp / Nov '96 / Prime / RTM/Disc

SELECTED AMBIENT WORKS 1985-1992
Xtal / Tha / Pulsewidth / Ageispolis / Green-calx / Heliospan / We are the music makers / Schotkey / Ptolemy / Hedphelym / Delphium / Actium
CD AMB 3922 CD
Apollo / Dec '92 / Vital

SELECTED AMBIENT WORKS VOL.2
CD WARPCD 21
Warp / Feb '94 / Prime / RTM/Disc

Aphrodite's Child

666
Aegean sea / All the seats were occupied / Altomont / Babylon / Battle of the beast / Beast / Break / Capture of the beast / Do it / Four horsemen / Hic-et-nunc / Infinity / Lamb / Lament / Loud loud / Marching beast / Ofis / Seven trumpets / Seventh seal / System / Tribulation / Wakening beast / Wedding of the lamb
CD 8384302
Phonogram / '92 / PolyGram

Apocalypse

APOCALYPSE
CD CDFLAG 23
Under One Flag / Aug '89 / Pinnacle

Apochrypha

AREA 54
Terrors holding on to you / Night in the fog / Instrubation #3 (instrumental) / Tian'anmen Square / Refuse the offer that you can't refuse / Catch 22 / Power elite / Area 54 / Detriment of man / Born to this world
CD RR 93452
Roadrunner / Nov '90 / PolyGram

EYES OF TIME
CD RR 9507 2
Roadrunner / Dec '88 / PolyGram

Apollo 2000

OUT OF THIS WORLD
CD CDSR 084
Telstar / Jun '97 / BMG

Apollo 440

ELECTRO GLIDE IN BLUE
Stealth overture / Ain't talkin' 'bout dub / Altamont super highway revisited / Electro glide in blue / Vanishing point / Tears of the the gods / Carrera rapida / Krupa / White man's throat / Pain in any language / Stealth mass in F sharp minor / Raw power
CD SSX 2440CDR
Stealth Sonic / Jul '97 / Sony
CD SSX 2440CD
Stealth Sonic / Mar '97 / Sony

MILLENNIUM FEVER
Rumble/Spirit of America / Liquid cool / Film me and finish me off / I need something stronger / Pain is a close up / Omega point / (Don't fear) the reaper / Astral America / Millenium fever / Stealth requiem
CD SSX 440 CD
Epic / Nov '94 / Sony

Appellation Controllee

APPELLATION CONTROLLEE
CD MWCD 1001
Music & Words / Jun '92 / ADA / Direct

TIZ
CD DIGIT 5679142
Dig It / Dec '95 / ADA / Direct

Appice, Carmine

CARMINE APPICE'S GUITAR ZEUS (Guitar Zeus)
CD 342622
No Bull / Dec '95 / Koch

Apple, Fiona

TIDAL
Sleep to dream / Sullen girl / Shadowboxer / Criminal / Slow like honey / First taste / Never is a promise / Child is gone / Pale September / Carrion
CD 4837502
Columbia / Sep '96 / Sony

Appleorchard

TACET
CD RSTR 007D
Rumblestrip / Nov '96 / Cargo

Apples

SCIENCE FAIRE
CD SPART 48CD
Spin Art / Nov '96 / Cargo

Apples In Stereo

FUN TRICK NOISEMAKER
CD SPART 42CD
Spin Art / Dec '96 / Cargo

Appleton, Jon

CONTES DE LA MEMOIRE
CD IMED 9635
Diffunzioni Musicali / Jun '97 / ReR Megacorp

Appleyard, Peter

BARBADOS COOL
Tangerine / Stompin' at the Savoy / Airmail special / Passion flower / Django / Prelude to a kiss / Memories of you / Fascinating rhythm / Broadway / Cherokee
CD CCD 4475
Concord Jazz / Aug '91 / New Note/ Pinnacle

BARBADOS HEAT
You stepped out of a dream / Body and soul / Take the 'A' train / Satin doll / Caravan nuages / Here's that rainy day / Sing sing sing
CD CCD 4436
Concord Jazz / Nov '90 / New Note/ Pinnacle

April March

PARIS IN APRIL
CD SFTRI 456CD
Sympathy For The Record Industry / Oct '96 / Cargo / Greyhound / Plastic Head

SINGS ALONG
CD SFTRI 434CD
Sympathy For The Record Industry / Apr '97 / Cargo / Greyhound / Plastic Head

Apu

SECRET OF THE ANDES
CD ANT 1CD
Antara / May '94 / ADA / Direct

Aqua Velvets

NOMAD
Nomad / Surf nouveau / Smoking panatelas on the blue / Mediterranean Sea / Holly tiki / Snorkel mask replica / Return to Paia / Ho'okipa / In a Spanish mood / Nervous on Neptune / Summer at dreampoint / Shakahoochie / Shrunken head
CD 74321408292
Milan / Sep '96 / Conifer/BMG / Silva Screen

Aquanettas

ROADHAUS
CD ROCK 61312
Rockville / Jun '93 / Plastic Head / SRD

Aquartet

ROUE LIBRE
CD DPCD 96014
Mustradem / Feb '96 / ADA

Aquasky

ORANGE DUST
CD 5378362
Polydor / Aug '97 / PolyGram

Aquaturbia

PSYCHEDELIC DRUGSTORE
CD HBG 122/15
Background / Apr '93 / Background / Greyhound

Aqueos

TALL CLOUDTREES
CD HERM 2222
Hermetic / Oct '96 / World Serpent

Aquila

AQUA DIVA
CD PSY 013CD
PSY Harmonics / Oct '95 / Plastic Head

Ar Braz, Dan

ACOUSTIC
CD GLCD 3035
Green Linnet / Oct '93 / ADA / CM / Direct / Highlander / Roots

MUSIQUE POUR LES SILENCES A VENIR/SEPTEMBRE BLEU/BORDERS OF (L'Essentiel Dan Ar Braz/3CD Set)
CD Set KM 022338
Keltia Musique / Jul '96 / ADA / Discovery

MUSIQUES POUR LES SILENCES A VENIR
CD KMCD 02
Keltia Musique / Aug '89 / ADA / Discovery

SONGS
CD KMCD 14
Red Sky / '91 / ADA / CM / Direct

Ar C'hoarezed Goadec

LES VOIX LEGENDARIES DE BRETAGNE
CD KMCD 11
Keltia Musique / '91 / ADA / Discovery

AR Kane

NEW CLEAR CHILD
Deep blue breath / Grace / Tiny little drop of perfumed time / Surf motel / Gather / Honey be (For Stella) / Cool as moons / Snow White's world / Pearl / Sea like a child
CD STONE 011CD
3rd Stone / Sep '94 / Plastic Head / Vital

Ar Menez, Diaouled

DIAOULED AR MENEZ
CD CD 318
Diffusion Breizh / May '93 / ADA

Ar Re Yaouank

BREIZH POSITIVE
CD STSC 02CD
Diffusion Breizh / Apr '95 / ADA

Ar-Log

AR-LOG VOL.4 & 5
CD SAIN 9068CD
Sain / Aug '94 / ADA / Direct / Greyhound

AR-LOG VOL.6
CD SCD 2119
Sain / Aug '96 / ADA / Direct / Greyhound

Arabesque

NIKRIZ (Arabesque & Hassan Erraji)
CD TUGCD 001
Riverboat / Aug '89 / New Note/Pinnacle / Stern's

TRADITIONAL ARABIC MUSIC (Arabesque & Hassan Erraji)
Longa / Taksim hussayni / Ansam (Breezes) / Redile guelbi / Hiwar (dialogue) / Sama'I thaqil / Sidi blal / Cerga / Alway mizan / Bab arraja (The door of hope)
CD CDSDL 387
Saydisc / Mar '94 / ADA / Direct / Harmonia Mundi

Aranbee Symphony Orchestra

ARANBEE POP SYMPHONY ORCHESTRA, THE (Under the Direction of Keith Richard)
There's a place / Rag doll / I got you babe / We can work it out / Play with fire / Mother's little helper / In the midnight hour / Take it or leave it / Sittin' on a fence / I don't want to go on without you
CD C5CD522
See For Miles/C5 / Sep '90 / Pinnacle

Arawi

DOCTRINE OF CYCLES, THE
CD NA 029
New Albion / Oct '90 / Cadillac / Harmonia Mundi

Arbete & Fritid

DEEP WOODS
Ganglat efter lejsme Per Larsson/Malung / Finsk sorgmarsch / Gabergsbrudens dodsmarsch / Arbete and Fritid / Esso motor hotel / Tva springare / Vals / Dorisk drone / Thuicandra / Harmageddon boogie / Jag ar inte som andra / European way / Smavarmt / Maklins brudmarsch/Orsa / Hin hales halling / Franska valsen
CD RESCD 501
Resource / Jul '97 / ADA / Direct

Arbuckle, Les

BUSH CREW, THE
CD AQ 1032
Audioquest / Apr '95 / ADA / New Note/ Pinnacle

ARC

12K
CD RA 011
Radikal Ambience / Jun '96 / Plastic Head

ARC

OUT OF AMBER
Early reflection / Distant window / Circadian rhythms / Snare in the woods / At the air's edge / Out of amber / Expecting to land / Radio pills / Snow dance / Goodbye dry land
CD SLAMCD 205
Slam / Oct '96 / Cadillac

Arcadia

SO RED THE ROSE
Election day / Keep me in the dark / Goodbye is forever / Flame / Missing / Rose arcana / Promise / El diablo / Lady Ice
CD CDPRG 1010
Parlophone / Aug '93 / EMI

Arcady

AFTER THE BALL
Hennessey's / River / Barn dances / Field behind the plow / Heaven's gate / Lullybye / Jackie Daly's reels / Breton reels / Trios matelots du Port - De - Brest / I'd cross the wild Atlantic / Tripping down the stairs / After the ball / Spinsters waltz
CD DARACD 037
Dara / Sep '93 / ADA / CM / Direct / Else / Grapevine/PolyGram

MANY HAPPY RETURNS
CD SHCD 79095
Shanachie / Aug '95 / ADA / Greensleeves / Koch
CD DARACD 080
Dara / Aug '96 / ADA / CM / Direct / Else / Grapevine/PolyGram

Arcane Device

FETISH
CD SR 9009
Silent / Jul '94 / Cargo / Plastic Head

Arcansiel

STILL SEARCHING
CD CONTECD 143
Contempo / Jun '90 / Plastic Head

Arceneaux, Fernest

ZYDECO STOMP (Arceneaux, Fernest & Thunders)
CD JSPCD 258
JSP / Jul '95 / ADA / Cadillac / Direct / Hot Shot / Target/BMG

Arch Enemy

BLACK EARTH
CD WAR 011CD
Wrong Again / Nov '96 / Plastic Head

Arch Rival

IN THE FACE OF DANGER
In the face of danger / Time won't wait / Me against the world / Rock the night away / Fortune hunter / God bless America / Revolution / Shotgun at Midnight / Siren's song / Can you tell me why
CD KILCD 1005
Killerwatt / Oct '93 / Kingdom

Archer, Tasmin

GREAT EXPECTATIONS
Sleeping satellite / Arienne / Lords of the new church / When it comes down to it / Steeltown / Higher you climb / In your care / Somebody's daughter / Hero / Ripped inside / Halfway to heaven
CD CDEMC 3624
EMI / Sep '92 / EMI

Archers Of Loaf

ALL THE NATION'S AIRSPORTS
Strangled by the stereo wire / All the nation's airsports / Scenic pastures / Worst defense / Attack of the killer bees / Rental sting / Assassination on Xmas eve / Chumming the ocean / Vocal shrapnel / Bones of her hands / Bumpo / Form & file / Acromegaly / Distance comes in droves / Bombs away
CD A 100CD
Alias / Sep '96 / Vital

ICKY METTLE
Web in front / Last word / Wrong / You and me / Might / Hate paste / Fat / Plumb line / Learo, you're a hole / Sick file / Toast / Backwash / Slow worm
CD A 049D
Alias / Sep '93 / Vital

SPEED OF CATTLE, THE
Wrong / South Carolina / Web in front / Bathroom / Tatyana / What did you expect / Ethel Merman / Funnelhead / Quinnbeast / Telepathic traffics / Don't believe / Smokin' pot / Mutes in the steeple / Revenge / Bacteria / I'll never / Power walker / Backlash
CD A 094D
Alias / Mar '96 / Vital

VEE VEE
Step into the light / Harnessed in slums / Nevermind the enemy / Greatest of all time

/ Underdogs if Nipomo / Floating friends / 1985 / Fabroch nostalgia / Let the loser melt / Death in the park / Worst has yet to come / Underacheivers march and fight song
CD A064 D
Alias / Mar '95 / Vital

Archetype

ARCHETYPE
CD CD 831
Diffusion Breizh / May '93 / ADA

Archey, Jimmy

DOCTOR JAZZ VOL.4 (1951-1952)
CD STCD 6044
Storyville / May '96 / Cadillac / Jazz Music / Wellard

JIMMY ARCHEY
CD BCD 310
GHB / Jun '94 / Jazz Music

Archies

SUGAR SUGAR
CD WMCD 5670
Woodford Music / Feb '93 / THE

SUGAR, SUGAR
CD CDSGP 0225
Prestige / Sep '97 / Else / Total/BMG

Archive

LONDINIUM
Old artist / All time / So few words / Headspace / Darkroom / Londinium / Man made / Nothing else / Skyscraper / Parvaneh / Beautiful love / Organ song / Last five / Untitled
CD ARKCD 1001
Island / Jan '97 / PolyGram

Archon Satani

IN SHELTER
CD DVLR 6CD
Dark Vinyl / Jan '95 / Plastic Head / World Serpent

Arckanum

KOSTOGHER
CD NR 011CD
Necropolis / May '97 / Plastic Head

Arcturus

ASPERA HIEMS SYMFONIA
CD ALC 002CD
Misanthropy / Apr '96 / Plastic Head

Arcwelder

ENTROPY
CD TG 158CD
Touch & Go / May '96 / SRD

PULL
CD TG 108CD
Touch & Go / Feb '93 / SRD

XERXES
CD TG 126CD
Touch & Go / Apr '94 / SRD

Arden, Jann

LIVING UNDER JUNE
Could I be your girl / Demolition love / Looking for it (finding heaven) / Insensitive / Gasoline / Wonderdrug / Living under June / Unloved / Good mother / It looks like rain / I would die for you
CD 5403362
A&M / Mar '95 / PolyGram

Arden, Victor

KEYBOARD WIZARDS OF THE GERSHWIN ERA VOL.3 (Arden, Victor & Phil Ohman)
CD GEMMCD 9203
Pearl / Dec '95 / Harmonia Mundi

Arditti String Quartet

ARDITTI VOL.1 (Beethoven/Nancarrow/Xenakis)
Grosse fugue op 133 / Quartet 1931 / Tetras / Quartet No. 3 / Coconino...a shattered landscape
CD GCD 79440
Gramavision / Jun '96 / Vital/SAM

ARDITTI VOL.2 (Bartok/Gubaidulina/Schnittke)
CD GCD 79439
Gramavision / Jun '96 / Vital/SAM

FERNEYHOUGH VOL.2 (Arditti String Quartet & Asko Ensemble/Magnus Andersson)
CD MO 782029
Montaigne / Dec '96 / Harmonia Mundi

Ardley, Neil

KALEIDOSCOPE OF RAINBOWS
Prologue / Rainbow one / Rainbow two / Rainbow three / Rainbow four / Rainbow five / Rainbow six / Rainbow seven / Epilogue
CD AMPCD 029
AMP / Apr '97 / Cadillac / Discovery / TKO Magnum

Ardoin, Amade

I'M NEVER COMIN' BACK
CD ARHCD 7007
Arhoolie / Jan '96 / ADA / Cadillac / Direct

Ardoin, Boisec

LA MUSIQUE CREOLE (Ardoin, Boisec & Canray Fontenot)
CD ARHCD 445
Arhoolie / Apr '96 / ADA / Cadillac / Direct

Ardoin, Chris

GON' BE JUS' FINE (Ardoin, Chris & Double Clutchin')
Lake Charles connection / Beauty in your eyes / When I'm dead and gone / Cowboy / Ardoin two step / Gon' be jus' fine / I believe in you / We are the boys / I don't want what I can't keep / Dimanche apres midi / Angel / Back door man / When the morning comes / We are the boys
CD ROUCD 2127
Rounder / Jul '97 / ADA / CM / Direct

Area

AGATE LINES
CD TMCD 59
Third Mind / Nov '90 / Pinnacle / Third Mind

Arecibo

TRANS PLUTONIAN TRANSMISSIONS
CD AT 02CD
Atmosphere / Mar '95 / Plastic Head

Arena

CRY
Theme / Cry / Offering / Problem line / Isolation / Fallen idols / Guidance / Only child / Stolen promise / Healer
CD VGCD 005
Verglas Music / Apr '97 / Pinnacle

PRIDE
Welcome to the cage / Crying for help V / Empire of a thousand days / Crying for help VI / Medusa / Crying for help VII / Fool's gold / Crying for help VIII / Sirens
CD VGCD 004
Verglas Music / Sep '96 / Pinnacle

SONGS FROM THE LIONS CAGE
Solomon / Crying for help IV / Midas vision / Jericho / Crying for help I / Out of the wilderness / Crying for help / Valley of the kings
CD VGCD 001
Verglas Music / Feb '95 / Pinnacle

Arena, Amy

EXCUSE ME
Excuse me / Addicted to dirt / Cheeseburger / Make love to myself / I will always love you / Shit / Perverts / Why / New religion / And then / Get to know me / Proud to be a woman
CD DOMO 710032
Domo / Sep '96 / Pinnacle

Arena, Tina

DON'T ASK
Chains / Heaven help my heart / Sorento moon (I remember) / Wasn't it good / Message / Love is the answer / Greatest gift / That's the way a woman feels / Baby be a man / Standing up / Show me heaven
CD 4778869
Columbia / Aug '96 / Sony

ARG

ONE WORLD WITHOUT THE END
CD BMCD 15
Black Mark / '92 / Plastic Head

Argent

ALL TOGETHER NOW
Hold your head up / Keep on rolling / Tragedy / I am the dance of ages / Be my lover, be my friend / He's a dynamo / Pure love / Fantasia / Prelude / Finale
CD 4773772
Epic / Aug '94 / Sony
CD 379412
Koch International / Jun '97 / Koch

ARGENT
Like honey / Liar / Be free / Schoolgirl / Dance in the smoke / Lonely hard road / Feelings inside / Freefall / Stepping stone / Bring you joy
CD BGOCD 110
Beat Goes On / Aug '91 / Pinnacle

ENCORE
Coming of Kohoutek / It's only money / God gave rock 'n' roll to you / Thunder and lightning / Music from the spheres / I don't believe in miracles / Dance of ages / Keep on rolling / Hold your head up / Time of the season
CD BGOCD 206
Beat Goes On / Sep '93 / Pinnacle

IN DEEP
CD 4805292
Columbia / May '95 / Sony

Arguelles, Julian

HOME TRUTHS
CD BDV 9503
Babel / Oct '95 / ADA / Cadillac / Diverse / Harmonia Mundi

PHAEDRUS
Phaedrus / Invisible thread / Duet / Forests / Maxine / Red rag / Wild rice / Everything I love / Hi Steve
CD AHUM 010
Ah-Um / Oct '91 / Cadillac / New Note/ Pinnacle

SCAPES (Arguelles, Julian & Steve)
CD BDV 9614
Babel / Oct '96 / ADA / Cadillac / Diverse / Harmonia Mundi

Arguelles, Steve

ARGUELLES
Redman / Don't tell me now / Lucky star / Dis at ease / Cherry waltz / Blessed light / Elderberries / My heart belongs to Daddy / Guara / Hermana guapa / Tin tin / Trimmings
CD AHUM 007
Ah-Um / Aug '90 / Cadillac / New Note/ Pinnacle

Argyle Park

MISGUIDED
CD REX 460132
Rex / Nov '95 / Cadillac

Arita, Yoshihiro

WHALE DANCE
CD SCR 28
Strictly Country / Aug '96 / ADA / Direct

Arizona Smoke Revue

BEST OF BLUEGRASS
Duelling banjos / Old Joe Clark / Earl's breakdown / Communications breakdown / Reuben's train / Foggy mountain breakdown / Old groundhog / Auld Lang Syne / Columbus George / Battle of New Orleans / Cannonball line / Black mountain rag / Teetotallers reel / Sailor's hornpipe / Orange blossom special
CD 3036300022
Country Skyline / Feb '96 / Carlton

Ark

SPIRITUAL PHYSICS
CD MC 301CD
Mutilation Corps / Jun '93 / Plastic Head

Ark

VOYAGE OF TRANQUILITY, A
Ark / Dawn of tranquility / Heavenly stars / Eternal skies / With a rhythm from the deep / Castaway / In earth's shadow / To sail through the universe / Drifting to love / Peace...your reality / In the garden of your mind / Through the forests of time / You are forever
CD CDMFP 6390
Music For Pleasure / Jun '97 / EMI

Arkarna

FRESH MEAT
House on fire / Eat me / Futures overrated / So little time / Block capital / Born yesterday part 1 / Born yesterday part 2 / Peace of mind / Direct dubit / R U ready
CD 3984200512
WEA / Aug '97 / Warner Music

Arkenstone, David

ANOTHER STAR IN THE SKY
Pool of radiance / Far far away / Light in the east / Under the canopy / Voices of the night / Another star in the sky / Taken by the wind / Canyon of the moon / Naked in the wind / Ride into midnight
CD ND 62012
Narada / May '94 / ADA / New Note/ Pinnacle

CHRONICLES
CD ND 64007
Narada / Jun '93 / ADA / New Note/ Pinnacle

CONVERGENCE (Arkenstone, David & David Lanz)
Madre de la tierra / Yosemite / Madrona / North wind / Dragon's daughter / Long way from home / Thousand small gold bells / Oaks / Cello's song / Love on the beach / Keeper of the flame
CD ND 64012
Narada / Feb '97 / ADA / New Note/ Pinnacle

IN THE WAKE OF THE WIND
Papillon (on the wings of the butterfly) / Dark dunes / Not too far to walk / Borderlands / Rug merchant / Firedance / Southern cross / Voyage of the stardancer / Overture / Stardancer / Morning sun on the sails / Lion's breath / Dances of the jankayla / Discovery
CD CD 4003
Narada / Aug '92 / ADA / New Note/ Pinnacle

QUEST OF THE DREAM WARRIOR
Prelude: Tallis the messenger / Rhythms of vision / Journey begins: Kyla's ride / Voice / Dance of the maidens / Magic forest / Road to the sea / Temple of vaal / Wings of the shadow / Homecoming
CD ND 64008
Narada / Jun '95 / ADA / New Note/ Pinnacle

RETURN OF THE GUARDIANS
Border journey / Trail of tears / Chosen voices / Winds of change / Forgotten lands / Two hearts / City in the clouds / Musk / Water of life - out of darkness transformation / Reunion
CD ND 64011
Narada / Feb '97 / ADA / New Note/ Pinnacle

SPIRIT OF OLYMPIA, THE (Arkenstone, David & Kostia/David Lanz)
Prelude: Let the games begin / Savannah runner / Memories of gold / Keeper of the flame / From the forge to the field / Heartfire / Celebration / Close without touching / Glory / Night in the village / Walk with the stars / Marathon man / Spirit of Olympia
CD CD 4006
Narada / May '92 / ADA / New Note/ Pinnacle

Arkkon

ARKKON
CD TK 01CD
Tonus Kozmetica / Oct '96 / World Serpent

Arlen, Harold

COME RAIN OR COME SHINE (The Harold Arlen Songbook) (McNair, Sylvia & Andre Previn/David Finck)
Over the rainbow / Stormy weather / Between the devil and the deep blue sea / It was written in the stars / As long as I live / That old black magic / Morning after / Sleepin' bee / Accentuate the positive / Goose never be a peacock / I wonder what becomes of me / It's only a paper moon / In the shade of the banana tree / Coconut sweet / Right as the rain / I've got the world on a string / Come rain or come shine / This time the dream's on me / Let's take a walk around the block / Last night when we were young
CD 4468182
Philips / Jun '96 / PolyGram

THAT OLD BLACK MAGIC (The Harold Arlen Songbook) (Various Artists)
CD 5375732
Verve / Jul '97 / PolyGram

Armacost, Tim

FIRE
Norwegian wood / Old familiar faces / Long haired girl / Pennies from heaven / Table master / Maconde / There's a lull in my life / Voyage / Imprint / Bailey's blues
CD CCD 4697
Concord Crossover / Jun '96 / New Note/ Pinnacle

Armagh Piper's Club

SONGS OF THE CHANTER
CD PTICD 3007
Pure Traditional Irish / Aug '96 / ADA / CM / Direct / Ross

Armagideon

EASE THE TENSION
CD ASCD 001
Armagideon Sounds / Jun '95 / Jet Star / SRD

STEPPIN' FORWARD
CD ASCD 003
Armagideon Sounds / Mar '95 / Jet Star / SRD

Armando

ONE WORLD ONE FUTURE
Welcome II the warehouse / Worldbeat / Real jazz / Future / Transaxual / Which way is up / Sweet love / Radikal bitch / Tunnelvision / Funky swing / Welcome 2 our world / Warning / Love will save the day / Bells 1996 / Long distance / 100% of dissin' U / Land of confusion
CD FEAR 023CD
Radikal Fear / May '96 / Vital

Armani, Robert

BLOW IT OUT
CD ACVCD 013
ACV / Nov '95 / Plastic Head / SRD

MADMAN STANDS
CD ACVCD 007
ACV / Apr '95 / Plastic Head / SRD

NEXT START
CD ACVCD 4
ACV / Nov '93 / Plastic Head / SRD

RIGHT TO SILENCE
CD ACVCD 6
ACV / Jul '94 / Plastic Head / SRD

SPECTACULAR
CD ACVCD 19
ACV / Sep '96 / Plastic Head / SRD

VII CHAPTER
CD CSCD 002
ACV / Mar '97 / Plastic Head / SRD

Armatrading, Joan

JOAN ARMATRADING
Down to zero / Help yourself / Water with the wine / Love and affection / Save me / Join the boys / People / Somebody who loves you / Like fire / Tall in the saddle
CD CDMID 104
A&M / Oct '92 / PolyGram

LOVE AND AFFECTION (Anthology/2CD Set)
Down to zero / True love / Talking to the wall / Show some emotion / I'm lucky / One more chance / Did I make you up / All a woman needs / Square the circle / Somebody who loves you / It could have been better / Alice / No love / Tall in the saddle (live) / Turn out the light / Shouting stage / One night / Save me / My family / City girl / Warm love / Power of dreams / Love by you / Weakness / More than one kind of love / Love and affection / Rosie / Bottom to the top / Drop the pilot / Me myself / Cool blue stole my heart / Water with the wine / Flight of the wild geese / Dry land / Always / Promise land / Can't get over (how I broke your heart)
CD Set 5404052
A&M / Feb '97 / PolyGram

ME, MYSELF, I
Me, myself and I / Ma me o beach / Friends / Is it tomorrow yet / Turn out the light / When you kissed me / All the way from America / Feeling in my heart (for you) / Simon / I need you
CD 5500582
Spectrum / Jun '93 / PolyGram

SHOW SOME EMOTION
Won'cha come on home / Show some emotion / Warm love / Never is too late / Peace in mind / Opportunity / Mama mercy / Get in the sun / Willow / Kissin' and a hugging
CD CDMID 105
A&M / Oct '92 / PolyGram

SQUARE THE CIRCLE
True love / Crazy / Wrapped around her / Sometimes I don't / Wanna go home / Square the circle / Weak woman / Can I get next to you / Can't get over you / (How I broke your heart) if women ruled the world / Cradled in your love
CD 3958882
A&M / Jun '92 / PolyGram

VERY BEST OF JOAN ARMATRADING
Love and affection / Down to zero / Drop the pilot / Show some emotion / Shouting stage / Willow / Rosie / I'm lucky / Me, myself and I / (I love it when you) call me names / Bottom to the top / More than one kind of love / Weakness in me / All the way from America
CD 3971222
A&M / Apr '91 / PolyGram

WHAT'S INSIDE
In your eyes / Everyday boy / Merchant of love / Shapes and sizes / Back on the road / Trouble / Shape of a pony / Can't stop loving you / Beyond the blue / Recommend my love / Would you like to dance / Songs / Lost the love
CD 74321272692
RCA / May '95 / BMG

Armchair Martian

ARMCHAIR MARTIAN
CD CDHED 062
Headhunter / Feb '97 / Cargo

Armed Forces

TAKE ON THE NATION
CD CDMFN 136
Music For Nations / Jun '92 / Pinnacle

Armitage Shanks

SHANK'S PONY
CD DAMGOOD 94CD
Damaged Goods / Jul '96 / Shellshock/ Disc

Armored Saint

SAINTS WILL CONQUER
Raising fear / Nervous man / Book of blood / Can U deliver / Mad house / No reason to live
CD 398414055CD
Metal Blade / May '96 / Pinnacle / Plastic Head

SYMBOL OF SALVATION
CD 398417014CD
Metal Blade / May '96 / Pinnacle / Plastic Head

Armoured Angel

MYSTERIUM
CD ID 000312CD
Modern Invasion / May '95 / Plastic Head

STIGMARTYR
CD NF 100012
Modern Invasion / Apr '95 / Plastic Head

Armstrong Family

WHEEL OF THE YEAR, THE
CD FF 594CD
Flying Fish / Feb '93 / ADA / CM / Direct / Roots

Armstrong, Frankie

FAIR MOON REJOICES, THE
Voices / London song / Earth, air, fire and water / Invitation / Flying high, feeling free/ Canaries in the mine / Still is the memory / Speech to Apollo / Out of the darkness / I feel that all the stars shine in me / Ballad of Marie Sanders / Whore and the holy one / Mourn not the dead/Song of Augustina Ruiz / Farewell my friends / Let the slave
CD HARCD 027
Harbour Town / Mar '97 / ADA / CM / Direct / Roots

TILL THE GRASS O'ERGREW THE CORN
Broomfield Hill / Lady Diamond / Hares on the mountain / Fair Lizzie / Young Orphy / Proud girl / Lover's ghost / Wife of Usher's well / John Blunt / Child waters / Well below the valley / Clerk Colven
CD FECD 116
Fellside / Mar '97 / ADA / Direct / Target/ BMG

WAYS OF SEEING
Ways of seeing / Meeting / Girl in a garden / Zaspo janko / Soothing croon / Low ground / Dead leaves / Message from Mother Earth / Bread and roses / I only believe in miracles / Seven gates / We are women / Trial / Pearl / Weave and mend / Shall there be womanly times
CD HARCD 009
Harbour Town / Nov '96 / ADA / CM / Direct / Roots

Armstrong, James

SLEEPING WITH A STRANGER
CD HCD 8068
Hightone / Dec '95 / ADA / Koch

Armstrong, Lil

CLASSICS 1936-1940
CD CLASSICS 564
Classics / Oct '91 / Discovery / Jazz Music

Armstrong, Louis

1924-1930 (6CD Set) (Armstrong, Louis & The Blues Singers)
CC rider / Jelly bean blues / Countin' the blues / Early in the morning / You've got the right key but the wrong keyhole / Of all the wrong you've done to me / Everybody loves my baby / Texas moaner blues / Papa, mama's all alone / Changeable daddy of mine / Baby, I can't use you no more / Trouble everywhere I roam / Poor house blues / Anybody here want to try my cabbage / Thunderstorm blues / If I lose, let me lose / Screamin' the blues / Good time flat blues / Mandy, make up your mind / I'm a little blackbird looking for a bluebird / Nobody knows the way I feel this morning / Early every morn' / Cake walkin' babies from home / Broken busted blues / Pickin' on your baby / St. Louis blues / Reckless blues / Sobbin' hearted blues / Cold in hand blues / You've been a good ole wagon / You've got to beat me to keep me / Mining camp blues / Cast away / Papa de da da / World's jazz crazy (and so am I) / Railroad blues / Shipwrecked blues / Court house blues / My John blues / Nashville woman's blues / Careless love blues / JC Holmes blues / I ain't gonna play no second fiddle / I miss my Swiss / You dirty mistreater / Come on coot do that thing / Have your chill, I'll be here when your fever rises / Find me at the greasy spoon / Just wait 'til you see my baby do the Charleston / Livin' high / Coal cart blues / Santa Claus blues / Squeeze me / You can't shush Katie (the grabbiest girl in town) / Lucy long / Low land blues / Kid man blues / Lazy woman blues / Lonesome lovesick blues / Gambler's dream / Sunshine baby / Adam and Eve had the blues / Put it where I can get it / Washwoman blues / I've stopped my man / Lonesome all alone blues / Trouble in mind / Georgia man / You've got to go home on time / What kind o' man is that / Deep water blues / G'man, I told you / Listen to ma / Lonesome hours / Jealous woman like me / Special delivery blues / Jack O'diamonds / Mail train blues / I feel good / Man for every day in the week / Bridwell blues / St. Peter blues / He likes it slow / Pleadin' for the blues / Pratt city blues / Mess, Katie, mess / Lovesick blues / Lonesome weary blues / Dead drunk blues / Have you ever been down / Lazy man blues / Flood blues / You're a real sweetheart / Too busy / Was it a dream / Last night I dreamed you kissed me / I can't give you anything but love / Baby / Sweetheart on parade / I must have that man / S'posin' / To be in love / Funny feathers / How do you do it that way / Ain't misbehavin' / Blue yodel no. 9 (Standing on the corner)
CD Set CDAFS 10186
Affinity / Sep '91 / Cadillac / Jazz Music / Koch

1957
CD CD 53153
Giants Of Jazz / Nov '95 / Cadillac / Jazz Music / Target/BMG

2 FACETS OF LOUIS
CD 4737542
Sony Jazz / Jan '95 / Sony

20 BLUES CLASSICS
Black and blue / Muskrat ramble / Dear old southland / Hobo you can't ride this train / I gotta right to sing the blues / I can't give you anything but love / Body and soul / Someday you'll be sorry / Heebie jeebies / Royal Garden blues / Tiger rag / Jeepers creepers / Baby won't you please come home / Harlem stomp / Wolverine blues / St. James infirmary / Do you know what it means to miss New Orleans / That lucky old sun / Brother Bill / Old rocking chair
CD SUMCD 4080
Summit / Nov '96 / Sound & Media

2ND ALLSTAR JAZZ FESTIVAL (Armstrong, Louis Allstars)
CD CD 09
Krazy Kat / Jul '93 / Hot Shot / Jazz Music

ALL STARS COLLECTION 1950-56, THE
CD CD 53091
Giants Of Jazz / Mar '92 / Cadillac / Jazz Music / Target/BMG

AMBASSADOR SATCH
CD 4718712
Sony Jazz / Jan '95 / Sony

AUDIO ARCHIVE
Jeepers creepers / Mame / On the sunny side of the street / Hello Dolly / Ain't misbehavin' / Basin Street blues / Cabaret / When the saints go marching in / Fly me to the moon / Tiger rag / Kiss to build a dream on / (Back home again in) Indiana / Please don't talk about me when I'm gone / St. Louis blues / Someday you'll be sorry / Back o' town blues / That's my desire / Jelly roll blues / Mack the knife / Blueberry Hill
CD CDAA 015
Tring / Jan '93 / Tring

BACK O'TOWN
CD 158732
Blues Archives / Apr '97 / Discovery

BASIN STREET BLUES
CD BLCD 760128
Black Lion / Jun '88 / Cadillac / Jazz Music / Koch / Wellard

BEST OF LOUIS ARMSTRONG VOL.1
CD DLCD 4001
Dixie Live / Mar '95 / TKO Magnum

BEST OF LOUIS ARMSTRONG VOL.2
CD CDSGP 055
Prestige / Apr '93 / Else / Total/BMG

BEST OF LOUIS ARMSTRONG VOL.2
CD DLCD 4014
Dixie Live / Mar '95 / TKO Magnum

BEST OF LOUIS ARMSTRONG, THE
CD CDSGP 038
Prestige / Jan '93 / Else / Total/BMG

BEST OF SATCHMO, THE
Struttin' with some barbecue / Confessin' / When the saints go marching in / Stardust / St. Louis blues / Basin Street blues / Mahogany Hall stomp / Georgia on my mind / Black and blue / All of me / Chinatown my Chinatown / Just you, just me
CD 399231
Koch Presents / May '97 / Koch

BIG BANDS VOL.1 1930-1931
CD JSPCD 305
JSP / Oct '88 / ADA / Cadillac / Direct / Hot Shot / Target/BMG

BIG BANDS, THE
CD PDSCD 534
Pulse / Aug '96 / BMG

C'EST SI BON
Mame / When the saints go marching in / Ain't misbehavin' / Cabaret / Kiss to build a dream on / Please don't talk about me when I'm gone / Blueberry Hill / Hello Dolly / St. Louis blues / That's my desire / Mack the knife / Back o' town blues / Fly me to the moon / (Back home again in) Indiana / Tiger rag / Black and blue / C'est si bon / St. James infirmary / Someday you'll be sorry / Sweethearts on parade / Jelly roll blues
CD GRF 036
Tring / '93 / Tring

CHICAGO CONCERT 1956
Memphis blues / Frankie and Johnny / Tiger rag / Do you know what it means to miss New Orleans / Basin Street blues / Black and blue / West End blues / On the sunny side of the street / Struttin' with some barbecue / Manhattan / When it's sleepy time down South / (Back home again in) Indiana / Gypsy / Faithful hussar / Rockin' chair / Bucket's got a hole in it / Perdido / Clarinet marmalade / Mack the knife / Tenderly / You'll never walk alone / Stompin' at the Savoy / Margie / Mama's back in town / That's my desire / Kokomo / I love you so
CD 4718702
Columbia / Nov '93 / Sony

CLASSICS 1925-1926 (Armstrong, Louis Hot Five)
CD CLASSICS 600
Classics / Sep '91 / Discovery / Jazz Music

CLASSICS 1926-1927
CD CLASSICS 585
Classics / Aug '91 / Discovery / Jazz Music

CLASSICS 1928-1929
CD CLASSICS 570
Classics / Oct '91 / Discovery / Jazz Music

CLASSICS 1929-1930
CD CLASSICS 557
Classics / Dec '90 / Discovery / Jazz Music

CLASSICS 1930-1931
CD CLASSICS 547
Classics / Dec '90 / Discovery / Jazz Music

CLASSICS 1931-1932
CD CLASSICS 536
Classics / Dec '90 / Discovery / Jazz Music

CLASSICS 1932-1933
CD CLASSICS 529
Classics / Dec '90 / Discovery / Jazz Music

CLASSICS 1934-1936
CD CLASSICS 509
Classics / Apr '90 / Discovery / Jazz Music

CLASSICS 1936-1937
CD CLASSICS 512
Classics / Apr '90 / Discovery / Jazz Music

CLASSICS 1937-1938
CD CLASSICS 515
Classics / Apr '90 / Discovery / Jazz Music

CLASSICS 1938-1939
CD CLASSICS 523
Classics / Apr '90 / Discovery / Jazz Music

CLASSICS 1940-1942 (Armstrong, Louis Orchestra)
CD CLASSICS 685
Classics / Mar '93 / Discovery / Jazz Music

CLASSICS 1944-1946
CD CLASSICS 928
Classics / Apr '97 / Discovery / Jazz Music

COLLECTION, THE
CD COL 001
Collection / Jan '95 / Target/BMG

COMPLETE CHICAGO CONCERT 1958, THE (2CD Set)
Flee as a bird to the mountain/Oh didn't he ramble / Memphis blues/Frankie and Johnny/Tiger rag / Do you know what it means to miss New Orleans / Basin Street blues / Black and blue / West End blues / On the sunny side of the street / Struttin' with some barbecue / When it's sleepy time down South / Manhattan/When it's sleepy time down South / Indiana / Gypsy / Faithful Hussar / Rockin' chair / Bucket's got a hole in it / Perdido / Clarinet marmalade / Mack the knife / Tenderly/You'll never walk alone / Stompin' at the Savoy / Margie / Big Mama's back in town / That's my desire / Ko ko mo (I love you so) / When the saints go marching in / Star spangled banner
CD Set C2K 65119
Sony Jazz / Jun '97 / Sony

COMPLETE RCA VICTOR RECORDINGS, THE (4CD Set)
That's my home / Hobo / I hate to leave you now / You'll wish you'd never been born / (I'll be glad when you're dead) you rascal you / When it's sleepy time down South / Nobody's sweetheart / When you're smiling / St. James Infirmary / Dinah / I've got the world on a string / I gotta right to sing the blues / Hustlin' and bustlin' for baby / Sittin' in the dark / High Society / He's a son of the South / Some sweet day / Basin Street blues / Honey do / Snowball / Mahogany Hall stomp / Swing you cats / Honey don't you love me anymore / Mississippi Basin / Laughin' Louie / Tomorrow night / Dusky

stevedore / There's a cabin in the pines / Mighty river / Sweet Sue, just you / I wonder who / St. Louis blues / Don't play me cheap / That's my home / Hobo, you can't ride this train / I hate to leave you now / You'll wish you'd never been born / When you're smiling / St. James Infirmary / Dinah / Mississippi Basin / Laughin' Louis / Tomorrow night / Blue yodel no.9 / Long, long journey / Snafu / Linger in my arms a little longer / Whatta ya gonna do / No variety blues / Joseph 'n' his brudders / Back o' town blues / I want a little girl / Sugar / Blues for yesterday / Blues in the South / Endie / Blues are brewin' / Do you know what it means to miss New Orleans / Where the blues were born in New Orleans / Mahogany Hall stomp / I wonder, I wonder, I wonder / I believe / Why doubt my love / It takes time / You don't learn that in school / Ain't misbehavin' / Rockin' chair / Back o' town blues / Pennies from heaven / Save it pretty Mama / St. James Infirmary / Jack Armstrong blues / Rockin' chair / Some day you'll be sorry / Fifty fifty blues / Song was born / Please stop playin' those blues boy / Before long / Lovely weather we're having / Rain, rain / Never saw a better day
CD Set ______ 07863666822
RCA Victor / Apr '97 / BMG

COMPLETE RECORDINGS 1924-1925 (2CD Set) (Armstrong, Louis & Fletcher Henderson Orchestra)
CD Set ______ F 38001/2/3
Forte / May '97 / Cadillac / Jazz Music

COMPLETE TOWN HALL CONCERT, THE
Cornet chop suey / Our Monday date / Dear old Southland / Big butter and egg man / Tiger rag / Struttin' with some barbecue / Sweethearts on parade / St. Louis blues / Pennies from Heaven / On the sunny side of the street / I can't give you anything but love / Back o' town blues / Ain't misbehavin' / Rockin' chair / Muskrat ramble / Save it pretty Mama / St. James Infirmary / Royal Garden blues / Do you know what it means to miss New Orleans / Jack Armstrong blues
CD ______ ND 897462
Jazz Tribune / Jun '94 / BMG

DO YOU KNOW WHAT IT MEANS TO MISS NEW ORLEANS (Live)
Do you know what it means to miss New Orleans / Mahogany Hall stomp / Someday you'll be sorry / That's my desire / When the saints go marching in / Bucket's got a hole in it / Struttin' with some barbecue / Kiss to build a dream on / Baby it's cold outside
CD ______ 8379192
Verve / Mar '94 / PolyGram

ESSENCE OF ARMSTRONG
CD ______ PHONTCD 9308
Phontastic / Dec '94 / Cadillac / Jazz Music / Wellard

ESSENTIAL HOT FIVE SIDES, THE
CD ______ JZCD 324
Suisa / Feb '91 / Jazz Music / THE

ESSENTIAL HOT SEVEN SIDES AND SOME RARITIES, THE
CD ______ JZCD 325
Suisa / Feb '91 / Jazz Music / THE

ESSENTIAL LOUIS ARMSTRONG, THE
CD ______ 4618702
Sony Jazz / Jan '95 / Sony

ESSENTIAL RECORDINGS 1925-1940 (4CD Set)
CD Set ______ CDDIG 17
Charly / Jun '95 / Koch

ESSENTIAL SATCHMO, THE
What a wonderful world / Blueberry Hill / Hello Dolly / La vie en rose / Cabaret / Lazy river / Whiffenpoof song / On the sunny side of the street / Georgia on my mind / When you're smiling / That lucky old sun / Home fire / Dream a little dream of me / Give me your kisses (I'll give you my heart) / Fantastic, that's you / Hellzapoppin' / Hello brother / Sunshine of love
CD ______ MCCD 088
Music Club / Dec '92 / Disc / THE

FIRST SOLOS (Armstrong, Louis & King Oliver's Jazzband)
CD ______ JZCD 323
Suisa / Feb '91 / Jazz Music / THE

FLETCHER HENDERSON & LOUIS ARMSTRONG 1924-1925 (Armstrong, Louis & Fletcher Henderson Orchestra)
Money blues / Why couldn't it be poor little me / I'll see you in my dreams / Tell me, dreamy eyes / My Rose Marie / Poplar Street blues / Shanghai shuffle / Mandy, make up your mind / Go 'long mule / Memphis bound / How come you do me like you do / Alabamy bound / Copenhagen / Meanest kind of blues / I miss my Swiss / Alone at last / Shanghai shuffle / When you do what you do / Words / Carolina stomp / Bye and bye / Naughty man / Play me slow / TNT / One of these days / Sugarfoot stomp
CD ______ CBC 1003
Timeless Historical / Jan '92 / New Note/ Pinnacle

GENIUS OF LOUIS ARMSTRONG (40 Jazz Classics From The Legendary Satchmo/2CD Set)
All of me / Chinatown, my Chinatown / I'm in the mood for love / Sweethearts on parade / You can depend on me / Jeepers creepers / West End blues / Melancholy baby / Struttin' with some barbecue / SOL blues / Wild man blues / St. James infirmary / Potato head blues / Squeeze me / Ain't misbehavin' / (What did I do to be so) black and blue / That rhythm man / Sweet Savannah Sue / Blue, turning grey over you / I hate to leave you now / Pennies from heaven: *Armstrong, Louis & Bing Crosby* / Flat foot floogie: *Armstrong, Louis & Mills Brothers* / You won't be satisfied (until you break my heart): *Armstrong, Louis & Ella Fitzgerald* / Coal cart blues: *Armstrong, Louis & Sidney Bechet* / Swing that music / Blue yodel No.9 / My sweet lovin' man / Sugar / Do you know what it means to miss New Orleans / Stardust / Memories of you / Shoe shine boy / When it's sleepy time down south / Shanghai shuffle / St. Louis blues: *Armstrong, Louis & Bessie Smith* / CC rider: *Armstrong, Louis & Ma Rainey* / Dead drunk blues / How do you do it that way / Pleadin' for the blues / Careless love blues: *Armstrong, Louis & Bessie Smith*
CD Set ______ 330342
Hallmark / Mar '97 / Carlton

GEORGIA ON MY MIND
Old rockin' chair / (I'll be glad when you're dead) you rascal you / Wild man blues / Confessin' / Lazy river / Dinah / I ain't got nobody / Georgia bo bo / You're lucky to me / Monday date / St. James infirmary / Georgia on my mind / West End blues / Ain't misbehavin' / Knocking a jug / I can't believe that you're in love with me / St. Louis blues / Chinatown, my Chinatown / Drop that sack / My sweet
CD ______ DBCD 17
Dance Band Days / Jun '88 / Prism

GITANES - JAZZ 'ROUND MIDNIGHT
Let's do it / Sweet Lorraine / That old feeling / East of the sun and West of the moon / Body and soul / Makin' whoopee / Blues in the night / Tin roof blues / I gotta right to sing the blues / Nobody knows the trouble I've seen / Stormy weather / I'll never be the same / We'll be together again
CD ______ 8434222
Verve / Mar '93 / PolyGram

GOLD COLLECTION, THE
CD ______ D2CD 04
Deja Vu / Dec '92 / THE

GREAT CONCERT, THE
CD ______ 401542CD
Musidisc / Jul '94 / Discovery

GREAT LOUIS ARMSTRONG 1937 - 1941, THE
Yes suh / Wolverine blues / Cut off my legs and call me shorty / Cain and Abel / When it's sleepy time down South / Hep cats' ball / Do you call that a buddy / Down in honky tonk town / You run your mouth, I'll run my business / Save it pretty Mama / Perdido street blues / Me and brother blues / Struttin' with some barbecue / 2.19 Blues / (I'll be glad when you're dead) you rascal you / Lazy 'Sippi steamers / I'll get mine bye and bye / Harlem stomp / Hey lawdy mama / I double dare you / Public melody number one / Yours and mine
CD ______ PASTCD 7002
Flapper / Jan '93 / Pinnacle

GUVNOR, THE
Mahogany hall stomp / St. Louis blues / I'm confessin' that I love you / Dinah / Chinatown, my Chinatown / Georgia on my mind / Lazy river / Rockin' chair / I hope Gabriel likes my music / Struttin' with some barbecue / I double dare you / Hear me talkin' to ya / Save it pretty Mama / Shoe shine boy / Red nose / West End blues / St. James infirmary / (I'll be glad when you're dead) you rascal you / You're luky to me / Wild man blues
CD ______ PAR 2015
Parade / Apr '95 / Disc

HAPPY FIFTIES, THE (3CD Set)
CD Set ______ CLA 19203
Ambassador / Jan '97 / Cadillac / Jazz Music / Wellard

HEAR ME TALKIN' TO YA
CD ______ MACCD 167
Autograph / Aug '96 / BMG

HIGH SOCIETY
Someday you'll be sorry / Dippermouth blues / Do you know what it means to miss New Orleans / Honeysuckle rose / Panama / Save it pretty Mama / High society / Rockin' chair / Back o' town blues / Tin roof blues / You can depend on me
CD ______ TCD 1046
Tradition / May '97 / ADA / Vital

HIGHLIGHTS FROM HIS DECCA YEARS
Wild man blues / Weary blues / Georgia bo bo / Shanghai shuffle / I'm in the mood for love / Ol man hose / Skeleton in the closet / She's the daughter of a planter from Havana / Jubilee / Struttin' with some barbecue / Jeepers creepers / I'm confessin' that I love you / Wolverine blues / Perdido street blues / When it's sleepy time down South / I never knew / Ronettes / Muskrat ramble / Black and blue / Song is ended (but the melody lingers on) / You won't be satisfied (Until you break my heart) / You can't lose a broken heart / (I'll be glad when you're dead) you rascal you / You can't lose a broken heart / Gone fishin' / That lucky old sun / My bucket's got a hole in it / La vie en rose / Someday / Baby, it's cold outside / Your cheatin' heart / Gypsy / Tin roof blues / Sometimes I feel like a Motherless child / When you're smiling / Memories of you / King of the Zulus
CD ______ GRP 26382
GRP / Oct '94 / New Note/BMG

HOT FIVE TO ALL-STARS (1925-1956)
Alligator crawl / Wild man blues / Melancholy blues / Willie the weeper / Ory's creole trombone / Struttin' with some barbecue / Hotter than that / West End blues / Potato head blues / Keyhole blues / Gully low blues / Basin Street blues / SOL blues / 12th Street rag / Savoy blues / Muskrat ramble / Cornet chop suey / Skid-dat-de-dat / Come back sweet Papa / Yes, I'm in the barrel / Weary blues / Put 'em down / Monday date / Rockin' chair / Jack / Armstrong blues / Mahogany hall stomp / Do you know what it means to miss New Orleans / Where the blues was born in New Orleans / Blues for yesterday / Sugar / Long long journey / (I'll be glad when you're dead) you rascal you / Perdido street blues / 2.19 blues / Down in honky tonk town / Coal cart blues / Wolverine blues / Cut off my legs and call me shorty / Satchel mouth swing / Loved walked in / On the sunny side of the street / Swing that music / Dusky stevedore / That's my home / I surrender dear / Blue turning grey over you / That rhythm man / What did I do to be so black and blue / Struttin' with some barbecue / All that meat and no potatoes / Ole Miss / Back o' town blues / (Back home again in) Indiana / That's my desire / Ain't misbehavin' / Aunt Hagar's blues / Tin roof blues / Panama / My bucket's got a hole in it / New Orleans function / Free as a bird / Didn't he ramble / When it's sleepy time down South
CD Set ______ CDB 1205
Giants Of Jazz / '92 / Cadillac / Jazz Music / Target/BMG

HOT FIVES AND HOT SEVENS
My heart / I'm in the barrel / Gut bucket blues / Come back sweet Papa / Georgia grind / Heebie jeebies / Cornet chop suey / Oriental strut / You're next / Muskrat ramble / Don't forget to mess around / I'm gonna gitcha / Droppin' shucks / Whosit / King of the Zulus / Big fat Ma and skinny Pa
CD ______ 4608212
CBS / May '90 / Sony

HOT FIVES AND HOT SEVENS
CD ______ CD 56010
Jazz Roots / Aug '94 / Target/BMG

HOT FIVES AND HOT SEVENS VOL.1 1925-1926
CD ______ 7810832
Jazztime / Aug '93 / Discovery

HOT FIVES AND HOT SEVENS VOL.1 1926-1927
Lonesome blues / Sweet little papa / Jazz lips / Skid-dat-de-dat / I want a big butter and egg man / Sunset cafe stomp / You made me love you / Irish black bottom / Willie the weeper / Wild man blues / Chicago breakdown / Alligator crawl / Potato head blues / Melancholy blues / Weary blues / 12th Street rag
CD ______ JSPCD 312
JSP / Apr '90 / ADA / Cadillac / Direct / Hot Shot / Target/BMG

HOT FIVES AND HOT SEVENS VOL.2
Willie the weeper / Wild man blues / Chicago breakdown / Alligator crawl / Potato head blues / Melancholy blues / Weary blues / 12th Street rag / Keyhole blues / SOL blues / Gully low blues / That's when I'll come back to you / Put 'em down blues / Ory's creole trombone / Last time / Struttin' with some barbecue / Got no blues / Once in a while / I'm not rough / Hotter than that / Savoy blues
CD ______ JSPCD 313
JSP / Apr '90 / ADA / Cadillac / Direct / Hot Shot / Target/BMG

HOT FIVES AND HOT SEVENS VOL.2
CD ______ 4630522
Sony Jazz / Apr '89 / Sony

HOT FIVES AND HOT SEVENS VOL.2 1926-1927
CD ______ 7810842
Jazztime / Aug '93 / Discovery

HOT FIVES AND HOT SEVENS VOL.3
CD ______ JSPCD 314
JSP / Feb '92 / ADA / Cadillac / Direct / Hot Shot / Target/BMG

HOT FIVES AND HOT SEVENS VOL.3
CD ______ 4651892
CBS / Jul '88 / Sony

HOT FIVES AND HOT SEVENS VOL.4
CD ______ JSPCD 315
JSP / Jun '92 / ADA / Cadillac / Direct / Hot Shot / Target/BMG

I GOT RHYTHM
I got rhythm / Honeysuckle rose / Jeepers creepers / Tiger rag / Muskrat ramble / Way down yonder in New Orleans / When the saints go marching in / Body and soul / Sweet hearts on parade / You're driving me crazy / Just a gigolo / Ain't misbehavin' / Back o' town blues / C'est si bon / Stompin' at the Savoy / Shine / On the sunny side of the street / La vie en rose / Hucklebuck / Memories of you
CD ______ PWK 137
Carlton / May '90 / Carlton

I WISH YOU WERE DEAD YOU RASCAL YOU
St Louis blues / West End blues / I've got the world on a string / Cornet chop suey / Save it pretty mama / Potato head blues / Heebie Jeebies / Knockin' a jug / Mahogany hall stomp / (I'll be glad when you're dead) you rascal you / When it's sleepy time down south / Hobo, you can't ride this train / Weather bird / I gotta right to sing the blues / Dear old southland / Lonesome road / I'm confessin' / Stardust
CD ______ CWNCD 2028
Javelin / Jul '96 / Henry Hadaway / THE

IMMORTAL CONCERTS (At the Symphony Hall-Boston, November 30, 1947) (Armstrong, Louis Allstars)
Mahogany Hall stomp / Black and blue / Royal Garden blues / That's my desire / C jam blues / Stars fell on Alabama / I cried for you / On the sunny side of the street / Tea for two / Baby, won't you please come home / Muskrat ramble / Lover / Body and soul / Steak face / High society / Boff boff
CD ______ ENTCD 235
Entertainers / Feb '88 / Target/BMG

IN CONCERT AT WASHINGTON THEATRE
CD ______ ATJCD 5957
All That's Jazz / '92 / Jazz Music / THE

INTRODUCTION TO LOUIS ARMSTRONG 1924-1938, AN
CD ______ 4004
Best Of Jazz / Dec '93 / Discovery

JAZZ CLASSICS MASTERWORKS (Armstrong, Louis & Sidney Bechet)
Yes, I'm in the barrel: *Armstrong, Louis* / Struttin' with some barbecue: *Armstrong, Louis* / Cornet shop suey: *Armstrong, Louis* / Wild man blues: *Armstrong, Louis* / SOL blues: *Armstrong, Louis* / Weary blues: *Armstrong, Louis* / Basin Street blues: *Armstrong, Louis* / Monday date: *Armstrong, Louis* / West End blues: *Armstrong, Louis* / Mahogany Hall stomp: *Armstrong, Louis* / On the sunny side of the street: *Armstrong, Louis* / Baby, won't you please come home: *Armstrong, Louis* / C jam blues: *Armstrong, Louis* / Kansas City man blues: *Bechet, Sidney* / Jazz me blues: *Bechet, Sidney* / Honeysuckle Rose: *Bechet, Sidney*
CD ______ 17051
Laserlight / Nov '95 / Target/BMG

JAZZ MASTERS
Just one of those things / That old feeling / I gotta right to sing the blues / Learnin' the blues / Let's do it / There's a boat that's leavin' soon for New York / Blues in the night / You're the top / Body and soul / When your lover has gone / Fine romance / Home / I've got the world on a string / I was dancing alright / When the saints go marchin' in
CD ______ 5198182
Verve / May '94 / PolyGram

JAZZ PORTRAITS
Can anyone explain / My sweet hunk o'trash / You won't be satisfied (until you break my heart) / Fifty fifty blues / You can't lose a broken heart / Frim fram sauce / (I'll be glad when you're dead) you rascal you / Oops / Life is so peculiar / Dream a little dream of me / Struttin' with some barbecue / Necessary evil / Lazybones / Long gone / Now you has jazz / Who walks in when I walk out / Boog it / Honeysuckle rose
CD ______ CD 14513
Jazz Portraits / May '94 / Jazz Music

LEGENDARY LOUIS ARMSTRONG, THE (4CD Set)
Jeepers creepers / Stompin' at the savoy / I got rhythm / On the sunny side of the street / Tea for two / New orleans stomp / Snake rag / Lover / Dippermouth blues / Just a gigolo / Muskat ramble / Way down yonder in New Orleans / I used to love you / Body and soul / Back o' town blues / Shine / Mame / When the saints go marching in / Ain't misbehavin' / Cabaret / Kiss to build a dream on / Blueberry hill / Hello dolly / St. Louis blues / That's my desire / Mack the knife / Big butter and egg man / Black and blue / C'est si bon / St. Jame's infirmary / Someday you'll be sorry / Sweethearts on parade / Heebie jeebies / Cornet chop suey / Muskrat ramble / Keyhole blues / Potato head blues / Hotter than that / Struttin' with some / Barbeque / West End blues / My monday date / Muggles / I can't give you anything but love / Dinah / I'm a ding dong daddy / I'm confessin' that I love you / Memories of you / You're lucky to me / Stardust / Sleepy time down south / Between the devil and the deep blue sea / Lawd you made the night too long / Hobo you can't ride this train / That's my home / I gotta right to sing the blues / I'm in the mood for love / I hope Gabriel likes my mu-

sic / Basin street blues / Coal cart blues / Perdido street blues / Some sweet day / Mahogany hall blues stomp / Ev'ntide / Swing that music
CD Set ____ QUAD 006
Tring / Nov '96 / Tring

LEGENDARY LOUIS ARMSTRONG, THE
Jeepers creepers / Basin Street blues / Stompin' at the Savoy / I got rhythm / On the sunny side of the street / Tea for two / New Orleans stomp / Lover / Dippermouth blues / Just a gigolo / Muskrat ramble / Way down yonder in New Orleans / Royal garden blues / La vie en rose / I used to love you / Body and soul / Back ole town blues / Shine
CD ____ QED 127
Tring / Nov '96 / Tring

LIVE 1938-1940 (Armstrong, Louis & Fats Waller)
CD ____ MM 31056
Music Memoria / Aug '93 / ADA / Discovery

LIVE AT EXHIBITION GARDEN - VANCOUVER CANADA (Armstrong, Louis Allstars)
Rockin' chair / Where did you stay last night / Baby, it's cold outside / C Jam blues / Stompin' at the Savoy / I used to love you / La vie en rose / Lover / I love the guy / That's my desire / Royal garden blues / Ain't misbehavin'
CD ____ CDINS 5046
Charly / Dec '92 / Koch

LIVE AT THE WINTER GARDEN, NEW YORK 1947/BLUE NOTE, CHICAGO (Armstrong, Louis Allstars)
CD ____ STCD 8242
Storyville / May '97 / Cadillac / Jazz Music / Wellard

LOUIS & LUIS (Original Recordings 1929-1940) (Armstrong, Louis & Luis Russell)
Baby, won't you please come home / Bessie couldn't help it / Blue turning grey over you / 2.19 blues / Bye and bye / Confessin' / Dallas blues / Mahogany hall stomp / On the sunny side of the street / Our Monday date / Perdido Street blues / Public Melody Number One / Rockin' chair / St. Louis blues / Savoy blues / Struttin' with some barbecue / Sweethearts on parade / Swing that music / Thanks a million / West End blues / When it's sleepy time down South / When the saints go marching in / Wolverine blues / You run your mouth, I'll run my business / You're a lucky guy
CD ____ CDAJA 5094
Living Era / Sep '92 / Select

LOUIS ARMSTRONG
CD ____ LECD 050
Dynamite / May '94 / THE

LOUIS ARMSTRONG
CD ____ 22701
Music / Nov '95 / Target/BMG

LOUIS ARMSTRONG (2CD Set)
CD Set ____ R2CD 4004
Deja Vu / Jan '96 / THE

LOUIS ARMSTRONG
Jeepers creepers / Kiss to build a dream on / When the stars go marchin' in / Mack the knife / C'est si bon / St. Louis blues / Black and blue / Dippermouth blues / Bye and bye / Rockin' chair / C jam blues / Stardust / Royal Garden blues / Indiana / I used to love her / Where did you stay last night / If I could be with you tonight / Way down yonder in New Orleans
CD ____ BN 004
Blue Nite / Feb '97 / Target/BMG

LOUIS ARMSTRONG (CD/CD Rom Set)
What a wonderful world / Hello dolly / Jeepers creepers / Foggy day: *Armstrong, Louis & Ella Fitzgerald* / Sweethearts on parade: *Armstrong, Louis & Frank Sinatra* / St. James Infirmary / Kiss to build a dream on / Blueberry Hill / Cabaret / Chimes blues / Jelly Roll blues / Mack The Knife / New Orleans stomp / Pretty little missy / Snake rag / When the Saints go marchin' in / Someday you'll be sorry
CD Set ____ WWCDR 002
Magnum Music / Apr '97 / TKO Magnum

LOUIS ARMSTRONG
Hello Dolly / When the Saints go marchin' in / Alligator crawl / Gipsy / New Orleans function / I've got a feeling I'm falling / Struttin' with some barbecue / C'est si bon / La vie en rose / Someday / When it's sleepy time down South / Black and blue / High society / Kiss to build a dream on / On the sunny side of the street / Only you
CD ____ 399527
Koch Presents / Jun '97 / Koch

LOUIS ARMSTRONG & EARL HINES (Armstrong, Louis & Earl Hines)
CD ____ 4663082
Sony Jazz / Jan '95 / Sony

LOUIS ARMSTRONG & HIS ALL STARS (Armstrong, Louis Allstars)
CD ____ 15773
Laserlight / Jul '92 / Target/BMG

LOUIS ARMSTRONG & HIS ALL STARS
CD ____ CD 14550
Jazz Portraits / Jul '94 / Jazz Music

LOUIS ARMSTRONG & HIS ALL STARS (Armstrong, Louis Allstars)
When it's sleepy time down South / Hello Dolly / Blueberry Hill / Volare / St. James infirmary / Girl from Ipanema / (Back home again in) Indiana / Muskrat ramble / Mack the knife / I love Paris / Time after time / Cabaret / Tiger rag / When the saints go marching in / This could be the start of something big / Please don't talk about me when I'm gone / Stompin' at the Savoy / That's my desire / Closer walk with thee / Them there eyes / Avalon / Kiss to build a dream on / Ole miss
CD ____ STCD 4095
Storyville / Feb '89 / Cadillac / Jazz Music / Wellard

LOUIS ARMSTRONG 1925-1928
CD ____ 15721
Laserlight / Apr '94 / Target/BMG

LOUIS ARMSTRONG 1926-1928
CD ____ KJ 151FS
King Jazz / Oct '93 / Cadillac / Discovery / Jazz Music

LOUIS ARMSTRONG 1928-1931
CD ____ HRM 6002
Hermes / Sep '88 / Nimbus

LOUIS ARMSTRONG 1931-1947 (Armstrong, Louis Orchestra/Hot Seven/ Dixieland Seven)
CD ____ CD 14563
Jazz Portraits / May '95 / Jazz Music

LOUIS ARMSTRONG 1946-1951 (When You & I Were Young Maggie)
CD ____ CLA 1915
Ambassador / Mar '94 / Cadillac / Jazz Music / Wellard

LOUIS ARMSTRONG 1949-1957 (Heavenly Music)
CD ____ CLA 1916
Ambassador / Mar '94 / Cadillac / Jazz Music / Wellard

LOUIS ARMSTRONG 1952-1956 (Moments To Remember)
CD ____ CLA 1917
Ambassador / Aug '95 / Cadillac / Jazz Music / Wellard

LOUIS ARMSTRONG AND EDMOND HALL'S ORCHESTRA (Live at Carnegie Hall, Feb 8 1947) (Armstrong, Louis & Edmond Hall Orchestra)
New Orleans function / St. Louis blues / Muskrat ramble / Ain't misbehavin'
CD ____ 20802
Laserlight / Mar '88 / Target/BMG

LOUIS ARMSTRONG AND HIS ALL STARS (1961-1962)
CD ____ STCD 4012
Storyville / Feb '89 / Cadillac / Jazz Music / Wellard

LOUIS ARMSTRONG AND HIS ALL STARS (1947-1950) (Armstrong, Louis Allstars)
CD ____ CD 53032
Giants Of Jazz / Sep '88 / Cadillac / Jazz Music / Target/BMG

LOUIS ARMSTRONG AND HIS ALL STARS (Armstrong, Louis Allstars)
CD ____ UCD 19002
Forlane / Jul '88 / Target/BMG

LOUIS ARMSTRONG AND HIS GREAT BIG BAND
CD ____ JCD 19
Jass / Feb '91 / ADA / Cadillac / CM / Direct / Jazz Music

LOUIS ARMSTRONG AND KING OLIVER
Just gone / Canal Street blues / Mandy Lee blues / I'm going to wear you off my mind / Chimes blues / Weatherbird rag / Dippermouth blues / Froggie Moore / Snake rag / Alligator hop / Zulu's ball / Workin' man blues / Krooked blues / Mabel's dream / Southern stomps (take 1) / Southern stomps (take 2) / Riverside blues / King Oliver / Jelly roll morton / Tom cat blues / Terrible blues / Santa Claus blues / Texas moaner blues / Of all the wrongs you've done to me / Nobody knows the way I feel this morning / Early every morn' / Cake walkin' babies from home
CD ____ MCD 47017 2
Milestone / Jun '93 / Cadillac / Complete/ Pinnacle / Jazz Music / Wellard

LOUIS ARMSTRONG AND THE ALL STARS
CD ____ 15728
Laserlight / Apr '94 / Target/BMG

LOUIS ARMSTRONG COLLECTION, THE
Mame / Stompin' at the Savoy / I got rhythm / Honeysuckle rose / When the saints go marching in / Muskrat ramble / Way down yonder in New Orleans / Ain't misbehavin' / Royal garden blues / La vie en rose / Cabaret / Hucklebuck / I used to love you / Kis to build a dream on / Hello Dolly / Please don't talk about me when I'm gone / Just a gigolo / I'm your ding dong daddy from Dumas / Blueberry hill / I'm in the market for you / Peanut vendor / Mahogany hall stomp / St. Louis blues / You're lucky to me / That's my desire / I'm confessin' that I love you / Mack the knife / If I could be with you one hour tonight / Jeepers creepers / Basin Street blues / Body and soul / Back o' town blues / Memories of you / You're driving me crazy / I want a big butter and egg man / Shine / On the sunny side of the street / (Back home again in) Indiana / Dear old southland / Tiger rag / Bye and bye / Black and blue / Tea for two / Jelly Roll blues / Chimes blues / Dippermouth blues / C'est si bon / Savoy stomp / I can't give you anything but love / St. James Infirmary / That rhythm man / Lover / Someday you'll be sorry / Snake rag / New Orleans stomp / Sweethearts on parade
CD Set ____ TFP 011
Tring / Nov '92 / Tring

LOUIS ARMSTRONG COLLECTORS' EDITION
CD ____ DVX 812
Deja Vu / Apr '95 / THE

LOUIS ARMSTRONG GOLD (2CD Set)
CD Set ____ D2CD 4004
Deja Vu / Jun '95 / THE

LOUIS ARMSTRONG GREAT ALTERNATIVES 1929-1937
CD ____ KJ 153FS
King Jazz / Oct '93 / Cadillac / Discovery / Jazz Music

LOUIS ARMSTRONG IN CONCERT
CD ____ RTE 10012CD
RTE / Apr '95 / ADA / Koch

LOUIS ARMSTRONG LIVE IN PARIS
CD ____ ACDCH 553
Milan / Jun '90 / Conifer/BMG / Silva Screen

LOUIS ARMSTRONG MEETS DUKE ELLINGTON 1961 (Armstrong, Louis & Duke Ellington)
It don't mean a thing (if it ain't got that swing) / Just squeeze me / Do nothin' 'til you hear from me / In a mellow tone / Solitude / Don't get around much anymore / Mooche / I'm beginning to see the light / Mood indigo / Beautiful American / I got it bad and that ain't good / Drop me off at Harlem / Black and tan fantasy / Cotton tail (shuckin' and stiffin') / I'm just a lucky so and so / Duke's place / Azalea
CD ____ CD 53148
Giants Of Jazz / Oct '96 / Cadillac / Jazz Music / Target/BMG

LOUIS ARMSTRONG PLAYS W.C. HANDY
St. Louis blues / Yellow dog blues / Loveless love / Aunt Hagar's blues / Louis Armstrong monologue / Long gone (from bowlin' green) / Memphis blues (or, Mister Crump) / Beale Street blues / Ole Miss / Chantez les bas (sing 'em low) / Hesitating blues / Atlanta blues (make me one pallet on your foot) / Interview with WC Handy / Loveless love / Hesitating blues / Louis Armstrong's alligator story / Long gone
CD ____ CK 64925
Sony Jazz / Apr '97 / Sony

LOUIS ARMSTRONG VOL.1 1925-1927
CD ____ KJ 146FS
King Jazz / Oct '93 / Cadillac / Discovery / Jazz Music

LOUIS ARMSTRONG VOL.1 1935 (Armstrong, Louis & Luis Russell/Victor Young)
Sunny side of the street / Ain't misbehavin' / I'm in the mood for love / You are my lucky star / I hope Gabriel likes my music / Solitude thanks a million / Shoe shine boy / Red sails in the sunset / On treasure island / Got a bran' new suit
CD ____ CLA 1901
Ambassador / Mar '94 / Cadillac / Jazz Music / Wellard

LOUIS ARMSTRONG VOL.2 1927-1928
CD ____ KJ 147FS
King Jazz / Oct '93 / Cadillac / Discovery / Jazz Music

LOUIS ARMSTRONG VOL.2 1936
Music goes 'round and around / Rhythm saved the world / I'm putting all my eggs in one basket / Yes yes, my my / Somebody stole my break / I come from a musical family / If we never meet again / Lyin' to myself / Eventide / Swing that music / Dinah
CD ____ CLA 1902
Ambassador / Mar '94 / Cadillac / Jazz Music / Wellard

LOUIS ARMSTRONG VOL.3 1928-1929
CD ____ KJ 148FS
King Jazz / Oct '93 / Cadillac / Discovery / Jazz Music

LOUIS ARMSTRONG VOL.3 1936-1937
CD ____ CLA 1903
Ambassador / Jul '96 / Cadillac / Jazz Music / Wellard

LOUIS ARMSTRONG VOL.4 1929-1931
CD ____ KJ 149FS
King Jazz / Oct '93 / Cadillac / Discovery / Jazz Music

LOUIS ARMSTRONG VOL.4 1938
CD ____ CLA 1904
Ambassador / Jun '96 / Cadillac / Jazz Music / Wellard

LOUIS ARMSTRONG VOL.5 1931-1932
CD ____ KJ 150FS
King Jazz / Oct '93 / Cadillac / Discovery / Jazz Music

LOUIS ARMSTRONG VOL.5 1938-1939
Naturally / I've got a pocketful of dreams / I can't give you anything but love / Ain't misbehavin' / 12th street rag / Swing that music / Flat foot floogie / Elder Eatmore's sermon on throwing stones / Elder Eatmore's sermon on generosity / Tiger rag / Jeepers creepers / I got rhythm / On the sunny side of the street / Blues / Honeysuckle rose / Shadrack / Nobody knows the trouble I've seen / Jeepers creepers / What is this thing called swing / Rockin' chair / Lazybones
CD ____ CLA 1905
Ambassador / Jun '94 / Cadillac / Jazz Music / Wellard

LOUIS ARMSTRONG VOL.6 1939-1940
CD ____ CLA 1906
Ambassador / Mar '94 / Cadillac / Jazz Music / Wellard

LOUIS ARMSTRONG VOL.7 1940-1941
CD ____ CLA 1907
Ambassador / Jun '95 / Cadillac / Jazz Music / Wellard

LOUIS ARMSTRONG/COUNT BASIE ESSENTIALS (Armstrong, Louis & Count Basie)
CD ____ LECDD 640
Wisepack / Aug '95 / Conifer/BMG / THE

LOUIS SINGS THE BLUES
CD ____ 07863662442
Novus / Jul '93 / BMG

MACK THE KNIFE
When it's sleepy time down South / (Back home again in) Indiana / Now you has jazz / High society calypso / Mahogany hall stomp / Blue moon / Sweet Georgia Brown / Riff blues / Mack the knife / Lazy river / Stompin' at the Savoy
CD ____ CD 2310 941
Pablo / Jun '93 / Cadillac / Complete/ Pinnacle

MACK THE KNIFE
Mame / When the saints go marching in / Ain't misbehavin' / Cabaret / Kiss to build a dream on / Blueberry hill / Hello Dolly / St. Louis blues / That's my desire / Mack The Knife / Back o' town blues / Big butter and egg man / Black and blue / C'est si bon / St. James infirmary / Someday you'll be sorry / Sweethearts on parade
CD ____ QED 033
Tring / Nov '96 / Tring

MAHOGANY HALL STOMP (Original Recordings 1927-1936)
Mahogany Hall stomp / Rockin' chair / Savoy blues / Sweethearts on parade / Swing that music / Lyin' to myself / Thankful / I come from a musical family / Eventide / Red nose / If we never meet again / Peanut vendor / You're lucky to me / St. James Infirmary / (I'll be glad when you're dead) you rascal you / Lazy river / I ain't got nobody / Ain't misbehavin'
CD ____ CDAJA 5049
Living Era / Nov '87 / Select

MASTERPIECES (Hot Five and Hot Seven 1925-1928)
CD ____ CD 53001
Giants Of Jazz / Mar '92 / Cadillac / Jazz Music / Target/BMG

MASTERPIECES 1926-41
CD ____ 158132
Masterpieces / Mar '94 / BMG

MASTERPIECES 1927-42
CD ____ 158142
Masterpieces / Mar '94 / BMG

NEW ORLEANS COLLECTION
When the Saints go marching in / Tiger rag / Nobody knows the trouble I've seen / I can't give you anything but love / Baby, won't you please come home / Way down yonder in New Orleans / Someday / Do you know what it means to miss New Orleans / New Orleans stomp / Ain't misbehavin' / That lucky old sun / Butter and egg man / Storyville blues / Muskrat ramble / Back o' town blues / Royal Garden blues / Ol' rocking chair / Swing that music / Brother Bill / Jeepers creepers / Dear old Southland
CD ____ 100512
CMC / May '97 / BMG

NEW ORLEANS FUNCTION
When it's sleepy time down South / (Back home again in) Indiana / Give me a kiss to build a dream on / My bucket's got a hole in it / Mack the knife / Ole Miss / C'est si bon / La vie en rose / New Orleans function / Free as a bird / Oh didn't he ramble
CD ____ ENTCD 206
Entertainers / Sep '87 / Target/BMG

ON THE ROAD
CD ____ 15798
Laserlight / Jan '93 / Target/BMG

ON THE SUNNY SIDE OF THE STREET
CD ____ JASSCD 19
Jass / Aug '90 / ADA / Cadillac / CM / Direct / Jazz Music

PLATINUM COLLECTION, THE
I got rhythm / Stardust / Between the devil and the deep blue sea / Ain't misbehavin' / I can't give you anything but love / Knockin' a jug / Lawd, you made the night too long / That's my home / Hobo, you can ride this train / I gotta right to sing the blues / Black and blue / That rhythm man / I ain't got nobody / Rockin' chair / Bessie couldn't help it / Dallas blues / Dear old Southland / Sugar foot strut / Basin Street blues / Once in a while / Sweet little Papa / You made me love you / Chicago breakdown / Coal cart blues / Down in Honky Tonk town / 2.19 blues / Perdido Street blues / Jeepers creepers / Dippermouth blues / Eventide / Swing that music / I'm in the mood for love / I can't believe that you're in love with me / I'm a ding dong Daddy (from Dumas) / I'm in the market for you / If I could be with you one hour tonight / Body and soul / Memories of you / You're lucky to me / Sweethearts on parade
CD Set ______ **PC 613**
Start / Jul '97 / Disc

PLAYS AND SINGS THE GREAT STANDARDS (1928-1932)
CD ______ **BLE 592262**
Black & Blue / Nov '92 / Discovery / Koch / Wellard

POCKET FULL OF DREAMS
Trumpet players lament / I double dare you / True confession / Let that be a lesson to you / Sweet as a song / So little time (so much to do) / Mexican swing / As long as you live, you'll be dead if you die / When the saints go marching in / On the sentimental side / 'S wonderful / Something tells me / Love walked in / Naturally (natch-ra-ly) / I've got a pocket full of dreams / I can't give you anyth'n but love / Ain't misbehavin' / Got a bran new suit
CD ______ **GRP 16492**
GRP / Nov '95 / New Note/BMG

PORGY AND BESS (Armstrong, Louis & Ella Fitzgerald)
Summertime / I got plenty o' nuttin' / My man's gone now / Bess you is my woman now / It ain't necessarily so / There's a boat that's leavin' soon for New York / Bess, oh where's my Bess / I'm on my way / I loves you Porgy / Woman is a sometime thing
CD ______ **8274752**
Verve / Feb '93 / PolyGram

PORTRAIT OF LOUIS ARMSTRONG, A
CD ______ **GALE 402**
Gallerie / May '97 / Disc / THE

PRICELESS JAZZ
I'm in the mood for love / Solitude / Ain't misbehavin' / You won't be satisfied (until you break my heart) / Rhythm saved the world / You can't lose a broken heart / Dream a little dream / You rascal you / La vie en rose / On the sunny side of the street / Perdido Street blues / Struttin' / With some barbecue / Gone fishin' / When it's sleept time down south / Dippermouth blues / What a wonderful world
CD ______ **GRP 98722**
GRP / Jul '97 / New Note/BMG

QUINTESSENCE VOL.2, THE (2CD Set)
Chimes blues / Tears / Texas moaner blues / Mandy, make up your mind / Cake walkin' babies (from home) / Cold in hand blues / You've been a good ole wagon / Skid-dat-de-dat / Big butter and egg man / Wild man blues / Chicago breakdown / Alligatoe crawl / Twelfth street rag / Keyhole blues / SOL blues / Gully low blues / Got no blues / Once in a while / Fireworks (a rhythmic explosion) / Skip the gutter / Two dueces / Knee drops / Symphonic raps / Hear me talkin' to ya / Some of these days / Dear old Southland / Body and soul / Hobo, you can't ride this train / I gotta right to sing the blues / Basin Street blues / Shoe shine boy / Ev'ntide / Thankful / I double dare you / You won't be satisfied / Do you know what it means to miss New Orleans
CD ______ **FA 221**
Fremeaux / Apr '97 / ADA / Discovery

QUINTESSENCE, THE (The Vocalist/2CD Set)
CD Set ______ **FA 230**
Fremeaux / Apr '96 / ADA / Discovery

QUINTESSENCE, THE (1925-1940/2CD Set)
CD Set ______ **FA 201**
Fremeaux / Oct '96 / ADA / Discovery

RADIO DAYS
CD ______ **MCD 0562**
Moon / Apr '94 / Cadillac / Harmonia Mundi

RARE BATCH OF SATCHMO, A
CD ______ **PLSCD 136**
Pulse / Apr '96 / BMG

SATCH PLAYS FATS
Honeysuckle rose / Blue turning grey over you / I'm crazy 'bout my baby / I've got a feeling I'm falling in love / Keepin' out of mischief now / All that meat and no potatoes / Squeeze me / Black and blue / Ain't misbehavin'
CD ______ **4509802**
CBS / Feb '88 / Sony

SATCHMO - WHAT A WONDERFUL WORLD
What a wonderful world / Nobody knows the trouble I've seen / Baby it's cold outside / Sweet Lorraine / Summertime / It ain't necessarily so / On the sunny side of the street / Tyree's blues / Cheek to cheek / Top hat, white tie and tails / Can't we be friends / Tin roof blues / Circle of your arms / Uncle Satchmo's lullaby / When the saints go marching in
CD ______ **0077002**
Verve / Jan '90 / PolyGram

SATCHMO 1931-1947
CD ______ **CD 56030**
Jazz Roots / Nov '94 / Target/BMG

SATCHMO AT SYMPHONY HALL
Mahogany hall stomp / Black and blue / Royal garden blues / Lover / Body and soul / Since I fell for you / Boff boff / Baby, won't you please come home / C jam blues / Tea for two / Steak face / On the sunny side of the street / High society / Stars fell on Alabama / Muskrat ramble
CD ______ **GRP 16612**
American Decca / Feb '96 / New Note/BMG

SATCHMO MEETS BIG T (1944-1958) (Armstrong, Louis & Jack Teagarden)
CD ______ **CD 53079**
Giants Of Jazz / Mar '92 / Cadillac / Jazz Music / Target/BMG

SATCHMO'S IMMORTAL PERFORMANCES 1929-1947
CD ______ **CD 53088**
Giants Of Jazz / Mar '90 / Cadillac / Jazz Music / Target/BMG

SATCHMO: A MUSICAL AUTOBIOGRAPHY VOL.1
CD ______ **JUCD 2003**
Jazz Unlimited / Jul '89 / Cadillac / Jazz Music / Wellard

SATCHMO: A MUSICAL AUTOBIOGRAPHY VOL.2
CD ______ **JUCD 2004**
Jazz Unlimited / Jun '89 / Cadillac / Jazz Music / Wellard

SATCHMO: A MUSICAL AUTOBIOGRAPHY VOL.3
CD ______ **JUCD 2005**
Jazz Unlimited / Dec '90 / Cadillac / Jazz Music / Wellard

SILVER COLLECTION, THE
Top hat, white tie and tails / Have you met Miss Jones / I only have eyes for you / Stormy weather / Home / East of the sun and west of the moon / You're blase / Body and soul / When your lover has gone / You're the top / Nobody knows the trouble I've seen / We'll be together again / I've got the world on a string / Do nothin' 'til you hear from me / I gotta right to sing the blues
CD ______ **8234462**
Verve / Mar '93 / PolyGram

SOMEDAY
CD ______ **MCD 080**
Moon / Dec '95 / Cadillac / Harmonia Mundi

SPOTLIGHT ON LOUIS ARMSTRONG
Mack the knife / I got rhythm / Just a gigolo / When the saints go marching in / That's my desire / Heebie jeebies / Ain't misbehavin' / On the sunny side of the street / Cabaret / Blueberry hill / Hello Dolly / I can't give you anything but love / Sweethearts on parade / Jeepers creepers / You're driving me crazy / Way down yonder in New Orleans
CD ______ **HADCD 140**
Javelin / Feb '94 / Henry Hadaway / THE

ST. LOUIS BLUES
Mahogany hall stomp / St. Louis blues / I'm confessin' that I love you / Dinah / Chinatown, my chinatown / Georgia on my mind / Lazy river / Rockin' chair / Wild man blues / You're lucky to me / (I'll be glad when you're dead) you rascal you / St. James infirmary / West End blues / Red nose / Shoe shine boy / Save it pretty Mama / Hear me talkin' to ya / I double dare you / Struttin' with some barbecue / I hope Gabriel likes my music
CD ______ **MUCD 9028**
Musketeer / Apr '95 / Disc

THANKS A MILLION
CD ______ **AMSC 574**
Avid / Jun '96 / Avid/BMG / Koch / THE

THIS IS JAZZ
Cornet chop suey / Heebie jeebies / Potato head blues / West End blues / Memories of you / Starbust / When you're smiling / Dinah / Tiger rag / Lazy river / Basin street blues / Big butter and egg man / Ain't misbehavin' / When it's sleepy time down south / I've got the world on a string / Between the devil and the deep blue sea
CD ______ **CK 64613**
Sony Jazz / May '96 / Sony

THIS IS JAZZ
I'm not rough / St Louis blues / On the sunnyside of the street / I surrender dear / Rockin' chair / All of me / Body and soul / Mack the knife / Love you funny thing / Just a gigolo / (What did I do to be so) Black and blue / Sweethearts on the parade / When your lover has gone / Memories of you / Summer song / When it's sleepy down south
CD ______ **CK 65039**
Sony Jazz / May '97 / Sony

TOGETHER AGAIN LIVE AT MONTREUX JAZZ FESTIVAL
CD ______ **CD 20005**
Pablo / May '86 / Cadillac / Complete/ Pinnacle

TRIBUTE TO THE LOUIS ARMSTRONG HOT FIVE, THE (Various Artists)
My heart / Yes I'm the barrel / Gutbucket blues / Come back sweet Papa / Georgia grind / Heebie jeebies / Cornet chop suey / Oriental strut / You're next / Muskrat ramble / Don't forget to mess around / I'm gonna gitcha / Dropping shucks / Who's it / King of the Zulus / Big fat Ma and skinny Pa / Lonesome blues / Sweet little Papa / 19 jazz lips / Skid-dat-de-dat
CD ______ **QED 225**
Tring / Nov '96 / Tring

ULTIMATE COLLECTION, THE
Blueberry hill / C'est si bon / Dream a little dream of me / Georgia on my mind / Hello Dolly / Jeepers creepers / Moon river / Only you / Up a lazy river / What a wonderful world / Basin Street blues / Rockin' chair / Someday you'll be sorry / Pennies from heaven / On the sunny side of the street / Tiger rag / Ain't misbehavin' / High society rag / St. Louis blues / What a wonderful world (II) / Do you know what it means to miss New Orleans / Faithful hussar / Mack the knife
CD ______ **74321197062**
Bluebird / May '94 / BMG

UNRELEASED MASTERS (Cornell University: Second Set)
Manhattan murals / Hy'a Sue / Fantazm / Tootin' through the roof / Brown Betty / Humouresque / How high the moon / Don't be so mean to baby / Lover come back to me / It's Monday everyday / Limehouse blues
CD ______ **MM 65162**
Music Masters / Feb '97 / Nimbus

VINTAGE MELLOW JAZZ (3CD Set) (Armstrong, Louis & Lionel Hampton/ Duke Ellington)
When the saints go marching in: *Armstrong, Louis* / I'm confessin': *Armstrong, Louis* / Our Monday date: *Armstrong, Louis* / You are my lucky star: *Armstrong, Louis* / As long as you live you'll be dead if you die: *Armstrong, Louis* / On the sunny side of the street: *Armstrong, Louis* / Lyin' to myself: *Armstrong, Louis* / Solitude: *Armstrong, Louis* / Shoe shine boy: *Armstrong, Louis* / So little time: *Armstrong, Louis* / I double dare you: *Armstrong, Louis* / Love walked in: *Armstrong, Louis* / Public melody number one: *Armstrong, Louis* / True confession: *Armstrong, Louis* / Thankful: *Armstrong, Louis* / Red sails in the sunset: *Armstrong, Louis* / Falling in love with you: *Armstrong, Louis* / Yours and mine: *Armstrong, Louis* / Hear me talkin' to ya: *Armstrong, Louis* / Save it pretty Mama: *Armstrong, Louis* / (I'll be glad when you're dead) you rascal you: *Armstrong, Louis* / When it's sleepy time down south: *Armstrong, Louis* / Hot mallets: *Hampton, Lionel* / Shufflin' at the Hollywood: *Hampton, Lionel* / Central Avenue breakdown: *Hampton, Lionel* / Dinah: *Hampton, Lionel* / Four or five times: *Hampton, Lionel* / Twelth street rag: *Hampton, Lionel* / Chasin' with chase: *Hampton, Lionel* / Rythm, rhythm: *Hampton, Lionel* / China stomp: *Hampton, Lionel* / Blue: *Hampton, Lionel* / Pig boot sonata: *Hampton, Lionel* / Three quarter boogie: *Hampton, Lionel* / Bouncing at the beacon: *Hampton, Lionel* / Ain't cha comin' home: *Hampton, Lionel* / Munson street breakdown: *Hampton, Lionel* / When the lights are low: *Hampton, Lionel* / Shoe shiners drag: *Hampton, Lionel* / Ring dem bells: *Hampton, Lionel* / I've found a new baby: *Hampton, Lionel* / Singin' the blues: *Hampton, Lionel* / Flying home: *Hampton, Lionel* / Take the 'A' train: *Ellington, Duke* / Perdido: *Ellington, Duke* / Five O'clock whistle: *Ellington, Duke* / Sidewalks of New York: *Ellington, Duke* / At a Dixie roadside diner: *Ellington, Duke* / Sophisticated lady: *Ellington, Duke* / Harlem air shaft: *Ellington, Duke* / Me and you: *Ellington, Duke* / Concerto for cootie: *Ellington, Duke* / My greatest mistake: *Ellington, Duke* / Johnny come lately: *Ellington, Duke* / Sepla panorama: *Ellington, Duke* / Cotton tail: *Ellington, Duke* / Don't get around much anymore: *Ellington, Duke* / Blue goose: *Ellington, Duke* / C Jam blues: *Ellington, Duke* / Pitter panther patter: *Ellington, Duke* / Raincheck: *Ellington, Duke* / Hayfoot, strawfoot: *Ellington, Duke* / Moon mist: *Ellington, Duke* / Morning glory: *Ellington, Duke* / Saratoga swing: *Ellington, Duke*
CD Set ______ **EMPRESS 1003**
Empress / Jul '96 / Koch

WE HAVE ALL THE TIME IN THE WORLD (The Pure Genius Of Louis Armstrong)
What a wonderful world / C'est si bon / Blueberry hill / It don't mean a thing if it ain't got that swing / Mack the knife / Cabaret / Tiger rag / I'm just a lucky so and so / Hello Dolly / Georgia on my mind / Moon river / Nobody knows the trouble I've seen / Back o' town blues / Faithful hussar / Mood indigo / Jeepers creepers / Go down Moses / Only you (and you alone) / When the saints go marching in / We have all the time in the world
CD ______ **CDEMTV 89**
EMI / Nov '94 / EMI

WEST END BLUES (Armstrong, Louis Hot Five)
CD ______ **CD 14530**
Jazz Portraits / Jan '94 / Jazz Music

WEST END BLUES (1926-1933)
CD ______ **IGOCD 2035**
Indigo / Dec '95 / ADA / Direct

WEST END BLUES 1926-1933
CD ______ **158722**
Archives / Apr '97 / Discovery

WHAT A WONDERFUL WORLD
What a wonderful world / Cabaret / Home fire / Dream a little dream of me / Give me your kisses (I'll give you my heart) / Sunshine of love / Hello brother / There must be a way / Fantastic, that's you / I guess I'll get the papers and go home / Hellzapoppin'
CD ______ **JHR 73507**
Jazz Hour / Sep '93 / Cadillac / Jazz Music / Target/BMG

WHAT A WONDERFUL WORLD
What a wonderful world / Everybody's talkin' (echoes) / Boy from New Orleans / We shall overcome / Creator has a master plan / Mood indigo / This black cat has nine lives / My one and only love / His father wore long hair / Give peace a chance
CD ______ **ND 88310**
Bluebird / Nov '88 / BMG

WHAT A WONDERFUL WORLD
What a wonderful world / Jeepers creepers / Georgia on my mind / On the sunny side of the street / Cabaret / Hello Dolly / Lazy river / When you're smiling / Whiffenpoof song / Blueberry Hill / La vie en rose / I can't give you anything but love / When it's sleepy time down South / Surrender dear / Some of these days / Exactly like you
CD ______ **PLATCD 304**
Platinum / Apr '88 / Prism

WHAT A WONDERFUL WORLD
Down by the riverside / Swing low, sweet chariot / What a wonderful world / Georgia on my mind / Moon river / Hello Dolly / C'est si bon / Cabaret / Mack the knife / Blueberry Hill / Basin Street blues / When the saints go marching in
CD ______ **12723**
Laserlight / Apr '96 / Target/BMG

YOU RASCAL YOU
When the saints go marching in / I'm confessin' that I love you / Our Monday date / You are my lucky star / As long as you'll be dead if you die / Red nose / Lyin' to myself / Solitude / Shoe shine boy / So little time / I double dare you / Love walked in / Public melody number one / True confession / I'm thankful / Red sails in the sunset / Eventide / Yours and mine / Hear me talkin' to ya / Save it pretty Mama / (I'll be glad when you're dead) you rascal you / When it's sleepy time down South
CD ______ **RAJCD 821**
Empress / Mar '97 / Koch

Army Air Forces Overseas ...

FAREWELL PERFORMANCES (Army Air Forces Overseas Orchestra)
CD ______ **HCD 248**
Hindsight / May '94 / Jazz Music / Target/ BMG

Army Of Lovers

GODS OF EARTH & HEAVEN
CD ______ **5191334**
Polydor / Jul '93 / PolyGram

Arnaz, Desi

BIG BANDS OF HOLLYWOOD (Arnaz, Desi Orchestra & Chico Marx Orchestra)
CD ______ **15767**
Laserlight / Jul '92 / Target/BMG

Arnaz, Lucie

JUST IN TIME
Lover / 'S Wonderful / Slow dancing / Sorry 'bout the whole darn thing / I love to dance/ I got lost in his arms / Things we did last summer / View from here / I'm beginning to see the light/Moonglow / My foolish heart / Just in time / Recipe for love / Another you / Witchcraft / Quiereme mucho / Make someone happy / Blue skies
CD ______ **CCD 4573**
Concord Jazz / Nov '93 / New Note/ Pinnacle

Arnez, Chico

ESSENTIAL SALSA (Arnez, Chico & His Cubana Brass)
Rhythm is gonna get you / Mama you can't go / Do the salsa / Get on your feet / Girl from Brazil / Jezebel / 1-2-3 / Live for loving you / That's my desire / Oye mi canto (hear my voice) / Cheeky Chico / What goes

around / 18th Century salsa / Specialization / Real wild house / Go away / Conga
CD CDMFP 6174
Music For Pleasure / Sep '95 / EMI

Arnold

BARN TAPES, THE
Float my boat / Calling Ira Jones / Face / Dog on the stairs / Windsor park / Sun / 2 Chairs / Medication time
CD CRECD 218
Creation / May '97 / 3mv/Vital

Arnold, Billy Boy

BACK WHERE I BELONG
CD ALCD 4815
Alligator / Nov '93 / ADA / CM / Direct

CHECKIN' IT OUT (The 1977 London Sessions)
Dirty mother fucker / Don't stay out all night / 1-2-99 / Riding the el / Just to know / Christmas time / I wish you would / Ah'w baby / Sweet Miss Bea / Blue and lonesome / Eldorado Cadillac / Mary Bernice / It's great to be rich / Just a dream / Catfish
CD NEBCD 850
Sequel / Aug '96 / BMG

ELDORADO CADILLAC
CD ALCD 4836
Alligator / Nov '95 / ADA / CM / Direct

GOING TO CHICAGO
CD TCD 5018
Testament / Jul '95 / ADA / Koch

Arnold, Eddy

CATTLE CALL/THEREBY HANGS A TALE
Streets of Laredo / Cool water / Cattle call / Leanin' on the old top rail / Ole faithful / Cowboy's dream / Wayward wind / Tumbling tumbleweeds / Cowpoke / Where the mountains meet the sky / Sierra Sue / Carry me back to the Lone Prairie / Jim I wore a tie today / Tom Dooley / Nellie sits a waitin' / Tennessee stud / Battle of Little Big Horn / Wreck of ol' 97 / Red headed stranger / Johnny Reb / Riders in the sky / Boot Hill / Ballad of Davy Crockett / Partners / Jesse James
CD BCD 15441
Bear Family / Apr '90 / Direct / Rollercoaster / Swift

ESSENTIAL EDDY ARNOLD, THE
It's a sin / I'll hold you my heart (till I can hold you in my arms) / Don't rob another man's castle / Eddy's song / I really don't want to know / Make the world go away / Molly darling / Just call me lonesome / Tip of my fingers / Cattle call / What's he doing in my world / Anytime / I want to go with you / Somebody like me / Take me in your arms and hold me / Lonely again / Turn the world around / Then you tell me goodbye / That's what I get for loving you / You don't miss a thing
CD 07863668542
RCA Nashville / Aug '96 / BMG

Arnold, Harry

HARRY ARNOLD
CD ANC 9097
Ancha / Aug '94 / Cadillac / Jazz Music / Wellard

PREMIARI - HARRY ARNOLD & HIS SWEDISH RADIO BAND
CD ANC 9501
Ancha / Dec '94 / Cadillac / Jazz Music / Wellard

Arnold, Kokomo

KING OF THE BOTTLENECK GUITAR 1934-1937
CD BLE 592502
Black & Blue / Nov '92 / Discovery / Koch / Wellard

Arnold, P.P.

BEST OF P.P. ARNOLD, THE (Kafunta/ First Lady Of Immediate)
(If you think) you're groovy / Something beautiful happened / Born to be together / Am I still dreaming / First cut is the deepest / Everything's gonna be alright / Treat me like a lady / Would you believe / Speak to me / God only knows / Eleanor Rigby / Yesterday / Angel of the morning / It'll never happen again / As tears go by / To love somebody / Dreamin' / If you see what I mean / Though it hurts me badly / Welcome home / Life is but nothing / Time has come
CD SEECD 235
See For Miles/C5 / Oct '88 / Pinnacle

Arnold, Wayne

TOUGH LIFE
She makes me feel good / Keep giving your love / Ready when you are / Just take me back / Lucky tough life / You got what I need / Love is on your side / Everything reminds me / Love storm / You're the reason / All or nothing / Right back into love / Closer / How long does it take
CD CD 013
ATR / Sep '92 / Beechwood/BMG

Arnoux, Viviane

CHEVAL ROUGE (Arnoux, Viviane & F. Michaud)
CD 829062
BUDA / Jul '95 / Discovery

Arnstrom, Kenneth

SAXCESS
CD NCD 8836
Phontastic / Dec '95 / Cadillac / Jazz Music / Wellard

Arranmore

BY REQUEST
CD FE 1418
Folk Era / Dec '94 / ADA / CM

LIVE
CD FE 1405
Folk Era / Nov '94 / ADA / CM

Arrested Development

3 YEARS, 5 MONTHS AND 2 DAYS IN THE LIFE OF...
Man's final frontier / Mama's always on stage / People everyday / Blues happy / Mr. Wendal / Children play with earth / Raining revolution / Fishin' for religion / Give a man a fish / U / Eave of reality / Natural / Dawn of the dreads / Tennessee / Washed away
CD CCD 1929
Cooltempo / May '92 / EMI

UNPLUGGED
Time / Give a man a fish / Gettin' / Natural / Searchin' for one soul / Raining revolution / Fishin' 4 religion / Mama's always on stage / U / Mr. Wendal / People everyday / Time / Give a man a fish (Instrumental) / Gettin' (instrumental) / Natural (Instrumental) / Searchin' for one soul (Instrumental) / Raining revolution (Instrumental) / Mama's always on stage (Instrumental) / U (Instrumental)
CD CTCD 33
Cooltempo / Apr '93 / EMI

ZINGALAMDUNI
WMFW (We must fight to win) / United minds / Ache'n for acres / United front / Africa's inside me / Pride / Shell / Mr. Landlord / Warm sentiments / Drum / In the sunshine / Kneelin' at my altar / Fountain of youth / Ease my mind / Praisin' u
CD CTCD 42
Cooltempo / Jun '94 / EMI

Arrow

BEST OF ARROW, THE
Slouch hat / Memories of Norway / Memories of Jaren / Evening breakfast / Kirsi
CD 100121 CD
Red Bullet / Sep '88 / Jet Star

CARRIBEAN PARTY, A (The Best Of Arrow)
CD AHLCD 45
Hit / May '97 / Grapevine/PolyGram

OUTRAGEOUS
CD 040 CD
Arrow / Jan '94 / Jet Star

PHAT
CD ARROW 0043CD
Arrow / Dec '95 / Jet Star

RIDE DE RIDDIM
CD ARROW 0045CD
Arrow / Jan '97 / Jet Star

Arroyo, Joe

REBELLION (Arroyo, Joe Y La verdad)
Yamulemao / Rebellion / Bam bam / Mary / La vuelta / Musa original / El coquero / El maletero / Son apretao / Echao pa'lante / Tumbatecho / En horabuena / Pan de arroz / De clavel / El barbero / Rosa Angelina
CD WCD 012
World Circuit / Jul '89 / ADA / Cadillac / Direct / New Note/Pinnacle

Arsenal FC

GOOD OLD ARSENAL (Various Artists)
Good old Arsenal / Boys from Highbury / Come on you gunners / Arsenal / Arsenal we're on your side / Here we go again / Arsenal rap / Highbury sunshine / Gooneroonie / Ooh ooh Tony Adams / Charlie George Calypso / Fever pitch / Arriverdici Liam / Gus Caesar rap / One night at Anfield / Roll out the red carpet / Kings of London / Victory song 1993 / Highbury heartbeat / Ian Wright Wright Wright / I wish I could play like Charlie George
CD CDGAFFER 1
Cherry Red / Nov '95 / Pinnacle

Arson Garden

WISTERIA
CD ASKD 66013
Vertebrae / Nov '92 / Vital

Art Bears

HOPES AND FEARS
CD RERABCD 2
ReR/Recommended / Aug '96 / ReR Megacorp / RTM/Disc

WINTER SONGS/THE WORLD AS IT IS TODAY
CD RERABCD
ReR/Recommended / Aug '96 / ReR Megacorp / RTM/Disc

Art Connection

STOLEN MOMENTS
CD BEST 1035CD
Acoustic Music / Nov '93 / ADA

Art Ensemble Of Chicago

ART ENSEMBLE OF CHICAGO (Art Ensemble Of Chicago & Fontella Bass)
CD 500172
Musidisc / Nov '93 / Discovery

DREAMING OF THE MASTERS SUITE
CD DIW 854
DIW / Mar '92 / Cadillac / Harmonia Mundi

EDA WOBU
CD JMY 10082
JMY / Aug '91 / Harmonia Mundi

FULL FORCE
CD 8291972
ECM / Oct '86 / New Note/Pinnacle

SPIRITUAL, THE
CD BLCD 760219
Black Lion / May '97 / Cadillac / Jazz Music / Koch / Wellard

THIRD DECADE
CD 8232132
ECM / Feb '85 / New Note/Pinnacle

TUTANKHAMUN
CD BLCD 760199
Black Lion / Apr '95 / Cadillac / Jazz Music / Koch / Wellard

URBAN BUSHMEN
CD 8293942
ECM / Jul '85 / New Note/Pinnacle

Art Ensemble Of Soweto

AMERICA-SOUTH AFRICA
CD DIW 848
DIW / Aug '91 / Cadillac / Harmonia Mundi

Art Lande

RUBISA PATROL
Celestial guests / Many chinas / Jaimi's birthday song / Romany / Corinthian melodies / For Nancy / Monk in his simple room
CD 5198752
ECM / Mar '94 / New Note/Pinnacle

Art Of Noise

AMBIENT COLLECTION, THE
Opus 4 / Nothing was going to stop them / Island / Ode to Don Jose / Roundabout 727/Ransom in the sand / Robinson Crusoe / Art of love / Opus for 4 / Crusoe / Camilla / Counterpoint / Eye of a needle / Nation rejects
CD WOLCD 1012
China / Apr '91 / Pinnacle

BEST OF THE ART OF NOISE, THE
Beat box / Moments in love / Close (to the edit) / Peter Gunn / Paranoimia / Legacy / Dragnet '88 / Kiss / Something always happens / Opus 4
CD WOLCD 1027
China / Aug '92 / Pinnacle

DAFT
Love / Time for fear, A (who's afraid) / Beatbox (diversion 1) / Army now / Donna / Memento / How to kill / Realization / Who's afraid (of the Art of Noise) / Moments in love / Bright noise / Flesh in armour / Comes and goes / Snapshot / Close (to the edit) / (Three fingers of) Love
CD 4509947472
ZTT / Mar '94 / Warner Music

DRUM 'N' BASS COLLECTION
CD WOLCD 1072
China / Oct '96 / Pinnacle

FON MIXES
CD WOLCD 1023
China / Nov '91 / Pinnacle

IN NO SENSE I NONSENSE
Galleons of stone / Dragnet / Fin du temps / How rapid / Opus for four / Debut / EFL / Ode to Don Jose / Day at the races / Counterpoint / Roundabout 727 / Ransom on the sand / Roller 1 / Nothing was going to stop them then, anyway / Crusoe / One earth
CD WOLCD 1017
China / Jul '91 / Pinnacle

IN VISIBLE SILENCE
Opus for four / Paranoimia / Eye of a needle / Legs / Slip of the tongue / Backbeat / Instruments of darkness / Peter Gunn: *Art Of Noise & Duane Eddy* / Camilla / Chameleon's dish
CD WOLCD 1016
China / Jul '91 / Pinnacle

STATE OF THE ART (3CD Set)
Opus / OPus for 4 / Nothing was going to stop / Crusoe / Island / Camilla / Ode to Don Jose / Counterpoint / Roundabout 727 / Eye of a neddle / Robinson Crusoe / Nation rejects / Art of love / Instruments of darkness / Yebo (interlude 1) / Roller 10 / Back to back beat / Shades of paranoimia / Ode to a DJ / Catwalk / Dragnet and Peter Gunn / Legs / LEF / I of the needle / Art of slow love / No sun / Something always happens / Ode to Don Jose / Art Of Love / Yebo / Opus 4 / Island / Camilla the old old story / Kiss / Eye of the needle / Peter Gunn / Crusoe
CD Set WOLCD 1075
China / Aug '97 / Pinnacle

WHO'S AFRAID OF THE ART OF NOISE
Time for fear / Beat box / Snapshot / Close / Who's afraid (of the Art of Noise) / Moments in love / Memento / Hard to kill / Realization / Liquid sky
CD 4509947462
ZTT / Mar '94 / Warner Music

Art Of Trance

WILDLIFE ON ONE
CD PLAT 25CD
Platipus / Nov '96 / Prime / SRD

Artaek, Lagun

SONGS FROM THE BASQUE COUNTRY (Artaek, Lagun Groupe)
CD ARN 64223
Arion / Jun '93 / ADA / Discovery

Artango

DOUBLES JEUX
CD ARN 62304
Arion / Jul '95 / ADA / Discovery

PIANO - BANDONEON
CD ARN 62245
Arion / Aug '93 / ADA / Discovery

Artch

ANOTHER RETURN
CD ACTCD 5
Active / Jul '91 / Pinnacle

Artefakto

DES CONSTRUCTION
CD CDZOT 113
Zoth Ommog / Oct '94 / Cargo / Plastic Head

Arthea

PASSAGES
CD SM 106550
Wergo / Apr '97 / ADA / Cadillac / Harmonia Mundi

Arthur

RIGHT OFF
CD TGT 014CD
Target / Jul '94 / SRD

Arthur, Dave

MORNING STANDS ON TIPTOE/THE LARK IN THE MORNING (Arthur, Dave & Toni)
Maiden came from London town / Morning stands on tiptoe / Female rambling sailor / Padstow drinking song / Guilty sea captain / Eynsham poaching song / Green grass / Barley grain for me / Jolly ploughboy / Blackburn poachers / John Peel / Bold Robinson / Green broom / Bendigo champion of England / Football match / All frolicking I'll give over / Death of Queen Jane / Creeping Jane / Merchant's daughter of Bristol / Bold dragoon / Cold blows the winter's wind / Lark in the morning / Poor old horse / Hey John Barleycorn / Bedlam / Admiral Benbow / Father father build me a boat / Press gang / Six jolly miners
CD HILLCD 18
Wooded Hill / May '97 / Direct / World Serpent

Arthur, Davey

CELTIC SIDE SADDLE
Celtic side saddle / Hail Mary full of grace / Galway farmer / Fair city set / Emigrant / Over the ocean / Slip 'n' slides / Euston station / Mad lady and me / Walk / Sit you down / Ness pipers / Sister Marcella
CD PRKCD 26
Park / Aug '94 / Pinnacle

Arthur, Joseph

BIG CITY SECRETS
Big city secret / Mercedes / Mikel K / Good about me / Daddy's on prozac / Marina / Birthday card / Crying like a man / Porcupine / Dessert / Haunted eyes / Bottle of you
CD CDRW 64
Realworld / Jun '97 / EMI

Arthur, Neil

SUITCASE
Breaking my heart / I love, I hate / Suitcase / Jumping like a kangaroo / I know these things about you / Heaven / That's what love is like / One day, one time / Jukebox theory / Beach
CD __________ **CDCHR 6065**
Chrysalis / Feb '94 / EMI

Artifacts

THAT'S THEM
Art of scratch / Arts of facts / 31 bumrush / To ya chest / Where yo skillz at / Collaboration of mics / Ultimate / It's gettin hot / This is da way / Interview / Break it down / Skwad training / Ingredients to time travel / Return to da wrongside / Who's this / Ultimate
CD __________ **7567927532**
Atlantic / Apr '97 / Warner Music

Artificial Peace

DISCOGRAPH
CD __________ **LF 038**
Plastic Head / Jun '92 / Plastic Head

Artillery

BY INHERITANCE
7.00 from Tashkent / Beneath the clay / Bombfood / Life in bondage / Razamanaz / Khomaniac / By inheritance / Don't believe / Equal at first / Back in the trash
CD __________ **RO 93972**
Roadrunner / May '90 / PolyGram

Artisan

BREATHING SPACE
CD __________ **FESTIVAL 9CD**
Festival / Oct '93 / ADA / CM / Discovery / Roots

BYGONE CHRISTMAS
CD __________ **BF 112CD**
Bygone Films / Nov '96 / ADA

OUR BACKYARD
CD __________ **BOING 9604CD**
Bedspring / Nov '96 / ADA

ROCKING AT THE END OF TIME
CD __________ **FESTIVAL 7CD**
Festival / '92 / ADA / CM / Discovery / Roots

WINGS
What's the use of wings / Talk to me / Curupay freijo / Feel the rhyme / Mabel / Trivia / Under the misteltoe / Mad old Mike / Buy and buy / One minute song
CD __________ **TERRCD 006**
Terra Nova / Feb '97 / Direct

Arts & Decay

TRAIL OF TEARS
CD __________ **HY 39100422CD**
Hyperium / Nov '92 / Cargo / Plastic Head

Artwoods

100 OXFORD STREET
Sweet Mary / If I ever get my hands on you / Goodbye sisters / Oh my love / I take what I want / Big city / She knows what to do / I'm looking for a saxophonist / Keep looking / I keep forgettin' / I feel good / One more heartache / Down in the valley / Be my lady / Stop and think it over / Don't cry no more
CD __________ **EDCD 107**
Edsel / Mar '83 / Pinnacle

Arundel, Jeff

RIDE THE RIDE
Ride the ride / Garden / Down on blue / Magdalena / Left at last / My last stand / Heart of stone / Harmon killebrew / Only gone / Slow train / Elmwood Avenue
CD __________ **FIENDCD 799**
Demon / Aug '97 / Pinnacle

Arvo Part

DE PROFUNDIS
CD __________ **HMU 907182**
Harmonia Mundi / Mar '97 / Cadillac / Harmonia Mundi

Arzachel

ARZACHEL
CD __________ **DOCD 1983**
Drop Out / Oct '96 / Pinnacle

As One

ART OF PROPHECY
Eclectricity / Relentless / Tomorrow people / Glow / Hideout / Space party ethics / Destination other / Theme from Op-Art / You who never arrived / Freefall / Hustler / Splendor solis / Return of the Kingpin / Farewell
CD __________ **SHLD 102CD**
Sheild / Mar '97 / Vital

CELESTIAL SOUL
Celestial soul / Ikiru / Interstellar / Dhyana / Laetoli / Hybrid / We no longer understand / Renaissance / Ariois / Return to Talimakan / What might have beeen
CD __________ **ELEC 26CD**
New Electronica / Apr '96 / Beechwood/ BMG / Plastic Head

IN WITH THEIR ARPS AND MOOGS...
Epic / Chiaro / Last of the almoravids / Electric hymn / Kiss / Sphere of the fixed stars / Triumphant / Queen constance / Message in Herbie's shirts / Short track about love / Hyeres
CD __________ **CLR 430CD**
Clear / May '97 / Prime / RTM/Disc

REFLECTIONS
Mihara / Meridian / Orchila / Shamballa / Dance of the uighurs / Majik jar / Star gaze / Soleil levant / Lunate / Asa nisi masa / Moon over the moab
CD __________ **ELEC 5CD**
New Electronica / Apr '96 / Beechwood/ BMG / Plastic Head

As Serenity Fades

EARTHBORN
CD __________ **CDAR 018**
Adipocre / May '94 / Plastic Head

Asana

TRIKUTI
CD __________ **NH 005**
Neu Harmony / Jun '97 / Cargo

Asante

ASANTE MODE
Intro...Asante mode / Look what you've done / All about you / Don't push me away / Why / Don't say goodnight / People get ready / Prelude...what goes on / What's the plan / Dopest Ethiopian / Interlude...the phone call / Cathin' feelins
CD __________ **4811342**
Columbia / Nov '95 / Sony

Ascension

BROADCAST (2CD Set)
CD Set __________ **SX 030CD**
Shock / Oct '96 / Cargo

Asgard

SONGS OF G
CD __________ **BEST 1042CD**
Acoustic Music / Nov '93 / ADA

Ash

1977
Lose control / Goldfinger / Girl from Mars / I'd give you anything / Gone the dream / Kung fu / Let it flow / Innocent smile / Angel interceptor / Lost in you / Dark side light side
CD __________ **INFECT 40CD**
Infectious / May '96 / RTM/Disc

INTERVIEW DISC
CD __________ **ASH 1CD**
Wax / Feb '97 / RTM/Disc / Total/BMG

LIVE AT THE WIRELESS
Darkside lightside / Girl from Mars / Oh yeah / T Rex / I'd give you anything / Kung fu / What Deaner was talking about / Goldfinger / Petrol / Clear invitation to the dance
CD __________ **DEATH 3**
Death Star / Feb '97 / RTM/Disc

TRAILOR
CD __________ **INFECT 14CD**
Infectious / Oct '94 / RTM/Disc

Ash, Daniel

COMING DOWN
Blue moon / Coming down fast / Walk this way / Closer to you / Day tripper / This love / Blue angel / Me and my shadow / Candy darling / Sweet little liar / Not so fast / Coming down
CD __________ **BEGA 114CD**
Beggars Banquet / Feb '91 / RTM/Disc / Warner Music

FOOLISH THINGS DESIRED
CD __________ **BBQCD 129**
Beggars Banquet / May '93 / RTM/Disc / Warner Music

Ash Ra Tempel

NEW AGE OF EARTH (Ashra)
Sunrain / Ocean of tenderness / Deep distance / Nightdust
CD __________ **CDV 2080**
Virgin / Jun '90 / EMI
CD __________ **14505**
Spalax / Feb '97 / ADA / Cargo / Direct / Discovery / Greyhound

SEVEN UP (Ash Ra Tempel & Timothy Leary)
CD __________ **14249**
Spalax / Oct '96 / ADA / Cargo / Direct / Discovery / Greyhound

STARRING ROSI
CD __________ **14247**
Spalax / Jan '97 / ADA / Cargo / Direct / Discovery / Greyhound

SUNRAIN (Ashra)
Sunrain / Midnight on mars / Morgana da capo / Oasis / Club cannibal / Screamer / Mistral / 77 Slightly delayed / Ice train / Deep distance / Ocean of tenderness / Phantasus / Blackouts
CD __________ **CDOVD 463**
Virgin / Jan '96 / EMI

TROPICAL HEAT (Ashra)
Mosquito dance / Tropical heat / Pretty papaya / Nights in sweat / Don't stop the fan / Monsoon
CD __________ **CDBT 138**
Thunderbolt / Feb '91 / TKO Magnum

WALKIN' THE DESERT (Ashra)
First movement / Second movement / Third movement / Fourth movement / Desert
CD __________ **CDTB 086**
Thunderbolt / Apr '90 / TKO Magnum

Ash, Vic

EYES HAVE IT, THE (Ash, Vic Quartet)
Touch of your lips / Bernie's tune / I thought about you / November rose / Between the devil and the deep blue sea / Silver minor / Namely you / Soon / Carnaval samba / Nancy with the laughing face / Eyes have it
CD __________ **ABCD 3**
AB / Oct '96 / Cadillac

Asha, Ras Imru

SPIRITUAL WARRIOR
CD __________ **ROTCD 010**
Reggae On Top / Jun '96 / Jet Star / SRD

Asha Vida

AS ONE OF ONE
CD __________ **IC 128CD**
Icon / Jul '97 / Pinnacle

Ashbrook, Karen

HILLS OF ERIN
CD __________ **MMCD 207**
Maggie's Music / Dec '94 / ADA / CM

Ashby, Harold

I'M OLD FASHIONED
CD __________ **STCD 545**
Stash / '92 / ADA / Cadillac / CM / Direct / Jazz Music

ON THE SUNNY SIDE OF THE STREET
Out of nowhere / There is no greater love / Honeysuckle rose / Pennies from heaven / It's the talk of the town / Satin doll / These foolish things / On the sunny side of the street / Scuffin' / In my solitude / Just squeeze me
CD __________ **CDSJP 385**
Timeless Jazz / Oct '92 / New Note/ Pinnacle

VIKING, THE
CD __________ **GEMCD 160**
Gemini / '87 / Cadillac

WHAT AM I HERE FOR (Ashby, Harold Quartet)
CD __________ **CRISS 1054CD**
Criss Cross / May '92 / Cadillac / Direct / Vital/SAM

Asher D

RAGAMUFFIN HIP-HOP (Asher D & Daddy Freddy)
CD __________ **MOLCD 999**
Music Of Life / Jan '95 / Grapevine/ PolyGram

STILL KICKIN'
CD __________ **ASHER 22CD**
Music Of Life / Jul '91 / Grapevine/ PolyGram

Asher, Meira

DISSECTED
Sida / Fair and ruddy / Give peace / Psalm 19 / Dissect me / Maligora the sand child / Daddy came / Taht a' shams
CD __________ **CRAM 094**
Crammed Discs / Mar '97 / Grapevine/ PolyGram / New Note/Pinnacle / Prime / RTM/Disc

Ashford & Simpson

BEEN FOUND (Ashford & Simpson/ Maya Angelou)
CD __________ **HOP 45122**
Ichiban / Nov '96 / Direct / Koch

GOSPEL ACCORDING TO...ASHFORD & SIMPSON (Count Your Blessings)
I'll be there for you / Love it away / Mighty mighty love / Make it work again / I'm not that tough / Street opera / Street opera / Street opera / Street opera / Street opera / Solid / Cherish forever more / Tonight we escape (we make love) / Still such a thing / Count your blessings
CD __________ **CTMCD 306**
EMI / Feb '97 / EMI

SOLID
Solid / Jungle / Honey I love you / Babies / Closest to love / Cherish forever more / Tonight we escape (we make love) / Outta the world
CD __________ **MUSCD 501**
MCI Original Masters / Sep '94 / Disc / THE

Ashkaru

MOTHER TONGUE
Maray-Wollelaye / Tigel / Ring my faith / Bellema / Sigh like you do / Labour of love / Must give back / Enat / If I chose / Know joy
CD __________ **3202142**
Triloka / Dec '95 / New Note/Pinnacle

Ashkhabad

CITY OF LOVE
Ayrylsa / Aglar men / Bayaty / Balam seni / Shalakho / Yaman ykbal / Bibining / Aisha / Kakan gyz / Ketshpelek / Garagum keshdeleri
CD __________ **CDRW 34**
Realworld / Apr '93 / EMI

Ashley, Steve

FAMILY ALBUM, THE
CD __________ **RGFCD 002**
Road Goes On Forever / Nov '91 / Direct

Ashtabula

RIVER OF MANY DEAD FISH, THE
CD __________ **SB 73CD**
Siltbreeze / Jun '97 / Cargo / Vital

Ashton, Susan

WAKENED BY THE WIND
Down on my knees / No one knows / My heart / Benediction / Ball and chain / I hear you / Land of nod / In my father's hands / In amazing grace land / Suffer in silence / Beyond justice to mercy
CD __________ **SPD 1259**
Alliance Music / Aug '95 / EMI

Ashtray Boy

EVERYMAN'S 4TH DIMENSION, THE
CD __________ **AJAX 057CD**
Ajax / Dec '96 / Cargo

HONEYMOON SUITE, THE
Ananda marga / Shirley MacLaine / Observatory Hill / There is a fountain / Time for a baby / How Charles destroyed the inland sea / Infidel / Little nature child / Hit / Love in a bakery / Honeymoon suite
CD __________ **SR 1003**
Scout / Jan '96 / Koch

Asia

ALPHA
Don't cry / Smile has left your eyes / Never in a million years / My own time (I'll do what I want) / Heat goes on / Eye to eye / Last to know / True colours / Midnight sun / Open your eyes
CD __________ **GED 04008**
Geffen / Nov '96 / BMG

AQUA
Aqua part 1 / Who will stop the rain / Back in town / Love under fire / Someday / Little rich boy / Voice of reason / Lay down your arms / Crime of the heart / Far cry / Don't call me / Heaven on earth / Aqua part 2
CD __________ **WKFMXD 180**
FM Coast To Coast / Feb '92 / Revolver

ARCHIVA VOL.1
Heart of gold / Tears / Fight against the tide / We fall apart / Mariner's dream / Boys from diamond city / ALO / Reality / I can't wait a lifetime / Dusty road / I believe / Ginger
CD __________ **LV 104CD**
Resurgence / Nov '96 / Pinnacle

ARCHIVA VOL.2
Obsession / Moon under the water / Love like the video / Don't come to me / Smoke that thunders / Satellite blues / Showdown / That season / Can't tell these walls / Higher you climb / Right to cry / Armenia
CD __________ **LV 105CD**
Resurgence / Dec '96 / Pinnacle

ARENA
CD __________ **CDVEST 69**
Bulletproof / Mar '96 / Pinnacle

ARIA
CD __________ **CDVEST 8**
Bulletproof / May '94 / Pinnacle

ASIA NOW (Live In Nottingham 1990)
Wildest dreams / Sole survivor / Don't cry / Voice of America / Time again / Prayin' 4 a miracle / Smile has left your eyes / Only time will tell / Days like these / Heat goes on / Go / Heat of the moment / Open your eyes
CD __________ **BP 253CD**
Blueprint / Mar '97 / Pinnacle

LIVE IN KOLN
Go / Back in town / Sad situation / Rememberance day / Someday / Heat goes on / Anytime / Sole survivor / Summer / Feels like love / Little rich boy / Desire / Who will stop the rain / Military man / Only time will tell / Heat of the moment

CD ________ BP 254CD
Blueprint / Jul '97 / Pinnacle

LIVE IN MOSCOW
Time again / Sole survivor / Don't cry / Only time will tell / Rock 'n' roll dream / Starless / Book of Saturday / Kari-Anne / Open your eyes / Heat of the moment / Heat goes on / Go / Smile has left your eyes (parts I &II)
CD ________ ESMCD 174
Essential / Aug '96 / BMG

LIVE IN OSAKA 1992 (2CD Set)
Go / Band intro / Lay down your arms / Love under fire / Rock 'n' roll dreams / Geoff Downes solo / Video kills radio star / Little rich boy / Voice of America / Aqua / Who will stop the rain / Wildest dreams / Back in town / Don't cry / Someday / Steve Howe solo / Voice of reason / Only time will tell / Heat goes on / Far cry
CD Set ________ BP 252CD
Blueprint / May '97 / Pinnacle

Asiabeat

ASIABEAT
CD ________ CDKUCK 11096
Kuckuck / Jun '92 / ADA / CM

DRUMUSIQUE
CD ________ DOM 0710162
Domo / Aug '97 / Pinnacle

Asian Dub Foundation

FACTS AND FICTIONS
CD ________ NATCD 58
Nation / Oct '95 / RTM/Disc

Askey, Arthur

BAND WAGGON (Askey, Arthur & Tommy Trinder & Richard Murdoch)
Adolf / (We're gonna hang out the) washing on the Siegfried Line / Big and stinkers moment musical / Worm / Big and stinkers parlour games / Chirrup / Seagull song / Proposal / Kiss me goodnight, Sergeant Major / How ashamed I was / Bee song
CD ________ PASTCD 9729
Flapper / Jan '91 / Pinnacle

BUSY BEE, THE
Bee song / Have a bit of pity on the crooner / Knitting / Chirrup / Two little doodlebugs / Worm / C'est la guerre / Guest / I pulled myself together / Ding dong bell / Ballad / She was very shy / Sarah Sarah / Follow the white line / FDR Jones / Seagull song / Minding the baby / Thingy mumm bob / Bandwagon
CD ________ RAJCD 885
Empress / May '97 / Koch

Askill/Cleworth/Lagos/Piper

TAIKO
CD ________ BSCD 15021
Black Sun / Apr '96 / ADA

Asleep At The Wheel

PASTURE PRIME
Across the valley from the Alamo / Switchin' in the kitchen / Write your own song / Cotton eyed Joe / Baby / Shorty / That chick's too young to fry / Big beaver / This is the way we make a broken heart / Deep water / Natural thing to do / Liars moon / That's your red wagon
CD ________ FIENDCD 44
Demon / Mar '91 / Pinnacle

VERY BEST OF ASLEEP AT THE WHEEL
Cherokee boogie / I'll never get out of this world alive / Space buggy / Letter that Johnny Walker read / Let me go home whiskey / Trouble in mind / Runnin' after fools / Miles and miles of Texas / Route 66 / My baby thinks she's a train / Am I high / Ragtime Annie / Somebody stole his body / When love goes wrong / Louisiana 1927 / Ain't nobody here but us chickens / One o'clock jump
CD ________ SEECD 81
See For Miles/C5 / Apr '93 / Pinnacle

Asmus Tietchens

ARCANE DEVICE
CD ________ SA 03
Stilleandacht / Nov '93 / Plastic Head

Asmussen, Svend

MUSICAL MIRACLE VOL.1 1935-1940
CD ________ PHONTCD 9306
Phontastic / Dec '94 / Cadillac / Jazz Music / Wellard

PHENOMENAL FIDDLER
CD ________ PHONTCD 9310
Phontastic / Jul '96 / Cadillac / Jazz Music / Wellard

SLUKAFTER IN THE TIVOLI-COPENHAGEN 1984
Believe it, beloved / Nadja / Exactly like you / Hot house / Body and soul / Coconut calypso / Someone to watch over me / Barney goin' / Out of nowhere / Pent-up house / Things ain't what they used to be
CD ________ PHONT CD 8804
Phontastic / Apr '90 / Cadillac / Jazz Music / Wellard

SVEND ASMUSSEN 1942 VOL.7
CD ________ THORANR 7
Hep / Oct '94 / Cadillac / Jazz Music / New Note/Pinnacle / Wellard

TWO OF A KIND (Asmussen, Svend & Stephane Grappelli)
CD ________ STCD 4088
Storyville / Feb '89 / Cadillac / Jazz Music / Wellard

Asocial

TOTAL ASOCIAL
CD ________ FINNREC 011CD
Finn / Jun '96 / Cadillac / Plastic Head

Asoj

SPIRIT OF KLEZMER
CD ________ 341052
Koch International / May '96 / Koch

Asphalt

257 KNOCK OUT
CD ________ DARK 0082
Dark Empire / Feb '95 / SRD

Asphyx

ASPHYX
CD ________ CM 770632
Century Media / May '94 / Plastic Head

CRUSH THE CENOTAPH
CD ________ CM 97232
Century Media / Sep '94 / Plastic Head

GOD CRIES
CD ________ CM 77117CD
Century Media / Mar '96 / Plastic Head

LAST ONE ON EARTH
CD ________ 8497342
Century Media / Nov '92 / Plastic Head

RACK, THE
CD ________ CM 97162
Century Media / Sep '94 / Plastic Head

Assad, Badi

ECHOES OF BRAZIL
CD ________ JD 154
Chesky / May '97 / Discovery / Goldring

Assad, Sergio & Odair

ALMA BRASILEIRA (Brazilian Music For Two Guitars)
CD ________ 7559791792
Nonesuch / Jul '90 / Warner Music

BAROQUE MUSIC FOR TWO GUITARS
CD ________ 7559792922
Nonesuch / Jul '93 / Warner Music

LATIN AMERICAN MUSIC FOR TWO GUITARS
CD ________ 7559792652
Nonesuch / Jan '94 / Warner Music

SAGA DOS MIGRANTES (Music Of The Americas)
CD ________ 7559793652
Nonesuch / Aug '96 / Warner Music

Assassin

DON'T WEAR SUITS
CD ________ JUCCD 01
Juce / May '95 / Grapevine/PolyGram

Asseccoires

VENDETTA
CD ________ EFA 063282
Ausfahrt / Nov '95 / SRD

Assfort

EJACULATION
CD ________ DISCCD 012
Discipline / Sep '95 / Plastic Head

Assia, Lys

SCHWEIZER MADEL
Ganz leis' erklingt musik / Ich habe mir fur heute nacht / Schweizer madel / Sowas tun die Herrn doch / Seit heut' bin ich verliebt / Marchen von Tahiti / Sing, kleiner Kolibri / Von gestern abend bis heute morgen / Tanz' diesen Walzer, Madeleine / Nachts in Paris / Erst kommt musik / Was kostet das Hundchen dort im Fenster / Holland madel / Heute klopft mein herz / Als der schnitter durch das korn ging / Bella Notte / Monsieur Taxi-Chauffeur / Wenn der Pierre tanz mit Madeleine / Refrain / Du bist musik / Die weissen bluten von Tahni / Traumkonzert / Dino / Der erste kuss / Die Welt war nie so schon fur mich / Nach vielen Jahren der Reise / Die Sterne von Venezia / I'll be waiting
CD ________ BCD 16108
Bear Family / Nov '96 / Direct / Rollercoaster / Swift

Associates

POPERA
Party fears two / Club country / Eighteen Carat love affair / Love hangover / Those first impressions / Waiting for the loveboat / Breakfast / Take me to the girl / Heart of glass / Country boy / Rhythm divine / Tell me Easter's on Friday / Q Quarters / Kitchen person / Message oblique speech / White car in Germany
CD ________ 9031724142
WEA / Jan '91 / Warner Music

SULK
It's better this way / Party fears two / Club country / Love hangover / Eighteen carat love affair / Arrogance gave him up / No / Skipping / White car in Germany / Gloomy Sunday / Associate
CD ________ K 2400052
WEA / Jul '88 / Warner Music

Association

1960'S FRENCH EPS COLLECTION, THE
CD ________ 175402
Magic / Jul '97 / Greyhound

DON'T LOOK BACK
CD ________ 60562
Enja / Nov '90 / New Note/Pinnacle / Vital/SAM

Assorted Jellybeans

ASSORTED JELLYBEANS
CD ________ KF 787602
Kung Fu / Jun '97 / Cargo

Assorted Phlavours

PATIENCE
Tell me / Hiding place / Make up your mind / Trust / What you gonna do / Patience / First you said / Don't let go / Tonight / Can't get you off my mind / Love so real / Love ballad / Don't stop / Farewell / Lovin' on the DI / Lovin' you / Patience
CD ________ 4853922
Epic / Mar '97 / Sony

Assuck

ANTICAPITAL
CD ________ CC 005CD
Common Cause / Jun '94 / Plastic Head / SRD

Assumpaco, Itamar

INTERCONTINENTAL
CD ________ MES 159912
Messidor / Apr '93 / ADA / Koch

SAMPA MIDNIGHT
CD ________ MES 158022
Messidor / Feb '93 / ADA / Koch

Astaire, Fred

ASTAIRABLE FRED
CD ________ CDMRS 911
DRG / '88 / Discovery / New Note/Pinnacle

ASTAIRE SINGS
CD ________ AVC 537
Avid / May '94 / Avid/BMG / Koch / THE

ASTAIRE STORY, THE (2CD Set)
Isn't this a lovely day (to be caught in the rain) / Puttin' on the ritz / I used to be colour blind / Continenetal / Let's call the whole thing off / Change partners / 'S wonderful / Lovely to look at / They all laughed / Cheek to cheek / Steppin' out with my baby / Way you look tonight / I've got my eyes on you / Dancing in the dark / Carioca / Nice work if you can get it / New sun in the sky / I won't dance / Fast dances / Top hat, white tie and tails / No strings / I concentrate on you / I'm putting all my eggs in one basket / Fine romance / Night and day / Fascinating rhythm / I love Louisa / Slow dances / Medium dance / They can't take that away from me / You're easy to dance with / Needle in a haystack / So near and yet so far / Foggy day / Oh lady be good / I'm building up to an awful letdown / Not my girl / Jam session
CD Set ________ 8356492
Verve / Apr '89 / PolyGram

CRAZY FEET
Night and day / My one and only / Fascinating rhythm / New sun in the sky / Louisiana / Swiss miss / I'd rather Charleston / High hat / Whichness of the whatness / I've got you on my mind / Puttin' on the Ritz / White heat / Dancing in the dark / Hang on to me / Oh gee, oh gosh / Not my girl / Half of it dearie blues / Babbitt and the bromide / I love Louisa / Funny face / Crazy feet
CD ________ CDAJA 5021
Living Era / Oct '88 / Select

CRAZY FEET
Crazy feet / I used to be colour blind / Fine romance / Yam / I'd rather lead a band / Let's call the whole thing off / Nice work if you can get it / Foggy day / We saw the sea / Let's face the music and dance / Let yourself go / Cheek to cheek / Yam step / They can't take that away from me / I'm putting all my eggs in one basket / Way you look tonight / I'm building up to a awful let down / Pick yourself up / Night and day / Wedding in the spring / You were never lovelier / Shorty George / I'm old fashioned / Dearly beloved
CD ________ RAJCD 856
Empress / Oct '95 / Koch

CREAM OF FRED ASTAIRE, THE
We saw the sea / I'm putting all my eggs in one basket / Puttin' on the Ritz / Way you look tonight / Let's call the whole thing off / Hoops / Hang on to me / I'd rather charleston / Night and day / Crazy feet / Shall we dance / Fine romance / Top hat, white tie and tails / Wedding cake walk / Dig it / Just like taking candy from a baby / I've got you on my mind / Let's face the music and dance / So near and yet so far / Who cares / They all laughed / Isn't this a lovely day (to be caught in the rain) / Slap that bass / Cheek to cheek / I'd rather lead a band
CD ________ PASTCD 7013
Flapper / Aug '93 / Pinnacle

FASCINATING RHYTHM
Shall we dance / Fascinating rhythm / Night and day / Crazy feet / Puttin' on the ritz / My one and only / Babbitt and the bromide / I've got you on my mind / Foggy day / Let's call the whole thing off / New sun in the sky / High hat / Hang on to me / Funny face / They can't take that away from me / Nice work if you can get it
CD ________ HADCD 163
Javelin / May '94 / Henry Hadaway / THE

FINE ROMANCE, A
CD ________ CDD 548
Progressive / May '91 / Jazz Music

FRED ASTAIRE COLLECTOR'S EDITION
CD ________ DVGH 7022
Deja Vu / Apr '95 / THE

FRED ASTAIRE IN HOLLYWOOD
CD ________ AMSC 570
Avid / Jun '96 / Avid/BMG / Koch / THE

LET'S FACE THE MUSIC
Let's face the music and dance / Things are looking up / Way you look tonight / Nice work if you can get it / Poor Mr. Chisolm / Let's call the whole thing off / They all laughed / Shall we dance / My one and only / I'm putting all my eggs in one basket / Piccolino / Pick yourself up / They can't take that away from me / Isn't this a lovely day / No strings I'm fancy free / Fascinating rhythm
CD ________ SUMCD 4049
Summit / Nov '96 / Sound & Media

LET'S FACE THE MUSIC AND DANCE
Change partners / Cheek to cheek / I used to be colour blind / I'm putting all my eggs in one basket / Let's face the music and dance / No strings / Top hat, white tie and tails / Yam / Foggy day / I can't be bothered now / I've got beginner's luck / Let's call the whole thing off / Nice work if you can get it / Shall we dance / Slap that bass / They all laughed / They can't take that away from me / Things are looking up / Poor Mr. Chisholm / Dearly Beloved / Fine romance / I'm old fashioned / Never gonna dance / Pick yourself up / Way you look tonight / You were never lovelier / Since I kissed my baby goodbye
CD ________ CDAJA 5123
Living Era / Mar '94 / Select

LET'S FACE THE MUSIC AND DANCE (All His Greatest Hits)
They can't take that away from me / Isn't this a lovely day / I'm putting all my eggs in one basket / They all laughed / Let's call the whole thing off / Shall we dance / Way you look tonight / Nice work if you can get it / Poor Mr, Chisholm / Let's face the music and dance / Piccolino / I used to be colour blind / Foggy day / My one and only / Pick yourself up / Yam / Let yourself go / Things are looking up / No strings (I am fancy free) / Fascinating rhythm
CD ________ 305512
Hallmark / Oct '96 / Carlton

LOVE OF MY LIFE
CD ________ DHDL 124
Halcyon / Sep '93 / Cadillac / Harmonia Mundi / Jazz Music / Swift / Wellard

PUTTIN' ON THE RITZ
CD ________ BSTCD 9108
Best Compact Discs / May '92 / Complete/Pinnacle

PUTTIN' ON THE RITZ
CD ________ RMB 75010
Remember / Nov '93 / Total/BMG

PUTTIN' ON THE RITZ
CD ________ MCCD 204
Music Club / May '95 / Disc / THE

SONGS FROM THE MOVIES
No strings / Isn't this a lovely day (to be caught in the rain) / Top hat, white tie and tails / Cheek to cheek / Piccolino / We saw the sea / Let yourself go / I'd rather lead a band / I'm putting all my eggs in one basket / Let's face the music and dance / Pick yourself up / Way you look tonight / Fine romance / Bojangles of Harlem / Never gonna dance / I've got beginner's luck / Slap that bass / They all laughed / Let's call the whole thing off / They can't take that away from me / Shall we dance / I can't be bothered now / Things are looking up / Foggy day / Nice work if you can get it
CD ________ PPCD 78115

Past Perfect / Feb '95 / Glass Gramophone Co.

STARRING FRED ASTAIRE
Top hat, white tie and tails / Cheek to cheek / Piccolino / No strings / Pick yourself up / Way you look tonight / Fine romance / Let's call the whole thing off / They can't take that away from me / Shall we dance / I can't be bothered now / Things are looking up / Foggy day / Nice work if you can get it / Let yourself go / Let's face the music and dance / Fascinating rhythm / Night and day / I used to be colour blind / Change partners
CD ___ CD 405
Entertainers / Oct '96 / Target/BMG

STEPPIN' OUT - ASTAIRE SINGS
Steppin' out with my baby / Let's call the whole thing off / Top hat, white tie and tails / They can't take that away from me / Dancing in the dark / 'S wonderful / Way you look tonight / They all laughed / I concentrate on you / Night and day / Fine romance / Nice work if you can get it / Continental / I won't dance / You're easy to dance with / Change partners / Cheek to cheek
CD ___ 5230062
Verve / Aug '94 / PolyGram

STEPPIN' OUT WITH MY BABY
CD ___ 15189
Laserlight / Aug '91 / Target/BMG

Asteroid B-612

ALL NEW HITS
CD ___ LRR 027
Lance Rock / Jun '97 / Greyhound

NOT MEANT FOR THIS WORLD
CD ___ ANDA 209
Au-Go-Go / Jul '97 / Cargo / Greyhound / Plastic Head

Astle, Jeff

SINGS
Back home / Sugar sugar / Lovey dovey / Lily the pink / You're in my arms / Puppet on a string / Congratulations / Ob-la-di ob-la-da / Glory O / Make me an island / Cinnamon stick / There'll always be an England / Sweet water / Summer sadness
CD ___ RETRO 805
RPM / Nov '95 / Pinnacle

Astley, Rick

BODY AND SOUL
Ones you love / Waiting for the bell to ring / Hopelessly / Dream for us / Body and soul / Enough love / Natures gift / Remember the days / Everytime / When you love someone
CD ___ 74321156332
RCA / Oct '93 / BMG

HOLD ME IN YOUR ARMS
She wants to dance with me / Take me to your heart / I don't want to lose her / Giving up on love / Ain't too proud to beg / Put yourself in my place / Till then / Dial my number / I'll never let you down / I don't want to be your lover / Hold me in your arms
CD ___ 74321369122
RCA / Jun '96 / BMG

WHENEVER YOU NEED SOMEBODY
Never gonna give you up / Whenever you need somebody / Together forever / It would take a strong, strong man / Love has gone / Don't say goodbye / Slippin' away / No more looking for love / You move me / When I fall in love
CD ___ ND 75150
RCA / Jan '92 / BMG

Aston, Michael

WHY ME
CD ___ TX 51205CD
Triple X / Oct '95 / Plastic Head

Aston Villa FC

COME ON YOU VILLA (Various Artists)
CD ___ CDGAFFER 9
Cherry Red / Nov '96 / Pinnacle

Astor, Peter

GOD AND OTHER STORIES
CD ___ DAN 9304CD
Danceteria / Feb '95 / ADA / Plastic Head / Shellshock/Disc

SUBMARINE
CD ___ CRELPCD 065
Creation / May '94 / 3mv/Vital

Astral Engineering

CHRONOGLIDE
CD ___ WI 01
Worm Interface / Feb '95 / Kudos / Pinnacle / Plastic Head

Astral Navigations

HOLYGROUND
CD ___ HBG 122/1
Background / Jun '97 / Background / Greyhound

Astral Pilot

ELECTRO ACUPUNCTURE
CD ___ HHCD 013
Harthouse / Aug '95 / Mo's Music Machine / Prime / Vital

Astral Projection

ASTRAL FILES (2CD Set)
Ionized / Zero / Enlightened evolution / Free Tibet / Maian dream / Kabalah dream / Time began with the universe / Utopia / Electronic / Ambience
CD Set ___ TRANR 607CD
Transient / Feb '97 / Prime / SRD / Total/BMG

Astralasia

ASTRALOGY
CD ___ MEYCD 10
Magick Eye / Nov '95 / Cargo / SRD

AXIS MUNDI
CD ___ MEYCD 9
Magick Eye / May '95 / Cargo / SRD

PITCHED UP AT THE EDGE OF REALITY
CD ___ EYELPCD 4
Magick Eye / Oct '93 / Cargo / SRD

SEVEN POINTED STAR, THE
CD ___ MEYCD 18
Magick Eye / Nov '96 / Cargo / SRD

SPACE BETWEEN, THE
CD ___ MEYCD 014
Magick Eye / May '96 / Cargo / SRD

WHATEVER HAPPENED TO UTOPIA
CD ___ EYECDLP 5
Magick Eye / May '94 / Cargo / SRD

Astream

WOODFISH
CD ___ BTR 009CD
Bad Taste / Sep '96 / Plastic Head

Astrocat

REALMS
CD ___ BINARY 0110101
TEQ / Jul '97 / Cargo / Plastic Head

Astronauts

EVERYTHING'S A-OK/ASTRONAUTS ORBIT CAMPUS
Bo Diddley / If I had a hammer / It's so easy / Dream lover / Wine, wine, wine / Money / Big boss man / Stormy Monday blues / Shortnin' bread / I need you / What'd I say / Johnny B Goode / Be bop a lula / Good golly Miss Molly / Let the good times roll / Linda Lou / Bony Moronie / Diddy wah diddy / Roll over Beethoven / Shop around / Greenback dollar / Summertime / Sticks and stones
CD ___ BCD 15443
Bear Family / Jul '89 / Direct / Rollercoaster / Swift

SURFIN' WITH THE ASTRONAUTS/ COMPETION COUPE
Baja / Surfin' USA / Miserlou / Surfer's stomp / Suzie Q / Pipeline / Kuk / Banzai pipeline / Movin' / Baby let's play house / Let's go trippin' / Batman / Little ford ragtop / Competition coupe / Hearse / Fifty five bird / Devil driver's theme / Happy ho Daddy / Our car club / Devil driver / Chevy scarfer / 4.56 Stingray / Aguila / 650 Scrambler
CD ___ BCD 15442
Bear Family / Jul '89 / Direct / Rollercoaster / Swift

astroPuppees

YOU WIN THE BRIDE
Underdog / She can't say no / Lower the line / Little weekend / Dead around here / Problem / Love is all that matters / Leave it alone / Rockets in my head / Dear John / Amanda / Stuck in the middle with you / Don't be / It's not me, it's her / You win the bride
CD ___ HCD 8076
Hightone / Dec '96 / ADA / Koch

Aswad

ANOTHER CHAPTER OF DUB VOL.2
CD ___ BUBBCD 3
Gut / Jun '95 / Total/BMG

ASWAD
Concrete slaves / Irie woman / Red up / Back to Africa / Natural progression / Ethiopian rhapsody / Can't stand the pressure / Rebel soul
CD ___ IMCD 58
Island / May '88 / PolyGram

BBC SESSIONS
CD ___ SFRSCD 002
Strange Fruit / Feb '97 / Pinnacle

BEST OF ASWAD, THE
CD ___ BUBBCD 4
Gut / Jul '95 / Total/BMG

BIG UP
CD ___ GUTCD 3
Gut / Aug '97 / Total/BMG

DISTANT THUNDER
Message / Don't turn around / Set them free / Smoky blues / I can't get over you / Give a little love / Tradition / Feelings / International melody / Bittersweet / Justice
CD ___ RRCD 27
Reggae Refreshers / Sep '91 / PolyGram / Vital

HULET
Behold / Sons of criminals / Judgement day / Not guilty / Can't walk the street / Corruption / Playing games / Hulet
CD ___ IMCD 56
Island / May '88 / PolyGram

LIVE AND DIRECT
Not guilty / Not satisfied / Your recipe / Roots rocking drum and bass line / African children / Soca rumba / Rockers medley / Love fire
CD ___ IMCD 54
Island / May '88 / PolyGram

NEW CHAPTER
African children / Natural progression / Ways of the Lord / I will keep on loving you / He gave the sun to shine / Tuff we tuff / Didn't know at the time / Zion / In a your rights / Candles / Love fire
CD ___ IMCD 55
Island / Jul '90 / PolyGram

REGGAE GREATS
Don't turn around / Woman / Justice / Give a little love / Message / Gave you my love / Babylon / Chasing for the breeze / Sons of criminals / 54-46 (was my number) / Hulet / Behold / Smoky blues / Bubbling
CD ___ 5500662
Spectrum / Jul '97 / PolyGram

RISE AND SHINE AGAIN
CD ___ BUBBCD 2
Gut / Mar '95 / Total/BMG

ROOTS ROCKIN' (The Island Anthology/ 2CD Set)
CD Set ___ 5243202
Island Jamaica / Aug '97 / Jet Star / PolyGram

SHOWCASE
Warrior charge / Babylon / Rainbow culture / It's not our wish / Three babylon / Back to Africa
CD ___ IMCD 57
Island / May '88 / PolyGram

TO THE TOP
Pull up / Wrapped up / Bubbling / Noh bada wid it / Gimme the dub / Nuclear soldier / Kool noh / Star of my show / Hooked on you
CD ___ IMCD 59
Island / Oct '89 / PolyGram

Asylum Street Spankers

SPANKS FOR THE MEMORIES
Introduction / If I had possession over judgement day / Superchief / Song with no words / Introduction / Lee Harvey / I'll see you in my dreams / Hesitation blues / Startin' to hate Country / Walkin' and whistlin' blues / Shave 'em dry / Brazil / Tradewinds / Introduction / Funny cigarette / Hometown boy
CD ___ WWCD 1060
Watermelon / Feb '97 / ADA / Direct

Async Sense

ASYNC SENSE
CD ___ EFA 127132
Imbalance / Apr '95 / SRD

At The Gates

GARDENS OF GRIEF
CD ___ BS 04CD
Dolores / Aug '95 / Plastic Head

RED IN THE SKY IS OURS/WITH FEAR I KISS THE BURNING DARKNESS
CD ___ CDVILE 59
Peaceville / May '95 / Pinnacle

SLAUGHTER OF THE SOUL
Blinded by fear / Slaughter of the soul / Cold / Under the serpent sun / Into the dead sky / Suicide nation / World of lies / Unto others / Nausea / Need / Flames of the end
CD ___ MOSH 143CD
Earache / Sep '97 / Vital

TERMINAL SPIRIT DISEASE
Swarm / Terminal spirit disease / World returned / Forever blind / Fevered circle / Beautiful wound / All life ends / Burning darkness / Kingdom gone
CD ___ CDVILE 47
Peaceville / Jun '94 / Pinnacle

Atabal

MUSICA MORENA
CD ___ ATABAL 93
Fresh Sound / Nov '96 / Discovery / Jazz Music

Ataraixa

MOON SANG, THE
CD ___ EFA 121622
Apollyon / Dec '95 / SRD

Atari Teenage Riot

1995
Start the riot / Into the death / Raver bashing / Speed / Sex / Midi junkies / Delete yourself you got no chance to wine / Helzajagd auf nazis / Cyberpunks are dead / Atari teenage riot / Kids are united / Riot 1995
CD ___ DHRCD 001
Digital Hardcore / Apr '95 / Vital

FUTURE OF WAR, THE
Get up while you can / Fuck all / Sick to death / PRESS / Deutschland (has gotta die) / Destroy 2000 years of culture / Not your business / You can't hold us back / Heatwave / Redefine the enemy / Deathstar / Future of war
CD ___ DHRCD 006
Digital Hardcore / Mar '97 / Vital

Ataris

ANYWHERE BUT HERE
CD ___ 787632
Kung Fu / Jun '97 / Cargo

Atcha Acoustic

FROM LHASA TO LEWISHAM
Pretty little thing / Lazy days / If you love her / Bar / Blue drag / Tibet blues / Manyatela / Another me / Night alone / Uncle in Harlem / Wintertime blues / Angel by my side
CD ___ TALENT 2001
Latent Talent / Jun '97 / Direct

Athamay

PLEASURE OF SIN
CD ___ NIGHT 011CD
Nightbreed / Sep '96 / Plastic Head

Atheist

ELEMENTS
Green / Water / Samba Briza / Air / Displacement / Animal / Mineral / Fire / Fractal point / Earth / See you again / Elements
CD ___ CDMFN 150
Music For Nations / Jul '93 / Pinnacle

PIECE OF TIME
Piece of time / Unholy war / Room with a view / On they slay / Beyond / I deny / Why brother / Life / No truth
CD ___ CDATV 8
Active / Jan '90 / Pinnacle

UNQUESTIONABLE PRESENCE
CD ___ CDATV 20
Active / Oct '91 / Pinnacle

Athena

GREEK PARTY/SYRTAKI DANCE
CD ___ CDSGP 0117
Prestige / Apr '95 / Else / Total/BMG

Athenians

12 OF THE MOST POPULAR SYRTAKIS
CD ___ EUCD 1058
ARC / '89 / ADA / ARC Music

ALEXIS SORBAS
CD ___ EUCD 1057
ARC / '89 / ADA / ARC Music

ATHENIANS LIFE
CD ___ EUCD 1036
ARC / '89 / ADA / ARC Music

BEST OF GREECE, THE
CD ___ EUCD 1091
ARC / '89 / ADA / ARC Music

GREEK POPULAR MUSIC
CD ___ EUCD 1024
ARC / '89 / ADA / ARC Music

REMBETIKO
CD ___ EUCD 1063
ARC / '89 / ADA / ARC Music

Atherton, Michael

AUSTRALIAN MADE, AUSTRALIAN PLAYED
CD ___ OZM 1008CD
Sounds Australian / Nov '95 / ADA

Atkins, Chet

ALMOST ALONE
Big foot / Waiting for Susie B / Little Mark musik / Jam man / I still write your name in the snow / Pu, uana hulu (Remembering Gabby) / Happy again / Sweet Alla Lee / Maybelle / Mr. Bo Jangles / Cheek to cheek / You do something to me / Ave Maria
CD ___ 4835242
Sony Music / Mar '96 / Sony

COLLECTION, THE
On the road again / Tenderly / Orange blossom special / Rodrigo's guitar concerto de Aranjuez / Take five / Caravan / Vincent / Mostly Mozart / Storms never last / Lime-

house blues / Over the waves / It don't mean a thing if it ain't got that swing / Brandenburg / Struttin' / I'll see you in my dreams / Heart of glass / Black and white/ Ragtime Annie/Hot Toddy
CD 74321140942
RCA / Jul '93 / BMG

DAY THE FINGER PICKERS TOOK OVER THE WORLD, THE
Borsalino / To 'B' or not to 'B' / Day the finger pickers took over the world / Tip toe through the bluegrass / News from the outback / Ode to Mel Bay / Dixie McGuire / Saltwater / Mr. Guitar / Road to Gundaghi/ Waltzing Matilda / Smokey mountain lullaby
CD 4868712
Columbia / Mar '97 / Sony

ESSENTIAL CHET ATKINS, THE
Mr. Sandman / Poor people of Paris / Boo boo stick beat / Alley cat / Travelin' / Yakety axe / Yesterday / Blue angel / Theme from Zorba the Greek / Snowbird / Steeplechase lane / Jerry's breakdown / Black mountain rag / Fiddlin' around / Somewhere my love / Entertainer / Londonderry air / On my way to Canaan's land / Tennessee rag/Beaumont rag / Chet's medley
CD 07863668552
RCA Nashville / Aug '96 / BMG

GALLOPIN' GUITAR
Guitar blues / Brown eyes cryin' in the rain / Ain'tcha tired of makin' me blue / I'm gonna get tight / Canned heat / Standing room only / Don't hand me that line / Bug dance / I know my baby loves me / Nashville jump / My guitar is my sweetheart / I'm pickin' the blues / Gone gone gone / Barnyard shuffle / Save your money / (I may be colour blind but) I know when... / I've been working on the guitar / Dizzy strings / Money, marbles and chalk / Wednesday night waltz / Guitar waltz / Telling my troubles to my old guitar / Dance of the goldenrod / Gallopin' guitar / Barber shop rag / Centipede boogie / Under the Hickory nut tree / I was bitten by the same bug twice / One more chance / Old buck dance / Boogie man boogie / Main street breakdown / Confusin' / Music in my heart / Indian love call / Birth of the blues / Mountain melody / You're always brand new / My crazy heart / Hybrid corn / Jitterbug waltz / One man boogie / Crazy rhythm (instrumental) / Crazy rhythm / Rustic dance / Rainbow / In the mood / Spanish fandango / Midnight / Goodbye blues / Your mean little heart / Sweet bunch of daisies / Blue gypsy / Third man theme / One man boogie (take D) / St. Louis blues / Listed knot / Lover come back to me / Stephen Foster medley / Hangover blues / Imagination / Black mountain rag / Guitar polka / Dream train / Meet Mr. Callaghan / Chinatown, my Chinatown / High rockin' swing / Pig leaf rag / Oh by jingo / Hello ma baby / Bells of St. Mary's / Country gentlemen / Memphis blues / Alice blue gown / 12th street rag / Peeping Tom / Three o'clock in the morning / Georgia camp meeting / City slicker / Dill pickle rag / Rubber doll rag / Beautiful Ohio / Kentucky derby / Wildwood flower / Guitars on parade / Simple Simon / Rubber doll rag (alternate version) / Get up and go / Pagan love song / Beautiful Ohio / Downhill drag / Avalon / Sunrise serenade / San Antonio rose / Set a spell / Mr. Misery / Get up and go / South / Alabama jubilee / Corine Corina / (Back home again in) Indiana / Red wing / Frankie and Johnny / Gay Ranchero / Ballin' the Jack / Honeysuckle rose / At the Darktown strutter's ball / Old spinning wheel / Silver bells / Under the double eagle / Have you ever been lonely / Caravan / Ol' man river / Mr. Sandman / New Spanish two-step
CD BCD 15714
Bear Family / Oct '93 / Direct / Rollercoaster / Swift

NECK AND NECK (Atkins, Chet & Mark Knopfler)
Poor boy blues / Sweet dreams / There'll be some changes made / Just one time / So soft / Your goodbye / Yakety axe / Tears / Tahitian skys / I'll see you in my dreams / Next time I'm in town
CD 4674352
CBS / Nov '90 / Sony

READ MY LICKS
Young thing / Mountains of Illinois / After you're gone / Every now and then / Somebody loves me now / Norway (Norwegian mountain song) / Read my licks / Take a look at her now / Around the bend / Dream / Vincent
CD 4746282
Sony Music / Jul '94 / Sony

Atkins, Juan

INFINITI COLLECTION
CD EFA 017942
Tresor / Jun '96 / 3mv/BMG / Prime / SRD

Atkins, Mark

DIDGERIDOO CONCERTO
CD LRF 338
Larrikin / Aug '96 / ADA / CM / Direct / Roots

Atlanta

DISCO SUCKAS
CD TKCD 35
2 Kool / Apr '97 / Pinnacle / SRD

Atlantic

POWER
It's only love / Power / War / Bad blood / Can't hold on / Hands of fate / Every beat of my heart / Dangerous games / Nothing to lose / Hard to believe
CD CDMFN 168
Music For Nations / Oct '94 / Pinnacle

Atlantic Ocean

WATERFALL
CD HFCD 41
PWL / Sep '94 / Warner Music

Atlantic Starr

LOVE CRAZY
CD 7599265452
WEA / Nov '91 / Warner Music

SECRET LOVERS (The Best Of Atlantic Starr)
Circles / Silver shadow / Send for me / Secret lovers / Love me down / Stand up / When love calls / Am I dreaming / Touch for a four leaf clover / One love / Gimme your lovin' / If your heart isn't in it / One love / Freak-a-Ristic
CD 5525412
Spectrum / Sep '96 / PolyGram

VERY BEST OF ATLANTIC STARR, THE
CD CDMID 152
A&M / Oct '92 / PolyGram

Atlas, Natacha

DIASPORA
CD NATCD 47
Nation / Jun '95 / RTM/Disc

HALIM
Marifnaash / Moustahil / Amulet / Leyli / Kidda / Sweeter than any sweets / Ya weledi / Enogoom wil amar / Andeel / Gafsa / Ya alibi ehda / Agib
CD NATCD 1087
Nation / May '97 / RTM/Disc

Atmosfear

JANGALA SPIRITS
Theme from higher communication / Hot sulpher boogie / Klatter klatter / Jangala spirits / Money / Dub to scratch / Return to whatever / Optical delusion / Galactic lifeboat
CD META 49701
Meta 4 / Apr '97 / Timewarp

Atom Bomb Yoga

IN PAST TIMES
She said tomorrow / Enough shame / Hubble / In past times / America / Lazy for you / London / Honey / Last night / 1000 Paths / Lifeguard / Lonely hearted / Final hour
CD MYSCD 116
Mystic / Sep '97 / Pinnacle

Atom Heart

BINARY AMPLIFIED SUPER STEREO
CD RI 032CD
Rather Interesting / Nov '95 / Plastic Head

Atom Heart Mother

SKIN 'EM UP, CHOP 'EM OUT RAWHIDE
CD ABT 095 CD
Abstract / Oct '92 / Cargo / Pinnacle / Total/BMG

Atom Seed

GET IN LINE
CD HMRXD 163
Heavy Metal / Nov '92 / Revolver / Sony

Atomic 61

PURITY OF ESSENCE
CD CSR 21CD
Cavity Search / Oct '95 / Plastic Head

TINNITUS IN EXTREMIS
CD CSR 106CD
Cavity Search / Oct '95 / Plastic Head

Atomic Rooster

BEST OF ATOMIC ROOSTER, THE
Devil's answer / Oh she, oh she's my woman / Tomorrow night / Play it again / Death walks behind you / Lose your mind / I don't need you anymore / He did it again / Who's looking for you / Show / No change by me / Hold it through the night
CD 12666
Laserlight / Apr '96 / Target/BMG

DEVIL HITS BACK, THE
CD DMCD 1023
Demi-Monde / Nov '89 / RTM/Disc / TKO Magnum

DEVIL'S ANSWER (2CD Set)
Banstead / And so to bed / Friday 13th / Broken wings / Tomorrow night / Play the game / Vug / Sleeping for years / Death walks behind you / Devil's answer / Rock / Breakthrough / Break the ice / Spoonful of bromide / Stand by me / Never to lose / Don't know what went wrong / Space cowboy / People you can't trust / All in Satan's name / Close your eyes / Save me / Can't find a reason / All across the country / Voodoo in you / Goodbye planet earth / Satan's wheel
CD Set SMDCD 128
Snapper / May '97 / Pinnacle

HEADLINE NEWS
Hold your fire / Headline news / Taking a chance / Metal minds / Land of freedom / Machine / Dance of death / Carnival / Time / Future shock / Watch out/Reaching out
CD BP 171CD
Blueprint / Jul '97 / Pinnacle

Atomic Spuds

GARBAGE SURFERS
CD AS 007
Bananajuice / Jan '96 / Nervous

Atomvinter

ATOMVINTER
CD DISTCD 12LF
Distortion / Jun '95 / Plastic Head

Atrocity

ART OF DEATH, THE
CD CORE 10CD
Metalcore / Feb '92 / Plastic Head

BLUT
CD MASSCD 033
Massacre / Nov '94 / Plastic Head

CALLING THE RAIN
CD MASSCD 071
Massacre / Aug '95 / Plastic Head

DIE LIEBE (Atrocity & Das Ich)
CD MASSCD 069
Massacre / Nov '95 / Plastic Head

HALLUCINATIONS
CD NB 038CD
Nuclear Blast / Jan '91 / Plastic Head

HUNT, THE
CD MASSCD 112
Massacre / Jan '97 / Plastic Head

INFECTED
CD CORE 3CD
Metalcore / Oct '90 / Plastic Head

WILLENSKRAFT
CD MASS 099CD
Massacre / Sep '96 / Plastic Head

Attacco Decente

CRYSTAL NIGHT
Never give in / Turn the magic on / Crystal night / Here comes my train / Future in your face / Chastity / When I'm in you (and you're in me) / Daydreams in mirrors / Shining angel / Catacombs of straw / Powerless
CD AON 005
All Or Nothing / Oct '94 / ADA / Direct

Attack

ZOMBIES
CD AHOY 22
Captain Oi / Nov '94 / Plastic Head

Attar, Bachir

IN NEW YORK (Attar, Bachir & Elliot Sharp)
CD EMCD 114
Enemy / Mar '90 / Grapevine/PolyGram

NEXT DREAM, THE
Ceremonies against the night of the devil / Under the shadow of liberty / 1001 nights / Here we stay / Mixed cultures / Full moon at the window / Next dream
CD CMPCD 57
CMP / Jun '93 / Cargo / Grapevine/PolyGram / Vital/SAM

Attia, Adolphe

JEWISH LITURGICAL FEASTS
CD LDX 2741033
Le Chant Du Monde / Sep '96 / Harmonia Mundi

JEWISH LITURGICAL MUSIC
CD CMT 274993
La Chant Du Monde / Oct '94 / ADA / Harmonia Mundi

Attica Blues

ATTICA BLUES
Intro / Blueprint / Atlanta / It's alright / Impulse / Medieval / 3ree (A means to be) / Tender (the final story) / 808 song / Pendulum being / Gone too far / REAL expense / Vybra / Questions / Enter
CD MW 080CD
Mo Wax / Sep '97 / PolyGram / Vital

Attika

WHEN HEROES FALL
CD MASSCD 023
Massacre / Feb '94 / Plastic Head

Attila The Stockbroker

SIEGE OF SHOREHAM
CD HELMETCD 1
Demi-Monde / Aug '96 / RTM/Disc / TKO Magnum

Attractions

MAD ABOUT THE WRONG BOY
Arms race / Damage / Little Miss Understanding / Straight jacket / Mad about the wrong boy / Motorworld / On the third stroke / Slow patience / La la la la la loved you / Single girl / Lonesome little town / Taste of poison / High rise housewife / Talk about me / Sad about girls / Camera camera
CD FIENDCD 25
Demon / Jul '91 / Pinnacle

Attrition

HIDDEN AGENDA, THE
CD HY 39100812
Hyperium / Dec '93 / Cargo / Plastic Head

Atwood, Eden

CAT ON A HOT TIN ROOF
For every man there's a woman / Twilight world / Silent movie / Cat on a hot tin roof / You've changed / My ship / Every time we say goodbye / Right as the rain / I'm glad there is you / Never let me go / Not while I'm around
CD CCD 4599
Concord Jazz / Jun '94 / New Note/ Pinnacle

NIGHT IN THE LIFE
When the sun comes out / I've grown accustomed to his face / Willow weep for me / Folks who live on the hill / If I love again / I could have told you / Spring can really hang you up the most / Lost in the stars/So many stars / You taught my heart to sing / Why did I choose you / Moon river
CD CCD 4730
Concord Jazz / Dec '96 / New Note/ Pinnacle

NO ONE EVER TELLS YOU
I didn't know what time it was / I was the last one to know / Is you is or is you ain't my baby / Ballad of the sad young men / Old devil moon / Cow cow boogie / No one ever tells you / Too late now / Gentle rain / Nothing's changed / Them there eyes
CD CCD 4560
Concord Jazz / Jul '93 / New Note/Pinnacle

THERE AGAIN
It never entered my mind / You're my thrill / Nearness of you / In love in vain / Music that makes me dance / I'm always drunk in San Francisco / Sonny boy / Everything I've got belongs to you / In the days of our love / Only you (and you alone) / You don't know what love is / Auld lang syne
CD CCD 4645
Concord Jazz / Jun '95 / New Note/ Pinnacle

Au Pairs

EQUAL BUT DIFFERENT
Pretty boys / Ideal woman / Come again / Monogamy / It's obvious / Love song / Repetition / Dear John / Set up / Headache / We're so cool / Armagh / Steppin' out / America / Sex without stress / Intact / Shakedown / Slider / Unfinished business
CD RPM 139CD
RPM / Jun '94 / Pinnacle

LIVE IN BERLIN
Diet / Headache for Michelle / Dear John / Love song / Set up / Inconvenience / Armagh / Repetition / We're so cool / Cum again / Piece of my heart
CD ESMCD 452
Essential / Oct '96 / BMG

PLAYING WITH A DIFFERENT SEX
CD RPM 107
RPM / Nov '92 / Pinnacle

SENSE AND SENSUALITY
CD RPM 111
RPM / Aug '93 / Pinnacle

Aube

CARDIAC STRAIN
CD ALIENCD 2
Alien8 / Mar '97 / Cargo / Harmonia Mundi

DAZZLE REFLECTION
CD IGLOO 007
Releasing Eskimo / Jun '97 / Cargo

MASCHINENWERK (Aube & Cock ESP)
CD CHCD 18
Charnel House / Jun '97 / Cargo / Greyhound

STARED GLEAM
CD ILIGHT 003CD
Iris Light / Aug '97 / Kudos

Auburn, Rachel

OUT OF HER BOX (Various Artists)
Unmanageable: *East Anglia* / Drop: *Mr. Whippy* / Circus beat: *Tecmania Rebel* / Jus' come: *Cool Jack* / Can't help it: *Happy Clappers* / You're no good: *Billabong* / Party groove: *DJ Kalpa* / Do it: *Trigger & Auburn* / No other love: *Blue Amazon* / U (I got a feeling): *Scot Project* / Secret worship: *Stone Factory* / Le voie le soleil: *Subliminal Cuts* / Big drum: *Digital Man* / Stuck on a Space Trip: *Demonic Emotions*
CD ______ FVRCD 4
Feverpitch / Sep '97 / EMI

Audience

AUDIENCE
Banquet / Waverley stage coach / River boat Queen / Harlequin / Heaven was an island / Too late I'm gone / Maidens cry / Troubles / Going song / Paper round / House on the hill / Man on box / Leave it unsaid / Pleasant conversation
CD ______ RPM 148
RPM / Oct '95 / Pinnacle

AUDIENCE UNCHAINED
Trombone gulch / Ain't the man you need / Indian summer / Raviole / I had a dream / Party games / In accord / I put a spell on you / Stand by the door / Nancy / It brings a tear / Thunder and lightnin' / Grief and disbelief / Hula girl / Belladonna / Moonshine / Barracuda Dan / Hard cruel world / Jackda W / You're not smiling
CD ______ CDVM 9007
Virgin / Aug '92 / EMI

FRIENDS, FRIENDS, FRIEND
CD ______ CASCD 1012
Charisma / Jun '92 / EMI

HOUSE ON THE HILL, THE
Jackdaw / You're not smiling / I had a dream / Raviole / Eye to eye / I put a spell on you / House on the hill / Nancy
CD ______ CASCD 1032
Charisma / Oct '90 / EMI

LUNCH
Stand by the door / Seven sore bruises / Hula girl / Ain't the man you need / In accord / Barracuda Dan / Thunder and lightning / Party games / Trombone gulch / Buy me an island
CD ______ CASCD 1054
Charisma / Feb '91 / EMI

Audio Active

HAPPY HAPPER
CD ______ ONUCD 77
On-U Sound / Jun '95 / Jet Star / SRD

HAPPY SHOPPING IN EUROPE
CD ______ EFA 186352
On-U Sound / Nov '95 / Jet Star / SRD

WAY OUT IS THE WAY IN, THE (Audio Active & Laraaji)
New laughter mode (the way in) / Music and cosmic (feel yourself) / Think cosmically / How time flies / Laaraajingle / Space visitors for tea - tat lump on your head / Hither and zither / Blooper's dance floor / New laugher mode (the way out)
CD ______ ASCD 026
All Saints / Nov '95 / Discovery / Vital

WE ARE AUDIO ACTIVE
CD ______ ONUCD 73
On-U Sound / Sep '94 / Jet Star / SRD

Audio Assault Squad

COMIN' UP OUTTA THIS BITCH
CD ______ TED 41742CD
Ichiban / May '94 / Direct / Koch

Audioweb

AUDIOWEB
Sleeper / Yeah / Into my world / Faker / Who's to blame / Time / Jah love / Bank robba sensi / Lover / Drip feed
CD ______ MUMXD 9604
CD ______ MUMCD 9604
Mother / Feb '97 / PolyGram

Auerbach, Loren

AFTER THE LONG NIGHT/PLAYING THE GAME (Auerbach, Loren & Bert Jansch)
Rainbow man / Frozen beauty / Christabel / So lonely / Journey of the moon through sorrow / Carousel / Weeping willow blues / Give me love / I can't go back / Smiling faces / Yarrow / Playing the game / Is it real / Sorrow / Days and nights
CD ______ CDLA 001
Christabel / Nov '96 / ADA / Direct

Auffret, Anne

ROUE GRALON NI HO SALUD (Auffret, Anne & Yann Fanch Kemener)
CD ______ KM 42CD
Keltia Musique / Feb '94 / ADA / Discovery

Auger, Brian

AUGERNIZATION (The Best Of Brian Auger)
Freedom jazz dance / Second wind / Maiden voyage / I want to take you higher / Don't look away / Happiness is just around the bend / Dawn of another day / Listen here / Foolish girl / Whenever you're ready
CD ______ TNGCD 008
Tongue 'n' Groove / Jul '95 / Vital

DEFINITELY WHAT (Auger, Brian & The Trinity)
CD ______ OW 30012
One Way / Sep '94 / ADA / Direct / Greyhound

Augscholl, Charly

BUS STOP
CD ______ 322 424
Koch / Oct '91 / Koch

August, Lynn

SAUCE PIQUANTE
CD ______ BT 1092CD
Black Top / Jul '93 / ADA / CM / Direct

Auld, Georgie

CANYON PASSAGE (Auld, Georgie & His Orchestra)
CD ______ MVSCD 57
Musicraft / '88 / Warner Music

JUMP GEORGIE JUMP
Short circuit / Mandrake root / Poinciana / Jivin with the jug / Yesterdays / I'll always be in love with you / Stompin' at the Savoy / Sentimental journey / Jump Georgie jump / I'm always chasing rainbows / I can't get started (with you) / Taps Miller / Concerto for tenor
CD ______ HEPCD 27
Hep / Jul '96 / Cadillac / Jazz Music / New Note/Pinnacle / Wellard

Auld Reekie Dance Band

CAPITAL REELS
Dashing white sergeant / Dashing white sergeant (encore) / Eightsome reel / Foursome reel / Scottish waltz / Hamilton House (jig) / Hamilton House (encore) / Duke of Perth / Duke of Perth (encore) / Strip the willow (Jig) / Strip the willow / Duke and Duchess of Edinburgh / Duke and Duchess of Edinburgh (Encore) / Gay Gordons / Scottish reform (jig) / Scottish reform / Reel of the 51st division / Reel of the 51st division (encore)
CD ______ LCOM 5190
Lismor / May '95 / ADA / Direct / Duncans / Lismor

Auldridge, Mike

EIGHT STRING SWING
Little rock getaway / Redskin rag / Bethesada / Swing scene / Caravan / Almost to Tulsa / Bluegrass boogie / Eight string swing / Brown's baggin' / Pete's place / Crazy red top / Stompin' at the Savoy
CD ______ SHCD 3725
Sugar Hill / '92 / ADA / CM / Direct / Koch / Roots

HIGH TIME (Auldridge, Mike & Lou Reid/T. Michael Coleman)
CD ______ SHCD 3776
Sugar Hill / Jan '90 / ADA / CM / Direct / Koch / Roots

MIKE AULDRIDGE
Southern rain / Tennessee traveller / Mountain slide / Blues for Barbara / Last train to Clarksville / California dreamin' / Dreaming my dreams / Indian summer / Carolina sunshine girl / All thumbs / Spanish grass / Lloyd's of Nashville / Georgia on my mind
CD ______ FF 70029
Flying Fish / May '97 / ADA / CM / Direct / Roots

TREASURES UNTOLD
CD ______ SH 3780
Sugar Hill / Jan '97 / ADA / CM / Direct / Koch / Roots

Auntie Christ

LIFE COULD BE A DREAM
CD ______ LOOKOUT 176CD
Lookout / May '97 / Cargo / Greyhound / Shellshock/Disc

Aura

BUTTERFLY CHRYSALIS CATERPILLAR
CD ______ INFECT 19CD
Infectious / May '95 / RTM/Disc

ORANGES ARE BLUE
CD ______ INFECT 26CD
Infectious / Jul '96 / RTM/Disc

SHATTERED DAWNBREAK
CD ______ HHR 005CD
Hammerheart / Nov '96 / Plastic Head

Aura Noir

DREAMS LIKE DESERTS
CD ______ HR 002CD
Hot / Feb '96 / Plastic Head

Aural Expansion

REMIXED SHEEP
CD ______ SSR 159
SSR / Jan '96 / Amato Disco / Grapevine/ PolyGram / Prime / RTM/Disc

SURREAL SHEEP
CD ______ SSR 143
SSR / Aug '95 / Amato Disco / Grapevine/ PolyGram / Prime / RTM/Disc

Aurora

PSYCHEDELIC TRANCE (2CD Set)
CD Set ______ DBCD 201
Dance Beat / Nov '96 / Total/BMG

Aurora

LAND OF HARM AND APPLETREES
CD ______ CDSATE 03
Talitha / Jul '93 / Plastic Head

Aurora Project

BALANCE OF RISK
CD ______ CENCD 011
Centaur / Feb '96 / Pinnacle

Aurora Sutra

DIMENSION GATE, THE
CD ______ CDSATE 10
Music Research / Oct '94 / Plastic Head

Austin, Claire

MEMORIES OF YOU (Austin, Claire & Don Ewell)
CD ______ ACD 143
Audiophile / Apr '93 / Jazz Music

Austin, Gene

GENE AUSTIN - THE VOICE OF THE SOUTHLAND (25 Vintage Hits)
Voice of the Southland / My blue heaven / When my sugar walks down the street / My bundle of love / Sweet child, I'm wild about you / Ya gotta know how to love / Ev'rything's made for love / Ain't she sweet / Lonesome road / Sweetheart of sigma chi / Girl of my dreams / Just like a melody from out of the sky / Carolina moon / I've got a feeling I'm falling / How am I to know / Rollin' down the river / When your lover has gone / Please don't talk about me when I'm gone / Without that gal / Love letters in the sand / I don't stand a ghost of a chance with you / Everything I have is yours / I cried for you / When I'm with you / Ramona
CD ______ CDAJA 5217
Living Era / Dec '96 / Select

Austin Lounge Lizards

CREATURES FROM THE BLACK SALOON
Golden triangle / Hot tubs of tears / Pflugerville / Car Hank died in / Swingin' from your crystal chandeliers / Kool whip / We are in control / Didn't go to college / Saquaro / Keeping up with the Joneses / War between the States / Old fat and drunk / Chester Woolah / Anahuac
CD ______ WM 1000
Watermelon / Jun '93 / ADA / Direct

HIGHWAY CAFE OF THE DAMNED
Highway Cafe of the Damned / Cornhusker refugee / Industrial strength tranquilizer / Wendell, the uncola man / Acid rain / I'll just have one beer / Dallas, Texas / Ballad of Ronald Reagan / When drunks go bad / Jalapeno Maria / Get a haircut Dad / Chester Ninitiz oriental garden waltz
CD ______ WM 1001
Watermelon / Jun '93 / ADA / Direct

SMALL MINDS
CD ______ WM 1034
Watermelon / Nov '95 / ADA / Direct

Austin, Lovie

CLASSICS 1924-1926
CD ______ CLASSICS 756
Classics / Aug '94 / Discovery / Jazz Music

Austin, Patti

ULTIMATE COLLECTION, THE
Hold me / Ability to swing / Givin' in to love / We fell in love / Heat of heat / Reach / I'll keep your dream alive / Soldier boy / Love is gonna getcha / Girl who used to be me / You who brought me love / Through the test of time
CD ______ GRP 98212
GRP / May '95 / New Note/BMG

Autechre

AMBER
CD ______ WARPCD 25
Warp / Nov '94 / Prime / RTM/Disc

CHIASTIC SLIDE
CD ______ WARPCD 49
Warp / Feb '97 / Prime / RTM/Disc

INCUNABULA
CD ______ WARPCD 17
Warp / Apr '96 / Prime / RTM/Disc

TRI REPETAE
CD ______ WARPCD 38
Warp / Nov '95 / Prime / RTM/Disc

Auteurs

AFTER MURDER PARK
Light aircraft on fire / Child brides / Land lovers / New brat in town / Everything you say will destroy you / Unsolved child murder / Married to a lazy lover / Buddha / Tombstone / Fear of flying / Dead sea navigators / After murder park
CD ______ DGHUT 33
Hut / Mar '96 / EMI

AUTEURS VS. U-ZIQ
Lenny Valentino 3 / Daughter of a child / Chinese bakery / Lenny Valentino 1 / Lenny Valentino 2 / Underground movies
CD ______ DGHUTM 20
Hut / Oct '94 / EMI

NEW WAVE
Show girl / Bailed out / American guitars / Junk shop clothes / Don't trust the stars / Starstruck / How could I be so wrong / Housebreaker / Valet parking / Idiot brother / Early years / Home again
CD ______ CDHUT 7
Hut / Mar '93 / EMI

NOW I'M A COWBOY
Modern history (Accoustic version) / Lenny Valentino / Brain child / I'm a rich man's toy / New french girlfriend / Upper classes / Chinese bakery / Sister like you / Underground movies / Life classes / Modern history / Daughter of a child
CD ______ CDHUT 16
Hut / May '94 / EMI

Authority

WHO KNOWS
CD ______ GMM 113
Gimmie My Money / Jul '97 / Cargo

Auto Creation

METTLE
CD ______ INTA 003CD
Intermodo / Aug '94 / RTM/Disc

Autoclave

AUTOCLAVE
CD ______ DIS 108CD
Dischord / Aug '97 / SRD

Autograph

MISSING PIECES
CD ______ USG 37651422
USG / Apr '97 / Cargo

Automatic Head Detonator

LIVE OUTSIDE THE HOLLYWOOD PALLADIUM SONIC YOUTH GIG
CD ______ LS 02
Lo-Fi Recordings / Jun '96 / SRD

WHAT THE FUCK DO YOU KNOW
CD ______ LF 001
Lo-Fi Recordings / Mar '95 / SRD

Automator

BETTER TOMORROW, A
CD ______ URCD 016
Ubiquity / Jul '96 / Cargo / Timewarp

Autonomex

EARLYMAN MEETS AUTONOMEX
CD ______ WOWCD 38
Words Of Warning / Oct '95 / SRD / Total/ BMG

Autopop

SELECTION BOX
Unhand me brother / Diamond / Crisis girl / Still hanging around / Bootboy remembers / Being seen / Wasted / Tristan
CD ______ MASKCD 69
Vinyl Japan / Apr '97 / Plastic Head / Vinyl Japan

Autopsia

KRISTALLMACHT
CD ______ HY 85921076
Hyperium / Apr '94 / Cargo / Plastic Head

MYSTERY SCIENCE
CD ______ 34502
Hypnobeat / Mar '97 / Plastic Head

REQUIM POUR UN EMPIRE
CD ______ HY 185000CD
Hypertension / Nov '92 / ADA / CM / Direct / Total/BMG

Autopsy

ACTS OF THE UNSPEAKABLE
CD ______ CDVILE 33
Peaceville / Apr '97 / Pinnacle

MENTAL FUNERAL
CD ______ CDMVILE 25
Peaceville / Jun '96 / Pinnacle

MENTAL FUNERAL/SEVERED SURVIVAL
CD ______ CDVILE 25
Peaceville / Aug '95 / Pinnacle

SEVERED SURVIVAL
CD ______ CDMVILE 12
Peaceville / Jun '96 / Pinnacle

SHITFUN
CD ______ CDVILE 49
Peaceville / Jul '95 / Pinnacle

Autry, Gene

BACK IN THE SADDLE AGAIN
CD ______ CTS 55430
Country Stars / Aug '94 / Target/BMG

BACK IN THE SADDLE AGAIN (25 Cowboy Classics)
Back in the saddle again / Blue yodel no.5 / Any old time / High steppin' Mama / Silver haired Daddy of mine / Tumbling tumbleweeds / Ridin' down the canyon / Mexicali Rose / Blue Hawaii / Dust / Old trail / Paradise in the moonlight / Rhythm of the hoofbeats / South of the border (Down Mexico way) / Blueberry Hill / Be honest with me / When swallows come back to Capistrano / You are my sunshine / Year ago tonight / I'll never let you go / I'll wait for you / After tomorrow / Lonely river / Have I told you lately that I love you / Goodbye little darlin' goodbye
CD ______ CDAJA 5188
Living Era / Apr '96 / Select

BEST OF GENE AUTRY, THE
CD ______ MACCD 219
Autograph / Aug '96 / BMG

Autumn Leaves

AUTUMN LEAVES
Building bridges / Light of your love / Right on / Keeping it cool / Vera cruz / Eye of the hurricane / Lies and alibis / Ten minutes romance / Thythm of the road / Together we're strong / Swing across Texas / Steppin' out on me / Thank you for the time / Blue water / Don't it make ya wanna dance
CD ______ BCD 15734
Bear Family / May '93 / Direct / Rollercoaster / Swift

Auzet, Roland

LA VIE C'EST MARRANT COMME CA CHANGE
CD ______ IMP 946
IMP / Jan '97 / ADA / Discovery

Ava & The Astronettes

PEOPLE FROM BAD HOMES
CD ______ GY 005
NMC / Mar '94 / Total/Pinnacle

Avail

4AM FRIDAY
CD ______ LOOKOUT 138CD
Lookout / Jun '96 / Cargo / Greyhound / Shellshock/Disc

Available Jelly

IN FULL FLAIL
CD ______ ECD 1013
Ear-Rational / Dec '90 / Cadillac / Impetus

MONUMENT
CD ______ RAMBOY 07
Bvhaast / Oct '94 / Cadillac

Avalon

HIGHER GROUND
Lion of the north / Sons of the sea / Into the mists / Soldier's dream / Palais de danse / Stretch the bowl / Wild cherry tree / Ellis isle
CD ______ IRCD 017
Lismor / Aug '92 / ADA / Direct / Duncans / Lismor

Avalon, Frankie

FABULOUS FRANKIE AVALON, THE
Venus / Why / Dede Dinah / Gingerbread / Bobby Sox to stockings / Boy without a girl / Just ask your heart / I'll wait for you / Don't throw away all those teardrops / Where are you / Togetherness / You are mine
CD ______ CDFAB 007
Ace / Sep '91 / Pinnacle

HIT SINGLE COLLECTABLES
CD ______ DISK 4501
Disky / Apr '94 / Disky / THE

Avatar

DEEP ARCHITECTURE
CD ______ SUB 32D
Subversive / Apr '97 / SRD

MEMORIAN DRACONIS
CD ______ WSR 002CD
Shiver / Jul '96 / Plastic Head

Ave Maria Avida

DISTANCE
CD ______ HY 39100652CD
Hyperium / Aug '93 / Cargo / Plastic Head

Avec Cholesterol

LU REVE DU DIABLE
CD ______ R2D2 105CD
R2D2 / Apr '96 / ADA

Average White Band

ABOVE AVERAGE
Pick up the pieces / Cut the cake / Queen of my soul / Person to person / You got it / Work to do / Walk on by / When will you be mine / Let's go round again / For you, for love / If I ever lose this Heaven / Schoolboy crush / Your love is a miracle / Love of your own / Cloudy / I heard it through the grapevine / Atlantic Avenue / Got the love
CD ______ CCSCD 438
Castle / Oct '96 / BMG

AVERAGE WHITE BAND (2CD Set)
Catch me before I have to testify / Let's go round again / Watcha gonna do for me / Help is on the way / Shine / For you for love / Into the night / Our time has come / If love only lasts for one night / Pick up the pieces / Person to person / Cut the cake / If I ever lose this heaven / Cloudy / TLC / I'm the one / Love your life / Schoolboy crush / I heard it through the grapevine
CD Set ______ SMDCD 173
Snapper / May '97 / Pinnacle

LET'S GO ROUND AGAIN - BEST OF THE AVERAGE WHITE BAND
CD ______ AHLCD 15
Hit / Mar '94 / Grapevine/PolyGram

SOUL TATTOO
CD ______ ARTFULCD 7
Artful / Feb '97 / Pinnacle / Total/BMG

VERY BEST OF AVERAGE WHITE BAND, THE
Pick up the pieces / Put it where you want it / Schoolboy crush / Queen of my soul / It's a mysterie / Work to do / Cut the cake / Groovin' the night away / How sweet can you get / Big city lights / She's a dream / Your love is a miracle / Into the night / You got it / When will you be mine / Person to person
CD ______ 12891
Laserlight / Feb '97 / Target/BMG

WHITE ALBUM, THE
You got it / Got the love / Pick up the pieces / Person to person / Work to do / Nothing you can do / Just wanna love you tonight / Keepin' it to myself / Just can't give you up / There's always someone waiting
CD ______ ESMCD 439
Essential / Oct '96 / BMG

Aversion

FALL FROM GRACE
CD ______ CDVEST 41
Bulletproof / Feb '95 / Pinnacle

Avery, Teodross

IN OTHER WORDS (Avery, Teodross Quartet)
High hopes / Our true love / One to love / Ancient civilisation / Edda / Possibilities are endless / What's new / Urban survival / Positive role models / In other words / Our struggle / Watching the sunrise
CD ______ GRP 97982
GRP / Mar '95 / New Note/BMG

MY GENERATION
Addis abeba / Mode for my father / Theme for Malcolm / Lover man / To the east / Mr. Wonsey / Salome / Sphere / My generation / Anytime, anyplace / It's about that time
CD ______ IMP 11812
Impulse Jazz / Jan '96 / New Note/BMG

Avia

AVIA
Wake up and sing out / Spring song of the masses / Russian lesson part 1 (goodbye) / Night watch / I don't love you / Russian lesson part 2 (home) / Celebration / Aviavial / Semaphore
CD ______ HNCD 1358
Hannibal / Jul '90 / ADA / Vital

Avulsed

CARNIVORACITY
CD ______ RPS 007MCD
Repulse / Oct '95 / Plastic Head

Awankana

FLAMBOYAN
CD ______ SM 18042
Wergo / Nov '93 / ADA / Cadillac / Harmonia Mundi

GENTLE RIVER
CD ______ SM 18022
Wergo / Feb '92 / ADA / Cadillac / Harmonia Mundi

KINGDOM IS NOT AFAR, THE
CD ______ SM 18012
Wergo / Aug '92 / ADA / Cadillac / Harmonia Mundi

RINGSEL
CD ______ SM 18052
Wergo / Nov '93 / ADA / Cadillac / Harmonia Mundi

Awful Truth

AWFUL TRUTH
It takes so long / I should have known all along / Ghost of heaven / Drowning man / Circle of pain / Higher / No good reason / Mary
CD ______ CDZORRO 3
Metal Blade / Aug '90 / Pinnacle / Plastic Head

AWOL

WHAT IT BE LIKE
CD ______ BRY 4175CD
Ichiban / Apr '94 / Direct / Koch

Axe

FIVE
Intro / Magic (in our eyes) / Heroes and legends / Sting of the rain / Life in the furnace / Burn me once (burn me twice) / Where there's smoke (there's fire) / Holding onto the night / Anyplace on this highway (is home) / Battles
CD ______ MTM 199617
MTM / Feb '97 / Cargo

Axiom

AXIOM DUB - MYSTERIES OF CREATION (Axiom Dub)
Maroon rebellion: *Ninja & Bill Laswell* / Return to the bass and trouble: *Sly & Robbie* / Revolution: *Sub Dub* / Cocksville USA: *Orb* / Illbient: *We & DJ Olive/Loop/Once 11* / Ghost light/Dread recall: *Material* / Dungeon of dub: *Wordsound & Powa* / Ariwa dub club: *Mad Professor* / Beta one/Assyrian dub: *Automaton* / Gun too hot: *Dub Syndicate* / Nev 12: *Wobble, Jah & Jaki Liebezeit/Neville Murray* / Cyborg dread: *Techno Animal* / Black falcon dub: *New Kingdom* / Fall of the towers of convention: *Scarab* / Anansi abstrakt: *DJ Spooky*
CD ______ 5243132
Axiom / Jan '97 / PolyGram / Vital

Axton, Hoyt

FREE SAILIN'
CD ______ EDCD 471
Edsel / Apr '96 / Pinnacle

SNOWBLIND FRIEND
You're the hangnail in my life / Little white moon / Water for my horse / Funeral of the king / I light this candle / Never been to Spain / You taught me how to cry / Snowblind friend / Pancho and Lefty / Seven come eleven / I don't know why I love you
CD ______ EDCD 426
Edsel / May '95 / Pinnacle

Ayers, Kevin

BANANAMOUR
Don't let it get you down / Shouting in a bucket blues / When your parents go to sleep / Interview / International anthem / Decadence / Oh wot a dream / Hymn / Beware of the dog
CD ______ BGOCD 142
Beat Goes On / Jun '92 / Pinnacle

CONFESSIONS OF DR DREAM
Day by day / See you later / Didn't feel lonely till I thought of you / Everybody's sometime and some people's all the time blues / It begins with a blessing / Once I awakened / But it ends with a curse / Ballbearing blues / Confessions of Dr. Dream / Irreversible neural damage / Invitation / One chance dance / Dr. Dream / Two goes into four
CD ______ BGOCD 86
Beat Goes On / Oct '90 / Pinnacle

FIRST SHOW IN THE APPEARANCE BUSINESS
CD ______ BOJCD 020
Band Of Joy / Nov '96 / Pinnacle

JOY OF A TOY
Joy of a toy continued / Clarietta rag / Song for insane times / Eleanor's cake which ate her / Oleh oleh bandu bandong / Town feeling / Girl on a swing / Stop this train / Lady Rachel / All this crazy gift of time
CD ______ BGOCD 78
Beat Goes On / '89 / Pinnacle

KEVIN AYERS
CD ______ CSAPCD 110
Connoisseur Collection / Sep '92 / Pinnacle

KEVIN AYERS COLLECTION
Lady Rachel / May I / Puis-je / Stranger in blue suede shoes / Caribbean moon / Shouting in a bucket blues / After the show / Didn't feel lonely till I thought of you / Once upon an ocean / City waltz / Blue star / Blaming it all on love / Strange song / Miss Hanaga / Money, money, money
CD ______ SEECD 117
See For Miles/C5 / Jun '97 / Pinnacle

RAINBOW TAKEAWAY
Blaming it all on love / Ballad of a salesman who sold himself / View from the mountain / Rainbow takeaway / Waltz for you / Beware of the dog / Strange song / Goodnight, goodnight / Hat song
CD ______ BGOCD 189
Beat Goes On / Apr '93 / Pinnacle

SHOOTING AT THE MOON (Ayers, Kevin & The Whole World)
May 1 / Colores para Dolores / Lunatics lament / Underwater / Red, green and blue you / Rheinhardt and Geraldine / Pisser dans un violon / Oyster and the flying fish / Clarence in Wonderland / Shooting at the moon
CD ______ BGOCD 13
Beat Goes On / Apr '90 / Pinnacle

SINGING THE BRUISE (Live At The BBC)
Why are we sleeping / You say you like my hat / Gemini chile / Lady Rachel / Derby day / Interview / We did it again / Oyster and the flying fish / Butterfly dance / Whatevershebringswesing / Falling in love again / Queen thing
CD ______ BOJCD 019
Band Of Joy / Aug '96 / Pinnacle

SOPORIFICS (June 1 1974) (Ayers, Kevin & John Cale/Nico/Brian Eno)
Driving me backwards / Baby's on fire / Heartbreak hotel / End / May I / Shouting in a bucket blues / Stranger in blue suede shoes / Everybody's sometime and some people's all the time blues / Two goes into four
CD ______ IMCD 92
Island / Feb '90 / PolyGram

SWEET DECEIVER
Observations / Guru banana / City waltz / Toujours la voyage / Sweet deceiver / Diminished but not finished / Circular letter / Once upon an ocean / Farewell again
CD ______ BGOCD 98
Beat Goes On / Aug '92 / Pinnacle

THAT'S WHAT YOU GET BABE
That's what you get / Where do I go from here / You never outrun your love / Given and taken / Idiots / Super salesman / Money, money, money / Miss Hanaga / I'm so tired / Where do the stars end
CD ______ BGOCD 190
Beat Goes On / Jun '93 / Pinnacle

WHATEVER SHE BRINGS WE SING
There is loving / Among us / Margaret oh my / Song from the bottom of a well / Whatever she brings we sing / Stranger in blue suede shoes / Champagne cowboy blues / Lullaby
CD ______ BGOCD 11
Beat Goes On / Apr '88 / Pinnacle

YES WE HAVE NO MANANAS
Star / Mr. Cool / Owl / love's gonna turn you round / Falling in love again / Help me / Ballad of Mr. Snake / Everyone knows the song / Yes I do / Blue
CD ______ BGOCD 143
Beat Goes On / Apr '93 / Pinnacle

Ayers, Roy

DRIVE
CD ______ ICH 1028CD
Ichiban / Mar '94 / Direct / Koch

ESSENTIAL GROOVE - LIVE
Everybody loves the sunshine / Hot / Red, black and green / Searchin' / Love will bring us back together / Don't wait for love / We live in London baby / Long time ago / Poo poo la la
CD ______ JHCD 035
Ronnie Scott's Jazz House / '88 / Cadillac / Jazz Music / New Note/Pinnacle / TKO Magnum

EVERYBODY LOVES THE SUNSHINE
Hey u / Golden rod / Keep on walking / You and me my love / Third eye / It ain't your sign / People and the world / Everybody loves the sunshine / Tongue power / Lonesome cowboy
CD ______ 8338442
Polydor / Sep '93 / PolyGram

FAST MONEY (Live at Ronnie Scott's)
Spirit of doo doo / I wanna touch you / Everybody loves the sunshine / Fast money / Battle of the vibes / Can't you see me / Running away / Don't stop the feeling
CD ______ CLACD 335
Castle / '93 / BMG

GOOD VIBRATIONS
Everybody loves the sunshine / Easy to move / Mission / Wrapped up in your love / X marks the spot / Poo poo la la / Ivory tower
CD ______ JHCD 028
Ronnie Scott's Jazz House / Jan '94 / Cadillac / Jazz Music / New Note/Pinnacle / TKO Magnum

HOT
Can't you see me / Running away / Love will bring us together / Lots of love / Everyone loves the sunshine / Hot / Pete King /

Sweet tears / Philadelphia mambo / We live in London baby
CD _______ **JHCD 021**
Ronnie Scott's Jazz House / Jan '94 / Cadillac / Jazz Music / New Note/Pinnacle / TKO Magnum

LIVE AT MONTREUX 1972 (Ayers, Roy Ubiquity)
CD _______ **5316412**
Verve / Jul '96 / PolyGram

NASTE
Naste / Mama Daddy / Your love / Treasure / Swirl / Fantasy / Ole Jose / Baby, set me free / No more trouble / Satisfaction / I like it like that / Last XT / Nonsense
CD _______ **07863666132**
Groovetown / Jun '95 / BMG

SEARCHIN'
Searchin' / Yes / You send me / Mystic voyage / Love will bring us together / Spirit of the Do Do / Long time ago / Can you see me
CD _______ **JHCD 013**
Ronnie Scott's Jazz House / Jan '94 / Cadillac / Jazz Music / New Note/Pinnacle / TKO Magnum

SHINING SYMBOL, A (The Ultimate Collection)
Running away / Love will bring us back together / Searching / Everybody loves the sunshine / Mystic voyage / Time and space / Evolution / He's a superstar / 2000 black / Red, black and green / We live in Brooklyn baby / He's coming / I wanna touch you baby / Can't you see me / Fire weaver / Shining symbol
CD _______ **5193782**
Polydor / May '93 / PolyGram

VIBESMAN (Live At Ronnie Scott's)
CD _______ **MCCD 215**
Music Club / Oct '95 / Disc / THE

VIBRANT
CD _______ **VSOPCD 179**
Connoisseur Collection / Feb '93 / Pinnacle

WAKE UP
Midnight after dark / Suave / Sweet talk / Spirit of dodo '89 / Crack is in the mirror (wake up) / You've got the power / Mystic vibrations
CD _______ **ICH 1040CD**
Ichiban / Oct '93 / Direct / Koch

Ayibobo

FREESTYLE
CD _______ **DIW 877**
DIW / Jan '94 / Cadillac / Harmonia Mundi

Ayler, Albert

FONDATION MAEGHT NIGHTS
CD _______ **COD 004**
Jazz View / Mar '92 / Harmonia Mundi

GOIN' HOME
CD _______ **BLCD 760197**
Koch / Nov '94 / Koch

LIVE IN EUROPE
CD _______ **LS 2902**
Lagoon / Mar '93 / Grapevine/PolyGram

MY NAME IS ALBERT AYLER
CD _______ **BLCD 760211**
Black Lion / Mar '96 / Cadillac / Jazz Music / Koch / Wellard

TRUTH IS MARCHING IN (Ayler, Albert Quintet)
CD _______ **30003**
Giants Of Jazz / Sep '92 / Cadillac / Jazz Music / Target/BMG

VIBRATIONS (Ayler, Albert & Don Cherry)
Ghosts / Children / Holy spirit / Vibrations / Mothers
CD _______ **FCD 41000**
Freedom / Sep '87 / Cadillac / Jazz Music / Koch / Wellard

WITCHES AND DEVILS
CD _______ **FCD 41018**
Freedom / Jan '87 / Cadillac / Jazz Music / Koch / Wellard

Aytekin, Ziya

ZIYA
CD _______ **SJE 8CD**
Sjelvar / Aug '96 / ADA

AZ

DOE OR DIE
Uncut raw / Gimme your's / Ho happy Jackie / Rather unique / I feel for you / Sugarhill / Mo money / Mo murder (homicide) / Doe or die / We can't win / Your world don't stop / Sugarhill (remix)
CD _______ **CTCD 51**
Cooltempo / Sep '97 / EMI

AZ

MUSIC FOR SCATTERED BRAINS
CD _______ **ALP 81CD**
Atavistic / Feb '97 / Cargo / SRD

Az Yet

AZ YET
Last night / Saved for someone else / Care for me / Every little bit / Hard to say I'm sorry / That's all I want / Secrets / Through my heart (the arrow) / I don't want to be lonely / Sadder than blue / Inseparable lovers / Time to end this story
CD _______ **73008260342**
LaFace / Jun '97 / BMG

Azaad

JUGNI
CD _______ **DMUT 1152**
Multitone / Nov '90 / BMG

Azalia Snail

DEEP MOTIF
CD _______ **CF 013**
Candy Floss / Nov '96 / Cargo

FUMAROLE RISING
CD _______ **CAT 007**
Catapult / May '97 / Cargo / Greyhound

Azar

SALAM KABYL DANCE
CD _______ **AAA 144**
Club Du Disque Arabe / Aug '97 / ADA / Harmonia Mundi

Azevedo, Geraldo

BEREKEKE
CD _______ **925632**
BUDA / Jun '93 / Discovery

Aznavour, Charles

20 CHANSONS D'OR
Je m'voyais deja / Trousse - chemise / Les plaisirs demodes / Qui / Les comediens / La mamma / For me... formidable / Non, je n'ai rien oublie / Le temps / Que c'est triste venise / Tu t'laisses aller / Et pourtant / La Boheme / Les deux guitares / Desormais / Il faut savoir / Comme Ils Disent / Hier encore / L'amour c'est comme un jour / Emmenez - moi
CD _______ **CDEMC 3716**
EMI / Jul '95 / EMI

LES COMEDIENS
CD _______ **CD 352072**
Duchesse / May '93 / Pinnacle

PARIS - PALAIS DES CONGRES (Aznavour, Charles & Liza Minnelli)
Prologue / Sound of your name / Mon emouvant amour / Les Comediens / Sa jeunesse / Napoli chante / Vous et tu / La Marguerite / Tu t'laisses aller / Non je n'ai rien oublie / Je bois / Comme ils disent / Les plaisirs demodes / La Boheme / Je m'voyais deja / Pour faire une jam / Bonjour Paris / God bless the child / Old friend / Liza with a Z / Sailor boys / Some people / J'ai deux amours / Stepping out / Losing my mind / I love a piano / Cabaret / New York, New York / Our love is here to stay / Song is you / Old devil moon / How high in the sky / Let's fall in love / I've got you under my skin / Dream / Unforgettable / I've grown accustomed to her face / These foolish things / Just a dream ago / How high the moon / Just in time / Le temps
CD _______ **CDEMD 1080**
EMI / Jul '95 / EMI

SHE (The Best Of Charles Aznavour)
She / Yesterday when I was young / Happy days / La Boheme / How sad Venice can be / No, I could never forget / Happy Anniversary / You've got to learn / I didn't see the time go by / And in my chair / Three is a time / You've let yourself go / Old fashioned way / Take me along / To my daughter / Sound of your name / It will be my day / Ave Maria / What makes a man / They fell
CD _______ **PRMTVCD 4**
Premier/EMI / Nov '96 / EMI

WE WERE HAPPY THEN
CD _______ **CDSL 5189**
DRG / '88 / Discovery / New Note/ Pinnacle

Azreal

THERE SHALL BE NO ANSWER
CD _______ **NBAZ 001CD**
Nuclear Blast / Nov '95 / Plastic Head

Azrie, Abed

AROMATES
CD _______ **7559792412**
Nonesuch / Jan '95 / Warner Music

Aztec Camera

FRESTONIA
CD _______ **0630119292**
WEA / Oct '95 / Warner Music

HIGH LAND, HARD RAIN
Oblivious / Boy wonders / Walk out to winter / Bugle sounds again / We could send letters / Pillar to post / Release / Lost outside the tunnel / Back on board / Down the dip / Haywire / Orchid girl / Queen's tattoos
CD _______ **4509928492**
WEA / Sep '93 / Warner Music

KNIFE
Just like the USA / Head is happy (heart's insane) / Backdoor to heaven / All I need is everything / Backwards and forwards / Birth of the true / Knife / Still on fire
CD _______ **K 2404832**
WEA / Sep '93 / Warner Music

LOVE
Deep and wide and tall / How men are / Everybody is a number one / More than a law / Somewhere in my heart / Working in a goldmine / One and one / Paradise / Killermont street
CD _______ **K 2422022**
WEA / Sep '93 / Warner Music

STRAY
Stray / Crying scene / Get outta London / Over my head / Good morning Britain / How it is / Gentle kind / Notting Hill blues / Song for a friend
CD _______ **9031716942**
WEA / Sep '93 / Warner Music

Azukx

EVERYTHING IS EVERYTHING
CD _______ **MNTCD 1**
Mantra / Oct '95 / RTM/Disc

Azuquita

LOS ORIGINALES
CD _______ **FA 407**
Fremeaux / Jul '96 / ADA / Discovery

Azusa Plane

TYCHO-MAGNETIC ANOMALY AND THE FULL CONSCIOUSNESS OF HIDDEN
CD _______ **CAM 002CD**
Camera Obscura / May '97 / Cargo

Azymuth

AZYMUTH
CD Set _______ **5230102**
ECM / Jul '94 / New Note/Pinnacle

AZYMUTH '85
Adios lony / Dream - lost song / Who are you / Breathtaking / Potion 1 / February daze / Till bakeblikk / Potion 2
CD _______ **8275202**
ECM / Dec '85 / New Note/Pinnacle

BEST OF AZYMUTH, THE
Club Morrocco / Cascades of the seven waterfalls / Textile factory / Right on / Somewhere in Brazil / Outubro / 500 miles high / Dear Limmertz / Song of the jet / Areiras / All the carnaval / Maracana
CD _______ **MCD 91602**
Milestone / Apr '94 / Cadillac / Complete/ Pinnacle / Jazz Music / Wellard

CARIOCA
CD _______ **MCD 9169**
Milestone / Oct '93 / Cadillac / Complete/ Pinnacle / Jazz Music / Wellard

CARNIVAL
Jazz carnival / Wuiema Roupa / Faca de conta / Esperando minha vez / Calma / Tudo que voce podia ser / Prefacio / Tempos atraz / Ausgang / Quem com quem
CD _______ **FARO 011CD**
Far Out / Oct '96 / Amato Disco / New Note/ Pinnacle

CRAZY RHYTHM
CD _______ **MCD 9156**
Milestone / Oct '93 / Cadillac / Complete/ Pinnacle / Jazz Music / Wellard

HOW IT WAS THEN...NEVER AGAIN
How it was then / Looking on / Whirlpool / Full circle / How deep is the ocean / Stango / Mindiatyr / Wintersweet
CD _______ **4238202**
ECM / Apr '95 / New Note/Pinnacle

JAZZ CARNIVAL - BEST OF AZYMUTH
Jazz carnival / Dear Limmertz / Estreito de taruma / Cascade of the seven waterfalls / Missing doto / Maracana / Samba da barra / Textile factory / Turma do samba / Papaia: *Malheiros, Alex* / Partido alto: *Bertrami, Jose Roberto* / Pantanal il swamp: *Conti, Ivan*
CD _______ **CDBGP 1007**
Beat Goes Public / Mar '88 / Pinnacle

Azzola, Marcel

L'ACCORDEONISTE (Homage A Edith Piaf)
L'accordeoniste / La vie en rose / L'Etranger / Les trois cloches / La goualante du pavre Jean / Mon legionnaire / Jezebel / Padam...padam / Milord / C'est un gars / Hymne a l'amour
CD _______ **5215002**
Verve / Jun '94 / PolyGram

Azzolini, Giorgio

SCICLUNA STREET, THE
CD _______ **RTCL 804CD**
Right Tempo / Jul '96 / New Note/ Pinnacle / Timewarp

B

B-Bumble & The Stingers

NUT ROCKER AND ALL THE CLASSICS
Nut rocker / Bumble boogie / School day blues / Boogie woogie / Near you / Bee hive / Caravan / Nautilus / Nola / Rockin' on 'n' off / Mashed / Apple knocker / Moon and the sea / All of me / Dawn cracker / Scales / 12th Street rag / Canadian sunset / Baby mash / Night time madness / In the mood / Chicken chow mein / Bumble bossa nova / Canadian sunset (Alt.)
CD ______ CDCHD 577
Ace / Jul '95 / Pinnacle

B-Girls

WHO SAYS THAT GIRLS CAN'T ROCK
CD ______ OPM 2111CD
Other People's Music / Feb '97 / Greyhound / Plastic Head

B Shops For The Poor

VISIONS AND BLUEPRINTS
CD ______ NWCD 2
No Wave / Oct '91 / Cadillac / ReR Megacorp

B So Global

WORLD IS COVERED IN WINDOWS, THE
CD ______ CHILLUM 002
Chill Um / Jan '96 / Plastic Head

B-12

ELECTRO-SOMA
CD ______ WARPCD 9
Warp / Apr '96 / Prime / RTM/Disc

B-52's

B-52'S
Planet Claire / Fifty two Girls / Dance this mess around / Rock lobster / Lava / There's a Moon in the sky (called Moon) / Hero worship / 6060 842 / Downtown
CD ______ IMCD 1
Island / May '90 / PolyGram

BOUNCING OFF THE SATELLITES
Summer of love / Girl from Ipanema goes to Greenland / Housework / Detour thru your mind / Wig / Theme for a nude beach / Juicy jungle / Communicate / She brakes for rainbows
CD ______ IMCD 105
Island / May '90 / PolyGram

COSMIC THING
Cosmic thing / Dead beat club / Junebug / Bush fire / Topaz / Dry county / Love shack / Roam / Channel Z / Follow your bliss
CD ______ K 9258542
WEA / Dec '96 / Warner Music

DANCE THIS MESS AROUND (The Best Of The B-52's)
Party out of bounds / Dirty back road / Wig / Rock lobster / Give me back my man / Planet Claire / Devil in my car / 6060 842 / Dance this mess around / Strobelight / Song for a future generation
CD ______ IMCD 238
Island / Mar '97 / PolyGram

GOOD STUFF
Tell it like it is / Hot pants explosion / Good stuff / Revolution earth / Dreamland / Is that you mo-dean / World's green laughter / Vision of a kiss / Breezin' / Bad influence
CD ______ 7599269432
WEA / Jun '92 / Warner Music

MESOPOTAMIA
Loveland / Mesopotamia / Throw that beat in the garbage can / Deep sleep / Cake / Nip it in the bud
CD ______ IMCD 107
Island / May '90 / PolyGram

PARTY MIX
Party out of bounds / Private Idaho / Give me back my man / Lava / Dance this mess around / Fifty two girls
CD ______ IMCD 106
Island / May '90 / PolyGram

PLANET CLAIRE
Planet Claire / Rock lobster / Lava / Downtown / 6060-842 / 52 Girls / Give me back my man / Strobe light / Dirty back road / Loveland / Nip it in the bud / Song for a future generation / Wig / Girl from Ipanema goes to Greenland
CD ______ 5512102
Spectrum / Aug '95 / PolyGram

WHAMMY
Legal tender / Whammy kiss / Song for a future generation / Butterbean / Trism / Queen of Las Vegas / Don't worry / Big bird / Work that skirt
CD ______ IMCD 109
Island / May '90 / PolyGram

WILD PLANET
Party out of bounds / Dirty back road / Running around / Give me back my man / Private Idaho / Quiche Lorraine / Strobelight / Fifty three miles West of Venus / Devils in my car
CD ______ IMCD 108
Island / May '90 / PolyGram

B-Movie

REMEMBRANCE DAY
Man on a threshold / Refugee / Drowning man / Soundtrack / Nowhere girl / Institution walls / This still life / Left out in the cold / Remembrance day / Aeroplanes and mountains / Remembrance day / Remembrance day
CD ______ CDMRED 137
Cherry Red / Mar '97 / Pinnacle

B-Tribe

SUAVE SUAVE
Suave suave / Que mala vida / Sensual / Ahoy / Hablando / Interlude / Albatros / Te siento / Nanita / Poesia / Yo quiero todo / Manha de carneval
CD ______ 0630175182
East West / Feb '97 / Warner Music

B12

TIME TOURIST
CD ______ WARPCD 37
Warp / Feb '96 / Prime / RTM/Disc

Baader Meinhof

BAADER MEINHOF
Baader Meinhof / Meet me at the airport / There's gonna be an accident / Mogadishu / Theme from Burn Warehouse Burn / GSG 29 / ...it's a moral issue / Back on the farm / Kill Ramirez / Baader Meinhof / I've been a fool for you
CD ______ CDHUT 36
Hut / Oct '96 / EMI

Baars, Ab

3900 CAROL COURT
CD ______ GEESTCD 12
Geest Gronden / Feb '89 / Cadillac

KRANG
CD ______ GEESTCD 02
Geest Gronden / Sep '87 / Cadillac

Baba Jam Band

KAYADA
CD ______ BEST 1036CD
Acoustic Music / Nov '93 / ADA

Babata

JJY MUSIC
CD ______ 122120
Long Distance / Jul '96 / ADA / Discovery

Babe The Blue Ox

(BOX)
Home / Honey do / Chicken head bone sucker / Gymkhana / Spatula / Waiting for water to boil / Booty / Born again / National Geographic / Tongue tied / Snicker
CD ______ RTD 15715752
World Service / Jun '93 / Vital

Babes In Toyland

FONTANELLE
CD ______ 185012
Southern / '92 / SRD

NEMESISTER
CD ______ 9362458682
Warner Bros. / Apr '95 / Warner Music

PAINKILLERS
CD ______ 185122
Southern / Jun '93 / SRD

Babs, Alice

ALICE BABS & DUKE ELLINGTON/NILS LINDBERG 1973 (Babs, Alice & Duke Ellington/Nils Lindberg)
CD ______ ABCD 005
Bluebell / Oct '96 / Cadillac / Jazz Music

ALICE BABS, RED MITCHELL, ARNE DOMNERUS & NILS LINDBERG
CD ______ ABC 052
Bluebell / Mar '94 / Cadillac / Jazz Music

FAR AWAY STAR (Babs, Alice & Duke Ellington/Nils Lindberg Orchestras)
Far away star / Serenade to Sweden / Spaceman / Jeep's blues / Daydream / Is God a three-letter word for love / Jump for joy / Warm valley / Blues for the maestro
CD ______ ABC 000005
Bluebell / Oct '90 / Cadillac / Jazz Music

SWING IT (1939-1953)
CD ______ PHONTCD 9302
Phontastic / Jun '94 / Cadillac / Jazz Music / Wellard

Baby Bird

BAD SHAVE
KW Jesus TV roof appeal / Bad jazz / Too handsome / Steam train / Bad shave / O my God, you're a king / Restaurant is guilty / Valerie / Shop girl / WBT / Hate song / 45 + Fat / Sha na na / Bug in a breeze / It's OK / Happy bus / Swinging from tree to tree
CD ______ BABYBIRDCD 002
Baby Bird / Oct '95 / Vital

FATHERHOOD
No children / Cooling towers / Cool and crazy thing to do / Bad blood / Neil Armstrong / May be / But love / Good weather / Not about a girl / Dustbin liner / Fatherhood / Failed old singer / Daisies / Godamn it, you're a kid / Aluminium beach / Iceberg / I didn't want to wake you up / Good night
CD ______ BABYBIRDCD 003
Baby Bird / Dec '95 / Vital

HAPPIEST MAN ALIVE, THE
Razor blade shower / Sundial in a tunnel / Little white man / Halfway up the hill / Horse sugar / Please don't be famous / Louse / Copper feel / Sea gullaby / Dead in love / Candy girl / Gunfingers / M-Word / Married / In the country / Plane crash xmas / Beautiful disease / You'll get a slap / In the morning
CD ______ BABYBIRDCD 004
Baby Bird / Apr '96 / Vital

I WAS BORN A MAN
Blow it to the moon / Man's tight vest / Lemonade baby / CFC / Corner shop / Kiss your country / Hong Kong blues / Dead bird sings / Baby bird / Farmer / Invisible tune / Alison / Love love love
CD ______ BABYBIRD 001
Baby Bird / Jul '95 / Vital

UGLY BEAUTIFUL
You're gorgeous / Farmer / Candy girl / Didn't want to wake you up / Dead bird sings / Goodnight / Hate song / Wife shirt beater / Cornershop / Bad shave 2 / Atomic soda / 45 & fat / You & me / King Bird / Ladybird in July / Too handsome to be homeless
CD ______ ECHCD 011
Echo / Oct '96 / EMI / Vital

Baby Buddah Heads

WHO KILLED ACID JAZZ
CD ______ CS 8522
Mic Mac / Mar '96 / Vital/SAM

Baby Chaos

LOVE YOUR SELF ABUSE
Hello / She's in pain / Mental bruising for beginners / Ignoramus / Sensual art of suffocation / Confessions of a teenage pervert / Penny dropped / Pink / Love your self abuse
CD ______ 0630146102
East West / Apr '96 / Warner Music

Baby D

DELIVERANCE (2CD Set)
Got to believe / So pure / Destiny / Come into my world / Casanova / Winds of love / I need your loving / Daydreaming / Euphoria / Nature's warning / Take me to heaven / Let me be your fantasy / Have it all / Daydreaming - Acenhallucination / So pure
CD ______ 8286832
CD Set ______ 8287202
Systematic / Jan '96 / PolyGram

Baby Doc

IN WORSHIP OF FALSE IDOLS (Baby Doc & The Dentist)
CD ______ TECLP 23CD
TEC / Jul '95 / SRD

Baby Ford

HEADPHONEASYRIDER
CD ______ BMI 1035CD
Black Market International / Apr '97 / Prime / Soul Trader / Vital

Baby Fox

NORMAL FAMILY, A
CD ______ COB 58992
Deep Blue / Jul '96 / PolyGram

Baby Mammoth

10,000 YEARS UNDER THE STREET
CD ______ PORK 035
Pork / Aug '96 / Kudos / Pinnacle / Prime

BRIDGING TWO WORLDS
CD ______ PORK 042
Pork / Feb '97 / Kudos / Pinnacle / Prime

ONE, TWO, FREAK
CD ______ PORK 044
Pork / Jul '97 / Kudos / Pinnacle / Prime

Baby Wayne

RAM DJ
CD ______ HBCD 147
Heartbeat / Jan '94 / ADA / Direct / Greensleeves / Jet Star

Babyface

CLOSER LOOK, A
Mary Mack / Two occasions / I love you babe / Chivalry / Lovers / It's no crime / Love saw it: *Babyface & Karyn White* / Love makes things happen: *Babyface & Pebbles* / My kinda girl / Whip appeal / Lovers
CD ______ 4693482
Epic / Feb '97 / Sony

DAY, THE
Every time I close my eyes / Talk to me / I said I love you / When your body gets weak / Simple days / All day thinkin' / Seven seas / Day (that you gave me a son) / How come, how long / This is for the lover in you
CD ______ 4853682
Epic / Nov '96 / Sony

FOR THE COOL IN YOU
For the cool in you / Lady lady / Never keeping secrets / Rock bottom / And our feelings / Saturday / When can I see you / Illusions / Bit old fashioned / You are so beautiful / I'll always love you / Well alright
CD ______ 4739492
Epic / Jan '94 / Sony

LOVERS
You make me feel brand new / Lovers / Chivalry / I love you / Mary Mack / Faithful / If we try / Take your time / I love you babe
CD ______ 4879282
Epic / Jul '97 / Sony

Babylon Dance Band

BABYLON DANCE BAND
When I'm home / Bold beginnings / Reckoning / Shively spleen / Roger / Leave / Resources / See that girl / Jacob's chain / ABC / Golden days / Someday / All radical / Shake
CD ______ OLE 0332
Matador / May '94 / Vital

Babylon Sad

KYRIE
CD ______ MASSCD 026
Massacre / Feb '94 / Plastic Head

Babylon Whores

COLD HEAVEN
Deviltry / Omega therion / Beyond the sun / Metatron / Enchiridion / In arcadia / Babylon astronaut / Flesh of a swine / Cold heaven
CD ______ CDMFN 226
Music For Nations / Aug '97 / Pinnacle

Babylon Zoo

BOY WITH THE X-RAY EYES, THE
Animal army / Spaceman / Zodiac sign / Paris green / Confused art / Caffeine / Boy with the x-ray eyes / Don't feed the animals / Fire guided light / Is your soul for sale / I'm cracking up I need a pill
CD ______ CDEMC 3742
EMI / Sep '97 / EMI

Bacan

CARA (Bacan & Lilian Vieira)
CD ______ CHR 70036
Challenge / Sep '96 / ADA / Direct / Jazz Music / Wellard

Bacan, Pedro

EN PUBLIC A BOBIGNY (Bacan, Pedro & Les Clan Des Pinini)
Sabeis ustedes Senores / Que quiere que tenga / Pobresito de aquel / Tu querer y mi querer / Gitania / Lo mucho que te quiero
CD ______ PW 011
Pee Wee / Jul '97 / New Note/Pinnacle

Bach Choir

IN DULCI JUBILO (Bach Choir & Philip Jones Brass Ensemble)
Fanfare / O come all ye faithful (adeste fidelis) / Gabriel's message / Angelus ad virginem / Ding dong merrily on high / Virgin most pure / God rest ye merry gentlemen / In dulci jubilo / Unto us is born a son / Nun seid ihr wohl gerochen / Lord Jesus hath a

garden / Come all ye shepherds / Wassail song / We three Kings / Il est ne / Jingle bells / Deck the hall / Holly and the ivy / We wish you a merry Christmas / Ach mein herzliebes Jesulein / Once in Royal David's city / Hush my dear, lie still and slumber / Shepherd's pipe carol / Away in a manger / Stille nacht / Sussex carol / Star carol / Hark the herald angels sing / Fanfare
CD _______________ 4489802
Decca / Nov '96 / PolyGram

Bach, Johnny

BACH ON THE BOTTLE AGAIN (Bach, Johnny & The Moonshine Boozers)
Lost John / Down the road / Move it / Wanted man / I don't wanna go home / Ice cold baby / Dissatisfied / Black rat swing / Hot lips baby / De bop / It ain't my job to tell you / Rock around the town / Jailhouse rock / I wanna bop / Move it / Hot lips baby
CD _______________ JRCD 30
Jappin' & Rockin' / May '97 / Swift / TKO Magnum

Bacharach, Burt

BACHARACH AND DAVID (They Write The Songs) (Various Artists)
Do you know the way to San Jose: *Warwick, Dionne* / Raindrops keep falling on my head: *Thomas, B.J.* / This guy's in love with you: *Distel, Sacha* / What the world needs now is love: *De Shannon, Jackie* / Message to Michael: *Deacon Blue* / 24 hours from Tulsa: *Pitney, Gene* / I'll never fall in love again: *Gentry, Bobbie* / (There's) Always something there to remind me: *Shaw, Sandie* / House is not a home: *Vandross, Luther* / (They long to be) Close to you: *Hayes, Isaac* / Alfie: *Monro, Matt* / Trains and boats and planes: *Kramer, Billy J.* / I say a little prayer: *Booker T & The MG's* / Only love can break your heart: *Yuro, Timi* / Anyone who had a heart: *Black, Cilla* / To wait for love: *Distel, Sacha* / Look of love: *Bassey, Shirley* / I just don't know what to do with myself: *Warwick, Dionne*
CD _______________ NTRCD 073
Nectar / Apr '97 / Pinnacle

BEST OF BURT BACHARACH, THE
CD _______________ 5404522
A&M / Apr '96 / PolyGram

BEST OF BURT BACHARACH, THE (RTE Concert Orchestra/Richard Hayman)
CD _______________ 8990051
Naxos / May '96 / Select

BURT BACHARACH/HAL DAVID SONGBOOK, THE (Various Artists)
I say a little prayer: *Warwick, Dionne* / What the world needs now is love: *De Shannon, Jackie* / Alfie: *Black, Cilla* / Message to Michael: *Warwick, Dionne* / I just don't know what to do with myself: *Springfield, Dusty* / Do you know the way to San Jose: *Warwick, Dionne* / Twenty four hours from Tulsa: *Pitney, Gene* / Close to you: *Monro, Matt* / You'll never get to heaven (If you break my heart): *Warwick, Dionne* / Anyone who had a heart: *Black, Cilla* / I'll never fall in love again: *Gentry, Bobbie* / Walk on by: *Van Dyke, Leroy* / Story of my life: *Holliday, Michael* / What's new pussycat: *Jones, Tom* / This guy's in love with you: *Distel, Sacha* / Trains and boats and planes: *Kramer, Billy J.* / Make it easy on yourself: *Walker Brothers* / House is not a home: *Bassey, Shirley* / Always something there to remind me: *Shaw, Sandie* / Look of love: *Warwick, Dionne* / Raindrops keep falling on my head: *Distel, Sacha* / Wishin' and hopin': *Merseybeats* / Only love can break a heart: *Yuro, Timi* / Promises, promises: *Warwick, Dionne*
CD _______________ VSOPCD 128
Connoisseur Collection / Jan '89 / Pinnacle

CLOSE TO YOU
CD _______________ MACCD 277
Autograph / Aug '96 / BMG

EASY LISTENING BACHARACH (Various Artists)
Promises, promises: *Faith, Percy* / Send me no flowers: *Day, Doris* / Alfie: *Bennett, Tony* / Wives and lovers: *Williams, Andy* / I'll never fall in love again: *Page, Patti* / Walk on by: *Torme, Mel* / Close to you: *Mathis, Johnny* / Trains and boats and planes: *Harris, Anita* / Do you know the way to San Jose: *Goulet, Robert* / House is not a home: *Fame, Georgie* / This girl's in love with you: *Jones, Salena* / Make it easy on yourself: *Bennett, Tony* / Blue on blue: *Vinton, Bobby* / Raindrops keep falling on my head: *Nero, Peter* / My little red book: *Torme, Mel* / I say a little prayer: *Harris, Anita* / Look of love: *Mathis, Johnny* / Story of my life: *Robbins, Marty* / If I could go back: *Williams, Andy* / What the world needs now is love: *Bennett, Tony*
CD _______________ 4851252
Columbia / Aug '96 / Sony

FOREVER BURT BACHARACH (Various Artists)
Walk on by: *Shapiro, Helen* / I say a little prayer: *Goodwin, Ron & His Orchestra* / Close to you: *Monro, Matt* / Alfie: *Cher* / Do you know the way to San Jose: *Manuel* / What the world needs now is love: *De Shannon, Jackie* / Raindrops keep falling on my head: *Gentry, Bobbie* / Trains and boats and planes: *Kramer, Billy J. & The Dakotas* / Magic moments: *Hilton, Ronnie* / Look of love: *Tarmey, Bill* / I'll never fall in love again: *Gentry, Bobbie* / House is not a home: *Bassey, Shirley* / This guy's in love with you: *O'Connor, Des* / Message to Martha: *Faith, Adam* / Once in a blue moon: *Cole, Nat 'King'* / Keep away from other girls: *Shapiro, Helen* / Make it easy on yourself: *Black, Cilla* / Anyone who had a heart: *Carr, Vikki* / Keep me in my mind: *Cogan, Alma*
CD _______________ CDMFP 6264
Music For Pleasure / Nov '96 / EMI

GOLD SERIES
Raindrops keep falling on my head / Look of love / I'll never fall in love again / Do you know the way to San Jose / What the world needs now is love / Alfie / Reach out / Promises, promises / This guy's in love with you / Close to you / Make it easy on yourself / I say a little prayer / April fools / Bond street / Any day now / Pacific coast highway / House is not a home / One less bell to answer / Wives and lovers / Living together, growing together / Knowing when to leave
CD _______________ CDMID 156
A&M / Oct '92 / PolyGram

I'LL NEVER FALL IN LOVE AGAIN
Do you know the way to San Jose / I say a little prayer / I'll never fall in love again / No one remembers my name / This guy's in love with you / Time and tenderness / Wives and lovers / Raindrops keep falling on my head / Close to you / Look of love / Alfie / Where are you / Us / Another spring will rise
CD _______________ 5500572
Spectrum / May '93 / PolyGram

MAGIC MOMENTS (The Classic Songs Of Burt Bacharach) (Various Artists)
Magic moments: *Como, Perry* / Raindrops keep fallin' on my head: *Como, Perry* / (They long to be) close to you: *Como, Perry* / House is not a home: *Como, Perry* / Look of love: *Simone, Nina* / Alfie: *Warwick, Dionne* / Sunny weather lover: *Warwick, Dionne* / Anyone who had a heart: *McGovern, Maureen* / There's always something there to remind me: *Feliciano, Jose* / I say a little prayer: *Davis, Skeeter* / Do you know the way to San Jose: *Ames, Ed* / Make it easy on yourself: *Ames, Ed* / What the world needs now is love: *Ames, Ed* / Wives and lovers: *Ames, Ed* / What's new pussycat: *Cramer, Floyd* / I just don't know what to do with myself: *Cramer, Floyd* / Any day now: *Milsap, Ronnie* / I'll never fall in love again: *Atkins, Chet* / This guy's in love with you: *Stuckey, Nat* / Blue on blue: *Anka, Paul* / Promises promises: *Hirt, Al*
CD _______________ 74321447232
Camden / Feb '97 / BMG

MAGIC MUSIC OF BURT BACHARACH (Various Artists)
CD _______________ GRF 195
Tring / Jan '93 / Tring

MAGIC OF BURT BACHARACH, THE (Various Artists)
CD _______________ CPCD 8227
Charly / Aug '96 / Koch

MUSIC OF BURT BACHARACH, THE (Various Artists)
24 hours from Tulsa: *Pitney, Gene* / Arthur's theme: *Bilk, Acker* / Raindrops keep fallin' on my head: *Thomas, B.J.* / Do you know the way to San Jose: *Coombe Music* / I say a little prayer: *Coombe Music* / I'll never fall in love again: *Coombe Music* / Make it easy on yourself: *Butler, Jerry* / Love that really counts: *Merseybeats* / Magic moments: *Coombe Music* / Alfie: *Coombe Music* / House is not a home: *Coombe Music* / Any day now: *Drifters* / Look of love: *Coombe Music* / Answer to everything: *Shannon, Del* / Only love can break your heart: *Pitney, Gene* / There's always something there to remind me: *Coombe Music* / What the world needs now is love: *Coombe Music* / This guy's in love with you: *Coombe Music* / Close to you: *Coombe Music* / Baby it's you: *Shirelles* / Walk on by: *Coombe Music* / Man who shot Liberty Valance: *Pitney, Gene* / Trains and boats and planes: *Kramer, Billy J.* / Wishin' and hopin': *Merseybeats*
CD _______________ QED 183
Tring / Nov '96 / Tring

REACH OUT
Reach out for me / Alfie / Bond street / Are you there (with another girl) / What the world need now is love / Look of love / House is not a home / I say a little prayer / Windows of the world / Lisa / Message to Michael
CD _______________ 3941312
A&M / Sep '95 / PolyGram

Bachelors

BEST OF THE BACHELORS, THE
Diane / I wouldn't trade you for the world / Whispering / Rose of Tralee / Marie / Sound of silence / Maggie / Unicorn / You'll never walk alone / Love me with all your heart / Ramona / Key to my heart / Danny Boy / Charmaine / No arms can ever hold you / Marta / Stay / He ain't heavy, he's my brother / I need love / I believe
CD _______________ CD 6041
Music / Oct '96 / Target/BMG

CLASSIC ARTISTS
CD _______________ JHD 049
Tring / Jun '92 / Tring

GOLDEN HITS & PRECIOUS MEMORIES
Diane / No arms can ever hold you / Charmaine / He's got the whole world in his hands / Whispering / Put your arms around me, honey / Moonlight and roses / I little white cloud that cried / Ramona / Only you / Pennies from heaven / Dream / Whispering grass / Saints (when the saints go marching in) / I wouldn't trade you for the world / Ten pretty girls / With all my heart / Whistle down the wind / Marie / Old Bill / Pagan love song / Faraway places / If / Always / True love for evermore / Skip to my Lou / Melody of love / I'm yours / I believe
CD _______________ 8444862
Deram / Jan '96 / PolyGram

WORLD OF THE BACHELORS, THE
I believe / Diane / I wouldn't trade you for the world / Whispering / I'll be with you in apple blossom time / Marie / He's got the whole world in his hands / No arms can ever hold you / Angel and the stranger / Ramona / With these hands / I'll see you in my dreams / Faraway places / Jailer, bring me water / When the saints go marching in / Stars will remember / True love for evermore / Whispering grass / Charmaine / You'll never walk alone
CD _______________ 5520172
Spectrum / May '96 / PolyGram

Bachicha, Bianco

ORIGINAL TANGOS
CD _______________ 995302
EPM / Jun '93 / ADA / Discovery

Bachir, Munir

MEDITATIONS
CD _______________ W 260071
Inedit / Sep '96 / ADA / Discovery / Harmonia Mundi

Bachman

ANY ROAD
CD _______________ 341082
Koch / Sep '93 / Koch

Bachman-Turner Overdrive

ANTHOLOGY (2CD Set)
CD Set _______________ 5149022
Phonogram / Jan '94 / PolyGram

GREATEST HITS
Lookin' out for no.1 / Hey you / Taking care of business / You ain't seen nothin' yet / Flat broke love / Rock 'n' roll nights / Roll on down the highway / Freeways / Down down / Let it ride / Can we all come together / Jamaica
CD _______________ 8300392
Phonogram / Jan '86 / PolyGram

NOT FRAGILE
Not fragile / Roll down the highway / You ain't seen nothin' yet / Free wheelin' / Sledgehammer / Blue moanin' / Second hand / Givin' it all away / Rock is my life, and this is my song
CD _______________ 8301782
Phonogram / '92 / PolyGram

ROLL ON DOWN THE HIGHWAY
You ain't seen nothin' yet / Roll on down the highway / Lookin' out for no.1 / Heartaches / Stayed awake all night / Just for you / Down and out man / Blue collar / Hey you / My wheel's won't turn / Takin' care of business / Stonegates / Not fragile / Away from home / Life still goes on (I'm lonely) / Take it like a man / Shotgun rider / Sledgehammer
CD _______________ 5504212
Spectrum / Aug '94 / PolyGram

VERY BEST OF BACHMAN-TURNER OVERDRIVE, THE
CD _______________ 10312
CMC / Jun '97 / BMG

Bachs

OUT OF THE BACHS
CD _______________ FLASH 43
Flash / Jul '97 / Greyhound

Bachue Cafe

BACHUE CAFE
CD _______________ HRM 001CD
Highlander / Mar '96 / ADA

Back Bay Ramblers

BACK BAY RAMBLERS
CD _______________ SOSCD 1262
Stomp Off / Dec '94 / Jazz Music / Wellard

MY MAMA'S IN TOWN (Back Bay Ramblers & Jimmy Mazzy)
CD _______________ SOSCD 1279
Stomp Off / Dec '94 / Jazz Music / Wellard

Back Porch Blues

BACK TO BASICS
CD _______________ BCD 00082
Burnside / Jul '96 / Koch

Back To The Future

PROGRESSIVELY FUNKY
CD _______________ HDHCD 502
HDH / Jul '91 / Pinnacle

Back To The Planet

MESSAGES AFTER THE BLEEP
Tidal motion / Electro Ray's / Flexing muscles / Elemental bliss / Immanent deities / Never let them / Meditational thoughts / Colour sex / Criminal / Super powers / Under your skin
CD _______________ BTTP 007CD
Arthur Mix / Mar '95 / Vital

Backbeats

BACKBEATS
CD _______________ NERCD 088
Nervous / Nov '96 / Nervous / TKO Magnum

Backhouse, Miriam

GYPSY WITHOUT A ROAD
Far away Tom / Widow / Farmers have gone East / Long lankin / Nasty spider / Dark side of the moon / John Riley / Keys of Canterbury / Gypsy without a road
CD _______________ DORIS 1
Vinyl Tap / Mar '95 / Cargo / Greyhound / Vinyl Tap

Backsliders

THROWIN' ROCKS AT THE MOON
My baby's gone / Throwin' rocks at the moon / Lonesome teardrops / Crazy wind / Paper doll world / Last wind / If you talk to my baby / Hey sheriff / If I was king / Broken wings / Cowboy boots
CD _______________ 927472
Mammoth / Feb '97 / Vital

Backstreet Boys

BACKSTREET BOYS
We've got it goin' on / Anywhere for you / Get down (you're the one for me) / I'll never break your heart / Quit playing games (with my heart) / Boys will be boys / Just to be close to you / I wanna be with you / Every time I close my eyes / Darlin' / Let's have a party / Roll with it / Nobody but you
CD _______________ CHIPX 169
CD _______________ CHIP 169
Jive / Feb '97 / Pinnacle

BACKSTREET'S BACK
CD _______________ CHIP 186
Jive / Aug '97 / Pinnacle

Backstrom, Ola

OLA BACKSTROM
CD _______________ GCD 21CD
Grappa / Apr '95 / ADA

Backtrack Blues Band

KILLIN' TIME
Killin' time / Heavy built woman / Cruesin' for a bluesin' / Like it or not / Work to do / Babe oh babe / Come on to me mama / Don't need nobody / I make my home in Florida / You'll come back someday
CD _______________ ICH 9005CD
Ichiban / Jun '94 / Direct / Koch

Backus, Gus

DIE SINGLES 1959-1961
CD _______________ BCD 15482
Bear Family / '88 / Direct / Rollercoaster / Swift

HILLBILLY GASTHAUS
Saginaw Michigan / Terribly pretty / Tennessee waltz / Oh Susanna / Laughin' and singin' / House I call my home / Don't fence me in / Home on the range / San Antonio rose / Long is the road / Reach for me / Paint and glue / On top of Old Smokey / I'm coming home / Deshalb ich nach Alaska / Das gross stadt m'dchen / Tennesse waltz (German) / Oh Susanna (German) / Nur in Tennessee / Der letzte trapper / Oh Cathrin / Heim will ich gehn / San Antonio rose (German) / Lang, lang, lang ist das her / He Alter John / Ese alles halb so schwer / Ein haus auf der Sierra / Es ist schon, Mutter
CD _______________ BCD 15765
Bear Family / May '94 / Direct / Rollercoaster / Swift

MY CHICK IS FINE
My chick is fine / You can't got it alone / Big Willie broke jail tonight / Short on love / Linda / Little kiss / Whisper / Queen of the stars / Listen / Priscilla / Happy end in Switzerland / Vaya con dios / For stealing her away / Just say goodbye (and you can go) / I'm coming home / Lost and found / Something you've got / Guess you'll have to do without / It feels so good / Blind man in our town / Need you all the time / Autumn breeze / Turn around / for I smile 'cause I

think of you / Touch on your heart / My scrapbook / Memories of Ofheidelberg / Wonderful rainbow
CD _______________ BCD 15769
Bear Family / Nov '95 / Direct / Rollercoaster / Swift

Backwater

ANGELS ARE COOL
CD _______________ CHE 57CD
Che / Oct '96 / SRD

Bacon, Max

HIGHER YOU CLIMB (Bacon, Max & His Orchestra)
CD _______________ NTHEN 023CD
Now & Then / Jan '96 / Plastic Head

Bacon, Paul

BACON, PAUL & HIS HOT COMBINATION (Bacon, Paul & His Hot Combination)
CD _______________ JCD 273
Jazzology / Mar '97 / Jazz Music

Bad Boys

BAD BOYS
CD _______________ BAD 001
Bad Boys / Nov '96 / Grapevine/PolyGram

Bad Boys Inc.

BAD BOYS INC.
Change your mind / Love here I come / I would give you forver / More to this world / Whenever you need someone / Falling for you girl / Take me away (I'll follow you) / Walking on air / You're my destiny / Honestly / Dream along with me tonight / Don't talk about love
CD _______________ 5402872
A&M / Oct '94 / PolyGram

TAKE ME HOME
You're my destiny / Falling for you girl / Whenever you need someone / Walking on air / I would give you forever / I'm gonna miss you / Don't talk about love / Honestly / Take me home / Ain't nothing gonna keep me from you / Dream along with me tonight / Second chance / Heaven knows / Hearts of fire
CD _______________ 5402002
A&M / Jan '94 / PolyGram

Bad Brains

BAD BRAINS
CD _______________ RUDCD 8223
ROIR / May '96 / Plastic Head / Shellshock/Disc

BLACK DOTS
Don't need it / At the Atlantis / Pay to cum / Supertouch/Shitfit / Regulator / You're a migraine / Don't bother me / Banned in DC / Why'd you have to go / Man won't annoy ya / Redbone in the city / Black dots / How low can a punk get / Just another damn song / Attitude / Send you no flowers
CD _______________ CAROL 005CD
Caroline / Sep '96 / Cargo / Vital

GOD OF LOVE
CD _______________ 9362458822
Warner Bros. / May '95 / Warner Music

I AGAINST I
CD _______________ SST 065CD
SST / May '93 / Plastic Head

LIVE
CD _______________ SST 160CD
SST / May '93 / Plastic Head

QUICKNESS
Soul craft / Voyage into infinity / Messengers / With the quickness / Gene machine / Don't bother me / Don't blow bubbles / Sheba / Yout juice / No conditions / Silent tears / Prophet's eye / Endtro
CD _______________ CAROLCD 1375
Caroline / Jun '97 / Cargo / Vital

ROCK FOR LIGHT
Big takeover / Attitude / Right brigade / Joshua's song / I and I survive / Banned in DC / Supertouch / Destroy Babylon / FVK / Meek / I / Coptic times / Sailin' on / Rock for light / Rally round jah throne / At the movies / Riot squad / How low can a punk get / We will not / Jam
CD _______________ CAROLCD 1613
Caroline / Jun '97 / Cargo / Vital

YOUTH ARE GETTING RESTLESS, THE (Live At The Paradiso Amsterdam 1987)
I / Rock for light / Right brigade / House of suffering / Day tripper / She's a rainbow / Coptic times / Sacred love / Re-ignition / Let me help / Youth are getting restless / Banned in DC / Sailin' on / Fearless vampire killer / At the movies / Revolution (dub) / Pay to cum / Big takeover
CD _______________ CAROLCD 1617
Caroline / Jun '97 / Cargo / Vital

Bad Company

10 FROM 6
Can't get enough / Feel like makin' love / Run with the pack / Shooting star / Movin' on / Bad company / Rock 'n' roll fantasy / Electric land / Ready for love / Live for the music
CD _______________ 7816252
Atlantic / Jan '86 / Warner Music

BAD COMPANY
Can't get enough / Rock steady / Ready for love / Don't let me down / Bad company / Way I choose / Movin' on / Seagull
CD _______________ 7567924412
Atlantic / Sep '94 / Warner Music

BURNIN' SKY
Burnin' sky / Leaving you / Like water / Morning sun / Knapsack / Heartbeat / Passing time / Man needs woman / Too bad / Master of ceremony / Peace of mind / Everything I need
CD _______________ 7567924502
Atlantic / Sep '94 / Warner Music

COMPANY OF STRANGERS
Company of strangers / Clearwater highway / Judas my brother / Gimme gimme / Down down down / Down and dirty / You're the only reason / Loving you out loud / Dance with the devil / Pretty woman / Abandoned and alone / Where I belong / Little Martha
CD _______________ 7559618082
Atlantic / Aug '95 / Warner Music

DESOLATION ANGELS
Rock 'n' roll fantasy / Crazy circles / Gone gone gone / Evil wind / Early in the morning / Lonely for your love / Oh, Atlanta / Take the time / Rhythm machine / She brings me love
CD _______________ 7567924512
Atlantic / Sep '94 / Warner Music

HERE COMES TROUBLE
How about that / Stranger than fiction / Here comes the trouble / This could be the one / Both feet in the water / Take this town / What about you / Little angel / Hold on to my heart / Broken hearted / My only one
CD _______________ 7567917592
Atlantic / Oct '92 / Warner Music

HOLY WATER
Holy water / Walk through fire / Stranger stranger / If you needed somebody / Fearless / Lay your love on me / Boys cry tough / With you in a heartbeat / I don't care / Never too late / Dead of the night / I can't live without you / Hundred miles
CD _______________ 7567913712
Atlantic / Jun '90 / Warner Music

RUN WITH THE PACK
Live for the music / Simple man / Honeychild / Love me somebody / Run with the pack / Silver blue and gold / Young blood / Do right by your woman / Sweet lil' sister / Fade away
CD _______________ 7567924352
Atlantic / Jul '94 / Warner Music

STRAIGHT SHOOTER
Good lovin' gone bad / Feel like makin' love / Weep no more / Shooting star / Deal with the preacher / Wild fire women / Anna / Call on me
CD _______________ 7567826372
Atlantic / Jun '94 / Warner Music

WHAT YOU HEAR IS WHAT YOU GET (The Best Of Bad Company - Live)
How about that / Holy water / Rock 'n' roll fantasy / If you needed somebody / Here comes trouble / Ready for love / Shooting star / No smoke without a fire / Feel like makin' love / Take this town / Movin' on / Good lovin' gone bad / Fist full of blisters / Can't get enough / Bad company
CD _______________ 7567923072
Atlantic / Dec '93 / Warner Music

Bad Examples

SLOW MUSIC
CD _______________ EFA 037652
Atatak / Nov '95 / SRD

Bad Influence

NEW AGE WITCH HUNT
CD _______________ SKULD 007
Skuld / Jan '97 / Cargo

Bad Livers

DELUSIONS OF BANJER
CD _______________ QS 14CD
Quarter Stick / Sep '92 / Cargo / SRD

HOGS ON THE HIGHWAY
CD _______________ SHCD 3862
Sugar Hill / Feb '97 / ADA / CM / Direct / Koch / Roots

HORSES IN THE MINES
CD _______________ QS 20CD
Quarter Stick / May '94 / Cargo / SRD

Bad Manners

BEST OF BAD MANNERS, THE
Lip up fatty / Special brew / Lorraine / Just a feeling / Can can / My girl lollipop / Walking in the sunshine / Skaville UK / This is ska / Midnight rider / You fat ... / Christmas time again / Gonna get along without you now
CD _______________ BBSCD 010
Blue Beat / Sep '90 / Grapevine/PolyGram

DON'T KNOCK THE BALDHEADS
CD _______________ RRCD 249
Receiver / Sep '97 / Grapevine/PolyGram

EAT THE BEAT
Since you've gone away / Return of the ugly / Stampede / Rosemary / Bonaza ska / Sally Brown / Skinhead girl / Non shrewd / Mafia / Pipeline / Big five / Viv la ska revolution / Dume batty / Gonna get along without you now / Johnny's knee / How big do you love me / Oh Jamaica / Gonna get along without you now
CD _______________ DOJOCD 248
Dojo / May '96 / Disc

FATTY FATTY
CD _______________ LG 21005
Lagoon / Jun '93 / Grapevine/PolyGram

GREATEST HITS LIVE
Echo 4 + 2 / Just a feeling / Wooly bully / Only funkin / My girl lollipop / Undersea adventures of Ivor the engine / Lorraine / Samson and Delilah / Walking in the sunshine / Inner London violence / Special brew / Magnificent seven / Lip up fatty / Can can / El pussy cat / Ne-ne na-na-na-na nu-nu
CD _______________ DOJOCD 111
Dojo / Mar '93 / Disc

INNER LONDON VIOLENCE
CD _______________ LG 21094
Lagoon / Apr '94 / Grapevine/PolyGram

SKINHEAD
CD _______________ LG 21026
Lagoon / Jul '93 / Grapevine/PolyGram

VIVE LA SKA REVOLUTION (2CD Set)
Skaville UK / Sally Brown / Bonanza ska / Return of the ugly / Skinhead love affair / Non shrewd / Big 5 / Stampede / Skinhead girl / Mafia / Pipeline / Viva la ska revolution / Gonna get along without you / How big do you love / Johnny Knee / This is ska / Oh Jamaica / Fatty fatty / Lip up fatty / Special brew / Walking in the sunshine / That'll do nicely / Since you've gone away / Can can / Samson and Delilah / Lorraine / My girl lollipop / Inner London violence / Wooly bully / Just a feeling
CD Set _______________ SMDCD 140
Snapper / May '97 / Pinnacle

Bad Moon Rising

BAD MOON RISING
Hands on / If it ain't dirty / Without your love / Full moon / Lie down / Old flames / Built for speed / Dark side of babylon / Sunset after midnight / Wayward son
CD _______________ CDFLAG 78
Under One Flag / Jan '93 / Pinnacle

BLOOD
Dangerous game / Servants of the sun / Devil's son (Where our children die) / Blood on the streets / Tears in the dark / Heart of darkness / Chains / Till the morning comes / Time will tell / Remember me
CD _______________ CDFLAG 79
Under One Flag / Apr '93 / Pinnacle

Bad News

CASH IN COMPILATION, THE
Hey hey bad news / Bad dreams / Warriors of Ghengis Khan / AGM / Bohemian rhapsody / Pretty woman / O levels / Life with Brian / Bad news / Masturbike / Double entendre / Drink till I die / Cashing in on Christmas
CD _______________ DOJOCD 152
Dojo / Sep '93 / Disc

Bad Religion

AGAINST THE GRAIN
CD _______________ 864092
Epitaph / Dec '90 / Pinnacle / Plastic Head

ALL AGES
CD _______________ 864432
Epitaph / Nov '95 / Pinnacle / Plastic Head

BAD RELIGION 1980-1985
CD _______________ 864072X
Epitaph / Nov '91 / Pinnacle / Plastic Head

FUCK ARMAGEDDON, THIS IS A BAD RELIGION TRIBUTE (Various Artists)
CD _______________ TR 003CD
Tribute / Dec '96 / Plastic Head

GENERATOR
CD _______________ 864162
Epitaph / Mar '92 / Pinnacle / Plastic Head

NO CONTROL
CD _______________ 864062
Epitaph / Jun '93 / Pinnacle / Plastic Head

STRANGER THAN FICTION
Incomplete / Leave mine to me / Stranger than fiction / Tiny voices / Handshake / Better off dead / Infected / Television / Individual / Hooray for me / Slumber / Marked / Inner logic / What it is / 21st Century (digital boy)
CD _______________ 4773432
Columbia / Sep '94 / Sony

Bad Sector

AMPOS
CD _______________ STCD 009
Staalplaat / Sep '95 / Vital/SAM

Bad Seed

BAD SEED
CD _______________ CDMFN 179
Music For Nations / Mar '95 / Pinnacle

Bad Seeds

BAD SEEDS/LIBERTY BELL (Bad Seeds/ Liberty Bell)
CD _______________ 642440
Arcade / Apr '97 / Discovery

Bad Yodellers

I WONDER
CD _______________ SR 30190CD
Semaphore / Jan '92 / Plastic Head

WINDOW
CD _______________ SR 330591CD
Semaphore / '91 / Plastic Head

Badarou, Wally

ECHOES
Keys / Hi life / Mambo / Voices / Canyons / Endless race / Chief inspector / Waltz / Jungle / Rain
CD _______________ CID 104
Island / May '85 / PolyGram

Badfinger

ASS
Apple of my eye / Get away / Icicles / Winner / Blind owl / Constitution / When I say / Cowboy / Can I love you / Timeless / Do you mind
CD _______________ CDSAPCOR 27
Apple / Feb '97 / EMI

BBC LIVE IN CONCERT
Come and get it / No matter what / Better days / Only you and I know / We're for the dark / Sweet Tuesday morning / Feelin' alright / Take it all / Suitcase / Love is easy / Blind owl / Constitution / Icicles / Mattered spam / I can't take it
CD _______________ SFRSCD 031
Strange Fruit / Jul '97 / Pinnacle

COME AND GET IT (Various Artists)
CD _______________ CPR 2181
Copper / Feb '97 / Cargo

COME AND GET IT - BEST OF BADFINGER
Come and get it / Maybe tomorrow / Rock of all ages / Dear Angie / Carry on till tomorrow / No matter what / Believe me / Midnight caller / Better days / Without you / Take it all / Money / Flying / Name of the game / Suitcase / Day after day / Baby blue / When I say / Icicles / I can love you / Apple of my eye
CD _______________ CDSAPCOR 28
Apple / Apr '95 / EMI

Badgeman

KINGS OF THE DESERT
Secret diary of Jim Morrison's bastard / Sean's seen the light / Cupid's exploding harpoon / King of the desert / Montezuma's revenge / My flash on you / Crystals / Extraordinary girl / False yellow eyes / Make me feel / Going sane gain / PAF
CD _______________ PAPCD 003
Paperhouse / Jul '90 / RTM/Disc

Badgewearer

THANK YOU FOR YOUR CUSTOM
CD _______________ GUIDE 7CD
Guided Missile / Aug '96 / Shellshock/Disc

Badjie, Saikouba

BOUGARABOU (Solo Drumming Of Casamance)
CD _______________ VPU 1005CD
Village Pulse / May '97 / ADA

Badland

BADLAND
CD _______________ BF 14
Bruce's Fingers / Sep '96 / Cadillac / Discovery

Badloves

GET ON BOARD
CD _______________ D 24025
Mushroom / Mar '94 / 3mv/Pinnacle

Badu, Erykah

BADUIZM
Rimshot (Intro) / On and on / Appletree / Otherside of the game / Sometimes / Certainly (Flipped it) / No love / 4 Leaf clover / Certainly
CD _______________ UND 53027
MCA/Kedar / Mar '97 / BMG

Baerwald, David

TRIAGE
Secret silken world / Got no shotgun hydra-head octopus blues / Nobody / Waiter / AIDS and armageddon / Postman / Bitter tree / China lake / Brand new morning / Born for love
CD _____ 395392
A&M / Mar '93 / PolyGram

Baez, Joan

BEST OF JOAN BAEZ, THE
Diamonds and rust / Forever young / Prison trilogy / Simpel twist of fate / Never dreamed you'd leave in summer / Love song to a stranger / Please come to Boston / Children and all that jazz / Sweeter for me / Imagine / Gracias a la vida (heres to life) / Night they drove old Dixie down
CD _____ CDMID 108
A&M / Oct '92 / PolyGram

BLESSED ARE... (2CD Set)
Blessed are / Night they drove old Dixie down / Salt of the Earth / Three horses / Brand new Tennessee waltz / Lost, lonely and wretched / Lincoln freed me today / Outside the Nashville city limits / San Francisco Mabel Joy / When time is stolen / Heaven help us all / Angeline / Help me make it through the night / Let it be / Put your hand in the hand / Gabriel and me / Milanese waltz/Marie Flore / Hitchhikers song / 33rd of August / Fifteen months / Plane wreck at Los Gatos (Deportee) / Maria Delores
CD Set _____ VCD2 6570
Vanguard / Jan '97 / ADA / Pinnacle

DIAMONDS (A Joan Baez Anthology/ 2CD Set)
Prison trilogy (Billy Rose) / Rainbow Road / Love song to a stranger / Myths / In the quiet morning / To Bobby / Son of Bangladesh / Tumbleweed / Imagine / Diamonds & rust / Fountain of sorrow / Never dreamed you'd leave in summer / Children and all that jazz / Simple twist of fate / Blue sky / Hello in there / Jesse / (Ain't gonna let nobody) Turn me around / Suzanne / I shall be released / Blowin' in the wind / Stewball / Ballad of Sacco & Vanzetti / Joe Hill / Love is just a four letter word / Forever young / Boulder to Birmingham / Swing low, sweet chariot / Oh happy day / Please come to Boston / Lily, Rosemary & the Jack of Hearts / Night they drove old Dixie down / Amazing Grace
CD Set _____ 5405002
A&M / Mar '96 / PolyGram

DIAMONDS AND RUST IN THE BULLRING
Diamonds and rust / No woman, no cry / Swing low, sweet chariot / El preso numero nuevo / Txoria txori / Gracias a la vida (Here's to life) / Ain't gonna let nobody turn me round / Famous blue raincoat / Let it be / Llego con tres heridas / Ellas danzan solas (cueca sola) / No nos moveran
CD _____ CDVIP 174
Virgin VIP / Apr '97 / EMI

FAREWELL ANGELINA
Farewell Angelina / Daddy, you've been on my mind / It's all over now baby blue / Baby blue / Wild mountain thyme / Rangers command / Colours / Satisfied mind / River in the pines / Pauvre rutebeuf / Sagt mir wo die blumen sind / Hard rain's gonna fall
CD _____ VMD 79200
Vanguard / Oct '95 / ADA / Pinnacle

GEMS
CD _____ 5501292
Spectrum / Oct '93 / PolyGram

GREATEST HITS AND OTHERS
Night they drove old Dixie down / Dangling conversation / Help me make it through the night / Blessed are / Eleanor Rigby / Let it be / There but for fortune / Brand new Tennessee waltz / I pity the poor immigrant / Love is just a four letter word / Heaven help us all
CD _____ VMD 79332
Vanguard / Oct '96 / ADA / Pinnacle

HONEST LULLABY
Let your love flow / No woman, no cry / Light a light / She sings at the end of the movie / Before the deluge / Honest lullaby / Michael / For Sasha / For all we know / Free at last
CD _____ 4736952
Columbia / Feb '97 / Sony

IMAGINE
Diamonds and rust / Night they drove old Dixie down / Simpel twist of fate / Imagine / In the quiet morning / Best of friends / Forever young / Prison trilogy / Jesse / Children and all that jazz / Please come to Boston / Never dreamed you'd leave in summer / Gracias a la vida (here's to life) / Sweeter for me / Love song to a stranger / Dida / Amazing grace
CD _____ CDMID 180
A&M / Mar '93 / PolyGram

JOAN
Be not too hard / Eleanor Rigby / Turquoise / La colombe / Dangling conversation / Lady came from Baltimore / North / Children of darkness / Greenwood side / If you were a carpenter / Annabel Lee / Saigon bride
CD _____ VMD 79240
Vanguard / Apr '97 / ADA / Pinnacle

JOAN BAEZ
Silver dagger / East Virginia / Ten thousand miles / House of the rising sun / All my trials / Wildwood flower / Donna Donna / John Riley / Rake and the rambling boy / Little Moses / Mary Hamilton / Henry Martin / El preso numero nuevo
CD _____ VMD 2077
Vanguard / Oct '95 / ADA / Pinnacle

JOAN BAEZ IN CONCERT
CD _____ VMD 2122
Vanguard / Jan '96 / ADA / Pinnacle

JOAN BAEZ IN CONCERT VOL.2
Once I had a sweetheart / Jackaroe / Don't think twice, it's alright / We shall overcome / Portland Town / Queen of hearts / Manha de carnaval / Te ador / Long black veil / Fennario / Ne belle cardillo / With God on our side / Three fishers / Hush little baby / Battle hymn of the Republic
CD _____ VMD 2123
Vanguard / Jan '96 / ADA / Pinnacle

JOAN BAEZ VOL.2
Wagoner's lad / Trees they do grow high / Lily of the West / Silkie / Engine 143 / Once I knew a pretty girl / Lonesome radio / Banks of the Ohio / Pal of mine / Barbara Allen / Cherry tree carol / Old blue / Railroad boy / Plaisir d'amour
CD _____ VMD 2097
Vanguard / Oct '95 / ADA / Pinnacle

JOAN BAEZ VOL.5
There but for fortune / Stewball / It ain't me babe / Death of Queen Jane / Child No.170 / Bachianas Brasileires No.5 / Go 'way from my window / I still miss someone / When you hear them cuckoos hollerin' / Birmingham Sunday / So we'll go no more a-roving / O'Cangaceiro / Unquiet grave / Child no.78
CD _____ VMD 79160
Vanguard / Apr '97 / ADA / Pinnacle

NOEL
O come, o come Emmanuel / Coventry carol / Good king Wencelas / Little drummer boy / Wonder as I wander, bring a torch Jeanette, Isabella / Down in yon forest / Carol of the birds / Angels we have heard on high / Ave maria / Mary's wandering / Away in a manger / Cantique de nord / What child is this / Silent night
CD _____ VMD 792330
Vanguard / Oct '96 / ADA / Pinnacle

ONE DAY AT A TIME
Sweet Sir Galahad / No expectations / Long black veil / Ghetto / Carry it on / Take me back to the sweet sunny south / Seven Bridges Road / Jolie blon / Joe Hill / Song for David / One day at a time
CD _____ VMD 79310
Vanguard / Oct '96 / ADA / Pinnacle

PLAY ME BACKWARDS
Play me backwards / Amsterdam / Isaac and Abraham / Stones in the road / Steal across the border / I'm with you / I'm with you (reprise) / Strange rivers / Through your hands / Dream song / Edge of glory
CD _____ CDVIP 164
Virgin VIP / Oct '96 / EMI

PLAY ME BACKWARDS
CD _____ VI 874842
Disky / Nov '96 / Disky / THE

RARE, LIVE & CLASSIC 1958-1989 (3CD Set)
Scarlet ribbons / Jimmy Brown / Careless love / Auctioneer / Black is the colour of my true love's hair / John Hardy / We are crossing River Jordan / John Riley / Silver dagger / House of the rising sun / Low down chariot / Wagoner's lad / Last night I had the strangest dream / Geordie / What have they down to the rain / Troubled and I don't know why / With God on our side / We shall overcome / Go 'way from my window / Mama, you've been on my mind / There but for fortune / Colours / River in the pines / Pack up your sorrows / Swallow song / Legend of a girl child Linda / Children of darkness / Catch the wind / I am a poor wayfaring stranger / Sweet Sir Galahad / Donna Donna / Long black veil / Mama tried / Sing me back home / Joe Hill / Night they drove old Dixie down / Blessed are... / Hello in there / Love song to a stranger / In the quiet morning / Angel band / Johnny, I hardly knew ya / Gracias a la vida / Diamonds and rust / Children and all that jazz / Blowin' in the wind / Swing low, sweet chariot / Jesse / Honest lullaby / Jackaroe / Marriott USA / Amazing grace / Forever young / Farewell Angelina / Hard rain's a-gonna fall / Here's to you / Blues improv / Ring them bells / El preso numero nueve / Speaking of dreams
CD Set _____ VCD 3125
Vanguard / Apr '96 / ADA / Pinnacle

RECENTLY
Brothers in arms / Recently / Asimbonanga / Moon is a harsh mistress / James and the gang / Let us break bread together / MLK / Do right woman, do right man / Biko
CD _____ CDVGC 1
Goldcastle / May '88 / EMI

RING THEM BELLS
CD _____ GRACD 208
Grapevine / Sep '95 / Grapevine/PolyGram

SPEAKING OF DREAMS
China / Warriors of the sun / Carrickfergus / Hand to mouth / Speaking of dreams / El Salvador / Rambler gambler / Whispering bells / Fairfax county / A mi manera (Comme d'habitude)
CD _____ CDVGC 12
Goldcastle / '90 / EMI

Bag

OF FEAR
CD _____ LOST 011
Lost / May '97 / Cargo

Bagad Bleimor

SONEREZH GELTIEK
CD _____ KMCD 12
Keltia Musique / '91 / ADA / Discovery

Bagad Brieg

DELC'H DA NOZ
CD _____ 433CD
Diffusion Breizh / Jul '95 / ADA

Bagad De Lann Bihoue

BAGAD DE LANN BIHOUE
CD _____ KMCD 09
Keltia Musique / '91 / ADA / Discovery

Bagad Kemper

BAGAD KEMPER
CD _____ KMCD 05
Keltia Musique / Jul '90 / ADA / Discovery

LIP AR MAOUT (Battering Rams)
CD _____ KMCD 50
Keltia Musique / Apr '95 / ADA / Discovery

Bagad Ronsed-Mor

AG AN DOUAR D'AR MOR
CD _____ CD 426
Diffusion Breizh / Apr '94 / ADA

Bagley, Bob

COVERING ALL THE BASS (Bagley, Bob & Friends)
CD _____ SBCD 3014
Sea Breeze / Jun '96 / Jazz Music

Baha Men

KALIK
CD _____ 7567923942
Warner Bros. / Sep '94 / Warner Music

Bahamadia

KOLLAGE
Intro / Word play / Spontaneity / Rugged / I confess / Unknowhowwedu / Total wreck / Innovation / Da jawn / Dat freak shit / Tha hard way / Biggest part of me / Path to rhythm
CD _____ CTCD 53
Cooltempo / May '96 / EMI

Bahia Black

BAHIA BLACK - RITUAL BEATING SYSTEM
Retrato calado / Capitao do asfalto / Seven powers / Uma viagem del baldes de Larry Wright / Olodum / Guia pro congal / Gwagwa o de / Follow me / Nina in the womb of the forest
CD _____ 5108562
Axiom / Mar '92 / PolyGram / Vital

Bailey, Admiral

REGGAE DANCEHALL SENSATION
CD _____ RRTGCD 7759
Rohit / Mar '90 / Jet Star

UNDISPUTED CHAMPION
CD _____ RNCD 2014
Rhino / Aug '93 / Grapevine/PolyGram / Jet Star

Bailey, Benny

BENNY BAILY & THE CZECH-NORWEGIAN QUARTET (Bailey, Benny & The Norwegian Quartet)
CD _____ GEMCD 69
Gemini / Dec '87 / Cadillac

BIG BRASS
Hard sock dance / Alison / Tipsy / Please say yes / Kiss to build a dream on / Maud's mood
CD _____ CCD 79011
Candid / Feb '97 / Cadillac / Direct / Jazz Music / Koch / Wellard

FOR HEAVEN'S SAKE (Bailey, Benny Quintet)
Little jazz / Blues East / Peruvian nights / Mood indigo / For heaven's sake / One for Wilton / No mo blues
CD _____ HHCD 1006
Hot House / May '95 / Cadillac / Harmonia Mundi / Wellard

PERUVIAN NIGHTS
Deep south / Reflectory / Caballeros / Hot house / No mo blues / Neptune / Peruvian nights / Blues easr / Set call
CD _____ TCB 96102
TCB / Jun '96 / New Note/Pinnacle

Bailey, Buster

CLASSICS 1925-1940
CD _____ CLASSICS 904
Classics / Nov '96 / Discovery / Jazz Music

INTRODUCTION TO BUSTER BAILEY 1924-1942, AN
CD _____ 4038
Best Of Jazz / Nov '96 / Discovery

Bailey, Chris

54 DAYS AT SEA
CD _____ DB 1145
Mushroom / Mar '94 / 3mv/Pinnacle

ENCORE
CD _____ 422009
Last Call / Oct '95 / Cargo / Direct / Discovery

WHAT WE DID ON OUR HOLIDAYS
CD _____ ROSE 30 CD
New Rose / Aug '90 / ADA / Direct / Discovery

Bailey, Craig

NEW JOURNEY, A
CB no.1 / What would I do without you / Laura / Bells / Cherokee / Soul flower / Casanova / Li'l darlin' / No hip hop / Love dreams / New journey
CD _____ CCD 79725
Candid / May '97 / Cadillac / Direct / Jazz Music / Koch / Wellard

Bailey, Derek

AIDA
CD _____ DEX 5
Dexter's Cigar / Apr '97 / Cargo

CYRO
CD _____ INCUSCD 01
Incus / '90 / Cadillac / Cargo

DEREK BAILEY & HAN BENNINK (Bailey, Derek & Han Bennink)
CD _____ CORTI 09
Cortical / Jul '97 / Harmonia Mundi

FIGURING (Bailey, Derek & Barre Phillips)
CD _____ INCUSCD 05
Incus / '90 / Cadillac / Cargo

GUITAR, DRUMS 'N' BASS (Bailey, Derek & DJ Ninj)
CD _____ AVAN 060
Avant / Oct '96 / Cadillac / Harmonia Mundi

HAN (Bailey, Derek & Han Bennik)
CD _____ INCUSCD 02
Incus / '90 / Cadillac / Cargo

INCUS TAPES
CD _____ CORTI 010
Cortical / Jul '97 / Harmonia Mundi

LACE
CD _____ EM 4013
Emanem / Dec '96 / Cadillac / Harmonia Mundi

Bailey, Mildred

BLUES SINGER 1929-1937, THE
CD _____ JZCD 353
Suisa / Jan '93 / Jazz Music / THE

BLUES SINGER 1937-1939, THE
CD _____ JZCD 354
Suisa / Jan '93 / Jazz Music / THE

FORGOTTEN LADY, A
CD _____ 158602
Jazz Archives / Sep '96 / Discovery

HARLEM LULLABY
Georgia on my mind / Concentratin' / Harlem lullaby / Junk man / Ol' Pappy / Squeeze me / Downhearted blues / Porter's love song / Smoke dreams / Rockin' chair / Moon got in my eyes / It's the natural thing to do / Worried over you / Thanks for the memory / More than ever / Please be kind / I let a song go out of my heart / Rock it for me / My melancholy baby / Lonesome road
CD _____ CDAJA 5065
Living Era / Dec '89 / Select

LA SELECTION 1931-1939
CD _____ 700092
Art Vocal / Nov '92 / Discovery

ROCKIN' CHAIR
CD _____ VJC 10062
Victorious Discs / Aug '90 / Jazz Music

THANKS FOR THE MEMORY (1935-1944)
Lover come back to me / It had to be you / I never knew / Please don't talk about me when I'm gone / I didn't know about you / I'll get by / St. Louis blues / Evaline / Thanks for the memory / Don't be that way / Gulf

coast blues / 'Tain't what you do / Barrelhouse music / Rock it for me / Arkansas blues / Darn that dream / I don't stand a ghost of a chance with you / Peace brother / I've got my love to keep me warm / There'll be some changes made / When day is done / Rockin' chair
CD _______________ CD 53282
Giants Of Jazz / Feb '97 / Cadillac / Jazz Music / Target/BMG

THAT ROCKIN' CHAIR LADY
CD _______________ TPZ 1007
Topaz Jazz / Oct '94 / Cadillac / Pinnacle

Bailey, Pearl

BEST OF PEARL BAILEY
CD _______________ ATJCD 8007
Disky / Jul '94 / Disky / THE

SOME OF THE BEST
As long as I live / Tired / I've got you under my skin / Easy street / Personality / Alla en el Rancho Grande / World weary / Hit the road to dreamland / I love my argentine / When the world was young / Supper time / In Spain they say si, si
CD _______________ 12643
Laserlight / May '97 / Target/BMG

Bailey, Richard

FIREDANCE
CD _______________ CMML 89007CD
M·sic Maker / Jul '94 / ADA / Grapevine/ PolyGram

Bailey, Roy

BUSINESS AS USUAL
CD _______________ CFCD 400
Fuse / Jul '94 / ADA / CM / Direct / Roots

NEVER LEAVE A SONG UNSUNG
CD _______________ CFCD 398
Fuse / Feb '88 / ADA / CM / Direct / Roots

NEW DIRECTIONS IN THE OLD
Poison train / Blackwaters / Migrant's lullaby / This old town / Brass band music / Language of the land / Calling Joe Hill / Here's to the juggler/Katherine / Lass of Lochroyan / Do you remember / Last house in our street / Light years away / Do you think that I do not know / Ballad maker's apprentice
CD _______________ CFCD 402
Fuse / May '97 / ADA / CM / Direct / Roots

WHAT YOU DO WITH WHAT YOU'VE GOT
What you do with what you've got / Ugly ones / Let your hair hang down / Patience Kershaw / See it come down / Send me back to Georgia / Rose of York / Day before the war / If they come in the morning / Song of the exile / Hard times of old England / Burning times / New Year's Eve / Everything possible / Rollin' home
CD _______________ CFCD 399
Fuse / Feb '89 / ADA / CM / Direct / Roots

WHY DOES IT HAVE TO BE ME
CD _______________ CFCD 396
Fuse / Jul '95 / ADA / CM / Direct / Roots

Bailongo

TANGOLEANDA
CD _______________ SYNCD 166
Syncoop / Jun '94 / ADA / Direct

Bailter Space

VORTURU
CD _______________ FNCD 295
Flying Nun / Apr '94 / RTM/Disc

WAMMO
Untied / Splat / At five we drive / Zapped / Colours / Retro / Glimmer / Voltage / D thing / Wammo
CD _______________ OLE 1422
Matador / Jul '95 / Vital

Bain, Aly

ALY BAIN AND FRIENDS (Bain, Aly & Various Artists)
Waiting for the federals: *Bain, Aly & Phil Cunningham* / Donald MacLean's farewell to Oban: *Bain, Aly & Phil Cunningham* / Sands of Burness: *Bain, Aly & Phil Cunningham* / Miller's reel: *Bain, Aly & Phil Cunningham* / Dean Cadalan Samhach: *Capercaillie* / Kerryman's daughter: *Boys Of The Lough* / O'Keefe's plough: *Boys Of The Lough* / Sligo maid: *Boys Of The Lough* / Humours of Ballinahinch: *Boys Of The Lough* / Gravel walk: *Boys Of The Lough* / Out by East Da Vong: *Boys Of The Lough* / Maiden's prayer: *Junior Daugherty* / Jimmy Mann's reel: *Hunter, William* / Aly's sound: *Hunter, William* / It's all just talk: *Gregson & Collister* / Pearl: *Cunningham, Phil* / Floggin': *Bain, Aly/Tulloch, Violet/John* / Chimes at midnight: *Bain, Aly* / Humours of Tulla: *O'Connor, Martin* / Fox Hunter's reel: *O'Connor, Martin* / St. Anne's reel: *O'Connor, Martin* / New road under my wheels: *Junior Daugherty* / Anne's tune: *Moore, Hamish & Dick Lee* / Love of the islands: *Hunter, William* / Compliments to Dan R MacDonald: *Hunter, William* / Marie MacLennan's reel: *Hunter, William* / Bonjour Tristesse: *Queen Ida & The Bon Temps Zydeco Band*
CD _______________ CDTRAX 026
Greentrax / Mar '89 / ADA / Direct / Duncans / Highlander

ALY BAIN WITH YOUNG CHAMPIONS
Dr. Donaldson/The anvil: *Bain, Aly & Violet Tulloch* / Ross Memorial Hospital: *Bain, ALy & Scott Williams* / Buain an Rainich/Brochan Lom/Cockle gatherers: *Ross, Gail & Vicki Ferguson* / Balkan Hills/Duke of Gordon/Deil and the dirk: *Lindsay, Bruce* / Pear tree: *Gardiner, Scott* / Mr. Michie/J.F. Dickie's delight/J.F. Dickie's reel: *Kostulin, Russell* / An Ataireachd Ard: *Ferguson, Vicki* / Aspen bank: *Williams, Scott* / Ardgualich/High road to Linton: *Thoumire, Simon* / Heaven's gate/Le Grande Chaine/Waiting for the Federals: *Bain, Aly & Russel Kostulin* / Conundrum/Mrs. Stewart of Grantully: *Bennett, Martyn* / Morning dew/Blarney pilgrim/Langstrom's pony: *Bennett, Martyn* / Helen Robertson: *Smith, Angie* / Humble tattie: *Gardiner, Scott* / Ballachulish Glen: *Ross, Gail* / Leaving Lismor/Heights of Dargai/Kilt is my delight: *Lindsay, Bruce* / Wee burr stuck tae ma apron: *Robertson, Nicole* / Midnight on the water/Bonaparte's retreat / Music of Spey / Sixereen/Barrowburn reel/ Fairy dance: *Bain, Aly & Violet Tulloch* / Margaret's waltz/Laird o'Drumblair/Deil among the tailors: *Bain, Aly & Young Champions*
CD _______________ SPRCD 1032
Springthyme / May '90 / ADA / CM / Direct / Duncans / Highlander / Roots

ALY MEETS THE CAJUNS (Bain, Aly & Various Artists)
Midland two step: *Bain, Aly & Doucet Cajun Band* / My friend: *Bain, Aly & Wayne Toups* / Mazuka: *Bain, Aly & Queen Ida* / Jongle a moi: *Bain, Aly & Doucet Cajun Band* / Sassy on step: *Bain, Aly & Boozoo Chavis* / Jolie blon: *Bain, Ain & Dewey Balfa* / La contre danse a perepere: *Bain, Aly & Harry LaFleur* / Water pump: *Bain, Aly & D L Menard* / J'ai ete au bal: *Bain, Aly & Wayne Toups* / Paper in my shoe: *Bain, Aly & Boozoo Chavis* / La vie est pas donne: *Bain, Aly & Harry LaFleur* / Back door: *Bain, Aly & D L Menard* / Chere toute toute: *Bain, Aly & Doucet Cajun Band* / Rosa majeur: *Bain, Aly & Queen Ida* / Devant ta porte: *Bain, Aly & D L Menard* / When I was poor: *Bain, Aly & Dewey Balfa*
CD _______________ LCOM 9009
Lismor / Oct '92 / ADA / Direct / Duncans / Lismor

DOWN HOME
CD _______________ LCOM 9027
Lismor / '90 / ADA / Direct / Duncans / Lismor

FIRST ALBUM
Peter Davidson/Jessica's tune/Barrowburn reel / Louis' waltz/Le grande chaine/The newly weds' reel / Waiting for the Federals / Dr. James Donaldson/The anvil reel / Auld noost / Barmaid/The carpenter/The reconcilliation / Hangman's reel / Calum Donaldson/The scholar/Maid in a box / Kevin MacCann's/Munster grass/Barclays / Margaret's waltz / Blaydon flats/Alamootie/ Dodd's farewell to Shetland / Da braaken baa/Violet Tulloch's hornpipe / Shack's farewell to the Workman's Club/Glen Farquhar/Reested
CD _______________ WHIRLIE 001CD
Whirlie / Dec '93 / ADA / CM / Direct / Duncans / Highlander / Roots / Whitetower

FOLLOW THE MOONSTONE
CD _______________ WHIRLIECD 4
Whirlie / Oct '95 / ADA / CM / Direct / Duncans / Highlander / Roots / Whitetower

LONELY BIRD
Gillan's reel/Charles Sutherland/Donald Stewart the piper / Mrs. Jamieson's favourite / Rosemary Brown / Spey in spate/Pottinger's reel/Dowd's reel / Beauty of the North/Pirates hornpipe / Midnight on the water/Bonaparte's retreat / Herr Roloff's farewell / Aly's waltz / Annalese Bain/Phil Cunningham's reel/Andy Brown's reel / Lonely bird / Weindia little/Da fashion o da delting lasses/Da black hat / Junior's waltz / Captain Campbell/Earl Grey/Largo's fairy dance
CD _______________ WHIRLIE 2CD
Whirlie / Oct '88 / ADA / CM / Direct / Duncans / Highlander / Roots / Whitetower

NORTH SEA MUSIC
CD _______________ HCD 7121
Helio / May '97 / ADA

PEARL, THE (Bain, Aly & Phil Cunningham)
Megan's wedding/The Herra Boys/The Barrowburn reel / Bonnie Nancy / Devant ta porte/Mamou two step / Jig runrig/The Swedish jig / Queendale Bay / Waltz of the little girls / Shores of Loch Bee/Headlands/ Floggin' reel / Music of Spey / Seud nan ceud bliadhna/Memories of Father Angus MacDonell/Br / Belle mere's waltz / Auld fiddler/B flat tune / Pearl
CD _______________ WHIRLIE 3CD
Whirlie / Oct '94 / ADA / CM / Direct / Duncans / Highlander / Roots / Whitetower

RUBY (Bain, Aly & Phil Cunningham)
CD _______________ WHIRLIECD 5
Whirlie / Sep '97 / ADA / CM / Direct / Duncans / Highlander / Roots / Whitetower

Bainbridge, Harvey

INTERSTELLA CHAOS
CD _______________ TASTE 40CD
Taste / Jan '95 / Plastic Head / SRD

RED SHIFT
CD _______________ TASTE 65CD
Taste Divine / May '97 / Cargo

Bainbridge, Merril

GARDEN, THE
Garden in my room / Under the water / Miss you / Mouth / Julie / Song for Neen / Sleeping dogs / Reasons why / Spinning / Being boring / State of mind / Power of one / Garden in my room
CD _______________ 74321431002
Arista / Jun '97 / BMG

Baird, Dan

BUFFALO NICKEL
Younger face / Cumberland river / I want you bad / On my way / Lil bit / Hell to pay / Woke up Jake / Birthday / Hush / Trivial as the truth / Hit me like a train / Frozen head state park
CD _______________ 74321295172
American / Jan '96 / BMG

LOVE SONGS FOR THE HEARING IMPAIRED
One I am / Julie and lucky / I love you period / Look what you started / Look at what you started / Seriously gone / Pick up the knife / Knocked up / Baby talk / Lost highway / Dixie beauxderaunt
CD _______________ 74321287582
American / Jun '95 / BMG

Baiza, Joe

PROSPEROUS AND QUALIFIED (Baiza, Joe & The Universal Congress)
CD _______________ SST 180CD
SST / May '93 / Plastic Head

Bajourou

BIG STRING THEORY
Hakilma / Mansa / Mankan / Fanta barana / I ka di nye / Sora / Bastan toure / Nkani / Jodoo
CD _______________ CDORBD 078
Globestyle / Mar '93 / Pinnacle

Baka Beyond

MEETING POOL, THE
Woosi / Ancestor's vice / Lupe / Ohureo / Lost dance of Atlantis / Journey / Ndaweh's dream / Booma lena
CD _______________ HNCD 1388
Hannibal / Oct '95 / ADA / Vital

SPIRIT OF THE FOREST (Baka Beyond & Martin Cradick)
Spirit of the forest / Man who danced too slowly / Canya jam / Ngombi / Baka play baka / Nahwia / Elephant song / Bounaka
CD _______________ HNCD 1377
Hannibal / Oct '93 / ADA / Vital

Baka Pygmies

HEART OF THE FOREST
Yelli 1 / Yelli 2 / Yelli 3 / Water drums 1 / Water drums 2 / Nursery rhyme / Venolouma / leta / Ngombi na peke 1 / Limbindi and voices / Earth bow / Limbindi / Water drums 3 / Welcome song / Banja's song / Ngombi na peke 2 / Ngombi na peke 3 / Acapella / Toji / Forest party / Distant yelli
CD _______________ HNCD 1378
Hannibal / Oct '93 / ADA / Vital

Bakardy, Vell

GENUINE LIQUA HITS
Drink wit me / Playa shit / Drunk bitches / Fantasy (it's reality) / Up in the hood / Deep sheet / Forever / FATHA / Liqua ndustry / Daddy's lil andgel / Typical day / Little kids / Life's so hard / Came up
CD _______________ 74321312652
RCA / Jan '96 / BMG

Bakdhi, Javed Salamat

QAWWALI - MUSIQUES DU PENDJAB VOL.3
CD _______________ ARN 64323
Arion / Nov '96 / ADA / Discovery

Baked Beans

BAKED BEANS
Bake daga / Desert bean / Heinz 1 / Has bean
CD _______________ 4509953462
Warner Bros. / Mar '94 / Warner Music
CD _______________ ROD 04
Recycle Or Die / Apr '96 / Kudos

BEAM ME UP SCOTTY
CD _______________ ROD 07
Recycle Or Die / Apr '96 / Kudos

I WANT I CAN'T
CD _______________ LF 272CD
Lost & Found / May '97 / Plastic Head

Baker, Anita

COMPOSITIONS
Talk to me / Whatever it takes / Lonely / More than you know / Fairy tales / Perfect love affair / Soul inspiration / No one to blame / Love you to the letter
CD _______________ 7559609222
Elektra / Jul '90 / Warner Music

GIVING YOU THE BEST THAT I GOT
Priceless / Lead me into love / Giving you the best that I got / Good love / Rules / Good enough / Just because I love you / You belong to me
CD _______________ 9608272
Elektra / Oct '88 / Warner Music

RAPTURE
Sweet love / You bring me joy / Caught up in the rapture / Been so long / Mystery / No one in the world / Same ole love / Watch your step
CD _______________ 9604442
Elektra / Apr '86 / Warner Music

RHYTHM OF LOVE
Rhythm of love / Look of love / Body and soul / Baby / I apologise / Plenty of room / It's been you / You belong to me / Wrong man / Only for a while / Sometimes I wonder why / My funny valentine
CD _______________ 7559615552
Elektra / Sep '94 / Warner Music

SONGSTRESS
Angel / You're the best thing yet / Feel the need / Squeeze me / No more tears / Sometimes / Will you be mine / Do you believe me
CD _______________ 7559611162
Elektra / Nov '91 / Warner Music

Baker Boys

FACING OUR TIME
CD _______________ SITCD 9221
Sittel / Nov '95 / Cadillac / Jazz Music

Baker, Chet

BALLADS FOR TWO (Baker, Chet & Wolfgang Lackerschmid)
Blue bossa / Five years ago / Why shouldn't you cry / Dessert / Softly as in the morning sunrise / You don't know what love is / Waltz for Susan
CD _______________ INAK 856CD
In Akustik / Jul '97 / Direct / TKO Magnum

BEST OF CHET BAKER
CD _______________ DLCD 4020
Dixie Live / Mar '95 / TKO Magnum

BEST OF CHET BAKER PLAYS, THE
Carson city stage / Imagination / All the things you are / Bea's flat / Happy little sunbeam / Pro defunctus / Moonlight becomes you / Stella by starlight / Darn the dream / Sweet Lorraine / Minor yours / CTA / To Mickey's memory / Jumpin' off a clef
CD _______________ CDP 7971612
Blue Note / Feb '92 / EMI

BEST OF CHET BAKER SINGS, THE
Thrill is gone / But not for me / Time after time / I get along without you very well / There will never be another you / Look for the silver lining / My funny valentine / I fall in love too easily / Daybreak / Just friends / I remember you / Let's get lost / Long ago (and far away) / You don't know what love is / That old feeling / It's always you / I've never been in love before / My buddy / Like someone in love / My ideal
CD _______________ CDP 7929322
Blue Note / Jan '90 / EMI

BOSTON 1954
CD _______________ UPCD 2735
Uptown / Apr '97 / Cadillac / Harmonia Mundi

BRUSSELS 1964
CD _______________ 449232
Landscape / Nov '92 / THE

BUT NOT FOR ME
CD _______________ STCD 584
Stash / Jun '94 / ADA / Cadillac / CM / Direct / Jazz Music

CARNEGIE HALL CONCERT (Baker, Chet & Gerry Mulligan)
Lion for Lyons / For an unfinished woman / My funny valentine / Song for strayhorn / It's sandy at the beach / Bernies tune / K-4 pacific / There will never be another you
CD _______________ ZK 64769
Columbia / Nov '95 / Sony

CHET
Alone together / How high the moon / It never entered my mind / 'Tis Autumn / If you could see me now / September song / You'd be so nice to come home to / Time on my hands / You, the night, and the music
CD _______________ OJCCD 87
Original Jazz Classics / Feb '92 / Complete/ Pinnacle / Jazz Music / Wellard

CHET BAKER IN CONCERT (Baker, Chet & Lee Konitz)
CD _______________ IN 1052CD
India Navigation / Jan '97 / Discovery / Impetus

CHET BAKER IN MILAN
CD _______________ OJCCD 370
Original Jazz Classics / Feb '92 / Complete/Pinnacle / Jazz Music / Wellard

CHET BAKER IN TOKYO
CD _______________ K 32Y6281
Concord Jazz / Jul '89 / New Note/ Pinnacle

CHET BAKER SINGS AGAIN
CD _______________ CDSJP 238
Timeless Jazz / '89 / New Note/Pinnacle

CHET IN PARIS (The Barclay Years 1955-1956)
CD Set _______________ FSR CD 1/2
Fresh Sound / May '88 / Discovery / Jazz Music

COOL CAT
Swift shifting / 'Round midnight / Caravelle / For all we know / Blue moon / My foolish heart
CD _______________ CDSJP 262
Timeless Jazz / Mar '90 / New Note/ Pinnacle

COOLS OUT (Baker, Chet Quintet)
Extra mild / Halema / Jumpin' off a cliff / Route / Lucius lou / Pawnee junction
CD _______________ CDBOP 013
Boplicity / Feb '89 / Pinnacle

DIANE (Baker, Chet & Paul Bley)
CD _______________ SCCD 31207
Steeplechase / Jul '88 / Discovery / Impetus

EMBRACEABLE YOU
Night we called it a day / Little girl blue (instrumental) / Embraceable you / They all laughed / There's a lull in my life / What is there to say / While my lady sleeps / Forgetful / How long has this been going on / Come rain or come shine / On Green Dolphin Street / Little girl blue / Travellin' light
CD _______________ CDP 8316762
Pacific Jazz / Jun '95 / EMI

GITANES - JAZZ 'ROUND MIDNIGHT
Easy living / Tenderly / Sweet Sue just you / Touch of your lips / You're, mine, you / You go to my head / Everything depends on you / There is no greater love / Exitus / When your lover has gone / Travellin' light / These foolish things / Alone together / Everything happens to me
CD _______________ 8409172
Verve / Mar '93 / PolyGram

HAIG '53 - THE OTHER PIANO-LESS QUARTET (Baker, Chet & Stan Getz)
CD _______________ CD 214W982
Philology / Mar '92 / Cadillac / Harmonia Mundi

HEART OF THE BALLAD (Baker, Chet & Enrico Pieranunzi)
CD _______________ W 202
Philology / Aug '92 / Cadillac / Harmonia Mundi

I REMEMBER YOU (The Legacy Vol.2)
But not for me / Broken wing / Nardis / You go to my head / Just friends
CD _______________ ENJ 90772
Enja / Dec '96 / New Note/Pinnacle / Vital/ SAM

IN A SOULFUL MOOD
On green Dolphin Street / 'Round Midnight / Milestones / Lucius Lu / Mr. B / Night bird / I'm old fashioned / Airegin
CD _______________ MCCD 269
Music Club / Nov '96 / Disc / THE

IN EUROPE - 1955
CD _______________ 214 W422
Philology / Aug '91 / Cadillac / Harmonia Mundi

IN ITALY (Unissued 1975-1988)
CD _______________ W 812
Philology / Apr '95 / Cadillac / Harmonia Mundi

IN NEW YORK
CD _______________ OJCCD 207
Original Jazz Classics / Feb '92 / Complete/Pinnacle / Jazz Music / Wellard

INTRODUCES JOHNNY
CD _______________ OJCCD 433
Original Jazz Classics / Feb '92 / Complete/Pinnacle / Jazz Music / Wellard

IT COULD HAPPEN TO YOU
CD _______________ OJCCD 303
Original Jazz Classics / Feb '92 / Complete/Pinnacle / Jazz Music / Wellard

ITALIAN MOVIES
CD _______________ IRS 00631CD
Liuto / Oct '90 / Cadillac / Harmonia Mundi

ITALIAN SESSIONS, THE
Well you needn't / These foolish things / Barbados / Star eyes / Somewhere over the rainbow / Pent-up house / Ballata in forma di blues / Blues in the closet
CD _______________ 09026685902
RCA Victor / Oct '96 / BMG

JAZZ MASTERS
CD _______________ 5169392
Verve / Apr '94 / PolyGram

JAZZ MASTERS
CD _______________ CDMFP 6306
Music For Pleasure / Mar '97 / EMI

JAZZ PORTRAITS
Line for lyons / Cherry / Thrill is gone / But not for me / My funny valentine / There will never be another you / Time after time / Daybreak / You don't know what love is / Let's get lost / Love / I fall in love too easily / Just friends / I remember you / Long ago and far away / That old feeling / My ideal / Everything happens to me
CD _______________ CD 14511
Jazz Portraits / May '94 / Jazz Music

JAZZ PROFILE
Bockbanal / That old feeling / Dot's groovy / Route / I get along without you very well / Russ Job / But not for me / Picture of health / I fall in love too easily / Lucius Lu / Halena
CD _______________ CDP 8549022
Blue Note / May '97 / EMI

LAST CONCERT VOL.1 & 2
CD _______________ ENJA 60742
Enja / Nov '91 / New Note/Pinnacle / Vital/ SAM

LEGACY, THE
Here's that rainy day / How deep is the ocean / Mr. B / In your own sweet way / All of you / Dolphin dance / Look for the silver lining / Django / All blues
CD _______________ ENJ 90212
Enja / Jun '95 / New Note/Pinnacle / Vital/ SAM

LET'S GET LOST
CD _______________ CD 56024
Jazz Roots / Aug '94 / Target/BMG

LIVE AT FAT TUESDAY'S
CD _______________ FSRCD 131
Fresh Sound / Sep '91 / Discovery / Jazz Music

LIVE AT NICK'S
CD _______________ CRISSCD 1027
Criss Cross / Mar '90 / Cadillac / Direct / Vital/SAM

LIVE AT ROSENHEIMER
CD _______________ CDSJP 233
Timeless Jazz / May '89 / New Note/ Pinnacle

LIVE IN EUROPE 1956
CD _______________ 556622
Accord / Apr '94 / Cadillac / Discovery

LIVE IN EUROPE 1956 VOL.2
CD _______________ COD 034
Jazz View / Aug '92 / Harmonia Mundi

LIVE IN ROSENHEIM/SINGS AGAIN/ HEARTBREAK (3CD Set)
Funk in deep freeze / I'm a fool to want you / Portrait in black and white / In a sentimental mood / If I should lose you / Arbor way / All of you / Body and soul / Look for the silver lining / I can't get started / My funny valentine / Alone together / Someone to watch over me / How deep is the ocean / Everything happens to me / Angel eyes / All of you / My funny valentine / Blue moon / I'm a fool to want you / You and the night and the music / As time goes by / 'Round midnight / My melancholy baby / My foolish heart
CD Set _______________ CDSJP 007
Timeless / Dec '96 / New Note/Pinnacle

LIVE IN SWEDEN
Lament / My ideal / Beatrice / You can't go home again / But not for me / Ray's idea / Milestones
CD _______________ DRCD 178
Dragon / Sep '89 / ADA / Cadillac / CM / Roots / Wellard

LONELY STAR (The Prestige Sessions)
Grade 'a' gravy / Serenity / Fine and dandy / Have you met miss Jones / Rearin' back / So easy / Madison avenue / Lonely star / Wee, too / Tan gaugin
CD _______________ PRCD 241722
Prestige / Jan '97 / Cadillac / Complete/ Pinnacle

MISTER B/AS TIME GOES BY/COOL CAT (3CD Set)
Dolphin dance / Ellen and David / Strollin' / In your own sweet way / Mister B / Beatrice / White blues / Father X-mas / You and the night and the music / As time goes by / My melancholy baby / I am a fool to want you / When she smiles / Sea breeze / You have been here all along / Angel eyes / You'd be so nice to come home to / 'Round midnight / Swift shifting / Round midnight / Caravelle / For all we know / Blue moon / My foolish heart
CD Set _______________ CDSJP 006
Timeless / Dec '96 / New Note/Pinnacle

MY FUNNY VALENTINE
My funny valentine / Someone to watch over me / Moonlight becomes you / This is always / I'm glad there is you / Time after time / Sweet Lorraine / It's always you / Let's get lost / Moon love / Like someone in love / I've never been in love before / Isn't it romantic / I fall in love too easily
CD _______________ CDP 8282622
Pacific Jazz / Jan '94 / EMI

NAIMA (Unusual Chet Vol.1)
CD _______________ 214 W522
Philology / Aug '91 / Cadillac / Harmonia Mundi

NEWPORT YEARS VOL.1, THE
CD _______________ 214 W512
Philology / Aug '91 / Cadillac / Harmonia Mundi

NIGHT AT THE SHALIMAR CLUB, A
CD Set _______________ 214 W592
Philology / Sep '91 / Cadillac / Harmonia Mundi

NIGHTBIRD (Live At Ronnie Scott's)
But not for me / Arboway / If I should lose you / My ideal / Nightbird / Love for sale / Shifting down / You can't go home again / Send in the clowns
CD _______________ CLACD 333
Castle / '93 / BMG

NO PROBLEM (Baker, Chet Quartet)
CD _______________ SCCD 31131
Steeplechase / '88 / Discovery / Impetus

ON A MISTY NIGHT (The Prestige Sessions)
Cut plug / Boudoir / Etude in three / Sleeping Susan / Go-go / Lament for the living / Pot luck / Bud's blues / Romas / On a misty night / Hurry
CD _______________ PRCD 241742
Prestige / Jan '97 / Cadillac / Complete/ Pinnacle

ONCE UPON SUMMERTIME
CD _______________ OJCCD 405
Original Jazz Classics / Feb '92 / Complete/Pinnacle / Jazz Music / Wellard

OUT OF NOWHERE
Fine and dandy / There will never be another you / Oh lady be good / Au privave / All the things you are / Out of nowhere / There is no greater love / Theme
CD _______________ MCD 91912
Milestone / Apr '94 / Cadillac / Complete/ Pinnacle / Jazz Music / Wellard

QUARTET (Baker, Chet & Russ Freeman)
Love nest / Fan Tan / Summer sketch / An afternoon at home / Say when / Lush life / Amblin' / Hugo Hurwhey
CD _______________ CDP 8554532
Pacific Jazz / Mar '97 / EMI

RISING SUN COLLECTION, THE
Milestones / Oh you crazy moon / There will never be another you / Snowbound / Love for sale
CD _______________ RSCD 0010
Just A Memory / May '96 / New Note/ Pinnacle

SHE WAS GOOD TO ME
CD _______________ 4509542
Sony Jazz / Jan '95 / Sony

SILENT NIGHTS
CD _______________ DCCD 04
Dinemec Jazz / Nov '96 / Koch

SILENT NIGHTS/CHRISTMAS JAZZ ALBUM (Baker, Chet & Christopher Mason)
CD _______________ CDVR 032
Varrick / '88 / ADA / CM / Direct / Roots

SONGS FOR LOVERS
Come rain or shine / My old flame / That old feeling / Lullaby of the leaves / There's a lull in my life / Moonlight in Vermont / Darn that dream / My ideal / Theres a lull in my life / Imagination / Embraceable you / Lush life / Goodbye
CD _______________ CDP 8571582
Pacific Jazz / Jul '97 / EMI

SPECIAL GUESTS (Baker, Chet & Wolfgang Lackerschmid)
Mr. Biko / Balzwaltz / Latin one / Rue Gregoire Du Tour / Here's that rainy day / Toku du
CD _______________ INAK 857CD
In Akustik / Jul '97 / Direct / TKO Magnum

STAIRWAY TO THE STARS (The Prestige Sessions)
Cherokee / Bevan beeps / Comin' on / Stairway to the stars / No fair lady / When you're gone / Choose now / Chabootie / Carpsie's groove / I waited for you / 490
CD _______________ PRCD 241732
Prestige / Jan '97 / Cadillac / Complete/ Pinnacle

STELLA BY STARLIGHT
CD _______________ BS 18006
Bandstand / Jul '96 / Swift

THERE'LL NEVER BE ANOTHER YOU (Baker, Chet & Philip Catherine)
Beatrice / There'll never be another you / Leaving / My foolish heart
CD _______________ CDSJP 437
Timeless / Aug '97 / New Note/Pinnacle

THIS IS JAZZ
Little duet / Love walked in / You don't know what love is / I'm through with love / You'd better go now / Wind / Autumn leaves / She was good to me / Tangerine / What'll I do
CD _______________ CK 64779
Sony Jazz / May '96 / Sony

TOGETHER - THE COMPLETE STUDIO RECORDINGS (Baker, Chet & Paul Desmond)
Tangerine / You can't go home again / How deep is the ocean / You'd be so nice to come home to / I'm getting sentimental over you/You've changed / Autumn leaves / Concierto de aranjuez
CD _______________ 4729842
Epic / Jan '93 / Sony

WEST COAST LIVE (2CD Set) (Baker, Chet & Stan Getz)
My funny valentine / Strike up the band / Way you look tonight / Yardbird suite / Yesterday's / Winter wonderland / Come out wherever you are / Move / What's new / Half nelson / Little Willie leaps / Soft shoe / Whispering / Bernie's tune / All the things you are / Winter wonderland / Gone with the wind / All the things you are / Darn that dream / Crazy rhythm
CD Set _______________ CDP 8356342
Parlophone / Apr '97 / EMI

WHEN SUNNY GETS BLUE
CD _______________ SCCD 31221
Steeplechase / Jul '88 / Discovery / Impetus

WHITE BLUES
Well you needn't / These foolish things / Star eyes / Somewhere over the rainbow / Blues in the closet / My one and only love / Almost blue / White blues / 'Round midnight / Swift shifting / Caravelle / Dolphin dance / Ellen and David
CD _______________ 74321451892
Camden / May '97 / BMG

WITCH DOCTOR (Baker, Chet & Lighthouse All Stars)
Loaded / I'll remember April / Winter wonderland / Pirouette / Witch doctor
CD _______________ OJCCD 609
Original Jazz Classics / Feb '92 / Complete/ Pinnacle / Jazz Music / Wellard

WITH STRINGS
You don't know what love is / I'm through with love / Love walked in / You'd better go now / I married an angel / Love / I love you / What a difference a day makes / Why shouldn't I / Little duet / Wind / Trickleydidlier
CD _______________ 4669682
Columbia / Apr '92 / Sony

YOUNG CHET
Look for the silver lining / But not for me / Time after time / My funny valentine / There will never be another you / Extra mild / Night on Bop Mountain / Down / Taboo / I can't get started (With you) / It's only a paper moon / Autumn in New York
CD _______________ CDP 8361942
Pacific Jazz / Feb '96 / EMI

Baker, Duck

AMERICAN TRADITIONAL (Baker, Duck & Molly Andrews)
CD _______________ DBMA 1CD
Dayjob / Jul '93 / ADA

CLEAR BLUE SKY
CD _______________ BEST 1065CD
Acoustic Music / Apr '95 / ADA

MOVING BUSINESS, THE (Baker, Duck & Molly Andrews)
CD _______________ DBMA 2CD
Dayjob / Oct '94 / ADA

OPENING THE EYES OF LOVE
CD _______________ SHAN 97025CD
Shanachie / May '93 / ADA / Greensleeves / Koch

SPINNING SONG (The Music Of Herbie Nichols)
CD _______________ AVAN 040
Avant / Jan '97 / Cadillac / Harmonia Mundi

THOUSAND WORDS, A (Baker, Duck & John Renbourn)
CD _______________ BEST 1021CD
Acoustic Music / Nov '93 / ADA

Baker, Etta

ONE DIME BLUES
CD _______________ ROUCD 2112
Rounder / Sep '91 / ADA / CM / Direct

Baker, George

STAR PORTRAIT: GEORGE BAKER SELECTION (Baker, George Selection)
CD _______________ 16029
Laserlight / '93 / Target/BMG

Baker, Ginger

AFRICAN FORCE
CD _______________ ITM 1417
ITM / '89 / Koch / Tradelink

HORSES AND TREES
Interlock / Dust to dust / Satou / Uncut / Mountain time / Makuta

CD ______________ MPG 74046
Movieplay Gold / Jul '97 / Target/BMG

MIDDLE PASSAGE
Mektoub / Under black skies / Time to be time / Alamout / Basil / South to the dust
CD ______________ 8467532
Axiom / Apr '91 / PolyGram / Vital

PALANQUIN'S POLE (Baker, Ginger & African Force)
CD ______________ ITM 1433
ITM / Apr '90 / Koch / Tradelink

Baker, Josephine

BLACK VENUS
J'ai deux amours / Le petite tonkinoise / La conga blicoti / Voulez vous de la canne a sucre / Dis-moi Josephine / Confessin' / Ram pam pam / Si j'etais blanche / Sans amour / Les mots d'amour / Mon reve c'etait vous / Pretty little baby / Suppose / Pardon si je t'importune / Aux iles Hawaii / Sleepy time gal / After I say I'm sorry / Blue skies / Breezing along with the breeze / Bye bye blackbird / He's the last word / I'm leaving for Alabamy
CD ______________ CD 394
Entertainers / Jun '96 / Target/BMG

EXOTIQUE
CD ______________ PASTCD 7059
Flapper / Apr '95 / Pinnacle

FABULOUS JOSEPHINE BAKER, THE
Paris ses amours / Le marchand de bonheur / Mo 'lo' / J'attendrai / Donnez moi la man / Je voudrais / La Seine / Sonny boy / Sous les toits de Paris / Mon p'tit bonhomme / En Avril a Paris / Sag beim Abschied leise 'Servus' / Don't touch my tomatoes
CD ______________ 09026616682
RCA Victor / Jun '95 / BMG

JOSEPHINE BAKER STORY, THE
CD ______________ CDD 3401
Concord Jazz / Jul '92 / New Note/ Pinnacle

LEGEND IN HER LIFETIME, A
CD ______________ WMCD 5674
Woodford Music / Feb '93 / THE

Baker, Kenny

BOSS IS HOME, THE
Swingin' the blues / Stumbling / Street dreams / Slightly latin / What am I here for / Threesome / When sunny gets the blue / Squatty roo / Golden cress / Sorta ragtime / Boss is home / More than you know / Harlem airshaft / It's alright with me / In a jam
CD ______________ ESJCD 538
Essential Jazz / Apr '97 / BMG

TRIBUTE TO THE GREAT TRUMPETERS
I can't get started (with you) / And the angels sing / Tenderly / You made me love you / Satchmo / Morning glory / How long has this been going on / Georgia / Memories of you / Little jazz / Music goes 'round and around / Carnival time / Won't you come home, Bill Bailey / What's new / Sugar blues / Davenport blues / Echoes of Harlem / Our love is here to stay
CD ______________ CDSIV 1124
Horatio Nelson / Jul '95 / Disc

Baker, LaVern

BLUES BALLADS
I cried a tear / If you love me / You're teasing me / Love me right / Dix-a-billy / So high so love / I waited too long / Why baby why / Humpty Dumpty heart / It's so fine / Whipper snapper / St. Louis blues / How often / Hurting inside / I didn't know I was crying / Help each other romance / You're the boss / I'll never be free
CD ______________ RSACD 911
Sequel / Mar '97 / BMG

LAVERN
Lots and lots of love / Of course I do / You'll be crying / Miracles / I'm in a crying mood / Mine all mine / Harbour lights / I'll never be free / Romance in the dark / Everybody is somebody's fool / How long will it be / Fool that I am / Living my life for you / I can't hold out any longer / Fee fi fo fum / I'll still do the same for you / Game of love
CD ______________ RSACD 909
Sequel / Mar '97 / BMG

LAVERN BAKER SINGS BESSIE SMITH
Gimme a pigfoot / Baby doll / On revival day / Money blues / I ain't gonna play no second fiddle / Backwater blues / Empty bed blues / There'll be a hot time in the old town tonight / Nobody knows you when you're down and out / After you've gone / Young woman's blues / Preaching the blues
CD ______________ RSACD 914
Sequel / Mar '97 / BMG

PRECIOUS MEMORIES
Precious memories / Carrying the cross for my boss / Just a little closer walk with thee / Touch me Lord Jesus / Didn't it rain / Precious Lord / Somebody touched me / In the other room / Journey to the sky / Everytime I feel the spirit / Too close / Without a God
CD ______________ RSACD 915
Sequel / Mar '97 / BMG

ROCK 'N' ROLL WITH LAVERN BAKER
Jim Dandy / Tra la la / I can't love you enough / Get up get up (you sleepy head) / That's all I need / Bop ting-a-ling / Tweedle dee / Still / Play it fair / Tomorrow night / That lucky old sun / Soul on fire / My happiness for ever / How can you leave a man like this / Learning to love / Jim Dandy got married / Substitute / Voodoo voodoo / Tiny Tim / If you love me
CD ______________ RSACD 910
Sequel / Mar '97 / BMG

SAVED
Saved / For love of you / Manana / My time will come / Shadows of love / Must I cry again / Bumble bee / Shake a hand / Don Juan / Wheel of fortune / Itty bitty girl / Eager beaver / You don't tell me / Loads of love / Hey Memphis / No love so true / Eternally / Senor big and fine
CD ______________ RSACD 912
Sequel / Mar '97 / BMG

SEE SEE RIDER
CC rider / You better stop / He's a real gone guy / Story of my love / You said / I'm leaving you / Don't let the stars get in your eyes / Trying / Half of your love / Little bird told me so / Endless love / All the time / Trouble in mind / Oh Johnny oh Johnny / Fly me to the moon / Go away / You better find yourself another fool / Ain't gonna cry no more
CD ______________ RSACD 913
Sequel / Mar '97 / BMG

SOUL ON FIRE
Soul on fire / Tomorrow night / Tweedlee dee / That's all I need / Bop-ting-a-ling / Play it fair / Jim Dandy / My happiness forever / Get up, get up (you sleepy head) / Sill / I can't love you enough / Jim Dandy got married / I cried a tear / Whippersnapper / I waited to long / Shake a hand / How often / You said / Saved / CC rider
CD ______________ 7567823112
WEA / Mar '93 / Warner Music

Baker, Lee

FRESH OIL (Baker, Lee & The Agitators)
CD ______________ BLW 5503CD
Blues Works / May '97 / Hot Shot

Baker, Marilyn

FACE TO FACE
Face to face / He is the rock / I know where you're coming from / Constantly amazed / Brand new heart / Lord I love you / He knows your sorrows / Don't deceive yourselves / When I think / Lord's my shepherd / O Lord you are so mighty / Open your ears / My God how great you are / I love to talk with Jesus
CD ______________ WSTCD 9722
Nelson Word / Apr '92 / Nelson Word

Baker, McHouston 'Mickey'

MISSISSIPPI DELTA BLUES
Good advice / High sheriff blues / Blues before sunrise / Terraplane blues / Animal farm / Alabama march / Spoonful / Sun is going down / Sweet home Chicago / My black woman / Can't find my baby / Trouble is / A woman / Lazy daisy / Drucilla
CD ______________ 5197282
Verve / Mar '94 / PolyGram

ROCK WITH A SOCK
Guitar mambo / Riverboat / Love me baby / Oh happy day / Where is my honey / I'm tired / Stranger blues / I wish I knew / Down to the bottom / You better heed my warning / Midnight hours / Please tell me / Shake walkin' / Greasy spoon / Bandstand stomp / Rock with a sock / Old devil moon / Guitarambo / Spinnin' rock boogie / I don't stand a ghost of a chance with you / Chloe / Man I love / Bobi, Mickey and Silvia / Hello stranger / My love / Woe woe is me / Can't get you on the phone / I'll always want you near
CD ______________ BCD 15654
Bear Family / Aug '93 / Direct / Rollercoaster / Swift

Baker-Baldwin Radiogram ...

OZARK BLUES (Baker-Baldwin Radiogram Washboards)
CD ______________ SOSCD 1243
Stomp Off / Jul '93 / Jazz Music / Wellard

Bal Sagoth

BLACK MOON BROODS OVER LEMURIA, A
Dreaming of Utlantean spires / Spellcraft and moonfire / Black moon broods over Lemuria / Enthroned in the Temple of the Serpent Kings / Shadows 'neath the black pyramid / Witch-storm / Ravening / Into the silent chambers of the Sapphirean Throne / Valley of silent paths
CD ______________ NIHIL 4CD
Cacophonous / Jun '97 / Plastic Head / RTM/Disc

STARFIRE BURNING
CD ______________ NIHIL 18CD
Cacophonous / Nov '96 / Plastic Head / RTM/Disc

Balaam & The Angel

PRIME TIME
Shame on you / Prime time / Next to me / What love is / Gathering dust / Eagle / She's not you / Mr. Business / Like a train / Burnin' / Just no good
CD ______________ CDBLEED 1
Bleeding Hearts / Apr '93 / Pinnacle

Balachander, S.

MUSIC OF THE VEENA VOL.1
CD ______________ VICG 50362
JVC World Library / Mar '96 / ADA / CM / Direct

Balafon Marimba Ensemble

BALAFON MARIMBA ENSEMBLE, THE
CD ______________ SHAN 670029CD
Shanachie / Feb '93 / ADA / Greensleeves / Koch

HARARE TO KISINGANI
CD ______________ SHCD 67004
Shanachie / Mar '94 / ADA / Greensleeves / Koch

Balalaika Ensemble Wolga

KALAKOLTSCHIK
CD ______________ EUCD 1064
ARC / '89 / ADA / ARC Music

KALINKA
CD ______________ EUCD 1054
ARC / '89 / ADA / ARC Music

POPULAR FOLK SONGS FROM RUSSIA
Cossack's dance / Bandura / Oriental dance / Legend of the 12 brigands / Katjusche / Ej uchnjem / Wass duli / Bajuschki baju / White acacia / Uri balki / Tears fall out of clouds / Roaring volga
CD ______________ EUCD 1126
ARC / '91 / ADA / ARC Music

SONGS FROM THE TAIGA
CD ______________ EUCD 1050
ARC / '89 / ADA / ARC Music

WOLGA (The Best Of Russian Folk Songs)
CD ______________ EUCD 1146
ARC / Jan '92 / ADA / ARC Music

Balalaikas Of Moscow

BALALAIKAS OF MOSCOW, THE
Pedlars / Shall we go to the river / Melody of Saratov / Song of the Volga boatmen / Bells / My joy is alive / Elegie / When I met you / Moon is shining / Tritsch-tratsch polka / Little comrade come and see me / Girl comes to see me in the evening / Russian ditties / Dark eyes / Long road / Kalinka / Lara's theme / Gypsy dance / O birch tree / Flight of the bumble bee / Katiusha
CD ______________ PS 65185
PlayaSound / Jun '97 / ADA / Harmonia Mundi

Bald

BALD
CD ______________ 132161
XIII Bis / Feb '97 / Discovery

Baldan, Bebo

EARTHBEAT (Baldan, Bebo & David Torn)
Desire / Earthbeat / Diving into the world / Niceday / San Isidro / Shakti no Brasil / Asoka's / On Namah Shivaya / Santoor / Ralph
CD ______________ MASOCD 90082
Materiali Sonori / Oct '95 / Cargo / Greyhound / New Note/Pinnacle

Baldry, Long John

IT AIN'T EASY
Conditional discharge / Don't try to lay no Boogie-Woogie / Black girl / It ain't easy / Morning morning / I'm ready / Let's burn down the cornfield / Mr. Rubin / Rock me when he's gone / Flying
CD ______________ LICD 901235
Line / Nov '96 / CM / Direct

IT STILL AIN'T EASY
It still ain't easy / Midnight in New Orleans / One step ahead / I never loved nobody / Get it while the gettin's good / What've I been drinking / Insane asylum / You wanna dance / Shake that thang / Like you promised / Busker / Can't keep from crying / No more / Soft and furry
CD ______________ SP 1163CD
Stony Plain / Sep '96 / ADA / CM / Direct

LET THE HEARTACHES BEGIN/WAIT FOR ME
Long and lonely nights / Stay with me baby / Every time we say goodbye / For all we know / Better by far / Let the heartaches begin / Wise to the ways of the world / Since I lost you baby / Smile / Annabella / We're together / I can't stop loving you / Sunshine of your love / Spanish Harlem / Henry Hannah's 42nd St. parking lot / Man without a dream / Cry like a baby / River deep, mountain high / How sweet it is (to be loved by you) / MacArthur Park / Brigadier McKenzie / Ligts of Cincinatti / Spinning wheel / Wait for me / Mexico / When the sun comes shining through
CD ______________ BGOCD 272
Beat Goes On / May '95 / Pinnacle

LONG JOHN'S BLUES/LOOKING AT LONG JOHN
You've lost that lovin' feelin' / Only a fool breaks his own heart / Make it easy on yourself / Let him go / Drifter / Cry me a river / Stop her on sight (SOS) / Turn on your love light / I love Paris / Keep on running' / Ain't nothin' you can do / Bad luck soul / Got my mojo working / Gee baby ain't I good to you / Rool 'em Pete / You're breaking my heart / Hoochie coochie / Everyday (I got the blues) / Dimples / Five long years / My babe / Times are getting tougher / Goin' down slow / Rock the joint
CD ______________ BGOCD 2
Beat Goes On / Dec '90 / Pinnacle

MEXICO
Let the heartaches begin / Every time we say goodbye / Lights of Cincinatti / Since I lost you baby / Spinning wheel / Annabella (Who flies to me when she's lonely) / Stay with me baby / Sunshine of your love / It's too late now / When the sun comes shining through / For all we know / Spanish Harlem / Cry like a baby / How sweet it is (to be loved by you) / MacArthur Park / Smile / River deep, mountain high / Mexico (Underneath the sun in)
CD ______________ 5507572
Spectrum / Feb '95 / PolyGram

RIGHT TO SING THE BLUES
CD ______________ HYCD 2917167
Hypertension / Feb '97 / ADA / CM / Direct / Total/BMG

ROCK WITH THE BEST
Midnight show / When you're ugly like me / Bad attitude / Twenty five years of pain / Rock with the best / Too late for crying / Love is where you find it / Stay the way you are / Passing glances / Let the heartaches stop / Iko iko / Hand jive / Got rhythm / Black girl
CD ______________ HYCD 296164
Hypertension / Nov '96 / ADA / CM / Direct / Total/BMG

VERY BEST OF LONG JOHN BALDRY, THE
Let the heartaches begin / Spinning wheel / It's too late now / Spanish Harlem / When the sun comes shining through / Mexico / River deep mountain high / Man without a dream / Cry like a baby / Lights of Cincinnati / Sunshine of your love / Wise to the ways of the world / Stay with me baby / Hold back the daybreak / Hey Lord you made the night too long / Macarthur Park / How sweet it is / For all we know / I can't stop loving you / Every time we say goodbye
CD ______________ MCCD 306
Music Club / Jun '97 / Disc / THE

Baldwin, Bob

COLD BREEZE
CD ______________ SH 5035
Shanachie / Jul '97 / ADA / Greensleeves / Koch

Balfa Brothers

NEW YORK CONCERTS PLUS, THE
Jolie blon / Les flames d'enfer / Les bars de la prison / Two step de lacassine / I don't want you anymore / La valse de grand bois / J'ai passe devant ta porte / Hippy ti yo / Madame Sostan / La valse criminel / You had some but you won't have anymore / Tee yeaux noir / Chanson de les mardi gras / Dying in misery / In my old wagon / Cowboy waltz / Texas two step / Coeur criminel / Les traces de mon bogue / J'etais au balle / Valse de kaplan
CD ______________ CDCHD 338
Ace / Oct '91 / Pinnacle

TRADITIONAL CAJUN MUSIC VOL.1 & 2
Drunkard's sorrow waltz / Lacassine special / My true love / La valse de Grand Bois / Family waltz / Newport waltz / Indian on a stomp / T'ai petite et t'ai meon / Two step a Hadley / Valse de Balfa / Parlez-nous a boire / Les blues de cajun / 'Tit galop pour mamou / Je suis Orphelin / T'en as eu mais t'en n'auras plus / Two step de l'anse a paille / La danse de Mardi Gras / Je me suis Marillie / Enterre moi pas / Chere joules roses / Chere bassette / J'ai passe devant ta porte / Les flames d'enfer / Madeleine / Drunkards sorrow waltz
CD ______________ CDCHD 955
Ace / Nov '90 / Pinnacle

Balfa, Dewey

SOUVENIRS/FAIT A LA MAIN (Balfa, Dewey & Friends)
Equand j'etais pauvre / La valse du Canada / La valse de deux familles / 1755 / Bienvenue au paradis / Fiddlesticks / J'ai pleure / Don't stop the music / La reel de joie / La mauvaise nouvelle / Watermelon reel / Grand mamou / Pauvre hobo / La jolie blonde / Back door / Valse de balfa / Blues a Leo Soileau / Two step a Nathan Abshire / Chere toute toute / J'ai passe devant ta

porte / Les veuves de la coulee / Les flames d'enfer / T'ai petite et t'ai meon / Perrodin two step
CD ______________ CDCHD 328
Ace / Jul '91 / Pinnacle

Balfa Toujours

A VIELLE TERRE HAUTRE
CD ______________ SW 6121CD
Swallow / Jul '95 / ADA

DEUX VOYAGES
Allons a Tepatate / Deux voyages / J'ai vu le loup, le Renard et le Belette / Chicot two-step / La Valse a Canray / Bee de la Manche / 73 special / Le Canard a Bois Sec / Le falcon gris / La Valse a Grandpere / Jeunes filles de la campagne / Galop a Wade Fruge / Cher petit monde / Octa's two-step / La musique de ma jeunesse / Le Reel de Nonc Will
CD ______________ ROUCD 6071
Rounder / Oct '96 / ADA / CM / Direct

NEW CAJUN TRADITION
La vielle terre haute / True love waltz / Madam boso / Apres nous esperer / J'ai perdu mes lunettes / Reel de deshotels / Old fashioned two step / Les fleurs du Printemps / Rodair special / La marrraine / Petite fille de la campagne / La valse de vieux vacher / Texas two step / Arrete pas la musique / Reel du melon d'eau / Pop, tu me parles toujours / L'anse aux pailles / La valse des Balfa / C'est tout perdu / Dans le coeur de basile / Two-step a tina / Tow truck blues
CD ______________ CDCHD 613
Ace / Jun '95 / Pinnacle

Balham Alligators

BAYOLI TECHE
CD ______________ PRPCD 51
Proper / Feb '97 / Grapevine/PolyGram

CAJUN DANCE PARTY (17 Sizzlers From The Swamp)
Cuvee cajun / Bayou pom pom / Guerre civille / Grand Texas / Wet and swampy / Rosie cheeks / Cher Mama / Colinda / Jole blon / Lacassine / Diggy liggy lo / Last waltz / Balham two step / Lache pas mes patats / Big Mamou / Hobo blues / Goodnight Irene
CD ______________ EMPRCD 719
Emporio / Jun '97 / Disc

GATEWAY TO THE SOUTH
Allons rock'n'roll / Hot rod / Bayou teche / Big bad dog / Malhereuse / You gotta have money / Cash on the barrelhead / Secret love / Too much / Honky tonk song / Last waltz / Johnny B Goode
CD ______________ PRPCD 001
Proper / Apr '96 / Grapevine/PolyGram

Balkana

MUSIC OF BULGARIA, THE
CD ______________ HNCD 1335
Hannibal / Oct '87 / ADA / Vital

Balke, Jon

FURTHER (Balke, Jon & The Magnetic North Orchestra)
Departure / Step one / Horizontal song / Flying thing / Shaded place / Taraf / Moving carpet / Eastern forest / Changing forest / Wooden voices / Arrival
CD ______________ 5217202
ECM / May '94 / New Note/Pinnacle

NONSENTRATION (Balke, Jon & Oslo 13)
Stealing space / Stealing space II / Stop / Blic / Constructing stop / Laws of freedom / Disappear here / Nord / Circling the square / Art of being
CD ______________ 8496532
ECM / Feb '92 / New Note/Pinnacle

Ball, E.C.

E.C. BALL WITH ORMA BALL (Ball, E.C./Orma Ball/Friendly Gospel Singers)
CD ______________ ROUCD 11577
Rounder / Mar '96 / ADA / CM / Direct

MOUNTAIN MUSIC
CD ______________ ROU 11577
Rounder / May '96 / ADA / CM / Direct

Ball, Ed

CATHOLIC GUILT
Mill Hill self hate club / Love is blue / Docklands blues / Controversial girlfriend / Hampstead therapist / Tilt / Trailblaze / Never live to love again / This is the story of my love / This is real
CD ______________ CRECD 200
Creation / May '97 / 3mv/Vital

IF A MAN EVER LOVED A WOMAN
CD ______________ CRECD 195
Creation / Jul '95 / 3mv/Vital

WONDERFUL WORLD OF ED BALL
CD Set ______________ CRECD 183
Creation / Feb '95 / 3mv/Vital

Ball, Kenny

BALL, BARBER & BILK (Ball, Kenny/ Chris Barber/Acker Bilk)
CD ______________ MATCD 300
Castle / Sep '93 / BMG

BEST OF KENNY BALL, THE (Hits & Requests) (Ball, Kenny & His Jazzmen)
March of the Siamese children / Muskrat ramble / I wanna be like you / Rondo / Sukiyaki / I ain't what you do (it's the way that you do it) / Kansas City stomps / Music goes 'round and around / Green leaves of summer / Acapulco 1922 / So do I / Midnight in Moscow / Samantha / Casablanca / Chimes blues / Hello Dolly / Original Dixieland one-step / Wild man blues / Basin Street blues / Ory's creole trombourne / When I'm sixty four / At the jazz band ball
CD ______________ TRTCD 147
TrueTrax / Oct '94 / THE

DIXIELAND CHRISTMAS, A
CD ______________ PWKS 4219
Carlton / Oct '95 / Carlton

GREENSLEEVES (Ball, Kenny & His Jazzmen)
Flow gently sweet Afton / Nobody knows you (when you're down and out) / I got rhythm / Ostrich walk / I shall not be moved / St. Louis blues / Greensleeves / My mother's eyes / I wanna be like you / Mood indigo / Them there eyes / Old folks / Sweet Georgia Brown
CD ______________ CDTTD 505
Timeless Traditional / Jul '94 / Jazz Music / New Note/Pinnacle

HELLO DOLLY
Midnight in Moscow / March of the Siamese children / Sukiyaki / Maple Leaf rag / Swing low, sweet chariot / Down by the riverside / When I'm sixty four / Puttin' on the Ritz / At the jazz band ball / American patrol / Hello Dolly / Cabaret / Green leaves of Summer / I got plenty o' nuttin' / Big noise from Winnetka / Acapulco 1922 / I love you Samantha / Washington Square / Lazy river / Alexander's ragtime band
CD ______________ 5507582
Spectrum / Feb '95 / PolyGram

IN DISNEYLAND
CD ______________ PLSCD 153
Pulse / Feb '97 / BMG

KENNY BALL & HIS JAZZMEN 1960-1961 (Ball, Kenny & His Jazzmen)
Hawaiian war chant / Them there eyes / Georgia swing / Riverside blues / Sorry / Original Dixieland one-step / Teddy bear's picnic / I got plenty of nuthin' / Dinah / Lazy river / 1919 / South Rampart Street parade / Savoy blues / Ostrich walk / Blue turning grey over you / Fingerbuster / Big noise from Winnetka / Potato head blues
CD ______________ LACD 76
Lake / Mar '97 / ADA / Cadillac / Direct / Jazz Music / Target/BMG

LIGHTING UP THE TOWN (Ball, Kenny & His Jazzmen)
CD ______________ ISCD 113
Intersound / Jul '93 / Jazz Music

STEPPIN' OUT (Ball, Kenny & His Jazzmen)
CD ______________ MATCD 209
Castle / Dec '92 / BMG

STRICTLY JAZZ (Ball, Kenny & His Jazzmen)
CD ______________ KAZCD 19
Kaz / Jul '92 / BMG

VERY BEST OF KENNY BALL, THE (Ball, Kenny & His Jazzmen)
I got plenty o'nuttin' / Pennies from heaven / Teddy bear's picnic / Your feet's too big / Preacher / Stevedore stomp / Pay off / I still love you all / Royal garden blues / Ol' man river / I want a big butter and egg man / Flying high / You are the sunshine of my life / I can't get started (With you) / Midnight in Moscow / Samantha
CD ______________ CDTTD 598
Timeless Jazz / Dec '95 / New Note/ Pinnacle

Ball, Marcia

BLUE HOUSE
CD ______________ ROUCD 3131
Rounder / Oct '94 / ADA / CM / Direct

HOT TAMALE BABY
CD ______________ ROUCD 3095
Rounder / '88 / ADA / CM / Direct

LET ME PLAY WITH YOUR POODLE
Let me play with your poodle / Why women cry / Crawfishin' / How big a fool / Right tool for the job / I'm just a prisoner / I still love you / Can't trust my heart / Story of my life / Something I can't do / For the love of a man / American dream / Louisiana 1927
CD ______________ ROUCD 3151
Rounder / Jul '97 / ADA / CM / Direct

SOULFUL DRESS
CD ______________ ROUCD 3078
Rounder / '88 / ADA / CM / Direct

Ball, Michael

ALWAYS
Song for you / House is not a home / If I can dream / Cry me a river / You don't have to say you love me / Someone to watch over me / On Broadway / Tell me there's a heaven / Always on my mind / You'll never know / Stormy weather / You made me love you
CD ______________ 5196662
Polydor / Jul '93 / PolyGram

COLLECTION, THE
Love changes everything / One step out of time / House is not a home / Cry me a river / You don't have to say you love me / Someone to watch over me / Stormy weather / As dreams go by / On Broadway / You made me love you / Secret of love / You'll never know (How much I love you) / Beautiful heartache / It's still you / Who needs to know / No one cries anymore / Holland Park / Simple affair of the heart / First man you remember
CD ______________ 5517712
Spectrum / Nov '95 / PolyGram

FIRST LOVE
Rose / Let the river run / Somewhere / If you could read my mind / (Something inside) So strong / How can I be sure / If you go away (Ne me quitte pas) / I'm gonna be strong / I'm so sorry / All by myself / Walk away / When you believe in love
CD ______________ 4835992
Columbia / Jan '96 / Sony

MICHAEL BALL
CD ______________ 5113302
Polydor / Mar '96 / PolyGram

MUSICALS
CD ______________ 5338922
PolyGram TV / Nov '96 / PolyGram

ONE CAREFUL OWNER
Wherever you are / From here to eternity / Lovers we were / Take my breath away / Leave a light on / When we began / My arms are strong / I wouldn't know / All for nothing / In this life / Give me love / I'll be there
CD ______________ 4772802
Columbia / Aug '94 / Sony

VERY BEST OF MICHAEL BALL, THE
Song for you / Sunset Boulevard / Holland Park / Love changes everything / No one cries anymore / One step out of time / We break our own hearts / Call on me / As dreams go by / Everyday everynight / No more steps to climb / House is not a home / Maria / Beautiful heartache / It's still you / If I can dream / Empty chairs at empty tables / Always on my mind / Simple affair of the heart / On Broadway
CD ______________ 5238912
Polydor / Nov '94 / PolyGram

Ball, Roger

STREET STRUTTIN'
CD ______________ EFZ 1013
EFZ / May '95 / Vital/SAM

Ball, Tom

BLOODSHOT EYES (Ball, Tom & Kenny Sultan)
CD ______________ FF 386CD
Flying Fish / Feb '93 / ADA / CM / Direct / Roots

DOUBLE VISION (Ball, Tom & Kenny Sultan)
Perfect woman / Your shoes don't fit my feet / No money, no honey / Automobile mechanic / I feel alright now / Sweet Georgia Brown/Bill Bailey / Sweet temptation / Sloppy Joe / Television / Roll of the tumblin' dice / Wing and a prayer / Ride that train / Back to California / Who drank my beer
CD ______________ CDFF 656
Flying Fish / Sep '96 / ADA / CM / Direct / Roots

GUITAR MUSIC
Estudio sin luz / Variation on forlorn hope fancy / Sweet Papa Lowdown / Fantasia no.30 / Joseph Spence medley / Cane break blues / Heigh ho holiday / Variation on a barrios prelude / Morley's pavan / Mirabella / Volt no.6 / Old time medley / Sarabande / Needed time / Lejania
CD ______________ CDKM 3906
Kicking Mule / Jan '97 / Pinnacle

TOO MUCH FUN (Ball, Tom & Kenny Sultan)
CD ______________ FF 532CD
Flying Fish / '92 / ADA / CM / Direct / Roots

Balla Et Ses Balladins

AFRICAN DANCE FLOOR CLASSICS
CD ______________ ADC 302
PAM / Feb '94 / ADA / Direct

Ballamy, Iain

ACME
Herpetology / Eggshells / Bliss off / Quandary / Battered this, battered that / Friendly ship / Cyclops / Chantries
CD ______________ BW 101
B&W / Nov '96 / New Note/Pinnacle / SRD / Vital/SAM

ALL MEN AMEN (Ballamy, Iain & Perfect Houseplants)
All men amen / Serendipity / Blennie / Haunted swing / Oaxaca / Meadow / This world / Further away
CD ______________ BW 065
B&W / Nov '96 / New Note/Pinnacle / SRD / Vital/SAM

Ballantine, David

PAINT
CD ______________ DTAB 16CD
Dtab / Nov '95 / ADA

Ballard, Hank

20 HITS (Ballard, Hank & The Midnighters)
CD ______________ KCD 5003
King / Apr '97 / Avid/BMG

SING 24 SONGS (Ballard, Hank & The Midnighters)
CD ______________ KCD 950
King / Mar '90 / Avid/BMG

Ballas, Corky

PASSION VOL.2 (Ballas, Corky & Shirley)
CD ______________ DLD 1061
Dance & Listen / Dec '95 / Savoy / Target/ BMG

Ballbusters

NO HANG UPS
CD ______________ 0090674DDX
Deep Distraxion/Profile / Oct '95 / Pinnacle

Ballero, Jimmy

JIMMY BALLERO AND THE RENEGADE BAND (Ballero, Jimmy & The Renegade Band)
CD ______________ SCD 27
Southland / Feb '93 / Jazz Music

Ballew, Michael

I LOVE TEXAS
Music is sweet / Greatest Texas song / Glenda Pearl / Ain't no future / I love Texas / Blue water / Country music / Rodeo cool / Hot spot / Lovin' me / Cheatin' / Take it slow / My family / Your daddy don't live in heaven / Pretending fool / Seminole County Jail / Crazy dreams / Dark side of the dancefloor / As precious as you are / Women love, love out there / Hazelwood Avenue
CD ______________ BCD 15669
Bear Family / Jun '92 / Direct / Rollercoaster / Swift

LIVE AT GRUENE HALL
Hot spot / Damned ol' beer / Whiskey's fine / I can't drive home / I can't do that (anymore) / Leavin' these honky tonks / I love to ride / Texas gal / Top of the world / Heavy on the blues / Where are the rangers / Sixteen tons / Music is sweet / Darkside on the dancefloor / Old cowboy / Cowboy and the preacher / Texas blue water / I love Texas
CD ______________ BCD 16167
Bear Family / May '97 / Direct / Rollercoaster / Swift

YOU BETTER HOLD ON
Blue to the bone / Livin' in limbo / Nothin' on me / Tiny fingers, tiny toes / Texas gal / Blue water / Boot scootin' / Your memory is better than mine / You better hold on / Hill country wine / For the honey / Dig in, get tough / Today will never end
CD ______________ BCD 15896
Bear Family / Jun '95 / Direct / Rollercoaster / Swift

Ballin, Chris

DO IT RIGHT
CD ______________ EMH 3CD
Intimate / Jun '96 / Jet Star / Total/BMG

Ballistic Brothers

LONDON HOOLIGAN SOUL
CD ______________ JBOCD 3
Junior Boys Own / May '97 / Mo's Music Machine / RTM/Disc

RUDE SYSTEM
Tuning up / Soul catcher / Marching on / Shiva's prelusion / Shiva's waltz / Conversation / Future James (Jack) / Streets are real / Blacker (4 the good times) / Rule of the bone / Love supreme / Silent runnings
CD ______________ SBCD 001
Soundboy / Jul '97 / Prime / RTM/Disc / Total/BMG

Balliu, Rudy

RUDY BALLIU'S SOCIETY SERENADERS (Balliu, Rudy & His Society Serenaders)
CD ______________ BCD 343
GHB / Jul '96 / Jazz Music

Ballochmyle

TOUCH OF COUNTRY, A
CD CDSLP 622
Klub / Aug '94 / ADA / CM / Direct / Duncans / Ross

Ballroom Dance Orchestra

COME DANCING RHUMBA
Have I told you lately / Another day in Paradise / And I love her / Spanish eyes / Europe / Feelings / Endless love / Most beautiful girl in the world / La isla bonita / I have a dream / It's too late / He ain't heavy he's my brother / I heard it through the grapevine / How deep is your love / Killingly me softly / All out of love
CD 306092
Hallmark / Jan '97 / Carlton

Ballyclare Male Voice Choir

MARVELLOUS AND WONDERFUL
CD CDPOL 906
Outlet / Jan '95 / ADA / CM / Direct / Duncans / Koch / Ross

WALKING WITH GOD
CD CDPOL 901
Outlet / Jan '95 / ADA / CM / Direct / Duncans / Koch / Ross

Balogh, Kalman

GIPSY CIMBALOM, THE
CD EUCD 1102
ARC / '91 / ADA / ARC Music

ROMA VANDOR
CD MWCD 4009
Music & Words / Apr '95 / ADA / Direct

Balogh, Meta

GYPSY MUSIC FROM THE HUNGARIAN VILLAGES (Balogh, Meta & Kalman)
CD EUCD 1373
ARC / Nov '96 / ADA / ARC Music

Balthaus, Dirk

TALES OF THE FROG
CD BEST 1082CD
Acoustic Music / Mar '96 / ADA

Baltic Quartet

BALTIC QUARTET
CD SITCD 9222
Sittel / Aug '95 / Cadillac / Jazz Music

Baltimore

THOUGHT FOR FOOD
CD SPV 08496112
SPV / Jul '94 / Koch / Plastic Head

Baltimores

BOOZE, BATTLE AND WOMEN
CD PEPCD 116
Pollytone / Oct '96 / Nervous / Pollytone

Bam Bam

BEST OF WESTBROOK CLASSICS
CD EFAO 17822
Tresor / Mar '95 / 3mv/BMG / Prime / SRD

Bamba, Amadu

DRUMS OF THE FIRDU FULA
CD VPU 1004CD
Village Pulse / May '97 / ADA

Bambaataa, Afrika

HIP HOP FUNK DANCE CLASSICS VOL.1
CD SPOCK 3CD
Music Of Life / Jul '91 / Grapevine/ PolyGram

HIP HOP FUNK DANCE CLASSICS VOL.2
CD SPOCK 4CD
Music Of Life / Aug '92 / Grapevine/ PolyGram

WARLOCKS, WITCHES, COMPUTERCHIPS
CD FILECD 464
Profile / Feb '96 / Pinnacle

Bambi

WARNING
CD DAMGOOD 118CD
Damaged Goods / Mar '97 / Shellshock/ Disc

Bana Maquis

LEILA
CD 2002968
Dakar Sound / Jan '97 / Stern's

Banana Slug String Band

PENGUIN PARADE
CD 9425892
Music For Little People / Aug '96 / Direct

Bananarama

BUNCH OF HITS
Love in the first degree / Bad for me / I heard a rumour / Ain't no cure / I can't let you go / Hooked on love / Young at heart / Robert De Niro's waiting / Hotline to heaven / Dance with a stranger / Scarlett / Ghost / Rough justice / Cheers then
CD 5500122
Spectrum / May '93 / PolyGram

GREATEST HITS
Venus / I heard a rumour / Love in the first degree / I can't help it / I want you back / Love, truth and honesty / Nathan Jones / Really saying something / Shy boy / Robert De Niro's waiting / Cruel summer / T'ain't what you do (it's the way that you do it) / Na na hey hey kiss him goodbye / Rough justice / Trick of the night / Aie a mwana / Venus (Mix) / Love in the first degree (mix)
CD 8281062
London / Jan '93 / PolyGram

PLEASE YOURSELF
CD 8283572
London / Nov '92 / PolyGram

Banchory Strathspey & Reel ...

GEOL NA FIDHLE (Banchory Strathspey & Reel Society)
CD CDTIV 605
Scotdisc / Aug '95 / Conifer/BMG / Duncans / Ross

Banco De Gaia

BIG MEN CRY
Drippy / Celestine / Drunk as a monk / Big men cry / Gates does Windows / One billion miles out / Starstation Earth
CD BARKCD 025
Planet Dog / Jul '97 / Pinnacle

LAST TRAIN TO LHASA
CD BARKCD 011
Planet Dog / May '95 / Pinnacle

LIVE AT GLASTONBURY
CD BARKCD 021
Ultimate / Jul '96 / Pinnacle

MAYA
CD BARKCD 3
Ultimate / Feb '94 / Pinnacle

Band

ACROSS THE GREAT DIVIDE (3CD Set)
Tears of rage / Weight / I shall be released / Chest fever / In a station / To kingdom come / Lonesome Suzie / Rag mama rag / Night they drove old dixie down / King Harvest (has surely come) / Rockin' chair / Whispering pines / Up on cripple creek / Across the great divide / Unfaithful servant / Shape I'm in / Daniel and the sacred harp / All la glory / Stage fright / When I paint my masterpiece / Moon struck one / Life is a carnival / River hymn / Don't do it / Calsonia mission / WS Walcott medicine show / Medicine show / Get up Jake / This wheel's on fire / Share your love with me / Mystery train / Acadian driftwood / Ophelia / It makes no difference / Living in a dream / Saga of Pepote Rouge / Right as rain / Who do you love / Do the honky tonk / He don't love you / katie's been gone / Bessie Smith / Orange juice blues / Ain't no cane on the brazos / Slippin' and slidin' / Twilight / Back to Memphis / Too wet to work / Loving you is sweeter than ever / Don't ya tell Henry / Endless highway / She knows / Evangeline / Out of the blue / Last waltz (refrain) / Last waltz (theme)
CD Set CDBAND 1
Capitol / Nov '94 / EMI

BAND, THE
Across the great divide / Rag mama rag / Night they drove old Dixie down / When you awake / Up on Cripple Creek / Whispering pines / Jemima surrender / Rockin' chair / Look out Cleveland / Jawbone / Unfaithful servant / King harvest (has surely come)
CD CZ 70
EMI / Aug '88 / EMI
CD CDP 7464932
EMI / Aug '97 / EMI

COLLECTION, THE
Weight / Night they drove old Dixie down / Ain't got no home / I shall be released / Change is gonna come / Third man theme / Don't do it / Stage fright / King Harvest has surely come / Long black veil / River hymn / Georgia on my mind / Great pretender / 4% Pantomine
CD CDGOLD 1075
EMI Gold / Feb '97 / EMI

HIGH ON THE HOG
CD TRACD 228
Transatlantic / Apr '96 / Pinnacle

JERICHO
Remedy / Blind Willie McTell / Caves of Jericho / Atlantic city / Too soon gone / Country boy / Move to Japan / Amazon (river of dreams) / Stuff you gotta watch / Same thing / Shine a light / Blues stay away from me
CD ESMCD 393
Essential / Feb '97 / BMG

LAST WALTZ, THE
Last waltz / Up on Cripple Creek / Who do you love / Helpless / Stage fright / Coyote / Dry your eyes / It makes no difference / Such a night / Night they drove old Dixie down / Mystery train / Mannish boy / Further on up the road / Shape I'm in / Down South in New Orleans / Ophelia / Tura lura larai (That's an Irish lullaby) / Caravan / Life is a carnival / Baby let me follow you down / I don't believe you (she acts like we never have met) / Forever young / I shall be released / Last waltz suite / Well / Evangeline / Out of the blue / Weight
CD K 266076
WEA / Mar '88 / Warner Music

LIVE AT WATKINS GLEN
Back to Memphis / Endless highway / I shall be released / Loving you is sweeter than ever / Too wet to work / Don't ya tell Henry / Rumour / Time to kill / Jam / Up on cripple creek
CD CDP 8317422
Capitol / Apr '95 / EMI

NORTHERN LIGHTS-SOUTHERN CROSS
Forbidden fruit / Hobo jungle / Ophelia / Acadian driftwood / Ring your bell / Rags and bones / It makes no difference / Jupiter hollow
CD CZ 404
Capitol / Mar '91 / EMI

TO KINGDOM COME
Back to Memphis / Tears of rage / To kingdom come / Long black veil / Chest fever / Weight / I shall be released / Up on Cripple Creek / Loving you is sweeter than ever / Rag mama rag / Night they drove old Dixie down / Unfaithful servant / King harvest (has surely come) / Shape I'm in / WS Walcott medicine show / Daniel and the sacred harp / Stage fright / Don't do it (baby don't you do it) / Life is a carnival / When I paint my masterpiece / 4% pantomime / River hymn / Mystery train / Endless highway / Get up Jake / It makes no difference / Ophelia / Acadian driftwood / Christmas must be tonight / Saga of Pepote Rouge / Knockin' lost John
CD Set CDS 792 169 2
Capitol / Sep '89 / EMI

WEIGHT, THE
Weight / Night they drove all dixie down / Ain't got no home / I shall be released / Change is gonna come / Third man theme / Don't do it (baby don't you do it) / Stage fright / King harvest (has surely come) / Long black veil / Rhythm hymn / Georgia on my mind / Great pretender / 4% pantomine
CD DC 867162
Disky / Nov '96 / Disky / THE

Band Ar Jazz

ZERO UN
CD CD 859
Escalibur / Aug '96 / ADA / Discovery / Roots

Band Of Holy Joy

TRACKSUIT VENDETTA, A (Holy Joy)
CD EQCD 004
Ecuador / Jun '92 / Vital

Band Of Hope

RHYTHMS AND REDS
CD MFCD 512
Musikfolk / Aug '94 / ADA / Direct / Roots

Band Of Outsiders

NO REFLECTION
CD EFA 15658CD
Repulsion / Oct '92 / SRD

Band Of Susans

HERE COMES SUCCESS
CD BFFP 114CD
Blast First / Apr '95 / RTM/Disc

HOPE AGAINST HOPE
Not even close / Learning to sin / Throne of blood / Elliott Abrams in hell / All the wrong reasons / I, the jury / No God / You were an optimist / Ready to bend / Hope against hope
CD FU 005CD
Furthur / Apr '88 / RTM/Disc

LOVE AGENDA
CD BFFP 43 CD
Blast First / Jan '89 / RTM/Disc

NOW
Pearls of wisdom / Following my heart / Trash train / Paint it black / Now is now (Remix) / Paint it black (instrumental)
CD RTD 15914912
World Service / Apr '93 / Vital

VEIL
Mood swing / Not in this life / Red and the black / Following my heart / Stained glass / Last temptation of Susan / Truce / Trouble spot / Out of the question / Pearls of wisdom / Trollbinder's theme / Blind
CD RTD 15715612
World Service / Jun '93 / Vital

WIRED FOR SOUND
CD Set BFFP 111CD
Blast First / Jan '95 / RTM/Disc

Band Of The Rising Sun

SETTING IT RIGHT
CD FSCD 37
Folksound / Jun '97 / CM / Roots

Banda Black Rio

BEST OF BANDA BLACK RIO, THE
Gafieira universal / Vidigal / Expresso madureira / Leblon via vaz lobo / Cravo e canela / Maria fumaca / Miss Sheryl / Mr. Funky Samba / Samboreando / Rio de fevereiro / Casta forte / Chega mais
CD USCD 3
Universal Sounds / May '96 / New Note/ Pinnacle / Timewarp

Banda De Gaites Mieres Del ...

EL TREBOLE DE SAN XUAN (Banda De Gaites Mieres Del Camin)
CD FA 8759CD
Fono Astur / Nov '96 / ADA

Banda Mantiquiera

ALDEIA
Linha de passe / Procura / Seis no choro / Carinhoso / Insensatez / Cubango / Aldeia
CD ACT 50082
Act / Sep '97 / New Note/Pinnacle

Banda Olodum

O MOVIEMENTO
Alegria geral / Rosa / Amor de eva / Mul mulher / Literatura faraonica / Luz celeste / Requebra / Papa furado / O falo da dala / Suenos lejos / Jazz E blues / Te amo / Cara preta / Tropicum / Ideologia / Bahia viva
CD 4509949122
East West / Feb '91 / Warner Music

Bandit Queen

HORMONE HOTEL
Scorch / Back in the belljar / Miss Dandys / Nailbiter / Give it to the dog / Petals and razorblades / Overture for beginners / Big sugar emotional thing / Essence vanilla / Oestrogen / Frida Kahlo / Hormone hotel / Blue black
CD AMUSE 26CD
Playtime / Feb '95 / Pinnacle

Bandoni, Mike

MIKE BANDONI
CD NOZACD 9
Ninebar / Sep '97 / Kudos / Prime / RTM/ Disc

Bands Of The British Army

MARCHING TO GLORY
CD MU 5009
Musketeer / Oct '92 / Disc

Bandulu

CORNERSTONE
CD 0630135472
East West / Mar '96 / Warner Music

GUIDANCE
CD INF 003CD
Infonet / Jun '93 / Pinnacle / Prime / Vital

Bandy, Moe

HONKY TONK AMNESIA
CD RAZCD 2096
Razor & Tie / Apr '96 / Koch

Bang Bang Machine

AMPHIBIAN
Breathless / Love and things / Tough Delilah / Fantasia / Slide / Show me your pain / Love it bleeds / When love comes down / Requiem of silence
CD TOPPCD 036
Ultimate / Mar '96 / Pinnacle

ETERNAL HAPPINESS
CD TOPPCD 009
Ultimate / Jun '94 / Pinnacle

Bang, Billy

LIVE AT CARLOS
CD 1211362
Soul Note / '88 / Cadillac / Harmonia Mundi / Wellard

RAINBOW GLADIATOR (Bang, Billy Quartet)
CD 1210162
Soul Note / Nov '92 / Cadillac / Harmonia Mundi / Wellard

TRIBUTE TO STUFF SMITH
CD 1212162
Soul Note / Nov '93 / Cadillac / Harmonia Mundi / Wellard

VALVE NO.10 (Bang, Billy Quartet)
CD 1211862
Soul Note / Nov '91 / Cadillac / Harmonia Mundi / Wellard

Bang On A Can

CHEATING, LYING, STEALING
CD SK 62254
Sony Classical / Aug '96 / Sony

INDUSTRY
CD SK 66483
Sony Classical / Jan '95 / Sony

Bang Tango

LOVE AFTER DEATH
CD CDMFN 174
Music For Nations / Feb '95 / Pinnacle

Bang The Party

BACK TO PRISON
CD WAFCD 4
Warriors Dance / Sep '90 / Pinnacle

Bangalore Choir

ON TARGET
Angel in black / Loaded gun / If the good die young (we'll live forever) / Doin' the dance / Hold on to you / All or nothin' / Slippin' away / She can't stop / Freight train rollin' / Just one night
CD 07599244332
Giant / Apr '92 / BMG

Bangash, Aman Ali

RAGA PURIYA KALYAN
Alap, jor and jhala / Gat composition
CD NRCD 0078
Navras / Jul '97 / New Note/Pinnacle

Bangles

ALL OVER THE PLACE
Hero takes a fall / Live / James / All about you / Dover beach / Tell me / Restless / Going down to Liverpool / He's got a secret / Silent treatment / More than meets the eye
CD 4879292
Columbia / Jul '97 / Sony

DIFFERENT LIGHT
Manic Monday / In a different light / Walking down your street / Walk like an Egyptian / Standing in the hallway / Return post / If she knew what she wants / Let it go / September gurls / Angels don't fall in love / Following / Not like you
CD 4844532
CBS / Aug '96 / Sony

EVERYTHING
In your room / Complicated girl / Bell jar / Something to believe in / Eternal flame / Be with you / Glitter years / I'll set you free / Watching the sky / Some dreams come true / Make a play for her now / Waiting for you / Crash and burn
CD 4629792
CBS / Jul '88 / Sony

GREATEST HITS
Hero takes a fall / Going down to Liverpool / Manic monday / If she knew what she wants / Walk like an Egyptian / Walking down your street / Following / Hazy shade of winter / In your room / Eternal flame / Be with you / I'll set you free / Everything I wanted / Where were you when I needed you
CD 4667692
CBS / Apr '95 / Sony

TWELVE INCH MIXES
If she knew what she wants / Walking down your street / In your room / Manic Monday / Walk like an Egyptian
CD 4689882
Columbia / Nov '92 / Sony

Banjo Express

OLD TIME COUNTRY MUSIC
CD PV 710 781
Disques Pierre Verany / '88 / Kingdom

Bank Statement

BANK STATEMENT
Throwback / Queen of darkness / Raincloud / Big man / More I hide it / I'll be waiting / That night / Border / House needs a roof / Thursday the twelfth
CD CDV 2600
Virgin / Apr '92 / EMI

Banks, Darrell

LOST SOUL OF DARRELL BANKS, THE
Open the door to your heart / Angel baby / You better go / Here comes the tears / I've got that feeling / I'm gonna hang my head and cry / Look into the eyes of a fool / Our love is in the pocket / Love of my woman / I'm knocking at your door / I wanna go home / Harder you love / I could never hate her / Don't know what to do / Only the strong survive / I'm the one who loves you / My love is strictly reserved / I will fear no evil / Baby whatcha got for me / Somebody somewhere needs you / Just because your love is gone / Forgive me / Beautiful feeling / Never alone / No one blinder / When a man loves a woman / We'll get over
CD GSCD 109
Goldmine / Mar '97 / Vital

Banks, Peter

INSTINCT
CD HTD CD 11
HTD / Feb '93 / CM / Pinnacle

LIVE
Small beginnings / Room with a view / Children of the universe / Dreams of heaven / Dead again / Pysco synch
CD BP 235CD
Blueprint / Jun '97 / Pinnacle

REDUCTION
Fade to blue / Dirty little secret / As night falls / Pirate's pleasure / Rosa nova / Fathat / Age of distortion / Sleep on it / Knuckle-dust / No strings / 2000 lies
CD HTDCD 76
HTD / Jul '97 / CM / Pinnacle

TWO SIDES OF PETER BANKS
CD OW S2118009
One Way / Sep '94 / ADA / Direct / Greyhound

Banks, R.C.

CHANKY CHANK MAN
Chanky chank man / I'm the one / Let's celebrate / That's my crowd / Hello raindrops / Bon amis / Hello big city / This town / I wish that you were mine / One and only / Jump / Grand promenade
CD MRCD 0596
Club De Musique / Feb '97 / Direct

Banks, Tony

CURIOUS FEELING, A
From the undertow / Lucky me / Lie / After the lie / Curious feeling / Forever morning / You / Somebody else's dream / Waters of Lethe / For a while / In the dark
CD CASCD 1148
Charisma / May '88 / EMI

DEAF FUGITIVE
This is love / Man of spells / And the wheels keep turning / Say you'll never leave me / Thirty three's / By you / At the edge of night / Charm / Moving under
CD TBCD 1
Charisma / '88 / EMI

SOUNDTRACKS
Shortcut to somewhere / Smilin' Jack Casey / Quicksilver suite / You call this victory / Lion of symmetry / Red wing suite
CD CASCD 1173
Charisma / Jul '87 / EMI

STILL
Red day on blue street / Angel face / Gift / Still it takes me by suprise / Hero for an hour / I wanna change the score / Water out of wine / Another murder of a day / Back to back / Final curtain
CD CDV 2658
Virgin / Jun '91 / EMI

Bannal

WAULKING SONGS
Bhean ud thall / Gu de th' orr' Aire / 'S muladach mi's air aineol / 'S I tir mo ruin sa ghaidhealtachd / He mandu / Latha dhomh's mi 'm beinn a' Cheathaich / Dh'eirich moch maduinn cheitein / Beir soiridh soiridh bhuam / Thug mi 'n oidhche ge b'fhad I / Chan eil mi gun mhulad orm / Clo mhiclllemhicheil / Gura mi tha trom duilich / Chunnaic mise 'n t-og uasal / Mile marbhphaisg air a' ghaol / Mhurchaidh bhig / He mo leannan ho mo leannan / Mo nighean donn ho gu / Chaidh mi 'na ghleannan as t-foghar / An long Eireannach
CD CDTRAX 099
Greentrax / Feb '96 / ADA / Direct / Duncans / Highlander

Bannerjee, Nikhil

RAGA AHIR
CD DSAV 1054
Multitone / Dec '95 / BMG

Bantam Rooster

DEAL ME IN
CD EFACD 12889
Crypt / Apr '97 / Shellshock/Disc

Baphomet

LATEST JESUS
CD MASSCD 007
Massacre / Apr '97 / Plastic Head

TRUST
CD MASSCD 027
Massacre / Apr '97 / Plastic Head

Bar-Kays

SOUL FINGER
Knucklehead / Soul finger / With a child's heart / Bar-kays boogaloo / Hell's Angels / You can't sit down / House shoes / Pearl high / I want someone / Hole in the wall / Don't do that
CD 8122702982
Atco / Jul '93 / Warner Music

Baraban

IL VALZER DEI DISERTORI
CD ACB 01
Robi Droli / Jan '94 / ADA / Direct

Barabas, Tom

CLASSICA NOUVEAU
CD SP 7152CD
Soundings Of The Planet / Jul '96 / Else

SEDONA SUITE
CD SP 7142CD
Soundings Of The Planet / Jul '96 / Else

Barachois

ACADIAN MUSIC FROM PRINCE EDWARD ISLAND
Pot pourri / Bartarache la rigondaine / Reel du pendu / La vieux soldat / Mon tour va venir un jour / Reel des Narcisse / Reel du barachois / J'aurais quelque chose a dire / Je mari jaloux / Les deux John / Envoyez d'l'avant / Le voyager / Marie Blanche / Le p'tit moine/La reel des acadiens
CD IRCD 048
Iona / May '97 / ADA / Direct / Duncans

Barazaz

ECHOUNDER
CD CD 828
Diffusion Breizh / May '93 / ADA

Barbarin, Paul

OXFORD SERIES VOL.15
CD AMCD 35
American Music / Jan '94 / Jazz Music

OXFORD SERIES VOL.16 (Barbarin, Paul Jazzband)
CD AMCD 36
American Music / Jul '96 / Jazz Music

SOUNDS OF NEW ORLEANS VOL.1 (Barbarin, Paul Band/Percy Humphrey)
CD STCD 6008
Storyville / Mar '97 / Cadillac / Jazz Music / Wellard

STREETS OF THE CITY (Barbarin, Paul & His New Orleans Band)
CD 504CD 9
504 / Jun '96 / Cadillac / Jazz Music / Target/BMG / Wellard

Barber, Chris

40 YEARS JUBILEE (Vol.1 1954-1955/ Vol.2 1955-1956 2CD Set)
Hiawatha rag / Jeep's blues / If I ever cease to love / Merrydown blues / Goin' to town / Lord, Lord, Lord / Someday sweetheart / When I move to the sky / On a Monday / Shout 'em Aunt Tillie / Spanish Mama / Please get him off my mind / CC rider / Black cat on the fence / In the evening / Midnight special / Papa de da da / Keystone blues / Jailhouse blues / High society / Bye and bye / Magnolia's wedding day / Jelly bean blues / Everywhere you go / Goin' down the road feelin' bad / Long gone lost John / Tiger rag / Can't afford to do it / Original tuxedo rag / Bogalousa strut / How long blues / Railroad Bill / Whistling Rufus / Reckell blues / Panama / Back water blues / Big house blues / Royal telephone
CD Set CDTTD 589
Timeless Traditional / Jul '95 / Jazz Music / New Note/Pinnacle

40 YEARS JUBILEE AT THE OPERAHOUSE NURNBERG
Isle of capri / We sure do need him now / It's tight like that / Old rugged cross / Hush-a-bye / Worried man blues / Down by the riverside / Ice cream / Workin' man blues / Petite fleur / Sweet Georgia Brown / Brown / Slap 'n' slide / Tiger rag / Mile end stomp / Wild cat blues
CD CDTTD 590
Timeless Traditional / Dec '94 / Jazz Music / New Note/Pinnacle

ACKER, KENNY AND CHRIS (Barber, Chris & Kenny Ball/Acker Bilk)
CD PLSCD 209
Pulse / Apr '97 / BMG

ALL THAT JAZZ (Barber, Chris/Acker Bilk/Kenny Ball)
CD KAZCD 18
Kaz / Jan '92 / BMG

BARBER, BALL & BILK (Barber, Chris/ Acker Bilk/Kenny Ball)
Big noise from Winnetka / Sweet Sue, just you / Livery stable blues / Careless love / Willie the weeper / 1919 March / Sweet Georgia Brown / Bourbon street parade / Dinah / Burgundy St. Blues / Marching through Georgia / Petite fleur / Temptation rag / Chelsea cakewalk / Yama yama man / South Rampart street parade / Bill Bailey, won't you please come home / Dardanella / Bugle boy march / Milenberg joys
CD TRTCD 130
TrueTrax / Oct '94 / THE

BARBER, BALL & BILK (Barber, Chris/ Acker Bilk/Kenny Ball)
CD SSLCD 205
Savanna / Jun '95 / THE

BEST OF BARBER AND BILK, THE (Barber, Chris Jazzband & Acker Bilk Paramount Jazzband)
April showers: *Barber, Chris Jazzband* / Doin' the crazy walk: *Barber, Chris Jazzband* / Hushabye: *Barber, Chris Jazzband* / Everybody loves my baby: *Barber, Chris Jazzband* / I can't give you anything but love: *Barber, Chris Jazzband* / Whistling Rufus: *Barber, Chris Jazzband* / Bugle call rag: *Barber, Chris Jazzband* / Beale Street blues: *Barber, Chris Jazzband* / Magnolia's wedding day: *Barber, Chris Jazzband* / Petite fleur: *Barber, Chris Jazzband* / Bye and bye: *Barber, Chris Jazzband* / Cre march: *Bilk, Acker & His Paramount Jazz Band* / Dardanella: *Bilk, Acker & His Paramount Jazz Band* / Franklin Street blues: *Bilk, Acker & His Paramount Jazz Band* / Blaze away: *Bilk, Acker & His Paramount Jazz Band* / Easter parade: *Bilk, Acker & His Paramount Jazz Band* / Marching through Georgia: *Bilk, Acker & His Paramount Jazz Band* / Louisian-i-ay: *Bilk, Acker & His Paramount Jazz Band* / El abanico: *Bilk, Acker & His Paramount Jazz Band* / Carry me back: *Bilk, Acker & His Paramount Jazz Band* / Travelling blues: *Bilk, Acker & His Paramount Jazz Band* / Delia gone: *Bilk, Acker & His Paramount Jazz Band* / Under the double eagle: *Bilk, Acker & His Paramount Jazz Band*
CD LACD 73
Lake / Oct '96 / ADA / Cadillac / Direct / Jazz Music / Target/BMG

BEST OF CHRIS BARBER & HIS JAZZ BAND, THE (Barber, Chris & His Jazz Band)
Petite fleur / When the saints go marching in / Bourbon Street parade / Bill Bailey won't you please come home / I wish I could shimmy like my sister Kate / Sweet Georgia Brown / Everybody loves my baby / Majorca / High society / April showers / Brown skin mama / Wild cat blues / Sweet Sue, just you / Jailhouse blues / Sheikh of Araby / New St. Louis blues
CD 21022
Laserlight / Jul '97 / Target/BMG

BEST SELLERS
CD STCD 200
Storyville / Oct '87 / Cadillac / Jazz Music / Wellard

CHRIS BARBER (Barber, Chris & The Zenith Hot Stompers)
Ole Miss rag / Riverside blues / Just a little while to stay here / Bugle boy march / Saratoga swing / Precious Lord, take my hand / Sweet Georgia Brown / Goin' home / Panama rag / Sweet Sue, just you / Creole love call / Bye and bye
CD CDTTD 582
Timeless Traditional / Feb '94 / Jazz Music / New Note/Pinnacle

CHRIS BARBER & HIS NEW ORLEANS FRIENDS
Birth of the blues / Coquette / Ma, she's making eyes at me / Over in the glory land / Sentimental journey / Yes sir that's my baby / Eyes of Texas are upon you / Mood indigo / My blue heaven / Let me call you sweetheart / Nobody's sweetheart / I ain't got nobody / Lord, lord, lord / Panama
CD CDTTD 573
Timeless Jazz / Oct '93 / New Note/ Pinnacle

CHRIS BARBER AND HIS JAZZ BAND IN CONCERT (Barber, Chris & His Jazz Band)
Bourbon Street Parade / New Blues / Willie the weeper / Mean mistreater / Yama yama man / Old man Mose / Mood indigo / Bearcat crawl / Lowland blues / Panama / Savoy blues / Lonesome Road / Sheikh of Araby
CD DM 23 CD
Dormouse / Aug '91 / Jazz Music / Target/ BMG

CHRIS BARBER CONCERTS, THE (2CD Set)
Bourbon street parade / New blues / Willy the weeper / Mean mistreater / Yama yama man / Old man mose / Mood indigo / Bearcat crawl / Lowland blues / Panama / Savoy blues / Lonesome road / Sheik or araby / Bill Bailey, won't you please come home / You took advantage of me / Sweet Sue, just you / Moonshine / (I'll be glad when you're dead) you rascal you / Bugle boy march / Pretty baby / Majorca / Indiana / Georgia grind / Rock in rhythm / My old kentucky home / Rent party blues / Careless love / Strange things happen everyday / Mama don't allow
CD Set LACDD 55/56
Lake / Nov '95 / ADA / Cadillac / Direct / Jazz Music / Target/BMG

COLLABORATION (Barber, Chris & Barry Martin)
CD BCD 40
GHB / Mar '93 / Jazz Music

COPENHAGEN CONCERT 1954
CD STCD 5527
Storyville / Jul '96 / Cadillac / Jazz Music / Wellard

DIXIE FROM THE ISLAND VOL.1 (Barber, Chris & Max Collie/Pete Allen/ Terry Lightfoot)
Texas moaner blues / Stevedore stomp / Immigration blues / Gospel train / Nobody knows you when you're down and out / After you've gone / Jazz me blues / That's a plenty / Mayfair blues / West End blues / Drum boogie / Honky tonk train blues
CD 8747022
DA Music / Jul '96 / Conifer/BMG

ECHOES OF ELLINGTON VOL.1 (Barber, Chris Jazz & Blues Band)
Stevedore stomp / Jeep's blues / I'm slapping Seventh Avenue with the sole of my shoe / In a mellow tone / Prelude to a kiss / Second line / Perdido / Moon indigo / Shout 'em Aunt Tillie
CD CDTTD 555
Timeless Traditional / Jun '91 / Jazz Music / New Note/Pinnacle

ECHOES OF ELLINGTON VOL.2 (Barber, Chris Jazz & Blues Band)
Squatty roo / Blues for Duke / Take the 'A' train / Warm valley / Caravan / Sophisticated lady / It don't mean a thing if it ain't got that swing / Just squeeze me / Mooche / Jeep is jumpin'
CD CDTTD 556
Timeless Traditional / May '91 / Jazz Music / New Note/Pinnacle

ELITE SYNCOPATIONS (Great British Traditional Jazzbands Vol. 2)
Swipsey cakewalk / Bohemia rag / Elite syncopations / Cole's moan / Peach / St. George's rag / Favourite / Reindeer ragtime two step / Entertainer / Georgia cake walk / Thriller rag / Whistling Rufus / Tuxedo rag / Bugle call rag
CD LACD 43
Lake / Feb '95 / ADA / Cadillac / Direct / Jazz Music / Target/BMG

ENTERTAINER, THE (Barber, Chris Jazzband)
Down home rag / Baby, won't you please come home / Entertainer / New St. Louis blues / Ory's creole trombone / Bourbon Street parade / High society / Stevedore stomp / Sheik of Araby / Georgia cakewalk / Lil' Liza Jane / Burgundy Street blues / On the sunny side of the street / When the saints go marching in
CD 8325932
Philips / Mar '94 / PolyGram

ESSENTIAL CHRIS BARBER (Featuring Ottilie Patterson & Monty Sunshine)
Panama rag / Petite fleur / Savoy blues / I wish I could shimmy like my sister Kate / Sweet Georgia Brown / Thriller rag / Beale Street blues / Bill Bailey, won't you please come home / Bourbon Street parade / New blues / Trombone cholly / Texas moaner / Willie the weeper / Careless love / Everybody loves my baby / High society / Jailhouse blues / Make me a pallet on the floor / One sweet letter from you / Tishomingo blues / Trouble in mind / When you and I were young / Whistling Rufus / Wildcat blues
CD KAZCD 13
Kaz / Oct '90 / BMG

GREAT REUNION CONCERT, THE
Bourbon Street parade / Saturday night function / Martinique / Isle of Capri / Hush-a-bye / It's tight like that / Fairfield reunion / Bobby Shaftoe / On a Monday / Bury my body / Long gone lost John / Jenny's ball / Chimes blues / Whistling Rufus / Jazz me blues / Just a sittin' and a rockin' / Stevedore stomp
CD CDTTD 553
Timeless Traditional / Jul '91 / Jazz Music / New Note/Pinnacle

GREATEST HITS
CD JW 77036
JWD / Jun '94 / Target/BMG

HE'S GOT THE WHOLE WORLD IN HIS HANDS
He's got the whole world in his hands / Topsy / When the saints go marching in / Mr. Sun / My old Kentucky home / Stormy Sunday / Just a little while to stay here / In come the blues / Mabel's dream / We shall walk through the streets of the city / Mama don't you think I know / Money blues / Fine time / Swanee River / 42nd Street / Down by the riverside / Morning order blues / Dippermouth blues
CD CDTTD 599
Timeless Jazz / Mar '96 / New Note/ Pinnacle

HOT GOSPEL 1963-1967 (Barber, Chris Jazzband)
CD LACD 39
Lake / Sep '94 / ADA / Cadillac / Direct / Jazz Music / Target/BMG

IN CONCERT (Barber, Chris Jazz & Blues Band)
Take the 'A' train / Just a sittin' and a rockin' / Blues for yesterday / Summertime / Oh Lady be good / When you're smiling / Just a closer walk with thee / Lord, lord, you've sure been good to me / Shady green pastures / They kicked him out of heaven / Precious Lord, take my hand
CD CDTTD 557
Timeless Traditional / Feb '91 / Jazz Music / New Note/Pinnacle

IN CONCERT VOL.2
Bill Bailey, won't you please come home / You took advantage of me / Sweet Sue, just you / Moonshine man / (I'll be glad when you're dead) you rascal you / Bugle boy march / Pretty baby / Majorca / Georgia grind / Rockin' in rhythm / My old Kentucky home / Careless love / Strange things happen every day / Mama don't allow
CD DM 24CD
Dormouse / '91 / Jazz Music / Target/BMG

IN HIS ELEMENT
CD Set CDTTD 572
Timeless Traditional / Jul '92 / Jazz Music / New Note/Pinnacle

JAZZ BAND FAVOURITES (Barber, Chris Jazzband)
Petite fleur / Whistling Rufus / When the saints go marching in (part 1) / When the saints go marching in (part 2) / Sweet Georgia Brown / High society / Bugle call rag / Mack the knife / Hamp's blues / Bill Bailey, won't you please come home / I shall not be moved / O Sole Mio / Wini Wini (let's do the Tamoure) / Bonsoir Mes souvenirs / Good morning blues / Bad luck blues / Morning train / Frankie and Johnny / If I had a ticket / Great bear / Jeeps blues / Sweetest little baby
CD CC 273
Music For Pleasure / Oct '91 / EMI

JAZZ HOLIDAY (Barber, Chris & Rod Mason's Hot Five)
CD CDTTD 524
Timeless Traditional / Sep '96 / Jazz Music / New Note/Pinnacle

JAZZ JAMBOREE (Barber, Chris/Acker Bilk/Kenny Ball)
CD Set DCDCD 214
Castle / Nov '95 / BMG

LIVE IN '85 (Barber, Chris Jazz & Blues Band)
CD CDTTD 527
Timeless Traditional / Jul '94 / Jazz Music / New Note/Pinnacle

LIVE IN EAST BERLIN
CD BLCD 760502
Black Lion / Oct '90 / Cadillac / Jazz Music / Koch / Wellard

LIVE IN MUNICH
Bourbon Street parade / All the girls go crazy about the way I walk / Tin roof blues / That's a plenty / Honeysuckle rose / Big noise from Winetka/Pitt's extract / Magnolia's wedding day / Take me back to New Orleans / Double check stomp / Stevedore stomp / Goin' to town / St. Louis blues / Harmonica harper
CD CDTTD 600
Timeless Jazz / Mar '96 / New Note/ Pinnacle

NEW ORLEANS SYMPHONY (2CD Set)
New Orleans overture / Bourbon street parade / Lead me on / Announcement / South Rampart Street parade / Music from the land of dreams / Announcement/Mood Indigo / Harlem rag / Announcement/Wild cat blues / Announcement/Ragtime / Blues / Stomp / Reprise stomp / Announcement: Introduction of the band / Announcement/ Take me back to New Orleans / Under the bamboo tree / Das gibt's nur einmal / Immigration blues / Announcement/Down by the riverside / Announcement/Ice Cream/Ice Cream
CD Set CDTTD 610
Timeless Traditional / Sep '96 / Jazz Music / New Note/Pinnacle

PANAMA (Barber, Chris & Wendell Brunious)
I wish I could shimmy like my sister Kate / Just a little while to stay here / Georgia on my mind / My blue heaven / Oh lady be good / Careless love / Anytime / That's my desire / Panama
CD CDTTD 568
Timeless Traditional / Oct '91 / Jazz Music / New Note/Pinnacle

PETITE FLEUR
Petite fleur / When the saints go marching in / Wild cat blues / April showers / Sweet Georgia Brown / Majorca / High society / Whistling Rufus / Bourbon street parade / Trouble in mind / Everybody loves my baby / Jailhouse blues / When you and I were young Maggie / Bill Bailey, won't you please come home / Beals Street blues / Mood indigo / (I'll be glad when you're dead) you rascal you / Bye and bye / Savoy blues
CD 5507442
Spectrum / Feb '95 / PolyGram

SOUTH RAMPART STREET PARADE
CD BLR 84 016
L&R / New Note/Pinnacle

STARDUST (Barber, Chris Jazz & Blues Band)
CD CDTTD 537
Timeless Traditional / May '89 / Jazz Music / New Note/Pinnacle

SWING IS HERE (European Concert Tour) (Barber, Chris & John Lewis/ Trummy Young)
Home folks / Time / Mood indigo / T'ain't what you do (it's the way that you do it) / Georgia / Someday you'll be sorry / Muskrat ramble / When the saints go marching in
CD BLCD 760517
Black Lion / Apr '96 / Cadillac / Jazz Music / Koch / Wellard

TAKE ME BACK TO NEW ORLEANS (Barber, Chris & Dr. John)
Take me back to New Orleans / Ti-pi-ti-na / Perdido street blues / New Orleans, Louisiana / Decatur drive / New Orleans / Meet me on the Levee / Harlem rag / Ride on / Big bass drum (on a mardi gras day) / At the cemetery / Concert on Canal Street / Bourbon Street scene / Basin Street / Just a little while to stay here / Oration by Dr. John / What a friend we have in Jesus / When the saints go marching in / Concert in Canal Street / Buddy Bolden's blues / South Rampart street parade / Burgandy Street Blues / Canal Street Blues / Bourbon Street Parade / Do you know what it means to miss New Orleans / Professor Longhair's tip / Brass band blues / Basin Street blues
CD BLC 760163
Black Lion / '92 / Cadillac / Jazz Music / Koch / Wellard

THAT'S IT THEM (Barber, Chris & Acker Bilk)
Just a closer walk with thee / Stranger on the shore / Bugle boy march / Wabash blues / On the sunny side of the street / South / Lou-easy-an-I-a / Panama / Poor butterfly / That's my home / High society
CD CDTTD 619
Timeless Jazz / Jul '97 / New Note/Pinnacle

ULTIMATE, THE (Barber, Chris/Acker Bilk/Kenny Ball)
I love you Samantha / Panama rag / Midnight in Moscow / Nobody knows you (when you're down and out) / Avalon / I wanna be like you / Christopher Columbus / Spanish harlem / That da da strain / Them there eyes / Stranger on the shore / That's my home / Good Queen Bess / Perdido street blues / Harlem rag / Mood indigo / Mary had a little lamb / When the saints go marching in / St. Louis blues / So do I / Muskrat ramble / Auf wiedersehen
CD Set KAZ CD 4
Kaz / May '88 / BMG

WHO'S BLUES
CD BLR 84 009
L&R / May '91 / New Note/Pinnacle

Barber, Damien

BOXED
CD NOF 002
Nof / May '96 / ADA

Barber, Patricia

CAFE BLUE
CD AIM 1058
Aim / Jun '96 / ADA / Direct / Jazz Music

Barbieri, Gato

CALIENTE
Fireflies / Fiesta / Europa (Earth's cry, Heaven's smile) / Don't cry / Rochelle / Adios / I want you / Behind the rain / Adios
CD 3945972
A&M / Mar '94 / PolyGram

CHAPTER THREE
CD MVCZ 126
MCA / Apr '97 / BMG

CHAPTER THREE: VIVA EMILIANO ZAPATA
Milongo triste / Lluvia azul / El sublime / La podrida / Cuando vuelva a tu lado / Viva Emiliano Zapata
CD GRP 1112
GRP / Jan '92 / New Note/BMG

GATO BARBIERI IN NEW YORK CITY
In search of the mystery / Michelle / Obsession no.2 / Cinematique
CD 30019
Giants Of Jazz / Sep '92 / Cadillac / Jazz Music / Target/BMG

GATO...PARA LOS AMIGOS
Llamerito tango / Carnavalito / Brazil / Viva Emiliano Zapata / Encuentros / Latino America / El arriero / Bolivia / Finale (medley)
CD 4880012
Sony Jazz / Aug '97 / Sony

PRICELESS JAZZ
India / Nunca mas / Marissea / Para nosotros / Milonga triste / Cuando vuelve a tu lado / Lluvia azul
CD GRP 98792
GRP / Jul '97 / New Note/BMG

QUE PASA
Straight into the sunshine / Blue gala / Mystica / Dancing with dolphins / Circulos / Guadeloupe / Cause we've ended as lovers / Indonesia / Woman I remember / Granada / Adentro
CD CK 67855
Sony Jazz / Apr '97 / Sony

TWO PICTURES (1965-1968)
CD IRS 00632CD
Liuto / Oct '90 / Cadillac / Harmonia Mundi

Barbieri, Richard

FLAME (Barbieri, Richard & Tim Bowness)
Night in heaven / Song of love and everything (parts 1 and 2) / Brightest blue / Flame / Trash talk / Time flown / Torch dance / Feel
CD TPLP 58CD
One Little Indian / Sep '94 / Pinnacle

Barbosa, Zelia

SERTAO E FAVELAS
CD LDX 2741002
La Chant Du Monde / Aug '95 / ADA / Harmonia Mundi

Barbosa-Lima, Carlos

CHANTS FOR THE CHIEF
A chamada dos ventos/Cancao naturna / Uirapuru do Amazonas / Cuhna-tan do Andira / Varando furos / Canto dos esquecidos/Yara levou o meu amor / Canto do missionario / Ventos do sertao / Canto da alvorada / Canto do verde-amado / Canoa furada/Cancao noturna/A chamada / Dos ventos - epilogo / Cajija de musica / Impressao de rua / Sonha yaya / Teotecacinte / Fantasy on an Hawaiian lullaby / Batucada / Entre olas / Panaderos / Cubanita / Corrion / De totana / Patio gitano / Alaiceria / Luna y clavel / Romance flamenco / Bailando
CD CCD 4489
Concord Picante / Jan '92 / New Note/ Pinnacle

FROM YESTERDAY TO PENNY LANE
Two ladies, one old, one new / Cumberland Road / Clio / Eleanor Rigby / She's leaving home / Yesterday / Ticket to ride / Got to get you into my life / Here, there and everywhere / Penny Lane / Etude in a menuet form / El colivri / Confession / Blue clouds / Embers / Rhapsody in blue
CD CCD 42041
Concord Concerto / Nov '96 / New Note/ Pinnacle

MUSIC OF THE AMERICAS (Barbosa-Lima, Carlos & Sharon Isbin)
Sambo Chorado / Chants for the chief No. 3 / Chants for the chief No. 7 / Carioquinha / Mazurka No. 3 / Caminho dos estados unidos / Brazil / Grande valsa / Lamento / Cochichando / Um a zero / Lullaby for Janine / Playful squirrels / Interlude dance / Vera cruz / Always / I got rhythm / Kathy's waltz / In your own sweet way / Duke / Timothy 'O'
CD CCD 4461
Concord Jazz / May '91 / New Note/ Pinnacle

TWILIGHT IN RIO
Twilight in Rio / Mi bossa blue (my blue bossa) / En la playa (at the beach) / Puerta de tierra / Etude on a theme by Mendelssohn / La alborada (dawn) / La mariposa (the butterfly) / Choro da saudade (choro of longing) / Danza paraguaya / Junto a tu corazon / Pais de abanico / El sueno de là munequita / Dinora / Um amor de valsa / Emerald / Sardius
CD CCD 42017
Concord Concerto / Mar '95 / New Note/ Pinnacle

Barboza, Raul

LA TIERRA SIN MAL
CD CDLLL 257
La Lichere / Mar '96 / ADA / Discovery

MUSIC AFTER THE GUARANI INDIANS
CD CDLLL 167
La Lichere / Aug '93 / ADA / Discovery

MUSIC FROM THE BORDER
CD 12453
Laserlight / Jul '95 / Target/BMG

Barclay James Harvest

ALONE WE FLY
Crazy city / Mockingbird / Our kid's kid / Loving is easy / Rock 'n' roll lady / Fifties child / Blow me down / He said love / Rock 'n' roll star / On the wings of love / For no one / Hymn / Berlin / Love on the line / Shades of B hill / Waiting for the right time / Sideshow / Guitar blues / Poor boy blues / You need love
CD VSOPCD 140
Connoisseur Collection / Dec '90 / Pinnacle

BARCLAY JAMES HARVEST LIVE
Summer soldier / Medicine man / Crazy city / After the day / Great 1974 mining disaster / Galadriel / Negative earth / She said / Paper wings / For no one / Mockingbird
CD VSOPCD 164
Connoisseur Collection / Jun '91 / Pinnacle

BEST OF BARCLAY JAMES HARVEST, THE
CD 5119322
Polydor / Jan '89 / PolyGram

BEST OF BARCLAY JAMES HARVEST, THE (Centenary Collection)
Taking some time on / Mother dear / Mocking bird / Vanessa Simmons / Early morning / Brother thrush / Medicine man / Someone there you know / Harry's song / Ursula (the swansea song) / Song with no meaning / Crazy over you / Delph town morn / Song for dying / Galadriel / I'm over you / Child of man / Child of the universe / Rock and roll woman / Thank you
CD CTMCD 309
EMI / Feb '97 / EMI

BJH & OTHER SHORT STORIES
Medicine man / Someone there you know / Harry's song / Ursula (the Swansea song) / Little lapwing / Song with no meaning / Blue John blues / Poet / After the day / Crazy (over you) / Delph Town morn / Summer soldier / Thank you / Hundred thousand smiles out / Moonwater
CD BGOCD 160
Beat Goes On / Nov '92 / Pinnacle

CAUGHT IN THE LIGHT
CD 5193032
Polydor / Jun '93 / PolyGram

CONCERT FOR THE PEOPLE, A
Berlin / Loving is easy / Mockingbird / Sip of wine / Nova lepidopter / In memory of the martyrs / Life is for living / Child of the universe / Hymn
CD 8000262
Polydor / Jan '89 / PolyGram

ENDLESS DREAM
CD VSOPCD 228
Connoisseur Collection / Aug '96 / Pinnacle

EVERYONE IS EVERYBODY ELSE
CD 8334482
Polydor / Feb '92 / PolyGram

FOUR BARCLAY JAMES HARVEST ORIGINALS (4CD Set)
Taking some time on / Mother dear / Sun will never shine / When the world was woken / Good love child / Iron maiden / Dark now my sky / Medicine man / Someone there you know / Harry's song / Ursula (The Swansea song) / Little lapwing / Song with no meaning / Blue John's blues / Poet / After the day / She said / Happy old world / Song for dying / Galadriel / Mockingbird / Vanessa Simmons / Ball and chain / Lady loves / Crazy (over you) / Delph Town morn / Summer soldier / Thank you / One hundred thousand smiles out / Moonwater
CD Set CDBARCLAY 1
Premier/EMI / Feb '96 / EMI

GONE TO EARTH
Hymn / Love is like a violin / Friend of mine / Poor man's moody blues / Hard hearted woman / Sea of Tranquility / Spirit on the water / Leper's song / Taking me higher
CD 8000922
Polydor / Jan '89 / PolyGram

HARVEST YEARS, THE
Early morning / Mr. Sunshine / Pools of blue / I can't go on without you / Eden unobtainable / Brother thrush / Poor wages / Taking some time on / When the world was woken / Good love child / Iron maiden / Dark now my sky / She said / Song for dying / Galadriel / Mocking bird / Vanessa Simmons / Happy old world (quad mix) / Ball and chain / Medicine man / Ursula (The Swansea song) / Someone there you know / Poet/After the day / I'm over you / Child of man / Breathless / When the city sleeps / Summer soldier / Hundred thousand smiles out / Moonwater / Joker / Good times
CD Set CDEN 5014
Harvest / May '91 / EMI

MOCKINGBIRD
Mocking bird / I can't go without you / Early morning / Ball and chain / Medicine man / Someone there you know / Joker / Summer soldier / When the city sleeps / Brother trush / Good love child / Iron maiden / Moonwater
CD DC 867212
Disky / Mar '97 / Disky / THE

OCTOBERON
World goes on / May day / Ra / Rock 'n' roll / Star / Polk street rag / Believe in me / Suicide
CD 8219302
Polydor / Oct '91 / PolyGram

ONCE AGAIN
She said / Happy old world / Song for dying / Galadriel / Mockingbird / Vanessa Simmons / Ball and chain / Lady loves
CD BGOCD 152
Beat Goes On / Nov '92 / Pinnacle

RING OF CHANGES
Fifties child / Looking from the outside / Teenage heart / Highwire / Midnight drug / Waiting for the right time / Just a day away / Paraiso des cavalos / Ring of changes
CD 8116382
Polydor / Oct '88 / PolyGram

Barde, Jerome

FELIZ
Marc / Dad's delight / No words / La Nina Cecile / Citrons / Barde bleue / Ombrage / Feliz / Lefru / I'll be seeing you
CD SSC 1042D
Sunnyside / Oct '91 / Discovery

Bardens, Pete

BIG SKY
China blue / Puerto Rico / Big sky / Gunblasters / On the air tonight / You got it / Brave new world / On a roll / Last waltz / For old time's sake
CD HTDCD 22
HTD / Sep '96 / CM / Pinnacle

WATER COLORS
Journey / De profundis / Higher ground / Yellowstone blue / Is it any wonder / Water colors / Shape of the rain / Timepiece / Ghostwater
CD MPCD 4001
Miramar / Jun '93 / New Note/Pinnacle

Bardo Pond

BUFO ALVARIUS
CD CHE 33CD
Che / Sep '95 / SRD

HIGH FREQUENCIES
Limerick / Sentence / Tantric porno / Wank / High frequency / Sometimes words / Yellow turbin / Rumination / Be a fish / Tapir song / RM
CD OLE 1802
Matador / Apr '96 / Vital

Bardot, Brigitte

LES PLUS BELLES (The Best Of Brigitte Bardot)
CD 5323502
Mercury / Nov '96 / PolyGram

Bardots

EYE-BABY
Pretty O / Chained up / Cruelty blonde / Sister Richard / Slow asleep / Sunsetted / My cute thought / Obscenity thing / Glorióle / Caterina / A / Shallow
CD CHEREE 031 CD
Cheree / Sep '92 / SRD

V-NECK
CD CHE 44CD
Che / May '96 / SRD

Bare, Bobby

ALL AMERICAN BOY
CD CTS 55428
Country Stars / Nov '94 / Target/BMG

ALL AMERICAN BOY, THE (4CD Set)
Darlin' don't / Another love has ended / Down on the corner of love / Life of a fool / Beggar / Livin' end / Vampira / Tender years / When the one you love / All American boy / What you gonna do now / I'm hanging up my rifle / That's where I want to be / Lynching party / Sweet singin' Sam / More than a poor boy could give / No letter from my baby / Book of love / Can can ladies / Lorena / Zig zag twist / Island of love / Sailor man / These tender years / Lovesick / Great big car / Brooklyn bridge / That mean old clock / Day my rainbow fell / Above and beyond / Shame on me / To whom it may concern / Wallflower / I don't believe I'll fall in love today / Dear waste basket / Baby, don't believe him / I'm gettin' lonely / Heart of ice / Candy coated kisses / Gods were angry with me / I'd fight the world / Is it wrong (for loving you) / Dear waste backet / Detroit city / Lonely town / She called me baby / 500 miles away from home / It all depends on Linda / Worried man blues / Homestead on the farm / Abilene / Gotta travel on / Noah's ark / I wonder where you are tonight / Let me tell you about Mary / What kind of bird is that / Jeannie's last kiss / Miller's cave / Sittin' and thinkin' / Have I stayed away too long / Long way back to Tennessee / Long black limousine / Down in Mexico / I was coming home to you / Another bridge to burn / I've lived a lot in my time / He was a friend of mine / Take me home / When I'm gone / Sweeter than the flowers / Four strong winds / When the wind blows in Chicago / Just to satisfy you / Let it be me / In the misty moonlight / I love you / Too used to being with you / Together again / We'll sing in the sunshine / Out of our minds / I don't care / That's all I want from you / Invisible tears / Dear John letter / True love / Rosalie / Alle glauben dass ich glucklich bin / Times are gettin' hard / I'm a long way from home / Deepening snow / I'm a man of constant sorrow / She picked a perfect day / One day at a time / So soon / Countin' the hours - countin' the days / Don't think twice, it's alright / Blowin' in the wind / Delia's gone / Lemon tree / It's alright / Salt Lake City / Changing my mind / Good old Tennessee / Das haus auf der sierra / Sixteen / Wilder wolfund brauner bar / Molly Brown / Little bit later on down the line / Got leavin' on her mind / Try to remember / All the good times are past and gone / Memories / Heaven help my soul / We helped each other out / In the same old way / Talk me some sense / You can't stop the wild wind from blowing / It ain't me babe / Long black veil / Passin' through / What color (is a man)
CD Set BCD 15663
Bear Family / Jan '94 / Direct / Rollercoaster / Swift

BOBBY BARE SINGS LULLABYS, LEGENDS & LIES
Lullabys, legends and lies / Paul / Marie Lavaau / Daddy what if / Wonderful soup stones / Winner / In the hills of Shiloh / She's my ever lovin' machine / Mermaid / Rest awhile / Bottomless well / True story / Sure hit songwriters pen / Rosalie's good eat's cafe
CD BCD 15683
Bear Family / Apr '93 / Direct / Rollercoaster / Swift

ESSENTIAL BOBBY BARE, THE
All American boy / Shame on me / Detroit City / 500 miles away from home / Miller's cave / Four strong winds / Dear John letter: *Bare, Bobby & Skeeter Davis* / It's alright / Streets of Baltimore / Game of triangles: *Bare, Bobby & Norma Jean/Liz Anderson* / Charleston railway tavern / Margie's at the Lincoln Park Inn / Bless America again / Your husband, my wife: *Bare, Bobby & Skeeter Davis* / Ride me down easy / Daddy what if / Marie Laveau / Winner / Dropkick me Jesus / Vegas: *Bare, Bobby & Jeanne*
CD 7863674052
RCA / May '97 / BMG

FOR THE GOOD TIMES
CD MACCD 220
Autograph / Aug '96 / BMG

GREATEST HITS
CD WMCD 5681
Disky / Nov '93 / Disky / THE

MERCURY YEARS 1970-1972, THE (3CD Set)
That's how I got to Memphis / Come sundown / I took a memory to lunch / I'm her hoss if I never win a race / Woman you've been a friend to me / It's freezing in El Paso / Mrs. Jones your daughter cried all night / Don't it make you wanna go home / Mary Ann regrets / Leaving on a jet plane / Fool / Waitress in the Main Street cafe / Please don't tell me how the story ends / How about you / Help me make it through the night / Rosalie / Dropping out of sight / Where have all the flowers gone / Travelling minstrel man / For the good times / Hello darlin' / Alabama rose / World is weighing heavy on my mind / Mama bake a pie (papa kill a chicken) / Coal river / Christian soldier / Don't you ever get tired of hurting me / West Virginia woman / New York City snow / Jesus is the only one that loves us / Loving her was easier (than anything I'll ever do again) / I need some good news bad / Me and Bobby McGee / Million miles to the city / Just the other side of nowhere / City boy country born / Short and sweet / Puppet and the parakeet / Great society talking blues / Year that Clayton Delaney died / Roses are red / Lonely street / Crazy arms / Jesus Christ what a man / Fallen star / That's alright / Pamela Brown / When I want to love a lady / Love forever / Darby's castle / Lot of soul / Just in case / What am I gonna do / When love is gone / Lorena / Don't ask me, ask Marie / Laying here lying in bed / Take some and give some / Sylvia's mother / Footprints in the snow / Lord let a lie come true / Under it all / Are you sincere / Even the bad times are good / High and dry / She gave her heart to Jethro / Music City USA
CD Set BCD 15417
Bear Family / Dec '87 / Direct / Rollercoaster / Swift

Bare Minimum

BARE MINIMUM
CD RXR 004CD
RX Remedy / Oct '96 / Cargo

NIGHT WE STREAK
CD RXR 008
RX Remedy / Nov '96 / Cargo

Bare Necessities

TAKE A DANCE
CD FF 564CD
Flying Fish / Apr '94 / ADA / CM / Direct / Roots

Barefoot

BAREFOOT
Barefoot / Gobi wind / Roundabout / Street strut / Serengeti / Shooz off / Black Noah / Gitano de Paraguay / Africa / Breath of life
CD 66052004
Global Pacific / Feb '91 / Pinnacle

Barefoot Contessa

BAREFOOT CONTESSA
CD LOLACD 1
Backs / Jun '95 / RTM/Disc

YOU CAN'T GO HOME AGAIN
CD LOLA 3CD
Indie 500 / Apr '97 / Shellshock/Disc

Barefoot Jerry

KEYS TO THE COUNTRY/BAREFOOTIN'
Battle of New Orleans / Summit ridge drive / Woes of the road / Wilma Lou / Appalachian fever / You can't say it all / Tonite's the nite I do / Georgia on my mind / Uncle Pen / My God (is alright with me) / Barefootin' / I ain't gettin' no touchin' / Keep on funkin' / Sentimental man / Dixie dancer / Hiroshima hole / Diana / Tokin' ticket / Headin' for the hills / Highland grass
CD SEECD 467
See For Miles/C5 / Jan '97 / Pinnacle

SOUTHERN DELIGHT/BAREFOOT JERRY
Hospitality song / I'm proud to be a redneck / Smokies / Quit while you're ahead (song of sensible compromise) / Blood is not the answer / Come to me tonight / Finishing touches / Minstrel is free at last / Nobody knows / That's OK, he'll be your brother someday / Castle rock / One woman / In god we trust / Message / Friends / Snuff queen / Little Maggie / Warm / Fish 'n' tits / Ain't it nice here / Ebeneezer
CD SEECD 485
See For Miles/C5 / Jul '97 / Pinnacle

WATCHING TV/YOU CAN'T GET OFF WITH YOUR SHOES ON
Watching TV (with the radio on) / Funny lookin' eyes / Pig snoots and nehi red / Hay Queen / Two mile pike / Faded love / There must be a better way / If there were only time for love / Violets and daffodils / Mother Nature's way of saying high / Ali Baba / Boogie woogie / Slowin' down / You can't get off with your shoes on / West side of Mississippi / Measure of your worth / Lucille / Hero Frodo / Sinkin' in the sea / Cades cove
CD SEECD 466
See For Miles/C5 / Jan '97 / Pinnacle

Barely Works

BEST OF BARELY WORKS
Byker hill / As a thoiseach / This fire / Liberty / Blackberry blossom / Cuckoo's nest / Big river / Bread and water / Maybe I'm a fool / June / Back to the mountains / Moving cloud / Cliff / Treen beach / Pull me up / Old Joe Clarke / Riddle me wry / Stand together
CD COOKCD 079
Cooking Vinyl / Feb '95 / Vital

Baren, Gasslin

OCCULT SONGS
CD 1C 567 1999 48
Harmonia Mundi / '88 / Cadillac / Harmonia Mundi

Barenaked Ladies

GORDON
Hello city / Enid / Grade 9 / Brian Wilson / Be my Yoko Ono / Wrap your arms around me / What a good boy / King of bedside manor / Box set / I love you / New kid (on the block) / Blame it on me / Flag / If I had one hundred thousand dollars / Crazy
CD 7599269562
East West / Aug '92 / Warner Music

MAYBE YOU SHOULD DRIVE
CD 9362457092
Warner Bros. / Aug '94 / Warner Music

Barenberg, Russ

HALLOWEEN REHEARSAL
CD ROUCD 11534
Rounder / '88 / ADA / CM / Direct

MOVING PICTURES
CD ROUCD 0249
Rounder / Aug '88 / ADA / CM / Direct

Barenboim, Daniel

MI BUENOS AIRES QUERIDO (Barenboim, Daniel & Rodolfo Mederos/ Hector Console)
CD 0630134742
Teldec Classics / Sep '96 / Warner Music

Baresi, Michelle

BERLIN & POGO
CD EFA 800402
Twah / Sep '95 / SRD

Bargad, Rob

BETTER TIMES (Bargad, Rob Sextet)
CD CRISS 1086CD
Criss Cross / May '94 / Cadillac / Direct / Vital/SAM

Barge, Gene

DANCE WITH DADDY G
I feel fine / Shake / Fine twine / Jerk / Way you do the things you do / In crowd / Twine time / Come see about me / Voice your choice / Monkey time / It's all over now / How sweet it is to be loved by you / Ain't too proud to beg / Chippie the hippie from Mississippi / Green tambourine / Little bit o' soul / Little boy blue / Quick getaway

CD SEECD 442
See For Miles/C5 / Apr '96 / Pinnacle

Bariu, Laver

SONGS FROM THE CITY
CD CDORBD 091
Globestyle / Jan '96 / Pinnacle

Bark Psychosis

GAME OVER
Blue / Three girl rhumba / I know / All different things / Manman / Bloodrush / Street scene / Murder city / Scum / Pendulum man
CD STONE 031CD
3rd Stone / May '97 / Plastic Head / Vital

HEX
Loom / Street scene / Absent friend / Big shot / Fingerspit / Eyes and smiles / Pendulum man
CD CIRCD 29
Circa / Apr '94 / EMI

INDEPENDENCY
I know / Nothing feels / All different things / By-blow / Manman / Blood rush / Tooled up / Scum
CD STONE 010CD
3rd Stone / Jul '94 / Plastic Head / Vital

Barker, 'Blue' Lu

CLASSICS 1938-1939
CD CLASSICS 704
Classics / Jun '93 / Discovery / Jazz Music

Barker, Dave

MONKEY SPANNER
Lucky boy / Lockjaw / Funky reggae / Sweeter she is / I've got to get a message to you / Follow your heart / Just my imagination / I got to get away / Girl in my dreams / Sex machine / Don't turn your back on me (blessed are the meek) / I feel alive / Double barrel / Lonely man / Heart of a man / Love love love / You ain't got a heart at all / Your love's a game / Baby I need your love / Monkey spanner / It's summer / Travelling man / Love is what I bring (I'm the one love forgot) / Only the strong survive / What a confusion
CD CDTRL 382
Trojan / Jun '97 / Direct / Jet Star

PRISONER OF LOVE
CD CDTBL 127
Trojan / Apr '96 / Direct / Jet Star

Barker, Guy

INTO THE BLUE
Into the blue / JJ swing / Oh Mr. Rex / Low down lullaby / Did it 'n' did it / Sphinx / Enigma / Ill wind / This is the life / Weatherbird rag
CD 5276562
Verve / Jun '95 / PolyGram

ISN'T IT
Sheldon the cat / Isn't it / In a mist / I get along without you very well / All or nothing / Amandanita / Good speed / Day and night / Lament for the black tower
CD SPJCD 545
Spotlite / Jul '93 / Cadillac / Jazz Music / New Note/Pinnacle / Swift

TIMESWING
Timeswing / Cat strut / Duke Ellington's sound of love / Whole bit / Sleeping in iridium / As and when / O subjectivo objectivo / Sometime soon / And all of that / Isn't it romantic
CD 5330292
Verve / Oct '96 / PolyGram

Barker, Les

CARDI AND A BLOKE, A
CD DOG 011
Mrs. Ackroyd / Dec '95 / ADA / Direct / Roots

EARWIGO
CD DOG 004CD
Mrs. Ackroyd / Apr '95 / ADA / Direct / Roots

GNUS & ROSES (Mrs. Ackroyd Band)
CD DOG 10CD
Mrs. Ackroyd / Jun '94 / ADA / Direct / Roots

INFINITE NUMBER OF OCCASIONAL TABLES, AN
CD DOG 008CD
Mrs. Ackroyd / Sep '94 / ADA / Direct / Roots

ORANGES AND LEMMINGS (Mrs. Ackroyd Band)
CD DOG 007CD
Mrs. Ackroyd / Sep '94 / ADA / Direct / Roots

PROBABLY THE BEST ALBUM EVER MADE BY ANYBODY IN OUR STREET
Cosmo revisited / Dachshunds with erections / Jason and the arguments / Weddell waddie penguin / Hard cheese of old England / King Harold was a ventriloquist / Everything glows / Stay go and fetch / Earwigo
CD TERRCD 007
Terra Nova / Jul '97 / Direct

UP THE CREEK WITHOUT A POODLE
CD DOG 012
Mrs. Ackroyd / Feb '97 / ADA / Direct / Roots

Barker, Sally

FAVOURITE DISH
Moses / Favourite dish / Blue moon / Landing light / Honeymoon is over / Hold on / Good woman / I know what I like (in your wardrobe) / Sleepy eyes / Wind, she carries
CD HYCD 296165
Hypertension / Feb '97 / ADA / CM / Direct / Total/BMG

IN THE SPOTLIGHT
CD PUP 1 CD
Old Dog / Aug '89 / CM / Roots

TANGO/MONEY'S TALKING
CD HYCD 200149
Hypertension / Mar '95 / ADA / CM / Direct / Total/BMG

THIS RHYTHM IS MINE
CD HY 200106CD
Hypertension / Sep '93 / ADA / CM / Direct / Total/BMG

Barking Tribe

SERPENT GO HOME
Pretty in print / Two important Pauls / White man's mind / Hide a prize / Breakaway / God knows what to do / Dammit to hell / Four fuses / Complain / With cretins as friends / Ain't as many girls as there used to be / Running down on my luck / City streets
CD RCD 10200
Rykodisc / Sep '91 / ADA / Vital

Barkmarket

EASY LISTENING
CD OUTCD 101
Brake Out / Aug '96 / Direct

Barley Bree

ANTHEM FOR THE CHILDREN
CD SH 52020 CD
Shanachie / '90 / ADA / Greensleeves / Koch

BEST OF BARLEY BREE, THE
CD SHCD 52039
Shanachie / Mar '95 / ADA / Greensleeves / Koch

Barleycorn

GREEN & GOLD
CD DOCDK 108
Dolphin / May '94 / CM / Else / Grapevine/PolyGram / Koch

MY LAST FAREWELL
CD DOCDX 9010
Dolphin / Sep '96 / CM / Else / Grapevine/PolyGram / Koch

SONG FOR IRELAND, A
Song for Ireland / Cavan Ireland / Portland Town / Dublin in my tears / Roseville fair / Long before your time / Over my mountains / Charlie on the MTA / Mary's song / Lakes of Coolfin
CD DOCDX 9004
Dolphin / Jul '96 / CM / Else / Grapevine/PolyGram / Koch

WALTZING FOR DREAMERS
CD DOCDK 104
Dolphin / May '94 / CM / Else / Grapevine/PolyGram / Koch

Barlow, Charles

BEST OF THE DANSAN YEARS VOL.9, THE (Barlow, Charles Orchestra & Irven Tidswell Orchestra)
CD DACD 009
Dansan / Mar '95 / Jazz Music / President / Target/BMG / Wellard

Barlow, Eric

BALLROOM FAVOURITES
Moonlight and roses / Tonight you belong to me / Avalon / Romany rose / Wyoming / Blue eyes / I've never been in love before / I left my heart in San Francisco / Sweetest song in the world / Mistakes / Dancing with tears in my eyes / Moonlight saunter / Underneath the stars / Mayfair quickstep / You're dancing on my heart / It's foolish but it's fun / First time I saw you / Luna rossa / Rosanna / You're still the only girl in the world / Girl of my dreams / In a shanty in old shanty town / Waltzing Matilda / Heart of my heart / Old mother Kelly's doorstep / Lily of laguna / Me and my shadow / If you knew Susie / Ma he's making eyes at me / Spanish eyes / Strangers in the night / Military two step / Hello hello who's your lady friend / Take me back to dear old blighty
CD EMPRCD 636
Emporio / Jun '96 / Disc

Barlow, Gary

OPEN ROAD
Love won't wait / So help me girl / My commitment / Hang on in there baby / Are you ready now / Everything I ever wanted / I fall so deep / Lay down for love / Forever love / Never knew / Open road / Always
CD 74321417202
RCA / May '97 / BMG

YOUTHOLOGY VOL.1 (2CD Set/ Documentary and Music)
CD Set OTR 1100036
Metro Independent / Jun '97 / Essential/ BMG

YOUTHOLOGY VOL.2 (2CD Set/ Documentary & Music)
CD Set OTR 1100037
Metro Independent / Jun '97 / Essential/ BMG

YOUTHOLOGY VOL.3 (Documentary & Music/2CD Set)
CD Set OTR 1100038
Metro Independent / Jun '97 / Essential/ BMG

Barmy Army

ENGLISH DISEASE
CD ONUCD 8
On-U Sound / Jun '94 / Jet Star / SRD

Barnard, Bob

BOB BARNARD & THE AUSTRALIAN JAZZ ALLSTARS 1977
CD LB 9511
La Brava / Jun '96 / Jazz Music

CORNET CHOP SUEY
CD OPUS3CD 19503
Opus 3 / Jul '96 / Direct / Jazz Music

NEW YORK NOTES 1995 (Barnard, Bob & Keith Ingham)
CD SKCD 23061
Sackville / Jan '97 / Cadillac / Jazz Music / Swift

Barnbrack

22 IRISH FOLK PUB SONGS
CD CDHRL 199
Outlet / Feb '95 / ADA / CM / Direct / Duncans / Koch / Ross

IRISH PUB FOLK SINGALONG
CD CDPUB 024
Outlet / May '96 / ADA / CM / Direct / Duncans / Koch / Ross

SLICE OF HOME, A
Belfast / Fields of Athenry / Whiskey in the jar/Coutin' in the kitchen/I'll tell me ma / My lagan softly flowing / If we only had one Ireland over here / I'll take you home again Kathleen / Galway boy / Mickey Marley's roundabout / Ringsend rose / Limerick you're a lady / Belfast mill / When I was a lad / Cockles and mussels/When Irish eyes are smiling/Galway shawl / Town I loved so well / Molly, my Irish Molly / Rose of Tralee / Carrickfergus / Rathlin island / Inn of Innisfree / Danny boy
CD MCVD 30004
Emerald Gem / Nov '96 / BMG

THREE OF THE BEST
Hannaghan's hooley / Boul O'Donaghue / If you're Irish / Lovely rose of Clare / Daisy a day / Two loves / Delaney's donkey / McNamara's band / My forever friend / Dublin in the rare oul times / You never learned to dance / Forty shades of green / Lannigan's ball / Cavan girl / Old rugged cross / Danny boy
CD CHCD 2008
Outlet / Mar '97 / ADA / CM / Direct / Duncans / Koch / Ross

Barnes, Alan

HERE COMES TROUBLE
Here comes trouble / SOS / Never let me go / Little Nemo / Clare's cares / Hushed tones / Quasimodo / East of the village / Arriving soon
CD FJCD 110
Fret / Jun '96 / Cadillac / New Note/ Pinnacle

LIKE MINDS (Barnes, Alan & David Newton)
'Round midnight / Blues in thirds / Batida differente / Poor butterfly / I'm just a lucky so and so / Lament for Javanette / Lull at dawn / Waltz for Sonny Criss / Walkin' shoes / Peacocks / Nobody else but me / Cotton tail
CD FJCD 105
Fret / Nov '94 / Cadillac / New Note/ Pinnacle

PLAY HAROLD ARLEN (Barnes, Alan & Brian Lemon)
CD ZECD 7
Zephyr / May '96 / Cadillac / Jazz Music / New Note/Pinnacle

THIRSTY WORK
Ecaroh / Stars fell on Alabama / Groovy samba / Sweet and lovely / Stay as sweet as you are / Double take and fade away / Go home / Solitude / Autumn in New York / Thirsty work
CD FJCD 106
Fret / Mar '95 / Cadillac / New Note/ Pinnacle

Barnes, Emile

EMILE BARNES & LOUISIANA JOYMAKERS
CD AMCD 13
American Music / Aug '95 / Jazz Music

Barnes, George

2 GUITARS & A HORN (Barnes, George & Carl Kress)
CD JCD 636
Jass / Jan '93 / ADA / Cadillac / CM / Direct / Jazz Music

PLAYS SO GOOD
Night and day / I'm coming Virginia / Days of wine and roses / Don't get around much anymore / On a clear day (You can see forever) / I've found a new baby / Honeysuckle rose / St. Louis blues / At sundown
CD CCD 4067
Concord Jazz / Apr '94 / New Note/ Pinnacle

Barnes, J.J.

BORN AGAIN, AGAIN
Can't see me leaving you / Time is love / Good men don't grow on trees / You are just a living doll / Wishful thinking / You owe it to yourself / No if's, and's or but's / (I just make believe I'm) touching you
CD NEMCD 936
Sequel / Jul '97 / BMG

KING OF NORTHERN SOUL
Whatever happend to our melody / On top of the world / Talk of the grapevine / Our love is in the pocket / Try it one more time / In and out of my life / Say it / Build a foundation / Sweet as a honey bee / Eternity / Happy road / That's just never enough / Please let me in / I've seen the light / Real humdinger / You can bet your love / Open the door to your heart / Sweet sherry
CD 3035990112
Motor City / Feb '96 / Carlton

Barnes, Jimmy

BARNESTORMING
CD D 245212
Mushroom / May '94 / 3mv/Pinnacle

BEST OF JIMMY BARNES, THE (2CD Set)
CD Set TVD 93465
Mushroom / Aug '97 / 3mv/Pinnacle

FLESH & WOOD
CD TVD 93390
Mushroom / Dec '94 / 3mv/Pinnacle

HEAT
CD TVD 93372
Mushroom / Jun '93 / 3mv/Pinnacle

PSYCLONE
CD TVD 93433
Mushroom / Jun '95 / 3mv/Pinnacle

SOUL DEEP
CD TVD 93344
Mushroom / Aug '94 / 3mv/Pinnacle

TWO FIRES
Lay down your guns / Let's make it last all night / Little darlin' / Love is enough / Hardline / One of a kind / Sister mercy / When your love is gone / Between two fires / Fade to black / Hold on
CD TVD 93318
Mushroom / May '94 / 3mv/Pinnacle

Barnes, Johnny

FANCY OUR MEETING
Samba rossi / Blue horizon / Boko's bounce / Hawk / Moonlight becomes you / Fascinating rhythm / Falling in love with you
CD CLGCD 019
Calligraph / Feb '89 / Cadillac / Jazz Music / New Note/Pinnacle / Wellard

LIKE WE DO (Barnes, Johnny & Roy Williams/Digby Fairweather)
But not for me / Nightingale sang in Berkeley Square / Serenade to a jobsworth / Fascinating rhythm / Kiss to build a dream on / Like we do / Once in a while / Wrap your troubles in dreams / Southern comfort / Struttin' with some barbecue / Please don't talk about me when I'm gone / One two button my shoe / I'm sorry I made you cry
CD LACD 69
Lake / Oct '96 / ADA / Cadillac / Direct / Jazz Music / Target/BMG

Barnes, Paul

PAUL BARNES & HIS POLO PLAYERS
CD AMCD 55
American Music / Aug '95 / Jazz Music

Barnes, Ricky

WELCOME TO HILLTOP USA (Barnes, Ricky & The Hootowls)

CD OK 33025CD
Okra / Feb '95 / ADA / Direct

Barnes, Roosevelt

HEARTBROKEN MAN, THE (Barnes, Roosevelt 'Booba' & The Playboys)
CD R 2623
Rooster / Jul '95 / Direct

Barnes, Will

TEXAS IN MY BLOOD
Texas music in my blood / My old truck / First show boat / Don't make me sing redneck mother again / Port Arkansas / Whiskyta / Speed of the race / Tupelo county jail / Sunshine lady / Rock 'n' roll roadie / My bike / She ran off with buck / Second fiddle in one man band / I always die in Dallas / Standing on the rock / Naked with the girl next door / Clap for me (But don't give me the claps) / Granpa was a farmer / Desperados waiting for a train / Marajuana polka
CD BCD 15991
Bear Family / Jul '96 / Direct / Rollercoaster / Swift

Barnet, Charlie

CHARLIE BARNET & RHYTHM MAKERS 1938
CD TAXCD 3715
Tax / Mar '94 / Cadillac / Jazz Music / Wellard

CHEROKEE
Cherokee/Redskin rhumba / Serenade to May / Moten swing / Pompton turnpike / East side, west side / Charleston Alley / Skyliner / Blue juice / Wild mab of the fish pond / Southern fried / Smiles
CD ECD 220652
Evidence / Nov '93 / ADA / Cadillac / Harmonia Mundi

CHEROKEE
Cherokee / Duke's idea / Count's idea / Right idea / Wrong idea / Ogoun Badagris (voodoo war God) / Oh what you said (We are burnt up) / Night clow / Ebony rhapsody / I never knew / Lament for a lost love (Solace) / All night record man (Stay up Stan) / Last jump (A jump to end all jumps) / Miss Annabelle Lee / Lazy bug / Echoes of Harlem / Afternoon of a moax (Shake, rattle, 'n roll) / Leapin' at the Lincoln / Swing street strut / Clap hands, here comes Charlie / Between 18th and 19th on Chestnutt Street / Only a rose / Scotch and soda
CD CD 53277
Giants Of Jazz / Jun '96 / Cadillac / Jazz Music / Target/BMG

INTRODUCTION TO CHARLIE BARNET 1935-1944, AN
CD 4039
Best Of Jazz / Nov '96 / Discovery

LIVE 1957-1959 (Barnet, Charlie Orchestra)
CD JH 3005
Jazz Hour / Mar '97 / Cadillac / Jazz Music / Target/BMG

MAKE BELIEVE BALLROOM 1936-1941 (Barnet, Charlie Orchestra)
CD RACD 7123
Aerospace / May '96 / Jazz Music / Montpellier

MORE (Barnet, Charlie Orchestra)
Evergreens / Stardust / Take the 'A' train / Goodbye / Early autumn / Flying home / I can't get started (with you) / Begin the beguine / Darn that dream / Midnight sun / One o'clock jump / Harlem nocturne
CD ECD 22112
Evidence / Jan '95 / ADA / Cadillac / Harmonia Mundi

SKYLINER
Gal from Joe's: *Barnet, Charlie Orchestra* / Night song: *Barnet, Charlie Orchestra* / Echoes of Harlem: *Barnet, Charlie Orchestra* / Lazy bug: *Barnet, Charlie Orchestra* / Midweek function: *Barnet, Charlie Orchestra* / Lament for a lost love: *Barnet, Charlie Orchestra* / Cherokee: *Barnet, Charlie Orchestra* / That all night record man: *Barnet, Charlie Orchestra* / Last jump: *Barnet, Charlie Orchestra* / Duke's idea: *Barnet, Charlie Orchestra* / Count's idea: *Barnet, Charlie Orchestra* / Wrong idea: *Barnet, Charlie Orchestra* / Right idea: *Barnet, Charlie Orchestra* / Things ain't what they used to be: *Barnet, Charlie Orchestra* / Washing whirligig: *Barnet, Charlie Orchestra* / Strollin': *Barnet, Charlie Orchestra* / Moose: *Barnet, Charlie Orchestra* / Pow-wow: *Barnet, Charlie Orchestra* / Great lie: *Barnet, Charlie Orchestra* / Drop me off in Harlem: *Barnet, Charlie Orchestra* / Gulf coast blues: *Barnet, Charlie Orchestra* / Skyliner: *Barnet, Charlie Orchestra* / Xango: *Barnet, Charlie Orchestra*
CD TPZ 1041
Topaz Jazz / Mar '96 / Cadillac / Pinnacle

THOSE SWINGING YEARS
Redskin rhumba / Jeep is jumpin' / In a mellow tone / Into each life some rain must fall / Yalta / Great lie / Blue moon / E-bob-o-lee-bob / Mellow mood / In there / You always hurt the one you love / Xango / Gulf coast blues / I like to riff / Bakiff / Drop me off in Harlem
CD HCD 264
Hindsight / Jun '97 / Jazz Music / Target/BMG

TRANSCRIPTION PERFORMANCES 1941, THE (Barnet, Charlie Orchestra)
Swing low, sweet chariot / Nowhere / It's a haunted town / Charleston alley / Lumby / Conga del moaxo / Redskin rhumba / Fantasia / Blue juice / Phyllysse / Wings over Manhattan / Little John ordinary / Little dip / Wild mab of the fish pond / Dutch kitchen stomp / Plowin' / Consider yourself kissed / Spanish kick (Habanera) / Barcarolle / Song of the Volga Boatmen / Reflections / Bar is now open / Ponce de Leon
CD HEPCD 53
Hep / Apr '97 / Cadillac / Jazz Music / New Note/Pinnacle / Wellard

WINGS OVER MANHATTAN 1941 (Barnet, Charlie Orchestra)
Swing low, sweet chariot / Afraid to say hello / Haunted town / Harmony haven / Nowhere / Blue juice / Buffy boy / Fantasia / Phylysee / Wings over Manhattan / Little dip / Little John ordinary / Why / Wild mab of the fish pond / Consider yourself kissed / Dutch kitchen stomp / Plowin' / Spanish kick / Herat you stole from me / Bar is open / Barcarolle / Ponce de Leon / Song of the Volga boatmen / Reflections
CD VN 1002
Viper's Nest / Nov '96 / ADA / Cadillac / Direct / Jazz Music

Barnett, Bobby

AMERICAN HEROES AND WESTERN LEGENDS
Oklahoma's OK / Hanging of Judge Parker / Ballad of Belle Starr / Cherokee Bill / Bill Doolin / Ballad of pretty boy Floyd / Sequoyah / Captain David L Paine / Iron horse / Gunfight at the OK Corral / Wyatt Earp / Ballad of Doc Holiday / Bat Masterson / Story of the Dalton gang / Three guardsmen / Run of '89 / Ballad of Geronimo / Chief Crazy Horse / Pawnee Bill / Bill Pickett of the 101 / Lost Dutchman mine / Tombstone Arizona / Tom Mix / Salute to Will Rogers / Jim Thorpe / Cowboy hall of fame / Tribute to Woody Guthrie
CD BCD 16121
Bear Family / Apr '97 / Direct / Rollercoaster / Swift

Barnshakers

HONKY TONK SESSION, A
CD GRCD 6048
Goofin' / Nov '96 / Nervous / TKO Magnum

STRING-O-RAMA
CD GRCD 6068
Goofin' / Sep '96 / Nervous / TKO Magnum

Baron, Christy

I THOUGHT ABOUT YOU
CD JD 152
Chesky / May '97 / Discovery / Goldring

Baron, Jean

BRITTANY
CD ARN 64302
Arion / Jul '95 / ADA / Discovery

DANSAL E BREIZ (Baron, Jean & Christian Anneix)
CD KMCD 41
Keltia Musique / Aug '93 / ADA / Discovery

DANSE DE BRETAGNE (Baron, Jean & Christian Anneix)
CD KMCD 07
Keltia Musique / Jul '90 / ADA / Discovery

E BRO ROUE MORVAN (Baron, Jean & Christian Anneix)
CD KMCD 68
Keltia Musique / Sep '96 / ADA / Discovery

SACRED MUSIC AND BRETON AIRS (Baron, Jean & Michel Ghesquiere)
CD KMCD 69
Keltia Musique / Nov '96 / ADA / Discovery

Baron, Joey

CRACKSHOT (Baron, Joey & Barondown)
CD AVAN 059
Avant / Feb '96 / Cadillac / Harmonia Mundi

RAISED PLEASURE DOT
CD 804492
New World / Apr '94 / ADA / Cadillac / Harmonia Mundi

TONGUE IN GROOVE
Blinky / Yow / Terra bina kia jeena / Guzzle / Spoo / But, cake / Archives / Shadow of your smile / Room service / I want a little girl / Sandbox / Response / Trunk / Go / Scottie Pippen / Mr. Pretension
CD 8491582
jMT / Mar '92 / PolyGram

Baroudi, Hamid

CITY NO MAD
CD EFA 042232
Vielklang / Aug '94 / SRD

MAD CT MIX
CD BARBARITY 014
Barbarity / Jan '97 / Stern's

Barra MacNeils

TIMESPAN
Row row row / Flower basket medley / Lone harper / My heart's in the highlands / Glenpark medley / Song for peace / Coaltown road / Highland exchange medley / Standing by the subway / Playhouse medley / One for Jeffy / Beautiful Point Aconi
CD IRCD 043
Iona / Mar '97 / ADA / Direct / Duncans

TRADITIONAL ALBUM, THE
Clumsy lover set / Celtic harp / tribute to Robert Stubbert / Visit medley / Maids of Arrochar / Brolum set / Twice a year fiddler / March/Strathspeys/Reels / Memories of Mary Ann MacKenzie / Wedding party medley / Toonik tyme / Twin fiddles / Neil Gow's lament for the death of his second wife
CD IRCD 047
Iona / Mar '97 / ADA / Direct / Duncans

Barracudas

COMPLETE BARRACUDAS
Barracuda wavers / Surfers are back / Rendezvous / I can't pretend / We're living in violent times / Don't let go / This ain't my time / I saw my death in a dream last night / Somewhere outside / On the strip / Chevy baby / Summer fun / His last summer / (I wish it could be) 1965 Again / Somebody / KGB (Made a man out of me) / Campus tramp / California lament / Codeine / My little red book / Neighbourhood girls / Tokyo rose
CD DOJOCD 99
Dojo / May '93 / Disc

DROP OUT WITH THE BARRACUDAS
I can't pretend / We're living in violent times / Don't let go / Codine / This ain't my time / I saw my death in a dream last night / Somewhere outside / Summer fun / His last summer / Somebody / Campus tramp / On the strip / California lament / (I wish it could be) 1965 again
CD VOXXCD 2009
Voxx / Jul '94 / Else / RTM/Disc

ENDEAVOUR TO PERSEVERE
Dealing with today / Leaving home again / Song for Lorraine / World turned upside down / See her eyes again / Black snake / Way we've changed / She knows / Man with money / Pieces broken / Losin' streak / Corine / Barracuda / Stolen heart / Laughing at you
CD MAUCD 642
Mau Mau / May '95 / Pinnacle

MEANTIME
Grammar of misery / Bad news / I ain't no miracle worker / Be my friend again / Shades of today / Dead skin / Middle class blues / You've come a long way / Ballad of a liar / When I'm gone / Eleventh hour / Hear me calling
CD MAUCD 641
Mau Mau / May '95 / Pinnacle

SURF AND DESTROY
CD 899027
New Rose / May '94 / ADA / Direct / Discovery

TWO SIDES OF A COIN
I want my woody back / Subway surfin' / Inside mind / Hour of degradation / Next time round / Take what he wants / Dead skin / Two sides of coin / Kingdom of pain / Twentieth Century myth / Very last day / Wastin time / Daggers of justice / There's a world out there / Seven and seven is / Codeine the strip / Song for Lorraine / Fortunate son
CD CDMGRAM 62
Anagram / May '95 / Cargo / Pinnacle

Barre, Martin

MEETING
CD SIVCD 0015
Red Steel / Mar '97 / Pinnacle

TRICK OF MEMORY, A
Bug / Way before your time / Bug bee / Empty cafe / Suspicion / I be thank you / Blues for all reasons / Trick of memory / Steal / Another view / Cold heart / Bug c / Morris minus / In the shade of the shadow
CD TT 5008
XYZ / Apr '94 / XYZ

Barrelhouse Jazz Band

DRIVING HOT JAZZ FROM THE 20'S
CD BCD 49
GHB / Apr '94 / Jazz Music

Barreto, Don

DON BARRETO ET SON ORCHESTRE CUBAIN 1932-1934 (Barreto, Don Et Son Orchestre Cubain)
La belle Creole / El beso / Negro bachatera / Chi chi biguine / Runidera / Biguine d'amour / Mi amor esta en el valle / A si pare / Lacrimas negras / Lamento esclavo / Marta / Negra consentida / Belle Melanie / Serenata Cubana / Nuestro cantar / La biguine qu'a pas fini / Mujer sonadora / Amor Cubano / Se acaba el mundo / Vengo por la Conga
CD HQCD 06
Harlequin / Oct '91 / Hot Shot / Jazz Music / Swift / Wellard

Barrett Sisters

HE'S GOT THE WHOLE WORLD IN HIS HANDS
CD BB 1982
Black & Blue / May '96 / Discovery / Koch / Wellard

Barrett, 'Wild' Willy

OPEN TOED AND FLAPPING
Jack o' diamonds / Crow that chicken / Open toed and flapping / HT blues / Hair across the frets / Father Jim / Chinatown / MK special / Notting Hill / Hot clubbing / Cowboy / Judge and the devil / Blacksmith's rope
CD PRKCD 29
Park / Apr '95 / Pinnacle

Barrett, Dan

JUBILESTA
CD ARCD 19107
Arbors Jazz / Nov '94 / Cadillac

Barrett, Emma

LAST RECORDINGS 1974 & 1978 (Barrett, Sweet Emma)
CD MG 9001
Mardi Gras / Feb '95 / Jazz Music

SWEET EMMA
CD OJCCD 183
Original Jazz Classics / Nov '95 / Complete/Pinnacle / Jazz Music / Wellard

Barrett, Greg

MEMPHIS HEAT
Into the mystic / Same old blues / Your love keeps me satisfied / Rainy night in Georgia / Worth her weight in gold / Since you've been gone / Standing next to rainbows / Until you come back to me (that's what I'm gonna do) / Before the light goes out tonight / That's all I want from you / Spanish Harlem / Goosebumps
CD INAK 9043CD
In Akustik / Jul '97 / Direct / TKO Magnum

Barrett, Larry

BEYOND THE MISSISSIPPI
CD GRCD 342
Glitterhouse / May '97 / Avid/BMG

FLOWERS
CD GRCD 298
Glitterhouse / Jan '94 / Avid/BMG

Barrett, Syd

BARRETT
Baby lemonade / Love song / Dominoes / It is obvious / Rats / Maisie / Gigolo aunt / Waving my arms in the air / Wined and dined / Wolfpack / Effervescing elephant / I never lied to you
CD CDGO 2054
Harvest / May '94 / EMI

CRAZY DIAMOND (The Complete Syd Barrett)
Terrapin / No good trying / Love you / No man's land / Dark globe / Here I go / Octopus / Golden hair / Long gone / She took a long cold look / Feel / If it's in you / Late night / Octopus (Take 1 and 2) / It's no use trying / Love you (Take 1) / Love you (Take 3) / She took a long cold look (Take 4) / Golden hair (Take 5) / Baby lemonade / Love songs / Dominoes / It is obvious / Rats / Maisie / Gigolo aunt / Waving my arms in the air / I never lied to you / Wined and dined / Wolfpack / Effervescing elephant / Baby lemonade / Waving my arms in the air (takes) / I never lied to you / Love song (Take 1) / Dominoes (take 1) / Dominoes (Take 2) / It is obvious (alt. takes) / Opel / Clowns and jugglers / Rats / Golden hair (vocal) / Dolly rocker / Word song / Wined and dined / Swan Lee (Silas Lang) / Birdie hop / Let's split / Lanky (Part 1) / Wouldn't you miss me / Milky way / Golden hair (Inst.) / Gigolo aunt (Take 9) / Clowns and jugglers (Octopus) / Late night (Take 2) / Effervescing elephant (Take 2)
CD Set SYDBOX 1
Harvest / Apr '93 / EMI

FISH OUT OF WATER (CD/Book Set)
CD Set SB 02
Sonik Book / Nov '96 / Cargo

MADCAP LAUGHS, THE
Terrapin / No good trying / Love you / No man's land / Here I go / Dark globe / Octopus / Golden hair / Long gone / She took a long cold look / Feel / If it's in you / Late night
CD CDGO 2053
Harvest / May '94 / EMI

OCTOPUS (The Best Of Syd Barrett)
Octopus / Swan Lee (Silas Lang) / Baby lemonade / Late night / Wined and dined / Golden hair / Gigolo aunt / Wolfpack / It is obvious / Lanky (part 1) / No good trying / Clowns and jugglers / Waving my arms in the air / Opel
CD CLEO 57712
Cleopatra / Oct '94 / Cargo / Greyhound / Plastic Head / RTM/Disc / SRD

OPEL
Opel / Clowns and jugglers / Rats / Golden hair / Dolly rocker / Word song / Wined and dined / Swan Lee (Silas Lang) / Birdie hop / Let's split / Lanky (part 1) / Wouldn't you miss me / Milky way / Golden hair (Inst.)
CD CDGO 2055
Harvest / May '94 / EMI

Barretto, Ray

ANCESTRAL MESSAGES
New world spirit / Song for Chano / Freedom jazz dance / On a sunday afternoon / Beautiful love / Killer Joe / Aquablue / Gabriela / My Latin New York / Ancestral messages
CD CCD 4549
Concord Picante / May '93 / New Note/ Pinnacle

BEYOND THE BARRIO
Nadie se salva la rumba / Tu proprio dolor / Lucretia the cat / Aguadilla / Vive y vacila / Canto abacua / Cancion para el nino / Lo tuyo lo mio / Aguardiente d cana / Ya no puede ser / Tin tin deo / Prestame tu mujer / Eras
CD CDHOT 518
Charly / Apr '95 / Koch

CARNAVAL
Manha de carnaval / Sugar's delight / Exodus / Descarga la moderna / Summertime / El negro y Ray / Mira que Linda / Concinando suave / Pachango oriental / Barretto en la tumbadora / Cumbamba / El Paso / Linda Mulata / Oye heck / Los Cueros / Pachanga suavecito / Ponte dura / Pachango para bailar
CD FCD 24713
Fantasy / Oct '93 / Jazz Music / Pinnacle / Wellard

INDESTRUCTIBLE
El hijo de obatalo / El Biablo / Yo tengo un amor / La familia / La orquestra / Llanto de coordrillo / Ay no / Indestructible / Adelante siempre voy / Algo nuevo
CD CDHOT 502
Charly / Oct '93 / Koch

LA CUNA
La cuna / Dolorosa / Mambotango / Old castle / Pastime paradise / Cocinado
CD ZK 66126
Sony Jazz / Feb '96 / Sony

LIVE AT THE BEACON THEATRE NEW YORK 1976
Intro / Vaya / Ahora si que vamo a gozar / Bab ban quere / Guarare / Night Flowers (flores de noche) / Slo flo / Cocinando / Que viva la musica
CD MES 159502
Messidor / Feb '93 / ADA / Koch

MY SUMMERTIME
CD 8358302
Owl / Apr '96 / Discovery

RAY BARRETTO 1939-1943
CD HQCD 36
Harlequin / Feb '94 / Hot Shot / Jazz Music / Swift / Wellard

TABOO (Barretto, Ray & New World Spirit)
Taboo / Bomba-Riquen / Work song / Cancion de'l yunque (Song for the rain forest) / Guaji-Rita / 99 MacDougal St / Montuno blue / Brother Tom / Lazy afternoon / Effendi
CD CCD 4601
Concord Picante / Jul '94 / New Note/ Pinnacle

Barrie, J.J.

NO CHARGE
Beunas dias senorita / My son / Where's the reason / I just fall in love again / While the feeling's good / It's too soon to know / Lady singer with a country music band / I love you / No charge / Lucille I got a honey of a deal / Husbands and wives / Sunday morning blues / Rainbows in my mind / I can't sing our love song / At my age / Very thought of you
CD SCD 28
Start / Feb '97 / Disc

Barrister

NEW FUJI GARBAGE (Barrister, Chief Dr. Sikiru Ayinde)
Refined Fuji garbage / Fuji worldwide
CD CDORBD 067
Globestyle / Feb '91 / Pinnacle

Barron, Bill

NEXT PLATEAU, THE
CD MCD 5368
Muse / Sep '92 / New Note/Pinnacle

Barron Knights

BEST OF THE BARRON KNIGHTS, THE
California girls / DIY / Mr. Bronski meets Mr. Evans / Air hostess song / All through the night / Street rhymes / Bohemian Rhapsody / Space oddity / Have you seen her / Wally song / Loan arranger / Superglue / Sister Josephine / Then he kicked me / Nellie the courier / Money for nothing / Stick to selling onions / Club erotica / Franksie / Don't let the Germans pinch your sunbeds / Little darling / Gas board bill / I'm anti biotics / Big bad bond / Ozone friendly
CD QED 103
Tring / Nov '96 / Tring

BEST OF THE BARRON KNIGHTS, THE
How about us / Olympic record / I've got you under my skin / Sunday shopping / Merry gentle pops / Can can / Traces / Chapel lead is missing / Cilla Black's hat / Under new management / Green knickers / Pop go the workers / Cold in my nose / Call up the groups '64 / Battle of Agincourt / All shock up
CD 306362
Hallmark / Jan '97 / Carlton

BEST OF THE BARRON KNIGHTS, THE
Cilla Black's hat / Can can / Chapel lead is missing / Bottle of Agincourt / Sunday shopping / Call up the groups / Call up the groups / Pop go the workers / Merry gentle pops / Under new management / Olympic record / Traces / I've got you under my skin / Come to the dance
CD CDSGP 0338
Prestige / Apr '97 / Else / Total/BMG

FUNNY IN THE HEAD
Taste of aggro / Get down Shep / Heaving on a jet plane / Sit song / Farewell to punk / Remember (decimalisation) / Little white bum / Funny in the head / Du wot / Buffalo Bill's last scratch / Live in trouble / Hands on the ear folk song / Big V (vasectomy) / Telephone line / Chapel lead is missing / Topical song / Never mind the presents
CD 4837232
Epic / May '96 / Sony

TWO SIDES OF THE SENSATIONAL BARRON KNIGHTS, THE
You are all I need / Before you leave / Bottle on the shelf / Lonely / You know what I mean / Don't let it die / Turning my back on you / Oh little girl / To the woods / Hey ho Europe / Beetroot song / I couldn't spell / You know what / Green knickers / With her head tucked underneath her arm / Three finger picker / What is a pop star / Cold in my nose / Peaceful life / Ballad of Frank Spencer / Nothin' doin' / Pardon me / I'm gonna give my love to you / I'm a nut
CD C5CD 572
See For Miles/C5 / Jun '97 / Pinnacle

Barron, Kenny

INVITATION
CD CRISS 1044CD
Criss Cross / Apr '91 / Cadillac / Direct / Vital/SAM

LEMURIA-SEASCAPE (Barron, Kenny Trio)
Ask me now / Sweet Lorraine / Fungii mama / Slow grind / Have you met Miss Jones / Maria Isabel / You go to my head / Magical look in your eyes / Seascape
CD CCD 79508
Candid / Feb '97 / Cadillac / Direct / Jazz Music / Koch / Wellard

LIVE AT MAYBECK RECITAL HALL VOL.10
I'm getting sentimental over you / Witchcraft / Bud-like / Spring is here / Well you needn't / Skylark / And then again / Sunshower
CD CCD 4466
Concord Jazz / Jun '91 / New Note/ Pinnacle

MOMENT, THE
CD RSRCD 121
Reservoir Music / Nov '94 / Cadillac

ONLY ONE, THE
CD RSRCD 115
Reservoir Music / Nov '94 / Cadillac

OTHER PLACES
Anywhere / Other places / Mythology / For Heaven's sake / Ambrosia / Wildlife / I should care / Nikara's song / Hey, it's me you're talkin' to
CD 5196992
Verve / Mar '94 / PolyGram

RED BARRON DUO, THE (Barron, Kenny & Red Mitchell Trio)
CD STCD 4137
Storyville / Feb '90 / Cadillac / Jazz Music / Wellard

RHYTHM-A-NING (Barron, Kenny & John Hicks Quartet)
Sunshower / Naima's love song / Blue monk / After the morning / Ghost of yesterday / Rhythm-a-ning
CD CCD 79044
Candid / Feb '97 / Cadillac / Direct / Jazz Music / Koch / Wellard

SAMBAO
Sambao / Yalele / Bacchanal / Belem encounter / Ritual / Gardenia / On the other side
CD 5127362
EmArCy / Mar '94 / PolyGram

WANTON SPIRIT
CD 5223642
Verve / Dec '94 / PolyGram

Barron, Ronnie

MY NEW ORLEANS SOUL
CD AIM 1038
Aim / Apr '95 / ADA / Direct / Jazz Music

Barros, Alberto

EL TITAN DE LA SALSA
Maldita duda / Vampiro / Confession / Perdi el control / Tu indiferencia / Fingiendo / Imagination / Sola quedaras / Reencarnado / Dosis pasional
CD 66058064
RMM / May '95 / New Note/Pinnacle

Barrow, Arthur

EYEBROW RAZOR
CD EFA 034192
Muffin / Aug '95 / SRD

Barrowside

HIDDEN CORNER, THE
CD RTMCD 73
Round Tower / Feb '96 / Avid/BMG

WISH & THE WAY, THE
CD RTMCD 66
Round Tower / Dec '94 / Avid/BMG

Barry, John

EMI YEARS VOL.1, THE
Let's have a wonderful time / Rockabilly boogie / Zip zip / Three little fishes / Every which way / You've gotta way / Big guitar / Rodeo / Farrago / bee's knees / When the saints go marching in / Pancho / Long John / Snap 'n' whistle / Little John / For Pete's sake / Rebel rouser / Mab mab / 12th Street rag / Christella / Rockin' already / Walk don't run / Saturday's child / Hideaway: *Barry, John Seven & Latin American Rhythm Accompaniment* / Good rockin' tonight: *Barry, John & Bob Miller & the Miller men* / Hit and miss: *Barry, John Four/Seven* / I'm movin' on: *Barry, John Four/Seven* / Main title: *Barry, John Orchestra* / Beat girl: *Barry, John Orchestra* / Beat for beatniks: *Barry, John Orchestra* / Big fella: *Barry, John Orchestra* / Blueberry Hill: *Barry, John Orchestra* / Never let go: *Barry, John Orchestra* / Black stockings: *Barry, John Seven* / Get lost Jack Frost: *Barry, John Seven* / Bee's knees: *Barry, John Seven & Latin American Rhythm Accompaniment* / Pancho: *Barry, John Seven & Latin American Rhythm Accompaniment*
CD CDEMS 1497
EMI / Jun '93 / EMI

EMI YEARS VOL.2, THE
Magnificent seven / Skid row / Twist it / Watch your step / Dark rider / Matter of who / Iron horse / It doesn't matter anymore / Sweet talk / Moon river / There's life in the old boy yet / Handful of songs / Like waltz / Rodeo / Donna's theme / Starfire / Baubles, bangles and beads / Zapata / Rum-de-dum-de-da / Spanish Harlem / Man from Madrid / Challenge / Menace / Satin smooth / Agressor / Rocco's theme / Spinnerree
CD CDEMS 1501
EMI / Jul '93 / EMI

HIT AND MISS
Hideaway / When the saints go marching in / Long John / Twelfth street rag / Hit and miss / Beat for beatniks / Blueberry hill / Never let go / WalkHit and miss / Walk don't run / Black stockings / Mgnificent seven / It doesn't matter anymore / Spanish Harlem / James Bond Theme / Cutty sark / Cherry pink and apple blossom white / Unchained melody / I'll be with you in apple blossom time / Voalre / That fatal kiss
CD CDMFP 6392
Music For Pleasure / Jul '97 / EMI

Barry, John

NASHVILLE STYLE
(Tonight we just might) fall in love again / Summer's comin' / Hey baby / Don't take the girl / Bobbie Ann Mason / Indian outlaw / If the world had a front porch / Gone country / One boy, one girl / You got it / Sold (the Grundy County auction incident) / I like it, I love it
CD HBCD 9501
Brewhouse / Feb '96 / ADA / Brewhouse Music

Barry, Margaret

HER MANTLE SO GREEN (Barry, Margaret & Michael Gorman)
CD TSCD 474
Topic / Aug '94 / ADA / CM / Direct

IRELAND'S OWN
CD PTICD 1029
Pure Traditional Irish / Aug '96 / ADA / CM / Direct / Ross

Barta, Steve

BLUE RIVER
Wish upon a canvas / Blue river / In another life / Like an old piano / Rossport / Carinho (dearest one) / High road / Asleep in the sweet light / Umtradah / On the edge
CD KOKO 1303
Kokopelli / Mar '96 / New Note/Pinnacle

Barth, Bruce

MORNING CALL
CD ENJACD 80842
Enja / Sep '95 / New Note/Pinnacle / Vital/ SAM

Barthelemy, Claude

MONSIEUR CLAUDE
CD ZZ 84124
Deux Z / Feb '97 / Cadillac / Harmonia Mundi

SOLIDE (Barthelemy, Claude & Pierre Ledic/Charles Biddle)
CD EVCD 316
Evidence / Feb '94 / ADA / Cadillac / Harmonia Mundi

Bartholomew, Dave

BASIN STREET BREAKDOWN
Basin street breakdown / Golden rule / Bad habit / In the alley / Twins / Lawdy Lawdy Lord (part 1) / Lawdy Lawdy Lord (part 2) / Country boy / Pyramid / Messy bessy / I'll never be the same / Mr. Fool / Stormy weather / Nickel wine / Sweet home blues / Mother knows best / High flying woman / My ding a ling
CD CDCHARLY 273
Charly / Jan '93 / Koch

Barton, Lou Ann

DREAMS COME TRUE (Barton, Lou Ann/Marcia Ball/Angela Strehli)
Fool in love / Good rockin' daddy / It hurts to be in love / Love sweet love / Gonna make it / You can if you think you can / I idolize you / Dreams come true / Bad thing / Turn the lock on love / Something's got a hold on me / Snake dance
CD ANTCD 0014
Antones / Mar '91 / ADA / Hot Shot

OLD ENOUGH
CD ANTCD 0021
Antones / Oct '95 / ADA / Hot Shot

Bartram & Holloway

FOUR RED FEET
CD WGSCD 268
Wild Goose / Feb '96 / ADA

Bartz, Gary

ALTO MEMORIES (Bartz, Gary & Sonny Fortune)
CD 5232682
Verve / Dec '94 / PolyGram

EPISODE ONE - CHILDREN OF HARLEM
CD CHR 70001
Challenge / May '96 / ADA / Direct / Jazz Music / Wellard

HARLEM BUSH MUSIC - TAIFA/UHURU (Bartz, Gary NTU Troop)
Rise / People dance / Du (rain) / Drinking song / Taifa / Parted / Warrior's song / Blue (a folk tale) / Uhuru sasa / Vietcong / Celestial blues / Planets
CD CDBGPD 108
Beat Goes Public / Jan '97 / Pinnacle

JULU STREET SONGS (Bartz, Gary NTU Troop)
CD PRCD 24181
Prestige / Aug '97 / Cadillac / Complete/ Pinnacle

THERE GOES THE NEIGHBORHOOD (Bartz, Gary Candid All Stars)
Racism (blues in double Bb minor) / On a misty night / Laura / Tadd's delight / Impressions / I've never been in love before / Flight path
CD CCD 79506
Candid / Feb '97 / Cadillac / Direct / Jazz Music / Koch / Wellard

WEST 42ND STREET (Live At Birdland 1990) (Bartz, Gary Quintet)
West 42nd Street / Speak low / It's easy to remember / Cousins / Night has a thousand eyes
CD CCD 79049
Candid / Feb '97 / Cadillac / Direct / Jazz Music / Koch / Wellard

Bartz, Richard

ESCAPE
CD ________ EFA 125462
Kurbel / Aug '96 / SRD

Bascomb, Paul

BAD BASCOMB
Blues and the beat / More blues-more beat / Black out / Pink cadillac / Soul and body / Coquette / Love's an old story / Nona / Mumble's blues / Indiana / Got cool too soon / Liza's blues / I know just how you feel / Soul and body / Blues and the beat / More blues-more beat / Pink cadillac
CD ________ DD 431
Delmark / Mar '97 / ADA / Cadillac / CM / Direct / Hot Shot

Baseball Annie

BASEBALL ANNIE
CD ________ LF 213CD
Lost & Found / May '96 / Plastic Head

Baseline

RETURNS
Though dreamers die / Avenger / Che cha / Northsea night / Strike again / Loudly at night / Magic kingdom / Returns / Wheeling
CD ________ CHR 70047
Challenge / Mar '97 / ADA / Direct / Jazz Music / Wellard

STANDARDS
CD ________ CHR 70023
Challenge / Feb '96 / ADA / Direct / Jazz Music / Wellard

Basement 5

1965-1980/BASEMENT 5 IN DUB
CD ________ IMCD 145
Island / Jul '92 / PolyGram

Bashful Brother Oswald

BROTHER OSWALD
CD ________ ROUCD 0013
Rounder / Jun '95 / ADA / CM / Direct

Basho, Robbie

GUITAR SOLI
Seal of the blue lotus / Mountain man's farewell / Dravidian Sunday / Grail and the lotus / Dharma prince / Oriental love song / Sansara in sweetness after sandstorm / Salangadou / Golden shamrock / Street dakini / Chung mei - the Chinese orchid
CD ________ CDTAK 8902
Takoma / Jan '97 / ADA / Pinnacle

SEAL OF THE BLUE LOTUS, THE
Seal of the blue lotus / Mountain man's farewell / Dravidian Sunday / Bardo blues / Sansara in sweetness after sandstorm / Black lotus - hymn to fugen
CD ________ CDTAK 1005
Takoma / Apr '96 / ADA / Pinnacle

Basia

TIME AND TIDE
Promises / Run for cover / Time and tide / Freeze thaw / From now on / New day for you / Prime time TV / Astrud / How dare you / Miles away / Forgive and forget
CD ________ CK 53791
Epic / Feb '95 / Sony

Basie Alumni

SWINGING FOR THE COUNT
Red bank shuffle / Snapper / Jive at five / Swinging for the count / Blue and sentimental / Kansas City Kitty / Basie like / Slow boat / Jumpin' at the Woodside
CD ________ CCD 79724
Candid / Jan '97 / Cadillac / Direct / Jazz Music / Koch / Wellard

Basie, Count

AIN'T MISBEHAVIN' (Basie, Count Orchestra)
CD ________ 15778
Laserlight / Jan '93 / Target/BMG

AMERICANS IN SWEDEN VOL.1 (Stockholm 1954) (Basie, Count Orchestra)
CD ________ TAX 37012
Tax / Aug '94 / Cadillac / Jazz Music / Wellard

AMERICANS IN SWEDEN VOL.2 (Stockholm 1954) (Basie, Count Orchestra)
CD ________ TAX 37022
Tax / Aug '94 / Cadillac / Jazz Music / Wellard

ANTHOLOGY
CD ________ EN 517
Encyclopaedia / Sep '95 / Discovery

APRIL IN PARIS (Basie, Count & Tony Bennett)
CD ________ MATCD 319
Castle / Dec '94 / BMG

APRIL IN PARIS
Jumpin' at the woodside / I guess I'll have to change my plan / 9.20 special / Jeepers creepers / Swingin' the blues / With plenty of money and you / Shorty George / Chicago / Broadway / I've grown accustomed to her face / Out the window / Poor little rich girl / Lester leaps in / Anything goes / Are you having any fun / Dickie's dream / Growing pains / Jive at five / Life is a song / April in Paris
CD ________ TRTCD 171
TrueTrax / Dec '94 / THE

APRIL IN PARIS
CD ________ PLSCD 146
Pulse / Apr '97 / BMG

AT NEWPORT
Swingin' at Newport / Polka dots and moonbeams / Lester leaps in / Sent for you yesterday and here you come today / Boogie woogie I may be wrong / Evenin' / Blee blop blues / Alright, OK you win / Comeback / Roll 'em Pete / Smack dab in the middle / One o'clock jump
CD ________ 8337762
Verve / Mar '94 / PolyGram

ATOMIC BAND LIVE IN EUROPE
CD ________ BS 18010
Bandstand / Jul '96 / Swift

ATOMIC MR. BASIE, THE (Basie, Count Orchestra)
Kid from Red Bank / Duet / After supper / Flight of the Foo birds / Double O / Teddy the toad / Whirly bird / Midnite blue / Splanky / Fantail / Li'l darlin'
CD ________ CDP 8286352
Blue Note / Mar '95 / EMI

ATOMIC MR. BASIE, THE (The Complete Atomic Basie) (Basie, Count Orchestra)
Kid from Red Bank / Duet / After supper / Flight of the Foo Birds / Double O / Teddy the toad / Whirly bird / Midnite blue / Splanky / Fantail / Li'l darlin' / Silks and satins / Sleepwalker's serenade / Sleepwalker's serenade / Late late show / Late late show
CD ________ CDROU 1055
Roulette / Feb '94 / EMI

ATOMIC MR. BASIE, THE (Basie, Count Orchestra)
CD ________ CD 53043
Giants Of Jazz / Jan '89 / Cadillac / Jazz Music / Target/BMG

AUDIO ARCHIVE
Lester leaps in / Going to Chicago / All of me / Platterbrains / I struck a match in the dark / Dance of the gremlins / Feather merchant / Everyday I have the blues / Stormy Monday blues / Swingin' the blues / Jumpin' at the woodside / One O'clock jump / Every tub / John's idea / Tom thumb / April in Paris / Fiesta in blue / Blues and sentimental / Down for double / Something new
CD ________ CDAA 013
Tring / Oct '92 / Tring

AUTUMN IN PARIS (Basie, Count Orchestra)
Whirly bird / Little pony / Corner pocket / Lovely baby / Blee blop blues / Nails / Kid from Red Bank / Spring is here / Why not / Well, alright, OK, you win / Roll 'em / Ol' man river / Duet / Gee baby ain't I good to you / One o'clock jump
CD ________ DAWE 13
Magic / Nov '93 / Cadillac / Harmonia Mundi / Jazz Music / Swift / Wellard

BASIC BASIE (Basie, Count Orchestra)
Idaho / Blues in my heart / I don't stand a ghost of a chance with you / Red roses for a blue lady / Moonglow / Ma, he's making eyes at me / M Squad / Sweet Lorraine / Ain't misbehavin' / Don't worry 'bout me / As long as I live / I've got the world on a string
CD ________ 8212912
MPS Jazz / Mar '94 / PolyGram

BASIE - ONE MORE TIME (Music From The Pen Of Quincy Jones)
For Lena and Lennie / Rat race / Quince / Meet B B / Big walk / Square at the round table / I needs to be bee'd with / Jessica's day / Midnite sun never sets / Muttnik
CD ________ CDROU 1035
Roulette / Aug '91 / EMI

BASIE AND FRIENDS
Easy does it / Zoot / Love me or leave me / NHOP / She's funny that way / Turnaround / Madame Fitz / Royal garden blues
CD ________ CD 2310925
Pablo / Apr '94 / Cadillac / Complete/ Pinnacle

BASIE AND ZOOT (Basie, Count & Zoot Sims)
I never knew / It's only a paper moon / Blues for Nat Cole / Captain Bligh / Honeysuckle rose / Hardav / Mean to me / Surrender dear
CD ________ OJCCD 822
Original Jazz Classics / Jun '95 / Complete/ Pinnacle / Jazz Music / Wellard

BASIE BOOGIE (Basie, Count Orchestra)
CD ________ JHR 73502
Jazz Hour / May '93 / Cadillac / Jazz Music / Target/BMG

BASIE IN LONDON (Basie, Count Orchestra)
Jumpin' at the Woodside / Shiny stockings / How high the moon / Nails / Flute juice / One o'clock jump / Alright, OK you win / Roll 'em Pete / Comeback / Blues backstage / Corner pocket / Blee blop blues / Yesterdays / Untitled / Sixteen men / Swinging / Plymouth rock
CD ________ 8338052
Verve / Jan '94 / PolyGram

BASIE IN SWEDEN
Little pony / Plymouth rock / Backwater blues / Who me / Corner pocket / Four, five, six / Splanky / In a mellow tone / April in Paris / Blues backstage / Good time blues / Peace pipe
CD ________ CDROU 1028
Roulette / Mar '91 / EMI

BASIE JAM VOL.1
Doubling blues / Hanging out / Red bank blues / One nighter / Freeport blues
CD ________ CD 2310 718
Pablo / May '94 / Cadillac / Complete/ Pinnacle

BASIE JAM VOL.2
Mama don't wear no drawers / Doggin' around / Kansas City line / Jump
CD ________ OJCCD 631
Original Jazz Classics / Feb '92 / Complete/ Pinnacle / Jazz Music / Wellard

BASIE JAM VOL.3
Bye bye blues / Moten swing / I surrender dear / Song of the Islands
CD ________ OJCCD 687
Original Jazz Classics / Feb '92 / Complete/ Pinnacle / Jazz Music / Wellard

BASIE RHYTHM (Basie, Count & Harry James)
Shoe shine boy / Evening / Boogie woogie / Oh lady be good / Jubilee / When we're alone / I can dream, can't I / Life goes to a party / Texas chatter / Song of the wanderer / Dreamer in me / One o'clock jump / My heart belongs to daddy / Sing for your supper / You can depend on me / Cherokee (part I) / Cherokee (part II) / Blame it on my last affair / Jive at five / Thursday / Evil blues / Oh lady be good
CD ________ HEPCD 1032
Hep / Jan '92 / Cadillac / Jazz Music / New Note/Pinnacle / Wellard

BASIE'S BAG (Basie, Count Orchestra)
Firm roots / Three in one / Hampton strut / For my lady / Way out Basie / Clarks / Basie's bag / Here's that rainy day / Count Basie rememberance suite
CD ________ CD 83358
Telarc / Jan '94 / Conifer/BMG

BEST OF BOOGIE
CD ________ DLCD 4069
Dixie Live / Mar '95 / TKO Magnum

BEST OF COUNT BASIE
Kid from Red Bank / Secret love / Cute / I cried for you / Blue and sentimental / Jumpin' at the woodside / Meet BB / Teach me tonight / Moten swing / One o'clock jump / Whirly bird / Hallelujah, I love her so / Makin' whoopee / Lullaby of Birdland / If I were a bell / Jackson County Jubilee / Sunset glow / Tickle toe / Ol' man river / Li'l darlin'
CD ________ CDMFP 6133
Music For Pleasure / Sep '94 / EMI

BEST OF COUNT BASIE
CD ________ DLCD 4024
Dixie Live / Mar '95 / TKO Magnum

BEST OF COUNT BASIE, THE
Tree frog / Sweet pea / Ticker / Flirt / Blues for Alfy / Billie's bounce / Festival blues / Jumpin' at the Woodside / Blue and sentimental / Red bank boogie / Shorty George / Rock-a-bye Basie / Every tub / Swingin' the blues / Sent for you yesterday / Boogie woogie / Broadway / Texas shuffle / Tickle toe / Doggin' around / Dickie's dream / Topsy / Lester leaps in / Out the window
CD ________ CD 2405408
Pablo / Apr '94 / Cadillac / Complete/ Pinnacle

BEST OF EARLY BASIE, THE
Honeysuckle rose / Roseland shuffle / Boogie woogie (I may be wrong) / One o'clock jump / John's idea / Good morning blues / Topsy / Oh lady be good / Jive at five / Panassie stomp / Shorty George / Jumpin' at the woodside / Texas shuffle / Doggin' around / Blues and sentimental / Swingin' the blues / Every tub / Sent for you yesterday / Blues in the dark / Don't you miss your baby / Out to the window
CD ________ GRP 16552
American Decca / Aug '96 / New Note/BMG

BEST OF THE BASIE BIG BAND, THE
Blues for Alfy / Heat's on / CB express / Sweet pea / Way out Basie / Featherweight / Katy / Prime time / Mr. Softie
CD ________ PACD 24054222
Pablo / Apr '94 / Cadillac / Complete/ Pinnacle

BIG BAND MONTREUX 1977
CD ________ OJCCD 377
Original Jazz Classics / Feb '92 / Complete/Pinnacle / Jazz Music / Wellard

BLUES ALLEY
All heart / Blues alley / Cherokee / Night in Tunisia / Goin' to chicago blues / Kid from red bank / Shiny stockings / Shadow of your smile / Splanky / Basie's thought / Blues in Hoss's flat / Magic flea / One o'clock jump
CD ________ CDC 9060
LRC / Apr '95 / Harmonia Mundi / New Note/Pinnacle

BROADCAST TRANSCRIPTIONS 1944-1945
CD ________ CD 884
Music & Arts / Sep '95 / Cadillac / Harmonia Mundi

CLASS OF 1954
CD ________ BLC 760924
Black Lion / Oct '94 / Cadillac / Jazz Music / Koch / Wellard

CLASSIC YEARS, THE
CD ________ CDSGP 0172
Prestige / Mar '96 / Else / Total/BMG

CLASSICS 1936-1938 (Basie, Count Orchestra)
Shoe shine boy / Evening / Boogie woogie / Oh lady be good / Honeysuckle rose / Pennies from Heaven / Swingin' at the daisy chain / Roseland shuffle / Exactly like you / Boo-hoo / Glory of love / Smarty / One o'clock jump / Listen my children / John's idea / Good morning blues / Our love was meant to be / Time out / Topsy / I keep remembering / Out the window / Don't you miss your baby / Let me dream / Georgianna
CD ________ CLASSICS 503
Classics / Apr '90 / Discovery / Jazz Music

CLASSICS 1938-1939 (Basie, Count Orchestra)
Blues in the dark / Sent for you yesterday / Every tub / Now will you be good / Swingin' the blues / Mama don't want no peas, no rice, no coconut oil / Blue and sentimental / Doggin' around / Stop beatin' around the mulberry bush / London Bridge is falling down / Texas shuffle / Jumpin' at the woodside / How long blues / Dirty dozen / Hey lawdy mama / Fives / Boogie woogie / Dark rapture / Shorty George / Blues I like to hear / Do you wanna jump children / Pansie stomp / My heart belongs to daddy / Sing for your supper / Old red
CD ________ CLASSICS 504
Classics / Apr '90 / Discovery / Jazz Music

CLASSICS 1939 VOL.1
CD ________ CLASSICS 513
Classics / Apr '90 / Discovery / Jazz Music

CLASSICS 1939 VOL.2
CD ________ CLASSICS 533
Classics / Dec '90 / Discovery / Jazz Music

CLASSICS 1939-1940
CD ________ CLASSICS 563
Classics / Oct '91 / Discovery / Jazz Music

CLASSICS 1940-1941 (Basie, Count Orchestra)
CD ________ CLASSICS 623
Classics / Sep '92 / Discovery / Jazz Music

CLASSICS 1941
CD ________ CLASSICS 652
Classics / Nov '92 / Discovery / Jazz Music

CLASSICS 1942
CD ________ CLASSICS 684
Classics / Mar '93 / Discovery / Jazz Music

CLASSICS 1943-1944
CD ________ CLASSICS 801
Classics / Mar '95 / Discovery / Jazz Music

CLASSICS 1945-1946
CD ________ CLASSICS 934
Classics / Apr '97 / Discovery / Jazz Music

CORNER POCKET (Basie, Count Orchestra)
CD ________ 15789
Laserlight / Aug '92 / Target/BMG

COUNT BASIE (2CD Set)
CD Set ________ R2CD 4012
Deja Vu / Jan '96 / THE

COUNT BASIE
CD ________ 22704
Music / Feb '96 / Target/BMG

COUNT BASIE
CD ________ 15704
Laserlight / Apr '94 / Target/BMG

COUNT BASIE & HIS GREAT VOCALISTS
I can't believe that you're in love with me / Don't worry 'bout me / If I can't be here with you (one hour tonight) / Goin' to Chicago blues / I want a little girl / My old flame / If I didn't care / Moon nocturne / Somebody stole my gal / All of me / Angels sing / Between the devil and the deep blue sea / Blue shadows and white gardenias / That

old feeling / Jivin' with Joe Jackson / Blue skies
CD CK 66374
Sony Jazz / Jul '95 / Sony

COUNT BASIE & SARAH VAUGHAN (Basie, Count & Sarah Vaughan)
Perdido / Lover man / I cried for you / Alone / There are such things / Mean to me / Gentleman is a dope / You go to my head / Until I met you / You turned the tables on me / Little man (you've had a busy day) / Teach me tonight / If I were a bell / Until I met you
CD CDP 8372412
Roulette / Apr '96 / EMI

COUNT BASIE 1937-1943 (Basie, Count Orchestra)
CD CD 53072
Giants Of Jazz / Mar '92 / Cadillac / Jazz Music / Target/BMG

COUNT BASIE 1944 (Basie, Count Orchestra)
CD HCD 224
Hindsight / Jul '94 / Jazz Music / Target/ BMG

COUNT BASIE AND THE KANSAS CITY SEVEN (Basie, Count & The Kansas City Seven)
I'll always be in love with you / Snooky / Blues for Charlie Christian / Jaws / I'm confessin' that I love you / I want a little girl / Blues in C / Brio
CD MCAD 5656
Impulse Jazz / '88 / New Note/BMG

COUNT BASIE AND THE KANSAS CITY SEVEN (Basie, Count & The Kansas City Seven)
Trey of hearts / Oh lady be good / Secrets / I want a little girl / Shoe shine boy / Count's place / Senator Whitehead / Tally-ho, Mr Basie / What'cha talkin'
CD IMP 12022
Impulse Jazz / May '97 / New Note/BMG

COUNT BASIE COLLECTION, THE
CD Set 55514
Laserlight / Sep '93 / Target/BMG

COUNT BASIE GOLD (2CD Set)
CD Set D2CD 4012
Deja Vu / Jun '95 / THE

COUNT BASIE SWINGS - JOE WILLIAMS SINGS (Basie, Count & Joe Williams)
Everyday I have the blues / Comeback / Alright, OK you win / In the evening / Roll 'em Pete / Teach me tonight / My baby upsets me / Please send me someone to love / Ev'ry day (I fall in love) / As I love you / Stop, don't / Too close for comfort
CD 5198522
Verve / Dec '93 / PolyGram

COUNT BASIE, ARTIE SHAW & TOMMY DORSEY (3CD Set) (Basie, Count/Artie Shaw/Tommy Dorsey)
CD Set MAK 102
Avid / Dec '93 / Avid/BMG / Koch / THE

COUNT ON THE COAST VOL.1 (Basie, Count & Joe Williams)
CD PHONTCD 7555
Phontastic / '88 / Cadillac / Jazz Music / Wellard

COUNT ON THE COAST VOL.2
CD PHONTCD 7575
Phontastic / Oct '92 / Cadillac / Jazz Music / Wellard

CREAM OF COUNT BASIE VOL.1, THE
Oh lady be good / Panassie stomp / Blame it on my last affair / My heart belongs to daddy / Thursday / Jive at five / Sing for your supper / Smarty (you know it all) / Our love was meant to be / Let me dream / One o'clock jump / Honeysuckle rose / Dark rapture / Roseland shuffle / Fives / Boo-hoo / Boogie woogie / Glory of love / Cherokee / Dirty dozens / Stop beatin' around the Mulberry bush
CD PASTCD 9774
Flapper / Feb '92 / Pinnacle

CREAM OF COUNT BASIE VOL.2, THE (Basie, Count Orchestra)
Clap hands, here comes Charlie / Riff interlude / I left my baby / Don't worry 'bout me / What goes up must come down / Pound cake / Lester leaps in / Dickie's dream / How long blues / Red wagon / Exactly like you / Pennies from heaven / Swinging at the Daisy Chain / Listen my children / Our love was meant to be / Now will you be good / Swingin' the blues / You can depend on me / Georgianna / Blues I like to hear / Oh Red / Good morning blues
CD PASTCD 9793
Flapper / Jun '92 / Pinnacle

DO YOU WANNA JUMP
Georgianna / Sent for you yesterday / Panassie stomp / Blues I like to hear / Stop beatin' around the mulberry bush / Swingin' the blues / Texas shuffle / Shorty George / Blue in the dark / Every tub / Nor will you be good / Mama don't want no peas, no rice, no coconut oil / Blue and sentimental / Doggin' around / London Bridge is falling down / Jumpin' at the woodside / Dark rapture / Do you wanna jump children
CD HEPCD 1027
Hep / Oct '89 / Cadillac / Jazz Music / New Note/Pinnacle / Wellard

ESSENTIAL COUNT BASIE VOL.1
Oh lady be good / Goin' to Chicago blues / Live and love tonight / Love me or leave me / Rock-a-bye Basie / Baby don't tell on me / If I could be with you one hour tonight / Taxi war dance / Jump for me / Twelfth street rag / Miss Thing (part 1) / Miss Thing (part 2) / Lonesome Miss Pretty / Nobody knows / Pound cake / How long blues
CD 4600612
Sony Jazz / Jan '95 / Sony

ESSENTIAL COUNT BASIE, THE
Clap hands, here comes Charlie / Tickle toe / Broadway / Jump the blues away / It's sand man / Ain't it the truth / For the good of your country / High tide / Queer street / Rambo / Stay cool / Stay on it / Golden bullet / Song of the Islands / One o'clock jump / Tootsie
CD 4671432
Columbia / Jul '93 / Sony

ESSENTIAL V-DISCS, THE
CD JZCD 303
Suisa / Feb '91 / Jazz Music / THE

FANCY PANTS (Basie, Count Orchestra)
Put it right there / By my side / Blue chip / Fancy pants / Hi five / Time stream / Samantha / Strike up the band
CD CD 2310920
Pablo / Apr '94 / Cadillac / Complete/ Pinnacle

FARMERS MARKET BARBEQUE
Way out Basie / St. Louis blues / Beaver Junction / Lester leaps in / Blues for the barbeque / I don't know yet / Ain't that something / Jumpin' at the Woodside
CD J33J 20056
Pablo / Apr '86 / Cadillac / Complete/ Pinnacle

FIVES 1936-1942, THE
How long blues / Bugle blues / Cafe society blues / Royal Garden blues / Sugar blues / Farewell blues / Way back blues / St. Louis blues / Boogie woogie / Dirty dozen / Fives / Oh Red / Hey lawdy Mama / Love me or leave me / Live and love tonight / I ain't got nobody / Shoe shine boy / Evenin' / Boogie woogie / Oh lady be good / Red wagon / Fare thee honey, fare thee well / Dupree blues / When the sun goes down
CD CD 53296
Giants Of Jazz / Feb '97 / Cadillac / Jazz Music / Target/BMG

FOR THE SECOND TIME (Basie, Count & Kansas City 3)
Sandman / If I could be with you one hour tonight / Draw / On the sunny side of the street / One I love (belongs to somebody else) / Blues for Eric / I surrender dear / Race horse
CD OJCCD 600
Original Jazz Classics / Feb '92 / Complete/ Pinnacle / Jazz Music / Wellard

FOUR TO A BAR (Basie, Count Orchestra)
Jive at five / Easy does it / Miss Thing / Love jumped out / If I could be with you one hour tonight / Between the devil and the deep blue sea / Don't worry 'bout me / You can depend on me / Clap hands, here comes Charlie / I left my baby / Swingin' the blues / Rock-a-bye Basie / Pound cake / Twelfth street rag / How long blues / Riff interlude / It's the same old south / One o'clock jump
CD PAR 2030
Parade / Sep '94 / Disc

FRANKLY BASIE (Count Basie Plays The Hits Of Frank Sinatra)
Second time around / Hey jealous lover / I'll never smile again / Saturday night is the loneliest night of the week / This love of mine / I thought about you / In the wee small hours of the morning / Come fly with me / On the road to Mandalay / Only the lonely / South of the border (Down Mexico way) / All of me / My kind of town (Chicago is) / Come rain or come shine / Hey jealous lover
CD 5198492
Verve / Mar '94 / PolyGram

FUN TIME (Basie, Count Orchestra)
Fun time / Why not / Li'l darlin' / In a mellow tone / Body and soul / Good time blues / I hate you baby / Lonesome blues / Whirly bird / One o'clock jump
CD CD 2310945
Pablo / Apr '94 / Cadillac / Complete/ Pinnacle

GET TOGETHER
Ode to pres / Basies bag / Like it used to be / Swinging on the cusp / My main men / I can't get started (with you) / What will i tell my heart / Talk of the town / I can't give you anything but love / I'm confessin' that I love you
CD CD 2310924
Pablo / Apr '87 / Cadillac / Complete/ Pinnacle

GOLD COLLECTION, THE
CD D2CD 12
Deja Vu / Dec '92 / THE

GOLDEN YEARS, THE (4CD Set)
Basie power / Meetin' / Blues in Hoss's flat / Why not / Good time blues / Festival blues / Splanky / More I see you / I needs to be bee'd with / Bookie blues / All of me / Shiny stockings / Basie / There will never be another you / Doubling blues / Baby Lawrence / Burning / Captain Bligh / Honeysuckle rose / Blues for Eric / I surrender dear / One o'clock jump / Memories of you / You got it / Ode to Pres / Honi coles / Opus six / Blues in C / Heat's on / Orange sherbert / Ticker / Swee' pea / Prime time / Corner pocket / Every tub / How sweet it us / CB express / Beaver junction / Way out Basie / Moten swing / Me and you / Time stream / Katy / Blues machine / I'm getting sentimental over you / My kind of trouble is you / Don't worry 'bout me / Lena and Lenny / Honeydripper / Blues around the clock / Flip, flop and fly / My jug and I / Cherry red / Wee baby / Blues for Joe Turner / Everyday I have the blues / Stormy Monday / I hate you baby / Lonesome blues / TV Momma / Corrine Corrina
CD Set 4PACD 4419
Pablo / Feb '97 / Cadillac / Complete/ Pinnacle

GREATEST, THE (Count Basie Plays - Joe Williams Sings Standards) (Basie, Count & Joe Williams)
Thou swell / There will never be another you / Our love is here to stay / 'S Wonderful / My baby just cares for me / Nevertheless / Singin' in the rain / I'm beginning to see the light / Fine romance / Come rain or come shine / I can't believe that you're in love with me / This cant be love
CD 8337742
Verve / Mar '93 / PolyGram

I TOLD YOU SO
Tree frog / Flirt / Blues for Alfy / Something to live for / Plain brown wrapper / Sweet pea / Too close for comfort / Told you so / Git
CD OJCCD 824
Original Jazz Classics / Jun '95 / Complete/ Pinnacle / Jazz Music / Wellard

IN CONCERT
CD Set RTE 15042
RTE / Aug '95 / ADA / Koch

INDISPENSABLE COUNT BASIE, THE
Bill's mill / Brand new wagon / One o'clock boogie / Futuile frustration / Swingin' the blues / St. Louis boogie / Basie's basement / Backstage at Stuff's / My buddy / Shine on harvest moon / Lopin' / I never knew / Sugar / Jungle king / I ain't mad at you / After you've gone / House rent boogie / South / Don't you want a man like me / Seventh Avenue express / Sophisticated swing / Guest in a nest / Your red wagon / Money is honey / Just a minute / Robbin's nest / Hey pretty baby / Bye bye baby / Just an old manuscript / She's a wine-o / Shoutin' blues / Wonderful thing / Mine too / Walking slow behind you / Normania / Rat race / Sweets
CD Set ND 89758
RCA / Mar '94 / BMG

INTRODUCTION TO COUNT BASIE 1936-1944, AN
CD 4026
Best Of Jazz / Nov '95 / Discovery

JAM SESSION AT MONTREUX 1975
Billie's bounce / Festival blues / Lester leaps in
CD CD 2310 750
Pablo / May '94 / Cadillac / Complete/ Pinnacle

JAZZ MASTERS
Big red / April in Paris / Two Franks / Shiny stockings / Royal Garden blues / Stereophonic / Blue and sentimental / Everyday / Paradise squat / Kansas City / Wrinkels / Midgets / KC organ blues / Every tub / Polka dots and moonbeams / Sent for you yesterday / One o'clock jump
CD 5198192
Verve / Apr '93 / PolyGram

JAZZ MASTERS
CD CDMFP 6296
Music For Pleasure / Mar '97 / EMI

JAZZ PORTRAITS (Basie, Count Orchestra)
Jumpin' at the woodside / One o'clock jump / Swingin' the blues / Tops / Every tub / Texas shuffle / Jive at five / Oh Lady be good / Twelfth street rag / Clap hands, here comes Charlie / Dickie's dream / Lester leaps in / Tickle toe / I never knew / Love jumped out / Super chief / Red bank boogie / Rhythm man
CD CD 14506
Jazz Portraits / May '94 / Jazz Music

JIVE AT FIVE
Blame it on my last affair / Blue and sentimental / Cherokee / Honeysuckle rose / How long blues / Jive at five / John's idea / Jumpin' at the woodside / Oh lady be good / Moten swing / One o'clock jump / Panassie stomp / Roseland shuffle / Shoe shine boy / Swingin' at the daisy chain / Texas shuffle / Time out / You can depend on me
CD CDAJA 5089
Living Era / '92 / Select

JUBILEE ALTERNATIVES (Basie, Count Orchestra)
Jumpin' at the woodside / I'm gonna move to the outskirts of town / I've found a new baby / Andy's blues / Avenue C / Basie's bag (Basie boogie) / More than you know / Let's jump / Harvard blues / One o'clock jump / Dinah / Baby, won't you please come home / Rock-a-bye Basie / Swing shift / Gee baby ain't I good to you / Beaver Junction / My what a fry
CD HEPCD 38
Hep / Mar '90 / Cadillac / Jazz Music / New Note/Pinnacle / Wellard

JUMPIN' AT THE WOODSIDE (Basie, Count Orchestra)
Jumpin' at the woodside / One o'clock jump / Swingin' the blues / Topsy / Every tub / Texas shuffle / Jive at five / Oh lady be good / Twelfth street rag / Clap hands / Here comes Charley / Dickie's dream / Lester leaps in / Tickle toe / I never knew / Love jumped out / Super Chief / Red bank boogie / Rhythm man
CD CD 56015
Jazz Roots / Aug '94 / Target/BMG

JUMPIN' AT THE WOODSIDE
CD JHR 73543
Jazz Hour / May '93 / Cadillac / Jazz Music / Target/BMG

KANSAS CITY 6
Walking the blues / Blues for little jazz / Vegas drag / Wee baby / Scooter / St. Louis blues / Opus six
CD OJCCD 449
Original Jazz Classics / Nov '95 / Complete/ Pinnacle / Jazz Music / Wellard

KANSAS CITY 7
Jaylock / Exactly like you / I'll always be in love with you / If I could be with you for one hour tonight / Honi coles / Blues for Norman / Count me in
CD CD 2310908
Pablo / Nov '95 / Cadillac / Complete/ Pinnacle

KANSAS CITY SHOUT (Basie, Count/ Joe Turner/Eddie Vinson)
My jug and I / Cherry red / Apollo daze / Standing on the corner / Stormy Monday / Signifying / Just a dream on my mind / Blues for Joe Turner / Blues for Joel / Everyday I have the blues / Blues au four
CD CD 2310859
Pablo / May '94 / Cadillac / Complete/ Pinnacle

KANSAS CITY SOUL (Basie, Count/Joe Turner/Eddie Vinson)
CD 1311252
Pablo / '88 / Cadillac / Complete/Pinnacle

LEGENDARY V-DISCS AND JUBILEE MASTERS (Basie, Count Orchestra)
CD VJC 1018 2
Vintage Jazz Classics / Oct '91 / ADA / Cadillac / CM / Direct

LIVE 1938-1939 (Basie, Count Orchestra & Lester Young)
CD VJC 1033
Vintage Jazz Classics / '91 / ADA / Cadillac / CM / Direct

LIVE 1954 AT THE SAVOY BALLROOM, NEW YORK (Basie, Count Orchestra)
CD 11089
Laserlight / '88 / Target/BMG

LIVE 1958-1959 (Unissued Recordings)
Why not / In a mellow tone / So young so beautiful / Splanky / Back to the apple / Yogi / Bag a' bones / Moon is not green / Rat race / G'wan away / Plymouth rock / Chestnut Street rumble
CD STATUSCD 110
Status / Oct '91 / Cadillac

LIVE AT MANCHESTER CRAFTSMEN'S GUILD (Basie, Count Orchestra & New York Voices)
Down for the count / Whirly bird / Cotton tail / In a mellow tone / Basie / Please send me someone to love / Bug out / Love makes the world go round / Farmer's market / Basie power
CD JAZZMCG 1002
Blue Jackel / Mar '97 / New Note/Pinnacle

LIVE AT MONTREUX 1977 (Basie, Count Orchestra)
CD CD 20019
Pablo / May '86 / Cadillac / Complete/ Pinnacle

LIVE AT THE EL MOROCCO (Basie, Count Orchestra)
Gone an' git it y'all / Night at El Morocco / Right on, right on / That's the kind of love I'm talking about / Corner pocket / Little Chicago fire / Shiny stockings / Angel eyes / Major Butts / Vignola express / Basie / One o'clock jump
CD CD 83312
Scorpio / Jul '92 / Complete/Pinnacle

LIVE AT THE FAMOUS DOOR 1938
CD JH 3003
Jazz Hour / Mar '97 / Cadillac / Jazz Music / Target/BMG

LIVE IN ANTIBES 1968
Vine Street rumble / Pleasingly plump / Cherokee / Good times blues / Lonely

Street / Night in Tunisia / Goin' to Chicago blues / I got rhythm / In a mellow tone / Basie's / Li'l darlin' / Blues in Hoss's flat / Everyday I have the blues / Wee baby blues / Stormy Monday blues / Magic flute / Jumpin' at the woodside
CD ____ **FCD 112**
France's Concert / Jun '88 / BMG / Jazz Music

LIVE IN JAPAN 1978
Heat's on / Freckle face / Ja da / Things ain't what they used to be / Bit of this and a bit of that / All of me / Shiny stockings / Left hand funk / John the III / Basie / Black velvet / Jumpin' at the Woodside
CD ____ **CD 2308246**
Pablo / May '94 / Cadillac / Complete/ Pinnacle

LIVE IN SWITZERLAND
CD ____ **LS 2907**
Landscape / Nov '92 / THE

LOOSE WALK (Basie, Count & Roy Eldridge)
Loose walk / In a mellow tone / Makin' whoopee / If I had you / I surrender dear / 5400 North
CD ____ **CD 2310928**
Pablo / Aug '94 / Cadillac / Complete/ Pinnacle

MAKIN' WHOOPEE
Ain't misbehavin' / Makin' whoopee / Shake rattle and roll / One o'clock jump / Summertime / Lester leaps in young / Jumpin' at the Woodside / These foolish things / I got it bad and that ain't good / Dance of the gremlins / Two for T blues / Ska-di-de-deedoo / Jazz me blues / Let's jump / Lullaby of Birdland / April in Paris
CD ____ **CDMT 026**
Meteor / Oct '96 / TKO Magnum

ME AND YOU
CD ____ **CD 2310891**
Pablo / May '86 / Cadillac / Complete/ Pinnacle

MOSTLY BLUES AND SOME OTHERS (Basie, Count & The Kansas City Seven)
I'll always be in love with you / Snooky / Blues for Charlie Christian / Jaws / I'm confessin' that I love you / I want a little girl / Blues in C / Brio
CD ____ **CD 2310919**
Pablo / Feb '87 / Cadillac / Complete/ Pinnacle

ON THE ROAD (Basie, Count Orchestra)
Wind machine / Blues for Stephanie / John the III / There'll never be another you / Bootie's blues / Splanky / Basie / Watch what happens / Work song / In a mellow tone
CD ____ **OJCCD 854**
Original Jazz Classics / Nov '95 / Complete/ Pinnacle / Jazz Music / Wellard

ON THE ROAD '79
CD ____ **CD 31121**
Pablo / May '86 / Cadillac / Complete/ Pinnacle

ON THE WEST COAST 1958 (Basie, Count Orchestra & Joe Williams)
CD ____ **NCD 8839**
Phontastic / Jul '96 / Cadillac / Jazz Music / Wellard

ONE O'CLOCK JUMP (Live) (Basie, Count Orchestra)
CD ____ **15797**
Laserlight / Jan '93 / Target/BMG

ONE O'CLOCK JUMP
Swingin' the blues / Oh lady be good / Topsy / One o'clock jump / Jumpin' at the woodside / Love jumped out / Dickie's dream / I never knew / Twelfth street rag / Lester leaps in / Super chief / Every tub / Tickle toe / Texas shuffle / Jive at five / Clap hands, here comes Charlie
CD ____ **HADCD 175**
Javelin / May '94 / Henry Hadaway / THE

OUR SHINING HOUR (Basie, Count & Sammy Davis Jr.)
My shining hour / Teach me tonight / Work song / Why try to change me now / Blues for Mr. Charlie / April in Paris / New York City blues / You're nobody till somebody loves you / She's a woman / Girl from Ipanema / Keepin' out of mischief now / Billy Bailey won't you please come home
CD ____ **8374462**
Verve / Aug '89 / PolyGram

PLAYS THE MUSIC OF NEAL HEFTI AND BENNY CARTER (Basie, Count Orchestra)
CD ____ **CD 53040**
Giants Of Jazz / Mar '92 / Cadillac / Jazz Music / Target/BMG

PRIME TIME
Prime time / Bundle o'funk / Sweet Georgia Brown / Featherweight / Reaching out / Ja da / Great debate / Ya gotta try
CD ____ **CD 2310797**
Pablo / Oct '92 / Cadillac / Complete/ Pinnacle

QUINTESSENCE, THE (1937-1941/2CD Set)
CD Set ____ **FA 202**
Fremeaux / Oct '96 / ADA / Discovery

ROUND TRIP
Ain't misbehavin' / Shake, rattle and roll / Jumpin' at the woodside / Makin' whoopee / Summertime / These foolish things / Lester leaps in / One o'clock jump / I got it bad and that ain't good / Ska-di-de-dee-doo / Two for the blues / Dance of the gremlins / Let's jump / Jazz me blues / April in Paris / Lullaby of Birdland
CD ____ **SUMCD 4045**
Summit / Nov '96 / Sound & Media

SHOUTIN' BLUES
Cheek to cheek / Just an old manuscript / Kayt / She's a wine-o / Shoutin' blues / Did you see Jackie Robinson hit that ball / St. Louis baby / After you've gone / Wonderful thing / Slider (take 1b) / Slider (take 1c) / Mine, too - Take 1C / Mine, too - Take 1d / Walking slow behind you / Normania (Bee bop blues) / Rocky mountain blues / Siler - take 2 / If you see my baby / Rat race / Sweets
CD ____ **07863661582**
Bluebird / Apr '93 / BMG

SONNY LESTER COLLECTION
CD ____ **CDC 9065**
LRC / Nov '93 / Harmonia Mundi / New Note/Pinnacle

SOPHISTICATED SWING
Sophisticated swing / Cheek to cheek / Hey pretty baby / Your red wagon / One o'clock boogie / Money is honey / Don't you want a man like me / Shoutin' blues / After you've gone / Jungle King South / Swinging the blues / Walking slowly behind you / Bye bye baby
CD ____ **74321451902**
Camden / Feb '97 / BMG

SWING MACHINE, THE (1937-1962) (Basie, Count Orchestra)
One o'clock jump / Swingin' the blues / Topsy / Every tub / Boogie woogie / Dickie's dream / 12th Street rag / Red wagon / Oh lady be good / Jive at five / Fives / Texas shuffle / Clap hands, here comes Charlie / Oh red / Tickle toe / I never knew / Sugar blues / Love jumped out / Super chief / Lester leaps in / Red bank boogie / Rhythm man / Fiesta in blue / Yeah man / What am I here for / April in Paris / There's a small hotel / Hob nail boogie / Blee blop blues / Basie talks / Paradise squat / Softly, with feeling / Beaver Junction / Nails / Did you see Jackie Robinson hit that ball / Seventh Avenue express / Mr. Roberts' roost / Mad boogie / King / Mutton leg / Patience and fortitude / Wild Bill's boogie / Stay cool / High tide / Jimmy's boogie woogie / Taps miller / Jumpin' at the woodside / Moten swing / Blue and sentimental / Sent for you yesterday / Blues in hoss's flat / Who me / Little pony / Legend / Goin' to Chicago blues / One o'clock junp / Shorty George / Duet / Double O / Splanky / Miss Missouri / Meetin' time / Stompin and jumpin'
CD Set ____ **CDB 1210**
Giants Of Jazz / '92 / Cadillac / Jazz Music / Target/BMG

SWINGIN' MACHINE LIVE, THE (Basie, Count Orchestra)
CD ____ **LEJAZZCD 17**
Le Jazz / Jun '93 / Cadillac / Koch

THIS IS JAZZ
One o'clock jump / Lester leaps in / 9:20 special / Oh lady be good / Goin' to Chicago blues / Red bank boogie / Dickie's dream / Miss thing / Tickle toe / How long blues / Broadway / Rock-a-bye Basie / Blow top / Let me see / Taxi war-dance / Moten swing / Jumpin' at the Woodside
CD ____ **CK 64966**
Sony Jazz / Oct '96 / Sony

TOPEKA, KANSAS 1955
CD ____ **JASSCD 17**
Jass / '88 / ADA / Cadillac / CM / Direct / Jazz Music

WARM BREEZE
CB express / After the rain / Warm breeze / Cookie / Flight to Nassau / How sweet it is (to be loved by you) / Satin doll
CD ____ **CD 311240**
Pablo / May '86 / Cadillac / Complete/ Pinnacle

YESSIR THAT'S MY BABY (Basie, Count & Oscar Peterson)
Blues for Roy / Teach me tonight / Joe Turner blues / Blues for cat / Yes sir that's my baby / After you've gone / Tea for two / Poor butterfly
CD ____ **CD 2310923**
Pablo / Dec '86 / Cadillac / Complete/ Pinnacle

Basil, Toni

MICKEY (The Best Of Toni Basil)
Mickey / Over my head / Street beat / Time after time / Spacewalkin' the dog / Do you wanna dance / Go for the burn / Nobody / You gotta problem / Space girls / Hanging around / Little in red book
CD ____ **301642**
Hallmark / Jun '97 / Carlton

Basin Brothers

LET'S GET CAJUN
CD ____ **FF 539CD**
Flying Fish / Jul '92 / ADA / CM / Direct / Roots

Basin Street Six

COMPLETE CIRCLE RECORDINGS, THE
CD ____ **BCD 103**
GHB / Aug '94 / Jazz Music

Baskett, Larry

QUALIOE (Baskett, Larry Trio)
ESP / I've never been in love before / Estate / Born to be blue / Lament / Blue gardenia / Black Nile / Spring can really hang you up the most / Indian summer / Nancy with the laughing face
CD ____ **AL 73047**
A / Nov '96 / Cadillac / Direct

POOR BOY BLUE
Beatrice / Haunted heart / Milestones / So in love / Theme for Denise / Poor boy blue / Northern lights / Child / Love letters / There's no you / Paradizer adieu / If you should leave me
CD ____ **AL 73086**
A / Jul '97 / Cadillac / Direct

Bass Dance

LOUD
CD ____ **REVXD 161**
FM / Oct '90 / Revolver / Sony

Bass, Fontella

NO WAYS TIRED
CD ____ **7599793572**
Nonesuch / Feb '95 / Warner Music

RESCUED (The Best Of Fontella Bass)
Rescue me / You'll never know / Don't you mess up a good thing / Soul of a man / You're gonna miss me / I surrender / Free at last / Baby what you want me to do / Joy of love / I can't rest / Oh no not my baby / Don't jump / Leave it in the hands of love
CD ____ **MCD 09335**
Chess/MCA / Apr '97 / BMG / New Note/ BMG

Bass X

HAPPY TO BE HARDCORE
CD ____ **EVCD 6**
Evolution / Jul '97 / Alphamagic

Bass-O-Matic

SET THE CONTROLS FOR THE HEART OF THE BASS
In the realm of the senses / Set the controls for the heart of the bass / Fascinating rhythm / Rat cut a bottle / Love catalogue / Zombie mantra / Freaky angel / Wicked love / Ease on by / My tears have gone
CD ____ **CDVIP 188**
Virgin VIP / Apr '97 / EMI

Bassett, Johnny

I GAVE MY LIFE TO THE BLUES
I'll get over you / Mean feeling / Drink muddy water / Blowing the horn / I love a good woman (but I like the bad ones too) / If the shoe is on the other foot / Too hot to trot / They call me lucky / Weed head woman / Same ol' blues / Tired of waiting / Mercedes woman / Double dealing / I gave my life to the blues
CD ____ **BM 9034**
Black Magic / Dec '96 / ADA / Cadillac / Direct / Hot Shot

Bassey, Shirley

20 OF THE BEST
As long as he needs me / You'll never know / Reach for the stars / Climb ev'ry mountain / I'll get by (as long as I have you) / Tonight / What now my love / What kind of fool am I / I (who have nothing) / My special dream / Gone / Goldfinger / No regrets / Big spender / Something / Fool on the hill / Where do I begin / For all we know / Diamonds are forever / Never never never
CD ____ **CDMFP 6252**
Music For Pleasure / Aug '96 / EMI

60TH ANNIVERSARY CONCERT, THE
CD ____ **ARTFULCD 10**
Artful / Sep '97 / Pinnacle / Total/BMG

ALL BY MYSELF
All by myself / This masquerade / If and when / He's out of my life / New York state of mind / Can you read my mind / Only when I laugh / Solitaire / New York medley / We don't cry out loud / That's what friends are for / Sorry seems to be the hardest word / Greatest love of all / Dio come ti amo
CD ____ **MOCD 001**
More Music / Feb '95 / Sound & Media

BASSEY - THE EMI/UA YEARS 1959-1979 (5CD Set)
'S Wonderful / As long as he needs me / You'll never know / So in love / Reach for the stars / Who are we / I'll get by / Tonight / What now my love / Above all others / It could happen to you / It all depends on you / I who have nothing / Gone / How do you believe / Goldfinger / My child / Seesaw of dreams / It's yourself / Secrets / Stay on the island / Once in a lifetime / Liquidator / Mr. Kiss Kiss Bang Bang / Boy from Ipanema / More / House is not a home / Don't take the lovers from the world / Take away / I've got a song for you / Shirley / Give him your love / We were lovers / Who could love me / Do I look like a fool / Big spender / Dangerous game / La vita / I must know / This is my life / Without a word / If he walked into my life / To give / My love has two faces / Clown town / Does anybody miss me / I'll never fall in love again / (You are) My way of life / Bus that never comes / Fa fa fa (live for today) / Something / Spinning wheel / Yesterday I heard the rain / Sea and sand / What about today / You and I / Light my fire / Yesterday when I was young / Fool on the hill / Where do I begin / Till love touches your life / For the love of him / Vehicle / Diamonds are forever / Way a woman loves / For all we know / Greatest performance of my life / Lost and lonely / Way of love / Day by day / Ballad of the sad young men / If I should love again / Let me be the one / Never never never / Somehow / Going going gone / Make the world a little younger / Everything I own / All that went to waste / I'm not anyone / Jesse / Living / Natalie / If I never sing another song / Can't take my eyes off you / You take my heart away / Come in from the rain / Tomorrow morning / Razzle dazzle / You made me love you / My man / Nature boy / Greatest love of all / Moonraker / Just one of those things / Burn my candle (at both ends) / All the things you are / If I were a bell / Lovely way to spend the evening / Lot of livin' to do / No regrets / Typically English / Fly me to the moon / Please Mr. Brown / I'm a fool to want you / You / Johnny one note / I could have danced all night / Lovely way to spend an evening
CD Set ____ **BASSEY 1**
Premier/EMI / Nov '94 / EMI

BORN TO SING
As I love you / Stormy weather / Love for sale / Birth of the blues / Hands across the sea / There's never been a night / Night and day / My funny valentine / Kiss me honey, honey kiss me / Gypsy in my soul / Crazy rhythm / How about you / Wayward wind / Born to sing the blues
CD ____ **5501852**
Spectrum / Mar '94 / PolyGram

CLASSIC TRACKS
CD ____ **5143472**
Phonogram / Jan '94 / PolyGram

COLLECTION, THE
Does anybody miss me / I'll never fall in love again / Never never no / Picture puzzle / I only miss him / As I love you / This is my life / Who am I / Funny girl / Sunny / I've been loved / Where is tomorrow / Think of me (You are) / My way of life / We / Give me you / It's always 4 am / Hold me, thrill me, kiss me / Now you want to be loved / Medley: Goin' out of my head/You go to my head / Softly as I leave you / Time for us / Joker / I must know / You're gonna hear from me / If you go away / Burn my candle (at both ends) / Shadow of your smile / Kiss me honey, honey kiss me / Impossible dream / Johnny one note / Summer wind / Walking happy / Strangers in the night / Look for me tomorrow (I'll be gone) / Let me sing and I'm happy / On a clear day (you can see forever) / It must be him / All or nothing at all / Dangerous games / I'm glad there is you / That's life / (You are) My way of life / You can have him / Lady is a tramp / You and I / Big spender / Sweet charity
CD Set ____ **CDDL 1239**
Music For Pleasure / Apr '93 / EMI

DEFINITIVE COLLECTION, THE
What now my love / Something / As long as he needs me / As I love you / Big spender / Send in the clowns / I who have nothing / All by myself / This masquerade / If and when / He's out of my life / New York state of mind / Can you read my mind / Only when I laugh / Solitaire / New York, New York / We don't cry out loud / Natalie
CD ____ **MDCD 3**
MMG Video / Jan '94 / TKO Magnum

DIAMONDS (The Best Of Shirley Bassey)
Diamonds are forever / Something / Big spender / I who have nothing / For all we know / Where do I begin / Who can I turn to / Far away / Reach for the stars / Climb every mountain / Goldfinger / Never never never / If you go away / As long as he needs me / With these hands / What now my love / What kind of fool am I / I'll get by / You'll never know / This is my life
CD ____ **CDP 7904692**
Premier/EMI / May '88 / EMI

DIAMONDS ARE FOREVER
CD ____ **PRS 23011**
Personality / Aug '93 / Target/BMG

DIAMONDS ARE FOREVER (3CD Set)
Diamonds are forever / Fly me to the moon / In other words / Nearness of you / You'll never know / Fool on the hill / Domage, domage(too bad, too bad) / For all we know / Ysterday when I was young / Just one of those things / Fools rush in (where angels fear to tread) / Moon river / Don't rain my parade / Sing / Send in the clowns / I don't know how to love him / Ave Maria / Killing

me softly with his sing / Where do I begin (Love story) / Never never never / Party's over / Let there be love / Gone / As long as he needs me / Everything's coming up roses / Day by day / Easy to love / I've got you under my skin / Jesse / Somewhere / Ev'ry time we say goodbye / You'll never walk alone / I get a kick out of you / (I) who have nothing / No regrets / What now my love / Tonight / Something / Light my fire / With these hands / Feel like making love / Lady is a tramp / Alone again (naturally) / There will never be another you / People / On a wonderful day like today / Nobody does it like me / This is my life / Big spender
CD Set SA 872582
Disky / Sep '96 / Disky / THE

FOUR DECADES OF SONG (3CD Set)
Something / As long as he needs me / Goldfinger / With these hands / Don't rain on my parade / In the still of the night / Feelings / You are the sunshine of my life / What are you doing the rest of your life / Cry me a river / You'd better love me / Imagination / All of me / Days of wine and roses / If you love me (hymn a l'amor) / Love is a many splendored thing / As if we never said goodbye / Don't cry for me Argentina / Look of love / Bridge over troubled waters / My way / Funny girl / It's impossible / Breakfast in bed / One less bell to answer / Greatest love of all / You never done it like that / Better off alone / As we fall in love once more / Night moves / Anyone who had a heart / Magic is you / How insensitive / Run on and on and on / I'll be your audience / All in love is fair / Way we were / What we did for love / Emotion / Good bad but beautiful / Where or when / Kiss me honey honey kiss me / Ave Maria / My special dream / Let there be love / I've got you under my skin / In other words (fly me to the moon) / Just one of those things / Secret love / Born to lose / Come back to me / If I were a bell / Something wonderful / He loves me
CD Set CDTRBOX 248
Trio / Oct '96 / EMI

GOLDFINGER
CD PRS 23010
Personality / Aug '93 / Target/BMG

GREATEST HITS COLLECTION
CD ST 5006
Star Collection / Nov '93 / BMG

HER GOLDEN VOICE
CD DC 862012
Disky / Mar '96 / Disky / THE

I AM WHAT I AM
Big spender / Goldfinger / Kiss me honey, honey kiss me / What now my love / Something / As long as he needs me / As I love you / Send in the clowns / I am what I am / I (who have nothing) / Natalie / And I love you so / Never never never / For all we know / This is my life / If you don't understand
CD ANT 003
Tring / Nov '96 / Tring
CD 100132
CMC / May '97 / BMG

I'M IN THE MOOD FOR LOVE
What now my love / Moon river / Fools rush in / No regrets / I wish you love / Liquidator / Nearness of you / This love of mine / Where are you / If love were all / There will never be another you / Days of wine and roses / People / Second time around / Tonight / Strange how love can be / I'm in the mood for love / I get a kick out of you / Angel eyes / To be loved by a man / Hold me tight / I believe in you / Let's start all over again / I'm a fool to want you
CD CC 241
Music For Pleasure / May '89 / EMI

LET ME SING AND I'M HAPPY
Send in the clowns / Don't cry for me Argentina / Can't help falling in love / Spinning wheel / That's life / Until it's time for you to go / On a clear day (You can see forever) / Something / Feel like makin' love / Shadow of your smile / Let me sing and I'm happy / Diamonds are forever / Alone again (naturally) / Killing me softly / Fool on the hill / Yesterday when I was young
CD CDP 7904222
Premier/EMI / May '88 / EMI

LIVE
Goldfinger / Where am I going / I Capricorn / Let me sing and I'm happy / Johnny One Note / For all we know / I'd like to hate myself in the morning / I who have nothing / Day by day / And I love you so / Diamonds are forever / Narration / Big spender / Never never never / You and I / Something / This is my life / Lovely way to spend an evening / Party's over / Lovely way to spend an evening / On a wonderful day like today / I get a kick out of you / Who can I turn to / You'd better love me / Other woman / He loves me / With these hands / Lot of livin' to do / I who have nothing / La Bamba / You can have him / Second time around / Lady is a tramp / Somewhere / Lovely way to spend an evening
CD Set CDDL 1221
Music For Pleasure / Apr '92 / EMI

LOVE ALBUM, THE
Something / What now my love / Where do I begin / Tonight / As long as he needs me / Time after time / As time goes by / With these hands / You'll never know / It must be him / Look of love / You made me love you / Softly as I leave you / I wish you love / Who can I turn to / Party's over / I'll never fall in love again / If you go away / I get a kick out of you / Nearness of you
CD CDMFP 5879
Music For Pleasure / Jan '92 / EMI

POWER OF LOVE, THE
CD 3036400172
Carlton / May '97 / Carlton

SHIRLEY
In the still of the night / Let there be love / All at once (deja) / For every man there's a woman / I'm in the mood for love / So in love / If I were a bell / There will never be another you / Hooray for love / Too late now / I'm shooting high / Every time we say goodbye
CD DORIG 101
EMI / Jul '97 / EMI

SHIRLEY BASSEY
CD DINCD 21
Dino / May '91 / Pinnacle

SHIRLEY BASSEY
CD HM 003
Harmony / Jun '97 / TKO Magnum

SHIRLEY BASSEY - 40 GREAT SONGS
CD DBP 102002
Double Platinum / Nov '93 / Target/BMG

SHIRLEY BASSEY SINGS ANDREW LLOYD WEBBER
Memory / All I ask of you / Starlight Express / Last man in my life / Chanson d'enfance / I don't know how to love him / With one look / Macavity / Don't cry for me Argentina / Tell me on a Sunday / Wishing you were somehow here again / As if we never said goodbye / Memory reprise
CD CDDPR 114
Premier/MFP / Nov '93 / EMI

SHIRLEY BASSEY: THE SINGLES
Something / Where do I begin / Diamonds are forever / Fool on the hill / Make the world a little younger / Big spender / Never never never / When you smile / If you go away / And I love you so / Does anybody miss me / For all we know / Goldfinger / No regrets / I who have nothing / What kind of fool am I
CD CDMFP 6004
Music For Pleasure / Aug '88 / EMI

SHOW MUST GO ON, THE
Slave to the rhythm / You'll see / Every breath you take / Can I touch you there / I'll stand by you / When I need you / All woman / He kills everything / Where is the love / We've got tonight / One day I'll fly away / Hello / Baby come home to / Show must go on
CD 5337122
PolyGram TV / Oct '96 / PolyGram

SINGS THE MOVIES
CD 5293992
PolyGram TV / Oct '95 / PolyGram

SINGS THE MOVIES
Goldfinger / Where do I begin / Tonight / Big spender / Diamonds are forever / As long as he needs me / Lady is a tramp / As time goes by / You'll never walk alone / Climb every mountain / Moon river / Funny girl / Just one of those things / S'Wonderful / You'll never know / More / Liquidator / I don't know how to love him
CD CDMFP 6205
Music For Pleasure / Nov '95 / EMI

SOMETHING
CD RMB 75079
Remember / Apr '95 / Total/BMG

SOMETHING
Diamonds are forever / Something / Strange how love can be / This love of mine / There will never be another you / Hold me tight / Make the world a little younger / When you smile / Does anybody miss me / Fools rush in / People / It must be him / Party's over / Liquidator
CD 16150
Laserlight / Apr '96 / Target/BMG

SONGS FROM THE SHOWS
Moon river / People / Tonight / If love were all / Days of wine and roses / I believe in you / I've never been in love before / Far away / Lady is a tramp / Somewhere / It might as well be Spring / Don't rain on my parade / I get a kick out of you / Just one of those things / As long as he needs me / Where or when / 'S Wonderful / Everything's coming up roses / He loves me / Something wonderful / If ever I would leave you / You'll never walk alone
CD CC 272
Music For Pleasure / Oct '91 / EMI

THIS IS SHIRLEY BASSEY
When you smile / Something / I get a kick out of you / Fly me to the moon / Sing / Lady is a tramp / Don't rain on my parade / Other side of me / I've got you under my skin / On a wonderful day like today / Somewhere / Lot of livin' to do / Once in a lifetime / Nobody does it like me / Goldfinger / As long as he needs me / Just one of those things / I who have nothing / Easy to love / Climb every mountain / Send in the clowns / Every time we say goodbye / Let there be love / What kind of fool am I / Everything's coming up roses / With these hands / Party's over / Tonight / Where do I begin / What now my love / No regrets / Big spender / Diamonds are forever
CD Set CDDL 1140
Music For Pleasure / Oct '88 / EMI

TOUCH OF CLASS, A
Something / As time goes by / With these hands / As long as he needs me / You'll never know / Party's over / Who can I turn to / I wish you love / Softly as I leave you / Tonight / What now my love / It must be him / I'll never fall in love again / If you go away / I get a kick out of you / Nearness of you / (Where do I begin) Love story / Look of love / You made me love you / Time after time
CD TC 865452
Disky / May '97 / Disky / THE

Bassholes

DEAF MIX VOL.3
CD ITR 49CD
In The Red / Jun '97 / Cargo / Greyhound

Bassline Generation

JUNGLE EXPLORERS
CD EFA 127192
Mask / Apr '95 / Vital

Bastaldua, Papi

SONGS OF PARAGUAY
CD VICG 53412
JVC World Library / Mar '96 / ADA / CM / Direct

Bastard

ZING BOOM
CD EFA 610542
Platten Meister / Mar '96 / SRD

Bastards

WORLD BURNS TO DEATH
CD LF 110CD
Lost & Found / Nov '94 / Plastic Head

Bastro

BASTRO DIABLO GUAPO
CD HMS 1322
Homestead / Jul '89 / Cargo / SRD

Bates

PSYCHO JUNIOR
CD SPV 08480702
SPV / Apr '96 / Koch / Plastic Head

Bates, Django

AUTUMN FIRES (Green Shoots)
Autumn leaves / Sweetie / Jetty / Ralf's trip / Is there anyone up there / Hollyhocks / Solitude / Loneliness of being right / Rat king / Dufy / Giant steps / Calm farm (for Paddy) / Infinity in a twinkling
CD 5140142
jMT / Mar '94 / PolyGram

GOOD EVENING...HERE IS THE NEWS (Bates, Django & London Sinfonietta)
CD 4520992
Argo / May '96 / PolyGram

SUMMER FRUITS (And Unrest)
Tightrope / Armchair march / Food for plankton (in detail) / Sad Afrika / Three architects called Gabrielle/Just what I expected / Queen of puddings / Hyphen / Nights at the circus / Discovering metal / Little Petherick / March hare dance
CD 5140082
jMT / Jan '94 / PolyGram

Bates, Martyn

IMAGINATION FEELS LIKE POISON
Mock sun / I can't look for you / Bones of your face / Years of salt / I forget you / God on the tree / Full sail / Flanaghan / Fully bright / Mystery seas / This wayward love / Fantacinni playground / Ellen Massey / Letters to a scattered family / Silvery images / No-one spoke / Mountain tomb
CD ASR 022
Ambivalent Scale / Apr '97 / World Serpent

LETTERS WRITTEN/RETURN OF THE QUIET
CD CDMRED 134
Cherry Red / Oct '96 / Pinnacle

LOVE SMASHED ON A ROCK
CD IR 002CD
Integrity / Jan '90 / SRD / Vital

Bathers

KELVINGROVE BABY
CD MA 22
Marina / Feb '97 / SRD

LAGOON BLUES
CD MAMCD 33962
Marina / Apr '94 / SRD

SUNPOWDER
CD MA 12
Marina / May '95 / SRD

Bathgate, Alec

GOLD LAME
CD FNCD 353
Flying Nun / Oct '96 / RTM/Disc

Bathory

BLOOD FIRE DEATH
Odens ride over Nordland / Golden wall of heaven / Pace 'til death / Dies irae / Fine day to die / Holocaust / For all those who died / Blood fire death
CD BMCD 6664
Black Mark / Oct '94 / Plastic Head

HAMMERHEART
CD BMCD 6665
Black Mark / Oct '94 / Plastic Head

JUBILEUM VOL.1
Rider at the gate of dawn / Crawl to your cross / Sacrifice / Dies irae / Through blood by thunder / You don't move me (I don't give a fuck) / Odens ride over Nordland / Fine day to die / War / Enter the eternal fire / Song to hall up high / Sadist / Under the runes / Equimanthorn / Blood fire death
CD BMCD 6667
Black Mark / Nov '92 / Plastic Head

OCTAGON
CD BMCD 66611
Black Mark / May '95 / Plastic Head

REQUIEM
CD BMCD 666
Black Mark / Nov '94 / Plastic Head

RETURN, THE
Revelation of doom / Total destruction / Born for burning / Wind of mayhem / Bestial lust / Possessed / Rite of darkness / Reap of evil / Son of the damned / Sadist / Return of the darkness and evil
CD BMCD 6662
Black Mark / May '92 / Plastic Head

TWILIGHT OF THE GODS
CD BMCD 6666
Black Mark / '92 / Plastic Head

Batimbos

MAITRES-TAMBOURS DU BURUNDI
Arrivee et salut a l'assistance / Offrande / Appel / Suite de danses rituelles / Suite de danses et d'appels rituels
CD ARN 64016
Arion / '87 / ADA / Discovery

Batin, Abdul Zahir

LIVE AT THE JAZZ CULTURAL
CD CJR 1029CD
Cadence / Sep '95 / Cadillac

Batiste, Alvin

BAYOU MAGIC
CD IN 1069CD
India Navigation / Jan '97 / Discovery / Impetus

Batiste, Milton

MILTON BATISTE
CD BCD 324
GHB / Aug '94 / Jazz Music

MILTON BATISTE & RUE CONTI JAZZ BAND
CD LA 031CD
Lake / Jan '94 / ADA / Cadillac / Direct / Jazz Music / Target/BMG

Batmobile

BAIL IS SET AT SIX MILLION DOLLARS
Kiss me now / Magic word called love / Can't find my way back home / Mystery Street / Calamity man / Shoot shoot / Gorilla rock / Gates of heaven / Girls, girls, girls / Hang on / 100 pounds of trouble / Ace of spades
CD NERCD 035
Nervous / '90 / Nervous / TKO Magnum

Batoh, Masaki

COLLECTED WORKS (Ghost From The Darkened Sea/Kikakubeshi)
CD NS 011
Now Sound / Feb '97 / Cargo

Bators, Stiv

DEAD BOYS, THE
CD 642002
New Rose / May '94 / ADA / Direct / Discovery

DISCONNECTED
CD BCD 4043
Bomp / Feb '94 / Cargo / Greyhound / RTM/Disc / Shellshock/Disc

LAST RACE
CD 7562819
Bond Age / Nov '96 / Direct

Bats

COUCHMASTER
CD ___ FNCD 301
Flying Nun / Oct '95 / RTM/Disc

DADDY'S HIGHWAY
CD ___ FNE 23CD
Flying Nun / Sep '88 / RTM/Disc

FEAR OF GOD
CD ___ R 2832
Rough Trade / Mar '92 / Pinnacle

SILVERBEET
CD ___ FNCD 260
Flying Nun / Sep '93 / RTM/Disc

Battalion Of Saints

DEATH R US
CD ___ T 103CD
Taang / Dec '96 / Cargo

Battery

ONLY THE DIEHARD REMAIN
CD ___ LF 089CD
Lost & Found / May '94 / Plastic Head

TILL THE END
CD ___ LF 216CD
Lost & Found / Mar '96 / Plastic Head

WE WON'T FALL
CD ___ LF 055
Lost & Found / Aug '93 / Plastic Head

Battiato, Franco

SHADOW, LIGHT
L'ombra della luce / Messa arcaica - Kyrie, Gloria, Credo, Sanctus, Agnus Dei / Haiku / Povera patria / Ricerca sul Terzo / Sacre sinfonie del tiemp
CD ___ CDHEMI 3
Hemisphere / Feb '96 / EMI

Battlefield Band

ACROSS THE BORDERS
Miss Sarah MacManus / Appropriate dipstick / Cafe Breton fiddlers welcome to Shetland / Tramps and hawkers / Snow on the hills / Xesus and Felisa / Concert reel / Green mountains / Arran convict / My home town / Kalabakan / Turieadh lain ruaidh / Trimdon grange explosion / Simon Thoumire's jig / Shake a leg / Ril gan ainm / Miss Kate Rusby / Green and the blue / Donnie McGregor / Clumsy lover / Woe be gone / Bubba's reel / Frank's reel / Six days on the road / In and out the harbour / Top tier / Sleepy maggie / Molly Rankin'
CD ___ COMD 2065
Temple / Jan '97 / ADA / CM / Direct / Duncans / Highlander

AFTER HOURS
CD ___ COMD 2001
Temple / Feb '94 / ADA / CM / Direct / Duncans / Highlander

ANTHEM FOR THE COMMON MAN
CD ___ COMD 2008
Temple / Feb '94 / ADA / CM / Direct / Duncans / Highlander

AT THE FRONT
Lady Carmichael / South of the Grampians / Mickie Ainsworth / Bachelor / Ge do theid mi do m'leabradh / Battle of Harlaw / Jenny Nettles / Grays of tongside / Tae the beggin' / Tamosher / Blackbird and the thrush / Moray club / Lang Johnnie More / Brown milkmaid / Dunnottar castle / Maid of Glengarrysdale / Disused railways / Lady Leroy / Stirling castle / Earl of Mansfield
CD ___ TP 56CD
Temple / Aug '94 / ADA / CM / Direct / Duncans / Highlander

BATTLEFIELD BAND
Silver spear / Humours of Tulla / Shipyard apprentice / Crossing the Minch / Minnie Hynd / Glasgow gaelic club / Brisk young lad / Birnie bouzie / Compliments of the band / AA Cameron's strathspey / Scott Skinner's compliments to Dr MacDonald / Bonnie Jean / Paddy Fahey's / Joseph's fancy / Hog's reel / It was a' for our rightful king / Inverness gathering / Marquis of Huntly's strathspey / John MacNeil's reel / Miss Margaret Brown's favourite / Deserts of Tulloch / Cruel brother
CD ___ TP 55CD
Temple / Aug '94 / ADA / CM / Direct / Duncans / Highlander

CELTIC HOTEL
Conway's farewell / Andy Renwick's Ferrett / Short coated Mary / Seacoalers / Return To Kashmagiro / Cuddly with the wooden leg / Jack the can / Rovin' dies hard / Muineira sul sacrato della chiesa / Hyoy Frwynen / E kostez an hebont / Celtic Hotel / Left handed fiddler / Floating crowbar / Ships are sailing / Lucy Campbell / June apple / We work the black seam / Tail o' the bank / Cran Tara / Madadh Ruadh
CD ___ COMD 2002
Temple / Feb '94 / ADA / CM / Direct / Duncans / Highlander

FAREWELL TO NOVA SCOTIA
CD ___ CD 802
Escalibur / May '96 / ADA / Discovery / Roots

HOME GROUND
CD ___ COMD 034
Temple / Feb '94 / ADA / CM / Direct / Duncans / Highlander

HOME IS WHERE THE VAN IS
CD ___ COMD 2006
Temple / Feb '94 / ADA / CM / Direct / Duncans / Highlander

NEW SPRING
CD ___ COMD 2045
Temple / Feb '94 / ADA / CM / Direct / Duncans / Highlander

ON THE RISE
CD ___ COMD 2009
Temple / Feb '94 / ADA / CM / Direct / Duncans / Highlander

OPENING MOVES
Silver spear/Humours of Tulla / Shipyard apprentice / Cruel brother / Ge do theid mi do m'leabradh / Battle of Harlaw / Jenny Nettles/Grays of tongside / Tae the beggin / Tamosher / Blackbird and the thrush/ Moray club / Lang Johnnie More / Brown milkmaid/Dunnottar castle / Maid of Glengarrysdale / Disused railway / Lady Leroy / Miss Drummond of Perth/Fiddler's joy / Traditional reel/Shetland fiddler / My last farewell to stirling/Cuidich'n right / I hae laid a herrin' in salt/My wife's a wanton wee thing / Banks of the allan / Battler of Falkirk Muir / Joe McGann's fiddle/Centre's bonnet
CD ___ TSCD 468
Topic / Sep '93 / ADA / CM / Direct

QUIET DAYS
CD ___ COMD 2050
Temple / Feb '94 / ADA / CM / Direct / Duncans / Highlander

STAND EASY/PREVIEW
CD ___ COMD 2052
Temple / Feb '94 / ADA / CM / Direct / Duncans / Highlander

THERE'S A BUZZ
CD ___ COMD 2007
Temple / Feb '94 / ADA / CM / Direct / Duncans / Highlander

Bauer, Konrad

THREE WHEELS FOUR DIRECTIONS (Bauer, Konrad Trio)
CD ___ VICTOCD 023
Victo / Nov '94 / Harmonia Mundi / ReR Megacorp

TORONTO TONE
CD ___ VICTOCD 017
Victo / Nov '94 / Harmonia Mundi / ReR Megacorp

Bauer, Stefan

BEST OF TWO WORLDS, THE (CD/CD-Rom)
Kayak / Don't take the 'A' train / Askale tulem / Look up / Cafe Orchidee / My favourite things / Priere / Kino / Kwiegesparach / I don't take the 'A' train again
CD ___ JL 111472
Jazz Line / Feb '97 / Vital/SAM

Bauer, Uschi

YODEL HITS FROM USCHI BAUER
CD ___ 399382
Koch / Sep '92 / Koch

Bauge, Andre

L'INOUBLIABLE
CD ___ UCD 19022
Forlane / Jun '95 / Target/BMG

Bauhaus

BAUHAUS 1979-1983
Kick in the eye / Hollow hills / In fear of fear / Ziggy Stardust / Silent hedges / Lagartija Nick / Third uncle / Spirit / All we ever wanted was everything / She's in parties / Sanity assassin / Crowds / Double dare / In the flat field / Stigmata martyr / Bela Lugosi's dead / Telegram Sam / St. Vitus dance / Spy in the cab / Terror couple kill colonel / Passions of lovers / Mask
CD ___ BEGA 64CD
Beggars Banquet / Feb '88 / RTM/Disc / Warner Music

BAUHAUS 1979-1983 VOL.2
CD ___ BEGA 64CD2
Beggars Banquet / Feb '88 / RTM/Disc / Warner Music

BELA (A Tribute To Bauhaus) (Various Artists)
CD ___ DOP 51
Doppelganger / Jul '97 / Total/BMG

BURNING FROM THE INSIDE
She's in parties / Antonin artaud / Wasp / King volcano / Who killed Mr. Moonlight / Slice of life / Honeymoon croon / Kingdom's coming / Burning from the inside / Hope / Lagartija Nick / Here's the dub / Departure / Sanity assassin
CD ___ BEGA 45CD
Beggars Banquet / Feb '88 / RTM/Disc / Warner Music
CD ___ BBL 45 CD
Lowdown/Beggars Banquet / Sep '88 / RTM/Disc / Warner Music

IN THE FLAT FIELD
CD ___ CAD 13CD
4AD / Apr '88 / RTM/Disc

MASK
Hair of the dog / Passion of lovers / Of lilies and remains / Hollow hills / Dancing / Kick in the eye / Muscle in plastic / In fear of fear / Man with the X-ray eyes / Mask
CD ___ BBL 29CD
Lowdown/Beggars Banquet / Oct '88 / RTM/Disc / Warner Music

PRESS THE EJECT AND GIVE ME THE TAPE
In the flat field / Rosegarden funeral of sores / Dancing / Man with the X-ray eyes / Bela Lugosi's dead / Spy in the cab / Kick in the eye / In fear of fear / Hollow hills / Stigmata martyr / Dark entries
CD ___ BBL 38CD
Lowdown/Beggars Banquet / '89 / RTM/ Disc / Warner Music

SINGLES 1981-1983
Passion of lovers / Kick in the eye / Spirit / Ziggy Stardust / Lagartija Nick / She's in parties
CD ___ BBP 4CD
Beggars Banquet / Dec '88 / RTM/Disc / Warner Music

SKY'S GONE OUT, THE
Third uncle / Silent hedges / In the night / Swing the heartache / Spirit / Three shadows (part 1) / Three shadows (part 2) / Three shadows (part 3) / All we ever wanted was everything / Exquisite corpse
CD ___ BBL 42 CD
Lowdown/Beggars Banquet / '89 / RTM/ Disc / Warner Music

SWING THE HEARTACHE
Hair of the dog / Telegram Sam / Double dare / Terror couple kill colonel / Ziggy Stardust / Third uncle / Silent hedges / Three shadows (pt. 2) / Party of the first part / Poison pen / Departure / Nightime / She's in parties / God in an alcove / In the flat field / In fear of fear / Swing the heartache / St. Vitus dance
CD ___ BEGA 103CD
Beggars Banquet / Jul '89 / RTM/Disc / Warner Music

TRIBUTE TO BAUHAUS (Various Artists)
CD ___ CLEO 9681CD
Cleopatra / Mar '96 / Cargo / Greyhound / Plastic Head / RTM/Disc / SRD

Baumann, Agnenta

TIME FOR LOVE, A
CD ___ TMCD 006
Touche / May '97 / Cadillac

Baumann, Peter

PHASE BY PHASE
Repeat repeat / Daytime logic / This day / Meridian moorland / Meadow of infinity (Part 1) / Meadow of infinity (part 2) / Romance / Home sweet home / MAN Series two / Bicentennial presentation / Phase by phase / White bench and black bench / Biking up the strand / Dance at dawn
CD ___ CDOVD 464
Virgin / Jan '96 / EMI

Bauza, Mario

944 COLUMBUS (Bauza, Mario & His Afro-Cuban Jazz Orchestra)
CD ___ MES 158282
Messidor / Apr '94 / ADA / Koch

MY TIME IS NOW (Bauza, Mario & His Afro-Cuban Jazz Orchestra)
CD ___ MES 158252
Messidor / Jun '93 / ADA / Koch

TANGA
CD ___ MES 158192
Messidor / Apr '96 / ADA / Koch

Bawl

YEAR ZERO
Approaching zero / Older and older / My spine hurts / Beyond safe ways / Mistake / Shallow / Sticky rock / Fake it / Ex-boyfriend / Mechanic from Rhyll / Girls = songs / Unfinished / Some people need others / He's all that's great about pop
CD ___ DEPAD 005
Dependent / Sep '96 / PolyGram / Vital

Baxter, Blake

H FACTOR, THE
CD ___ EFA 122952
Disko B / Jun '97 / SRD

VAULT, THE
CD ___ EFA 122762
Tresor / Oct '95 / 3mv/BMG / Prime / SRD

Baxter, Les

BY POPULAR REQUEST
CD ___ BA 0014
Bacchus Archives / Dec '96 / Cargo / Plastic Head

COLOURS OF BRAZIL/AFRICAN BLUE
Felicidade / Canta de ossanha / Balan samba / Day of the roses / Man and a woman / Who will buy / Somewhere in the hills / Goin' out of my head / Insteza / Berimbau / Laia ladaia / Banda / Born free / Yellow sun / Flame tree / Zebra / Dark river / Topaz / Tree of life / Girl of Uganda / Magenta mountain / Johannesburg blues / Jalaba / Azure sands Kalahari
CD ___ GNPD 2036
GNP Crescendo / Oct '95 / ZYX

EXOTIC MOODS OF LES BAXTER, THE (2CD Set)
Quiet village / Jungalero / Temple of gold / Hong Kong cable car / Oasis of Dakhla / Taboo / Amazon falls / Jungle flower / Ancient galleon / Zambezi / Tahiti / Summer night at sea / Congo trail / Acapulco / Stone God / Voodoo dreams / Mozambique / City of veils / Bacoa / Mombassa after midnight / Bom bom/Mood tattooed / Simba / High priest of the Aztecs/Pyramids of the sun / Harem silks from Bombay / Papagayo / Jungle river boat / Temptation / Pantan / Lost City / Pool of love / Busy port / Spice Islands sea birds / Go chango / Nightingale / Love dance / Safari / Sunken City / Tehran / Blue jungle / Left arm of Buddha / Procesion of the princes
CD Set ___ PRDCD 5
Premier/EMI / Aug '96 / EMI

Bay B Kane

GUARDIAN OF RUFF, THE
CD ___ WHSCD 1
Whitehouse / Jan '95 / Grapevine/ PolyGram / Jet Star / Mo's Music Machine / Target/BMG

HAVE A BREAK
CD ___ WHSCD 3
Whitehouse / Nov '95 / Grapevine/ PolyGram / Jet Star / Mo's Music Machine / Target/BMG

Bay City Rollers

ABSOLUTE ROLLERS
(Dancing) on a Saturday night / Shang-a-lang / Remember (sha la la) / Bye bye baby / I only want to be with you / All of me love all of you / Give a little love / Summer love sensation / Rebel rebel / Money honey / Keep on dancing / Love me like I love you / Once upon a star / Be my baby / You made me believe in magic / Way I feel tonight / Another rainy day in New York City / It's a game / There goes my baby / Rock 'n' roll love letter / Bay City Rollers megamix
CD ___ 74321265752
Arista / Aug '95 / BMG

BAY CITY ROLLERS
CD ___ 295588
Ariola Express / Dec '92 / BMG

BYE BYE BABY
Keep on dancing / Remember / Shang a lang / Summerlove sensation / Bye bye baby / Give a little love / Money honey / Love me like I love you / I only wanna be with you / You made me believe in magic / Rock 'n' roll love letter
CD ___ QED 106
Tring / Nov '96 / Tring

GREATEST HITS
CD ___ JHD 025
Tring / Jun '92 / Tring

GREATEST HITS
Remember (sha la la) / Give a little love / Shang a lang / Yesterday's hero / I only wanna be with you / Summerlove sensation / Bye bye baby / It's a game / Saturday night / Rock 'n' roll love letter / You made me believe in magic
CD ___ RM 1551
BR Music / Apr '97 / Target/BMG

VERY BEST OF THE BAY CITY ROLLERS, THE
Remember (sha la la) / Give a little love / Shang-a-lang / Yesterday's hero / I only wanna be with you / Summer love sensation / Bye bye baby / It's a crime / Saturday night / Rock 'n' roll letter / You made me believe in magic / Megamix
CD ___ 100602
CMC / May '97 / BMG

Bay Laurel

UNDER A CLOUDED SKY
CD ___ NOX 003CD
Noxious / May '95 / Plastic Head

Bayer Sager, Carole

CAROLE BAYER SAGER
Come in from the rain / Until the next time / Don't wish too hard / Sweet alibis / Aces / I'd rather leave while I'm in love / Steal away again / You're moving out today / Shy as a violet / Home to myself

CD 7559606172
Elektra / Jan '96 / Warner Music

Bayete

AFRICA UNITE
Mmalo-we / Africa unite / Amasoka / Ungayingeni / Mmangwane / Inkinobho / Umkhaya-lo / Umbugwala / Amadlozi / Jabula time
CD CIDM 1119
Mango / Mar '97 / PolyGram / Vital

Baylor, Helen

LOOK A LITTLE
CD DAYCD 4215
Nelson Word / May '93 / Nelson Word

Bayou Gumbo

BALD ON THE BAYOU
CD BEANDOG 47CD
Beandog / May '93 / ADA

Bazooka

BLOWHOLE
CD SST 308CD
SST / Oct '94 / Plastic Head

CIGARS, OYSTERS AND BOOZE
CD SST 325CD
SST / Jan '96 / Plastic Head

PERFECTLY SQUARE
CD SST 296CD
SST / May '93 / Plastic Head

Bazzle, Germaine

NEW NEW ORLEANS MUSIC VOL.3 (Bazzle, Germaine & Friends)
CD ROUCD 2067
Rounder / '88 / ADA / CM / Direct

BB & The Blues Shacks

FEELIN' FINE TODAY
CD CDST 01
Stumble / Nov '95 / Direct

BBC Big Band

AGE OF SWING VOL.1, THE
CD EMPRBX 003
Empress / Sep '94 / Koch

AGE OF SWING VOL.2, THE
Moonlight sonata / South Rampart Street parade / King Porter stomp / Little brown jug / Solitude / Eager beaver / Serenade in blue / I know why / On the Alamo / Hornet / Listen to my music / Wrappin' it up the lindy / Chattanooga choo choo / Caravan / Apple honey / I'm getting sentimental over you / Harlem nocturne / Leave us leap / You made me love you / Boogie woogie Maxine
CD EMPRCD 534
Emporio / Sep '94 / Disc

AGE OF SWING VOL.3, THE
Down south camp meeting / Don't be that way / Anvil chorus / St. Louis blues march / Mood indigo / Intermission riff / Jersey bounce / Hot toddy / 'S wonderful / Oh lady be good / Chloe / Leap frog / Pennysylvania 6-5000 / Opus no.1 / I got it bad and that ain't good / String of pearls / Sweet Georgia Brown / I'll never smile again / Stardreams / I get a kick out of you / Long John Silver
CD EMPRCD 535
Emporio / Sep '94 / Disc

AGE OF SWING VOL.4, THE
Moonlight serenade / After you've gone / Pompton turnpike / On the sunny side of the street / Do nothin' 'til you hear from me / At last / Flying home / Cotton tail / Body soul / Painted rhythm / Tuxedo junction / Take the 'A' train / Swanee river / Don't sit under the apple tree / Sophisticated lady / Swingin' the blues / Memories of you / I can't get started / Poor Butterfly / Song of the Volga boatmen / Woodchoppers ball
CD EMPRCD 536
Emporio / Sep '94 / Disc

BBC BIG BAND
Don't count / Song of the Volga boatmen / Street scene / King Porter stomp / Camptown races / Ol' man river / Herman's habit / Crescendo in blue / Alfresco / Say it isn't so / Opus in pastel / Magic time
CD RBBCD 001
Radio Big Band / Feb '95 / New Note/ Pinnacle

CITY LIFE
Strike up the band / I still care about us / I've got it bad, and that ain't good / But not for me / Singer / I let a song go out of my heart / Cotton tail / Declaration of love / Drop me off in Harlem / When my dreamboat comes home / I put a spell on you / City life / Blues and me / It don't mean a thing if it ain't got that swing
CD RBBCD 003
Radio Big Band / Nov '93 / New Note/ Pinnacle

SHOWSTOPPERS
CD BBB 004
BBC Big Band / Nov '96 / Jazz Music

BBE

EARLY WORKS
CD ZYX 204342
ZYX / May '97 / ZYX

BBM

AROUND THE NEXT DREAM
Waiting in the wings / City of gold / Where in the world / Can't fool the blues / High cost of living / Glory days / Why does love (Have to go wrong) / Naked flame / I wonder (Why are you so mean to me) / Wrong side of town
CD CDV 2745
Virgin / Jun '94 / EMI

BC Kid

STOP THOSE MF'S
CD EFA 008772
Shockwave / Jun '96 / SRD

Be Sharp

NIGHT BY NIGHT
CD RMCCD 0186
Red Steel / Aug '96 / Pinnacle

PIER PRESSURE
CD RMCCD 0184
Red Steel / Sep '96 / Pinnacle

PLAY THIS
CD RMCCD 0185
Red Steel / Aug '96 / Pinnacle

Be-Bop Deluxe

AIR AGE (Be-Bop Deluxe Anthology/ 2CD Set)
Axe victim / Love with the madman / Sister seagull / Heavenly homes / Ships in the night / Twilight capers / Kiss of light / Crying to the sky / Sleep that burns / Life in the air age / Electrical language / Panic in the world / Maid in heaven / Between the worlds / Blazing apostles / Lovers are mortal / Down on terminal street / Darkness (l'immoraliste) / Adventures in a Yorkshire landscape / Night creatures / Music in dreamland / Jean Cocteau / Beauty secrets / Life in the air age / Speed of the wind / Modern music / Dancing in the moonlight / Honeymoon on mars / Lost in the neon world / Dance of the Uncle Sam humanoids / Modern music (reprise) / Fair exchange / Autosexual / New mysteries / Surreal estate / Islands of the dead / Visions of endless hopes / Bird charmers destiny / Gold at the end of my rainbow
CD Set CDEM 1602
Premier/EMI / Feb '97 / EMI

AXE VICTIM
Axe victim / Love is swift arrows / Jet silver and the dolls of venus / Third floor heaven / Night creature / Rocket cathedrals / Adventures in a Yorkshire landscape / Jets at dawn / No trains to heaven / Darkness (L'immoraliste) / Piece of mine (live) / Mill Street junction / Adventures in a Yorkshire landscape (live)
CD CDP 7947262
Premier/EMI / Feb '91 / EMI

LIVE - IN THE AIR-AGE
Life in the air age / Ships in the night / Piece of mind / Fair exchange / Mill Street junction / Adventures in a Yorkshire landscape / Blazing apostles / Shine / Sister seagull / Maid in heaven
CD CDP 7947322
Premier/EMI / Feb '91 / EMI

RAIDING THE DIVINE ARCHIVES (Best Of Be-Bop Deluxe)
Jet Silver and the Dolls of Venus / Adventures in a Yorkshire landscape / Maid in Heaven / Ships in the night / Life in the air age / Kiss of light / Sister Seagull / Modern music / Japan / Panic in the world / Bring back the spark / Forbidden lovers / Electrical Language / Fair exchange / Sleep that burns / Between the worlds / Music in dreamland
CD CDP 7941582
Premier/EMI / Apr '90 / EMI

SUNBURST FINISH
Fair exchange / Heavenly homes / Ships in the night / Crying to the sky / Sleep that burns / Beauty secrets / Life in the air age / Like an old blues / Crystal gazing / Blazing apostles / Shine / Speed of the wind / Blue as a jewel
CD CDP 7947272
Premier/EMI / Feb '91 / EMI

Beach Boys

20 GOLDEN GREATS: BEACH BOYS
Surfin' USA / Fun, fun, fun / I get around / Don't worry baby / Little deuce coupe / When I grow up (to be a man) / Help me Rhonda / California girls / Barbara Ann / Sloop John B / You're so good to me / God only knows / Wouldn't it be nice / Good vibrations / Then I kissed her / Heroes and villains / Darlin' / Do it again / I can hear music / I break away
CD CDP 7467382
Capitol / Nov '87 / EMI

20 GREAT LOVE SONGS
CD LS 863072
Disky / Nov '96 / Disky / THE

ALL SUMMER LONG
Good vibrations / Help me Rhonda / Surfin' USA / California girls / I get around / Surfin' safari / Surfer girl / Catch a wave / Warmth of the sun / Be true to your school / Little deuce coupe / In my room / Shut down fun, fun, fun / Girls on the beach / Wendy / Let him run wild / Don't worry baby / Girl don't tell me / You're so good to me / All summer long
CD DC 878682
Disky / Mar '97 / Disky / THE

BEACH BOYS TODAY/SUMMER DAYS AND SUMMER NIGHTS
Do you wanna dance / Don't hurt my little sister / Help me Rhonda / Please let me wonder / Kiss me baby / In the back of my mind / Girl from New York City / Then I kissed her / Girl don't tell me / Let him run wild / Summer means new love / And your dreams come true / I'm so young (alt. take) / Graduation day / Good to my baby / When I grow up (to be a man) / Dance, dance, dance / I'm so young / She knows me too well / Bull session with Big Daddy / Amusement Parks USA / Salt Lake City / California girls / You're so good to me / I'm bugged at my ole man / Little girl I once knew / Let him run wild (alternate take) / Help me Rhonda (LP version) / Dance, dance, dance (alt. take)
CD CDP 7936942
Capitol / Jul '90 / EMI

BEACH BOYS/JAN & DEAN (Beach Boys/Jan & Dean)
CD CD 115
Timeless Treasures / Oct '94 / THE

BEST OF THE BEACH BOYS, THE (2CD Set)
California girls / Surfin' USA / Little deuce coupe / Fun, fun, fun / Surfer girl / I get around / Girls on the beach / Don't worry baby / When I grow up (to be a man) / All summer long / Wendy / Do you wanna dance / Dance, dance, dance / In my room / Help me Rhonda / Then I kissed her / Little girl I once knew / Barbara Ann / Sloop John B / You're so good to me / Caroline no / God only knows / Wouldn't it be nice / Heroes and villains / Good vibrations / Darlin' / Wild honey / Friends / Do it again / Blue birds over the mountain / I can hear music / Break away / Cotton fields / Forever / Tears in the morning / Disney girls / Surf's up / Sail on sailor / Rock 'n' roll music / Here comes the night / Lady Lynda / Sumahama / California dreamin' / Kokomo
CD Set CDESTVD 3
Capitol / Jun '95 / EMI

CHRISTMAS ALBUM
Little Saint Nick / Man with all the toys / Santa's beard / Merry Christmas baby / Christmas day / Frosty the snowman / We three kings of Orient are / Blue Christmas / Santa Claus is coming to town / White Christmas / I'll be home for Christmas / Auld Lang Syne
CD CDMFP 6150
Music For Pleasure / Oct '94 / EMI

ENDLESS SUMMER
Surfin' safari / Surfer girl / Catch a wave / Warmth of the sun / Surfin' USA / Be true to your school / Little deuce coupe / In my room / Shut down / Fun, fun, fun / I get around / Girls on the beach / Wendy / Let him run wild / Don't worry baby / California girls / Girl don't tell me / Help me Rhonda / You're so good to me / All summer long / Good vibrations
CD CDMFP 50528
Music For Pleasure / Jul '91 / EMI

FRIENDS/20-20
Meant for you / Friends / Wake the world / Be here in the morning / When a man needs a woman / Passing by / Anna Lee, the healer / Little bird / Be still / Busy doing nothing / Diamond head / Transcendental meditation / Do it again / I can hear music / Bluebirds over the mountain / Be with me / All I want to do / Nearest faraway place / Cotton fields / I went to sleep / Time to get alone / Never learn not to love / Our prayer / Cabinessence / Breakaway / Celebrate the news / We're together again / Walk on by / Old folks at home/Ol' man river
CD CDP 7936972
Capitol / Sep '90 / EMI

FUN FUN FUN
CD 15164
Laserlight / Aug '91 / Target/BMG

GOOD VIBRATIONS - 30 YEARS OF THE BEACH BOYS (5CD Set)
Surfin' USA (demo) / Little surfer girl / Surfin' (rehearsal) / Surfin' / Their hearts were full of spring (demo) / Surfin' safari / 409 / Punchline (instrumental) / Surfin' USA / Shut down / Surfer girl / Little deuce coupe / In my room / Catch a wave / Surfer moon / Be true to your school / Spirit of America / Little saint Nick (45RPM) / Things we did last summer / Fun, fun, fun / Don't worry baby / Why do fools fall in love / Warmth of the sun / I get around / All summer long / Little Honda / Wendy / Don't back down / Do you wanna dance / When I grow up to be a man / dance, dance, dance / Please let me wonder / She knows me too well / Radio station jingles/Honda 55 / Concert promo/hushabye (live) / California girls / Help me Rhonda / Then I kissed her / And your dreams come true / Little girl I once knew (45 version) / Barbara Ann (45 version) / Ruby baby (party outtake) / Koma (radio promo spot) / Sloop John B / Wouldn't it be nice / You still believe in me / God only knows / Hang on to your ego (alternative version) / I just wasn't made for these times / Pet sounds / Caroline no / Good vibrations (45 version) / Our prayer / Heroes and villains / Heroes and villains (sections) / Wonderful / Cabinessence / Wind chimes / Heroes and villains (intro) / Do you like worms / Vegetables / I love to say da da / Surf's up / With me tonight / Heroes and villains (45 version) / Darlin' / Wild honey / Let the wind blow / Can't wait too long / Cool cool water / Meant for you / Friends / Little bird / Busy doin' nothin' / Do it again / I can hear music / I went to sleep / Time to get alone / Breakaway / Cotton fields / San Miguel / Games two can play / I just got my pay / This whole world / Add some music / Forever / Our sweet love / HELP is on the way / 4th of July / Long promised road / Disney girls / Till I die / Sail on sailor / California / Trader / Funky pretty / Fairy tale music / You need a mess of help to stand alone / Marcella / All this is that / Rock 'n' roll music / It's over now / It's OK / Had to phone ya / That same song / Still I dream of it / Let us go on this way / Night was so young / I'll bet he's nice / Airplane / Come go with me / Our team / Baby blue / Good timin' / Goin' on / Getcha back / Kokomo / In my room (demo) / Radio spot / I get around (track) / Radio spot / Dance, dance, dance (track) / Hang on to your ego (tracking session) / God only knows (training session) / Good vibrations (sessions) / Heroes and villains (track) / Cabinessence (track) / Surf's up (track) / Radio spot / All summer long (vocals) / Wendy (vocals) / Hush-a-bye (vocals) / When I grow up to be a man (vocals) / Wouldn't it be nice (vocals) / California girls (vocals) / Radio spot / Concert intro/surfin' USA (live 1964) / Surfer girl (live 1964) / Be true to your school (live 1964) / Good vibrations (live 1966) / Surfer girl (live in Hawaii rehearsals 1967) / Blue birds over the mountain / Tears in the morning / Here comes the night / Lady Lynda / Sumahama
CD Set CDS 7812942
Capitol / Oct '93 / EMI

I LOVE YOU
Good vibrations / Then I kissed her / God only knows / Darlin' / Help me Rhonda / All summer long / Wendy / Don't worry baby / You're so good to me / Why do fools fall in love / I can hear music / Wouldn't it be nice / Surfer girl / Devoted to you / I'm so young / There's no other (like my baby) / She knows me too well / Good to be my baby / Please let me wonder / I was made to love her
CD CDMFP 5988
Music For Pleasure / Jun '93 / EMI

PET SOUNDS
Caroline no / Wouldn't it be nice / You still believe in me / That's not me / Don't talk / I'm waiting for the day / Let's go away for awhile / Sloop John B / God only knows / I know there's an answer / Here today / I just wasn't made for these times / Pet sounds / Hang on to your ego / Trombone dixie
CD CDFA 3298
Fame / Nov '93 / EMI

PET SOUNDS SESSIONS (4CD Set)
CD Set PRDDCD 2
Premier/EMI / May '96 / EMI

SMILEY SMILE/WILD HONEY
Heroes and villains / Vegetables / Fall breaks and back to winter / She's goin' bald / Little pad / Good vibrations / With me tonight / Wind chimes / Gettin' hungry / Wonderful / Whistle in / Wild honey / Aren't you glad / I was made to love her / Country air / Thing or two / Darlin' / I'd love just once to see you / Here comes the night / Let the wind blow / How she boogaloed it / Mama says / Heroes and villains (alt. take) / Good vibrations (various sessions) / Good vibrations (early take) / You're welcome / Their hearts were full of spring / Can't wait too long
CD CDP 7936962
Capitol / Jul '90 / EMI

SUMMER DREAMS
I get around / Surfin' USA / In my room / Fun, fun, fun / Little deuce coupe / Warmth of the sun / Surfin' safari / Help me Rhonda / Good vibrations / Sloop John B / You're so good to me / God only knows / Then I kissed her / Wouldn't it be nice / Heroes and villains / Wild honey / California girls / Don't worry baby / All summer long / Wendy / When I grow up (to be a man) / Dance, dance, dance / Little girl I once knew / Barbara Ann / Do it again / Friends / Darlin' / Bluebirds over the mountain / I can hear music / Breakaway / Cotton fields / California dreamin'
CD CDP 7946202
Capitol / Jun '90 / EMI

SUMMER IN PARADISE
Hot fun in the summertime / Surfin' / Summer of love / Island fever / Still surfin' / Slow

summer dancin' (One summer night) / Strange things happen / Remember / Walking in the sand / Lahaina Aloha / Under the boardwalk / Summer in paradise / Forever
CD CDFA 3321
Fame / Apr '95 / EMI

SURFIN' BACK TO BACK (Beach Boys/ Jan & Dean)
Surfin' safari: *Beach Boys* / Surfin': *Beach Boys* / Judy: *Beach Boys* / Surfer girl: *Beach Boys* / Beach boy stomp: *Beach Boys* / Barbie: *Beach Boys* / Luau: *Beach Boys* / What is a young girl made of: *Beach Boys* / Surf city: *Jan & Dean* / Ride the wild surf: *Jan & Dean* / Baby talk: *Jan & Dean* / Help me Rhonda: *Jan & Dean* / I get around: *Jan & Dean* / Fun fun fun: *Jan & Dean* / Sidewalk surfin': *Jan & Dean* / Cindy: *Jan & Dean*
CD ECD 3214
K-Tel / Mar '95 / K-Tel

TODAY/SUMMER DAYS AND SUMMER NIGHTS/SMILEY SMILE (The Originals/ 3CD Set)
Do you wanna dance / Good to my baby / Don't hurt my little sister / When I grow up (to be a man) / Help me Rhonda / Dance, dance, dance / Please let me wonder / I'm so young / Kiss me baby / She knows me too well / In the back of my mind / She knew me too well / Girl from New York City / Amusement parks USA / Then I kissed her / Salt Lake City / Girl don't tell me / Help me Rhonda / California girls / Let him run wild / You're so good to me / Summer means new love / I'm bugged at my ol' man / Your dream comes true / Heroes and villains / Vegetables / Fall breaks and back to winter (W Woodpecker symphony) / She's goin' bald / Little pad / Good vibrations / With me tonight / Wind chimes / Gettin' hungry / Wonderful / Whistle in
CD Set CDOMB 018
EMI / Mar '97 / EMI

Beach Buddha

GILDING THE LILY
CD AQUACD 3
Aquarius / Feb '97 / Arabesque / Prime

Beacon Street Union

EYES OF THE BEACON STREET UNION, THE/THE CLOWN DIED IN MARGI
CD 3497
Head / Jun '97 / Greyhound

Beaker, Norman

INTO THE BLUES (Beaker, Norman Band)
CD JSPCD 230
JSP / Oct '89 / ADA / Cadillac / Direct / Hot Shot / Target/BMG

Beamer, Kapono

PARADISE FOUND
CD ISCD 117
Intersound / Oct '91 / Jazz Music

Beamer, Keola

WOODEN BOAT
CD DCT 38024CD
Dancing Cat / Mar '96 / ADA

Bear

BEAR TRACKS
CD BGR 010
BGR / Mar '95 / Plastic Head

Bear, Keith

ECHOES OF THE UPPER MISSOURI
CD SPALAX 14962
Spalax / Oct '96 / ADA / Cargo / Direct / Discovery / Greyhound

Beard, Chris

BAR WALKIN'
You ain't all that / Barwalkin' / Everything man / I'm your man / All night long / Caught up / I had a dream / Get yo self a life / Delivery man / It's about time / Playing the blues for a living / I need it all
CD JSPCD 288
JSP / Jul '97 / ADA / Cadillac / Direct / Hot Shot / Target/BMG

Beard, Jim

LOST AT THE CARNIVAL
CD LIP 890272
Lipstick / May '95 / Vital/SAM

SONG OF THE SUN
Camieff / Parsley trees / Songs of the sun / Holodeck waltz / Diana / Baker's annex / Haydel Bay / Lucky charms / Long bashels / Sweet bumps / Crossing troll bridge
CD ESJCD 231
Essential Jazz / Oct '94 / BMG

TRULY
Big pants / Tandoori taxi / Gone was, gone will be / In all her finery / Social climate / Side two / Hand to hand / Gonna tell on you / Major Darlings' impossible halftime show
CD ESC 036522
Escapade / Apr '97 / New Note/Pinnacle

Beasley, Walter

TONIGHT WE LOVE
CD SHCD 5032
Shanachie / May '97 / ADA / Greensleeves / Koch

Beastiality

DEHYDRATED SPLIT
CD METALAGE 1CD
Clay / Apr '94 / Cargo

Beastie Boys

CHECK YOUR HEAD
Jimmy James / Funky boss / Pass the mic / Gratitude / Lighten up / Finger lickin' good / So what'cha want / Biz Vs. the nuge / Time for livin' / Something's got to give / Blue nun / Stand together / Pow / Maestro / Groove Holmes / Live at PJ's / Mark on the bus / Professor Booty / In 3's / Mamaste
CD CDP 7989382
Grand Royal / Apr '92 / EMI

DEF AND DUMB (Interview)
CD DIST 005
Disturbed / Mar '96 / Total/BMG

ILL COMMUNICATION
Sure shot / Tough guy / B boys makin' with the freak freak / Bobo on the corner / Root down / Sabotage / Get it together / Sabrosa / Update / Futterman's rule / Alright hear this / Eugene's lament / Flute loop / Do it / Ricky's theme / Heart attack man / Scoop / Shamballa / Bodhisattva vow / Transitions
CD CDEST 2229
Grand Royal / May '94 / EMI

IN SOUND FROM WAY OUT, THE
Groove Holmes / Sabrosa / Namaste / Pow / Son of Neckbone / In 3's / Eugene's lament / Bobo on the corner / Shambala / Lighten up / Ricky's theme / Transition / Drinkin' wine
CD CDEST 2281
Grand Royal / Apr '96 / EMI

LICENSED TO ILL
Rhymin and stealin' / New style / She's crafty / Posse in effect / Slow ride / Girls / (You gotta) Fight for your right (to party) / No sleep till Brooklyn / Paul Revere / Hold it, now hit it / Brass monkey / Slow and low / Time to get ill
CD 5273512
Def Jam / Jul '95 / PolyGram

PAUL'S BOUTIQUE
To all the girls / Shake your rump / Johnny Ryall / Egg man / High plains drifter / Sounds of science / Three minute rule / Hey ladies / Five piece chicken dinner / Looking down the barrel of a gun / Car thief / What comes around / Shadrach / Ask for Janice / B boy bouillabaisse
CD CDP 7917432
Grand Royal / May '92 / EMI

ROOT DOWN
Root down / Root down / Root down / Time to get ill / Heart attackman / Maestro / Sabrosa / Fluteloop / Time for livin' / Something's got to give
CD CDEST 2262
Grand Royal / May '95 / EMI

SOME OLD BULLSHIT
Egg raid on mojo (demo) / Beastie Boys / Transit cop / Jimi / Holy snappers / Riot fight / Ode to... / Michelle's farm / Egg raid on mojo / Transit cop (demo) / Cooky puss / Bonus batter / Beastie revolution / Cooky puss (censored version)
CD CDEST 2225
Grand Royal / Mar '94 / EMI

TOUR SHOT
CD TOCP 8417
Mushroom / Nov '96 / Cargo

Beasts Of Bourbon

AXEMAN'S JAZZ
CD REDCD 4
Red Eye / Mar '94 / Direct

BLACK MILK
CD REDCD 12
Red Eye / Mar '94 / Direct

FROM THE BELLY OF THE BEASTS
CD REDCD 30
Red Eye / Mar '94 / Direct

GONE
Saturated / Fake / Makem cry / Mullett / Get on / I s'pose / What a way to live / That sinking feeling again / So long / Is that love / This day is over / Unfolded
CD REDCD 58
Red Eye/Australia / Feb '97 / Cargo

JUST RIGHT
CD REDCD 20
Red Eye / Mar '94 / Direct

LOW ROAD, THE
CD REDCD 26
Red Eye / Mar '94 / Direct

SOUR MASH
CD REDCD 5
Red Eye / Mar '94 / Direct

Beat

BPM (The Very Best Of The Beat)
Mirror in the bathroom / Hands off...she's mine / Twist and crawl / Jackpot / Tears of a clown / Ranking fullstop / Rough rider / Best friend / Stand down Margaret / Too nice to talk to / All out to get you / Door of your heart / Drowning / Can't get used to losing you / I confess / Save it for later
CD 74321231952
Arista / Jan '96 / BMG

DANCE HALL ROCKERS (International Beat)
CD CDBM 109
Blue Moon / Jan '96 / Cadillac / Discovery / Greensleeves / Jazz Music / Jet Star / TKO Magnum

LIVE IN JAPAN (Special Beat)
Concrete jungle / Monkey man / Tears of a clown / Rough rider / Too much too young / Get a job / Rat race / Spar wid me / Too nice to talk to / Too hot / Do nothing / Nite club / Noise in this world / Gangsters / Ranking full stop / Mirror in the bathroom / Doesn't make it alright / Enjoy yourself / Jackpot / Message to you Rudy / Save it for later / You're wondering now
CD DOJOCD 146
Dojo / Jun '94 / Disc

Beat Angels

RED BADGE OF DISCOURAGE
CD EP 1820
Epiphany / Jun '97 / Cargo

Beat Brothers

LEGEND (Documentray/Live)
CD OTR 1100011
Metro Independent / Apr '97 / Essential/ BMG

Beat Farmers

MANIFOLD
CD SECT2 10019
Sector 2 / Oct '95 / Cargo / Direct

TALES OF THE NEW WEST
Bigger stones / There she goes again / Reason to believe / Lost weekend / California kid / Never goin' back / Goldmine / Showbiz / Lonesome hound / Where do they go / Selfish heart
CD FIENDCD 39
Demon / Sep '90 / Pinnacle

VIKING LULLABYS
CD SECT2 10013
Sector 2 / Apr '95 / Cargo / Direct

Beat Happening

JAMBOREE
CD SP 62B
Sub Pop / Mar '94 / Cargo / Greyhound / Shellshock/Disc

Beatlerape

BEATLERAPE, THE
CD CI 9204
Staalplaat / Dec '95 / Vital/SAM

Beatles

1962-1966 (2CD Set)
Love me do / Please please me / From me to you / She loves you / I want to hold your hand / All my loving / Can't buy me love / Hard day's night / And I love her / Eight days a week / I feel fine / Ticket to ride / Yesterday / Help / You've got to hide your love away / We can work it out / Day tripper / Drive my car / Norwegian wood / Nowhere man / Michelle / In my life / Girl / Paperback writer / Eleanor Rigby / Yellow submarine
CD Set CDPCSP 717
Apple / Feb '94 / EMI

1967-1970 (2CD Set)
Strawberry Fields forever / Penny Lane / Sergeant Pepper's lonely hearts club band / With a little help from my friends / Lucy in the sky with diamonds / Day in the life / All you need is love / I am the walrus / Hello goodbye / Fool on the hill / Magical mystery tour / Lady Madonna / Hey Jude / Revolution / Back in the USSR / While my guitar gently weeps / Ob-la-di ob-la-da / Get back / Don't let me down / Ballad of John and Yoko / Old brown shoe / Here comes the sun / Come together / Something / Octopus's garden / Let it be / Across the universe / Long and winding road
CD Set CDPCSP 718
Apple / Feb '94 / EMI

ABBEY ROAD
Come together / Something / Maxwell's silver hammer / Oh darling / Octopus's garden / I want you (she's so heavy) / Here comes the sun / Because / You never give me your money / Sun king / Mean Mr Mustard / Polythene Pam / She came in through the bathroom window / Golden slumbers / Carry that weight / End Her Majesty
CD CDP 7464462
Apple / Nov '88 / EMI

AND YOUR BIRD CAN SING (36 Classic Interpretations Of Beatles Standards/ 2CD Set) (Various Artists)
Ob-la-di ob-la-da: *Marmalade* / Good day sunshine: *Tremeloes* / Michelle: *Overlanders* / You've got to hide your love away: *Silkie* / Bad to me: *Kramer, Billy J.* / Nowhere man: *Three Good Reasons* / Things we said today: *Sandpipers* / Fool on the hill: *Mendes, Sergio* / Girl: *St. Louis Union* / Norwegian wood: *London Jazz Four* / World without love: *Peter & Gordon* / Got to get you into my life: *Bennett, Cliff* / I call your name: *Mamas & The Papas* / Drive my car: *Campbell, Junior* / Rocky racoon: *Fairweather-Low, Andy* / I'll cry instead: *Cocker, Joe* / Something: *Bassey, Shirley* / Here comes the sun: *Harley, Steve* / Lucy in the sky with diamonds: *John, Elton* / Get back: *Stewart, Rod* / Yesterday: *Charles, Ray* / Hey Jude: *Pickett, Wilson* / Come together: *Ross, Diana* / Let it be: *Knight, Gladys* / Imagine: *Baez, Joan* / And I love her: *Robinson, Smokey* / Can't buy me love: *Fitzgerald, Ella* / Eleanor Rigby: *Havens, Richie* / Here, there and everywhere: *Harris, Emmylou* / I'm a loser: *Faithfull, Marianne* / She's leaving home: *Ferry, Bryan* / Do you want to know a secret: *Fairground Attraction* / Tomorrow never knows: *Monsoon* / Revolution: *Thompson Twins* / Dear Prudence: *Siouxsie & The Banshees* / Getting better: *Status Quo*
CD Set 5531102
Debutante / Jan '97 / PolyGram

ASK YOU ONCE AGAIN (Interview)
CD 3D 002
Network / Nov '96 / Total/BMG

BEATLES ANTHOLOGY VOL.1 (2CD Set)
Free as a bird / That'll be the day / In spite of all the danger / Hallelujah / I love her so / You'll be mine / Cayenne / My bonnie / Ain't she sweet / Cry for a shadow / Searchin' / Three cool cats / Sheik of Araby / Like dreamers do / Hello little girl / Besame mucho / Love me do / How do you do it / Please please me / One after 909 (sequence) / One after 909 (complete) / Lend me your comb / I'll get you / I saw her standing there / From me to you / Money (that's what I want) / You really got a hold on me / Roll over Beethoven / She loves you / Till there was you / Twist and shout / This boy / I want to hold your hand / Moonlight bay / Can't buy me love / All my loving / You can't do that / I love her / Hard's day night / I wanna be your man / Long tall Sally / Boys / Shout / I'll be back (take 2) / I'll be back (take 3) / You know what to do / No reply (demo) / Mr. Moonlight / Leave my kitten alone / No reply / Eight days a week / Hey hey hey / Kansas City / Eight days a week (complete)
CD Set CDPCSP 727
Apple / Nov '95 / EMI

BEATLES ANTHOLOGY VOL.2 (2CD Set)
Real love / Yes it is / You've got to hide your love away / If you've got trouble / That means a lot / I'm down / Yesterday / It's only love / I feel fine / Ticket to ride / Yesterday / Help / Everybody's trying to be my baby / Norwegian wood / I'm looking through you / 12-bar original / Tomorrow never knows / Got to get you into my life / And your bird can sing / Taxman / Eleanor Rigby / I'm only sleeping (rehearsal) / I'm only sleeping / Rock 'n' roll music / She's a woman / Strawberry Fields forever (demo) / Strawberry Fields forever (take 1) / Strawberry Fields forever / Penny Lane / Day in the life / Good morning, good morning / Only a northern song / Being for the benefit of Mr. Kite / Being for the benefit of Mr. Kite / Lucy in the sky with diamonds / Within you without you / Sgt. Pepper's Lonely Hearts Club Band (reprise) / You know my name (look up the number) / I am the walrus / Fool on the hill / Your mother should know / Fool on the hill (Take 4) / Hello goodbye / Lady Madonna / Across the universe
CD Set CDPCSP 728
Apple / Mar '96 / EMI

BEATLES ANTHOLOGY VOL.3 (2CD Set)
Beginning / Happiness is a warm gun / Helter skelter / Mean Mr. Mustard / Polythene Pam / Glass onion / Junk / Piggies / Honey pie / Don't pass me by / Ob-la-di ob-la-da / Good night / Cry baby cry / Blackbird / Sexy Sadie / While my guitar gently weeps / Hey Jude / Not guilty / Mother nature's son / Glass onion / Rocky Raccoon / What's the new Mary Jane / Step inside love / I'm so tired / I will / Why don't we do it in the road / Julia / I've got a feeling / She came in through the bathroom window / Dig a pony / Two of us / For you blue / Teddy boy / Medley / Long and winding road / Oh darling / All things must pass / Mailman, bring me no more blues / Get back / Old brown shoe / Octopus's garden / Maxwell's silver hammer / Something / Come together / Come and get it / Ain't she sweet / Because / Let it be / I me mine / End
CD Set CDPCSP 729
Apple / Nov '96 / EMI

BEATLES BOX SET (From Please Please Me To Past Masters 2/16CD Set)
I saw her standing there / Misery / Anna (go to him) / Chains / Ask me why / Please please me / Love me do / PS I love you / Baby it's you / Do you want to know a se-

cret / Taste of honey / There's a place / Twist and shout / It won't be long / All I've got to do / All my loving / Don't bother me / Little child / Till there was you (The music man) / Please Mr. Postman / Roll over Beethoven / Hold me tight / You really got a hold on me / I wanna be your man / Devil in her heart / Not a second time / Money (that's what I want) / Hard day's night / I should have known better / If I fell / I'm happy just to dance with you / And I love her / Tell me why / Can't buy me love / Any time at all / I'll cry instead / Things we said today / When I get home / You can't do that / I'll be back / No reply / I'm a loser / Baby's in black / Rock 'n' roll music / I'll follow the sun / Mr. Moonlight / Kansas City / Eight days a week / Words of love / Honey don't / Every little thing / I don't want to spoil the party / What you're doing / Everybody's trying to be my baby / Help / Night before / You've got to hide your love away / I need you / Another girl / You're going to lose that girl / Ticket to ride / Act naturally / It's only love / You like me too much / Tell me what you see / I've just seen a face / Yesterday / Dizzy Miss Lizzy / Drive my car / Norwegian wood / You won't see me / Nowhere man / Think for yourself / Word / Michelle / What goes on / Girl / I'm looking through you / In my life / Wait / If I needed someone / Run for your life / Taxman / Eleanor Rigby / I'm only sleeping / Love you to / Here there and everywhere / Yellow submarine / She said she said / Good day sunshine / And your bird can sing / For no one / Doctor Robert / I want to tell you / Got to get you into my life / Tomorrow never knows / Sgt. Pepper's Lonely Hearts Club Band / With a little help from my friends / Lucy in the sky with diamonds / Getting better / Fixing a hole / She's leaving home / Being for the benefit of Mr. Kite / Within you without you / When I'm sixty four / Lovely Rita / Good morning good morning / Sgt. Pepper's Lonely Hearts Club Band / Day in the life / Back in the USSR / Dear Prudence / Glass onion / Ob-la-di ob-la-da / Wild honey pie / Continuing story of Bungalow Bill / While my guitar gently weeps / Happiness is a warm gun / Martha my dear / I'm so tired / Blackbird / Piggies / Rocky Raccoon / Don't pass me by / Why don't we do it in the road / I will / Julia / Birthday / Yer blues / Mother nature's son / Everybody's got something to hide except me and my monkey / Sexy Sadie / Helter skelter / Long long long / Revolution 1 / Honey pie / Savoy truffle / Cry baby cry / Revolution 9 / Goodnight / Yellow submarine / Only a northern song / All together now / Hey bulldog / It's all too much / All you need is love / Pepperland / Sea of time / Sea of holes / Sea of monsters / March of the meanies / Pepperland laid waste / Yellow submarine in Pepperland / Magical mystery tour / Fool on the hill / Flying / Blue Jay way / Your mother should know / I am the walrus / Hello goodbye / Strawberry fields forever / Penny Lane / Baby you're a rich man / All you need is love / Come together / Something / Maxwell's silver hammer / Oh darling / Ocotpus's garden / I want you (she's so heavy) / Here comes the sun / Because / You never give me your money / Sun King / Mean Mr. Mustard / Polythene Pam / She came in through the bathroom window / Golden slumbers / Carry that weight / End / Her Majesty / Two of us / Dig a pony / Across the universe / I me mine / Dig it / Let it be / Maggie Mae / I've got a feeling / One after 909 / Long and winding road / For you blue / Get back / Love me do / From me to you / Thank you girl / She loves you / I'll get you / I want to hold your hand / This boy / Komm gib mir deine hand / Sie liebt dich / Long tall Sally / I call your name / Slow down / Matchbox / I feel fine / She's a woman / Bad boy / Yes it is / I'm down / Day tripper / We can work it out / Paperback writer / Rain / Lady Madonna / Inner light / Hey Jude / Revolution / Get back / Don't let me down / Ballad of John and Yoko / Old brown shoe / Across the universe / Let it be / You know my name (look up the number)
CD Set _____ CDS 7913022
Apple / Dec '88 / EMI

BEATLES CLASSICS PERFORMED ON PAN PIPES, THE (Various Artists)
Free as a bird / Lucy in the sky with diamonds / Michelle / Blackbird / And I love her / Yesterday / Eleanor Rigby / Strawberry Fields forever / Penny Lane / Hey Jude / Something / All my loving / Norwegian wood / She loves you / With a little help from my friends / If I fell / Long and winding road / Here, there and everywhere / Let it be
CD _____ SUMCD 4060
Summit / Nov '96 / Sound & Media

BEATLES FOR SALE
No reply / I'm a loser / Baby's in black / Rock 'n' roll music / I'll follow the sun / Mr. Moonlight / Kansas City / Eight days a week / Words of love / Honey don't / Don't want to spoil the party / What you're doing / Everybody's tryin' to be my baby
CD _____ CDP 7464382
Apple / Nov '88 / EMI

BEATLES INTERVIEW PICTURE DISC (Beatles Conquer The USA)
CD _____ CBAK 4001
Baktabak / Feb '88 / Arabesque

BEATLES SAX MOODS (Evolution)
Something / Free as a bird / Michelle / If I fell / My love / You've got to hide your love away / Let it be / Long and winding road / Lady Madonna / Strawberry fields forever / In my life / Across the universe / I will / For no one / Yesterday / Here, there and everywhere / Real love / Eleanor Rigby / Hey Jude
CD _____ 3036000422
Carlton / May '96 / Carlton

BEATLES TALK DOWNUNDER VOL.1 (Australia 1964)
CD _____ CBAK 4024
Baktabak / Jun '91 / Arabesque

BEATLES TALK DOWNUNDER VOL.1
CD _____ 12679
Laserlight / Mar '96 / Target/BMG

BEATLES TALK DOWNUNDER VOL.2
CD _____ CBAK 4034
Baktabak / Jun '91 / Arabesque

BEATLES TALK DOWNUNDER VOL.2
CD _____ 12680
Laserlight / Mar '96 / Target/BMG

BEATLES TAPES (David Wigg Interviews 1969-1973)
Interview (part 1) June 1969: *Lennon, John & Yoko Ono* / Give peace a chance: *Lennon, John & Yoko Ono* / Interview (Part 2) June 1969: *Lennon, John & Yoko Ono* / Imagine: *Lennon, John* / Interview (Part 3) June 1969: *Lennon, John & Yoko Ono* / Come together: *Lennon, John & Yoko Ono* / Interview October 1971: *Lennon, John & Yoko Ono* / Interview (Part 1) March 1970: *McCartney, Paul* / Because: *McCartney, Paul* / Interview (Part 2) March 1970: *McCartney, Paul* / Hey Jude: *McCartney, Paul* / Interview (Part 1) March 1969: *Harrison, George* / Here comes the sun: *Harrison, George* / Interview (Part 2) March 1969: *Harrison, George* / Something: *Harrison, George* / Interview December 1968: *Starr, Ringo* / Interview July 1970: *Starr, Ringo* / Interview (Part 1) December 1973: *Starr, Ringo* / Octopus's Garden: *Starr, Ringo* / Interview (Part 2) December 1973: *Starr, Ringo* / Yellow submarine: *Starr, Ringo*
CD Set _____ 8471852
Polydor / Oct '90 / PolyGram

BEATLES, THE (The White Album) (2CD Set)
Back in the USSR / Dear Prudence / Glass onion / Ob-la-di ob-la-da / Wild honey pie / Continuing story of bungalow Bill / While my guitar gently weeps / Happiness is a warm gun / Martha my dear / I'm so tired / Blackbird / Piggies / Rocky raccoon / Don't pass me by / Why don't we do it in the road / I will / Julia / Yer blues / Mother nature's son / Everybody's got something to hide except me and my monkey / Sexy Sadie / Helter skelter / Long long long / Revolution 1 / Honey pie / Savoy truffle / Cry baby cry / Revolution 9 / Goodnight
CD Set _____ CDS 7464438
Apple / Nov '88 / EMI

CLASSIC BEATLES (Symphonic Rock Orchestra)
CD _____ 322879
Koch / Mar '93 / Koch

COME TOGETHER VOL.2 (Various Artists)
Tomorrow never knows: *Krantz, Wayne* / Strawberry fields: *De Gruy, Philip* / Drive my car: *Hunter, Charlie* / I am the walrus: *Rogers, Adam* / Not a second time: *Rypdal, Terje* / Yes it is: *Quine, Robert* / Because: *Tronzo, David* / Golden slumbers: *Ford, Robben* / If I needed someone: *Hedges, Michael*
CD _____ NYC 60142
NYC / Apr '95 / New Note/Pinnacle

DOWNTOWN DOES THE BEATLES (Various Artists)
CD _____ KFWCD 113
Knitting Factory / Nov '94 / Cargo / Plastic Head

EXOTIC BEATLES VOL.2, THE (Various Artists)
Let it be: *Squirrels* / I saw her standing there: *Valley, Joah* / Nowhere man: *Masotoshi, Tsunema* / Sergeant Pepper's lonely hearts club band: *Sewll, Brian* / Yesterday: *Mullard, Arthur* / Rain: *Grupo 15* / Can't buy me love: *Baga, Ena* / Lady Madonna: *Geesin, Ron* / Yellow submarine: *Chevalier, Maurice* / Flying: *Sidebottom, Frank* / Hard day's night: *Beatle Barkers* / From me to you: *Pracatan, Margarita* / Desert island discs: *Peel, John & Kenny Everett* / It's for you: *Velvelettes* / We love rock 'n' roll: *Fisher & Marks* / Ob-la-di ob-la-da: *Prytko, Johnny & The Connecicut Hi-Tones* / Hey Jude: *Templeton Twins* / Piggies: *Pietsch, R.A.M.* / I am the walrus: *Coxhill, Lol* / Give peace a chance: *Beyer, Klaus* / All my loving: *Fernandos, Lili* / Continuing story of Bungalow Bill: *Beyer, Klaus* / Day tripper: *West, Mae* / Nostalgia: *Peel, John & Friends*
CD _____ PELE 007CD
Exotica / Oct '94 / SRD / Vital

EXOTIC BEATLES, THE (Various Artists)
Yellow submarine: *Enright, Derek MP* / Yellow submarine ondo: *Kanazawa, Akiko* / Lucy in the sky with diamonds: *Shatner, William* / I should have known better: *Dino E ! Kings* / I wanna be your man: *Sewell, Brian* / Penny Lane: *Malone, Wilson Voice Band* / She loves you: *Bonilla, Emi* / Come together: *Dekker, Desmond* / Step inside love: *Henderson, Dickie* / In my life: *Fairground Organ* / When I'm sixty four: *Metropolitan Police choir* / Please please me: *Los Mustang* / There's a place: *Les Surfs* / Things we said today: *OS Vips* / Fool on the hill: *Valente, Caterina & Edmondo Ros* / Paperback writer: *Lefty On The Right* / I want to hold your hand: *Balsara & His Singing Stars* / Eleanor Rigby: *Enright, Derek MP* / We can work it out: *Sandro* / I am the walrus: *Otway, John* / And I love her: *Fairground Organ* / I'll be back: *Quests* / Her majesty: *Sewell, Brian* / Goodnight: *Moog Beatles*
CD _____ PELE 003CD
Exotica / May '93 / SRD / Vital

FOREVER LENNON & MCCARTNEY (Various Artists)
Can't buy me love: *Martin, George Orchestra* / All my loving: *Monro, Matt* / Ticket to ride: *Cogan, Alma* / Eleanor Rigby: *Strings For Pleasure* / Do you want to know a secret: *Kramer, Billy J. & The Dakotas* / I want to hold your hand: *Martin, George Orchestra* / Hey Jude: *Loss, Joe Orchestra* / Michelle: *David & Jonathan* / World without love: *Peter & Gordon* / I feel fine: *Cogan, Alma* / Get back: *Shadows* / Yesterday: *Seekers* / Sgt. Peppers Lonely Hearts Club Band: *Palmer, David & The London Symphony Orchestra* / Got to get you into my life: *Bennett, Cliff* / With a little help from my friends: *Young Idea* / Day tripper: *Lulu* / Fool on the hill: *Bassey, Shirley* / Paperback writer: *Shadows* / Back in the USSR: *Bennett, Cliff*
CD _____ CDMFP 6276
Music For Pleasure / Nov '96 / EMI

GEORGE HARRISON INTERVIEW
CD _____ GEORGE 1
UFO / Jun '96 / Pinnacle

HARD DAY'S NIGHT, A
I should have known better / If I fell / I'm happy just to dance with you / And I love her / Tell me why / Can't buy me love / Hard day's night / Anytime at all / I'll cry instead / Things we said today / When I get home / You can't do that / I'll be back
CD _____ CDP 7464372
Apple / Nov '88 / EMI

HELP (Film Soundtrack)
Help / Night before / You've got to hide your love away / I need you / Another girl / You're going to lose that girl / Ticket to ride / Act naturally / It's only love / You like me too much / Tell me what you see / I've just seen a face / Yesterday / Dizzy Miss Lizzy
CD _____ CDP 7464392
Apple / Nov '88 / EMI

HITS OF THE BEATLES (Various Artists)
CD _____ DCD 5276
Disky / Aug '92 / Disky / THE

IN WORDS AND MUSIC (2CD Set) (McCartney, Paul)
CD Set _____ OTR 110029
Metro Independent / Apr '97 / Essential/ BMG

INSIDE INTERVIEWS
CD _____ 15981
Laserlight / Mar '96 / Target/BMG

INTERVIEW 1980
CD _____ FABFOUR 5
Wax / Jun '97 / RTM/Disc / Total/BMG

INTERVIEW DISC
CD _____ SAM 7001
Sound & Media / Nov '96 / Sound & Media

INTERVIEW DISC - GEORGE HARRISON
CD _____ FABFOUR 3
Wax / Aug '96 / RTM/Disc / Total/BMG

INTERVIEW DISC - RINGO STARR
CD _____ FABFOUR 4
Wax / Aug '96 / RTM/Disc / Total/BMG

INTERVIEW DISC VOL.1
CD _____ BEAT 1
Wax / May '96 / RTM/Disc / Total/BMG

INTERVIEW DISC VOL.2
CD _____ BEAT 2
Wax / May '96 / RTM/Disc / Total/BMG

INTERVIEW DISC VOL.3
CD _____ BEAT 3
Wax / May '96 / RTM/Disc / Total/BMG

INTERVIEW DISC VOL.4
CD _____ BEAT 4
Wax / May '96 / RTM/Disc / Total/BMG

INTERVIEWS VOL.2
CD _____ CBAK 4009
Baktabak / Apr '88 / Arabesque

INTERVIEWS: ALL TOGETHER NOW
CD _____ 12677
Laserlight / Mar '96 / Target/BMG

INTERVIEWS: BEATLEMANIA
CD _____ 12678
Laserlight / Mar '96 / Target/BMG

INTERVIEWS: IN MY LIFE
CD _____ 12676
Laserlight / Mar '96 / Target/BMG

INTROSPECTIVE: BEATLES
Twist and shout / I saw her standing there / Till there was you / Interview part one / Roll over Beethoven / Hippy hippy shake / Taste of honey / Interview part two
CD _____ CINT 5004
Baktabak / Jun '91 / Arabesque

JOHN LENNON INTERVIEW
CD _____ JOHN 1
UFO / Jun '96 / Pinnacle

LEGEND BEGINS, THE (Sheridan, Tony & The Beatles)
Sweet Georgia Brown / Let's dance / Take out some insurance / Why (can't you love me again) / Cry for a shadow / Ya ya / Ruby baby / What'd I say
CD _____ 305492
Hallmark / Oct '96 / Carlton

LENNON AND MCCARTNEY SONGBOOK VOL.2, THE (Various Artists)
It's only love: *Bonds, Gary 'US'* / Misery: *Flamin' Groovies* / Blackbird: *Preston, Billy* / Lady Madonna: *Domino, Fats* / I want to hold your hand: *Crickets* / I'll cry instead: *Cocker, Joe* / Love me do: *Shaw, Sandie* / Help: *Deep Purple* / There's a place: *Flamin' Groovies* / You won't see me: *Ferry, Bryan* / She's leaving home: *Bragg, Billy* / And I love him: *Phillips, Esther* / For no one: *Harris, Emmylou* / With a little help from my friends: *Wet Wet Wet* / This boy: *Nylons* / Drive my car: *Bo Street Runners* / One and one is two: *Shannon, Mike & The Strangers* / Like dreamers do: *Applejacks* / Don't let me down: *Dillard, Doug & Gene Clark* / I am the walrus: *Spooky Tooth* / Rain: *Rundgren, Todd* / Nobody I know: *Peter & Gordon* / Hello little girl: *Fourmost* / Ticket to ride: *Vanilla Fudge*
CD _____ VSOPCD 162
Connoisseur Collection / Nov '91 / Pinnacle

LET IT BE
Two of us / Dig a pony / Across the universe / I me mine / Dig it / Let it be / Maggie Mae / I've got a feeling / One after 909 / Long and winding road / Get back
CD _____ CDP 7464472
Apple / Nov '88 / EMI

LOST FAB FOUR TAPES, THE (Interview/2CD Set)
CD Set _____ OTR 1100026
Metro Independent / Jun '97 / Essential/ BMG

MAGICAL MYSTERY TOUR
Magical mystery tour / Fool on the hill / Flying / Blue jay way / Your mother should know / I am the walrus / Hello goodbye / Strawberry fields forever / Penny Lane / Baby, you're a rich man / All you need is love
CD _____ CDP 7480622
Apple / Nov '88 / EMI

ORCHESTRAL SGT. PEPPER (Arranged/ Conducted By David Palmer) (Royal Academy Symphony Orchestra)
Sergeant Pepper's lonely hearts club band / With a little help from my friends / Lucy in the sky with diamonds / Getting better / Fixing a hole / She's leaving home / Being for the benefit of Mr. Kite / When I'm sixty four / Lovely Rita / Sergeant Pepper's lonely hearts club band (reprise) / Day in the life
CD _____ CDDPR 125
Premier/MFP / Jun '97 / EMI

PAST MASTERS VOL.1
Love me do / From me to you / Thank you girl / She loves you / I'll get you / I want to hold your hand / This boy / Komm gib mir deine hand / Sie liebt dich / Long tall Sally / I call your name / Slow down / Matchbox / I feel fine / She's a woman / Bad boy / Yes it is / I'm down
CD _____ CDP 7900432
Apple / Aug '88 / EMI

PAST MASTERS VOL.2
Day tripper / We can work it out / Paperback writer / Rain / Lady Madonna / Inner light / Hey Jude / Revolution / Get back / Don't let me down / Ballad of John and Yoko / Old brown shoe / Across the universe / Let it be / You know my name (look up the number)
CD _____ CDP 7900442
Apple / Aug '88 / EMI

PAUL MCCARTNEY INTERVIEW
CD _____ PAUL 1
UFO / Jun '96 / Pinnacle

PLAY THE BEATLES BALLADS (Various Artists)
For no one / Michelle / Strawberry fields forever / Here, there and everywhere / In my life / And I love her / If I fell / Long and winding road / Something / Fool on the hill / Free as a bird / Real love / You've got to hide your love away / Imagine / My love / Blackbird / Mother nature's son / Across the universe / Yesterday / I will
CD _____ 3036000262
Carlton / Jan '96 / Carlton

PLEASE PLEASE ME
Taste of honey / I saw her standing there / Misery / Anna / Chains / Boys / Ask me why / Please please me / Love me do / I love you / Baby it's you / Do you want to know a secret / There's a place / Twist and shout

CD _____ CDP 7464352
Apple / Nov '88 / EMI

PRESS CONFERENCE 1979
CD _____ FABFOUR 6
Wax / Jun '97 / RTM/Disc / Total/BMG

PRESS CONFERENCE JAPAN 1991
CD _____ FABFOUR 7
Wax / Jun '97 / RTM/Disc / Total/BMG

PRESS CONFERENCE LONDON
CD _____ FABFOUR 8
Wax / Jun '97 / RTM/Disc / Total/BMG

REGGAE TRIBUTE TO THE BEATLES VOL.1, A (Various Artists)
Yesterday: *Livingstone, Dandy* / Hey Jude: *Holt, John* / Come together: *Israelites* / Something: *Dillon, Phyllis* / Let it be: *Thomas, Nicky* / Get back: *Anonymously Yours* / My Jude: *Joe's All Stars* / My sweet Lord: *Lynn, Keith, Brendon Lee & The Dragonaires* / World without love: *Davis, Del* / Give peace a chance: *Maytals* / Lady Madoona: *Crystalites* / Isn't it a pity: *Thomas, Nicky* / Don't let me down: *Harry J All Stars* / Blackbirds singing: *Sweet, Roslyn & The Paragons* / Eleanor Rigby: *Seaton, B.B.* / World without love: *Arthey, Johnny Orchestra*
CD _____ EMPRCD 584
Emporio / Oct '95 / Disc

REGGAE TRIBUTE TO THE BEATLES VOL.2, A (Various Artists)
Ob-la-di ob-la-da: *Heptones* / Hard day's night: *Minott, Sugar* / Yesterday: *Taylor, Tyrone* / My love: *Boothe, Ken* / You won't see me: *Smith, Ernie* / And I love her: *Mohawks* / Norwegian wood: *Williams, Marshall* / My sweet Lord: *Sterling, Fitzroy* / Don't let me down: *Griffiths, Marcia* / Here comes the sun: *Penn, Dawn* / In my life: *Robinson, Jackie* / Imagine: *Cadogan, Susan* / Hey Jude: *Dynamites* / Let it be: *Soulettes* / Carry that weight: *Dobson, Dobby* / Happy Xmas (war is over): *Holt, John*
CD _____ EMPRCD 718
Emporio / Jun '97 / Disc

REVOLVER
Taxman / Eleanor Rigby / I'm only sleeping / Love you to / Here, there and everywhere / Yellow submarine / She said she said / Good day sunshine / And your bird can sing / For no one / Dr. Robert / I want to tell you / Got to get you into my life / Tomorrow never knows
CD _____ CDP 7464412
Apple / Nov '88 / EMI

RINGO STARR INTERVIEW
CD _____ RINGO 1
UFO / Jun '96 / Pinnacle

ROCK AND POP REVIVAL PLAYS THE BEATLES (Rock & Pop Revival)
CD _____ RPR 9403
Scratch / Mar '95 / Koch / Scratch/BMG

ROCKUMENTARY - IN THEIR OWN WORDS (5CD Set)
CD Set _____ 15968
Laserlight / Dec '95 / Target/BMG

ROCKUMENTARY NO.1 - THE LOST BEATLES INTERVIEWS
CD _____ 12591
Laserlight / Dec '95 / Target/BMG

ROCKUMENTARY NO.2 - THINGS WE SAID TODAY (Talking With The Beatles)
CD _____ 12592
Laserlight / Dec '95 / Target/BMG

ROCKUMENTARY NO.3 - JOHN LENNON FOREVER
CD _____ 12593
Laserlight / Dec '95 / Target/BMG

ROCKUMENTARY NO.4 - PAUL MCCARTNEY: BEYOND THE MYTH
CD _____ 12594
Laserlight / Dec '95 / Target/BMG

ROCKUMENTARY NO.5 - THE SECRET LIFE OF GEORGE HARRISON
CD _____ 12595
Laserlight / Dec '95 / Target/BMG

RUBBER SOUL
Drive my car / Norwegian wood / You won't see me / Nowhere man / Think for yourself / Word / Michelle / What goes on / Girl / I'm looking through you / In my life / Wait / If I needed someone / Run for your life
CD _____ CDP 7464402
Apple / Nov '88 / EMI

SGT. PEPPER'S LONELY HEARTS CLUB BAND
Sergeant Pepper's lonely hearts club band / With a little help from my friends / Lucy in the sky with diamonds / Getting better / Fixing a hole / She's leaving home / Being for the benefit of Mr. Kite / Within you without you / When I'm sixty four / Lovely Rita / Good morning good morning / Day in the life
CD _____ CDP 7464422
Apple / Jun '92 / EMI

SPIRIT OF LENNON & MCCARTNEY, THE (Instrumental Versions) (Various Artists)
Strawberry fields forever / Fool on the hill / Here there and everywhere / Dear Prudence / Let it be / Because / Nowhere man / Yesterday / In my life / She's leaving home / If I fell / For no one / This boy / Michelle / Across the universe / And I love her / Julia / Mother Nature's son
CD _____ RECD 508
REL / Oct '96 / CM / Duncans / Highlander

STRAWBERRY FIELDS (Various Artists)
Come together: *Reeves, Dianne & Cassandra Wilson* / Stawberry fields forever: *Wilson, Cassandra* / Tomorrow never knows: *Reeves, Dianne* / I'm only sleeping: *Cole, Holly* / Get back: *Jahlisa & Junko Onishi* / Fool on the hill: *Reeves, Dianne* / I've just seen a face: *Cole, Holly* / Hey Jude: *Jahlisa & Osby, Greg* / Lady Madonna: *Ford, P* / Let it be: *Hemwell, S*
CD _____ CDP 8539202
Blue Note / Nov '96 / EMI

WITH THE BEATLES
It won't be long / All I've got to do / All my loving / Don't bother me / Little child / Till there was you / Please Mr. Postman / Roll over Beethoven / Hold me tight / You really got a hold on me / I wanna be your man / Devil in her heart / Not a second time / Money
CD _____ CDP 7464362
Apple / Nov '88 / EMI

YELLOW SUBMARINE
Yellow submarine / Only a northern song / All you need is love / Hey bulldog / It's all too much / All together now / Pepperland / Sea of time / Sea of holes / Sea of monsters / March of the meanies / Pepperland laid to waste / Yellow submarine in Pepperland
CD _____ CDP 7464452
Apple / Nov '88 / EMI

YESTERDAY VOL.1 (16 Fab Beatle Reggae Classics) (Various Artists)
CD _____ CDTRL 294
Trojan / Mar '94 / Direct / Jet Star

YESTERDAY VOL.2 (The Black Album) (Various Artists)
CD _____ CDTRL 338
Trojan / Apr '94 / Direct / Jet Star

YESTERDAY VOL.3 (Various Artists)
CD _____ CDTRL 365
Trojan / Oct '96 / Direct / Jet Star

Beatnigs

BEATNIGS
CD _____ VIRUS 65CD
Alternative Tentacles / Oct '88 / Cargo / Greyhound / Pinnacle

Beatnik Filmstars

ALL POPSTARS ARE TALENTLESS SLAGS
CD _____ SCRATCH 27
Scratch / Jun '97 / Koch / Scratch/BMG

LAID BACK & ENGLISH
CD _____ LADIDA 027CD
La-Di-Da / Jul '94 / Vital

PHASE 3
CD _____ MOBSTAR 008CD
Mobstar / Jan '97 / Cargo

Beatnuts

STONE CRAZY
World famous intro / Bless the MIC / Intermission / Here's a drink / Off the books / Be proud/Interlude / Do you believe / Finger smoke / Stone crazy / Niggaz know / Horny horns / Find that / Supa supreme / Thinkin' 'bout cash / Uncivilized / Give me tha ass / Strokes
CD _____ 4869042
Relativity / Jun '97 / Sony

Beaton, Alex

20 HITS OF SCOTLAND
Scots wha hae / Dumbarton's drums / These are my mountains / Annie Laurie / Wee castanettes / Man's a man for a' that / Ae fond kiss / Killiecrankie / Skye boat song / Hey Johnny Cope / Amazing grace / Stoutest man in the forty twa / Glencoe / Scottish soldier / Flowers of the forest / Loch Lomond / Big Nellie May / Rowan tree / Fower of Scotland / Bonnie Galloway / Scotland the brave
CD _____ LCDM 9031
Lismor / Aug '90 / ADA / Direct / Duncans / Lismor

Beats

UP UNTIL NOW
CD _____ CDCOT 102
Cottage / Oct '94 / Koch / THE

Beats The Hell Out Of Me

BEATS THE HELL OUT OF ME
Painfully / Buzz / Told / Behind my back / Intro / Act like a man
CD _____ CDZORRO 66
Metal Blade / Feb '94 / Pinnacle / Plastic Head

ROLLING THUNDER MUSIC
CD _____ 148072
Metal Blade / Oct '95 / Pinnacle / Plastic Head

Beau

BEAU/CREATION
Welcome / 1917 Revolution / Fising song / Pillar of economy / Sundancer / Morning sun / Ways of winter / Nine minutes / Spider / Is this your day / Blind faith / Release / Silence returns / Imagination / Soldier of the willow / Painted vase / Nations pride / Rain / Summer has gone / Welcome tag piece / There was once a time / April meteor / Creation / Ferris street / Reason to be
CD _____ SEECD 421
See For Miles/C5 / May '95 / Pinnacle

Beau Brummels

AUTUMN IN SAN FRANCISCO
Laugh laugh / Just a little / You tell me why / Don't talk to strangers / In good time / Sad little girl / Still in love with you baby / Stick like glue / That's if you want me to / Can it be / When it comes to your love / Gentle wanderin' ways / I grow old / Lonely man / She sends me
CD _____ EDCD 141
Edsel / Aug '90 / Pinnacle

AUTUMN OF THEIR YEARS
She sends me / Tomorrow is another day / She loves me / Woman / Dream on / Cry some / I grow old / No lonelier man / This is love / She's my girl / I'll tell you / Let me in / Love is just a game / Till the day / I will go / Stay with me awhile / I'm alone again / Down on me / Can't be so / Fine with me / Coming home / That's all that matter / Laugh laugh / Still in love with you baby / Just a little / When it comes to your love
CD _____ CDWIKD 127
Big Beat / Feb '94 / Pinnacle

BRADLEY'S BARN
Turn around / Added attraction / Deep water / Long walking down to misery / Little bird / Cherokee girl / I'm a sleeper / Loneliest man in town / Love can fall a long way down / Jessica / Bless you California
CD _____ 7599268872
WEA / Jan '96 / Warner Music

SIXTIES GEMS
Just a little / Don't talk to strangers / When it comes to your love / In good time / Fine with me / Sad little girl / Still in love with you baby / You tell me why / They'll make you cry / Good time music / Laugh laugh / Woman / She loves me
CD _____ HADCD 213
Spotlight On / Jun '97 / Henry Hadaway

TRIANGLE
CD _____ 7599268862
WEA / Jan '96 / Warner Music

Beaumont Hannant

BASIC DATA MANIPULATION
CD _____ GPRCD 2
GPR / Nov '93 / 3mv/Vital

SCULPTURED
CD _____ GPRCD 9
GPR / Oct '94 / 3mv/Vital

TEXTUROLOGY
CD _____ GPR 4CD
GPR / Apr '94 / 3mv/Vital

Beaumont, Howard

HIGHLIGHTS
CD _____ CDGRS 1277
Grosvenor / May '95 / Grosvenor

JUBILEE
Best of times / I am what I am / Nice and easy / Where or when / Tender trap / These foolish things / Mairi's wedding / Scotch on the rocks / Scottish solider / Loch Lomond / Roaming' in the gloamin' / Scotland the Brave / Manana / Enjoy yourself / Big brass band from Brazil / Coffee song / In my life / Quando, quando, quando / Eso beso / Moon river / Charade / It don't mean a thing if it ain't got that swing / Happy feet / After you've gone / Shine / When day is done / On a slow boat to China / At last / I know why / Losing my mind / When I fall in love / Fool on the hill / Watch what happens / Blue velvet / Hey there / Norwegian wood / I've got a gal in Kalamazoo / Stompin' at the Savoy / Auntie Maggie's remedy / Fanlight fanny / With my little ukulele in my hand / When I'm cleaning windows (The window cleaner) / Leaning on a lamp-post / Thorn birds (Theme from) / My wild Irish rose / How can you buy Killarney / Come back Erin / Here's that rainy day / Love letters / My foolish heart / Stella by Starlight / World of our own / There's a kind of hush / It might as well rain until September / I only want to be with you / Raining in my heart
CD _____ CDGRS 1256
Grosvenor / Feb '95 / Grosvenor

SHALL WE DANCE
Take the 'A' train / Dancing in the dark / Deep in my heart / Perhaps, perhaps, perhaps / Once in a while / Makin' whoopee / La Rosita / Blue skies / Hey good lookin' / Bye bye blues
CD _____ CDGRS 1295
Grosvenor / May '97 / Grosvenor

Beaumont, Tex

ONE-EYED JACKS
One-eyed Jacks / Dancing in dreamland / Guess I'll be going soon / Bells of Shoreditch / Powder blue Chevrolet / Baby I just want to get on your nerves / Who would I love / Poor girl's Elvis, poor man's Marilyn Monroe / Lolita / Honky tonk eyes / Closing time
CD _____ FIENDCD 792
Demon / Apr '97 / Pinnacle

Beausoleil

ALLONS A LAFAYETTE
CD _____ ARHCD 308
Arhoolie / Apr '95 / ADA / Cadillac / Direct

BAYOU BOOGIE
Zydeco gris gris / Fais pas ca / It's you I love / Dimanche apres-midi / Madame Bozo / Kolinda / Maman Rosin Boudreaux / Chez Seychelles / Jongle a moi / Flame will never die / La vaise de malchanceaux / Beausoleil boogie
CD _____ ROUCD 6015
Rounder / '88 / ADA / CM / Direct

CAJUN CONJA
Sophie / Tortue perdue / Conja (New Orleans 1786) / Vieux crowley / Sur le pont de Lyon / Cajun telephone stomp / Nuit de clifton chenier (Clifton's night) / Le reel de nez pique / Ti monde / Le chanky chank francais / La valse de la poussiere / Tasso / McGee's ree
CD _____ FIENDCD 704
Demon / Sep '91 / Pinnacle

HOT CHILI MAMA (Beausoleil & Michael Doucet)
CD _____ ARHCD 5040
Arhoolie / Apr '95 / ADA / Cadillac / Direct

L'ECHO
CD _____ 8122718082
Warner Bros. / Nov '94 / Warner Music

LA DANSE DE LA VIE
La danse de la vie / Dans le Grand Brouillard / L'ouragon / Dis-moi pas / Jeunes filles de la campagne / Quelle belle vie / RD special / Chanson pour Ezra / Menage a trois reels / Zydeco X / Je tombe aux Genoux / Attrape mes larmes / La fille de quatorze ans
CD _____ 8122712212
Atlantic / Jun '93 / Warner Music

PARLEZ-NOUS A BOIRE
CD _____ ARHCD 322
Arhoolie / Apr '95 / ADA / Cadillac / Direct

THEIR SWALLOW RECORDINGS
J'ai vu le loup / Valse a Beausoleil / Two-step des freres Mathieu / Travailler c'est trop dur / Potpourri cadjin / He, Mom / Valse des Balfa / Zydeco gris gris / Les barres de la prison / Hommage aux freres Balfa / Chanson / Love bridge waltz / Tu peux cognai / Contredanse de mamou / Reel de Dennis McGee / Blues a bebe / Talle du ronces / Blues de morse / Fi fi a Poncho / J'ai fait la tour de grand bois / Je m'endors, je m'endors / La valse de grand bois / Trinquez, trinquez
CD _____ CDCHD 379
Ace / Sep '92 / Pinnacle

Beautiful South

0898 BEAUTIFUL SOUTH
Old red eyes is back / We are each other / Rocking chair / We'll deal with you later / Domino man / 36D / Here it is again / Something that you said / I'm your No.1 fan / Bell-bottomed tear / You play glockenspiel, I'll play drums / When I'm 84
CD _____ 8283102
Go Discs / Apr '92 / PolyGram

BLUE IS THE COLOUR
Don't marry her / Little blue / Mirror / Blackbird on the wire / Sound of north America / Have fun / Liars bar / Rotterdam (or anywhere) / Foundations / Artificial flowers / One god / Alone
CD _____ 8288452
Go Discs / Oct '96 / PolyGram

CARRY ON UP THE CHARTS (The Best Of The Beautiful South)
Song for whoever / You keep it all in / I'll sail this ship alone / Little time / My book / Let love speak up for itself / Old red eyes is back / We are each other / Bell bottomed tear / 36D / Good as gold (stupid as mud) / Everybody's talkin' / Prettiest eyes / One last love song / Dream a little dream
CD _____ 8285722
Go Discs / Nov '94 / PolyGram

CHOKE
Tonight I fancy myself / Let love speak up itself / I've come for my award / I think the answer's yes / Mother's pride / Rising of Grafton Street / My book / Should've kept my eyes shut / Lips / Little time / I hate you (but you're interesting)
CD _____ 8282332
Go Discs / Oct '90 / PolyGram

MIAOW
Hold on to what / Good as gold / Especially for you / Everybody's talkin' / Prettiest eyes / Worthless lie / Hooligans don't fall in love

/ Hidden jukebox / Hold me close / Tattoo / Mini correct / Poppy
CD _______________ 8285072
Go Discs / Mar '94 / PolyGram

Beautiful World

IN EXISTENCE
In the beginning / In existence / Evolution / Magicien du bonheur / I know / Silk road / Love song / Journey of the ancestors / Revolution of the heart / Coming of age / Spoken word / Wonderful world / Final emotion
CD _______________ 4509951202
WEA / Mar '94 / Warner Music

Beauvoir, Jean

ROCKIN' IN THE STREET
Jacknifed / Feel the heat / Rockin' in the street / Standing on my own two feet / Dyin' at your door / Same song plays on and on / Sorry I missed your wedding day / If love could only / Spend your life with me / Find my way home / Never went down / Alone again / Searching for a light / Drive you home / If I was me / Missing the young days / Gamblin' man / Nina
CD _______________ CDOVD 465
Virgin / Jan '96 / EMI

Beaven, Nancy

WILD GARDEN, THE
CD _______________ SCD 195
Starc / Mar '96 / ADA / Direct

Becaud, Gilbert

ET MAINTENANT
CD _______________ CD 352127
Duchesse / Jul '93 / Pinnacle

Because

MAD SCARED DUMB AND GORGEOUS
CD _______________ HAVENCD 1
Haven / May '92 / Pinnacle / Shellshock/ Disc

Bechegas, Carlos

FLUTE SOLOS/MOVEMENT SOUNDS (Bechegas, Carlos Trio)
CD _______________ LEOLABCD 032
Leo Lab / May '97 / Cadillac

Bechet, Leonard

LEONARD BECHET & ALTON PURNELL 1973 (Bechet, Leonard & Alton Purnell)
CD _______________ BCD 236
GHB / Apr '97 / Jazz Music

Bechet, Sidney

AMERICAN FRIENDS
CD _______________ VGCD 655623
Vogue / Jan '93 / BMG

BECHET
Kansas City man blues: *Bechet, Sidney & Clarence Williams Blue Five* / Old fashioned love: *Bechet, Sidney & Clarence Williams Blue Five* / Texas moaner blues: *Bechet, Sidney & Clarence Williams Blue Five* / Mandy, make up your mind: *Bechet, Sidney & Clarence Williams Blue Five* / Papa de da da: *Bechet, Sidney & Clarence Williams Blue Five* / Wild cat blues: *Bechet, Sidney & Clarence Williams Blue Five* / Coal cart blues: *Bechet, Sidney & Clarence Williams Blue Five* / Sweetie dear: *Bechet, Sidney & His New Orleans Feetwarmers* / I want you tonight: *Bechet, Sidney & His New Orleans Feetwarmers* / Ja da: *Bechet, Sidney & Tommy Ladnier Orchestra* / Really the blues: *Bechet, Sidney & Tommy Ladnier Orchestra* / I've found a new baby: *Bechet, Sidney & His New Orleans Feetwarmers* / When you and I were young Maggie: *Bechet, Sidney & Tommy Ladnier Orchestra* / Shake it and break it: *Bechet, Sidney & His New Orleans Feetwarmers* / Old man blues: *Bechet, Sidney & His New Orleans Feetwarmers* / Wild man blues: *Bechet, Sidney & His New Orleans Feetwarmers* / Nobody knows the way I feel this morning: *Bechet, Sidney & His New Orleans Feetwarmers* / Blues in thirds: *Bechet, Sidney Trio* / Blues for you Johnny: *Bechet, Sidney & His New Orleans Feetwarmers* / Ain't misbehavin': *Bechet, Sidney & His New Orleans Feetwarmers* / Save it pretty Mama: *Bechet, Sidney & His New Orleans Feetwarmers* / Stompy Jones: *Bechet, Sidney & His New Orleans Feetwarmers*
CD _______________ PASTCD 9772
Flapper / Jan '92 / Pinnacle

BECHET-MEZZROW QUINTET
CD _______________ 401172CD
Musidisc / Jul '94 / Discovery

BEST OF CHARLESTON (Bechet, Sidney & Claude Luter)
CD _______________ DLCD 4070
Dixie Live / Mar '95 / TKO Magnum

BEST OF SIDNEY BECHET
CD _______________ DLCD 4025
Dixie Live / Mar '95 / TKO Magnum

BLUES IN THIRDS
CD _______________ LEJAZZCD 30
Le Jazz / Aug '94 / Cadillac / Koch

BLUES IN THIRDS 1940-1941
Blues in thirds / Ain't misbehavin' / Save it, pretty mama / Stompy Jones / You're the limit / Perdido Street blues / Down in honky-tonk town / Old man blues / Shake it and break it / Strange fruit / Wild man blues / Mooche / I ain't gonna give nobody / Blues in the air / China boy / Dear old southland / Egyptian fantasy / Baby, won't you please come home / Slippin' and slidin' / I know that you know / I'm comin' Virginia / Georgia cabin / Limehouse blues / Texas moaner blues
CD _______________ CD 53105
Giants Of Jazz / May '97 / Cadillac / Jazz Music / Target/BMG

CENTENARY CELEBRATION 1997 (Great Original Performances 1924-1946)
Indian summer: *Bechet, Sidney & His New Orleans Feetwarmers* / Sweetie Dear: *Bechet, Sidney & His New Orleans Feetwarmers* / I've found a new baby: *Bechet, Sidney & His New Orleans Feetwarmers* / Maple leaf rag: *Bechet, Sidney & His New Orleans Feetwarmers* / Shag: *Bechet, Sidney & His New Orleans Feetwarmers* / One o'clock jump: *Bechet, Sidney & His New Orleans Feetwarmers* / Old man blues: *Bechet, Sidney & His New Orleans Feetwarmers* / Swing parade: *Bechet, Sidney & His New Orleans Feetwarmers* / Blues in the air: *Bechet, Sidney & His New Orleans Feetwarmers* / Bugle call rag - ole Miss: *Bechet, Sidney & His New Orleans Feetwarmers* / Make up your mind: *Williams, Clarence Blue Five* / Early every morning: *Red Onion Jazzband* / Okey doke: *Sissle, Noble* / Characteristic blues: *Sissle, Noble* / Viper mad: *Sissle, Noble* / Blackstick: *Sissle, Noble* / When the sun sets down south: *Sissle, Noble* / Sweet papootie: *Sissle, Noble* / Really the blues: *Ladnier, Tommy* / Weary blues: *Ladnier, Tommy* / Blues in thirds: *Bechet, Sidney Trio* / Muskrat ramble: *Levine, Henry* / Blues of Bechet
CD _______________ RPCD 632
Robert Parker Jazz / Apr '97 / Conifer/BMG / New Note/Pinnacle

CLASSICS 1923-1936
CD _______________ CLASSICS 583
Classics / Oct '91 / Discovery / Jazz Music

CLASSICS 1937-1938
CD _______________ CLASSICS 593
Classics / Sep '91 / Discovery / Jazz Music

CLASSICS 1938-1940
CD _______________ CLASSICS 608
Classics / Oct '92 / Discovery / Jazz Music

CLASSICS 1940
CD _______________ CLASSICS 619
Classics / Sep '92 / Discovery / Jazz Music

CLASSICS 1940-1941
CD _______________ CLASSICS 638
Classics / Nov '92 / Discovery / Jazz Music

CLASSICS 1941-1944
CD _______________ CLASSICS 860
Classics / Mar '96 / Discovery / Jazz Music

COMPLETE SIDNEY BECHET VOL.1 & 2 1932-1941, THE
One o'clock jump / Preachin' blues / Old man blues / Blues in thirds / Ain't misbehavin' / Save it pretty Mama / Stompy Jones / Muskrat ramble / Coal black shine / Sweetie dear / Lay your racket / Maple leaf rag / Ja da / Really the blues / Weary blues / Indian summer / I want you tonight / I've found a new baby / When you and I were young Maggie / Maggie / Sidney's blues / Shake it and break it / Wild man blues / Nobody knows the way I feel this morning / Make a pallet on the floor / St. Louis blues / Blues for you / Johnny / Egyptian fantasy
CD Set _______________ ND 89760
Jazz Tribune / May '94 / BMG

COMPLETE SIDNEY BECHET VOL.3 & 4 1941, THE
I'm coming Virginia / Limehouse blues / Georgia cabin: Y / Texas moaner / Strange fruit / You're the limit / Rip up the joint / Suey / Blues in the air / Mooche / Laughin' in rhythm / 12th Street rag / I know that you know / Egyptian fantasy / Baby, won't you please come home / Slippin' and slidin' / Sheikh of Araby / Blues of Bechet / Swing parade / When it's sleepy time down South / I ain't gonna give nobody none o' this jelly roll
CD _______________ ND 89759
Jazz Tribune / Jun '94 / BMG

COMPLETE SIDNEY BECHET VOL.5, THE
Mood indigo / Oh lady be good / What's this thing called love / After you've gone / Bugle call rag/Ole Miss rag / St. Louis blues / Revolutionary blues / Comin' on with the come on / Careless love / Royal Garden blues / Everybody loves my baby / I ain't gonna give nobody none o' this Jelly Roll / If you see me comin' / Gettin' together / Rosetta / Minor jive / World is waiting for the sunrise / Who / Blues my baby gave to me / Rompin'
CD _______________ 74321155192
Jazz Tribune / Jun '94 / BMG

FREIGHT TRAIN BLUES
Sweetie dear / I want you tonight / I've found a new baby / Lay your racket / Maple leaf rag / Shag / Okey doke / Characteristic blues / Viper mad / Blackstick / When the sun sets down south (Southern sunset) / Sweet patootie / Freight train blues / Trixie blues / My Daddy rocks me (Part I) / My Daddy rocks me (Part II) / What a dream / Hold tight / Jungle drums / Chant in the night / Ja da / Really the blues / When you and I were young Maggie / Weary blues
CD _______________ GRF 100
Tring / '93 / Tring

GENIUS OF SIDNEY BECHET, THE
CD _______________ JCD 35
Jazzology / Aug '95 / Jazz Music

INTRODUCTION TO SIDNEY BECHET 1923-1941, AN
CD _______________ 4017
Best Of Jazz / Mar '95 / Discovery

JAZZ AT STORYVILLE
CD _______________ BLCD 760902
Black Lion / Jun '88 / Cadillac / Jazz Music / Koch / Wellard

JAZZ PORTRAITS
Shag / Maple leaf rag / Sweetie dear / I've found a new baby / Lay your racket / I want you tonight / Polka dot rag / T'ain't a fit night out for man or beast / When the sun sets down south (southern sunset) / Freight train blues / Chant in the night / Characteristic blues / Black stick blues / Jungle drums / Really the blues / Weary blues / When you and I were young Maggie / Ja da
CD _______________ CD 14517
Jazz Portraits / May '94 / Jazz Music

LEGENDARY SIDNEY BECHET, THE
Maple leaf rag: *Bechet, Sidney & His New Orleans Feetwarmers* / I've found a new baby: *Bechet, Sidney & His New Orleans Feetwarmers* / Weary blues: *Bechet, Sidney & Tommy Ladnier* / Really the blues: *Bechet, Sidney & Tommy Ladnier* / High society: *Bechet, Sidney & Jelly Roll Morton* / Indian summer / Sidney's blues / Shake it and break it / Wild man blues / Save it pretty Mama / Stompy Jones / Muskrat ramble: *Bechet, Sidney & Levine Henry* / Baby, won't you please come home / Sheikh of Araby / When it's sleepy time down South / I'm coming Virginia / Strange fruit / Blues in the air / Mooche / Twelfth St. rag / Mood indigo / What is this thing called love
CD _______________ ND 86590
Bluebird / Apr '89 / BMG

LIVE IN SWITZERLAND 1951 & 1954
CD _______________ 449012
Landscape / Aug '93 / THE

MASTERS OF JAZZ VOL.4
CD _______________ STCD 4104
Storyville / May '93 / Cadillac / Jazz Music / Wellard

OLYMPIA CONCERT 1954
CD _______________ VGCD 655625
Vogue / Jan '93 / BMG

PLEYEL CONCERTS PARIS 1952
CD _______________ CD 53177
Giants Of Jazz / Sep '94 / Cadillac / Jazz Music / Target/BMG

QUINTESSENCE, THE (1932-1943/2CD Set)
CD Set _______________ FA 206
Fremeaux / Oct '96 / ADA / Discovery

RARE SOPRANO SAX RECORDINGS (The Golden Age of Jazz)
CD _______________ JZCD 364
Suisa / May '92 / Jazz Music / THE

REALLY THE BLUES (Original Recordings 1932-1941)
Baby, won't you please come home / 2.19 blues / Blues in thirds / China boy / Egyptian fantasy / Four or five times / High society / I ain't gonna give nobody none o' this jelly roll / I thought I heard Buddy Bolden say / Indian summer / Lay your racket / Maple leaf rag / Mooche / Muskrat ramble / Nobody knows the way I feel this morning / Perdido Street blues / Preachin' blues / Really the blues / Sheikh of araby / When it's sleepy time down South / Stompy Jones / Strange fruit / Texas moaner / When you and I were young Maggie / Wild man blues
CD _______________ CDAJA 5107
Living Era / Jul '93 / Select

REVOLUTIONARY BLUES 1941-1951
Shimme-sha wabble / I wish I could shimmy like my sister Kate / Fidgety feet / Jelly roll blues / Mood indigo / Laura / St. Louis blues / Love for sale / At a Georgia camp meeting / Groovin' the minor / I had it but it's all gone now / Old stack o'lee blues / Darktown strutter's ball / Revolutionary blues / Out of the gallion / Changes made / Blame it on the blues / Blue horizon / Rose room / Oh, lady be good / What is this thing called love / Bugle call rag / Ole Miss Blues
CD _______________ CD 53106
Giants Of Jazz / May '97 / Cadillac / Jazz Music / Target/BMG

SIDNEY BECHET & HIS NEW ORLEANS FEETWARMERS 1940-1941
CD _______________ 882442
Music Memoria / Aug '93 / ADA / Discovery

SIDNEY BECHET & HIS NEW ORLEANS FEETWARMERS 1941-1943
CD _______________ 882452
Music Memoria / Aug '93 / ADA / Discovery

SIDNEY BECHET & MUGGSY SPANIER/ DON EWELL/DOC EVANS VOL.1
CD _______________ DD 226
Delmark / Feb '95 / ADA / Cadillac / CM / Direct / Hot Shot

SIDNEY BECHET & PEE WEE RUSSELL (Bechet, Sidney & Pee Wee Russell)
Crazy rhythm / Jazz me blues / Indiana / Bugle blues / On the sunny side of the street / Missy / Sugar / Sweet Georgia Brown / If I had you / I want a little girl
CD _______________ 8747142
DA Music / Jul '96 / Conifer/BMG

SIDNEY BECHET 1932-1951
CD Set _______________ CDB 1214
Giants Of Jazz / Jul '92 / Cadillac / Jazz Music / Target/BMG

SIDNEY BECHET 1937-1938
CD _______________ CD 593
Classic Jazz Masters / Sep '91 / Wellard

SIDNEY BECHET 1944-1945 (2CD Set)
CD _______________ 414682
Music Memoria / Mar '96 / ADA / Discovery

SIDNEY BECHET IN CONCERT
CD _______________ 710440
RTE / Apr '95 / ADA / Koch

SIDNEY DE PARIS 1943-1944
CD _______________ 409392
Music Memoria / Nov '95 / ADA / Discovery

SLIPPIN' AND SLIDIN' (The Bluebird Sessions)
Slippin' and slidin' / 12th St. rag / Shake it and break it / Old man blues / Ain't misbehavin' / Stompy Jones / Muskrat ramble / Coal black shine / Baby won't you please come home / Sweetie dear / Weary blues / One o'clock jump / Swing parade / I ain't gonna give nobody none of this jelly roll / Limehouse blues / Texas moaner blues / Blues in the air / I'm coming, Virginia / You're the limit / Rose bloom / Bugle call rag/Ole Miss Blues / St. Louis blues
CD _______________ 74321487302
Camden / May '97 / BMG

SUMMERTIME 1932-1940
I've found a new baby / Sweetie dear / Shag / Maple leaf rag / Really the blues / Weary blues / Lay your racket / I want you tonight / Ja-da / When you and I were young, Maggie / Oh, didn't he ramble / I thought, I heard Buddy Bolden say / High society / Winnin' boy blues / Tain't a fit night out for man or beast / Black stick blues / When the sun sets down south / Indian summer / Preachin' blues / Characteristic blues / Jungle drums / Chant in the night / Polka dot rag / Summertime
CD _______________ CD 53104
Giants Of Jazz / May '97 / Cadillac / Jazz Music / Target/BMG

WEARY BLUES
CD _______________ CD 56052
Jazz Roots / Mar '95 / Target/BMG

WEARY BLUES
CD _______________ JHR 73553
Jazz Hour / Jan '93 / Cadillac / Jazz Music / Target/BMG

Beck

MELLOW GOLD
Loser / Pay no mind (snoozer) / Fuckin' with my head (Mountain dew rock) / Whiskeyclone / Hotel City 1997 / Soul suckin' jerk / Truckdrivin' neighbours downstairs / Sweet sunshine / Beercan / Steal my body home / Nightmare hippy girl / Motherfucker / Blackhole
CD _______________ GED 24634
Geffen / Mar '94 / BMG

ODELAY
Devils haircut / Hotwax / Lord only knows / New pollution / Derelict / Novacane / Jackass / Where it's at / Minus / Sissyneck / Readymade / High 5 (rock the Catskills) / Ramshackle / Diskobox
CD _______________ GED 24926
CD _______________ GED 24908
Geffen / Jun '96 / BMG

ONE FOOT IN THE GRAVE
CD _______________ KLP 28CD
K / Jun '97 / Cargo / Greyhound / SRD

Beck, Elder Charles

ELDER BECK & ELDER CURRY 1930-1939
CD _______________ BDCD 6035

Blues Document / Apr '93 / ADA / Hot Shot / Jazz Music

ELDER CHARLES BECK VOL.2 1946-1956
CD _______________ DOCD 5524
Document / Apr '97 / ADA / Hot Shot / Jazz Music

Beck, Gordon

ONCE IS NEVER ENOUGH
CD _______________ FMRCD 20
Future / Sep '96 / ADA / Harmonia Mundi

ONE FOR THE ROAD
Good times, sometimes / Out of the shadows into the sun / Thoughts / Long, lean and lethal / What's this / Beautiful, but / One for the road / Shhhh / Pay now, live later
CD _______________ JMS 186752
JMS / Nov '95 / New Note/BMG

Beck, Jeff

BECKOLOGY (3CD Set)
Trouble in mind: *Tridents* / Nursery rhyme: *Tridents* / Wandering man blues: *Tridents* / Steeled blues: *Yardbirds* / Heart full of soul: *Yardbirds* / I'm not talking: *Yardbirds* / I ain't done wrong: *Yardbirds* / I'm a man: *Yardbirds* / Shapes of things: *Yardbirds* / Over under sideways down: *Yardbirds* / Happenings ten years time ago: *Yardbirds* / Hot house of Omagararshid: *Yardbirds* / Lost women: *Yardbirds* / Rack myh mind: *Yardbirds* / Nazz are blue: *Yardbirds* / Psycho daisies: *Yardbirds* / Jeff's boogie: *Yardbirds* / Too much monkey business: *Yardbirds* / Sun is shining: *Yardbirds* / You're a better man than I: *Yardbirds* / Love me like I love you: *Yardbirds* / Hi ho silver lining / Tallyman / Beck's bolero / I ain't superstitious: *Beck, Jeff Group* / Rock my plimsoul: *Beck, Jeff Group* / Jailhouse rock: *Beck, Jeff Group* / Plynth (water down the drain): *Beck, Jeff Group* / I've been drinking: *Beck, Jeff Group* / Definitely maybe: *Beck, Jeff Group* / New ways/train train: *Beck, Jeff Group* / Going down: *Beck, Jeff Group* / I can't give back the love I feel for you: *Beck, Jeff Group* / Superstition: *Beck, Bogert, Appice* / Black cat moan: *Beck, Bogert, Appice* / Blues deluxe BBA boogie: *Beck, Bogert, Appice* / Jizz whizz: *Beck, Bogert, Appice* / 'Cause we've ended as lovers / Goodbye Pork Pie Hat / Love is green / Diamond dust / Freeway jam: *Beck, Jeff & Jan Hammer Group* / Pump / People get ready: *Beck, Jeff & Rod Stewart* / Escape / Gets us all in the end / Back on the street / Wild thing / Train kept a rollin' / Sleepwalk / Stumble / Big block: *Beck, Jeff/Terry Bozzio/Tony Hymas* / Where were you: *Beck, Jeff/Terry Bozzio/Tony Hymas*
CD Set _______________ 4692622
Legacy / May '94 / Sony

BEST OF JEFF BECK, THE
Shapes of things / Morning dew / You shook me / I ain't superstitious / All shook up / Jailhouse rock / Plynth (water down the drain) / Hi ho silver lining / Tallyman / Love is blue / I've been drinking / Rock my plimsoul / Beck's bolero / Rice pudding / Greensleeves / Spanish boots
CD _______________ CDMFP 6202
Music For Pleasure / Nov '95 / EMI

BEST OF JEFF BECK, THE
Hi-ho silver lining / Beck's Bolero / Greensleeves / You shook me / Tallyman / Rock my plimsoul / Jailhouse rock / Shapes of things / All shook up / I ain't superstitious / Plynth (water down the drain) / Love is blue / Morning dew / Spanish boots / Rice pudding / I've been drinking
CD _______________ CDGOLD 1060
EMI Gold / Oct '96 / EMI

BLOW BY BLOW
It doesn't really matter / She's a woman / Constipated duck / Air blower / Scatterbrain / 'Cause we've ended as lovers / Thelonious / Freeway jam / Diamond dust
CD _______________ 4690122
Epic / Apr '94 / Sony

FLASH
Ambitious / Gets us all in the end / Escape / People get ready / Stop, look and listen / Get workin' / Ecstacy / Night after night / You know, we know / Get us all in the end / Ecstasy
CD _______________ 4688672
Epic / Feb '97 / Sony

JEFF BECK/ERIC CLAPTON ESSENTIALS (Beck, Jeff & Eric Clapton)
CD _______________ LECDD 639
Wisepack / Aug '95 / Conifer/BMG / THE

LEGENDS IN MUSIC
CD _______________ LECD 080
Wisepack / Jul '94 / Conifer/BMG / THE

THERE AND BACK
Star cycle / Too much to lose / You never knew / Pump / El Becko / Golden road / Space boogie / Final peace
CD _______________ 4777812
Epic / Feb '97 / Sony

TRUTH/BECKOLA (Beck, Jeff Group)
Shapes of things / Let me love you / Morning dew / You shook me / Ol' man river / Greensleeves / Rock my plimsoul / Beck's bolero / Blues deluxe / I ain't superstitious / All shook up / Spanish boots / Girl from Mill Valley / Jailhouse rock / Plynth (water down the drain) / Hangman's knee / Rice pudding
CD _______________ CDP 7954692
Premier/EMI / Feb '91 / EMI

Beck, Joe

BECK AND SANBORN
CD _______________ ZK 40805
Sony Jazz / Aug '97 / Sony

FINGER PAINTING
CD _______________ EFA 034532
Wavetone / Nov '95 / SRD

LIVE AT SALISHAN (Beck, Joe & Red Mitchell)
CD _______________ 174033
Capri / Nov '93 / Cadillac / Wellard

Becker, David

IN MOTION
Westward ho / Intro / In motion / Outta towner / Forgotten friends / Time has fun / Pepe / From the right side / Cobalt blue / Passion dance / Just because
CD _______________ R27 91672
Bluemoon / Oct '92 / New Note/Pinnacle

Becker, Jason

PERPETUAL BURN
Altitudes / Perpetual blues / Mabel's fatal fable / Temple of the absurd / Eleven blue Egyptians / Dweller in the cellar / Opus pocus
CD _______________ RR 9528 2
Roadrunner / Sep '88 / PolyGram

Becker, Walter

ELEVEN TRACKS OF WHACK
Down in the bottom / Junkie girl / Surf and or die / Book of liars / Lucky Henry / Hard up case / Cringemaker / Girlfriend / My Waterloo / This moody bastard / Hat too flat
CD _______________ 74321226092
Giant / Nov '94 / BMG

FOUNDERS OF STEELY DAN (Becker, Walter & Donald Fagen)
CD _______________ RMB 75004
Remember / Nov '93 / Total/BMG

PEARLS FROM THE PAST (Becker, Walter & Donald Fagen)
CD _______________ KLMCD 022
BAM / Jul '94 / Koch / Scratch/BMG

ROOT OF STEELY DAN, THE (Becker, Walter & Donald Fagen)
Android warehouse / Parker's band / You go where I go / Little with sugar / Stone piano / Roaring of the lamb / Charlie freak / This seal's been taken / More to come / Oh wow it's you / Take it out on me / Ida lee / Barrytown / Any world / Caves of Altamira / Horse in town / Sun mountain
CD _______________ 306152
Hallmark / Jan '97 / Carlton

YOU GOTTA WALK IT LIKE YOU TALK IT (Or You'll Loose That Beat/Original Soundtrack) (Becker, Walter & Donald Fagen)
You gotta walk it like you talk it / Flotsam and jetsam / War and peace / Roll back the meaning / You gotta walk it like you talk it (reprise) / Dog eat dog / Red giant/white dwarf / If it rains
CD _______________ SEECD 357
See For Miles/C5 / Jun '97 / Pinnacle

Beckett, Harry

ALL FOUR ONE
White sky / Time of day / One for all / Enchanted / Shadowy light / Happy 96 / Images of clarity / Better git it in your soul
CD _______________ SPJCD 547
Spotlite / May '93 / Cadillac / Jazz Music / New Note/Pinnacle / Swift

COMPARED 2 WHAT (Beckett, Harry Quintet)
CD _______________ BASIC 50008
ITM / Apr '96 / Koch / Tradelink

IMAGES OF CLARITY (Beckett, Harry & Didier Levallet/Tony Marsh)
CD _______________ EVCD 315
Evidence / Feb '94 / ADA / Cadillac / Harmonia Mundi

Beckingham, Keith

HAMMOND SHOWCASE REVISITED
There's no business like show business / Medley / Medley / Medley / Medley / Smile to smile / This heart of mine / This is my lovely day / Smoke gets in your eyes / Medley / Donkey serenade / Stormy weather / I have dreamed / Serenade in the night / My Fair Lady selection / Medley / Michael Legrand medley / Medley / Green cockatoo / Twilight time / Jerry Allen tribute / Branch line / Medley
CD _______________ OS 220
OS Digital / May '96 / Conifer/BMG

Becton, William

BROKEN (Becton, William & Friends)
Broken / Still in love with you / Fall afresh / Sure won't forget / No turning back / In your arms of love / 'Til the end / Joy / Be encouraged / Closer to you / Courage to journey on / 'Til you take the pain away / Let the healing again / Since the Lord changed my life / 'Til the end (jazz version)
CD _______________ CDK 9145
Alliance Music / Oct '95 / EMI

Bede, Arran

GOSSAMER MANSION
CD _______________ CDLCDL 1221
Lochshore / Nov '94 / ADA / Direct / Duncans

Bedford, David

GREAT EQUATORIAL
Great equatorial (Part 1 to part 6)
CD _______________ VP 156CD
Voiceprint / Oct '94 / Pinnacle

INSTRUCTIONS FOR ANGELS
Theme / Wanderers of the pale wood / Dazzling burden / Be music, night / First came the lion rider / Instructions for angels / Alleujah tympanis
CD _______________ CDV 2090
Virgin / Jun '97 / EMI

NURSES SONG WITH ELEPHANTS
It's easier than it looks / Nurses song with elephants / Some bright stars from Queens College / Trona / Sad and lonely faces
CD _______________ BP 116CD
Blueprint / Aug '96 / Pinnacle

ODYSSEY, THE
Penelope's shroud / King Aeolus / Penelope's shroud / Phaeacian games / Penelope's shroud / Sirens / Scylla and Charybdis / Penelope's shroud / Circe's island / Penelope's shroud completed / Battle in the hall
CD _______________ CDOVD 444
Virgin / Apr '94 / EMI

RIGEL 9
Forest / Anders' capture / City / Anders and the red one / Kapper and Lee in the forest / Death of the orange one / Funeral procession / Anders alone in the city / Ritual song / Anders flight through the forest / At the ship: countdown and lift-off / Finale
CD _______________ CDOVD 484
Charisma / Jun '97 / EMI

SONG OF THE WHITE HORSE, THE
Prelude: Wayland's Smithy / White horse / Blowing stone / Song of the white horse / Postlude / Text / Choir 1 / Choir 2
CD _______________ VP 110 CD
Voiceprint / Feb '93 / Pinnacle

STAR'S END
Side one / Side two
CD _______________ CDV 2020
Virgin / Jun '97 / EMI

VARIATIONS ON A RHYTHM
CD _______________ VP 180CD
Voiceprint / Feb '95 / Pinnacle

VARIATIONS ON A RHYTHM OF MIKE OLDFIELD (Bedford, David Tom Newman & Mike Oldfield)
CD _______________ VP 191CD
Voiceprint / Mar '95 / Pinnacle

Bedhead

BEHEADED
CD _______________ R 4052
Rough Trade / Oct '96 / Pinnacle

WHAT FUN LIFE WAS
CD _______________ TR 21CD
Trance / Apr '94 / SRD

Bedlam Rovers

FROTHING GREEN
CD _______________ NORM 171CD
Normal / Mar '94 / ADA / Direct

LAND OF NO SURPRISE
CD _______________ NORMAL 191CD
Normal / Aug '95 / ADA / Direct

SQUEEZE YOUR INNER CHILD
CD _______________ RTS 16
Return To Sender / Apr '95 / ADA / Direct

WALLOW
CD _______________ NORMAL 151CD
Normal / Mar '94 / ADA / Direct

Bedouin Ascent

MUSIC FOR PARTICALS
CD _______________ RSNCD 37
Rising High / Jul '95 / 3mv/Sony

SCIENCE, ART & RITUAL
CD _______________ RSNCD 27
Rising High / Nov '94 / 3mv/Sony

Bee Gees

CHILDREN OF THE WORLD
You should be dancing / You stepped into my life / Love so right / Lovers / Can't keep a good man down / Boogie child / Love me / Subway / Way it was / Children of the world
CD _______________ 8236582
Polydor / Nov '89 / PolyGram

CLAUSTROPHOBIA
CD _______________ CDSGP 0307
Prestige / Aug '97 / Else / Total/BMG

CUCUMBER CASTLE
If I only had my mind on something else / Then you left me / I was the child / Sweet heart / My thing / Turning tide / IOIO / Lord / I lay down and die / Bury me down by the river / Chance of love / Don't forget to remember
CD _______________ 8337832
Polydor / Nov '89 / PolyGram

ESP
ESP / You win again / Live or die / Giving up the ghost / Longest night / This is your life / Angela / Overnight / Crazy for your love / Backtafunk
CD _______________ 9255412
WEA / Feb '95 / Warner Music

EVER INCREASING CIRCLES
Three kisses of love / Batle of the blue and grey / Take hold of that star / Claustrophobia / could it be / Turn around and look at me / Theme from Jamie McPheeters / You wouldn't know / How many birds / Big chance / I don't think it's funny / How love was true / Glasshouse
CD _______________ CDTB 132
Thunderbolt / '91 / TKO Magnum

HORIZONTAL
World / And the sun will shine / Lemons never forget / Really and sincerely / Birdie told me / With the sun in my eyes / Massachusetts / Harry Braff / Daytime girl / Earnest of being George / Change is made / Horizontal
CD _______________ 8336592
Polydor / Mar '90 / PolyGram

IDEA
Let there be love / In the Summer of his years / Down to earth / I've gotta get a message to you / When the swallows fly / I started a joke / Swansong / Kitty can / Indian gin and whisky dry / Such a shame / Idea / I have decided to join the airforce / Kilburn towers
CD _______________ 8336602
Polydor / Nov '89 / PolyGram

LEGEND BEGINS, THE
Spicks and specks / You wouldn't know / I was a lover, a leader of men / How love was true / To be or not to be / Theme from Jamie McPhetter's / I want home / I am the world / Could it be I'm in love / I don't think it's funny / Every day I have to cry / Wine and women / Claustrophobia / Turn around, look at me
CD _______________ 307662
Hallmark / Jul '97 / Carlton

LIFE IN A TIN CAN
Saw a new morning / I don't wanna be the one / South Dakota morning / Livin in Chicago / While I play / My life has been a song / Come home Johnny Bridie / Method in my madness
CD _______________ 8337882
Polydor / Jul '92 / PolyGram

ONE
Ordinary lives / Bodyguard / Tears / Flesh and blood / House of shame / One / It's my neighbourhood / Tokyo nights / Wish you were here / Will you ever let him
CD _______________ 9258872
WEA / Feb '95 / Warner Music

SIZE ISN'T EVERYTHING
Paying the price of love / Kiss of life / How to fall in love Pt 1 / Omega man / Haunted house / Heart like mine / Anything for you / Blue island / Above and beyond / For whom the bell tolls / Fallen angel / Decadance
CD _______________ 5199452
Polydor / Sep '93 / PolyGram

SPICKS AND SPECKS
CD _______________ RMB 75068
Remember / Aug '93 / Total/BMG

SPIRITS HAVING FLOWN
Tragedy / Too much heaven / Love you inside out / Reaching out / Spirits (having flown) / Living together / I'm satisfied / Until
CD _______________ 8273352
Polydor / Nov '89 / PolyGram

SPOTLIGHT ON BEE GEES
Wine and women / Turn around, look at me / How many birds / Claustrophobia / Three kisses of love / To be or not to be / I don't think it's funny / Spicks and specks / How love was true / Follow the wind / Take hold of that star / I was a lover, a leader of men / I am the world / Second hand people / Every day I have to cry / Monday's rain
CD _______________ HADCD 105
Javelin / Feb '94 / Henry Hadaway / THE

STILL WATERS
Alone / I surrender / I could not love you more / Still waters run deep / My lover's prayer / With my eyes closed / Irresistible force / Closer than close / I will / Obsessions / Miracles happen / Smoke and mirrors
CD _______________ 5373022
Polydor / Mar '97 / PolyGram

TALES FROM THE BROTHERS GIBB (A History In Song)
New York mining disaster 1941 / I can't see nobody / Holiday / Massachusetts / Barker of the UFO / World / Sir Geoffrey saved the world / Sun will shine / Words / Sinking ships / Jumbo / Singer sang his song / I've got to get a message to you / I started a joke / First of May / Melody fair / Tomorrow tomorrow / Sun in the morning / Saved by the bell / Don't forget to remember / If I only had my mind on something else / IOIO / Railroad / I'll kiss your memory / Lonely days / Morning of my life / How can you mend a broken heart / Country women / My world / On time / Run to me / Alive / Saw a new morning / Wouldn't it be someone / Elisa / King and country / Mr. Natural / Country woman / Don't want to live inside myself / It doesn't matter too much to me / Throw a penny / Charade / Jive talkin' / Nights on broadway / Fanny (Be tender with my love) / You should be dancing (Long version) / Love so right / Boogie child / Edge of the universe / How deep is your love / Stayin' alive / Night fever / More than a woman / If I can't have you / Don't throw it all away / Too much heaven / Tragedy / Love you inside out / He's a liar / Another lonely night in New York / Woman in you / Someone belonging to someone / Toys / My eternal love / Where tomorrow is / Letting go / ESP / You win again / Ordinary lives / One / Juliet / To love somebody
CD Set 8439112
Polydor / Nov '90 / PolyGram

TO BE OR NOT TO BE
Three kings of love / Battle of the blue and grey / Take hold of that star / Claustrophobia / Could it be / Turn around look at me / Theme from Jamie McPheeters / You wouldn't know / How many birds / Big chance / I don't think it's funny / How love was true / Glasshouse / Everyday I have to cry / Wine and women / Follow the wind / I was a lover / Children laughing / I want home / Spicks and specks / I am the world / Playdown / I don't know why I bother myself / Monday's rain / To be or not to be / Swcond hand people
CD CDTB 170
Thunderbolt / Oct '95 / TKO Magnum

TOMORROW THE WORLD
Everyday I have to cry / Wine and women / Follow the wind / I was a lover / And the children laughing / I want home / Spicks and specks / I am the world / Playdown / I don't know why I bother myself / Monday's rain / To be or not to be / Second hand people
CD CDTB 135
Magnum Music / Jan '92 / TKO Magnum

TRAFALGAR
How can you mend a broken heart / Israel / Greatest man in the world / It's just the way / Remembering / Somebody / Stop the music / Trafalgar / Don't wanna live inside myself / When do I / Dearest / Lion in winter / Walking back to Waterloo
CD 8337862
Polydor / Mar '90 / PolyGram

TWO YEARS ON
Two years on / Portrait of Louise / Man for all seasons / Sincere relation / Back home / First mistake I made / Lonely days / Alone again / Tell me why / Lay it on me / Every second, every minute / I'm weeping
CD 8337852
Polydor / Mar '90 / PolyGram

VERY BEST OF THE BEE GEES
You win again / How deep is your love / Night fever / Tragedy / Massachusetts / I've gotta get a message to you / You should be dancing / New York mining disaster 1941 / World / First of May / Don't forget to remember / Saved by the bell / Run to me / Jive talkin' / More than a woman / Stayin' alive / Too much heaven / Ordinary lives / To love somebody / Nights on Broadway
CD 8473392
Polydor / Nov '90 / PolyGram

YOU WOULDN'T KNOW
CD JHD 006
Tring / Jun '92 / Tring

Beebe, Jim

SULTRY SERENADE, A (Beebe, Jim Chicago Jazz)
Chicago / Canal St. blues / Blue prelude / This joint is jumpin' / Sultry serenade / Travellin' light / Bye and bye / Drummin' man / Buddy Bolden's blues / Just a closer walk with thee / Night train
CD DE 230
Delmark / Jun '97 / ADA / Cadillac / CM / Direct / Hot Shot

Beechman, Laurie

NO ONE IS ALONE
CD VSD 5623
Varese Sarabande / Nov '96 / Pinnacle

TIME BETWEEN THE TIME
Another hundred people / It might be you / Look at that face / Very precious love / Long before I knew you / Look of love / House is not a home / I'll never stop loving you / Shining sea/Shadow of your smile / Soon it's gonna rain/Rain sometimes / Music that makes me dance / Time between the time / Never never land / Home
CD DRGCD 5230
DRG / Nov '93 / Discovery / New Note/ Pinnacle

Beef Masters

SECRET PLACE
CD VIRION 103
Sound Virus / Sep '94 / Plastic Head

Beenie Man

BEENIE MAN GOLD
CD CRCD 32
Charm / May '94 / Jet Star

BEENIE MAN MEETS MAD COBRA (Beenie Man & Mad Cobra)
CD VPCD 1413
VP / Aug '95 / Greensleeves / Jet Star / Total/BMG

DEFEND IT
CD SVCD 3
Shocking Vibes / Feb '94 / Jet Star

DIS UNU FI HEAR
CD HCD 7010
Hightone / Nov '94 / ADA / Koch

MAESTRO
Intro / Heights of great man / Nuff gal / Yaw yaw / Be my lady / Maestro / Old dog / Jerusalem / Blackboard / Any Mr. man / Broadway: *Beenie Man & Little Kirk* / Man royal / Oh Jah Jah: *Beenie Man & Silver Cat* / His-story / Africans / Girl's way / Nuh lock: *Beenie Man & Little Kirk* / One big road / Si mi ya / Never been down / Outro/Special thanks
CD GRELCD 234
Greensleeves / Jan '97 / Jet Star / SRD

REGGAE MAX
CD JSRNCD 14
Jet Star / Mar '97 / Jet Star

RUFF & RUGGED STRICTLY RAGGA
CD RNCD 2041
Rhino / Jan '94 / Grapevine/PolyGram / Jet Star

Beer, Phil

ALLANZA (Beer, Phil & Incantation)
CD RGFCD 012
Road Goes On Forever / Nov '90 / Direct

HARD HATS
Fireman's song / Chance / This far / Blinded by love / More / Blind fiddler / This year / Hard hats / She could laugh / Think it over
CD HTDCD 24
HTD / Sep '96 / CM / Pinnacle

SHOW OF HANDS
CD RGFCD 010
Road Goes On Forever / Nov '91 / Direct

WORKS, THE
CD OCOCD 1
Old Court / Feb '96 / ADA

Beers Family

SEASONS OF PEACE
Run like a deer / Seasons of peace / Song of the virgin / Blue spring rain / Three little drummers from Africa / I got a bird that whistles / Ladybug song / Simple gifts / Fiddler's green / two foxes / Kitty alone / Dumbarton's drums / Green gravel / Peace carol / Blackhawk waltz
CD BCD 146
Biograph / Jun '97 / ADA / Cadillac / Direct / Hot Shot / Jazz Music / Wellard

Bees, Andrew

MILITANT
CD ML 818112
Music / Sep '95 / Jet Star

Beesley, John

INSPIRATION
CD CDGRS 1275
Grosvenor / Feb '95 / Grosvenor

ORCHESTRALLY ORGANISED
Cabaret / All the things you are / Take five / Yellow submarine / Caravan / Gigue fugue / Whiter shade of pale / Waterloo march / Henry Mancini medley / I dreamed a dream / Bohemian rhapdosy / Power of love / Olympic flame / Morning / Blue rondo a la Turk / Summertime / Stars and stripes forever
CD OS 204
OS Digital / Mar '94 / Conifer/BMG

PERFORMANCE
Trumpet blues and cantabile / Think twice / Songs of praise / I got rhythm / Bridge over troubled water / Jurassic park / Intermezzo from Cavalleria Rusticana / Night in Tunisia / Overture to the light Cavalry / Can you feel the love tonight / Nutcracker suite - characteristic dances / Eleanor Rigby
CD CDGRS 1282
Grosvenor / Nov '95 / Grosvenor

Beeston Pipe Band

AMAZING GRACE
CD EUCD 1189
ARC / Apr '92 / ADA / ARC Music

Beevar, Brian

ONCE IN A LIFE
CD RM 2222
Real / Aug '96 / Else

BEF

MUSIC OF QUALITY AND DISTINCTION VOL.1
Ball of confusion: *Turner, Tina* / Secret Life of Arabia: *MacKenzie, Billy* / There's a Ghost in my House: *Jones, Paul* / These Boots are made for Walking: *Yates, Paula* / Suspicious Minds: *Glitter, Gary* / You keep me hangin' on: *Nolan, Bernie* / Wichita Lineman: *Gregory, Glen* / Anyone who had a Heart: *Shaw, Sandie* / Perfect Day: *Gregory, Glen* / It's Over: *MacKenzie, Billy*
CD CDBEF 1
Virgin / Aug '92 / EMI

Beggar's Opera

FINAL CURTAIN, THE
CD SCRCD 015
Scratch / Sep '96 / Koch / Scratch/BMG

Beggars & Thieves

LOOK WHAT YOU CREATE
CD MTMCD 199619
MTM / Apr '97 / Cargo

Begley, Philomena

COUNTRY QUEEN FOR 30 YEARS
Every second / Look at us / Walkin', talkin', cryin', barely beatin' broken heart / Picture of me (without you) / Bright lights and country music / Start living again / Bed you made for me / Home I'll be / Our wedding day / Just one time / If my heart had windows / Family tree / Last rose of summer / Life is not always a rainbow / Gold and silver days / Bing bang boom
CD RITZRCD 522
Ritz / Nov '92 / Pinnacle

IN HARMONY (Begley, Philomena & Mick Flavin)
No love left / Just between you and me / I'm wasting your time you're wasting mine / Till a tear becomes a rose / Always, always / We're strangers again / We'll get ahead someday / All you've got to do is dream / Daisy chain / Don't believe me I'm lying / You can't break the chains of love / Let's pretend we're not married tonight / How can I (help you forgive me) / Somewhere between
CD RITZCD 0061
Ritz / Apr '91 / Pinnacle

SILVER ANNIVERSARY ALBUM
Key is in the mailbox / Here today and gone tomorrow / Rose of my heart / Behind the footlights / Jeannie's afraid of the dark / Red is the rose / Dark island / Leavin' on your mind / Queen of the silver dollar / Blanket on the ground / Truck drivin' woman / One is one too many / Galway Bay / Old arboe
CD RITZCD 505
Ritz / '90 / Pinnacle

SIMPLY DIVINE (Begley, Philomena & Ray Lynam)
You don't know love / Simply divine / Together alone / Near you / Don't cross over an old love / Making plans / Sweetest of all / I'll never need another you / She sang the melody / As long as we're dreaming / Hold on / Fire of two old flames
CD RITZSCD 425
Ritz / Apr '93 / Pinnacle

Begley, Seamus

MEITHEAL (Begley, Seamus & Stephen Cooney)
CD HBCD 0004
Hummingbird / Jul '93 / ADA / Direct / Grapevine/PolyGram

Begnagrad

BROKEN DANCE, A
CD AAYACDT 1190
Ayaa Disques / Apr '91 / ReR Megacorp

Beguiled

BLUE DIRGE
CD EFA 115742
Crypt / Apr '94 / Shellshock/Disc

Behan, Kathleen

WHEN ALL THE WORLD WAS YOUNG
CD CLUNCD 046
Mulligan / Aug '86 / ADA / CM

Beherit

DRAWING DOWN THE MOON
CD SP 1014CD
Spinefarm / May '96 / Plastic Head

ELECTRIC DOOM
CD SPI 028CD
Spinefarm / Mar '96 / Plastic Head

H4180V21C
CD SP 119CD
Spinefarm / Jun '94 / Plastic Head

Beiderbecke, Bix

20 CLASSIC TRACKS
Jazz me blues / Somebody stole my gal / Ol man river / Wringin' and twistin' / Clarinet marmalade / Ostrich walk / Mississippi mud / Baby, won't you please come home / Goose pimples / Margie / Louisiana / Rhythm king / Three blind mice / Krazy cat / Good man is hard to find / Thou swell / Wa-da-da / Louise / Japanese sandman / Dusky stevedore
CD CDMFP 6163
Music For Pleasure / May '95 / EMI

AT THE JAZZ BAND BALL (1924-1928)
Fidgety feet / Tiger rag / Flock o'blues / I'm glad / Toddlin' blues / Davenport blues / In a mist / Riverboat shuffle / Ostrich walk / At the jazz band ball / Clementine / Deep down South / For no reason at all / From Monday on / I'm coming Virginia / Jazz me blues / Krazy kat / Mississippi mud / San / Since my best gal turned me down / Singin' the blues / Way down yonder in New Orleans
CD CDAJA 5080
Living Era / Apr '91 / Select

BEIDERBECKE AFFAIR, THE
Riverboat shuffle / Tiger rag / Davenport blues / I'm looking over a four leaf clover / Trumbology / Clarinet marmalade / Ostrich walk / Way down yonder in New Orleans / Three blind mice / Clementine / Royal garden blues / Coquette / When / Lovable / Is it gonna be long / Oh you have no idea / Felix the cat / T'ain't so honey, t'ain't so / I'd rather cry over you / Louisiana / Futuristic rhythm / Raisin' the roof / Rockin' chair / Strut Miss Lizzie / Georgia on my mind
CD GRF 079
Tring / '93 / Tring

BEIDERBECKE COLLECTION, THE (20 Classics From The Jazz Genius)
I'm coming Virginia / Rhythm king / At the jazz band ball / Ostrich walk / Somebody stole my gal / Goose pimples / Royal garden blues / Cryin' all day / Good man is hard to find / Trumbology / Singing the blues / Since my best gal turned me down / Louisianna / Clarinet marmalade / Sorry / Riverboat shuffle / Thou swell / Ol' man river / Wa-da-da (Everybody's doin' it now) / Jazz me blues
CD 306302
Hallmark / Jan '97 / Carlton

BIX
CD CD 14532
Jazz Portraits / Jan '94 / Jazz Music

BIX 'N' BING (Recordings From 1927-1929) (Beiderbecke, Bix/Bing Crosby/ Paul Whiteman Orchestra)
Changes / Mary / There ain't no sweet man that's worth the salt of my tears / Sunshine / Mississippi mud / High water / From Monday on / Loveable / My pet / Louisiana / Do I hear you saying I love you / You took advantage of me / That's my weakness now / Because my baby don't mean maybe now / I'm in seventh heaven / Reaching for someone (and not finding anyone there) / Oh Miss Hannah / Your mother and mine / Waiting at the end of the road / T'ain't so honey, t'ain't so
CD CDAJA 5005
Living Era / Oct '88 / Select

BIX BEIDERBECKE
CD DVX 08062
Deja Vu / May '95 / THE

BIX BEIDERBECKE (2CD Set)
CD Set R2CD 4023
Deja Vu / Jan '96 / THE

BIX BEIDERBECKE & THE WOLVERINES
CD CBC 10013
Timeless Jazz / Feb '94 / New Note/ Pinnacle

BIX BEIDERBECKE 1924
CD CBC 1013
Bellaphon / Jun '93 / New Note/Pinnacle

BIX BEIDERBECKE AND THE CHICAGO CORNETS
Fidgety feet / Jazz me blues / Oh baby / Copenhagen / Riverboat shuffle / Susie / Royal garden blues / Tiger rag / I need some pettin' / Sensation / Lazy daddy / Tia Juana / Big boy / I'm glad / Flovk o' blues / Toddlin' blues / Davenport blues / Prince of Wails / When my sugar walks down the street / Steady roll blues / Mobile blues / Really a pain / Chicago blues / Hot mittens / Buddy's habit
CD MCD 47019 2
Milestone / Jun '93 / Cadillac / Complete/ Pinnacle / Jazz Music / Wellard

BIX BEIDERBECKE GOLD (2CD Set)
CD Set D2CD 4023
Deja Vu / Jun '95 / THE

BIXOLOGY
Jazz me blues / At the jazz band ball / Royal garden blues / Sorry / Singin' the blues / I'm coming Virginia / Way down yonder in New Orleans / For no reason at all in C / Goose pimples / Trumbology / Ostrich walk / Riverboat shuffle / Davenport blues / Copenhagen / Fidgety feet / Tiger rag / In a mist / Clementine / Thou swell / Ol' man river / Wa-da-da / Louisiana / Margie / I'll be a friend with pleasure / Bessie couldn't help it
CD _____ CD 53017
Giants Of Jazz / Jun '88 / Cadillac / Jazz Music / Target/BMG

CLASSIC YEARS, THE
CD _____ CDSGP 0178
Prestige / Nov '95 / Else / Total/BMG

CLASSICS 1924-1927
CD _____ CLASSICS 778
Classics / Mar '95 / Discovery / Jazz Music

CLASSICS 1927-1930
CD _____ CLASSICS 788
Classics / Nov '94 / Discovery / Jazz Music

COMPLETE BIX BEIDERBECKE, THE
CD Set _____ BIX BOX
IRD / Jul '91 / Cadillac / Harmonia Mundi

FIDGETY FEET
Fidgety feet / Jazz me blues / Copenhagen / Riverboat shuffle / Oh baby / Susie / Sensation rag / Lazy daddy / Tiger rag / Big boy / Tia juana
CD _____ BIX 1
IRD / Jul '91 / Cadillac / Harmonia Mundi

FROM MONDAY ON
CD _____ BIX 5
IRD / Jul '91 / Cadillac / Harmonia Mundi

GENIUS OF BIX BEIDERBECKE
Jazz me blues / Thou swell / Royal garden blues / At the jazz band ball / Mississippi mud / Riverboat shuffle / T'ain't so honey, t'ain't so / Clementine / Lonely melody / There ain't no sweet man that's worth the salt of my tears / Dardanella / Sugar / Since my best gal turned me down / Wa-da-da / Rhythm king / Clarinet marmalade / I'm coming Virginia / Crying all day / Deep down South / I'll be a friend with pleasure
CD _____ PASTCD 9765
Flapper / Oct '91 / Pinnacle

GOOSE PIMPLES
CD _____ BIX 4
IRD / Jul '91 / Cadillac / Harmonia Mundi

I LIKE THAT
CD _____ BIX 8
IRD / Jul '91 / Cadillac / Harmonia Mundi

I'M COMING VIRGINIA
CD _____ BIX 3
IRD / Jul '91 / Cadillac / Harmonia Mundi

IN THE DARK
CD _____ BIX 9
IRD / Jul '91 / Cadillac / Harmonia Mundi

INDISPENSABLE BIX BEIDERBECKE 1924-1930, THE
I didn't know / Idolizing / Sunday / I'm proud of a baby like you / I'm looking over a four leaf clover / I'm gonna meet my sweetie now / Hoosier sweetheart / My pretty girl / Slow river / In my merry Oldsmobile / Clementine / Washboard blues / Changes / Mary / Lonely melody / San / Back in your own backyard / There ain't no sweet man that's worth the salt of my tears / Dardanella / From Monday on / Mississippi mud / Sugar / Coquette / When / Lovable / My pet / Forget me not / Louisiana / You took advantage of me / Rockin' chair / Barnacle Bill the sailor / Deep down south / I don't mind walking in the rain / I'll be a friend with pleasure / Georgia on my mind / Bessie couldn't help it
CD Set _____ ND 89572
RCA / Mar '94 / BMG

INTRODUCTION TO BIX BEIDERBECKE 1924-1930, AN
CD _____ 4012
Best Of Jazz / Aug '94 / Discovery

JAZZ MASTERS
CD _____ CDMFP 6297
Music For Pleasure / Mar '97 / EMI

JAZZ ME BLUES
CD _____ JHR 73517
Jazz Hour / '91 / Cadillac / Jazz Music / Target/BMG

JAZZ ME BLUES
CD _____ CDD 490
Progressive / Jul '91 / Jazz Music

LEON BISMARCK 'BIX' BEIDERBECKE
Singin' the blues / Jazz me blues / All the jazz band hall / Royal garden blues / Sorry / I'm coming Virginia / Trumbology / Goose pimples / Riverboat shuffle / For no reason at all in C / Fidgety feet / Thou swell / Margie / Clementine / Ol' man river / Louisiana / In a mist / I'll be a friend with pleasure
CD _____ CD 56016
Jazz Roots / Aug '94 / Target/BMG

MY MELANCHOLY BABY
CD _____ BIX 7
IRD / Jul '91 / Cadillac / Harmonia Mundi

QUINTESSENCE, THE (1924-1930/2CD Set)
CD Set _____ FA 215
Fremeaux / Oct '96 / ADA / Discovery

SINGIN' THE BLUES
Trumbology / Clarinet marmalade / Singin' the blues / Ostrich walk / Riverboat shuffle / I'm going Virginia / Way down yonder in New Orleans / For no reason at all / Three blind mice / Blue river / There's a cradle in Caroline / In a mist / Wringin' and twistin' / Humpty and dumpty / Krazy kat / Baltimore / There ain't no land like Dixieland to me / Just an hour of love / I'm wondering who
CD _____ 4663092
Sony Jazz / '91 / Sony

SUNDAY
CD _____ BIX 2
IRD / Jul '91 / Cadillac / Harmonia Mundi

THOU SWELL
CD _____ BIX 6
IRD / Jul '91 / Cadillac / Harmonia Mundi

TIGER RAG
CD _____ TKCD 020
Magnum America / Nov '96 / TKO Magnum

Being

SELECTED TRANSMISSIONS (2CD Set)
Mune / McLaren / Fotts / Mavebeep Pt.3 / Flee / Ayemooth / Foamy / Ryam / Toobit / Aquapan / Eeeshab / Toyled / Quickie
CD Set _____ SE 006CD
Special Emissions / Feb '96 / Vital

TIDES
CD _____ EFA 290092
Spacefrog / Nov '95 / SRD / Vital

Beirach, Richie

ANTARCTICA
Ice shelf / Neptune's bellows / Penguins on parade / Deception island / Mirage / Water lilies (The cloud) / Empress
CD _____ ECD 220862
Evidence / Jun '94 / ADA / Cadillac / Harmonia Mundi

DOUBLE EDGE (Beirach, Richie & David Liebman)
CD _____ STCD 4091
Storyville / Feb '89 / Cadillac / Jazz Music / Wellard

ELEGY FOR BILL EVANS
CD _____ STCD 4151
Storyville / Feb '90 / Cadillac / Jazz Music / Wellard

EXPLORATIONS AND IMPRESSIONS (Beirach, Richie & Francois Moutin/ Steve Davis)
Pendulum / Blue and green / Softly as in a morning sunrise / Elm / Nardis / Free/Stella by star light/Solar
CD _____ DTRCD 123
Double Time / Apr '97 / Express Jazz

LEAVING
CD _____ STCD 4149
Storyville / Feb '90 / Cadillac / Jazz Music / Wellard

LIVE AT MAYBECK RECITAL HALL
CD _____ CCD 4518
Concord Jazz / Aug '92 / New Note/ Pinnacle

OMERTA
CD _____ STCD 4154
Storyville / Feb '90 / Cadillac / Jazz Music / Wellard

SELF PORTRAITS
CD _____ CMPCD 51
CMP / Jun '92 / Cargo / Grapevine/ PolyGram / Vital/SAM

TRUST (Beirach, Richie Trio)
What are the rules / Trust / Moor / Jamala / Boston Harry / Gargoyles / Nefertiti / Johnny B / Rectilinear
CD _____ ECD 221432
Evidence / Mar '96 / ADA / Cadillac / Harmonia Mundi

Beken, Munir Nurettin

ART OF THE TURKISH UD, THE
Karce / Fihrist taksimi / Pesrev / Taksim / Pesrev / Taksim / Saz semaisi / Kocekeler / Cecen kizi / Son pesrev/Son yuruk semaii / Kapris / Ege de yagmur sevinci / Susamurunun aski / Dugun evinde / Fantaisie / Konser etudu / Kervan
CD _____ ROUCD 1135
Rounder / May '97 / ADA / CM / Direct

Bel Biv Devoe

POISON
Dope / BBD (I thought it was me) / Let me know something / Do me / Ronnie, Bobby, Ricky, Mike / Ralph and Johnny (word to the Mutha) / Poison / Ain't nut'in changed / When will I see you smile / Again / I do need you

CD _____ MCLD 19299
MCA / Oct '95 / BMG

Bel Canto

BIRDS OF PASSAGE
CD _____ CRAM 065
Crammed Discs / '88 / Grapevine/ PolyGram / New Note/Pinnacle / Prime / RTM/Disc

MAGIC BOX
Kiss of Spring / Bombay / Rumour / Magic box / Freelaunch in the jungle / Sleepwalker / Big belly butterfly / Magic box
CD _____ 7567926172
Atlantic / May '96 / Warner Music

SHIMMERING, WARM AND BRIGHT
CD _____ CRAM 077
Crammed Discs / Apr '92 / Grapevine/ PolyGram / New Note/Pinnacle / Prime / RTM/Disc

WHITE OUT CONDITION
CD _____ CRAM 57
Crammed Discs / Aug '93 / Grapevine/ PolyGram / New Note/Pinnacle / Prime / RTM/Disc

Bel, M'Bilia

BAMELI SOY
CD _____ SHCD 43025
Shanachie / Jul '91 / ADA / Greensleeves / Koch

Belafonte, Harry

BEST OF HARRY BELAFONTE
CD _____ DLCD 4003
Dixie Live / Mar '95 / TKO Magnum

CALYPSO FROM JAMAICA
Man smart, woman smarter / Kingston market / Come back Liza / Calypso war / Island in the sun / I do adore her / Belinda / Not me / Hosanna / Jackass song / Kitch cavalcade / Mahalia, I want back my dollar / Brown skin girl / Dolly dawn / Donkey city / Coconut woman
CD _____ CD 62072
Saludos Amigos / Apr '95 / Target/BMG

FOLK SONGS FROM THE WORLD
CD _____ CD 12518
Music Of The World / Feb '95 / ADA / Target/BMG

HARRY BELAFONTE
Mama look a boo boo / Day-O (Banana boat song) / Angelina / Matilda, Matilda / Coconut woman / John Henry / Jamaica farewell / Scarlet ribbons / Jump in the line / Jump down, spin around / Hava Nagila / Danny boy / Kingston market / Manha de carnival / Island in the sun / Shenandoah / When the saints go marching in
CD _____ 399544
Koch Presents / Jun '97 / Koch

HARRY BELAFONTE RETURNS TO CARNEGIE HALL
Jump down, spin around / Suzanne / Little lyric of great importance / Chickens / Vaichazkem / I do adore her / Ballad of Sigmund Freud / I've been driving on bald mountain / Waterboy / Hole in the bucket / Click song / One more dance / Ox drivers / Red rosy bush / Didn't it rain / Hene ma tov / I know where / I'm going / Old King Cole / La bamba
CD _____ 09026626902
RCA Victor / Jun '95 / BMG

ISLAND IN THE SUN
CD _____ WMCD 5643
Disky / May '94 / Disky / THE

STATIONEN
CD _____ 16092
Laserlight / Jul '94 / Target/BMG

VERY BEST OF HARRY BELAFONTE, THE
CD _____ MCCD 059
Music Club / '92 / Disc / THE

Belanger, Jean-Francois

CAP-AUX-SORCIERS
CD _____ JFB 01CD
JFB / Apr '96 / ADA

Belden, Bob

WHEN DOVES CRY (The Music Of Prince) (Belden, Bob Ensemble)
Diamonds and pearls / Purple rain / Kiss / When doves cry / Arms of Orion / Nothing compares 2 U / 1999 / Little red corvette / Question of U / When 2 R in love / Baby I'm a star
CD _____ CDP 8295152
Blue Note / Oct '94 / EMI

Belew, Adrian

EXPERIMENTAL GUITAR SERIES VOL.1
CD _____ DGM 9611
Discipline / Feb '97 / Pinnacle

OP ZOP TOO WAH
CD _____ DGM 9609
Discipline / Dec '96 / Pinnacle

Belgium

CUMBERLAND'S TREE
Cumberland's tree / Rico / Static music no.6 / Rain / Lost colour blue / Static music no.5 / Static music no.8 / Molly had a job / Wey / Ozone / In the spoon house / Deathwish / Rue Des Lemmenardes
CD _____ KLB 30032
Extreme / Nov '96 / Vital/SAM

Belial

NEVER AGAIN
CD _____ LRC 666
Lethal / Feb '94 / Plastic Head

Belile, Elspeth

YOUR ONLY OTHER OPTION
CD _____ NAR 111CD
New Alliance / Sep '94 / Plastic Head

Belisha Beacon

GOODBYE
CD _____ LF 245CD
Lost & Found / Jul '96 / Plastic Head

Bell, Alan

WITH BREAD & FISHES
CD _____ DRGNCD 942
Dragon / Apr '94 / ADA / Cadillac / CM / Roots / Wellard

Bell, Carey

CAREY BELL'S BLUES HARP
CD _____ DE 622
Delmark / Dec '95 / ADA / Cadillac / CM / Direct / Hot Shot

DEEP DOWN
I got to let go / Let me stir in your pot / When I get drunk / Low down dirty shame / Borrow your love / Lonesome stranger / After you / I got a rich man's woman / Jawbreaker / Must I holler / Tired of giving you my love
CD _____ ALCD 4828
Alligator / Feb '95 / ADA / CM / Direct

DYNASTY (Bell, Carey & Lurrie)
Brought up the hard way / (I shoulda did) What my mama told me / Sail on / I'll be your 44 / Gladys shuffle / I need you so bad / 1215 W. Belmont / Second hand man / New harp in town / Going back to Louisiana / No picks / I don't need no woman
CD _____ JSPCD 276
JSP / Jan '97 / ADA / Cadillac / Direct / Hot Shot / Target/BMG

HARPSLINGER
What my Mama told me / Pretty baby / Blues with a feeling / 85% / Sweet little woman / It's so easy to love you / Strange woman / Last night
CD _____ JSPCD 264
JSP / Nov '95 / ADA / Cadillac / Direct / Hot Shot / Target/BMG

HEARTACHES AND PAIN
Carey bell rocks / Heartaches and pain / One day your gonna get lucky / Black-eyed peas / So hard to leave you alone / Stop that train conductor / Everything's gonna be alright / Capri crash
CD _____ DD 666
Delmark / Mar '97 / ADA / Cadillac / CM / Direct / Hot Shot

Bell, Chris

I AM THE COSMOS
CD _____ RCD 10222
Rykodisc / Mar '97 / ADA / Vital

Bell, Clive

SHAKUHACHI
CD _____ EUCD 1135
ARC / '91 / ADA / ARC Music

Bell, Derek

ANCIENT MUSIC FOR THE IRISH HARP
Reminiscences of Sean O Riada / Colonel O'Hara / Little Molly O / Love in secret / Soft mild morning / Wexford bells / Lady Blaney / Within a mile of Edinburgh town / An buachaill Caol Dubh / Lady Iveagh/Black rose bud / Dawning of the day/Green woods of truagh/Captivating youth / Carolan's devotion / Lonesome/An paistin fionn / Churchyard of Creagan/Brown sloe bush/Benevolent Father Dona / Untitled air/Thomas a Burca / Lulaby/Bardic hornpipe / Harp serenade/Paraguayan dance in G / Dances from the Quechua Indians
CD _____ CC 59CD
Claddagh / Feb '93 / ADA / CM / Direct

CAROLAN'S FAVOURITE (Music Of Carolan Vol.2)
Carolan's favourite jig/Carolan's fancy / Squire Wood's lamentation on ye refusal of his halfpence / Sean Jones / Lady St. John / David Poer/Seamus Plunkett / Lament for Terence O'Connor / Lady Dillon / Michael O'Connor / Carolan's welcome/Madam Keel / Right Reverend Lord bishop MacMahon of Clogher / Carolan's variations on cock up your beaver

CD CC 28CD
Claddagh / Jan '90 / ADA / CM / Direct

CAROLAN'S RECEIPT
Sidh Beag / Carolan's receipt for drinking / Lady Athenry / Fanny Poer / Blind Mary / Sir Festus Burke / Carolan's quarrel with the landlady / Carolan's ramble to Cashel / Mrs. Poer / John O'Connor / Ode to Whiskey / George Brabazon / Mable Kelly / Madam Maxwell/Carolan's nightcap/Lady Gethin / Brighid Cruis / John O'Reilly / Carolan's farewell to music
CD CC 18CD
Claddagh / Nov '90 / ADA / CM / Direct

DEREK BELL'S MUSICAL IRELAND
She moved through the fair / Boys of Bluehill/Hillsborough Castle/Greencastle hornpipe / Carrickfergus / Little white cat / Gartan mothers lullaby / Im aonar seal / Down by the Sally Gardens / Eileen my secret love / Piper through the meadow straying / Limerick's lamentation / Christ the seed / I wish the shepherd's pet were mine
CD CC 35CD
Claddagh / Nov '90 / ADA / CM / Direct

Bell, Ed

ED BELL 1927-1930
CD DOCD 5090
Document / '92 / ADA / Hot Shot / Jazz Music

Bell, Eric

LIVE TONITE
Songs / Stumble / Oh pretty woman / Things I used to do / Madame George / Walk on water / Three o'clock blues / Hold that plane / Whiskey in the jar / Rocker / Baby please don't go
CD BMAC 0315
BMA / Sep '97 / Pinnacle

Bell, Freddy

ROCKIN' IS OUR BUSINESS (Bell, Freddy & The Bellboys)
Hound dog / Move me baby / Five-ten fifteen hours / Old town hall / Big bad wolf / I said it and I'm glad / Rockin' the polonaise / Giddy up and ding dong / Alright, OK you win / Hucklebuck / Rompin' and stompin' / Stay loose, Mother goose / Hey there you / Take the first train out of town / Voo doo / Teach you to rock / I'm advertising / You're gonna be sorry / Variety / Rockin' is my business
CD BCD 15901
Bear Family / Mar '96 / Direct / Rollercoaster / Swift

Bell, Lurrie

700 BLUES
I've got papers on you baby / How many more years / All over again / 700 blues / She walks right in / Honey bee / You got to stop this mess / Found love / Million miles from nowhere / You got me dizzy / I'll be your 44 / Sadie / Baby take it easy
CD DE 700
Delmark / Jun '97 / ADA / Cadillac / CM / Direct / Hot Shot

EVERYBODY WANTS TO WIN
CD JSPCD 227
JSP / May '93 / ADA / Cadillac / Direct / Hot Shot / Target/BMG

MERCURIAL SON
CD DE 679
Delmark / Dec '95 / ADA / Cadillac / CM / Direct / Hot Shot

Bell, Maggie

QUEEN OF THE NIGHT
CD RR 4661
Repertoire / Jun '97 / Greyhound

Bell, Paddie

MAKE ME WANT TO STAY
CD ALACD 102
Alauda / Mar '97 / Duncans

Bell, T.D.

IT'S ABOUT TIME (Bell, T.D. & Erbie Bowser)
CD BMCD 9019
Black Magic / Apr '93 / ADA / Cadillac / Direct / Hot Shot

Bell Tower

POP DROPPER
CD TOPPCD 002
Ultimate / Jul '94 / Pinnacle

Bell, Vince

PHOENIX
CD CD 1027
Watermelon / Sep '94 / ADA / Direct

Bell, William

BEST OF WILLIAM BELL, THE
I forgot to be your lover / Private number / Born under a bad sign / My kind of girl / Lonely soldier / Save us / Penny for your thoughts / My baby specializes / My whole world is falling down / All for the love of a woman / 'Til my back ain't got no bone / I'll be home / Smile can't hide (a broken heart) / Gettin' what you want (losin' what you got)
CD CDSXE 113
Stax / Jul '97 / Pinnacle

BOUND TO HAPPEN/WOW
I forgot to be your lover / Hey Western union man / My whole world is falling down / Everyday people / Johnny I love you / All God's children got soul / Happy / By the time I get to Phoenix / Bring the curtain down / Smile can't hide a broken heart / Born under a bad sign / I got a sure thing / I can't make it (all by myself) / Till my back ain't got no bone / All for the love of a woman / My door is always open / Penny for your thoughts / You'll want diamonds / Winding winding road / Somebody's gonna get hurt / I'll be home
CD CDSXD 970
Stax / Apr '91 / Pinnacle

LITTLE SOMETHING EXTRA, A
She won't be like you / All that I am / Let's do something together / Forever wouldn't be too long / You got me where you want me / Quittin' time / That's my love / You need a little something extra / There's a love / Never let me go / We got something good / Will you still love me tomorrow / Love will find a way / What did I do wrong / Sacrifice / Love is after me / Life I live / Wait / You're never too old
CD CDSXD 037
Stax / Sep '91 / Pinnacle

PHASES OF REALITY
Save us / True love don't come easy / Fifty dollar habit / What I don't know won't hurt me / Phases of reality / If you really love him / Lonely for your love / Man in the street
CD CDSXE 058
Stax / Jul '92 / Pinnacle

SOUL OF A BELL, THE
Everybody loves a winner / You don't miss your water / Do right woman, do right man / I've been loving you too long / Nothing takes the place of you / Then you can tell me goodbye / Eloise (hang on in there) / Any other way / It's happening all over / Never like this before / You're such a sweet thing
CD 7567822522
Atlantic / Apr '95 / Warner Music

Bella Bella

PLUS GRANDS SUCCES VOL.1 1971-1975 (Bella Bella & Freres Soki)
CD NG 029
Ngoyarto / Jan '97 / Stern's

PLUS GRANDS SUCCES VOL.2 1971-1975 (Bella Bella & Freres Soki)
CD NG 030
Ngoyarto / Jan '97 / Stern's

Bellamy Brothers

BEST OF THE BEST
Let your love flow / If I said you had a beautiful body (would you hold it agains / Old hippie / You ain't just whistlin' Dixie / Dancin' cowboys / Sugar daddy / Lovers live longer / Crazy from the heart / Feelin' the feelin' / Do you love as good as you look / For all the wrong reasons / Redneck girls / When I'm away from you / I'd lie to you for your love / You'll never be sorry / Santa Fe / I need more of you / Big love / Kids of the baby boom / Get into reggae cowboy / Cowboy beat
CD SCD 22
Start / Feb '97 / Disc

CRAZY FROM THE HEART/REBELS WITHOUT A CLUE
Crazy from the heart / I'll give you all my love tonight / Santa Fe / It's rainin' girls / Ying yang / Melt down / Ramblin' again / We don't wanna got for it / Your name / White trash / Rebels without a clue / I'll help you hurt him / Fountain of middle age / Stayin' in love / Get your priorities in line / Big love / When the music meant everything / Courthouse / Andy Griffith Show / Little naive
CD SCD 24
Start / Feb '97 / Disc

DANCIN'
Redneck girl / Reggae cowboy / Shine them buckles / Cowboy beat / Rip off the knob / Hard way to make an easy livin' / Big hair / Twang town / Get a little crazy / We dared the lightning / If I said you had a beautiful body
CD SCD 29
Start / Feb '97 / Disc

HEARTBREAK OVERLOAD
Rip off the knob / Not / Heartbreak overload / Blame it on the fire in my heart / On a summer night / Sweet nostalgia / Bubba / Stayin' in love / D-D-D-D-Divorce / Can I come on home to you / Hemingway hideaway / Andy Griffith Show / Hard on a heart / Nobody's perfect
CD SCD 23
Start / Feb '97 / Disc

LET YOUR LOVE FLOW
Let your love flow / If I said you had a beautiful body / Sugar Daddy / Lovers live longer / Get into reggae cowboy / Redneck girl / I need more of you / Old hippie / Lie to you for your love / Feelin' the feelin' / Kids of the baby boom / Crazy from the heart / Rip off the knob / No.1 / Miami moon / Life is a beach / Cowboy beat / Can I come home to you / Hard way to make an easy living / She's gone with the wind
CD CTS 55432
Country Stars / Jan '96 / Target/BMG

OVER THE LINE
Over the line / Slow hurry / Afterglow / Guilty of the crime / Catahoula / Passions thunder / Tough love / Mama likes to reggae / Hurricane Alley / Wonderful mistake / Hanging in / My wife left me for my girlfriend
CD SCD 30
Start / Jul '97 / Disc

REALITY CHECK/ROLLIN' THUNDER
Too late / I could be persuaded / Have a little compassion / Was there life before this love / Makin' promises / What's this world coming to / Forever ain't long enough / How can you be everywhere at the same time / I don't wanna lose you / Reality check / All in the name of love / Down to you / She don't know that she's perfect / Strength of the weaker sex / Anyway I can / Rollin' thunder / What's the dang deal / Our love / Lonely eyes / I make her laugh
CD SCD 25
Start / Feb '97 / Disc

SONS OF BEACHES
Shine them buckles / Big hair / Pit bulls and chain saws / Blue rodeo / Twang town / She's awesome / Old hippie (the sequel) / Native American / Feel free / Too much fun / We dared the lightening / Elvis, Marilyn and James Dean / Gotta get a little crazy / Jesus is coming
CD SCD 27
Start / Feb '97 / Disc

Bellamy, Peter

TRANSPORTS, THE
Overture / Ballad of Henry and Susannah: *Bellamy, Peter & Dave Swarbrick* / Us poor fellows: *Jones, Nic* / Robber's song: *Jones, Nic* / Ballad of Henry and Susannah (part 2): *Jones, Nic* / I once lived in service: *Waterson, Norma* / Norwich gaol: *Winsor, Martin* / Sweet loving friendship: *Winsor, Martin* / Black and bitter night: *Waterson, Mike* / Humane turnkey: *Carthy, Martin* / Plymouth mail: *Legg, Vic* / Green fields of England: *Watersons* / Roll down: *Tawney, Cyril* / Still and silent ocean: *Waterson, Mike & Norma* / Ballad of Henry and susannah (parts 3,4and5): *Bellamy, Peter & Dave Swarbrick* / Convict's wedding dance: *Bellamy, Peter & Dave Swarbrick*
CD TSCD 459
Topic / Aug '92 / ADA / CM / Direct

Belle & Sebastian

IF YOU'RE FEELING SINISTER
Stars of track and field / Seeing other people / Me and the Major / Like Dylan in the movies / Fox in the snow / Get me away from here / If you're feeling sinister / Mayfly / Boy done wrong again / Judy and the dream of horses
CD JPRCD 001
Jeepster / Nov '96 / 3mv/Vital

Belle, Regina

REACHIN' BACK
Reachin' back / Could it be I'm falling in love / Love TKO / You make me feel brand new / Hurry up this way again / Whole town's laughing / You are everything / Let me make love to you / I'll be around / Just don't want to be lonely / Didn't I blow your mind this time
CD 4807622
Columbia / Sep '95 / Sony

Belle Stars

HIT SINGLE COLLECTABLES
CD DISK 4514
Disky / Apr '94 / Disky / THE

SIGN OF THE TIMES
CD 12365
Laserlight / May '94 / Target/BMG

VERY BEST OF THE BELLE STARS, THE
CD STIFFCD 5
Disky / Apr '94 / Disky / THE

Bellson, Louie

AIR BELLSON (Bellson, Louie Magic 7)
Air Jordan / Lou's blues / Tito / Tempo de carlo / Ballade / Groove blues / 150 pounds of bones / Bassiano / Mele Kalikimaka / Smooth and mellow / Another shade of the blues / Waltz a-way / PMH
CD CCD 47422
Concord Jazz / Feb '97 / New Note/ Pinnacle

AT THE FLAMINGO HOTEL 1959 (Bellson, Louie & Big Band)
CD JH 1026
Jazz Hour / Feb '93 / Cadillac / Jazz Music / Target/BMG

DON'T STOP NOW
CD 710002
Capri / Oct '94 / Cadillac / Wellard

DUKE ELLINGTON - BLACK, BROWN AND BEIGE (Bellson, Louie & His All Star Orchestra)
Hawk talks / Skin deep / Work song / Come Sunday / West Indian dance / Emancipation proclamation / Ellington-Strayhorn suite / European skallyhoppin' / Portrait of Billy Strayhorn / Sketches
CD 5224292
Limelight / Mar '94 / PolyGram

EAST SIDE SUITE (Bellson, Louie & His Jazz Orchestra)
Tenor time / What makes Moses run
CD MM 5009
Music Masters / Oct '94 / Nimbus

HOT
CD MM 5008
Music Masters / Oct '94 / Nimbus

LIVE AT JAZZ SHOWCASE (Bellson, Louie Four)
Sonny side / Duke's blues / 3 p.m. / I hear a rhapsody / Jam for your bread / Warm alley / Cherokee
CD CCD 4350
Concord Jazz / Jul '88 / New Note/Pinnacle

LIVE AT THE CONCORD SUMMER FESTIVAL
Now and then / Here's that rainy day / My old flame / It might as well be spring / These foolish things / Body and soul / True blue / Roto blues / Starship concord / Dig
CD CCD 4025
Concord Jazz / May '95 / New Note/ Pinnacle

LIVE FROM NEW YORK (Bellson, Louie & Big Band)
Soar like an eagle / Louie shuffle / Blow your horn / LA suite / Louie and Clark expedition / Francine / Santos
CD CD 83334
Telarc / Jul '94 / Conifer/BMG

LOUIE BELLSON & HIS BIG BAND
CD CCD 4036
Concord Jazz / Nov '96 / New Note/ Pinnacle

LOUIE IN LONDON
Carnaby Street / Proud Thames / London suite / Kings Road boogaloo / Hyde Park 2am / Limehouse blues / Sketches from the National Gallery
CD DRGCD 8471
DRG / Jul '96 / Discovery / New Note/ Pinnacle

ORIGINALS, THE
CD STBCD 2509
Stash / Mar '96 / ADA / Cadillac / CM / Direct / Jazz Music

PEACEFUL THUNDER
CD MM 65074
Music Masters / Oct '94 / Nimbus

PRIME TIME
Step lighty / Space ship 2 / I remember Clifford / With you in mind / What's new / Cotton tail / Let me dream / Thrash in / And then she stopped / Collaborations
CD CCD 40642
Concord Jazz / May '97 / New Note/ Pinnacle

RAINCHECK
Raincheck / Alone together / I thought about you / Blue moon / Body and soul / Oleo / Song is you / Tristamente / Funky blues / More I see you
CD CCD 4073
Concord Jazz / Nov '95 / New Note/ Pinnacle

SALUTE (Bellson, Louie Quintet)
CD CRD 329
Chiaroscuro / Nov '95 / Jazz Music

THEIR TIME WAS THE GREATEST
Hallelujah / Liza / 24th Day / Brush taps / Well alright then / Y-not / Stix and bones / Zig zag / It's those magical drums in you / Acetnam / Our Manne Shelly / All about Steve
CD CCD 4683
Concord Jazz / Apr '96 / New Note/ Pinnacle

Belly

KING
Puberty / Seal my fate / Red / Silverfish / Super connected / Bees / King / Now they'll sleep / Untitled and unsung / Li'l Ennio / Judas my heart
CD CAD 5004CD
CD CADD 5004CD
4AD / Feb '95 / RTM/Disc

STAR
CD CAD 3002CD
4AD / Jan '93 / RTM/Disc

Belmez

BESERKER
CD SPV 08407952
Candlelight / Apr '95 / Plastic Head

Belmonde, Pierre

101% PAN PIPES (4CD Set)
Love changes everything / Riverdance / Windmills of your mind / We have all the time in the world / I believe / From a distance / Greensleeves / Bunch of thyme / Waterfalls / It must have been love / Annie's song / Lady in red / Without you / Unchained melody / Sky boat song / Fernando / Danny boy / Scarlet ribbons / Beautiful dreamer / Theme from Love Story / Up where we belong / Dirty old town / Bless this house / Ave Maria / Amazing grace / Change the world / I will always love you / Holding back the years / Love is all around / Wonderful tonight / Perfect year / Constant craving / Summer in the city / Caribbean blue / Summer of '42 / Summer love / All I have to do is dream / Good day sunshine / El condor pasa / Theme from Harry's game / Someday / Beauty and the beast / House of the rising sun / Sunshine after the rain / I never dreamed you'd leave in summer / Wonderful world / You are the sunshine of my life / All by myself / You are my sunshine / Unforgettable / When I fall in love / Orinoco flow / Back for good / Wind of change / Fields of gold / Sailing / Morning has broken / I can't stop loving you / You don't bring me flowers / Bright eyes / Don't cry for me Argentina / Whiter shade of pale / Time after time / Careless whisper / When you and I were young, Maggie / Green leaves of summer / Mull of Kintyre / Colours of the wind / Forbidden colours / Aria / Miss you nights / Feelings / Stranger on the shore / Concerto de aranjuez / Forever autumn / Nights in white satin / Free as a bird / Think twice / Sacrifice / No more "I love yous" / I swear / Power of love / I'm not in love / Show me heaven / Eternal flame / Local hero / Happy ever after / Love hurts / Stay another day / Streets of Philadelphia / Wonderwall / Kiss from a rose / Get here / Take my breath away / Don't give up / Sadness (Part 1) / Road / Up on the roof / Heaven for everyone / Anywhere is / Jealous guy
CD Set ______ ECD 3320
K-Tel / Mar '97 / K-Tel

CHANGE THE WORLD
Change the world / I will always love you / Holding back the years / Love is all around / Wonderful tonight / Perfect year / Constant craving / Summer in the city / Carribean blue / Summer of '42 / Summer love / All I have to do is dream / Good day sunshine / El condor pasa / Theme from Harry's game / Someday / Beauty and the beast / House of the rising sun / Sunshine after the rain / I never dreamed you'd leave in summer / Wonderful world / You are the sunshine of my life / When I fall in love / Unforgettable / You are my sunshine / All by myself
CD ______ ECD 3324
K-Tel / Mar '97 / K-Tel

FREE AS A BIRD
Free as a bird / Think twice / Sacrifice / No more "I love yous" / I swear / Power of love / I'm not in love / Stay another day / Love hurts / Happy ever after / Local hero / Eternal flame / Show me heaven / Streets of Philadelphia / Wonderwall / Kiss from a rose / Get here / Jealous guy / Anywhere is / Heaven for everyone / Up on the roof / Road / Sadness (Part 1) / Don't give up / Take my breath away
CD ______ ECD 3322
K-Tel / Mar '97 / K-Tel

FROM A DISTANCE
Love changes everything / Riverdance / Windmills of your mind / We have all the time in the world / I believe / From a distance / Greensleeves / Bunch of thyme / Waterfalls / It must have been love / Annie's song / Lady in red / Without you / Unchained melody / Sky boat song / Fernando / Danny boy / Scarlet ribbons / Beautiful dreamer / Theme from Love story / Up where we belong / Dirty old town / Bless this house / Ave Maria / Amazing grace
CD ______ ECD 3321
K-Tel / Mar '97 / K-Tel

HALCYON DAYS (The Sound Of The Pan Pipes)
Bunch of thyme / From a distance / Skye boat song / Mull of Kintyre / Danny boy / Beautiful dreamer / Maggie / Scarlet ribbons / Dirty old town / Bless this house / Isle of Innisfree / Those endearing young charms / Greensleeves / Morning has broken / Green leaves of summer / Lord's my shepherd / Ave Maria / Amazing grace
CD ______ ECD 3298
K-Tel / Feb '97 / K-Tel

MISS YOU NIGHTS
Orinoco flow / Back for good / Wind of change / Fields of gold / Careless whisper / Time after time / Whiter shade of pale / Don't cry for me Argentina / Bright eyes / You don't bring me flowers / I can't stop loving you / Morning has broken / Sailing / When you and I were young Maggie / Green leaves of summer / Aria / Miss you nights / Feelings / Stranger on the shore / Concerto de aranjuez / Forever autumn / Nights in white satin / Forbidden colours / Colours of the wind / Mull of Kintyre
CD ______ ECD 3323
K-Tel / Mar '97 / K-Tel

PAN-PIPE DREAMS
We have all the time in the world / Think twice / Sacrifice / No more I love you's / I swear / Power of love / I'm not in love / Stay another day / Love changes everything / Love hurts / Windmills of your mind / Happy ever after / Local hero / Fernando / Eternal flame / Show me heaven / Without you / Lady in red
CD ______ ECD 3206
K-Tel / Mar '95 / K-Tel

Belmondo Quintet

FOR ALL FRIENDS
CD ______ CHR 70016
Challenge / Aug '95 / ADA / Direct / Jazz Music / Wellard

Belmont, Martin

BIG GUITAR
CD ______ FMCD 3
Demon / Feb '95 / Pinnacle

Belmont, Sarah

DREAMLAND MAGIC FLUTE
If you leave me now / I will always love you / Wind of change / Tears in heaven / Everything I do / All I have to do is dream / Massachussetts / Fly away / Air that I breathe / When a man loves a woman / California dreamin' / One moment in time / I just called to say I love you / San Francisco / All that she wants / Half a minute / Dreamland / Tenderness / It's no longer just a dream / Air
CD ______ 12708
Laserlight / Feb '96 / Target/BMG

Beloved

BLISSED OUT
Up, up and away (happy sexy mix) / Wake up soon / Pablo (special K dub) / It's alright now (back to basics) / Hell (honky tonk) / Time after time (muffin mix) / Sun rising / Your love takes me higher
CD ______ 9031729072
East West / Nov '90 / Warner Music

CONSCIENCE
Spirit / Sweet harmony / Outerspace girl / Lose yourself in me / Paradise found / You've got me thinking / Celebrate your life / Rock to the rhythm of love / Let the music take you / 1000 Years from today / Dream on
CD ______ 4509914832
East West / Dec '96 / Warner Music

HAPPINESS
Hello / Your love takes me higher / Time after time / Don't you worry / Scarlet beautiful / Sun rising / I love you more / Wake up soon / Up, up and away / Found
CD ______ 2292462532
East West / Feb '95 / Warner Music

SINGLE FILE (The Best Of The Beloved)
Sun rising / Sweet harmony / Your love takes me / Satellite / Outerspace girl / Time after time / Hello / Ease the pressure / It's alright now / You've go thinking / Deliver me / Mark's deep house
CD ______ 0630199322
East West / Aug '97 / Warner Music

X
CD ______ 0630133162
East West / Mar '96 / Warner Music

Belton, Richard

MODERN SOUNDS IN CAJUN MUSIC
Cajun stripper / I'll have to forget you / Just a dream / Un autre soir d'ennui (Another sleepless night) / Cajun waltz / San Antonio rose / Madamme Sostan / Chrokee waltz / Who-diggie / Oh yea yi-yi / La jolie blonde / For the last time / Musician's paradise / Laisser les cajun danser / Give me another chance / J'ai pleurer pour toi / Oh lucille / I'm not a fool anymore / Cajun Fugitive / Won't be satisfied / Chere toute toute / Cette la j'aime / Roll on wagon wheel / She didn't know I was married / Heartbroken waltz / Cajun streak
CD ______ CDCHD 378
Ace / Jan '93 / Pinnacle

Beltram, Joey

CLASSICS
Energy flash / Jazz 303 / Subsonic trance / Psychobase / My sound / Melody / Subbass experience / Reflex / Mind to mind / Mentasm / Fuck you all MF / Get into life / She ain't coming home
CD ______ RS 96100CD
R&S / Jun '96 / Vital

PLACES (2CD Set)
CD Set ______ EFA 292782
Tresor / Aug '97 / 3mv/BMG / Prime / SRD
CD Set ______ 74321299132
Tresor / Jul '97 / 3mv/BMG / Prime / SRD

Beltran, John

EARTH & NIGHTFALL
Blue world / Pluvial interlude / Synaptic transmission / Sub surface / Earth and nightfall / Mutualism / Dawn / Anticipation / Nitric / Fragile interlude / Aquatic / Vienna
CD ______ RS95072CD
R&S / Jun '95 / Vital

TEN DAYS OF BLUE
Flex / Collage of dreams / Guitaris breeze / Ten days of blue / Venlin and wonder / Deluge / Decembers tragedy / Soft summer / Collage of dreams (Outro)
CD ______ PF 049CD
Peacefrog / Aug '96 / Mo's Music Machine / Prime / RTM/Disc / Vital

Belvin, Jesse

BLUES BALLADEER, THE
Daddy loves baby / My love comes tumbling down / Dream girl / Confusin' blues / Baby don't go / Blues has got me / Hang your tears out to dry / Don't stop / Love me / Puddin' 'n' tane / Open up your heart / What's the matter / Ding dong baby / One little blessing / Gone / Love love of my life / Where's my girl / Let's try romance / Come back / Love of my life
CD ______ CDCHD 305
Ace / Nov '93 / Pinnacle

GOODNIGHT MY LOVE
Goodnight my love / (I love you) for sentimental reasons / I'll mess you up medley / Don't close the door / Senorita / Let me love you tonight / I need you so / My satellite / Just to say hello / Dream house / I'm not free / You send me / By my side / Let's make up / Summertime / I want you with me Christmas / Goodnight my love (alt take) / Sad and lonesome / Beware / What can I do without you / I'll make a bet
CD ______ CDCHD 336
Ace / Nov '93 / Pinnacle

Beme Seed

FUTURE IS ATTACKING
Future is attacking
CD ______ BFFP 50 CD
Blast First / Jul '89 / RTM/Disc

Ben, Jorge

PAIS TROPICAL - FILHO MARAVILHA
CD ______ 1917482
EPM / Apr '97 / ADA / Discovery

Ben, Kaira

SINGA
CD ______ ST 1072
Stern's / May '96 / ADA / CM / Stern's

Benaiah

CHILDREN OF ISRAEL
CD ______ CAPS 002CD
Sphinx / May '96 / Jet Star

WE NAH GIVE UP
CD ______ CAPS 001CD
Sphinx / May '96 / Jet Star

Benatar, Pat

BEST SHOTS
Hit me with your best shot / Love is a battlefield / We belong / We live for love / Sex as a weapon / Invincible / Shadows of the night / Heartbreaker / Fire and ice / Treat me right / If you think you know how to love me / You better run
CD ______ CCD 1538
Chrysalis / Sep '97 / EMI

VERY BEST OF PAT BENATAR
Heartbreaker / We live for love / Promises in the dark / Fire and ice / Ooh ooh song / Hit me with your best shot / Shadows of the night / Anxiety (get nervous) / I want out / Lipstick lies / Love is a battlefield / We belong / All fired up / Hell is for children / Invincible / Somebody's baby / Everybody lay down / True love
CD ______ CDCHR 6070
Chrysalis / Apr '94 / EMI

Bender

JEHOVAH'S ALLSTARS
CD ______ WOWCD 48
Words Of Warning / Jun '96 / SRD / Total/BMG

LOST CITY OF DALSTON
CD ______ WOWCD 43
Words Of Warning / Jun '95 / SRD / Total/BMG

Benediction

DARK IS THE SEA
CD ______ NB 059CD
Nuclear Blast / Apr '92 / Plastic Head

DREAMS YOU DREAD, THE
CD ______ NB 120CD
Nuclear Blast / Jun '95 / Plastic Head

GRAND LEVELLER
CD ______ NB 241CD
Nuclear Blast / Apr '97 / Plastic Head

GROTESQUE ASHEN EPITAPH, THE
CD ______ NB 0882
Nuclear Blast / May '94 / Plastic Head

SUBCONSCIOUS TERROR
CD ______ NB 165CD
Nuclear Blast / Jun '96 / Plastic Head

TRANSCEND THE RUBICON
CD ______ NB 073CD
Nuclear Blast / Jun '93 / Plastic Head

Beneke, Tex

DANCERS DELIGHT
CD ______ DAWE 79
Magic / Mar '97 / Cadillac / Harmonia Mundi / Jazz Music / Swift / Wellard

JUKEBOX SATURDAY NIGHT (Beneke, Tex & The Glenn Miller Orchestra)
CD ______ VJC 1039
Vintage Jazz Classics / Nov '92 / ADA / Cadillac / CM / Direct

PALLADIUM PATROL
CD ______ AERO 1031
Aerospace / Jul '96 / Jazz Music / Montpellier

Benet, Eric

TRUE TO MYSELF
True to myself / I'll be there / If you want me to stay / Let's stay together / Just friends / Femininity / While you where here / Spiritual thang / Chains / All in the game / More than just a girlfriend / What if we was cool / Let's stay together
CD ______ 9362462702
Warner Bros. / Apr '97 / Warner Music

Benford, Mac

WILLOW
CD ______ ROUCD 0371
Rounder / Feb '96 / ADA / CM / Direct

Benighted Leams

CALIGINOUS ROMANTIC MYTH
CD ______ AURA 001CD
Supernal / Dec '96 / RTM/Disc

Benito, Oscar

FOLKLORE DE PARAGUAY
CD ______ EUCD 1221
ARC / Sep '93 / ADA / ARC Music

Benjamin, Sathima Bea

MORNING IN PARIS
Dam that dream / I got it bad and that ain't good / I could write a book / I should care / Spring will be a little late this year / Solitude / Man I love / Your love has faded / I'm glad there is you / Soon / Lover man / Nightingale sang in Berkeley Square
CD ______ ENJ 93092
Enja / Mar '97 / New Note/Pinnacle / Vital/SAM

Bennet

SUPER NATURAL
CD ______ RR 88662
CD ______ RR 88662N
Roadrunner / Sep '96 / PolyGram

Bennett, Billy

ALMOST A GENTLEMAN
Nell / My mother doesn't know I'm on the stage / Mandalay / I'll be thinking of you / Ogul mogul - a kanakanese love lyric / No power on earth / She was poor but she was honest / Family secrets / Please let me sleep on your doorstep tonight / Christmas day in the cookhouse / Club raid / Mottoes / Green tie on the little yellow dog
CD ______ TSCD 780
Topic / Jul '97 / ADA / CM / Direct

Bennett, Brian

CHANGE OF DIRECTION/ILLUSTRATED LONDON NOISE
Slippery Jim De Grize / Canvas / Whisper not / Memphis / Tricycle / Sunshine superman / On Broadway / Sunny afternoon / Little old lady / 98.6 / Con Alma / Change of direction / Love and occasional rain / I heard it through the grapevine / Chameleon / Just lookin' / Rocky raccoon / Ticket to ride
CD ______ SEECD 205
See For Miles/C5 / Nov '87 / Pinnacle

MISTY
Wave / Laura / Misty / Close to you / Madrid / Love for sale / Who can I turn to / Shadow of your smile / What are you doing the rest of your life / Blue hankerchief
CD ______ C5CD 610
See For Miles/C5 / Sep '95 / Pinnacle

Bennett, Don

CHICAGO CALLING (Bennett, Don Sextet)
About time / Sleeping child / Love found me / Makin' whoopee / Dance of the night child / Au privave / Prayer for Sean / Steven's song / All the things you are

CD ________ CCD 79713
Candid / Feb '97 / Cadillac / Direct / Jazz Music / Koch / Wellard

SOLAR (Bennett, Don Trio)
Blues for Nikki / Since I fell for you / Solar / You don't know what love is / If I should lose you / Tune up / Afternoon in Paris / In search of... / It's you or no one / Blue moon / Night in Tunisia
CD ________ CCD 79723
Candid / Feb '97 / Cadillac / Direct / Jazz Music / Koch / Wellard

Bennett, Duster

JUMPIN' AT SHADOWS
CD ________ IGOCD 2010
Indigo / Nov '94 / ADA / Direct

OUT IN THE BLUE
CD ________ IGOCD 2018
Indigo / Apr '95 / ADA / Direct

Bennett, Elinor

TELYNAU A CHAN/FOLK SONGS & HARPS
Clychau Aberdyfi / Ar lan y mor / Paid a deud / Merch y melinydd / Meillionen / Morfa Rhuddlan / Syr Harri Ddu / Codiad yr ehedydd / Ar hyd y nos / Gwyr Harlech / Dafydd y Garreg Wen / Y bore glas / Gwcw fach / Ei di'r deryn du / Y deryn pur / Cainc Dafydd broffwyd / Annhawdd ymadael / Pant corlan yr wyn / Hen benillion / Marwnad Sion Eos / Bugeilio'r gwenith gwyn / Huna blentyn / Y gwydd / Migildi magildi
CD ________ SCD 4041
Sain / Feb '95 / ADA / Direct / Greyhound

Bennett, Gordon

ENGLISH PUBSONGS (Bennett, Gordon & The Good Times)
CD ________ CNCD 5980
Disky / Apr '94 / Disky / THE

Bennett, Martyn

MARTYN BENNETT
CD ________ ECLCD 9614
Eclectic / Mar '96 / ADA / New Note/ Pinnacle

Bennett, Richard

WALKING DOWN THE LINE
Sounds of winter / Greensleeves / Banks of the Ohio / Walking down the line / Pallet on the floor / If I could go back home again / True love is hard to find / Roan mountain rag / Johnstown flood / Rain pours down
CD ________ REBCD 1738
Rebel / Jul '97 / ADA / Direct

Bennett, Richard Rodney

HAROLD ARLEN'S SONGS
CD ________ ACD 168
Audiophile / Oct '93 / Jazz Music

SPECIAL OCCASIONS
Civil war ballet / Hero ballet / Within the quota / Ghost town
CD ________ DRGCD 6102
DRG / Apr '94 / Discovery / New Note/ Pinnacle

SURE THING, A (A Tribute To Jerome Kern) (Bennett, Richard Rodney & Barry Tuckwell/Neil Richardson)
CD ________ CDEMX 2270
Eminence / Apr '96 / EMI

Bennett, Samm

BIG OFF, THE
CD ________ KFWCD 126
Knitting Factory / Nov '94 / Cargo / Plastic Head

HISTORY OF THE LAST FIVE MINUTES
CD ________ KFWCD 166
Knitting Factory / Oct '96 / Cargo / Plastic Head

LIFE OF CRIME (Bennett, Samm & Chunk)
CD ________ KFWCD 110
Knitting Factory / Nov '94 / Cargo / Plastic Head

Bennett, Steve

STEVE BENNETT'S BLUESBUSTERS (Bennett, Steve Bluesbusters)
CD ________ SMV 002CD
Smallville / May '97 / CM / Smallville Records

Bennett, Tony

16 MOST REQUESTED SONGS
Because of you / Stranger in paradise / Rags to riches / Boulevard of broken dreams / Cold cold heart / Just in time / I left my heart in San Francisco / I wanna be around / Who can I turn to / For once in my life / This is all I ask / Smile / Tender is the night / Shadow of your smile / Love story
CD ________ 4724182
Columbia / Nov '92 / Sony

ALL TIME GREATEST HITS
Something / Love story / Maybe this time / Just in time / For once in my life / I left my heart in San Francisco / Because of you / Boulevard of broken dreams / Stranger in paradise / I wanna be around / Time for love / Who can I turn to / This is all I ask / Smile / Sing you sinners / Firefly / Put on a happy face / Love look away / Rags to riches / Where do I begin / Shadow of your smile
CD ________ 4688432
Columbia / Sep '91 / Sony

BLUE VELVET
CD ________ BMCD 3013
Blue Moon / Apr '97 / Cadillac / Discovery / Greensleeves / Jazz Music / Jet Star / TKO Magnum

CHICAGO (Bennett, Tony & Count Basie Orchestra)
CD ________ CDSGP 0220
Prestige / Aug '97 / Else / Total/BMG

HERE'S TO THE LADIES
People / I'm so in love again / Somewhere over the rainbow / My love went to London / Poor butterfly / Sentimental journey / Cloudy morning / Tenderly / Down in the depths / Moonlight in Vermont / Tangerine / God bless the child / Day break / You showed me the way / Honeysuckle Rose / Maybe this time / I got rhythm / My ideal
CD ________ 4812662
Columbia / Nov '95 / Sony

HOLLYWOOD AND BROADWAY
CD ________ CDSIV 6145
Horatio Nelson / Jul '95 / Disc

I LEFT MY HEART IN SAN FRANCISCO/I WANNA BE AROUND
I left my heart in San Francisco / Once upon a time / Tender is the night / Smile / Love for sale / Taking a chance on love / Candy kisses / Have I told you lately that I love you / Rules of the road / Marry young / I'm always chasing rainbows / Best is yet to come / Good life / If I love again / I wanna be around / Love look away / Let's face the music and dance / Once upon a summertime / If you were mine / I will live my life for you / Someone to love / It was me / Quiet nights
CD ________ 4775922
Columbia / Oct '94 / Sony

IN PERSON (Bennett, Tony & Count Basie)
Just in time / When I fall in love / Taking a chance on love / Without a song / Fascinating rhythm / Solitude / Pennies from Heaven / Lost in the stars / Firefly / There will never be another you / Lullaby of Broadway / Ol' man river
CD ________ CK 642763
Mastersound / Jan '96 / Sony

MOVIE SONG ALBUM, THE
Maybe September / Girl talk / Gentle rain / Emily / Pawnbroker / Samba de orfeu / Shadow of your smile / Smile / Second time around / Days of wine and roses / Never too late / Trolley song
CD ________ 4879472
Columbia / Jul '97 / Sony

ON HOLIDAY
Solitude / All of me / When a woman loves a man / Me myself and I (Are all in love with you) / She's funny that way (I got a woman, crazy for me) / If I could be with you (One hour tonight) / Willow weep for me / Laughing at life / I wished on the moon / What a little moonlight can do / My old flame / That olde devil called love / Ill wind (you're blowin' me no good) / These foolish things (remind me of you) / Some other spring / Crazy she calls me / Good morning, heartache / Trav'lin light / God bless the child
CD ________ 4872632
Columbia / May '97 / Sony

PERFECTLY FRANK
Time after time / I fall in love too easily / East of the sun and west of the moon / Nancy / I thought about you / Night and day / I've got the world on a string / I'm glad there is you / Nightingale sang in Berkeley Square / I wished on the moon / You go to my head / Lady is a tramp / I see your face before me / Day in, day out / Indian summer / Call me irresponsible / Here's that rainy day / Last night when we were young / I wanna be in love again / Foggy day / Don't worry 'bout me / One for my baby (and one more for the road) / Angel eyes / I'll be seeing you
CD ________ 4722222
Columbia / Aug '94 / Sony

RODGERS & HART SONGBOOK (Bennett, Tony & Ruby Braff/George Barnes Quartet)
This can't be love / Blue moon / Lady is a tramp / Lover / Manhattan / Spring is here / Have you met Miss Jones / Isn't it romantic / Wait till you see her / I could write a book / Thou swell / Most beautiful girl in the world / There's a small hotel / I've got five dollars / You took advantage of me / I wish I were in love again / This funny world / My heart stood still / My romance / Mountain greenery
CD ________ CDSIV 1129
Horatio Nelson / Jul '95 / Disc

SINGING AND SWINGING (Bennett, Tony & Count Basie)
CD ________ HADCD 184
Javelin / Nov '95 / Henry Hadaway / THE

SNOWFALL (The Tony Bennett Christmas Album)
Snowfall / My favourite things / Christmas song / Santa Claus is coming to town / We wish you a Merry Christmas / Silent night / O come all ye faithful (Adeste Fidelis) / Jingle bells / Where is love / Christmasland / I love the winter weather / I've got my love to keep me warm / White Christmas / Winter wonderland / Have yourself a merry little Christmas / I'll be home for Christmas
CD ________ 4775972
Columbia / Nov '96 / Sony

SONGS FROM THE HEART
CD ________ MCCD 238
Music Club / Mar '96 / Disc / THE

SPECIAL MAGIC OF TONY BENNETT
What is this thing called love / Love for sale / I'm in love again / You'd be so nice to come home to / Easy to love / It's all right with me / Night and day / Dream dancing / I've got you under my skin / Get out of town / Experiment / One / This funny world / Lost in the stars / As time goes by / I used to be colour blind / Mr. Magic
CD ________ JHD 053
Tring / Mar '93 / Tring

TOGETHER AGAIN (Bennett, Tony & Bill Evans)
Child is born / Make someone happy / Bad and the beautiful / Lucky to be me / You're near me / Two lonely people / You don't know what love is / Maybe September / Lonely girl / You must believe in spring
CD ________ CDMRS 901
DRG / '88 / Discovery / New Note/Pinnacle
CD ________ CDSIV 1122
Horatio Nelson / Jul '95 / Disc

TONY BENNETT/BILL EVANS ALBUM, THE (Bennett, Tony & Bill Evans)
CD ________ OJCCD 439
Original Jazz Classics / Feb '92 / Complete/Pinnacle / Jazz Music / Wellard

UNPLUGGED
Old devil moon / Speak low / It had to be you / I love a piano / It amazes me / Girl I love / Fly me to the moon / You're the world to me / Rags to riches / When Joanna love me / Good life/I wanna be around / I left my heart in San Francisco / Steppin' out with my baby / Moonglow: *Bennett, Tony & k.d. Lang* / They can't take that away from me: *Bennett, Tony & Elvis Costello* / Foggy day / All of you / Body and soul / It don't mean a thing if it ain't got that swing / Autumn leaves
CD ________ 4771702
Columbia / Aug '94 / Sony

Bennett, Winston

PRISONER OF YOUR LOVE (Bennett, Winston & Merger)
Prisoner of your love / You to me are as love / Shine on / Young generation / On the road again / If I was a baby / Ain't gonna do it / Ask them / Jenny / Andria / Lost a friend / Glad to be alive / Happiness
CD ________ PRCD 604
President / May '96 / Grapevine/PolyGram / President / Target/BMG

Benoit, Bernard

GUITARE AND BOMBARDE - BARZAZ BREIZH
CD ________ GRI 190832
Griffe / Sep '96 / ADA / Discovery

Benoit, Blue Boy

PARLEZ-VOUS FRANCAIS
CD ________ CDLLL 87
La Lichere / Aug '93 / ADA / Discovery

PLUS TARD DANS LA SOIREE
CD ________ CDLLL 187
La Lichere / Aug '93 / ADA / Discovery

Benoit, David

BENOIT/FREEMAN PROJECT (Benoit, David & Russ Freeman)
Reunion / When she believed in me / Mediterranean nights / Swept away / End of our season / After the love has gone / Smartypants / It's the thought that counts / Mirage / That's all I could say
CD ________ GRP 97392
GRP / Feb '94 / New Note/BMG

BEST OF DAVID BENOIT, THE
Drive time / Every step of the way / Cast your fate to the wind / Searching for June / MWA / Linus and Lucy / Kei's song / Key to you / Freedom at midnight / Still standing / Wailea / Letter to Evan / Urban daydreams / Mediterranean nights
CD ________ GRP 98312
GRP / Oct '95 / New Note/BMG

REMEMBERING CHRISTMAS
Skating / Santa Claus is coming to town / Angels we have heard on high / Christmas time is here / Jesu, joy of man's desiring / Hark the herald angels sing / Do you hear what I hear / Christmas is coming / Silent night / Remembering Christmas / First Noel / Christmas song
CD ________ GRP 98522
GRP / Oct '96 / New Note/BMG

SHAKEN, NOT STIRRED
Wailea / I went to bat for you / Any other time / Carmel / Sparks flew / Shaken, not stirred / Chi Chi's eyes / Days of old / Jacqueline / Sarah's theme
CD ________ GRP 97872
GRP / Oct '94 / New Note/BMG

Benoit, Tab

NICE AND WARM
CD ________ JR 12012
Justice / Apr '93 / Koch

WHAT I LIVE FOR
CD ________ JR 12022
Justice / Oct '94 / Koch

Benson, Brendan

ONE MISSISSIPPI
Tea / Bird's eye view / Sittin' pretty / I'm blessed / Crosseyed / Me just purely / Got no secrets / How 'bout you / Emma J / Insects rule / Imaginary girl / House in Virginia / Cherries / Strawbearry rhubarb pie
CD ________ CDVUS 117
Virgin / May '97 / EMI

Benson, George

20/20
No one emotion / Please don't walk away / I just wanna hang around you / Nothing's gonna change my love for you / La mer / New day / You are the love of my life / Hold me / Stand up / 20/20 / Shark bite
CD ________ 9251782
WEA / Feb '92 / Warner Music

A&M GOLD SERIES
Last train to Clarksville / Jama Joe / Footin' it / Don't cha hear me callin' to ya / Chattanooga choo choo / Durham's turn / Shape of things that are and were / Face it boy, it's over / My cherie amour / Oh darling / She went a little bit further / Tell it like it is / My woman's good to me / Out of the blue / I got a woman / Something/Octopus's garden/The End / I worry 'bout you
CD ________ 3970732
A&M / Mar '93 / PolyGram

BEST OF GEORGE BENSON, THE
California dreamin' / Gentle rain / One rock don't make no boulder / Take five / Summertime / Theme from good king bad / Body talk / Summer of '42 / My latin brothers / Ode to a Kudu / I remember Wes / From now on
CD ________ 4654052
Columbia / Oct '92 / Sony

BEST, THE
Shape of things to come / My woman's good to me / Here comes the sun / Water brother / Tell it like it is / Oh darling / My cherie amour / Golden slumbers / You never give me your money / Footin' it / Don't let me lose this dream
CD ________ 3932032
A&M / Mar '94 / PolyGram

BODY TALK
CD ________ 239206
Musidisc / Dec '86 / Discovery

BREEZIN'
This masquerade / Six to four / Breezin' / So this is love / Lady / Affirmation
CD ________ 256199
WEA / Jun '89 / Warner Music

COLLABORATION (Benson, George & Earl Klugh)
Mount Airey groove / Mimosa / Brazilian stomp / Dreamin' / Since you're gone / Collaboration / Jamaica / Romeo and Juliet
CD ________ 9255802
WEA / Feb '95 / Warner Music

GEORGE BENSON COLLECTION, THE
Turn your love around / Love all the hurt away / Give me the night / Cast your fate to the wind / Love ballad / Nature boy / Last train to Clarksville / Livin' inside your love / Never give up on a good thing / On Broadway / White rabbit / This masquerade / Here comes the sun / Breezin' / Moody's mood / We got the love / Greatest love of all
CD ________ K 266107
WEA / Jul '88 / Warner Music

GEORGE BENSON COOKBOOK, THE
Cooker / Benny's back / Bossa rocka / All of me / Big fat lady / Benson's rider / Ready and able / Borgia stick / Return of the prodigal son / Jumpin' with symphony Sid
CD ________ 4769032
Columbia / Sep '94 / Sony

GIVE ME THE NIGHT
What's on your mind / Dinorah, Dinorah / Love dance / Star of the story / Midnight love affair / Turn out the lamplight / Love x love / Off Broadway / Moody's mood / Give me the night
CD ________ 256823
WEA / Apr '84 / Warner Music

GUITAR GENIUS OF GEORGE BENSON, THE
Love for sale / This masquerade is over / Witchcraft / There will never be another you / All blues / Blue bossa / Oleo / Li'l darlin'
CD ____ QED 075
Tring / Nov '96 / Tring

IMMORTAL CONCERTS (Live San Francisco 1972)
All blues / Love for sale / Oleo / Blue bossa / All the things you are / Lil' darlin' / Dahlin's delight
CD ____ CD 53284
Giants Of Jazz / Oct '96 / Cadillac / Jazz Music / Target/BMG

IN FLIGHT
Nature boy / Wind and I / World is a ghetto / Gonna love you more / Valdez in the country / Everything must change
CD ____ 256327
WEA / '86 / Warner Music

IN YOUR EYES
Feel like makin' love / Inside love (so personal) / Lady love me (one more time) / Love will come again / In your eyes / Never too far to fall / Being with you / Use me / Late at night / In search of a dream
CD ____ 9237442
WEA / Jul '88 / Warner Music

IT'S UPTOWN WITH THE GEORGE BENSON QUARTET (Benson, George Quartet)
Clockwise / Summertime / Ain't that peculiar / Jaguar / Willow weep for me / Foggy day / Hello birdie / Bullfight / Stormy weather / Eternally / Myna bird blues
CD ____ 4769022
Columbia / Sep '94 / Sony

JAZZ MASTERS
Thunder walk / Sack o' woe / Tuxedo junction / Billie's bounce / Something/Octopus's garden / What's new / Shape of things to come / Low down and dirty / I remember Wes / Boss
CD ____ 5218612
Verve / Feb '94 / PolyGram

LEGENDS IN MUSIC
CD ____ LECD 068
Wisepack / Jul '94 / Conifer/BMG / THE

LIL' DARLIN'
Witchcraft / Blue bossa / Oleo / Li'l darlin'
CD ____ CDTB 078
Thunderbolt / Sep '90 / TKO Magnum

LIVE AT CASA CARIBE (Benson, George Quartet)
CD ____ COD 011
Jazz View / Mar '92 / Harmonia Mundi

LIVE AT CASA CARIBE VOL.2 (Benson, George Quartet)
CD ____ COD 035
Jazz View / Jun '92 / Harmonia Mundi

LIVE AT CASA CARIBE VOL.3 (Benson, George Quartet)
CD ____ COD 036
Jazz View / Aug '92 / Harmonia Mundi

LOVE FOR SALE
Love for sale / L'il darlin' / There will never be another you / Blue bossa / All blues / Oleo
CD ____ 100722
CMC / May '97 / BMG

LOVE REMEMBERS
I'll be good to you / Got to be there / My heart is dancing / Love of my life / Kiss and make up / Come into my world / Love remembers / Willing to fight / Somewhere Island / Lovin' on borrowed time / Lost in love / Calling you
CD ____ 7599266852
WEA / Dec '96 / Warner Music

LOVE WALKED IN
All the things you are / Invitation / Love walked in / Dahlin's delight
CD ____ CDTB 088
Thunderbolt / Dec '90 / TKO Magnum

MASQUERADE
Love for sale / This masquerade / There will never be another you / All blues
CD ____ CDTB 072
Thunderbolt / Oct '89 / TKO Magnum

NEW BOSS GUITAR OF GEORGE BENSON, THE (Benson, George & 'Brother' Jack McDuff Quartet)
Shadow dancers / Sweet Alice blues / I don't know / Just another Sunday / Will you still be mine / Easy living / Rock-a-bye / My three sons
CD ____ OJCCD 461
Original Jazz Classics / Apr '92 / Complete/Pinnacle / Jazz Music / Wellard

QUARTET ALL BLUES
CD ____ CDSGP 034
Prestige / Jul '92 / Else / Total/BMG

QUARTET BLUE BOSSA
CD ____ CDSGP 035
Prestige / Jul '92 / Else / Total/BMG

SHAPE OF THINGS TO COME
Footin' it / Face it boy it's over / Shape of things that are and were / Chattanooga choo choo / Don't let me lose this dream / Last train to Clarksville / Shape of things to come
CD ____ 3969952
A&M / Mar '94 / PolyGram

SILVER COLLECTION, THE
Billie's bounce / Low down and dirty / Thunder walk / Doobie doobie blues / What's new / I remember Wes / Windmills of your mind / Song for my father / Carnival joys / Giblet gravy / Walk on by / Sack o' woe / Groovin'
CD ____ 8234502
Verve / Sep '92 / PolyGram

SPOTLIGHT ON GEORGE BENSON
Witchcraft / Love for sale / There will never be another you / All blues / Li'l darlin' / Oleo
CD ____ HADCD 102
Javelin / Feb '94 / Henry Hadaway / THE

TELL IT LIKE IT IS
Soul limbo / Are you happy / Tell it like it is / Land of 1000 dances / Jackie all / Don't cha hear me callin' to ya / Water brother / My woman's good to me / Jama Joe / My cherie amour / Out in the cold again
CD ____ 3930202
A&M / Mar '94 / PolyGram

THAT'S RIGHT
That's right / Thinker / Marvin said / True blue / Hold'n on / Song for my brother / Johnnie Lee / Summer love / P Park / Footprints in the sand / When love comes calling / Where are you now
CD ____ GRP 98242
GRP / Jun '96 / New Note/BMG

THIS IS JAZZ
Clockwise / Myna bird blues / Willow weep for me / Stormy weather / Cooker / Borgia stick / Ode to a kudu / Take five / I remember Wes / Good King Bad / Summertime / From now on
CD ____ CK 64631
Sony Jazz / May '96 / Sony

TWICE THE LOVE
Twice the love / Starting all over / Good habit / Everybody does it / Living on borrowed love / Let's do it again / Stephanie / Tender love / You're still my baby / Until you believe
CD ____ K 9257052
WEA / Dec '96 / Warner Music

WHILE THE CITY SLEEPS
Shiver / Love is here tonight / Teaser / Secrets in the night / Too many times / Did you hear the thunder / While the city sleeps / Kisses in the moonlight
CD ____ 9254752
WEA / Feb '95 / Warner Music

WITCHCRAFT
CD ____ JHR 73523
Jazz Hour / Sep '93 / Cadillac / Jazz Music / Target/BMG

Bensusan, Pierre

2
CD ____ ROUCD 3037
Rounder / Mar '96 / ADA / CM / Direct

BAMBOULE
CD ____ BEST 1040CD
Acoustic Music / Nov '93 / ADA

MUSIQUES
CD ____ ROUCD 3038
Rounder / Mar '96 / ADA / CM / Direct

PRES DE PARIS
CD ____ ROUCD 3023
Rounder / Mar '96 / ADA / CM / Direct

SOLILAI
Nice feeling / Bamboule / Au jardin d'amour / Santa Monica / Suite flamande aux pommes / Milton / Solilai / Doa tea
CD ____ CMA 945CD
La Chant Du Monde / Jan '95 / ADA / Harmonia Mundi
CD ____ ROUCD 3068
Rounder / Mar '96 / ADA / CM / Direct

SPICES
Femme cambree / Mille vallees / Le bateau fiction / Shi big, shi mhor / Agadiramadan / La cour interieure / Last pint / Les voiles catalanes / Montsegur / Four am
CD ____ CMA 944CD
Danceteria / Jan '95 / ADA / Plastic Head / Shellshock/Disc
CD ____ ROUCD 3128
Rounder / Mar '96 / ADA / CM / Direct

WU WEI
CD ____ CMA 942
Danceteria / Oct '94 / ADA / Plastic Head / Shellshock/Disc
CD ____ ROUCD 3138
Rounder / Mar '96 / ADA / CM / Direct

Bente's Gammaldansorkester

I GODLYNT LAG
CD ____ B 1011CD
Musikk Distribujson / Dec '94 / ADA

Bentley Rhythm Ace

BENTLEY RHYTHM ACE
Let there be flutes / Midlander (There can only be one) / Why is a frog too / Mind that gap / Run on the spot / Bentley's gonna sort you out / Ragtopskodacarchaser / Whoosh / Who put the bom in the bom bom diddleye bom / Spacehopper / Return of the harbour carbootechodisco roadshow
CD ____ BRASSIC 5CD
Skint / May '97 / 3mv/Vital / Mo's Music Machine / Prime

Bentley, Alison

ALISON BENTLEY QUARTET (Bentley, Alison Quartet & Mornington Lockett)
Fairly normal / Bit of a risk / Harlequin cat / Maybe / Rabbits / Angels on a pin / Mink / Making time / Pigs / Sonnet blues
CD ____ SLAMCD 211
Slam / Oct '96 / Cadillac

Bentley, Ed

BOLLA KEYBOARD BLUES
CD ____ CDSGP 003
Prestige / Jan '94 / Else / Total/BMG

METROPOLIS
CD ____ CDSGP 0137
Prestige / Sep '95 / Else / Total/BMG

Benton, Brook

20 GREATEST HITS
CD ____ RMB 75041
Remember / Nov '93 / Total/BMG

COLLECTION, THE
CD ____ COL 047
Collection / Jan '95 / Target/BMG

ESSENTIAL COLLECTION, THE
CD Set ____ LECD 622
Wisepack / Apr '95 / Conifer/BMG / THE

RAINY NIGHT IN GEORGIA
CD ____ MSCD 031
Music De-Luxe / May '96 / TKO Magnum

RAINY NIGHT IN GEORGIA, A
Rainy night in Georgia / It's just a matter of time / Boll weevil song / Baby, you got what it takes / Rockin' good way / Lie to me / So many ways / Hotel happiness / Kiddio / Endlessly / Revenge / Same one / Think twice
CD ____ CDSGP 033
Prestige / Sep '92 / Else / Total/BMG

THAT OLD FEELING
That old feeling / Second time around / Nightingale sang in Berkeley Square / Impossible, incredible, but true / Moon river / Love is a many splendoured thing / Hawaiian wedding song / There I've said it again / Once in love with Amy / Try a little tenderness / More / Just as much as ever / Hey there / Peg o' my heart / I only have eyes for you / Goodnight my love / Call me irresponsible / Blue moon / There goes my heart / Unforgettable
CD ____ 74321432542
Camden / Feb '97 / BMG

Benton, Buster

BLUES AT THE TOP
You're my lady / Blues and trouble / It's good in my neighbourhood / Lonesome for a dime / I wish't I knew / From Missouri / Dangerous woman / That's your thing / Can't wait to see my baby's face / In the ghetto / Honey bee / Hawk is coming / I must have a hole in my head / Cold man ain't no good / Money's the name of the game
CD ____ ECD 260302
Evidence / Feb '93 / ADA / Cadillac / Harmonia Mundi

Benzie, Ian F.

SO FAR
CD ____ CDLDL 1228
Lochshore / May '95 / ADA / Direct / Duncans

Beowulf

2 CENTS
Throw your rock / Bullet hole / 140 Days / Two cents / Jumped in / Life ain't, life's only / Lack of knowledge / Superstar / No one knows no one / Only human / Badge abuse / Dope bag
CD ____ 727722
Restless / Apr '95 / Vital

BEP

RIPPER
CD ____ KI 57CD
Konkurrel / Jan '95 / SRD

Berard, Al

DANSE LA LOUISIANE (Berard, Al & The Basin Brothers)
CD ____ ROUCD 6065
Rounder / Aug '96 / ADA / CM / Direct

Berendsen, Ben

AMONG THE TREES (Berendsen, Ben & Marcel Van Der Heyden)
CD ____ 322801
Koch / Mar '93 / Koch

Beresford, Steve

CUE SHEETS
CD ____ TZ 7501
Tzadik / Oct '96 / Cargo

SHORT IN THE UK
CD ____ INCUSCD 27
Incus / Mar '97 / Cadillac / Cargo

SIGNALS FOR TEA
CD ____ AVAN 039
Avant / Apr '95 / Cadillac / Harmonia Mundi

Berezan, Jennifer

BORDERLINES
CD ____ FF 615CD
Flying Fish / Apr '94 / ADA / CM / Direct / Roots

Berg, Bob

ENTER THE SPIRIT
Second sight / Snapshot / Promise / Nature of the beast / Sometime ago / No moe / Night moves / Blues for Bella / I loves you Porgy / Angles
CD ____ SCD 90042
Stretch / Mar '97 / New Note/Pinnacle

RIDDLES
Morning star (A primeira estrela) / Something in the way she moves / Ramiro's dream / Children of the night / Riddle me this / Ebony eyes / Ahmed-6 / Coaster / For little Mia
CD ____ SCD 90082
Stretch / Mar '97 / New Note/Pinnacle

Berg, Matraca

SPEED OF GRACE, THE
Slow poison / Tall drink of water / Let's face it, baby / I won't let go / Jolene / Guns in my head / Waiting for the sky to fall / Lying on the moon / Come on momma / River of no return
CD ____ 74321192302
RCA / Mar '94 / BMG

Berg, Rene

LEATHER, THE LONELINESS
CD ____ CMG 005CD
Communique / Nov '92 / Plastic Head

Bergalli, Gustavo

ON THE WAY
CD ____ DRCD 212
Dragon / Oct '93 / ADA / Cadillac / CM / Roots / Wellard

Bergens, Sodra

KAMARINSKAYA (Bergens, Sodra Balalaika Orchestra)
Skomorosina / Pod dugoj kolokolclk pojot / Slbirskaja polka / Ja krolla rubasku / U zari, u zorenki / U vorot, vorot / Korobejniki / Kak na gorke / Trava moja travuska / Russkaja vesiolaja / Vspomni, vspomni / Ocesxvel / Na otdyche / Zaigraj moja volynka / Kamarinskaya / Ty poduj / Ech da uz vy noci / Valenki
CD ____ XOUCD 103
Xource / May '97 / ADA / Direct

Berger, Bengt

BITTER FUNERAL BEER BAND
In a Balinese bar / Two ewe songs / Upper region / Twisted pattern / Ammasu / Pire for Palme / Dar-Kpen: Gan da Yina / Praise drumming for ANC
CD ____ 8393082
ECM / '89 / New Note/Pinnacle

Berger, Karl

AROUND (Berger, Karl & Friends)
CD ____ 1201122
Black Saint / May '91 / Cadillac / Harmonia Mundi

NO MAN IS AN ISLAND (Berger, Karl Orchestra)
CD ____ ADC 4
Douglas Music / Jul '97 / Cadillac / New Note/Pinnacle

Bergeron, Shirley

FRENCH ROCKING BOOGIE
French rocking boogie / J'ai fait mon idee / Old home waltz / Quel etoile / New country waltz / Perrodin two step / Chez Tanie / Mama and papa / Since that first time / True love waltz / J'ai passe devant ta porte / Poor hobo / La valse a August breaux / Eunice two step / La valse de cherokee / Bosco blues / Madam Sostan / La crepe a nazare / Chere bassette / Vermillion two step / La valse de grand bois / Chere toute toute
CD ____ CDCHD 353
Ace / Apr '92 / Pinnacle

Bergh, Totti

WARM VALLEY
CD ____ GMCD 91
Gemini / May '97 / Cadillac

Bergin, Johnny

COME DANCING
Everything's in rhythm with my heart / Please don't talk about me when I'm gone / Dream of me/Dreamy melody/Dream lover / Where the blue of the night/Sailing by / You brought a new kind of love to me/Undecided/A sky blue sh / Alexander's ragtime band / September in the rain/I'll string along with you / In a shady nook/Love letters in the sand / 'Deed I do / Goodbye blues / Blueberry hill/Goodnight sweetheart / We'll meet again/I don't want to walk without you / Breezin' along with the breeze / I saw stars/Auf weidersehn, sweetheart / Deep purple/Moonlight bay / Here's that rainy day / More I see you, The/Red sails in the sunset / Play to me gipsy / Ecstasy / When the red red robin/Glory of love / You're driving me crazy/Makin' whoopee/Roamin' in the Glomin
CD _______________ SAV 173CD
Savoy / Jun '92 / Savoy / THE / TKO Magnum

COME DANCING VOL.2
Ma, he's making eyes at me/Moonstruck / You always hurt the one you love / Five foot two, eyes of blue / Some of these days/My blue heaven / If I had a talking picture of you / If I had my way/Pennies from heaven / Dancing with my shadow/Everything stops for tea / There's a land of begin again / Let us be sweethearts over again / I'll always be in love with you / Tennessee waltz/Far away places / Tell me I'm forgiven / Golden tango / Till there was you / I hear a rhapsody/Come back to Sorrento / All I do is dream of you/Ukelele lady/Soldiers of the Queen / Elmer's tune/Battle of New Orleans/Davy Crockett / You made me love you/A slow boat to China / Me and my shadow / Carolina in the morning / Maybe it's because I'm a Londoner/Lambeth walk / Japanese sandman/Old father Thames / Seven lonely days/Exactly like you/Glad rag doll / Lida rose/You are my everything/ Spread a little happiness / Black hills of Dakota / Bye bye blues / 'S Wonderful
CD _______________ SAV 192CD
Savoy / Jun '93 / Savoy / THE / TKO Magnum

Bergin, Mary

FEADOGA STAIN
CD _______________ CEFCD 071
Gael Linn / '89 / ADA / CM / Direct / Grapevine/PolyGram / Roots

FEADOGA STAIN VOL.2
CD _______________ CEFCD 149
Gael Linn / Feb '93 / ADA / CM / Direct / Grapevine/PolyGram / Roots

Bergin, Sean

LIVE AT THE BIMHUIS
CD _______________ BVHAASTCD 9202
Bvhaast / Oct '93 / Cadillac

Bergman, Borah

HUMAN FACTOR, THE (Bergman, Borah & Andrew Cyrille)
CD _______________ 1212122
Soul Note / Apr '93 / Cadillac / Harmonia Mundi / Wellard

NEW FRONTIER, A
CD _______________ 1210302
Soul Note / May '94 / Cadillac / Harmonia Mundi / Wellard

REFLECTIONS ON ORNETTE COLEMAN & THE STONE HOUSE (Bergman, Borah & Hamid Drake)
CD _______________ 1212802
Soul Note / Jan '96 / Cadillac / Harmonia Mundi / Wellard

Bergonzi, Jerry

LINEAGE
CD _______________ 1232372
Red / Mar '91 / ADA / Cadillac / Harmonia Mundi

SIGNED BY... (Bergonzi, Jerry & Joachim Kuhn)
CD _______________ ZZ 84104
Deux Z / Feb '94 / Cadillac / Harmonia Mundi

TILT (Bergonzi, Jerry Quartet)
CD _______________ 1232452
Red / Mar '92 / ADA / Cadillac / Harmonia Mundi

Bergstrom, Totte

TOTTE BERGSTROM
CD _______________ FE 1433
Folk Era / Aug '96 / ADA / CM

Berigan, Bunny

1936-38 (Berigan, Bunny & His Rhythm Makers)
Take my word: *Berrigan,Bunny* / Rendezvous with a dream: *Berrigan,Bunny* / On a coconut island: *Berrigan,Bunny* / On the beach at Bali-Bali: *Berrigan,Bunny* / But definitely: *Berrigan,Bunny* / Sing sing sing: *Berrigan,Bunny* / I'm an old cowhand: *Berrigan,Bunny* / Empty saddles: *Berrigan,Bunny* / On your toes: *Berrigan,Bunny* / Did I remember: *Berrigan,Bunny* / San Francisco: *Berrigan,Bunny* / I can't escape from you: *Berrigan,Bunny* / I can't pull a rabbit out of my hat: *Berrigan,Bunny* / When I'm with you: *Berrigan,Bunny* / Dardanella: *Berrigan,Bunny* / When did you leave heaven: *Berrigan,Bunny* / You're not the kind: *Berrigan,Bunny* / You've got to eat your spinach baby: *Berrigan,Bunny* / Sweet misery of love: *Berrigan,Bunny* / That's a plenty: *Berrigan,Bunny* / Now it can be told: *Berrigan,Bunny* / My walking stick: *Berrigan,Bunny* / Wacky dust: *Berrigan,Bunny* / A sky of blue and so forth: *Berrigan,Bunny* / Flat foot floogie: *Berrigan,Bunny* / Shanghai shuffle: *Berrigan,Bunny* / I got a guy: *Berrigan,Bunny* / Tonight will live: *Berrigan,Bunny* / Cowboy from Brooklyn: *Berrigan,Bunny* / Devil's holiday: *Berrigan,Bunny* / Easy to find and hard to lose: *Berrigan,Bunny* / The wearing of the green: *Berrigan,Bunny* / The pied piper: *Berrigan,Bunny* / Sunday: *Berrigan,Bunny* / Frankie and johnny: *Berrigan,Bunny* / Don't wake up my heart: *Berrigan,Bunny* / I'll always be in love with you: *Berrigan,Bunny* / I never knew I could love anybody: *Berrigan,Bunny* / How to make love in 10 easy lessons: *Berrigan,Bunny* / Black bottom: *Berrigan,Bunny* / There's a brand new picture in my picture frame: *Berrigan,Bunny* / There's something about an old love: *Berrigan,Bunny* / Small fry: *Berrigan,Bunny* / Sing you sinners: *Berrigan,Bunny* / Meet the beat of my heart: *Berrigan,Bunny* / T'aint so honey t'aint so: *Berrigan,Bunny* / Where in the world: *Berrigan,Bunny* / Peg o' my herat: *Berrigan,Bunny* / Hi-yo silver: *Berrigan,Bunny* / Mahogany hall stomp: *Berrigan,Bunny*
CD _______________ JASSCD 627
Jass / Oct '92 / ADA / Cadillac / CM / Direct / Jazz Music

1938 BROADCASTS-PARADISE RESTAURANT
CD _______________ JH 1022
Jazz Hour / Feb '93 / Cadillac / Jazz Music / Target/BMG

BUNNY BERIGAN & HIS RHYTHM MAKERS 1936-1938 (2CD Set) (Berigan, Bunny & His Rhythm Makers)
Take my word / Rendevous with a dream / On a coconut island / On the beach at Bali Bali / But definitely / Sing sing sing / I'm old cowhand / Empty saddles / On your toes / Did I remember / San Francisco / I can't escape from you / I can't pull a rabbit out of a hat / When I'm with you / Dardanella / When did you leave heaven / You're not the kind / You've gotta eat your spinach baby / Sweet misery of love / That's a plenty / Now it can be told / My walking stick / Wacky dust / (A sky of blue) and so forth / Flat foogie Shanghai shuffle / I got a guy / Tonight will live / Cowboy from Brooklyn / Devil's holiday / Easy to find hard to lose / Wearing of the green / Pied piper / Sunday / Frankie and Johnny / Don't wake up my heart / I'll always be in love with you / I never knew (I could love anybody) / (How to make love)in 10 easy lessons / Black bottom / There's a brand new picture in my picture frame / There's something about an old love / Small fry / Sing you sinners / Will you remember tonight tomorrow / So help me / Meet the beat of my heart / T'aint so honey ain't so / Where in the world / Peg o' my heart / Hi-ho silver / Mahogany hall stomp
CD Set _______________ CDJZCL 5016
Jazz Classics / Aug '97 / Cadillac / Direct / Jazz Music

BUNNY BERIGAN 1936-38
CD _______________ JCD 627
Jass / Feb '91 / ADA / Cadillac / CM / Direct / Jazz Music

BUNNY BERIGAN AND HIS RHYTHM MAKERS 1936 (Berigan, Bunny & His Rhythm Makers)
CD _______________ TAX 37102
Tax / Aug '94 / Cadillac / Jazz Music / Wellard

BUNNY BERIGAN AND HIS RHYTHM MAKERS VOL.2 - 1938 (Berigan, Bunny & His Rhythm Makers)
CD _______________ JASSCD 638
Jass / May '94 / ADA / Cadillac / CM / Direct / Jazz Music

CLASSICS 1935-1936
CD _______________ CLASSICS 734
Classics / Jan '94 / Discovery / Jazz Music

CLASSICS 1936-1937
CD _______________ CLASSICS 749
Classics / Aug '94 / Discovery / Jazz Music

CLASSICS 1937
CD _______________ CLASSICS 766
Classics / Aug '94 / Discovery / Jazz Music

CLASSICS 1937-1938
CD _______________ CLASSICS 785
Classics / Nov '94 / Discovery / Jazz Music

CLASSICS 1938
CD _______________ CLASSICS 815
Classics / May '95 / Discovery / Jazz Music

CLASSICS 1938-1942
CD _______________ CLASSICS 844
Classics / Nov '95 / Discovery / Jazz Music

DEVIL'S HOLIDAY
CD _______________ JCD 638
Jass / Jan '93 / ADA / Cadillac / CM / Direct / Jazz Music

GANG BUSTERS 1938-1939
When a prince / Livery stable blues / Let this be a warning / Why doesn't somebody / High society / Father dear father / Button, button / Rockin' rollers / Jubilee / Sobbin' blues / I cried for you / 'Deed I do / In a mist / Flashes / Davenport blues / Candlelights / In the dark / Walking the dog / Patty cake / Jazz me blues / You had it comin' to you / There'll be some changes made / Little gate's special / Gangbuster's holiday
CD _______________ HEPCD 1036
Hep / May '92 / Cadillac / Jazz Music / New Note/Pinnacle / Wellard

INTRODUCTION TO BUNNY BERIGAN 1935-1939, AN
CD _______________ 4021
Best Of Jazz / May '95 / Discovery

PIED PIPER 1935, THE
Nothin' but the blues / Troubled / Sometimes I'm happy / King Porter stomp / Jingle bells / Santa Claus came in spring / Honeysuckle rose / Blues / Song of India / Marie Liebestraum / Mendelssohn's spring song / Blue Lou / I can't get started (with you) / Prisoner's song / Trees / Russian lullaby / Wearing of the green / Pied piper / Jelly roll blues / Candelights / I've found a new baby
CD _______________ 07863666152
Bluebird / Aug '95 / BMG

PORTRAIT OF BUNNY BERIGAN
Me minus you / She reminds me of you / Troubled / Plantation moods / In a little Spanish town / Solo hop / Nothin' but the blues / Squareface / King Porter stomp / Buzzard / Tillie's downtown now / You took advantage of me / Chicken and waffles / I'm coming Virginia / Blues / Swing Mister Charlie / Blue Lou / Marie / Black bottom / Prisoner's song / I can't get started (with you)
CD _______________ CDAJA 5060
Living Era / Apr '89 / Select

SWINGIN' HIGH
CD _______________ TPZ 1013
Topaz Jazz / Feb '95 / Cadillac / Pinnacle

Berio, Luciano

ACOUSMATRIX 7, ELECTRONIC WORKS (Berio, Luciano & Bruno Maderna)
CD _______________ BVHAASTCD 9109
Bvhaast / Oct '94 / Cadillac

Berk, Dick

EAST COAST STROLL
CD _______________ RSRCD 128
Reservoir Music / Nov '94 / Cadillac

LET'S COOL ONE
CD _______________ RSRCD 122
Reservoir Music / Nov '94 / Cadillac

Berki, Lazlo

GYPSY VIOLIN
CD _______________ VICG 52702
JVC World Library / Mar '96 / ADA / CM / Direct

Berlin

COUNT THREE AND PRAY
Will I ever understand you / You don't know / Like flames / Heartstrings / Take my breath away / Trash / When love goes to war / Hideaway / Sex me, talk me / Pink and velvet
CD _______________ 5509012
Spectrum / Jan '95 / PolyGram

Berlin Contemporary Jazz ...

BERLIN CONTEMPORARY JAZZ ORCHESTRA (Berlin Contemporary Jazz Orchestra)
CD _______________ 8417772
ECM / Oct '90 / New Note/Pinnacle

LIVE IN JAPAN '96 (Berlin Contemporary Jazz Orchestra)
CD _______________ DIW 922
DIW / Feb '97 / Cadillac / Harmonia Mundi

Berlin, Irving

BLUE SKIES (The Irving Berlin Songbook) (Various Artists)
Let yourself go: *Fitzgerald, Ella* / You're just in love: *Vaughan, Sarah & Billy Eckstine* / Say it isn't so: *Holiday, Billie* / Remember: *Hartman, Johnny & Errol Garner* / No strings (I'm fancy free): *Astaire, Fred* / I used to be colour blind: *O'Day, Anita* / How deep is the ocean: *Williams, Joe* / This year's kisses: *Fitzgerald, Ella* / Supper time: *Waters, Ethel* / Blue skies: *Washington, Dinah* / Always: *Vaughan, Sarah & Billy Eckstine* / Top hat, white tie and tails: *Astaire, Fred* / Isn't this a lovely day: *Fitzgerald, Ella & Louis Armstrong* / Let's face the music and dance: *O'Day, Anita* / Waiting at the end of the road: *Laine, Frankie* / All by myself: *Fitzgerald, Ella*
CD _______________ 5316362
Verve / Jul '96 / PolyGram

FOREVER IRVING BERLIN (Various Artists)
Let's face the music and dance: *Cole, Nat 'King'* / I've got my love to keep me warm: *Martin, Dean* / All by myself: *Darin, Bobby* / Easter paradise: *Garland, Judy* / I've got the sun in the morning: *Riddle, Nelson & Orchestra* / Cheek to cheek: *Monro, Matt* / If I had you: *Vaughan, Sarah* / Say it isn't so: *Washington, Dinah* / Blue skies: *Cogan, Alma* / Change partners: *Crosby, Bing* / Happy birthday: *Lee, Peggy* / Isn't this a lovely day: *Haymes, Dick* / Late, late show: *Cole, Nat 'King'* / Let me sing a happy song: *Monro, Matt* / Puttin' on the ritz: *Garland, Judy* / Supper time: *Wilson, Nancy* / There's no business like show business: *Wilson, Nancy* / Maybe it's because (I love you too much): *Lee, Peggy* / Always: *Darin, Bobby* / White Christmas: *Martin, Dean*
CD _______________ CDMFP 6262
Music For Pleasure / Nov '96 / EMI

HOW DEEP IS THE OCEAN (The Irving Berlin Songbook) (Various Artists)
CD _______________ 5377012
Verve / Aug '97 / PolyGram

IRVING BERLIN'S
CD _______________ VJC 10102
Victorious Discs / Feb '91 / Jazz Music

TOP HAT, WHITE TIE AND TAILS (Various Artists)
CD _______________ MACCD 192
Autograph / Aug '96 / BMG

UNSUNG IRVING BERLIN
CD _______________ VSD 5770
Varese Sarabande / Apr '97 / Pinnacle

Berline, Byron

DAD'S FAVORITES
Coming down from Denver / New broom / Grey eagle / B and B rag / Redbird / Ragtime Annie / Lime rock / Stones rag / Miller's reel / Arkansas traveller / Sweet memories waltz / Birmingham fling
CD _______________ ROUCD 0100
Rounder / Jul '97 / ADA / CM / Direct

DOUBLE TROUBLE (Berline, Byron & John Hickman)
CD _______________ SHCD 3750
Sugar Hill / Aug '95 / ADA / CM / Direct / Koch / Roots

FIDDLE AND A SONG
Sally goodin / Rose of old Kentucky / My dixie darling / Roly poly / Faded love / Skippin' along on top / Sweet memory waltz / Fiddle faddle / Second fiddle / Fiddle's dream / Were you there / Cajun medley
CD _______________ SHCD 3838
Sugar Hill / Sep '96 / ADA / CM / Direct / Koch / Roots

JUMPIN' THE STRINGS
CD _______________ SHCD 3787
Sugar Hill / Jan '97 / ADA / CM / Direct / Koch / Roots

NOW THEY ARE FOUR (Berline, Byron & Dan Crary/John Hickman)
Big dog / Train of memory / Weary blues from waiting / Moonlight motor inn / They don't play George Jones on MTV / Speak softly you're talking to my heart / Santa Anna / Leave me the way I am / Kodak 1955 / Hallelujah Harry
CD _______________ SHCD 3773
Sugar Hill / Jul '90 / ADA / CM / Direct / Koch / Roots

OUTRAGEOUS
Barndance / Fall creek / Passin' by / Don't put it away / Coming home / Jack rabbit / Stampede / Byron's barn / Outrageous / Skippin' around / Oklahoma stomp / Funky deer
CD _______________ FF 70227
Flying Fish / Sep '96 / ADA / CM / Direct / Roots

Berman, Sonny

WOODCHOPPER'S HOLIDAY (Berman, Sonny & Serge Chaloff)
CD _______________ C&BCD 111
Cool & Blue / Oct '93 / Discovery / Jazz Music

Bermejo, Mili

CASA CORAZON (Bermejo, Mili Quartet)
CD _______________ GLCD 4016
Green Linnet / May '94 / ADA / CM / Direct / Highlander / Roots

IDENTIDAD
CD _______________ XENO 4020CD
Xenophile / Apr '96 / ADA / Direct

Bernard, Alison

FUNKIFINO
CD TRIP 7716
Ruf / Sep '96 / Pinnacle

Bernard, James

ATMOSPHERICS
CD RSNCD 14
Rising High / Mar '94 / 3mv/Sony

Bernard, Rod

SWAMP ROCK 'N' ROLLER
Pardon Mr Gordon / Recorded in England / Memphis / Gimme back my cadillac / Who's gonna rock my baby / Forgive / My old mother in law / I might as well / Boss man's son / Fais do do / Loneliness / Colinda / I want somebody / Diggy liggy lo / Lawdy Miss Clawdy / Prisoner's song / Thirty days / That's alright mama / Lover's blues / Maybellene / Midnight special / My babe / Jambalaya / Big mamou / New Orleans / Give me love / Shake, rattle and roll / This should go on forever
CD CDCHD 488
Ace / May '94 / Pinnacle

Bernard-Smith, Simon

PRAISE HIM ON THE PANPIPES
CD SOPD 2050
Spirit Of Praise / May '92 / Nelson Word

Berne, Tim

ANCESTORS, THE (Berne, Tim Sextet)
CD 1210612
Soul Note / Oct '90 / Cadillac / Harmonia Mundi / Wellard

BLOODCOUNT UNWOUND (3CD Set)
Bro' ball / No Ma'am / Yes Dear / Loose ends / Bloodcount / Mr. Johnson's blues / Other / What are the odds
CD Set SCREWU 70001
ScrewGun / Apr '97 / New Note/Pinnacle

DIMINUTIVE MYSTERIES (Mostly Hemphill)
Sounds in the fog / Serial abstractions / Out the regular / Unknown / Writing love lines / Rites / Maze / Mystery to me
CD 5140032
jMT / Jan '93 / PolyGram

FRACTURED FAIRY TALES
Now then / SEP / Hong Kong sad song/ More coffee / Evolution of a pearl / Lightnin' bug boute / Telex blues
CD 8344312
jMT / Jan '91 / PolyGram

FULTON STREET MAUL
CD 378262
Koch Jazz / Nov '96 / Koch

MEMORY SELECT (Berne, Tim & Bloodcount)
CD 5140292
jMT / Apr '96 / PolyGram

NICE VIEW (Berne, Tim Caos Totale)
It could have been a lot worse / Third rail / Impacted wisdom
CD 5140132
jMT / Jul '93 / PolyGram

SANCTIFIED DREAMS
Velcho man / Hip doctor / Elastic lad / Blue alpha (for alpha) / Mag's groove / Terre haute
CD 378252
Koch Jazz / Jun '97 / Koch

Bernelle, Agnes

FATHER'S LYING DEAD ON THE IRONING BOARD
Homecoming / Chansonette / Bertha de Sade / Hafen-kneipe / Tootsies / Horse / Girl with brown mole / Night elegy / Ballad of the poor child / Hurdy gurdy / Nightingale
CD DIAB 815
Diabolo / Jul '95 / Pinnacle

Bernie

I SAW THE LIGHT
I saw the light / This world is not my home / Me and Jesus / One day at a time / Morning has broken / Tramp on the streets / Precious memories / Fly away / Daddy sang bass / Why me Lord / Old rugged cross / Amazing grace / Rivers of Babylon / Swing low, sweet Chariot / He's got the whole world in his hands / Old country church / Safe in the arms of Jesus / Go tell it on the mountain / Will the circle be unbroken / When the saints go marching in / Count your blessings / Family bible / Rock of ages / How great thou art
CD PLATCD 339
Platinum / Mar '93 / Prism

Bernstein, Peter

BRAIN DANCE (Bernstein, Peter Quintet)
Brain dance / Chant / Means and ends / Dual nature / While we're young / You leave me breathlesss / Lady bug / Danger zone
CD CRISS 1130CD
Criss Cross / Jul '97 / Cadillac / Direct / Vital/SAM

SIGNS
CD CRISS 1095
Criss Cross / Apr '95 / Cadillac / Direct / Vital/SAM

SOMETHIN'S BURNIN' (Bernstein, Peter Quartet)
CD CRISS 1079CD
Criss Cross / Nov '93 / Cadillac / Direct / Vital/SAM

Bernstein, Steven Jesse

PRISON
CD SPCD 37195
Sub Pop / Jul '92 / Cargo / Greyhound / Shellshock/Disc

Beron, Paul

TRASNOCHANDO
CD BMT 009
Blue Moon / Jul '97 / Cadillac / Discovery / Greensleeves / Jazz Music / Jet Star / TKO Magnum

Berrios, Steve

AND THEN SOME (Berrios, Steve & Son Bacheche)
Son bacheche / Leri eyo / Al mundo de los recuerdos / Bemsha swing / Chamalongo / Blues for sarka / Un ecobio / With the sweetness / Fire and brimstone / Mojiganga / Hominaje a un trovador / Uncle Toms
CD MCD 92552
Milestone / Sep '96 / Cadillac / Complete/ Pinnacle / Jazz Music / Wellard

Berry, Bill

HELLO REV (Berry, Bill LA Big Band)
Hello rev / Star crossed lovers / Bink / And how / Earl / Little song for Mex / Be your own best friend / Tulip or turnip / Boy meets horn / Cotton tail
CD CCD 4027
Concord Jazz / Aug '90 / New Note/ Pinnacle

SHORTCAKE
Avalon / Betty / Bloose / I didn't know about you / Royal Garden blues / Moon song / I'm getting sentimental over you / I hadn't anyone till you
CD CCD 4075
Concord Jazz / Feb '95 / New Note/ Pinnacle

Berry, Chuck

20 GREAT TRACKS
Maybellene / Roll over Beethoven / Reelin' and rockin' / Rock 'n' roll music / Sweet little sixteen / Johnny B Goode / No particular place to go / Memphis, Tennessee / Wee wee hours / You never can tell / Go go go / Downbound train / No money down / Havana moon / House of blue lights / Crying steel / I'm just a lucky so and so / Promised land / My Mustang Ford / Drifting heart
CD CDMFP 5936
Music For Pleasure / Apr '92 / EMI

BEST OF CHUCK BERRY, THE
Roll over Beethoven / No particular place to go / Memphis, Tennessee / Tulane / Havana moon / Wee wee hours / Nadine / Let it rock / Sweet little sixteen / Maybellene / Back in the USA / Little queenie / Almost grown / Johnny B Goode / School day / Oh baby doll / Sweet little rock 'n' roller / Reelin' and rockin' / Promised land / Rock 'n' roll music / Downbound train / Brown eyed handsome man / Merry Christmas baby / Bye bye Johnny / Around and around / No money down
CD MCCD 019
Music Club / May '91 / Disc / THE

BEST OF CHUCK BERRY, THE
Roll over Beethoven / Sweet little sixteen / Johnny B Goode / You never can tell / You can't catch me / Downbound train / Too much monkey business / Havana moon / School day / Oh baby doll / Beautiful Delilah / Sweet little rock'n'roller / Antony boy / Little Queenie / Almost grown / Let it rock / Back in the USA / Reelin' and rockin' / Around and around / Brown eyed handsome man / Maybelline / No particular place to go / Rock 'n' roll / Run randolph run / Jo Jo Gunne / Carol / Confessin' the blues / Jaguar and thunderbird / Down the road apiece / Thirty days / Merry christmas baby / My ding-a-ling / I'm talking about you / Too pooped to pop / Bye bye Johnny / Promised land / Tulane / Come on / Nadine (is it you) / Memphis, Tennessee
CD MCD 11560
MCA / Nov '96 / BMG

CHESS MASTERS VOL.2
Around and around / Beautiful Delilah / Carol / Memphis, Tennessee / Sweet little rock 'n' roller / Little Queenie / Almost grown / Back in the USA / Let it rock / Bye bye Johnny / Come on / Nadine / You never can tell / Promised land / No particular place to go / It wasn't me
CD CDMF 080
Magnum Force / Nov '91 / TKO Magnum

CHUCK BERRY
CD CD 111
Timeless Treasures / Oct '94 / THE

CHUCK BERRY
Rock 'n' roll music / Johnny B Goode / Maybellene / Reelin' and rockin' / You never can tell / Sweet little sixteen / Let it rock / Roll over Beethoven / Back in the USA / Little Queenie / No particular place to go / No money down / Memphis Tennessee / Nadine / I got to find my baby / School days / Wee wee hours / Too much monkey business
CD 399537
Koch Presents / May '97 / Koch

CHUCK BERRY COLLECTION
CD COL 002
Collection / Jun '95 / Target/BMG

CHUCK BERRY IN CONCERT
CD CDSGP 0155
Prestige / Mar '95 / Else / Total/BMG

CHUCK BERRY IS ON TOP
CD CHLD 19250
Chess/MCA / Oct '94 / BMG / New Note/ BMG

CHUCK BERRY/GENE VINCENT ESSENTIALS (Berry, Chuck & Gene Vincent)
CD LECDD 625
Wisepack / Aug '95 / Conifer/BMG / THE

EP COLLECTION, THE
CD SEECD 320
See For Miles/C5 / Jul '91 / Pinnacle

FRUIT OF THE VINE
Downbound train / Wee wee hours / No money down / Drifting heart / Brown eyed handsome man / Havana moon / Oh baby doll / Anthony boy / Merry Christmas baby / Jo Jo Gunne / Childhood sweetheart / I got to find my baby / Worried life blues / Jaguar and the thunderbirds / Confessin' the blues / Thirteen question method / Things I used to do / You two / Little Marie / Dear Dad / It wasn't me / Ramona say yes / Tulane / Have mercy judge
CD CDRED 19
Charly / Jun '90 / Koch

GREAT 28 HITS, THE
CD CHLD 19116
Chess/MCA / Jan '94 / BMG / New Note/ BMG

HIS BEST VOL.1
CD MCD 09371
Chess/MCA / Aug '97 / BMG / New Note/ BMG

LEGENDS IN MUSIC
CD LECD 037
Wisepack / Nov '94 / Conifer/BMG / THE

LIVE ON STAGE
Schooldays / Sweet little sixteen / Roll over Beethoven / Everyday I have the blues / Bio / Maybellene/Mountain dew / Let it rock / Carol/Little Queenie / Keys to the highway / Got my mojo working / Reelin' and rockin' / Johnny B Goode
CD CDMF 092
Magnum Force / Mar '95 / TKO Magnum

ON THE BLUES SIDE
Confessin' the blues / runaround / Worried life blues / Things that I used to do / Blues for Hawaiians / Wee wee hours / I still got the blues / Down the road apiece / No money down / Stop and listen / Blue on blue / Sweet sixteen / I got to find my baby / I just want to make love to you / Merry Christmas baby / Deep feeling / Wee hour blues / Don't you lie to me / Ain't that just like a woman / Driftin' blues / Blue feeling
CD CDCH 397
Ace / Sep '93 / Pinnacle

PACKET OF THREE VOL.3 (3CD Set) (Berry, Chuck/Bo Diddley/Various Artists)
Brown eyed handsome man: *Berry, Chuck* / Roll over Beethoven: *Berry, Chuck* / Too much monkey business: *Berry, Chuck* / School days: *Berry, Chuck* / Rock 'n' roll music: *Berry, Chuck* / Sweet little sixteen: *Berry, Chuck* / Reelin' and rockin': *Berry, Chuck* / Johnny B Goode: *Berry, Chuck* / Around and around: *Berry, Chuck* / Carol: *Berry, Chuck* / Memphis Tennessee: *Berry, Chuck* / Sweet little rock and roller: *Berry, Chuck* / Little Queenie: *Berry, Chuck* / Back in the USA: *Berry, Chuck* / Let it rock: *Berry, Chuck* / Nadine: *Berry, Chuck* / You never can tell: *Berry, Chuck* / Promised land: *Berry, Chuck* / I'm looking for a woman: *Diddley, Bo* / Before you accuse me: *Diddley, Bo* / You can't judge a book by the cover: *Diddley, Bo* / Bo's guitar: *Diddley, Bo* / She's mine, she's fine: *Diddley, Bo* / Diddley Daddy: *Diddley, Bo* / Story of Bo Diddley: *Diddley, Bo* / Hey Bo Diddley: *Diddley, Bo* / I'm a man: *Diddley, Bo* / You don't love me: *Diddley, Bo* / I'm sorry: *Diddley, Bo* / Cops and robbers: *Diddley, Bo* / Diddley wah diddy: *Diddley, Bo* / Say man: *Diddley, Bo* / Mona: *Diddley, Bo* / Bring it to Jerome: *Diddley, Bo* / Bo Diddley: *Diddley, Bo* / Blueberry Hill: *Domino, Fats* / Roadrunner: *Diddley, Bo* / Sweet little sixteen: *Berry, Chuck* / Let there be drums: *Nelson, Sandy* / Great balls of fire: *Lewis, Jerry Lee* / Jailhouse rock: *Perkins, Carl* / She's got it: *Little Richard* / Yakety yak: *Coasters* / Shake, rattle and roll: *Haley, Bill* / At the hop: *Danny & The Juniors* / Moody river: *Boone, Pat* / Hey baby: *Shannon, Del* / Lotta lovin': *Vincent, Gene* / Stroll: *Diamonds* / Red river rock: *Johnny & The Hurricanes* / Keep a-knockin': *Little Richard*
CD Set KLMCD 303
BAM / Nov '96 / Koch / Scratch/BMG

SWEET LITTLE EIGHTEEN
CD 3001052
Scratch / Jul '95 / Koch / Scratch/BMG

SWEET LITTLE ROCK 'N' ROLLER
Carol / Back in the USA / Sweet little rock 'n' roller / Little queenie / School days / Promised land / Maybeline / Nadine / Blues for Hawaiians / No money down / Fraulein / Roll over Beethoven / Memphis Tennessee / Sweet little sixteen / Johnny B Goode / No particular place to go / Down the road a piece / Let it rock / You never can tell / My ding-a-ling
CD MCD 80245
Chess/MCA / Apr '97 / BMG / New Note/ BMG

TWO GREAT GUITARS/SUPER SUPER BLUES BAND (Berry, Chuck & Bo Diddley/Howlin' Wolf/Muddy Waters)
Liverpool drive / Chuck's beat / When the Saints go marching in / Bo's beat / Long distance call / Medley / Sweet little angel / Spoonful / Diddley daddy / Little red rooster / Going down slow
CD BGOCD 334
Beat Goes On / Feb '97 / Pinnacle

VERY BEST OF CHUCK BERRY, THE
CD MCBD 19536
MCA / Apr '97 / BMG

VERY BEST OF CHUCK BERRY, THE
Johnny B Goode / Sweet little sixteen / Hail, hail rock 'n' roll / Hoochie coochie man / Reelin' 'n' rockin' / My ding a ling / Johnny B Goode (reprise) / Nadine (is it you) / Maybelline / In the wee, wee hours / Bon soire Cherie / Memphis / Rock 'n' roll music / Carol
CD 100362
CMC / May '97 / BMG

Berry, Dave

VERY BEST OF DAVE BERRY, THE
Memphis Tennessee / My baby left me / Baby it's you / Crying game / One heart between two / Little things / This strange effect / Mama / Can I get it from you / I'm gonna take you there / If you wait for love / Stranger / Heartbeat / Change our minds / Suspicions (in your mind) / I got the feeling / Girl from the Fair Isle / Sticks and stones / I love you babe / Coffee song
CD 5520192
Spectrum / Jan '97 / PolyGram

Berry, Heidi

BELOW THE WAVES
CD CRECD 048
Creation / May '94 / 3mv/Vital

HEIDI BERRY
CD CAD 3009CD
4AD / Jun '93 / RTM/Disc

LOVE
CD CADCD 1012
4AD / Aug '91 / RTM/Disc

MIRACLE
Mountain / Time / Holy grail / Darkness / Miracle / Californian / Queen / Only human / Northern country
CD CAD 6011CD
4AD / Jul '96 / RTM/Disc

Berry, Iris

LIFE ON THE EDGE IN STILETTOS
CD NAR 108CD
New Alliance / Jul '95 / Plastic Head

Berry, Jan

SECOND WAVE
CD OW 34524
One Way / Jun '97 / ADA / Direct / Greyhound

Berry, John

FACES
She's taken a shine / Change my mind / I will if you will / He doesn't even know her / Faithfully / Livin' on love / Time to be a man / Forty again / Love is everything / I give my heart
CD PRMDCD 14
Premier/EMI / Sep '96 / EMI

FAITHFULLY
Your love amazes me / You and only you / Fire / Faithfully / Standing on the edge of goodbye / If I had any pride at all / Kiss me in the car / I give my heart
CD PRMCD 7
Premier/EMI / Jun '96 / EMI

STANDING ON THE EDGE
Every time my heart calls your name / Standing on the edge of goodbye / Prove me wrong / I think about it all the time / If I had any pride left at all / Desperate meas-

ures / What are we fighting for / There's no cross that love won't bear / Ninety miles an hour / I never lost you / You and only you
CD CDEST 2265
Capitol / Jun '95 / EMI

Berry, Leon 'Chu'

BLOWING UP A BREEZE
CD TPZ 1024
Topaz Jazz / Jul '95 / Cadillac / Pinnacle

CLASSICS 1937-1941
CD CLASSICS 784
Classics / Nov '94 / Discovery / Jazz Music

Berry, Mike

ROCK 'N' ROLL BOOGIE... PLUS
I'm a rocker / Don't fight it / Love rocket / Don't ever change / Stay close to me / Hard times / Take me high / It's a hard hard world / Tribute to Buddy Holly / Boogaloo dues / Midnight train / Hey Joe / One by one / Rebel without a cause / Take a heart / Dial my number / New Orleans / Wake up Suzy / Baby boy / Low country woman / Hey baby / Think it over / Don't be cruel
CD C5CD 541
See For Miles/C5 / Oct '92 / Pinnacle

TRIBUTE TO BUDDY HOLLY, A
Tribute to Buddy Holly / Only rock 'n' roll / Heaven out of hell / Peggy Sue got married / Dreams can come true / Think it over / Raining in my heart / That'll be the day / Peggy Sue / Rave on / Stay close to me / Fool's paradise / I'm gonna love you too / Holly
CD 302512
Hallmark / Jul '97 / Carlton

Berry, Richard

GET OUT OF THE CAR
Mad about you / Angel of my life / Yama yama pretty mama / Next time / Rockin' man / Oh oh, get out of the car / Crazy lover / I'm still in love with you / Jelly roll / Big John / One little prayer / Big break
CD CDCH 355
Ace / Mar '92 / Pinnacle

Berry, Robert

PILGRIMAGE TO A POINT
No one else to blame / You've changed / Shelter / Another man / Love we share / Blame / Otherside / Freedom / Last ride into the sun
CD CYCL 019
Cyclops / Apr '95 / Pinnacle

Berryhill, Cyndi Lee

NAKED MOVIE STAR
CD AWCD 1016
Awareness / Jul '89 / ADA

Bert, Eddie

HUMAN FACTOR, THE (Bert, Eddie Sextet)
CD FSR 5005CD
Fresh Sound / Nov '95 / Discovery / Jazz Music

LIVE AT BIRDLAND (Bert, Eddie & J.R. Monterose)
CD FSRCD 198
Fresh Sound / Dec '92 / Discovery / Jazz Music

Bertoncini, Gene

BOSSA NOVA COLLECTION, A (Bertoncini, Gene & Michael Moore)
Once I loved / No more blues / Zingaro / Rio Pindare / O grand amor / Quiet nights of quiet stars / Let go / Pensativa
CD VN 1004
Viper's Nest / Nov '96 / ADA / Cadillac / Direct / Jazz Music

JOBIM - SOMEONE TO LIGHT UP MY LIFE
CD CRD 343
Chiaroscuro / Jan '97 / Jazz Music

TWO IN TIME (Bertoncini, Gene & Michael Moore)
CD CRD 308
Chiaroscuro / Mar '96 / Jazz Music

Bertone, Bruno

LA MUSICA FROM ITALY (Bertone, Bruno Mandoline Orchestra)
CD 15209
Laserlight / '91 / Target/BMG

NIGHTS IN WHITE SATIN
Love story (where do I begin) / Strangers in the night / Something / Bright eyes / Woman / You are the sunshine of my life / Michelle / Lara's theme (somewhere my love) / To all the girls I've loved before / Spanish eyes / Don't it make my brown eyes blue / Tara's theme / Feelings / Annie's song / Love is blue / If you leave me now / Unchained melody / Memory / Nights in white satin
CD CD 6005
Music / Apr '96 / Target/BMG

SONG SUNG BLUE
Song sung blue / Don't cry for me Argentina / Oh happy day / Fool on the hill / September wind / Yesterday / Bilitis / Last farewell / Sailing / Greensleeves / Eleanor Rigby / House of the rising sun / Banks of the Ohio / Around the world / Cast your face to the wind / Whiter shade of pale / My way
CD CD 6008
Music / Apr '96 / Target/BMG

STRICTLY DANCING: FOX-TROT (Bertone, Bruno Ballroom Orchestra)
CD 15337
Laserlight / Jun '92 / Target/BMG

Besses O' The Barn

HYMNS AND THINGS
Praise my soul the King of heaven / Eventide / Dem bones / Ave Maria / Simple gifts / Nun's chorus / Deep harmony / Jerusalem / Hymn tune medley / Aurelia / O, for the wings of a dove / God be in my head / Dear Lord and the father of mankind / Sandon / Thanks be to God
CD CHAN 4529
Chandos / Aug '93 / Chandos

SHOWCASE FOR BRASS
Three figures / In memoriam RK / Summer scherzo / Belmont variations / Northwest passage
CD CHAN 4525
Chandos / May '93 / Chandos

Best, Barbara

SWING LOW (Best, Barbara Singers)
CD BB 1992
Black & Blue / May '96 / Discovery / Koch / Wellard

Best, Pete

BACK TO THE BEAT (Best, Pete Band)
My Bonnie / Roll over Beethoven / Dancing in the streets / Dizzie Miss Lizzie / Money / Love me do / Stand by me / Long tall Sally / I saw her standing there / Twist and shout / Hippy hippy shake / Johnny B Goode / C'mon everybody
CD PBSCD 2000
Splash / Apr '96 / BMG / Else

BEYOND THE BEATLES 1963-1968 (Best, Pete Combo)
All aboard / Why did you leave me baby / Shimmy like my sister Kate / I need your lovin' / I can't do without you now / I don't know why I do / I'll try anyway / I'm checking out now baby / Keys to my heart / She's alright / I'm blue / Castin' my spell / Off the hook / Pete's theme / Everybody / I wanna be there / Rock 'n' roll music / Don't play with me / Way I feel about you / I'll have everything too / How do you get to know her name / She's not the only girl in town / If you can't get her / More than I need myself
CD CDMRED 124
Cherry Red / Feb '96 / Pinnacle

LIVE AT THE ADELPHI/INTERVIEW (Best, Pete Band)
CD CDMRED 136
Cherry Red / Sep '96 / Pinnacle

Bestial Warlust

BLOOD AND VALOUR
CD MIM 7321CD
Modern Invasion / Jul '96 / Plastic Head

VENGEANCE WAR TIL DEATH
CD MIN 73162
Modern Invasion / Feb '95 / Plastic Head

Bethania, Maria

CANTO DO PALE
Abertura/Texto/O canto do paje / Tocando em frente / Maria/Linda flor logrador / Quase / Pronta pra cantar tomara / Flor de ir embora / Awo/Inhansa / Palavra
CD 8480222
Philips / Jan '94 / PolyGram

LAS CANCIONES QUE HICISTE PARA MI
Las canciones que hiciste para mi / Olha / Fiera herida / Palabras / Costumes / Detalhes / Tu no sabes / Necesito de tu amor / Seu sorpo / Tu / Emocione
CD 5187872
Verve / Jan '95 / PolyGram

MEL
Mel / Ela e eu / Cherio de amor / Da cor Brasileira / Loucura / Gota de sangua / Grito de sangua / Grito de alerta / Labios del Mel / Amando sobre os jornais / Nenhum verao / Infinito desejo / Queda d'agua
CD 8382872
Verve / Jan '95 / PolyGram

MEMORIA DA PELE
Reconvexo / Tenha calma / Confesso / Junho / Morena / Salve as folhas / Memoria da pele / A mais bonita / Guerra no mar / Vinganca / Paiol do ouro vinheta
CD 8389282
Verve / Mar '94 / PolyGram

OLHO D'AGUA
Sodade meu bem sodade / Vida va / Invisivel / Ilumina / Medalha de sao Jorge / O tempo e a cancao / Bilhete de despedida / Olho d'agua / Louvacao a oxum / Rainha negra buzio / Modinha / Alem da ultima estrela / Sodade meu bem sodade
CD 5120522
Philips / Jan '94 / PolyGram

Bethlehem

DARK METAL
CD CDAR 022
Adipocre / Jul '94 / Plastic Head

Beto & The Fairlanes

SALSAFIED
CD DOS 7009
Dos / Sep '94 / ADA / CM / Direct

Betrayer

CALAMITY
CD MNO 2CD
Nuclear Blast / Nov '94 / Plastic Head

Betsy

ROUGH AROUND THE EDGES
All over my heart / If I don't stay the night / Love me like you mean it / Draggin' it back / Bits and pieces / Hard to believe / You can look (but you can't touch) / Southern wind / Passage / This house
CD 7567924282
Warner Bros. / Nov '94 / Warner Music

Bettencourt, Nuno

SCHIZOPHONIC
Gravity / Swollen princess / Crave / What you want / Fallen angels / 2 weeks in dizkneelande / Pursuit of happiness / Fine by me / Karmalaa / Confrontation / Note on the screen door / I wonder / Got to have you / You / Severed
CD 5405932
A&M / Feb '97 / PolyGram

Better Daze

ONE STREET OVER
CD URCD 017
Ubiquity / Jul '96 / Cargo / Timewarp

Bettie Serveert

DUST BUNNIES
Geek / Link / Musher / Dust bunnies / What friends / Misery galore / Story in a nutshell / Sugar the pill / Rudder / Pork and beans / Fallen foster / Co-coward / Heaven
CD BBQCD 189
Beggars Banquet / Mar '97 / RTM/Disc / Warner Music

LAMPREY
CD BBQCD 169
Beggars Banquet / Jan '95 / RTM/Disc / Warner Music

SOMETHING SO WILD
CD BBQ 58CD
Beggars Banquet / Jun '95 / RTM/Disc / Warner Music

Betty & The Bops

BETTY & THE BOPS
CD 622592
Skydog / Apr '97 / Discovery

Beuf, Sylvian

IMPRO PRIMO (Beuf, Sylvian Quartet)
CD BBRC 9311
Big Blue / Jan '94 / Harmonia Mundi

Bevan, Tony

ORIGINAL GRAVITY (Bevan, Tony & Greg Kingston & Matt Lewis)
CD INCUSCD 03
Incus / '90 / Cadillac / Cargo

TWISTERS (Bevan, Tony & Steve Noble)
CD 06CD
Scatter / May '97 / Cadillac

Beverley Sisters

GREEN FIELDS
Together wherever we go / Hold me / English muffins & Irish stew / We have to be so careful / Green fields / Skye boat song / Oh wishing star / Water or the wine / Sultan / Sphinx won't tell / I was never loved by anyone else / Undecided / Teasin' / Yell for your Mama / String along / I wish I wuz / Wheel of fortune / Poor Whip poor Will (move over, move over) / For you / In the wee small hours of the morning / Once in a while / When the boys talk about the girls / I'm always chasing rainbows / No one but you
CD CDMFP 6220
Music For Pleasure / Apr '96 / EMI

SING AND SWING (Beverley Sisters & Syd Lawrence Orchestra)
Roll out the barrel: *Beverley Sisters* / Army, the Navy and the Air Force: *Beverley Sisters* / St. Louis blues: *Lawrence, Syd Orchestra* / I know why and so do you: *Foxes* / I'll be seeing you: *Wright, Babette* / Woodchopper's ball: *Lawrence, Syd Orchestra* / Alexander's ragtime band: *Foxes* / In the mood: *Lawrence, Syd Orchestra* / Yankee doodle boy: *Beverley Sisters* / Guam: *Beverley Sisters* / I'll be with you in apple blossom time: *Beverley Sisters* / Oh what a lovely war: *Beverley Sisters* / Skyliner: *Lawrence, Syd Orchestra* / Keep the home fires burning: *Beverley Sisters*
CD 3036001112
Carlton / Jul '97 / Carlton

SISTERS, SISTERS
CD QPRM 601D
Polyphonic / Aug '93 / Complete/Pinnacle

VERY BEST OF THE BEVERLEY SISTERS, THE
Willie can / I dreamed / Little drummer boy / Little donkey / Have you ever been lonely / Sisters / Left right out of your heart / Mr. Wonderful / Long black nylons / Strawberry fair / Morning has broken / It's illegal, it's immoral, or it makes you fat / If anybody finds this, I love you / Greensleeves / I saw Mommy kissing Santa Claus / Naughty lady of shady lane / Little things mean a lot / Somebody bad stole de wedding bell / We like to do things like that / Mama doll song / Triplets / Changing partners
CD 5523692
Spectrum / Jan '97 / PolyGram

Bevis Frond

ANY GAS FASTER
Lord Plentiful reflects / Rejection day (am) / Ear song (olde world) / This corner of England / Legendary / When you wanted me / Lost rivers / Somewhere else / These dark days / Head on a pole / Your mind's gone grey / Old sea dog / Rejection day (pm) / Good old fashioned pain / Olde worlde
CD CDRECK 18
Reckless / Jan '90 / RTM/Disc

AUNTIE WINNIE ALBUM, THE
CD CDRECK 17
Reckless / Jul '89 / RTM/Disc

GATHERING OF FRONDS, A
CD CDRECK 25
Reckless / Mar '92 / RTM/Disc

INNER MARSHLAND
CD CDRECK 14
Reckless / Jul '89 / RTM/Disc

IT JUST IS
CD WO 21CD
Woronzow / Oct '93 / Pinnacle

MIASMA
CD CDRECK 13
Reckless / Jul '89 / RTM/Disc

NEW RIVER HEAD
CD WO 16CD
Woronzow / Sep '91 / Pinnacle

SON OF WALTER
CD W 028CD
Woronzow / Oct '96 / Pinnacle

SPRAWL
CD Set WO 22CD
Woronzow / Oct '94 / Pinnacle

SUPERSEEDER
CD WO 26CD
Woronzow / Oct '95 / Pinnacle

TRIPTYCH
CD CDRECK 15
Reckless / Mar '89 / RTM/Disc

Bevoir, Paul

DUMB ANGEL
CD TANGCD 8
Tangerine / May '94 / RTM/Disc

HAPPIEST DAYS OF YOUR LIFE, THE
CD TANGCD 2
Tangerine / Aug '92 / RTM/Disc

Bewitched

DIABOLICAL DESECRATION
CD OPCD 034
Osmose / May '96 / Plastic Head

ENCYCLOPEDIA OF EVIL
CD OPCD 041
Osmose / Jul '96 / Plastic Head

Bey, Andy

BALLADS, BLUES & BEY
Someone to watch over me / You'd be so nice to come home to / I let a song go out of my heart / In a sentimental mood / Willow weep for me / Yesterdays / If you could see me now / I'm just a lucky so and so / Daydream / Embraceable you
CD ECD 221622
Evidence / Oct '96 / ADA / Cadillac / Harmonia Mundi

Bey, Ronnell

NEARNESS OF YOU, THE (Bey, Ronnell & Eartha Kitt/Clark Terry)
CD BASIC 50017
ITM / Apr '96 / Koch / Tradelink

Beyer, Adam

RECODED (2CD Set)
CD Set PRRUKCD 002
Planet Rhythm UK / Sep '97 / Prime

Beyond

CHASM
CD CDMFN 147
Music For Nations / Jul '93 / Pinnacle

Beyond Belief

RAVE THE ABYSS
CD SHARK 102CD
Shark / Jun '95 / Plastic Head

Beyond Dawn

LONGING FOR SCARLET DAYS
CD CDAR 019
Adipocre / May '94 / Plastic Head

PITY LOVE
CD CANDLE 012CD
Candlelight / Nov '95 / Plastic Head

BF Trike

BF TRIKE
CD BFT 1001
Rockadelic / May '97 / Greyhound

BFM

CITY OF DOPE
City of dope / Go amazen' (do yo' thang) / Can't slow down / Am I black enough / Let yourself go / Why ya "p" ain't tight / Gimme a bottle / Larceny / Give it up / Pass the joint
CD ICH 1118CD
Ichiban / Sep '91 / Direct / Koch

BGK

NOTHING CAN GO WRONG
CD VIRUS 52CD
Alternative Tentacles / '92 / Cargo / Greyhound / Pinnacle

Bhatt, Krishna

KIRWANI (Bhatt, Krishna & Zakir Hussain)
CD ARNR 0495
Amiata / Aug '97 / Harmonia Mundi

Bhatt, Vishnwa Mohan

BOURBON AND ROSEWATER
CD WLACS 47CD
Waterlilly Acoustics / Nov '95 / ADA

GATHERING RAINCLOUDS
CD WLAES 22CD
Waterlilly Acoustics / Nov '95 / ADA

JUGALBANDI
CD CDA 92059CD
Music Today / Jan '95 / ADA

SANGEET TRIO IN CONCERT (Sangeet Trio)
CD C 560091
Ocora / Dec '96 / ADA / Harmonia Mundi

SARADAMANI
CD WLAES 23CD
Waterlilly Acoustics / Feb '96 / ADA

Bhattacharya, Pandit Amit

CLASSIC MUSIC FROM NORTH INDIA
CD KMCD 54
Keltia Musique / Jul '95 / ADA / Discovery

Bhawalker, Uday

RAGAS PURIYA AND JOG
CD NRCD 0058
Navras / May '96 / New Note/Pinnacle

Bhundu Boys

FRIENDS ON THE ROAD
Radio Africa / Pombi / Ring of fire / Gonzo nachin'ai / Bitter to the south / Foolish harp/ Waerara / Anna / Church on fire / Don't forget Africa / Anyway / My best friend / Lizzie
CD COOKCD 053
Cooking Vinyl / Feb '93 / Vital

MUCHIYEDZA (OUT OF THE DARK)
Kachembere / Hazvisekanwe / Satan ngaaparadzwe / Tamba wega / Misodzi pamatama / Pafunge / Dorica / Mumhanzi we jit / Mhunza musha
CD COOKCD 118
Cooking Vinyl / Feb '97 / Vital

TRUE JIT
Jit jive / My foolish heart / Chemedzevana / Rugare / Vana / Wonderful world / Ndoitasei / Susan / African woman / Happy birthday / Jekesa / I don't think that man should sleep alone / Over you / Loving you / You shoulda kept a spare / Past / You make my nature dance / Perfect lovers / After midnite / I love your daughter / After dark
CD 2422032
WEA / Sep '87 / Warner Music

Bi Kyo Ran

PARALLAX (2CD Set)
CD Set BELLE 95186
Belle Antique / Jun '97 / ReR Megacorp

Biafra, Jello

SKY IS FALLING, THE (Biafra, Jello & No Means No)
CD VIRUS 85CD
Alternative Tentacles / Feb '01 / Cargo / Greyhound / Pinnacle

Bianchi, Maurico

AKTIVITAT
CD DVLR 02
Dark Vinyl / Jan '94 / Plastic Head / World Serpent

Bianco Bachicha

TANGOS IN PARIS 1926-1941
CD HQCD 66
Harlequin / Jun '96 / Hot Shot / Jazz Music / Swift / Wellard

Bibb, Eric

GOOD STUFF
CD OPUS3CD 19603
Opus 3 / Mar '97 / Direct / Jazz Music

SPIRIT AND THE BLUES (Bibb, Eric & Needed Time)
Lonesome valley / In my father's house / Needed time / I am blessed / Just keep goin' on / Where shall I be / Woke up this mornin' / I want Jesus to walk with me / You're gonna need somebody on your bond / Braggin' / Water under the bridge / Tell ol' Bill / Satisfied mind / Meetin' at the buildin'
CD OPUS3CD 19401
Opus 3 / Nov '96 / Direct / Jazz Music

Bible

EUREKA
Skywriting / Honey be good / Skeleton crew / November brides / Cigarette girls / Crystal Palace / Wishing game / Red Hollywood / Tiny lights / Blue shoes stepping
CD HAVENCD 5
Haven / Nov '95 / Pinnacle / Shellshock/ Disc

RANDOM ACTS OF KINDNESS
CD HAVENCD 8
Haven / Nov '95 / Pinnacle / Shellshock/ Disc

WALKING THE GHOST BACK HOME
CD HAVENCD 4
Haven / Nov '95 / Pinnacle / Shellshock/ Disc

Bick-Clark, Nancy

CROSSING TO IRELAND (Bick-Clark, Nancy & Sara Johnson)
CD RS 00113CD
Rising Star / May '96 / ADA

Biddleville Quintette

BIDDLEVILLE QUINTETTE VOL.1 1926-1929
CD DOCD 5361
Document / Jun '95 / ADA / Hot Shot / Jazz Music

BIDDLEVILLE QUINTETTE VOL.2 1929
CD DOCD 5362
Document / Jun '95 / ADA / Hot Shot / Jazz Music

Biddu Orchestra

SUMMER OF '42
Summer of '42 / Blue eyed soul / Exodus / Black magic woman / Concierto de Aranjuez / Couldn't we be friends / Rain forest / Jump for joy / Laura / I could have danced all night / Trippin' on a soul cloud / Girl you'll be a woman soon / Nirvana / Love's serenade
CD QED 130
Tring / Nov '96 / Tring

Biddulph, Rick

SECOND NATURE
CD VP 178CD
Voiceprint / Jan '95 / Pinnacle

Biff Bang Pow

ACID HOUSE ALBUM, THE
CD CRECD 046
Creation / May '94 / 3mv/Vital

DEBASEMENT TAPES
CD CRECD 125
Creation / Jun '93 / 3mv/Vital

L'AMOUR, DEMURE, STENHOUSEMUIR
CD CRECD 099
Creation / May '94 / 3mv/Vital

ME
CD CRECD 071
Creation / May '94 / 3mv/Vital

SONGS FOR THE SAD EYED GIRL
CD CRECD 058
Creation / Jan '90 / 3mv/Vital

Big Al

DA BUDDAH KLAN
TWCTFW / Texas niggas / Zoota bang / Breaking fools down / You too near me / Neighborhood drug dealer / Tony montana / Walk with me / Fenna grab the AK / Strictly conversation / Kickin' it like big players / Clockhound AKA gorilla pimpin / Hard dick no conscious / Exit the dragon / Texas G's
CD PCD 1468
Profile / Mar '97 / Pinnacle

Big Ass Truck

BIG ASS TRUCK
CD UPSTART 024
Upstart / Nov '95 / ADA / Direct

KENT
CD UPSTART 027
Upstart / Mar '96 / ADA / Direct

Big Audio Dynamite

F-PUNK
CD RAD 11280
Radioactive / Jun '95 / BMG / Vital

THIS IS BIG AUDIO DYNAMITE
Medicine show / Sony / E=MC2 / Bottom line / Sudden impact / Stone Thames / BAD / Party
CD 4629992
CBS / Nov '88 / Sony

TIGHTEN UP VOL.88
Rock non stop (all night long) / Other 99 / Funny names / Applecart / Esquerita / Champagne / Mr. Walker said / Battle of All Saints Road / Battle of New Orleans / Duellin' banjos / Hip neck and thigh / Two thousand shoes / Tighten up vol. 88 / Just play music
CD 4611992
CBS / Sep '94 / Sony

Big Bad Smitty

MEAN DISPOSITION
CD AIM 1037
Aim / Apr '95 / ADA / Direct / Jazz Music

Big Band All Stars

SWITCHED ON SWING
CD PLSCD 197
Pulse / Apr '97 / BMG

Big Band De Lausanne

COSMOS (Big Band De Lausanne & Kenny Werner/Joe Lovano)
Fort Worth / Portrait of Jenny / Naked in the Cosmos / Turn out the stars / In the land of Ephesus / Sasumi
CD TCB 96502
TCB / Feb '97 / New Note/Pinnacle

Big Ben Banjo Band

BIG BEN BANJO PARTY
Rolling around the world/The best things in life are free / Who takes care of the caretaker's daughter/ Somebody loves / Man on the flying trapeze/In the twi-twi-twilight/ Mee / Is it true what they say about Dixie / Give me the moonlight give me the girl/ Ain't misbehavin'/ S / I've never seen a straight banana / You must have been a beautiful baby/ In a shanty in old Shan / Cheek to cheek/ Anything you can do/ You keep coming back li / Lady in red/Fare thee well Annabelle/Oh you beautiful / California here I come/ Are you from Dixie/ Ain't we got fun / Rose Rose I love you/ Buttons and bows/ In the middle of the / Leave the pretty girls alone/She wore a little jacket / I'll be with you in apple blossom time / Put your arms around me honey/ Me and my shadow/ You were me / Band played on/ I'm forever blowing bubbles / Let's face the music and dance/ No strings (I'm fancy free)/ / Lullaby of Broadway/Jeepers creepers/42nd Street / Maybe it's because I'm a Londoner/ Strollin'/ Lily of Laguna / There's something about a soldier/ I want a girl/ Any old ir / Lulu's back in town
CD CC 290
Music For Pleasure / Dec '92 / EMI

BIG BEN BANJO PARTY
CD MATCD 230
Castle / Dec '92 / BMG

BIG BEN BANJO PARTY
CD PLSCD 224
Pulse / Jul '97 / BMG

Big Big Train

GOODBYE TO THE AGE OF STEAM
CD GEPCD 1007
Giant Electric Pea / May '94 / Pinnacle

Big Black

BIG BLACK: LIVE
CD BFFP 49CD
Blast First / Oct '89 / RTM/Disc

HAMMER PARTY
CD HMS 044 CD
Homestead / Jul '89 / Cargo / SRD

PIGPILE
CD TG 81CD
Touch & Go / Nov '92 / SRD

RICH MAN'S EIGHT TRACK
CD BFFP 23CD
Blast First / Jun '88 / RTM/Disc

SONGS ABOUT FUCKING
Power of independent trucking / Model / Bad penny / L dopa / Precious thing / Columbian necktie / Kitty empire / Ergot / Kasimir S Pulaski Day / Fish fry / Tiny, King of the Jews / Bombastic intro / He's a whore
CD TG 24CD
Touch & Go / '94 / SRD

Big Brother & The Holding ...

CHEAPER THRILLS (Big Brother & The Holding Company)
Let the good times roll: *Joplin, Janis & Big Brother & The Holding Company* / I know you rider / Moanin' at midnight / Hey baby / Down on me / Whisperman / Women is losers / Blow my mind / Ball and chain / Coo coo / Gutra's garden / Harry
CD EDCD 135
Edsel / Aug '90 / Pinnacle

Big Car

NORMAL
Not the tunnel of love / Rosalita / Venus / Get started / Mad at the world / Amazing contradiction / Cats / Day by day / Shut up / Easy street
CD 07599244432
Giant / May '92 / BMG

Big Catholic Guilt

JUDGEMENT
CD CHERRY 228902
Cherrydisc / Jun '94 / Plastic Head

Big Chief

BIG CHIEF BRAND PRODUCT
CD SPCD 89260
Sub Pop / Apr '93 / Cargo / Greyhound / Shellshock/Disc

MACK AVENUE SKULL GAME
CD SP 109/285CD
Sub Pop / Sep '93 / Cargo / Greyhound / Shellshock/Disc

SHOUT OUT (Big Chief & Thornett)
CD SPCD 135322
Sub Pop / Sep '94 / Cargo / Greyhound / Shellshock/Disc

Big Chill

HALFWAY TO HEAVEN
CD CDMFN 142
Music For Nations / Sep '92 / Pinnacle

Big Country

CROSSING, THE
In a big country / Inwards / Chance / Thousand stars / Storm / Harvest home / Lost patrol / Close action / Fields of fire / Porroh man
CD 5323232
Mercury / Mar '96 / PolyGram

ECLECTIC
River of hope / King of emotion / Big yellow taxi / Buffalo skinners / Summertime / Dixie / Eleanor Rigby / Winter sky / Sing it / I'm on fire / Where the rose is sown / Come back to me / Ruby Tuesday
CD TRACD 234
Transatlantic / Aug '96 / Pinnacle

GREATEST HITS LIVE, THE
Harvest home / Peace in our time / Just a shadow / Broken hearts (13 valleys) / Storm / Chance / Look away / What are you working for / Steeltown / Ships / Wonderland / Long way home / In a big country / Lost patrol
CD DC 878632
Disky / Mar '97 / Disky / THE

IN A BIG COUNTRY
In a big country / Thousand stars / Tracks of my tears / Giant / One great thing / Hold the heart / Look away / Honky tonk woman / Restless natives / Longest day / Everything I need / Black skinned blue eyed boys / Fly like an eagle / Kiss the girl goodbye / Keep on dreaming / Freedom song
CD 5508792
Spectrum / Jul '95 / PolyGram

KINGS OF EMOTION (2CD Set)
CD Set SMDCD 101
Snapper / Jul '97 / Pinnacle

LEGENDS IN MUSIC
CD LECD 043
Wisepack / Jul '94 / Conifer/BMG / THE

NO PLACE LIKE HOME
We're not in Kansas / Republican party reptile / Dynamite lady / Keep on dreaming / Beautiful people / Hostage speaks / Beat the devil / Leap of faith / Ships / Into the fire

CD 5323272
Mercury / Mar '96 / PolyGram

PEACE IN OUR TIME
King of emotion / Broken hearts / Thousand yard stare / From here to eternity / Everything I need / Peace in our time / Time for leaving / River of hope / In this place
CD 5323262
Mercury / Mar '96 / PolyGram

SEER, THE
Eiledon / Hold the heart / Look away / One great thing / Remembrance day / Red fox / Sailor / Seer / Teacher / I walk the hill
CD 5323252
Mercury / Mar '96 / PolyGram

SEER, THE/THE CROSSING (2CD Set)
Look away / Seer / Teacher / I walk the hill / Eiledon / One great thing / Hold the heart / Remembrance day / Red fox / Sailor / In a big country / Inwards / Chance / Thousand stars / Storm / Harvest home / Lost patrol / Close action / Fields of fire / Porroh man
CD Set 5286072
Mercury / Aug '95 / PolyGram

STEELTOWN
Flame of the west / East of Eden / Steeltown / Where the rose is sown / Come back to me / Tall ships go / Girl with grey eyes / Raindance / Great divide / Just a shadow
CD 5323242
Mercury / Mar '96 / PolyGram

THROUGH A BIG COUNTRY (Greatest Hits)
In a big country / Fields of fire / Chance / Wonderland / Where the rose is sown / Just a shadow / Look away / King of emotion / East of Eden / One great thing / Teacher / Broken heart (thirteen valleys) / Peace in our time / Eiledon / Seer / Harvest home
CD 5323282
Mercury / Mar '96 / PolyGram

WHY THE LONG FACE
CD TRACD 109
Transatlantic / Apr '96 / Pinnacle

WITHOUT THE AID OF A SAFETY NET
Harvest home / Just a shadow / Thirteen valleys / Storm / Chance / Look away / Steeltown / Ships / Wonderland / In a big country / Peace in our time / What are you working for / Long way home / Lost patrol
CD CDGOLD 1082
EMI Gold / Feb '97 / EMI

Big Dish

RICH MAN'S WARDROBE
Christina's world / Wishing time / Swimmer / Life / Big new beginning / Jealous / Faith healer / Jean / Where do you live / Waiting for the parade / European rain / Loneliest man in the world / Voodoo baby / Slide / Prospect street
CD VI 874882
Disky / Nov '96 / Disky / THE

Big Dogs

LIVE AT THE BIRCHMERE
CD SCR 24
Strictly Country / Jul '95 / ADA / Direct

Big Drill Car

ALBUM/TAPE/CD TYPE THING
CD CRZ 008CD
Cruz / Jan '90 / Plastic Head

SMALL BLOCK
CD CRZ 014CD
Cruz / May '93 / Plastic Head

Big E The Black

LIVIN' BIG E
CD 50533
Raging Bull / Jun '97 / Prime / Total/BMG

Big Elastic Band

WHEN BIG ROY SANG ON ANNIE MCGREGOR'S JUKE BOX
Jimmy Shand's on the wireless / Old folk / Frontiersong / Meet me on the landing / On golden streets / Along came rock 'n' roll / When Big Roy sang on Annie McGregor's juke box / Blue lagoon / All stood up / Here we go again / Sunday morning - Saturday night / Accordion under the bed
CD LCOM 5254
Lismor / Nov '96 / ADA / Direct / Duncans / Lismor

Big Electric Cat

DREAMS OF A MAD KING
CD CLEO 94952
Cleopatra / Jan '95 / Cargo / Greyhound / Plastic Head / RTM/Disc / SRD

Big Eye

HIDDEN CORE, THE
CD DUKE 027
Hydrogen Dukebox / Nov '95 / 3mv/Vital / Kudos / Prime

Big Fat Love

HELL HOUSE
CD GR 041CD
Grand Royal / May '97 / Cargo / Plastic Head

Big Flame

RIGOUR
CD DC 19
Drag City / Dec '96 / Cargo / Greyhound

Big Head Todd

BEAUTIFUL WORLD (Big Head Todd & The Monsters)
Resignation superman / Caroline / Crazy Mary / Helpless / Tower / Please don't tell her / Beautiful world / True lady / Heart of wilderness / If you can't slow down / Boom boom: *Big Head Todd & The Monsters/John Lee Hooker* / These days without you
CD 74321441092
Revolution / May '97 / BMG

SISTER SWEETLY
Broken hearted saviour / Sister sweetly / Turn the light out / Tomorrow never comes / It's alright / Groove thing / Soul for every cowboy / Ellis island / Bittersweet / Circle / Brother John
CD 74321147992
Giant / Jun '94 / BMG

STRATAGEM (Big Head Todd & The Monsters)
Kensington line / Stratagem / Wearing only flowers / Neckbreaker / Magdalena / Angel leads me on / In the morning / Candle / Ninety nine / Greyhound / Poor miss / Shadowlands
CD 74321229042
Giant / Oct '94 / BMG

Big House

BIG HOUSE
Dollar in my pocket (pretty things) / All nite / Refuse 2 run / baby doll / Can't cry anymore / Devil's road / Nothing comes 4 free / Happiness / LA / Angel on my arm
CD MCD 11446
MCA / Apr '97 / BMG

Big Joe

COOL DYNAFLOW (Big Joe & The Dynaflows)
CD TRCD 9915
Tramp / Apr '93 / ADA / CM / Direct

LAYIN' IN THE ALLEY (Big Joe & The Dynaflows)
CD BT 1098CD
Black Top / Feb '94 / ADA / CM / Direct

Big Maceo

BLUEBIRD RECORDINGS 1941-1942, THE
Worried life blues / Ramblin' mind blues / County jail blues / Can't you read / So long baby / Texas blues / Tuff luck blues / I got the blues / It's all up to you / Bye bye, baby / Why should I hang around / Poor Kelly blues / Some sweet day / Anytime for you / My last go around / Since you been gone
CD 07863667152
Bluebird / Feb '97 / BMG

Big Maybelle

MAYBELLE SINGS THE BLUES
CD CDRB 14
Charly / Nov '94 / Koch

Big Miller

LAST OF THE BLUES SHOUTERS, THE
CD SCD 42
Southland / Feb '93 / Jazz Music

Big Mountain

RESISTANCE
Hooligans / Resistance / Rise Rasta rise / Get together / Caribbean blue / Sweet and deadly / Troddin' / Know your culture / Soul teacher / Where do the children play / Retire / Inner city youth / Wante wante / Love is the only way / Bobbin' & weavin' / Hooligans dub
CD 74321299882
RCA / Oct '95 / BMG

UNITY
Fruitful days / Revolution / Bordertown / Upful and right / Sweet sensual love / I would find a way / Tango ganas / Baby, I love your way / Young revolutionaries / Time has come / Big mountain / Baby I love your way (Spanish version) / Sweet sensual love (Spanish version)
CD 74321219642
Giant / Jun '96 / BMG

WAKE UP
Light'n up / Reggae inna summertime / Peaceful revolution / Rastaman / Back in the hill / Once again / Let you go / Touch my light / Beautiful day / Amor de lejos / Llena mi Vida / Reggae inna summertime (Spanglish) / Lick up tup
CD 74321267482
Giant / Jun '95 / BMG

Big Noyd

EPISODES OF A HUSTLA
It's on you / Precinct / Recognize and realize / All pro / Infamous mobb / Interrogation / Usual suspect / Episodes of a hustla / Recognize and realize / I don't wanna love again: *Big Noyd & Se'Kou* / Usual suspect
CD TBCD 1156
Tommy Boy / Feb '97 / RTM/Disc

Big Red Kite

SHORT STORIES
CD SR 1010
Scout / May '96 / Koch

Big Rhythm Combo

TOO SMALL TO DANCE
CD BM 9025CD
Black Magic / Aug '94 / ADA / Cadillac / Direct / Hot Shot

Big Road Breaker

DISINTERPRETITIONED
CD MUZA 09CD
Muzamuza / Jun '97 / Cargo

Big Sandy

ON THE GO (Big Sandy & The Flyrite Trio)
CD NOHITCD 006
No Hit / Jan '94 / Cargo / SRD

SWINGIN' WEST (Big Sandy & The Flyrite Trio)
CD HCD 8064
Hightone / Oct '95 / ADA / Koch

Big Sky

BIG SKY
CD FERCD 025
Future Earth / Nov '96 / Future Earth/ Konexion / Grapevine/PolyGram

Big Soul

HIPPY HIPPY SHAKE
Sweet thang / Funky Caroline / Rumble and roll / Lost my girl / Sister Caroline / Mystery jazz / Give it up / Hippy hippy shake / Le bri / Shot of love / John Lee Booger / All your requests
CD 4816362
Epic / Aug '96 / Sony

Big Star

BIG STAR LIVE
CD RCD 10221
Rykodisc / Mar '97 / ADA / Vital

NO.1 RECORD/RADIO CITY
Feel / Ballad of El Goodo / In the street / Thirteen / Don't lie to me / India song / When my baby's beside me / My life is right / Give me another chance / Try again / Watch the sunrise / O my soul / Life is white / Way out west / What's goin' ahn / You get what you deserve / Mod lang / Back of a car / Daisy glaze / She's a mover / September gurls / Morpha too / I'm in love with a girl
CD CDWIK 910
Big Beat / Jan '90 / Pinnacle

THIRD/SISTER LOVERS
Kizza me / You can't have me / Jesus Christ / Downs / Whole lotta shakin' goin' on / Thank you friends / O'Dana / Femme fatale / Stroke it, Noel / Holocaust / Nightime / Kangaroo / For you / Take care / Blue mood / Dream lover / Big black car
CD RCD 10220
Rykodisc / Mar '97 / ADA / Vital

Big Stick

CRACK 'N' DRAG
CD BFFP 25CD
Blast First / Nov '93 / RTM/Disc

PRO-DRAG
CD PWD 7456CD
IFA / Oct '95 / Plastic Head

Big Three

CAVERN STOMP
Some other guy / I'm with you / Let true love begin / By the way / Cavern stomp / Peanut butter / Bring it on home to me / What'd I say / Don't start running away / Zip a dee doo dah / Reelin' and rockin' / You've got to keep her under hand / High School confidential
CD 8440062
Mercury / Jan '96 / PolyGram

Big Three

BIG THREE FEATURING MAMA CASS, THE
I may be right / Anna Fia / Tony and Delia / Grandfather's clock / Silkie / Ringo / Down in the valley / Wild women / All the pretty little horses / Glory glory / Come away Melinda / Young girl's lament / Banjo song / Winken blinken and nod / Ho honey ho / Nora's dove (Dink's song) / Come along / Rider / It makes a long time man feel bad / Sing hallelujah / Dark as a dungeon
CD NEMCD 755
Sequel / Oct '95 / BMG

Big Time Sarah

BLUES IN THE YEAR 1D1
Blues in the year 1D1 / Hound dog / Ain't nobody's business / Woke up this morning / Long tall daddy / You don't love me baby / Cadillac assembly line / Steal away / Chicken heads / Down home blues / Bouncin' and breakin' / Little red rooster / I don't want no man
CD DE 692
Delmark / Jun '97 / ADA / Cadillac / CM / Direct / Hot Shot

LAY IT ON 'EM GIRLS
CD DD 659
Delmark / Jul '93 / ADA / Cadillac / CM / Direct / Hot Shot

Big Tom

25 GOLDEN GREATS (Big Tom & The Mainliners)
Back in my baby's arms / Gentle mother / Old rustic bridge / I'll settle for old Ireland / Wheels fell off the wagon / Isle of Innishfree / My own washing / Kentucky waltz / Be careful of stones that you throw / Bunch of violet blues / From summer to winter / Sing me back home / Carroll county accident / Blue eyes crying in the rain / Sunset years of my life / Wedding bells / Flowers for mama / My world's come down / Old log cabin for sale / Please mama please / Before I met you / Tears on a bridal bouquet / They covered the old swimming hole / Cold hard facts of life / Give my love to rose
CD MCVD 30006
Emerald Gem / Nov '96 / BMG

I'LL SETTLE FOR OLD IRELAND
CD SWCD 1006
TC / Aug '92 / Pinnacle / Prism

Big Town Playboys

HIP JOINT
Ain't no big deal on you / When it rains it pours / Shake your hips / Glamour girl / I don't care who knows / Kiddio / Forever true / Rock me again / Girls all over the world / My heart is mended / No place to go
CD CDBLUH 017
Blue Horizon / Jun '96 / Pinnacle

PLAYBOY BOOGIE
Hurry baby / Chicken shack boogie / Happy payday / Walkin' / She walked right in / What more do you want me to do / Playboy boogie / Come on / Down the road apiece / I done it / Shake your hips / Roomin' house boogie / Driftin'
CD SPINCD 203
Making Waves / Aug '96 / CM

Big Twist

BIGGER THAN LIFE (Live From Chicago) (Big Twist & The Mellow Fellows)
CD ALCD 4755
Alligator / May '93 / ADA / CM / Direct

PLAYING FOR KEEPS (Big Twist & The Mellow Fellows)
300 pounds of heavenly joy / Flip flop / I want your love / Polk salad Annie / Pouring water on a drowning man / I've got a problem / I brought the blues on myself / We're gonna make it / Just one woman
CD ALCD 4732
Alligator / Jun '91 / ADA / CM / Direct

Big Wheel

SLOWTOWN
You shine, And / Down / Lied / Vicious cirle / Pete Rose / Birthday / Down the line / Daddy's at the wheel / Storm / Tuff skins / Bug bites / Lazy days
CD MR 00472
Mammoth / Apr '93 / Vital

Big Wheeler

BONE ORCHARD (Big Wheeler & The Ice Cream Men)
Bad bacon baby / I got a feeling I got the blues / Bone orchard / You got me messed up / Hell bound man / She loves another man / Evil woman / Down in Virginia / Katie Blues / Damn good mojo / Everybody needs somebody / Man or mouse / Chains of love / Bad bacon baby
CD DE 661
Delmark / Mar '97 / ADA / Cadillac / CM / Direct / Hot Shot

Big Youth

A LUTA CONTINUA
CD HBCD 28
Heartbeat / Sep '85 / ADA / Direct / Greensleeves / Jet Star

DJ ORIGINATORS (Big Youth & Dillinger)
CD RGCD 020
Rocky One / Dec '95 / Jet Star

DREADLOCKS DREAD
Train to Rhodesia / House of dreadlocks / Lightning flash / Weak heart / Natty dread she want / Some like it dread / Marcus Garvey / Big Youth special / Dread organ / Blackman message / You don't care / Moving away
CD _____ CDFL 9006
Frontline / Sep '90 / EMI / Jet Star

HIGHER GROUND
CD _____ VPCD 1440
VP / Oct '95 / Greensleeves / Jet Star / Total/BMG

HIT THE ROAD JACK
What's going on / Hit the road Jack / Wake up everybody / Get up stand up / Jah man of Syreen / Ten against one / Hotter fire / Way of the light / Dread high ranking / Dread is the best
CD _____ CDTRL 137
Trojan / Sep '95 / Direct / Jet Star

JAMMING IN THE HOUSE OF DREAD
CD _____ DANCD 112
Danceteria / Jun '97 / ADA / Plastic Head / Shellshock/Disc

MANIFESTATION
No nukes / Love fighting so / Turn me on / Mr. Right / Like it like that / Conqueror / Spiderman meet the Hulk / No way to treat a lady
CD _____ HBCD 46
Heartbeat / Apr '88 / ADA / Direct / Greensleeves / Jet Star

REGGAE PHENOMENON
CD _____ CDTRD 411
Trojan / Mar '94 / Direct / Jet Star

SAVE THE WORLD
CD _____ 504002
Declic / Nov '95 / Jet Star

SCREAMING TARGET
Screaming target / Pride and joy rock / Be careful / Tippertone rock / One of these fine days / Screaming target / Killer / Solomon A Gunday / Honesty / I am alright / Lee a low / Concrete jungle
CD _____ CDTRL 61
Trojan / Mar '94 / Direct / Jet Star

SOME GREAT BIG YOUTH
World War III / Living / Roots foundation / Get on up / Dancing mood / Time alone will tell / Suffering / Love Jah with all of my heart / Green bay killing / We can work it out
CD _____ CDBM 015
Blue Moon / Jul '92 / Cadillac / Discovery / Greensleeves / Jazz Music / Jet Star / TKO Magnum

Bigard, Barney

BARNEY BIGARD & THE PELICAN TRIO
CD _____ JCD 228
Jazzology / Oct '93 / Jazz Music

BARNEY BIGARD AND THE LEGENDS OF JAZZ
CD _____ BCD 338
GHB / Jun '95 / Jazz Music

BARNEY BIGARD STORY 1929-1945, THE
CD _____ 158502
Jazz Archives / Jul '96 / Discovery

CLARINET LAMENT
Saturday night function / Turtle twist / Clarinet lament / Clouds in my heart / Pigeons and peppers / Barney going easy / Just another dream / Early mornin' / Honey hush / Watch the birdie / Solid rock / Diga diga doo / Lament for Javanette / Lull at dawn / Ready Eddy / World is waiting for the sunrise / Big eight blues / Moonglow / Tea for two / Step steps up, steps step down / Rose room / Coquette
CD _____ TPZ 1055
Topaz Jazz / Oct '96 / Cadillac / Pinnacle

CLASSICS 1944
CD _____ CLASSICS 896
Classics / Oct '96 / Discovery / Jazz Music

CLASSICS 1944-1945
CD _____ CLASSICS 930
Classics / Apr '97 / Discovery / Jazz Music

INTRODUCTION TO BARNEY BIGARD 1928-1941, AN
CD _____ 4028
Best Of Jazz / Feb '96 / Discovery

Bigband Orchestra

LEGEND OF GLENN MILLER, THE
CD _____ 500582
Musidisc / Jan '94 / Discovery

Bigeneric

MYRIADES
CD _____ EFA 698262
Spacefrog / Jul '95 / SRD / Vital

Bigeou, Esther

ESTHER BIGEOU 1921-1923
CD _____ DOCD 5489
Document / Nov '96 / ADA / Hot Shot / Jazz Music

Bigger The God

VARIETY
He broke it off / She's coming out / Pentonville / Shagged / Twice a week / Cow / Three of a kind / Double deckers / Miss Pritchard / Let's pretend we care / Mum steals boyfriend / Spiral / Front page news / Tina's haircut / Unbudgeable
CD _____ OUTD 9604
Outdigo / Nov '96 / Vital

Biggie Tembo

OUT OF AFRICA
CD _____ COOKCD 039
Cooking Vinyl / Feb '92 / Vital

Biggs, Barry

SIDESHOW
CD _____ JMC 200117
Jamaican Gold / Jun '95 / Grapevine/ PolyGram / Jet Star

Biggun, Ivor

MORE FILTH DIRT CHEAP
Cockerel song / My shirt collar (it won't go stiff) / Southern breeze / Burglars holler / Gums and plums / John Thomas Allcock / I have a dog his name is Rover / My brothers magazine / Richard the third / Walking your blues away / Are mice electric / I can be the hot dog and you can be the bun / I wanna be a bear / I woke up dis moanin' / Terrific Teddy sings the blues / Ah feel so bad / Other educated monkey
CD _____ BBL 3 CD
Lowdown/Beggars Banquet / Sep '88 / RTM/Disc / Warner Music

PARTNERS IN GRIME (Biggun, Ivor & Ivors Jivers)
Hide the sausage / Nobody does it like the ukelele man / Chantilly lace / Halfway up Virginia / Pussy song / Probing Andromeda / Majorca song / Sixty minute man / Toolbag Ted from Birkenhead / Where did the lead in my pencil go / Cue for a song / I've got a monster
CD _____ BBL 79 CD
Lowdown/Beggars Banquet / Jan '89 / RTM/Disc / Warner Music

WINKERS ALBUM, THE
I've parted / Great grandad John / My brother's got files / Oh oh oh / Cucumber number / Underground music / Winker's paradise / Charabanc
CD _____ BBL 1 CD
Lowdown/Beggars Banquet / Jul '88 / RTM/ Disc / Warner Music

Bigjig

FEET TO THE FLOOR
CD _____ SMALLCD 9404
Smallworld / Apr '94 / ADA / Cadillac / Direct / Total/BMG

Biglight

NOWHERE
CD _____ SPV 08544422
SPV / Nov '96 / Koch / Plastic Head

Big'N

DISCIPLINE THROUGH SOUND
CD _____ GR 23CD
Skingraft / Aug '96 / SRD

Bigod 20

SUPERCUTE
CD _____ CDZOT 122
Zoth Ommog / Nov '94 / Cargo / Plastic Head

Bijlsma, Masha

LEBO
Work song / Lebo / Suddenly / Low down / Deep song / Way you look tonight / La vie en rose / Man from Tollund / First peace / Long as you're living / Alone together / Leaving / Africa / Zimbabwe
CD _____ JL 111452
Lipstick / Oct '96 / Vital/SAM

Bijma, Greetje

BAREFOOT
Barefoot / Bosnia / Painter at work / As I drive by / Glazed frost / Lonely walk / Katsjima / Sings with strings / Duck pond / Guess where it's coming from / Vortex
CD _____ ENJ 80382
Enja / Oct '93 / New Note/Pinnacle / Vital/ SAM

Bikaye, Bony

COMPUTER'S DREAMS
CD _____ 926602
BUDA / Oct '96 / Discovery

Bikini Kill

PUSSY WHIPPED
Blood one / Alien she / Magnet / Speed heart / L'il red / Tell me so / Sugar / Starbellied boy / Hamster baby / Rebel girl / Starfish / For Tammy Rae
CD _____ WIJ 028CD
Wiiija / Oct '93 / RTM/Disc

REJECTS ALL AMERICAN
CD _____ KRS 260CD
Kill Rock Stars / Apr '96 / Cargo / Greyhound / Plastic Head

YEAH YEAH YEAH YEAH
Double dare ya / Liar / Carnival / Suck my left one / Feels blind / Thurston hearts the who / White boy / This is not a test / Don't need you / Jigsaw youth / Resist psychic death / Rebel girl / Outta me
CD _____ KRS 204CD
Kill Rock Stars / Mar '94 / Cargo / Greyhound / Plastic Head

Bila, Vila

ROM POP
CD _____ 7422510
WMD / Jan '97 / Discovery

Bile

TEKNO WHORE
CD _____ 0086822CTR
Edel / Jul '97 / Pinnacle

Bilezikjian, John

MUSIC FROM THE ARMENIAN DIASPORA PLAYED ON THE OUD
CD _____ GV 809CD
Global Village / May '94 / ADA / Direct

Bilk, Acker

ACKER BILK AND HIS PARAMOUNT JAZZ BAND (Bilk, Acker & His Paramount Jazz Band)
CD _____ LACD 36
Lake / Oct '94 / ADA / Cadillac / Direct / Jazz Music / Target/BMG

ACKER BILK IN HOLLAND
I can't believe that you're in love with me / Clarinet marmalade / Mood indigo / Them there eyes / Take the 'A' train / World is waiting for the sunrise / Just a closer walk with thee / Jeepers creepers / Lover man / Watermelon man / I don't want to set the world on fire / St. Thomas / Georgia / Senora Signora / Blues walk / Stranger on the shore / Nobody's sweetheart / Once in a while / Old music master
CD Set _____ CDTTD 506/7
Timeless Traditional / Aug '94 / Jazz Music / New Note/Pinnacle

ACKER BILK SONGBOOK
Just when I needed you most / I want to know what love is / I just called to say I love you / Longfellow serenade / Truly / Hundred ways / Still / Always on my mind / Memory / Ships / Arthur's tree / Do that to me one more time / This masquerade / Stuck on you / If ever you're in my arms again / Could I have this dance / To all the girls I've loved before / Three times a lady / Hello / Just once
CD _____ QED 112
Tring / Nov '96 / Tring

AFTER MIDNIGHT
Stranger on the shore / Right here waiting / Room in your heart / Smack a Latin / Another day in paradise / Don't know much / After midnight / Don't wanna lose you / How am I supposed to live without you / I'm not in love / Best of me / Anything for you / Disney girls / If leaving is easy / When summer comes / Traces of dreams
CD _____ PWKM 4019
Carlton / Feb '96 / Carlton

AT SUNDOWN (Bilk, Acker & Humphrey Lyttelton)
At Sundown / When you and I were young Maggie / You're exceptional to me / Lower than low / Just a little while to stay here / You're a lucky guy / Red beans and rice / Wabash blues / Carry me back to old Virginny / Summertime / I used to love you / Lonesome blues / Jazz me blues / Southern sunset
CD _____ CLGCD 027
Calligraph / May '92 / Cadillac / Jazz Music / New Note/Pinnacle / Wellard

BLAZE AWAY (Bilk, Acker & His Paramount Jazz Band)
Riverboat shuffle / I'm gonna sit right down and write myself a letter / Black and tan fantasy / Spain / Blaze away / Wabash blues / Way down yonder in New Orleans / Aria / Keepin' out of mischief now / Jazz me blues / Memphis blues / Exactly like you / Is you is or is you ain't my baby / Singin' the blues / Please don't talk to me... / Stranger on the shore
CD _____ CDTTD 543
Timeless Traditional / Mar '90 / Jazz Music / New Note/Pinnacle

BRIDGE OVER TROUBLED WATER
Bridge over troubled water / Stranger on the shore / Touch me in the morning / Evergreen / She / When I need you / You're my best friend / Way we were / Raindrops keep falling on my head / Amazing Grace / Raining in my heart / September song / Don't cry for me Argentina / Aria / Talking in your sleep / Misty / Without you / This guy's in love with you / Forever autumn / Ebony and ivory
CD _____ 5507322
Spectrum / Mar '95 / PolyGram

CAN'T SMILE WITHOUT YOU (Bilk, Acker, His Clarinet & Strings)
CD _____ TRTCD 129
TrueTrax / Oct '94 / THE

CLARINET MOODS
Stranger on the shore / Summertime / Night and day / I wonder who's kissing her now / Long ago and far away / Fly me to the moon / Body and soul / Embraceable you / I'll get by / That ole buttermilk sky / Pennies from heaven / South of the border / Try a little tenderness
CD _____ CDMFP 6394
Music For Pleasure / Jul '97 / EMI

COLLECTION, THE
CD _____ COL 070
Collection / Mar '95 / Target/BMG

FEELINGS
CD Set _____ MBSCD 403
Castle / Nov '93 / BMG

HEARTBEATS
Get here / Unchained melody / Somerset skies / Crazy for you / Close to you / When I'm back on my feet again / Rio nights / I've got you under my skin / Sacrifice / Walk on by / Cuts both ways / It's easy now / Here we are / On Takapuna Beach / You've lost that lovin' feelin' / Heartbeats
CD _____ PWKS 4084
Carlton / Feb '96 / Carlton

HITS, BLUES AND CLASSICS (Bilk, Acker & His Paramount Jazz Band)
Louisian-i-ay / Black and tan fantasy / My baby just cares for me / Papa dip / That's my home / Semper fidelis / Basin Street blues / White cliffs of Dover / Blaze away / Nairobi / When it's sleepy time down South / Savoy blues / Just a closer walk with thee / South / Mood indigo / Buona sera / Ain't misbehavin' / Aria / Beale Street blues / Stranger on the shore
CD _____ KAZ CD 10
Kaz / Aug '88 / BMG

IMAGINE
Mull of Kintyre / Norwegian wood / Sailing / Send in the clowns / Stranger on the shore / Yesterday / Windmills of your mind / You are the sunshine of my life / Aranjuez mon amour / Aria / Ebony and ivory / Feelings / Fool on the hill / Imagine / Michelle / Missing you
CD _____ PLS CD 511
Pulse / Jun '95 / BMG

IN A MELLOW MOOD
CD _____ MATCD 213
Castle / Dec '92 / BMG

IN A MELLOW MOOD
CD _____ PLSCD 163
Pulse / Apr '97 / BMG

JAZZ TODAY COLLECTION
CD _____ LACD 48
Lake / Jun '95 / ADA / Cadillac / Direct / Jazz Music / Target/BMG

LOVE ALBUM, THE
When I fall in love / Groovy kind of love / Silvery nights / Could've been / My love / He ain't heavy, he's my brother / Good times / One moment in time / Till I loved you / Candle in the wind / Tune for melody / Take my breath away / Love changes everything / Sweet crystal / Lady in red / Every time we say goodbye
CD _____ PWKS 534
Carlton / Feb '96 / Carlton

MAGIC CLARINET OF ACKER BILK
CD _____ EMPRCD 513
Emporio / Jul '94 / Disc

MELLOW MOODS
CD _____ MACCD 162
Autograph / Aug '96 / BMG

NEW ORLEANS DAYS
CD _____ LA 36CD
Lake / Jun '94 / ADA / Cadillac / Direct / Jazz Music / Target/BMG

OSCAR WINNERS
When you wish upon a star / For all we know / Three coins in the fountain / Love story / Last time I saw Paris / Swinging on a star / Mona Lisa / Love is a many splendoured thing / Can you feel the love tonight / Up where we belong / All the way / You'll never know / Days of wine and roses / It might as well be spring / Hello Dolly / Over the rainbow
CD _____ 3036000022
Carlton / Oct '95 / Carlton

REFLECTIONS
Stranger on the shore / Petit fleur / Georgia on my mind / Ain't misbehavin' / I left my heart in San Francisco / La paloma / Greensleeves / Sentimental journey / Moon river / I'm in the mood for love / Creole love call / Dinah / Shenandoah / Only you

CD 5500462
Spectrum / Jun '93 / PolyGram

STRANGER ON THE SHORE (Bilk, Acker & Leon Young String Chorale)
Stranger on the shore / It had to be you / Petite fleur / Ain't misbehavin' / Greensleeves / Only you / Sentimental journey / I'm in the mood for love / La mer / Moon river / Shenandoah / I left my heart in San Francisco
CD 8307792
Philips / Mar '94 / PolyGram

STRANGER ON THE SHORE
CD MATCD 282
Castle / May '94 / BMG

STRANGER ON THE SHORE (The Best Of Acker Bilk)
Stranger on the shore / Windmills of your mind / Cavatina / Magnificent Mog / If / Bilitis / Amazing Grace / For the good times / Lazy serenade / Shepherd's song / When I need you / Pescadores / Aria / As time goes by / Love letters / Pacelbel Canon / Skylark / Autumn leaves / Love said goodbye / First of Spring / Colours of my life / Clair / She's leaving home
CD PLSCD 202
Pulse / Feb '97 / BMG

TOGETHER AGAIN (Bilk, Acker & Ken Colyers Jazzmen)
CD LACD 53
Lake / Oct '95 / ADA / Cadillac / Direct / Jazz Music / Target/BMG

UNCHAINED MELODY (32 Great Love Songs From The King Of Clarinet/2CD Set)
Unchained melody / Traces of dreams/Wind beneath my wings / He ain't heavy he's my brother / Close to you / Love story / Over the rainbow / Disney girls / You've lost that loving feeling / Up where we belong / Don't wanna lose you / Cuts both ways / When I fall in love / I'm not in love / Lady in red / Sacrifice / My love / Can you feel the love tonight / Love changes everything / Another day in paradise / Groovy kind of love / If leaving me is easy / Take my breath away / Candle in the wind / I've got you under my skin / Every time we say goodbye / Crazy for you / Heartbeats / Right here waiting / Best of me / Walk on by / Room in your heart / It might as well be Spring
CD Set 330382
Hallmark / Mar '97 / Carlton

Bill Ding

AND THE SOUND OF...
CD HEFTY 003
Hefty / May '97 / Cargo

TRUST IN GOD, BUT TIE UP YOUR CAMEL
CD HEFTY 05
Hefty / Apr '97 / Cargo

Billy & The Lucky Boys

ROBBER
CD PT 605002
Part / Jun '96 / Nervous

WILD TRAIN
CD PT 605001
Part / Jun '96 / Nervous

Billy Tipton's Memorial ...

SAXHOUSE (Billy Tipton's Memorial Saxophone Quartet)
CD KFWCD 143
Knitting Factory / Feb '95 / Cargo / Plastic Head

Billys

ROCKABILLY REBELS
Boppin' the blues: *Billys & Carl Perkins/The Jordanaires* / Matchbox: *Billys & Carl Perkins* / Honey don't: *Billys & Carl Perkins* / Blue suede shoes: *Billys & Carl Perkins/The Jordanaires* / Blue jean bop: *Billys & Carl Perkins/The Jordanaires* / So glad you're mine / Baby what you want me to do / Drinking wine spo-dee-o-dee / Dream girl / Warm beer in the morning: *Billys & The Jordanaires* / No longer no more / That's why I know: *Billys & The Jordanaires* / Cadillac queen / I just wonder why / Sweet little baby: *Billys & The Jordanaires*
CD 303902
Hallmark / Jun '97 / Carlton

Bim Skala Bim

AMERICAN PLAYHOUSE
CD DOJOCD 209
Dojo / Jul '96 / Disc

Bina, Sima

MUSIC OF NORTH KHORASSAN, IRAN
CD 926362
BUDA / Feb '96 / Discovery

PERSIAN CLASSICAL MUSIC
CD NI 5391
Nimbus / Apr '95 / Nimbus

Bindstouw, Af

LIVE AT THE FEMO JAZZ 1995 (Bindstouw, Af Jazz Men)
CD MECCACD 1084
Music Mecca / May '97 / Cadillac / Jazz Music / Wellard

Bingert, Hector

CANDOMBE
CD ADCD 7
ADCD / May '97 / Cadillac

Bingham, Mark

I PASSED FOR HUMAN
CD DOG 006CD
Wild Dog / Sep '94 / Koch

Bingo Trappers

SIERRA
CD SHR 91CD
Shrimper / Mar '97 / Cargo

Bingy Bunny

KINGSTON 12 TOUGHIE (A Tribute To Bingy Bunny)
CD RASCD 3189
Ras / Sep '96 / Direct / Greensleeves / Jet Star / SRD

Binney, David

LUXURY OF GUESSING, THE
CD AQ 1030
Audioquest / Apr '95 / ADA / New Note/ Pinnacle

Biochip C

INSIDE VOL.2
CD EFA 008302
Anodyne / Jul '95 / SRD

Biohazard

BIOHAZARD
CD MCD 1067
MCA / Aug '94 / BMG
CD SPV 07646502
SPV / Dec '96 / Koch / Plastic Head

MATELEAO
CD 9362462082
Warner Bros. / May '96 / Warner Music

NO HOLDS BARRED
Shades of grey / What makes us tick / Authority / Urban discipline / Modern democracy / Business / Tales from the hardside / Better days / Victory / Lot to learn / How it is / After forever / Tears of blood / Chamber spins three / Wrong side of the tracks / Waiting to die / These eyes / Punishment / Hold my own
CD RR 88032
Roadrunner / Aug '97 / PolyGram

STATE OF THE WORLD ADDRESS
State of the world address / Down for life / What makes us tick / Tales from the hard side / How it is / Remember / Five blocks to the subway / Each day / Failed territory / Lack there of / Pride / Human animal / Cornered / Love denied
CD 9362455952
WEA / May '94 / Warner Music

URBAN DISCIPLINE
Chamber spins three / Punishment / Shades of grey / Business / Black and white and red all over / Man with a promise / Disease / Hold my own / Urban disciple / Loss / Wrong side of the tracks / Mistaken identity / We're only gonna die (From our own arrogance) / Tears of blood / Shades of grey / Punishment
CD RR 91122
Roadrunner / Sep '96 / PolyGram

Biomuse

WRONG
4 Rubber feet / Race / Sine God / Very approximately / Convolvotron / Medral / Anaural / Ursonate / Ba-Umf / Wrong / X
CD WORDD 002
Language / Nov '95 / Grapevine/PolyGram / Prime / Vital

Biosinites

FIRST TAKE
CD FMPCD 80
FMP / May '97 / Cadillac

Biosphere

MICROGRAVITY
Microgravity / Baby satellite / Tranquillizer / Fairy tale / Cloudwalker 11 / Chromosphere / Cygnus-A / Baby interphase / Biosphere
CD AMBCD 3921
Apollo / Jun '93 / Vital

PATASHNIK
Phantasm / Startoucher / Decryption / Novelty waves / Patashnik / Mir / Shield / Seti project / Mestigoth / Botanical dimensions / Caboose / En-trance
CD AMB 3927CD
Apollo / Feb '94 / Vital

SUBSTRATA
As the sun kissed the horizon / Poa alpina / Chukhung / Things I tell you / Times when I know you'll be sad / Hyperborea / Kobresia / Antennaria / Uva-ursi / Sphere of no-form / Silene
CD ASCD 033
All Saints / May '97 / Discovery / Vital

Biota

ALMOST NEVER
CD RERBCD 3
ReR/Recommended / Oct '96 / ReR Megacorp / RTM/Disc

BELLOWING ROOM/TINCT
CD RERBCD 2
ReR/Recommended / Apr '90 / ReR Megacorp / RTM/Disc

OBJECT HOLDER
CD RERBCD 4
ReR/Recommended / Oct '96 / ReR Megacorp / RTM/Disc

TUMBLE
CD RERBCD
ReR/Recommended / Apr '90 / ReR Megacorp / RTM/Disc

Bird, Ted

MADE IN AMERICA
Dirty little town / Land o' plenty / Drivin' in Rhode Island / Still in your power / Hurricane / Sadness in my eyes / Daddy's diamonds / Philadelphia kid / Southern Ohio / Lady crystal / That far to fall / When she gets drinkin' whiskey / On the radio / Dollar bill / Allyson's waltz
CD CDSL 5219
DRG / Aug '92 / Discovery / New Note/ Pinnacle

Bird, Tony

SORRY AFRICA
CD CDPH 1135
Philo / Dec '90 / ADA / CM / Direct

Birdsong Mesozoic

SONIC ECOLOGY
CD RCD 20073
Rykodisc / Apr '92 / ADA / Vital

Birkin, Jane

BEST OF JANE BIRKIN, THE
Je t'aime moi non plus / Ex fan des sixties / Ballade de Johnny Jane / La gadoue / Yesterday yes a day / Di doo dah / Fuir le bonheur de peur qu'il ne se sauve / Baby alone in Babylon / Les dessous chics / Quoi / These foolish things / Avec le temps / Et quand bien meme / Baby Lou / Les yeux fermes / Je suis venu te dire que je m'en vais / La javanaise
CD 5346912
Mercury / Mar '97 / PolyGram

Birkin Tree

CONTINENTAL REEL
CD NT 6753CD
New Tone / Aug '96 / ADA / Impetus

Birmingham 6

ERROR OF JUDGEMENT
CD CLP 9748
Cleopatra / Oct '96 / Cargo / Greyhound / Plastic Head / RTM/Disc / SRD

YOU CANNOT WALK HERE
CD CLP 9887
Cleopatra / Jun '97 / Cargo / Greyhound / Plastic Head / RTM/Disc / SRD

Birmingham City FC

HAPPY COS I'M BLUE (Birmingham City FC & Supporters)
Keep right on: *Lauder, Harry* / Happy cos I'm blue: *Hockey, Trevor* / Home and away: *Andrews, Harvey* / Lads from the Tilton: *Phillips, Colin Combo* / Keep right on: *Blues Players 1968* / Birmingham blues: *Phillips, Colin Combo* / Beau brummie: *Green, Roy* / Bobby Latchford: *Saint, Andrew* / Louie Louie: *Rockin' Berries* / Davey boy: *Holmes, John* / Blue nose: *Kop Dis* / Trevor's blues: *Saint, Andrew* / My colour is blue: *Small Heath Alliance* / Keep right on: *Team Of '91* / Barry Fry Song: *Austin, Steve* / You'll never walk alone: *Francis, Trevor & Viv Anderson* / Keep right on: *Small Heath Alliance* / When the blues win the cup: *Andrews, Harvey*
CD CDGAFFER 10
Cherry Red / Aug '97 / Pinnacle

Birmingham Jubilee Singers

1926-1927 VOL.1
CD DOCD 5345
Document / May '95 / ADA / Hot Shot / Jazz Music

Birmingham Sunlights

FOR OLD TIME'S SAKE
CD FF 588CD
Flying Fish / Nov '94 / ADA / CM / Direct / Roots

Biro, Daniel

COMPARATIVE ANATOMY OF ANGELS
CD SCD 28022
Sargasso / Sep '96 / SRD

Birth Control

BACKDOOR POSSIBILITIES
CD RR 7054
Repertoire / Jun '97 / Greyhound

Birtha

BIRTHA/CAN'T STOP THE MADNESS
Free spirit / Fine talking man / Tuesday / Feeling lonely / She was good to me / Work on a dream / Too much woman (for a hen pecked man) / Judgement day / Forgotten soul / Can't stop the madness / My pants are too short / Freedom / Let us sing / Don't let it get you down / (When will ya) understand / Rock me / All this love / Sun / My man told me
CD SEECD 474
See For Miles/C5 / Feb '97 / Pinnacle

Birthday Party

HITS
Friend catcher / Happy birthday / Mr. Clarinet / Nick the stripper / Zoo music girl / King Ink / Release the bats / Blast off / She's hit / Gold blade / Hamlet (pow pow pow) / Dead Joe / Junkyard / Big Jesus trash can / Wild world / Sonny's burning / Deep in the woods / Swampland / Jennifer's veil / Mutiny in Heaven
CD DAD 2016CD
4AD / Oct '92 / RTM/Disc

JUNKYARD
She's hit / Dead Joe / Dim locator / Hamlet pow pow pow / Several sins / Big Jesus trash can / Kiss me black / Six inch gold blade / Kewpie doll / Junkyard
CD CAD 207 CD
4AD / Apr '88 / RTM/Disc

MUTINY/BAD SEED
CD CAD 301CD
4AD / Jul '89 / RTM/Disc

PRAYERS ON FIRE
CD CAD 104CD
4AD / Apr '88 / RTM/Disc

Birtwistle, Harrison

PANIC/EARTH DANCES
Panic: *Birtwistle, Harrison & John Harle/Paul Clavis/BBC SO* / Earth dances: *Birtwistle, Harrison & The Cleveland Orchestra*
CD 4521042
Argo / Oct '96 / PolyGram

Biry, Daniel

FEATHERED SNAKE, THE
CD AMPCD 009
AMP / Feb '95 / Cadillac / Discovery / TKO Magnum

Bis

NEW TRANSISTER HEROES
Tell it to the kids / Sweet shop avengers / Starbright boy / Popstar kill / Mr. important / Antiseptic poetry / Popyura / Skinny tie sensurround / Poster parent / Monstarr / Everybody thinks they're going to get theirs / Rebel soul / Photo shop / X-Defect / Lie detector test / Dinosaur germs / Troubled land: *King Loser*
CD WIJCD 1064
Wiiija / Apr '97 / RTM/Disc

Biscuit, Karl

AKTUALISMUS
CD MTM 28
Made To Measure / Dec '92 / New Note/ Pinnacle

Bishop, Duffy

BACK TO THE BONE (Bishop, Duffy Band)
CD BCD 00232
Burnside / Aug '96 / Koch

BOTTLED ODDITIES (Bishop, Duffy Band)
CD BCD 00182
Burnside / May '96 / Koch

Bishop, Elvin

ACE IN THE HOLE
Another mule kickin' in your stall / Driving wheel / Give me some of that money / Ace in the hole / Party 'til the cows come home / Think / Home of the blues / Pigmeat on the line / Ain't that love / Fishin' / Blue flame / Talkin' mood / Fooled around and fell in love
CD ALCD 4833
Alligator / Aug '95 / ADA / CM / Direct

BIG FUN
CD ALCD 4767
Alligator / Aug '92 / ADA / CM / Direct

DON'T LET THE BOSSMAN GET YOU DOWN
Fannie Mae / Don't let the bossman get you down / Murder in the first degree / Kissing in the dark / My whiskey head buddies / Stepping up in class / You got to rock 'em / Come on in this house / Soul food / Rollin' with my blues / Devil's slide / Just your fool
CD ALCD 4791
Alligator / Apr '91 / ADA / CM / Direct

Bishop, Joni

ENDLESS CHRISTMAS (Bishop, Joni & Electra Reed)
CD CDSGP 0213
Prestige / Dec '96 / Else / Total/BMG

EVERYDAY MIRACLES
When God made you / I'd hardly noticed you were gone / Mojave rose / Everyday miracles / Rest assured / Money tree / Art of flying / Sequoia / Thief of hearts / Living love
CD CDSGP 0134
Prestige / Nov '95 / Else / Total/BMG
CD BWE 91CD
BWE / Nov '96 / ADA

THREADS
CD BWE 0094CD
BWE / May '97 / ADA

Bishop, Stephen

INTRODUCTION TO STEPHEN BISHOP, AN
CD HMNCD 011
Half Moon / Jun '97 / BMG

Bishop, Walter Jr.

MILESTONES
CD BLCD 760109
Black Lion / Feb '89 / Cadillac / Jazz Music / Koch / Wellard

Bishops

BEST OF THE BISHOPS, THE
Train train / Baby you're wrong / Stay free / I want candy / I take what I want / Mr. Jones / I need you / Down in the bottom / You're in my way / Talk to you / Taste and try / Someone's got my number / Good times / Your Daddy won't mind / What's your number / Till the end of the day / These arms of mine / Rolling man / Paul's blues / No lies / Too much, too soon / Sometimes good guys don't wear white / Don't start me talkin' / Somebody's gonna get their head kicked in tonight / I don't like it / Route 66 / Train, train
CD CDWIKD 150
Chiswick / Aug '95 / Pinnacle

Bisi, Martin

SEE YA IN TIAJUANA
CD NAR 123CD
New Alliance / Jul '95 / Plastic Head

Bisiker, Mick

HOME AGAIN
Home again / Don't you go / Jigs / Katy Jane / Si beag si mor / Rose of Allendale / Maid from the shore / Mossy green banks of the lea / Jigs and reels / Downhills of life / Rainbows end
CD FE 083CD
Fellside / Feb '88 / ADA / Direct / Target/ BMG

Bisk

STRANGE OR FUNNY HA HA
CD SR 118
Sub Rosa / Jun '97 / Direct / RTM/Disc / SRD / Vital

TIME
CD SR 112
Sub Rosa / Sep '96 / Direct / RTM/Disc / SRD / Vital

Bismillah

ETERNAL SPIRIT
Alap / Vilambit / Gat composition
CD NRCD 0080
Navras / Jul '97 / New Note/Pinnacle

Bison, Fred

BEATROOTS
CD WO 19CD
Woronzow / Apr '94 / Pinnacle

Bisserov Sisters

PIRIN WEDDING AND RITUAL SONGS
CD PAN 7005CD
Pan / Nov '95 / ADA / CM / Direct

Bitch

BITCH IS BACK
Do you wanna rock / Hot and heavy / Me and the boys / Storm raging up / Bitch is back / Head banger / Fist to face / Turns me on / Skullcrusher
CD 398414218CD
Metal Blade / Jan '97 / Pinnacle / Plastic Head

DAMNATION
CD 398414213CD
Metal Blade / Jan '97 / Pinnacle / Plastic Head

ROSE BY ANY OTHER
CD 398414214CD
Metal Blade / Jan '97 / Pinnacle / Plastic Head

Bitch Funky Sex Machine

LOVE BOMB
CD CDVEST 39
Bulletproof / Jan '95 / Pinnacle

Bitch Magnet

BEN HUR
CD COMM 21CD
Communion / Dec '96 / Cargo

UMBER
CD COMM 12CD
Communion / Dec '96 / Cargo

Bitchcraft

DON'T COUNT ON IT
CD IT 0062
Iteration / Feb '95 / SRD

Bitches Brue

WE MIGHT NOT BE AMERICAN BUT STILL WE FK**
CD HMRXD 131
Heavy Metal / Aug '89 / Revolver / Sony

Bitter End

HARSH REALITIES
CD CDZORRO 10
Metal Blade / Jul '89 / Pinnacle / Plastic Head

Bitter Grin

DESTINATION
CD WWRCD 024
Walzwerk / Nov '96 / Cargo

Bittersweets

LESSON ONE
CD THEN 029CD
Thats Entertainment / Nov '96 / Plastic Head

Bivouac

TUBER
Good day song / Big question mark / Dragging your weight around / Rue / Deadend friend / Drank / Steel strung / Need / Bell foundry / Bad day song
CD ELM 11 CDX
Elemental / Jun '93 / RTM/Disc

Bizarre Inc.

SURPRISE
Keep the music strong / Feel is real / Surprise / Get up (Sunshine Street) / Never give you up / Love groove / Soul fire / Porcelain cafe / Breakaway / Miracle / Take a look / Shout it out
CD 5148192
Some Bizarre/Mercury / Sep '96 / PolyGram

Bjork

BEST MIXES FROM THE ALBUM DEBUT (For All The People Who Don't Buy White Labels)
Human behaviour / One day / Come to me / Anchor song
CD MUMCD 59
Mother / Oct '94 / PolyGram

DEBUT
Human behaviour / Crying / Venus as a boy / There's more to life than this / Like someone in love / Big time sensuality / One day / Aeroplane / Come to me / Violently happy / Anchor song / Play dead: *Bjork & David Arnold*
CD TPLP 31CDX
One Little Indian / Nov '93 / Pinnacle

GLING GLO
CD TPLP 61CD
One Little Indian / Mar '97 / Pinnacle

INTERVIEW DISC
CD ICE 1CD
Wax / Feb '97 / RTM/Disc / Total/BMG

POST
Army of me / Hyperballad / Modern things / It's oh so quiet / Enjoy / You've been flirting again / Isobel / Possibly maybe / I miss you / Cover me / Headphones
CD TPLP 51CD
One Little Indian / Jun '95 / Pinnacle

TELEGRAM
CD TPLP 51CDT
One Little Indian / Nov '96 / Pinnacle

Bjorkenheim, Raoul

RITUAL (Bjorkenheim, Raoul & Krakatu)
CD RUNE 86
Cuneiform / Jun '97 / ReR Megacorp

Bjorkman, Erik

SVARDSJO SPELMANSLAG
CD GCD 33
Giga / May '97 / ADA / Total/BMG

Bjornstad, Ketil

RIVER, THE (Bjornstad, Ketil & David Darling)
River
CD 5311702
ECM / Feb '97 / New Note/Pinnacle

SEA, THE
CD 5217182
ECM / Sep '95 / New Note/Pinnacle

WATER STORIES
Glacial reconstruction / Levels and degrees / Surface movements / View (part one) / Between memory and presentiment / Ten thousand years later / Waterfall / Flotation and surroundings / Riverscape / Approaching the sea / View (part two) / History
CD 5190762
ECM / Sep '93 / New Note/Pinnacle

BKA

CLEVER
CD FILERCD 405
Profile / Jun '91 / Pinnacle

Blab Happy

BOAT
CD XXCD 20
F-Beat / Oct '91 / Pinnacle

Black & Farrell

CATARACT JUMP
CD FR 9520141
Blueprint / Dec '96 / Pinnacle

Black & White Gospel Singers

LOOK TO GOD
CD FA 405
Fremeaux / Nov '95 / ADA / Discovery

Black & White Minstrels

30 GOLDEN GREATS (Black & White Minstrels & The Joe Loss Orchestra)
Baby face / Ain't she sweet / Good ole mammy song / Nostalgia, Home town, Strollin', Underneath the arches / Y viva Espana / Happy feet/I want to be happy/ Happy days are here again / Consider yourself / Mame / Tzena, tzena, tzena / Hava Nagila / Bring me sunshine / Paloma blanca / Old fashioned way / You are my sunshine / Laugh a happy laugh / Continental / Piccolino / When the red, red robin comes bob, bob, bobbin' along / Hopscotch / Mexican shuffle / Tijuana Taxi / La Bamba / (We're gonna) rock around the clock
CD CDMFP 5720
EMI / Mar '93 / EMI

Black

TURN LOOSE THE IDIOTS
CD NORMAL 196CD
Normal / Jan '96 / ADA / Direct

WONDERFUL LIFE
Ravel in the rain / Sixteens / Leave yourself alone / It's not you Lady Jane / Hardly star crossed lovers / Wonderful life / Everything's coming up roses / Sometimes for the asking / Finder / Paradise / I'm not afraid / I just grew tired / Blue / Just making memories / Sweetest smile
CD CDMID 166
A&M / Aug '91 / PolyGram

Black

BLACK BLOOD
CD NR 012CD
Necropolis / Sep '96 / Plastic Head

Black Ace

I'M THE BOSS CARD IN YOUR HAND
CD ARHCD 374
Arhoolie / Apr '95 / ADA / Cadillac / Direct

Black, Alastair

BALANDA DANCING (Black, Alastair & Stephen Richter)
CD LARRCD 317
Larrikin / Nov '94 / ADA / CM / Direct / Roots

Black, Andrea

JUMPING FROM THE WALL
CD AKRCDA 38
AKR / Mar '95 / Pinnacle

Black, Barry

BARRY BLACK
Train of pain / Mighty fields of tabacco / Broad majestic haw / Sandviken stomp / Fisherman thugs / Cockroaches / Vampire lounge / Staticus von carrborus / I can't breathe / Cowboys and thieves / Boo Barry blip / Animals are for eating / Rabid dog / Golden throat
CD A 085D
Alias / Oct '95 / Vital

TRAGIC ANIMAL STORIES
Horrible truth about plankton / When sharks smell blood / Duelling elephants / Derelict vultures / Iditarod sled dogs / Chimps / Slow loris' lament / Drowning spider / Tropical fish revival / Snail trail of tears
CD A 122D
Alias / Aug '97 / Vital

Black, Bill

GOES WEST AND PLAYS (Black, Bill Combo)
CD HIUKCD 124
Hi / Jun '93 / Pinnacle

GREATEST HITS (Black, Bill Combo)
Do it rat / Josephine / Rollin' / Hearts of stone / Yogi / White silver sands / Blue tango / Willie / Ole buttermilk sky / Royal blue / Don't be cruel / Smokie part 2 / School days / Sweet little sixteen / Roll over Beethoven / Maybellene / Carol / Little queenie / Brown eyed handsome man / Nadine / Thirty days / Johnny B Goode / Reelin' and rockin' / Memphis, Tennessee
CD HIUKCD 115
Hi / '91 / Pinnacle

LET'S TWIST HER/THE UNTOUCHABLE SOUND (Black, Bill Combo)
CD HIUKCD 131
Hi / Jun '92 / Pinnacle

SOLID AND RAUNCHY AND MOVIN' (Black, Bill Combo)
Don't be cruel / Singin' the blues / Blueberry Hill / I almost lost my mind / Cherry pink / Mona Lisa / Honky Tonk / Tequila / Raunchy / You win again / Bo Diddley / Mack the knife / Movin' / What'd I say / Hey Bo Diddley / Witchcraft / Work with me Annie / Be bop a lula / My babe / Forty miles of bad road / Ain't that lovin' you baby / Honky train / Walk / Torquay
CD HIUKCD 112
Hi / '91 / Pinnacle

THAT WONDERFUL FEELING (Black, Bill Combo)
CD HIUKCD 145
Hi / Aug '94 / Pinnacle

WONDERFUL WORLD OF BILL BLACK, THE
CD HILOCD 22
Hi / Aug '96 / Pinnacle

Black, Bill

DAWNING, THE (Black, Bill & His Scottish Dance Band)
CD SPRCD 1037
Springthyme / May '96 / ADA / CM / Direct / Duncans / Highlander / Roots

Black Box

DREAMLAND
Everybody everybody / I don't know anybody else / Open your eyes / Fantasy / Dreamland / Ride on time / Hold on / Ghost box / Strike it up
CD 74321158672
De-Construction / Sep '93 / BMG

Black Brothers

WHAT A TIME (Black, Shay/Michael/ Martin)
CD DARTECD 192
Dolphin / Mar '96 / CM / Else / Grapevine/ PolyGram / Koch

Black Cat Bones

BARBED WIRE SANDWICH
Chauffeur / Death Valley blues / Feelin' good / Please tell me baby / Coming back / Save my love / Four women / Sylvester's blues / Good lookin' woman
CD SEECD 405
See For Miles/C5 / May '96 / Pinnacle

Black, Cilla

BEST OF THE EMI YEARS, THE
You're my world / Anyone who had a heart / Love of the loved / It's for you / You've lost that lovin' feelin' / I've been wrong before / Goin' out of my head / Love's just a broken heart / Alfie / Fool am I / Sing a rainbow / Don't answer me / When I fall in love / Yesterday / Make it easy on yourself / What good am I / I only live to love you / Step inside love / Where is tomorrow / What the world needs now is love / Conversatikons / Surround yourself with sorrow / If I thought you'd ever change your mind / Something tells me (something's gonna happen tonight) / Liverpool lullaby / Baby we can't go wrong

CD ______ CDEMS 1410
EMI / Jun '91 / EMI

CILLA BLACK 1963-1973 (The Abbey Road Decade/3CD Set)
Love of the loved / Shy of love / Anyone who had a heart / Just for you / You're my world / Suffer now I must / It's for you / He won't ask me / You've lost that loving feeling / Is it love / I've been wrong before / I don't want to know / Love's just a broken heart / Yesterday / Alfie / Night time is here / Don't answer me / Right one is left / Fool am I / For no one / What good am I / Over my head / I only live to love you / From now on / Step inside love / I couldn't take my eyes off you / Where is tomorrow / Work is a four letter word / Surround yourself with sorrow / London bridge / Conversations / Liverpool lullaby / If I thought you'd ever change your mind / It feels so good / Child of mine / That's why I love you / Something tells me (something's gonna happen tonight) / La la la lu / World I wish for you / Down in the city / You you you / Silly wasn't I / Abyssinian secret / Trees and lonliness / There I go / Time / M'Innamoro / Mon C'e Domani / Fever / Shot of rhythm and blues / (Love is like a) heatwave / Some things you never get used to / Poor boy / Shotgun / Cherry song / Please don't teach me to love you / Any time you need me / Only you can free my mind / All my love / Step inside love / Work is a four letter word / Step inside love / Your heart is free (just like the wind) / On a street called hope / Changes / Surround yourself with sorrow
CD Set ______ CILLA 1
EMI / Aug '97 / EMI

Black, Clint

GREATEST HITS
Like the rain / Summer's comin' / Good run of bad luck / State of mind / Bad goodbye: *Black, Clint & Wynonna* / Better man / Killin' time / We tell ourselves / Half way up / Burn one down / Cadillac Jack favor / Put yourself in my shoes / Wherever you go / Life get's away / No time to kill / Desperado
CD ______ 07863666712
RCA Nashville / Oct '96 / BMG

NO TIME TO KILL
No time to kill / Thinking again / Good run of bad luck / State of mind / Bad goodbye / Back to back / Half the man / I'll take Texas / Happiness alone / Tuckered out
CD ______ 07863662392
RCA / Jul '93 / BMG

NOTHIN' BUT THE TAILIGHTS
CD ______ 7863675152
RCA / Aug '97 / BMG

ONE EMOTION
You walked by / Life gets away / One emotion / Summer's comin' / Untanglin' my mind / Hey hot rod / Change in the air / I can get by wherever you go / You made me feel / Good run of bad luck / Bad goodbye
CD ______ 74321229572
RCA / Oct '94 / BMG

PUT YOURSELF IN MY SHOES
Put yourself in my shoes / Gulf of Mexico / One more payment / Where are you now / Old man / This nightlife / Loving blind / Heart like mine / Good night loving
CD ______ PD 90544
RCA / Jan '90 / BMG

Black Crowes

AMORICA
Gone / Conspiracy / High head blues / Cursed diamond / Non-fiction / She gave good / Sunflower / P25 London / Ballad in urgency / Wiser time / Downtown money waster / Descending / Tied up and swallowed
CD ______ 74321236822
American / Oct '94 / BMG

SHAKE YOUR MONEY MAKER
Twice as hard / Jealous again / Sister luck / Could I've been so blind / Seeing things / Hard to handle / Thick 'n' thin / She talks to angels / Struttin' blues / Stare it cold
CD ______ 74321248392
American / Dec '94 / BMG

SOUTHERN HARMONY AND MUSICAL COMPANION, THE
Sting me / Remedy / Thorn in my pride / Bad luck blue eyes goodbye / Sometimes salvation / Hotel illness / Black moon creepin' / No speak, no slave / My morning song / Time will tell
CD ______ 74321248402
American / Dec '94 / BMG

THREE SNAKES AND ONE CHARM
Under a mountain / Good Friday / Nebakanezer / One mirror too many / Blackberry / Girl from a pawnshop / (Only) Halfway to everywhere / Bring on, bring on / How much for your wings / Let me share the ride
CD ______ 74321384842
American / Jul '96 / BMG

Black Crucifixion

PROMEATHEAN GIFT
CD ______ LMCD 222
Lethal / Nov '93 / Plastic Head

Black, Dick

KEEP THE MUSIC GOING (Black, Dick Scottish Dance Band)
CD ______ CDKBP 517
Klub / Mar '95 / ADA / CM / Direct / Duncans / Ross

Black Dog

BYTES
CD ______ WARPCD 8
Warp / Apr '96 / Prime / RTM/Disc

MUSIC FOR ADVERTS
CD ______ PUPCD 2
Warp / Jul '96 / Prime / RTM/Disc

SPANNERS
CD ______ PUPCD 1
Warp / Jan '95 / Prime / RTM/Disc

TEMPLE OF TRANSPARENT BALLS
CD ______ GPRCD 1
GPR / Jul '93 / 3mv/Vital

Black, Donald

WESTWIND (Scottish Mouth Organ Music)
Pipe jigs / J Scott Skinner slow airs / Cape Breton set / Slow airs / Welcome Christmas morning / Shetland reels / Pipe slow air and marches / Hebridean duet / Shores of Loch Linnhe / Slow air and pipe marches / Touch of the Irish / Lewis danns a rathad
CD ______ CDTRAX 091
Greentrax / Jul '95 / ADA / Direct / Duncans / Highlander

Black Dyke Mills Band

BLITZ
Blitz / Pageantry / Journey into freedom / Tam O'Shanter's ride
CD ______ CHAN 8370
Chandos / Aug '85 / Chandos

BROADWAY BRASS
There's no business like show business / Oklahoma / Medley from West Side Story / I have a love / Somewhere / I don't know how to love him / Colours of my life / Where is my love / Music of the night / Starlight express / Bring him home / Wunderbar / How to handle a woman / Summertime / Medley from South Pacific / There is nothin' like a dame / Wonderful guy / Some enchanted evening / That's entertainment
CD ______ CDMFP 5947
Music For Pleasure / Oct '92 / EMI

COMPLETE CHAMPIONS
Contest music / Royal parks / Salute to youth / Cloudcatcher fells
CD ______ CHAN 4509
Chandos / Apr '92 / Chandos

ESSENTIAL DYKE
Queensbury / Le roi d'ts / Pandora / Deep harmony / Galop / Macushla / Capriccio Italien / Knight templar / Cornet carillon / Rule Britannia / Abide with me / Angels guard thee / Hungarian rhapsody No. 1
CD ______ DOYCD 034
Doyen / Oct '94 / Conifer/BMG

GREAT BRITISH MARCHES
Queensbury / Roll away Bet / Battle Abbey / ORB / Senator / Invincible / Pompous main / Cossack / Imperioso / Raby / Captain / Olympus / Knight templar
CD ______ DOYCD 039
Doyen / May '95 / Conifer/BMG

GREAT BRITISH TRADITION, THE
Endeavour / West country fantasy / North country fantasy / Sir Roger De Coverley / Sally in our alley / On Ilkley Moor baht'at / Fifth of August / Lincolnshire poacher / Carnival of the animals suite / Carmen fantasy
CD ______ CHAN 4524
Chandos / May '93 / Chandos

GREGSON - BRASS MUSIC VOL.2
Prelude for an occasion / Plantagenets / Essay / Laudate dominum / Prelude and capriccio / Concerto grosso / Partita
CD ______ DOYCD 044
Doyen / Nov '95 / Conifer/BMG

LION AND THE EAGLE, THE
Yeoman of the guard / Phil the fluter's ball / Land of my fathers (Hen wlad fy nhadau) / Fantasia on the dargason / Scottish lament / Will ye no' come back again / Auld lang syne / Pomp and circumstance march No.4 / Stars and stripes forever / Rhapsody on negro spirituals / Go down Moses / Peter, go ring dem bells / Every time I feel de spirit / I'm a rollin' through an unfriendly world / Stephen Foster fantasy / Camptown races / My old Kentucky home / Beautiful dreamer / Jeanie with the light brown hair / Old folks at home (Swanee river) / Oh Susanna / Old black Joe / Strike up the band / Embraceable you / They can't take that away from me / Someone to watch over me / Oh lady be good / Rhapsody in blue / Man I love
CD ______ CHAN 4528
Chandos / Aug '93 / Chandos

MORE OF THE WORLD'S MOST BEAUTIFUL MELODIES
Your tiny hand is frozen / Celeste Aida / Skye boat song / Bruch and Mendelssohn violin concerto themes / Flower song / Holy city / I hear you calling me / Ave Maria
CD ______ CHAN 8513
Chandos / '87 / Chandos

PLANETS, THE/THE MOORSIDE SUITE (Black Dyke Mills Band & The Halle Chorus)
CD ______ DOYCD 050
Doyen / Dec '96 / Conifer/BMG

REVELATIONS
Toccata / Revelation / Symphony for brass on a theme of Purcell / Paragon / Amparito roca / Ted Heath Big Band Set / Impromptu for tuba / Ave Maria / Carnival of Venice / March
CD ______ DOYCD 046
Doyen / Jun '96 / Conifer/BMG

RHAPSODY IN BRASS
Frogs / Academic festival overture / Rhapsody in brass / Prometheus unbound / Symphonic suite / Resurgam
CD ______ QPRL 061D
Polyphonic / Sep '93 / Complete/Pinnacle

SACRED SYMPHONIES (Black Dyke Mills Band & Fresno Wind Ensemble)
Dawnflight / Lowry sketchbook / Toccata brillante / Revelation / Concert gallop / Symphonia sacra
CD ______ DOYCD 053
Doyen / Jun '96 / Conifer/BMG

Black Eagle Jazz Band

BLACK EAGLE JAZZ BAND VOL.7
CD ______ SOSCD 1224
Stomp Off / Oct '92 / Jazz Music / Wellard

BLACK EAGLE JAZZ BAND VOL.9
CD ______ SOSCD 1303
Stomp Off / Jul '96 / Jazz Music / Wellard

DON'T MONKEY WITH IT
CD ______ SOSCD 1147
Stomp Off / Oct '92 / Jazz Music / Wellard

SOME SWEET DAY
In the sweet bye & bye / Careless love / Perfect rag / Perdido Street blues / Ponchartrain blues / Martha / Purple rose of Cairo / Love song of the Nile / Some sweet day / Misty morning / Dreaming the hours away / Baby o' mine / Lina blues
CD ______ LACD 65
Lake / Aug '96 / ADA / Cadillac / Direct / Jazz Music / Target/BMG

Black Eg

BLACK EG
CD ______ CRECD 086
Creation / May '94 / 3mv/Vital

Black Family

BLACK FAMILY, THE
Broom o'the Cowdenknowes / Colannon / Motorway song / Tomorrow is a long time / Donkey riding / Will ye gang, love / Bramble and the rose / Ploughboy lad / Warlike lads of Russia / Dark and roving eye / James Connolly / Wheel the perambulator
CD ______ DARACD 023
Dara / Jan '94 / ADA / CM / Direct / Else / Grapevine/PolyGram

TIME FOR TOUCHING HOME
Alabama John Cherokee / Rough ride / Old bones / Farewell to the gold / Sweet liberty / Peat bog soldiers / Weave and mend / Time alone / Song of the diggers / Since Maggie went away / First Christmas / Eliza Lee / This love will carry
CD ______ DARACD 035
Dara / Jan '94 / ADA / CM / Direct / Else / Grapevine/PolyGram

Black Flag

DAMAGED
CD ______ SST 007CD
SST / May '93 / Plastic Head

EVERYTHING WENT BLACK
CD ______ SST 015CD
SST / May '93 / Plastic Head

FAMILY MAN
CD ______ SST 026CD
SST / May '93 / Plastic Head

FIRST FOUR YEARS, THE
CD ______ SST 021CD
SST / May '93 / Plastic Head

IN MY HEAD
CD ______ SST 045CD
SST / May '93 / Plastic Head

LOOSE NUT
CD ______ SST 035CD
SST / May '93 / Plastic Head

MY WAR
CD ______ SST 023CD
SST / May '93 / Plastic Head

PROCESS OF WEEDING OUT
CD ______ SST 037CD
SST / May '93 / Plastic Head

SLIP IT IN
CD ______ SST 029CD
SST / May '93 / Plastic Head

WASTED...AGAIN
Wasted / TV party / Six pack / I don't care / I've had it / Jealous again / Slip it in / Annihilate this week / Loose nut / Gimmie gimmie / Louie Louie / Drinking and driving
CD ______ SST 166CD
SST / May '93 / Plastic Head

WHO'S GOT THE 10%
CD ______ SST 060CD
SST / May '93 / Plastic Head

Black Fork

ROCK FOR LOOT
CD ______ LOOKOUT 172CD
Lookout / Aug '97 / Cargo / Greyhound / Shellshock/Disc

Black, Frances

FRANCES BLACK & KIERAN GOSS (Black, Frances & Kieran Goss)
CD ______ TRACD 112
Transatlantic / Apr '96 / Pinnacle

SKY ROAD, THE
CD ______ DARA 068CD
Dara / Aug '97 / ADA / CM / Direct / Else / Grapevine/PolyGram

SMILE ON YOUR FACE, THE
CD ______ TORCD 084
Dara / Jul '97 / ADA / CM / Direct / Else / Grapevine/PolyGram

TALK TO ME
All the lies that you have told me / Don't be a stranger / On Grafton Street / Soldiers of destiny / Talk to me while I'm listening / Intuition / Colder than Winter / Always will / Time of inconvenience / World of our own / If love had wings
CD ______ 7567827362
Warner Bros. / Apr '95 / Warner Music
CD ______ DARA 056CD
Dara / Aug '97 / ADA / CM / Direct / Else / Grapevine/PolyGram

Black, Frank

CULT OF RAY, THE
Marsist / Men in black / Punk rock city / You ain't me / Jesus was right / I don't want to hurt you (every single time) / Mosh, don't pass the guy / Kicked in the taco / Creature crawling / Adventure and the resolution / Dance war / Cult of Ray / Last stand of Shazeb Andleeb
CD ______ 4816472
CD ______ 4816479
Dragnet / Jan '96 / Sony

FRANK BLACK
CD ______ CAD 3004CD
4AD / Mar '93 / RTM/Disc

TEENAGER OF THE YEAR
CD ______ DAD 4009CD
4AD / May '94 / RTM/Disc

Black Grape

IT'S GREAT WHEN YOU'RE STRAIGHT... YEAH
Reverend Black Grape / In the name of the father / Tramazi parti / Kelly's heroes / Yeah yeah brother / Big day in the North / Shake well before opening / Submarine / Shake your money / Little Bob
CD ______ RAD 11224
Radioactive / Aug '95 / BMG / Vital

Black Harmony

BLACK HARMONY
Party with Jesus / La cite / Aurore / Les elans du coeur / Nous tous / Esprit divin / Loue ton dieu / When the saints go marching in / Meci / La cite (dance in heaven mix)
CD ______ FA 413
Fremeaux / Oct '96 / ADA / Discovery

Black, Ika

SPECIAL LOVE
CD ______ KMCD 004
Keyman / Oct '88 / Greensleeves / Jet Star / SRD

Black Ivory

BATTLE OF THE BANDS (Black Ivory/ Odds & Ends)
Don't turn around: *Black Ivory* / Surrender: *Black Ivory* / I'll find a way: *Black Ivory* / Got to be there: *Black Ivory* / Spinning around: *Black Ivory* / I keep asking you questions: *Black Ivory* / Time is love: *Black Ivory* / Find the one who loves you: *Black Ivory* / Our future: *Black Ivory* / We made it: *Black Ivory* / Just leave me some: *Black Ivory* / You and I (see today): *Black Ivory* / Foot track: *Odds & Ends* / Who could doubt my love: *Odds & Ends* / Apples, peaches, pumpkin pie: *Odds & Ends* / Let me try: *Odds & Ends* / Give me something: *Odds & Ends* / Talk that talk: *Odds & Ends* / Love makes the world go round: *Odds & Ends* / Yesterday my love: *Odds & Ends*
CD ______ NEMCD 731
Sequel / Jul '97 / BMG

Black Lace

20 ALL TIME PARTY FAVOURITES
Agadoo / Hands up / Atmosphere / DISCO / We danced we danced / Wig wam bam / I just called to say I love you / Viva Espana / I am the music man / Dancing in the street / Superman / Simon says / Birdie song / Brown girl in the ring / Soaking up the sun / Let's twist again / Sailing/You'll never walk alone / Hokey cokey / Do the conga / YMCA/In the navy
CD ____ **BLPFCD 1**
Connoisseur Collection / Nov '89 / Pinnacle

ACTION PARTY
Agadoo / I am the music man / Wig wam bam / Hi ho silver lining / Penny arcade / Superman / Do the conga / Locomation / Hippy hippy shake / Good golly Miss Molly / Twist and shout / Do you love me / Bump / Come on Eileen / Let's dance / Do wah diddy diddy / Mandolin jivin' / Dancin' party / (We're gonna) Rock around the clock / This ole house / Birdie song / Teardrops / Knock three times / We danced we danced / Time warp
CD ____ **PLATCD 3915**
Platinum / Apr '93 / Prism

SATURDAY NIGHT
CD ____ **LACECD 2**
Flair / Dec '94 / Total/BMG

Black Lodge

COVET
CD ____ **HNF 010CD**
Head Not Found / Mar '95 / Plastic Head

Black Lodge Singers

POW WOW WOW
CD ____ **SPA 14286**
Spalax / Nov '94 / ADA / Cargo / Direct / Discovery / Greyhound

Black Lung

DEPOPULATION BOMB, THE
CD ____ **NZ 036CD**
Nova Zembla / May '95 / Plastic Head

SILENT WEAPONS FOR QUIET WARS
CD ____ **DOROBO 005CD**
Dorobo / Oct '95 / Plastic Head

Black, Marc

BIG DONG DHARMA
CD ____ **ESP 30112**
ESP / Jan '93 / Jazz Music

Black, Mary

BABES IN THE WOOD
CD ____ **GRACD 008**
Grapevine / Jan '95 / Grapevine/PolyGram

BY THE TIME IT GETS DARK
By the time it gets dark / Schoolday's over / Once in a very blue moon / Farewell farewell / Sparks might fly / Katy / Leaving the land / There is a time / Jamie / Leaboy's lassie / Trying to get the balance right
CD ____ **GRACD 004**
Grapevine / Jan '95 / Grapevine/PolyGram

CIRCUS
CD ____ **GRACD 014**
Grapevine / Sep '95 / Grapevine/PolyGram

COLLECTED
Mo Ghile Mear / Fare thee well my own / True love / Men o' worth / She moved through the fair / Love's endless war / Both sides of the Tweed / My youngest son came / Home today / Isle of St. Helena / Don't explain / Everything that touches me
CD ____ **GRACD 002**
Grapevine / Jan '95 / Grapevine/PolyGram

COLLECTION, THE
Moon and St. Christopher / No frontiers / Babes in the wood / Carolina rua / Katie / Columbus / Adam at the window / Ellis island / Bright blue rose / Vanities / Only a woman's heart / Song for Ireland / Tearing up the town / There's a train that leaves tonight
CD ____ **GRACD 10**
Grapevine / Jan '95 / Grapevine/PolyGram

HOLY GROUND, THE
CD ____ **GRACD 011**
Grapevine / Jan '95 / Grapevine/PolyGram

MARY BLACK
Rose of Allendale / Loving you / Loving Hannah / My Donald / Crusader / Anachie Gordon / Home / God bless the child / Rare's hill
CD ____ **GRACD 001**
Grapevine / Jan '95 / Grapevine/PolyGram

NO FRONTIERS
CD ____ **GRACD 009**
Grapevine / Jan '95 / Grapevine/PolyGram

SHINE
CD ____ **GRACD 015**
Grapevine / Mar '97 / Grapevine/PolyGram

WITHOUT THE FANFARE
There's a train that leaves tonight / State of heart / Night time / Crow on the cradle / Greatest dream / Water is wild / Ellis island / Strange thing / Without the fanfare / As I leave behind Neidin / Diamond days / Going gone
CD ____ **GRACD 003**
Grapevine / Jan '95 / Grapevine/PolyGram

Black Nasty

TALKING TO THE PEOPLE
Talking to the people / I must be in love / Nasty soul / Getting funky round here / Black nasty boogie / We're doin' our thing / I have no choice / It's not the world / Rushin' sea / Booger the hooker
CD ____ **CDSXE 091**
Stax / Nov '93 / Pinnacle

Black, Neal

BLACK POWER (Black, Neal & The Healers)
CD ____ **DFGCD 8435**
Dixie Frog / Jun '96 / Direct / TKO Magnum

Black Oak Arkansas

AIN'T LIFE GRAND
Taxman / Fancy Nancy / Keep on / Good stuff / Rebel / Back door man / Love can be found / Diggin' for gold / Crying shame / Let life be good to you
CD ____ **RSACD 830**
Sequel / Jun '95 / BMG

EARLY TIMES
Someone something / When I'm gone / Let us pray / Sly fox / Mean woman / No one and the sun / Theatre / Collective thinking / Older than grandpa
CD ____ **CDSXE 067**
Stax / Nov '92 / Pinnacle

HIGH ON THE HOG
Swimmin' in quicksand / Back to the band / Movin' / Happy hooker / Red hot lovin' / Jim Dandy / Moonshine sonata / Why shouldn't I smile / High 'n' dry / Madman
CD ____ **RSACD 832**
Sequel / Jun '95 / BMG

HOT & NASTY
Mean woman (if you ever blues) / Uncle Lijah / Hot and nasty / Lord have mercy on my soul / When electricity came to Arkansas / Keep the faith / Fever in my mind / Hot rod / Gravel roads / Mutants of the monster / Jim Dandy / Happy hooker / Son of a gunn / Dixie / Everybody wants to see heaven / Diggin' for gold / Taxman / So you want to be a rock 'n' roll star
CD ____ **8122711462**
WEA / Mar '93 / Warner Music

IF AN ANGEL CAME
Gravel roads / Fertile woman / Spring vacation / We help each other / Full moon ride / Our mind's eye / To make us what we are / Our eyes are on you / Mutants of the monster
CD ____ **RSACD 831**
Sequel / Jun '95 / BMG

KEEP THE FAITH
Keep the faith / Revolutionary all American boys / Feet on earth, head in sky / Fever in my mind / Big one's still coming / White headed woman / We live on day to day / Short life line / Don't confuse what you don't know
CD ____ **RSACD 828**
Sequel / Jun '95 / BMG

STREET PARTY
Dancing in the street / Sting me / Good good woman / Jailbait / Sure been working hard / Son of a gun / Brink of creation / I'm a man / Goin' home / Dixie / Everybody wants to see heaven / Hey y'all
CD ____ **RSACD 829**
Sequel / Jun '95 / BMG

Black Ocean Drowning

BLACK OCEAN DROWNING
CD ____ **EFA 08439CD**
Dossier / Oct '92 / Cargo / SRD

Black, Paul

KING DOLLAR (Black, Paul & The Flip Kings)
Moo goo / Malted milk / Last time / Murder my baby / (Makes her way) The hard way / G-baby / Factory girl / Cross eyed baby / Honeymoon blues / Fixer / Dead shrimp blues / Paulie's little nightmare
CD ____ **70010870092**
House Of Blues / Jun '96 / ADA / BMG

Black Rock Coalition

HISTORY OF OUR FUTURE
Son talkin' (intro) / HOPE / Make it my world / Bluestime in America / Tough times / M.L.K...check / It will all / Think twice / Didn't live long / Hustler man / Son talkin' / Dadahdoodahda / Royal pain / Good guys / Michael Hill's Bluesband / Jupiter / Blue print / JJ Jumpers / Blackasaurus mex / PBR Streetgang / Shock counsel
CD ____ **RCD 20211**
Rykodisc / Sep '91 / ADA / Vital

Black Roots

DUB FACTOR VOL.2 (The Dub Judah Mixes)
Take heed / Not into war / Just look back / People dub / Moving dub / Jah Jah dub / Mash them dub / Dub the youth / Warning from Jah / Now is the time / Chant it dub / Show them dub / Take heed 2 (Outro mix)
CD ____ **NRCD 010**
Nubian / Jul '94 / Jet Star / Vital

DUB FACTOR: THE MAD PROFESSOR MIXES (Black Roots & Mad Professor)
CD ____ **NRCD 007**
Nubian / Nov '91 / Jet Star / Vital

Black Rose

ROOM INSIDE
CD ____ **CONTECD 168**
Contempo / Oct '91 / Plastic Head

Black, Roy

GRAFIN MARIZA/DIE BLUME VON HAWAII
Zardas / Schwesterlein / Komm mit nach varasdin / Komm czigan / Wo wohnt die liebe / Ich mochte traumen / Gruss mir mein Wien / Braunes madel von der pussta / Sag ja mein lieb / Juliska Rosika / Eh ein kurzer mond / Einmal mocht ich wieder tanzen / Ein paradies am meeresstrand / My little boy / Blum von Hawaii / Wir singen zur jazzband / Will dir die welt zu fussen legen / Ich muss madel seh'n / My golden baby / Kann nicht kussen ohne liebe / Heute' hab' ich ein schwipserl / Ich hab' ein diwnapuppchen / Traumschone perle de Sudsee / Bin nur ein Jonny
CD ____ **BCD 15829**
Bear Family / Jan '97 / Direct / Rollercoaster / Swift

Black Sabbath

BLACK SABBATH
Black Sabbath / Wizard / Behind the wall of sleep / NIB / Evil woman / Sleeping village / Warning
CD ____ **ESMCD 301**
Essential / Feb '96 / BMG

BLACK SABBATH VOL.4
Wheels of confusion / Tomorrow's dream / Changes / FX / Supernaut / Snowblind / Cornucopia / Laguna sunrise / St. Vitus dance / Under the sun
CD ____ **ESMCD 304**
Essential / Feb '96 / BMG

BORN AGAIN
Trashed / Stonehenge / Disturbing the priest / Park / Hot line / Zero the hero / Digital bitch / Born again / Keep it warm
CD ____ **ESMCD 334**
Essential / Apr '96 / BMG

COLLECTION, THE
Paranoid / Behind the wall of sleep / Sleeping village / Warning / War pigs / Hand of doom / Planet caravan / Electric funeral / Rat salad / Iron man / After forever / Supernaut / St. Vitus dance / Wheels of confusion / Snowblind / Killing yourself to live / Sabbra cadabra / Writ
CD ____ **CCSCD 109**
Castle / Nov '85 / BMG

CROSS PURPOSES
I witness / Cross of thorns / Psychophobia / Virtual death / Immaculate deception / Dying for love / Back to Eden / Hand that rocks the cradle / Cardinal sin / Evil eye
CD ____ **EIRSCD 1067**
IRS/EMI / Jan '94 / EMI

ETERNAL IDOL, THE
Shining / Ancient warrior / Hard life to love / Glory ride / Born to lose / Scarlet Pimpernel / Lost forever / Eternal idol
CD ____ **ESMCD 336**
Essential / Apr '96 / BMG

HEADLESS CROSS/TYR/DEHUMANIZER (3CD Set)
Gates of hell / Headless cross / Devil & daughter / When death calls / Kill in the spirit world / Call of the world / Black moon / Rightwing / Anno mundi / Law maker / Jerusalem / Sabbath stones / Battle of Tyr / Odin's court / Valhalla / Feels good to me / Heaven in black / Computer God / After all / TV crimes / Letters from Earth / Master of insanity / Time machine / Sins of the father / Too late / I / Buried alive
CD Set ____ **CDOMB 014**
IRS/EMI / Oct '95 / EMI

HEAVEN AND HELL
Neon knights / Children of the sea / Lady evil / Heaven and hell / Wishing well / Die young / Walk away / Lonely is the word
CD ____ **RAWCD 104**
Raw Power / Apr '96 / Pinnacle

HEAVEN AND HELL
Neon knights / Children of the sea / Lady evil / Heaven and hell / Lonely is the word / Wishing well / Die young / Walk away
CD ____ **ESMCD 330**
Essential / Jan '96 / BMG

INTERVIEW, THE
CD ____ **CBAK 4071**
Baktabak / Feb '94 / Arabesque

IRON MAN
Sabbath bloody Sabbath / Wizard / Sweet leaf / Electric funeral / Into the void / Wheels of confusion / Paranoid / Iron man / Am I going insane (Radio) / Killing yourself to live / Snowblind / Hole in the sky / Laguna sunrise / War pigs
CD ____ **5507202**
Spectrum / Sep '94 / PolyGram

LIVE AT LAST
Tomorrow's dream / Sweet leaf / Killing yourself to live / Cornucopia / War pigs / Laguna sunrise / Paranoid / Wicked world
CD ____ **ESMCD 331**
Essential / Aug '96 / BMG

LIVE EVIL
E 5150 / Neon knights / NIB / Children of the sea / Voodoo / Black Sabbath / War pigs / Iron man / Mob rules / Heaven and hell / Sign of the Southern cross / Paranoid / Children of the grave / Fluff
CD ____ **ESMCD 333**
Essential / Apr '96 / BMG

MASTER OF REALITY
Sweet leaf / After forever / Embryo / Children of the grave / Lord of this world / Solitude / Into the void / Orchid
CD ____ **ESMCD 303**
Essential / Feb '96 / BMG

MASTERS OF MISERY (A Black Sabbath Tribute) (Various Artists)
Shock wave: *Cathedral* / Snowblind: *Sleep* / Zero the hero: *Godflesh* / Hole in the sky: *Confessor* / Changes: *Fudge Tunnel* / Who are you: *Old* / Lord of this world: *Brutal Truth* / NIB: *Pitch Shifter* / Wizard: *Scorn* / Sweet leaf: *Cadaver* / Solitude: *Cathedral*
CD ____ **TFCK 88607**
Toys Factory / Jan '95 / Greyhound / Plastic Head

MOB RULES
Turn up the night / Voodoo / Sign of the Southern Cross / E5150 / Mob rules / Country girl / Slippin' away / Falling off the edge of the world / Over and over
CD ____ **ESMCD 332**
Essential / Jan '96 / BMG

NATIVITY IN BLACK (A Tribute To Black Sabbath) (Various Artists)
After forever: *Biohazard* / Children of the grave: *White Zombie* / Paranoid: *Megadeth* / Supernaut: *1000 Homo DJ's* / Iron man: *Osbourne, Ozzy* / Lord of this world: *Corrosion Of Conformity* / Solitude: *Cathedral* / Symptom of the universe: *Sepultura* / Wizard: *Bullring Brummies* / Sabbath bloody Sabbath: *Dickinson, Bruce* / NIB: *Ugly Kid Joe* / War pigs: *Faith No More* / Black Sabbath: *Type O Negative*
CD ____ **4776712**
Sony Music / Oct '94 / Sony

NEVER SAY DIE
Never say die / Johnny Blade / Junior's eyes / Hard road / Shock wave / Air dance / Over to you / Breakout / Swinging the chain
CD ____ **ESMCD 329**
Essential / Jan '96 / BMG

PARANOID
War pigs / Planet caravan / Iron man / Electric funeral / Hand of doom / Rat salad / Fairies wear boots / Wicked world / Paranoid
CD ____ **ESMCD 302**
Essential / Feb '96 / BMG

SABBATH BLOODY SABBATH
Sabbath bloody Sabbath / National acrobat / Fluff / Sabbra cadabra / Killing yourself to live / Who are you / Looking for today / Spiral architect
CD ____ **ESMCD 305**
Essential / Feb '96 / BMG

SABBATH STONES, THE (The IRS Years)
Headless cross / When death calls / Devil and daughter / Sabbath stones / Battle of Tyr / Odin's court / Valhalla / TV crimes / Virtual death / Evil eyes / Kiss of death / Guilty as hell / Loser gets it all / Disturbing the priest / Heart like a wheel / Shining
CD ____ **EIRSCD 1076**
IRS/EMI / Apr '96 / EMI

SABOTAGE
Hole in the sky / Don't start (too late) / Symptom of the universe / Megalomania / Thrill of it all / Supertzar / Am I going insane (Radio) / Writ
CD ____ **ESMCD 306**
Essential / Feb '96 / BMG

SEVENTH STAR
In for the kill / No stranger to love / Turn to stone / Sphinx (The guardian) / Seventh star / Danger zone / Heart like a wheel / Angry heart / In memory
CD ____ **ESMCD 335**
Essential / Apr '96 / BMG

TECHNICAL ECSTASY
All moving parts (stand still) / Backstreet kids / Dirty women / Gypsy / It's alright / Rock 'n' roll doctor / She's gone / You won't change me
CD ____ **ESMCD 328**
Essential / Jan '96 / BMG

UNDER THE WHEELS OF CONFUSION (Black Sabbath 1970-1987/4CD Set)
Black Sabbath / Wizard / Nib / Evil woman / Wicked world / War pigs / Paranoid / Iron man / Planet caravan / Hand of doom / Sweet leaf / After forever / Children of the grave / Into the void / Lord of this world / Orchid / Supernaut / Tomorrow's dream / Wheels of confusion / Am I going insane / Changes / Snowblind / Laguna surprise / Cornucopia / Sabbath bloody Sabbath / Kill yourself to live / Hole in the sky / Writ / Symptom of the universe / Dirty woman / Backstreet kids / Rock 'n' roll doctor / She's gone / Hard road / Never say die / Neon knights / Heaven and hell / Die young / Lonely is the word / Digital bitch / Trashed / Hotline / Mob rules / Voodoo / Turn up the night / Sign of the cross / Falling off the edge of the world / In for the kill / Seventh star / Heart like a wheel / Shining / Eternal idol
CD Set ESFCD 419
Essential / Nov '96 / BMG

Black Science Orchestra

WALTER'S ROOM
CD JBOCD 5
Junior Boys Own / May '97 / Mo's Music Machine / RTM/Disc

Black Scorpio

BLACK SCORPIO ALL STARS (Various Artists)
CD 794522
Melodie / Dec '95 / ADA / Discovery / Grapevine/PolyGram / Greensleeves / Jet Star

Black Sheep

WOLF IN SHEEPS CLOTHING, A
Intro / U mean I'm not / Butt in the meantime / Have UNE pull / Strobelite honey / Are U mad / Choice is yours / To whom it may concern / Similak child / Try counting sheep / Flavor of the month / La menage / LASM / Gimme the finga / Hoes we knows / Go to hail / Black with NV / Pass the 40 / Blunted / For Doz that slept
CD 8483682
Mercury / Oct '91 / PolyGram

Black Slate

AMIGO (The Best Of Black Slate)
Amigo / Boom boom / Sticks man '80 / Freedom time (black star liner) / Rocker's palace / Live a life / Losing game / Mind your motion / Thin line between love and hate / Sirens in the city / Legalise collie herb / Reggae everytime / Reggae music / Amigo
CD CDRRS 036
Jayrem / Oct '96 / CM / Jet Star

GET UP AND DANCE
CD EXRCD 002
Elixir / Nov '95 / Jet Star

Black Sorrows

BETTER TIMES
CD TIMBCD 601
Timbuktu / Aug '93 / Pinnacle

LUCKY CHARM
CD TIMBCD 603
Timbuktu / Mar '95 / Pinnacle

Black Star

TRIBUTE TO HAILE SELASSIE 1, A (King Of Kings)
CD Set RASTA 3
Jungle / Jul '95 / RTM/Disc / SRD

Black Star Liner

YEMEN CUTTA CONNECTION
Duggie dhol / Killah connection / Ottoman Empire strikes back / Hooba hooba / Inverse / Harmon session special / None stop to the border / Soft sitar / Ga ga
CD EXPCD 006
EXP / Aug '96 / 3mv/Pinnacle / RTM/Disc

Black State Choir

PACHAKUTI
CD PDCD PPP119
Head / May '95 / Total/BMG

PERMACULTURE
CD PPP 116
PDCD / Apr '94 / Plastic Head

Black, Stanley

TOUCH OF LATIN, A (18 Lush & Lovely Latin American Favourites) (Black, Stanley & His Orchestra)
Granada / La macarenas / Carmen fantasy / Cancion del mar / Mexican hat dance / Siboney / Estrelita / Tropical / Cherry pink and apple blossom white / Malaguena / Cavaquinho / Solamente una vez / La bamba / Samba de orfeo / Valencia / Ay ay ay / Nostalgia / Breeze and I
CD 306222
Hallmark / Jan '97 / Carlton

Black Sun Ensemble

LAMBENT FLAME
CD CDRECK 11
Reckless / Oct '89 / RTM/Disc

Black Swan Network

LATE MUSIC VOL.1, THE
CD CAM 003CD
Camera Obscura / Jul '97 / Cargo

Black Syndrome

ZARATHUSTRA
CD MIN 05CD
Minority/One / Jul '96 / Pinnacle

Black Tape For A Blue Girl

TEARDROP
CD HY 39100262
Hyperium / Nov '92 / Cargo / Plastic Head

Black Train Jack

YOU'RE NOT ALONE
Handouts / Not alone / Joker / What's the deal / Struggle / Alright then / Lottery / Regrets / Back up / Reason / Mr. Walsh blues / That reminds me
CD RR 90172
Roadrunner / Sep '96 / PolyGram

Black Uhuru

ANTHEM
What is life / Party next door / Try it / Black Uhuru anthem / Botanical roots / Somebody's watching you / Bull in the pen / Elements
CD RRCD 41
Reggae Refreshers / Jul '92 / PolyGram / Vital

BLACK SOUNDS OF FREEDOM
I love King Selassie / Satan Army Band / Time to unite / Natural mystic / Edan out deh / Love crisis / African love / Hard ground / Willow tree / Sorry for the man
CD GRELCD 23
Greensleeves / Feb '97 / Jet Star / SRD

BLACK UHURU
Shine eye girl / Leaving to Zion / General penitentiary / Guess who's coming to dinner / Abortion / Natural reggae beat / Plastic smile
CD CDVX 1004
Virgin / Jun '89 / EMI

BRUTAL
Let us pray / Dread in the mountain / Brutal / City vibes / Great train robbery / Uptown girl / Vision / Reggae with you / Conviction or fine / Fit you haffe fit
CD RASCD 3015
Ras / Jun '95 / Direct / Greensleeves / Jet Star / SRD

BRUTAL DUB
Let us dub / Dub in the mountain / Brutalize me with dub / City dub / Dub you haffe dub / Robbery dub / Uptown dub / Visions of dub / Dub it with you / Conviction or a dub
CD RASCD 3020
Ras / Nov '92 / Direct / Greensleeves / Jet Star / SRD

CHILL OUT
Chill out / Darkness / Eye market / Right stuff / Mondays / Fleety foot / Wicked act / Moya (Queen of I jungle) / Emotional slaughter
CD RRCD 43
Reggae Refreshers / Jun '88 / PolyGram / Vital

DUB FACTOR, THE
Ion storm / Youth / Big spliff / Boof n baff b biff / Puffed out / Android rebellion / Apocalypse back breaker / Sodom / Slaughter
CD RRCD 28
Reggae Refreshers / Sep '91 / PolyGram / Vital

GUESS WHO'S COMING TO DINNER
CD HBCD 18
Heartbeat / Apr '88 / ADA / Direct / Greensleeves / Jet Star

IRON STORM
CD R 279035
Mesa / Mar '94 / Total/BMG

LIBERATION: THE ISLAND ANTHOLOGY
Chill out / Party next door / Black Uhuru anthem / Guess who's coming to dinner / Shine eye gal (live) / Sponji reggae / Wicked act / Botanical roots / Somebody's watching you / Utterance / Slaughter / I love King Selassie / Darkness-dubness / Elements / What is life / Youth of Eglington / Youth right stuff / World is Africa / Happiness (live) / Mondays-killer / Tuesday / Solidarity / Ion storm / Try it / Bull in the pen / Sinsemilla / Puff she puff / Party in session
CD Set CRNCD 1
Mango / Feb '94 / PolyGram / Vital

LIVE
CD SONCD 0080
Sonic Sounds / Nov '95 / Jet Star

LIVE IN NEW YORK
CD RBUCD 88000
Rohit / Aug '88 / Jet Star

POSITIVE DUB
Cowboy town / Firecity / Positive / My concept / Space within my heart / Dry weather house / Pain / Create
CD RE 159CD
ROIR / Nov '94 / Plastic Head / Shellshock/ Disc

RAS PORTRAITS
Brutal / Fire city / Great train robbery / Dub in the mountain / Positive / Fit you haffe fit / Cowboy town / Dread in the mountain / Robbery dub / Space within your heart / Dub it with you / Painfully dub
CD RAS 3312
Ras / Jul '97 / Direct / Greensleeves / Jet Star / SRD

RED
Youth of Eglington / Sponji reggae / Sistren / Journey / Utterance / Puff she puff / Rock stone / Carbine
CD RRCD 18
Reggae Refreshers / Nov '90 / PolyGram / Vital

REGGAE GREATS
Happiness / World is Africa / Sponji reggae / Youth of Eglington / Darkness / What is life / Bull in the pen / Elements / Push push / Right stuff
CD 5525822
Spectrum / Jul '97 / PolyGram

SINSEMILLA
Happiness / World is Africa / Push push / There is fire / No loafing / Sinsemilla / Every dreadlocks / Vampire
CD RRCD 12
Reggae Refreshers / Sep '90 / PolyGram / Vital

Black Umfolosi

FESTIVAL - UMDLALO
Bazali bethu jazz song / Phetsheya kwezilwandle over the seas / Ingoma yakwethu catch our song / Inobembela njiba / Emthimbeni wedding / When shall wars / Sawelu umfula ushangane / Salu 'randela / Gumboot dance / Helele mama Afrika / Side of the city / Take me home
CD WCD 037
World Circuit / Sep '93 / ADA / Cadillac / Direct / New Note/Pinnacle

UNITY
CD WCD 020
World Circuit / Oct '91 / ADA / Cadillac / Direct / New Note/Pinnacle

Black Voices

SPACE TO BREATHE
CD T&M 005
Tradition & Moderne / Dec '95 / ADA / Direct

WOMEN IN (E)MOTION FESTIVAL
CD T&M 103
Tradition & Moderne / Nov '94 / ADA / Direct

Black Watch Band

PIPES AND DRUMS 1ST BATTALION (The Black Watch)
CD CC 293
EMI / May '93 / EMI

SCOTCH ON THE ROCKS
Scotch on the rocks / Sands of time / Hundred pipers / Caller herrin' / Ye banks and braes / Will ye no' come back again / Song on the wind / Charlie is my darling / Afton water / Robin Adair / Skye boat song / Dream of peace / Papa's got a brand new bagpipe
CD SUMCD 4055
Summit / Nov '96 / Sound & Media

Black Widow

SACRIFICE
In ancient days / Way to power / Come to the Sabbat / Conjuration / Seduction / Attack of the demon / Sacrifice
CD CLACD 262
Castle / '91 / BMG

Blackalicious

MELODICA
Swan lake / Lyric fathom / Attica black / Forty ounce / Rhymes for the deaf / Deep in the jungle
CD MWSSCD 001
Mo Wax / Apr '96 / PolyGram / Vital

Blackbyrds

ACTION/BETTER DAYS
Supernatural feeling / Lookin' ahead / Mysterious vibes / Something special / Street games / Soft and easy / Dreaming about you / Dancin' dancin' / Loneliness for your love / Better days / Do it girl / Without your love / Do you wanna dance / Love don't strike twice / What's on your mind / Don't know what to say / What we have is right
CD CDBGPD 090
Beat Goes Public / Nov '94 / Pinnacle

BEST OF THE BLACKBYRDS, THE
Blackbyrds' theme / Rock creek park / Time is movin' / Don't know what to say / Love don't strike twice / Supernatural feeling / Soft and easy / Do it fluid / Walking in rhythm / Happy music / Something special / Baby / Gut level / Dreaming about you / Mysterious vibes
CD CDBGP 918
Beat Goes Public / Jun '88 / Pinnacle

BLACKBYRDS/FLYING START
Do it fluid / Gut level / Reggins / Runaway / Funkie junkie / Summer love / Life styles / Hot day today / I need you / Baby / Love is love / Blackbyrds' theme / Walking in rhythm / Future children, future hopes / April showers / Spaced out
CD CDBGPD 86
Beat Goes Public / Jul '94 / Pinnacle

CITY LIFE/UNFINISHED BUSINESS
Rock creek park / Thankful 'bout yourself / City life / All I ask / Happy music / Love so fine / Flying high / Hash and eggs / Time is movin' / In life / Enter in / You've got that somwthing / Party land / Lady / Unfinished business
CD CDBGPD 089
Beat Goes Public / Sep '94 / Pinnacle

Blackeyed Biddy

HIGH SPIRITS
CD DUNCD 014
Dunkeld / Jun '88 / ADA / CM / Direct

PEACE, ENJOYMENT & PLEASURE
CD CDTRAX 056
Greentrax / May '93 / ADA / Direct / Duncans / Highlander

Blackfoot

AFTER THE REIGN
CD CDVEST 15
Bulletproof / Jun '94 / Pinnacle

MEDICINE MAN
Doin' my job / Stealer / Sleazy world / Not gonna cry any more / Runnin' runnin' / Chilled to d'bone / Guitar slingers song and dance
CD CDMFN 106
Music For Nations / Oct '90 / Pinnacle

Blackfoot Sue

BEST OF BLACKFOOT SUE, THE
CD CSAPCD 123
Connoisseur Collection / Jul '96 / Pinnacle

Blackgirl

TREAT U RIGHT
Krazy / Treat U right / Can U feel it / Where did we go wrong / Chains / Ooh yeh (Smooth) / 90's Girl / Nubian prince / Things we used to do / Can't live without U / Let's do it again / Home
CD 07863663592
Arista / Jul '94 / BMG

Blackhawk

BLACKHAWK
CD 07822187082
Arista / Sep '94 / BMG

LOVE AND GRAVITY
CD 7822188372
Arista / Aug '97 / BMG

STRONG ENOUGH
Big guitar / Like there ain't no yesterday / Cast iron heart / I'm not strong enough to say no / Almost a memory now / King of the world / Bad love gone good / Any man with a heartbeat / Kiss is worth a thousand words / Hook, line and sinker
CD 07822187922
Arista / Sep '95 / BMG

Blackhouse

5 MINUTES AFTER I DIE
CD BHCD 5
Nuclear Blast / Aug '93 / Plastic Head

HOPE LIKE A CANDLE
CD DV 12
Nuclear Blast / Aug '93 / Plastic Head

PRO LIFE
CD MHCD 006
Massacre / Nov '93 / Plastic Head

SHOCK THIS NATION
CD DISC 028
Discordia / Oct '96 / Cargo

Blackmadrid

ATLANTIC CROSSING: THE PEOPLE'S JOURNEY
CD NAR 056CD
New Alliance / May '93 / Plastic Head

Blackman, Cindy

ARCANE
CD MCD 5341
Muse / Sep '92 / New Note/Pinnacle

TRIO (Blackman, Cindy/Santi Debriano/ Dave Fiuczynski)
CD ______ FRLCD 015
Freelance / Oct '92 / Cadillac / Koch

Blackmore, Ritchie

ROCK PROFILE VOL.1 (Various Artists)
Return of the outlaws: *Outlaws* / Texan spiritual: *Outlaws* / If you gotta pick a baby: *Collins, Glenda* / Big fat spider: *Heinz* / Doo dah day: *Outlaws* / Thou shalt not steal: *Collins, Glenda* / I'm not a bad guy: *Heinz* / Ritchie Blackmore interview: *Blackmore, Ritchie* / Been invited to a party: *Collins, Glenda* / Shake with me: *Outlaws* / Movin' in: *Heinz* / Keep a knockin': *Outlaws* / I shall be released: *Boz* / Playground: *Deep Purple* / Wring that neck: *Deep Purple* / Why didn't Rosemary: *Deep Purple* / Living wreck: *Deep Purple* / Guitar job: *Blackmore, Ritchie* / No, no, no: *Deep Purple* / Highway star: *Deep Purple* / A200: *Deep Purple* / Gypsy: *Deep Purple* / Hold on: *Deep Purple* / Show me the way to go home: *Blackmore, Ritchie*
CD ______ RPVSOPCD 143
Connoisseur Collection / Oct '89 / Pinnacle

ROCK PROFILE VOL.2 (Various Artists)
Getaway: *Blackmore, Ritchie* / Little brown jug: *Blackmore, Ritchie* / Honey hush: *Sutch, Screaming Lord* / Train kept a rollin': *Sutch, Screaming Lord* / Gemini suite: guitar movement: *Lord, Jon* / Bullfrog: *Green Bullfrog* / Good golly Miss Molly: *Sutch, Screaming Lord* / Great balls of fire: *Sutch, Screaming Lord* / Hurry to the city: *Pie, Randy & Family* / Still I'm sad: *Rainbow* / Man on the silver mountain: *Rainbow* / Lady of the lake: *Rainbow* / Sixteenth century greensleeves: *Rainbow* / I call, no answer: *Green, Jack* / Son of Alerik: *Deep Purple*
CD ______ RPVSOPCD 157
Connoisseur Collection / Apr '91 / Pinnacle

SESSION MAN
CD ______ RPM 120
RPM / Oct '93 / Pinnacle

Blacknote

NOTHIN' BUT THE SWING
Core / Mahonisms / Double indemnity / Saturday night / For someone so beautiful / An open letter (to Vanessa) / J'ai beaucoup de chance (I'm so lucky) / Getting your trane on / West coastings / Two souls coalesce / I saw her first / Allergic reaction / Early morning (before dawn)
CD ______ IMP 11772
Impulse Jazz / Jun '96 / New Note/BMG

Blacknuss

ALLSTARS
Dinah / Seventh heaven / Disco fantasy / Roll with me / Intimate friends / Doreen / Earmeal / Dreams / Last night ADJ saved my last / Blacknuss blues / Hell / Loungtangyaa
CD ______ 74321428762
RCA / Jun '97 / BMG

Blackout

BLACKOUT
CD ______ SHCD 6017
Sky High / Jul '95 / Direct / Jet Star

Blackstone Edge

GYPSY
CD ______ GRACD 001
Granite / Feb '96 / Pinnacle

Blackstones

OUTBURST
CD ______ CDSGP 0219
Prestige / Nov '95 / Else / Total/BMG

RIDIN' HIGH
CD ______ CDSGP 0274
Prestige / Sep '96 / Else / Total/BMG

SOMEBODY OUGHT TO WRITE ABOUT IT
CD ______ CDSGP 0334
Prestige / Mar '97 / Else / Total/BMG

Blackstreet

ANOTHER LEVEL
Black & Street intro / This is how we roll / No diggity: *Blackstreet & Dr. Dre* / Fix / Good lovin' / Let's stay in love / We gonna take you back/Don't leave me / Never gonna let you go / I wanna be your man / Taja's lude / My paradise / Deja's poem / (Money can't) Buy me love / Blackstreet on the radio / I can't get you (out of my mind) / I'll give it to you / Happy song (tonite) / Motherlude / Lord is real (time will reveal)
CD ______ IND 90071
Interscope / Oct '96 / BMG

BLACKSTREET
Intro (Blackstreet philosophy) / Baby be mine / U blow my mind / Hey love (keep it real) / I like the way you work / Good life / Physical thing / Make U wet / Booti call / Love's in need / Joy / Before I let you go / Confession (interlude) / Tonight's the night / Happy home / Wanna make love / Once in a lifetime / Givin' you all my lovin' / Falling in love again / Candlelight night
CD ______ IND 92351
Interscope / Aug '96 / BMG

Blackthorne

AFTERLIFE
Cradle of the grave / Afterlife / We won't be forgotten / Breaking the chains / Over and over / Hard feelings / Baby you're the blood / Sex crime / Love from the ashes / All night long
CD ______ CDMFN 148
Music For Nations / May '93 / Pinnacle

VERY BEST OF IRISH TRADITIONAL FOLK MUSIC, THE
CD ______ CDBALLAD 007
Outlet / Mar '97 / ADA / CM / Direct / Duncans / Koch / Ross

Blacktop

I GOT A BAAD FEELIN
CD ______ ITR 027CD
In The Red / Dec '96 / Cargo / Greyhound

Blacktop Rockets

WHAT'LL YA HAVE
CD ______ BR 001
Straight 8 / Apr '97 / Nervous

Blackwell

TRIBUTE TO BLACKWELL (Various Artists)
CD ______ 1201132
Black Saint / Nov '90 / Cadillac / Harmonia Mundi

Blackwell, Ed

WALLS-BRIDGES (Blackwell, Ed Trio)
CD ______ 1201532
Black Saint / Mar '97 / Cadillac / Harmonia Mundi

WHAT IT BE LIKE
Nebula / Grandma's shoes / Pentahouve / First love / Lito (Part 1,2,3,)
CD ______ ENJ 80542
Enja / Jul '94 / New Note/Pinnacle / Vital/ SAM

Blackwell, Otis

BRACE YOURSELF (A Tribute To Otis Blackwell) (Various Artists)
CD ______ SHCD 5705
Shanachie / Apr '94 / ADA / Greensleeves / Koch

OTIS BLACKWELL 1953-1955 (The Complete Joe Davis Sessions)
CD ______ FLYCD 26
Flyright / Feb '91 / Hot Shot / Jazz Music / Wellard

Blackwell, Scrapper

VIRTUOSO GUITAR
CD ______ YAZCD 1019
Yazoo / Apr '91 / ADA / CM / Koch

Blackwood Singers

GREATEST GOSPEL
I believe / Spirit of the living God / Glory glory clear the road / First day in heaven / House of God / This olde house / When the saints go marching in / Jonah / Amazing grace / I'll fly away / Yesterday / No further than your knees
CD ______ HADCD 171
Javelin / May '94 / Henry Hadaway / THE

Blad, Nikolai

NIKOLAI BLAD
CD ______ EICD 4
Eino / Mar '96 / ADA

Blade

PLANNED AND EXECUTED
CD ______ BLADE 1208CD
Move/691 Influential / Jan '96 / Plastic Head

Blade Fetish

ABSINTHE
CD ______ EFA 064802
Tess / Mar '94 / SRD

Blades, Ruben

AGUA DE LUNA
Isobel / No te Duermas / Blackaman / Ojos de Perro Azul / Claro Oscuro / Laura Farina / La cita / Agua de luna
CD ______ 15964
Messidor / Sep '89 / ADA / Koch

ANTECEDENTE (Blades, Ruben Y Son Del Solar)
Juana mayo / 'Tas caliente / La marea / Contrabando / Patria / Noches del ayer / Nuestro adios / Nacer de ti / Plaza herrera
CD ______ 15993
Messidor / Aug '89 / ADA / Koch

ESCENAS
Cuentas del alma / Tierra dura / La cancion del final del mundo / La sorpresa / Caina / Silencois / Muevete
CD ______ 1115939
Messidor / Jan '87 / ADA / Koch

POETA LATINA
Mucho major / Anor pa'que / Ya no te Puedo Querer / Siembra / El Corrido / Del Caballa / Blanco / Usted / Noe / Cabeza de Hacha / Si yo pudier a andar / Tu me acostumbraste / Ganas / La pasado no perdona / Te odio y te Quiero / Para ser rumbero
CD ______ CDHOT 503
Charly / Oct '93 / Koch

POETRY
Tiburon / Ganas / Plastico / Solo / Paula / Buscando guyaba / Juan Gonzalez / Dime / Siembra / Manuela / Pablo Pueblo / Sin tu carino
CD ______ CDCHARLY 261
Charly / Jan '91 / Koch

Blaenavon Male Voice Choir

NEW DAY, A
Sailor's chorus / You are the new day / Diolch i'r lor / Oh Isis and Osiris / There is nothing like a dame / Sometimes / A ca / Pan fo'r nos yn hir / George Jones / Myfanwy / Rhythm of life / Sanctus / Men of Harlech / Softly as I leave you / Migildi magildi / Tydi a roddaist / When the saints go marching in / Nidaros
CD ______ OS 222
OS Digital / Jul '96 / Conifer/BMG

Blaggers ITA

FUCK FASCISM
CD ______ KONCD 002
Knock Out / Mar '97 / Cargo

ON YER TOEZ (Blaggers)
On yer toez / Crazy / Bronco bullfrog / Nice one blaggers / Britain's dreams / Young blaggers / Weekend warriors / Save your hate / Jailhouse doors
CD ______ MBC 001
M-Butcher / Mar '97 / Cargo

UNITED COLOURS
CD ______ WOWCD 27
Words Of Warning / '94 / SRD / Total/ BMG

Blahzay Blahzay

BLAH BLAH BLAH
CD ______ 5329672
Mercury Black Vinyl / Sep '96 / PolyGram

Blaine, Terry

IN CONCERT (Blaine, Terry & Mark Shane Quintet)
CD ______ JJZ 9502
Jukebox / Nov '96 / Jazz Music

WHOSE HONEY ARE YOU
CD ______ JJZ 9201
Jukebox / Nov '96 / Jazz Music

Blair 1523

BEAUTIFUL DEBRIS
CD ______ VOXXCD 2060
Voxx / Mar '93 / Else / RTM/Disc

Blak Twang

DETTWORK SOUTH EAST
CD ______ ANTICDLP 3
Anti-Static / Jan '97 / Pinnacle / Vital

Blake Babies

INNOCENCE AND EXPERIENCE
Wipe it up / Rain / Boiled potato / Lament / Cesspool / You don't give up / Star / Sanctify / Out there / Girl in a box / I'm not your mother / Temptation eyes / Downtime / Over and over
CD ______ MR 0582
Mammoth / Oct '93 / Vital

NICELY, NICELY
Wipe it up / Her / Tom and Bob / Sweet burger LP / Bye / Let them eat chewy granola bars / Julius fast body / Bitter n you / Swill and the cocaine sluts
CD ______ MR 0862
Mammoth / Oct '94 / Vital

Blake, Eubie

MEMORIES OF YOU
Charleston rag / Chevy chase / Mirandy / Fizz water / Crazy blues / Memphis blues / Dangerous blues / Arkansas blues / Down home blues / Good fellow blues / Don't tell your monkey man / Boll weevil blues / If you don't want me blues / I'm just wild about Harry / Memories of you
CD ______ BCD 112
Biograph / Jul '91 / ADA / Cadillac / Direct / Hot Shot / Jazz Music / Wellard

Blake, Karl

MANDIBLES
CD ______ SHP 616131/01CD
Swordex Hieroglyph Proper / Oct '96 / World Serpent

PAPER THIN RELIGION
CD ______ USEO 13102CD
Pro-Evil Pro-Devil / Oct '96 / World Serpent

Blake, Kenny

INTERIOR DESIGN
Hey mister / Take five / What can I say / Irene / Little stars / Harlem nocturne / Alladin / Babylon sisters / Soulmates / Oasis
CD ______ 101S 71342
101 South / Jun '93 / New Note/Pinnacle

INTIMATE AFFAIR, AN
Intimate affair / Sunday serenade / European underground / Stand a little closer / ABC / Contemplation swing / Heartland to soulville / Every time I think of u / Constantinople strut / Shady side / Steeltown
CD ______ INAK 30372CD
In Akustik / Jul '97 / Direct / TKO Magnum

Blake, Michael

KINGDOM OF CHAMPA
Champa theme / Dislocated in Natran / Folksong / Purple city / Mekong / Hue is hue / Perfume river
CD ______ INT 31892
Intuition / Jun '97 / New Note/Pinnacle

Blake, Norman

BACK HOME IN SULPHUR SPRINGS
CD ______ ROUCD 0012
Rounder / Nov '95 / ADA / CM / Direct

BLAKE AND RICE (Blake, Norman & Tony Rice)
CD ______ ROUCD 0233
Rounder / Aug '88 / ADA / CM / Direct

BLIND DOG (Blake, Norman & Nancy)
CD ______ ROUCD 0254
Rounder / '90 / ADA / CM / Direct

FIELDS OF NOVEMBER/OLD & NEW
CD ______ FF 004CD
Flying Fish / May '93 / ADA / CM / Direct / Roots

HOBO'S LAST RIDE, THE (Blake, Norman & Nancy)
CD ______ SHCD 6020
Shanachie / Sep '96 / ADA / Greensleeves / Koch

JUST GIMME SOMETHIN' I'M USED TO (Blake, Norman & Nancy)
CD ______ SHCD 6001
Shanachie / Apr '92 / ADA / Greensleeves / Koch

NATASHA'S WALTZ (Blake, Norman & Nancy)
CD ______ ROUCD 11530
Rounder / '88 / ADA / CM / Direct

NORMAN & NANCY BLAKE COMPACT DISC
Hello stranger / New bicycle hornpipe / Marquis Huntley / Florida rag / Jordan am a hard road to travel / Belize / Elzic's farewell / Lighthouse on the shore / Grand junction / Butterfly weed / President Garfield's hornpipe / In Russia (we have parking lots too) / Wroxall / If I lose I don't care / Chrysanthemum / Lima road jig / Boston boy / Last night's joy / My love is like a red rose / Wildwood flower / Tennessee mountain fox chase
CD ______ ROUCD 11505
Rounder / '88 / ADA / CM / Direct

NORMAN BLAKE & TONY RICE VOL.2 (Blake, Norman & Tony Rice)
It's raining here this morning / Lost Indian / Georgie / Father's hall / Two soldiers / Blackberry blossom / Eight more miles to Louisville / Lincoln's funeral train (The sad journey to Springfield) / Molly Bloom / D-18 Song (Thank you, Mr. Martin) / Back in yonder's world / Bright days / Salt creek
CD ______ ROUCD 0266
Rounder / Jul '90 / ADA / CM / Direct

SLOW TRAIN THROUGH GEORGIA
CD ______ ROUCD 11526
Rounder / '88 / ADA / CM / Direct

WHILE PASSING ALONG THIS WAY (Blake, Norman & Nancy)
CD ______ SHAN 6012CD
Shanachie / Apr '95 / ADA / Greensleeves / Koch

WHISKEY BEFORE BREAKFAST
Hand me down my walking cane / Under the double eagle / Six white horses / Salt river / Old grey mare / Down at Mylow's house / Sleepy eyed Joe / Indian creek / Arkansas traveller / Girl I left in Sunny Tennessee / Mistrel boy to war has gone / Ash grove / Church Street blues / Macon rag / Fiddler's dream / Whiskey before breakfast / Slow train through Georgia
CD ______ ROUCD 0063
Rounder / Aug '93 / ADA / CM / Direct

Blake, Peter

PRIVATE DAWN
CD ______ WCL 110082
White Cloud / May '95 / Select

Blake, Ran

BREAKTHRU (Solo piano)
CD ______ 1238422
IAI / Mar '92 / Cadillac / Harmonia Mundi

DUKE DREAMS
CD ______ RN 1210272
Soul Note / Oct '94 / Cadillac / Harmonia Mundi / Wellard

EPISTROPHY
CD ______ 1211772
Soul Note / Sep '92 / Cadillac / Harmonia Mundi / Wellard

THAT CERTAIN FEELING
CD ______ ARTCD 6077
Hat Art / Jul '91 / Cadillac / Harmonia Mundi

UNMARKED VAN (A Tribute To Sarah Vaughan)
Sarah / My reverie / Sometimes I feel like a Motherless child / Tenderly / Make yourself comfortable / Tenderly / Solitary Sunday / My man's gone now / Old devil moon / Homage to Roy Haynes / Whatever Lola wants / Wallflower waltz / Tenderly / April / April / Call me / Moonlight on the Ganges / Girl from Ipanema / Stompin' at the Savoy / Little tear / Septembro / Unmarked man / Tenderly
CD ______ 1212272
Soul Note / May '97 / Cadillac / Harmonia Mundi / Wellard

Blake, Seamus

CALL, THE
CD ______ 1088CD
Criss Cross / Jan '95 / Cadillac / Direct / Vital/SAM

Blake, Tomcat

I'VE BEEN WONDERING
CD ______ DTCD 3037
Double Trouble / Jan '97 / CM / Hot Shot

Blakey, Art

1958: PARIS OLYMPIA (Blakey, Art & The Jazz Messengers)
Just by myself / I remember Clifford / Are you real / Moanin' / Justice / Blues march / Whisper not
CD ______ 8326592
Fontana / Feb '92 / PolyGram

ART BLAKEY & THE JAZZ MESSENGERS (Blakey, Art & The Jazz Messengers)
Alamode / Invitation / Circus / You don't know what love is / I hear a rhapsody / Gee baby ain't I good to you
CD ______ IMP 11752
Impulse Jazz / Feb '96 / New Note/BMG

ART BLAKEY IN CONCERT
CD Set ______ RTE 15022
RTE / Apr '95 / ADA / Koch

ART COLLECTION (The Best Of Art Blakey)
Fuller love / Oh, by the way / Webb City / Second thoughts / In walked Bud / Dark side, light side / Jody
CD ______ CCD 4495
Concord Jazz / Jan '92 / New Note/ Pinnacle

ART OF JAZZ, THE
CD ______ IOR 770282
In & Out / Mar '96 / Vital/SAM

BEST OF ART BLAKEY & THE JAZZ MESSENGERS, THE (Blakey, Art & The Jazz Messengers)
Moanin' / Blues march / Lester's left town / Night in Tunisia / Dat dere / Mosaic / Free for all
CD ______ CDP 7932052
Blue Note / Dec '95 / EMI

BEST OF ART BLAKEY, THE
Generique / No problem / Moanin' / I remember Clifford / Whisper not / Night in Tunisia / My romance / Blues march
CD ______ 8482452
EmArCy / Jun '91 / PolyGram

BIG BAND
CD ______ BET 6002
Bethlehem / Jan '95 / ADA / ZYX

BIG BEAT, THE (Blakey, Art & Max Roach/Elvin Jones/Philly Joe Jones)
Caravan / High priest / Theme / Conversation / Jody's cha-cha / Larry-Larue / Lady luck / Buzz-at / Pretty Brown / Six and four / Stablemates / Carioca ("El Tambores") / Battery blues / Gone gone gone / Tribal message
CD ______ MCD 47016 2
Milestone / Apr '94 / Cadillac / Complete/ Pinnacle / Jazz Music / Wellard

BLUES MARCH (Blakey, Art & The Jazz Messengers)
Blues march / Uranus / Whisper not / Backgammon / Georgia on my mind / Third world express / Nam fulay / I can't get started (with you)
CD ______ ATJCD 8009
All That's Jazz / Aug '94 / Jazz Music / THE

BLUES MARCH (Blakey, Art & The Jazz Messengers)
CD ______ JHR 73539
Jazz Hour / May '93 / Cadillac / Jazz Music / Target/BMG

DAY WITH ART BLAKEY VOL.1
Summit / Breeze and I / Blues march / Moanin' / It's only a paper moon
CD ______ PRCDSP 201
Prestige / Aug '93 / Else / Total/BMG

DRUM KINGS (Blakey, Art & Max Roach)
Transfiguration / Exhibit A / Scotch blues / Rhapsody in blue / Summertime / Someone to watch over me / Man I love / Flight to Jordan / That old devil called love again / Four x / Crackle hut / CM / Speculate / Audio blues
CD ______ 306292
Hallmark / Jan '97 / Carlton

DRUM SUITE
Sacrifice / Cubano chant / Oscarlypso / Nica's tempo / D's dilemma / Just for Marty
CD ______ 809882
Columbia / Mar '96 / Sony

HARD DRIVE, THE (Out Of This World...And The Next World Too) (Blakey, Art & The Jazz Messengers)
CD ______ BET 6001
Bethlehem / Jan '95 / ADA / ZYX

I GET A KICK OUT OF BU (Blakey, Art & The Jazz Messengers)
CD ______ 1211552
Soul Note / Nov '90 / Cadillac / Harmonia Mundi / Wellard

IN SWEDEN (Blakey, Art & The Jazz Messengers)
Webb City / How deep is the ocean / Skylark / Gypsy folk tales
CD ______ ECD 22044
Evidence / Mar '93 / ADA / Cadillac / Harmonia Mundi

JAZZ MESSENGERS (Blakey, Art & The Jazz Messengers)
Sacrifice / Cubano chant / Oscalypso / Nica's tempo / D's dilemma / Just for Marty
CD ______ 4809882
Sony Jazz / Dec '95 / Sony

JAZZ PROFILE
Wee dot / Moanin' / Along came Betty / Down under / Up jumped Spring / Jodi
CD ______ CDP 8548992
Blue Note / May '97 / EMI

KYOTO
CD ______ OJCCD 145
Original Jazz Classics / Feb '92 / Complete/Pinnacle / Jazz Music / Wellard

LAUSANNE 1960 VOL.1 (Blakey, Art & The Jazz Messengers)
Now's the time / Announcement / Lester left town / Noise in the attic / Dat dere / Kozo's waltz
CD ______ TCB 02022
TCB / Jul '95 / New Note/Pinnacle

LAUSANNE 1960 VOL.2 (Blakey, Art & The Jazz Messengers)
Announcement / It's only a paper moon / 'Round midnight / Summit / Night in Tunisia / This here
CD ______ TCB 02062
TCB / Jul '96 / New Note/Pinnacle

LIKE SOMEONE IN LOVE (Blakey, Art & The Jazz Messengers)
Like someone in love / Johnny's blue / Noise in the attic / Sleeping dancer sleep on / Giants / Sleeping dancer sleep on (alt. take)
CD ______ CDP 7842452
Blue Note / Feb '97 / EMI

LIVE AT BUBBA'S
Moanin' / My funny valentine / Soulful Mister Timmons / Au privave / Free for all
CD ______ CDGATE 7003
Kingdom Jazz / Oct '90 / Kingdom

LIVE AT RONNIE SCOTT'S
On the Ginza / Dr. Jekyll / Two of a kind / I want to talk about you
CD ______ CLACD 332
Castle / '93 / BMG

LIVE IN EUROPE 1959 (Blakey, Art & The Jazz Messengers)
CD ______ LS 2916
Landscape / Nov '92 / THE

LIVE IN STOCKHOLM 1959
CD ______ DRGCD 182
Dragon / Oct '88 / ADA / Cadillac / CM / Roots / Wellard

MELLOW BLUES (Blakey, Art & The Jazz Messengers)
CD ______ MCD 0322
Moon / Jan '92 / Cadillac / Harmonia Mundi

MOANIN' (Blakey, Art & The Jazz Messengers)
Moanin' / Moanin' / Are you real / Along came Betty / Drum thunder suite / Blues march / Come rain or come shine / Slide's delight / You don't know what love is / Blues for Eros / Blue moon / Theme song
CD ______ CDP 7465162
Blue Note / Mar '95 / EMI

MOANIN'
Slide's delight / You don't know what love is / Blues for Eros / Moanin' / Blue moon / Theme
CD ______ 17127
Laserlight / May '97 / Target/BMG

NIGHT IN TUNISIA, A (Blakey, Art & The Jazz Messengers)
Night in Tunisia / Moanin' / Blues march
CD ______ 8000642
Philips / Jul '88 / PolyGram

OH BY THE WAY (Blakey, Art & The Jazz Messengers)
Oh by the way / Duck soup / Tropical breeze / One by one / Sudan blue / My funny valentine / Alicia
CD ______ CDSJP 165
Timeless Jazz / Feb '92 / New Note/ Pinnacle

ONE FOR ALL (Blakey, Art & The Jazz Messengers)
Here we go / One for all (and all for one) / Theme for Penny / You've changed / Accidentally yours / Medley / Green is mean / I'll wait and pray / Logarhythms / Bunyip / Polka dots and moonbeams / Nica's tempo
CD ______ 3953292
A&M / Mar '94 / PolyGram

ORGY IN RHYTHM
Buhaina chant / Ya ya / Toffi / Split skins / Amuck / Elephant walk / Abdullah's delight
CD ______ CDP 8565862
Blue Note / Jun '97 / EMI

RUCERDO (Blakey, Art & The Jazz Messengers)
CD ______ CDSGP 0108
Prestige / May '96 / Else / Total/BMG

STRAIGHT AHEAD
Falling in love with love / My romance / Webb City / How deep is the ocean / ETA / Theme
CD ______ CCD 4168
Concord Jazz / Oct '90 / New Note/ Pinnacle

THEORY OF ART (Blakey, Art & The Jazz Messengers)
Night in Tunisia / Off the wall / Couldn't it be you / Theory of Art / Evans / Night at Tony's / Social call
CD ______ 09026687302
RCA Victor / Mar '97 / BMG

THIS IS JAZZ
Moanin / Nica's dream / Little Melonae / Hank's symphony / Nica's tempo / I remember Clifford
CD ______ CK 65044
Sony Jazz / May '97 / Sony

UGETSU
One by one / Ugetsu / Time off / Ping pong / I didn't know what time it was / On the ginza
CD ______ OJCCD 90
Original Jazz Classics / Feb '92 / Complete/ Pinnacle / Jazz Music / Wellard

Blakey, Rev. Johnny

1927-1929 (Blakey, Rev. Johnny & Rev. M.L. Gipson)
CD ______ DOCD 5363
Document / Jul '95 / ADA / Hot Shot / Jazz Music

Blame

LOGICAL PROGRESSION VOL.2 (Mixed/ Compiled By Blame - 2CD Set) (Various Artists)
Visions of Mars: *Blame* / Expressions: *Odyssey* / Seafarer: *Artemis* / Solitude: *Blame* / West side blues: *Intense* / Dreams: *Tayla* / Breeze: *Nookie* / Global access: *Blu Mar Ten* / Cuban Lynx: *Blame* / Close your eyes: *Chameleon* / Love and happiness: *PFM* / Positive notions: *Intense* / Universal music: *Seba* / In the area: *Ils & Solo* / Atlantis (I need you): *LTJ Bukem* / 360 Click: *Blame* / Complexities: *Source Direct* / Dark skies: *Intense*
CD Set ______ GLRCDX 002
CD Set ______ GLRCD 002
Good Looking / Apr '97 / Prime / Vital

Blanc Estoc

MISTUCK
CD ______ WB 1164CD
We Bite / Jun '97 / Plastic Head

Blanca, Peres

STRICTLY DANCING: RHUMBA (Blanca, Peres Band)
CD ______ 15338
Laserlight / Jun '92 / Target/BMG

Blanchard, Terence

HEART SPEAKS, THE
Aparecida / Antes que seja tarde / Meu pais (my country) / Valse Mineira / Heart speaks / Congada blues / Nocturna / Just for Nana / Orizimba and Rosicler / Choros das aguas / Love dance/Comecar de novo / Menino / Aparecida reprise
CD ______ 4836382
Sony Jazz / Mar '96 / Sony

NEW YORK SECOND LINE (Blanchard, Terence & Donald Harrison)
New York second line / Oliver Twist / I can't get started (with you) / Duck steps / Dr. Drums / Isn't it so / Subterfuge
CD ______ CCD 43002
Concord Jazz / '88 / New Note/Pinnacle

ROMANTIC DEFIANCE
Premise / Unconditional / Betrayal of my soul / Divine order / Romantic defiance / Focus / Romantic processional / Morning after / Celebration
CD ______ 4804892
Sony Jazz / Jun '95 / Sony

Blancmange

BEST OF BLANCMANGE, THE
CD ______ VSOPCD 226
Connoisseur Collection / Jun '96 / Pinnacle

MANGE TOUT
Don't tell me / Game above my head / Blind vision / Time became the tide / That's love that it is / Murder / See the train / All things are nice / My baby / Day before you came
CD ______ 5521082
Spectrum / Mar '96 / PolyGram

SECOND HELPINGS (Best Of Blancmange)
God's kitchen / I've seen the world / Feel me / Living on the ceiling / Waves / Game above my head / Blind vision / That's love that it is / Don't tell me / Day before you came / What's your problem
CD ______ 8280432
London / Jun '90 / PolyGram

THIRD COURSE, THE
Feel me / I've seen the world / God's kitchen / I can't explain / Waves / Lose your love / No wonder they never made it back / Day before you came / All things are nice / Running thin / Game above my head / Wasted / Get out of that / Lorraine's my nurse
CD ______ 5501942
Spectrum / Mar '94 / PolyGram

Bland, Bobby

BLUES IN THE NIGHT
Blue moon / If I hadn't called you back / Ask me 'bout nothin' (but the blues) / Jelly jelly / When you put me down / Blind man / Chains of love / Fever / Blues in the night / Loneliness hurts / Feeling is gone / I'm too far gone (to turn around) / Black night / Share your love with me
CD ______ CD 14531
Jazz Portraits / Jan '94 / Jazz Music

CALIFORNIA ALBUM
This time I'm gone for good / Up and down world / It's not the spotlight / (If loving you is wrong) I don't want to be right / Going down slow / Right place at the right time / Help me through the day / Where baby went / Friday the 13th child / I've got to use my imagination
CD ______ BGOCD 64
Beat Goes On / Jan '89 / Pinnacle

DREAMER
Ain't no love in the heart of the city / I wouldn't treat a dog (the way you treated me) / Lovin' on borrowed time / End of the road / I ain't gonna be the first to cry / Dreamer / Yolanda / Twenty four hour blues / Cold day in hell / Who's foolin' who
CD ______ BGOCD 63
Beat Goes On / Oct '89 / Pinnacle

LIVE AT LONG BEACH
CD ______ CDBL 750
Charly / Nov '94 / Koch

MASTER OF THE BLUES
CD ______ NTRCD 025
Nectar / Jun '94 / Pinnacle

TOGETHER AGAIN - LIVE (Bland, Bobby & B.B. King)
Let the good times roll / Strange things happen / Feel so bad / Mother in law blues / Mean ol' world / Everyday I have the blues / Thrill is gone / I ain't gonna be the first to cry
CD ______ BGOCD 162
Beat Goes On / Feb '93 / Pinnacle

TWO STEPS FROM THE BLUES
Cry cry cry / Two steps from the blues / I pity the fool / I'll take care of you / I'm not ashamed / Don't cry no more / Lead me on / I've just got to forget you / Little boy blue / St. James infirmary
CD ______ BGOCD 163
Beat Goes On / Feb '93 / Pinnacle

VOICE, THE (Duke Recordings 1959-1969)
Who will the next fool be / I pity the fool / Don't cry no more / Ain't that lovin' you / I'm not ashamed / Cry cry cry / I'll take care of you / Call on me / Blue moon / Turn on your love light / Stormy Monday blues / Two steps from the blues / Ain't nothin' you can do / Ain't doing too bad Part 1 / Sometimes you gotta cry a little / Ain't no tellin' / Yield not to temptation / I'm too far gone (to turn around) / These hands / Good time Charlie Part 1 / Ask me 'bout nothin' (but the blues) / Share your love with me / That did it / Shoes / Back in the same old bag again / Chains of love
CD ______ CHCD 323
Ace / Nov '93 / Pinnacle

Blanks 77

KILLER BLANKS
CD ______ 700122
Radical / Mar '97 / Cargo

TANKED AND POGOED
CD ______ RAD 700152
Radical / Jul '97 / Cargo

Blanston, Gern

GERN BLANSTON
CD ______ CSR 014CD
Cavity Search / Oct '95 / Plastic Head

Blarney Lads

SEVEN DRUNKEN NIGHTS
Bold O'Donaghue / Paddle me own canoe / Molly Malone / Doherty's reel / Paddy Ryan's dream / McGinnelly's reel / Ferryman / Cod liver oil / Coolies / Home boys home / Father O'Flynn / Irish washerwoman / Blackberry blossom / Lannigan's ball / All for me grog / Wild rover / Galway races / An dearig dun / Welcoming / Mursheen durkin / Paddy Cathy's reel / Dinny's fancy / Spanish lady / Maid behind the bar / Gravel walk / Holy ground / Finnegan's wake / Irish Rover / Rakes of mallow / Seven drunken nights
CD ______ CD 6023
Music / Jun '96 / Target/BMG

Blasnost

BLASNOST
CD ______ BEST 1023CD
Acoustic Music / Nov '93 / ADA

Blast

POWER OF EXPRESSION, THE
CD ______ SST 148CD
SST / May '93 / Plastic Head

TAKE THE MANIC RIDE
CD ______ SST 225CD
SST / May '93 / Plastic Head

Blast Off Country Style

C'MON AND ...
CD ______ TEENBEAT 131CD
Teenbeat / Mar '94 / Cargo / SRD / Vital

Blastula

BLASTULA
CD ______ ALP 40CD
Atavistic / Mar '97 / Cargo / SRD

Blatz

SHIT SPLIT (2CD Set) (Blatz/Filth)
CD Set ______ LOOKOUT 43CD
Lookout / May '97 / Cargo / Greyhound / Shellshock/Disc

Blaze

BASIC BLAZE
CD ______ SLIPCD 61
Slip 'n' Slide / Jul '97 / Amato Disco / Prime / RTM/Disc / Vital

Blazers

EAST SIDE SOUL
CD ______ ROUCD 9053
Rounder / Jul '95 / ADA / CM / Direct

GOING UP THE COUNTRY
CD ______ CRCDM 3
CRS / Jun '96 / ADA / Direct / Jet Star

JUST FOR YOU
CD ______ ROUCD 9063
Rounder / Aug '97 / ADA / CM / Direct

SHORT FUSE
CD ______ ROUCD 9043
Rounder / Apr '94 / ADA / CM / Direct

Blazing Rains

BLAZING RAINS
CD ______ SF 002CD
Sugar Free / Mar '97 / Cargo

Blazing Redheads

BLAZING REDHEADS
Paradise drive / Cienega / Sea level / In search of... / Cha cha slippers / February song / Santa Fe / Get down (and stay down) / Final segment / Mozambo / Street dreamin' / My Picasso
CD ______ RR 26CD
Reference Recordings / May '96 / Jazz Music / May Audio

CRAZED WOMEN
CD ______ RR 41CD
Reference Recordings / May '96 / Jazz Music / May Audio

Bleachbath

BLEACHBATH
CD ______ VIRION 102
Sound Virus / Sep '94 / Plastic Head

Bleasdale, Paul

CREAM SEPARATES VOL.3 (Mixed By Les Ryder & Paul Bleasdale) (Various Artists)
Illegal gunshot: *Ragga Twins* / Gettin' stupid: *Dirty Beatniks* / We wanna go back: *Word Up* / There's gonna be a riot: *Dub Pistols* / Trickshot: *Ceasefire* / Karaoke with Buddah: *Eboman* / King of the beats: *Mantronix* / Loose caboose: *Electroliners* / Wrecktify: *Laidback* / Scared: *Slacker* / Psychic bounty killaz: *DJ Sneak & Armand Van Helden* / Jack another day: *Innocent* / Fat cow: *Fiasco* / Body music: *Wulf n' Bear* / Theme from OP Art: *As One*
CD ______ 74321462022
De-Construction / Mar '97 / BMG

Bleed

ACTION MAN
CD ______ BLEED 7CD
Bleed / Jun '97 / Cargo / Pinnacle

GOOD TIMES ARE KILLING ME, THE
CD ______ BLEED 6CD
Bleed / Jul '95 / Cargo / Pinnacle

Bleedin' Hearts

SECONDS TO GO
CD ______ CSCCD 1003
CRS / Sep '95 / ADA / Direct / Jet Star

Bleep & Booster

WORLD OF BLEEP & BOOSTER
Technotropolis / Sexy / Electro city / Genk / Find the light / Boosterdrome / Glock / Amber to atoms / Wonder of the world / Piano 1
CD ______ 8285112
London / Sep '94 / PolyGram

Blegvad, Peter

DOWNTIME
CD ______ RERPBCD
ReR/Recommended / Jul '88 / ReR Megacorp / RTM/Disc

JUST WOKE UP
CD ______ RERPB 2
ReR/Recommended / Jun '96 / ReR Megacorp / RTM/Disc

NAKED SHAKESPEARE, THE
How beautiful you are / Karen / Lonely too / First blow struck / Weird monkeys / Naked Shakespeare / Irma / Like a baby / Powers in the air / You can't miss it / Vermont / Blue eyed William
CD ______ CDV 2284
Virgin / Jun '91 / EMI

Bleiming, Christian

JIVIN' TIME
CD ______ BEST 1010CD
Acoustic Music / Nov '93 / ADA

Bleizi Ruz

MUSIQUES & DANSES DE BRETAGNE
CD ______ PL 3355/65CD
Diffusion Breizh / Jun '94 / ADA

Blender

RETURN OF THE BLENDER
CD ______ XBR 001CD
Dolores / Jun '96 / Plastic Head

Blenner, Serge

VISION ET POESIE
CD ______ SKYCD 3053
Sky / Sep '95 / Greyhound / Koch / Vital/SAM

Blessed Ethel

WELCOME TO THE RODEO
CD ______ 2DMCD 012
2 Damn Loud / Nov '95 / Pinnacle

Blessid Union Of Souls

HOME
I believe / Let me be the one / All along / Oh Virginia / Nora / Would you be there / Home / End of the world / Heaven / Forever for tonight / Lucky to be here
CD ______ CDEMC 3708
EMI / Jun '95 / EMI

Bley, Carla

BIG BAND THEORY
On the stage in cages / Birds of paradise / Goodbye Pork Pie Hat / Fresh impression
CD ______ 5199662
Watt / Oct '93 / New Note/Pinnacle

DINNER MUSIC
CD ______ 8258152
ECM / Jan '94 / New Note/Pinnacle

DUETS (Bley, Carla & Steve Swallow/ Andy Sheppard)
Baby baby / Walking batteriewoman / Utviklingssang / Ladies in Mercedes / Romantic notions / Remember / Ups and downs / Reactionary tango parts 1/2/3 / Soon I will be done with the troubles of this world
CD ______ 8373452
ECM / Nov '88 / New Note/Pinnacle

ESCALATOR OVER THE HILL
CD Set ______ 8393102
ECM / Jan '90 / New Note/Pinnacle

FLEUR CARNIVORE
CD ______ 8396622
Watt / Nov '89 / New Note/Pinnacle

GO TOGETHER (Bley, Carla & Steve Swallow/Andy Sheppard)
Sing me softly of the blues / Mother of the dead man / Masquerade / Ad infinitum / Copyright royalties / Peau douce / Doctor / Fleur carnivor
CD ______ 5176732
Watt / May '93 / New Note/Pinnacle

GOES TO CHURCH (Bley, Carla Big Band)
Setting Calvin's waltz / Exaltaion/Religious experience/Major / One way / Beads / Permanent wave / Who will rescue you
CD ______ 5336822
Watt / Nov '96 / New Note/Pinnacle

HEAVY HEART
Light or dark / Talking hearts / Joyful noise / Ending it / Starting again / Heavy heart
CD ______ 8178642
ECM / Jan '94 / New Note/Pinnacle

I HATE TO SING
Internationale / Murder / Very very simple / I hate to sing / Piano lesson / Lone arranger / Battleship
CD ______ 8238652
Watt / Jul '96 / New Note/Pinnacle

LIVE
Blunt object / Lord is listenin' to ya, hallelujah / Time and us / Still in the room / Real life hits / Song sung long
CD ______ 8157302
ECM / Feb '86 / New Note/Pinnacle

MUSIQUE MECANIQUE
CD ______ 8393132
ECM / Sep '89 / New Note/Pinnacle

NIGHT-GLO
Pretend you're in love / Night-glo / Rut / Crazy with you / Wildlife
CD ______ 8276402
ECM / Dec '85 / New Note/Pinnacle

SEXTET
More Brahms / Houses and people / Girl who cried champagne / Brooklyn Bridge / Lawns / Healing power
CD ______ 8316972
ECM / Apr '87 / New Note/Pinnacle

SOCIAL STUDIES
CD ______ 8318312
ECM / Jul '87 / New Note/Pinnacle

SONGS WITH LEGS (Bley, Carla & Steve Swallow/Andy Sheppard)
Real life hits / Lord is listenin' to ya, hallelujah / Chicken / Misterioso / Wrong key donkey / Crazy with you
CD ______ 5270692
Watt / Feb '95 / New Note/Pinnacle

Bley, Paul

ALONE AGAIN
CD ______ 1238402
IAI / May '94 / Cadillac / Harmonia Mundi

ANNETTE (Bley, Paul/Various Artists)
CD ______ ARTCD 6118
Hat Art / Nov '92 / Cadillac / Harmonia Mundi

AXIS
CD ______ 1238532
IAI / Jan '93 / Cadillac / Harmonia Mundi

BLUES FOR RED
CD ______ 1232382
Red / Mar '91 / ADA / Cadillac / Harmonia Mundi

CHANGING HANDS
CD ______ JUST 402
Justin Time / Jul '92 / Cadillac / New Note/Pinnacle

FABULOUS PAUL BLEY QUINTET, THE (Bley, Paul Quintet)
CD ______ 500542
Musidisc / Sep '96 / Discovery

FRAGMENTS
CD ______ 8292802
ECM / Sep '86 / New Note/Pinnacle

HANDS ON
Remembering / Points / Ram dance / Three fifth / Hands on / If / Cowhand
CD ______ ECD 221842
Evidence / Jul '97 / ADA / Cadillac / Harmonia Mundi

IN A ROW
CD ______ ARTCD 6081
Hat Art / Aug '91 / Cadillac / Harmonia Mundi

IN THE EVENINGS OUT THERE
Afterthoughts / Portrait of a silence / Soft touch / Speak easy / Interface / Allignment / Fair share / Article four / Married alive / Spe-cul-lay-ting / Tomorrow today / Note police
CD ______ 5174692
ECM / Sep '93 / New Note/Pinnacle

JAPAN SUITE
CD ______ 1238492
IAI / Sep '92 / Cadillac / Harmonia Mundi

LIVE AT SWEET BASIL (Bley, Paul Group)
CD ______ 1212352
Soul Note / Jun '91 / Cadillac / Harmonia Mundi / Wellard

MEMOIRS (Bley, Paul, Charlie Haden & Paul Motian)
CD ______ 1212402
Soul Note / May '92 / Cadillac / Harmonia Mundi / Wellard

OUTSIDE IN (Bley, Paul & Sonny Greenwich)
CD ______ JUST 692
Justin Time / Apr '95 / Cadillac / New Note/Pinnacle

PAUL BLEY QUARTET (Bley, Paul Quartet)
CD ______ 8352402
ECM / May '88 / New Note/Pinnacle

PAUL BLEY WITH GARY PEACOCK (Bley, Paul Trio)
Blues / Getting started / When will the blues leave / Long ago and far away / Moor / Gary / Big Foot / Albert's love theme
CD ______ 8431622
ECM / Oct '90 / New Note/Pinnacle

PAUL BLEY, NIELS HENNING, ORSTED PEDERSON (Bley, Paul, Niels Henning & Orsted Pederson)
CD ______ SCCD 31005
Steeplechase / Nov '90 / Discovery / Impetus

RAMBLIN'
CD ______ 1231172
Red / Feb '96 / ADA / Cadillac / Harmonia Mundi

SWEET TIME
CD ______ JUST 56
Justin Time / Oct '94 / Cadillac / New Note/Pinnacle

TIME WILL TELL (Bley, Paul, Evan Parker & Barre Philips)
Poetic justice / Time will tell / Above the treeline / You will, Oscar, you will / Sprung / No questions / Vine laces / Clawback / Marsh tides / Instance / Burlesque
CD ______ 5238192
ECM / Feb '95 / New Note/Pinnacle

TOUCHING
CD ______ BLCD 760195
Black Lion / Jun '94 / Cadillac / Jazz Music / Koch / Wellard

Blige, Mary J.

MY LIFE
Intro / Mary Jane / You bring me joy / Marvin interlude / I'm the only woman / K Murray interlude / My life / You gotta believe / I never wanna live without you / I'm going down / My life interlude / Be with you / Mary's joint / Don't go / I love you / No one else / Be happy / (You make me feel like) a natural woman
CD ______ MCD 11398
MCA / Jan '96 / BMG

SHARE MY WORLD
Intro / I can love you / Love is all we need / Round and round / Share my world / Share my world (interlude) / Seven days / It's on / Thank you Lord (interlude) / Missing you / Everything / Keep your head / Can't get you off my mind / Get to know you better / Searching / Our love / Not gon' cry / (You make me feel like a) Natural woman
CD ______ MCD 11619
MCA / Apr '97 / BMG

WHAT'S THE 411
Leave a message / Reminisce / Real love / You remind me / Intro' talk / Sweet thing / Love no limit / I don't want to do anything / Slow down / My love / Changes I've been going through / What's the 411
CD ______ MCLD 19315
MCA / Jul '96 / BMG

WHAT'S THE 411 (Remix)
Leave a message / You don't have to worry / My love / Real love / What's the 411 / Reminisce / Mary and Andre / Sweet thing / Love no limit / You remind me / Changes

I've been going through / I don't want to do anything
CD MCLD 19338
MCA / Oct '96 / BMG

Blind Alley

RUBY KENNEL CLUB
CD FRR 022
Freek / Sep '96 / RTM/Disc / SRD

Blind Blake

BLIND BLAKE VOL.1
CD DOCD 5024
Document / Nov '93 / ADA / Hot Shot / Jazz Music

MASTER OF RAGTIME GUITAR, THE
CD IGOCD 2046
Indigo / Aug '96 / ADA / Direct

Blind Faith

BLIND FAITH
Had to cry today / Can't find my way home / Well alright / Presence of the Lord / Sea of joy / Do what you like
CD 8250942
Polydor / Nov '90 / PolyGram

Blind Guardian

BATTALIONS OF FEAR
CD 859810
SPV / Sep '89 / Koch / Plastic Head

Blind Idiot God

BLIND IDIOT GOD
CD SST 104CD
SST / May '93 / Plastic Head

UNDERTOW
CD EMY 1072
Enemy / Nov '89 / Grapevine/PolyGram

Blind Illusion

SANE ASYLUM, THE
Sane asylum / Vengeance is mine / Kamikaze / Vicious vision / Bloodshower / Death noise / Smash the crystal / Metamorphosis of a monster
CD CDFLAG 18
Under One Flag / Mar '88 / Pinnacle

Blind Light

ABSENCE OF TIME, THE
CD EFA 275012
Alda / Feb '97 / SRD

Blind Melon

BLIND MELON
Soak the sin / Tones of home / Ronettes / Paper scratcher / Dear ol' dad / Change / No rain / Deserted / Sleepyhouse / Holy man / Seed to a tree / Drive / Time
CD CDEST 2188
Capitol / Mar '93 / EMI

SOUP
Galaxie / Two times four / Vernie / Skinned / Toes across the floor / Walk / Dumptruck / Car seat (God's presents) / Wilt / Duke / St. Andrew's fall / New life / Mouthful of cavities / Lemonade
CD CDEST 2261
Capitol / Sep '97 / EMI

Blind Mr. Jones

STEREO MUSICALE
Sisters / Spooky Vibes / Regular Disease / Small caravan / Flying With Lux / Henna And Swayed / Lonesome Boatman / Unforgettable Waltz / Going on cold / Spook Easy / One Watt Above darkness / Dolores / Against The Glass
CD CDBRED 100
Cherry Red / Oct '92 / Pinnacle

TATOOINE
Hey / Disneyworld / Viva fisher / See you again / Big plane / Drop for days / Surfer baby / Please me / What's going on / Mesa
CD CDBRED 113
Cherry Red / May '94 / Pinnacle

Blind Passengers

DESTROYKA
CD CD 08561292
SPV / Apr '96 / Koch / Plastic Head

Blink 182

CHESHIRE CAT
CD GRL 001CD
Grilled Cheese / Oct '96 / Cargo

DUDE RANCH
CD CRGD 11624
Cargo / Jul '97 / Cargo

Blink Twice

OTHER LOCATIONS
CD EFA 129662
Glasnost / Apr '97 / SRD

Blissed

RITE OF PASSAGE
CD PODCD 029
Pod Communications / Aug '95 / Plastic Head

Blithe

HEAD IS MIGHTY
CD A 104CD
Alias / Nov '96 / Vital

VERSE CHORUS VERSE
I guess yes / Haven / Now you know / Losefer / Hell of man / Allegiance / Mother Goose / Mind dent / Hardliner / Man / 2 Spring clean / Early risers
CD A 106
Alias / May '97 / Vital

Blitz

BEST OF BLITZ
Attack / Fight to live / Forty five revolutions / Someone's gonna die / Time bomb / 4Q / Never surrender / Razors in the night / Voice of a generation / Nation on fire / Youth / Warriors / Bleed / New age / Fatigue / Suffragette city / Overdrive / Those days / Killing dream / Walkaway
CD DOJOCD 123
Dojo / Mar '93 / Disc

BLITZED ON ALL OUT ATTACK
Warriors / 4Q / Time bomb / Criminal damage / Razors in the night / Attack / Escape / Never surrender / Nation on fire / Warriors (Live) / Someone's gonna die / Forty five revolutions / Fight to live / Youth / I don't need you / Propaganda / Closedown / Your revolution / New age / Bleed / Caberet / Vicious / Escape (demo) / Youth (demo) / Bleed (demo) / Crimianl damage
CD DOJOCD 93
Dojo / Apr '93 / Disc

COMPLETE BLITZ SINGLES COLLECTION
Someone's gonna die / Attack / Fight to live / Forty five revolutions / Never surrender / Razors in the night / Voice of a generation / Warriors / Youth / New age / Fatigue / Bleed / Telecommunication / Teletron / Solar / Husk
CD CDPUNK 25
Anagram / Dec '93 / Cargo / Pinnacle

Blitz Babiez

ON THE LINE
CD SPENTUNIT 002CD
Spentunit / Aug '95 / Plastic Head

THOUGHT SPAWN
CD 35520162
Onefoot / Oct '96 / Cargo

Blitzkrieg

FUTURE MUST BE OURS
CD RRCD 010
Retch / Oct '96 / Cargo / Plastic Head

UNHOLY TRINITY
CD NM 002CD
Neat Metal / Nov '95 / Pinnacle

Blizard, Ralph

SOUTHERN RAMBLE
CD ROUCD 0352
Rounder / Aug '95 / ADA / CM / Direct

Block

LEAD ME NOT INTO PENN STATION
CD INDIGO 58532
Zensor / Dec '96 / Cargo

MEAN MACHINE
CD CDZOT 101
Zoth Ommog / Nov '93 / Cargo / Plastic Head

Block, Brandon

BRANDON BLOCK LIVE VOL.1
CD QPM 7
QPM / Nov '96 / Beechwood/BMG

Block, Rory

AIN'T I A WOMAN
Silver wings / Faithless world / Sisters / Ain't I a woman / Come on in my kitchen / Rolling log / Maggie Campbell / Never call your name / Road to Mexico / Cool drink of water / Walk in Jerusalem / Never called your name
CD NETCD 0038
Network / Nov '92 / Direct / Greensleeves / SRD

ANGEL OF MERCY
CD NET 47CD
Network / Apr '94 / Direct / Greensleeves / SRD

BEST BLUES AND ORIGINALS - VOL.1
CD MRCD 137
Munich / Jun '93 / ADA / CM / Direct / Greensleeves

BEST BLUES AND ORIGINALS - VOL.2
Uncloudy day / Devil got my man / Down in the dumps / Since you been gone / Achin' heart / Hilarity rag / Kind hearted man / Love my blues away / Elder green is gone / Just like a man / Swing low, sweet chariot / Ecstasy / Feel just like going on / Frankie and Albert / No place like home / Midnight light / I might find a way / Dr. Make it right / No way for me to get along / Back to the woods / I've got a rock in my sock / Highland overture (for Wendy) / Long journey
CD NETCD 43
Network / Jul '93 / Direct / Greensleeves / SRD

BLUE HORIZON
CD ROUCD 3073
Polydor / Aug '88 / PolyGram

GONE WOMAN BLUES (The Country Blues Collection)
Big road blues / Preaching blues / Joliet bound / Maggie Campbell / Hellhound on my trail / Bye bye blues / Gone woman blues / Pea vine blues / Rolling log / I let my Daddy do that / Tallahatchie bles / Tain't long fo day / Terraplane blues / Come on in my kitchen / Be ready when he comes / Cypress grove / Railroadin' some / Hawkins blues / Cool drink of water / Do your duty / Rowdy blues / On the wall / Devil got my man / Take my heart again
CD ROUCD 11575
Rounder / Mar '97 / ADA / CM / Direct

HIGH HEELED BLUES
CD ROUCD 3061
Rounder / '88 / ADA / CM / Direct

HOUSE OF HEARTS
CD ROUCD 3104
Rounder / '88 / ADA / CM / Direct

I'VE GOT A ROCK IN MY SOCK
CD ROUCD 3097
Rounder / '88 / ADA / CM / Direct

MAMA'S BLUES
Terraplane blues / Bye bye blues / Big road blues / Do your duty / Spirit returns / Got to shine / Mama's blues / Ain't no shame / Hawkins blues / Weepin' willow blues / Sing good news
CD NETCD 22
Network / May '91 / Direct / Greensleeves / SRD
CD ROUCD 3117
Rounder / Mar '97 / ADA / CM / Direct

RHINESTONE AND STEEL STRINGS
CD ROUCD 3085
Rounder / Aug '88 / ADA / CM / Direct

TORNADO
CD ROUCD 314
Rounder / May '96 / ADA / CM / Direct

TURNING POINT
Turning point / Holdin' on / Far away / All of my life / Spiderboy / Gedachentrein / All as one / Heather's song / Old times are gone / Leavin' here / Down the highway / Tomorrow
CD MRCD 145
Munich / Aug '94 / ADA / CM / Direct / Greensleeves

WHEN A WOMAN GETS THE BLUES
CD ROUCD 3139
Rounder / Apr '95 / ADA / CM / Direct

WOMEN IN (E)MOTION FESTIVAL
CD T&M 107
Tradition & Moderne / Jan '95 / ADA / Direct

Blodwyn Pig

AHEAD RINGS OUT
It's only love / Sing me a song that I know / Up and coming / Change song / Dear Jill / Modern alchemist / Leave it with me / Ain't ya coming home, babe
CD BGOCD 54
Beat Goes On / Aug '94 / Pinnacle

GETTING TO THIS
Drive me / Variations on Nainos / See my way / Long lamb blues / Squirreling must go on / San Francisco sketches / Beach scape / Fisherman's wharf / Telegraph hill / Close the door, I'm falling out of the room / Worry / Toys / To Rassman / Send your son to die
CD BGOCD 81
Beat Goes On / Aug '94 / Pinnacle

LIES
CD CDVEST 12
Bulletproof / May '94 / Pinnacle

MODERN ALCHEMIST, THE
It's only love / Modern alchemist / Change song / Summers day / Cat squirrel / Dear Jill / See my way / Drive me / Slow down / Ain't you coming home babe
CD IGOXCD 507
Indigo / May '97 / ADA / Direct

Bloedow, Oren

OREN BLOEDOW
CD KFWCD 115
Knitting Factory / Nov '94 / Cargo / Plastic Head

Blonde On Blonde

CONTRASTS
Ride with Captain Max / Spinning wheel / No sleep blues / Goodbye / I need my friend / Mother Earth / All day and all night / Eleanor Rigby / Conversationally making the grade / Regency / Island on an island / Don't be too long / Jeanette Isabella / Country life
CD SEECD 406
See For Miles/C5 / Jul '94 / Pinnacle

REFLECTIONS ON A LIFE
CD 14526
Spalax / Feb '97 / ADA / Cargo / Direct / Discovery / Greyhound

Blonde Redhead

FAKE CAN BE JUST AS GOOD
CD TG 169CD
Touch & Go / Apr '97 / SRD

Blondie

AUTOAMERICAN
Europa / Live it up / Here's looking at you / Tide is high / Angels on the balcony / Go through it / Do the dark / Rapture / Faces / T-Birds / Walk like me / Follow me
CD CDCHR 6084
Chrysalis / Sep '94 / EMI

BEAUTIFUL (The Remix Album)
Union city blue / Dreaming / Rapture / Heart of glass / Sunday girl / Call me / Atomic / Tide is high / Hanging on the telephone / Fade away and radiate
CD CDCHR 6105
Chrysalis / Jul '95 / EMI

BEST OF BLONDIE, THE
Denis / Tide is high / In the flesh / Sunday girl / (I'm always touched by your) presence dear / Dreaming / Hanging on the telephone / Rapture / Picture this / Union city blue / Call me / Atomic / Rip her to shreds / Heart of glass
CD CCD 1371
Chrysalis / Jan '88 / EMI

BLONDIE
X offender / Rifle range / Look good in blue / In the sun / Shark in Jet's clothing / Man overboard / Rip her to shreds / Little girl lies / In the flesh / Kung fu girls / Attack of the giant ants
CD CDCHR 6081
Chrysalis / Sep '94 / EMI

BLONDIE AND BEYOND
Underground girl / English boys / Sunday girl (French version) / Susie and Jeffrey / Shayla / Denis / X offender / Poets problem / Scenery / Picture this / Angels on the balcony / Once I had a love / I'm gonna love you too / Island of lost souls / Call me (Spanish version) / Heart of glass / Ring of fire / Bang a gong (get it on) / Heroes
CD CDCCHR 6063
Chrysalis / Jan '94 / EMI

COMPLETE PICTURE, THE (The Best Of Deborah Harry & Blondie)
Heart of glass / I want that man: *Harry, Deborah* / Call me / Sunday girl / French kissin' in the USA: *Harry, Deborah* / Denis / Rapture / Brite side: *Harry, Deborah* / (I'm always touched by your) presence dear / Well did you evah: *Harry, Deborah & Iggy Pop* / Tide is high / In love with love: *Harry, Deborah* / Hanging on the telephone / Island of lost souls / Picture this / Dreaming / Sweet and low: *Harry, Deborah* / Union City Blue / Atomic / Rip her to shreds
CD CCD 1817
Chrysalis / Mar '91 / EMI

DENIS
Denis / Tide is high / Hanging on the telephone / Rip her to shreds / Picture this / X Offender / Rifle range / For your eyes only / Susie and Jeffrey / Die young stay pretty / Island of lost souls / Platinum blonde / War child / In the flesh
CD DC 867192
Disky / Nov '96 / Disky / THE

EAT TO THE BEAT
Dreaming / Hardest part / Union city blue / Shayla / Eat to the beat / Accidents never happen / Die young stay pretty / Slow motion / Atomic / Sound asleep / Victor / Living in the real world
CD CPCD 1225
Chrysalis / Nov '92 / EMI

ESSENTIAL COLLECTION, THE
Denis / Tide is high / Hanging on the telephone / Rip her to shreds / Picture this / X Offender / Rifle range / For your eyes only / Susie and Jeffrey / Die young stay pretty / Island of lost souls / Platinum blonde / War child / In the flesh
CD CDGOLD 1091
EMI Gold / Feb '97 / EMI

HUNTER, THE
Orchid club / Island of lost souls / Dragonfly / For your eyes only / Beast / War child / Little Caesar / Danceway / Can I find the right words (to say) / English boys / Hunter gets captured by the game
CD CDCHR 6083
Chrysalis / Sep '94 / EMI

PARALLEL LINES
Fade away / Hanging on the telephone / One way or another / Picture this / Pretty baby / I know but I don't know / 11.59 / Will anything happen / Sunday girl / Heart of glass / I'm gonna love you too / Just go away
CD ____ CCD 1192
Chrysalis / Jul '94 / EMI

PLASTIC LETTERS
Fan mail / Denis / Bermuda triangle / Youth nabbed as sniper / Contact in Red Square / (I'm always touched by your) presence dear / I'm on / I didn't have the nerve to say no / Love at the pier / No imagination / Kidnapper / Detroit 442 / Cautious lip
CD ____ CDCHR 6085
Chrysalis / Sep '94 / EMI

PLATINUM COLLECTION, THE (2CD Set)
X offender / In the flesh / Man overboard / Rip her to shreds / Denis / Contact in red square / Kung fu girls / I'm on E / (I'm always touched by your) presence dear / Poets problem / Detroit 442 / Picture this / Fade away and radiate / I'm gonna love you too / Just go away / Hanging on the telephone / Will anything happen / Heart of glass / Rifle range / 11.59 / Sunday girl / I know but I don't know / One way or another / Dreaming / Sound asleep / Living in the real world / Union city blue / Hardest part / Atomic / Die young stay pretty / Slow motion / Call me / Tide is high / Susie and Jeffrey / Rapture / Walk like me / Island of lost souls / Dragon fly / War child / Little Caesar / Out in the streets / Platinum blonde / Thin line / Puerto Rico / Once I had a love / Atomic (remix) / Rapture (remix)
CD Set ____ CDCHR 6089
Chrysalis / Oct '94 / EMI

Blood

METAL CONFLICTS
CD ____ SPV 08412412
SPV / Apr '95 / Koch / Plastic Head

Blood Farmers

BLOOD FARMERS
CD ____ H 00372
Hellhound / Apr '95 / Koch

Blood Feast

CHOPPING BLOCK BLUES
CD ____ FLAME 1016CD
Flametrader / Nov '90 / Plastic Head

KILL FOR PLEASURE
CD ____ SHARK 013 CD
Shark / Apr '90 / Plastic Head

Blood From The Soul

TO SPRITE THE GLAND THAT BREEDS
Painted life / Image and the helpless / On fear and prayer / Guinea pig / Nature's hole / Vascular / To spite / Suspension of my disbelief / Yet to be savoured / Blood from the soul
CD ____ MOSH 089CD
Earache / Oct '93 / Vital

Blood On The Saddle

NEW BLOOD
CD ____ 422062
Last Call / Feb '97 / Cargo / Direct / Discovery

Blood Or Whiskey

BLOOD OR WHISKEY
CD ____ SUN 24CD
Sound / May '97 / ADA

Blood Shanti

PURE SPIRIT
CD ____ ABACD 002
Aba Shanti / Aug '96 / SRD

Blood, Sweat & Tears

BLOOD, SWEAT & TEARS
Variations on a theme by Satie / Smiling phases / Sometimes in winter / More and more / And when I die / God bless the child / Spinning wheel / You've made me so very happy / Blues
CD ____ BGOCD 28
Beat Goes On / Dec '88 / Pinnacle

WHAT GOES UP (The Best Of Blood, Sweat & Tears/2CD Set)
Refugee from Yuhupitz / I can't quit her / House in the country / I love you more than you'll ever know / You've made me so very happy / More and more / And when I die / Sometimes in winter / Smiling phases / Spinning wheel / God bless the child / Children of the wind / Hi de ho / Lucretia / Mac evil / He's a runner / Something's coming on / 40,000 headmen / Go down gamblin' / Mama gets high / Lisa, listen to me / Valentine's day / John the baptist (Holy John) / So long Dixie / Snow queen / Maiden voyage / I can't move to the mountains / Time remembered / Roller coaster / Tell me that I'm wrong / Got to get you into my life / You're the one / Mean ole world

CD Set ____ 4810192
Columbia / Jan '96 / Sony

Bloodbath

LIVE
CD ____ PP 002
Phenotype / Jan '97 / Harmonia Mundi

Bloodfire Posse

PRIMO
CD ____ RASCD 3108
Ras / Nov '92 / Direct / Greensleeves / Jet Star / SRD

Bloodgood

ALL STAND TOGETHER
SOS / All stand together / Escape from the fire / Say goodbye / Out of love / Kingdom come / Fear no evil / Help me / Rounded are the rocks / Lies in the dark / Streelight dance / I want to live in your heart
CD ____ CD 08793
Broken / Jan '92 / Broken

Bloodlet

ELETIC
CD ____ VR 031CD
Victory Europe / Jan '96 / Plastic Head

Bloodstar

ANYTIME ANYWHERE
CD ____ RR 90982
Roadrunner / Feb '93 / PolyGram

Bloom, Jane Ira

ART & AVIATION
Gateway to progress / Further into the night / Hawkin's parallel universe / Straight no chaser/Miro / Oshumare / Art and aviation / Most distant galaxy / I believe Anita / Lost in the stars
CD ____ AJ 0107
Arabesque / Jun '93 / New Note/Pinnacle

MODERN DRAMA
CD ____ 378282
Koch Jazz / Nov '96 / Koch

NEARNESS, THE
Nearly summertime / Midnight round / 'Round midnight / B6 Bop / Middnight's measure / In the wee small hours of the morning / Painting over Paris / Wing dining / Panosonic / White tower / It's a corrugated world / Monk's tale / Nearness of you / Lonely house / All diesel kitchen of tomorrow / Yonder
CD ____ AJ 0120
Arabesque / Apr '96 / New Note/Pinnacle

SLALOM
CD ____ 378272
Koch Jazz / Jun '97 / Koch

Bloom, Luka

ACOUSTIC MOTORBIKE, THE
CD ____ 7599266702
Reprise / Dec '96 / Warner Music

RIVERSIDE
Delerious / Dreams in America / Gone to pablo / Man is alive / Irishman in Chinatown / Rescue mission / One / Hudson lady / This is your life / You couldn't have come at a better time / Hill of Allen
CD ____ 7599260922
Reprise / Dec '96 / Warner Music

TURF
Cold comfort / True blue / Diamond mountain / Right here, right now / Sunny sailor boy / Black is the colour of my true love's hair / To begin to / Freedom song / Holding back the river / Background noise / Fertile rock / I did time / Sanctuary
CD ____ 9362456082
Reprise / Jun '94 / Warner Music

Bloomfield, Mike

AMERICAN HERO
Hully gully / Wings of an angel / Walking the floor / Don't you lie to me / Junko partner / Knockin' myself out / Women lovin' each other / Cherry red / RX for the blues / You must have Jesus
CD ____ CDBT 009
Thunderbolt / Feb '90 / TKO Magnum

BETWEEN A HARD PLACE AND THE GROUND
Eyesight to the blind / Linda Lou / Kansas City blues / At the Darktown strutter's ball / Mop mop / Call me a dog / I'm glad I'm jewish / Great gifts from heaven / Lo though I am with thee / Jockey blues / Between a hard place and the ground / Uncle Bon's barrelhouse blues / Wee wee hours / Vamp in C / One of these days
CD ____ CDTB 076
Thunderbolt / Sep '90 / TKO Magnum

BLUES, GOSPEL & RAGTIME INSTRUMENTALS
CD ____ SHCD 99007
Shanachie / Mar '94 / ADA / Greensleeves / Koch

DON'T SAY THAT I AIN'T YOU MAN (Essential Blues 1964-1969)
I've got you in the palm of my hand / Last night / Feel so good / Goin' down slow / I got my mojo working / Born in Chicago / Work song / Killing floor / Albert's shuffle / Stop / Mary Ann / Don't throw your love on me so strong / Don't think about it baby / It takes time / Carmelita skiffle
CD ____ 4767212
Columbia / May '94 / Sony

GOSPEL TRUTH
Cruisin' for a bruisin' / Linda Lu / Papa mama / Rompha stompin' / Junker's blues / Midnight / It'll be me / Motorised blues / Mathilda / Winter moon / Snow blind / Lights out / Your friend / Orphan blues / Juke joint / Knockin' myself out
CD ____ CDTB 179
Thunderbolt / Oct '96 / TKO Magnum

I'M WITH YOU ALWAYS
Eyesight to the blind / Frankie and Johnny / I'm with you always / Jockey blues / Some of these days / Don't you lie to me / Hymn tune / At the Darktown strutter's ball / Stagger Lee / I'm glad I'm Jewish / A flat boogaloo
CD ____ FIENDCD 92
Demon / Aug '90 / Pinnacle

KNOCKIN' MYSELF OUT
CD ____ CDSGP 0216
Prestige / Mar '96 / Else / Total/BMG

LIVE ADVENTURES OF MIKE BLOOMFIELD AND AL COOPER (2CD Set) (Bloomfield, Mike & Al Kooper)
Opening speech / 59th Street Bridge song / I wonder why / Her holy modal highness / Weight / Mary Ann / Together / That's alright / Green onions
CD Set ____ 4851512
Columbia / Mar '97 / Sony

TRUE SOUL BROTHER, A
CD ____ 8400892
Affinity / May '96 / Cadillac / Jazz Music / Koch

Bloss, Rainer

AMPSY
Oracle / From long ago / Energy / Adoring multitudes / Psyche / I'm the heat / He's an angel / Who the hell is she / Lights out baby / Love is a beginning
CD ____ CDTB 032
Thunderbolt / May '87 / TKO Magnum

Blount

TRAUMA
CD ____ F 018CD
Fearless / Apr '97 / Cargo / Plastic Head

Blount, Chris

NEW ORLEANS IMPRESSIONS (Blount, Chris & The Delta Four)
CD ____ PKCD 042
PEK / May '96 / Cadillac / Jazz Music / Wellard

NEW ORLEANS JAZZ BAND
CD ____ PKCD 031
PEK / Oct '94 / Cadillac / Jazz Music / Wellard

OLD RUGGED CROSS, THE (Blount, Chris New Orleans Jazz Band)
Mary wore a golden chain / Amazing grace / Lord, Lord, Lord / Only a look / Royal telephone / Old rugged cross / In the sweet bye and bye / Hands of God / Lead me saviour / It is no secret / Walking with the King / Evening prayer / Yes Lord I'm crippled / His eye is on the sparrow / End of a perfect day
CD ____ LACD 16
Lake / Nov '93 / ADA / Cadillac / Direct / Jazz Music / Target/BMG

BLOW

FLESHMACHINE
CD ____ PA 004CD
Paragoric / Mar '95 / Cargo / Plastic Head

KISS LIKE CONCRETE
CD ____ COTINDCD 8
Cottage Industry / May '96 / Total/BMG

MAN AND GOAT ALIKE
CD ____ COTINDCD 1
Cottage Industry / Mar '95 / Total/BMG

PIGS
CD ____ COTINDCD 10
Cottage Industry / Aug '96 / Total/BMG

Blow Monkeys

CHOICES (The Singles Connection)
Wait: *Howard, Robert & Kym Mazelle* / Choice / Slaves no more / Celebrate the day (after you) / Wicked ways / Diggin' your scene / It doesn't have to be this way / Out with her / This is your life / It pays to belong / Wait / Choice / Man from Russia / Atomic lullaby / Wildflower / Forbidden fruit
CD ____ 74321137072
RCA / Apr '93 / BMG

FOR THE RECORD (The Best Of The Blow Monkeys)
Digging your scene / Springtime for the world / Out with her / Wicked ways / Wait / No woman is an island / Squaresville / Some kind of wonderful / It doesn't have to be this way / (Celebrate) The day after you / It pays to belong / Atomic lullaby / Choice / This is the way it has to be / This is your life / Digging your scene / Celebrate
CD ____ 74321393342
Camden / Jun '96 / BMG

Blowpipe

FIRST CIRCLE
Conc / Kucou / Chixalub / Toba / Trench / First circle / Prop / Unkindness
CD ____ STITCH 6CD
Needlework / Jul '97 / SRD

Blowzabella

BEST OF BLOWZABELLA, THE
Blowzabella/Marriage marches / L'enfant de dieu/Faerie dance / Jenny pluck pears/ Half hannikin / Polka piquee / Bourees three and four / Shave the monkey/Boys of the mill / Eglantine/Man in the brown hat/Schottishe fran havero/Minah / Eight step waltz/ Lisa/Stukka gruppa / Glass island / Newbury jig/Moll in the wood/Sword dance/Old wife of Coverda / New jigs / Death in a Fen/ Bruton town/Our Captain cried / Spaghetti panic / Jan mijne man/Go mauve / Horizonto
CD ____ OSMOCD 001
Osmosys / Oct '95 / Direct

RICHER DUST, A
Wars of the roses / Death in a fen/Bruton Town/Our Captain cried / Moth / Man in the brown hat / Diamond / New hornpipes / All things are quite silent
CD ____ OSMOCD 010
Osmosys / Jan '97 / Direct

VANILLA
CD ____ GLCD 3050
Green Linnet / Feb '95 / ADA / CM / Direct / Highlander / Roots

WALL OF SOUND
Kopenitsa / Eight step wa' z/Lisa/Stukka gruppa / Hallowed ground / Newbury jig/ Moll in the wood/Sword dance (ghost tune)/ Old wi / Sideways glance / Roger De Coverley/Trip o'er Tweed / Finnish Scottish / Last chance bouree / Glass island / Sinfonia
CD ____ OSMOCD 005
Osmosys / Jul '96 / Direct

Blue

ANOTHER NIGHT TIME FLIGHT
Another night time flight / Fantasy / Women / Shepherd / Strange thing / Bring back the love / I'm alone / Tired of loving you / Capture your heart / I understand / Don't wanna make you cry
CD ____ SPINCD 2001
Making Waves / Nov '96 / CM

Blue

MEXICAN CHURCH
Small bones / Gorgon / Dark blue / Mass / Simononian / Cut me free / She's machine / Lower / Metal / Slow wave / Sand stone / Staff announcement
CD ____ SOP 008CD
Sabres Of Paradise / Jun '96 / Vital

RESISTANCE
Diamandra / Doctor / External / Black stone / Circle line / Division dub / Still moving / Golden / Prisoner
CD ____ SOP 004CD
Sabres Of Paradise / Apr '95 / Vital

Blue 101

FROZENLAND
CD ____ OOR 19CD
Out Of Romford / Jun '95 / Pinnacle / SRD

Blue Aeroplanes

FRIENDLOVERPLANE
CD ____ FIRE 33015
Fire / Oct '91 / Pinnacle / RTM/Disc

FRUIT
CD ____ FIRECD 057
Fire / Jun '96 / Pinnacle / RTM/Disc

HUH (The Best Of The Blue Aeroplanes)
Jacket hangs / Huh / Colour me / Razor walk / Growing up, growing down / Fun / Weightless / ...And stones / You (are loved) Jack leaves and back spring / Anti-pretty / Disney head / Your own world / What it is / Lovething/Higherthing / Sixth continent
CD ____ CDCHRM 101
Chrysalis / Feb '97 / EMI

LIFE MODEL
CD ____ BBQCD 143
Beggars Banquet / Feb '94 / RTM/Disc / Warner Music

ROUGH MUSIC
CD ____ BBQCD 167
Beggars Banquet / Jan '95 / RTM/Disc / Warner Music

SPITTING OUT MIRACLES
CD FIRE 33010
Fire / Oct '91 / Pinnacle / RTM/Disc

TOLERANCE
CD FIRE 33003
Fire / Oct '91 / Pinnacle / RTM/Disc

WARHOL'S 15 (The Very Best Of The Blue Aeroplanes)
Lover and confidence / Veils of colour / Cowardice and caprice / Action painting / Up / Warhol's 15 / Ceiling roses / King of the soap box / Weird heart / Julie / Bury your love like treasure / Arriving / Severn beach / Season ticket to a bad place / Tolerance / Journal of an airman / When the wave comes / Spitting out miracles / Breaking my heart / Soul
CD NTMCD 530
Nectar / Feb '97 / Pinnacle

Blue, Barry

GREATEST HITS
(Dancing) on a Saturday night / If I show you I can dance / Heads I win, tails you lose / Hot shot / Problem child / Behind my eyes / Miss hit and run / Do you wanna dance / New day / Girl next door / Hobo man / Life jacket round my heart / Back to the wall / School love
CD 305782
Hallmark / Oct '96 / Carlton

VERY BEST OF BARRY BLUE, THE
CD MCCD 103
Music Club / May '93 / Disc / THE

Blue Blood

BIG NOISE, THE
CD CDMFN 93
Music For Nations / Oct '89 / Pinnacle

UNIVERSAL LANGUAGE
CD CDMFN 112
Music For Nations / Apr '91 / Pinnacle

Blue Brass Connection

COOL AFFAIRS
Endless flight / Vine City / Va ja jo / Mama Laura / Impulse / Latine Lee / Rhythm-a-ning / For Loui
CD 5132772
Amadeo / Jan '92 / PolyGram

Blue By Nature

BLUE TO THE BONE
CD SHA 0092
Shattered / Nov '96 / Cargo / Nervous

Blue Caps

HEP TO THE BEAT
CD PEPCD 119
Pollytone / Jan '97 / Nervous / Pollytone

LEGENDARY BLUE CAPS, THE
Wrapped up in rockabilly / Baby blue / Yes I love you baby / I got a baby / Blue cap man / I lost an angel / Silly song / Lotta lovin' / Say Mama / Down at the in den / Dance to the bop / Johnny's boogie / Be bop a Lula / Rap / Unchained melody / Jealous heart / September in the rain / Am I that easy to forget / Jezebel / I dreamed of an old love affair
CD CDMF 089
Magnum Force / Jun '93 / TKO Magnum

Blue Cats

TUNNEL, THE
CD NERCD 069
Nervous / Sep '92 / Nervous / TKO Magnum

Blue Cheer

BLITZKRIEG OVER NUREMBERG
Babylon / Girl next door / Ride with me / Just a little bit / Summertime blues / Out of focus / Doctor please / Hunter
CD CDTB 091
Thunderbolt / Sep '90 / TKO Magnum

HIGHLIGHTS AND LOWLIVES
Urban soldiers / Hunter of love / Girl from London / Blues steel dues / Big trouble in paradise / Flight of the enola gray / Hoochie coochie man / Down and dirty
CD CDTB 125
Thunderbolt / Jun '91 / TKO Magnum

LIVE AND UNRELEASED 1968-1974
CD CTCD 023
Captain Trip / Jul '97 / Greyhound

LIVE AND UNRELEASED VOL.2
CD CTCD 026
Captain Trip / Jul '97 / Greyhound

Blue Crystal

INNER PEACE
CD BCCD 001
Blue Crystal / Feb '96 / Else

SPIRIT DANCER
CD BCCD 004
Blue Crystal / Feb '96 / Else

Blue Dog

WHAT IS ANYTHING
CD KFWCD 152
Knitting Factory / Feb '95 / Cargo / Plastic Head

Blue Environment

ECHOSPACE
CD AQDCD 002
Aquadar / Jul '95 / SRD

SEA, SPACE, OCEAN
CD AQUADAR 1CD
Aquadar / Sep '94 / SRD

Blue For Two

SEARCH AND ENJOY
CD RA 91392
Roadrunner / Sep '92 / PolyGram

Blue Hawaiians

CHRISTMAS ON BIG ISLAND
Christmas time is here / Jingle jangle / White Christmas / Jungle bells / Blue Christmas / Christmas on Big Island / Have yourself a quiet little Christmas / Mele Kalikmaka / We four kings (little drummer boy) / Enchanted Xmas
CD 7729212
Restless / Nov '95 / Vital

Blue Hearts

HEART'S ABOUT TO BREAK
CD 3 BC
Big Cactus / Nov '95 / ADA / Direct

Blue Highway

IT'S A LONG, LONG ROAD
CD REB 1719CD
Rebel / Apr '96 / ADA / Direct

WIND TO THE WEST
CD REB 1731CD
Rebel / Aug '96 / ADA / Direct

Blue Humans

CLEAR TO HIGHER TIME (Blue Humans & Rudolph Grey)
CD NAR 077CD
New Alliance / May '93 / Plastic Head

Blue Jam

RAPPER'S PARADISE (Blue Jam & The Ghetto Street Fighters)
Gangsta's paradise / Tonite's the night / I got 5 on it / Hey lover / Big poppa / Player's anthem / Ain't nuthin' but a 'she' thing / 1st Of the month / Too hot / Ice cream / Craziest / Danger / Keep their heads ringin' / Sugar hill / Dear Mama / How high
CD 12839
Laserlight / May '96 / Target/BMG

Blue Law

GONNA GETCHA
CD HNRCD 02
Hengest / Apr '96 / Grapevine/PolyGram

Blue Magic

BLUE MAGIC
Sideshow / Look me up / What's come over me / Just don't want to be lonely / Stop to start / Welcome to the club / Spell / Answer to my prayer / Tear it down
CD 7567804132
Atlantic / Jan '96 / Warner Music

Blue Meanies

FULL THROTTLE
CD THK 048CD
Thick / Jun '97 / Cargo

Blue Mink

BLUE MINK ARCHIVE
Melting pot / Randy / I wanna be around (with you) / Good morning freedom / Yesterday's gone / By the devil I was tempted / Our world / Stop us / Let him stay / Stay with me / Banner man / Song for Madeline / Non commercial blues / Morning glory / Mind your business / Mary Jane / Country chick / But not forever / Chopin up stix / Over the top
CD RMCD 210
Rialto / Sep '96 / Disc / Total/BMG

VERY BEST OF BLUE MINK
CD MCCD 117
Music Club / Aug '93 / Disc / THE

Blue Mountain

HOMEGROWN
Bloody 98 / Myrna Lee / Pretty please / Black dog / Generic America / Last words of Midnight Clyde / Babe / It ain't easy to love a liar / Ira Magee / Town clown / Dead end street / Rain
CD RR 88302
Roadrunner / Sep '97 / PolyGram

Blue Mountain Panpipe ...

CHRISTMAS PANPIPE FAVOURITES (Blue Mountain Panpipe Ensemble)
Little drummer boy / Christmas song / We three kings / Stop the cavalry / I saw three ships / Jingle bells / Mistletoe and wine / Sleigh ride / Have yourself a merry little Christmas / Good King Wenceslas / Silent night / When a child is born / Deck the halls with boughs of holly / Little donkey / Winter wonderland / Silver bells / Jolly old St. Nicholas / Let it snow, let it snow, let it snow / Happy holiday / White Christmas
CD CDMFP 6179
Music For Pleasure / Oct '96 / EMI

PAN PIPE FAVOURITES (3CD Set)
Whiter shade of pale / Live and let die / True love ways / Spanish eyes / Wichita lineman / Wooden heart / When I'm sixty four / Unchained melody / Imagine / All time high / Save the last dance for me / Help me make it through the night / Whatever will be will be (Que sera sera) / Hey Jude / Sailing / Silly love songs / Smoke gets in your eyes / Michelle / Rhinestone cowboy / Yesterday / And I love you so / We've only just begun / Unforgettable / I just called to say I love you / Fool on the hill / Green green grass of home / Can't help falling in love / I've never been to me / Let it be / My guy / Nobody's child / And I love her / Close to you / Something's gotten hold of my heart / It's now or never / Mull of Kintyre / Any dream will do / Wonder of you / Tears on my pillow / When the girl in your arms (is the girl in your heart) / Long and winding road / My way
CD Set CDTRBOX 196
Trio / Sep '95 / EMI

PAN PIPE LOVE SONGS (Blue Mountain Panpipe Ensemble)
Without you / To much love will kill you / Sometimes when we touch / Lady in red / When I fall in love / Whole new world / I'm not in love / Get here / Love us all around / You need me / Always on my mind / Wind beneath my wings / Love lifted me / Power of love / On the wings of love / It must have been love / Greatest love of all / Everything I do (I do it for you) / Secret love
CD CDMFP 6169
Music For Pleasure / Jun '95 / EMI

Blue Nile

HATS
Downtown lights / Over the hillside / Let's go out tonight / Headlights on the parade / From a late night train / Seven am / Saturday night
CD LKHCD 2
Linn / Apr '92 / PolyGram

PEACE AT LAST
CD 9362458482
Warner Bros. / Jun '96 / Warner Music

WALK ACROSS THE ROOFTOPS, A
Walk across the rooftops / Tinsel Town in the rain / From rags to riches / Stay / Easter parade / Heatwave / Automobile noise
CD LKHCD 1
Linn / '88 / PolyGram

Blue Note Six

FROM VIENNA WITH SWING
CD JCD 243
Jazzology / Jun '95 / Jazz Music

Blue Oyster Cult

AGENTS OF FORTUNE
This ain't the summer of love / True confessions / (Don't fear) the reaper / ETI (Extra Terrestrial Intelligence) / Revenge of Vera Gemini / Sinful love / Tattoo vampire / Morning final / Tenderloin / Debbie Denise
CD 4680192
Columbia / Apr '95 / Sony

BAD CHANNELS
CD IRSCD 993018
Intercord / Nov '96 / Plastic Head

BLUE OYSTER CULT
Transmission MC / I'm the lamb but I ain't no sheep / Then came the last days of May / Stairway to the stars / Before the kiss / Redcap / Screams / She's as beautiful as a foot / Cities on flame / Workshop of the telescopes / Redeemed
CD 4688742
Epic / Feb '97 / Sony

CLUB NINJA
White flags / Dancin' in the ruins / Rock not war / Perfect water / Spy in the house of the night / Beat 'em up / When the war comes / Shadow warrior / Madness to the method
CD 379432
Koch International / Jun '97 / Koch

CULT CLASSICS
(Don't fear) the reaper / ETI (Extra Terresstial Intelligence) / ME 262 / This ain't the summer of love / Burning for you / OD'd on life itself / Flaming telepaths / Godzilla / Astronomy / Cities on flame with rock 'n' roll / Harvester of eyes / Buck's boogie
CD CDFRL 003
Fragile / Oct '94 / Grapevine/PolyGram

LIVE 1976
Stairway to the stars / Harvester of eyes / Cities on flame / ME262 / Dominance and submission / Astronomy / ETI (Extra Terrestrial Intelligence) / Buck's boogie / This ain't the summer of love / (Don't fear) the reaper
CD CLACD 269
Castle / Oct '91 / BMG

SOME ENCHANTED EVENING
R U ready 2 rock / ETI (Extra Terrestrial Intellegence) / Astronomy / Kick out the jams / Godzilla / (Don't fear) the reaper / We gotta get out of this place
CD 4879312
Columbia / Jul '97 / Sony

WORKSHOP OF THE TELESCOPES (2CD Set)
Cities on flame with rock and roll / Transmaniacon MC / Before the kiss / Redcap / Stairway to the stars / Buck's boogie / Workshop of the telescopes / Red and the black / 7 screaming diz-busters / Career of evil / Flaming telepaths / Astronomy / Subhuman / Harvester of eyes / ME 262 / Born to be wild / (Don't fear) the reaper / This ain't the summer of love / ETI (Extra Terrestrial Intelligence) / Godzilla / Goin' through the motions / Golden age of leather / Kick out the james / We gotta get out of this place / In thee / Marshall plan / Veteran of the psychic wars / Burnin' for you / Dominance and submission / Take me away / Shooting shark / Dancin' in the ruins / Perfect water
CD Set 4809492
Columbia / Jan '96 / Sony

Blue People

BLUE
CD JVC 90012
JVC / Feb '96 / Direct / New Note/ Pinnacle / Vital/SAM

Blue Pillar Organ

STREET ORGAN FAVOURITES
CD SOW 90135
Sounds Of The World / Jan '95 / Target/ BMG

Blue Rhythm Boys

AT LAST
That's the stuff you gotta watch / I'll go crazy / Person to person / I'm walkin' / It isn't right / Cajun love affair / Trace of you / Crazy mixed up world / Ride 'n' roll / Babie's comin' home / Mother earth / I'll try / Hoochie coochie man / Come on back / Wang dang doodle / Breathless / Blue rhythm boogie / Go on ahead / Catfish
CD CDWIK 105
Big Beat / Apr '92 / Pinnacle

Blue Rose

BLUE ROSE
CD SHCD 3768
Sugar Hill / Jan '97 / ADA / CM / Direct / Koch / Roots

Blue Sky Boys

IN CONCERT 1964
CD ROUCD 11536
Rounder / ADA / CM / Direct

Blue Stingrays

SURF 'N' BURN
CD 60012
Epitaph / Sep '97 / Pinnacle / Plastic Head

Blue Tip

DISCHORD NO.101
CD DIS 101CD
Dischord / Jun '96 / SRD

Blue Wisp Big Band

ROLLIN'
CD SB 2077
Sea Breeze / Jan '97 / Jazz Music

Bluebells

BEST OF THE BLUEBELLS, THE
CD 82840522
London / Apr '93 / PolyGram

Blueberry Hill

D-DAY FAVOURITES 1944
CD SOW 510
Sound Waves / May '94 / Target/BMG

IT'S PARTY TIME
CD SOW 520
Sound Waves / May '95 / Target/BMG

ONE STEP FORWARD (Blueberry Hill & Sheila G. White)
My baby loves me / Dream baby / One more last chance / On the road / Mercury blues / Wild one / Achy breaky heart / Live till I die / Honey (Won't you open that door) / You make me feel like a man / Chattahoochie / One step forward / Blue roses / Bootscootin boogie / Ancient history / Cotton Eye Joe / When will I be loved / Loves

gotta hold on you / I swear / Guitars and cadillacs
CD 3036300162
Country Skyline / Aug '96 / Carlton

OUR KINDA COUNTRY (Blueberry Hill & Sheila G. White)
Ghost riders in the sky / Blue moon over Kentucky / Do what you do do well / Good hearted woman / Folsom prison / Truck driving man / Wild side of life / Peaceful easy feeling / Take it easy / When I was yours / Six days on the road / Walk on by / I love you because / Take these chains from my heart / Ramblin' rose / Walking after midnight / From a Jack to a King / Tonight the bottle let me down / Running bear / Delta dawn / I really had a ball last night / Jambalaya / Me and Bobby McGee / Your cheating heart / Paper roses / Don't fence me in / Hello Mary Lou / I'm gonna be a country girl again / Walk tall / On top of the world / San Quentin / Sea of heartbreak / Blanket on the ground / Gypsy woman / Okie from Muskogee / Take me home country roads / Together again / Sweet dreams / You're my best friend / Today I started loving you again / Oh lonesome me / I walk the line / Turn out the light / Let's think about living / Leaving on a jet plane / What I've got in mind / Single girl / If I said you had a beautiful body / Harper valley PTA / Sloop John B
CD SOW 523
Sound Waves / Aug '96 / Target/BMG

Bluebird Society Orchestra

MUSIC OF HIGH SOCIETY
CD ST 583
Stash / Jul '94 / ADA / Cadillac / CM / Direct / Jazz Music

Bluebirds

SOUTH FROM MEMPHIS
CD ICD 9420
Icehouse / Oct '96 / Hot Shot

SWAMP STOMP
CD ICD 9407
CD TX 1012CD
Taxim / Jul '95 / ADA

Blueboy

IF WISHES WERE HORSES
CD SARAH 612CD
Sarah / Mar '95 / Vital

UNISEX
So catch him / Cosmopolitan / Marble Arch / Joy of living / Fleetway / Also ran / Boys don't matter / Self portrait / Lazy thunderstorms / Finistere / Always there / Imipramine
CD SARAH 620CD
Sarah / Apr '94 / Vital

Bluegills

BLUEGILLS, THE
Real gone / Waiting for the big one / Don't gimme that gimme / Tell tale signs / Don't tell me that / Bluegills / We hang on / Soul full of blues / Rock bottom / My funky valentine / I'm a little mixed up / In a funk in a phone booth
CD ATM 123
Atomic Theory / Nov '96 / ADA / Direct

Bluegrass Album Band

BLUEGRASS INSTRUMENTALS VOL.6
CD ROUCD 0330
Rounder / Aug '96 / ADA / CM / Direct

SONGS OF BILL MONROE, THE
On my way back to the old home / I believe in you darling / Cheyenne / Letter from my darlin' / Lonesome moonlight waltz / When you are lonely / Sitting alone in the moonlight / Molly and Tenbrooks / On the old Kentucky shore / Brown County breakdown / Toy heart / River of death
CD EDCD 7003
Easydisc / Oct '96 / Direct

SONGS OF FLATT & SCRUGGS, THE
I'll never shed another tear / Down that road / Don't this road look rough and rocky / Is it too late now / Your love is like a flower / Old home town / Come back darling / I'm waiting to hear you call me darling / Somehow tonight / I'd rather be alone / Head over heals / So happy I'll be
CD EDCD 7002
Easydisc / Aug '96 / Direct

Bluejean

TRY MY LOVIN'
CD EBCD 28
Eightball / Jan '95 / Vital

Bluerunners

CHATEAU CHUCK, THE
CD MON 6118CD
Ichiban / Mar '94 / Direct / Koch

Blues Band

BACK FOR MORE
Normal service / Victim of love / Not me / Blue collar / Can't get my ass in gear / Great crash / When I itches I scratch / Don't buy the potion / Bad boy / Down in the bottom / Leaving
CD COBM 6
Cobalt / Sep '95 / Grapevine/PolyGram

BRAND LOYALTY
Seemed like a good idea at the time / Rolling log / I want to be loved / Might as well be / What do you want / Big fine girl / Sure feels good / Little baby / Grits ain't groceries / Funny money / Take me home / Ooo-ee / So bad / Ain't it tough
CD COBCM 5
Cobalt / Sep '95 / Grapevine/PolyGram

EIGHTEEN YEARS AND ALIVE
CD COBCD 2
Cobalt / Feb '97 / Grapevine/PolyGram

FAT CITY
Fat city / Longing for you baby / Help me / I can't tell it all / Down to the river / Country blues / Cold emotions, frozen hearts / Killing me by degrees / Duisburg blues / So lonely / Too bad you're no good / Long time gone
CD COBCM 1
Cobalt / Mar '95 / Grapevine/PolyGram

ITCHY FEET
Talkin' woman blues / Who's right, who's wrong / Rock 'n' roll radio / Itchy feet / Ultimatum time / So lonely / Come on / Turn around / I can't be satisfied / Got to love you baby / Nothin' but the blues / Let your bucket down
CD COBCM 4
Cobalt / Sep '95 / Grapevine/PolyGram

LIVE
Come on in / Hey hey little girl / Death letter / Grit's ain't groceries / Flatfoot Sam / Don't lie to me / Can't hold on much longer / It might as well be me / Nadine / Big boss man / Maggie's farm / Treat her right / Find youself another fool / Big fine girl / Someday baby / Rolling log / Greenstuff / Boom boom (out go the lights)
CD MAUCD 629
Mau Mau / Feb '95 / Pinnacle

OFFICIAL BLUES BAND BOOTLEG ALBUM
Talk to me baby / Flatfoot Sam / Two bones and a pick / Someday baby / Boom boom (out go the lights) / Come in / Death letter / Going home / I don't know / Diddy wah diddy
CD COBCM 2
Cobalt / Mar '95 / Grapevine/PolyGram

READY
Twenty nine ways / I'm ready / Hallelujah, I love her so / Sus blues / Noah Lewis blues / Treat her right / Lonely Avenue / Find yourself another fool / Hey hey little girl / Green stuff / Can't hold on / Cat / That's alright / Nadine
CD COBCM 3
Cobalt / Mar '95 / Grapevine/PolyGram

THESE KIND OF BLUES
Tobacco Road / Doin' alright / Time after time / Stealing / That's it, I quit / Bad penny blues / Let the four winds blow / Bad luck / Hard working man / These kind of blues / Smokestack lightnin'
CD COBCM 7
Cobalt / Feb '96 / Grapevine/PolyGram

WIRE-LESS
CD COBCD 1
Cobalt / Mar '95 / Grapevine/PolyGram

Blues Boy Willie

BE WHO VOL.1
Why are you cheatin' on me / Same ol' fishing hole / Crack up / Stealing your love tonight / Let me funk with you / Can we talk before we separate / Highway blues / Be who
CD ICH 1064CD
Ichiban / Oct '93 / Direct / Koch

BE WHO VOL.2
Party all night / I still care / Break away / Rest of my life / Where is Leroy / Love darling love / Let's get closer / Be who, two
CD ICH 1119CD
Ichiban / Jun '94 / Direct / Koch

Blues Brothers

BEST OF THE BLUES BROTHERS
Expressway / Everybody needs somebody to love / I don't know / She caught the Katy / Soul man / Rubber biscuit / Goin' back to Miami / Gimme some lovin' / B Movie / Boxcar blues / Flip flop fly
CD 7815862
Atlantic / Jun '89 / Warner Music

BLUES BROTHERS - MUSIC FROM THE FILM (Original Soundtrack)
Minnie the moocher / Jailhouse rock / Sweet home chicago / Theme from rawhide / Peter Gunn / Gimme some lovin' / She caught the Katy / Old landmark / Shake a tail feather / Everybody needs somebody to love / Think
CD 7567827872
Atlantic / Nov '95 / Warner Music

BRIEFCASE FULL OF BLUES
I can't turn you loose / Hey bartender / Messin' with the kid / I got everything I need / Shot gun blues / Rubber biscuit / Groove me / Soul man / Flip flop and fly / B Movie / Boxcar blues
CD 250556
Atlantic / Mar '87 / Warner Music

LIVE IN MONTREUX (Blues Brothers Band)
Hold on I'm comin' / In the midnight hour / She caught the katy / Thrill is gone / I can't turn you loose / Sweet home Chicago / Knock on wood / Rasie your hand / Peter Gunn / Soul finger / Hey bartender / Soul man / Everybody needs somebody to love / Green onions
CD 9031716142
Atlantic / Feb '95 / Warner Music

MADE IN AMERICA
Soul finger / Funky Broadway / Who's making love / Do you love me / Guilty / Perry Mason (theme from) / Riot in cell block 9 / Green onions / I ain't got you / From the bottom / Going to Miami
CD 7567814782
Atlantic / Jun '89 / Warner Music

Blues Busters

IN MEMORY OF THE BLUES BUSTERS
CD JMC 200114
Jamaican Gold / Sep '93 / Grapevine/ PolyGram / Jet Star

Blues Company

PUBLIC RELATIONS
Public relations / Red blood / Dance all night / Midnight train / Just can't keep from crying / She's gone / I've got the blues / Rhythm of Zydeco / Cry for me / Big bad wolf / Gambler / Blow Jay blow / Change / Crippled mind
CD INAK 9018
In Akustik / Aug '95 / Direct / TKO Magnum

SO WHAT
What's wrong / Cold blue moon / Stay with me / Downhome blues / Mean woman blues / Rattlesnake blues / Pension blues / Look here baby / Good times boogie / Teeny weeny bit / Drinkin' blues / Mr. TNT / Black nite
CD INAK 8803CD
In Akustik / Jul '97 / Direct / TKO Magnum

VINTAGE
CD INAK 9036
In Akustik / Nov '95 / Direct / TKO Magnum

Blues Mobile Band

NEW DAY YESTERDAY, A
CD PRD 70772
Provogue / May '95 / Pinnacle

OUT IN THE BLUE
What I do / She's gone / I'm going home / I can't stand it / Try hard / Leave this town / I've got dreams to remember / Leave me alone / Tell me why / Helpless without you / Too late
CD PRD 70852
Provogue / Nov '95 / Pinnacle

Blues 'n' Trouble

BAG FULL OF BOOGIE
Bag full of boogie / Riding in my cadillac / Deep blue feeling / You got me spinnin' / Blues because of you / Breaking the ice / Good morning little school girl / Serenade for a wealthy widow / Slim's chance / Drug store woman / Lookin' for my baby / Lowdown / Down in Dallas
CD BAMCD 2
Barking Mad / Jul '94 / Conifer/BMG

HAT TRICK
I got your number / Why / Cherry peaches / Travelling light / When the lights go down / Comin' home / What's the matter / Be mine tonight / Rockin' with you Jimmy / TNT / See my baby shake it / I don't need no doctor
CD CDBLUH 001
Blue Horizon / Feb '92 / Pinnacle

POOR MOON
CD BAMCD 1
Barking Mad / Feb '93 / Conifer/BMG

Blues Project

ANTHOLOGY (2CD Set)
CD Set 5297852
Polydor / Jun '97 / PolyGram

LIVE AT TOWN HALL
CD OW 30010
One Way / Jul '94 / ADA / Direct / Greyhound

Blues Section

BLUES SECTION
CD LRCD 3
Love / Dec '94 / ADA / Direct / Greyhound

BLUES SECTION VOL.2
CD LXCD 604
Love / Aug '95 / ADA / Direct / Greyhound

Blues Traveller

FOUR
Runaround / Stand / Look around / Fallible / Mountains win again / Freedom / Crash burn / Price to pay / Hook / Good, the bad and the ugly / Just wait / Brother John
CD 5402652
Polydor / Nov '94 / PolyGram

STRAIGHT ON 'TILL MORNING
Carolina blues / Felicia / Justify the thrill / Canadian rose / Business as usual / Yours / Psycho JOe / Great big world / Battle of someone / Most precarious / Gunfighter / Last night I dreamed / Make my way
CD 5407502
A&M / Jun '97 / PolyGram

Bluetones

EXPECTING TO FLY
Talking to Clarry / Bluetonic / Cut some rug / Things change / Fountainhead / Carnt be trusted / Slight return / Putting out fires / Vampire / Parting gesture / Time & again
CD BLUE 004CD
Superior Quality / Feb '96 / Vital

INTERVIEW DISC
CD TONE 10CD
Wax / Jan '97 / RTM/Disc / Total/BMG

Bluezeum

PORTRAIT OF A GROOVE
Portrait of a groove / Can I get that funk / Luv uncondishunal / Dreamtyme / Every day and every minute / Just anotha day / Swing / Strange love last night / Soundscape
CD CD 83331
Telarc Jazz / Nov '96 / Conifer/BMG

Bluiett, Hamiet

BIRTHRIGHT
CD IN 1030CD
India Navigation / Jan '97 / Discovery / Impetus

EBU
CD SNCD 1088
Soul Note / Jan '86 / Cadillac / Harmonia Mundi / Wellard

IM/POSSIBLE TO KEEP
CD IN 1072CD
India Navigation / Jan '97 / Discovery / Impetus

LIVE AT CARLOS VOL.1 (Bluiett, Hamiet & Concept)
Mighty denn / Full, deep and mellow / Nalikoal / Oleo / Night in Tunisia
CD JAM 9129
Just A Memory / Jun '97 / New Note/ Pinnacle

SANKOFA/REAR GARDE
CD 1212382
Soul Note / Sep '93 / Cadillac / Harmonia Mundi / Wellard

Blum, Eberhard

ALEA
CD ARTCD 6180
Hat Art / Feb '96 / Cadillac / Harmonia Mundi

Blumfeld

LETAT AT MOI
CD ABB 73CD
Big Cat / Feb '95 / 3mv/Pinnacle

Blunderbuss

CONSPIRACY
CD HMS 2192
Homestead / Aug '95 / Cargo / SRD

Blunstone, Colin

GREATEST HITS
Say you don't mind / Old and wise / Caroline goodbye / Andorra / I don't believe in miracles / She's not there / Tell her no / Time of the season / What becomes of the broken hearted / Tracks of my tears / Still burning bright / Don't feel no pain
CD CLACD 351
Castle / Aug '93 / BMG

LIVE AT THE BBC
Misty roses / Say you don't mind / Brother love / Something happens when you touch me / She's not there / Time of the season / Andorra / Caroline goodbye / I don't believe in miracles / Wonderful
CD WINCD 079
Windsong / Dec '95 / Pinnacle

SOME YEARS IT'S THE TIME OF
She loves the way they love her / Misty roses / Caroline goodbye / Though you are far away / Mary won't you warm my bed / Let me come closer to you / Say you don't mind / I don't believe in miracles / How wrong can one man be / Andorra / How could we dare to be wrong / Wonderful / Beginning / Keep the curtains closed today / You who are lonely / It's magical / This is your captain calling

CD ____________ EK 66449
Columbia / Jul '95 / Sony

Blur

BLUR
Beetlebum / Song 2 / Country sad ballad man / MOR / On your own / Theme from retro / You're so great / Death of a party / Chinese bombs / I'm just a killer for your love / Look inside America / Strange news from another star / Movin' on / Essex dogs
CD ____________ FOODCD 19
Food / Jun '97 / EMI

GREAT ESCAPE, THE
Stereotypes / Country house / Best days / Charmless man / Fade away / Top man / Universal / Mr. Robinson's quango / He thought of cars / It could be you / Ernold Same / Globe alone / Dan Abnormal / Entertain me / Yoko and Hiro
CD ____________ FOODCD 14
Food / Sep '95 / EMI

LEISURE
She's so high / Bang / Slow down / Repetition / Bad day / Sing / There's no other way / Fool / Come together / High cool / Birthday / War me down
CD ____________ FOODCD 6
Food / Aug '91 / EMI

MODERN LIFE IS RUBBISH
For tomorrow / Advert / Colin Zeal / Pressure on Julian / Star shaped / Blue jeans / Chemical world / Intermission / Sunday Sunday / Oily water / Miss America / Villa Rosie / Coping / Turn it up / Resigned / Commercial break
CD ____________ FOODCD 9
Food / May '93 / EMI

PARKLIFE
Girls and boys / Tracy Jacks / End of a century / Parklife / Bank holiday / Debt collector / Far out / To the end / London loves / Trouble in the message centre / Clover over Dover / Magic America / Jubilee / This is a low
CD ____________ FOODCD 10
Food / Apr '94 / EMI

Blurt

PAGAN STRINGS
CD ____________ 14988
Spalax / Feb '97 / ADA / Cargo / Direct / Discovery / Greyhound

Blyth Power

OUT FROM UNDER THE KING
CD ____________ DR 004CD
Downwarde Spiral / Sep '96 / ADA / Direct

PARADISE RAZED
CD ____________ DR 003CD
Downwarde Spiral / Feb '95 / ADA / Direct

PASTOR SKULL
Pastor skull / Man who came in third / Gabriel the angel / In the lines of graves / Breitenfeld / General Winter / Sunne in splendour / Stonehaven / Vane tempest / Pandora's people / Stitching in time
CD ____________ DR 002CD
Downwarde Spiral / Sep '96 / ADA / Direct

Blythe, Arthur

CALLING CARD
As of yet / Blue blues / Naima's love song / Hip dripper / Odessa / Elaborations / Jitterbug waltz / Break tune
CD ____________ ENJ 90512
Enja / Feb '96 / New Note/Pinnacle / Vital/ SAM

METAMORPHOSIS/THE GRIP
CD ____________ IN 1029CD
India Navigation / Jan '97 / Discovery / Impetus

RETROFLECTION
Jana's delight / JB blues / Peacemaker / Light blue / Lenox avenue breakdown / Faceless woman / Break tune
CD ____________ ENJ 80462
Enja / Mar '94 / New Note/Pinnacle / Vital/ SAM

BM EX

APPOLONIA
CD ____________ UCRCD 14
Union City / Jan '93 / EMI

BMX Bandits

C-86 AND MORE
CD ____________ ER 1048
Elefant / Jul '97 / Greyhound / SRD

GETTING DIRTY
CD ____________ CRECD 174
Creation / May '95 / 3mv/Vital

LIFE GOES ON
CD ____________ CRECD 133
Creation / Sep '93 / 3mv/Vital

STAR WARS
CD ____________ ASK 7CD
Vinyl Japan / '92 / Plastic Head / Vinyl Japan

THEME PARK
CD ____________ CRECD 202
Creation / Oct '96 / 3mv/Vital

BNFL Band

BY REQUEST (BNFL Band/Richard Evans)
Toccata / Revelation / Paragon / Amparito roca / Ted Heath big band set / Impromptu for tuba / Ave Maria / Carnival of Venice / March
CD ____________ QPRL 078D
Polyphonic / May '96 / Complete/Pinnacle

COME FOLLOW THE BAND
Come follow the band / Arcadians / Summertime / Cheek to cheek / I got rhythm / I dreamed a dream / Pie Jesu / Slaughter on 10th Avenue / Another opening another show / Overture to Phantom of the Opera / Anything goes / Memory / West Side story / Till there was you / You'll never walk alone / Oklahoma
CD ____________ DOYCD 018
Doyen / Oct '92 / Conifer/BMG

MUSIC OF PHILIP SPARKE VOL.1, THE (Cambridge Variations) (BNFL Band/ Richard Evans)
Jubilee overture / Music for a festival / Serenade for horns / Malvern suite / Concerto grosso / Mountains song / Cambridge variations
CD ____________ QPRL 081D
Polyphonic / Aug '96 / Complete/Pinnacle

PARTITE
CD ____________ QPRL 062D
Polyphonic / Sep '93 / Complete/Pinnacle

ROMANCE IN BRASS VOL.2
Kiss me again / Spread a little happiness / Just the way you are / Somewhere out there / Serenade for Toni / Annie Laurie / Girl with the flaxen hair / Meditation from thais / Li'l darlin' / Indian summer / Aubade / Love on the rocks / Romance de l'amour / Passing by / Myfanwy / Sweet shepherdess / Georgia on my mind / Folks who live on the hill / Memory
CD ____________ QPRL 063D
Polyphonic / Apr '94 / Complete/Pinnacle

TRAVELLIN' LIGHT (BNFL Band & Russel Gray/Intrada Brass/Waitakere Brass)
Charivari / Apres un reve / Napoli / Solveig's song / Jubilance / Song of the seashore / Songs of Erin / Higgin's hornpipe/The Kildare fancy / David of the white rock / Grand Russian fantasia / Dark haired Marie / Zelda / My love is like a red, red rose / Phantasy
CD ____________ QPRL 079D
Polyphonic / Aug '96 / Complete/Pinnacle

UN VIE DE MATELOT
Un vie de matelot / Snowdon fantasy / Little suite for brass / Rococo variations / Land of the long white cloud
CD ____________ QPRL 069D
Polyphonic / Oct '94 / Complete/Pinnacle

Bo, Eddie

BEST OF EDDIE BO, THE
Hook and sling / If it's good to you (it's good for you) / Getting to the middle / Check your bucket / Getting to the middle / Don't turn me loose / We're doing it / Disco party
CD ____________ HUBCD 16
Hubbub / Apr '97 / Beechwood/BMG / SRD / Timewarp

CHECK MR POPEYE
Check Mr. Popeye / Now let's Popeye / It must be love / Dinky doo / I'll do anything for you / Warm daddy / Roamin-itis / Hey there baby / I need someone / Tell it like it is / You got your mojo working / Ain't you ashamed / Baby I'm wise / Every dog has his day
CD ____________ ROUCD 2077
Rounder / '88 / ADA / CM / Direct

Boat Band

BURNING THE WATER
CD ____________ HARCD 030
Harbour Town / Apr '95 / ADA / CM / Direct / Roots

Boatman, James

MAIN STREET USA
CD ____________ CCS 9896
Channel Classics / Nov '96 / Select / Vital/ SAM

Boatman, Tooter

ROCKIN' TOOTER BOATMAN
CD ____________ CLCD 4408
Collector/White Label / Jan '97 / TKO Magnum

Bob & Earl

DANCETIME USA (Bob & Earl/The Olympics)
Baby, your time is my time: *Bob & Earl* / Big brother: *Bob & Earl* / Land of 1000 dances: *Bob & Earl* / I can't get away: *Bob & Earl* / My little girl: *Bob & Earl* / I'll keep running back: *Bob & Earl* / Dancin' everywhere: *Bob & Earl* / Send for me I'll be there: *Bob & Earl* / Ooh honey babe: *Bob & Earl* / Harlem shuffle: *Bob & Earl* / Bounce: *Olympics* / Mine exclusively: *Olympics* / Baby, do the philly dog: *Olympics* / Duck: *Olympics* / Same old thing: *Olympics* / I'll do a little bit more: *Olympics* / We go together: *Olympics* / Secret agent: *Olympics*
CD ____________ GSCD054
Goldmine / Jul '95 / Vital

Bob & Ray

STEREO SPECTACULAR, A (Various Artists)
Bob and Ray visit Dr Akhbar at the castle: *Bob & Ray* / Bob and Ray in the round room: *Bob & Ray* / Thing: *Bob & Ray* / Bob and Ray in the laboratory: *Bob & Ray* / End: *Bob & Ray* / Riders in the sky: *Melachrino, George* / Minute on the rocks: *Henderson, Skitch* / Buck dance: *Schory, Dick* / New fangled tango: *Horne, Lena* / Second Hungarian rhapsody: *Guckenheimer Sour Kraut Band* / First Noel: *Lieber, Richard* / We'll gather lilacs in the spring: *Andrews, Julie* / Song of the Volga boatmen: *Sauter-Finegan Orchestra* / Whatever Lola wants: *Lane, Abbe* / Ox drivers: *Belafonte Singers*
CD ____________ 743212574929
RCA / Jul '96 / BMG

Bob & The Bearcats

HIGH HEELS AND HOMICIDE
CD ____________ PEPCD 115
Pollytone / Sep '96 / Nervous / Pollytone

Bob Delyn

GEDON
Gortoz pell zo gortoz gwell / Poeni dim / Llys Ifor Haul / Ffair y Bala / Corsydd Fyrjinia / Mil harddach wyt / Beaj iskis / Seance Watcyn Wynn / Y swn / Tren bach y sgwarnogod / Blodau haearn blodau glo / Y clewr olaf / Llewg zotrog oz llep zotrog (Kig ejen c'hoazh)
CD ____________ CRAICD 021
Crai / Aug '94 / ADA / Direct

GWBADE BACH COCHLYD
CD ____________ CRAICD 49
Crai / Oct '96 / ADA / Direct

Bobbejaan

ICH STEH AN DER BAR UND HABE KEIN GELD
Ich steh on der bar und habe kein geld / Roy old boy / Ich weine in mein bier / Ein hauschen auf der heide / Vie biitre tranen / Marina / Kili watch / Die letzte rose / Ich muss ein cowboy sein / Spiel gitarre spiel / Ach war ich nur / Wie ne kneipe ohne bier / Und das hat mir g'rad noch gefenlt / O-la-la Luise / Dein herz kommt mir vor wie ein wanderpokal / Was kohn ich denn dafur / Zwischen Tennessee und Oklahoma / Schon langsam und nur nicht zu schnell / Die katz kam wieder / Ein voles glas und ein volles pomemon / Naie / Was meine frau alles wissen will / Der weg nach Winnepeg / Texas rangers abschied / Ich hab kein geld fur ein orchester / Das treibt den Mann an die Theke / Der verliebte pfeifer / Der pfeifer und sein schatten
CD ____________ BCD 15921
Bear Family / Jul '96 / Direct / Rollercoaster / Swift

Bobby & Steve

BREAKBEAT SESSIONS VOL.2 (Black Trax)
Black trax / Night grooves / Fantasy / Benji / Midnight / Everybody / Hustle / I wanna / Soul / Groove on / Don't you / Tell me / Tribe
CD ____________ 343712
Koch Dance Force / May '96 / Koch

Bobo, Willie

TALKIN' VERVE
CD ____________ 5375752
Verve / Jul '97 / PolyGram

UNO DOS TRES
CD ____________ 5216642
Verve / Feb '95 / PolyGram

Bobs

COVER THE SONGS OF...
CD ____________ ROUCD 9049
Rounder / Nov '94 / ADA / CM / Direct

PLUGGED
CD ____________ ROUCD 9059
Rounder / Oct '95 / ADA / CM / Direct

SHUT UP AND SING
CD ____________ ROUCD 9039
Rounder / Jan '94 / ADA / CM / Direct

TOO MANY SANTA'S
CD ____________ ROUCD 9060
Rounder / Sep '96 / ADA / CM / Direct

Bobs Your Uncle

CAGES
CD ____________ ZULU 009CD
Zulu / Oct '95 / Plastic Head

Bobvan

WATER DRAGON
Ay triste / Eyebrow and curved hair / Water dragon / Branle poitevin / Serendipity / Careful with that fax Eugene / Labbra Rosse / Shrinking of the gigantic / Perky Pat's lament / Memory
CD ____________ SSR 127
SSR / Jan '94 / Amato Disco / Grapevine/ PolyGram / Prime / RTM/Disc

Bocage, Peter

PETER BOCAGE & HIS CREOLE SERENADERS
CD ____________ AMCD 93
American Music / Nov '96 / Jazz Music

Bocelli, Andrea

ROMANZA
Con te partiro / Vivere: *Bocelli, Andrea & Gerardina Trovato* / Per amore / Il mare calmo della sera / Caruso / Macchine da guerra / La tue parole / Vivo per lei / Romanza / La luna che non c'e / Rapsodia / Voglio restare cosi / E chiove / Miserere: *Bocelli, Andrea & John Miles* / Time to say goodbye: *Bocelli, Andrea & Sarah Brightman*
CD ____________ 4564562
Philips / May '97 / PolyGram

Bocian, Michael

REVERENCE
CD ____________ ENJACD 80962
Enja / Sep '95 / New Note/Pinnacle / Vital/ SAM

Bock, Wolfgang

BISCAYA SUNSET
CD ____________ SKYCD 3054
Sky / Sep '95 / Greyhound / Koch / Vital/ SAM

Boddy, Ian

CLIMB
CD ____________ SER 005
Something Else / Jun '96 / Pinnacle

CONTINUUM (2CD Set)
CD Set ____________ SER 011
Something Else / Apr '97 / Pinnacle

DEEP, THE
Standing at the edge / Dark descent / Deep / In the realm of poseidon / Leviathan / Flow current flow / Sirens call / Aquanaut / Re-emergence / Surface flight / Sub aquiem
CD ____________ SER 006
Something Else / Sep '94 / Pinnacle

PHOENIX
CD ____________ SER 009
Something Else / Jun '96 / Pinnacle

SPIRITS
CD ____________ SER 007
Something Else / Jun '96 / Pinnacle

UNCERTAINTY PRINCIPLE, THE
Times arrow / Virtual journey / Chromazone / Space cadet / Interstellar interlude No.1 / Cassiopeia's dream / Interstellar interlude No.2 / Sopernova / Uncertainty principle 1 / Uncertainty principle 2 / Uncertainty principle 3 / Beyond the event horizon / Times end
CD ____________ SER 004
Something Else / Sep '94 / Pinnacle

Bodimead, Jackie

DON'T BELIEVE IN LOVE
CD ____________ ASBCD 007
Scratch / Dec '96 / Koch / Scratch/BMG

Bodner, Phil

FINE AND DANDY
CD ____________ JHR 73511
Jazz Hour / May '93 / Cadillac / Jazz Music / Target/BMG

NEW YORK JAM
CD ____________ STB 2505
Stash / Sep '95 / ADA / Cadillac / CM / Direct / Jazz Music

Body Count

BODYCOUNT
Smoked pork / Body Count's in the house / Now sports / Body Count / Statistic / Bowels of the devil / Real problem / KKK Bitch / Note / Voodoo / Winner loses / There goes the neighborhood / Oprah / Evil dick / Body Count anthem / Momma's gotta die tonight / Ice T/Freedom of speech
CD ____________ 9362451392
WEA / Mar '94 / Warner Music

BORN DEAD
Body m/f count / Masters of revenge / Killin' floor / Necessary evil / Drive-by / Last breath / Hey Joe / Shallow graves / Who are you / Street lobotomy / Born dead
CD ____________ RSYND 2
Rhyme Syndicate / Sep '94 / EMI

VIOLENT DEMISE - THE LAST DAYS
Interview / My way: *Body Count & Raw Breed* / Strippers intro / Strippers / Truth or death / Violent demise / Bring it to pain / Music business / I used to love her / Root of all evil / Dead man walking / Interview end / You're fuckin' with BC / Ernie's intro / Dr. K / Last days
CD ______ **CDV 2813**
Virgin / Mar '97 / EMI

Bodychoke

FIVE PROSTITUTES
CD ______ **FRR 010**
Freek / Jul '96 / RTM/Disc / SRD

MINDSHAFT
CD ______ **FRR 003**
Freek / Mar '94 / RTM/Disc / SRD

Bodyjar

TAKE A LOOK INSIDE
CD ______ **BHR 035CD**
Burning Heart / Feb '96 / Plastic Head

TIME TO GROW UP
CD ______ **BHR 036CD**
Burning Heart / Jul '96 / Plastic Head

Boe, Knut Ivar

FERDAMANN
CD ______ **HCD 7100**
Musikk Distribujson / Dec '94 / ADA

Boehmer, Conrad

ACOIUSMATRIX VOL.5
CD ______ **BVHAASTCD 9011**
Bvhaast / Oct '93 / Cadillac

IN ILO TEMPORE
CD ______ **BVHAASTCD 9008**
Bvhaast / Oct '93 / Cadillac

WOUTERJE PIETERSE
CD ______ **BVHAASTCD 9401/2**
Bvhaast / Oct '94 / Cadillac

Bofill, Angela

LOVE IN SLOW MOTION
All she wants is love / Love in slow motion / Real love / Galaxy of my love / Guess you didn't know / Sail away / Are you leaving me now / Let them talk / Soul of mine / Love changes / Black angel
CD ______ **XECD 8**
Expansion / Jun '96 / 3mv/Sony

Bogan, Lucille

LUCILLE BOGAN
CD ______ **SOB 32352**
Story Of The Blues / Dec '92 / ADA / Koch

LUCILLE BOGAN VOL.1 1923-1930
CD ______ **BDCD 6036**
Blues Document / Apr '93 / ADA / Hot Shot / Jazz Music

LUCILLE BOGAN VOL.3 1934-1935
CD ______ **BDCD 6038**
Blues Document / Apr '93 / ADA / Hot Shot / Jazz Music

Bogart, Deanna

CROSSING BORDERS
CD ______ **FF 601CD**
Flying Fish / Feb '93 / ADA / CM / Direct / Roots

Bogguss, Suzy

ACES
Outbound plane / Aces / Someday soon / Let goodbye hurt like it should / Save yourself / Yellow river road / Part of me / Letting go / Music on the wind / Still hold on
CD ______ **CDP 7985472**
Capitol / Feb '92 / EMI

COUNTRY CLASSICS
Under the gun / My side of the story / Moment of truth / All things made new again / Wild horses / Fear of flying / As if I didn't know / Blue days / Burning down / Friend of mine
CD ______ **CDMFP 6330**
Music For Pleasure / Apr '97 / EMI

GIVE ME SOME WHEELS
Give me some wheels / Feeling ,bout you / Let's get real / Travelling light / Live to love another day / No way out / Fall / Saying goodbye to a friend / She said, he heard / Far and away
CD ______ **PRMDCD 10**
Premier/EMI / Jul '96 / EMI

SOMETHING UP MY SLEEVE
Diamonds and tears / Just like the weather / Just keep comin' back to you / You never will / You'd be the one / Take it to the limit / Hey Cinderella / Souvenirs / You wouldn't say that to a stranger / Take it like a man / No green eyes / Something up my sleeve: *Bogguss, Suzy & Billy Dean*
CD ______ **CDEST 2211**
Capitol / Sep '93 / EMI

VOICES IN THE WIND
Heartache / Drive south / Don't wanna / How come you go to her / Other side of the hill / In the day / Love goes without saying / Eat at Joe's / Lovin' a hurricane / Letting go / Cold day in July
CD ______ **CDP 7985852**
Liberty / Oct '92 / EMI

Boghall & Bathgate ...

INTERCONTINENTAL DRUMMERS FANFARE, THE (Boghall & Bathgate Caledonia Pipe Band)
CD ______ **LCOM 9042**
Lismor / Jul '91 / ADA / Direct / Duncans / Lismor

RUBIC CUBE, THE (Boghall & Bathgate Caledonia Pipe Band)
2/4 marches / Hornpipes / March, strathspey and reel / Slow air and 9/8 jigs / Selection / Reels / Hornpipe and jig / March and strathspey and reel / Slow air and 6/8 jigs / Strathspeys and reels / 6/8 marches / Jigs
CD ______ **LCOM 5181**
Lismor / Aug '96 / ADA / Direct / Duncans / Lismor

Boghandle

STEP ON IT
Miserable and ugly / Get off / Hey mom / High toned son of a bitch / Hold back the tears / Don't give me that shit / Far from home / Loaded 'n' fucked / Only son / Fuck fun / Intoxicated
CD ______ **BMCD 024**
Black Mark / Jun '92 / Plastic Head

Bogle, Eric

EMIGRANT AND THE EXILE, THE (Bogle, Eric & John Munro)
Poacher's moon / Were you there / Strangers / World cup fever / Ballard of Charles Devenport / Progress / Marking time / Campbell's daughter / One small star / Listen to the old ones / End of an auld song / Cuddy river reverie / Old and in the way / Kissing English arses talking blues / Standing in the light
CD ______ **CDTRAX 121**
Greentrax / Feb '97 / ADA / Direct / Duncans / Highlander

ERIC BOGLE SONGBOOK VOL.1
Reason for it all / Nobody's moggy now / Hard hard times / Scraps of paper / If wishes were fishes / Front row cowboy / And the band played waltzing Matilda / Little Gomez / Aussie Bar-b-q / When the wind blows
CD ______ **CDTRAX 028**
Greentrax / Aug '89 / ADA / Direct / Duncans / Highlander

ERIC BOGLE SONGBOOK VOL.2
Now I'm easy / Glasgow lullaby / No man's land / Do you know any Bob Dylan / My youngest son came home today / Belle of Broughton / Leaving Nancy / Singing the spirit home / Wee china pig / Leaving the land / Rosie / All the fine young men / Across the hills of home
CD ______ **CDTRAX 051**
Greentrax / Apr '92 / ADA / Direct / Duncans / Highlander

HARD, HARD TIMES
CD ______ **TUT 72162**
Wundertute / Jan '94 / ADA / CM / Duncans

I WROTE THIS WEE SONG (Live - 2CD Set)
Sound of singing / Leaving the land / Silly slang song / Mirrors / Reason for it all / Flying finger filler / Vanya / Don't you worry about that / Somewhere in America / Them old song writing blues / Rosie / Feed the children / Singing the spirit home / Leaving Nancy / Now I'm easy / Plastic Paddy / No man's land / Never again- remember / Short white blues / Welcome home / Daniel smiling / Eric and the informers / Shelter / Gift of years
CD Set ______ **CDTRAX 082D**
Greentrax / Jan '95 / ADA / Direct / Duncans / Highlander

MIRRORS
Refugee / One small life / Plastic Paddy / Welcome home / Flat stony broke waltz / Vanya / Don't you worry about that / Mirrors / Song / Big (in a small way) / At risk / Never again - remember / Somewhere in America / Wouldn't be dead for quids / Wishing is free
CD ______ **CDTRAX 068**
Greentrax / Nov '93 / ADA / Direct / Duncans / Highlander

NOW I'M EASY
CD ______ **LRF 041CD**
Larrikin / Mar '89 / ADA / CM / Direct / Roots

SCRAPS OF PAPER
CD ______ **LARRCD 104**
Larrikin / Jun '94 / ADA / CM / Direct / Roots
CD ______ **FF 70311**
Flying Fish / Mar '97 / ADA / CM / Direct / Roots

SINGING THE SPIRIT HOME
Old song / Lifeline / Singing the spirit home / Twenty years ago / All the fine young men / Leaving the land / Australian through and through / Lancelot and Guinevere / Silo / Shelter
CD ______ **LRF 186CD**
Larrikin / '88 / ADA / CM / Direct / Roots

SMALL MIRACLES
Small miracles / Digger's legacy / Dedication day / Ekka's silver jubilee song / Always back to you / Blessing / Here in the green / Sayonara Australia / Golden city / Somebody's daughter / Keeper of the flame / Romeo and juliet in Sarajevo / Red heart / Troy's song / Unsung hero / Heart of the land / One small star
CD ______ **CDTRAX 130**
Greentrax / Jun '97 / ADA / Direct / Duncans / Highlander

VOICES IN THE WILDERNESS
Peace has broken out / Lily and the poppy / Blues for Alex / What kind of man / Wilderness / Feed the children / Amazon / Silly slang song / Fences and walls / It's only Tuesday / Gift of years
CD ______ **CDTRAX 040**
Greentrax / Apr '91 / ADA / Direct / Duncans / Highlander

WHEN THE WIND BLOWS
CD ______ **LARRCD 144**
Larrikin / Jun '94 / ADA / CM / Direct / Roots

Bohannon, Hamilton

ESSENTIAL DANCEFLOOR ARTISTS VOL.4
CD ______ **DGPCD 699**
Deep Beats / Jun '94 / BMG

Bohinta

SESSIONS
CD ______ **AMCD 001**
Aarde / May '97 / Direct

WISHES
CD ______ **NORA 001CD**
Nora / Aug '96 / ADA

Boiled In Lead

ANTLER DANCE
CD ______ **OMM 2007CD**
Omnium / Dec '94 / ADA

OLD LEAD
CD ______ **OMM 2001CD**
Omnium / Dec '94 / ADA

SONGS FROM THE GYPSY
CD ______ **OMM 2013CD**
Omnium / Jul '95 / ADA

Boilermaker Jazz Band

BURGUNDY STREET BLUES
CD ______ **BCD 140**
Biograph / Apr '96 / ADA / Cadillac / Direct / Hot Shot / Jazz Music / Wellard

HONKY TONK TOWN
Meet you there / Coquette / Over in Glory land / Trust in me / When we danced at the Mardi Gras / Lonesome blues / Honky Tonk town / My sweeet southern belle / You always hurt the one you love / Whinin' boy blues
CD ______ **BCD 148**
Biograph / Jun '97 / ADA / Cadillac / Direct / Hot Shot / Jazz Music / Wellard

Boine, Mari

EALLIN (Mari Boine Live)
CD ______ **5337992**
Antilles/New Directions / Nov '96 / PolyGram

GOASKINVIELLJA/EAGLE BROTHER
Cuvges vuovttat / Duodalas calbmi / Sami eatnan duoddarat / Modjas Katrin / Das aiggun cuozzut / Dolgesuorbmageziiguin / Skadja / Goaskinviellja / Rahkesvuodain / Mu ahkku / Ale ale don
CD ______ **5213882**
Verve / Jan '94 / PolyGram

LIEHKASTIN
CD ______ **MB 94CD**
Lean / Dec '94 / ADA

SALMER PA VEIEN HJEM (Paus, Boine Persen, Bremmnes)
CD ______ **FXC 105**
Kirkelig Kultuverksted / Jul '93 / ADA

Boingo

BOINGO
Insanity / Hey / Mary / Can't see (useless) / Pedestrian wolves / Lost like this / Spider / War again / I am the walrus / Tender lumplings / Change / Helpless
CD ______ **74321189712**
Giant / Oct '94 / BMG

Bojan Z

BOJAN Z QUARTET (Bojan Z Quartet)
No name valse / Play ball / Zilbra / Mashala / Ginger pickles / Les instants / Grand od bora / Nishka bania / Spirito
CD ______ **LBLC 6565**
Label Bleu / Nov '95 / New Note/Pinnacle

YOPLA
Yopla / Beyond the frame / Un demi-porc et deaux caisses de bierre / Zajdi, Zajdi / Night thing / Multi don kulti / Ingenuity / Post it / Dugan evinde / She-dance
CD ______ **LBLC 6590**
Label Bleu / Jun '96 / New Note/Pinnacle

Boksch

OCKER 1-8
CD ______ **EFA 610522**
Platten Meister / Jun '96 / SRD

Bolan, Marc

BOLAN'S ZIP GUN (T-Rex)
Light of love / Solid baby / Precious star / Spaceboss / Token of my love / Think zinc / Till dawn / Girl in the thunderbolt suit / Golden belt / I really love you babe / Zip gun boogie / Do you wanna dance / Dock of the bay
CD ______ **EDCD 393**
Edsel / May '94 / Pinnacle

CAT BLACK
CD ______ **CLP 9803**
Cleopatra / Oct '96 / Cargo / Greyhound / Plastic Head / RTM/Disc / SRD

COMPLETE BBC SESSIONS, THE (2CD Set) (T-Rex)
CD Set ______ **PILOT 017**
Burning Airlines / Sep '97 / Total/Pinnacle

DANDY IN THE UNDERWORLD (T-Rex)
Dandy in the underworld / Crimson moon / Universe / I'm a fool for you girl / I love to boogie / Visions of domino / Jason B Sad / Groove a little / Soul of my suit / Hang ups / Pain and love / Teen riot structure / To know him is to love him / City port / Dandy in the underworld / Tame my tiger / Celebrate Summer
CD ______ **EDCD 395**
Edsel / May '94 / Pinnacle

DAZZLING RAIMENT (The Alternate 'Futuristic Dragon') (T-Rex)
Futuristic dragon / Chrome sitar / All alone / New York City / My little baby / Sensation Boulevard / Dreamy lady / Dawn storm / Casual agent / London boys / Life's an elevator / Futuristic dragon / Dreamy lady / Casual agent / All alone / All alone / Dreamy lady / London boys / Life's an elevator
CD ______ **EDCD 522**
Edsel / Jun '97 / Pinnacle

DEFINITIVE TYRANNOSAURUS REX, THE (Tyrannosaurus Rex)
Deborah / Weilder of words / Mustang Ford / One inch rock / Conesuela / Friends / Juniper suction / Warlord of the royal crocodiles / Chariots of silk / Iscariot / King of the rumbling spires / Once upon the seas of Abyssinia / By the light of the magical moon / Day laye / Great horse / Elemental child / Child star / Chateau in Virginia Waters / Salamanda paraganda / Stacey Grove / Eastern spell / Pewter suitor / Cat black (the wizards hat) / Seal of seasons / Misty coast of Albany / Do you remember / Blessed wild apple girl / Find a little wood / Pavilions of the sun / Lofty skies
CD ______ **NEXCD 250**
Sequel / Nov '93 / BMG

DIRTYSWEET VOL.1 (T-Rex)
CD ______ **FELD 1**
Demon / Aug '97 / Pinnacle

DIRTYSWEET VOL.2 (T-Rex)
CD ______ **FELD 2**
Demon / Aug '97 / Pinnacle

EARLY RECORDINGS
Your scare me to death / You've got the power / Eastern spell / Charlie / I'm weird / Hippy gumbo / Mustang Ford / Observations / Jasmine '49 / Cat black / Black and white incident / Perfumed garden of Gulliver Smith
CD ______ **EMPRCD 545**
Emporio / Nov '94 / Disc

ELECTRIC BOOGIE (2CD Set) (T-Rex)
Cadillac / Beltane Walk / One inch rock / Debora / Ride a white swan / Girl / Cosmic dancer / Hot love / Get it on / Jewel / Elemental child / Jam session
CD Set ______ **PILOT 013**
Burning Airlines / Aug '97 / Total/Pinnacle

ELECTRIC WARRIOR SESSIONS, THE (T-Rex)
Get it on / Monolith / Cosmic dancer / Life's a gas / Honey don't / Woodland rock / Monolith / Summertime blues / Jeepster / Baby strange / Jewel / Get it on
CD ______ **PILOT 004**
Burning Airlines / Jan '97 / Total/Pinnacle

ESSENTIAL COLLECTION, THE (Bolan, Marc & T-Rex)
CD ______ **5259612**
PolyGram TV / Sep '95 / PolyGram

FUTURISTIC DRAGON (T-Rex)
Futuristic dragon / Jupiter liar / Chrome sitar / All alone / New York City / My little baby / Calling all destroyers / Theme for a dragon / Sensation boulevard / Ride my wheels / Dreamy lady / Dawn storm / Casual agent / London boys / Laser love / Life's an elevator
CD ______ **EDCD 394**
Edsel / May '94 / Pinnacle

GET IT ON
CD ______ **MASQCD 1010**
Masquerade / Jul '97 / BMG

GREAT HITS 1972-1977 (The A-Sides) (T-Rex)
Telegram Sam / Metal guru / Children of the revolution / Solid gold easy action / 20th century boy / Groover / Truck on / Teenage dream / Light of love / Zip gun boogie / New York City / Dreamy lady / London boys / I love to boogie / Laser love / To know you is to love you / Soul of my suit / Dandy in the underworld / Celebrate Summer
CD ______ **EDCD 401**
Edsel / Oct '94 / Pinnacle
CD ______ **REXLUX 1013**
Demon / Aug '97 / Pinnacle

GREAT HITS 1972-1977 (The B-Sides) (T-Rex)
Cadillac / Baby strange / Thunderwing / Lady / Jitterbug love / Sunken rags / Xmas riff / Born to boogie / Free angel / Midnight / Sitting here / Satisfaction pony / Explosive mouth / Space boss / Chrome sitar / Do you wanna dance / Dock of the bay / Solid baby / Baby boomerang / Life's an elevator / City port / All alone / Groove a little / Tame my tiger / Ride my wheels
CD ______ **EDCD 402**
Edsel / Oct '94 / Pinnacle

LEFT HAND LUKE (The Alternate Tanx) (T-Rex)
Tenement lady darling / Rapids / Mister mister / Broken hearted blues / Country honey / Mad Donna / Born to boogie / Life is strange / Street and the babe shadow / Highway knees / Left hand Luke / Children of the revolution / Solid gold easy action / Free angel / Mister mister / Broken hearted blues / Street and the babe shadow / Tenement lady / Tenement lady / Broken hearted blues / Mad Donna / Street and the babe shadow / Left hand Luke
CD ______ **EDCD 410**
Edsel / May '95 / Pinnacle

LEGEND LIVES, THE (Various Artists)
Children of the revolution / Telegram sam / Ride a white swan / Debora / 20th century boy / Salamanda palaganda / Child star / Metal guru / Get it on / Solid gold easy action / By the light of the magical moon / Jeepster / Life's an elevator / Hot love / Ain't no square with crowscrew hair
CD ______ **305482**
Hallmark / Oct '96 / Carlton

LIGHT OF LOVE (T-Rex)
Light of love / Solid baby / Precious star / Token of my love / Space boss / Think zinc / Till dawn / Teenage dream / Girl in the thunderbolt suit / Explosive mouth / Venus moon
CD ______ **EDCD 413**
Edsel / May '95 / Pinnacle

LIVE (2CD Set) (T-Rex)
Jeepster / Visions of domino / New York City / Soul of my suit / Groove a little / Telegram Sam / Hang ups / Debora / I love to boogie / Teen riot structure / Dandy in the underworld / Hot love / Get it on: *T-Rex & The Damned* / Jeepster / Telegram Sam / Token of my love / Teenage dream / Zip gun boogie
CD Set ______ **EDCD 530**
Edsel / Jun '97 / Pinnacle

LIVE AT THE BBC (T-Rex)
CD ______ **BOJCD 016**
Band Of Joy / May '96 / Pinnacle

LOVE AND DEATH
You scare me to death / You've got the power / Eastern spell / Charlie / I'm weird / Hippy gumbo / Mustang Ford / Observations / Jasmine '49 / Cat black (the wizard's hat) / Black and white incident / Perfumed garden of Gulliver Smith / Wizard / Beyond the rising sun / Rings of fortune
CD ______ **CDMRED 70**
Cherry Red / Jan '91 / Pinnacle

MARC BOLAN ACOUSTIC
CD ______ **TCD 2858**
Telstar / Sep '96 / BMG

MESSING WITH THE MYSTIC (Unissued Songs 1972-1977) (T-Rex)
Is it true / Over the flats / Jet tambourine / Children of the world / Mr. Motion / Hope you enjoy the show / All of my love / Saturday night / Down home lady / Sky church music / Plateau skull / Bolan's zip gun / Magical moon / Bust my ball / Savage Beethoven / Reelin' an' a rockin' an' a boppin' an' a Bolan / Christmas bop / Funky London childhood / Love drunk / Foxy boy / 20th century boy / Sing me a song / Endless sleep / Messing with the mystic
CD ______ **EDCD 404**
Edsel / Oct '94 / Pinnacle

MISSING LINK TO T-REX, THE (Peregrine-Took, Steve)
CD ______ **95282**
Cleopatra / May '97 / Cargo / Greyhound / Plastic Head / RTM/Disc / SRD

PRECIOUS STAR (T-Rex)
CD ______ **EDCD 443**
Edsel / Jun '96 / Pinnacle

PREHISTORIC
Jasper C Debussy / Beyond the rising sun / Eastern sun / Mustang Ford / One inch rock / CCat black / Hot rod mama / Rings of fortune / Black and white incident / You got the power / Jasmine '49 / Sarah crazy child / Sally was an angel / Charlie / Pictures of purple people
CD ______ **EMPRCD 589**
Emporio / Oct '95 / Disc

PROPHETS, SEERS & SAGES (T-Rex)
CD ______ **CUCD 10**
Disky / Oct '94 / Disky / THE

RABBIT FIGHTER (The Alternate Slider) (T-Rex)
Metal guru / Mystic lady / Rock on / Slider / Thunderwing / Spaceball ricochet / Buick MacKane / Telegram Sam / Rabbit fighter / Baby strange / Ballrooms of Mars / Cadillac / Main man / Lady / Sunken rags
CD ______ **EDCD 403**
Edsel / Oct '94 / Pinnacle

SLIDER, THE (T-Rex)
Metal guru / Mystic lady / Rock on / Slider / Baby boomerang / Spaceball ricochet / Buick McKane / Telegram Sam / Rabbit fighter / Baby strange / Ballrooms of Mars / Chariot choogle / Main man / Cadillac / Thunderwing / Lady
CD ______ **EDCD 390**
Edsel / May '94 / Pinnacle

TANX (Bolan, Marc & T-Rex)
Tenement lady / Rapids / Mister mister / Broken hearted blues / Shock rock / Country honey / Electric slim and the factory hen / Mad Donna / Born to boogie / Life is strange / Street and the babe shadow / Highway knees / Left hand Luke and the beggar boys / Children of the revolution / Jitterbug love / Sunken rags / Solid gold easy action / Xmas message / 20th century boy / Free angel
CD ______ **EDCD 391**
Edsel / May '94 / Pinnacle

UNCHAINED: UNRELEASED RECORDINGS VOL.1 (1972 - Part 1) (Bolan, Marc & T-Rex)
Over the flats / Sugar baby / Children of the world / Did you ever / Alligator man / Shame on you / Guitar blues / Shadow blues / Cry baby (Acoustic/Electric) / Rollin' stone / What do I see / Shame on you little girl / Always / Auto machine / Unicorn horn (A thousand Mark Field charms) / Jam / Sailors of the highway (wah wah)
CD ______ **EDCD 411**
Edsel / May '95 / Pinnacle

UNCHAINED: UNRELEASED RECORDINGS VOL.2 (1972 - Part 2) (Bolan, Marc & T-Rex)
Wouldn't I be the one / Meadows of the sea / Mr. Motion (Versions 1 and 2) / City port / Just like me / Is it true / Zinc rider / Canyon / Fast blues - easy action / Bolan's blues / Shake it wind one / Work with me baby / Spaceball boot / Electric lips / Slider blues / Ellie May / My baby's new Porsche / Darklipped woman
CD ______ **EDCD 412**
Edsel / May '95 / Pinnacle

UNCHAINED: UNRELEASED RECORDINGS VOL.5 (Bolan, Marc & T-Rex)
CD ______ **EDCD 444**
Edsel / Jun '96 / Pinnacle

UNCHAINED: UNRELEASED RECORDINGS VOL.6 (Bolan, Marc & T-Rex)
CD ______ **EDCD 445**
Edsel / Jun '96 / Pinnacle

UNCHAINED: UNRELEASED RECORDINGS VOL.7 (Bolan, Marc & T-Rex)
Riff / Freeway / I'm a voodoo man / Decadent priestess / Midnight creeps across your window / Demon grave / Memphis highway / Bombs out of London / Funky London childhood / London boys / Savage deception of love / Angel when I'm mad / Over you babe / Mellow love / 20th century baby / Shy boy / Love drunk / Foxy boy / 20th century baby / Hot George / Write me a song / Mellow love / Endless sleep / Sing me a song / Riff
CD ______ **EDCD 524**
Edsel / Jun '97 / Pinnacle

UNICORN (T-Rex)
Unicorn / Chariots of silk / 'Pon a hill / Seal of seasons / Throat of winter / Cat black (the wizard's hat) / Stones for Avalon / She was born to be my unicorn / Like a white star, tangled and far / Tulip, that's what you are / Warlord of the royal crocodiles / Evenings of Damask / Sea beasts / Iscariot / Nijinsky hind / Pilgrim's tale / Misty coast of Albany / Romany soup
CD ______ **CUCD 11**
Disky / Oct '94 / Disky / THE

US RADIO TOURS 1971-1972 (2CD Set) (T-Rex)
Spaceball ricochet / Jeepster / Cosmic dancer / Main man / Ballrooms of Mars / Mystic lady / Girl / Baby strange / Left hand Luke / Slider / Spaceball ricochet / Cosmic dancer / Planet Queen / Elemental child / Jewel / Hot love / Cosmic dancer / Honey don't / Planet Queen / Get it on blues
CD Set ______ **PILOT 021**
Burning Airlines / Aug '97 / Total/Pinnacle

VERY BEST OF MARC BOLAN AND T-REX (T-Rex)
Telegram Sam / Metal guru / Children of the revolution / Solid gold easy action / Twentieth century boy / Truck on (tyke) / Teenage dream / Light of love / New York City / London boys / I love to boogie / Laser love / Lady / Born to boogie / Dandy in the underworld / Life's an elevator / All alone / Celebrate summer / Buick Mckane / Chariot choogle
CD ______ **MCCD 030**
Music Club / May '91 / Disc / THE

WIZARD, A TRUE STAR, A (3CD Set) (Bolan, Marc & T-Rex)
Interview / Telegram Sam / Spaceball ricochet / Cadillac / Metal guru / Baby strange / Over the flats / Thunderwing / Is it true / Interview / Rabbit fighter / Jingle/Pepsi ad / Sunken rags / Slider / Buick MacKane / Would I be the one / Rock on / Children of the revolution / Painted pony / Solid gold easy action / 20th century boy / Street and the babe shadow / I wanna go / Interview / You got the look / Electric slim / Groover / Sure enough / Interview / Highway knees / Midnight poem / Left hand Luke / Interview / Change / Delanie / Interview / Venus loon / All my love / Leopards / Interstellar soul / Carsmile Smith / Interview / Saturation syncopation / Down home lady / Sky church music / Teenage dream / Till dawn / Jitterbug love / Are you ready Steve / Light of love / Satisfied / Think zinc / Solid baby / Bust my ball / Token of my love / Children of Rarn / Interview / Interview / Brain police / Futuristic dragon / New York City / Reelin' and a wheelin' / Dreamy lady / Christmas bop / Rip it up / Teenager in love / Capital Radio jingle / Jupiter liar / Pale horse riding / Chrome sitar / Piccadilly radio jingle / Jeepster rap / Funky London childhood / Dawn storm / casual agent / 20th century baby / I love to boogie / Interview (10) / London boys / Life's an elevator / Funky riff / Pain and love / Dandy in the underworld / Hang ups / Teen riot structure / Hot George / 21st century stance / Interview (11) / Celebrate summer / Interview (12)
CD Set ______ **FBOOK 17**
Demon / Feb '97 / Pinnacle

ZINC ALLOY AND THE HIDDEN RIDERS OF TOMORROW (Bolan, Marc & T-Rex)
Venus loon / Sound pit / Explosive mouth / Galaxy / Change / Nameless wildness / Teenage dream / Liquid gang / Carsmile Smith and the old one / You got to live to stay alive / Interstellar soul / Painless persuasion v the meathawk imm / Avengers / Leopards featuring gardenia and the mighty slug / Groover / Midnight / Truck on (tyke) / Sitting here / Satisfaction pony
CD ______ **EDCD 392**
Edsel / May '94 / Pinnacle

Boland, Francy

TWO ORIGINALS (Boland, Francy & Kenny Clarke)
CD ______ **5235252**
PolyGram Jazz / Jan '95 / PolyGram

Bolek

MEMORIES OF POLAND
CD ______ **MCD 71409**
Monitor / Jun '93 / CM

Bolin, Tommy

FROM THE ARCHIVES VOL.1
CD ______ **RPM 158**
RPM / Jan '96 / Pinnacle

PRIVATE EYES
Bustin' out of Rosey / Sweet burgundy / Post toastee / Shake the devil / Gypsy soul / Someday we'll bring our love home / Hello again / You told me that you loved me
CD ______ **4723702**
Epic / Feb '97 / Sony

TEASER
Grind / Homeward / Strut / Dreamer savannah woman / Teaser / People, people / Marching powder / Wild dogs / Lotus
CD ______ **4680162**
Epic / May '94 / Sony

Boll Weevils

HEAVYWEIGHT
CD ______ **DSRCD 35**
Dr. Strange / Sep '95 / Cargo / Greyhound / Plastic Head

WEEVIL LIVE
CD ______ **DSR 048CD**
Dr. Strange / Oct '96 / Cargo / Greyhound / Plastic Head

Bolland, C.J.

4TH SIGN, THE
Mantra / Nightbreed / Thrust / Aquadrive / Pendulum / Spring yard / Camargue / Inside out / Jungle man
CD ______ **RS 92024CD**
R&S / Jul '93 / Vital

ANALOGUE THEATRE, THE
Obsidion / Pesticide / Analogue theatre / On line / Prophet / People of the universe / There can be only one / Kung kung ka / Sugar is sweeter
CD ______ **TRUCD 13**
Internal / Oct '96 / Pinnacle / PolyGram

ANALOGUE THEATRE, THE (New Version)
Obsidion / Pesticide / Analogue theatre / On line / Prophet / People of the universe / There can be only one / Kung kung ka / Counterpoint / Sugar is sweeter / Electro power / Sugar is sweeter
CD ______ **8289092**
FFRR / May '97 / PolyGram

DJ KICKS
CD ______ **K7 038CD**
Studio K7 / Sep '95 / Prime / RTM/Disc

ELECTRONIC HIGHWAY
Tower of Naphtali / Drum tower / Neural paradox / Spoof / Con Spirito / Bones / Zenith / Nec plus ultra / Catharsis
CD ______ **RS 95011CD**
R&S / Oct '95 / Vital

Bollin, Zuzu

TEXAS BLUES MAN
Big legs / Hey little girl / Blues in the dark / Kidney stew / Cold cold feeling / Why don't you eat where you slept last night / Headlight blues / How do you want your rollin' done / Leary blues / Rebecca / Zu's blues
CD ______ **ANTCD 0018**
Antones / Feb '92 / ADA / Hot Shot

Bolling, Claude

BLACK, BROWN AND BEIGE
CD ______ **74321162782**
Milan / May '96 / Conifer/BMG / Silva Screen

CINEMADREAMS
CD ______ **74321355012**
Milan / Jul '96 / Conifer/BMG / Silva Screen

RAGTIME BOOGIE-WOOGIE JAZZ CLASSICS
3-4 6-8 boogie / Mississippi rag / Death ray boogie / On the Mississippi / Louisiana glide / Maple leaf rag / Tiger rag / Man that got away / Yesterdays / Begin the beguine / Tea for two / Dardanella / Honky tonk train blues / Harlem strut / Pinetop's boogie woogie / Entertainer's rag / Waiting for the Robert E Lee / Perfect rag
CD ______ **8225062**
Philips / Jan '93 / PolyGram

VICTORY CONCERT, THE
CD ______ **887971**
Milan / Aug '94 / Conifer/BMG / Silva Screen

VINTAGE BOLLING
Baroque and blue / Sentimentale / Fugace / Hispanic dance / Mexicaine / Romance / Gavotte / Slavonic dance / Cross over the USA / Way down yonder in New Orleans / Do you know what it means to miss New Orleans / Back home again in Indiana
CD ______ **74321331202**
Milan / Apr '96 / Conifer/BMG / Silva Screen

WARM UP THE BAND
CD ______ **4684132**
Sony Jazz / Jan '95 / Sony

Bollock Brothers

BEST OF THE BOLLOCKS, THE
CD ______ **CDCRM 1011**
Charly / Jul '93 / Koch

FOUR HORSEMEN OF THE APOCALYPSE, THE
Legend of the snake / Woke up this morning and found myself dead / Mistress of the macabre / Faith healer / King Rat / Four horsemen of the Apocalypse / Return to the garden of Eden / Loud, loud, loud / Seventh seal
CD ______ **CDCRH 109**
Charly / Feb '97 / Koch

LAST SUPPER, THE
Horror movies / Enchantment / Reincarnation of Bollock Brothers / Save our souls / Face in the mirror / Last supper / Act became real / Gift
CD ______ **CDCRH 103**
Charly / Feb '97 / Koch

LIVE - IN PUBLIC IN PRIVATE
Woke up this morning and found myself dead / Drac's back / Four horsemen of the Apocalypse / Count Dracula where's yar troosers / King Rat / Midnight Moses / Faith healer / Rock 'n' roll
CD ______ **CDCRH 105**
Charly / Feb '97 / Koch

LIVE PERFORMANCES (Official Bootleg)
Slow removal of Vincent Van Gogh's left ear / Loose / Horror movies / Bunker / Last supper / Reincarnation of Bollock Brothers / New York / Holidays in the sun / Problems / Vincent: *Fagan, Michael* / Pretty vacant: *Fagan, Michael* / God save the queen: *Fagan, Michael*
CD ______ CDCRH 102
Charly / Feb '97 / Koch

NEVER MIND THE BOLLOCKS 1983
Holidays in the sun / Problems / No feelings / God save the queen / Pretty vacant / Submission / New York / Seventeen / Anarchy in the UK / Liar / Bodies / EMI
CD ______ CDCRH 104
Charly / Feb '97 / Koch

Bolo, Yami

BORN AGAIN
CD ______ RASCD 3174
Ras / Sep '96 / Direct / Greensleeves / Jet Star / SRD

COOL AND EASY
CD ______ DSRCD 442
Tappa / Aug '93 / Jet Star

FIGHTING FOR PEACE
CD ______ RAS 3141
Ras / Jun '94 / Direct / Greensleeves / Jet Star / SRD

RANSOM
Ransom of a man's life / Take time to know / What make the world taste good / Definitely / Memories / She loves me so / World of confusion / Jah is life / Star time - fun time / One has to be real strong
CD ______ GRELCD 125
Greensleeves / Apr '89 / Jet Star / SRD

WAR MONGER
Johanna / Warmonger / Show me / Call me / African woman / Satr of love / Mind games / Maximum greedium / Spread jah love / Mr. Big and in crime
CD ______ RFCD 002
Record Factory / Sep '95 / Jet Star

Bolthrower

4TH CRUSADE
CD ______ MOSH 070CD
Earache / Sep '94 / Vital

FOR VICTORY
War / Remembrance / When glory beckons / For victory / Graven image / Lest we forget / Silent demise / Forever fallen / Tank (MK1) / Armageddon bound
CD ______ MOSH 120CD
Earache / Nov '94 / Vital

REALM OF CHAOS
Eternal war / Through the eye of terror / Dark millenium / All that remains / Lost souls domaine / Plague bearer / World eater / Drowned in torment / Realm of chaos
CD ______ MOSH 013CD
Earache / Sep '97 / Vital

WAR MASTER
CD ______ MOSH 029CD
Earache / Sep '97 / Vital

Bolton, Michael

EARLY YEARS, THE (Bolotin, Michael)
Lost in the city / Everybody needs a reason / Your love / It's just a feelin' / Dream while you can / Take me as I am / These eyes / You mean more to me / If I had your love / Give me a reason / Tell me how you feel / Time is on my side
CD ______ ND 90593
RCA / Feb '97 / BMG

EVERYBODY'S CRAZY
Everybody's crazy / Save our love / Can't turn it off / Call my name / Everytime / Desperate heart / Start breaking my heart / You don't want me bad enough / Don't tell me it's over
CD ______ 4666622
Columbia / May '91 / Sony

GREATEST HITS 1985-1995
Soul provider / (Sittin' on the) dock of the bay / How am I supposed to live without you / How can we be lovers / When I'm back on my feet again / Georgia on my mind / Time, love and tendernes / When a man loves a woman / Missing you now / Steel bars / Said I loved you but I lied / Lean on me / Can I touch you there / I promise you I found someone / Love so beautiful / This river
CD ______ 4810022
Columbia / Sep '95 / Sony

HUNGER, THE
Hot love / Wait on love / (Sittin' on the) dock of the bay / Gina / That's what love is all about / Hunger / You're all I need / Take a look at my face / Walk away
CD ______ 4844682
Columbia / Aug '96 / Sony

MICHAEL BOLTON
Fool's game / She did the same thing / Home town hero / Can't hold on, can't let go / Fighting for my life / Paradise / Back in my arms again / Carrie / I almost believed you
CD ______ 4667422
Columbia / Apr '92 / Sony

MICHAEL BOLTON/EVERYBODY'S CRAZY/THE HUNGER (3CD Set)
CD Set ______ 4683272
Columbia / Jul '93 / Sony

ONE THING, THE
Said I loved you but I lied / I'm not made of steel / One thing / Soul of my soul / Completely / Lean on me / Ain't got nothing if you ain't got love / Time for letting go / Never get enough of your love / In the arms of love / Voice of my heart
CD ______ 4743552
Columbia / Nov '93 / Sony

SOUL PROVIDER
Soul provider / Georgia on my mind / It's only my heart / How am I supposed to live without you / How can we be lovers / You wouldn't know love / When I'm back on my feet again / From now on: *Bolton, Michael & Suzie Benson* / Love cuts deep / Stand up for love
CD ______ 4635432
Columbia / Jun '96 / Sony

THIS IS THE TIME - THE CHRISTMAS COLLECTION
Silent night / Santa claus is coming to town / Have yourself a merry little Christmas / Joy to the world / Ave maria: *Bolton, Michael & Placido Domingo* / Christmas song / O holy night / White Christmas / This is the time: *Bolton, Michael & Wynonna* / Love is the power: *Bolton, Michael & Wynonna*
CD ______ 4850192
Columbia / Nov '96 / Sony

TIME, LOVE AND TENDERNESS
Love is a wonderful thing / Time, love and tenderness / Missing you now / Forever isn't long enough / Now that I found you / When a man loves a woman / We're not makin' love anymore / New love / Save me / Steel bars
CD ______ 4678122
Columbia / Apr '91 / Sony

TIMELESS (The Classics)
Since I fell for you / To love somebody / Reach out, I'll be there / You send me / Yesterday / Hold on / I'm coming / Bring it on home to me / Knock on wood / Drift away / White Christmas
CD ______ 4723022
Columbia / Apr '95 / Sony

Bolton, Polly

LOVELIEST OF TREES (Bolton, Polly Band & Nigel Hawthorne)
CD ______ SHEPCD 1
Shepherd Music / Aug '96 / ADA / Direct

SONGS FROM A COLD OPEN FIELD
CD ______ PBBCD 02
PBB / May '93 / ADA

Bom

BOM BOM SHEVAYA
CD ______ OCH 2CD
Ochre / Aug '96 / SRD

Bomb Bassets

TAKE A TRIP WITH...
CD ______ LK 165CD
Lookout / Aug '97 / Cargo / Greyhound / Shellshock/Disc

Bomb Everything

ALL POWERFUL FLUID, THE
CD ______ CDDVN 10
Devotion / Jul '92 / Pinnacle

Bomb Party

FISH
CD ______ NORMAL 103CD
Normal / May '89 / ADA / Direct

Bomb The Bass

CLEAR
Bug powder dust / Sleepyhead / One to one religion / Dark heart / If you reach the border / Brain dead / 5ml Barrel / Somewhere / Sandcastles / Tidal wave / Empire
CD ______ IMCD 239
Island / Mar '97 / PolyGram

Bomboras

IT CAME FROM PIER 13
CD ______ ID 123345CD
Dionysus / Feb '97 / Cargo / Greyhound / Plastic Head

Bon

FULL CIRCLE COMING HOME
CD ______ EFA 130022
Ozone / Oct '94 / Mo's Music Machine / Pinnacle / SRD

Bon Jovi

7800 DEGREES FAHRENHEIT
In and out of love / Price of love / Only lonely / King of the mountain / Silent night / Tokyo road / Hardest part is the night / Always run to you / To the fire / Secret dreams
CD ______ 8245092
Vertigo / Jan '90 / PolyGram

BON JOVI
Runaway / She didn't know me / Shot through the heart / Love lies / Burning for love / Breakout / Come back / Get ready
CD ______ 8149822
Vertigo / Apr '84 / PolyGram

BON JOVI: INTERVIEW PICTURE DISC
CD ______ CBAK 4004
Baktabak / Apr '88 / Arabesque

CROSS ROAD
CD ______ 5229362
Jambco / Oct '94 / PolyGram

INTERVIEW DISC
CD ______ SAM 7004
Sound & Media / Nov '96 / Sound & Media

INTERVIEWS VOL.2, THE
CD ______ CBAK 4070
Baktabak / Feb '94 / Arabesque

KEEP THE FAITH
I believe / Keep the faith / I'll sleep when I'm dead / In these arms / Bed of roses / If I was your mother / Dry county / Woman in love / Fear / I want you / Blame it on the love of rock and roll / Little bit of soul / Save a prayer
CD ______ 5141972
Jambco / Nov '92 / PolyGram

NEW JERSEY
Lay your hands on me / Bad medicine / Born to be my baby / Living in sin / Blood on blood / Stick to your guns / Homebound train / I'll be there for you / Ninety nine in the shade / Love for sale / Wild is the wind / Ride cowboy ride
CD ______ 8363452
Vertigo / Sep '88 / PolyGram

SLIPPERY WHEN WET
Let it rock / You give love a bad name / Livin' on a prayer / Social disease / Wanted dead or alive / Raise your hands / Without love / I'd die for you / Never say goodbye / Wild in the streets
CD ______ 8302642
Vertigo / Sep '90 / PolyGram

THESE DAYS
Hey God / Something for the pain / This ain't a love song / These days / Lie to me / Damned / My guitar lies bleeding in my arms / (It's hard) Letting you go / Hearts breaking even / Something to believe in / If that's what it takes / Diamond ring / All I want is everything / Bitter wine
CD ______ 5282482
Jambco / Jun '95 / PolyGram

THESE DAYS (2CD Tour Pack Set)
Hey God / Something for the pain / This ain't a love song / These days / Lie to me / Damned / My guitar lies bleeding in my arms / (It's hard) Letting you go / Hearts breaking even / Something to believe in / If that's what it takes / Diamond ring / All I want is everything / Bitter wine / Fields of fire / I thank you / Mrs. Robinson / Let's make it baby / I don't like Mondays / Crazy / Tumblin' dice / Heaven help us
CD Set ______ 5326442
Jambco / Jun '96 / PolyGram

Bon Jovi, Jon

BLAZE OF GLORY - YOUNG GUNS II
Billy get your guns / Blaze of glory / Santa Fe / Never say die / Bang a drum / Guano City / Miracle / Blood money / Justice in the barrel / You really got me now / Dyin' ain't much of a livin'
CD ______ 8464732
Vertigo / Aug '90 / PolyGram

DESTINATION ANYWHERE
CD ______ 5360112
Mercury / Jun '97 / PolyGram

POWER STATION YEARS 1980-1983, THE (Bongiovi, John)
Who said it would last forever / Open your heart / Stringin' a line / Don't leave me tonight / More than we bargained for / For you / Hollywood dreams / All talk no action / Don't keep me wondering / Head over heels / No one does it like you / What you want / Don't you believe him / Talkin' in your sleep
CD ______ MASQCD 1011
Masquerade / Jul '97 / BMG

Bonano, Sharkey

SHARKEY & HIS KINGS OF DIXIELAND (Bonano, Sharkey & His Kings Of Dixieland)
CD ______ BCD 122
GHB / Jul '96 / Jazz Music

SHARKEY BONANO 1928-1937
Panama / Dippermouth blues / Sizzling the blues / High society / Git wit it / Ideas / Everybdoy loves my baby / Yes she do - no she don't / I'm satisfied with my gal / High society / Mudhole blues / Swing in, swing out / Blowin' off steam / Mr. Brown goes to town / Wash it clean / When you're smiling / Swingin' on the Swanee shore / Old fashioned swing / Big boy blue / Swing like a rusty gate / Doodlebug / Magnolia blues / I never knew what a gal could do / Never had a reason to believe in you
CD ______ CBC 1001
Timeless Historical / Jan '92 / New Note/ Pinnacle

Bond, Eddie

ROCKIN' DADDY (2CD Set)
Double duty lovin' / Talking off the wall / Love makes a fool (Everyday) / Your eyes / I got a woman / Rockin' Daddy / Slip, slip slippin in / Baby, baby, baby (What am I gonna do) / Flip flop Mama / Boppin' Bonnie / You're part of me / King on your throne / They say we're too young / Backslidin / Love love love / Lovin' you, lovin' you / Hershey bar / One step close to you / Show me (Without sax) / Broke my guitar / This old heart of mine / Show me (With sax) / One more memory / I can't quit / My bucket's got a hole in it / (Back home again in) Indiana / They'll never take her love from me / Day I found you / Standing in the window / Back street affair / Our secret rendezvous / I'd just be fool enough / You nearly lose your mind / I thought I heard you calling my name / Big boss man / In my solitude / Most of all I want to see Jesus / Where could I go but to the Lord / Satisfied / When they ring those golden bells / If we never meet again / Will I be lost or will I be saved / Just a closer walk with thee / Pass me not, o gentle saviour / I saw the light / Letter to God / Precious memories / Hallelujah way
CD Set ______ BCD 15708
Bear Family / May '93 / Direct / Rollercoaster / Swift

ROCKIN' DADDY
Rockin' daddy / Big boss man / Can't win for losing / When the jukebox plays / Hey Joe / Monkey and the baboon / Blues got me / Standing in your window / Look like a monkey / I'll step aside / Memphis, Tennessee / My bucket's got a hole in it / Winners circle / Juke joint Johnny / You'll never be a stranger to me / Boo bop da caa caa / Heart full of heartaches / Here comes the train / Someday I'll sober up / Double duty lovin' / Let's make the parting sweet / Tomorrow I'll be gone / One more memory / Country shindig / When the jukebox plays / Raunchy / Cold dark waters / Your eyes / It's been so long darling / Your old standby / This old heart of mine
CD ______ STCD 1
Stomper Time / '92 / TKO Magnum

Bond, Graham

TWO HEADS ARE BETTER THAN ONE...PLUS (Bond & Brown)
Lost tribe / Ig the pig / Oobati / Amazing grass / Scunthorpe crabmeat train sideways boogie shuffle stomp / CFDT (Colonel Fright's Dancing Terrapins) / Mass debate / Looking for time / Milk is turning sour in my shoes / Macumbe / Beginning / Aeroplane drinking man / Italian song / Spend my nights in armour / Fury of war / Magpie man / Drum roll / Swing song / Sailor's song / Ending
CD ______ SEECD 345
See For Miles/C5 / Apr '92 / Pinnacle

Bond, Joyce

CALL ME
CD ______ OCD 33
Orbitone / Jan '90 / Jet Star

NICE TO HAVE YOU BACK AGAIN
Nice to have you back again / Nothing ever comes easy / Love me and leave me / Lonesome Road / You've been gone too long / If I ever fall in love again / No other one is sweeter than you
CD ______ SPCD 06
Spindle / Dec '95 / Else / Jet Star

YOU TOUCH MY HEART
CD ______ SPCD 04
Spindle / Dec '95 / Else / Jet Star

Bondi Cigars

BAD WEATHER BLUES
CD ______ LRF 258
Larrikin / Oct '93 / ADA / CM / Direct / Roots

Bonds, Gary 'US'

BEST OF GARY 'US' BONDS, THE
CD ______ MCCD 111
Music Club / Jun '93 / Disc / THE

GREATEST HITS
CD ______ TRLGCD 100
Timeless Jazz / Sep '90 / New Note/ Pinnacle

TAKE ME BACK TO NEW ORLEANS
Take me back to New Orleans / Send her to me / Shine on lover's moon / Please forgive me / Workin' for my baby / Give me one more chance / My little room / What a dream / Don't go to strangers / Food of love / Girl next door / What a crazy world / I'm that kind of guy / Call me for Christmas / Guida's Romeo and Juliet / Million tears / Time ol' story / My sweet Ruby Rose / I know why dreamers cry / I walk the line /

Oh yeah oh yeah / Nearness of you / I love you so / I don't wanna wait (why wait 'til Saturday night)
CD ______ CDCHD 549
Ace / Aug '94 / Pinnacle

Bone Machine

DISAPPEARING INC.
CD ______ BM 004
Big Disc / Oct '96 / Cargo

SEARCH AND DESTROY
CD ______ NTHEN 022CD
Now & Then / Jan '96 / Plastic Head

Bone Structure

BONE STRUCTURE
On Green Dolphin Street / Vatican roulette / Modal T / Lush life / Doodlin' / Bone idle rich / Latin line / Shades of blue and green / Last minute waltz / Spanish white
CD ______ CLGCD 020
Calligraph / Jun '92 / Cadillac / Jazz Music / New Note/Pinnacle / Wellard

Bone Thugs n' Harmony

ART OF WAR, THE
Retaliation / Handle the vibe / Look into my eyes / Body rott / It's all mo'thug / Ready 4 war / Ain't nothin' changed / Clog up yo mind / Thug in me / Hardtimes / Mind of a Souljah / If I could teach the world / Family tree / Mo thug / Thug luv / Hatin' nation / 7 sign / Wasteland warriors / Neighbourhood slang / U ain't Bone / Get cha thug on / All original / Blaze it / Let the law end / Whom die they lie / Friends / Evil paradise / Mo thug family tree
CD ______ 4880802
Ruthless / Jul '97 / Sony

E 1999 ETERNAL
Da introduction / East 1999 eternal / Crept and we came down / Down 71 (the getaway) / Mr. Bill Collector / Budsmokers only / Tha crossroads / Me killa / Land of the heartless / No shorts, no losses / 1st of tha month / Buddah lovaz / Die die die / Mr. Ouija 2 / Mo murda / Shortz to tha double glock
CD ______ 4810386
Epic / Aug '96 / Sony

E1999 ETERNAL
Da introduction / East 1999 / Eternal / Crept and we came down '71 (the getaway) / Mr. Bill Collector / Budsmokers only / Crossroads / Me killa / Land of the heartless / No shorts, no losses / First of the month / Budds lovaz / Die die die / Mr. Ouija 2 / Mo murda / Shots to the double glock
CD ______ 4810382
Ruthless / Jul '95 / Sony

Bonecrushin'

ALL BILLS PAID
CD ______ TIN 46002
Tin Can Discs / May '97 / Total/Pinnacle

Bonesaw

ABANDONED
CD ______ LF 099CD
Lost & Found / Jun '94 / Plastic Head

SHADOW OF DOUBT
CD ______ LF 189CD
Lost & Found / Jan '96 / Plastic Head

WRITTEN IN STONE
CD ______ LF 140CD
Lost & Found / May '95 / Plastic Head

Boneshakers

BOOK OF SPELLS
CD ______ VPBCD 40
Virgin / Apr '97 / EMI

Bonewire

THROWN INTO MOTION
CD ______ NIHIL 3CD
Cacophonous / Mar '95 / Plastic Head / RTM/Disc

Boney M

20 GREATEST CHRISTMAS SONGS
Christmas medley / Oh Christmas tree / Hark the herald angels sing / Zion's daughter / First Noel / O come all ye faithful (adeste fidelis) / Petit Papa Noel / Darkness is falling / Joy to the world / White Christmas / Jingle bells / Feliz Navidad / When a child is born / Little drummer boy / Medley / Auld lang syne
CD ______ 258116
Hansa / Nov '96 / BMG

ALL THE HITS
Rivers of Babylon / Daddy cool / Sunny / Brown girl in the ring / Rasputin / Ma Baker / Hooray hooray it's a holi-holiday / Painter man / Belfast / No woman, no cry / Mary's boy child / Gotta go home / Boney M megamix
CD ______ 74321128892
Arista / Jan '93 / BMG

BEST OF BONEY M, THE
Rivers of babylon / Ma Baker / Rasputin / He was a steppenwolf / Daddy cool / Motherless child / Brown girl in the ring / Sunny / No woman, no cry / Mary's boy child / Hooray hooray it's a holi-holiday / Never change lovers in the middle of the night / Voodoonight / Still I'm sad / Nightflight to Venus / Heart of gold / Gotta go home
CD ______ 74321476812
Camden / Apr '97 / BMG

COLLECTION, THE
CD ______ 261670
Arista / Aug '92 / BMG

DADDY COOL (Greatest Hits)
CD ______ 290 799
Ariola Express / Jun '92 / BMG

GREATEST HITS
CD ______ JHD 032
Tring / Jun '92 / Tring

GREATEST HITS
CD ______ TCD 2656
Telstar / Mar '93 / BMG

NIGHT FLIGHT TO VENUS
Night flight to venus / Rasputin / Painter man / He was a steppenwolf / King of the road / Rivers of Babylon / Voodoo night / Brown girl in the ring / Never change lovers in the middle of the night / Heart of gold
CD ______ 74321212692
Arista / Jun '94 / BMG

Bonfa, Luiz

SAMBOLERO - GUITARRA DO BRASIL
CD ______ BMCD 3059
Blue Moon / Apr '97 / Cadillac / Discovery / Greensleeves / Jazz Music / Jet Star / TKO Magnum

Bonfanti, Paolo

TRYIN' TO KEEP THE WHOLE THING ROCKIN'
On my best behaviour / Blues don't pay / Dead end / Look ka py py / Two steps from the blues / Changes I'm goin' thru / Route one / Stream of your love / I'm just tryin' / You were right
CD ______ MRCD 1096
Club De Musique / Feb '97 / Direct

Bonga, Ntshuk

URBAN RITUAL (Bonga, Ntshuk Tsisha)
Burning myths / City escapes / Ancient whispers / Urban precipice / Ritual reality / Rites of speech / Mzangwa mzangwa / Song unsung / Before the snow
CD ______ SLAMCD 213
Slam / Oct '96 / Cadillac

Bongshang

CRUDE
Le introducement / Things to come / Floggin set / If and when / Lee highway blues / Phosphene / Tamlinn / Hangmans reel / Dig a hole / Scotland / Frosty morning / AKA Crude / Wedding row / Reprise
CD ______ DOOVFCD 1
Doovf / Oct '94 / ADA / CM
CD ______ IRCD 032
Iona / Nov '95 / ADA / Direct / Duncans

HURRICANE JUNGLE
CD ______ DOOVFCD 2
Doovf / May '97 / ADA / CM

Bonham, Jason

IN THE NAME OF MY FATHER (The Zep Set) (Bonham, Jason Band)
In the evening / Ramble on / Song remains the same / What is and what should never be / Ocean / Since I've been loving you / Communication breakdown / Ten years gone / Rain song / Whole lotta love
CD ______ 4874432
Epic / Mar '97 / Sony

Bonham, Tracy

BURDEN OF BEING UPRIGHT, THE
CD ______ 5241872
Island Red / Jun '96 / PolyGram / Vital

Boni, Raymond

LE GOUT DU JOUR (Boni, Raymond Octet)
CD ______ CELP C18
CELP / Feb '92 / Cadillac / Harmonia Mundi

Bonilla, Luis

PASOS GIGANTES (Bonilla, Luis Latin Jazz All Stars)
Pasos gigantes (giant steps) / Deluge / Panama / Caravan / Dolphin / If you could see me now / Irazu / Eva / Mambo Barbara
CD ______ CCD 79507
Candid / Feb '97 / Cadillac / Direct / Jazz Music / Koch / Wellard

Bonilla, Marc

EE TICKET
Entrance / White noise / Mannequin highway / Commotion / Lycanthrope / Hit and run / Afterburner / Hurling blues skyward / Antonio's love jungle / Razor back / Slaughter on Memory Lane / Exit
CD ______ 7599267252
Reprise / Apr '92 / Warner Music

Bonner, Joe

IMPRESSIONS OF COPENHAGEN
CD ______ ECD 220242
Evidence / Aug '92 / ADA / Cadillac / Harmonia Mundi

MONKISMS
CD ______ 74030
Capri / Nov '93 / Cadillac / Wellard

Bonner, Juke Boy

JUKE BOY BONNER 1960-1967 (Bonner, Weldon 'Juke Boy')
Look out Lightning / Jumpin' with Juke Boy / Dust my broom / That a while ago / Three ring circus / Look out your window / True love darling / Jumpin' at the studio / I'm going up / Life is a dirty deal / Nine below zero
CD ______ FLYCD 38
Flyright / Oct '91 / Hot Shot / Jazz Music / Wellard

LIFE GAVE ME A DIRTY DEAL (Bonner, Weldon 'Juke Boy')
CD ______ ARHCD 375
Arhoolie / Apr '95 / ADA / Cadillac / Direct

Bonnet, Graham

HERE COMES THE NIGHT
CD ______ PCOM 1114
President / Jul '91 / Grapevine/PolyGram / President / Target/BMG

Bonnet, Guy

CANTE (Bonnet Sings Trenet)
A la porte du garage / Mes jeunes annees / Y'a-d'la joie / La mer / Route N7 / Je chante / La java du Diable / Une noix / Le soleil et la lune / Que reste-t-il de nos amours / La jolie Sardane / Longtemps / Boum / Pour finir
CD ______ UCD 19112
Forlane / Nov '95 / Target/BMG

Bonney, Graham

GRAHAM BONNEY
CD ______ 16008
Laserlight / Aug '91 / Target/BMG

Bonney, Simon

EVERYMAN
CD ______ CDSTUMM 114
Mute / Mar '96 / RTM/Disc

FOREVER
CD ______ CDSTUMM 99
Mute / May '92 / RTM/Disc

Bonzo Dog Band

BESTIALITY OF BONZO DOG BAND
Intro and the outro / Canyons of your mind / Trouser press / Postcard / Mickey's son and daughter / Sport (the odd boy) / Tent / I'm the urban spaceman / Mr. Apollo / Shirt / Bad blood / Readymades / Rhinocratic oaths / Can blue men sing the whites / Mr. Slater's parrot / Strain / We are normal / My pink half of the drainpipe / Jazz, delicious hot, disgusting cold / Big shot / Jollity farm / Humanoid boogie
CD ______ CDP 7926752
Premier/EMI / Apr '90 / EMI

CORNOLOGY (The Intro/The Outro/Dog Ends) (3CD Set)
CD Set ______ CDS 7995952
Premier/EMI / Jun '92 / EMI

DOG ENDS
My brother makes the noises for the talkies / I'm going to bring a watermelon to my girl tonight / Alley oop / Button up your overcoat / Mr. Apollo / Ready mades / Strain / Turkeys / King of Scurf / Waiting for the wardrobe / Straight from my heart / Rusty / Rawlinson end / Don't get me wrong / Fresh wound / Bad blood / Slush / Labio-dental fricative / Recycled vinyl blues / Trouser freak
CD ______ CDP 7995982
Premier/EMI / Jun '92 / EMI

FOUR BONZO ORIGINALS (Gorilla/Doughnut/Tadpoles/Keynsham) (4CD Set)
Cool Britannia / Equestrian statue / Jollity Farm / (I left my heart) in San Francisco / Look out, there's a monster coming / Jazz, delicious hot, disgusting cold / Death cab for cutie / Narcissus / Intro and the outro / Mickey's son and daughter / Big shot / Music for the head ballet / Piggy bank love / I'm bored / Sound of music / We are normal / Postcard / Beautiful Zelda / Can blue men sing the whites / Hello Mabel / Kama Sutra / Humanoid boogie / Trouser press / My pink half of the drainpipe / Rockaliser baby / Rhinocratic oaths / Eleven mustachioed daughters / Hunting tigers out in "Indiah" / Shirt / Tubas in the moonlight / Dr. Jazz / Monster mash / I'm the urban spaceman / Ali Baba's camel / Laughing blues / By a waterfall / Mr. Apollo / Canyons of your mind / You done my brain in / Keynsham / Quiet talks and summer walks / Tent / We were wrong / Joke shop man / Bride stripped bare by Bachelors / Look at me I'm wonderful / What do you do / Mr. Slater's parrot / Sport (The odd boy) / I want to be with you / Noises for the leg / Busted
CD Set ______ CDBONZO 1
Premier/EMI / Feb '96 / EMI

GORILLA
Cool Britannia / Equestrian statute / Jollity farm / I left my heart in San Francisco / Look out there's a monster coming / Jazz, delicious hot, disgusting cold / Death cab for a cutie / Narcissus / Intro and the outro / Mickey's son and daughter / Big shot / Music for head ballet / Piggy bank love / I'm bored / Sound of music
CD ______ BGOCD 82
Beat Goes On / Jul '95 / Pinnacle

INTRO, THE (Gorilla/Doughnut)
Cool Britannia / Equestrian statute / Jollity farm / I left my heart in San Francisco / Look out there's a monster coming / Jazz, delicious hot, disgusting cold / Death cab for cutie / Narcissus / Intro and the outro / Mickey's son and daughter / Big shot / Music for the head ballet / Piggy bank love / I'm bored / Sound of music / We are normal / Postcard / Beautiful Zelda / Can blue men sing the whites / Hello Mabel / Kama Sutra / Humanoid boogie / Trouser press / Pink half of the drainpipe / Rockaliser baby / Rhinocratic oaths / Mustachioed daughters
CD ______ CDP 7995962
Premier/EMI / Jun '92 / EMI

OUTRO, THE (Tadpoles/Keynsham)
Hunting tigers out in Indiah / Shirt / Tubas in the moonlight / Dr. Jazz / Monster mash / I'm the urban spaceman / Ali Baba's camel / By a waterfall / Mr. Apollo / Canyons of your mind / You've done my brain in / Keynsham / Quiet talks and summer walks / Tent / We were wrong / Joke shop man / Bride stripped bare by "bachelors" / Look at me I'm wonderful / What do you do / Mr. Slater's parrot / Sport (the odd boy) / I want to be with you / Noises for the leg / Busted
CD ______ CDP 7995972
Premier/EMI / Jun '92 / EMI

Boo Radleys

C'MON KIDS
C'mon kids / Meltin's worm / Melodies for the deaf (colours for the blind) / Get on the bus / Everything is sorrow / Bullfrog green / What's in the box (see watcha got) / 4 saints / New Brighton promenade / Fortunate sons / Shelter / Ride the tiger / One last hurrah
CD ______ CRECD 194
Creation / Sep '96 / 3mv/Vital

EVERYTHING'S ALRIGHT FOREVER
CD ______ CRECD 120
Creation / Mar '92 / 3mv/Vital

GIANT STEPS
I hang suspended / Upon 9th and fairchild / Wish I was skinny / Leaves and sand / Butterfly McQueen / Rodney King / Thinking of ways / Barney (and me) / Spun around / If you want it, take it / Best lose the fear / Take the time around / Lazarus / One is for / Run my way runway / I've lost the reason
CD ______ CRECD 149
Creation / Aug '93 / 3mv/Vital

LEARNING TO WALK
CD ______ R 3012
Rough Trade / Nov '93 / Pinnacle

WAKE UP
CD ______ CRECD 179
Creation / Mar '95 / 3mv/Vital

Boo-Yaa TRIBE

ANGRY SAMOANS
Skarred for life / Breakin life sykos / Buried alive / Full metal Jack / Kill for the family / Retaliate / Boogie man / Where U want it / Gang bangin' / Mr Mister Redeyes / Angry Samoans / No free ride
CD ______ CDVEST 81
Bulletproof / May '97 / Pinnacle

DOOMSDAY
CD ______ CDVEST 20
Bulletproof / Jul '94 / Pinnacle

METALLY DISTURBED
CD ______ CDMVEST 76
Bulletproof / Aug '96 / Pinnacle

Boogalusa

BOOGALUSA
Goodnight Bob / Hunger / Dead man sing / To the water / Rednecks on the radio / Shakedown zydeco / Silent phrases / Big lights / Heart jump / Way you say
CD ______ CDLDL 1223
Lochshore / Feb '97 / ADA / Direct / Duncans

CARELESS ANGELS & CRAZY CAJUNS
CD ______ LDLCD 1208
Lochshore / Oct '93 / ADA / Direct / Duncans

Boogie Down Productions

CRIMINAL MINDED
CD ______ MIL 47872
Multimedia / Jun '97 / Jet Star

Boogiemen

BOOGIE TIME
CD ______ BLRCD 033
Blue Loon / May '97 / Hot Shot

Book Of Wisdom

CATACOMBS
CD ______ NACD 201
Nature & Art / Oct '95 / Plastic Head

Bookbinder, Roy

LIVE BOOK - DON'T START ME TALKIN'
CD ______ ROUCD 3130
Rounder / May '94 / ADA / CM / Direct

ROY BOOKBINDER
CD ______ ROUCD 3107
Rounder / '88 / ADA / CM / Direct

Booker, Chuckii

NIICE 'N' WIILD
Spinnin / Love is medicine / Out of the dark / You don't know / With all my heart / I git around / Games / Deep c diiver / Soul triilogy 1 / Soul triilogy 11 / Soul triilogy 111 / Niice n wiild / I should have loved you
CD ______ 7567824102
WEA / Nov '92 / Warner Music

Booker, James

JUNCO PARTNER
Black minute waltz / Goodnight Irene / Pixie / On the sunny side of the street / Make a better world / Junco partner / Put out the light / Medley / Pop's dilemma / I'll be seeing you
CD ______ HNCD 1359
Hannibal / Feb '93 / ADA / Vital

KING OF THE NEW ORLEANS KEYBOARD
How do you feel / Going down slow / Classified / One hell of a nerve / Blues rhapsody / Rockin' pneumonia and the boogie woogie flu / Please send me someone to love / All by myself / Ain't nobody's business if I do / Something you got / Harlem in Hamburg
CD ______ CDJP 1
JSP / Apr '92 / ADA / Cadillac / Direct / Hot Shot / Target/BMG

NEW ORLEANS PIANO WIZARD (Live)
CD ______ ROUCD 2027
Rounder / '88 / ADA / CM / Direct

RESURRECTION OF THE BAYOU MAHARAJAH
CD ______ ROUCD 2118
Rounder / Aug '93 / ADA / CM / Direct

SPIDERS ON THE KEYS
CD ______ ROUCD 2119
Rounder / Oct '93 / ADA / CM / Direct

Booker, Steve

FAR CRY FROM HERE, A
CD ______ RMRCD 1
JVO / Aug '96 / Pinnacle

Booker T & The MG's

AND NOW
My sweet potato / Jericho / No matter what shape / One mint julep / In the midnight hour / Summertime / Working in the coal mine / Don't mess up a good thing / Think / Taboo / Soul jam / Sentimental journey
CD ______ 8122702972
Atlantic / Jul '93 / Warner Music

BEST OF BOOKER T AND THE MG'S, THE
Green onions / Slim Jenkins' place / Hip hug-her / Soul dressing / Summertime / Bootleg / Jelly bread / Tic-tac-toe / Can't be still / Groovin' / Mo' onions / Red beans and rice / Terrible thing / My sweet potato / Be my lady / Booker-loo
CD ______ 7567812812
Atlantic / Jan '93 / Warner Music

BEST OF BOOKER T AND THE MG'S, THE
Time is tight / Soul limbo / Heads or tails / Over easy / Hip hug-her / Hang 'em high / Johnny I love you / Slum baby / Horse / Soul clap '69 / Sunday sermon / Born under a bad sign / Mrs. Robinson / Something / Light my fire / It's your thing / Fuquawi / Kinda easy like / Meditation / Melting pot
CD ______ CDSX 46
Stax / Apr '93 / Pinnacle

DOIN' OUR THING
I can dig it / Expressway to your heart / Doin' our thing / You don't love me / Never my love / Exodus song / Beat goes on / Ode to Billie Joe / Blue on green / You keep me hangin' on / Let's go get stoned
CD ______ 8122710142
Atlantic / Jul '93 / Warner Music

GREEN ONIONS
Green onions / Rinky dink / I got a woman / Mo' onions / Twist and shout / Behave yourself / Stranger on the shore / Lonely avenue / One who really loves you / You can't sit down / Woman, a lover, a friend / Comin' home baby
CD ______ 7567822552
Atlantic / Oct '94 / Warner Music

HIP HUG HER
Hip hug-her / Slim Jenkin's place / Soul sanction / Get ready / More / Double or nothing / Carnaby street / Slim Jenkins' joint / Pigmy / Groovin' / Booker's notion / Sunny
CD ______ 8122710132
Atlantic / Jul '93 / Warner Music

IN THE CHRISTMAS SPIRIT
Jingle bells / Santa Claus is coming to town / Winter wonderland / White Christmas / Christmas song / Silver bells / Merry Christmas baby / Blue Christmas / Sweet little Jesus boy / Silent night / We three kings / We wish you a Merry Christmas
CD ______ 7567823382
Atlantic / Jul '93 / Warner Music

MCLEMORE AVENUE
Golden slumbers / Here comes the sun / Come together / Because / Mean Mr Mustard / She came in through the bathroom window / Carry that weight / End / Something / You never give me your money / Polythene Pam / Sun king / I want you
CD ______ CDSXE 016
Stax / Nov '88 / Pinnacle

MELTING POT
Melting pot / Back home / Chicken pox / Fuquawi / Kinda easy like / Hi ride / LA jazz song / Sunny Monday
CD ______ CDSXE 055
Stax / Sep '92 / Pinnacle

PLAY THE HIP HITS
Baby scratch my back / Harlem shuffle / Hi-heel sneakers / Downtown / I was made to love her / Georgia on my mind / Wade in the water / Fannie Mae / Day tripper / You left the water running / Every beat of my heart / Ain't that peculiar / You can't do that / Wang dang doodle / On a Saturday night / Letter / Oo wee baby, I love you / Spoonful / I hear a symphony / You're so fine / Raunchy / You are my sunshine / Soul man / Gimme some lovin' / When something is wrong with my baby
CD ______ CDSXD 065
Stax / Apr '95 / Pinnacle

SOUL DRESSING
Soul dressing / Tic-tac-toe / Big train / Jelly bread / Aw' mercy / Outrage / Night owl walk / Chinese checkers / Home grown / Mercy mercy / Plum Nellie / Can't be still
CD ______ 7567823372
Atlantic / Feb '95 / Warner Music

Booker T Trio

GO TELL IT ON THE MOUNTAIN
CD ______ SHCD 114
Silkheart / Oct '92 / Cadillac / CM / Jazz Music / Wellard

Boom, Barry

LIVING BOOM, THE
CD ______ FADCD 016
Fashion / Nov '90 / Jet Star / SRD

TRUST ME
CD ______ MERCD 010
Merger / Jan '93 / Jet Star

Boom Boyz

BOTTOM, THE
CD ______ BRY 4185CD
Ichiban / Mar '94 / Direct / Koch

Boom Shaka

FREEDOM NOW
CD ______ KFWCD 501
Stone Mountain Entertainment / Oct '96 / Grapevine/PolyGram

Boomtown Rats

TONIC FOR THE TROOPS
Like clockwork / Blind date / I never loved Eva Braun / Living in an island / Don't believe what you read / She's so modern / Me and Howard Hughes / Can't stop / Watch out for the normal people / Rat trap
CD ______ 5140532
Mercury / Jul '93 / PolyGram

Boon Man

TIN MAN
Tin man / Don't walk away / Kick or the kiss / Baby I know / Ever the way / Sleepy people / Every day / One from the heart / How deep (is your heart) / Growing wild in the desert / Tears me down / Knight
CD ______ RES 106CD
Resurgence / Apr '97 / Pinnacle

Boondocks

STRAIGHT FROM NOWHERE
CD ______ 50572
Raging Bull / Jun '97 / Prime / Total/BMG

Boone Creek

ONE WAY TRACK
One way rider / Head over heels / Little community church / Mississippi Queen / In the pines / Can't you hear me callin' / No Mother or Dad / Blue and lonesome / Daniel prayed / Sally Goodun
CD ______ SHCD 3701
Sugar Hill / Jan '97 / ADA / CM / Direct / Koch / Roots

Boone, Daniel

BEAUTIFUL SUNDAY
CD ______ 12550
Laserlight / Jun '95 / Target/BMG

VERY BEST OF DANIEL BOONE, THE
CD ______ MCCD 247
Music Club / Jun '96 / Disc / THE

Boone, Pat

APRIL LOVE
Love letters in the sand / I love you more and more / I almost lost my head / Friendly persuasion / Mr. Blue / April love / Speedy Gonzales / Ain't that a shame / Tutti frutti / Don't forbid me / Wonderful time up there / I believe in music / I'll be home / Moody River / She fights that lovin' feelin' / Jambalaya / You lay so easy on my mind / Bernadine / Where there's a heartache / Poetry in motion
CD ______ HADCD 162
Javelin / May '94 / Henry Hadaway / THE

APRIL LOVE
CD ______ RMB 75070
Remember / Apr '94 / Total/BMG

BABY OH BABY
Baby, oh baby / Rose Marie / Baby sonnenschein / Wie eine lady / Ein goldener stern / Komm zu mir wenn du einsam bist / Oh lady / Nein nein valentina / Mary Lou / Wo find ich meine traume / Que pasa contigo / Y te quiero / Recuerdame siempre / Amor al reves / En cualquier lugar / Cartas en la arena / Tu che non hai amato mai / E fuori la pioggia cade / Se tu non fossi qui
CD ______ BCD 15645
Bear Family / Jun '92 / Direct / Rollercoaster / Swift

BEST OF PAT BOONE, THE
CD ______ MATCD 306
Castle / Oct '94 / BMG

COLLECTION, THE
CD ______ COL 036
Collection / Jan '95 / Target/BMG

FAMILY CHRISTMAS
CD ______ 12289
Laserlight / Nov '95 / Target/BMG

FIFTIES, THE - COMPLETE (12CD Set)
Until you tell me so / (I'll never be free) my heart belongs to you / Remember to be mine / Halfway chance / I need someone / Loving you madly / Two hearts / Tra-la-la / Ain't that a shame / Angel eyes / Tennessee Saturday night / Take the time / Now I know / No arms can ever hold you (no other arms) / Rich in love / You're gonna be sorry / At my front door / Gee Whittakers / Tutti frutti / I'll be home / Hoboken baby / Just as long as I'm with you / I almost lost my mind / Long tall Sally / Am I seeing angels / Bingo / Money honey / Treasure of love / I'm in love with you / Friendly persuasion (thee I love) / King for a day / When you help a friend in need / All I do is dream of you / Ev'ry little thing / Would you like to take a walk / Chains of love / Harbour lights / Sunday / Hummin' the blues / I'm waiting just for you / Beg your pardon / Chattanooga shoe shine boy / With you / Forgive me / Begin the beguine / Mocking bird / Indiana holiday / Coax me a little / Marry me, marry me / That lucky old sun / Scattered toys / Old fashioned Christmas / Why did I choose you / Honey hush / Tomorrow night / Rock me baby / Anastasia / Poem / Gold / Don't forbid me / Flip, flop and fly / Pledging my love / Ain't nobody here but us chickens / Shake a hand / Please send me someone to love / I'm in love again / Rock around the clock / Shot gun boogie / Five, ten, fifteen hours / Too soon to know / Love letters in the sand / Fat man / When I write my song / Great googa mooga / Why, baby why / Peace in the valley / He'll understand and say well done / Technique / Bernadine / Talking to myself about you / Just a closer walk with thee / Steal away / Louella / Without my love / Louella / There's a goldmine in the sky / Sweet hour of prayer / Old rugged cross / In the garden / Now the day is over / Too soon to know / Love letters in the sand / Beyond the sunset / It is no secret / My God is real / Softly and tenderly / Will the circle be unbroken / Have thine own way Lord / Yield not temptation / Whispering hope / There's a goldmine in the sky / Cathedral in the pines / From a Jack to a King / Remember you're mine / How deep is the ocean / Pretty girl is like a melody / Say it isn't so / Cheek to cheek / Always / They say it's wonderful / All alone / What'll I do / All by myself / Remember / Soft lights and sweet music / Be careful, it's my heart / Girl that I marry / Say it with music / Count your blessings / Clover in the meadow / April love / Wonderful time up there / My little red book / I've got you on my mind / Sugar moon / Count your blessings / When the swallows come back to Capistrano / Terry / Great Googa Mooga / Santa Claus is coming to town / Jingle bells / White Christmas / Silent night / Give me a gentle girl / Clover in the meadow / April love / Wonderful time up there / Too soon to know / My little red book / I've got you on my mind / Call it stormy Monday / Keep your heart / Cherie, I love you / Peace on Earth / Have faith / If dreams come true / Baby has gone bye bye / If dreams come true / That's how much I love you / If dreams come true / That's how much I love you / September song / Ebb tide / I'll walk alone / To each his own / Autumn leaves / Anniversary song / Stardust / Cold, cold heart / Solitude / Deep purple / Blueberry hill / St. Louis blues / Heartaches / Her hand in mine / He / I believe / Ave Maria / Lord's prayer / They can't take that away from me / Yes indeed / Don't worry 'bout me / Lazy river / Lonesome road / American beauty / Rose / Little white lies / Sweet Sue, just you / It's a pity to say goodnight / Sweet Georgia Brown / Gone fishin' / My baby just cares for me / I'll build a stairway to paradise / Robins and roses / I've heard that song before / Frenesi / Sweet Georgia Brown / Two little kisses / Gee, but it's lonely / For my good fortune / Gee, but it's lonely / Wait for me Mary / Havin' fun spo-dee-o-dee / I'll remember tonight / Mardi Gras march / Bourbon Street blues / Fiddle, a rifle, an axe and a bible / Bigger than Texas / Loyalty / Yes indeed / For my good fortune / Jingle bells / Here comes Santa Claus / My happiness / You can't be true, dear / Side by side / Midnight / Silver bells / I'll be home for Christmas / It came upon a midnight clear / Rudolph the red-nosed reindeer / Santa Claus is coming to town / O little town of Bethlehem / Adeste fidelis / Joy to the world / Hark, the herald angels sing / First Noel / Wait for me Mary / Bewildered / Good rockin' tonight / How soon / With the wind and rain in your hair / Shake a hand / Money honey / 'Tis sweet to be remembered / Rock boll weevil / Brightest wishing star / Beulah / Rock boll weevil / Anytime / True love / I'm in the mood for love / Fascination / Secret love / How soon / Because of you / Maybe you'll be there / Tenderly / You belong to me / Why don't you believe me / Nearness of you / More than you know / You're my girl / You just can't plan these things / Goodnight, sleep tight / Do I worry / Wang dang taffy apple tango / Bewildered / For a penny / Alone / Walking the floor over you / Oh what a feeling / Last night was the end of the world / Drifting and dreaming / Tumbling tumblweeds / Beside me / I'll never be free / Sentimental me / Let the rest of the world go by / Melody of love / Let me call you sweetheart / Vaya con dios / Twixt, twelve and twenty / All at once / Brightest wishing star / Why don't you haul off and love me / It's a sin / Didn't it rain / No middle ground / (Remember me) I'm the one who loves you / Fools hall of fame / This girl is mine / I've got a dream on my mind / God be with you / Take the name of Jesus / I love to tell a story / Blessed assurance / Saviour, like a shepherd lead us / He leadeth me / God will take care of thee / I'll be home for Christmas / White Christmas / Joy to the world / Silent night / O little town of Bethlehem / It came upon a midnight clear / First Noel / Adeste fidelis / O holy night / God rest ye merry gentlemen / Hark, the herald angels sing / Santa's coming in a whirly bird / That's all / I want to be there / To the centre of the Earth / Many dreams ago / Wait for me Mary / Faithful heart / Boone's rock'n'roll / Too marvellous for words / My love is like a red, red rose / Twice as tall / Come Spring / What a friend we have in Jesus / I am thine, O Lord / Let the lower lights be burning / Nearer my God to thee / Rock of ages / Loving you madly / Money honey / Friendly persuasion (thee I love) / Ev'ry little thing / Love letters in the sand / Pledging my love / I'm waiting just for you / Walking the floor over you / Love letters in the sand / Beyond the sunset / Louella / Baby has gone, bye bye / St. Louis blues / Two little kisses / For my good fortune / Bigger than Texas / Wait for me Mary / How soon / It's a sin / Didn't it rain / I almost lost my mind / Don't forbid me / Love letters in the sand / Why baby why / Bernadine / There's a goldmine in the sky / I'm in love with you / Chains of love / Remember you're mine / Anastasia / I'm waiting just for you / Friendly persuasion (thee I love) / Wonderful time up there / Too soon to know / That's how much I love you
CD Set ______ BCD 15884
Bear Family / Jun '97 / Direct / Rollercoaster / Swift

GOLDEN GREATS
April love / Don't forbid me / I almost lost my mind / At my front door / Friendly persuassion (Thee I love) / Sugar moon / Moody river / I'll be home / Love letters in

the sand / Gospel boogie / Remember your mine / Ain't that a shame / Main attraction / It's too soon to know / Why baby why / Speedy Gonzalez
CD _______ MCLD 19182
MCA / Mar '93 / BMG

LOVE LETTERS (20 Classics)
Love letters in the sand / I love you more and more / I almost lost my head / Friendly persuasion / Mr. Blue / April love / Speedy Gonzalez / Ain't that a shame / Tutti frutti / Don't forbid me / Wonderful time up there / I believe in music / I'll be home / Moody river / She fights that lovin' feelin' / Jambalaya / You lay so easy on my mind / Bernadine / Where there's a heartache / Poetry in motion
CD _______ SUMCD 4081
Summit / Nov '96 / Sound & Media

LOVE LETTERS IN THE SAND (Pat Boone At His Best)
CD _______ PLSCD 211
Pulse / Apr '97 / BMG

ULTIMATE HIT COLLECTION, THE
CD _______ 12387
Laserlight / Mar '95 / Target/BMG

VERY BEST OF PAT BOONE, THE
Ain't that a shame / Bernadine / Don't forbid me / Friendly persuasion / I almost lost my mind / Jambalaya (on the bayou) / Moody river / Remember your mine / Speedy Gonzales / Love letters in the sand / Tutti frutti / Hey good lookin' / I believe in music / I love you more and more every day / Oh boy / Poetry in motion / Three bells / April love
CD _______ 12999
Laserlight / Jul '97 / Target/BMG

Boone, Richard

MAKE SOMEONE HAPPY (Boone, Richard & Bent Jaedig Quintet)
CD _______ STCD 8282
Storyville / May '97 / Cadillac / Jazz Music / Wellard

Boot Camp Clik

FOR THE PEOPLE
1-900 get da boot / Down by law / Night riders / Headz are reddee / Watch your step / Illa noyz / Rag time / Blackout / Ohkeedoke / Rugged terrain / Dugout / Go for yours / Likkle youth man dem / Last time
CD _______ CDPTY 145
Priority/Virgin / Jun '97 / EMI

Booth, Tim

BOOTH & THE BAD ANGEL (Booth, Tim & Angelo Badalamenti)
I believe / Dance of the bad angels / Hit parade / Fall in love with me / Old ways / Life gets better / Heart / Rising / Butterfly's dream / Stranger / Hands in the rain
CD _______ 5268522
Fontana / Jul '96 / PolyGram

Booth, Webster

MOONLIGHT AND YOU (Webster Booth Sings Songs Of Romance)
World is mine tonight / Pale moon / Vienna / Stay with me forever / I love the moon / Always as I close my eyes / Moonlight and you / Brown bird singing / Princess Elizabeth / This year of theatreland / At dawning / Mifanwy / Song for you and me / Moon of romance / Serenade in the night / Way you look tonight / Serenata / In old Madrid / Elégie / Hindu song
CD _______ PASTCD 9709
Flapper / '90 / Pinnacle

THREE GREAT TENORS (Booth, Webster & Josef Locke/Richard Tauber)
Lovely maid in the moonlight: *Booth, Webster & Joan Cross* / My heart and I: *Tauber, Richard* / Soldier's dream: *Locke, Josef* / English rose: *Booth, Webster* / Hear my song: *Locke, Josef* / Take a pair of sparkling eyes: *Booth, Webster* / Song of songs: *Tauber, Richard* / When the stars are brightly shining: *Booth, Webster* / Serenade: *Tauber, Richard* / March of the grenadiers: *Locke, Josef* / Wandering minstrel: *Booth, Webster* / Break of day: *Tauber, Richard* / One alone: *Tauber, Richard* / If I can help somebody: *Locke, Josef* / Faery song: *Booth, Webster & John T. Cockerill* / You are my heart's delight: *Tauber, Richard* / I'll walk beside you: *Locke, Josef* / Love is my reason: *Tauber, Richard* / Goodbye: *Locke, Josef* / Lost chord: *Booth, Webster*
CD _______ CDSL 8248
EMI / Jul '95 / EMI

Boothe, Ken

ACCLAIMED
CD _______ UPCD 004
Upstairs / May '97 / Jet Star

COLLECTION, THE
CD _______ RNCD 2124
Rhino / Nov '95 / Grapevine/PolyGram / Jet Star

EVERYTHING I OWN
One that I love / You left the water running / Say you / Can't see you / Lady with the starlight / Somewhere / Live good / Old fashion way / Can't fight me down / I'm not for sale / Why baby why / Freedom street / It's gonna take a miracle / Now I know / Artibella / Stop your crying / I wish it would be peaceful again / Your feeling and mine / Make me feel alright / So nice / Rasta never fail / Second chance / Silver words / Is it because I'm black / Everything I own / Crying over you
CD _______ CDTRL 381
Trojan / Jun '97 / Direct / Jet Star

FREEDOM ST.
CD _______ 0444052
Rhino / Mar '97 / Grapevine/PolyGram / Jet Star

I AM JUST A MAN
CD _______ LG 21101
Lagoon / Mar '95 / Grapevine/PolyGram

KEN BOOTHE COLLECTION
CD _______ CDTRL 249
Trojan / Mar '94 / Direct / Jet Star

SINGS HITS FROM STUDIO ONE AND MORE
I'm in a dancing mood / I'm in a dancing mood dub / My heart is gone / My heart is gone dub / Take my hands / Take my hands dub / When I fall in love / When I fall in love dub / Do you love me / Do you love me dub / Got to tell you goodbye / Got to tell you goodbye dub / Without love / Without love dub / Train is coming / Train is coming dub / Moving away / Moving away dub / Puppet on a string / Puppet on a string dub / You are no good / You are no good dub / Now you come running / Now you come running dub
CD _______ RN 7012
Rhino / Feb '97 / Grapevine/PolyGram / Jet Star

Boots & His Buddies

CLASSICS 1935-1937
CD _______ CLASSICS 723
Classics / Dec '93 / Discovery / Jazz Music

CLASSICS 1937-1938
CD _______ CLASSICS 738
Classics / Feb '94 / Discovery / Jazz Music

Bootstrappers

BOOTSTRAPPERS
CD _______ NAR 046CD
New Alliance / May '93 / Plastic Head

Booty, Charlie

AFTER HOURS
CD _______ SACD 108
Solo Art / Mar '95 / Jazz Music

Booze & Blues

MOTORWAY LIGHTS
CD _______ BOO 003
B&B / Nov '94 / Else / Jet Star

Booze Brothers

BREWERS DROOP
CD _______ CLACD 428
Castle / Mar '97 / BMG

Bop Brothers

STRANGE NEWS
Thrill me / Cruisin' and coastin' / One mint julep / Big bad beautiful blues / Strange news / Money is getting cheaper / Long slow ride down / Little finger / Georgia on my mind / Chicken and the hawk
CD _______ ABACACD 1
Abacabe / Jul '95 / Direct / Hot Shot

Bop City

BOP CITY - HIP STRUT
No problem / Hip strut / New rhumba / Funk in deep freeze / Duid deed / Another kind of soul / Squirrel / Bop city / Ahmad's blues / Squirrel
CD _______ HIBD 8013
Hip Bop / Oct '96 / Koch / Silva Screen

Bop Fathers

BOP FATHERS VOL.2
CD _______ COD 027
Jazz View / Jul '92 / Harmonia Mundi

Borderlands

FROM CONJUNTO TO CHICKEN SCRATCH
CD _______ SFWCD 40418
Smithsonian Folkways / Oct '94 / ADA / Cadillac / CM / Direct / Koch

Bore, Sergio

INTUICAO DE TUPA
CD _______ EX 3582
Instinct / Jun '97 / Cargo

TAMBORES URBANOS
Adivinhacao / Voices of percussion / Rumbata / Tambores urbanos / El cogollo / Chama criolla / Stop killing the Amazon / El poliangito / Lamento Africano / Pingentes / Luz de lua / Marimba / Suite Brasila part 1
CD _______ ME 000342
Soulciety/Bassism / Oct '95 / EWM

Boredoms

ONANIE BOMB MEETS THE SEX PISTOLS
Wipe out shock / Shoppers / Boredom Vs.SDI / We never sleep / Bite my bollocks / Young assouls / Call me God / No core punk / Lick'n cock boatpeople / Melt down boogie / Feedbackfuck / Anal eater / God from anal / Born to anal
CD _______ EN 001
Earthnoise / Sep '94 / Vital

SOUL DISCHARGE '99
Your name is limitless / Bubblebop shot / Fifty two boredom / Sun, gun, run / Z and U and T and A / TV Scorpion / Pow wow now / JB Dick and Tina Turner pussy / GIL '77 / Jup-na-keeeeel / Catastro mix '99 / Milky way / Songs without electric guitars / Hamaiin disco bollocks / Hamaiin disco without bollocks
CD _______ EN 002
Earthnoise / Sep '94 / Vital

WOW VOL.2
CD _______ AVANT 026
Avant / Nov '93 / Cadillac / Harmonia Mundi

Borenius, Louis

LAST OF THE AZTECS (Borenius, Louis Coup D'Etat)
CD _______ LOTCD 4304
Loose Tie / May '97 / Timewarp

Borgat, Stephane

DIATONICOEUR
CD _______ CNAI 55388
Le Cire Jaune / Mar '96 / ADA

Borge, Victor

COMEDY IN MUSIC
CD _______ 4840422
Columbia / May '96 / Sony

Borghi, Emmanuel

ANECDOTES
CD _______ A XXII
Seventh / Oct '96 / Cadillac / Harmonia Mundi / ReR Megacorp

Boris & His Bolshie Balalaika

PSYCHIC REVOLUTION
Toadstool soup / Onward christian soldiers / Purple haze / Burnin' with the fire / Blacklisted blues / Voodoo chile / Moonsong / Goin' nowhere / Psychic revolution (sunsong)
CD _______ DELECCD 014
Delerium / Nov '94 / Cargo / Pinnacle / Vital

Borknagar

BORKNAGAR
CD _______ MR 012CD
Malicious / Oct '96 / Plastic Head

Borland, Adrian

CINEMATIC
Dreamfuel / Bright white light / When can I be me / Cinematic / Night cascade / Neon and stone / Long dark train / Antartica / Western veil / We are the night / Dreamfuel 2 / I can't stop the world / Heading emotional / South / Spanish hotel / March
CD _______ RES 002
Resolve / Mar '96 / Prime / Vital

Born Against

PATRIOTIC BATTLE HYMNS
CD _______ VMFM 612
Vermiform / Nov '94 / Cargo / Greyhound / Plastic Head

Born For Bliss

ARABIA EP
CD _______ DW 0213CD
Deathwish / Dec '96 / Plastic Head

Born Jamericans

KIDS FROM FOREIGN
Instant death interlude / Warning sign / So ladies / Sweet honey / Informa fe dead / Cease and seckle / Ain't no stoppin' / Why do girls / Oh gosh / Nobody knows / Boom shak-a-tack
CD _______ 7567923492
Warner Bros. / Jun '94 / Warner Music

Bornkamp, Arno

REED MY MIND
CD _______ BVHAASTCD 9304
Bvhaast / Oct '94 / Cadillac

Borrfors, Monica

SECOND TIME AROUND
CD _______ 1397
Caprice / Jun '85 / ADA / Cadillac / CM / Complete/Pinnacle

YOUR TOUCH
CD _______ 1350
Caprice / Oct '90 / ADA / Cadillac / CM / Complete/Pinnacle

Borstlap, Michiel

MICHIEL BORSTLAP LIVE
CD _______ CHR 70030
Challenge / Nov '95 / ADA / Direct / Jazz Music / Wellard

Bosco, Joao

AFROCANTO GUITAR
CD _______ 68909
Tropical / Apr '97 / Discovery

CORACAO TROPICAL
CD _______ 68969
Tropical / Apr '97 / Discovery

DA LICENCA MEU SENHOR
Pagodespell / Forro em limoeiro / Se voca juras / Pai grande / Peixe vivo/O verto / Tico tico no fuba / Desafinado / Espinha de bacalhau / Expresso 2222 / No tabuleiro da baiana / Um gago apaixonado / Melodia sentimental / Rio De Janeiro / Herois da liberdade
CD _______ 4792132
Sony Jazz / Jul '96 / Sony

Bose, Miguel

SIGN OF CAIN, THE
One touch / Fire and forgiveness / They're only words / Home / Sign of cain / Hunter and the prey / Wako-shamen / I hold only you / mayo / Nada particular
CD _______ 4509950532
East West / Feb '95 / Warner Music

Boson, Higgs

HIGGS BOSON
CD _______ FHPCD 1
FHP / Sep '96 / Discovery

Boss

BORN GANGSTAZ
Call from mom / Deeper / Comin' to getcha / Mai sister is a bitch / Thelma and Louise / Drive-by / Progress of elimination / Livin' loc'd / Recipe of a hoe / Blind date with Boss / Catch a bad one / Born gansta / 1800 body bags / Diary of a mad bitch / 2 to da head / I don't give a fuck / Call from dad
CD _______ 4740742
Columbia / Aug '93 / Sony

Boss Hog

BOSS HOG
Winn coma / Sick / Beehive / Ski bunny / Green shirt / I dig you / Try one / What the fuck / I idolize you / Punkture / Strawberry / Walk in / Texas / Sam
CD _______ GED 24811
Geffen / Oct '95 / BMG

COLD HANDS
CD _______ EFA 08127CD
Amphetamine Reptile / Jan '91 / Plastic Head

Boss Martians

13 EVIL TALES
CD _______ ID 123344CD
Dionysus / Jan '97 / Cargo / Greyhound / Plastic Head

JETAWAY SOUNDS OF...
CD _______ HILLS 1
Hillsdale / Jun '97 / Greyhound

Bostic, Earl

14 HITS
CD _______ KCD 5010
King / Apr '97 / Avid/BMG

BEST OF BOSTIC, THE
Flamingo / Always / Deep purple / Smoke rings / What, no pearls / Jungle drums / Serenade / I can't give you anything but love / Seven steps / I'm gettin' sentimental over you / Don't you do it / Steamwhistle jump
CD _______ KCD 500
King / Mar '90 / Avid/BMG

BLOWS A FUSE
Night train / 8.45 stomp / That's the groovy thing / Special delivery stomp / Moonglow / Mambostic / Earl blows a fuse / Harlem nocturne / Who snuck the wine in the gravy / Don't you do it / Disc jockey's nightmare / Flamingo / Steam whistle jump / What, no pearls / Tuxedo Junction
CD _______ CDCHARLY 241
Charly / Oct '90 / Koch

BOSTIC FOR YOU
Sleep / Moonglow / Velvet sunset / For you / Very thought of you / Linger awhile / Cherokee / Smoke gets in your eyes / Memories / Embraceable you / Wrap your troubles in dreams (and dream your troubles away) / Night and day

CD KCD 503
King / Mar '90 / Avid/BMG

FLAMINGO (Charly R&B Masters Vol. 16)
Flamingo / Sleep / Always / Moonglow / Ain't misbehavin' / You go to my head / Cherokee / Streamwhistle jump / What, no pearls / Deep purple / Mambostic / Sweet Lorraine / Where or when / Harlem nocturne / 720 in the books / Tuxedo junction / Night train / Special delivery stomp / Song of the Islands / Liebestraum / Liszt
CD CDRB 16
Charly / Mar '95 / Koch

JAZZ TIME
CD LEJAZZCD 52
Le Jazz / Jan '96 / Cadillac / Koch

Boston

BOSTON
More than a feeling / Peace of mind / Foreplay (long time) / Rock 'n' roll band / Smokin' / Hitch a ride / Something about you / Let me take you home tonight
CD CD 81611
Epic / Mar '87 / Sony

DON'T LOOK BACK
Journey / It's easy / Man I'll never be / Feeling satisfied / Part / Used to bad news / Don't be afraid
CD CD 86057
Epic / Mar '87 / Sony

FOR REAL
CD MCD 10973
MCA / May '94 / BMG

GREATEST HITS
Tell me / Higher power / More than a feeling / Peace of mind / Don't look back / Cool the engines / Livin' for you / Feelin' satisfied / Party / Foreplay long time / Amanda / Rock 'n' roll band / Smokin' / Man I'll never be / Star spangled banner/4th of July reprise / Higher power
CD 4843332
Epic / Jun '97 / Sony

THIRD STAGE
Amanda / We're ready / Launch / Cool the engines / My destination / New world / To be a man / I think I like it / Can'tcha say / Still in love / Hollyann
CD MCLD 19066
MCA / Oct '92 / BMG

Boston, Rick

NUMB
CD WD 00402
World Domination / Oct '96 / Pinnacle / RTM/Disc

Bostonian Friends

PEACE FROM AFRICA
CD 151472
EPM / Nov '92 / ADA / Discovery

Boswell Sisters

AIRSHOTS AND RARITIES 1930-1935
Here comes the sun / Liza Lee / Down the river of golden dreams / Rarin' to go / There's a wah wah girl in Agua Caliente / Let me sing and I'm happy/Crazy rhythm/Farewell blues/Mammy / My mad moment / Gee but I'd like to make you happy / I'm in training for you / When the little red roses get the blues for you / Does my baby love / Song of the dawn / Liza Lee / Rainy days / At the Darktown strutter's ball / Sleep come on and take me / Heebie jeebies / Why don't you practice what you preach / Fare the well Annabelle / Lullaby of Broadway
CD RTR 79009
Retrieval / Feb '97 / Cadillac / Direct / Jazz Music / Swift / Wellard

ANTHOLOGY 1930-1940
CD EN 518
Encyclopaedia / Sep '95 / Discovery

BOSWELL SISTERS 1931-1935
CD CD 56082
Jazz Roots / Mar '95 / Target/BMG

BOSWELL SISTERS COLLECTION VOL.1 (1931-1932)
CD COCD 21
Collector's Classics / Mar '95 / Cadillac / Complete/Pinnacle / Jazz Music

IT'S THE GIRLS (Boswell Sisters & Connee Boswell)
It's the girls / That's what I like about you / Heebie jeebies / Concentratin' on you / Wha'd ja do to me / I'm all dressed up with a broken heart / When I take my sugar to tea / Don't tell him what happened to me / Roll on Mississippi roll on / I'm gonna cry (cryin' blues) / This is the missus / That's love / Life is just a bowl of cherries / My future just passed / What is it / Shine on harvest moon / Gee but I'd like to make you happy / We're on the highway to Heaven / Time on my hands / Nights when I'm lonely / Shout, sister, shout / It's you
CD CDAJA 5014
Living Era / Jun '88 / Select

IT'S YOU
CD PASTCD 7087
Flapper / May '96 / Pinnacle

Boswell, Connee

DEEP IN A DREAM
CD HQCD 80
Harlequin / Sep '96 / Hot Shot / Jazz Music / Swift / Wellard

HEART AND SOUL (25 Hits 1932-1942)
All I do is dream of you / Amapola / Basin Street blues: *Boswell, Connee & Bing Crosby* / Bob White: *Boswell, Connee & Bing Crosby* / Carioca / Deep in a dream / Gipsy love song / Heart and soul / I cover the waterfront / I hear a rhapsody / I let a song go out of my heart / In the middle of a kiss / It's the talk of the town / Little man you've had a busy day / Me minus you / On the isle of May / One dozen roses / Sand in my shoes / Stormy weather / Sunrise serenade / That old feeling / They can't take that away from me / Under a blanket of blue / You forgot to remember / You grow sweeter as the years go by
CD CDAJA 5221
Living Era / Aug '97 / Select

Boswell, Eve

EMI PRESENTS THE MAGIC OF EVE BOSWELL
Pickin' a chicken / I believe / True love / Heatwave / Dear hearts and gentle people / All my love / If / Transatlantic lullaby / Hi-Lili, Hi-Lo / Sugar bush / Here in my heart / Moon above Malaya / I'm yours / Bridge of Sighs / If you love me / Bewitched / Little shoemaker / More than ever / Skokiaan / On the waterfront / These are the things we'll share / Ready, willing and able / Blue star / Young and foolish / Gypsy in my soul
CD CDMFP 6370
Music For Pleasure / May '97 / EMI

Bothy Band

AFTER HOURS (Live In Paris)
Kesh jig / Butterfly / Casadh an tsugain / Farewell to Erin / Heathery hills of Yarrow / Queen Jane / Pipe on the hob / Mary Willies / How can I live at the top of a mountain / Rosie Finn's favourite / Green groves of Erin
CD GL 3016CD
Green Linnet / Jul '94 / ADA / CM / Direct / Highlander / Roots

BEST OF THE BOTHY BAND, THE
Salamanca / Banshee / Sailor's bonnet / Petty peg / Craig's pipes / Blackbird / Maids of Mitchelstown / Casadh an tsugain / Music in the glen / Fionnghuala / Old hag you have killed me / Do you love an apple / Rip the calico / Death of Queen Jane / Green groves of Erin / Flowers of Red Hill
CD GL 3001CD
Green Linnet / Jul '94 / ADA / CM / Direct / Highlander / Roots

BOTHY BAND
Kesh jig / Give us a drink of water / Flowers of the flock / Famous Ballymote / Green groves of Erin / Flowers of Red Hill / Do you love an apple / Julia Delaney / Patsy Geary's / Coleman's cross / Is trua nack bhfuil me in Eirinn / Navvy on the line / Rainy day / Tar road to Sligo / Paddy Clancy's jig / Martin Wynn's / Lonford tinker / Pretty peg / Craig's pipes / Hector the hero / Laird of Drumblair / Traveller / Humors of Lissade / Butterfly / Salamanca / Banshee / Sailor's bonnet
CD GL 3011CD
Green Linnet / Jul '94 / ADA / CM / Direct / Highlander / Roots

OLD HAG YOU HAVE KILLED ME
Music in the Glen / Fionnghuala / Kid on the mountain / Farewell to Erin / Summer will come / Laurel tree / Sixteen come next Sunday / Old hag you have killed me / Calum Sgaire / Ballintore fancy / Maid of Coolmore / Michael Gorman's reel
CD GL 3005CD
Green Linnet / Jul '94 / ADA / CM / Direct / Highlander / Roots

OUT OF THE WIND INTO THE SUN
Morning star / Maids of Mitchelstown / Rip the Calico / Streets of Derry / Pipe on the hob / Sailor boy / Blackbird / Strayaway child / Factory girl / Slides
CD GL 3013CD
Green Linnet / Jul '94 / ADA / CM / Direct / Highlander / Roots

Bottcher, Gerd

FUR GABI TU' ICH ALLES
Fur gabi tu ich alles / Du schaust mich an / Deine roten lippen / Adieu lebewohl goodbye (Tonight is so right for love) / Goodbye rock a hula baby / Wine nicht um mich / Geld wie heu / Man geht so leicht am gluck vorbei Tina Lou / Jambalaya / Ein dutzend and're manner / Oh Billy Billy Black / Sing / Sing denn mein zuhause das bist du / Susanna ich kenn' die / Strassen der weiten / Ay ay ay ay oh / Signorina / Ich such' dich auf allen Wegen / Ich komme wieder / Du heut nacht / Carolin, Carolin / Meine braut, die kann das besser / Bing bang bungalow / Lady Lou / Ich finde nichts dabei
CD BCD 15402
Bear Family / Dec '87 / Direct / Rollercoaster / Swift

PRETTY WOMAN
Pretty woman / Wer wird der nachste sein / Weil du meine grosse liebe bist: *Bottcher, Gerd & Detlef Engel* / Aber du darling dear / In der twist spelunke von McMiller: *Bottcher, Gerd & Detlef Engel* / Oh Katherin / So wie ein Indianer / Heim heim mocht ich ziehn: *Bottcher, Gerd & Detlef Engel* / Blue lady / Mach nicht nochzeit ohne mich / Sailor boy: *Bottcher, Gerd & Detlef Engel* / Weil du himmelblaue augen hast / Wo ist mein baby heut nacht / Lorelei / Uber die prarie: *Bottcher, Gerd & Detlef Engel* / Schenk mir dein vertauen / Nur keine Beatle-frisur / Nur Anne-Marie kommt in frage / Zwei caballeros: *Bottcher, Gerd & Detlef Engel* / Ich stehe zu dir / Madchen gibt's wie sand am meer / Stern von Samoa: *Bottcher, Gerd & Detlef Engel* / Niemals darfst du mich verlassen / Eine gefiel mir am allerbesten / Crazy little bluebird / Eine welte ohne liebe: *Bottcher, Gerd & Detlef Engel* / Tschau / Auf wiedersehn
CD BCD 16107
Bear Family / Dec '96 / Direct / Rollercoaster / Swift

Botti, Chris

MIDNIGHT WITHOUT YOU
CD 5371322
Verve/Forecast / May '97 / PolyGram

Bottle Rockets

BOTTLE ROCKETS
Early in the morning / Gas girl / Trailer Mama / Wave that flag / Kerosene / Every kinda everything / Got what I wanted / Manhattan countryside / Rural route / Bud Nanney theme / Lonely cowboy
CD ESD 80772
East Side Digital / Mar '96 / Vital

BROOKLYN SIDE, THE
Welfare music / Gravity falls / I'll be comin' around / Radar gun / Sunday sports / Pot of gold / 1000 dollar car / Idiots revenge / Young lovers in town / Take me to the bank / Stuck in a rut / I wanna come home now / Queen of the world
CD ESD 81002
East Side Digital / Mar '96 / Vital

Bottom 12

DANCE OR BE SHOT (Remixes)
CD EFA 032592
Noise-O-Lution / Aug '97 / SRD

SONGS FOR THE DISGRUNTLED POSTMAN
CD EFA 032502
Noise-O-Lution / Dec '95 / SRD

Bottom Feeders

BIG SIX
Big six / Wrecked / Can't stand you / Here come squeenie / 69 drags pack / Better of dead / I love you / Strange muscle / Out of it / Potty mouth / Five forty one / Giant gurl / Iatlaians are pretty fucking cool / Beer song
CD PO 15CD
Scooch Pooch / Oct '96 / Cargo / Greyhound / Pinnacle
CD 206152
Epitaph / Jul '97 / Pinnacle / Plastic Head

Bouchard, Dominic

HEOL DOUR (Bouchard, Dominic & Cyrille Colas)
CD KMCD 40
Keltia Musique / Aug '93 / ADA / Discovery

VIBRATIONS
CD KMCD 03
Keltia Musique / Jul '90 / ADA / Discovery

Boucher, Judy

CAN'T BE WITH YOU TONIGHT
CD OCD 024
Orbitone / Sep '86 / Jet Star

DEVOTED TO YOU
CD KU 106CD
Kufe / Apr '94 / Jet Star

TAKE ME AS I AM
CD KUCD 113
Kufe / Mar '96 / Jet Star

TEARS ON MY PILLOW
CD KUCD 100
Kufe / Jul '92 / Jet Star

Boud Deun

ASTRONOMY MADE EASY
CD RUNE 91
Cuneiform / Jun '97 / ReR Megacorp

Boudreaux, Helene

UNE DEUXIEME (Boudreaux, Helene & Pete Bergeron)
CD SW 6120CD
Swallow / Jul '95 / ADA

Bouffard, Patrick

MUSIC FOR HURDY GURDY FROM AUVERGNE
CD C 560007
Ocora / Nov '90 / ADA / Harmonia Mundi

REVENANT DE PARIS
CD 49502CD
Acousteak / Apr '96 / ADA / Discovery

Boukan Ginen

JOU A RIVE
CD XENO 4024
Xenophile / Feb '95 / ADA / Direct

REV AN NOU
Salouwe / Afrika / Zanfan nago / Se yo ki lakoz / Kouman napfe / Neg yo danjere / Timounyo / Je'n la nape gade / Ma doute / Rev an nou / Move fanmi
CD XENO 4027CD
Xenophile / Oct '96 / ADA / Direct

Boulevard Of Broken Dreams

IT'S THE TALK OF THE TOWN
CD HNCD 1345
Hannibal / May '89 / ADA / Vital

Boulton, Laura

NAVAJO SONGS
CD SFWCD 40403
Smithsonian Folkways / Dec '94 / ADA / Cadillac / CM / Direct / Koch

Bouncing Souls

GOOD, THE BAD...
CD BYO 031CD
BYO / Jan '97 / Cargo

MANIACAL LAUGHTER
CD BYO 037CD
BYO / Jan '97 / Cargo

Bounty Killer

DOWN IN THE GHETTO
CD GRELCD 210
Greensleeves / Jan '97 / Jet Star / SRD

GHETTO GRAMMA
Ancient day killing / Convince / Smoke the herb / Fat and sexy / Book book book / Gal fi get wock / No no no (world a respect): *Bounty Killer & Dawn Penn* / Report you missing / Fear no evil / Mi heart beat / Run-around girl: *Bounty Killer & Chuck Turner* / Down grade mi gun / I'll be back: *Bounty Killer & Colin Roach* / Income / Wedding done arrange / You've got me waiting: *Bounty Killer & Nitty Kutchie/Angel Doolas* / War is not a nice thing / Mangoose / This world's too haunted: *Bounty Killer & Junior Reid* / Time to realize: *Bounty Killer & Dirtsman*
CD GRELCD 238
Greensleeves / Aug '97 / Jet Star / SRD

GUNS OUT
CD GRELCD 206
Greensleeves / Jan '97 / Jet Star / SRD

JAMAICA'S MOST WANTED
CD GRELCD 195
Greensleeves / Jan '97 / Jet Star / SRD

MY XPERIENCE VOL.1
Fed up / Lord is my light and salvation / Hip-hopera ("Mr Punk") / Guns and roses / Mama / Change like the weather / War beyond the stars / Living dangerously / War face (ask fi war) / Marathon ("To Chicago") / Revolution III / Gun down / Mi nature / Virgin Island / Who send dem / Seek God / Maniac / Suicide or murder / Benz and the Bimma / My experience
CD CDV 2823
Virgin / Dec '96 / EMI

NO ARGUMENT
CD GRELCD 222
Greensleeves / Jan '97 / Jet Star / SRD

Bourbonese Qualk

BOURBONESE QUALK
CD PRAXIS 5CD
Praxis / Feb '94 / Plastic Head

FEEDING THE HUNGRY GHOST
CD FUNFUNDVIERZ 69
Funfundvierz / Jun '94 / Cargo / Greyhound

MY GOVERNMENT
CD CD 34
Funfundvierz / Feb '90 / Cargo / Greyhound

UNPOP
CD 2TF 13CD
TFI / Jul '95 / Plastic Head

Bourbons

HOUSE PARTY 1964-1966
CD AA 058
Arf Arf / Jul '97 / Greyhound

Bourelly, Jean-Paul

ROCK THE CATHARTIC SPIRITS (Vibe Music & The Blues)

CD DIW 911
DIW / Oct '96 / Cadillac / Harmonia Mundi

TRIPPIN'
CD EMY 1272
Enemy / Mar '92 / Grapevine/PolyGram

Bournet, P.

PLAY JOHN MCLAUGHLIN AND ASTOR PIAZZOLLA (Bournet, P. & Enrique Alberti)
CD IMP 948
IMP / Jan '97 / ADA / Discovery

Boutouk, Ian

GIPSY CLASSICS (The Soul Of The Gipsy Violin) (Boutouk, Ian & Batalonia Gipsy Orchestra)
CD 995552
EPM / Jul '95 / ADA / Discovery

Boutte, Lillian

JAZZ BOOK, THE
Now baby or never / Comes love / On revival day / Don't worry 'bout me / Lover come back to me / Muddy water / Tennessee waltz / That old feeling / Embraceable you / Barefootin'
CD BLU 10202
Blues Beacon / Dec '94 / New Note/ Pinnacle

LILLIAN BOUTTE
Teardrops from my eyes / 'Tis autumn / Meet me at the station / My one and only love / You hit the spot / Funghi Mama / Who can I turn to / Almost like being in love / Meet me at no special place / Hold it / When you wish upon a star
CD FJCD 111
Fret / Jul '96 / Cadillac / New Note/Pinnacle

LILLIAN BOUTTE WITH HUMPHREY LYTTLETON AND BAND (Boutte, Lillian/ Humphrey Lyttelton & His Band)
Back in your own backyard / Miss Otis regrets / Squiggles / I double dare you / Lillian
CD CLGCD 018
Calligraph / Oct '88 / Cadillac / Jazz Music / New Note/Pinnacle / Wellard

LIVE IN TIVOLI (Boutte, Lillian & Her American Band)
CD MECCACD 1030
Music Mecca / Jun '93 / Cadillac / Jazz Music / Wellard

Bouzouki Ensemble

SONGS OF GREECE
CD SOW 90131
Sounds Of The World / Sep '94 / Target/ BMG

Bovell, Dennis

DUB DEM SILLY
CD ARKCD 107
Arawak / Oct '95 / Jet Star

DUB OF AGES
CD LKJCD 015
LKJ / Apr '97 / Grapevine/PolyGram / Jet Star

DUBMASTER
CD JMC 200210
Jamaican Gold / Jan '94 / Grapevine/ PolyGram / Jet Star

STRICTLY DUBWISE (Bovell, Dennis Dub Band)
CD 14808
Spalax / Jun '97 / ADA / Cargo / Direct / Discovery / Greyhound

TACTICS
CD LKJCD 010
LKJ / Mar '95 / Grapevine/PolyGram / Jet Star

Bow Wow Wow

APHRODISIAC (The Best Of Bow Bow Wow)
I want candy / Roustabout / Cowboy / Baby oh no / Lonesome tonight / Joy of eating raw flesh / See jungle (jungle boy) / Louis Quatorze / Mario (your own way to Paradise) / Prince of darkness / Quiver (arrows in my) / Rikki Dee / (I'm a) TV savage / Do you wanna hold me / What's the time (hey buddy) / Elimination dancing / El boss dicho / Love, peace and harmony / Chihuahua / Aphrodisiac / Go wild in the country
CD 74321419672
Camden / Oct '96 / BMG

GO WILD - THE BEST OF BOW WOW WOW
I want Candy / Go wild in the country / Prince of darkness / Cowboy / Baby, oh no / Do you wanna hold me / Golly golly go buddy / Louis Quatorze / What's the time (Hey buddy) / Joy of eating raw flesh / Elimination dancing / Aphrodsiac / Mile high club / TV savage / See jungle (See jungle boy) / Chihuahua (12" version) / Go wild in the country (12" Version) / Chihuahua
CD 74321213362
Arista / Jun '94 / BMG

LIVE IN JAPAN
(I'm a) TV savage / Golly golly go buddy / Mickey put it down / Orang-outang / See jungle / Go wild in the country / Baby, oh no / Elimination dancing / Louis quatorze / I want candy / C30 C60 C90 go / Prince of darkness / GSBT / Sun, sea and piracy
CD RRCD 233
Receiver / Feb '97 / Grapevine/PolyGram

SEE JUNGLE SEE JUNGLE GO JOIN YOUR GANG YEAH...
Jungle boy / Chihuahua / Sinner sinner sinner / Mickey put it down / TV savage / Elimination dancing / Golly golly / Go buddy / King Kong / Go wild in the country / I am not a know it all / Why are babies so wise / Orang-utan / Hello hello daddy
CD OW 34502
One Way / Jun '97 / ADA / Direct / Greyhound

WHEN THE GOING GETS TOUGH, THE TOUGH GET GOING
Aphrodisiac / Do you wanna hold me / Roustabout / Lonesome tonight / Love me / What's the time / Mario (your own way to paradise) / (Arrows in my) quiver / Man mountain / Rikki Dee / Tommy Tucker / Love peace and harmony
CD OW 34503
One Way / Jun '97 / ADA / Direct / Greyhound

Bowden, Chris

TIME CAPSULE
Epsilon / Time capsule / Telescopic / Epsilon transmission / Mothers and daughters now Mothers / Retrospective / Sane
CD SJRCD 031
Soul Jazz / Jun '96 / New Note/Pinnacle / Timewarp / Vital

Bowdler, John

LET'S FACE THE MUSIC AND DANCE
CD JB 001CD
Key / Oct '94 / ADA / CM

Bowen, Ralph

MOVIN' ON (Bowen, Ralph Quintet)
CD CRISS 1066CD
Criss Cross / Oct '92 / Cadillac / Direct / Vital/SAM

Bowen, Robin Huw

HARP MUSIC OF WALES
CD CDSDL 412
Saydisc / Oct '95 / ADA / Direct / Harmonia Mundi

HUNTING THE HEDGEHOG
CD RHB 002CD
Teires / Jun '94 / ADA

Bowers, Bryan

VIEW FROM HOME, THE
CD FF 70037
Flying Fish / Mar '89 / ADA / CM / Direct / Roots

Bowers, Graham

OF MARY'S BLOOD
CD RWCD 001
Extreme / May '95 / Vital/SAM

Bowery Electric

BEAT
Beat / Empty words / Without stopping / Under the sun / Fear of flying / Looped / Black light / Inside out / Coming out / Post script / Low density
CD BBQCD 188
Warp / Feb '97 / Prime / RTM/Disc

BOWERY ELECTRIC
CD KRANK 007CD
Kranky / Mar '97 / Cargo / Greyhound

VERTIGO
CD BBQ 315CDD
Beggars Banquet / Aug '97 / RTM/Disc / Warner Music

Bowie, David

1966
I'm not losing sleep / I dig everything / Can't help thinking about me / Do anything you say / Good morning girl / And I say to myself
CD CLACD 154
Castle / Dec '89 / BMG

ALADDIN SANE
Watch that man / Aladdin Sane / Drive-in Saturday / Panic in Detroit / Cracked actor / Time / Prettiest star / Let's spend the night together / Jean Genie / Lady grinning soul
CD CDP 7947682
Premier/EMI / Sep '97 / EMI

BLACK TIE, WHITE NOISE
Wedding / You've been around / I feel free / Black tie, white noise / Jump they say / Nite flights / Pallas Athena / Miracle goodnight / Don't let me down / Looking for Lester / I know it's gonna happen someday / Wedding song / Lucy can't dance
CD 74321136972
Arista / Jul '96 / BMG

CHANGESBOWIE
Space oddity / John I'm only dancing / Changes / Ziggy Stardust / Suffragette City / Jean Genie / Diamond dogs / Rebel rebel / Young Americans / Fame '90 / Golden years / Heroes / Ashes to ashes / Fashion / Let's dance / China girl / Modern love / Blue Jean / Starman / Life on Mars / Sound and vision
CD CDP 7941802
Premier/EMI / Apr '90 / EMI

DAVID BOWIE
Uncle Arthur / Sell me a coat / Rubber band / Love you till Tuesday / There is a happy land / We are hungry men / When I live my dream / Little bombardier / Silly boy blue / Come and buy my toys / Join the gang / She's got medals / Maid of Bond street / Please Mr. Gravedigger
CD 8000872
Deram / Apr '91 / PolyGram

DAVID BOWIE SONGBOOK, THE (Various Artists)
CD VSOPCD 236
Connoisseur Collection / Apr '97 / Pinnacle

DAVID LIVE (At Tower Theatre Philadelphia) (2CD Set)
1984 / Rebel rebel / Moonage daydream / Sweet thing / Changes / Suffragette city / Aladdin Sane / All the young dudes / Cracked actor / Rock 'n' roll with me / Watch that man / Knock on wood / Diamond dogs / Big brother / Width of a circle / Jean Genie / Rock 'n' roll suicide / Band introduction / Here today, gone tomorrow / Time
CD Set CDDBLD 1
EMI / Jun '95 / EMI

DIAMOND DOGS
Future legend / Diamond dogs / Sweet thing / Candidate / Rebel rebel / Rock 'n' roll with me / We are the dead / 1984 / Big brother / Chant of the ever circling skeletal family / Dodo / Candidate (demo)
CD CDP 7952112
Premier/EMI / Oct '90 / EMI

EARTH CALLING ZIGGY (2CD Set/ Documentary and Music)
CD Set OTR 1100048
Metro Independent / Jun '97 / Essential/ BMG

EARTHLING
Little wonder / Looking for satellites / Battle for Britain / Seven years in Tibet / Dead man walking / Telling lies / Last think you should do / I'm afraid of Americans / Law (earthlings on fire)
CD 74321449442
RCA / Feb '97 / BMG

HEROES
Beauty and the beast / Joe the lion / Sons of the silent age / Blackout / V2 Schneider / Sense of doubt / Moss garden / Neukoln / Secret life of Arabia / Heroes / Abdulmajid / Joe the lion ('91 Mix)
CD CDP 7977202
Premier/EMI / Aug '91 / EMI

HUNKY DORY
Changes / Oh you pretty things / Eight line poem / Life on Mars / Kooks / Quicksand / Fill your heart / Andy Warhol / Song for Bob Dylan / Queen bitch / Bewlay Brothers / Bombers / Supermen / Quicksand (demo version) / Bewlay brothers (alternative mix)
CD CDP 7918432
Premier/EMI / Aug '97 / EMI

INTERVIEW COMPACT DISC: DAVID BOWIE
CD CBAK 4040
Baktabak / Sep '90 / Arabesque

INTERVIEW DISC
CD TELL 03
Network / Dec '96 / Total/BMG

INTROSPECTIVE: DAVID BOWIE
I'm not losing sleep / I dig everything / Can't help thinking about me / Interview part one / Do anything you say / Good morning girl / And I say to myself / Interview part two
CD CINT 5001
Baktabak / Nov '90 / Arabesque

LET'S DANCE
Modern love / China girl / Let's dance / Without you / Ricochet / Criminal world / Cat people (putting out fires) / Shake it / Under pressure: *Queen & David Bowie*
CD CDVUS 96
Virgin / Nov '95 / EMI

LODGER
Fantastic voyage / African night flight / Move on / Yassassin / Red sails / DJ / Look back in anger / Boys keep swinging / Repetition / Red money / I pray ole / Look back in anger (1988 version)
CD CDP 7977242
Premier/EMI / Aug '91 / EMI

LONDON BOY
Space oddity (original version) / Did you ever have a dream / There is a happy land / Rubber band / Let me sleep beside you / Maid of Bond Street / We are hungry men / When I live my dream / Karma man / Laughing knome / She's got medals / Little bombardier / Please Mr. Grave Digger / Gospel according to Tony Day / Sell me a coat / Join the gang / Love you til Tuesday / London boys
CD 5517062
Spectrum / Mar '96 / PolyGram

LOW
Speed of life / Breaking glass / What in the world / Sound and vision / Always crashing in the same car / Be my wife / New career in a new town / Warszawa / Art decade / Weeping wall / Subterraneans / Some are / All saints / Sound and vision (1991 remix)
CD CDP 7977192
Premier/EMI / Aug '90 / EMI

MAN WHO SOLD THE WORLD, THE
Width of a circle / All the madmen / Black country rock / After all / Running gun blues / Saviour machine / She shook me cold / Man who sold the world / Supermen / Lightning frightening / Holy holy / Moonage daydream / Hang on to yourself
CD CDP 7918372
Premier/EMI / Sep '97 / EMI

NEVER LET ME DOWN
New York's in love / Too dizzy / Bang bang / Day in, day out / Time will crawl / Beat of your drum / Never let me down / Zeroes / Glass spider / Shining star (making my love) / '87 and cry / Julie / Girls / When the wind blows
CD CDVUS 98
Virgin / Nov '95 / EMI

OUTSIDE
Leon take us outside / Outside / Heart's filthy lesson / Small plot of land / Baby Grace (a horrid cassette) / Hallo spaceboy / Motel / I have not been to Oxford town / No control / Algeria touchshriek / Voyeur of utter destruction / Ramona A Stone/I am with name / Wishful beginnings / We prick you / Nathan Adler / I'm deranged / Thru' these architects eyes / Strangers when we meet
CD 74321307022
RCA / Sep '95 / BMG

PIN UPS
Rosalyn / Here comes the night / I wish you would / See Emily play / Everything's alright / I can't explain / Friday on my mind / Sorrow / Don't bring me down / Shapes of things / Anyway anyhow anywhere / Where have all the good times gone / Growin' up / Amsterdam
CD CDP 7947672
Premier/EMI / Jul '90 / EMI

RARESTONEBOWIE
All the young dudes / Queen bitch / Sound and vision / Time / Be my wife / Footstompin' / Ziggy Stardust / My death / I feel free
CD GY 014
NMC / May '95 / Total/Pinnacle

RISE AND FALL OF ZIGGY STARDUST & THE SPIDERS FROM MARS, THE
Five years / Soul love / Moonage daydream / Starman / It ain't easy / Lady Stardust / Star / Hang on to yourself / Ziggy Stardust / Suffragette city / Rock 'n' roll suicide / John I'm only dancing / Velvet goldmine / Sweet head / Ziggy Stardust / Lady Stardust
CD CDP 7944002
Premier/EMI / Jun '90 / EMI

SANTA MONICA '72
Ziggy Stardust / Changes / Superman / Life on mars / Five years / Space oddity / Andy Warhol / My death / Width of a circle / Queen bitch / Moonage daydream / John I'm only dancing / Waiting for the man / Jean genie / Suffragette city / Rock 'n' roll suicide
CD GY 002
NMC / Mar '94 / Total/Pinnacle

SCARY MONSTERS
It's no game / Up the hill backwards / Scary monsters (and super creeps) / Ashes to ashes / Fashion / Teenage wildlife / Scream like a baby / Kingdom come / Because you're young / It's no game (part 2) / Space oddity / Panic in Detroit / Crystal Japan / Alabama song
CD CDP 7993312
Premier/EMI / May '92 / EMI

SINGLES COLLECTION, THE (2CD Set)
Space oddity / Changes / Starman / Ziggy Stardust / Suffragette city / John I'm only dancing / Jean genie / Drive-in Saturday / Life on Mars / Sorrow / Rebel rebel / Rock 'n' roll suicide / Diamond dogs / Knock on wood / Young Americans / Fame / Golden years / TVC 15 / Sound and vision / Heroes / Beauty and the beast / Boys keep swinging / DJ / Alabama song / Ashes to ashes / Fashion / Scary monsters (and super creeps) / Under pressure: *Queen & David Bowie* / Wild is the wind / Let's dance / China girl / Modern love / Blue jean / This is not America / Dancing in the street: *Bowie, David & Mick Jagger* / Absolute beginners / Day in, day out
CD Set CDEM 1512
Premier/EMI / Nov '95 / EMI

SPACE ODDITY
Space oddity / Unwashed and somewhat slightly dazed / Letter to Hermione / Cygnet committee / Janine / Wild eyed boy from

Freecloud / God knows I'm good / Memory of a free festival / Occasional dream
CD CDP 7918352
Premier/EMI / Sep '97 / EMI

STAGE (2CD Set)
Hang on to yourself / Ziggy Stardust / Five years / Soul love / Star / Station to station / Fame / TVC 15 / Warszawa / Speed of life / Art decade / Sense of doubt / Breaking glass / Heroes / What in the world / Blackout / Beauty and the beast / Alabama song
CD Set CDS 7986172
Premier/EMI / Feb '92 / EMI

STATION TO STATION
Station to station / Golden years / Word on a wing / TVC 15 / Stay / Wild is the wind / Word on a wing (live) / Stay (live)
CD CDP 7964352
Premier/EMI / Apr '91 / EMI

TONIGHT
Loving the alien / Don't look down / God only knows / Tonight / Neighbourhood threat / Blue Jean / Tumble and twirl / I keep forgetting / Dancing with the big boys / This is not America: *Bowie, David & Pat Metheny Group* / As the world falls down / Absolute beginners
CD CDVUS 97
Virgin / Nov '95 / EMI

YOUNG AMERICANS
Young Americans / Win / Fascination / Right / Somebody up there likes me / Across the universe / Can you hear me / Fame / Who can I be now / It's gonna be me / John I'm only dancing again
CD CDP 7964362
Premier/EMI / Apr '91 / EMI

ZIGGY STARDUST THE MOTION PICTURE
Watch that man / Moonage daydream / Suffragette city / Changes / Time / All the young dudes / Space oddity / White light, white heat / My death / Wild eyed boy from Freecloud / Oh you pretty things / Hang on to yourself / Ziggy Stardust / Cracked actor / Width of a circle / Let's spend the night together / Rock 'n' roll suicide
CD CDP 7804112
Premier/EMI / Sep '92 / EMI

Bowie, Lester

ALL THE MAGIC
For Louie / Spacehead / Ghosts / Trans traditional suite / Let the good times roll / Organic echo / Dunce dance / Charlie M (part II) / Thirsty / Almost Christmas / Down home / Okra influence / Miles Davis meets Donald Duck / Deb Deb's face / Monkey waltz / Fraudulent fanfare / Organic echo (part II)
CD Set 8106252
ECM / Nov '91 / New Note/Pinnacle

AVANT POP (Bowie, Lester Brass Fantasy)
CD 8295632
ECM / Sep '86 / New Note/Pinnacle

BRAZZY VOICES (Bowie, Lester & The Brazz Brothers)
CD IOR 770292
In & Out / Jun '96 / Vital/SAM

FUNKY T COOL T (Bowie, Lester New York Organ Ensemble)
CD DIW 853
DIW / Feb '92 / Cadillac / Harmonia Mundi

GREAT PRETENDER
Great pretender / It's howdy doody time / When the doom (moon) comes over the mountain / Rios negroes / Rose drop / Oh how the ghost sings
CD 8293692
ECM / '90 / New Note/Pinnacle

I ONLY HAVE EYES FOR YOU
I only have eyes for you / Think / Lament / Coming back Jamaica / Nonet / When the spirit returns
CD 8259022
ECM / '90 / New Note/Pinnacle

ORGANIZER, THE (Bowie, Lester New York Organ Ensemble)
CD DIW 821
DIW / Mar '91 / Cadillac / Harmonia Mundi

WORKS: LESTER BOWIE
Charlie M / Rose drop / B funk / When the spirit returns / Let the good times roll
CD 8372742
ECM / Jun '89 / New Note/Pinnacle

Bowles, Paul

BLACK STAR AT THE POINT OF DARKNESS
CD SUBCD 01437
Sub Rosa / Jul '91 / Direct / RTM/Disc / SRD / Vital

Bowlfish

BISCUIT
CD NECKCD 13
Roughneck / Oct '93 / RTM/Disc

Bowlly, Al

AL BOWLLY
Love is the sweetest thing / Dark eyes / Careless / Goodnight sweetheart / Over the rainbow / Moon love / Close your eyes / When you wear your Sunday blue / Man and his dream / What do you know about love / Marie / You're as pretty as a picture / Romany / Small town / Dreaming / Little rain must fall / Give me my ranch / I'm madly in love with you / I miss you in the morning / It was a lover and his lass / Blow blow thou winter wind / Au revoir but not goodbye / South of the border / Bella bambina / Ridin' home
CD CDMFP 6355
Music For Pleasure / Jun '97 / EMI

AL BOWLLY AND THE GREAT BRITISH BANDS
Actions speak louder than words / To be worthy of you / Thanks / Is I in love I is / Looking on the bright side of life / Night on the desert / Hurt / Linda / Dinah / When Mother Nature sings her lullaby / Good evening / What do you know about love / Proud of you / Heart and soul / Is that the way to treat a sweetheart / Smile when you say goodbye / Small town / My own / Home town / Bei mir bist du schon / Girl in the Alice blue gown / My Capri serenade
CD PASTCD 7088
Flapper / Aug '97 / Pinnacle

JUST A BOWL OF CHERRIES
Lady of Spain / Smile, darn ya, smile / Adeline / Save the last dance for me / Goodnight Vienna / All of me / My sweet Virginia / Auf wiedersehen my dear / Rain on the roof / Can't we talk it over / Just humming along / One more kiss / By the fireside / Weep no more my baby / Dinner at eight / This is romance / And so, goodbye / Wagon wheels / I idolize my baby's eyes / Falling in love / Life is just a bowl of cherries / You call it madness / Was that the human thing to do / Now that you're gone / You ought to see Sally on Sunday / Pied piper of Hamlin
CD PASTCD 7003
Flapper / Feb '93 / Pinnacle

LOVE IS THE SWEETEST THING
Love is the sweetest thing / When you wear your Sunday blue / You're a sweetheart / Dreaming / Bi mir bist du schoen / Man and his dream / Over the rainbow / Have you ever been lonely / Marie / It was a lover and his lass / What do you know about love / Something to sing about / Moon love / Little rain must fall / Bella bambina / Au revoir (but not goodbye) / I'll string along with you / In my little red book / Blow, blow thou winter wind / Goodnight sweetheart
CD PAR 2024
Parade / Jul '94 / Disc

PROUD OF YOU
Marie / Sweet someone / Colorado sunset / Is that the way to treat a sweetheart / When Mother Nature sings her lullaby / Two sleepy people / Sweet as a song / Goodnight angel / Any broken hearts to mend / Al Bowlly remembers (medley) / Very thought of you / You're as pretty as a picture / Proud of you / True / Summer's end / There's rain in my eyes / Bei mir bist du schon / When the organ played 'O promise me' / While the cigarette was burning / Penny serenade
CD CDAJA 5064
Living Era / Sep '89 / Select

SWEET SOMEONE
CD CDMOIR 307
Memoir / Apr '94 / Jazz Music / Target/BMG

TWO SLEEPY PEOPLE
Two sleepy people / Goodnight angel / Any broken hearts to mend / Sweet as a song / When Mother Nature sings her lullaby / Is that the way to treat a sweetheart / Marie / Sweet someone / Colorado sunset / Al Bowlly remembers (Medley) / Very thought of you / You're as pretty as a picture / Proud of you / True / Penny serenade / While the cigarette was burning / When the organ played 'O promise me' / Bei mir bist du schon / There's rain in my eyes / Summer's end
CD GRF 097
Tring / '93 / Tring

VERY THOUGHT OF YOU, THE
Whispering / Faded summer love / Tell me (you love me) / You didn't know the music / Dinah / Time alone will tell / Foolish facts / Eleven more months and ten more days / If I have to go on without you / My sweet Virginia / Out of nowhere / I'm so used to you now / Hurt / Leave the rest to nature / From me to you / Just another dream of you / In London on a night like this / Night and day / Night on the Desert / Judy / Madonna mine / Very thought of you
CD RAJCD 837
Empress / Oct '94 / Koch

VERY THOUGHT OF YOU, THE
Time on my hands / Goodnight sweetheart / Sweet and lovely / Pied Piper of Hamlin / By the fireside / Love is the sweetest thing / How could we be wrong / Weep no more my baby / Love locked out / You ought to see Sally on Sunday / One morning in May / Very thought of you / Isle of Capri / Blue Hawaii / In my little red book / Penny serenade / They say / South of the border (Down Mexico way) / Over the rainbow / Somewhere in France with you / When you wish upon a star / Who's taking you home tonight / Blow, blow thou winter wind / It was a lover and his lass
CD CDP 7943412
Premier/EMI / May '90 / EMI

VERY THOUGHT OF YOU, THE
Top hat, white tie and tails / Lover come back to me / Where the lazy river goes by / Be still my heart / I've got you under my skin / Maria, my own / Soon / Carelessly / Touch of your lips / Eadie was a lady / Very thought of you / Why dream / My canary has circles under it's eyes / True / Dinner for one please James / Little Dutch mill / On a little dream ranch / Blue Hawaii / Down by the river / Goodnight sweetheart
CD PLCD 540
President / Jul '95 / Grapevine/PolyGram / President / Target/BMG

Bowman, Gill

CITY LOVE
Your average woman / Very good year / Verses / Ballad of the four Mary's / Make it good / City love / Psychics in America / Story today / Lang-a-growing / Different game / If I didn't love you
CD FE 080CD
Fellside / Feb '91 / ADA / Direct / Target/BMG

PERFECT LOVER
Take me home / Walking away / Rantin' dog / Dear friend / Comin' thro' the rye / This time / To be like you / Ae fond kiss / Dream Angus / Making friends / Somebody's baby
CD CDTRAX 081
Greentrax / Sep '94 / ADA / Direct / Duncans / Highlander

TOASTING THE LASSIES
Green grow the rashes / Now westlin' winds / Banks o'Doon / Sweet Tibbie Dunbar / Rantin' dog / Sweet afton / Auld lang syne / This in no my ain lassie / Rosebud by my early walk / Lea rig / De'il's awa' wi' tha exciseman / Ae fond kiss / Comin' thro' the rye
CD CDTRAX 085
Greentrax / Feb '95 / ADA / Direct / Duncans / Highlander

Bown, Alan

KICK ME OUT
My friend / Strange little friend / Elope / Perfect day / All I can do / Friends in St Louis / Still as stone / Prisoner / Kick me out / Children of the night / Gypsy girl / Wrong idea
CD SEECD 393
See For Miles/C5 / Oct '93 / Pinnacle

LISTEN/STRETCHING OUT
Wanted man / Crash landing / Loosen up / Pyramid / Forever / Curfew / Make us all believe / Make up your mind / Get myself straight / Messenger / Find a melody / Up above my hobby horse's head / Turning point / Build me a stage / Stretching out
CD EDCD 362
Edsel / Jan '93 / Pinnacle

Bowne, Dougie

ONE WAY ELEVATOR
CD DIW 920
DIW / Jan '97 / Cadillac / Harmonia Mundi

Bowyer, Brendan

IRELAND'S BRENDAN BOWYER
CD DOCX 9012
Dolphin / Jul '96 / CM / Else / Grapevine/PolyGram / Koch

Box & Banjo Band

DANCING PARTY
Hello Dolly / Margie / When you wore a tulip / Bye bye love / Heart of myself / I'm gonna sit right down and write myself a letter / Singin' the blues / Bless 'em all / After the ball was over / Oh dear what can the matter be / Locomotion / How do you do it / Roll out the barrel / Pack up your troubles / Who were you with last night / Happy wanderer / Yankee doodle boy / Dixie / She'll be coming round the mountains / Please help me, I'm falling / Crystal chandeliers / I can't stop loving you / Laughing samba / Wedding samba / Bluebell polka / You're free to go / Anna Marie / He'll have to go / Can Can / Nightingale sang in Berkeley Square / Birth of the blues / Once in a while / Peggy O'Neil / Garden where the praties grow / Teddy O'Neil / Wild rover / Loch Lomond / Bluebells of Scotland / Bonnie lass o'Fyvie / Mormond Braes / New York, New York
CD LCOM 5209
Lismor / May '92 / ADA / Direct / Duncans / Lismor

GO DANCING
Bye bye blackbird / At the Darktown strutter's ball / Alexander's ragtime band / You made me love you / Oh you beautiful doll / On the sunny side of the street / When Irish eyes are smiling / Lily McNally McNair / Too-ra-loo-ra-loo-ra / Let's twist again / Birdie dance / I love a lassie / Roamin' in the gloamin' / Stop your ticklin' Jock / Just a wee deoch an' Doris / Anniversary song / Bicycle built for two / I'll be your sweetheart / Alley cat / El Cumbanchero / Charleston / I wonder where my baby is tonight / Yes sir that's my baby / Side by side / Lily of Laguna / Carolina in the morning / Me and my gal / Isle of Capri / Jealousy / O sole mio / Camptown races / Steamboat Bill / Oh Susanna / Beautiful Sunday / Una paloma blanca / Amarillo / California here I come / Waiting for the Robert E Lee / Baby face / Swanee / Come back to Sorrento / Edelweiss / Lara's theme / Quickstep / Breakaway blues / Pride of Erin / Twist and tweet / Gay Gordons / Old time waltz / Samba / Madison / Foxtrot / Tango / Barn dance / Slosh / Mississippi dip / Modern waltz
CD LCOM 9020
Lismor / Sep '95 / ADA / Direct / Duncans / Lismor

SINGALONGA SCOTLAND
Hundred thousand welcomes / Northern lights / Wee Cooper o' Fife / Skye boat song / Come in, come in / Strip the willow / Scottish soldier / Sailing up the Clyde / Annie Laurie / Star of Rabbie Burns / Dark island / Lassie come and dance with me / Auld hoose / Roses of Prince Charlie / Gay Gordons / Song of the Clyde / Wachlin' hame / Bonnie Dundee / Auld lang syne
CD LCOM 9017
Lismor / Sep '95 / ADA / Direct / Duncans / Lismor

Box Office Poison

BEYOND THE TWILIGHT ZONE
Think for yourself / Checkmate / Mysteries / magic / Love on the phone / Cry out the pain / Sad world / 1995 / Backstreet Boulevard / 16 year old / We're all insane / Alien / We are the future
CD FLEGCD 4
Future Legend / Jun '97 / Future Legend / Pinnacle

Boxcar

ALGORHYTHM
CD PULSE 24CD
Pulse 8 / Sep '96 / BMG

VERTIGO
Gas stop (who do you think you are) / Insect / Vertigo / Freemason (you broke the promise) / Comet / Hit and run / 900 hours / Lelore / Cruel to you / This is the town / Index
CD VOLTCD 024
Volition / Mar '92 / Pinnacle / Vital

Boxcar Willie

ACHY BREAKY HEART
Rockin' bones / Sally let your bangs hang down / Train of love / Maybellene / That's alright Mama / Sixteen chickens and a tamborine / Mystery train / Pipeliner blues / No help wanted / Haunted house / Hank you're like your Daddy / Caribbean / Boney Maronie / Memphis / Achy breaky heart
CD 5501342
Spectrum / Oct '93 / PolyGram

BEST OF BOXCAR WILLIE, THE
Waiting for a train / From a Rolls to the rails / Lord made a hobo out of me / Take me home / I wake up every morning with a smile on my face / I came so close to calling you last night / I'm so lonesome I could cry / (I heard that) Lonesome whistle / Daddy was a railroad man / Hot box blues / I can't help it (if I'm still in love with you) / Day Elvis died / Hank, you still make me cry / Train medley
CD 307862
Hallmark / Jul '97 / Carlton

BOXCAR WILLIE & SPECIAL GUESTS
CD MU 5061
Musketeer / Oct '92 / Disc

COUNTRY FAVOURITES
King of the road / Wabash cannonball / You are my sunshine / Boxcar blues / Don't let the stars get in your eyes / Your cheatin' heart / I saw the light / Wreck of the old '97 / Hank and the hobo / Peace in the valley / Mule train / Hey good lookin' / Kaw-Liga / Move it on over / London leaves / Rollin' in my sweet babies arms / Divorce me COD / Red river valley / Heaven / San Antonio Rose / Train melody
CD RM 1540
BR Music / Apr '97 / Target/BMG

COUNTRY GREATS
Freightline fever / Truck driving man / Phantom 309 / Truck drivin' son-of-a-gun / Six days on the road / Teddy bear / White line fever / Girl on the billboard / How fast them trucks will go / Trucker's prayer / Give me 40 acres (to turn this rig around) / Convoy / Spirit of America / Old Kentucky home / Dixie / Thank you old flag of mine / America / North to Alaska / Play the star spangled / Battle hymn of the republic / There's a star-spangled banner waving somewhere / Yankee doodle / Battle of New Orleans
CD QED 035
Tring / Nov '96 / Tring

HEART BREAKIN' HILLBILLY SONGS
Only in my mind / Lonesome old town / Long black veil around my heart / Forty nine nights / Why do you want me / Long black limousine / I don't feel like doing anything /

Danny boy / Reflections of an old man / Cody, Wyoming / Nothing but memories / Long long train / If I didn't love you / Old King Cole
CD RITZRCD 536
Ritz / Oct '93 / Pinnacle

KING OF THE RAILROAD
CD CTS 55431
Country Stars / Sep '94 / Target/BMG

KING OF THE ROAD
King of the road / Wabash cannonball / You are my sunshine / Boxcar blues / Don't let the stars get in your eyes / Your cheatin' heart / I saw the light / Wreck of ol' 97 / Hank and the hobo / Peace in the valley / Mule train / Hey good lookin' / Kaw-liga / Move it on over / London leaves / Rollin' in my sweet baby's arms / Divorce me COD / Red river valley / Heaven / San Antonio rose
CD PLATCD 23
Platinum / Apr '88 / Prism

KING OF THE ROAD
King of the road / Wabash cannonball / You are my sunshine / Boxcar blues / Don't let the stars get in your eyes / Your cheatin' heart / I saw the light / Wreck of the old '97 / Hank and the hobo / Peace in the valley / Mule train / Hey good lookin' / Kaw-Liga / Move it on over / London leaves / Rollin' in my sweet baby's arms / Divorce me COD / Red river valley / Heaven / San Antonio rose
CD WB 870962
Disky / Mar '97 / Disky / THE

TWO SIDES OF BOXCAR
Freightline fever / Truck drivin' man / Phantom 309 / Truck drivin' son of a gun / Six days on the road / Teddy bear / Whiteline fever / Girl on a billboard / How fast them trucks will go / Truckers' prayer / Forty acres / Convoy / Spirit of America / Old Kentucky home / Dixie / Thank you old flag of mine / America / North to Alaska / Play the star spangled banner over me / Battle hymn of the Republic / Star spangled banner waving somewhere / Yankee doodle / America the beautiful / Battle of New Orleans
CD GRF 151
Tring / Feb '93 / Tring

Boxer

BELOW THE BELT
Shooting star / All the time in the world / California calling / Hip kiss / More than meets the eye / Waiting for a miracle / Loony Ali / Save me / Gonna work out fine / Town drunk
CD CDV 2049
Virgin / Jun '97 / EMI

BLOODLETTING
Hey bulldog / Blizzard / Rich man's daughter / Big city fever / Loner / Why pick on me / Love has got me / Dinah-low / Teachers
CD CDV 2073
Virgin / Jun '97 / EMI

Boy George

AT WORST... THE BEST OF BOY GEORGE AND CULTURE CLUB
Do you really want to hurt me: *Culture Club* / Time (clock of the heart): *Culture Club* / Church of the poison mind: *Culture Club* / Karma chameleon: *Culture Club* / Victims: *Culture Club* / I'll tumble 4 ya: *Culture Club* / It's a miracle: *Culture Club* / Miss me blind: *Culture Club* / Move away: *Culture Club* / Love is love / Love hurts / Everything I own / Don't cry / After the love / More than likely / Crying game / Generations of love / Bow down mister / Sweet toxic love
CD VTCD 19
Virgin / Oct '93 / EMI

CHEAPNESS AND BEAUTY
Fun time / Blindman / Genocide peroxide / Sad / Satan's butterfly ball / Same thing in reverse / Cheapness and beauty / If I could fly / God don't hold a grudge / Evil is so civilised / Your love is what I am / Unfinished business / Il adore
CD CDV 2780
Virgin / May '95 / EMI

EVERYTHING I OWN
Everything I own / Sold / To be reborn / Keep me in mind / What becomes of the brokenhearted / Whisper / Where are you now when I need you / I'll adore / Something strange called love / If I could fly / Don't cry / Freedom / I love you / Cheapness and beauty
CD VI 867222
Disky / Nov '96 / Disky / THE

SOLD
Sold / I asked for love / Keep me in mind / Everything I own / Freedom / Just ain't enough / Where are you now / Little ghost / Next time / We've got the right / To be reborn
CD CDV 2430
Virgin / Jun '87 / EMI

Boyack, Pat

BREAKIN' IN (Boyack, Pat & The Prowlers)
CD BBCD 9557
Bullseye Blues / Dec '94 / Direct

SUPER BLUE AND FUNKY (Boyack, Pat & The Prowlers)
For you my love / I'll be the joker / Longwallin' / Why must I suffer / Mexican vodka / Louisiana love shack / Can't you see / Sweet redemption / Think (before you do) / Ol' blondie swings again / Way you do / Righteous love / Poppa stoppa / Look at me look at you
CD CDBB 9587
Bullseye Blues / Jul '97 / Direct

Boyce, Max

LIVE AT TREORCHY
9-3 / Scottish trip / Ballad of Morgan the moon / Outside-half factory / Asso asso yagoshi / Duw it's hard / Ten thousand instant Christians / Did you understand / Hymns and arias
CD CDSL 8251
EMI / Jul '95 / EMI

Boyd, Eddie

7936 SOUTH RHODES
You got to reap / Just the blues / She is real / I'll never stop (I can't stop loving you) / She's gone / Thank you baby / Third degree / You are my love / Blues is here to stay / Ten to one / Be careful / Blackslap
CD BGOCD 195
Beat Goes On / May '95 / Pinnacle

EDDIE BOYD & HIS BLUES BAND (Boyd, Eddie Blues Band)
Too bad / Dust my broom / Unfair lovers / Key to the highway / Vacation from the blues / Steakhouse rock / Letter missin' blues / Ain't doing too bad / Blue coat man / Save her doctor / Rack 'em back / Too bad (part 2) / Big bell / Pinetop's boogie woogie / Night time is the right time / Train is coming
CD 8440122
Deram / Jan '94 / PolyGram

FIVE LONG YEARS
Five long years / Hello stranger / Where you belong / I'm comin' home / My idea / Big question / Come on home / Blue Monday blues / Eddie's blues / All the way / Twenty four hours of fear / Rock the rock / Rosa Lee / Hound dog
CD ECD 260512
Evidence / Sep '94 / ADA / Cadillac / Harmonia Mundi

LIVE IN SWITZERLAND
I'm coming home to you / Early in the morning / I ain't doing too bad at all / Mr. Highwayman / Little red rooster / I'm sitting here waiting / Third degree / Hotel blues / I got a woman / Cool kind treatment / Five long years / She's the one / It's miserable to be alone / Save her doctor / Rattlin' and runnin' around / Reel good feeling / Her picture in the frame
CD STCD 8022
Storyville / Mar '95 / Cadillac / Jazz Music / Wellard

Boyer, Jacqueline

MITSOU
Tom Pilibi / Gruss mir die liebe / Mademoiselle de Paris in Tirol / Ich sag: oui, oui, oui / Liebe-liebelei: *Boyer, Jacqueline & Lucienne* / Frederick / Du bist das grosse los: *Boyer, Jacqueline & Francois Lubiana* / In der kleinen bar auf dem Grand Boulevard: *Boyer, Jacqueline & Francois Lubiana* / Mitsou / Mon cher Robert / Happy sing-song: *Boyer, Jacqueline & Dany Mann/Peter Weck* / Regenschirm song: *Boyer, Jacqueline & Paul Kuhn* / Hongkong madchen / Wenn du sie liebst, dann sag es ihr / Ganz in der nah' von den Champs-Elysees / Suleika / Jacques mit dem frack / Butterfly / Hor das signal, korporal / Ein weekend in Paris / Mademoiselle / Little, little china girl / Urlaub an der Cote D'Azur / C'est la vie / Comme au premier jour / Il bat mon coeur / Loin (greensleeves) / Melodie
CD BCD 16147
Bear Family / Apr '97 / Direct / Rollercoaster / Swift

Boyer, Jean Pierre

GRILLER PISTACHE
CD PS 65146CD
PlayaSound / Jul '95 / ADA / Harmonia Mundi

Boyer, Lucienne

CHANSOPHONE 1926-1931
CD 701262
Chansophone / Jun '93 / Discovery

PARLEZ-MOI D'AMOUR
Parlez-moi d'amour / Prenez mes roses / Dans la fumee / Gigolette / C'est un chagrin de femme / La barque d'Yves / Quand tu seras dans mes bras / Ne dis pas toujours / Moi, j'crache dans l'eau / Si petite / Sans toi / Parle-moi d'autre chose / L'etoile d'amour / C'est ma faute / Comme une femme / Ta main / En se regardant / Estampe Marocaine / Parle-moi de toi / Mon rendez-vous / Je t'aime / Embrasse-moi / Mon p'tit kaki
CD CDAJA 5226
Living Era / May '97 / Select

Boyes, Jim

OUT OF THE BLUE
CD NMV 1CD
No Master's Voice / Feb '93 / ADA / Direct

Boyfriend

HAIRY BANJO
CD RUST 003CD
Creation / Mar '93 / 3mv/Vital

RUBBER EAR
CD RUST 006CD
Creation / Jun '94 / 3mv/Vital

Boyle, Gary

ELECTRIC GLIDE
Snap crackle / Electric glide / Gaz / Hayabusa / Grumble / Morning father joys / Brat No.2 / It's almost light again
CD NAIMCD 002
Naim Audio / Apr '97 / Koch

Boymerang

BALANCE OF THE FORCE
Soul beat runna / Mind control / River (VIP) / You like it like that / ACID / Where it's at / Secret life / Still / Lazarus
CD REG 13CD
Regal / May '97 / Prime / RTM/Disc

Boyoyo Boys

BACK IN TOWN
Back in town / Maraba start 500 / Dayeyton special / Duba duba / Mapetla / Pulukwani centre / Brakpan no.2 / Dube station / Arcie special / Vezunyawo
CD ROUCD 5026
Rounder / Jan '88 / ADA / CM / Direct

Boyracer

WE ARE MADE OF THE
CD SLR 048
Slumberland / Dec '96 / Cargo

Boys

BEST OF THE BOYS, THE
CD DOJOCD 137
Dojo / Mar '95 / Disc

COMPLETE PUNK SINGLES COLLECTION
CD CDPUNK 85
Anagram / Nov '96 / Cargo / Pinnacle

LIVE AT THE ROXY
CD RRCD 135
Receiver / Nov '90 / Grapevine/PolyGram

Boys Life

DEPARTURES AND LANDFALLS
CD HED 063CD
Headhunter / Oct '96 / Cargo

Boys Next Door

DOOR, DOOR
CD DOORCD 1
The Grey Area / Mar '93 / RTM/Disc

Boys Of The Lough

DAY DAWN
CD LOUGH 006CD
Lough / Dec '94 / ADA / CM / Direct / Duncans

FAIR HILLS OF IRELAND
Bonnie labouring boy / Mickey Doherty's highland/Banks of the Allan/Maurice O'Keeff / Ban chnoic erin o / Wandering minstrel/Fasten the leg in her/Coleman's cross / Ook pick waltz / Midsummer's night/Tinker's daughter/Over the moor to Maggie / Father Brian MacDermott Roe / Boys of the lough/Lucky in love/Sleep sound in the morning / Pinch of snuff / Erin gra mo chroi / Ross memorial hospital / Lancers/Petronella/Ger the rigger / Wind that shakes the barley / Hunt
CD LOUGHCD 005
Lough / Oct '89 / ADA / CM / Direct / Duncans

FAREWELL AND REMEMBER ME
Sean Bui/Tommy Peoples/The lark in the morning / Leitrim queen / Lucky can du link ony/Pottinger's/Billy Nicholson / Farewell and remember me / Angus polka No.1/Angus polka No.2/Donegal barn dance / An spailpin fanach/The one-horned buck / Valencia harbour/The jug of punch/MacArthur Road / Lovely Ann / Holly bush/The new ships are sailing / Waterford waltz/The stronsay waltz
CD LOUGHCD 002
Lough / Oct '90 / ADA / CM / Direct / Duncans

GOOD FRIENDS GOOD MUSIC
Crook of gold / Midsummer's night / Tinker's daughter / Flail / Paddy Doory's / Pride of Leinster / Kitty's gone a milking / Master McDermott's / Roll her in the rye grass / First house in Connaught / Humours of ennistymon / Leather britches / Dennis Murphy's hornpipe / Hop high ladies / Canadain waltz / New riggit ship / Kitchen girl / Newlyweds reel / La grand chaine / Bretton wedding march / Wild irishman / Scholar / Down the broom / Gatehouse maid / Gaelic mouth music / Farewell to Gibaltar / Captain Horne / High road to Linton / Far from home / Da road to Houll / Robertson's reel / Bonnie lass of Bonne Accord
CD CDPH 1051
Philo / Mar '97 / ADA / CM / Direct

IN THE TRADITION
Out on the ocean / Padeen O'Rafferty / Isabelle Blackley / Kiss her under the coverlet / Lads of Alnwick / Road to Cashel / Paddy Kelly's brew / Lord Gregory / Dark woman of the glen / LO Forbes Esq of Corse / Hawk / Charles Sutherland / Eddie Kelly's jigs / Green fields of Glentown / Eclipse / Tailor's twist / Biddy from Sligo / Sunset / Peoples / Padraig O'Keefe's / Con Cassidy's highland reel / Sea apprentice / Miss McDonald / For Ireland I'd not tell her name
CD OSSCD 70
Ossian / Apr '93 / ADA / CM / Direct / Highlander

LIVE AT CARNEGIE HALL
Garrison Keillor / Maho snaps/Charlie Hunter/The mouse in the cupboard/The rose / I'll buy boots for Maggie/Brendan Begley's polka/O'Connor's / Leaving Glasgow/The Killarney boys of pleasure / Forest flower/ James Byrne's reel/Jenny dang the weaver / Margaert's waltz/Captain Caswell/The jig of slurs / Flower of Magherally / Glencoe bridge march/Stirling castle/O'Keefe's polkas / On Raglan Road / Donegal jig No.1/ Donegal jig No.2 / Hanged man's reel / Kerryman's daughter/O'Keefe's plough/The sligo maid
CD LOUGHCD 004
Lough / Oct '89 / ADA / CM / Direct / Duncans
CD SA 001 CD
Sagem / Jul '90 / CM / Duncans / Roots

LIVE IN PASSIM
CD CDPH 1026
Philo / Feb '97 / ADA / CM / Direct

SWEET RURAL SHADE
Out on the ocean/Mooney's jig/Isabelle Blackley / Forest flower/Kitty the hare/ Jenny Dang the weaver / Maro snaps/Charlie Hunter/The mouse in the cupboard/ Rosewood / Hills of Donegal / Todd's sweet rural shade / Once I loved / Tim O'Leary's waltz / Captain Carswell/Green hills of Tyrol/Trip to Windsor / Humours of Flinn
CD LOUGH 003CD
Lough / Nov '96 / ADA / CM / Direct / Duncans

WELCOMING PADDY HOME
When sick is it tea you want / Cape Breton wedding reel no 1 / Teelin march / Welcoming Paddy home / Miss Rowan Davies / Eugene Stratton / Antrim rose / Alexander's / Rose of Ardee / Tonbigbee waltz / Irish washerwoman
CD LOUGHCD 001
Lough / Dec '94 / ADA / CM / Direct / Duncans

Boystown Gang

CRUISIN' THE STREETS/DISCHARGE
Remember me/Ain't no mountain high enough suite / Cruisin' the streets / Can't take my eyes off you / Come and get your love / Signed, sealed, delivered (I'm yours) / You're the one / Disco kicks / Can't take my eyes off you (reprise)
CD MOCD 3004
More Music / Feb '95 / Sound & Media

Boyz II Men

COOLEYHIGHHARMONY
Please don't go / Lonely heart / This is my heart / Uhh ahh / It's so hard to say goodbye to yesterday / Motownphilly / Under pressure / Sympin' / Little things / Your love / End of the road
CD 5300892
Motown / Oct '92 / PolyGram

REMIX COLLECTION, THE
Under pressure / Vibin' / I remember / Water runs dry / U know / I'll make love to you / Uhh ahh / Motownphilly / On bended knee / Brokenhearted / Thank you / Sympin'
CD 5305982
Motown / Oct '95 / PolyGram

Boyzone

DIFFERENT BEAT, A
Paradise / Different beat / Melting pot / Ben / Don't stop looking for love / Isn't it a wonder / Words / It's time / Games of love / Strong enough / Heaven knows / Crying in the night / Give a little / She moves through the fair
CD 5337422
CD 5338762
Polydor / Dec '96 / PolyGram

SAID AND DONE
CD 5278012
Polydor / Aug '95 / PolyGram

BR5-49

BR5-49
Even if it's wrong / Cherokee boogie / Honk tonk song / Lifetime to prove / Little Ra-

mona / Crazy arms / I ain't never / Chains of this town / Are you getting tired of me / Hickory wind / One long Saturday night
CD _______________ 07822188182
Arista / Sep '96 / BMG

LIVE FROM ROBERT'S
Hillbilly thang / 18 wheels & a crowbar / Bettie Bettie / Me 'n' Opie (down by the duckpond) / Knoxville girl / Ole Stewfoot
CD _______________ 7822108002
Arista / Jun '96 / BMG

Braam, Bentje

BENTJE BRAAM (Braam, Bentje & Michiel)
CD _______________ BVHAASTCD 9007
Bvhaast / Oct '93 / Cadillac

Brackeen, Charles

ATTAINMENT (Brackeen, Charles Quartet)
CD _______________ SHCD 110
Silkheart / May '89 / Cadillac / CM / Jazz Music / Wellard

Brackeen, Jo Anne

FI-FI GOES TO HEAVEN
Estilo magnifico / Stardust / Fi Fi goes to heaven / Zingaro / I hear a rhapsody / Cosmonaut / Dr. Chang
CD _______________ CCD 4316
Concord Jazz / Jul '87 / New Note/Pinnacle

HAVIN' FUN (Brackeen, Jo Anne Trio)
Thinking of you / I've got the world on a string / Emily / Just one of those things / This is always / Everything she wants / Manha de carnaval / Day by day
CD _______________ CCD 4280
Concord Jazz / Jan '87 / New Note/Pinnacle

INVITATION
CD _______________ BLCD 760218
Black Lion / May '96 / Cadillac / Jazz Music / Koch / Wellard

LIVE AT MAYBECK RECITAL HALL VOL.1
Thou swell / Dr. Chu Chow / Yesterdays / Curved space / My foolish heart / Calling Carl / I'm old fashioned / Strike up the band / Most beautiful girl in the world / It could happen to you / African Aztec
CD _______________ CCD 4409
Concord Jazz / Mar '90 / New Note/Pinnacle

NEW TRUE ILLUSION (Brackeen, Jo Anne & Clint Houston)
Steps what was / Search for peace / New true illusion / My romance / Freedent / Solar
CD _______________ CDSJP 103
Timeless Jazz / Jun '91 / New Note/Pinnacle

SIX ATE
Six ate / Circle / Old devil moon / C-sri / Nefertiti / Snooze / I didn't know what time it was / Zulu
CD _______________ CHCD 71009
Candid / Mar '97 / Cadillac / Direct / Jazz Music / Koch / Wellard

TAKE A CHANCE
Recado bossa nova / Children's games / Estate / Cancao do sal / Frevo / Mountain flight / Island / Take a chance / Ponta de areia / Duduka / Mist on a rainbow
CD _______________ CCD 4602
Concord Picante / Jul '94 / New Note/Pinnacle

TURNAROUND
There is no greater love / Rubies and diamonds / Picasso / Bewitched, bothered and bewildered / Turnaround / Tricks of the trade
CD _______________ ECD 221232
Evidence / Sep '95 / ADA / Cadillac / Harmonia Mundi

WHERE LEGENDS DWELL
Where legends dwell / Oahu lizard / Picasso / Helen song / Consmic ties or mud pies / Doris and Anders / Edgar Irving Poe / For Stan / Can this Mcbee / Asian spell / Jump in Jack / How to think like a millionaire
CD _______________ 66056021
Ken Music / Nov '92 / New Note/Pinnacle

Bracken, Mark

CELTIC DAWN
CD _______________ MCD 1752
Midsummer / Aug '96 / Else

Bracket

4 WHEEL VIBE
Circus act / Cool aid / Happy to be sad / John Wilkes isolation booth / Tractor / Green apples / Closed caption / Trailer park / Fresh air / PC / G vibe / Warren's song part 4 / Two hotdogs for 99c / Metal one / Pessimist / Lazy / My stepson
CD _______________ CAROLCD 1787
Caroline / Jun '97 / Cargo / Vital

924 FORESTVILLE STREET
Get it rite / Dodge ball / Missing link / Sleep / Huge balloon / Stalking stuffer / Why should eye / Warren's song / Can't make me / Skanky love song / J Weed / Rod's post
CD _______________ CAROLCD 1754
Caroline / Jun '97 / Cargo / Vital

E IS FOR EVERYTHING
CD _______________ FAT 548CD
Fatwreck Chords / Nov '96 / Plastic Head

Brad

INTERIORS
Secret girl / Day brings / Lift / I don't know / Upon my shoulders / Sweet Al George / Funeral song / Circle and line / Some never come home / Candles / Those three words
CD _______________ 4879212
Epic / Jun '97 / Sony

Braden, Don

AFTER DARK (Braden, Don Septet)
CD _______________ CRISS 1081CD
Criss Cross / May '94 / Cadillac / Direct / Vital/SAM

OPEN ROAD
Open road / Sundown / April in Paris / I thought about you / Maiden voyage / Storm / Alone together / Someday my Prince will come / Scrapple from the apple / Lush life
CD _______________ DTRCD 114
Double Time / Dec '96 / Express Jazz

ORGANIC
Moonglow / Saving all my love / Walking / Brighter days / Cousin Esan / Twister / Belief / It might as well be spring / Plain ol'blues
CD _______________ 4812582
Sony Jazz / Oct '95 / Sony

TIME IS NOW, THE (Braden, Don Quintet)
CD _______________ CRISS 1051CD
Criss Cross / Nov '91 / Cadillac / Direct / Vital/SAM

VOICE OF THE SAXOPHONE, A
Soul station / Speak no evil / Winelight / After the rain / Dust kicker / Monk's hat / Cozy / Face I love / Point of many returns / Voicce of the saxophone
CD _______________ 09026687972
RCA Victor / Sep '97 / BMG

Bradford

SHOUTING QUIETLY
CD _______________ FOUND 001CD
Foundation 2000 / Feb '90 / Plastic Head

Bradford, Alex

RAINBOW IN THE SKY
Packing up / Rainbow in the sky / Too close to heaven / I've found someone / Take the Lord along with you / Bells keep on ringing / I won't sell out / Oh my loving mother / Oh Lord, save me / Holy ghost / Let Jesus lead you / Captain Jesus / Life's candlelight / Feel like I'm running for the Lord / Dinner, Mr Rupe / It all belongs to him / Steal away / Over in Beulah land / I've got a job / Man is wonderful / Great consolation / What makes a man turn his back on God / Don't you want Jesus / See if I care
CD _______________ CDCHD 413
Ace / Nov '93 / Pinnacle

TOO CLOSE
Too close to heaven / Lord, Lord, Lord / He lifted me / I don't care what the world may do / He leads me safely through / God is all / Just the name of Jesus / Right now / Don't let Satan turn you 'round / Life's candlelight / He'll wash you whiter than snow / Oh Lord, save me / Holy ghost / Crossing over Jordan / If mother knew / I dare you / I can't tarry / Without a God / Safe in Jesus' arms / Meeting ground / What did John do / There's only one way (to get to heaven) / What folks say about me / Truth will set you free / God searched the world / Lifeboat / Man is wonderful / Move upstairs / This may be the last time
CD _______________ CDCHD 480
Ace / Jul '93 / Pinnacle

TOO CLOSE TO HEAVEN
One step / Walk through the streets / Just in time / Left my sins behind me / Let the Lord be seen in you / Climbing up the mountain / I wasn't gonna tell nobody / What about you / Lord looks out for me / Oh my Lord / Too close / Angel on vacation / When you pray / He always keeps his promises / They came out shouting / Let your conscience be your guide / Nothing but the holy ghost / Daniel is a prayin' man / Just to know / I made it in / I made God a promise
CD _______________ CPCD 8114
Charly / Jul '95 / Koch

Bradford, Carmen

FINALLY YOURS
Destiny (prelude) / Destiny / Maybe September / Rough ridin' / Right to love / I believe to my soul / I love you more than you'll ever know / Chicago hello / You must believe in spring / More than a trial
CD _______________ ECD 22186
Evidence / May '97 / ADA / Cadillac / Harmonia Mundi

WITH RESPECT
Even Steven / Mr. Paganini / Look who's mine / High wire / Finally / Maybe now / Little Esther / Ain't no use / Was I in love alone / He comes to me in comfort / Nature boy
CD _______________ ECD 22115
Evidence / Jun '95 / ADA / Cadillac / Harmonia Mundi

Bradford, Geoff

RETURN OF A GUITAR LEGEND, THE
Going down slow / Broke and hungry / Dark side / Pontiac / Keys to the highway / Paris strut / Alimony / Red's piece / Hallelujah, I love her so / Blind Blake's rag / Blues jumped the devil / Auto-mechanics blues
CD _______________ RNCD 001
Beat Goes On / Jun '95 / Pinnacle

Bradford, Perry

PERRY BRADFORD & THE BLUES SINGERS 1923-1927
CD _______________ DOCD 5353
Document / Jun '95 / ADA / Hot Shot / Jazz Music

Bradford, Terry

HANDS ACROSS THE OCEAN
CD _______________ RITZRCD 556
Ritz / Mar '96 / Pinnacle

Bradley, Clint

THIS HOUR
Guilty heart / Barbed wire round the meadow / Love is to blame / Insane / This hour / You feed the devil / Forever forever / Purple land / When will I learn / Alright Mary / Years / Has not been kind (the man from the shire)
CD _______________ MAGCD 1059
M&G / Apr '97 / 3mv/Sony

Bradley, Josephine

FIRST LADY OF THE BALLROOM (Bradley, Josephine & Her Ballroom Orchestra)
CD _______________ PASTCD 7092
Flapper / Aug '96 / Pinnacle

Bradley, Tommie

TOMMIE BRADLEY & JAMES COLE
CD _______________ DOCD 5189
Document / Oct '93 / ADA / Hot Shot / Jazz Music

Bradley, Will

BASIN STREET BOOGIE (1941-1942) (Bradley, Will & Orchestra)
CD _______________ RACD 7110
Aerospace / May '96 / Jazz Music / Montpellier

FAMOUS DOOR BROADCASTS 1940 (Bradley, Will & Ray McKinley)
Fatal fascination / Flying home / All the things you are / When you wish upon a star / Old Doc Yak / In a little Spanish town / It's a blue world / Starlit hour
CD _______________ TAX 37132
Tax / Aug '94 / Cadillac / Jazz Music / Wellard

FIVE O'CLOCK WHISTLE (1939-1941) (Bradley, Will & Orchestra)
CD _______________ RACD 7101
Aerospace / May '96 / Jazz Music / Montpellier

ROCK-A-BYE THE BOOGIE (1940-1941) (Bradley, Will & Orchestra)
CD _______________ RACD 7112
Aerospace / May '96 / Jazz Music / Montpellier

Brady, Paul

BACK TO THE CENTRE
CD _______________ 8268092
Mercury / Apr '86 / PolyGram

PRIMITIVE DANCE
Steal your heart away / Soul commotion / Paradise is here / It's gonna work out fine / Awakening / Eat the peach / Don't start knocking / Just in case of accidents / Game of love: *Brady, Paul & Mark Knopfler*
CD _______________ 8321332
Mercury / Apr '87 / PolyGram

TRICK OR TREAT
Soul child / Blue world / Nobody knows / Can't stop wanting you / You and I / Trick or treat / Don't keep pretending / Solid love / Love goes on / Dreams will come
CD _______________ 8484542
Mercury / Apr '91 / PolyGram

TRUE FOR YOU
Great pretender / Let it happen / Helpless heart / Dance the romance / Steel claw / Take me away / Not the only one / Interlude / Trouble round the bend
CD _______________ 8108932
Mercury / May '89 / PolyGram

WELCOME HERE KIND STRANGER
CD _______________ LUNCD 024
Mulligan / Aug '94 / ADA / CM

Brady, Shane

LIVING ROOM, THE
CD _______________ HY 200120CD
Hypertension / Feb '95 / ADA / CM / Direct / Total/BMG

Brady, Tim

IMAGINARY GUITARS
CD _______________ JTR 84402
Justin Time / Nov '92 / Cadillac / New Note/Pinnacle

INVENTIONS
CD _______________ JTR 84332
Justin Time / Apr '92 / Cadillac / New Note/Pinnacle

SCENARIO
CD _______________ JTR 84452
Justin Time / Apr '94 / Cadillac / New Note/Pinnacle

Braff, Ruby

AS TIME GOES BY
Shoe shine boy / Lonely moments / This is all I ask / Love me or leave me / Liza / As long as I live / Jeepers creepers / My shining hour / Sugar / As time goes by / You're sensational / I love you, Samantha / True love / Basin street blues / Linger awhile
CD _______________ CCD 79741
Candid / Jul '97 / Cadillac / Direct / Jazz Music / Koch / Wellard

BRAVURA ELOQUENCE (Braff, Ruby Trio)
Ol' man river / Smile (who'll buy my violets) / Lonely moments / Here's Cari / God bless the child / It's bad for me / I've grown accustomed to her face / Make sense / I'm shooting high / Orange / Persian rug / Travellin' light / Royal Garden blues / Judy medley
CD _______________ CCD 4423
Concord Jazz / Aug '90 / New Note/Pinnacle

CALLING BERLIN VOL.2 (Braff, Ruby & Ellis Larkins)
CD _______________ ARCD 19140
Arbors Jazz / May '97 / Cadillac

CORNET CHOP SUEY
Cornet chop suey / Nancy with the laughing face / Ooh, that kiss / Do it again / Love me or leave me / It's the same old South / It had to be you / I must have that man / sweet and slow / Shoe shine boy / You're sensational/I love you Samantha/True love / Lover come back to me
CD _______________ CCD 4606
Concord Jazz / Aug '94 / New Note/Pinnacle

EASY NOW
My walking stick / Willow weep for me / When my sugar walks down the street / Song is ended (but the melody lingers on) / Give my regards to broadway / This is my lucky day / Someday you'll be sorry / Yesterdays / For now / I just couldn't take it baby / Little man you've had a busy day / Swinging on a star / Old folks / Did you ever see a dream walking / Pocket full of dreams / Moonlight becomes you / Pennies from Heaven / Go fly a kite / Please / All alone / You're sensational / Too-ra-loo-ra-loo-ra / White Christmas
CD _______________ 74321185222
RCA / Jul '94 / BMG

FIRST, A (Braff, Ruby & Scott Hamilton)
CD _______________ CCD 4274
Concord Jazz / Jan '89 / New Note/Pinnacle

HEAR ME TALKIN'
You've changed / Hear me talkin' to ya / Don't blame me / No one else but you / Nobody knows you (when you're down and out) / Buddy Bolden's blues / Mean to me / Where's Freddy
CD _______________ BLC 760161
Black Lion / Apr '92 / Cadillac / Jazz Music / Koch / Wellard

HUSTLIN' AND BUSTLIN'
Hustlin' and bustlin' / There's a small hotel / What's the reason / 'S wonderful / When it's sleepy time down South / Flaky / Fine and mellow / Ad lib blues
CD _______________ BLCD 760908
Black Lion / Sep '88 / Cadillac / Jazz Music / Koch / Wellard

INSIDE AND OUT (Braff, Ruby & Roger Kellaway)
Love walked in / Yesterdays / Memories of you / I want to be happy / I got rhythm / Always / Between the devil and the deep blue sea / Basin Street blues / Exactly like you
CD _______________ CCD 4691
Concord Jazz / Apr '96 / New Note/Pinnacle

LIVE AT THE NEW SCHOOL (Braff, Ruby & George Barnes)
CD ____ CRD 126
Chiaroscuro / Aug '94 / Jazz Music

LIVE AT THE REGATTABAR
Persian rug / 'S wonderful / Louisiana / Sweet Sue, just you / Do it again / No one else but you / Crazy rhythm / Where are you / Between the devil and the deep blue sea / Orange / Give my regards to Broadway
CD ____ ARCD 19131
Arbors Jazz / Nov '94 / Cadillac

ME, MYSELF AND I (Braff, Ruby Trio)
Muskrat ramble / You've changed / Honey / Me, myself and I / When I fall in love / That's my home / Let me sing and I'm happy / You're a lucky guy / No one else but you / When you're smiling / Swan lake / Jubilee
CD ____ CCD 4381
Concord Jazz / Jul '89 / New Note/Pinnacle

MR. BRAFF TO YOU (Braff, Ruby Quintet)
CD ____ PHONT CD 7568
Phontastic / Apr '88 / Cadillac / Jazz Music / Wellard

MUSIC FROM MY FAIR LADY (Braff, Ruby & Dick Hyman)
Wouldn't it be loverly / With a little bit of luck / I'm just an ordinary man / Rain in Spain / I could have danced all night / Ascot gavotte / On the street where you live / Show me / Get me to the church on time / Without you / I've grown accustomed to her face
CD ____ CCD 4393
Concord Jazz / '89 / New Note/Pinnacle

MUSIC FROM SOUTH PACIFIC (Braff, Ruby & Dick Hyman)
Bali Ha'i / Some enchanted evening / Cock-eyed optimist / Wonderful guy / Happy talk / Dites moi / This nearly was mine / There is nothin' like a dame / Honeybun / Younger than Springtime / Bali Ha'i (final version)
CD ____ CCD 4445
Concord Jazz / Feb '91 / New Note/ Pinnacle

PIPE ORGAN RECITAL PLUS ONE (Braff, Ruby & Dick Hyman)
When it's sleepy time down South / When I fall in love / When my sugar walks down the street / As long as I live / America the beautiful / High society / I ain't got nobody / Louisiana / I'll be with you in apple blossom time / This is all I ask
CD ____ CCD 43003
Concord Jazz / Mar '90 / New Note/ Pinnacle

PLAYS GERSHWIN (Braff, Ruby & George Barnes)
CD ____ CCD 6005
Concord Jazz / Jul '88 / New Note/ Pinnacle

PLAYS WIMBLEDON - THE FIRST SET
Someday sweetheart / Very thought of you / Wouldn't it be loverly / I've got a feeling I'm falling / Take the 'A' train / This is all I ask / It's the same Old South / When I fall in love / China boy
CD ____ ZECD 15
Zephyr / Apr '97 / Cadillac / Jazz Music / New Note/Pinnacle

RODGERS & HART (Braff, Ruby & George Barnes)
CD ____ CCD 6007
Concord Jazz / Jul '88 / New Note/ Pinnacle

RUBY BRAFF & BUDDY TATE WITH THE NEWPORT ALLSTARS (Braff, Ruby & Buddy Tate & Newport Allstars)
Mean to me / Body and soul / I surrender dear / Lullaby of the leaves / Take the 'A' train / Don't blame me
CD ____ BLC 760138
Black Lion / Oct '90 / Cadillac / Jazz Music / Koch / Wellard

RUBY BRAFF VOL.1 (Braff, Ruby & His New England Songhounds)
CD ____ CCD 4478
Concord Jazz / Sep '91 / New Note/ Pinnacle

RUBY BRAFF VOL.2 (Braff, Ruby & His New England Songhounds)
Indian summer / Thousand Islands / What's new / Heartaches / Cabin in the sky / You're a sweetheart / Please / All alone / Lullaby of birdland / Nice work if you can get it / As time goes by / Keepin' out of mischief now
CD ____ CCD 4504
Concord Jazz / May '92 / New Note/ Pinnacle

RUBY GOT RHYTHM
There's a small hotel / 'S wonderful / I wish I could shimmey like my sister Kate / Flaky / Shoe shine boy / Fine and mellow / Hear me talkin' to ya / Ruby got rhythm / When my sugar walks down the street / Smart Alex blues / Between the devil and the deep blue sea
CD ____ 8747162
DA Music / Jul '96 / Conifer/BMG

SAILBOAT IN THE MOONLIGHT (Braff, Ruby & Scott Hamilton)
Lover come back to me / Where are you / 'Deed I do / When lights are low / Jeepers creepers / Milkman's matinee / Sweethearts on parade / Sailboat in the moonlight
CD ____ CCD 4296
Concord Jazz / Apr '86 / New Note/ Pinnacle

Braganca, Paulo

AMAI
Prelude / Janary, night, full moon / Farewell / Sorrow's child / Vox populis / Interlude / Lighthouse (of cruz de sal) / Spirit of the flesh / Hero's fado parts 1 and 2 / Sin I / Fatigue / Epilogue
CD ____ 9362463342
East West / Feb '97 / Warner Music

Bragg, Billy

BACK TO BASICS
Milkman of human kindness / To have and have not / Richard / Lover's town revisited / New England / Man in the iron mask / Busy girl buys beauty / It says here / Love gets dangerous / From a Vauxhall Velox / Myth of trust / Saturday boy / Island of no return / This guitar says sorry / Like soldiers do / St. Swithins day / Strange things happen / Lover sings / Between the wars / World turned upside down / Which side are you on
CD ____ COOKCD 060
Cooking Vinyl / Nov '93 / Vital

BREWING UP WITH BILLY BRAGG
It says here / Love gets dangerous / Myth of trust / From a Vauxhall Velox / Saturday boy / Island of no return / St. Swithin's day / Like soldiers do / This guitar says sorry / Strange things happen / Lover sings
CD ____ COOKCD 107
Cooking Vinyl / Sep '96 / Vital

DON'T TRY THIS AT HOME
Accident waiting to happen / Moving the goalposts / Everywhere / Cindy of a thousand lives / You woke up my neighbourhood / Trust / God's footballer / Few / Mother of the bride / Tank park salute / Dolphins / North Sea bubble / Rumours of war / Wish you were her / Body of water / Sexuality
CD ____ COOKCD 062
Cooking Vinyl / Nov '93 / Vital
CD ____ COOKCD 110
Cooking Vinyl / Sep '96 / Vital

INTERNATIONALE, THE
Internationale / I dreamt I saw Phil Ochs last night / March of the covert battalions / Red flag / My youngest son came home today
CD ____ UTILCD 011
Utility / May '90 / Grapevine/PolyGram

LIFE'S A RIOT WITH SPY VS. SPY/ BETWEEN THE WARS
Milkman of human kindness / To have and to have not / Richard / New England / Man in the iron mask / Busy girl buys beauty / Lovers town revisited / Between the wars / Which side are you on / World time upside down / It says here
CD ____ COOKCD 106
Cooking Vinyl / Sep '96 / Vital

TALKING WITH THE TAXMAN ABOUT POETRY
Greetings to the new brunette / Train train / Marriage / Ideology / Levi Stubbs' tears / Honey I'm a big boy now / There is power in a union / Help save the youth of America / Wishing the days away / Passion / Warmest room / Home front
CD ____ COOKCD 108
Cooking Vinyl / Sep '96 / Vital

VICTIM OF GEOGRAPHY
Greetings to the new brunette / Train train / Marriage / Ideology / Levi Stubbs' tears / Honey I'm a big boy now / There is power in a union / Help save the youth of America / Wishing the days away / Passion / Warmest room / Home front / She's got a new spell / Must I paint you a picture / Tender Comrade / Price I pay / Little time bomb / Rotting on remand / Valentine's day is over / Life with the lions / Only one / Short answer / Waiting for the great leap forwards
CD ____ COOKCD 061
Cooking Vinyl / Nov '93 / Vital

WILLIAM BLOKE VOL.2
Boy done good / Just one victory / Qualifications / Sugardaddy / Never had no one ever / Run out of reasons / Rule nor reason / Thatcherites
CD ____ COOKCD 127
Cooking Vinyl / Jun '97 / Vital

WORKERS PLAYTIME
She's got a new spell / Must I paint you a picture / Tender comrade / Price I pay / Little time bomb / Rotting on remand / Valentine's day is over / Life with the lions / Only one / Short answer / Waiting for the great leap forwards
CD ____ COOKCD 109
Cooking Vinyl / Sep '96 / Vital

Brahaspati, Sulochana

RAG BIULASKHANI TODI/RAGA MISHRA BHAIRAVI
CD ____ NI 5305
Nimbus / Sep '94 / Nimbus

Brahem, Anouar

BARZAKH
Raf raf / Barzakh / Sadir / Ronda / Hou / Sarandib / Souga / Parfum de Gitane / Bou naouara / Kerkenah / La nuit des yeux / Le belvedera assiege / Oaf
CD ____ 8475402
ECM / May '91 / New Note/Pinnacle

CONTE DE L'INCROYABLE AMOUR
Etincelles / Le chien sur les genoux de la devineresse / L'oiseau de bois / Lumiere du silence / Conte de l'incroyable amour / Peshrev Hidjaz Homayoun / Diversion / Nayzak / Battements / En souvenir d'Iram retrouvee / Epilogue
CD ____ 5119592
ECM / Jun '92 / New Note/Pinnacle

KHOMSA
CD ____ 5270932
ECM / Feb '95 / New Note/Pinnacle

Brahmachari, Prahlad

SONGS OF THE BAULS (Brahmachari, Prahlad & Kumkum)
CD ____ VICG 50312
JVC World Library / Mar '96 / ADA / CM / Direct

Brahms 'n' Liszt

CLASSICAL COCKNEY
Set sail / This is the 90's / Madame Belle Fruit / Music / Going nowhere / Miss Tu Tu / Flash the plastic / Daddy wouldn't buy me a pit bull / Henry VIII / China ship / Strollin' / Far too many love songs / Dagenham dustbins / Bill Bailey, Won't you please come home / Mabely Street / Pulling on a rope / Breezing along / All things bright and beautiful
CD ____ URCD 109
Upbeat / Jun '93 / Cadillac / Target/BMG

Brain Bats

BRAIN BATS, THE
CD ____ CYCD 101
Cyclone / Jul '96 / Cargo / Nervous / TKO Magnum

Brain Pilot

BRAIN PILOT
CD ____ N 20072
Nova Zembla / Apr '94 / Plastic Head

ILLEGAL ENTRY
CD ____ NZ 043
Nova Zembla / Oct '96 / Plastic Head

MIND FUEL
CD ____ NZ 037
Nova Zembla / Jul '95 / Plastic Head

Brain Police

DRAIN
CD ____ BGR 004CD
BGR / Mar '95 / Plastic Head

FUEL
CD ____ BGR 011CD
BGR / May '95 / Plastic Head

Brainbox

PRIMORDIA
CD ____ W 230069
Nettwerk / Jun '95 / Greyhound / Pinnacle / Vital

Brainbox

BRAINBOX (Brainbox & Jan Akkerman)
CD ____ CDP 1033DD
Pseudonym / Jun '97 / Greyhound

Braincell

LUCID DREAMING
CD ____ HHSP 007CD
Harthouse / May '95 / Mo's Music Machine / Prime / Vital

MAN OF MANY THEORIES
CD ____ HHCD 21
Harthouse / Oct '96 / Mo's Music Machine / Prime / Vital

Braindance

BRAINIAC
CD ____ HOO 20CD
Helen Of Oi / Mar '97 / Cargo

Braindead Sound Machine

BRAINDEAD VOL.2
CD ____ EFA 007602
Shockwave / Apr '95 / SRD

Brainiac

BONSAI SUPERSTAR
CD ____ GROW 462
Grass / Jan '95 / Pinnacle / SRD

HISSING PRIGS IN STATIC COUTURE
CD ____ TG 155CD
Touch & Go / Apr '97 / SRD

SMACK BUNNY BABY
I, fuzzbot / Ride / Smack bunny baby / Martian dance invasion / Cultural zero / Brat girl / Hurting me / I could own you / Anesthetize / Draag / Get away
CD ____ GROW 0042
Grass / Oct '93 / Pinnacle / SRD

Brainiac 5

WORLD INSIDE, THE
CD ____ CDRECK 1
Reckless / Jun '88 / RTM/Disc

Brainless

SUPERPUNKTUESDAY
CD ____ CDHOLE 005
Golf / Oct '95 / Plastic Head

Brainstorm

SEMI-DETACHED HOUSE MUSIC
CD ____ TBCD 06
T&B / Apr '97 / Plastic Head

Brainstorm

SMILE AWHILE
CD ____ FGBG 4215
Musea / Jun '97 / ADA / Greyhound

Brainticket

CELESTIAL OCEAN
CD ____ CLP 9935
Cleopatra / Mar '97 / Cargo / Greyhound / Plastic Head / RTM/Disc / SRD

Bramhall, Doyle

BIRD NEST ON THE GROUND
CD ____ ANT 0027CD
Antones / Oct '95 / ADA / Hot Shot

Branagan, Geraldine

GOLD AND SILVER DAYS
Gold and silver days / Candle / Sonny / Ain't that a shame / Tonight as we dance / What's another year / Troubled times / Water is wide / Woman's heart / Stay with me / Will ye go, iassie go / Love me tender / Don't fly too high / Take me back
CD ____ KCD 460
Irish / Mar '97 / Target/BMG

Branca, Glenn

SYMPHONIES NO.8 AND 10
CD ____ BFFP 106CD
Blast First / Oct '96 / RTM/Disc

SYMPHONY NO.1
CD ____ RE 125CD
ROIR / Nov '94 / Plastic Head / Shellshock/Disc

Branch, Billy

MISSISSIPPI FLASHBACK (Branch, Billy & The Sons Of Blues)
CD ____ GBWCD 005
GBW / Sep '92 / Harmonia Mundi

WHERE'S MY MONEY (Branch, Billy & The Sons Of Blues)
Where's my money / You want it all / Third degree / Small town baby / Son of Juke / Sons of blues / Tell me what's on your mind / (Get up I feel like being a) sex machine / Eyesight to the blind / Take out the time
CD ____ ECD 26069
Evidence / Jul '95 / ADA / Cadillac / Harmonia Mundi

Branch Manager

ANYTHING TRIBAL
CD ____ DIS 107CD
Dischord / Jul '97 / SRD

Branco, Walter

MEU BALANEO
CD ____ MRBCD 002
Mr. Bongo / May '95 / New Note/Pinnacle / RTM/Disc / SRD

Brand, Kelly

DREAM IN STONE, A (Brand, Kelly Sextet)
CD ____ 378182
Koch Jazz / Sep '96 / Koch

Brand New Heavies

BRAND NEW HEAVIES, THE
Dream come true / Stay this way / People get ready / Never stop / Put the funk back in it / Ride in the sky / Brand new heavies / Gimme one of those / Got to give / Sphynx / Dream come true (Mix)
CD ____ 8283002
Acid Jazz/FFRR / Mar '92 / PolyGram
CD ____ JAZIDCD 023
Acid Jazz / Feb '95 / Disc

BROTHER SISTER
Back to love / Ten ton take / Mind trips / Spend some time / Keep together / Snake hips / Fake / People giving love / World keeps spinning / Forever / Daybreak / Midnight at the Oasis / Dream on dreamer / Have a good time / Brother sister
CD 8285572
Acid Jazz/FFRR / Apr '94 / PolyGram

HEAVY RHYME EXPERIENCE VOL.1
Bona fied funk / It's getting hectic / Who makes the loot / Wake me when I'm dead / Jump 'n' move / Death threat / State of yo / Do what I gotta do / Whatgabothat / Soul Flower
CD 8283352
Acid Jazz/FFRR / Jul '92 / PolyGram

SHELTER
I like it / Sometimes / Shelter / You are the universe / Crying water / Day by day / Feels like right / Highest high / Stay gone / You've got a friend / Once is twice enough / After forvever / Last to know
CD 8288872
CD 8288902
FFRR / Apr '97 / PolyGram

Brand New Unit

LOOKING BACK AGAIN
CD BYO 43
BYO / Jun '97 / Cargo

UNDER THE BIG TOP
CD EXC 0102
Excursion / May '94 / SRD

Brand Nubian

EVERYTHING IS EVERYTHING
Word is bond / Straight of da head / Nubian jam / Weed vs weaves / What the fuck / Return of the dread / Down for the real / Gang bang / Claimin' I'm a criminal / Lick dem muthaphuckas / Sweatin' bullets / Step into da cipher / Hold on / Alladat
CD 7559616822
WEA / Oct '94 / Warner Music

IN GOD WE TRUST
Allah u akbar / Ain't no mystery / Meaning of the 5% / Pass the gat / Black star line / Allah and justice / Godz / Travel jam / Brand Nubian rock the set / Love me or leave me alone / Steal ya ho / Steady bootleggin' / Black and blue / Punks get up to get beat down
CD 7559613812
WEA / Feb '93 / Warner Music

ONE FOR ONE
All for one / Concerto in X minor / Ragtime / To the right / Dance to my ministry / Drop the bomb / Wake up / Step to the rear / Slow down / Try to do me / Who can get busy like this man / Grand puba / Positive and LG dedication / Feels so good / Brand nubian
CD 7559609462
WEA / Feb '91 / Warner Music

Brand, Oscar

PIE IN THE SKY
CD TCD 1021
Tradition / Aug '96 / ADA / Vital

Brand-X

BRAND-X
Nuclear burn / Touch wood / Hate zone / Euthanasia waltz / Running of three / Sun in the night / Born ugly / Why should I lend you mine / Unorthodox behaviour / Malaga virgen / Smacks of euphoric hysteria / Macrocosm
CD VI 867242
Disky / Nov '96 / Disky / THE

DO THEY HURT
Noddy goes to Sweden / Voidarama / Act of will / Fragile / Cambodia / Triumphant limp / DMZ
CD CASCD 1151
Charisma / May '89 / EMI

IS THERE ANYTHING ABOUT
Ipanaemia / Longer April / Modern, noisy and effective / Swansong / Is there anything about / Tmiu'atga
CD 4844372
Columbia / Jul '96 / Sony

LIVE AT THE ROXY
CD ZCDBX 010
Zok / Oct '96 / Grapevine/PolyGram / Total/BMG

LIVESTOCK
Nightmare patrol / Ish / Euthanasia waltz / Isis mourning / Malaga virgen
CD CLACD 5
Virgin / May '89 / EMI

MANIFEST DESTINY
True to the Clik / Stellerator / Virus / XXL / Worst man / Manifest destiny / Five drops / Drum dbu / Operation hearts and minds / Mr. Bubble goes to Hollywood
CD OUTER 2CD
CD CLP 9940
Cleopatra / Jun '97 / Cargo / Greyhound / Plastic Head / RTM/Disc / SRD

MASQUES
Poke / Masques / Black moon / Deadly nightshade / Earth dance / Access to data / Ghost of Mayfield Lodge
CD CASCD 1138
Charisma / May '89 / EMI

MOROCCAN ROLL
Sun in the night / Why should I lend you mine / Maybe I'll lend you mine after all / Hate zone / Collapsar / Disco suicide / Orbits / Malaga virgen / Machocosm
CD CASCD 1126
Charisma / May '89 / EMI

PLOT THINS, THE (A History Of Brand X)
Nuclear burns / Born ugly / Why should I lend you mine / Disco suicide / Malaga virgen / Isis mourning / Poke / Ghost of Mayfield lodge / Dance of the illegal aliens / Algon / Cambodia / Triumphant limp
CD CDVM 9005
Virgin / Oct '92 / EMI

PRODUCT
Don't make waves / Dance of the illegal aliens / Soho / Not good enough - see me / Algon / Rhesus perplexus / Wal to wal / And so to F / April
CD CASCD 1147
Charisma / May '89 / EMI

UNORTHODOX BEHAVIOUR
Nuclear burn / Euthanasia waltz / Born ugly / Smacks of euphoric hysteria / Unorthodox behaviour / Running on three / Touch wood
CD CASCD 1117
Charisma / May '89 / EMI

Brandon, Kirk

STONE IN THE RAIN
Stone in the rain / Communication / How long / Satellite / Children of the damned / Europa / Psycho woman / Revolver / Propaganda / Heroes / Future world / Spirit tribe
CD CDGRAM 92
Anagram / Mar '95 / Cargo / Pinnacle

Brandon, Mary-Ann

EVERYTHING I TOUCH
CD APCD 091
Appaloosa / Jun '92 / ADA / Direct / TKO Magnum

SELF APPOINTED HOMECOMING QUEEN
CD APCD 070
Appaloosa / '92 / ADA / Direct / TKO Magnum

Brandos

PASS THE HAT
CD SPV 08544202
SPV / Sep '96 / Koch / Plastic Head

Brandwein, Naftule

KING OF THE KLEZMER CLARINET
Heiser Bulgar / Freit sich, Yiddelach / Der Turkisher-Bulgar tanz / Kolomeika / Naftule spielt far dem Rebin / Nifty's freilach / Oi Tate, S'is gut / Der Terk in America / Wie bist die Gewesen vor prohibition / Das Teureste in Bukowina / Der Heisser / A Hora mit tzibeles / Fun tashlach / Leben zol Palastina / Dem Rabin's Chusid / Der Yid in Jerusalem / Bulgar ala Naftule / Kleine Princessin / Turkishe Yale Vey Uve / Naftule, shpiel es noch amol / Araber tanz / Nifty's eigene / Fufzehn yahr fon der heim awek / Vie tsvie is Naftule der driter / Freilicher yontov
CD ROUCD 1127
Rounder / Feb '97 / ADA / CM / Direct

Brandy

BRANDY
I wanna be down / I dedicate / I'm yours / As long as you're here / Sunny day / I dedicate / Give me you / Love is on my side / I dedicate / Always on my mind / Brokenhearted / Best friend / Movin' on / Baby
CD 7567826102
Atlantic / Nov '94 / Warner Music

Brandywine Bridge

AND SO TO THE FAIR (Brandywine Bridge Play The Music Of Warwick Castle)
Horses brawl / Lavender blue / Ballad of Moll Bloxham / Jaunty John / English meadow / Dancing boy/Donkey riding/ Bobby Shaftoe / Weekend in Warwick / Bernard of Clairvaux / Salisbury Plain / Beggar's song / When a knight won his spurs / Over the hills and far away / Boar's head carol / Rose of Allendale / Lorna of Wychwood / Unto the fair / Hi ho bendigo / Billy the budgie
CD SAMLSCD 503
Soundalive / Nov '96 / Complete/Pinnacle

Brandywine Singers

WORLD CLASS FOLK
CD FE 1402
Folk Era / Nov '94 / ADA / CM

Branigan, Laura

SELF CONTROL
Lucky one / Self control / Ti amo / Heart / Will you still love me tomorrow / Satisfaction / Silent partners / Breaking out / Take me / With every beat of my heart
CD 7801472
Atlantic / '87 / Warner Music

Brasilia

RIVER WIDE
A chamada do Rio / Angel voices / River wide / Tudo joia / Sanctuary / Seeds of joy / With open arms / Voce ja foi a Bahia / Samba em preludio / Song of praise
CD KOKO 1304
Kokopelli / Mar '96 / New Note/Pinnacle

Brass Construction

BRASS CONSTRUCTION
Movin' / Peekin' / Changin' / Love / Talkin' / Dance
CD MUSCD 510
MCI Original Masters / May '95 / Disc / THE

GET UP TO GET DOWN
Get up to get down / Can you see the light / L-o-v-e u / What's on your mind / Talkin' / Dancin' / Right place / Walkin' the line / We can work it out / Startin' all over again / Watch out / Partyline / Renegades
CD CTMCD 325
EMI / Jul '97 / EMI

Brass Monkey

COMPLETE BRASS MONKEY, THE
CD TSCD 467
Topic / Sep '93 / ADA / CM / Direct

Brass Pennies

PRIDE OF ENGLAND
Rule Britannia / Rose of England / Oh I do like to be beside the seaside / All the nice girls love a sailor / Man who broke the bank at Monte Carlo / We'll meet again / White cliffs of Dover / Over the sticks / Sing as we go / Wish me luck as you wave me goodbye / Sally / Knees up Mother Brown / Bless them all / English country garden / John Peel / Robin Hood / Billy Boy / British grenadiers / There's a tavern in the town
CD CDITV 581
Scotdisc / Aug '94 / Conifer/BMG / Duncans / Ross

Brass Tracks Jazz Orchestra

FIRST TRACK
CD SB 2083
Sea Breeze / Jan '97 / Jazz Music

Brasshoppers

VA VA VOOM
Froogie doogie / Big bottom / Dan's samba / Last night / Top boiler / Maria of my soul / Diver's boot / Carmen Miranda's hat / Afro trip / Mo' better blues / Bop bee oo / Va va voom / Weird moment
CD 33WM 102
33 Jazz / Aug '96 / Cadillac / New Note/ Pinnacle

Brassil

BRASSIL PLAYS BRAZIL (Brass Music From NE Brazil)
CD NI 5462
Nimbus / Feb '96 / Nimbus

Bratland/Opheim

DAM (Bratland/Opheim & The Oslo Chamber Choir)
CD FX 147CD
Musikk Distribujson / Apr '95 / ADA

Bratmobile

REAL JANELLE, THE
Real Janelle / Brat girl / Yeah, huh / Die / I live in a town where the boys amputate their hearts / Where eagles dare
CD KRS 219CD
Kill Rock Stars / Aug '94 / Cargo / Greyhound / Plastic Head

Braun, Grace

IT WON'T HURT
Do right / Mermaid and the sailor / It won't hurt / O my ladies / Bittersweet / Lover's dream / What wondrous love is this / Stand by me / Carter's lullaby / Hopeless / Liftin' up me / Jenny Wren
CD SRRCD 026
Slow River / Jul '97 / Cargo

Brave Boys

NEW ENGLAND TRADITIONS IN FOLK MUSIC
CD 802392
New World / Sep '95 / ADA / Cadillac / Harmonia Mundi

Brave Combo

BRAVE COMBO
CD ROUCD 9019
Rounder / '88 / ADA / CM / Direct

GROUP DANCE EPIDEMIC
Hokey pokey / Mexican hat dance / Never on Sunday / Limbo rock/Hand jive / Hustle / Chicken dance / Mana vu / Jeffrey / Peanut vendor / Jeopardy / Hokey pokey / Bunny hop
CD ROUCD 9055
Rounder / Jun '97 / ADA / CM / Direct

KISS OF FIRE
Kiss of fire / I get ideas / Way to say goodbye / Burn slow / I could have danced all night / J'ai faim, toujours / Eyes of Santa Lucia / Candles / Serendipity / Take a deep breath / Day in the life of a fool / Under Paris skies
CD WMCD 1058
Watermelon / Feb '97 / ADA / Direct

MOOD SWING MUSIC
Three ducks waltz / Little bit of soul / Conmigo no quires nada / Skin / Volare / Three ducks polka / Come back to Sorrento / Sombras nada mas / Walking stick / Pirate Captain's quickstep / Burn slow / Three ducks ondo / Besos Besitos / Herrgard's polka / Girl / Tales from the Vienna Woods / Mas tequila / Three ducks cha cha / Always Vienna (the last words of Sigmund Freud) / Polka overture
CD ROUCD 11574
Rounder / Nov '96 / ADA / CM / Direct

MUSICAL VARIETIES
CD ROUCD 11546
Rounder / '88 / ADA / CM / Direct

NO NO NO CHA CHA CHA
CD ROUCD 9035
Rounder / Apr '93 / ADA / CM / Direct

POLKAS FOR A GLOOMY WORLD
CD ROUCD 9045
Rounder / Jul '95 / ADA / CM / Direct

POLKATHARSIS
Happy wanderer / Crazy Serbian butchers dance / Old country polka / Anniversary song / Who stole the kishka / La Rufalina / Lovesick / Atotonilco / New mind polka / Jeusita en chihuahua / Westphalia waltz / Pretty dancing girl / Hey ba ba re bop
CD ROUCD 9009
Rounder / '88 / ADA / CM / Direct

Brave Old World

BEYOND THE PALE
CD ROUCD 3135
Rounder / Jul '94 / ADA / CM / Direct

Bravo, Soledad

VOLANDO VOY
CD MES 159662
Messidor / Apr '93 / ADA / Koch

Braxton, Anthony

11 COMPOSITIONS (Braxton, Anthony & Brett Larner)
CD CDLR 244
Leo / May '97 / Cadillac / Impetus / Wellard

2 COMPOSITIONS (ENSEMBLE) 1989/ 1991
CD ARTCD 606
Hat Art / Apr '92 / Cadillac / Harmonia Mundi

4 COMPOSITIONS 1992
CD 1201242
Black Saint / Nov '93 / Cadillac / Harmonia Mundi

5 COMPOSITIONS 1986
CD 1201062
Black Saint / Nov '92 / Cadillac / Harmonia Mundi

6 COMPOSITIONS 1984
CD BSR 0086
Black Saint / Jan '86 / Cadillac / Harmonia Mundi

6 MONK COMPOSITIONS
CD 1201162
Black Saint / Aug '88 / Cadillac / Harmonia Mundi

8 DUETS, HAMBURG 1991
CD CD 710
Music & Arts / Jun '92 / Cadillac / Harmonia Mundi

ANTHONY BRAXTON: TOWN HALL 1972
CD ARTCD 6119
Hat Art / Nov '92 / Cadillac / Harmonia Mundi

COMPOSITION NO.165
CD NA 050
New Albion / Nov '92 / Cadillac / Harmonia Mundi

COMPOSITION NO.174
CD CDLR 217
Leo / May '95 / Cadillac / Impetus / Wellard

COMPOSITION NO.96
CD ____ CDLR 169
Leo / Mar '94 / Cadillac / Impetus / Wellard

CREATIVE ORCHESTRA (Koln 1978)
CD ____ ARTCD 26171
Hat Art / Apr '95 / Cadillac / Harmonia Mundi

CREATIVE ORCHESTRA 1987 (Pieces 1-6)
CD ____ ND 86579
Bluebird / Jun '88 / BMG

DORTMUND 1976
CD ____ ARTCD 6075
Hat Art / Jul '91 / Cadillac / Harmonia Mundi

DUET - MERKIN HALL, NEW YORK (Braxton, Anthony & Richard Teitelbaum)
CD ____ CD 949
Music & Arts / Oct '96 / Cadillac / Harmonia Mundi

DUETS (Braxton, Anthony & Mario Pavone)
CD ____ CD 786
Music & Arts / Nov '93 / Cadillac / Harmonia Mundi

DUO (Braxton, Anthony & Evan Parker)
CD ____ CDLR 193
Leo / Mar '94 / Cadillac / Impetus / Wellard

DUO 1976 (Braxton, Anthony & George Lewis)
CD ____ ART 6150CD
Hat Art / Jul '94 / Cadillac / Harmonia Mundi

EIGHT (3): TRISTANO COMPOSITIONS 1989
CD ____ ARTCD 6052
Hat Art / Nov '90 / Cadillac / Harmonia Mundi

ENSEMBLE - VICTORIAVILLE 1988
CD ____ VICTOCD 07
Victo / Nov '94 / Harmonia Mundi / ReR Megacorp

EUGENE (1989) (Braxton, Anthony & Northwest Creative Orchestra)
CD ____ 1201372
Black Saint / Jan '92 / Cadillac / Harmonia Mundi

KNITTING FACTORY 1994 VOL.1 (2CD Set)
CD Set ____ CDLR 222/3
Leo / Oct '95 / Cadillac / Impetus / Wellard

LEIPZIG 1993 (Braxton, Anthony & Ted Reichman)
CD ____ CD 848
Music & Arts / Feb '96 / Cadillac / Harmonia Mundi

MOMENT PRECLEUX (Braxton, Anthony & Derek Bailey)
CD ____ VICTOCD 02
Victo / Nov '94 / Harmonia Mundi / ReR Megacorp

OPEN ASPECTS
CD ____ ARTCD 6106
Hat Art / Nov '93 / Cadillac / Harmonia Mundi

PIANO MUSIC 1968-1988
CD ____ ARTCD 4619414
Hat Art / Jan '97 / Cadillac / Harmonia Mundi

QUARTET (LONDON) 1985 (Braxton, Anthony Quartet)
CD ____ CDLR 200/201
Leo / '90 / Cadillac / Impetus / Wellard

SANTA CRUZ 1993 (Braxton, Anthony Quartet)
CD ____ ARTCD 6190
Hat Art / Jul '97 / Cadillac / Harmonia Mundi

SILENCE/TIME ZONES (Braxton, Anthony & Richard Teitelbaum)
CD ____ BLCD 760221
Black Lion / May '97 / Cadillac / Jazz Music / Koch / Wellard

TOGETHER ALONE (Braxton, Anthony & Joseph Jarman)
CD ____ DD 428
Delmark / Dec '94 / ADA / Cadillac / CM / Direct / Hot Shot

TRIO (Braxton, Anthony & Evan Parker/ Paul Rutherford)
CD ____ CDLR 197
Leo / Nov '94 / Cadillac / Impetus / Wellard

VICTORIAVILLE 1992 (Braxton, Anthony Quartet)
CD ____ VICTOCD 021
Victo / Nov '94 / Harmonia Mundi / ReR Megacorp

WESLEYAN
CD ____ ARTCD 6128
Hat Art / Sep '93 / Cadillac / Harmonia Mundi

WILLISAU 1991
CD ____ ARTCD 46100
Hat Art / Jul '92 / Cadillac / Harmonia Mundi

Braxton, Toni

SECRETS
Come on over here / You're makin' me high / There's no me without you / Unbreak my heart / Talking in his sleep / How could an angel break my heart / Find me a man / Let it flow / Why should I care / I don't want to / I love me some him / In the late of night
CD ____ 73008260202
Arista / Jul '96 / BMG

TONI BRAXTON
Another sad song / Breathe again / Seven whole days / Love affair / Candlelight / Spending my time with you / Love shoulda brought you home / I belong to you / How many ways / You mean the world to me / Best friend / Breathe again (Reprise)
CD ____ 74321162682
Arista / Feb '97 / BMG

Braxtons

BRAXTONS, THE
So many ways / Where's the good in goodbye / Slow flow / Girl on the side / I'd still say yes / LADI / Never say goodbye / Take me home to Momma / Boss
CD ____ 7567828752
Atlantic / Sep '96 / Warner Music

Brazen Abbot

EYE OF THE STORM
CD ____ USG 37437422
USG / Apr '97 / Cargo

Brazil, Noel

LAND OF LOVE, THE
CD ____ TORCD 090
Dara / Jul '97 / ADA / CM / Direct / Else / Grapevine/PolyGram

Breach

FRICTION
CD ____ BHR 026CD
Burning Heart / Oct '95 / Plastic Head

IT'S ME GOD
CD ____ BHR 057CD
Burning Heart / Jun '97 / Plastic Head

OUTLINES
CD ____ BHR 014CD
Burning Heart / Oct '94 / Plastic Head

Breach, Joyce

CONFESSIONS
CD ____ ACD 269
Audiophile / Apr '93 / Jazz Music

JOYCE BREACH & JERRY MELAGI TRIO (Breach, Joyce & Jerry Melagi)
CD ____ ACD 199
Audiophile / Aug '95 / Jazz Music

LOVERS AFTER ALL
CD ____ ACD 282
Audiophile / Oct '93 / Jazz Music

THIS MOMENT (Breach, Joyce & William Roy)
CD ____ ACD 293
Audiophile / Mar '97 / Jazz Music

Bread

BREAD
CD ____ 0349735022
Elektra / Jan '96 / Warner Music

DAVID GATES & BREAD ESSENTIALS
CD ____ 7559619612
Elektra / Sep '96 / Warner Music

LET YOUR LOVE GO
CD ____ RMB 75063
Remember / Aug '92 / Total/BMG

MANNA
Let your love go / Take comfort / Too much love / If / Be kind to me / He's a good lad / She was my lady / Live in your love / What a change / I say again / Come again / Truckin'
CD ____ 0349735042
Elektra / Jan '96 / Warner Music

ON THE WATERS
Why do you keep me waiting / Make it with you / Blue satin pillow / Look what you've done / I am that I am / Been too long on the road / I want you with me / Coming apart / Easy love / In the afterglow / Call on me / Other side of love
CD ____ 0349735032
Elektra / Jan '96 / Warner Music

Breadmakers

COOL
CD ____ CORD 024CD
Corduroy / Apr '97 / Cargo / Greyhound

Breakers

MILAN
CD ____ FWBR 1
Fast Western / May '95 / Grapevine/ PolyGram

Breakstone, Joshua

LET'S CALL THIS MONK
Let's call this / Work / We see / Reflections / Monk's dream / I mean you / Ruby my dear / Eronel / Brilliant corners / Humph
CD ____ DTRCD 121
Double Time / Mar '97 / Express Jazz

SITTIN' ON THE THING WITH MING
CD ____ 740422
Capri / Oct '94 / Cadillac / Wellard

WALK DON'T RUN (Breakstone, Joshua Quartet)
Lullaby of the leaves / Telstar / Ram-bunk-shush / Perfidia / Walk don't run / Taste of honey / Apache / Caravan / Slaughter on 10th Avenue / Blue star
CD ____ ECD 22058
Evidence / Oct '93 / ADA / Cadillac / Harmonia Mundi

Breath Of Life

LOST CHILDREN
CD ____ DW 076CD
Deathwish / Nov '95 / Plastic Head

TASTE OF SORROW
CD ____ DW 1032CD
Deathwish / Jan '95 / Plastic Head

Breathin' Canyon Band

HARMONY OF A COUPLE, THE
CD ____ 642085MAN85
Mantra / Nov '94 / Cargo / Direct / Discovery

MOTHER AND CHILD
CD ____ 642086MAN86
Mantra / Nov '94 / Cargo / Direct / Discovery

Breathless

BETWEEN HAPPINESS AND HEARTACHE
CD ____ BREATHCD 10
Tenor Vosa / Oct '91 / Pinnacle

HEARTBURST
CD ____ SAT 70012
Tenor Vosa / Feb '94 / Pinnacle

Breathnach, Maire

ANGEL'S CANDLES
Mystic's slipjigs / Eist / Angel's candles / Carillion's/Moling / West ocean waltz / Swans at Coole / Beta/Carnival / Breatnaigh abu / Roundabout/Parallel / Goban/Hallow-een jig / Dreamer / Cuimhne / Aisling Samhna / Hop, skip, jump
CD ____ SCD 593
Starc / Jul '93 / ADA / Direct

CELTIC LOVERS
CD ____ SC 696
Starc / Aug '96 / ADA / Direct

VOYAGE OF BRAN
CD ____ 7567827342
Warner Bros. / Apr '95 / Warner Music

Breathnach, Siobhan

CELTIC HARP
CD ____ OSS 33CD
Ossian / Mar '94 / ADA / CM / Direct / Highlander

Breaux, Zachary

GROOVIN'
Coming home baby / Impressions / Picadillo / Alice / Where is the love / Red, black and green / Lagos / Thinking of Alexis
CD ____ JHCD 023
Ronnie Scott's Jazz House / Jan '94 / Cadillac / Jazz Music / New Note/Pinnacle / TKO Magnum

LAIDBACK
Small town in Texas / Laid back / West side worry / Find a place / Going out of my head / Intro / Remember the sixties / Ten days before / Midnight cowboy / In the midst of it all / On 6th street
CD ____ NYC 60092
NYC / Oct '94 / New Note/Pinnacle

UPTOWN GROOVE
Breakfast at the Epiphany / Cafe Reggio / I told you / Never can say goodbye / Thrill is gone / After 2am on the West coast / All blues / Back into time / Uptown groove / Flavours of my mind / 135th Street theme / After 2am on the East coast / I love this life
CD ____ ZD 44002
Zebra / Mar '97 / New Note/Pinnacle

Brechin, Sandy

OUT OF HIS BOX
CD ____ CDBAR 6001
Brechin All / Apr '96 / Direct / Duncans

Brecker Brothers

COLLECTION, THE
Skunk funk / Sponge / Squids / Funky sea, funky dew / Bathsheba / Dream theme / Straphangin' / East river
CD ____ ND 90442
RCA / Apr '90 / BMG

HEAVY METAL BE BOP
CD ____ OW 31447
One Way / Jun '97 / ADA / Direct / Greyhound

OUT OF THE LOOP
Slang / Ecovation / Scrunch / Secret heart / African skies / When it was / Harpoon / Night crawler / Then she wept
CD ____ GRP 97842
GRP / Sep '94 / New Note/BMG

RETURN OF THE BRECKER BROTHERS
Above and below / That's all there is to it / On the backside / Big idea / Bikutsi / Funk / Good gracious / New Guinea / Roppongi / Sozinho (alone) / Sperical
CD ____ GRP 96842
GRP / Aug '92 / New Note/BMG

Brecker, Michael

TALES FROM THE HUDSON
Slings and arrows / Midnight voyage / Song for Bilbao / Beau rivage / African skies / Introduction to naked soul / Naked soul / Willie T / Cabin fever
CD ____ IMP 11912
Impulse Jazz / Jun '96 / New Note/BMG

Brecker, Randy

LIVE AT SWEET BASIL
Sleaze factor / Thrifty man / Ting chang / Incidentally / Hurdy gurdy / Moontide / Mojoe
CD ____ GNPD 2210
GNP Crescendo / Jun '95 / ZYX

Breeders

LAST SPLASH
CD ____ CAD 3014CD
4AD / Jun '93 / RTM/Disc

POD
Glorious / Happiness is a warm gun / Hellbound / Fortunately gone / Opened / Limehouse / Doe / Oh / When I was a painter / Iris / Only in 3's / Metal man
CD ____ CAD 0006CD
4AD / May '90 / RTM/Disc

Breeding Fear

CHASE IS ON, THE
CD ____ SPV 08487092
SPV / Dec '96 / Koch / Plastic Head

Breen, Ann

BEST OF FRIENDS
Blue forever / Silver threads among the gold / Killarney / Runaround angel / May the good lord / You'll never get to heaven / Sonny / Close to you
CD ____ PLAYCD 1038
Play / Mar '96 / Avid/BMG / Koch

EVENING WITH ANN BREEN, AN
CD ____ PLACD 100
Play / Oct '94 / Avid/BMG / Koch

SAVE THE LAST DANCE
CD ____ DHCD 725
Homespun / Nov '96 / ADA / CM / Direct / Koch / Ross

SINCERELY
CD ____ APLCD 1040
Avid / Dec '96 / Avid/BMG / Koch / THE

SPECIALLY FOR YOU MOTHER
CD ____ PHCD 509
Outlet / Jan '95 / ADA / CM / Direct / Duncans / Koch / Ross

VERY BEST OF ANN BREEN, THE
CD ____ DHCD 724
Homespun / Nov '96 / ADA / CM / Direct / Koch / Ross

Breeze

INTIMATE MOMENTS
CD ____ TJCD 001
TJ / Nov '92 / Jet Star

Brel, Jacques

GREATEST HITS
CD ____ CD 352111
Duchesse / Jul '93 / Pinnacle

JACQUES BREL ALBUM, THE (Various Artists)
CD ____ ITM 1455
ITM / Apr '92 / Koch / Tradelink

NE ME QUITTE PAS
Ne me quitte pas / Marieke / On n'oublie rien / Les flamandes / Les prenoms de Paris / Quand on n'a l'amour / Les biches / Le prochain amour / Le moribond / La valise a mille temps / Je ne sais pas pourquoi
CD ____ 8130092
ECM / Jul '90 / New Note/Pinnacle

Bremnes, Kari

GATE VED GATE
CD FXCD 143
Musikk Distribujson / Jan '95 / ADA

Brennan, Dave

TAKE ME TO THE MARDI GRAS (Brennan, Dave Jubilee Jazzband)
Don't go 'way nobody / Dauphine Street blues / Bright star blues / Move the body over / Ride red ride / Roses of Picardy
CD LACD 20
Lake / Nov '93 / ADA / Cadillac / Direct / Jazz Music / Target/BMG

Brennan, Dennis

IODINE IN THE WINE
Familiar surroundings / Mighty long time / Blue sky red road / Lies / Pill of love / Iodine in the wine / Youngstown / Ones and fours / Worried man / Call your rider / River rise up / Lemmy go down
CD UPST 036
Upstart / Feb '97 / ADA / Direct

JACK IN THE PULPIT
CD UPSTART 016
Upstart / May '95 / ADA / Direct

Brennan, Maire

MAIRE
Ce leis / Against the wind / Oro / Voices of the land / Jealous heart / Land of youth / I believe (deep within) / Beating heart / No easy way / Atlantic shore
CD 74321228212
RCA / Sep '94 / BMG

Brennan, Paul

FIRE IN THE SOUL (Brennan, Paul Band)
CD FE 090CD
Fellside / Apr '93 / ADA / Direct / Target/ BMG

Breuer, Carolyn

ACQUAINTANCE
Let's face the music and dance / I got it bad and that ain't good / Zest for life / Simply be / Where can I go without you / I'm old fashioned / I know you / Murphy's law / Aspire / Hale bop
CD AL 73073
A / Jul '97 / Cadillac / Direct

FAMILY AFFAIR (Breuer, Carolyn & Hermann)
Prost / My ideal / Blue rock / Fidelidade / That silver hilversum / Lyrical excursion / Sunset one
CD ENJACD 80022
Enja / Oct '93 / New Note/Pinnacle / Vital/ SAM

SIMPLY BE (Breuer, Carolyn & Fee Claassen Quintet)
CD CHR 70017
Challenge / Sep '95 / ADA / Direct / Jazz Music / Wellard

Breuker, Willem

BAAL/BRECHT/BREUKER
CD BVHAASTCD 9006
Bvhaast / Oct '93 / Cadillac

BOB'S GALLERY
CD BVHAASTCD 8801
Bvhaast / Oct '93 / Cadillac

DEZE KANT OP DAMES
CD BVHAASTCD 9301
Bvhaast / Oct '93 / Cadillac

HEIBEL
CD BVHAASTCD 9102
Bvhaast / Oct '93 / Cadillac

KOLLEKTIEF - TO REMAIN
CD BVHAASTCD 8904
Bvhaast / Oct '93 / Cadillac

METROPOLIS
CD BVHAASTCD 8903
Bvhaast / Oct '93 / Cadillac

MONDRIAAN STRINGS- PARADE
CD BVHAASTCD 9101
Bvhaast / Oct '93 / Cadillac

MUSIC FOR FILMS OF FREAK DE JONGE
CD BVHAASTCD 9205
Bvhaast / Oct '93 / Cadillac

OVERTIME/UBERSTUNDEN
CD 92042
NM Classics / Feb '95 / Impetus

VERA BETHS & MONDRIAAN STRINGS
CD BVHAASTCD 8802
Bvhaast / Oct '93 / Cadillac

Brewer & Shipley

ARCHIVE ALIVE
CD 80006
Archive / Jun '97 / Greyhound

Brewer, Gary

LIVE IN EUROPE
CD COPP 0144CD
Copper Creek / Dec '96 / ADA

Brewer, Jack

HARSH WORLD (Brewer, Jack Band)
CD NAR 063CD
New Alliance / May '93 / Plastic Head

RHYTHM OR SUICIDE
CD NAR 078CD
New Alliance / Jun '95 / Plastic Head

ROCKIN' ETHEREAL (Brewer, Jack Band)
CD NAR 039CD
New Alliance / Sep '90 / Plastic Head

Brewer, Teresa

MEMORIES OF LOUIS
CD 4692832
Sony Jazz / Nov '92 / Sony

TEENAGE DANCE PARTY
Hula hoop song / Ricky ticky song / Why baby why / Teardrops in my heart / Tweedle dee / After school / Rock love / Pledging my love / Lula rock a hula / On Treasure Island / If were a train / Gone / Empty arms / Since you went away / Dark moon / So shy / It's the same old jazz / Bobby / Jingle bell rock / Born to love
CD BCD 15440
Bear Family / Apr '89 / Direct / Rollercoaster / Swift

VERY BEST OF TERESA BREWER
CD SOW 710
Sound Waves / Jun '93 / Target/BMG

Brian Jonestown Massacre

METHODRONE
CD BCD 4050
Bomp / Aug '95 / Cargo / Greyhound / RTM/Disc / Shellshock/Disc

TAKE IT FROM THE MAN
CD BCD 4055
Bomp / Jan '97 / Cargo / Greyhound / RTM/Disc / Shellshock/Disc

THANK GOD FOR MENTAL ILLNESS
CD BCD 4061
Bomp / Nov '96 / Cargo / Greyhound / RTM/Disc / Shellshock/Disc

Briar, Celia

DARK ROSE
CD WCL 11005
White Cloud / May '94 / Select

Brick Layer Cake

TRAGEDY - TRAGEDY
CD TG 127D
Touch & Go / Oct '94 / SRD

Brickell, Edie

GHOST OF A DOG (Brickell, Edie & New Bohemians)
Mama help me / Black and blue / Carmelito / He said / Times like this / 10,000 angels / Ghost of a dog / Strings of love / Woyaho / Oak cliff bra / Stwisted / This eye / Forgiven / Me by the sea
CD GFLD 19269
Geffen / Feb '95 / BMG

PICTURE PERFECT MORNING
Tomorrow comes / Green / When the lights go down / Good times / Another woman's dream / Stay awhile / Hard times / Olivia / In the bath / Picture perfect morning / Lost in the moment
CD GFLD 19332
Geffen / Sep '96 / BMG

SHOOTING RUBBERBANDS AT THE STARS (Brickell, Edie & New Bohemians)
What I am / Little Miss S / Air of December / Wheel / Love like we do / Circle / Beat the time / She / Nothing / Now / Keep coming back
CD GFLD 19268
Geffen / Feb '95 / BMG

Brickman, Jim

PICTURE THIS
Dream come true / Sun, moon and stars / Sound of your voice / Picture this / Edgewater / You never know / Coming home / Frere Jacques / Secret love / First step / Valentine: *Brickman, Jim & Martina McBride* / Sweet dreams: *Brickman, Jim & Martina McBride* / Hero's dreams: *Brickman, Jim & Martina McBride*
CD 01934112112
Windham Hill / Mar '97 / BMG

Bricktop's Jazz Babes

STOMPIN' AT THE JAZZ CAFE
CD BCD 326
GHB / Jan '94 / Jazz Music

Bride

SILENCE IS MADNESS
CD CMGCD 002
Communique / Nov '90 / Plastic Head

SNAKES IN THE PLAYGROUND
CD CDMFN 156
Music For Nations / Nov '93 / Pinnacle

Brides Of Funkenstein

BRIDES OF FUNKENSTEIN - LIVE
Introduction / War ship touchante / Birdie / Ride on / Bridesmaids / Vanish in our sleep / Together / Disco to go / James Wesley Jackson comedy spot: *Jackson, James Wesley*
CD NEMCD 719
Sequel / Nov '94 / BMG

Bridewells

CAGE
CD EXPALCD 14
Expression / Oct '92 / Pinnacle

Bridget

BRIDGET OF CALIFORNIA
CD GROW 0402
Grass / Feb '95 / Pinnacle / SRD

Bridgewater, Dee Dee

IN MONTREUX
All of me / How insensitive / Just friends / Child is born / Strange fruit / Night in Tunisia / Sister Sadie/Next time I fall in love/Senor Blues
CD 8479132
Polydor / Jan '92 / PolyGram

KEEPING TRADITION
Just one of those things / Fascinating rhythm / Island / Angel eyes / What is this thing called love / Les feuilles mortes/Autumn leaves / I'm a fool to want you/I fall in love too easily / Lullaby of Birdland / What a little moonlight can do / Love vibrations / Polka dots and moonbeams / Sister Sadie
CD 5196072
Verve / Mar '93 / PolyGram

LIVE IN PARIS
All blues / Misty / On a clear day (You can see forever) / Dr. Feelgood / There is no greater love / Here's that rainy day / Medley blues / Cherokee
CD CDCHARLY 24
Charly / Jun '87 / Koch

PRECIOUS THINGS (Featuring Ray Charles)
CD CDSGP 053
Prestige / Aug '92 / Else / Total/BMG

Brier

BALLADS AND CRAIC
Fairy tale of New York / First of May / Dingle bay / Primrose polka / Black is the colour / Finnegan's wake / Home boys home / Peace song / Town I loved so well / Flight of the earls / Liberty boy (Home again in Dublin) / Dreams of tomorrow / Waltz medley / Dirty old town / Streets of New York / Lotto song / Lonesome boatman / Dear little town in old county down
CD PHCD 540
Outlet / Mar '97 / ADA / CM / Direct / Duncans / Koch / Ross

BEST OF IRISH FOLK, THE
CD CHCD 1038
Chyme / Aug '94 / ADA / CM / Direct / Koch

Brier, Tom

RISING STAR
CD SDSCD 1274
Stomp Off / Jun '94 / Jazz Music / Wellard

Brigades

TILL LIFE US DO PART
CD DANCD 011
Danceteria / Apr '90 / ADA / Plastic Head / Shellshock/Disc

Brigadier Jerry

HAIL HIM
CD CDTZ 014
Tappa / Aug '93 / Jet Star

ON THE ROAD
CD RAS 3071CD
Ras / Feb '91 / Direct / Greensleeves / Jet Star / SRD

Briggs, Anne

CLASSIC ANNE BRIGGS (The Complete Topic Recordings)
Recruited collier / Doffin mistress / Lowlands away / My bonny boy / Polly Vaughan / Rosemary Lane / Gathering rushes in the month of May / Whirly whorl / Stonecutter boy / Martinmas time / Blackwater side / Snow it melts the soonest / Willie o' Winsbury / Go your way / Thorneymoor woods / Cuckoo / Reynardine / Young Tambling / Living by the water / My bonny lad
CD FE 078CD
Fellside / Nov '95 / ADA / Direct / Target/ BMG

SING A SONG FOR YOU
Hills of Greenmoor / Sing a song for you / Sovay / I thought I saw you again / Summer's in / Travelling's easy / Bonambuie / Tongue in cheek / Bird in the bush / Sullivan's John
CD FLED 3008
Fledg'ling / Feb '97 / ADA / CM / Direct

Briggs, Arthur

HOT TRUMPET IN EUROPE 1927-1933
CD 158472
Jazz Archives / Feb '96 / Discovery

Brighouse & Rastrick Band

COMPOSER'S CHOICE, THE
CD HARCD 1122
Harlequin / Jul '95 / TKO Magnum

EVENING WITH BRIGHOUSE & RASTRICK BAND, AN
Floral dance / Overture to Mack and Mabel / Amazing grace / Great little army / Because / Le carnaval Romain (The Roman carnival) / Marching through Georgia / Nimrod / Army of the nile / Lento from Eurphoria concerto (1972) / Eriskay love lilt / Poet and peasant
CD CDMFP 6151
EMI / Feb '95 / EMI

FLORAL DANCE, THE
CD 295941
Ariola / Oct '94 / BMG

MARCHES & WALTZES
King cotton / Waltz of the flowers / Radetzky march / Westminster waltz / Espana / French military march / Waltz (Symphonie Fantastique) / Old comrades / West riding / Gold and silver / Cornish cavalier / Morning papers / BB and CF / Waltz from Sleeping Beauty / Colonel Bogey
CD DOYCD 032
Doyen / Oct '94 / Conifer/BMG

MUSIC OF ERIC BALL
CD HARCD 1124
Harlequin / Jul '95 / TKO Magnum

Bright, Larry

SHAKE THAT THING
CD DFCD 71253
Del-Fi / May '97 / Cargo / Koch

Brightman, Sarah

AS I CAME OF AGE
River cried / As I came of age / Some girls / Love changes everything / Alone again or / Bowling green / Something to believe in / Take my life / Brown eyes / Good morning starshine / Yesterday / It must be tough to be that cool
CD 8435632
Polydor / May '90 / PolyGram

DIVE
Dive / Captain Nemo / Second element / Ship of fools / Once in a lifetime / Cape horn / Salty dog / Siren / Seven seas / Johnny wanna live / By now / Island / When it rains in America / La mer
CD 5400832
A&M / Apr '93 / PolyGram

Brightside

FACE THE TRUTH
CD LF 127
Lost & Found / Mar '95 / Plastic Head

PUNCHLINE
CD LF 185CD
Lost & Found / Apr '96 / Plastic Head

Brignola, Nick

IT'S TIME
CD RSRCD 123
Reservoir Music / Nov '94 / Cadillac

LIVE AT SWEET BASIL
CD RSRCD 125
Reservoir Music / Nov '94 / Cadillac

ON A DIFFERENT LEVEL
CD RSRCD 112
Reservoir Music / Nov '94 / Cadillac

RAINCHECK
Raincheck / Tenderly / Hurricane Connie / My ship / I wish I knew / Hesitation blues / Jo Spring / Jitterbug waltz / Darn that dream / North Star
CD RSRCD 108
Reservoir Music / '89 / Cadillac

TRIBUTE TO GERRY MULLIGAN (Brignola, Nick & Sal Salvador)
CD STCD 574
Stash / Feb '94 / ADA / Cadillac / CM / Direct / Jazz Music

WHAT IT TAKES
CD RSRCD 117
Reservoir Music / Nov '94 / Cadillac

Brilliant Corners

CREAMY STUFF
CD MCQCD 006
McQueen / Sep '91 / Cargo

HISTORY OF WHITE TRASH, A
Get it up / Around the bend / You make the days seem longer / Death of a protest singer / I like it here / Gushing / Electric slam no. 1 / La / Jukebox junk / He likes to be with you / Closer / Always on a sunday / Electric slam no. 6
CD CMPCD 005
CMP / Oct '96 / Cargo / Grapevine/PolyGram / Vital/SAM

JOYRIDE
You don't know how lucky you are / This girl / Grow cold / I didn't see you / Emily / Nothing / Hemingway's back / Accused by the angels
CD MCQCD 004
McQueen / May '89 / Cargo

Brim, John

ICE CREAM MAN, THE
CD CDTC 1150
Tonecool / May '94 / ADA / Direct

Brimble, Allister

SOUNDS DIGITAL
CD AMBCD 1
AMB / Jun '94 / Plastic Head

Brinsley Schwarz

BRINSLEY SCHWARZ/DESPITE IT ALL
Hymn to me / Shining brightly / Rock 'n' roll women / Lady Constant / What do you suggest / Mayfly / Ballad of a has been Beauty Queen / Country girl / Slow one / Funk angel / Piece of home / Love song / Starship / Edbury Down / Old Jarrow
CD BGOCD 239
Beat Goes On / Jun '94 / Pinnacle

NERVOUS ON THE ROAD
Nervous on the road / It's been so long / Happy doing what we're doing / Surrender to the rhythm / Feel a little funky / I like it like that / Brand new you, brand new me / Home in my hand / Why why why
CD BGOCD 289
Beat Goes On / Oct '95 / Pinnacle

PLEASE DON'T EVER CHANGE
Hooked on love / I worry / Home in my hand / I won't make it without you / Speedoo / Why do we hurt the one we love / Don't ever change / Play that fast thing / Down in Mexico / Version
CD EDCD 237
Edsel / Sep '90 / Pinnacle

SILVER PISTOL
Dry land / Merry go round / One more day / Nightingales / Silver pistol / Last time I was fooled / Unknown number / Range war / Egypt / Niki Hoeke speedway / Ju ju man / Rockin' chair
CD EDCD 190
Edsel / Sep '90 / Pinnacle

Brise Glace

WHEN IN VANITAS
CD GR 17CD
Skingraft / Sep '94 / SRD

Brisker, Gordon

GIFT, THE (Brisker, Gordon Quartet)
CD 860012
Naxos Jazz / Jun '97 / Select

Brislin, Kate

OUR TOWN (Stecher, Jody & Kate Brislin)
Going to the west / Home / Old country stomp / In between dreams / Showerbread reel/The twisted arm / Too late, too late / Bramble and the rose / Our town / Twilight is stealing / Curtains of the night / Queen of the Earth and child of the stars / Roving on last winter's night / Henry the true machine / Won't you come and sing for me
CD ROUCD 0304
Rounder / Jul '93 / ADA / CM / Direct

SLEEPLESS NIGHTS
CD ROUCD 0374
Rounder / Feb '96 / ADA / CM / Direct

Brissett, Annette

ANNETTE (Brissett, Annette & The Taxi Gang)
CD RASCD 3088
Ras / Apr '92 / Direct / Greensleeves / Jet Star / SRD

Bristol Citadel Choir

MIGHTY TO SAVE (Salvation Army Hymns) (Bristol Citadel Choir/Bristol Easton Songsters Choirs)
Why are you doubting and fearing / I bring my heart to Jesus / My life must be Christ's broken bread / I know thee who thou art saviour / Hear me while before thy feet / Yet once again / By God's abundant mercy / With my heart shone bright in Heavenly light / Life is a journey, long is the road / Once on a day / Was Christ led forth to die / Let me love thee / Thou art claiming / In the secret of my presence / Blessed Lord, in thee is refuge
CD KMCD 865
Kingsway / May '96 / Complete/Pinnacle

Brit Pops Orchestra

IT MUST BE...
It must be love / Waterloo Sunset / Line up / Live forever / There's no other way / Worlds apart / True faith / I go to sleep / See my friends / Stereotypes / Without words / Creep / Portrait of my love / Rock on
CD PCOM 1146
President / Jun '96 / Grapevine/PolyGram / President / Target/BMG

Britannia Building Society ...

ANTHOLOGY (Britannia Building Society Foden Band)
White knuckle ride / Here's that rainy day / Four pieces for four trombones / Consecration / Blue John / Whisper a prayer / Scarborough Fair / Street fair / Elegy for Mippy / Nightingale sang in Berkeley Square / Concert piece for trombone / Bluesleeves / Londonderry air / Adagio / Every time we say goodbye / Eternal quest
CD QPRL 076D
Polyphonic / May '96 / Complete/Pinnacle

BAND OF THE YEAR (Britannia Building Society Foden Band)
Spanish dance / Winter / You'll never walk alone / Tea for two / Solvejg's song / Eighteenth variation from a rhapsody on a theme of Paganini / American in Paris / Postcard from Mexico / Pretty girl is like a melody / Puttin' on the ritz / Sweet and low / In the wood / Bolero
CD GRCD 33
Grasmere / Oct '88 / Highlander / Savoy / Target/BMG

BEST OF BRASS AND VOICES, THE (Britannia Building Society Foden Band/ Halifax Choral Society)
Hallelujah chorus / Praise my soul / Swing low, sweet chariot / Oh God our help in ages past / Fantasy on North Country tunes / Onward, Christian soldiers / Chorus of the Hebrew slaves / Crimond / Grand march from Aida / Day thou gavest Lord is ended / Jerusalem / Pomp and circumstance
CD DOYCD 041
Doyen / Aug '95 / Conifer/BMG

FESTIVAL OF BRASS 1992 (Britannia Building Society Foden Band)
CD DOYCD 019
Doyen / Jan '93 / Conifer/BMG

MUSIC OF JOHN MCCABE (Britannia Building Society Foden Band)
Salamander / Cloudcatcher fells / Desert 11 horizons / Images / Northern lights
CD DOYCD 030
Doyen / May '95 / Conifer/BMG

PINES OF ROME (Britannia Building Society Foden Band/Howard Snell)
Pines of the Villa Borghese / Pines close to a catacomb / Pines of the Gianicolo / Pines of the Appian Way / Dawn / Chloe's dance / Bacchanale / Circuses / Jubilee / October festival / La befana - the Epiphany festival
CD DOYCD 045
Doyen / Aug '96 / Conifer/BMG

YEAR OF THE DRAGON (Britannia Building Society Foden Band)
CD DOYCD 021
Doyen / May '93 / Conifer/BMG

British North American Act

IN THE BEGINNING
CD AFT 005
Afterglow / Jun '97 / Greyhound

British Saxophone Quartet

EARLY OCTOBER
Early October / Neologie musicale / Time to go now
CD SLAMCD 216
Slam / Oct '96 / Cadillac

British Tuba Quartet

MARCH TO THE SCAFFOLD
Thunderer / Hava nagila / Dance of the sugar plum fairy / On the sunny side of the street / Glyder landscape / Sortie in E flat / Triplet for four tubas / Fugue / Battle royal / Dido's lament / Minitures for four valve instruments / Turkish march / In memoriam / April is in my mistress' face / Sonatina for tuba quartet / March to the scaffold
CD QPRZ 013D
Polyphonic / Jul '94 / Complete/Pinnacle

Broadbent, Alan

CONCORD DUO SERIES (Broadbent, Alan & Gary Foster)
Ode to the road / Speak low / Wonder why / Lady in the lake / 317 East 32nd / What is this thing - hot house / If you could see me now / In your own sweet way / One morning in May / Relaxin' at Camarillo
CD CCD 4562
Concord Jazz / Jul '93 / New Note/Pinnacle

LIVE AT MAYBECK RECITAL HALL VOL.14
I hear a rhapsody / Oleo / You've changed / Lennie's pennies / Nardis / Sweet and lovely / Don't ask why / Parisian thoroughfare
CD CCD 4488
Concord Jazz / Dec '91 / New Note/ Pinnacle

PACIFIC STANDARD TIME
Summer night / This one's for Bud / Easy living / Easy to love / I should care / Django / Beautiful love / In love in vain / Someday my prince will come / I've never been in love before / Reets and I
CD CCD 4664
Concord Jazz / Sep '95 / New Note/ Pinnacle

PERSONAL STANDARDS
Consolation / Ballad impromptu / Long goodbye / Everytime I think of you / Song of home / North / Chris craft / Idyll / Uncertain terms
CD CCD 47572
Concord Jazz / May '97 / New Note/ Pinnacle

Broadcast

WORK AND NON WORK
Accidentals / Book lovers / Message from home / Phantom / We've got time / Living room / According to no plan / World backwards / Lights out
CD WARPCD 52
Warp / Jun '97 / Prime / RTM/Disc

Broadside Band

ENGLISH COUNTRY DANCES
Cuckolds all in a row / Shepherd's Holyday or Labour in Vaine / Newcastle / Beggar boy / Picking of sticks / Faine I would if I could or Parthenia / Gathering peascods / Nightpeece or The shaking of the sheets / Chelsey Reach or Buckingham-House / Jameko / Epping Forest / Well-Hall / Fits come on me now or Bishop of Chester's jig / Mad robin / Red house / Mr. Beveridge's magot / Geud man of Ballangigh / To a new Scotch jigg / Childgrove / Wooly and Georgey / Portsmouth / Whitehall minuet / Bloomsberry market
CD CDSDL 393
Saydisc / Mar '94 / ADA / Direct / Harmonia Mundi

ENGLISH NATIONAL SONGS (Broadside Band & John Potter/Lucie Skeaping)
Greensleeves / Gather ye rosebuds while ye may / When the King enjoys his own again / Northern lass / Harvest home / Sally in our alley / Roast beef of old England / Vicar of Bray / Rule Britannia / God save the King / Nancy Dawson / Miller of the Dee / British Grenadiers / Hunting we will go / Drink to me only with thine eyes / Chapter of Kings / Lass of Richmond Hill / Begone dull care / Tom Bowling / Early one morning / Home sweet home
CD CDSDL 400
Saydisc / Mar '94 / ADA / Direct / Harmonia Mundi

JOHN PLAYFORD'S POPULAR TUNES
Greenwood / Heart's ease / Excuse me / Lady Catherine Ogle / Scotchman's dance / In the Northern lass / Never love thee more / Miller's jig / Granadees march / Saraband by Mr.Simon Ives / Lady Hatton's almaine / Prins Robbert Masco / Prince Rupert's march / Daphne / Lilliburlero / Parthenia / La chabott / Jocobella / Paul's steeple / Lady Nevils delight / Whisk / New rigaudon / Italian rant / Bouzar castle / Childgrove / Mr. Lane's minuet / Up with aily / Cheshire rounds / Hunt the squirrel
CD CDSAR 28
Amon Ra / Jul '94 / Harmonia Mundi

OLD ENGLISH NURSERY RHYMES (Broadside Band & Tim Laycock/Vivien Ellis)
Girls and boys come out to play / Polly put the kettle on/Lucy Locket / Jack and Jill went up the hill / Tom, he as the piper's son / Little boy blue come blow your horn / Little Miss Muffet, she sat on a tuffet / Oh dear what can the matter be / Here we go round the mulberry bush / Oranges and lemons / Oats and beans and barley grow / Farmer's in the den / Dance to your Daddy / Ring o'roses / Hey diddle diddle/Humpty Dumpty / I had four brothers over the sea / I saw a ship a-sailing / There was a man who lived in the moon / If all the world were paper / Lavender's blue / Sing a song of sixpence / I had a little nut tree / Oliver Cromwell lay buried and dead / Old King Cole was a merry old soul / Grand old Duke of York/ Lion and the unicorn / Ding dong bell, pussy's in the well / Hickery dickery dock / Three blind mice / There were three little kittens / I love little pussy / Pussy cat, pussy cat, where have you been / Three mice went into a hole to spin / My Daddy is dead, but I can't tell you how / Jolly fat frog lived in the river / North wind doth blow / Who killed cock robin / Frog he would a wooing go / Mary had a little lamb / Baa baa black sheep / Litle Bo Peep / Hot cross buns / Little Jack Horner / Dame get up and bake your pies / Pat a cake, pat a cake, baker's man / Oh what have you got for dinner Mrs. Bond / Hush a bye baby on the tree top / Dance a baby diddy / Hey diddle dumpling, my son John / Twinkle twinkle little star / Sleep, baby, sleep / Boys and girls come out to play
CD CDSDL 419
Saydisc / Sep '96 / ADA / Direct / Harmonia Mundi

POPULAR 17TH CENTURY DANCE TUNES
CD HMA 1901039CD
Musique D'Abord / Oct '94 / Harmonia Mundi

SONGS & DANCES FROM SHAKESPEARE (Broadside Band & Deborah Roberts/John Potter)
Full fathom five thy Father lies / Where the bee sucks / O Mistress mine where are you roaming / Poor soul sat sighing / It was a lover and his lass / Sellengers round / Scottish jigge / Hoboken brawl / Staines morris / How should I your true love know / Tomorrow is St. Valentine's day / And will he not come again / In youth when I did love / Woosell cock, so black of hue / O sweet Oliver / When daffodils begin to peer / Jog on, jog on, the footpath way / Kemp's jig / Passamezzo pavan / Bargamasca / Queen Mary's dumpe / As you came from that holy land / I loathe that I did love / Bonny sweet robin / Come live with me / There dwelt a man / Farewell dear love / Fortune my foe / Earl of Essex measure / La volta / Sinkapace galliard / Coranto / Take , o take those lips away / Sigh no more ladies / Hark, hark, the lark / Lawn as white as driven snow / Get ye hence / When that I was and a little tiny boy
CD CDSDL 409
Saydisc / Feb '95 / ADA / Direct / Harmonia Mundi

Broberg, Basse

WEST OF THE MOON (Broberg, Basse & Red Mitchell)
CD DRCD 235
Dragon / Oct '94 / ADA / Cadillac / CM / Roots / Wellard

Broccoli

BROCCOLI
CD SEEP 19CD
Rugger Bugger / Nov '96 / Shellshock/ Disc

Brock, Dave

AGENT OF CHAOS (Brock, Dave & The Agents Of Chaos)
CD SHARP 042CD
Flicknife / Apr '88 / Pinnacle

STRANGE DREAMS
CD EBSCD 116
Emergency Broadcast System / Dec '96 / BMG

STRANGE TRIPS AND PIPE DREAMS
Hearing aid test / White zone / UFO Line / Space / Pipe dream / Self / Something going on / Bosnia / Parasites are here on earth / Gateway / It's never too late / La forge / Encounter
CD EBSSCD 116
Emergency Broadcast System / Jul '95 / BMG

Brock, Jim

LETTERS FROM THE EQUATOR
CD RR 56CD
Reference Recordings / May '96 / Jazz Music / May Audio

TROPIC AFFAIR
Pass-a-grill / Ladies of the calabash / Tropic affair / Anya / Quo qui's groove / Sidewalk / Palm-palm girls / O vazio
CD RR 31CD
Reference Recordings / May '96 / Jazz Music / May Audio

Brock, Paul

MO CHAIRDIN
CD CEFCD 155
Gael Linn / Jan '94 / ADA / CM / Direct / Grapevine/PolyGram / Roots

Brodie, Mark

SHORES OF HELL, THE (Brodie, Mark & Beaver Patrol)
CD SH 031CD
Shreder / Nov '95 / Plastic Head

Brodsky Quartet

BRODSKY QUARTET
Chromatic fantasy / Concertino / String quartet no.1 Op.8 (1923)
CD SILKD 6014
Silva Classics / Jun '97 / Koch / Silva Screen

Brodsky, Chuck

LETTERS IN THE DIRT
CD ____ **RHRCD 87**
Red House / Oct '96 / ADA / Koch

Broggs, Peter

RAS PORTRAITS
Rastafari liveth / You've got to be wise / Jah Jah voice is calling / Cheer up / Rastaman chant Nyahbingi / Just can't stop praising Jah / Cease the war / Military man / Don't let the children cry / Just because I'm a Rastaman / International farmer / Leggo me hand / 400 years
CD ____ **RAS 3304**
Ras / Jun '97 / Direct / Greensleeves / Jet Star / SRD

RASTAFARI LIVETH
CD ____ **RASCD 3001**
Ras / Nov '92 / Direct / Greensleeves / Jet Star / SRD

REASONING
CD ____ **RASCD 3051**
Ras / Jul '90 / Direct / Greensleeves / Jet Star / SRD

RISE AND SHINE
You got to be wise / Rise and shine / I admire you / International farmer / Leggo mi hand / Bloodstain / Fuss and fight / I love to play reggae / Jah is the ruler / Rastaman chant Nyahbingi
CD ____ **RASCD 3011**
Ras / Sep '93 / Direct / Greensleeves / Jet Star / SRD

Broken Arrow

BROKEN ARROW
CD ____ **74321348652**
RCA / Apr '96 / BMG

Broken Bones

BRAIN DEAD
CD ____ **CDJUST 19**
Rough Justice / Oct '92 / Pinnacle

COMPLETE SINGLES
CD ____ **CLP 96872**
Cleopatra / Jan '97 / Cargo / Greyhound / Plastic Head / RTM/Disc / SRD

DEATH IS IMMINENT
CD ____ **CLEO 93092**
Cleopatra / Dec '93 / Cargo / Greyhound / Plastic Head / RTM/Disc / SRD

DEM BONES
CD ____ **FALLCD 028**
Fallout / Dec '90 / RTM/Disc

FOAD/BONECRUSHER
CD ____ **FALLCD 041**
Fallout / May '93 / RTM/Disc

LOSING CONTROL
Killing fields / Nowhere to run / Jump / Going down / Shutdown / Brain dead / Life's to fast / Bitching / Mercy / Maniac / Lesson
CD ____ **HMRXD 133**
Heavy Metal / Aug '89 / Revolver / Sony

STITCHED UP
CD ____ **CDJUST 18**
Rough Justice / Oct '91 / Pinnacle

TRADER IN DEATH
Traders in death / Money, pleasure and pain / Who cares about the cost / Stabbed in the back (still bleeding) / Booze for free / Crack attack / Trader in death / Blue lie blue life
CD ____ **HMRCD 141**
Heavy Metal / Mar '90 / Revolver / Sony

Broken Dog

BROKEN DOG
CD ____ **ABB 122CD**
Big Cat / Mar '97 / 3mv/Pinnacle

Broken Hearts Are Blue

TRUTH ABOUT LOVE
CD ____ **CR 025CD**
Caulfield / May '97 / Cargo

Broken Hope

BOWELS OF REPUGNANCE
CD ____ **CDZORRO 64**
Metal Blade / Sep '93 / Pinnacle / Plastic Head

LOATHING
CD ____ **398414120CD**
Metal Blade / Mar '97 / Pinnacle / Plastic Head

SWAMPED IN GORE
CD ____ **140962**
Metal Blade / Nov '95 / Pinnacle / Plastic Head

Broken Pledge

MUSIQUE IRLANDAISE
CD ____ **BCD 6801**
Auvidis/Ethnic / Jan '95 / ADA / Harmonia Mundi

Brokesch, Susanne

SHARING THE SUNHAT
CD ____ **EFA 123002**
Disko B / Apr '97 / SRD

Brokken, Corry

LA MAMMA
La Mamma / Das gluck kam zu mir wie ein Traum / La boheme / Nimm meine hand / Alle meine Traume / Heiss ist der kaffee in San Jose / Kind nummer zehn / Und doch / Van deinen Traumen kannst du nict leben / Spiel Zigeuner / Menschen / Was wird aus mir / Vorbei / Ich bin glucklich obwohl ich weine / Und sie trug eine Rose im Haar / Was weisst du von mi / Ouzo / Femde strassen / Da ist die Andere / Warum machst du dir das so leicht / Mylady / Der mann, den ich will / Deine Mutter ist da / Meine Leibesmelodie / Die letzten sieben Tage
CD ____ **BCD 15883**
Bear Family / Dec '96 / Direct / Rollercoaster / Swift

MILORD
Damals war alles so schon / Seit wir uns seh'n / Milord / Bonjour Paris / Er sah aus wie ein lord / Du bist durchschaut / Maurice, der altecharmeur / Er macht musik am montparnasse / Wie der traum meiner schlaflosen nachte / Es war im fruhling, cherie / Wenn ich nur wusst / Gluck und glas / Flomarkt melodie / Moro / Gib mir die hand / Doch nur dann hab'ich weh getan / Venedig in grau / So ist die liebe, mon ami / Don Juan / Es kann si viel gesch'n / 14 April / Ich traum so gern von San Francisco / Ich bin girl und du bist boy / Ein haus ist kein / Zuhaus / Sag lieber nein / Ohne mich wird morgen hochezeit zein / Gut nacht, mein schatz, gut nacht
CD ____ **BCD 15877**
Bear Family / Jul '96 / Direct / Rollercoaster / Swift

Bromberg, Brian

BASSICALLY SPEAKING
CD ____ **NOVA 9031**
Nova / Jan '93 / New Note/Pinnacle

IT'S ABOUT TIME
CD ____ **NOVA 9146**
Nova / Jan '93 / New Note/Pinnacle

Bromide

ISCARIOT HEART
CD ____ **SR 61652**
Scratchy / Feb '97 / Pinnacle

Bronner, Till

GERMAN SONGS (Bronner, Till & Deutsches Symphonieorchester)
CD ____ **MM 801057**
Minor Music / Oct '96 / Vital/SAM

MY SECRET LOVE
CD ____ **MM 801051**
Minor Music / Sep '95 / Vital/SAM

Bronski Beat

AGE OF CONSENT, THE
Why / It ain't necessarily so / Screaming / No more war / Love and money / Smalltown boy / Heatwave / Junk / Need a man blues / I feel love / I feel love/Medley: *Bronski Beat & Marc Almond* / Run from love / Hard rain / Memories / Puit d'amour / Heatwave
CD ____ **8288242**
London / Jul '96 / PolyGram

HUNDREDS AND THOUSANDS
Cadillac car / Heatwave / Why / Run from love / Hard rain / Smalltown boy / Junk / Infatuation / Close to the edge / I feel love
CD ____ **5500432**
Spectrum / Jun '93 / PolyGram

Bronzemen

RADIO TRANSCRIPTIONS 1939
CD ____ **DOCD 5501**
Document / Nov '96 / ADA / Hot Shot / Jazz Music

Brood

HITSVILLE
CD ____ **IDI 2330CD**
Dionysus / Sep '95 / Cargo / Greyhound / Plastic Head

Brook, Michael

ALBINO ALLIGATOR
Arrival / Doggie dog / Slow town / Preparation / Miscalculation / Aftermath / Tunnel / Albo gator / Promise / City / Kicker / Exit / Ill wind (you're blowing me no good)
CD ____ **CAD 7003CD**
4AD / Feb '97 / RTM/Disc

COBALT BLUE
CD ____ **CAD 2007CD**
4AD / Jun '92 / RTM/Disc

SHONA
CD ____ **SINE 002**
Sine / Sep '95 / Grapevine/PolyGram

Brooker, Gary

NO MORE FEAR OF FLYING
CD ____ **RR 4659**
Repertoire / Jun '97 / Greyhound

Brooklyn Allstars

BEST OF THE BROOKLYN ALLSTARS, THE
CD ____ **NASH 4504**
Nashboro / Feb '96 / Pinnacle

Brooklyn Funk Essentials

COOL, STEADY & EASY
Take the L train (to Brooklyn) / Creator has a master plan / Revolution was postponed because of rain / Brooklyn recycles / Madame Zzaj / Headnaddas journey to the planet Addiskizm / Big apple boogaloo / Blow your brains out / Stickman crossing the Broklyn bridge / Dilly dally / Take the L train (to 8 ave)
CD ____ **DOR 22CD**
Dorado / Jun '94 / Pinnacle

Brookmeyer, Bob

BOB BROOKMEYER & FRIENDS (Brookmeyer, Bob & Stan Getz)
Jive hoot / Misty / Wrinkle / Bracket / Skylark / Sometime ago / I've grown accustomed to her face / Who cares
CD ____ **468413 2**
Columbia / Nov '93 / Sony

BOB BROOKMEYER WITH STOCKHOLM JAZZ ORCHESTRA (Brookmeyer, Bob & Stockholm Jazz Orchestra)
Cats / Lies / Tick tock / Dreams / Missing work / Ceremony
CD ____ **DRCD 169**
Dragon / Sep '89 / ADA / Cadillac / CM / Roots / Wellard

ELECTRICITY
Farewell, New York / Ugly music / White blues / Say ah / No song / Crystal Palace
CD ____ **892192**
Act / Sep '94 / New Note/Pinnacle

PARIS SUITE (Brookmeyer, Bob New Quartet)
CD ____ **CHR 70026**
Challenge / Sep '95 / ADA / Direct / Jazz Music / Wellard

Brooks & Dunn

BORDERLINE
My Maria / Man this lonely / Why would I say goodbye / Mama don't get dressed up for nothing / I am that man / More than a Margarita / Redneck / Rhythm & blues / My love will follow you / One heartache at a time / Tequila town / White line Casanova
CD ____ **07822188102**
Arista / Apr '96 / BMG

BRAND NEW MAN
Brand new man / My next broken heart / Coll drink of water / Cheating on the blues / Neon moon / Lost and found / I've got a lot to learn / Boot scootin' boogie / I'm no good / Still in love with you
CD ____ **07822186582**
Arista / Jul '91 / BMG

WAITIN' ON SUNDOWN
Little Miss Honky Tonk / She's not the cheatin' kind / Silver and gold / I'll never forgive my heart / You're gonna miss me when I'm gone / My kind of crazy / Whiskey under the bridge / If that's the way you want it / She's the kind of trouble / Good few rides away
CD ____ **7822187652**
RCA / Jun '97 / BMG

Brooks, Bernard

CHEERS
CD ____ **DLD 1017**
Dance & Listen / Jul '93 / Savoy / Target/ BMG

MOVING ON
CD ____ **DLD 1060**
Dance & Listen / Dec '95 / Savoy / Target/ BMG

SWING AND SWAY VOL.1
CD ____ **DLD 1005**
Dance & Listen / '92 / Savoy / Target/ BMG

SWING AND SWAY VOL.10
CD ____ **DLD 1024**
Dance & Listen / '92 / Savoy / Target/ BMG

SWING AND SWAY VOL.11
All of me / Some of these days / Beautiful dreamer / Ramona / Love letters in the sand / 'Deed I do
CD ____ **DLD 1026**
Dance & Listen / May '92 / Savoy / Target/ BMG

SWING AND SWAY VOL.12
That certain party/When you're smiling / If I had a talking picture of you/Clementine / King of the road/The man who comes around / On mother Kelly's doorstep/Underneath the arches / Babette/Charmaine / Dancing with tears in my eyes/I love you truly / Stars will remember / Hernando's hideaway / My melancholy baby/Taking a chance on love / Just walking in the rain/ On a slow boat to China / There's a boy coming home on leave/Blue skies/Playmates / Rose Rose I love you/Nursie nursie / Always in my hair/There will never be another you / Stranger on the shore/More than ever / It's the talk of the town/Dance of the hours / Just walking in the rain/Singin' in the rain / Jingle jangle jingle/Who's been polishing the sun / I wonder where my baby is tonight / Silver wings/You always hurt the one you love / You, you, you/Too young / Snowbird/Don't sweetheart me / I'm thinking tonight of my blue eyes / Beautiful Ohio/ The shadow waltz / Just for a while/Santa Lucia
CD ____ **DLCD 1029**
Dance & Listen / Jul '92 / Savoy / Target/ BMG

SWING AND SWAY VOL.16
CD ____ **DLD 1039**
Dance & Listen / Jul '93 / Savoy / Target/ BMG

SWING AND SWAY VOL.2
CD ____ **DLD 1007**
Dance & Listen / '92 / Savoy / Target/ BMG

SWING AND SWAY VOL.3
Rose Marie / Only a rose / At the Balalaika / Blue tango / Don't get around much anymore / Makin' whoopee / Sunny side of the street / It's magic / Maybe / Sierra Sue / Marie Elena / I'm in the mood for love / Just one more chance / Carolina in the morning / You're driving me crazy / So what's new / 12th Street rag / Charleston / Are you lonesome tonight / Wonderful one / When you and I were seventeen / I wonder who's kissing her now / Carolina moon / Alice blue gown / You are my sunshine / Baby face / My blue heaven / Yes sir that's my baby / Sugartime / I'm looking over a four leaf clover / Oh what it seemed to be / Where are you / Please be kind / Music maestro please / Oh my papa / I wish you love / My special angel / Moving south
CD ____ **DLD 1008**
Dance & Listen / '92 / Savoy / Target/BMG

SWING AND SWAY VOL.4
CD ____ **DLD 1011**
Dance & Listen / '92 / Savoy / Target/ BMG

SWING AND SWAY VOL.5
CD ____ **DLD 1012**
Dance & Listen / Dec '92 / Savoy / Target/ BMG

SWING AND SWAY VOL.6
CD ____ **DLD 1015**
Dance & Listen / '92 / Savoy / Target/ BMG

SWING AND SWAY VOL.7
CD ____ **DLD 1018**
Dance & Listen / '92 / Savoy / Target/ BMG

SWING AND SWAY VOL.8
CD ____ **DLD 1021**
Dance & Listen / '92 / Savoy / Target/ BMG

SWING AND SWAY VOL.9
CD ____ **DLD 1022**
Dance & Listen / '92 / Savoy / Target/ BMG

Brooks, Big Leon

LET'S GO TO TOWN
CD ____ **CD 4931**
Earwig / Feb '95 / ADA / CM

Brooks, Buppa

BIG SOUND OF BUPPA BROOKS, THE
Blues for Tina / Mood indigo / Robin's nest / Willow weep for me / Harvard blues / Pocket corner / Body and soul / I let a song out of my heart / Moon river
CD ____ **501395**
Claves / Jun '96 / Complete/Pinnacle

Brooks, Elkie

AMAZING (Brooks, Elkie & The Royal Philharmonic Orchestra)
Nights in white satin / One more heartache / Our love / Lilac wine / From the heart / Paint your pretty picture / Gasoline alley / Minutes / Will you write me a song / Don't cry out loud / Growing tired / 'Round midnight / It all comes back on you / We've got tonight / Off the beaten track / No more the fool / Only women bleed
CD ____ **3036000282**
Carlton / Apr '96 / Carlton

BEST OF ELKIE BROOKS, THE
Pearl's a singer / Sunshine after the rain / Don't cry out loud / Nights in white satin / Gasoline alley / I guess that's why they call it the blues / Growing tired / Ain't misbehavin' / Goin' back / Fool if you think it's over / Our love / Only love can break your heart / Runaway / Money / If you leave me now / Blue moon / Minutes / Lilac wine

CD 5513292
Spectrum / Nov '95 / PolyGram

BOOKBINDER'S KID
Sail on / Stairway to heaven / You ain't leavin' / Keep it a secret / When the hero walks alone / What's the matter baby / Can't wait all night / Kiss me for the last time / Love is love / Foolish games / Only love will set you free / I can dream, can't I
CD CLACD 327
Castle / May '93 / BMG

ELKIE BROOKS
CD MATCD 258
Castle / Apr '93 / BMG

EVENING WITH ELKIE BROOKS, AN
CD ARTFULCD 8
Artful / Aug '97 / Pinnacle / Total/BMG

FROM THE HEART
Last teardrop / Don't go changing your mind / We are all your children / One of a kind / Tell her / You and I (are you lonely) / Free to love / Suits my style / Got to get better / From the heart
CD MSCD 1
Magnum Music / May '94 / TKO Magnum

NO MORE THE FOOL
No more the fool / Only women bleed / Blue jay / Break the chain / We've got tonight
CD CLACD 326
Castle / May '93 / BMG

NOTHIN' BUT THE BLUES
I ain't got nothin' but the blues / Baby get lost / Blues for Mama / Baby what do you want me to do / Tell me more then some / I'd rather go blind / I wonder who / Ain't no use / Nobody but you / I love your lovin' ways / Bad bad whiskey / Fine and mellow / Me and my gin / Mean and evil / Trouble in mind / Please send me someone to love
CD ESMCD 402
Essential / Jan '97 / BMG

ONE OF A KIND
CD MSCD 1
Music De-Luxe / Apr '94 / TKO Magnum

PEARLS
Superstar / Fool (if you think it's over) / Giving it up for your love / Sunshine after the rain / Warm and tender love / Lilac wine / Pearl's a singer / Don't cry out loud / Too busy thinking about my baby / If you leave me now / Paint your pretty picture / Dance away
CD CDA 20116
A&M / Apr '84 / PolyGram

PEARLS VOL.2
Goin' back / Our love / Gasoline Alley / I just can't go on / Too much between us / Giving us hope / Money / Nights in white satin / Loving arms / Will you write me a song
CD 5500602
Spectrum / Jun '93 / PolyGram

PEARLS VOL.3
CD MER 007
Tring / Mar '93 / Tring

PEARLS/TWO DAYS AWAY (2CD Set)
CD Set CDA 24122
A&M / Jan '92 / PolyGram

ROUND MIDNIGHT
'Round midnight / Cry me a river / Just for a thrill / Travelling light / Don't explain / Rainy day / All night long / What kind of man are you
CD CLACD 403
Castle / '95 / BMG

VERY BEST OF ELKIE BROOKS, THE
Pearl's a singer / No more the fool / Don't cry out loud / Fool if you think it's over / I just can't go on / Sunshine after the rain / I guess that's why they call it the blues / Nights in white satin / Only love can break your heart / Ain't misbehavin' / Lilac wine / Blue moon / If you leave me now / Goin' back / Gassoline alley / We've got tonight / Our love / Loving arms / Runaway / Growing tired
CD 5407122
PolyGram TV / Mar '97 / PolyGram

WE'VE GOT TONIGHT
CD TRTCD 200
TrueTrax / Jun '95 / THE

WE'VE GOT TONIGHT
CD PLSCD 159
Pulse / Apr '97 / BMG

Brooks, Ernie

FALLING, THEY GET YOU
CD 422501
New Rose / Nov '94 / ADA / Direct / Discovery

Brooks, Garth

BEYOND THE SEASON
Go tell it on the mountain / God rest ye merry gentlemen / Old man's back in town / Gift / Unto you this night / White Christmas / Friendly beasts / Santa looks a lot like Daddy / Silent night / Mary's dream / What child is this
CD CDP 7987422
Liberty / Sep '92 / EMI

CHASE, THE
That summer / Somewhere other than the night / Face to face / Every now and then / Mr. Right / Learning to live again / Walkin' after midnight / Dixie chicken / Night rider's lament
CD CDESTU 2184
Liberty / Sep '92 / EMI

FRESH HORSES
Old stuff / Cowboys and angels / Fever / That ol' wind / Rollin' / Change / Beaches of Cheyenne / It's midnight Cinderella / She's every woman / Ireland
CD CDGB 1
Capitol / Nov '95 / EMI

HITS
Ain't going down (til the sun comes up) / Friends in low places / Burning bridges / Callin' Baton Rouge / River / Much too young (to feel this damn old) / Thunder rolls / American Honky-Tonk Bar Association / If tomorrow never comes / Unanswered prayers / Standing outside the fire / Rodeo / What she's doing now / We shall be free / Papa loved Mama / Shameless / Two of a kind, workin' on a full house / That summer / Red strokes / Dance
CD CDEST 2247
EMI / Dec '94 / EMI

IN PIECES
Standing outside / Night I called the old man out / American honky-tonk bar association / One night a day / Kickin' and screamin' / Ain't going down (til the sun comes up) / Red strokes / Callin' baton rouge / Night will only know / Cowboy song / Fire
CD CDEST 2212
Liberty / Aug '93 / EMI

NO FENCES
If tomorrow never comes / Not counting you / Much too young (to feel this damn old) / Dance / Thunder rolls / New way to fly / Two of a kind, workin' on a full house / Victim of the game / Friends in low places / Wild horses / Unanswered prayers / Same old story / Mr. Blue / Wolves
CD CDEST 2136
Capitol / Nov '90 / EMI

ROPIN' THE WIND
Against the grain / Rodeo / What she's doing now / Burning bridges / Papa loved Mama / Shameless / Cold shoulder / We bury the hatchet / In lonesome dove / River / Alabama clay / Everytime that it rains / Nobody gets off in this town / Cowboy Bill
CD CDESTU 2162
Capitol / Jan '92 / EMI

Brooks, Hadda

ANYTIME, ANYPLACE, ANYWHERE
Anytime anyplace anywhere / That's my desire / Don't go to strangers / Don't you think I ought to know / Man with the horn / But not for me / Rain sometime / heart of a clown / Ol' man river / Dream / Foggy day / Trust in me / Please be kind/I'm blue / Stolen love / All of me
CD DRGCD 91423
DRG / Sep '94 / Discovery / New Note/ Pinnacle

ROMANCE IN THE DARK
Variety bounce / That's my desire / Romance in the dark / Bully wully boogie / Out of the blue / Honey, honey, honey / Keep your hand on your heart / Bewildered / Jukebox boogie / Trust in me / Don't take your love from me / Schubert's serenade in boogie / Tough on my heart / When a woman cries / Say it with a kiss / I've got my love to keep me warm / I feel so good / It all depends on you / Don't call it love / Honky tonk boogie / Don't you think I ought to know / You won't let me go / Tootsie timesie
CD CDCHD 453
Ace / Jun '93 / Pinnacle

TIME WAS WHEN
Time was when / My romance / You won't let me go / I must have that man / I'm a fool to want you / I feel so good / Miss Brown to you / Can you look me in the eye / You go your way and I'll go crazy / Close your eyes (and I'll be there) / Thrill is gone / Mama's blues / How do you speak to an angel / I hadn't anyone till you / I need a little sugar in my bowl
CD VPBCD 30
Pointblank / Feb '96 / EMI

Brooks, Lonnie

BAYOU LIGHTNING
Voodoo daddy / Figure head / Watchdog / Breakfast in bed / Worked up woman / Alimony / Watch what you got / I ain't superstitious / You know what my body needs / In the dark
CD ALCD 4717
Alligator / May '93 / ADA / CM / Direct

HOT SHOT
Don't take advantage of me / Wrong number / Messed up again / Family rules / Back trail / I want all my money back / Mr. hot shot / One more shot
CD ALCD 4731
Alligator / May '93 / ADA / CM / Direct

LET'S TALK IT OVER
CD DD 660
Delmark / Jan '94 / ADA / Cadillac / CM / Direct / Hot Shot

LIVE FROM CHICAGO
Two headed man / Trading post / In the dark / Got me by the tail / One more shot / Born with the blues / Eyeballin' / Cold lonely nights / Hideaway
CD ALCD 4759
Alligator / May '93 / ADA / CM / Direct

ROADHOUSE BLUES
CD ALCD 4843
Alligator / Aug '96 / ADA / CM / Direct

SATISFACTION GUARANTEED
Temporary insanity / Man's gotta do / Feast or famine / Lyin' time / Little RR and CB / Wife for tonight / Family curse / Horoscope / Like Father, like son / Holding on to the memories / Accident / Price is right
CD ALCD 4799
Alligator / May '93 / ADA / CM / Direct

SWEET HOME CHICAGO
CD BLE 595542
Black & Blue / Apr '91 / Discovery / Koch / Wellard

TURN ON THE NIGHT
Eyeballin' / Inflation / Teenage boogie man / Heavy traffic / I'll take care of you / TV mama / Mother nature / Don't go to sleep on me / Something you got / Zydeco
CD ALCD 4721
Alligator / May '93 / ADA / CM / Direct

WOUND UP TIGHT
Got lucky last night / Jealous man / Belly rubbin' music / Bewitched, bothered and bewildered / End of the rope / Wound up tight / Boomerang / Musta' been dreaming / Skid row / Hush mouth money
CD ALCD 4751
Alligator / May '93 / ADA / CM / Direct

Brooks, Meredith

BLURRING THE EDGES
I need / Bitch / Watched you fall / Pollyanne / Shatter / My little town / What would happen / It don't get better / Birthday / Stop / Wash my hands
CD CDEST 2298
Parlophone / Aug '97 / EMI

Brooks, Paul

HOOKED ON THE USA
Tara's theme / Oh Susannah / Swanee River / When Johnny comes marching home / Shenandoah / Camptown races / Beautiful dreamer / Dixie / Some folks / Battle hymn of the republic / Swing low, sweet chariot
CD ECD 3312
K-Tel / Mar '97 / K-Tel

PIANO MOODS (18 Romantic Instrumentals)
How deep is your love / Free as a bird / Jesus to a child / Living years / Exhale / Lifted / Take a bow / Heaven for everyone / My old piano / Earth song / Piano in the dark / Jealous guy / Smoke gets in your eyes / Fever / Don't give up / I am blessed / If you don't know me by now / Search for a hero
CD ECD 3280
K-Tel / Jan '97 / K-Tel

SAX SEDUCTION (18 Sensual Instrumentals)
Killing me softly with his song / Je t'aime / Move closer / Lovin' you / Sexual healing / Love letters / Have I told you lately / One more night / How deep is your love / Fever / Private dancer / First time ever I saw your face / When a man loves a woman / Touch me in the morning / Summer (the first time) / Way you look tonight / Where is the love / Make it with you
CD ECD 3303
K-Tel / Feb '97 / K-Tel

SOUL OF SPAIN, THE
La paloma / Spanish Harlem / Chiquitita / Spanish eyes / In a little Spanish town / Man without love / Spanish flea / Maria Elena / Quando, quando, quando / Lady of Spain / Boy from nowhere / Guantanamera / Fernando / Concierto de Aranjuez / Spanish romance / Una paloma blanca / La isla bonita / Granada
CD ECD 3372
K-Tel / Jun '97 / K-Tel

Brooks, Randy

RANDY BROOKS 1945-1947 (Brooks, Randy & His Orchestra)
CD CCD 35
Circle / Mar '95 / Jazz Music / Swift / Wellard

RANDY BROOKS 1945-1947
CD JH 1049
Jazz Hour / Jul '96 / Cadillac / Jazz Music / Target/BMG

Broom, Bobby

NO HYPE BLUES
CD CRISS 1109
Criss Cross / Dec '95 / Cadillac / Direct / Vital/SAM

Broom, Mark

ANGIE IS A SHOPLIFTER
CD PP 08CD
Pure Plastic / Oct '96 / Kudos / Pinnacle / Vital

Broonzy, 'Big' Bill

ALL TIME BLUES CLASSICS
CD 8420292
Music Memoria / Oct '96 / ADA / Discovery

BIG BILL BROONZY 1935-1940
CD BLE 592532
Black & Blue / Dec '92 / Discovery / Koch / Wellard

BIG BILL BROONZY 1955 LONDON SESSIONS, THE
When do I get to be called a man / Partnership woman / Southbound train / St. Louis blues / Minding my own business / It feels so good / Saturday evening / Glory of love / Southern saga inc Joe Turner blues / In the evening / Going down this road feeling bad
CD NEXCD 119
Sequel / Apr '90 / BMG

BIG BILL BROONZY VOL.10 (1940)
CD DOCD 5132
Document / Oct '92 / ADA / Hot Shot / Jazz Music

BIG BILL BROONZY VOL.12 (1945-1947)
CD BDCD 6047
Blues Document / Sep '94 / ADA / Hot Shot / Jazz Music

BIG BILL BROONZY VOL.4 (1935-1936)
CD DOCD 5126
Document / Oct '92 / ADA / Hot Shot / Jazz Music

BIG BILL BROONZY VOL.5 (1936-1937)
CD DOCD 5127
Document / Oct '92 / ADA / Hot Shot / Jazz Music

BIG BILL BROONZY VOL.6 (1937)
CD DOCD 5128
Document / Oct '92 / ADA / Hot Shot / Jazz Music

BIG BILL BROONZY VOL.7 (1937-1938)
CD DOCD 5129
Document / Oct '92 / ADA / Hot Shot / Jazz Music

BIG BILL BROONZY VOL.8 (1938-1939)
CD DOCD 5130
Document / Oct '92 / ADA / Hot Shot / Jazz Music

BIG BILL BROONZY VOL.9 (1939)
CD DOCD 5131
Document / Oct '92 / ADA / Hot Shot / Jazz Music

BIG BILL'S BLUES
Too too train blues / Mistreatin' mama blues / Bull cow blues / Long tall mama / I'll be back home again / Keep your hands off her / Big Bill blues / I'm a Southern man / Southern flood blues / You do me any old way / New shake 'em on down / Let me dig it / Baby I done got wise / Just a dream / Just got to hold you tight / Oh yes / Looking up at down / You better cut that out / Lonesome road blues / When I had been drinking / All by myself / Night watchman blues / Tell me baby / I'm gonna move to the outskirts of the town
CD TPZ 1038
Topaz Jazz / Feb '96 / Cadillac / Pinnacle

BLACK, BROWN AND WHITE
Get back / Black, brown and white / Hey hey (baby) / Stump blues / Willie Mae / Walkin' down a lonesome road / Mopper's blues / I know she will / Hollerin' and cryin' / Blues / Leavin' day / Southbound train / Tomorrow / You changed / Bunny hop / John Henry / Crawdad hop sound / Bill Bailey, won't you please come home / Make my getaway / Jimmy crack corn / Blue tail fly / Blackwater blues / Bessie Smith / In the evening / Trouble in mind
CD 8427432
Mercury / Jan '93 / PolyGram

BLUES, THE (Chicago 1937-1945)(2CD Set)
CD FA 252
Fremeaux / Feb '96 / ADA / Discovery

EVENING WITH BIG BILL BROONZY VOL.1 (Club Montmartre, Copenhagen 1956)
CD STCD 8016
Storyville / May '95 / Cadillac / Jazz Music / Wellard

EVENING WITH BIG BILL BROONZY VOL.2
CD STCD 8017
Storyville / May '95 / Cadillac / Jazz Music / Wellard

GOOD TIME TONIGHT
I can't be satisfied / Long tall Mama / Worrying you off my mind - Part 1 / Too too

train blues / Come home early / Hattie blues / I want my hands on it / Made a date with an angel (got no walking shoe / Horny frog / I believe I'll go back home / Good time tonight / Flat foot Susie with her flat yes yes / WPA rag / Going back to Arkansas / It's a low down dirty shame / Too many drivers / Woodie woodie / Whiskey and good time blues / Merry go round blues / You've got to hick the right lick
CD 4672472
CBS / Oct '90 / Sony

HISTORICAL RECORDINGS 1932-1937
CD 157422
Blues Collection / Feb '93 / Discovery

HOUSE RENT STOMP
Big Bill blues / Little city woman / Back water blues / Guitar shuffle / Romance without finance / Jacqueline / Lonesome / House rent stomp / Willie Mae blues / Saturday evening blues / Louise Louise blues / Key to the highway / Swing low, sweet chariot / Stump blues / Makin' my getaway / Boogie woogie / CC rider / Going down the road feelin' bad / Plowhand blues / I'm gonna move to the outskirts of town / How long blues
CD CD 52007
Blues Encore / '92 / Target/BMG

I CAN'T BE SATISFIED
CD CBCD 005
Collector's Blues / Jun '96 / TKO Magnum

I FEEL SO GOOD
CD IGOCD 2006
Indigo / Nov '94 / ADA / Direct

REMEMBERING BIG BILL BROONZY (The Greatest Minstrel Of The Authentic Blues)
John Henry / Bill Bailey, won't you please come home / Blue tail fly / Leroy Carr / Trouble in mind blues / Stump blues / Get back / Willie Mae / Hey hey / Tomorrow / Walkin' down a lonesome road
CD BGOCD 91
Beat Goes On / Dec '90 / Pinnacle

SINGS FOLK SONGS
CD SFWCD 40023
Smithsonian Folkways / Mar '95 / ADA / Cadillac / CM / Direct / Koch

SOUTHERN BLUES (Charly Blues - Masterworks Vol. 49)
CD CDBM 49
Charly / Jun '93 / Koch

TREAT ME RIGHT
CD TCD 1005
Tradition / Feb '96 / ADA / Vital

YOUNG BIG BILL BROONZY 1928-1935
CD YAZCD 1011
Yazoo / Jun '91 / ADA / CM / Koch

Bros

INTERVIEW COMPACT DISC: BROS
CD CBAK 4017
Baktabak / Nov '89 / Arabesque

Brosnan, John

COOK IN THE KITCHEN, THE
CD JB 01CD
JB / Nov '96 / ADA

Brostrom, Hakan

CELESTIAL NIGHTS
CD DRCD 257
Dragon / Oct '94 / ADA / Cadillac / CM / Roots / Wellard

DARK LIGHT
CD DRAGON 190
Dragon / May '89 / ADA / Cadillac / CM / Roots / Wellard

Brother Boys

BROTHERS BOYS
CD NHD 1101
Zu Zazz / Aug '90 / Rollercoaster

PLOW
Gonna row my boat / I got over the blues / Kiss the dream girl / Alone with you / Twist you up / Then and only then / Hoping that you're hoping / I see love / Blue guitar / Little box / Darkest day / Satellite shack / What will be in the fields tomorrow
CD SHCD 3805
Sugar Hill / Jul '92 / ADA / CM / Direct / Koch / Roots

PRESLEY'S GROCERY
CD SHCD 3844
Sugar Hill / Oct '95 / ADA / CM / Direct / Koch / Roots

Brother Cane

SEEDS
Horses and needles / Hung on a rope / Fools shine on / Kerosene / Breadmaker / Rise on water / 20/20 Faith / Bad seeds / Stain / Intempted / Voice of Eujena / High speed freezin'
CD CDVUS 95
Virgin / Mar '96 / EMI

Brother JT

DOOMSDAY ROCK (Brother JT & Vibrolux)
CD SB 65CD
Siltbreeze / May '97 / Cargo / Vital

MUSIC FOR THE OTHER HEAD (Brother JT & Vibrolux)
Comet / Music for the other head / Blur / Mind (Rot)
CD SB 41
Siltbreeze / Feb '97 / Cargo / Vital

RAINY DAY FUN
CD DFR 030
Drunken Fish / Dec '96 / Cargo

Brother Most

MOOD & INTENSITY
Red rover parts 1&2 / Dead man walking / Dreamscape / Wasn't in the plan / Ready / Bunga nattural
CD GRS 45012
Ichiban / May '96 / Direct / Koch

Brotherhood

ELEMENTALZ
One 3 / Alphabetical response / Nothing in particular / Mad headz / On the move / Goin' undaground / Punk funk / You gotta life / One shot / Incredible / Clunk click / Nominate / Dark stalkers / British accent / Pride (revisited)
CD CDBHOOD 1
Bite It / Feb '96 / EMI

XXIII
CD CDBITE 7
Bite It / Aug '93 / RTM/Disc

Brotherhood Of Breath

LIVE AT WILLISAU
CD OGCD 001
Ogun / Sep '94 / Cadillac / Jazz Music / Wellard

Brotherhood Of Man

20 GREAT HITS
CD CDPT 817
Prestige / May '96 / Else / Total/BMG

BEST OF BROTHERHOOD OF MAN (16 Super Hits)
CD 12210
Laserlight / May '94 / Target/BMG

UNITED WE STAND
CD 8206232
Deram / Jan '96 / PolyGram

VERY BEST OF THE BROTHERHOOD OF MAN
Save your kisses for me / United we stand / Angelo / My sweet Rosalie / When will I see you again / We don't talk anymore / Cahnson d'amour / Bright eyes / Together we are beautiful / Dancing queen / Figaro / Oh boy (the mood I'm in) / Middle of the night / Where are you going to my love / Beautiful lover / How deep is your love / When I need you / Sailing / Without you / Don't go breaking my heart
CD EMPRCD 654
Emporio / Jun '96 / Disc

Brother's Keeper

CONTINUUM
CD WN 1147CD
We Bite / Sep '96 / Plastic Head

Brothers Brooks

BROTHERS BROOKS, THE
CD DOS 7011
Dos / Dec '94 / ADA / CM / Direct

Brothers Johnson

AIN'T WE FUNKIN' NOW
CD VSOPCD 229
Connoisseur Collection / Jun '96 / Pinnacle

Brotzmann, Caspar

HOME
CD BFFP 110CD
Blast First / Jan '95 / RTM/Disc

KOKSOFEN
CD ABBCD 052
Big Cat / Aug '95 / 3mv/Pinnacle

TRIBE, THE
CD ZSCM 08
Special Delivery / Jul '92 / ADA / CM / Direct

ZULU TIME
CD BFFP 129CD
Blast First / Jul '96 / RTM/Disc

Brotzmann, Peter

DARE DEVIL
CD DIW 857
DIW / May '92 / Cadillac / Harmonia Mundi

DIE LIKE A DOG
CD FMPCD 64
FMP / Oct '94 / Cadillac

MACHINE GUN
CD FMPCD 24
FMP / Mar '94 / Cadillac

MARTZ COMBO - LIVE IN WUPPERETAL, THE
CD FMPCD 47
FMP / May '89 / Cadillac

RESERVE
CD FMPCD 17
FMP / Apr '87 / Cadillac

SPREADING BLUSHES OR ACCELERATING ORIGINAL SIN (Brotzmann, Peter & Keiji Haino)
CD PSFD 79
PSF / Oct '96 / Harmonia Mundi

WIE DES LIEBEN SO SPIELD (Brotzmann, Peter & Werner Ludi)
CD FMPCD 22
FMP / Jul '85 / Cadillac

Brou, Roland

CHANTS AND COMPLAINTS DE HAUTE BRETAGNE
CD RS 220
Keltia Musique / May '96 / ADA / Discovery

TROIS GARCONS DU LION D'OR
CD RSCD 220
Keltia Musique / Jul '96 / ADA / Discovery

Broughton, Ben

CONTINUING ADVENTURES OF... (Broughton, Ben & Joe)
CD 101REC 5CD
101 / Dec '96 / ADA

Broughton, Edgar

BANDAGES (Broughton, Edgar Band)
CD CLACD 261
Castle / Jun '92 / BMG

EDGAR BROUGHTON BAND (Broughton, Edgar Band)
CD CSAPCD 109
Connoisseur Collection / Oct '92 / Pinnacle

EDGAR BROUGHTON BAND/IN SIDE OUT (Broughton, Edgar Band)
Evening over rooftops / Birth / Piece of my mind / Poppy / Don't even know what day it is / House of turnabout / Madhatter / Getting hard / What is a woman for / Thinking of you / For Dr Spock (part one) / For Dr Spock (Part two) / Get out of bed / There's nobody there / Side by side / Sister Angela / I got mad / They took it away / Homes fit for heroes / Gone blue / Chilly morning mamma / Rake / Totin this guitar / Double agent / It's not you / Rock 'n' roll
CD BGOCD 179
Beat Goes On / Mar '93 / Pinnacle

LIVE HITS HARDER (Broughton, Edgar Band)
CD 0884948906
CTE / Dec '95 / Koch

OORAH (Broughton, Edgar Band)
CD BGOCD 114
Beat Goes On / Sep '91 / Pinnacle

SING BROTHER SING (Broughton, Edgar Band)
CD BGOCD 7
Beat Goes On / Feb '92 / Pinnacle

SUPERCHIP...PLUS (Broughton, Edgar Band)
Metal Sunday / Superchip / Who only fade away / Curtain / Outrageous behaviour / Not so funny farm / Night hogs / Pratfall / Overdose / Do you wanna be immortal / Subway information / Last electioneer / Ancient homeland / Innocent bystanders / Fourteen the virus
CD SEECD 464
See For Miles/C5 / Oct '96 / Pinnacle

WASA WASA (Broughton, Edgar Band)
CD BGOCD 129
Beat Goes On / Feb '92 / Pinnacle

Broussard, Donny

UNDER THE LOUISIANA MOON
Under the Louisianna moon / Raised like a cajun / Mom and Pop spoke only in French / With her heart / Open the door / Mom, the prettiest rose / Waltz of poor parents / House dance / Music in French / Bayou vermilion / Tears fall like rain
CD SOC 90252
Cajun Sound / Jul '96 / Target/BMG

Brown & Black

BROWN, BLACK AND BLUE
CD VP 162CD
Voiceprint / Nov '96 / Pinnacle

Brown

BROWN
CD RI 036
Rather Interesting / May '96 / Plastic Head

Brown, Angela

ANGELA BROWN LIVE
CD BEST 1038CD
Acoustic Music / Nov '93 / ADA

BREATH TAKING BOOGIE SHAKING (Brown, Angela & A. Humphrey/C. Christl)
CD BEST 1004CD
Acoustic Music / Nov '93 / ADA

WILD TURKEY (Brown, Angela & C. Christl)
CD BEST 1017CD
Acoustic Music / Nov '93 / ADA

Brown, Ari

ULTIMATE FRONTIER
Big V / Lester Bowie's gumbo stew / One for Luba / Meeting time / Ultimate frontier / Sincerity / Motherless child
CD DE 486
Delmark / Jun '97 / ADA / Cadillac / CM / Direct / Hot Shot

Brown, Arthur

CHISHOLM IN MY BOSOM/DANCE
Need to know / Money walk / Let a little sunshine (into your life) / I put a spell on you / She's on my mind / Lord is my saviour / Chisholm in my bosom / We gotta get out of this place / Helen with the sun / Take a chance / Crazy / Hearts and minds / Dance / Out of time / Quietely with tact / Soul garden / Lord will find a way / Is there nothing beyond God
CD SEECD 431
See For Miles/C5 / Aug '95 / Pinnacle

CRAZY WORLD OF ARTHUR BROWN, THE
Nightmare / Fanfare - fire poem / Fire / Come and buy / Time / I put a spell on you / Spontaneous apple creation / Rest cure / I've got money / Child of my kingdom
CD 8337362
Polydor / Feb '91 / PolyGram

GALACTIC ZOO DOSSIER (Kingdom Come)
Internal messenger / Space plucks / Galactic zoo / Metal monster / Simple man / Night of the pigs / Sunrise / Trouble / Brains / Galactic zoo / Space plucks / Galactic zoo / Creep / Creation / Gypsy escape / No time
CD BP 135CD
Blueprint / Nov '96 / Pinnacle

JOURNEY (Kingdom Come)
Time captives / Triangles / Gypsy / Superficial roadblocks / Conception / Spirit of joy / Come alive
CD BP 137CD
Blueprint / Mar '97 / Pinnacle

KINGDOM COME (Kingdom Come)
Teacher / Scientific experiment / Whirl pool / Hymn / Water / City melody / Traffic light song
CD BP 136CD
Blueprint / Aug '96 / Pinnacle

ORDER FROM CHAOS
CD BP 144CD
Blueprint / Sep '96 / Pinnacle

ORDER FROM CHAOS - LIVE 1993
When you open the door / When you open the door / King of England / Juices of love / Nightmare / Fire poem / Fire / Come and buy / Pick it up / Mandela / Time captains / I put a spell on you
CD VP 144CD
Voiceprint / Mar '94 / Pinnacle

REQUIEM
Chant / Shades / Animal people / Spirits take flight / Gabriel / Requiem / Machanicla masseur / Busha-busha / Fire ant and the cockroaches / Tear down the wall / Santa put a spell on me / Pale stars / Chromatic alley / Falling up
CD VP 125 CD
Voiceprint / Feb '93 / Pinnacle

SPEAK NO TECH
King of England / Conversations / Strange romance / Not fade away / Morning was cold / Speak no tech / Names are names / Love lady / Big guns don't die / Take a picture / You don't know / Old friend my colleage / Lost my soul in London / Joined forever / Mandala / Desert floor
CD VPCD 124 CD
Voiceprint / Feb '93 / Pinnacle

STRANGELANDS, THE
CD CDRECK 2
Reckless / Jun '88 / RTM/Disc

Brown, Arthur

MARYLAND TO MOSCOW (Brown, Arthur Jazz Band)
CD RSCD 653
Raymer / Sep '96 / Jazz Music

Brown, Barry

FAR EAST
CD 78249700030
Channel One / Apr '95 / Jet Star

LOVE AND PROTECTION
CD _______________ CDSGP 0182
Prestige / Sep '96 / Else / Total/BMG

Brown, Bessie

BESSIE BROWN 1925-1929/LIZA BROWN 1929 (Brown, Bessie & Liza Brown)
CD _______________ DOCD 5456
Document / Jun '96 / ADA / Hot Shot / Jazz Music

Brown, Bobby

BOBBY
Humpin' around (Prelude) / Humpin' around / Two can play that game / Get away / Till the end of time / Good enough / Pretty little girl / Lovin' you down / One more night / Something in common / That's the way love is / College girl / Storm away / I'm your friend / Humpin' around (mix) / Humpin' around (Epilogue)
CD _______________ MCLD 19300
MCA / Oct '95 / BMG

DON'T BE CRUEL
Don't be cruel / My prerogative / Roni / Rock wit'cha / Every little step / I'll be good to you / All day, all night / Take it slow
CD _______________ MCLD 19212
MCA / Aug '93 / BMG

DON'T BE CRUEL/BOBBY (2CD Set)
Don't be cruel / My perogative / Roni / Rock witcha / Every little step / I'll be good to you / All day, all night / Take it slow / Humpin' around / Two can play that game / Get away / Til the end of time / Good enough / Pretty little girl / Lovin' you down / One more night / Something in common / That's the way love is / College girl / Storm away / I'm your friend
CD Set _______________ MCD 33730
MCA / Jul '96 / BMG

Brown, Bobby

CAPE BRETON FIDDLE COMPANY (Brown, Bobby & Cape Breton Fiddlers)
Selection of reels / Selection of jigs / Clog strathspey & reel / Hornpipe medley / Pastoral strathspey / Polk medley no.2 / March and reel medley / Slow air / Strathspey & reel medley / Clog & hornpipe medley
CD _______________ LCOM 5251
Lismor / Feb '96 / ADA / Direct / Duncans / Lismor

Brown, Bundy

DIRECTIONS IN MUSIC (Brown, Bundy & Doug Scharin/James Warden)
CD _______________ THRILL 033CD
Thrill Jockey / Jul '97 / Cargo / Greyhound

Brown, Charles

CHARLES BROWN LIVE
Quicksand / Saving my love for you / Seven days long / Just the way you are / Black night / So long / Cottage for sale / Brown's boogie
CD _______________ CDCBL 757
Charly / Oct '95 / Koch

CLASSICS 1944-1945
CD _______________ CLASSICS 894
Classics / Sep '96 / Discovery / Jazz Music

COOL CHRISTMAS BLUES
CD _______________ BBCD 9561
Bullseye Blues / Nov '94 / Direct

DRIFTING AND DREAMING (Brown, Charles & Johnny Moore's Three Blazers)
Travellin' blues / I'll get along somehow / Copyright on your love / If you should ever leave / When your lover has gone / Blues because of you / Sail on blues / More than you know / You should show me the way / It had to be you / You are my first love / You won't let me go / Make believe land / So long / Warsaw concerto (part 1) / Warsaw concerto (part 2) / You left me forsaken / How deep is the ocean / Nutmeg / It's the talk of the town / What do you know about love
CD _______________ CDCHD 589
Ace / Jan '96 / Pinnacle

HONEYDRIPPER, THE
CD _______________ 5298482
Verve / Apr '96 / PolyGram

I'M GONNA PUSH ON (Live at Nosebacke) (Brown, Charles & Hjartslag)
Teardrops from my eyes / Black night / Please don't drive me away / Trouble blues / Please come home for Christmas / Just the way you are / Bad bad whiskey / I'm gonna push on / I wanna go back home to Gothenburg / I'll do my best
CD _______________ RBD 200
Stockholm / Jan '91 / CM / Swift

JUST A LUCKY SO 'N' SO
CD _______________ BB 9521CD
Bullseye Blues / Feb '94 / Direct

THESE BLUES
These blues / Honey / May I never love again / I got it bad and that ain't good / Is you is or is you ain't my baby / Hundred years from today / Save your love for me / I did my best for you / Sunday kind of love
CD _______________ 5230222
Verve / Oct '94 / PolyGram

Brown, Clarence

GATE SWINGS (Brown, Clarence 'Gatemouth')
CD _______________ 5376172
Verve / Jul '97 / PolyGram

GATE'S ON THE HEAT (Brown, Clarence 'Gatemouth')
Gate's on the heat / Man and his environment / Funky Mama / Please Mr. Nixon / St. Louis blues / Jelly jelly / Drifter / One mint julep / Dollar got the blues / River's invitation / Never ending love for you / Louisiana breakdown
CD _______________ 5197302
Verve / Feb '94 / PolyGram

LIVE (Brown, Clarence 'Gatemouth')
CD _______________ CDCBL 753
Charly / Jan '95 / Koch

LONG WAY HOME (Brown, Clarence 'Gatemouth')
CD _______________ 5294652
Verve / Mar '96 / PolyGram

MAN, THE (Brown, Clarence 'Gatemouth')
CD _______________ 5237612
PolyGram Jazz / Feb '95 / PolyGram

NO LOOKING BACK (Brown, Clarence 'Gatemouth')
Better off with the blues / Digging new ground / Dope / My own prison / Stop time / C jam blues / Straighten up and fly right / Peeper / Blue gummed catahoula (alligator eating boy) / I will be your friend / We're outta here
CD _______________ ALCD 4804
Alligator / May '93 / ADA / CM / Direct

ONE MORE MILE (Brown, Clarence 'Gatemouth')
Information blues / Song for Renee / Stranded / Sunrise cajun style / Big yard / Ain't that dandy / One more mile / Ronettes / Flippin' out / Neat baku
CD _______________ ROUCD 2034
Rounder / '88 / ADA / CM / Direct

ORIGINAL PEACOCK RECORDINGS (Brown, Clarence 'Gatemouth')
CD _______________ ROUCD 2039
Rounder / '88 / ADA / CM / Direct

PRESSURE COOKER (Brown, Clarence 'Gatemouth')
CD _______________ ALCD 4745
Alligator / May '93 / ADA / CM / Direct

REAL LIFE (Brown, Clarence 'Gatemouth')
Real Life / Okie Dokie stomp / Frankie and Johnny / Next time you see me / Take the 'A' train / Please send me someone to love / Catfish / St. Louis blues / What a shame what a shame
CD _______________ ROUCD 2054
Rounder / '88 / ADA / CM / Direct

STANDING MY GROUND (Brown, Clarence 'Gatemouth')
CD _______________ ALCD 4779
Alligator / May '93 / ADA / CM / Direct

TEXAS SWING (Brown, Clarence 'Gatemouth')
CD _______________ ROUCD 11527
Rounder / '88 / ADA / CM / Direct

Brown, Cleo

LEGENDARY CLEO BROWN, THE
(Lookie lookie) here comes Cookie / You're a heavenly thing / (You take the East, take the West, take the North) I'll take / Stuff is here and it's mellow / Pinetop's boogie woogie / Pelican stomp / Never too tired for love / Give a broken heart a break / Mama don't want no peas an' rice an' coconut oil / Me and my wonderful one / When Hollywood goes black and tan / When / You're my fever / Breakin' in a pair of shoes / Latch on / Love in the first degree / My gal Mezzanine
CD _______________ PLCD 548
President / Nov '96 / Grapevine/PolyGram / President / Target/BMG

LIVING IN THE AFTERGLOW (Brown, Cleo & Marian McPartland)
CD _______________ ACD 216
Audiophile / Jun '96 / Jazz Music

Brown, Clifford

BEGINNING AND THE END, THE
I come from Jamaica / Ida red / Walkin' / Night in Tunisia / Donna Lee
CD _______________ 4777372
Columbia / Oct '94 / Sony

BIRDLAND 21/2/1954 (Brown, Clifford & Art Blakey)
CD _______________ CD 53033
Giants Of Jazz / Mar '90 / Cadillac / Jazz Music / Target/BMG

BROWNIE (The Complete EmArCy Recordings Of Clifford Brown/10CD Set)
Delilah / Darn that dream / Parisian thoroughfare / Jordu / Sweet Clifford / Sweet Clifford (Clifford's fantasy) / I don't stand a ghost of a chance with you / I don't stand a ghost of a chance with you / Stompin' at the Savoy / I get a kick out of you / I get a kick out of you / I'll string along with you / Joy spring / Joy spring / Mildama / Mildama / Mildama mildama / Mildama / Mildama mildama / These foolish things / Daahoud / Daahoud / Coronado / Coronado / Coronado / You go to my head / Caravan / Caravan (the boss man) / I've got you New York / What is this thing called love / I've got you under my skin / No more / Darn that dream / You go to my head / My funny valentine / Don't worry 'bout me / Bess you is my woman now / It might as well be Spring / Lover come back to me / Alone together / Summertime / Come rain or come shine / Crazy he calls me / There is no greater love / I'll remember April / September song / Lullaby of Birdland / Lullaby of Birdland / I'm glad there is you / You're not the kind / Jim / He's my guy / April in Paris / It's crazy / Embraceable you / Don't explain / Born to be blue / You'd be so nice to come home to / 'S wonderful / Yesterdays / Falling in love with love / What's new / Gerkin for perkin / Take the 'A' train / Land's End / Land's End / Swingin' / George's dilemma / If I love again / Blues walk / Blues walk / What am I here for / Cherokee / Jacqui / Sandu / Gertrude's bounce / Step / Lightly (Junior's arrival) / Powell's prances / I'll remember April / I'll remember April / I'll remember April / Time / Scene is clean / Flossie Lou / Flossie Lou / Flossie Lou / What is this thing called love / What is this thing called love / Love is a many splendored thing / Love is a many splendored thing / Love is a many splendored thing
CD Set _______________ 8383062
EmArCy / Jul '93 / PolyGram

CLIFFORD BROWN MEMORIAL (Various Artists)
Stockholm sweetnin' / 'Scuse these blues / Falling in love with love / Lover come back to me / Philly JJ / Dial B for beauty / Theme of no repeat / Choose now
CD _______________ OJCCD 1729
Original Jazz Classics / Mar '94 / Complete/ Pinnacle / Jazz Music / Wellard

COMPLETE BLUE NOTE AND PACIFIC JAZZ RECORDINGS, THE (4CD Set)
Bellarosa / Carvin' the rock / Carvin' the rock / Cookin' / Cookin' / Brownie speaks / De-dah / You go to my head / Carvin' the rock / Wail bait / Wail bait / Hymn of the Orient / Brownie eyes / Cherokee / Cherokee / Easy living / Minor mood / Hymn of the Orient / Capri / Capri / Lovr man / Turnpike / Turnpike / Sketch one / It could happen to you / Get happy / Get happy / Daahoud / Finders keepers / Joy spring / Gone with the wind / Bones for Jones / Blueberry hill / Tiny capers / Tiny capers / Split kick / Once in a while / Quicksilver / Wee dot / Blues / Night in Tunisia / Mayreh / Wee dot / If I had you / Quicksilver / Way you look tonight / Lou's blues / Now's the time / Confirmation
CD Set _______________ CDP 8341952
Blue Note / Oct '95 / EMI

COMPLETE PARIS SESSIONS VOL.1, THE (Original Vogue Masters)
Brown skins / Deltitnu / Keeping up with Joneses / Conception / All the things you are / I cover the waterfront / Goofin' with me
CD _______________ 74321457282
Vogue / May '97 / BMG

COMPLETE PARIS SESSIONS VOL.2, THE
Minority / Salute to the band box / Strictly romantic / Baby / Quick step / Bum's rush / No start, no end
CD _______________ 74321154622
Vogue / Oct '93 / BMG

JAZZ MASTERS (Brown, Clifford & Max Roach)
CD _______________ 5281092
Verve / Mar '96 / PolyGram

WITH STRINGS
Yesterdays / Laura / Blue moon / Can't help lovin' dat man / Embraceable you / Willow weep for me / Smoke gets in your eyes / Portrait of Jennie / Memories of you
CD _______________ 8146422
EmArCy / Mar '93 / PolyGram

Brown, D.R.

LIVE IN THE MIND'S EYE
CD _______________ BEARD 005CD
Beard / Oct '92 / Pinnacle

Brown, Dennis

20 GOLDEN GREATS
CD _______________ CDSGP 0104
Prestige / Oct '94 / Else / Total/BMG

20 MAGNIFICENT HITS
CD _______________ DBP 1CD
Dennis Brown Productions / Jul '93 / Jet Star

ANOTHER DAY IN PARADISE
(Sittin' on the) dock of the bay / Last thing on my mind / Just a guy / My girl / Everybody needs love / Ain't that lovin' you / Another day in paradise / Queen Majesty / I'm still waiting / Conversation / Green green grass of home / Girl I got a date
CD _______________ CDTRL 310
Trojan / Mar '94 / Direct / Jet Star

AT THE PENTHOUSE (Brown, Dennis & Leroy Smart)
CD _______________ RN 7024
Rhino / Jun '97 / Grapevine/PolyGram / Jet Star

BEAUTIFUL MORNING
CD _______________ WRCD 002
World / Jun '97 / Jet Star / TKO Magnum

BEST OF DENNIS BROWN VOL.1, THE
CD _______________ 60042
Declic / Nov '95 / Jet Star

BEST OF DENNIS BROWN VOL.2, THE
CD _______________ 60052
Declic / Nov '95 / Jet Star

BEST OF DENNIS BROWN, THE
CD _______________ JMGL 6048
Joe Gibbs / Jan '94 / Jet Star

BEST OF DENNIS BROWN, THE
CD _______________ CB 6004
Caribbean / Jan '96 / TKO Magnum

BLAZING
CD _______________ GRELCD 171
Greensleeves / May '92 / Jet Star / SRD

BROWN SUGAR
CD _______________ RASCD 3207
Ras / '88 / Direct / Greensleeves / Jet Star / SRD

CLASSIC HITS
CD _______________ SONCD 0022
Sonic Sounds / Apr '92 / Jet Star

COSMIC FORCE
CD _______________ HBCD 135
Heartbeat / Apr '93 / ADA / Direct / Greensleeves / Jet Star

COULD IT BE
CD _______________ VPCD 1478
VP / May '96 / Greensleeves / Jet Star / Total/BMG

CROWN PRINCE OF REGGAE
Westbound train / Wolf and leopards / Cassandra / Silhouettes / No more will I roam / Tribulation / Let me down easy / Without you / Rock with me Deborah / Rolling down / Black magic woman / Go now / Melting pot / Song my Mother used to sing / You're no good / How could I let you get away / Love you madly / I didn't know / Only a smile / Africa
CD _______________ CPCD 8187
Charly / Oct '96 / Koch

CROWN PRINCE, THE
CD _______________ WRCD 015
World / Jun '97 / Jet Star / TKO Magnum

DENNIS BROWN LIVE AT MONTREUX
So jah say / Wolves and leopards / Ain't that lovin' you / Words of wisdom / Drifter / Milk and honey / Yabby you / Don't feel no way / Whip them Jah / Money in my pocket
CD _______________ CDBM 016
Blue Moon / Apr '91 / Cadillac / Discovery / Greensleeves / Jazz Music / Jet Star / TKO Magnum

FACTS OF LIFE
CD _______________ DIACD 0002
Diamond / Feb '95 / Discovery

FOUL PLAY
CD _______________ JGMLCD 4850
Joe Gibbs / Jan '94 / Jet Star

FRIENDS FOR LIFE
CD _______________ SHCD 45004
Shanachie / Jun '93 / ADA / Greensleeves / Koch

GIVE PRAISES
CD _______________ CDTZ 012
Tappa / Aug '93 / Jet Star

GOOD TONIGHT
CD _______________ GRELCD 152
Greensleeves / Aug '90 / Jet Star / SRD

GREATEST HITS
CD _______________ RRTGCD 7709
Rohit / '88 / Jet Star

HEAVEN
CD _______________ 8412952
Declic / May '96 / Jet Star

HIT AFTER HIT
CD _______________ RGCD 027
Rocky One / Feb '95 / Jet Star

HOTTER FLAMES (Brown, Dennis & Frankie Paul)
CD _______________ VPCD 1310
VP / Aug '93 / Greensleeves / Jet Star / Total/BMG

I DON'T KNOW
CD ______ DGVCD 1600
Dynamite & Grapevine / Oct '95 / Grapevine/PolyGram / Greensleeves / Jet Star

IF I DIDN'T LOVE
CD ______ JMC 200202
Jamaican Gold / Dec '92 / Grapevine/PolyGram / Jet Star

IT'S THE RIGHT TIME
CD ______ RNCD 2021
Rhino / Sep '93 / Grapevine/PolyGram / Jet Star

JOSEPH'S COAT OF MANY COLOURS
Slave driver / Open your eyes / Creator / Cup of tea / Together brothers / Oh what a day / Well without water / Three meals a day / Home sweet home / Man next door
CD ______ CDBM 010
Blue Moon / Nov '88 / Cadillac / Discovery / Greensleeves / Jazz Music / Jet Star / TKO Magnum

JOY IN THE MORNING
CD ______ LG 21106
Lagoon / Mar '95 / Grapevine/PolyGram

JUDGE NOT (Brown, Dennis & Gregory Isaacs)
Crazy list: *Brown, Dennis* / Judge not: *Brown, Dennis* / Deceiving girl: *Brown, Dennis* / Live and love: *Isaacs, Gregory* / Street walker: *Isaacs, Gregory* / Inner city lady: *Isaacs, Gregory*
CD ______ GRELCD 72
Greensleeves / Sep '88 / Jet Star / SRD

LIGHT MY FIRE
CD ______ CDHB 154
Heartbeat / May '94 / ADA / Direct / Greensleeves / Jet Star

LIMITED EDITION
CD ______ GRELCD 177
Greensleeves / Nov '92 / Jet Star / SRD

LIVE IN MONTEGO BAY
CD ______ SONCD 0039
Sonic Sounds / Jan '93 / Jet Star

LOVE LIGHT
Little bit more / Tribulation / Rocking time / Caress me girl / Love light / Hold on to what you've got / Little village / Have you ever been in love
CD ______ CDBM 102
Blue Moon / Apr '95 / Cadillac / Discovery / Greensleeves / Jazz Music / Jet Star / TKO Magnum

LOVER'S PARADISE
CD ______ CDSGP 068
Prestige / Oct '93 / Else / Total/BMG

MILK AND HONEY
CD ______ RASCD 3193
Ras / Feb '96 / Direct / Greensleeves / Jet Star / SRD

MONEY IN MY POCKET
Money in my pocket / Ah so we stay / Changing times / Silhouettes / Africa / Yagga yagga (you'll suffer) / I am the conqueror / Show us the way / Cassandra / No more will I roam
CD ______ CDTRL 197
Trojan / Mar '94 / Direct / Jet Star

MUSICAL HEATWAVE
Baby don't do it / What about the half / Don't you cry / Cheater / Let love in / Concentration / Silhouettes / He can't spell / Musical heatwave / I don't know / How could I let you get away / Lips of wine / Let me down easy / Changing times / Black magic woman / Money in my pocket / It's too late / Song my mother used to sing / Westbound train / Cassandra / I am the conqueror / No more will I roam / Why seek more / Moving away
CD ______ CDTRL 327
Trojan / Mar '94 / Direct / Jet Star

MY TIME
CD ______ RRTGCD 7713
Rohit / Jan '89 / Jet Star

NO CONTEST (Brown, Dennis & Gregory Isaacs)
CD ______ GRELCD 133
Greensleeves / Jul '89 / Jet Star / SRD

NOTHING LIKE THIS
There's nothing like this / Have you ever been in love / Rock 'n' roll lady / Dance nah keep / Come home / Slave driver / Come let me love you / Street kid / Give love a chance / People of the world / It's not a one man thing
CD ______ GRELCD 199
Greensleeves / Feb '94 / Jet Star / SRD

ONE OF A KIND
CD ______ 111912
Musidisc / Mar '94 / Discovery

OPEN THE GATE (Greatest Hits Vol.2)
Words: *Davis, Anthony 'Sangie' & Lee 'Scratch' Perry* / Vampire: *Irons, Devon & Dr. Alimantado* / Babylon falling: *Heptones* / Babylon falling version: *Upsetters* / Mistry Babylon: *Heptones* / Mistry Babylon version: *Upsetters* / Garden of life: *Sibbles, Leroy* / History: *Jackson, Carlton* / Sons of slaves: *Delgado, Junior* / Open the gate: *Burnett, Watty* / Talk about it: *Diamonds* / Yama-ky: *Upsetters* / Cherry oh baby: *Donaldson, Eric* / Rainy night in Portland: *Burnett, Watty* / Ruffer ruff: *Smart, Horace* / Ruffer dub: *Upsetters* / Neckodeemus: *Congos* / Know love: *Twin Roots* / City too hot: *Perry, Lee 'Scratch'* / Bionic rats: *Perry, Lee 'Scratch'* / Bad weed: *Murvin, Junior*
CD ______ CDHB 177
Heartbeat / Apr '95 / ADA / Direct / Greensleeves / Jet Star

OVERPROOF
CD ______ SHCD 43086
Shanachie / Jun '91 / ADA / Greensleeves / Koch

PRIME OF DENNIS BROWN, THE
CD ______ MCCD 118
Music Club / Aug '93 / Disc / THE

RAS PORTRAITS
Milk and honey / Sitting and watching / Should I / Give thanks to the Father / Revolution / Your love / Easy / Sea of love / Victory is mine / Wisdom / Hold on to what you've got
CD ______ RAS 3322
Ras / Jul '97 / Direct / Greensleeves / Jet Star / SRD

REGGAE MAX
CD ______ JSRNCD 11
Jet Star / Mar '97 / Jet Star

SARGE
CD ______ JASCD 4
Sarge / Mar '97 / Jet Star

SLOW DOWN
Slow down / Woman / Joy in the morning / They fight / Let's build our dreams / Love by the score / Can't keep a good man down / Icy road / Now and forever / Come on over / Africa we want to go
CD ______ GRELCD 80
Greensleeves / Feb '87 / Jet Star / SRD

SMILE LIKE AN ANGEL
Let me live / Pretend you're happy / Westbound train / Don't expect me to be your friend / Play girl / Smile like an angel / Poorer side of town / We will be free / Summertime / Silver words / My kind / Golden streets
CD ______ CDBM 034
Blue Moon / Jun '95 / Cadillac / Discovery / Greensleeves / Jazz Music / Jet Star / TKO Magnum

SO AMAZING (Brown, Dennis & Janet Kay)
CD ______ CDTRL 315
Trojan / Mar '94 / Direct / Jet Star

SOME LIKE IT HOT
CD ______ HBCD 107
Heartbeat / Nov '92 / ADA / Direct / Greensleeves / Jet Star

SONGS OF EMANUEL
CD ______ SONCD 0082
Sonic Sounds / Apr '96 / Jet Star

TEMPERATURE RISING
CD ______ CDTRL 353
Trojan / Jun '95 / Direct / Jet Star

TOGETHER AS ONE
CD ______ RGCD 043
Rocky One / Apr '97 / Jet Star

TRAVELLING MAN VOL.2, THE
CD ______ CB 6005
Caribbean / Jan '96 / TKO Magnum

UNCHALLENGED
CD ______ GRELCD 138
Greensleeves / Oct '89 / Jet Star / SRD

UNFORGETTABLE
CD ______ CRCD 24
Charm / Sep '93 / Jet Star

VICTORY IS MINE
Victory is mine / Call me / We are in love / Don't give up / Everyday people / Sea of love / Just because / Should I / Jah can do it / Sad news
CD ______ CDBM 084
Blue Moon / Apr '91 / Cadillac / Discovery / Greensleeves / Jazz Music / Jet Star / TKO Magnum

VISION OF THE REGGAE KING
CD ______ GOLDCD 001
Goldmine / Jun '94 / Jet Star

WOLVES AND LEOPARDS
Wolves and leopards / Emanuel / Here I come / Whip them Jah / Created by the Father / Party time / Rolling down / Boasting / Children of Israel / Lately girl
CD ______ CDBM 046
Blue Moon / Apr '87 / Cadillac / Discovery / Greensleeves / Jazz Music / Jet Star / TKO Magnum

YOU GOT THE BEST OF ME
CD ______ SAXCD 004
Saxon Studio / Oct '95 / Jet Star

Brown, Earl

SYNERGY
CD ______ ARTCD 6177
Hat Art / Dec '95 / Cadillac / Harmonia Mundi

TWENTY FIVE PAGES
CD ______ WER 66122
Wergo / Jul '97 / ADA / Cadillac / Harmonia Mundi

Brown, Florie

IRISH FIDDLE TUNES
CD ______ EUCD 1308
ARC / Jul '95 / ADA / ARC Music

Brown, Foxy

ILL NA NA
Intro chicken coop / (Hol matrimony) Letter to the firm / Foxy's bell / Get me home / Promise / Interlude the set up / If I / Chase / Ill na na / No on'es / Fox boogie / I'll be / Outro
CD ______ 5336842
Def Jam / Dec '96 / PolyGram

Brown, Gabriel

MEAN OLD BLUES 1943-1949
CD ______ FLYCD 59
Flyright / Jun '96 / Hot Shot / Jazz Music / Wellard

Brown, Gerry

LIVE AT THE EXCISE HOUSE (Brown, Gerry Mission Hall Jazzband)
CD ______ RSCD 656
Raymer / Mar '97 / Jazz Music

Brown, Glen

CHECK THE WINNER
CD ______ GRELCD 603
Greensleeves / May '90 / Jet Star / SRD

SENSI DUB VOL.6 (Brown, Glen & Roots Radics)
CD ______ OMCD 26
Original Music / Feb '93 / Jet Star / SRD

TERMINATION DUB (Glen Brown 1973-1979) (Brown, Glen & King Tubby)
CD ______ BAFCD 15
Blood & Fire / Mar '97 / Vital

WAY TO MOUNT ZION, THE
CD ______ RUSCD 8215
ROIR / Oct '95 / Plastic Head / Shellshock/Disc

Brown, Greg

44 AND 66
CD ______ RHRCD 02
Red House / Oct '96 / ADA / Koch

BATH TUB BLUES
CD ______ RHRCD 42
Red House / Oct '96 / ADA / Koch

DOWN IN THERE
CD ______ RHRCD 35
Red House / Oct '96 / ADA / Koch

FURTHER IN
CD ______ RHRCD 88
Red House / Oct '96 / ADA / Koch
CD ______ 8425802
Sky Ranch / Apr '97 / Discovery

IN THE DARK WITH YOU
CD ______ RHRCD 08
Red House / Oct '96 / ADA / Koch

IOWA WALTZ, THE
CD ______ RHRCD 01
Red House / Oct '95 / ADA / Koch

LIVE ONE, THE
CD ______ RHRCD 78
Red House / Dec '95 / ADA / Koch

ONE BIG TOWN
CD ______ RHRCD 28
Red House / Oct '96 / ADA / Koch

ONE MORE GOODNIGHT KISS
CD ______ RHRCD 23
Red House / Oct '96 / ADA / Koch

POET GAME, THE
CD ______ RHRCD 68
Red House / May '95 / ADA / Koch
CD ______ 8401422
Sky Ranch / Sep '96 / Discovery

SONGS OF INNOCENCE AND EXPERIENCE
CD ______ RHRCD 14
Red House / Oct '96 / ADA / Koch

Brown, Herschel

COMPLETE HERSCHEL BROWN 1928-1929, THE
CD ______ DOCD 8001
Document / Jan '97 / ADA / Hot Shot / Jazz Music

Brown, Horace

HORACE BROWN
Why why why / How can we stop: *Brown, Horace & Faith Evans* / Things we do for love / I want your baby / One for the money / Taste your love / Trippin' / I like / Just let me know / Gotta find a way / You need a man / Enjoy
CD ______ 5306942
Motown / Jun '96 / PolyGram

Brown, Hylo

HYLO BROWN 1954-1960 (2CD Set) (Brown, Hylo & The Timberliners)
Flower blooming in the wildwood / Put my little shoes away / Blue eyed darling / Will the angels play their harps for me / Old home town / Love and wealth / I'll be all smiles tonight / Gathering flowers from the hillside / Little Joe / Darling Nellie across the sea / When it's lamplighting time in the valley / Why do you weep dear willow / Test of love / Dark as a dungeon / Lost to a stranger / Sweethearts or strangers / In the clay beneath the tomb / Wrong kind of life / I'll be broken hearted / Let's stop fooling our hearts / Lovesick and sorrow / Get lost, you wolf / One sided love affair / Only one / Prisoner's song / Nobody's darlin' but mine / One way train / Foolish pride / John Henry / There's more pretty girls than one / Stone wall (around my heart) / Shuffle of my feet / Your crazy heart / You can't relive the past / I've waited as long as i can / It's all over but the crying / Thunder clouds of love / Just any old love / Darlin' how can you forget so soon / Sweethearts and strangers: *Brown, Hylo & The Jordanaires*
CD Set ______ BCD 15572
Bear Family / Mar '92 / Direct / Rollercoaster / Swift

Brown, James

BEST OF JAMES BROWN, THE
CD ______ MACCD 228
Autograph / Aug '96 / BMG

COLD SWEAT
Give it up or turn it loose / Too funky in here / Gonna have a funky good time / Try me / Get on the good foot / Get up offa that thing / Georgia on my mind / Hot pants / I got the feelin' / It's a man's man's man's world / Cold sweat / I can't stand it / Papa's got a brand new bag / I feel good / Please please please / Jam
CD ______ HADCD 164
Javelin / May '94 / Henry Hadaway / THE

COLD SWEAT (The Best Of James Brown Live)
Introduction/Give it up or turn it loose / It's too funky here / Doing it to death / Try me / Get on the good foot / Get up offa that thing / Georgia on my mind / Hot pants / I got the feelin' / It's a man's man's man's world / Cold sweat / I can't stand myself (when you touch me) / Papa's got a brand new bag / I got you (I feel good) / Please, please, please / Jam
CD ______ 305802
Hallmark / Oct '96 / Carlton

COLLECTION, THE
CD ______ COL 003
Collection / Mar '95 / Target/BMG

EARLY STUDIO HITS (2CD Set)
Bells / I don't mind / Just you and me darling / Lost someone / I love you yes I do / Come over here / Dancin' little thing / I do just what I want / So long / Tell me what you're gonna do / Love don't love nobody / You don't have to go / Papa's got a brand new pig bag / Sex machine / Bodyheat / Gonna have a funky good time / Give it up, or turn it loose / It's too funky in here / Doing it to death / Try me / Get on the good foot / Get up offa that thing / Georgia on my mind / Hot pants / I got the feelin / It's a man's man's man's world / Cold sweat / I can't stand myself (when you touch me) / I got you (I feel good) / Please please please / I am
CD Set ______ DBG 53045
Double Gold / May '96 / Target/BMG

ESSENTIAL COLLECTION, THE
CD Set ______ LECD 623
Wisepack / Apr '95 / Conifer/BMG / THE

FUNKY GOODTIME (Live In Atlanta 1984)
It's a man's man's man's world / Super bad / Disco rap / Turn it loose (Give it up) / It's too funky in here / Gonna have a funky good time / Try me / I got the feeling / Get on the good foot / Prisoner of love / Get up offa that thing / Georgia on my mind / Cold sweat / When you touch me (I can't stand myself) / Papa's got a brand new bag / I got you (I feel good)
CD ______ PLATCD 153
Platinum / Mar '96 / Prism

FUNKY PRESIDENT (The Very Best Of James Brown Vol.2)
Funky President / Try me / My thang / Body heat / Talkin' loud and sayin' nothing / There was a time / Doing it to death / Payback / Soul power / I got the feeling / Honky tonk / Get up, get into it and get involved / I got ants in my pants / Funky drummer / It's a new day
CD ______ 5198542
Polydor / Mar '96 / PolyGram

GODFATHER OF SOUL, THE
It's a man's man's man's world / Papa's got a brand new bag / Nature boy / Think / Signed, sealed, delivered (I'm yours) / Please please please / How do you stop / Call me super bad / Spinning wheel / Mona Lisa / This old heart / Good good lovin' / Bewildered / (Get up I feel like being a) sex machine

CD 5500402
Spectrum / May '93 / PolyGram

GODFATHER OF SOUL, THE
CD 100099
Scratch / Mar '95 / Koch / Scratch/BMG

GODFATHER OF SOUL, THE
It's a man's man's man's world / Super bad / Disco rap / Turn it loose (give it up) / It's too funky in here / Gonna have a funky good time / Try me / I got the feelin' / Get on the good foot / Prisoner of love / Get up offa that thing / Georgia on my mind
CD MUCD 9009
Musketeer / Apr '95 / Disc

GODFATHER RETURNS, THE
Get up offa that thing / Hey America / Stormy Monday / Body heat / For once in my life / What the world needs now is love / Back stabbin' / Hot pants / Stagger Lee / Need your love so bad / Woman / Never can say goodbye / Time after time / Georgia on my mind
CD 5501992
Spectrum / Sep '94 / PolyGram

I'M REAL
Tribute / I'm real / Static / Time to get busy / She looks all types a good / Keep keepin' / Can't get enuff / It's your money / Godfather running the joint
CD 8347552
Polydor / Jun '88 / PolyGram

IN THE JUNGLE GROOVE
It's a new day / Funky drummer / Give it up or turn it loose(remix) / I got to move / Talking loud and saying nothing(remix) / Get up, get into it and get involved / Soul power (re-edit) / Hot pants
CD 8296242
Urban / May '88 / PolyGram

JAMES BROWN
CD EXP 003
Experience / May '97 / TKO Magnum

JAMES BROWN AT STUDIO 54
Gonna have a funky good time / Get up offa that thing / Body heat / (Get on up I feel like being a) Sex machine / Try me / Papa's got a brand new bag / Get on the good foot / Medley / Medley
CD CPCD 8031
Charly / Jan '95 / Koch

JAMES BROWN LIVE
Give it up or turn it loose / It's a man's man's man's world / I got the feelin' / I can't stand it / Hot pants / Try me / I feel good today / Get up offa that thing / Please please please / Jam / Cold sweat / Georgia on my mind / It's too funky in here / Gonna have a funky good time / Get on the good foot / (Get up I feel like being a) sex machine
CD 15136
Laserlight / Jun '93 / Target/BMG

JAMES BROWN LIVE (The Godfather Of Soul & Funk)
CD IMT 100099
Scratch / Sep '96 / Koch / Scratch/BMG

JAMES BROWN LIVE
Give it up, turn it loose / Too funky in here / Gonna have a funky good time / Try me / Get on the good foot / Get up offa that thing / Hot pants / I got the feeling / It's a man's man's man's world / Cold sweat / I can't stand it / Papa's got a brand new bag / I feel good / Please please please / Jam
CD SUMCD 4027
Summit / Nov '96 / Sound & Media

LIVE AT THE APOLLO VOL.1
Intro/Opening fanfare / Try me / I don't mind / Lost someone / Night train / I'll go crazy / Think / Medley / Outro/Closing fanfare
CD 8434792
Polydor / Jul '90 / PolyGram

LIVE IN CONCERT
Give it up or turn it loose / It's too funky in here / Doing it to death (gonna have a funky good time) / Try me / Get on the good foot / Prisoner of love / Get up offa that thing / Georgia on my mind / I got the feelin' / It's a man's man's man's world / Super bad / Disco rap / Cold sweat / I can't stand myself (when you touch me) / Papa's got a brand new bag / I got you (I feel good)
CD QED 028
Tring / Nov '96 / Tring

MESSIN' WITH THE BLUES (2CD Set)
Like it is, like it was / Don't cry baby / Caldonia / Somebody done changed the lock on my door / Ain't nobody here but us chickens / Good rockin' tonight / I love you, yes I do / Messing with the blues / Waiting in vain / For you, my love / Blues for my baby / Every day I have the blues / Love don't love nobody / Goin' home / Have mercy baby / Bells / Don't deceive me / Things that I used to do / Need your love so bad / Like a baby / Honky tonk / Suffering with the blues / Further on up the road / Radio spot / Talk to me / Kansas City / Wonder when you're coming home
CD Set 8472582
Polydor / Dec '90 / PolyGram

ON STAGE (2CD Set)
Gonna have a funky good time (doing it to death) / Get up offa that thing / Body heat / Sex machine / Try me / Papa's got a brand new bag / Get on the good foot / Medley / I got the feeling / Cold sweat / Please, please, please / Jam / Medley / Introduction/Give it up or turn it loose / It's too funky in here / Doing it to death / Try me / Get on the good foot / Get up offa that thing / Georgia on my mind / Hot pants / I got the feelin' / It's a man's man's man's world / Cold sweat / I can't stand myself (when you touch me) / Papa's got a brand new bag / I got you (I feel good) / Please, please, please / Jam
CD Set CPCD 82562
Charly / Nov '96 / Koch

PEARLS FROM THE PAST
CD KLMCD 018
BAM / Apr '94 / Koch / Scratch/BMG

SEX MACHINE (The Very Best Of James Brown Vol.1)
Please please please / Think / Night train / Out of sight / Papa's got a brand new bag (part 1) / I got you (I feel good) / It's a man's man's man's world / Cold sweat / Say it loud, I'm black and I'm proud / Hey America / Make it funky / (Get up I feel like being a) sex machine / I'm a greedy man / Get on the good foot / Get up offa that thing / It's too funky in here / Livin' in America / I'm real / Hot pants / soul power
CD 8458282
Polydor / Nov '91 / PolyGram

SLAUGHTER'S BIG RIP OFF (Original Soundtrack)
Slaughter theme / Tryin' to get over / Transmografication / Happy for the poor / Brother rap / Big strong / Really really really / Sexy sexy sexy / To my brother / How long can I keep it up / Peole get up and drive your funky soul / King slaughter / Straight ahead
CD 3145171362
Polydor / Aug '96 / PolyGram

SOUL JUBILEE (Live At Chastain Park/ 25th Anniversary Concert) (Brown, James & The Soul G's)
Give it up or turn it loose / It's too funky in here / Try me / Get on the good foot / Get up offa that thing / Georgia on my mind / Hot pants / I got the feelin' / It's a man's man's man's world / Cold sweat / I can't stand myself (when you touch me) / Papa's got a brand new bag / I got you (I feel good) / Please please please / Jam
CD CDBM 081
Blue Moon / Apr '90 / Cadillac / Discovery / Greensleeves / Jazz Music / Jet Star / TKO Magnum

STAR TIME (4CD Set)
Please please please / Why do you do me / Try me / Tell me what I did wrong / Bewildered / Good good lovin' / I'll go crazy / I know it's true / Do the mashed potato / Think / Baby you're right / Lost someone / Night train / I've got money / I've got no money / I don't mind / Prisoner of love / Devil's den / Out of the blue / Out of sight / Grits / Maybe the last time / Papa's got a brand new bag (parts 1, 2 & 3) / Papa's got a brand new bag (part 1) / I got you (I feel good) / Ain't that a groove / It's a man's man's man's world / Money won't change you / Don't be a dropout / Bring it up (Hipster's avenue) / Let yourself go / Cold sweat / Get it together / I can't stand myself (when you touch me) / I got the feelin' / Lickin' stick / Say it loud, I'm black and I'm proud / There was a time / Give it up or turn it loose / I don't want nobody to give me nothing / Mother popcorn / Funky drummer / (Get up I feel like being a) sex machine / Super bad / Talkin' loud and sayin' nothing / Get up, get into it and get involved / Soul power, parts 1 and 2 / Brother rapp/Ain't it funky now / Hot pants / I'm a greedy man / Make it funky / It's a new day / I got ants in my pants / King Heroin / There it is, part 1 / Public enemy no.1 / Get on the good foot / I got a bag of my own / Doing it to death / Payback / Papa don't take no mess, part 1 / Stoned to the bone, part 1 / My thang / Funky president / Hot (I need to be loved, loved, loved) / Get up offa that thing / Body heat (part 1) / It's too funky in here / Rapp payback / Unity, part 1
CD Set 8491082
Polydor / May '91 / PolyGram

TELL ME WHAT YOU'RE GONNA DO (Brown, James & The Famous Flames)
Just you and me darling / I love you, yes I do / I don't mind / Come over here / bells / Love don't love nobody / Dancin' little thing / Lost someone / And I do just what I want / So long / You don't have to go / Tell me what you're gonna do
CD CPCD 8053
Charly / Mar '95 / Koch

Brown, Jeri

APRIL IN PARIS
Gentle piece / Once upon a summertime / Twelfth of never / When April comes again / Who can I turn to / Morning lovely / I could have loved you / Summertime / Poem - as the mist leaves no scar / Greensleeves / Windmills of your mind
CD JUST 922
Justin Time / Feb '97 / Cadillac / New Note/ Pinnacle

FRESH START
Come, come play with me / Wandering love / Nothing else but you / Fresh start / Moment I look at you / Bohemia after dark / Moonray / You're a joy / Vision is the key / Orange sky / Shall we gather at the river / Fresh start (reprise)
CD JUST 782
Justin Time / May '96 / Cadillac / New Note/ Pinnacle

UNFOLDING - THE PEACOCKS
CD JUST 452
Justin Time / Apr '93 / Cadillac / New Note/Pinnacle

Brown, Jim

BACK TO THE COUNTRY (Brown, Jimmy & Willy Lee Harris)
CD TCD 5013
Testament / Dec '94 / ADA / Koch

Brown, Jocelyn

ABSOLUTELY
CD BR 1402
BR Music / Mar '95 / Target/BMG

Brown, Joe

56 AND TALLER THAN YOU THINK
56 and taller than you think / You'll remember me / Without love / When I write my book / Corner of our street / It's a sin to tell a lie / Do it all over again / Early in the morning / Brother, can you spare a dime / You woke the dreamer in me / Old chunk of coal / Rose of England / All worked out / I'll see you in my dreams
CD FIENDCD 790
Demon / Jun '97 / Pinnacle

JOE BROWN STORY, THE (Brown, Joe & The Bruvvers)
People gotta talk / Comes the day / Savage / At the Darktown strutter's ball / Swagger / Jellied eels / Shine / Switch / Crazy mixed up kid / I'm Henery the Eighth (I am) / Good luck and goodbye / Popcorn / Picture of you / Layabout's lament / Talking guitar / Lonely Island pearl / Your tender look / Other side of town / It only took a minute / All things bright and beautiful / That's what love will do / What's the name of the game / Casting my spell / What a crazy world we're living in / Hava Nagila / You can't lie to a liar / Sweet little sixteen / Nature's time for love / Spanish bit / Sally Ann / There's only one of you / Walkin' tall / Hercules unchained / You do things to me / Everybody calls me Joe / Don't / Just like that / Teardrops in the rain / Lonely Circus / Sicilian tarantella / Sea of heartbreak / Mrs. O's theme / Little ray of sunshine / Your loving touch / Satisfied mind / Th' wife / Rich man's son and the poor man's daughter / With a little help from my friends / Show me around
CD NEDCD 235
Sequel / Oct '93 / BMG

LIVE AND IN THE STUDIO
CD C5MCD 612
See For Miles/C5 / Jun '94 / Pinnacle

PICTURE OF YOU, A
Picture of you / That's what love will do / It only took a minute / Sea of heartbreak / English country garden / Shine / With a little help from my friends / Alley oops (live) / Little ray of sunshine / What a crazy world we're livin' in (live) / Sweet little sixteen (live) / Hallelujah I love her so (live) / I'm Henry the eighth I am / Just like that / My favourite occupation / Hava nagila (the hora) / All things bright and beautiful / Nature's time for love
CD 5507592
Spectrum / Apr '95 / PolyGram

Brown, Junior

12 SHADES OF BROWN
My baby don't dance to nothing but Ernest Tubb / Baby let the bad times be / Free born man / They don't choose to live that way / Too many nights in a roadhouse / Hillbilly hula gal / Way to survive / Broke down South of Dallas / What's left just won't go right / Moan all night long / Coconut Island / Don't sell the farm
CD FIENDCD 205
Demon / Oct '90 / Pinnacle

SEMI-CRAZY
CD CURCD 025
Curb / May '96 / Grapevine/PolyGram

Brown, Kevin

ROAD DREAMS
CD HNCD 1340
Hannibal / May '88 / ADA / Vital

RUST
Don't quit / Hey Joe Louis / Write a bible of your own / Telephone tears / We'll be with you / If I had my way / You don't have to tell me / Southern Streets / Meltdown / Sunny side up
CD HNCD 1344
Hannibal / May '89 / ADA / Vital

Brown, Lee

LEE BROWN 1937-1940 (Piano Blues Rarities)
CD DOCD 5344
Document / May '95 / ADA / Hot Shot / Jazz Music

Brown, Les

22 ORIGINAL BIG BAND RECORDINGS
CD HCD 408
Hindsight / Sep '92 / Jazz Music / Target/ BMG

BIG BAND CLASSICS (Brown, Les & Billy May)
CD ISCD 129
Intersound / Jul '93 / Jazz Music

DIGITAL SWING (Brown, Les & His Band Of Renown)
How high the moon / I can't get started (with you) / Blue skies / For all we know / What is this thing called love / Just friends / Perky / One more blues / St. Louis blues / Come rain or come shine / Misty / You're nobody 'til somebody loves you / Yo Henry
CD FCD 9650
Fantasy / Apr '94 / Jazz Music / Pinnacle / Wellard

ELITCH GARDENS, DENVER 1959 VOL.1
CD DSTS 1002
Status / Harmonia Mundi / Jazz Music / Wellard

ELITCH GARDENS, DENVER 1959 VOL.2 (Brown, Les & His Band Of Renown)
CD DSTS 1006
Status / Feb '95 / Harmonia Mundi / Jazz Music / Wellard

GREAT LES BROWN, THE
CD HCD 330
Hindsight / May '95 / Jazz Music / Target/ BMG

HEATWAVE (Brown, Les & His Band Of Renown)
CD DAWE 54
Magic / Nov '93 / Cadillac / Harmonia Mundi / Jazz Music / Swift / Wellard

LES BROWN & JOHNNY MERCER/ MARGARET WHITING
CD DAWE 68
Magic / Apr '94 / Cadillac / Harmonia Mundi / Jazz Music / Swift / Wellard

LES BROWN AND HIS BAND OF RENOWN (Brown, Les & His Band Of Renown)
CD HCD 252
Hindsight / May '94 / Jazz Music / Target/ BMG

LES BROWN AND HIS GREAT VOCALISTS
Robin Hood / Lament to love / I guess I'll have to dream the rest / Good man is hard to find / I got it bad and that ain't good / 'Tis autumn / Sentimental journey / Sleigh ride in July / My dreams are getting better all the time / Day by day / I guess I'll get the papers and go home / OH how I miss you tonight / Comes the sandman (a lullaby) / Just a gigolo / Crosstown trolley / Rock me to sleep
CD CK 66373
Columbia / Jul '95 / Sony

LES BROWN AND THE DUKE (Brown, Les & Duke Ellington)
CD 15760
Laserlight / Apr '94 / Target/BMG

RIDIN' HIGH
CD BMCD 3058
Blue Moon / Apr '97 / Cadillac / Discovery / Greensleeves / Jazz Music / Jet Star / TKO Magnum

SENTIMENTAL JOURNEY
CD 8254932
Polydor / '88 / PolyGram

Brown, Lloyd

STRAIGHT NO CHASER
CD CRDCD 002
Groove & A Quarter / Jul '96 / Jet Star

Brown, Marion

AFTERNOON OF A GEORGIA FAUN
CD 5277102
ECM / Jul '96 / New Note/Pinnacle

BACK TO PARIS
CD FRLCD 002
Freelance / Oct '92 / Cadillac / Koch

GEECHEE RECOLLECTIONS
CD MVCZ 120
MCA / Apr '97 / BMG

PORTO NOVO
Similar limits / Sound and structure / Improvisation / Qbic / Porto novo / And then they danced / Rhythmus
CD BLCD 760200
Black Lion / Apr '95 / Cadillac / Jazz Music / Koch / Wellard

SWEET EARTH FLYING
CD MVCZ 119
MCA / May '97 / BMG

VISTA
CD __________ MVCZ 118
MCA / Apr '97 / BMG

WHY NOT (Brown, Marion Quartet)
CD __________ ESP 10402
ESP / Jan '93 / Jazz Music

Brown, Marty

HERE'S TO THE HONKY TONKS
CD __________ HCD 8075
Hightone / Oct '96 / ADA / Koch

Brown, Maxine

OH NO NOT MY BABY
Since I found you / Gotta find a way / I wonder what my baby's doing tonight / Let me give you my lovin' / It's torture / One in a million / Oh no not my baby / You're in love / Anything for a laugh / Coming back to you / Yesterday's kisses / Ask me / All in my mind / Little girl lost / I want a guarantee / Secret of livin' / Baby cakes / One step at a time / I've got a lot of love left in me / I don't need anything / Oh Lord what are you doing to me / I cry alone / Funny / Misty morning eyes / Love that man / Losing my touch / Put yourself in my place / It's gonna be alright
CD __________ CDKEND 949
Kent / Oct '90 / Pinnacle

Brown, Nappy

AW, SHUCKS
You know it ain't right / Let love take care (of the rest) / Aw shucks baby / Still holding on / It's not what you do / Mind your own business / True love / Chickadee / Night time (live jam version)
CD __________ ICH 9006CD
Ichiban / Jun '94 / Direct / Koch

BLACK TOP BLUES-A-RAMA VOL.2 (Live At Tipitina's)
CD __________ CD 1045
Black Top / '88 / ADA / CM / Direct

I DONE GONE OVER (Brown, Nappy & The Roosters)
CD __________ RBD 205
Mr. R&B / Apr '91 / CM / Swift / Wellard

JUST FOR ME
Night time / Bye bye baby / Things have changed / Just for me / We need to love one another / What more can I say / You must be crazy woman / Deep sea diver
CD __________ JSPCD 274
JSP / Jan '97 / ADA / Cadillac / Direct / Hot Shot / Target/BMG

SOMETHING'S GONNA JUMP OUT THE BUSHES
CD __________ CD 1039
Black Top / '88 / ADA / CM / Direct

TORE UP (Brown, Nappy & The Heartfixers)
CD __________ ALCD 4792
Alligator / May '93 / ADA / CM / Direct

Brown, Norman

AFTER THE STORM
Take me there / After the storm / That's the way love goes / Any love / Lydian / For the love of you / Trashman / It costs to love / Let's come together / Acoustic time / El dulce sol / Family
CD __________ 5303012
MoJazz / Mar '94 / PolyGram

BETTER DAYS AHEAD
CD __________ 5306642
MoJazz / Jul '96 / PolyGram

JUST BETWEEN US
Stormin' / Just between us / East meets West / Love's holiday / It's a feelin' / Too high / Something just for you / Here to stay / Moonlight tonight / Sweet taste / Inside
CD __________ 5300912
MoJazz / Feb '93 / PolyGram

Brown, Oscar Jr.

SIN AND SOUL...AND THEN SOME
Work song / But I was cool / Bid 'em in / Signifyin' monkey / Watermelon man / Somebody buy me a drink / Rags and old iron / Dat dere / Brown baby / Humdrum blues / Sleepy / Afro blue / Mr. Kicks / Hazel's hips / World of grey / Forbidden fruit / Straighten up and fly right
CD __________ CK 64994
Sony Jazz / Nov '96 / Sony

Brown, Peggy

DENN SIE FAHREN HINAUS AUF DAS MEER
Denn sie fahren hinaus auf das Meer / Honeymoon mit dir allein / Sag, ist das die liebe / Gegen liebe gibt es keine medizin / Jeden Sonntag eine Rose von dir / Melodie aus Germany / Meine reklame boy / Schiffe ohne Hafen# / Wenn es abend wird / Ein tango in der Hafenbar / Zahlen jeden Stunde / Spiel nicht mit der liebe / Eine trane fiel ins Meer / Lieber Jonny, komm doch wieder / Gondola d'amore / Lass mich nie wieder weinen / Das lexicon d'amour / Die Berge von Dakota / Ein mann wie du / Du bist meine Welt / Silberweisse Wogen / Don Carlos / Keiner weiss ob sie sich wiedersehn / Ein wiedersehn mit Jacky / Jedes gluck auf der Welt / Komm doch wieder / Das kann nur liebe sein / Bitte sag's nicht weiter / Gehn am Kai die lichter aus / Alone on the shore
CD __________ BCD 16110
Bear Family / Nov '96 / Direct / Rollercoaster / Swift

Brown, Pete

ARDOURS OF THE LOST RAKE (Brown, Pete & Phil Ryan)
CD __________ AUL 736
Aura / Apr '91 / Cadillac

Brown, Phil

WHISTLING FOR THE MOON
Bowland air / Teddy O'Neill / Women of Ireland / Old man Quinn/Alexander's hornpipe / Lonesome boatman / Danny boy / Dark island / Copy nook / Endearing young charms / King of the fairies / Terminal love song / As I roved out / Leaboy's lassie / Down by the Sally Gardens / Whalley roundabout
CD __________ FSCD 34
Folksound / Oct '95 / CM / Roots

Brown, Phil

DISCOVERY
At the sign of the swinging cymbal / Romance for violin and orchestra no.2 in F / Vienna is Vienna / Girl from Corsica / Up to the races / So eine liebe gibt es einmal nur / Carmen medley / Missing / London kid / At the woodchopper's ball / Eine kleine nachtmusik / Dizzy fingers / Mornings at seven / Taste of honey / Rare auld times / Abba medley / Discovery / Who cares
CD __________ CDRS 1284
Grosvenor / Nov '95 / Grosvenor

Brown, Polly

BEWITCHED - THE POLLY BROWN STORY
That same old feeling: *Pickettywitch* / (It's like a) sad old kinda movie: *Pickettywitch* / All those days: *Pickettywitch* / Baby I won't let you down: *Pickettywitch* / To love somebody / Crazy love / Wild night / Amoreuse / Honey honey / Best of everything: *Sweet Dreams* / That's the way love grows: *Sweet Dreams* / Up in a puff of smoke / Special delivery / SOS / You're my number one / One girl too late / Short down in flames / I need another song / Do you believe in love at first sight / Bewitched, bothered and bewildered / Believe in me / Angel / It's me you're leaving / Writing you a letter / Precious to me
CD __________ RPM 143
RPM / Apr '95 / Pinnacle

Brown, Pud

PUD BROWN & NEW ORLEANS JAZZMEN
CD __________ JCD 216
Jazzology / Apr '94 / Jazz Music

PUD BROWN & THE SPIRIT OF NEW ORLEANS JAZZ BAND (Brown, Pud & The Spirit Of New Orleans Jazz Band)
CD __________ BCD 247
GHB / Aug '94 / Jazz Music

PUD BROWN PLAYS CLARINET
CD __________ JCD 166
Jazzology / Apr '94 / Jazz Music

Brown, Ray

BASS FACE (Brown, Ray Trio)
Milestones / Bass face / In the wee small hours of the morning / Tin Tin Deo CRS - CRAFT / Takin' a chance on love / Remember / Makin' whoopee / Phineas can be
CD __________ CD 83340
Telarc / Oct '93 / Conifer/BMG

BLACK ORPHEUS
Days of wine and roses / I thought about you / Balck Orpheus / How insensitive / My foolish heart / Please send me someone to love / Ain't misbehavin' / When you wish upon a star / Things ain't what they used to be
CD __________ ECD 220762
Evidence / Feb '94 / ADA / Cadillac / Harmonia Mundi

BROWN'S BAG
Blues for Eddie Lee / Keep on pumpin' / You are my sunshine / Time for love / Surrey with the fringe on top / Emily
CD __________ CCD 6019
Concord Jazz / Aug '91 / New Note/ Pinnacle

DON'T GET SASSY (Brown, Ray Trio)
Tanga / Con alma / Brown's new blues / Don't get sassy / Good life / Everything I love / Kelly's blues / When you go / Raincheck / In a sentimental mood / Squatty roo
CD __________ CD 83368
Telarc / Sep '94 / Conifer/BMG

LIVE AT THE CONCORD JAZZ FESTIVAL - 1979 (Brown, Ray Trio)
Blue bossa / Bossa nova do marilla / Manha de carnaval / St. Louis blues / Fly me to the moon / Georgia on my mind / Here's that rainy day / Please send me someone to love / Honeysuckle rose
CD __________ CCD 4102
Concord Jazz / Mar '90 / New Note/ Pinnacle

MOORE MAKES 4 (Brown, Ray Trio)
CD __________ CCD 4477
Concord Jazz / Oct '91 / New Note/ Pinnacle

MUCH IN COMMON (2CD Set) (Brown, Ray & Milt Jackson)
CD Set __________ 5332592
Verve / Jan '97 / PolyGram

RAY BROWN THREE, A (Brown, Ray & Monty Alexander/Sam Most)
I wish you love / I can't stop loving you / Jamento / Blue monk / Candy man / Too late now / You're my everything / There is no greater love
CD __________ CCD 42132
Concord Jazz / May '97 / New Note/ Pinnacle

SEVEN STEPS TO HEAVEN (Brown, Ray Trio)
Two RB's / Seven steps to heaven / Dejection blues / Thumb / My romance / Cotton tail / Samba de orfeu / There is no greater love / In a sentimental mood / Stella by starlight / Things ain't what they used to be
CD __________ CD 83384
Telarc / Feb '96 / Conifer/BMG

SOLAR ENERGY
Exactly like you / Cry me a river / Teach me tonight / Take the 'A' train / Mistreated but undefeated blues / That's all / Easy does it / Sweet Georgia Brown
CD __________ CCD 4268
Concord Jazz / Jul '89 / New Note/Pinnacle

SOME OF MY BEST FRIENDS ARE...
Lover / Ray of light / Just a gigolo / St. Louis blues / Bag's groove / Love walked in / Nearness of you / Close your eyes / Giant steps / My romance / How come you do me like you do / If I love again / St Tropez
CD __________ CD 83373
Telarc / Apr '95 / Conifer/BMG

SOME OF MY BEST FRIENDS ARE...THE SAX PLAYERS (Brown, Ray Trio)
How high the moon / Love walked in / Polka dots and moonbeams / Crazeology / Port of Rico / Moose the mooche / Easy living / Just you, just me / Fly me to the moon / When it's sleepy time down South / These foolish things / God bless the child
CD __________ CD 83388
Telarc / Jun '96 / Conifer/BMG

SOMETHING FOR LESTER
CD __________ OJCCD 412
Original Jazz Classics / Feb '93 / Complete/Pinnacle / Jazz Music / Wellard

SUPERBASS (Recorded Live At Sculler's) (Brown, Ray & John Clayton/ Christian McBride)
SuperBass theme / Blue Monk / Bye bye blackbird / Lullaby of birdland / Who cares / Mack The Knife / Centrepiece / Sculler blues / Brown funk / SuperBass theme
CD __________ CD 83393
Telarc Jazz / Aug '97 / Conifer/BMG

TASTY (Brown, Ray & Jimmy Rowles)
Sleepin' bee / I'm gonna sit right down and write myself a letter / Night is young and you're so beautiful / My ideal / Come Sunday / Close your eyes / Nancy with the laughing face / Smile
CD __________ CCD 4122
Concord Jazz / Jul '95 / New Note/Pinnacle

THREE DIMENSIONAL (Brown, Ray Trio)
Ja da / Paradise / You are my sunshine / Nancy / Gumbo hump / Classical in G / My romance / Take me out to the ball game / Ellington medley / Equinox / Time after time
CD __________ CCD 4520
Concord Jazz / Sep '92 / New Note/ Pinnacle

TWO BASS HITS
CD __________ 74034
Capri / Nov '93 / Cadillac / Wellard

Brown, Roy

BLUES DELUXE
Cadillac baby / Hard luck blues / New Rebecca / Sweet peach / Love don't love nobody / Dreaming blues / Good man blues / Too much lovin' ain't no good / Teenage jamboree / Train time blues / Bar room blues / Long about sundown / Beautician blues / Drum boogie / Double crossin' woman / Swingin' with Johnny / Wrong woman blues / Good rockin' man / I've got the last laugh now / Big town / Brown angel / Rock-a-bye baby / Lonesome lover / Answer to Big Town
CD __________ CDCHARLY 289
Charly / Nov '93 / Koch

MIGHTY, MIGHTY MAN
Mr. Hound Dog's in town / Bootleggin' baby / Trouble at midnight / Everything's alright / This is my last goodbye / Don't let it rain / Up jumped the devil / No love at all / Ain't it a shame / Ain't no rockin' no more / Queen of diamonds / Gal from Kokomo / Fannie Brown got married / Worried life blues / Black diamond / Letter to baby / Shake 'em up baby / Rinky dinku doo / Adorable one / School bell rock / Ain't got no blues today / Good looking and foxy too
CD __________ CDCHD 459
Ace / Sep '93 / Pinnacle

Brown, Roy 'Chubby'

FAT OUT OF HELL
Rockin' good Christmas / It's a condom / Protect your bum de de bum / Play your funky horn / Stunt / Awful / Toss me off / Play your funky horn / Santa, where's me fucking bike / Rockin' good Christmas
CD __________ 5370602
PolyGram TV / Nov '96 / PolyGram

TAKE FAT AND PARTY
CD __________ 5297482
PolyGram TV / Nov '95 / PolyGram

Brown, Rula

RULA
CD __________ BCR 1002
Bee Cat / Nov '95 / Jet Star

Brown, Ruth

BEST OF THE REST OF RUTH BROWN, THE
Hello little boy / Please don't freeze / Bye bye young men / I still love you / When I get you baby / Show me / New love / I hope we meet / Look me up / Just too much / Book of lies / I'll step aside / Mama he treats your daughter mean / 5-10-15 hours / Papa Daddy / Jack O' Diamonds / What I wouldn't give / Door is still open / I burned your letter / Honey boy / It tears me all to pieces / Sure nuff / Here he comes / Mama he treats your daughter mean / Oh what a dream
CD __________ RSACD 864
Sequel / Mar '97 / BMG

BLUES ON BROADWAY
Nobody knows you (When you're down and out) / Good morning heartache / If I can't sell it I'll keep sittin' on it / Ain't nobody's business if I do / St. Louis blues / Am I blue / I'm just a lucky so and so / I don't break dance / Come Sunday
CD __________ FCD 9662
Fantasy / Mar '94 / Jazz Music / Pinnacle / Wellard

HAVE A GOOD TIME
CD __________ FCD 9661
Fantasy / Nov '95 / Jazz Music / Pinnacle / Wellard

LIVE IN LONDON
I've got the world on a string / I'm a lucky so and so / Have a good time / Fine and mellow / Lover man / Good morning heartache / Secret love / Fine Brown frame / It could happen to you / 5-10-15 Hours / Be anything (but be mine) / Since I fell for you / He's a real gone guy
CD __________ JHCD 042
Ronnie Scott's Jazz House / Sep '95 / Cadillac / Jazz Music / New Note/Pinnacle / TKO Magnum

MISS RHYTHM
CD __________ 7567820612
Atlantic / Jul '93 / Warner Music

MISS RHYTHM (The Greatest Hits/2CD Set)
CD Set __________ RSDCD 816
Sequel / Oct '94 / BMG

SONGS OF MY LIFE
CD __________ FCD 9665
Fantasy / Jun '94 / Jazz Music / Pinnacle / Wellard

Brown, Sam

BOX
Box / Ebb and flow / Whisper / I forgive you / They're the ones / Liberty in reality / Embrace the darkness / Toes / Intuition / As the crow flies / What's the use / Bert and Flo
CD __________ FIENDCD 789
Demon / Apr '97 / Pinnacle

KISSING GATE
Can I get a witness / Hypnotised / With a little love / Once in your life / April moon / Mind works / Contradictions / Kissing gate / S'envolver / Where are you / As one / Eye for an eye / Troubled soul / This feeling
CD __________ 5501132
Spectrum / Oct '93 / PolyGram

STOP
Walking back to me / Your love is all / It makes me wonder / This feeling / Tea / Piece of my luck / Ball and chain / Wrap me up / I'll be in love / Merry go round / Sometimes / Can I get a witness / High as a kite / Nutbush City Limits
CD __________ CDMID 181
A&M / Jul '93 / PolyGram

Brown, Sandy

MCJAZZ & FRIENDS
CD ______ **LACD 58**
Lake / Feb '96 / ADA / Cadillac / Direct / Jazz Music / Target/BMG

Brown, Sarah

SAYIN' WHAT I'M THINKIN'
CD ______ **BPCD 5030**
Blind Pig / Apr '96 / ADA / CM / Direct / Hot Shot

Brown, Sawyer

GREATEST HITS
CD ______ **CURCD 013**
Curb / Jan '95 / Grapevine/PolyGram

OUTSKIRTS OF TOWN
Boys and me / Farmer tan / Outskirts of town / Thank God for you / Listenin' for you / Eyes of love / Hard to say / Drive away / Heartbreak highway / Love to be wanted / Hold on
CD ______ **CURCD 006**
Curb / Mar '94 / Grapevine/PolyGram

SIX DAYS ON THE ROAD
CD ______ **CURCD 44**
Curb / May '97 / Grapevine/PolyGram

WANTIN' AND HAVIN' IT ALL
CD ______ **CURCD 17**
Curb / Sep '95 / Grapevine/PolyGram

Brown, Scott

THEORY OF EVOLUTION, THE
CD ______ **EVCD 5**
Evolution / Nov '96 / Alphamagic

Brown, Shirley

DIVA OF SOUL
CD ______ **DOMECD 7**
Dome / Oct '95 / 3mv/Sony

FOR THE REAL FEELING
When, where, what time / Crowding in on my mind / After a night like this / Dirty feelin' / Hang on Louie / Eyes can't see / Move me, move me / Love starved
CD ______ **CDSXE 082**
Stax / Nov '92 / Pinnacle

WOMAN TO WOMAN
Woman to woman / Yes sir brother / It ain't no fun / As long as you love me / Stay with me baby / I've got to go on without you / It's worth a whipping / So glad to have you / Passion / I can't give you up / I need you tonight / Between you and me
CD ______ **CDSXE 002**
Stax / Aug '87 / Pinnacle

Brown, Steven

DAY IS GONE, THE
CD ______ **SUBCD 00921**
Sub Rosa / '89 / Direct / RTM/Disc / SRD / Vital

Brown, Teacher Ras Sam

HISTORY PAST AND PRESENT
CD ______ **RASCD 3199**
Ras / Feb '97 / Direct / Greensleeves / Jet Star / SRD

Brown, Tom

TOM BROWN & HIS NEW ORLEANS JAZZ BAND (Brown, Tom & His New Orleans Jazz Band)
CD ______ **BCD 3**
GHB / Aug '94 / Jazz Music

Brown/Crane

FASTER THAN THE SPEED OF LIGHT
CD ______ **BP 228CD**
Blueprint / Oct '96 / Pinnacle

Browne, Duncan

TRAVELLING MAN, THE (Browne, Duncan & Sebastian Graham Jones)
CD ______ **CDSGP 0114**
Prestige / Sep '95 / Else / Total/BMG

Browne, Jackson

FOR EVERYMAN
Take it easy / Our Lady of the Well / Colours of the sun / I thought I was a child / These days / Redneck friend / Times you come / Ready or not / Sing my songs to me / For everyman
CD ______ **243003**
Asylum / Jan '87 / Warner Music

HOLD OUT
Disco apocalypse / Hold on, hold out / Of missing persons / Call it a loan / That girl could sing / Hold out / Boulevard
CD ______ **2522262**
Asylum / Jan '87 / Warner Music

I'M ALIVE
I'm alive / My problem is you / Everywhere I go / I'll do anything / Miles away / Too many angels / Take this rain / Two of me, two of you / Sky blue and black / All good things
CD ______ **7559615242**
Asylum / Oct '93 / Warner Music

JACKSON BROWNE
Jamaica say you will / Child in these hills / Song for Adam / Doctor my eyes / From silver lake / Something fine / Under the falling sky / Looking into you / Rock me on the water / My opening farewell
CD ______ **253022**
Asylum / Dec '86 / Warner Music

LATE FOR THE SKY
Late for the sky / Fountain of sorrow / Farther on / Late show / Road and the sky / For a dancer / Walking slow / Before the deluge
CD ______ **243007**
Asylum / Jan '87 / Warner Music

LAWYERS IN LOVE
For a rocker / Lawyers in love / On the day / Cut it away / Downtown / Tender is the night / Knock on any door / Say it isn't true
CD ______ **9602682**
Asylum / Jul '87 / Warner Music

LIVES IN THE BALANCE
For America / Soldier of plenty / In the shape of a heart / Candy / Lawless Avenue / Lives in the balance / Till I go down / Black and white
CD ______ **K 9604572**
Asylum / Dec '96 / Warner Music

LOOKING EAST
CD ______ **7559618672**
Asylum / Feb '96 / Warner Music

PRETENDER, THE
Fuse / Your bright baby blues / Linda Paloma / Here come those tears again / Only child / Daddy's time / Sleep's dark and silent gate / Pretender
CD ______ **253048**
Asylum / Dec '86 / Warner Music

RUNNING ON EMPTY
Running on empty / Road / Rosie / You love the thunder / Cocaine / Shaky town / Love needs a heart / Nothing but time / Load-out / Stay
CD ______ **253070**
Asylum / Jan '87 / Warner Music

WORLD IN MOTION
World in motion / Enough of the night / Chasing you into the night / How long / Anything can happen / When the stone begins to turn / Word justice / My personal revenge / I am a patriot / Lights and virtues
CD ______ **9608322**
Asylum / Feb '95 / Warner Music

Browne, Kirk

CIVIL WAR GUITAR - CAMPFIRE MEMORIES
CD ______ **SLCD 9002**
Starline / Dec '94 / Jazz Music

Browne, Ronan

SOUTH WEST WIND, THE (Browne, Ronan & Peter O'Loughlin)
Jenny picking cockles/Colliers' reel / Frieze breeches jig / Shaskeen/Five mile chase / Banks of Lough Gowna/Willie Clancy's Paidin O Raifeartaigh / Paidin O Raifeartaigh jig / Connaught heifers/Corney is coming / Bold trainer O / Dublin reel/Steampacket/ Hand me down the tackle / An ghaoth aniar aneas/Petticoat loose / Spike Island lassies/ Farewell to Connaught / Drunken gauger / Queen of the rushes/Chorus / Byrne's and Alfie's rambles / Bridie's joy/The spinner's delight / Thrush in the morning/Crooked road
CD ______ **CC 47CD**
Claddagh / Feb '93 / ADA / CM / Direct

Browne, Ronnie

SCOTTISH LOVE SONGS
Dumarton's drums / My love is like a red red rose / Come all ye fair and tender maidens / Touch and the go / Bonnie lass o'Fyvie / Loch Lomond / Bonnie Earl o'Moray / Canvas of my life / Kate Dalrymple / Massacre of Glencoe / Mary Hamilton / Queen's Maries / Leezie Lindsay / Gin I were a Baron's heir / Willie's gan tae Melville Castle / Parting glass
CD ______ **CDITV 602**
Scotdisc / Oct '95 / Conifer/BMG / Duncans / Ross

Browne, Tom

ANOTHER SHADE OF BROWNE
Bluesanova / Philly twist / Sleepy lagoon / Pove / Bee Tee's / Minor plea / In a sentimental mood / Eighty one
CD ______ **HIBD 8011**
Hip Bop / Sep '96 / Koch / Silva Screen

Browns

THREE BELLS, THE (8CD Set)
Rio de Janeiro / Looking back to see / Itsy witsy bitsy me / Why am I fallin' / Draggin' Main Street / You're love is as wild as the west wind / Cool green / Do memories haunt me / It's love I guess / I'm your man, I'm your gal / Set the dawgs on 'em / Jungle magic / You thought, I thought / Here today and gone tomorrow / Grass is green / Lookin' on / I take the chance / I can't see for lookin' / I'm in heaven / Goo goo dada / Just as long as you love me / Getting used to being lonely / Man with a plan / Sweet talk / Don't tell me your troubles / Last thing that I want / Preview of the blues / My Isle of golden dreams / I'm in heaven / Guess I'm crazy / Sky princess / I'll hold you in my heart / How can it be imagination / I heard the bluebirds sing / It takes a long, long train with a red caboose / Don't use the word lightly / Waltz of the angels / Table next to me / Money / You'll always be in my heart / Behave yourself, Jose / Just in time / Man in the moon / Ain't no way in this world / Crazy dreams / True love goes far beyond / Only one way to love you / Be my love / Land of golden dreams / Love is in season / Would you care / Trot / Beyond the shadow / This time I would know / Three bells / Wake up Jonah / Be my love / Heaven fell last night / Your pretty blue eyes / Unchained melody / Indian love call / Blues stay away from me / Dream on / Where did the sunshine go / We should be together / Bye bye love / I still do / Only the lonely / Hi de ank tum / Love me tender / Put on an old pair of shoes / Blue bells ring / Scarlet ribbons / Red sails in the sunset / That's my desire / That little boy of mine / Halfway to heaven / Teen-ex / Oh my Papa / Margo / Cool water / True love / Enchanted sea / Old lamplighter / Billy McCoy / Am I that easy to forget / Whiffenpoof song / Streamlined cannonball / My adobe hacienda / Pledge of love / Wabash blues / Who's gonna buy you ribbons / Margo / Chandelier of stars / Eternally / Brighten the corner where you are / Blue skirt waltz / Have you ever been lonely / Lonely little robin / Wayward wind / Old village choir / High noon / Lavender blue / Blues in my heart / Chandelier of stars / Whiffenpoof song / Blue christmas / This land is your land / In the pines / Brighten the corner where you are / Greenwillow christmas / Remember me / Twelfth of never / Nevada / Where I was (when we became strangers) / You're so much a part of me / Revenge / Bandit / Send me the pillow that you dream on / Down in the valley / Shenandoah / Columbus Stockade blues / Clementine / Poor wayfaring stranger / Ground hog / Poor wildwood flower / Who's gonna shoe your pretty little feet / John B Sails / My pretty quadroon / Down on the old plantation / My baby's gone / Alpha and omega / Foolish pride / Angel's dolly / Alpha and omega / My baby's gone / Whispering wine / Remember me / Lord I'm coming home / How great thou art / Child of the King / Just as I am / Church in the wildwood / Evening prayer / In the garden / Whispering hope / When they ring those golden bells / Where no one stands alone / My latest sun is sinking fast / Faith unlocks the door / It's just a little heartache / No love at all / Buttons and bows / Old master painter / They call the wind Maria / Forty shades of green / Is it make believe / Everlasting / Twelfth rose / Watching my world fall apart / Oh no / Dear Teresa / Rumba boogie / Great speckled bird / Don't let the stars get in your eyes / Sugarfoot rag / Fair and tender ladies / Tragic romance / Four walls / You nearly lose your mind / Mansion on the hill / Wondering / Mommy please stay home with me / Anna / Pirogue / Happy fool / Grass is red / Circuit ridin' preacher / Half breed / Young land / Gun, the gold, the girl / Mister and Mississippi / Blowin' in the wind / Tobacco road / Then I'll stop loving you / You're easy to remember / I know my place / My baby doesn't love me anymore / Love didn't pass me by / Outskirts of town / Tangled web / My destiny / Johnny I hardly knew you / Three hearts in a tangle / Everybody's darlin' plus mine / Meadow green / One take away one / No sad songs for me / I feel like crying / Big blizzard / Watch the roses grow / Little too much to dream / Little boy blue / Maybe tomorrow / I can stand it (as long as you can) / Gone / This heart of mine / I'm so lonesome I could cry / Yesterday's gone / You can't grow peaches on a cherry tree / Two of a kind / Spring time / When I stop dreaming / Too soon to know / Now I can live again / I will bring you water / June is as cold as Decmeber / I'd just be fool enough / Maker of raindrops and roses / Making plans / Born to be with you / Million miles from nowhere / Big daddy / Where does a little tear come from / Coming back to you / Do not ask for love / Gigawackem / Rhythm of the rain / Greener pastures / After losing you / Tip of my fingers / Four strong winds / Sorry I never knew you / Old country church / They tore the old country church down / Though your sins be as scarlet / He will set your fields on fire / Night watch / When I lift up my head / Taller than trees / Mocking bird / Jezebel / Rusty old halo / Weapon of prayer / I hear it now / Ride ride ride / Country boy's dream / All of me belongs to you / Where does the good times go / I'm a lonesome fugitive / Once / Walk through this world with me / Happy tracks / Misty blue / If the whole world stops lovin'
CD Set ______ **BCD 15665**
Bear Family / Dec '93 / Direct / Rollercoaster / Swift

Brownstone

FROM THE BOTTOM UP
Party wit me / Grapevyne / If you love me / Sometimes dancin' / I can't tell you why / Don't cry for me / Pass the lovin' / Fruit of life / True to me / Wipe it up / Deeper feelings / Half of you
CD ______ **4773622**
MJJ Music / Jan '95 / Sony

STILL CLIMBING
Let's get it started / 5 Miles to empty / Love me like you do / In the game of love / Foolish pride / Kiss and tell / Baby love / Around you / Revenge / All I do / If you play your cards right / You give good love
CD ______ **4853882**
MJJ Music / May '97 / Sony

Brozman, Bob

BLUE HULA STOMP
C stomp blues / Body and soul / Hilo march / Ukelele spaghetti / Do you call that a buddy / Chili blues / Paauau waltz / Short man's vindication / Wasting my love on you / Hano hano hanlei / Blue hula stomp / Hilo hula / Agogostein's lament
CD ______ **CDKM 3905**
Kicking Mule / Jan '97 / Pinnacle

BLUES 'ROUND THE BEND
CD ______ **847162**
Sky Ranch / Apr '96 / Discovery

DEVIL'S SLIDE
CD ______ **ROUCD 11557**
Rounder / '88 / ADA / CM / Direct

GOLDEN SLIDE
CD ______ **8441862**
Sky Ranch / Jun '97 / Discovery

Brubeck, Darius

GATHERING FORCES VOL.1 (Brubeck, Darius & Dan)
Earthrise / Three mile island / Kearsage strut / Just think about what happens / Tugela rail / Parrot / I say there's hope
CD ______ **BW 022**
B&W / Sep '93 / New Note/Pinnacle / SRD / Vital/SAM

GATHERING FORCES VOL.2
Kitu / Friendship ragga and boogie / Hariji / Mamazala / Amaselesele emvuleni (frogs) / October / Gathering forces
CD ______ **BW 046**
B&W / Feb '95 / New Note/Pinnacle / SRD / Vital/SAM

LIVE AT THE NEW ORLEANS & HERITAGE FESTIVAL 1990 (Afro Cool Concept) (Brubeck, Darius & Victor Ntoni)
Kwela mama / Lakutshon ilanga / Daveyton special / Mokotedi / Kilamanjaro
CD ______ **BW 024**
B&W / Oct '93 / New Note/Pinnacle / SRD / Vital/SAM

Brubeck, Dave

24 CLASSIC RECORDINGS (Brubeck, Dave Trio)
CD ______ **CDJZD 005**
Fantasy / Jan '91 / Jazz Music / Pinnacle / Wellard

25TH ANNIVERSARY REUNION (Brubeck, Dave Quartet)
St. Louis blues / Three to get ready / African times suite / First movement (African theme) / Second movement (African breeze) / Third movement / Salute to Stephen Foster / Take five / Don't worry 'bout me
CD ______ **3969982**
A&M / Mar '94 / PolyGram

75TH BIRTHDAY CELEBRATION
CD ______ **83349CD**
Telarc / Nov '95 / Conifer/BMG

ALL THE THINGS WE ARE
Like someone in love / In your own sweet way / All the things you are / Deep in a dream / Here's that rainy day / Polka dots and moonbeams / It could happen to you / Don't get around much anymore
CD ______ **7567813992**
Atlantic / Mar '93 / Warner Music

BACK HOME
Cassandra / (I'm afraid) the masquerade is over / Hometown blues / Two-part contention / Caravan
CD ______ **CCD 4103**
Concord Jazz / Jul '94 / New Note/Pinnacle

BLUE RONDO (Brubeck, Dave Quartet)
How does your garden grow / Festival hall / Easy as you go / Blue rondo a la Turk / Dizzy's dream / I see, Satie / Swing bells / Strange meadowlark / Elana Joy
CD ______ **CCD 4317**
Concord Jazz / Aug '90 / New Note/ Pinnacle

CONCORD ON A SUMMER NIGHT (Brubeck, Dave Quartet)
Benjamin / Koto Song / Black And Blue / Take five / Softly, William, softly
CD ______ **CCD 4198**
Concord Jazz / Nov '86 / New Note/ Pinnacle

DAVE BRUBECK & PAUL DESMOND (Brubeck, Dave Octet & Paul Desmond)
Jeepers creepers / On a little street in Singapore / Trolley song / I may be wrong, but I think you're wonderful / Blue moon / My heart stood still / Let's fall in love / Over the rainbow / You go to my head / Crazy Chris / Give a little whistle / Oh lady be good / Tea for two / This can't be love
CD ______ **OJCCD 101**
Original Jazz Classics / Nov '95 / Complete/ Pinnacle / Jazz Music / Wellard

DAVE BRUBECK CHRISTMAS, A
'Homecoming' jingle bells / Santa Claus is coming to town / Joy to the world / Away in a manger / Winter wonderland / O little town of Bethlehem / What child is this (Greensleeves) / To us is given / O tannenbaum / Silent night / Cantos para pedir las posadas / Run, run, run to Bethlehem / 'Farewell' jingle bells / Christmas song
CD ______ **CD 83410**
Telarc Jazz / Nov '96 / Conifer/BMG

DAVE BRUBECK IN CONCERT (Brubeck, Dave Quartet)
Perdido / These foolish things / Stardust / Way you look tonight / I'll never smile again / I remember you / For all we know / All the things you are / Lullaby in rhythm
CD ______ **FCD 60013**
Fantasy / Mar '94 / Jazz Music / Pinnacle / Wellard

DAVE BRUBECK QUARTET (With Paul Desmond) (Brubeck, Dave Quartet)
Maria / I feel pretty / Somewhere / Tonight / Quiet girl / Dialogues for jazz combo and orchestra
CD ______ **CD 53031**
Giants Of Jazz / Aug '88 / Cadillac / Jazz Music / Target/BMG

DAVE DIGS DISNEY (Brubeck, Dave Quartet)
Alice in Wonderland / Give a little whistle / Heigh ho / When you wish upon a star / Someday my Prince will come / One song
CD ______ **4712502**
Sony Jazz / Jan '95 / Sony

ESSENTIAL DAVE BRUBECK QUARTET, THE (Brubeck, Dave Quartet)
CD ______ **4737342**
Sony Jazz / Jan '95 / Sony

GONE WITH THE WIND
Swanee river / Lonesome road / Georgia on my mind / Camptown races / Sort'nin' bread / Basin Street blues / Ol' man river / Gone with the wind
CD ______ **4509842**
Columbia / May '93 / Sony

GREAT CONCERTS, THE
Pennies from Heaven / Blue rondo a la Turk / Take the 'A' train / Wonderful Copenhagen / Tangerine / For all we know / Take five / Real ambassador / Like someone in love
CD ______ **4624032**
CBS / May '90 / Sony

GREATEST HITS
Take five / I'm in a dancing mood / In your own sweet way / Camptown races / Duke / It's a raggy waltz / Bossa nova USA / Trolley song / Unsquare dance / Blue rondo a la Turk / Mr. Broadway
CD ______ **CD 32046**
CBS / Jun '89 / Sony

IN THEIR OWN SWEET WAY (Brubeck, Dave & Chris/Dan/Darius/Matthew)
In your own sweet way / Bifocal blues / Sermon on the mount / Michael my second son / Ode to a cowboy / Dave 'n' Darius / We will all remember Paul / Sixth sense / My one bad habit / Sweet Georgia Brown
CD ______ **CD 83355**
Telarc Jazz / Jun '97 / Conifer/BMG

JAZZ AT COLLEGE OF THE PACIFIC (Brubeck, Dave Quartet)
CD ______ **OJCCD 47**
Original Jazz Classics / Feb '92 / Complete/Pinnacle / Jazz Music / Wellard

JAZZ AT OBERLIN (Brubeck, Dave Quartet)
These foolish things / Perdido / Stardust / Way you look tonight / How high the moon
CD ______ **OJCCD 46**
Original Jazz Classics / Sep '93 / Complete/ Pinnacle / Jazz Music / Wellard

JAZZ COLLECTION (2CD Set)
Le souk / Stompin' for Mili / In your own sweet way / History of a boy scout / Home at last / Someday my Prince will come / Tangerine / Golden horn / Georgia on my mind / Three to get ready / Blue rondo a la Turk / Take five / Darktown strutters ball / There'll be some changes made / Somewhere / Weep no more / Unsquare dance / Summer song / Non-sectarian blues / Bossa nova USA / It's a raggy waltz / World's fair / Fujiyama / Upstage rumba / My favourite things / La paloma azul / Recuerdo / St. Louis Blues
CD Set ______ **4804632**
Columbia / Jul '95 / Sony

JAZZ GOES TO COLLEGE
Balcony rock / Out of nowhere / Le souk / Take the 'A' train / Song is you / Don't worry 'bout me / I want to be happy
CD ______ **4656822**
CBS / Feb '93 / Sony

JAZZ IMPRESSIONS OF EURASIA
Nomad / Brandenburg Gate / Golden horn / Thank you / Marble arch / Calcutta blues
CD ______ **4712492**
Columbia / Apr '92 / Sony

JAZZ IMPRESSIONS OF NEW YORK
CD ______ **4669712**
Sony Jazz / Jan '95 / Sony

JUST YOU, JUST ME
Just you, just me / Strange meadowlark / It's the talk of the town / Brother can you spare a dime / Lullaby / Tribute / I married an angel / Music maestro please / Briar bush / Newport waltz / I understand / More than you know
CD ______ **CD 83363**
Telarc / Sep '94 / Conifer/BMG

LAST SET AT NEWPORT
Introduction / Blues for Newport / Take five / Open the gates
CD ______ **7567813822**
Atlantic / Mar '93 / Warner Music

LATE NIGHT BRUBECK (Live From Blue Note)
These foolish things / Here's that rainy day / Theme for June / Duke / Thing's ain't what they used to be / C Jam blues / Don't get around much anymore / Who will take care of me / Koto song / So wistfully sad / Mean to me
CD ______ **CD 83345**
Telarc / Mar '94 / Conifer/BMG

LIVE (Brubeck, Dave Quartet)
CD ______ **BS 18009**
Bandstand / Jul '96 / Swift

LIVE AT MONTREUX 1982 (Brubeck, Dave Quartet)
CD ______ **DM 15015**
DMA Jazz / Jul '96 / Jazz Music

LIVE AT THE BERLIN PHILHARMONIC (Brubeck, Dave & Gerry Mulligan)
Things ain't what they used to be / Blessed are the poor / Duke of New Orleans / Indian song / Limehouse blues / Lullaby de Mexico / St. Louis blues / Out of the way of the people / Basin street blues / Take five / Out of nowhere / Mexican jumpin' bean
CD ______ **4814152**
Sony Jazz / Nov '95 / Sony

MOSCOW NIGHT
CD ______ **CCD 4353**
Concord Jazz / Jul '88 / New Note/ Pinnacle

NEW QUARTET AT MONTREUX
CD ______ **269 613 2**
Tomato / Mar '90 / Vital

NIGHTSHIFT
Yesterdays / I can't give you anything but love / Travellin' blues / Thank you you go to my head / Blues for Newport / Ain't misbehavin' / Knives / River stay 'way from my door
CD ______ **CD 83351**
Telarc / May '95 / Conifer/BMG

PAPER MOON
Music maestro please / I hear a rhapsody / Symphony / I thought about you / It's only a paper moon / Long ago and far away / St. Louis blues / Music, Maestro, Please
CD ______ **CCD 4178**
Concord Jazz / Aug '92 / New Note/ Pinnacle

PLAYS AND PLAYS AND PLAYS
CD ______ **OJCCD 716**
Original Jazz Classics / Nov '95 / Complete/Pinnacle / Jazz Music / Wellard

PLAYS MUSIC FROM WEST SIDE STORY (Brubeck, Dave Quartet)
CD ______ **4504102**
Sony Jazz / Jan '95 / Sony

QUARTET, THE
Castillian drums / Three to get ready / St. Louis Blues / Forty days / Summer song / Someday my Prince will come / Brandenburg Gate / In your own sweet way
CD ______ **17080**
Laserlight / Jan '97 / Target/BMG

QUIET AS THE MOON
Bicycle built for two / Linus and Lucy / Forty days / When I was a child / Quiet as the moon / Cast your fate to the wind / Benjamin / Looking at a rainbow / Desert and the parched land / Travellin' blues / Unisphere / When you wish upon a star
CD ______ **8208452**
Limelight / Dec '91 / PolyGram

SOMEDAY MY PRINCE WILL COME (Brubeck, Dave Quartet)
CD ______ **JHR 73572**
Jazz Hour / Nov '93 / Cadillac / Jazz Music / Target/BMG

STARDUST
Mam'selle / Stardust / Frenesi / Me and my shadow / At a perfum counter / Crazy Chris / Foggy day / Somebody loves me / Lyons busy / Look for the silver lining / Alice in wonderland / All the things you are / Lulu's back in town / My romance / Just one of those things
CD ______ **FCD 24728**
Fantasy / Jun '94 / Jazz Music / Pinnacle / Wellard

TAKE FIVE
Take five / Bossa nova USA / Unsquare dance / Someday my Prince will come / I'm in a dancing mood / It's a raggy waltz / Blue rondo a la Turk / Kathy's waltz / My favourite things / Castillian drums / Duke / Trolley song
CD ______ **VN 160**
Viper's Nest / May '95 / ADA / Cadillac / Direct / Jazz Music

TAKE FIVE
Take five / Unsquare dance / Bossa nova USA / Duke / Ain't misbehavin' / All by myself / Blues in the dark / Evenin' / I never know / My melancholy baby / River stay away from my door / There'll be some changes made / You can depend on me / Flamingo / C jam blues / Am I blue
CD ______ **BN 006**
Blue Nite / Nov '96 / Target/BMG

TAKE THE "FIVE" TRAIN
CD ______ **MCD 0522**
Moon / Apr '94 / Cadillac / Harmonia Mundi

THIS IS JAZZ
Take five / Gone with the wind / Someday my prince will come / Blue rondo a la Turk / Pennies from heaven / When you wish upon a star / Jeepers creepers / For all we know
CD ______ **CK 64615**
Sony Jazz / May '96 / Sony

TIME FURTHER OUT (Brubeck, Dave Quartet)
It's a raggy waltz / Bluesette / Charles Matthew hallelujah / Far more blues / Far more drums / Maori blues / Unsquare dance / Bru's boogie woogie / Blue shadows in the street / Slow and easy / It's a raggy waltz (live)
CD ______ **CK 64668**
Sony Jazz / Nov '96 / Sony

TIME IN
CD ______ **4746352**
Sony Jazz / Jan '95 / Sony

TIME OUT (Brubeck, Dave Quartet)
Blue rondo a la Turk / Strange meadowlark / Take five / Three to get ready / Kathy's waltz / Everybody's jumpin' / Pick up sticks
CD ______ **CK 65122**
Sony Jazz / Apr '97 / Sony

TO HOPE - A CELEBRATION (Recorded Live At The Washington National Cathedral) (Brubeck, Dave Quartet & Cathedral Choral Society Chorus)
To hope - a celebration / Lord have mercy / Desert and the parched land / Peace of Jerusalem / Alleluia / Father all powerful / Holy holy holy while he was at supper / When we eat this bread / Through him, with him / Great Amen / Our Father / Lamb of God / All my hope / Gloria
CD ______ **CD 80430**
Telarc / Sep '96 / Conifer/BMG

TRIO BRUBECK (Brubeck, Dave & Chris Brubeck/Dan Brubeck)
I cried for you / Broadway bossa nova / King for a day / Autumn / One moment worth years / Calcutta blues / Waltz limp / Jazzanians / Over the rainbow / Bossa nova USA / Some day my prince will come
CD ______ **8443372**
Limelight / Mar '93 / PolyGram

TRITONIS
Brother can you spare a dime / Like someone in love / Theme for June / Lord, Lord / Mr. Fats / Tritonis
CD ______ **CCD 4129**
Concord Jazz / Jul '95 / New Note/Pinnacle

WE'RE ALL TOGETHER AGAIN FOR THE FIRST TIME (Brubeck, Dave & Friends)
Truth / Unfinished woman / Koto song / Take five / Rotterdam blues / Sweet Georgia Brown
CD ______ **7567813902**
Atlantic / Mar '93 / Warner Music

Brubeck, Matthew

REALLY (Brubeck, Matthew & David Widelock)
CD ______ **CDJP 1030**
Jazz Point / Nov '91 / Cadillac / Harmonia Mundi

Bruce, Ed

PUZZLES
Puzzles / Blue denim eyes / By route of New Orleans / Shadows of her mind / Lonesome is me / Tiny golden locket / If I could just go home / Walker's woods / Give me more than you take / I'm getting better / Painted girls and wine / Price I pay to stay / Something else to mess your mind / I know better / Memphis morning / Blue bayou / Why can't I come home / Last train to Clarksville / Her sweet love and the baby / I'll take you away / Ninety seven more to go / I'd be best leaving you / Ballad of the drummer boy / Best be leaving you
CD ______ **BCD 15830**
Bear Family / Mar '95 / Direct / Rollercoaster / Swift

Bruce, Ian

BLODWEN'S DREAM
John / Factory life / Eldorado / Classical music / Ghost of the chair / Farewell deep blue / No noise / This peaceful evening / I can play you anything / Black fog / Blodwen's dream
CD ______ **FE 076CD**
Fellside / Nov '95 / ADA / Direct / Target/ BMG

FREE AGENT
Scarborough settlers lament / Bizzie Lizzie / Hearts of Ohio / Find out who your friends are / Please be here / Out of sight (Rolling Stones) / Corners / No satisfaction / Bad bet / Anchor line / Dawn of a brand new day / Free agents / Ladies left behind / Find out who your friends are (reprise)
CD ______ **IRCD 026**
Iona / Jul '94 / ADA / Direct / Duncans

KIND AND GENTLE NATURE
CD ______ **WGS 277CD**
Wild Goose / Nov '96 / ADA

OUT OF OFFICE
CD ______ **FE 085CD**
Fellside / Jul '92 / ADA / Direct / Target/ BMG

Bruce, Jack

CITIES OF THE HEART
Can you follow / Running thro' our hands / Over the cliff / Statues / First time I met the blues / Smiles and grins / Bird alone / Neighbor, neighbor / Born under a bad sign / Ships in the night / Never tell your Mother she's out of tune / Theme from an imaginary western / Golden days / Life on earth / NSU / Sittin' on top of the world / Politician / Spoonful / Sunshine of your love
CD Set ______ **CMPCD 1005**
CMP / Mar '96 / Cargo / Grapevine/ PolyGram / Vital/SAM

COLLECTOR'S EDITION, THE
CD ______ **CMPCD 1013**
CMP / Aug '96 / Cargo / Grapevine/ PolyGram / Vital/SAM

MONKJACK
Third degree / Boy / Shouldn't we / David's harp / Know one blues / Time repairs / Laughing on music / Street / Folksong / Weird of Hermiston / Tightrope / Food / Immoral ninth
CD ______ **CMPCD 1010**
CMP / Sep '95 / Cargo / Grapevine/ PolyGram / Vital/SAM

TRUCE (Bruce, Jack & Robin Trower)
Gonna shut you down / Gone too far / Thin ice / Last train to the stars / Take good care of yourself / Falling in love / Fat gut / Shadows touching / Little boy lost
CD ______ **S21 17609**
One Way / May '94 / ADA / Direct / Greyhound

Bruce Lee Band

BRUCE LEE BAND
CD ______ **AM 004CD**
Asian Man / Feb '97 / Cargo / Greyhound / Plastic Head

Bruce, Michael

IN MY OWN WAY
CD ______ **OW 34486**
One Way / Jun '97 / ADA / Direct / Greyhound

Bruce, Vin

CAJUNS OF THE BAYOU, THE
Les cadjins du bayou / He' jolie / La valse de la belle riviere / La cle'de mon coeur / Le del aisse / Troler / Appelle-moi sur le telephone / Ma vie da muscicien / C'est malheur reux / Ma belle du bayou / Prends ces chaines de mon coeur / Si j'aurais des ailes
CD ______ **SOC 90251**
Cajun Sound / Jul '96 / Target/BMG

Bruford, Bill

EARTHWORKS
Thud / Making a song and dance / Up North / Pressure / My heart declares a holiday / Emotional shirt / It needn't end in tears / Shepherd is eternal / Bridge Of Inhibition
CD ______ **EEGCD 48**
EG / Mar '87 / EMI

EARTHWORKS LIVE
Nerve / Up north / Stone's throw / Pilgrim's way / Emotional shirt / It needn't end in tears / All heaven broke loose / Psalm / Old song / Candles still flicker in Romania's dark / Brige of inhibition
CD ______ **CDVE 922**
Virgin / Apr '94 / EMI

HEAVENLY BODIES (A Collection) (Bruford, Bill Earthworks)
Stromboli kicks / Making a song and dance / Up north / Candles still flicker in Romania's darkness / Pigalle / My heart declares a holiday / Temple of the winds / Nerve /

Gentle persuasion / It needn't end in tears / Libreville / Dancing on Frith street / Bridge of inhibition
CD ______ CDVE 934
Venture / Jul '97 / EMI

MASTER STROKES 1978-85
Hell's bells / Gothic 17 / Travels with myself / And someone else / Fainting in coils / Beelzebub / One of a kind / Drum also waltzes / Joe Frazier / Sahara of snow / Palewell park / If you can't stand the heat / Five G / Living space / Split seconds
CD ______ EGCD 67
EG / Dec '88 / EMI

STAMPING GROUND
CD ______ 72438394762
Venture / Aug '94 / EMI

Bruisers

CRUISIN' FOR A BRUISIN'
CD ______ LP 095
Lost & Found / Jul '94 / Plastic Head

SOCIETY'S FOOLS
CD ______ LF 142CD
Lost & Found / May '95 / Plastic Head

STILL STANDING UP
CD ______ LF 280CD
Lost & Found / May '97 / Plastic Head

UP IN FLAMES
CD ______ LF 215CD
Lost & Found / Apr '96 / Plastic Head

Brujeria

MATANDO GUEROS
Para de Venta / Leyes narcos / Sacrificio / Santa Lucia / Matando Gueros / Seis seis seis / Cruza la Frontera / Grenudos Locos / Chingo de Mecos / Narcos-Satanicos / Desperado / Culeros / Misas Negras (sacrificio III) / Chinga tu Madre / Verga del Brujo/Estan Chingados / Molestando Ninos Muertos / Machetazos / Castigo del Brujo / Christa de la Roca
CD ______ RR 90612
Roadrunner / Sep '96 / PolyGram

RAZA ODIADA
CD ______ RR 89232
Roadrunner / Sep '96 / PolyGram

Brume Vs. Aphasia

SERIES ONE: ROUND ONE
CD ______ ATMOCD 1
Atmoject / Jan '97 / Cargo / ReR Megacorp

Brunel, Bunny

DEDICATION
CD ______ 500362
Musidisc / Nov '93 / Discovery

Bruner, Cliff

CLIFF BRUNER & HIS TEXAS WANDERERS 1937-1950 (5CD Set) (Bruner, Cliff Texas Wanderers)
So tired / Milk cow blues / Right key / You got to hi de hi / Shine / Can't nobody truck like me / Bringin' home the bacon / Under the silvery moon / Corrine Corrina / Four or five times / In the blue of the night / Oh you pretty woman / I ain't gonna give nobody none o' this jelly / Old fashioned love / Oh how I miss you tonight / One sweet letter from you / Dream train / Sun bonnet Sue / Tonight you belong to me / By a window at the end of the lane / Girl of my dreams / I saw your face in the moon / Red lips kiss my blues away / You can depend on me / In the blue of the night / Shine / Can't nobody truck like me / Sugar / My Daddy, my Mother and me / Truckin' on down / River stay away from my door / Baby won't you please come home / Beaumont rag / Annie Laurie / Bring it on home to Grandma / Ease my wearied mind / Remember / It makes no difference now / My bonnie lies over the ocean / Over moonlit waters / Draggin' the bow / Yearning just for you / Old Joe Turner blues / When you're smiling / Sister Kate / Sittin' on the moon / Kangaroo blues / I'll keep on loving you / I hate to lose you / Jessie / Over the hill / I'll keep on smiling / Truck driver's blues / I'm tired of you / Because / I'll forgive you / I'm still in love with you / Stardust / Other way / Peggy Lou / Singin' the low down blues down low / It's all over now / Tell me why little girl tell me why / Girl that you loved long ago / Little white lies / Kelly swing / San Antonio rose / Take me back again / You don't love me but I'll always care / I'm heading for that ranch in the sky / Over the trail / Ten pretty girls / Sorry / Sparkling blue eyes / New falling rain blues / I'll keep thinking of you / 'Neath the purple on the hills / 'Neath the purple on the hills / Draft board blues / I'll be faithful / Jesse's sister / Let me smile my last smile at you / Tequila rag / Red river rose / My time will come someday / Sun has gone down on our love / If it's wrong to love you / Born to be blue / Baby won't you tell me what you're doing to... / Snowflakes / That's what I like about the South / You took everything / My pretty blonde / You always hurt the one you love / Don't make me blue / Mother gave a son / I'll try not to cry / Won't you mend my aching heart / Roadhouse rag / Too wet to plow / Jessie / Lucille from mobile / You were all the world to me / You took advantage of a lonely heart / Honey what you doing to me / Santa Fe waltz / Rio Grande polka / Unfaithful one / San Antonio blues / Out of business / Mr. Postman / Ouch / You took advantage of a lonely heart / You better do better baby / Hard luck blues / Sweetest little Danny / I was a gambler in Texas / You've got to give me what's mine / I'm dying by pieces dear
CD Set ______ BCD 15932
Bear Family / Apr '97 / Direct / Rollercoaster / Swift

Brunet, Alain

ROMINUS
CD ______ LBLC 6541
Label Bleu / Jan '92 / New Note/Pinnacle

Bruninghaus, Ranier

CONTINUUM
Strahlenspur / Stille / Continuum / Raga rag / Schattenfrei / Innerfern
CD ______ 8156792
ECM / '90 / New Note/Pinnacle

FREIGEWEHT
Stufen / Spielraum / Radspuren / Die flusse hinauf / Freigeweht
CD ______ 8473292
ECM / Feb '96 / New Note/Pinnacle

Brunning Sunflower Blues ...

TRACKSIDE BLUES (Brunning Sunflower Blues Band)
CD ______ APCD 031
Appaloosa / Jun '94 / ADA / Direct / TKO Magnum

Bruno, Francisco

EL LUGAR (THE PLACE) (Bruno, Francisco & Richie Havens)
CD ______ CDSGP 063
Prestige / Aug '92 / Else / Total/BMG

Bruno, Jimmy

BURNIN
Eternal triangle / Pastel / One for Amos / Our love is here to stay / Burnin' / Moonlight in Vermont / Central Park West / Giant steps / Witchcraft / On the sunny side of the street / Rose for a peg / That's all
CD ______ CCD 4612
Concord Jazz / Sep '94 / New Note/ Pinnacle

LIKE THAT
EV / Raezer's edge / Waltz for Nancy / There is no greater love / Uguana's uncle / Pat's house / Night dreamer / Way you look / Tonight / Like that / Stars fell on Alabama / Unit seven
CD ______ CCD 4698
Concord Jazz / Jun '96 / New Note/ Pinnacle

LIVE AT BIRDLAND
F8 / Move / Groove yard / Valse hot / Segment / Au privava / These foolish things remind me of you / For JT / Anthropology / My one and only love
CD ______ CCD 47682
Concord Jazz / Jul '97 / New Note/Pinnacle

SLEIGHT OF HAND (Bruno, Jimmy Trio)
Egg plant pizza / Stompin' at the Savoy / Body and soul / Wheat thins / Night mist / Big shoes / Mandha de carnaval / Tenderly / Song for Jimmy and Susanna / All the things you are / Lionel's hat / Here's that rainy day
CD ______ CCD 4532
Concord Jazz / Nov '92 / New Note/ Pinnacle

Bruno's Salon Band

LUCKY DAY
CD ______ SOSCD 1251
Stomp Off / May '93 / Jazz Music / Wellard

Brunsden, Martin

OUT OF THE WOOD
CD ______ IS 01CD
Isis / Apr '94 / ADA / Direct

Bruntnell, Peter

CAMELOT IN SMITHEREENS
CD ______ ALMCD 14
Almost / Sep '97 / Pinnacle

CANNIBAL - THE PETER BRUNTNELL COLLECTION
CD ______ ALMCD 002
Almo Sounds / Feb '96 / Pinnacle

Brus Trio

AIM
CD ______ DRCD 214
Dragon / Nov '87 / ADA / Cadillac / CM / Roots / Wellard

Brutal Juice

I LOVE THE WAY THEY SCREAM WHEN THEY DIE
CD ______ VIRUS 157CD
Alternative Tentacles / Nov '94 / Cargo / Greyhound / Pinnacle

Brutal Obscenity

IT'S BECAUSE OF THE BIRDS AND THE FLOWERS
Death is a damn good solution / Straight and stoned / Mom or dad / 1-2-3 / God is just a fairy tale / No more feelings left / Overtaking / It's because of the birds and the flowers / Emotion suicide / It's cruel (part 2) / Useless immortality / Defensor minor / Hangover DDD
CD ______ CMFT 2CD
CMFT / Jun '89 / Plastic Head

Brutal Truth

EXTREME CONDITIONS...
CD ______ MOSH 069CD
Earache / Sep '92 / Vital

KILL TREND SUICIDE
CD ______ RR 69482
Relapse / Feb '97 / Pinnacle / Plastic Head

NEED TO CONTROL
Collapse / Black door mine / Turn face / God player / I see red / Iron lung / Bite the hand / Ordinary madness / Media blitz / Judgement / Brain trust / Choice of a new generation / Mainliner / Displacement / Crawlspace / BTITB / Bethroned / Painted clowns / Wish you were here
CD ______ MOSH 110CD
Earache / Sep '97 / Vital

Brutality

SCREAMS OF ANGUISH
CD ______ NB 075CD
Nuclear Blast / Jul '93 / Plastic Head

WHEN THE SKY TURNS BLACK
CD ______ NB 1152
Nuclear Blast / Jan '95 / Plastic Head

Bruton, Stephen

RIGHT ON TIME
CD ______ DOS 7013
Dos / Jul '95 / ADA / CM / Direct

WHAT IT IS
CD ______ DOSCD 7002
Dos / Sep '94 / ADA / CM / Direct

Bruynel, Ton

LOOKING EARS
CD ______ BVHAASTCD 9214
Bvhaast / Oct '93 / Cadillac

Bryan, Morgan

ASLEEP WHILE THE RAIN FALLS
CD ______ DCD 01
Dox Music / Oct '93 / Dox Music

THORN
CD ______ DT 11
Dox Music / '94 / Dox Music

UNDER EVERY SKY
CD ______ DCD 02
Dox Music / '94 / Dox Music

Bryant, Dana

WISHING FROM THE TOP
CD ______ 9362456422
Warner Bros. / Jul '96 / Warner Music

Bryant, Don

COMIN' ON STRONG
CD ______ HIUKCD 133
Hi / Aug '92 / Pinnacle

Bryant, Jimmy

SUNTIDE DESERT JAM (Bryant, Jimmy & Jody Reynolds & Les Paul)
Out of nowhere / Jammin' the blues / Caravan / (Back home again in) Indiana / Rose of desert view / Speedo / I can't get started (with you) / Yakety axe / Undecided / Market street blues / Rose room / How high the moon
CD ______ C5CD 611
See For Miles/C5 / Feb '94 / Pinnacle

Bryant, Leon

FINDERS KEEPERS/MIGHTY BODY (HOTSY TOTSY)
Finders keepers / Your kind of loving / I'm gonna put a spell on you / Are you ready (until tonight) / You're my everything / Honey / I can see me loving you / Never / Mighty body (hotsy totsy) / Come and get it / Just the way you like it / Something more / You can depend on me / Can I / I promise / In the heat of the night
CD ______ DEEPM 011
Deep Beats / Jan '97 / BMG

Bryant, Ray

ALL MINE...AND YOURS
Walrus walk / Samba elegante / Darlin' / Marilyn / Adalia / Reflection / I don't care / Nuts and bolts / Pawn ticket / Big buddy
CD ______ 5104232
EmArCy / Jan '93 / PolyGram

BLUE MOODS
Sometimes I feel like a Motherless child / Good morning heartache / Blues in the closet / Bag's groove / Blue Monk / Since I fell for you / Lush life / Blues in G
CD ______ 8424382
EmArCy / Mar '93 / PolyGram

HOT TURKEY
CD ______ BB 881
Black & Blue / Apr '97 / Discovery / Koch / Wellard

MONTREUX 1977
CD ______ OJCCD 371
Original Jazz Classics / Nov '95 / Complete/Pinnacle / Jazz Music / Wellard

PLAYS BASIE AND ELLINGTON
Jive at five / Swingin' the blues / 9.20 special / Teddy the toad / Blues for Basie / I let a song go out of my heart / It don't mean a thing if it ain't got that swing / Things ain't what they used to be
CD ______ 8322352
ECM / Mar '88 / New Note/Pinnacle

RAY BRYANT TRIO (Bryant, Ray Trio)
CD ______ OJCCD 793
Original Jazz Classics / Nov '95 / Complete/Pinnacle / Jazz Music / Wellard

THROUGH THE YEARS VOL.1 (60th Birthday Special)
Autumn leaves / Cubano chant / Prayer song / St. Thomas / Moanin' / Blues changes / Cry me a river / Blue bossa / Django / Little Susie
CD ______ 5127642
EmArCy / May '92 / PolyGram

THROUGH THE YEARS VOL.2 (60th Birthday Recording)
You and the night and the music / Shake a lady / Satin doll / Oleo / Lil' darlin' / Whisper not / Cold turkey / 'Round midnight / So in love / Misty
CD ______ 5129332
EmArCy / May '92 / PolyGram

Bryant, Rusty

FIRE EATER
Fire eater / Free at last / Hooker / Mister S
CD ______ PCD 10014
Prestige / Jun '96 / Cadillac / Complete/ Pinnacle

FRIDAY NIGHT FUNK FOR SATURDAY NIGHT BROTHERS
Friday night funk for Saturday night brothers / Down by the Cuyahoga / Have you seen her / Mercy mercy mercy / Blues for a brother
CD ______ PCD 10054
Prestige / Jun '96 / Cadillac / Complete/ Pinnacle

LEGENDS OF ACID JAZZ, THE
Cootie boogaloo / Funky Mama / Funky rabbits / Night train / With these hands / Home fries / Cold duck time / Ballad of Oren Bliss / Lou Lou / Soul liberation / Freeze-dried soul
CD ______ PRCD 24168
Prestige / Oct '96 / Cadillac / Complete/ Pinnacle

Bryant, Willie

BLUE AROUND THE CLOCK
CD ______ DEL 685CD
Delmark / Feb '96 / ADA / Cadillac / CM / Direct / Hot Shot

BLUES AROUND THE CLOCK
Amateur night in Harlem / Blues around the country / Blues around the country / Naggin' wife blues: *Pomus, Doc* / Blues without booze: *Pomus, Doc* / Sneaky Pete / Because your baby is on your mind / Honey in a hurry: *Watson, Laurel* / Blues around the clock / Blues around the clock / Alley alley blues: *Pomus, Doc* / Blues in the red: *Pomus, Doc* / Reboppin' for red: *Smith, Ben* / I found out: *Range, Bob* / Tell me: *Range, Bob* / Algiers blues / Phungie phungie an' stchew / Kangaroo blues: *Watson, Laurel* / I can't sleep: *Range, Bob* / You'll never miss the water 'til the well runs dry: *Range, Bob* / It's over because we're through: *Range, Bob*
CD ______ DE 685
Delmark / Jun '97 / ADA / Cadillac / CM / Direct / Hot Shot

CLASSICS 1935-1936
CD ______ CLASSICS 768
Classics / Aug '94 / Discovery / Jazz Music

Bryant's Jubilee Quartet

BRYANT'S JUBILEE QUARTET/ QUINTET 1928-1931
CD ______ DOCD 5437
Document / May '96 / ADA / Hot Shot / Jazz Music

Bryars, Gavin

FAREWELL TO PHILOSOPHY (Bryars, Gavin & English Chamber Orchestra/ James Judd)
Farewell to philosophy / One last bar, then Joe can sing / By the vaar
CD 4541262
Point Music / Sep '96 / PolyGram

HOMMAGES
My first hommage / English mail coach / Vespertine park / Hi-tremelo
CD TWI 0272
Les Disques Du Crepuscule / Oct '93 / Discovery

SINKING OF THE TITANIC
CD TWI 9222
Les Disques Du Crepuscule / Oct '93 / Discovery

Bryden, Beryl

BERYL BYRDEN 1975 & 1984
CD ACD 113
Audiophile / Aug '94 / Jazz Music

I'VE GOT WHAT IT TAKES (A BBC Radio Celebration Of The Music Of Bessie Smith) (Bryden, Beryl & The Blue Boys)
Sunset Cafe stomp / Beale Street blues / Downhearted blues / I've got what it takes / St. Louis blues / Hotter than that / Trombone cholly / Nobody knows you when you're down and out / Cakewalking babies / Froggie more / Wild man blues / There'll be a hot time in the old town tonight / Gimme a pigfoot and a bottle of beer / Kitchen man / Forty and tight / Good man is hard to find / Young woman's blues / Alexander's ragtime band
CD LACD 71
Lake / Oct '96 / ADA / Cadillac / Direct / Jazz Music / Target/BMG

Bryson, Jeanie

I LOVE BEING HERE WITH YOU
CD CD 83336
Telarc / May '93 / Conifer/BMG

Bryson, Peabo

I'M SO INTO YOU
Feel the fire / Reaching for the sky / Love walked out on me / Crosswinds / I'm so into you / Don't touch me / Let's fall in love/ You send me: *Bryson, Peabo & Natalie Cole* / Love will find you: *Bryson, Peabo & Natalie Cole* / I love the way you love me: *Bryson, Peabo & Natalie Cole* / Turn the hands of time: *Bryson, Peabo & Natalie Cole* / Let the feeling flow: *Bryson, Peabo & Natalie Cole* / Give me your love: *Bryson, Peabo & Natalie Cole* / I believe in you: *Bryson, Peabo & Natalie Cole* / Tonight I celebrate my love: *Bryson, Peabo & Natalie Cole*
CD CTMCD 326
EMI / Jul '97 / EMI

Brythoniaid Male Voice Choir

20 OF THE BEST
CD SCD 2018
Sain / Feb '93 / ADA / Direct / Greyhound

BSG

WARM INSIDE
CD XM 031CD
X-Mist / Apr '92 / Cargo / SRD

BT

IMA
CD 0630123452
Perfecto/East West / Oct '95 / Warner Music

Buarque, Chico

SONHO DE UM CARNAVAL (2CD Set)
CD Set 1917492
EPM / Apr '97 / ADA / Discovery

Bubble Puppy

GATHERING OF PROMISES, A
Hot smoke and sasafrass / Todds tune / I've got to reach you / Lonely / Gathering of promises / Hurry sundown / Elizabeth / It's safe to say / Road to St Stephens / Beginning
CD 642038
EVA / Jun '94 / ADA / Direct

Bubonique

TRANCE ARSE VOL.3
You can't fool the dead / Cod is love / Pianna / Truck turner / Sermon / Freestyle masterclass 1 - sawing / Talking' about talkin' about / Freebird / I've always liked hunting / Oi copper / Return of the nice age / What's E saying / Hey, handsome / Industrial woman / Rainbow buffalo cornwoman / Freestyle masterclass 2 - drilling / Q magazine / Kind of pure / George aid suite / Abbabortion / Sven of Newcastle
CD KWCD 028
Kitchenware/Vital / Sep '95 / Vital

Buccaneer

CLASSIC
Intro - Moonlight Sonata / Bad man sonata / Gal sink fi bore: *Buccaneer & Red Rat* / Hold on pon him / Brick wall: *Buccaneer & Richie Stephens/Dennis Brown* / Nowadays woman / Poverty: *Buccaneer & Papa San* / Vintage old bruk: *Buccaneer & Papa San* / Skettel concerto / Hotter this year / Good director / Second place / Punky brewster / Stop light / Buccaneer medley / Real ganja man / Man tief sonata / Outro - Blue danube waltz
CD GRELCD 235
Greensleeves / Mar '97 / Jet Star / SRD

THERE GOES THE NEIGHBOURHOOD
CD MAINCD 1
Main Street / Dec '94 / Jet Star

Buchanan, Brian

AVENUES
CD JFCD 002
Jazz Focus / Dec '94 / Cadillac

Buchanan, Isobel

SONGS OF SCOTLAND
John Anderson, My Jo / I'm owre young tae marry yet / Ye banks and braes o' bonnie Doon / Aye waukin' o / Comin' thro' the rye / Queen's mairies / My heart is sair / Deirdre's farewell to Scotland / Durisdeer / Rowan tree / Oor ain fireside / Mairi's wedding / Bonnie Earl O'Moray / Charlie is my darling / My ain folk
CD LCOM 6038
Lismor / Sep '95 / ADA / Direct / Duncans / Lismor

WHITE CLIFFS OF DOVER, THE (Songs and Music of the 40's) (Buchanan, Isobel & English Chamber Orchestra)
Calling all workers / Dambusters march / Knightsbridge march / Spitfire prelude and fugue / There'll always be an England / We'll meet again / White cliffs of Dover / Nightingale sang in Berkeley square / When I grow too old to dream / Would you please oblige us with a Bren Gun / It's a lovely day tomorrow / I'll be seeing you / Love is the sweetest thing / All the things you are / Long ago and far away / So in love / Every time we say goodbye / I only have eyes for you / Always
CD CDDCA 598
ASV / Nov '87 / Select

Buchanan, Jack

ELEGANCE
Night time / Living in clover / Fancy our meeting / Oceans of time / Like Monday follows Sunday / When we get our divorce / Not bad / Dancing honeymoon / And her mother came too / Who / Now that I've found you / You forgot your gloves / One I'm looking for / Sweet so an so / I think I can / Dapper Dan / Alone with my dreams / Two little bluebirds / Goodnight Vienna / It's not you / There's always tomorrow
CD CDAJA 5033
Living Era / Apr '91 / Select

JACK BUCHANAN
Fancy our meeting / You forgot your gloves / I've looked for trouble / This year, next year / Goodnight Vienna / Chirp chirp / Leave a little for me / Dapper Dan / One good tune deserves another / Let's say goodnight till the morning / Stand up and sing / Alone with my dreams / Weep no more baby / Who / Take a step / I think I can / Now that I've found you / Yes Mr. Brown / Don't love you / Living in clover / Jack Buchanan medley
CD PASTCD 9763
Flapper / Nov '91 / Pinnacle

THIS'LL MAKE YOU WHISTLE
CD CMSCD 010
Movie Stars / Oct '91 / Conifer/BMG

Buchanan, Roy

DANCING ON THE EDGE
Peter Gunn / Chokin' kind / Jungle gym / Drowning on dry land / Petal to the metal / You can't judge a book by the cover / Cream of the crop / Beer drinking woman / Whiplash / Baby, baby, baby / Matthew
CD ALCD 4747
Alligator / May '93 / ADA / CM / Direct

HOT WIRES
High wire / That did it / Goose grease / Sunset over broadway / Ain't no business / Flash Gordon / 25 miles / These arms of mine / Country boogie / Blues lover
CD ALCD 4756
Alligator / May '93 / ADA / CM / Direct

MALAGUENA
CD 11132
Annecillo / Jul '97 / Greyhound

ROY BUCHANAN LIVE
Short fuse (instrumental) / Green onions (instrumental) / Strange kind of feeling / Pressure (instrumental) / Peter Gunn (instrumental) / Chicago smoke shop (instrumental) / Blues in E (instrumental) / Hey Joe / Foxy lady / Fantasia (instrumental)
CD CDCBL 758
Charly / May '95 / Koch

SWEET DREAMS (The Roy Buchanan Anthology)
CD 5170862
Polydor / Apr '96 / PolyGram

WHEN A GUITAR PLAYS THE BLUES
When a guitar plays the blues / Mrs. Pressure / Nickel and a nail / Short fuse / Why don't you want me / Country boy / Sneaking Godzilla through the alley / Hawaiian punch / Chicago smokeshop
CD ALCD 4741
Alligator / Aug '92 / ADA / CM / Direct

Buchman, Rachel

JEWISH HOLIDAY SONGS FOR CHILDREN
CD ROUCD 8028
Rounder / Jan '94 / ADA / CM / Direct

SING A SONG OF SEASONS
CD ROUCD 8042
Rounder / May '97 / ADA / CM / Direct

Buck O Nine

TWENTY EIGHT TEETH
CD TVT 57602
TVT / Apr '97 / Cargo / Greyhound

Buck Pets

TO THE QUICK
Living is the biggest thing / Shave / Walk it to the payphone / To the quick / Nothing's ever gonna be alright again / Smiler with a knife / C'mon baby / Crutch / Rocket to you / Car chase / Worldwide smile / Manatee / Bargain
CD 727262
Restless / Nov '93 / Vital

Buck Wild

BEAT ME SILLY
CD LOBSTER 1003CD
Lobster/Fat Wreck Chords / Jul '96 / Plastic Head

Bucketheads

ALL IN THE MIND
Bomb (these sounds fall into my mind) / Sayin' dope / Sunset (new at) / Time and space / You're a runaway / Come and be gone / Got myself together / Jus' plain funky / I wanna know / Went / Little Louie Bonus / Bucketheads outro
CD CDTIVA 1010
Positiva / Jan '96 / EMI

Buckingham Banjos

BANJO SPECTACULAR (Buckingham Banjos & Fred Hartley)
CD 4524942
Decca / Mar '97 / PolyGram

Buckley, Jeff

GRACE
Mojo Pin / Grace / Last Goodbye / Lilac Wine / So real / Hallelujah / Lover / You should've come over / Corpus christi carol / Eternal life / Dream brother
CD 4759282
Columbia / Aug '94 / Sony

LIVE AT SIN-E
CD ABB 61CD
Big Cat / Mar '94 / 3mv/Pinnacle

Buckley, Jimmy

COUNTRY FAVOURITES
CD RITZCD 557
Ritz / Apr '96 / Pinnacle

Buckley, Tim

DREAM LETTER (Live In London 1968/ 2CD Set)
Introduction / Buzzin' fly / Phantasmagoria in two / Morning glory / Dolphins / I've been out walking / Earth is broken / Who do you love / Pleasant street / Love from room 109 - Strange feelin' / Carnival song / Hallucinations / Troubadour / Dream letter / Happy time / Wayfaring stranger / You got me runnin' / Once I was
CD Set PT 340703
Manifesto / Feb '97 / Vital

GREETINGS FROM LA
Move with me / Get on top / Sweet surrender / Night hawkin' / Devil eyes / Hong Kong bar / Make it right
CD 7599272612
Elektra / Jan '96 / Warner Music

HAPPY SAD
Strange feeling / Buzzin' fly / Love from room 109 at the islander / Dream letter / Gypsy woman / Sing a song for you
CD 7559740452
WEA / Feb '92 / Warner Music

HONEY MAN
CD ED 450CD
Edsel / Nov '95 / Pinnacle

LIVE AT THE TROUBADOUR 1969
Strange feelin' / Venice mating call / I don't need it to rain / I had a talk with my woman / Gypsy woman / Blue melody / Chase the blues away / Driftin' / Nobody walkin'
CD PT 340705
Manifesto / May '97 / Vital

LOOK AT THE FOOL
Look at the fool / Bring it on up / Helpless / Freeway blues / Tijuana moon / Ain't it peculiar / Who could deny you / Mexicali voodoo / Down the street / Wanda Lu
CD PT 340702
Manifesto / Feb '97 / Vital

SEFRONIA
Dolphins / Honey man / Because of you / Peanut man / Martha / Quicksand / Stone in love / Sefron after Asklepiades after Kafka / Sefronia, the Kings chain / Sally go round the roses / I know I'd recognise your face
CD P 2340701
Manifesto / Feb '97 / Vital

Buckner, Milt

GREEN ONIONS
CD BLE 590872
Black & Blue / Oct '94 / Discovery / Koch / Wellard

MILT BUCKNER & ILLINOIS JACQUET (Buckner, Milt & Illinois Jacquet)
CD PCD 7017
Progressive / Aug '94 / Jazz Music

Buckner, Richard

BLOOMED
CD GRCD 340
Glitterhouse / May '97 / Avid/BMG

Bucks Fizz

BEST AND THE REST, THE
CD MER 010
Tring / Mar '93 / Tring

BEST OF BUCKS FIZZ
Land of make believe / Making your mind up / Piece of the action / I hear talk / Run for your life / Talking in your sleep / Now those days are gone / My camera never lies / If you can't stand the heat / Heart of stone / Magical / London town / One of those nights / Golden days
CD 74321183272
Ariola Express / Feb '94 / BMG

BEST OF BUCKS FIZZ
CD 74321292792
RCA / Jul '95 / BMG

GREATEST HITS OF BUCKS FIZZ, THE
Land of make believe / My camera never lies / If you can't stand the heat / Piece of the action / Now those days are gone / Run for your life / Golden days / I hear talk / When we were young / Talking in your sleep / Heart of stone / One of those nights / Rules of the game / London town / Thief in the night / Making your mind up
CD 74321446722
Camden / Feb '97 / BMG

Buckshot Lefonque

MUSIC EVOLUTION
Here we go again / Music evolution / Wasineveritis / James Brown / Another day / Try these on / Buckshot rebuttal / My way (doin' it) / Better than I am / Paris is burning / Jungle grove / Weary with oil / Black Monday / Phoenix / Samba hop / ...And we out / One block past it
CD 4841952
Columbia / May '97 / Sony

Buckwheat Zydeco

100% FORTIFIED ZYDECO
CD CD 1024
Black Top / '88 / ADA / CM / Direct

BUCKWHEAT ZYDECO & THE 11'S SONT PARTIS BAND (Buckwheat Zydeco & The 11's Sont Partis Band)
CD ROUCD 11528
Rounder / '88 / ADA / CM / Direct

TURNING POINT
CD ROUCD 2045
Rounder / '88 / ADA / CM / Direct

WAITIN' FOR MY YA-YA
CD ROUCD 251
Rounder / '88 / ADA / CM / Direct

Bucky

LIVE AT THE VINEYARD THEATRE (Bucky & John Pizzarelli)
CD CHR 70025
Challenge / Feb '96 / ADA / Direct / Jazz Music / Wellard

Budapest Gypsy Orchestra

BUDAPEST GYPSY ORCHESTRA
CD CDODE 1310
ODE / Feb '90 / CM / Discovery

Budapest Klezmer Band

FOLKLORE YIDDISH
CD QUI 903070
Quintana / Apr '92 / Harmonia Mundi

YIDDISH FOLKLORE
CD HMA 1903070CD
Musique D'Abord / Aug '94 / Harmonia Mundi

Budapest Ragtime Band

ELITE SYNCOPATIONS
CD CDPAN 122
Pan / Apr '93 / ADA / CM / Direct

Budd, Harold

AGUA
CD SINE 003
Sine / Sep '95 / Grapevine/PolyGram

GLYPH
CD MTM 37
Made To Measure / Jul '96 / New Note/ Pinnacle

LOVELY THUNDER
Gunfighter / Sandtreader / Ice floes in Eden / Olancha farewell / Flowered knife shadows (for Simon Raymonde) / Gypsy violin
CD EEGCD 46
EG / Oct '86 / EMI

LUXA
Sidelong glance from my round neggertiti / Agnes Martin / Anish Kapoor / Paul McCarthy / Serge Poliakoff / Djion / Porphyry / How dark the response to our slipping away / Nove Alberi / Chet / Mandan / Ferai / Grace Marion Brown (sweet earth flying) / Steven Brown (pleasure)
CD ASCD 030
All Saints / Sep '96 / Discovery / Vital

MOON AND THE MELODIES, THE (Budd, Harold & The Cocteau Twins)
Sea, swallow me / Memory gongs / Why do you love me / Eyes are mosaics / She will destroy you / Ghost has no home / Bloody and blunt / Ooze out and away, one how
CD CAD 611CD
4AD / Nov '86 / RTM/Disc

MUSIC FOR 3 PIANOS (Budd, Harold & Ruben Garcia & Daniel Lentz)
Pulse, pause, repeat / La muchacha de los suenos dorados / Iris / Somos tres / Messenger / La casa bruja
CD ASCD 014
All Saints / Dec '92 / Discovery / Vital

PAVILION OF DREAMS, THE
Bismallahi'rrahmani'rrahim / Let us go into the House of The Lord / Butterfly Sunday / Madrigals of the rose ange / Juno
CD CDOVD 482
EG / Jun '97 / EMI

PEARL, THE (Budd, Harold & Brian Eno)
Late October / Stream with bright fish / Silver ball / Against the sky / Lost in the humming air / Dark eyed sister / Their memories / Pearl / Foreshadowed / Echo of night / Still return
CD EEGCD 37
EG / Jan '87 / EMI

SERPENT IN QUICKSILVER/ ABANDONED CITIES
Afar / Wanderer / Rub with ashes / Children on the Hill / Widows charm / Serpent in quicksilver / Dark star / Abandoned cities
CD ASCD 08
All Saints / Jun '92 / Discovery / Vital

WHITE ARCADES, THE
White arcades / Balthus bemused by colour / Child with a lion / Real dream of sails / Algebra of darkness / Totems of the red sleeved warrior / Room / Coyote / Kiss
CD ASCD 03
All Saints / Jun '92 / Discovery / Vital

Budd, Roy

REBIRTH OF THE BUDD
Fear is the key / Birth of the Budd / Get Carter / Soldier blue / Theme to Mr. Rose / Aranjeuz mon amour / Jesus Christ superstar / Whizz ball / In my hole / Too much attention / Lead on / Zeppelin / Carey treatment / Envy, greed and gluttony / Girl talk / Pavanne / Call me / Play thing / Little boat / So nice / Wonderful life is / Fields of green, skies of blue / Lust / Hurry to me / This hostage escapes
CD NEMCD 927
Sequel / Apr '97 / BMG

Buddah On The Moon

STRATOSPHERIC
CD DRIVE 12
Drive-In / Jun '97 / Cargo

Buddy & Ghost Riders

FOR FOOLS ONLY
CD BRAM 1992322
Brambus / Nov '93 / ADA

Budgie

BEST OF BUDGIE
Breadfan / I ain't no mountain / I can't see my feelings / Baby, please don't go / Zoom club / Breaking all the house rules / Parents / In for the kill / In the grip of a tyre-fitter's hand
CD MCLD 19067
MCA / Oct '92 / BMG

ORNITHOLOGY VOL.1 (Six Ton Budgie)
Southern girl / Three legged race / Say it like it is / In the grip of a tyrefitter's hand / You know I will return / Martin John shuffle / Pink cadillac / Oh so far / Our life / Motorbiking / Young is a world / Dead to rights
CD AXEL/VINTAP 2
Axel/Vinyl Tap / Jul '97 / Cargo

PANZER DIVISION DESTROYED (Live At The Reading Festival 1980/1982 - 2CD Set)
Breaking all the house rules / Crime against the world / Napoleon Bona / Forearm smash / Panzer division destroyed / Wildfire / I turned to stone / You're a superstar / She used me up / Breadfan / Forearm smash / Crime against the world / I turned to stone / Truth drug / You're a superstar / She used me up / Panzer division destroyed / In the grip of a tyrefitters hand / I turned to stone / You're a superstar / She used me up
CD Set PILOT 014
Burning Airlines / Jul '97 / Total/Pinnacle

UNPLUCKED (Six Ton Budgie)
CD AXEL/VINTAP 1
Axel/Vinyl Tap / Jan '96 / Cargo

Budha Building

SOUNDS FROM THE ABNORMAL HEART
CD DSCD 001
TEQ / Jul '97 / Cargo / Plastic Head

Bue, Papa

40 YEARS JUBILEE CONCERT (Bue, Papa Viking Jazz Band)
CD MECCACD 2010
Music Mecca / May '97 / Cadillac / Jazz Music / Wellard

COLLECTION, THE (2CD Set) (Bue, Papa Viking Jazz Band)
CD Set MECCACD 2101
Music Mecca / May '97 / Cadillac / Jazz Music / Wellard

DOWN BY THE RIVERSIDE 1969-1971 (Bue, Papa Viking Jazz Band)
CD STCD 5503
Storyville / May '97 / Cadillac / Jazz Music / Wellard

EVERYBODY LOVES SATURDAY NIGHT (Bue, Papa Viking Jazz Band)
Everybody loves Saturday night / Yellow dog blues / Blueberry Hill / Song was born / Weary blues / Tin roof blues / New Orleans / Mack the knife / Oh baby / I'm confessin' that I love you / Basin Street blues / Big butter and egg man / Maple leaf rag
CD CDTTD 590
Timeless Traditional / Nov '93 / Jazz Music / New Note/Pinnacle

ICE CREAM (Bue, Papa Viking Jazz Band)
CD MECCAVCD 1000
Music Mecca / Jul '93 / Cadillac / Jazz Music / Wellard

LIVE AT SLUKEFTER (Bue, Papa Viking Jazz Band)
CD MECCACD 1028
Music Mecca / Jun '93 / Cadillac / Jazz Music / Wellard

ON STAGE (Bue, Papa Viking Jazz Band)
CD CDTTD 511
Timeless Traditional / Sep '86 / Jazz Music / New Note/Pinnacle

TIVOLI BLUES (Bue, Papa Viking Jazz Band)
CD MECCACD 1001
Music Mecca / Aug '90 / Cadillac / Jazz Music / Wellard

Buen, Knut

AS QUICK AS FIRE
CD HSR 0002
Henry Street / Mar '96 / Direct

SAMSPEL
CD BK 12CD
Buen / Mar '96 / ADA

Buffalo Daughters

CAPTIN VAPOUR ATHLETES
CD GR 030CD
Grand Royal / Apr '97 / Cargo / Plastic Head

SOCKS, DRUGS AND ROCK 'N' ROLL EP
CD GR 043CD
Grand Royal / Jun '97 / Cargo / Plastic Head

Buffalo Road

HOTEL INCIDENT
CD OLKCD 002
Backwater / Apr '95 / SRD

Buffalo Springfield

AGAIN
Mr. Soul / Child's claim to fame / Everydays / Expecting to fly / Bluebird / Hung upside down / Sad memory / Good time boy / Rock 'n' roll woman / Broken arrow
CD 7903912
Atlantic / '88 / Warner Music

BUFFALO SPRINGFIELD
For what its worth / Sit down I think I love you / Nowadays Clancy can't even sing / Go and say goodbye / Pay the price / Burned / Out of my mind / Mr. Soul / Bluebird / Broken arrow / Rock 'n' roll woman / Expecting to fly / Hung upside down / Child's claim to fame / Kind woman / On the way home / I am a child / Pretty girl why / Special care / Uno mundo / In the hour of not quite rain / Four days gone / Questions
CD 756903892
Atlantic / Feb '92 / Warner Music

LAST TIME AROUND
On the way home / It's so hard to wait / Pretty girl why / Four days gone / Carefree country day / Special care / Hour of not quite rain / Questions / I am a child / Merry go round / Uno mundo / Kind woman
CD 7567903932
Atlantic / Mar '94 / Warner Music

RETROSPECTIVE (The Best Of Buffalo Springfield)
For what it's worth / Hello Mr. Soul / Sit down I think I love you / Kind woman / Bluebird / On the way home / Nowadays Clancy can't even sing / Broken arrow / Rock 'n' roll woman / I am a child / Go and say goodbye / Expecting to fly
CD K 7904172
Atlantic / Mar '88 / Warner Music

Buffalo Tom

BIG RED LETTER DAY
Sodajerk / I'm allowed / Tree house / Would not be denied / Latest monkey / My responsibility / Dry land / Torch singer / Late at night / Suppose / Anything that way
CD BBQCD 142
Beggars Banquet / Sep '93 / RTM/Disc / Warner Music

BIRD BRAIN
Bird brain / Caress / Enemy / Fortune teller / Directive / Skeleton key / Guy who is me / Crawl / Baby / Bleeding heart
CD BBL 31CD
Beggars Banquet / Sep '95 / RTM/Disc / Warner Music

BUFFALO TOM
Sunflower suit / Plank / Impossible / 500,000 warnings / Bus / Racine / In the attic / Flushing stars / Walk away / Reason why
CD SST 250CD
SST / Jul '89 / Plastic Head

LET ME COME OVER
CD SITU 36CD
Situation 2 / Mar '92 / Pinnacle

SLEEPY EYED
Tangerine / Summer / Kitchen door / Rules / It's you / When you discover / Sunday night / Your stripes / Sparklers / Clobbered / Sundress / Twenty points / Souvenir / Crueler
CD BBQCD 177
Beggars Banquet / Jul '95 / RTM/Disc / Warner Music

Buffalo, Norton

LOVIN' IN THE VALLEY OF THE MOON/ DESERT HORIZON
Lovin' in the valley of the moon / One kiss to say goodbye / Ghetto hotel / Nobody wants me / Puerto de azul / Hangin' tree / Another day / Rosalie / Jig is up / Eighteen wheels / Sea of key / Echoes of the last stampede / Desert horizon / Age old puppet / Wasn't it bad enough / Thinkin' 'bout you babe / Hopin' you'll come back / High tide in wingo / Walkin' down to Suzy's / Cold, cold city nights / Where has she gone / Sun comes in the morning / Anni in the morning
CD EDCD 431
Edsel / Jul '95 / Pinnacle

Buffett, Jimmy

ALL TIME GREAT HITS
Margaritaville / Fins / Come Monday / Volcano / Changes in latitudes / Cheeseburger in paradise / Son of a son of a sailor / Stars fell on Alabama / Miss you so badly / Why don't we all get drunk / Pirate looks at forty / We went to Paris / Grapefruit - juicy fruit / Pencil thin mustace / Boat drinks / Chanson pour les petits enfants / Banana republic / Lat mango in Paris
CD PLATCD 4903
Platinum / Sep '94 / Prism

Bufford, Mojo

STATE OF THE (BLUES) HARP
CD JSPCD 233
JSP / Mar '90 / ADA / Cadillac / Direct / Hot Shot / Target/BMG

Bug

TAPING THE CONVERSATION
CD WSCD 018
Word Sound Recordings / Jun '97 / Cargo / SRD

Bug Guts

BIG BOWL OF WARM FUR
CD VC 102
Vinyl Communication / Nov '96 / Cargo / Greyhound / Plastic Head

Bug, Steve

RELEASED TRACKS
CD RAW 610CD
Raw Elements / Dec '96 / Plastic Head / SRD

Bugbear

PLAN FOR THE ASSASINATION OF THE BUGBEAR
Theme from the bugbear / (I got a) New crush / Ride roughshod / Punkist / Mystic boy / Marlin / Damaged III / Dando motherfucker / Fucking through / Triple-brrr / Panik / I love the girl with the money shot face / Teen city intrigue / I like violence / 22 Boy whore / I hate my band
CD MASKCD 049
Vinyl Japan / Jun '95 / Plastic Head / Vinyl Japan

Bugskull

CROCK
CD DRL 029
Darla / Jan '97 / Cargo

CROCK OMPST
CD DRL 028
Darla / Jan '97 / Cargo

DISTRACTED SNOWFLAKE VOL.1
CD DRL 031
Darla / Jun '97 / Cargo

SNAKLAND
CD SCR 020
Scratch / Dec '96 / Cargo

Buhlan, Billy

LINKS EIN MADCHEN, RECHTS EIN MADCHEN
Rauber rock / Links ein madchen, rechts ein madchen / Du wirst niemals ein cowboy sein / Mir ist so dideldadeldum / Eine frau muss man kussen / Leo, Leo, Leo / Irgendwann, irgendwie, irgendwo / So schon ist Melanie / Signorina aus Messina / Sowas wie dich / Wie lange das noch gut geht / Heute abend ball (im alten ballhaus) / Ich schreibe meiner frau heut' einen liebsb / Kannst du das vergessen / Einmal blond, einmal braun / Fragen sie den fachmann / Ja, der Tobby (choo choo eisenbahn) / Du bist ja viel zu schade / Das war der scchinderhannes / Eine marchenweise / Wenn der regen nicht war / Damals waren wir sechzehn / Dieser tag / Liber leierlastenmann / Ich hab' mich so an dich gewohnt / Ich hab' noch einen koffer in Berlin / Das war sein milljoh / Lass mich dein primaner auf der 'prima' sein
CD BCD 16136
Bear Family / Apr '97 / Direct / Rollercoaster / Swift

Buick 6

CYPRESS GROVE
CD TX 1003CD
Taxim / Jan '94 / ADA

JUICE MACHINE
CD TX 1014CD
Taxim / Apr '96 / ADA

Buick MacKane

PAWN SHOP YEARS, THE
End / Falling down again / Black shiny beast / Edith / Queen Anne / Say goodnight / Big shoe head / John Conquest, you've got enough dandruff on / Wandering eye / Loose
CD RCD 10361
Rykodisc / Feb '97 / ADA / Vital

Built To Spill

NORMAL YEARS, THE
CD KLP 52CD
K / May '96 / Cargo / Greyhound / SRD

PERFECT FROM NOW ON
Randy described eternity / I would hurt a fly / Stop the show / Made up dreams / Velvet waltz / Out of site / Kicked it in the sun / Untrustable/Part 2
CD EFA 0499226
City Slang / Feb '97 / RTM/Disc

THERE'S NOTHING WRONG WITH LOVE
CD _______________ EFA 049632
City Slang / Oct '95 / RTM/Disc

Buju Banton

BUJU BANTON MEETS GARNETT SILK AND TONY REBEL (Buju Banton & Friends)
CD _______________ RNCD 2033
Rhino / Oct '93 / Grapevine/PolyGram / Jet Star

MR. MENTION
Batty rider / Love how the gal dem flex / Long black woman / Love how you sweet / Woman no fret / Have to get you tonight / Dickie / Love me brownin' / Buju movin' / Who say / How the world a run / Bona fide love
CD _______________ 5220222
Mercury / Jan '94 / PolyGram
CD _______________ PHCD 18
Penthouse / Jun '97 / Jet Star

TIL SHILOH
Shiloh / Till I'm glad to rest / Murderer / Champion / Untold stories / Not an easy road / Only man / Complaint / Chuck it so / How could you / Wanna be loved / It's all over / Hush baby hush / What you're gonna do / Rampage
CD _______________ 5241192
Loose Cannon / Jul '95 / Jet Star / PolyGram

VOICE OF JAMAICA
Searching / Red rose / Commitment / Deportees / No respect / If loving was a crime / Good body / Wicked act / Tribal war / Little more time / Him take off / Willy (don't be silly) / Gone a lead / Make my day / Operation ardent
CD _______________ 5180132
Mercury / Aug '93 / PolyGram

Bulag, Ci

MORIN HUUR
CD _______________ VICG 52122
JVC World Library / Feb '96 / ADA / CM / Direct

Bulba, Taras

SKETCHS OF BABEL
CD _______________ HY 39100782
Hyperium / Nov '93 / Cargo / Plastic Head

Bulgarian National Folk ...

PIRIN FOLK (Bulgarian National Folk Ensemble)
CD _______________ CDPT 827
Prestige / Jun '94 / Else / Total/BMG

Bulgarka Junior Quartet

FETES TRADITIONNELLES BULGARES
CD _______________ D 2550
Studio SM / Nov '96 / Discovery

LEGEND OF THE BULGARIAN VOICES
CD _______________ EUCD 1331
ARC / Nov '95 / ADA / ARC Music

Bull

GORDON ZONE
CD _______________ HMS 1972
Homestead / Jun '93 / Cargo / SRD

Bull City Red

COMPLETE RECORDINGS 1935-1939
CD _______________ SOB 035272
Story Of The Blues / Dec '92 / ADA / Koch

Bull, Geoff

VINTAGE GEOFF BULL
CD _______________ BCD 356
GHB / Nov '96 / Jazz Music

Bulldog Breed

MADE IN ENGLAND
CD _______________ SPMWRCD 0052
Worldwide / Jun '97 / Greyhound

Bullet In The Head

JAWBONE OF AN ASS
CD _______________ ORGAN 0112
Lungcast / May '94 / SRD

Bullet LaVolta

GIFT, THE
CD _______________ TAANG 29CD
Taang / Nov '92 / Cargo

Bullhead, Earl

LAKOTA SONGS, THE
CD _______________ SPALAX 14871
Spalax / Oct '96 / ADA / Cargo / Direct / Discovery / Greyhound

Bullitnuts

1ST OF THE DAY
CD _______________ PORK 036
Pork / Sep '96 / Kudos / Pinnacle / Prime

Bumble Bees

BUMBLE BEES
CD _______________ HBCD 0012
Hummingbird / Jun '97 / ADA / Direct / Grapevine/PolyGram

Bunch, John

JOHN BUNCH PLAYS KURT WEILL
CD _______________ CRD 144
Chiaroscuro / Mar '96 / Jazz Music

STRUTTIN' (Bunch, John & Phil Flanagan)
CD _______________ ARCD 19157
Arbors Jazz / May '97 / Cadillac

Bundrick, John 'Rabbit'

DREAM JUNGLE
CD _______________ RMCCD 0199
Red Steel / May '96 / Pinnacle

RUN FOR COVER
CD _______________ RMCCD 0198
Red Steel / Jul '96 / Pinnacle

SAME OLD STORY
CD _______________ RMCCD 0182
Red Steel / Aug '96 / Pinnacle

TOUR GUIDE
CD _______________ RMCCD 0204
Red Steel / Jul '96 / Pinnacle

Bunka, Roman

COLOUR ME CAIRO
CD _______________ ENJACD 90832
Enja / Dec '95 / New Note/Pinnacle / Vital/SAM

Bunn, Teddy

SPIRITS OF RHYTHM
CD _______________ JSPCD 307
JSP / Apr '89 / ADA / Cadillac / Direct / Hot Shot / Target/BMG

Bunnett, Jane

RENDEZ VOUS BRAZIL/CUBA
Baiao do porao / Pam Pam / Ritos de angola / Choro de pere / Barreto / For you / Forro na vovo / Um a zero / Rendez-vous / Sweet melody
CD _______________ JUST 742
Justin Time / Aug '96 / Cadillac / New Note/Pinnacle

WATER IS WIDE, THE
Elements of freedom / Time again / Real truth / Serenade to a cuckoo / You must believe in spring / Influence peddling / Pannonica / Brakes' sake / Burning tear / Lucky strike / Water is wide / Rockin' in rhythm
CD _______________ ECD 220912
Evidence / Jul '94 / ADA / Cadillac / Harmonia Mundi

Bunny Rugs

TALKING TO YOU
CD _______________ GRELCD 215
Greensleeves / May '95 / Jet Star / SRD

Bunter, Billy

FUTURE OF HARD DANCE VOL.1, THE (2CD Set) (Bunter, Billy 'Daniel')
CD Set _______________ ALPHACD 1
Alpha Projects / Jun '97 / Alphamagic

Burach

BORN TIRED
How on Earth / Funky fat challenge / Nothing left to say / Highfield set / Drop my body / Born tired / Ring around the moon / Antidote / Sleep of the dead / Smuggler's skull and cross bones / You're not the only one / Destitution / Lullaby
CD _______________ CDTRAX 136
Greentrax / Jul '97 / ADA / Direct / Duncans / Highlander

WEIRD SET, THE
All I ask / Boiling black kettle / Curve / Post-conscious modernisation of space / Candlelight reel / Jar o'lentils / Zombie song / Return to Milltown / Tarbolton lodge / Oni bucharesti / Green Loch / Vincent black lightening 1952 / Rest of your life / January the 8th / Concertina / Dick Gossips / Earl's chair / Halfway round / Walking the line / What shall we drink to tonight
CD _______________ CDTRAX 093
Greentrax / Jul '95 / ADA / Direct / Duncans / Highlander

Burbank, Albert

CREOLE CLARINETS (Burbank, Albert & Raymond Burke)
CD _______________ MG 9005
Mardi Gras / Feb '95 / Jazz Music

Burch, Elder J.E.

COMPLETE RECORDED WORKS 1927-29 (Burch, Elder J.E. & Rev. Beaumont)
CD _______________ DOCD 5329
Document / Mar '95 / ADA / Hot Shot / Jazz Music

Burchell, Chas

UNSUNG HERO
Juicy Lucy / Bobbin' / Gone into it / Have you met Miss Jones / It's you or no one/ Shades / Marsh bars / Which way / Just squeeze me / Blue monk / Tickle toe / Come back / Sometimes / Sonnymoon for two / Solea
CD _______________ IOR 70262
In & Out / Sep '95 / Vital/SAM

Burdett, Phil

PATCHOULI ELECTRIC
CD _______________ CDSGP 0291
Prestige / Jul '96 / Else / Total/BMG

Burdon, Eric

BIG HITS (2CD Set)
CD Set _______________ CPCD 82882
Charly / Jul '97 / Koch

CRAWLING KING SNAKE
No more elmore / Crawling king snake / Take it easy / Dey won't / Wall of silence / Street walker / It hurts me too / Lights out / Bird on the beach
CD _______________ CDTB 017
Magnum Music / Nov '92 / TKO Magnum

ERIC BURDON DECLARES WAR
Vision of Rassan / Dedication / Roll on Kirk / Tobacco Road / I have a dream / Blues for the Memphis Slim / Birth / Mother Earth / Mr. Charlie / Danish pastry / You're no stranger
CD _______________ 74321305262
Avenue / Sep '95 / BMG

ERIC BURDON LIVE
CD _______________ RRCD 220
Receiver / Jul '96 / Grapevine/PolyGram

GREATEST HITS
House of the rising sun / Spill the wine / San Franciscan nights / Help me girl / Bring it on home to me / We gotta get out of this place / Don't let me be misunderstood / White houses / Anything / Monterey / When I was young / CC rider / Boom boom / I'm crying / It's my life / Don't bring me down
CD _______________ RM 1542
BR Music / Apr '97 / Target/BMG

LOST WITHIN THE HALLS OF FAME
CD _______________ JETCD 1011
Jet / Apr '95 / Total/Pinnacle

MISUNDERSTOOD
CD _______________ AIM 1054
Aim / Oct '95 / ADA / Direct / Jazz Music

RARE MASTERS VOL.1
CD _______________ SPV 08589992
SPV / Mar '96 / Koch / Plastic Head

RARE MASTERS VOL.2
CD _______________ SPV 08544232
SPV / Aug '96 / Koch / Plastic Head

SOLDIER OF FORTUNE
Heart attack / Power company / Highway mover / Wicked man / Ghetto child / Portrait of a soldier / Devil's daughter / Comeback / You can't kill my spirit / Yes indeed, yeah / House of the rising sun / ghetto child (reprise)
CD _______________ CDTB 180
Thunderbolt / Feb '97 / TKO Magnum

THAT'S LIVE (Burdon, Eric & The Band)
CD _______________ INAK 854 CD
In Akustik / '88 / Direct / TKO Magnum

Burgess, John

KING OF THE HIGHLAND PIPERS
CD _______________ TSCD 466
Topic / May '93 / ADA / CM / Direct

Burgess, Mark

PARADYNING (Burgess, Mark & Yves Altana)
CD _______________ GOODCD 8
Dead Dead Good / Oct '95 / Pinnacle

SPRING BLOOMS TRA LA LA (2CD Set)
CD Set _______________ INDIGO 11742
Indigo / Oct '96 / Cargo

Burgess, Sally

OTHER ME, THE
CD _______________ DMHCD 7
Timbre / Oct '96 / Koch

SALLY BURGESS SINGS JAZZ
CD _______________ CDVIR 8308
TER / Dec '89 / Koch

Burgess, Sonny

1956 - 1959
We wanna boogie / Red headed woman / Prisoner's song / All night long / Life's too short to live / Restless / Ain't got a thing / Daddy blues / Fannie Brown / Ain't gonna do it / You / Hand me down my walking cane / Please listen to me / Gone / My babe / My bucket's got a hole in it / Sweet misery / What'cha gonna do / Oh mama / Truckin' down the avenue / Feelin' good / So glad you're mine / One night / Always will / Little town baby / You're not mine / Mr. Blues / Find my baby for me / Tomorrow night / Tomorrow never comes / Skinny Ginny / So soon / Mama Loochie / Mama Loochie / Itchy / Thunderbird / Kiss goodnight / Sadie's back in town / Smoochin' Jill / My baby loves me / One broken heart
CD Set _______________ BCD 15525
Bear Family / Jul '91 / Direct / Rollercoaster / Swift

ARKANSAS WILD MAN, THE
We wanna boogie / Red headed woman / Prisoner's song / Restless / Ain't got a thing / Daddy blues / Hand me down my walking cane / Fannie Brown / One broken heart / Gone / Please listen to me / My babe / Sweet misery / Oh mama / Truckin' / Down tha avenue / What'cha gonna do / So glad you're mine / One night / My little town baby / Mr. Blues / Find my baby for me / Tomorrow night / Skinny Ginny / Mama Loochie / Sadie's back in town
CD _______________ CPCD 8103
Charly / Jun '95 / Koch

RAZORBACK TAPES, THE (Burgess, Sonny & The Pacers/Bobby Crafford)
CD _______________ CLCD 4405
Collector/White Label / Oct '96 / TKO Magnum

SONNY BURGESS
CD _______________ ROUCD 3144
Rounder / Jun '96 / ADA / CM / Direct

Burgos, 'Wild' Bob

HOMETOWN ROCKIN'
CD _______________ PT 606001
Part / Jun '96 / Nervous

REBEL KEEPS ROCKIN', THE
Right behind you / White lightning / Salt Box Hill / Hypnotised / Dreamland boogie / Long live rock'n'roll / Emma / Reedin' the blues / It's been a long time / Whatever will be will be (que sera sera) / Back seat driver / Beware of the hound / Ride on rebels / Forever rockin' / Taste of wild berries / Mumbo jumbo / Beat the clock / I'm telling you now
CD _______________ RAUCD 024
Raucous / Jun '97 / Nervous / RTM/Disc / TKO Magnum

Burke, Joe

BUCKS OF ORANMORE, THE (Burke, Joe & Charlie Lennon)
Yellow tinker/The Sally Gardens / Connachtman's rambles/The cat in the corner / Dillon's fancy/Toss the feathers / Frieze breeches / Beeswing/Tailor's twist / Paddy Kelly's reels / Rambles of Kitty/Sacko's jig / High level/Western / Master Crowley's/Jug of punch / Golden eagle/Fiddler's contest / Trim the velvet / PJ Moloneys/Paddy Fahy's / Mullingar Lea/Crooked road to Dublin / Job of Journeywork/The blackbird / Humours of Ennistymon/Larry O'Gaff / Wonder/Liverpool hornpipe / Willie Coleman's/ Dinny O'Brien's / Bucks of Oranmore
CD _______________ GLCD 1165
Green Linnet / Feb '97 / ADA / CM / Direct / Highlander / Roots

HAPPY TO MEET, SORRY TO PART
CD _______________ GLCD 1069
Green Linnet / Feb '93 / ADA / CM / Direct / Highlander / Roots

PURE IRISH TRADITIONAL MUSIC ON THE ACCORDION
Lambert's jig / Knockagow / Richard Dwyer's / Paddy Kelly's / Morrison's / Molly's / Jackson's jig / Ivy leaf / Ginley's fancy / Last night's fun / Hut in the bog / Music in the glen / Green fields of America / Paddy Fahy's / Pigeon on the gate / Bunch of key's / Ballinasloe fair / Drunken tinker / Fahy's / Port padraig na carra / Frost is all over / Spike island lassies / Farewell to Leitrim / Return from Camden Town / Ton Moyland's frolic / Limestone rock / Boyne hunt
CD _______________ PTICD 1015
Pure Traditional Irish / Mar '97 / ADA / CM / Direct / Ross

TAILOR'S CHOICE, THE
Dark woman of the Glen / Mills are grinding/ Paddy Doorhy's reel / Green blanket / Dean Brig of Edinburgh / Jack Coughlan's fancy / Coolin' / Sean Reid's fancy/Kerry reel / Mama's pet/Tailor's choice / Blind Mary / Humours of Quarry Cross/Jackson's bottle of brandy / Roisin Dubh / Fort of Kincora/ Caroline O'Neill's hornpipe / Were you at the Rock / Limestone rock/Banshee reel / O'Rahilly's grave
CD _______________ GLCD 1045
Green Linnet / Aug '93 / ADA / CM / Direct / Highlander / Roots

TRADITIONAL MUSIC OF IRELAND
Bucks of Oranmore/Wind that shakes the barley / Dogs among the bushes/Gorman's / Trip to the cottage/Tatter Jack Walsh / Minny Foster/The banks / Sporting Nell/ Boyne hunt / Murray's fancy/Smell of the

bog / Patsy Touhey's/Molly Ban / College groves/Flogging reel / Jackson's reel / Grey goose/Sixpenny money / Bonnie Kate/Jenny's chickens / Galway bay/Contradiction / Pat burke's jigs/Fraher's jigs / Longford spinster/Paddy Lynn's delight
CD _______________ GLCD 1048
Green Linnet / Jun '93 / ADA / CM / Direct / Highlander / Roots

Burke, Kevin

CELTIC FIDDLE FEST (Burke, Kevin & Johnny Cunningham/C. Lemaitre)
CD _______________ GLCD 1133
Green Linnet / Oct '93 / ADA / CM / Direct / Highlander / Roots

EAVESDROPPER (Burke, Kevin & Jackie Daly)
CD _______________ LUNCD 039
Mulligan / Aug '94 / ADA / CM

HOOF AND MOUTH (Burke, Kevin & Open House)
Tour de taille / Drag her round the road / Sporting Paddy / Connemara stockings / Jame's Keanes / Okarina / Tattoo / Hoof and mouth / Oedipus rex / Split rock / Pipe on the hob / Blue adder / When I die / Paddy the caffler / Glen cottage polka / Tolka polka / Dueino kolo / Tour de traille / Kivatasaluevalssie / Bright sunny south
CD _______________ GLCD 1169
Green Linnet / Mar '97 / ADA / CM / Direct / Highlander / Roots

IF THE CAP FITS
Kerry reel/Michael Coleman's reel/Wheels of the world / Dinney Delaney's/Yellow wattle / Mason's apron/Laington's reel / Paddy Fahy's jigs/Cliffs of Moher / Star of Munster / Biddy Martin's and Bill Sullivan's polkas/ Ger the Rigger / Bobby Casey's hornpipe / Toss the feathers / College groves/Pinch of snuff/Earl's chair / Woman of the house/Girl that broke my heart/Drunken tinker / Paddy Cronin/McFadden's handsome daughter / Hunter's purse/Toss the feathers
CD _______________ GLCD 3009
Green Linnet / Aug '92 / ADA / CM / Direct / Highlander / Roots

OPEN HOUSE
CD _______________ GLCD 1122
Green Linnet / Jun '92 / ADA / CM / Direct / Highlander / Roots

PORTLAND (Burke, Kevin & Michael O'Dohmnhaill)
Maudabawn chapel/Wild Irishman/Moher reel / Eirigh a shiuir / Breton Gavottes / Rolling waves/Market town/Scatter the mud / Aird ui chumhaing / Paddy's return/Willy Coleman's/Up in the air / Lucy's fling/ S'iomadh rud a chunnaic mi/Some say the Devil i / Is fada Liom Uaim I / Tom Morrison's/Beare Island reel/George White's favourite / Dipping the sheep
CD _______________ GLCD 1041
Green Linnet / Oct '88 / ADA / CM / Direct / Highlander / Roots

PROMENADE
CD _______________ LUNCD 028
Mulligan / Aug '94 / ADA / CM

SWEENEY'S DREAM
CD _______________ OSS 18CD
Ossian / Mar '94 / ADA / CM / Direct / Highlander

UP CLOSE
Lord Gordon's reel / Finnish polka/Jessica's polka / Thrush in the straw/Health to the ladies/Boys of the town / Tuttle's reel/Bunch of green rushes/Maids of Mitchelstown / Shepherd's daughter/Jerusalem ridge / Michael Kennedy's reel / Bloom of youth/Molloy's favourite/Cabin hunter / Boys of Ballycastle/Stack of barley / Raheen medley / Rambler/Chapel bell / Peeler's jacket/Flax in bloom/Eileen curran / Orphan/Mist on the mountain/Stolen purse
CD _______________ GLCD 1052
Green Linnet / Feb '90 / ADA / CM / Direct / Highlander / Roots

Burke, Malena

SALSEANDO
Homenaje a matamoros / Longina / Chencha la gamba / Comprension / Me voy p'al pueblo / Bruca manigua / Capullito de aleli / De noche / Realidad y fantasia / Que bella es Cuba / El madrugador / Seguire sin sonar
CD _______________ PSCCD 1006
Pure Sounds From Cuba / Feb '95 / Henry Hadaway / THE

Burke, Raymond

IN NEW ORLEANS (Burke, Raymond & Cie Frazier)
Gypsy love song / Hindustan / Dead bug blues / Wonderful one / I want somebody to love / At sundown / Oh daddy / All that I ask is love / I surrender dear / Sweet little you / Honky tonk town / Maybe you're mine / Blues in A flat / Dirty rag / All by myself
CD _______________ 504CDS 27
504 / Sep '94 / Cadillac / Jazz Music / Target/BMG / Wellard

RAYMOND BURKE & HIS SPEAKEASY BOYS
CD _______________ AMCD 47
American Music / Jan '94 / Jazz Music

Burke, Solomon

DEFINITION OF SOUL, THE
CD _______________ VPBCD 38
Virgin / Jan '97 / EMI

GREATEST HITS
Down in the valley / Just out of reach / How many times / Baby (I wanna be loved) / Gotta travel on / Looking for my baby / I'm hanging up my heart for you / Cry to me / I almost lost my mind / Tear fell / Be bop Grandma / Keep the magic working
CD _______________ RSACD 859
Sequel / Jan '97 / BMG

HOME IN YOUR HEART (Best of Solomon Burke)
Home in your heart / Down in the valley / Looking for my baby / I'm hanging up my heart for you / Cry to me / Just out of reach / Goodbye baby (baby goodbye) / Words / Stupidity / Send me some lovin' / Go on back to him / Baby (I wanna be loved) / Can't nobody love you / Got to get you off my mind / Someone to love me / You're good for me / dance, dance, dance / Everybody needs somebody to love / Tonight's the night / Baby, come on home / If you need me / Price / Get out of my life woman / Save it / Take me (just as I am) / When she touches me / I wish I knew (how it would feel to be free) / Party people / Keep a light in the window / I feel a sin coming on / Meet me in the church / Someone is watching / Detroit city / Shame on me / I stayed away too long / It's just a matter of time / Since I met you baby / Time is a thief / Woman how do you make me love you like I do / It's been a change / What'd I say
CD _______________ 8122702842
Atlantic / Jul '93 / Warner Music

I WISH I KNEW
I wish I knew (How it would feel to be free) / Get out of my life woman / Meet me in church / By the time I get to Phoenix / Then you can tell me goodbye / What'd I say / Since I met you baby / Save it / Shame on me / Why, why, why / I feel a sin coming on / Lawdy Miss Clawdy / Mountain of pride / Suddenly / Keep lookin' / I stayed away too long / I need your love so bad
CD _______________ RSACD 863
Sequel / Mar '97 / BMG

IF YOU NEED ME
If you need me / Words / Stupidity / Go on back to him / I said I was sorry / It's alright / Home in your heart / I really don't want to know / You can make it if you try / Send me some lovin' / This little ring / Tonight my heart she is crying
CD _______________ RSACD 860
Sequel / Jan '97 / BMG

KING OF ROCK 'N' SOUL, THE
Good rockin' tonight / My babe / Lonesome highway / Letter from my darling / Sweet walkin' woman / Everybody needs somebody to love / If you need me/Tonight's the night/I almost lost my mind / Down in the valley / Got to get you off my mind
CD _______________ CDBTEL 7006
Black Top / May '97 / ADA / CM / Direct

KING OF SOUL
Boo hoo hoo / Hold on I'm comin' / Sweeter than sweetness / Sidewalks, fences and walls / Let the love flow / More / Lucky / Please come back home to me
CD _______________ CPCD 8014
Charly / Feb '94 / Koch

KING SOLOMON (The Soul Sounds Of Solomon Burke)
It's been a change / Take me as I am / Time is a thief / Keep a light in the window / Baby, come on home / Detroit city / Someone is watching / Party people / When she touches me / Woman how do you make me / It's just a matter of time / Presents for Christmas / Only love can save me now / I don't want you anymore / Can't stop loving you now
CD _______________ RSACD 862
Sequel / Mar '97 / BMG

LIVE AT HOUSE OF BLUES
CD _______________ BT 1108CD
Black Top / Dec '94 / ADA / CM / Direct

ROCK 'N' SOUL
Goodbye baby goodbye / Cry to me / Won't you give him (one more) / If you need me / Hard, ain't it hard / Can't nobody love you / Just out of reach / You're too good for me / You can't love them all / Someone to love me / Beautiful brown eyes / He'll have to go / Everybody needs somebody / Yes I do / Price / Got to get you off my mind / Peepin' / Little girl that loves me / Dance dance dance / Maggie's farm
CD _______________ RSACD 861
Sequel / Mar '97 / BMG

SOUL ALIVE
Everybody needs somebody to love / I almost lost my mind / Just out of reach / If you need me / Tonight's the night / You're good for me / What am I living for / Monologue / Take me (just as I am) / Down in the valley / Proud Mary / Tonight's the night (reprise) / Beautiful brown eyes / Just a matter of time / Hold what you've got / He'll have to go / Cry to me / Gotta get you off my mind / Meet me in the church / Price / Words / Send me some lovin' / Having a party / Amen
CD _______________ ROUCD 11521
Rounder / Oct '96 / ADA / CM / Direct

SOUL OF THE BLUES
CD _______________ BT 1095CD
Black Top / Jan '94 / ADA / CM / Direct

YOU CAN RUN BUT YOU CAN'T HIDE
To thee / What do that to me / This is it / My heart is a chapel / Picture of you / You can run but you can't hide / Friendship ring / I'm not afraid / Don't cry / Christmas presents / I'm in love / Leave my kitten alone / No man walks alone / I'm all alone / I need you tonight / Walking in a dream / You are my one love / For you and you alone
CD _______________ RBD 108
Mr. R&B / Apr '91 / CM / Swift / Wellard

Burland, Dave

BENCHMARK
CD _______________ FC 004CD
Fat Cat / Jul '94 / ADA / CM / Direct

HIS MASTERS CHOICE
CD _______________ RGFCD 009
Road Goes On Forever / '92 / Direct

Burman, Karin & Peter

GROWING GREEN
CD _______________ GIM 003
Gimli / May '97 / Cadillac

Burn

SO FAR, SO BAD
CD _______________ FONECD 001
Formula One / Aug '95 / Plastic Head

SPARK TO A FLAME
CD _______________ FONECD 003
Formula One / Jan '96 / Plastic Head

Burn, Chris

HENRY COWELL CONCERT, A
CD _______________ ACTA 7
Acta / Oct '94 / Acta / Cadillac / Impetus

Burnell, Kenny

MOON AND SAND
Moon and sand / My ship / For once in my life / UMMG / Blue bossa / Stolen moments / Love for sale / Lost in the stars
CD _______________ CCD 4121
Concord Jazz / Jun '92 / New Note/ Pinnacle

Burnett, T-Bone

B52 BAND & THE FABULOUS SKYLARKS
CD _______________ MCAD 22140
One Way / Sep '94 / ADA / Direct / Greyhound

BEHIND THE TRAP DOOR
Strange combination / Amnesia and jealousy (oh Lana) / Having a wonderful time wish you were here / Law of average / My life and the women who lived it / Welcome home, Mr.Lewis
CD _______________ VEXCD 3
Demon / Aug '92 / Pinnacle

TRUTH DECAY
Quicksand / Talk talk talk talk / Boomerang / Love at first sight / Madison Avenue / Drivin' wheel / Come home / Power of love / House of mirrors / Tears, tears, tears / Pretty girls / I'm coming home
CD _______________ FIENDCD 71
Demon / Jun '97 / Pinnacle

Burnette, Dorsey

GREAT SHAKIN' FEVER
Great shakin' fever / Don't let go / Dying ember / raining in my heart / Sad boy / He gave me my hands / Good good lovin' / Full house / Feminine touch / It's no sin / Creator / Biggest lover in town / Buckeye road / That's me without you / No one but him / Cry for your love / Rains came down / Country boy in the army / Somebody nobody wants / It could've been different / Little child / With all your heart / Look what you've missed / Gypsy magic / I would do anything
CD _______________ BCD 15545
Bear Family / '93 / Direct / Rollercoaster / Swift

Burnette, Johnny

BURNETTE BROTHERS, THE (Burnette, Johnny & Dorsey)
CD _______________ RSRCD 005
Rockstar / Dec '94 / Direct / Nervous / Rollercoaster / TKO Magnum

DREAMIN'/JOHNNY BURNETTE
Dreamin' / Lovesick blues / Please help me, I'm falling / Haul off and love me one more time / Love me / Kaw-Liga / Settin' the woods on fire / I want to be with you always / Cincinnati fireball / My special angel / Finders keepers / I really don't want to know / You're sixteen / Crying in the chapel / Dream lover / Oh lonesome me / I beg your pardon / I love you baby / Little boy sad / It's only make believe / Singin' the blues / You're so fine / I go down to the river / Let's think about living
CD _______________ BGOCD 329
Beat Goes On / Dec '96 / Pinnacle

ROCK 'N' ROLL TRIO/TEAR IT UP (Burnette, Johnny Rock 'N' Roll Trio)
Honey hush / Lonesome train (on a lonesome track) / Sweet love on my mind / Rockabilly boogie / Lonesome tears in my eyes / All by myself / Train kept a rollin' / I just found out / Your baby blue eyes / Chains of love / I love you so / Drinkin' wine spo-dee-o-dee / Tear it up / You're undecided / Oh baby babe / Eager beaver baby / Touch me / Midnight train / If you want it enough / Blues stay away from me / Shattered dreams / My love, you're a stranger / Rock therapy / Please don't leave me
CD _______________ BGOCD 177
Beat Goes On / Jun '93 / Pinnacle

ROCKABILLY BOOGIE (The Complete Recordings) (Burnette, Johnny Rock 'N' Roll Trio)
Rockabilly boogie / Please don't leave me / Rock therapy / Lonesome train (on a lonesome track) / Sweet love on my mind / My love, you're a stranger / Your baby blue eyes / I love you so / Train kept a rollin' / All by myself / Drinkin' wine spo-dee-o-dee / Blues stay away from me / Honey hush / Lonesome tears in my eyes / I just found out / Chains of love / Lonesome train (on a lonesome track) / I love you so (master) / If you want it enough / Butterfingers / Eager beaver baby / Touch me / Tear it up / Oh baby babe / You're undecided / Midnight train / Shattered dreams
CD _______________ BCD 15474
Bear Family / '88 / Direct / Rollercoaster / Swift

THAT'S THE WAY I FEEL
CD _______________ RSRCD 006
Rockstar / Dec '94 / Direct / Nervous / Rollercoaster / TKO Magnum

Burnin' Chicago Blues Machine

BOOGIE BLUES
CD _______________ GBW 003
GBW / Mar '92 / Harmonia Mundi

Burnin' Rain

RITUAL MEDICINE SHOW
CD _______________ ME 1001
Mind Eye / May '97 / Cargo

Burning Flames

FAN DE FLAMES
CD _______________ BF 015
JW / Jul '97 / Jet Star

WORKEY WORKEY (Highlights From The 9th Cartagena Festival)
CD _______________ CPCD 8134
Charly / Jan '96 / Koch

Burning Orange

13
CD _______________ CDMFN 209
Music For Nations / Dec '96 / Pinnacle

Burning Sky

CREATION
CD _______________ CR 7027CD
Canyon / Nov '96 / ADA

Burning Spear

APPOINTMENT WITH HIS MAJESTY
Appointment with His Majesty / Play Jerry / Reggae physician / Music / African Jamaican / Loving you / My island / Don't sell out / Commercial development / Glory be to Jah / Clean it up / Come in peace
CD _______________ HBCD 20605
Heartbeat / Jun '97 / ADA / Direct / Greensleeves / Jet Star

CHANT DOWN BABYLON (The Island Anthology/2CD Set)
Marcus Garvey / Slavery days / I & I survive / Old Marcus Garvey / Tradition / Invasion / Door peep / No more war / Black soul / Man in the hills / Cultivation / Sun / Throw down your arms / It's a long way round / Dry and heavy / Black disciples / Lion / Jordan river / Jah no dead / Marcus children suffer / Social living / Marcus say Jah no dead / Nyah Keith / Civilize reggae / Mek we dweet / My roots / Recall some great men / Great men's dub / One people / African woman / Jah kingdom / Praise him / Should I / Estimated prophet / Thank you
CD Set _______________ 5241902
Island Jamaica / Jul '96 / Jet Star / PolyGram

DRY AND HEAVY
Any river / Sun / It's a long way around / IWIN / Throw down your arms / Dry and heavy / Wailing / Disciples / Shout it out
CD _______________ RRCD 40

Reggae Refreshers / Jul '93 / PolyGram / Vital

FAR OVER
CD _______________ HBCD 11
Heartbeat / '88 / ADA / Direct / Greensleeves / Jet Star

FITTEST OF THE FITTEST, THE
Fittest of the fittest / Fireman / Bad to worst / Repatriation / Old Boy Garvey / 2000 years / For you / In Africa / Vision
CD _______________ HBCD 22
Heartbeat / '88 / ADA / Direct / Greensleeves / Jet Star

HAIL HIM
African teacher / African postman / Cry blood Africa / Hail HIM / Jah a go raid / Columbus / Road foggy / Follow Marcus Garvey / Jah see and know
CD _______________ HBCD 145
Heartbeat / Jun '94 / ADA / Direct / Greensleeves / Jet Star

JAH KINGDOM
CD _______________ CIDM 1089
Mango / Aug '91 / PolyGram / Vital

KEEP THE SPEAR BURNING
CD _______________ CIDD 9377
Island / '89 / PolyGram

LIVE 1993
CD _______________ 503582
Declic / Sep '94 / Jet Star

LIVING DUB VOL.1
CD _______________ HBCD 131
Heartbeat / Jun '93 / ADA / Direct / Greensleeves / Jet Star

LIVING DUB VOL.2
CD _______________ HBCD 132
Greensleeves / Jan '94 / Jet Star / SRD

LOVE AND PEACE (Live)
CD _______________ CDHB 175
Heartbeat / Jan '95 / ADA / Direct / Greensleeves / Jet Star

MEK WI DWEET
Mek wi dweet / Garvey / Civilization / Elephants / My roots / Great man / African woman / Take a look / One people / Mek we dweet in dub
CD _______________ CIDM 1045
Mango / Jun '90 / PolyGram / Vital

ORIGINAL BURNING SPEAR, THE
CD _______________ SONCD 0023
Sonic Sounds / Apr '92 / Jet Star

RASTA BUSINESS
CD _______________ 406042
Declic / Nov '95 / Jet Star

REGGAE GREATS
Door peep / Slavery days / Lion / Black disciples / Man in the hills / Tradition / Throw down your arms / Social living / Marcus Garvey / Dry and heavy / Black wa-da-da (Invasion) / Sun
CD _______________ 5525852
Spectrum / Jul '97 / PolyGram

RESISTANCE
CD _______________ HBCD 33
Heartbeat / '88 / ADA / Direct / Greensleeves / Jet Star

SOCIAL LIVING
Marcus children suffer / Social living / Nayah Keith / Institution / Marcus senior / Civilised reggae / Mr. Garvey / Come / Marcus say Jah no dead
CD _______________ BAFCD 4
Blood & Fire / Oct '94 / Vital

WORLD SHOULD KNOW, THE
CD _______________ HBCD 119
Greensleeves / Feb '93 / Jet Star / SRD
CD _______________ 8412122
Declic / May '96 / Jet Star

Burns, Eddie

DETROIT (Burns, Eddie Band)
Orange driver / When I get drunk / Kidman / Bottle up and go / Inflation blues / Detroit / Butterfly / Boom boom / Time out / New highway 61 / Blue jay
CD _______________ ECD 260242
Evidence / Feb '92 / ADA / Cadillac / Harmonia Mundi

Burns, Hugh

DEDICATION
CD _______________ BRGCD 15
Bridge / Nov '95 / Grapevine/PolyGram

Burns, Jerry

JERRY BURNS
Pale red / Casually unkind / Hardly me / Fall for lovers / Sometimes I'm wild / Crossing over / Simple heart / Completely my dear / Safe in the rain / Stepping out slowly
CD _______________ 4716452
Columbia / Jun '92 / Sony

Burns, Jimmy

LEAVING HERE WALKING
Leaving here walking / Twelve year old boy / Miss Annie Lou / Whiskey headed woman / One room country shack / Shake your boogie / Better know what you're doing / Rollin' and tumblin' / Gypsy woman / How many times / Mean mistreating mama / Notoriety woman / Talk to me / Catfish blues
CD _______________ DE 694
Delmark / Jun '97 / ADA / Cadillac / CM / Direct / Hot Shot

Burns Sisters

CLOSE TO HOME
CD _______________ CDPH 1178
Philo / Aug '95 / ADA / CM / Direct

IN THIS WORLD
Dance upon this Earth / I won't turn my back / Old friend / My father's blue eyes / Far from my home / Working girl blues / Can I walk away tonight / Heavenly blue / In this world / Stay away from me / Owl / Johnny's got a gun / No more silence
CD _______________ CDPH 1198
Philo / Feb '97 / ADA / CM / Direct

Burnside, R.L.

ASS POCKET 'O' WHISKEY
Goin' down south / Boogie chillen / Poor boy / 2 Brothers / Snake drive / Shame'n on down / Criminal inside me / Walkin' blues / Tojo told Hitler / Have you ever been lonely
CD _______________ OLE 2142
Matador / Jun '96 / Vital

BAD LUCK CITY
Talking about the ghetto / Bad luck city, friend of mine / Shake for me / Boogie chillen / All she do / Long haired doney, poor boy long way from home / Burnside's blues / Crosscut saw / Outskirts of town / My eyes keep me in trouble / Look on yonder's wall / Jumper on the line / No place to go / Bad sign / Killing floor / You don't love me
CD _______________ FIENDCD 741
Demon / May '97 / Pinnacle

MR. WIZARD
Going over the hill / Alice May / Georgia woman / Snake drive / Rolling tumbling / Out on the road / Highway 7 / Tribute to Fred / You gotta' move
CD _______________ 03012
Epitaph / Mar '97 / Pinnacle / Plastic Head

Burrage, Ronnie

SHUTTLE
CD _______________ SSCD 8052
Sound Hills / Apr '94 / Cadillac / Harmonia Mundi

Burrell, Dave

HIGH WON - HIGH TWO
CD _______________ BLCD 760206
Black Lion / Nov '95 / Cadillac / Jazz Music / Koch / Wellard

IN CONCERT (Burrell, Dave & David Murray)
CD _______________ VICTOCD 016
Victo / Nov '94 / Harmonia Mundi / ReR Megacorp

WINDWARD PASSAGES
CD _______________ ARTCD 6138
Hat Art / Feb '94 / Cadillac / Harmonia Mundi

Burrell, Kenny

BEST OF KENNY BURRELL, THE
Now see how you are / Cheetah / DB Blues / Phinupi / Chitlins con carne / Midnight blue / Love your spell is everywhere / Loie / Daydream / Togethering / Summertime / Jumpin' blues / Jeannine
CD _______________ CDP 8304932
Blue Note / Apr '95 / EMI

BLUE LIGHTS (2CD Set)
Phinupi / Yes baby / Scotch blues / Man I love / I never knew / Caravan / Chuckin' / Rock salt / Autumn in New York
CD Set _______________ CDP 8571842
Blue Note / Aug '97 / EMI

BLUESY BURRELL (Burrell, Kenny & Coleman Hawkins)
Tres palabras / No more / Guilty / Monotono blues / I thought about you / Out of this world / It's getting dark / I never knew
CD _______________ OJCCD 926
Original Jazz Classics / Jun '97 / Complete/ Pinnacle / Jazz Music / Wellard

ELLINGTON A LA CARTE
Take the 'A' train / Sultry serenade / Flamingo / In a mellow tone / Don't worry 'bout me / Azure / I ain't got nothin' but the blues / Do nothin' 'til you hear from me / Mood indigo
CD _______________ MCD 5435
Muse / Jul '95 / New Note/Pinnacle

GUITAR FORMS (Burrell, Kenny & Gil Evans)
Greensleeves / Last night when we were young / Breadwinner / Downstairs / Lotus land / Prelude No.2 / Moon and sand / Loie / Terrace theme
CD _______________ 8255762
Verve / Oct '88 / PolyGram

JAZZ MASTERS
CD _______________ 5276522
Verve / Mar '96 / PolyGram

LIVE AT THE BLUE NOTE
Tones for Joan's bones / Entertainer / Embraceable you / Quasi Modo / Dear Ella / Birk's works / I've got a crush on you / Take the 'A' train / All blues / Groove merchant
CD _______________ CCD 4731
Concord Jazz / Nov '96 / New Note/ Pinnacle

LIVE AT THE VILLAGE VANGUARD (Burrell, Kenny Trio)
All night long / Will you still be in my mind / I'm a fool to want you / Trio / Broadway / Soft winds / Just a sittin' and a rockin' / Well you needn't / Second balcony jump / Willow weep for me / Work song / Woody 'n' you / In the still of the night / Don't you know I care (or don't you care to) / Love you madly / It's getting dark
CD _______________ LEJAZZCD 22
Le Jazz / Feb '94 / Cadillac / Koch

LOTUS BLOSSOM
Warm valley / I don't stand a ghost of a chance with you / If you could see me now / Lotus blossom / Once upon a summertime / For once in in my life / Minha saudade / Young and foolish / Old folks / They can't take that away from me / There will never be another you / Night has a thousand eyes / I'm falling for you / Satin doll
CD _______________ CCD 4668
Concord Jazz / Oct '95 / New Note/ Pinnacle

MIDNIGHT BLUE
Chitlins con carne / Mule / Soul lament / Midnight blue / Wavy gravy / Gee baby ain't I good to you / Saturday night blues
CD _______________ CDP 7463992
Blue Note / Sep '92 / EMI

PRESTIGE 7088
Don't cry baby / Drum boogie / Strictly confidential / All of you / Perception
CD _______________ OJCCD 19
Original Jazz Classics / Jun '96 / Complete/ Pinnacle / Jazz Music / Wellard

SOULERO
Hot bossa / Mother in law / People / Sabella / Girl talk / Suzy / Tender gender / La petite mambo / If someone had told me / I'm confessin' that I love you / My favourite things / I want my baby back / Con alma / Soulero / Wild is the wind / Blues fuse
CD _______________ GRP 18082
GRP / Oct '95 / New Note/BMG

TIN TIN DEO
Tin Tin Deo / Old folks / Have you met Miss Jones / I remember you / Common ground / If you could see me now / I hadn't anyone till you / La petite mambo
CD _______________ CCD 4045
Concord Jazz / Jul '94 / New Note/Pinnacle

WHEN LIGHTS ARE LOW
CD _______________ CCD 4083
Concord Jazz / Jul '96 / New Note/ Pinnacle

Burri, Jessica

WEIHNACHTSLIEDER AUS DEUTSCHLAND, ENGLAND UND AMERIKA
Maria durch ein Dornwald ging / Es flog ein voglen leise / O komm Emmanuel / Oh Heiland, reiss die Himmel auf / Sunny bank / Nowel syng we bothe al and som / Coventry carol / What child is this / First noel / Holly & the ivy / Twelve days of Christmas / Ich steh' an deine Krippen hier / O Jesuslein suss / Nun singet und seid froh / Es ist ein ros' entsprungen / O du frohliche / Stille nacht / Mary wrote three links of chain / O Mary / Mary had a baby / Sweet little Jesus boy / Little drummer boy / Go tell it on the mountain
CD _______________ BCD 16012
Bear Family / Nov '96 / Direct / Rollercoaster / Swift

Burroughs, Chris

WEST OF TEXAS
CD _______________ ROSE 203 CD
New Rose / Jul '90 / ADA / Direct / Discovery

Burroughs, William S.

ELVIS OF LETTERS (Burroughs, William S. & Gus Van Sant)
Burroughs break / Word is virus / Millions of images / Hipster be-bop junkie
CD _______________ TK91CD 001
T/K / Jun '94 / Pinnacle

SPARE ASS ANNIE AND OTHER TALES (Burroughs, William S. & Disposable Heroes Of Hiphoprisy)
CD _______________ BRCD 600
4th & Broadway / Oct '93 / PolyGram
CD _______________ IMCD 240
Island / Mar '97 / PolyGram

Burrowes, Roy

LIVE AT THE DREHER - PARIS 1980 (Burrowes, Roy Sextet)
CD _______________ 151992
Marge / Jun '93 / Discovery

Burrows, Stuart

FAVOURITE SONGS OF WALES
CD _______________ SCD 2032
Sain / Dec '94 / ADA / Direct / Greyhound

Burtnick, Glenn

RETROSPECTACLE
CD _______________ MTM 199613
MTM / Nov '96 / Cargo

Burton, Abraham

MAGICIAN, THE
I can't get started (With you) / Little Melonae / Addition to the family / It's to you / Mari's soul / Gnossienne # 1 / Magician
CD _______________ ENJ 90372
Enja / Nov '95 / New Note/Pinnacle / Vital/ SAM

Burton, Aron

PAST, PRESENT AND FUTURE
CD _______________ EARWIGCD 4927
Earwig / Oct '93 / ADA / CM

Burton, Gary

CRYSTAL SILENCE (Burton, Gary & Chick Corea)
Senor Mouse / Arise, her eyes / I'm your pal / Desert air / Crystal silence / Falling grace / Feelings and things / Children's song / What game shall we play today
CD _______________ 8313312
ECM / Mar '88 / New Note/Pinnacle

DEPARTURE (Burton, Gary & Friends)
September song / Poinciana / Depk / Tenderly / If I were a bell / For all we know / Japanese waltz / Tossed salads and scrambled eggs / Born to be blue / Ecaroh
CD _______________ CCD 47492
Concord Jazz / Apr '97 / New Note/ Pinnacle

DREAMS SO REAL (Music Of Carla Bley) (Burton, Gary Quintet)
CD _______________ 8333292
ECM / Jul '88 / New Note/Pinnacle

DUET (Burton, Gary & Chick Corea)
CD _______________ 8299412
ECM / Oct '88 / New Note/Pinnacle

GARY BURTON & THE BERKLEE ALL STARS (Burton, Gary & The Berklee All Stars)
CD _______________ JD 3301
JVC / Jul '88 / Direct / New Note/Pinnacle / Vital/SAM

GARY BURTON COLLECTION, THE
Quick and running / Huba huba / Last to know / Sing sing sing / Moonglow / My funny valentine / Redial / Our love is here to stay / Solitude / My romance
CD _______________ GRP 98512
GRP / Sep '96 / New Note/BMG

HOTEL HELLO (Burton, Gary & Steve Swallow)
CD _______________ 8355862
ECM / '90 / New Note/Pinnacle

LIVE IN CANNES
My foolsih heart / One / No more blues / Night has a 1000 eyes / Autumn leaves / African flower / Bogota
CD _______________ JWD 102214
JWD / Apr '95 / Target/BMG

NEW QUARTET, THE
Open your eyes you can fly / Coral / Tying up loose ends / Brownout / Olhos de gato / Mallet man / Four or less / Nonsequence
CD _______________ 8350022
ECM / Sep '88 / New Note/Pinnacle

NEW VIBE MAN IN TOWN
Joy spring / Over the rainbow / Like someone in love / Minor blues / Our waltz / So many things / Sir John / You stepped out of a dream
CD _______________ 74321218282
RCA / Jan '95 / BMG

PASSENGERS (Burton, Gary Quartet & Eberhard Weber)
CD _______________ 8350162
ECM / Oct '88 / New Note/Pinnacle

REAL LIFE HITS (Burton, Gary Quartet)
Syndrome: *Burton, Gary* / Beatle: *Burton, Gary* / Fleurette Africaine (the African flower): *Burton, Gary* / Ladies in Mercedes: *Burton, Gary* / Real life hits: *Burton, Gary* / I need you here: *Burton, Gary* / Ivanushka Durachok: *Burton, Gary*
CD _______________ 8252352
ECM / '88 / New Note/Pinnacle

RING (Burton, Gary Quintet & Eberhard Weber)
Mevlevia: *Burton, Gary Quintet* / Unfinished sympathy: *Burton, Gary Quintet* / Tunnel of love: *Burton, Gary Quintet* / Intrude: *Burton, Gary Quintet* / Silent spring: *Burton, Gary*

Quintet / Colours of chloe: *Burton, Gary Quintet*
CD 8291912
ECM / Oct '86 / New Note/Pinnacle

THROB (Burton, Gary & Keith Jarrett)
Grow your own / Moonchild / In your quiet place / Como en Vietnam / Fortune smiles / Raven speaks
CD 8122715942
Atlantic / Mar '94 / Warner Music

TIMES SQUARE
CD 5219822
ECM / Jul '94 / New Note/Pinnacle

WHIZ KIDS (Burton, Gary Quintet)
Last clown: *Burton, Gary Quartet* / Yellow fever: *Burton, Gary Quartet* / Soulful Bill: *Burton, Gary Quartet* / La divetta: *Burton, Gary Quartet* / Cool train: *Burton, Gary Quartet* / Loop: *Burton, Gary Quartet*
CD 8311102
ECM / Feb '87 / New Note/Pinnacle

WORKS: GARY BURTON
Olhos de gato / Desert air / Tunnel of love / Vox humana / Three / Brotherhood / Chelsea bells / Coral / Domino biscuit
CD 8232672
ECM / Jun '89 / New Note/Pinnacle

Burton, Gary

TENNESSEE FIREBIRD (Burton, Gary & Friends)
Gone / Tennessee firebird / Just like a woman / Black is the colour of my true love's hair / Faded love / Panhandle rag / I can't help it / I want you / Alone and forsaken / Walter L / Born to lose / Beauty contest / Epilogue
CD BCD 15458
Bear Family / Jun '89 / Direct / Rollercoaster / Swift

Burton, James

CORN PICKIN' AND SLICK SLIDIN' (Burton, James & Ralph Mooney)
Columbus Stockade blues / Texas waltz / It's such a pretty world today / Moonshine / Laura / There goes my everything / I'm a lonesome fugitive / My elusive dreams / Corn pickin' / Your cheatin' heart / Spanish eyes / Sneaky strings
CD SEECD 377
See For Miles/C5 / Aug '97 / Pinnacle

GUITAR SOUNDS OF JAMES BURTON, THE
Polk salad Annie / Susie-Q / Fire and rain / Fools rush in / Johnny B Goode / I know (you don't want me no more) / Delta lady / Mystery train / Rock and raunch / Hound dog / Hi-heel sneakers / Long reach
CD 5405532
A&M / Jun '97 / PolyGram

Burton, Joe

ST. LOUIS BLUES
CD PS 012CD
P&S / Sep '95 / Discovery

SUBTLE SOUND
CD PS 006CD
P&S / Sep '95 / Discovery

TASTY TOUCH OF JOE BURTON, THE
CD PS 013CD
P&S / Sep '95 / Discovery

Burton, Larry

HUSTLER'S PARADISE
CD BRAM 1992332
Brambus / Nov '93 / ADA

Burton, Rahn

POEM, THE (Burton, Rahn Trio)
CD DIW 610
DIW / Nov '92 / Cadillac / Harmonia Mundi

Burton, W.E. 'Buddy'

BUDDY BURTON & ED 'FATS' HUDSON 1928-1936 (Burton, W.E. 'Buddy' & Ed 'Fats' Hudson)
CD JPCD 1511
Jazz Perspectives / Dec '94 / Hot Shot / Jazz Music

Burzum

BURZUM/ASKE
CD AMAZON 003CD
Misanthropy / May '95 / Plastic Head

DET SOMEGAG VAR
CD AMAZON 002CD
Misanthropy / Oct '94 / Plastic Head

FILOSOFEM
CD AMAZON 009BK
Misanthropy / Jan '96 / Plastic Head

HVIS LYSET TAR OSS
CD AMAZON 001
Misanthropy / Aug '94 / Plastic Head

Busaras, David

SMEGMA 'STRUCTIONS DON'T RHYME
CD SR 1008
Scout / Jan '96 / Koch

Busby, Colin

BIG SWING BAND FAVOURITE (Busby, Colin Big Swing Band)
At the woodchoppers' ball / Sing sing sing / April in Paris / Take the 'A' train / String of pearls / Begin the beguine / One o'clock jump / Skyliner / In the mood / St. Louis blues march / Satin doll / Little brown jug
CD CDSIV 1117
Horatio Nelson / Jul '95 / Disc

Busby, Sid

PORTRAITS (Busby, Sid & The Berkeley Orchestra)
Portrait of my love / With a song in my heart / Days of wine and roses / I can't get started (with you) / My son, my son / Serenade in blue / Java / Stardust / As time goes by / Serenata / And this is my beloved / Love changes everything / Violino tzigano / When a love affair has ended
CD PCOM 1105
President / Aug '90 / Grapevine/PolyGram / President / Target/BMG

SO MANY STARS (Busby, Sid & The Berkeley Orchestra)
Nessun dorma / Cuban Pete / Memories of you / Tango desiree / Estrellita / Deep purple / Just the way you are / Dindi / Cool cool Luke / Wave / Easy does it / Bess you is my woman now / Someday my prince will come / Inter city 125 / Going home / So many stars
CD PCOM 1138
President / Dec '94 / Grapevine/PolyGram / President / Target/BMG

Bush

RAZORBLADE SUITCASE
Personal Holloway / Greedy fly / Swallowed / Insect kin / Cold contagious / Tendency to start fires / Mouth / Straight no chaser / History / Synapse / Communicator / Bonedriven / Distant voices
CD IND 90091
Interscope / Feb '97 / BMG

SIXTEEN STONE
Everything zen / Swim / Bomb / Little things / Comedown / Body / Machinehead / Testosterone / Monkey / Glycerine / Alien / X-girlfriend
CD IND 90001
Interscope / Aug '96 / BMG

Bush Chemists

DUB CONVENTION (Bush Chemists & The Dub Organiser)
CD FDCD 001
Fashion / Aug '96 / Jet Star / SRD

DUBS FROM ZION VALLEY (Bush Chemists & Jonah Dan)
CD JKPD 001CD
JKP / Apr '97 / SRD

LIGHT UP YOUR SPLIFF
CD DNCD 005
Conscious Sounds / Jan '96 / Jet Star / SRD

MONEY RUN TINGS (Bush Chemists & King General)
CD DNCD 006
Conscious Sounds / Jun '96 / Jet Star / SRD

STRICTLY DUBWISE
CD WWCD 6
Wibbly Wobbly / Jul '94 / SRD

Bush, Kate

DREAMING, THE
Sat in your lap / There goes a tenner / Pull out the pin / Suspended in Gaffa / Leave it open / Dreaming / Night of the swallow / All the love / Houdini / Get out of my house
CD CDP 7463612
EMI / Mar '91 / EMI

HOUNDS OF LOVE
Running up that hill / Hounds of love / Big sky / Mother stands for comfort / Cloudbusting / And dream of sheep / Under ice / Waking the witch / Watching you without me / Jig of life / Hello earth / Morning fog / Big sky / Running up that hill / Be kind to my mistakes / Under the ivy / Burning bridge / My lagan love
CD CDCNTAV 3
EMI / Jun '97 / EMI

KATE BUSH: INTERVIEW DISC
CD CBAK 4011
Baktabak / Apr '88 / Arabesque

KICK INSIDE, THE
Moving / Saxophone song / Strange phenomena / Kite / Man with the child in his eyes / Wuthering Heights / James and the cold gun / Feel it / Oh to be in love / L'amour looks something like you / Them heavy people / Room for the life / Kick inside
CD CDEMS 1522
EMI / Sep '94 / EMI

LIONHEART
Symphony in blue / In search of Peter Pan / Wow / Don't push your foot on the heartbrake / Oh England my lionheart / Full house / In the warm room / Kashka from Baghdad / Coffee homeground / Hammer horror
CD CDEMS 1523
EMI / Sep '94 / EMI

NEVER FOR EVER
Babooshka / Delius / Blow away / All we ever look for / Egypt / Wedding list / Violin / Infant kiss / Night scented stock / Army dreamers / Breathing
CD CDP 7463602
EMI / Oct '90 / EMI

NEVER FOR EVER
CD Set KB 2
UFO / Oct '92 / Pinnacle

RED SHOES, THE
Rubber band girl / And so is love / Eat the music / Moments of pleasure / Song of Solomon / Lily / Red shoes / Top of the city / Constellation of the heart / Big stripey lie / Why should I love you / You're the one
CD CDEMD 1047
EMI / Nov '93 / EMI

SENSUAL WORLD, THE
Sensual world / Love and anger / Fog / Reaching out / Heads we're dancing / Deeper understanding / Between a man and a woman / Never be mine / Rocket's tail / This woman's work / Walk straight down the middle
CD CDP 7930782
EMI / Oct '89 / EMI

WHOLE STORY, THE
Wuthering Heights / Cloudbusting / Man with the child in his eyes / Breathing / Wow / Hounds of love / Running up that hill / Army dreamers / Sat in your lap / Experiment IV / Dreaming / Babooshka / Big sky
CD CDP 7464142
EMI / Nov '86 / EMI

Bush League Allstars

OLD NUMBERS
CD GRCD 401
Glitterhouse / Apr '97 / Avid/BMG

Bush, Sam

GLAMOUR AND GRITS
CD SHCD 3849
Sugar Hill / Jul '96 / ADA / CM / Direct / Koch / Roots

LATE AS USUAL
CD ROUCD 0195
Rounder / Aug '88 / ADA / CM / Direct

Bush, Stan

DIAL 818 888 8638
I got it bad for you / One kiss away / Total surrender / Come to me / Hold your head up high / Are you over me / Come on / In the name of love / Hero of the heart / Take this heart / Take my love
CD CDVEST 7
Bulletproof / Mar '94 / Pinnacle

Bushberry Mountain Devils

PEACE AND JUSTICE
CD ENI 101CD
Enigma / Apr '96 / Else

Bushfire

DIDGERIDOO MUSIC OF THE AUSTRALIAN ABORIGINEES
CD EUCD 1224
ARC / Sep '93 / ADA / ARC Music

Bushgiants

NEWLANDING
CD BUSH 96001
Knock On Wood / Apr '97 / Discovery

Bushkin, Joe

ROAD TO OSLO/PLAY IT AGAIN, JOE
Now you has jazz / Hallelujah / Bess, you is my woman now / How long has this been going on / Man I love / Yesterday / Ain't been the same since the Beatles / There'll be a hot time in the town of Berlin / Oh look at me now / I love a piano / Phone call to the past / I've grown accustomed to her face / Someday I'll be sorry / Sunday of the Shepherdess / Sail away from Norway / I can't get started (with you) / Someday you'll be sorry / Man that got away / One for my baby (and one more for the road) / It had to be you / Learnin' the blues / There's always the blues / Our love is here to stay / What's new
CD DRGCD 8490
DRG / Feb '95 / Discovery / New Note/ Pinnacle

Bushman

NYAH MAN CHANT
Nayh man chant / Cannabis / Man a lion / Rude boy life / Remember the days / Black starliner / She's gone / Grow your natty / My day / Anything for your love / Call the hearse / Poor people power
CD GRELCD 239
Greensleeves / Aug '97 / Jet Star / SRD

Bushwick Bill

PHANTOM OF THE RAPRA
Phantom's theme / Wha cha gonna do / Times is hard / Who's the biggest / Ex-girlfriend / Only God knows / Already dead / Bushwicken / Subliminal criminal / Inhale exhale / Mr. President / Phantom's reprise
CD CDVUS 91
Virgin / Jun '95 / EMI

Business

BEST OF THE BUSINESS
Out in the cold / Streets where you live / Harry May / NJ Blacklist / Suburban rebels / Product / Smash the disco / Disco girls / H-Bomb / Blind justice / Get out while you can / Guttersnipe / Real enemy / Loud, proud and punk / Get out of my house / Outlaw / Saturday's heroes / Front line / Spanish jails / Freedom / Coventry / No emotions / Do a runner / Welcome to the real world / Fear in your heart / Never say never / Look at him now / Drinking and driving
CD DOJOCD 124
Dojo / Apr '93 / Disc

COMPLETE SINGLES COLLECTION
Harry May / National insurance blacklist / Step into Christmas / Dayo / Disco girls / Smash the discos / Loud, proud and punk / H-bomb / Last train to Clapham Junction / Law and order / Do they owe us a living / Tell us the truth / Get out of my house / All out tonight / Foreign girl / Out law / Drinking and driving / Hurry up Harry / H-bomb (live) / Do a runner / Coventry / Welcome to the real world / No emotions / Anywhere but here / All out / (You're) Going down in history
CD CDPUNK 57
Anagram / Jun '95 / Cargo / Pinnacle

KEEP THE FAITH
CD CM 770832
Century Media / Oct '94 / Plastic Head

SINGALONG-A-BUSINESS (The Best Of The Business)
Suburban rebels / Blind justice / Loud, proud and punk / Real enemy / Spanish jails / Product / National insurance blacklist (employers blacklist) / Get out of my house / Saturday's heroes / Out in the cold / Smash the discos / Harry May / Drinking and driving / Hurry up Harry
CD AHOY 19
Captain Oi / Nov '94 / Plastic Head

SUBURBAN REBELS
CD AHOYCD 7
Captain Oi / Oct '93 / Plastic Head

WELCOME TO THE REAL WORLD
Mouth an' trousers / Do a runner / Ten years / We'll take 'em on / Fear in your heart / Welcome to the real world / Never say never / Hand ball / Living in day dreams / Look at him now / We gotta go / Never say never (reprise) / Coventry / No emotions / Tina Turner / Welcome to the real world
CD AHOYCD 2
Captain Oi / May '93 / Plastic Head

Buskirk, Paul

NACOGDOCHES WALTZ
CD JR 17012
Justice / Apr '94 / Koch

Busstra, Marnix

ON THE FACE OF IT (Busstra, Marnix Quartet)
Strega / Brandon head / That's a fact / Snake and the hammer / On the face of it / Little Big Mama / Searching for silence
CD 9920072
Via Jazz / Oct '96 / New Note/Pinnacle

Busta Rhymes

COMING, THE
Coming / Do my thing / Abandon ship / Everything remains raw / Hot fudge/Interlude / Flipmode squad meets def squad / Keep it movin' / End of the world / Finish line / Still shining / Ill vibe / It's a party / Woo hah got you all in check
CD 7559617422
WEA / Mar '96 / Warner Music

FLIPMODE REMIXES
Woo hah got you all in check / It's a party / Do my thing / Abandon ship
CD 7559639922
Elektra / Jul '97 / Warner Music

Bustan Abraham

PICTURES THROUGH THE PAINTED WINDOW

Gipsy soul / Jazz kar-kurd / Fountain head / Here comes (Muwashah) / Longa / Walls of Jerico / Samai nahawand / Wallah / Pictures through the painted window
CD CRAW 17
Cramworld / May '97 / New Note/Pinnacle

Busters

94 ER HITS
CD WL 2478CD
Weser / Jul '95 / Plastic Head

CHEAP THRILLS LIVE
CD WL 2461CD
Weser / Jul '95 / Plastic Head

COUCH POTATOES
CD WL 2449CD
Weser / Jul '95 / Plastic Head

DEAD OR ALIVE
CD WL 2457CD
Weser / Jul '95 / Plastic Head

LIVE IN MONTREUX
CD WL 24902CD
Weser / Nov '95 / Plastic Head

RUDER THAN RUDE
CD WL 2453CD
Weser / Jul '95 / Plastic Head

RUDER THAN YOU
CD PHZCD 27
Unicorn / Sep '93 / Plastic Head

SEXY MONEY
CD WL 2477CD
Weser / Jul '95 / Plastic Head

Busy Going Crazy

INFUSION
Six summer suns / Talking with myself / Heavenly / Wetspot / Magnesia nights / Halfway in light / Analogue ID / Arcades / Analogue snobs / (Stole some sky) / Gone to our end
CD LINE 003CD
White Lines / Jun '97 / Vital

Butera, Sam

BY REQUEST (Butera, Sam & The Wildest)
When you're smiling / Just a gigolo/I ain't got nobody / For once in my life / Up a lazy river / Ol' man mose / Night train / Lover is a 5 letter word / Alexander's ragtime band / Margie / Come to the cabaret / Mariyootch / St. Louis blues / Your rascall you / French poodle / My first, my last / Closer to the bone / Greenback dollar bill
CD JASCD 314
Jasmine / Aug '95 / Conifer/BMG / Hot Shot / TKO Magnum

HOT NIGHTS IN NEW ORLEANS
Shine the buckle / Chicken scratch / Sam's clan / Easy rocking / Wailin' walk / Screw driver / Things I love / Do you care / I don't want to set the world on fire / Tout / Long ago / Giddyap baby / Sweep up / Sam's reverie / Who's got the key / Ooh / Linda / Tout, The (version) / Ooh (version)
CD BCD 15449
Bear Family / Apr '89 / Direct / Rollercoaster / Swift

SHEER ENERGY (Butera, Sam & The Wildest)
Let the good times roll / For you / I can't get started (with you) / Jump, jive and wail / Glow worm / Closer to the bone / Hard hearted Hannah / Body and soul / Night train / Rosetta / You ain't no ordinary woman / Pennies from heaven / Kansas City / Why not / Ol' man river
CD JASCD 313
Jasmine / Jul '95 / Conifer/BMG / Hot Shot / TKO Magnum

TRIBUTE TO LOUIS PRIMA
Josephine / Please no lean on the bell / That old black magic / Please no squeeza da banana / Medley: Robin Hood / Buona sera / White cliffs of Dover / I got you under my skin / Angelina / Oh Marie / Felicia / No capicia / Medley / Tiger rag / Just the way you are / Romance without finance / Exodus / Che-la-luna
CD JASCD 319
Jasmine / Mar '95 / Conifer/BMG / Hot Shot / TKO Magnum

TRIBUTE TO LOUIS PRIMA VOL.2, A
CD JASCD 320
Jasmine / Apr '95 / Conifer/BMG / Hot Shot / TKO Magnum

Butler, Carl

CRYING MY HEART OUT OVER YOU (Butler, Carl & Pearl)
Crying my heart out over you / Fools like me / Garden of shame / Dog eat dog / If teardrops were pennies / Holding on with open arms / Take me back to Jackson / Don't let me cross over / Blue eyes and waltzes / My joy / Precious memories / I hope we walk the last mile together
CD BCD 15739
Bear Family / Jul '93 / Direct / Rollercoaster / Swift

Butler, Freddy

WITH A DAB OF SOUL
There was a time / That's when I need you / I like your style / I fell in love / Never let love go / They say I'm afraid / This thing / Just because you've been hurt / You'd better get hip girl / Give me lots of lovin' / She's foolin' you / Deserted
CD SSCD 003
Goldmine / Feb '97 / Vital

Butler, George

KEEP ON DOING WHAT YOU'RE DOING (Butler, George 'Wild Child')
CD BMCD 9015
Black Magic / Nov '93 / ADA / Cadillac / Direct / Hot Shot

STRANGER
CD BB 9539CD
Bullseye Blues / Aug '94 / Direct

Butler, Jerry

ICE MAN
CD CDRB 30
Charly / Nov '95 / Koch

TIME & FAITH
CD ICH 1151CD
Ichiban / Feb '94 / Direct / Koch

WHATEVER YOU WANT
Rainbow Valley / Lonely soldier / Thanks to you / When trouble calls / Aware of love / Isle of sirens / It's too late / Moon River / Woman with soul / Let it be whatever it is / I almost lost my mind / Good times / Give it up / Believe in me / Just for you / For your precious love
CD CDSGP 083
Prestige / Sep '93 / Else / Total/BMG

Butler, Jonathan

BEST OF JONATHAN BUTLER, THE
CD CHIP 133
Jive / Mar '93 / Pinnacle

Butler, Lester

13
CD HCD 8078
Hightone / Jun '97 / ADA / Koch

RED DEVIL
CD WENCD 013
When / Sep '96 / Pinnacle

Butler, Margie

CELTIC LULLABY
CD EUCD 1191
ARC / Apr '92 / ADA / ARC Music

MAGIC OF THE CELTIC HARP, THE
CD EUCD 1316
ARC / Jul '95 / ADA / ARC Music

Butler Twins

NOT GONNA WORRY ABOUT TOMORROW
Finally found me a girl / My Baby's coming home / Not gonna worry about tomorrow / I know you don't love me baby / 1-900 / You don't need me / Going down a long country road / Crackhouse baby / That old devil (crossroads) / Bring it on back to me / Travellin' down south
CD JSPCD 257
JSP / Apr '95 / ADA / Cadillac / Direct / Hot Shot / Target/BMG

PURSUE YOUR DREAMS
My old Tom cat / I'm talkin' about love / Livin' in paradise / Jack Daniels and me / Pursue your dreams / Hey baby / How long / Blues walked in this morning / Tribute to Little Walter / Inner city blues / What's a poor man's supposed to do / Take a little walk with me / Cold winter nights
CD JSPCD 268
JSP / May '96 / ADA / Cadillac / Direct / Hot Shot / Target/BMG

Butt, Clara

HEART OF THE EMPIRE
Enchantress / O lovely night / Abide with me / Land of Hope and Glory / Softly and gently / Sweetest flower / Kashmiri song / O rest the Lord / Lost chord / Annie Laurie / Rosary / Home sweet home / Barbara Allen / Trees / Shenandoah / Minstrel boy / Swanee river / Love's old sweet song / Handel's Largo / Keys of Heaven / Softly awakes my heart / Rule Britannia
CD PASTCD 7012
Flapper / Aug '93 / Pinnacle

Butt Steak

MEN WHO PAUSE
CD GKCD 017
Go-Kart / Sep '97 / Greyhound / Pinnacle

Butter 08

BUTTER
CD GR 029CD
Grand Royal / Apr '97 / Cargo / Plastic Head

Butterbeans

BUTTERBEANS & SUSIE VOL.1 (1924-1925) (Butterbeans & Susie)
CD DOCD 5544
Document / Jul '97 / ADA / Hot Shot / Jazz Music

BUTTERBEANS & SUSIE VOL.2 (1924-1927) (Butterbeans & Susie)
CD DOCD 5545
Document / Jul '97 / ADA / Hot Shot / Jazz Music

Butterfield, Paul

EAST-WEST (Butterfield Blues Band)
Walkin' blues / Get out of my life woman / I got a mind to give up living / All these blues / Work song / Mary mary / Two trains running / Never say no / East West: *Strongman, Jay*
CD 7559607512
Atlantic / Jan '93 / Warner Music

EAST-WEST LIVE (Butterfield Blues Band)
CD WINNER 447
Winner / Jun '97 / Greyhound

KEEP ON MOVING
CD 7559611562
Elektra / Jan '97 / Warner Music

OFFER YOU CAN'T REFUSE, AN (Butterfield, Paul & Walter Horton)
Easy / Have a good time / Mean mistreater / In the mood / West side blues / Louise / Tin pan alley / Walters boogie / Everything's gonna be alright / Poor boy / Got my mojo working / Last night / Loaded / One room country shack
CD CLACD 429
Castle / Apr '97 / BMG

PAUL BUTTERFIELD BLUES BAND (Butterfield Blues Band)
Born in Chicago / Shake your moneymaker / Blues with a feeling / Thank you Mr. Poobah / I got my mojo working / Mellow down easy / Screamin' / Our love is drifting / Mystery train / Last night / Look over yonder's wall
CD 7559606472
WEA / Nov '94 / Warner Music

STRAWBERRY JAM (Butterfield Blues Band)
CD WINNER 446
Winner / Jun '97 / Greyhound

Butterfly Child

HONEYMOON SUITE, THE
Mother have mercy / Passion is the only fruit / Ghost on your shoulder / Flaming burlesque / Unwashed, uncool / Carolina and the be bop review / Deep south / Louis as Anna / Six urchins / Botany bay / Towns come tumblin' / I shall hear in heaven
CD DEDCD 019
Dedicated / Apr '96 / BMG / Vital

ONOMATOPOEIA
CD R 3082
Rough Trade / Aug '93 / Pinnacle

Butterglory

ARE YOU BUILDING A TEMPLE IN HEAVEN
CD K 167
Konkurrel / May '96 / SRD

Butthole Surfers

ELECTRICLARRYLAND
Birds / Cough syrup / Pepper / Thermador / Ulcer breakout / Jingle of a dog's collar / TV star / My brother's wife / Ah ha / Lord is a monkey / Let's talk about cars / LA / Space
CD CDEST 2285
Capitol / May '96 / EMI

HAIRWAY TO STEVEN
CD BFFP 29CD
Blast First / Feb '88 / RTM/Disc

HOLE TRUTH AND NOTHING BUTT, THE
CD TR 35CD
Trance / Mar '95 / SRD

INDEPENDENT WORM SALOON
Who was in my room last night / Wooden song / Tongue / Chewin' George Lucas' chocolate / Goofy's concern / Alcohol / Dog inside your body / Strawberry / Some dispute over T-shirt sales / Dancing fool / You don't know me / Annoying song / Dust devil / Leave me alone / Edgar / Ballad of naked men / Clean it up
CD CDP 7987982
Capitol / Mar '93 / EMI

LOCUST ABORTION TECHNICIAN
Sweat loaf / Graveyard / Graveyard / Pittsburgh to Lebanon / Weber / Hay / Human cannonball / USSA / O-men / Kuntz / Twenty two going on twenty three
CD BFFP 15CD
Blast First / Jun '87 / RTM/Disc

PIOUHGD
CD DAN 069CD
Danceteria / Dec '94 / ADA / Plastic Head / Shellshock/Disc

Buttons & Bows

FIRST MONTH OF SUMMER, THE
John D McGurk's / I les de la Madeleine / First month of summer / Fitmaurice's polka / Sir Sidney Smith / Man from Bundoran / Humours of Kinvara / Green garters / Inisheer / Gypsy hornpipe / Margaret's waltz / Four courts / Joyous waltz / Piper's despair
CD GLCD 1079
Green Linnet / Feb '92 / ADA / CM / Direct / Highlander / Roots

GRACE NOTES
CD CEFCD 151
Gael Linn / Jan '94 / ADA / CM / Direct / Grapevine/PolyGram / Roots

Buzzcocks

ALL SET
Totally from the heart / Without you / Give it to me / Your love / Point of no return / Hold me close / Kiss and tell / What am I supposed to do / Some kind of wonderful / (What you) Mean to me / Playing for time / Pariah / Back with you
CD EIRSCD 1078
IRS/EMI / Apr '96 / EMI

ANOTHER MUSIC IN A DIFFERENT KITCHEN
Fast cars / No reply / You tear me up / Get on our own / Love battery / Sixteen / I don't mind / Fiction romance / Autonomy / I need / Moving away from the pulsebeat
CD PRDFCD 3
Premier/EMI / Jul '96 / EMI

CHRONOLOGY
Boredom / Sixteen / Fast cars / No reply / Whatever happened to / Oh shit / I need / Fiction romance / Autonomy / Just lust / ESP / Lipstick / Promises / Mother of turds / You say you don't love me / I don't know what to do with my life / I don't know / Runaway from home / Drive system / Jesus made me feel guilty / You know you can't help it / I believe / No friend of mine
CD CDGO 2073
EMI Gold / Jun '97 / EMI

ENTERTAINING FRIENDS (Live At The Hammersmith Odeon - March 1979)
Ever fallen in love / I don't mind / Harmony in my head / Promises / Orgasm addict / Breakdown / What do I get / Fiction romance / Fast cars / Oh shit / Autonomy
CD CDGOLD 1029
EMI Gold / May '96 / EMI

I DON'T MIND
CD CDGOLD 1093
EMI Gold / Apr '97 / EMI

LEST WE FORGET
CD RE 158CD
ROIR / Nov '94 / Plastic Head / Shellshock/Disc

LIVE AT THE ROXY 2ND APRIL 1977
Orgasm addict / Get on your own / What do I get / Sixteen / Oh shit / No reply / Fast cars / Friends of mine / Time's up / Boredom
CD RRCD 131
Receiver / Jul '93 / Grapevine/PolyGram

LOVE BITES
Real world / Ever fallen in love / Operator's manual / Nostalgia / Just lust / Sixteen again / Walking distance / Love is lies / Nothing left / ESP / Late for the train
CD PRDFCD 4
Premier/EMI / Jul '96 / EMI

OPERATORS MANUAL (Buzzcocks Best)
Orgasm addict / What do I get / I don't mind / Autonomy / Fast cars / Get on our own / Sixteen / Fiction romance / Love you more / Noise annoys / Ever fallen in love / Operators manual / Nostalgia / Walking distance / Nothing left / ESP / Promises / Lipstick / Everybody's happy nowadays / Harmony in my head / You say you don't love me / I don't know what to do with my life / I believe / Are everything / Radio nine
CD CDP 7975342
Premier/EMI / Mar '96 / EMI

PRODUCT (3CD Set)
Fast cars / No reply / You tear me up / Get on your own / Love battery / Sixteen / I don't mind / Fiction romance / Autonomy / I need / Moving away from the pulsebeat / Real world / Ever fallen in love / Operator's manual / Nostalgia / Just lust / Walking distance / Love is lies / Nothing left / ESP / Late for the train / Paradise / Sitting 'round at home / You say you don't love me / You know you can't help it / Mad mad Judy / Raison D'etre / I don't know what to do with my life / Money / Hollow inside / Different kind of tension / I believe / Radio nine / Orgasm addict / Love you more / Promises / Everybody's happy nowadays / Harmony in my head / Whatever happened to / Oh shit / Noise annoys / Lipstick / Why can't I touch it / Something's gone wrong again / Breakdown / What do I get / Times up / Are

everything / Strange thing / What do you know / Why she's a girl from the chainstore / Airwaves dream / Running free / I look alone
CD Set PRODUCT 1
Premier/EMI / May '95 / EMI

SINGLES GOING STEADY
Orgasm addict / What do I get / I don't mind / Love you more / Ever fallen in love / Promises / Everybody's happy nowadays / Harmony in my head / Whatever happened to / Oh shit / Autonomy / Noise annoys / Just lust / Lipstick / Why can't I touch it / Something's gone wrong again
CD CDFA 3241
Fame / Oct '90 / EMI

Buzzkill

UP
CD VIRUS 188CD
Alternative Tentacles / Dec '96 / Cargo / Greyhound / Pinnacle

Buzzoven

CHOKEHOLD
CD ALLIED 84
Allied / Mar '97 / Cargo / Greyhound / Plastic Head

GOSPEL ACCORDING, THE
CD ALLIED 84CD
Allied / Mar '97 / Cargo / Greyhound / Plastic Head

BWF

UNSENTIMENTAL
Cast away / Up-lifted / Unsentimental / Victim of riches / POW / Articles / Special one / Last days / Hole in my pocket / Said a prayer / Wish your life / Ain't no place like home
CD 727152
Restless / May '94 / Vital

Byard, Jaki

BLUES FOR SMOKE
Excerpts from European episode / Aluminum baby / Pete and Thomas / Spanish tinge no.1 / Flight of the fly / Blues for smoke / Jaki's blues next / Diane's melody / One two five
CD CCD 9018
Candid / Feb '97 / Cadillac / Direct / Jazz Music / Koch / Wellard

EMPIRICAL
CD MCD 6010
Muse / Sep '92 / New Note/Pinnacle

PHANTASIES (Byard, Jaki & The Apollo Stompers)
CD SNCD 1075
Soul Note / Dec '86 / Cadillac / Harmonia Mundi / Wellard

PHANTASIES VOL.2 (Byard, Jaki & The Apollo Stompers)
CD 1211752
Soul Note / Jun '91 / Cadillac / Harmonia Mundi / Wellard

Byas, Don

ALL THE THINGS YOU ARE
CD JHR 73541
Jazz Hour / Sep '93 / Cadillac / Jazz Music / Target/BMG

CLASSICS 1944-1945
CD CLASSICS 882
Classics / Jul '96 / Discovery / Jazz Music

CLASSICS 1945
CD CLASSICS 910
Classics / Jan '97 / Discovery / Jazz Music

INTRODUCTION TO DON BYAS 1935-1945, AN
CD 4044
Best Of Jazz / Apr '97 / Discovery

INTRODUCTION TO DON BYAS, AN
CD 4045
Best Of Jazz / Jun '97 / Discovery

LIVING MY LIFE
CD VGCD 650122
Vogue / Jan '93 / BMG

LOVER MAN
If I had you / Lover man / I can't give you anything but love / Remember my forgotten man / GDB / Time on my hands / Blues for Don Carlos / Sweet Lorraine / April in Paris / Don't blame me / Unknown original / No one but you / Darling je vous aime beaucoup / Le musicien / Lover come back to me / I can't get started (with you) / Athena / Sincerely / Minor encamp / Cerisier rose et pommier blanc / Hold my hand / Un jour tu verras / Just one of those things / Anatole
CD 74321154702
Vogue / Oct '93 / BMG

NIGHT IN TUNISIA, A
CD BLCD 760136
Black Lion / Oct '90 / Cadillac / Jazz Music / Koch / Wellard

ORIGINAL 1945 RECORDINGS
CD TAXS 82
Tax / Mar '97 / Cadillac / Jazz Music / Wellard

THREE TENORS, THE (Byas, Don & Paul Gonsalves/Ben Webster)
I'll remember April / Lady Bird / Yesterdays / Just a-sittin' and a-rockin' / Hi ya Sue / I'm in the market for you / Tea for two / Stardust / What's new / Autumn leaves / Easy to love
CD 8747062
DA Music / Jul '96 / Conifer/BMG

WALKIN'
CD BLCD 760167
Black Lion / Oct '93 / Cadillac / Jazz Music / Koch / Wellard

Bygraves, Max

CHEERS
It had to be you / I'll string along with you / I'll be seeing you / Sit right down and write myself a letter / My very good friend the milkman / When somebody thinks you're wonderful / He's got the whole world / Michael row the boat ashore / Amen amen / Who's sorry now / You made me love you / For me and my gal / We'll meet again / Hometown / In old shanty town / Underneath the arches / (My) Mammy / Sonny boy / Rockabye your baby / Mistakes / Dancing with tears in my eyes / Are you lonesome tonight / When I grow to old to dream / It's a long way to Tipperary / Pack up your troubles / Kiss me goodnight Sgt. Major / Run rabbit run / We're gonna hang out the washing / Bless 'em all / She loves you / All my loving / Hard day's night / Can't buy me love / I love a lassie / Just a wee doech and Doris / Keep right on to the end of the road / Knees up Mother Brown / Robert E Lee / Australia / Shuddaup your face / Maybe it's because I'm a Londoner / When the saints go marching in / John Brown's body / D'ye ken John Peel / Grand old Duke of York / She'll be coming round the mountain / Comrades / Two lovely black eyes / Lassie from Lancashire / Let's all sing like the birdies / Down at the old bull and bush / Swanee river / Poor old Joe / My Bonnie lies over the ocean / If you knew Susie
CD CDSIV 1143
Horatio Nelson / Jul '95 / Disc

GOLDEN MEDLEYS
I don't know why I love you / You made me love you / Me and my shadow / Moonlight and roses / You were meant for me / You are my sunshine / Let the rest of the world go by / Let me call you sweetheart / Girl of my dreams / Where the blue of the night meets the gold of the day / Everybody loves somebody / Just one more chance / What a wonderful world / Nightingale sang in Berkeley Square / I left my heart in San Francisco / One of those songs / Baby face / Toot toot tootsie goodbye / Swanee / Happy days are here again / Powder your face with sunshine / I'm looking over a four leaf clover / When you're smiling / Put your arms around me honey / Wyoming Lullaby / What'll I do / When your hair has turned to silver / Till we meet again / It had to be you / I'll get by / I'll string along with you / I'll be seeing you / You'd be so nice to come home to / I love you because / True love / Charmaine / I'll be your sweetheart / When I grow too old to dream / Who's taking you home tonight / You need hands / Au revoir / Auf wiedersehen sweetheart / Arrivederci Roma / Goodbye blues
CD 5507602
Spectrum / Mar '95 / PolyGram

I WANNA SING YOU A SONG
CD MACCD 172
Autograph / Aug '96 / BMG

I WANNA SING YOU A SONG
CD PLSCD 196
Pulse / Apr '97 / BMG

SINGALONG YEARS, THE
Don't bring Lulu / Ma, he's making eyes at me / Yes sir that's my baby / I wonder where my baby is tonight / Who's sorry now / Amy, wonderful Amy / Underneath the arches / Home town / South of the border (Down Mexico way) / Is it true what they say about Dixie / Baby face / California here I come / I've got a lovely bunch of coconuts / You're a pink toothbrush / Who wants to be a millionaire / Beatles medley / What a wonderful world / Tie a yellow ribbon round the ole oak tree / Dance in the old-fashioned way / Neighbours / It's bad / Repeats
CD 74321183232
Ariola Express / Sep '96 / BMG

SINGALONGACHRISTMAS PARTY
We wish you a merry Christmas / Oh come all ye faithful / Once in royal David's city / While shepherds watched their flocks / First noel / Good King Wenceslas / Hark the herald angels sing / Christmas island / I saw Mummy kissing Santa Claus / Rudolph the red nosed reindeer / Little drummer boy / Have yourself a merry little Christmas / Jingle bells / Sleigh ride / Deck of cards / Jingle bell rock / White Christmas / Winter wonderland / Mary's boy child / Christmas song / I love Lassie / Wee Doc and Doris / Keep right on to the end of the road / Auld lange syne
CD TOTCD 5
Total / Dec '95 / Total/BMG

SINGALONGAMAX
CD PLSCD 228
Pulse / Jul '97 / BMG

SINGALONGAWARYEARS
CD MCCD 102
Music Club / May '93 / Disc / THE

SINGALONGAWARYEARS VOL.2
This is the army Mr. Jones / Fleet's in port again / Army, Navy and Airforce / Roll out the barrel / I'm going to get lit up (when the lights go on in London) / Chattanooga choo choo / Jeepers creepers / I've got a gal in Kalamazoo / Three little fishes / You'd be so nice to come home to / If I should fall in love again / You don't have to tell me / One day when we were young / I remember you / Don't sit under the apple tree / Yes my darling daughter / Woodpecker song / Put your arms around me honey / That lovely weekend / It's been a long, long time / You must have been a beautiful baby / Blueberry hill / Sentimental journey / Pennies from heaven / Hokey cokey / Horsey horsey / Under the spreading chestnut tree / Lambeth walk / White Christmas
CD MCCD 159
Music Club / May '94 / Disc / THE

SINGALONGWITHMAX
CD MATCD 289
Castle / Mar '94 / BMG

SONGS LIKE THEY USED T'BE
Fing's ain't what they used to be / You need hands / Who made the morning / When you come to the end of a lollipop (Live) / Little train / Every streets a coronation street / (In) a shanty in old Shanty Town / Lazybones / Bells of Avignon / Ain't that a grand and glorious feeling / Over the rainbow / I'd do anything / They're changing guards at Buckingham Palace / You're a pink toothbrush / O mein Papa (Oh my Papa) / Little white lies / Gotta have rain
CD 5500952
Spectrum / Oct '93 / PolyGram

Byles, Junior

BEAT DOWN BABYLON (The Upsetter Years)
Beat down Babylon / Da-da / I've got a feeling / Don't know why / Demonstration / Coming home / Joshua's desire / Place called Africa / Poor chubby / Matter of time / Fun and games (motion dub) / Pretty fe true (pretty dub) / King of Babylon / Pharaoh hiding
CD UPCD 003
Upsetter / Dec '96 / SRD

CURLY LOCKS
Da da / Come da da / Fever / Lick the pipe Peter: *Byles, Junior & Jah-T/Errol Thompson* / Place called Africa / Africa stand: *Byles, Junior & Dennis Alcapone* / Long way / When will better come / Informer man / Curly locks / Curly locks / Curly locks / Fun and games / Education rock / Got the tip / What is this world coming to / Demonstration / Cutting razor: *Byles, Junior & The Versatiles* / Now generation / Thanks we get / Matter of time / Are you leading me on
CD CDHB 208
Heartbeat / Feb '97 / ADA / Direct / Greensleeves / Jet Star

JORDAN
CD CDHB 45
Heartbeat / Oct '95 / ADA / Direct / Greensleeves / Jet Star

BYOB

BYOB
Too good to let go / Ramifications of shaking one's ass / Change it / Distances / Go jazz go / Outerspacegetthithang / Ramblifications of getting and saying high / Rackett / Day off in the life / Where ya going to
CD RCD 10310
Rykodisc / Oct '94 / ADA / Vital

Byrd, Charlie

AQUARELLE
Concerto grosso / Canta mais / In a mist / 'S wonderful / Man I love / I got rhythm / Quintet (Mozart K 581) / Los Angeles aquarelle suite / In the dark / Modinha / Candlelights
CD CCD 42016
Concord Concerto / Apr '94 / New Note/ Pinnacle

BLUEBYRD
It don't mean a thing if it ain't got that swing / Vou vivendo / Nice work if you can get it / Jitterbug waltz / Soft light and sweet music / Ain't got nothing but the blues / This can't be love / Carinhoso / Mama I'll be home someday / Isn't it a lovely day / Saturday night fish fry
CD CCD 4082
Concord Jazz / Oct '91 / New Note/ Pinnacle

BOSSA NOVA - GUITAR JUBILEE (Byrd, Charlie & Joao Gilberto)
CD CD 62006
Jasmine / Oct '93 / Conifer/BMG / Hot Shot / TKO Magnum

BOSSA NOVA YEARS, THE (Byrd, Charlie Trio)
Meditation / One note samba / Corcovado / Triste / Dindi / O pato / Girl from Ipanema / Samba d'Orpheus / How insensitive / Wave / P'ra dizer adeus / O nosso amor
CD CCD 4468
Concord Jazz / Jul '91 / New Note/Pinnacle

DU HOT CLUB DE CONCORD
Swing '59 / Golden earrings / Lamentos / Carinhoso / Till the clouds roll by / Jubilee / Frenesi / At the seaside (na praia) / Gypsy boots (sapatos novos) / Old New Orleans Blues / Cotton tail / Perfidia / Moon river / Besame mucho / They didn't believe me
CD CCD 4674
Concord Jazz / Nov '95 / New Note/ Pinnacle

GREAT GUITARS VOL.2 (Byrd, Charlie & Barney Kessel)
Lover / Makin' whoopee / Body and soul / Outer drive / On green dolphin street / Nuages: Going out of my head
CD CCD 4023
Concord Jazz / Mar '95 / New Note/ Pinnacle

I'VE GOT THE WORLD ON A STRING
I'm gonna sit right down and write myself a letter / Blue skies / How deep is the ocean / Gee baby ain't I good to you / I've got the world on a string / Goody goody / They can't take that away from me / Avalon / Just you, just me / One to nothing / Don't get around much anymore / Satin doll / Travellin' on / Someone to light up my life / So danco samba / Imagination / Straight no chaser
CD CDSJP 427
Timeless Jazz / May '95 / New Note/ Pinnacle

ISN'T IT ROMANTIC (Byrd, Charlie Trio)
Isn't it romantic / I could write a book / Cheek to cheek / Very thought of you / Thou swell / One morning in May / I didn't know what time it was / There's a small hotel / Someone to watch over me / Thought about me / Last night when we were young
CD CCD 4252
Concord Jazz / Aug '92 / New Note/ Pinnacle

IT'S A WONDERFUL WORLD (Featuring Scott Hamilton) (Byrd, Charlie Trio & Scott Hamilton)
CD CCD 4374
Concord Jazz / May '89 / New Note/ Pinnacle

JAZZ 'N' SAMBA
CD HCD 606
Hindsight / Aug '95 / Jazz Music / Target/ BMG

LATIN BYRD
Duck / Amor flamengo / Azul tiple / Cancion di Argentina / Manha de carnaval / Homage a villa Lobos / Bogota / Mexican song / Mexican song / Galopera / Vals / Outra vez / Presente de Natal / Insensatez / Three note samba / Samba da minha terra / Limehouse blues / Saudade da Bahia / Anna / Socegadamente / Chega de saudade / Cancao de ninar para Carol
CD MCD 470052
Milestone / Aug '96 / Cadillac / Complete/ Pinnacle / Jazz Music / Wellard

MOMENTS LIKE THIS
Little girls at play / Si tu vois ma mere / My ideal / Rose of the Rio Grande / Too late now / Rosetta / Russian lullaby / As long as I live / Wang wang blues / Prelude to a kiss / Soon / Polka dots and moonbeams / Moments like this / Don't explain
CD CCD 4627
Concord Jazz / Jan '95 / New Note/ Pinnacle

TAMBU (Byrd, Charlie & Cal Tjader)
CD FCD 6169453
Fantasy / Jun '87 / Jazz Music / Pinnacle / Wellard

Byrd, Donald

AT THE HALF NOTE CAFE (2CD Set)
My girl Shirl / Child's play / Chan / Portrait of Jennie / Cecile / Jeannine / Between the devil and the deep blue sea / Theme from Mr. Lucky / Kinyas / When Sunny gets blue
CD Set CDP 8571872
Blue Note / Aug '97 / EMI

BEST OF DONALD BYRD
Change (makes you want to hustle) / You and music / Black Byrd / Think twice / Onward 'til morning / Lanasana's priestess / Street lady / Flight time / Places and spaces / Wind parade / Dominoes / Steppin' into tomorrow / Just my imagination / Love's so far away / Dominoes (Live)
CD CDP 7986382
Blue Note / Feb '92 / EMI

EARLY BYRD - THE BEST OF THE JAZZ SOUL YEARS
Slow drag / West of Pecos / Books Bossa / Jelly roll / Mustang / Blackjack / Weasil / Dude / Emperor / Little rasti
CD ______ CDP 7896062
Blue Note / Jun '93 / EMI

ELECTRIC BYRD
Estavanico / Essence / Xibaba / Dude
CD ______ CDP 8361952
Blue Note / Mar '96 / EMI

FIRST FLIGHT
CD ______ DELMARK 407
Delmark / Feb '87 / ADA / Cadillac / CM / Direct / Hot Shot

GROOVIN' FOR NAT
Hush / Child's play / Angel eyes / Smoothie / Suede / Friday's child / Out of this world / Groovin' for Nat
CD ______ BLCD 760134
Black Lion / '88 / Cadillac / Jazz Music / Koch / Wellard

PLACES AND SPACES
Change (makes you want to hustle) / Wind parade / (Fallin' like) dominoes / Places and spaces / You and the music / Night whistler / Just my imagination
CD ______ CDP 8543262
Blue Note / Feb '97 / EMI

STREET LADY
Lansana's priestess / Miss Kane / Sister love / Street lady / Witch hunt / Woman of the world
CD ______ CDP 8539232
Blue Note / Jan '97 / EMI

Byrd, Joe

AMERICAN METAPHYSICAL CIRCUS (Byrd, Joe & The Field Hippies)
CD ______ OW 26792
One Way / Jun '97 / ADA / Direct / Greyhound

Byrd, John

COMPLETE RECORDINGS 1929-1931 (Byrd, John & Walter Taylor)
CD ______ SOB 035172
Story Of The Blues / Dec '92 / ADA / Koch

Byrd, Tracy

BIG LOVE
Big love / Cowgirl / Good ol' fashioned love / Don't take her she's all I got / If I stay / Don't love make a diamond shine / Tucson too soon / I don't believe that's how you feel / Driving me out of your mind / I love you that's all / Lifestyles of the not so rich and famous / Keeper of the star
CD ______ MCD 11546
MCA / Oct '96 / BMG

TRACY BYRD
That's the thing about a memory / Back in the swing of things / Someone to give my love to / Holdin' heaven / Why / Out of control raging fire / Hat trick / Why don't that telephone ring / Edge of a memory / Talk to me Texas
CD ______ MCAD 10649
MCA / Mar '94 / BMG

Byrds

20 ESSENTIAL TRACKS FROM THE BOXED SET
Mr. Tambourine Man / I'll feel a whole lot better / All I really want to do / Turn turn turn / 5-D / Eight miles high / Mr. Spaceman / So you want to be a rock 'n' roll star / Have you seen her face / Lady friend / My back pages / Goin' back / Ballad of Easy Rider / Jesus is just alright / Chestnut mare / I wanna grow up to be a politician / He was a friend of mine / Paths of victory / From a distance / Love that never dies
CD ______ 4716652
Columbia / Jul '91 / Sony

BALLAD OF EASY RIDER
Ballad of Easy Rider / Fido / Oil in my lamp / Tulsa County / Jack Tarr the sailor / Jesus is just alright / It's all over now, baby blue / There must be someone (I can talk to) / Deportee (Plane wreck at Los Gatos) / Armstrong, Aldrin and Collins / Way beyond the sun / Mae Jean goes to Hollywood / Oil in my lamp / Tulsa County / Fiddler a dram (Moog experiment) / Ballad of Easy Rider / Build it up
CD ______ 4867542
Columbia / Mar '97 / Sony

BYRDS PLAY DYLAN, THE
Mr. Tambourine man / All I really want to do / Chimes of freedom / Spanish Harlem incident / Time they are a changin' / Lay down your weary tune / My back pages / You ain't goin' nowhere / Nothing was delivered / This wheel's on fire / It's all over now baby blue / Baby blue / Lay lady lay / Positively 4th street
CD ______ 4767572
Columbia / Feb '96 / Sony

BYRDS, THE
Full circle / Sweet Mary / Changing heart / For free / Born to rock 'n' roll / Things will be better / Cowgirl in the sand / Long live the King / Borrowing time / Laughing / See the sky about to rain
CD ______ 7559609552
WEA / Jan '93 / Warner Music

BYRDS, THE
Mr. Tambourine Man / Turn turn turn / All I really want to do / You ain't going nowhere / Eight miles high / Chestnut mare / It won't be wrong / Time and place / Do you remember / Tell Sarah / He was a friend of mine / Home again / Out of sight / Quit this
CD ______ EXP 004
Experience / May '97 / TKO Magnum

BYRDS, THE
CD ______ GFS 077
Going For A Song / Jul '97 / Else / TKO Magnum

DR. BYRDS AND MR. HYDE
This wheel's on fire / Old blue / Your gentle way of loving me / Child of the universe / Nashville West / Drug store truck drivin' man / King Apathy III / Candy / Bad night at the whiskey / Medley: My back pages / BJ blues / Baby, what you want me to do
CD ______ BGOCD 107
Beat Goes On / Aug '91 / Pinnacle

DR. BYRDS AND MR. HYDE
This wheel's on fire / Old Blue / Your gentle way of loving me / Child of the universe / Nashville West / Drug store truck drivin' man / King Apathy III / Candy / Bad night at the whisley / Medley / Stanley's song / Lay lady lay / This wheel's on fire / Medley
CD ______ 4867532
Columbia / Mar '97 / Sony

FIFTH DIMENSION
5-D (fifth dimension) / Wild mountain thyme / Mr. Spaceman / I see you / What's happening / I come and stand at every door / Eight miles high / Hey Joe (where you gonna go) / Captain soul / John Riley / 2-4-2 foxtrot (the lear jet song)
CD ______ BGOCD 106
Beat Goes On / Sep '91 / Pinnacle

FIFTH DIMENSION
5D (fifth dimension) / Wild mountain thyme / Mr. Spaceman / I see you / What's happening / I come and stand at every door / Eight miles high / Hey Joe (where you gonna go) / Captain soul / John Riley / 2-4-2 fox trot (The lear jet song) / Why / I know my rider / Psychodrama City / Eight miles high / Why / John Riley
CD ______ 4837072
Columbia / May '96 / Sony

GREATEST HITS
Mr. Tambourine man / I'll feel a whole lot better / Bells of Rhymney / Turn turn turn / All I really want to do / Chimes of freedom / Eight miles high / Mr. Spaceman / 5-D (fifth dimension) / So you want to be a rock 'n' roll star / My back pages
CD ______ 4678432
Columbia / Feb '91 / Sony

MR. TAMBOURINE MAN
Mr. Tambourine Man / I'll feel a whole lot better / Spanish Harlem incident / You won't have to cry / Here without you / Bells of Rhymney / All I really want to do / I knew I'd want you / It's no use / Don't doubt yourself babe / Chimes of freedom / We'll meet again / She has a way / I'll feel a whole lot better / It's no use / You won't have to cry / All I really want to do / You and me
CD ______ 4837052
Columbia / May '96 / Sony

NOTORIOUS BYRD BROTHERS, THE
Artificial energy / Goin' back / Natural harmony / Draft morning / Wasn't born to follow / Get to you / Change is now / Old John Robertson / Tribal gathering / Dolphin's smile / Space odyssey / Moog raga / Bound to fall / Triad / Goin' back / Universal mind decoder / Draft morning
CD ______ 4867512
Columbia / Mar '97 / Sony

SWEETHEART OF THE RODEO
You ain't goin' nowhere / I am a pilgrim / Christian life / You don't miss your water / You're still on my mind / Pretty boy Floyd / Hickory wind / Hundred years from now / Blue Canadian Rockies / Life in prison / Nothing was delivered
CD ______ 4681782
Columbia / Aug '93 / Sony

SWEETHEART OF THE RODEO
You ain't going nowhere / I am a pilgrim / Christian life / You don't miss your water / You're still on my mind / Pretty Boy Floyd / Hickory wind / One hundred years from now / Blue Canadian Rockies / Life in prison / Nothing was delivered / You got a reputation / Lazy days / Pretty Polly / Christian life / Life in prison / You're still on my mind / One hundred years from now / All I have is memories
CD ______ 4867522
Columbia / Mar '97 / Sony

TURN TURN TURN
Turn turn turn / It won't be long / Set you free this time / Lay down your weary tune / He was a friend of mine / World turns all around her / Satisfied mind / If you're gone / Times they are a changin' / Wait and see / Oh Susannah / She don't care about time / Times they are a changin' / It's all over now baby blue / Day walk (never before) / World turns all around her / Stranger in a strange land
CD ______ 4837062
Columbia / May '96 / Sony

ULTIMATE BYRDS, THE (4CD Set)
Mr. Tambourine man / I'll feel a whole lot better / Chimes of freedom / She has a way / All I really want to do / Spanish harlem incident / Bells of Rhymney / It's all over now baby blue / She don't care about time / Turn, turn, turn / It won't be wrong / Lay down your weary tune / He was a friend of mind / World turns all around her / Day walk (never before) / Times are a-changing / 5-D (Fifth dimension) / I know my rider / Eight miles high / Why / Psychodrama City / I see you / Hey Joe (where you gonna go) / Mr. Spaceman / John Riley / Roll over Beethoven / So you want to be a rock 'n' roll star / Have you seen her face / My back pages / Time between / It happens each day / Renaissance Fair / Everybody's been burned / Girl with no name / Triad / Lady friend / Old John Robertson / Goin' back / Draft morning / Wasn't born to follow / Dolphin's smile / Reputation / You ain't goin' nowhere / Christian life / I am a pilgrim / Pretty boy Floyd / You don't miss your water / Hickory wind / Nothing was delivered / Hundred years from now / Pretty Polly / Lazy days / This wheel's on fire / Nashville West / Old blue / Drug store truck drivin' man / Bad night at the whiskey / Lay lady lay / Mae Jean goes to Hollywood / Easy rider theme / Oil in my lamp / Jesus is just alright / Way beyond the sun / Tulsa county / Deportee / Lover of the Bayou / Willin' / Black mountain rag / Positively 4th Street / Chestnut mare / Just a season / Kathleen's song / Truck stop girl / Just like a woman / Stanley's song / Glory glory / I trust / I wanna grow up to be a politician / Green apple quick step / Tiffany Queen / Bugler / Lazy waters / Farther along / White's lightning / He was a friend of mine / Paths of victory / From a distance / Love that never dies
CD Set ______ 4676112
Columbia / Dec '90 / Sony

VERY BEST OF THE BYRDS, THE
Mr. Tambourine man / All I really want to do / Chimes of freedom / I'll feel a whole lot better / Turn turn turn / Times they are a-changin' / World turns all around her / It won't be wrong / He was a friend of mine / Eight miles high / 5D / Mr. Spaceman / So you want to be a rock 'n' roll star / My back pages / Renaissance Fair / Goin' back / Wasn't born to follow / Dolphin's smile / You ain't goin' nowhere / One hundred years from now / You're still on my mind / Hickory wind / Ballad of Easy Rider / Jesus is just alright / It's all over now baby blue / Lay lady lay / Chesnut Mare
CD ______ 4879952
Columbia / Jun '97 / Sony

YOUNGER THAN YESTERDAY
So you want to be a rock 'n' roll star / Have you seen her face / CTA - 102 / Renaissance fair / Time between / Everybody's been burned / Thoughts and words / Mind gardens / My back pages / Girl with no name / Why / It happens each day / Don't make waves / My back pages / Lady friend / Old John Robertson / Mind gardens
CD ______ 4837082
Columbia / May '96 / Sony

Byrne, David

DAVID BYRNE
Long time ago / Angels / Crash / Self made man / Back in the box / Sad song / Nothing at all / My love is you / Lillies of the valley / You and eye / Strange ritual / Buck naked
CD ______ 9362455582
Sire / May '94 / Warner Music

FEELINGS
Fuzzy freaky / Miss America / Soft seduction / Dance on vaseline / Gates of paradise / Amnesia / You don't know me / Daddy go down / Finite alright / Wicked little doll / Burnt by the sun / Civil wars / They are in love
CD ______ 9362466052
Sire / May '97 / Warner Music

FOREST, THE
Ur / Kish / Dura europus / Nineveh / Ava / Machu picchu / Teotihuacan / Asuka / Samara / Tula
CD ______ 7599265842
Sire / Jun '91 / Warner Music

REI MOMO
Independence day / Make believe mambo / Call of the wild / Dirty old town / Rose tattoo / Dream police / Don't want to be part of your world / Marching through the wilderness / Lie to me / Women vs. men / Carnival eyes / I know sometimes a man is a wrong / Loco de amor / Good and evil / Office cowboy
CD ______ 9259902
Sire / Feb '95 / Warner Music

UH-OH
Now I'm your mom / Girls on my mind / Something ain't right / She's mad / Hanging upside down / Twistin' in the wind / Walk in the dark / Cowboy's mambo / Tiny town / Somebody
CD ______ 7599267992
Sire / Feb '95 / Warner Music

Byrne, Dermot

DERMOT BYRNE
CD ______ HBCD 0007
Hummingbird / Mar '96 / ADA / Direct / Grapevine/PolyGram

Byrne, Donna

LET'S FACE THE MUSIC AND DANCE
CD ______ ST 579
Stash / Jun '94 / ADA / Cadillac / CM / Direct / Jazz Music

Byrne, James

ROAD TO GLENLOUGH, THE
CD ______ CC 52CD
Claddagh / Nov '95 / ADA / CM / Direct

Byron

BYRON
CD ______ WKFMXD 173
FM Coast To Coast / Mar '92 / Revolver

Byron, Don

BUG MUSIC
CD ______ 7559794382
Nonesuch / Mar '97 / Warner Music

MUSIC FOR SIX MUSICIANS
CD ______ 7559793542
Nonesuch / '95 / Warner Music

NO VIBE ZONE (Byron, Don Quintet)
CD ______ KFWCD 191
Knitting Factory / Oct '96 / Cargo / Plastic Head

PLAYS THE MUSIC OF MICKEY KATZ
CD ______ 7559793132
Nonesuch / Jul '96 / Warner Music

TUSKEGEE EXPERIMENT
CD ______ 7559792802
Nonesuch / May '92 / Warner Music

Bystanders

BIRTH OF MAN
That's the end / (You're gonna) hurt yourself / My love - come home / 98.6 / Royal blue summer sunshine day / Make up your mind / Green grass / Cave of clear light / Painting the time / This time / Have I offended the girl / If you walk away / Stubborn kind of fellow / Pattern people / When jezamine goes / This world is my world
CD ______ SEECD 301
See For Miles/C5 / '90 / Pinnacle

Byzar

GAIATRONYK
CD ______ EFA 709732
Asphodel / Jun '97 / Cargo / SRD

C

C&C Music Factory

GONNA MAKE YOU SWEAT
Gonna make you sweat / Here we go / Things that make you go hmmmm / Just a touch of love (everyday) / Groove of love (what's this world called love) / Live happy / Ooh baby / Let's get funkee / Givin' it to you / Bang that beat
CD _______ 4678142
Columbia / Apr '94 / Sony

ULTIMATE, THE
Gonna make you sweat (everybody dance now) / Here we go let's rock and roll / Things that make you go hmmmm / Just a touch of love / Robi-robs boriqua anthem / Deeper love / Keep it comin' / Do you wanna get funky / Take a toke / I found love
CD _______ 4811172
Columbia / Feb '97 / Sony

C. Gibbs Review

SINCERITY'S GROUND
CD _______ CDEAR 016
Earth Music / Jan '97 / Cargo

CA Quintet

TRIP THRU HELL
CD _______ 852126
EVA / May '94 / ADA / Direct

Caballero, Don

FOR RESPECT
CD _______ EFA 049292
City Slang / Oct '93 / RTM/Disc

Cabaret Voltaire

2 X 45
CD _______ CABS 9CD
Mute / Oct '90 / RTM/Disc

8 CREPUSCULE TRACKS
Sluggin for Jesus (part 1) / Sluggin for Jesus (part 2) / Fools game-sluggin for Jesus (part 3) / Yashar / Your agent man / Gut level / Invocation / Shaft
CD _______ TWI 7492
Les Disques Du Crepuscule / Mar '96 / Discovery

CABARET VOLTAIRE 1974-1976
CD _______ CABS 15CD
Mute / Mar '92 / RTM/Disc

CONVERSATION, THE
Exterminating angel / Brutal but clean / Message / Let's start / Night rider / I think / Heat / Harmonic parallel / Project 80 / Exterminating angel (Outro)
CD Set _______ AMB 4934CD
Apollo / Jul '94 / Vital

COVENANT, THE SWORD AND THE ARM OF THE LORD, THE
L 21st / I want you / Hell's home / Kick back / Arm of the Lord / Warm / Golden halos / Motion rotation / Whip blow / Web
CD _______ CVCD 3
Some Bizarre/Virgin / Sep '91 / EMI

CRACKDOWN, THE
24-24 / In the shadows / Talking time / Animation / Over and over / Just fascination / Why kill time (when you can kill yourself) / Haiti / Crackdown / Diskono / Double vision / Badge of evil / Moscow
CD _______ CVCD 1
Some Bizarre/Virgin / Apr '86 / EMI

JOHNNY YES NO
CD _______ CABSCD 10
Mute / Oct '90 / RTM/Disc

LISTEN UP WITH CABARET VOLTAIRE
CD _______ CABS 5CD
Mute / Jun '90 / RTM/Disc

LIVE AT THE LYCEUM
CD _______ CABS 13CD
Mute / '88 / RTM/Disc

LIVE AT THE YMCA
CD _______ CABS 4CD
Mute / Jun '90 / RTM/Disc

LIVING LEGENDS
CD _______ CABS 6CD
Mute / Jun '90 / RTM/Disc

MICROPHONIES
Do right / Operative / Digital rasta / Spies in the wires / Earthshaker (Theme) / James Brown / Slammer / Blue heat / Sensoria
CD _______ CVCD 2
Some Bizarre/Virgin / Sep '91 / EMI

MIX UP
CD _______ CABS 8CD
Mute / Oct '90 / RTM/Disc

PLASTICITY
CD _______ TWI 9752
Les Disques Du Crepuscule / Mar '96 / Discovery

RED MECCA
CD _______ CABS 3CD
Mute / Jun '90 / RTM/Disc

THREE MANTRAS
CD _______ CABS 7CD
Mute / Jun '90 / RTM/Disc

VOICE OF AMERICA
CD _______ CABS 2CD
Mute / Jun '90 / RTM/Disc

Cabazz

FAR AWAY
CD _______ DRCD 194
Dragon / Jan '89 / ADA / Cadillac / CM / Roots / Wellard

KAOTIKA
CD _______ DRCD 241
Dragon / Oct '94 / ADA / Cadillac / CM / Roots / Wellard

Cable

DOWN-LIFT THE UP-TRODDEN
CD _______ INFECT 32CD
Infectious / Mar '96 / RTM/Disc

WHEN ANIMALS ATTACK
Souvenir / Bluebirds are blue / Signature tune / Freeze the atlantic / Ultra violet / I'm always right / Colder climate / Whisper firing line / God gave me gravity / From here you can see yourself / Do the tube
CD _______ INFECT 35CD
CD _______ INFECT 35CDX
Infectious / May '97 / RTM/Disc

Cable Regime

ASSIMILATE AND DESTROY
CD _______ PPP 110CD
PDCD / Sep '93 / Plastic Head

KILL LIES ALL
CD _______ STC 17CD
Sentrax Corporation / Aug '94 / Plastic Head

LIFE IN THE HOUSE OF THE ENEMY
CD _______ PPP 108CD
PDCD / Nov '92 / Plastic Head

Cables, George

BY GEORGE
Bess you is my woman now / My man's gone now / I got rhythm / Embraceable you / Someone to watch over me / Foggy day / Summertime
CD _______ CCD 14030
Contemporary / Apr '94 / Cadillac / Complete/Pinnacle / Jazz Music / Wellard

DARK SIDE, LIGHT SIDE (Cables, George Trio)
CD _______ SCCD 31405
Steeplechase / Apr '97 / Discovery / Impetus

INTRODUCING JEFF JEROLAMON
CD _______ CCD 79522
Candid / Feb '97 / Cadillac / Direct / Jazz Music / Koch / Wellard

LIVE AT MAYBECK RECITAL HALL VOL.35
Over the rainbow / Helen's song / Bess you is my woman now / Someone to watch over me / You don't know what love is / Lullaby / Everything happens to me / Goin' home / Little B's poem
CD _______ CCD 4630
Concord Jazz / Jan '95 / New Note/ Pinnacle

NIGHT AND DAY (Cables, George Trio)
CD _______ DIW 606
DIW / Sep '91 / Cadillac / Harmonia Mundi

PERSON TO PERSON
CD _______ SCCD 31369
Steeplechase / Feb '96 / Discovery / Impetus

Cabo Verde Show

SANTO CATARINA
CD _______ 012331
Sun / Jan '97 / Stern's

Cabrette

CORNEMUSE D'AUVERGNEL 1895-1976
CD _______ Y 225104
Silex / Aug '93 / ADA / Harmonia Mundi

Cacavas, Chris

DWARF STAR
CD _______ RTS 14
Return To Sender / Dec '94 / ADA / Direct

GOOD TIMES
CD _______ NORMAL 140CD
Normal / Sep '93 / ADA / Direct

NEW IMPROVED PAIN (Cacavas, Chris & Junkyard Love)
CD _______ NORMAL 200CD
Normal / Oct '95 / ADA / Direct

PALE BLONDE HELL
CD _______ NORMAL 170CD
Normal / Mar '94 / ADA / Direct

Cactus

CACTOLOGY
Evil / Parchman farm / You can't judge a book by the cover / One way or another / Alaska / Long tall Sally / Let me swim / Bro Bill / Rock 'n' roll children / Song for Aries / Restrictions / Oleo / Feel so good / Rumblin' man / Bad stuff / Parchman farm
CD _______ 8122724112
Atlantic / Jul '96 / Warner Music

CACTUS
You can't judge a book by the cover / Parchman farm / My lady from south of Detroit / Let me swim / Oleo / No need to worry / Feel so good / Bro Bill
CD _______ 7567802902
Atlantic / Jan '96 / Warner Music

Cadaver

HALLUCINATING ANXIETY
CD _______ NECRO 4 CD
Necrosis / Dec '90 / Vital

Cadaverous Condition

IN MELANCHOLY
CD _______ LRC 008
Lethal / Feb '94 / Plastic Head

Caddick, Bill

WINTER WITH FLOWERS
CD _______ FLED 3004
Fledg'ling / Jul '95 / ADA / CM / Direct

Cadets

STRANDED IN THE JUNGLE (The Legendaray Modern Recordings)
Let's rock 'n' roll / Fools rush in / My clumsy heart / Annie met Henry / Rollin' stone / Don't be angry / Hands across the table / Smack dab in the middle / Pretty Evey / Love can do most anything / Baby ya know / Love bandit / Why did I fall in love / Church bells may ring / Car crash / Ring chimes / Heartbreak hotel / Dancin' Dan / Rum Jamaica rum / Don't / I got loaded / I'll be spinning / Sugar baby / Stranded in the jungle
CD _______ CDCHD 534
Ace / Sep '94 / Pinnacle

Cadicamo, Enrique

HOMENAJE A LOS POETAS DEL TANGO
CD _______ EBCD 74
El Bandoneon / Jul '96 / Discovery

LITTO NEBIA QUINTETO
CD _______ KAR 980
IMP / Sep '96 / ADA / Discovery

Cadillac Blues Band

LIVE 1996
CD _______ INAK 9042
In Akustik / Feb '97 / Direct / TKO Magnum

Cadillac Tramps

IT'S ALRIGHT
CD _______ CDVEST 28
Bulletproof / Aug '94 / Pinnacle

Cadillacs

BEST OF THE CADILLACS
Gloria / No chance / Down the road / Window lady / Speedoo / Zoom / You are / Woe is me / Betty my love / Girl I love / Sugar sugar / My girl friend / Speedo is back / Peek-a-boo / Zoom boom zing / Please Mr. Johnson / Romeo / Tell me today
CD _______ NEMCD 604
Sequel / Aug '90 / BMG

COMPLETE JOSIE SESSIONS, THE
Gloria / I wonder why / Wishing well / Carelessly / I want to know about love / No chance / No chance (alt) / Sympathy sympathy / Party for two / Party for two (alt) / Corn whiskey / Down the road / Window lady / Speedoo (alt) / Speddoo / Zoom boom zing / Let me explain (alt) / Let me explain / You are (version 1) / Zoon (version 3) / Oh wahtcha do / Shock-a-doo / You are / Why / (That's) All I need / Baby's coming home to me baby / Girl I love / Betty my love / Woe is me / Rudolph the red nosed reindeer / Don't take your love from me / If you want to be a woman of mine / About that girl named Lou / Sugar sugar / Broken heart / C'mon home baby / Hurry home / Lucy / From this day on / My girlfriend / Don't be mad with my heart / Buzz buzz buzz / Yeah yeah baby / Holy smoke baby / I want to know / Ain't you gonna / It's spring / Speedoo is back / Look-a-here / Great googly moo / Copy cat / Oh oh Lolita / Peek-a-boo / Jelly bean / Please Mr. Johnson / Your heart is so blind / Cool it fool / Jay Walker / Who ya gonna kiss / Vow / Naggity nag / You're not in love with me / Bad Dan McGoon / Romeo Romeo / Always my darling / Dumbell / Still you left me baby / Dum dee dum dum / Frankenstein / I want to be loved / I'm in love / Tell me today / Let me down easy / It's love / That's why / Louise / Rock 'n' roll is here to stay / Boogie man / I'll never let you go / Wayward wanderer
CD Set _______ BCD 15648
Bear Family / Mar '95 / Direct / Rollercoaster / Swift

Cadogan, Susan

HURT SO GOOD
CD _______ CDTRL 122
Trojan / Jun '95 / Direct / Jet Star

Caducity

WEILIAON WIELDER
CD _______ SHR 012CD
Shiva / Nov '95 / Plastic Head

Caedmon

CAEDMON
CD _______ KSCD 9450
Kissing Spell / Jun '97 / Greyhound

Caesar

LIVE AT CAESAR'S PALACE
CD _______ E 12251CD
Disko B / Sep '93 / SRD

Caesars Palace

ROCK DU MUTA
CD _______ DOL 036CD
Dolores / Jun '96 / Plastic Head

Caetano, Gal, Gil & Bethania

COLLECTION, THE
CD _______ 883720
Milan / May '97 / Conifer/BMG / Silva Screen

Cafe Jacques

ROUND THE BACK
Meaningless / Ain't no love in the heart of the city / Sands of Singapore / Farewell my lovely / Eberehtel / Dark eyed Johnny / Sandra's a phonie / None of your business / Crime passionelle / Lifeline
CD _______ 4872362
Columbia / Mar '97 / Sony

Cafe Orchestra

TOPAZ
CD _______ GRACD 221
Grapevine / Jun '97 / Grapevine/PolyGram

Cage, John

SIXTY EIGHT/QUARTETS I-VIII
CD _______ ARTCD 6168
Hat Art / Dec '95 / Cadillac / Harmonia Mundi

SIXTY-TWO MESOSTICS RE MERCE CUNNINGHAM
CD Set _______ ARTCD 26095
Hat Art / Jan '92 / Cadillac / Harmonia Mundi

SONATAS AND PRELUDES
CD _______ MODE 50
Mode / Jun '97 / Harmonia Mundi / ReR Megacorp

TWO, FIVE AND SEVEN (2CD Set)
CD Set _______ CD 6192
Hat Hut / Feb '97 / Harmonia Mundi

Cagney & Lacee

SIX FEET OF CHAIN
CD _______ KAR 041
No.6 / May '97 / Greyhound

Caillier, Jackie

FRONT PORCH CAJUN MUSIC
CD ZNCD 1011
Zane / Oct '96 / Pinnacle

Cain & Abel

CAIN AND ABEL
CD 35699
Sphinx Ministry / Nov '96 / Cargo

Cain, Chris

SOMEWHERE ALONG THE WAY
CD BPCD 5024
Blind Pig / Dec '95 / ADA / CM / Direct / Hot Shot

Cain, Jackie

JACKIE & ROY FOREVER (Cain, Jackie & Roy Kral)
CD 01612651282
Music Masters / Dec '95 / Nimbus

Cain, Michael

CIRCA (Cain, Michael & Ralph Alessi/ Peter Epstein)
Siegfried and Roy / Social drones / Ped cruc / Miss M / Circa / Egg / Top o' the dunes / ...And their white tigers / Red rock rain / Suchness of Dory Philpott / Marche
CD 5370472
ECM / Feb '97 / New Note/Pinnacle

STRANGE OMEN
Emanations / Strange omen / Follow through / Bestido al cielo de noche / Piano sketch no.1 / Piano sketch no.2 / Piano sketch no.3 / Piano sketch no.4 / Way things work / Heroine's serenity / Facing North
CD CCD 790505
Candid / Feb '97 / Cadillac / Direct / Jazz Music / Koch / Wellard

WHAT MEANS THIS
As I gazed / What means this / Meander / Two Kims / How so / Clearly / Figure of speech / Ginnette
CD CCD 79529
Candid / Feb '97 / Cadillac / Direct / Jazz Music / Koch / Wellard

Caine, Jackie

ALEC WILDER COLLECTION (Caine, Jackie & Roy Kral)
CD ACD 257
Audiophile / Oct '92 / Jazz Music

TRIBUTE TO ALAN J. LERNER, A (Caine, Jackie & Roy Kral)
CD ACD 230
Audiophile / Oct '92 / Jazz Music

Caine, Marti

MARTI
Still crazy after all these years / Not like this / Waters of March / Guess who I saw today / When the sun comes out / Why did I choose you / Send in the clowns / Looking for the right one / It never entered my mind / What does a woman see in a man / Some cats know / Everything must change / Evert time we say goodbye / Goodbye / I'll be around / Les boys / I've loved these days / Thank song
CD 1731070042
Carlton / Aug '96 / Carlton

Caine, Uri

SPHERE MUSIC
Mr. BC / This is a thing called love / When the world is given / 'Round midnight / Let me count the ways / Jelly / Just in time / We see / Jan fan
CD 5140072
JMT / May '94 / PolyGram

TOYS
CD 5140222
JMT / May '96 / PolyGram

Cajun, Richard

CAJUN TRACKS (Cajun, Richard & The Zydeco Brothers)
CD BCAT 04CD
Bearcat / Jun '94 / ADA / Direct

NO KNOWN CURE (Cajun, Richard & The Zydeco Brothers)
CD BCAT 03CD
Bearcat / Jun '93 / ADA / Direct

THAT CAJUN THING (Cajun, Richard & The Zydeco Brothers)
CD BCAT 05CD
Bearcat / Aug '94 / ADA / Direct

Cajuns Denbo

STOMPIO
Yr uffern hon / Llond fy mol / Jole blon / Ffwl fel fi / Sut fath o foi / Elen / Deugam acadien / Y drws cefn / Walts hefo fi / Puntan yn fy llaw / Diggy diggy lo / Dawnsia nawr / Cajun cwins / Tit galop
CD SCD 2155
Sain / Feb '97 / ADA / Direct / Greyhound

Cake

FASHION NUGGET
Frank Sinatra / Distance / Friend is a four letter word / Open book / Daria / Race car ya ya's / I will survive / Stickshifts and safety belts / Perhaps, perhaps, perhaps / It's coming down / Nugget / She'll come back to me / Italian leather sofa / Sad songs and waltzes
CD 5328672
Capricorn / Mar '97 / PolyGram

MOTORCADE OF GENEROSITY
Comanche / Up so close / Jolene / You part the waters / Jesus wrote a blank cheque / I bombed Korea / Ain't no good / Ruby sees all / Pentagram / Haze of love / Is this love / Rock 'n' roll lifestyle / Mr. Mastodon Farm
CD 5325062
Capricorn / Jul '97 / PolyGram

Cake Kitchen

FAR FROM THE SUN
CD HMS 1982
Homestead / Jul '93 / Cargo / SRD

Cake Like

BRUISER QUEEN
New girl / Wendy / Mr. Fireman / Groovy / Latin lover / Pretty new / Lorraine's car / Franchise / Cancer / American woman / Truck stop hussy / Destroyed
CD 9362466012
Warner Bros. / Jun '97 / Warner Music

Calabash Case

PARADING CONSTANTLY
CD WR 8
Wrenched / Jan '97 / Cargo

Calazans, Teca

FIROLIU
CD 829302
BUDA / Oct '96 / Discovery

Calcutta Cyber Cafe

DRUM 'N' SPACE
CD OMNICD 001
Omni / Jul '96 / RTM/Disc

Cale, J.J.

CLOSER TO YOU
Long way home / Sho-biz blues / Slower baby / Devil's nurse / Like you used to / Borrowed time / Rose in the garden / Brown dirt / Hard love / Ain't love funny / Closer to you / Steve's song
CD CDV 2746
Virgin / Jun '94 / EMI

EIGHT
Money talks / Losers / Hard times / Reality / Takin' care of business / People lie / Unemployment / Trouble in the city / Teardrops in my tequila / Livin' here too
CD 8111522
Mercury / Sep '89 / PolyGram

FIVE
Thirteen days / Boilin' pot / I'll make love to you anytime / Don't cry sister / Too much for me / Sensitive kind / Friday / Lou easy Ann / Let's go to Tahiti / Katy Kool lady / Fate of a fool / Mona
CD 8103132
Mercury / Jul '93 / PolyGram

GRASSHOPPER
City girls / Devil in disguise / One step ahead of the blues / You keep me hangin' on / Downtown LA / Can't live here / Grasshopper / Drifter's wife / Thing going on / Nobody but you / Mississippi river / Does your mama like to reggae / Dr. Jive
CD 8000382
Mercury / Nov '84 / PolyGram

GUITAR MAN
Death in the wilderness / It's hard to tell / Day's go by / Low down / This town / Guitar man / If I had a rocket / Perfect woman / Old blue / Doctor told me / Miss Ol St.Louie / Nobody knows
CD CDVIR 48
Virgin / Apr '96 / EMI

NATURALLY
Call me the breeze / Call the doctor / Don't go to strangers / Woman I love / Magnolia / Clyde / Crazy mama / Nowhere to run / After midnight / River runs deep / Bringing it back / Crying eyes
CD 8300422
Mercury / Jan '87 / PolyGram

OKIE
Crying / I'll be there (if you ever want me) / Starbound / Rock 'n' roll records / Old man and me / Ever lovin' woman / Cajun moon / I'd like to love you baby / Anyway the wind blows / Precious memories / Okie / I got the same old blues
CD 8421022
Mercury / May '90 / PolyGram

REALLY
Lies / Everything will be alright / I'll kiss the world goodbye / Changes / Right down here / If you're ever in Oklahoma / Riding home / Going down / Soulin' / Playin' in the streets / Mo Jo / Louisiana woman
CD 8103142
Mercury / Aug '89 / PolyGram

SHADES
Carry on / Deep dark dungeon / Wish I had not said that / Pack my jack / If you leave her / Mama don't / What do you expect / Cloudy day / Love has been and gone
CD 8001052
Mercury / Aug '89 / PolyGram

SPECIAL EDITION
Cocaine / Don't wait / Magnolia / Devil in disguise / Sensitive kind / Carry on after midnight / Money talks / Call me the breeze / Lies / City girls / Cajun moon / Don't cry sister / Crazy mama
CD 8186332
Mercury / Jun '84 / PolyGram

TEN
CD ORECD 523
Silvertone / Sep '92 / Pinnacle

WHEN THE WIND BLOWS (The Anthology) (2CD Set)
CD Set 5329012
Mercury / Jun '97 / PolyGram

Cale, John

23 SOLO PIECES
CD YMCD 007
Yellow Moon / Nov '95 / Vital

ARTIFICIAL INTELLIGENCE
Every time the dogs bark / Dying on the vine / Sleeper / Vigilante lover / Chinese takeaway / Song of the valley / Fade away tomorrow / Black rose / Satellite walk
CD BBL 68CD
Lowdown/Beggars Banquet / Mar '96 / RTM/Disc / Warner Music

CHURCH OF ANTHRAX (Cale, John & Terry Riley)
Church of Anthrax / Hall of mirrors in the Palace of Versailles / Soul of Patrick Lee / Ides of march / Protege
CD 4746042
Columbia / Mar '96 / Sony

FEAR
Fear is a man's best friend / Buffalo ballet / Barracuda Emily / Ship of fools / Gun / Man who couln't afford to orgy / You know we more than I know / Momma scuba
CD IMCD 140
Island / Aug '91 / PolyGram

FRAGMENTS OF A RAINY SEASON
CD HNCD 1372
Hannibal / Oct '92 / ADA / Vital

GUTS
Guts / Mary Lou / Helen of Troy / Pablo Picasso / Leaving it up to you / Fear is a man's best friend / Gun / Dirty-ass rock and roll / Rock 'n' roll / Heartbreak hotel
CD IMCD 203
Island / Jul '94 / PolyGram

HELEN OF TROY
My Maria / Helen of Troy / China Sea / Engine / Save us / Cable hogue / I keep a close watch / Pablo Picasso / Coral moon / Baby, what you want me to do / Sudden death / Leaving it up to you / Sylvia said
CD IMCD 177
Island / Mar '94 / PolyGram

HONI SOIT
Honi soit / Dead or alive / Strange times in Casablanca / Fighter pilot / Wilson Joliet / Streets of Laredo / River bank / Russian roulette / Magic and lies
CD CDMID 1936
A&M / Jul '94 / PolyGram

ISLAND YEARS ANTHOLOGY, THE (2CD Set)
Fear is a man's best friend / Buffalo ballet / Barracuda / Emily / Ship of fools / Gun / Man couldn't afford to orgy / You know me more than I know / Momma scuba / Sylvia said / All I want is you / Bamboo floor / Mr. Wilson / Talking it all away / Dirty-ass rock 'n' roll / Darling I need you / Rollaroll / Heartbreak hotel / Ski patrol / I'm not the loving kind / Guts / Jeweller / My Maria / Helen Of Troy / China Sea / Engine / Save us / Cable hogue / I keep a close watch / Pablo Picasso / Leaving it up to you / Baby, what you want me to do / Sudden death / You and me / Coral moon / Mary Lou
CD Set 5242352
Island / Sep '96 / PolyGram

LA NAISSANCE DE L'AMOUR
La naissance de l'amour / If you love me no more / And if I love you still / Judith / Converging themes / Opposites attract / I will do it, I will keep it / Keep it to yourself / Walk towards the sea / Unquiet heart / Waking up to love / Mysterious relief / Never been so happy / Beyond expectations / Conversations in the garden / La naissance de l'amour III / Secret dialogue / Roma / On the dark side / La naissance de l'amour II / Eye to eye / Maria's car crash and hotel rooms / La naissance de l'amour IV
CD TWI 9542
Les Disques Du Crepuscule / Nov '93 / Discovery

MUSIC FOR A NEW SOCIETY
Taking your life / Thoughtless kind / Sanities / If you were still around / Close watch / Broken bird / Chinese envoy / Changes made / Damn life / Rise Sam and Rimsky Korsakov / Library of force
CD YMCD 003
Yellow Moon / Mar '96 / Vital

PARIS 1919
Child's Christmas in Wales / Hanky panky no how / Endless plain of furtune / Andalucia / MacBeth / Paris 1919 / Graham Greene / Half past France / Antarctica starts here
CD 7599259262
WEA / Oct '93 / Warner Music

SLOW DAZZLE
Mr. Wilson / Taking it all away / Dirty-ass rock and roll / Darling I need you / Rollaroll / Heartbreak Hotel / Ski patrol / I'm not the loving kind / Guts / Jeweller
CD IMCD 202
Island / Jul '94 / PolyGram

WALKING ON LOCUSTS
Dancing undercover / Set me free / So what / Crazy Egypt / So much for love / Tell me why / Indistinct notion of cool / Secret corrida / Circus / Gatorville and points east / Some friends / Entre nous
CD HNCD 1395
Hannibal / Sep '96 / ADA / Vital

WORDS FOR THE DYING
Introduction / There was a saviour / On a wedding anniversary / Interlude II / Lie still, sleep becalmed / Do not go gentle into that good night / Songs without words I / Songs without words II / Soul of Carmen Miranda
CD ASCD 009
All Saints / Oct '95 / Discovery / Vital

Caledon

NOBLE TROUSERS, THE
CD HYCD 297169
Hypertension / Feb '97 / ADA / CM / Direct / Total/BMG

Calennig

TRADE WINDS
CD SCD 2091
Sain / Jun '95 / ADA / Direct / Greyhound

Calglia

MUSIC OF THE BALKANS & ANATOLIA VOL.2
CD PANCD 2007
Pan / May '93 / ADA / CM / Direct

Caliche

MUSIC OF THE ANDES
Festival of the flowers / Andean dawn / Memories of the lake / Flight of the Condor / Bell bird / Returning to a new time / Winds from the South / Silver paper / She left my crying
CD CDSDL 388
Saydisc / Mar '94 / ADA / Direct / Harmonia Mundi

California

TRAVELER
Rocker arm reel / Walk in the Irish rain / Scissors, paper and stone / My sweet blue eyed darling / Spurs / Farmers son / California traveler / I'll dry every tear that falls / Whiplash / Sasquatch / Uncle Pen / Band of angels
CD SHCD 3803
Sugar Hill / Oct '92 / ADA / CM / Direct / Koch / Roots

California Cajun Orchestra

NONC ADAM TWO-STEP
CD ARHCD 436
Arhoolie / Sep '95 / ADA / Cadillac / Direct

NOT LONESOME ANYMORE
CD ARHCD 356
Arhoolie / Apr '95 / ADA / Cadillac / Direct

California Guitar Trio

INVITATION
Train to lamy suite / Punta patri / Toccata and fugue in d minor / Fratres / Train to Lamy / Apache / Above the clouds / Prelude circulation / Good, the bad and the ugly
CD DGM 9501
Discipline / Apr '95 / Pinnacle

YAMANASHI BLUES
Yamanashi blues / Melrose Avenue / Corrente / Walk don't run / Ricercar / Pipeline / Beeline / Chromatic fugue in D minor / Tenor madness / Sleepwalk / Carnival / Prelude in C minor / Ciaccona / Blockhead / Kan-non power
CD DGM 9301
Discipline / Aug '94 / Pinnacle

California, Randy

KAPT. KOPTER AND THE (FABULOUS) TWIRLY BIRDS
Downer / Devil / Day tripper / Mother and child reunion / Things yet to come / Rain / Rainbow / I don't want nobody

CD EDCD 164
Edsel / May '97 / Pinnacle

KAPT. KOPTER AND THE (FABULOUS) TWIRLY BIRDS
Downer / Devil / I don't want nobody / Day tripper / Mother and child reunion / Things yet to come / Rain / Rainbow / Live for the day / Walkin' the dog / Rebel
CD 4875792
Epic / Jun '97 / Sony

Calle, Ed

DOUBLE TALK (2CD Set)
Mr. Slick / Hot sauce / You're the one / Island girl / Mowtown melody / Double talk / Autumn / Antes que seja tarde (Before it's too late) / Blocks / Me and Mrs Jones
CD Set 4697992
Sony Jazz / Jun '96 / Sony

Callier, Terry

NEW FOLK SOUND OF TERRY CALLIER, THE
900 Miles / Oh dear, what can the matter be / Johnny be gay if you can / Cotton eyed Joe / It's about time / Promenade in green / Spin spin spin / I'm a drifter
CD CDBGPM 101
Beat Goes Public / Nov '95 / Pinnacle

VERY BEST OF TERRY CALLIER
CD CDARC 514
Charly / Apr '94 / Koch

Calliope

I CAN SEE YOU WITH MY EYES
CD THK 031
Thick / Nov '95 / Cargo

I CAN SEE YOU WITH MY EYES CLOSED
CD THK 0312
Thick / May '97 / Cargo

Calloway, Blanche

CLASSICS 1925-1935
CD CLASSICS 783
Classics / Nov '94 / Discovery / Jazz Music

Calloway, Cab

BEST OF CAB CALLOWAY, THE
Aw you dog / Ghost of Smokey Joe / Tarzan of Harlem / Reefer man / I ain't gettin' nowhere fast / I gotta right to sing the blues / FDR Jones / Queen Isabella / Swing swing swing / Black rhythm / Jiveinformation please / Mister Paganini swing for Minnie / Pickin' the cabbage / Beale Street Mama / Do you wanna jump children / Kicking the gong around / Minnie the moocher / Jumpin' jive / Eadie was a lady / Hi-de-ho Romeo
CD 306522
Hallmark / May '97 / Carlton

CAB CALLOWAY & HIS ORCHESTRA 1939-1940
CD CD 595
Classic Jazz Masters / Sep '91 / Wellard

CAB CALLOWAY & HIS ORCHESTRA 1939-1942 (Calloway, Cab Orchestra)
CD CD 14567
Jazz Portraits / May '95 / Jazz Music

CAB CALLOWAY ON FILM 1934-1950
CD FLYCD 944
Flyright / Feb '95 / Hot Shot / Jazz Music / Wellard

CLASSICS 1930-1931
CD CLASSICS 516
Classics / Apr '90 / Discovery / Jazz Music

CLASSICS 1931-1932
CD CLASSICS 526
Classics / Apr '90 / Discovery / Jazz Music

CLASSICS 1932
CD CLASSICS 537
Classics / Dec '90 / Discovery / Jazz Music

CLASSICS 1932-1934
CD CLASSICS 544
Classics / Dec '90 / Discovery / Jazz Music

CLASSICS 1934-1937
CD CLASSICS 554
Classics / Dec '90 / Discovery / Jazz Music

CLASSICS 1937-1938
CD CLASSICS 568
Classics / Oct '91 / Discovery / Jazz Music

CLASSICS 1938-1939
CD CLASSICS 576
Classics / Oct '91 / Discovery / Jazz Music

CLASSICS 1939-1940
CD CLASSICS 595
Classics / Sep '91 / Discovery / Jazz Music

CLASSICS 1940 (Calloway, Cab Orchestra)
CD CLASSICS 614
Classics / Feb '92 / Discovery / Jazz Music

CLASSICS 1940-1941 (Calloway, Cab Orchestra)
CD CLASSICS 629
Classics / Nov '92 / Discovery / Jazz Music

CLASSICS 1940-1942
CD CLASSICS 682
Classics / Mar '93 / Discovery / Jazz Music

CRUISIN' WITH CAB (Calloway, Cab Orchestra)
Get with it / That old black magic / Airmail stomp / Jealous / I've got a girl named Netty / Bassically blue / You got it / Blue Serge suit / One o'clock jump / This is always / All by myself in the moonlight / Jumpin' jive / Everybody eats when they come to my house / I don't want to love you / Yesterdays / Cruisin' with Cab / Stormy weather / Duck trot
CD TPZ 1010
Topaz Jazz / Oct '94 / Cadillac / Pinnacle

FRANTIC IN THE ATLANTIC
I got a girl named Netty / This is always / Jealous / Blue serge suit / One o'clock jump / Frantic in the Atlantic / Jumpin' jive / Airmail stomp / Cruisin' with cab / You got it / That old black magic / Everybody eats when they come to my house / Duck trot
CD DBCD 10
Dance Band Days / Dec '88 / Prism

GET WITH CAB
CD WWCD 2403
West Wind / Apr '92 / Koch

HI DE HO MAN, THE
Minnie the moocher / Smooth one / Miss Hallelujah Brown / There's a sunny side to everything / Some of these days / Jumpin' jive / Man from Harlem / Pluckin' the bass / St. James infirmary / St. Louis blues / Boogie woogie / Viper's drag / Ain't that something / I've got you under my skin / Ratamacue / Come on with the come on
CD 74321267292
Milan / Aug '97 / Conifer/BMG / Silva Screen

HI-DE-HI-DE-HO
Hi de ho man / I'll be around / Summertime / It ain't necessarily so / Kicking the gong around / (I'll be glad when you're dead) You rascal you / Minnie the Moocher / I see a million people / St. James Infirmary / Stormy weather / Jumpin' jive
CD 74321185242
RCA Victor / Oct '94 / BMG

HI-DE-HO (Calloway, Cab Orchestra)
Minnie the moocher / Long about midnight / Moonglow / Margie / Scar song / (I'll be glad when you're dead) you rascal you / Harlem camp meeting / There's a cabin in the cotton / Father's got his glasses on / Nobody's sweetheart / Between the devil and the deep blue sea / Kicking the gong around / Hotcha razz ma tazz / Jitterbug / Harlem hospitality / Lady with the fan / Zaz zuh zaz
CD PAR 2008
Parade / Apr '95 / Disc

HI-DE-HO MAN, THE
St. Louis blues / Minnie the moocher / St. James infirmary / Nobody's sweetheart / Six or seven times / (I'll be glad when you're dead) you rascal you / Kicking the gong around / Between the devil and the deep blue sea / Minnie the moocher's wedding day / Seat song / Bugle call rag / Blues in my heart / Sweet Georgia Brown / Mood Indigo / Dinah / Aw you dawg
CD HADCD 174
Javelin / May '94 / Henry Hadaway / THE

HIS BEST SIDE
Minnie the moocher / Scat song / Reefer man / Calling all bars / Doin' the new low down / Bugle call rag / Margie / Wedding of Mr. and Mrs. Swing / Six or seven times / Jonah joins the Cab / Corinne Corrina / Hey Doc / Keep that hi-de-hi in your soul / St. James infirmary / Man from Harlem / Jumpin' jive
CD SUMCD 4034
Summit / Nov '96 / Sound & Media

INTRODUCTION TO CAB CALLOWAY 1930-1942, AN
CD 4011
Best Of Jazz / Aug '94 / Discovery

KICKING THE GONG AROUND
Minnie the moocher / Without rhythm / Aw you dog / Bugle call rag / Downhearted blues / Nightmare / Black rhythm / Yaller / Between the Devil and the deep blue sea / Nobody's sweetheart / Trickeration / St. Louis blues / Mood indigo / Farewell blues / (I'll be glad when you're dead) you rascal you / My honey's lovin' arms / Some of these days / Six or seven times / Somebody stole my gal / Kicking the gong around
CD CDAJA 5013
Living Era / Sep '90 / Select

KING OF HI-DE-HO (Calloway, Cab Orchestra)
Minnie the moocher / Man from Harlem / Chinese rhythm / Jumpin' jive / Scat song / Trickeration / Kicking the gong around / Lonesome nights / Run little rabbit / Bye bye blues / Ad-de-day
CD CDHD 260
Happy Days / Feb '97 / Conifer/BMG

KING OF HI-DE-HO 1934-1947, THE
CD CD 53096
Giants Of Jazz / Mar '92 / Cadillac / Jazz Music / Target/BMG

KINGS OF THE COTTON CLUB, THE (Calloway, Cab & Scatman Crothers)
CD 15378
Laserlight / Jan '93 / Target/BMG

LIVE IN 1944
CD MRCD 123
Magnetic / Sep '91 / TKO Magnum

MINNIE THE MOOCHER
Nagaski / Hoy hoy / Jumpin' jive / Give baby give / I want to rock / Minnie the moocher / Honey dripper / Hi de ho man / Jungle king / Calloway boogie / Two blocks down town to the left / Chicken ain't nothin' but a bird / I can't give you anything but love / Stormy weather / You got it / Everybody eats when they come to my house / Afternoon moon / This is always / Duck trot / That old black magic / How big can you get / Hey now hey now / Birth of the blues / We the cats shall help you / Foo a little ballyhoo
CD CD 56073
Jazz Roots / Mar '95 / Target/BMG

MINNIE THE MOOCHER
CD GRF 077
Tring / '93 / Tring

MINNIE THE MOOCHER
Nagasaki / Hoy hoy (Hep-hep) the jumpin' jive / Give, baby, give / I want to rock / Minnie the moocher / Honeydripper / Hi-de-ho man / Jungle swing / Calloway boogie / Two blocks down turn left / Chicken ain't nothin' but a bird / Stormy weather / Evreybody eats when they come to my house / Afternoon moon / This is always / Duck trot / That old black magic / How big can you get / Birth of the blues / We the cats / Foo a little ballyhoo
CD QED 043
Tring / Nov '96 / Tring

RADIO YEARS 1940-1945, THE
CD JUCD 2027
Jazz Unlimited / May '97 / Cadillac / Jazz Music / Wellard

SOUNDTRACKS AND BROADCASTS 1943-1944 (Calloway, Cab Orchestra)
Bojangles steps in / Easy Joe / Ain't that something / Everybody dance / Honeydripper / Let's go Joe / Jumpin' jive / Angels sing / Birth of the blues / Fiesta in brass / I've got you under my skin / Lady whistle bait / Russian lullaby / Foo a little bally-hoo / 9.20 Special
CD 550232
Jazz Anthology / Feb '94 / Cadillac / Discovery / Harmonia Mundi

Calvary

ACROSS THE RIVER OF LIFE
CD DREAM 001MCD
Polyphemus / Jul '96 / Plastic Head

Calvert, Eddie

EMI YEARS, THE
Oh mein papa / Poor people of Paris / Stranger in paradise / April in Portugal / On a slow boat to China / Love is a many splendoured thing / I'm getting sentimental over you / Sucu sucu / My son, my son / malaguena / Cherry pink and apple blossom white / Mandy (the pansy) / Around the world / Forgotten dreams / My Yiddishe Momme / Summertime / John and Julie / Little serenade (Piccolossima serenata) / I love Paris / Zambesi
CD CDP 7801372
Premier/EMI / Aug '92 / EMI

GOLDEN SOUNDS OF EDDIE CALVERT, THE
CD GS 863572
Disky / Mar '96 / Disky / THE

OH MEIN PAPA
Oh mein Papa / Love is a many splendored thing / April in Portugal / Forgotten dreams / What is this thing called love / Why do I love you / Free and easy / Love is the sweetest thing / And the angels sing / My son, my son / Zambesi / Georgia on my mind / Holiday night / Cherry pink and apple blossom white / Whispering / Taking a chance on love / Carnival of Venice / John and Julie / Roses of Picardy / They didn't believe me
CD CDMFP 6210
Music For Pleasure / Feb '96 / EMI

Calvert, Robert

BLUEPRINTS FROM THE CELLAR
CD BGOCD 135
Beat Goes On / Oct '92 / Pinnacle

CAPTAIN LOCKHEAD AND THE STARFIGHTERS
CD BGOCD 5
Beat Goes On / Oct '88 / Pinnacle

FREQ REVISITED
Ned ludd / Talk one / Acid rain / Talk two / All the machines are quiet / Talk three / Picket line / Talk four / Cool courage of the bomb / Squad / Talk five / Work song / Lord of the Hornets / Greenfly and the rose
CD CDMGRAM 55
Anagram / Jun '92 / Cargo / Pinnacle

HYPE
Over my head / Ambitious / It's the same / Hanging out on the seafront / Sensitive / Evil rock / We like to be frightened / Teen ballad of Deano / Flight 105 / Luminous green glow of the dashboard / Greenfly and the rose / Lord of the hornets
CD SEECD 278
See For Miles/C5 / '89 / Pinnacle

LIVE AT THE QUEEN ELIZABETH HALL
Evil rock / Catch a falling starfighter / Gremlins / Aerospace age inferno / Test tube conceived / Working down a diamond mine / All the machines are quiet / Work song / Telekinesis / Acid rain / Lord of the hornets
CD BGOCD 187
Beat Goes On / Apr '93 / Pinnacle

TEST TUBE CONCEIVED
Telekinesis / I hear voices / Fanfare for the perfect race / On line / Save them from the scientists / Fly on the wall / Thanks to the scientists / Test tube conceived / In vitro breed / Rah rah man
CD CDTB 113
Thunderbolt / '91 / TKO Magnum

Calvin Party

LIES, LIES & GOVERNMENT
Tell me about poverty / Lies, lies & government 1 / Lies, lies & government 2 / Caspers ballroom / Flowers / Looking at me for / Life and other sex tragedies / Repetition no.2 / Pomo Gothic / Heart and soul / First thing / Celebration / Sweetest dream
CD PROBE 043CD
Probe Plus / Feb '96 / SRD

LIFE AND OTHER SEX TRAGEDIE, THE
All messed up / Monster / Song from England / Messalina / Gun / Alphabet song / Look back in angst uh / Taxi man / None the less / Less is more / Mass
CD PROBE 038CD
Probe Plus / Sep '94 / SRD

Camacho, Wichy

LA ROMANCE
Desilucionado / Todo por amor / Dime carino / Me das libertad / Me pides que te ame / Amor de fantasia / Dosis del amor / Solicito un amor
CD 66058079
RMM / Nov '95 / New Note/Pinnacle

Camara, Ladsi

AFRICA, NEW YORK (Master Drummer)
CD LYRCD 7345
Lyrichord / Jul '94 / ADA / CM / Roots

Camber

BEAUTIFUL CHARADE
CD DER 359
Deep Elm / Apr '97 / Cargo

Camel

BREATHLESS
Breathless / Echoes / Wing and a prayer / Down on the farm / Starlight ride / Summer lightning / You make me smile / Sleeper / Rainbow's end
CD 8207262
Deram / Jun '92 / PolyGram

CAMEL
Slow yourself down / Mystic queen / Six ate / Separation / Never let go / Curiosity / Arubaluba
CD CP 002CD
Camel Productions / Jul '93 / Pinnacle

DUST & DREAMS
CD CP 001CD
Camel Productions / Jul '93 / Pinnacle

HARBOUR OF TEARS
CD CP 006CD
Camel Productions / Jan '96 / Pinnacle

NEVER LET GO
CD Set CP 004CD
Camel Productions / Oct '93 / Pinnacle

ON THE ROAD 1972
CD CP 003CD
Camel Productions / Jul '93 / Pinnacle

ON THE ROAD 1981
CD CP 007CD
Camel Productions / Mar '97 / Pinnacle

ON THE ROAD 1982
Sasquatch / Highways of the sun / Hymn of her / Neon magic / You are the one / Drafted / Lies / Captured / Heart's desire / Heroes / Who we are / Manic / Wait and never let go

CD ____ CP 005CD
Camel Productions / Jan '95 / Pinnacle

RAIN DANCES
First light / Metrognome / Tell me / Highways of the sun / Unevensong / One of these days I'll get an early night / Skylines / Elke / Rain dances
CD ____ 8207252
Deram / Jan '93 / PolyGram

SNOW GOOSE
Great marsh / Rhayader / Rhayader goes to town / Sanctuary / Fritha / Snow goose / Friendship / Rhayader alone / Flight of the snow goose / Preparation / Dunkirk / Epitaph / Fritha alone / La princesse perdue / Pressure points / Refugee / Stationary traveller
CD ____ 8000802
Deram / Jul '93 / PolyGram

Camelia Jazz Band

THAT'S MY HOME
CD ____ JCD 249
Jazzology / Aug '95 / Jazz Music

Cameo

BEST OF CAMEO, THE
Word up / Single life / Candy / Shake your pants / Rigor mortis / Attack me with your love / Talkin' out the side of your neck / Sparkle / Back and forth / Flirt / She's strange / I just want to be / Skin I'm in / It's over / She's mine
CD ____ 5149292
Club / Jun '93 / PolyGram

NASTY
Intro / Flirt / She's strange / Back and forth / Skin I'm in / Why have I lost you / Sparkle / Candy / Shake your pants / I just want to be / Keep it hot / Word up / Come fly with me / Nasty / Mega-mix
CD ____ ESMCD 445
Essential / Oct '96 / BMG

WORD UP
Word up / Urban warrior / Candy / Back and forth / Don't be lonely / She's mine / Fast, fierce and funny / You can have the world
CD ____ 8302652
Club / Sep '86 / PolyGram

Cameron Highlanders Of ...

ADVANCE (Cameron Highlanders Of Ottawa)
CD ____ BNA 5108
Bandleader / Jan '95 / Conifer/BMG

Cameron, John Allan

GLENCOE STATION
Getting dark again / Parlour sessions / Saban the woodfitter / Cape Breton shore / Emigrant eyes / Islanders / Miners song / Roving gyspy song / Heading for Halifax / Evangeline / Kitchen session
CD ____ IRCD 051
Iona / May '97 / ADA / Direct / Duncans

Camilla's Little Secret

STEPS, THE
CD ____ SNRCD 944
S&R / May '95 / Pinnacle

Camilo, Michel

MICHEL CAMILO
Suite sandrine part 1 / Nostalgia / Dreamlight / Crossroads / Sunset (Interlude/Suite sandrine) / Yarey / Pra voce / Blue brossa / Caribe
CD ____ 4633302
Sony Jazz / Dec '90 / Sony

ON FIRE
CD ____ 4658802
Sony Jazz / Jan '95 / Sony

ONE MORE ONCE
One more once / Why not / Resolution / Suite sandrine / Dreamlight / Just kidding / Caribe / Suntan / On the other hand / Not yet
CD ____ 4777532
Columbia / Oct '94 / Sony

RENDEZVOUS
CD ____ 4737722
Sony Jazz / Jan '95 / Sony

Camp Lo

UPTOWN SATURDAY NIGHT
CD ____ FILECD 470
Profile / Feb '97 / Pinnacle

Camp, Manuel

ROSEBUD (Camp, Manuel & M. Simon)
CD ____ FSNT 011CD
Fresh Sound / Sep '96 / Discovery / Jazz Music

Campbell Family

SINGING CAMPBELLS, THE
Fur does bonnie lorna lie / Sleep till yer mammy / Nicky tams / Road and the miles to Dundee / Drumdelgie / I ken faur I'm gaun / My wee man's a miner / Fa, fa, fa wid be a bobby / Foul Friday / Me an' mi mither / We three kings of Orient are / Bogie's bonnie belle / Cruel mother / Lang-a-growing / Lady Eliza / Will ye gang love / I wish I wish / McGinty's meal and ale
CD ____ OSS 97CD
Ossian / Aug '94 / ADA / CM / Direct / Highlander

Campbell, Al

BOUNCE BACK
CD ____ ALCD 002
Al Campbell / Jun '94 / Jet Star

IT'S MAGIC
CD ____ ALCD 001
Al Campbell / Jun '94 / Jet Star

RASTA TIME
CD ____ LG 21056
Lagoon / Feb '93 / Grapevine/PolyGram

ROAD BLOCK
CD ____ EXTCD 5
Exterminator / May '97 / Jet Star

SOULFUL, THE
CD ____ RNCD 2067
Rhino / Jul '94 / Grapevine/PolyGram / Jet Star

Campbell, Ali

BIG LOVE
Big love (intro) / Happiness / That look in your eyes / Let your yeah be yeah / You can cry on my shoulder / Somethin' stupid / Big love / You could meet somebody / Talking blackbird / Pay the rent / Drive it home / Stop the guns
CD ____ CDV 2783
Kuff / Jun '95 / EMI

Campbell, Anthony

YOUR SPECIAL GIFT
CD ____ CAMCD 3
Stringbean / Oct '95 / Jet Star

Campbell, Blind James

BLIND JAMES CAMPBELL
CD ____ ARHCD 438
Arhoolie / Jun '95 / ADA / Cadillac / Direct

Campbell, Chris

MEETINGS WITH REMARKABLE ALLOYS
CD ____ JHR 2021
Larrikin / Feb '95 / ADA / CM / Direct / Roots

RINGS OF FIRE
CD ____ JHR 2022
Larrikin / Nov '94 / ADA / CM / Direct / Roots

Campbell, Cornell

NATTY DREAD IN A GREENWICH FARM
CD ____ TSL 104CD
Striker Lee / Jul '95 / Jet Star

TELL THE PEOPLE
CD ____ CDSGP 072
Prestige / May '94 / Else / Total/BMG

Campbell, Don

ALBUM, THE
CD ____ JGLGCD 01
Juggling / May '94 / Jet Star

Campbell, Eddie C.

BADDEST CAT ON THE BLOCK, THE
Hye baby / Nineteen years old / I'm in love with you baby / Tears are for losers / Early in the morning / Same thing / Cha cha blues / Cheaper to keep her
CD ____ JSPCD 216
JSP / Jul '88 / ADA / Cadillac / Direct / Hot Shot / Target/BMG

KING OF THE JUNGLE
CD ____ R 2602
Rooster / Feb '96 / Direct

LET'S PICK IT
Messin' with my pride / Don't throw your love on me so strong / All my whole life / All of my life / Double dutch / Red light / Cold and hungry / Love me with a feeling / Dream / Let's pick it / Big leg mama / That will never do
CD ____ ECD 260372
Evidence / Sep '93 / ADA / Cadillac / Harmonia Mundi

THAT'S WHEN I KNOW
CD ____ BPCD 5014
Blind Pig / Dec '94 / ADA / CM / Direct / Hot Shot

Campbell, Gary

INTERSECTION
CD ____ MCD 9236
Milestone / Apr '96 / Cadillac / Complete/ Pinnacle / Jazz Music / Wellard

THICK AND THIN
Light stokes / Final decision / Would-be blues / Three-four fable / We'll be together again / Con alma / Thick and thin / Veils / You stepped out of a dream / Good bait
CD ____ DTRCD 115
Double Time / Dec '96 / Express Jazz

Campbell, Gene

GENE CAMPBELL & WILLIE REED 1928-1935 (Campbell, Gene & Willie Reed)
CD ____ BDCD 6043
Blues Document / May '93 / ADA / Hot Shot / Jazz Music

Campbell, Glen

20 GREATEST HITS (The Concert Collection)
Rhinestone cowboy / Gentle on my mind / Wichita lineman / Galveston / Country boy / By the time I get to Phoenix / Dreams of the everyday housewife / Heartache number three / Please come to Boston / Trials and tribulation / It's only make believe / Crying / Bluegrass medley / Milk cow blues / Rollin' (in my sweet baby's arms) / I'm so lonesome I could cry / Southern nights / Amazing grace / Try a little tenderness / In your loving arms / It's your world (boys and girls) / Mull of Kintyre
CD ____ PLATCD 139
Platinum / Feb '97 / Prism

BEST OF GLEN CAMPBELL, THE
Rhinestone cowboy / Gentle on my mind / Medley: *Campbell, Glen & Wichita Lineman* / Galveston / Country boy (got your feet in LA) / By the time I get to Phoenix / Dreams of the everyday housewife / Heartache number three / Please come to Boston / It's only make believe / Cryin' / Bluegrass medley / Milk cow blues / Rollin' in my sweet baby's arms / I'm so lonesome I could cry / Southern nights / Amazing grace / Try a little kindness / Mull of kintyre
CD ____ MATCD 303
Castle / Oct '94 / BMG

BEST OF GLEN CAMPBELL, THE
CD ____ MACCD 266
Autograph / Aug '96 / BMG

BOY IN ME, THE
Boy in me / Living the legacy / Where time stands still / Call it even / Come harvest time / Best is yet to come / Something to die for / Mercy's eyes / All I need is you / Amazing grace
CD ____ 8441875372
Alliance Music / May '95 / EMI

COUNTRY CLASSICS
Honey come back / By the time I get to Phoenix / Country girl / Gentle on my mind / Reason to believe / One last time / (I'm getting used) to the crying / It's only make believe / How high did we go / If this is love / Love is not a game / For my woman's love / Last thing on my mind / Everything a man could ever need / Dream baby / Hey little one / Your cheatin' heart / This is Sarah's song / Let go / God only knows
CD ____ CDMFP 6321
Music For Pleasure / Apr '97 / EMI

GLEN CAMPBELL COLLECTION, THE (2CD Set)
CD Set ____ RE 2129
Razor & Tie / Mar '97 / Koch

GLEN CAMPBELL IN CONCERT
Rhinestone cowboy / Gentle on my mind / Medley / By the time I get to Phoenix / Dreams of an everyday housewife / Heartache number three / Please come to Boston / It's only make believe / Crying / Bluegrass medley / Milk cow blues / Rollin' in my sweet baby's arms / I'm so lonesome I could cry / Southern nights / Amazing grace / Try a little kindness / Mull of Kintyre
CD ____ TRTCD 163
TrueTrax / Dec '94 / THE

GLEN CAMPBELL IN CONCERT
CD ____ 15346
Laserlight / Aug '91 / Target/BMG

GLEN CAMPBELL LIVE
Rhinestone cowboy / Gentle on my mind / Wichita lineman / Galveston / Country boy / By the time I get to Phoenix / Dreams of the everyday housewife / Heartache no.3 / Please come to Boston / It's only make believe / Crying / Bluegrass medley / Milk cow blues / Rollin' (in my sweet baby's arms) / I'm so lonesome I could cry / Southern nights / Amazing grace / Try a little kindness / Mull of Kintyre / In your loving arms again / It's your world boys and girls / Trials and tribulations
CD ____ EMPRCD 523
Emporio / Sep '94 / Disc

GLEN CAMPBELL LIVE 1994
CD ____ 12437
Laserlight / Mar '95 / Target/BMG

GREATEST HITS LIVE
Rhinestone cowboy / Gentle on my mind / Medley / By the time I get to Phoenix / Dreams of an everyday housewife / Heartache number two / Please come to Boston / It's only make believe / Crying / Bluegrass medley / Milk cow blues / Rollin' in my sweet baby's arms / I'm so lonesome I could cry / Southern nights / Amazing grace / Try a little kindness / Mull of Kintyre / In your loving arms again / It's your world girls and boys / Trials and tribulations
CD ____ GRF 182
Tring / Feb '93 / Tring

GREATEST HITS LIVE
Rhinestone cowboy / Gentle on my mind / Medley / By the time I get to Phoenix / Dreams of the everyday housewife / Heartache number three / Please come to Boston / It's only make believe / Crying / Medley / Milk cow blues / Rollin' in my sweet baby's arms / I'm so lonesome I could cry / Southern nights / Amazing Grace / Try a little kindness / Mull Of Kintyre
CD ____ CDSD 081
Sundown / Nov '96 / TKO Magnum

GREATEST HITS LIVE
Rhinestone cowboy / Gentle on my mind / Medley / By the time I get to Phoenix / Dreams of the everyday housewife / Heartache number three / Please come to Boston / It's only make believe / Crying / Bluegrass medley / Milk cow blues / Rollin' (in my sweet baby's arms) / I'm so lonesome I could cry / Southern nights / Amazing grace / Try a little kindness / Mull of Kintyre / In your loving arms again / It's your world girls and boys / Trials and tribulations
CD ____ QED 185
Tring / Nov '96 / Tring

IN CONCERT: GLEN CAMPBELL
Rhinestone cowboy / Gentle on my mind / Wichita lineman / Galveston / Country boy / By the time I get to Phoenix / Dreams of an everyday housewife / Heartache number three / Please come to Boston / Trials and tribulations / Crying/Blue grass medley / Milk cow blues / Rollin' in my sweet baby's arms / I'm so lonesome I could cry / Southern nights / Amazing grace / Try a little kindness / In your loving arms again / It's your world girls and boys / Mull of Kintyre
CD ____ CPCD 8003
Charly / Oct '93 / Koch

LOVE SONGS
Gentle on my mind / Reason to believe / By the time I get to Phoenix / It's only make believe / Honey come back / Country girl / One last time / I'm getting used to the crying / Last thing on my mind / Everything a man could ever need / Dream baby / Hey little one / Your cheatin' heart / This is Sarah's song / Let go / God only knows / How high did we go / If this is love / Love is not a game / For my woman's love
CD ____ CDMFP 5881
Music For Pleasure / Apr '90 / EMI

MAGIC OF GLEN CAMPBELL, THE
CD ____ TKOCD 001
TKO / '92 / TKO

RHINESTONE COWBOY
CD ____ WMCD 5666
Disky / Oct '94 / Disky / THE

RHINESTONE COWBOY
CD ____ MU 5027
Musketeer / Oct '92 / Disc

RHINESTONE COWBOY (Live In Concert)
Rhinestone cowboy / Gentle on my mind / Wichita lineman/Galveston/Country boy / By the time I get to Phoenix / Dreams of the everyday housewife / Heartache number three / Please come home to Boston / Crying / It's only make believe / Bluegrass medley / Milk cow blues / Rollin' (in my sweet baby's arms) / I'm so lonely I could cry / Southern nights / Amazing grace / Try a little kindness / Mull of Kintyre
CD ____ SUMCD 4021
Summit / Nov '96 / Sound & Media

RHINESTONE COWBOY (Greatest Hits Live)
Gentle on my mind / By the time I get to Phoenix / Galveston / Kentucky means paradise / Wichita lineman / Mansion in Branson / Here in the real world / Classical gas / Rhinestone cowboy / Medley / Dreams of the everyday housewife/Sunflower / Let it be me / No more nights / Southern nights
CD ____ CTS 55444
Country Stars / Feb '97 / Target/BMG

THAT CHRISTMAS FEELING
Christmas is for children / Old toy trains / Little altar boy / It must be getting close to Christmas / Have yourself a merry little Christmas / Blue Christmas / Christmas song / Pretty paper / There's no place like home / I'll be home for Christmas / Christmas day
CD ____ CDMFP 6243
Music For Pleasure / Oct '96 / EMI

TWENTY GOLDEN GREATS
Rhinestone cowboy / Both sides now / By the time I get to Phoenix / Too many mornings / Wichita lineman / One last time / Don't pull your love, then tell me goodbye / Reason to believe / It's only make believe / Honey come back / Give me back that old familiar feeling / Galveston / Dreams of an everyday housewife / Last thing on my mind / Where's the playground / Try a little kindness / Country boy / All I have to do is dream / Amazing grace
CD ____ CDP 7486132
Liberty / Oct '90 / EMI

WITCHITA LINEMAN
CD ______ PLSCD 210
Pulse / Apr '97 / BMG

Campbell, Ian

THIS IS THE IAN CAMPBELL FOLK GROUP/ACROSS THE HILLS (Campbell, Ian Folk Group)
TWA recruiting sergeants / Keel row / Unquiet grave / To hear the nightingale sing / Drover's dream / Traditional medley / Rocking the cradle / Jute Mill song / Johnny lad / Blow boys blow / Down in the coal mine / Garton mother's lullaby / Bells of Rhymney / Apprentice's song / Rocky road to Dublin/ Drops of brandy / Homeward bound / Waters of Tyne / Wee cooper of Fife / Across the hills / Come kiss me love / Blind man, he could see / I know my love / Derby ram / Mary Mild / Remember me / Cockfight / Gypsy rover / Chocho Losa / Keeper / Collier laddie / We're nae awa' to bide awa'
CD ______ ESMCD 357
Essential / Jan '96 / BMG

Campbell, Jo Ann

ALL THE HITS
CD ______ MAR 116
Marginal / Jun '97 / Greyhound

Campbell, John

LIVE AT MAYBECK RECITAL HALL VOL.29
Just friends / You and the night and the music / Invitation / Easy to love / Emily / I wish I knew / Darn that dream / Touch of your lips
CD ______ CCD 4581
Concord Jazz / Nov '93 / New Note/ Pinnacle

ONE BELIEVER
Devil in my closet / Angel of sorrow / Wild streak / Couldn't do nothin' / Tiny coffin / World of trouble / Voodoo edge / Person to person / Take me down / One believer
CD ______ 7559610862
Elektra / Oct '91 / Warner Music

Campbell, Kate

MOONPIE DREAMS
When panthers roamed in Arkansas / Moonpie dreams / See Rock City / Bud's See-Mint boat / Bascom's blues / Tupelo's too far / Older angel / Delmus Jackson / Signs following / Galaxie 500 / Waiting for the weather to break / Wrought iron fences
CD ______ FIENDCD 791
Demon / Feb '97 / Pinnacle

SONGS FROM THE LEVEE
CD ______ FIENDCD 780
Demon / Apr '96 / Pinnacle

Campbell, Kenna

CURAIDH SINTE
CD ______ WHFP 0001
WHFP / Dec '96 / CM

Campbell, Mike

LOVING FRIENDS
CD ______ ACD 279
Audiophile / May '95 / Jazz Music

ONE ON ONE
CD ______ ACD 259
Audiophile / Jun '93 / Jazz Music

Campbell, Mont

MUSIC FROM A ROUND TOWER
Shen Nong's miracle herbs / In pursuit of a gazelle / Eunuch's song / Tarak Totoosh / Driftwood biographies / Kua Fu races with the sun / When the rain comes, roses dance on gold / Makoma / Ernest Scott pursues a theory / Anyphylaxis / Mwamburi dies manfully at the hands of a thousand Thracians / Travels over a black Earth / Ikhwan el Safa / What the rose said to the cypress / Dede Korkut at the Boma / Moment to listen to the audience / Wise King Konuzion / Evening over Hickling Broad / Serenitsa / Enormous colony of peewits takes flight from Brickett's Poin
CD ______ RES 120CD
Resurgence / Jan '97 / Pinnacle

Campbell, Phil

DREAMING
CD ______ SCD 1036
Spring / Nov '96 / ADA / Direct

Campbell, Rocky

VALLEY OF TEARS
CD ______ ANGELLA 001CD
Angella / May '95 / Jet Star

Campbell, Rory

MAGAID A PHIPIR (The Piper's Whim)
Lachie and the tractor / Careau Llaniscu / Cutting down the privet hedge / Donachd head / An Islay melody / Medley / Barlinnie highlander / Medley / Medley / Shepherd's crook / Mirren's pyjamas / Calum fighader agus Calum taillear (Malcolm the weaver and M / Mo shuiridhach, bi suigartach (My woer, be merry) / Trad reel / Medley / Breton andro (nouvelle suite d'an dros pour pipes) / Medley / I hae a wife o' my ain / Tending the cattle with a heavy heart / Medley / Medley / Magaid a phipir (piper's whim) / Trad jig / Medley / Oiseanbeag reel / Sloe jig / Clementina / Medley / Medley (10)
CD ______ CDLDL 1250
Lochshore / Mar '97 / ADA / Direct / Duncans

Campbell, Roy

NEW KINGDOM
Jahne's waltz / Booker's lament / Straight on up straight on down / Charmaine / La tierra del fuego suite / Losaida / Sermon
CD ______ DE 469
Delmark / Mar '97 / ADA / Cadillac / CM / Direct / Hot Shot

Campbell, Sarah Elizabeth

LITTLE TENDERNESS, A
Mexico / I never meant to fall / Part of a story / Waltz with you / Geraldine and Ruthie Mae / Heartache / Tell me baby / To remember / My heart can't seem to forget / I could use a little tenderness
CD ______ DJD 3220
Dejadisc / Nov '95 / ADA / Direct

RUNNING WITH YOU
CD ______ DJD 3210
Dejadisc / May '94 / ADA / Direct

Campbell, Tevin

BACK TO THE WORLD
CD ______ 9362460032
Qwest / Jul '96 / Warner Music

I'M READY
Can we talk / Don't say goodbye girl / Interlude / Halls of desire / I'm ready / What do I say / Uncle sam / Paris 1798430 / Always in my heart / Shhh / Brown eyed girl / Infant child
CD ______ 9362453882
Qwest / Dec '96 / Warner Music

TEVIN
Interlude/over the rainbow and on to the sun / Tell me what you want me to do / Li'l brother / Strawberry letter 23 / One song / Round and round / Just asking me to / Perfect world / Look what we'd have (if you were mine) / She's all that
CD ______ 7599262912
Qwest / Apr '92 / Warner Music

Campbells

POWER & HONESTY
CD ______ IRVCD 562
Scotdisc / Apr '93 / Conifer/BMG / Duncans / Ross

Campi, Ray

EAGER BEAVER BOY
Hot dog / All the time / Boogie boogie boo / Rock it / Thought of losing / Waffle stompin' mama / Blue ranger / Ballin' keen / Let 'er roll / Dobro daddio from Del Rio / Born to be wild / How low can you feel / Where my sweet baby goes / Tribute to 'You know who' / Eager beaver boy / Pretty mama / One part stops where the other begins / Pinball millionaire / When two ends meet / Good time woman / It ain't me / Chug-a-lug / Parts unknown / Wicked wicked woman / Shelby county penal farm / Don't give your heart to a rambler / Play anything / Major label blues
CD ______ BCD 15501
Bear Family / Sep '90 / Direct / Rollercoaster / Swift

HOLLYWOOD CATS
CD ______ PT 613001
Part / Jun '96 / Nervous

ORIGINAL ROCKABILLY ALBUM, THE
Caterpillar / It ain't me / Let go of Louise / Livin' on love / My screamin' screamin' Mimi / Long tall Sally / Johnny's jive / Play it cool / Give that love to me / You can't catch me / I didn't mean to be mean / Crossing / Loretta
CD ______ CDMF 063
Magnum Force / Jul '90 / TKO Magnum

PERPETUAL STOMP (The Ray Campi Anthology 1957-1996)
CD ______ BA 12CD
Bacchus Archives / Nov '96 / Cargo / Plastic Head

ROCKABILLY ROCKET
Second story man / Don't get pushy / Cravin' / Separate ways / Gonna bid my blues goodbye / How can I get on top / Little young girl / Chew tobacco rag / You don't rock and roll at all / Ruby Ann / I don't know why you still come around / Runnin' after fools / Jimmie skins the blues
CD ______ CDMF 046
Magnum Force / May '94 / TKO Magnum

TAYLOR, TEXAS 1988
Curtain of tears / Haunted hungry heart / Woods are full of them now / Dessau waltz / When they operated on papa / Butterball bounce / Wild side of live / That's that / Million tears / Honk your horn / Love for sale / Honky tonk women / Bermuda grass waltz
CD ______ BCD 15486
Bear Family / Nov '89 / Direct / Rollercoaster / Swift

Campoli, Alfredo

ALDREDO CAMPOLI AND HIS SALON ORCHESTRA (Campoli, Alfredo & His Salon Orchestra)
Mosquitoes' parade / Shadow waltz / Elgar's serenade / Little valley in the mountains / Snowman / Czardas / Liszt, Chopin and Mendelssohn / Mouse in the clock / Simonetta / Musical box / Wild violets / Parade of the pirates / Cavatina / Moths around the candle flame / Waltzing to Archibald Joyce / Serenade / Love in idleness / Knave of diamonds / Fairy tale / In old Vienna / La petite tonkinoise / Garden of roses
CD ______ PASTCD 9707
Flapper / '90 / Pinnacle

CAMPOLI'S CHOICE
CD ______ PASTCD 7744
Flapper / Jun '91 / Pinnacle

SALON MUSIC OF THE THIRTIES
Ah sweet mystery of life / Butterfly / Canary / Czardas / Daddy long legs / Goodnight waltz: *Campoli, Alfredo & Cavan O'Connor* / Grasshoppers dance: *Campoli, Alfredo & Cavan O'Connor* / Gypsy love song: *Campoli, Alfredo & Cavan O'Connor* / Her first dance / Hiawatha / Moths around the candle flame / Old Spanish tango / Old spinning wheel: *Campoli, Alfredo & Cavan O'Connor* / Old violin: *Campoli, Alfredo & Olive Groves* / Only my song: *Campoli, Alfredo & Olive Groves* / Pale Volga moon: *Campoli, Alfredo & Cavan O'Connor* / La petite tonkinoise / Popular Viennese waltzes / Softly awakes my heart / Song of paradise / Tell me tonight / Waltzing to Irving Berlin
CD ______ CDAJA 5135
Living Era / Jul '94 / Select

Can

ANTHOLOGY
CD Set ______ SPOONCD 30/31
The Grey Area / Oct '94 / RTM/Disc

CAN
All gates open / Safe / Sunday jam / Sodom / Spectacle / E.F.S. No.99 / Ping pong / Can be
CD ______ SPOONCD 28
The Grey Area / Jan '95 / RTM/Disc

CAN DELAY 1968
Butterfly / Pnoom / Nineteen century man / Thief / Man named Joe / Uphill / Little star of Bethlehem
CD ______ SPOONCD 12
The Grey Area / Jul '89 / RTM/Disc

CANNIBALISM VOL.1
Father cannot yell / Soup / Mother Sky / She brings the rain / Mushroom / One more night / Outside my door / Spoon / Hallelujah / Aumgn / Dizzy dizzy / Yoo doo right
CD Set ______ SPOONCD 1/2
The Grey Area / Jul '89 / RTM/Disc

CANNIBALISM VOL.2
CD ______ SPOONCD 21
The Grey Area / Jan '95 / RTM/Disc

CANNIBALISM VOL.3
CD ______ SPOONCD 22
The Grey Area / Jan '95 / RTM/Disc

EGE BAMYASI
Pinch / Sing swan song / One more night / Vitamin C / Soup / I'm so green / Spoon
CD ______ SPOONCD 8
The Grey Area / Jul '89 / RTM/Disc

FLOW MOTION
I want more / Cascade waltz / Laugh till you cry... live till you die / And more / Babylonian pearl / Smoke (E.F.S. No.59) / Flow motion
CD ______ SPOONCD 26
The Grey Area / Jan '95 / RTM/Disc

FUTURE DAYS
Future days / Spray / Moonshake / Bel-air
CD ______ SPOONCD 9
The Grey Area / Jul '89 / RTM/Disc

INNER SPACE
All gates open / Safe / Sunday jam / Sodom / Spectacle / Can can / Ping pong / Can be
CD ______ CDTB 020
Thunderbolt / '88 / TKO Magnum

LANDED
Full moon on the highway / Half past one / Hunters and collectors / Vernal equinox / Red hot Indians / Unfinished
CD ______ SPOONCD 25
The Grey Area / Jan '95 / RTM/Disc

MONSTER MOVIE
Father cannot yell / Mary Mary so contrary / Outside my door / Yoo doo right
CD ______ SPOONCD 4
The Grey Area / Jul '89 / RTM/Disc

OUT OF REACH
Surpentine / Pauper's daughter and I / November / Seven days awake / Give me no 'roses' / Like inobe God / One more day
CD ______ CDTB 025
Thunderbolt / Nov '88 / TKO Magnum

RITE TIME
CD ______ SPOONCD 29
The Grey Area / Oct '94 / RTM/Disc

SACRILEGE (2CD Set)
Pnoom / Blue bag (inside paper) / Tango whiskey man / TV Spot / Vitamin C / Hallelujah / Oh yeah / Unfinished / Future days / More / Father cannot yell / Dizzy spoon / Yoo doo right / Flow motion
CD Set ______ SPOONCD 39/40
The Grey Area / May '97 / RTM/Disc

SAW DELIGHT
Don't say no / Sunshine day and night / Call me / Animal waves / Fly by night
CD ______ SPOONCD 27
The Grey Area / Jan '95 / RTM/Disc

SOON OVER BABALUMA
Dizzy dizzy / Come sta, la luna / Splash / Chain reaction / Quantom physics
CD ______ SPOONCD 10
The Grey Area / Jul '89 / RTM/Disc

SOUNDTRACKS
Deadlock / Tango whiskeyman / Don't turn the light on, leave me alone / Soul desert / Mother sky / She brings the rain
CD ______ SPOONCD 5
The Grey Area / Jul '89 / RTM/Disc

TAGO MAGO
Paperhouse / Mushroom / Oh yeah / Hallelujah / Aumgn / Peking O / Bring me coffee or tea
CD Set ______ SPOONCD 6/7
The Grey Area / Jul '89 / RTM/Disc

UNLIMITED EDITION
CD ______ SPOONCD 23/24
The Grey Area / Jan '95 / RTM/Disc

Canadian All Stars

EUROPEAN CONCERT
CD ______ SKCD 23055
Sackville / Oct '94 / Cadillac / Jazz Music / Swift

Canadian Brass

RENAISSANCE MEN
CD ______ 09026681082
RCA Victor / Nov '95 / BMG

SWINGTIME
Artistry in rhythm / Blue rondo a la Turk: *Bernhardt, Warren & Gordon Gottlieb* / Back home in Indiana: *Sims, Zoot Quartet* / 'Round midnight: *Stoltzman, Richard & Canadian Brass* / AT the Woodchopper's ball: *Stoltzman, Richard & Canadian Brass* / Lady is a tramp: *Mulligan, Gerry Quartet* / Sugar blues: *Eldridge, Roy* / Man I love: *Eldridge, Roy* / Whatever happened to the dream / Concierto de Aranjuez / I found love / Ellington medley / One o'clock jump: *Taylor, Joe & Canadian Brass* / Night and day: *Sims, Zoot Quartet*
CD ______ 09026683152
RCA Victor / Oct '95 / BMG

Canambu

SON CUBANO: THE RHYTHM STICKS
CD ______ CORA 123
Corason / Apr '95 / ADA / CM / Direct

Canavan, Josie

O AIRD GO HAIRD (Canavan, Josie & Tommy)
CD ______ CICD 044
Clo Iar-Chonnachta / Dec '94 / CM

Cancer

BLACK FAITH
CD ______ 0630107522
East West / Jul '95 / Warner Music

Candid Jazz Masters

FOR MILES
Milestones / All blues / Nardis / My funny valentine / Walkin' / So what / If I were a bell / Milestrane
CD ______ CCD 79710
Candid / Mar '97 / Cadillac / Direct / Jazz Music / Koch / Wellard

Candido

DANCIN' AND PRANCIN'
Dancin' and prancin' / Jingo / Thousand finger man / Rock and shuffle
CD ______ CPCD 8074
Charly / Mar '95 / Koch

Candiria

BEYOND REASONABLE DOUBT
CD ______ TDH 0022
Too Damn Hype / Jun '97 / Cargo / SRD

Candlebox

CANDLEBOX
Don't you / Change / You / No sense / Far behind / Blossom / Arrow / Rain / Mothers dream / Cover me / He calls home

CD 9362453132
Maverick / Jul '93 / Warner Music

WIDELUX
CD 9362459622
Maverick / Aug '95 / Warner Music

Candlemass

ANCIENT DREAMS
CD CDATV 7
Active / Feb '90 / Pinnacle

AS IT IS, AS IT WAS (The Best Of Candlemass) (2CD Set)
Solitude / Bewitched / Dying illusion / Demon's gate / Mirror mirror / Samaritan / Into the unfathomed tower / Bearer of pain / Where the runes still speak / At the gallows end / Mourner's lament / Tale of creation / Ebony throne / Under the oak / Well of souls / Dark are the veils of death / Darkness in paradise / End of pain / Sorcerer's pledge / Solitude '87 / Crystal ball '87 / Bullfest '93
CD Set CDMFN 166
Music For Nations / Oct '94 / Pinnacle

CANDLEMASS LIVE IN STOCKHOLM 9TH JUNE 1990
Well of souls / Bewitched / Dark reflections / Demon's gate / Through the infinitive halls of death / Mirror mirror / Sorceror's pledge / Dark are the veils / Solitude / Under the oak / Bells of Acheron / Samaritan / Gallows end
CD CDMFN 109
Music For Nations / Nov '90 / Pinnacle

CHAPTER SIX
CD CDMFN 128
Music For Nations / May '92 / Pinnacle

EPICUS DOOMICUS METALLICA
CD BD 013
Black Dragon / Apr '95 / Else

NIGHTFALL
CD CDATV 3
Active / Jun '88 / Pinnacle

TALES OF CREATION
CD CDMFN 95
Music For Nations / Sep '89 / Pinnacle

Candler, Norman

MAGIC DREAMS (Candler, Norman Strings)
CD ISCD 116
Intersound / Oct '91 / Jazz Music

MAGIC STRINGS VOL.1
CD ISCD 001
Intersound / Jul '93 / Jazz Music

MAGIC STRINGS VOL.2
CD ISCD 002
Intersound / Jul '93 / Jazz Music

SOFT MAGIC, THE (Candler, Norman & The Magic Strings)
CD ISCD 101
Intersound / Oct '89 / Jazz Music

Candy Snatchers

CANDY SNATCHERS
CD SH 21272
Safe House / Dec '96 / Cargo

Candyskins

FUN
Wembley / Fun / House at the top of the hill / Tired of being happy / Land of love / Everybody loves you / Everything just falls apart on me / You are here / Grass / Dig it deep / Let's take over the world / All over now
CD GED 24494
Geffen / Nov '96 / BMG

SUNDAY MORNING FEVER
Mrs. Hoover / 24 hours / Car crash / Monday morning / Get on / Europe and Japan / Hang myself on you / Disco hell / Circles / Face the day / DRUNK / No no no / Help me / In my hair
CD TOPPCD 054
Ultimate / Mar '97 / Pinnacle

Cannata

WATCHING THE WORLD
CD NTHEN 3
Now & Then / Sep '95 / Plastic Head

Canned Heat

BEST OF CANNED HEAT, THE
On the road again / Amphetamine Annie / My crime / Time was / Goin' up the country / Sugar bee / Whiskey headed woman / Bullfrog blues / Let's work together / World in a jug / Fried hockey boogie / Rollin' and tumblin' / I'm her man / Parthenogenesis
CD DC 878652
Disky / Mar '97 / Disky / THE

BIG ROAD BLUES
CD CDSGP 079
Prestige / Feb '96 / Else / Total/BMG

BOOGIE UP THE COUNTRY
Ansage / Mercury blues / Take me to the river / Rollin' and tumblin' / Amphetamine Annie / Bullfrog blues / Sweet home Chicago / Kidman blues / Going up the country / Let's work together / Trouble no more / Younderswall / Boogie / Absage
CD INAK 8804CD
In Akustik / Jul '97 / Direct / TKO Magnum

BURNIN' LIVE
CD AIM 1033CD
Aim / Oct '93 / ADA / Direct / Jazz Music

CANNED HEAT
CD EXP 005
Experience / May '97 / TKO Magnum

CANNED HEAT '70 CONCERT (Live In Europe)
CD BGOCD 12
Beat Goes On / Sep '89 / Pinnacle

FUTURE BLUES
CD BGOCD 49
Beat Goes On / Sep '89 / Pinnacle

HISTORICAL FIGURES AND ANCIENT HEADS
Sneakin' around / Rockin' with the king / Long way from LA / That's alright Mama / Hill's stomp / I don't care what you tell me / Cherokee dance / Utah
CD BGOCD 83
Beat Goes On / Aug '90 / Pinnacle

INTERNAL COMBUSTION
CD AIM 1044
Aim / Apr '95 / ADA / Direct / Jazz Music

LET'S WORK TOGETHER (The Best Of Canned Heat)
On the road again / Bullfrog blues / Rollin' and tumblin' / Amphetamine Annie / Fried hockey boogie / Sic 'em pigs / Poor moon / Let's work together / Going up the country / Boogie music / Same all over / Time was / Sugar bee / Rockin' with the king / That's alright mama / My time ain't long / Future blues / Pony blues / So sad (the world's in a tangle) / Chipmunk song
CD CDP 7931142
Liberty / Sep '89 / EMI

LIVE IN AUSTRALIA
CD AIM 1003CD
Aim / Oct '93 / ADA / Direct / Jazz Music

NEW AGE, THE
Keep it clean / Harley Davidson blues / Don't deceive me / You can run but you sure can't hide / Lookin' for my rainbow / Rock 'n' roll music / Framed / Election blues / So long wrong
CD BGOCD 85
Beat Goes On / Dec '90 / Pinnacle

ON THE ROAD AGAIN
On the road again / Amphetamine Annie / My crime / Time was / Going up the country / Sugar bee / Whiskey headed woman / Bullfrog blues / Let's work together / World in a jug / Fried hockey boogie / Rollin' and tumblin' / I'm her man / Dust by broom / Parthenogenesis
CD CDGOLD 1076
EMI Gold / Feb '97 / EMI

PEARLS FROM THE PAST
CD KLMCD 015
BAM / May '94 / Koch / Scratch/BMG

RE-HEATED
CD SPV 858805
SPV / Mar '96 / Koch / Plastic Head

STRAIGHT AHEAD
Big road blues / Got my mojo working / Pretty thing / Louise / Dimples / Talk to me baby / Straight ahead / Rollin' and tumblin' / I'd rather be a devil / It hurts me too / Bullfrog blues / Sweet sixteen / Dust my broom
CD CDTB 130
Thunderbolt / Apr '97 / TKO Magnum

TIES THAT BIND
CD ACH 80002
Archive / Jul '97 / Greyhound

UNCANNED (The Best Of Canned Heat) (2CD Set)
On the road again (Alternate take) / Nine below zero / TV Mama / Rollin' and tumblin' / Bullfrog blues / Evil is going on / Goin' down slow / Dust my broom / Help me / Story of my life / Hunter / Whiskey and wimmen / Shake, rattle and roll / Mean ol' world / Fannie Mae / Gotta boogie (The world boogie) / My crime / On the road again / Evil woman / Amphetamine Annie / Old owl song / Christmas blues / Going up the country / Time was / Low down (and high up) / Same all over / Big fat (The fat man) / It's alright / Poor moon / Sugar bee / Shake it and break it / Future blues / Let's work together / Wooly bully / Human condition / Long way from LA / Hill's stomp / Rockin' with the king / Harley Davidson blues / Rock 'n' roll music
CD CDEM 1543
Liberty / Aug '94 / EMI

Cannibal Corpse

BLEEDING
Staring through the eyes of the dead / Fucked with a knife / Stripped, raped and strangled / Pulverized / Return to flesh / Pick-axe murders / She was asking for it / Bleeding / Force fed broken glass / Experiment in homicide
CD 398414137CD
Metal Blade / Feb '97 / Pinnacle / Plastic Head

BUTCHERED AT BIRTH
CD 398414072CD
Metal Blade / Mar '96 / Pinnacle / Plastic Head

EATEN BACK TO LIFE
Shredded humans / Put them to death / Scattered remains, splattered brains / Rotting head / Bloody chunks / Buried in the backyard / Edible autopsy / Mangled / Born in a casket / Undead will feast / Skull full of maggots
CD 398414024CD
Metal Blade / Mar '96 / Pinnacle / Plastic Head

HAMMER SMASHED FACE
Hammer smashed face / Exorcist / Zero the hero / Meat hook sodomy / Shredded humans
CD CDMZORRO 57
Metal Blade / Apr '93 / Pinnacle / Plastic Head

TOMB OF THE MUTILATED
CD 398414010CD
Metal Blade / Mar '96 / Pinnacle / Plastic Head

VILE
CD 398414104CD
Metal Blade / Apr '96 / Pinnacle / Plastic Head

Cannibals

BREAST OF THE CANNIBALS
CD CDHIT 2
Hit / Feb '95 / RTM/Disc

Canning, Francis

MY DREAMS OF LONG AGO
After all these years / Let the rest of the world go by / Village where I went to school / Old rugged cross / If those lips could only speak / If I had my life to live over / Fool such as I / True love / Mother's love's a blessing / I will love you all my life / When I grow too old to dream / Old rustic bridge by the mill / My dreams of long ago / Maggie / Sunshine of your smile / Pal of my cradle days / Silver threads among the gold / I'll be your sweetheart
CD LCOM 3006
Lismor / Sep '95 / ADA / Direct / Duncans / Lismor

Cannon, Ace

ACES HI/PLAYS THE GREAT SHOW TUNES
CD HIUKCD 125
Hi / Jun '93 / Pinnacle

ROCKIN' ROBIN
CD HADCD 198
Javelin / Nov '95 / Henry Hadaway / THE

TUFF SAX/MOANING SAX
Tuff sax / Trouble in mind / St. Louis blues / Wabash blues / Basin Street blues / Cannonball / Blues in my heart / Blues stay away from me / Lonesome Road / Careless love / Kansas City / I've got a woman / Moanin' the blues / Trouble in mind (version 2) / Prisoner's song / I love you because / Last date / Singin' the blues / It's all in the game / No letter today / I left my heart in San Francisco / I can't get started (with you) / Prisoner of love / Moanin'
CD HIUKCD 121
Hi / Sep '91 / Pinnacle

Cannon, Gus

COMPLETE (Cannon, Gus & His Jug Stompers)
CD YAZCD 1082
Yazoo / Apr '91 / ADA / CM / Koch

GUS CANNON VOL.1 (1927-1928)
CD DOCD 5032
Document / Feb '92 / ADA / Hot Shot / Jazz Music

GUS CANNON VOL.2 (1929-1930) (Cannon, Gus & Noah Lewis)
CD DOCD 5033
Document / Feb '92 / ADA / Hot Shot / Jazz Music

Cano, Nacho

WORLD SPLIT BY THE SAME GOD, A
Patio / Dance instructor / Waltz of the mad / Land of cement / Piano (Piano) / World split by the same God / Wounded water / Piano violin and guitar / Battle / Vaikuntha / Battle (Piano) / Battle (Orchestra) / World split by the same God (End)
CD CDVIR 40
Virgin / Jun '96 / EMI

Canorous Quintet

SILENCE OF THE WORLD BEYOND
CD NFR 019CD
No Fashion / Jan '97 / Plastic Head

Cantairi Oga Atha Cliath Choir

FIVE CENTURIES OF SONG
CD AC 6456
Chorus / Dec '96 / Harmonia Mundi

Canter, Robin

OBOE COLLECTION
CD CDSAR 22
Amon Ra / '88 / Harmonia Mundi

Canterbury Cathedral Choir

CANTERBURY CAROLS
O come, all ye faithful / Sussex carol / Stille nacht (Silent night) / Once in Royal David's City / Ding dong merrily on high / Candlelight carol / God rest ye merry Gentlemen / Three kings / O little town of Bethlehem / Gaudete, Christus natus est / In the bleak midwinter / While shepherds watched their flocks by night / Away in a manger / Hark the herald angels sing / Toccata for organ
CD YORKCD 109
York Ambisonic / Oct '95 / Complete/ Pinnacle

Canticle

COLLECTION, THE
If you're Irish / Holy ground / Green glens of Antrim / Mick McGilligan's ball / I'll take you home again Kathleen / Courtin' in the kitchen / Come back Paddy Reilly / Let him go let him tarry / I know where I'm goin' / Rose of Tralee
CD EMPRCD 720
Emporio / Jun '97 / Disc

Canticum Fuebris

ENDLESS
CD CDSATE 14
Music Research / Jan '95 / Plastic Head

Cantovivo

ANTOLOGIA
CD BRAM 1991202
Brambus / Nov '93 / ADA

Cantuaria, Vinicius

SOL NA CARA
Sem pisar no chao / Rio negro / Samba de estrela / Ludo real / Sutis diferencas / Sol na cara / O nome dela / Corre campo / O grande lance e fazer romance / O vento / Este sej olhar / Labrea
CD GCD 79518
Gramavision / Jun '97 / Vital/SAM

Cao, Emilio

CARTAS MARINAS
CD F 1021CD
Sonifolk / Jun '94 / ADA / CM

Capability Green

53310761
CD CDHOLE 011
Golf / Jun '96 / Plastic Head

Capaldi, Jim

OH HOW WE DANCED
Eve / Big thirst / Love is all you can try / Last day of dawn / Don't be a hero / Open your heart / How much can a man really take / Oh how we danced
CD EDCD 502
Edsel / Nov '96 / Pinnacle

SHORT CUT DRAW BLOOD
Goodbye love / It's all up to you / Love hurts / Johnny too bad / Short cut draw blood / Living on a marble / Boy with a problem / Keep on trying / Seagull
CD EDCD 504
Edsel / Nov '96 / Pinnacle

WHALE MEAT AGAIN
It's all right / Whale meat again / Yellow sun / I've got so much lovin' / Low rider / My brother / Summer is fading
CD EDCD 503
Edsel / Nov '96 / Pinnacle

Capart, Louis

MARIE-JEANNE GABRIELLE
CD KMCD 06
Keltia Musique / '91 / ADA / Discovery

PATIENCE
CD KMCD 13
Keltia Musique / '91 / ADA / Discovery

Capella Cordina

MISSA L'HOMME ARME
CD LEMS 8009
Lyrichord / Aug '94 / ADA / CM / Roots

TWO THREE VOICE MASSES, THE
CD LEMS 8010
Lyrichord / Aug '94 / ADA / CM / Roots

Capercaillie

BEAUTIFUL WASTELAND
CD SURCD 021
Survival / Aug '97 / ADA / Pinnacle

BLOOD IS STRONG, THE
Aignish / Arrival / Iona / Calum's road / Fear / Dean Cadalan samhach / Grandfather mountain / An atairreachd ard / 'S fhada leam an oidhche gheamhraidh / Hebrides / Lordship of the isles / Arrival reprise / Columcille / Downtown Toronto
CD SURCD 014
Survival / Jul '95 / ADA / Pinnacle

CAPERCAILLIE
Miracle of being / When you return / Grace and pride / Tobermory / Take the floor / Stinging rain / Aladsair / Crime and passion / Bonaparte / When you return
CD SURCD 018
Survival / May '95 / ADA / Pinnacle

CROSSWINDS
Puirt-a-beul / Soraidh bhuam gu barraidh / Glenorchy / Am buachaille ban / Haggis / Brenda Stubbert's set / Ma theid mise tuilleagh / David Glen's / Urnaigh a 'bhan-thigreach / My laggan love/Fox on the town / An ribhinn donn
CD GLCD 1077
Green Linnet / May '92 / ADA / CM / Direct / Highlander / Roots

DELIRIUM
Rann na mona / Waiting for the wheel to turn / Aodann Strathbain / Cape Breton song / You will rise again / Kenny MacDonald's jigs / Dean saor an spiorad / Coisich a ruin (walk my beloved) / Dr. MacPhail's reel / Heart of the highland / Brelsleach / Islay Ranter's reels / Servant to the slave
CD SURCD 015
Survival / May '95 / ADA / Pinnacle

GET OUT
Waiting for the wheel to turn / Pige ruadh / Silver spear reels / Outlaws / Coisich a ruin (walk my beloved) / Fear a'bhata / Dr. MacPhail's trance
CD SURCD 016
Survival / May '95 / ADA / Pinnacle

SECRET PEOPLE
Bonaparte / Grace and pride / Tobar Mhoire (Tobermory) / Miracle of being / Crime of passion / Whinney hills jigs / An eala bhan (the white swan) / Selce Ruairidh (Roddy's drum) / Stinging rain / Hi rim bo / Four stone walls / Harley ashtray / Oran / Black fields
CD SURCD 017
Survival / May '95 / ADA / Pinnacle

SIDEWAULK
Alasdair Mhic Cholla Ghasda / Balindore / Fisherman's dream / Sidewaulk reels / Iain Ghlinn'Cuaich / Fosgail an Dorus / Turnpike / Both sides of the tweed / Weasel / Oh mo Dhuthaich
CD CDGL 1094
Green Linnet / Feb '89 / ADA / CM / Direct / Highlander / Roots

TO THE MOON
To the moon / Claire in heaven / Wanderer / Price of fire / Rob Roy reels / Ailein Duinn / Nil si / Crooked mountain / God's alabi / Collector's daughter / Only you
CD SURCD 019
Survival / Oct '95 / ADA / Pinnacle

Capital Letters

HEADLINE NEWS
Fire / Daddy was no murderer / President Amin / Smoking my ganja / Unemployed / Rejoice / Buzzrock / Run run run / Out of Africa
CD GRELCD 7
Greensleeves / Nov '92 / Jet Star / SRD

Capitalist Casualties

COLLECTION, THE
CD SAH 35
Slap A Ham / May '97 / Cargo / Greyhound / Plastic Head

Capitol Punishment

FIRST LINE-UP, THE
CD WB 078166CD
We Bite / Sep '93 / Plastic Head

MESSIAH COMPLEX
CD WB 2102CD
We Bite / Apr '94 / Plastic Head

Capleton

ALMS HOUSE
CD GRELCD 182
Greensleeves / Mar '93 / Jet Star / SRD

CAPLETON AND FRIENDS (Capleton & Friends)
CD KPCRCD 59
Charm / Jan '97 / Jet Star

PROPHECY
Tour / Big time / Obstacle / Leave Babylon / Heathen reign / Don't dis the trinity / No competition / Wings of the morning / See from afar
CD 5292642
RAL / Oct '95 / PolyGram

Cap'n Jazz

KITES, KUNG FU AND TROPHIES
CD MWG 002CD
Man With Gun / Apr '97 / Cargo

Capone & Noreaga

WAR REPORT, THE
Intro / Bloody money / Driver's seat / Stick you / Patrol violators / Iraq (see the world) / Live on live long / Neva die alone / TONY / cHANNEL 10 / Capone phone home / Stay tuned / Capone bone / Halfway thugs / LA LA / Capone-n-Noreaga / Illegal life / Black gangstas / Closer / Capone phone home outro
CD PENCD 3041
Tommy Boy / Jun '97 / RTM/Disc

Capone, Eddie

EXPERIENCE
CD TR 12CD
Treatment / Jul '96 / Jet Star

Capp, Frank

CAPP-PIERCE JUGGERNAUT (Capp-Pierce Juggernaut)
Avenue C / All heart / Moten swing / Basie / Mr. Softie / It's sand man / Dickie's dream / Take the 'A' train / Wee baby blues / Roll 'em Pete
CD CCD 4040
Concord Jazz / Jun '91 / New Note/ Pinnacle

FRANK CAPP TRIO PRESENTS RICKEY WOODWARD (Capp, Frank Trio)
Oleo / Au privave / If I should lose you / Speak low / Sweet Lorraine / Polka dots and moonbeams / Doxy / Three bears / You tell me
CD CCD 4469
Concord Jazz / Jul '91 / New Note/Pinnacle

IN A HEFTI BAG (Capp, Frank Juggernaut)
I'm shoutin' again / Cherry point / Flight of the Foo birds / Kid from Red Bank / Splanky / Fantail / Li'l darlin' / Duet / Whirly bird / Cute / Awful nice to be with you / Bag a' bones / Midnight blue / Dinner with my friends / Teddy the toad / Scoot / Late date
CD CCD 4655
Concord Jazz / Jul '95 / New Note/Pinnacle

JUGGERNAUT STRIKES AGAIN (Capp-Pierce Juggernaut)
One for Marshall / I remember Clifford / New York shuffle / Chops, fingers and sticks / You are so beautiful / Parker's mood / Word from Bird / Charade / Things ain't what they used to be / Little Pony
CD CCD 4183
Concord Jazz / Aug '90 / New Note/ Pinnacle

PLAY IT AGAIN SAM (Capp, Frank Juggernaut)
Heat's on / Warm breeze / Ja da / Sweet Georgia Brown / Katy / Wind machine / Soft as velvet / Ya gotta try / Freckle face / Satin 'n' glass / 88 Basie Street / Night flight
CD CCD 47472
Concord Jazz / Mar '97 / New Note/ Pinnacle

QUALITY TIME
Dip stick / Back to Brea / I've never been in love before / Daahoud / There you have it / Tadd's delight / 9:20 Special / Sophisticated lady / Things ain't what they used to be
CD CCD 4677
Concord Jazz / Dec '95 / New Note/ Pinnacle

Cappelletti, Arrigo

TRANSFORMATION (Cappelletti, Arrigo Quartet)
CD Y225024
Silex / Jun '93 / ADA / Harmonia Mundi

Capris

CAPRIS 1954-1958
CD FLYCD 56
Flyright / Oct '93 / Hot Shot / Jazz Music / Wellard

Captain & Tennille

SCRAPBOOK
Do that to me one more time / Love on a shoestring / You've never done it like that before / Lonely night (Angel face) / No love in the morning / Baby I still got it / Keeping our love warm / Love will keep us together / Can't stop dancing / Until you come back to me / Shop around / You need a woman tonight / Happy together (A fantasy) / Way I want to touch you
CD 5501212
Spectrum / Oct '93 / PolyGram

Captain Barkey

GO GO WINE
CD KPSTONECD 1
Stone Love / Jan '97 / Jet Star

Captain Beefheart

BLUE JEANS AND MOONBEAMS
Captain's holiday / Pompadour swamp / Party of special things to do / Blue jeans and moonbeams / Twist ah luck / Further than we've gone / Rock 'n' roll's evil doll / Observatory quest / Same old blues
CD CDV 2023
Virgin / Jun '88 / EMI

CARROT IS AS CLOSE AS A RABBIT GETS TO A DIAMOND
Sugar bowl / Past sure is tense / Happy love song / Floppy boot stomp / Blue jeans and moonbeams / Run paint run run / This is the day / Tropical hot dog night / Observatory crest / Host the ghost the most holy O / Harry Irene / I got love on my mind / Pompadour swamp / Love lies / Sheriff of Hong Kong / Further than we've been / Candle mambo / Light reflected off the oceans of the moon / Carrot is as close as a rabbit gets to a diamond
CD CDVM 9028
Virgin / Jul '93 / EMI

DOC AT THE RADAR STATION
Hothead / Ashtray heart / Carrot is as close as a rabbit gets to a diamond / Run paint run run / Sue Egypt / Brickbats / Dirty blue gene / Best batch yet / Telephone / Flavour bud living / Sheriff of Hong Kong / Making love to a vampire with a monkey on my knee
CD CDV 2172
Virgin / Jun '88 / EMI

ICE CREAM FOR CROW
Ice cream for crow / Host the ghost the most holy O / Semi-multicoloured caucasian / Hey Garland, I dig your tweed coat / Evening bells / Cardboard cut-out sundown / Past sure is tense / Ink mathematics / Witch doctor love / 81 poop hatch / Thousanth and tenth day of the human totem pole / Skeleton makes good
CD CDV 2237
Virgin / Apr '88 / EMI

LEGENDARY A&M SESSIONS, THE
Diddy wah diddy / Who do you think you're fooling / Moonchild / Frying pan / Here I am I always am
CD BLIMPCD 902
Edsel / Mar '92 / Pinnacle

LONDON 1974
CD MPG 74025
Movieplay Gold / Nov '93 / Target/BMG

SAFE AS MILK (Captain Beefheart & His Magic Band)
Sure nuff 'n' yes I do / Zig zag wanderer / Call on me / Dropout boogie / I'm glad / Electricity / Yellow brick road / Abba zaba / Plastic factory / Where there's a woman / Grown so ugly / Autumn's child
CD CLACD 234
Castle / May '91 / BMG

SHINY BEAST (BAT CHAIN PULLER)
Floppy boot stomp / Tropical hot dog night / Ice rose / Harru Irene / You know you're a man / Bat chain puller / When I see mummy I feel like a mummy / Owed t Alex / Candle mambo / Love lies / Suction prints / Apes-ma
CD CDV 2149
Virgin / Jul '87 / EMI

SPOTLIGHT KID/CLEAR SPOT (Captain Beefheart & His Magic Band)
I'm gonna booglariza you baby / White jam / Blabber 'n smoke / When it blows it's stacks / Alic in blunderland / Spotlight kid / Click clack / Grow fins / There ain't no Santa Claus / Glider / Low yo yo stuff / Nowadays a woman's gotta hit a man / Too much time / Circumstances / My head is my only house unless it rains / Sum zoom spark / Clear spot / Crazy little thing / Long neck bottles / Her eyes are a blue million miles / Big eyes beans from Venus / Goldne birdies
CD 7599262492
Warner Bros. / Aug '90 / Warner Music

STRICTLY PERSONAL
Ah feel like acid / Safe as milk / Trust us / Son of mirror man-mere man / On tomorrow / Beatle bones n' smokin' stones / Gimme dat harp boy / Kandy korn
CD CZ 529
Premier/EMI / Jul '94 / EMI

TROUT MASK REPLICA
Hair pie: Bake II / Pena / Well / When Big Joan sets up / Fallin' ditch / Sugar 'n' spikes / Ant man bee / Orange claw hammer / Wild life / She's too much for my mirror / Hobo chang ba / Blimp (mousetrapreplica) / Steal softly thru snow / Old fart at play / Veteran's day poppy
CD 7599271962
Warner Bros. / Sep '94 / Warner Music

UNCONDITIONALLY GUARANTEED
Upon the my-o-my / Sugar bowl / New electric ride / Magic be / Happy love song / Full moon hot sun / I got love on my mind / This is the day / Lazy music / Peaches
CD CDV 2015
Virgin / Jun '88 / EMI

ZIG ZAG WANDERER (The Best Of The Buddah Years)
Sure nuff 'n' yes I do / Zig zag wanderer / Dropout boogie / I'm glad / Electricity / Yellow brick road / Abba zabba / Plastic factory / Tarot plane / Kandy korn / Trust us / Beatle bones 'n' smokin' stones / Safe as milk / Gimme dat harp boy
CD HILLCD 6
Wooded Hill / Nov '96 / Direct / World Serpent

Captain Gumbo

BACK A LA MAISON
CD MWCD 2006
Music & Words / Apr '93 / ADA / Direct

CHANK-A-CHANK
CD MWCD 2012
Music & Words / Aug '94 / ADA / Direct

ONE MORE TWO STEP
CD MWCD 2001
Music & Words / Jun '92 / ADA / Direct

Captain Hollywood

ANIMALS & HUMANS
CD PULSE 20CD
Pulse 8 / Apr '95 / BMG

Captain Rizz

MANIFESTO
Voodoo Rizz / Rizz's radio song / Rizz's anthem / City of angels / St. Cecelia / Rizz's radio song (instrumental) / Voodoo Rizz (instrumental)
CD EBSCD 112
Emergency Broadcast System / Nov '96 / BMG

Captain Sensible

BEST OF CAPTAIN SENSIBLE, THE
CD CLP 0041
Cleopatra / Aug '97 / Cargo / Greyhound / Plastic Head / RTM/Disc / SRD

CAPTAIN'S BOX (2CD Set)
CD Set BAH 32
Humbug / Jun '97 / Total/Pinnacle

LIVE AT THE MILKY WAY
Interstella overcoat / Jet boy jet girl / Smash it up / Back to school / Come on Geoffrey Brown / Happy talk / Kamikaze millionaire / Exploding heads and teapots / Love song / Neat neat neat / New rose / Wot / Looking at you / Hey Joe / Glad it's all over
CD BAH 12
Humbug / Aug '94 / Total/Pinnacle

MAD COWS AND ENGLISHMEN
CD SCRCD 017
Scratch / Dec '96 / Koch / Scratch/BMG

MEATHEAD
CD Set BAH 14
Humbug / Aug '95 / Total/Pinnacle

REVOLUTION NOW
CD BAH 3
Humbug / Jul '96 / Total/Pinnacle

SLICE OF CAPTAIN SENSIBLE, A
CD BAH 30
Humbug / Jun '97 / Total/Pinnacle

UNIVERSE OF GEOFFREY BROWN, THE
CD BAH 4
Humbug / Mar '93 / Total/Pinnacle

Captive Heart

ONLY THE BRAVE
CD MTM 199614
MTM / Nov '96 / Cargo

Captor

DROWNED
CD PCD 034
Progress / Jul '96 / Cargo / Plastic Head

Carabelli, Adolfo

CUATRO PALABRAS
CD EBCD 87
El Bandoneon / Apr '97 / Discovery

Caramia, Tony

PIANO
CD SOSCD 1313
Stomp Off / Jul '96 / Jazz Music / Wellard

Caravan

ALBUM, THE
Heartbreaker / Corner of me eye / What'cha gonna tell me / Piano player / Make yourself at home / Golden mile / Bright shiny day / Clear blue sky / Keepin' up de fences
CD CDKVL 9003
Kingdom / Jan '87 / Kingdom

ALL OVER YOU
CD HTDCD 57
HTD / Apr '96 / CM / Pinnacle

ALL OVER YOU (Re-Recorded Special Edit)
If I could do it all over again, I'd do it all over you / Place of my own / Love in your eye/To catch me a brother / In the land of grey and pink / Golf girl / Disassociation (nine feet underground) / Hello hello / As-forteri 25 / For Richard / Memory Iain Hugh / Headloss / Be alright/Chance of a lifetime / If I could do it all over again, I'd do it all over you
CD HTDCD 57L
HTD / Apr '97 / CM / Pinnacle

BACK TO FRONT
Back to Herne Bay front / Bet you wanna take it all / Hold on hold on / Videos of Hollywood / Sally don't change it / Take my breath away / Proper job / Back to front / All aboard / AA man
CD ________ **CDKVS 5011**
Kingdom / Jan '87 / Kingdom

BATTLE OF HASTINGS
CD ________ **HTDCD 41**
HTD / Oct '95 / CM / Pinnacle

BEST OF CARAVAN
And I wish I were stoned again / Don't worry / Francoise-for Richard-Warlock / Can't be long now / Warlock / No backstage pass / Dog, the dog, he's at it again / Love in your eye / To catch me a brother / In the land of grey and pink / Memory lain Hugh
CD ________ **C5CD505X**
See For Miles/C5 / Apr '93 / Pinnacle

BLIND DOG AT ST. DUNSTAN'S
Here I am / Chiefs and indians / Very smelly, grubby little oik / Bobbing wide / Come on back / Very smelly, grubby little oik, A (reprise) / Jack and Jill / Can you hear me / All the way
CD ________ **HTDCD 60**
HTD / May '96 / CM / Pinnacle

CANTERBURY COLLECTION, THE
It's never too late / What'cha gonna tell me / All aboard / Piano player / Sally don't change it / Bright shiny day / Clear blue sky / Bet you wanna take it all / Hold on hold on / Corner of me eye / Taken my breath away
CD ________ **CDKVL 9028**
Kingdom / Jan '87 / Kingdom

CARAVAN
Place of my own / Ride / Policeman / Love song with flute / Cecil runs / Magic man / Grandma's lawn / Where but for Caravan would I be
CD ________ **HTDCD 65**
HTD / Sep '96 / CM / Pinnacle

COOL WATER
CD ________ **HTDCD 18**
HTD / Feb '94 / CM / Pinnacle

CUNNING STUNTS
Show of our lives / Stuck in a hole / Lover / No backstage pass / Dabsong conshirtoe / Fear and loathing in Tollington Park rag
CD ________ **HTDCD 52**
HTD / Jan '96 / CM / Pinnacle

EVENING OF MAGIC, AN (Sinclair, Richard)
In the land of grey and pink / Only the brave/plan it earth / Share it / Videos / Heather / Going for a song / O Caroline / Nine feet underground / Felafel shuffle / Cruising / Emily / Halfway between heaven and earth / It didn't matter anyway / Golf girl
CD ________ **HTDCD 17**
HTD / Jan '94 / CM / Pinnacle

IN THE LAND OF GREY AND PINK
Golf girl / Winter wine / Love to love you / In the land of grey and pink / Nine feet underground: Nigel blows a tune / Love's a friend / Make it 76 / Dance of the seven paper hankies- hold grandad by the nose / Honest I did - disassociation / 100% proof
CD ________ **8205202**
Deram / Apr '89 / PolyGram

LIVE 1990
CD ________ **NINETY 2**
Demon / Mar '93 / Pinnacle

Caravans

ACTION OR SLANDER
(I'm gonna) mainline baby / Mobile Alabama / Killer boogie / Ballad of Lucy Jordan / All messed up / Nothin' 'bout nothin'
CD ________ **RAUCD 028**
Raucous / May '97 / Nervous / RTM/Disc / TKO Magnum

Caravans

AMAZING GRACE
Amazing grace / Just like him / Nobody knows like the Lord / Sacred Lord / Lord stay with me / To whom shall I turn / I'm ready to serve the Lord / No coward soldier / Till I meet the Lord / Jesus will save / Till you come / Lord don't leave us now / Jesus and me / One of these old days / Everything you need / What will tomorrow bring / I don't mind / It must not suffer loss / I'm going thru' / Place like that
CD ________ **CPCD 8088**
Charly / Apr '95 / Koch

Caravensari

PIG
CD ________ **SZDATCD 02**
Samizdat / Jul '93 / ADA

SHOCK HORO
CD ________ **SAMIZDAT 03CD**
Samizdat / Apr '95 / ADA

Carawan Family

HOMEBREW
CD ________ **FF 609CD**
Flying Fish / Apr '94 / ADA / CM / Direct / Roots

Carawan, Guy

TREE OF LIFE
CD ________ **FF 525CD**
Flying Fish / '92 / ADA / CM / Direct / Roots

Carbo, Chuck

BARBER'S BLUES, THE
CD ________ **ROUCD 2140**
Rounder / Feb '96 / ADA / CM / Direct

Carbo, Gladys

STREET CRIES
CD ________ **1211972**
Soul Note / Oct '90 / Cadillac / Harmonia Mundi / Wellard

Carbon

LARYNX
CD ________ **SST 194CD**
SST / May '93 / Plastic Head

TRUTHTABLE
CD ________ **HMS 2022**
Homestead / Jul '93 / Cargo / SRD

Carbon, Lisa

OPTO FREESTYLE
CD ________ **PODUKCD 037**
Pod Communications / Sep '96 / Plastic Head

POLYESTER
CD ________ **CAT 026CD**
Rephlex / Jan '96 / Prime / RTM/Disc

TRIO
CD ________ **RI 043CD**
Rather Interesting / Mar '97 / Plastic Head

Carbonell, Augustin

AUGUSTIN 'BOLA' CARBONELL
CD ________ **MES 158142**
Messidor / Apr '93 / ADA / Koch

CARMEN
Alegrias de cascorro / Travesia la comadre / Minerico / Gina / Esencia jonda / Galicia / Coral / Alchacon / Carmen / Improvisation
CD ________ **158142**
Messidor / Aug '92 / ADA / Koch

Carbonized

DISHARMONIZATION
CD ________ **FDN 2006CD**
Foundation 2000 / Sep '93 / Plastic Head

SCREAMING MACHINES
CD ________ **FDN 2013CD**
Foundation 2000 / Sep '96 / Plastic Head

Carcamo, Pablo

20 BEST OF CARIBBEAN TROPICAL MUSIC (Carcamo, Pablo & Jaime Mella)
CD ________ **EUCD 1112**
ARC / '91 / ADA / ARC Music

BEST OF CARIBBEAN TROPICAL MUSIC
CD Set ________ **EUCD 1322**
ARC / Nov '95 / ADA / ARC Music

CARIBBEAN TROPICAL MUSIC VOL.2
CD ________ **EUCD 1162**
ARC / '91 / ADA / ARC Music

CARIBBEAN TROPICAL MUSIC VOL.3
CD ________ **EUCD 1201**
ARC / Sep '93 / ADA / ARC Music

CUMBIA DANCE PARTY (Carcamo, Pablo & Enrique Ugarte)
CD ________ **EUCD 1234**
ARC / Nov '93 / ADA / ARC Music

FLY AWAY HOME
CD ________ **EUCD 1128**
ARC / '91 / ADA / ARC Music

IT'S TIME FOR MAMBO (Carcamo, Pablo & Vanessa Lawicki/Miguel Castro)
CD ________ **EUCD 1225**
ARC / Sep '93 / ADA / ARC Music

MAGIC OF THE PARAGUAYAN AND THE INDIAN FLUTES (Carcamo, Pablo & Oscar Benito)
CD ________ **EUCD 1245**
ARC / Nov '93 / ADA / ARC Music

MI CHILOE
CD ________ **EUCD 1095**
ARC / '91 / ADA / ARC Music

MOST POPULAR SONGS FROM CHILE, THE
CD ________ **EUCD 1217**
ARC / Sep '93 / ADA / ARC Music

MY INSPIRATION
CD ________ **EUCD 1181**
ARC / Apr '92 / ADA / ARC Music

SAMBA BOSSA (Carcamo, Pablo, Hossam Ramzy & Ulrick Stiegler)
CD ________ **EUCD 1142**
ARC / '91 / ADA / ARC Music

Carcass

HEARTWORK
Buried dreams / Carnal fudge / No love lost / Heartwork / Embodiment / This mortal coil / Albeit macht fleisch / Blind bleeding the blind / Doctrinal expletives / Death certificate
CD ________ **MOSH 097CD**
Earache / Sep '97 / Vital

NECROTICISM - DESCANTING THE INSALUBRIOUS
Inpropgation / Corporeal jigsore quandary / Symposium of sickness / Pedigree butchery / Incarnated solvent abuse / Carneous cacoffin / Lavaging expectorate of Lysergide composition / Forensic clinicism - The Sanguine article
CD ________ **MOSH 042CD**
Earache / Sep '94 / Vital

REEK OF PUTRIFICATION
Genital grinder / Regurgitation of giblets / Pyosisified (still rotten to the gore) / Carbonized eye-sockets / Frenzied detruncation / Vomited anal tract / Festerday / Fermenting innards / Excreted alive / Suppuration / Foeticide / Microwaved uterogestation / Splattered cavities / Psychopathologist / Burnt to a crisp / Pungent excruciation / Manifestation of verrucose urethra / Oxidised razor masticator / Malignant defecation
CD ________ **MOSH 006CD**
Earache / Sep '94 / Vital

SWANSONG
Keep on rotting in the free world / Tomorrow belongs to nobody / Black star / Cross my heart / Child's play / Room 101 / Polarized / Generation hexed / Firm hand / Go to hell / Don't believe a word / Rock the vote
CD ________ **MOSH 160CDL**
Earache / Jun '96 / Vital
CD ________ **MOSH 160CD**
Earache / Sep '97 / Vital

SYMPHONIES OF SICKNESS
CD ________ **MOSH 018CD**
Earache / Sep '94 / Vital

WAKE UP AND SMELL THE CARCASS
Edge of darkness / Emotional flatline / Ever increasing circles / Blood splattered banner / I told you S (corporate rock really does suck) / Buried dreams / No love lost / Rot 'n' roll / Edge of darkness / This is your life / Rot 'n' roll / Pyosisified (still rotten to the core) / Hepatic tissue fermentation / Genital grinder II / Hepatic tissue fermentation / Exhume to consume
CD ________ **MOSH 161CD**
Earache / Oct '96 / Vital

Carcrash International

FRAGMENTS OF A JOURNEY IN HELL
CD ________ **CLEO 94612**
City Slang / Apr '94 / RTM/Disc

Cardiacs

ALL THAT GLITTERS IS A MARE'S NEST
CD ________ **ALPHCD 018**
Alphabet Business Concern / May '95 / Plastic Head

ARCHIVE CARDIACS
CD ________ **ALPHCD 000**
Alphabet Business Concern / May '95 / Plastic Head

BELLEYE
CD ________ **ORGAN 011CD**
Org / Apr '95 / Pinnacle

CARDIACS LIVE
Icing on the world / In a city lining / Tarred and feathered / Loosefish scapegrace / Is this the life / To go off and things / Gina Lollibrigida / Goosegash / Cameras / Big ship
CD ________ **ALPHCD 010**
Alphabet Business Concern / May '95 / Plastic Head

LITTLE MAN AND A HOUSE AND THE WHOLE WORLD WINDOW, A
Back to the cave / Little man and a house / In a city lining / Is this the life / Interlude / Dive / Icing on the world / Breakfast line / Victory / RES / Whole world window / I'm eating in bed
CD ________ **ALPHCD 007**
Alphabet Business Concern / May '95 / Plastic Head

ON LAND AND IN THE SEA
CD ________ **ALPHCD 012**
Alphabet Business Concern / May '95 / Plastic Head

RUDE BOOTLEG
CD ________ **ALPHCD 005**
Alphabet Business Concern / May '95 / Plastic Head

SAMPLER
CD ________ **ALPHCD 019**
Alphabet Business Concern / May '95 / Plastic Head

SEASIDE
CD ________ **ALPHCD 013**
Alphabet Business Concern / May '95 / Plastic Head

SING FOR GOD (2CD Set)
CD Set ________ **ALPHCD 022**
Alphabet Business Concern / Jun '96 / Plastic Head

SING FOR GOD VOL.1
CD ________ **ALPHCD 023**
Alphabet Business Concern / Jun '96 / Plastic Head

SING FOR GOD VOL.2
CD ________ **ALPHCD 024**
Alphabet Business Concern / Jun '96 / Plastic Head

SONGS FOR SHIPS AND IRONS
CD ________ **ALPHCD 014**
Alphabet Business Concern / May '95 / Plastic Head

Cardigans

COMPLETE SINGLES COLLECTION (10CD Single Box Set)
CD Set ________ **CARDSIN 1**
Border / May '97 / Cargo

EMMERDALE
CD ________ **5232152**
Stockholm / Jan '97 / PolyGram

FIRST BAND ON THE MOON
Your new cuckoo / Been it / Heartbreaker / Happy meal II / Never recover / Step on me / Love fool / Loser / Iron man / Great divide / Choke
CD ________ **5331172**
Stockholm / Sep '96 / PolyGram

LIFE
Carnival / Gordon's garden party / Daddy's car / Sick and tired / Tomorrow / Rise and shine / Beautiful one / Travelling with Charley / Fine / Celia inside / Hey, get out of my way / After all / Sabbath bloody Sabbath
CD ________ **5235562**
Stockholm / Jun '95 / PolyGram

TRIBUTE TO THE CARDIGANS (Various Artists)
Losers: *Anywhen* / After all: *Red Sleeping Beauty* / Hey, get out of my way: *Mobyletters* / Gordon's garden party: *Groove Tunnel* / Daddy's car: *Lonos* / Been it: *Inbetweendays* / Sick and tired: *Dilemmas* / Step on me: *Elvis Ellington* / Fire and shine: *Sulky* / Tomorrow: *Flow*
CD ________ **TR 012CD**
Tribute / Jun '97 / Plastic Head

Cardinal Sin

SPITEFUL INTENTS
CD ________ **WAR 010CD**
Wrong Again / Jan '97 / Plastic Head

Cardona, Milton

BEMBE
Salute to Eleuga / Eleuga / Ogun / Ochosi / Ebioso / Babalu aye / Obatala / Chango / Ochun / Yemaya
CD ________ **AMCL 10042**
American Clave / Jun '96 / ADA / Direct / New Note/Pinnacle

Cardwell, Joi

JUMP FOR JOI
CD ________ **EBCD 51**
Eightball / Jan '95 / Vital

TROUBLE (The Remix Compilation)
CD ________ **EBCD 58**
Eightball / Jan '95 / Vital

Care

DIAMONDS AND EMERALDS
Diamonds and emeralds / Evening in the ray / Chandeliers / Flaming sword / Cymophone / Love crowns and crucifies / Temper temper / White cloud / Caretaking / My boyish days / Sad day for England / Soldiers and sailors / Whatever possesed you / Such is life / What kind of world / Nature prayed upon / Misericorde / Besides 1 and 2
CD ________ **74321500232**
Camden / Jun '97 / BMG

Care, Simon

TWO'S UP (Care, Simon & Gareth Turner)
CD ________ **OC 02CD**
Old Court / May '97 / ADA

Carey, Mariah

DAYDREAM
Fantasy / Underneath the stars / One sweet day: *Carey, Mariah & Boyz II Men* / Open arms / Always be my baby / I am free / When I saw you / Long ago / Melt away / Forever / Daydream interlude / Looking in
CD ________ **4813672**
Columbia / Sep '95 / Sony

EMOTIONS
Emotions / And you don't remember / Can't let go / Make it happen / If it's over / You're

so cold / So blessed / To be around you / Till the end of time / Wind / Vanishing
CD _______________ 4688512
Columbia / Oct '91 / Sony

HER STORY (2CD Set)
CD Set _______________ OTR 1100033
Metro Independent / Jun '97 / Essential/ BMG

MARIAH CAREY
Vision of love / There's got to be a way / I don't wanna cry / Someday / Vanishing / All in your mind / Alone in love / You need me / Sent from up above / Prisoner / Love takes time
CD _______________ 4668152
Columbia / Aug '90 / Sony

MARIAH CAREY UNPLUGGED
Emotions / If it's over / Someday / Vision of love / Make it happen / I'll be there / Can't let go
CD _______________ 4718692
Columbia / Jul '92 / Sony

MERRY CHRISTMAS
Silent night / All I want for Christmas is you / O holy night / Christmas (Baby please come home) / Miss you most (at Christmas time) / Joy to the world / Jesus born on this day / Santa Claus is coming to town / Hark the herald angels sing/Gloria (In Excelsis Deo) / Jesus oh what a wonderful child / God rest ye merry gentlemen
CD _______________ 4773422
Columbia / Nov '96 / Sony

MUSIC BOX
Dream lover / Hero / Anytime you need a friend / Music box / Now that I know / Never forget you / Without you / Just to hold you once again / I've been thinking about you / All I've ever wanted / Everything fades away
CD _______________ 4742702
Columbia / Sep '93 / Sony

Carey, Mutt

MUTT CAREY & LEE COLLINS (Carey, Mutt & Lee Collins)
CD _______________ AMCD 72
American Music / Jan '94 / Jazz Music

Caribbean Clan

ULTIMATE IN REGGAE
CD _______________ HADCD 176
Javelin / Nov '95 / Henry Hadaway / THE

Caribbean Jazz Project

ISLAND STORIES
Bluellespie / Sadie's dance / Calabash / Tjader motion / Zigzag / Shadowplay / Libertango / Lost voice / Grass roots
CD _______________ INAK 30392
In Akustik / Jul '97 / Direct / TKO Magnum

Carioca

CARIOCA
Revoada / Pitanga / Alvorada / Briza / Branca / Despertar / Brilho / Caminho do sol / Bemtev / Revoada final
CD _______________ 5177092
Carmo / Jul '93 / New Note/Pinnacle

Carisma

1825
CD _______________ HGDSRRR 3
Escape / Nov '96 / Cargo

Carle, Frankie

1946 BROADCASTS (Carle, Frankie & His Orchestra)
CD _______________ JH 1008
Jazz Hour / '91 / Cadillac / Jazz Music / Target/BMG

FRANKIE CARLE 1944-1946 (Carle, Frankie & His Orchestra)
CD _______________ CCD 43
Circle / Jul '93 / Jazz Music / Swift / Wellard

FRANKIE CARLE 1944-1949 (Carle, Frankie & His Orchestra)
CD _______________ CCD 146
Circle / Jul '93 / Jazz Music / Swift / Wellard

GOLDEN TOUCH, THE (Frankie Carle At The Piano)
CD _______________ CCD 138
Circle / Mar '97 / Jazz Music / Swift / Wellard

Carless, Dorothy

THAT LOVELY WEEKEND
Daddy / It can't be wrong / My sister and I / Room 504 / That lovely weekend / You too can have a lovely romance / Love stay in my heart / We three / Until you fall in love / Where's my love / I want to be in Dixie / This is no laughing matter / When the sun comes out / Our love affair / I can't love you anymore / I'll always love you / I'd know you anywhere / I guess I'll have to dream the rest / I'm sending my blessing / Ragtime cowboy Joe / Never a day goes by / Walkin' by the river
CD _______________ RAJCD 849
Empress / Jan '97 / Koch

Carlin, Bob

BANGING AND SAWING
Too young to marry / Walk along John / Ninety degrees / Ora Lee / Far in the mountain / Geese honking / Old sledge / Ten yards of calico / Paddy on the turnpike / Indian on a stump / Hosses in the cane-break / Cuttin' at the Point / Grasshopper sitting on a sweet potato vine / Chinese breakdown / Cider / Back step Cindy / Farewell Trion / Black snake bit me on the toe / Little boy, little boy / Big footed man in the sandy lot / Pretty Polly Ann / Spring creek gal / Old bunch of keys / Cherokee shuffle
CD _______________ ROUCD 0197
Rounder / Oct '96 / ADA / CM / Direct

FUN OF OPEN DISCUSSION (Carlin, Bob & John Hartford)
CD _______________ ROUCD 0320
Rounder / Apr '95 / ADA / CM / Direct

Carlisle, Belinda

BELINDA
Mad about you / I need a disguise / Since you're gone / I feel the magic / I never wanted a rich man / Band of gold / Gotta get to you / From the heart / Shot in the dark / Stuff and nonsense
CD _______________ IRLD 19002
IRS/MCA / Apr '92 / BMG

BEST OF BELINDA VOL.1, THE
Heaven is a place on Earth / Same thing / Circle in the sand / Leave a light on for me / Little black book / Summer rain / Vision of you / I get weak / La luna / I plead insanity / World without you / Do you feel like I feel / Half the world / Runaway horses
CD _______________ BELCD 1
Offside / Sep '92 / EMI

HEAVEN ON EARTH
Heaven is a place on Earth / Circle in the sand / I feel free / Should I let you in / World without you / I get weak / We can change / Fool for love / Nobody owns me / Love never dies
CD _______________ CDV 2496
Virgin / Dec '87 / EMI

LIVE YOUR LIFE BE FREE
Live your life be free / Do you feel like I feel / Half the world / You came out of nowhere / You're nothing without me / I plead insanity / Emotional highway / Little black book / Love revolution / World of love / Loneliness game
CD _______________ CDV 2680
Virgin / Oct '91 / EMI

REAL
Goodbye day / It's too real (big scary animal) / Too much water / Lay down your arms / Where love hides / One with you / Wrap my arms / Tell me / Windows of the world / Here comes my baby
CD _______________ CDVIP 165
Virgin VIP / Oct '96 / EMI

RUNAWAY HORSES
Leave a light on for me / Runaway horses / Vision of you / Summer rain / La luna / Same thing / Deep deep ocean / Valentine / Whatever it takes / Shades of Michaelangelo
CD _______________ CDV 2599
Virgin / Oct '89 / EMI

WOMAN AND A MAN, A
In too deep / California / Remember September / Listen to love / Always breaking my heart / Love doesn't live here / He goes on / Kneel at your feet / Love in the key of C / My heart goes out to you
CD _______________ CDCHR 6115
Chrysalis / Sep '96 / EMI

Carlisle, Cliff

BLUES YODELER AND STEEL GUITAR WIZARD
Memphis yodel / No Daddy blues / Hobo blues / Columbus stockade blues / Shanghai rooster yodel / I don't mind / High steppin' Mama / It ain't no fault of mine / That nasty swing / Get her by the tail on the down hill grade / My lovin' Kathleen / Wild cat woman and a tom cat man / You'll miss me when I'm gone / Rambling yodeler / When the evening sun goes down / Handsome blues / My rockin' Mama / Payday flight / My travellin' night / Trouble minded blues / Pan-American blues / I'm saving Saturday night for you / Footprints in the snow / Black Jack David
CD _______________ ARHCD 7039
Arhoolie / Nov '96 / ADA / Cadillac / Direct

Carlisle, Una Mae

UNA MAE CARLISLE & SAVANNAH CHURCHILL 1944 (Carlisle, Una Mae & Savannah Churchill)
T'ain't yours / Without you baby / I'm a good good woman / Ain't nothin' much / I like it 'cause I love it / You gotta take your time / He's the best little Yankee to me / I speak so much about you / Teasin' me / You and your heart of stone / You're gonna change your mind / Rest of my life: *Carlisle, Una Mae* / He's commander in chief of my heart / Two faced man / Tell me your blues / Fat meat is good meat: *Churchill, Savannah* / That glory day: *Carlisle, Una Mae* / Crying need for you: *Carlisle, Una Mae* / I carry the torch for you: *Carlisle, Una Mae* / Behavin' myself for you: *Carlisle, Una Mae*
CD _______________ HQCD 19
Harlequin / Jun '94 / Hot Shot / Jazz Music / Swift / Wellard

Carlo & The Belmonts

CARLO AND THE BELMONTS
We belong together: *Belmonts* / Such a long way: *Belmonts* / Santa Margherita: *Belmonts* / My foolish heart: *Belmonts* / Teenage Clementine: *Belmonts* / Little orphan girl: *Carlo* / Five minutes more: *Carlo* / Write me a letter: *Carlo* / Brenda the great pretender: *Carlo* / Ring-a-ling: *Carlo* / Baby doll: *Carlo* / Mairzy doats and dozy doats: *Carlo* / Story of love: *Carlo* / Kansas City: *Carlo*
CD _______________ CHCHD 251
Ace / Jun '91 / Pinnacle

Carlotti, Jean-Marie

PACHIQUELI VEN DE NEUCH (PROVENCE)
CD _______________ Y225034
Silex / Jun '93 / ADA / Harmonia Mundi

Carlton, Larry

GIFT, THE
Ridin' the treasure / Things we said today / Goin' nowhere / Gift / Shop 'til you drop / Pammie dear / Osaka cool / My old town / Mourning dove / Buddy
CD _______________ GRP 98542
GRP / Oct '96 / New Note/BMG

KID GLOVES
Kid gloves / Preacher / Michele's whistle / Oui oui si / Heart to heart / Just my imagination / Where be Mosada / Farm jazz / Terry T / If I could I would
CD _______________ GRP 96832
GRP / Aug '92 / New Note/BMG

RENEGADE GENTLEMAN
Crazy Mama / RCM / Sleep medicine / Cold day in hell / Anthem / Amen AC / Never say naw / Farm jazz / Nothin' comes / Bogner / Red hot poker / I gotta right
CD _______________ GRP 97442
GRP / Aug '93 / New Note/BMG

SINGING/PLAYING
CD _______________ EDCD 439
Edsel / Oct '95 / Pinnacle

SLEEPWALK
Last nite / Blues bird / Song for Katie / Frenchman's flat / Upper kern / 10 p.m. / You gotta get it while you can / Sleepwalk
CD _______________ GRP 01262
GRP / Aug '92 / New Note/BMG

WITH A LITTLE HELP FROM MY FRIENDS
CD _______________ EDCD 480
Edsel / Jun '96 / Pinnacle

Carman, Jenks Tex

HILLBILLY HULA
Hillbilly hula / Another good dream gone wrong / Hilo march / Gosh I miss you all the time / Locust hill rag / Calssons go rolling along / Samoa stomp / Dixie cannonball / Sweet luwanna / My lonely heart and I / Indian polka / I'm a poor lonesome fellow / Don't feel sorry for me / My trusting heart / Gonna stay right here / (I've recieved) A penny postcard / Ten thousand miles (Away from home) / I could love you darling / You tell her, I s-t-u-t-t-e-r / Blue memories
CD _______________ BCD 15574
Bear Family / Mar '92 / Direct / Rollercoaster / Swift

Carmel

COLLECTED (A Collection Of Work 1983-1990)
And I take it for granted / Sally / It's all in the game / I'm not afraid of you / Every little bit / I have fallen in love (Je suis tombee amoureuse) / More, more, more / You can have him / Bad day / J'oublierai ton nom / I'm over you
CD _______________ 8282192
London / May '92 / PolyGram

LIVE IN PARIS
Bad day / I'm not afraid / Stand together / Sticks and stones / Sugar you're sweet / It's all in the game / More more more / Lullaby / Rekindle your youth / If birds can fly / Sally / Tracks of my tears
CD _______________ 120752
Musidisc UK / Mar '97 / Grapevine/ PolyGram

Carmello, Janusz

PORTRAIT
When the saints go marching in / Some time ago / Fun run / Song for Babyshka / Tiny capers / Li'l darlin' / Joy spring / Day-dream / Lover man
CD _______________ HEPCD 2044
Hep / Sep '90 / Cadillac / Jazz Music / New Note/Pinnacle / Wellard

Carmen, Eric

GREATEST HITS
All by myself / Never gonna fall in love again / That's rock'n'roll / Hey Deanie / Hungry eyes / Make me lose control / Change of heart / She did it / It hurts too much / No hard feelings / Boats against the current
CD _______________ 258999
Arista / Jun '96 / BMG

Carmen, Phil

BACK FROM LA LIVE
CD _______________ HYCD 200148
Hypertension / Mar '95 / ADA / CM / Direct / Total/BMG

Carmichael's Ceilidh

CARMICHAEL'S CEILIDH
CD _______________ CDLOC 1081
Lochshore / Jul '94 / ADA / Direct / Duncans

Carmichael, Anita

ANITA CARMICHAEL
Lying in the sun / Come with me/Love me / Footloose / Shibuya sunset / Take your time / Move it / Destination Bali / Soothe me / One in a million / Walk to groove
CD _______________ LIP 89442
Lipstick / Oct '96 / Vital/SAM

COME WITH ME
CD _______________ SAXCD 004
Saxology / May '94 / Cadillac / Harmonia Mundi

Carmichael, Hoagy

ART VOCAL 1927-1942
CD _______________ 700182
Art Vocal / Sep '96 / Discovery

HOAGY CARMICHAEL 1927-1944
Washboard blues / Stardust / Rockin' chair / Georgia / Lazy river / Lazybones / Moon country / Two sleepy people / Little old lady
CD _______________ CBC 1011
Timeless Jazz / Jun '93 / New Note/ Pinnacle

HOAGY CARMICHAEL 1951
CD _______________ FLYCD 912
Flyright / Oct '92 / Hot Shot / Jazz Music / Wellard

HOAGY CARMICHAEL SONGBOOK (Various Artists)
Stardust: *Cole, Nat 'King'* / Washboard blues: *Dorsey, Tommy* / Rockin' chair: *Armstrong, Louis* / Little old lady: *Hutchinson, Leslie 'Hutch'* / Lamplighter's serenade: *Miller, Glenn Orchestra* / Lazybones: *Carmichael, Hoagy* / Georgia on my mind: *Jones, Tom* / Skylark: *Shore, Dinah* / Old music master: *Mercer, Johnny* / Nearness of you: *Fitzgerald, Ella* / Old buttermilk sky: *Four Freshmen* / I should have known you years ago: *Davis, Beryl* / One morning in May: *Monro, Matt* / Blue orchids: *Vaughan, Sarah* / I get along without you very well: *Newley, Anthony* / In the cool, cool, cool of the evening: *Mancini, Henry* / Doctor, lawyer, indian chief: *Hutton, Betty* / Judy: *Laine, Frankie* / My resistance is low: *Sarstedt, Robin* / When love goes wrong: *Whiting, Margaret & Jimmy Wakely* / Memphis in June: *Skellern, Peter* / Ivy: *Stafford, Jo* / How little it matters, how little we know: *Monro, Matt*
CD _______________ VSOPCD 123
Connoisseur Collection / Oct '88 / Pinnacle

HOAGY CARMICHAEL VOL.1
CD _______________ HOAGY 1
JSP / Jul '94 / ADA / Cadillac / Direct / Hot Shot / Target/BMG

JAZZ PORTRAIT
CD _______________ CD 14585
Complete / Nov '95 / THE

MR. MUSIC MASTER
Mr. Music Master / Stardust / Rockin' chair / Moon country / Riverboat shuffle / Two sleepy people / Judy / Skylark / Moonburn / Hong Kong blues / One morning in May / Lazy river / I get along without you very well / Blue orchids / Little old lady / Georgia on my mind / Sing me a swing song / Lazybones / Washboard blues / Snowball / Small fry / Sing it way down low
CD _______________ PASTCD 7004
Flapper / Mar '93 / Pinnacle

STARDUST (1927-1960)
CD _______________ CD 53192
Giants Of Jazz / May '95 / Cadillac / Jazz Music / Target/BMG

STARDUST
Darktown strutters ball / Hong kong blues / Old music master / Casanova cricket / Rockin' chair / I may be wrong (but I think you're wonderful) / Memphis in June / Who killed 'er (who killed the black widder) / Georgia on my mind / Huggin' and chakin' / Don't forget to say no baby / Old piano roll blues / Doctor, lawyer, indian, chief / For every man there's a woman / Old buttermilk

sky / Shh the old man's sleeping / Riverboat shuffle / Put yourself in my place baby / Old man Harlem / Tune for humming / My resistance is low / Monkey song / Stardust
CD _______________ 3035900052
Essential Gold / Apr '96 / Carlton

Carmichael, John

MORE CARMICHAEL'S CEILIDH
CD _______________ CDLOC 1095
Lochshore / Aug '96 / ADA / Direct / Duncans

Carmona, Juan

BORBOREO
CD _______________ ED 13055
L'Empreinte Digitale / May '96 / ADA / Harmonia Mundi

FALLA LORCA (Carmona, Juan & Francoise Atlan)
Anda laleo / El pano moruno / Asturiana / Nana del caballo grande / Los cuatro muleros / La Tarara / Nana del carino / Zorongo / Las tres hojas / Romance de Don Boyso / Los mozos de Monleon / El Vito / Los pelegrinitos / Nana / Sevillana del siglo XVIII / Los reyes de la baraja / Las morillas de Jaen / El cafe de Chinitas / Nana de Sevilla
CD _______________ ED 13062
L'Empreinte Digitale / May '97 / ADA / Harmonia Mundi

Carnage

DARK RECOLLECTIONS
CD _______________ NECRO 3 CD
Necrosis / Dec '90 / Vital

Carnahan, Danny

CUT & RUN (Carnahan, Danny & Robin Petrie)
CD _______________ FLE 1006CD
Fledg'ling / Jun '94 / ADA / CM / Direct

Carne, Jean

LOVE LESSONS
Don't stop doin' whatcha doin' / Make love / Good thing goin' on / So I can love you / Have I told you that I love you / No one does it better / Fallin' for you / It's not for me to say / Misty / Someone to watch over me
CD _______________ XECD 6
Expansion / Dec '95 / 3mv/Sony

Carnegie Hall Jazz Band

CARNEGIE HALL JAZZ BAND
In the mood / It never entered my mind / Shiny stockings / Giant steps / Frame for the blues / Sing sing sing / Getting sentimental over you / South Rampart Street parade
CD _______________ CDP 8367282
Blue Note / Jun '96 / EMI

Carneiro, Nando

VIOLAO
Violao / Charada / Poromim / Juliana / As gralhas / GRES luxo artezanal / O compones / Liza
CD _______________ 8492122
Carmo / May '91 / New Note/Pinnacle

Carnes, Kim

BETTE DAVIS EYES
Bette Davis eyes / Divided hearts / Invisible hands / Mistaken identity / Abadabadango / More love / Bon voyage / You make my heart beat faster / Cry like a baby / Does it make you remember / I pretend / Young love / Invitation to dance / Crazy in the night
CD _______________ DC 867252
Disky / Nov '96 / Disky / THE

MISTAKEN IDENTITY
Bette Davis eyes / Hit and run / Mistaken identity / When I'm away from you / Draw of the cards / Break the rules tonite / Still hold on / Don't call it love / Miss you tonite / My old pals
CD _______________ MUSCD 507
MCI Original Masters / Nov '94 / Disc / THE

SWEET LOVE SONG OF MY SOUL
Sweet love song of my soul / Everything has got to be free / Do you want to dance / I won't call you back / To love / To love somebody / Fell in love with a poet / One more river to cross / You can do it to me anytime / Rest on me
CD _______________ CDTB 084
Thunderbolt / '89 / TKO Magnum

Carnivore

CARNIVORE
Predator / Male supremacy / Legion of doom / Thermonuclear warrior / Carnivore / Armageddon / God is dead / World wars III and IV
CD _______________ RR 97542
Roadrunner / Apr '86 / PolyGram

RETALIATION
CD _______________ RR 95972
Roadrunner / Apr '89 / PolyGram

Carol, Rene

HAFENMARIE
Hafenmarie / Ein vagabundenherz / Gruss mir die sterne von Montana / Solang es liebe gibt / Solang du freunde hast / Der rote Wien / Auf der insel bell'amore / Das macht der sonnenschein / Jonny komm wieder / Strassenmusikant / Ich hab nur dich / Prinzessin Sonnenschein / Im hafen von San Remo / Carina / Bianca rosa / Ich mocht' mit dir mal ein Marchen erleben / Die schonen marchen / Sieben meere und kein kuss / Tief in deinen augen / Unter Palmen und Cypressen / Du darfst nicht weinen / Schones madchen lass' das weinen / Schenk' mir deine freundschaft / Sonne, wind und sterne / Wo meine sterne Bundeswehr parodie / Bildzeitungs parodie
CD _______________ BCD 16137
Bear Family / Jan '97 / Direct / Rollercoaster / Swift

KEIN LAND KANN SCHONER SEIN
Kein land kann schoner sein / Ich hab' ein herz gefunden / Ich muss dich wiedersehn / Nicoletta / Das lied der Geigen / Der goldschmied von Toledo / Lass mich nicht zu lang allein / Wann kommst du wieder nach hause / Marchenland Hawaii / Serenata di Napoli / Sieben nachte blieb der Jos, in Santa Fe / Ich mochte stundenlang in deine augen sehn / Am blauen Gardasee (Angeli) / Die Mondscheinserenade / Ich will immer an dich denken / Romanita / Meine Heimat ist die liebe / Vergiss nicht, dass ich bei dir bin / Schau zu den sternen der liebe / An wen denkst du / Verlieb dich in mich / Leb' wohl, Marie / Viola-Violetta / Musikant / Chicita May / Du braune Madonna der Sudsee / Das schiff deine Sehnsucht / Mitten im Meer / Wo ist mein Zuhause
CD _______________ BCD 15985
Bear Family / May '96 / Direct / Rollercoaster / Swift

Caron, Alain

RHYTHM 'N' JAZZ
Bump / Fat cat / District 6 / Slam the clown / Little Miss March / I C U / Cherokee drive / Flight of the bebop bee / Donna Lee / Intuitions
CD _______________ JMS 186782
JMS / Nov '95 / New Note/BMG

Carousel

ABCDEFGHIJKLMNOPQRSTUVWXYZ
CD _______________ MASKCD 050
Vinyl Japan / Feb '95 / Plastic Head / Vinyl Japan

Carpathian Forest

THROUGH CHASMS, CAVES
CD _______________ AV 011
Avant Garde / Jul '95 / Plastic Head / RTM/Disc

Carpathian Full Moon

SERENADES IN BLOOD
CD _______________ AV 006
Avant Garde / Sep '94 / Plastic Head / RTM/Disc

Carpendale, Howard

HELLO AGAIN
Hello again / Du lachst nicht mehr / Schade / (Sittin' on the) dock of the bay / Liebe von gestern / Bitte nenn' mich immer daddy / Ghandi / Sandy river / Augen wie asphalt / Joshua fit the battle of Jericho / Hello how are you / Wie du es willst / Happy birthday rock 'n' roll / Verloscht dann das licht
CD _______________ DC 875422
Disky / Mar '97 / Disky / THE

Carpenter, Mary-Chapin

COME ON, COME ON
Hard way / He thinks he'll keep her / Rhythm of the blues / I feel lucky / Bug / Not too much to ask / Passionate kisses / Only a dream / I am a town / Walking through fire / I take my chances / Come on come on
CD _______________ 4718982
Columbia / Feb '97 / Sony

HOMETOWN GIRL
Lot like me / Other streets and other towns / Hometown girl / Downtown train / Family hands / Road is just a road / Come on home / Waltz / Just because / Heroes and heroines
CD _______________ 4739152
Columbia / Jun '93 / Sony
CD _______________ 4879322
Columbia / Jul '97 / Sony

PLACE IN THE WORLD, A
Keeping the faith / Hero in your own hometown / I can see it now / I want to be your girlfriend / Let me into your heart / What if we went to Italy / That's real / Ideas are like stars / Naked to the eye / Sudden gift of fate / Better to dream of you / Place in the world
CD _______________ 4851822
Columbia / Oct '96 / Sony

SHOOTING STRAIGHT IN THE DARK
Going out tonight / Right now / More things change / When she's gone / Middle ground / Can't take love for granted / Down at the twist and shout / When Halley came to Jackson / What you didn't say / You win again / Moon and St Christopher
CD _______________ 4674682
Columbia / Sep '96 / Sony

STATE OF THE HEART
How do / Something of a dreamer / Never had it so good / Read my lips / This shirt / Quittin' time / Down in Mary's land / Goodbye again / Too tired / Slow country dance / It don't bring you
CD _______________ 4666912
Columbia / Apr '90 / Sony

STONES IN THE ROAD
Why walk when you can fly / House of cards / Stones in the road / Keeper for every flame / Tender when I want to be / Shut up and kiss me / Last word / End of my private days / John Doe No.24 / Jubilee / Outside looking in / Where time stands still / This is love
CD _______________ 4776792
Columbia / Apr '95 / Sony

Carpenters

CARPENTERS
Rainy days and Mondays / Saturday / Let me be the one / (A place to) hideaway / For all we know / Superstar / Druscilla penny / One love / Bacharach and David medley / Sometimes
CD _______________ 5500632
Spectrum / May '93 / PolyGram

CARPENTERS PERFORMED ON PANPIPES, THE (Various Artists)
We've only just begun / For all we know / Rainy days and mondays / Those good old dreams / Look to your dreams / I need to be in love / Please Mr Postman / Top of the world / Only yesterday / Sing / Superstar / Now / I just fall in love again / Yesterday once more / Close to you
CD _______________ SUMCD 4083
Summit / Nov '96 / Sound & Media

CARPENTERS, THE
CD _______________ HM 004
Harmony / Jun '97 / TKO Magnum

CHRISTMAS COLLECTION (2CD Set)
O come o come Emmanuel / Overture / Christmas waltz / Sleigh ride / It's Christmas time/Sleep well little children / Have yourself a merry Christmas / Santa Claus is comin' to town / Christmas song / Silent night / Jingle bells / First snowfall/Let it snow / Carol of the bells / Merry Christmas darling / I'll be home for Christmas / Christ is born / Winter wonderland/Silver bells/ White Christmas / Ave Maria / It came upon a Midnight clear / Overture / Old fashioned Christmas / O Holy night / (There's no place like) home for the holidays / Medley / Little altar boy / Do you hear what I hear / My favourite things / He came here for me / Santa Claus is comin' to town / What are you doin' New Year's eve / Nutcracker / I heard the bells on Christmas day
CD Set _______________ 5406032
A&M / Nov '96 / PolyGram

CHRISTMAS PORTRAIT
O come, o come Emmanuel / Overture / Christmas waltz / Sleigh ride / It's Christmas time / Sleep well little children / Have yourself a merry little Christmas / Santa Claus is coming to town / Christmas song / Silent night / Jingle bells / First snowfall / Merry Christmas darling / I'll be home for Christmas
CD _______________ CDMID 147
A&M / Oct '92 / PolyGram

CLOSE TO YOU
We've only just begun / Love is surrender / Maybe it's you / Reason to believe / Help / Close to you / Baby it's you / I'll never fall in love again / Crescent moon / Mr. Guder / I kept on loving you / Another song
CD _______________ CDMID 138
A&M / Oct '92 / PolyGram

FROM THE TOP (4CD Set)
CD Set _______________ 3968752
A&M / Oct '91 / PolyGram

HORIZON
Aurora / Only yesterday / Desperado / Please Mr. Postman / I can dream, can't I / Solitaire / Happy / Goodbye and I love you (I'm caught between) / Love me for what I am / Eventide
CD _______________ CDMID 141
A&M / Oct '92 / PolyGram

IF I WERE A CARPENTER (A Tribute To The Carpenters) (Various Artists)
Goodbye to love: *American Music Club* / Top of the world: *Shonen Knife* / Superstar: *Sonic Youth* / Close to you: *Cranberries* / For all we know: *Bettie Serveert* / It's going to take some time: *Dishwalla* / Solitaire: *Crow, Sheryl* / Hurting each other: *Napolitano, Johnette & Marc Moreland* / Yesterday once more: *Redd Kross* / Calling occupants of interplanetary craft: *Babes In Toyland* / Rainy days and Mondays: *Cracker* / Let me be the one: *Sweet, Matthew* / Bless the beasts and children: *4 Non Blondes* / We've only just begun: *Grant Lee Buffalo*
CD _______________ 5402582
A&M / Sep '94 / PolyGram

INTERPRETATIONS (A 25th Anniversary Celebration)
Without a song / Sing / Bless the beasts and children / When I fall in love / From this moment on / Tryin' to get the feeling again / When it's gone / Where do I go from here / Desperado / Superstar / Rainy days and Mondays / Ticket to ride / If I had you / Please Mr. Postman / We've only just begun / Calling occupants of interplanetary craft / Little girl blue / You're the one / Close to you
CD _______________ 5402512
A&M / Oct '94 / PolyGram

KAREN CARPENTER (Carpenter, Karen)
Lovelines / All because of you / If I had you / Making love in the afternoon / If we try / Remember when lovin' took all night / Still in love with you / My body keeps changing my mind / Make believe it's your first time / Guess I just lost my head / Still crazy after all these years / Last one singin' the blues
CD _______________ 5405882
A&M / Nov '96 / PolyGram

LOVELINES
Lovelines / Where do I go from here / Uninvited guest / If we try / When I fall in love / Kiss me the way you did last night / Remember when lovin' took all night / You're the one / Honolulu City lights / Slow dance / If I had you / Little girl blue
CD _______________ CDMID 148
A&M / Oct '92 / PolyGram

NOW AND THEN
Sing / This masquerade / Heather / Jambalaya / I can't make music / Yesterday once more / Fun, fun, fun / End of the world / Da doo ron ron / Dead man's curve / Johnny angel / Night has a thousand eyes / Our day will come / One fine day
CD _______________ CDMID 140
A&M / Oct '92 / PolyGram

ONLY YESTERDAY (Richard & Karen Carpenter's Greatest Hits)
Yesterday once more / Superstar (remix) / Rainy days and mondays / Top of the world / Ticket to ride / Goodbye to love (remix) / This masquerade / Hurting each other / Solitaire / We've only just begun / Those good old dreams / Please Mr. Postman / I won't last a day without you / Touch me when we're dancing / Jambalaya / For all we know / All you get from love is a love song / Close to you / Only yesterday / Calling occupants of interplanetary craft
CD _______________ CDA 1990
A&M / Mar '90 / PolyGram

PASSAGE
B'wana she no home / All you get from love is a love song / I just fell in love again / On the balcony of the Casa Rosada / Don't cry for me Argentina / Sweet sweet smile / Two sides / Man smart, woman smarter / Calling occupants of interplanetary craft
CD _______________ CDMID 143
A&M / Oct '92 / PolyGram

REFLECTIONS
I need to be in love / I just fall in love again / Baby it's you / Can't smile without you / Beechwood 45789 / Eve / All of my life / Reason to believe / Your baby doesn't love you anymore / Maybe it's you / Ticket to ride / Sweet sweet smile / Song for you / Because we are in love (The wedding song)
CD _______________ 5515932
Spectrum / Nov '95 / PolyGram

SINGLES 1969-73, THE
We've only just begun / Top of the world / Ticket to ride / Superstar / Rainy days and Mondays / Goodbye to love / Yesterday once more / It's going to take some time / Sing / For all we know / Hurting each other / Close to you
CD _______________ CDA 63601
A&M / Jun '84 / PolyGram

SINGLES 1974-1978, THE
Sweet sweet smile / Jambalaya / Can't smile without you / I won't last a day without you / All you get from love is a love song / Only yesterday / Solitaire / Please Mr. Postman / I need to be in love / Happy / There's a kind of hush / Calling occupants of interplanetary craft
CD _______________ CDA 19748
A&M / '88 / PolyGram

SONG FOR YOU, A
Song for you / Top of the world / Hurting each other / It's going to take some time / Goodbye to love / Intermission / Bless the beasts and children / Flat baroque / Piano picker / I won't last a day without you / Crystal lullaby / Road ode
CD _______________ CDMID 139
A&M / Oct '92 / PolyGram

TICKET TO RIDE
Invocation / Your wonderful parade / Someday / Get together / All of my life / Turn away / Ticket to ride / Don't be afraid / What's the use / All I can do / Eve / Nowadays Clancy can't even sing / Benediction
CD _______________ CDMID 137
A&M / Oct '92 / PolyGram

VOICE OF THE HEART
Now / Sailing on the tide / Make believe it's your first time / Two lives / At the end of a song / Ordinary fool / Your baby doesn't love you anymore / Look to your dreams
CD ____ **CDMID 144**
A&M / Oct '92 / PolyGram

Carpetbaggers

SIN NOW...PRAY LATER
CD ____ **HCD 8071**
Hightone / May '96 / ADA / Koch

Carpettes

BEST OF THE CARPETTES, THE
CD ____ **CDPUNK 80**
Anagram / Jun '96 / Cargo / Pinnacle

Carr, Ian

SOUNDS AND SWEET AIRS (Carr, Ian & John Taylor)
CD ____ **130642**
Celestial Harmonies / May '96 / ADA / Select

Carr, James

ESSENTIAL JAMES CARR, THE
CD ____ **RE 2060**
Razor & Tie / Sep '96 / Koch

SOUL SURVIVOR
Soul survivor / Man worth knowing / Put love first / I can't leave your love alone / Things a woman need / Daydreaming / All because of your love / I'm into something / Memphis after midnight / That's how strong a woman's love is
CD ____ **CDCH 487**
Ace / Oct '93 / Pinnacle

TAKE ME TO THE LIMIT
Take me to the limit / Sugar shock / Love attack / You gotta love your woman / High on your love / She's already gone / Our garden of Eden / I can't leave your love alone / What's a little love between friends / Lack of attention
CD ____ **CDCH 310**
Ace / Jan '91 / Pinnacle

Carr, Leroy

BLACK BOY SHINE 1934-1937
CD ____ **DOCD 5465**
Document / Jul '96 / ADA / Hot Shot / Jazz Music

DON'T CRY WHEN I'M GONE
Barrelhouse woman / Alabama women blues / You left me crying / 11.29 blues / How long has that evening train been gone / Suicide blues / Sloppy drunk blues / 'Fore day rider / Rocks in my bed
CD ____ **PYCD 07**
Magpie / Apr '90 / Hot Shot / Jazz Music

HURRY DOWN SUNSHINE
CD ____ **IGOCD 2016**
Indigo / Mar '95 / ADA / Direct

NAPTOWN BLUES
CD ____ **ALB 1011CD**
Aldabra / Mar '94 / CM / RTM/Disc

PIANO BLUES 1929-1935
CD ____ **PYCD 17**
Magpie / Nov '92 / Hot Shot / Jazz Music

REMAINING TITLES, THE (Carr, Leroy & Scrapper Blackwell)
CD ____ **SOB 035382**
Story Of The Blues / Oct '92 / ADA / Koch

Carr, Mike

GOOD TIMES AND THE BLUES
Good times / Blues for Mr. B / One that got away / Harlem waltz / Battery blues / Mexican samba / Freedom song / Viva Victor / Baron of bop / Theme for Cliff
CD ____ **CGCD 191**
Cargo Gold / Apr '96 / Wellard

Carr, Romey

ROBERT BURNS, A WOMAN'S MAN
CD ____ **ALBACD 02**
Alba / Jul '96 / Pinnacle

WOMAN KNOWS, A
Bonny banks of Loch Lomond / Nae luck about the house / Ae fond kiss / Wee willie winkie / My love is like a red red rose / Eriskay love lilt / Whistle and I'll come to you my lad / Queen's Marines / Charlie is my darling / Amazing grace (the lord is my shepherd) / Ca' the yowes / Ye banks and brae's o'bonnie doon / In praise of Islay / Cockle gatherer / Hush-a-bye-baby / Bonnie wee thing / Wee Cooper o' Fife / I left my dearie lying here / Peat-fire flame / Auld lang syne
CD ____ **ALBACD 01**
Alba / Sep '95 / Pinnacle

Carr, Sister Wynona

DRAGNET FOR JESUS
Each day / Lord Jesus / I want to go to heaven and rest / I'm a pilgrim traveller / I heard the news (Jesus is coming again) / Our father / He said he would / I see Jesus / Don't miss that train / I heard mother pray one day / Good old way / See his blessed face / Did he die in vain / I know someday God's gonna call me / Conversation with Jesus / Ball game / Letter to heaven / In a little while / Untitled instrumental / Operator, operator / Dragnet for Jesus / Fifteen rounds for Jesus / Nobody but Jesus / Just a few more days
CD ____ **CDCHD 411**
Ace / Nov '93 / Pinnacle

JUMP JACK JUMP
Jump Jack jump / Till the well runs dry / Boppity bop (boogity boog) / Should I ever love again / I'm mad at you / Old fashioned love / Hurt me / It's raining outside / Nursery rhyme rock / Ding dong daddy / Someday, somewhere, somehow / Act right / What do you know about love / Now that I'm free / Heartbreak melody / Please Mr. Jailer / Weatherman / If these walls could speak / Touch and go / If I pray / Finders keepers / Things you do to me / How many times / Give me your hand to hold
CD ____ **CDCHD 513**
Ace / Jan '94 / Pinnacle

Carr, Vikki

IT MUST BE HIM/THE WAY OF TODAY
It must be him / None but the lonely heart / Her little heart went to loveland / Laila Ladala (Reza) / Look again / Cuana callente el sol / Hoe does the wine taste / Should I follow / May I come in / Toys / San Francisco / Can I trust you (Lot Ti Daro Di Piu) / Anyone who had a heart / My prayer / My heart reminds me / You don't have to say you love me / Nowhere man / If you love me, really love me / Strangers in the night / I will wait for you / My world is empty without you / I hear a rhapsody
CD ____ **CTMCD 102**
EMI / Nov '96 / EMI

UNFORGETTABLE, THE
He's a rebel / Mirror / Only love can break a heart / Bye bye blackbird / How does the wine taste / Unforgettable / It must be him / With pen in hand / Alfie / Can't take my eyes off you / By the time I get to Phoenix / Never my love / All my love / Singing my song / Sunday morning coming down / Yesterday when I was young / Walk away / If you love me (I won't care) / Poor butterfly / Everything I touch turns to tears
CD ____ **CDSL 8255**
Music For Pleasure / Sep '95 / EMI

Carrack, Paul

21 GOOD REASONS
How long: *Ace* / Real feeling: *Ace* / No future in your eyes: *Ace* / You're all that I need: *Ace* / Tempted: *Squeeze* / Do me lover: *Carrack, Paul & Carlene Carter* / Oh how happy: *Carrack, Paul & Carlene Carter* / Rumour / I need you / Always better with you / Little unkind / One good reason / Don't shed a tear / Button off my shirt / When you walk in the room / I live by the groove / Only my heart can tell / Battlefield / Loveless / Silent running: *Mike & The Mechanics* / Living years: *Mike & The Mechanics*
CD ____ **CDCHR 6067**
Chrysalis / Feb '94 / EMI

BLUE VIEWS
Eyes of blue / For once in our lives / No easy way out / Oh oh oh my my my / Only a breath away / Nothing more than a memory / Somewhere in your heart / Love will keep us alive / Always have always will / Don't walk over me / How long
CD ____ **EIRSCD 1075**
IRS/EMI / Jan '96 / EMI
CD ____ **ARKK 10007**
ARKK / May '97 / Greyhound

Carrasco, Joe 'King'

BANDIDO ROCK (Carrasco, Joe 'King' Y Las Coronas)
CD ____ **ROUCD 9012**
Rounder / '88 / ADA / CM / Direct

BORDER TOWN (Carrasco, Joe 'King' & The Crowns)
Escondido / Hola coca cola / Who bought the guns / Are you Amigo / Put me in jail / Mr. Bogota / Walk it like you talk it / Current events (are making me tense) / Cucaraca taco / Baby let's go to Mexico / Vamos a bailar / Tamale baby
CD ____ **ROSE 40CD**
New Rose / '88 / ADA / Direct / Discovery

Carreg Lafar

YSBRYD Y WERIN
CD ____ **SCD 2102**
Sain / Jan '96 / ADA / Direct / Greyhound

Carreras, Jose

BEST OF JOSE CARRERAS, THE
CD ____ **TRTCD 187**
TrueTrax / Jul '96 / THE

BRILLIANT VOICE, THE
CD ____ **MU 5042**
Musketeer / Oct '92 / Disc

CELEBRATION OF CHRISTMAS, A (Carreras, Jose & Natalie Cole/Placido Domingo)
I walked today where Jesus walked / Panis angelicus: *Carreras, Jose* / O joyful children: *Domingo, Placido* / Christmas song, the: *Cole, Natalie* / Ay para navidad / Holly and the ivy: *Cole, Natalie & Jose Carreras* / I'll be home for christmas / Agnus Dei: *Domingo, Placido* / Lord's prayer: *Carreras, Jose* / Winter wonderland: *Cole, Natalie* / Navidad: *Carreras, Jose & Placido Domingo* / White christmas / What child is this / Pero mira como beben los peces en el rio / May each day / Cantique de noel / Amazing grace / Oh, du frochliche / Sleigh ride
CD ____ **0630146402**
Erato / Nov '96 / Warner Music

JOSE CARRERAS SINGS ANDREW LLOYD WEBBER
Memory / Phantom of the opera / Music of the night / You / Pie Jesu / Tell me on a Sunday / Half a moment / There's me / Starlight express / Unexpected song / Love changes everything
CD ____ **2569242**
WEA / Nov '89 / Warner Music

MY ROMANCE
All the things you are / Drinking song / Lippen schweigen / This nearly was mine / Rose Marie / If I loved you / Lover come back to me / Indian love call / Wolgalied / Softly as in a morning sunrise / Deep in your heart dear / Cancion del gitano / Dein ist mein ganzes herz
CD ____ **0630177892**
Erato / Sep '97 / Warner Music

ROMANTICA
CD ____ **PLSCD 117**
Pulse / Apr '96 / BMG

WHITE CHRISTMAS
White Christmas / O come all ye faithful (Adeste fidelis) / Agnus dei / Caro mio ben / Maria / Pieta, Signore / What child is this / Mille cherubini / Pregaria / Panis angelicus / El romanc / Andantino / Silent night
CD ____ **DSHCD 7010**
D-Sharp / Nov '95 / Pinnacle

Carrere, Tia

DREAM
State of grace / I wanna come home with you tonight / Innocent side / I never even told you / Gift of perfect love / Surrender / Love is a cannibal / We need to belong / Our love / Dream a perfect dream
CD ____ **9362453002**
WEA / Oct '93 / Warner Music

Carrick, Brian

1995 BUDE FESTIVAL (Carrick, Brian & The New City Stompers)
CD ____ **PKCD 054**
PEK / Jul '96 / Cadillac / Jazz Music / Wellard

BRIAN CARRICK & HIS HERITAGE STOMPERS
CD ____ **BCD 345**
GHB / Jun '96 / Jazz Music

SPIRIT OF NEW ORLEANS (Carrick, Brian Heritage Hall Stompers)
CD ____ **PKCD 050**
PEK / May '96 / Cadillac / Jazz Music / Wellard

Carrier, Chubby

DANCE ALL NIGHT (Carrier, Chubby & Bayou Swamp Band)
CD ____ **BP 5007CD**
Blind Pig / Mar '94 / ADA / CM / Direct / Hot Shot

WHO STOLE THE HOT SAUCE
CD ____ **BLPCD 5032**
Blind Pig / Sep '96 / ADA / CM / Direct / Hot Shot

Carrier, Roy

AT HIS BEST
CD ____ **ZNCD 1010**
Zane / Nov '95 / Pinnacle

SOULFUL SIDE OF ZYDECO (Carrier, Roy & Joe Walker)
CD ____ **ZNCD 1003**
Zane / Oct '95 / Pinnacle

Carroll, Baikida

DOOR OF THE CAGE
CD ____ **1211232**
Soul Note / Apr '95 / Cadillac / Harmonia Mundi / Wellard

Carroll, Barbara

EVERYTHING I LOVE
You'd be so nice to come home to / Ace in the hole / I wish I could forget you / As long as I live / Song for Griffin / Hundred years from today / Now's the time / Everything I love / Heavenly / That face / Chelsea bridge
CD ____ **DRGCD 91438**
DRG / Dec '95 / Discovery / New Note/ Pinnacle

OLD FRIENDS
CD ____ **ACD 254**
Audiophile / Feb '91 / Jazz Music

THIS HEART OF MINE
Way you look tonight / I wanna be yours / Sweet lilacs / On second thought/Why can't I / Lester leaps in / Some other time / Rain sometimes / Whenever a soft rain falls / It's like reaching for the moon / Never let me go / In some other world / This heart of mine
CD ____ **91416**
DRG / Jul '94 / Discovery / New Note/ Pinnacle

Carroll, Cath

TRUE CRIME MODEL
Easter bunny song / Into day / I know / True crime model / Mississippi factory town / Jimmy's candy / Just once / L'amour c'est ca / Lullaby for a steeplejack / Breathe for me
CD ____ **TB 1672**
Matador / Aug '95 / Vital

Carroll, Dina

ONLY HUMAN
Escaping / Only human / Give me the right / World come between us / Love will always bring you back to me / I didn't mean to hurt you / Living for the weekend / Mind, body & soul / Run to you / Do you think I'm in love / I don't want to talk about it / Perfect year
CD ____ **5340962**
Mercury / Oct '96 / PolyGram

SO CLOSE
Special kind of love / Hold on / This time / Falling / So close / Ain't no man / Express / Heaven sent / You'll never know / Don't be a stranger / Why did I let you go / If I knew you then
CD ____ **5400342**
A&M / Jan '93 / PolyGram

Carroll, Jeanne

TRIBUTE TO WILLIE DIXON (Carroll, Jeanne & C. Christi/Willie Dixon)
CD ____ **BEST 1014CD**
Acoustic Music / Nov '93 / ADA

Carroll, Johnny

ROCK BABY, ROCK IT
Hearts of stone / Why cry / Love is a merry go round / Stingy thing / Crazy little Mama / Sexy ways / Cut out / You two timed me two times too often / You made me love you / Hot rock / Rock'n'roll Ruby / Wild wild women / Corrina, Corrina / Crazy, crazy lovin' / Tryin' to get to you / That's the way I love / I'll wait / Rock baby, rock it / Swing / Bandstand doll / Sugar / Lost without you / Rag mop / Little Otis / Trudy / Run come see / Sally Ann / Run come see / Crazy, crazy lovin' / Wild wild women / You made me love you / Rockin' Maybelle / Sugar baby
CD ____ **BCD 15928**
Bear Family / May '96 / Direct / Rollercoaster / Swift

Carroll, Karen

GOSPEL
Glory glory since I laid my burdens down / I want to be a christian / He's got the whole world in his hands / Peace, be still / Amazing grace / Oh happy day / Walk with me / Jesus is on the mainline / Doxology / When the saints go marching in
CD ____ **HFCD 002**
Hot Fox / Jun '93 / New Note/Pinnacle

HAD MY FUN
CD ____ **DE 680**
Delmark / Dec '95 / ADA / Cadillac / CM / Direct / Hot Shot

Carroll, Kevin

REDEMPTION DAY (Carroll, Kevin & The Sleestacks)
CD ____ **MRCD 0995**
Club De Musique / Jun '96 / Direct

Carroll, Liane

CLEARLY
CD ____ **BRGCD 19**
Bridge / Oct '95 / Grapevine/PolyGram

DOLLY BIRD
CD ____ **JHCD 051**
Ronnie Scott's Jazz House / May '97 / Cadillac / Jazz Music / New Note/Pinnacle / TKO Magnum

Carroll, Liz

FRIEND INDEED, A
CD ____ **SHCD 34013**
Shanachie / Aug '95 / ADA / Greensleeves / Koch

KISS ME KATE (Carroll, Liz & Tommy McGuire)
CD ____ **SHCD 34012**
Shanachie / Dec '95 / ADA / Greensleeves / Koch

LIZ CARROLL
Reel Beatrice/Abbey reel / Out on the road/ Princess Nancy / For Eugene/Gravity hill / Clarke's favourite/Pigeon on the gate / Tune for Mairead and Anna Ni Mhaonaigh / Sock in the hole/Hole in the sock / Mrs. Carroll's Strathspey/Chapter 16 / Helicopters/ Crossing the Delaware / Sister's reel/Wynding the hay / Lacey's jig/Tune for Charles/ Geese in the bog / Par cark/Baiting the hook/Jumping the white nut eater / Greenleaf Strathspey/Setting sun / Wee dollop/ Houseboat / G reel/Merle's tune / Western reel/Road to recovery
CD ______ GLCD 1092
Green Linnet / Feb '91 / ADA / CM / Direct / Highlander / Roots

TRION
CD ______ FF 70586
Flying Fish / Jul '92 / ADA / CM / Direct / Roots

Carroll, Ronnie

ROSES ARE RED (The Ronnie Carroll Story)
Last love / Walk hand in hand / Wisdom of a fool / Around the world / April love / To be loved / Wonder of you / Footsteps / Chain gang / (You've got to) move two mountains / Ring a ding girl / Roses are red (my love) / If only tomorrow (could be like today) / Say wonderful things / Mary Rose / Let's fall in love: *Carroll, Ronnie & Millicent Martin* / Love is a ball: *Carroll, Ronnie & Millicent Martin* / Twelfth of never / Tears and roses / Clinging vine / Dear heart / Without love / Endlessly / House is not a home / My heart cries for you / I'll never fall in love again: *Carroll, Ronnie & Aimi McDonald*
CD ______ GEMCD 004
Diamond / Nov '96 / Pinnacle

Carroll, Toni

CELEBRITY
CD ______ ACD 122
Audiophile / Nov '96 / Jazz Music

Carry Nation

PROTECT AND SURVIVE
CD ______ LF 211CD
Lost & Found / Apr '96 / Plastic Head

Cars

CARS, THE
Good times roll / My best friend's girl / Just what I needed / I'm in touch with your world / Don't cha stop / You're all I've got tonight / Bye bye love / Moving in stereo / All mixed up
CD ______ K 252088
Elektra / Jan '84 / Warner Music

GREATEST HITS
Just what I needed / Since you're gone / You might think / Good time roll / Touch and go / Drive / Tonight she comes / My best friend's girl / Heartbeat city / Let's go / Magic / Shake it up
CD ______ 9604642
Elektra / Nov '85 / Warner Music

HEARTBEAT CITY
Looking for love / Jackie / Not the night / Drive / Shooting for you / Why can't I / Magic / You might think / I do refuse / Stranger eyes / Hello again
CD ______ 9602962
Elektra / Jul '84 / Warner Music

JUST WHAT I NEEDED - ANTHOLOGY (2CD Set)
CD Set ______ 0349735062
Elektra / Jan '96 / Warner Music

Carson, Ernie

ERNIE CARSON & GOOSE HOLLOW GANG
CD ______ BCD 297
GHB / Apr '94 / Jazz Music

OLD BONES (Carson, Ernie & Castle Jazz Band)
CD ______ SOSCD 1283
Stomp Off / Mar '95 / Jazz Music / Wellard

WHER'M I GONNA LIVE (Carson, Ernie & Castle Jazz Band)
CD ______ SOSCD 1277
Stomp Off / Dec '94 / Jazz Music / Wellard

Carson, Lori

WHERE IT GOES
Down here / Waking to the dream of you / You won't fall / Petal / Twisting my words / Where it goes / Through the cracks / Fell into the loneliness / Anyday / Christmas
CD ______ 727872
Restless / Apr '95 / Vital

Carson, Sam

NO SURRENDER (14 Great Loyalist Songs)
Derry's walls / No surrender / Auld orange flute / Green grassy slopes of the Boyne / Lily O / Dolly's brae / Protestant boys / Sash / Battle of Garvagh / Orange and blue / Aghalee heroes / Blackman's dream / Boyne water / Sprigs of Kilrea
CD ______ CDUCD 3
Ulster Music / Apr '97 / ADA / CM / Direct / Duncans / Koch / Ross

Carsten, Mannie

JUST A KISS (Mannie Carsten's Hot Jazz Syndicate)
CD ______ CD 1201
Hep / Oct '94 / Cadillac / Jazz Music / New Note/Pinnacle / Wellard

Carstensen, Dee

REGARDING THE SOUL
Time / Before you / Underneath my skin / Love thing / Angel / What a little love can do / To you from me / Hemingway's shotgun / Stay / This time around / Light
CD ______ 120252
Musidisc UK / Jun '97 / Grapevine/ PolyGram

Carter, Anita

RING OF FIRE
Ring of fire / Fair and tender ladies / Satan's child / Fly pretty swallow / As the sparrow goes / All my trials / Voice of the bayou / Sour grapes / Johnny I hardly knew you / My love / Kentuckian song / Five short years ago / No my love, no farewell / Running back / Take me home / John John John / John Hardy / I never will marry / In the highways / Bury me beneath the willow / Beautiful isle o'er the sea / Wildwood flower
CD ______ BCD 15434
Bear Family / '88 / Direct / Rollercoaster / Swift

Carter, Benny

3-4-5 (The Verve Small Group Sessions)
Little girl blue / June in January / Jeepers creepers / Rosetta / Birth of the blues / When your lover has gone / Moon is low / This love of mine / Moonglow / My one and only love / Our love is here to stay / This can't be love / Tenderly / Unforgettable / Ruby / Moon song / Don't you think / Will you still be mine / We'll be together again
CD ______ 8493952
Verve / Mar '91 / PolyGram

ALL THAT JAZZ - LIVE AT PRINCETON
Introduction / Hackensack / I'm beginning to see the light / Misty / Now's the time / Almost like being in love / When Sunny gets blue / All that jazz / We were in love / Blues walk / All of me
CD ______ 8208412
Limelight / Jun '91 / PolyGram

BENNY CARTER IN EUROPE 1936-1937
Black bottom / Mighty like the blues / Pardon me pretty baby / Just a mood / Royal garden blues / Rambler's rhythm / Lazy afternoon / I ain't got nobody / Waltzin' the blues / When day is done / Bugle call rag / There'll be some changes made / If only I could read your mind / Gin and jive / New street swing / I'll never give in / Skip it / Somebody loves me / Blues in my heart / My buddy / Nightfall / I've got two lips
CD ______ PASTCD 7023
Flapper / Sep '93 / Pinnacle

BENNY CARTER MEETS OSCAR PETERSON
CD ______ CD 2310926
Pablo / Jan '92 / Cadillac / Complete/ Pinnacle

CLASSICS 1929-1933
CD ______ CLASSICS 522
Classics / Apr '90 / Discovery / Jazz Music

CLASSICS 1933-1936
CD ______ CLASSICS 530
Classics / Dec '90 / Discovery / Jazz Music

CLASSICS 1936
CD ______ CLASSICS 541
Classics / Dec '90 / Discovery / Jazz Music

CLASSICS 1937-1939
CD ______ CLASSICS 552
Classics / Dec '90 / Discovery / Jazz Music

CLASSICS 1939-1940
CD ______ CLASSICS 579
Classics / Oct '91 / Discovery / Jazz Music

CLASSICS 1940-1941
CD ______ CLASSICS 631
Classics / Mar '92 / Discovery / Jazz Music

CLASSICS 1943-1946
CD ______ CLASSICS 923
Classics / Apr '97 / Discovery / Jazz Music

COMPLETE RECORDINGS VOL.1 (3CD Set)
Goodbye blues / Cloudy skies / Got another sweetie now / Bugle call rag / Dee blues / Do you believe in love at first sight / Wrap your troubles in dreams (and dream your troubles away) / Tell all your daydreams to me / Swing it / Synthetic love / Six bells stampede / Love you're not the one for me / Blue interlude / I never knew / Once upon a time / Krazy kapers / Devil's holiday / Lonesome nights / Symphony in riffs / Blue Lou / Shoot the works / Dream lullaby / Everybody shuffle / Swingin' at Maida vale / Night fall / Big Ben blues / These foolish things / When day is done / I've got two lips / Just a mood / Swingin' the blues / Scandal in flat / Accent on swing / You understand / If I could only read your mind / I gotta go / When lights are low / Waltzing the blues / Tiger rag / Blue / Some of these days / Gloaming / Poor butterfly / Drop in next time your passing / Man I love / That's how the first song was born / There'll be some changes made / Jingle bells / Royal garden blues / Carry me back to old Virginny / Gin and jive / Nagasaki / There's a small hotel / I'm in the mood for swing / Rambling in C / Black bottom / Rambler's rhythm / New street swing / I'll never give in
CD ______ CDAFS 10223
Affinity / Oct '92 / Cadillac / Jazz Music / Koch

COOKIN' AT CARLOS VOL.1
You'd be so nice to come home to / All the things you are / Key Largo / Just friends / My romance / 'S Wonderful / Time for the blues
CD ______ 8208232
Limelight / Oct '90 / PolyGram
CD ______ MM 5033
Music Masters / Oct '94 / Nimbus

COSMOPOLITE (The Oscar Peterson Verve Sessions)
Gone with the wind / I got it bad and that ain't good / Long ago (and far away) / I've got the world on a string / Street scene / Imagination / Pick yourself up / I get a kick out of you / Laura / That old black magic / Angel eyes / Song is you / Foggy day / You took advantage of me / Poinciana / Prisoner of love / Frenesi / Gone with the wind / I got it bad and that ain't good / Long ago (and far away) / I've got the world on a string
CD ______ 5216732
Verve / Oct '94 / PolyGram

FURTHER DEFINITIONS
Honeysuckle rose / Midnight sun will never set / Crazy rhythm / Blue star / Cotton tail / Body and soul / Cherry / Doozy / Fantastic that's you / Come on back / We were in love / If dreams come true / Prohibido / Rock bottom / Titmouse
CD ______ IMP 12292
Impulse Jazz / Apr '97 / New Note/BMG

GENTLEMAN AND HIS MUSIC, A
Sometimes I'm happy / Blues for George / Things ain't what they used to be / Lover man / Idaho / Kiss from you
CD ______ CCD 4285
Concord Jazz / Jan '87 / New Note/ Pinnacle

GROOVIN' IN LA 1946
CD ______ HEPCD 15
Hep / Nov '92 / Cadillac / Jazz Music / New Note/Pinnacle / Wellard

HARLEM RENAISSANCE - NEW CLASSICS FOR BIG BAND & ORCHESTRA (85th Birthday Celebration/2CD Set) (Carter, Benny Big Band)
Vine Street rumble / Sao Paolo / I can't get started (with you) / Stockhom sweetnin' / Evening star / How high the moon / Tales of the rising sun suite / August moon / Teatime / Song of long ago / Samurai song / Chow chow / Harlem renaissance suite / Lament for Langston / Sugar Hill slow drag / Happy feet / Sunday morning / Happy feet (reprise)
CD Set ______ 8442992
Limelight / Aug '92 / PolyGram

IN RIFFS 1930-1937
Bugle call rag / Everybody shuffle / Shoot the works / Dee blues / Swing it / Nightfall / Bream lullaby / Pardon me pretty baby / Lazy afternoon
CD ______ CDAJA 5704
Living Era / Jan '91 / Select

INTRODUCTION TO BENNY CARTER 1929-1940, AN
CD ______ 4001
Best Of Jazz / Dec '93 / Discovery

JAZZ GIANT
Old fashioned love / I'm coming Virginia / Walkin' thing / Blue Lou / Ain't she sweet / How can you lose / Blues my naughty sweetie gives to me
CD ______ OJCCD 167
Original Jazz Classics / Oct '92 / Complete/ Pinnacle / Jazz Music / Wellard

JAZZ PORTRAIT
CD ______ CD 14583
Complete / Nov '95 / THE

KING, THE
Walkin' thing / My kind of trouble is you / Easy money / Blue star / I still love him so / Green wine / Malibu / Blues in D flat
CD ______ PACD 2310768
Pablo / Mar '94 / Cadillac / Complete/ Pinnacle

LEGENDS
More I see you / I was wrong / Wonderland / Blues in my heart / You are / People time / There is no greater love / Sunset love / Little things that mean so much / Legend / Honeysuckle rose
CD ______ 5186272
Limelight / Mar '93 / PolyGram

LIVE BROADCASTS 1939-1941 (Carter, Benny & His Orchestra)
CD ______ JH 1005
Jazz Hour / Oct '91 / Cadillac / Jazz Music / Target/BMG

MASTERPIECES ARCHIVES
CD ______ 158672
Jazz Archives / Jan '97 / Discovery

MONTREUX 1977 (Carter, Benny Quartet)
CD ______ OJCCD 374
Original Jazz Classics / Nov '95 / Complete/Pinnacle / Jazz Music / Wellard

MY MAN BENNY, MY MAN PHIL (Carter, Benny & Phil Woods)
Reet's neet / Just a mood (II) / Sultry serenade / We were in love / My man Benny / My man Phil / Just a mood / MA blues / People time / I'm just wild about Harry
CD ______ 8208252
Limelight / Feb '91 / PolyGram

NEW JAZZ SOUNDS (2CD Set)
CD Set ______ 5316372
Verve / Jul '96 / PolyGram

NEW YORK NIGHTS
What is this thing called love / Easy money / But beautiful / Just in time / Shadow of your smile / Secret love / When lights are low / Perdido / Green Dolphin Street
CD ______ MM 65154
Music Masters / Mar '97 / Nimbus

OVER THE RAINBOW (Carter, Benny All Star Sax Ensemble)
Blues for lucky lovers / Straight talk / Over the rainbow / Out of nowhere / Gal from Atlanta / Pawnbroker / Easy money / Ain't misbehavin'
CD ______ 8208102
Limelight / Aug '90 / PolyGram

SKYLAND DRIVE & TOWARDS
CD ______ PHONTCD 9305
Phontastic / Apr '94 / Cadillac / Jazz Music / Wellard

SONGBOOK
Only trust your heart / All that jazz / I was wrong / Rain / Cow-cow boogie / Fresh out of love / Speak now / Kiss from you / I see you / We were in love / Key largo / Lonely woman / When lights are low / My kind of trouble is you / You bring out
CD ______ MM 65134
Music Masters / Mar '96 / Nimbus

SWINGIN' THE 1920'S
Thou swell / My blue Heaven / Just imagine / If I could be with you / Sweet Lorraine / Who's sorry now / Laugh clown laugh / All alone / Mary Lou / In a little Spanish town / Someone to watch over me / Monday date
CD ______ OJCCD 339
Original Jazz Classics / Jan '94 / Complete/ Pinnacle / Jazz Music / Wellard

SYMPHONY IN RIFFS
Blue interlude / Blues in my heart / Bugle call rag / Dee blues / Devil's holiday / Dream lullaby / Everybody shuffle / Just a mood / Lazy afternoon / Lonesome nights / Nightfall / Once upon a time / Pardon me pretty baby / Pastoral / Shoot the works / Skip it / Swing it / Swingin' with Mezz / Symphony in riffs / Waltzing the blues / When lights are low / You understand
CD ______ CDAJA 5075
Living Era / '91 / Select

THESE FOOLISH THINGS
Blue interlude / How come you like me like you do / Once upon a time / Devil's holiday / Lonesome nights / Shoot the works / Dream lullaby / Blue Lou / Krazy kapers / Symphony in riffs / I never knew / Music at sunrise / Firebird / Everybody shuffle / Synthetic love / Swingin' at Maida Vale / These foolish things / When day is done / I've got two lips / Swingin' the blues / Just a mood / Big Ben blues / Nightfall
CD ______ GRF 087
Tring / '93 / Tring

Carter, Betty

AT THE VILLAGE VANGUARD
By the bend of the river / Ego / Body and soul / Heart and soul / Surrey with the fringe on top / Girl talk / I didn't know what time it was / All the things you are / I could write a book / Sun died / Please do something
CD ______ 5195812
Verve / Dec '93 / PolyGram

AUDIENCE WITH BETTY CARTER, THE (2CD Set)
Sounds (movin' on) / I think I got it now / Caribbean sun / Trolley song / Everything I have is yours / I'll buy you a star / I could write a book / Can't we talk it over / Either it's love or it isn't / Deep night / Spring can

really hang you up the most / Tight / Fake / So / My favourite things / Open the door
CD 8356842
Verve / Mar '93 / PolyGram

DROPPIN' THINGS
30 years / Stardust/Memories of you / What's the use / Open the door / Droppin' things / I love music / Why music / Dull day (In Chicago)
CD 8439912
Verve / Mar '91 / PolyGram

FEED THE FIRE
CD 5236002
Verve / Oct '94 / PolyGram

I'M YOURS, YOU'RE MINE
CD 5331822
Verve / Nov '96 / PolyGram

IT'S NOT ABOUT THE MELODY
Naima's love song / Stays as sweet as you are / Make him believe / I should care / Once upon a summertime / You go to my head / In the still of the night / When it's sleepy time down South / Love we had yesterday / Dip bag / You're mine you
CD 5138702
Verve / Apr '92 / PolyGram

MEET BETTY CARTER & RAY BRYANT (Carter, Betty & Ray Bryant)
Let's fall in love / Social call / Run away / Frenesi / Moonlight in Vermont / Thou swell / I could write a book / Gone with the wind / Way you look tonight / Tell him I said hello / Can't we be friends / Sneaking around / Old devil moon / Willow weep for me / What is this thing called love / Threesome / No moon at all / Bryant's folly / Get happy
CD 4850992
Sony Jazz / Sep '96 / Sony

ROUND MIDNIGHT
CD Set ATJCD 8008
All That's Jazz / Aug '94 / Jazz Music / THE

Carter, Bo

BANANA IN YOUR FRUIT BASKET
CD YAZCD 1064
Yazoo / Apr '91 / ADA / CM / Koch

BO CARTER VOL.2 (1931-1934)
CD DOCD 5079
Document / Mar '95 / ADA / Hot Shot / Jazz Music

BO CARTER VOL.3 (1934-1936)
CD DOCD 5080
Document / Mar '95 / ADA / Hot Shot / Jazz Music

BO CARTER VOL.4 (1936-1938)
CD DOCD 5081
Document / Mar '95 / ADA / Hot Shot / Jazz Music

BO CARTER VOL.5 (1938-1940)
CD DOCD 5082
Document / Mar '95 / ADA / Hot Shot / Jazz Music

RAREST BO CARTER VOL.1 (1928-1931)
CD DOCD 5078
Document / Mar '95 / ADA / Hot Shot / Jazz Music

Carter, Carlene

ACTS OF TREASON
Love like this / Lucky ones / Little acts of treason / He will be mine / Come here you / Change / Hurricane / Go wild / You'll be the one / All night long / Come here you (reprise)
CD 74321294872
Giant / Aug '95 / BMG

HINDSIGHT 20/20
Sweet meant to be / I fell in love / Every little thing / Unbreakable heart / Come on back / Me and Wildwood Rose / Never together but close sometimes / Cry / Sweetest thing / Baby ride easy / I love you cause I want to / I'm so cool / He will be mine / Hurricane / Change / Trust yourself / One tender night / It's no wonder / Love like this / Do it in a heartbeat
CD 74321360122
Giant / Sep '96 / BMG

I FELL IN LOVE
I fell in love / Come on back / Sweetest thing / My Dixie darling / Goodnight Dallas / One love / Leaving side / Guardian angel / Me and the wildwood rose / You are the one / Easy from now on
CD 7599261392
Reprise / Jan '96 / Warner Music

LITTLE ACTS OF TREASON
CD 74321259892
Giant / Aug '95 / BMG

LITTLE LOVE LETTERS
Little love letter / Every little thing / Wastin' time with you / Unbreakable heart / Sweet meant to be / Nowhere train / Long hard fall / Little love letter / I love you 'cause I want to / World of miracles / First kiss / Hallelujah in my heart / Rain / Heart is right
CD 74321156062
Giant / Sep '96 / BMG

MUSICAL SHAPES/BLUE NUN
Cry / Madness / Baby ride easy / Bandit of love / I'm so cool / Appalachian eyes / Ring of fire / Too bad about Sandy / That very first kiss / Foggy mountain top / Too drunk / Oh how happy / Love is a four-letter verb / That boy / 300 pounds of hungry / Tougher stuff / I need a hit / Rock-a-baby / Me and my 38 / Do me lover / Too many teardrops / Billy / C'mon feets / Think dirty / If the shoe fits / Home run hitter / When you comin' back
CD FIENDCD 703
Demon / Sep '91 / Pinnacle

Carter, Clarence

BEST OF CLARENCE CARTER, THE
CD RSACD 801
Sequel / Oct '94 / BMG

DOCTOR CC
Dr. CC / I stayed away too long / If you let me take you home / Leftover love / You been cheatin' on me / Try me / Let's funk / Strokin'
CD ICH 1003CD
Ichiban / Oct '93 / Direct / Koch

DOCTOR'S GREATEST PRESCRIPTIONS, THE (The Best Of Clarence Carter)
Strokin' / Trying to sleep tonight / Messin' with my mind / I was in the neighbourhood / Dr. C.C. / Love me with a feeling / I'm not just good, I'm the best / I'm the best / Slip away / Grandpa can't fly his kite / Kiss you all over / I've got a thing for you baby / I'm between a rock and a hard place
CD ICH 1116CD
Ichiban / Feb '94 / Direct / Koch

DYNAMIC CLARENCE CARTER, THE
I'd rather go blind / Think about it / Road of love / You've been a long time comin' / Light my fire / That old time feeling / Steal away / Let me comfort you / Look what I got / Too weak to fight / Harper Valley PTA / Weekend love
CD 7567803772
Atlantic / Jan '96 / Warner Music

DYNAMIC CLARENCE CARTER, THE
I'd rather go blind / Think about it / Road of love / You've been a long time comin' / Light my fire / That old time feeling / Steal away / Let me comfort you / Look what I got / Too weak to fight / Haper Valley PTA / Weekend love / Don't make my baby cry / Take if off him (and put it on me) / Few troubles I've had
CD RSACD 904
Sequel / Jan '97 / BMG

HAVE YOU MET CLARENCE CARTER...YET
CD ICH 1141CD
Ichiban / Nov '92 / Direct / Koch

HOOKED ON LOVE
CD ICH 1016CD
Ichiban / Mar '94 / Direct / Koch

I GOT CAUGHT MAKING LOVE (The ABC Years)
I got caught making love / I thought it was over / Warning / Come back baby / Just one more day / Don't bother me / Take it all off / Real / On your way down / Fine love / Take a taste of your love / Let's start doing (what we came here to do) / Danger point
CD SCL 21162
Ichiban Soul Classics / Jun '96 / Koch

LONELINESS AND TEMPTATION
Love ain't here no more / Take a taste of your love / Glad to see you walking in / Just one more day / Lets start doing what we came here to do / Lets live for ourselves / I got caught making love / Is it alright / Daer abby / Take it all off / All messed up / Heart full of song / Danger point / Jennings alley / Shoulder to cry on / That's what your love means to me / Nothing ventured nothing gained / Come back baby / I thought it was over / Don't bother me
CD EDCD 489
Edsel / Jul '96 / Pinnacle

PATCHES
Willie and Laura Mae Jones / Say man / I'm just a prisoner (of your good lovin') / Let it be / I can't leave your love alone / Your love lifted me / Till I can't take it anymore / Patches / It's all in your mind / Changes / CC blues / Getting the bills (but no merchandise) / Scratch my back / I'm the one / If you can't beat 'em / Lonesomest lonesome
CD RSACD 906
Sequel / Mar '97 / BMG

PATCHES (The Best Of Clarence Carter)
CD CDSGP 0131
Prestige / Dec '94 / Else / Total/BMG

SNATCHING IT BACK (The Best Of Clarence Carter)
Tell Daddy / Slipped, tripped and fell in love / I can't see myself / Too weak to fight / Looking for a fox / Step by step / Patches / Soul deep / Kind woman / Making love / Back door Santa
CD 8122702862
WEA / Jul '93 / Warner Music

TESTIFYIN'
Bad news / Snatching it back / Soul deep / I smell a rat / Doin' our thing / You can't miss what you can't measure / Instant reaction / Making love / Feeling is right / Back door Santa / I can't do without you / Devil woman / Court room / Slipped, tripped and fell in love / I hate to love and run
CD RSACD 905
Sequel / Mar '97 / BMG

THIS IS CLARENCE CARTER
Do what you gotta do / Looking for a fox / Slippin' around / I'm qualified / I can't see myself / Wind it up / Part time love / Thread the needle / Slip away / Funky fever / She ain't gonna do right / Set me free / Step by step / Rooster knees and rice / I stayed away too long / Tell Daddy
CD RSACD 903
Sequel / Jan '97 / BMG

TOUCH OF THE BLUES
I'm not just good, I'm the best / Rock me baby / Why do I stay here / It's a man down there / All night, all day / Kiss you all over / Stormy Monday blues / Dance to the blues
CD ICH 1032CD
Ichiban / Oct '93 / Direct / Koch

Carter, Dean

PERSISTENCE OF VISION
CD THEBES 002CD
Oedipus / Nov '92 / Plastic Head

Carter, Deana

DID I SHAVE MY LEGS FOR THIS
Angel without a prayer / Rita Valentine / I've loved enough to know / I can't shake you / Are you coming home today / Did I shave my legs for this / Turn those wheels around / Graffiti Bridge / Before we ever heard goodbye / We share a wall / Don't let go / Just what you need
CD CDEST 2249
Capitol / Mar '95 / EMI

Carter, Derrick

COSMIC DISCO, THE
Prayer: *Guillaume, Jephte* / Big knockers: *Jedi Knights* / Chord symbols: *Glitch City* / 2 Stupid dogs: *Trouble* / Republic Earthshaker EP: *Earthshaker* / Turntable brothers Mk II EP: *Get Ready* / Gimme some horns: *Essentials* / You can't hide from your bud: *DJ Sneak* / Visions of the future: *Farris, Gene* / Only 4 U: *Cajmere* / Land of the lost: *Green Velvet* / Bozz eyes: *Fandango Widewheels & Huggy Bear* / Answering machine: *Green Velvet* / Keep on groovin': *House 'N' Control* / Life is changing: *Castelli, Cricco* / Get down: *X-OR* / Hot music: *Soho* / Action 78: *DJ 78*
CD MMLCD 023
Mixmag Live / May '97 / Pinnacle

Carter Family

ANCHORED IN LOVE
CD ROUCD 1064
Rounder / Jan '94 / ADA / CM / Direct

HISTORIC REUNION, AN
CD 379252
Koch International / Jun '97 / Koch

MY CLINCH FAMILY HOME
CD ROUCD 1065
Rounder / Jan '94 / ADA / CM / Direct

ON BORDER RADIO VOL.1
CD ARHCD 411
Arhoolie / Jan '96 / ADA / Cadillac / Direct

WHEN THE ROSES BLOOM IN DIXIELAND
CD ROUCD 1066
Rounder / Nov '95 / ADA / CM / Direct

WORRIED MAN BLUES
CD ROUCD 1067
Rounder / Nov '95 / ADA / CM / Direct

Carter, James

CONVERSIN' WITH THE ELDERS
CD 7567829082
Atlantic / Jan '96 / Warner Music

JURASSIC CLASSICS
Take the 'A' train / Out of nowhere / Epistrophy / Ask me now / Equinox / Sansu / Oleo
CD 4786122
Sony Jazz / Jun '95 / Sony

ON THE SET
CD DIW 875
DIW / Nov '93 / Cadillac / Harmonia Mundi

Carter, Jason

ON THE MOVE
CD ROUCD 0387
Rounder / Aug '97 / ADA / CM / Direct

Carter, Joe

DUETS
CD ST 578
Stash / Jul '94 / ADA / Cadillac / CM / Direct / Jazz Music

Carter, John

SEEKING (Carter, John & Bobby Bradford)
CD ARTCD 6085
Hat Art / Aug '91 / Cadillac / Harmonia Mundi

TANDEM VOL.1 (Carter, John & Bobby Bradford)
Tandem / Petals / Angels / Portrait of JBG / Circle / Woodman's Hall blues / Woman / Echoes from Rudolph's
CD EM 4011
Emanem / Oct '96 / Cadillac / Harmonia Mundi

TANDEM VOL.2 (Carter, John & Bobby Bradford)
CD EM 4012
Emanem / Jan '97 / Cadillac / Harmonia Mundi

Carter, John

SPIRIT FLYING FREE (Carter, John & Martin Barre)
Student / Winter setting / No easy way / Spirit flying free / Melody of words / Laugh it off / Don't mess around with me / I can't forget / Exciting eyes / I'll make a stand this time / Your dry land
CD ANDCD 16
A New Day / May '97 / Direct

Carter, Lisa

COUNTRY ROADS
CD SOV 017CD
Sovereign / Jan '93 / Target/BMG

Carter, Mabel

WILDWOOD PICKIN'
CD VCD 77021
Vanguard / May '97 / ADA / Pinnacle

Carter, Ron

AD IDEM
Stellarator / Hip no twist / Away / Force 10 / Midnight sun / Save the best till last / Terraformimg / Stealth rider / Ad idem / Ready to rise / Blasted funk
CD QFM 007
Steady On / Jun '97 / New Note/Pinnacle

NEW YORK SLICK
Slight smile / Tierra Espanola / Aromatic / Alternate route / NY slick
CD OJCCD 916
Original Jazz Classics / May '97 / Complete/ Pinnacle / Jazz Music / Wellard

PASTELS
Woolaphant / Ballad / One bass rag / Pastels / Twelve plus twelve
CD OJCCD 665
Original Jazz Classics / Sep '93 / Complete/ Pinnacle / Jazz Music / Wellard

PEG LEG
CD OJCCD 621
Original Jazz Classics / Oct '95 / Complete/Pinnacle / Jazz Music / Wellard

RON CARTER PLAYS BACH
CD 8308902
ECM / Mar '88 / New Note/Pinnacle

THIRD PLANE (Carter, Ron, Tony Williams & Herbie Hancock)
Third plane / Quiet times / Lawra / Stella by starlight / United blues / Dolphin dance
CD OJCCD 754
Original Jazz Classics / Apr '94 / Complete/ Pinnacle / Jazz Music / Wellard

UPTOWN CONVERSATION
CD 7567819552
Atlantic / Apr '95 / Warner Music

WHERE (Carter, Ron & Eric Dolphy/Mal Waldron)
Rally / Bass duet / Softly as in a morning sunrise / Where / Yes indeed / Saucer eyes
CD OJCCD 432
Original Jazz Classics / May '93 / Complete/ Pinnacle / Jazz Music / Wellard

Carter, Sara

SARA & MAYBELLE (Carter, Sara & Maybelle)
Lonesome pine special / Hand that rocked the cradle / Goin' home / Ship that never returned / Three little strangers / Sun of the soul / Weary prodigal son / While the band is playing Dixie / Farther on / No more goodbyes / Happiest day of all / Charlie Brooks / I told them what you're fighting for / We all miss you Joe / San Antonio rose / Mama's Irish jig / Black mountain rag / Let's be lover's again / Give me your love and I'll give mine / Letter from home / There's a mother always waiting / Tom cat's kitten / Kitty Puss
CD BCD 15471
Bear Family / Jul '93 / Direct / Rollercoaster / Swift

Carter USM

101 DAMNATIONS
Road to domestos / Every time a church bell rings / Twenty four minutes from Tulse

Hill / All American national sport, An / Sheriff Fatman / Taking of Peckham 123 / Crimestoppers A go-go / Good grief Charlie Brown / Midnight on the murder mile / Perfect day to drop the bomb / GI blues
CD ______ **ABBCD 101**
Big Cat / Aug '95 / 3mv/Pinnacle

1992 - THE LOVE ALBUM
1993 / Is wrestling fixed / Only living boy in New Cross / Suppose you gave a funeral and nobody came / England / Do re me, so far so good / Look mum, no hands / While you were out / Skywest and crooked / Impossible dream
CD ______ **CCD 1946**
Chrysalis / May '92 / EMI

30 SOMETHING
My second to last will and testament / Anytime anyplace anywhere / Prince in a pauper's grave / Shoppers' paradise / Billy's smart circus / Bloodsport for all / Sealed with a Glasgow kiss / Say it with flowers / Falling on a bruise / Final comedown
CD ______ **CCD 1897**
Chrysalis / Feb '92 / EMI

POST HISTORIC MONSTERS
Two million years BC / Music that nobody likes / Midday crisis / Cheer up, it might never happen / Stuff the jubilee / Bachelor for Baden Powell / Spoilsports personality of the year / Suicide isn't painless / Being here / Evil / Sing fat lady sing / Travis / Lean on me I won't fall over / Lenny and Terence / Under the thumb and over the moon
CD ______ **CDCHR 7090**
Chrysalis / Sep '93 / EMI

STRAW DONKEY - THE SINGLES
Sheltered life / Sherrif Fatman / Rubbish / Anytime, anyplace, anywhere / Bloodsport for all / After the watershed / Only living boy in New Cross / Do re me, so far so good / Impossible dream / Lean on me I won't fall over / Lenny and Terence / Glam rock cops / Let's get tattoos / Young offender's mum / Born on the 5th of November
CD ______ **CDCHR 6110**
Chrysalis / Sep '97 / EMI

WORLD WITHOUT DAVE, A
Broken down in broken town / World without Dave / Before the war / Nowhere fast / Johnny cash / And God created Brixton
CD ______ **COOKCD 120**
Cooking Vinyl / Mar '97 / Vital

WORRY BOMB
Cheap 'n' cheesy / Airplane food/Airplane fast food / Young offender's mum / Gas (man) / Life and soul of party dies / My defeatist attitude / Worry bomb / Senile delinquent / Me and Mr. Jones / Let's get tattoos / Going straight / God, Saint Peter and the Guardian Angel / Only looney left in town / Ceasefire / Alternative Alf Garnet / Do re me, so far so good / Bachelor for Baden Powell / Re-educating Rita / Only living boy in New Cross / Lean on me I won't fall over / Granny farming in the UK / Travis / Sing fat lady sing / Lenny and Terence / Commercial fucking suicide (part 1)
CD ______ **CDCHR 6096**
Chrysalis / Feb '95 / EMI

Carter, Wilf

COWBOY SONGS (8CD Set)
My Swiss moonlight lullaby / Capture of Albert Johnson / Hobo's blues / Twilight on the prairie / Roundup in the fall / Cowboy's best friend is his pony / He rode the strawberry roan / Little silver haired sweetheart of mine / Take me back to old Montana / Sway back Pinto Pete / Yodelling trailrider / Cowboy, don't forget your Mother / Cowboy blues / Smoke went up the chimney just the same / Moonlight prison blues / Prairie blues / Down the old cattle trail / I miss my Swiss / Cowboy's high toned dance / Hobo's dream of heaven / My little Swiss and me / Lover's lullaby yodel / Awaiting the chair / Life and death of John Dillinger / Cowhand's guiding star / Hobo's song of the Mounties / By the silvery moonlight trail / Dying mother's prayer / I long for old Wyoming / How my yodelling days began / I'm hittin' the trail / Lonesome for my baby tonight / I'm gonna ride to heaven on a streamlined train / Sundown blues / Cowboy lullaby / Yodelling hillbilly / Two-gun cowboy / Hillbilly valley / Returning to my old prairie home / Pete Knight, the King of the cowboys / Cowboy's mother / Calgary roundup / Trail to home sweet home / My blues have turned to sunshine / Dear old Daddy of mine / My little grey haired Mother in the West / Little log shack I can always call home / Rescue from the Moose River goldmine / Keep smiling old pal / Don't let me down old pal / Won't you be the same old pal / Last ride down Lariat Trail / Rose of my heart / Memories of my grey haired Mother in the West / Broken down cowboy / That tumbledown shack by the trail / Covered wagon headed west / Midnight, the unconquered outlaw / Fate of old Strawberry Road / Cowboy's wedding in May / Sweetheart of my childhood days / Ridin' a maverick / There'll be no blues up yonder / Goodbye little pal of my dreams / I loved her till she done me wrong / Under the light of the Texas moon / I'm still waiting for you / Longing for my Mississippi home / Old Alberta plains / Cowboy's heavenly dream / My old Montana home (my old Montana blues) / Why did I ever start roaming/Roaming my whole life away / Hobo's yodel / Yodelling cowgirl / Fate of Sunset Trail / Prairie sunset / I just can't forget you old pal / Roundup time in heaven / Put my little shoes away / When the bright prairie moon is rolling by / Roll on dreamy Texas moon / Old barn dance / Dreamy prairie moon / Roundup time in sunny old Alberta / Roll along moonlight yodel / My faithfull Pinto pal / Preacher and the cowboy / When the sun says goodnight to the prairie / Where is my boy tonight / There's a loveknot in my lariat / My little Yoho lady / Answer to my Swiss moonlight lullaby / Hindenburg disaster / Pete Knight's last ride / I wish I had never seen sunshine / Everybody's been some mother's darlin' / You'll always be mine in my dreams / Dusty trails / By the grave of nobody's darlin' / What a friend we have in mother / Martins and McCoys/Nobody's darling but mine / Little red patch on the seat of my trousers / Golden memories of Mother and Dad / My Honeymoon Bridge brokedown / Down the yodelling trail at twilight / I'm only a dude in cowboy clothes / My Lulu / Rootin' tootin' cowboy / Little red patch on the seat of my trousers / We'll meet again in Peaceful Valley / My brown eyed prairie rose / I'll meet you at the roundup in the Spring / Down on the prairie / My yodelling sweetheart / Yodelling memories / Cowboy's airplane ride / Memories of my little old log shack / My last old yodel song / My yodelling days are through / Headin' for that land of gold / Wilf Carter blues / Golden lariat / Cowboy who never returned / When it's twilight over Texas / My only memories of you / When I say hello to the Rockies / When I bid the prairie goodbye / My dreams come true / You left your brand on my heart / Yodelling love call / It makes no difference now / What difference does it make / Answer to it makes no difference now / Roll along Kentucky moon / Blue Ridge Mountain blues/Birmingham Jail / Red River Valley blues / When the white azales start blooming / My ramblin' days are through / I still think of you, sweet Nellie Dean / He left the one who loved him for another / When it's roll call in the Bunkhouse / My true and earnest prayer / Beautiful girl of the prairie / It's all over now / Rattlin' cannonball / My old Canadian home / I'll get mine by and by / Dad's little Texas lad / Thinking what a wonderful Mother of mine / You are my sunshine / My Texas sweetheart / Echoing hills yodel back to me / You were with me in the waltz of my dreams / When that somebody else were you / My Missoula Valley moon / Old chuck wagon days / It's a cowboy's night to howl / Back ridin' trails again / Let's go back to the Bible / Why should I feel sorry for you now / I bought a rock for a Rocky Mountain gal / It's great to be back in the saddle again / If you don't really care / Why did we ever part / La Verne my brown eyed rose / Last letter / Ride for the open range / Call of the range / Streamlined yodel song / My old lasso is headed straight for you / Memories that never die / I'm thinking tonight of my blue eyes / Prisoner's song / I may be wrong / Old buddies / Sweetheart's farewell / Sittin' by the old Corral / I'll always keep smilin' for you / First love of mine / Waiting for a train / West of Rainbow Trail / Yodelling my babies to sleep / Just one more ride / Rescue from the Moose River goldmine
CD Set ______ **BCD 15939**
Bear Family / Jun '97 / Direct / Rollercoaster / Swift

DYNAMITE TRAIL - THE DECCA YEARS 1954-1958
One golden curl / My mountain high yodel song / I'm gonna tear down the mailbox / Maple leaf waltz / There's a tree on every road / I bought a rock for a rocky mountain gal / Shoo shoo sh'lala / Sunshine bird / Kissing on the sly / Alpine milkman / Dynamite trail / Strawberry road / Ragged but right / There's a padlock on your heart / Yodelin' song / On a little two acre farm / Strawberry road / My little lady / Silver bell yodel / Away out on the mountain / Blind boy's prayer / X's from down in Texas / Let a little sunshine in your heart / There's a bluebird on your windowsill / My French Canadian girl / Sick, sober and sorry / Sinner's prayer / My prairie rose / Yodeling my babies to sleep / Born to lose
CD Set ______ **BCD 15507**
Bear Family / Jul '90 / Direct / Rollercoaster / Swift

PRAIRIE LEGEND, A (4CD Set)
Farewell, sweetheart, farewell: *Carter, Wilf & Montana Slim* / Old Shep: *Carter, Wilf & Montana Slim* / I've hung up my chaps and saddle: *Carter, Wilf & Montana Slim* / You'll get used to it: *Carter, Wilf & Montana Slim* / I ain't gonna hobo no more: *Carter, Wilf & Montana Slim* / Don't be mean, I wasn't mean to you: *Carter, Wilf & Montana Slim* / Sinner's prayer: *Carter, Wilf & Montana Slim* / Plant some flowers by my graveside: *Carter, Wilf & Montana Slim* / There's a goldstar in her window: *Carter, Wilf & Montana Slim* / My blue skies: *Carter, Wilf & Montana Slim* / Put me in your pocket: *Carter, Wilf & Montana Slim* / Smilin' through tears: *Carter, Wilf & Montana Slim* / Born to lose: *Carter, Wilf & Montana Slim* / No letter today: *Carter, Wilf & Montana Slim* / Our Canadian flag: *Carter, Wilf & Montana Slim* / So hard to start all over again: *Carter, Wilf & Montana Slim* / I'll never die of a broken heart: *Carter, Wilf & Montana Slim* / Dreaming of my blue eyes: *Carter, Wilf & Montana Slim* / Memories bring heartaches to me: *Carter, Wilf & Montana Slim* / My Queen of the prairies: *Carter, Wilf & Montana Slim* / Rye whiskey: *Carter, Wilf & Montana Slim* / One golden curl: *Carter, Wilf & Montana Slim* / Hang the key on the bunkhouse door: *Carter, Wilf & Montana Slim* / I'm a fool for foolin' around: *Carter, Wilf & Montana Slim* / There's a loveknot in my lariat: *Carter, Wilf & Montana Slim* / It's later than you think: *Carter, Wilf & Montana Slim* / Too many blues: *Carter, Wilf & Montana Slim* / Singing on borrowed time: *Carter, Wilf & Montana Slim* / Just an old forgotten letter: *Carter, Wilf & Montana Slim* / She lost her cowboy pal: *Carter, Wilf & Montana Slim* / Ol' lonely: *Carter, Wilf & Montana Slim* / If we can't be sweethearts, why can't we be...: *Carter, Wilf & Montana Slim* / Don't cry over me: *Carter, Wilf & Montana Slim* / Sharing your love with somebody new: *Carter, Wilf & Montana Slim* / Don't wait till Judgement Day: *Carter, Wilf & Montana Slim* / Cowboy days ain't ramblin' days no more: *Carter, Wilf & Montana Slim* / 'Neath a blanket of stars: *Carter, Wilf & Montana Slim* / I never knew that I could be so blue: *Carter, Wilf & Montana Slim* / It's just a wild rose I'm sending: *Carter, Wilf & Montana Slim* / Where the sleepy Rio's flowing: *Carter, Wilf & Montana Slim* / You'll be sorry you turned me down: *Carter, Wilf & Montana Slim* / Dream lullaby yodel: *Carter, Wilf & Montana Slim* / It's hard to forget you: *Carter, Wilf & Montana Slim* / Tramp's mother: *Carter, Wilf & Montana Slim* / Take away those blues around my heart: *Carter, Wilf & Montana Slim* / Midnight train: *Carter, Wilf & Montana Slim* / I'm gonna tear down the mailbox: *Carter, Wilf & Montana Slim* / It can't be done: *Carter, Wilf & Montana Slim* / All I need is some more lovin': *Carter, Wilf & Montana Slim* / (There's a) Bluebird on your windowsill: *Carter, Wilf & Montana Slim* / When the iceworms nest again: *Carter, Wilf & Montana Slim* / Shackles and chains: *Carter, Wilf & Montana Slim* / No, no, don't ring those bells: *Carter, Wilf & Montana Slim* / Give a little, take a little: *Carter, Wilf & Montana Slim* / Unfaithful one: *Carter, Wilf & Montana Slim* / Little shirt my mother made for me: *Carter, Wilf & Montana Slim* / Guilty conscience: *Carter, Wilf & Montana Slim* / Take it easy blues: *Carter, Wilf & Montana Slim* / My heart's closed for repairs: *Carter, Wilf & Montana Slim* / My wife is on a diet: *Carter, Wilf & Montana Slim* / Let's go back to the bible: *Carter, Wilf & Montana Slim* / She'll be there: *Carter, Wilf & Montana Slim* / I wish there were only three days in the year: *Carter, Wilf & Montana Slim* / When that love bug bites you: *Carter, Wilf & Montana Slim* / Just a woman's smile: *Carter, Wilf & Montana Slim* / Rudolph the red nosed reindeer: *Carter, Wilf & Montana Slim* / Apple, cherry, mince and choc'late cream: *Carter, Wilf & Montana Slim* / Jolly old St. Nicholas: *Carter, Wilf & Montana Slim* / KP blues: *Carter, Wilf & Montana Slim* / Blue Canadian Rockies: *Carter, Wilf & Montana Slim* / Dear Evalina: *Carter, Wilf & Montana Slim* / My Oklahoma rose: *Carter, Wilf & Montana Slim* / What cigarette is best: *Carter, Wilf & Montana Slim* / Sick, sober and sorry: *Carter, Wilf & Montana Slim* / Teardrops don't always mean a broken heart: *Carter, Wilf & Montana Slim* / Wha hoppen: *Carter, Wilf & Montana Slim* / Punkinhead (The little bear): *Carter, Wilf & Montana Slim* / Night before Christmas in Texas that is: *Carter, Wilf & Montana Slim* / Goodbye Maris (I'm off to Korea): *Carter, Wilf & Montana Slim* / Driftwood on the river: *Carter, Wilf & Montana Slim* / Manhunt: *Carter, Wilf & Montana Slim* / (All you gave me) Mockingbird love: *Carter, Wilf & Montana Slim* / Square dance boogie: *Carter, Wilf & Montana Slim* / Sweet little lover: *Carter, Wilf & Montana Slim* / Huggin', squeezin', kissin', teasin': *Carter, Wilf & Montana Slim* / Sleep one little sleep: *Carter, Wilf & Montana Slim* / Alabama Saturday night: *Carter, Wilf & Montana Slim* / Hot foot boogie: *Carter, Wilf & Montana Slim* / I remember the rodeo: *Carter, Wilf & Montana Slim* / Pete Knight, the King of the cowboys: *Carter, Wilf & Montana Slim* / When the iceworms nest again: *Carter, Wilf & Montana Slim* / My little grey haired Mother in the west: *Carter, Wilf & Montana Slim* / He rode the strawberry roan: *Carter, Wilf & Montana Slim* / Rattlin' cannonball: *Carter, Wilf & Montana Slim* / Calgary roundup: *Carter, Wilf & Montana Slim* / That silver haired daddy of mine: *Carter, Wilf & Montana Slim* / Smoke went up the chimney just the same: *Carter, Wilf & Montana Slim* / Capture of Albert Johnson: *Carter, Wilf & Montana Slim* / Beautiful girl of the prairie: *Carter, Wilf & Montana Slim* / Singing in my last roundup: *Carter, Wilf & Montana Slim*
CD Set ______ **BCD 15754**
Bear Family / Nov '93 / Direct / Rollercoaster / Swift

Carthy, Eliza

ELIZA CARTHY & NANCY KERR (Carthy, Eliza & Nancy Kerr)
Waterloo fair (The Henryco)/Speed the plow / Lucy's waltz/Liza's favourite / Alistair's / Unquiet grave / March of the Kings of Laoise / Old man came courting / Swedish wedding march / Whittingham Fair/For Whittingham Fair / Bushes and briars / Tune / Wrong favour / Prague/Polly Bishop's slip jig/The storyteller / Black and white rag
CD ______ **MCR 3991CD**
Mrs. Casey / Nov '93 / ADA / Direct

ELIZA CARTHY & THE KINGS OF CALICUTT (Carthy, Eliza & The Kings Of Calicutt)
Trip / Whirly / Bonaparte's / Tractor / Mother / Mr. Walker / Sea / Sheffield / Fisher / Storyteller
CD ______ **TSCD 489**
Topic / Jul '97 / ADA / CM / Direct

HEAT LIGHT AND SOUND
CD ______ **TSCD 482**
Topic / Feb '96 / ADA / CM / Direct

SHAPE OF SCRAPE (Carthy, Eliza & Nancy Kerr)
Edward Corcoran/Black joke / I know my love / Low down in the broom/The sukebind / Downfall of Paris / Keek (or ride) in the creel / Mary custy air / Growling (The trees they do grow high) / Poor and young single sailor / Balter Svens Parapolkett / Bonny light horseman/Michael Turner's waltz / Wanton wife of Castlegate/Princess Royal / Gypsy hornpipe/The hawk/Indian Queen
CD ______ **MCR 5992CD**
Mrs. Casey / Jul '95 / ADA / Direct

Carthy, Martin

BECAUSE IT'S THERE
Nothing rhymed / May song / Swaggering Boney / Lord Randal / Long John, old John and Jackie North / Jolly tinker / Lovely Joan / Three cripples / Siege of Delhi / Death of young Andrew
CD ______ **TSCD 389**
Topic / May '95 / ADA / CM / Direct

BUT TWO CAME BY (Carthy, Martin & Dave Swarbrick)
Ship in distress / Banks of the sweet primroses / Long lankin / Brass band music
CD ______ **TSCD 343**
Topic / May '94 / ADA / CM / Direct

COLLECTION, THE
CD ______ **GLCD 1136**
Green Linnet / Jan '94 / ADA / CM / Direct / Highlander / Roots

CROWN OF HORN
Bedmaking / Locks and bolts / King Knapperty / Geordie / Willie's lady / Virginny / Worcestershire wedding / Bonnie lass o'Anglesey / William Taylor the poacher / Old Tom of Oxford / Palaces of gold
CD ______ **TSCD 300**
Topic / Oct '95 / ADA / CM / Direct

LANDFALL
Here's adieu to all judges and juries / Brown Adam / O'er the hills / Cruel mother / Cold haily windy night / His name is Andrew / Bold poachers / Dust to dust / Broomfield hill / January man
CD ______ **TSCD 345**
Topic / Apr '96 / ADA / CM / Direct

MARTIN CARTHY
High Germany / Trees they do grow high / Sovay / Ye mariners all / Queen of hearts / Broomfield hill / Springhill mine disaster / Scarborough Fair / Lovely Joan / Barley and the rye / Wind that shakes the barley / Two magicians / Handsome cabin boy / And a begging I will go
CD ______ **TSCD 340**
Topic / May '93 / ADA / CM / Direct

OUT OF THE CUT
Devil and the feathery wife / Reynard the fox / Song of the lower classes / Rufford Park poachers / Molly Oxford / Rigs of the time / I sowed some seeds / Frair in the well / Jack Rowland / Old horse
CD ______ **TSCD 426**
Topic / Aug '94 / ADA / CM / Direct

PRINCE HEATHEN (Carthy, Martin & Dave Swarbrick)
Arthur McBride / Salisbury Plain / Polly on the shore / Rainbow / Died for love / Staines Morris / Reynardine / Seven yellow gypsies / Little Musgrave / Wren
CD ______ **TSCD 344**
Topic / Jun '94 / ADA / CM / Direct

RIGHT OF PASSAGE
Ant and the grasshopper / Eggs in her basket / Stitch in time / McVeagh / Hommage a roche proulx / All in green / Company policy / Banks of the Nile / La carde use / Bill Norrie / Sleepwalker / Cornish young man / Dominion of the sword
CD ______ **TSCD 452**
Topic / Dec '88 / ADA / CM / Direct

RIGS OF THE TIMES (The Best Of Martin Carthy)
Skewball / Ant and the grasshopper / Foxhunt / Devil and the feathery wife / Sheepstealer / Begging song / Geordie / Billy boy / Lovely Joan / Sovay / Bill Norrie / Question

of sport / Old horse / All of a row / Work life out to keep life in / Rigs of the time / Such a war has never been / Dominion of the sword / Byker hill
CD _______________ MCCD 145
Music Club / Dec '93 / Disc / THE

SECOND ALBUM
Two butchers / Ball o'yarn / Farewell Nancy / Lord Franklin / Rambling sailor / Lowlands of Holland / Fair maid on the shore / Bruton town / Box on her head / Newlyn town / Brave Wolfe / Peggy and the soldier / Sailor's life
CD _______________ TSCD 341
Topic / Sep '93 / ADA / CM / Direct

SWEET WIVELSFIELD
Shepherd O shepherd / Billy boy / Three jolly sneaksmen / Trimdon grange / All of a row / Skewball / Mary Neal / King Henry / John Barleycorn / Cottage in the wood
CD _______________ TSCD 418
Topic / Apr '96 / ADA / CM / Direct

Cartland, Barbara

GREAT ROMANTIC SONGS
CD _______________ CDSIV 6132
Horatio Nelson / Jul '95 / Disc

Cartwright, Deirdre

DEBUT (Cartwright, Deirdre Group)
Spartia / Slipper 15s 8d / I thought of you / Trap / When pushing comes to shoving / Grand loup / Pisces moon / One more / Walk with me
CD _______________ BTF 9401
Blow The Fuse / Oct '94 / New Note/ Pinnacle

Carty, John

CAT THAT ATE THE CRADLE (Carty, John & Brain McGrath)
CD _______________ CICD 099
Clo Iar-Chonnachta / Aug '94 / CM

LAST NIGHT'S FUN
CD _______________ SH 79098
Shanachie / May '96 / ADA / Greensleeves / Koch

Carty, Paddy

TRADITIONAL IRISH MUSIC
CD _______________ SHCD 34017
Shanachie / Apr '97 / ADA / Greensleeves / Koch

Carvenius, Rolf

ROLF CARVENIUS & HIS SINGING CLARINET
CD _______________ CCCD 2
Cloetta / Feb '95 / Cadillac / Jazz Music

Carvin, Michael

EACH ONE TEACH ONE
Surrey with the fringe on top/Eternal triangle / Waltz for Gina / Nails (to Michael Carvin) / Smoke gets in your eyes / Recife's blues / I don't stand a ghost of a chance with you / One by one
CD _______________ MCD 5485
Muse / Feb '95 / New Note/Pinnacle

Cary, Marc

CARY ON
Vibe / Afterthought / When I think of you / So gracefully / We learn as we go / Trial / Melody in C / He who hops around
CD _______________ ENJ 90232
Enja / May '95 / New Note/Pinnacle / Vital/ SAM

LISTEN
Runnin out of time (Epilogue) / In another way (Part 1) / Throw it away / In another way (Part II) / Conditional statement / Fallacy / Leaving home / New blues / Mr Lucky / Down de road / Spiritual / Runnin out of time (Prologue)
CD _______________ AJ 0125
Arabesque / Apr '97 / New Note/Pinnacle

Casa Loma Orchestra

CASA LOMA STOMP
Love is a dreamer / Lucky me, loveable you / Happy days are here again / Sweeping the clouds away / Anytime's the time to fall in love / China girl / San Sue strut / When the little red roses (Get the blues for you) / Exactly like you / Dust / Leave it that way / On the sunny side of the street / Alexander's ragtime band / Casa Loma stomp / Overnight / Put on your grey bonnet / Little did I know / Royal garden blues
CD _______________ HEPCD 1010
Hep / Mar '97 / Cadillac / Jazz Music / New Note/Pinnacle / Wellard

MANIACS BALL
Alexander's ragtime band / Put on your old grey bonnet / I wanna be around my baby all the time / I'm crazy 'bout my baby / White jazz / Black jazz / Maniac's ball / Clarinet marmalade / I never knew / Indiana / Blue jazz / Thanksgivin' / Lady from St Paul / Dame of the lame duck / Rhythm man / New Orleans / Wild goose chase / Moon country / Milenberg joys / Out of space / Copenhagen / Royal garden blues / Rose of the Rio Grande / Jungle jitters / Bugle call rag / Study in Brown
CD _______________ HEPCD 1051
Hep / Jul '96 / Cadillac / Jazz Music / New Note/Pinnacle / Wellard

Cascade

LET IT BE ME
CD _______________ CDOK 3007
OK / Nov '88 / Ross

Case

CASE
CD _______________ 5331342
Def Jam / Aug '96 / PolyGram

Case, John Carol

FAVOURITE CHRISTMAS CAROLS (Case, John Carol & The Bach Choir/ Jacques Orchestra)
Hark the herald angels sing / I saw three ships / in the bleak midwinter / We've been awhile a-wandering / Past three o'clock / Up good Christian folk, and listen / I sing of a maiden / Tomorrow shall be my dancing day / It came upon a midnight clear / Sussex carol / Ding dong merrily on high / God rest ye merry gentlemen / Away in a manger / O little one sweet / Unto us is born a son / Wassail / When Christ was born / Infant holy / When an angel host entuned / Born in a manger / Patapan / Carol with lullaby / Christmas carol / Masters in this hall / Gabriel's message / See amid the winter's snow / Child is born / Rocking / Coventry carol / While shepherds watched their flocks by night
CD _______________ CDCFP 4629
Classics For Pleasure / Oct '96 / EMI

Case, Peter

SINGS LIKE HELL
CD _______________ GRCD 351
Glitterhouse / Nov '96 / Avid/BMG
CD _______________ VMD 79476
Vanguard / Apr '97 / ADA / Pinnacle

Casey, Al

JIVIN' AROUND
Surfin' hootenanny / El aguila / Thunder beach / Baja / Surfin' blues / Lonely surfer / Guitars, guitars, guitars / Hearse / Ramrod / Caravan / Surfin' blues part II / Surfs you right / Cookin' / Hot food / Indian love call / Jivin' around / Doin' the shotish / Doin' it / Hucklebuck / Full house / Laughin' / Monte carlo / Huckleberry hound / Chicken feathers / Easy pickin' / What are we gonna do in '64
CD _______________ CDCHD 612
Ace / Aug '95 / Pinnacle

JUMPIN' WITH AL
CD _______________ BB 8732
Black & Blue / Jan '97 / Discovery / Koch / Wellard

SIDEWINDER
Undecided / You come a long way from St. Louis / Sidewinder / Ashokan farewell / Endless sleep / Limeshouse blues / Saguaro sunrise / Route 1 / Plectrum banjo medley / Fool
CD _______________ BCD 15889
Bear Family / Aug '95 / Direct / Rollercoaster / Swift

TRIBUTE TO FATS, A
CD _______________ 1044
Jazz Point / Jan '95 / Cadillac / Harmonia Mundi

Casey, Karan

SONGLINES
CD _______________ SHANCD 87007
Shanachie / May '97 / ADA / Greensleeves / Koch

Casey, Nollaig

CAUSEWAY (Casey, Nollaig & Arty McGlynn)
Causeway / Cabbage and cale / Sel Le Thoil / Jack Palance's reel / Tra an phearla / Rainy summer / Stor mo chiroi / Comanche moon / Trip to Tokyo / Dun na sead / Murals / Lois na banrfona
CD _______________ TARA 3035
Tara / Aug '95 / ADA / CM / Conifer/BMG / Direct

Cash Crew

FROM AN AFROPEAN PERSPECTIVE
Introlude - my resume (peep it) / Bounce back / Afropean prelude / Play 4 U / Notting 'ill shit / Who's to blame / Turn it out / Ruffie / Original freaky Flo / Time is now / 2 da start prelude / Back 2 da start / Codes of honour / Nothing is impossible / Turn it out / Turn it out / Conclusion
CD _______________ 74321380202
RCA / Nov '96 / BMG

Cash, Johnny

18 ORIGINAL COUNTRY CLASSICS
Sunday morning coming down / Get rhythm / Cry cry cry / Tennessee flat top box / I still miss someone / Blue train / Don't take your guns to town / Home of the blues / Guess things happen that way / I get stripes / Hey porter / Ballad of teenage Queen / Wanted man / Let him roll / Backstage pass / Ballad of Ira Hayes / Greatest cowboy of them all / W Lee O'Daniel and the light crust doughboys
CD _______________ 5525582
Spectrum / Sep '96 / PolyGram

AMERICAN RECORDINGS
Delia's gone / Let the rain blow the whistle / Beast in me / Drive on / Why me Lord / Thirteen / Oh bury me not / Bird on the wire / Tennessee stud / Down there by the train / Redemption / Like a soldier / Man who couldn't cry
CD _______________ 74321236852
American / Oct '94 / BMG

AT FOLSOM PRISON/JOHNNY CASH AT SAN QUENTIN
Folsom Prison blues / Dark as the dungeon / I still miss someone / Cocaine blues / 25 minutes to go / Orange blossom special / Long black veil / Send a picture of Mother / Wall / Dirty old egg-sucking dog / Flushed from the bathroom of your heart / Jackson / Give my love to rose / I got stripes / Green green grass of home / Greystone chapel / Wanted man / Wreck of the old '97 / I walk the line / Darlin' companion / Starkville City / San Quentin / Boy named Sue / There'll be peace in the valley / Folsom Prison blues
CD _______________ 4814002
Columbia / Jan '95 / Sony

BEST OF JOHNNY CASH, THE
Boy named Sue / Thing called love / Busted / Daddy sang bass / Don't take your guns to town / Folsom prison blues / Ghost riders in the sky / Hey porter / I'm so lonely I could cry / I walk the line / It ain't me babe / Jackson / One piece at a time / Orange blossom special / Ring of fire / Ballad of Ira Hayes
CD _______________ 4837252
Columbia / Feb '96 / Sony

BEST OF JOHNNY CASH, THE
CD _______________ PLSCD 132
Pulse / Apr '96 / BMG

BEST OF JOHNNY CASH, THE
CD _______________ MACCD 145
Autograph / Aug '96 / BMG

BEST OF THE SUN YEARS 1955-1961
CD _______________ MCCD 082
Music Club / Sep '92 / Disc / THE

BIGGEST HITS
Don't take your guns to town / Ring of fire / Understand your man / One on the right is on the left / Rosanna's going wild / Folsom Prison blues / Baddy sand bass / Boy named Sue / Sunday morning coming down / Flesh and blood / Thing called love / One piece at a time / There ain't no good chain gang / Riders in the sky / Baron
CD _______________ CD 32304
Columbia / Jun '91 / Sony

CLASSIC CASH
Get rhythm / Long black veil / I still miss someone / Blue train / Five feet high and rising / Don't take your guns to town / Guess things happen that way / I walk the line / Ballad of Ira Hayes / Folsom Prison blues / Tennessee flat top box / Thing called love / Cry cry cry / Sunday morning coming down / Peace in the valley / Home of the blues / I got stripes / Ring of fire / Ways of a woman in love / Suppertime
CD _______________ 8345262
Mercury / Mar '89 / PolyGram

COLLECTION, THE
Wide open road / Cry cry cry / Folsom Prison blues / So doggone lonesome / Mean eyed cat / New Mexico / I walk the line / I love you because / Straight A's in love / Home of the blues / Rock Island line / Country boy / Doin' my time / Big river / Ballad of a teenage queen / Oh lonesome me / You're the nearest thing to heaven / Always alone / You win again / Hey good lookin' / Blue train / Katy too / Fools hall of fame / Ways of a woman in love / Down the street to 301
CD _______________ CCSCD 146
Castle / Feb '93 / BMG

COLLECTION, THE
CD _______________ COL 004
Collection / Jan '95 / Target/BMG

COME ALONG AND RIDE THIS TRAIN (4CD Set)
Come along and ride this train / Loading coal / Slow rider / Lumberjack / Dorraine of ponchartrain / Going to Memphis / When papa played the dobro / Boss Jack / Old Doc Brown / Legend of John Henry's hammer / Tell him I'm gone / Another man done gone / Casey Jones / Nine pound hammer / Chain gang / Busted / Waiting for a train / Roughneck / Pick a bale of cotton / Cotton pickin' hands / Hiawatha's vision / Hammer and nails / Shifting whispering sands / Ballad of Boot Hill / I ride an old paint / Hardin wouldn't run / Mr. Garfield / Streets of Laredo / Johnny Reb / Letter from home / Bury me not on the lone prairie / Mean as hell / Sam Hall / Twenty five minutes to go / Blizzard / Sweet Betsy from Pike / Green grow the lilacs / Rodeo hand / Stampede / Remember the Alamo / Reflections / Big foot / As long as the grass shall grow / Apache tears / Custer / Talking leaves / Ballard of Ira Hayes / Drums / White girl / Old apache squaw / Vanishing race / Paul Revere / Road to Kaintuck / Battle of New Orleans / Lorena / Gettysburg address / Big battle / Come and take a trip in my airship / These are my people / From the sea to shining sea / Whirl and the suck / Call daddy from the mine / Frozen four hundred pound to middin' cotton picker / Walls of a prison / Masterpiece / You and Tennesse / She came from the mountains / Another song to sing / Flint arrowhead / Cisco Clifton's fillin' station / Shrimpin' sailin' / From sea to shining sea / Hit the road and go / If it wasn't for the Wabash river / Lady / After the ball / No earthly good / Wednesday car / My cowboy's last ride
CD Set _______________ BCD 15563
Bear Family / May '91 / Direct / Rollercoaster / Swift

COUNTRY CHRISTMAS
CD _______________ 15417
Laserlight / Nov '95 / Target/BMG

COUNTRY CLASSICS (2CD Set)
I walk the line / Country boy / Get rhythm / Oh lonesome me / Train of love / Give my love to Rose / Ballad of a teenage queen / Blue train / You win again / Hey porter / Wide open road / There you go / Cry cry cry / So doggone lonesome / Mean eyed cat / Rock Island line / Two timin' woman / Big river / Folsom prison blues / Doin' my time / I was there when it happened / Luther played the boogie / Home of the blues / I just thought you'd like to know / Remember me / Come in stranger / Thr ways of a woman in love / Guess things happen that way / You're the nearest thing to heaven / Straight 'A's in love / I heard that lonesome whistle blow / Goodbye little darling / Story of a broken heart / Down the street to 301 / Next in line / It's just about time
CD Set _______________ 330232
Hallmark / Jul '96 / Carlton

FOLSOM PRISON BLUES (Original Sun Hits)
Cry cry cry / Folsom prison blues / So doggone lonesome / I walk the line / Get rhythm / There you go / Train of love / Next in line / Don't make me go / Home of the blues / Give my love to Rose / Ballad of a teenage queen / Big river / Guess things happen that way / Come in stranger / Ways of a woman in love / You're the nearest thing to heaven / It's just about time / Luther played the boogie / Thanks a lot / Katy too / Goodbye little darling / Straight A's in love / I love you because / Mean eyed cat / Oh lonesome me / Rock Island line / Down the street to 301
CD _______________ CPCD 8101
Charly / Jun '95 / Koch

GOLDEN YEARS, THE
I walk the line / Guess things happen that way / Ballad of a teenage Queen / Folsom Prison blues / Hey good lookin' / I can't help it / I forgot to remember to forget / You're the nearest thing to Heaven / Big river / Born to lose / You win again / Get rhythm / Rock Island line / Thanks a lot / Next in line / There you go / Oh lonesome me / Ways of a woman in love
CD _______________ NTMCD 536
Nectar / Feb '97 / Pinnacle

GREATEST HITS
CD _______________ WMCD 5661
Woodford Music / Aug '92 / THE

HEROES (Cash, Johnny & Waylon Jennings)
Folks out on the road / I'm never gonna roam again / American by birth / Field of diamonds / Heroes / Even cowgirls get the blues / Love is the way / Ballad of forty dollars / I'll always love you - in my own crazy way / One too many mornings
CD _______________ RE 2078
Razor & Tie / Aug '96 / Koch

I WALK THE LINE
CD _______________ CTS 55406
Country Stars / Jan '92 / Target/BMG

ITCHY FEET (20 Foot-Tappin' Greats)
Folsom prison blues / I walk the line / Ring of fire / Forty shades of green / I still miss someone / There ain't no good chain gang / Busted / Twenty five minutes to go / Orange blossom special / It ain't me babe / Boy named Sue / San Quentin / Don't take your guns to town / One on the right is on the left / Jackson / Hey porter / Daddy sang bass / I got stripes / Thing called love / One piece at a time
CD _______________ 4681162
Columbia / Apr '95 / Sony

JOHNNY CASH
CD _______________ 12373
Laserlight / Oct '95 / Target/BMG

JOHNNY CASH
Cry cry cry / I'm so doggone lonesome / Next in line / There you go / Home of the blues / Give my love to Rose / Ballad of a

teenage Queen / Come in stranger / Katy too / You are the nearest thing to Heaven / Straight A's in love / Get rhythm / Rock Island line / Hey Porter / Way of a woman in love / Mean eyed cat
CD _______________ 12786
Laserlight / Feb '97 / Target/BMG

JOHNNY CASH (CD/CD Rom Set)
Going by the book / Ballad of a teenage queen / Guess things happen that way / Folsom prison blues / I walk the line / Ways of a woman in love / Rock Island line / You're the nearest thing to heaven / Next in line / I just thought you'd like to know / Straight A's in love / Hey porter / Get rhythm / Big river / Born to lose / Sugartime / I love you because / Thanks a lot
CD Set _______________ WWCDR 001
Magnum Music / Apr '97 / TKO Magnum

JOHNNY CASH 1958-1986 (The CBS Years)
Oh what a dream / I still miss someone / Pickin' time / Don't take your guns to town / Five feet high and rising / Seasons of my heart / Legend of John Henry's hammer / Ring of fire / Ballad of Ira Hayes / Orange Blossom special / Folsom Prison blues / San Quentin / Boy named Sue / Sunday morning coming down / Man in black / One piece at a time / Riders in the sky / Without love / Baron / Highway patrolman
CD _______________ 4504662
CBS / Apr '87 / Sony

JOHNNY CASH IN CONCERT
CD _______________ TRTCD 188
TrueTrax / Jun '95 / THE

JOHNNY CASH LIVE
Get rhythm / Ring of fire / Rock island line / Peace in the valley / Sunday morning coming down / Boy named Sue / Folsom prison blues / Highwayman / Big river / Sixteen tons / Wall / I still miss someone / I got stripes / City of New Orleans / Jackson / If I were a carpenter / Orange blossom special / Casey Jones / I walk the line
CD _______________ 12888
Laserlight / May '97 / Target/BMG

JOHNNY CASH VOL.1
CD _______________ DS 001
Desperado / Jun '97 / TKO Magnum

JOHNNY CASH VOL.2
CD _______________ DS 002
Desperado / Jun '97 / TKO Magnum

LIVE - IN THE RING OF FIRE
Folsom Prison blues / These hands / Peace in the valley / Rock Island line / Wall / I still miss someone / Ring of fire / Sunday morning coming down / Highwayman / Big river / Sixteen tons / Boy named Sue / Help me / City of New Orleans / If I were a carpenter / Orange blossom special
CD _______________ SUMCD 4020
Summit / Nov '96 / Sound & Media

MAN IN BLACK VOL.1, THE (5CD Set)
Wide open road / You're my baby / My treasure / Hey porter / Folsom Prison blues / My two timin' woman / Cry cry cry / Port of lonely hearts / I couldn't keep from crying / New Mexico / So doggone lonesome / Mean eyed cat / Luther played the boogie / Rock 'n' roll Ruby / I walk the line / Brakeman's blues / Get rhythm / Train of love / There you go / One more ride / I love you because / Goodbye little darling / Straight A's in love / Don't make me go / Next in line / Home of the blues / Give my love to Rose / Rock Island line / Wreck of ol' 97 / Belshazar / Country boy / Leave that junk alone / Doin' my time / If the good Lord's willing / (I heard that) lonesome whistle / I was there when it happened / Remember me / Big river / Ballad of a teenage queen / Goodnight Irene / Come in stranger / Guess things happen that way / Sugartime / Born to lose / You're the nearest thing to heaven / Story of a broken heart / Always alone / Story of a broken heart (false starts) / You tell me / Life goes on / You win again / I could never be ashamed of you / Hey good lookin' / I can't help it / Cold cold heart / Blue train / Katy too / Ways of a woman in love / Fools hall of fame / Thanks a lot / It's just about time / I forgot to remember to forget / I just thought you'd like to know / Down the street to 301 / Oh what a dream / I'll remember you / Drink to me / What do I care / Suppertime / It was Jesus / Mama's baby / Troubador / Run softly blue river / All over again / That's all over / Frankie's man / Johnnie / Walking the blues / Lead me father / That's enough / I still miss someone / Pickin' time / Don't take your guns to town / I'd rather die young / Shepherd of my heart / Cold shoulder
CD Set _______________ BCD 15517
Bear Family / Sep '90 / Direct / Rollercoaster / Swift

MAN IN BLACK VOL.2, THE (1959-1962/ 5CD Set)
Snow in his hair / I saw a man / Lead me gently home / Are all the children in / Swing low, sweet chariot / I call him / Old account / He'll be a friend / These things shall pass / It could be you / God will / Great speckled bird / Were you there / He'll understand and say well done / God has my fortune laid away / When I've learned / I got shoes / Let the lower lights be burning / If we never meet again / When I take my vacation in heaven / When he reached down his hand for me / Taller than trees / I won't have to cross Jordan alone / My god is real / These hands / Peace in the valley / Day in the Grand Canyon / I'll remember you / I got stripes / You dreamer you / Five feet high and rising / Rebel Johnny Yuma / Lorena / Second honeymoon / Fable of Willie Brown / Smiling Bill McCall / Johnny Yuma / Man on the hill / Hank and Joe and me / Caretaker / Clementine / I want to go home / Old Apache squaw / Don't step on mother's roses / My grandfather's clock / I couldn't keep from crying / My shoes keep walking back to you / I will miss you when you go / I feel better all over / Bandana / Wabash blues / Viel zu spat / Woistzuhause, mama / Heartbeat / Hello again / Tall man / Girl in Saskatoon / Locomotive man / Losing kind / Five minutes to live / Forty shades of green / Big battle / Blues for two / Jeri and Nina's melody / Why do you punish me / Just one more / Seasons of my heart / Honky tonk girl / I'm so lonesome I could cry / Time changes everything / I'd just be fool enough / Transfusion blues / Lovin' locomotive man / Mr. Lonesome / Folsom Prison blues / I walk the line / Hey porter / I forgot more than you'll ever know / There's a mother always waiting / Tennessee flat top box / Sing it pretty Sue / Little at a time / So do I / Bonanza / Shamrock doesn't grow in California / I'm free from the chain gang now / Delia's gone / Lost on the desert / Accidentally on purpose / You remember me / In the jailhouse now / Let me down easy / In them cottonfields back home / You won't have to go far / No one will ever know / Danger zone / I'll be all smiles tonight / Send a picture of Mother / Hardin wouldn't run / Blue bandana / So doggone lonesome / Johnny Reb
CD Set _______________ BCD 15562
Bear Family / Aug '91 / Direct / Rollercoaster / Swift

MAN IN BLACK VOL.3, THE (1963-1969/ 6CD Set)
Ring of fire / Matador / I'd still be there / Still in town / El matador (spanish) / Fuego d'amour (spanish) / My old faded rose / It ain't me babe / Don't think twice it's alright / One too many mornings / Mama, you've been on my mind / Long black veil / Wall / Orange blossom special / Troublesome waters / I walk the line / Folsom prison blues / Wreck of the old '97 / Hey porter / Big river / All God's children ain't free / Amen / When it's springtime in Alaska / You wild Colorado / Danny Boy / I still miss someone / Give my love to Rose / Goodbye little darlin' goodbye / Dark as a dungeon / Bottom of the mountain / Understand your man / Time and time again / Hardin wouln't run / Certain kinda hurtin / How did you get away from me / Bad news / Cup of coffee / Dirty old egg sucking hound / One on the right is one on the left / Concerning your new song / Bug that tried to crawl around the world / Flushed from the bathroom of your heart / Dirty old egg sucking dog / Take me home / Song of the coward / Please don't play red river valley / Foolish questions / Singing stars queen / Austin prison / Boa constrictor / Everybody loves a nut / Sound of laughter / Joe Bean / Frozen lagger / Baby is mine / Happy to with with you / For lovin' me / You'll be alright / Fast boat to Sidney / Long legged guitar pickin' man / Pack up your sorrows / Jackson / Is this my destiny / Wound time can't erase / You comb her hair / Ancient history / Happiness is you / Guess things happen that way / I got a woman / What I'd say / Oh, what a good thing we had / No, no, no / Shanty town / What'd I say / Matador (original) / Wer kennt den weg / In Virginia / Kleine Rosmarie / Besser so, Jenny Jo / Thunderball / Sons of Katie Elder / Put the sugar to bed / Red velvet / Rosanna's going wild / Wind changes / On the line / Roll call / You beat all I ever saw / I tremble for you / Cattle call / Bill's theme / Spanish Harlem / Folk singer / Southwind / Devil to pay / 'Cause I love you / See Ruby fall / Rout # 1 / Box 144 / Sing a travelling song / If I were a carpenter / To beat the devil / Blisterd / Wrinkled, crinkled, wadded dollar bill / I've got a thing about trains / Six white horses / Jesus was a carpenter / Man in black / Christmas spirit / I heard the bells on Christmas day / Blue Christmas / Gifts they gave / Here was a man / Christmas as I knew it / Silent night / Little drummer boy / It came upon a midnight clear / Ringing the bells for jim / We are the shepherds / Who kept the sheep / Ballad of the harpweavers / Wildwood flowers / Engine 143 / Keep on the sunnyside / Single girl, married girl / Banks of the Ohio / My clinch mountain home / Lonesome valley / Worried man blues / Brown hearted lover / Brown eyes / I'm working on a building / Gathering flowers from the hillside / When the roses bloom again / I taught the weeping willow / Rock Island line / Ballad of Ira Hayes
CD Set _______________ BCD 15588
Bear Family / Nov '95 / Direct / Rollercoaster / Swift

MAN IN BLACK, THE
Ring of fire / I walk the line / Get rhythm / It Ain't Me Babe / I still miss someone / Ghost riders in the sky / Baron / Sunday morning coming down / Daddy sang bass / Jackson / One piece at a time / Orange blossom special / Folsom prison blues / San Quentin / Boy named Sue / Thing called love / Don't take your guns to town / Wanted man / Big river / Without love / No expectations / Highway patrolman / Singin' in
CD _______________ MOODCD 35
Columbia / Aug '94 / Sony

PERSONAL CHRISTMAS COLLECTION
Christmas spirit / I heard the bells on Christmas day / Blue Christmas / Christmas as I knew it / Little drummer boy / Christmas with you / Silent night / Joy to the world / Away in a manger / O little town of Bethlehem / Hark the herald angels sing / O come all ye faithful (Adeste Fidelis)
CD _______________ 4777692
Columbia / Nov '96 / Sony

RING OF FIRE
Ring of fire / Thing called love / I walk the line / Long black veil / Cats in the cradle / Goin' by the book / As long as I live / Ways of a woman in love / Night Hank Williams came to town / Folsom Prison blues / Five feet high and rising / Mystery of life / That's one you owe me / Suppertime / Family bible / Big light / Sixteen tons / Peace in the valley
CD _______________ 5509322
Spectrum / Mar '95 / PolyGram

SUN YEARS, THE (3CD Set)
Wide open road / You're my baby / Folsom Prison blues / Two timin' woman / Goodnight Irene / Port of lonely hearts / My treasure / Cry cry cry / Hey porter / Luther played the boogie / So doggone lonesome / Mean eyed cat / I couldn't keep from crying / New Mexico / Rock 'n' roll Ruby / Get rhythm / I walk the line / Train of love / There you go / One more ride / Goodbye little darling / I love you because / Straight A's in love / Don't make me go / Next in line / Give my love to Rose / Home of the blues / Wreck of ol' 97 / Rock Island line / Belshazar / Leave that junk alone / Country boy / Doin' my time / If the good Lord's willing / (I heard that) lonesome whistle / Remember me / I was there when it happened / Come in stranger / Big river / Ballad of a teenage queen / Oh lonesome me / Guess things happen that way / You're the nearest thing to Heaven / Sugartime / Born to lose / Always alone / Story of a broken heart / You tell me / Life goes on / You win again / I could never be ashamed of you / Cold cold heart / Hey good lookin' / I can't help it / Blue train / Katy too / Ways of a woman in love / Thanks a lot / It's just about time / I just thought you'd like to know / I forgot to remember to forget / Down the street to 301
CD Set _______________ CDSUNBOX 5
Charly / Oct '95 / Koch

TENNESSEE TOPCAT
CD _______________ CTJCD 1
Stomper Time / Apr '95 / TKO Magnum

UNCHAINED
Rowboat / Sea of heartbreak / Rusty cage / One rose / Country boy / Memories are made of this / Spiritual / Kneeling drunkards plea / Southern accents / Mean eyed cat / Meet me in heaven / I never picked cotton / Unchained / I've been everywhere
CD _______________ 74321397422
American / Nov '96 / BMG

UP THROUGH THE YEARS 1955-1957
Cry cry cry / Hey Porter / Folsom Prison blues / Luther played the boogie / So doggone lonesome / I walk the line / Get rhythm / Train of love / There you go / Goodbye little darling / I love you because / Straight A's in love / Next in line / Don't make me go / Home of the blues / Give my love to Rose / Rock Island line / Wreck of ol' 97 / Ballad of a teenage queen / Big river / Guess things happen that way / Come in stranger / You're the nearest thing to heaven / Blue train
CD _______________ BCD 15247
Bear Family / Nov '86 / Direct / Rollercoaster / Swift

VERY BEST OF JOHNNY CASH, THE (2CD Set)
Cry, cry, cry / So doggone lonesome / Folsom prison blues / I walk the line / Get rhythm / There you go / Train of love / Next in line / Don't make me go / Home of the blues / Give my love to Rose / Ballad of a teenage queen / Big river / Guess things happen that way / Come in stranger / Ways of a woman in love / You're the nearest thing to heaven / It's just about time / Luther played the boogie / Thanks a lot / Katy too / Goodbye little darlin' / I love you because / Straight A's in love / Mean-eyed cat / Oh, lonesome me / Rock Island line / Two timin' woman / Wide open road / Hey porter / Wreck of the old '97 / Balshazar / Country boy / Doin' my time / If the good Lord's willing / I heard that lonesome whistle cry / Remember me (I'm the one who loves you) / I was there when it happened / Born to lose / Life goes on / Blue train / Goodnight Irene / Fool's hall of fame / I forgot to remember to forget / I can't help it (if I'm still in love with you) / Always alone / I could never be ashamed of you / Story of a broken heart / You win again / I thought you'd like to know

CD Set _______________ CPCD 82412
Charly / Oct '96 / Koch

Cash Money

BLACK HEARTS AND BROKEN WILLS
CD _______________ TG 177CD
Touch & Go / Apr '97 / SRD

Cash, Rosanne

RETROSPECTIVE
Our little angel / On the surface / All come true / Wheel / Sleeping in Paris / 707 / Runaway train / I'm only sleeping / It hasn't happened yet / On the inside / What we really want / I count the tears / Pink bedroom / Seventh Avenue / Lover is forever
CD _______________ 4816132
Columbia / Nov '95 / Sony

Casino Steel

CASINO STEEL & HOLLYWOOD BRATS/ THE BOYS/GARY HOLTON (Various Artists)
Little ole wine drinker me: *Hollywood Brats* / You can't hurt a memory: *Boys* / Ruby: *Holton, Gary & Casino Steel* / Cajun invitation: *Claudia/Big Hand/Casino* / Strange brew: *CCCP* / Ballad of the sad cafe: *Scott & Steel* / Dust of the angels wings: *Steel, Casino & The Bandits* / Waiting for the lady: *Boys* / Candy: *Holton, Gary & Casino Steel* / Suckin' on Suzie: *Hollywood Brats* / Independent girl: *Boys* / Ghost riders in the sky: *Holton, Gary & Casino Steel* / Honky tonk night: *Claudia/Big Hand/Casino* / Chez Maximes: *Hollywood Brats* / This ain't America: *Scott & Steel* / Little rebel: *Steel, Casino & The Bandits* / Gotta serve somebody: *Claudia/Big Hand/Casino*
CD _______________ MISSCD 1993
Mission Discs / Apr '97 / Pinnacle

Casiopea

WORLD LIVE 1988 (Brazil/Australia/ Japan/Mexico/USA)
Doo loo doo / Bayside express / Taiyo fu / Red zone / Princess Moon / Inshie / Sold swing / Magnetic vibration / Mei mu / Supersonic / Movement / Access
CD _______________ 8378292
Polydor / Mar '94 / PolyGram

Cassandra Complex

SEX AND DEATH
Kneel (to the Boss) / Mouth of heaven / War against sleep / Come out / Satisfy me / Give me what I need / Devil's advocate / You make me sick / Voices / Realm of the senseless / Frankie teardrop / In memoriam JC / You still make me sick
CD _______________ BIAS 255CD
Play It Again Sam / Nov '93 / Discovery / Plastic Head / Vital

Cassiber

BEAUTY AND THE BEAST
CD _______________ RERCCD 3
ReR/Recommended / Feb '97 / ReR Megacorp / RTM/Disc

FACE WE ALL KNOW, A
This was the way it was / Remember / Old Gods / Two o'clock in the morning / Philosophy / Gut / Start the show / Screaming comes across the sky / They go in under archways / They have begun to move / Time gets faster / It's never quiet / Philosophy / Screaming holds / Philosophy / I was old / Way it was / To move
CD _______________ RERCCD
ReR/Recommended / Jun '97 / ReR Megacorp / RTM/Disc

MAN OR MONKEY
CD _______________ RERCCD 2
ReR/Recommended / Oct '96 / ReR Megacorp / RTM/Disc

PERFECT WORLDS
CD _______________ RERB 0000CD
ReR/Recommended / Oct '96 / ReR Megacorp / RTM/Disc

Cassidy, David

DAYDREAMER
CD _______________ ST 5004
Star Collection / Nov '93 / BMG

WHEN I'M A ROCK 'N' ROLL STAR (The David Cassidy Collection)
CD _______________ RE 21172
Razor & Tie / Dec '96 / Koch

Cassidy, Jane

MARY ANN MCCRACKEN (Cassidy, Jane & Maurice Leyden)
CD _______________ ASH 004CD
Ash / Apr '95 / ADA

Cassidy, Patrick

CHILDREN OF LIR, THE
CD _______________ 7567827442
Warner Bros. / Apr '95 / Warner Music

CRUIT
CD _____ CEFCD 130
Gael Linn / Jan '94 / ADA / CM / Direct / Grapevine/PolyGram / Roots

Cast

COLOURS OF LICHEN
CD _____ CUL 109CD
Culburnie / Jul '96 / ADA / CM / Direct / Duncans / Highlander / Ross

WINNOWING
CD _____ CUL 104CD
Culburnie / Oct '95 / ADA / CM / Direct / Duncans / Highlander / Ross

Cast

ALL CHANGE
Alright / Promised land / Sandstorm / Mankind / Tell it like it is / Four walls / Fine time / Back of my mind / Walkaway / Reflections / History / Two of a kind
CD _____ 5293122
Polydor / Sep '95 / PolyGram

MOTHER NATURE CALLS
Free me / On the run / Live the dream / Soul tied / She sun shines / I'm so lonely / Mad hatter / Mirror me / Guiding star / Never gonna tell you what to do (revolution) / Dance of the stars
CD _____ 5375672
Polydor / Apr '97 / PolyGram

Cast Iron Hike

WATCH IT BURN
CD _____ VR 052CD
Victory / Jun '97 / Plastic Head

Cast Of Thousands

PASSION
This is love / Passion / September / Tear me down / Girl / Immaculate deception / Colour fields / This experience / Thin line / Nothing is forever
CD _____ CDAFTER 6
Fun After All / Jun '88 / Pinnacle

Castle, Ben

BIG CELEBRATION (Castle, Ben & Roy)
CD _____ KMCD 735
Kingsway / Jun '94 / Complete/Pinnacle

Castle, Geoff

EXPANDED
CD _____ FORT 1
Turret / Mar '96 / Cadillac / Turret / Wellard

Castle, Joey

ROCK 'N' ROLL DADDY-O
CD Set _____ BCD 15560
Bear Family / Apr '92 / Direct / Rollercoaster / Swift

Castle, Pete

FALSE WATERS
CD _____ MATS 012CD
Steel Carpet / Nov '95 / ADA

Castro, Miguel

EXOTIC RHYTHMS OF LATIN AMERICA
CD _____ EUCD 1214
ARC / Sep '93 / ADA / ARC Music

Castro, Tommy

CAN'T KEEP A GOOD MAN DOWN
Can't keep a good man down / You knew the job was dangerous / Suitcase full of blues / You gotta do what you gotta do / I want to show you / My time after awhile / Take the highway down / High on the hog / You only go around once / Nobody loves me like my baby / Hycodan / Can't you see what you're doing to me
CD _____ BPCD 5041
Blind Pig / May '97 / ADA / CM / Direct / Hot Shot

EXCEPTION TO THE RULE
CD _____ BPCD 5029
Blind Pig / Feb '96 / ADA / CM / Direct / Hot Shot

Castro-Neves, Oscar

BRAZILIAN SCANDALS
Brazilian scandals / Pendando / Romancing lorry / Sugarloaf skyride / Cafe Copacabana / Return to Rio / Your eyes / Carioca rap / Ocean drive / Tropical dream / Ipanema afternoon
CD _____ JVC 20182
JVC / Aug '96 / Direct / New Note/Pinnacle / Vital/SAM

MARACUJA
Maracuja / Love in the afternoon / Scandal No.2 / El groove del segundo de mayo / Caiu no samba / Seresta / Buzios / Must it be now / Wiggle / Vea LA / Water circles / Ballad rocks and snow
CD _____ JVC 20192
JVC / Aug '96 / Direct / New Note/Pinnacle / Vital/SAM

TROPICAL HEART
Holding with an open hand / You are my romance / New hope / If the dance is over / Envelope / I still do / My heart surrenders / Maya's gift / I have seen tomorrow / Jasmina's perfume / Souvenirs / Tropical heart / Lullaby for a magical child
CD _____ JVC 20262
JVC / Dec '93 / Direct / New Note/Pinnacle / Vital/SAM

Casual

FEAR ITSELF
CD _____ CHIP 148
Jive / Feb '94 / Pinnacle

Casuals

VERY BEST OF THE CASUALS, THE
Jesamine / Toy / Fool's paradise / Hey hey hey / Hello it's me / Sunflower eyes / Now you can be / Daddy's song / Love me tonight / Someday man / Seven times seven / Weather vane / Never my love / My name is love / Adios amour / I've got something too / Caroline / Someday rock 'n' roll lady / Naughty boy
CD _____ 5520882
Spectrum / Jan '97 / PolyGram

Casus Belli

TAILGUNNRANGELES
CD _____ ARRCD 64007
Amphetamine Reptile / Aug '95 / Plastic Head

Cat Power

WHAT WOULD THE COMMUNITY THINK
In this hole / Good clean fun / What would the community think / Nude as the news / They tell me / Taking people / Fate of the human carbine / King rides by / Bathosphere / Water and air / Enough / Coat is always on
CD _____ OLE 2020
Matador / Sep '96 / Vital

Cat Rapes Dog

GOD, GUNS AND GASOLINE
CD _____ KK 034CD
KK / Sep '90 / Plastic Head

MAXIMUM OVERDRIVE
CD _____ KK 031
KK / Nov '89 / Plastic Head

RARITIES (Best Of Cat Rapes Dog - 2CD Set)
CD Set _____ KK 134DCD
KK / Jul '95 / Plastic Head

Cat Scratch Fever

DEATH WESTERN
CD _____ WOWCD 03
Words Of Warning / Feb '97 / SRD / Total/ BMG

Cat Sun Flower

CHILDISH
CD _____ EFA 127752
Freak Scene / Oct '95 / SRD

Catalogue

PENETRATION
CD _____ QRTCD 6187
Hat Art / Oct '96 / Cadillac / Harmonia Mundi

Catatonia

CATATONIA
CD _____ CRAI 039CDS
Crai / Dec '93 / ADA / Direct

WAY BEYOND BLUE
CD _____ 0630163052
Blanco Y Negro / Sep '96 / Warner Music

Catchers

MUTE
Beauty No.3 / Cotton dress / Apathy / Country freaks / Worm out / Jesus spaceman / Song for Autumn / Hollowed / Shifting / Sleepy head / La luna / Epitaph
CD _____ SETCD 018
Setanta / Oct '94 / Vital

Caterpillar

THOUSAND MILLION MICRONAUGHTS
CD _____ CPS 021CD
Compulsive / Jun '94 / SRD

Catfish Hodge Band

ADVENTURES AT CATFISH POND
CD _____ 9425872
Music For Little People / Aug '96 / Direct

Catfish Keith

CHERRY BALL
Mr. Catfish's advice / Cool can of beer / Your head's too big / By and by I'm going see the King / Cherry ball / Rabbits in your drawers / Swim deep, pretty mama / Hawaiian cowboy / Deep sea moan / Goin' up north to get my hambone boiled / Ramblin' blues / Leave my wife alone / Mama don't you sell it, papa don't you give it away / That ain't no way for me to get along
CD _____ FTRCD 003
Fish Tail / Sep '93 / Hot Shot

JITTERBUG SWING
Jitterbug swing / Slap a suit on you / Come back old devil / Blues at midnight / 12th street rag / Move to Louisiana / Gonna give that life / Preachin' the blues / Goin' down to Memphis / Texas tea party / Oh, captain / Fistful of riffs / Police and a sergeant / Tell everybody / Takin' my time
CD _____ FTRCD 002
Fish Tail / Nov '93 / Hot Shot

PEPPER IN MY SHOE
Jealous hearted see / Knockin' myself out / Saturday night stroll / Oh Mr Catfish / Daddy, where you been / Pepper in my shoe / You got to move / Tell me, baby / Nineteen bird dogs / Howling tom cat
CD _____ FTRCD 001
Fish Tail / Nov '93 / Hot Shot

Catharsis

ET S'AIMER...ET MOURIR
CD _____ SPA 14280
Spalax / Nov '94 / ADA / Cargo / Direct / Discovery / Greyhound

Cathedral

CARNIVAL BIZARRE, THE
Vampire sun / Hopkins (witchfinder general) / Utopian blaster / Night of the seagulls / Carnival bizarre / Electric grave / Palace of the fallen majesty / Blue light / Fangalactic supergoria / Interias cave
CD _____ MOSH 130CD
Earache / Sep '97 / Vital

ETHEREAL MIRROR, THE
Violet vortex / Ride / Enter the worms / Midnight mountain / Fountain of innocence / Grim luxuria / Jaded entity / Ashes you leave / Phantasmagoria / Imprisoned in flesh
CD _____ MOSH 077CD
Earache / May '93 / Vital

FOREST OF EQUILIBRIUM
CD _____ MOSH 043CD
Earache / Sep '94 / Vital

IN MEMORIAM
Mourning of a new day / All your sins / Ebony tears / March
CD _____ RISE 008CD
Rise Above / Apr '94 / Plastic Head / Vital

SUPERNATURAL BIRTH MACHINE
Cybertron 71/Eternal countdown / Urko's conquest / Stained glass horizon / Cyclops revolution / Birth machine 2000 / Nightmare castle / Fireball demon / Phaser quest / Suicide asteroid / Dragon ryder / Magnetic hole
CD _____ MOSH 156CD
Earache / Oct '96 / Vital

Catherine

HOT SAKI AND BEDTIME STORIES
Whisper / It's gonna get worse / Cotton candy high / Milkshake / Four leaf clover / Vegas glam / Punch me out / Make me smile / Blacklight / Don't touch me there / Sign of the cross / Angels / Pink Floyd poster / Good luck charm
CD _____ 4874362
Epic / Mar '97 / Sony

Catherine Wheel

CHROME
Kill rhythm / I confess / Crank / Broken head / Pain / Strange fruit / Chrome / Nude / Ursa Major space station / Fripp / Half life / Show me Mary
CD _____ 5180392
Fontana / Jul '93 / PolyGram

FERMENT
Texture / I wanna touch you / Black metallic / Indigo is blue / She's my friend / Shallow / Ferment / Flower to hide / Tumble down / Bill and Ben / Salt
CD _____ 5109032
Fontana / Feb '92 / PolyGram

HAPPY DAYS
God inside my head / Way down / Little muscle / Heal / Empty head / Receive / My exhibition / Eat my dust you insensitive fuck / Shocking / Love tips up / Judy staring at the sun / Hole / Fizzy love / Kill my soul / Glitter
CD _____ 5147172
Fontana / Nov '95 / PolyGram

LIKE CATS AND DOGS
CD _____ 5324562
Fontana / Sep '96 / PolyGram

Catherine's Cathedral

EQUILIBRIUM
CD _____ NOX 004CD
Noxious / Sep '95 / Plastic Head

INTOXICATION
CD _____ NOX 001CD
Noxious / Oct '94 / Plastic Head

Catherine, Philip

I REMEMBER YOU (Catherine, Philip Trio)
CD _____ CRISS 1048CD
Criss Cross / Nov '91 / Cadillac / Direct / Vital/SAM

MOODS VOL.1 (Catherine, Philip Trio)
CD _____ CRISS 1060CD
Criss Cross / Oct '92 / Cadillac / Direct / Vital/SAM

MOODS VOL.2
CD _____ CRISS 1061CD
Criss Cross / Nov '93 / Cadillac / Direct / Vital/SAM

TRANSPARENCE
Transparence / Dance for victor / Nem um talvez / L'eternel desir / Father Christmas / Rene Thomas / Galerie St. Hubert / Ozone / Goodbye / April blue
CD _____ INAK 8701CD
In Akustik / Jul '97 / Direct / TKO Magnum

TWIN HOUSE (Catherine, Philip & Larry Coryell)
Ms. Julie / Homecoming / Airpower / Twin house / Mortgage on your soul / Gloryell / Nuages / Twice a week
CD _____ 92022
Act / Apr '94 / New Note/Pinnacle

Catley, Marc

FINE DIFFERENCE (Catley, Marc & Geoff Mann)
We are one / One of the green things / Keep on / Calling / Love is the only way / This time / Freedom / Closer to you / True riches / War is won / Growth / All along the way / Weep for the city / Theospeak / Somewhere here / Hosea / Hello
CD _____ PCDN 133
Plankton / Apr '92 / Plankton

MAKE THE TEA
Make the tea / Jesus stops traffic / Ethnic praise / All glory to the wealthy / Newpraise / This is the day after yesterday / Times seven / P-r-r-raise the-e-e Lord / Jesus was so nice / Jesus you really are just God / Come to the quiet / Come and fill me with your power holy spirit / Lying in the spirit / Shepherding song / Lord I still just want to praise you / Now Lord in the outgoing faith situation / Lord / Hard livin' guy / If I had a rhyming dictionary / Gonna rock you tonite / Legend of ham 'n' egg / Hundred miraculous things before breakfast
CD _____ PCDN 135
Plankton / May '92 / Plankton

OFF THE END OF THE PIER SHOW, THE (Catley, Marc & Geoff Mann)
Over the edge / River - blue water / River - white water / River - delta / Twittering machine / Terence the termite stares down his underpants in growing am / In the wilderness / Europe after the rain
CD _____ PCDN 130
Plankton / Aug '91 / Plankton

Catney, Dave

FIRST FLIGHT
CD _____ JR 004012
Justice / Sep '92 / Koch

JADE VISIONS
CD _____ JR 004022
Justice / Nov '92 / Koch

REALITY ROAD
CD _____ JR 04032
Justice / Jun '94 / Koch

Cato, Pauline

BY LAND AND SEA (Cato, Pauline & Tom McConville)
CD _____ TCCD 01
Tomcat / Sep '96 / ADA / Direct

CHANGING TIDES (Cato, Pauline & Tom McConville)
Go to Berwick Johnny/High road to Linton / Omnibus/Beeswing / Gypsy's lullaby/Billy Pigg's hornpipe / Gardebylaten/Rejnlaender/Trettondagsmarschen / Keel row / South shore/De'il amang the tailors / Hector the hero/Iron man / Willafjord/Miss McLeods/Sleep soond in da mornin' / Ned of the hill / I'll get wedded in my auld claes/ Coffee bridge / Golden eagle/Alexander's hornpipe / Roslin Castle/Jump at the sun / Forth bridge/Easy club reel / Peacock follows the hen/(Another) peacock follows the hen / Peacock's revenge
CD _____ PCCD 02
Cato / Jul '94 / ADA / Direct

WANSBECK PIPER, THE
Calliope house/Tripping upstairs / Captain Ross/Cuckold come out of the amrey (Variations) / Piper's weird / Carrick hornpipe/

Happy hours / Lament for Ian Dickson / Acrobat / Wild hills o' Wannies / Town green polka/Bluebell polka / Exhibition/The hawk / Neil Gow's lament for the death of his second wife / Rowley burn/Remember me / Lady's well/Random (Variations) / Wallington Hall/Locomotive / Moving cloud/New high level (Whinham)/Mason's apron
CD _______ PCCD 01
Cato / Aug '92 / ADA / Direct

Cats Cradle

CATS CRADLE
Invisible man / Time and again / Scribbling / Cold comfort / D(S)ribbling / Raining down / Niagra / Sense of ourselves / One move ahead / Dynamite dream / Music is the magic / Gift of our time / Your rules
CD _______ 33WM 104
33 Jazz / Sep '97 / Cadillac / New Note/ Pinnacle

Cat's Miaow

KISS AND A CUDDLE, A
CD _______ BUS 10152
Bus Stop / Mar '97 / Cargo / Vital

Cattanach, Dave

DANCING IN THE SHADOWS
CD _______ CDLDL 1252
Lochshore / May '97 / ADA / Direct / Duncans

Cattle Company

HERO
CD _______ JHS 003
Bunny / Dec '94 / Bunny

Caudel, Stephen

IMPROMPTU ROMANCE
CD _______ CDSGP 9023
Prestige / Apr '95 / Else / Total/BMG

Caught In The Act

RELAPSE OF REASON
CD _______ NTHEN 025CD
Now & Then / Jan '96 / Plastic Head

VIBE
CD _______ ZYX 204504
ZYX / Jun '97 / ZYX

Caught On The Hop

NATION OF HOPKEEPERS
CD _______ HARCD 024
Harbour Town / Oct '93 / ADA / CM / Direct / Roots

Cauld Blast Orchestra

DURGA'S FEAST
CD _______ ECLCD 9410
Eclectic / Jan '96 / ADA / New Note/ Pinnacle

SAVAGE DANCE
Reels within wheels / Tower of babel stomp / Cauld blast / Savage dance / Oyster wives' rant / Tarbolton lodge / Railyard band / Rantin' reel / Green shutters / Bottle hymn of the republic / Quaich
CD _______ ECLCD 9002
Eclectic / Jan '96 / ADA / New Note/ Pinnacle

Cause For Alarm

CAUSE FOR ALARM
CD _______ VE 19CD
Victory / Mar '95 / Plastic Head

CAUSE FOR ALARM/WARZONE (Split CD) (Cause For Alarm/Warzone)
CD _______ VR 0126
Victory / Jan '96 / Plastic Head

CHEATERS AND THE CHEATED
CD _______ VR 049CD
Victory / Apr '97 / Plastic Head

Causing Much Pain

SOUTHERN POINT OF VIEW, A
CD _______ THT 4211CD
Ichiban / Aug '95 / Direct / Koch

Cavallaro, Carmen

UNCOLLECTED 1946, THE (Cavallaro, Carmen & His Orchestra)
CD _______ HCD 112
Hindsight / Nov '94 / Jazz Music / Target/ BMG

Cavanagh, Page

DIGITAL PAGE VOL.2, THE
CD _______ SLCD 9006
Starline / Jun '94 / Jazz Music

Cavatina

SOUND OF CHRISTMAS, THE
Sleigh ride / Ding dong merrily on high / Good King Wenceslas / First Noel / Ave Maria / What child is this / God rest ye merry gentlemen / Little drummer boy / Holly and the ivy / Golden bells / Past three o'clock / O Little town of Bethlehem / Christmas song / Walking in the air / Little shepherd boy / In the bleak midwinter / Trio from l'enfance du Christ, Opus 25 / Coventry carol / We three kings of Orient are / Holy boys / Interlude from Ceremony Of Carols, Opus 28 / Amid the roses Mary sits / Rudolph the red nosed reindeer / White Christmas / Silent night
CD _______ PWK 123
Carlton / Oct '95 / Carlton

Cave, Nick

BOATMAN'S CALL (Cave, Nick & The Bad Seeds)
Into my arms / Time tree arbour / People ain't no good / Brompton oratory / There is a kingdom / (Are you) The one I've been waiting for / Where do we go now but nowhere / West country girl / Black hair / Idiot prayer / Far from me / Green eyes
CD _______ CDSTUMM 142
Mute / Mar '97 / RTM/Disc

FIRST BORN IS DEAD, THE (Cave, Nick & The Bad Seeds)
CD _______ CDSTUMM 21
Mute / Apr '88 / RTM/Disc

FROM HER TO ETERNITY (Cave, Nick & The Bad Seeds)
Avalanche / Cabin fever / Well of misery / From here to eternity / In the ghetto / Moon in the ghetto / St. Huck / Wings off flies / Box for black Paul / From here to eternity (1987)
CD _______ CDSTUMM 17
Mute / '87 / RTM/Disc

GOOD SON, THE (Cave, Nick & The Bad Seeds)
Foi na cruz / Good son / Sorrow's child / Weeping song / Ship song / Hammer song / Lament / Witness song / Lucy
CD _______ CDSTUMM 76
Mute / Apr '90 / RTM/Disc

HENRY'S DREAM (Cave, Nick & The Bad Seeds)
Papa won't leave you, Henry / I had a dream, Joe / Straight to you / Brother my cup is empty / Christina the astonishing / When I first came to town / John Finns' wife / Loom of the land / Jack the ripper
CD _______ CDSTUMM 92
Mute / Apr '92 / RTM/Disc

KICKING AGAINST THE PRICKS (Cave, Nick & The Bad Seeds)
CD _______ CDSTUMM 28
Mute / Aug '86 / RTM/Disc

LET LOVE IN (Cave, Nick & The Bad Seeds)
Do you love me / Nobody's baby now / Lover man / Jangling Jack / Red right hand / I let love in / Thirsty dog / Ain't gonna rain anymore / Lay me low / Do you love me part 2
CD _______ CDSTUMM 123
Mute / Apr '94 / RTM/Disc

LIVE SEEDS (Cave, Nick & The Bad Seeds)
CD _______ CDSTUMM 122
Mute / Sep '93 / RTM/Disc
CD _______ LCDSTUMM 122
Mute / Aug '96 / RTM/Disc

MURDER BALLADS (Cave, Nick & The Bad Seeds)
Song of joy / Stagger Lee / Henry Lee / Lovely creature / Where the wild roses grow / Curse of Millhaven / Kindness of strangers / Crow Jane / O'Malley's bar / Death is not the end
CD _______ LCDSTUMM 138
Mute / Jan '96 / RTM/Disc

TENDER PREY (Cave, Nick & The Bad Seeds)
CD _______ CDSTUMM 52
Mute / Sep '88 / RTM/Disc

YOUR FUNERAL, MY TRIAL (Cave, Nick & The Bad Seeds)
CD _______ CDSTUMM 34
Mute / Feb '87 / RTM/Disc

Caveman

POSITIVE REACTION
CD _______ FILERCD 406
Profile / Apr '91 / Pinnacle

WHOLE 9 YARDS
CD _______ FILERCD 429
Profile / May '92 / Pinnacle

Caveman Shoestore

FLUX
Knife edge / Pond at night / Actualize / Four year old / Ticket to obscurity / Kurtain / All this air / Lightning / Henzyme / Underneath the water / Underneath the city / Cold
CD _______ TK 93CD056
T/K / Jun '94 / Pinnacle

Cavendish Dance Band

ST. ANDREW'S BALL
CD _______ SAB 200
BMG / May '94 / BMG

Cavour, Ernesto

EL VUELO DEL PICAFLOR
Padre viento / Rosario de uvas / Danza agraria / Matraca de quena y charango / Carnaval de san luis / Leyenda de la kantuta / Las mamalitas / El vuelo del picaflor / La yegua y el arroyo / La cueca destrozada / Hailon en chiceria / Tres pastores / Chulupi / Ida y vuelta / Rio choqueyapu / Bailecitos desairados / Te amare despues te muerto
CD _______ 68953
Tropical / Apr '97 / Discovery

Cazazza, Monte

WORST OF MONTE
CD _______ MONTE 1CD
The Grey Area / Jun '92 / RTM/Disc

CBQ

CIRCLES AND TRIPLETS
CD _______ DRCD 230
Dragon / May '87 / ADA / Cadillac / CM / Roots / Wellard

CCCC

FLASH
CD _______ CSR 15CD
Cold Spring / Sep '96 / Plastic Head / RTM/Disc

Cecil

BOMBAR DIDDLAH
Dream awake / Plastics keep coming / Spirit level / Upside down smile / Fishes / My neck / No excuses / Poshinalagweedy
CD _______ CDPCS 7384
Parlophone / Oct '96 / EMI

Ceddo

UNCHAINED
CD _______ ITMP 970052
ITM / Jan '91 / Koch / Tradelink

Cee Bee Beaumont

PRE-STRESSED
Micro-cycle offensive / Wormhole / Deadshot / After the slide / Gumkick / Swamp drag / Weeny roast / York Way rumble / Continental cooler / Led pedal / Scooter Joe / Zero agenda / N19 mudslide / Roscoe monstertruck / Mad dog glove compartment / Mansize / Dumpsterville patrol vehicle / Slap dunk / Offord Road divide / Zippo raid
CD _______ DAMGOOD 66CD
Damaged Goods / Jul '95 / Shellshock/Disc

Cee Mix

HOME IS WHERE THE BASS IS
CD _______ INCCD 3311
Incoming / Jul '96 / Pinnacle

Ceiver, Jiri

HEADPHONE
CD _______ HHCD 014
Harthouse / Oct '95 / Mo's Music Machine / Prime / Vital

JIG, AMBLE AND LISP
Valve / Poke / Ttsys (me4u) / Stitch / Fastloom / CAT / Vex / Pigeons OSL / Plaque / Poke / Gt bosse / Miller / Ycool
CD _______ HHCD 024
Harthouse / Apr '97 / Mo's Music Machine / Prime / Vital

Celea

WORLD VIEW (Celea & Liebman/ Reisinger)
Acid birds / Nadir / Witches groove / Village / Jungle / City / Desert / Sky / Unity / Sixteen tones / Piano trio / Dirgis
CD _______ LBLC 6592
Label Bleu / Jun '97 / New Note/Pinnacle

Celestial Season

FOREVER SCARLET
CD _______ CDAR 015
Adipocre / Feb '94 / Plastic Head

ORANGE
CD _______ IS 779990CD
I Scream Music / Jun '97 / Plastic Head

SOLAR LOVERS
CD _______ D 00038CD
Displeased / Apr '95 / Plastic Head / RTM/ Disc

Celestin, Oscar 'Papa'

1950'S RADIO BROADCASTS, THE
Sheik of Araby / Eh la bas / Lil' Liza Jane / Just a closer walk with thee / Bill Bailey / Mama don't allow / Jazz it blues / It don't mean a thing if it ain't got that swing / Panama / San / Sister Kate / Dippermouth blues / Tiger rag / Maryland my Maryland / Milenburg joys / War cloud / Woodchopper's ball / High society / Fidgety feet / Ballin' the jack / Oh didn't he ramble / When the saints go marching in
CD _______ ARHCD 7024
Arhoolie / Nov '96 / ADA / Cadillac / Direct

NEW ORLEANS CLASSICS (Celestin, Oscar 'Papa' & Sam Morgan)
Original tuxedo rag: *Celestin, Oscar 'Papa' Original Tuxedo Orchestra* / Careless love / Black rag / I'm satisfied you love me / My Josephine / Station calls / Give me some more / Dear Almanzoer / Papa's got the jim-jams / As you like it / Just for you dear, I'm crying / When I'm with you / It's jam up / Sweetheart of TKO / Ta ta daddy / Steppin' on the gas / Everybody's talking about Sammy / Mobile stomp / Sing on / Short dress gal / Bogalousa strut / Down by the riverside / Over in the glory land
CD _______ AZCD 12
Azure / Nov '92 / Azure / Cadillac / Jazz Music / Swift / Wellard

Celetia

CELETIA
Are U ready / Missing your love / Work me over / All my loving / This feelings killing me / Be my honey / It rains in my heart / Candelight / Way U make me feel / Up and down / Excited / Gonna get down
CD _______ DESCD 03
Diesel / Jan '96 / Jet Star

Celias, Elyane

ETOILES DE LA CHANSON
CD _______ 414722
Music Memoria / Mar '96 / ADA / Discovery

Celibate Rifles

BLIND EAR
Johnny / Worlds keep turning / Electravision mantra / Dial om / Wonderful life '88 / Sean O'Farell / Belfast / Cycle / They're killing us all (to make the world safe) / O salvation / El Salvador / Fish and trees
CD _______ HOT 1046CD
Hot / Oct '94 / Hot Records

CELIBATE RIFLES, THE
CD _______ HOT 1007CD
Hot / Nov '92 / Hot Records

HEAVEN ON A STICK
CD _______ HOT 1038CD
Hot / May '97 / Hot Records

KISS KISS BANG BANG
Back in the red / Temper, temper / JNS / Pretty colours / Nether world / Some kinda feeling / New mistakes / Carmine vattelly (NYNYC) / City of fun / Conflict of instinct / Sometimes / Burn my eye / SOS
CD _______ HOT 1029CD
Hot / Nov '92 / Hot Records

PLATTERS DU JOUR
Kent's theme / Let's get married / Twenty four hours / Tubular greens / Pretty pictures / Out in the west again / Summer holiday blues / Merry Christmas blues / Wild desire / I'm waiting for the man / Sometimes / E=MC2 / Six days on the road / Groupie girl / Eddie / Ice blue / Thank you America / Back in the red / Rainforest / Dancing barefoot / Jesus on TV / More things change / Junk
CD _______ HOT 103334CD
Hot / Oct '94 / Hot Records

ROMAN BEACH PARTY
CD _______ HOT 1030CD
Hot / Nov '92 / Hot Records

SIDEROXYLON
CD _______ HOT 1001CD
Hot / Mar '93 / Hot Records

SOFA
Killing time / Wild desire / Sometimes / Bill Bonney regrets / Jesus on TV / Johnny / Electravision mantra / Wonderful life / More things change / Oceanshore / New mistakes / Back in the red / Ice blue / This week / Nether world / Glasshouse / Frank Hyde (slight return) / Darlinghurst confidential / Pretty pictures / Gonna cry
CD _______ HOT 1043CD
Hot / Jul '95 / Hot Records

SPACEMAN IN A SATIN SUIT, A
Spirits / Kev the Head / Brickin' around / Living what I dream / City of hope / Seams / Big world / Whatever you want / Kathy says / Diamond sky / Cuttin' it fine / This gift / Let's do it again / Spaceman in a satin suit
CD _______ HOT 1047CD
Hot / Apr '96 / Hot Records

TURGID MIASMA OF EXISTENCE, THE
CD _______ HOT 1024CD
Hot / Nov '92 / Hot Records

YIZGARNNOFF
Brickin' around / Word about Jones / Cycle / Downtown / Johnny / Happy house / Dream of night / Groovin' in the land of love / S and MTV / Electravision mantra / 2000 light years from home / More things change / Tubular greens / Invisible man / Glasshouse / O salvation / Oceanshore / Baby, please don't go
CD _______ HOT 1041CD
Hot / Jul '95 / Hot Records

Cell

LIVING ROOM
CD EFA 049332
City Slang / Feb '94 / RTM/Disc

SLO-BLO
CD EO 4909CD
City Slang / Nov '92 / RTM/Disc

Cello

ALVA
CD BIOCD 04
Messerschmitt / Mar '94 / Plastic Head

Cellophane

HANG UPS
CD MINTCD 10
Mint Tea / Oct '94 / RTM/Disc

Celtarabia

ANCIENT FORCES
Ride / Oro / Corvus / Lark / Ancient forces / Armenian / Eight step trance / She moved through the fair/Wedding day
CD OSMOCD 011
Osmosys / Mar '97 / Direct

Celtic Frost

IN MEMORY OF CELTIC FROST (Various Artists)
CD DWELL 1006CD
Dwell / Jul '96 / Plastic Head

MORBID TALES/EMPERORS RETURN
CD NCD 3
Noise / '88 / Koch

PARCHED WITH THIRST AM I, AND DYING (1984-1992)
Idols of Chagrin / A... descent to Babylon / Return to the Eve / Juices like wine / Inevitable factor / Heart beneath / Cherry orchards / Tristesses de la lune / Wings of solitude / Usurper / Journey into fear / Downtown Hanoi / Circle of the tyrants / In the chapel in the moonlight / I won't dance / Name of my bride / Mexican radio / Under Appolyon's sun
CD N 01912
Noise / Mar '92 / Koch

TO MEGA THERION
CD N 00313
Noise / Jul '92 / Koch

VANITY/NEMESIS
Heart beneath / Wine in my hand (third from the sun) / Wings of solitude / Name of my bride / This island earth / Restless seas / Phallic tantrum / Kiss or a whisper / Vanity / Nemesis / Heroes
CD N 01992
Noise / Jul '92 / Koch

Celtic Orchestra

CELTIC REFLECTIONS (Instrumental Airs & Melodies Of Ireland)
Carrickfergus / My Lagan love / Spancil Hill / Go lassie go / Sally Garden / Water is wide / Buachail on Eirne / Ag Chriost an Siol / West's awake / Bruach na carraige baine / Mo gheale mear / Believe me if all those endearing young charms / Clare to here
CD DOCDK 109
Dolphin / Aug '96 / CM / Else / Grapevine/ PolyGram / Koch

Celtic Spirit

CELTIC SPIRIT
CD MCCD 243
Music Club / Jun '96 / Disc / THE

Celtic Thunder

LIGHT OF OTHER DAYS, THE
CD GLCD 1086
Green Linnet / Jan '90 / ADA / CM / Direct / Highlander / Roots

Celtus

MOONCHILD
Strange day in the country / Moonchild / Every step of the way / Some kind of wonder / Brother's lament / Beyond the dark / Love turns to dust / Rosa-ree / Pilgrim / Trikuti / We two are one
CD 4877152
Sony Soho2 / Jun '97 / Sony

Cement

CEMENT
Living sound delay / Shout / I feel / Four / Prison love / Six / Blue / Too beat / Take it easy / Old days / Reputation shot / Chip away / KCMT
CD RTD 15715732
World Service / Jun '93 / Vital

MAN WITH THE ACTION HAIR, THE
Man with the action hair / Killing an angel / Pile driver / Crying / Dancing from the depths of the fire / Life on the sun / Sleep / Train / King Arthur / Hotel Aiablo / Bonnie Brae / Magic number / Power and the magic
CD RTD 15717452
World Service / Aug '94 / Vital

Cemetary

BLACK VANITY
CD BMCD 59
Black Mark / Oct '94 / Plastic Head

EVIL SHADE OF GREY, AN
Dead red / Where the rivers of madness stream / Dark illusions / Evil shade of grey / Sidereal passing / Scars / Nightmare lake / Souldrain
CD BMCD 020
Black Mark / Jun '92 / Plastic Head

Cenotaph

RIDING OUR BLACK OCEANS
CD CYBERCD 13
Cyber / Feb '95 / Amato Disco / Arabesque / Plastic Head

THIRTEEN THRENODIES
CD KK 001CD
Planet K / May '95 / Plastic Head

Centinex

REFLECTIONS
CD RRS 954CD
Centinex / Mar '97 / Plastic Head

Central Nervous System

6 DEGREES
CD WB 1158CD
We Bite / Apr '97 / Plastic Head

REALITY CHECK
CD WB 1122CD
We Bite / Jul '95 / Plastic Head

Centry In Dub

THUNDER MOUNTAIN
CD WWCD 10
Wibbly Wobbly / Mar '95 / SRD

Century

RELEASE THE CHAINS
CD DNCCD 4
Conscious Sounds / May '95 / Jet Star / SRD

Ceolbeg

FIVE
Mother Farquhar / Skate in the hand / Gillie's favourite / Willie Wastle / Chow man / Catriona Og / Cadal Cha / Cockerel in the creel / Duncan Finlay / Black cocks of Berriedale / Presence / Old Maid's dream / Borderline / Les freres Denis / India / Nodding song / Gude'en tae ye kimmer / Skye Bridge dance / Duncan Cla's / Gaberlunzie man
CD CDTRAX 100
Greentrax / Apr '96 / ADA / Direct / Duncans / Highlander

NOT THE BUNNY HOP
Big parcel / Not the bunny hop / Queen of Argyll / Tam Billy's jig / Archie Beag and Calum Mor / Miss Donella Beaton / High and mighty / Arthur Gillies / Farewell tae the haven / It was long ago / Three wheeled rabbit / My lass has a lovely red schleppack / De'il's awa' wi' tha exciseman / Seagull / Soft horse reel / Pumpkin's fancy / Snug in the blanket / Otago River / Iain Ghlinn Cuaich / Shores of Loch Bea
CD CDTRAX 053
Greentrax / Feb '93 / ADA / Direct / Duncans / Highlander

SEEDS TO THE WIND
Mazurka set / Senorita Ana Rocio / Seeds to the wind / Coupit yowe set / Glenlivet / A the airts / Here's a health tae the sauters / Cajun two-step / Johnny Cope / See the people run / Lord Galloway's lamentation
CD CDTRAX 048
Greentrax / Dec '91 / ADA / Direct / Duncans / Highlander

UNFAIR DANCE, AN
Zito the bubbleman / Galicia revisited / Jolly beggar / Gale warning / Collier's way / Stand together / Wild west waltz / Ceol beag / Seton's lassie / Train journey north / My love is like a red red rose / Sleeping tune
CD CDTRAX 058
Greentrax / Jul '93 / ADA / Direct / Duncans / Highlander

Ceoltoiri

CELTIC LACE
CD MMCD 203
Maggie's Music / Dec '94 / ADA / CM

SILVER APPLES OF MOON
CD MMCD 202
Maggie's Music / Dec '94 / ADA / CM

Cephas, John

COOL DOWN (Cephas, John 'Bowling Green' & Phil Wiggins)
CD ALCD 4838
Alligator / Feb '96 / ADA / CM / Direct

DOG DAYS OF AUGUST
CD FF 394CD
Flying Fish / May '93 / ADA / CM / Direct / Roots

FLIP, FLOP AND FLY (Cephas, John 'Bowling Green' & Phil Wiggins)
CD FF 58CD
Flying Fish / May '93 / ADA / CM / Direct / Roots

GUITAR MAN (Cephas, John 'Bowling Green' & Phil Wiggins)
Black cat on the line / Richmond blues / Weeping willow / Guitar man / Police dog blues / Corrine / Careless love / Brownsville
CD FF 70470
Flying Fish / Oct '96 / ADA / CM / Direct / Roots

SWEET BITTER BLUES (Cephas, John 'Bowling Green' & Phil Wiggins)
Bittersweet blues / St. James infirmary / I saw the light / Sickbed blues / Piedmont rag / Dog days of August / Roberta-a-thousand miles from home / Highway 301 / Hoodoo woman / Louisiana chase / Bowling green rag / Bye bye baby / Last fair deal gone down / Big boss man / Burn your bridges / Running and hiding
CD ECD 260502
Evidence / Sep '94 / ADA / Cadillac / Harmonia Mundi

Cerbone, Lisa

CLOSE YOUR EYES
Amber / Blue frog / Asbury Park / My little sister and me / Manic depressive jubilation / Close your eyes / Tears / Three boys in the schoolyard / Painful smile (New Year's Day) / Dead end street
CD INDIGO 12102
Strange Ways / Jul '97 / Cargo / Pinnacle

Cerebral Fix

DEATH EROTICA
Death erotica / World machine / Clarissa / Haunted eyes / Mind within mine / Splintered wings / Creator of outcasts / Angel's kiss / Still in mind / Raft of Medusa / Never again / Too drunk to funk / Burning / Living after midnight
CD CDFLAG 75
Under One Flag / Nov '92 / Pinnacle

Cerebros Exprimidos

DEMENCIA
CD GRITA 33994CD
Grita / Jun '96 / Plastic Head

Ceremonial Oath

CARPET
CD BS 02CD
Black Sun / Apr '95 / Plastic Head

Cerrone

BEST OF THE REMIXES, THE
CD 3020712
Arcade / Jul '97 / Discovery

Cervenka, Exene

SURFACE TO AIR SERPENTS
CD 213CD 004
2.13.61 / Jun '96 / Pinnacle

Cetera, Peter

SOLITUDE/SOLITAIRE
Big mistake / They don't make 'em like they used to / Glory of love / Queen of the masquerade ball / Daddy's girl / Next time I fall / Wake up love / Solitude/Solitaire / Only love knows why
CD 92547422
WEA / Aug '90 / Warner Music

WORLD FALLING DOWN
Restless heart / Even a fool can see / Feels like heaven / Wild ways / World falling down / Man in me / Where there's no tomorrow / Last place God made / Dip your wings / Have you ever been in love
CD 7599268942
WEA / Jun '92 / Warner Music

Ceyleib People

TANYET
Aton 1: Leyshem / Zendan / Ceyladd beyta / Becal / Ddom / Toadda BB / Aton 11: Dyl / Ralin / Tygstyl / Pendyl / Jacayl / Menyatt dyl com
CD DOCD 1991
Drop Out / Jan '92 / Pinnacle

Chabenat, Giles

DE L'EAU ET DES AMANDES (Chabenat, Giles & Frederic paris)
CD Y 225060CD
Silex / Nov '95 / ADA / Harmonia Mundi

Chabez, Carlos Hernandez

SONGS OF MEXICO (Chabez, Carlos Hernandez & Los Trovadores)
CD VICG 53352
JVC World Library / Mar '96 / ADA / CM / Direct

Chacksfield, Frank

MUSIC OF COLE PORTER, THE (Chacksfield, Frank Orchestra)
Night and day / Begin the beguine / I love Paris / My heart belongs to Daddy / Every time we say goodbye / Wunderbar / Just one of those things / You'd be so nice to come home to / Friendship / In the still of the night / Blow, Gabriel, blow
CD 4524912
Decca / Mar '97 / PolyGram

Chad & Jeremy

CHAD AND JEREMY SING FOR YOU
CD 14524
Spalax / Jan '97 / ADA / Cargo / Direct / Discovery / Greyhound

Chadbourne, Eugene

CAMPER VAN CHABOURNE (Chadbourne, Eugene & Camper Van Beethoven)
Reason to believe / I talk to the wind / Fayettenam / Evil filthy preacher / Games people play / Zappa medley / Ba-lue bolivar balues are / Boy with the coins / Psychedelic basement / Hum-allah hum-allah / Careful with that axe, Eugene / They can make it rain bombs
CD HYMN 7
Fundamental / Aug '97 / Cargo / Plastic Head / Shellshock/Disc

END TO SLAVERY
CD INTAKTCD 047
Intakt / May '97 / Cadillac

LOCKED IN A DUTCH COFFEE SHOP (Chadbourne, Eugene & Jimmy Carl Black)
CD HYMN 2
Fundamental / Aug '97 / Cargo / Plastic Head / Shellshock/Disc

PATRIZIO (Chadbourne, Eugene & Paul Lovens)
CD VICTOCD 046
Victo / Mar '97 / Harmonia Mundi / ReR Megacorp

TERROR HAS SOME STRANGE KINFOLK (Chadbourne, Eugene & Evan Johns)
CD VIRUS 119CD
Alternative Tentacles / Jun '93 / Cargo / Greyhound / Pinnacle

Chadima, Mikolas

PSEUDODEMOKRITUS
CD P 00982
Black Point / Jun '97 / ReR Megacorp

Chain Gang

PERFUMED
Dead at the Meadowlands / Metallands / Kill for you / Beijing / Cut of the drug Czar's head / Satanic rockers / Pal / Kill the bouncers at the Ritz / Nam / Brother and sister / That's how strong my love is / Rockland / Born in Brazil / Prostitute / Guts boss / My fly / Cannibal him / Piss your pants / Son of Sam / Murder for the millions / Wrestler / OTB / Label this
CD OLE 0192
Matador / Mar '94 / Vital

Chain Of Strength

ONE THING, THE
CD REVCD 010
Revelation / Apr '96 / Plastic Head

Chain, Paul

ALKAHEST
CD GOD 013CD
Rise Above / Feb '96 / Plastic Head / Vital

Chainsaw Kittens

POP HEIRESS
Sore on the floor / Pop heiress dies / Dive into the sea / I ride free / Media star hymn / Silver millionaire / We're like / Justine find heaven / Soldier on my shoulder / Burn you down / Closet song / Loneliest China place
CD 7567923182
Atlantic / Feb '95 / Warner Music

Chainsaw Sisters

HOT SAUCE
CD NM 7CD
No Master's Voice / Apr '95 / ADA / Direct

Chairmen Of The Board

BEST OF CHAIRMEN OF THE BOARD, THE
CD CCSCD 810
Renaissance Collector Series / Mar '97 / BMG

Chaix, Henri

JIVE AT FIVE
CD SKCD 22035
Sackville / Jun '94 / Cadillac / Jazz Music / Swift

JUMPIN' PUMPKINS (Chaix, Henri Trio)
CD ________ **SKCD 22020**
Sackville / Jun '93 / Cadillac / Jazz Music / Swift

Chaka Demus

BAD BAD CHAKA
CD ________ **792112**
Jammy's / Jan '94 / Jet Star

CHAKA DEMUS & PLIERS GOLD (Chaka Demus & Pliers)
Bogle dance / Thief / Nuh me / World a girls / Winning machine / You send come call me / Blood in a eyes / Sweet Jamaica / Love up de gal / Terror girl wine / Pretty face
CD ________ **CRCD 11**
Charm / Apr '92 / Jet Star

CHAKA DEMUS MEETS SHABBA RANKS
CD ________ **RNCD 2101**
Rhino / Apr '95 / Grapevine/PolyGram / Jet Star

CONSCIOUSNESS A LICK (Chaka Demus & Pliers)
CD ________ **080902**
Melodie / Jun '96 / ADA / Discovery / Grapevine/PolyGram / Greensleeves / Jet Star

FOR EVERY KINDA PEOPLE (Chaka Demus & Pliers)
Every kinda people / We pray / Boom smilin' / Witness stand / Posse come jump around / In the mood / What's the move / Searching / Man smart, woman smarter / Hurry up and come / Comin' home / War a gwaan (down the lane)
CD ________ **IJCD 3008**
Island Jamaica / Jan '97 / Jet Star / PolyGram

GAL WINE (Chaka Demus & Pliers)
CD ________ **VYDCD 7**
Vine Yard / Sep '95 / Grapevine/PolyGram

GAL WINE WINE (Chaka Demus & Pliers)
CD ________ **GRELCD 173**
Greensleeves / Jul '92 / Jet Star / SRD

RUFF THIS YEAR (Chaka Demus & Pliers)
CD ________ **RASCD 3112**
Ras / Apr '93 / Direct / Greensleeves / Jet Star / SRD

TEASE ME (Chaka Demus & Pliers)
Tease me / She don't let nobody / Nuh betta nuh deh / Bam bam / Friday evening / Let's make it tonight / One nation under a groove / Tracy / Sunshine day / Murder she wrote / Roadrunner / I wanna be your man / Twist and shout / Gal wine
CD ________ **CIDMX 1102**
Mango / Jan '94 / PolyGram / Vital

WORLD ENTERPRISE (Chaka Demus & Pliers)
CD ________ **RNCD 2028**
Rhino / Nov '93 / Grapevine/PolyGram / Jet Star

Chako

EBB & FLOW
CD ________ **DDE 3931**
Scout / May '96 / Koch

Chalice

CHALICE DUB
CD ________ **ROTCD 006**
Reggae On Top / Feb '95 / Jet Star / SRD

Challengers

MAN FROM UNCLE
More / Cast your fate to the wind / Taste of honey / Walk don't run / Only the young / Work song / Born free / Telstar / Stranger on the shore / Memphis / Lonely bull / Penetration / Summer place / In crowd rebel rouser / Somewhere my love / Mr. Moto / Alley cat / Tequila / Man from UNCLE / Pipeline / Strangers in the night / Out of limits / Raunchy / Wipeout
CD ________ **EDCD 350**
Edsel / Jul '92 / Pinnacle

Challis, Bill

BILL CHALLIS AND HIS ORCHESTRA 1936 (Challis, Bill & Orchestra)
CD ________ **CCD 71**
Circle / Jun '95 / Jazz Music / Swift / Wellard

Chaloff, Serge

FABLE OF MABEL, THE
You brought a new kind of love to me / Fable of Mabel / Let's jump / Zdot / On baby / Salute to tiny / Sherry / Easy Street / All I do is dream of you
CD ________ **BLCD 760923**
Black Lion / Oct '90 / Cadillac / Jazz Music / Koch / Wellard

Chamber Jazz Sextet

PLAYS PAL JOEY
I could write a book / My funny valentine / I didn't know what time it was / Zip / Lady is a tramp / Bewitched / There's a small hotel / Terrific rainbow
CD ________ **CCD 79030**
Candid / Feb '97 / Cadillac / Direct / Jazz Music / Koch / Wellard

Chambers, Joe

PHANTOM OF THE CITY
Phantom of the city / Fun / For miles / Nuevo mundo / El Gaucho / You've changed / In and out
CD ________ **CCD 79517**
Candid / Feb '97 / Cadillac / Direct / Jazz Music / Koch / Wellard

Chambers, Ken

ABOVE YOU
CD ________ **TAANG 83**
Taang / Aug '94 / Cargo

Chambers, Paul

JUST FRIENDS (Chambers, Paul & Cannonball Adderley)
Ease it / Just friends / I got rhythm / Julie Ann / Awful mean / There is no greater love
CD ________ **LEJAZZCD 24**
Le Jazz / Feb '94 / Cadillac / Koch

Chamblee, Eddie

CHAMBLEE, EDDIE & JULIAN DASH/ JOE THOMAS 1951-1955 (Chamblee, Eddie & Julian Dash/Joe Thomas)
CD ________ **BMCD 1052**
Blue Moon / Apr '97 / Cadillac / Discovery / Greensleeves / Jazz Music / Jet Star / TKO Magnum

EDDIE CHAMBLEE 1947-1952
CD ________ **BMCD 1049**
Blue Moon / Apr '97 / Cadillac / Discovery / Greensleeves / Jazz Music / Jet Star / TKO Magnum

Chameleons

FAN AND THE BELLOWS, THE
CD ________ **GOODCD 9**
Dead Dead Good / Sep '96 / Pinnacle

LIVE AT THE GALLERY CLUB
CD ________ **VICD 007**
Visionary/Jettisoundz / Jun '96 / Cargo / Pinnacle / RTM/Disc / THE

RADIO 1 EVENING SHOW SESSIONS
CD ________ **CDNT 1**
Night Tracks / Jan '93 / Grapevine/ PolyGram / Pinnacle

RETURN OF THE ROUGHNECKS, THE (The Best Of The Chameleons/2CD Set)
CD ________ **GOODCD 12**
CD Set ________ **GOODCD 12X**
Dead Dead Good / May '97 / Pinnacle

SCRIPT OF THE BRIDGE
Don't fall / Here today / Monkeyland / Seal skin / Up the down escalator / Less than human / Pleasure and pain / Thursday's child / As high as you can go / Person isn't safe anywhere these days / Paper tiger / View from a hill / Nostalgia / In shreds
CD ________ **GOODCD 6**
Dead Dead Good / Sep '96 / Pinnacle

STRANGE TIMES
Mad Jack / Caution / Soul in isolation / Swamp thing / Time / End of time / Seriocity / In answer / Childhood / I'll remember / Tears / Paradiso / Inside out / Ever after / John I'm only dancing / Tomorrow never knows
CD Set ________ **GFLDD 19207**
Geffen / Jun '93 / BMG

WHAT DOES ANYTHING MEAN BASICALLY
CD ________ **GOODCD 7**
Dead Dead Good / Sep '96 / Pinnacle

Champion, Simon

CAMPFIRES AND DREAMTIME
Campfires / Echoes / Turu-etya / Storyteller / Valley of the kings / Set sail / Far away
CD ________ **EUCD 1218**
ARC / Sep '93 / ADA / ARC Music

Champs

EARLY SINGLES, THE (30 Great A & B Sides)
Tequila / Train to nowhere / El rancho rock / Midnighter / Chariot rock / Subway / Turnpike / Rockin' Mary / Gone train / Beatnik / Caramba / Moonlight bay / Night train / Rattler / Sky high / Double eagle rock / Too much tequila / Twenty thousand leagues / Red eye / Little Matador / Alley cat / Coconut drive / Tough train / Face / Hokey pokey / Jumping bean / Sombrero / Shoddy shoddy / Cantina / Panic button
CD ________ **CDCHD 525**
Ace / Jun '96 / Pinnacle

GO CHAMPS GO/EVERYBODY'S ROCKIN'
Go champs go / El rancho rock / I'll be there / Sky high / What's up buttercup / Lollipop / Tequilla / Train to nowhere / Midnighter / Robot walk / Just walking in the rain / Night beat / Everybody's rockin' / Chariot rock / Caterpillar / Turnpike / Lavenia / Mau mau stomp / Rockin' Mary / Subway / Toast / Bandido / Ali baba / Foggy river
CD ________ **CDCHD 451**
Ace / Jun '93 / Pinnacle

LATER SINGLES, THE
Tequila twist / Limbo rock / Experiment in terror / La cucuracha / Limbo dance / Latin limbo / Varsity rock / That did it / Mr. Cool / 3/4 mash / Nik nak / Shades / Cactus juice / Roots / San Juan / Jalisco / Only the young / Switzerland / Kahlua / Fraternity waltz / Bright lights, big city / French 75 / Man from Durango / Red pepper / Anna / Buckaroo
CD ________ **CDCHD 631**
Ace / Feb '97 / Pinnacle

TEQUILA
Tequila / Train to nowhere / Sombrero / Experiment in terror / La cucaracha / Too much tequila / Turn pike / Beatnik / El rancho rock / Midnighter / Chariot rock / Subway / Limbo rock / Red eye / Gone train / Caramba
CD ________ **CDCH 227**
Ace / Jan '94 / Pinnacle

TEQUILA
CD ________ **MCCD 283**
Music Club / Dec '96 / Disc / THE

WING DING
Wing ding / TNT / Percolator / Swanee river blues / Baja / Roughneck / Istanbul / Stampede / Shiverin' and shakin' / Lowdown / Siesta / Volkswagen / Suicide / Cherokee stomp / Shiver / Rockin' crickets / Fireball / Hot line / You are my sunshine / Wildwood flower / Clubhouse / Eternal love / Rattler / 20,000 leagues / Double eagle rock / Jumping bean / Man from Durango / Roots
CD ________ **CDCHD 460**
Ace / Oct '93 / Pinnacle

Chance, James

LIVE IN NEW YORK (Chance, James & the Contortions)
CD ________ **DANCD 082**
Danceteria / Nov '94 / ADA / Plastic Head / Shellshock/Disc

LOST CHANCE
CD ________ **RUSCD 8214**
ROIR / Oct '95 / Plastic Head / Shellshock/Disc

SOUL EXORCISM
CD ________ **RE 191CD**
ROIR / Nov '94 / Plastic Head / Shellshock/Disc

Chancey, Vincent

NEXT MODE
CD ________ **DIW 914**
DIW / Jan '97 / Cadillac / Harmonia Mundi

Chandeen

SHOCKED BY LEAVES
CD ________ **HY 39100942**
Hyperium / Apr '94 / Cargo / Plastic Head

Chandell, Tim

LOVE LETTERS
CD ________ **PILPCD 115**
Pioneer / May '93 / Jet Star

Chandler, Gene

NOTHING CAN STOP ME (Greatest Hits)
CD ________ **VSD 5515**
Varese Sarabande / Apr '95 / Pinnacle

Chandler, Kerri

SHAKE YOUR ASS
CD ________ **BB 042142CD**
Broken Beat / Jan '96 / Plastic Head

Chandler, Omar

PIECES OF MY HEART
I know what's on your mind / Ecstasy / Later tonite / Buckwild / Let's settle down / Show me / Tell me what you're feeling / Guess who's back / For the love of you
CD ________ **XECD 10**
Expansion / Feb '97 / 3mv/Sony

Chandra, Sheila

ABONECRONEDRONE
CD ________ **CDRW 56**
Realworld / Sep '96 / EMI

WEAVING MY ANCESTORS' VOICES
Speaking in tongues / Dhyana and donalogue / Ever so lonely/Eyes/Ocean / Enchantment / Call / Bhajan / Speaking in tongues II / Sacred stones / Om namaha shiva
CD ________ **CDRW 24**
Realworld / May '92 / EMI

ZEN KISS, THE
La sagesse (Women, I'm calling you) / Speaking in tongues III / Waiting / Shehnai song / Love it is a killing thing / Speaking in tongues IV / Woman and child / En mireal del penal / Sailor's life / Abbess Hildegard / Kafi noir
CD ________ **CDRW 45**
Realworld / May '94 / EMI

Change

GLOW OF LOVE, THE
Lover's holiday / It's a girl's affair / Angel in my pocket / Glow of love / Searching / End
CD ________ **7599234382**
WEA / Jan '96 / Warner Music

Change Of Season

COLD SWEAT
CD ________ **RTN 41205**
Rock The Nation / Feb '95 / Plastic Head

Changelings

CHANGELINGS, THE
Pomegranate / Season of mist / Earthquake at Versailles / Sony of the Sephardim / Pranam / Into this divide / Incantation / Solitude / Awakening / Seraphim / 11:59 / October 30 / Sunday morning
CD ________ **WSCD 015**
World Serpent / Jan '97 / World Serpent

Changing Faces

ALL DAY, ALL NIGHT
Intro / GHETTOUT / My lovely / Thinkin' about you / I apologize / Time after time / All of my days: *Changing Faces & Jay-Z* / All day, all night / GHETTOUT part 2 / My heart can't take much more / To get somebody else / Goin' nowhere / No stoppin' this groove / All that / Baby tonight
CD ________ **7567927202**
Big Beat/Atlantic / Jun '97 / Warner Music

CHANGING FACES
Stroke you up / Foolin' around / Lovin' ya boy / One of those things / Keep it right there / Am I wasting my time / Feeling all this love / Thoughts of you / Come closer / Baby your love / Movin' on / Good thing / All is not gone
CD ________ **7567923692**
Warner Bros. / Oct '94 / Warner Music

Changui

AHORA SI - HERE COMES CHANGUI
CD ________ **CORACD 121**
Corason / Feb '95 / ADA / CM / Direct

Channel 3

HOW DO YOU OPEN THE DAMN THING
CD ________ **LP 098**
Lost & Found / Jul '94 / Plastic Head

I'VE GOT A GUN/AFTER THE LIGHTS GO OUT
Fear of life / Out of control / I've got a gun / Wetspots / Accident / You make me feel cheap / You lie / Catholic boy / Waiting in the wings / Strength in numbers / Double standard boys / Life goes on / What about me / Separate peace / No love / After the lights go out / Truth and trust / I'll take my chances / All my dreams / Can't afford it / I didn't know / Manzanar / Mannequin
CD ________ **CDPUNK 2**
Anagram / Jun '94 / Cargo / Pinnacle

Channel Light Vessel

AUTOMATIC
Testify / Train travelling north / Dog day afternoon / Ballyboots / Place we pray for / Bubbling blue / Duende / Flaming creatures / Bill's last waltz / Thunderous accordions / Fish owl moon / Little luminaries
CD ________ **ASCD 019**
All Saints / Apr '97 / Discovery / Vital

EXCELLENT SPIRITS
Invisible spectator / Footsteps / Haiku detour / Birdie / Loose connections / Eternal lightbulbs / Slow jig and whirligig / Stone in your palm / Accordian night / Offering / Same shape different meaning / Everything everywhere / Century that dared to dream
CD ________ **ASCD 027**
All Saints / Jun '96 / Discovery / Vital

Channel Zero

BLACK FUEL
Black fuel / Mastermind / Call on me / Fool's parade / Self control / Misery / Hill / Love/Hate satellite / Caveman / Put it in / Wasted / Outro
CD ________ **BIAS 350CD**
Play It Again Sam / May '97 / Discovery / Plastic Head / Vital

STIGMATIZED FOR LIFE
Chrome dome / Repetition / Stigmatized for life / America / Play a little / Gold / Testimony / Unleash the dog / Big now / Last gasp
CD ________ **BIAS 259CD**
Play It Again Sam / Jun '94 / Discovery / Plastic Head / Vital

UNSAFE
Suck my energy / Heroin / Bad to the bone / Help / Lonely / Run WTT / Why / No more / Unsafe / Dashboard devils / As a boy / Man on the edge
CD BIAS 290CD
Play It Again Sam / Feb '95 / Discovery / Plastic Head / Vital

Channing, Carol

JAZZ BABY
Jazz baby / Thoroughly modern Millie / Join us in a cup of tea / Doin' the old yahoo step / Little game of tennis / Teeny little weeny nest of two / Ain't misbehavin' / You've got to see Mama ev'ry night / Ma, he's making eyes at me / You're the cream in my coffee / Baby, won't you please come home / Good man is hard to find / Button up your overcoat / Wouldn't you like to lay your head upon my pillow / Little girl from Little Rock / Bye bye baby / Homesick blues / Diamonds are a girl's best friend
CD DRGCD 13112
DRG / Apr '94 / Discovery / New Note/ Pinnacle

Chantan

PRIMARY COLOURS
Gloomy winter's noo awa / John Anderson my Jo / Slaves lament / Darn that dream / Collier laddie / Donal og / Witches reel / Dowie dens o'Yarrow / Ribbonbow / Wha'll mow me noo / Braes O'Killiecrankie / Boser girls / Hishey bah / Down in the jungle
CD CUL 108CD
Culburnie / Jan '97 / ADA / CM / Direct / Duncans / Highlander / Ross

Chantays

PIPELINE
CD VSD 5491
Varese Sarabande / Oct '94 / Pinnacle

Chantel

CLUB GUERILLA
CD SDW 0212
Shadow / Feb '97 / Cargo / Plastic Head

Chantels

BEST OF THE CHANTELS
He's gone / Plea / Maybe / I've lied: *Wilson, Willie & The Chantels* / So real / Every night (I pray) / Whoever you are / I love you so / How could you call it off / Prayee / Sure of love / Memories / If you try / I can't take it (there's our song again) / Goodbye to love: *Barrett, Richard & The Sevilles* / Look in my eyes / Well I told you
CD NEMCD 605
Sequel / Oct '90 / BMG

Chanteurs Du Pays De Vilaine

DANSES EN ROND, DANSES EN CHENE
CD RSCD 215
Keltia Musique / Feb '96 / ADA / Discovery

Chanticleer

WONDROUS LOVE
Dulaman / Fengyang ge / Nelly bly / Oy polna, polna korobushka / Brigg Fair / El Manisero / Molihua / Die vogelhochzeit / Wondrous love / Na bahia tem / La Villanella / Loch Lomond / Domaredansen / Arirang / La vasija de barro / South Australia / La petenera / Sakura / Or'cha BaMidbar / Diu, diu deng / L'amour de moy / Sohran bushi / American folk medley
CD 0630166762
Teldec Classics / Mar '97 / Warner Music

Chantre, Teofilo

TERRA & CRETCHEU
CD 086722
Melodie / Jul '95 / ADA / Discovery / Grapevine/PolyGram / Greensleeves / Jet Star

Chaos UK

ENOUGH TO MAKE YOU SICK/THE CHIPPING SODBURY TAPES
Head on a pole / Vicious cabaret / Kettlehead / Midas touch / Loser / Drink thudd / 2010 (The day they made contact) / Urban nightmare / Cider I up landlord / Down on the farm / C-rap / Intro / World stock market / Indecision / Kill / Uniform choice / No taxi / Think / Rises from the rubble / Brain bomb / Too cool for school, too stupid for the real world / Courier / Farmyard
CD CDPUNK 12
Anagram / May '93 / Cargo / Pinnacle

FLOGGIN THE CORPSE
Intro / Maggie / Hate / Police protection / No security / Kill your baby / Selfish few / False prophets / End is nigh / Parental love / Victimised / Four minute warning / Farmyard / Victimised part 2
CD CDPUNK 65
Anagram / Oct '95 / Cargo / Pinnacle

LIVE IN JAPAN
Kill your baby / Indecision / Four Minute warning / Too cool for school, too stupid for the real world / Head on a pole / Farmyard boogie / Vicious / Lawless Britain / Detention centre / Mid touch / 2010 (The day they made contact) / Crap song / Cider I up landlord / Down on the farm / Police story / Speed (Encore)
CD DOJOCD 114
Dojo / Feb '94 / Disc

MORNING AFTER THE NIGHT BEFORE
CD CDMGRAM 109
Anagram / Jan '97 / Cargo / Pinnacle
CD CLP 9982
Cleopatra / Jun '97 / Cargo / Greyhound / Plastic Head / RTM/Disc / SRD

SHORT SHARP SHOCK (Lawless Britain)
Lawless Britain / Living in fear / Detention centre / Suport / Control / People at the top / Global domination / No one seems to really care / Farmyard stomp (again)
CD CDPUNK 71
Anagram / Feb '96 / Cargo / Pinnacle

TOTAL CHAOS
Selfish few / Fashion change / You'll never own me / End is nigh / Victimised / Parental love / Leech / Chaos / Mentally insane / Urban guerilla / Farmyard boogie / Four minute warning / Kill your baby / Army / No security / What about a future / Hypocrite / Senseless conflict
CD CDPUNK 26
Anagram / Feb '94 / Cargo / Pinnacle

TWO FINGERS IN THE AIR PUNK ROCK
CD CM 770532
Century Media / Jan '94 / Plastic Head

Chaotic Dischord

FUCK RELIGION, FUCK POLITICS.../ DON'T THROW IT ALL AWAY
Rock 'n' roll swindle / Don't throw it all away / Stab your back / Sausage, beans and chips / Who killed ET (I killed the fucker) / 22 Hole Doc Martens / Anarthy in Woolworths / Batcave benders meet / Alien durex machine / City claustraphobia / Boy Bill / Wild mohicans (for wattie) / SOAHC / Sound of music / Cider 'n' dogs / Destroy peace 'n' freedom / Boring bastards / Shadow / Anti christ / 77 in 82 (What's it got to do with you) / There woz cows / Alternative culture / Loud, tuneless 'n thick (Ugly's too good for you)
CD CDPUNK 72
Anagram / Feb '96 / Cargo / Pinnacle

GOAT FUCKING VIRGIN KILLERZ FROM HELL
CD CDPUNK 84
Anagram / Oct '96 / Cargo / Pinnacle

THEIR GREATEST FUCKIN' HITS
Fuck religion, fuck politics, fuck the lot of you / Fuck the world / Fuck off and die / Loud, tuneless and thick / Are students safe / Anarchy in woolworths / You bastards can't fuck us around / Psycho hippy skateboard punx / Destroy peace and freedom / Sausage beans and chips / Anti-christ / Life of Brian / Never trust a friend / City claustrophobia / Who killed ET (I killed the fucker) / I am the sturgeon / There was cows / Get off my fuckin' allotment / Me and my girl (seal clubbing) / Goat fuckin' virgin killerz from hell / Sound of music / Pop stars / Twenty two hole Doc Martens / Boy Bill / Sold out to the GPO / Soach / Glue accident / Great rock 'n' roll swindle / Don't throw it all away / Stab your back
CD CDPUNK 27
Anagram / Mar '94 / Cargo / Pinnacle

Chaouqi, Si Mohamed

TIKTOU
Takadoum / Casamance blues / Feast of tranquility / Naar O Lilla day and night / Tiktou / Hajouj locura / Gnawa sarewa / Tbel trance / Lala Mary-Am chlha
CD SMGNA 1
Sakti / Jun '96 / New Note/Pinnacle

Chaperals

ANOTHER SHOW
Hello everybody / Lucky guy / Falling leaves / Lover's question / Sh-boom / White cliffs of Dover / Motorbiene / Angels listened / Jitterbug Mary / Sitting in my room / Zoom, zoom, zoom / So allein / In gee-home is where the heart is
CD BCD 15573
Bear Family / Jul '91 / Direct / Rollercoaster / Swift

Chapin, Harry

GREATEST STORIES-LIVE
Dreams go by / WOLD / Saturday morning / I wanna learn a love song / Mr. Tanner / Better place to be / Let time go lightly / Cats in the cradle / Taxi / Circle / 30,000 pounds of bananas / She is always seventeen / Love is just another world / Shortest story
CD 9606302
Elektra / '89 / Warner Music

TRIBUTE TO HARRY CHAPIN, A (Various Artists)
CD 4677262
Epic / May '91 / Sony

Chapin, Thomas

ANIMA (Chapin, Thomas Trio)
CD KFWCD 121
Knitting Factory / Nov '94 / Cargo / Plastic Head

HAYWIRE (Chapin, Thomas Trio)
CD KFWCD 176
Knitting Factory / Oct '96 / Cargo / Plastic Head

I'VE GOT YOUR NUMBER
I've got your number / Drinkin' / Time waits / Moon ray / Don't look now / Present / Walking wounded / Rhino
CD AJ 0110
Arabesque / Nov '93 / New Note/Pinnacle

INSOMNIA (Chapin, Thomas Trio)
CD KFWCD 132
Knitting Factory / Feb '95 / Cargo / Plastic Head

MENAGERIE DREAMS (Chapin, Thomas Trio & John Zorn)
CD KFWCD 167
Knitting Factory / Oct '96 / Cargo / Plastic Head

THIRD FORCE (Chapin, Thomas Trio)
CD KFWCD 103
Knitting Factory / Nov '94 / Cargo / Plastic Head

YOU DON'T KNOW ME
Izzit / Kaokoland / Kunene / Opuwo / Namibian sunset / Kura kura / Goodbye / You don't know me
CD AJ 0115
Arabesque / Jun '95 / New Note/Pinnacle

Chapman, Michael

BEST OF MICHAEL CHAPMAN 1969-1971, THE
Naked ladies and electric ragtime / Rainmaker / You say / In the valley / Kodak ghosts / Postcards of Scarborough / It didn't work out / Last lady song / Wrecked again / First leaf of autumn / Soulful lady / Polar bear fandango / All in all / Fennario / Shuffle boat river farewell / Small stones
CD SEECD 230
See For Miles/C5 / Sep '88 / Pinnacle

DREAMING OUT LOUD
Overture from strange places / Cowboy phase / Hell to pay / Gamelan 1 / All is pride / Sensimilia / Fool in the night / Gamelan 2 / Only pretend / Overture reprise / For once
CD FIENDCD 796
Demon / Jun '97 / Pinnacle

FULLY QUALIFIED SURVIVOR
Fishbeard sunset / Soulful lady / Rabbit hills / March rain / Kodak ghosts / Andru's easy rider / Trinkets and rings / Aviator / Naked ladies and electric ragtime / Stranger in the room / Postcards of Scarborough
CD C5CD 527
See For Miles/C5 / Apr '96 / Pinnacle

LIFE ON THE CEILING
Blue season / Lescudjack / No thanks to me / High, wide and handsome / Gamblers on the shoreline / Life on the ceiling / Babe / Prospector / Theme from the movie of the same name / Early cortina / End of the line / Midas in reverse
CD EDCD 495
Edsel / Oct '96 / Pinnacle

LOOKING FOR 11
White night starlight / Black dark / Spain one to four / Great gifts from Heaven / East coast / Dead man's handle / White out E79 / Fireside hound / Common knowledge / Aquamarine / Easy way / Health food / Nuages
CD EDCD 496
Edsel / Oct '96 / Pinnacle

NAVIGATION
CD PLANCD 07
Planet / Mar '96 / Direct

Chapman, Owen 'Snake'

UP IN CHAPMAN'S HOLLOW
CD ROUCD 0378
Rounder / Aug '96 / ADA / CM / Direct

Chapman, Roger

HE WAS SHE WAS YOU WAS WE WAS
Higher round / Ducking down / Making the same mistake / Blood and sand / King bee / That same thing / Face of stone / Hyenas only laugh for fun
CD CLACD 373
Castle / Apr '94 / BMG

HYENAS ONLY LAUGH FOR FUN
Prisoner / Hyenas only laugh for fun / Killing time / Wants nothing chained / Long goodbye / Blood and sand / Common touch / Goodbye (reprise) / Hearts on the floor / Step up / Take a bow / Jukebox mama
CD CLACD 305
Castle / Jun '92 / BMG

KICK IT BACK
Walking the cat / Cops in shades / House behind the sun / Chicken fingers / Kick it back / Son of Red Moon / Someone else's clothes / Hideaway / Toys / Do you / Hot night to rhumba / Stranger than strange / Just a step away (let's go) / Jesus and the Devil
CD ESMCD 175
Essential / Aug '96 / BMG

KISS MY SOUL
CD ESMCD 382
Essential / May '96 / BMG

LIVE IN BERLIN
Shadow on the wall / How how how / Let me down / Mango crazy
CD CLACD 313
Castle / Nov '92 / BMG

LIVE IN HAMBURG
Moth to a flame / Keep forgettin' / Midnite child / Who pulled the nite down / Talking about you / Going down / Short list / Can't get in / Keep a knockin' / Hoochie coochie man / Let's spend the night together
CD CLACD 320
Castle / Nov '92 / BMG

MANGO CRAZY
Mango crazy / Toys: do you / I read your file / Los los Bailadores / Blues breaker / Turn it up loud / Let me down / Hunt the man / Rivers run dry / I really can't go straight / Room service / Hegoshegoyougoamigo
CD CLACD 304
Castle / Jun '92 / BMG

SHADOW KNOWS, THE
Busted loose / Leader of man / Ready to roll / I think of you now / Sitting up pretty / How how how / Only love is in the red / Sweet vanilla / I'm a good boy now
CD CLACD 370
Castle / Mar '94 / BMG

TECHNO PRISONERS
Drum / Wild again / Techno prisoners / Black forest / We will touch again / Run for your love / Slap bang in the middle / Who's been sleeping in my bed / Ball of confusion
CD CLACD 371
Castle / Mar '94 / BMG

WALKING THE CAT
Kick it back / Son of Red Moon / Stranger than strange / Just a step away (let's go) / Fool / Walking the cat / J and D / Come the dark night / Hands off / Jivin' / Saturday night kick back
CD CLACD 372
Castle / '94 / BMG

Chapman, Steven Curtis

HEAVEN IN THE REAL WORLD
Heaven in the real world / King of the jungle / Dancing with the dinosaur / Mountain / Treasure of you / Love and learn / Burn the ships / Remember your chains / Heartbeat of heaven / Still listening / Facts are facts / Miracle of mercy
CD SPD 1408
Alliance Music / Jul '95 / EMI

SIGNS OF LIFE
Lord of the dance / Children of the burning heart / Signs of life / Walk / Let us pray / Free / Only natural / Rubber meets the road / What could I say / Celebrate you / Land of opportunity / Hold on to Jesus
CD SPD 1554
Alliance Music / Oct '96 / EMI

Chapman, Topsy

TOPSY CHAPMAN & MAGNOLIA JAZZBAND
CD BCD 320
GHB / Apr '94 / Jazz Music

Chapman, Tracy

CROSSROADS
Crossroads / Freedom now / Be careful of my heart / Born to fight / This time / Bridges / Material world / Sub city / Hundred years / All that you have is your soul
CD K 960 8882
Elektra / Sep '89 / Warner Music

MATTERS OF THE HEART
Bang bang bang / So / I used to be a sailor / Love that you had / Woman's work / If these are the things / Short supply
CD 7559612152
Elektra / Jun '92 / Warner Music

NEW BEGINNINGS
CD 7559618502
Elektra / Nov '95 / Warner Music

TRACY CHAPMAN
Talkin' bout a revolution / Fast car / Across the lines / Behind the wall / Baby can I hold you / Mountains O' things / She's got her ticket / Why / For my lover / If not now... / For you
CD 9607742
Elektra / Apr '88 / Warner Music

Chapterhouse

ROWNDERBOWT
CD Set _______________ DEDCD 025
Dedicated / Nov '96 / BMG / Vital

Chardiet, Simon

BUG BITE DADDY
Gerbil on the wheel of love / Bug bite Daddy / Different way to live / Surf octopus / Taking up space / What's new pussycat / Lesson in love / All by myself / Truth hearts / No soul / Have love, will travel / Rik-a-tik (ikety pikety) / I'd be grateful / Left wing fascist / Broke, bored and lonesome / Rock my blues away / Bop-a-lena / Panic button / Run chicken run / Goldfinger / Surf 2000 / Dr. No / Attack of the little ones / Good, the bad and the ugly
CD _______________ UPSTART 037
Upstart / Mar '97 / ADA / Direct

Charge

CHARGE
CD _______________ KSCD 9419
Kissing Spell / Jun '97 / Greyhound

Charivari Trio

ROMANCE DE BARRIO
CD _______________ MWIC 8000CD
1Cub4t / Nov '96 / ADA

Charlap, Bill

ALONG WITH ME
CD _______________ CRD 326
Chiaroscuro / Mar '96 / Jazz Music

DISTANT STAR (Charlap, Bill Trio)
Along the way / While we're young / Last night when we were young / Here I'll stay / Distant star / Bon ami / '39 Worlds fair / Starlight / The heather on the hill
CD _______________ CRISS 1131CD
Criss Cross / Jul '97 / Cadillac / Direct / Vital/SAM

MULLIGAN
CD _______________ CRD 349
Chiaroscuro / May '97 / Jazz Music

PIANO & BASS (Charlap, Bill & Sean Smith)
CD _______________ PCD 7092
Progressive / Jan '94 / Jazz Music

SOUVENIR (Charlap, Bill Trio)
CD _______________ CRISS 1108
Criss Cross / Dec '95 / Cadillac / Direct / Vital/SAM

Charlatans

BETWEEN 10TH AND 11TH
CD _______________ SITU 37CD
Situation 2 / Mar '92 / Pinnacle

CHARLATANS, THE
CD _______________ BBQCD 174
Beggars Banquet / Aug '95 / RTM/Disc / Warner Music

SOME FRIENDLY
You're not very well / White shirt / Only one I know / Opportunity / Then / 109 / Polar bear / Believe you me / Flower / Sonic / Sproston green
CD _______________ BBL 30CD
Beggars Banquet / Sep '95 / RTM/Disc / Warner Music

TELLIN' STORIES
With no shoes / North country boy / Tellin' stories / One to another / You're a big girl now / How can you leave us / Area 51 / How high / Only teethin' / Get on it / Rob's theme
CD _______________ BBQCD 190
Beggars Banquet / Apr '97 / RTM/Disc / Warner Music

UP TO OUR HIPS
Come in number 21 / I never want an easy life if me and he were ever to get ther / Can't get out of bed / Feel flows / Autograph / Jesus Hairdo / Up to our hips / Patrol / Another rider up in flames / Inside looking out
CD _______________ BBQCD 147
Beggars Banquet / Mar '94 / RTM/Disc / Warner Music

Charlatans

AMAZING CHARLATANS, THE
Baby won't you tell me / Number one / Blues ain't nothin' / Jack of diamonds / Codeine blues / I saw her / 32-20 / Shadow knows / Alabama bound / 'Long come a viper / Sidetrack / By hook or by crook / Devil got my man / Alabama bound / I always wanted a girl like you / How can I miss you when you won't go away / Walkin' / We're not on the same trip / Sweet Sue just you / East Virginia / Steppin' in society / I got mine / Groom 'n' clean ad
CD _______________ CDWIKD 138
Big Beat / Aug '96 / Pinnacle

FIRST ALBUM/ALABAMA BOUND
CD _______________ 842020
EVA / Jun '94 / ADA / Direct

Charles & Eddie

CHOCOLATE MIX
Keep on smilin' / Jealousy / 24-7-365 / Wounded bird / Peace of mind / Sunshine and happiness / Smile my way / She's so shy / I can't find the words / Little piece of heaven / Dear God / To someone else / Zarah / Your love / Best place in the world / Goodbye song
CD _______________ CDEST 2256
Capitol / May '95 / EMI

DUOPHONIC
House is not a home / NYC / Would I lie to you / Hurt no more / I understand / Unconditional / Love is a beautiful thing / Where do we go from here / Father to son / December 2nd / Be a little easy on me / Vowel song / Shine / Bonus cut
CD _______________ CDESTU 2186
Capitol / May '95 / EMI

Charles River Valley Boys

BEATLE COUNTRY
CD _______________ ROUCDSS 41
Rounder / Apr '95 / ADA / CM / Direct

Charles, Bobby

LOUISIANA RHYTHM & BLUES MAN
CD _______________ CDRB 31
Charly / Nov '95 / Koch

SMALL TOWN TALK
Street people / Long face / I must be in a good place now / Save me Jesus / He's got all the whisky / Let yourself go / Grow too old / I'm that way / Tennessee blues
CD _______________ SEECD 218
See For Miles/C5 / Mar '88 / Pinnacle

WISH YOU WERE HERE RIGHT NOW
CD _______________ SPCD 1203
Stony Plain / May '95 / ADA / CM / Direct

Charles, Christophe

UNDIRECTED 1986-1996
CD _______________ EFA 006832
Mille Plateau / Feb '97 / SRD

Charles, Ray

ALONE IN THE CITY
CD _______________ RMB 75009
Remember / Nov '93 / Total/BMG

AUDIO ARCHIVE
I wonder who's kissing her now / Let's have a ball / Goin' down slow / Sittin' on top of the world / Alone in the city / Blues is my middle name / This love of mine / Now she's gone / Can anyone ask for more / CC rider / Rockin' chair blues / Hey now / Sentimental blues / Can't you see darling / Tell me baby / Baby, let me hold your hand / I won't let you go / I'm gonna drown myself / Snow is fallin' / If I give you my love
CD _______________ CDAA 003
Tring / Jan '92 / Tring

BERLIN 1962 (Jazz At The Philharmonic)
Band intro / Strike up the band / One mint julep / I got a woman / Georgia on my mind / Margie / Danger zone / Hallelujah I love her so / Come rain or come shine / Hide nor hair / Alexander's ragtime band / I believe my soul / Hit the road Jack / Right time / Bye bye love / Unchain my heart / What'd I say
CD _______________ PACD 5301
Pablo / Jun '96 / Cadillac / Complete/ Pinnacle

BEST OF RAY CHARLES
CD _______________ DLCD 4008
Dixie Live / Mar '95 / TKO Magnum

BEST OF RAY CHARLES - THE ATLANTIC YEARS
It should've been me / Don't you know / Blackjack / I've got a woman / What would I do without you / Greenbacks / Come back / Fool for you / This little girl of mine / Hallelujah, I love her so / Lonely avenue / It's alright / Ain't that love / Swanee river rock / That's enough / What I'd say / (Night time) is the right time / Drown in my own tears / Tell the truth / Just for a thrill
CD _______________ 8122717222
Atlantic / Aug '94 / Warner Music

BEST OF RAY CHARLES, THE
Hard times / Rock house / Sweet sixteen bars / Doodlin' / How long blues / Blues waltz
CD _______________ 7567813682
Atlantic / Mar '93 / Warner Music

BLUES & JAZZ ANTHOLOGY
Someday / Sun's gonna shine again / Midnight hour / Worried life blues / Low society / Losing hand / Sinner's prayer / Funny (but I still love you) / Feelin' sad / I wonder who / Nobody cares / Ray's blues / Mr. Charles blues / Black jack / Come back / Fool for you / hard times (no one knows better than I) / Drown in my own tears / What would I without you / I want a little girl / Early in the morning / Night time is the right time / Two years of torchure / I believe to my soul / Man I love / Music music music / I surrender dear / Hornful soul / Ain't misbehavin' / Doodlin' / Sweet sixteen bars / Undecided / Rock house / X-ray blues / Love on my mind / Fathead / Bill for Bennie / Hard times / Willow weep for me / Spirit feel
CD _______________ 8122716072
Atlantic / Mar '94 / Warner Music

BLUES BEFORE SUNRISE
Blues / I've had my fun / CC rider / Walkin' and talkin' / Baby let me hold your hand / Why did you go / Blues before sunrise / Ain't that fine / Don't put all your dreams in one basket / This love of mine / All to myself / If I give you my love / Late in the evening blues / Sittin' on top of the world / Back home / Kiss me baby
CD _______________ SUMCD 4044
Summit / Nov '96 / Sound & Media

BLUES IS MY MIDDLE NAME
Goin' down slow / Alone in the city / Now she's gone / Rockin' chair blues / Sentimental blues / Can anyone ask for more / Let's have a ball / This love of mine / Can't you see darling / If I give you my love / Sittin' on top of the world / Kiss me baby / I'm gonna drown myself / Snow is fallin' / Blues is my middle name / I wonder who's kissing her now / CC rider / Hey now / Tell me baby / All to myself alone / Baby, let me hold your hand / I won't let you go / I'm glad for your sake / Walkin' and talkin' / I'm wonderin' and wonderin' / I found my baby there
CD _______________ GRF 033
Tring / '93 / Tring

BLUES IS MY MIDDLE NAME
Baby won't you please come home / She's on the ball / Hallelujah I love her so / Margie / Ego song / I believe to my soul / If I give you my love / You always miss the water (when the well runs dry) / What'd I say / Come rain or come shine / I've had my fun (going down slow) / CC rider / I love you, I love you (I will never let you go) / Baby let me hold your hand / This love of mine / Ain't that fine / Let the good times roll / Blues is my middle name
CD _______________ ECD 3341
K-Tel / May '97 / K-Tel

BLUES IS MY MIDDLE NAME
Blues is my middle name / Walkin' and talkin' / Hey now / Going away blues / CC Rider / Alone in the city / Sitting on top of the world / Rocking chair blues / How long / You won't let me go / Sentimental blues / Can anyone ask for more / Kiss me baby / I wonder who's kissing her now / I'm going down to the river / Tell me baby / Easy riding gal / All the girls in town
CD _______________ CWNCD 2039
Crown / Jun '97 / Henry Hadaway

CLASSIC YEARS, THE
Sticks and stones / Georgia on my mind / Ruby / Hard hearted Hannah / Theme that got / One mint julep / I've got news for you / Hit the road Jack / Unchain my heart / Hide nor hair / At the club / I can't stop loving you / Born to lose / You don't know me / You are my sunshine / Your cheatin' heart / Don't set me free / Take these chains from my heart / No one / Without love (there is nothing) / Busted / That lucky old sun / Baby don't you cry / My heart cries for you / My baby don't dig me / No one to cry to / Smack dab in the middle / Makin' whoopee / Cry / Crying time / Together again / Let's go get stoned / Please say you're fooling / I don't need no doctor / In the heat of the night / Yesterday / Eleanor Rigby / Understanding and nine more
CD _______________ ESBCD 144
Essential / Jul '91 / BMG

CLASSIC YEARS, THE
CD _______________ CDSGP 0121
Prestige / Jun '94 / Else / Total/BMG

COLLECTION VOL.1, THE
Your cheatin' heart / Hit the road Jack / Georgia on my mind / Unchain my heart / One mint julep / Take these chains from my heart / I can't stop loving you / Busted / You are my sunshine / Makin' whoopee / Let's go get stoned / My heart cries for you / Feel so bad / Lucky old sun / Smack dab in the middle / Crying time / If it wasn't for bad luck / In the heat of the night / Eleanor Rigby / Born to lose / No one / Hard hearted Hannah / Yesterday
CD _______________ CCSCD 241
Castle / Mar '90 / BMG

COLLECTION VOL.2, THE
Here we go again / Makin' whoopee / At the club / My baby don't dig me / Sticks and stones / No one to cry to / I choose to sing the blues / I've got news for you / I gotta woman part 1 / Without love (there is nothing) / I'm gonna move to the outskirts of town / You don't know me / Ruby / What have they done to my song ma / Don't set me free / Them that got / What am I living for / Understanding / If you were mine / Cry / Hide nor hair
CD _______________ CCSCD 328
Castle / Apr '92 / BMG

COLLECTION, THE
What'd I say / CC rider / Tell me how so you feel / Sentimental blues / Heartbreaker / I'm wonderin' and wonderin' / I wonder who's kissing her now / This love of mine / I love you, I love you (I won't let you go) / Can't you see darling / Goin' down slow / Let's have a ball / Hey now / I found my baby there / You be my baby / Kiss me baby / Oh baby / Rockin' chair blues / Sittin' on top of the world / Walkin' and talkin' / I'm glad for your sake / If I give you my love / I'm movin' on / Talkin' bout you / Leave my woman alone
CD _______________ COL 005
Collection / Jul '96 / Target/BMG

EARLY YEARS, THE
CD _______________ KCD 5011
King / Apr '97 / Avid/BMG

ESSENTIAL COLLECTION, THE
CD Set _______________ LECD 607
Wisepack / Apr '95 / Conifer/BMG / THE

GENIUS + SOUL = JAZZ
From the heart / I've got news for you / Moanin' / Let's go / One mint julep / I'm gonna move to the outskirts of town / Stompin' room only / Mr. C / Strike up the band / Birth of the blues / Alabamy bound / Basin Street blues / New York's my home
CD _______________ CLACD 339
Castle / Aug '93 / BMG

GENIUS + SOUL = JAZZ
CD _______________ JZCD 310
Suisa / Feb '91 / Jazz Music / THE

GENIUS OF RAY CHARLES, THE
CD _______________ 7567813382
Atlantic / Jun '93 / Warner Music

GENIUS OF RAY CHARLES, THE
Blues is my middle name / Rocking chair blues / Sentimental blues / Can anyone ask for more / Let's have a ball / This love of mine / Can't you see darling / If I give you my love / Sitting on top of the world / Kiss me baby / I'm going to drown myself / Snow is falling / I wonder who's kissing her now / CC rider / Hey now / Tell me baby / All to myself / Baby let me hold your hand / I'm glad for your sake
CD _______________ QED 017
Tring / Nov '96 / Tring

GOING DOWN SLOW
Goin' down slow / Honey honey / Can anyone ask for more / Can't see you darling / Let's have a ball / Ain't that fine / Rocking chair blues / Sentimental blues / How long / Tell me baby / Misery in my heart / Alone in the city / She's on the ball / Don't put all your dreams in one basket / You always miss the water / Baby won't you please come home
CD _______________ CDBM 120
Blue Moon / Sep '96 / Cadillac / Discovery / Greensleeves / Jazz Music / Jet Star / TKO Magnum

GOLD COLLECTION, THE
CD _______________ D2CD 05
Deja Vu / Dec '92 / THE

GREAT RAY CHARLES, THE
Ray / Melancholy baby / Black coffee / There's no you / Doodlin' / Sweet sixteen bars / I surrender dear / Undecided
CD _______________ 7567817312
Atlantic / Jun '93 / Warner Music

GREATEST COUNTRY AND WESTERN HITS
CD _______________ PRS 23002
Personality / Jun '95 / Target/BMG

GREATEST HITS
CD _______________ PRS 23005
Personality / '93 / Target/BMG

HEY NOW
I'm going down to the river / Rocking chair blues / Walkin' and talkin' / Can anyone ask for more / I'm glad for your sake / If I give you my love / Hey now / Baby tell me what I have done / Snow is fallin' / Blues is my middle name / Sentimental blues / This love of mine / Sittin' on top of the world / Crazy about me / Goin' down slow
CD _______________ 100312
CMC / May '97 / BMG

LIVE
Hot rod / Blues waltz / In a little Spanish town / Sherry / Right time / Fool for you / I got a woman / Talkin' 'bout you / Swanee river rock / Yes indeed / Frenesi / Spirit feel / Tell the truth / Drown in my own tears / What'd I say
CD _______________ 7567817322
Atlantic / Jun '93 / Warner Music

MY WORLD
My world / Song for you / None of us are free / So help me God / Let me take over / One drop of love / If I could / Love has a mind of its own / I'll be there / Still crazy after all these years
CD _______________ 7599267352
WEA / Mar '93 / Warner Music

RAY CHARLES
CD _______________ LECD 049
Dynamite / May '94 / THE

RAY CHARLES (2CD Set)
CD Set _______________ R2CD 4005
Deja Vu / Jan '96 / THE

RAY CHARLES
I can't stop loving you / I've got a woman / What'd I say / Makin' believe / Makin' whoopee / Unchain my heart / Ruby / Crying time / Together again / Mess around / Georgia on my mind / Born to lose / Busted

/ Take these chains from my heart / Yesterday / Hit the road Jack / Eleanor Rigby
CD ________ 399526
Koch Presents / Jun '97 / Koch

RAY CHARLES AND BETTY CARTER (Charles, Ray & Betty Carter)
Every time we say goodbye / You and I / Goodbye we'll be together again / People will say we're in love / Cocktails for two / Side by side / Baby, it's cold outside / Together / For all we know / It takes two to tango / Alone together / Just you and me / But on the other hand baby / I never see Maggie alone / I like to hear it sometimes
CD ________ CLACD 340
Castle / '93 / BMG

RAY CHARLES AND BETTY CARTER (Charles, Ray & Betty Carter)
CD ________ PRS 23003
Personality / '93 / Target/BMG

RAY CHARLES GOLD (2CD Set)
CD Set ________ D2CD 4005
Deja Vu / Jun '95 / THE

ROCK + SOUL = GENIUS
CD ________ JMY 10092
JMY / Aug '91 / Harmonia Mundi

ROCKIN' CHAIR BLUES
CD ________ MACCD 227
Autograph / Aug '96 / BMG

SEE SEE RIDER
CC rider / Sentimental blues / She's on the ball / This love of mine / How long blues / You never miss the water / Someday / Baby, let me hold your hand / Baby, won't you please come home / Ain't that fine / Don't put all your dreams in one basket / Why did you go / Let me hear you call my name / Sittin' on top of the world / Going down slow (I've had my fun) / Can't you see darling / What have I done / Money honey / Blues before sunrise / Snow is fallin' / Baby, won't you please come home
CD ________ MUCD 9011
Musketeer / Apr '95 / Disc

SOUL MEETING (Charles, Ray & Milt Jackson)
Hallelujah, I love her so / Blue genius / X-ray blues / Soul meeting / Love on my mind / Bags of blues
CD ________ 7567819512
Atlantic / Mar '93 / Warner Music

STRONG LOVE AFFAIR
CD ________ 9362461072
Qwest / Feb '96 / Warner Music

TWO IN ONE (Charles, Ray & Nat 'King' Cole)
CD ________ CDTT 8
Charly / Apr '94 / Koch

Charles, Teddy

JAZZ AT THE MUSEUM OF MODERN ART
CD ________ FSRCD 212
Fresh Sound / Oct '96 / Discovery / Jazz Music

ON CAMPUS (Charles, Teddy & Zoot Sims)
CD ________ FSCD 43
Fresh Sound / Oct '90 / Discovery / Jazz Music

Charles, Tina

TINA CHARLES
CD ________ HM 006
Harmony / Jun '97 / TKO Magnum

VERY BEST OF TINA CHARLES, THE
I love to love (but my baby loves to dance) / Dr. Love / I'll go where your music takes me / Dance little lady dance / You set my heart on fire / Love bug / World of emotion / This is the moment / Foundation of love / Time for a change / You can do magic / Smarty pants / Band of gold / You're so vain / Don't play that song (you lied) / Stoney end / River deep, mountain high / Tina's medley
CD ________ SUMCD 4052
Summit / Nov '96 / Sound & Media

Charleston Chasers

PLEASURE MAD
CD ________ SOSCD 1287
Stomp Off / Aug '95 / Jazz Music / Wellard

Charlesworth, Bob

MUSIC FOR THE 3RD EAR
CD ________ WWCD 12
Wibbly Wobbly / Sep '95 / SRD

Charlesworth, Dick

DICK CHARLESWORTH & HIS CITY GENTS
CD ________ BCD 272
GHB / Aug '95 / Jazz Music

Charley's War

1000 YEARS OF CIVILISATION
CD ________ SRC 10CD
Snoop / Nov '92 / Koch / Plastic Head

Charlie & His Orchestra

GERMAN PROPAGANDA SWING VOL.1 1941-1943
You're driving me crazy / You can't stop me from dreaming / St. Louis blues / Slumming on Park Avenue / Dinah / Daisy / FDR Jones / Who'll buy my bublitchky / I'm putting all my eggs in one basket / King's horses / I've got a pocketful of dreams / Three little fishes / Why'd ya make me fall in love with you / Miss Annabelle Lee / South of the border / Hold tight / Man with the big cigar / I'm sending you the Siegfried Line / Bye bye blackbird / Japanese sandman / Who's afraid of the big bad wolf / Unter'n linden
CD ________ HQCD 03
Harlequin / Oct '91 / Hot Shot / Jazz Music / Swift / Wellard

GERMAN PROPAGANDA SWING VOL.2 1941-1944
Nice people / Thanks for the memory / Indian love call / Sheik of Araby / Let's put out the lights / Bei mr bist du schon / Lili Marlene / Elmer's tune / Picture me without you / I double dare you / MacPherson is rehearsin' / I can't give you anything but love / Daisy stardust / United air man / I got rhythm / And so another lovely day is over / Roll on the blue funnel / Under an umbrella in the evening / Calling invasion forces / Atlantic wall / Submarine
CD ________ HQCD 09
Harlequin / Oct '91 / Hot Shot / Jazz Music / Swift / Wellard

Charlie Chaplin

20 SUPER HITS
CD ________ SONCD 0003
Sonic Sounds / Oct '90 / Jet Star

CHARLIE CHAPLIN MEETS PAPA SAN (Charlie Chaplin & Papa San)
CD ________ RNCD 2068
Rhino / Aug '94 / Grapevine/PolyGram / Jet Star

LIVE AT CLARENDON (Charlie Chaplin & King Sturgav Sounds)
CD ________ DHV 1CD
Tamoki Wambesi / Nov '95 / Greensleeves / Jet Star / Roots Collective / SRD

OLD AND NEW TESTAMENT
CD ________ RASCD 3090
Ras / Apr '92 / Direct / Greensleeves / Jet Star / SRD

QUENCHIE
CD ________ TWCD 1028
Tamoki Wambesi / Jun '92 / Greensleeves / Jet Star / Roots Collective / SRD

RAS PORTRAITS
Ruffian / License to kill / DJ roll call / Send Ninjaman home / Rappin' Chaplin / Don't touch crack / Charlie in the party / Not a bag of locks / Chalice contest / From a distance / Through some corn / Promise land / Obeah business
CD ________ RAS 3318
Ras / Jun '97 / Direct / Greensleeves / Jet Star / SRD

RED POND/CHAPLIN CHANT
CD ________ TWCD 1014
Tamoki Wambesi / Apr '94 / Greensleeves / Jet Star / Roots Collective / SRD

TAKE TWO
CD ________ RASCD 3060
Ras / Jul '90 / Direct / Greensleeves / Jet Star / SRD

Charlottes

THINGS COME APART
Liar / Prayer song / See me, feel me / By my side / Mad girls love song / Beautify / Love in the emptiness / We're going wrong / Blue / Venus
CD ________ CDBRED 92
Cherry Red / Jan '91 / Pinnacle

Charming Prophets

ALIENS AND ME
CD ________ SISSY 005
Sticksister / Jun '97 / Cargo

Chartbusters

MATING CALL
Kirk's works / Mambo bounce / 245 / Minor march / Mating call / Jugsville / Oleo / Don't go to strangers / Back on the farm / Doxy
CD ________ PRCD 110022
Prestige / Jun '96 / Cadillac / Complete/ Pinnacle

Chas & Dave

AIN'T NO PLEASING YOU
Ain't no pleasing you / That's what I like / My melancholy baby / Sunday / One o' them days / Poor old Mr. Woogie / Bored stiff / Turn that noise down / Behave yourself / Rabbit / Wish I could write a love song / That old piano / Nobody / Miss you all the time / Flying / Stop dreaming / London girls / There in your eyes / I miss ya gel / Mustn't grumble
CD ________ TRTCD 149
TrueTrax / Oct '94 / THE

AIN'T NO PLEASING YOU
CD ________ PLSCD 157
Pulse / Apr '97 / BMG

ALL TIME JAMBOREE BAG
CD ________ DCDCD 218
Castle / Nov '95 / BMG

BEST OF CHAS & DAVE
Poor old Mr. Woogie / Bored stiff / Don't anyone speak English / Turn that noise down / Beer belly / Behave yourself / Ain't no pleasing you / I miss ya gel / Lonnie D / Wallop / Rabbit / That old piano / That's what I like / London girls / Give it some stick, Mick / Nobody / Flying / Margate / Musn't grumble / Word from Anne / Stop dreaming / Give it gavotte / Wish I could write a love song
CD ________ MATCD 207
Castle / Dec '92 / BMG

CHAS & DAVE'S ROCK 'N' ROLL PARTY
CD ________ CDSR 082
Telstar / Jul '97 / BMG

Chase, Allan

DARK CLOUDS WITH SILVER LININGS (Chase, Allan Quartet)
Dark clouds with silver linings / Poinciana / Comin' up / How little we know / Borderick / Close your eyes / East of the sun / Routine / Of thee I sing / Dismal / Yeah / Clamdiggers
CD ________ AC 5013
Accurate / Jul '97 / Direct

Chassagnite, Francois

SAMYA CYNTHIA
CD ________ CDLLL 97
La Lichere / Aug '93 / ADA / Discovery

Chastain

IN DEMENTIA
CD ________ MASSCD 122
Massacre / May '97 / Plastic Head

SICK SOCIETY
CD ________ MASSCD 076
Massacre / Nov '95 / Plastic Head

Chastain, David T.

7TH OF NEVER, THE
CD ________ MASSCD 077
Massacre / Oct '95 / Plastic Head

MOVEMENTS THROUGH TIME
Thunder and lightning / 827 / Fortunate and happenstance / Citizen of hell / Blitzkrieg / Oracle within / New York rush / We must carry on / Capriccio / In E minor / No man's land / Seven Hills groove / Now or never / Trapped in the wind / Zoned in danger / Bargin
CD ________ KILCD 1002
Killerwatt / Oct '93 / Kingdom

NEXT PLANET PLEASE
CD ________ CDVEST 9
Bulletproof / May '94 / Pinnacle

Chateau Neuf Spelemannslag

SPELL
CD ________ HCD 7104CD
Helio / Apr '95 / ADA

Chattaway, Jay

SPACE AGE
CD ________ ND 66003
Narada / Nov '92 / ADA / New Note/ Pinnacle

Chatuye

HEARTBEAT IN THE MUSIC
CD ________ ARHCD 383
Arhoolie / Apr '95 / ADA / Cadillac / Direct

Chaurand, Anne

CELTIA
CD ________ ECLCD 9613
Eclectic / Feb '96 / ADA / New Note/ Pinnacle

Chaurasia, Hariprasad

ABOVE AND BEYOND
CD Set ________ IMUT 1064
Multitone / Jul '96 / BMG

RAG AHIR BHAIRAV
CD ________ NI 5111
Nimbus / Sep '94 / Nimbus

RAG BHIMPALASI
CD ________ NI 5298
Nimbus / Sep '94 / Nimbus

RAG KAUNSI KANHRA
CD ________ NI 5182
Nimbus / Sep '94 / Nimbus

RAG LALIT
CD ________ NI 5152
Nimbus / Sep '94 / Nimbus

RAGA DARBARI KANADA/DHUN IN RAGA
CD ________ NI 5638
Nimbus / Sep '94 / Nimbus

RAGA PATDIP/PAHADI DHUN (Chaurasia, Hariprasad & Shib Sankar Ray)
CD ________ NI 5469
Nimbus / Aug '96 / Nimbus

Chavela

CHAVELA VARGAS
CD ________ 68983
Tropical / Jul '97 / Discovery

Chaves, Guillermo

EL SUSPIRO DEL MORO (Chaves, Guillermo & Marc Loopuyt/Adel Shamseddin)
CD ________ AUB 006777
Auvidis/Ethnic / Apr '93 / ADA / Harmonia Mundi

Chavez

GONE GLIMMERING
Nailed to the blank / Spot / Break up your band / Ghost by the sea / Relaxed fit / Wakeman's air / Flaming gong / In our pools / Pentagram ring / Laugh track
CD ________ OLE 1332
Matador / Jul '95 / Vital

RIDE THE FADER
Top pocket man / Guard attacks / Unreal is here / New room / Tight around the jaws / Lions / Our boys will shine / Tonight / Memorize this face / Cold joys / Flight '96 / Ever overpsyched / You must be stopped
CD ________ OLE 2002
Matador / Nov '96 / Vital

Chavis, Boozoo

BOOZOO CHAVIS
Boozoo's theme song / I'm ready me / Dog hill / Keep your dress tail down / Johnnie billy goat / Goin' to la maison / Forty one days / Oh yae yae / Tee black / Zydeco hee haw / Don't worry about Boozoo / Berandette
CD ________ 7559611462
Nonesuch / Jul '91 / Warner Music

BOOZOO, THAT'S WHO
CD ________ ROUCD 2126
Rounder / Jan '94 / ADA / CM / Direct

LEGENDS OF ZYDECO: SWAMP MUSIC VOL.7
CD ________ US 0203
Trikont / Apr '95 / ADA / Direct

LIVE AT RICHARD'S ZYDECO DANCE HALL VOL.1 (Chavis, Boozoo & The Majic Sounds)
CD ________ ROUCD 2069
Rounder / '88 / ADA / CM / Direct

LIVE AT THE HABIBI TEMPLE
CD ________ ROUCD 2130
Rounder / Sep '94 / ADA / CM / Direct

Cheap 'n' Nasty

BEAUTIFUL DISASTER
CD ________ WOLCD 1002
China / May '91 / Pinnacle

Cheap Seats

CALL IT WHAT YOU WILL
Something in the water / It's just love / Sometimes they do / Drop me gently / I'll get over you / From where I stand / Can't stop my heart / Water into wine / She wears the clown / If I lose you (I lose you) / Broken heart attack / After the rain / Rambling man
CD ________ GEMINI 02
JVO / Jul '97 / Pinnacle

LITTLE LESS TALK, A
CD ________ GEMINI 01
JVO / Aug '96 / Pinnacle

Cheap Trick

CHEAP TRICK
Hot love / Speak now or forever hold your peace / He's a whore / Mandocello / Ballad of TV violence / Ello kiddies / Daddy should have stayed in High School / Taxman / Mr. Thief / Cry cry / Oh Candy / Surrender / California / High roller / Auf wiedersehen / Takin' me back / On the radio / Heaven tonight / Stiff competition / How are you
CD ________ 4879332
Epic / Jul '97 / Sony

CHEAP TRICK
Anytime / Hard to tell / Carnival game / Shelter / You let a lotta people down / Baby no more / Yeah yeah / Say goodbye / Wrong all along / Eight miles low / It all comes back to you
CD ________ RAACD 002
Red Ant / Jun '97 / Pinnacle

GREATEST HITS
Magical mystery tour / Dream police / Don't be cruel / Tonight it's you / She's tight / I want you to want me / If you want my love / Ain't that a shame (live) / Surrender /

Flame / I can't take it / Can't stop fallin' into love / Voices
CD 4690862
Epic / Apr '94 / Sony

SEX, AMERICA, CHEAP TRICK
Hello there / ELO kiddies / Hot love / Oh, Candy / Mandocello / Lovin' money / I want you to want me / Southern girls / So good to see you / Down on the bay / Mrs. Henry / Violins / Ballad of TV violence / You're all talk / Fan club / Surrender / High roller / On top of the world / Auf Wiedersehen / I want you to want me / Clock strikes ten / Dream police / Way of the world / Gonna raise hell / Voices / Stop this game / Just got back / Baby loves to rock / Everything works if you let it / World's greatest lover / Waitin' for the man/Heroin / Daytripper / I need love / World's greatest lover / I'm the man / Born to raise hell / Ohm sweet ohm / She's tight / Love's got a hold on me / If you want my love / Lookin' out for / Don't make our love a crime / All I really want / I can't take it / Twisted heart / Invaders of the heart / Y O Y O Y / Tonight it's you / Cover girl / This time around / A place in France / Funk / Take me to the top / Money is the route of all fun / Fortune cookie / You want it / Flame / Through the night / Stop that thief / I know what I want / Had to make you mine / I can't understand it / Can't stop falling into love / Come on Christmas
CD Set E4K 649384
Columbia / Aug '96 / Sony

WOKE UP WITH A MONSTER
My gang / Woke up with a monster / You're all I wanna do / Never runout of love / Didn't know I had it / Ride the pony / Girlfriends / Let her go / Tell me everything / Cry baby / Love me for a minute
CD 9362454252
WEA / Mar '94 / Warner Music

Cheater Slicks

DON'T LIKE YOU
CD ITR 030CD
In The Red / Dec '96 / Cargo / Greyhound

Cheatham, Doc

AT THE BERNE JAZZ FESTIVAL (Cheatham, Doc & Jim Galloway)
CD SKCD 23045
Sackville / Jun '93 / Cadillac / Jazz Music / Swift

DOC CHEATHAM LIVE
CD NI 4023
Natasha / Feb '94 / ADA / Cadillac / CM / Direct / Jazz Music

DUETS AND SOLOS (2CD Set) (Cheatham, Doc & Sammy Price)
CD Set SK2CD 5002
Sackville / Mar '97 / Cadillac / Jazz Music / Swift

HEY DOC
CD BLE 590902
Black & Blue / Apr '91 / Discovery / Koch / Wellard

SWINGING DOWN IN NEW ORLEANS
CD JCD 233
Jazzology / Dec '95 / Jazz Music

YOU'RE A SWEETHEART
CD SKCD 2038
Sackville / Jul '96 / Cadillac / Jazz Music / Swift

Cheatham, Jeannie

BASKET FULL OF BLUES (Cheatham, Jeannie & Jimmy)
Blues like Jay McShann / Heaven or hell blues / Buddy Bolden's blues / Song of the wanderer / Basket full of blues / All the time / Baby, where have you been / Band rat blues / Little girl blue/Am I blue / Bye 'n' bye blues / Ballad of the wannabes / Don't cha boogie with your black drawers off
CD CCD 4501
Concord Jazz / Mar '92 / New Note/ Pinnacle

BLUES AND THE BOOGIE MASTERS
What we do for fun / Lead dog blues / Little bitty bluebird blues / Don't let me wake up / Blues and the boogie masters / Lonesome road / Line in the sand / Too many goodbyes / Up in Rickey's room / Leave that woman blues / Please send me someone to love
CD CCD 4579
Concord Jazz / Nov '93 / New Note/ Pinnacle

GUD NUZ BLUZ (Cheatham, Jeannie & Jimmy)
Mr. CP / Low lines blues / Shop-o-holic / Careless love / That ain't right / What a fool I was / Few good men / Coal yard and ice house blues / Fine and mellow / Go down go down / Gud nuz bluz
CD CCD 4690
Concord Jazz / Apr '96 / New Note/ Pinnacle

MIDNIGHT MAMA
Wrong direction blues / CC rider / Worried life blues / Big fat daddy blues / Midnight mama / Piney Brown / Finance company / How long blues / Reel ya' deel ya dee dee dee
CD CCD 4297
Concord Jazz / Nov '96 / New Note/ Pinnacle

Checker, Chubby

ALL THE HITS VOL.1
CD MAR 020
Marginal / Jun '97 / Greyhound

ALL THE HITS VOL.2
CD MAR 025
Marginal / Jun '97 / Greyhound

LEGENDS IN MUSIC
CD LECD 062
Wisepack / Jul '94 / Conifer/BMG / THE

LET'S TWIST AGAIN
CD RMB 75058
Remember / Nov '93 / Total/BMG

PEARLS FROM THE PAST
CD KLMCD 014
BAM / Apr '94 / Koch / Scratch/BMG

ULTIMATE COLLECTION, THE (16 All Time Classics)
Twist / Limbo rock / Dancin' party / Hey babba needle / Loddy lo / Slow twistin' / Fly / Party time / Let's twist again / Let's limbo some more / Birdland / Dance the mess around / Popeye (The hitchiker) / Twenty miles / Twist it up / Hucklebuck
CD ECD 3045
K-Tel / Jan '95 / K-Tel

Checkists

NEVER MIND THE ELECTRODES
CD WSCD 009
World Serpent / Oct '96 / World Serpent

Cheech & Chong

GREATEST HIT
Earache my eye / Dave / Let's make a dope deal / Basketball Jones / Blin melon chitlin' / Sister Mary elephant / Sergeant Stadanko / Dave / Cruisin' / Continuing adventures of Pedro De Pacas / Pedro and man at the drivein / Trippin' in court
CD 7599236142
WEA / Jan '93 / Warner Music

Cheeks, Judy

RESPECT
Reach / So in love (The real deal) / Could it be (Falling in love) / This time / Forgive and forget / You're the story of my life / Respect / Joy to the world / As long as you're good to me / Different love / I'm only here / Wishing on the same star / Single tear
CD CDTIVA 1005
Positiva / Jun '95 / EMI

Cheer Accident

DUMB ASK
CD NM 001CD
Neat Metal / Nov '95 / Pinnacle

Chelsea

ALTERNATIVE, THE
Alternative / Weirdos in wonderland / More than a giro / Wasting time / Ever wonder / Where is everything / You can be there too / What's wrong with you / Oh no / Too late / Dreams of dreams / Ode to the travellers
CD WLO 24662
Weser / Oct '94 / Plastic Head

FOOLS AND SOLDIERS
I'm on fire / Come on / No flowers / Urban kids / 12 men / Trouble is the day / Your toy / Decide / Curfew / Look at the outside / Don't get me wrong / Fools and soldiers / Bring it on home / No admission / Loner / Route 66 / Right to work
CD RRCD 242
Receiver / Jul '97 / Grapevine/PolyGram

LIVE AND WELL
Tribal song / Evacuate / No admission / How do you know / No flowers / Only thinking / Running wild / Urban kids / Last time / Right to work
CD PUNXCD 1
Punx / Oct '95 / Total/BMG

LIVE AT THE MUSIC MACHINE 1978
CD REM 016 CD
Released Emotions / Mar '92 / RTM/Disc

TRAITORS GATE
CD WL 24802
Weser / Aug '94 / Plastic Head

Chelsea F.C.

BLUE IS THE COLOUR
Blue is the colour / Chirpy chirpy cheep cheep / Football is / Give me back my soccer boots / Maybe it's because I'm a Londoner / Let's all go down the Strand / On mother Kelly's doorstep / Strollin' / Let's all sing together / Song sung blue / Stop and take a look / Son of my father / Alouette
CD MONDE 19CD
Cherry Red / Oct '94 / Pinnacle

Chemical Brothers

DIG YOUR OWN HOLE
Block rockin' beats / Dig your own hole / Elektrobank / Piku / Setting sun / It doesn't matter / Don't stop the rock / Get up on it like this / Lost in the K-hole / Where do I begin / Private psychedelic reel
CD XDUSTCD 2
Freestyle Dust / Apr '97 / EMI

EXIT PLANET DUST
Leave home / In dust we trust / Song to the siren / Three little birdies down beats / Fuck up beats / Chemical beats / Life is sweet / Playground for a wedgeless firm / Chico's groove / One too many mornings / Alive: alone
CD XDUSTCD 1
Freestyle Dust / Jun '95 / EMI

Chemical People

ANGELS 'N' DEVILS
CD CRZ 019CD
Cruz / May '93 / Plastic Head

CHEMICAL PEOPLE
CD CRZ 023CD
Cruz / May '93 / Plastic Head

LET IT GO
CD CRZ 025CD
Cruz / May '93 / Plastic Head

RIGHT THING, THE
CD CRZ 013CD
Cruz / Aug '90 / Plastic Head

SO SEXIST
CD CRZ 002CD
Cruz / Jan '90 / Plastic Head

SOUNDTRACKS
CD CRZ 020CD
Cruz / May '93 / Plastic Head

TEN-FOLD HATE
CD CRZ 007CD
Cruz / Jan '90 / Plastic Head

Chemirani, Djamchid

TRADITION CLASSIQUE DE L'IRAN VOL.1 (Le Zarb)
CD HMA 190388
Musique D'Abord / Nov '93 / Harmonia Mundi

Chemlab

BURN OUT AT THE HYDROGEN BAR
Codeine, glue and you / Suicide jag / Chemical halo / Neurozone / Elephant man / Rivethead / Derailer / Summer of hate
CD CDDVN 21
Devotion / Jun '93 / Pinnacle

EAST SIDE MILITIA
CD 398414115CD
Metal Blade / Oct '96 / Pinnacle / Plastic Head

Chen, Sisi

TIDES AND SAND
CD HSR 0001
Henry Street / Mar '96 / Direct

Cheneour, Paul

TIME HAS COME, THE
Med mig sjalv / Time has come / First find an angel / Glass bead game / Who will cry / Rain / Moontide / Village / Sowena / Shroud / Fantasie I / Fantasie II / Fantasie III / Knots / Rain / Nasrudin
CD RGM 294CD
Red Gold Music / Feb '95 / Red Gold Music

Chenier, C.J.

BIG SQUEEZE, THE
CD ALCD 4844
Alligator / Sep '96 / ADA / CM / Direct

Chenier, Clifton

60 MINUTES WITH THE KING OF ZYDECO
CD ARCD 301
Arhoolie / Apr '95 / ADA / Cadillac / Direct

BOGALUSA BOOGIE
CD ARHCD 347
Arhoolie / Apr '95 / ADA / Cadillac / Direct

BON TON ROULET
CD ARHCD 345
Arhoolie / Apr '95 / ADA / Cadillac / Direct

CAJUN SWAMP
CD 2696062
Tomato / May '88 / Vital

CAJUN SWAMP MUSIC LIVE
CD 269 621 2
Tomato / Mar '90 / Vital

CLIFTON CHENIER IN NEW ORLEANS
Boogie Louisiana / Cotton picker blues / J'aime pain de mais / Pousse cafe waltz / Hello Rosa-Lee / Jusque parce que je t'aime / Boogie in Orleans / Rumblin' on the bayou / I'm gonna take you home tonite / Mon vieux buggy / Crying my heart out to you / Tous les jours / Mardi gras boogie
CD GNPD 2119
GNP Crescendo / Sep '95 / ZYX

CLIFTON CHENIER SINGS THE BLUES (Home Cookin' & Prophesy Sides From 1969)
CD ARHCD 351
Arhoolie / Apr '95 / ADA / Cadillac / Direct

FRENCHIN' THE BOOGIE
Caldonia / Laissez le bon temps roulez / Tu peux cogner mais tu peux pas rentrer / Blues de la vache a lait / Moi j'ai une petite femme / Tous les jours mon coeur est blue / Je veux faire l'amour a toi / Choo choo ch' boogie / La valse de Paris / Shake, rattle and roll / Going down slow (in Paris) / Aye, aye mama / Don't you lie to me
CD 5197242
Verve / Apr '93 / PolyGram

KING OF THE BAYOUS
CD ARHCD 339
Arhoolie / Apr '95 / ADA / Cadillac / Direct

KING OF ZYDECO LIVE AT MONTREUX
CD ARHCD 355
Arhoolie / Apr '95 / ADA / Cadillac / Direct

LIVE AT LONG BEACH & SAN FRANCISCO BLUES FESTIVAL
CD ARHCD 404
Arhoolie / Apr '95 / ADA / Cadillac / Direct

LIVE AT ST. MARK'S
CD ARHCD 313
Arhoolie / Apr '95 / ADA / Cadillac / Direct

LOUISIANA BLUES AND ZYDECO
CD ARHCD 329
Arhoolie / Apr '95 / ADA / Cadillac / Direct

MY BABY DON'T WEAR NO SHOES
CD ARHCD 1098
Arhoolie / Apr '95 / ADA / Cadillac / Direct

ON TOUR
CD 157722
Blues Collection / Feb '93 / Discovery

OUT WEST
CD ARHCD 350
Arhoolie / Apr '95 / ADA / Cadillac / Direct

TOO MUCH FUN (Chenier, Clifton & His Red Hot Louisiana Band)
CD ALCD 4830
Alligator / Apr '95 / ADA / CM / Direct

ZODICO BLUES & BOOGIE
Boppin' the rock / Ay tet fee / Cat's dreamin' / Squeeze box boogie / Things I did for you / Think it over / Zodico stomp / Yesterday (I lost my best friend) / Chenier's boogie / I'm on my way (back home to you) / All night long / Opelousas hop / Wherever you go I'll go / Clifton's dreamin'
CD CDCHD 389
Ace / May '92 / Pinnacle

Chenille Sisters

HAUTE CHENILLE (A Retrospective)
CD RHRCD 81
Red House / Jan '96 / ADA / Koch

TRUE TO LIFE
CD RHRCD 67
Red House / May '95 / ADA / Koch

Cher

ALL I REALLY WANT TO DO/SONNY SIDE OF CHER/CHER (3CD Set)
All I really want to do / I go to sleep / Needles and pins / Don't think twice / She thinks I still care / Dream baby / Bells of Rhymney / Girl don't come / CC rider / Come and stay with me / Cry myself to sleep / Blowin' in the wind / Bang bang (my baby shot me down) / Young girl (une enfante) / Where do you go / Our day will come / Elusive butterfly / Like a rolling stone / Ol' man river / Come to your window / Girl from Ipanema / It's not unusual / Time / Milord / Twelfth of never / You don't have to say you love me / I feel something in the air / Will you love me tomorrow / Until it's time for you to go / Cruel war / Catch the wind / Pied piper / Homeward bound / I want you / Alfie
CD Set CDOMB 005
EMI / Oct '95 / EMI

BANG BANG (MY BABY SHOT ME DOWN)
Dream baby / All I really want to do / I go to sleep / Come & stay with me / Where do you go / See see blues / Bang bang (my baby shot me down) / Needles & pins / Come to your window / Alfie / She's no better than me / Behind the door / Magic in the air (I feel something in the air) / Mama (when my dollies have babies) / You better sit down kids / Click song number one / But I can't love you any more / It all adds up now / I wasn't ready / Take me for a little while / Song called children / Reason to believe
CD CDP 7927732
EMI / Sep '96 / EMI

CHER
I found someone / We all sleep alone / Bang bang (my baby shot me down) / Main man / Give our love a fightin' chance / Perfection / Dangerous times / Skin deep / Working girl / Hard enough getting over you
CD GED 24164
Geffen / Nov '96 / BMG

CHER'S GREATEST HITS 1965-1992
Oh no not my baby / Whenever you're near / Many rivers to cross / Love and understanding / Save up all your tears / It's in his kiss (The shoop shoop song) / If I could turn back time / Just like Jesse James / Heart of stone / I found someone / We all sleep alone / Bang bang (my baby shot me down) / dead ringer for love / Dark lady / Gypsies, tramps and thieves / I got you babe
CD ____ GED 24439
Geffen / Nov '92 / BMG

CHER/FOXY LADY
Way of love / Gypsies, tramps and thieves / He'll never know / Fire and rain / When you find out where you're goin' let me know / He ain't heavy, he's my brother / I hate to sleep alone / I'm in the middle / Touch and go / One honest man / Living in a house divided / It might as well stay Monday (from now on) / Song for you / Down down down / Don't try to close a rose / First time / Let me down easy / If I knew then / Don't hide your love / Never been to Spain
CD ____ MCLD 19208
MCA / Jul '93 / BMG

HALF BREED/DARK LADY
My love / Two people clinging to a thread / Half breed / Greatest song I ever heard / How can you mend a broken heart / Carousel man / David's song / Melody / Long and winding road / God-forsaken day / Chastity's sun / Train of thought / I saw a man and he danced with his wife / Make the man love me / Just what I've been lookin' for / Dark lady / Miss subway of 1952 / Dixie girl / Rescue me / What'll I do / Apples don't fall far from the tree
CD ____ MCLD 19209
MCA / Oct '95 / BMG

HEART OF STONE
If I could turn back time / Just like Jesse James / You wouldn't know love / Heart of stone / Still in love with you / Love on a rooftop / Emotional fire / All because of you / Does anybody really fall in love anymore / Starting over / Kiss to kiss / After all
CD ____ GEFD 24239
Geffen / Jan '91 / BMG

HOLDIN OUT FOR LOVE
CD ____ JHD 021
Tring / Jun '92 / Tring

IT'S A MAN'S WORLD
Don't come around tonite / What about the moonlight / Same mistake / Gunman / Sun ain't gonna shine anymore / Shape of things to come / It's a man's man's man's world / Walking in Memphis / Not enough love in the world / One by one / I wouldn't treat a dog (the way you treated me) / Angels running / Paradise is here / I'm blowin' away
CD ____ 0630126702
WEA / Nov '95 / Warner Music

LOVE HURTS
Save up all your tears / Love hurts / Love and understanding / Fires of Eden / I'll never stop loving you / One small step / World without heroes / Could've been you / When love calls your name / When lovers become strangers / Who you gonna believe / It's in his kiss (The shoop shoop song)
CD ____ GFLD 19266
Geffen / Feb '95 / BMG

TAKE ME HOME/PRISONER
Take me home / Wasn't it good / Say the word / Happy was the day we met / Git down / Love and pain / Let this be a lesson to you / It's too late to love me now / My song (too far gone) / Prisoner / Holdin' out for love / Shoppin' / Boys and girls / Mirror image / Hell on wheels / Holy smoke / Outrageous
CD ____ 5500382
Spectrum / May '93 / PolyGram

Cherish The Ladies

BACK DOOR, THE
Character's Polka/The Warlock/The Volunteer/The Donegal Trav / Back door / Redican's/Sean Ryan's/Take the bull by the horns / Galway Hornpipe/Dessie O'Connor/ Mother reel / Coal Quay market/Happy days/Rabbit in the field / Maire Mhor / If ever you were mine / Paddy O'Brien's/Toss the feathers/Jenny Dang the weaver / My own native land / Pepin Arsenault/The Shepherd's daughter/A bunch in the dark / Three weeks we were wed / Jessica's polka / Tear the Calico/I have no money / Carrigdhoun / Redican's mother / Humours of Westport/The morning dew/The glass of beer/Yougha
CD ____ GLCD 1119
Green Linnet / Nov '92 / ADA / CM / Direct / Highlander / Roots

CHERISH THE LADIES
Callan lassies / Flowing bowl / Donegal jig / Cherish the ladies / Scully Casey's / O'Bryne's / Boys of the 25 / Farrel O'Gerbhaigh / Dark slender boy / Bonnie Prince Charlie / Dairy maid / Heathery breeze / Dublin reel / Trip to Athlone / Gold ring / Murphy's / O'Rourke's / Pinch of snuff / Hewlett / Sonny Mazurka / Churn of buttermilk / O'Kennedy's / Tom Ward's down fall
CD ____ PTICD 1043
Pure Traditional Irish / Aug '96 / ADA / CM / Direct / Ross

IRISH WOMEN MUSICIANS IN AMERICA
CD ____ SHCD 79053
Shanachie / Mar '95 / ADA / Greensleeves / Koch

NEW DAY DAWNING
Highway to Kilkenny / Green grow the rushes oh / Barrel Rafferty's jigs / A Neansai mhile gra / Crowley's reels/Tom Ward's downfall / Green cottage polkas / Lord Mayo / Galway rover / Joe Ryan's barn dance set / Ned of the hill / Broken wings / Rayleen's reel / Keg of brandy
CD ____ GLCD 1175
Green Linnet / Oct '96 / ADA / CM / Direct / Highlander / Roots

OUT & ABOUT
Old favourite/Flogging reel/Leave my way/ The Kerryman / Spoon river / Ladies of Carrick/Kinnegad slashers/Old man Dillon / Declan's waltz/Waltz Duhamel / Cameronian set / Inisheer / O'Keefe's/Shepherd's lamb/ Johnny O'Leary / Roisin dubh / Le voyage de Camouret/House of Hamill / Cat rambles to the child's saucepan/Maire O'Keefe/ Harry Brad / Missing piece / Out and about set
CD ____ GLCD 1134
Green Linnet / Oct '93 / ADA / CM / Direct / Highlander / Roots

Cherry, Don

ART DECO
Art deco / Body and soul / Maffy / Blessing / I've grown accustomed to her face / When will the blues leave / Bemsha swing / Folk medley / Passing / Compute
CD ____ 3952582
A&M / Jul '94 / PolyGram

DONA NOSTRA
In memoriam / Fort cherry / Arrows / M'bizo / Race face / Prayer / What reason could O give / Vienna / Ahaye-da
CD ____ 5217272
ECM / Apr '94 / New Note/Pinnacle

IN ANKARA/THE ETERNAL NOW (The Sonet Recordings/2CD Set)
Gandalf's travels / Ornette's concert / Ornette's tune / St. John and the dragon / Efeler / Anadolu havasi / Discovery of bhupala / Waterboy / Yaz geldi / Tamzara / Kara deniz / Kocekce / Man on the moon / Creator has a master plan / Two flutes / Gamla stan / Old town by night / Love train / Piano piece for two pianos and three piano players / Moving pictures for the ear
CD Set ____ 5330492
Verve / Dec '96 / PolyGram

MU (The Complete Session)
Brilliant action / Amejelo / Total vibrations / Sun of the east / Terrestrial beings / Mystics of my sound / Dollar brand / Spontaneous composing / Exert / Man on the moon / Bamboo night / Teo-teo can / Smiling faces / Going places / Psycho drama / Theme albert heath / Theme dollar brand / Babyrest / Time for
CD ____ LEJAZZCD 56
Le Jazz / Aug '96 / Cadillac / Koch

SYMPHONY FOR IMPROVISERS
CD ____ CDP 8289762
Blue Note / Sep '94 / EMI

Cherry, Ed

FIRST TAKE
Jean Pauline / Little sunflower / Lorenzo's wings / Third stone from the sun / Serious / In a sentimental mood / Inner circle / Rachel's step / Blue interrogation
CD ____ 5199422
Groovin' High / Jun '94 / PolyGram

Cherry, Neneh

HOMEBREW
Sassy / Money love / Move with me / I ain't gone under yet / Twisted / Buddy X / Somedays / Trout: *Cherry, Neneh & Michael Stipe* / Peace in mind / Red paint
CD ____ CIRCD 25
Circa / Oct '92 / EMI

MAN
Woman / Feel it / Hornbeam / Trouble man / Golden ring / 7 seconds: *Cherry, Neneh & Youssou N'Dour* / Kootchi / Beastiality / Carry me / Together now / Everything
CD ____ CDHUT 38
Hut / Sep '96 / EMI

RAW LIKE SUSHI
Buffalo stance / Manchild / Kisses on the wind / Inna city mamma / Next generation / Love ghetto / Heart / Phoney ladies / Outre risque locomotive / So here I come / My bitch / Heart (it's a demo) / Buffalo stance (sukka mix) / Manchild (Mix)
CD ____ CIRCD 8
Circa / Apr '92 / EMI

Cherry People

CHERRY PEOPLE, THE
And suddenly / Girl on the subway / On to something new / Imagination / Mr. Hyde / Do something to me / Ask the children / I'm the one who loves you / Don't hang me up girl / Light of love
CD ____ NEMCD 723
Sequel / May '95 / BMG

Cherub

SARC ART
CD ____ MASSCD 045
Massacre / Jan '95 / Plastic Head

Cherubs

HEROIN MAN
CD ____ TR 24CD
Trance / Jun '94 / SRD

SHORT FOR POPULAR
CD ____ TR 48CD
Trance Syndicate / Aug '96 / SRD

Chesapeake

FULL SAIL
CD ____ SHCD 3941
Sugar Hill / Dec '95 / ADA / CM / Direct / Koch / Roots

RISING TIDE
CD ____ SHCD 3827
Sugar Hill / May '95 / ADA / CM / Direct / Koch / Roots

Chescoe, Laurie

LAURIE CHESCOE'S GOOD TIME JAZZ
I wanna girl / Dans les rues D'Antibes / Is you is or is you ain't my baby / My blue heaven / Limehouse blues / I want a little girl / Bloodshot eyes
CD ____ JCD 002
Jazzology / Oct '90 / Jazz Music

LONDON PRIDE 1994 (Chescoe, Laurie Good Time Jazz Band)
CD ____ JCD 244
Jazzology / Jan '97 / Jazz Music

Chesney, Kenny

ME AND YOU
CD ____ 07863669082
RCA / Jun '96 / BMG

Chesnutt, Mark

GREATEST HITS
Bubba shot the jukebox / Too cold at home / Blame it on Texas / Almost goodbye / It's a little too late / Ol' country / Brother jukebox / Gonna get a life / Let it rain / It sure is Monday / Goin' through the big D / I'll think of something
CD ____ MCD 11529
MCA / Feb '97 / BMG

Chesnutt, Vic

ABOUT TO CHOKE
CD ____ PLR 0052
CD ____ PLR 0055
Texas Hotel / Nov '96 / Pinnacle

DRUNK
Sleeping man / Bourgeois and biblical / One of many / When I ran off and left her / Dodge / Gluefoot / Free of hope / Naughty fatalist / Super Tuesday / Kick my ass
CD ____ TXH 0222
Texas Hotel / Jul '96 / Pinnacle

IS THE ACTOR HAPPY
Gravity of the situation / Sad Peter Pan / Strange language / Onion soup / Doubting woman / Wrong piano / Free of hope / Betty lonely / Thumbtack / Thailand / Guilty by association
CD ____ TXH 0232
Texas Hotel / Jul '96 / Pinnacle

LITTLE
Isadora Duncan / Danny Carlisle / Giupetto / Bakersfield / Mr. Riely / Rabbit box / Speed racer / Soft Picasso / Independence Day / Stevie Smith
CD ____ TXH 0202
Texas Hotel / Jul '96 / Pinnacle

SAMPLER
CD ____ TXHO 213
Texas Hotel / Jul '94 / Pinnacle

SWEET RELIEF VOL.2 (Various Artists)
Kick my ass: *Garbage* / Sponge: *REM* / Gravity of the situation: *Griffith, Nanci & Hootie & the Blowfish* / When I ran off and left her: *Soul Asylum* / Dodge: *Dog's Eye View* / Supernatural: *Live* / Sad Peter Pan: *Smashing Pumpkins & Red Red Meat* / West of Rome: *Sparklehorse* / Guilty by association: *Henry, Joe & Madonna* / Panic pure: *Hersh, Kristin* / Withering: *Cracker* / Free of hope: *Indigo Girls* / Florida: *O'Hara, Mary Margaret* / God is good: *Chestnutt, Vic & Williams, Victoria*
CD ____ 4841372
Columbia / Aug '96 / Sony

WEST OF ROME
Latent blatant / Withering away / Sponge / Where were you / Lucinda Williams / Florida / Stupid pre-occupation / Panic / Miss Mary / Steve Willougby / West of Rome / Big huge valley / Soggy tongues / Fuge
CD ____ TXH 0212
Texas Hotel / Jul '96 / Pinnacle

Chessa, Totore

OGANITTOS
CD ____ NT 6743CD
Newtone / Mar '96 / ADA

Chester, Bob

BOB CHESTER & HIS ORCHESTRA 1940-41
CD ____ CCD 44
Circle / Jan '94 / Jazz Music / Swift / Wellard

OCTAVE JUMP 1939-1942 (Chester, Bob & His Orchestra)
CD ____ RACD 7103
Aerospace / May '96 / Jazz Music / Montpellier

Chester, Paul Vernon

SUITE DJANGO
Naissence / Valse des enfants / Flame of destiny / Redemption / Nin nin / Broadbrimmed hat / Baro and matelo / Hotel claridge / Selmer swing / American dream / Naguine's tears
CD ____ FJCD 112
Fret / Jan '97 / Cadillac / New Note/ Pinnacle

Chesterfields

KETTLE
Nose out of joint / Ask Johnny Dee / Two girls and a treehouse / Shame about the rain / Everything a boy could ever need / Kiss me stupid / Thumb / Storm Nelson / Holiday hymn / Oh Mr. Wilson / Boy who sold his suitcase / Completely and utterly
CD ____ ASKCD 030
Vinyl Japan / Sep '93 / Plastic Head / Vinyl Japan

Chesterman, Charlie

HIT THIS AND KICK THAT
Sexy Rickenbacker / Lonesome cowboy's lament / Mister Blue / Hello Judy / So long now / New lease on life (parts 1 & 2) / Short brown hair brown eyes / Mona's prayer / Jackhammers / Trash / Theo's El Camino / I've got time / Got you bad
CD ____ RCD 10367
Rykodisc / Sep '96 / ADA / Vital

Chestnut, Mark

ALMOST GOODBYE
It sure is Monday / Woman, sensuous woman / Almost goodbye / I just wanted you to know / April's fools / Texas is bigger than it used to be / My heart's too broke (To pay attention) / Vickie Vance gotta dance / Till a better memory comes along / Will
CD ____ MCAD 10851
MCA / Mar '94 / BMG

Chevalier, Maurice

CHARMER, THE
Paris sera toujours Paris / You took the words right out of my mouth / Appelez ca comme vous voulez / Hello beautiful / Ma pomme / Walkin' my baby back home / Notre espoir / Oh, come on, be sociable / Mimi / On top of the world alone / Toi et moi / Mama Inez / Nouveau bonheur / Sweepin' the clouds away / La chanson du macon / March de menilmontant
CD ____ HADCD 158
Javelin / May '94 / Henry Hadaway / THE

ENCORE MAURICE
Hello beautiful / Up on top of a rainbow (sweepin' the clouds away) / Ca m'est egal / On top of the world alone / Mais ou est ma Zou-Zou / It's a great life / Mama Inez / Toi et moi / Savez-vous / Bon soir / Goodnight Cherie / Paris je t'aime d'amour / Walkin' my baby back home / Mon coeur / Nobody's using it now / Vous etes mon nouveau bonheur / Right now / Les ananas / O come on be sociable / Lovin' in the moonlight / Paris stay the same / You brought a new kind of love to me / Mon cocktail d'amour / Dites moi ma mere
CD ____ CDAJA 5016
Living Era / Feb '87 / Select

FLEUR DE PARIS
Ma pomme / Paris sera toujourd Paris / Fleur de Paris / Le chanson de Macon / Ca s'est passe un Dimanche / Ca sent si bon la France / Prosper / Appelez ca comme vous le voulez / Partout c'est l'amour / Le chapeau do zozo / Donnez-moi la main / Y A d'la joie / Mimile / Dites-moi ma mere / Ca fait d'excellents Francais / Quand un viconte / Notre Espoir / Mon vieux Paris
CD ____ 306272
Hallmark / Jan '97 / Carlton

FRENCH MONUMENT, A
CD ____ 995692
EPM / Jul '96 / ADA / Discovery

IMMORTAL MAURICE CHEVALIER, THE
CD ____ CD 118
Timeless Treasures / May '95 / THE

LE ROI DU MUSIC HALL
Valentine / Paris, je t'aime d'amour / La romance de la plune / Mimi / Quand un vi-

comte / Donnez-moi la Main Mam'zelle / Prosper / Le chapeau de Zozo / L'amour est passe pres de vous / Un p'tit air / Ah si vous connaissiez ma poule / Ca s'est passe un dimanche / Il pleurait / Ca fait d'excellents Francais / Ma pomme / Appelez-ca comme vous voulez / Paris ser toujours Paris / On est comme on est / Y a du bonheur pour tout le monde
CD _____ UCD 19055
Forlane / Mar '96 / Target/BMG

MAURICE CHEVALIER'S PARIS
What would you do / You brought a new kind of love to me / Le chapeau de Zozo (Zozo's new hat) / Livin' in the sunlight, livin' in the moonlight / Rhythm of the rain / Ma pomme (my apple) / You've got that thing / You look so sweet, Madame / Oh cette mitzi (oh that mitzi) / Singing a happy song / Paris, je t'aime d'amour (Paris, stay the same) / Valentine / Tzinga-doodle-day / Wait 'til you see ma cherie / Donnez-moi la main, Mam'zelle / Mimi / Quand un vicompte / My love parade / Les mots qu'on voudrait dire / All I want is just one girl / Personne ne s'en sert maintenant (nobody's using it now) / Louise
CD _____ QED 061
Tring / Nov '96 / Tring

ON TOP OF THE WORLD
Valentine / It's a habit of mine / Wait till you see Ma cherie / On top of the world alone / Sweepin' the clouds away / All I want is just one girl / mama Inez / Toi et moi / You brought a new kind of love / Living in the sunlight / Paris stay the same / My love parade / Dites moi ma mere / Quand on est tout seul / Walkin' my baby back home / Oh, come on, be sociable / You took the words right out of my mouth / Hello beautiful / Mimi / Ma pomme / Ah Si vous connaissiez ma poule / Singing a happy song / Rhythm of the rain
CD _____ PASTCD 9711
Flapper / '90 / Pinnacle

PARIS SERA TOUJOURS PARIS
Paris, Je t'Aime d'Amour / Mais ou est ma Zou-Zou / Toi et moi / Ca m'est Egal / Louise / Mon Coeur / Vous etes mon Nouveau Bonheur / Les Ananas / Ma Pomme / Paris sera toujours Paris / Ca Fait d'excellents Francais / Fleur de Paris / Mimi / La Marche de Menilmontant / Ca c'est passe un dimanche / Bon soir / Savez-vous / Valentine / Hello beautiful / La Choupetta
CD _____ MDF 102608
Mudisque / Nov '96 / Target/BMG

SUCCES ET RARETES 1920-1928
CD _____ 701552
Chansophone / Sep '96 / Discovery

Chi-Lites

BEST OF THE CHI-LITES
Give it away / Let me be the man my daddy was / Twenty four hours of sadness / I like your lovin' / Are you my woman (tell me so) / For god's sake give more power to the people / Have you seen her / Oh girl / Coldest day of my life / We need order / Letter to myself / Stoned out of my mind / I found sunshine / Homely girl / Too good to be forgotten / There will never be any peace (until God is seated at the... / Toby / It's time for love / You don't have to go
CD _____ CDKEN 911
Kent / Jun '87 / Pinnacle

BEST OF THE HITS, THE
Homely girl / Toby / For god's sake give more power to the people / I want to pay you back (For loving me) / Too good to be forgotten / Twenty four hours of sadness / Lonely man / Coldest day of my life / You don't have to go / There will never be any peace (Until God is seated at the co / I found sunshine / It's time for love / Give it away / Oh girl / Stoned out of my mind / Have you seen her / Letter to myself / Let me be the man my Daddy was / We are neighbours
CD _____ CPCD 8051
Charly / Mar '95 / Koch

CHI-LITES COLLECTION, THE
Have you seen her / Oh girl / Heavenly body / Strung out / Round and round / All I wanna do is make love to you / Give me a dream / Super mad / Men and you / Tell me where it hurts / Whole lot of good good loving / Get down with me / Try my side / Hot on a thing / Never speak to a stranger
CD _____ SUMCD 4116
Sound & Media / May '97 / Sound & Media

GREATEST HITS
CD _____ KWEST 5402
Kenwest / Mar '93 / THE

HAVE YOU SEEN HER (The Very Best Of The Chi-Lites)
CD _____ PWKS 4240
Carlton / Feb '95 / Carlton

JUST SAY YOU LOVE ME
Happy music / Solid love affair / Just you and I tonite / Just say you love me / Inner city blues / There's a change / Eternity / Only you
CD _____ ICH 1057CD
Ichiban / Mar '94 / Direct / Koch

SWEET SOUL MUSIC
Have you seen her / Heavenly body / Strung out / Round and round / Give me a dream / Super mad / All I wanna do is make love to you / Love shock / Me and you / Tell me where it hurts / Oh girl / Get down with me / Hot on a thing (called love) / Never speak to a stranger / Whole lot of good loving / Try my side (of love)
CD _____ CPCD 8019
Charly / Feb '94 / Koch

VERY BEST OF THE CHI-LITES, THE
Have you seen her / For god's sake give more power to the people / Oh girl / Coldest day of my life / Homely girl / Are you my woman (tell me so) / Let me be the man my daddy was / There will never be any peace (until god is se / I found sunshine / Too good to be forgotten / It's time for love / You don't have to go / I like your lovin' / Stoned out of my mind / Give it away / Letter to myself
CD _____ MCCD 029
Music Club / May '91 / Disc / THE

Chiarelli, Rita

JUST GETTING STARTED
CD _____ HYCD 200151
Hypertension / Jul '95 / ADA / CM / Direct / Total/BMG

Chiasson, Warren

GOOD VIBES FOR KURT WEILL
CD _____ ACD 236
Audiophile / Jun '93 / Jazz Music

Chiavola, Kathy

HARVEST
CD _____ FIENDCD 779
Demon / Apr '96 / Pinnacle

Chic

BEST OF CHIC VOL.2, THE
Rebels are we / What about me / Twenty six / Will you cry (when you hear this song) / Stage fright / Real people / Hangin' / Give me the lovin' / At last I am free / Just out of reach / When you love someone / Your love is cancelled / Believer / You are beautiful / Flash back / You can't do it alone / Tavern on the green
CD _____ 8122710862
Atlantic / Mar '93 / Warner Music

C'EST CHIC
Le freak / Chic cheer / I want your love / Happy man / Dance, dance, dance / Savoir faire / At last I am free / Sometimes you win / Funny bone / Everybody dance
CD _____ 7567815522
Atlantic / Feb '93 / Warner Music

CHIC
Dance, dance, dance / Sao Paulo / You can get by / Everybody dance / Est-ce que c'est chic / Falling in love with you / Strike up the band
CD _____ 7567804072
Atlantic / Feb '92 / Warner Music

MEGACHIC (The Best Of Chic Vol. 1)
Megachic (medley) / Chic cheer / My feet keep dancing / Good times / I want your love / Everybody dance / Le freak / Dance, dance, dance
CD _____ 2292417502
Atlantic / Aug '90 / Warner Music

Chicago

25 OR 6 TO 4
CD _____ CDSGP 0126
Prestige / Oct '94 / Else / Total/BMG

CHICAGO
Feelin' stronger everyday / Just you and me / Rediscovery / What's this world comin' to / Darlin' dear / Hollywood / Jenny / In terms in two / Something in this city changes people / Critic's choice / 25 or 6 to 4 / I'm a man / Questions 67 & 68 / Does anybody really know what time it is / Beginnings / Purple song
CD _____ EXP 006
Experience / May '97 / TKO Magnum

CHICAGO 17
Stay the night / We can stop the hurtin' / Hard habit to break / Only you / Remember the feeling / Along comes a woman / You're the inspiration / Please hold on / Prima donna / Once in a lifetime
CD _____ 9250602
WEA / Apr '84 / Warner Music

CHICAGO 20
Explain it to my heart / If it were you / You come to my senses / Somebody / Somewhere / What does it take / One from the heart / Chasin' the wind / God save the queen / Man to woman / Only time can heal the wounded / Who do you love / Holdin' on
CD _____ 7599263912
WEA / Dec '96 / Warner Music

CHICAGO TRANSIT AUTHORITY, THE (Chicago Transit Authority)
Does anybody really know what time it is / Beginnings / Questions 67 and 68 / Listen / Poem 58 / Free form guitar / South California purples / I'm a man / Prologue, August 29 / Someday / Liberation / Introduction
CD _____ 4747882
Columbia / May '94 / Sony

GREATEST HITS
25 or 6 to 4 / Does anybody really know what time it is / Colour my world / Just you 'n' me / Saturday in the park / Never been in love before / Feeling stronger every day / I'm a man / Make me smile / Wishing you were here / Call on me / I've been searchin' so long / Beginnings
CD _____ CD 32535
Columbia / Mar '91 / Sony

GROUP PORTRAIT
CD Set _____ 4692092
Legacy / May '94 / Sony

HEART OF CHICAGO, THE
If you leave me now / Baby what a big surprise / Take me back to Chicago / Hard to say I'm sorry / Love me tomorrow / Hard habit to break / You're the inspiration / Along comes a woman / Remember the feeling / If she would have been faithful / What kind of man would I be / Look away / Where did the loving go / Only you / Will you still love me
CD _____ WX 328CD
WEA / Feb '94 / Warner Music

I'M A MAN
25 or 6 to 4 / I'm a man / Purple song / Beginnings / Liberation / Questions / Does anybody know what time it is
CD _____ 305652
Hallmark / Jul '97 / Carlton

IN CONCERT
Beginnings / Purples / I'm a man / Questions 67 and 68 / Does anybody really know what time it is / 25 or 6 to 4 / Liberation
CD _____ HADCD 172
Javelin / May '94 / Henry Hadaway / THE

LEGENDS IN MUSIC
CD _____ LECD 075
Wisepack / Jul '94 / Conifer/BMG / THE

LIVE IN TORONTO
Beginnings / Purples / 25 or 6 to 4 / Does anybody really know what time it is / I'm a man / Questions 67 and 68 / Liberation
CD _____ CDTB 103
Thunderbolt / Jul '95 / TKO Magnum

Chicago All Stars

WHEN I LOST MY BABY
CD _____ CM 10003
Magnum Music / Oct '92 / TKO Magnum

Chicago Beau

CHICAGO BEAU & FRIENDS
CD _____ GBW 009
GBW / Feb '94 / Harmonia Mundi

MY ANCESTORS
CD _____ GBW 004
GBW / Mar '92 / Harmonia Mundi

Chicago String Band

CHICAGO STRING BAND
CD _____ TCD 5006
Testament / Oct '94 / ADA / Koch

Chicken Bones

HARDROCK IN CONCERT
CD _____ SB 023
Second Battle / Jul '97 / Greyhound

Chicken Chest

ACTION PACKED (Chicken Chest & Leslie Thunder)
CD _____ RE 174CD
ROIR / Jun '97 / Plastic Head / Shellshock/Disc

Chickenpox

DINNER DANCE AND LATE NIGHT MUSIC
CD _____ BHR 025CD
Burning Heart / Jul '95 / Plastic Head

Chicory Tip

CHICORY TIP
CD _____ 12377
Laserlight / May '95 / Target/BMG

VERY BEST OF CHICORY TIP, THE (20 Original Recordings)
Son of my father / What's your name / Cigarettes, women and wine / I see you / Future is past / Big wheels rolling / Join our gang / Me and Stan Foley / Good grief Christina / Move on / IOU / Take your time Caroline / Sweat, dust and red wine / Lodi / Pride comes before a fall / Excuse me baby / Friend of mine / Whta she thinks about / I can here you calling / Memory
CD _____ SUMCD 4099
Sound & Media / Mar '97 / Sound & Media

Chief Groovy Loo

GOT 'EM RUNNING SCARED
CD _____ WRA 8116CD
Wrap / Jan '94 / Koch

Chieftains

ANOTHER COUNTRY
Wabash cannonball / Morning dew/Father Kelly's reels / I can't stop loving you / Heartbreak hotel / Heartbreak hotel/Cliffs of Moher / Cotton eyed Joe / Nobody's darlin' but mine / Goodnight Irene
CD _____ 09026609392
RCA / Nov '92 / BMG

BEST OF THE CHIEFTAINS
Up against the Buachalawns / Boil the breakfast early / Friel's kitchen / No.6 the Coombe / O'Sullivan's march / Sea image / Speic seoigheach / Dogs among the bushes / Job of journeywork / Oh the breeches full of stitches / Chase around the windmill / Toss the feathers / Ballinasloe Fair / Cailleach an airgid / Cuil addha slide / Pretty girl / Wind that shakes the barley / Reel with the Beryle
CD _____ 4716662
Columbia / May '92 / Sony

CHIEFTAINS LIVE
Morning dew / George Brabazon / Kerry slides / Carrickfergus / Carolan's concerto / Foxhunt / Round the house and mind the dresser / Caitlin trial / For the sakes of old decency / Carolan's farewell to music / Banish misfortune / Tarbolton/The pinch of snuff / Star of munster/Flogging reel / Limerick's lamentation / O'Neill's march / Ril mhor
CD _____ CC 21CD
Claddagh / Apr '89 / ADA / CM / Direct

CHIEFTAINS VOL.1
Se fath mo Bhuartha / Lark on the Strand / An fhallaingin mhuimhneagh / Trim the velvet / An combra Donn/Murphy's hornpipe / Cailin na Gruaige Doinne / Comb your hair or curl it/Boys of Ballisodare / Musical priest/Queen of May / Walls of Liscarroll jig / Dhruimfhion donn dilis / Connemara stocking/Limestone rock/Dan Breen's reel / Casadh an tSugain / Boy in the Gap / St. Mary's / Church Street polka / Garrett Barry/The battering ram / Kitty goes milking/Rakish Paddy
CD _____ CC 2CD
Claddagh / Nov '90 / ADA / CM / Direct

CHIEFTAINS VOL.10
Christmas reel / Salut a la Compagnie / My love is in America / Manx music / Master Crowley's reels / Pride of Pimlico / An Faire / Turtle dove / Sir Arthur Shaen/Madam Cole / Garech's wedding / Cotton eyed Joe
CD _____ CC 33CD
Claddagh / Nov '90 / ADA / CM / Direct

CHIEFTAINS VOL.2
Banish misfortune/Gillian's apples / Planxty George Brabazon / Bean an fhir rua / O'Farrell's welcome to Limerick / An paistin Fionn/Mountain top / Foxhunt / An mhaighdean mhara / Tie the bonnet/O'Rourke's reel / Callaghan's and Byrne's hornpipes / Pigtown/Tie the ribbons/Bag of potatoes / Humours of whiskey/Hardiman the fiddler / Donald Og / Brian Boru's march / Sweeney's polka/Denis Murphy's polka / Scartagien polka
CD _____ CC 7CD
Claddagh / Aug '92 / ADA / CM / Direct

CHIEFTAINS VOL.3
Strike the gay harp / Lord Mayo / Lady on the island / Sailor on the rock / Sonny's mazurka / Tommy Hunt's jig / Eibi gheal chiuin ni chearbhaill / Defahunty's hornpipe / Hunter's purse / March of the King of Laois / Carolan's concerto / Tom Billy's / Road to Lisdoonvarna / Merry sisters / An ghaoth aneas / Lord Inchiquin / Trip to Sligo / An raibh tu ag an Gcarraig / John Kelly's / Merrily kiss the Quaker / Dennis Murphy's
CD _____ CC 10CD
Claddagh / Jan '93 / ADA / CM / Direct

CHIEFTAINS VOL.4
Drowsy Maggie / Morgan Magan / Tip of the whistle / Bucks of Oranmore / Battle of Aughrium / Morning dew / Carrickfergus / Hewlett / Cherish the ladies / Lord Mayo / Mna ban / Star above the garter / Weavers
CD _____ CC 14CD
Claddagh / Oct '88 / ADA / CM / Direct

CHIEFTAINS VOL.5
Timpan reel / Tabhair dom do lamh / Three Kerry polkas / Ceol Bhriotanach / Chieftains knock on the door / Robber's glen / An ghe agus an gra geal / Humours of Carolan / Sambradh Sambradh (Summertime Summertime) / Kerry slides
CD _____ CC 16CD
Claddagh / '88 / ADA / CM / Direct

CHIEFTAINS VOL.6
Chattering magpie / First Tuesday of Autumn/Green grow the rushes O / Bonaparte's retreat / Away with ye / Caledonia / Princess Royal/Blind Mary/John Drury / Rights of man / Round the house and mind the dresser
CD _____ CC 20CD
Claddagh / Nov '90 / ADA / CM / Direct

CHIEFTAINS VOL.7
Away we go again / Dochas / Hedigan's fancy / John O'Connor / Friel's kitchen / No. 6 The Coombe / O'Sullivan's march / Ace and deuce of pipering / Fairies / Lamentation and dance / Oh the breeches full of stitches

CD 4838512
Columbia / Mar '96 / Sony

CHIEFTAINS VOL.8
Session / Dr. John Hart / Sean sa cheo / Fairies' hornpipe / Sea image / If I had Maggie in the wood / An speic seogheach / Dogs among the bushes / Miss Hamilton the job of journeywork / Wind that shakes the barley / Reel with the Beryle
CD CC 29CD
Claddagh / Dec '93 / ADA / CM / Direct

CHIEFTAINS VOL.9
Boil the breakfast early / Mrs. Judge / March: Oscar and Malvina / When a man's in love / Path through the wood / Travelling through Blarney / Carolan's welcome / Up against the Buachalawns / Gol na mBan san Ar / Chase around the windmill
CD CC 30CD
Claddagh / '88 / ADA / CM / Direct

FILM CUTS
O'Sullivan's march / Dublin / You're the one / Treasure island / Barry Lyndon love theme / Tristan and Isolde / Grey fox / Fighting for dough / Ireland moving
CD 09026684382
RCA / Jul '96 / BMG

GREATEST HITS
Millenium celtic suite / Wexford carol / Iron man / Stray away child / Here's a health to the company / Coolin' medley / Boffyflow and Spike / O'Mahoney's frolics / Dan tros fisel / Heulliadenn tonniou breizh-izel
CD 74321339452
Camden / Jan '96 / BMG

IRISH EVENING, AN
CD RD 60916
RCA / Jun '92 / BMG

LIVE IN CHINA
Full of joy / In a suzhow garden / If I had Maggie in the wood / Reason for my sorrow / Chieftains in China / Planxty irwin / Off the great wall / Tribute to O'Carolan / Wind from the south / China to Hong kong
CD CC 42CD
Claddagh / Aug '85 / ADA / CM / Direct

LONG BLACK VEIL, THE
Mo ghile mear / Long black veil / Foggy dew / Have I told you lately that I love you / Changing your demeanor / Lily of the west / Coast of Malabar / Dunmore lassies / Ferny Hill / Tennessee waltz / Tenessee mazurka / Rocky road to Dublin
CD 74321251672
RCA / Jan '95 / BMG

MAGIC OF THE CHIEFTAINS
O'Mahoney's frolics / Coolin' medley / Wexford carol / Marches / Boffyflow and Spike / Celtic wedding / Here's a health to the company / Strayaway child / Iron man / Millennium celtic suite / Dans tro fisel / Heuliadenn toniou breizh-izel
CD MCCD 048
Music Club / Jan '92 / Disc / THE

SANTIAGO (Chieftains & Linda Ronstadt/Los Lobos/Ry Cooder/Carlos Nunez)
Txalaparta / Arku-Dantza/Arin-Arin / El besu (the kiss) / Nao vas ao mar, Toino (don't go to sea, Toino) / Dum paterfamilias/Ad honorem / Dueling chanters (sixpenny money/ Polka de Vilagarcia) / Galician Overture / Guadalupe / Minho Waltz / Setting sail/Muineira de frexido / Maneo / Santiago de Cuba / Galleguita/Tutankhamen / Tears of stone / Duublin in Vigo / Alboreda gallega / Miudino / Lola / Jackson's morning brush / Muineira de Cabana / Muineira de Chantada
CD 09026686022
RCA Victor / Nov '96 / BMG

Chiffons

BEST OF THE CHIFFONS
Sweet talking guy / One fine day / He's so fine / Tonight I'm gonna dream / Out of this world / I have a boyfriend / Nobody knows what's going on / When the boy's happy (the girl's happy too) / Tonight I met an angel / Love so fine / Open your eyes / Sailor boy / Stop, look & listen / My block / Oh my lover / Just for tonight / My boyfriend's back / Why am I so shy / I'm gonna dry my eyes / Did you ever go steady
CD CDMFP 6219
Music For Pleasure / Apr '96 / EMI

ONE FINE DAY
CD RMB 75071
Remember / Apr '94 / Total/BMG

Chihabi, Abou

FOLKOMOR OCEAN
CD PS 65188
PlayaSound / Jul '97 / ADA / Harmonia Mundi

Chiky(u)u

JAPANESE COLLECTION
CD ASH 36
Ash International / May '97 / Kudos / Pinnacle

Child, Jane

HERE NOT THERE
Mona Lisa smiles / Do whatcha do / Monument / All I do / Sshhh / Perfect love / I do not feel as good as you / Heavy smile / Calling / Step out of time / Sarasvati / Here not there
CD 9362452962
Warner Bros. / Sep '93 / Warner Music

Childe Rolande

FOREIGN LAND
Walk a lonely road / Fair wind / Aranmor / Just landed / Out of the dream / Living in a game of chance / More fool you / Time and the tide / Dead reckoning / Poison pen / Ghost / Foreign land
CD CDLDL 1251
Lochshore / Mar '97 / ADA / Direct / Duncans

Childers, Buddy

ARTISTRY IN JAZZ (Childers, Buddy & The Russ Garcia Strings)
Come home again / Shadow of your smile / Stardust / You are too beautiful / Body and soul / 'Round midnight / My Diane / Lush life / Stars fell on Alabama / Sophisticated lady / Angel eyes / Din di (jin je)
CD CCD 79735
Candid / Jan '97 / Cadillac / Direct / Jazz Music / Koch / Wellard

WEST COAST QUINTET
Straight no chaser / My funny valentine / Buffy / Street of dreams / Scam / What's new / All the things you are / Lament / Cotton tail
CD CCD 79722
Candid / May '97 / Cadillac / Direct / Jazz Music / Koch / Wellard

Childish, Billy

AT THE BRIDGE (Childish, Billy & The Singing Loins)
CD DAM 22CD
Damaged Goods / Apr '94 / Shellshock/ Disc

CAPTAIN CALYPSO'S HOODOO PARTY/LIVE IN THE NETHERLANDS (Childish, Billy & The Black Hands)
CD SCRAG 3UP
Hangman's Daughter / Sep '94 / Shellshock/Disc / SRD

Children

EVERY SINGLE DAY
CD SKYCD 2015
Sky / Sep '94 / Greyhound / Koch / Vital/ SAM

Children Of Dub

CHAMELEON
CD MEYCD 15
Magick Eye / Aug '96 / Cargo / SRD

SILENT POOL
CD BACCYCD 002
Diversity / Oct '95 / 3mv/Vital

Children Of Judah

WAITING BY THE GATES OF EDEN
CD TRIBE 001CD
Wall Of Sound / Jun '95 / Prime / Soul Trader / Vital

Children Of Selma

WHO WILL SPEAK FOR THE CHILDREN
CD ROUCD 8008
Rounder / '88 / ADA / CM / Direct

Children Of The Bong

SIRIUS SOUNDS
Polyphase / Ionosperic state / Interface reality / Veil / Underwater / Life of plant earth / Squigglasonica / Visitor
CD BARKCD 012
Planet Dog / Jul '95 / Pinnacle

Children On Stun

MONDO WEIRD
CD MACDL 953
Resurrection / Apr '97 / Plastic Head

TORNIQUETS OF LOVE DESIRE
CD CLEO 72082
Cleopatra / Aug '94 / Cargo / Greyhound / Plastic Head / RTM/Disc / SRD

Children's Choir

CHRISTMAS CAROLS
Star carol / O little town of Bethlehem / Infant holy infant lowly / Candlelight carol / Once in Royal David's city / In the winter darkness / Silent night / Carol of the children / Here comes Christmas / Silver sleigh / Christmas cheer / Away in a manger / Nativity carol / I saw three ships / In the bleak mid-winter / Mary had a baby / Sussex carol / Little Jesus sweetly slept / While shepherds watched / Child in the manger / Unto us is born a son / Cowboy carol
CD XMAS 003
Tring / Nov '96 / Tring

Children's Company

POLLY POCKET - POLLY'S DISCO PARTY
CD LFPK 2006
Listen For Pleasure / Jul '96 / EMI

Childs Brothers

EUPHONIUM MUSIC
CD DOYCD 002
Doyen / Nov '92 / Conifer/BMG

WELSH WIZARDS (Childs Brothers & The Tredegar Town Band)
CD DOYCD 022
Doyen / May '93 / Conifer/BMG

Childs, Billy

CHILD WITHIN, THE
CD SHCD 5023
Shanachie / Sep '96 / ADA / Greensleeves / Koch

I'VE KNOWN RIVERS
I've known rivers / Starry night / Lament / Way of the new world / This moment / Realism / Somewhere I have never travelled / Siren serenade
CD SCD 90102
Stretch / Mar '97 / New Note/Pinnacle

Childs, Toni

HOUSE OF HOPE
CD 3971492
A&M / Aug '91 / PolyGram

UNION
Don't walk away / Walk and talk like angels / Stop you're fussin' / Dreamer / Let the rain come down / Zimbabwe / Hush / Tin drum / Where's the ocean
CD 3951752
A&M / Apr '95 / PolyGram

WOMAN'S BOAT
Womb / Welcome to the world / Predator / I just want affection / I met a man / Woman's boat / Wild bride / Sacrifice / Lay down your pain / Long time coming / death
CD GFLD 19341
Geffen / Oct '96 / BMG

Chilli Willi

I'LL BE HOME (Chilli Willi & Red Hot Peppers)
CD PRPCD 002
Proper / Jan '97 / Grapevine/PolyGram

Chillingworth, Sonny

SONNY SOLO
CD DCT 38005CD
Dancing Cat / Mar '96 / ADA

Chills

KALEIDOSCOPE WORLD
Kaleidoscope world / Satin doll / Frantic drift / Rolling moon / Bite / Flame thrower / Pink frost / Purple girl / This is the way / Never never go / Don't even know her name / Bee bah bee bah bee boe / Whole weird world / Dream by dream / Doledrums / Hidden bay / I love my leather jacket / Great escape
CD FNE 013CD
Flying Nun / Mar '94 / RTM/Disc

SUNBURNT
CD FNCD 303
Flying Nun / Sep '96 / RTM/Disc

Chilton, Alex

ALEX CHILTON
CD 422051
New Rose / May '94 / ADA / Direct / Discovery

ALEX CHILTON 1970
CD CREV 044CD
Rev-Ola / Apr '96 / 3mv/Vital

BACH'S BOTTOM
CD RE 2010
Razor & Tie / Mar '97 / Koch

CLICHES
CD NR 422481
New Rose / Jan '94 / ADA / Direct / Discovery

FEUDALIST TARTS/NO SEX
CD RE 2032
Razor & Tie / Mar '97 / Koch

HIGH PRIEST/BLACKLIST
CD RE 2033
Razor & Tie / Mar '97 / Koch

LIKE FLIES ON SHERBERT
Boogie shoes / My rival / Hey little child / Hook or crook / I've had it / Rock hard / Girl after girl / Waltz across Texas / Alligator man / Like flies on sherbert
CD COOKCD 095
Cooking Vinyl / Jan '96 / Vital
CD 422445
Last Call / Feb '97 / Cargo / Direct / Discovery

LIVE IN LONDON
CD CREV 015CD
Rev-Ola / Jun '93 / 3mv/Vital

MAN CALLED DESTRUCTION, A
CD RRCD 901312
Ruf / May '95 / Pinnacle

TOP 30
CD 3021082
Arcade / Jun '97 / Discovery

Chimes

CHIMES
Love so tender / Heaven / True love / 1-2-3 / Underestimate / Love comes to mind / I still haven't found what I'm looking for (street mix) / Don't make me wait / Stronger together / Stay / I still haven't found what I'm looking for
CD 4664812
CBS / Jun '90 / Sony

China Beach

SIX BULLET RUSSIAN ROULETTE
CD RTN 41213
Rock The Nation / Aug '95 / Plastic Head

China Crisis

CHINA CRISIS COLLECTION
African and white / No more blue horizons / Christian / Tragedy and mystery / Working with fire and steel / Wishful thinking / Hanna Hanna / Black man ray / King in a catholic style / You did cut me / Arizona sky / Best kept secret / It's everything / St. Saviour square / Scream down at me / Cucumber garden / Golden handshake for every daughter / Some people I know / Instigator / Little Italy / Greenacre Bay / No ordinary lover / Dockland / Forever I and I / Performing seals / This occupation / Watching over burning fields / Animalistic
CD CDV 2613
Virgin / Sep '90 / EMI

DIARY (A Collection)
Black man Ray / Animalistic / Hampton beach / Red letter day / Diary of a hollow horse / Strength of character / When the piper calls / Christian / Golden handshake for every daughter / Hanna Hanna / African and white / Here comes a raincloud / King in a catholic style / Blue sea / Tragedy and mystery / Wishful thinking
CD CDVIP 109
Virgin VIP / Nov '93 / EMI

DIFFICULT SHAPES AND PASSIVE RHYTHMS (Some People Think It's Fun To Entertain)
Seven sports for all / No more blues horizons / Feel to be driven away / Some people I know to lead fantastic lives / Christian / African and white / Are we a worker / Red sails / You never see it / Temptations big blue eyes / Jean walks in fresh fields
CD CDV 2243
Virgin / Jul '87 / EMI

FLAUNT THE IMPERFECTION
Highest high / Strength of character / You did cut me / Black man Ray / Wall of God / Gift of freedom / King in a catholic style / Bigger the punch I'm feeling / World spins, The, I'm part of it / Blue sea
CD CDV 2342
Virgin / Jan '90 / EMI

WARPED BY SUCCESS
CD STACD 001
Stardumb / Sep '96 / Koch

WHAT PRICE PARADISE
It's everything / Arizona sky / Safe as houses / World's apart / Hampton beach / Understudy / Best kept secret / We do the same / June bride / Days work for the days done / Trading in gold
CD CDVIP 167
Virgin VIP / Dec '96 / EMI

WISHFUL THINKING (2CD Set)
African and white / No more blue horizons / Wishful thinking / Everyday the same / It's everything / Christian / Good again / Hands on the wheel / Black Man Ray / King in a Catholic style / Thank you / Singing the praises of finer things / Working with fire and steel / Diary of a hollow horse / Hands on wheel / Always / Everyday the same / Without the love / Thank you / Hard to be around / One wish too many / Wishing time / Good again / Real tears / Does it pay / Way we are made / Tell me what it is
CD Set SMDCD 117
Snapper / May '97 / Pinnacle

WORKING WITH FIRE AND STEEL-POSSIBLE POP SONGS VOL.2
Working with fire and steel / When the piper calls / Hanna Hanna / Animals in the jungle / Here comes a raincloud / Wishful thinking / Tragedy and mystery / Papua / Gates of door to door / Soulful awakening
CD CDV 2286
Virgin / Sep '84 / EMI

China Drum

GOOSE FAIR
CD MNTCD 1002
Mantra / Apr '96 / RTM/Disc

Chinafrica

CREATION
CD ______ CACD 01
Graylan / Jul '95 / Grapevine/PolyGram / Jet Star

Chinatown

PLAY IT TO DEATH
CD ______ ETHEL 6
Vinyl Tap / Mar '97 / Cargo / Greyhound / Vinyl Tap

Chinchilla

101 ITALIAN HITS
CD ______ CRISIS 011CD
Crisis / Oct '96 / Plastic Head

Chino XL

HERE TO SAVE YOU ALL
Here to save you all / Deliver / No complex / Partner to swing / It's all bad / Freestyle rhymes / Riiiot / Waiting to exhale / What am I / Feelin' evil again / Thousands / Kreep / Many different ways / Shabba doo conspiracy / Ghetto vampire / Rise / My hero
CD ______ 74321302782
American / Apr '96 / BMG

Chipmunks

CLUB CHIPMUNK - THE DANCE MIXES
Macarena / Vogue / Stayin alive / Play that funky music / Chipmunk / I'm too sexy / Turn the beat around / Witch doctor / Love shack
CD ______ 4867022
Chipmunk/Sony / Dec '96 / Sony

Chipolata 5

SKINLESS
Intro / Sweet lassi set / Old Joe Clarke / Two men / Three around three / Boa constrictor / Rambling sailor / Lake Arthur / Bacca pipes
CD ______ HOODCD 001
Hoodlum / May '97 / Direct

Chirag Penchan

RAIL GADDI
CD ______ DMUT 1039
Multitone / Mar '96 / BMG

Chirgilchin

WOLF AND THE KID, THE
CD ______ SH 64070
Shanachie / Oct '96 / ADA / Greensleeves / Koch

Chisholm, George

WITH MAXINE DANIELS & JOHN PETTERS BAND (Chisholm, George/ Maxine Daniels & John Petters)
Swinging down memory lane / Riverboat shuffle / Happiness is a thing called Joe / Do nothin' 'til you hear from me / I've got my love to keep me warm / Zing went the strings of my heart
CD ______ CMJCD 011
CMJ / Mar '90 / Jazz Music / Wellard

Chittison, Herman

CLASSICS 1933-1941
CD ______ CLASSICS 690
Classics / May '93 / Discovery / Jazz Music

PS WITH LOVE
CD ______ IAJRCCD 1006
IAJRC / Jun '94 / Jazz Music / Wellard

Chiweshe, Stella

AMBUYA/NDIZVOZVO (Chiweshe, Stella & The Earthquake)
Chachimurenga / Nehondo / Njuzu / Mugomba / Chamakuwende / Kasahwa / Chipindura / Ndinogarochema / Sarura Wako
CD ______ CDORB 029
Globestyle / May '89 / Pinnacle

Chixdiggit

CHIXDIGGIT
CD ______ SPCD 355
Sub Pop / Jun '96 / Cargo / Greyhound / Shellshock/Disc

Choates, Harry

FIDDLE KING OF CAJUN SWING
CD ______ ARHCD 380
Arhoolie / Apr '95 / ADA / Cadillac / Direct

Choc Stars

EPAKA MASASI/CODE 007 (Choc Stars/ Ben Nyambo)
CD ______ KL 150
Gefraco / Jan '97 / Stern's / Triple Earth

Chocolate

HUNG, GIFTED AND SLACK
CD ______ CDWOOS 1
Out Of Step / Apr '96 / Pinnacle

SUBSTITUTE FOR SEX
CD ______ DPROMCD 15
Dirter Promotions / Aug '93 / Cargo / Pinnacle / World Serpent

Chocolate Watch Band

44
Don't need your lovin' / No way out / It's all over now baby blue / I'm not like everybody else / Misty lane / Loose lip sync ship / Are you gonna be there (at the love in) / Gone and passes by / Sitting there standing / She weaves a tender trap / Sweet young thing / I ain't no miracle worker / Blues theme
CD ______ CDWIK 25
Big Beat / May '90 / Pinnacle

INNER MYSTIQUE/ONE STEP BEYOND
Voyage of the triste / In the past / Inner mystique / I'm not like everybody else / Medication / Let's go, let's go (Aka Thrill on the hill) / It's all over now baby blue / I ain't no miracle worker / Uncle Morris / How ya been / Devil's motorcycle / I don't need no doctor / Flowers / Fireface / And she's lonely
CD ______ CDWIKD 111
Big Beat / Apr '93 / Pinnacle

NO WAY OUT...PLUS
Let's talk about girls / In the midnight hour / Come on / Dark side of the mushroom / Hot dusty road / Are you gonna be there (at the love in) / Gone and passes by / No way out / Expo 2000 / Gossamer wings / Sweet young thing / Baby blue / Misty lane / She weaves a tender trap / Milk cow blues / Don't let the sun catch you crying / Since you broke my heart / Misty lane (Remix)
CD ______ CDWIKD 118
Big Beat / Jun '93 / Pinnacle

Chodack, Walter

RAGTIME (The Best Of Scott Joplin)
CD ______ MAN 4838
Mandala / Oct '94 / ADA / Harmonia Mundi / Mandala

Choeurs D'Enfants

CHANTS DE NOEL (Chants Of Christmas)
CD ______ 74321408322
Milan / Nov '96 / Conifer/BMG / Silva Screen

Choir

CHOIR PRACTICE
I'd rather you leave me / It's cold outside / When you were with me / Don't change your mind (rehersal version) / Dream of one's life / In love's shadow (mod's demo) / I'm slippin' / Leave me be (mod's demo) / I'd rather you leave me (rehearsal version) / Treeberry / Smile / A to F / I only did it 'cause I felt so lonely / Don't change your mind / Anyway I can / Boris' lament / David Watts / These are men
CD ______ CDSC 11018
Sundazed / Apr '94 / Cargo / Greyhound / Rollercoaster

Chokebore

ANYTHING NEAR WATER
CD ______ ARRCD 61004
Amphetamine Reptile / May '95 / Plastic Head

MOTIONLESS
CD ______ ARRCD 43/289
Amphetamine Reptile / Aug '93 / Plastic Head

TASTE FOR BITTERS, A
CD ______ ARRCD 77020
Amphetamine Reptile / Dec '96 / Plastic Head

Chop Shop

RECOVERED PIECES
Intro / Six buckets / Sunny days / Carnival ride / Kick the ballistics / Stoop / Drop da new flavor / X-break / Dab'l do ya / Shaolin shoot out
CD ______ ME 000362
Soulciety/Bassism / Sep '95 / EWM

Chopper

DID YOU HEAR THAT
CD ______ CRACKLE 001
Crackle / Aug '97 / Shellshock/Disc

Chorale Iroise

D'IROISE ET D'AILLEURS
CD ______ CI 20
Keltia Musique / May '96 / ADA / Discovery

Chordettes

FABULOUS CHORDETTES, THE
Lollipop / Born to be with you / Eddie my love / Wedding / Mr. Sandman / Teenage goodnight / Just between you and me / Soft sands / Zorro / No other arms, no other lips / Lay down your arms / Never on Sunday
CD ______ CDFAB 005
Ace / Sep '91 / Pinnacle

MAINLY ROCK'N'ROLL
True love goes on and on / Mr. Sandman / Lonely lips / Hummingbird / Wedding / Eddie my love / Born to be with you / Lay down your arms / Teenage goodbye / Echo of love / Just between you and me / Soft sands / Photographs / Lollipop / Baby come-a-back-a / Zorro / Love is a two way street / No other arms, no other lips / Girl's work is never done / No wheels / Lonely boy / Charlie Brown / I cried a tear / Pink shoelaces / Tall Paul / To know him is to love him / My heart stood still / For me and my gal / Broken vow / Never on Sunday / Faraway star / In the deep blue sea
CD ______ CDCHD 934
Ace / Jul '90 / Pinnacle

Chorus Of Disapproval

CHORUS OF DISAPPROVAL
CD ______ NA 021CD
New Age / Jul '96 / Plastic Head

Chosen

SOMETHING FOR THE WEEKEND
Girl called Tuesday / Give it up / Bargain basement lover / Angel / Don't ask me / Slide / Monday Friday man / My medicine / Check out the checkout girl / Old enough to notice / Blue and white / Mr. Weekender
CD ______ DRCD 009
Detour / Sep '96 / Detour / Greyhound

Chosen Gospel Singers

LIFEBOAT, THE
Before this time another year / Ananais / Don't you know the man / Come by here / Family prayer / Leaning on the Lord / 1-2-3 / Lord will make a way somehow / It's getting late in the evening / No room at the hotel / Watch ye therefore / I'm going back with him / I've tried / Lifeboat is coming / What a wonderful sight / Don't worry 'bout me / When I get home / On the main line / Stay with Jesus / Prayer for the doomed
CD ______ CDCHD 414
Ace / Nov '93 / Pinnacle

Chowdhury, Subroto Roy

BAGESHREE
Raga brageshree parts 1 to 4 / Raga sindhi bhairavi part 1 to 2
CD ______ 8888212
Tiptoe / Dec '95 / New Note/Pinnacle

MORNING
CD ______ CDJP 1033
Jazz Point / Feb '93 / Cadillac / Harmonia Mundi

Chraibi, Said

OUD
Souleimane / Awjara / Awjara Ghouzoud / Hitaz kar kurdi / Pensees andalouses / Likaa / Raast danjikah / Ya ommou abaya / Longa nakryse / Nouzha
CD ______ CP 10196
Cinq Planetes / May '97 / Harmonia Mundi

Chris & Carla

LIFE FULL OF HOLES
CD ______ GRCD 360
Glitterhouse / Feb '95 / Avid/BMG

SHELTER FOR AN EVENING
CD ______ SPCD 92/264
Sub Pop / Jul '93 / Cargo / Greyhound / Shellshock/Disc

Chris & Cosey

CHRONOMANIC
CD ______ CTI 93002
Conspiracy / Oct '96 / World Serpent

COLLECTIV VOL.1
CD ______ CTICD 001
Conspiracy / '89 / World Serpent

COLLECTIV VOL.2
CD ______ CTICD 002
Conspiracy / '89 / World Serpent

COLLECTIV VOL.3
CD ______ CTICD 007
Conspiracy / '89 / World Serpent

COLLECTIV VOL.4
CD ______ CTICD 008
Conspiracy / '89 / World Serpent

HEARTBEAT (Creative Technology Instite)
CD ______ CTICD 004
Conspiracy / Aug '88 / World Serpent

IN CONTINUUM
CD ______ CTI 95003
Conspiracy / Oct '96 / World Serpent

METAPHYSICAL (Creative Technology Instite)
CD ______ CTI 93001
Conspiracy / Oct '96 / World Serpent

MUZIK FANTASTIQUE
CD ______ BIAS 221CD
Play It Again Sam / Oct '92 / Discovery / Plastic Head / Vital

SKIMBLE SKAMBLE
CD ______ CC 1096
Conspiracy / Jan '97 / World Serpent

SONGS OF LOVE AND LUST
CD ______ CTICD 006
Conspiracy / Jul '88 / World Serpent

SPACE BETWEEN (Carter, Chris)
CD ______ ICC 1CD
The Grey Area / Jan '92 / RTM/Disc

TECHNO PRIMITIV
CD ______ CTICD 003
Conspiracy / Jan '86 / World Serpent

TRANCE
CD ______ CTICD 005
Conspiracy / Jul '88 / World Serpent

Chris & James

DJ'S IN A BOX VOL.5 (Mixed By Chris & James) (Various Artists)
CD ______ UCCD 005
Urban Collective / Mar '97 / Amato Disco / RTM/Disc / Total/BMG / Vital

Chrissos, Theo

WHITE ROSE OF ATHENS, THE
CD ______ CNCD 5952
Disky / Jul '93 / Disky / THE

Christ Agony

DAEMOONSETH ACT II
CD ______ CDAR 024
Fringe / Mar '95 / Plastic Head

DARKSIDE
CD ______ HHR 010CD
Hammerheart / Jun '97 / Plastic Head

Christ Analogue

IN RADIANT DECAY
No daughter icon / This shall not breathe / Optima / Grain / Cradle and debase / Wear / Rigor / Unclean / Cold magnetic sun
CD ______ CRGD 84054
Re-Constriction / May '97 / Cargo

Christ Denied

...GOT WHAT HE DESERVED
Banish the vanished / Monk's wetdream / Pay to pray / Deserved no less / Useless sinless life / No salvation / Misery / Angels of death / Body of Christ / Hierarchy of hipocrisy
CD ______ SPV 08457772
SPV / Feb '97 / Koch / Plastic Head

Christdriver

EVERYTHING BURNS
CD ______ EXISTSKULD 032CD
Profane Existence / Apr '97 / Cargo

Christian Death

AMEN (2CD Set)
CD Set ______ CM 77107
Century Media / Nov '95 / Plastic Head

ANTHOLOGY OF BOOTLEGS
CD ______ NOS 1006 CD
Nostradamus / May '88 / RTM/Disc

ASHES
CD ______ NORMAL 15CD
Normal / May '94 / ADA / Direct

ATROCITIES
CD ______ NORMAL 18CD
Normal / May '94 / ADA / Direct

CATASTROPHE BALLET
CD ______ N 181CD
Normal / Jan '96 / ADA / Direct

DEATHWISH
CD ______ NORMAL 84CD
Normal / May '94 / ADA / Direct

DOLL'S THEATRE
CD ______ CLEO 62082
Cleopatra / Jun '94 / Cargo / Greyhound / Plastic Head / RTM/Disc / SRD

INSANUS, ULTIO, MISERICORDIAQUE
CD ______ FREUDCD 48
Jungle / Jan '95 / RTM/Disc / SRD

JESUS POINTS THE BONE
CD ______ FREUDCD 39
Jungle / Mar '92 / RTM/Disc / SRD

PATH OF SORROW, THE
CD ______ CLEO 39932
Cleopatra / Mar '94 / Cargo / Greyhound / Plastic Head / RTM/Disc / SRD

PROPHECIES
CD ______ FREUDCD 053
Jungle / Feb '96 / RTM/Disc / SRD

RAGE OF ANGELS, THE
CD ______ CLEO 81252
Cleopatra / May '94 / Cargo / Greyhound / Plastic Head / RTM/Disc / SRD

SCRIPTURES
CD ____ NORMAL 65
Normal / May '94 / ADA / Direct

SEX, DRUGS AND JESUS CHRIST
CD ____ FREUDCD 050
Jungle / Aug '95 / RTM/Disc / SRD

SEXY DEATH GOD
CD ____ CDVEST 26
Bulletproof / Aug '94 / Pinnacle

TALES OF INNOCENCE
CD ____ CLEO 91092
Cleopatra / Dec '93 / Cargo / Greyhound / Plastic Head / RTM/Disc / SRD

WIND KISSED PICTURES
CD ____ NORMAL 76CD
Normal / Jan '96 / ADA / Direct

Christian Tabernacle Baptist ...

RIVER OF LIFE (Christian Tabernacle Baptist Choir)
Congregation arrives / Welcome (what a friend we have in Jesus) / Prayer / Victory today is mine / Jesus said / Great change in me / Leave it there / I'm delivered / Jesus can work it out / I won't leave here like I came / Something about the lord is mighty sweet / Lily of the valley / River of life
CD ____ VICG 53952
JVC World Library / May '97 / ADA / CM / Direct

Christian, Charlie

1939-1941 (Christian, Charlie & Benny Goodman)
CD ____ CD 56059
Jazz Roots / Mar '95 / Target/BMG

AIRCHECKS AND PRIVATE RECORDINGS
CD ____ JZCD 379
Suisa / Jun '93 / Jazz Music / THE

CHARLIE CHRISTIAN WITH BENNY GOODMAN (Christian, Charlie & Benny Goodman)
CD ____ CD 14545
Jazz Portraits / Jan '94 / Jazz Music

GENIUS OF THE ELECTRIC GUITAR
Rose room / Seven come eleven / Till Tom special / Gone with "what" wind / Grand slam / Six appeal / Wholly cats / Royal Garden blues / As long as I live / Benny's bugle / Breakfast feud / I found a new baby / Solo flight / Blue in B / Waiting for Benny / Airmail special
CD ____ 4606122
Sony Jazz / Jan '95 / Sony

GENIUS OF THE ELECTRIC GUITAR
CD ____ CD 53049
Giants Of Jazz / May '90 / Cadillac / Jazz Music / Target/BMG

GUITAR WIZARD
CD ____ LEJAZZCD 11
Le Jazz / Jun '93 / Cadillac / Koch

IMMORTAL, THE
CD ____ 17032
Laserlight / Jul '94 / Target/BMG

INTRODUCTION TO CHARLIE CHRISTIAN 1939-1941, AN
CD ____ 4032
Best Of Jazz / Jul '96 / Discovery

JAZZ GUITAR VOL.2, THE
CD ____ CD 56027
Jazz Roots / Nov '94 / Target/BMG

LIVE AT MINTONS
CD ____ DM 15001
DMA Jazz / Jul '96 / Jazz Music

QUINTESSENCE, THE (1939-1941/2CD Set)
CD Set ____ FA 218
Fremeaux / Jul '96 / ADA / Discovery

SOLO FLIGHT (Christian, Charlie/Benny Goodman Sextet & Orchestra)
CD ____ TPZ 1017
Topaz Jazz / Feb '95 / Cadillac / Pinnacle

SOLO FLIGHT (2CD Set)
Flying home / Rose room / Memories of you / AC/DC current no.1 / Dinah / Till tom special / Gone with 'what' wind / Sheik of Araby / Soft winds / Six appeal (my daddy rocks me) / AC/DC current / Ad-lib blues / I never knew / Charlie's dream / Wholly cats no.1 / Lester's dream / Benny's bugle no.1 / Wholly cats no.2 / Honeysucle rose / Flying home / Air mail special / Ida, sweet as apple cider / Benny's bugle / Solo flight / Swing to bop / Stompin' at the savoy / Up on Teddy's hill / Star dust no.1 / Kerouac / Star dust no.2 / Guy's got to go / Lips flips
CD Set ____ JZCL 5005
Jazz Classics / Nov '96 / Cadillac / Direct / Jazz Music

SWING TO THE BOP
CD ____ NI 4020
Natasha / Feb '94 / ADA / Cadillac / CM / Direct / Jazz Music

Christian, Emma

BENEATH THE TWILIGHT
CD ____ EM 001CD
Manx Productions / Oct '94 / ADA / Direct

Christian, Frank

FROM MY HANDS
CD ____ PM 2011
Palmetto / Nov '95 / Direct

Christian, Garry

YOUR COOL MYSTERY
CD ____ 0630189162
Coalition / May '97 / Warner Music

Christian, James

RUDE AWAKENING
CD ____ NTHEN 12
Now & Then / Sep '95 / Plastic Head

Christian, Jodie

EXPERIENCE
Bluesing around / Mood indigo / Faith / End of a love affair / They can't take that away from me / If I could let you go / Reminiscing / Blues holiday / All the things you are / Goodbye
CD ____ DD 454
Delmark / Nov '92 / ADA / Cadillac / CM / Direct / Hot Shot

FRONT LINE
In a mellow tone / Willow weep for me / Lester left town / Front line / Don't get around much anymore / Chelsea Bridge / Mood indigo / All blues / Faith / Splanky
CD ____ DE 490
Delmark / Jun '97 / ADA / Cadillac / CM / Direct / Hot Shot

RAIN OR SHINE
Let's try / Song for Atala / Ballad medley / Yardbird suite / Coltrane's view / Mr. Freddie / Chromatically speaking / Come rain or come shine / Cherokee
CD ____ DE 467
Delmark / Mar '97 / ADA / Cadillac / CM / Direct / Hot Shot

Christian, Neil

NEIL CHRISTIAN & THE CRUSADERS 1962-1973 (With Jimmy Page, Ritchie Blackmore and Nicky Hopkins) (Christian, Neil & The Crusaders)
Road to love / Little bit of something else / Honey hush / She's got the action / Wanna lover / She said yeah / Count down / You're all things bright and beautiful / My baby left me / I remember / Feel in the mood / What would your mamma say / I like it / All last night / One for the money / Get a load of this / Give the game away / Two at a time / Oops / Bit by bit / Bad girl / Gonna love you baby / Yakety yak / Crusading / That's nice / Dedicated follower of fashion / Let me in / Big beat in
CD ____ SEECD 342
See For Miles/C5 / Feb '97 / Pinnacle

Christians

BEST OF THE CHRISTIANS, THE
CD ____ CIDTV 6
Island / Nov '93 / PolyGram

CHRISTIANS, THE
Forgotten town / When the fingers point / Born again / Ideal world / Save a soul in every town / And that's why / Hooverville / One in a million / Sad songs
CD ____ IMCD 162
Island / Mar '93 / PolyGram

COLOUR
Man don't cry / I found out / Greenbank Drive / All talk / Words / Community of spirit / There you go again / One more baby in black / In my hour of need
CD ____ IMCD 181
Island / Mar '94 / PolyGram

HAPPY IN HELL
CD ____ IMCD 182
Island / Mar '94 / PolyGram

Christianson, Denny

SUITE MINGUS (Christianson, Denny Big Band)
CD ____ JUST 152
Justin Time / Jun '92 / Cadillac / New Note/Pinnacle

Christie Brothers

CHRISTIE BROTHERS STOMPERS (Christie Brothers Stompers)
CD ____ SGC/MELCD 20/1
Cadillac / Jan '94 / Cadillac / Jazz Music / Wellard

Christie Front Drive

CHRISTIE FRONT DRIVE
CD ____ CR 024CD
Caulfield / Apr '97 / Cargo

Christie, Lou

GLORY RIVERS (Buddah Years)
Genesis and the third verse / Rake up the leaves / Johnstown kite / Canterbury road / I'm gonna make you mine / I'm gonna get married / Are you getting any sunshine / She sold me magic / Life is what you make it / I got love / Boys lazed on the veranda / Tell her / Indian lady / Glory river / Wood child / Paper song / Chuckie wagon / Campus rest / Lighthouse / Look out the window / Paint America love / Shuffle on down ot Pittsburgh
CD ____ NEX CD 187
Sequel / Jul '92 / BMG

HIT SONGS AND MORE
CD ____ HADCD 204
Javelin / Jul '96 / Henry Hadaway / THE

LIGHTNING STRIKES
CD ____ RMB 75048
Remember / Nov '93 / Total/BMG

Christie, Tony

BEST OF TONY CHRISTIE
CD ____ MCCD 185
Music Club / Nov '94 / Disc / THE

BEST OF TONY CHRISTIE, THE
CD ____ MCLD 19204
MCA / May '93 / BMG

Christlieb, Pete

CONVERSATIONS WITH WARNE (Christlieb, Pete & Warne Marsh)
CD ____ CRISS 1103
Criss Cross / Oct '95 / Cadillac / Direct / Vital/SAM

Christmas, Keith

LOVE BEYOND DEALS
CD ____ HTDCD 61
HTD / Jun '96 / CM / Pinnacle

WEATHERMAN ONE
CD ____ RRACD 0016
Run River / Jul '92 / ADA / CM

Christ's Hospital Choir

CHRISTMAS CAROLS
Break forth, o beautious heavenly light / O come all ye faithful (adeste fidelis) / Tommow shall be my dancing day / Nativity carol / Hymn to the virgin / Of the fathers heart begotten / Von himmel hoch / Maiden most gentle / Noel nouvelet / Eastern monarchs / Puer nayus in Bethlehem / God rest ye merry gentlemen / In dulci jubilo / O little town of Bethlehem / Ding dong merrily on high / Once in Royal David's City / No small wonder / Out of your sleep / Lo he comes with clouds / Descending / Hark the herald angels sing
CD ____ 3037600012
Carlton / Oct '95 / Carlton

CHRISTMAS CAROLS FROM CHRIST'S HOSPITAL (Christ's Hospital Choir & Peter Allwood/Mark Wardell)
Break forth O beauteous Heavenly light / O come all ye faithful (adeste fidelis) / Tomorrow shall be my dancing day / Eastern monarchs / Noel nouvelat / Maiden most gentle / Choral preludes / Peur natus in Bethlehem / In dulci jubilo / O come o come Emmanuel final descant / In the bleak midwinter / Of the Father's heart begotten / Hymn to the virgin / Nativity carol / God rest ye merry gentlemen / O little town of Bethlehem / Ding dong merrily on high / Once in Royal David's city / No small wonder / Out of your sleep / Lo he comes with clouds ascending / Hark the herald angels sing
CD ____ 3036700012
Carlton / Nov '96 / Carlton

Christy, June

DAY DREAMS
I let a song go out of my heart / If I should lose you / Daydream / Little grass skirt / Skip rope / I'll bet you do / Way you look tonight / Everything happens to me / I'll remember April / Get happy / Somewhere (if not in heaven) / Mile down the highway (there's a toll bridge) / Do it again / He can come back anytime he wants to / Body and soul / You're blase
CD ____ CDP 8320832
Capitol Jazz / Aug '95 / EMI

IMPROMPTU (Christy, June & Lou Levy Sextet)
My shining hour / Once upon a summertime / Show me / Everything must change / Willow weep for me / I'll remember April / Trouble with hello is goodbye / Autumn serenade / Sometime ago / Angel eyes
CD ____ DSCD 836
Discovery / Jun '93 / Warner Music

JAZZ SESSIONS, THE (The Best Of June Christy)
Something cool / I want to be happy / Remind me / Looking for a boy / My ship / Rock me to sleep / Day dream / Baby all the time / It's a most unusual day / Midnight sun / Fly me to the moon / Get happy / When sunny gets blue / Willow weep for me / Make someone happy / How high the moon / Spring really can hang you up the most / It don't mean a thing
CD ____ CDP 8539222
Capitol Jazz / Jan '97 / EMI

SONG IS JUNE, THE
Spring can really hang you up the most / One I love (belongs to somebody else) / Nobody's heart / My shining hour / I remember you / Night time was my mother / I wished on the moon / Song is you / As long as I live / Saturday's children / Remind me / Out of this world / You wear love so well / Off beat / Bad and the beautiful / Who cares about April / You care you say / Out of the shadows / Sleepin' bee / Somewhere if not in heaven
CD ____ CDP 8554552
Capitol Jazz / Mar '97 / EMI

THROUGH THE YEARS
CD ____ HCD 260
Hindsight / Aug '95 / Jazz Music / Target/BMG

UNCOLLECTED JUNE CHRISTY & THE KEYTONES VOL.1 1946
CD ____ HCD 219
Hindsight / Jun '94 / Jazz Music / Target/BMG

UNCOLLECTED JUNE CHRISTY & THE KEYTONES VOL.2 1957
CD ____ HCD 235
Hindsight / Sep '94 / Jazz Music / Target/BMG

Chrome

3RD FROM THE SUN
Third from the Sun / Firebomb / Future ghosts / Armageddon / Heartbeat / Off the line / Shadows of 1,000 years
CD ____ CLEO 95332
Cleopatra / Aug '95 / Cargo / Greyhound / Plastic Head / RTM/Disc / SRD

BLOOD ON THE MOON/ETERNITY
CD ____ EFA 7490 CD
Dossier / Jun '89 / Cargo / SRD

CHROME SAMPLER VOL.1
CD ____ EFA 084612
Dossier / Feb '95 / Cargo / SRD

CHRONICLES VOL.1 & 2
CD ____ EFA 7499
Dossier / Jun '89 / Cargo / SRD

CLAIRAUDIENT SYNDROME, THE
CD ____ EFA 084562
Dossier / Jul '94 / Cargo / SRD

HALF MACHINE LIP MOVES
TV as eyes / Zombie warfare (can't let you down) / March of the chrome police (a cold clamey bombing) / You've been duplicated / Mondo anthem / Half machine lip moves / Abstract nympho / Turned around / Zero time / Creature eternal / Critical mass
CD ____ DCD 9009
Dossier / '85 / Cargo / SRD

HAVING A WONDERFUL TIME IN THE JUICE DOME
CD ____ EFA 084622
Dossier / Mar '95 / Cargo / SRD

INTO THE EYES OF THE ZOMBIE KINGS (Chrome & Damon Edge)
CD ____ DCD 9004
Dossier / Aug '88 / Cargo / SRD

LYON CONCERT, THE/ANOTHER WORLD
If you come around / I found out today / Our good dreams / Stranger from another world / Moon glow / Sky said / Loving lovely lover / We are connected / Saniby / As we stand here in time / March of the rubber people / Ghosts of the long forgotten future / Version two (raining milk) / Source improves / Frankenstein's party
CD ____ EFA 7709CD
Dossier / Jun '89 / Cargo / SRD

THIRD FROM THE SUN
CD ____ DCD 9012
Dossier / Mar '89 / Cargo / SRD

Chrome Cranks

CHROME CRANKS, THE
Dark room / Subway man / Driving bad / Eight track mind / No. 1 girl / Doll in a dress / Backdoor maniac / Stuck in a cave / Loend buzz / Outta my heart
CD ____ PCP 0162
PCP / Jan '95 / Vital

DEAD COOL
Dead cool / Desperate friend / Shine it on / Nightmare in pink / Burn baby burn / Bloodshot eye / Down so low / Way out lover
CD ____ EFA 115902
Crypt / May '95 / Shellshock/Disc

LOVE IN EXILE
CD ____ K 172CD
Konkurrent / Dec '96 / SRD

Chrome Molly

SLAP HEAD
Out of our minds / Gimme that line again / Red hot red rock / Shotgun / Loosen up / Caught with the bottle again / Sitter the chil-

dren / Assinine nation / Pray with me / Now / Little voodoo magic
CD CDMFN 98
Music For Nations / May '90 / Pinnacle

Chron Gen

BEST OF CHRON GEN
CD AHOY 18
Captain Oi / Nov '94 / Plastic Head

LIVE AT THE WARDORF IN SAN FRANCISCO
CD PUNXCD 3
Punx / Oct '95 / Total/BMG

Chubb Rock

MIND, THE
CD 08516672
Black Jam / Aug '97 / Essential/BMG

Chubbies

TRES FLORES
CD SFTRI 472CD
Sympathy For The Record Industry / May '97 / Cargo / Greyhound / Plastic Head

Chuchuk, Raymond

LET'S DANCE
CD SAV 190CD
Savoy / Jun '93 / Savoy / THE / TKO Magnum

Chuck D

AUTOBIOGRAPHY OF MISTACHUCK
MistaChuck / Free Big Willie / No / Generation wrekked / Niggativity...do I dare disturb the universe / Talk show created the fool / But can you kill the nigger in you / Underdog / Paid / Endonesia / Pride / Horizontal heron
CD 5329442
Mercury / Oct '96 / PolyGram

Chug

SASSAFRAS
CD FNCD 300
Flying Nun / Nov '94 / RTM/Disc

Chul, Kim Suk

SHAMANISTIC CEREMONIES OF THE EASTERN SEABOARD (Chul, Kim Suk Ensemble)
CD VICG 52612
JVC World Library / Mar '96 / ADA / CM / Direct

Chum

DEAD TO THE WORLD
CD CM 77113CD
Century Media / Jun '96 / Plastic Head

Chumbawamba

ANARCHY
Give the anarchist a cigarette / Timebomb / Homophobia / On being pushed / Heaven/Hell / Love me / Georgina / Doh / Blackpool rock / This years thing / Mouthful of shit / Never do what you are told / Bad dog / Enough is enough / Rage
CD TPLP 46CD
One Little Indian / Apr '94 / Pinnacle

ENGLISH REBEL SONGS 1381-1914
Cutty wren / Digger's song / Collier's march / Triumph of General Ludd / Chartist anthem / Song on the times / Smashing of the van / World turned upside down / Poverty knock / Idris strike song / Hanging on the old barbed wire
CD TPLP 64CD
One Little Indian / Feb '95 / Pinnacle

LOVE/HATE
CD TPLP 66CD
One Little Indian / Oct '95 / Pinnacle

PICTURES OF STARVING CHILDREN/ NEVER MIND THE BALLOTS
How to get your band on the television / British colonialism and the BBC / Commercial break / Unilever / More whitewashing / Interlude: Beginning to take it back / Dutiful servants and political masters / Cocacolonisation / In a nutshell invasion / Always tell the voter what the voter wants to hear / Come on baby (let's do the revolution) / Wasteland / Today's sermon / Ah-men / Mr. Heseltine meets his public / Candidates find common ground
CD TPLP 63CD
One Little Indian / Feb '95 / Pinnacle

SHHH
CD 185152
Southern / Oct '94 / SRD

SHOWBUSINESS
Never do what you are told / Rappoport / Give the anarchist a cigarette / Heaven/Hell / Hungary / Homophobia / Morality / Bad dog / Stitch that / Mouthful of shit / Nazi / Jimbomb / Slad aid
CD TPLP 56CD
One Little Indian / Oct '95 / Pinnacle

SLAP
Ulrike / Tiananmen square / Cartrouble / Chase PC'd flee attack by own dog / Ruben's has been shot / Rappoport's testament: I never gave up / Slap / That's how grateful we are / Meinhof
CD TPLP 65CD
One Little Indian / Feb '95 / Pinnacle

TUBTHUMPER
Tubthumping / Amnesia / Drip drip drip / Big issue / Good ship lifestyle / One by one / Outsider / Creepy crawling / Mary MaryGood ship lifestyle / Small town / I want more / Scapegoat
CD CDEMC 3773
EMI / Aug '97 / EMI

Church

ALMOST YESTERDAY 1981-1990
CD RVCD 43
Raven / Dec '94 / ADA / Direct

MAGICIAN AMONG THE SPIRITS
CD D 31562
Roadrunner / Feb '97 / Cargo

SOMETIME ANYWHERE
Day of the dead / Lost my touch / Loveblind / My little problem / Maven / Angelica / Lullaby / Eastern / Places at once / Business woman / Authority / Fly home / Dead man's dream
CD 07822187272
Arista / Jun '94 / BMG

Church Of God

IN HIM I LIVE (Church Of God & Saints Of Christ)
CD LYRCD 7423
Lyrichord / Dec '94 / ADA / CM / Roots

CIA

ATTITUDE
CD CDFLAG 68
Under One Flag / Jul '91 / Pinnacle

IN THE RED
Extinction / In the red / NASA / Flight 103 / Turn to stone / Natas / Buried alive / Mind over matter / Moby Dick (part 2) / Samantha
CD CDFLAG 40
Under One Flag / May '90 / Pinnacle

Ciani, Suzanne

NEVERLAND
Neverland / Tuscany / Mosaic / Aegean wave / Summer's day / Life in the moonlight / When love dies / Adagio / Mother's song / Lumiere
CD 259758
Private Music / Aug '89 / BMG

Cibo Matto

VIVA LA WOMAN
CD 9362459892
WEA / Mar '96 / Warner Music

Ciccu, Bianca

GUSCH, THE (Ciccu, Bianca & Randy Brecker)
CD ITM 1440 CD
ITM / Apr '90 / Koch / Tradelink

Cicek, Ali Ekbar

BEKTACHI MUSIC
CD D 8069
Unesco / Nov '96 / ADA / Harmonia Mundi

Cicion Tropical Orchestra La ...

CYCLONE TROPICAL (Cicion Tropical Orchestra La Colegiala)
CD UCD 19108
Forlane / Jul '95 / Target/BMG

Ciel, Red

JUMP TO THE MOON
CD RCL 1
RCL / Mar '96 / ADA

Ciletti, Miles

LONG DAYS & MONSTER NIGHTS
CD NAR 091CD
New Alliance / Sep '94 / Plastic Head

Cimarons

BEST OF CIMARONS
CD CC2 703
Crocodisc / Nov '92 / Grapevine/PolyGram

MAKA
CD CC 2704
Crocodisc / Jun '93 / Grapevine/PolyGram

PEOPLE SAY
CD LG 21006
Lagoon / Jun '93 / Grapevine/PolyGram

Cinderella

LONG COLD WINTER
Falling apart at the seams / Gypsy road / Last mile / Long cold winter / If you don't like it / Coming home / Fire and ice / Take me back / Bad seamstress blues / Don't know what you got (til it's gone) / Second wind
CD 8346122
Vertigo / Jul '88 / PolyGram

Cindytalk

CAMOUFLAGE HEART
CD TOUCH 3CD
Touch / Oct '96 / World Serpent

IN THIS WORLD
CD TOUCH 2CD
Touch / Oct '96 / World Serpent

WAPPINSCHAW
CD TOUCH 1CD
Touch / Oct '96 / World Serpent

Cinorama

GARDEN, THE GARDEN
CD D 63
PSF / Aug '95 / Harmonia Mundi

Ciotti, Roberto

ROAD 'N' RAIL
CD CDSGP 039
Prestige / Jan '93 / Else / Total/BMG

Circle

PARIS CONCERT (2CD Set)
Nefertitti / Song for the newborn / Duet / Lookout farm / Kalvin 73, variation - 3 / Toy room / There is no greater love
CD Set 8434632
ECM / Oct '90 / New Note/Pinnacle

Circle

HISSI
CD FDMETCD 1
Fourth Dimension / Mar '97 / Cargo

Circle Jerks

GROUP SEX
Deny everything / I just want some skank / Beverly Hills / Operation / Back against the wall / Wasted / Behind the door / World up my ass / Paid vacation / Don't care / Live fast die young / What's your problem / Group sex / Red tape
CD 01012
Frontier / Jun '97 / Plastic Head / Vital

GROUP SEX/WILD IN THE STREETS
CD FR 002CD
Frontier / Apr '97 / Plastic Head / Vital

WILD IN THE STREETS
Wild in the streets / Leave me alone / Stars and stripes / 86'd (good as gone) / Meet the press / Trapped / Murder the disturbed / Letter bomb / Question authority / Defamation innuendo / Moral majority / Forced labor / Political Stu / Just like me / Put a little love in your heart
CD 01052
Frontier / Jun '97 / Plastic Head / Vital

Circle Of Dust

CIRCLE OF DUST
CD REX 460112
Rex / Nov '95 / Cadillac

Circle X

CELESTIAL
Kyoko / Pulley / Crow's ghost / Gothic fragment / Some things don't grow back / Tell my horse / Big picture / Cabin 9 / Waxed fruit / Celestial / They come prancing
CD OLE 0912
Matador / Jul '94 / Vital

CIRCLE X EP
CD DEX 3
Dexter's Cigar / Dec '96 / Cargo

Circus

BRISTOL STREET
Godwhat / My daughter / In limbo / Bristol Street / Cold Alice / Weekdays / Weekdays / Things you left / Island / What can I say / Wave in the night / Bristol Street (instrumental) / Things you left
CD PCOM 1143
President / Oct '95 / Grapevine/PolyGram / President / Target/BMG

Circus Lupus

SOLID BRASS
CD DIS 79D
Dischord / Jul '93 / SRD

Cissoko, Sunjul

SONGS OF THE GRIOTS VOL.2
CD VICG 52272
JVC World Library / Mar '96 / ADA / CM / Direct

CITA

HEAT OF EMOTION
CD 19968
MTM / Oct '96 / Cargo

Citania

CITANIA
CD H 002CD
Sonifolk / Jun '94 / ADA / CM

O ASUBIO DO PADRINO
CD J 101CD
Sonifolk / Jun '94 / ADA / CM

Citizen Cain

SOMEWHERE BUT YESTERDAY
Jonny had another face (parallel lines) / Junk and donuts (an afterthought) / To dance the enamel faced queen (beyond the boundaries) / Somewhere but yesterday / Owls / Obsessions / Ballad of Creepy John / Echoes, the labyrinth penumbra / All the sin's men / Farewell (a word in your ear) / Strange barbarians (the mother's shroud)
CD CYCL 049
Cyclops / Feb '97 / Pinnacle

Citizen Fish

FREE SOULS IN A TRAPPED
CD FISH 24CD
Bluurg / Apr '94 / Shellshock/Disc

LIVE FISH
CD FISH 29CD
Bluurg / Nov '93 / Shellshock/Disc

MILLENNIA MADNESS
CD FISH 34CD
Bluurg / Sep '95 / Shellshock/Disc

Citizen Z

FLUXUS AND THE FIST EP (Citizen Z Vs The Continuum)
CD BLAZE 92CD
Fire / Oct '95 / Pinnacle / RTM/Disc

Citizen's Arrest

CITIZEN ARREST
CD LF 086CD
Lost & Found / Jun '94 / Plastic Head

Citizens' Utilities

LOST AND FOUNDERED
CD CDSTUMM 135
Mute / Nov '96 / RTM/Disc

Citroen, Soesja

SONGS FOR LOVERS AND LOSERS
CD CHR 70034
Challenge / Sep '96 / ADA / Direct / Jazz Music / Wellard

City Waites

GHOSTS, WITCHES AND DEMONS (From The Castle To The Graveyard)
Soulcake / Devil's dream / Two daughters of this aged stream / Mermaid / Dead man's moan / Where the bee sucks / Satyr's dance / Widdecombe Fair / Shaking of the sheets / Lunatick lover / But e're we this perform / Gelding of the devil / Miss Bailey's ghost / Full fathom five / Tale of Sir Eglamore and how he slew the wondrous dragon / Witches dance / Finnigan's wake / Song for the sprite Ariel and Ferdinanad / Fairie galliard / Unquiet grave / Wonder of wonders / Witches dance
CD SAMPPCD 401
Soundalive / Aug '96 / Complete/Pinnacle

LADS & LASSES (The Music Of The English Countryside) (City Waites & The Noise Minstrels)
Chirping of the lark / Parson's farewell / You lasses and lads / Branles / Newcastle / Country lass / Rufty tufty / Spanish gypsy / Millfield / Argeers / Nonsuch / Great booby / Maiden Lane / Couple of pigeons / Parson in boots / One misty moisty morning / Ward's brae / Merry merry milkmaids / All in a garden green / Bobbing Joan / Sellinger's round / Wilson wilde / Hulichan's jig / Stanes morris / Blue cap / Nine pins / Jenny pluck pears / Half hanekin / Paul's wharf / Grimstock / Heart's ease
CD SAMPPCD 403
Soundalive / Aug '96 / Complete/Pinnacle

LOW AND LUSTY SONGS (Songs From 17th Century England)
Brooms for old shoes / Trader's medley / Lavender's green / We be soldiers three / Hey, jolly broom man / Give me my yellow hose again / Oak and the ash / Tobacco is an Indian weed / Lumps of pudding / Farmer's cursed wife / Over the hills and far away / Tomorrow the fox will come to town / My dog and I / Baffled knight / Three ravens / Crossed couple / Back and sides go bare / Broom of the cowdenknowes / Song of the cutpurse
CD SAMHSCD 202
Soundalive / Aug '96 / Complete/Pinnacle

MADRIGAL FOR ALL SEASONS, A (Songs Of Tudor England)
To shorten Winter's sadness / Silver swan / Fair Phyllis I saw sitting all alone / Dear love be not unkind / Since my tears and lamenting / On the plains, fairy trains / Bianco fiori / Fine knacks for ladies / April is in my Mistress face / Let us not that young man be / Have you seen the bright

lily grow / Little pretty bonny lass / La caccia / Sing we and chant it / Most sacred Queen Elizabeth, her galliard / In going to my naked bed / Aminitas with his Phyllis fair / Say gentle nymphs / Tell me dearest, what is love / Adieu, sweet Amaryllis / Weep you no more sad fountains / Galliard / Say love if ever / Ah, the sighs / Now, oh now / There is a lady sweet and kind / If love be blind
CD SAMHSCD 201
Soundalive / Aug '96 / Complete/Pinnacle

MUSIC FROM THE TIME OF CHARLES II
Ayre/Sarabande/Courante/Allemand / Oh my Clarissa / This mossy bank they prest / Broken consort in C major / La chitarra royale / In the merry month of May / King's jig / Among thy fancies / Overture/Gavote / Here's a health unto His Majesty / Armoni concerti / Gather your rosebuds / Mateis suite / Long look't for now may come at last / Overture from Le Bourgeois Gentilhomme / Wanton trick / Matachia/Espanleta/Pavana/Forneo/Canarios / Shepherd well met / Ah Heav'n / What is't I hear / Fine young folly / 29th May / Dialogue between a lover and his friend
CD SAMFNCD 302
Soundalive / Aug '96 / Complete/Pinnacle

MUSIC FROM THE TIME OF HENRY VIII (City Waites & His Majesty's Sagbutts & Cornets)
CD SAMFNCD 301
Soundalive / Aug '96 / Complete/Pinnacle

MUSIC OF THE MIDDLE AGES
Oh admirabile / Miri it is / Brid on a brier / English dance / Edi bi thu / Isle of Rea / Fast stantipes / La rotta / Lamento di Tristan / Dance royale / Angelus and Virginem / Sancta mari gratia / Trotto / Mirth of all this lond / Fors seulement / Tapster, drinker
CD SAMMTCD 102
Soundalive / Jun '96 / Complete/Pinnacle

MUSIC OF THE STUART AGE
Trumpet tune / Chirping of the lark / Air / Parson's farewell / Newcastle / Sefauchi's farewell / Tomorrow the fox will come to town / First act tune / Cuckolds all in a row / Fairest isle / Mortlack's ground / Grimstock / Harvest home / Fantasy suite / Heartsease / Jenny pluck pears / How blest are the shepherds / Song tune / Maiden Lane / Lavena / Aire / Martin said to his man
CD SAMMTCD 105
Soundalive / Aug '96 / Complete/Pinnacle

MUSIC OF THE TUDOR AGE, THE
Pastime with good company / Galliard / Bransall / Runden / Taundernaken / Pavan / Now is the month of Maying / Galliard / Sing we and chant it / Tourdion / Tree ravens / Thomas Ravenscroft / Honeysuckle / Regina galliard / Oh Mistress mine / Woodycock / Dolent depart / Nightwatch / Galliard Lombardo / Mohrentanz / Heigh ho holiday / Tourdion / Mille regrets / Greensleeves / Daphne / Ballo Lomabardo / Earl of Salisbury's pavan / Now oh now
CD SAMMTCD 104
Soundalive / Aug '96 / Complete/Pinnacle

MUSICIANS OF GROPE LANE, THE (Music Of Brothels & Bawdy Houses Of Purcell's England)
Diddle diddle or The kind country lovers: *Terry, Clark* / Fair maid of Islington / Green stockings / Jovial lass or Dol & Roger / Mundanga Was / Lady of pleasure / Old wife / Beehive / Blue petticoats or green garters / Gelding of the Devil / Maid's complaint for want of a Dil Doul / Oyster Nan / Frolic / Husband who met his match / Jovial broom man / Disappointment / Lusty young Smith / Greensleeves & yellow lace / Jolly brown turd / Two rounds / Tom making a Manteau / When Celia was learning / Lady lie near me / Oh how you protest / Ditty delightful of Mother Watkin's ale / Miss Nelly
CD 070969
Musica Oscura / Dec '96 / Complete/Pinnacle

PILLS TO PURGE MELANCHOLY (City Waites & Richard Wistreich)
Blowzabella, my bouncing dixie / As oyster nan stood by her tub / There was a lass of Islington / Would ye have a young virgin / With my strings of small wire / Like a ring without a finger / When for air I take my mare / Young Colin cleaving of a beam / Do not rumple my top knot / Come jug my honey let's to bed
CD CDSDL 382
Saydisc / Mar '94 / ADA / Direct / Harmonia Mundi

City West Quartet

CHATTERBOX
CD BRAM 1992302
Brambus / Nov '93 / ADA

CIV

SET YOUR GOALS
So far so good so what / United kids / Don't got to prove it / Trust slips through your hands / Set your goals / Do something / State of grace / Gang opinion / Solid bond / Marching goals / Soundtrack for violence / Boring summer / All twisted / Choices made / Can't wait one mimute more / Et tu Brute
CD 7567926032
Atlantic / Nov '95 / Warner Music

Civil Defiance

FISHERS FOR SOULS, THE
CD CD 2
Dream Circle / Nov '96 / Cargo / Plastic Head

Ciyo

SOMEWHERE OUT THERE
Off the cuff / Somewhere out there / Little sunflower / Sun city / Sincerely yours / Si-militude / It don't matter / Thoughts and feelings
CD DESCD 02
Diesel / Aug '96 / Jet Star

Clair Obscur

ANTIGONE
CD AFACD 1567
Apocalyptic Vision / Jul '96 / Cargo / Plastic Head / SRD

COLLECTION OF ISOLATED TRACKS 1982-1988, A
CD EFA 015602
Apocalyptic Vision / Oct '95 / Cargo / Plastic Head / SRD

IN OUT
CD AV 001CD
Apocalyptic Vision / Oct '93 / Cargo / Plastic Head / SRD

PLAY
CD EFAO 15542
Apocalyptic Vision / Apr '95 / Cargo / Plastic Head / SRD

ROCK
CD EFA 015502
Apocalyptic Vision / Oct '95 / Cargo / Plastic Head / SRD

SANS TITRE
CD AV 022
Apocalyptic Vision / Jun '97 / Cargo / Plastic Head / SRD

Clan Sutherland Pipe Band

CLAN SUTHERLAND PIPE BAND
CD EUCD 1311
ARC / Jul '95 / ADA / ARC Music

Clan/Destine

CLAN/DESTINE
CD CR 7037CD
Canyon / Nov '96 / ADA

Clancy, Aoife

IT'S ABOUT TIME
CD BM 559CD
Beaumex / Jul '95 / ADA

Clancy Brothers

28 SONGS OF IRELAND (Clancy Brothers & Tommy Makem)
O'Donnell aboo / Croppy box / Rising of the moon / Foggy dew / Ministrel boy / Wind that shakes the barley / Tipperary far away / Kelly, the boy from Killane / Kevin Barry / Whack for the diddle / Men of the West / Eamonn an chnuic (Ned of the hills) / Nell Flaherty's Drake / Boulavogue / Whisky you're the devil / Maid of the sweet brown knowe / Moonshiner / Bold thady quill / Rosin the beau / Finnegan's wake / Real old mountain dew / Courtin' in the kitchen / Mick McGuire / Jug of punch / Johnny McEldoo / Cruiscin lan / Partlairge / Parting glass
CD IHCD 10
Irish Heritage / Jul '89 / Prism

CLANCY BROTHERS & TOMMY MAKEM, THE (Clancy Brothers & Tommy Makem)
CD TCD 1022
Tradition / Aug '96 / ADA / Vital

CLANCY BROTHERS IN CONCERT (Clancy Brothers & Tommy Makem)
Isn't it grand boys / Mountain dew / Whistling gypsy rover / Finnegan's wake / Carrickfergus / Haul away Joe / Wild rover / Red haired Mary / Jug of punch / Leaving of Liverpool / Wild colonial boy / Holy ground / Wild mountain thyme
CD PLATCD 335
Platinum / Jul '92 / Prism

IRISH DRINKING SONGS (Clancy Brothers & Tommy Makem/Dubliners)
Whiskey in the jar: *Dubliners* / Beer, beer, beer: *Clancy Brothers* / Water is alright in tay: *Clancy Brothers* / Mountain dew: *Clancy Brothers & Tommy Makem* / Jug of this: *Clancy Brothers & Tommy Makem* / Pub with no name: *Dubliners* / Drink it up men: *Dubliners* / Maloney wants a drink: *Dubliners* / All for me grog: *Clancy Brothers & Tommy Makem* / Galway Bay: *Clancy Brothers & Tommy Makem* / Jug of punch: *Clancy Brothers & Tommy Makem* / Tim Finnegan's wake: *Clancy Brothers & Tommy Makem* / Moonshiner: *Clancy Brothers & Tommy Makem* / Juice of the barley: *Clancy Brothers & Tommy Makem* / Whiskey, you're the divil: *Clancy Brothers & Tommy Makem* / Parting glass: *Clancy Brothers & Tommy Makem*
CD CK 52833
Columbia / Mar '97 / Sony

MEN OF THE WEST, THE
Will ye go lassie go / As I roved out / Cruise of the calabar / Irish girl / B is for blarney / Green gravel / Maid of ballydoo / See saw and others / All around the lonely o / When I was single / I'll tell my Ma / Doffin mistress / I know my love / Dark eyed gypsy / Barnyards of Dalgety / Bard of Armagh / Bold tenant farmer / Johnny I Hardly knew you / Real old mountain dew / O'Donnell aboo / Finnegan's wake / Portlairge / Boulavogue / Courting in the kitchen / Tipperary so far away / Men of the West
CD SUMCD 4073
Summit / Nov '96 / Sound & Media

OLDER BUT NO WISER (Clancy Brothers & Robbie O'Connell)
Ramblin' gamblin' Willie / When the ship comes in / Lily Marlene / Roll on the day / Let no man steal your thyme / Salonika / Flower of Scotland / Curragh of Kildare / Boys of Wexford / Final trawl / Lads of the fair / Those were the days
CD VCD 79488
Vanguard / Mar '96 / ADA / Pinnacle

REUNION (Clancy Brothers & Tommy Makem)
Isn't it grand / Mountain dew / Whistling gypsy rover / Finnegan's wake / Carrickfergus / Haul away Joe / Wild rover / Red haired Mary / Jug of punch / Leaving of Liverpool / Wild colonial boy / Holy ground / Wild mountain thyme
CD CD 5009
Ogham / Apr '88 / CM / Duncans / Roots

TUNES & TALES OF IRELAND LIVE
CD FE 2061
Folk Era / Dec '94 / ADA / CM

TUNES 'N' TALES
CD FE 20612
Frantic / Dec '96 / Cargo

WRAP THE GREEN FLAG (Clancy Brothers & Tommy Makem)
Paddy West / Heave away my Johnny / Bold tenant farmer / Fare thee well Enniskillen / Bold Fentan men / Jennifer Gentle / New South Wales / Wrap the green flag 'round me boys / Johnson's motor car / Valley of Knockanure / Nation once again / Rising of the moon / Leaving of Liverpool / Galway races / Johnny I hardly knew ye / Irish rover
CD CK 48866
Columbia / Mar '97 / Sony

Clancy Children

SO EARLY IN THE MORNING
CD TCD 1053
Tradition / Jul '97 / ADA / Vital

Clancy, Willie

MINSTREL FROM CLARE, THE
Langstern pony uilleann pipes / Templehouse / Over the moor to Maggie whistle / Bruachna carraige baine pipes / Erin's lovely lea / Killavil fancy / Dogs among the bushes / Family ointment vocal / Dear Irish boy / Caoineadh an spailpin whistle / Pipe on the hob / Gander vocal / Legacy jig whistle / Flogging reel pipes / Song of the riddles vocal / Spailpin a ruin pipes
CD GL 3091CD
Green Linnet / Sep '94 / ADA / CM / Direct / Highlander / Roots

PIPERING OF WILLIE CLANCY VOL.1, THE
West wind/Sean Reid's fancy / Rocks of Bawn / Old bush / Will you come down to Limerick / Bold trainer O / Rolling wave / An Ghaoth Aniar-Aneas / Garrett Barry's Mazurka / Jenny picking cockles/My love is in America / Bright lady / Lady's pantaletts/ Ravelled Hank of Yarn / Purty Molly Brannigan/Green fields of America / Kitty got a clinking coming from the fair / Bonny bunch of roses / Down the back lane / Paidin O Raifeartaigh / Clancy's jig / Jenny tie the bonnet/Corney is coming
CD CC 32CD
Claddagh / Jul '93 / ADA / CM / Direct

PIPERING OF WILLIE CLANCY VOL.2, THE
Sean O Duibhir a Ghleanna / Caislean dhun guaire / McKenna's / Casadh an tSugain / Harvest home / I buried my wife and danced on her grave / Chaillgh, do mhairis me / Fowler on the moor / Bimis as ol s ag pogadh na mban / Milliner's daughter / Trip o'er the mountain / Connaught heifers / Steampacket / Gold ring / Kitty goes milking / Banish misfortune / An buachaill caol dubh / As phis fhliuch / Rakish paddy / Fraher's jig / Garrett Barry's / Dark is the colour of my true love's hair / Chief O'Neill's favourite / Jenny's welcome to Charlie
CD CC 39CD
Claddagh / Jul '93 / ADA / CM / Direct

Clannad

AN AM
Ri na cruinne / An am (soul) / In fortune's hand / Poison glen / Wilderness / Why worry / Uirchill an chreagain / Love and affection / You're the one / Dobhar
CD 74321330682
RCA / Feb '96 / BMG

ATLANTIC REALM
Atlantic realm / Predator / Moving thru / Berbers / Signs of life / In flight / Ocean of light / Drifting / Under Neptune's cape / Voyager / Primeval sun / Child of the sea / Kirk pride
CD 74321318672
RCA / Jun '96 / BMG

BACK2BACK
CD Set 74321206932
RCA / Sep '95 / BMG

BANBA
Na leatha bhi / Banba oir / There for you / Mystery game / Struggle / I will find you / Soul searcher / Ca de sin don te sin / Other side / Sunset dreams / Gentle place
CD 74321139612
RCA / Aug '96 / BMG

CLANNAD
Theme from Harry's Game / Closer to your heart / Lady Marian / Newgrange / Mhorag's no Horo Gheallaidh / Nil Sen La / Caislean Oir / In a life time / Now is here / Na Buachailli Alainn / Down by the Sally Gardens / Dulaman / Robin (the hooded man)
CD KCD 400
Celtic Collections / Jan '97 / Target/BMG

CLANNAD IN CONCERT
CD SHANCD 79030
Shanachie / Oct '88 / ADA / Greensleeves / Koch

CLANNAD IN CONCERT
CD TFCB 5001
Third Floor / Oct '94 / ADA / Direct / Total/ BMG

CLANNAD VOL.2
An gabhar ban / Eleanor Plunkett / Coinleach glas an fhomhair / Rince Philib a Cheoil / By chance it was / Rince Briotanach / Dheanainn sugradh / Gaoth barra na d'tonn / Teidhm abhaile riu / Fairly shot of her / Chuaigh me 'na rosann
CD CEFCD 041
Gael Linn / Jan '94 / ADA / CM / Direct / Grapevine/PolyGram / Roots

CRANN ULL
Ar a ghabhail 'n a 'chuain damh / Last rose of Summer / Cruscin lan / Bacach Shile Andai / La coimhthioch fan dtuath / Crann ull / Gathering mushrooms / Bunan bui / Planxty Browne
CD TARACD 3007
Tara / Nov '90 / ADA / CM / Conifer/BMG / Direct

DULAMAN
CD CEFCD 058
Gael Linn / Jan '94 / ADA / CM / Direct / Grapevine/PolyGram / Roots

FUAIM
Na Buachailli Alainn / Mheall Si Lena Glorthai Me / Bruachna carraige baine pipes / La Brea Fan Dtuath / An tull / Strayed away / Ni La Na Gaoithe La Na Scoib / Lish young buy a broom / Mhorag's Na Horo Ghealaidh / Green fields of Gaothdobhair / Buaireadh / An Phosta
CD COOKCD 035
Cooking Vinyl / Apr '90 / Vital

LEGEND
Robin (the hooded man) / Now is here / Herne / Together we / Darkmere / Strange land / Scarlet inside / Lady Marian / Battles / Ancient forest
CD ND 71703
RCA / Aug '88 / BMG

LORE
Croi croga / Seanchas / Bridge (that carries us over) / From your heart / Alasdair Maccolla / Broken pieces / Trathnona beag areir / Trail of tears / Dealramh go Deo / Farewell love / Fonn mharta
CD 74321300802
RCA / Mar '96 / BMG

LORE/THEMES AND DREAMS (2CD Set)
Croi croga / Seanchas / Bridge (that carries us over) / From your heart / Alasdair Maccolla / Broken pieces / Trathnona beag areir / Trail of tears / Dealramh go Deo / Farewell love / Fonn mharta / Theme from Harry's Game / Robin (the hooded man) / In a lifetime / I will find you / Something to believe in / New Grange
CD Set 74321357952
RCA / Mar '96 / BMG

MACALLA
Caislean oir / Wild cry / Closer to your heart / Almost seems (too late to turn) / In a lifetime / Buachaill an Eirne / Blackstairs / Journey's end / Northern skyline
CD 74321160352
RCA / Sep '93 / BMG

MAGICAL RING
Harry's Game / Tower hill / Searchran charn tsail / I see red / Passing time / Coinleach

glas an fhomair / Ta 'me mo shui / New grange / Fairy queen / Thios fa'n chosta
CD ________________ ND 71473
RCA / Aug '95 / BMG

PAST PRESENT
Harry's Game / Closer to your heart / Almost seems (too late to turn) / Hunter / Lady Marian / Sirius / Coinleach glas an fhomair / Second nature / World of difference / In a lifetime / Robin (the hooded man) / Something to believe in / Newgrange / Buachaill an eirne / White fool / Stepping stone
CD ________________ 74321289812
RCA / May '97 / BMG

SIRIUS
In search of a heart / Second nature / Turning tide / Skellig / Stepping stone / White fool / Something to believe in / Live and learn / Many roads / Sirius
CD ________________ ND 75149
RCA / Jan '92 / BMG

ULTIMATE COLLECTION, THE
Dulaman / Two sisters / Siuil a run (Irish love song) / Nil sen la / Down by the Sally Gardens / An tull: *Clannad & Enya* / Na buachaili alainn: *Clannad & Enya* / Green fields of Gaothdobhar: *Clannad & Enya* / Mhorag's na horo ghealladh: *Clannad & Enya* / Theme from Harry's Game / New Grange / Robin (the hooded man) / In a lifetime: *Clannad & Bono* / Closer to your heart / Something to believe in: *Clannad & Bruce Hornsby* / Hunter / I will find you / Mystery game / Seanchas / Bridge (that carries us over)
CD ________________ 74321486742
RCA / May '97 / BMG

Clapton, Eric

24 NIGHTS (Eric Clapton Live)
Badge / Running on faith / White room / Sunshine of your love / Watch yourself / Have you ever loved a woman / Worried life blues / Hoodoo man / Pretending / Bad love / Old love / Wonderful tonight / Bell bottom blues / Hard times / Edge of darkness
CD ________________ 7599264202
Warner Bros. / Nov '90 / Warner Music

461 OCEAN BOULEVARD
Get ready / Give me strength / I can't hold out much longer / I shot the sheriff / Let it grow / Mainline Florida / Motherless children / Please be with me / Steady rollin' man / Willie and the hand jive
CD ________________ 8116972
RSO / Jul '83 / PolyGram

ANOTHER TICKET
Something special / Black rose / Another ticket / I can't stand it / Hold me Lord / Floating bridge / Catch me if you can / Rita Mae / Blow wind blow
CD ________________ 5318302
Polydor / Sep '96 / PolyGram

AUGUST
It's in the way that you use it / Run / Tearing us apart: *Clapton, Eric & Tina Turner* / Bad influence / Hung up on your love / I take a chance / Hold on / Miss you / Holy Mother / Behind the mask
CD ________________ 9254762
Duck/Warner Bros. / Feb '95 / Warner Music

BACKLESS
Early in the morning / Golden ring / If I don't be there by morning / I'll make love to you anytime / Promises / Roll it / Tell me that you love me / Tulsa time / Walk out in the rain / Watch out for Lucy
CD ________________ 5318262
Polydor / Sep '96 / PolyGram

BACKTRACKIN' (22 Tracks Spanning The Career Of A Rock Legend)
Cocaine / Strange brew / Spoonful / Let it rain / Have you ever loved a woman / Presence of the Lord / Crossroads / Roll it over / Can't find my way home / Blues power / Further on up the road / I shot the Sheriff / Knockin' on Heaven's door / Lay down Sally / Promises / Swing low, sweet chariot / Wonderful tonight / Sunshine of your love / Tales of brave Ulysses / Badge / Little wing / Layla
CD ________________ 8219372
Polydor / Feb '85 / PolyGram

BEHIND THE SUN
She's waiting / See what love can do / Same old blues / Knock on wood / Something's happening / Forever man / It all depends / Tangles in love / Never make you cry / Just like a prisoner / Behind the sun
CD ________________ 9251662
Duck/Warner Bros. / Apr '85 / Warner Music

CREAM OF ERIC CLAPTON, THE
Layla / Badge / I feel free / Sunshine of your love / Strange brew / White room / Cocaine / I shot the sheriff / Behind the mask / Forever man / Lay down Sally / Knockin' on Heaven's door / Wonderful tonight / Let it grow / Promises / I've got a rock 'n' roll heart / Heart / Crossroads
CD ________________ 5218812
Polydor / Jan '95 / PolyGram

CROSSROADS (4CD Set)
Boom boom: *Yardbirds* / Honey in your hips: *Yardbirds* / Baby what's wrong: *Yardbirds* / I wish you would: *Yardbirds* / Certain girl: *Yardbirds* / Good morning little schoolgirl: *Yardbirds* / Ain't got you: *Yardbirds* / For your love: *Yardbirds* / Got to hurry: *Yardbirds* / Lonely years: *Mayall, John & The Bluesbreakers* / Bernard Jenkins: *Mayall, John & The Bluesbreakers* / Hideaway: *Mayall, John & The Bluesbreakers* / All your love: *Mayall, John & The Bluesbreakers* / Ramblin' on my mind: *Mayall, John & The Bluesbreakers* / Have you ever loved a woman: *Mayall, John & The Bluesbreakers* / Wrapping paper: *Cream* / I feel free: *Cream* / Spoonful: *Cream* / Lawdy Mama: *Cream* / Strange brew: *Cream* / Sunshine of your love: *Cream* / Tales of brave Ulysses: *Cream* / Steppin' out: *Cream* / Anyone for tennis: *Cream* / White room: *Cream* / Crossroads: *Cream* / Badge: *Cream* / Presence of the Lord: *Blind Faith* / Can't find my way home: *Blind Faith* / Sleeping in the ground: *Blind Faith* / Comin' home: *Delaney & Bonnie* / Tell the truth: *Derek & The Dominoes* / Roll it over: *Derek & The Dominoes* / Layla: *Derek & The Dominoes* / Mean old world: *Derek & The Dominoes* / Key to the highway: *Derek & The Dominoes* / Crossroads: *Derek & The Dominoes* / Got to get better in a little while: *Derek & The Dominoes* / Evil: *Derek & The Dominoes* / One more chance: *Derek & The Dominoes* / Mean old Frisco blues: *Derek & The Dominoes* / Snake Lake blues: *Derek & The Dominoes* / Blues power / After midnight / Let it rain / Let it grow / Ain't that lovin' you / Motherless children / I shot the sheriff / Better make it through today / Sky is crying / I found a love / (When things go wrong) things hurt me too / Whatcha gonna do / Knockin' on Heaven's door / Someone like you / Hello my old friend / Sign language / Further on up the road / Lay down Sally / Wonderful tonight / Cocaine / Promises / If I don't be there by morning / Double trouble / I can't stand it / Shape you're in / Heaven is one step away / She's waiting / Too bad / Miss you / Wanna make love to you / After midnight
CD Set ________________ 8352612
Polydor / Nov '96 / PolyGram

CROSSROADS VOL.2 (Live In The Seventies)
CD Set ________________ 5293052
Polydor / Mar '96 / PolyGram

EC WAS HERE
Have you ever loved a woman / Presence of the Lord / Driftin' blues / Can't find my way home / Ramblin' on my mind / Further on up the road
CD ________________ 5318232
Polydor / Sep '96 / PolyGram

ERIC CLAPTON
Slunky / Bad boy / Lonesome and a long way from home / After midnight / Easy now / Blues power / Bottle of red wine / Lovin' you loving me / I've told you for the last time / I don't know why / Let it rain
CD ________________ 5318192
Polydor / Sep '96 / PolyGram

ERIC CLAPTON & THE YARDBIRDS
CD ________________ CD 12337
BR Music / Apr '94 / Target/BMG

ERIC CLAPTON & THE YARDBIRDS (Clapton, Eric & The Yardbirds)
CD ________________ IMT 100100
Scratch / Sep '96 / Koch / Scratch/BMG

ERIC CLAPTON AND FRIENDS
CD ________________ GFS 062
Going For A Song / Jul '97 / Else / TKO Magnum

ERIC CLAPTON VOL.1
I'm your Witch Doctor / For your love / Boom boom / Good morning little schoolgirl / Miles road / I ain't got you / Certain girl / Tribute to Elmore / Train kept a rollin' / Talking about you / I wish you would / Got to hurry / Freight loader / Let it rock / She's so respectable / You can't judge a book by looking at the cover / Louise / Smokestack lightning
CD ________________ EXP 007
Experience / May '97 / TKO Magnum

ERIC CLAPTON VOL.2
CD ________________ EXP 008
Experience / May '97 / TKO Magnum

FROM THE CRADLE
Blues before sunrise / Third degree / Reconsider baby / Hoochie coochie man / Five long years / I'm tore down / How long blues / Goin' away baby / Blues leave me alone / Sinner's prayer / Motherless child / It hurts me too / Someday after a while / Standing around crying / Driftin' / Groaning the blues
CD ________________ 9362457352
Warner Bros. / Sep '94 / Warner Music

IN WORDS AND MUSIC (2CD Set)
CD Set ________________ OTR 1100028
Metro Independent / Jun '97 / Essential/BMG

INTERVIEW DISC
CD ________________ SAM 7018
Sound & Media / Nov '96 / Sound & Media

JOURNEYMAN
Pretending / Anything for your love / Bad love / Running on faith / Hard times / Hound dog / No alibis / Run so far / Old love / Breaking point / Lead me on / Before you accuse me
CD ________________ 92620742
Warner Bros. / Oct '89 / Warner Music

JUST ONE NIGHT
Tulsa time / Early in the morning / Lay down Sally / Wonderful tonight / If I don't be there by morning / All our past times / Worried life blues / Blues power / Knockin' on Heaven's door / Double trouble / Setting me up / After midnight / Ramblin' on my mind / Cocaine / Further on up the road
CD ________________ 5318272
Polydor / Sep '96 / PolyGram

MONEY AND CIGARETTES
Everybody oughta make a change / Shape you're in / Ain't going down / I've got a rock 'n' roll heart / Man overboard / Pretty girl / Man in love / Crosscut saw / Slow down Linda / Crazy country hop
CD ________________ 9237732
Warner Bros. / Feb '95 / Warner Music

NO REASON TO CRY
Beautiful things / County jail / Carnival / Sign language / Country jail blues / All our past times / Hello old friend / Double trouble / Innocent times / Hungry / Black summer rain
CD ________________ 5318242
Polydor / Sep '96 / PolyGram

RAINBOW CONCERT
Badge / Roll it over / Presence of the Lord / Pearly queen / After midnight / Little wing
CD ________________ 5274722
Polydor / May '95 / PolyGram

RUSH (Original Soundtrack)
New recruit / Tracks and lines / Realization / Kristen and Jim / Preludin fugue / Cold turkey / Will gaines / Help me up / Don't know which way to go / Tears in heaven
CD ________________ 7599267942
WEA / Oct '94 / Warner Music

STAGES OF CLAPTON (Various Artists)
Stepping out: *Mayall, John & The Bluesbreakers* / Ramblin' on my mind: *Mayall, John & The Bluesbreakers* / Hideaway: *Mayall, John & The Bluesbreakers* / Have you heard: *Mayall, John & The Bluesbreakers* / Outside woman blues: *Cream* / Crossroads: *Cream* / They call it stormy Monday: *Mayall, John & The Bluesbreakers* / Well alright: *Blind Faith* / Bell bottom blues: *Derek & The Dominoes* / Blues power: *Derek & The Dominoes* / Driftin' blues: *Clapton, Eric* / Mean ol' Frisco: *Clapton, Eric*
CD ________________ 5500282
Spectrum / May '93 / PolyGram

STRICTLY THE BLUES
CD ________________ PLSCD 103
Pulse / Aug '96 / BMG

SURVIVOR
I wish you would / For your love / Certain girl / Got to hurry / Too much monkey business / I don't care no more / Bye bye bird / Twenty three hours too long / Baby don't worry / Take it easy baby
CD ________________ CDTB 013
Thunderbolt / Mar '95 / TKO Magnum

THERE'S ONE IN EVERY CROWD
We've been told (Jesus coming soon) / Swing low, sweet chariot / Little Rachel / Don't blame me / Sky is crying / Singin' the blues / Better make it through the day / Pretty blue eyes / High / Opposite
CD ________________ 5318222
Polydor / Sep '96 / PolyGram

TIME PIECES VOL.1 (The Best Of Eric Clapton)
I shot the sheriff / After midnight / Wonderful tonight / Layla / Willie and the hand jive / Knockin' on Heaven's door / Let it grow / Swing low, sweet chariot / Cocaine / Lay down Sally / Promises
CD ________________ 8000142
RSO / '83 / PolyGram

TIME PIECES VOL.2 (The Best Of Eric Clapton Live In The Seventies)
Tulsa time / Knockin' on Heaven's door / If I don't be there by morning / Ramblin' on my mind / Presence of the Lord / Can't find my way home / Smile / Blues power
CD ________________ 8118352
RSO / Jul '88 / PolyGram

UNPLUGGED
Signe / Before you accuse me / Hey hey / Tears in heaven / Lonely stranger / Nobody knows you (when you're down and out) / Layla / Running on faith / Walkin' blues / Alberta / San Francisco Bay blues / Malted milk / Old love
CD ________________ 9362450242
Warner Bros. / Aug '92 / Warner Music

Clare, Allen

ALLEN CLARE & LENNY BUSH (Clare, Allen & Lenny Bush)
CD ________________ CHECD 00108
Master Mix / Nov '93 / Jazz Music / New Note/Pinnacle / Wellard

Clarinet Summit

CLARINET SUMMIT
CD ________________ IN 1062CD
India Navigation / Jan '97 / Discovery / Impetus

Clarinette Quintet

BAZH DU
CD ________________ Y 225031CD
Silex / Dec '93 / ADA / Harmonia Mundi

Clarion

FROM THE OAK
CD ________________ BAK 002CD
Bakkus / Jul '95 / ADA

Clarissa

SILVER
For you / Out of flight / High horses / Sail away / Slow punch / Charms / Butterfly / This necklace / Bandits / Stange voices
CD ________________ MR 1102
Mammoth / May '96 / Vital

Clark, Anne

LAW IS AN ANAGRAM OF WEALTH, THE
CD ________________ SPV 08492702
SPV / Aug '95 / Koch / Plastic Head

NINETIES, THE (A Fine Collection)
Abuse / Counter act / Empty me / If I could / Windmills of your mind / Haunted road / Fragility / Seize the vivid sky / Elegy for a lost summer / Echoes remain forever / Dream made real / Letter of thanks to a friend / Our darkness / Sleeper in metropolis
CD ________________ SPV 08544632
SPV / Feb '97 / Koch / Plastic Head

PSYCHOMETRY
CD ________________ SPV 08489282
SPV / Aug '95 / Koch / Plastic Head

TO LOVE AND BE LOVED
CD ________________ SPV 08589542
SPV / Mar '96 / Koch / Plastic Head

Clark, Chris

SOUL SOUNDS
CD ________________ MAR 049
Marginal / Jun '97 / Greyhound

Clark, Dave Five

GLAD ALL OVER AGAIN
Glad all over / Do you love me / Bits and pieces / Can't you see that she's mine / Don't let me down / Anyway you want it / Catch us if you can / Having a wild weekend / Because / I like it like that / Over and over / Reelin' and rockin' / Come home / You got what it takes / Everybody knows / Try too hard / I'll be yours my love / Good old Rock 'N' Roll Medley / Here comes summer / Live in the sky / Red Balloon / Sha-na-na hey hey kiss him goodbye / More good old Rock 'N' Roll Medley / Put a little love in your heart / Everybody get together
CD ________________ CDEMTV 75
EMI / Apr '93 / EMI

Clark, David Anthony

AUSTRALIA BEYOND THE DREAMTIME
CD ________________ WCL 11013
White Cloud / May '95 / Select

TERRA INHABITATA
CD ________________ WCL 11007
White Cloud / May '94 / Select

Clark, Dee

HEY LITTLE GIRL
I just can't help myself / When I call on you / Just like a fool / Seven nights / Oh little girl / Wondering / Nobody but you / Just keep it up / Hey little girl / How about that / Blues get off my shoulder / At my front door / You're looking good / Your friends / Because I love you / Raindrops / (Don't) walk away from me / I'm going back to school / Shook up over you / I'm a soldier boy
CD ________________ CDRB 19
Charly / Apr '95 / Koch

Clark, Gary

TEN SHORT SONGS ABOUT LOVE
This is why, J / We sail on stormy waters / St. Jude / Short song about love / Make a family / Freefloating / Baby blue No.2 / Nancy / Any Sunday morning / Making people cry / Sail on / Jackson in your kitchen
CD ________________ CIRCD 23
Circa / Apr '93 / EMI

Clark, Gene

AMERICAN DREAMER 1964-1974
CD ________________ RVCD 21
Raven / Feb '93 / ADA / Direct

GENE CLARK & THE GOSDIN BROTHERS (Clark, Gene & The Gosdin Brothers)
Echoes / Think I'm gonna feel better / Tried so hard / Is yours is mine / Keep on pushing / I found you / So you say you lost your

baby / Elevator operator / Same one / Couldn't believe her / Needing someone
CD EDCD 529
Edsel / Jun '97 / Pinnacle

ROADMASTER
She's the kind of girl / One in a hundred / Here tonight / Full circle song / In a misty morning / Rough and rocky / Roadmaster / I really don't want to know / I remember the railroad / She don't care about time / Shooting star
CD ED CD 198
Edsel / Jun '90 / Pinnacle

SILHOUETTED IN LIGHT (Clark, Gene & Carla Olsen)
Your fire burning / Number one is to survive / Love wins again / Fair and tender ladies / Photograph / Set you free this time / Last thing on my mind / Gypsy rider / Train leaves here this morning / Almost Saturday night / Del Gato / I'll feel a whole lot better / She don't care about time / Speed of the sound of loneliness / Will the circle be unbroken
CD FIENDCD 710
Demon / Feb '92 / Pinnacle

SO REBELLIOUS A LOVER (Clark, Gene & Carla Olsen)
Drifter / Gypsy rider / Every angel in heaven / Del gato / Deportees / Fair and tender ladies / Almost Saturday night / I'm your toy / Why did you leave me / Don't it make you wanna go home / Are we still making love
CD FIENDCD 89
Demon / Aug '87 / Pinnacle

THIS BYRD HAS FLOWN
Tambourine man / Vanessa / Rainsong / C'est la bonne rue / If you could read my mind / Dixie flyer / Feel a whole lot better / Rodeo rider / All I want / Something about you / Made for love / Blue raven
CD EDCD 436
Edsel / Jul '95 / Pinnacle

Clark, Glen

LOOKING FOR A CONNECTION
CD DOSCD 7006
Dos / Sep '95 / ADA / CM / Direct

Clark, Graham

ISTHMUS (Clark, Graham & Jon Thorne/ Milo Fell)
Duende / Bang on / System x / Lonestar / Buffalo wings / Dagobert / Isthmus / Ragsville / Second thought / When in Rome... / Secret shortbread
CD AGASCD 012
GAS / Jul '97 / Pinnacle

Clark, Guy

BOATS TO BUILD
Baton Rouge / Picasso's mandolin / How'd you get this number / Boats to build / Too much / Ramblin' Jack and Mahan / I don't love you much do I / Jack of all trades / Madonna w/Child ca 1969 / Must be my baby
CD 7559614422
Nonesuch / Jul '93 / Warner Music

CRAFTSMAN
Fool on the roof / Fools for each other / Shade of all greens / Vila an american dream / One paper kid / In the jailhouse now / Comfort and crazy / Don't you take it too bad / Houston kid / Fool on the roof blues / Who do you think you are / Crystelle / New cut road / Rita Ballou / South coast of Texas / Heartbroke / Partner nobody chose / She's crazy for leaving / Calf rope / Lone star hotel / Blowin' like a bandit / Better days / Home grown tomatoes / Supply and demand / Randall knife / Carpenter / Uncertain Texas / No deal / Tears / Fool in the mirror
CD CDPH 118485
Philo / Jun '95 / ADA / CM / Direct

ESSENTIAL GUY CLARK, THE
Texas 1947 / Desperadoes waiting for a train / Like a coat from the cold / Instant coffee blues / Let him roll / Rita Ballou / LA freeway / She ain't going nowhere / Nickel for the fiddler / That old time feelin' Texas cookin' / Anyhow I love you / Virginia's real / Broken hearted people / Black haired boy / Me I'm feeling the same / Ballad of Laverne and Captain Flint / Don't let the sunshine fool you / Last gunfighter ballad / Fools for each other
CD 7863674042
RCA / May '97 / BMG

KEEPERS
CD SHCD 1055
Sugar Hill / Apr '97 / ADA / CM / Direct / Koch / Roots

OLD FRIENDS
CD SHCD 1026
Sugar Hill / Aug '95 / ADA / CM / Direct / Koch / Roots

OLD NUMBER ONE
Rita Ballou / LA freeway / She ain't goin' nowhere / Nickel for the fiddler / That old time feeling / Texas - 1947 / Desperados waiting for the train / Like a coat from the cold / Instant coffee blues / Let him roll
CD EDCD 285
Edsel / Apr '96 / Pinnacle
CD SHCD 1030
Sugar Hill / Jan '97 / ADA / CM / Direct / Koch / Roots

TEXAS COOKIN'
Texas cookin' / Anyhow I love you / Virginia's real / It's about time / Good to love you lady / Broken hearted people / Black haired boy / Me I'm feelin' the same / Ballad of Laverne and Captain Flint / Last gunfighter ballad
CD EDCD 287
Edsel / Apr '96 / Pinnacle
CD SHCD 1031
Sugar Hill / Jan '97 / ADA / CM / Direct / Koch / Roots

Clark, John

Il SUONO
Mustang Sally / Buster's move / Groove from the Louvre / Hot fired fish / Miradita / Il suono delle ragazze che ridono / Pretty loose
CD CMPCD 59
CMP / Oct '93 / Cargo / Grapevine/PolyGram / Vital/SAM

Clark, Mike

FUNK STOPS HERE, THE (Clark, Mike, Paul Jackson, Kenny Garrett & Jeff Pittson)
CD TIP 8888112
Enja / Jul '92 / New Note/Pinnacle / Vital/SAM

MASTER DRUMMERS VOL.3
CD URCD 011
Ubiquity / Jul '96 / Cargo / Timewarp

MIKE CLARK SEXTET (Clark, Mike Sextet / Ricky Ford & Jack Walrath)
CD STCD 22
Stash / Oct '91 / ADA / Cadillac / CM / Direct / Jazz Music

Clark, Nigel

WORLDWIDE SOUND (Clark, Nigel Quintet)
Batfunk the worlwide sound / 2000 giraffes / Over the moon / No romance / Ice / 26th samba / Only a dream / Highwire / ECT
CD SNA 1001
Sienna / Feb '97 / Vital/SAM

Clark, Petula

BEST OF PETULA CLARK, THE
CD MATCD 206
Castle / Dec '92 / BMG

CLASSIC COLLECTION, THE (4CD Set)
Downtown / My love / Who am I / I know a place / Don't sleep in the subway / Other man's grass is always greener / Look at mine / Round every corner / Cat in the window (the bird in the sky) / Happy heart / Thank you / You're the one / Don't give up / I will follow him / Baby it's me / You'd better come home / I couldn't live without your love / True love never runs smooth / I want to sing with your band / Valentino / This is my song / Sailor / Romeo / My friend the sea / I'm counting on you / Something missing / Road / Jumble sale / Ya ya twist / American boys / Sign of the times / No one better than you / Kiss me goodbye / Chariot / Cinderella Jones / Let me tell you / In love / Whistlin' for the moon / Welcome home / Colour my world / Groovy kind of love / Days / Black coffee / Homeward bound / Elusive butterfly / Here, there and everywhere / Reach out, I'll be there / Cherish / Every little bit hurts / Nobody I know (partir il nous faut) / Answer me, my love / I want to hold your hand / You belong to me / Dancing in the street / San Francisco (be sure to wear some flowers in your hair) / Well respected gentleman (un jeune homme bien) / Please please me (tu perds ton coeur) / Let it be me / Am I that easy to forget (tu reviendras a ta maison) / Foot tapper (mon bonheur danse) / Call me / Just say goodbye / Heart / Life and soul of the party / There goes my love, there goes my life / Marie De Vere / Close to you / Tiny bubbles (dans mon lit) / Two rivers / Hello Mr Brown / This is goodbye / L'amour viendra / Cranes flying south / Cala di volpe / Crying through a sleepless night / Conversations in the wind / If ever you're lonely / Where did we go wrong / Qu'est ce qui fait courir le monde / Show is over
CD Set PBXCD 404
Pulse / Jul '97 / BMG

DOWNTOWN
Downtown / Sign of the times / This is my song / I couldn't live without your love / You're the one / I know a place / Kiss me goodbye / Colour my world / Mad about you / Don't sleep in the subway / Good life / Other man's grass / My love / Give it a try / Strangers in the night / Call me
CD 15103
Laserlight / Jun '93 / Target/BMG

DOWNTOWN
True love never runs smooth / Baby it's mine / Now that you've gone / Tell me (that it's love) / Crying through a sleepless night / In love / Music / Be good to me / This is goodbye / Let me tell you / You belong to me / Downtown / I will follow him / Darling Cheri / You'd better love me
CD NEBCD 661
Sequel / Oct '93 / BMG

DOWNTOWN
Downtown / Don't sleep in the subway / Romeo / I don't know how to love him / If / For all we know / I couldn't live without your love / Where do I go from here / Welcome home / Thank you / This is my song / Sailor / Colour my world / Fly me to the moon / Memories are made of this / I get along without you very well / Night has a thousand eyes / Chariot / Happy heart / My love
CD 5507332
Spectrum / Mar '95 / PolyGram

DOWNTOWN
CD PDSCD 529
Pulse / Aug '96 / BMG

EP COLLECTION VOL.2, THE
I know a place / Tell me / In love / Let me tell you / You'd better love me / Every little bit hurts / Time for love / This is my song / Monday, Monday / I'm begging you / On the path of glory / Resist / Winchester Cathedral / Homeward bound / Jack and John / Music / Forgetting you / Be good to me / My love / Where am I going / 31st of June / Show is over / Colour my world / Here comes the morning / Fancy dancin' man / Bang bang / Groovy kind of love
CD SEECD 381
See For Miles/C5 / Oct '93 / Pinnacle

EP COLLECTION, THE
Cinderella Jones / With your love / Who needs you / While the children play / Slumming on Park Avenue / I've grown accustomed to his face / Love me again / Here, there and everywhere / Welcome home / My favourtie things / Sailor / Don't sleep in the subway / Have I the right / Downtown / Gotta tell the world / Everything in the garden / Hold on to what you've got / Life and soul of the party / I couldn't live without your love / Long before I knew you / In a little moment / Baby it's me / True love never runs smooth / Strangers and lovers / We can work it out / Wasn't it you / Come rain or come shine / What would I be
CD SEECD 306
See For Miles/C5 / Dec '90 / Pinnacle

GOLD
CD GOLD 207
Disky / Apr '94 / Disky / THE

GREATEST HITS
Downtown / This is my song / Colour my world / My love / I couldn't live without your love / It's a sign of the times / I know a place / Kiss me goodbye / Don't sleep in the subway darling / Other man's grass / You're the one / Give it a try / Mad about you
CD 100522
CMC / May '97 / BMG

HER GREATEST HITS (2CD Set)
CD Set SMDCD 195
Snapper / Jul '97 / Pinnacle

I COULDN'T LIVE WITHOUT YOUR LOVE/COLOUR MY WORLD
Strangers in the night / Groovy kind of love / Rain / Wasn't it you / There goes my love, there goes my life / Monday Monday / Bang bang (my baby shot me down) / Homeward bound / Two rivers / Come rain or come shine / Elusive butterfly / I couldn't live without your love / Your way of life / England swings / Cherish / Please don't go / What would I be / While the children play / Who am I / Winchester Cathedral / Las Vegas / Reach out, I'll be there / Special people / Here, there and everywhere / Colour my world / I'm begging you (take me home again) / Love is a long journey / What would I be
CD RPM 170
RPM / Sep '96 / Pinnacle

I KNOW A PLACE
Dancing in the street / Strangers and lovers / Everything in the garden / In crowd / Heart / You're the one / Foggy day / Gotta tell the world / Every little bit hurts / Call me / Goin' out of my head / I know a place / Jack and John / You'd better come home / Sound of love / Round every corner
CD NEBCD 660
Sequel / Jan '95 / BMG

I LOVE TO SING
Madamoiselle de paris / On the atchison, topeka and the Santa Fe / I get along without you very well / Fly me to the moon / Gotta have me go with you / George / There's nothing more to say / Nighty-night / Valentino / Imagination / Thankyou / Saturday sunshine / You'd better love me / Forgetting you / Round about / Never will I / Sound of love / Look at me / Nothing much matters / Make way for love / At the crossroads / Without a song / Only when to love me / Big love sale / Make a time for loving / What I did for love / Downtown / Sailor / Romeo / My friend the sea / I love to sing / I will follow him / I know a place / Things go better with coca-cola / You'd better come home / Round every corner / You're the one / My love / Just say goodbye / Sign of the times / I couldn't live without your love / Who am I / Colour my world / This is my song / Don't sleep in the subway / High / Other man's grass / Kiss me goodnight / Don't give up / Look at mine / You and I / I don't know how to love him / Superstar / Take good care of your heart / Love will find a way / Gotta be better than this / After you / Gotta be love / Theme from a dream / Goodbye Mr. Chips / Things to do / Conversations in the wind / Support your nearest love / Cranes flying south / Melody man / Beautiful sounds / Song is love / I've got to know / I think of you / Lifetime of love / Coming back to you again / On the road / Goin' out of my head / Maybe
CD Set NXTCD 265
Sequel / Jul '95 / BMG

JUMBLE SALE
CD Set NEDCD 198
Sequel / Feb '92 / BMG

JUST PET
Lights of night / Fill the world with love: *Clark, Petula & Jimmy Joyce Singers/Boys Chorus* / Houses / Happy together / Things bright and beautiful / Hey Jude / For those in love / Butterfly / If I only had time / Fool on the hill / No one better than you / Look at mine / You and I / Fill the world with love / Happy together
CD NEBCD 902
Sequel / Sep '96 / BMG

LIVE AT THE COPACABANA
Put on a happy face / I've seen that face before / My love / Our love is here to stay / Come rain or come shine / I know a place / Typically English / I couldn't live without your love / Santa Lucia / Hello Dolly / Call me / M'sieure m'sieure / My name is Petula / (In) a shanty in old Shanty Town / So nice top come home to / Dear hearts
CD NEBCD 653
Sequel / Jun '93 / BMG

MY GREATEST
Downtown / If you ever go away / I couldn't live without your love / This is my song / Got it / Turn to me / Song of my life / Send away the clowns / We'll still be friends / Don't sleep in the subway / My love / All my life / Other man's grass / Colours of love / Kiss me goodbye / Show is over
CD CDMFP 6053
Music For Pleasure / Jan '89 / EMI

MY LOVE
My love / Hold on to what you've got / We can work it out / Time for love / Just say goodbye / Life and soul of the party / Sign of the times / 31st of June / Where did we go wrong / I can't remember (ever loving you) / Dance with me / If I were a bell / Rain / Love is a long journey / Your way of life
CD NEBCD 658
Sequel / Jun '94 / BMG

NIXA YEARS VOL.1, THE
Suddenly there's a valley / Band of gold / Memories are made of this / Fortune teller / To you, my love / Another door opens / Million stars above / With all my heart / 'Allo mon coeur / Papayer / Tout ce que veut Lola / Histoire D'un amour / Guitare et tambourin / Java pour Petula / Mon couer danse avec la chance / Tango au L'esquimau / Prends mon couer / Lune de miel / Che sbadato / Ne joue pas / Que voulez vous de plus / Je t'aime / Liebe in St. Tropez / Du bist mein anfang und mein schluss / Hark the herald angels sing / List our merry carol / Once in Royal David's City / Little Jesus / Holly and the ivy / Away in a manger
CD RPM 138
RPM / Aug '94 / Pinnacle

NIXA YEARS VOL.2, THE
Gonna find me a bluebird / Alone / Baby lover / Little blue man / Devotion / St. Tropez / Fibbin' / Where do I go from here / Dear Daddy / Through the lovelong day / Let's get lost / I love to sing / All through the day / You're a sweetheart / Don't blame me / More I see you / Moi j'prefere l'amour a tout ca / Dis-moi / T es ma pluie et mon beau temps / Grand-mere / Non et non / Garde ta derniere danse pour moi / Sur un tapis volent / Calcutta (ma fete a moi) / Marin / Les gens diront / Calender girl / Ya ya twist / Si c'est oui, c'est oui / Bye bye mon amour
CD RPM 144
RPM / Nov '94 / Pinnacle

OTHER MAN'S GRASS IS ALWAYS GREENER, THE/PETULA-KISS ME GOOD
Smile / Black coffee / Answer me my love / Other man's grass is always greener / Today, tomorrow / I could have danced all night / At the crossroads / Ville de france / Cat in the window (bird in the sky) / For love / Ballad of a sad young man / Don't give up / Have another dream on me / Your love is everywhere / One in a million / Beautiful in the rain / This girl's in love with you / Kiss me goodbye / Sun shines out of your shoes / We're falling in love again / Days / Why can't I cry / Good life
CD SEECD 435
See For Miles/C5 / Oct '95 / Pinnacle

PETULA CLARK IN MEMPHIS
I wanna see morning with him / Nothing's as good as it used to be / Goodnight sweet

dreams / Right on / Neon rainbow / It don't matter to me / How we gonna live to be a hundred / Years old together / When the world was round / That old time feeling / That's what life is all about / People get ready / When the world was round / Beautiful sounds / Song is love
CD NEBCD 901
Sequel / Sep '96 / BMG

POLYGON YEARS VOL.1
You go to my head / Out of a clear blue sky / Music music music / Blossoms on the bough / Silver dollar / Talky talky talky / Who spilt coffee on the carpet / You are my true love / You're the sweetest in the land / Beloved be faithful / Fly away Peter, fly away Paul / Tennessee waltz / Sleepy eyes / Teasin' / Black note serenade / May kway / Clickety clack / Mariandl / Broken heart / That's how a love song is born / Cold cold heart / Tell me truly / Song of the mermaid / It had to be you / Card / Boy in love / Where did my snowman go / Teasin'
CD RPM 130
RPM / Jun '94 / Pinnacle

POLYGON YEARS VOL.2
Anytime is teatime now / Made in heaven / Temptation rag / My love is a wanderer / Take care of yourself / Christopher Robin at Buckingham Palace / Three little kittens / Poppa Piccolino / Who-is-it song / Little shoemaker / Helpless / Meet me in Battersea Park / Long way to go / Smile / Somebody / Christmas cards / Little Johnny Rainbow / Majorca / Fascinating ryhthm / Get well soon / Romance in Rome / Chee Chee oo chee / Crazy Otto rag / Pendulum song / How are things with you / Tuna puna Trinidad / Chee chee oo chee
CD RPM 131
RPM / Jun '94 / Pinnacle

PORTRAIT OF PETULA
Happy heart / If ever you're lonely (Lontago dagli occhi) / Games people play / Love is the only thing / When I was a child / Ad / My funny valentine / Lovin' things / When I give my heart / Let it be me / Some / Windmills of your mind / When you return / Have another dream on me / One in a million / Your love is everywhere
CD NEBCD 659
Sequel / Jan '95 / BMG

PYE YEARS VOL.1 (Don't Sleep In The Subway)
Never on a Sunday / You can't keep me from loving you / What now my love / Why don't they understand / Have I the right / Volare / One more sunrise / I want to hold your hand / Love me with all your heart / Boy from Ipanema / I who have nothing / Hello Dolly / This is my song / Groovin' / Lover man / San Francisco / Eternally / Resist / Don't sleep in the subway / Imagine / Love is here / How insensitive / I will wait for you / On the path of glory / High / Here comes the morning / Show is over
CD RPM 146
RPM / Jun '95 / Pinnacle

PYE YEARS VOL.2
CD RPM 159
RPM / Mar '96 / Pinnacle

THESE ARE MY SONGS
Downtown / It's a sign of the times / This is my song / I couldn't live without you / You're the one (un mal pour un bien) / I know a place / Kiss me goodbye / Colour my world / Mad about you / Don't sleep on the subway darling / Good life / Other man's grass is always greener / My love / Give it a try / Call me / Strangers in the night
CD STFCD 5
Start / Feb '97 / Disc

VERY BEST OF PETULA CLARK, THE
CD PLSCD 156
Pulse / Feb '97 / BMG

YOU ARE MY LUCKY STAR
It's foolish but it's fun / Sonny boy / Zing went the strings of my heart / Alone / I, yi, yi, yi, yi / Goodnight my love / I wish I knew / Slumming on Park Avenue / As time goes by / It's the natural thing to do / Afraid to dream / You are my lucky star / I yi yi yi yi (I like you very much)
CD C5CD 551
See For Miles/C5 / Jan '90 / Pinnacle

Clark, Roy

MAKIN' MUSIC (Clark, Roy & Clarence 'Gatemouth' Brown)
CD MCAD 22125
One Way / Jul '94 / ADA / Direct / Greyhound

Clark, Sanford

FOOL, THE
Fool / Man who made an angel cry / Love charms / Cheat / Lonesome for a letter / Ooh baby / Darling dear / Modern romance / Travellin' man / Swanee river rock / Lou be doo / Usta be my baby / Nine pound hammer / Glory of love / Don't care / Usta be my baby
CD BCD 15549
Bear Family / Jun '92 / Direct / Rollercoaster / Swift

SHADES
Better go home (throw that blade away) / Pledging my love / Girl on Death Row / Step aside / (They call me) Country / Shades / Fool / Climbin' the walls / Once upon a time / It's nothing to me / Where's the door / Big lie / Calling all hearts / Black Jack county chain / Big big day tomorrow / Bad case of you / Wind will blow (demo) / Streets of San Francisco / Oh Julie / Kung Fu U / Mother Texas (you've been a mother to me) / Taste of you / Movin' on / Wind will blow / Feathers / Now I know I'm not in Kansas / Nine pound hammer
CD BCD 15731
Bear Family / Jul '93 / Direct / Rollercoaster / Swift

Clark Sisters

MIRACLE
It's gonna be alright / Miracle / Simply yes / Call me / I don't know why / He's a real friend / Amazing grace / Jesus is the best thing / No doubt about it / Work to do
CD SPD 1368
Alliance Music / Aug '95 / EMI

Clark, Sonny

COOL STRUTTIN'
Cool struttin' / Blue minor / Sippin' at bells / Deep night / Royal flush / Lover
CD CDP 7465132
Blue Note / Mar '95 / EMI

DIAL S FOR SONNY
Dial S for Sonny / Bootin' it / It could happen to you / Sonny's mood / Shoutin' on a riff / Love walked in / Bootin' it 5:1
CD CDP 8565852
Blue Note / Jun '97 / EMI

SONNY CLARK, MAX ROACH, GEORGE DUVIVIER (Clark, Sonny/Max Roach/ George Duvivier)
CD COD 009
Jazz View / Mar '92 / Harmonia Mundi

Clark, Terri

JUST THE SAME
Emotional girl / Poor, poor pitiful me / Just the same / Something in the water / Neon flame / Any woman / Twang thang / You do or you don't / Keeper of the flame / Not what I wanted to hear / Hold your horses
CD 5328792
Mercury / Nov '96 / PolyGram

TERRI CLARK
CD 5269912
Mercury / Feb '96 / PolyGram

Clark, Terry

COLOR CHANGES
Blue waltz (la valse bleue): *Terry, Clark* / Brother Terry: *Terry, Clark* / Flutin' and fluglin': *Terry, Clark* / No problem: *Terry, Clark* / La rive gauche: *Terry, Clark* / Nahstye blues: *Terry, Clark* / Chat qui peche (A cat that fishes): *Terry, Clark*
CD CCD 79009
Candid / Jan '89 / Cadillac / Direct / Jazz Music / Koch / Wellard

Clark, Thais

THAIS CLARK & FESSOR'S FUNKY NEW ORLEANIANS (Clark, Thais & Ole 'Fessor' Lindgren)
CD MECCACD 2011
Music Mecca / May '97 / Cadillac / Jazz Music / Wellard

Clark, W.C.

HEART OF GOLD
CD BT 1103CD
Black Top / May '94 / ADA / CM / Direct

Clarke, Alex

SAX
CD SPLCD 030
Sloane / Apr '96 / Grapevine/PolyGram

Clarke, Ann

UNSTILL LIFE
CD 0888362
SPV / May '91 / Koch / Plastic Head

Clarke, Anthony John

SIDEWAYS GLANCE, A
Irish eyes / Tuesday night is always karaoke / Journey home / Seven in Ireland / Ireland's burning / Savin' the best till last / Patrick / Hawk / Irish visit '91 / Turning the corner now / But then I'm Irish / Even at the beat of times
CD TERRCD 008
Terra Nova / Jul '97 / Direct

Clarke, Buddy

ONCE AND FOR ALWAYS
CD JCD 631
Jass / '92 / ADA / Cadillac / CM / Direct / Jazz Music
CD JZCL 6003
Jazz Classics / Feb '97 / Cadillac / Direct / Jazz Music

Clarke, Dave

ARCHIVE ONE
Rhapsody in red / Protective custody / No one's driving / Woki / Southside / Wisdom to the wise / Tales of two cities / Storm / Miles away / Thunder / Splendour
CD 74321361102
De-Construction / Jun '96 / BMG

X-MIX VOL.7 (Electro Boogie) (Various Artists)
Phox: *SEM* / We come to dub: *Imperial Brothers* / I am: *Lockstep* / Electronic warfare/The mixes/Aux 88: *Underground Resistance* / Demented spirit: *Octagon Man* / DJ: *Aux 88* / Midnight drive: *Elecktroids* / Future: *Model 500* / Future tone: *Elecktroids* / Subsonic soundscape: *Shiver* / Ignition: *Dynamix II* / We are back: *LFO* / Sole waves: *Detrechno* / Technicolor: *Channel One* / Voice activated: *Dopplereffekt* / I do because I couldn't care less: *I-F* / Primrose path: *Hashim*
CD K7 050CD
Studio K7 / Jan '97 / Prime / RTM/Disc

Clarke, Gilby

PAWNSHOP GUITARS
Cure me... or kill me / Black / Tijuana jail / Skin and bones / Johanna's chopper / Let's get lost / Pawnshop guitar / Dead flowers / Jail guitar doors / Hunting dogs / Shut up
CD CDVUS 76
Virgin / Jul '94 / EMI

Clarke, Johnny

20 MASSIVE HITS
CD 3021462
Arcade / Jun '97 / Discovery
CD RN 7020
Rhino / May '97 / Grapevine/PolyGram / Jet Star

AUTHORISED ROCKERS
Rockers time now / It's green and cold / African roots / Be holy my brothers and sisters / Satta a masagana / Stop the tribal war / Declaration of rights / Let's give jah jah praises / Wish it would go on forever / Natty dreadlocks stand up right / Prophesy a fulfilled / Marcus Garvey / Roots, natty roots, natty congo / Wrath of jah / Legalize it / I'm still waiting / Let go violence / Academy award version / Cry tough / Crazy baldheads / Simmer down / Jah jah see them come / Freedom blues
CD CDFL 9014
Frontline / Jun '91 / EMI / Jet Star

GOLDEN HITS
CD SONCD 0081
Sonic Sounds / Nov '95 / Jet Star

LIFT YOURSELF UP
CD CDSGP 0275
Prestige / Sep '96 / Else / Total/BMG

Clarke, Mick

ALL THESE BLUES (Clarke, Mick Band)
CD APCD 058
Appaloosa / '92 / ADA / Direct / TKO Magnum

HAPPY HOME (Clarke, Mick & Lou Martin)
CD BCD 0026
Burnside / Mar '97 / Koch

LOOKING FOR TROUBLE (Clarke, Mick Band)
CD APCD 038
Appaloosa / '92 / ADA / Direct / TKO Magnum

NO COMPROMISE (Clarke, Mick Band)
CD TX 1006CD
Taxim / Dec '93 / ADA

TELL THE TRUTH (Clarke, Mick Band)
CD TX 1001CD
Taxim / Dec '93 / ADA

WEST COAST CONNECTION
CD BRAM 1988012
Brambus / Aug '95 / ADA

Clarke Sisters

TRIBUTE TO THE GREAT SINGING GROUPS, A (The Clarke Sisters Swing Again)
My blue Heaven / Until the real thing comes along / Bei mir bist du schon / Paper doll / I'll get by / I've got a gal in Kalamazoo / Dream / Sugartime / I'm getting sentimental over you / Undecided / I'm forever blowing bubbles / When I take my sugar to tea / St. Louis blues march / Hot toddy / Song of India / I've got my love to keep me warm / I can't get started / Trumpet blues / In the mood / When day is done / Mole
CD JASCD 603
Jasmine / Oct '96 / Conifer/BMG / Hot Shot / TKO Magnum

Clarke, Stanley

CLARKE/DUKE PROJECT VOL.1 (Clarke, Stanley & George Duke)
CD 4682232
Sony Jazz / Jan '95 / Sony

CLARKE/DUKE PROJECT VOL.2 (Clarke, Stanley & George Duke)
Put it on the line / Atlanta / Trip you in love / You're gonna love it / Good times / Great danes / Every reason to smile / Try me baby / Heroes
CD EK 38934
Sony Jazz / Jul '95 / Sony

EAST RIVER DRIVE
CD 4737972
Sony Jazz / Jan '95 / Sony

FIND OUT (Clarke, Stanley Band)
Find out / What if I should fall in love / Born in the USA / Sky's the limit / Don't turn the lights out / Campo Americano / Stereo typica / Psychedelic / My life
CD EK 40040
Sony Jazz / Aug '97 / Sony

HIDEAWAY
Overjoyed / My love, her inspiration / Where do we go / Boys of Johnson Street / Old friends / When it's cold outside / Listen to the beat of your heart / Basketball / I'm here to stay
CD EK 40275
Sony Jazz / Aug '97 / Sony

I WANNA PLAY FOR YOU
Rock 'n' roll jelly / All about / Jamaican boy / Christopher Ivanhoe / My greatest hits / Strange weather / I wanna play for you / Just a feeling / Streets of Philadelphia / School days / Quiet afternoon / Together again / Blues for Mingus / Off the planet / Hot fun
CD 4773132
Sony Jazz / Jan '95 / Sony

IF THIS BASS COULD ONLY TALK
If this bass could talk / I wanna play for you / Funny how time flies / Bassically taps / Working man / Come take my hand / Stories to tell / Tradition
CD 4608832
Epic / Jan '92 / Sony

JOURNEY TO LOVE
Silly putty / Journey to love / Hello, Jeff / Song to John / Concerto for jazz-rock orchestra
CD 4682212
Sony Jazz / Jan '95 / Sony

LIVE 1976-1977
CD 4689592
Sony Jazz / Jan '95 / Sony

LIVE AT THE GREEK
CD 4766022
Sony Jazz / Jan '95 / Sony

RITE OF SPRING, THE (Clarke, Stanley & Al Di Meola/Jean-Luc Ponty)
CD 8341672
Gai Saber / Dec '95 / Vital

ROCKS, PEBBLES AND SAND
Danger street / All hell broke loose / Rocks, pebbles and sand / You / Me together / Underestimation / We supply / Story of a man and a woman / She thought I was Stanley Clarke / Fool again / I nearly went crazy (until I realised what had occurred)
CD 4682222
Sony Jazz / Jan '95 / Sony

SCHOOL DAYS
School days / Quiet afternoon / Danger / Desert song / Hot fun / Life is just a game / Dancer
CD 4682192
Sony Jazz / Jan '95 / Sony

STANLEY CLARKE
Vulcan princess / Yesterday Princess / Lopsy lu / Power / Spanish phases for strings and bass / Life suite (part 1) / Life suite (part 2) / Life suite (part 3) / Life suite (part 4)
CD 4682182
Sony Jazz / Jan '95 / Sony

TIME EXPOSURE
Play the bass 103 / Are you ready / Speedball / Heaven sent you / Time exposure / Future shock / Future / Spacerunner / I know just how you feel
CD EK 38688
Sony Jazz / Aug '97 / Sony

Clarke, Terry

HEART SINGS
Rocks of Ireland / Roll away / Detroit to dingle / Back to the wall / Shelly river / Walk with me / Looking for you / Heart sings / Blue honey / Bruce Channel in this town / Edge of shamrock city / American lipstick / Irish rockabilly blues / Last rhythm
CD TRACD 226
Transatlantic / May '97 / Pinnacle

Clarke, William

BLOWIN' LIKE HELL
CD ALCD 4788
Alligator / Mar '93 / ADA / CM / Direct

GROOVE TIME
CD ALCD 4827
Alligator / Dec '94 / ADA / CM / Direct

HARD WAY, THE
CD ALCD 4842
Alligator / Aug '96 / ADA / CM / Direct

SERIOUS INTENTIONS
Pawnshop bound / Trying to stretch my money / Educated fool / Going down this highway / I know you're fine / Driving my life away / Chasin' the gator / With a tear in my eye / It's been a long time / Work song / I feel like jumping / Soon forgotten
CD ALCD 4806
Alligator / May '93 / ADA / CM / Direct

Clash

CLASH, THE
Janie Jones / Remote control / I'm so bored with the USA / White riot / Hate and war / What's my name / Deny / London's burning / Career opportunities / Cheat / Protex blue / Police and thieves / 48 hours / Garage land
CD 4687832
Columbia / Jun '91 / Sony

CLASH, THE (American Version)
Clash city rockers / I'm so bored with the USA / Remote control / Complete control / White riot / Hate & war / White man in Hammersmith Palais / London's burning / I fought the law / Janie Jones / Career opportunities / What's my name / Police & thieves / Jail guitar doors / Garageland
CD CD 32232
Columbia / Jan '95 / Sony

COMBAT ROCK
Inoculated city / Know your rights / Car jamming / Should I stay or should I go / Rock the Casbah / Red angel dragnet / Straight to hell / Overpowered by funk / Atom tan / Sean Flynn / Ghetto defendant / Death is a star
CD CD 32787
Columbia / Jul '92 / Sony

CUT THE CRAP
Dictator / Dirty punk / We are The Clash / Are you ready / Cool under heat / Movers and shakers / This is England / Three card trick / Play to win / Finger poppin' / North and South / Life is wild
CD 4651102
CBS / '91 / Sony

GIVE 'EM ENOUGH ROPE
Safe European home / English civil war / Tommy gun / Julie's been working for the drug squad / Last gang in town / Guns on the roof / Drug stabbing time / Stay free / Cheapstakes / All the young punks (new boots and contracts)
CD CD 32444
CBS / '91 / Sony

LONDON CALLING
London calling / Brand new Cadillac / Jimmy Jazz / Hateful / Rudie can't fail / Spanish bombs / Right profile / Lost in the supermarket / Clampdown / Guns of Brixton / Wrong 'em / Boyo / Death or glory / Koka cola / Card cheat / Lover's rock / I'm not down / Revolution rock / Four horsemen
CD 4601142
CBS / '91 / Sony

ON BROADWAY (3CD Set)
CD Set 4693082
Legacy / May '94 / Sony

SANDINISTA
Hitsville UK / Junco partner / Leader / Rebel waltz / Look here / One more time / Corner soul / Equaliser / Call up / Broadway / Junkie slip / Version city / Crooked beat / Up in heaven / Midnight log / Lose this skin / Kingston advice / Let's go crazy
CD Set 4633642
Columbia / Apr '89 / Sony

SINGLES, THE
White riot / Remote control / Complete control / Clash city rockers / White man in Hammersmith Palais / Tommy gun / English Civil War / I fought the law / London calling / Train in vain / Bankrobber / Call up / Hitsville UK / Magnificent seven / This is radio clash / Know your rights / Rock the casbah / Should I stay or should I go
CD 4689462
Columbia / Nov '91 / Sony

STORY OF THE CLASH VOL.1, THE (2CD Set)
Magnificent seven / This is Radio Clash / Straight to hell / Train in vain / I fought the law / Somebody got murdered / Bankrobber / Rock the Casbah / Should I stay or should I go / Armagideon time / Guns of Brixton / Clampdown / Lost in the supermarket / White man in Hammersmith Palais / London's burning / Janie Jones / Tommy gun / Complete control / Capital radio / White riot / Career opportunities / Clash city rockers / Safe European home / Stay free / London calling / Spanish bombs / English civil war / Police and thieves
CD Set 4602442
Columbia / Oct '95 / Sony

SUPER BLACK MARKET CLASH
1977 / Protex blue / Deny / Cheat / 48 Hours / Listen / Jail guitar doors / City of the dead / Prisoner / Pressure drop / One-two crush on you / Groovy times / Gates of the west / Capital radio two / Time is tight / Kick it over / Bankrobber / Stop the world / Cool out / First night back in London / Long time jerk / Cool confusion / Magnificent dance / This is radio clash / Mustapha dance
CD 4745462
Columbia / Sep '96 / Sony

Classen, Martin

STOP AND GO (Classen, Martin Quartet)
CD BEST 1033CD
Acoustic Music / Nov '93 / ADA

Classic Jazz Quartet

COMPLETE RECORDINGS
CD JCD 138
Jazzology / Jun '95 / Jazz Music

COMPLETE RECORDINGS VOL.2
CD JCD 139
Jazzology / Jun '95 / Jazz Music

Clastrier, Valentin

PALUDE (Clastrier, Valentin & Michael Riessler/Carlo Rizzo)
CD WER 8009
Wergo / Dec '95 / ADA / Cadillac / Harmonia Mundi

Clatterbox

EAZY DOES IT
CD CLR 422CD
Clear / Apr '96 / Prime / RTM/Disc

Clau De Lluna

CERCLE DE GAL-LA
CD H 039CD
Sonifolk / Jun '94 / ADA / CM

FICA-LI, NOIA
CD 20049CD
Sonifolk / Jun '94 / ADA / CM

Clawfinger

DEAF, DUMB, BLIND
Nigger / Truth / Rosegrove / Don't get me wrong / I need you / Catch me / Warfair / Wonderful world / Sad to see your sorrow / I don't care
CD 4509933212
WEA / Aug '93 / Warner Music

USE YOUR BRAIN
CD 4509996312
WEA / Apr '95 / Warner Music

Clawhammer

PABLUM
CD E 864252
Epitaph / Nov '92 / Pinnacle / Plastic Head

Clay, Joe

DUCKTAIL
Duck tail / Did you mean jelly bean (what you said cabbage head) / Crackerjack / Goodbye goodbye / Sixteen chicks / Slipping out and sneaking in / Doggone it / Get on the right track baby / You look good to me
CD BCD 15516
Bear Family / Jul '90 / Direct / Rollercoaster / Swift

Clay, Judy

BILLY VERA AND JUDY CLAY (Clay, Judy & Billy Vera)
CD SCL 2101
Ichiban Soul Classics / May '95 / Koch

Clay, Otis

GOSPEL TRUTH, THE
CD BP 5005CD
Blind Pig / May '94 / ADA / CM / Direct / Hot Shot

OTIS CLAY 45'S
CD HILOCD 1
Hi / Dec '93 / Pinnacle

THAT'S HOW IT IS
CD HIUKCD 110
Hi / Jul '91 / Pinnacle

Clay People

STONE TEN STITCHES
CD CDRED 026
Re-Constriction / Jan '97 / Cargo

Clayderman, Richard

BALLERINA
CD MSCD 15
Music De-Luxe / Mar '95 / TKO Magnum

CARPENTERS COLLECTION, THE
Yesterday once more / There's a kind of hush (all over the world) / We've only just begun / Superstar / Top of the world / Rainy days and Mondays / Close to you / Only yesterday / For all we know / Please Mr. Postman / I won't last a day without you / Solitaire / Meldley: For all we know, We've only just begun / Sing
CD 8286882
Delphine / Oct '95 / PolyGram

CHRISTMAS
White Christmas / Medley / Silent night / Christmas concerto / Little red-nosed reindeer / Little drummer boy / Moonlight sonata / Jingle bells / Snow falls slowly / Largo / Romance / O tannenbaum / Medley / Jesus will always be my joy / Ave Maria
CD 5506442
Spectrum / Nov '96 / PolyGram

CLASSIC TOUCH
Dream of Olwen / Variation of a theme of Paganini / Pathetique / Liebestraum / Warsaw concerto / Piano concerto in A minor / Cornish rhapsody / Piano concerto no.2 / Rhapsody in blue / Clair de Lune / Concerto No. 1/ B flat minor Op. 23 / Piano concerto No.21 in C major
CD 8202992
Delphine / Oct '90 / PolyGram

COLLECTION, THE
Ballade pour Adeline / Yesterday / Moon river / Don't cry for me Argentina / Souvenirs d'enfance / Love is blue / Fur Elise / Only you / Exodus / Rondo pour un tout petit enfant / Moonlight sonata / Bridge over troubled water / Largo / Lettre a ma mere / Woman in love / Lady Di / Liebestraum / Romeo and Julia
CD AMC 51022
BR Music / May '97 / Target/BMG

LITTLE NIGHT MUSIC, A (12 Classic Love Songs)
I just called to say I love you / I'm not in love / Sailing / For all we know / We've only just begun without you / Nights in white satin / Careless whisper / Power of love / Whiter shade of pale / Nothing's gonna change my love for you / Just the way you are / Princess of the night
CD 5501332
Spectrum / Oct '93 / PolyGram

LOVE SONGS
CD 8287382
Delphine / Mar '96 / PolyGram

MY CLASSIC COLLECTION
Four seasons: spring / Swan / Italian symphony no.1 - A sharp/opus 90 / Aria / Waltz in A flat / Cavalleria rusticana / Barcarolle / Nocturne - D flat major/ opus 27 / Forever green / Hill Street Blues / Mahogany / Sleepy shores / Evergreen / Tara's theme / Over the rainbow / Medley: Four Seasons
CD 8282282
Delphine / Jun '92 / PolyGram

RICHARD CLAYDERMAN
Libestraum / Barcarolle / Lettre a ma mere / Pour Elise / Feelings / Ballade pour Adeline / Don't cry for me Argentina / Elizabethan serenade / My way / Hymne a la joie / Le mer / Romeo and Julia / Blue eyes / Woman in love
CD AMC 55109
BR Music / May '97 / Target/BMG

SONGS OF LOVE
Medley / Nikita / Do you know where you're going to / Lady in red / Take my breath away / You are my world / We are the world / I know him so well / Eleana / Colin Maillard / Eroica / La sorellina / All by myself / I dreamed a dream / All I ask of you
CD 5518202
Spectrum / May '96 / PolyGram

SUN AND THE FLOWER, THE
CD MSCD 10
Magnum Music / Oct '94 / TKO Magnum

TOGETHER AT LAST (Clayderman, Richard & James Last)
From a distance / Everything I do (I do it for you) / Sacrifice / Moonfire / Careless whisper / Pretty ballerina / Chancer (theme) / Wind beneath my wings / Any dream will do / Unchained melody / Indigo bay / Promise me / Reflections / Candle in the wind
CD 5115252
Polydor / Oct '91 / PolyGram

Claypool, Philip

CIRCUS LEAVING TOWN, A
CD CURCD 18
Curb / Nov '95 / Grapevine/PolyGram

Clayton Brothers

MUSIC, THE
CD 74037
Capri / Nov '93 / Cadillac / Wellard

Clayton, Buck

BADEN-SWITZERLAND
CD SKCD 22028
Sackville / Jul '93 / Cadillac / Jazz Music / Swift

BASEL 1961, SWISS RADIO DAYS JAZZ SERIES VOL.7 (Clayton, Buck All Stars)
Swinging at the coppers' rail / Robbins' nest / Outer drive / Moon glow / Swingin' the blues / Night train / Saint-Louis blues
CD TCB 02072
TCB / Feb '97 / New Note/Pinnacle

BLOW THE BLUES (Clayton, Buck & Buddy Tate)
CD OJCCD 850
Original Jazz Classics / Nov '95 / Complete/Pinnacle / Jazz Music / Wellard

BUCK CLAYTON & BUDDY TATE (Clayton, Buck & Buddy Tate)
CD OJCCD 757
Original Jazz Classics / Jun '95 / Complete/Pinnacle / Jazz Music / Wellard

BUCK CLAYTON ALL STARS 1961 (Clayton, Buck All Stars)
CD STCD 8231
Storyville / May '97 / Cadillac / Jazz Music / Wellard

BUCK CLAYTON JAM SESSION, A
CD CRD 132
Chiaroscuro / Jul '96 / Jazz Music

BUCK CLAYTON LIVE (Clayton, Buck Swing Band)
Scorpio / Swingin' on the state line / Horn o'plenty / Rise 'n' shine / One for me / BC special / Black sheep blues / Sparky / Song for Sarah / Cadillac taxi / What a beautiful yesterday / Bowery bunch
CD CD 030
Nagel Heyer / Jan '97 / Jazz Music

BUCK CLAYTON STORY 1937-1945, THE
CD 158682
Jazz Archives / Jun '97 / Discovery

COPENHAGEN CONCERT (Clayton, Buck All Stars)
CD SCCD 36006/7
Steeplechase / Nov '90 / Discovery / Impetus

DOCTOR JAZZ VOL.3 (Clayton, Buck Band)
CD STCD 6043
Storyville / Jul '96 / Cadillac / Jazz Music / Wellard

INTRODUCTION TO BUCK CLAYTON, AN
CD 4046
Best Of Jazz / Jun '97 / Discovery

JAM SESSION 1975
CD CRD 143
Chiaroscuro / Nov '95 / Jazz Music

SWINGIN' DREAM, A (Clayton, Buck Swing Band)
CD STCD 16
Stash / Oct '92 / ADA / Cadillac / CM / Direct / Jazz Music

Clayton, Dr. Peter

DOCTOR PETER CLAYTON (1935-1942)
CD DOCD 5179
Document / Oct '93 / ADA / Hot Shot / Jazz Music

DR. CLAYTON & HIS BUDDY
CD SOB 035392
Story Of The Blues / Apr '93 / ADA / Koch

Clayton, Jay

JAZZ ALLEY TAPES, THE (Clayton, Jay & Don Lamphere)
You're a weaver of dreams / Nearness of you / Softly as in a morning sunrise / I remember Clifford / New stores / Love for sale / I've grown accustomed to her face / My silent love / Mr. PC / AC
CD HEPCD 2046
Hep / Sep '92 / Cadillac / Jazz Music / New Note/Pinnacle / Wellard

Clayton, John

GROOVE SHOP (Featuring Hamilton Jazz Orchestra) (Clayton, John & Jeff)
CD 740212
Capri / '90 / Cadillac / Wellard

HEART AND SOUL (Clayton-Hamilton Orchestra)
CD 74028
Capri / Nov '93 / Cadillac / Wellard

SUPER BASS (Clayton, John & Ray Brown)
CD 740182
Capri / '90 / Cadillac / Wellard

Clayton, Lee

ANOTHER NIGHT
CD PRLD 700812
Provogue / Nov '89 / Pinnacle

BORDER AFFAIR/NAKED CHILD
Silver stallion / If you can touch her at all / Back home in Tennessee / Border affair / Old number nine / Like a diamond / My woman my love / Tequila is addictive / My true love / Rainbow in the sky / Saturday night special / I ride alone / 10000 alone / Sexual moon / I love you / Jaded virgin / Little cocaine / If I can do it (so can you)
CD EDCD 434
Edsel / Oct '95 / Pinnacle

LEE CLAYTON
CD EDCD 475
Edsel / Apr '96 / Pinnacle

SPIRIT OF TWILIGHT
CD _______ PRD 70652
Provogue / Sep '94 / Pinnacle

Clayton, Steve

LOVE IS SAID IN MANY WAYS
CD _______ STCD 559
Stash / Oct '93 / ADA / Cadillac / CM / Direct / Jazz Music

Clayton, Vikki

MIDSUMMER CUSHION
CD _______ CDSGP 008
Prestige / Jun '94 / Else / Total/BMG

MOVERS AND SHAKERS
Pilgrim / 10 years / Africa was calling / My Donald / Kisses in the dark / Movers and shakers / Wild nights / Payback / I want something / Girlie press gang / My bonny light horseman / Sir Hugh of Lincoln / Beguiled
CD _______ ANDCD 15
A New Day / May '97 / Direct

Clayton, Willie

AT HIS BEST
CD _______ ICH 1503CD
Ichiban / Dec '95 / Direct / Koch

CHICAGO SOUL GREATS (Clayton, Willie & Otis Clay)
It's time you made up your mind: *Clayton, Willie* / I must be losing you: *Clayton, Willie* / Baby you're ready: *Clayton, Willie* / Too much of nothing: *Clayton, Willie* / Gotta have money: *Clayton, Willie* / Hello, how have you been: *Clayton, Willie* / Say yes to love: *Clayton, Willie* / Abracadabra: *Clayton, Willie* / When I'm gone: *Clayton, Willie* / That wall: *Clayton, Willie* / If I could reach out: *Clay, Otis* / Let me be the one: *Clay, Otis* / I didn't know the meaning of pain: *Clay, Otis* / Woman don't live here no more: *Clay, Otis* / You can't escape the hands of love: *Clay, Otis* / You did something to me: *Clay, Otis* / It was jealousy: *Clay, Otis*
CD _______ HILOCD 16
Hi / Jul '95 / Pinnacle

FEELS LIKE LOVE
CD _______ ICH 1155CD
Ichiban / Feb '94 / Direct / Koch

NO GETTING OVER ME
CD _______ ICH 1182CD
Ichiban / Aug '95 / Direct / Koch

Clean

COMPILATION
CD _______ FNCD 154
Flying Nun / Jun '95 / RTM/Disc

GREAT UNWASHED
CD _______ FNCD 208
Flying Nun / Jun '95 / RTM/Disc

MODERN ROCK
CD _______ FNCD 292
Flying Nun / Feb '95 / RTM/Disc

ODDITIES
CD _______ FNCD 223
Flying Nun / Jun '95 / RTM/Disc

UNKNOWN COUNTRY
CD _______ FNCD 349
Flying Nun / Oct '96 / RTM/Disc

VEHICLE
CD _______ FNCD 147
Flying Nun / Jun '95 / RTM/Disc

Cleaners From Venus

BACK FROM THE CLEANERS
CD _______ TANGCD 014
Tangerine / Oct '95 / RTM/Disc

GOLDEN CLEANERS
CD _______ TANGCD 3
Tangerine / Aug '93 / RTM/Disc

Clear Light

FOREVER BLOWING BUBBLES
Chanson / Without words / Way / Ergotrip / Et pendent ce temps la / Narcisse et Goldmund / Jungle bubbles
CD _______ CDV 2039
Virgin / Jun '97 / EMI

Clearwater, Eddy

BLUES HANGOUT
CD _______ ECD 260082
Evidence / Jan '92 / ADA / Cadillac / Harmonia Mundi

BOOGIE MY BLUES AWAY
Muddy Waters goin' to run clear / Boogie my blues away / Came up the hard way / Blues at Theresa's / I don't know why / Tore up all the time / Real fine woman / Mayor Daley's blues
CD _______ DD 678
Delmark / Mar '97 / ADA / Cadillac / CM / Direct / Hot Shot

CHIEF, THE
Find you a job / Blues for breakfast / Blue blue blue over you / One day at a time / I wouldn't lay my guitar down / Chills / Bad dream / I'm tore up / Lazy woman / Blues for a living
CD _______ R 2615
Rooster / Feb '97 / Direct

LIVE AT THE KINGSTON MINES, CHICAGO
Last nite / Black night / Just a little bit / Pretty baby / Hoochie coochie man / Everything's gonna be alright / Sweet little sixteen / Reelin' and rockin' / Kansas city / Honky tonk
CD _______ 422213
Last Call / Feb '97 / Cargo / Direct / Discovery

MEAN CASE OF THE BLUES
Mean case of the blues / Send for me / Check up on my baby / Love being loved by you / Make it if you try / Hard way to make an easy living / Look whatcha done / Come on down / Party at my house / Don't take my blues
CD _______ CDBB 9584
Bullseye Blues / Jul '97 / Direct

TWO TIMES NINE
CD _______ 422226
Last Call / Feb '97 / Cargo / Direct / Discovery

Cleary, Jon

ALLIGATOR LIPS AND DIRTY RICE
Go ahead baby / Long distance lover / C'mon second line / Groove me / In the mood / Big chief / Let them talk / Pick up the pieces / Burnt mouth boogie
CD _______ CDCH 377
Ace / Mar '93 / Pinnacle

Cleaver, Robinson

EARFUL OF MUSIC, AN (Wurlitzer Organ Favourites)
Earfull of music / Legend of the glass mountain / Masaniello overture / Things to come / Rondo / To a wild rose / Walk in the Black Forest / Man and a woman / Canadian capers / Alligator crawl / Goldfinger / Black canary hora / Moonlight serenade / Music to watch girls by / Fiddle faddle / Spanish gypsy dance / Skyscraper fantasy / In a persian market / Blaze away / Earful of music
CD _______ PLCD 544
President / Aug '96 / Grapevine/PolyGram / President / Target/BMG

Cleaves, Slaid

NO ANGEL KNOWS
Not going down / No angel knows / Dance around the fire / Jennie's alright / Look back at me / Wrecking ball / River runs / Don't tell me / Skunk juice / Last of the V8's / 29 3.32
CD _______ CDP 1201
Philo / Feb '97 / ADA / CM / Direct

Cleftones

BEST OF THE CLEFTONES
CD _______ NEMCD 603
Sequel / Aug '90 / BMG

Clegg, Johnny

IN MY AFRICAN DREAM
CD _______ SHAKACD 3
Safari / Aug '94 / Pinnacle

Clement, Giles

WES SIDE STORIES (Clement, Giles Quartet)
CD _______ 500492
Musidisc / Nov '93 / Discovery

Clements, Vassar

GRASS ROUTES
Beats me / Westport Drive / Come on home / Florida blues / Other end / Rain rain rain / Rambling / Rounder's blues / Fiddlin' will / Non-stop / Flame of love / Turkey in the straw
CD _______ ROUCD 0287
Rounder / Feb '92 / ADA / CM / Direct

HILLBILLY JAZZ
CD _______ FF 101CD
Flying Fish / Jul '92 / ADA / CM / Direct / Roots

HILLBILLY JAZZ RIDES AGAIN
Hillbilly jazz / Don't hop don't skip / Airmail special / Say goodbye to the blues / Swing street / Woodsheddin' / Be a little discreet / Your mind is on vacation / Caravan / How can I go on without you / Triple stop boogie / Take a break
CD _______ FF 385CD
Flying Fish / May '93 / ADA / CM / Direct / Roots

Clemons, Clarence

PEACEMAKER
Peace prayer / Into the blue forest / Abraxas / Miracle / Serenity / Spirit dance
CD _______ 72445110322
Zoo Entertainment / Jun '95 / BMG

Click

GAME RELATED
CD _______ CHIP 171
Jive / Jul '96 / Pinnacle

Cliff, Dave

PLAY TADD DAMERON (Cliff, Dave & Geoff Simkins 5)
Ladybird / Squirrel / Blue time / If you could see me now / Flossie Lou / Jahbero / Hot house / Soultrane / Casbah / Good bait / Our delight / Interview
CD _______ SPJCD 560
Spotlite / Feb '97 / Cadillac / Jazz Music / New Note/Pinnacle / Swift

SIPPIN' AT BELLS (Cliff, Dave & Geoff Simkins)
Back to back / Sal's line / How deep is the ocean / Easy to love / Nobody knows the trouble I've caused / I guess I'll hang my tears out to dry / Nightingale sang in Berkeley Square / Lester's blues / Sippin' at bells / Conception / Once I loved / Touch of your lips / That old feeling / Indian summer
CD _______ SPJCD 553
Spotlite / Jul '95 / Cadillac / Jazz Music / New Note/Pinnacle / Swift

Cliff, Jimmy

100% PURE REGGAE
Samba reggae / I'm a winner / Breakout / Oneness / Peace / War a Africa / Roll on rolling stone / Be ready / Jimmy Jimmy / Haunted / Baby let me feel it / Stepping out of limbo / True story / Shout for freedom
CD _______ 74321491702
Milan / Jul '97 / Conifer/BMG / Silva Screen

BEST OF JIMMY CLIFF
Hard road to travel / Sooner or later / Sufferin' in the land / Keep your eye on the sparrow / Struggling man / Wild world / Vietnam / Another cycle / Wonderful world, beautiful people / Harder they come / Let your yeah be yeah / Synthetic world / I'm no immigrant / Give and take / Many rivers to cross / Going back west / Sitting in limbo / Come into my life / You can get it if you really want / Goodbye yesterday
CD _______ RRCD 50
Reggae Refreshers / Mar '96 / PolyGram / Vital

CLIFF HANGER
Hitting with music / American sweet / Arrival / Brown eyes / Reggae Street / Hotshot / Sunrise / Dead and awake / Now and forever / Nuclear war
CD _______ 4712202
Columbia / Feb '97 / Sony

COOL RUNNER LIVE IN LONDON, THE
Intro (Jimmy Jimmy) / Africa / Yeah ho / Rub-a-dub / Peace / Rock steady / Save the planet / Many rivers to cross / Limbo / Third world people / Harder they come / Samba reggae / Rebel in me / Wonderful world, beautiful people / Justice / Higher and deeper love / Baby let me feel it / True story / Shout for freedom
CD _______ MOCD 3010
More Music / Feb '95 / Sound & Media

FOLLOW MY MIND
Look at the mountains / News / I'm gonna live, I'm gonna love / Going mad / Dear mother / Who feels it, knows it / Remake the world / No woman, no cry / Wahjahka man / Hypocrite / If I follow my mind / You're the only one
CD _______ 7599263112
WEA / Jan '96 / Warner Music

FUNDAMENTAL REGGAY
Fundamental reggae / Under the sun, moon and stars / Rip off / On my life / Commercialization / You can't be wrong and get right / Oh Jamaica / No. 1 rip off man / Brother / House of exile / Long time no see / My love is as solid as rock / My people / Actions speak louder than words / Brave warrior
CD _______ SEECD 83
See For Miles/C5 / Apr '93 / Pinnacle

JIMMY CLIFF
Many rivers to cross / Vietnam / My ancestors / Hard road to travel / Wonderful world, beautiful people / Sufferin' in the land / Hello sunshine / Use what I got / That's the way life goes / Come into my life
CD _______ CDTRL 16
Trojan / Mar '94 / Direct / Jet Star

JIMMY CLIFF
CD _______ EXP 009
Experience / May '97 / TKO Magnum

MANY RIVERS TO CROSS
CD Set _______ CDTRL 342
Trojan / Jun '94 / Direct / Jet Star

REGGAE GREATS
Vietnam / Sitting in limbo / Struggling man / Let your yeah be yeah / Bongo man / Harder they come / Sufferin' in the land / Many rivers to cross / Hard road to travel / You can get it if you really want / Sooner or later
CD _______ RRCD 22
Reggae Refreshers / Nov '90 / PolyGram / Vital

SAVE OUR PLANET EARTH
CD _______ 106552
Musidisc / Oct '90 / Discovery

Clifford, Billy

BILLY CLIFFORD
CD _______ OSS 11CD
Ossian / Mar '88 / ADA / CM / Direct / Highlander

Clifford, Linda

IF MY FRIENDS COULD SEE ME NOW
If my friends could see me now / You are, you are / Runaway love / Broadway gypsy lady / I feel like falling in love / Please darling, don't say goodbye / Gypsy lady
CD _______ CPCD 8158
Charly / Jan '96 / Koch

RIGHT COMBINATION (Clifford, Linda & Curtis Mayfield)
Rock you to your socks / Right combination / I'm so proud / Ain't no love lost / It's lovin' time / Love's sweet sensation / Between you baby and me
CD _______ CPCD 8072
Charly / Jun '94 / Koch

Clifton, Bill

EARLY YEARS 1957-1958, THE
Girl I left in Tennessee / Dixie darlin' / You don't need to think about me ... / I'll be there Mary dear / Paddy on the turnpike / I'll wander back someday / Darling Corey / When you kneel at my mother's grave / Blue ridge mountain blues / Are you alone / Springhill disaster / I'm living the right life now / Lonely heart blues / Cedar Grove / You go to your church / Walking in my sleep / Pal of yesterday / Just another broken heart / Little white washed chimney
CD _______ ROUCD 1021
Rounder / '92 / ADA / CM / Direct

Clifton, Ian

MUSIC FOR LIFE
CD _______ DLD 1033
Dance & Listen / Mar '93 / Savoy / Target/BMG

MUSIC FOR LIFE VOL.2
Blackpool belle / I've told every little star / Aria / Yellow bird / Friends and neighbours / Put on a happy face
CD _______ DLD 1041
Dance & Listen / Nov '93 / Savoy / Target/BMG

Clikatat Ikatowi

LIVE 29-30/8/1995
CD _______ GRAVITY 26CD
Gravity / Apr '97 / Cargo / Greyhound / Plastic Head

Climax Blues Band

BEST OF THE CLIMAX BLUES BAND, THE
Couldn't get it right / Gotta have more love / I love you / California sunshine / Berlin blues / Briefcase / Like Uncle Charlie / Everyday / Rollin' home / Mighty fire / Mean ol' world / Hey Mama / Little girl / Crazy' bout my baby / Louisiana blues / Mole on the dole
CD _______ 12540
Laserlight / Apr '96 / Target/BMG

BLUES FROM THE ATTIC
CD _______ HTDCD 15
HTD / Oct '93 / CM / Pinnacle

CLIMAX CHICAGO BLUES BAND
Mean ol' world / Insurance / Going down this road / You've been drinking / Don't start me talkin' / Wee baby blues / Twenty past one / Stranger in your town / How many more years / Looking for my baby / Lonely, And / Entertainer
CD _______ C5CD 555
See For Miles/C5 / Oct '92 / Pinnacle

COULDN'T GET IT RIGHT...PLUS
Couldn't get it right / Berlin blues / Chasing change / Losin' the humbles / Shopping bag people / Sense of direction / Before you reach the grave / Reaching out / Right now / Cobra / Rollin' home / Sav'ry gravy / Sky high / Loosen up / Running out of time / Mr. Goodtime / I am constant / Mighty fire
CD _______ SEECD 222
See For Miles/C5 / Oct '96 / Pinnacle

DRASTIC STEPS
California sunshine / Lonely avenue / Deceiver / Ordinary people / Winner / Couldn't get it right / Fool for the bright times / Good times / Trouble / American dream / Couldn't get it right (Mix)
CD _______ C5CD 573
See For Miles/C5 / Sep '91 / Pinnacle

FM/LIVE...PLUS
All the time in the world / Flight / Seventh son / Let's work together / Standing by a river / So many roads, so many trains / You make me sick / Shake your love / Going to New York / I am constant / Mesopopmania / Country hat
CD _______ SEECD 279
See For Miles/C5 / Sep '89 / Pinnacle

HARVEST YEARS, THE (1969-1972)
Please don't help me / Hey baby everything's gonna be alright / Yeh yeh yeh / Everyday / Towards the sun / You make me sick / Reap what I've sowed / Shake your love / Looking for my baby / Flight / Mole on the dole / That's all / Insurance / Wee baby blues / Crazy about my baby / All right blue / Cut you loose
CD ______ SEECD 316
See For Miles/C5 / Jun '91 / Pinnacle

LOT OF BOTTLE, A
Country hat / Everyday / Reap what I've sowed / Brief case / Alright blue / Seventh son / Please don't help me / Morning, noon and night / Long lovin' man / Louisiana blues / Cut you loose
CD ______ C5CD 548
See For Miles/C5 / Oct '92 / Pinnacle

PLAYS ON
Flight / Hey baby's everything gonna be alright yeah yeah yeah / Cubano chant / Little girl / Mum's the word / Twenty past two / Temptation rag / So many roads / City ways / Crazy about my baby
CD ______ C5CD 556
See For Miles/C5 / Oct '92 / Pinnacle

RICH MAN
Rich man / Mole on the dole / You make me sick / Standing by a river / Shake your love / All the time in the world / If you wanna know / Don't you mind people grinning in your face
CD ______ C5CD553
See For Miles/C5 / '90 / Pinnacle

TIGHTLY KNIT
Hey mam / Shoot her if she runs / Towards the sun / Come on in my kitchen / Who killed McSwiggen / Little link / St. Michael's blues / Bide my time / That's all
CD ______ C5CD557
See For Miles/C5 / Jun '90 / Pinnacle

Climax Golden Twins

IMPERIAL HOUSEHOLD ORCHESTRA
CD ______ SCRATCH 23
Scratch / Nov '96 / Cargo

Climax Reunion Jazz Band

RETRO JAZZ DOWN UNDER
CD ______ CRJS 95
Retro Jazz / Jul '96 / Jazz Music

Climie, Simon

SOUL INSPIRATION
Soul inspiration / Does your heart still break / Love in the right hands / Dream with me / Oh how the years go by / Don't give up so easy / Spell / Don't waste time (Make your move) / Losing you / Life goes on
CD ______ 4722202
Epic / Jan '93 / Sony

Cline, Nels

CHEST
CD ______ LB 006CD
Little Brother / Apr '97 / Cargo

Cline, Patsy

BEST OF PATSY CLINE
CD ______ DCD 5323
Disky / Dec '93 / Disky / THE

BEST OF PATSY CLINE
CD ______ WMCD 5656
Woodford Music / Jun '92 / THE

COLLECTION, THE
CD ______ COL 007
Collection / Oct '95 / Target/BMG

CRAZY DREAMS
CD ______ TRTCD 177
TrueTrax / Jun '95 / THE

CRAZY DREAMS (2CD Set)
I love you honey / Stop, look and listen / Come on in / He will do for you / Walkin' after midnight / Stranger in my arms / I've loved and lost again / Honky tonk merry go round / Turn the cards slowly / Hidin' out / I cried all the way to the altar / Church, a courtroom and then goodbye / Heart you break may be your own / Today, tomorrow and forever / Pick you up on your way down / Too many secrets / Poor man's roses or rich man's gold / Fingerprints / Don't ever leave me / Three cigarettes in an ashtray / Try again / Then you'll know / I can't forget / In care of the blues / Dear God I go to church on a Sunday / Walking dream / Stop the world / I don't wanta / Hungry for love / Cry not for me / Just out of reach / I'm moving along / If I could see the world / Let the teardrops fall / I can see an angel / Lovesick blues / There she goes / I'm blue again / If I could only stay asleep / That wonderful someone / Ain't no wheels on this ship / Never no more / Yes I understand / Just a closer walk with thee / Love me, love me honey do / Gotta lot of rhythm in my soul / Life's railway to Heaven / Crazy dreams / How can I face tomorrow
CD Set ______ CPCD 82672
Charly / Dec '96 / Koch

CRY NOT FOR ME
If I could only stay sleeping / Heart you break may be your own / Try again / Three cigarettes in a ashtray / If I could see the world / Cry not for me / Yes, I understand / Dear God / I'm blue again / Love, love, love me honey / Stop, look and listen / Don't ever leave me again / Gotta lot of rhythm in my soul / I'm moving along / Honky tonk merry go round / I cried all the way to the alter / Turn the cards slowly / Pick me up on your way down / Come on in / Then you'll know
CD ______ CDSB 005
Starburst / Feb '96 / TKO Magnum

DEFINITIVE PATSY CLINE, THE
CD ______ ARC 94992
ARC / Sep '92 / ADA / ARC Music

DISCOVERY
I don't wanta / Then you'll know / Don't ever leave me again / Two cigarettes in an ashtray / In care of the blues / Your cheatin' heart / Man upstairs / Stop the world (and let me off) / Try again / Walkin' dream / Too many secrets / Down by the riverside / Come on in / Ain't no wheels on this ship / Hungry for love / Walkin' after midnight
CD ______ PLATCD 5902
Platinum / Sep '94 / Prism

DREAMING
Sweet dreams / I fall to pieces / Crazy / Heartaches / Tra le la le la triangle / Have you ever been lonely / Faded love / Your cheatin' heart / She's got you / Walkin' after midnight / San Antonio rose / Three cigarettes in an ashtray / When I need a laugh / Always
CD ______ PLATCD 303
Platinum / Apr '88 / Prism

ESSENTIAL COLLECTION, THE
CD Set ______ MCAD 410421
MCA / Nov '91 / BMG

ESSENTIAL COLLECTION, THE
CD Set ______ LECD 608
Wisepack / Apr '95 / Conifer/BMG / THE

JUST OUT OF REACH
CD ______ MU 5072
Musketeer / Oct '92 / Disc

LEGENDS IN MUSIC
CD ______ LECD 052
Wisepack / Aug '94 / Conifer/BMG / THE

LIVE AT THE CIMARRON BALLROOM
CD ______ MCD 11579
MCA / Aug '97 / BMG

LOVE COUNTRY
True love / Heartaches / Your cheatin' heart / Half as much / I love you so much it hurts / Love letters in the sand / Seven lonely days / Why can't he be you / Your kinda love / Sweet dreams / That's how a heartache begins / There he goes again / Have you ever been lonely / He called me baby / I'll sail my ship alone / You belong to me / Someday (you'll want me to want you) / Lovin' in vain / I fall to pieces / Leavin' on your mind
CD ______ MCLD 19240
MCA / May '94 / BMG

LOVE SONGS
CD ______ CDMFP 5957
Music For Pleasure / Jan '92 / EMI

ONE AND ONLY PATSY CLINE, THE
Stop the world / Walkin' after midnight / Just a closer walk with thee / Just out of reach / I've loved and lost again / Fingerprints / Stranger in my arms / Poor man's roses / I can see an angel / If I could only stay asleep / I'm blue again / Today, tomorrow and forever / I love you honey / Never no more / Love love love me honey / Let the teardrops fall / I'm moving alone / Stop, look and listen
CD ______ ECD 3086
K-Tel / Jan '95 / K-Tel

PATSY CLINE
Just a closer walk with thee / Never no more / Ain't no wheels on this ship / He'll do for you / Honky tonk merry go round / Poor man's roses / Pick me up / Turn the cards slowly / Dear God / I love you honey / I can't forget you / Crazy dreams
CD ______ CD 102
Timeless Treasures / Oct '94 / THE

PATSY CLINE
CD ______ DVAD 6072
Deja Vu / May '95 / THE

PATSY CLINE
CD ______ GOLD 058
Gold / Jul '96 / Else

PATSY CLINE (3CD Set)
Walking after midnight / Fingerprints / Honky tonk merry-go-round / Life's railway to heaven / I can see an angel walkin' / Ain't no wheels on this ship / If I could see the world / I don't wanna / Pick me up on the way down / Come on in / Hidin' out / Hungry for love / If I could only stay asleep / Cry not for me / I cried all the way to the altar / Three cigarettes in the ashtray / Heart you break may be your own / I can't forget / Secrets / I love you honey / I've loved and lost again / Try again / Let the teardrops fall / Stop the world and let me off / Too many secrets / Turn the cards slowly / Just out of reach / Today, tomorrow & forever / Crazy dreams / I'm blue again / I'm moving along / Poor man's roses (or a rich man's gold) / Then you'll know / Hungry for love / How can I face tomorrow / Church, a courtroom & then goodbye / Got a lot of rhythm in my soul / Just a closer walk with thee / Stranger in my arms / That wonderful someone / Lovesick blues / Don't ever leave me
CD Set ______ KBOX 357
Collection / Nov '96 / Target/BMG / TKO Magnum

PATSY CLINE VOL.1
CD ______ DS 003
Desperado / Jun '97 / TKO Magnum

PATSY CLINE VOL.2
CD ______ DS 004
Desperado / Jun '97 / TKO Magnum

PATSY CLINE/BRENDA LEE ESSENTIALS (Cline, Patsy & Brenda Lee)
CD ______ LECDD 628
Wisepack / Aug '95 / Conifer/BMG / THE

PLATINUM COLLECTION, THE (2CD Set)
Church, a courtroom and then goodbye / Honky tonk merry-go-round / Hidin' out / I cried all the way to the altar / I've loved and lost again / Dear God / Walkin' after midnight / Fingerprints / Stranger in my arms / Try again / Then you'll know / Three cigarettes in an ashtray / He will do for you / Poor man's roses (or a rich man's gold) / Hungry for love / I can't forget you / That wonderful someone / Stop the world / If I could see the world (through the eyes of a child) / Cry not for me / Just out of reach (of my two open arms) / Never no more / Walking dream / In the care of the blues / Turn the cards slowly / Gotta lot of rhthm in my soul / Ain't no wheels on this ship / I don't wanna / I love you, honey / Love me honey do / Too many secrets / Let the teardrops fall / I'm moving along / Stop, look and listen / I can see an angel / If I could only stay asleep / I'm blue again / Yes, I understand / Life's railway to heaven / Today, tomorrow and forever
CD Set ______ PC 615
Start / Jul '97 / Disc

SPOTLIGHT ON PATSY CLINE
Walkin' after midnight / I cried all the way to the altar / In care of the blues / I can't forget you / I love you honey / Just out of reach / Walking dream / Today, tomorrow and forever / Let the teardrops fall / Hungry for love / Too many secrets / Never no more / Stop the world / I don't wanna / Turn the cards slowly / I've loved and lost again
CD ______ HADCD 130
Javelin / Feb '94 / Henry Hadaway / THE

STOP THE WORLD
In care of the blues / Stop the world / Too many secrets / Ain't no wheels on this ship / If I could only stay asleep / Never no more / Love me honey do / Three cigarettes in an ashtray / Honky tonk merry go round / Life's railway to heaven / Try again / Fingerprints / Turn the cards slowly / I cried all the way to the altar / Cry not for me / I love you honey / I'm blue again / Let the teardrops fall / Hidin' out
CD ______ MUCD 9029
Musketeer / Apr '95 / Disc

THINKING OF YOU
I don't wanna / I can't forget / If I could see the world / Too many secrets / Hidin' out / Let the teardrops fall / Hungry for love / Walkin' dream / Three cigarettes in an ashtray / I cried all the way to the altar / Stop the world (and let me off) / I love you honey / Fingerprints / Just out of reach / Never no more / Pick me up on your way down / Today tomorrow forever / Honky tonk merry go round / Ain't no wheels on this ship
CD ______ SUMCD 4023
Summit / Nov '96 / Sound & Media

TODAY, TOMORROW AND FOREVER
Walkin' after midnight / Stop, look and listen / Yes I understand / I can see an angel / Just out of reach / Walking dream / Then you'll know / Don't ever leave me again / I can't forget you / I'm hungry, hungry for your love / I don't wanna / I'm moving along / Gotta lot of rhythm in my soul / Just a closer walk with thee / I've loved and lost again / Todya, tomorrow and forever / If I could see the world / Come on in / Pick me up on your way down / Heart you break may be your own / In care of the blues / Stop the world / Too many secrets / Ain't no wheels on this ship / If only I could stay asleep / Never no more / Love me honey do / Three cigarettes in an ashtray / Honky tonk merry go round / Life's railway to heaven / Try again / Fingerprints / Turn the cards slowly / I cried all the way to the altar / Cry not for me / I love you honey / I'm blue again / Let the teardrops fall / Hidin' out
CD Set ______ PAR 2305
Parade / Mar '95 / Disc

TOO MANY SECRETS
Walkin' after midnight / I've loved and lost again / I love you honey / Fingerprints / Never no more / Hidin' out / Walking dream / Let the teardrops fall / Just out of reach / Ain't no wheels on this ship / I can't forget / Too many secrets / In care of the blues / Hungry for love / I don't wanna / If I could see the world / Stop the world (and let me off) / I can see an angel / Today, tomorrow and forever / Life's railway to heaven
CD ______ CDSB 013
Starburst / Jun '96 / TKO Magnum

UNFORGETTABLE
Gotta lot of rhythm in my soul / In care of the blues / Hungry for love / Lovesick blues / Stranger in my arms / Crazy dreams / Honky tonk merry go round / I cried all the way to the altar / Church, a courtroom and then goodbye / I've loved and lost again / Three cigarettes in an ashtray / I can't forget you / Just out of reach / I love you honey / Poor man's roses / Pick me up on your way down / Heart you break may be your own / Turn the cards slowly / That wonderful someone / Don't ever leave me again / Just a closer walk with thee / Dear God / He'll do for you / Never no more
CD ______ PWK 017
Carlton / Feb '96 / Carlton

UNFORGETTABLE CLASSICS VOL.1
CD ______ MACCD 173
Autograph / Aug '96 / BMG

UNFORGETTABLE CLASSICS VOL.2
CD ______ MACCD 223
Autograph / Aug '96 / BMG

VERY BEST OF PATSY CLINE, THE
CD ______ DCDCD 207
Castle / Aug '96 / BMG

VERY BEST OF PATSY CLINE, THE
Sweet dreams / Walking after midnight / Crazy / I fall to pieces / Back in baby's arms / He called me baby / She's got you / When you need a laugh / Heartaches / Faded love / So wrong / Strange / Leavin' on your mind / Why can't he be you / You're stronger than me / When I get thru with you (you'll love me too) / Crazy arms / I can't help it (if I'm still in love with you) / I love you so much it hurts / Anytime / Always lonely street / Your cheatin' heart / Just out of reach / Three cigarettes in an ashtray
CD ______ MCD 11483
MCA / Jun '96 / BMG

WALKIN' AFTER MIDNIGHT (28 Country Classics)
Walkin' after midnight / I've loved and lost again / Poor man's roses / Turn the cards slowly / I cried all the way to the altar / Pick me up on your way down / Stranger in my arms / Honky tonk merry go round / Church a courtroom and then goodbye / Three cigarettes in an ashtray / Never no more / Dear God / Lovesick blues / If I could stay asleep / Just out of reach / Then you'll know / I love honey / Fingerprints / There he goes he'll do for you (what he's done for me) / I can't forget you / Today, tomorrow and forever / Crazy dreams / I can see an angel / If I could see the world
CD ______ PLATCD 27
Platinum / Jul '89 / Prism

WALKIN' AFTER MIDNIGHT
CD ______ CTS 55404
Country Stars / Jan '92 / Target/BMG

WALKIN' AFTER MIDNIGHT
Church, a courtroom then goodbye / Honky tonk merry go round / Hidin' out / I cried all the way to the alter / I've loved and lost again / Dear God / Walkin' after midnight / Fingerprints / Stranger in my arms / Try again / Then you'll know / Three cigarettes in an ashtray / He will do for you / Poor man's roses (or a rich man's gold) / Hungry for love / I can't forget / That wonderful someone / Stop the world (and let me off) / If I could see the world (through the eyes of a child) / Cry not for me / Just out of reach (of my two open arms) / Never no more / Walking dream / In care of the blues / Turn the cards slowly
CD ______ CD 6014
Music / Apr '96 / Target/BMG

WALKIN' AFTER MIDNIGHT
CD ______ PLSCD 111
Pulse / Apr '96 / BMG

Clint Eastwood

AFRICAN ROOTS
CD ______ LG 21054
Lagoon / Mar '93 / Grapevine/PolyGram

STOP THAT TRAIN (Clint Eastwood & General Saint)
Stop Jack / True vegetarian / Everything crash / Monkey man / HAPPY / Stop that train / Vote for me / Nuclear crisis / Rock with me / Shame and scandal
CD ______ GRELCD 53
Greensleeves / Feb '87 / Jet Star / SRD

TWO BAD DJ'S (Clint Eastwood & General Saint)
Can't take another world war / Another one bites the dust / Talk about run / Sweet sweet Matilda / Special request to all prisoner / Dance have fi nice / Gal pon the front line / Jack Spratt / Tribute to General Echo / Hey Mr. DJ
CD ______ GRELCD 24
Greensleeves / '89 / Jet Star / SRD

Clinton, Bill

BILL CLINTON JAM SESSION
CD **PRES 001CD**
Pres / Nov '94 / Direct

Clinton, George

COMPUTER GAMES
Get dressed / Man's best friend / Loopzilla / Pot sharing totts / Computer games / Atomic dog / Free alterations / One fun at a time
CD **MUSCD 511**
MCI Original Masters / May '95 / Disc / THE

FIFTH OF FUNK
Flatman and Robin / Count Funkula (I didn't know that funk was loaded) / Thumparella (Oh Kay) / Eyes of a dreamer / I found you / Ice melting in your heart / Clone ranger / Who do you love / Up up and away / Can't get over losing you / Rat kissed the cat / Too tight for light / Every little bit hurts
CD **ESMCD 490**
Essential / Apr '97 / BMG

GEORGE CLINTON FAMILY SERIES VOL.1 (Various Artists)
Go for yer funk: *Parliament* / Funk it up: *Sterling Silver Starship* / Funkin' for my momma's rent: *Fabulous, Gary & Black Slack* / Send a gram: *Cleaves, Jessica* / Who in the funk do you think you are: *Cleaves, Jessica* / Better days: *Foxxe, Andre* / Chong song: *Collins, Bootsy* / Michelle: *Flastic Brain Flam* / Sunshine of your love: *Blackbyrds* / Interview: *Clinton, George*
CD **ESMCD 383**
Essential / Jul '96 / BMG

GEORGE CLINTON FAMILY SERIES VOL.2 (Various Artists)
May Day (SOS): *Funkadelic* / These feet are made for dancin' (footstranger): *Dunbar, Ron* / Booty body ray for the plush funk: *Sterling Silver Starship* / I really envy the sunshine: *Cleaves, Jessica* / Lickety split: *Wesley, Fred & The Horny Horns* / Common law wife: *Flo* / Superspirit: *Morrison, Junie* / Love don't come easy: *Brides Of Funkenstein* / I can't stand it: *Lewis, Tracey & Andre Fox/Flastic Brain Flam* / Monster dance: *Ford, Ron* / We're just funkers: *Hampton, Michael* / Interview: *Clinton, George*
CD **ESMCD 384**
Essential / Jul '96 / BMG

GEORGE CLINTON FAMILY SERIES VOL.3 (P Is The Funk) (Various Artists)
Clone communicado / Does disc with dat / Shove on / Rock jam / Love is something / Every booty (get on down) / Personal problems / Bubblegum gangster / She's crazy / Think right / In the cabin of my Uncle Jam (P is the funk) / My love / Interview / Commercials
CD **ESMCD 385**
Essential / Jul '96 / BMG

GEORGE CLINTON FAMILY SERIES VOL.4 (Testing Positive For The Funk) (Various Artists)
Live up (to what she thinks of me): *Parliament* / Secrets: *Barnes, Sidney* / She never do's things: *Lewd, Trey* / Take my love: *Brides Of Funkenstein* / Just for play: *Brides Of Funkenstein* / Off the wall: *Cleaves, Jessica* / Get it on: *Jimmy G* / Triune: *Morrison, Junie* / Superstar madness: *Maruga & the Soda Jerks* / One angle: *Funkadelic* / Twenty bucks: *Brides Of Funkenstein* / To care: *Four Tops* / Comin' down from your love: *Savannah, Nick & Dwarf* / Interview: *Clinton, George*
CD **ESMCD 392**
Essential / Jul '96 / BMG

GEORGE CLINTON'S BAG 'O' FUNK (Various Artists)
Atomic dog: *Clinton, George* / Hollywood: *Red Hot Chili Peppers* / May the cube be with you: *Dolby's Cube* / Break my heart: *Jimmy G. & The Tackheads* / Last dance: *Clinton, George* / Get lucky: *Well Red* / Work that sucker to death: *Xavier & George Clinton & Bootsy* / Walk the dinasour: *Goombas & George Clinton* / You and your folks: *Day, Otis & The Knights* / Lies: *Jimmy G. & The Tackheads* / Leave my monkey alone: *Zevon, Warren* / Cool Joe: *Clinton, George* / Checkin' you checkin' yourself out: *Hall, Eramus*
CD **DC 880902**
Disky / Jul '97 / Disky / THE

GREATEST FUNKIN' HITS, THE
Atomic dog: *Clinton, George & Coolio* / Flashlight: *Clinton, George & Q-Tip/Busta Rhymes/Ol' Dirty Bastard* / Booty body ready for the plush funk / Bop gun (one nation): *Clinton, George & Ice Cube* / Break my heart / Mothership connection / Knee deep: *Clinton, George & Digital Underground* / Hey good lookin' / Do fries go with that shake / Atomic / Knee deep: *Clinton, George & Digital Underground* / Mothership connection starchild
CD **PRMDCD 20**
Premier/EMI / Mar '97 / EMI

HEY MAN, SMELL MY FINGER
Martial law / Paint the white house black / Way up / Dis beat disrupts / Get satisfied / Hollywood / Rhythm and rhyme / Big pump / If true love / High in my hello / Maximumisness / Kick back / Flag was still there / Martial law (Hey man, smell my finger)
CD **NPG 60532**
New Power Generation / Mar '95 / EMI

HYDRAULIC FUNK (P-Funk All Stars)
Pump up and down / Pumpin' it up / Copy cat / Hydraulic pump / Throw your hands up in the air / Generator pop / Acupuncture / One of those summers / Catch a keeper / Pumpin' you is so easy / Generator pop (mix)
CD **CDSEWD 097**
Westbound / Jun '95 / Pinnacle

SAMPLE SOME OF DISC, SAMPLE SOME OF DAT
CD **MOLCD 36**
Music Of Life / Nov '94 / Grapevine/ PolyGram

SAMPLE SOME OF DISC, SAMPLE SOME OF DAT VOL.2
CD **MOLCD 33**
Music Of Life / Sep '93 / Grapevine/ PolyGram

TAPOAFOM (Clinton, George & The P-Punk Allstars)
If anybody gets funked up (It's gonna be you) / Summer swim / Funky kind (Gonna knock it down) / Mathematics / Hard as steel / New spaceship / Underground angel / Let's get funky / Flatman and Bobbin / Sloppy seconds / Rock the party / Get your funk on / TAPOAFOM (Fly away)
CD **4838332**
MJJ Music / Jun '96 / Sony

Clinton, Larry

1941 - 1949 (Clinton, Larry & His Orchestra)
CD **CCD 58**
Circle / '92 / Jazz Music / Swift / Wellard

FEELING LIKE A DREAM
Feeling like a dream / Jump Joe / I want to rock / Because of you / Nobody knows the trouble I've seen / Taboo / Sahara / Dance of the reed flutes / Arab dance / I may be wrong / Do you call that a buddy / Rockin' chair / Camptown races
CD **HEPCD 1047**
Hep / Nov '95 / Cadillac / Jazz Music / New Note/Pinnacle / Wellard

SHADES OF HADES (Clinton, Larry & Bea Wain)
Big dipper / Snake charmer / Midnight in the madhouse / I double dare you / I cash clo'es / Two dreams got together / Swing lightly / Military madcaps / I've got my heart set on you / Mr. Jinx stay away from me / True confession / Shades of Hades / Abba dabba / Dr. Rhythm / Campbells are swingin' / Always and always / Jubilee / I was doing all right / One rose (that's left in my heart) / Our love is here to stay / Wolverine blues / Oh Lady be good / Scrapin' the toast
CD **HEPCD 1037**
Hep / Oct '93 / Cadillac / Jazz Music / New Note/Pinnacle / Wellard

STUDIES IN CLINTON
Martha / Study in blue / Night shades / My reverie / Boogie woogie blues / Milenburg joys / Dippermouth blues / Jitterbug / Over the rainbow / Deep purple
CD **HEPCD 1052**
Hep / Nov '96 / Cadillac / Jazz Music / New Note/Pinnacle / Wellard

Clinton, Michelle T.

BLACK ANGELES (Clinton, Michelle T. & Wanda Coleman)
CD **NAR 031CD**
New Alliance / May '93 / Plastic Head

Clique

SELF PRESERVATION SOCIETY
CD **DRCD 003**
Detour / Jul '95 / Detour / Greyhound

Clive Natural

NATURAL MAN
CD **GRCD 9**
Graylan / Jul '97 / Grapevine/PolyGram / Jet Star

Clivilles & Cole

GREATEST REMIXES VOL.1 (Various Artists)
C and C Music Factory MTV medley: *C&C Music Factory* / Because of you: *Cover Girls* / Don't take your love away: *Love, Lydia Lee* / Two to make it right: *Seduction* / Pride (in the name of love): *Clivilles & Cole* / Let the beat hit 'em: *Lisa Lisa & Cult Jam* / Mind your business: *Clivilles & Cole* / You take my breath away: *Cole, David* / Deeper love: *Clivilles & Cole* / Clouds: *Khan, Chaka* / True love: *Billy* / Notice me: *Sandee* / Do it properly: *Two Puerto Ricans & A Black Man/ Dominican*
CD **4879492**
Columbia / Jul '97 / Sony

Clock

IT'S ABOUT TIME VOL.2
Oh what a night / It's over / Whoomph (There it is) / Everybody / You give me love (Rap version) / Axel F / Everybody jump around / Fly away / C'mon everybody / Don't go away / September / Finest / On the beach / Holding on 4 U / Gave you my love / Lonely snowman
CD **MCD 60032**
MCA / Mar '97 / BMG

IT'S TIME
Axel F / Whoomp (There it is) / Everybody / Holding on in the house / Keep the fires burning / Rythm holding on / Keep pushin' / Clock carnival / Secret / Clock ten to two megamix
CD **MCD 11355**
MCA / Sep '95 / BMG

Clock DVA

BLACK WORDS ON WHITE PAPER
CD **CONTECD 172**
Contempo / Oct '93 / Plastic Head

COLLECTIVE
CD Set **HY 39100**
Hyperium / Aug '94 / Cargo / Plastic Head

DIGITAL SOUNDTRACKS
Sensual engine / Cycom / Presence / Sound sweep / Chemicals / Delta machines / Stills in emotion / Inversion / Operator / E-Wave / Diminishing point / Stations of the mind
CD **CONTECD 217**
Contempo / Jan '93 / Plastic Head

MAN AMPLIFIED
CD **CONTECD 182**
Contempo / Mar '92 / Plastic Head

SIGN
CD **CONTECD 225**
Contempo / Sep '93 / Plastic Head

THIRST
CD **CONTECD 192**
Contempo / May '92 / Plastic Head

WHITE SOULS IN BLACK SUITS
CD **CONTECD 157**
Contempo / May '92 / Plastic Head

Clockwise

NOSTALGIA
CD **ERCD 1034**
Empire / Feb '97 / Cargo

Clooney, Rosemary

BEST OF ROSEMARY CLOONEY
Half as much / This ole house / Hey there / Come on a my house / Botch-a-me (ba-ba-baciami piccina) / You're just in love / Mangos / It might as well be spring / In the cool, cool, cool of the evening / Blues in the night / Mambo Italiano / You'll never know / Too old to cut the mustard: *Clooney, Rosemary & Marlene Dietrich* / Beautiful brown eyes / Where will the dimple be / Be my life's companion / Mixed emotions / If teardrops were pennies / I could have danced all night / Tenderly
CD **4840432**
Columbia / May '96 / Sony

BOTCH-A-ME
CD **WW 88020**
World Music / May '93 / Pinnacle

DEDICATED TO NELSON
Foggy day / We're in the money / It's so peaceful in the country / Limehouse blues / Do you know what it means to miss New Orleans / I got it bad and that ain't good / Continental / Mean to me / You're in Kentucky / As time goes by / Haven't got a worry / Mangos / At sundown / Woman likes to be told / What is this thing called love / Come rain or come shine
CD **CCD 4685**
Concord Jazz / Feb '96 / New Note/ Pinnacle

DEMI-CENTENNIAL
Danny boy / Coffee song / I'm confessin' that I love you / I left my heart in San Francisco / Old friends / White Christmas / There will never be another you / Falling in love again / Sophisticated lady / How will I remember you / Mambo italiano / Promise (I'll never say goodbye) / Heart's desire / We'll meet again / Time flies / Dear departed past
CD **CCD 4633**
Concord Jazz / Mar '95 / New Note/ Pinnacle

EVERYTHING'S COMING UP ROSIE (Clooney, Rosemary & Nat Pierce Quintet)
I cried for you / I can't get started (with you) / Do you know what it means to miss New Orleans / I've got such a crush on you / As time goes by / More than you know / Foggy day / Hey there
CD **CCD 4047**
Concord Jazz / Jun '89 / New Note/ Pinnacle

EVERYTHING'S ROSIE
CD **HCD 255**
Hindsight / Nov '94 / Jazz Music / Target/ BMG

FOR THE DURATION
No love, no nothin' / Don't fence me in / I don't want to walk without you / Every time we say goodbye / You'd be so nice to come home to / Sentimental journey / For all we know / September song / These foolish things / They're either too young or too old / More I see you / White cliffs of Dover / Saturday night is the loneliest night of the week / I'll be seeing you
CD **CCD 4444**
Concord Jazz / Feb '91 / New Note/ Pinnacle

GIRL SINGER
Nice 'n' easy / Sweet Kentucky ham / Autumn in New York / Miss Otis regrets / Let there be love / Lovers after all / From this moment on / More than you know / Wave / We fell in love anyway / It don't mean a thing if it ain't got that swing / I'm checkin' out (goodbye) / Of course it's crazy / Straighten up and fly right / Best is yet to come
CD **CCD 4496**
Concord Jazz / Feb '92 / New Note/ Pinnacle

MOTHERS AND DAUGHTERS
Thank heaven for little girls / Always / Face / Baby mine / Best gift / Maria / God bless the child / Look to the rainbow / Turn around / Hello young lovers / Wrap your troubles in dreams / And I'll be there / Sisters / Child is only a moment / Funny face / Look for the silver lining / Pick yourself up
CD **CCD 47542**
Concord Jazz / May '97 / New Note/ Pinnacle

ROSEMARY CLOONEY SINGS BALLADS
CD **CCD 4282**
Concord Jazz / Nov '85 / New Note/ Pinnacle

ROSEMARY CLOONEY SINGS COLE PORTER
CD **CCD 185**
Concord Jazz / '89 / New Note/Pinnacle

ROSEMARY CLOONEY SINGS HAROLD ARLEN
Hooray for love / Happiness is a thing called love / One for my baby (and one more for the road) / Get happy / Ding dong the witch is dead / Out of this world / My shining hour / Let's take the long way home / Stormy weather
CD **CCD 4210**
Concord Jazz / Nov '92 / New Note/ Pinnacle

ROSIE AND BING (Clooney, Rosemary & Bing Crosby)
CD **CD 6018**
Music / Apr '96 / Target/BMG

ROSIE SINGS BING
CD **CCD 4060**
Concord Jazz / Jul '96 / New Note/ Pinnacle

SHOW TUNES
I wish I were in love again / I stayed too long at the fair / How are things in Glocca Morra / When do you start / I'll see you again / Guys and dolls / Manhattan / Everything I've got / Come back to me / Taking a chance on love / All the things you are
CD **CCD 4364**
Concord Jazz / '91 / New Note/Pinnacle

SINGS RODGERS, HART & HAMMERSTEIN
OH what a beautiful morning / People will say we're in love / Love look away / Gentleman is a dope / It might as well be Spring / Sweetest sounds / I could write a book / You took advantage of me / Lady is a tramp / Little girl blue / My romance / Yours sincerely
CD **CCD 4405**
Concord Jazz / Mar '90 / New Note/ Pinnacle

SINGS THE LYRICS OF IRA GERSHWIN
But not for me / Nice work if you can get it / How long has this been going on / Fascinating rhythm / Our love is here to stay / Strike up the band / Long ago and far away / They all laughed / Man that got away / They can't take that away from me
CD **CCD 4112**
Concord Jazz / Mar '90 / New Note/ Pinnacle

SINGS THE LYRICS OF JOHNNY MERCER
CD **CCD 4333**
Concord Jazz / Nov '87 / New Note/ Pinnacle

SINGS THE MUSIC OF IRVING BERLIN
It's a lovely day today / Be careful it's my heart / Cheek to cheek / How about me / Best thing for you would be me / I got lost in his arms / There's no business like show business / Better luck next time / What'll I do / Let's face the music and dance
CD **CCD 4255**
Concord Jazz / Jul '88 / New Note/Pinnacle

SINGS THE MUSIC OF JIMMY VAN HEUSEN
Love won't let you get away / I thought about you / My heart is a hobo / Second time around / It could happen to you / Imagination / Like someone in love / Call me irresponsible / Walking happy / Last dance
CD _____ **CCD 4308**
Concord Jazz / Jan '87 / New Note/ Pinnacle

SOMETHING TO REMEMBER ME BY
This can't be love / Half as much / Tenderly / Zing a little zong / Who kissed me last night / You'll never know / Merry-go-run-around / Blues in the night / I do I do I do / Chicago style / South Rampart Street / Lovely weather for ducks / Something to remember you by / Haven't got a worry to my name / It's only a paper moon / Only forever / Lonely am I / You're in Kentucky sure as you're born / Medley / It's a most unusual day / You're just in love / Bad news / You make me feel so young / Man and woman / Tomorrow I'll dream and remember
CD _____ **JASCD 335**
Jasmine / May '97 / Conifer/BMG / Hot Shot / TKO Magnum

STILL ON THE ROAD
Take me back to manhattan / Rules of the road / On the road again / Let's get away from it all / Road to Morocco / Let's eat home / Till we meet again / Still crazy after all these years / Ol' man river / Moonlight Mississippi / (Back home again in) Indiana / Corcovado / How deep is the ocean / How are things in Glocca Morra / Still on the road
CD _____ **CCD 4590**
Concord Jazz / Mar '94 / New Note/ Pinnacle

TRIBUTE TO BILLIE HOLIDAY - "HERE'S TO MY LADY"
CD _____ **CCD 4081**
Concord Jazz / Jul '92 / New Note/ Pinnacle

WITH LOVE
Just the way you are / Way we were / Alone at last / Come in from the rain / Meditation / Hello, young lovers / Just in time / Tenderly / Will you still be mine
CD _____ **CCD 4144**
Concord Jazz / '89 / New Note/Pinnacle

Close Lobsters

HEADACHE RHETORIC
CD _____ **FIRE 33017**
Fire / Oct '91 / Pinnacle / RTM/Disc

Closedown

NEARFIELD
CD _____ **SR 9469CD**
Silent / Jan '95 / Cargo / Plastic Head

Clouds

SCRAPBOOK/WATERCOLOUR DAYS
CD _____ **BGOCD 317**
Beat Goes On / Jul '96 / Pinnacle

Clout

CLOUT
CD _____ **12366**
Laserlight / May '94 / Target/BMG

Cloven Hoof

DOMINATOR
Rising up / Nova battlestar / Reach for the sky / Warrior of the wasteland / Invaders / Fugitive / Dominator / Road of eagles
CD _____ **HMRXD 113**
FM / Jul '88 / Revolver / Sony

SULTAN'S RANSOM, A
Astral rider / Forgotten heroes / DVR / Jekyll and Hyde / 1001 Nights / Silver surfer / Notre dame / Mad mad world / Highlander / Mistress of the forest
CD _____ **HMRXD 129**
Heavy Metal / Aug '89 / Revolver / Sony

Cloverleaf

BORN A RIDER
CD _____ **HY 200129CD**
Hypertension / Mar '95 / ADA / CM / Direct / Total/BMG

Clovers

CLOVERS, THE
Love love love / Lovey dovey / Yes it's you / Ting-a-ling / I played the fool / Hey Miss Fannie / Don't you know I love you / Middle of the night / Blue velvet / Little Mama / Crawlin' / Here goes a fool / I got my eyes on you / Devil or angel / Skylark / Needless / Comin' on / One mint julep / Wonder where my baby's gone / Good lovin' / I confess / Feeling is good / Down in the alley / Your cash ain't nothing but trash
CD _____ **RSACD 857**
Sequel / Jan '97 / BMG

DANCE PARTY
Lovebug / All about you / If I could be loved by you / So young / Down in the alley / Nip sip / I, I love you / In the morning time / Your tender love / Fool fool fool / Wishing for your love / There's no tomorrow / Your cash ain't nothing but trash / Alrighty oh sweetie / If you love me (why don't you tell me so) / Love love love / Hey doll baby / Baby baby oh my darling / Bring me love / I'm a lonely fool / From the bottom of my heart / You good lookin' woman / Here comes romance / Bootie green / Drive it home
CD _____ **RSACD 858**
Sequel / Jan '97 / BMG

DOWN IN THE ALLEY
One mint julip / Good lovin' / Don't you know I love you / Wonder where my baby's gone / Ting a ling / Crawlin' / Hey Miss Fannie / Lovey dovey / Middle of the night / Fool fool fool / I've got my eyes on you / I confess / Your cash ain't nothin' but trash / Little Mama / Down in the alley / Nip slip / Devil or angel / Blue velvet / In the morning time / Love bug / If I could be loved by you
CD _____ **7567823122**
Atlantic / Mar '93 / Warner Music

Clusone Trio

CLUSONE 3
CD _____ **RAMBOY 05**
Bvhaast / Oct '94 / Cadillac

I AM AN INDIAN
CD _____ **GCD 79505**
Gramavision / Oct '95 / Vital/SAM

LOVE HENRY
Introduction / Improvisation no.1 / When I lost you / Improvisation no.2 / It's you / Improvisation no.6 / Cuckoo in the clock / Uninhabited island / Improvisation no.4 / Bilbao song / Restless in pieces / Love Henry / In the company of angels / Comodo / Pilar/Moeder / White Christmas / Ao velho Pedro / Goodbye
CD _____ **GCD 79517**
Gramavision / Mar '97 / Vital/SAM

SOFT LIGHTS AND SWEET MUSIC
CD _____ **ART 6153CD**
Hat Art / Jul '94 / Cadillac / Harmonia Mundi

Cluster

CLUSTER
CD _____ **SOUL 17**
Soul Static Sound / Feb '97 / SRD

CLUSTER & BRIAN ENO (Cluster & Brian Eno)
CD _____ **SKYCD 3010**
Sky / Nov '94 / Greyhound / Koch / Vital/ SAM

CLUSTER VOL.2
CD _____ **14864**
Spalax / Oct '96 / ADA / Cargo / Direct / Discovery / Greyhound

CURIOSUM
CD _____ **SKYCD 3063**
Sky / May '95 / Greyhound / Koch / Vital/ SAM

ERUPTION
CD _____ **MT 365**
Marginal Talent / May '97 / Greyhound

FIRST ENCOUNTER TOUR (2CD Set)
CD Set _____ **CLP 9933**
Cleopatra / Mar '97 / Cargo / Greyhound / Plastic Head / RTM/Disc / SRD

GROSSES WASSER
CD _____ **SKYCD 3027**
Sky / Nov '94 / Greyhound / Koch / Vital/ SAM

ONE HOUR
CD _____ **105865**
Clear Spot / Dec '96 / Cargo / SRD

SOWIESOSO
CD _____ **SKYCD 3005**
Sky / Nov '94 / Greyhound / Koch / Vital/ SAM

ZUCKERZEIT
Hollywood / Caramel / Rote Riki / Rosa / Caramba / Fotschi tong / James / Marzipan / Rotor / Heisse Lippen
CD _____ **14865**
Spalax / Oct '96 / ADA / Cargo / Direct / Discovery / Greyhound

Clutch

TRANS NATIONAL SPEEDWAY LEAGUE
Shogun named Marcus / El Jefe speaks / Binge and purge / Twelve Ounce epilogue / Bacchanal / Milk of human kindness / Rats / Earthworm / Heirloom 13 / Walking in the great shining path of monster trucks / Effigy
CD _____ **7567922812**
Warner Bros. / Oct '93 / Warner Music

Clydesiders

CROSSING THE BORDERS
CD _____ **RECD 502**
REL / Mar '96 / CM / Duncans / Highlander

CMU

SPACE CABARET/OPEN SPACES
Space cabaret / Song from the 4th era / Doctor am I normal / Light shine / Voodoo man / Japan / Mystical sounds / Archway 272 / Distand thought, a point of light / Dream / Henry / Slow and lonesome blues / Clown / Open spaces
CD _____ **SEECD 373**
See For Miles/C5 / Jun '93 / Pinnacle

Coal Chamber

COAL CHAMBER
Loco / Oddity / Bradley / Unspoiled / Sway / Big truck / First / Maricon puto / I / Clock / My frustration / Amir of the desert / Dreamtime / Pig
CD _____ **RR 88632**
Roadrunner / Mar '97 / PolyGram

Coal Porters

LAND OF HOPE & CROSBY
CD _____ **SID 002**
Prima / Sep '94 / Direct

REBELS WITHOUT APPLAUSE
CD _____ **RUB 17**
Rubber / Jul '95 / ADA / CM / Direct / Jazz Music / Roots

Coast

BIG JET RISING
CD _____ **SUGA 13CD**
Sugar / Apr '97 / RTM/Disc

Coasters

COAST ALONG WITH THE COASTERS
(Ain't that) just like me / Keep on rollin' / Wait a minute / Stewball / Snake and the bookworm / What about us / Little Egypt / Wake me, shake me / Run run run / My babe / Bad blood / Girls girls girls / Crazy baby / Bell bottom slacks and a chinese kimono / Ladylike / Thumbin' a ride / Ridin' hood / Hongry / Teach me how to shimmy / Bull tick waltz / PTA / Slime / I'm a hog for you / Hey sexy
CD _____ **RSACD 871**
Sequel / Mar '97 / BMG

COASTERS, THE
One kiss led to another / Brazil / Turtle dovin' / Smokey Joe's cafe / Wrap it up / Riot in cell block no.9 / Loop de loop mambo / One kiss / I must be dreamin' / Lola / Framed / Down in Mexico / Hatchet man / Just like a fool / I love Paris / Whadaya want / If teardrops were kisses / Sweet Georgia Brown / My baby comes to me / Idol with the golden head / What is the secret of your success / Wait a minute / Dance / Gee golly / Three cool cats
CD _____ **RSACD 868**
Sequel / Mar '97 / BMG

GREATEST HITS
Poison Ivy / Along came Jones / Shadow knows / I'm a hog for you baby / Charlie Brown / Yakety yak / Zing went the strings of my heart / That's rock 'n' roll / Searchin' / Youngblood / She's a yum yum / Saturday night fish fry / What about us / Run red run / Keep on rollin' / Three cool cats / Bad blood / Little Egypt / Girls girls girls / Sorry but I'm gonna have to pass / Besame mucho / Shoppin' for clothes / Bad detective / Lovey dovey
CD _____ **RSACD 869**
Sequel / Mar '97 / BMG

JUST COASTIN'
I got to boogie / If I had a hammer / Poison ivy / Young blood / Along came Jones / Searchin' / Charlie Brown / Yakety yak / Benjamin and Loretta / Chick is guilty
CD _____ **C5CD 579**
See For Miles/C5 / Feb '92 / Pinnacle

LEGENDS IN MUSIC
CD _____ **LECD 076**
Wisepack / Jul '94 / Conifer/BMG / THE

ONE BY ONE
But beautiful / Satin doll / Gee baby ain't I good to you / Autumn leaves / You'd be so nice to come home to / Moonlight in Vermont / Moonglow / Easy living / Way you look tonight / Don't get around much anymore / Willow weep for me / On the sunny side of the street / Girls girls girls / Climb / T'ain't nothing to me / Speedo's back in town / I must be dreamin' / Money money / Let's go get stoned / Along came Jones / Charlie Brown / That is rock and roll / Stewball / Wild one / Riding hood
CD _____ **RSACD 870**
Sequel / Mar '97 / BMG

VERY BEST OF THE COASTERS, THE
Riot in cell block 9 / Smoky Joe's cafe / Down in mexico / Searchin' / Idol with the golden head / Young blood / yakety yak / Charlie Brown / Along comes Jones / That is rock and roll / I'm a hog for you / Poison ivy / What about us / Run red run / Little Eygpt / Shoppin' for clothes / Sorry but I'm gonna have to pass
CD _____ **9548326562**
Atlantic / Mar '94 / Warner Music

WHAT IS THE SECRET TO YOUR SUCCESS, 1957-64
My baby comes to me / Gee Golly / Sorry but I'm gonna have to pass / Teach me how to shimmy / PTA
CD _____ **RBD 102**
Mr. R&B / Jan '91 / CM / Swift / Wellard

Coates, Eric

ERIC COATES
CD _____ **GEMMCD 9973**
Pearl / Sep '92 / Harmonia Mundi

THREE ELIZABETHS, THE
Three Elizabeths suite / Music everywhere / Last love / Jester at the wedding / Fanfare no.1 - Salute the soldier / Summer afternooon idyll / Footlights concert waltz / Seven seas / From meadow to Mayfair / Music of the night / Green hills o' Somerset / Stonecracker John / Bird songs at Eventide / Four centuries suite / Impression of a princess / London calling / Moon magic / Joyous youth / Eighth Army march / Mirage / I pitch my lonely caravan at night / Sweet seventeen / Selfish giant / Holborn march / Under the stars / Moresque / Dancing nights / Over to you
CD _____ **75605523902**
Happy Days / Jul '96 / Conifer/BMG

Cobb, Arnett

AGAIN WITH MILT BUCKNER (Cobb, Arnett & Milt Buckner)
CD _____ **BLE 590522**
Black & Blue / Apr '91 / Discovery / Koch / Wellard

ARNETT BLOWS FOR 1300
Arnett blows for 1300 / Go, red go / Walkin' with Sid / Dutch kitchen bounce / Running with Ray / Big league blues / Cobb's idea / When I grow too old to dream / Pay it no mind / Cobb's boogie / Flower garden blues / Cobb's corner / Top flight / Chick she ain't nowhere / Still flying
CD _____ **DD 471**
Delmark / Mar '97 / ADA / Cadillac / CM / Direct / Hot Shot

BLUE AND SENTIMENTAL (Cobb, Arnett & Red Garland Trio)
CD _____ **PCD 24122**
Prestige / Nov '95 / Cadillac / Complete/ Pinnacle

DEEP PURPLE
CD _____ **BB 8642**
Black & Blue / Apr '96 / Discovery / Koch / Wellard

IT'S BACK
CD _____ **PCD 7037**
Progressive / '91 / Jazz Music

LIVE IN PARIS, 1974 (Cobb, Arnett & Tiny Grimes)
CD _____ **FCD 133**
France's Concert / '89 / BMG / Jazz Music

SMOOTH SAILING
CD _____ **OJCCD 323**
Original Jazz Classics / Dec '95 / Complete/Pinnacle / Jazz Music / Wellard

TENOR TRIBUTE (Cobb, Arnett & Jimmy Heath/Joe Henderson)
CD _____ **1211842**
Soul Note / Oct '90 / Cadillac / Harmonia Mundi / Wellard

Cobb, Jimmy

ENCOUNTER
CD _____ **PHIL 662**
Philology / Oct '94 / Cadillac / Harmonia Mundi

Cobb, Junie C.

COLLECTION 1926-1929, THE
CD _____ **COCD 14**
Collector's Classics / Oct '91 / Cadillac / Complete/Pinnacle / Jazz Music

Cobbs, Willie

DOWN TO EARTH
CD _____ **R 2628**
Rooster / Nov '94 / Direct

Cobham, Billy

BEST OF BILLY COBHAM, THE
Quadrant 4 / Snoopy's search / Red baron / Spanish moss / Moon germs / Stratus / Pleasant pheasant / Solo panhandler / Do whatcha wanna
CD _____ **7567815582**
Atlantic / Jan '93 / Warner Music

FLIGHT TIME (Billy Cobham Live)
Flight time / Antares / 6 persimmons / Day grace / Whisperer / Princess / Jackhammer
CD _____ **INAK 8616CD**
In Akustik / Jul '97 / Direct / TKO Magnum

NORDIC
CD _____ **RHYTHM 101**
Rhythm / Feb '97 / Discovery

SPECTRUM
Quadrant 4 / Searching for the right door / Spectrum / Anxiety / Taurian matador / Stratus / To the women in my life / Le lis / Snoopy's search / Red Baron
CD _______________ 7567814282
Atlantic / Jan '93 / Warner Music

STRATUS
Drum solo intro/Stratus / AC/DC / Kasia / All Hallows Eve / Wrapped in a cloud / Drum solo / Total eclipse / Brooze
CD _______________ INAK 813CD
In Akustik / Jul '97 / Direct / TKO Magnum

TRAVELLER, THE
Alfa waves / All that your soul provides / Balancing act / What if / Dipping the biscuits in the soup / Fragolino / Just one step away / Mushu Creole blues / On the inside track / Soul provider
CD _______________ ECD 220982
Evidence / Jul '94 / ADA / Cadillac / Harmonia Mundi

Cobra

GOLDMINE (Mad Cobra)
CD _______________ RASCD 3110
Ras / Apr '93 / Direct / Greensleeves / Jet Star / SRD

MAD COBRA
CD _______________ CSCD 001
Graylan / Oct '92 / Grapevine/PolyGram / Jet Star

SEXPERIENCE (Mad Cobra)
Real men / Sexperience / Never forget / Just party / Sex drive / Change position / Respect / Justice / Wish you were here / Def rock
CD _______________ VERSCD 1
Versatal / Jan '96 / Jet Star

SHOOT TO KILL (Mad Cobra)
CD _______________ RNCD 2020
Rhino / Aug '93 / Grapevine/PolyGram / Jet Star

VENOM (Mad Cobra)
Platinum / Mark 10 / Mr. Pleasure / Wife and darling / RIP / Length and bend / Hotness / To the max / Gal a model / Heartless / Fat and buff / Mate no ready
CD _______________ GRELCD 202
Greensleeves / Mar '94 / Jet Star / SRD

YOUR WISH
CD _______________ LG 21059
Lagoon / Nov '92 / Grapevine/PolyGram

Cobra Verde

EGOMANIA (LOVE SONGS)
CD _______________ SCAT 67
Scat / Jun '97 / Greyhound

VIVA LA MUERTE
Was it good / Gimme your heart / Montenegro / Despair / Debt / Already dead / Until the killing time / I thought you knew (what pleasure was) / Cease to exist
CD _______________ SCT 0362
Matador / Oct '94 / Vital

Cobras

ONCE BITTEN
CD _______________ PEPCD 117
Pollytone / Nov '96 / Nervous / Pollytone

Cochabamba

GREATEST HITS
CD _______________ PV 758 11
Disques Pierre Verany / '88 / Kingdom

Cochise

BEST OF COCHISE
Past loves / Trafalgar day / Moment and the end / Watch this space / China / That's why I sing the blues / Strange image / Down country girls / Home again / Another day / Love's made a fool of you / Cajun girl / Diamonds / Blind love / Thunder in the crib / Midnight moonshine
CD _______________ EDCD 254
Edsel / Sep '92 / Pinnacle

Cochran, Charles

HAUNTED HEART
CD _______________ ACD 177
Audiophile / May '95 / Jazz Music

Cochran, Eddie

BEST OF EDDIE COCHRAN, THE
Summertime blues / C'mon everybody / Three steps to heaven / Sittin' in the balcony / Drive in show / Jeanie, Jeanie, Jeanie / Teenage heaven / Somethin' else / My way / Cut across Shorty / Twenty flight rock / Weekend / Hallelujah I love her so / Lonely / Sweetie Pie / Three stars / Skinny Jim / Nervous breakdown / Completely sweet / Rock'n'roll blues
CD _______________ CDMFP 6268
Music For Pleasure / Sep '96 / EMI

CRUISIN' THE DRIVE IN
CD _______________ RSRCD 009
Rockstar / Jan '96 / Direct / Nervous / Rollercoaster / TKO Magnum

EARLY YEARS, THE
Skinny Jim: *Capehart, Jerry* / Half loved: *Capehart, Jerry* / Tired and sleepy: *Capehart, Jerry* / That's what it takes to make a man: *Capehart, Jerry* / Pink pegged slacks: *Cochran Brothers* / Open the door: *Cochran Brothers* / Country jam: *Stone, Albert* / Don't bye bye baby me: *Stone, Albert* / My love to remember: *Stone, Albert* / Guybo: *Stone, Albert* / Dark lonely street: *Stone, Albert* / If I were dying: *Stone, Albert* / Jelly bean / Latch on: *Capehart, Jerry* / Slow down: *Cochran Brothers* / Fool's paradise: *Cochran Brothers* / Bad baby doll: *Weaver, Darry* / Itty bitty Betty: *Weaver, Darry* / Heart of a fool: *Capehart, Jerry* / Instrumental blues
CD _______________ CDCH 237
Ace / Nov '93 / Pinnacle

EDDIE COCHRAN BOX SET, THE (4CD Set)
Tired and sleepy / Fool's paradise / Open the door / Slow down / Pink peg slacks / Latch on / My love to remember / Yesterday's heartbreak / I'm ready / Blue suede shoes / Long tall Sally / Half loved / Skinny Jim / I almost lost my mind / Twenty flight rock / That's my desire / Completely sweet / Cotton picker / Sittin' in the balcony / Dark lonely street / One kiss / Mean when I'm mad / Drive-in show / Cradle baby / Undying love / Am I blue / Tell me why / Sweetie pie / I'm alone because I love you / Stockings 'n' shoes / Proud of you / Lovin' time / Teenage cutie / Never / Jeannie Jeannie Jeannie / Pocket full of hearts / Little Lou / Pretty girl / Teresa / Nervous breakdown / Summertime blues / Love again / Let's get together / Lonely / C'mon everybody / Don't ever let me go / Teenage heaven / I've waited so long / My way / I remember / Three stars / Rock 'n' roll blues / Weekend / Think of me / Boll weevil song / Three steps to heaven / Cut across shorty / Cherished memories / Guybo / Strollin' guitar / Eddie's blues / Jam sandwich / Hammy blues / Fourth man theme / Country jam / Hallelujah, I love her so / Something else / Money honey / Have I told you lately that I love you / Milk cow blues / I don't like you no more / Sweet little sixteen / White lightning / Jelly bean / Little angel / Don't bye bye baby me / You oughta see grandma rock / Heart-breakin' mama / Slowly but surely / Keeper of the key / Let's coast awhile / I want Elvis for Christmas / How'd ja do / Don't wake up the kids / Willa Mae / It happened to me / Chicken shot blues
CD Set _______________ CDECB 1
Liberty / Mar '91 / EMI

EP COLLECTION, THE
Skinny Jim / Twenty flight rock / Sittin' in the balcony / Blue suede shoes / Pink peg slacks / Mean when I'm mad / Stockin's 'n' shoes / Jeannie Jeannie Jeannie / Pretty girl / Teresa / Sweetie pie / C'mon everybody / Summertime blues / I remember / Rock 'n' roll blues / Milk cow blues / Little angel / Cherished memories / Three steps to heaven
CD _______________ SEECD 271
See For Miles/C5 / Jan '91 / Pinnacle

LA SESSIONS
Jelly bean / Don't bye bye baby me / Half loved / My love to remember / Dark lonely Street / Guybo / Strollin' guitar / Fourth man theme / Chicken shot blues / Bad baby doll / Lovin' I'm wastin' / Itty bitty Betty / Seriously in love / Fontella / It's Heaven / My baby she loves me / Take my hand / Once more / Bread Fred / Hide and go seek / If I were dying / I wanna know / Uh oh little girl / I can't let you go
CD _______________ RSRCD 003
Rockstar / Apr '94 / Direct / Nervous / Rollercoaster / TKO Magnum

MIGHTY MEAN
CD _______________ RSRCD 008
Rockstar / May '95 / Direct / Nervous / Rollercoaster / TKO Magnum

ONE MINUTE TO ONE
CD _______________ RSRCD 010
Rockstar / Oct '96 / Direct / Nervous / Rollercoaster / TKO Magnum

ROCK 'N' ROLL (3CD Set/The Originals) (Cochran, Eddie/Fats Domino/Gene Vincent)
Singin' to my baby: *Cochran, Eddie* / Sittin' in the balcony: *Cochran, Eddie* / Completely sweet: *Cochran, Eddie* / Undying love: *Cochran, Eddie* / I'm alone: *Cochran, Eddie* / Because I love you: *Cochran, Eddie* / Lovin' time: *Cochran, Eddie* / Proud of you: *Cochran, Eddie* / Am I blue: *Cochran, Eddie* / Twenty flight rockers: *Cochran, Eddie* / Drive in show: *Cochran, Eddie* / Mean when I'm mad: *Cochran, Eddie* / Stockins'n'shoes: *Cochran, Eddie* / Tell me why: *Cochran, Eddie* / Have I told you lately that I love you: *Cochran, Eddie* / Cradle baby: *Cochran, Eddie* / One kiss: *Cochran, Eddie* / My blue heaven: *Domino, Fats* / Swanee river hop: *Domino, Fats* / Second line jump: *Domino, Fats* / Goodbye: *Domino, Fats* / Careless love: *Domino, Fats* / I love her: *Domino, Fats* / I'm in love again: *Domino, Fats* / When my dreamboat comes home: *Domino, Fats* / Are you going my way: *Domino, Fats* / If you need me: *Domino, Fats* / My heart is in your hands: *Domino, Fats* / Fats frenzy: *Domino, Fats* / Blue jean bop: *Vincent, Gene* / Jezebel: *Vincent, Gene* / Who slapped John: *Vincent, Gene* / Ain't she sweet: *Vincent, Gene* / I flipped: *Vincent, Gene* / Waltz of the wind: *Vincent, Gene* / Jump back: *Vincent, Gene* / Wedding bells: *Vincent, Gene* / Jumps, giggles and shouts: *Vincent, Gene* / Lazy river: *Vincent, Gene* / Bop street: *Vincent, Gene* / Pet o' my heart: *Vincent, Gene*
CD Set _______________ CDOMB 006
EMI / Mar '97 / EMI

ROCK 'N' ROLL LEGEND
Pink peg slacks / Latch on (version 1) / My love to remember / Heart of a fool / Yesterday's heartbreak / Latch on (version 2) / Tired and sleepy / Fool's paradise / Slow down / Open the door / Skinny Jim / Half loved / Drownin' all my sorrows / Let's coast awhile / Dark lonely street / Guybo / Take my hand / Jelly bean / Don't bye bye baby me / Chicken shot blues
CD _______________ RSRCD 001
Rockstar / Apr '94 / Direct / Nervous / Rollercoaster / TKO Magnum

SUMMERTIME BLUES
CD _______________ RMB 75054
Remember / Nov '93 / Total/BMG

SUMMERTIME BLUES
C'mon everybody / Summertime blues / Yesterday's heartbreak / That's my desire / Completely sweet / Mean when I'm mad / Undying love / I'm alone because I love you / Stockin's 'n' shoes / Lovin' time / Never / Nervous breakdown / Rock 'n' roll blues / Fourth man theme
CD _______________ 16151
Laserlight / Sep '96 / Target/BMG

VERY BEST OF EDDIE COCHRAN, THE (The Anniversary Album)
C'mon everybody / Three steps to heaven / Weekend / Skinny Jim / Completely sweet / Milk cow blues / Cut across shorty / Hallelujah, I love her so / Something else / Blue suede shoes / Eddie's blues / Sittin' in the balcony / Summertime blues / Twenty flight rock / Three stars / Cherished memories
CD _______________ CDFA 3019
Fame / Mar '90 / EMI

Cochrane, Brenda

VOICE, THE
You're the voice / Pearl's a singer / Right here waiting for you / New York, New York / You've lost that lovin' feelin' / You make lovin' fun / I want to know what love is / Wind beneath my wings / Easy to love / Put the weight on my shoulders / All night long
CD _______________ 8431412
Polydor / Mar '90 / PolyGram

Cochrane, Michael

IMPRESSIONS
De ja vu / There will never be another you / Cinco / Impressions / Ballade / Bud Powell / Raindrops / Escape / Blues for Gwen
CD _______________ LCD 15482
Landmark / Jun '96 / New Note/Pinnacle

SONG OF CHANGE (Cochrane, Michael Trio)
CD _______________ 1212512
Soul Note / Nov '93 / Cadillac / Harmonia Mundi / Wellard

Cochrane, Tom

RAGGED ASS ROAD
I wish you well / Wildest dreams / Just scream / Paper tiger / Crawl / Ragged Ass Road / Flowers in the concrete / Dreamer's dream / Message / Best waste of time / Will of the gun / Song before I leave
CD _______________ CDEST 2268
Capitol / Oct '95 / EMI

Cock 'n' Bull Band

BELOW THE BELT
CD _______________ C & B 104CD
Cock & Bull / Dec '93 / ADA

PUMPED UP AND LOADED
CD _______________ MCRCD 6992
Mrs. Casey / Jun '96 / ADA / Direct

Cock Sparrer

SHOCK TROOPS
CD _______________ AHOYCD 4
UN Recordings / Aug '93 / Plastic Head

SHOCK TROOPS/RUNNIN RIOT IN 84
CD _______________ SLOG CD 4
Slogan / Aug '92 / BMG

Cockburn, Bruce

BIG CIRCUMSTANCE
If a tree falls / Shipwrecked at the stable door / Gospel of bondage / Don't feel your touch / Tibetan side of town / Understanding nothing / Where the death squad lives / Radium rain / Pangs of love / Gift / Anything can happen
CD _______________ REVXD 122
FM / Jan '89 / Revolver / Sony

CHARITY OF THE NIGHT
Night train / Get up Jonah / Pacing the cage / Mistress of storms / Whole night sky / Coming rains / Birmingham shadows / Mines of Mozambique / Live on my mind / Charity of night / Strange waters
CD _______________ RCD 10366
Rykodisc / Feb '97 / ADA / Vital

DANCING IN THE DRAGON'S JAWS
Creation dream / Hills of the morning / Badlands flashback / Northern lights / After the rain / Wondering where the lions are / Incandescent blue / No footprints
CD _______________ REVXD 127
FM / Jul '89 / Revolver / Sony

HUMANS
Grim travellers / Rumours of glory / More not more / You get bigger as you go / What about the bond / How I spent my fall vacation / Guerilla betrayed / Tokyo / Fascist architecture / Rose above the sky
CD _______________ REVXD 124
FM / Jul '89 / Revolver / Sony

LIVE
Silver wheels / World of wonders / Rumours of glory / See how I miss you / After the rain / Call it democracy / Wondering where the lions are / Nicaragua / Broken wheel / Stolen land / Always look on the bright side of life / Tibetan side of town / To raise the morning star / Maybe the poet
CD _______________ COOKCD 034
Cooking Vinyl / Apr '90 / Vital

STEALING FIRE
CD _______________ REVXD 125
FM / Jul '89 / Revolver / Sony

TROUBLE WITH NORMAL
Trouble with normal / Candy man's gone / Hoop dancer / Waiting for the moon / Tropic moon / Going up against chaos / Put our hearts together / Civilization and its discontents / Planet of the clowns
CD _______________ REVXD 126
FM / Jul '89 / Revolver / Sony

WAITING FOR A MIRACLE (Singles 1970-1987)
Mama just wants to barrelhouse all night long / All the diamonds in the world / Burn / Silver wheels / Laughter / Wondering where the lions are / Tokyo / Fascist architecture / Trouble with normal / Rumours of glory / Coldest night of the year / You pay your money and take your chance / Lovers in a dangerous time / If I had a rocket launcher / Peggy's kitchen wall / People see through you / Call it democracy / Stolen land / Waiting for a miracle / One day I walk / It's going down slow
CD _______________ REVXD 90
Revolver / May '87 / Revolver / Sony

WORLD OF WONDERS
They call it democracy / Lily of the midnight sky / World of wonder / Berlin tonight / People see through you / See how I miss you / Santiago dawn / Dancing in paradise / Down here tonight
CD _______________ REVXD 73
Revolver / Mar '87 / Revolver / Sony

Cocker, Joe

BEST OF JOE COCKER, THE
Unchain my heart (90's version) / You can leave your hat on / When the night comes / Up where we belong / Now that the magic has gone / Don't you love me anymore / I can hear the river / Sorry seems to be the hardest word / Shelter me / Feels like forever / Night calls / Don't let the sun go down on me / Now that you're gone / Civilised man / When a woman cries / With a little help from my friends
CD _______________ CDESTU 2187
Capitol / Oct '92 / EMI

CIVILISED MAN/COCKER/UNCHAIN MY HEART (The Originals/3CD Set)
Civilzed man / There goes my baby / Come on in / Tempted / Long drag off a cigarette / I love the night / Crazy in love / Girl like you / Hold on (I feel our love is changing) / Even a fool would let go / You can leave your hat on / Heart of the matter / Inner city blues / Love is on a fade / Heaven / Shelter me / A to z / Don't you love me any more / Livin' without your love / Don't drink the water / Unchain my heart / One / Two wrongs don't make a right / I stand in wonder / River's rising / Isolation / All our tomorrows / Woman loves a man / Trust in me / Satisfied / You can leave your hat on
CD Set _______________ CDOMB 024
EMI / Mar '97 / EMI

CIVILIZED MAN
Civilized man / There goes my baby / Come on in / Tempted / Long drag off a cigarette / I love the night / Crazy in love / Girl like you / Hold on (I feel our love is changing) / Even a fool would let go
CD _______________ EJ 2401392
Capitol / Apr '92 / EMI

COCKER
You can leave your hat on / Heart of the matter / Inner city blues / Love is on a fade / Heaven / Shelter me / A to Z / Don't you love me anymore / Livin' without your love / Don't drink the water

CD ____ CDEST 2009
Capitol / Jul '94 / EMI

COCKER HAPPY
Hitchcock railway / She came in through the bathroom window / Marjorine / She's so good to me / Hello little friend / With a little help from my friends / Delta lady / Darling be home soon / Do I still figure in your life
CD ____ CUCD 01
Disky / Oct '94 / Disky / THE

ESSENTIAL, THE
Up where we belong / Sweet lil' woman / Easy rider / Threw it away / Ruby Lee / Many rivers to cross / Taking back the night / Honky tonk woman / Sticks and stones / Cry me a river / Please give peace a chance / She came in thru the bathroom window / Letter / Delta lady
CD ____ 5514082
Spectrum / Nov '95 / PolyGram

FAVOURITE RARITIES
CD ____ RA 95022
BR Music / Sep '94 / Target/BMG

FIRST TIME
CD ____ 5501262
Spectrum / Oct '93 / PolyGram

HAVE A LITTLE FAITH
Let the healing begin / Have a little faith in me / Simple things / Summer in the city / Great divide / Highway highway / Too cool / Soul time / Out of the blue / Angeline / Hell and high water / Standing knee deep in a river / Take me home
CD ____ CDEST 2233
Capitol / Sep '97 / EMI

HITCHCOCK RAILWAY
CD ____ JHD 030
Tring / Jun '92 / Tring

JOE COCKER LIVE
Feeling alright / Shelter me / Hitchcock railway / Up where we belong / Guilty / You can leave your hat on / When the night comes / Unchain my heart / With a little help from my friends / You are so beautiful / Letter / She came in through the bathroom window / High time we went / What are you doing with a fool like me / Living in the promised land
CD ____ CDESTSP 25
Capitol / May '90 / EMI

LEGEND, THE ESSENTIAL COLLECTION
Up where we belong: *Cocker, Joe & Jennifer Warnes* / With a little help from my friends / Delta lady / Letter / She came in through the bathroom window / Whiter shade of pale / Love the one you're with / You are so beautiful / Let it be / Just like a woman / Many rivers to cross / Talking back to the night / Fun time / I heard it through the grapevine / Please give peace a chance (live) / Don't let me be misunderstood / Honky tonk women / Cry me a river (live)
CD ____ 5154112
Polydor / Jun '92 / PolyGram

LONG VOYAGE HOME, THE (4CD Set)
With a little help from my friends / I'll cry instead / Those precious words / Marjorine / Bye bye blackbird / Just like a woman / Don't let me be misunderstood / Do I still figure in your life / Feelin' alright / I shall be released / I don't need no doctor / Let it be / Delta lady / She came in through the bathroom window / Hitchcock railway / Dear landlord / Darling be home soon / Something / Wake up little Susie / Letter / Space Captain / Cry me a river / Let's go get stoned / Please give peace a chance / Blue medley / Weight / High time we went / Black-eyed blues / Midnight rider / Woman to woman / Something to say / She don't mind / Pardon me Sir / Put out the light / I can stand a little rain / Moon is a harsh Mistress / You are so beautiful / Guilty / I think it's going to rain today / Jamaica say you will / Jealous kind / Catfish / Song for you / Fun time / I'm so glad I'm standing here today / Ruby Lee / Many rivers to cross / So good so right / Up where we belong / I love the night / Civilized man / Edge of a dream / You can leave your hat on / Unchain my heart / I've got to use my imagination / I'm your man / When the night comes / Can't find my way home / Don't let the sun go down on me / You've got to hide your love away / Love is alive / With a little help from my friends
CD Set ____ 5402362
A&M / Dec '95 / PolyGram

MAD DOGS AND ENGLISHMEN
Honky tonk women / Sticks and stones / Cry me a river / Bird on the wire / Feeling alright / Superstar / Let's go get stoned / I'll drown in my own tears / When something is wrong with my baby / I've been loving you too long / Girl from the North Country / Give peace a chance / She came in through the bathroom window / Space captain / Letter / Delta lady
CD Set ____ CDA 6002
A&M / '88 / PolyGram
CD ____ 3960022
A&M / Jan '97 / PolyGram

MIDNIGHT RIDER
CD ____ WMCD 5701
Disky / Oct '94 / Disky / THE

NIGHT CALLS
Feels like forever / I can hear the river / Now that the magic has gone / Unchain my heart (90's version) / Night calls / There's a storm coming / Can't find my way home / Don't let the sun go down on me / When the night comes / Five women / Love is alive / Please no more / Out of the rain / You've got to hide your love away / When a woman cries
CD ____ CDESTU 2167
Capitol / Feb '92 / EMI

ON AIR (Cocker, Joe & The Grease Band)
Run shakers life / With a little help from my friends / Majorine / Change in Louise / Can't be so bad / Let's get stoned / That's your business / Delta lady / Hitchcode highway / Lawdy Miss Clawdy / Darlin' be home soon / Hello little friend
CD ____ SFRSCD 036
Strange Fruit / Jul '97 / Pinnacle

ONE NIGHT OF SIN
When the night comes / I will live for you / I've got to use my imagination / Letting go / Just to keep from drowning / Unforgiven / Another mind gone / Fever / You know it's gonna hurt / Bad bad sign / I'm your man / One night
CD ____ CDEST 2098
Capitol / Feb '94 / EMI

ORGANIC
Into the mystic / Bye bye blackbird / Delta lady / Heartful of rain / Don't let me be misunderstood / Many rivers to cross / High lonesome blue / Sail away / You and I / Darlin' be home soon / Dignity / You can leave your hat on / You are so beautiful / Can't find my way home
CD ____ CDESTD 6
Parlophone / Oct '96 / EMI

SHEFFIELD STEEL
Look what you've done / Shocked / Seven days / Marie / Ruby Lee / Many rivers to cross / Talking back to the night / Just like always / Sweet little woman / So good, so right
CD ____ IMCD 149
Island / Jul '92 / PolyGram

SIMPLY THE BEST
CD ____ WMCD 5705
Disky / Oct '94 / Disky / THE

UNCHAIN MY HEART
Unchain my heart / One / Two wrongs don't make a right / I stand in wonder / River's rising / Isolation / All our tomorrows / Woman loves a man / Trust in me / Satisfied / You can leave your hat on
CD ____ CDEST 2045
Capitol / Aug '92 / EMI

VERY BEST OF JOE COCKER, THE (The Voice)
With a little help from my friends / Honky tonk women / Delta lady / Marjorine / Don't let me be misunderstood / Something / Pardon me sir / Talking back to the night / Up where we belong / She came in through the bathroom window / Letter / Just like a woman / Jamaica say you will / Cry me a river / Midnight rider / Let it be
CD ____ BRCD 104
BR Music / Jun '94 / Target/BMG

Cockersdale

BEEN AROUND FOR YEARS
CD ____ FE 101CD
Fellside / Jul '94 / ADA / Direct / Target/BMG

Cockney Rejects

BEST OF THE COCKNEY REJECTS, THE
Flares n slippers / Police car / I'm not a fool / East end / Bad man / Headbanger / Join the rejects / Where the hell is Babylon / War on the terraces / Oi oi oi / Hate of the city / Rocker / Greatest cockney rip off / We can do anything / We are the firm / I'm forever blowing bubbles / Here we go again / Motorhead / Easy life / On the streets again / Power and the glory / Teenage fantasy
CD ____ DOJOCD 82
Dojo / May '93 / Disc

GREATEST HITS VOL.1
I'm not a fool / Headbanger / Bad man / Fighting in the streets / Shitter / Here they come again / Join the rejects / East End / New song / Police car / Someone like you / They're gonna put me away / Are you ready to ruck / Where the hell is Babylon / I'm forever blowing bubbles / West side boys
CD ____ DOJOCD 136
Dojo / Feb '94 / Disc

GREATEST HITS VOL.2
War on the terraces / In the underworld / Oi oi oi / Hate of the city / With the boys / Urban guerilla / Rocker / Greatest cockney rip off / Sitting in a cell / On the waterfront / We can do anything / It's alright / Subculture / Blockbuster / Fifteen nights / We are the firm
CD ____ DOJOCD 138
Dojo / Feb '94 / Disc

LETHAL
CD ____ NEATCD 1049
Neat / Jan '96 / Pinnacle

POWER AND THE GLORY
Power and the glory / Because I'm in love / On the run / Lemon / Friends / Van Bollocks / Teenage fantasy / It's over / On the streets again / BYC / Greatest story ever told
CD ____ DOJOCD 174
Dojo / Nov '93 / Disc

PUNK SINGLES COLLECTION
Flares 'n' slippers / Police car / I wanna be a star / I'm not a fool / East end / Bad man / New song / Greatest cockney rip off / Hate of the city / I'm forever blowing bubbles / West side boys / We can do anything / Nights / We are the firm / On the terraces / Easy life / Motorhead / Hang 'em high / On the streets again / Lomdob / Till the end of the day / Rock 'n' roll dream
CD ____ CDPUNK 90
Anagram / Mar '97 / Cargo / Pinnacle

Coco Steel & Lovebomb

IT
CD ____ WARPCD 24
Warp / Aug '94 / Prime / RTM/Disc

NEW WORLD
Great Ocean Road / Park Central / Pacific power / Press zero / On the beach / La Isla / Indurain / This is London / New world / Sun / Last call / Neon Madonna / On the beach / Pianopella
CD ____ THECD 108
Other / Jul '97 / Mo's Music Machine / Pinnacle

Cocoa T

CAN'T LIVE SO
CD ____ SHCD 45016
Shanachie / May '94 / ADA / Greensleeves / Koch

COME LOVE ME
CD ____ VPCD 1395
VP / Feb '95 / Greensleeves / Jet Star / Total/BMG

ISRAEL KING
CD ____ KPCRCD 61
Charm / Jan '97 / Jet Star

KINGSTON HOT
CD ____ GRELCD 174
Greensleeves / Nov '92 / Jet Star / SRD

LOVE ME
CD ____ DBTXCD 1
Digital B / Mar '95 / Jet Star

ONE UP
Africa here I come / If it's not you / Yard away home / One up / Stop your nagging / Grow your locks / Virus / Mr. Fisherman / Earthquake / I put my trust in Jah / Grow your locks (With Tony Rebel) / Getting closer / Beware (With Mutabaruka)
CD ____ GRELCD 187
Greensleeves / Sep '93 / Jet Star / SRD

RAS PORTRAITS
Rocking dolly / Bust outta hell / Gotta know rastafari / Jah made them that way / Kingston hot / Dancehall night / I lost my soul / Pose up / I'm going home / Louisiana / No wanted man
CD ____ RAS 3324
Ras / Jul '97 / Direct / Greensleeves / Jet Star / SRD

RIKERS ISLAND
CD ____ GRELCD 156
Greensleeves / Dec '90 / Jet Star / SRD

SWEET LOVE
CD ____ RASCD 3161
Ras / Mar '95 / Direct / Greensleeves / Jet Star / SRD

TUNE IN
CD ____ GRELCD 200
Greensleeves / May '94 / Jet Star / SRD

Coctails

COCTAILS, THE
CD ____ EFA 121182
Moll / Mar '96 / SRD

LIVE AT LOUNGE AX
CD ____ SAKI 013
Carrot Top / Jul '97 / Cargo

PEEL
CD ____ EFA 121142
Moll / Aug '95 / SRD

Cocteau Twins

BLUE BELL KNOLL
Blue bell knoll / Athol brose / Carolyn's fingers / For Phoebe still a baby / Itchy Glowbo / Cico buff / Suckling The Mender / Spooning good singing gum / Kissed out red floatboat / Ella megalast burls forever
CD ____ CAD 807CD
4AD / Sep '88 / RTM/Disc

FOUR CALENDAR CAFE
CD ____ 5182592
Fontana / Oct '93 / PolyGram

GARLANDS
Blood bitch / Wax and wane / But I'm not / Blind dumb deaf / Gail overfloweth / Shallow than hallow / Hollow men / Garlands
CD ____ CAD 211 CD
4AD / '86 / RTM/Disc

HEAD OVER HEELS
When mama was moth / Sugar hiccup / In our angelhood / Glass candle grenades / Multifoiled / In the gold dust rush / Tinderbox, The (of a heart) / My love paramour / Musette and drums / Five ten fiftyfold
CD ____ CAD 313 CD
4AD / '86 / RTM/Disc

HEAVEN OR LAS VEGAS
Cherry coloured funk / Pitch the baby / Iceblink luck / Fifty fifty clown / Heaven or Las Vegas / I wear your ring / Fotzepolitic / Wolf in the breast / River, road and rail / Frou-frou foxes in the midsummer fires
CD ____ CAD 0012 CD
4AD / Sep '90 / RTM/Disc

MILK AND KISSES
Violaine / Serpentskirt / Tishbite / Half gifts / Calfskin smack / Rilkean heart / Ups / Eperdu / Treasure hiding / Seekers who are lovers
CD ____ 5145012
CD ____ 5323632
Fontana / Apr '96 / PolyGram

PINK OPAQUE
CD ____ CAD 513 CD
4AD / Jan '86 / RTM/Disc

TINY DYNAMITE/ECHOES IN A SHALLOW BAY
CD Set ____ BAD 510/511 CD
4AD / Oct '86 / RTM/Disc

TREASURE
Ivo / Lorelei / Beatrix / Persephone / Pandora - for Cindy / Amelia / Aloysius / Cicely / Otterley / Donimo
CD ____ CAD 412 CD
4AD / '86 / RTM/Disc

VICTORIA LAND
Lazy calm / Fluffy tufts / Throughout the dark months of April and May / Whales tales / Oomingmac / Little spacey / Feet-like fins / How to bring a blush to the snow / Thinner the air
CD ____ CAD 602 CD
4AD / '86 / RTM/Disc

Code Indigo

FOR WHOM THE BELL
For whom the bell
CD ____ AD 16CD
AD / Dec '96 / Disc

Codeine

WHITE BIRCH, THE
CD ____ SPCD 118299
Sub Pop / May '94 / Cargo / Greyhound / Shellshock/Disc

Codona

CODONA
Like that of sky / Codona / Colemanwonder: race face, sortie, Sir Duke / Mumakata / New light
CD ____ 8293712
ECM / '90 / New Note/Pinnacle

CODONA VOL.2
Que faser / Godumaduma / Malinye / Drip dry / Walking on eggs / Again and again, again
CD ____ 8333322
ECM / Jul '88 / New Note/Pinnacle

CODONA VOL.3
Goshakabuch / Hey da ba doom / Travel by night / Trayra boia / Clicky clacky / Inner organs
CD ____ 8274202
ECM / Feb '86 / New Note/Pinnacle

Cody, Robert Tree

WHITE BUFFALO
CD ____ CRCD 555
Canyon / Mar '96 / ADA

Coe, David Allan

COMPASS POINT/I'VE GOT SOMETHING TO SAY
Heads or tails / Three times loser / Gone (like) / Honey don't / Lost Merle and me / Loving her (will make you lose your mind) / Fish aren't bitin' today / X's and O's (kisses and hugs) / I've got something to say / Back to Atlanta / I could never give you up (for someone else) / Take it easy rider / Great Nashville railroad disaster / Hank Williams Junior Junior / Get a little dirt on my hands / If you hold the ladder (I'll climb to) / This bottle (in my hand) / Take this job and shove it too / Lovin' you comes so natural
CD ____ BCD 15841
Bear Family / Mar '95 / Direct / Rollercoaster / Swift

HUMAN EMOTIONS/SPECTRUM VII
Would you lay with me (in a field of stone) / If this is just a game / You can count on me / Mississippi river queen / Tomrrow is another day / Human emotions / Love's

cheatin' line / Whiskey and women / Jack Daniels if you please / Suicide / Rollin' with the punches / On my feet again / Fall in love with you / What can I do / Sudden death / Fairytale morning / Seven mile bridge / Now's the time / Love is just a porpoise / Please come back to Boston
CD _______ BCD 15840
Bear Family / Mar '95 / Direct / Rollercoaster / Swift

INVICTUS (MEANS) UNCONQUERED/ TENNESSE WHISKEY
Rose knows / Ain't it funny / Way love can do ya / If you ever think of me / Purple heart / London homesick blues / Stand by your man / As far as this feeling will take us / Someplace to come when it rains / Best game in town / I love robbing banks / Tennessee whiskey / I knew I've given bout all I can take / Pledging my love / I'll always be a fool for you / (Sittin' on the) dock of the bay / Juanita / We've got a bad thing goin' / D-R-U-N-K / Little orphan Annie / Bright morning light
CD _______ BCD 15842
Bear Family / Mar '95 / Direct / Rollercoaster / Swift

LONGHAIRED REDNECK/ RIDES AGAIN
Long haired redneck / When she's got me (Where she wants me) / Revenge / Texas lullaby / living on the run / Family reunion / Rock 'n' roll holiday / Free born rambling man / Spotlight / Dakota the dancing bear, Part 2 / Willie, Waylon and me / House we've been calling home / Young Dallas cowboy / Sense of humour / Pumkin certer barn dance / Willie, Waylon and Me (Reprise) / Lately I've been thinking too much lately / Laid back and wasted / Under Rachel's wings / Greener than the grass we laid on / If that ain't country
CD _______ BCD 15707
Bear Family / Mar '93 / Direct / Rollercoaster / Swift

MYSTERIOUS RHINESTONE COWBOY, THE/ ONCE UPON A RHYME
Sad country song / Crazy Mary / River / 33rd of August / Bossier city / Atlanta song / Old men tell me / Desperados waiting for the train / I still sing the old songs / Old grey goose is dead / Would you lay with me (In a field of stone) / Jody like a melody / Loneliness in Ruby's eyes / Would you be my lady / Sweet vibrations / Another pretty country song / Piece of wood and steel / Fraulein / Shine it on / You never even called me by my name
CD _______ BCD 15706
Bear Family / Mar '93 / Direct / Rollercoaster / Swift

TATTOO/FAMILY ALBUM
Just to prove my love for you / Face to face / You'll always live inside of me / Play me a sad song / Daddy was a god fearin' man / Canteen of water / Maria is a mystery / Just in time / San Francisco Mabel Joy / Hey gypsy / Family album / Million dollar memories / Divers do it deeper / Guilty footsteps / Take this job and shove it / Houston, Dallas, San Antone / I've got to have you / Whole lot of lonesome / Bad impressions / Heavenly Father, Holy Mother
CD _______ BCD 15839
Bear Family / Mar '95 / Direct / Rollercoaster / Swift

Coe, Pete

LONG COMPANY
Bring the new year in / Across the Western ocean / Fireman's song / East Boldon/Ann Frazer MacKenzie / PR man from hell / Juniper, gentle and rosemary / What's it worth / William Taylor / As I roved out / Kings and Queens of England / I courted a wee girl / None so steady / Barleycorn / We'll have a May day / Bill Hall's no.1 and no.2
CD _______ BASHCD 45
Backshift / May '97 / Direct / Roots

Coe, Tony

BLUE JERSEY (Live At The 10th Jersey Jazz Festival) (Coe, Tony & Horler/ Ganley/Horler/Creese)
I got rhythm / Three / You stepped out of a dream / Solid silver / What is this thing called love / Blue Jersey / Chrissie / This heart of mine / Royal blues
CD _______ ABCD 4
AB / Oct '96 / Cadillac

CANTERBURY SONG
Canterbury song / How beautiful is the night / Light blue / Sometime ago / Re: person I knew / I guess I'll hang my tears out to dry / Lagos / Blue in green
CD _______ HHCD 1005
Hot House / Jun '89 / Cadillac / Harmonia Mundi / Wellard

JAZZPAR 1995 (Coe, Tony & Bob Brookmeyer)
CD _______ STCD 4206
Storyville / May '96 / Cadillac / Jazz Music / Wellard

SOME OTHER AUTUMN
Aristotle blues / Some other autumn / Line up blues / Body and soul / Reka / Together / Regrets / Perdido / When your lover has gone / In a mellow tone / UMMG
CD _______ HEPCD 2037
Hep / Jan '96 / Cadillac / Jazz Music / New Note/Pinnacle / Wellard

Coen, Jack

BRANCH LINE, THE (Irish Traditional Music From Galway to New York) (Coen, Jack & Charlie)
Scatter the mud / Larry Redigan's jig / Sailor's cravat / Repeal of the union / John Conroy's jig / Peach blossom / Fiddler's contest / Jim Conroy's reel / Pullet / Redican's mother / Humours of Kilkenny / Mike Coen's polka / Branch line / Have a drink with me / Blarney pilgrim / Two woodford flings / Waddling gander / O'Connell's jig on top of Mount Everest / Lads of Laois / Green groves of Erin / Tongs by the fire / Spinning wheel / Whelan's reel / Jenny dang the weaver / Jack Coen's jig / Paddy O'Brien's jig
CD _______ GLCD 3067
Green Linnet / Oct '93 / ADA / CM / Direct / Highlander / Roots

WARMING UP (Coen, Jack/Martin Mulhaire/Seamus Connolly)
CD _______ GL 1135CD
Green Linnet / Mar '94 / ADA / CM / Direct / Highlander / Roots

Coex

ASCENTS METEORA
Soul fragments / Interlude / Two figures / Drance / Ascents meteora / Dark
CD _______ DNDC 010CD
De Nova Da Capo / Jul '97 / World Serpent

SYNAESTHESIA
CD _______ DNDC 004CD
De Nova Da Capo / Oct '96 / World Serpent

Coffee Sergeants

MOONLIGHT TOWERS
CD _______ DJD 3204
Dejadisc / May '94 / ADA / Direct

Coffin Break

NO SLEEP TILL STARDUST MOTEL
CD _______ CZ 038
C/Z / Sep '94 / Plastic Head

Coffin Nails

FISTFUL OF BURGERS
CD _______ GREYCD 01
Greystone / May '96 / Else / Nervous

WRECKERS YARD
CD _______ GREYCD 02
Greystone / Dec '96 / Else / Nervous

Cogan, Alma

EMI PRESENTS THE MAGIC OF ALMA COGAN
Bell bottom blues / This old house / I can't tell a waltz from a tango / Dreamboat / Banjo's back in town / Go on by / Twenty tiny fingers / Never do a tango with an eskimo / Willie can / Birds and the bees / Why do fools fall in love / In the middle of the house / You, me and us / Whatever Lolo wants / Just couldn't resist her with her pocket transistor / Story of my life / Sugartime / Cheek to cheek / Last night on the back porch / We got love / Dream talk / Train of love / Cowboy Jimmie Joe / When I fall in love
CD _______ CDMFP 6290
Music For Pleasure / May '97 / EMI

EMI YEARS, THE
You, me and us / Bell bottom blues / Mambo Italiano / Got 'n idea / Last night on the back porch / It's all been done before: *Cogan, Alma & Ronnie Hilton* / Lucky lips / Fly away lovers / Little shoemaker / Chiqu chaqui / I can't tell a waltz from a tango / Ricochet / I love you bit: *Cogan, Alma & Lionel Bart* / Never do a tango with an eskimo / Little things mean a lot / Gettin' ready for Freddy / Mama says / Dreamboat / Said the little moment / In the middle of the house
CD _______ CDEMS 1378
EMI / Jan '91 / EMI

HOUR OF ALMA COGAN, AN
To be worthy of you / Till I waltz again with you / Till they've all gone home / Bell bottom blues / Jilted / Canoodlin / Rag / This ole house / I can't tell a waltz from a tango / (Don't let the) Kiddygeddin / Softly, softly / Dreamboat / Willie can / Lizzie Borden / Birds and the bees / Why do fools fall in love / Whatever Lola wants (Lola gets) / Cahntez, chantez / Fabulous / Party time / Please Mr. Brown / Sugartime / Sorry, sorry, sorry / Pink shoelaces / We got love / Train of love / Just couldn't resist her with her pocket transistor
CD _______ CC 8240
EMI / Nov '94 / EMI

WITH LOVE IN MIND
Somebody loves me / Can't help falling in love / Hello, young lovers / Our love affair / Love me as though there were no tomorrow / Love is just around the corner / Let me love you / If love were all / With you in mind / I dream of you / Let's fall in love / In other words / My heart stood still / But beautiful / You'll never know / All I do is dream of you / What is there to say / Don't blame me / Falling in love with love / More I see you / I can't give you anything but love / I've never been in love before / Lady's in love with you / I'm in the mood for love
CD _______ CDB 906582
Music For Pleasure / Sep '88 / EMI

Cohen, Ben

JAZZ LIPS (Cohen, Ben Hot Five & Hot Seven)
CD _______ PKCD 057
PEK / Jan '97 / Cadillac / Jazz Music / Wellard

Cohen, Greg

WAY LOW
CD _______ DIW 918
DIW / Jan '97 / Cadillac / Harmonia Mundi

Cohen, Leonard

COHEN LIVE
Dance me to the end of love / Bird on the wire / Everybody knows / Loan of arc / There is a war / Sisters of mercy / Hallelujah / I'm your man / Who by fire / One of us cannot be wrong / If it be your will / Heart with no companion / Suzanne
CD _______ 4771712
Columbia / Aug '94 / Sony

FUTURE, THE
Future / Waiting for the miracle / Be for real / Closing time / Anthem / Democracy / Light as the breeze / Always / Tacoma trailer
CD _______ 4724982
Columbia / Nov '92 / Sony

GREATEST HITS
Suzanne / Sisters of mercy / So long, Marianne / Bird on the wire / Lady Midnight / Partisan / Hey, that's no way to say goodbye / Famous blue raincoat / Last year's man / Chelsea Hotel no.2 / Who by fire / Take this longing
CD _______ CD 32644
Columbia / Jun '89 / Sony

I'M YOUR FAN (The Songs Of Leonard Cohen) (Various Artists)
Who by fire: *House Of Love* / Hey, that's no way to say goodbye: *McCulloch, Ian* / I can't forget: *Pixies* / Stories of the street: *That Petrol Emotion* / Bird on the wire: *Lilac Time* / Suzanne: *Oryema, Geoffrey* / So long, Marianne: *James* / Avalanche IV: *Murat* / Don't go home with your hard-on: *McComb, David & Adam Peters* / First we take Manhattan: *REM* / Chelsea hotel: *Cole, Lloyd* / Tower of song: *Forster, Robert* / Take this longing: *Astor, Peter* / True love leaves no traces: *Dead Famous People* / I'm your man: *Pritchard, Bill* / Singer must die: *Fatima Mansions* / Hallelujah: *Cale, John* / Tower of song: *Cave, Nick & The Bad Seeds*
CD _______ 9031755982
East West / Sep '91 / Warner Music

I'M YOUR MAN
First we take Manhattan / Ain't no cure for love / Everybody knows / I'm your man / Take this waltz / Jazz police / I can't forget / Tower of song
CD _______ 4606422
Columbia / Feb '88 / Sony

LIVE SONGS
Minute prologue / Passing through / You know who I am / Bird on the wire / Nancy / Improvisation / Story of Isaac / Please don't pass me by (a disgrace) / Tonight will be fine / Queen Victoria
CD _______ 4844542
Columbia / Feb '97 / Sony

NEW SKIN FOR OLD CEREMONY
Is this what you wanted / Chelsea Hotel no.2 / Lover lover lover / Field Commander Cohen / Why don't you try / There is a war / Singer must die / I tried to leave you / Leaving green sleeves / Who by fire / Take this longing
CD _______ CD 32660
Columbia / Mar '96 / Sony

RECENT SONGS
Guests / Humbled in love / Window / Came so far for beauty / Lost Canadian (Un Canadien errant) / Traitor / Our lady of solitude / Gypsy's wife / Smoky life / Ballad of the absent mare
CD _______ 4747502
Columbia / Apr '94 / Sony

SO LONG, MARIANNE
Who by fire / So long, Marianne / Chelsea Hotel no.2 / Lady midnight / Sisters of mercy / Bird on the wire / Suzanne / Lover lover lover / Winter lady / Tonight will be fire / Partisan / Diamonds in the mine
CD _______ 4605002
Columbia / Oct '95 / Sony

SONGS FROM A ROOM
Bird on the wire / Story of Isaac / Bunch of lonesome heroes / Seems so long ago / Nancy / Old revolution / Butcher / You know who I am / Lady Midnight / Tonight will be fine
CD _______ 32072
Columbia / May '90 / Sony

SONGS FROM A ROOM/SONGS OF LOVE AND HATE (2CD Set)
Bird on the wire / Story of Isaac / Bunch of lonesome heroes / Seems so long ago / Nancy / Old revolution / Butcher / You know who I am / Lady Midnight / Tonight will be fine / Avalanche / Last year's man / Dress rehearsal rag / Diamonds in the mine / Love calls you by your name / Famous blue raincoat / Sing another song / Boys / Joan of Arc
CD Set _______ 4784802
Columbia / Mar '95 / Sony

SONGS OF LEONARD COHEN, THE
Suzanne / Master song / Winter lady / Stranger song / Sisters of mercy / So long, Marianne / Hey, that's no way to say goodbye / Stories of the street teachers / One of us cannot be wrong
CD _______ 4686002
Columbia / Oct '91 / Sony

SONGS OF LOVE AND HATE
Avalanche / Last year's man / Dress rehearsal rag / Diamonds in the mine field / Love calls you by your name / Famous blue raincoat / Sing another song / Joan of Arc
CD _______ 4767992
Columbia / May '94 / Sony

TOWER OF SONG (A Tribute To Leonard Cohen) (Various Artists)
Everybody knows: *Henley, Don* / Coming back to you: *Yearwood, Trisha* / Sisters of mercy: *Sting & The Chieftains* / Hallelujah: *Bono* / Famous blue raincoat: *Amos, Tori* / Ain't no cure for love: *Neville, Aaron* / I'm your man: *John, Elton* / Bird on a wire: *Nelson, Willie* / Suzanne: *Gabriel, Peter* / Light as the breeze: *Joel, Billy* / If it be your will: *Arden, Jann* / Story of Isaac: *Vega, Suzanne*
CD _______ 5402592
A&M / Sep '95 / PolyGram

VARIOUS POSITIONS
Dance me to the end of love / Coming back to you / Law / Night comes on / Hallelujah / Captain / Hunter's lullaby / Heart with no companion / If it be your will
CD _______ 4655692
Columbia / Nov '89 / Sony

Cohen, Porky

RHYTHM AND BONES
CD _______ CDBB 9572
Bullseye Blues / Aug '96 / Direct

Cohn, Al

BODY AND SOUL (Cohn, Al & Zoot Sims)
CD _______ MCD 5356
Muse / Sep '92 / New Note/Pinnacle

KEEPER OF THE FLAME (Cohn, Al & The Jazz Seven)
Bilbo baggins / Mood indigo / Casa 50 / Keeper of the flame / High on you / Feel more like I do now
CD _______ JHCD 022
Ronnie Scott's Jazz House / Jan '94 / Cadillac / Jazz Music / New Note/Pinnacle / TKO Magnum

NONPAREIL
Take four / Unless it's you / El Cajon / Raincheck / Mr. George / Girl from Ipanema / This is new / Blue hodge / Expense account
CD _______ CCD 4155
Concord Jazz / Nov '92 / New Note/ Pinnacle

OVERTONES
P-Town / Woody's lament / High on you / I love you / Vignette / Pensive / I don't want anybody at all / Let's be buddies
CD _______ CCD 4194
Concord Jazz / Nov '96 / New Note/ Pinnacle

SKYLARK (2CD Set)
You stepped out of a dream / Woody's lament / America the beautiful / Lover man / Skylark / What is this thing called love / Tune / I love you / Do nothin' 'til you hear from me / Fred / Sophisticated lady / Danielle / Girl from Ipanema / Tickle toe
CD Set _______ JLR 103606
Live At EJ's / May '96 / Target/BMG

TOUR DE FORCE (Cohn, Al & Scott Hamilton/Buddy Tate)
Blues up and down / Tickle toe / Let's get away from it all / Soft winds / Stella by starlight / Broadway / Do nothin' 'til you hear from me / Jumpin' at the woodside / Bernie's tune / Rifftide / If
CD _______ CCD 4172
Concord Jazz / Aug '90 / New Note/ Pinnacle

Cohn, Marc

MARC COHN
Walking in Memphis / Ghost train / Silver Thunderbird / Dig down deep / Walk on water / Miles away / Saving the best for last / Strangers in a car / Twenty nine ways / Perfect love / True companion
CD _______ 7567821782
Atlantic / Apr '91 / Warner Music

RAINY SEASON, THE
Walk through the world / Rest for the weary / Rainy season / Mama's in the moon /

Don't talk to her at night / Paper walls / From the station / Medicine man / Baby king / She's becoming gold / Things we've handed down
CD 7567824912
Atlantic / Feb '95 / Warner Music

Cohn, Steve

ITTEKIMASU
CD ITM 970059
ITM / Apr '91 / Koch / Tradelink

Coil

ANGELIC CONVERSATION
CD LOCICD 6
Threshold House / Oct '96 / SRD / World Serpent

BLACK LIGHT DISTRICT
CD ESKATON 8
Threshold House / Oct '96 / SRD / World Serpent

GOLD IS THE METAL
CD NORMAL 77
Normal / May '94 / ADA / Direct
CD LOCICD 11
Threshold House / Oct '96 / SRD / World Serpent

HELLRAISER
CD COILCD 001
Solar Lodge / Feb '89 / SRD

HOW TO DESTROY ANGELS
CD LOCICD 5
Threshold House / Oct '96 / SRD / World Serpent

STOLEN AND CONTAMINATED
CD LOCICD 4
Threshold House / Oct '96 / SRD / World Serpent

UNNATURAL HISTORY VOL.1
CD LOCICD 2
Threshold House / Jan '89 / SRD / World Serpent

UNNATURAL HISTORY VOL.2
CD LOCICD 10
Threshold House / Oct '96 / SRD / World Serpent

UNNATURAL HISTORY VOL.3 (Joyful Participation In The Sorrows Of The World)
First dark ride / Baby food / Music for commercials / Panic / Neither his nor yours / Feeder / Wrong eye / Meaning what exactly / Scope / Lost rivers of London
CD LOCICD 12
Threshold House / Jul '97 / SRD / World Serpent

WINDOW PANE/THE SNOW
CD LOCICD 7
Threshold House / Oct '96 / SRD / World Serpent

Coila

GET REEL
Jigs / Hornpipes / Hoedown / Slow air / Reel / Gaelic waltzes / Jig / Reels / Slow air / Pipe hornpipe and 6/8 marches / Waltzes / Jigs / Pipe reels
CD LCOM 5258
Lismor / May '97 / ADA / Direct / Duncans / Lismor

Coinneach

LIFE IN A SCOTTISH GREENHOUSE
How many battles / (Life in a) Scottish greenhouse / Rhythm method / No time to cry / Gloomy summer / Energy rising / Coinneach / Sound of the sound / Animal song / Phantom fiddler
CD CDLDL 1254
Lochshore / Mar '97 / ADA / Direct / Duncans

Cojazz

COJAZZ PLUS (Cojazz & Alice Day)
Sometimes I'm happy / Mr. Ugly / Never make your move too soon / Mascarade is over / Man I love / Harbor bridge / What a wonderful world / Black coffee / Milestones
CD TCB 96052
TCB / Apr '96 / New Note/Pinnacle

Colaiuta, Vinnie

VINNIE COLAIUTA
I'm tweeked / Attack of the 20lb pizza / Private earthquake: Error 7 / Chauncey / John's blues / Slink / Darlene's song / Momoska (dub mix) / Bruce Lee / If one was one
CD SCD 90072
Stretch / Mar '97 / New Note/Pinnacle

Colcannon

LIFE OF RILEY'S BROTHER
CD ORP 401CD
Oxford Road / Aug '96 / ADA

Colclough, Phil

PLAYERS FROM A DRAMA (Colclough, Phil & June)
CD CMCD 060
Celtic Music / '91 / CM

Cold Chisel

EAST
Standing on the outside / Never before / Choir girl / Rising sun / My baby / Tomorrow / Cheap wine / Best kept lies / ITA / Star hotel / Four walls / My turn to cry
CD 2292549302
East West / Jan '96 / Warner Music

Cold Cold Hearts

COLD COLD HEARTS
CD KRS 287CD
Kill Rock Stars / Apr '97 / Cargo / Greyhound / Plastic Head

Cold Sweat

COLD SWEAT PLAYS JAMES BROWN
Brown's France / Give it up or turn it loose / It's a man's man's man's world / I got the feelin' / Brown's dance / Showtime medley / I got the feelin' / I can't stand it / Licking stick / There was a time / Please please please / Try me / Cold sweat / Funky good time
CD 8344262
jMT / May '93 / PolyGram

Coldcut

COLD KRUSH CUTS (Coldcut & DJ Food)
CD TFCK 87910
Toys Factory / Jun '97 / Greyhound / Plastic Head

JOURNEYS BY DJ VOL.8
CD JDJCD 8
JDJ / Oct '95 / 3mv/Pinnacle / SRD

LET US PLAY (CD/CD-ROM Set)
Return to the margin / Atomic moog / More beats and pieces / Rubaiyat / Pan opticon / Music for no musicians / Noah's toilet / Space journey / Timber / Every home a prison / Cloned again / I'm wild about that thing / Playtime / My little funkit / Coldcut's A-Z / Pic pump / Coldcut infobone videosyncrasy
CD Set ZENCD 030
Ninja Tune / Sep '97 / Kudos / Pinnacle / Prime / Vital

Coldstream Guards

LONDON SALUTE
London salute / State procession / Cockney lover / Bank holiday / Westminster waltz / Birdcage walk / Clarinet on the town / Royal windsor / Covent garden / Knightsbridge march / Nightingale sang in Berkley Square / Cockney cocktail / Foggy day in Camden town / Overture 'Cockaigne (In London town) / March finale / Boys in the old brigade / When the guards are on parade / Coldstream march 'Milanollo
CD BNA 5119
Bandleader / Oct '95 / Conifer/BMG

MARCHE MILITARE (Coldstream Guards Band)
CD MATCD 260
Castle / Apr '93 / BMG

MUSIC OF ANDREW LLOYD WEBBER (Coldstream Guards Band)
Phantom of the opera / Think of me / All I ask of you / Music of the night / Pie Jesu / Hosanna / Cats overture / Skimbleshanks the railway cat / Old gumbie cat / Macavity / Memory / I am the starlight / Engine of love / Only you / Race is on / Make up my heart / Light at the end of the tunnel / Starlight express / I'm very you / You're very me / Capped teeth and Caesar salad / Tell me on a Sunday / Take that look off your face / Variations 1-4 / Andrew Lloyd Webber - Symphonic Study
CD BNA 5025
Bandleader / '88 / Conifer/BMG

OUT THE ESCORT (Coldstream Guards Band)
CD BNA 5052
Bandleader / Feb '92 / Conifer/BMG

TROOPING THE COLOUR (Coldstream Guards Massed Bands)
Royal salute/God save the Queen / King William IV / Melodies from the North / Les Hugenots / Third battalion / Escort for the colour / Grenadiers march / Medley / Liberton pipe band / Long live Elizabeth / Regimental slow march of the Royal Horse Guards / Regimental slow march of the Life Guards / To your guard / God save the Queen
CD SUMCD 4072
Summit / Nov '96 / Sound & Media

Cole, B.J.

HEART OF THE MOMENT
In at the deep end / Icarus enigma / Eastern cool / Indian willow / Three piece suite / Sands of time / Promenade and arabesque / Kraken wakes / Forever amber / Adagio in blue
CD RES 107CD
Resurgence / Apr '97 / Pinnacle

TRANSPARENT MUSIC
CD HNCD 1325
Hannibal / May '89 / ADA / Vital

Cole, Bobby

DANCE-DANCE-DANCE
Diana / Thorn birds / Look for the silver lining / Music maestro please / Whispering / On Mother Kelly's doorstep / Rock-a-bye your baby with a DIxie melody / Don't bring Lulu / Put your arms around me honey / My blue Heaven / Bring me sunshine / Sheikh of Araby / Powder your face with sunshine / Memories / For ever and ever / I'm always chasing rainbows / Something tells me / All my loving / Hey Jude / I love Paris / Serenata / Melancholy baby / Sleepy time gal
CD SAV 187CD
Savoy / May '93 / Savoy / THE / TKO Magnum

Cole, Cozy

CLASSICS 1944
CD CLASSICS 819
Classics / May '95 / Discovery / Jazz Music

CLASSICS 1944-1945
CD CLASSICS 865
Classics / Mar '96 / Discovery / Jazz Music

Cole, Freddy

CIRCLE OF LOVE, A
You're nice to be around / Manha de carnaval / They didn't believe me / How little we know / I wonder who my Daddy is / Circle of love / Never let me go / All too soon / If I had you / Angel eyes / Temptation / September morn
CD FCD 967
Fantasy / Jun '96 / Jazz Music / Pinnacle / Wellard

I'M NOT MY BROTHER, I'M ME
CD SSC 1054D
Sunnyside / Jan '92 / Discovery

LIVE AT BIRDLAND WEST
My hat's the size of my head / I almost lost my mind / Am I blue / Walkin' my baby back home / This heart of mine / Send for me / Somewhere along the way / Ballerina / I'm not my brother, I'm me / He was the king / Copacabana ripple
CD 17015
Laserlight / Dec '95 / Target/BMG

TO THE ENDS OF THE EARTH
To the ends of the Earth / I didn't mean to love you / In the still of the night / Candy / For all we know / I'll buy you a star / You don't have to say you're sorry / One at a time / Once you've been in love / Love walked in / Should've been / I'll be seeing you / Two for the road / Close enough for love
CD FCD 9675
Fantasy / Jun '97 / Jazz Music / Pinnacle / Wellard

Cole, Holly

BLAME IT ON MY YOUTH (Cole, Holly Trio)
Trust in me / I'm gonna laugh you right out of my life / If I were a bell / Smile / Purple Avenue / Calling you / God will / On the street where you live / Honeysuckle rose
CD CDP 7973492
Metro Blue / Feb '97 / EMI

DON'T SMOKE IN BED (Cole, Holly Trio)
I can see clearly now / Don't let the teardrops rust your shining heart / Get out of town / So and so / Tennessee waltz / Everyday will be like a holiday / Blame it on youth / Ev'rything I've got / Je ne t'aime pas / Cry (if you want to) / Whatever will be will be (Que sera sera) / Don't smoke in bed
CD CDP 7811982
Metro Blue / Feb '97 / EMI

IT HAPPENED ONE DAY
Get out of town / Cry (If you want to) / Train song / Losing my mind / Tango til they're sore / Don't let the teardrops rust your shining heart / Whatever will be will be (Que sera sera) / Calling you
CD CDP 8526990
Metro Blue / Nov '96 / EMI

TEMPTATION
Take me home / Train song / Jersey girl / Temptation / Falling down / Invitation to the blues / Cinny's waltz / Frank's theme / Little boy blue / I don't wanna grow up / Tango 'til they're sore / Looking for the heart of Saturday night / Soldier's things / I want you / Good old world / Briar and the rose / Shiver me timbers
CD CDP 8343482
Capitol Jazz / Sep '95 / EMI

Cole, Jude

VIEW FROM 3RD STREET
Hallowed ground / House full of reasons / Time for letting go / This time it's us / Compared to nothing / Baby, it's tonight / Get me through the night / Stranger to myself / Heart of blues / Prove me wrong
CD 7599261642
WEA / Aug '90 / Warner Music

Cole, Lloyd

1984 - 1989 (Cole, Lloyd & The Commotions)
CD 8377362
Polydor / Mar '89 / PolyGram

BAD VIBES
Morning is broken / So you'd like to save the world / Holier than thou / Love you so what / Wild mushrooms / My way to you / Too much of a good thing / Fall together / Mr. Wrong / Seen the future / Can't get arrested
CD 5183182
Fontana / Oct '93 / PolyGram

DON'T GET WEIRD ON ME BABE
CD 5110932
Polydor / Mar '96 / PolyGram

EASY PIECES (Cole, Lloyd & The Commotions)
Rich / Why I love country music / Pretty gone / Grace / Cut me down / Brand new friend / Lost weekend / James / Minor character / Perfect blue / Her last fling / Big world / Nevers end
CD 8276702
Polydor / Mar '96 / PolyGram

LOVE STORY
Trigger happy / Sentimental fool / I didn't know that you cared / Love ruins everything / Baby / Be there / June bride / Like lovers do / Happy for you / Traffic / Let's get lost / For crying out loud
CD 5285292
Fontana / Sep '95 / PolyGram

MAINSTREAM (Cole, Lloyd & The Commotions)
My bag / Twenty nine / Mainstream / Jennifer she said / Mr. Malcontent / Sean Penn blues / Big snake / Hey rusty / These days
CD 8336912
Polydor / Oct '87 / PolyGram

RATTLESNAKES (Cole, Lloyd & The Commotions)
Perfect skin / Speedboat / Rattlesnakes / Down on Mission Street / Forest fire / Charlotte Street / 2 CV / Four flights up / Patience / Are you ready to be heartbroken
CD 8236832
Polydor / Jan '92 / PolyGram

Cole, Nat 'King'

18 SONGS
CD CD 62052
Saludos Amigos / May '94 / Target/BMG

1943-49 VOCAL SIDES, THE (Cole, Nat 'King' Trio)
CD 11044
Laserlight / Jun '86 / Target/BMG

1949-1951
CD CD 53160
Giants Of Jazz / Aug '95 / Cadillac / Jazz Music / Target/BMG

1949-1960
CD CD 53166
Giants Of Jazz / Nov '95 / Cadillac / Jazz Music / Target/BMG

20 GOLDEN GREATS: NAT KING COLE
Sweet Lorraine / Straighten up and fly right / Nature boy / Dance, ballerina, dance / Mona Lisa / Too young / Love letters / Smile / Around the world / For all we know / When I fall in love / Very thought of you / On the street where you live / Unforgettable / It's all in the game / Ramblin' rose / Portrait of Jennie / Let there be love / Somewhere along the way / Those lazy, hazy, crazy days of summer
CD CDEMTV 9
Capitol / Dec '87 / EMI

20 GREATEST LOVE SONGS
Stardust / Answer me / Autumn leaves / Walkin' my baby back home / These foolish things / There goes my heart / Nightingale sang in Berkeley Square / You made me love you / Blossom fell / More / Love letters / OH how I miss you tonight / Brazilian love song / You're my everything / Love is a many splendoured thing / You'll never know / He'll have to go / Stay as sweet as you are / More I see you / Party's over
CD CDEMTV 35
EMI / Dec '87 / EMI

36 UNFORGETTABLE MEMORIES (2CD Set)
Nature boy / Stardust / You stepped out of a dream / You're the cream in my coffee / Sand and the sea / Too marvellous for words / Darling, je vous aime beaucoup / Don't get around much anymore / Embraceable you / Love is a many splendoured thing / It's crazy but I'm in love / Call the police / Thou swell / Are you fer it / Slow down / Route 66 / Honeysuckle rose

/ Hit the ramp / Unforgettable / Gee baby ain't I good to you / Mona Lisa / Hit that jive, Jack / For all we know / I like to riff / When you're smiling / End of a beautiful friendship / Scotchin' with the soda / That ain't right / Babs / Coquette / It's only a paper moon / Early American / Cuba / Somebody loves me / To the ends of the Earth / This side up
CD Set **TNC 96221**
Natural Collection / Aug '96 / Target/BMG

ANATOMY OF A JAM SESSION
Black market stuff / Laguna leap / I'll never be the same / Swingin' on central / Kicks
CD **BLC 760137**
Black Lion / Oct '90 / Cadillac / Jazz Music / Koch / Wellard

ANY OLD TIME (Cole, Nat 'King' Trio)
Little joy from Chicago / Sunny side of the street / Candy / Any old time / (Back home again in) Indiana / Man I love / Trio grooves in Brooklyn / That'll just about knock me out / Too marvellous for words / Besame mucho / Wouldn't you like to know
CD **GOJCD 1031**
Giants Of Jazz / Mar '95 / Cadillac / Jazz Music / Target/BMG

AUDIO ARCHIVE
You're the cream in my coffee / Bugle call rag / Sweet Georgia Brown / Too marvellous for words / Sweet Lorraine / Yes sir that's my baby / Frim fram sauce / It's only a paper moon / If you can't smile and say yes / Cole's bop blues / Trouble with me is you / Miss thing / Man on the keys / Satchel mouth baby / On the sunny side of the street / Last but not least / Tea for two / Nat meets June / Don't cry crybaby
CD **CDAA 002**
Tring / Jan '93 / Tring

BEST OF NAT KING COLE, THE
CD **DLCD 4004**
Dixie Live / Mar '95 / TKO Magnum

BEST OF THE NAT KING COLE ORCHESTRA, THE
CD **CDP 7982882**
Capitol Jazz / Jan '93 / EMI

BEST OF THE NAT KING COLE TRIO, THE (The Vocal Classics 1942-1946) (Cole, Nat 'King' Trio)
All for you / Straighten up and fly right / Gee baby ain't I good to you / If you can't smile and say yes / Sweet Lorraine / Embraceable you / It's only a paper moon / I realize now / I'm a shy guy / You're nobody 'til somebody loves you / What can I say after I say I'm sorry / I'm thru with love / Come to baby / Do / Frim fram sauce / How does it feel / Route 66 / Baby, baby all the time / But she's my buddy's chick / You call it madness (but I call it love) / Best man / (I love you) for sentimental reasons / You're the cream in my coffee
CD **CDP 8335712**
Capitol Jazz / Nov '95 / EMI

BEST OF THE VOCAL CLASSICS 1947-1950, THE (Cole, Nat 'King' Trio)
Meet me at no special place (and I'll be there at no particu / Naughty Angeline / I miss you so / That's what / When I take my sugar to tea / What I'll do / This is my night to dream / Makin' whoopee / There I've said it again / I'll string along with you / Too marvellous for words / Love nest / Dream a little dream of me / Little girl / No moon at all / If I had you / For all we know / 'tis autumn / Yes sir, that's my baby / I used to love you (but it's all over now) / Don't let your eyes go shopping (for your heart) / Ooh kickeroonie
CD **CDP 8335722**
Capitol Jazz / Jan '97 / EMI

CAPITOL COLLECTORS SERIES: NAT 'KING' COLE
Straighten up and fly right: *Cole, Nat 'King' & King Cole Trio* / Route 66: *Cole, Nat 'King' & King Cole Trio* / (I love you) for sentimental reasons: *Cole, Nat 'King' & King Cole Trio* / Christmas song: *Cole, Nat 'King' & King Cole Trio* / Nature boy: *Cole, Nat 'King' & Frank Devol Orchestra* / Too young / Walkin' my baby back home: *Cole, Nat 'King' & Billy May Orchestra* / Pretend: *Cole, Nat 'King' & Nelson Riddle Orchestra* / Answer me: *Cole, Nat 'King' & Nelson Riddle Orchestra* / Darling je vous aime beaucoup: *Cole, Nat 'King' & Nelson Riddle Orchestra* / Blossom fell / Send for me: *Cole, Nat 'King' & Billy May Orchestra* / Non dimenticar (Don't forget): *Cole, Nat 'King' & Nelson Riddle Orchestra* / Ramblin' rose: *Cole, Nat 'King' & Belford Hendricks Orchestra* / Dear lonely hearts / All over the world / Those lazy-hazy-crazy days of summer / LOVE / Mona Lisa / Unforgettable
CD **CZ 303**
Capitol / Apr '90 / EMI

CHRISTMAS WITH NAT & DEAN (Cole, Nat 'King' & Dean Martin)
Christmas song / Let it snow, let it snow, let it snow / White Christmas / Frosty the snowman / Winter wonderland / Happiest Christmas tree / Deck the halls with boughs of holly / O tannenbaum / Silent night / Brahms lullaby / Buon natale / O come all ye faithful (Adeste fidelis) / Rudolph the red nosed reindeer / Little boy that Santa Claus forgot / Cradle in Bethlehem / Christmas blues / Mrs. Santa Claus / Caroling, caroling / O little town of Bethlehem / O holy night / Joy to the world / God rest ye merry gentlemen
CD **CDMFP 5902**
Music For Pleasure / Dec '94 / EMI

CLASSICS 1936-1940
CD **CLASSICS 757**
Classics / Aug '94 / Discovery / Jazz Music

CLASSICS 1940-1941
CD **CLASSICS 773**
Classics / Aug '94 / Discovery / Jazz Music

CLASSICS 1941-1943
CD **CLASSICS 786**
Classics / Nov '94 / Discovery / Jazz Music

CLASSICS 1943-1944
CD **CLASSICS 804**
Classics / Mar '95 / Discovery / Jazz Music

CLASSICS 1944-1945
CD **CLASSICS 861**
Classics / Mar '96 / Discovery / Jazz Music

CLASSICS 1945
CD **CLASSICS 893**
Classics / Sep '96 / Discovery / Jazz Music

CLASSICS 1946
CD **CLASSICS 938**
Classics / Jun '97 / Discovery / Jazz Music

COLLECTION, THE
Sweet Lorraine / Our love is here to stay / Autumn leaves / Dance, ballerina, dance / September song / Beautiful friendship / Fly me to the moon / Let there be love / Mona Lisa / Pick yourself up / More I see you / Just one of those things / Let's fall in love / Love is the thing / Stay as sweet as you are / Love letters / When I fall in love / Stardust / Around the world / Too young / Very thought of you / On the street where you live / Ramblin' rose / Almost like being in love / Don't get around much anymore / Once in a while / These foolish things / I'm gonna sit right down and write myself a letter / This can't be love / For all we know / Lush life / Jet / Somewhere along the way / Because you're mine / Pretend / Mother Nature and Father Time / Can't I / Tenderly / Smile / Blossom fell / Dreams can tell a lie / Too young to go steady / Love me as though there were no tomorrow / To the ends of the earth / Time and the river / That's you / That Sunday that summer / Look no further / People / Song is ended (but the melody lingers on) / Azure te / Serenata / Party's over / Cottage for sale / There goes my heart / Ain't misbehavin'
CD Set **CDMFPBOX 5**
Music For Pleasure / Dec '92 / EMI

COLLECTION, THE
CD **COL 008**
Collection / Apr '95 / Target/BMG

COMPLETE AFTER MIDNIGHT SESSIONS
CD **CDP 748 328 2**
Capitol / Feb '88 / EMI

COMPLETE EARLY TRANSCRIPTIONS
CD **VJC 1026/7/8/9**
Vintage Jazz Classics / Oct '92 / ADA / Cadillac / CM / Direct

DESTINATION MOON
CD **BMCD 3024**
Blue Moon / Mar '96 / Cadillac / Discovery / Greensleeves / Jazz Music / Jet Star / TKO Magnum

EARLY FORTIES
CD **FSRCD 139**
Fresh Sound / Dec '90 / Discovery / Jazz Music

EARLY TRANSCRIPTIONS 1938-1941, THE (2CD Set) (Cole, Nat 'King' Trio)
Mutiny in the nursery / Swanee river / Don't blame me / Lullaby in rhythm / Flea hop / Chopsticks / Liza / Three blind mice / Caravan / Ta-de-ah / Undecided / T'ain't what you do (it's the way that you do it) / Do you want to jump children / Riffin' in F minor / Blue Lou / Georgie porgie / Limp / Liebestraum / Some like it hot / I like to riff / Moon song / Baby won't you please come home / Sweet Lorraine / Rosetta / Trompin' / Hoy soy / Black spider stomp / Rhythm serenade / Slew foot Joe / Crazy about rhythm / King Cole blues / Vine street jump / B-Flat / You send me / Gone with the draft / Scotchin' with the soda / Windy city boogie woogie / This side up / Ode to a wild clam
CD Set **JZCL 5013**
Jazz Classics / Nov '96 / Cadillac / Direct / Jazz Music

EMBRACEABLE YOU
Sweet Lorraine / Besame mucho / Too marvellous for words / This will make you laugh / Wouldn't you like to know / That'll just 'bout knock me out / It only happens once / Baby won't you please come home / Baby / Embraceable you / I love you for sentimental reasons / Do nothin' 'til you hear from me / Candy / What can I say after I say I'm sorry / Please consider me / Is you is or is you ain't my baby / Shoo shoo baby / Trouble with me is you / Yes sir that's my baby / If you can't smile and say yes (please don't cry and say no) / Don't cry baby / You call it madness but I call it love / On the sunny side of the street / I love to make love to you / I wanna turn out my light / It's only a paper moon
CD **PASTCD 7816**
Flapper / Apr '97 / Pinnacle

ESSENTIAL V-DISCS, THE
CD **JZCD 342**
Suisa / Jan '93 / Jazz Music / THE

FOR SENTIMENTAL REASONS (25 Early Vocal Classics) (Cole, Nat 'King' Trio)
(I love you) for sentimental reasons / This will make you laugh / That ain't right / Beautiful moons ago / I'm lost / Straigten up and fly right / Gee baby ain't I good to you / Sweet Lorraine / Embraceable you / It's only a paper moon / Look what you've done to me / I realize now / Don't blame me / I'm thru with love / It only happens once / It is better to be by yourself / I'm in the mood for love / I don't know why, I just do / Route 66 / What can I say after I say I'm sorry / But she's my buddy's chick / You call it madness but I call it love / I want to thank you folks / You don't learn that in school / Christmas song (merry christmas to you)
CD **CDAJA 5236**
Living Era / Mar '97 / Select

FOR SENTIMENTAL REASONS (Cole, Nat 'King' Trio)
I'm in the mood for love / I don't know why (I just do) / Everyone is saying hello again (why must we say goodbye) / Route 66 / I've got the world on a string / Just you, just me / What can I say after I say I'm sorry / To a wild rose / Too marvellous for words / Loan me two till Tuesday / How does it feel / Could-ja / Baby, baby all the time / Rex rhumba (rhumba a la king) / On the sunny side of the street / I'd like to make love to you / How deep is the ocean / You call it madness but I call it love / But she's my buddy's chick / Best man / (I love you) for sentimental reasons / In the cool of the evening / You're the cream in my coffee / Christmas song
CD **PLCD 555**
President / Feb '97 / Grapevine/PolyGram / President / Target/BMG

GOLD COLLECTION, THE
CD **D2CD 10**
Deja Vu / Dec '92 / THE

GOT A PENNY
I'm lost / Let's spring one / Beautiful moons / Got a penny / All for you / Fine sweet and tasty / My lips remember your kisses / Vom vim veedle / Bugle call rag / Let's pretend / Melancholy Madeline / Pitchin' up the boogie / Honky tonk town
CD **CDSGP 047**
Prestige / May '93 / Else / Total/BMG

GREAT BEGINNINGS
CD **AMSC 569**
Avid / Jun '96 / Avid/BMG / Koch / THE

GREAT GENTLEMEN OF SONG - SPOTLIGHT ON NAT KING COLE
She's funny that way / Sunday, Monday or always / Crazy she calls me / Spring is here / You'll never know / Funny (not much) / I want a little girl / Am I blue / Until the real thing comes along / Embraceable you / Should I / Say it isn't so / Too marvellous for words / Mood indigo / For you / I remember you / That's all / Lights out
CD **CDP 8293932**
Capitol / Aug '95 / EMI

GREAT NAT KING COLE 1940-1956
CD **11086**
Laserlight / '88 / Target/BMG

HIT THAT JIVE, JACK
Sweet Lorraine / Honeysuckle rose / Gone with the draft / Gone with the draft (alternate) / This side up / Babs / Scotchin' with soda / Slow down / Early morning blues / This will make you laugh / Stop, the red light's on / Hit the ramp / I like to riff / Call the police / Are you fer it / That ain't right / Hit that jive Jack / Honey rush / Honey rush (Alternate) / Stompin' at the Panama / Bedtime sleep, baby sleep / Thunder
CD **GRP 16622**
American Decca / Jul '96 / New Note/BMG

HIT THAT JIVE, JACK (Cole, Nat 'King' Trio)
Sweet Lorraine / Honeysuckle rose / Scotchin' with soda / Two against one / With plenty of money and you / Stop the red light's on / Call the police / Don't blame me / Hit that jive, Jack / Early morning blues
CD **CWNCD 2032**
Crown / Jun '97 / Henry Hadaway

IT'S ALMOST LIKE BEING IN LOVE (Cole, Nat 'King' Trio)
It's almost like being in love / It's only a paper moon / Jumpy jitters / Nothing ever happens / Let's do things / Sentimental blue / What'cha doing to my heart / Love me sooner / I'm through with love / Flo and Joe / Go bongo / Yes sir that's my baby / Tiny's excercise / Gee baby ain't I good to you / Baby I need you / Bop kick
CD **DBCD 15**
Dance Band Days / Jul '89 / Prism

JAZZMAN, THE
CD **TPZ 1012**
Topaz Jazz / Feb '95 / Cadillac / Pinnacle

JAZZY - THE BEGINNING (Cole, Nat 'King' Trio)
Honeysuckle rose / Gone with the draft / This will make you laugh / That ain't right / Trio groove / Blue because of you / All of you / My tips / Sweet Lorraine / Scotchin' with the soda / Call the police / Hit that jive Jack / Sunny side of the street / Tea for two / I'm lost / Got a penny
CD **74321329632**
Milan / Aug '97 / Conifer/BMG / Silva Screen

JUST LOVE SONGS (An Everlasting Collection Of 18 Memorable Tracks)
(I love you) for sentimental reasons / Embraceable you / It's only a paper moon / I don't know why / Besame mucho / Just you just me / What can I say after I say I'm sorry / If yesterday could only be tomorrow / Too marvellous for words / I'm in the mood for love / That'll just about knock me out / If you can't smile and say yes / Straighten up and fly right / Laura / I realise now / You must be blind / I thought you ought to know / Sweet Lorraine
CD **ECD 3306**
K-Tel / Feb '97 / K-Tel

LAURA
CD **BMCD 3040**
Blue Moon / Mar '96 / Cadillac / Discovery / Greensleeves / Jazz Music / Jet Star / TKO Magnum

LEGEND OF NAT 'KING' COLE, THE (2CD Set)
Straighten up and fly right / Gee baby ain't I good to you / If you can't smile and say yes / Sweet Lorraine / Embraceable you / It's only a paper moon / I just can't see for lookin' / What is this thing called love / Vom, vim, veedle / Darling, je vous aime beaucoup / It's crazy but I'm in love / Sand and the sea / Crazy rhythm / Thou swell / End of a beautiful friendship / You stepped out of a dream / Somebody loves me / Mona Lisa / (I'll be seeing you) In Cuba / To the ends of the earth / Autumn leaves / Route 66 / When you're smiling / Unforgettable / Frim fram sauce / I'm a shy guy / I'm in the mood for love / Too young / I've grown accustomed to her face / Sweet Sue, just you / House with love in it / Pick yourself up / Take me back to toyland / Just in time / This can't be love / Tea for two / Two different worlds / Early American / Little girl / Night lights
CD Set **MUCD 9504**
Musketeer / May '96 / Disc

LEGENDS IN MUSIC
CD **LECD 070**
Wisepack / Jul '94 / Conifer/BMG / THE

LET'S FACE THE MUSIC AND DANCE
Let's face the music and dance / Let there be love / Route 66 / Something makes me want to dance with you / More I see you / Answer me / These foolish things / Dance, ballerina, dance / Midnight flyer / Sweet Lorraine / Straighten up and fly right / Fly me to the moon / Just one of those things / I'm gonna sit right down and write myself a letter / Ain't misbehavin' / Girl from Ipanema / Papa loves mambo / Baby, won't you please come home / Blue moon / Party's over
CD **CDEST 2228**
Capitol / Apr '94 / EMI

LET'S FALL IN LOVE
When I fall in love / Stardust / Around the world / Too young / Very thought of you / On the street where you live / Ramblin' rose / Just one of those things / Let's fall in love / Almost like being in love / Don't get around much anymore / Once in a while / These foolish things / I'm gonna sit right down and write myself a letter / This can't be love / For all we know / Somewhere along the way / Cottage for sale / There goes my heart / Ain't misbehavin'
CD **CDMFP 5895**
Music For Pleasure / Oct '90 / EMI

LIVE AT THE SANDS
Ballerina / Funny (not much) / Continental / I wish you love / You leave me breathless / Thou swell / My kind of love / Surrey with the fringe on top / Where or when / Miss Otis regrets / Joe Turner blues
CD **CDEMS 1110**
Capitol / Mar '91 / EMI

LOVE IS THE THING
When I fall in love / End of a love affair / Stardust / Stay as sweet as you are / Where can I go without you / Maybe it's because I love you too much / Love letters / Ain't misbehavin' / I thought about Marie / At last / It's all in the game / When Sunny gets blue / Love is the thing
CD **BU 11**
Capitol / Mar '88 / EMI

NAT 'KING' COLE CHRISTMAS ALBUM, THE
Christmas song / Deck the halls with boughs of holly / Frosty the snowman / I saw three ships / Buon Natale (Merry Christmas to you) / O come all ye faithful (Adeste fidelis) / O little town of Bethlehem / Little boy that Santa Claus forgot / O'Tannenbaum / First Noel / Little Christmas / Joy to the world / O holy night / Caroling, caroling / Cradle in Bethlehem / Away in a manger / God rest ye merry gentlemen / Silent night
CD ____ CDMFP 5976
EMI / Dec '94 / EMI

NAT 'KING' COLE COLLECTION, THE
Straighten up & fly right / Sweet Lorraine / Embraceable you / It's only a paper moon / Mona Lisa / To the end of the Earth / Autumn leaves / Unforgettable / Too young / Just in time / This can't be love / Tea for two / Gee baby ain't I good to you / If you can't smile and say yes / I just can't see for lookin' / Vom, vim, veedle / Crazy rhythm / Thou swell / End of a relationship / Somebody loves me / What is this thing called love
CD ____ PAR 2069
Parade / Nov '96 / Disc

NAT 'KING' COLE GOLD (2CD Set)
CD Set ____ D2CD 4010
Deja Vu / Jun '95 / THE

NAT 'KING' COLE LIVE (Cole, Nat 'King' & Nelson Riddle Orchestra)
Two different worlds / Thou swell / Mona Lisa / Night lights / Too young / That's my girl / But not for me / Repeat after me / True love / Little girl / Love letters / Just in time / Unforgettable / Love me tender / My foolish heart / Sweet Sue, just you / Somewhere along the way / This can't be love / I'm sitting on top of the world / You are my first love / It's just a little street / Toyland
CD ____ DATOM 1
A Touch Of Magic / Apr '94 / Harmonia Mundi

NAT 'KING' COLE SHOWS VOL.1
CD ____ OTA 101902
On The Air / Mar '95 / Target/BMG

NAT 'KING' COLE SHOWS VOL.2
CD ____ OTA 101903
On The Air / Mar '95 / Target/BMG

NAT 'KING' COLE SHOWS VOL.3
CD ____ OTA 101904
On The Air / Mar '95 / Target/BMG

NAT 'KING' COLE STORY
Straighten up and fly right / Sweet Lorraine / It's only a paper moon / Route 66 / (I love you) for sentimental reasons / Christmas song / Nature boy / Lush life / Calypso blues / Mona Lisa / Orange coloured sky / Too young / Unforgettable / Somewhere along the way / Walkin' my baby back home / Pretend / Blue gardenia / I am in love / Answer me / Smile / Darling je vous aime beaucoup / Sand and the sea / If I may / Blossom fell / To the ends of the earth / Night lights / Ballerina / Stardust / Send for me / St. Louis blues / Looking back / Non dimenticar / Paradise / Oh, Mary, don't you weep
CD Set ____ CDS 7951292
Capitol / May '91 / EMI

NAT 'KING' COLE TRIO (Cole, Nat 'King' Trio)
CD ____ CD 53005
Giants Of Jazz / Mar '92 / Cadillac / Jazz Music / Target/BMG

NAT 'KING' COLE TRIO 1943-1947 (Cole, Nat 'King' & Oscar Moore/Johnny Miller)
CD ____ CD 14566
Jazz Portraits / May '95 / Jazz Music

NAT 'KING' COLE TRIO 1947-1948 (Cole, Nat 'King' & Pearl Bailey/Duke Ellington)
CD ____ VJC 1011 2
Vintage Jazz Classics / Oct '91 / ADA / Cadillac / CM / Direct

NAT 'KING' COLE TRIO WITH OSCAR MOORE & JOHNNY MILLER (1943-1945) (Cole, Nat 'King' Trio & Oscar Moore/ Johnny Miller)
Sweet Lorraine / Sweet Georgia Brown / Embraceable you / It's only a paper moon / I just can't see for lookin' / I'm thru with love / Jumpin' at Capitol / Don't blame me / You're nobody 'til somebody loves you / Man I love / Katusha / I realize now / Prelude in C sharp minor / Gee baby ain't I good to you / Bring another drink / I'm a shy guy / Look what you done to me / If you can't smile and say yes / I tho't you ought to know / Barcarolle / It only happens once
CD ____ CD 53144
Giants Of Jazz / Oct '96 / Cadillac / Jazz Music / Target/BMG

NAT KING COLE
Sweet Lorraine / It's only a paper moon / Gone with the draft / Route 66 / You're the cream in my coffee / Too marvellous for words / Honeysuckle rose / Sweet Georgia Brown / Easy listening blues / What is this thing called love / This autumn / Babs / Early morning blues / Jumpin' at capitol / Stompin' down broadway / Somebody loves me / Tea for two
CD ____ 22713
Music / Dec '95 / Target/BMG

NAT KING COLE
Sweet Lorraine / It's only a paper moon / Gone with the draft / Route 66 / You're the cream in my coffee / Too marvellous for words / Honeyusuckle rose / Sweet Georgia Brown / Easy listening blues / What is this thing called love / This autumn / Babs / Early morning blues / Jumpin' at capitol / Stompin' down Broadway / Somebody loves me / Tea for two
CD ____ DVX 08092
Deja Vu / May '95 / THE

NAT KING COLE (2CD Set)
CD Set ____ R2CD 4010
Deja Vu / Jan '96 / THE

NAT KING COLE
Open up the doghouse (Two cat's are comin' in) / Send for me / When Sunny gets blue / Caravan / To the ends of the earth / Candy / My baby just cares for me / Can I come in for a second / I'll never say never again / Wish I were somebody else / Ev'ry day (I fall in love) / It's crazy / Where were you / Land of love (Come my love and live with me) / That's my girl / Roses and wine / Looking back / Orange coloured sky / Hey, not now (I'll tell you when) / Get out and get under the moon / You can't make me love you / It's a man every time / Poor Jenny is a-weepin' / Your voice
CD ____ CD 372
Entertainers / Jun '96 / Target/BMG

ONE AND ONLY NAT 'KING' COLE, THE
Sweet Lorraine / Our love is here to stay / Autumn leaves / Dance, ballerina, dance / September song / Beautiful friendship / Fly me to the moon / Let there be love / Mona Lisa / Pick yourself up / More I see you / Just one of those things / Let's fall in love / Love is the thing / Stay as sweet as you are / Love letters / Azure te / Serenata / Party's over
CD ____ CDMFP 6082
Music For Pleasure / Aug '96 / EMI

QUINTESSENCE, THE (1936-1944/2CD Set)
CD Set ____ FA 208
Fremeaux / Oct '96 / ADA / Discovery

RAMBLIN' ROSE
When I fall in love / Stardust / Around the world / Too young / Very thought of you / On the street where you live / Ramblin' rose / Just one of those things / Let's fall in love / Almost like being in love / Don't get around much anymore / Once in a while / These foolish things (remind me of you) / I'm gonna sit right down and write myself a letter / This can't be love / For all we know / Somewhere along the way / Cottage for sale / There goes my heart / Ain't misbehavin'
CD ____ DC 879672
Disky / Mar '97 / Disky / THE

RARE RADIO RECORDINGS
CD ____ JZCD 343
Suisa / Oct '93 / Jazz Music / THE

SINCERELY/THE BEAUTIFUL BALLADS
Sweethearts on parade / You are mine / Let me tell you, babe / No other heart / Because you love me / Cappucina / Let true love begin / Baby blue / Silver bird / Nothing in the world / Take a fool's advice / Felicia / Miss me / Marnie / Here's to my lady / Fool was I / Bend a little my way / You'll see / If I knew / Back in my arms / When it's summer / I'll always be remembering (things)
CD ____ CTMCD 103
EMI / Nov '96 / EMI

SINGLES
Lush life / Jet / Somewhere along the way / Because you're mine / Faith can move mountains / Pretend / Mother Nature and Father Time / Can't I / Tenderly / Smile / Blossom fell / Dreams can tell a lie / Too young to go steady / Love me as though there were no tomorrow / To the ends of the earth / Time and the river / That's you / That Sunday that summer / Look no further / People
CD ____ CDMFP 5939
Music For Pleasure / Dec '92 / EMI

SUNNY SIDE OF THE STREET, THE (2CD Set) (Cole, Nat 'King' Trio)
Straighten up & fly right / Is you is or is you ain't my baby / Gee baby ain't I good to you / Vom vim veedle / What is this thing called love / I just can't see for looking / Let's spring one / If you can't smile & say yes / Embraceable you / Sweet Lorraine / Prelude in 'c' sharp minor / Beautiful moons ago / It's only a paper moon / Body and soul / FST (fine, sweet & tasty) / Man I love / Jumpin' at capitol / On the sunny side of the street / Lester leaps in / You must be blind / Indiana / Little Joe from Chicago / After you've gone / Mexican Joe / This will make you laugh / Rhythm Sam / Old music master / Wild goose chase / Too marvellous for words / Shoo, shoo baby / I can't give you anything but love / Just another blues / I realise now / I may be wrong / Miss thing / Have fun / Solid potato salad / Do nothin' 'til you hear from me
CD Set ____ 330062
Hallmark / Jul '96 / Carlton

SWEET GEORGIA BROWN
CD ____ GRF 038
Tring / Jun '92 / Tring

TELL ME ABOUT YOURSELF/THE TOUCH OF YOUR LIPS
Tell me about yourself / Until the real thing comes along / Best thing for you / When you walked by / Crazy she calls me / You've got the Indian sign on me / For you / Dedicated to you / You are my love / This is always / My life / (I would do) anything for you / Touch of your lips / I remember you / Illusion / You're mine, you / Funny (not much) / Poinciana / Sunday, Monday, or always / Not so long ago / Nightingale sung in Berkeley square / Only forever / My need for you / Lights out
CD ____ CTMCD 106
EMI / Jan '97 / EMI

THIS IS NAT KING COLE (2CD Set)
When I fall in love / On the street where you live / Ramblin' Rose / Gee baby ain't I good to you / I'm an errand boy for rhythm / Honeysuckle rose / End of a love affair / When the world was young / Where can I go without you / Nightingale sang in Berkeley Square / Let's fall in love / Arriverderci Roma / Best thing for you / Tangerine / Late late show / I got it bad and that ain't good / Open up the doghouse / For you my love / Autumn leaves / More I see you / Dance ballerina dance / Mona Lisa / Fly me to the moon / Get out and get under the moon / Miss Otis regrets / Continental / Surrey with the fringe on top / Girl from Ipanema / My kind of girl / Pretend / Smile / Breezin' along with the breeze / Les feuilles mortes / Aqui se hable en Amore / Make believe land / Day isn't long enough / Happy new year / Miss me / Blossom fell / Too young to go steady
CD Set ____ CDDL 1305
Music For Pleasure / Nov '95 / EMI

TOUCH OF CLASS, A
When I fall in love / Stardust / Around the world / Too young / Very thought of you / On the street where you live / Ramblin' rose / Just one of those things / Let's fall in love / Almost like being in love / Don't get around much anymore / Ain't misbehavin' / There goes my heart / Cottage for sale / Somewhere along the way / For all we know / This can't be love / I'm gonna sit right down and write myself a letter / These foolsih things / Once in a while
CD ____ TC 877032
Disky / May '97 / Disky / THE

TRIO CLASSICS (2CD Set) (Cole, Nat 'King' Trio)
Sweet Lorraine / Honeysuckle rose / Early morning blues / This will make you laugh / That ain't right / On the sunny side of the street / Back home in Indiana / Too marvellous for words / I may be wrong / Shoo, shoo baby / Miss Thing / Little Joe from Chicago / Do nothin' 'til you hear from me / Old music master / After you've gone / Is you is or is you ain't my baby / Vom, vim, veedle / All for you / Pitchin' up a boogie / Beautiful moons ago / I'm lost / FST (Fine, sweet and tasty) / Straighten up and fly right / Gee baby ain't I good to you / Jumpin' at Capitol / If you can smile and say yes / Embraceable you / It's only a paper moon / I just can't see for lookin' / Man I love / Body and soul / Prelude in C sharp minor / What is this thing called love / Easy listening blues / I'm a shy guy / Barcarolle / Sweet Georgia Brown / I tho't you ought to know / It only happens once / (I call my papa) Fla-ga-la-pa / It's better to be by yourself / Come to baby, do / Frim fram sauce / Homeward bound / I'm an errand boy for rhythm / This way out / I know that you know / But she's my buddy's chick / Oh, but I do / How does it feel
CD Set ____ CPCD 82612
Charly / Dec '96 / Koch

TRIO RECORDINGS VOL.1, THE
CD ____ 15746
Laserlight / Aug '92 / Target/BMG

TRIO RECORDINGS VOL.1-5, THE
CD Set ____ 15915
Laserlight / Aug '92 / Target/BMG

TRIO RECORDINGS VOL.3, THE
CD ____ 15748
Laserlight / Aug '92 / Target/BMG

TRIO RECORDINGS VOL.4, THE
CD ____ 15749
Laserlight / Aug '92 / Target/BMG

TRIO RECORDINGS VOL.5, THE
CD ____ 15750
Laserlight / Aug '92 / Target/BMG

UNBELIEVABLE
CD ____ BMCD 3036
Blue Moon / Mar '96 / Cadillac / Discovery / Greensleeves / Jazz Music / Jet Star / TKO Magnum

UNFORGETTABLE
Unforgettable / Too young / Mona Lisa / (I love you) for sentimental reasons / Pretend / Answer me / Portrait of Jennie / What'll I do / Lost April / Red sails in the sunset / Make her mine / Hajji baba
CD ____ CDEMS 1100
Capitol / Mar '91 / EMI

UNFORGETTABLE (The Velvet Voice Of Nat King Cole)
Darling Je vous aime beaucoup / It's crazy but I'm in love / Sand and the sea / Crazy rhythm / Thou swell / End of a beautiful relationship / It's only a paper moon / You stepped out of a dream / Somebody loves me / Mona Lisa / Cuba / To the ends of the Earth / Autumn leaves / Route 66 / When you're smiling / Unforgettable / I'm in the mood for love / Embraceable you
CD ____ PLATCD 154
Platinum / Mar '96 / Prism

UNFORGETTABLE NAT KING COLE, THE
Unforgettable / Dance, ballerina, dance / It's all in the game / Let there be love / St. Louis blues / Beautiful friendship / Let's fall in love / Those lazy hazy crazy days of Summer / Pretend / Mona Lisa / When I fall in love / Nature boy / Ramblin' rose / Smile / Serenata / Tenderly / Love is a many splendoured thing / Stay as sweet as you are / Love letters / Christmas song
CD ____ CDEMTV 61
EMI / Nov '91 / EMI

UNFORGETTABLE NAT KING COLE, THE
Somewhere along the way / Love me tender / But not for me / Mona Lisa / Too young / Unforgettable / True love / Love letters / You are my first love / Take me back to Toyland / This can't be love / Two different worlds / Just in time / It's only a paper moon / To the ends of the earth / Tea for two / Somebody loves me / Sweet Lorraine
CD ____ BSTCD 9113
Best Compact Discs / Apr '94 / Complete/ Pinnacle

VERY BEST OF NAT 'KING' COLE, THE
Sweet Georgia Brown / Yes Sir that's my baby / On the sunny side of the street / Paper moon / Body and soul / Tea for two / Sweet Lorraine / Old piano plays the blues / Don't cry crybaby / If you can't smile and say yes / Miss Thing / Nat meets June / Blues / Satchel mouth baby / Cole's bop blues / Last but not least / Trouble with me is you / Greatest inventor / Frim fram sauce / I'm lost
CD ____ 100372
CMC / May '97 / BMG

VOCAL SIDES, THE
CD ____ 15718
Laserlight / Sep '92 / Target/BMG

Cole, Natalie

GOOD TO BE BACK
Safe / As a matter of fact / Rest of the night / Miss you like crazy / I do / Good to be back / Gonna make you mine / Starting over again / Don't mention my heartache / I can't cry / Someone's rocking my dreamboat / Wild women do
CD ____ 7559611152
Elektra / Jul '91 / Warner Music

HOLLY & IVY
CD ____ 7559617042
Elektra / Nov '94 / Warner Music

I'VE GOT LOVE ON MY MIND
CD ____ JD 1236
Jazz Door / Oct '96 / Koch

SOPHISTICATED LADY
This will be / Good morning heartache / Touch me / Unpredictable you / Sophisticated lady / Joey / I've got love on my mind / Needing you / Your face stays in my mind / Can we get together again / Heaven is with you / Our love / I love you so / Keep smiling / Not like mine / Be thankful / Who will carry on / You / Oh daddy / Stand by
CD ____ CDMFP 5984
Music For Pleasure / Jun '93 / EMI

SOUL OF NATALIE COLE, THE (1975-1980)
This will be / Lovers / Mr. Melody / Annie Mae / I can't break away / La costa / Peaceful living / (I've seen) Paradise / Stairway to the stars / Inseparable / I love him so much / Be mine tonight / What you won't do for love / Still i love / Love will find you / Party lights / This will be (remix)
CD ____ CDEST 2157
Capitol / Oct '91 / EMI

STARDUST
CD ____ 7559619902
Elektra / Nov '96 / Warner Music

TAKE A LOOK
I wish you love / I'm beginning to see the light / Swingin' shepherd blues / Crazy he calls me / Cry me a river / Undecided / Fiesta in blue / I'm gonna laugh you right out of my life / Let there be love / It's sand man / Don't explain / As time goes by / Too close for comfort / Calypso blues / This will make you laugh / Lovers / All about love / Take a look
CD ____ 7559614962
Elektra / Jun '93 / Warner Music

UNFORGETTABLE
Very thought of you / It's only a paper moon / Route 66 / Mona lisa / LOVE / This can't be love / Smile / Lush life / That Sunday /

That summer / Orange coloured sky / (I love you) for sentimental reasons / Straighten up and fly right / Avalon / Don't get around much anymore / Too young / Nature boy / Darling / Je vous aime beaucoup / Almost like being in love / Thou swell / Non dimenticar / Our love is here to stay
CD 7559610492
Elektra / Jun '91 / Warner Music

Cole, Paula

HARBINGER
CD 9362460412
Warner Bros. / Jan '96 / Warner Music

THIS FIRE
Tiger / Where have all the cowboys gone / Throwing stones / Carmen / Mississippi / Nietzche's eyes / Road to dead / Me / Feelin' love / Hush hush hush / I don't want to wait
CD 9362464242
Reprise / Jul '97 / Warner Music

Cole, Richie

ALTO MADNESS
Price is right / Common touch / Last tango in Paris / Island breeze / Big Bo's paradise / Remember your day off... / Moody's mood
CD MCD 5155
Muse / Sep '92 / New Note/Pinnacle

BOSSA INTERNATIONAL
CD MCD 9180
Milestone / Oct '93 / Cadillac / Complete/ Pinnacle / Jazz Music / Wellard

HOLLYWOOD MADNESS
Hooray for Hollywood / Hi fly / Tokyo rose sing the Hollywood blues / Relaxin' at Camarillo / Malibu breeze / I love Lucy / Waiting for Waits / Hooray for Hollywood (reprise)
CD MCD 5207
Muse / Feb '86 / New Note/Pinnacle

MUSIC OF DIZZY GILLESPIE, THE
CD INAK 3032
In Akustik / Oct '96 / Direct / TKO Magnum

NEW YORK AFTERNOON
Dorothy's den / Waltz for a rainy be-bop evening / Alto madness / New York afternoon / It's the same thing everywhere / Stormy weather / You'll always be my friend
CD MCD 5119
Muse / Sep '92 / New Note/Pinnacle

POPBOP
Overjoyed / Eddie Jefferson / On a misty night / LDorado kaddy / La bamba / When you wish upon a star / Spanish harlem / Star trek 1 / Sonomascope / Saxophobia / Straight no chaser
CD MCD 91522
Milestone / Jan '94 / Cadillac / Complete/ Pinnacle / Jazz Music / Wellard

SIGNATURE
Sunday in New York / Trade winds / Doing the jungle walk / Occasional man / Rainbow lady / Take the cole train / If ever I would leave you / Peggy's blue skylight / America the beautiful
CD MCD 91622
Milestone / Jan '94 / Cadillac / Complete/ Pinnacle / Jazz Music / Wellard

YAKETY MADNESS (Cole, Richie & Boots Randolph)
CD 15473
Laserlight / Jan '94 / Target/BMG

Coleman, Anthony

DISCO BY NIGHT
CD AVAN 011
Avant / Nov '92 / Cadillac / Harmonia Mundi

Coleman, Bill

AN INTRODUCTION TO BILL COLEMAN
CD 4043
Best Of Jazz / Apr '97 / Discovery

BILL COLEMAN
CD JCD 196
Jazzology / Apr '94 / Jazz Music

BILL COLEMAN IN PARIS VOL.2 1936-1938
After you've gone / I'm in the mood for love / Joe Louis stomp / Coquette / Exactly like you / Hangover blues / Rose room / (Back home again in) Indiana / Bill street blues / Merry go round broke down / I ain't got nobody / Baby, won't you please come home / Big boy blues / Swing guitars / Bill Coleman blues / In a little Spanish town / I double dare you / Way down yonder in New Orleans / I wish I could shimmy like my sister Kate
CD DRGCD 8402
DRG / Sep '93 / Discovery / New Note/ Pinnacle

CLASSICS 1936-1938
CD CLASSICS 764
Classics / Jun '94 / Discovery / Jazz Music

FONSEQUE/FLEUR
CD 873121
Milan / Aug '92 / Conifer/BMG / Silva Screen

HANGIN' AROUND
Feeling the spirit / Rosetta / Star dust / I'm in the mood for love / After you've gone / Joe Louis stomp / Coquette / Between the devil and the deep blue sea / I got rhythm / Hangin' around Boudon / Ol' man river / Swing time / Indiana / Bill Street blues / Rose room / Merry go round broke down / Way down yonder in New Orleans / (I wish I could shimmy like my) Sister Kate / Wandering man blues / Three o'clock jump / Reunion in Harlem / Hawkins' barrel house / Stumpy
CD TPZ 1040
Topaz Jazz / Mar '96 / Cadillac / Pinnacle

MEETS GUY LAFITTE
CD BLCD 760182
Black Lion / Apr '93 / Cadillac / Jazz Music / Koch / Wellard

Coleman, Bob

CINCINNATI BLUES 1928-1936 (Coleman, Bob Cincinnati Jug Band)
CD SOB 035192
Story Of The Blues / Dec '92 / ADA / Koch

Coleman, Cy

WHY TRY TO CHANGE ME NOW
CD PS 003CD
P&S / Sep '95 / Discovery

Coleman, Deborah

I CAN'T LOSE
CD BPCD 5038
Blind Pig / Feb '97 / ADA / CM / Direct / Hot Shot

Coleman, Gary B.B.

BEST OF GARY B.B. COLEMAN, THE
One eyed woman / Baby scratch my back / Cloud 9 / Word of warning / I fell in love on a one night stand / Merry Christmas baby / Watch where you stroke / Think before you act / If you can beat me rockin' / St. James infirmary / I won't be your fool / Christmas blues
CD ICH 1065CD
Ichiban / Jun '94 / Direct / Koch

ONE NIGHT STAND
Baby scratch my back / Sitting and waiting / I just can't lose this blues / I'll take care of you / I wrote this song for you / As the years go passing by / I fell in love on a one night stand / Going down
CD ICH 1034CD
Ichiban / Oct '93 / Direct / Koch

ROMANCE WITHOUT FINANCE IS A NUISANCE
She ain't ugly / Don't give away that recipe / If you see my one eyed woman / Dealin' from the bottom of the deck / Romance without finance / Food stamp Annie / Mr. Chicken Stew / Mr. B's frosting
CD ICH 1107CD
Ichiban / Oct '93 / Direct / Koch

Coleman, George

AMSTERDAM AFTER DARK
Amsterdam after dark / New arrival / Lo-Joe / Autumn in New York / Apache dance / Blondie's waltz
CD CDSJP 129
Timeless Jazz / Mar '91 / New Note/ Pinnacle

AT YOSHI'S
They say it's wonderful / Good morning heartache / Laig gobblin' blues / Ten / Up jumped Spring / Father / Soul eyes
CD ECD 220212
Evidence / Aug '92 / ADA / Cadillac / Harmonia Mundi

BLUES INSIDE OUT (Coleman, George Quintet)
CD JHCD 046
Ronnie Scott's Jazz House / Nov '96 / Cadillac / Jazz Music / New Note/Pinnacle / TKO Magnum

BONGO JOE
CD ARHCD 1040
Arhoolie / Apr '95 / ADA / Cadillac / Direct

MANHATTAN PANORAMA
CD ECD 220192
Evidence / Jun '92 / ADA / Cadillac / Harmonia Mundi

MY HORNS OF PLENTY (Coleman, George Quartet)
Lush life / Conrad / My romance / Sheikh of Araby / You mean so much to me / Old folks
CD 8372782
Birdology / Jan '92 / PolyGram

PLAYING CHANGES
Laura / Siorra / Moment's notice
CD JHCD 002
Ronnie Scott's Jazz House / Jan '94 / Cadillac / Jazz Music / New Note/Pinnacle / TKO Magnum

Coleman, Michael

1891-1945
CD CEFCD 161
Gael Linn / Jan '94 / ADA / CM / Direct / Grapevine/PolyGram / Roots

Coleman, Naimee

SILVER WRISTS
Care about you / Control / Better than this / Silver wrists / Still she sings / Ruthless affection / Sometimes / Remind me / True / Hold tight
CD CDCHR 6119
Chrysalis / Jun '97 / EMI

Coleman, Ornette

ART OF THE IMPROVISERS
CD 7567909782
Atlantic / Apr '95 / Warner Music

AT THE GOLDEN CIRCLE VOL.2
Snowflakes and sunshine / Morning song / Riddle / Antiques
CD BNZ 181
Blue Note / Aug '89 / EMI

BEAUTY IS A RARE THING (Complete Atlantic Recordings - 6CD Set)
Focus on sanity / Chrology / Peace / Congeniality / Lonely woman / Monk and the nun / Just for you / Eventually / Una muy bonita / Bird food / Change of the century / Music always / Face of the bass / Forerunner / Free / Circle with a hole in the middle / Ramblin' / Little symphony / Tribes of New York / Kaleidoscope / Rise and shine / Mr. and Mrs. People / Blues connotation / I heard it over the radio / P.S Unless one has (Blues connotation No.2) / Revolving doors / Brings goodness / Joy of a toy / To us / Humpty dumpty / Fifth of Beethoven / Motive for its use / Moon inhabitatnts / Legend of bebop / Some other / Embraceable you / All / Folk tale / Poise / Beauty is a rare thing / First take / Free jazz / Proof readers / Wru / Check up / Alchemy of Scott La Faro / Eos / Enfant / Ecars / Cross breeding / Harlem's Manhattan / Mapa / Abstraction / Variants on a theme of Thelonious Monk (criss-cross)
CD Set 8122714102
Atlantic / Feb '94 / Warner Music

BODY META
Voice poetry / Homegrown / Macho woman / Fou amour / European echoes
CD 5319162
Harmolodic/Verve / Oct '96 / PolyGram

CHANGE OF THE CENTURY
Ramblin' / Free / Face of the bass / Forerunner / Bird food / Una muy bonita / Change of the century
CD 7567813412
Atlantic / Jun '93 / Warner Music

CHAPPAQUA SUITE (2CD Set)
Part one / Part two / Part three / Part four
CD 4805842
Sony Jazz / Dec '95 / Sony

COLOURS (Coleman, Ornette & Joachim Kuhn)
Faxing / House of stained glass / Refills / Story writing / Three ways to one / Passion cultures / Night plans / Cyber cyber
CD 5377892
Harmolodic/Verve / Jul '97 / PolyGram

DEDICATION TO POETS AND WRITERS
CD 30010
Giants Of Jazz / Sep '92 / Cadillac / Jazz Music / Target/BMG

FREE
Chronology / Eventually / Change of the century / Peace / Congeniality / Monk and the nun / Forerunner / Free / Music always / Una muy bonita / Ramblin'
CD CD 53212
Giants Of Jazz / Oct '96 / Cadillac / Jazz Music / Target/BMG

FREE JAZZ
Little symphony / Rise and shine / Kaleidoscope / Revolving doors / Legend of bebop / Embraceable you / Folk tale / Free jazz
CD CD 53214
Giants Of Jazz / Jan '96 / Cadillac / Jazz Music / Target/BMG

FREE JAZZ - THAT'S JAZZ
Free jazz (part 1) / Free jazz (part 2)
CD 7567813472
Atlantic / Mar '93 / Warner Music

IN ALL LANGUAGES
Peace warriors / Feet music / Africa is the mirror of all colours / Word for Bird / Space church / Latin genetics / In all mercury / Sound manual / Mothers of the veil / Cloning / Music news / Art of love is happiness / Today, yesterday and tomorrow / Listen up / Feet up / Biosphere / Storytellers
CD 5319152
Harmolodic/Verve / Jul '97 / PolyGram

ORNETTE ON TENOR
Cross breeding / Mapa / Enfant / Eos / Ecars
CD 8122714552
Atlantic / Jul '96 / Warner Music

SHAPE OF JAZZ TO COME, THE
Lonely woman / Eventually / Peace / Focus on sanity / Congeniality / Chronology
CD 7567813392
Atlantic / Jun '93 / Warner Music

SOAPSUDS SOAPSUDS (Coleman, Ornette & Charlie Haden)
Mary Hartman, Mary Hartman / Human being / Soapsuds / Sex spy / Some day
CD 5319172
Harmolodic/Verve / Oct '96 / PolyGram

SOMETHING ELSE
CD OJCCD 163
Original Jazz Classics / Feb '93 / Complete/Pinnacle / Jazz Music / Wellard

SONG X (Coleman, Ornette & Pat Metheny)
Song X / Mob job / Endangered species / Video games / Kathelin Gray / Trigonometry / Song X / Long time no see
CD GFLD 19195
Geffen / Mar '93 / BMG

SOUND MUSEUM (Hidden Man)
CD 5319142
Harmolodic/Verve / Aug '96 / PolyGram

SOUND MUSEUM (Three Women)
CD 5316572
Verve / Aug '96 / PolyGram

TOMORROW IS THE QUESTION
Tomorrow is the question / Tears inside / Mind and time / Compassion / Giggin' / Rejoicing / Lorraine / Turnaround / Endless
CD OJCCD 342
Original Jazz Classics / Apr '89 / Complete/ Pinnacle / Jazz Music / Wellard

TONE DIALING (Coleman, Ornette & Prime Time)
Street blues / Search for life / Guadalupe / Bach prelude / Sound is everywhere / Miguel's fortune / La capella / OAC / If I knew as much about you (as you know about me) / When will I see you again / Kathelin Gray / Badal / Tone dialing / Family reunion / Local instinct / Ying yang
CD 5274832
Harmolodic/Verve / Mar '96 / PolyGram

Coleman, Steve

CURVES OF LIFE (Coleman, Steve & Five Elements)
Multiplicity of approaches / Country bama / Streets / 'Round midnight / Drop kick live / Gypsy / I'm burning up
CD 74321316932
RCA Victor / Oct '96 / BMG

DEF TRANCE BEAT (Modalities Of Rhythm) (Coleman, Steve & Five Elements)
Flint / Verifiable / pedagogy / Dogon / Multiplicity of approachs / Khu / Pad thai / Jeannine's sizzling patterns of force / Mantra / Salt peanuts
CD 01241631812
Novus / Apr '95 / BMG

FLASHBACK ON M-BASE (Coleman, Steve & Robin Eubanks/Greg Osby/ Cassandra Wilson)
Micro move / Never give up / To perpetuate the funk / Silent attitude / Rock this calling / Gyrhythmitoid / I'm going home / Mischief makers / Never midtown / Another level
CD 5140102
jMT / Mar '93 / PolyGram

MOTHERLAND PULSE (Coleman, Steve Group)
Irate blues / Another level / Cud ba rith / Wights waits for weights / No good time fairies / On this / Glide was in the ride / Motherland pulse
CD 8344012
jMT / Oct '93 / PolyGram

MYTHS, MODES AND MEANS
Mystic dub / Finger of God / Initiate / Madra / Song of the beginnings / Numerology / Transits
CD 74321316922
RCA Victor / Nov '96 / BMG

ON THE EDGE OF TOMORROW (Coleman, Steve & Five Elements)
Fire revisited / Fat lay back / I'm going home / It is time / (In order to form) a more perfect union / Little one I miss you / T-T Tim / Metaphysical phunktion / Nine to five / Profile man / Stone bone (so can't go wrong) / Almost there / Change the guard
CD 8345042
jMT / Oct '93 / PolyGram

PHASE = SPACE (Coleman, Steve & Dave Holland)
CD DIW 865
DIW / Jan '93 / Cadillac / Harmonia Mundi

SIGN AND THE SEAL, THE (Transmissions Of The Metaphysics Of A Culture) (Coleman, Steve Mystic Rhythm Society & Afro Cuba De Matanzas)
Diurnal Lord (for Agayu) / Seal / Passage of the river / Oya natureza / Secretos del Aba-

cua / Saudade / Metamorphosis of Amalia / Mystery of seven (the guaguanco in progression) / Prologue / Guaguanco / Abacua/ Obatala / Son abacua/Obatala / Montuno / Epilogue
CD 74321407272
RCA Victor / Aug '97 / BMG

TALE OF THREE CITIES EP (Coleman, Steve & Metrics)
Be bop / I am who I am / Science / Get open / Slow burn / Left to right
CD 74321247472
Novus / Jul '95 / BMG

WAY OF THE CIPHER, THE
Freestyle / Fast lane / Slow lane / S-ludes / Black Genghis / Chaos (tech jump) / Hyped laxed and warped / Night breed
CD 74321316902
RCA Victor / Nov '96 / BMG

WORLD EXPANSION (BY THE M-BASE NEOPHYTE) (Coleman, Steve & Five Elements)
Desperate move / Stone bone Jr / Mad monkey / Dream state / Tang lung / Yo ho / And they parted ... / In the park / Just a funky old song / Urilai Thrane / To perpetuate the funk / Koshine Koji / Tlydor's bane
CD 8344102
jMT / Jan '94 / PolyGram

Coleman, Wanda

BERSERK ON HOLLYWOOD BOULEVARD
CD NAR 059CD
New Alliance / May '93 / Plastic Head

HIGH PRIESTESS OF WORD
CD NAR 048CD
New Alliance / May '93 / Plastic Head

Coles, Johnny

NEW MORNING (Coles, Johnny Quartet)
CD CRISS 1005CD
Criss Cross / Oct '92 / Cadillac / Direct / Vital/SAM

WARM SOUND, THE
CD 378042
Koch / Jan '96 / Koch

Colianni, John

LIVE AT MAYBECK RECITAL HALL VOL.37
Blue and sentimental / Stardust / What's your story Morning Glory / It never entered my mind / Londonderry air / Don't stop the carnival / When your lover has gone / Ja da / Basin Street blues / I never knew / Baby, won't you please come home / Tea for two / Goodbye / Heart shaped box
CD CCD 4643
Concord Jazz / May '95 / New Note/ Pinnacle

Colin, Daniel

PRESTIGE DE L'ACCORDEON VOL.1
CD 242052
Wotre Music / Nov '92 / Discovery / New Note/Pinnacle

Colina, Michael

SHADOW OF URBANO
Joy dancing / Shades / Shadow of Urbano / Hong Kong flu / Doctor of desire / Fast break / Lady and the tramp / Drifter
CD 259967
Private Music / Nov '89 / BMG

Coll, Brian

AT HOME IN IRELAND
CD CDBC 505
Outlet / Jan '95 / ADA / CM / Direct / Duncans / Koch / Ross

Collage

GET IN TOUCH/SHINE THE LIGHT
Get in touch with me / Love is for everyone / Simple / Near to me / Young girls / Move in time / Alien Zzz / Kickin' it / Romeo where's Juliet / Winners and losers / Shine the light / In the mix / Step right up / Here and now
CD DEEPM 034
Deep Beats / Aug '97 / BMG

Collapsed Lung

COOLER
London tonight / Lungs collapse / Ballad night / Sense / Codename: Omega / One foot up the rude ladder / Board game / 25 years / Casino kisschase / TV is life Elvis / Maclife / Connection / Eat my goal / Codename: Omega (instrumental) / Ballad night (instrumental) / Lungs collapse (instrumental) / Casino kisschase (instrumental)
CD BLUFF 031CD
CD BLUFF 031CDS
Deceptive / Jun '96 / Vital

JACKPOT GOALIE
Maclife intro / Maclife / Down with the plaid fad / Eat my goal / Interactive / I may not know the score but / Something ordinary / Burn rubber soul / Filthy's fix / Dis MX / Begrudgit / Slack agenda
CD BLUFF 015CD
Deceptive / Apr '95 / Vital

Collectif Mu

LIVE AU CRESCENT
CD AXX 111
Seventh / Jan '97 / Cadillac / Harmonia Mundi / ReR Megacorp

Collective Quartet

ORCA
CD LEOLABCD 031
Leo Lab / May '97 / Cadillac

Collective Soul

COLLECTIVE SOUL
CD 7567827452
Atlantic / Jun '95 / Warner Music

DISCIPLINED BREAKDOWN
Precious declaration / Listen / Maybe / Full circle / Blame / Disciplined breakdown / Forgiveness / Link / Giving / In between / Crowded head / Everything
CD 7559829842
Atlantic / Mar '97 / Warner Music

HINTS, ALLEGATIONS & THINGS LEFT UNSOLVED
Shine / All / Scream / Breath / Reach / Pretty Donna / Heaven's already here / In a moment / Love lifted me / Burning bridges / Goodnight good guy / Sister don't cry / Wasting time
CD 7567825962
Atlantic / Aug '94 / Warner Music

Collectors

ASTRONAUT GIRL
CD CITREC 02
Citizen / Oct '93 / Plastic Head

DESOLATION ANGELS
CD CITRE 03
Citizen / Oct '94 / Plastic Head

Collet, Danny

LOUISIANA SWAMP CATS
CD FF 628CD
Flying Fish / Dec '93 / ADA / CM / Direct / Roots

Collette

ATTITUDE
CD REVXD 135
FM / Mar '93 / Revolver / Sony

Collette, Buddy

BUDDY'S BEST (Collette, Buddy Quintet)
Soft touch / Walkin' Willie / Changes / My funny valentine / Cute monster / Orlando blues / Blue sands / It's you
CD CDBOP 020
Boplicity / Jul '96 / Pinnacle

SOFT TOUCH
CD FSRCD 214
Fresh Sound / Jan '97 / Discovery / Jazz Music

TASTY DISH (Collette, Buddy Quartet/ Quintet)
CD FSRCD 213
Fresh Sound / Jan '97 / Discovery / Jazz Music

Collide

BENEATH THE SKIN
CD SPV 08543152
SPV / Sep '96 / Koch / Plastic Head

Collie, Max

ACES HIGH (Collie, Max Rhythm Aces)
CD RCD 114
Reality / Jun '96 / Cadillac / Jazz Music / New Note/Pinnacle / Wellard

FRONTLINE BACKLINE (Collie, Max Rhythm Aces)
Royal Garden blues / Kinklets / Down by the river / Gatemouth / Muskrat ramble / St. Louis blues / Isle of Capri / Ory's Creole trombone / Mahogany hall stomp / Lazy river / (I'll be glad when you're dead) you rascal you / Sing on / Oh you beautiful doll / You always hurt the one you love / Sweet Sue, just you
CD CDTTD 504
Timeless Jazz / Feb '95 / New Note/ Pinnacle

HIGH SOCIETY SHOW, THE (Collie, Max Rhythm Aces)
CD RCD 108
Reality / Oct '92 / Cadillac / Jazz Music / New Note/Pinnacle / Wellard

MAX COLLIE & FRIENDS PART 2
CD R 113C
Reality / Aug '94 / Cadillac / Jazz Music / New Note/Pinnacle / Wellard

MAX COLLIE'S RHYTHM ACES VOL.2 (Collie, Max Rhythm Aces)
CD BCD 83
GHB / Jun '96 / Jazz Music

MAX COLLIE'S RHYTHM ACES VOL.3 (Collie, Max Rhythm Aces)
CD BCD 98
GHB / Nov '96 / Jazz Music

SENSATION
CD CDTTD 530
Timeless Traditional / Jan '88 / Jazz Music / New Note/Pinnacle

THRILL OF JAZZ, THE (Collie, Max Rhythm Aces)
CD RCD 111
Reality / Mar '90 / Cadillac / Jazz Music / New Note/Pinnacle / Wellard

WORLD CHAMPIONS OF JAZZ (Collie, Max Rhythm Aces)
Too bad / Sweet like this / Salutation march / 'S wonderful / I'm crazy 'bout my baby / Didn't he ramble / Ragtime dance / Dans les rues D'Antibes / Fidgety fingers
CD BLCD 760512
Black Lion / Nov '95 / Cadillac / Jazz Music / Koch / Wellard

Collier, Graham

CHARLES RIVER FRAGMENTS
Hackney five / Charles river fragments
CD BHR 004
Boathouse / Apr '96 / New Note/Pinnacle

Collins Kids

HOP, SKIP AND JUMP
Go away don't bother me / Rock 'n' roll polka / Move a little closer / My first love / Hush money / I wish / Cuckoo rock / Beetle bug bop / I'm in my teens / Rockaway rock / They're still in love / Make him behave / Hop, skip and jump / Shortnin' bread rock / Just because / Hoy hoy / Hot rod / Heartbeat / Mama worries / Party / Walking the floor over you / Missouri waltz / You are my sunshine / Soda poppin' around / Young heart / Ain't you ever / What'cha gonna do now / Waitin' and watchin' / Home of the blues / Lonesome road / Early American / Rockin' gypsy / Bye bye / Hurricane / Mercy / Rock boppin' baby / Whistle bait / Sweet talk / Spur of the moment / Rebel / Johnny Yuma / There'll be some changes made / Fireball mail / T-bone / What about tomorrow / Get along home Cindy / You've been gone too long / One step down / There stands the one / Wild and wicked love / Hey mama boom a lacka / More than a friend / Pied piper poodle / Blues in the night / Another man done gone / Sugar plum / Kinda like love / Are you certain / That's your affair
CD Set BCD 15537
Bear Family / Aug '91 / Direct / Rollercoaster / Swift

ROCKIN' ON TV 1957-1961
CD KKCD 14
Krazy Kat / Oct '93 / Hot Shot / Jazz Music

Collins, Albert

ALBERT COLLINS & BARRELHOUSE LIVE (Collins, Albert & Barrelhouse)
CD BMCD 225
Munich / '90 / ADA / CM / Direct / Greensleeves

ALBERT COLLINS LIVE
You're so high / You accuse me / I get the feeling / Angel mercy / Icy blue / Trouble was money / Playing with my mind / Too many dirty dishes / Things I used to do / Black cat bone
CD CDCBL 756
Charly / Oct '95 / Koch

COLD SNAP
Cash talkin' / Bending like a willow tree / Good fool is hard to find / Lights are on but nobody's home / I ain't drunk / Hooked on you / Too many dirty dishes / Snatchin' it back / Fake ID
CD ALCD 4752
Alligator / May '93 / ADA / CM / Direct

COLLINS MIX
There's gotta be a change / Honey hush / Master charge / If trouble was money / Don't lose your cool / If you love me like you say / Frosty / Tired man / Moon is full / Collin's mix / Same old thing
CD VPBCD 17
Pointblank / Nov '93 / EMI

DON'T LOSE YOUR COOL
Got togettin' / My mind is trying to leave me / I'm broke / Don't lose your cool / When a guitar plays the blues / But I was cool / Melt down / Ego trip / Quicksand
CD ALCD 4730
Alligator / May '93 / ADA / CM / Direct

FROSTBITE
If you love me like you say / Blue Monday hangover / I got a problem / Highway is like a woman / Brick / Don't go reaching across my plate / Give me my blues / Snowed in
CD ALCD 4719
Alligator / May '93 / ADA / CM / Direct

FROZEN ALIVE
Frosty / Angel of mercy / I got that feeling / Caledonia / Things I used to do / Got a mind to travel / Cold cuts
CD ALCD 4725
Alligator / May '93 / ADA / CM / Direct

ICE PICKIN'
Talking woman blues / When the welfare turns its back on you / Ice pick / Cold cold feeling / Too tired / Master charge / Conversation with Collins / Avalanche
CD ALCD 4713
Alligator / May '93 / ADA / CM / Direct

ICEMAN
Mr. Collins, Mr. Collins / Iceman / Don't mistake kindness for weakness / Travellin' South / Put the shoe on the other foot / I'm beginning to wonder / Head rag / Hawk / Blues for Gabe / Mr. Collins, Mr. Collins (reprise)
CD VPBCD 3
Pointblank / Feb '91 / EMI

IN CONCERT
CD CLACD 427
Castle / Mar '97 / BMG

LIVE 1992-1993 (Collins, Albert & The Icebreakers)
Iceman / Lights are on but nobody's home / If you love me (like you say) / Put the shoe on the other foot / Frosty / Travellin' South / Talkin' woman / My woman has a black cat bone / I ain't drunk / T-bone shuffle
CD VPBCD 27
Pointblank / Oct '95 / EMI

LIVE IN JAPAN (Collins, Albert & The Icebreakers)
Listen here: *Collins, Albert* / Tired man: *Collins, Albert* / If trouble was money: *Collins, Albert* / Jealous man: *Collins, Albert* / Stormy Monday: *Collins, Albert* / Skatin': *Collins, Albert* / All about my girl: *Collins, Albert*
CD ALCD 4733
Alligator / May '93 / ADA / CM / Direct

SHOWDOWN (Collins, Albert/Johnny Copeland/Robert Cray)
T-Bone shuffle / Moon is full / Lion's den / She's into something / Bring your fine self home / Black cat bone / Dream / Albert's alley / Black Jack
CD ALCD 4743
Alligator / May '93 / ADA / CM / Direct

Collins, Bootsy

AHH...THE NAME IS BOOTSY BABY (Bootsy's Rubber Band)
Ahh the name is Bootsy, baby / Pinocchio theory / Rubber dickie / Preview side too / What's a telephone bill / Munchies for your love / Can't stay away / We want Bootsy (reprise)
CD 7599229722
WEA / Jan '96 / Warner Music

BACK IN THE DAY - THE BEST OF BOOTSY COLLINS
Ahh...the name is Bootsy baby / Stretchin' out (in a rubber band) / Pinocchio theory / Hollywood squares / I'd rather be with you / What so never the dance / Can't stay away / Jam fan (hot) / Mug push / Body slam / Scenery / Vanish in our sleep / Psychoticbumpschool
CD 7599265812
WEA / Aug '94 / Warner Music

BLASTERS OF THE UNIVERSE (Bootsy's New Rubber Band)
Blasters of the universe / JR / Funk express card / Bad girls / Back n the day / Where r the children / Female troubles (The national anthem) / Wide track / Funk me dirty / Blasters of the universe 2 (The sequel) / Goodnight Eddie / Sacred place / Half pass midnight / It's a silly serious world
CD Set RCD 9030708
Rykodisc / Aug '94 / ADA / Vital

BOOTSY PLAYER OF THE YEAR (Bootsy's Rubber Band)
Bootsy (whats the name)... / As in (I love you) / Roto-rooter / Very yes / Bootzilla / May the force be with you / Hollywood squares
CD 7599263352
Warner Bros. / Jan '96 / Warner Music

JUNGLE BASS (Bootsy's Rubber Band)
Jungle bass / Disciples of funk / Interzone / Jungle bass (Mix)
CD BRECD 550
4th & Broadway / Jul '90 / PolyGram

KEEPIN' DAH FUNK ALIVE 4 1995 (Bootsy's New Rubber Band)
Intro / Ahh the name is Bootsy, baby / Bootsy (What's the name of this town) / Psychoticbumpschool / Pinocchio theory / Hollywood squares / Bernie solo / One nation under a groove / P Funk (wants to get funked up) / Cosmic slop / Flash light / Bootzilla / Roto-rooter / I'd rather be with you / Sacred place / Stretchin' out (In a rubber band) / Touch somebody / Night of the thumpasaurus peoples / Keepin' da funk alive 1994-5
CD Set RCD 9032324
Rykodisc / Aug '95 / ADA / Vital

LORD OF THE HARVEST (Zillatron)
Bugg light / Fuzz face / Exterminate / Smell the secrets / Count zero / Bootsy and the beast / No fly zone the devils playground / Passion continues
CD RCD 10301
Black Arc / Jun '94 / Vital

ONE GIVETH, THE COUNT TAKETH AWAY, THE
Shine o'Myte (rap popping) / Landshark / Count Dracula / Funkateer, I / Lexicon (of love) / So nice you name him twice / What's wrong radio / Music to smile by / Play on playboy / Take a lickin' and keep on kickin' / Funky funkateer
CD 7599236672
WEA / Jan '96 / Warner Music

STRETCHIN' OUT (Bootsy's Rubber Band)
Stretchin' out (In a rubber band) / Psychotic bum school / Another point of view / I'd rather be with you / Love vibes / Physical love / Vanish in our sleep
CD 7599263342
WEA / Jan '96 / Warner Music

THIS BOOT IS MADE FOR FONK-N (Bootsy's Rubber Band)
Under the influence of a groove / Bootsy get live / O boy gorl / Jam fan / Chug-a-lug / Shejam / Reprise
CD 7559232952
WEA / Jan '96 / Warner Music

ULTRA WAVE
CD 7599263362
WEA / Jan '96 / Warner Music

Collins, Cal

INTERPLAY (Collins, Cal & Herb Ellis)
Besame mucho / I'll be seeing you / People will say we're in love / That's your head / Tricia's fantasy / I got it bad and that ain't good / Lime house blues
CD CCD 41372
Concord Jazz / May '97 / New Note/ Pinnacle

OHIO STYLE (Collins, Cal Quartet)
Falling in love with love / East of the sun and west of the moon / Be anything / Bag's groove / Affair to remember / Skylark / I've got the world on a string / I don't stand a ghost of a chance with you / Tumbling tumbleweeds / Ill wind / Sweet Sue, just you / Until the real thing comes along
CD CCD 4447
Concord Jazz / Feb '91 / New Note/ Pinnacle

Collins, Dave & Ansell

DOUBLE BARREL
CD RASCD 3225
Ras / Jan '96 / Direct / Greensleeves / Jet Star / SRD

Collins, Edwyn

GORGEOUS GEORGE
Campaign for real rock / Girl like you / Low expectations / Out of this world / If you could love me / North of heaven / Gorgeous George / It's right in front of you / Make me feel again / You got it all / Subsidence / Occupy your mind
CD SETCD 014
Setanta / Jul '95 / Vital

HELLBENT ON COMPROMISE
Means to an end / You poor deluded fool / It might as well be you / Take care of yourself / Graciously / Someone else besides / My girl has gone / Now that it's love / Everything and more / What's the big idea / Time of the preacher - long time gone
CD FIENDCD 195
Demon / Oct '90 / Pinnacle

HOPE AND DESPAIR
Coffee table song / Fifty shades of blue / You're better than you know / Pushing it to the back of my mind / Darling they want it all / Wheels of love / Beginning of the end / Measure of the man / Testing time / Let me put your arms around you / Wide eyes child in me / I don't stand a ghost of a chance with you
CD FIENDCD 144
Demon / Aug '95 / Pinnacle

I'M NOT FOLLOWING YOU
It's a steal / Magic piper / Seventies night / No one waved goodbye / Downer / Keep on burning / Running away with myself / Country rock / For the rest of my life / Superficial cat / Adidas world / I'm not following you
CD SETCD 039
Setanta / Sep '97 / Vital

Collins, Glenda

BEEN INVITED TO A PARTY (1963-1966)
I lost my heart at the fairground / I feel so good / If you gotta pick a baby / Baby it hurts / Nice wasn't it / Lollipop / Everybody got to fall in love / Johnny loves me / Paradise for two / Thou shalt not steal / Been invited to a party / Something I got to tell you / My heart didn't lie / It's hard to believe it / Don't let it rain on Sunday / In the first place
CD CSAPCD 108
Connoisseur Collection / Aug '90 / Pinnacle

GLENDA COLLINS STORY, THE (The Joe Meek Collection)
CD GEMCD 014
Diamond / Feb '97 / Pinnacle

Collins, Johnny

SHANTIES AND SONGS OF THE SEA
Blow the man down (flying fish sailor) / Haul boys haul / Blood red roses / South Australia / Leave her Johnny / Randy Dandy O / Fire marengo / Shallow brown / Eliza Lee / Goodbye fare thee well / Maul / Old Billy Riley / Bold Reilly-O / Down the bay to Julianna / Wild goose / Hard on the beach oar / Roll the wood pile down / Dodger bank / Sailor prayer / Farewell shanty
CD GRCD 75
Grasmere / Apr '96 / Highlander / Savoy / Target/BMG

Collins, Joyce

SWEET MADNESS
CD ACD 262
Audiophile / Sep '91 / Jazz Music

Collins, Judy

AMAZING GRACE
CD TCD 2265
Telstar / Jul '87 / BMG

COLORS OF THE DAY - THE BEST OF JUDY COLLINS
Someday soon / Since you asked / Both sides now / Sons of / Suzanne / Farewell to Tarwathie / Who knows where the time goes / Sunny Goodge Street / My father (always promised) / Albatross / In my life / Amazing grace
CD 9606812
Elektra / Feb '92 / Warner Music

LIVE AT NEWPORT 1959-1966
Introduction / Greenland whale fisheries / Anathea / Bonny ship The Diamond / Turn turn turn / Blowin' in the wind / Hey Nelly Nelly / Great silkie / Carry it on / Hard lovin' loser / Coming of the roads / Silver dagger / Get together / Bullgine run
CD VCD 77013
Vanguard / Oct '95 / ADA / Pinnacle

SANITY AND GRACE
History / Lovin' and leavin' / Sanity and grace / Daughters of time / Born to the breed / Moonfall / Morning has broken / When a child is born / Jerusalem / Life you dream
CD 12701
Laserlight / Nov '96 / Target/BMG

WIND BENEATH MY WINGS
CD 15451
Laserlight / May '94 / Target/BMG

Collins, Kathleen

TRADITIONAL MUSIC OF IRELAND
CD SHAN 34010CD
Shanachie / Apr '95 / ADA / Greensleeves / Koch

Collins, Lui

BAPTISM OF FIRE
CD GLCD 1060
Green Linnet / '92 / ADA / CM / Direct / Highlander / Roots

MADE IN NEW ENGLAND
CD GLCD 1056
Green Linnet / Feb '89 / ADA / CM / Direct / Highlander / Roots

THERE'S A LIGHT
CD GLCD 1061
Green Linnet / Feb '92 / ADA / CM / Direct / Highlander / Roots

Collins, Phil

BOTH SIDES
Both sides of the story / Can't turn back the years / Everyday / I've forgotten everythin' / We're sons of our fathers / Can't find my way / Survivors / We fly so close / There's a place for us / We want and we wonder / Please come out tonight
CD CDV 2800
Virgin / Oct '93 / EMI

BUT SERIOUSLY
Hang in long enough / That's just the way it is / Do you remember / Something happened on the way to heaven / Colours / I wish it would rain down / Another day in paradise / Heat on the street / All of my life / Saturday night and Sunday morning / Father to son / Find a way to my heart
CD CDV 2620
Virgin / Nov '89 / EMI

DANCE INTO THE LIGHT
CD 0630160002
Face Value / Oct '96 / Warner Music

DEEP GREEN (Collins, Phil & Gary Moore/Rod Argent/Friends)
CD 74321475372
Milan / Aug '97 / Conifer/BMG / Silva Screen

FACE VALUE
In the air tonight / This must be love / Behind the lines / Roof is leaking / Droned / Hand in hand / I missed again / You know what I mean / I'm not moving / If leaving me is easy / Tomorrow never knows / Thunder and lightning
CD CDV 2185
Virgin / Jan '84 / EMI

HELLO I MUST BE GOING
I don't care anymore / I cannot believe it's true / Like China / Do you know, do you care / You can't hurry love / It don't matter to me / Thru these walls / Don't let him steal your heart away / West side / Why can't it wait till morning
CD CDV 2252
Virgin / Jun '88 / EMI

HITS OF PHIL COLLINS (Various Artists)
CD DCD 5260
Disky / Aug '92 / Disky / THE

NO JACKET REQUIRED
Sussudio / Only you know and I know / Long long way to go / Don't want to know / One more night / Don't lose my number / Who said I would / Doesn't anybody stay together anymore / Inside out / Take me home / We said hello goodbye
CD CDV 2345
Virgin / Feb '85 / EMI

SERIOUS HITS LIVE
Something happened on the way to heaven / Against all odds / Who said I would / One more night / Don't lose my number / Do you remember / Another day in paradise / Separate lives / In the air tonight / You can't hurry love / Two hearts / Sussudio / Groovy kind of love / Easy lover / Take me home
CD PCVCD 1
Virgin / Nov '90 / EMI

SERIOUSLY ORCHESTRAL (The Hits Of Phil Collins) (Royal Philharmonic Orchestra)
In the air tonight / Groovy kind of love / Easy lover / Do you remember / I wish it would rain down / Against all odds / Another day in paradise / Two hearts / One more night / Take me home
CD CDVIP 122
Virgin VIP / Sep '93 / EMI

Collins, Sam

JAILHOUSE BLUES
CD YAZCD 1070
Yazoo / Apr '91 / ADA / CM / Koch

Collins, Shirley

ANTHEMS IN EDEN SUITE (Collins, Shirley & Dolly)
Meeting - searching for lambs / Courtship, A - the wedding song / Denying / Foresaking - our captain cried / Dream - lowlands / Leavetaking (pleasant and delightful) / Awakening / New beginning, A - the staines morris / Rembleaway / Ca' the yowes / God dog / Bonnie cuckoo / Nellie / Gathering rushes in the month of May / Gower wassail / Beginning
CD CDEMS 1477
Harvest / Jul '93 / EMI

FOR AS MANY AS WILL (Collins, Shirley & Dolly)
Lancashire lass / Never again / Lord Allenwater / Beggar's opera medley / O Polly you might have toy'd and kist / Oh what pain it is to part / Miser thus a shilling sees / Youth's the season made for joys / Hither dear husband, turn your eyes / Lumps of plum pudding / Gilderoy / Rockley firs / Sweet Jenny Jones / German tune / Moon shines bright / Harvest home medley (Peas, beans, oats and the barley) / Mistress's health / Poor Tom
CD FLE 1003CD
Fledg'ling / Jan '94 / ADA / CM / Direct

FOUNTAIN OF SNOW
CD DURTRO 010CD
Durtro / Jan '92 / World Serpent

SWEET PRIMROSES
All things are quite silent / Cambridgeshire May Carol / Spencer the rover / Rigs of time / Cruel Mother / Bird in the bush / Streets of Derry/False bride / Locks and bolts rambleaway / Brigg fair / Higher Germaine / George Collins / Babes in the wood / Down in yon forest / Magpie's nest / False true love / Sweet primroses
CD TSCD 476
Topic / Aug '95 / ADA / CM / Direct

Collins, Tommy

LEONARD (5CD Set)
Campus boogie / Too beautiful to cry / Smooth sailin' / Fool's gold / You gotta have a license / Let me love you / There'll be no other / I love you more and more each day / Boob-i-lak / You better not do that / I always get a souvenir / High on a hilltop / Untied / What'cha gonna do now / Love-a-me, s'il vous plait / You're for me / I'll be gone / Wait a little longer / Let down / It tickles / It's nobody's fault but yours / I guess I'm crazy / You oughta see pickles now / Those old love letters from you / I wish I had died in my cradle / I'll never, never let you go / I'll always speak well of you / What kind of sweetheart are you / No love have I / All of the monkeys ain't in the zoo / That's the way love is / How do I say goodbye / Man we all ought to know / Are you ready to go / Think it over boys / I think of you yet / Upon this rock / Feet of the traveler / Don't you love me anymore / Retirement in heaven / What have you done / Love is born / I'm nobody's fool but yours / O Mary don't you weep / Did you let your light shine / In the shadow of the cross / When I survey the wondrous cross / Who at my door is standing / My saviour's love / Where could I go but to the Lord / What a friend we have in Jesus / Each step of the way / Softly and tenderly / That's why I love him / Jesus keep me near the cross / Amazing grace / Old rugged cross / Hearts don't break / You belong in my arms / Hundred years from now / Little June / My last chance with you / Sidewalks of New York / Last letter / Oklahoma hills / Great speckled bird / Broken engagement / Wreck of ol' 97 / I'm just here to get my baby out of jail / Have I told you lately that I love you / It makes no difference now / Let's live a little / I'll keep on loving you / I overlooked an orchard / I wonder if you feel the way I do / Juicy fruit / Black cat / We kissed again with tears / Keep dreaming / Don't let me stand in his footsteps / Summer's almost gone / Take me back to the good old days / Oh what a dream / Let her go / When did right become wrong / If I could just go back / I got mine / You'd better be nice / I can do that / I got mine (live) / Shindig in the barn / Million miles / Good goody gumdrop / Clock on the wall / Bee that gets the honey / It's a big jump / It's a pretty good ol' world after all / Take me back to the good old days (With chorus) / Oh what a dream (Without chorus) / Klipps kloppa / If you can't bite, don't growl / Man gotta do what a man gotta do / Man machine / Girl on sugar pie lane / Poor, broke, mixed up mess of a heart / Be serious Ann / Fool's castle / Little time for a little love / I'm not getting anywhere with you / Two sides of life / You're everything to me / Big dummy / There's no girl in my life anymore / Skinny / I'm not looking for an angel / Don't wipe the tears that you cry / Birmingham / Put me irons, lock me up (Throw away the key) / Sam Hill / It's to much like lonesome / Wine take me away / General delivery USA / Roll truck roll / If that's the fashion / Piedras negras / Laura / Branded man / Cincinnati, Ohio / Break my mind / I made a prison band / Best thing I've done in my life / Woman you have been told / Sunny side of life / He's gonna have to catch me first
CD Set BCD 15577
Bear Family / Jan '93 / Direct / Rollercoaster / Swift

Collinson, Dean

LIFE AND TIMES
Hello hello / Words to that effect / Life and times / This time / Louise / Russian roulette / Game for losers (she is out there) / Runaways / Measure upon measure / Welcome to the club
CD 74321134682
Arista / Sep '93 / BMG

Collinson, Lee

SLIP THE DRIVER A FIVER
CD FLED 3003
Fledg'ling / May '95 / ADA / CM / Direct

Collister, Christine

BLUE ACONITE
How far to the horizon / Private storm / Can't win / Paper wings / Kicking in my stall / Heart like a wheel / Forever he said / Midnight feast / Blue moon on the rise / Harvest for the world / Broken bicycles
CD FLED 3010
Fledg'ling / Oct '96 / ADA / CM / Direct

HORIZON EP
How far to the horizon / Harvest for the world / How will I ever be simple again / Guilty / Mirage
CD CING 4001
Fledg'ling / Mar '97 / ADA / CM / Direct

LIVE
CD FLECD 1004
Fledg'ling / Sep '94 / ADA / CM / Direct

Colm

SERUM
CD NR 422480
New Rose / Jan '94 / ADA / Direct / Discovery

Cologne

EARLY ELECTRONIC MUSIC
CD BVHAASTCD 9106
Bvhaast / Oct '93 / Cadillac

Colombo

COMPOSITIONS 1924-1942
CD FA 009CD
Fremeaux / Nov '95 / ADA / Discovery

Colombo, Lou

I REMEMBER BOBBY
It all depends on you / I don't stand a ghost of a chance with you / Octopus rag / Memories of you / (I'm afraid) the masquerade is over / My romance / I remember Bobby / Three little words / Emily / Gypsy / Avalon / Easy living / I let a song go out of my heart
CD ______ **CCD 4435**
Concord Jazz / Nov '90 / New Note/ Pinnacle

Colon, Willie

CONTRABANDO
Bailando asi / Manana amor / Contrabando / Che che cole / Barrunto / Te conozco / Calle luna calle sol / Lo que es de juan / Pregunta por ahi / Especial no.5 / Soltera / Quien eres
CD ______ **MES 159592**
Messidor / Apr '93 / ADA / Koch

TIEMPO PA'MATAR
El diablo / Tiempo pa'matar / Noche de lose enmascarados / Callejon sin salido / Volo / Falta de consideracion / Gitana / Serenata
CD ______ **MES 159272**
Messidor / Feb '93 / ADA / Koch

TOP SECRETS (Colon, Willie & Legal Alien)
CD ______ **MES 159802**
Messidor / Jun '93 / ADA / Koch

Colone

ACID SCIENCE TRACKS
CD ______ **DBM 2042**
Death Becomes Me / Oct '96 / Grapevine/ PolyGram / Pinnacle / SRD

Color Me Badd

TIME & CHANCE
Intro / Time and chance / Groovy now / Let me have it all / Roseanna's little sister / How deep / La tremenda (Intro) / In thee / Sunshine choose / Bells / Wildflower / Living without her / Close to heaven / Trust me / Let's start with forever / God is love / God is love (Outro) / C'est la vie / I remember
CD ______ **74321166742**
RCA / Nov '93 / BMG

Colorblind James Experience

SOLID BEHIND THE TIMES
CD ______ **RHRCD 52**
Red House / Oct '95 / ADA / Koch

Colorvine

COLORVINE
CD ______ **MAR 001**
Mark Avenue / May '97 / Cargo

Colossamite

ALL LINGO'S CLAMOUR
CD ______ **GR 34CDEP**
Skingraft / Mar '97 / SRD

Colosseum

COLLECTION, THE
CD ______ **CCSCD 287**
Castle / May '91 / BMG

COLLECTORS COLOSSEUM, THE
Jumping off the sun / Those about to die / I can't live without you / Beware the Ides of March / Walking in the park / Bolero / Rope ladder to the moon / Grass is greener
CD ______ **NEXCD 255**
Sequel / Sep '93 / BMG

COLOSSEUM (Live)
Rope ladder to the moon / Walking in the park / Skelington / Tanglewood '63 / Encore... / Stormy Monday blues / Lost angeles / I can't live without you
CD ______ **NEXCD 201**
Sequel / Feb '92 / BMG

DAUGHTER OF TIME
Three score and ten, Amen / Time lament / Take me back to doomsday / Daughter of time / Theme for an imaginary western / Bring out your dead / Downhill and shadows / Time machine
CD ______ **NEXCD 256**
Sequel / Sep '93 / BMG

EPITAPH
Walking in the park / Bring out your dead / Those about to die / Beware the Ides of March / Daughter of time / Valentine suite
CD ______ **RAWCD 014**
Raw Power / Apr '86 / Pinnacle

IDES OF MARCH, THE
Those about to die / Beware the ides of March / Machine demands a sacrifice / Elegy / Walking in the park / Backwater blues / Time machine / Bring out your dead / Theme for an imaginary Western / Daughter of time / Rope ladder to the moon / Bolero / Encore... Stormy Monday blues
CD ______ **5507342**
Spectrum / May '95 / PolyGram

REUNION CONCERT 1994
Those about to die / Elegy / Valentine suite / January's search / February's valentyne / Grass is always greener / Theme for an imaginary western / Machine demands a sacrifice / Solo colinia / Lost Angeles / Stormy Monday blues
CD ______ **INT 31602**
Intuition / May '95 / New Note/Pinnacle

STRANGE NEW FLESH (Colosseum II)
Dark side of the Moog / Down to you / Gemini and Leo / Secret places / On second thoughts / Winds
CD ______ **CLACD 104**
Castle / '86 / BMG

THOSE WHO ARE ABOUT TO DIE.../ VALENTYNE SUITE
Walking in the park / Plenty hard luck / Madarin / Debut / Beware the Ides of March / Road she walk / Before / Backwater blues / Those about to die / Kettle / Elegy / Butty's blues / Machine demands a sacrifice / Sacrifice / Valentine suite
CD ______ **NEXCD 161**
Sequel / Dec '90 / BMG

Colour Club

COLOUR CLUB
Welcome to the Colour Club / Scene / Freedom words / Great issue: Freedom / Trust in me / Consumption / Scene II / On and on / Scene III / Chicago / Cultures of jazz / Scene IV / Howbotsuntinkikdis / Scene V / State of mind / Don't wait too long
CD ______ **JVC 20342**
JVC / Aug '94 / Direct / New Note/Pinnacle / Vital/SAM

Colour Of Memory

OLD MAN & THE SEA, THE
Grace / Rigmarole / Rain parade / Emotional fish / Changed days / Into my own / Always with me / Days on end / Sun fire majestic / Old man and the sea
CD ______ **IRCD 028**
Iona / Jan '95 / ADA / Direct / Duncans

Colour Trip

COLOURTRIP
CD ______ **MASSCD 014**
Massacre / Feb '94 / Plastic Head

FULL TIME FUNCTION
CD ______ **08436272**
SPV / Dec '95 / Koch / Plastic Head

GROUND LEVEL SEX TYPE THING
CD ______ **SPV 08436222**
SPV / Dec '94 / Koch / Plastic Head

GROUNDLEVELSEXTYPE
CD ______ **SPV 8436222**
SPV / Dec '96 / Koch / Plastic Head

Colourbox

COLOURBOX
Suspicion / Arena / Say you / Just give 'em whiskey / You keep me hangin' on / Moon is blue / Manic / Sleepwalker / Inside informer / Punch
CD ______ **CAD 508 CD**
4AD / '86 / RTM/Disc

COLOURBOX MINI LP
CD ______ **MAD 315 CD**
4AD / Nov '86 / RTM/Disc

Colourhaus

WATER TO THE SOUL
Moving mountains / We talk to the angels / Stone roses / Innocent child / Missing the beat / Ghost train / I would walk the earth / Colour me you / Waves / Feather in the fire / All the way to Marakesh / Oxygen (Nosferatu-the seduction)
CD ______ **7567921232**
East West / Aug '92 / Warner Music

Coltrane, Alice

JOURNEY IN SATCHIDANANDA
Journey in Satchidananda / Shiva-loka / Stover Bombay / Something about John Coltrane / Isis and Osiris
CD ______ **IMP 12282**
Impulse Jazz / Apr '97 / New Note/BMG

MONASTIC TRIO, A
CD ______ **MVCZ 125**
MCA / Apr '97 / BMG

PTAH, THE EL DAOUD
Ptah, the El Daoud / Turiya and Ramakrishna / Blue Nile / Mantra
CD ______ **IMP 12012**
Impulse Jazz / Sep '96 / New Note/BMG

Coltrane, John

AFRICA BRASS VOL.1 & 2
Africa / Blues minor / Greensleeves / Greensleeves / Song of the underground railroad / Africa
CD ______ **MCAD 42001**
Impulse Jazz / Jun '89 / New Note/BMG

AFRO BLUE IMPRESSIONS
Lonnie's lament / Naima / Chasin' the trane / My favourite things / Afro blue / Cousin Mary / I want to talk about you / Spiritual / Impressions
CD Set ______ **2620101**
Pablo / '94 / Cadillac / Complete/Pinnacle

AVANT GARDE, THE (Coltrane, John & Don Cherry)
CD ______ **7567900412**
Atlantic / Jul '93 / Warner Music

BAGS AND TRANE (Coltrane, John & Milt Jackson)
Bags and trane / Three little words / Night we called it a day / Be bop / Late late blues
CD ______ **7567813482**
Atlantic / Jun '93 / Warner Music

BAHIA
CD ______ **OJCCD 415**
Original Jazz Classics / Feb '92 / Complete/Pinnacle / Jazz Music / Wellard

BELIEVER, THE
Believer / Nakatini serenade / Do I believe you because you're beautiful / Filidia / Paul's pal
CD ______ **OJCCD 876**
Original Jazz Classics / Jun '96 / Complete/ Pinnacle / Jazz Music / Wellard

BEST OF JOHN COLTRANE, THE (Live)
Afro blue / Promise / Every time we say goodbye / Bye bye blackbird / Chasin' the trane
CD ______ **CD 2310886**
Pablo / Apr '94 / Cadillac / Complete/ Pinnacle

BEST OF JOHN COLTRANE, THE
My favourite things / Naima / Giant steps / Equinox / Cousin Mary / Central Park West
CD ______ **7567813662**
Atlantic / Jun '93 / Warner Music

BLACK PEARLS
Black pearls / Lover come back to me / Sweet sapphire blues / Believer / Nakatini serenade / Do I love you because you're beautiful
CD ______ **OJCCD 352**
Original Jazz Classics / Feb '92 / Complete/ Pinnacle / Jazz Music / Wellard

BLUE TRAIN (Enhanced CD)
Blue train / Moment's notice / Locomotion / I'm old fashioned / Lazy bird / Blue train / Lazy bird
CD ______ **CDP 8534280**
Blue Note / Mar '97 / EMI

BLUE TRANE (John Coltrane Plays The Blues)
Slow trane / Traneing / Billie's bounce / Real McCoy / Big Paul / Sweet sapphire blues
CD ______ **PRCD 11005**
Prestige / Jun '97 / Cadillac / Complete/ Pinnacle

BYE BYE BLACKBIRD
Bye bye blackbird / Traneing in
CD ______ **OJCCD 681**
Original Jazz Classics / Feb '92 / Complete/ Pinnacle / Jazz Music / Wellard

CATTIN' WITH C & Q (Coltrane, John & Paul Quinichette)
CD ______ **OJCCD 460**
Original Jazz Classics / Apr '92 / Complete/Pinnacle / Jazz Music / Wellard

CHIM CHIM CHEREE AND OTHER RARITIES
CD ______ **JZCD 318**
Suisa / Feb '91 / Jazz Music / THE

COAST TO COAST (Coltrane, John Quartet)
CD ______ **MCD 0352**
Moon / Jan '92 / Cadillac / Harmonia Mundi

COLLECTION VOL.2, THE
CD ______ **CCSCD 435**
Castle / May '95 / BMG

COLLECTION, THE
CD ______ **CCSCD 418**
Castle / May '95 / BMG

COLTRANE
Bakai / Violets for your furs / Time was / Straight street / While my lady sleeps / Chronic blues
CD ______ **OJCCD 20**
Original Jazz Classics / Oct '92 / Complete/ Pinnacle / Jazz Music / Wellard

COLTRANE JAZZ
Little old lady / Village blues / My shining hour / Fifth house / Harmonique / Like Sonny / I'll wait and pray / Some other blues / Like Sonny / I'll wait and pray
CD ______ **7567813442**
Atlantic / Feb '92 / Warner Music

COLTRANE PLAYS THE BLUES
Blues to Elvin / Blues to Bechet / Blues to you / Mr. Day / Mr. Syms / Mr. Knight / Untitled original
CD ______ **7567813512**
Atlantic / Jun '93 / Warner Music

COLTRANE TIME
CD ______ **CDP 7844612**
Blue Note / Feb '92 / EMI

COLTRANE'S SOUND
Night has a thousand eyes / Central Park West / Liberia / Body and soul / Equinox / Satellite / 26-2 / Body and soul
CD ______ **7567813582**
Atlantic / Mar '93 / Warner Music

COLTRANE/LUSH LIFE
Lush life / I love you / Trane's slow blues / I hear a rhapsody / Violets for your furs / Time was / Straight street / While my lady sleeps / Chronic blues
CD ______ **CDJZD 001**
Prestige / Jan '91 / Cadillac / Complete/ Pinnacle

COMPLETE 1961 VILLAGE VANGUARD RECORDINGS, THE (4CD Set)
India / Chasin' the train / Impressions / Spiritual / Miles mode / Naima / Braslia / Chasin' another train / India / Spiritual / Softly as in the morning sunrise / Chasin' the train / Greensleeves / Impressions / Spiritual / Naima / Impressions / India / Greensleeves / Miles Mode / India / Spiritual
CD Set ______ **IMPD 4232**
Impulse Jazz / Sep '97 / New Note/BMG

COMPLETE AFRICA BRASS VOL.1 & 2 (2CD Set)
Greensleeves / Song of the underground railroad / Greensleeves / Damned don't cry / Africa (first version) / Blues minor / Africa (alternate take) / Africa
CD Set ______ **IMP 21682**
Impulse Jazz / Oct '95 / New Note/BMG

COMPLETE GRAZ CONCERT, THE (2CD Set)
Bye bye blackbird / Inchworm / Autumn leaves / Everytime we say goodbye / Mr. PC / I want to talk about you / Impressions / My favourite things
CD Set ______ **CPCD 8262**
Charly / Jan '97 / Koch

COUNTDOWN (Coltrane, John & Wilbur Harden)
Wells Fargo - take 1 / Wells Fargo - take 2 / EFFPH / Countdown / Rhodomagnetics 1 / Rhodomagnetics 2 / Snuffy / West 42nd street
CD ______ **VGCD 650102**
Vogue / Oct '93 / BMG

CRESCENT (Coltrane, John Quartet)
Crescent / Wise one / Bessie's blues / Lonnie's lament / Drum thing
CD ______ **IMP 12002**
Impulse Jazz / Sep '96 / New Note/BMG

DAKAR
Dakar / Mary's blues / Route 4 / Velvet scene / Witches' pet / Cat walk / CTA / Interplay / Anatomy / Light blue / Soul eyes
CD ______ **OJCCD 393**
Original Jazz Classics / Feb '92 / Complete/ Pinnacle / Jazz Music / Wellard

DIG IT (Coltrane, John & Red Garland Quintet)
Billie's bounce / Crazy rhythm / CTA / Lazy Mae
CD ______ **OJCCD 392**
Original Jazz Classics / Apr '93 / Complete/ Pinnacle / Jazz Music / Wellard

EUROPEAN TOUR, THE
Promise / I want to talk about you / Naima / Mr. PC
CD ______ **PACD 23082222**
Pablo / Jul '94 / Cadillac / Complete/ Pinnacle

EVERYTIME WE SAY GOODBYE (Coltrane, John Quartet)
CD ______ **NI 4003**
Natasha / Jun '93 / ADA / Cadillac / CM / Direct / Jazz Music

GIANT STEPS
Giant steps / Cousin Mary / Countdown / Spiral / Syeeda's song flute / Naima / Mr. PC
CD ______ **7813372**
Atlantic / '87 / Warner Music

IN A SOULFUL MOOD
In a sentimental mood / Tunji / Soul eyes / Inchworm / Nancy / Blues minor / After the rain / You don't know what love is / I want to talk about you / Alabama / Naima / Afro blue
CD ______ **MCCD 170**
Music Club / Sep '94 / Disc / THE

JAZZ PORTRAITS
Trane's blues / Sweet Sue, just you / Soultrane / Mating call / Monk's mood / Chronic blues / While my lady sleeps / Straight street / Bakay
CD ______ **CD 14507**
Jazz Portraits / May '94 / Jazz Music

JOHN COLTRANE & KENNY BURRELL (Coltrane, John & Kenny Burrell)
CD ______ **OJCCD 300**
Original Jazz Classics / Oct '92 / Complete/Pinnacle / Jazz Music / Wellard

JOHN COLTRANE AND THE JAZZ GIANTS
CD ______ **FCD 60014**
Fantasy / Oct '93 / Jazz Music / Pinnacle / Wellard

JOHN COLTRANE MEETS ERIC DOLPHY (Coltrane, John & Eric Dolphy)
CD ______ **MCD 0692**
Moon / Aug '95 / Cadillac / Harmonia Mundi

JOHN COLTRANE QUARTET PLAYS, THE (Coltrane, John Quartet)
Chim chim cheree / Brazilia / Nature boy / Song of praise / Feelin' good
CD _______________ IMP 12142
Impulse Jazz / Apr '97 / New Note/BMG

JOHN COLTRANE QUARTET, THE
Out of this world / Soul eyes / Inch worm / Tunji / Miles mode / Big nick / Up against the wall
CD _______________ IMP 12152
Impulse Jazz / Apr '97 / New Note/BMG

JUAN LES PINS JAZZ FESTIVAL (Antibes July 1965)
CD _______________ CD 53068
Giants Of Jazz / May '92 / Cadillac / Jazz Music / Target/BMG

LAST TRANE
CD _______________ OJCCD 394
Original Jazz Classics / Feb '92 / Complete/Pinnacle / Jazz Music / Wellard

LIVE AT BIRDLAND
Mr. PC / Miles mode / My favourite things / Body and soul
CD _______________ CDCHARLY 68
Charly / Jun '87 / Koch

LIVE AT BIRDLAND (Coltrane, John Quartet)
Afro blue / I want to talk about you / Promise / Alabama / Your lady / Vilia
CD _______________ IMP 11982
Impulse Jazz / Sep '96 / New Note/BMG

LIVE AT BIRDLAND
Mr. PC / Miles' mode / My favourite things / Body and soul
CD _______________ LEJAZZCD 58
Le Jazz / Nov '96 / Cadillac / Koch

LIVE AT THE VILLAGE VANGUARD AGAIN
Naima / My favourite things
CD _______________ IMP 12132
Impulse Jazz / Apr '97 / New Note/BMG

LIVE IN ANTIBES 1965
CD _______________ LEJAZZCD 10
Le Jazz / Jun '93 / Cadillac / Koch

LIVE IN COMBLAIN-LA-TOUR 1965
CD _______________ LS 2922
Landscape / Feb '93 / THE

LIVE IN EUROPE 1960 (Coltrane, John & Miles Davis)
CD _______________ LS 2910
Landscape / Nov '92 / THE

LIVE IN JAPAN (4CD Set)
Afro blue / Peace on Earth / Crescent / Peace on Earth / Leo / My favourite things
CD Set _______________ GRP 41022
GRP / Jul '91 / New Note/BMG

LIVE IN PARIS
Naima / Impressions / Blue valse / Afro blue / Impressions (2nd version)
CD _______________ LEJAZZCD 31
Le Jazz / Sep '94 / Cadillac / Koch

LIVE IN SEATTLE (2CD Set)
Cosmos / Out of this world / Body and soul / Tapestry in sound / Evolution / Afro blue
CD Set _______________ GRP 21462
GRP / Nov '94 / New Note/BMG

LIVE IN STOCKHOLM 1961
My favourite things / Blue train / Naima / Impressions
CD _______________ LEJAZZCD 57
Le Jazz / Sep '96 / Cadillac / Koch

LIVE IN STOCKHOLM 1963
Mr. PC / Traneing in / Spiritual / I want to talk about you
CD _______________ LEJAZZCD 59
Le Jazz / Jan '97 / Cadillac / Koch

LOVE SUPREME, A
Acknowledgement (part 1) / Resolution (part 2) / Pursuance (part 3) / Psalm (part 4)
CD _______________ MCLD 19029
MCA / Apr '92 / BMG

LOVE SUPREME, A (Live)
CD _______________ JZCD 317
Suisa / Oct '92 / Jazz Music / THE

MAJOR WORKS OF JOHN COLTRANE, THE (2CD Set)
Ascension I / Ascension II / Om / Kula se mama / Selflessness
CD Set _______________ GRP 21132
Impulse Jazz / Jan '92 / New Note/BMG

MAN MADE MILES
CD _______________ CDSGP 0265
Prestige / Jan '97 / Else / Total/BMG

MEDITATIONS
Love / Consequences / Serenity / Father and the Son and the Holy Ghost / Compassion
CD _______________ IMP 11992
Impulse Jazz / Sep '96 / New Note/BMG

MY FAVOURITE THINGS
My favourite things / Every time we say goodbye / Summertime / But not for me
CD _______________ 7567813462
Atlantic / Mar '93 / Warner Music

MY FAVOURITE THINGS
CD _______________ JHR 73538
Jazz Hour / May '93 / Cadillac / Jazz Music / Target/BMG

MY FAVOURITE THINGS IN CONCERT AND OTHER RARITIES
CD _______________ JZCD 320
Suisa / Feb '91 / Jazz Music / THE

NEW WAVE IN JAZZ (Coltrane, John & Archie Shepp)
Nature boy / Ham bone / Brilliant corners / Plight / Blue free / Intellect
CD _______________ GRP 11372
GRP / Mar '94 / New Note/BMG

OLE COLTRANE
Ole / Dahomey dance / Aisha / To her ladyship
CD _______________ 7813492
Atlantic / Feb '94 / Warner Music

OM
CD _______________ MCAD 39118
Impulse Jazz / Jun '89 / New Note/BMG

ON STAGE 1962
CD _______________ 556632
Accord / Mar '96 / Cadillac / Discovery

PARIS CONCERT, THE
Mr. PC / Inchworm / Every time we say goodbye
CD _______________ OJCCD 781
Original Jazz Classics / Jun '94 / Complete/ Pinnacle / Jazz Music / Wellard

PRESTIGE RECORDINGS, THE (16CD Set)
Tenor madness / Weeja / Polka dots and moonbeams / On it / Avalon / Tenor conclave / Hoe deep is the ocean / Just you, just me / Bob's boys / Mating call / Soultrane / Grind / Super jet / On a misty night / Romas / Soul eyes / Anatomy / Interplay / Light blue / CTA / Eclypso / Solacium / Minor mishap / Tommy's time / Dakar / Route 4 / Velvet scene / Witches' pit / Cat walk / Pot pourri / JM's dream doll / Don't explain / Falling in love with love / Blue calypso / Way you look tonight / From this moment on / One by one / Cattin' / Anatomy / Vodka / Sunday / Straight street / While my lady sleeps / Chronic blues / Bakai / Violets for your furs / Time was / I hear a rhapsody / Trane's slo blues / Slowtrane / Like someone in love / I love you / Dealin' / Wheelin' / Robbin's nest / Things ain't what they used to be / You leave me breathless / Bass blues / Soft lights and sweet music / Traneing in / Slow dance / Our delight / They can't take that away from me / Woody 'n' you / I got it bad and that ain't good / Undecided / Soul junction / What is there to say / Birk's works / Hallelujah / All morning long / Billie's bounce / Solitude / Two bass hit / Soft winds / Lazy Mae / Under Paris skies / Two sons / Clifford's kappa / Filide / Paul's pal / Ammon joy / Grove blues / Real McCoy / It might as well be Spring / Lush life / Believer / Nakatini serenade / Come rain or come shine / Lover / Russian lullaby / Theme for Ernie / You say you care / Good bait / I want to talk about you / Lyresto / Why was I born / Freight Trane / I never knew / Big Paul / Rise 'n' shine / I see your face before me / If there is something lovelier than you / Little Melonae / By the number / Black pearls / Lover come back to me / Sweet sapphire blues / Spring is here / Invitation / I'm a dreamer / Aren't we all / Love thy neighbour / Don't take your love from me / Stardust / My ideal / I'll get by / Do I love you because you're beautiful / Then I'll be tired of you / Something I dreamed last night / Bahia / Goldsboro express / Time after time
CD Set _______________ 16PCD 44052
Prestige / Nov '96 / Cadillac / Complete/ Pinnacle

PRICELESS JAZZ
Bessie's blues / Dear Lord / Big Nick / Alabama / Love supreme / Naima / Mile's mode / Crescent / After the rain
CD _______________ GRP 98742
GRP / Jul '97 / New Note/BMG

PRIVATE RECORDINGS - 1951-58
CD _______________ JZCD 316
Suisa / Feb '91 / Jazz Music / THE

ROY AND OTHER RARITIES
CD _______________ JZCD 319
Suisa / Feb '91 / Jazz Music / THE

SAX IMPRESSIONS
Blue train / Naima / Spiritual / Traneing in / My favourite things / Impressions
CD _______________ BN 007
Blue Nite / Nov '96 / Target/BMG

SETTIN' THE PACE
I see your face before me / If there's someone lovelier than you / Little Melonae / Rise and shine
CD _______________ OJCCD 78
Original Jazz Classics / Feb '92 / Complete/ Pinnacle / Jazz Music / Wellard

STANDARD COLTRANE
CD _______________ OJCCD 246
Original Jazz Classics / Feb '92 / Complete/Pinnacle / Jazz Music / Wellard

STARDUST
Stardust / Time after time / Love thy neighbour / Then I'll be tired of you
CD _______________ OJCCD 920
Original Jazz Classics / Jun '97 / Complete/ Pinnacle / Jazz Music / Wellard

STARDUST SESSION, THE
Spring is here / Invitation / I'm a dreamer (aren't we all) / Love thy neighbour / Don't take your love from me / My ideal / Stardust / I'll get by
CD _______________ PRCD 24056
Prestige / Jul '94 / Cadillac / Complete/ Pinnacle

STELLAR REGIONS
Creation / Sun star / Stellar regions / Iris / Offering / Configuration / Jimmy's mode / Tranesonic / Stellar regions (alternate take) / Sun star (alternate take) / Tranesonic (alternate take)
CD _______________ IMP 11692
Impulse Jazz / Oct '95 / New Note/BMG

SUNSHIP
Sun ship / Dearly beloved / Amen / Attending / Ascent
CD _______________ IMP 11672
Impulse Jazz / Nov '95 / New Note/BMG

TENOR CONCLAVE (Coltrane, John & Hank Mobley/Al Cohn/Zoot Sims)
CD _______________ OJCCD 127
Original Jazz Classics / Jul '94 / Complete/Pinnacle / Jazz Music / Wellard

TRANE'S BLUES - 1955-57
CD _______________ CD 53058
Giants Of Jazz / Mar '90 / Cadillac / Jazz Music / Target/BMG

TRANEING IN - WITH THE RED GARLAND TRIO
Traneing in / Slow dance / Bass blues / You leave me breathless / Soft lights and sweet music
CD _______________ OJCCD 189
Original Jazz Classics / Mar '92 / Complete/ Pinnacle / Jazz Music / Wellard

TURNING POINT (The Bethlehem Years)
CD _______________ BET 6003
Bethlehem / Jan '95 / ADA / ZYX

WHEELIN' & DEALIN'
CD _______________ OJCCD 672
Original Jazz Classics / May '93 / Complete/Pinnacle / Jazz Music / Wellard

Columbia Corina

DEEP FLITE
CD _______________ DFDCD 7
Defender / Mar '97 / Essential/BMG / Prime / SRD

Colvin, Shawn

COVER GIRL
CD _______________ 4772402
Columbia / Aug '94 / Sony

FAT CITY
Polaroids / Tennessee / Tenderness on the block / Round of blues / Monopoly / Orion in the sky / Climb on (a back that's strong) / Set the prairie on fire / Object of my affection / Kill the messenger / I don't know why
CD _______________ 4679612
Columbia / Apr '93 / Sony

FEW SMALL REPAIRS, A
Sunny came home / Get out of this house / Facts about Jimmy / You and the Mona Lisa / Trouble / I want it back / If I were brave / Wichita skyline / 84,000 different delusions / Suicide alley / What I get paid for / New thing now / Nothin' on me
CD _______________ 4843272
Columbia / Oct '96 / Sony

LIVE 1988
CD _______________ PLUCD 002
Plump / Mar '96 / Grapevine/PolyGram

STEADY ON
Steady on / Diamonds in the rough / Shotgun down the avalanche / Stranded another long one / Cry like an angel / Something to believe in / Story / Ricochet in time / Dead of the night
CD _______________ 4661422
Columbia / Aug '95 / Sony

Colyer, Ken

AT THE DANCING SLIPPER 1969
CD _______________ AZCD 25
Azure / Nov '96 / Azure / Cadillac / Jazz Music / Swift / Wellard

COLYER'S PLEASURE (Colyer, Ken Jazzmen)
Teasing rag / After you've gone / Highway blues / Dardanella / I can't escape from you / You always hurt the one you love / Creole bo bo / Honeysuckle rose / Barefoot boy / Mahogany Hall stomp / Gettysburg march / La Harpe St. blues / Thriller rag / I'm travelling / Virginia strut
CD _______________ LACD 34
Lake / Nov '94 / ADA / Cadillac / Direct / Jazz Music / Target/BMG

DARKNESS ON THE DELTA (The Hague 1979)
Lord, Lord you've sure been good to me / Darkness on the delta / Yaaka hula hickey dula / Gettysburg march / Deep Bayou blues / Shine / Auf wiedersehen
CD _______________ BLCD 760518
Black Lion / May '97 / Jazz Music

DECCA YEARS 1953-1954, THE (Colyer, Ken Jazzmen)
CD _______________ LACD 14
Lake / Sep '94 / ADA / Cadillac / Direct / Jazz Music / Target/BMG

DECCA YEARS 1955-59, THE (Colyer, Ken Jazzmen)
CD _______________ LA 001CD
Lake / Jan '94 / ADA / Cadillac / Direct / Jazz Music / Target/BMG

IN HOLLAND (Colyer, Ken & Butch Thompson)
CD _______________ MECCACD 1032
Music Mecca / Nov '94 / Cadillac / Jazz Music / Wellard

JUST A LITTLE WHILE TO STAY HERE
Just a little while to stay here / Saturday night function / Lead me on / Lily of the valley / Sometimes my burden is so hard to bear / Lord, Lord, Lord / Just a closer walk with thee / Nobody's fault but mine
CD _______________ CMJCD 012
CMJ / Oct '90 / Jazz Music / Wellard

KEN COLYER & CHRIS BLOUNT
CD _______________ KCT 5CD
Ken Colyer Trust / Oct '92 / Jazz Music / Wellard

KEN COLYER & RAYMOND BURKE 1952-1953 (Colyer, Ken & Raymond Burke)
CD _______________ 504CD 23
504 / Oct '93 / Cadillac / Jazz Music / Target/BMG / Wellard

KEN COLYER IN CONCERT 1959 (Colyer, Ken Jazzmen)
CD _______________ DJCD 001
Dine-a-mite / Jun '96 / Jazz Music

KEN COLYER IN NEW YORK 1953
CD _______________ 504CD 53
504 / Mar '97 / Cadillac / Jazz Music / Target/BMG / Wellard

KEN COLYER TRUST BAND PLAY NEW ORLEANS JAZZ (Colyer, Ken Trust Band)
Yes Lord I'm crippled / Alexander's ragtime band / Over the waves / Breeze / Salutation march / Panama rag / Lights out / Bogalousa strut / Amazing Grace / Darktown strutters ball / San Jacinto blues / Precious Lord / Silver bell / Sing on / Washington and Lee swing / My life will be sweeter some day
CD _______________ URCD 112
Upbeat / Aug '94 / Cadillac / Target/BMG

LIVE AT THE PIZZA EXPRESS, LONDON, FEBRUARY 1985 (Colyer, Ken Jazz Quartet)
Blame it on the blues / How long blues / Willie the weeper / Dinah / Dallas blues / (Back home again in) Indiana / Scatterbrain, Liza / Sweet Lorraine / Weary blues
CD _______________ AZCD 33
Azure / Jan '95 / Azure / Cadillac / Jazz Music / Swift / Wellard

MORE OF KEN COLYER & HIS JAZZMEN 25/1/72 (Colyer, Ken & His Hand Picked Jazzmen)
Pretty baby / Sing on / Snag it / Wabash blues / Louisian-I-Ay / Tishomingo blues / Black cat on the fence / High society
CD _______________ KCT 3CD
Ken Colyer Trust / Jun '96 / Jazz Music / Wellard

ONE FOR MY BABY (Colyer, Ken Jazzmen)
Royal Garden blues / High society / Drop me off in Harlem / Bogalousa strut / One for my baby (and one more for the road) / Stardust / Tiger rag
CD _______________ JOYCD 1
Joy / Aug '91 / Jazz Music / President / Wellard

PAINTING THE CLOUDS WITH SUNSHINE
CD _______________ BLCD 760501
Black Lion / Oct '90 / Cadillac / Jazz Music / Koch / Wellard

SERENADING AUNTIE (BBC Recordings 1955-1960)
Carolina moon / In the evening / Papa dip / Tell me your dreams / My blue heaven / Perdido street blues / Clarinet marmalade / When I leave the world behind / Eccentric rag / Riverside blues / Thriller rag / Hilarity rag / Yancey stomp / Heliotrope bouquet / Creole song / Chrysanthemum rag / You've got to see mama ev'ry night / Ice cream / Dinah / Going home / World is waiting for the sunrise
CD _______________ URCD 111
Upbeat / Apr '94 / Cadillac / Target/BMG

SPIRITUALS VOL.1 (Colyer, Ken Jazzmen)
We shall walk through the streets of the city / Darkness on the Delta / It's nobody's fault

but mine / My life will be sweeter someday / Were you there when they satisfied my soul / Sometimes my burden is so hard to bear / Old rugged cross
CD JOYCD 5
Joy / Aug '91 / Jazz Music / President / Wellard

STUDIO 51 REVISITED (Colyer, Ken Jazzmen)
Oh lady be good / Dusty rag / Fidgety feet / Perdido street blues / Ace in the hole / Muskrat ramble / Yes Lord I'm crippled / Riverside blues / In the sweet bye and bye / Wolverine blues
CD LACD 25
Lake / Jan '95 / ADA / Cadillac / Direct / Jazz Music / Target/BMG

SUNNY SIDE OF KEN COLYER, THE (Colyer, Ken All Stars)
Sunny side of the street / Yaaka hula hickey dula / Canal Street blues (Slow) / Canal street blues (Fast) / Royal garden blues / Bill Bailey, Won't you please come home / Chloe / You always hurt the one you love / Everywhere you go the sunshine follows you
CD URCD 113
Upbeat / Oct '94 / Cadillac / Target/BMG

TOO BUSY (Harlow 1985)
Tunes too busy / My old Kentucky home / Tishomingo blues / Down home rag / Old rugged cross / One sweet letter from you / Bogalousa strut / Snag it / Nobody's fault but mine / Home sweet home
CD CMJCD 008
CMJ / Jul '89 / Jazz Music / Wellard

UP JUMPED THE DEVIL
Sensation rag / Milnburg joys / When you wore a tulip / Mazie (Martha) / Up jumped the devil / Moose march / Breeze / Bourbon street parade / Red sails in the sunset / Dr. Jazz / Tiger rag
CD URCD 114
Upbeat / Apr '95 / Cadillac / Target/BMG

URGENT REQUEST (Colyer, Ken & Chris Blount Band)
CD BCD 184
GHB / Nov '96 / Jazz Music

WANDERING (Crown Hotel Twickenham, July 1965) (Colyer, Ken Skiffle Group)
I'm going to walk and talk with Jesus / No letters today/Colorado trail / Ella speed / Poor Howard / I can't sleep / Muleskinner blues / Wandering / If I could hear my mother pray again / Good morning blues / Drop down mama / Easy ridin' boogie / New York town / Green corn / Casey Jones
CD LACD 68
Lake / Sep '96 / ADA / Cadillac / Direct / Jazz Music / Target/BMG

WHEN I LEAVE THE WORLD BEHIND (Colyer, Ken & Sammy Rimington)
CD BCD 152
GHB / Jun '96 / Jazz Music

Coma Virus

HIDDEN
CD DFX 027CD
Side Effects / Apr '97 / Plastic Head / World Serpent

Combelle, Alix

CLASSICS 1935-1940
CD CLASSICS 714
Classics / Jul '93 / Discovery / Jazz Music

CLASSICS 1940-1941
CD CLASSICS 751
Classics / May '94 / Discovery / Jazz Music

CLASSICS 1942-1943
CD CLASSICS 782
Classics / Nov '94 / Discovery / Jazz Music

Combustible Edison

I, SWINGER
Cadillac / Millionaire's holiday / Breakfast at Denny's / Intermission / Cry me a river / Impact / Guadaloupe / Carnival of souls / Veldt / Surabaya Johnny / Spy Vs. spy / Theme from The Tiki Wonder Hour
CD EFA 049342
City Slang / Mar '94 / RTM/Disc

SCHIZOPHONIC
CD RTD 34600022
City Slang / Feb '96 / RTM/Disc

Come

DON'T ASK, DON'T TELL
CD BBQCD 160
Beggars Banquet / Sep '94 / RTM/Disc / Warner Music

NEAR LIFE EXPERIENCE
CD WIGCD 25
Domino / May '96 / Vital

Comecon

CONVERGING CONSPIRACIES
CD CM 770752
Century Media / Jan '94 / Plastic Head

FABLE FROLIC
CD CM 77094CD
Century Media / Sep '95 / Plastic Head

Comedy Harmonists

AUF WIEDERSEHEN
Das alte spinnrad / Am brunnen vor dem tore / An der schonen blauen donau / Auf wiederseh'n, my dear / Barber of Seville overture / Barcarolle / Ein bisschen leichtsinn kann nicht schaden / Congo lullaby / Creole love call / Hein spielt abends so schon auf dem schifferklavier / Heute nacht oder nie / Holzhackerlied / Humoreske / Ich traum' von eine marchennacht / In stiller nacht / Komm im traum / Liebling mein herz / Muss I' denn zum stadtle hinaus / Night and day / Perpetuum mobile / Puppenhochzeit / Sah ein knab' ein roslein steh'n / Tea for two / Wenn die Sonnja russisch tanzt / Whispering
CD CDAJA 5204
Living Era / Nov '96 / Select

COMEDIAN HARMONISTS
Barber of Seville / Must I, then / When Sonia danced in Russian style / Sleep my little Prince / Good moon, you go so gently / Minuet / Creole love call / Little lightness / Blue Danube waltz / Court serenade / Marie Marie / Auf wiedersehen my dear / Liebesleid / Boy saw a rosebush / Woodcutter's song / Village music / Old ship piano / Let's have another beer / In the hayloft / Perpetuum mobile
CD PASTCD 7000
Flapper / Jan '93 / Pinnacle

Comelade, Pascal

MUSIC FOR FILMS VOL.2
CD DSA 54042
CDSA / Dec '96 / Harmonia Mundi / ReR Megacorp

Comet

CHANDELIER MUSINGS
Rocket flare / Day at the races / She's a mastermind / Soundtrack to the short film: Lifelines / Shogun girl / Birds are little dinosaurs / Formula one driver blues / American flyer
CD DEDCD 030
Dedicated / Apr '97 / BMG / Vital

Comet, Al

COMET
Saturne / Krishna 88 / Basse pression / L'envol du canard / XTC for ya / Platform H / One three seven / L22 / Over the hills
CD BIAS 349CD
Play It Again Sam / Jul '97 / Discovery / Plastic Head / Vital

Comet Gain

CASINO CLASSICS
Footstompers / Million and nine / Turnpike county blue / Last night / Original arrogance / Another girl / Music upstairs / Villain / Stay with me / Charlie / Just seventeen / Ghost of the roman empire / Intergalactic starbed / Chevron action flash
CD WIJ 042CD
Wiiija / Apr '95 / RTM/Disc

Coming Up Roses

I SAID BALLROOM
CD UTIL 005 CD
Utility / Jul '89 / Grapevine/PolyGram

Comite Imaginaire

HOLZ FOR EUROPA
CD FMPCD 84
FMP / May '97 / Cadillac

Commander Cody

BAR ROOM CLASSICS
CD AIM 1024CD
Aim / Sep '93 / ADA / Direct / Jazz Music

LET'S ROCK
Let's rock / Rockin' over China / Midnight on the strand / Do you mind / Angel got married / Truckstop at the end of the world / One more ride / Your cash ain't nothin' but trash / Rockabilly funeral / Transfusion / Home of rock 'n' roll
CD BPCD 72086
Blind Pig / Dec '94 / ADA / CM / Direct / Hot Shot

TOUR FROM HELL 1973, THE (Commander Cody & His Lost Planet Airmen)
I took three bennies and my semi truck won't start / Smoke smoke smoke / Four five times / What's the matter now / Down to seeds and stems again / Truck stop rock / Goin' back to Tennessee / Mama tried / All I have to offer is me / Git it / Sister Sue / Lost in the ozone again
CD AIM 1059
Aim / Nov '96 / ADA / Direct / Jazz Music

VERY BEST OF COMMANDER CODY AND HIS LOST PLANET AIRMEN (Commander Cody & His Lost Planet Airmen)
Back to Tennessee / Wine do yer stuff / Seeds and stems (again) / Daddy's gonna treat you right / Family Bible / Lost in the ozone / Hot rod Lincoln / Beat me Daddy, eight to the bar / Truckstop rock / Truck drivin' man / It should've been me / Watch my 38 / Everybody's doin' it now / Rock that boogie / Smoke, smoke, smoke / Honeysuckle honey / Sunset on the sage (live) / Cryin' time (live)
CD SEECD 64
See For Miles/C5 / Oct '96 / Pinnacle

WORST CASE SCENARIO (Commander Cody & His Lost Planet Airmen)
Big rock / Lights go out / Lose it tonight / Real gone / Green light / Good morning judge / Working mans blues / New radio / They kicked me out of the band / River city / Buddy's cafe / Crash pad blues / Keys to my cadillac / King of the honky tonks / Mansion on the hill / Death ray boogie
CD AIM 1043
Aim / Apr '95 / ADA / Direct / Jazz Music

Commando

BATTLE OF THIS WEEK
CD MNWCD 190
MNW / Mar '90 / ADA / Vital

Commodores

ALL THE GREAT LOVE SONGS
Sweet love / Just to be close to you / Easy / Three times a lady / Say yeah / Still / Loving you / Sail on / Old fashioned love / Jesus is love / Lady (you bring me up) / Oh no / This love / Lucy
CD 5301512
Motown / Jan '93 / PolyGram

COMMODORES, THE
CD 12465
Laserlight / Oct '95 / Target/BMG

COMPACT COMMAND PERFORMANCES (14 Greatest Hits)
Machine gun / Slippery when wet / Sweet love / Fancy dancer / Easy / Brick house / Too hot ta trot / Three times a lady / X-rated movie / Sail on / Still / Wonderland / Old-fashioned love / Lady (you bring me up)
CD 5300962
Motown / Jan '93 / PolyGram

RISE UP
Cowboys to girls / Rise up / Losing you / Who's making love / Sing a simple song / Baby this is forever / Love canoe / Come by here / Keep on dancing
CD CDBM 035
Blue Moon / Apr '87 / Cadillac / Discovery / Greensleeves / Jazz Music / Jet Star / TKO Magnum

VERY BEST OF THE COMMODORES, THE
Easy / Three times a lady / Nightshift / Brick house / Machine gun / Zoom / Old fashion love / Sail on / Lady (you bring me up) / Oh no / Too hot ta trot / Zoo (the human zoo) / Still / Sweet love / Janet / Flying high / Only you / Animal instinct / Just to be close to you / Wonderland
CD 5305472
Motown / Jul '95 / PolyGram

Common Cause

SAUSALITO
CD BB 721202
Backbeat / Mar '97 / Jet Star / Timewarp

Common Language

FLESH IMPACT
CD BFFP 84CD
Blast First / Sep '93 / RTM/Disc

Communards

COMMUNARDS
Don't leave me this way / La dolarosa / Disenchanted / Reprise / So cold the night / You are my world / Lover man / Don't slip away / Heaven's above / Forbidden love / Breadline Britain / Disenchanted
CD 8288632
London / Jan '97 / PolyGram

HEAVEN
You are my world / Czardas / So cold the night / Tomorrow / Annie / Hold on tight / If I could tell you / There's more to love (than boy meets girl) / Zing went the strings of my heart / I do it all for love / Sanctified / Judgement day / Heaven's above / Victims (Live)
CD 5500932
Spectrum / Oct '93 / PolyGram

Como, Perry

20 GREATEST HITS VOL.1
Magic moments / Caterina / Catch a falling star / I know / When you were sweet sixteen / I believe / Try to remember / Love makes the world go round / Prisoner of love / Don't let the stars get in your eyes / Hot diggity (dog ziggity boom) / Round and round / If I loved you / Hello, young lovers / Delaware / Moonglow / Killing me softly / More / Dear hearts and gentle people / I love you and don't you forget it
CD ND 89019
RCA / Apr '90 / BMG

20 GREATEST HITS VOL.2
And I love you so / For the good times / Close to you / Seattle / Tie a yellow ribbon / Walk right back / What kind of fool am I / Days of wine and roses / Where do I begin / Without a song / It's impossible / I think of you / If / We've only just begun / I want to give / Raindrops keep falling on my head / You make me feel so young / Temptation / Way we were / Sing
CD ND 89020
RCA / Apr '92 / BMG

BEST OF PERRY COMO, THE
Best of times / Days of wine and roses / What's new / Something / For all we know / Very thought of you / I left my heart in San Francisco / It's impossible / Where do I begin / What kind of fool am I / Without a song / Quiet nights of quiet stars / Close to you / You are the sunshine of my life / I think of you / When I need you / If / For the good times / Most beautiful girl in the world / Wind beneath my wings
CD 74321378382
RCA / Jul '96 / BMG

GREATEST VOCALIST, THE
CD CDSR 067
Telstar / May '95 / BMG

INCOMPARABLE, THE (20 Outstanding Classics)
Blue skies / I love you / Goodbye Sue / Aren't you glad you're mine / Here comes Heaven again / All through the day / You won't be satisfied / I can't begin to tell you / I'm always chasing rainbows / Till the end of time / Love letters / Cynthia's in love / It's the talk of the town / You must have been a beautiful baby / It's been a long long time / Te quiero dijiste / Don't blame me / Song of songs / Prisoner of love / So long ago and far away
CD PLATCD 149
Platinum / Mar '96 / Prism

LOVE COLLECTION, THE
Best of times / Days of wine and roses / What's new / Something / For all we now / Very thought of you / (I left my heart) in San Francisco / It's impossible / Where do I belong / What kind of fool am I / Without a song / (They long to be) close to you / You are the sunshine of my life / I think of you / When I need you / If / For the good times / Most beautiful girl / Wind beneath my wings
CD 74321393422
Camden / Jan '97 / BMG

LOVE LETTERS
Love letters / Blue skies / Cynthia's in love / Long ago and far away / Te quiero dijiste / It's the talk of the town / You won't be satisfied / Aren't you glad your mine / Prisoner of love / Here comes heaven again / Don't blame me / Till the end of time / You must have been a beautiful baby / It's been a long long time / I love you / Song of songs / I can't begin to tell you / Goodbye Sue / All through the day / I'm always chasing rainbows
CD 300112
Hallmark / Jul '96 / Carlton

LOVE SONGS
Blue skies / I love you / Goodbye Sue / Aren't you glad you're you / Here comes heaven again / All through the day / You won't be satisfied / I can't begin to tell you / I'm always chasing rainbows / Till the end of time / Love letters / Cynthia's in love / It's the talk of the town / You must have been a beautiful baby / It's been a long long time / Te quiero dijiste / Don't blame me / Song of songs / Prisoner of love / Long ago and far away
CD CD 6036
Music / Sep '96 / Target/BMG

LOVE SONGS, THE
CD MCCD 125
Music Club / Sep '93 / Disc / THE

PERRY COMO SHOWS 1943 VOL.1, THE
CD OTA 101905
On The Air / Mar '96 / Target/BMG

PERRY COMO SHOWS 1943 VOL.2, THE
For a little while / Do I know what I'm doing / More than you know / Now we know / My blue heaven / Goodbye Sue / Girl of my dreams / I have faith / I heard you cried last night (and so did I) / Don't get around much anymore / Hit the road to Dreamland / As time goes by / I'm thinking tonight of my blue eyes / Temptation / My ideal / You took advantage of me / It's always you / For me and my gal / Take me in your arms / Johnny Zero / You'd be so nice to come home to
CD OTA 101906
On The Air / Mar '96 / Target/BMG

PERRY COMO SHOWS 1943 VOL.3, THE
For a little while / Thank your lucky stars / Lazybones / No love, no nothin' / Paper doll / Beard / I've had this feeling before (but never like this) / Put your arms around me honey / It's breaking my heart to keep away

from you / 627 South / I'll be home for Christmas / All or nothing at all / Violins were playing / I lost my sugar in Salt Lake City / In an 18th Century drawing room / You'll never know / If that's the way you want it baby / I kiss your hand madame / In the blue of evening / Shine on harvest moon / Secretly
CD OTA 101907
On The Air / Mar '96 / Target/BMG

TAKE IT EASY
Bridge over troubled water / El condor pasa / Way we were / When I need you / Feelings / Wind beneath my wings / Michelle / Yesterday / For the good times / You are so beautiful / Killing me softly / Most beautiful girl / You are the sunshine of my life / Sunrise sunset / Sing / Close to you / We've only just begun / And I love you so
CD ND 90490
RCA / Nov '90 / BMG

TILL THE END OF TIME (The Early Hits 1936-1945)
Deep in the heart of Texas / Did you ever get that feeling in the moonlight / Faithful forever / Fooled by the moon / Goodbye Sue / Have I stayed away too long / I dream of you / I wonder who's kissing her now / I'm always chasing rainbows / I'm confessin' that I love you / I'm gonna love that girl / If I loved you / In my little red book / Lili Marlene / Long ago and far away / May I never love again / Mr. Meadowlark / Prisoner of love / Rainbow on the river / Temptation / Till the end of time / Until today / You can't pull the wool over my eyes / You won't be satisfied
CD CDAJA 5196
Living Era / Apr '96 / Select

WORLD OF DREAMS
World of dreams / Jason / Long life, lots of happiness / Wonderful baby / Someone who cares / What's one more time / Love looks so good on you / Meditation / There'll never be another night like this / That's you / Beats there a heart so true / I thought about you / Unchained melody / When she smiles / So it goes / Where you're concerned / You're following me / Stand beside me / How insensitive / Hawaiian wedding song / Dancin' / Everybody is looking for an answer / You are my world / Bless the beasts and the children
CD 74321278492
RCA / Aug '95 / BMG

Compagnia Sonadur Di ...

PAS EN AMUR (Compagnia Sonadur Di Ponte Caffaro)
CD ACB 05
Robi Droli / Jan '94 / ADA / Direct

Company

COMPANY 91 - VOL.1
CD INCUSCD 16
Incus / Oct '94 / Cadillac / Cargo

COMPANY 91 - VOL.2
CD INCUSCD 17
Incus / Oct '94 / Cadillac / Cargo

COMPANY 91 - VOL.3
CD INCUSCD 18
Incus / Oct '94 / Cadillac / Cargo

ONCE
CD INCUSCD 04
Incus / '90 / Cadillac / Cargo

Complicity

PLAYING GOD
CD FETISH 016CD
Grave News / Apr '97 / Plastic Head

Compostella

WADACHI
CD TZA 7211
Tzadik / Feb '97 / Cargo

Compression

COMPRESSION
CD TOL 9701
Tolerance / Jun '97 / Cargo

Compton, Mike

CLIMBING THE WALLS (Compton, Mike & David Grier)
Climbin' the walls / Honky tonk swing / Waters street waltz / Black mountain rag / Bye bye blue / Going up Caney / Huffy / Over the waterfall / Flop eared mule / New five cents / Paul's blues / Fun's all over
CD ROUCD 0280
Rounder / '91 / ADA / CM / Direct

Compulsion

FUTURE IS MEDIUM
CD TPLP 79CD
One Little Indian / May '96 / Pinnacle

Comsat Angels

FICTION
After the rain / Zinger / Now I know / Not a word / Ju ju money / More / Pictures / Birdman / Don't look now / What else / It's history / After the rain / Private party / Mass
CD RPM 157
RPM / Jan '96 / Pinnacle

GLAMOUR
CD CSA 103
RPM / Jun '95 / Pinnacle

SLEEP NO MORE
Eye dance / Sleep no more / Be brave / Gone / Dark parade / Diagram / Restless / Goat of the West / Light years / Our secret / Eye of the lens / Another world / At sea / (Do the) Empty house / Red planet revisited
CD RPM 156
RPM / Jan '96 / Pinnacle

TIME CONSIDERED (BBC Sessions)
CD RPM 106
RPM / Nov '92 / Pinnacle

UNRAVELLED (Dutch Radio Sessions Vol.1)
After the rain / Always near / Beautiful monster / Cutting edge / Field of tall flowers / SS 100X / Our secret / Storm of change / Citadel / Driving / My mind's eye / Shiva descending
CD RPM 123
RPM / Jul '94 / Pinnacle

WAITING FOR A MIRACLE
Missing in action / Baby / Independence day / Waiting for a miracle / Total war / On the beach / Monkey pilot / Real story / Map of the world / Postcard / Home is the range / We were
CD RPM 155
RPM / Jan '96 / Pinnacle

Comus

FIRST UTTERANCE
Diana / Herald / Drip drip / Song to Comus / Bite / Bitten / Prisoner
CD BGOCD 275
Beat Goes On / Aug '95 / Pinnacle

Con Funk Shun

LIVE FOR YA
Ffun / Chase me / Shake and dance with me / Let me put love on your mind / I'm leaving baby / Too tight / Straight from the heart / Baby I'm hooked / By your side / Love's train / Ffun / Throw it up / Head to toe / Mega-mix
CD ESMCD 444
Essential / Oct '96 / BMG

Concept In Dance

DIGITAL ALCHEMY
CD DICD 123
Beggars Banquet / Oct '94 / RTM/Disc / Warner Music

TRIBAL SCIENCE
CD DICCD 124
Beggars Banquet / Aug '95 / RTM/Disc / Warner Music

Conception

LAST SUNSET
Prevision / Building a force / War of hate / Bowed down with sorrow / Fairy's dance / Another world / Elegy / Last sunset / Live to survive / Among the Gods
CD N 02322
Noise / Jan '94 / Koch

PARALLEL MINDS
CD N 02182
Noise / Oct '93 / Koch

Concord Jazz All Stars

AT THE NORTHSEA FESTIVAL VOL.2
Vignette / Emily / That's your red wagon / Sweet Lorraine / Can't we be friends / Out of nowhere / Once in a while / In a mellow tone
CD CCD 4205
Concord Jazz / '83 / New Note/Pinnacle

ON CAPE COD
Man I love / This is always / Recado bossa nova / It never entered my mind / Cherokee / All my tomorrows / Bewitched, bothered and bewildered / As long as I live / Time after time
CD CCD 4530
Concord Jazz / Feb '93 / New Note/ Pinnacle

OW
Ow / Fungi mama / My shining hour / I'll close my eyes / Why did I choose you / Blue hodge / I love being here with you / All blues / Down home blues
CD CCD 4348
Concord Jazz / Jul '88 / New Note/Pinnacle

TAKE EIGHT
CD CCD 4347
Concord Jazz / Jul '88 / New Note/ Pinnacle

Concrete Blonde

RECOLLECTION
God is a bullet / Tomorrow Wendy / Joey / Scene of a perfect crime / Someday / Ghost of a Texas ladies man / Dance along the edge / Bloodletting / Happy birthday / Caroline / Cold part of town / Walking in London / Heal it up / Everybody knows / True / Mexican moon / Still in Hollywood / Mercedez Benz
CD EIRSCD 1077
IRS/EMI / Apr '96 / EMI

Concrete Sox

NO WORLD ORDER
CD LF 048
Lost & Found / Aug '93 / Plastic Head

Condell, Sonny

SOMEONE TO DANCE WITH
CD SCD 295CD
Starc / Jan '95 / ADA / Direct

Condemned 84

BOOTS GO MARCHING IN
CD GMM 111
GMM / Jun '97 / Cargo

FACE THE AGGRESSION
CD GMM 110
GMM / Jun '97 / Cargo

Condon, Eddie

CHICAGO STYLE (His Greatest Recordings 1927-1940)
Ballin' the jack / Carnegie jump / China boy / Easy to get / Good man is hard to find / Harlem fuss / Home cooking / I ain't gonna give nobody none of my jelly roll / I'm gonna stomp Mr. Henry Lee / I've found a new baby / Indiana / Jazz me blues / Love is just around the corner / Madame Dynamite / Margie / Minor drag / Nobody's sweetheart / Oh baby / Oh Peter you're so nice / Sugar / That's a serious thing / There'll be some changes made / Who's sorry now / Wolverine blues
CD CDAJA 5192
Living Era / Mar '96 / Select

CLASSICS 1927-1938
CD CLASSICS 742
Classics / Feb '94 / Discovery / Jazz Music

CLASSICS 1938-1940
CD CLASSICS 759
Classics / Aug '94 / Discovery / Jazz Music

CLASSICS 1942-1943
CD CLASSICS 772
Classics / Aug '94 / Discovery / Jazz Music

CONDON TOWN HALL CONCERT VOL.10
CD JCD 1019/20
Jazzology / Jul '96 / Jazz Music

DIXIELAND AT THE JAZZ BAND BALL (Condon, Eddie & George Wettling)
CD CD 53175
Giants Of Jazz / Jan '95 / Cadillac / Jazz Music / Target/BMG

DOCTOR JAZZ VOL.5 (Condon, Eddie Band & 'Wild' Bill Davison)
CD STCD 6045
Storyville / May '97 / Cadillac / Jazz Music / Wellard

DOCTOR JAZZ VOL.8
CD STCD 6048
Storyville / Jul '96 / Cadillac / Jazz Music / Wellard

EDDIE CONDON 1928-1931
One step to heaven / Shimme Sha Wabble / Oh baby (rain or shine) / Indiana / I'm sorry I made you cry / Makin' friends / I'm gonna stomp, Mr Henry Lee / That's a serious thing / Firehouse blues / Tailspin blues / Never had a reason / Hello Lola / One hour / Girls like you were meant for boys like me / Arkansas blues / Georgia on my mind / I can't believe that you're in love with me / Darktown strutters ball / (I'll be glad when you're dead) you rascal you
CD CBC 1024
Timeless / Sep '96 / New Note/Pinnacle

EDDIE CONDON 1930-1944
CD CD 53183
Giants Of Jazz / Nov '95 / Cadillac / Jazz Music / Target/BMG

EDDIE CONDON 1933-1940
CD CD 56078
Jazz Roots / Jul '95 / Target/BMG

EDDIE CONDON BAND & 'WILD' BILL DAVISON 1951-1952 (Condon, Eddie Band & 'Wild' Bill Davison)
CD STCD 6056
Storyville / Mar '97 / Cadillac / Jazz Music / Wellard

EDDIE CONDON LIVE IN 1944 VOL.3 (Condon, Eddie & His All Stars)
CD JCD 634
Jass / '92 / ADA / Cadillac / CM / Direct / Jazz Music

HIS JAZZ CONCERT
CD STCD 530
Stash / Feb '91 / ADA / Cadillac / CM / Direct / Jazz Music

IN JAPAN
CD CRD 154
Chiaroscuro / Dec '95 / Jazz Music

JAZZ ON THE AIR - EDDIE CONDON FLOOR SHOW
Them there eyes / Blues in my heart / Riverboat shuffle
CD 20803
Laserlight / Mar '88 / Target/BMG

LIVE AT THE NEW SCHOOL (Condon, Eddie & Kenny Davern/Gene Krupa)
CD CRD 110
Chiaroscuro / Jul '96 / Jazz Music

TOWN HALL BLUE (3CD Set)
CD Set JCD 1021/22/23
Jazzology / Nov '96 / Jazz Music

TOWN HALL CONCERTS VOL.1 (Condon, Eddie & His All Stars)
Jazz me blues / Cherry / I'm coming Virginia / Love nest / Big butter and egg man / Oh Katharina / Impromptu ensemble / Sugar / It's been so long / Mandy, make up your mind / September in the rain / Song of the wanderer / Walking the dog
CD JCECD 1001/2
Jazzology / Oct '92 / Jazz Music

TOWN HALL CONCERTS VOL.2
CD Set JCECD 1003/4
Jazzology / Jazz Music

TOWN HALL CONCERTS VOL.3
CD JCECD 1005/6
Jazzology / Oct '92 / Jazz Music

TOWN HALL CONCERTS VOL.4
CD JCECD 1007/8
Jazzology / Oct '92 / Jazz Music

TOWN HALL CONCERTS VOL.5
CD Set JCECD 1009/10
Jazzology / Oct '91 / Jazz Music

TOWN HALL CONCERTS VOL.6
CD Set JCECD 1011/12
Jazzology / Oct '91 / Jazz Music

TOWN HALL CONCERTS VOL.8
CD Set JCD 1015/16
Jazzology / Jul '93 / Jazz Music

TOWN HALL CONCERTS VOL.9
CD JCD 1017/18
Jazzology / Jan '94 / Jazz Music

TRANSCRIPTION OF THE TOWN HALL CONCERT (2CD Set) (Condon, Eddie & His All Stars)
Ballin' the jack / That's a plenty / Cherry/ alternate take/breakdown take/master take / Sweet Georgia / At the Jazz band ball / When my sugar walks down the street / Uncle Sam's blues / Someone to watch over me / One I love belongs to somebody else / Where ever there's love (there's you and I) / What's new / Ja da / Time on my hands / Royal garden blues / Muskrat ramble / It's been so long / Man I love / 'S wonderful / Just you just me / Old folks / You're lucky to me / At the darktown strutter's ball / Eddie Condon speaks / St. Louis blues / Honeysuckle rose / She's funny that way / It's been so long / Nobody knows (nobody seems to care) / Uncle Sam's Blues / Serenade in thirds / Untitled original / China boy / Impromptu ensemble
CD Set JZCL 5008
Jazz Classics / Nov '96 / Cadillac / Direct / Jazz Music

WINDY CITY JAZZ
CD TPZ 1026
Topaz Jazz / Aug '95 / Cadillac / Pinnacle

Conemelt

CONFUSE AND DESTROY
Misty traincrash / Flashermac / Cuckoo clock rock / Joys of surface noises / Big up hte conemelt / Overbite nightmare / Espionage / Big and clever track / Pushbutton twist / Motorskating
CD SOP 007CD
Emissions / Jan '96 / Amato Disco / Vital

Conexion Latina

LA CONEXION
Llegue a la cima / Maravilla / La clave / La conexion / Yo quiero tambien / Palmira / Ritmo internacional / Ataconda / Fiesta de despedida
CD ENJ 90652
Enja / Sep '96 / New Note/Pinnacle / Vital/ SAM

Confederate Railroad

WHEN AND WHERE
CD 7567827742
Atlantic / Jun '94 / Warner Music

Confessor

CONDEMNED
CD MOSH 044CD
Earache / Oct '91 / Vital

Confetti

RETROSPECTIVEL EP
Who's big and clever now / It's kinda funny / Yes please / Tomorrow who knows / Warm / Jenny / Bridge 61 / Diet / Whatever

became of Alice and Jane / Here again / River island / Nothing II / Corduroy / Anyone can make a mistake / Once more
CD ASKCD 039
Vinyl Japan / Sep '94 / Plastic Head / Vinyl Japan

Conflict

CONCLUSION
CD MORTCD 100
Mortarhate / Dec '93 / RTM/Disc

DEPLOYING ALL MEANS NECESSARY
CD CLP 99322
Cleopatra / Apr '97 / Cargo / Greyhound / Plastic Head / RTM/Disc / SRD

EMPLOYING ALL MEANS NECESSARY
CD CLEO 1023CD
Cleopatra / Jul '94 / Cargo / Greyhound / Plastic Head / RTM/Disc / SRD

FINAL CONFLICT, THE
You cannot win / Ungovernable farce / Piss in the ocean / Crass / Custom rock / 1986 the struggle continues / Mental mania / Ungovernable force / They said that / Force or service / Arrest / Statement / Day before / This is the ALF / To be continued
CD MORTCD 50
Mortarhate / Dec '96 / RTM/Disc

IN THE VENUE
CD MORTCD 120
Mortarhate / Feb '97 / RTM/Disc

IT'S TIME TO SEE WHO'S WHO NOW
CD MORTCD 110
Mortarhate / May '94 / RTM/Disc

ONLY STUPID BASTARDS USE EMI
CD MORTCD 130
Mortarhate / Jan '95 / RTM/Disc

STANDARD ISSUE VOL.2 1988-1994
CD MORTCD 170
Mortarhate / Jan '96 / RTM/Disc

THESE COLOURS DON'T RUN
CD MORTCD 080
Mortarhate / Oct '93 / RTM/Disc

TURNING REBELLION INTO MONEY
Banned in the UK / Piss in the ocean / Increased pressure / Serenade is dead / They said that / From protest to resistance / Big hand / G song / I ain't thick, it's just a trick / So what / Punk is dead / Rival tribal / Statement
CD MORTCD 30
Mortarhate / Dec '96 / RTM/Disc

WE WON'T TAKE NO MORE
CD MORTCD 150
Mortarhate / Aug '95 / RTM/Disc

Confront

ONE LIFE - DRUG FREE
CD LF 097CD
Lost & Found / Aug '94 / Plastic Head

Confront, James

TEST ONE REALITY
CD SST 305CD
SST / Mar '95 / Plastic Head

Confrontation

CONFRONTATION
CD LF 139CD
Lost & Found / Mar '95 / Plastic Head

Confuse

COLLECTION, THE
CD JPC 03
Japan Punk Collection / Nov '96 / Cargo

Confusions

EVERYONES INVITED
CD EFA 054012
Clear Spot / Feb '97 / Cargo / SRD

Congaline

DE CONGALINE CARNIVA
CD CCD 0023
CRS / Apr '96 / ADA / Direct / Jet Star

Conglomerate

PRECISELY THE OPPOSITE OF WHAT WE NOW KNOW TO BE TRUE
CD DIS 004
FMR/Dissenter / Oct '95 / Cadillac / Harmonia Mundi

Congos

HEART OF THE CONGOS
Fisherman / Congo man / Open up the gate / Children crying / La la bam bam / Can't come in / Sodom and Gomorrah / Wrong thing / Ark of covenant / Solid foundation
CD 14805
Spalax / Jun '97 / ADA / Cargo / Direct / Discovery / Greyhound

HEART OF THE CONGOS (2CD Set)
CD Set BAFCD 9
Blood & Fire / Jan '96 / Vital

NATTY DREAD RISE AGAIN
Rock of Gibraltar / Step aside / Music is the key / Seeking a favour / Judgement day / Natty dread rise again / Vibration / This could not be happening / Love is the answer / Apartheid / Sent to Babylon
CD RASCD 3238
Ras / Feb '97 / Direct / Greensleeves / Jet Star / SRD

Congregation

EGHAM
CD FIREMCD 55
Fire / Oct '95 / Pinnacle / RTM/Disc

Conjunto Alma De Apatzingan

ARRIBA TIERRA CALIENTE
CD ARHCD 426
Arhoolie / Apr '95 / ADA / Cadillac / Direct

Conjunto Bernal

MI UNICO CAMINO
CD ARHCD 344
Arhoolie / Apr '95 / ADA / Cadillac / Direct

Conjunto Casino

MAMBO CON CHA CHA CHA 1953-1955
CD TCD 080
Tumbao Cuban Classics / Jul '96 / Discovery

MOLIENDA CAFE
CD CCD 507
Caney / Nov '95 / ADA / Discovery

Conjunto Cespedes

UNA SOLA CASA
CD GLCD 4007
Green Linnet / Jul '93 / ADA / CM / Direct / Highlander / Roots

VIVITO Y COLEANDO
CD XENO 4033CD
Xenophile / Jun '95 / ADA / Direct

Conjunto Clasico

CLASICO DE NUEVO
Tu mi estrella / Hipocresia / Gracias amor / Se que volvera / Une dia de abril / No te quiero como amiga / Contigo me voy / Me enamore
CD 66058092
RMM / Feb '96 / New Note/Pinnacle

Conjunto De Luis Santi

MAMBO INFIERNO
CD TCD 075
Tumbao / Feb '97 / Discovery

Conjunto Explosao Do Samba

BEST OF CARNIVAL IN RIO VOL.3, THE
CD EUCD 1137
ARC / '91 / ADA / ARC Music

Conjunto Libre

SIEMPRE SERE GUAJIRO
CD CDGR 154
Charly / May '97 / Koch

Conjunto Matamoros

BAILARE TU SON
CD TCD 070
Tumbao Cuban Classics / Jul '96 / Discovery

Conjunto Niagara

QUE NO SE ACABE EL BONGO 1945-1947
CD TCD 068
Tumbao Cuban Classics / Jul '96 / Discovery

Conklin, Larry

POET'S ORCHESTRA
CD INAK 9020CD
In Akustik / Jun '93 / Direct / TKO Magnum

SNOW TIGER, THE
CD INAK 8901
In Akustik / Jul '95 / Direct / TKO Magnum

Conley, Arthur

SOUL DIRECTIONS
Funky Street / Burning fire / Otis sleep on / Hearsay / This love of mine / Love comes and goes / People sure act funny / How to hurt a guy / Get another fool / Put our love together
CD 7567803862
Atlantic / Jan '96 / Warner Music

SWEET SOUL MUSIC (The Best Of Arthur Conley)
I'm a lonely stranger / Who's foolin' who / In the same old way / I can't stop (no no no) / Take me (just as I am) / Sweet soul music / Let's go steady / Wholesale love / Shake, rattle and roll / Whole lotta woman / People sure act funny / Funky Street / Get yourself another fool / Run on / Otis sleeps on / Put our love together / Aunt Dora's love soul shack / Ob-la-di ob-la-da / Star review / They call the wind Maria / God bless / Nobody's fault but mine
CD Set SCL 2105
Ichiban Soul Classics / Nov '95 / Koch

SWEET SOUL MUSIC
CD 7567802842
Atlantic / Jan '96 / Warner Music

Conley, Brian

STAGE TO STAGE (2CD Set)
CD Set TCD 2870
Telstar / Oct '96 / BMG

Conlon, Bill

WITH YOU IN MIND
Lucille / I know one / Cowboys don't get lucky all the time / I don't have far to fall / Please please / Chair / Carmen / Not counting you / She's holding her own now / That ain't like your memory / Let's start forever / Streets of Bakersfield
CD ETCD 189
Etude / Apr '96 / Grapevine/PolyGram

Conlon, Eddie

1933-40
CD CD 14557
Jazz Portraits / Jul '94 / Jazz Music

Conn, Bobby

BOBBY CONN
CD ALP 302
Atavistic / May '97 / Cargo / SRD

Connacht Ramblers

CONNACHT RAMBLERS
CD RR 001CD
RR / Jan '95 / ADA

Conneff, Kevin

WEEK BEFORE EASTER, THE
Ellen Brown / Hornpipes / I'm here because I'm here / John Barber / McAuliffe's polkas / Flower of Magherally / Salt / Dark eyed gipsies / Fair maid wont' you call me your Darling / Cape breton reel / Green fields of America / Gathering mushrooms / Estonian waltz / Week before Easter
CD CCF 23CD
Claddagh / Feb '93 / ADA / CM / Direct

Connells

RING
Slackjawed / Carry my picture / Doin' you / Find out / Eyes on the ground / Spiral / Hey you / New boy / Disappointed / Burden / Any day now / Running Mary / Logan street / Wonder why / Living in the past
CD 8286602
London / Aug '95 / PolyGram

Connelly, Chris

PHENOBARB BAM-BA-LAM
CD CDDVN 13
Devotion / Jul '92 / Pinnacle

WHIPLASH BOYCHILD
CD CDDVN 14
Devotion / Oct '92 / Pinnacle

Connemara

SIREN SONG
CD BLX 10031CD
Blix Street / Nov '96 / ADA

Connick, Harry Jr.

25
Stardust / Music, maestro, please / On the street where you live / After you've gone / I'm an old cowhand (from the Rio Grande) / Moments notice / Tangerine / Didn't he ramble / Caravan / Lazybones / Muskrat ramble / This time the dream is on me / On the Atchison, Topeka and the Santa Fe
CD 4728092
Columbia / Jan '93 / Sony

BLUE LIGHT, RED LIGHT
Blue light, red light / Blessing and a curse / You didn't know me when / Jill / He is they are / With imagination (I'll get there) / If I could give you more / Last payday / It's time / She belongs to me / Sonny cried / Just kiss me
CD 4690872
Columbia / Apr '95 / Sony

ELEVEN
Sweet Georgia Brown / Tin roof blues / Wolverine blues / Jazz me blues / Dr. Jazz / Muskrat ramble / Lazy river / Joe Avery's place / Way down yonder in New Orleans
CD 4728082
Columbia / Mar '93 / Sony

FOREVER FOR NOW
It had to be you / Our love is here to stay / Forever for now / Stardust / Do you know what it means to miss New Orleans / Recipe for love / One last pitch / Heavenly / Blue light, red light / But not for me / Little clown / Where or when / Don't get around much anymore / You don't know me when / It's all right with me / We are in love
CD 4738732
Columbia / Jun '93 / Sony

HARRY CONNICK JR
Our love is here to stay / Little clown / Zealousy / Sunny side of the street / I mean you / Vocation / On Green Dolphin Street / Little waltz / E / Love is here to stay / Zealou
CD 4604904
Columbia / Aug '94 / Sony
CD 4879352
Columbia / Jul '97 / Sony

SHE
She / Between us / Here comes the big parade / Trouble / (I could only) whisper your name / Follow the music further / Joe slam and the spaceship / To love the language / Honestly now (safety's just danger out of place) / She blessed be the one / Funky dunky / That party / Booker
CD 4768162
Columbia / Aug '94 / Sony

STAR TURTLE
Star turtle / How do ya'll know / Hear me in the morning / Reason to believe / Just like me / Star turtle 2 / Little Farley / Eyes to the seeker / Nobody like you to me / Booze hound / Star turtle 3 / Never young / Mind on the matter / City beneath the sea / Star turtle 4
CD 4843262
Columbia / Jul '96 / Sony

WE ARE IN LOVE
We are in love / Only 'cause I don't have you / Recipe for love / Drifting / Forever for now / nightingale sang in berkeley square / Heavenly / Just a boy / I've got a great idea / I'll dream of you again / It's all right with me / Buried in blue
CD 4667362
Columbia / Apr '94 / Sony

Connie & Babe

DOWN THE ROAD TO HOME (Connie & Babe/The Backwoods Boys)
CD ROUCD 0298
Rounder / Nov '95 / ADA / CM / Direct

Conniff, Ray

'S WONDERFUL/'S MARVELOUS
'S wonderful / Dancing in the dark / Speak low / Wagon wheels / Sentimental journey / Begin the beguine / September song / I get a kick out of you / Stardust / I'm an old cowhand / Sometimes I'm happy / That old black magic / Way you look tonight / I hear rhapsody / They can't take that away from me / Moonlight serenade / I love you / I've told ev'ry little star / You do something to me / As time goes by / In the still of the night / Someone to watch over me / Be my lover / Where or when
CD 4840302
Columbia / Jun '96 / Sony

16 MOST REQUESTED SONGS
'S wonderful / Sometimes I'm happy / You do something to me / They can't take that away from me / I'd like to teach the world to sing / A time for us (Theme from Romeo and Juliet) / Lara's (Theme from Dr. Zhivago) / Ravel's Bolero / Where do I begin / Way we were / Speak softly love (Theme from The Godfather) / We've only just begun / I write the songs / Just the way you are / Emotion / How deep is your love / You light up my life
CD 4720462
Columbia / Jan '94 / Sony

CANCION DE AMOR
Brasil / Extrano en el paraiso / Te llevo dentro de mi / Noche y dia / Tentacion / Joven para amar / Gigi / La rueda de la fortuna / Moulin rouge / That old feeling / Di que no es asi / Abril en Paris / Solitario / Los ninos del pireo / Cancion de amor / Purpura real
CD CD 62094
Saludos Amigos / Jul '97 / Target/BMG

ENCORE - 16 MOST REQUESTED SONGS
Begin the beguine / Besame mucho / Thanks for the memory / Love is a many splendoured thing / It's been a long, long time / Memories are made of this / Midnight lace, part 1 / Hi Lili hi Lo / Invisible tears / Try to remember / This is my song / Red roses for a blue lady / It's impossible / First time I ever saw her face / Seasons in the sun / Memory
CD 4805142
Columbia / May '95 / Sony

FRIENDLY PERSUASION
CD CT 9010
Columbia / Jan '94 / Sony

INVISIBLE TEARS
CD CT 9064
Columbia / Jan '94 / Sony

RAY CONNIFF
CD CD 326
Entertainers / Apr '94 / Target/BMG

SPEAK TO ME OF LOVE
CD CT 8950
Columbia / Jan '94 / Sony

TICO TICO
Tico tico / Lisboa Antigua / Aquellos Ojos Verdes / El continental / La mar (la mer) / Extrana musica / La Colina de blueberry / Llorar / RogarParadiso / Todo lo que tu eres / El humo ciega tus ojos / Volare / Rapsodia en blue / Suave como el Amanecer / Una de esas cosas
CD — CD 62090
Saludos Amigos / Mar '97 / Target/BMG

WE WISH YOU A MERRY CHRISTMAS (Conniff, Ray & Singers)
Jolly old St. Nicholas / Little drummer boy / Holy night / We three kings of Orient are / Deck the halls with boughs of holly / Ring Christmas bells / Let it snow, let it snow, let it snow / Count your blessings (instead of sheep) / We wish you a Merry Christmas / Twelve days of Christmas / First Noel / Hark the herald angels sing / O come all ye faithful (Adeste Fidelis)
CD — 4814372
Columbia / Nov '96 / Sony

Connolly, John

AN TOILEAN AERACH
CD — CICD 063
Clo Iar-Chonnachta / Jan '94 / CM

Connolly, Kevin

LITTLE TOWN
CD — RTMCD 74
Round Tower / Jun '96 / Avid/BMG

MY MY MY
CD — EFR 103
Eastern Front / Feb '94 / ADA / Direct

Connolly, Rita

RITA CONNOLLY
Venezuela / Miracles / Factory girl/Same old man / Alice in Jericho / Fanny Hawke / It's really pouring / Two of us / Amiems / Red dust / Dreams in the morning / Close your eyes
CD — TARACD 3029
Tara / Jul '92 / ADA / CM / Conifer/BMG / Direct

VALPARAISO
Ocean floor / Valparaiso / Lizzie Finn / Ripples in the rockpools / Piccadilly / His name is Elvis / Two white horses / Shakin' the blues away / Sun song / Rio / Great guns roar / Quiet land of Erin
CD — TARACD 3033
Tara / Nov '95 / ADA / CM / Conifer/BMG / Direct

Connolly, Seamus

HERE AND THERE
Reel le blanc / Pat the budgie / Le reel / Reel of the blindmen / Larry's delight / Dominick McCarthy's Irish barndance/ Saunder's fort / I'll always remember you / Dr. Gilbert/Flax in bloom / Sheila Coyle's reel / Bells of congress/Dance for the haymaker/Kitty O'Brien / Marian McCarthy/ Jockey to the fair / Thirteen arches/ Thoughts of Carignan / Man in the bog/ O'Brien from Newtown / Carraigin Ruadh / Earl gray/Mrs. Macinroy of Lude/Spey in spate
CD — GLCD 1098
Green Linnet / Feb '92 / ADA / CM / Direct / Highlander / Roots

NOTES FROM MY MIND
CD — GLCD 1087
Green Linnet / Jan '88 / ADA / CM / Direct / Highlander / Roots

Connor, Chris

ALL ABOUT RONNIE
Jeepers creepers / If I should lose you / And the bull walked around, olay / All about Ronnie / I get a kick out of you / Where flamingos fly / Miser's serenade / Ask me / Chiquita from Chi-wah-wah / Blue silhouette / Everything I love / Gone with the wind / How long has this been going on / Stella by starlight / Lullaby of Birdland / I hear music / Out of this world / Lush life / From this moment on / In other words / Cottage for sale / Spring is here / Indian summer / Goodbye
CD — CD 53230
Giants Of Jazz / Feb '97 / Cadillac / Jazz Music / Target/BMG

AS TIME GOES BY
Falling in love with love / As time goes by / September in the rain / Gone with the wind / Strike up the band / Lovely way to spend an evening / Foggy day / Goodbye
CD — ENJ 70612
Enja / Nov '92 / New Note/Pinnacle / Vital/ SAM

CHRIS (Bethlehem Jazz Classics)
All about Ronnie / Mad miser man / Everything I love / Indian Summer / I hear music / Come back to Sorrento / Out of this world / Lush life / From this moment on / Good man is a seldom thing / Don't wait up for me / In other words
CD — CDGR 136
Charly / Apr '97 / Koch

LONDON CONNECTION
CD — ACD 246
Audiophile / Jun '93 / Jazz Music

SINGS LULLABYS OF BIRDLAND
CD — CDGR 125
Charly / Mar '97 / Koch

SWEET & SWINGING
CD — ACD 208
Audiophile / Aug '94 / Jazz Music

Connor, Joanna

BIG GIRL BLUES
CD — BPCD 5037
Blind Pig / Dec '96 / ADA / CM / Direct / Hot Shot
CD — RUF 1010
Ruf / Feb '97 / Pinnacle

LIVING ON THE ROAD
CD — INAK 9022
In Akustik / Jul '95 / Direct / TKO Magnum

ROCK 'N' ROLL GYPSY
CD — RRCD 901315
Ruf / May '95 / Pinnacle

Connors, Bill

OF MIST & MELTING
Melting / Not forgetting / Face in the water / Aubade / Cafe vue / Unending
CD — 847324 2
ECM / Jun '93 / New Note/Pinnacle

STEP IT
Lydia / Pedal / Step it / Cookies / Brody / Twinkle / Titan / Flickering lights
CD — ECD 220802
Evidence / Mar '94 / ADA / Cadillac / Harmonia Mundi

SWIMMING WITH A HOLE IN MY BODY
Feet first / Wade / Sing and swim / Frog stroke / Surrender to the water / Survive / With strings attached / Breath
CD — 8490782
ECM / Mar '92 / New Note/Pinnacle

Connors, Bob

BRAHMIN BELLHOPS
CD — SOSCD 1305
Stomp Off / Nov '96 / Jazz Music / Wellard

Connors, Loren Mazzacane

HELL, HELL, HELL
CD — TLS 003CD
Lotus Sound / Apr '97 / Cargo

IN PITTSBURGH
CD — DEX 7CD
Dexter's Cigar / Dec '96 / Cargo

Connors, Norman

BEST OF NORMAN CONNORS (The Buddah Collection)
Once I've been there / You are my starship / Mother of the future / Captain Connors / Be there in the morning / Kwasi / This is your life / Betcha by golly wow / Valentine love / Stella / Butterfly / Kingston / We both need each other / Romantic journey
CD — NEXCD 118
Sequel / Aug '90 / BMG

SATURDAY NIGHT SPECIAL/YOU ARE MY STARSHIP
Saturday night special / Dindi / Maiden voyage / Valentine love / Akia / Skin diver / Kwasi / We both need each other / Betcha by golly wow / Bubbles / You are my starship / Just imagination / So much love / Creator has a master plan
CD — NEXCD 186
Sequel / May '92 / BMG

THIS IS YOUR LIFE
Stella / This is your life / Wouldn't you like to see / Listen / Say you love me / Captain Connors / You make me feel brand new / Butterfly / Creator / Captain Connors (Mix)
CD — NEMCD 637
Sequel / Mar '93 / BMG

Conrad, Tony

SLAPPING PYTHAGORAS
CD — VANADIUM 23
Table Of The Elements / Jun '97 / Cargo

Consolers

BEST OF THE CONSOLERS, THE
CD — NASH 4502
Nashboro / Feb '96 / Pinnacle

Consolidated

BUSINESS OF PUNISHMENT
Cutting / Business of punishment / Born of a woman / Das habe ich nicht gewusst / No answer for a dancer / Meat, meat, meat and meat / Dog and pony show / Today is my birthday / Butyric acid / Woman shoots John / Consolidated buries the mammoth / Worthy victim / Recuperation / Empowerless / Emancipate yourself
CD — 8285142
London / Jun '94 / PolyGram

FRIENDLY FASCISM
CD — NET 033CD
Nettwerk / May '91 / Greyhound / Pinnacle / Vital

PLAY MORE MUSIC
Industrial music is fascism / Tool and die / CNN / Praxis 'Bold as love' / We came here for music, play it / Accept me for what I am / Veggie beat manifesto / Why I'm in the klan / Hello are you there / Infomodities 92 / Animal rights/Abortion rights / Wendy O Matic / One more song / He / I reckon you should shut the fuck up and play some music / You suck / Men's movement / Gone fishing / Labor vs. Leisure / Day on the green / More music/Hip O crats / Industry corporate / This isn't a fuckin' press conference / Crackhouse / More music please
CD — NET 040CD
Nettwerk / Sep '92 / Greyhound / Pinnacle / Vital

THIS IS FASCISM (2CD Set)
CD Set — PROCD 14
MC Projects / May '96 / Pinnacle / Prime

Conspiracy Of Silence

FACELESS
CD — SHR 013MCD
Shiva / Nov '95 / Plastic Head

Conte, Paolo

900
Novecento / Il treno va / Una di queste notti / Pesce veolce del baltico / La Donna della tua vita / Per quel che vale / Inno in re bemolle / Gong oh / I giardini pensil hanno fatto li loro tempo / Schiava del politeama / Chiamami adesso / Brillantina / Do do
CD — 4509910332
East West / Jun '93 / Warner Music

BEST OF PAOLO CONTE, THE
CD — 0630194052
Warner Bros. / Jul '97 / Warner Music

Contemporary Piano Ensemble

FOUR PIANOS FOR PHINEAS
Fond times with Junior / While my lady sleeps / Sweet and lovely / Newborn spirit / Moonlight in Vermont / Salt peanuts / Back home / Pass me not / It don't mean a thing if it ain't got that swing
CD — ECD 221562
Evidence / Sep '96 / ADA / Cadillac / Harmonia Mundi

KEY PLAYERS, THE
CD — DIW 616
DIW / Feb '94 / Cadillac / Harmonia Mundi

Conti, Ivan

BATIDA DIFERENTE
CD — ITM 94004
ITM / Nov '92 / Koch / Tradelink

Continental Drifters

CONTINENTAL DRIFTERS
CD — MON 6123
Monkey Hill / Sep '94 / Direct / Koch

Continentals

REASON WE SING, THE
CD — WSTCD 9696
Nelson Word / '88 / Nelson Word

Contours

VERY BEST OF THE CONTOURS, THE
Storm warning / Revenge / I'm coming home to you / Running in circles / When it rains it pours / Face up to the fact / Magic lady / Head over heels / Blinded by the light / One day too late / Look out for the stop sign / Under loves control / Flashback / Rise above it / Gonna win you back / Spread the news around / Ready or not here I come / Heaven sent
CD — 3035990052
Carlton / Oct '95 / Carlton

Contraband

DE RUYTER SUYTE
CD — BVHAASTCD 9104
Bvhaast / Jun '87 / Cadillac

LIVE AT THE BIMHUIS
CD — BVHAASTCD 8906
Bvhaast / Jun '88 / Cadillac

Contrastate

ENGLISH EMBERS
CD — DPROMCD 38
Dirter Promotions / Oct '96 / Cargo / Pinnacle / World Serpent

Control Freak

LOW ANIMAL CUNNING
CD — CSR 021CD
Cavity Search / Oct '95 / Plastic Head

Controlled Bleeding

BODY SAMPLES
CD — EFA 5321 D
Dossier / Mar '93 / Cargo / SRD

CONTROLLED BLEEDING
CD — CLEO 1022CD
Cleopatra / Jan '94 / Cargo / Greyhound / Plastic Head / RTM/Disc / SRD

CURD
CD — EFA 7726 D
Dossier / Mar '93 / Cargo / SRD

GILDED SHADOWS
CD — CLP 0027
Hypnotic / Aug '97 / Cargo / SRD

KNEES AND BONES
CD — EFA 084842
Dossier / May '97 / Cargo / SRD

MUSIC FROM THE VAULTS
CD — DV 21
Dark Vinyl / Mar '94 / Plastic Head / World Serpent

PETS FOR MEAT (Controlled Bleeding & Doc Wor Mirran)
CD — EFA 122052
Crypt / Apr '94 / Shellshock/Disc

SONGS FROM THE DRAIN
CD — EFA 085472
Dossier / Jun '94 / Cargo / SRD

Conundrum

TOMORROW TRADITION
CD — CDLOC 1085
Lochshore / Apr '95 / ADA / Direct / Duncans

Convoy Crew

TRUCKING GREATS
Convoy / Eighteen wheels / How fast them trucks can go / Movin' on / Me and old CB / Ode to 10-33 / Six days on the road / Teddy bear / Truck drivin' man / Rhythm of the road / Big city / Freightliner fever / Hold everything / I'll have another cup of coffee (then I'll go) / Phantom 309 / Tennessee is home to me / Dixie winds / Trucker's way of life / Wolf creek pass / Trucker's lady / Highway 40 blues
CD — QED 047
Tring / Nov '96 / Tring

Convulse

REFLECTIONS
CD — NB 114CD
Nuclear Blast / Jan '95 / Plastic Head

Conway, Francis

WAKE UP
Wake up (introduction) / New York skyline / It's a bedsit / Sweet Carronlaoe / Not even the president / Wake up / Striking it rich / Your drug is Hollywood / Somebody stole my gal / Walking on seashells / Spanish nights / She haunts me / Somewhere in heaven / To the edge of time / One night in Amsterdam
CD — RTMCD 22
Round Tower / Jan '91 / Avid/BMG

Conway, Russ

BEST OF RUSS CONWAY
CD — MATCD 212
Castle / Dec '92 / BMG

EP COLLECTION, THE
Call of the sea / Side saddle / It's my mother's birthday today / That's a plenty / Soho fair / Darktown strutters ball / Falling tears / Wedgewood blue / Rocking horse cowboy / Empty saddles / Ragtime cowboy Joe / Pixillated penguin / Let the big wheel keep turning / Pal Joey pops (medley) / Musical chairs / Musical chairs (Medley more party pops) / Part 2 Even more party pops part 1 (Medley) / More and more party pops - part 2 (Medley) / Scots pops (Medley) / I'll be seeing you / Twelth street rag / Temptation rag
CD — SEECD 310
See For Miles/C5 / Feb '91 / Pinnacle

GOLDEN SOUNDS OF RUSS CONWAY, THE
CD — GS 863562
Disky / Mar '96 / Disky / THE

GREATEST HITS
Side saddle / Mack the knife / Westminster waltz / Pixillated penguin / Snow coach / Sam's song / Always / Wedding of the painted doll / World outside / China tea / Lesson one / When you're smiling / I'm looking over a four leaf clover / When you wore a tulip / Row row row / For me and my gal / Shine on harvest moon / By the light of the silvery moon / Side by side / Roulette / Toy balloons / Pepe / Royal event / Lucky five / Passing breeze / Got a match / Always you and me / Pablo / Fings ain't wot they used t'be / Polka dots / Where do little birds go / Forgotten dreams / Music music music / If you were the only girl in the world / I'm nobody's sweetheart now / Yes sir that's my baby / Some of these days / Honeysuckle and the bee / Hello hello,

who's your lady friend / (In) a shanty in old Shanty Town
CD _______ CC 203
Music For Pleasure / May '88 / EMI

WALK IN THE BLACK FOREST, A (The Best Of Russ Conway)
CD _______ PLSCD 162
Pulse / Apr '97 / BMG

Cooder, Ry

BOOMER'S STORY
Boomer's story / Cherry ball blues / Crow black chicken / Axe sweet Mama / Maria Elena / Dark end of the street / Rally round the flag / Coming in on a wing and a prayer / President Kennedy / Good morning Mr. Railway man
CD _______ 7599263982
WEA / Jan '93 / Warner Music

BOP TILL YOU DROP
Little sister / Go home girl / Very thing that makes you rich makes me poor / I think it's gonna work out fine / Down in Hollywood / Look at granny run run / Trouble / Don't mess up a good thing / I can't win
CD _______ 256691
WEA / '83 / Warner Music

BORDERLINE
634 5789 / Speedo is back / Why don't you try me / Down in the boondocks / Johnny Porter / Way we make a broken heart / Crazy about an automobile / Girls from Texas / Borderline / Never make a move too soon
CD _______ 256864
WEA / '88 / Warner Music

BUENA VISTA SOCIAL CLUB (Cooder, Ry & Ochoa/Compay Segundo/Ibrahim Ferrer)
Chan chan: *Cooder, Ry* / Camino por vereda: *Cooder, Ry* / Veinte anos: *Cooder, Ry* / Pueblo nuevo: *Cooder, Ry* / Dos gardinerias: *Cooder, Ry* / El carretero: *Cooder, Ry* / Candela: *Cooder, Ry* / Amor de loca juventud: *Cooder, Ry* / Orgullecida: *Cooder, Ry* / Murmullo: *Cooder, Ry* / El cuarto de tula: *Cooder, Ry* / Y tu que has hecho: *Cooder, Ry* / Buena vista social club: *Cooder, Ry* / La bayamesa: *Cooder, Ry*
CD _______ WCD 050
World Circuit / Jun '97 / ADA / Cadillac / Direct / New Note/Pinnacle

CHICKEN SKIN MUSIC
Bourgeois blues / I got mine / Always lift him up / He'll have to go / Smack dab in the middle / Stand by me / Yellow roses / Chloe / Goodnight Irene
CD _______ 254083
WEA / '88 / Warner Music

GET RHYTHM
Get rhythm / Low commotion / Going back to Okinawa / Thirteen question method / Women will rule the world / All shook up / I can tell by the way you smell / Across the borderline / Let's have a ball
CD _______ 9256392
WEA / Dec '87 / Warner Music

INTO THE PURPLE VALLEY
How can you keep on moving / Billy the kid / Money honey / FDR in Trinidad / Teardrops will fall / Denomination blues / On a Monday / Hey porter / Great dreams of heaven / Taxes on the farmer feeds us all / Vigilante man
CD _______ 244142
WEA / '88 / Warner Music

JAZZ
Big bad Bill is sweet William now / Face to face that I shall meet him / Pearls / Tia Juana / Dream / Happy meeting in glory / In a mist / Flashes / Davenport blues / Shine / Nobody / We shall be happy
CD _______ 256488
WEA / '88 / Warner Music

LAST MAN STANDING (Original Soundtrack)
CD _______ 5334152
Verve / Oct '96 / PolyGram

MEETING BY THE RIVER, A (Cooder, Ry & V.M. Bhatt)
CD _______ WLACS 029
Topic / Apr '93 / ADA / CM / Direct

MUSIC BY RY COODER (2CD Set)
CD Set _______ 9362459872
WEA / Jun '95 / Warner Music

PARADISE AND LUNCH
Tamp 'em up solid / Tattler / Married man's a fool / Jesus on the mainline / It's all over now / Fool about a cigarette / Feeling good / If walls could talk / Mexican divorce / Ditty wa ditty
CD _______ 244260
WEA / Oct '87 / Warner Music

RY COODER
Alimony / France chance / One meat ball / Do re mi / Old Kentucky home / How can a poor man stand such times and live / Available space / Pig meat / Police dog blues / Goin' to Brownsville / Dark is the night
CD _______ 7599275102
WEA / May '95 / Warner Music

SHOW TIME
School is out / Alimony / Jesus on the mainline / Dark end of the street / Viva sequin / Do re mi / Volver, volver / How can a poor man stand such times and live / Smack dab in the middle
CD _______ 7599273192
WEA / Aug '92 / Warner Music

SLIDE AREA, THE
UFO has landed in the ghetto / I need a woman / Gypsy woman / Blue suede shoes / Mama don't treat your daughter mean / I'm drinking again / Which came first / That's the way love turned out for me
CD _______ K2 56976
WEA / Jul '88 / Warner Music

WHY DON'T YOU TRY ME TONIGHT
How can a poor man stand such times and live / Available space / Money honey / Tattler / He'll have to go / Smack dab in the middle / Dark end of the street / Down in Hollywood / Little sister / I think it's gonna work out fine / Crazy about an automobile / 634 5789 / Why don't you try me
CD _______ K 2408642
WEA / '86 / Warner Music

Cook, Barbara

BARBARA COOK SINGS THE WALT DISNEY SONG BOOK
When you wish upon a star / Give a little whistle / Pink elephants on parade / When I see an elephant fly / With a smile and a song / Lavender blue / Zip a dee doo dah / Dream is a wish your heart makes / Second star to the right / Baby mine / Someone's waiting for you / Sooner or later / I'm late / Someday my Prince will come
CD _______ PWK 090
Carlton / Feb '89 / Carlton

CLOSE AS PAGES IN A BOOK
It's not where you start / Close as pages in a book / I can't give you anything but love / Make the man love me / Exactly like you / April snow / Don't blame me / I'm in the mood for love / on the sunny side of the street / Way you look tonight / Bojangles of Harlem / I must have that man / April fooled me/I'm way ahead
CD _______ DRGCD 91412
DRG / Nov '93 / Discovery / New Note/ Pinnacle

I HAVE DREAMED
CD _______ DRGCD 91448
DRG / Mar '97 / Discovery / New Note/ Pinnacle

LIVE FROM LONDON
Sing a song with me / Let me sing and I'm happy / Beauty and the beast / Never never land / Can you read my mind / Come rain or come shine / Ship in a bottle / Sweet dreams / I see your face before me / Change partners / I'm beginning to see the light / I had myself a true love / Sweet Georgia Brown / Errol Flynn / Love don't need a reason / He was too good to me / Losing my mind / Accentuate the positive / Why did I choose you / In between goodbyes
CD _______ DRGCD 91430
DRG / Oct '94 / Discovery / New Note/ Pinnacle

TILL THERE WAS YOU (Broadway Years)
CD _______ 379052
Koch / Aug '95 / Koch

Cook, Jesse

GRAVITY
Mario takes a walk / Azul / Gravity / Closer to madness / Into the dark / Brio / Falling from grace / Olodum / Rapture / Gipsy / Lluna Llena
CD _______ ND 63037
Narada / Nov '96 / ADA / New Note/ Pinnacle

TEMPEST
Tempest / Cascada / Breeze from Saintes Maries / Baghdad / Parasol / Dance of spring / Soledad / Orbit / Fate (parasol reprise) / Jumpstart
CD _______ ND 63035
Narada / Dec '95 / ADA / New Note/ Pinnacle

Cook, Marty

NIGHT WORK
CD _______ ENJACD 50332
Enja / May '95 / New Note/Pinnacle / Vital/ SAM

Cooke, Sam

HEAVEN IS MY HOME (Cooke, Sam & The Soul Stirrers)
That's heaven to me / Deep river / I thank God / Heaven is my home / God is standing by / Pass me not / Steal away / Must Jesus bear his cross alone / Lead me Jesus / Trouble in mind / Sometimes / Somebody
CD _______ C5CD523
See For Miles/C5 / Jul '88 / Pinnacle

HITS OF THE 50'S
Hey there / Mona Lisa / Too young / Great pretender / You, you, you / Unchained melody / Wayward wind / Secret love / Song from Moulin Rouge / I'm walking behind you / Cry / Venus / All the way / Since I met you baby / I wish you love / Cry me a river
CD _______ 74321260562
RCA / Jun '95 / BMG

IN THE BEGINNING (Cooke, Sam & The Soul Stirrers)
He's my friend / I'm gonna build on that shore / Jesus wash away my troubles / Must Jesus bear the cross alone / Jesus I'll never forget / Nearer to thee / Any day now / Touch the hem of his garment / I don't want to cry / Lovable / Forever (alternative take) / I'll come running back to you / Happy in love / I need you now / That's all I need to know / One more river / He's so wonderful / Jesus gave me water / That's all I need to know (alternative take) / I don't want to cry (alternative take) / Forever / Lovable (alternative take)
CD _______ CDCHD 280
Ace / Nov '89 / Pinnacle

MAGIC OF SAM COOKE, THE
You send me / Only sixteen / Stealing kisses / Talk of the town / I love you most of all / Comes love / Lover come back to me / Everybody loves to cha cha / Little things you do / Good morning heartache / Win your love for me / Moonlight in Vermont / There, I've said it again / Stealaway / All of my life / That lucky old sun / God bless this child / When I fall in love
CD _______ MCCD 021
Music Club / May '91 / Disc / THE

MAN AND HIS MUSIC, THE
Meet me at Mary's place / Good times / Shake / Sad mood / Bring it on home to me / That's where it's at / That's heaven to me / Touch the hem of his garment / You send me / I'll come running back to you / Win your love for me / Wonderful world / Cupid / Just for you / Chain gang / Only sixteen / When a boy falls in love / Rome wasn't built in a day / Everybody loves to cha cha / Nothing can change this love / Love will find a way / Another Saturday night / Having a party / Twistin' the night away / Somebody have mercy / Ain't that good news / Soothe me / Change is gonna come
CD Set _______ PD 87127
RCA / Apr '86 / BMG

SAM COOKE WITH THE SOUL STIRRERS (Cooke, Sam & The Soul Stirrers)
Peace in the valley / It won't be very long / How far am I from Canaan / Just another day / Come and go to that land / Any day now / He'll make a way / Nearer to thee / Be with me, Jesus / One more river / I'm so glad (trouble don't last always) / Wonderful / Farther along / Touch the hem of his garment / Jesus wash away my troubles / Must Jesus bear the cross alone / That's heaven to me / Were you there / Mean ol' world / Lord remember me / Lovable / Forever / I'll come running back to you / That's all I need to know / I don't want to cry
CD _______ CDCHD 359
Ace / Nov '91 / Pinnacle

SAM COOKE'S NIGHT BEAT
Lost and lookin' / Mean old world / Nobody knows the trouble I've seen / Please don't drive me away / I lost everything / Get yourself another fool / Little red rooster / Laughin' and clownin' / Trouble blues / You gotta move / Fool's paradise / Shake, rattle and roll
CD _______ 5285672
London / Sep '95 / PolyGram

TWO ON ONE (Cooke, Sam & Jackie Wilson)
CD _______ CDTT 1
Charly / Apr '94 / Koch

WONDERFUL WORLD (The Best Of Sam Cooke)
You send me / Only sixteen / Everybody loves to cha cha / (I love you) for sentimental reasons / Wonderful world / Summertime / Chain gang / Cupid / Twistin' the night away / Sad mood / Having a party / Bring it on home to me
CD _______ ND 89903
RCA / Aug '95 / BMG

WONDERFUL WORLD
There, I've said it again / Let's go steady again / When I fall in love / Little things you do / You send me / Ol' man river / Moonlight in Vermont / Around the world / Danny boy / Ain't misbehavin' / Summertime / Wonderful world / Everybody loves to cha cha / Along the Navajo trail / Someday you'll want me to want you / I cover the waterfront / Mary Mary Lou / Love you most of all / Only sixteen / Win your love for me
CD _______ CDFA 3195
Fame / May '88 / EMI

Cookie & The Cupcakes

KINGS OF SWAMP POP
Got you on my mind / Mathilda / I'm twisted / Great pretender / I've been so lonely / I cried / Breaking up is hard to do / Betty and Dupree / I almost lost my mind / Feel so good / Charged with cheating / Sea of love / Close up the back door / Until then / Even though / Honey hush / Belinda / Trouble in my life / Who would have thought it / I had the blues / Walking down the aisle / Franko-Chinese cha cha cha / Shake 'em up / Mary Lou doin' the Pop-Eye / Just one kiss / Since your love has grown cold / Cindy Lou / Such as love / Married life / Mathilda
CD _______ CDCHD 142
Ace / Jul '97 / Pinnacle

Cookies

COMPLETE COOKIES
Chains / Don't say nothin' bad about my baby / Girls grow up faster than boys / Will power / Old crowd / Stranger in my arms / Softly in the night / Foolish little girl / I want a boy for my birthday / On Broadway / Only to other people / I never dreamed / I'm into something good / We love and learn / Randy / They're jealous of me
CD _______ NEMCD 649
Sequel / Jun '94 / BMG

Cool Breeze

ASSIMILATION
CD _______ DOR 38CD
Dorado / Apr '95 / Pinnacle

Cooley, Joe

COOLEY
CD _______ CEFCD 044
Gael Linn / Jan '94 / ADA / CM / Direct / Grapevine/PolyGram / Roots

Coolidge, Rita

ALL TIME HIGH
We're all alone / I don't want to talk about it / Loving arms / Closer you get / You're so fine / (Your love has lifted me) Higher and higher / Way you do the things you do / All time high / We've got tonight / Wishin' and hopin' / You / One fine day / I'd rather leave while I'm in love / Words
CD _______ 5500792
Spectrum / May '93 / PolyGram

COLLECTION, THE
We're all alone / I'd rather leave while I'm in love / (Your love has lifted me) higher and higher / Crazy love / Seven bridges road / I believe in you / Bird on the wire / I'll be your baby tonight / I don't want to talk about it / Words / One fine day / Fool that I am / Tempted / All time high / Walk on in / Wishin' and hopin' / Slow dancer / You / Sweet inspiration / You're so fine
CD _______ 5518162
Spectrum / Nov '95 / PolyGram

GREATEST HITS
We're all alone / I'd rather leave while I'm in love / (Your love has lifted me) higher and higher / One fine day / Only you know and I know / Bye bye love / Fever / Am I blue / Words / Slow dancer / Way you do the things you do / Let's go dancing / Keep the candle burning / I don't want to talk about it / Fool that I am / Mean to me
CD _______ CDMID 109
A&M / Oct '92 / PolyGram

OUT OF THE BLUES
Mean to me / Am I blue / Hallelujah I love him so / Call it stormy Monday / For the good times / Black coffee / Bring it on home to me / Nobody wins / Man I love / When the night rolls in / Out of the blues
CD _______ MA 1804100
Music Avenue / Jun '97 / Pinnacle

Coolio

GANGSTA'S PARADISE
That's how it goes / Geto highlites / Gangsta's paradise / Too hot / Cruisin' / Exercise yo' game / Sumpin' new / Smilin' / Fuck Coolio / Kinda high, kinda drunk / For my sistas / Is this me / Thing goin' on / Bright as the sun / Recoup this / Revolution / Get up, get down
CD _______ TBCD 1141
Tommy Boy/MCA / Dec '95 / BMG

IT TAKES A THIEF
Fantastic voyage / County line / Mama I'm in love with a gangsta / Hand on my nutsac / Ghetto cartoon / Smokin' / Can-o-corn / U know hoo / It takes a thief / Bring back somethin' / Fo da hood / N da closet / On my way to Harlem / Sticky fingers / Thought you knew / Ugly woman / I remember
CD _______ TBCD 1099
Tommy Boy / Oct '94 / RTM/Disc

MY SOUL
CD _______ TBCD 1180
Tommy Boy / Aug '97 / RTM/Disc

Coolman, Todd

LEXICON
Con alma / Caravan / I'm getting sentimental over you / All too soon / Summer serenade / Cancion para cadiz / You go to my head / One for Walton
CD _______ DTRCD 104
Double Time / Nov '96 / Express Jazz

Coon, Jackie

BACK IN HIS OWN BACKYARD
CD _______ ARCD 19109
Arbors Jazz / Nov '94 / Cadillac

Coon-Sanders Orchestra

EVERYTHING IS HOTSY-TOTSY NOW (Coon-Sanders Original Nighthawk Orchestra)
Nighthawk blues / Red-hot Mama / I'm gonna Charleston back to Charleston / Alone at last / Yes, Sir that's my baby / Everything is hotsy-totsy now / Flamin' mamie / Deep Henderson / My baby knows how / Slue foot / Mine, all mine / Wail / Hallucinations / Stay out of the south / Oh you have no idea / Here comes my ball and chain / Little orphan Annie / Rhythm King / We love us / Alone in the rain / After you've gone / Darktown strutters ball / Keepin' out of mischief now
CD ___ CDAJA 5199
Living Era / Sep '96 / Select

Cooney, Andy

IRISH INFLUENCE
CD ___ SHCD 52044
Shanachie / May '97 / ADA / Greensleeves / Koch

Coope, Boyes & Simpson

FALLING SLOWLY
CD ___ NMCD 9
No Master's Cooperative / Aug '96 / CM / Direct

FUNNY OLD WORLD
CD ___ NMCD 3
No Master's Voice / Feb '96 / ADA / Direct

HERE
CD ___ NMCDS 1
No Master's Voice / Jul '95 / ADA / Direct

Cooper

DO YOU NOT KNOW
CD ___ KIS 6CD
Konkurrel / Jan '95 / SRD

NO.2
CD ___ CDWOOS 3
Out Of Step / Aug '96 / Pinnacle

Cooper, Al

CLASSICS 1938-1941 (Cooper, Al & His Savoy Sultans)
CD ___ CLASSICS 728
Classics / Dec '93 / Discovery / Jazz Music

Cooper, Alice

ALICE COOPER
CD ___ EXP 010
Experience / May '97 / TKO Magnum

ALICE COOPER
CD ___ GFS 071
Going For A Song / Jul '97 / Else / TKO Magnum

ALICE COOPER LIVE 1968
CD ___ EDCD 320
Edsel / Feb '92 / Pinnacle

BEAST OF ALICE COOPER, THE
School's out / Under my wheels / Billion dollar babies / Be my lover / Desperado / Is it my body / Only women bleed / Elected / Eighteen / Hello hooray / No more Mr. Nice Guy / Teenage lament '74 / Muscle of love / Department of youth
CD ___ 2417812
WEA / Nov '89 / Warner Music

BILLION DOLLAR BABIES
Hello hooray / Raped and freezin' / Elected / Unfinished sweet / No more Mr. Nice Guy / Generation landslide / Sick things / Mary Ann / I love the dead / Billion dollar babies
CD ___ 7599272692
WEA / Jan '93 / Warner Music

CLASSICKS
Poison / Hey stoopid / Feed my Frankenstein / Love's a loaded gun / Stolen prayer / House of fire / Lost in America / It's me / Under my wheels / Billion dollar babies / Eighteen / No more Mr. Nice Guy / Only women bleed / School's out / Fire
CD ___ 4808452
Epic / Oct '95 / Sony

CONSTRICTOR
CD ___ MCLD 19068
MCA / Jan '94 / BMG

CONSTRICTOR/RAISE YOUR FIST AND YELL (2CD Set)
CD Set ___ MCD 33004
MCA / Jul '96 / BMG

FISTFUL OF ALICE, A
School's out / Under my wheels / I'm eighteen / Desperado / Lost in America / Teenage lament '74 / I never cry / Poison / No more Mr. Nice guy / Welcome to my nightmare / Only women bleed / Feed my Frankenstein / Elected / Is elected home
CD ___ CTMCD 331
EMI / Jun '97 / EMI

GOES TO HELL
Go to hell / You gotta dance / I'm the coolest / Didn't we meet / I never cry / Give the kid a break / Guilty / Wake me gently / Wish you were here / I'm always chasing rainbows / Going home
CD ___ 7599272992
Warner Bros. / May '94 / Warner Music

HEY STOOPID
Hey stoopid / Love's a loaded gun / Snakebite / Burning our bed / Dangerous tonight / Might as well be on Mars / Feed my Frankenstein / Hurricane years / Little by little / Die for you / Dirty dreams / Wind up toys
CD ___ 4684162
Epic / Mar '96 / Sony

KILLER
Under my wheels / Be my lover / Halo of flies / Desperado / You drive me nervous / Yeah yeah yeah / Dead babies / Killer
CD ___ K 9272552
WEA / Sep '89 / Warner Music

LADIES MAN
Freak out / Painting a picture / I've written home to mother / Science fiction / For Alice / Nobody likes me / Going to the river / Ain't that just like a woman
CD ___ CDTB 090
Thunderbolt / Feb '91 / TKO Magnum

LEGENDS IN MUSIC
CD ___ LECD 085
Wisepack / Sep '94 / Conifer/BMG / THE

RAISE YOUR FIST AND YELL
Lock me up / Give the radio back / Freedom / Step on you / Not that kind of love / Prince of Darkness / Time to kill / Chop chop chop / Gail / Roses on white lace
CD ___ MCLD 19137
MCA / Nov '91 / BMG

SCHOOL'S OUT
Luney tune / Gutter Cats vs The Jets / Blue turk / My stars / Public animal no. 9 / Alma master / Grand finale / School's out
CD ___ 9272602
WEA / Jun '89 / Warner Music

SNAKES AND DEAD BABIES
CD ___ CBAK 4037
Baktabak / Apr '90 / Arabesque

TRASH
Poison / Spark in the dark / House of fire / Why trust you / Only my heart talkin' / Bed of nails / This maniac's in love with you / Trash / Hell is living without you / I'm your gun
CD ___ 4651302
Epic / Aug '89 / Sony

Cooper, Bob

MOSAIC
CD ___ 74026
Capri / Nov '93 / Cadillac / Wellard

Cooper Clarke, John

DISGUISE IN LOVE
I don't want to be nice / Psyche sluts 1 and 2 / (I've got a brand new) tracksuit / Teenage werewolf / Readers' wives / Post-war glamour girl / (I married) a monster from outerspace / Salome Maloney health fanatic / Strange bedfellows / Valley of the lost women
CD ___ 4805302
Epic / May '95 / Sony

OU EST LA MAISON DE FROMAGE
Serial (part 1) / Letter to Fiesta / Film extra's extra / Majorca / Action man / Kung fu international / Sperm test / Missing persons / Split beans / Dumb row laughs / Bunch of twigs / Trains / Cycle accident / Gimmix / Readers wives / Ten years in an open neck shirt (part 1) / Nothing / (I married a) monster from outer space / Ten years in an open neck shirt (part 2) / Daily Express (you'll never see a nipple in) / Ten years in an open neck shirt (part 3) / Salome Malone / Psycle sluts
CD ___ RRCD 110
Receiver / Nov '96 / Grapevine/PolyGram

SNAP CRACKLE AND BOP
Evidently chickentown / Conditional discharge / Sleepwalk / 23rd / Beasley Street / Thirty six hours / Belladonna / It man / Limbo / Distant relation
CD ___ 4773802
Epic / Aug '94 / Sony

Cooper, Jim

NUTVILLE
Nutville / Mallethead / Mija / Bemsha swing / Cantor da noite / Sui fumi / Autumn nocturne / Cabbie patch / Tanga
CD ___ DD 457
Delmark / Mar '97 / ADA / Cadillac / CM / Direct / Hot Shot

TOUGH TOWN
Cheryl / Waltz for Betty / I waited for you / Tough town / Dolphin / Shades of light / Town sound/She'd be so nice to come home to
CD ___ DD 446
Delmark / Mar '97 / ADA / Cadillac / CM / Direct / Hot Shot

Cooper, Lindsay

MUSIC FOR OTHER OCCASIONS
CD ___ NML 8603CD
No Man's Land / Oct '93 / ReR Megacorp

OH MOSCOW
CD ___ VICTOCD 015
Victo / Nov '94 / Harmonia Mundi / ReR Megacorp

PIA MATER (Cooper, Lindsay & Charles Gray)
Pia mater
CD ___ RES 124CD
Resurgence / Sep '97 / Pinnacle

RAGS/THE GOLDDIGERS
CD ___ RERLCD
ReR/Recommended / Apr '91 / ReR Megacorp / RTM/Disc

Cooper, Mike

AVANT ROOTS (Cooper, Mike & Vivienne Dogan Corringham)
CD ___ MASHCD 0022
Mash / Dec '93 / Cadillac

CONTINUOUS PREACHING BLUES, THE (Cooper, Mike & Ian A. Anderson)
CD ___ APCD 037
Appaloosa / Mar '97 / ADA / Direct / TKO Magnum

DO I KNOW YOU/TROUT STEEL
Link / Journey to the East / First song / Theme in C / Thinking back / Think she knows me now / Too late now / Wish she was with me / Do I know you / Start of a journey / Looking back / That's how / Sitting here watching / Goodtimes / I've got mine / Don't talk too fast / Trout steel / In the mourning / Hope you see / Pharoah's march / Weeping rose
CD ___ BGOCD 276
Beat Goes On / Nov '95 / Pinnacle

PLACES I KNOW/THE MACHINE GUN COMPANY
Country water / Three - Forty Eight / Night journey / Time to time / Paper and smoke / Broken bridges / Now I know / Goodbye blues, goodbye / Places I know / Song for Abigail / Singing tree / Midnight words / So glad (that I found you) / Lady Anne
CD ___ BGOCD 294
Beat Goes On / May '96 / Pinnacle

Cooper, Pete

WOUNDED HUSSAR, THE
CD ___ FFS 002CD
Fiddling From Scratch / Oct '93 / ADA / Direct

Cooper, Roger

GOING BACK TO OLD KENTUCKY
Nine miles out of Louisville / Pine Creek / Cauliflower / New money / Growling old man, fussing old woman / Boatin' up Sandy / Bostony / Warfield / Paddy / Susan's gone / Morris Allen's Brickyard Joe / Weddington's reel / Greek melody / Salt lick / Something sweet to tell / Charleston / Snakewinder / Chillicothe beauty / Portsmouth / Meg Gray / Bumble bee in a jug / Coon dog / Jimmy Arthurs / Going back to old Kentucky / Bear Creek hop
CD ___ ROUCD 0380
Rounder / Oct '96 / ADA / CM / Direct

Cooper, Wilma Lee

WILMA LEE COOPER COLLECTION
CD ___ REB 1122CD
Rebel / Apr '96 / ADA / Direct

Cop Shoot Cop

ASK QUESTIONS LATER
CD ___ ABBCD 045
Big Cat / Apr '93 / 3mv/Pinnacle

CONSUMER REVOLT
CD ___ ABB 033CD
Big Cat / Apr '92 / 3mv/Pinnacle

RELEASE
CD ___ ABB 69CD
Big Cat / Aug '95 / 3mv/Pinnacle

WHITE NOISE
CD ___ ABB 029CD
Big Cat / Oct '91 / 3mv/Pinnacle

Cope, Julian

20 MOTHERS
CD ___ ECHCD 005
Echo / Sep '95 / EMI / Vital

AUTOGEDDON
CD ___ ECHCD 001
Echo / Jul '94 / EMI / Vital

FLOORED GENIUS VOL.1 (The Best Of Julian Cope)
Reward / Treason / Sleeping gas / Bouncing babies / Passionate friend / Great dominions / Greatness and perfection of love / Elegant chaos / Sunspots / Reynard the fox / World shut your mouth / Trampolene / Spacehopper / Charlotte Anne / China doll
CD ___ CID 8000
Island / Aug '92 / PolyGram

FOLLOWERS OF SAINT JULIAN, THE
Transporting / World shut your mouth / I've got levitation / Non-alignment pact / Umpteenth unnatural blues / Trainsporting / Trampolene / Disaster / Mock turtle / Warwick the kingmaker / Almost beautiful child / Eve's volcano (covered in sin)/Vulcano lungo / Pulsar nx / Shot down
CD ___ IMCD 251
Island / Jun '97 / PolyGram

FRIED
Reynard the fox / Bill Drummond said / Laughing boy / Me singing / Sunspots / Bloody assizes / Search party / O king of chaos / Holy love / Torpedo / I went on a chourney / Mic mak mok / Land of fear
CD ___ 8228322
Mercury / Mar '96 / PolyGram

INTERPRETER
I come from another planet baby / I've got my TV and my pills / Planetary sit-in / Since I lost my head, it's awl-right / Cheap age new fix / Battle for the trees / Arthur / Spacerock with me / Re-directed male / Maid of constant sorrow / Loveboat / Dust
CD ___ ECHCD 012
Echo / Oct '96 / EMI / Vital

JEHOVAHKILL
Soul desert / No hard shoulder to cry on / Akhenaten / Mystery trend / Upwards at 45 / Cut my friends down / Necropolis / Slow rider / Gimme back my flag / Poet is priest / Julian H Cope / Subtle energies commission / Fa-fa-fa-fine / Fear loves this place / Tower / Peggy Suicide is missing
CD ___ IMCD 189
Island / Mar '94 / PolyGram

MY NATION UNDERGROUND
Five o'clock world / Charlotte Anne / China doll / I'm not losing sleep / Vegetation / My nation underground / Someone like me / Great white hoax
CD ___ IMCD 138
Island / Aug '91 / PolyGram

PEGGY SUICIDE
Pristeen / Double vegetation / East easy rider / Promised land / Hanging out and hung up on the line / Safesurfer / If you loved me at all / Drive she said / Soldier blue / You... / Not raving but drowning / Head / Leperskin / Beautiful love / Western front 1992 CE / Hung up and hanging out to dry / American lite / Las Vegas basement
CD ___ IMCD 188
Island / Mar '94 / PolyGram

SAINT JULIAN/ MY NATION UNDERGROUND
CD Set ___ ITSCD 11
Island / Nov '92 / PolyGram

ST. JULIAN
Crack in the clouds / Trampoline / Shot down / Eve's volcano (covered in sin) / Space hopper / Planet ride / World shut your mouth / St. Julian / Pulsar / Screaming secrets
CD ___ IMCD 137
Island / Aug '91 / PolyGram

WORLD SHUT YOUR MOUTH
Bandy's first jump / Greatness and perfection of love / Elegant chaos / Kolly Kibber's birthday / Head hang low / Metranil vavin / Sunshine playroom / Lunatic and fire pistol / Strasbourg / Quizmaster / Pussyface / Wreck my car / High class butcher / Eat the poor
CD ___ 8183652
Mercury / Mar '96 / PolyGram

Copeland, Johnny

AIN'T NOTHIN' BUT A PARTY (Live in Houston, Texas)
CD ___ ROUCD 2055
Rounder / '88 / ADA / CM / Direct

FLYIN' HIGH
Flyin' high / Yesterday / Hooked, hog-tied and collared / Greater man / Jambalaya / San Antone / Thigpen / Promised myself / Love song / Circumstances / Around the world
CD ___ 5175122
EmArCy / Jan '92 / PolyGram

FURTHER ON UP THE ROAD
CD ___ AIM 1032CD
Aim / Oct '93 / ADA / Direct / Jazz Music

TEXAS TWISTER
Midnight fantasy / North Caroline / Don't stop by the creek son / Excuses / Jessanne / Houston / When the rain starts fallin' / I de go now / Early in the morning / Twister / Idiom / Easy to love / Media / Morning coffee / Jelly roll / Where or when
CD ___ ROUCD 11504
Rounder / '88 / ADA / CM / Direct

WHEN THE RAIN STARTS FALLIN'
CD ___ ROUCD 11515
Rounder / '88 / ADA / CM / Direct

Copeland, Ruth

SELF PORTRAIT/I AM WHAT I AM (Copeland, Ruth & Parliament)
Prologue: child of the North / Thanks for the birthday card / Your love been so good to me / Music box / Silent boatman / To William in the night / No commitment / I got a

thing for you Daddy / Gift of me / Medal / Crying has made me stronger / Hare Krishna / Suburban family lament / Play with fire / Don't you wish you had (what you had when you had it) / Gimme shelter
CD ________________ DEEPM 022
Deep Beats / Jun '97 / BMG

Copernicus

NO BORDERLINE
CD ________________ MCD 2089
Humbug / Jun '94 / Total/Pinnacle

Coping Saw

OUTSIDE NOW
CD ________________ HBOIS 004CD
House Of Dubois / Aug '97 / SRD

Copland, Marc

AT NIGHT
CD ________________ 500592
Sunnyside / Nov '92 / Discovery

Copley, Al

GOOD UNDERSTANDING (Copley, Al & The Fabulous Thunderbirds)
CD ________________ SECD 754
Suffering Egos / Apr '94 / Direct

LIVE AT MONTREUX
CD ________________ OMCD 1201
One Mind / Nov '94 / Direct

ROYAL BLUE (Copley, Al & Hal Singer)
CD ________________ BT 1054CD
Black Top / '92 / ADA / CM / Direct

Copper Family

COPPERSONGS VOL.2
CD ________________ COPP 002CD
Coppersongs / Nov '95 / ADA

Copper, Monique

BABAR & DOOS MEL SPEELGOOD
CD ________________ BVHAASTCD 8907
Bvhaast / Apr '89 / Cadillac

Copperfield, David

I GOT VARIETY
Big enough for me and you / Augusta's song / Buzz / Toys / Medallion man / Like a tune I can't forget / Independent lady / Don't sink your claws into me / I drink to your memory / Big dipper / I got variety
CD ________________ OWNL 60001
Own Label / May '96 / Else

Copperpot, Chester

SHORTCUTS
CD ________________ DOL 019CD
Dolores / Apr '95 / Plastic Head

Coppin, Johnny

COUNTRY CHRISTMAS, A
CD ________________ RSKCD 114
Red Sky / Jan '96 / ADA / CM / Direct

EDGE OF DAY (Music & Poetry) (Coppin, Johnny & Laurie Lee)
CD ________________ RSKCD 108
Red Sky / May '89 / ADA / CM / Direct

FORCE OF THE RIVER
River song / Reach out for you / Just for you / Shining stars / Full force of the river / All depends on you / May not be far away / Rise with the dawn / Border county road / On a hill in Shropshire / LOng lost love
CD ________________ RSKCD 112
Red Sky / Oct '93 / ADA / CM / Direct

GLOUCESTERSHIRE COLLECTION, THE (Forest & Vale & High Blue Hill/English Morning)
In Flanders / Song of Gloucestershire / Piper's wood / Fisherman of Newnham / Cotswold love / Briar roses / Legacy / Warning / High road / Field of Autumn / Cotswold lad / Song of Minsterworth Perry / Have wondered / Cotswold farmers / This night the stars / English morning / Everlasting mercy / Dover's hill / Hill / Tom Long's post / High hill / Holy brook / East wind / Winter / Cotswold tiles / Roads go down
CD ________________ RSKCD 015/107
Red Sky / Feb '95 / ADA / CM / Direct

SONGS AND CAROLS FOR A WEST COUNTRY CHRISTMAS
Intro: Lord of all this Revelling / Gloucestershire Wassail / Song for loders / My dancing day / Sans Day carol / Come all you worth Christian friends / Sailor's carol / Glastonbury thorn (theme) / Oxen / Innocent's song / O little town of Bethlehem / Wiltshire carol / Virgin most pure / Birth / Campden carol / Flowering of the thorn
CD ________________ RSKCD 111
Red Sky / Nov '90 / ADA / CM / Direct

Coptic Rain

11/11
CD ________________ DY 142
Dynamica / Jul '95 / Koch

CLARION'S END
Haunt / Devil in disguise / In to the sun / And all I loved / Rejoice / Selvas / Midgard / Cortex wave / Scanner / Slepnir / Even closer
CD ________________ DY 022CD
Dynamica / Sep '96 / Koch

DIES IREA
CD ________________ DY 22
Dynamica / Oct '93 / Koch

Cor Godre'r Aran

EVVIVA
Evviva beviam / Y blodyn a holltodd y maen / Berwyn / De animals a-comin' / A llawenydd cenwch / Majesty / Ach Fraulein Zart / Creation / Rhythm of life / Mae'r dydd yn cilio / Morte criste / Clychau'r gog / Jerusalem / Ar lan y mor / Gwyr Harlech
CD ________________ SCD 2120
Sain / May '97 / ADA / Direct / Greyhound

Cor Meibion Llanelli

YR YNYS DDIRGEL
Cragen ddur / Nkosi sikelel'i Afrika / Mae hon yn fyw / Llanfair / Unwaith eto / Yr ynys ddrigel / Draw dros y don / Y Greadigaeth / Ysbryd y nos / Yr anthem geltaidd / Gwawrio mae'r bore / Ffarwel I ddociau lerpwl / Gwawrio geltaidd
CD ________________ SCD 2126
Sain / Nov '96 / ADA / Direct / Greyhound

Corbett, Jon

ANOTHER FINE MESS (Corbett, Jon & Steve Done)
Commence to dancing / Acrobat / Glove for sale / Millstones / Tapdancer / Waltz for debris / Square midnight / Little weed / ...and there's an end to it
CD ________________ SLAMCD 217
Slam / Oct '96 / Cadillac

Cordas Et Cannas

PLACE OF WINDS
Abbas abbadas / Su testamentu / Nanneddu / Tancus serrada / Intr'a duos abbas / Mamma no keret / Tula et pula / Filugnana / Notti d'ea / Procurade 'e moderare / Su falkittu / Abba a bula / Scalmentu / Sos pirates barbarescos / Ninna nanna pizzinnu / In s'abba / Non si poni risisti / Terra de'entos
CD ________________ TERRCD 002
Terra Nova / Nov '96 / Direct

Cordelia's Dad

COMET
CD ________________ 179CD
Normal / Apr '95 / ADA / Direct

CORDELIA'S DAD
CD ________________ OKRACD 011
Okra / Mar '94 / ADA / Direct

HOW CAN I SLEEP
CD ________________ OKRACD 33019
Okra / Mar '94 / ADA / Direct

JOY FUN GARDEN, THE
CD ________________ RTS 3CD
Normal / Mar '94 / ADA / Direct

ROADKILL
CD ________________ SCOF 1004CD
Scenescof / Apr '96 / ADA

Cordell, Frank

SWEET AND DRY/THE MELODY LINGERS ON (Cordell, Frank & His Orchestra)
Get happy / April in Paris / Pick yourself up / 'Round midnight / Sing for your supper / There's a lull in my life / Summertime / Gone with the wind / Nobody's heart / What is this thing called love / Lover / You stepped out of a dream / Dance little lady / Man I love / Cherokee / You go to my head / Continental / Yesterdays / Just one of those things / Song is ended
CD ________________ CDMFP 6391
Music For Pleasure / Jul '97 / EMI

Cordner, Rodney

IRELAND - A SENSE OF PLACE
CD ________________ 12513
Music Of The World / Sep '93 / ADA / Target/BMG

Cordola, Lanny

ELECTRIC WARRIOR, ACOUSTIC SAINT
Intro (a new beginning) / Behold this dreamer cometh / Angry candy / Looney tunes / Ish kabibble / When shiloh comes / Birenbau / Farbage valves / Marriage of figaro (sort of) / Slappy white / Zulu jam / Shadows over my heart / Neesh taps / Jalapeno man / Django / Hungry hallow / Plymouth rock / Sadako / Jabberwocky / Vindaloo / Fripp / Summertime / Echo boy / Groom Lake / All the things you are / Amazing grace
CD ________________ FLD 9274
Frontline / Apr '92 / EMI / Jet Star

Cords

HEAR SEE FEEL TASTE
CD ________________ CORDS 001
Konkurrent / May '96 / SRD

Corduroy

NEW YOU, THE
Evolver / Joker is wild / Winky wagon / Supercrime / Season of the rich / Designosaur / Hand that rocks the cradle / (I know where the) Good times (have gone) / Data 70 / Crossfire / Fisherman's wharf / New you
CD ________________ ABB 139CD
Big Cat / Apr '97 / 3mv/Pinnacle

Core Foundation

READY TO FLY (2CD Set)
Ready to fly / You got it / This beat kicks / Freedom / Mortal combat / Time for change / Raise the Titantic / Let the rhythm unwind / New generation / Welcome to the future / In control / Forever and a day / Global sounds / Let yourself go / 20mm / Time to start pumpin'
CD Set ________________ ALPHACD 1
Alpha Projects / Mar '97 / Alphamagic

Corea, Chick

AKOUSTIC BAND, THE
Autumn leaves / So in love / Morning sprite / Circles / Spain
CD ________________ GRP 95822
GRP / Feb '89 / New Note/BMG

ALIVE (Corea, Chick Akoustic Band)
On Green Dolphin Street / 'Round midnight / Hackensack / Sophisticated lady / UMMG / Humpty dumpty / How deep is the ocean / Morning sprite
CD ________________ GRP 96272
GRP / Dec '90 / New Note/BMG

ARC (Corea, Chick & Holland & Altschul)
Nefertiti / Ballad for Tillie / ARC / Vedana / Thanatos / Games
CD ________________ 8336782
ECM / Mar '88 / New Note/Pinnacle

BEGINNING, THE
Drone / Percussion piece / Ballad II / Blues connotation / Balham III
CD ________________ 17083
Laserlight / Jan '97 / Target/BMG

BENEATH THE MASK (Corea, Chick Elektric Band)
Beneath the mask / Little things that count / One of us is over 40 / Wave goodbye / Lifescape / Jammin' E Cricket / Charged particles / Free step / Ninety nine flavours / Illusions
CD ________________ GRP 96492
GRP / Aug '91 / New Note/BMG

BEST OF RETURN TO FOREVER (Corea, Chick & Return To Forever)
Musician / Romantic warrior / So long Mickey Mouse / Majestic dance / Music magic / Hello again / Sorceress
CD ________________ 4682062
Sony Jazz / Jan '95 / Sony

CHICK COREA
CD ________________ 15751
Laserlight / Apr '94 / Target/BMG

CHICK COREA IN CONCERT (Corea, Chick & Gary Burton)
Senor Mouse / Bud Powell / Crystal silence / Tweak / Falling grace / Mirror mirror / Song to Gayle / Endless trouble, endless pleasure
CD ________________ 8214152
ECM / '84 / New Note/Pinnacle

CHILDREN'S SONGS
CD ________________ 8156802
ECM / Apr '84 / New Note/Pinnacle

EARLY DAYS
Brain / Converge / Waltz for Bill Evans / Sundance / Dave / Vamp / Jamala
CD ________________ 17082
Laserlight / Mar '97 / Target/BMG

EXPRESSIONS
Lush life / This nearly was mine / It could happen to you / My ship / I didn't know what time it was / Monk's mood / Oblivion / Panonica / Someone to watch over me / Armando's rhumba / Blues for art / Stella by starlight / Anna / I want to be happy / Smile
CD ________________ GRP 97732
GRP / May '94 / New Note/BMG

FRIENDS
One step / Waltse for Dave / Children's song / Samba song / Friends / Sicily / Children's song (15) / Cappucino
CD ________________ 8490712
Polydor / Jun '92 / PolyGram

HYMN OF THE SEVENTH GALAXY, THE (Corea, Chick & Return To Forever)
Hymn of the seventh galaxy / After the cosmic rain / Captain senor mouse / Theme to the mothership / Space circus Part 1-3 / Game maker
CD ________________ 8253362
Polydor / Apr '92 / PolyGram

JAZZ MASTERS
You're everything / Lenore / Space circus / Friends / Night streets / Children's song (15) / Spain / Interplay / Nite sprite / Light as a feather / Tweedle dee / Wind dance / My Spanish heart / Captain Marvel
CD ________________ 5198202
Verve / May '94 / PolyGram

LEPRECHAUN, THE
Imp's welcome / Lenore / Reverie / Looking at the world / Nite sprite / Soft and gentle / Pixiland rag / Leprechaun's dream
CD ________________ 5197982
Verve / Dec '93 / PolyGram

LIGHT AS A FEATHER (Corea, Chick & Return To Forever)
You're everything / Light as a feather / Captain Marvel / 500 miles high / Children's song / Spain
CD ________________ 8271482
Polydor / Mar '93 / PolyGram

LIVE IN MONTREUX (Corea, Chick & Joe Henderson)
Introduction / Hairy canary / Folk song / Psalm / Quintet / Up, up and... / Trinkle, tinkle / So in love / Drum interlude / Slippery when wet
CD ________________ SCD 90092
Stretch / Mar '97 / New Note/Pinnacle

MAD HATTER, THE
Woods / Tweedle dee / Trial / Humpty dumpty / Prelude to falling Alice / Falling Alice / Tweedle dum / Dear Alice / Mad hatter rhapsody
CD ________________ 5197992
Verve / Mar '93 / PolyGram

MOZART SESSIONS, THE (Corea, Chick & St. Paul Chamber Orchestra/Bobby McFerrin)
Piano concerto no.23/K488 / Piano concerto no.20/K466 / Song for Amadeus
CD ________________ SK 62601
Sony Classical / Nov '96 / Sony

MUSIC FOREVER AND BEYOND (The Selected Works Of Chick Corea/5CD Set)
Matrix / Chick's tune / Litha / Windows / Starp / Spain / No mystery / Hymn of the 7th galaxy / Captain senor mouse / Nite sprite / Leprechaun's dream, part 1 / Leprechaun's dream, part 2 / Duel of the jester and the tyrant / Armando's rhumba / Humpty dumpty / Sicily / Quartet No.2 part 1 / Central park / Rumble / Cool weasle boogie / Got a match / Light years / Eternal child / Trance dance / Make a wish part 1 / Make a wish part 2 / 99 Flavors / Blue miles / Ished / I don't see me in your eyes / Anymore / Lush life / Soft and gentle / Liza / Bautiful love / Yellow numbus / Crystal silence / O solo mio on the lone / Prairie / Even from me / I fall in love so easily / 'Round midnight / That old feeling / Trinkle tinkle (Monk) / Monk's mood / Stella by starlight / Summer nights / Straight no chaser / Story
CD Set ________________ GRD 59819
GRP / Jun '96 / New Note/BMG

MUSIC MAGIC (Return To Forever)
CD ________________ CK 34682
Sony Jazz / Aug '97 / Sony

MY SPANISH HEART
Love castle / Gardens / Day danse / My Spanish heart / Night streets / Hilltop / Wind danse / Armando's rhumba / El Bozo / Spanish fantasy
CD ________________ 8256572
Polydor / Jan '93 / PolyGram

PAINT THE WORLD (Corea, Chick Elektric Band)
Paint the world / Blue miles / Tone poem / CTA / Silhouette / Space / Ant and the elephant / Tumba island / Ritual / Ished / Spanish sketch / Final frontier / Reprise
CD ________________ GRP 97412
GRP / Feb '94 / New Note/BMG

PIANO IMPROVISATIONS
Noon Song / Song for Sally / Ballad for Anna / Song of the wind / Sometime ago / Where are you now
CD ________________ 8119792
ECM / '88 / New Note/Pinnacle

PIANO IMPROVISATIONS VOL.2
CD ________________ 8291902
ECM / New Note/Pinnacle

PRICELESS JAZZ
Trance dance / Spain / Cool weasel boogie / Got a match / Light years / Eternal child / Make a wish / Make a wish / 99 flavors / Blue Miles
CD ________________ GRP 98782
GRP / Jul '97 / New Note/BMG

REMEMBERING BUD POWELL (Corea, Chick & Friends)
Bouncin' with Bud / Mediocre / Willow grove / Desk in Sandi / Oblivion / Bud Powell / I'll keep loving you / Glass enclosure / Tempus fugit / Celia
CD ________________ SCD 90122
Stretch / Feb '97 / New Note/Pinnacle

RETURN TO FOREVER
Return to forever / Crystal silence / What game shall we play today / Sometime ago - la fiesta

CD 8119782
ECM / Mar '88 / New Note/Pinnacle

RETURN TO THE 7TH GALAXY (The Return To Forever Anthology/2CD Set) (Corea, Chick & Return To Forever)
CD Set 5331082
Verve / Oct '96 / PolyGram

ROMANTIC WARRIOR (Corea, Chick & Return To Forever)
Medieval overture / Sorceress / Romantic warrior / Majestic dance / Magician / Duel of the jester and the tyrant (Part 1 and 2)
CD 4682052
Columbia / Nov '93 / Sony

SEPTET
First movement / Second movement / Third movement / Fourth movement / Fifth Movement / Temple of Isfahan
CD 8272582
ECM / New Note/Pinnacle

TAP STEP
Samba LA / Embrace / Tap step / Magic carpet / Slide / Grandpa blues / Flamenco
CD SCD 90062
Stretch / Mar '97 / New Note/Pinnacle

THIS IS JAZZ (Corea, Chick & Return To Forever)
Romantic warrior / Sorceress / Music magic / So long Mickey Mouse / On Green Dolphin Street
CD CK 64967
Sony Jazz / Oct '96 / Sony

THREE QUARTETS
Quartet / Folk song / Hairy canary / Slippery when wet / Confirmation
CD SCD 90022
Stretch / Mar '97 / New Note/Pinnacle

TIME WARP
New life / Wish / Terrain / Day danse / That old feeling / New waltz / 'Round midnight
CD GRP 98292
GRP / Aug '95 / New Note/BMG

TOUCHSTONE
Touchstone / Procession / Ceremony / Departure / Yellow nimbus / Duende / Compadres / Estancia / Dance of chance
CD SCD 90032
Stretch / Mar '97 / New Note/Pinnacle

TRIO MUSIC
Trio improvisations 1,2,3 / Duet improvisation 1,2,3,4,5 / Slippery when wet / Rhythm-a-ning / 'Round midnight / Eronel / Think of one / Little rootie tootie / Reflections / Hackensack / Music of Thelonious Monk
CD Set 8277022
ECM / May '87 / New Note/Pinnacle

TRIO MUSIC LIVE IN EUROPE
Loop / I hear a rhapsody / Night and day / Summer night / Prelude no.2 / Mock up / Hittin' it / Microvisions
CD 8277692
ECM / Dec '86 / New Note/Pinnacle

VOYAGE
Mallorca / Diversions / Star Island / Free fall / Hong Kong
CD 8234682
ECM / New Note/Pinnacle

WALTZ FOR BILL EVANS
CD 500782
Musidisc / Sep '96 / Discovery

WHERE HAVE I KNOWN YOU BEFORE (Corea, Chick & Return To Forever)
Beyond the seventh galaxy / Earth juice / Shadow of Lo / Song to the Pharoah Kings / Vulcan worlds / Where have I danced with you before / Where have I known you before / Where have I loved you before
CD 8252062
Polydor / Feb '92 / PolyGram

WORKS: CHICK COREA
Where are you now / Noon song / Children's song / Brasilia / Slippery when wet / Duet improvisation / New place / La Fiesta / Return to forever / Song of the wind / 'Round midnight / Rhythm-a-ning / Senor Mouse / Sometime ago / Addendum
CD 8254262
ECM / Jun '89 / New Note/Pinnacle

Coria, Enrique

GUITAR ARTISTRY OF ENRIQUE CORIA, THE (Solos From South America)
CD ACD 6
Acoustic Disc / Jun '97 / ADA / Koch

Cormack, Arthur

NUAIR BHA MI OG
CD COMD 2016
Temple / Feb '94 / ADA / CM / Direct / Duncans / Highlander

RUITH NA GAOITH (CHASING THE WIND)
CD COMD 2032
Temple / Feb '94 / ADA / CM / Direct / Duncans / Highlander

Cormann, Enzo

MINGUS CUERNAVACA (Cormann, Enzo & Jean-Marc Padovani)
CD LBLC 6549
Label Bleu / Apr '92 / New Note/Pinnacle

Cormier, John Paul

RETURN TO THE CAPE
Haggis/Caber feidh / Cowie's clog/Winston tune / Jerry Sullivan's strathspey/Tammy Sullivan's reel / Flannigan's favourite/Ole French reel/Kelly's reel / Slow air/Moving cloud / Horseshoe reel/Winter carnival reel/ Pigeon on the gate / Hilda Chasson-Cormier's reel/Temperence reel / Shetland hornpipe/The E flat tune / Holland wedding reel/Stool of repentance/Sleepy Maggie / Niel Gow's lament/Niel Gow march/Slieveman's clog / Highland dream / Reel made with Hilda/Miss Watson's return to the cape
CD IRCD 041
Iona / Mar '97 / ADA / Direct / Duncans

Corn Dollies

EVERYTHING BAG
CD MC 015CD
Medium Cool / Jul '88 / Vital

Cornelius Brothers

TOO LATE TO TURN BACK NOW (Cornelius Brothers & Sister Rose)
Too late to turn back now / I'm never gonna be alone anymore / Don't ever be lonely (a poor little fool like me) / Treat her like a lady / Big time lover / Since I found my baby / Let me down easy / Got to testify (love) / Think it over / Come on let's be happy forever / I just can't stop loving you / Can't stand to be lonely / Just ain't no love (like a lady's) / I keep falling deeper and deeper
CD CTMCD 313
EMI / Apr '97 / EMI

Cornell

SILVER JUBILEE
CD RNCD 2024
Rhino / Sep '93 / Grapevine/PolyGram / Jet Star

Cornershop

WOMAN'S GOTTA HAVE IT
6 a.m. Jullander shere / Honk Kong book of Kung Fu / My dancing days are gone / Call all destroyer / Camp orange / Never leave yourself (vocal overload mix) / Jamsimran King / Wog / Looking for a way in / 7.20 a.m. Jullander shere
CD WIJ 045CD
Wiiija / Apr '95 / RTM/Disc

Cornerstone

OUT OF THE VALLEY
CD FE 1411
Folk Era / Dec '94 / ADA / CM

Cornerstone

BEATING THE MASSES
CD LF 159CD
Lost & Found / Jul '95 / Plastic Head

Cornfield, Klaus

LITTLE TIGERS (Cornfield, Klaus & Lotzi Lapislazuli)
CD EFA 11312CD
Musical Tragedies / Aug '93 / SRD

Cornucopia

FULL HORN
CD RR 7049
Repertoire / Jun '97 / Greyhound

Cornwell, Francoise

LE PEUPLE MAGIQUE
CD 860CD
Escalibur / Nov '96 / ADA / Discovery / Roots

Cornwell, Hugh

CORNWELL, COOK AND WEST (Cornwell, Cook & West)
CD UFO 009CD
UFO / Jun '92 / Pinnacle

GUILTY
One burning desire / Snapper / Nerves of steel / Black hair, black eyes, black suit / Hot head / Endless day, endless night / Five miles high / Sravandrabellagola / Long dead train / Torture garden / House of sorrow
CD SMACD 501
Snapper / May '97 / Pinnacle

Corona

RHYTHM OF THE NIGHT
Baby baby / Try me out / Get up and boogie / I don't wanna be a star / I want your love / In the name of love / I gotta keep dancin' / Rhythm of the night / Baby I need your love / Don't go breaking my heart / When I give my love / Do you want me / You gotta be movin'
CD 0630103322
Eternal / May '95 / Warner Music

Coronado, Florencio

ANDEAN HARP
CD PS 65159
PlayaSound / Feb '96 / ADA / Harmonia Mundi

Coronado, Joe

FINAL WARNING (Coronado, Joe & The Texas Beat)
She is fine as wine / Bet you do it real good / Sunrise sorrow / You got to walk on baby / What this woman is doing to me / Final warning / Know who your friends are / Let me tell you about my baby / Wasp / You know and I know
CD JSPCD 279
JSP / Feb '97 / ADA / Cadillac / Direct / Hot Shot / Target/BMG

Coroner

CORONER
CD N 02122
Noise / Apr '95 / Koch

GRIN
Dream path / Lethargic age / Internal conflicts / Cavaet (To the coming) / Serpent moves / Status: Still thinking / Theme for silence / Paralized, mesmerized / Grin (Nails hurt) / Host
CD N 02102
Noise / May '93 / Koch

MENTAL VORTEX
CD N 01772
Noise / Aug '91 / Koch

Corpolongo, Rich

JUST FOUND JOY (Corpolongo, Rich Quartet)
Valse / Time impulse / LA blues / Hey, what's happening / Just found joy / Try to, if you can / Time sense / Way it is
CD DE 489
Delmark / Jun '97 / ADA / Cadillac / CM / Direct / Hot Shot

Corporal Punishment

INTO THE NERVE OF PAIN
CD SPI 018CD
Spinefarm / Jun '95 / Plastic Head

Corporate Art

CORPORATE ART
Blood sugar 360 degress centigrade / Twenty one / Mutations / Skin / Chiaroscuro / Heitere gelassenheit / Bass minotaur / Same but different / Theme for W
CD 8491552
jMT / Oct '91 / PolyGram

Corps Of Drums

BEAT OF BATTLE, THE
Drum and bugle display / Under the double eagle / Salamanca day / Great escape / Flag and empire / La paloma / Yellow bird / Ode to joy / Sheik of Araby / Galanthia / Light of foot / Drum display / Resistance / Seven tears / Drummer's lilt / Marantha / Moray Firth / Trelawny and glo-pri-arg / Wotan's thunder / Vendetta / Victory beatings
CD 303782
Hallmark / Jun '97 / Carlton

Corpus

CREATION OF A CHILD
CD FLASH 45
Flash / Jul '97 / Greyhound

Corpus Delicti

OBSESSIONS
CD NIGHTCD 013
Nightbreed / Apr '97 / Plastic Head

Corrette, Michel

LE NOUVEAU QUATUOR
CD CSAR 57
Saydisc / Nov '92 / ADA / Direct / Harmonia Mundi

Corries

BONNET, BELT AND SWORD
Hot asphalt / Cam ye o'er frae France / Joy of my heart / Jolly beggar / Bring back my granny to me / Glenlyon lament / Johnny Cope / Gaberlunzie king / Haughs o' Cromdale / Banks of Newfoundland / Parcel o' rogues / North sea holes / Katie Bairdie / Oor wee school / I once loved a lass / Blow ye winds in the morning / My brother Bill's a fireman
CD BGOCD 271
Beat Goes On / Mar '95 / Pinnacle

COMPACT COLLECTION, THE
Flower of Scotland / Dumbarton's drums / Portree kid / Glencoe / Bricklayer's song / Come o'er the stream / MacPherson's rant / Roses of Prince / Lammas tide / Massacre of Glencoe / Ettrick lady / Turn ye tae me / Sherramuir fight / Dark Lochnagar / King fareweel / Man's a man for a' that
CD LCOM 9006
Lismor / Mar '88 / ADA / Direct / Duncans / Lismor

FLOWER OF SCOTLAND
Stirling brig / Kelvingrove / Vicar and the frog / Bona line / Loo song / Black Douglas / Bonnie ship the Diamond / Mothers, daughters, wives / Tibbie dunbar / Shenandoah / Castle of Dromore / Food blues / Flower of Scotland
CD MOICD 002
Moidart / Jun '94 / Conifer/BMG

IN CONCERT/SCOTTISH LOVE SONGS
Johnny lad / Lord of the dance / Flower of Scotland / Wild mountain thyme / Ca' the yowes / Bonnie lass o'Fyvie / Skye boat song / Wild rover / Kid songs / Hills of Ardmorn / Tiree love song / Annie Laurie / Ae fond kiss / Nut brown maiden / Sally free and easy / Liverpool Judies / Granny's in the cellar / Road to Dundee / Hunting tower / Lowlands of Holland
CD BGOCD 267
Beat Goes On / Feb '95 / Pinnacle

LIVE FROM SCOTLAND VOL.1
CD CDPA 002
CML / Oct '96 / Duncans

SCOTS WHA'HAE
Stirling Brig / Black Douglas / Scots wha hae / Lammas tide / Battle of Harlaw / Lock the door Lariston / Haughs o' Cromdale / Bonnie Dundee / Braes o'Killiecrankie / Sherramuir fight / News from Moidart / Johnny Cope / King Fareweel
CD MOICD 009
Moidart / Apr '94 / Conifer/BMG

SILVER COLLECTION
Killiecrankie / Rise rise / News from Moidart / Johnny Cope / Lock the door Lariston / Scots wha hae / I will go / Loch Lomond / Skye boat song / Welcome Royal Charlie / Parcel o' rogues / Barrett's privateers / Queen's Maries / Jock O'Braidislee / Bonnie lass o'Fyvie / Haughs o' Cromdale / Rose of Allendale / Westering home / Twa recruiting sergeants / Wild mountain thyme
CD MOICD 005
Moidart / Jun '93 / Conifer/BMG

SINGING GAMES, THE (The Dawning Of The Day) (Corrie Folk Trio & Paddy Bell)
Singing games / Lock the door, Lariston / Jock o' Braidislee / Doodle let me go / Lass o' Fyvie / Itinerant cobbler / Lord Gregory / McPherson's farewell / Coorie Doon / Greenland fisheries / My love she's but a lassie yet / Shoals o' herrin' / Trooper and the maid / Whistling gypsy / Queen Mary / Leaving of Liverpool / Uist tramping song / Johnnie lad / Roddy McCorly / Verdant braes o' Screen / Around Cape Horn / Fear a' Bhata / Killiecrankie / Jock Hawk's adventure in Glasgow
CD MOICD 013
Moidart / Apr '97 / Conifer/BMG

THOSE WILD CORRIES/KISHMUL'S GALLEY
Maid of Amsterdam / There are no pubs in Kirkintilloch / Quiet lands of Erin / Gentleman soldier / Lammas tide / Galway races / Lowlands low / Riever's galley / Kerry recruit / I'm a rover / Cam ye by atholl / Kishmul's galley / Roving journeyman / Lewis bridal song / Spanish shawl / Cruel brother / Gallus bloke / Highland lament / Twa corbies / Night visitor's song / Doran's favourite / Toon o' Kelso / October song / Shamrock and the thistle
CD BGOCD 326
Beat Goes On / Oct '96 / Pinnacle

VERY BEST OF THE CORRIES, THE
Black Douglas / Wha wadna fecht for Charlie / Isle of Skye / I will go / Sound the pibroch / Derwentwater's farewell / Flood Garry / Bonnie Dundee / Peggy Gordon / Boys of Barehill and Derry hornpipe / Abigail / Tartan mother's lullaby / Maids, when you're young never wed an old man / Rose of Allendale / Kiss the children for me Mary / Westering home
CD CDSL 8285
EMI Gold / Feb '97 / EMI

Corrigan, Briana

WHEN MY ARMS WRAP AROUND YOU
CD 0630142712
East West / Jun '96 / Warner Music

Corringham, Vivienne Dogan

POPULAR TURKISH FOLK SONGS (Corringham, Vivienne Dogan & George Hadjineophytou)
CD EUCD 1166
ARC / '91 / ADA / ARC Music

Corrosion Of Conformity

ANIMOSITY
Loss for words / Mad world / Consumed / Holier / Positive outlook / Prayer / Intervention / Kill death / Hungry child / Animosity
CD 398414078CD
Metal Blade / Apr '96 / Pinnacle / Plastic Head

DELIVERANCE
Heaven's not overflowing / Albatross / Clean my wounds / Without wings / Broken man / Senor Limpio / Man de mono / Seven

days / 2121313 / My grain / Deliverance / Shake like you / Shelter / Pearls before swine
CD 4776832
Columbia / Oct '94 / Sony

EYE FOR AN EYE
Tell me / Indifferent / Rabid dogs / Redneckkk / Minds are controlled / Broken will / LS / Co-exist / Dark thoughts / What / Positive outlook / College town / Eye for an eye / Poison planet / Negative outlook / No drunk / Not safe / Nothing's gonna change
CD INCDD 002/3
Product Inc. / Jun '94 / Vital

TECHNOCRACY
Technocracy / Hungry child / Happily ever after / Crawling / Ahh blugh / Intervention / Technocracy / Crawling / Happily ever after
CD 398417019CD
Metal Blade / May '96 / Pinnacle / Plastic Head

WISEBLOOD
King of the rotten / Long whip/Big America / Wiseblood / Goodbye windows / Born again for the last time / Drowning in a daydream / Snake has no head / Door / Man or ash / Redemption city / Wishbone (some tomorrow) / Fuel / Bottom / Feeder (elque come abajo)
CD 4843282
CD 4843289
Columbia / Sep '96 / Sony

Corrs

FORGIVEN NOT FORGOTTEN
CD 7567926122
Atlantic / Feb '96 / Warner Music

Cortes, Amparo

ENRIQUE DE MELCHOR
CD MW 4015CD
Music & Words / Nov '96 / ADA / Direct

Cortes, Joaquin

GIPSY PASSION BAND (Cortes, Joaquin & The Gipsy Passion Band)
CD CDEMD 1106
EMI / Apr '97 / EMI

PASION GITANA (Gypsy Passion)
Perdidos / Levenda ambiguedad / Naciente / Irradian / Oscura luz
CD 92402
Act / Jun '96 / New Note/Pinnacle

Cortes, Jose Luis

EN DIRECTO DESIDE EL PATIO DE MI CASA (Cortes, Jose Luis Y NG La Banda)
CD 74321401382
Milan / Sep '96 / Conifer/BMG / Silva Screen

Cortez, Dave 'Baby'

DAVE 'BABY' CORTEZ
Shake / Watermelon man / Boy from New York City / Can't buy me love / How sweet it is (to be loved by you) / Twine time / Stagger Lee / Yeh, yeh / Searchin' / Come see about me / Where did our love go / Paper tiger / Tweetie pie / Things ain't what they used to be / Count down part 1 / Count down part 2 / Belly rub part 1 / Belly rub part 2 / Do any dance / Peg leg / Sticks and stones / My sweet baby parts 1 and 2 / In orbit / Summertime / You talk too much / Hula hoop / Come back
CD NEMCD 751
Sequel / Aug '95 / BMG

HAPPY ORGANS, WILD GUITARS AND PIANO SHUFFLES
Happy organ / Piano shuffle / Cat nip / Hey hey hey / Mardi gras / Fiesta / Love me as I love you / Whistling organ / Hurricane / Deep in the heart of Texas / Do the slop / You're just right / Red sails in the sunset / Calypso love song / Dave's special / I'm happy / Summertime / Tootsie / It's a sin to tell a lie / Boogie piano / Boogie organ / Shift / Organ bounce / Swinging piano / Riffin'
CD CDCHD 386
Ace / Jun '93 / Pinnacle

Cortez, Jayne

TAKING THE BLUES BACK HOME
CD 5319182
Harmolodic/Verve / Nov '96 / PolyGram

WOMEN IN (E)MOTION FESTIVAL (Cortez, Jayne & The Firespitters)
CD T&M 106
Tradition & Moderne / Nov '94 / ADA / Direct

Coryell, Larry

BOLERO (Coryell, Larry & Brian Keane)
Improvisation on Bolero / Nothing is forever / Something for Wolfgang Amadeus / Tombeau de couperin (Prelude from) / Elegancia del sol / Fancy frogs / 6 Watch hill road / Blues in Madrid / Motel time / At the airport / Brazilia / Piece for Larry / La pluie / Patty's song
CD ECD 22046
Evidence / Mar '93 / ADA / Cadillac / Harmonia Mundi

BOLERO AND SCHEHERAZADE
CD 8100242
Philips / May '93 / PolyGram

COMING HOME
Good citizen swallow / Glorielle / Twelve and twelve / Confirmation / It never entered my mind
CD MCD 5303
Muse / Jan '86 / New Note/Pinnacle

ELEVENTH HOUSE
Birdfingers / Funky waltz / Low-lee-tah / Adam smasher / Joy ride / Yin / Theme for a dream / Gratitude / Ism-ejericico / Right on y'all
CD VMD 79342
Vanguard / Oct '95 / ADA / Pinnacle

EQUIPOISE
Unemployed Floyd / Tender tears / Equipoise / Christina / Joy Spring / First things first
CD MCD 5319
Muse / Feb '87 / New Note/Pinnacle

ESSENTIAL LARRY CORYELL, THE
CD VCD 75
Vanguard / Oct '96 / ADA / Pinnacle

FALLEN ANGEL
Inner city blues / Pieta / Fallen / Thus spoke z / Never never / Stella by starlight / Angel in sunset / Monk's corner / Stardust / Westerly winds / Misty / Moors / I remember bill
CD ESJCD 237
Essential Jazz / Oct '94 / BMG

QUIET DAY IN SPRING, A (Coryell, Larry & Urbaniak, Michal)
CD SCCD 31187
Steeplechase / '88 / Discovery / Impetus

SKETCHES OF CORYELL
CD SH 5024CD
Shanachie / Oct '96 / ADA / Greensleeves / Koch

SPACES
Spaces / Rene's theme / Gloria's step / Wrong is right / Chris / New year's day in Los Angeles-1968
CD VMD 79345
Vanguard / Oct '95 / ADA / Pinnacle

SPACES REVISITED
CD SH 5033
Shanachie / Jun '97 / ADA / Greensleeves / Koch

TOGETHER (Coryell, Larry & Emily Remler)
Arabian nights / Joy Spring / Ill wind / How my heart sings / Six beats, six strings / Geri's blues / First things first
CD CCD 4289
Concord Jazz / Nov '86 / New Note/ Pinnacle

TOKUDO
CD MCD 5350
Muse / Sep '92 / New Note/Pinnacle

TWELVE FRETS TO ONE OCTAVE
CD CD 322657
Koch International / Jul '97 / Koch

Coryell, Murall

EYES WIDE OPEN
CD BIGMO 30232
Big Mo / Aug '95 / ADA / Direct

Cosa

MAP OF LOVE
CD INCCD 3309
Incoming / May '96 / Pinnacle

Cosa Nostra

LOVE THE MUSIC
CD 99 2143
Ninetynine / Jul '96 / Timewarp

MIND SONGS
CD 99 2128
Ninetynine / Jul '96 / Timewarp

WORLD PEACE
CD 992156CD
Ninetynine / Nov '96 / Timewarp

Cosby, Bill

MY APPRECIATION
Camille / Trinkle tinkle / Wholly Holy / Have a little talk with Jesus / 3rd Avenue jog / All blues / Come Sunday / Wholly Holy / Have a little talk with Jesus / If I had my way / If I had my way
CD 8478922
Verve / Feb '92 / PolyGram

WHERE YOU LAY YOUR HEAD (Cosby, Bill & Friends)
Ursalina / Where you lay your head / Four Queens and a King / Mouth of the blowfish / Why is it I can never find anything in the closet
CD 8419302
Verve / May '90 / PolyGram

Cosmetic

SO TRANQUILIZIN
All things must change / Be my girl / Take it to the top / All my love / N-er-gize me / About the money / So tranquilizin / Jet set
CD 1883102
Gramavision / '85 / Vital/SAM

Cosmic Baby

THINKING ABOUT MYSELF
Thinking about myself / Treptow / Tag 20000 / Another day in another city / Brooklyn / Au dessous des nuages / Comic greets Florida....in Berlin / Fantasia / Loops of infinity (contemplative) / Movements in love
CD 74321196052
RCA / Apr '94 / BMG

Cosmic Couriers

OTHER PLACES
CD CLP 9823
Cleopatra / Oct '96 / Cargo / Greyhound / Plastic Head / RTM/Disc / SRD

Cosmic Jokers

LIFE AS ONE
CD IYFCD 07
In Yer Face / Apr '97 / Else

SCI FI PARTY
CD SPA 14884
Spalax / Nov '94 / ADA / Cargo / Direct / Discovery / Greyhound

Cosmic Psychos

PALOMINO PIZZA
CD EFA 0492409
City Slang / May '93 / RTM/Disc

SELF TOTALLED
CD ARRCD 63006
Amphetamine Reptile / May '95 / Plastic Head

Cosmic Trigger

SOLAR ECLIPSE
CD SR 9345
Silent / Jan '94 / Cargo / Plastic Head

Cosmic Twins

COSMIC TWINS
CD GRCD 312
Glitterhouse / Sep '94 / Avid/BMG

Cosmonauts Hail Satan

CAPE CANNIBAL
CD FDCD 47/DPROMCD 32
4th Dimension/Dirter / Nov '96 / Cargo

Cosmosis

COSMOLOGY
CD TRANR 604CD
Transient / Aug '96 / Prime / SRD / Total/ BMG

Cosmotheka

KEEP SMILING THROUGH (Hit Songs Of World War II)
Smiling through / Wish me luck as you wave me goodbye / I love to sit with Sophie in the shelter / I did what I could with my gas mask / Whitehall warriors / Lili Marlene / D-day dodgers / Roll me over / We'll meet again / Follow the white line / I get along without you very well / Hey little hen / Dig dig dig to victory / They're all under the counter / I'm gonna get lit up (when the lights go on in London) / Knees up Mother Brown / Medley
CD EMPRCD 509
Emporio / Apr '94 / Disc

Cosse, Ike

LOWDOWN THROWDOWN, THE
Bang bang girls / I just wanna rent / Let it happen / Doggy style / Dog dang shoot / Hell to pay / When I get home / She's expensive / My baby's so cynical / Hubba bubba brother / Let it happen
CD JSPCD 283
JSP / Jul '97 / ADA / Cadillac / Direct / Hot Shot / Target/BMG

Costa, Angela

SOUL DISEASE
Middle of the day / Circus beserk / Stars began to fall / Mothering Sunday / Disillusion / Inside the kiss / Being born / I just don't know / Sisters of mercy / Waiting for my angel / Empty chair / Oh my heart / Soul disease / Wait a minute / Rebirth of wonder
CD PLANCD 10
Planet / Feb '97 / Direct

Costa, Ercilia

ERCILIA COSTA & ARMANDINHO (Costa, Ercilia & Armandinho)
CD HTCD 32
Heritage / Nov '96 / ADA / Direct / Hot Shot / Jazz Music / Swift / Wellard

Costa, Gal

MEU NOM E GAL
Luz do sol / Acai / London London / Neu nome e Gal / Nao identificado / Meu bem meu mal / Folhetim / Modinha para Gabriella / Forca estranha / Canta Brasil / India / So louco / Dom de iludir / Baby / Oracao de mae Menininha / Teco teco / Bloco do prazer / Pegando fogo / Balance / Festa do interior
CD 8368412
Verve / Mar '93 / PolyGram

Costa, Johnny

CLASSIC COSTA
CD CRD 205
Chiaroscuro / Mar '96 / Jazz Music

DREAM (Johnny Costa Plays Johnny Mercer)
CD CRD 341
Chiaroscuro / Jan '97 / Jazz Music

FLYING FINGERS
CD CRD 317
Chiaroscuro / Mar '96 / Jazz Music

PORTRAIT OF GERSHWIN, A
CD CRD 335
Chiaroscuro / Mar '96 / Jazz Music

Costanzo, Sonny

PROMISES TO KEEP (Costanzo, Sonny & Czech Radio Big Band)
CD CR 00022
Czech Radio / Nov '95 / Czech Music Enterprises

Costello, Elvis

ALL THIS USELESS BEAUTY
CD 9362461982
Warner Bros. / May '96 / Warner Music

ALMOST BLUE (Remastered) (Costello, Elvis & The Attractions)
Why don't you love me (like you used to do) / Sweet dreams / Success / I'm your toy / Tonight the bottle let me down / Brown to blue / Good year for the roses / Sittin' and thinkin' / Colour of the blues / Too far gone / Honey hush / How much I lied / He's got you / Cry cry cry / There won't be anymore / Sittin' and thinkin' / Honey hush / Psycho / Your angel steps out of Heaven / Darling you know I wouldn't lie / Shoes keep walking back to you / Tears before bedtime / I'm your toy
CD DPAM 7
Demon / Oct '94 / Pinnacle

ARMED FORCES (Remastered) (Costello, Elvis & The Attractions)
Accidents will happen / Senior service / Oliver's army / Big boys / Green shirt / Party girl / Goon squad / Busy bodies / Sunday's best / Moods for moderns / Chemistry class / Two little Hitlers / My funny Valentine / Tiny steps / Clean money / Talking in the dark / Wednesday week / Accidents will happen / Alison / Watching the detectives
CD DPAM 3
Demon / Oct '93 / Pinnacle

BLOOD AND CHOCOLATE (Remastered) (Costello, Elvis & The Attractions)
Uncomplicated / I hope you're happy now / Tokyo storm warning / Home is anywhere you hang your head / I want you / Honey, are you straight or are you blind / Blue chair / Battered old bird / Crimes of Paris / Poor Napoleon / Next time round / Seven day weekend: *Costello, Elvis & The Attractions/ Jimmy Cliff* / Forgive her anything / Blue chair / Baby's got a brand new hairdo / American without tears / Town called big nothing
CD DPAM 12
Demon / Jul '95 / Pinnacle

BRUTAL YOUTH
Pony St. / Kinder murder / Thirteen steps lead down / This is hell / Clown strike / You tripped at every step / Still too soon to know / 20% amnesia / Sulky girl / London's brilliant parade / My science fiction twin / Rocking horse road / Just about glad / All the rage / Favourite hour
CD 9362455352
Warner Bros. / Mar '94 / Warner Music

GET HAPPY (Remastered) (Costello, Elvis & The Attractions)
Love for tender / Opportunity / Imposter / Secondary modern / King Horse / Possession / Men called Uncle / Clowntime is over / New Amsterdam / High fidelity / I can't stand up for falling down / Black and white world / Five gears in reverse / B movie / Motel matches / Human touch / Beaten to the punch / Temptation / I stand accused / Riot act / Girls talk / Clowntime is over / Getting mighty crowded / So young / Just a memory / Hoover factory / Ghost train / Dr. Luther's assistant / Black and white world / Riot act
CD DPAM 5
Demon / Apr '94 / Pinnacle

GIRLS, GIRLS, GIRLS (2CD Set)
Watching the detectives / (I don't want to go to) Chelsea / Alison / Shipbuilding / I want you / Oliver's army / This year's girl /

Lover's walk / Pump it up / Strict time / Temptation / High fidelity / Loveable / Mystery dance / Big tears / Uncomplicated / Lipstick vogue / Man out of time / Brilliant mistake / New lace sleeves / Accidents will happen / Beyond belief / Black and white world / Green shirt / Loved ones / New Amsterdam / Angels want to wear my red shoes / King horse / Big sister's clothes / Man called Uncle / Party girl / Shabby doll / Motel matches / Tiny steps / Almost blue / Riot act / Love field / Possession / Poisoned rose / Indoor fireworks / Pills and soap / Sunday's best / Watch your step / Less than zero / Clubland / Tokyo storm warning / Girl's talk / Home is anywhere you hang your head / Honey, are you straight or are you blind / I hope you're happy now / I'll wear it proudly / Poor Napoleon / Sleep of the just / Stranger in the house / Turning the town red
CD Set DFIENDCD 160
Demon / Sep '96 / Pinnacle

GOODBYE CRUEL WORLD (Remastered) (Costello, Elvis & The Attractions)
Only flame in town / Home truth / Room with no number / Inch by inch / Worthless thing / Love field / I wanna be loved / Comedians / Joe Porterhouse / Sour milk cow blues / Great unknown / Deportees club / Peace in our time / Turning the town red / Baby it's you: *Costello, Elvis & The Attractions/Nick Lowe* / Get yourself another you / I hope your happy now / Only flame in town / Worthless thing / Motel matches / Sleepless nights / Deportees club
CD DPAM 10
Demon / Feb '95 / Pinnacle

IMPERIAL BEDROOM (Remastered) (Costello, Elvis & The Attractions)
Beyond belief / Tears before bedtime / Shabby doll / Long honeymoon / Man out of time / Almost blue / And in every home / Loved ones / Human hands / Kid about it / Little savage / Boy with a problem / Pidgin English / You little fool / Town cryer / From head to toe / World of broken hearts / Night time / Really mystified / I turn around / Seconds of pleasure / Stamping ground / Shabby doll / Imperial bedroom
CD DPAM 8
Demon / Oct '94 / Pinnacle

JULIET LETTERS (Costello, Elvis & Brodsky Quartet)
Jacksons, Monk and Rowe / This sad burlesque / Romeo's seance / I thought I'd write to Juliet / Last post / First to leave / Damnation's cellar / Birds will still be singing / Deliver us / For other eyes / Swine / Expert rites / Dead letter / I almost had a weakness / Why / Who do you think you are / Taking my life in your hands / This offer is unrepeatable / Dear sweet filthy world / Letter home
CD 9362451802
WEA / Dec '96 / Warner Music

KING OF AMERICA (Remastered) (Costello Show)
Brilliant mistake / Lovable / Our little angel / Don't let me be misunderstood / Glitter gulch / Indoor fireworks / Little palaces / I'll wear it proudly / American without tears / Eisenhower blues / Poisoned rose / Big light / Jack of all parades / Suit of lights / Sleep of the just / People's limousine: *Coward Brothers* / They'll never take her love from me: *Coward Brothers* / Suffering face / Shoes without heels / King of confidence
CD DPAM 11
Demon / Jul '95 / Pinnacle

KOJAK VARIETY
Strange / Hidden charms / Remove this doubt / I threw it all away / Leave my kitten alone / I've been wrong before / Must you throw dirt in my face / Everybody's cryin' mercy / Bama lama bama loo / Pouring water on a drowning man / Payday / Very thought of you / Please stay / Runnin' out of fools / Days
CD 9362459032
Warner Bros. / Dec '96 / Warner Music

MIGHTY LIKE A ROSE
Other side of summer / Hurry down doomesday / How to be dumb / All grown up / Invasion hit parade / Harpies bizzare / After the fall / Georgie and her rival / So like Candy / Couldn't call it unexpected No. 2 / Playboy to a man / Sweet pear / Broken / Couldn't call it unexpected No. 4
CD 7599265752
Warner Bros. / Feb '95 / Warner Music

MY AIM IS TRUE (Remastered) (Costello, Elvis & The Attractions)
Welcome to the working week / Miracle man / No dancing / Blame it on Cain / Alison / Sneaky feelings / (The angels wanna wear my) red shoes / Less than zero / Mystery dance / Pay it back / I'm not angry / Waiting for the end of the world / Radio sweetheart / Stranger in the house / Imagination (is a powerful deceiver) / Mystery dance / Cheap reward / Jump up / Wave a white flag / Blame it on Cain / Poison moon
CD DPAM 1
Demon / Oct '93 / Pinnacle

OUT OF OUR IDIOT (Costello, Elvis & The Attractions)
Blue chair / Seven day weekend: *Costello, Elvis & The Attractions/Jimmy Cliff* / Turning the town red / Heathrow Town / People's limousine: *Coward Brothers* / So young / American without tears / Get yourself another fool / Walking on thin ice / Baby it's you: *Costello, Elvis & The Attractions/Nick Lowe* / From head to toe / Shoes without heels / Baby's got a brand new hairdo / Flirting kind / Black sails in the sunset / Imperial bedroom / Stampling grams
CD FIENDCD 67X
Demon / Mar '93 / Pinnacle

PUNCH THE CLOCK (Remastered)
Let them all talk / Everyday I write the book / Greatest thing / Element within her / Love went mad / Shipbuilding / TKO (Boxing day) / Charm school / Invisible man / Mouth almighty / King of thieves / Pills and soap / World and his wife / Heathen town / Flirting kind / Walking on thin ice / Town where time stood still / Shatterproof / World and his wife / Everyday I write the book
CD DPAM 9
Demon / Feb '95 / Pinnacle

SPIKE
This town / Let him dangle / Deep dark truthful mirror / Veronica / God's comic / Chewing gum / Tramp the dirt down / Stalin Malone / Satellite / Pads, paws and claws / Baby plays around / Miss Macbeth / Any king's shilling / Coal train robberies / Last boat leaving
CD 9258482
Warner Bros. / Jan '89 / Warner Music

TEN BLOODY MARYS AND TEN HOW'S YOUR FATHERS (Costello, Elvis & The Attractions)
Clean money / Girls talk / Talking in the dark / Radio sweetheart / Big tears / Crawling to the USA / Just a memory / Watching the detectives / Stranger in the house / Clowntime is over (no.2) / Getting mighty crowded / Hoover factory / Tiny steps / Peace, love and understanding / Dr. Luther's assistant / Radio radio / Black and white world / Wednesday week / My funny valentine / Ghost train
CD FIENDCD 27
Demon / '86 / Pinnacle
CD FIENDCD 27X
Demon / Mar '93 / Pinnacle

THIS YEAR'S MODEL (Remastered) (Costello, Elvis & The Attractions)
No action / This year's girl / Beat / Pump it up / Little triggers / You belong to me / Hand in hand / (I don't want to go to) Chelsea / Lip service / Living in paradise / Lipstick vogue / Night rally / Radio radio / Big tears / Crawling to the USA / Running out of angels / Green shirt / Big boys
CD DPAM 2
Demon / Oct '93 / Pinnacle

TRUST (Remastered) (Costello, Elvis & The Attractions)
Clubland / Lovers' walk / You'll never be a man / Pretty words / Strict time / Luxembourg / Watch your step / New lace sleeves / From a whisper to a scream / Different finger / White knuckles / Shot with his own gun / Fish 'n' chip paper / Big sister's clothes / Black sails in the sunset / Big sister / Sad about girls / Twenty five to twelve / Love for sale / Weeper's dream / Gloomy Sunday / Boy with a problem / Seconds of pleasure
CD DPAM 6
Demon / Apr '94 / Pinnacle

TWO & HALF YEARS - THE ELVIS COSTELLO BOXSET (My Aim Is True/ This Years Model/Armed Forces/Live CD)
CD Set DPAMBOX 1
Demon / Oct '93 / Pinnacle

VERY BEST OF ELVIS COSTELLO & THE ATTRACTIONS, THE (Costello, Elvis & The Attractions)
Alison / Watching the detectives / (I don't want to go to) Chelsea / Pump it up / Radio radio / (What's so funny 'bout) peace, love and understanding / Oliver's army / Accidents will happen / I can't stand up for falling down / New Amsterdam / High fidelity / Clubland / Watch your step / Good year for the roses / Beyond belief / Man out of time / Everyday I write the book / Shipbuilding / Love field / Brilliant mistake / Indoor fireworks / I want you
CD DPAM 13
Demon / Oct '94 / Pinnacle

Costello, Julian

TEA AND SCANDAL (Costello, Julian Quintet)
Sitting on the fence / Figment / Mr Palomar / Ermentrude / Pilgrim / Naggar castle / Olives / Merry go round / Apothecary's chest / Fruit and fruition / Gerald the goose
CD JCQCD 001
Avid / Mar '96 / Avid/BMG / Koch / THE

Costello, Sean

CALL THE COPS (Costello, Sean Jivebombers)
CD BLUESUN 1017
Blue Sun / May '97 / Hot Shot

Coster, Tom

FORBIDDEN ZONE, THE
In the beginning / Jazz lament / Shall me / Father-daughter / Lover man / Voyage to nowhere / Waste land/Jam / Blue and cool / Group / Blues for DC / Fix / Closing thought
CD JVC 20402
JVC / Nov '94 / Direct / New Note/Pinnacle / Vital/SAM

FROM THE STREET
Can't we all just get along / Monk-E Shines / From the street / Dennis the meanace / Amazon life / Pharoah's jig / What's the deal / Spankin' / Funky Joe / She said she didn't
CD JVC 20532
JVC / May '96 / Direct / New Note/Pinnacle / Vital/SAM

LET'S SET THE RECORD STRAIGHT
To be or not to be / Slick / Dance of the spirits / Then and now / Thinking of you / Mr. MD / Best of friends / Turkish delight / Blue blues / Welcome to my chambers / Caribbean sunset / For the folks back home
CD JVC 20252
JVC / Nov '93 / Direct / New Note/Pinnacle / Vital/SAM

Cotten, Elizabeth

FREIGHT TRAIN (North Carolina Folk Songs & Tunes)
CD SFWCD 40009
Smithsonian Folkways / May '95 / ADA / Cadillac / CM / Direct / Koch

Cotter, Eamonn

TRADITIONAL IRISH MUSIC FROM COUNTY CLARE
CD EC 001CD
EC / Apr '96 / ADA

Cotton, Billy

SMILE, DARN YA SMILE
CD PASTCD 7085
Flapper / Oct '96 / Pinnacle

THINGS I LOVE ABOUT THE 40'S, THE (Cotton, Billy & His Band)
Bottle party / I'm gonna get lit up (when the lights go on in London) / Yeah man / That lovely weekend / You'll be happy little sweetheart in the spring / Shine / Hold tight, hold tight / Toy trumpet / Things I love / Dere's jazz in dem dere horns / Margie / Hut sut song / Man with the mandolin / Lights out / Bon voyage cherie / Aurora / Fifty million robins can't be wrong / Man who comes around / Never took a lesson in my life / Woe is me / Shoe shine boy / Mammy bong
CD RAJCD 814
Empress / May '97 / Koch

WAKEE WAKEE (Cotton, Billy & His Band)
Somebody stole my gal / Bugle call rag / I'm just wild about Harry / Third tiger / Mood indigo / Fancy our meeting / So green / Ooo-la-la / It's only a paper moon / Rhapsody in blue / Skirts / Best wishes / Sweep / Mrs. Bartholomew / You don't understand / Why has a cow got four legs / St. Louis blues / She was only somebody's daughter / Night owl / Young and healthy / You're getting to be a habit with me / Shuffle off to Buffalo / Forty second steet / Smile, darn ya, smile
CD C5CD513
See For Miles/C5 / Aug '90 / Pinnacle

Cotton, James

100% COTTON (Cotton, James Band)
Boogie thing / One more mile / All walks of life / Creeper creeps again / Rocket 88 / How long can a fool go wrong / I don't know / Burner / Infatuation / Fever
CD OW 27670
One Way / May '94 / ADA / Direct / Greyhound

DEALIN' WITH THE DEVIL (The Best Of James Cotton)
I need you so bad / Don't start me talking / Dealin' with the devil / Creeper / V8 Ford blues / Turn on your lovelight / Southside boogie / There is something on your mind / Knock on wood / So glad you're mine / Diggin' my potatoes / You know it ain't right / Jelly jelly
CD AIM 2005CD
Aim / May '97 / ADA / Direct / Jazz Music

DEEP IN THE BLUES
CD 5298492
Verve / Jun '96 / PolyGram

HARP ATTACK (Cotton, James/Junior Wells/Carey Bell/Billy Branch)
Down home blues / Who / Keep your hand out of my pocket / Little car blues / My eyes keep me in trouble / Broke and hungry / Hit man / Black night / Somebody changed the lock / Second hand man / New kid on the block
CD ALCD 4790
Alligator / May '93 / ADA / CM / Direct

HIGH COMPRESSION
Diggin' my potatoes / Ying yang / Twenty three hours too long / No more doggin' / No cuttin' loose / Ain't doing too bad / Sunny road / Superharp / Easy loving / High compression
CD ALCD 4737
Alligator / Oct '93 / ADA / CM / Direct

HIGH ENERGY (Cotton, James Band)
Hot and cold / Chicken heads / Hard time blues / I got a feeling / Weather report (the weather man said) / Rock 'n' roll music (ain't nothing new) / Fannie Mae / Caldonia / James theme / Keep cooking mama
CD OW 27671
One Way / May '94 / ADA / Direct / Greyhound

LIVE AND ON THE MOVE
Cotton boogie / One more mile / All walks of life / Born in Missouri / Flip flop and fly / Mojo / Rocket 88 / Goodbye my lady / I don't know / Caldonia / Boogie thing / Good morning little school girl / Oh baby you don't have to go / Help me / Fannie Mae / Hot and cold / Teeny weeny bit / Blow wind blow / How long can a fool go wrong
CD NEMCD 865
Sequel / Nov '96 / BMG

LIVE AND ON THE MOVE VOL.1 (Cotton, James Band)
CD OW 24835
One Way / May '94 / ADA / Direct / Greyhound

LIVE AT ANTONES
CD ANTCD 0007
Antones / Jan '93 / ADA / Hot Shot

LIVE AT ELECTRIC LADY (Cotton, James Band)
Back at the chicken shack / Off the wall / Rocket 88 / Don't start me talkin' / Georgia swing / One more mile / I got my mojo working / How long can a fool go wrong / Blow wind blow / Mean ol' world / I don't know / Boogie thing / Stormy Monday / Fever
CD NEXCD 224
Sequel / Nov '92 / BMG

LIVE FROM CHICAGO (Mr Superharp Himself)
Here I am / Part time love / Just to be with you / Hard headed / When it rains it really pours / Cross your heart / Come back baby / Born in Chicago / Creeper
CD ALCD 4746
Alligator / May '93 / ADA / CM / Direct

MIGHTY LONG TIME
Straighten up baby / Everything gonna be alright / Black nights / Blow wind blow / Sugar sweet / Moanin' at midnight / Baby please / Hold me in your arms / Stormy Monday / 300 pounds of joy / Northside cadillac / Mighty long time
CD ANTCD 0015
Antones / Mar '91 / ADA / Hot Shot

TAKE ME BACK
CD CD 72587
Blind Pig / '88 / ADA / CM / Direct / Hot Shot

Cottone, F.P.

DREAM IN YOUR HEAD, THE
CD INAK 79500
In Akustik / Jan '97 / Direct / TKO Magnum

Cougars

COUGARS, THE
CD SFTRI 395CD
Sympathy For The Record Industry / Apr '96 / Cargo / Greyhound / Plastic Head

Coughlan, Cathal

GRAND NECROPOLITAN
This building / Unbroken bones / On the parish / New "Royal" / Eerin go braghag / We are the sinister world / Government / Big lukewarm / Straying away / Irrational falsifier / Two grotesques, embracing / Angy white snail / Free and worthless / Garrai na muic / Last lamplight / Grand necropolitan promenade / Waiting for wood, Captain
CD KWCD 029
Kitchenware/Vital / Jul '96 / Vital

Coughlan, Mary

AFTER THE FALL
Woman undone / Sunburn / Still in love / Lucy's dream / John fell off the work-around / Dilmma / Poison words / Run away Teddy / That face / Nobody / Black crow / Saint Judy / When I am laid in earth
CD ABB 123CD
Big Cat / Mar '97 / 3mv/Pinnacle

LIVE IN GALWAY
CD ABB 116CD
Big Cat / Oct '96 / 3mv/Pinnacle

LOVE FOR SALE
CD FIENDCD 730
Demon / May '93 / Pinnacle

LOVE ME OR LEAVE ME
Ancient rain / Double cross / I'd rather go blind / Invisible to you / Ride on / Leaf from

a tree / Delaney's gone back on the wine / Sunday mornings / Red ribbon / Ice cream man / There is a bed / Francis of Assisi / Beach / Man of the world / Seduced / Ain't nobody's business if I do / I get along without you very well / Handbags and gladrags / Whiskey didn't kill the pain
CD 4509940362
WEA / Dec '96 / Warner Music

SENTIMENTAL KILLER
There is a bed / Hearts / Magdalen laundry / Francis of Assisi / Love in a shadow / Ain't no cure for love / Handbags and gladrags / Just a friend of mine / Ballad of a sad young man / Not up to scratch / Sentimental killer
CD 9032771752
WEA / Dec '96 / Warner Music

TIRED AND EMOTIONAL
Double cross / Beach / Meet me where they play the blues / Delaney's gone back on the wind / Sense of silence (SOS) / Nobody's business - the tango / Mama just wants to barrelhouse all night long / Country fair dance (The cowboy song) / Lady in green / Seduced
CD 2420942
WEA / Mar '87 / Warner Music

UNCERTAIN PLEASURES
Man of the world / I can dream, can't I / Whiskey didn't kill the pain / Leaf from a tree / Little death / Invisible to you / I get along without you very well / Heartbreak hotel / Red ribbon / Mother's little helper
CD 9031711002
WEA / Dec '96 / Warner Music

UNDER THE INFLUENCE
Laziest girl / Ice cream van / Parade of clowns / My land is too green / Ride on / Good morning heartache / Fifteen only / AWOL / Dice / Don't smoke in bed / Blue surrender / Sunday morning / Copa
CD 2421852
WEA / Feb '95 / Warner Music

Coulibaly Brothers

ANKA DIA : SONGS & DANCES FROM BURKINA FASO
CD AUB 006775
Auvidis/Ethnic / Apr '93 / ADA / Harmonia Mundi

Coulter, Phil

AMERICAN TRANQUILITY
CD KCD 376
Irish / Jul '95 / Target/BMG

CELTIC TRANQUILITY
Planxty Irwin / Tears on the heather / Ar Eirinn ni Nosfhainn ce hi / Battle of Kinsale/ The great O'Neill / Before the battle / Valley of tears / Road to Glenaan / Ghost ships of Tory / Year of the French / A thiarna dean trocaire / Wounded hussar / House of the planter / Tune for a found harmonium
CD KCD 465
Irish / Mar '97 / Target/BMG

CLASSIC TRANQUILITY
CD FSCD 001
Four Seasons / Jan '93 / ADA / Direct

COLLECTION, THE
CD DINCD 2
Telstar / May '92 / BMG

ESSENTIAL COLLECTION, THE
CD KCD 367
Irish / Jul '95 / Target/BMG

LOCAL HEROES
CD RTECD 165
Four Seasons / Jan '95 / ADA / Direct

PEACE AND TRANQUILITY
CD FSCD 003
Four Seasons / Jan '93 / ADA / Direct

PHIL COULTER'S CHRISTMAS
CD FSCD 005
Four Seasons / Sep '94 / ADA / Direct

SCOTTISH TRANQUILITY
Flower of Scotland / Skye boat song / Will ye no' come back again / Loch Lomond / Dark Island / I belong to Glasgow / Ye banks and braes o' bonnie Doon / Wild mountain thyme / Annie Laurie / Rowan tree / Lochnagar / Amazing grace / Eriskay love lilt/Westering home / Red red rose/Bonnie Mary of Argyll / No awa' tae bid awa'/Scotland the brave / Auld lang syne
CD MCCD 071
Music Club / Jun '92 / Disc / THE

SEA OF TRANQUILITY
CD FSCD 002
Four Seasons / Jan '93 / ADA / Direct

SERENITY
CD FSCD 004
Four Seasons / Jan '93 / ADA / Direct

ULTIMATE CELTIC JOURNEY, THE
Derry air (Danny Boy) / Carrickfergus / Meeting of the waters/The rose of Mooncoin / Rose of Tralee / Spancil Hill / Green Glens of Antrim / Raglan Road / Mountains of Mourne / I'll tell me Ma / Anniversary song / Sally Gardens / Water is wide / Spinning wheel / Fields of Athenry / Dear Sarah / One day at a time / Emmigrant's letter/ Eamon an Chnuic / Soldier's song
CD KCD 410
Celtic Collections / Jan '97 / Target/BMG

WORDS & MUSIC
CD FSCD 007
Four Seasons / Sep '94 / ADA / Direct

Coulter, William

MUSIC ON THE MOUNTAIN (Coulter, William & Barry Phillips)
CD GM 123CD
Gourd Music / Aug '96 / ADA

Counce, Curtis

EXPLORING THE FUTURE (Counce, Curtis Quintet)
So nice / Angel eyes / Into the orbit / Move / Race for space / Someone to watch over me / Countdown / Exploring the future / Foreplay / Riffin' / Move / Countdown
CD CDBOP 007
Boplicity / Jul '96 / Pinnacle

YOU GET MORE BOUNCE WITH CURTIS COUNCE
CD OJCCD 159
Original Jazz Classics / Jan '95 / Complete/Pinnacle / Jazz Music / Wellard

Count Bass-D

PRE-LIFE CRISIS
Dozens / Sandwiches (I got a feeling) / T-boz (part 1/2) / Shake / T-boz tried to talk to me / Carmex / I got needs / Broke Thursday / Agriculture / Brown / Hate game / Pink tornado / Sunday school / Baker's dozen
CD 4783732
Columbia / Oct '95 / Sony

Count Bishops

SPEEDBALL + 11
Route 66 / I ain't got you / Beautiful Delilah / Teenage letter / Cry to me / Buzz me babe / Sweet little sixteen / Honey I need / Carol / Don't start crying now / Mercy mercy / Reelin' and rockin' / Down the road apiece / I'm a man / I want candy
CD CDWIKM 161
Chiswick / Nov '95 / Pinnacle

Count Five

PSYCHOTIC REACTION
Double decker bus / Pretty big mouth / World / Psychotic reaction / Peace of mind / They're gonna get you / Morning after / Can't get your lovin' / You must believe me / Teeny bopper, teeny bopper / Merry go round / Contrast / Revelation in slow motion / Declaration of independence
CD EDCD 225
Edsel / Oct '87 / Pinnacle

Count Raven

DESTRUCTION OF THE VOID
Until death do us part / Hippies triumph / Destruction of the void / Let the dead bury the dead / Northern lights / Leaving the warzone / Angel of death / Final journey / On ones hero / Europa
CD HELL019CD
Hellhound / Apr '94 / Koch

HIGH ON INFINITY
Jen / Children's holocaust / In honour / Madman from waco / Masters of all evil / Ode to Rebecca / High on infinity / Ordinary loser / Traitor / Dance / Coming / Lost world / Cosmos
CD HELL 026
Hellhound / Apr '94 / Koch

STORM WARNING
Intro (Count Raven) / Inam naudemina / True revelation / In the name of rock 'n' roll / Sometimes a great nation / Within the garden of mirrors / Devastating age / How can it be / Social warfare
CD HELL 009CD
Hellhound / Apr '94 / Koch

Count Zero

AFFLUENZA
CD K 169CD
Konkurrel / Aug '96 / SRD

Countdown Dance Band

CHART DANCE MANIA
Gangsta's paradise / Shy guy / Stayin' alive / Love rendezvous / Boombastic / La la la hey hey / Sunshine after the rain / Lick it / Move your ass / Scatman's world / Try me out / Shimmy shake / Another night / Bomb / Boom boom boom / 3 is family
CD QED 229
Tring / Nov '96 / Tring

Counterblast

BALANCE OF PAIN
CD EB 010CD
Elderberry / Oct '96 / Cargo

Counting Crows

AUGUST AND EVERYTHING AFTER
Round here / Omaha / Mr. Jones / Perfect blue buildings / Anna begins / Time and time again / Rain King / Sullivan Street / Ghost train / Raining in Baltimore / Murder of one
CD GED 24528
Geffen / Feb '94 / BMG

RECOVERING THE SATELLITES
Catapult / Angels of the silences / Daylight fading / I'm not sleeping / Goodnight Elizabeth / Children in bloom / Have you seen me lately / Miller's angels / Another horsedreamers blues / Recovering the satellites / Monkey / Mercury / Long December / Walkaways
CD GED 24975
Geffen / Oct '96 / BMG

Country All Stars

JAZZ FROM THE HILLS
Stompin' at the Savoy / Tennessee rag / Do something / Indiana march / Sweet Georgia Brown / Midnight train / In a little Spanish town / My little girl / Lady in red / Marie / It goes like this / What's the reason I'm not pleasin' you / When it's darkness on the delta / Vacation train / Fiddle patch / Fiddle sticks
CD BCD 15728
Bear Family / Oct '93 / Direct / Rollercoaster / Swift

Country Dance Kings

COUNTRY DANCE CLUB: DENIM DANCIN'
CD 33112
Irish / Jun '95 / Target/BMG

COUNTRY DANCE NIGHT (18 Country Line Dancing Favourites)
Rock my world (little country girl) / Chattahoochee / Trashy women / One more last chance / Prop me up beside the jukebox (if I die) / My baby loves me / Blame it on your heart / Live until I die / State of mind / I swear / What's it to you / Fast as you / That's my story / Wild one / Reckless / Mercury blues / Cowboy boogie / Ain't going down (Til the sun comes up)
CD ECD 3197
K-Tel / Mar '95 / K-Tel

COUNTRY LINE DANCE JUBILEE VOL.2
Bubba shot the jukebox / Papa loved Mama / I'm in a hurry (And I don't know why) / What part of no / One more payment / Jukebox with a country song / Whatcha gonna do with a cowboy / I want you bad (And that ain't good) / My next broken heart / Boom it was over
CD 32322
Irish / Jun '96 / Target/BMG

DANCE ALL NIGHT
Good run of bad luck / Before you kill us all / That ain't no way to go / Why haven't I heard from you / Rope the moon / Lovebug / Walking away a winner / Your love amazes me / Addicted to a dollar / Don't take the girl
CD 33122
Dominion / Feb '96 / Target/BMG

Country Gazette

HELLO OPERATOR...THIS IS COUNTRY GAZETTE
Saro Jane / Virginia boys / Love, lost and found / Don't let nobody tie you down / Sweet Allis Chalmers / You can't get the hell out of Texas / Charlotte breakdown / Great Joe Bob (a regional tragedy) / Still feeling blue / Uncle Clooney played the banjo (but mostly out of time) / Molly and tenbrooks / Kentucky waltz / Blue light / Tallahassee / Highland dream / Last thing on my mind / Hello operator / Great American banjo tune / Nothing is left but the blues / Cabin on a mountain / Done gone
CD FF 70112
Flying Fish / May '97 / ADA / CM / Direct / Roots

KEEP ON PUSHING
Rosa Lee McFall / Forgive and forget / Get up there and dance / Lovely lovely world / Anywhere the wind blows / Keep on pushing / Pretty boy Floyd / Picking at Snuffy's / Going back to Alabam' / Lucky dog / Marching through Georgia / Live and love / We've got a good fire going / Durang's hornpipe
CD FF 70561
Flying Fish / May '97 / ADA / CM / Direct / Roots

TRAITOR IN OUR MIDST/DON'T GIVE UP YOUR DAY JOB
Lost indian / Keep on pushin' / I wish you knew / Hot burrito breakdown / I might take you back again / Forget me not / Tried so hard / Anna / If you're ever gonna love me / Aggravation / Sound of goodbye / Swing low, sweet chariot / Huckleberry hornpipe / Fallen eagle / I don't believe you met my baby / Deputy Dalton / Teach your children / My Oklahoma / Down the road / Winterwood / Honky cat / Snowball / Lonesome blues / Singin' all day and dinner on the ground
CD BGOCD 298
Beat Goes On / Nov '95 / Pinnacle

Country Gentlemen

CLASSIC COUNTRY GENTS REUNION
Fare thee well / Stewball / I'll be there in the morning / Champagne breakdown / Here today, gone tomorrow / Gonna get there soon / Hey Lala / Casey's last ride / Wild side of life / Wait a little longer / Say won't you be mine
CD SHCD 3772
Sugar Hill / Oct '89 / ADA / CM / Direct / Koch / Roots

COUNTRY GENTLEMEN SUGAR HILL COLLECTION, THE
CD SHCD 2207
Sugar Hill / Aug '95 / ADA / CM / Direct / Koch / Roots

COUNTRY SONGS OLD AND NEW
CD SFCD 40004
Smithsonian Folkways / Dec '94 / ADA / Cadillac / CM / Direct / Koch

Country Teasers

COUNTRY TEASERS
CD EFA 115942
Crypt / Apr '95 / Shellshock/Disc

SATAN IS REAL AGAIN
CD EFA 128772
Crypt / Jul '96 / Shellshock/Disc

Counts

IT'S WHAT'S IN THE GROOVE
Medley / Dedicated man / Tecalli / Flies over watermelon / Riding high / Jazzman / Since we said goodbye / Magic ride / At the fair / I'm the music / Funk / Funk pump / Too bad (you don't love me) / Chicken pox / Munchies / Short cut / Sacrifice / Love sign / Just you, just me / Counts say goodbye
CD CDSEWD 109
Southbound / Aug '96 / Pinnacle

WHAT'S UP THE FRONT THAT - COUNTS
What's up front that counts / Rhythm changes / Thinking single / Why not start all over again / Pack of lies / Bills / Motor city / What's it all about
CD CDSEWM 063
Southbound / Nov '94 / Pinnacle

County, Jayne

DEVIATION
CD CSA 105
RPM / Jul '95 / Pinnacle

LET YOUR BACKBONE SLIP
Max's / Are you a boy or are you a boy / '28 Model T / Berlin / Lady Dye twist / Time machine (I wish I had) / Mr. Normal / Fun in Amerika / Where Queens collide (part 1) / No one woman can satisfy no one man all the time / Tomorrow is another day / Plain of nazca / I fell in love with a Russian soldier / Love lives in lies / Black black window / Midnight pal / Waiting for the marines / Bad in bed
CD RPM 145
RPM / Jul '95 / Pinnacle

ROCK 'N' ROLL CLEOPATRA (From Sneakers To Stilettos) (County, Wayne & The Electric Chairs)
Eddie and Sheena / Rock 'n' roll Cleopatra / (If you don't want to fuck me) fuck off / Toilet love / Mean mutha fuckin' man / Night time / Trying to get on the radio / Evil minded momma / I had too much to dream last night / Crest / Waiting for the marines / Midnight pal / Berlin / Storm the gates of heaven / Cry of angels / Speed demon / Mr. Norman / Man enough to be a woman / Tomorrow is another day / Wonder woman / Wall city girl / Boy with the stolen face / C3 / Think straight
CD RPM 119
RPM / Oct '93 / Pinnacle

Coupland, Gary

A' THE BEST FAE SCOTLAND
CD GCD 1
Gary Coupland / May '96 / Duncans

Couple Of Swells

COUPLE OF SWELLS, A
CD CDSR 089
Telstar / Aug '96 / BMG

Courage Of Lassie

SING OR DIE
CD TMCD 055
Third Mind / Oct '90 / Pinnacle / Third Mind

THIS SIDE OF HEAVEN
CD BBQCD 146
Beggars Banquet / Oct '94 / RTM/Disc / Warner Music

Course Of Empire

INITIATION
Hiss / White vision blowout / Gear / Breed / Apparition / Infested / Invertebrate / Sacrifice / Minions / Initiation / Chiluahaphile

CD 72445110542
Zoo Entertainment / Aug '94 / BMG

Court Music Ensemble Of Hue

MUSIC FROM HUE (Music From Vietnam)
CD W 260073
Inedit / Dec '96 / ADA / Discovery / Harmonia Mundi

Courtney Melody

COURTNEY MELODY CLASH WITH SANCHEZ (Courtney Melody & Sanchez)
CD RNCD 2072
Rhino / Jul '94 / Grapevine/PolyGram / Jet Star

Courvoisier, Sylvie

OCRE
Gugging / Anecdote 1 / La goulante de l'idiot / Andecdote 2 / Machines a sons / Ensorcelirradiant / Triton et demi / Anecdote 3 / Curio in Trivia / Anecdote 4 / Terre d'agala / Viable / Paradiso perduto / Tabular / Gnou gnou valse
CD ENJ 93232
Enja / Jun '97 / New Note/Pinnacle / Vital/SAM

Cousens

CORNER OF THE SKY
CD OCRCD 6043
First Night / Jun '96 / Pinnacle

Cousin Joe

BAD LUCK BLUES
Boxcar shorty / Life is a one way ticket / Take a lesson from your teacher / Bad luck blues / I'm living on borrowed time / That's enough / Goin' down slow / Chicken and the hawk / Levee blues / Railroad porter blues / I don't want no second hand love / Tore down
CD ECD 260462
Evidence / Mar '94 / ADA / Cadillac / Harmonia Mundi

COMPLETE VOL.1 1945-1947, THE
CD BMCD 6001
Blue Moon / Sep '95 / Cadillac / Discovery / Greensleeves / Jazz Music / Jet Star / TKO Magnum

COMPLETE VOL.2 1946-1947, THE
CD BMCD 6002
Blue Moon / Sep '95 / Cadillac / Discovery / Greensleeves / Jazz Music / Jet Star / TKO Magnum

Cousins, Dave

BRIDGE, THE (Cousins, Dave & Brian Willoughby)
CD RGFCD 020
Road Goes On Forever / Aug '94 / Direct

OLD SCHOOL SONGS (Cousins, Dave & Brian Willoughby)
CD RGFCD 004
Road Goes On Forever / '92 / Direct

Couturier, Francois

PASSAGIO
CD LBLC 6543
Label Bleu / Jun '92 / New Note/Pinnacle

Couvez, Remy

ITINERANCES
CD 829392
BUDA / Apr '97 / Discovery

Couza, Jim

APPALACHIAN BEACH PARTY (Couza, Jim & Durberville)
CD DRGNCD 922
Dragon / Jan '93 / ADA / Cadillac / CM / Roots / Wellard

JUBILEE
Mississippi jubilee (year of jubilo) / You've joined our hearts / My old man / Invention No. 13 / Gallo del cielo / Cranes over Hiroshima / Puncheon floor (Oklahoma rooster) / St. Paul's song / Poor wayfaring stranger / There were roses / If you don't love your neighbour / Jubilee
CD FSCD 6
Folksound / Aug '89 / CM / Roots

MUSIC FOR THE HAMMERED DULCIMER
Jenny Lind polka / Johnny get your hair cut / Intrada and Minuet / Londonderry Air / Maid at the spinning / Nola / High cauled cap / As I roved out / Miss Hamilton / Christine's Waltz / Bells of St. Mary's / Devil's dream / Enchanted valley / La belle Katherine / Fisher's hornpipe / Swinging on a gate / Norwegian wood / Flower of England / Snowflake / Los ejes de mi carreta / Perfect cure me / Starry night for a ramble / Peel the carrot / Take five
CD CDSDL 335
Saydisc / Mar '94 / ADA / Direct / Harmonia Mundi

OUT OF THE SHADOWLAND
Canon in D / Song of the whale / Falls of Richmond / Hard love / Kitchen girl / I'll tickle Nancy / Christmas concerto / Forever / Green Willis / Out of the Shadowland / Concerto no. 1 / Jonah and the whale / Wish I could fall in love / William Tell overture / St. Francis prayer / Seek ye first
CD FSCD 14
Folksound / Jun '97 / CM / Roots

Covenant

SPECTRES AT THE FEAST
CD COVCD 0002
Covenant / Nov '94 / Else

Coverdale, David

WHITESNAKE/NORTHWINDS
Lady / Time on my side / Blindman / Goldies place / Whitesnake / Peace lovin' man / Sunny days / Hole in the sky / Celebration / Keep on giving me love / Northwinds / Give me kindness / Time and again / Queen of hearts / Only my soul / Say you love me / Breakdown
CD VSOPCD 118
Connoisseur Collection / Nov '88 / Pinnacle

Coverdale-Page

COVERDALE PAGE (Coverdale, David & Jimmy Page)
Shake my tree / Waiting on you / Take me for a little while / Pride and joy / Over now / Feeling hot / Easy does it / Take a look at yourself / Don't leave me this way / Absolution blues / Whisper a prayer for the dying
CD CDEMD 1041
EMI / Jul '94 / EMI

Covington, Robert

BLUES IN THE NIGHT
Trust in me / I just want to make love to you / Better watch your step / I Don't care / Playing on me / Blues in the night / I want to know / Mean mistreater / I want to thank ya
CD ECD 260742
Evidence / Oct '95 / ADA / Cadillac / Harmonia Mundi

Coward, Noel

CLASSIC RECORDINGS 1928-1938
CD CDCHD 168
Happy Days / Jul '90 / Conifer/BMG

I'LL SEE YOU AGAIN (His Greatest Recordings)
Could you please oblige me with a Bren Gun / Dearest love / Dream is over / I travel alone / I'll see you again / Imagine the duchess's feelings / Let's say goodbye / London pride / Lorelei / Lover of my dreams / Mad dogs and Englishmen / Mary Make-Believe / Most of ev'ry day / Mrs. Worthington / Medley / Private lives: *Coward, Noel & Gertrude Lawrence* / Shadow play: *Coward, Noel & Gertrude Lawrence* / Stately homes of England / We were dancing / Where are the songs we sung / World weary
CD CDAJA 5126
Living Era / Mar '94 / Select

LIVE IN LAS VEGAS AND NEW YORK
CD CD 47253
Sony Classical / Nov '91 / Sony

LONDON PRIDE
Lorelei / Dream is over / Zigeuner / World weary / Let's say goodbye / We were dancing / Parisian Pierrot / Poor little rich girl / Room with a view / Dance little lady / Someday I'll find you / Any little fish / If you could only come with me / I'll see you again / London pride / Last time I saw Paris / Could you please oblige us with a bren gun / Imagine the Duchess's feelings / Private Lives / Shadowplay / Red peppers / Family album
CD CDHD 216
Happy Days / Feb '97 / Conifer/BMG

MASTER
Room with a view / Dance little lady / Poor little rich girl / Something to do with spring / Where are the songs we sung / We were so young / Just let me look at you / Dearest love / Play orchestra play / Don't lets be beastly to the Germans / Mad dogs and Englishmen / Stately homes of England / London pride / Don't put your daughter on the stage Mrs. Worthington / I'm old fashioned / Lover of my dreams / Fare thee well / Half caste women / Gyspy melody / I'll see you again
CD 300692
Hallmark / Jul '96 / Carlton

MASTER'S VOICE, THE (His HMV Recordings 1928-1953)
Room with a view / Dance little lady / Mary make-believe / Try to learn to love / Lorelei / Dream is over / Zigeuner / World weary / Private lives / Half caste woman / Any little fish / Cavalcade prologue / Cavalcade - vocal selection / Lover of my dreams / Cavalcade vocal selection part 2 / Cavalcade epilogue / Noel Coward medley part 1 / Noel Coward medley part 2 / Let's say goodbye / Party's over now / Something to do with Spring / Mad dogs and Englishmen / Medley / I'll follow my secret heart / Melanie's aria part 1 / Melanie's aria part 2 / I travel alone / Most of ev'ry day / Love in bloom / Fare thee well / Mrs. Worthington / We were so young / Then play, orchestra, play / You were there / Has anybody seen our ship / Man about town / Family album / Parisian Pierrot / We were dancing / Dearest love / Where are the songs we sung / Stately homes of England / Gypsy melody / Dearest love (Operetta) / I'll see you again / Just let me look at you / Poor little rich girl / London pride / Last time I saw Paris / Could you please oblige us with a bren gun / There have been songs in England / Imagine the Duchess's feelings / It's only you / Don't let's be beastly to the Germans / Welcoming land / I'm old fashioned / You'd be so nice to come home to / Sigh no more ladies / I wonder what happened to him / Matelot / Nina / Never again / Wait a bit Joe / Bright was the day / This is a changing world / His excellency regrets / 1-2-3 / Uncle Harry / I never knew / I saw no shadow / Josephine / Don't make fun of the fair / Sail away / Why does love get in the way / I like America / Time and again / There are bad times just around the corner
CD Set COWARD 1
EMI / Sep '92 / EMI

MORE COMPACT COWARD
Room with a view / Shadow play / We were dancing / Something to do with Spring / I'll see you again / Poor little rich girl / Zigeuner / Stately homes of England / Dearest love / World weary / Uncle Harry / Half caste woman / Family album / Dance little lady / Don't let's be beastly to the Germans / Nina / Matelot / Don't make fun of the festival / Wait a bit Joe / Sail away
CD CDEMS 1417
EMI / Aug '91 / EMI

ROOM WITH A VIEW, A
CD CDGFR 098
Tring / Jun '92 / Tring

SONGS OF NOEL COWARD, THE (Various Artists)
Mrs. Worthington: *Coward, Noel* / Parisian Pierrot: *Coward, Noel* / There's life in the old girl yet: *Coward, Noel* / Poor little rich girl: *Coward, Noel* / I'll see you again: *Coward, Noel* / If love were all: *Coward, Noel* / Zigeuner: *Coward, Noel* / Room with a view: *Coward, Noel* / Dance little lady: *Coward, Noel* / I'll follow my secret heart: *Coward, Noel* / Regency rakes: *Coward, Noel* / There's always something fishy about the french: *Coward, Noel* / Has anybody seen our ship: *Coward, Noel* / You were there: *Coward, Noel* / Someday I'll find you: *Coward, Noel* / Dearest love: *Coward, Noel* / Stately homes of England: *Coward, Noel* / London pride: *Coward, Noel* / Any little fish: *Coward, Noel* / Mad about the boy: *Coward, Noel* / Mad dogs and englishmen: *Coward, Noel* / Party's over now: *Coward, Noel*
CD PASTCD 7080
Flapper / Jul '96 / Pinnacle

TOGETHER WITH MUSIC (Coward, Noel & Mary Martin)
CD CDXP 1103
DRG / '88 / Discovery / New Note/Pinnacle

Cowboy Junkies

200 MORE MILES (2CD Set)
Blue moon revisited (A song for Elvis) / 200 More miles / Me and the devil / State trooper / Sun comes up, it's Tuesday morning / Oregon hill / Where are you tonight / Casue cheap is how I feel / Floorboard blues / Murder, tonight, in the trailer park / Sweet Jane / If you were the woman and I was the man / Pale sun / Hunted / Lost my driving wheel / Forgive me / Misguided angel / I'm so lonesome I could cry / Walking after midnight
CD Set 74321296432
RCA / Feb '96 / BMG

CAUTION HORSES, THE
Sun comes up, it's Tuesday morning / 'Cause cheap is how I feel / Thirty summers / Mariner's song / Powder finger / Where are you tonight / Witches / Rock and bird / Escape is so easy / You will be loved again
CD 74321183572
RCA / Feb '94 / BMG

LAY IT DOWN
Something more besides you / Common disaster / Lay it down / Hold on to me / Come calling / Just want to see / Lonely sinking feeling / Angel mine / Bea's song / Musical key / Speaking confidentially / Come calling / Now I know
CD GED 24952
Geffen / Feb '96 / BMG

PALE SUN, CRESCENT MOON
Crescent moon / First recollection / Ring on the sill / Anniversary song / White sail / Seven years / Pale sun / Post / Cold tea blues / Hard to explain / Hunted / Floorboard blues
CD 74321168082
RCA / Feb '96 / BMG

TRINITY SESSION, THE
Mining for gold / I don't get it / To love is to bury / Dreaming my dreams with you / Postcard blues / Misguided angel / I'm so lonesome I could cry / 200 more miles / Sweet Jane / Walkin' after midnight / Blue moon revisited (song for Elvis) / Working on a building
CD 74321183562
RCA / Feb '94 / BMG

Cowboy Killers

DAI LAUGHING
CD DISC 9
Discipline / Jan '94 / Pinnacle

Cowboy Mouth

LIFE AS A DOG
CD MA 8
Marina / Jan '95 / SRD

LOVE IS DEAD
CD MA 17
Marina / Mar '96 / SRD

Cowboy Nation

COWBOY NATION
RPM / Remember the Alamo / Cowboy way / Old paint / Cowboy nation / Way out west / Blizzard / Tender foot / Revolution / Cowboy's lament / Big train / Rifle, pony and me / Clock
CD FIENDCD 793
Demon / May '97 / Pinnacle

Cowdrey, Lewis

IT'S LEWIS
CD ANT 0029CD
Antones / Jul '94 / ADA / Hot Shot

Cowell, Henry

PIANO MUSIC
CD SFCD 40801
Smithsonian Folkways / Jul '93 / ADA / Cadillac / CM / Direct / Koch

Cowell, Stanley

BACK TO THE BEAUTIFUL
Theme for Ernie / Wall / It don't mean a thing if it ain't got that swing / But beautiful / Sylvia's place / Come Sunday / Carnegie six / St. Croix / Prayer for peach / Nightingale sang in Berkeley Square
CD CCD 4398
Concord Jazz / Nov '89 / New Note/Pinnacle

HEAR ME ONE (Cowell, Stanley Quartet)
CD SCCD 31407
Steeplechase / Apr '97 / Discovery / Impetus

SUCH GREAT FRIENDS (Cowell, Stanley, Billy Harper, Reggie Workman & Billy Hart)
Sweet song / Destiny is yours / Layla joy / East harlem nostalgia
CD 66051008
Strata East / May '91 / New Note/Pinnacle

TRAVELLIN' MAN
CD BLCD 760178
Black Lion / Mar '93 / Cadillac / Jazz Music / Koch / Wellard

WE THREE
CD DIW 807
DIW / Jul '94 / Cadillac / Harmonia Mundi

Cowie, Charlie

UNSQUARE DANCE
Le reel de grandmere / Centennial jig / Joys of Quebec / Paris waltz / American rag / Maitland River / Ned Kendall / Snowshoer / Spin and glow / McDowall's breakdown / Mamou two step / Coryn Street / Rocky mountain / Kinloss clog / Cowal gathering / Duncan Johnstone / Silver spear / Salley Gardens / Jackie Coleman's / Knotted chord / Last cheater's waltz / Turnpike reek / Schottische / Lilting fisherman / Rose wood / Syracuse / Snug in the blanket / Spanish two step / Mouth of the tobique / Janet's piano lesson / Mrs. Forbes Leith / Little house on the hill / Paddy Carey's / Pet of the pipers / House in the garden / Rowe's division / Baker's breakdown
CD LCOM 5207
Lismor / '91 / ADA / Direct / Duncans / Lismor

Cowlan, Paul F.

PAPER DEVILS & SPIRITS OF FIRE
CD BRAM 1992362
Brambus / Nov '93 / ADA

SECOND CLASS HOTEL
CD BRAM 1989042
Brambus / Nov '93 / ADA

Cows

OLD GOLD 1989-1991
CD ARRCD 68011
Amphetamine Reptile / Jan '96 / Plastic Head

ORPHAN'S TRAGEDY
CD ARRCD 55/335
Amphetamine Reptile / Sep '94 / Plastic Head

WHORN
CD ARR 70013CD
Amphetamine Reptile / Mar '96 / Plastic Head

COWWS Quintet

GROOVES 'N' LOOPS
CD FMPCD 59
FMP / Oct '94 / Cadillac

Cox, Bruce

STICK TO IT
CD MM 801055
Minor Music / Jun '96 / Vital/SAM

Cox, Carl

CARL COX FACT VOL.1 (2CD Set) (Various Artists)
Hot the heels of love: *DJ Hell* / Late night: *Mills, Jeff* / Secrets of meditation: *Trancesetters* / Cactus: *Union Jack* / Ego acid: *Pump Panel* / Hope: *Quench* / Orange theme: *Cygnus X* / Amphetamine: *Heckman, Thomas* / Psycho trip: *Gorl, Robert* / Elektra: *Source* / Phat man: *Wild, Morgen* / Like that: *DJ Hell* / Drum: *Aloof* / Singularity: *Brainchild Vol.2* / Kosmos: *Semisphere* / Raz: *Borealis, Aurora* / Pulsar cycle: *Galactic Spiral Sound* / Fuzz: *Beltram, Joey* / Sacred circles: *Lazonby, Peter* / First question: *Sister Cyrex* / Deep in you: *Stone Circle* / Phosphene: *Heckman, Thomas* / Tonight: *Stone Circle* / No more worry: *Lesamis* / Coda back again: *Coda* / Motorway: *Cox, Carl* / Meet my modern: *Bassxpansion*
CD Set REACTCD 056
React / Feb '95 / Arabesque / Prime / Vital

FANTAZIA VOL.3 (Made In Heaven - The Carl Cox Remix) (Various Artists)
Montana (Let yourself go): *Way Out West* / Natural high: *Q-Tex* / Mayorca: *Nevins, Jason* / Move on: *Secret Society* / Space: *Omer & Crooks* / Musika: *Lost Tribe* / We gonna funk: *DJ Pierre* / Space child: *Megwana* / Too high: *KOTT* / Power of love: *Q-Tex* / Time to let go: *KOTT* / You got me: *NRG* / Free the feeling: *Ellis Dee & Krome & Time* / In the machines: *Machines* / Let me see ya move: *Visa* / Big band: *Luxor* / War path: *Anti Visor* / Moon: *Megwana* / Aah yeah: *Anti Visor*
CD FANTA 005CDR
Fantazia / Aug '94 / 3mv/Sony / Prime

Cox, Derek

20 PIANO FAVOURITES (Cox, Derek & His Music)
As time goes by / One day I'll fly away / Canadian sunset / With one more look at you / Impossible dreams / Can't smile without you / Three times a lady / Eleanor Rigby / Michelle / With a little help from my friends / Memory / I know him so well / Serenata / Hello / Moonlight serenade / She's out of my life / Greensleeves / How deep is your love / I just called to say I love you / My way
CD CDSIV 1126
Horatio Nelson / Jul '95 / Disc

MAGIC OF ANDREW LLOYD WEBBER
Phantom of the opera / All I ask of you / Music of the night / Memory / King Herod's song / Any dream will do / Jesus Christ superstar / I don't know how to love him / Don't cry for me Argentina / Mr. Mistoffelees / Starlight express / Close every door / Unexpected song
CD CDSIV 1113
Horatio Nelson / Jul '95 / Disc

VIVA BRAZIL (Cox, Derek & his Bossa Nova Rhythm)
One Note Samba / Desafinado / Quiet nights and quiet stars / Once I Loved / So many stars / Wave / Someone to light up my life / Girl From Ipanema / How Insensitive / Dindi / Tristeza / manha de carnaval / Surfboard / Abanda / Meditation / Sheila's Theme / Just a little bossa nova / Samba d'Orpheus / Adieu Tristeza / Brazil
CD CDSIV 1136
Horatio Nelson / Jul '95 / Disc

Cox Family

BEYOND THE CITY
CD ROUCD 0327
Rounder / May '95 / ADA / CM / Direct

EVERYBODY'S REACHING OUT FOR SOMEONE
Standing by the bedside of a neighbour / Look me up by the ocean door / Everybody's reaching out for someone / Little white washed chimney / Cry baby cry / I've got that old feeling / But I do / Why not confess / Pardon me / My favorite memory / When God dips his pen of love in my heart / Backroads
CD ROUCD 0297
Rounder / May '93 / ADA / CM / Direct

Cox, Ida

I CAN'T QUIT MY MAN
CD CDAFS 1015
Affinity / Sep '91 / Cadillac / Jazz Music / Koch

IDA COX VOL.1 1923
CD DOCD 5322
Document / Mar '95 / ADA / Hot Shot / Jazz Music

IDA COX VOL.2 1924-1925
CD DOCD 5323
Document / Mar '95 / ADA / Hot Shot / Jazz Music

IDA COX VOL.3 1927-1938
CD DOCD 5324
Document / Mar '95 / ADA / Hot Shot / Jazz Music

IDA COX VOL.4 1927-1938
CD DOCD 5325
Document / Mar '95 / ADA / Hot Shot / Jazz Music

UNCROWNED QUEEN OF THE BLUES, THE
CD BBCD 7
Black Swan / Nov '96 / Jazz Music

Coxhill, Lol

EAR OF BEHOLDER
Introduction / Hungerford / Deviation dance / Two little pigeons / Don Alfonso / Open Piccadilly / Feedback / How insensitive / Conversation / Mango walk / Piccadilly with hoofs / Rasa moods / Collective improvisation / I am the walrus / Rhythmic hooter / Lover man / Zoological fun / Little trip one shoot / Dat's why darkies were born / Series of superbly played mellotron codas
CD SEECD 414
See For Miles/C5 / Oct '94 / Pinnacle

HOLYWELL CONCERT, THE (Coxhill, Lol & George Haslam/Paul Rutherford/ Howard Riley)
In transit / Half pisced / No how / Bliss / Gliss / Duet for trombone and piano / Oxford
CD SLAMCD 302
Slam / Jan '90 / Cadillac

SLOW MUSIC (Coxhill, Lol & Morgan-Fisher)
Que en paz descanse / Flotsam / Vase / Jetsam / Matt finish / Slow music / Pretty little girl
CD BP 160CD
Blueprint / Nov '96 / Pinnacle

THREE BLOKES (Coxhill, Lol & Evan Parker/Steve Lacy)
CD FMPCD 63
FMP / Oct '94 / Cadillac

TOVERBAL SWEET
Five to four / Clompen stomp / Spirit of Maasluis / Association / Or alternatively nine / One to three / PC one / Toverbal / Toverbal sweet / Jasper and out / Un-tempered klavier and heavy friends / Toverbal revisited
CD SEECD 480
See For Miles/C5 / Jul '97 / Pinnacle

Coyle & Sharp

ON THE LOOSE
CD 213CD 005
2.13.61 / Jun '96 / Pinnacle

Coyle, Peter

SEASON
CD TLGCD 008
Telegraph / Jan '97 / Total/BMG

Coyne, Kevin

ADVENTURES OF CRAZY FRANK, THE
Born crazy / Drunk again / Moon madness / You're so wonderful / Crazy dream / Devil calling / Married / Deep the darkness / I stood up / Playing the fool / Heart of hearts / Perversion / Frankies dream No.1 / Frankies dream No.2 / Time for tears / Blast of glory / Never ending
CD CD 388701742
Rockport / Oct '95 / Pinnacle

BURSTING BUBBLES
Only one / Children's crusade / No melody / Learn to swim - learn to drown / Mad boy No. 2 / Dark dance hall / I don't know what to do / Little piece of heaven / Day to day / Golden days / Old fashioned love song
CD CDV 2152
Virgin / Jun '91 / EMI

CASE HISTORY ...PLUS
God bless the bride / White horse / Uggy's song / Need somebody / Evil island home / Araby / My message to the people / Mad boy / Sand all yellow / I'm all aching / Leopard never changes it's spots
CD SEECD 410
See For Miles/C5 / Sep '94 / Pinnacle

DYNAMITE DAZE
Dynamite daze / Brothers of mine / Lunatic / Are we dreaming / Take me back to Dear old Blighty / I really live round here (false friends) / I am / Amsterdam / I only want to see you smile / Juliet and Mark / Woman, woman, woman / Cry / Dance of Bourgeoise
CD CDV 2096
Virgin / Jun '91 / EMI

ELVIRA: SONGS FROM THE ARCHIVES 1979-83
Stand up for England / I'm a girl / Debutante / Leopard never changes it's spots / Golden days / Bad boys / Long arm of the law / Think of sunshine / Elvira / Better than you / Rambling Germany blues / Bimbo / Up North / Born in 1944 / Blood in the night
CD GH 70122
Golden Hind / Mar '95 / Pinnacle

EVERYBODY'S NAKED
Millionaires song / I couldn't love you / Not the way / We don't talk too much / Here comes the morning / City crazy / Take me back in your arms / Last time blues / Slave / Old hippie / Radio / Everybody's naked (in their way)
CD IMC 57218023CK
Zabo / Nov '94 / Vital

LEGLESS IN MANILA
Big money man / Gina's song / Money machine / Raindrop on the river / Nigel in Napoli / Zoo wars / Black cloud / Legless in Manila / Don't raise an argument / Cycling
CD GH 70062
Golden Hind / Nov '94 / Pinnacle

MARJORY RAZORBLADE
Marjory Razorblade / Marlene / Talking to no one / Eastbourne ladies / Old soldier / I want my crown / Nasty, lonesome valley / House on the hill / Cheat me / Jack and Edna / Everybody says / Mummy / Heaven in my view / Karate king / Dog Latin / This is Spain / Chairman's ball / Good boy / Chicken wing
CD CDVM 2501
Virgin / Sep '90 / EMI

MATCHING HEAD AND FEET
Saviour / Lucy / Lonely lovers / Sunday morning sunrise / Rock 'n' roll hymn / Mrs. Hooley go home / It's not me / Turpentine / Tulip / One fine day
CD CDV 2033
Virgin / Jun '91 / EMI

POINTING THE FINGER
There she goes / As I recall / Children of the deaf / One little moment / Let love reside / Sleeping, waking / Pointing the finger / You can't do that / Song of the womb / Old lady
CD MAUCD 640
Mau Mau / Aug '94 / Pinnacle

RABBITS (Coyne, Kevin & Siren)
Stride / Mandy Lee / Marilyn / Why why why / Cheat me / Whole lotta shakin' goin' on / Flowering cherry / Trouble in mind / God bless the bride / Bottle up and go / Blues before sunrise / I need you / John the baptist / Lunatic laughs / Big pistol Mama / Hot potato / Start walking / Let's dance / Forked lightening / Wait until dark
CD DJC 001
DJC / Oct '94 / Direct

ROMANCE ROMANCE (Coyne, Kevin & The Paradise Band)
Ready for love / Happy, happy / Chances / It's all over / Seventeenth Floor / Theresa / No kindness, no pity / Heaven song / Lovers and friends / Wild eyes / Best friend / Impossible child / Neighbourhood girl
CD SPV 8492602
Voiceprint / Dec '94 / Pinnacle

SIGN OF THE TIMES
CD CDVM 9029
Virgin / Aug '92 / EMI

STUMBLING ONTO PARADISE
I'm still here / Pack of lies / How is your luck / Sunshine home / Tear me up / No revolution / Victoria smiles / Charming / Winter into summer / Love for five minutes / Back home boogie
CD GH 70102
Golden Hind / Nov '94 / Pinnacle

TOUGH AND SWEET
Little Miss Dynamite / Precious love / Burning head II / Really in love / Ponytail song / Elvis is dead / Totally naked II / Walls have ears / Baby blue / Talking money / Slow burner / All the loving / No lullabies / It's amazing II / Tell me Tony / Now's the time / Getting old / Some day / Love and money / Let's get romantic / Creeper
CD GH 70092
Golden Hind / Jun '94 / Pinnacle

WILD TIGER LOVE (Coyne, Kevin & The Paradise Band)
Bungalow / Sensual / Cafe crazy / Looking in your eyes / Open up the gates / Go Sally go / American girls / Fish brain / Fooled again / Don't you look (that way) / Raindrops on the window / Passions pleasure
CD CD 3887001240
Golden Hind / Oct '94 / Pinnacle

Coyotes

COYOTES, THE
CD RTMCD 85
Round Tower / Nov '96 / Avid/BMG

Cozens, Chris

SYNTHESIZER GREATEST HITS
Eve of the war / Chariots of fire / Oxygene / Axel F / Crockett's theme / Magic fly / Autobahn / Telstar / Toccata / Chung kuo / Tokyo rendezvous / Miami Vice / Pulstar / Love theme from Bladerunner / Equinoxe / Birdland / Sweet lullaby / Moments in love / Friends of Mr. Cairo
CD CDMFP 6134
Music For Pleasure / Sep '94 / EMI

Crabs

BRAINWASHED
CD KLP 56CD
K / Sep '96 / Cargo / Greyhound / SRD

Crack

SO 92
Happy birthday / For he's a jolly good fellow / For she's a jolly good lady / Auld lang syne / Congratulations / Happy anniversary / Christmas megamix / Irish national anthem / Number one (jingle)
CD SUNCD 5
Sound / Sep '94 / ADA

Crack Up

FROM THE GROUND
CD NB 257CD
Nuclear Blast / Jun '97 / Plastic Head

Cracker

CRACKER
Teen angst (what the world needs now) / Happy birthday to me / This is cracker soul / I see the light / St. Cajetan / Mr. Wrong / Someday / Can I take my gun to heaven / Satisfy you / Another song about the rain / Don't fuck me up (with peace and love) / Dr. Bernice
CD CDVUS 48
Virgin / Apr '92 / EMI

KEROSENE HAT
Low / Movie star / Get off this / Kerosene hat / Take me down to the infirmary / Nostalgia / Sweet potato / Sick of goodbyes / I want everything / Lonesome Johnny blues / Let's go for a ride / Loser / Hi-desert biker meth lab / Euro-trash girl / I ride my bike / Kerosene hat (Accoustic)
CD CDVU 67
Virgin / Jun '94 / EMI

Crackerbash

TIN TOY
CD EFA 11397CD
Musical Tragedies / Aug '93 / SRD

Cracknell, Sarah

LIPSLIDE
Ready or not / Desert baby / Coastal town / Home / Anymore / How far / Goldie / Taxi / Taking off for France / If you leave me / Penthouse girl basement boy / Can't stop now
CD GUTCD 2
Gut / May '97 / Total/BMG

Craddock, Billy

CRASH'S SMASHES (The Hits Of Billy 'Crash' Craddock)
CD RAZCD 2095
Razor & Tie / Apr '96 / Koch

WELL DON'T YOU KNOW
Sweet pie / School day dreams / Lulu Lee / Ah poor little baby / I miss you so much / Blabbermouth / Am I to be the one / Sweetie Pie / Well don't you know / Boom boom baby / Don't destroy me / (What makes you) Treat me like you do / I want that / Since she turned seventeen / All I want is you / Letter of love / One last kiss / Is it true or is it false / Report card of love / Heavenly love / Goodtime Billy
CD BCD 15610
Bear Family / Jun '92 / Direct / Rollercoaster / Swift

Cradle

BABA YAGA
CD TOPPCD 042
Ultimate / Jun '96 / Pinnacle

Cradle Of Filth

DUSK & HER EMBRACE
Human inspired to nightmare / Heaven torn asunder / Funeral in Carpathia / Gothic romance / Malice through the looking glass / Dusk and her embrace / Graveyard moonlight / Beauty sleeps in sodom / Haunted shores / Hell awaits / Camilla's masque
CD CDMFNX 208
CD CDMFN 208
Music For Nations / Nov '96 / Pinnacle

VEMPIRE
CD NIHIL 6CD
Cacophonous / Apr '96 / Plastic Head / RTM/Disc

Cradle Of Spoil

SOLAR ECLIPSE
CD EFA 125192
Celtic Circle / Apr '95 / SRD

Craig, Carl

DJ KICKS
CD ______ K7 042CD
Studio K7 / Apr '96 / Prime / RTM/Disc

LANDCRUISING
CD ______ 4509998652
Blanco Y Negro / Dec '96 / Warner Music

MORE SONGS ABOUT FOOD AND REVOLUTIONARY ART
Es30 / Televised green smoke / Goodbye world / Alien talk / Red lights / Dreamland / Butterfly / Act 2 / Dominas / At Les / Suspiria / As time goes by (sitting under a tree) / Attitude / Frustration / Food and art (in the spirit of revolution)
CD ______ SSR 188CD
Crammed Discs / Mar '97 / Grapevine/ PolyGram / New Note/Pinnacle / Prime / RTM/Disc

Craig, Cathryn

CATHRYN CRAIG
Runnin from love / talk to you / Are you out there / Never / Colorado / Love coming down on me / My window faces the south / New Paint / Voyager / If you don't weaken
CD ______ GOLDCD 002
Goldrush / Aug '97 / Direct

PORCH SONGS
CD ______ GOLDCD 001
Goldrush / Jul '95 / Direct

Craig, Sara

SWEET EXHAUST
CD ______ 0072112ATT
Edel / Jul '95 / Pinnacle

Crain

HEATER
Foot sanding / Save me your head / Valium and alcohol / Waste kings / Blistering / Knock your daylights out / Hey cops / Bricks / One who hangs / Broken heart of a neutron star
CD ______ 727512
Restless / Apr '94 / Vital

Cramer, Floyd

ESSENTIAL FLOYD CRAMER, THE
Last date / Fancy pants / I'm so lonesome I could cry / San Antonio rose / Flip flop and bop / Your last goodbye / Corrina corrina / Drown in my own tears / I need you now / On the rebound / Georgia on my mind / Lovesick blues / Chattanooga choo choo / Losers weepers / Java / Shrum / (These are) the young ears / All keyed up / Stood up / What'd I say
CD ______ 74321665912
RCA / Feb '96 / BMG

KING OF COUNTRY PIANO
CD ______ PWKS 4222
Carlton / Nov '94 / Carlton

Cramps

BIG BEAT FROM BADSVILLE
CD ______ 65162
Epitaph / Sep '97 / Pinnacle / Plastic Head

DATE WITH ELVIS, A
How far can too far go / Hot pearl snatch / People ain't no good / What's inside a girl / Kizmiaz / Cornfed dames / Chicken / Womanneed / Aloha from hell / It's just that song
CD ______ CDWIK 46
Big Beat / Apr '86 / Pinnacle

FLAMEJOB
Mean machine / Ultra twist / Let's get fucked up / Nest of cuckoo birds / I'm customized / Sado county auto show / Naked girl falling down the stairs / How come you do me / Upside down and upside down / Trapped love / Swing the big eyed rabbit / Strange love / Blues blues blues / Sinners / Route 66
CD ______ CRECD 170
Creation / Oct '94 / 3mv/Vital

ROCKIN NREELININ AUCKLAND NEWZEALANDXXX
Hot pearl snatch / People ain't no good / What's inside a girl / Cornfed Dames / Sunglasses after dark / Heartbreak Hotel / Chicken / Do the clam / Aloha from Hell / Can your pussy do the dog / Blue moon baby / Georgia Lee Brown / Lonesome town
CD ______ CDWIKD 132
Big Beat / Aug '94 / Pinnacle

SMELL OF FEMALE
Most exalted potentate of love / You got good taste / Call of the wig hat / Faster pussycat / I ain't nothin' but a gorehound / Psychotic reaction
CD ______ CDWIKM 95
Big Beat / Feb '91 / Pinnacle

SONGS THE CRAMPS TAUGHT US (Various Artists)
CD ______ APECALL 007
Jungle Noise / Mar '97 / Cargo

STAY SICK
Bop pills / God damn rock 'n' roll / Bikini girls with machine guns / All women are bad / Creature from the black leather lagoon / Shortnin' bread / Daisys up your butterfly / Everything goes / Journey to the center of a girl / Mama oo pow pow / Saddle up a buzz buzz / Mule skinner blues / Her love rubbed off
CD ______ CDWIKD 126
Big Beat / Jan '94 / Pinnacle

Cran

CROOKED STAIR
CD ______ CBM 002CD
Cross Border Media / Oct '93 / ADA / Direct / Grapevine/PolyGram

Cranberries

CRANBERRIES, THE (Fully Illustrated Book & Interview Dics)
CD ______ SAM 7034
Sound & Media / Jun '97 / Sound & Media

EVERYBODY ELSE IS DOING IT, SO WHY CAN'T WE
CD ______ CID 8003
Island / Feb '94 / PolyGram

EVERYBODY ELSE IS DOING IT, SO WHY CAN'T WE/NO NEED TO ARGUE (2CD Set)
I still do / Dreams / Sunday / Pretty / Waltzing back / Not sorry / Linger / Wanted / Still can't... / I will always / How / Put me down / Ode to my family / I can't be with you / Twenty one / Zombie / Empty / Everything I said / Icicle melts / Disappointment / Ridiculous thoughts / Dreaming my dreams / Yeats' grave / Daffodil lament / No need to argue
CD Set ______ ISDCD 1
Island / Nov '95 / PolyGram

NO NEED TO ARGUE
Ode to my family / I can't be with you / Twenty one / Zombie / Empty / Everything I said / Icicle melts / Disappointment / Ridiculous thoughts / Dreaming my dreams / Yeats grave / Daffodils lament / No need to argue
CD ______ CID 8029
Island / Aug '94 / PolyGram

TO THE FAITHFUL DEPARTED
Hollywood / Salvation / When you're gone / Free to decide / Warchild / Forever yellow skies / Rebels / I just shot John Lennon / Electric blue / I'm still remembering / Will you remember / Joe / Bosnia
CD ______ CID 8048
Island / Apr '96 / PolyGram

Crane

345S
CD ______ ELM 7CD
Elemental / Jan '93 / RTM/Disc

Crane River Jazz Band

CRANE RIVER JAZZ BAND
CD ______ SGC/MELCD 202
Cadillac / Nov '96 / Cadillac / Jazz Music / Wellard

GREAT BRITISH TRADITIONAL JAZZBANDS VOL.5
Balling the Jack / Maryland my Maryland / After dark / Moose march / Canal street blues / Down by the riverside / Winnin' boy blues / You tell me your dream / Tishomingo blues / When I leave the world behind / Saturday night function / Ain't gonna give nobody none of my jellyroll / I'm travelling / Washington and Lee swing / South
CD ______ LACD 57
Lake / Dec '95 / ADA / Cadillac / Direct / Jazz Music / Target/BMG

Crane, Tony

FEEL LIKE DANCING
CD ______ DLD 1020
Dance & Listen / '92 / Savoy / Target/ BMG

GEE BUT IT'S GOOD
CD ______ DLD 1036
Dance & Listen / May '93 / Savoy / Target/BMG

Cranes

FOREVER
Forever / Cloudless / Jewel / Far away / Adrift / Clear / Sun and sky / And ever / Golden / Rainbows
CD ______ DEDCD 009
Dedicated / Apr '93 / BMG / Vital

LOVED
CD ______ DEDCD 016
Dedicated / Sep '94 / BMG / Vital

POPULATION FOUR
Tangled up / Fourteen / Breeze / Can't get free / Stalk / Sweet unknown / Angel bell / On top of the world / Brazil / Let go / To be / Lemon tree
CD ______ DEDCD 026
CD ______ DEDCD 026S
Dedicated / Feb '97 / BMG / Vital

Cranioclast

ICONCLASTER
CD ______ EEE 09CD
Musica Maxima Magnetica / Sep '93 / Cargo / Plastic Head

Cranitch, Matt

ANY OLD TIME
CD ______ CLUNCD 047
Mulligan / Oct '83 / ADA / CM

IRISH FIDDLE BOOK, THE
CD ______ OSS 4CD
Ossian / Jan '87 / ADA / CM / Direct / Highlander

SMALL ISLAND, A (Cranitch, Milne & Sullivan)
CD ______ OSS 70CD
Ossian / Dec '94 / ADA / CM / Direct / Highlander

TAKE A BOW
CD ______ CDOSS 05
Ossian / Apr '93 / ADA / CM / Direct / Highlander

Crank

PICKING UP THE PIECES
Lonely man / Why did you go / You as well / Punk a'a'right
CD ______ SEMAPHORE 35662
Onefoot / Nov '96 / Cargo

Craobh Rua

MORE THAT'S SAID THE LESS THE BETTER
CD ______ CDLDL 1215
Lochshore / Jul '94 / ADA / Direct / Duncans

NO MATTER HOW COLD AND WET YOU ARE
CD ______ CDLDL 1237
Lochshore / Mar '96 / ADA / Direct / Duncans

SOH IT IS
Red crow / Dawn / Bianzano / Ye lovers all / Paddy Fahey's / Handy with the bottle / Wearing the britches / Cook in the kitchen / Na' tar ach san oiche / Tosa waltz / My charming Nancy Bell / Lads of Laois / London lasses / Miss McClouds / High road to Linton / Shore 'neath the tide / Ivy leaf / Fox on the town
CD ______ CDLDL 1259
Lochshore / Mar '97 / ADA / Direct / Duncans

Crary, Dan

BLUEGRASS GUITAR
CD ______ SHCD 3806
Sugar Hill / Jan '97 / ADA / CM / Direct / Koch / Roots

GUITAR
Cotton patch rag / Stanley Brothers medley / Sweet laree / Memories of Mozart / Green in the blue medley / Tom and Jerry / Bill Monroe medley
CD ______ SHCD 3730
Sugar Hill / Jan '97 / ADA / CM / Direct / Koch / Roots

JAMMED IF I DO
CD ______ SHCD 3824
Sugar Hill / Oct '94 / ADA / CM / Direct / Koch / Roots

LADY'S FANCY
Huckleberry hornpipe / Lime rock / If the devil dreamed about playing flamenco / With a flatpick / Jenny's waltz / Sally Goodin / Julie's reel / Dill pickle rag / Pretty little indian / Grey eagle / Lady's fancy
CD ______ ROUCD 0099
Rounder / Dec '94 / ADA / CM / Direct

TAKE A STEP OVER
Bugle call rag / Take a step over / Great tunes/Dumb names medley / Raleigh and special / Come hither / Willow, the wandering gypsy / Hot canary / Traditional suite in "E" medley / Lord build me a cabin
CD ______ SHCD 3770
Sugar Hill / Jan '89 / ADA / CM / Direct / Koch / Roots

THUNDERATION
Banderilla / Depoe Bay / West O' the moon / Amsterdance / Songs of Makoraka-o / Thunderation / Lady's fantasy / Lime rock / Andante in steel / Denouement
CD ______ SHCD 1135
Sugar Hill / Oct '91 / ADA / CM / Direct / Koch / Roots

Crash Test Dummies

GHOST THAT HAUNTS ME, THE
Winter song / Comin' back song (The bereft man's song) / Superman's song / Country life / Here on earth (I'll have my cake) / Ghost that haunts me / Thick necked man / Androgynous / Voyage / At my funeral
CD ______ 74321283342
RCA / Aug '95 / BMG

GOD SHUFFLED HIS FEET
God shuffled his feet / Afternoons and coffespoons / Mmm mmm mmm mmm / In the days of the cinema / Swimming in you ocean / Here I stand before me / I think I've disappeared / How does a duck know / When I go out with artists / Psychic / Two knights and maidens / Untitled
CD ______ 74321201522
RCA / May '94 / BMG

WORM'S LIFE, A
Overachievers / He liked to feel it / Worm's life / Our driver gestures / My enemies / There are many dangers / I'm outlived by that thing / All of this ugly / An old scab / My own sunrise / I'm a dog / Swatting flies
CD ______ 74321402012
RCA / Sep '96 / BMG

Crash Worship

ADRV
CD ______ CHCD 3
Charnel House / Jun '97 / Cargo / Greyhound

ASESINOS
CD ______ RUSCD 8212
ROIR / Jul '95 / Plastic Head / Shellshock/ Disc

Crass

BEST BEFORE 1984
CD ______ CRASS 5CD
Crass / Oct '90 / SRD

CHRIST THE ALBUM
CD ______ BOLLOX2U2 CD
Crass / Oct '90 / SRD

CHRIST THE BOOTLEG
CD ______ ALLIED 76CD
Allied / Nov '96 / Cargo / Greyhound / Plastic Head

FEEDING OF THE 5,000
CD ______ 621984 CD
Crass / Oct '90 / SRD

PENIS ENVY
CD ______ 321984 CD
Crass / Oct '90 / SRD

STATIONS OF THE CRASS
Stations of the crass / Mother Earth / White punks on hope / You've got big hands / Darling / System / Bigman / Hurry up Gary / Gas man cometh / Democrats / Contaminational power / Time out / I ain't thick, it's just a trick / Fun going on / Crutch of society / Heard too much about / Chairman of the board / Tired / Walls / Upright citizen / System / Big man / Banned from the Roxy / Hurry up Gary / Middle class, working class / Fight war, not wars / Shaved women / Fun going on / Unknown songs / Do they owe us a living / Punk is dead
CD ______ 521984 CD
Crass / Oct '90 / SRD

YES SIR I WILL
CD ______ 121984/2 CD
Crass / Oct '90 / SRD

Craven, Beverley

BEVERLEY CRAVEN
Promise me / Holding on / Woman to woman / Memories / Castle in the clouds / You're not the first / Joey / Two of a kind / I listen to the rain / Missing you
CD ______ 4670532
Epic / Jul '90 / Sony

LOVE SCENES
Love scenes / Love is the light / Look no further / Mollie's song / In those days / Feels like the first time / Blind faith / Lost without you / Winner takes it all
CD ______ 4745172
Epic / Sep '93 / Sony

Cravens, Red

419 WEST MAIN (Cravens, Red & Bray Brothers)
WHOW introduction / This train / Glory in the meeting house / Bluegrass breakdown / Cora is gone / East Virginia blues / Jingle bell breakdown / Blue eyed darling / Little darling pal of mine / Pass me by / Cumberland gap / I never shall marry / Lost love / Sally Goodin / Gentle blues / Rawhide / Angel with the golden hair / Buckin' mule / Our darling's gone / Hazel Dell
CD ______ ROUCD 0015
Rounder / May '97 / ADA / CM / Direct

Craw

CRAW
CD ______ CHK 002
Choke Inc. / Feb '94 / SRD

MAP, MONITOR, SURGE
CD ______ CAM 004
Cambodia / Jun '97 / Greyhound

Crawdaddys

CRAWDADDY EXPRESS
I'm a lover not a fighter / You can't judge a book by the cover / Down the road apiece / Let's make it / Raining in my heart / I'm movin' on / Mystic eyes / Oh baby doll /

Bald headed woman / Come see me / Got you in my soul / Times are getting tougher than tough / Down in the bottom / Crawdaddy Express / I wanna put a tiger in your tank
CD VOXXCD 2001
Voxx / Oct '94 / Else / RTM/Disc

HERE TIS
CD VOXXCD 2046
Voxx / Oct '94 / Else / RTM/Disc

Crawford, Hank

SOUTH CENTRAL
Falling in love with love / I should care / South Central / I want to talk about you / In a mellow tone / Conjunction Mars / Fool that I am / Splanky / O holy night
CD MCD 9201
Milestone / Oct '93 / Cadillac / Complete/ Pinnacle / Jazz Music / Wellard

Crawford, Hugh

READY OR NOT
CD DIVCD 04
Diverse / Nov '94 / Grapevine/PolyGram

Crawford, Johnny

BEST OF JOHNNY CRAWFORD, THE
Cindy's birthday / Rumours / Your nose is gonna grow / Proud / Patti Ann / Daydreams / Cindy's gonna cry / Judy loves me / Janie please believe me / What happened to Janie / Lonesome town / Lucky star / Devil or angel / Sandy / Debbie / Your love is growing old / That's all I want from you / Cry on my shoulder / I don't need you / Mr. Blue / Girl next door (Once upon a time) / We belong together / No one really loves a clown / Sittin' and watchin'
CD CDCHD 429
Ace / Oct '92 / Pinnacle

Crawford, Kevin

'D' FLUTE ALBUM
CD KBSCD 77
Kerbstone / Oct '94 / ADA / Direct

RAISE THE RAFTERS
CD CCD 002
Celtic Prime / Feb '96 / ADA

Crawford, Michael

EFX
CD TCD 2810
Telstar / Dec '95 / BMG

LOVE SONGS
CD TCD 2748
Telstar / Nov '94 / BMG

MICHAEL CRAWFORD - STAGE AND SCREEN
West Side story / What'll I do / Unexpected song / If loved you / Before the parade passes by / When you wish upon a star / In the still of the night / Memory / Not a day goes by / Bring him home / You'll never walk alone
CD CDSR 060
Telstar / Aug '94 / BMG

PERFORMS ANDREW LLOYD WEBBER
CD TCD 2544
Telstar / Nov '91 / BMG

TOUCH OF MUSIC IN THE NIGHT, A
CD TCD 2676
Telstar / Oct '93 / BMG

WITH LOVE
CD CDSR 061
Telstar / Aug '94 / BMG

Crawford, Randy

ABSTRACT EMOTIONS
Can't stand the pain / Actual emotional love / World of fools / Betcha / Higher than anyone can count / Desire / Getting away with murder / Overnight / Almaz / Don't wanna be normal
CD 9254232
WEA / Jul '86 / Warner Music

EVERYTHING MUST CHANGE
Everything must change / I let you walk away / I'm easy / I had to see you one more time / I've never been to me / Don't let me down / Something so right / Soon as I touched him / Only your love song lasts / Gonna give lovin a try
CD 7599273072
WEA / Feb '92 / Warner Music

NAKED AND TRUE
Cajun moon / Give me the night / Glow of love / Purple rain / Forget me nots / I'll be around / Joy inside my tears / Come into my life / What a difference a day makes / Holding back the years / All the king's horses
CD 0630109612
WEA / Jul '95 / Warner Music

NOW WE MAY BEGIN
Now we may begin / Blue flame / When your life was low / My heart is not as young as it used to be / Last night at danceland / Tender falls the rain / One day I'll fly away / Same old story (same old song)
CD 7599234212
WEA / Feb '92 / Warner Music

RAW SILK
I stand accused / Declaration of love / Someone to believe in / Endlessly / Love is like a newborn child / Where there was darkness / Nobody / I hope you'll be very unhappy without me / I got myself a happy song / Just to keep you satisfied / Blue mood
CD 7599273862
WEA / Feb '93 / Warner Music

RICH AND POOR
Knockin' on heaven's door / Every kinda people / Wrap U up / This is love / Seperate lives / Believe that love can change the world / Rich and poor / Cigarette in the rain / Love is / I don't feel much like crying / All it takes is love
CD 9260022
WEA / Oct '89 / Warner Music

SECRET COMBINATION
You might need somebody / Rainy night in Georgia / That's how heartaches are made / Two lives / You bring the Sun out / Rio De Janeiro blue / Secret combination / When I lose my way / Time for love / Trade winds
CD K2 56904
WEA / Mar '87 / Warner Music

THROUGH THE EYES OF LOVE
Who's crying now / It's raining / When love is new / If i were (in your shoes) / Rhythm of romance / Shine / Hold on, be strong / Lot that you can do / If you'd only believe / Like the sun out of nowhere / Just a touch / Diamante
CD 7599267362
WEA / Dec '96 / Warner Music

Crawford, Ray

SMOOTH GROOVE
Compendium suite / Miss April / Impossible / I knew prez / Smooth groove
CD CCD 9028
Candid / Feb '97 / Cadillac / Direct / Jazz Music / Koch / Wellard

Crawford, Stephanie

TIME FOR LOVE, A (Crawford, Stephanie & Michel Graillier)
CD BBRC 9103
Big Blue / Nov '92 / Harmonia Mundi

Crawler

PASTIME DREAMER
CD RMCCD 0206
Red Steel / Apr '97 / Pinnacle

Crawley

SUPERSONIC
CD SPV 08436202
SPV / Oct '94 / Koch / Plastic Head

Crawlpappy

DELUXE
CD WB 2094CD
We Bite / Nov '92 / Plastic Head

Cray, Robert

BAD INFLUENCE (Cray, Robert Band)
Phone booth / Grinder / Got to make a comeback / So many women, so little time / Where do I go from here / Waiting for a train / March on / Don't touch me / No big deal / Bad influence / Share what you've got, keep what you need / I got loaded
CD HCD 8001
Hightone / Apr '96 / ADA / Koch

DON'T BE AFRAID OF THE DARK (Cray, Robert Band)
Don't be afraid of the dark / Your secret's safe with me / Acting this way / Don't you even come / I can't go home / Across the line
CD 8349232
Mercury / Aug '88 / PolyGram

FALSE ACCUSATIONS (Cray, Robert Band)
Porch light / Change of heart, change of mind / She's gone / Playin' in the dirt / I've slipped her mind / False accusations / Last time / Payin' for it now / Sonny
CD HCD 8005
Hightone / Apr '96 / ADA / Koch

I WAS WARNED (Cray, Robert Band)
Just a loser / I'm a good man / I was warned / Price I pay / Won the battle / On the road down / Whole lotta pride / Picture of a broken heart / He don't live here anymore / Our last time
CD 5127212
Mercury / Jan '93 / PolyGram

MIDNIGHT STROLL (Cray, Robert Band & Memphis Horns)
CD 8466522
Mercury / Sep '90 / PolyGram

NEW BLUES
Who's been talkin' / Nice as a fool can be / If you're thinkin' what I'm thinkin' / Welfare (turns its back on you) / I'm gonna forget about you / Sleeping on the ground / Too many cooks / I'd rather be a wino / Score / That's what I'll do
CD 306642
Hallmark / Jun '97 / Carlton

SCORE, THE (Charly Blues - Masterworks Vol. 16)
Too many cooks / Score / Welfare / That's what I'll do / I'd rather be a wino / Who's been talkin' / Sleeping in the ground / I'm gonna forget about you / Nice as a fool can be / If I'm thinkin' what I'm thinkin'
CD CDBM 16
Charly / Apr '92 / Koch

SHAME & SIN
CD 5185172
Mercury / Oct '93 / PolyGram

STRONG PERSUADER (Cray, Robert Band)
Smoking gun / I guessed I showed her / Right next door (because of me) / Nothin' but a woman / Still around / More than I can stand / Foul play / Ronettes / Fantasized / New blood
CD 8305682
Mercury / Nov '86 / PolyGram

SWEET POTATO PIE (Cray, Robert Band)
CD 5346982
Mercury / May '97 / PolyGram

TOO MANY COOKS
Too many cooks / Score / When the welfare turns it back on you / That's what I'll do / I'd rather be a wino / Who's been talkin' / Sleeping in the ground / I'm gonna forget about you / Nice as a fool can be / If you're thinkin' what I'm thinkin'
CD 2696532
Tomato / Oct '91 / Vital

Crayton, Pee Wee

BLUES AFTER HOURS
Win-o / Hurry hurry / Runnin' wild / I got news for you / Don't break my heart / Blues before dawn / Don't go / Telephone is ringing / Mistreated so bad / Poppa stoppa / Phone call from my baby / Tired of travellin' / California women / Blues for my baby / Rosa Lee / Guitar boogie / Dedicating the blues / Brand new woman / I love you so / Texas hop / Blues after hours / After hours boogie
CD CD 52045
Blues Encore / Oct '96 / Target/BMG

MODERN LEGACY, THE
Texas hop / Central Avenue blues / Bounce Pee Wee / T for Texas (mistreated blues) / Rosa Lee / Blues after hours / I'm still in love with you / Pee Wee's boogie / Louella Brown / From blues to boogie / Please come back / Rock Island blues / Rockin' the blues / Change your way of lovin' / Pee Wee's wild / Black gal / Boogie woogie upstairs / When darkness falls / Bop hop / My everything / Blues for my baby / Tired of travellin' / Austin boogie
CD CDCHD 632
Ace / Aug '96 / Pinnacle

THINGS I USED TO DO
Every night / But on the other hand / Peace of mind / Let the good times roll / Blues after hours / You were wrong / Things I used to do / Little bitty things / SK blues / Long tall Texan / My kind of woman
CD VMD 65662
Vanguard / Oct '95 / ADA / Pinnacle

Crazy

CRAZIAH THAN EVER
CD JW 056CD
Soca / Feb '94 / Jet Star

CRAZY FOR YOU
CD JW 067CD
JW / Feb '95 / Jet Star

Crazy Alice

WHEEL
CD EVRCD 14
Eve / Nov '92 / Grapevine/PolyGram

Crazy Backward Alphabet

CRAZY BACKWARD ALPHABET
Blood and the ink / Det Enda Raka / Get it you / Welfare elite / Ghosts / Lobster on the rocks / Sarayushka (La Grange) / Dropped D / Book of Joel / Bottoms up / We are in control / Maran II
CD SST 110CD
SST / May '93 / Plastic Head

Crazy Cavan

COOL AND CRAZY
CD 107352
Musidisc / Mar '94 / Discovery

HEY, TEENAGER
CD 107332
Musidisc / Mar '94 / Discovery

ROLLIN' THROUGH THE NIGHT
CD 107342
Musidisc / Mar '94 / Discovery

ROUGH, TOUGH & READY
CD 107072
Musidisc / Mar '94 / Discovery

WILD, WEIRD AND CRAZY (Crazy Cavan & The Rhythm Rockers)
CD CRCD 01
Crazy Rhythm / Nov '96 / Nervous

Crazy Gods Of Endless Noise

HEAVY PLANET
CD CRAZY 26
Blind / Nov '96 / 3mv/Vital

Crazy Horse

CRAZY HORSE
Gone dead train / Dance, dance, dance / Look at all the things / beggar's day / I don't want to talk about it / Carolay / Dirty, dirty / Nobody / I'll get by / Crow Lady Jane
CD 7599268082
Reprise / Apr '94 / Warner Music

LEFT FOR DEAD
CD SERV 009CD
World Service / Nov '89 / Vital

Crazy Rhythm Daddies

CRAZY RHYTHM DADDIES
CD IR 001
Igloo / Sep '96 / Nervous

Crazyhead

SOME KIND OF FEVER
Big sister / Above those things / Everything's alright / Magic eye / I can do anything / Movie theme / Talk about you / Rome / Train / Some kinda fever
CD REVXD 162
Black / Oct '90 / Revolver / Sony

Creach, Papa John

I'M THE FIDDLE MAN
CD OW 30004
One Way / Jul '94 / ADA / Direct / Greyhound

ROCK FATHER
CD OW 30005
One Way / Jul '94 / ADA / Direct / Greyhound

Cream

ALTERNATIVE ALBUM, THE
CD ITM 960002
ITM / Oct '92 / Koch / Tradelink

CREAM BOX SET
CD Set CR 1
UFO / Oct '92 / Pinnacle

CREAM LIVE VOL.2
Deserted cities of the heart / White room / Politician / Tales of brave Ulysses / Sunshine of your love / Steppin' out
CD 8236612
Polydor / May '88 / PolyGram

DISRAELI GEARS
Strange brew / Sunshine of your love / World of pain / Dance the night away / Blue condition / Tales of brave Ulysses / We're going wrong / Outside woman blues / Take it back / Mother's lament
CD 8236362
Polydor / Nov '90 / PolyGram

FRESH CREAM
I feel free / NSU / Sleepy time time / Dreaming / Sweet wine / Spoonful / Cat's squirrel / Four until late / Rollin' and tumblin' / I'm so glad / Toad / Coffee song / Wrapping paper
CD 8275762
Polydor / Nov '90 / PolyGram

THOSE WERE THE DAYS (4CD Set)
CD Set 5390022
Polydor / Sep '97 / PolyGram

VERY BEST OF CREAM, THE
White room / I feel free / Tales of brave Ulysses / I'm so glad / Toad / Sunshine of your love / Strange brew / NSU / Born under a bad sign / Badge / Crossroads
CD 5237522
Polydor / Jan '95 / PolyGram

WHEELS OF FIRE (In The Studio - Live At The Fillmore)
White room / Sittin' on top of the world / Passing the time / As you said / Pressed rat and warthog / Politician / Those were the days / Born under a bad sign / Deserted cities of the heart / Crossroads / Spoonful / Train time / Toad
CD Set 8275782
Polydor / Nov '90 / PolyGram

Cream 8

EMERALD TOUCH, THE
CD SPV 08423622
SPV / May '95 / Koch / Plastic Head

Creaming Jesus

END OF AN ERROR
CD FREUDCD 52
Jungle / Oct '96 / RTM/Disc / SRD

TOO FAT TO RUN, TO STUPID TO HIDE
CD FREUDCD 36
Jungle / Dec '90 / RTM/Disc / SRD

Creation

HOW DOES IT FEEL TO FEEL
How does it feel to feel / Life is just beginning / Through my eyes / Ostrich man / I am the walker / Tom Tom / Girls are naked / Painter man / Try and stop me / Biff bang pow / Making time / Cool jerk / For all that I am / Nightmares / Midway down / Can I join your band
CD EDCD 106
Edsel / Aug '90 / Pinnacle

LAY THE GHOST
CD COCRD 001
Cohesion / Oct '93 / Grapevine/PolyGram

MARK FOUR/THE CREATION (Mark Four/Creation)
CD 842058
EVA / May '94 / ADA / Direct

PAINTER MAN
CD NESTCD 904
Demon / Apr '93 / Pinnacle

POWER SURGE
CD CRECD 176
Creation / Jun '96 / 3mv/Vital

Creation Of Death

PURIFY YOUR SOUL
CD CDFLAG 62
Under One Flag / Sep '91 / Pinnacle

Creation Of Sunlight

CREATION OF SUNLIGHT
CD MYSTIC 7
Mystic / Jun '97 / Cargo / Greyhound / Plastic Head

Creation Rebel

HISTORIC MOMENTS VOL.1 (Dub From Creation Rebel Vibrations)
CD ONUCD 72
On-U Sound / Jul '94 / Jet Star / SRD

HISTORIC MOMENTS VOL.2
CD ONUCD 74
On-U Sound / Mar '95 / Jet Star / SRD

LOWS AND HIGHS
Independent man / Rebel party / Reasoning / No peace / Love I can feel / Rubber skirt / Creation rebel / Creative involvements
CD CDBRED 33
Cherry Red / Sep '97 / Pinnacle

THREAT TO CREATION (Creation Rebel & New Age Steppers)
Chemical specialists / Threat to creation / Eugenic device / Last sane dream / Pain staker / Earthwire line / Ethos design / Final frontier
CD CDBRED 21
Cherry Red / Sep '97 / Pinnacle

Creative Music Studio

WOODSTOCK JAZZ FESTIVAL VOL.1
Waltz / Isfahan / Stella by stralight / Round mignight
CD ADC 8
Douglas Music / Jul '97 / Cadillac / New Note/Pinnacle

WOODSTOCK JAZZ FESTIVAL VOL.2
Impressions / No greater love / All blues
CD ADC 9
Douglas Music / Jul '97 / Cadillac / New Note/Pinnacle

Creator, Carlos

PURE GUITAR
Radio guitar / Snake dance / Wet blues / Mad kisses / Making satanic train / Grand Prix / Bound for Istanbul / European guitars / Elixir of life / ET calling / 711Q / Nightmare continutes
CD PCOM 1113
President / Jul '91 / Grapevine/PolyGram / President / Target/BMG

Creators

HAVE A MASTERPLAN
CD BS 002CD
Blindside / Feb '96 / RTM/Disc

Credit To The Nation

DADDY ALWAYS WANTED ME TO GROW A PAIR OF WINGS
CD TPLP 54CD
One Little Indian / Feb '96 / Pinnacle

Credo

FIELD OF VISION
Rules of engagement / Goodboy / Don't look back / Alicia / Power to the Nth degree / Phantom / Sweet scarlet whisper / Party / Kindness
CD CYCL 012
Cyclops / Jun '97 / Pinnacle

Creedence Clearwater Revival

BAYOU COUNTRY
Born on the bayou / Bootleg / Graveyard train / Good golly Miss Molly / Penthouse pauper / Proud Mary / Keep on chooglin'
CD CDFE 502
Fantasy / Aug '87 / Jazz Music / Pinnacle / Wellard

CHOOGLIN'
I heard it through the grapevine / Keep on chooglin' / Suzie Q / Pagan baby / Born on the bayou
CD CDFE 517
Fantasy / Jun '93 / Jazz Music / Pinnacle / Wellard

CHRONICLE (20 Greatest Hits)
Suzie Q / I put a spell on you / Proud Mary / Bad moon rising / Lodi / Green river / Commotion / Down on the corner / Fortunate son / Travellin' band / Who'll stop the rain / Up around the bend / Run through the jungle / Lookin' out my back door / Long as I can see the light / I heard it through the grapevine / Have you ever seen the rain / Hey tonight / Sweet hitch hiker / Some day never comes
CD CDCCR 2
Fantasy / Jun '87 / Jazz Music / Pinnacle / Wellard

CHRONICLE VOL.2
Walk on the water / Suzie Q (Part 2) / Born on the Bayou / Good golly Miss Molly / Tombstone shadow / Wrote a song for everyone / Night time is the right time / Cotton fields / It came out of the sky / Don't look now / Midnight special / Before you accuse me / My baby left me / Pagan baby / I wish I could hide away / It's just a thought / Molina / Born to move / Lookin' for a reason / Hello Mary Lou
CD CDCCR 3
Fantasy / Jun '87 / Jazz Music / Pinnacle / Wellard

COLLECTION, THE (10CD Set)
I put a spell on you / Working man / Suzie Q / Ninety nine and a half (won't do) / Get down woman / Porterville / Gloomy / Walk on the water / Born on the bayou / Bootleg / Graveyard train / Good golly miss molly / Penthouse pauper / Proud Mary / Keep on chooglin' / Green river / Commotion / Tombstone shadow / Wrote a song for everyone / Bad moon rising / Lodi / Sinister purpose / Night time is the right time / Down on the corner / It came out of the sky / Cotton fields / Poorboy shuffle / Feelin' blue / Don't look now / Midnight special / Side of the road / Effigy / Ramble tamble / Before you accuse me / Ooby dooby / Lookin' out my back door / Run through the jungle / Up around the bend / My baby left me / Who'll stop the rain / I heard it through the grapevine / Long as I can see the light / Pagan baby / Sailor's lament / Chameleon / Have you ever seen the rain / I wish I could hide away / Born to move / Hey tonight / It's just a thought / Molina / Rude awakening / Lookin' for a reason / Hello Mary Lou / Cross tie walker / Take it like a friend / Need someone to hold / Tearin' up the country / Someday never comes / What are you gonna do / Sail away / Door to door / Sweet Hitch-Hiker / Born on the bayou (live) / Green river (live) / Suzie Q (Live) / It came out of the sky (live) / Travellin' Band / Fortunate son / Commotion (live) / Lodi (live) / Bad moon rising (live) / Proud Mary (live) / Up around the bend (live) / Hey tonight (live) / Keep on chooglin' (live)
CD Set FCDCCR 10
Fantasy / Oct '92 / Jazz Music / Pinnacle / Wellard

CONCERT, THE
Born on the bayou / Green river / Tombstone shadow / Don't look now / Travellin' band / Who'll stop the rain / Bad moon rising / Proud Mary / Fortunate son / Commotion / Midnight special / Night time (is the right time) / Down on the corner / Keep on chooglin'
CD CDFE 511
Fantasy / Jul '89 / Jazz Music / Pinnacle / Wellard

COSMO'S FACTORY
Ramble tamble / Before you accuse me / Lookin' out my back door / Run through the jungle / Up around the bend / My baby left me / Who'll stop the rain / I heard it through the grapevine / Long as I can see the light / Travellin' band / Ooby dooby
CD CDFE 505
Fantasy / Aug '87 / Jazz Music / Pinnacle / Wellard

CREEDENCE CLEARWATER REVIVAL
I put a spell on you / Working man / Suzie Q / Ninety nine and a half (won't do) / Get down, woman / Porterville / Gloomy / Walk on the water
CD CDFE 501
Fantasy / Jul '87 / Jazz Music / Pinnacle / Wellard

CREEDENCE COUNTRY
Lookin' for a reason / Don't look now / Lodi / My baby left me / Hello Mary Lou / Ramble tamble / Cotton fields / Before you accuse me / Wrote a song for everyone / Ooby dooby / Cross tie walker / Lookin' out my back door
CD CDFE 518
Fantasy / Sep '92 / Jazz Music / Pinnacle / Wellard

CREEDENCE GOLD
Proud Mary / Down on the corner / Bad moon rising / I heard it through the grapevine / Midnight special / Have you ever seen the rain / Born on the Bayou / Suzie Q
CD CDFE 515
Fantasy / Aug '91 / Jazz Music / Pinnacle / Wellard

GREEN RIVER
Bad moon rising / Cross tie walker / Sinister purpose / Night time is the right time / Green River / Commotion / Tombstone Shadow / Wrote a song for everyone / Lodi
CD CDFE 503
Fantasy / '88 / Jazz Music / Pinnacle / Wellard

LIVE IN EUROPE
Born on the bayou / It came out of the sky / Fortunate son / Lodi / Proud Mary / Hey tonight / Green River / Suzie Q / Travellin' band / Commotion / Bad moon rising / Up around the bend / Keep on chooglin'
CD CDFE 514
Fantasy / Feb '90 / Jazz Music / Pinnacle / Wellard

MARDI GRAS
Lookin' for a reason / Take it like a friend / Need someone to hold / Tearin' up the country / Some day never comes / What are you gonna do / Sail away / Hello Mary Lou / Door to door / Sweet hitch hiker
CD CDFE 513
Fantasy / Aug '89 / Jazz Music / Pinnacle / Wellard

MORE CREEDENCE GOLD
Hey tonight / Run through the jungle / Fortunate son / Bootleg / Lookin' out my back door / Molina / Who'll stop the rain / Sweet hitch-hiker / Good golly Miss Molly / I put a spell on you / Don't look now / Lodi / Porterville / Up around the bend
CD CDFE 516
Fantasy / Aug '91 / Jazz Music / Pinnacle / Wellard

PENDULUM
Pagan baby / I wish I could hide away / It's just a thought / Rude awakening number two / Sailor's lament / Chameleon / Born to move / Hey tonight / Molina / Have you ever seen the rain
CD CDFE 512
Fantasy / Aug '89 / Jazz Music / Pinnacle / Wellard

WILLY AND THE POORBOYS
Down on the corner / It came out of the sky / Cotton fields / Poor boy shuffle / Feelin' blue / Fortunate son / Don't look now / Midnight special / Side of the road / Effigy
CD CDFE 504
Fantasy / Aug '87 / Jazz Music / Pinnacle / Wellard

Creedle

WHEN THE WIND BLOWS
CD HED 057
Headhunter / Oct '96 / Cargo

Creek

STORM THE GATE
Storm the gate / Foxy / I love / Passion / Fountain of youth / On my way / Rock me tonight / Girl is crying / Hanky panky / Climb / Bad light
CD CDMFN 102
Music For Nations / Jul '90 / Pinnacle

Creep

NO PAIN
CD SPCD 90262
Sub Pop / May '93 / Cargo / Greyhound / Shellshock/Disc

Creepmine

CHIAROSCURO
CD M 7015CD
Mascot / Oct '95 / Vital

Crematory

ILLUSIONS
CD MASSCD 080
Massacre / Oct '95 / Plastic Head

JUST DREAMING
CD MASSCD 031
Massacre / Jun '94 / Plastic Head

TRANSMIGRATION
CD MASSCD 016
Massacre / Nov '93 / Plastic Head

Crenshaw, Marshall

MIRACLE OF SCIENCE
CD GRACD 231
Grapevine / Jun '97 / Grapevine/PolyGram

Creolé Unit

LATITUDES 30
CD KAR 993
IMP / Apr '97 / ADA / Discovery

Crepillon, Pierre

DREUZ KRIEZ BREIZ (Crepillon, Pierre & L. Bigot)
CD KMCD 56
Keltia Musique / Jul '95 / ADA / Discovery

Crescent

ELECTRONIC SOUND CONSTRUCTIONS
CD CLK 001CD
Snap Shot / Jul '97 / Cadillac / New Note/ Pinnacle

Crescent City

ULTIMATE SESSION, THE
CD 72902103242
High Street / Feb '96 / BMG

Crescent City Maulers

SCREAMIN'
CD CCM 001
Pollytone / Oct '96 / Nervous / Pollytone

Cresent

NOW
CD PUNK 011CD
Planet / Dec '95 / SRD

Crests

BEST OF THE CRESTS, THE (Crests & Johnny Maestro)
Sixteen candles / Step by step / Trouble in Paradise / Angels listened in / Pretty little angel / Model girl / Six nights a week / I thank the moon / Journey of love / It must be love / Mr. Happiness / What a surprise / Gee (but I'd give the world) / Flower of love / Isn't it amazing / Year ago tonight / Young love / I'll remember in the still of the night
CD CDCHD 297
Ace / May '90 / Pinnacle

BEST OF THE REST, THE
Learning 'bout love / Molly Mae / IOU / I do / Keep away from Carol / Paper crown / Way you look tonight / Earth angel / Let me be the one / Beside you / Always you / Test of love / Six nights a week / Let true love begin / My special angel / Step by step / Say it isn't so / Isn't it amazing / Out in the cold again / Besame baby / Strangelove / Rose and a baby Ruth / If my heart could write a letter / We've got to tell them / Silhouettes / Angels listened in / You took the joy out of Spring / Dream maker / Warning voice
CD CDCHD 322
Ace / Apr '91 / Pinnacle

Crew Cuts

BEST OF THE CREW CUTS, THE (The Mercury Years)
Crazy 'bout ya baby / Sh-boom / I spoke too soon / Oop shoop / Do me good baby / Ko ko mo (I love you so) / Earth angel / Chop chop boom / This is my story / Two hearts, two kisses (make one love) / Don't be angry / Mostly Martha / Story untold / Angels in the sky / Gum drop / Seven days / Honey hair, sugar lips, eyes of blue / Out of the picture / Tell me why / Young love / Be my only love / I like it like that
CD 5527622
Spectrum / Feb '97 / PolyGram

Crickets

COLLECTION, THE/CALIFORNIA SUN - SHE LOVES YOU
La Bamba / All over you / Everybody's got a little problem / I think I've caught the blues / We gotta get together / Playboy / Lonely avenue / My little girl / Teardrops fall like rain / Right or wrong / You can't be in between / Don't try to change me / Lost and alone / I'm not a bad guy / I want to hold your hand / California sun / She loves you / Fool never learns / Slippin' and slidin' / I saw her standing there / Lonely avenue / Please please me / Money / From me to you / You can't be in between / Come on
CD BGOCD 251
Beat Goes On / Mar '95 / Pinnacle

ROCK 'N' ROLL MASTERS (Best of The Crickets)
My little girl / Teardrops fall like rain / Lost and alone / Little Hollywood girl / What'd I say / Right or wrong / Blue Monday / La Bamba / Lonely Avenue / Don't ever change / Willie and the hand jive / I think I've caught the blues / Summertime blues / Love is strange / I'm not a bad guy / Now hear this / Thoughtless / Slippin' and slidin' / Someday: *Crickets & Bobby Vee* / I believe in you
CD CZ 155
Liberty / Aug '89 / EMI

SOMETHING OLD, SOMETHING NEW
Willie and the hand jive / Don't ever change / Summertime blues / Searchin' / Little Hol-

lywood girl / Pretty blue eyes / What I'd say / Parisienne girl / Blue blue day / Love is strange / He's old enough to know better / Blue Monday / La bamba / Lonely adventure / Teardrops fall like rain / Thoughtless / My little girl / Playboy
CD ____ **BGOCD 242**
Beat Goes On / Sep '94 / Pinnacle

TOO MUCH MONDAY MORNING
As good as gone / Do you want to be loved: *Crickets & Nanci Griffith* / Picture this / Goin' out lovin' / Betty Sue's still breaking Jimmy Lee's heart / Letter of love / Say it isn't so / No kidding / (Get a little) closer / I gotta pass / Playing by the rules / Best in me / I had a dream / Too much Monday morning
CD ____ **3036000332**
Carlton / Mar '97 / Carlton

Crime & The City Solution

ADVERSARY - LIVE
CD ____ **CDSTUMM 110**
Mute / Sep '93 / RTM/Disc

BRIDE SHIP, THE
Shadow of no man / Stone / Keepsake / Free world / Greater head / Dangling man / Bride ship / New world
CD ____ **CDSTUMM 65**
Mute / Apr '89 / RTM/Disc

PARADISE DISCOTHEQUE
CD ____ **CDSTUMM 78**
Mute / Aug '90 / RTM/Disc

ROOM OF LIGHTS
CD ____ **CDSTUMM 36**
Mute / '88 / RTM/Disc

SHINE
All must be love / Fray so slow / Angel / On every train (grain will bear grain) / Hunter / Steal to the sea / Home is far from here / On every train (grain will bear grain)(12") / All must be love (early version)
CD ____ **CDSTUMM 59**
Mute / Apr '88 / RTM/Disc

Crime Boss

CONFLICTS AND CONFUSION (Crime Boss & The Fedz)
Intro / Conflicts and confusion / No friends / Chemical imbalance / Warning / Back to the streets / Life is crying / What does it mean (to be a real crime boss) / Close range / Please stop / Get up in your ass (skit) / Death notes / Get mine
CD ____ **4869032**
Epic / Jun '97 / Sony

Criminals

NEVER BEEN CAUGHT
CD ____ **LOOKOUT 170CD**
Lookout / May '97 / Cargo / Greyhound / Shellshock/Disc

Crimson Glory

CRIMSON GLORY
CD ____ **RR 349655**
Roadrunner / Dec '88 / PolyGram

TRANSCENDENCE
CD ____ **RR 9508 2**
Roadrunner / Nov '88 / PolyGram

Crimson Relic

PURGATORY'S REIGN
CD ____ **RAD 005CD**
Radiation / Apr '96 / Plastic Head

Criptanite

TALEZ FROM THE CRYPT
CD ____ **WRA 8130CD**
Wrap / May '94 / Koch

Crisis

NOUS SOMMES TOUS LES JUIFS ET DES ALLEMANDS
Holocaust / PC 1984 / No town hall / White youth / UK 78 / Brukwood Hospital / Alienation / Laughing afraid / Red brigades / On TV / Back in the USSR / Frustration kanada kommando / Militant / Kill kill kill
CD ____ **CR 16CD**
Crisis / Mar '97 / World Serpent

Crisis

8 CONVULSIONS
CD ____ **TOODAMNHY 72**
Too Damn Hype / Jan '95 / Cargo / SRD

DEATHSHED
CD ____ **398414108CD**
Metal Blade / Mar '96 / Pinnacle / Plastic Head

Crisis Children

I'D LIKE TO PAINT AN AEROPLANE
CD ____ **NEATCD 63**
Neat / Oct '92 / Pinnacle

ONE MORE TIME FOR THE STUPID PEOPLE
CD ____ **NEAT 1058CD**
Neat / May '96 / Pinnacle

Crisis NTI

ALIEN CONSPIRACY, THE
CD ____ **SPV 08461262**
SPV / Jun '96 / Koch / Plastic Head

Crisis Of Faith

LAND OF THE FREE
CD ____ **LF 059CD**
Lost & Found / Aug '93 / Plastic Head

Crisp, Rufus

CHICKENS ARE A-CROWING (Crisp, Rufus Experience)
In this ring two ladies fair / Betty Lickens / Green beds / Needle case / Omie Wise / Train on the island / June apple / Sherman's march / Fly around my pretty Miss / Sandy river belles / Cold rain and snow / Old grey mare / Chickens are a-crowing / Angeline the baker / I'm going to join the army / Sadie at the backdoor
CD ____ **FECD 113**
Fellside / Feb '97 / ADA / Direct / Target/BMG

Crispell, Marilyn

CASCADES (Crispell, Marilyn & Barry Guy/Gerry Hemingway)
CD ____ **CD 853**
Music & Arts / Jan '96 / Cadillac / Harmonia Mundi

CIRCLES
CD ____ **VICTOCD 012**
Victo / Nov '94 / Harmonia Mundi / ReR Megacorp

CRISPELL & HEMINGWAY (Crispell, Marilyn & Hemingway)
CD ____ **KFWCD 117**
Knitting Factory / Oct '92 / Cargo / Plastic Head

GAIA (Crispell, Marilyn/Reggie Workman/Doug James)
CD ____ **CDLR 152**
Leo / Feb '89 / Cadillac / Impetus / Wellard

HIGHLIGHTS FROM THE 1992 AMERICAN TOUR (Crispell, Marilyn Trio)
CD ____ **CD 758**
Music & Arts / Apr '93 / Cadillac / Harmonia Mundi

HYPERION (Crispell, Marilyn & Peter Brotzmann/Hamid Drake)
CD ____ **CD 852**
Music & Arts / Dec '95 / Cadillac / Harmonia Mundi

INFERENCE (Crispell, Marilyn & Tim Berne)
CD ____ **CD 851**
Music & Arts / Dec '95 / Cadillac / Harmonia Mundi

LABYRINTHS
CD ____ **VICTOCD 06**
Victo / Nov '94 / Harmonia Mundi / ReR Megacorp

LIVE IN BERLIN
CD ____ **1200692**
Black Saint / Nov '93 / Cadillac / Harmonia Mundi

LIVE IN ZURICH (Crispell, Marilyn Trio)
CD ____ **CDLR 122**
Leo / '90 / Cadillac / Impetus / Wellard

NOTHING EVER WAS ANYWAY (2CD Set) (Crispell, Marilyn & Gary Peacock/ Paul Motian)
Nothing ever was anyway / Butterflies that I feel inside of me / Open to love / Cartoon / Albert's love theme / Dreams (if time weren't) / Touching / Both / You've left me / Miracles / Ending / Blood
CD Set ____ **5372222**
ECM / Sep '97 / New Note/Pinnacle

OVERLAPPING HANDS (Crispell, Marilyn & Irene Schweizer)
CD ____ **FMPCD 30**
FMP / Aug '87 / Cadillac

SANTUERIO
CD ____ **CDLR 191**
Leo / Feb '94 / Cadillac / Impetus / Wellard

Criss, Sonny

OUT OF NOWHERE
All the things you are / Dreamer / El tiante / My ideal / Out of nowhere / Brother can you spare a dime / First one
CD ____ **MCD 5089**
Muse / Sep '92 / New Note/Pinnacle

THIS IS CRISS
CD ____ **OJCCD 430**
Original Jazz Classics / Nov '95 / Complete/Pinnacle / Jazz Music / Wellard

Critchinson, John

FIRST MOVES (Critchinson, John & Art Themen Quartet)
CD ____ **JHCD 052**
Ronnie Scott's Jazz House / Feb '97 / Cadillac / Jazz Music / New Note/Pinnacle / TKO Magnum

Critics

BRAINTREE
CD ____ **BV 160952**
Black Vinyl / Nov '96 / Cargo

Crivits

DRIVE
Drive
CD ____ **LF 068**
Lost & Found / Jan '94 / Plastic Head

STARE
CD ____ **LF 148CD**
Lost & Found / May '95 / Plastic Head

Cro Magnon

BULL
CD ____ **LOW 008**
Lowlands / Jun '97 / Greyhound / ReR Megacorp / SRD

Cro-Mags

ALPHA OMEGA
CD ____ **CM 9730CD**
Century Media / Jun '92 / Plastic Head

HARD TIMES IN AN AGE OF QUARREL
CD ____ **CM 770722**
Century Media / Jun '94 / Plastic Head

NEAR DEATH EXPERIENCE
CD ____ **CM 770502**
Century Media / Sep '93 / Plastic Head

Croce, A.J.

THAT'S ME IN THE BAR
That's me in the bar / Pass me by / Checkin' in / Music box / Some people call it love / I mean what I said / Night out on the town / Callin' home / I confess / Sign on the line / Maybe I'm to blame / Digin' a hole / She's waiting for me / I meant what I said
CD ____ **01005821272**
Private Music / Jul '95 / BMG

Croce, Jim

50TH ANNIVERSARY
Spin, spin, spin / Vespers / Big wheel / Searchin' / He don't love you / Chain gang / Chain gang medley / Hey tomorrow / Long time ago / Cigarettes, whiskey and wild, wild women / (And) I remember her / Cottom mouth river / More than that tomorrow / Migrant worker / Child of midnight / Stone walls / King's song / Mississipi lady / Which way are you goin' / Rapid Roy (the stcok car boy) / You don't mess around with Jim / Tomorrow's gonna be a brighter day / New York's not my home / Hard times losin' man / Photographs and memories / Walkin' back to Georgia / Operator (That's not the way it feels) / Time in a bottle / Box (10)
CD Set ____ **ESDCD 188**
Essential / Dec '92 / BMG

BAD BOY LEROY BROWN (The Definitive Collection/2CD Set)
You don't mess around with Jim / Photographs amd memories / New York's not my home / Operator (that's not the way it feels) / Time in a bottle / Rapid Roy (the stock car boy) / Hey tomorrow / One less set of footsteps / Roller derby queen / Alabama rain / Bad, bad Leroy Brown / These dreams / Speedball tucker / It doesn't have to be that way / I got a name / Lover's cross / Working at the car wash blues / I'll have to say I love you in a song / Salon and saloon / Chain gang medley / Spin, spin, spin / Tomorrow's gonna be a bright new day / Hard time losin' man / Walkin' back to Georgia / Box 10 / Long time ago / Dreamin' again / Careful man / Good time man like me ain't got no business (singing the blu / Next time, this time / Five short minutes / Ages / Thursday / Top hat bar and grill / Recently / Hard way / Every time / Ol' man river / Which way are you goin' / Mississippi lady
CD Set ____ **SMDCD 102**
Snapper / May '97 / Pinnacle

BEST OF JIM CROCE, THE
I got a name / Bad, bad, Leroy Brown / Operator (that's not the way it feels) / You don't mess around with Jim / One less set of footsteps / Time ina bottle / Workin' at the car wash blues / Lover's cross / New York's not my home / I'll have to say I love you in a song / Chain gang medley / Rapid Roy (The stock car boy) / Photographs and memories / These dreams / Box no.10 / Age / Dreamin' again / Speedball tucker / It doesn't have to be that way
CD ____ **MCCD 295**
Music Club / May '97 / Disc / THE

BOMBS OVER PUERTO RICO (Croce, Jim & Ingrid)
Age / Spin, spin, spin / I am who I am / What do people do / Another day, another town / Vespers / Big wheel / Just another day / Next man that I marry / What the hell / Man that is me
CD ____ **BCD 15894**
Bear Family / May '96 / Direct / Rollercoaster / Swift

COLLECTION, THE
Time in a bottle / Operator (that's not the way it feels) / Salon Saloon / Alabama rain / Dreamin' again / It doesn't have to be that way / I'll have to say I love you in a song / Lover's cross / Thursday / These dreams / Long time ago / Photographs and memories
CD ____ **CCSCD 154**
Castle / Jan '86 / BMG

DOWN THE HIGHWAY
I got a name / Mississippi lady / New York's not my home / Chain gang medley / Chain gang / He don't love you / Searchin' / You don't mess around with Jim / Ol' man river / Which way are you going / Bad, Bad Leroy Brown / Walkin' back to Georgia / Box no.10 / Speedball Tucker / Alabama rain
CD ____ **CLACD 118**
Castle / '88 / BMG

FINAL TOUR, THE
Operator (that's not the way it feels) / Roller derby queen dialogue / Roller derby queen / Next time,this time / Trucker dialogue / Speedball trucker / New York's not my home / Hard time losin' man / Ball of Kerrymuir dialogue / Ball of Kerrymuir / You don't mess around with Jim / It doesn't have to be that way / Careful man dialogue / Careful man / Shopping for clothes / These dreams
CD ____ **CLACD 341**
Castle / Jun '94 / BMG

LEGEND OF JIM CROCE, THE
CD ____ **RR 34 9841**
Roadrunner / '88 / PolyGram

PHOTOGRAPHS AND MEMORIES (His Greatest Hits)
Bad, Bad Leroy Brown / Operator (that's not the way it feels) / Photographs and memories / Rapid Roy (The stock car boy) / Time in a bottle / New York's not my home / Workin' at the car wash blues / I got a name / I'll have to say I love you in a song / You don't mess around with Jim / Lover's cross / One less set of footsteps / These dreams / Roller Derby Queen
CD ____ **CLACD 119**
Castle / Jun '88 / BMG

SIMPLY THE BEST
CD ____ **WMCD 5703**
Disky / Oct '94 / Disky / THE

TIME IN A BOTTLE
Time in a bottle / Operator (that's not the way it feels) / Salon and saloon / Alabama rain / Dreamin' again / It doesn't have to be that way / I'll have to say I love you in a song / Lover's cross / Thursday / These dreams / Long time ago / Photographs and memories
CD ____ **CLACD 117**
Castle / Nov '86 / BMG

Crocker, Barry

EMOTIONS
CD ____ **HADCD 192**
Javelin / Nov '95 / Henry Hadaway / THE

Crocker, John

ALL OF ME
Smiles / Don't blame me / My gal Sal / I love you / All of me / Between the devil and the deep blue sea / Tangerine / Poor butterfly / She's funny that way / Exactly like you / Stealin' apples
CD ____ **CDTTD 585**
Timeless Traditional / May '94 / Jazz Music / New Note/Pinnacle

EASY LIVING (Crocker, John Quartet)
Avalon / I can't get started (with you) / Oh lady be good / Shine / Fine time / I hadn't anyone till you / Have you met Miss Jones / Easy living / Rose room / After you've gone
CD ____ **CDTTD 561**
Timeless Traditional / Aug '91 / Jazz Music / New Note/Pinnacle

Crockett, Valerie

UNBUTTON YOUR HEART (Crockett, Valerie & Walter)
Unbutton your heart / On the road to Cleveland / Starlight / Apron of care / My heartache, my heartache / As I fall in love with you / Southbound trucker / Tell me now / Don't make her afraid / Nobody / I never thought about it / Computer song / I said goodbye
CD ____ **DARINGCD 3030**
Daring / Feb '97 / ADA / CM / Direct

Crofts, Jamie

CUTTING EDGE, THE (50 Years Of British Fashion 1947-1997)
Romantic style / Tailoring traditions / Country fashion / Bohemian fashion
CD ____ **PCOM 1147**
President / Mar '97 / Grapevine/PolyGram / President / Target/BMG

Croker, Brendan

REDNECK STATE OF THE ART
CD ____ WFRCD 004
World Famous / Oct '95 / Grapevine/ PolyGram

Crombie, Tony

ATMOSPHERE (Crombie, Tony & His Rockets)
Beryl's bounce / Ninth man / St. James Infirmary / Invitation / Stompin' at the Savoy / Duke's joke / Panic stations / I'll close my eyes / Small talk / Perpetual lover / Shapes / Copy cats
CD ____ CDREN 002
Renaissance / Jul '89 / Jazz Music / Wellard

SWEET, WILD AND BLUE
Cocktails for two / Wrap your troubles in dreams (and dream your troubles away) / So near, so far / I've got the world on a string / Embraceable you / Tulip or turnip / To each his own / Tender trap / Hold my hand / All the way / It's magic / High and mighty / So rare / Percussion staccato / I should care / For you alone / Summertime / You are my lucky star
CD ____ CDREN 003
Renaissance / '89 / Jazz Music / Wellard

TONY CROMBIE AND FRIENDS
Tango '89 / Sophisticated lady / Moonglow / Twelve note samba / Raising the temperature / Fallen bird / I don't stand a ghost of a chance with you / Serenade in blue / Alison Adamant / Autumn rustle / Prelude to a kiss / So near, so far / Rabbit pie / Child of fancy / Viva Rodriguez
CD ____ CDREN 001
Renaissance / Jul '89 / Jazz Music / Wellard

Cromwell, Rodney

LET THE PICTURE PAINT ITSELF
Let the picture paint itself / Give my heart a rest / Stuff that works / Big heart / Loving you makes me strong / Best years of our lives / I don't fall in love so easy / That ol'door / Rose of Memphis / Once in a while
CD ____ MCD 11042
MCA / Aug '94 / BMG

Cronos

DANCIN' IN THE FIRE
CD ____ NEAT 1048
Neat / May '96 / Pinnacle

ROCK 'N' ROLL DISEASE
Message of war / Rock 'n' roll disease / Midnight eye / Lost and found / Love is infectious / Sexploitation / Super power / Aphrodisiac / Sweet savage sex / Bared to the bone / Dirty tricks dept.
CD ____ NEATCD 1051
Neat / Jan '96 / Pinnacle

VENOM
CD ____ NM 003CD
Neat Metal / Nov '95 / Pinnacle

Cronos Train

BRIDES OF CHRIST
CD ____ TATCD 23
Tatra / Aug '95 / Plastic Head

Cronshaw, Andrew

ANDREW CRONSHAW CD, THE
Voice of silence / Wexford carol / Andro and his cutty gun / Galician processional / Harry Bloodgood's famous jig/American Boot dance / Blacksmith / Fingal's cave / Yowe came to our door / Ships in distress/St Kilda rowing song/Go to sea no more / Pandeirada de entrimo/Gentle dark eyed Mary / Empty places / Dark haired youth/Taladh ar slanair / Freumh as craobh taigh challadair / Wasps in the woodpile / Turning the tide / Seana Mheallan / Giullan nam bo / Ho ho nighean donn/First of May/Prince of Wale's jig / Saratoga hornpipe / Old highland air
CD ____ TSCD 447
Topic / Sep '89 / ADA / CM / Direct

LANGUAGE OF SNAKES, THE
CD ____ SPDCD 1050
Special Delivery / Sep '93 / ADA / CM / Direct

Crooked Jack

AUDIENCE WITH CROOKED JACK & BILLY MCGUIRE, AN (A Night In A Scottish Pub) (Crooked Jack & Billy McGuire)
Bonnie lass o'Tyvie / Barnyards of Dalgety / It's good to see you / Alan McPherson of Mosspark / Auld fiddler / Massacre of Glencoe / Continental Ceili / Sook blaw / Crooked Jack / Mary Mack / Heart song / John McMillan meets the Cajuns / When I'm 64 / Don't call me early in the morning / Red rose cafe / I'm my own Grandpa / Royal Scots Polka / Fairy dance / Piper O'Dundee / A the wae fae Dysart / Love is teasing / Pheasant plucker / Rolling home / Atholl Highlanders / Mrs. McLeod's reel
CD ____ CDLOC 1098
Lochshore / Nov '96 / ADA / Direct / Duncans

TOMORROW MUST WAIT
Rambling rover / Hermless / Magie cockabendie / Jigs and reels / Belfast mill / Working man / Auchtertool / Loch tay boat song / New teacher / March, strathspey and reel / Come by the hills / In search of you
CD ____ LCOM 5224CD
Lismor / Jan '94 / ADA / Direct / Duncans / Lismor

Crooklyn Dub Consortium

CERTIFIED DOPE VOL.1
CD ____ WSCD 003
Word Sound Recordings / Nov '95 / Cargo / SRD

CERTIFIED DOPE VOL.2
CD ____ WSCD 012
Word Sound Recordings / Feb '97 / Cargo / SRD

Crooks

LIVE IN NOVOSIBIRSK
CD ____ PAN 151CD
Pan / Mar '95 / ADA / CM / Direct

Crooks, Richard

ALL OF MY HEART
All of my heart / My song goes round the world / Ah' fuyez / Douce image / Mother o' mine / Thora / E Lucevan le stelle / Ah / Moon of my delight / Neapolitan love song (t'amo) / Il mio tesoro / Until una furtive lagrima / Little love / Little kiss (Un peu d'amour) / Preislied / Songs my mother taught me / Nirvana / O song divine
CD ____ CDHD 167
Happy Days / Oct '89 / Conifer/BMG

FOR YOU ALONE
CD ____ CDMOIR 431
Memoir / Oct '95 / Jazz Music / Target/ BMG

Cropdusters

IF THE SOBER GO TO HEAVEN
CD ____ DOJOCD 202
Dojo / Nov '94 / Disc

Cropper, Steve

WITH A LITTLE HELP FROM MY FRIENDS
Crop dustin' / Land of 1000 dances / ninety nine and a half (won't do) / Boogaloo down Broadway / Funky Broadway / With a little help from my friends / Oh pretty woman / I'd rather drink muddy water / Way I feel tonight / In the midnight hour / Rattlesnake
CD ____ CDSXE 008
Stax / Aug '92 / Pinnacle

Crosby, Bing

20 GOLDEN GREATS: BING CROSBY
Swinging on a star / Gone fishin' / White Christmas / You are my sunshine / Moonlight bay / Pennies from Heaven / MacNamara's band
CD ____ MCLD 19218
MCA / Jan '95 / BMG

50TH ANNIVERSARY CONCERT AT THE LONDON PALLADIUM
Where the blue of the night meets the gold of the day / Pleasure of your company / Mary Lou / Where the morning glories grow / At my time of life / On a slow boat to China / By myself / Tenderly / 50 ways to leave your lover / Send in the clowns / Gone fishin': *Crosby, Bing & Ted Rogers* / Now you has jazz / Man that got away/Hallelujah / Great day / Just one of those things / I surrender, dear / Swinging on a star / Wrap your troubles in dreams / True love / Don't fence me in / Pennies from heaven / Blue Hawaii / Sweet Leilani / Too-ra-loo-ra-loo-ra that's an Irish lullaby / Just one more chance / Them there eyes / Moonlight becomes you / You are my sunshine / I'll be seeing you / White cliffs of Dover / When the lights go on again all over the world / Accentuate the positive / Please / Baby face / South of the border / Galway boy / Dinah / San Fernando valley / I found a million dollar baby / San Antonio rose / I'm an old cowhand / In a little Spanish town / Wait till the sun shines, Nellie: *Crosby, Bing & Kathryn* / Easy to remember / Blue skies / It's been a long, long time / Mississippi mud / Ol' man river / That's what life is all about / Where the blue of the night meets the gold of the day
CD ____ CDMFP 6389
Music For Pleasure / Jun '97 / EMI

ALL THE CLOUDS WILL ROLL AWAY (Crosby, Bing & Judy Garland/Andrews Sisters)
CD ____ JSPCD 702
JSP / May '93 / ADA / Cadillac / Direct / Hot Shot / Target/BMG

ANYTHING GOES
CD ____ PDSCD 532
Pulse / Aug '96 / BMG

BEST OF BING CROSBY, THE
CD ____ ENTCD 248
Entertainers / Mar '92 / Target/BMG

BEST OF BING CROSBY, THE (2CD Set)
Swinging on a star / Alexander's ragtime band / Moonlight becomes you / Gone fishin' / Busy doing nothing / So would I / Friend of yours / Gigi / I've never been in love before / Among my souvenirs / Weaver of dreams / Where the blue of the night meets the gold of the day / I whistle a happy tune / Wrap your troubles in dreams / Dear hearts and gentle people / Very though of you / Sweet leilani / Give me the simple life / San Antonio rose / Spaniard that blighted my life / People will say we're in love / Follk's that live on the hill / Sentimental music / Moonlight on a white picket fence / Blue skies / Anything you can do / Embraceable you / Fella with an umbrella / McNamara's band / Now is the hour / Getting to know you / Galway bay / Don't fence me in / Just one of those things / Sam's song / Like someone in love / Stardust / In the cool cool cool of evening / Too ra loo ra loo ra / Oh, what a beautiful morning / Pennies from heaven / Play a simple melody / Things we did last summer / Just for you / I can't begin to tell you / Marrying for love / Nightingale sang in Berkeley Square / Silent night, holy night / Deck the halls/ away in a manger/I saw three ships / White Christmas
CD Set ____ MCD 11561
MCA / Nov '96 / BMG

BING CROSBY
Beautiful dreamer / Darling Nellie Gray / Ah sweet mystery of life / Deep purple / Sweethearts / Where the blue of the night meets the gold of the day / Pennies from heaven / Out of nowhere / How deep is the ocean / Street of dreams / Brother can you spare a dime / Ghost of chance / Please / Dancing in the dark / Stardust / I found a million dollar baby / Goodnight sweetheart / White Christmas
CD ____ BSTCD 9114
Best Compact Discs / Apr '94 / Complete/ Pinnacle

BING CROSBY & FRIENDS
Gone fishin' / Couple of song and dance men / Swinging on a star / Pennies from heaven / Zing a little zong / You are my sunshine / Moonlight bay / In the cool, cool, cool of the evening / Where the blue of the night meets the gold of the day / Anything you can do / White Christmas / Road to Bali / Spaniard that blighted my life / Whiffenpoof song / Life is so peculiar / MacNamara's band / Too ra loo ra loo ra / Moon came up with a great idea / Mr. Gallagher and Mr. Shean / Connecticut
CD ____ MCCD 089
Music Club / Nov '92 / Disc / THE

BING CROSBY 1926-1932
Pretty lips / Muddy water / I'm coming Virginia / Mississippi mud/I left my sugar standing in the rain / Changes / Mary / Ol' man river / Make believe / From Monday on / Lovable / Louisiana / You took advantage of me / T'ain't so honey, t'ain't so / Susianna / Spell of the blues / Let's do it / My kinda love / So the bluebirds and the blackbirds got together / If I had a talking picture of you / Happy feet / Three little words / One more time / Dinah / St. Louis blues
CD ____ CBC 1004
Timeless Historical / Jan '92 / New Note/ Pinnacle

BING CROSBY COLLECTION, THE
(There'll be bluebirds over) The white cliffs of Dover / Yankee doodle dandy / I don't want to walk without you baby / You'd be so nice to come home to / As time goes by / I'll be seeing you / Bless 'em all / I'll get by (as long as I have you) / Basin Street blues / You belong to my heart / Swingin' on a star / Temptation / Too marvellous for words / June in January / I'm an old cowhand (from the Rio Grande) / Pennies from heaven / Mr. Gallagher & Mr. Shean / You must have been a beautiful baby / Sunday, Monday or always / Sierra Sue / Deep in the heart of Texas / Long ago (and far away)
CD ____ PAR 2067
Parade / Sep '96 / Disc

BING CROSBY/NAT KING COLE ESSENTIALS (Crosby, Bing & Nat 'King' Cole)
CD ____ LECDD 641
Wisepack / Aug '95 / Conifer/BMG / THE

BING SINGS BERLIN, RODGERS AND HART
Soft lights and sweet music / On a roof in Manhattan / How deep is the ocean / I'm playing with fire / Soon / Down by the river / It's easy to remember / Alexander's ragtime band / Now it can be told / When I lost you / God bless America / Bombardier song / Angels of mercy / I'll capture your heart / Lazy / Happy holiday / Let's start the New Year right / Abraham / Be careful it's my heart / Easter Parade / Song of freedom / I've got plenty to be thankful for / White Christmas
CD ____ CDHD 232
Happy Days / Feb '97 / Conifer/BMG

BING SWINGS WITH JOHN SCOTT TROTTER ORCHESTRA (Crosby, Bing & John Scott Trotter Orchestra)
Painting the clouds with sunshine / Shanghai / Oh lady be good / Everywhere you go / So tired / Easter parade / Bali Ha'i / Lazybones
CD ____ DAWE 48
Magic / Nov '93 / Cadillac / Harmonia Mundi / Jazz Music / Swift / Wellard

BING'S BUDDIES (1951 Crosby & Guests)
Bright eyes / Painting the clouds with sunshine / Sweet violets / Wang wang blues / Domino / I only have eyes for you / Buttermilk sky
CD ____ DAWE 41
Magic / Sep '93 / Cadillac / Harmonia Mundi / Jazz Music / Swift / Wellard

BLUE OF THE NIGHT, THE
Where the blue of the night meets the gold of the day / Sweet and lovely / Dinah / Shine / Sweet georgia Brown / Cabin in the cotton / Some of these days / You're beautiful tonight my dear / You're getting to be a habit with me / You've got me crying again / Temptation / May I / June in January / With every breath I take / I'm an old cowhand (from the Rio Grande) / Mr. Gallagher and Mr. Shean / You must have been a beautiful baby
CD ____ MSCD 12
Music De-Luxe / '90 / TKO Magnum

BLUE SKIES
Waiting for the evening mail / I wish you love / Chances are / Where or when / What is there to say / Sunday / They didn't believe me / This can't be love / I can't get started (with you) / I guess I'll have to change my plan / Try a little tenderness / What is this thing called love / Mandy / My ideal / Don't take your love from me / Tender trap / Love is just around the corner / Crazy rhythm / I've grown accustomed to her face / Come rain or come shine / She's funny that way / We're in the money / Little man you've had a busy day / At sundown
CD ____ TRTCD 151
TrueTrax / Dec '94 / THE

CHRISTMAS SONGS (Wartime Christmas Broadcasts)
CD ____ VJC 1017 2
Vintage Jazz Classics / Oct '91 / ADA / Cadillac / CM / Direct

CHRISTMAS WITH BING CROSBY
CD ____ MCCDX 002
Music Club / Nov '93 / Disc / THE

COLLECTION, THE
CD ____ COL 009
Collection / Jan '95 / Target/BMG

EP COLLECTION, THE
Road to Morocco / That's a plenty / Moments to remember / Suddenly there's a valley / Oh loneliness of evening / Sailing down the Chesapeake Bay / Sing soft, sing sweet, sing gentle / Me and the moon / Got the moon in my pocket / Young at heart / Mademoiselle de Paris / Morgen / Domenica / It had to be you / Something in common / Look at your heart / Possibility's there / Longest walk / Sweetheart waltz / Moon was yellow / Pale moon / Chicago style / Oh baby mine I get so lonely / La mer / Under Paris skies / White Christmas / Road to Morocco: *Crosby, Bing & Bob Hope*
CD ____ SEECD 360
See For Miles/C5 / Aug '97 / Pinnacle

ESSENTIAL COLLECTION, THE
CD Set ____ LECD 612
Wisepack / Apr '95 / Conifer/BMG / THE

EVERYTHING I HAVE IS YOURS
Blacksmith blues / Come what may / I dreamt I dwelt in Marble Hall / Glow worm / Feet up / Pittsburgh, Pennsylvania / Please Mr. Sun / Cockeyed optimist / When the red roses grow / Girl in the bonnet of blue / Everything I have is yours / Thousand violins / Dark moon / Now that I need you / Maybe it's because / When the midnight choo choo leaves for Alabam' / If I had my way / Blues my naughty sweetie gives to me / Down yonder / Lady of Spain / Zip a dee doo dah / PS I love you / If this isn't love / Ole buttermilk sky / Great day / I git the sun in the morning / It's a good day / You go to my head / Old lamp lighter
CD ____ GRF 016
Tring / '93 / Tring

EVERYTHING I HAVE IS YOURS
Blacksmith blues / Come what may / Glow worm / Feet up / Pitsburgh pennsylvania / Please Mr. Sun / Cockeyed optimist / Everything I have is yours / Thousand violins / Dark moon (come out from the clouds above) / Now that I need you / Maybe it's because / Blues my naughty sweetie gives to me / Down yonder / Lady of spain / Zip a dee doo dah / Ps I love you / If this isn't love / Ole buttermilk sky / Great day / I got the sun in the morning / It's a good day / You go to my head / Old lamplighter
CD ____ QED 111
Tring / Nov '96 / Tring

GREAT MOMENTS WITH BING CROSBY (2CD Set)
Theme from Where the blue of the night meets the cold of the / Don't fence me in / Moonlight becomes you / Accentuate the positive: *Crosby, Bing & The Charioteers* / Philco advertisement: *Crosby, Bing & The Charioteers* / Moonlight bay: *Crosby, Bing & The Charioteers* / Hut song: *Crosby, Bing*

& Connie Boswell / Sleigh ride in July: Crosby, Bing & Connie Boswell / It makes no difference now / Amor / Maybe you'll be there: Crosby, Bing & Peggy Lee / Sentimental journey: Crosby, Bing & The Charioteers / Where the blue of the night meets the gold of the day: Crosby, Bing & The Charioteers / Way you look tonight: Crosby, Bing & Trudy Erwin / Please / Lazy bones: Crosby, Bing & Louis Armstrong / It's always you / Ghost riders in the sky / Remember me / Connecticut: Crosby, Bing & Judy Garland / Home on the range: Crosby, Bing & Judy Garland / If I had my way: Crosby, Bing & The Charioteers / You don't have to know the language: Crosby, Bing & The Rhythmaires / I'm always chasing rainbows: Crosby, Bing & Eddy Duchin / Night train to Memphis: Crosby, Bing & The Charioteers / People will say we're in love: Crosby, Bing & Trudy Erwin / More and more / White Christmas: Crosby, Bing & The Charioteers/Music Maids/Trudy Erwin / Pistol packin' mama: Crosby, Bing & The Charioteers / Oh what a beautiful mornin': Crosby, Bing & Trudy Erwin / Deep in the heart of Texas: Crosby, Bing & The Music Maids / Poinciana / Thank your lucky stars: Crosby, Bing & The Music Maids / All my love (bolero): Crosby, Bing & The Music Maids / Manhattan: Crosby, Bing & Connie Boswell / Now is the hour / I've got a crush on you: Crosby, Bing & Peggy Lee / Easter parade: Crosby, Bing & Jeannie Durelle / War bonds message: Crosby, Bing & Jeannie Durelle / I used to love you but it's all over now: Crosby, Bing & Jeannie Durelle / You've got me where you want me: Crosby, Bing & Eugenie Baird / Medley from Missisippi / Some enchanted evening / Between 18th and 19th on Chestnut Street: Crosby, Bing & Connie Boswell / Loch Lomond: Crosby, Bing & The Music Maids / Put it there pal: Crosby, Bing & Bob Hope / Whistle while you work / As time goes by / Maybe it's because: Crosby, Bing & Judy Garland / It's only a paper moon / Kraft advertisement / Marie Elena / I'll be home for Christmas: Crosby, Bing & The Charioteers/Music Maid / Mona Lisa: Crosby, Bing & The Charioteers/Music Maid / Goodnight Irene: Crosby, Bing & Bob Hope/Judy Garland
CD Set ____ OTA 101978
On The Air / Jun '97 / Target/BMG

GREAT YEARS, THE
Deep in the heart of Texas / White Christmas / Wait till the sun shines Nellie / Moonlight becomes you / Road to Morocco / You are my sunshine / Walking the floor over you / Yes indeed / Mr. Meadowlark / Where the blue of the night meets the gold of the day / Let's all meet at my house / Do you ever think of me / Between a kiss and a sigh / When day is done / Be honest with me / Sing me a song of the Islands / Tea for two / Tumbling tumbleweeds / Miss you / Along the Santa Fe trail / Start the day right / I want my Mama
CD ____ PASTCD 7027
Flapper / Nov '93 / Pinnacle

HERE LIES LOVE (A Selection of Love Songs)
Very thought of you / Love thy neighbour / June in January / You've got me crying again / May I / With every breath I take / Temptation / Let me call you sweetheart / Sweet and lovely / Love in bloom / You're getting to be a habit with me / I love you truly / Someday, sweetheart / You're beautiful tonight my dear / Love is just around the corner / Just a wearyin' for you / It must be true / Here lies love
CD ____ CDAJA 5043
Living Era / Sep '90 / Select

HEY, LOOK US OVER (Crosby, Bing & Rosemary Clooney)
Introduction / Isn't it a lovely day / Anything you can do / They say it's wonderful / Ain't we got fun / Let's take a walk around the block / Summertime / Let's call the whole thing off / People will say we're in love / Lover / Hey look me over / Let's put out the lights / They can't take that away from me / Everytime I see you I'm in love again / Paris medley
CD ____ JASCD 318
Jasmine / Nov '93 / Conifer/BMG / Hot Shot / TKO Magnum

HOLIDAY INN (Crosby, Bing & Fred Astaire)
CD ____ VJC 1012 2
Vintage Jazz Classics / Oct '91 / ADA / Cadillac / CM / Direct

HOLLYWOOD GUYS AND DOLLS VOL.1
CD ____ PARCD 005
Parrot / Dec '94 / BMG / Jazz Music / THE / Wellard

HOLLYWOOD GUYS AND DOLLS VOL.2
CD ____ PARCD 006
Parrot / Dec '94 / BMG / Jazz Music / THE / Wellard

I'M AN OLD COWHAND
Don't fence me in: Crosby, Bing & Andrews Sisters/Vic Schoen Orchestra / Home on the range: Crosby, Bing & Lennie Hayton Orchestra / I'm an old cowhand (from the Rio Grande): Crosby, Bing & Jimmy Dorsey Orchestra / Take me back to my boots and saddle: Crosby, Bing & Victor Young Orchestra / Silver on the sage: Crosby, Bing & John Scott Trotter Orchestra / When the bloom is on the sage: Crosby, Bing & Foursome/John Scott Trotter Five / Tumbling tumbleweeds: Crosby, Bing & John Scott Trotter Orchestra / After sundown: Crosby, Bing & Lennie Hayton Orchestra / El rancho grande: Crosby, Bing & Foursome/John Scott Trotter Orchestra / Singing hills: Crosby, Bing & John Scott Trotter Orchestra / Along the Sante Fe trail: Crosby, Bing & John Scott Trotter Orchestra / Clementine: Crosby, Bing & Music Maids/Hal Hoppe/ John Scott Trotter / San Antonio rose: Crosby, Bing & Bob Crosby Orchestra / Deep in the heart of Texas: Crosby, Bing & Woody Herman/Woodchoppers / Who calls: Crosby, Bing & John Scott Trotter Orchestra / Pistol packin' Mama: Crosby, Bing & Andrews Sisters/Vic Schoen Orchestra / Ridin' down the canyon: Crosby, Bing & Victor Young Orchestra / San Fernando valley: Crosby, Bing & John Scott Trotter Orchestra / Empty saddles (In the old corral): Crosby, Bing & Victor Young Orchestra / Round up lullaby: Crosby, Bing & Victor Young Orchestra / Old oaken bucket: Crosby, Bing & Music Maids/Hal Hoppe/ John Scott Trotter / We'll rest at the end of the trail: Crosby, Bing & Victor Young Orchestra / Twilight on the trail: Crosby, Bing & Victor Young Orchestra / Goodbye little darlin' goodbye: Crosby, Bing & John Scott Trotter Eight / Last round-up: Crosby, Bing & Lennie Hayton Orchestra
CD ____ CDAJA 5160
Living Era / Apr '96 / Select

IMMORTAL BING CROSBY
CD ____ AVC 535
Avid / May '94 / Avid/BMG / Koch / THE

JAZZIN' BING CROSBY 1927-1940, THE (2CD Set)
I'm coming Virginia / Side by side / Mississippi mud / I left my sugar standing in the rain (and she melted away) / Mary / There ain't no sweet man that's worth the salt of my tears / From Monday on / High water / Louisiana / T'ain't so honey, t'ain't so / Because my baby don't mean maybe now / Rhythm king / I'm crazy over you / Susianna / If I had you / Spell of the blues / Let's do it / My kinda love / So the bluebirds and the blackbirds got together / Oh Miss Hannah / Waiting at the end of the road / After you've gone / One more time / I'm sorry dear / Dinah / St. Louis blues / Shine / Shadows on the window / Cabin in the cotton e / How deep is the ocean / Sweet Sue, just you / My honey's lovin' arms / Somebody stole Gabriel's horn / Stay on the right side of the road / Blue prelude / I'm hummin', I'm whistlin', I'm singin' / Someday sweetheart / Moonburn / Pennies from heaven / Don't be that way / Mr. Gallagher and Mr. Shean / You must have been a beautiful baby / Yodelin' jive / Rhythm on the river / Yes indeed
CD Set ____ CDAFS 10212
Affinity / Jun '93 / Cadillac / Jazz Music / Koch

JUST BREEZIN' ALONG
Breezin' along with the breeze / How are things in Glocca Morra / Heatwave / Best things in life are free / My heart stood still / I got rhythm / Good old times / Cabaret / Send in the clowns / Only way to go / Have a nice day / Some sunny day / At my time of life / With a song in my heart / Razzle dazzle / That's what life is all about
CD ____ CZ 5
EMI / Oct '87 / EMI

KING OF THE CROONERS
Dinah / Temptation / Please / I've got the world on a string / Pennies from heaven / How deep is the ocean / Blue Hawaii / Thanks / Did you ever see a dream walking / I'm an old cowhand / St. Louis blues / Where the blue of the night / Wrap your troubles in dreams / Some of these days / I don't stand a ghost of a chance with you / Someday sweetheart
CD ____ HADCD 219
Spotlight On / Jun '97 / Henry Hadaway

L'ART VOCAL 1928-1945
CD ____ 700202
L'Art Vocal / Jul '97 / Discovery

LIVE DUETS 1947-1949
Then I'll be happy: Crosby, Bing & Ethel Merman / Your all time flop parade: Crosby, Bing & Ethel Merman / Chidabee chidabee chidabee: Crosby, Bing & Jimmy Durante / Clementine: Crosby, Bing & Dinah Shore/ Burl Ives / You was: Crosby, Bing & Kay Starr / Little bird told me: Crosby, Bing & Hattie McDaniel/Ernie Whiteman / Just a gigolo: Crosby, Bing & Bob Burns / When it's night time in little Italy: Crosby, Bing & Groucho Marx / April showers / Ma blushin' Rosie: Crosby & Jolson / Swannee: Crosby & Jolson / One I love (belongs to somebody else): Crosby, Bing & Al Jolson / So in love: Crosby, Bing & Peggy Lee / Blue shadows: Crosby, Bing & The Four Crosby Brothers / If you stubb your toe on the moon: Crosby, Bing & Jud Conlon's Rhythmaires / Once and for all: Crosby, Bing & Peggy Lee / For your all time flop parade: Crosby, Bing & Ethel Merman / There's a flaw in my flue: Crosby, Bing & Ethel Merman / Your all time flop parade: Crosby, Bing & Ethel Merman / Lazybones: Crosby, Bing & Louis Armstrong
CD ____ VN 1003
Viper's Nest / Nov '96 / ADA / Cadillac / Direct / Jazz Music

OLD LAMPLIGHTER, THE
CD ____ CDSGP 0127
Prestige / Dec '94 / Else / Total/BMG

ON THE SENTIMENTAL SIDE (20 Classic Tracks Of The 30's)
Black moonlight / How deep is the ocean / Stardust / Dancing in the dark / I'm through with love / Sweet is the word for you / Between a kiss and a sigh / Funny old hills / I found a million dollar baby / I have eyes / If you should ever need me / I'm building a sailboat of dreams / Joobalai / My heart is taking lessons / On the sentimental side / Our big love scene / Sing a song of sunbeams / That sly old gentleman / Thine alone / You're a sweet little headache
CD ____ CDAJA 5072
Living Era / Aug '90 / Select

ON THE SENTIMENTAL SIDE, THE
My heart is taking lessons / Funny old hills / Joobalai / East side of heaven / Hang your heart on a hickory limb / On the sentimental side / This is my night to dream / I have eyes / You're a sweet little headache / That sly old gentleman / Apple for the teacher / Man and his dream / Still the bluebird sings / April played the fiddle / I haven't time to be a millionaire / In my merry oldsmobile / Medley of Gus Edwards / Go fly a kite / Meet the sun halfway / Moon and the willow tree
CD ____ MUCD 9030
Musketeer / Apr '95 / Disc

ON TREASURE ISLAND
CD ____ JSPCD 703
JSP / May '93 / ADA / Cadillac / Direct / Hot Shot / Target/BMG

ONLY FOREVER
Only forever / Rhythm on the river / That's for me / When the moon comes over Madison Square / You're dangerous / Birds of a feather / Apple for the teacher / Still the bluebird sings / Go fly a kite / If I had my way / Too romantic / Sweet potato piper / April played the fiddle / I haven't time to be a millionaire / Meet the sun halfway / Man and his dream / I have eyes / You're a sweet little headache / It's always you / Birth of the blues / My melancholy baby / Waiter and the porter and the upstairs maid
CD ____ RAJCD 802
Empress / Oct '93 / Koch

PORTRAIT OF BING CROSBY, A
CD ____ GALE 403
Gallerie / May '97 / Disc / THE

SPOTLIGHT ON BING CROSBY & ROSEMARY CLOONEY (Crosby, Bing & Rosemary Clooney)
White Christmas: Crosby, Bing / Have yourself a merry little Christmas: Clooney, Rosemary / Silent night: Crosby, Bing / It came upon a midnight clear: Clooney, Rosemary / Away in a manger: Crosby, Bing / Christmas song: Clooney, Rosemary / O'litte town of Bethlehem: Crosby, Bing / Little drummer boy: Clooney, Rosemary / Rudolph the red nosed reindeer: Crosby, Bing / Jingle bells: Clooney, Rosemary / O come all ye faithful (Adeste fidelis): Crosby, Bing
CD ____ HADCD 110
Javelin / Feb '94 / Henry Hadaway / THE

START OFF EACH DAY WITH A SONG (Crosby, Bing & Jimmy Durante)
CD ____ JSPCD 701
JSP / May '93 / ADA / Cadillac / Direct / Hot Shot / Target/BMG

SWINGIN' ON A STAR (2CD Set)
(There'll be bluebirds over) The white cliffs of Dover / Yankee doodle dandy / I don't want to talk without you baby / You'd be so nice to come home to / It's all over now / As time goes by / I'll be seeing you / Shoo shoo baby / Long ago (and far away) / Bless'em all / I'll get by (as long as I have you) / Is you is or is you ain't my baby / Saturday night / Wait for me Mary / It's always you / Basin Street Blues / You belong to my heart / Too ra loo ra loo ra (that's an Irish lullaby) / Swingin' on a star / Trade winds / New San Antonio Rose / Dinah / I love you / Sweet Georgia Brown / You're getting to be a habit with me / Temptation / Too marvellous for words / May I / June in January / With every breath I take / I'm an old cowhand (from the Rio Grande) / Pennies from heaven / Mr. Gallagher and Mr. Shean / You must have been a beautiful baby / Sunday, Monday or always / Sierra Sue / Deep in the heart of Texas / I'll be home for Christmas / White Christmas
CD Set ____ MUCD 9515
Musketeer / May '96 / Disc

SWINGING ON A STAR
CD ____ PASTCD 7065
Flapper / Jun '95 / Pinnacle

THAT'S JAZZ
St. Louis blues / Please / Temptation / Did you ever see a dream walking / I don't stand a ghost of a chance with you / Down the old ox road / Black moonlight / Where the blue of the night meets the gold of the day / Last round-up / Someday sweetheart / How deep is the ocean / Our big love scene / Song of the Islands / Dinah / I'm an old cowhand (from the Rio Grande) / Wrap your troubles in dreams (and dream your troubles away) / Blue Hawaii / Sailor beware / Sweet Leilani / Pennies from heaven / Happy go lucky you and broken hearted me / Thanks
CD ____ PASTCD 9739
Flapper / Mar '91 / Pinnacle

THOSE GREAT WORLD WAR II SONGS
CD ____ DBG 53042
Double Gold / Apr '95 / Target/BMG

TOO MARVELLOUS FOR WORDS (25 Chart Toppers)
CD ____ CDGR 105
Charly / Jan '96 / Koch

TWO ON ONE: BING CROSBY & FRANK SINATRA (Crosby, Bing & Frank Sinatra)
CD ____ CDTT 6
Charly / Apr '94 / Koch

VISIT TO THE MOVIES, A
CD ____ 15411
Laserlight / Jan '93 / Target/BMG

Crosby, Bob

1937 - 1938 (Crosby, Bob & His Bobcats)
CD ____ SWAGGIECD 501
Swaggie / Jun '93 / Jazz Music

1939 (Crosby, Bob & His Bobcats)
CD ____ SWAGGIECD 502
Swaggie / Jan '94 / Jazz Music

1940 (Crosby, Bob & His Bobcats)
CD ____ SWAGGIECD 503
Swaggie / Jun '93 / Jazz Music

22 ORIGINAL BIG BAND RECORDINGS
CD ____ HCD 409
Hindsight / Sep '92 / Jazz Music / Target/ BMG

BIG APPLE 1936-1940, THE (Crosby, Bob & His Orchestra)
CD ____ RACD 7111
Aerospace / May '96 / Jazz Music / Montpellier

BIG NOISE STATUS, THE
CD ____ DHDL 126
Halcyon / Dec '94 / Cadillac / Harmonia Mundi / Jazz Music / Swift / Wellard

BOB CROSBY & HIS BOB CATS VOL.4
CD ____ SWAGGIECD 504
Swaggie / Dec '94 / Jazz Music

BOB CROSBY & HIS DIXIELAND BOBCATS 1939-1942 (Crosby, Bob & His Bobcats)
CD ____ JH 1043
Jazz Hour / Jun '95 / Cadillac / Jazz Music / Target/BMG

BOB CROSBY & HIS ORCHESTRA (Crosby, Bob & His Orchestra)
CD ____ HCD 245
Hindsight / Sep '94 / Jazz Music / Target/ BMG

BOB CROSBY ORCHESTRA VOL.11 (Crosby, Bob Orchestra)
CD ____ HDL 131
Halcyon / Mar '97 / Cadillac / Harmonia Mundi / Jazz Music / Swift / Wellard

BOB CROSBY'S BOB CATS VOL.1
Stumbling / Who's sorry now / Coquette / Fidgety feet / You're driving me crazy / Can't we be friends / Loopin' the loop / Mama's gone goodbye / March of the bob cats / Palesteena / Slow mood / Big foot jump / Big crash from China / Five point blues / Way down yonder in New Orleans / Do you ever think of me
CD ____ CD 501
Swaggie / Oct '91 / Jazz Music

DIXIELAND FAVOURITES
Big noise from Winnetka / Washington & Lee swing / I don't stand a ghost of a chance with you / Sugarfoot stomp / Stomp, Mr. Henry Lee / March of the Mustangs / High society / Mississippi mud / What's new / On the Alamo / San Antonio shout / March of the Bob Cats
CD ____ HCD 332
Hindsight / Mar '96 / Jazz Music / Target/ BMG

EYE OPENER
Savoy blues / Royal garden blues / Gin mill blues / Little Rock getaway / Who's sorry now / Coquette / Fidgety feet / South Rampart Street parade / Dogtown blues / Panama / Wolverine blues / Yancey special / Big foot jump / I hear you talking / Call me a taxi / Big noise from Winnetka / I'm free (what's new) / Diga diga doo / Eye opener / Mournin' blues / Till we meet again / Jazz me blues / Vultee special / Tin roof blues
CD ____ TPZ 1054
Topaz Jazz / Sep '96 / Cadillac / Pinnacle

HIGH SOCIETY VOL.10
CD ____ DHDL 130
Magic / Oct '96 / Cadillac / Harmonia Mundi / Jazz Music / Swift / Wellard

HOW CAN YOU FORGET (Crosby, Bob & His Orchestra)
CD ______ DHDL 125
Halcyon / Nov '93 / Cadillac / Harmonia Mundi / Jazz Music / Swift / Wellard

I REMEMBER YOU - THE BOB CROSBY MEMORIAL ALBUM
CD ______ VJC 1046
Vintage Jazz Classics / Aug '93 / ADA / Cadillac / CM / Direct

JAZZ ME BLUES (Crosby, Bob & The Bobcats)
South rampart street parade / Washington & Lee swing / Gin mill blues / Yancey special / Love nest / I'm praying humble / All by myself / I hear you talking / Jazz me blues / Squeeze me / Till we meet again / Call me a taxi / Mournin' blues / Who's sorry now / Tin roof blues / Spain
CD ______ 305152
Hallmark / Jul '97 / Carlton

MARCH OF THE BOBCATS (Crosby, Bob & The Bop Cats)
CD ______ JHR 73534
Jazz Hour / May '93 / Cadillac / Jazz Music / Target/BMG

MARCH OF THE BOBCATS (Crosby, Bob & The Bobcats)
Dixieland shuffle / Muskrat ramble / Can't we be friends / Squeeze me / Coquette / Fidgety feet / Stumbling / You're driving me crazy / Who's sorry now / South Rampart Street parade / Big Foot jump / March of the Bobcats / Slow mood / Big crash from China / Big noise from Winnetka / What's new
CD ______ CWNCD 2037
Crown / Jun '97 / Henry Hadaway

REMINISCING TIME
CD ______ DHDL 131
Halcyon / Apr '97 / Cadillac / Harmonia Mundi / Jazz Music / Swift / Wellard

STOMP OFF, LET'S GO
Big noise from Winnetka / Call me a taxi / Diga diga doo / Dixieland shuffle / Dogtown blues / Gin mill blues / Gypsy love song: *Crosby, Bob & Connie Boswell* / Grand terrace rhythm / I'm free / March of the bob cats / Milk cow blues / Muskrat ramble / Ooh looka there, ain't she pretty / Panama / Savoy blues / Smoky Mary / South Rampart Street parade / Spain / Stomp off, let's go / Stumbling / Swing Mister Charlie: *Crosby, Bob & Judy Garland* / Till we meet again / Wolverine blues / Yancey special
CD ______ CDAJA 5097
Living Era / Nov '92 / Select

STRANGE ENCHANTMENT (Vol.8/1938-39) (Crosby, Bob & His Orchestra)
My inspiration / Your lovely, Madame / Deep in a dream / Summertime / Loopin' the loop / Skater's waltz / Stomp off and let's go / Smoky Mary / South Rampart Street parade / Song of the wanderer / Cherry / Eye opener / Begin the beguine / Hindustan / Long time no see / Mournin' blues / Don't worry 'bout me / I never knew heaven could speak / If I were sure of you / Strange enchantment
CD ______ DHDL 127
Halcyon / May '95 / Cadillac / Harmonia Mundi / Jazz Music / Swift / Wellard

STRANGE NEW RHYTHM IN MY HEART VOL.4 (Crosby, Bob Orchestra)
CD ______ DHDL 122
Halcyon / Nov '93 / Cadillac / Harmonia Mundi / Jazz Music / Swift / Wellard

SUGARFOOT STOMP 1936-1942 (Crosby, Bob & His Orchestra)
CD ______ RACD 7121
Aerospace / May '96 / Jazz Music / Montpellier

THEM THERE EYES
CD ______ DHDL 128
Halcyon / Jul '96 / Cadillac / Harmonia Mundi / Jazz Music / Swift / Wellard

YOU CAN CALL IT SWING (Crosby, Bob & His Orchestra)
CD ______ DHDL 121
Halcyon / Sep '93 / Cadillac / Harmonia Mundi / Jazz Music / Swift / Wellard

YOU'RE DRIVING ME CRAZY (Crosby, Bob & His Orchestra)
CD ______ DHDL 123
Halcyon / Mar '93 / Cadillac / Harmonia Mundi / Jazz Music / Swift / Wellard

Crosby, David

IF I COULD ONLY REMEMBER MY NAME
Music is love / Cowboy movie / Tamalpais high at about 3 / Laughing / What are their names / Traction in the rain / Song with no words / Tree with no leaves / Orleans / I'd swear there was somebody here
CD ______ 7567814152
Rhino / May '95 / Warner Music

THOUSAND ROADS
Hero / Too young to die / Old soldier / Through your hands / Yvette in english / Thousand roads / Columbus / Helpless heart / Coverage / Natalie
CD ______ 7567824842
Atlantic / May '93 / Warner Music

WIND ON THE WATER (Crosby, David & Graham Nash)
Carry me / Mamma Lion / Bittersweet / Take the money and run / Naked in the rain / Love work out / Low down payment / Cowboy of dreams / Homeward through the haze / Fieldworker / To the last whale / Wind on the water
CD ______ NTMCD 550
Nectar / Mar '97 / Pinnacle

Crosby, Stills & Nash

4 WAY STREET (2CD Set) (Crosby, Stills, Nash & Young)
On the way home / Cowgirl in the sand / Southern man / Teach your children / Don't let it bring you down / Ohio / Triad / Forty nine bye byes / Carry on / Lee shore / Love the one you're with / Find the cost of freedom / Chicago / Pre-road downs / Right between the eyes / Long time gone / Suite: Judy blue eyes / King Midas in reverse / Black Queen / Loner/Cinnamon girl/Down by the river
CD Set ______ K 260003
Atlantic / Mar '87 / Warner Music
CD Set ______ 7567824082
Atlantic / May '95 / Warner Music

AFTER THE STORM
CD ______ 7567826542
Atlantic / May '95 / Warner Music

AMERICAN DREAM (Crosby, Stills, Nash & Young)
American dream / Got it made / Name of love / Don't say goodbye / This ole house / Nighttime for the generals / Shadowland / Drivin' thunder / Clear blue skies / That girl / Compass / Soldiers of peace / Feel your love / Night song
CD ______ 7818862
Atlantic / Nov '88 / Warner Music

BEST OF CROSBY, STILLS & NASH (4CD Set)
Suite: Judy blue eyes / Helplessly hoping / You don't have to cry / Wooden ships / Guinevere / Marrakesh express / Long time gone / Blackbird / Lady of the island / Song with no words (tree with no leaves) / Almost cut my hair / Teach your children / Horses through a rainstorm / Deja vu / Helpless / Four plus twenty / Laughing / Carry on/ questions / Woodstock / Ohio / Love the one you're with / Our house / Old times good times / Lee shore / Music is love / I'd swear there was somebody here / Man in the mirror / Black queen / Military madnesss / Urge for going / I used to be a king / Simple man / Southbound train / Change partners / My love is a gentle thing / Word game / Johnny's garden / So begins the task / Turn back the pages / See the changes / It doesn't matter / Immigration man / Chicago/We can change the world / Homeward through the haze / Where will I be / Page 43 / Carry me / Cowboy of dreams / Bittersweet / To the last whale...a critical mass/Wind on water / Prison song / Another sleep song / Taken at all / In my dreams / Just a song before I go / Shadow captain / Dark star / Cathedral / Wasted on the way / Barrel of pain (half life) / Southern cross / Daylight again/Find the cost of freedom / Thoroughfare gap / Wild tales / Cold rain / Got it more / Tracks in the dust / As I come of age / 50/50 / Drive my car / Delta / Soldiers of peace / Yours and mine / Haven't we lost enough / After the dolphin / Find the cost of freedom
CD ______ 7567823192
Atlantic / Dec '91 / Warner Music

CARRY ON
Woodstock / Marrakesh express / You don't have to cry / Teach your children / Love the one you're with / Almost cut my hair / Wooden ships / Dark star / Helpless / Chicago/We can change the world / Cathedral / Four plus twenty / Our house / AMass/BWind on the water / Change partners / Just a song before I go / Ohio / Wasted on the way / Southern cross / Suite: Judy blue eyes / Carry on/questions / Horses through a rainstorm / Johnny's garden / Guinevere / Helplessly hoping / Lee shore / Taken at all / Shadow captain / As I come of age / Drive my car / Dear Mr. Fantasy / In my dreams / Yours and mine / Haven't we lost enough / After the dolphin / Find the cost of freedom
CD ______ 7567804872
Atlantic / Dec '91 / Warner Music

CROSBY, STILLS AND NASH
Suite: Judy blue eyes / Marrakesh express / Guinevere / You don't have to cry / Pre-road downs / Wooden ships / Lady of the island / Helplessly hoping / Long time gone / Forty nine bye byes
CD ______ 7567826512
Atlantic / Aug '94 / Warner Music

CSN
Shadow captain / See the changes / Carried away / Fair game / Anything at all / Cathedral / Dark star / Just a song before I go / Run from tears / Cold rain / In my dreams / I give you give blind
CD ______ 7567826502
Atlantic / Jan '95 / Warner Music

DAYLIGHT AGAIN
Turn your back on love / Wasted on the way / Southern cross / Into the darkness / Delta / Since I met you / Too much love to hide / Song for Susan / You are alive / Might as well have a good time / Daylight again
CD ______ 7567826722
Atlantic / Oct '94 / Warner Music

DEJA VU (Crosby, Stills, Nash & Young)
Carry on / Teach your children / Almost cut my hair / Helpless / Woodstock / Deja vu / Our house / Four plus twenty / Country girl / Everybody I love you
CD ______ 7567826492
Atlantic / Aug '94 / Warner Music

LIVE IT UP
Live it up / If anybody had a heart / Tomboy / Haven't we lost enough / Yours and mine / (Got to keep) open / Straight line / House of broken dreams / Arrows / After the dolphin
CD ______ 7567821072
Atlantic / Jun '90 / Warner Music

REPLAY
Carry on / Marrakesh express / Just a song before I go / First things first / Shadow captain / To the last whale / Love the one you're with / Pre-road downs / Change partners / I give you give blind / Cathedral
CD ______ 7567826792
Atlantic / Dec '94 / Warner Music

SO FAR (Crosby, Stills, Nash & Young)
Deja vu / Helplessly hoping / Wooden ships / Teach your children / Ohio / Find the cost of freedom / Woodstock / Our house / Helpless / Guenevere / Suite: Judy Blue eyes
CD ______ 7567826482
Atlantic / Sep '94 / Warner Music

Crosland, Ben

NORTHERN RUN, THE
Blues for Lex / Sunshower / Away too long / Don't you dare / Northern run / Break a leg / Pause for thought / Blue / Take the coltrane / Confluence
CD ______ JCCD 101
Jazz Cat / Sep '95 / New Note/Pinnacle

Cross

SHOVE IT
Shove it / Heaven for everyone / Love on a tightrope (like an animal) / Cowboys and indians / Stand up for love / Love lies bleeding / Rough justice / Second shelf mix / Contact
CD ______ CDV 2477
Virgin / '88 / EMI

Cross

DREAM REALITY
Changing / Fire / Armoury show / Uncovered heart / Courage / Run for rescue / Fake / Dream reality / Fanfare song / Poison into medicine / Yearning
CD ______ CYCL 054
Cyclops / Aug '97 / Pinnacle

GAZE
CD ______ CYCL 039
Cyclops / Aug '96 / Pinnacle

Cross, Christopher

BEST OF CHRISTOPHER CROSS, THE
CD ______ 9548306562
WEA / Nov '96 / Warner Music

CHRISTOPHER CROSS
Say you'll be mine / I really don't know anymore / Spinning / Never be the same / Poor Shirley / Ride like the wind / Light is on / Sailing / Minstrel gigolo
CD ______ 256789
WEA / Jul '89 / Warner Music

RENDEZVOUS
Rendezvous / Deputy Dan / Night across the world / Angry young men / In the blink of an eye / Is there something / Isn't it love / Nothing will change / Driftin' away / Fisherman's tale
CD ______ 74321102912
Arista / Jun '97 / BMG

WINDOW
Been there, done that / Wild wild West / Wishing well / Thinkin' bout you / Jan's tune / Open up my window / Nature's way / Uncharted hearts / Before I go / Love is calling
CD ______ 74321246542
Arista / Jun '97 / BMG

Cross, David

BIG PICTURE, THE
CD ______ CDR 104
Red Hot / Mar '94 / THE

MEMOS FROM PURGATORY
Poppies / Meantime / First policeman / Animal / New dawn / Postscript / Bizarre bazaar / Basking in the blue
CD ______ CDR 103
Red Hot / Mar '94 / THE

TESTING TO DESTRUCTION (Cross, David Band)
CD ______ CDR 107
Red Hot / Nov '94 / THE

Cross, Mike

BEST OF THE FUNNY STUFF, THE (Creme De La Cross)
CD ______ SHCD 1010
Sugar Hill / Mar '94 / ADA / CM / Direct / Koch / Roots

BOUNTY HUNTER
CD ______ SHCD 1003
Sugar Hill / Jan '97 / ADA / CM / Direct / Koch / Roots

CAROLINA SKY
CD ______ SHCD 1006
Sugar Hill / Jan '97 / ADA / CM / Direct / Koch / Roots

HIGH POWERED, LOW FLYING
CD ______ SHCD 1011
Sugar Hill / Nov '94 / ADA / CM / Direct / Koch / Roots

IRREGULAR GUY
CD ______ SHCD 1009
Sugar Hill / Jan '97 / ADA / CM / Direct / Koch / Roots

LIVE AND KICKIN'
CD ______ SHCD 1005
Sugar Hill / Jan '97 / ADA / CM / Direct / Koch / Roots

PRODIGAL SON
CD ______ SHCD 1008
Sugar Hill / Jan '97 / ADA / CM / Direct / Koch / Roots

Cross, Sandra

100% LOVERS ROCK
CD ______ ARCD 096
Ariwa Sounds / Jun '94 / Jet Star / SRD

COMET IN THE SKY
Who's finally won / Comet in the sky / Blinded by love / White wash / I need a man / My only desire / Styler boy / Why oh why / Free South Africa / I want you so badly
CD ______ ARICD 034
Ariwa Sounds / Oct '88 / Jet Star / SRD

COUNTRY LIFE
CD ______ ARICD 026
Ariwa Sounds / Feb '89 / Jet Star / SRD

FOUNDATION OF LOVE
CD ______ ARICD 047
Ariwa Sounds / Jun '92 / Jet Star / SRD

Cross, Tim

CLASSIC LANDSCAPE
CD ______ NAGE 3CD
Art Of Landscape / Jan '86 / Sony

Crouch, Andrae

MERCY
Say so / Give it all back to me / Lord is my light / Love somebody like me / Nobody else like you / Mercy / This is the Lord's doing / We love it here / He's the light / Mercy interlude / God still loves me
CD ______ 9362454322
Warner Bros. / Jul '95 / Warner Music

Crow, Dan

OOPS
CD ______ ROUCD 8007
Rounder / '88 / ADA / CM / Direct

Crow, Rob

LACTOSE ADEPT
CD ______ EAR 017
Earth Music / Oct '96 / Cargo

Crow, Sheryl

SHERYL CROW
Maybe angels / Change / Home / Sweet Rosalyn / If it makes you happy / Redemption day / Hard to make a stand / Everyday is a winding road / Love is a good thing / Oh Marie / Superstar / Book / Ordinary morning / Free man
CD ______ 5405902
A&M / Sep '96 / PolyGram

TUESDAY NIGHT MUSIC CLUB
Run baby run / Leaving Las Vegas / Strong enough / Can't cry anymore / Solidity / Na-na song / No-one said it'd be easy / What can I do for you / All I wanna do / We do what we can / Reach around jerk / Can't cry anymore (live) / What can I do for you (live) / Leaving Las Vegas (live) / No-one said it would be easy (live) / Volvo cowgirl
CD ______ 5401262
A&M / Oct '93 / PolyGram
CD Set ______ 5403682
A&M / May '95 / PolyGram

Crowbar

CROWBAR/LIVE + 1
High rate extinction / All I had (I gave) / Will that never dies / No quarter / Self inflicted / Negative pollution / Existance is punishment / Holding nothing / I have failed / Self inflicted (Live) / Fixation / I have failed (Live) / All I had (Live) / Numb sensitive
CD ______ CDVEST 5
Bulletproof / Apr '94 / Pinnacle

OBEDIENCE THRU SUFFERING
CD CDVEST 42
Bulletproof / Feb '95 / Pinnacle

TIME HEALS NOTHING
CD CDVEST 51
Bulletproof / May '95 / Pinnacle

Crowbar

BROKEN GLASS
Conquering / Like broken glass / (Can't) Turn away from dying / Wrath of time / Nothing / Burn your world / I am forever / Above, below and in between / You know (I'll live again) / Reborn thru me
CD CDVEST 77
Bulletproof / Oct '96 / Pinnacle

Crowd Of Isolated

MEMORIES & SCARS
CD XM 025CD
X-Mist / Apr '92 / Cargo / SRD

Crowded House

CROWDED HOUSE
World where you live / Now we're getting somewhere / Don't dream it's over / Mean to me / Love you till the day I die / Something so strong / Hole in the river / I walk away / Tombstone / That's what I call love
CD CDEST 2016
Capitol / Feb '94 / EMI

CROWDED HOUSE/TEMPLE OF LOW MEN/WOODFACE (The Originals/3CD Set)
World where you live / Now we're getting somewhere / Don't dream it's over / Mean to me / Love you 'til the day I die / Something so strong / Hole in the river / I walk away / Tombstone / That's what I call love / I feel possessed / Kill eye / Into temptation / Mansion in the slums / When you come / Never be the same / Love this life / Sister madly / In the lowlands / Better be home soon / Chocolate cake / It's only natural / Fall at your feet / Tall trees / Weather with you / Whispers and moans / Four seasons in one day / There goes God / Fame is / All I ask / As sure as I am / Italian plastic / She goes on / How will you go
CD Set CDOMB 001
EMI / Mar '97 / EMI

INTERVIEW 1991
CD NEW 1CD
Wax / Jun '97 / RTM/Disc / Total/BMG

RECURRING DREAM (The Very Best Of Crowded House)
Weather with you / World where you live / Fall at your feet / Locked out / Don't dream it's over / Into temptation / Pineapple head / When you come / Private universe / Not the girl you think you are / Instinct / I feel possessed / Four seasons in one day / It's only natural / Distant sun / Something so strong / Mean to me / Better be home soon / Everything is good for you
CD CDEST 2283
Capitol / Jun '96 / EMI

RECURRING DREAM (The Very Best Of Crowded House/2CD Set)
Weather with you / World where you live / Fall at your feet / Locked out / Don't dream it's over / Into temptation / Pineapple head / When you come / Private universe / Not the girl you think you are / Instinct / I feel possessed / Four seasons in one day / It's only natural / Distant sun / Something so strong / Mean to me / Better be home soon / Everything is good for you / There goes God / Newcastle jam / Love U 'til the day I die / Hole in the river / Pineapple head / Private universe / How will you go / Left hand / Whispers and moans / Kill eye / Fingers of love / Don't dream it's over / When you come / Sister Madly / In my command
CD Set CDESTX 2283
Capitol / Nov '96 / EMI

TEMPLE OF LOW MEN
I feel possessed / Kill eye / Into temptation / Mansion in the slums / When you come / Never be the same / Love this life / Sister madly / In the lowlands / Better be home soon
CD CDEST 2064
Capitol / Jul '88 / EMI

TOGETHER ALONE
Kare kare / In my command / Nails in my feet / Black and white boy / Fingers of love / Pineapple head / Locked out / Private Universe / Walking on the spot / Distant sun / Catherine wheels / Skin feeling / Together alone
CD CDESTU 2215
Capitol / Sep '97 / EMI

WOODFACE
Chocolate cake / It's only natural / Fall at your feet / Tall trees / Weather with you / Whispers and moans / Four seasons in one day / There goes God / Fame is / All I ask / As sure as I am / Italian plastic / She goes on / How will you go
CD CDEST 2144
Capitol / Jun '91 / EMI

Crowe, Bobby

SHORES OF LOCH ALVIE, THE (Crowe, Bobby & His Scottish Band)
CD GRCD 48
Grasmere / '92 / Highlander / Savoy / Target/BMG

Crowe, J.D.

FLASHBACK (Crowe, J.D. & The New South)
CD ROUCD 0322
Rounder / Nov '94 / ADA / CM / Direct

GOING BACK (Crowe & McLaughlin)
CD ROUCD 314
Rounder / Jan '94 / ADA / CM / Direct

J.D. CROWE AND THE NEW SOUTH (Crowe, J.D. & The New South)
Old home place / Some old day / Rock salt and nails / Sally Goodin / Ten degrees / Nashville blues / You are what I am / Summer wages / I'm walkin' / Home sweet home revisited / Cryin' Holly
CD ROUCD 0044
Rounder / '88 / ADA / CM / Direct

STRAIGHT AHEAD
CD ROUCD 0202
Rounder / Jun '87 / ADA / CM / Direct

Crowell, Rodney

DIAMONDS AND DIRT
Crazy baby / I couldn't leave you if I tried / She's crazy for leaving / After all this time / I know you're married / Above and beyond / It's such a small world / I didn't know I could lose you / Brand new rag / Last waltz
CD 4608732
CBS / Apr '89 / Sony

Crowforce

CROWFORCE
CD CDDVN 1
Devotion / Jul '92 / Pinnacle

Crowley, Jimmy

CAMP HOUSE BALLADS (Crowley, Jimmy & Stoker's Lodge)
CD CLUNCD 031
Mulligan / Jan '92 / ADA / CM

Crown Heights

MORE PRICKS THAN KICKS
Greed kicks in / More pricks than kicks / Foxy looser / Learn to breathe / Unkind / Margaret / Dear Sir / Call king sour / Wired for sound / Moving from the small room to the big room / Out of Carolina
CD 74321438312
American / May '97 / BMG

Crown Heights Affair

ESSENTIAL DANCEFLOOR ARTISTS VOL.1
Dreaming a dream / Foxy lady / Dancin' / Far out / I'm gonna love you forever / Galaxy of love / You gave me love / Use your body and soul / Say a prayer for two
CD DGPCD 665
Deep Beats / Mar '94 / BMG

STRUCK GOLD (The Best Of Crown Heights Affair)
CD DEEPM 014
Deep Beats / Mar '97 / BMG

Crown Of Thorns

21 THORNS (2CD Set)
CD Set IRSCD 993026
Hengest / Nov '96 / Grapevine/PolyGram

BREAKTHROUGH
CD NTHEN 28
Now & Then / Apr '96 / Plastic Head

BREAKTHROUGH
CD IRSCD 993025
Hengest / Nov '96 / Grapevine/PolyGram

BURNING, THE
CD BS 005CD
Black Sun / Jan '96 / Plastic Head

CROWN OF THORNS
CD NTHEN 8
Now & Then / Apr '96 / Plastic Head

ETERNAL DEATH
CD BS 010CD
Burning Sun / Mar '97 / Plastic Head

RAW THORNS
CD NTHEN 13
Now & Then / Apr '96 / Plastic Head

Crown Of Thornz

TRAIN YARD BLUES
CD LF 151CD
Lost & Found / May '95 / Plastic Head

Crown Royals

ALL NIGHT BURNER
CD ES 1236CD
Estrus / May '97 / Cargo / Greyhound / Plastic Head

Crowsdell

DREAMETTE
CD ABB 83CD
Big Cat / Apr '95 / 3mv/Pinnacle

WITHIN THE CURVE OF AN ARM
Popsick / Five stars / Mooncalf / Lurking in sagas / You want me dead / Floridian lamb / WC Haley / Pharmeceutical fingers / Patches / Sunny sparkle / Cut and paste / Wake the lass / Foul
CD ABB 125CD
Big Cat / Jun '97 / 3mv/Pinnacle

Cru

DA DIRTY 30
CD 5376072
Mercury / Aug '97 / PolyGram

Crucial Robbie

CRUCIAL VIEW
CD ARICD 056
Ariwa Sounds / Oct '90 / Jet Star / SRD

Crucial Vibes

CONTROL YOURSELF
CD CDSGP 061
Prestige / Jun '93 / Else / Total/BMG

Crucifix

DEHUMANIZATION
CD 18523 2
Southern / Sep '94 / SRD

Crucifixion

DESERT OF SHATTERED HOPES
CD 9040172
Mausoleum / Apr '95 / Grapevine/PolyGram

Crucifucks

OUR WILL BE DONE
CD VIRUS 111
Alternative Tentacles / '92 / Cargo / Greyhound / Pinnacle

Crude

INNER CITY GUITAR PERSPECTIVES
CD FNCD 363
Flying Nun / Nov '96 / RTM/Disc

Crudup, Arthur

ARTHUR 'BIG BOY' CRUDUP MEETS THE MASTER BLUES BASSISTS (Crudup, Arthur 'Big Boy')
CD DD 621
Delmark / Mar '95 / ADA / Cadillac / CM / Direct / Hot Shot

ARTHUR 'BIG BOY' CRUDUP VOL.1 (Crudup, Arthur 'Big Boy')
CD DOCD 5201
Document / Oct '93 / ADA / Hot Shot / Jazz Music

ARTHUR 'BIG BOY' CRUDUP VOL.2 (Crudup, Arthur 'Big Boy')
CD DOCD 5202
Document / Oct '93 / ADA / Hot Shot / Jazz Music

ARTHUR 'BIG BOY' CRUDUP VOL.3 (Crudup, Arthur 'Big Boy')
CD DOCD 5203
Document / Oct '93 / ADA / Hot Shot / Jazz Music

ARTHUR 'BIG BOY' CRUDUP VOL.4 (Crudup, Arthur 'Big Boy')
CD DOCD 5204
Document / Oct '93 / ADA / Hot Shot / Jazz Music

FATHER OF ROCK 'N' ROLL, THE
I'm in the mood / Ethel Mae / My mama don't allow me / Look no yonder wall / Too much competition / My baby left me
CD CD 52025
Blues Encore / Feb '93 / Target/BMG

LOOK ON YONDER'S WALL (Crudup, Arthur 'Big Boy')
Look on yonder's wall / Questionnaire blues / Keep your hands off that woman / That's all right / Rock me mama / Katie Mae / Dust my broom / Landlord blues / Coal black mare / Life is just a gamble / Walk out on the road / I'm all alone / You'll be old before your time / Ramblin' blues / When I lost my baby (I almost lost my mind)
CD DE 614
Delmark / Jul '97 / ADA / Cadillac / CM / Direct / Hot Shot

MEAN OL' FRISCO (Charly Blues - Masterworks Vol. 50)
CD CDBM 50
Charly / Jun '93 / Koch

Cruel Frederick

BIRTH OF THE CRUEL
CD SST 127CD
SST / May '93 / Plastic Head

WE ARE THE MUSIC WE PLAY
CD SST 290CD
SST / May '93 / Plastic Head

Cruel Sea

THIS IS NOT THE WAY HOME
CD REDCD 25
Red Eye / Aug '94 / Direct

THREE-LEGGED DOG
CD 5275372
Polydor / Jun '95 / PolyGram

Cruise, Julee

FLOATING INTO THE NIGHT
Floating / Falling / I remember / Mysteries of love / Into the night / I float alone / Nightingale / Swan / World spins
CD 7599258592
WEA / Feb '90 / Warner Music

VOICE OF LOVE, THE
This is our night / Space for love / Movin' in on you / Friends for life / Up in flames / Kool kat walk / Until the end of the world / She would die for love / In my other world / Questions in a world of blues / Voice of love
CD 9362453902
WEA / Oct '93 / Warner Music

Crumbs

CRUMBS
CD LOOKOUT 161CD
Lookout / Jan '97 / Cargo / Greyhound / Shellshock/Disc

Crumbsuckers

LIFE OF DREAMS
CD CDJUST 4
Rough Justice / Aug '91 / Pinnacle

Crumit, Frank

MOUNTAIN GREENERY
Bride's lament / Mountain greenery / Abdul Abulbul Amir / Thanks for the buggy ride / Kingdom coming and the year of Jubilo / Ukelele lady / Jack is every inch a sailor / Oh by jingo, oh by gee / Prune song / Girlfriend / Billy boy / King of Borneo / Get away old man get away / Down in the cane break / Crazy words crazy tune / Gay caballero / Insurance man
CD CDAJA 5001
Living Era / Oct '93 / Select

RETURN OF THE GAY CABELLERO
I'm bettin' the roll on roamer / Donald the dub / Lady of my dreams taught me how to play second fiddle / I learned about women from her / Pretty little dear / O'Hooligans ball / Return of the Gay Cabellero / My grandfather's clock / My little bimbo down on the bamboo isle / Granny's old armchair / I'm a specialist / Would you like to take a walk / And then he took up golf / Wake Nicodemus / Oh, baby (don't say no say maybe) / Dolan's poker party / I married the Bootlegger's daughter / Little brown jug / Return of Abdul Abulbul Amir
CD CDAJA 5012
Living Era / Oct '93 / Select

Crumly, Pat

BEHIND THE MASK (Crumly, Pat Quartet)
Behind the mask / Voyage / I'll remember April / You don't know what love is / Island / Carib-blue / This heart of mine / Tears inside / Little off beat / Polka dots and moonbeams / Contemplation / If I should lose you / Behind the mask (Second version)
CD SPJCD 549
Spotlite / May '93 / Cadillac / Jazz Music / New Note/Pinnacle / Swift

FLAMINGO
Nightwalk / Beautiful love / Bewitched, bothered and bewildered / Slow burn / Flamingo / Here's that rainy day / Eucalpyso / Days of wine and roses / Three little words / My old flame / Flamebirds / Two degrees East - three degrees West / It might as well be spring / Way you look tonight
CD SPJCD 550
Spotlite / Jun '94 / Cadillac / Jazz Music / New Note/Pinnacle / Swift

Crunt

CRUNT
CD TR 19CD
Trance / Feb '94 / SRD

Crusaders

COLLECTION, THE
CD CCSCD 420
Castle / Mar '95 / BMG

CRUSADERS AND BEYOND, THE
Street life / Inherit the wind / Stomp and buck dance / Burnin' up the carnival / (No matter how high I get) I'll still be looking up to you / Keep that same old feeling / Snowflakes / Brazos river / Breakdown / Soul shadows / Let's dance together / Time bomb / Voices in the rain

CD MCCD 163
Music Club / Jul '94 / Disc / THE

CRUSADERS BEST, THE
Street life / Way back home / Feeling funky / Tough talk / Do you remember when / Message from the inner city / Eleanor Rigby / Carnival of the night / My Mama told me / I'm so glad I'm standing here today / Put it where you want it
CD PWKS 4231
Carlton / Nov '94 / Carlton

GREATEST CRUSADE, THE
Street life: *Crusaders & Randy Crawford* / Hustler / Rodeo drive (High steppin') / Marcella's dream / Rainbow seeker: *Sample, Joe* / Burning up the carnival: *Sample, Joe & Josie James* / Snowflake / Spiral / Nite crawler / Rainbow visions / Hold on (I feel our love is changing): *Crusaders & B.B. King* / Chain reaction: *Crusaders & B.B. King* / Carnival of the night / Ballad for Joe (Louis) / Inherit the wind: *Felder, Wilton & Bobby Womack* / Some people just never learn / (No matter how high I get) I'll still be looking up to you: *Felder, Wilton & Bobby Womack/ Altrina Grayson* / Oasis: *Sample, Joe* / It happens every day / Fly with the wings of love: *Sample, Joe* / Soul caravan / Fairy tales / I'm so glad I'm standing here today: *Crusaders & Joe Cocker* / Put it where you want it / Elegant evening / Free as the wind / Search for soul / Survivor: *Sample, Joe & Phyllis Hyman*
CD CLBCD 5501
Calibre / Feb '95 / Sound & Media

HAPPY AGAIN (Jazz Crusaders)
Lock it down / When your so far away / Midnite moods / Top of the world / Fool's rush in / Are you a part of me / Slyzappit / Rockslide / La luz el dia / Jamaica / Travellin' inside your love / Young rabbits / Uh huh oh yea
CD 9950322
Sin-Drome / Jul '95 / New Note/Pinnacle

HEALING THE WOUNDS
Pessimisticism / Mercy mercy mercy / Little things mean a lot / 'Cause we've ended as lovers / Shake dance / Maputo / Running man / Healing the wounds
CD GRD 9638
GRP / May '91 / New Note/BMG

HOLLYWOOD
CD 5303062
Verve / Apr '94 / PolyGram

LIVE IN JAPAN
Rainbow seeker / Hustler / Sweet gentle love / Spiral / Melodies of love / Carmel / So far away / Brazos river breakdown / In all my wildest dreams / Put it where you want it
CD GRP 97462
GRP / Nov '93 / New Note/BMG

OLD SOCKS, NEW SHOES
CD 5303072
Verve / Apr '94 / PolyGram

PASS THE PLATE
CD 5303082
PolyGram Jazz / Nov '94 / PolyGram

SAMPLE A DECADE
So far away / Bayou bottoms / Soul shadows / Don't let it get you down / My mama told me so / I'm so glad I'm standing here today / Soul caravan / Nite crawler / Fairytales / Honky tonk struttin' / Chain reaction / And then there was the blues / Street life / Hold on / Snow flake / Rhapsody and blues / Sweet 'n' sour / Night ladies / Rodeo drive (high steppin') / Free as the wind
CD VSOPCD 131
Connoisseur Collection / Jan '89 / Pinnacle

SOUL SHADOWS
Night theme / Stomp and buck dance / Spiral / Street life / Feel it / 'Cause we've ended as lovers / Ballad for Joe (Louis) / Destiny / I felt the love / Soul shadows / Way it goes / Night ladies
CD VSOPCD 212
Connoisseur Collection / Feb '95 / Pinnacle

STREET LIFE
Street life / My lady / Rodeo drive (high steppin') / Carnival of the night / Hustler / Night faces / Inherit the wind: *Felder, Wilton*
CD MCLD 19004
MCA / Apr '92 / BMG

STREET LIFE RHAPSODY
CD GRP 50132
GRP / Jul '96 / New Note/BMG

ULTIMATE COLLECTION
CD NTRCD 035
Nectar / Mar '95 / Pinnacle

WAY BACK HOME (The Complete Authorised Collection) (4CD Set)
Young rabbits / Freedom sound / Brother Barnard / Tough talk / Scratch / Blues up tight / Eleanor Rigby / Inside the outside / Jazz / Thank you / Golden slumber / Way back home / Put it where you want it / So far away / Sweet revival / That's how I feel / Three children / Mosadi / Shade of blue / Don't let it get you down / Message from the inner city / Search for soul / Scratch / Hard times / Stomp and buck dance / Double bubble / Crossfire / Lilies of the Nile / When there's love around / Ballad for Joe (Louis) / Whispering pines / Chain reaction / Creole / Free as the wind / Sweet 'n' sour / I felt the love / Spiral / Night crawler / Keep that same old feeling / It happens every day / Snowflake / Fairy tales / Street life / Way back home
CD Set BTD 4700
Blue Thumb / Sep '96 / New Note/BMG

Crusaders For Real Hip Hop

DEJA VU/ IT'S '82
CD PCD 1428
Profile / Jul '92 / Pinnacle

Crush, Bobby

DOUBLE DECKER PARTY
CD PLATCD 5920
Platinum / Jul '92 / Prism

HOLLYWOOD AND BROADWAY
Why God / Bohemian rhapsody / I dreamed a dream / Tears in heaven / Love moves in mysterious ways / Everything I do (I do it for you) / Beauty and the beast / Love can't happen / Places that belong to you / Any dream will do / Music of the night / Someone to watch over me
CD PLATCD 3919
Platinum / Apr '93 / Prism

Crusher

ACT 2-UNDERMINE
CD N 02312
Noise / Nov '93 / Koch

Crust

CRUSTY LOVE
CD TR 23CD
Trance / May '94 / SRD

Cruz, Celia

CUBAN LEGEND
Pa la paloma / Burundanga / Con mucho cachet / Baila yemaya / Cao cao mani picao / Lo tuyo es mio / Chango ta veni / La guagua / Esperame en el cielo / Sun sun babae / La negrita sandunguera / Bambolalle / Vengan a la charanga / Cha cha guere / Me voy a pinar del rio / Quien sera / Mambo del amor / Agua pa mi / El barracon / Elegua quiere tambo
CD CDHOT 610
Charly / Jan '97 / Koch

EL MERENGUE
CD CD 62002
Saludos Amigos / Apr '94 / Target/BMG

IRREPETIBLE
Que le den candela / Bembelequa / Limon Y menta / Marion ague / Drume negrita / Caballero y dama / Enamorada de ti / La guagua / Cuando cuba se acabe de liberar
CD 66058054
RMM / Feb '95 / New Note/Pinnacle

MADRE RUMBA
CD CD 62016
Saludos Amigos / Apr '94 / Target/BMG

MADRE RUMBA (Cruz, Celia & La Sonora Matancera)
CD CD 3557
Cameo / Jul '95 / Target/BMG

MAMBO DEL AMOR
CD CD 62007
Saludos Amigos / Apr '94 / Target/BMG

QUEEN OF THE RUMBA
CD CDHOT 601
Charly / Jun '96 / Koch

RITMOY Y CALOR DE CUBA CON
CD BMB 504CD
Blue Moon / Nov '95 / Cadillac / Discovery / Greensleeves / Jazz Music / Jet Star / TKO Magnum

SALSA SUPERSTAR (2CD Set)
Agua pa' mi / Reina rumba / La Mucura / Suavecito / Guede Zaina / Pa' La Paloma / Cao, Cao Mani Picao / Sun, sun babae / Me voy a pinar Del Rio / Quien sera / El Merengue / Ritmo / Tambo Y Flores / Mi bomba sono / Tamborilero / Baila Balla Vicente / Chango ta veni / Vengan a la Charanga / Rock and roll / Rumbanacao / Pila Pilandera / Mi Soncito / Juancito Trucupey / Mango mangue / Tumba La Cana Jibarito / Baila Yemaya / Melao de cana / Pepe Antonio / Los Ritmos Cambian / Matiagua / Mambo del amor / Hay comentario / Tatalibaba / El pai y la mai / Madre rumba / Vamos a Guarachar / Elegua quiere tambo / Saoco / Cha cha guere / Tu voz / Lalle lalle
CD Set CPCD 82532
Charly / Nov '96 / Koch

SALSA Y MERENGUUE
CD CD 62054
Saludos Amigos / May '94 / Target/BMG

Cryner, Bobbie

GIRL OF YOUR DREAMS
Son of a preacher man / I didn't know my own strength / Girl of your dreams / Vision of loneliness / Lesson in leaving / You'd think he'd know me better / I just can't stand to be unhappy / Nobody leaves / Oh to be the one / Just say so
CD MCD 11324
MCA / Jan '96 / BMG

Crypt Of Kereberos

WORLD OF MYTHS
CD CDAR 013
Adipocre / Feb '94 / Plastic Head

Cryptic Slaughter

SPEAK YOUR PEACE
Born too soon / Insanity by the numbers / Death styles of the poor and lonely / Divided minds / Killing time / Still born, again / Co-exist / One thing or another / Speak your piece
CD CDZORRO 6
Metal Blade / Jul '90 / Pinnacle / Plastic Head

STREAM OF CONSCIOUSNESS
Circus of fools / Aggravated / Last laugh / Overcome / Deteriorate / See through you / Just went back / Drift / Altered visions / One last thought / Whisker biscuit / Addicted
CD RR9 521 2
Roadrunner / Nov '88 / PolyGram

Cryptopsy

BLASPHEMY MADE FLESH
CD IR 011CD
Invasion / Apr '95 / Plastic Head

Crystal Palace FC

GLAD ALL OVER (A Tribute To Crystal Palace FC & Supporters) (Various Artists)
Glad all over: *Crystal Palace FC FA Cup Final Squad 1990* / Claret and blue: *Crystal Palace FC 1972* / Power to the Palace: *Palace* / Why can't we all get together: *Crystal Palace FC 1972 & Wives* / Bye bye blackbird: *Venables, Terry & Friends* / Flying high: *Palace* / Gonna build a Palace: *Gary's Construction Company* / Our Crystal Palace: *Crystal Band* / Where eagles fly: *Crystal Palace FC FA Cup Final Squad 1990* / Follow the eagles: *Universal* / We all follow the Palace: *Eastern Eagles* / We are the eagles: *Eastern Eagles* / Eagles are flying high: *Garage Mechanics* / I'm in love with Harry Bassett: *Lady Helen Of Selhurst* / Where's Joyce: *Lower Tier* / We're back where we belong: *Eddie Eagle* / Yes we're back: *Back Five*
CD CDGAFFER 19
Cherry Red / Aug '97 / Pinnacle

Crystal Trip

CRYSTAL TRIP
CD GULL 2CD
Seagull / Sep '93 / SRD

Crystals

ULTIMATE COLLECTION, THE
CD MAR 063
Marginal / Jun '97 / Greyhound

Csardas, Slovak

DANCE TUNES FROM THE PENNSYLVANIA COAL MINES
CD HTCD 37
Heritage / Jun '97 / ADA / Direct / Hot Shot / Jazz Music / Swift / Wellard

Cua, Rick

TIMES TEN
CD CD 58002
Salt / Apr '96 / Else

Cuarteto Caney

CUARTETO CANEY 1936-1939
CD HQCD 75
Harlequin / Jun '96 / Hot Shot / Jazz Music / Swift / Wellard

Cuarteto Marcano

CUARTETO MARCANO 1939-1945
CD HQCD 74
Harlequin / Jun '96 / Hot Shot / Jazz Music / Swift / Wellard

Cuarteto Patria

UNA COQUETA, A
CD CO 106
Corason / Jan '94 / ADA / CM / Direct

Cub

MAULER
CD ANDA 214
Au-Go-Go / Feb '97 / Cargo / Greyhound / Plastic Head

Cuba, Joe

SALSA Y BEMBE (Cuba, Joe Sextet)
CD CDHOT 606
Charly / Aug '96 / Koch

Cuban All Stars

PASSPORTE
Presentation / Rumberos de ayer / Descarga pa' gozar / Donde va mulata / Anga / Blem blem blem / Tata se ha vuelto loco / La clave de los primros
CD ENJ 90192
Enja / Apr '95 / New Note/Pinnacle / Vital/ SAM

Cubanate

ANTIMATTER
Blackout / Bodyburn / Revolution time / Autonomy / Junky / Exert / Disorder / Sucker / Switch / Forceful / Bodyburn (remix) / Kill or cure
CD DYCD 12
Dynamica / Sep '93 / Koch

BARBAROSSA
Vortech 1 / Barbarossa / Joy / Why are you here / Exultation / Musclemen / Come alive / Vortech 2 / Lord of the flies
CD DY 172
Dynamica / Jun '96 / Koch

CYBERIA
CD DY 82E
Dynamica / Nov '95 / Koch

SUCK TASTE SPIT
CD DY 202
Dynamica / Jul '96 / Koch

Cubanismo

MALEMBE
Mulence / Salsa pilon / Montuno allegre / El prugunton / Now in Marinao / Cubanismo lleho / Danson Daulen / Mar y tierra / Malembe
CD HNCD 1411
Hannibal / Apr '97 / ADA / Vital

Cuber, Ronnie

SCENE IS CLEAN, THE
Scene is clean / Adoracion / Song for Pharoah / Arroz con pollo / Mazambo / Fajardo / Tee's bag / Flamingo
CD MCD 92182
Milestone / Jul '94 / Cadillac / Complete/ Pinnacle / Jazz Music / Wellard

Cucchi, Flavio

FLAVIO CUCCHI PLAYS BARRIOS & VILLA-LOBOS
CD EUCD 1096
ARC / Jan '92 / ADA / ARC Music

FROM YESTERDAY TO PENNY LANE
CD EUCD 1247
ARC / Mar '94 / ADA / ARC Music

GUITAR - CROSSING OVER
CD EUCD 1326
ARC / Nov '95 / ADA / ARC Music

PLAYS BROUWER
CD EUCD 1192
ARC / Apr '92 / ADA / ARC Music

Cuchulainn

THREE MONTHS IN WINTER
CD PTICD 3006
Pure Traditional Irish / Aug '96 / ADA / CM / Direct / Ross

Cuckooland

POP SENSIBILITY
CD DAMGOOD 67CD
Damaged Goods / Jun '95 / Shellshock/ Disc

Cud

ASQUARIUS
CD 3953902
A&M / Apr '95 / PolyGram

SHOWBIZ
Somebody snatched my action / ESP / Waving and drowning / Sticks and stones / Mystery deepens / Slip away / One giant love / I reek of chic / Not neccessarily evil / You lead me / Tourniquet / Neurotica
CD 5402112
A&M / Apr '95 / PolyGram

Cudgels

GOD'S CHILDREN
CD BULL 90CD
Bring On Bull / Jul '92 / SRD / Vital

Cuenca, Juanita

NINA BONITA TE ILAMAN
CD ALCD 045
Alma Latina / Jul '97 / Discovery

Cues

WHY
Yes sir / Why / Crackerjack / Burn that candle / Poppa loves momma / Charlie Brown / Crazy crazy party / You're on my mind / Ladder / Destination 2100 and 65 / Prince or pauper / Rock 'n' roll Mr. Oriole / Warm spot / Girl I love / Oh my darlin' / Killer diller / I pretend / Be my wife / Don't make be-

lieve / Only you / Fell for your loving, I / Hot rotten soda pop / So near and yet so far / Forty leven dozen ways / Schoochie schoochie / Yes sir / Ol' man river
CD BCD 15510
Bear Family / May '91 / Direct / Rollercoaster / Swift

Cuesta, Ivan

A TI, COLOMBIA (Cuesta, Ivan Y Sus Baltimore Vallent)
CD ARHCD 388
Arhoolie / Apr '95 / ADA / Cadillac / Direct

Cueva, Julio

DESTINTEGRANDO
CD TCD 083
Tumbao Cuban Classics / Apr '97 / Discovery

Cuevas, Sergio

LA HARPE INDIENNE DU PARAGUAY
Camino de San Juan / Maquinita / Feliz Navidad / Harpa serenata / Pajaro campana / A mi dos amores / Nuevo baile / Poncho cuatro colores / Golpe llanero / Danza india / Barrio rincon / Magnolia / Balada de mi sueno / Pa i Zacaria
CD ARN 64040
Arion / '88 / ADA / Discovery

Cuffe, Tony

WHEN FIRST I WENT TO CALEDONIA
When first I went to Caledonia / Miss Wharton Duff/The mare / Iron horse / Caledonia / Dr. MacInnes' fancy / Buchan turnpike / Lass o' paties mill / Weary pund o' tow / Paddy Kelly's brew / Otterburn / Scalloway lasses / Humours of Tulla / Miss Forester
CD IRCD 011
Iona / Feb '94 / ADA / Direct / Duncans

Cugat, Xavier

CONGAS, CHIHUAHUAS & RUMBAS 1940-1945
CD HQCD 83
Harlequin / Sep '96 / Hot Shot / Jazz Music / Swift / Wellard

CUBAN MAMBO
CD CD 62003
Saludos Amigos / Apr '94 / Target/BMG

CUGAT IN FRANCE
Ciao ciao bambina / Souvenir d'Italie / Under Paris skies / Symphony / La boda de luis alonso / Valencia / Vola colomba (Fly dove) / Comme faccette mammeta / Sea / My man / Andalucia / Si vas a calatayud / El beso / El gato montes / Clavelitos / Malaguena
CD 74321357482
RCA / Jun '96 / BMG

DANCING PARTY VOL.5 (2CD Set)
CD Set 1917552
EPM / Jul '97 / ADA / Discovery

EL AMERICANO
El Americano / Yo quiero un mambo / Strangers in the dark / Que rico el mambo / Uuuh / Anything can happen - mambo / Mambo ay ay ay / Riviera mambo / Jamay / Maracaibo / Humpty dumpty / Mambo mania / Flute nightmares / Mambo gitano / Mambo OK / El Marijuano / Mondongo / Mambo at the Waldorf
CD CD 62078
Saludos Amigos / Jan '96 / Target/BMG

LE GRAN ORQUESTA DE XAVIER CUGAT
CD BM 513
Blue Moon / Feb '97 / Cadillac / Discovery / Greensleeves / Jazz Music / Jet Star / TKO Magnum

ME GUSTA LA CONGA (Cugat, Xavier & His Orchestra)
CD CD 62009
Saludos Amigos / Jan '93 / Target/BMG

PARA VIGO ME VAY (Cugat, Xavier & His Orchestra)
CD CD 62044
Saludos Amigos / Nov '93 / Target/BMG

SOUTH AMERICA, TAKE IT AWAY (24 Latin Hits) (Cugat, Xavier & His Waldorf-Astoria Orchestra)
Lady in red / Jalouise / Estrellita / Ahi viene la conga / Cielito lindo / La paloma / Night must fall / Perfida / Yours / La cumparsita / Jungle drums / Breeze and I / Frenesi / Green eyes / I yi yi yi yi I like you very much / Brazil / Tico tico / Siboney / Baia / Hasta manana / You belong to my heart / No can do / South America, take it away
CD CDAJA 5223
Living Era / Mar '97 / Select

TO ALL MY FRIENDS
New Cucaracha / Golden sunset / La Bamba / Que lindas in Mexicanas / Despedida / Cielito lindo / Banana boat song (Day O) / Cuban holiday / Adius marquita Linda / Barbados baila / Diamante negro / Braziliana
CD ISCD 146
Intersound / Jun '95 / Jazz Music

XAVIER CUGAT (Cugat, Xavier & His Band)
CD HQCD 14
Harlequin / '92 / Hot Shot / Jazz Music / Swift / Wellard

XAVIER CUGAT & DINAH SHORE 1939-1945 (Cugat, Xavier & Dinah Shore)
CD HQCD 29
Harlequin / Oct '93 / Hot Shot / Jazz Music / Swift / Wellard

XAVIER CUGAT 1944 & 1945 (Cugat, Xavier & His Orchestra)
CD CCD 59
Circle / Aug '94 / Jazz Music / Swift / Wellard

XAVIER CUGAT ON THE RADIO 1935-1942
CD HQCD 95
Harlequin / Apr '97 / Hot Shot / Jazz Music / Swift / Wellard

Cujo

ADVENTURES IN FOAM
CD NOZACD 03
Ninebar / Sep '96 / Kudos / Prime / RTM/Disc

Cul De Sac

CHINA GATE
CD FNCD 376
Flying Nun / Jun '96 / RTM/Disc

I DON'T WANT TO GO TO BED
CD FNCD 330
Flying Nun / Jun '95 / RTM/Disc

Cullum, Jim

BATTLE OF THE BANDS (Cullum, Jim Jazz Band & Banv Gibson)
CD RWCD 4
Riverwalk / Jun '96 / Jazz Music

BOOGIE WOOGIE (Cullum, Jim Jazz Band & David Holt/Dick Hyman)
CD RWCD 2
Riverwalk / Jun '96 / Jazz Music

HOORAY FOR HOAGY (Cullum, Jim Jazz Band)
CD ACD 251
Audiophile / '91 / Jazz Music

MUSIC OF JELLY ROLL MORTON (Cullum, Jim Jazz Band)
CD SOSCD 1254
Stomp Off / Jul '93 / Jazz Music / Wellard

SUPER SATCH (Cullum, Jim Big Band)
CD SOSCD 1148
Stomp Off / Jan '88 / Jazz Music / Wellard

Cult

CEREMONY
CD BEGA 122CD
Beggars Banquet / Oct '91 / RTM/Disc / Warner Music

COMPLETE RECORDINGS (Death Cult)
God's zoo / Brothers grimm / Ghost dance / Horse nation / Christians / God's zoo (these times)
CD SIT 2329CD
Situation 2 / '91 / Pinnacle

CULT
CD BBQCD 164
Beggars Banquet / Sep '94 / RTM/Disc / Warner Music

DREAMTIME
Horse nation / Butterflies / Flower in the desert / Bad medicine waltz / Spiritwalker / 83rd dream / Go West / Gimmick / Dreamtime / Rider in the snow
CD BBL 57 CD
Lowdown/Beggars Banquet / Oct '88 / RTM/Disc / Warner Music

ELECTRIC
Wild flower / Peace dog / Li'l devil / Aphrodisiac jacket / Electric ocean / Bad fun / King country man / Born to be wild / Love removal machine / Outlaw / Memphis hip shake
CD BBL 80CD
Beggars Banquet / Apr '97 / RTM/Disc / Warner Music

GHOST DANCE (Death Cult)
CD BBL 2008CD
Beggars Banquet / Sep '96 / RTM/Disc / Warner Music

INTERVIEW DISC
CD CBAK 4027
Baktabak / Sep '90 / Arabesque

LOVE
Nirvana / Big neon glitter / Love / Brother wolf, sister moon / Rain / Phoenix / Hollow man / Revolution / She sells sanctuary / Black angel
CD BBL 65CD
Beggars Banquet / Apr '97 / RTM/Disc / Warner Music

PURE CULT (The Best Of The Cult)
CD BEGA 130CD
Beggars Banquet / Jan '93 / RTM/Disc / Warner Music

SONIC TEMPLE
Fire woman / Sun king / Sweet soul sister / Soul asylum / Soldier blue / Edie (ciao baby) / American horse / Automatic blues / Wake up time for freedom / New York City
CD BBL 98CD
Beggars Banquet / Apr '97 / RTM/Disc / Warner Music

SOUTHERN DEATH CULT (Southern Death Cult)
All glory / Fat man / Today / False faces / Crypt / Crow / Faith / Vivisection / Apache / Moya
CD BBL 2009CD
Beggars Banquet / Sep '96 / RTM/Disc / Warner Music

Cult Maniax

LIVE AT ADAM & EVE'S
CD RRCD 012
Retch / May '97 / Cargo / Plastic Head

Cultural Roots

PRETTY WOMAN
CD LG 21073
Lagoon / Mar '93 / Grapevine/PolyGram

Culture

BALDHEAD BRIDGE
Them a payaka / How can I leave jah / Bald head bridge / Behold I come / Love shine bright / Jah love / Zion gate / So long babylon / Fool I (and I)
CD SHCD 44017
Shanachie / Mar '94 / ADA / Greensleeves / Koch

CULTURE AT WORK
CD SHANCD 43047
Shanachie / '89 / ADA / Greensleeves / Koch

CULTURE IN DUB - 15 DUB SHOTS
CD HBCD 173
Heartbeat / Aug '94 / ADA / Direct / Greensleeves / Jet Star

CUMBOLO
They never love in this time / Innocent blood / Cumbolo / Poor Jah people / Natty never get weary / Natty dread naw run / Down in Jamaica / This train / Payday / Mind who you beg for help
CD SHANCD 44005
Shanachie / '88 / ADA / Greensleeves / Koch

GOOD THINGS
Hand 'a' bowl / Good things / Love music / Psalm of Bob Marley / Cousin rude boy / Youthman move / Righteous loving / Chanting on
CD RASCD 3048
Ras / Aug '96 / Direct / Greensleeves / Jet Star / SRD

LION ROCK
CD NETCD 1005
Network / Apr '95 / Direct / Greensleeves / SRD

ONE STONE
CD RASCD 3188
Ras / Apr '96 / Direct / Greensleeves / Jet Star / SRD

PEACE AND LOVE
CD CPCD 8024
Charly / Feb '94 / Koch

PEACE AND LOVE
CD RN 7023
Rhino / Jun '97 / Grapevine/PolyGram / Jet Star

RAS PORTRAITS
One stone / Youth man move / Addis Ababa / Good things / Lazybones / Chanting on / Mark of the beast / I tried / Psalm of Bob Marley / Stoned again / Slice of Mount Zion / Righteous dub
CD RAS 3321
Ras / Jun '97 / Direct / Greensleeves / Jet Star / SRD

STONED
Dubbing in the capital / Eye of the needle / Stoned again / We need answers / And the river ran red / Determined / Lazybones / Firm up yourself / Mark of the beast / Can't get we out / It's about time / One track mind
CD RAS 3177
Ras / Feb '97 / Direct / Greensleeves / Jet Star / SRD

STRICTLY CULTURE
CD MCCD 158
Music Club / May '94 / Disc / THE

TOO LONG IN SLAVERY
Behold / Poor jah people / Stop the fussing and fighting / Cumbolo / Work on Natty / Tell me where you get it / Iron sharpening iron / International herb / Too long in slavery / Shepherd / Holy mount zion / Never get weary / Citizen as a peaceful dub
CD CDFL 9011
Frontline / Sep '90 / EMI / Jet Star

TOO LONG IN SLAVERY/DREAD IN A BABYLON/DREADLOCKS (3CD Set) (Culture & U-Roy/Gladiators)
CD Set TPAK 14
Virgin / Oct '90 / EMI

TROD ON
CD HBCD 137
Heartbeat / Jun '93 / ADA / Direct / Greensleeves / Jet Star

TWO SEVENS CLASH
Callin' rasta for I / I'm alone in the wilderness / Pirate days / Two sevens clash / I'm not ashamed / Get ready to ride the lion to Zion / Black starliner / Jah pretty face / See them a-come / Natty dread taking over
CD SHANCD 44001
Shanachie / '88 / ADA / Greensleeves / Koch

WINGS OF A DOVE
Marcus / Why worry about them / Marriage in canaan / Wings of a dove / Freedom time / Rub-a-dub style / Pass on / Campyard / Too much pressure / England fireplace
CD SHCD 43097
Shanachie / Jul '92 / ADA / Greensleeves / Koch

Culture Beat

CULTURE BEAT
Inside out / Intro / Walk the same line / Get it right / Troubles / Nothing can come ... take me away / Miracle / Crying in the rain / Do I have you / Under my skin / Worth the wait / In the mood
CD 4874042
Epic / Jun '96 / Sony

SERENITY
Serenity (prolog) / Mr. Vain / Got to get it / World in your hands / Adelante / Rocket to the moon / Anything / Key to your heart / Other side of me / Hurt / Mother Earth / Serenity (epilog) / ID Tania / ID Jay
CD 4741012
Epic / Sep '96 / Sony

Culture Ceilidh Band

AFTER THE CEILIDH
CD CDITV 543
Scotdisc / May '93 / Conifer/BMG / Duncans / Ross

Culture Club

BEST OF CULTURE CLUB, THE
Do you really want to hurt me / White boy / Church of the poison mind / Changing everyday / War song / I'm afraid of me / It's a miracle / Dream / Time (Clock of the heart) / Dive / Victims / I'll tumble 4 ya / Miss me blind / Mistake no. 3 / Medal song / Karma chameleon
CD CDVIP 102
Virgin / Sep '94 / EMI

BEST OF CULTURE CLUB, THE (18 Original Hits/3CD Set)
Karma chameleon / Church of the poison mind / It's a miracle / White boy / Dream (from electric dreams) / Victims / Do you really want to hurt me / Time (clock of the heart) / Mistake no.3 / Changing everyday / Dive / Move away / War song / I'll tumble 4 ya / Medal song / I'm afraid of me / Miss me blind / God thank you woman
CD Set LAD 873182
Disky / Nov '96 / Disky / THE

COLLECT 12" MIXES PLUS
Move away / Miss me blind/It's a miracle / God thank you woman / I'll tumble 4 ya / Love is cold / Do you really want to hurt me / Everything I own / Colour by numbers / From luzury to heartache / Time / Black money / Love is love / Man shake / War song
CD CDVIP 116
Virgin VIP / Mar '94 / EMI

COLOUR BY NUMBERS
Karma chameleon / It's a miracle / Black money / Changing everyday / That's the way / Church of the poison mind / Miss me blind / Mr. Man / Storm keeper / Victims
CD CDV 2285
Virgin / Feb '92 / EMI

KISSING TO BE CLEVER
White boy / You know I'm not crazy / I'll tumble 4 ya / Take control / Love twist / Boy boy (I'm the boy) / I'm afraid of me / White boys can't control it / Do you really want to hurt me
CD VI 874792
Disky / Nov '96 / Disky / THE
CD CDVIP 158
Virgin VIP / Oct '96 / EMI

THIS TIME
Do you really want to hurt me / Move away / I'll tumble 4 ya / Love is love / Victims / Karma chameleon / Church of the poison mind / Miss me blind / Time (Clock of the heart) / It's a miracle / Black money / War song / I'll tumble 4 ya (US 12" mix) / Miss me blind (US 12" mix)
CD CDVTV 1
Virgin / Apr '92 / EMI

WAKING UP WITH THE HOUSE ON FIRE
Dangerous man / War song / Unfortunate thing / Crime time / Mistake no.3 / Dive / Medal song / Don't talk about it / Mannequin / Hello goodbye
CD ______ CDV 2330
Virgin / Oct '84 / EMI

Culture Musical Club

TAARAB MUSIC OF ZANZIBAR VOL.4
Sibadili / Mwiko / Bingwa amekwenda kapa / Subalkheri mpenzi / Kupendana kwetu sisi / Sasa sinaye / Jipeleleze / Nimtakaye hataki / Mbuzi / Nieye / Umenita azizi
CD ______ CDORBD 041
Globestyle / May '89 / Pinnacle

Culturemix

CULTUREMIX (Culturemix & Bill Nelson)
Luna park / Radio head / Housewives on drugs / Dancematic / Four postcards home / Zebra / Exile / Tangram / Cave paintings
CD ______ RES 113CD
Resurgence / Apr '97 / Pinnacle

Cultus Sanguine

CULTUS SANGUINE
CD ______ WLR 006CD
Wounded Love / Jul '95 / Plastic Head

Cunliffe, Bill

PAUL SIMON SONG BOOK, A
You can call me Al / I do it for your love / Oh, Marion / One trick pony / Scarborough Fair / Jonah / Still crazy after all these years / Mrs. Robinson / America / Boxer / 59th Street Bridge song / Bridge over troubled water
CD ______ 77005
Discovery / Nov '93 / Warner Music

RARE CONNECTION, A
Stella by starlight / Chick it out / Jamaican lounge lizards / Cityscape / Rare connection / Big slide / Joyous dance / Minnesota / Miyako / Nobody else but me
CD ______ 77007
Discovery / Apr '94 / Warner Music

Cunningham, David

WATER
Stars / Next day / Once removed / Fourth sea / White, blue and grey / Shade creek / Short winter's day / Blue river / Beneath the vines / Yellow river / Low sun / Only shadows / Liquid hand / Dark ocean / Same day
CD ______ MTM 31
Made To Measure / Sep '96 / New Note/ Pinnacle

Cunningham, Deirdre

CITY OF TRIBES
City of tribes / Dig for water / Mystical island / Secret pathway / Stormy heart / Fire on the line / Terror times / Darlin' Corey / September 1913 / Stoney fingers and star of Munster
CD ______ CDLDL 1246
Lochshore / Jan '97 / ADA / Direct / Duncans

Cunningham, John

FAIR WARNING
Celtic society's quickstep/42nd Highlander's farewell / Archibald MacDonald of Keppoch / Planxty Drew/Planxty Wilkinson / Sad is my fate / Lord Drummond/Lady Margaret Stewart/Crarae / Logan water / Drovers lads/Mug of brown ale / Waulkin o' the fauld / Fair warning
CD ______ GLCD 1047
Green Linnet / Oct '88 / ADA / CM / Direct / Highlander / Roots

Cunningham, John

SHANKLY GATES
CD ______ LADIDA 020
La-Di-Da / Jul '94 / Vital

Cunningham, Larry

AT HIS BEST
Good old country music / They wouldn't do it now / Ballybunion by the sea / Night coach to Dallas / I love you because / 90 years on / My Kathleen / Is his love any better than mine / Forty shades of green / Pretty little girl from Omagh / Emerald Isle Express / Come back to Erin / Blue side of lonesome / Lough Gowna / Me ould tamborine / Lovely Leitrim / There's been a change in you / Seems like I'm always leaving / I used to be a railroad bum / Old Bog road / Annaghdown
CD ______ 3036000922
Carlton / Feb '97 / Carlton

Cunningham, Phil

AIRS AND GRACES
CD ______ GLCD 3032
Green Linnet / Nov '93 / ADA / CM / Direct / Highlander / Roots

PALOMINO WALTZ, THE
Bombardier beetle/Webbs wonderful / Ross Memorial Hospital / Palomino waltz/Donna's waltz / Four stroke reel/Martin O'Connor's flying clog / Leaving Glen Affric / Ceilidh funk / Wedding / Violet Tulloch's welcome to the Crask of Aigas / Laird of Drumblair / Ciara McCarthy's lullaby
CD ______ GLCD 1102
Green Linnet / Nov '92 / ADA / CM / Direct / Highlander / Roots

REBOX
CD Set ______ GLCD 200
Green Linnet / May '94 / ADA / CM / Direct / Highlander / Roots

RELATIVITY (Cunningham, Phil & Johnny/M. O Domhnaill/T. Ni Dhomhnail)
Hut on Staffin Island / Sandy MacLeod of Garafad / Soft horse reel / There was a lady / Gile Mear / Gracelands / When Barney flew over the hills / Leaving Brittany / Pernod waltz / An seanduine doite / John Cunningham's return to Edinburgh / Heather bells/Bell reel / Limerick lasses / Ur-Chill an Chreagain
CD ______ GLCD 1059
Green Linnet / Feb '88 / ADA / CM / Direct / Highlander / Roots

Cunningham, Woody

NEVER SAY NEVER
Highways of my life / Animal / Forgive me / Body to body / Remove your halo / Tonite / You fooled me / Love is taking over / Hung up on your love / Never say never
CD ______ EXCDP 15
Expansion / May '97 / 3mv/Sony

Cuppini, Gil

WHATS NEW VOL.2 (Cuppini, Gil Quintet)
CD ______ RTCL 811CD
Right Tempo / Jul '96 / New Note/ Pinnacle / Timewarp

Curbelo, Jose

LIVE AT THE CHINA DOLL, NEW YORK 1946
CD ______ TCD 074
Tumbao Cuban Classics / Jul '96 / Discovery

Curd Duca

MINIMALISTIC MOOD (Switched On Wagner)
CD ______ EFA 006812
Mille Plateau / Nov '96 / SRD

Cure

100 YEARS - A TRIBUTE TO THE CURE (Various Artists)
CD ______ CLP 0001
Cleopatra / Jun '97 / Cargo / Greyhound / Plastic Head / RTM/Disc / SRD

BOYS DON'T CRY
Boys don't cry / Plastic passion / 10.15 Saturday night / Accuracy / Object / Jumping someone else's train / Subway song / Killing an arab / Fire in Cairo / Another day / Grinding halt / World War / Three imaginary boys
CD ______ 8150112
Fiction / Jun '92 / PolyGram

CONCERT - THE CURE LIVE
Shake dog shake / Primary / Charlotte sometimes / Hanging gardens / Give me it / Walk / Hundred years / Forest / 10.15 Saturday night / Killing an arab / Heroin face / Boys don't cry / Subway song / At night / In your house / Drowning man / Other voices / Funeral party / All mine / Forever
CD ______ 8236822
Fiction / Jun '92 / PolyGram

CURE (Interview Disc)
CD ______ 3D 003
Network / Dec '96 / Total/BMG

CURE 16CD BOX SET
CD Set ______ 5135992
Fiction / Jan '92 / PolyGram

CURE: INTERVIEW PICTURE DISC
CD ______ CBAK 4003
Baktabak / Apr '88 / Arabesque

DISINTEGRATION
Plainsong / Closedown / Last dance / Fascination Street / Same deep water as you / Homesick / Pictures of you / Love song / Lullaby / Prayers for rain / Disintegration / Untitled
CD ______ 8393532
Fiction / Jun '92 / PolyGram

ENTREAT
Pictures of you / Closedown / Last dance / Fascination Street / Prayers for rain / Disintegration / Homesick / Untitled
CD ______ 8433592
Fiction / Jun '92 / PolyGram

FAITH
All cats are grey / Carnage visors / Doubt / Drowning man / Faith / Funeral party / Holy hour / Other voices / Primary
CD ______ 8276872
Fiction / Jun '92 / PolyGram

HEAD ON THE DOOR, THE
In between days / Kyoto song / Blood / Six different ways / Push / Baby screams / Close to me / Night like this / Screw / Sinking
CD ______ 8272312
Fiction / Jun '92 / PolyGram

JAPANESE WHISPERS
Let's go to bed / Walk / Love cats / Dream / Just one kiss / Upstairs room / Lament / Speak my language
CD ______ 8174702
Fiction / Jun '92 / PolyGram

KISS ME, KISS ME, KISS ME
Kiss / Catch / Torture / If only tonight we could sleep / Why can't I be you / How beautiful you are... / Snakepit / Just like heaven / Hot hot hot / All I want / One more time / Like cockatoos / Icing sugar smooth / Perfect girl / Thousand hours / Shiver and shake / Fight
CD ______ 8321302
Fiction / Jun '92 / PolyGram

MIXED UP
Lullaby / Close to me / Fascination Street / Walk / Love song / Forest / Pictures of you / Hot hot hot / Why can't I be you / Caterpillar / In between days / Never enough
CD ______ 8470002
Fiction / Jun '92 / PolyGram

PARIS
CD ______ 5199942
Fiction / Oct '93 / PolyGram

PORNOGRAPHY
Pornography / Hanging gardens / Hundred years / Siamese twins / Figurehead / Strange day / Cold / Short term effect
CD ______ 8276882
Fiction / Jun '92 / PolyGram

SEVENTEEN SECONDS
At night / Final sound / Forest / In your house / M / Play for today / Reflection / Secrets / Seventeen seconds / Three
CD ______ 8253542
Fiction / Jun '92 / PolyGram

SHOW
Tape / Open / High / Pictures of you / Lullaby / Just like heaven / Fascination Street / Night like this / Trust / Doing the unstuck / Walk / Let's go to bed / Friday I'm in love / In between days / From the edge of the deep green sea / Never enough / Cut / End
CD ______ 5199512
Fiction / Sep '93 / PolyGram

STARING AT THE SEA
Killing an Arab / 10.15 Saturday night / Boys don't cry / Jumping someone else's train / Forest / Play for today / Primary / Other voices / Charlotte sometimes / Hanging gardens / Let's go to bed / Walk / Love cats / I'm cold / Caterpillar / In between days / Another journey by train / Close to me / Descent / Night like this / Splintered in her head / Mr. Pink eyes / Happy the man / Throw your foot / Exploding boy / Few hours after this / Man inside my mouth / Stop dead / New day
CD ______ 8292392
Fiction / May '86 / PolyGram

THREE IMAGINARY BOYS
Accuracy / Another day / Fire in Cairo / Foxy lady / Grinding halt / It's not you / Meat hook / Object / So what / Subway / 10.15 Saturday night / Three imaginary boys
CD ______ 8276862
Fiction / Jun '92 / PolyGram

TOP, THE
Caterpillar / Piggy in the mirror / Empty world / Bananafishbones / Top / Shake dog shake / Bird mad girl / Wailing wall / Give me it / Dressing up
CD ______ 8211362
Fiction / Jun '92 / PolyGram

WILD MOOD SWINGS
Want / Club America / This is a lie / 13th / Strange attraction / Mint car / Jupiter crash / Round and round and round / Gone / Numb / Return / Trap / Treasure / Bare
CD ______ FIXCD 28
Fiction / Apr '96 / PolyGram

WISH
Open / High / Apart / From the edge of the deep green sea / Wendy time / Doing the unstuck / Friday I'm in love / Trust / Letter to Elise / Cut / To wish impossible things / End
CD ______ FISCD 20
Fiction / May '92 / PolyGram

Curiosity Killed The Cat

BACK TO FRONT (Curiosity)
Work it out / Hang on in there baby / Gimme the sunshine (Original) / Vibezin' / Addict / Killing me softly / Call on me / Gimme the sunshine (Ron's reprise) / Music's a mystery / Spice it up / Fall in again / Work it out
CD ______ 74321166572
RCA / Oct '93 / BMG

VERY BEST OF CURIOSITY KILLED THE CAT, THE
Down to Earth / Name and number / Free / Misfit / First place / Go go ahead / Keep on trying / Ball & chain / Cascade / Curiosity killed the cat / Treat you so well / Who are you / Bullet / Mile high / We just gotta do it (for us) / Something new, something blue / Shallow memory / Ordinary day
CD ______ 5525482
Spectrum / Sep '96 / PolyGram

Curless, Dick

TOMBSTONE EVERY MILE, A (7CD Set)
Coat of Maine / Ida dance / Jelly doughnuts / Fiddlers dance / Cottage in the pines / Cupid's arrow / Baby darling / Naponee / Rocky mountain queen / Streets of Laredo / Foggy foggy dew / China nights / Blues in my mind / Lovin' Dan sixty minute man / Blue yodle # 6 / Bright lights and blonde / Travellin' man / I'm ragged but I'm right / St. James infirmary / I am a pilgrim / Tuck me to sleep in my old kentucky home / I ain't got nobody / Rainbow in my heart / Something's wrong with you / Evil hearted man blues / I dreamed of a hillbilly heaven / Deck of cards / High noon / Strawberry roan / Red river valley / Cowboy Jack / On top of old smokey / Home on the range / Bury me not on the lone prairie / Chisholm trail / I ride an old paint / Whoopie ti yi yo / Green grow the lilacs / Last roundup / Crawdad song / Rock Island line / Don't fence me in / Big rock candy mountain / Rovin' gambler / Molly darlin' / Yellow rose of texas / Liza Jane / Careless love / Buffalo girl / San Antonio Rose / What a friend we have in Jesus / Whispering hope / My old kentucky home / Beautiful dreamer / I was seeing Nellie home / You tell me your dream, I'll tell you mine / Silver threads among the gold / I've been working on the railroad / Little brown jug / Rock of ages / Church in the wildwood / Bring them in / Onward Christian soldiers / Nearer my God to thee / In the garden / Jesus loves me / I love to tell the story / Old rugged cross / Tombstone every mile / Heart talk / King of the road / Uncle Tom / Six times a day / Down by the old river / Teardrops in my heart / Nine pound hammer / Sunny side of the mountain / Tater raisin / Down by the river / Tater raisin' man / Friend that makes it four / Mama's hand / Mom and Dad's waltz / Mama's hands / Daddy and home / I'm going home / Buckaroo / Little Terry / Please don't make me go / You, you only you / Terrible tangles web / Devil like me needs / No fool like an old fool / Old standby / Too late / I can't stop (lovin' you) / For ever and ever / Congratulations, you're absolutely / Highwayman / Baron / Memories / Old picture and a ring / Good job hunting and fishing / How do I say goodbye / I didn't know love was this way / House of memories / All of me belongs to you / My side of the night / Game of love and poker / Try and leave me / On the outside looking in / Hello honey / Hobo / Tears of Saint Ann / I went bad for a pretty girl / Tornado tillie / Life goes on / Big foot / Mumble boogy / You can't go back again / Shoes / When Dad was around / End of the road / Bury the bottle with me / Wrinkled, crinkled, wadded dollar bill / Just for the record / I'm worried about me / Heartline special / Secret of your heart / Bummin' on track E / Wild side of town / Nobody knows you (when you're down and out) / Things / Easy woman / Down at the corner at Kelly's / Tonight's the night my angels halo fell / Maybe I'll cry over you / It's nothing to me / Good old days / Over the edge / Blue is a beautiful color / Good year for the wine / Tears instead of cheers / All I need is you / Brand new bed of roses / Be here to love me / Kentucky boy / Fanning the flame / Sun / Somebody else / Jamaica farewell / Golden rocket / Just a closer walk with thee / I'm in love again / I walk the line / Marianne / Down by the riverside / Oh, lonesome me / Where is your heart tonight / I can get along without you now / What do I care / There's been a change in me / After all I ain't got much to lose / Monday night / Just a little lovin' / Tuck me to sleep / Montreal express / Station breaks / Tumbleweed kid
CD Set ______ BCD 15882
Bear Family / Feb '96 / Direct / Rollercoaster / Swift

TRAVELLING THROUGH
CD ______ ROUCD 3137
Rounder / Aug '95 / ADA / CM / Direct

WELCOME TO MY WORLD
CD ______ RRCD 007
Rocade / Aug '93 / ADA / Direct

Curlew

BEAUTIFUL WESTERN SADDLE, A
CD ______ RUNE 50
Cuneiform / Nov '87 / ReR Megacorp

Current 93

ALL THE PRETTY LITTLE HORSES
CD ______ DURTRO 030CD
Durtro / Oct '96 / World Serpent

AS THE WORLD DISAPPEARS
CD ______ DURTRO 007CD
Durtro / Oct '96 / World Serpent

CHRIST AND THE PALE QUEENS
CD MAL 666CD
Maldoror / Oct '96 / Pinnacle / World Serpent

CROOKED CROSSES FOR THE NODDING
CD UD 033CD
United Dairies / Sep '90 / World Serpent

CROWLEYMASS
Crowleymass / As for the other side (Christmassacre) / Crowleymass / I arise
CD DURTRO 418CD
Durtro / Jul '97 / World Serpent

DAWN
CD DURTRO 002CD
Durtro / Oct '96 / World Serpent

DOG'S BLOOD RISING
CD DURTRO 027CD
Durtro / Oct '96 / World Serpent

EARTH COVERS EARTH
CD DURTRO 012CD
Durtro / Oct '96 / World Serpent

HITLER AS KHALKI
CD DURTRO 014CD
Durtro / Oct '96 / World Serpent

HORSEY
Diana / Death of the corn / Tree / Broken birds fly / Horsey
CD DURTRO 032
Durtro / Apr '97 / World Serpent

IMPERIUM
CD DURTRO 008CD
Durtro / Oct '96 / World Serpent

IN A FOREIGN TOWN, IN A FOREIGN LAND (Current 93 & Thomas Ligotti)
His shadow shall rise to a higher place / Bells shall sound forever / Soft voice whispers nothing / When you hear the singing you will know it is time
CD DURTRO 035CD
Durtro / Jul '97 / World Serpent

ISLAND
CD DURTRO 006CD
Durtro / Oct '96 / World Serpent

LIVE AT THE BAR MALDOROR
CD DURTRO 001CD
Durtro / Jan '89 / World Serpent

LIVE IN FRANKFURT 1991 (Current 93 & Death In June/Sol Invictus)
CD WSBLCD 001
World Serpent / Oct '96 / World Serpent

LOONEY RUNES
CD DURTRO 004CD
Durtro / Oct '96 / World Serpent

MENSTRUAL NIGHT
CD DURTRO 020CD
Durtro / Oct '96 / World Serpent

MENSTRUAL YEARS (2CD Set)
CD Set DURTRO 016CD
Durtro / Oct '96 / World Serpent

NATURE UNVEILED
CD DURTRO 009CD
Durtro / Oct '96 / World Serpent

OF RUINE...
CD DURTRO 018CD
Durtro / Oct '96 / World Serpent

SWASTIKAS FOR NODDY
Benediction / Blessing / North / One eye / Black sun bloody moon / Oh coal black Smith / Panzer rune / Black flowers please / Final church / Summer of love / Hey ho the Noddy (oh) / Beau soleil / Scarlet woman / Stair song / Angel / Since yesterday / Valediction / Malediction
CD DURTRO 017CD
Durtro / Oct '96 / World Serpent

THUNDER PERFECT MIND
CD DURTRO 011CD
Durtro / Oct '96 / World Serpent

Curry, Clifford

CLIFFORD'S BLUES
CD APCD 122
Appaloosa / May '97 / ADA / Direct / TKO Magnum

Curse

TEENAGE MEAT
CD OPM 2110CD
Other People's Music / May '97 / Greyhound / Plastic Head

Cursed

RHAPSODY
CD DW 20629CD
Deathwish / Jan '92 / Plastic Head

Curson, Ted

PLENTY OF HORN
Caravan / Nosruc / Things we did last summer / Dem's blues / Ahma (see ya) / Flatted fifth / Bali Ha'i / Antibes / Mr. Teddy
CD CDBOP 018
Boplicity / Mar '94 / Pinnacle

TEARS FOR DOLPHY
CD BLCD 760190
Black Lion / Jun '94 / Cadillac / Jazz Music / Koch / Wellard

TED CURSON GROUP FEATURING ERIC DOLPHY
CD COD 016
Jazz View / Jun '92 / Harmonia Mundi

Curtin, Dan

ART AND SCIENCE
Airport martini / America / Ride / A 23 / Art and science / One evening at Mrs. Applebee's / Lunar groove / Mist / More
CD PF 051CD
Peacefrog / Oct '96 / Mo's Music Machine / Prime / RTM/Disc / Vital

DECEPTION
I'll take you there / My mystery / Plot and deceive / There and gone (parts 1 and 2) / Horizontal momentum / Horizontal momentum / Voices from another age / Greengirl
CD SBLCD 5010
Sublime / Mar '97 / Vital

WEB OF LIFE
Matter of sound / Quantum / Biotic / Intersellar perception / Out of sight and mind / Path / Subconscious / Awareness / 3rd from the sun / Envision
CD PF 038CD
Peacefrog / Sep '95 / Mo's Music Machine / Prime / RTM/Disc / Vital

Curtin, Glen

WILD COLONIAL BOY
CD MACCD 316
Autograph / Aug '96 / BMG

Curtis, Amy

PEACE FOR LOVE
CD FSR 5004CD
Fresh Sound / Mar '95 / Discovery / Jazz Music

Curtis, Mac

BLUE JEAN HEART
Grandaddy's rockin' / Just so you call me / Half hearted love / If I had me a woman / Low road / That ain't nothing but right / Don't you love me / You ain't treatin' me right / I'll be gentle / Say so / Blue jean heart / Goosebumps / You are my very special baby / What you want / Little Miss Linda / Missy Ann
CD CDCHARLY 164
Charly / Feb '91 / Koch

Curtis, Ronald

THANKS FOR THE MEMORY
There's a blue ridge round my heart / Old pianna rag / I can't give you anything but love / Liza / Flamingo / Sylvia / Ma curly headed baby / Oh lady be good / Sweet Sue, just you / Happy feet / Bye bye blues / Love is / O' my beloved father / Crackin' corn / Memories of you / Thanks for the memory / I've got a pocketful of dreams / Cabaret / I've got my love to keep me warm / Powder your face with sunshine / Dambuster's march / Butterflies in the rain / Happy wanderer / Dixie / De camptown races / Old black Joe / Swanee river / Turkey in the straw / Marching through Georgia / Out of the blue / Storm at sea / Anchors aweigh / What shall we do with a drunken sailor / Hornpipe / Life on the ocean wave / Skye boat song / Eternal father / Strong to save / Comedian's galop / Tiger rag / Lucky old sun / Cactus polka / Here's to the next time / When day is done
CD CDGRS 1287
Grosvenor / May '96 / Grosvenor

Curtis, Yvonne

BEST OF YVONNE CURTIS
CD BROWNCD 002
Brown / Mar '96 / Jet Star

Curved Air

AIR CONDITIONING
It happened today / Stretch / Screw / Blind man / Vivaldi / Hide and seek / Propositions / Rob one / Situation
CD 7599264332
WEA / Jan '96 / Warner Music

LIVE
CD HTDCD 49
HTD / Dec '95 / CM / Pinnacle

LOVECHILD
Exsultate Jubilate / Lovechild / Seasons / Flasher / Joan / Dancer / Widow / Paris by night
CD CLACD 342
Castle / Jun '94 / BMG

MIDNIGHT WIRE
Woman on a one night stand / Day breaks my heart / Pipe of dreams / Orange Street blues / Dance of love / Midnight wire / It happened today
CD HTDCD 50
HTD / Dec '95 / CM / Pinnacle

SECOND ALBUM
Young mother / Backstreet luv / Jumbo / You know / Puppets / Everdance / Bright summer's day / Piece of mind
CD 7599264342
WEA / Jan '96 / Warner Music

Cusack, Michael

PIPERS OF DISTINCTION
CD CDMON 807
Monarch / Jul '90 / ADA / CM / Direct / Duncans

Cusan Tan

RIDGE, THE
CD SCD 2116
Sain / Jan '96 / ADA / Direct / Greyhound

Cusp

SPACE AND TIME LIQUIDS AND METAL
CD WM 8
Swim / Nov '95 / Kudos / RTM/Disc / SRD

Custy, Mary

MARY CUSTY BAND, THE (Custy, Mary Band)
CD MCB 003CD
MCB / Nov '96 / ADA

Custy, Tola

SETTING FREE (Custy, Tola & Cyril O'Donoghue)
CD CICD 098
Clo Iar-Chonnachta / Aug '94 / CM

Cutler, Chris

DOMESTIC STORIES (Cutler, Chris & Lutz Glandien)
CD RERLSMCD
ReR/Recommended / Mar '93 / ReR Megacorp / RTM/Disc

LIVE IN MOSCOW, PRAGUE AND WASHINGTON (Cutler, Chris & Fred Frith)
CD RERCCFFCD
ReR/Recommended / Apr '90 / ReR Megacorp / RTM/Disc

LIVE IN TRONDHEIM, BERLIN AND LIMOGES (Cutler, Chris & Fred Frith)
CD RERCCFF 2
ReR/Recommended / Oct '96 / ReR Megacorp / RTM/Disc

Cutler, Ivor

LIFE IN A SCOTCH SITTING ROOM
CD CREV 035CD
Rev-Ola / May '95 / 3mv/Vital

LUDO
CD CREV 49CD
Creation / Mar '97 / 3mv/Vital

WET HANDLE, A
Her tissues / An American drink / One day / Out of decency / My disposition / No I won't / It's stupid / By the bus / Thatcher generation / My vest / Goosie / When it warts / Her Zimmer / Farmers wife / Bets / Just in time / Specific sundry / Just listen / Breaking point / Spring back / Hell / Man / Place / Hello explorer / Not asking / His slow hand / Local creatures / Heptagon / Where's my razor / One side / Singing to my foot / Ride off / Great albatross / Berd / Half and half / Get off the road / Fine example / Face of people / Stand well clear / Naughty Sydney / Perverse / Bargain / Space sandwich / Baked beetle / Taking hands / Entitles / It / Kitchen knife / Not from Hens / Carpet / Beyond / Way out / To take / Do you call that living / On holiday / Taste of gunny / Blunt yashmak / Kiddies / I give up / My window box / Pain in the neck / Not even / Tablets / Flat thin chests / Good girl / He himself / Uncrossing her legs / Crete/Greece / Squeaky / Oddly comforting / Original sweet / Bridge / Butterfly / Snaps / Just / Hummed and hawed / Thursday / Cosy nest / Slice of seedcake / What a funny room / Heavy rock / Whole forest / Little Hetty
CD CRECD 217
Creation / May '97 / 3mv/Vital

Cutting Crew

BEST OF CUTTING CREW, THE
(I just) died in your arms / Any colour / Fear of falling / Everything but my pride / Contact high / Tip of your tongue / One for the mockingbird / I've been in love before / Life in a dangerous time / Don't look back / Scattering / Christians / (I just) died in your arms (mix) / Reach for the sky / (Between a) rock and a hard place / If that's the way you want it
CD CDVIP 121
Virgin VIP / Dec '93 / EMI

Cutting Edge

TURNING THE TIDE
Turning the tide / Seagate salsa / Beechgrove / Jig of slurs / When she sleeps / Sniffer's delight / Ass in the graveyard / Silver spire / O'Keefe's no.7 / Ceilidh Dave / Miss Rowan Davies / Shandon bells / Gorgon's Ola / Rudy's reggae / Lilly
CD NGCD 1007
Ninegates Music / Jan '95 / ADA

Cutty Ranks

60 MILLION WAYS TO DIE
CD P 253871
Priority / Nov '96 / Jet Star

FROM MI HEART
CD SHCD 45001
Shanachie / Jun '93 / ADA / Greensleeves / Koch

Cutty Wren

PARSON'S HAT
CD CICD 101
Clo Iar-Chonnachta / Dec '94 / CM

Cuzner, Kate

FLY BY WIRE
Tell me know / Snake in the grass / Metamorphosis / Savannah song / Jim'll mix it / Fly by wire / Contemplation / Rain dance / Twisting shadows / Ballad for Paul / Rodent rap
CD FMRCD 28
Future / Jun '97 / ADA / Harmonia Mundi

Cwithe

ILLEGAL (2CD Set)
CD Set BR 028CD
Blue Room Released / Mar '97 / Essential/ BMG / SRD

CWS Band

LAND OF THE MOUNTAIN AND THE FLOOD
CD HARCD 1123
Harlequin / Sep '93 / TKO Magnum

Cyan Kills E Boli

DO NOT OPEN
CD EFA 155862
Gymnastic / Nov '95 / SRD

Cyber-Tec

LET YOUR BODY DIE
CD SPV 07661112
SPV / Jan '96 / Koch / Plastic Head

Cybermen

CYBERMEN, THE
CD ES 111CD
Estrus / Nov '96 / Cargo / Greyhound / Plastic Head

Cybertron

INTERFACE (The Roots Of Techno)
Clear / Eden / Enter / Techno city / Cosmic cars / Alleys of your mind / Megiddo / R 9 / Cosmic raindance / El Salvador / Vision
CD CDSEWD 069
Southbound / Jan '94 / Pinnacle

Cyborg

CHRONICLES
CD RRS 951CD
Die Hard/Progress / Sep '96 / Plastic Head

Cyco Mike

LOST MY BRAIN... (ONCE AGAIN)
I love destruction / All I ever get / FUBAR / All kinda crazy / Gonna be alright / Save a peace for me / Nothing to lose / Ain't gonna get me / Lost my brain once again / It's always something / Cyco Mike wants you / Ain't mess'n around
CD 4811362
Epic / Oct '95 / Sony

Cygnus X

HYPERMETRICAL
CD EYEUKCD 006
Eye Q / Jan '96 / Vital

Cylob

CYLOBIAN SUNSET
CD CAT 033CD
Rephlex / Jul '96 / Prime / RTM/Disc

Cymande

CYMANDE
Message / Brothers on the slide / Dove / Bra / Fug / For baby woh / Rickshaw / Equitorial forest / Listen / Getting it back / Anthracite / Willy's headache / Genevieve / 'Pon de jungle / Rastafarian folk song / One more / Zion I
CD NEX CD 202
Sequel / Jul '92 / BMG

Cypher In The Snow

BLOW AWAY THE GLITTER DIAMONDS
CD CAR 24
Candy Ass / Jul '97 / Cargo

Cypress Hill

BLACK SUNDAY
I wanna get high / I ain't goin' out like that / Insane in the brain / When the ship goes down / Lick a shot / Cock the hammer / Interlude / Li'l Putos / Legalize it / Hits from the bong / What go around come around, kid / A to the K / Hand on the glock / Break 'em off some
CD 474075 2
Ruff House / Jul '93 / Sony

CYPRESS HILL
Pigs / How I could just kill a man / Hand on the pump / Hole in the head / Ultraviolet dreams / Light another / Phuncky feel one / Break it up / Real estate / Stoned is the way of the walk / Psycobetabuckdown / Something for the blunted / Latin lingo / Funky Cypress Hill shit / Tres eqyis / Born to get busy
CD 4688932
Ruff House / Feb '97 / Sony

TEMPLE OF BOOM
Spark another owl / Throw your set in the air / Stoned raiders / Illusions / Killa hill niggas / Boom biddy bye bye / No rest for the wicked / Make a move / Killafornia / Funk freakers / Locotes / Red light visions / Strictly hip hop / Let it rain / Everybody must get stoned
CD 4781272
CD Set 4781279
Ruff House / Oct '95 / Sony

UNRELEASED AND REVAMPED
Boom biddy bye bye / Throw your hands in the air / Intellectual dons: *Cypress Hill & Call O Da Wild* / Hands on the pump / Whatta you know / Hits from the bong / Illusions / Latin lingo / When the ship goes down
CD 4852302
Columbia / Aug '96 / Sony

Cyrille, Andrew

METAMUSICIANS' STOMP (Cyrille, Andrew & Maono)
CD 1200252
Black Saint / Nov '93 / Cadillac / Harmonia Mundi

MY FRIEND LOUIS (Cyrille, Andrew Quintet)
CD DIW 858
DIW / Jun '92 / Cadillac / Harmonia Mundi

NAVIGATOR, THE
CD 1210622
Soul Note / May '94 / Cadillac / Harmonia Mundi / Wellard

NUBA
CD 1200302
Black Saint / May '94 / Cadillac / Harmonia Mundi

X MAN
CD RN 1210982
Soul Note / Oct '94 / Cadillac / Harmonia Mundi / Wellard

Cyrka, Jan

BEYOND THE COMMON GROUND
CD CDGRUB 22
Food For Thought / Mar '92 / Pinnacle

PRICKLY PEAR
Back in the saddle / In a broken dream / Yours is mine / Hard rain falls / Gonna make it happen / This land / Road to glory / Je t'embrasse / Scratching the fixtures / One whole heart
CD CDGRUB 32
Food For Thought / Feb '97 / Pinnacle

SPIRIT
CD CDGRUB 29
Food For Thought / Oct '93 / Pinnacle

Cyrus, Billy Ray

COVER TO COVER (The Best Of Billy Ray Cyrus)
It's all the same to me / Cover to cover / Bluegrass state of mind / Trail of tears / One last thrill / Storm in the heartland / Words by heart / Somebody new / In the heart of a woman / She's not cryin' anymore / Could've been me / Achy breaky heart
CD 5348372
Mercury / Aug '97 / PolyGram

IT WON'T BE THE LAST
CD 514758242
Mercury / Jul '93 / PolyGram

SOME GAVE ALL
Could've been me / Achy breaky heart / She's not cryin' anymore / Wher'm I gonna live / These boots are made for walkin' / Someday, somewhere, somehow / Never thought I'd fall in love with you / Ain't no good goodbye / I'm so miserable / Some gave all
CD 5106352
Mercury / Mar '92 / PolyGram

STORM IN THE HEARTLAND
CD 5260812
Mercury / Mar '95 / PolyGram

TRAIL OF TEARS
CD 5328292
Mercury / Aug '96 / PolyGram

Cythara

CYTHARA
CD GLCD 001
Realwood / Feb '96 / ADA

CYTHARA
Sherwood forest / Alfonso XIII el Sabio / Brittany / Star of county down / For Ireland I'd not tell her name / Maids of Mounre Shore / Xchanter / Carolans concerto / Scarborough fair / Watkins ale / Planxty Irwin/Planxty Howard glasser / Mwynder maldwyn / Hachas / Grenadier and the lady / Canon
CD CDLDL 1245
Lochshore / Mar '97 / ADA / Direct / Duncans

PLUCKIN' HAMMERED
CD CDLDL 1253
Lochshore / Jul '97 / ADA / Direct / Duncans

Czech Army Central Band

PRAGUE PANORAMA
CD CQ 00092
Clarton / Mar '96 / Czech Music Enterprises

Czukay, Holger

CANAXIS
CD SPOONCD 15
The Grey Area / Jan '95 / RTM/Disc

FULL CIRCLE (Czukay, Holger/Jah Wobble/Jaki Liebezeit)
How much are they / Where's the money / Full circle R.P.S. (No. 7) / Mystery R.P.S. (No. 8) / Trench warfare / Twilight world
CD CDOVD 437
Virgin / May '92 / EMI

MOVING PICTURES
CD CDSTUMM 125
Mute / May '93 / RTM/Disc

ROME REMAINS ROME
Hey ba ba re bop / Blessed Easter / Sudetenland / Hit hit flop flop / Perfect world / Music in the air / Der osten ist rot (the east is red) / Das massenmedium / Photo song / Ronrad / Michy / Esperanto socialiste / Traum mal wieder
CD CDV 2408
Virgin / '88 / EMI

D-Maximillian

MY STORY
CD BLKMCD 10
Blakamix / Oct '94 / Jet Star / SRD

D:Ream

BEST OF D:REAM, THE
Things can only get better / U R The best thing / Take me away / Shoot me with your love / Unforgiven / I like it / Party up the world / Power / Blame it on me / Heart of gold / Star / Hold me now
CD 0630190692
Magnet / May '97 / Warner Music

D:REAM ON VOL.1
Take me away / U R the best thing / Unforgiven / I like it / Glorious / So long movin' on / Picture my world / Blame it on me / Things can only get better / Star
CD 4509933712
Magnet / Dec '96 / Warner Music

WORLD
Power (of all the love in the world) / Shoot me with your love / You've saved my world / Miracle / Call me / Enough is enough / You can't tell me you cannot buy me love / Party up the world / Hold me now / Heart of gold
CD 0630117962
Magnet / Sep '95 / Warner Music

D+

D PLUS
CD KCD 72
K / Aug '97 / Cargo / Greyhound / SRD

D-Influence

GOOD 4 WE
Good lover / I'm the one / Funny (how things change) / Good 4 we / No illusions / Journey / Changes / For you I sing this song / Sweetest things
CD 7567951882
East West / Aug '92 / Warner Music

PRAYER 4 UNITY
Waiting / I will / Should I / You're all I need / Afrojam / Brasilia interview interlude / Prayer for unity / Break up / Midnight / Phuncky times / Simmer down / Always
CD 7559617512
East West / Jul '95 / Warner Music

D-Note

BABEL
Judgement / Babel / Now's the time / Aria / Bronx bull / Rain / Pharoah / More I see / Message / Lychia / Scheme of things / D votion
CD DOR 12CD
Dorado / Aug '97 / Pinnacle

COMING DOWN (The Soundtrack)
Lost and found / Short goodbye / 'Avin' it / Deep water / Just a little chaser / Coming down / Kite hill
CD VCRD 19
Virgin / Mar '97 / EMI

CRIMINAL JUSTICE
CD DOR 32CD
Dorado / Aug '97 / Pinnacle

D-NOTE
Moody / Lost and found / Coming up / Waiting hopefully / Long goodbye / Say what you mean / Tri-cyclic / Black dog / Changeless
CD CDVCR 2
Virgin / Jul '97 / EMI

D-Roc

ENGLEWOOD 4 LIFE
CD WRA 8152
Wrap / Jan '96 / Koch

D-Train

D-TRAIN - THE COLLECTION
CD CCSCD 387
Castle / Oct '93 / BMG

GO FOR IT BABY
CD TRCD 9916
Tramp / Nov '93 / ADA / CM / Direct

MUSIC/SOMETHING'S ON YOUR MIND
I treasure your pleasure / Something's on your mind / You're the reason / Hustle and bustle of the city / Thank you / I'll do anything / So far away / Keep giving me love / Shadow of your smile / Are you ready for me / Music / Children of the world / Let me show you / Don't you wanna ride
CD DEEPM 012
Deep Beats / Mar '97 / BMG

YOU'RE THE ONE FOR ME
You're the one for me / Walk on by / Tryin' to get over / Lucky day / D-Train theme / Keep on / Love vibrations / You're the one for me / You're the one for me / Keep on / D-Train dub / You're the one for me
CD DEEPM 010
Deep Beats / Jan '97 / BMG

Da Beat Goes

NEW FRATERNITY OF HOUSE
CD DST 305102
House Nation / Nov '96 / ZYX

Da Brat

ANUTHATANTRUM
Anuthatantrum / My beliefs / Sittin' on top of the world / Let's all get high / West Side interlude / Just a little bit more / Keepin' it live / Ghetto love / Lyrical molestation / Live it up / Make it happen
CD 4841982
Columbia / Oct '96 / Sony

FUNKDAFIED
Da shit you can't fuck wit / Fa all y'all / Fire it up / Celebration time / Funkdafied / May da funk be wit'cha / Ain't no thang / Come and get some / Mind blowin' / Give it to you
CD 4769802
Columbia / Feb '97 / Sony

Da Costa, Paulino

SUNRISE
Taj Mahal / I'm going to Rio / African sunrise / Walkman / O mar e meu chao / You came into my life / My love / You've got a special kind of love / Carioca / Groove
CD CD 2312143
Pablo / Apr '94 / Cadillac / Complete/ Pinnacle

Da Costa, Tico

BRAZIL ENCANTO
CD CDC 211
Music Of The World / Jun '93 / ADA / Target/BMG

Da Lench Mob

GUERILLAS IN THE MIST
Capital punishment in America / Buck tha devil / Lost in the system / You and your heroes / All on my nut sac / Guerillas in tha mist / Lenchmob also in tha group / Ain't got no class / Freedom got an AK / Ankle blues / Who ya gonna shoot wit that / Lord have mercy / Inside tha head of a black man
CD 7567922062
Street Knowledge / Nov '92 / Warner Music

PLANET OF DA APES
Scared lil' nigga / Chocolate city / Cut throats / King of the jungle / Who is it / Planet of da apes / Goin' bananas / Mellow madness / Enviromential terrorist / Set the shit straight / Trapped / Final call
CD CDPTY 110
Priority/Virgin / Dec '94 / EMI

Da Silva, Jorginho

EL BOSSA NOVA
CD 12385
Strictly Dancing / Feb '95 / Target/BMG

Da Steppas Project

MOON STEPPIN'
CD ONER 005CD
One Drop / Nov '96 / Timewarp / Vital

Da Vila, Martinho

MEU SAMBA FELIZ
Mangueirense feliz / Vai ou nao vai / Casa de bamba / Calango longo / Choro chorao / Al que saudade que en tenho / Ao povo em forma de arte / Canta canta minha gente / Mudiakime / Camafeu / Minha com-adre / Isto e o amor / Meu pais
CD 68911
Tropical / Jul '97 / Discovery

Da Willys

SATUHDAY NITE PALSY
CD OUTCD 105
Brake Out / Aug '96 / Direct

Da Youngstas

NO MERCY
CD 7567923702
WEA / Nov '94 / Warner Music

Daams, Menno

MY CHOICE (Daams, Menno Sextet)
CD CHR 70031
Challenge / Sep '96 / ADA / Direct / Jazz Music / Wellard

Dabagian, Gevorg

MUSIC OF ARMENIA VOL.3, THE (The Duduk)
CD 131172
Celestial Harmonies / Sep '96 / ADA / Select

Dabany, Patience

CENTRAL AFRICAN REPUBLIC
Levekisha / Pitie / Sango ya mawa / Opoungou andimba / Abagui alobi / Jalousie / Ayangal kelio / Ne t'inquietes pas / Patience II / Fly girl
CD CDEMC 3677
Hemisphere / May '94 / EMI

Daboa

FROM THE GEKKO
CD TRECD 115
Triple Earth / Feb '97 / Grapevine/ PolyGram / Stern's

DAD

RISKIN' IT ALL
Bad craziness / D Law / Day of the wrong moves / Rock 'n' rock radar / I won't cut my hair / Down that dusty 3rd world road / Makin' fun of money / Smart bot can't tell ya / Riskin' it all / Laugh 'n' a 1/2
CD 7599267722
WEA / Oct '91 / Warner Music

Dada

EL SUBLIMINOSO
Time is your friend / Sick in Santorini / Bob the drummer / I get high / Spirit of 2009 / Star you are / Trip with my Dad / You won't know me / Rise / No one / Fleecing of America / Hollow man / California dreamin'
CD EIRSCD 1080
IRS/EMI / Jun '96 / EMI

Dadamah

THIS IS NOT A DREAM
CD KRANK 002
Kranky / Mar '97 / Cargo / Greyhound

Daddy Freddie

BIG ONE, THE
CD MDLCD 35
Music Of Life / Aug '95 / Grapevine/ PolyGram

NOW OR NEVER
Haul and pull / Now or never / Respect due / Vibe up (break 1) / Jah Jah gives me vibes / Give me a little lovin' / Don number 1 / Rappin' music
CD FREDDY 2CD
Music Of Life / Oct '92 / Grapevine/ PolyGram

STRESS
CD FREDDY 1CD
Music Of Life / Feb '91 / Grapevine/ PolyGram

Daddy Rings

STAND OUT
Stand out / Herb fi bun / Cat and the fiddle / Can I trust a stranger / Rumours / Stick to the man / Stand out / Secret life / Tell me what yuh dealing / Religion / Bonifide / Judgement day / Friend enemy / Don't you cry again / Mothers cry
CD GRELCD 237
Greensleeves / Jul '97 / Jet Star / SRD

Dadi, Marcel

COUNTRY GUITAR FLAVOURS
CD 982532
EPM / Nov '92 / ADA / Discovery

Daemion

DARK OPERA OF THE ANCIENT WAR SPIRIT
CD CDAR 020
Adipocre / May '94 / Plastic Head

SEVEN DEADLY SINS
CD RRS 947CD
Progress / Dec '96 / Cargo / Plastic Head

Daemon

ENTRANCE TO HELL, THE
CD KSCD 9491
Kissing Spell / Jun '97 / Greyhound

Daemyon, Jerald

THINKING ABOUT YOU
You make me feel brand new / Thinking about you / Africa / Paradigms / Summer madness / 13 / For the love in your eyes (prelude) / For the love in your eyes / Peace of mind
CD GRP 98292
GRP / Feb '96 / New Note/BMG

Daere, Kim

SHAMANISTIC CEREMONIES OF CHINDO
CD VICG 52142
JVC World Library / Mar '96 / ADA / CM / Direct

DAF

DIE KLEINEN UN DIE BOSEN (Deutsch Amerikanische Freundschaft)
CD CDSTUMM 1
Mute / Apr '92 / RTM/Disc

Daft Punk

HOMEWORK
Daftendirekt / WDPK 837 FM / Revolution 909 / Da funk / Phoenix / Fresh / Around the world / Rollin' and scratchin' / Teachers / High fidelity / Rock 'n' roll / Oh yeah / Burnin' / Indo silver club / Alive / Funk AD
CD CDV 2821
Virgin / Jan '97 / EMI

Dafunkshun

ALBUM, THE
CD CDSPV 08516522
SPV / Jul '97 / Koch / Plastic Head

Dag Nasty

1985 - 1986
CD SFLS 52
Selfless / Nov '92 / SRD

FIELD DAY
CD WB 3040CD
We Bite / Sep '93 / Plastic Head

Dagar Brothers

DHRUPAD (The Vocal Art Of Hindustan)
Alap / Dhamar Raga / Alap / Dhrupad
CD JVC 53902
JVC World Library / Sep '96 / ADA / CM / Direct

RAG KAMBHOJI
CD CDT 114
Topic / Apr '93 / ADA / CM / Direct

Dagar, Zia Mohiuddin

RUNDRA VINA
CD NI 5402CD
Nimbus / Jul '94 / Nimbus

Dagir, Abdu

MALIK AT-TAQASIM
Longa nahawand / Layali zaman / Samai kurd / Longa agam / Quartertone bycicle / Nidaa / Nil
CD ENJACD 80122
Enja / Oct '93 / New Note/Pinnacle / Vital/ SAM

D'Agostino, Peppino

CLOSE TO THE HEART
CD BEST 1039CD
Acoustic Music / Nov '93 / ADA

Dagradi, Tony

DREAMS OF LOVE
CD ROUCD 2071
Rounder / '88 / ADA / CM / Direct

Dahl, Jeff

ULTRA UNDER
CD TX 93172
Roadrunner / Apr '91 / PolyGram

Dahlander, Nils-Bertil

FROM SWEDEN WITH LOVE
CD ECD 102
Everyday / Jun '95 / Cadillac / Jazz Music

Dahlgren, Chris

SLOW COMMOTION
CD 378132
Koch Jazz / Oct '96 / Koch

Daigrepont, Bruce

PETIT CADEAU
CD ROUCD 6060
Rounder / May '94 / ADA / CM / Direct

STIR UP THE ROUX
Laissez-faire / La valse de la riviere rouge / Disco et fais do-do / Les traces de mon bogue / Le two-step de marksville / Les filles

cajines / Un autre soir ennuyant / Frisco zydeco / Stir up the roux
CD ROUCD 6016
Rounder / '88 / ADA / CM / Direct

Daily Planet

CLARK'S SECRET
CD GRP 003CD
Get Real / Dec '96 / ADA

Dairo, I.K.

ASHIKO
CD GL 4018CD
Green Linnet / Aug '94 / ADA / CM / Direct / Highlander / Roots

DEFINITIVE DAIRO
Okin omo ni / Baba ngbo ti wa / Omo Owa o Ijesa / Ta lo ba mi ri / Labondo / Omo alaro / Chief Okeyemi Otubusin / Ore arakunrin temi / Congo kinshasa / President Mobutu
CD XENO 4045CD
Xenophile / Oct '96 / ADA / Direct

I REMEMBER (Dairo, I.K. & His Blue Spots)
CD CDC 212
Topic / Apr '93 / ADA / CM / Direct

JUJU MASTER
CD OMCD 009
Original Music / Nov '90 / Jet Star / SRD

Daisy Chainsaw

ELEVENTEEN
CD TPLP 100CD
One Little Indian / Sep '92 / Pinnacle

FOR THEY KNOW NOT WHAT THEY DO
Future free / Belittled and beaten down / Sleeping with heaven / Love me forever / Candyfloss / Life tomorrow / Zebra head / Unit shifter / Diamond of the desert / Mosquito / Greatest God's divine / Voice of a generation / Looking for an angel
CD TPLP 111CD
One Little Indian / Jun '94 / Pinnacle

Daisy Cutter

SHITHAMMER DELUXE
CD ROCK 60802
Rockville / Mar '93 / Plastic Head / SRD

TRUCK FIST
CD ROCK 61342
Rockville / Apr '94 / Plastic Head / SRD

Dako, Del

BALANCING ACT
CD SKCD 22021
Sackville / Jun '93 / Cadillac / Jazz Music / Swift

Dalakopa

EVI ALLE IHOPA
CD HCD 7109
Helio / Nov '95 / ADA

Dalal, Yair

AL OL (Ud, Clarinet & Voices)
CD ALCD 202
Al Sur / Sep '96 / ADA / Discovery

Dalaras, George

GREEK SPIRIT, THE
CD 68966
Tropical / Apr '97 / Discovery

GREEK VOICE, THE
CD 68954
Tropical / Apr '97 / Discovery

Dalby, Graham

GREAT LEGENDS OF JAZZ AND SWING, THE (Dalby, Graham & The Grahamophones)
Because my baby don't mean maybe now / Makin' whoopee / Cotton club stomp / Mooche / Sing, sing, sing / Blues in the night / I can't get started / Stompin' at the Savoy / Pennsylvania 6500 / Moonlight serenade / Fools rush in / Who (stole my heart away) / Deep purple / Eager beaver / Mack the knife
CD CDMFP 6397
Music For Pleasure / May '97 / EMI

LET'S DANCE FOXTROT (Dalby, Graham & The Grahamophones)
CD LTD 102702
Let's Dance / Apr '95 / Target/BMG

LET'S DANCE LATIN AMERICAN
CD LTD 102705
Let's Dance / May '95 / Target/BMG

LET'S DANCE THE BOSSA NOVA (Dalby, Graham & The Grahamophones)
Carol's theme / Te ame / Sweet inspiration / Bahia bosa nova / Cinnamon and clove / Latin snowfall / Way you look tonight / Pink polo / Desafinado / Soul bossa / Il silenzio
CD LTD 102713
Let's Dance / Apr '96 / Target/BMG

LET'S DANCE THE CHA CHA CHA (Dalby, Graham & The Grahamophones)
Cha cha Mama Brown / Makin' whoopee / Ida, sweet as apple cider / Eternally / Last night on the back porch / Isle of Capri / If you knew Susie / Little serenade / C'est si bon / Christopher Columbus / L'Abeille et la Papillon / El canguro / In the mood / In a shady nook / My prayer / Chestnut tree / South of the border / How wonderful to know / Calcutta / Sucu Sucu / Any old iron cha cha / Isn't this a lovely day / Eye level / Dancin' easy / Rivers of Babylon / Sunny / Daddy Cool / Rasputin
CD LTD 102712
Let's Dance / Nov '96 / Target/BMG

LET'S DANCE THE JIVE (Dalby, Graham & The Grahamophones)
Copper coloured girl / Is you is or is you ain't my baby / Little brown jug / Steppin' out with my baby / Jersey bounce / Don't sit under the apple tree / (I'll be glad when you're dead) you rascal you / Chicago / When I see an elephant fly / Hold tight hold tight / Bugle call rag / Eager beaver / Boogie woogie bugle boy / Can't buy me love / (We're gonna) Rock around the clock / See you later alligator / Hound dog / Under the moon of love / When / Dancing party
CD LTD 102711
Let's Dance / Apr '96 / Target/BMG

LET'S DANCE THE PASO DOBLE (Dalby, Graham & The Grahamophones)
El pico / Islas canarias / Ven a bailir / Valencia / Viva el rumbo / Rafaelillo / Bizas andaluzas / Manolo vazquez / El nino de jerez / Gallito / Gitaneria andaluza / Jeronimo pimentel
CD LTD 102714
Let's Dance / Apr '96 / Target/BMG

LET'S DANCE THE RUMBA (Dalby, Graham & The Grahamophones)
Savoy rumba medley / Angela Mia / Miami Beach rumba / Begin the beguine / You do something to me / Once in a while / Green eyes / Hill Street blues / I am a song / Laughter in the rain / That's when the music takes me / Lady in red / Romantica
CD LTD 102715
Let's Dance / Nov '96 / Target/BMG

LET'S DANCE THE SLOW FOXTROT (Dalby, Graham & The Grahamophones)
CD LTD 102704
Let's Dance / Apr '95 / Target/BMG

LET'S DANCE THE TANGO (Dalby, Graham & The Grahamophones)
CD LTD 102703
Let's Dance / Apr '95 / Target/BMG

LET'S DANCE THE WALTZ (Dalby, Graham & The Grahamophones)
CD LTD 102701
Let's Dance / Apr '95 / Target/BMG

LET'S DANCE VOL.1 (Dalby, Graham & The Grahamophones)
CD LTD 102706
Let's Dance / Jun '95 / Target/BMG

LET'S DANCE VOL.2 (Dalby, Graham & The Grahamophones)
CD LTD 102707
Let's Dance / Jun '95 / Target/BMG

LET'S DANCE VOL.3 (Dalby, Graham & The Grahamophones)
CD LTD 102708
Let's Dance / Jun '95 / Target/BMG

LET'S DANCE VOL.4 (Dalby, Graham & The Grahamophones)
CD LTD 102709
Let's Dance / Jun '95 / Target/BMG

LET'S DANCE VOL.5 (Dalby, Graham & The Grahamophones)
CD LTD 102710
Let's Dance / Jun '95 / Target/BMG

MAD DOGS AND ENGLISHMEN (Dalby, Graham & The Grahamophones)
CD PCOM 1097
President / Feb '89 / Grapevine/PolyGram / President / Target/BMG

TRANSATLANTIQUE (Dalby, Graham & The Grahamophones)
Jeeves and Wooster / La mer / Anything goes / Easy come, easy go / Mackie Messer / My canary has circles under his eyes / Top hat, white tie and tails / Ces petites choses / 42nd Street / Once in a while / Crazy words crazy tune / I would sooner be a crooner / Ill wind / Hollywood's got nothing on you / Let's misbehave
CD PCOM 1128
President / Aug '93 / Grapevine/PolyGram / President / Target/BMG

Dalcan, Dominique

ENTRE L'ETOILE & LE CARRE
Typical blues / Entre l'etoilr and le carre / Promesse celeste / Un jour sur deux / Une epee dans le dos / Comment faut-il faire / Up and down / Les annees bleues / Naked and so shy / Une direction contraire
CD CRAM 074
Crammed Discs / Nov '93 / Grapevine/ PolyGram / New Note/Pinnacle / Prime / RTM/Disc

Dale, Colin

OUTER LIMITS VOL.1 (Various Artists)
CD KICKCD 10
Kickin' / Jun '94 / Prime / SRD

OUTER LIMITS VOL.2 (Various Artists)
CD KICKCD 21
Kickin' / May '95 / Prime / SRD

Dale, Dick

CALLING UP SPIRITS
CD BBQCD 184
Beggars Banquet / May '96 / RTM/Disc / Warner Music

GREATEST HITS (Dale, Dick & His Del-Tones)
Victor / Surf beat / Sloop John B / King of the surf guitar / Wedge / Let's go trippin' / Peppermint man / Misirlou / Those memories of you / Scavenger / Surf buggy / Hot rod racer / Grudge run / Mr. Eliminator / Surfin' drums / Night rider / Del-tone rock / Mag wheels / Death of a gremmie
CD GNPD 2095
GNP Crescendo / '88 / ZYX

TRIBAL THUNDER
CD HCD 8046
Hightone / Mar '95 / ADA / Koch

UNKNOWN TERRITORY
CD HCD 8055
Hightone / Mar '95 / ADA / Koch

Daley & Lorien

DREAMS OF THE YES MEN
CD EUCD 1193
ARC / Apr '92 / ADA / ARC Music

Daley, Lloyd

IT'S SHUFFLE 'N' SKA TIME
CD JMC 200221
Jamaican Gold / Jun '95 / Grapevine/ PolyGram / Jet Star

Daley, Martin

ARCHITECTS OF TIME (Daley, Martin & Duncan Lorien)
Structure / Bermuda / Architects of time / Into the oasis / Eleven days / Thank you / Waiting for Karl / Spirit warrior
CD EUCD 1154
ARC / Jun '91 / ADA / ARC Music

Dalienst, Ntesa

BEST OF NTESA DALIENST VOL.1, THE
CD CD 36563
Sonodisc / Jan '97 / Stern's

BEST OF NTESA DALIENST VOL.2, THE
CD CD 36564
Sonodisc / Jan '97 / Stern's

Dali's Car

WAKING HOUR
Dali's car / His box / Cornwall stone / Artemis / Create and melt / Moonlife / Judgement is the mirror
CD BBL 52CD
Lowdown/Beggars Banquet / Jan '89 / RTM/Disc / Warner Music

Dall, Cindy

CINDY DALL
CD WIGCD 23
Domino / Mar '96 / Vital

Dallas Jazz Orchestra

THANK YOU, LEON
Back in town / Anand / Miami beach / Willow weep for me / Latin dream / Alison's tune / Basin Street blues / Reggae blues / Tickle toe / Yesterdays / Bikini beach / Thank you, Leon
CD SBCD 2041
Sea Breeze / Oct '91 / Jazz Music

Dalli, Toni

BEST OF TONI DALLI, THE
CD C5CD 570
See For Miles/C5 / Jul '91 / Pinnacle

Dallwitz, Dave

HOOKED ON RAGTIME VOL.1 (Dallwitz, Dave Euphonic Ragtime Ensemble)
CD BCD 321
GHB / Jan '94 / Jazz Music

HOOKED ON RAGTIME VOL.2 (Dallwitz, Dave Euphonic Ragtime Ensemble)
CD BCD 322
GHB / Jan '94 / Jazz Music

Dalriada

ALL IS FAIR
Haughs o' Cromdale / Scots wha hae / Green grow the rashes / Jock o'Hazeldean / Ye Jacobites by name / Will ye no' come back again / Johnny Cope / Loch Lomond / Macphersons' farewell / Ae fond kiss / Caledonia / Grey man
CD IR 015 CD
Iona / Nov '91 / ADA / Direct / Duncans

Dalseth, Laila

TIME FOR LOVE, A
CD GEMCD 151
Gemini / Oct '90 / Cadillac

Dalton, Joe

I STILL DO
CD FCRCD 201
Flat Canyon / Mar '96 / ADA

Dalton, Karen

IT'S SO HARD TO TELL WHO'S GOING TO LOVE YOU THE BEST
CD CD 379182
Koch International / Jul '97 / Koch

Daltrey, Roger

BEST OF ROGER DALTREY
Martyrs and madmen / Say it isn't so Joe / Oceans away / Treasury / Free me / Without your love / It's a hard life / Giving it all away / Avenging Annie / Proud / You put something better inside me
CD 8478552
Polydor / May '91 / PolyGram

DALTREY
One man band / Way of the world / You are yourself / Thinking / You and me / It's a hard life / Giving it all away / Story so far / When the music stops / Reasons / Reprise - One man band
CD 5272592
Polydor / Apr '95 / PolyGram

Daltry, Peter

DREAM ON
Dust / Going back to Bohemia / Fitzgerald / Tender is the night / Ravenswing / Richard and I / Nothing more than this / Felt like the moon / Unicorn / Eighteen summers / Dream on / Roundway Hill
CD BP 182CD
Blueprint / May '97 / Pinnacle

Daly, Jackie

BUTTONS AND BOWS (Daly, Jackie/ Seamus & Manus McGuire)
Blue Angel / Esther's reel/Trip to Kinvara / Old resting chair / Crowley's reels / Norwegian waltz/Liza Lynn / Dionne reel / Waltz from Orsa / Barn dances / My love is an Arbutus / Waltz clog / La Bastringue / Bog carrot
CD GLCD 1051
Green Linnet / Jun '93 / ADA / CM / Direct / Highlander / Roots

JACKIE DALY
CD OSS 30CD
Ossian / Mar '94 / ADA / CM / Direct / Highlander

JACKIE DALY & SEAMUS CREAGH (Daly, Jackie & Seamus Creagh)
CD CEFCD 057
Gael Linn / Jan '94 / ADA / CM / Direct / Grapevine/PolyGram / Roots

MANY'S A WILD NIGHT
CD CEFCD 176
Gael Linn / Dec '95 / ADA / CM / Direct / Grapevine/PolyGram / Roots

MUSIC FROM SLIABH LUACHRA
Tom Sullivan's / Johnny Leary's / Jim Keefe's / Keefe's / Clog / Tir na nog / Callaghan's hornpipe / Rising sun / Pope's toe / Glin cottage polkas / Paddy scully's / Gallant tipperay / Walsh's / Ballyvourine polka / Johnny Mickey's / Trip to the Jacks / Where is the cat / Banks of Sullane / Biddy Martin's / Ger the rigger / Glenside cottage / Tdim gan airgead / Willie Reilly / Murphy's / Going to the well for water
CD GLCD 3065
Green Linnet / Jun '92 / ADA / CM / Direct / Highlander / Roots

Daly, Vic

SO AM I
CD ADITZ 1
Album Zutique / Dec '95 / Else

Dama & D'Gary

LONG WAY HOME
CD SH 64052CD
Shanachie / Oct '94 / ADA / Greensleeves / Koch

Damad

RISE AND FALL
CD PRANK 011CD
Prank / Feb '97 / Cargo / Plastic Head

Damage

FOREVER
Love II love / Love guaranteed / Girlfriend / Let it be me / Wonderful tonight / By my baby / Love lady / Anything / Forever / Do me that way / Storyteller / In your eyes
CD BLRCD 31X

Big Life / Apr '97 / Mo's Music Machine / Pinnacle / Prime

Dambert No Bacon

UNFAIRYTALE, THE
CD _______________ SEEP 16CD
Rugger Bugger / Apr '97 / Shellshock/Disc

D'Ambrosio, Meredith

IT'S YOUR DANCE
Giant steps / Once upon a tempo / Listen little girl / Devil may care / August moon / Nobody else but me / Humpty dumpty heart / It's your dance / Underdog / It isn't so good it couldn't be better / Off again on again / No one remembers but me / Miss Harper goes bizarre / Strange meadowlark
CD _______________ SSC 1011 D
Sunnyside / Feb '86 / Discovery

LOVE IS NOT A GAME
Daybreak / In April / Autumn serenade / Young and foolish / I love you / You, I love / Quiet now / Get used to it baby / That old sweet song / Heaven sent / All or nothing at all / This lament / Indian summer / Peace / Oh look at me now / But now look at me / Love is not a game
CD _______________ SSC 1051D
Sunnyside / Jun '91 / Discovery

MEREDITH....ANOTHER TIME
All of us in it together / Aren't you glad you're you / It's so peaceful in the country / Rain rain (don't go away) / Dear Bix / Lazy afternoon / Where's the child I used to hold / Love is a simple thing / You are there / While we're young / Small day tomorrow / Child is born / Piano player / Someday my Prince will come / Such a lonely girl am I / Wheelers and dealers / I was doing all right / Skylark
CD _______________ SSC 1017D
Sunnyside / Nov '90 / Discovery

SHADOWLAND
CD _______________ 500602
Sunnyside / Nov '92 / Discovery

SILENT PASSION
CD _______________ SSC 1075
Sunnyside / Apr '97 / Discovery

Dambuilders

GOD DAMBUILDERS BLESS AMERICA
CD _______________ CTX 066CD
Cortex / Feb '97 / Cargo

Dameron, Tadd

MAGIC TOUCH, THE (Dameron, Tadd Orchestra)
On a misty night / Fontainebleau / Just plain talkin' / If you could see me now / Our delight / Dial b for beauty / Look, stop and listen / Bevan's birthday / You're a joy / Swift as the wind
CD _______________ OJCCD 143
Original Jazz Classics / Jan '97 / Complete/ Pinnacle / Jazz Music / Wellard

MATING CALL
CD _______________ OJCCD 212
Original Jazz Classics / Oct '92 / Complete/Pinnacle / Jazz Music / Wellard

Damia

1928-35
CD _______________ 123
Chansophone / Nov '92 / Discovery

LA TRAGEDIENNE DE LA CHANSON
CD _______________ UCD 19075
Forlane / Jun '95 / Target/BMG

LA TRAGEDIENNE DE LA CHANSON
CD _______________ 701622
Chansophone / Nov '96 / Discovery

Damiano, Peter

MERRY XMAS AND A HAPPY NEW YEAR
White Christmas / Jingle bells / Do they know it's Christmas / Stille nacht / Notte d'amore / Last Christmas / Oh happy day / Once upon a long ago / This is the night / Bonne Noel / Happy Xmas (war is over) / Tanti auguri
CD _______________ CDSGP 0116
Prestige / Feb '96 / Else / Total/BMG

Damn Yankees

DAMN YANKEES
Coming of age / Bad reputation / Runaway / High enough / Damn yankees / Come again / Mysified / Rock city / Tell me how you want it / Pile driver
CD _______________ 7599261592
WEA / Mar '94 / Warner Music

Damnation

BURIED ALIVE
CD _______________ BJR 96001
Black Jack / Mar '97 / Cargo

DAMNATION
CD _______________ LRR 021
Last Resort / Oct '96 / Cargo

NO MORE DREAMS OF HAPPY ENDINGS
CD _______________ JT 1020CD
Jade Tree / Sep '95 / Cargo / Greyhound / Plastic Head

Damned

BALLROOM BLITZ - LIVE
CD _______________ RRCD 159
Receiver / Jul '93 / Grapevine/PolyGram

BBC RADIO 1 SESSIONS
CD _______________ CDNT 011
Strange Fruit / Jun '96 / Pinnacle

BEST OF THE DAMNED
New rose / Neat neat neat / I just can't be happy today / Jet boy jet girl / Hit and miss / There ain't no sanity clause / Smash it up (parts 1 and 2) / Plan 9 channel 7 / Ra bid (over you) / Wait for the blackout / History of the world (part 1)
CD _______________ CDDAM 1
Big Beat / Oct '87 / Pinnacle

BLACK ALBUM, THE
Wait for the blackout / Lively arts / Silly kids games / Drinking about my baby / Hit and miss / Dr. Jekyll and Mr. Hyde / Thirteenth floor vendetta / Curtain call / Twisted nerve / Sick of this and that / History of the world (part 1) / Therapy
CD _______________ CDWIK 906
Big Beat / '87 / Pinnacle

BORN TO KILL (2CD Set)
Thanks for the night / Billy bad breaks / Disco man / I think I'm wonderful / Lovely money / Some girls are ugly / Ignite / Generals / Dozen girls / Bad time for Bonzo / Gun fury / Fun factory / Neat neat neat / Fan club / Wait for the blackout / I fall / Noise noise noise / last time / I just can't be happy today / Smash it up / I feel alright / Love song / In a rut / Dr. Jeckyll and Mr. Hyde / Plan 9 channel 7 / Teenage dream / Problem child / Born to kill / Ballroom blitz / Stretcher case baby / Melody Lee / Suicide / New rose / Looking at you / Ignite / Disco man
CD Set _______________ SMDCD 143
Snapper / May '97 / Pinnacle

CHAOS YEARS, THE
CD _______________ CLP 9960
Cleopatra / Mar '97 / Cargo / Greyhound / Plastic Head / RTM/Disc / SRD

COLLECTION, THE
Ignite / Generals / Dozen girls / Bad time for Bonzo / Gun fury / Thanks for the night / History of the world (part 1) / Lively arts / There ain't no sanity clause / White rabbit / Melody Lee / Lovely money / Disco man / I think I'm wonderful / Help / I just can't be happy today / Love song / Neat neat neat / New rose / Noise noise noise / Smash it up / Wait for the blackout
CD _______________ CCSCD 278
Castle / Dec '90 / BMG

DAMNED BUT NOT FORGOTTEN
Dozen girls / Lovely money / I think I'm wonderful / Disguise / Take that / Torture me / Disco man / Thanks for the night / Take me away / Some girls are ugly / Nice cup of tea / Billy bad breaks
CD _______________ ESMCD 472
Essential / Feb '97 / BMG

DAMNED, DAMNED, DAMNED
Neat neat neat / Fan club / I fall / Born to kill / Stab your back / Feel the pain / New rose / Fish / See her tonite / One of the two / So messed up / I feel alright
CD _______________ FIENDCD 91
Demon / Apr '87 / Pinnacle

ETERNALLY DAMNED (The Very Best Of The Damned)
Neat neat neat / New rose / Problem child / Don't cry wolf / Stretcher case baby / Sick of being sick / Love song / Smash it up / I just can't be happy today / History of the world (Part 1) / White rabbit / Disco man / Nasty / There ain't no sanity clause / Shadow of love / Grimly fiendish / Eloise / Is it a dream / Alone again or / Gigolo
CD _______________ MUSCD 017
MCI Music / May '94 / Disc / THE

FIENDISH SHADOWS
CD _______________ CLP 9804
Cleopatra / Oct '96 / Cargo / Greyhound / Plastic Head / RTM/Disc / SRD

FINAL DAMNATION
See her tonite / Neat neat neat / Born to kill / I fall / Fan club / Fish / Help / New rose / I feel alright / I just can't be happy today / Wait for the blackout / Melody Lee / Noise noise noise / Love song / Smash it up / Looking at you / Last time
CD _______________ CLACD 338
Castle / '94 / BMG

I'M ALRIGHT JACK AND THE BEANSTALK
CD _______________ MOCDR 1
The Record Label / Apr '97 / Pinnacle

LIGHT AT THE END OF THE TUNNEL (2CD Set)
CD Set _______________ MCLDD 19007
MCA / Apr '92 / BMG

LIVE AT SHEPPERTON
Love song / Second time around / I just can't be happy today / Melody Lee / Help / Neat neat neat / Looking at you MC / Smash it up (parts 1 and 2) / New rose / Plan 9 channel 7
CD _______________ CDWIKM 27
Big Beat / Jun '88 / Pinnacle

MACHINE GUN ETIQUETTE
Love song / Machine gun etiquette / I can't be happy today / Melody Lee / Anti-pope / These hands / Plan 9 channel 7 / Noise noise noise / Looking at you / Liar / Smash it up (Part 1) / Smash it up (Part 2) / Ballroom blitz / Suicide / Rabid (over you) / White rabbit
CD _______________ CDWIK 905
Big Beat / '86 / Pinnacle

MCA SINGLES A'S AND B'S, THE
CD _______________ VSOPCD 174
Connoisseur Collection / Jul '92 / Pinnacle

MUSIC FOR PLEASURE
Problem child / Don't cry wolf / One way love / Politics / Stretcher case baby / Idiot box / You take my money / Alone / Your eyes / Creep (you can't fool me) / You know
CD _______________ FIENDCD 108
Demon / Apr '88 / Pinnacle

NEAT NEAT NEAT (3CD Set)
I feel alright / Neat neat neat / Don't cry wolf / Born to kill / Alone / Stab your back / Fish / So messed up / One of the two / Your eyes / You take my money / Politics / New rose / Sick of being sick / I fall / Fan club / Problem child / Creep / New rose / One way love / Fan club / Singalonga Scabies / You know / Help / See her tonite / Stretcher case baby / Creep / I fall / Idiot box / Problem child / Love song / Suicide / I just can't be happy today / Plan 9 channel 7 / Rabid (over you) / Lively arts / History of the world / Tailspin / Testify / I need a life / No moer tears
CD Set _______________ FBOOK 14
Demon / Feb '97 / Pinnacle

NOISE (The Best Of The Damned Live)
New rose / In a rut / Dr. Jeckyl and Mr. Hyde / Ballroom blitz / Love song / Born to kill / Generals / Melody lee / Drinking about my baby / Looking at you / Problem child / I feel alright / Stretcher case baby / Plan 9-channel 7 / Shakin' all over
CD _______________ EMPRCD 592
Emporio / Oct '95 / Disc

NOT THE CAPTAIN'S BIRTHDAY PARTY
You take my money / Creep (you can't fool me) / Fan club / Problem child / I fall / So messed up / New rose / Feel alright / Born to kill
CD _______________ VEXCD 7
Demon / Oct '91 / Pinnacle

PHANTASMAGORIA
Street of dreams / Shadow of love / There'll come a day / Sanctum sanctorum / Is it a dream / Grimly fiendish / Edward the bear / Eighth day / Trojans / I just can't be happy today
CD _______________ MCLD 19069
MCA / Oct '91 / BMG

SKIP OFF TO SCHOOL TO SEE THE DAMNED
New rose / Help / Neat neat neat / Stab your back / Singalongascabies / Stretcher case baby / Sick of being sick / Problem child / You take my money / Don't cry wolf / One way love
CD _______________ VEXCD 12
Demon / Sep '92 / Pinnacle

STRAWBERRIES
Ignite / Generals / Stranger on the town / Dozen girls / Dog / Gun fury / Pleasure and pain / Life goes on / Bad time for Bonzo / Under the floor again / Don't bother me
CD _______________ CLEO 10292
Cleopatra / Dec '93 / Cargo / Greyhound / Plastic Head / RTM/Disc / SRD
CD _______________ ESMCD 473
Essential / Mar '97 / BMG

TALES FROM THE DAMNED
CD _______________ CLEO 71392
Cleopatra / Oct '94 / Cargo / Greyhound / Plastic Head / RTM/Disc / SRD

TOTALLY DAMNED
Fun factory / Generals / Stranger / On the town / Gun fury / Born to kill / I fall / Fish / Help / New rose / I just can't be happy today / Wait for the blackout / Noise noise noise / Looking at you / Disguise / Take that / Torture me / Take me away / Some girls are ugly / Billy bad breaks
CD _______________ DOJOCD 65
Dojo / Feb '94 / Disc

Damon & Naomi

WONDEROUS WORLD OF...
CD _______________ SP 322B
Sub Pop / Nov '95 / Cargo / Greyhound / Shellshock/Disc

Damone, Vic

16 MOST REQUESTED SONGS
On the street where you live / War and peace / Almost like being in love / Smoke gets in your eyes / Do I love you because you're beautiful / Affair to remember / You're breaking my heart / Angela mia / Maria / Gigi / Separate tables / But beautiful / Pleasure of her company / Serenade in blue / In the blue of evening
CD _______________ 4721972
Columbia / Nov '92 / Sony

BEST OF VIC DAMONE LIVE, THE
CD _______________ RCD 8204
Ranwood / May '89 / Jazz Music

BEST OF VIC DAMONE, THE (The Mercury Years)
I have but one heart / You do / Again / You're breaking my heart / Four winds and the seven seas / My bolero / Why was I born / Vagabond shoes / Tzena tzena tzena / Just say I love her / Cincinatti dancing pig / My heart cries for you / Music by the angels / Night is young and you're so beautiful / My truly truly fair / Longing for you / Calla calla / Here in my heart / Rosanne / Sugar / April in Portugal / Eternally / Ebb tide / Breeze and I / In my own quiet way
CD _______________ 5527572
Spectrum / Feb '97 / PolyGram

BEST OF VIC DAMONE, THE
Goin' out of my head / Time after time / More I see you / Shadow of your smile / It makes no difference / Why can't I walk away / Stardust / Watch what happens / Meditation / On the South side of Chicago / Make me rainbows / Quiet tear / Stay with me / I never go there anymore / Stay / What is a woman / Two for the road / I got it bad and that ain't good / When you've laughed all your laughter / You don't have to say you love me
CD _______________ 74321451912
Camden / Feb '97 / BMG

CLOSER THAN A KISS/THIS GAME OF LOVE
Closer than a kiss / Out of nowhere / I kiss your hand / Madame / We kiss in a shadow / Cuddle up a little closer / Toujours / You and the night and the music / Prelude to a kiss / How deep is the ocean / Day by day / As time goes by / Close as pages in a book / Game of love / Alone together / My romance / Ain't misbehavin' / But beautiful / End of a love affair / Things we did last summer / Am I blue / I'll be around / It's a lonesome old town / Me and my shadow / I like the likes of you / Fellow needs a girl
CD _______________ 4871902
Columbia / Mar '97 / Sony

FEELINGS
Feelings / Lazy afternoon / Ghost riders in the sky / Softly / Windmills of your mind / People / Top of the world / Farewell to paradise / Over the rainbow
CD _______________ MU 3004
Musketeer / Oct '92 / Disc

ON THE STREET WHERE YOU LIVE
CD _______________ MU 5074
Musketeer / Oct '92 / Disc

ON THE STREET WHERE YOU LIVE
When lights are low / Close your eyes / Tender is the night / No strings / Once upon a time / Little girl / Alright, OK you win / What kind of fool am I / Ooh looka there, ain't she pretty / Affair to remember / Call me irresponsible / Wives and lovers / Again / I'm gonna miss you / Cathy / Vieni vieni / Dearly beloved / Maria / Lost in the stars / On the street where you live
CD _______________ CDSL 8277
Music For Pleasure / Nov '95 / EMI

THAT TOWERING FEELING/YOUNG AND LIVELY
You stepped out of a dream / Wait till you see her / Song is you / Spring is here / Let's fall in love / Smoke gets in your eyes / Time on your hands / I'm glad there is you / Touch of your lips / All the things you are / Cheek to cheek / Last night when we were young / We could make such beautiful music / It had to be you / In the blue of evening / I got it bad and that ain't good / Serenade in blue / Very thought of you / Spring will be a little late this year / Imagination / Solitude / What is there to say / Evert time we say goodbye
CD _______________ 4810142
Columbia / Aug '95 / Sony

VIC DAMONE COLLECTOR'S EDITION
CD _______________ DVAD 6022
Deja Vu / Apr '95 / THE

Dan Air Scottish Pipe Band

BEST OF SCOTTISH PIPES AND DRUMS, THE
CD _______________ EUCD 1150
ARC / '91 / ADA / ARC Music

Dan Ar Bras

SEPTEMBER BLEU
CD _______________ KMCD 38
Keltia Musique / May '94 / ADA / Discovery

THEME FOR THE GREEN LANDS
CD _______________ KMCD 48
Keltia Musique / May '94 / ADA / Discovery

Dan 'n' Dad

DAYLIGHT
Years go by / Skiing wild / Don't look over your shoulder / Surfer's paradise / Guiding light / Strike while the iron's hot / Mon ami / It all takes time / Tender zone / Daylight
CD ____ ZYZCD 2
Pink Whistle / May '96 / Pink Whistle

Dan, Teddy

UNITED STATES OF AFRICA
CD ____ RMCD 013
Roots Man / Nov '94 / Jet Star

Dana

DANA THE COLLECTION
Fairytale / Never gonna fall in love again / Right back where we started / Girl is back / Something's cooking in the kitchen / Can't find a way / Far away / Rainy days and mondays / If you leave me now / All kinds of everything / Magic / I feel love / Who put the lights out / Cold cold Christmas / Please tell him I said hello / Baby come back / Dream lover / Bridge over troubled water
CD ____ 3036400112
Carlton / Mar '96 / Carlton

Dance 2 Trance

REVIVAL
Surrealistic pillow / Purple onions / Neil's aurora / Land of Oz / Enuf Eko / Christopher / Mrs. Canabis / Morning star / Fly, fly dragonfly / Warrior
CD ____ 74321260282
Logic / Feb '95 / 3mv/BMG

Dance Hall Crashers

OLD RECORD
CD ____ DON 002
Fatwreck Chords / Dec '96 / Plastic Head

Dance, Heather

HIGHLAND WELCOME
CD ____ CDLOC 1083
Lochshore / Oct '94 / ADA / Direct / Duncans

Danceable Weird Shit

HERE'S THE RECORD
CD ____ WD 6662CD
World Domination / Sep '90 / Pinnacle / RTM/Disc

Dancefloor Virus

BALLROOM, THE
Message in a bottle / De do do do de da da da / Bed's too big without you / When the world is running down / Walking on the moon / Synchronicity / Every breath you take / Spirits in a material world / Don't stand so close to me
CD ____ 4804872
Epic / Nov '95 / Sony

Dancetime Orchestra

OLD TIME CHAMPIONSHIP DANCES
CD ____ SAV 183CD
Savoy / May '93 / Savoy / THE / TKO Magnum

Dancing Feet

IN THAT LAND ACROSS THE SEA
CD ____ DFO 2CD
Diffusion Breizh / Apr '94 / ADA

Dancing French Liberals

POWERLINE
CD ____ SKIP 342
Broken Rekids / May '95 / Cargo / Plastic Head

Dancing Strings

ENCORE
CD ____ LCOM 5225
Lismor / Oct '93 / ADA / Direct / Duncans / Lismor

Dando Shaft

REAPING THE HARVEST
Coming home to me / Railway / Magnetic beggar / Pass it on / Kalyope driver / Prayer / Sometimes / Waves upon the ether / Dewet / Riverboat / Harp lady I bombed / Black prince of paradise / When I'm weary / Till the morning comes / Whispering Ned / Road song / Is it me / It was good / Rain / Cold wind / In the country / End of the game
CD ____ SEECD 291
See For Miles/C5 / Jan '90 / Pinnacle

SHADOWS ACROSS THE MOON
CD ____ HT 001CD
Happy Trail / Oct '94 / ADA

D'Andrea, Franco

ENROSADIRA (D'Andrea, Franco & Luis Agudo)
CD ____ 1232432
Red / Nov '91 / ADA / Cadillac / Harmonia Mundi

Dandridge, Putney

CLASSICS 1935-1936
CD ____ CLASSICS 846
Classics / Nov '95 / Discovery / Jazz Music

CLASSICS 1936 (Dandridge, Putney & His Orchestra)
CD ____ CLASSICS 869
Classics / Mar '96 / Discovery / Jazz Music

PUTNEY DANDRIDGE 1935-1936
CD ____ CBC 1023
Timeless Jazz / Sep '95 / New Note/ Pinnacle

Dandruff Deluxe

DEAL WITH THE DEVIL, THE
CD ____ EFA 043762
Crippled Dick Hot Wax / Jan '97 / SRD

Dandy Jack

DANDY JACK AND THE COSMIC TROUSERS
CD ____ RI 033CD
Rather Interesting / Jan '96 / Plastic Head

Dane, Barbara

SOMETIMES I BELIEVE SHE LOVES ME (Dane, Barbara & Lightnin' Hopkins)
I'm going back baby / I know you got another man / Sometimes I believe she loves me / Baby shake that thing / It's a lonesome old town / Don't push me / Let me be your rag doll / Mother Earth / Mama told Papa / Careless love / Love with a feeling / Betty and Dupree / Don't you push me down / Bury me in my overalls / Deportees / Hold on / Jesus won't you come by here
CD ____ ARHCD 451
Arhoolie / Nov '96 / ADA / Cadillac / Direct

Danemo, Peter

BARABAN
CD ____ DRAGON 206
Dragon / Sep '89 / ADA / Cadillac / CM / Roots / Wellard

D'Angelo

BROWN SUGAR
Brown sugar / Alright / Jonz in my bonz / Me and those dreaming eyes of mine / Shit, damn Motherfucker / Smooth / Cruisin' / When we get by / Lady / Higher
CD ____ CTCD 46
Cooltempo / Jun '95 / EMI

Danger Gens

LIFE BETWEEN CIGARETTES
CD ____ CMR 1022
Crunch Melody / Jul '95 / 3mv/Vital

Dangerous Toys

PISSED
CD ____ CDVEST 30
Bulletproof / Sep '94 / Pinnacle

Daniels, Bebe

FEMALE VOCALISTS (3CD Set) (Daniels, Bebe & Dorothy Carless/Anne Shelton)
While the mucic plays on: *Shelton, Anne* / Daddy: *Shelton, Anne* / Better not roll those blue blue eyes: *Shelton, Anne* / Minnie from Trinidad: *Shelton, Anne* / Russian rose: *Shelton, Anne* / St. Louis blues: *Shelton, Anne* / Yes my darling daughter: *Shelton, Anne* / Until you fall in love: *Shelton, Anne* / Little steeple pointing to a star: *Shelton, Anne* / Let there be love: *Shelton, Anne* / Amapola: *Shelton, Anne* / Tomorrow's sunrise: *Shelton, Anne* / Fools rush in: *Shelton, Anne* / Always in my heart: *Shelton, Anne* / How about you: *Shelton, Anne* / How green was my valley: *Shelton, Anne* / I don't want to walk without you: *Shelton, Anne* / My devotion: *Shelton, Anne* / Taxi driver's serenade: *Shelton, Anne* / South wind: *Shelton, Anne* / Only you: *Shelton, Anne* / My yiddishe Momme: *Shelton, Anne* / Daddy: *Carless, Dorothy* / It can't be wrong: *Carless, Dorothy* / My sister and I: *Carless, Dorothy* / Room 504: *Carless, Dorothy* / That lovely weekend: *Carless, Dorothy* / You too can have a lovely romance: *Carless, Dorothy* / Love stay in my heart: *Carless, Dorothy* / We three: *Carless, Dorothy* / Where's my love: *Carless, Dorothy* / I want to be in Dixie: *Carless, Dorothy* / This is no laughing matter: *Carless, Dorothy* / When the sun comes out: *Carless, Dorothy* / Our love affair: *Carless, Dorothy* / I can't love you anymore: *Carless, Dorothy* / I'll always love you: *Carless, Dorothy* / I'd know you anywhere: *Carless, Dorothy* / I guess I'll have to dream the rest: *Carless, Dorothy* / I'm sending my blessing: *Carless, Dorothy* / Ragtime cowboy Joe: *Carless, Dorothy* / Never a day goes by: *Carless, Dorothy* / Walkin' by the river: *Carless, Dorothy* / Deep purple: *Daniels, Bebe* / Stop it's wonderful: *Daniels, Bebe* / As round and round we go: *Daniels, Bebe* / Start the day right: *Daniels, Bebe* / Your company's requested: *Daniels, Bebe* / It's a small world: *Daniels, Bebe* / Give me a little whistle: *Daniels, Bebe* / I'm singing to a million: *Daniels, Bebe* / There I go: *Daniels, Bebe* / Rio Rita: *Daniels, Bebe* / Little Swiss whistling song: *Daniels, Bebe* / Imagination: *Daniels, Bebe* / Nursie nursie: *Daniels, Bebe* / Somewhere in France with you: *Daniels, Bebe* / Mother's prayer at twilight: *Daniels, Bebe* / Our love: *Daniels, Bebe* / Three little fishes: *Carless, Dorothy* / With the wind and rain in your hair: *Carless, Dorothy* / Little Sir Echo: *Carless, Dorothy* / Masquerade is over: *Daniels, Bebe* / Ling ring on your doorstep: *Daniels, Bebe* / Little boy who never told a lie: *Daniels, Bebe*
CD Set ____ EMPRESS 1002
Empress / Jul '96 / Koch

STOP, IT'S WONDERFUL
Deep purple / Stop it's wonderful / As round and round we go / Start the day right / Your company's requested / It's a small world / Give a little whistle / I'm singing to a million / There I go / Rio Rita / Little swiss whistling / Imagination / Nursie Nursie / Somewhere in France with you / Mother's prayer at twilight / Our love / Three little fishes / With the wind and rain in your hair / Little Sir Echo / Little boy who never told a lie / Ling'ring on your doorstep / (I'm afraid) the masquerade is over
CD ____ RAJCD 850
Empress / May '95 / Koch

Daniels, Chris

IS MY LOVE ENOUGH
CD ____ FIENDCD 744
Demon / Nov '93 / Pinnacle

Daniels, Dee

LETS TALK BUSINESS
CD ____ 740272
Capri / '90 / Cadillac / Wellard

Daniels, Eddie

BEAUTIFUL LOVE (Intimate Jazz Portraits)
CD ____ SH 5029
Shanachie / Mar '97 / ADA / Greensleeves / Koch

BLUE BOSSA
Blue bossa / Wistful moment / Emily / Samia / Etude no.14 in F minor Op.25 no.2 / Variations on an Autumn theme / As long as I live / Shine / Two for the road / Entr'acte / Afterthought / Samia / Flower for all seasons / Blue bossa
CD ____ CHCD 71002
Candid / May '97 / Cadillac / Direct / Jazz Music / Koch / Wellard

BRIEF ENCOUNTER
Brief encounter / Child is born / Path / Sway / There is no greater love / Ligia
CD ____ MCD 5154
Muse / Sep '92 / New Note/Pinnacle

FIVE SEASONS, THE
CD ____ SHCD 5017
Shanachie / Nov '96 / ADA / Greensleeves / Koch

MEMO'S FROM PARADISE
Spectralight / Dreaming / Heartline / Love of my life / Homecoming / Memo's from Paradise / Seventh heaven / Capriccio twilight / Impressions from ancient dreams / Flight of the dove / Eight-pointed star
CD ____ GRPD 9651
GRP / May '88 / New Note/BMG

Daniels, Joe

SWING IS THE THING (Daniels, Joe & His Hotshots)
Avalon / Basin Street blues / It don't mean a thing if it ain't got that swing / Power house / Who / Crashing through / Somebody stole my gal / No name jive / Swing is the thing / Steepin' out to swing / Darktown strutters ball / Red light / Whirlwind / Downbeat / Oh lady be good / Red robin rag / When you're smiling / Swing fan / Honeysuckle rose / Time on my hands / Drum boogie / Jammin' sessions / Beat me Daddy, eight to the bar / Fats' in the fire
CD ____ RAJCD 853
Empress / Jan '97 / Koch

Daniels, Luke

LUKE DANIELS & FRANK KILKELLY (Daniels, Luke & Frank Kilkenny)
CD ____ ACS 019CD
Acoustics / Aug '94 / ADA / Koch

TARANTELLA
Patsy Denning set / Musette a Teresa / Golden eagle / Tommy Peoples' jigs / King of Prussia / Wednesday's tune / Baby, Isle of Ewe/The snoring barber / Bandolim / Badinerie / Wounded Hussar / Reels for Nadine / Tarantella sonata
CD ____ CDACS 023
Acoustics / May '97 / ADA / Koch

Daniels, Maxine

MEMORY OF TONIGHT, A
Memory of tonight / Miss you / My one and only love / Moving into Spring / Everybody loves my baby / Ill wind / Cottage for sale / Blues for Holly Ann / That's the way it is / I'm nobody's baby / Come rain or come shine / Waltzing round the moon / Smoke gets in your eyes / I've got a crush on you / Who knows how much I love you / They can't take that away from me / Everything happens to me / I fall in love with you every day / You keep coming back like a song
CD ____ CLGCD 032
Calligraph / Sep '96 / Cadillac / Jazz Music / New Note/Pinnacle / Wellard

POCKETFUL OF DREAMS, A
I've got a pocketful of dreams / With you in mind / Deep purple / Seems like old times / Change partners / Sunshine of love / Something 'bout you baby I like / When you wish upon a star / Leaning on a lamp-post / Into each life some rain must fall / Broken doll / For all we know / Over the rainbow / Talk to the animals
CD ____ CLGCD 016
Calligraph / Oct '93 / Cadillac / Jazz Music / New Note/Pinnacle / Wellard

Danielsson, Lars

CONTINUATION
Hit man / Continuation / Long ago and far away / Flykt / Falin' down / Hymn / It never entered my mind / Namtih / Fatima / Solar / Postludium
CD ____ CDLR 45085
L&R / Aug '94 / New Note/Pinnacle

NEW HANDS
CD ____ DRAGON 125
Dragon / Jan '89 / ADA / Cadillac / CM / Roots / Wellard

POEMS
CD ____ DRAGON 209
Dragon / May '87 / ADA / Cadillac / CM / Roots / Wellard

Danish Radio Big Band

CRACKDOWN (1st UK Tour 1987)
Mr. CT / Vismanden / Ballad for Benny / Crackdown / From one to another / Say it / Malus scorpio ritus / Cherry juice / Big dipper
CD ____ HEPCD 2041
Hep / Apr '90 / Cadillac / Jazz Music / New Note/Pinnacle / Wellard

SUITE FOR JAZZ BAND
Nervous Charlie / November / Daydream / Suite for jazz band / This is all I ask / On Green Dolphin Street / Groove merchant / Well you needn't
CD ____ HEPCD 2051
Hep / May '92 / Cadillac / Jazz Music / New Note/Pinnacle / Wellard

Danko, Harold

AFTER THE RAIN
CD ____ SCCD 31356
Steeplechase / Sep '95 / Discovery / Impetus

TIDAL BREEZE
CD ____ SCCD 31411
Steeplechase / Jul '97 / Discovery / Impetus

Danko, Rick

DANKO/FJELD/ANDERSEN (Danko, Rick & Jonas Fjeld/Eric Andersen)
Driftin' away / Blue hotel / One more shot / Mary I'm comin' back home / Blue river / Judgement day / When morning comes to America / Wrong side of town / Sick and tired / Angels in the snow / Blaze of glory / Last thing on my mind
CD ____ RCD 10270
Rykodisc / Oct '93 / ADA / Vital

RICK DANKO
What a town / Brainwash / New Mexico / Tired of waiting / Sip the wine / Java blues / Sweet romance / Small town talk / Shake it / Once upon a time
CD ____ ED CD 317
Edsel / Apr '90 / Pinnacle

RIDIN' ON THE BLINDS (Danko, Rick & Jonas Fjeld/Eric Andersen)
CD ____ GR 4080CD
Grappa / Apr '95 / ADA

Dankworth, Jacqui

FIRST CRY (Dankworth, Jacqui & Anthony Kerr)
CD ____ EFZ 1010
EFZ / Jan '95 / Vital/SAM

FIVE HOUSMAN SETTINGS (Dankworth, Jacqui & New Perspectives)
On Green Dolphin Street / Bachiana brasileiras No.5 / Sinner's rose / Terence this is stupid stuff / On the idle hill of summer / White in the moon the long road lies / When summer's end is nighing / Creole love call / Reflections in D / Maids of Cadiz / Down hill all the way
CD ____ SPJCD 559

Spotlite / Jul '96 / Cadillac / Jazz Music / New Note/Pinnacle / Swift

Dankworth, John

NEBUCHADNEZZAR (Dankworth Generation Big Band)
Maggot / It ain't necessarily so / Early June / Song for my lad / Day I met Kenny G / Every time we say goodbye / Black narcissus / Ida Lupino / Down to earth / Up for an oscar / Emily / Song for my lady
CD JHCD 029
Ronnie Scott's Jazz House / Mar '94 / Cadillac / Jazz Music / New Note/Pinnacle / TKO Magnum

RHYTHM CHANGES (Dankworth Generation Big Band)
I got rheumatics / Just once more / Around the track / Jelly mould blues / Going back, going on / Thoughts / Pigs head copanitza / All things
CD JHCD 043
Ronnie Scott's Jazz House / Nov '95 / Cadillac / Jazz Music / New Note/Pinnacle / TKO Magnum

Danleers

ONE SUMMERNIGHT
One summer night / My flaming heart / Perlude to love / Wheelin' and dealin' / Picture of you / Really love you, I / You're everything / Whole mess of trouble / Just look around / Can't sleep, I / Your love / (I live) half a block from an angel / If you don't care / Little lover / I'll always believe in you / Light of love / I'll be forever yours / I'm looking around / Foolish / Angels sent you / Were you there / If / Where is love / Think it over baby / Love you better leave me alone
CD BCD 15503
Bear Family / May '91 / Direct / Rollercoaster / Swift

Danny & Dusty

LOST WEEKEND, THE
CD SID 006
Prima / Mar '96 / Direct

Danny & The Juniors

BACK TO THE HOP (Original Swan Recordings 1960-1962)
CD RCCD 3005
Rollercoaster / Sep '92 / Rollercoaster / Swift

Danny Wilson

BEBOP MOPTOP
Imaginary girl / Second summer of love / I can't wait / If you really love me (let me go) / If everything you said was true / Loneliness / I was wrong / Charlie boy / Never gonna be the same / Desert hearts / NYC Shanty / Goodbye Shanty Town / Ballad of me and Shirley MacLaine
CD CDV 2594
Virgin / Aug '91 / EMI

BEST OF DANNY WILSON, THE
Davy / Mary's prayer / Girl I used to know / I won't forget / Second summer of love / Get happy / Never gonna be the same / I'll be waiting / Living to learn / Nothing ever goes to plan / Broken china
CD CDVIP 139
Virgin VIP / Sep '95 / EMI

MEET DANNY WILSON
Davy / Mary's prayer / Lorraine parade / Aberdeen / Nothing ever goes to plan / Broken china / Steamtrains to the milkyway / Spencer Tracey / You remain an angel / Ruby's golden wedding / Girl I used to know / Five friendly aliens / I won't be here when you get home
CD CDV 2419
Virgin / '87 / EMI

SWEET DANNY WILSON
Never gonna be the same / Ballad of me and Shirley MacLaine / If you really love me (Let me go) / Mary's prayer / Girl I used to know / Pleasuer to pleasure / Davy / Ruby's golden wedding / I can't wait / I won't be here when you get home / Second Summer of love / From a boy to a man
CD CDV 2669
Virgin / Aug '92 / EMI

Dantalian's Chariot

CHARIOT RISING
CD WHCD 005
Wooden Hill / Mar '97 / Wooden Hill

Dante Fox

UNDER SUSPICION
CD NTHEN 30CD
Now & Then / Oct '96 / Plastic Head

Danzas Panama

INSTRUMENTAL FOLK MUSIC OF PANAMA
CD VICG 53382
JVC World Library / Mar '96 / ADA / CM / Direct

Danzig

BLACK ACID DEVIL
CD 1620842
Polydor / Oct '96 / PolyGram

DANZIG
Twist of Cain / Not of this world / She rides / Soul on fire / Am I demon / Mother / Possession / End of time / Hunter / Evil thing
CD 74321248412
American / Apr '95 / BMG

DANZIG VOL.4
Brand new God / Little whip / Cantspeak / Going down to die / Until you call on the dark / Dominion / Bringer of death / Sadistikal / Son of the morning star / I don't mind the pain / Stalker song / Let it be captured
CD 74321236812
American / Oct '94 / BMG

HOW THE GODS KILL
CD 74321248432
American / Apr '95 / BMG

LUCIFUGE
Long way back from hell / Killer wolf / I'm the one / Devil's plaything / Blood and tears / Pain in the world / Snakes of Christ / Tired of being alone / Her black wings / 777 / Girl
CD 74321248422
American / Apr '95 / BMG

THRALL/DEMONSWEATLIVE
It's coming down / Violet fire / Trouble / Snakes of Christ / Am I demon / Sistinas / Mother
CD 74321248442
American / Apr '95 / BMG

Daphne's Flight

DAPHNE'S FLIGHT
CD FLE 1005CD
Fledg'ling / Apr '96 / ADA / CM / Direct

Dapogny, Jim

JAMES DAPOGNY & HIS CHICAGOANS
CD SOSCD 1263
Stomp Off / Oct '93 / Jazz Music / Wellard

Darby, Blind Teddy

BLIND TEDDY DARBY 1929-1937
CD BDCD 6042
Blues Document / May '93 / ADA / Hot Shot / Jazz Music

D'Arby, Terence Trent

INTRODUCING THE HARDLINE ACCORDING TO TERENCE TRENT D'ARBY
If you all get to Heaven / If you let me stay / Wishing well / I'll never turn my back on you (fathers words) / Dance little sister / Seven more days / Let's go forward / Rain / Sign your name / As yet untitled / Who's loving you
CD 4509112
CBS / Apr '95 / Sony

TERENCE TRENT D'ARBY'S SYMPHONY OR DAMN (Exploring The Tension Inside The Sweetness)
Welcome to the Monasteryo / She kissed me / Do you love me like you say / Baby let me share my love / Delicate / Neon messiah / Penelope please / Wet your lips / Turn the page / Castilian blues / TITS/FandJ / Are you happy / Succumb to me / I still love you / Seasons / Let her down easy
CD 4735612
Columbia / Sep '96 / Sony

TERENCE TRENT D'ARBY'S VIBRATOR
Vibrator / Supermodel sandwich / Holding onto you / Read my lips (I dig your scene) / Undeniably / We don't have that much time / Together / Epilog / CYFLAY / If you go before me / Surrender / TTD's recurring dream / Supermodel sandwich with cheese / Resurrection / It's been said
CD 4785052
Columbia / May '95 / Sony

TOUCH WITH TERENCE TRENT D'ARBY, THE
CD 8393082
Polydor / Aug '89 / PolyGram

Darby, Tom

COMPLETE RECORDINGS (Darby, Tom & Jimmie Tarlton)
Down in Florida on a hog / Birmingham town / Birmingham jail / Columbus Stockade blues / Gamblin' Jim / Lonesome in the pines / After the ball / I can't tell you why / I love you / Irish police / Hobo tramp / Alto waltz / Mexican rag / Birmingham jail # 2 / Rainbow division / Country girl valley / Lonesome railroad / If you ever learn to love me / If I had listened to my Mother / Travelling yodel blues / Heavy hearted blues / New York hobo / All bound down in Texas / Touring yodel blues / Slow wicked blues / Black Jack moonshine / Ain't gonna marry no more / Down in the old cherry orchid / When the bluebirds nest again / Beggar Joe / When you're far away from home / Birmingham rag / Sweet Sarah blues / Little Bessie / I left her heart at the river / Jack and May / Captain won't you let me go home / Going back to my Texas home / Whistling songbird / Freight train ramble / Lonesome Frisco line / Down among the sugar cane / Black sheep / Little ola / Once I had a sweetheart / Maple on the hill / My father died a drunkyard / Franke Dean / Pork chops / On the banks of a lonely river / Faithless husband / Hard time blues / Rising sun blues / My little blue heaven / Careless love / By the old oaken bucket / Louise / Lowe Bonnie / After the sinking of the Titanic / New Birmingham jail / Roy Dixon / Moonshine blues / She's waiting for me / That lonesome Frisco line / Thirteen years in Kilbie prison / Once I had a fortune / Dixie mail / Weaver's blues / Sweetheart of my dreams / Ooze up to me / Let's be friends again / By the oaken bucket
CD Set BCD 15764
Bear Family / Jun '95 / Direct / Rollercoaster / Swift

Darc, Daniel

PARCE QUE (Darc, Daniel & Bill Pritchard)
CD BIAS 100CD
Play It Again Sam / '90 / Discovery / Plastic Head / Vital

Dardanelle

COLORS OF MY LIFE, THE
CD STCD 544
Stash / '91 / ADA / Cadillac / CM / Direct / Jazz Music

DARDANELLE & DAG WALTON'S BIG BAND (Dardanelle & Dag Walton)
CD ACD 227
Audiophile / Oct '92 / Jazz Music

DOWN HOME
CD ACD 214
Audiophile / Oct '92 / Jazz Music

ECHOES SINGING LADIES
CD ACD 145
Audiophile / Mar '95 / Jazz Music

NEW YORK NEW YORK
CD STCD 547
Stash / '92 / ADA / Cadillac / CM / Direct / Jazz Music

SWINGIN' IN LONDON
CD ACD 278
Audiophile / Jan '94 / Jazz Music

Darensbourg, Joe

N'ORLEANS STATESMEN
CD BCD 313
GHB / Aug '94 / Jazz Music

D'Arienzo, Juan

JUAN D'ARIENZO 1937-1944
CD HQCD 71
Harlequin / Jul '96 / Hot Shot / Jazz Music / Swift / Wellard

TIPICA 1935-1939
CD EBCD 84
El Bandoneon / Jan '97 / Discovery

Darin, Bobby

AS LONG AS I'M SINGIN'
CD JASSCD 4
Jass / Oct '91 / ADA / Cadillac / CM / Direct / Jazz Music

BEST OF BOBBY DARIN VOL.1, THE
CD 7567917942
Atlantic / Dec '96 / Warner Music

DREAM LOVER
La mer / Clementine / That's the way love is / I got a woman/What'd I say/When the saints go marching in / Mack the knife / By myself/When your lover has gone / Splish splash / Queen of the hop / Quarter to nine / You're nobody till somebody loves you / Girl who stood beside me / Dream lover / This could be the start of something big/ Just in time / I wish I were in love again / Don't rain on my parade / Toot toot tootsie goodbye/Don't worry 'bout me / Plain Jane / Early in the morning / Swing low, sweet chariot/Lonesome road/When the saints / If I were a carpenter / That's all
CD CD 6040
Music / Sep '96 / Target/BMG

DREAM LOVER (The Concert Collection)
Mack the knife / Dream lover / Splish splash / If I were a carpenter / Queen of the hop / Early in the morning / Plain Jane / Girl who stood beside me / Funny what love can do / Quarter to nine / Once upon a time / I wish I were in love again
CD PLACD 111
Platinum / Feb '97 / Prism

GREATEST HITS
Mack the knife / Dream lover / Splish splash / If I were a carpenter / Queen of the hop / Early in the morning / Plain Jane / Girl who stood beside me / Funny what love can do / Quarter to nine / Once upon a time / I wish I were in love again
CD HADCD 152
Javelin / May '94 / Henry Hadaway / THE

I GOT RHYTHM
Eighteen yellow roses / If a man answers / True true love / I wonder who's kissing her now / Hello Dolly / All by myself / Roses of Picardy / You'll never know / You made me love you (I didn't want to do it) / Nightingale sang in Berkeley Square / Days of wine and roses / Goodbye Charlie / Softly as I leave you / Call me irresponsible / I got rhythm / All of you / Fly me to the moon / In a world without you / I'm sitting on top of the world / Party's over
CD CDMFP 6247
Music For Pleasure / Aug '96 / EMI

LIVE
Mack the knife / Dream lover / Splish splash / Funny what love can do / Quarter to nine / I wish I were in love again / Early in the morning / Queen of the hop / Plain jane / If I were a carpenter / Girl who stood beside me / Once upon a time
CD 305772
Hallmark / Jul '97 / Carlton

SPOTLIGHT ON BOBBY DARIN
Alabamy bound / Blue skies / You'll never know / Standing on the corner / I'm beginning to see the light / Good life / Oh look at me now / Just in time / You made me love you / All of you / There's a rainbow 'round my shoulder / Fly me to the moon / I got rhythm / All by myself / I wanna be around / Nightingale sang in Berkley Square / Call me irresponsible / My buddy / Always / I'm sitting on top of the world
CD CDP 8285122
Capitol / Apr '95 / EMI

TOUCH OF CLASS, A
18 Yellow roses / If a man answers / True true love / I wonder who's kissing her now / Hello Dolly / All by myself / Roses of Picardy / You'll never know / You made me love you / Nightingale sang in Berkley Square / Days of wine and roses / Goodbye Charlie / Softly as I leave you / Call me irresponsible / I got rhythm / All of you / Fly me to the moon / In a world without you / I'm sitting on top of the world / Party's over
CD TC 877052
Disky / May '97 / Disky / THE

Darius

DARIUS
CD FLASH 009
Flashback / Jun '97 / Greyhound

Dark

ENDLESS DREAMS OF SADNESS
CD GUN 117CD
Gun / Mar '97 / Plastic Head

ZYEZN GAMBALLE & MENTALWORLD
CD MABCD 008
MAB / Sep '94 / Plastic Head

Dark

DARK
CD KSCD 9204
Kissing Spell / Jun '97 / Greyhound

Dark Angel

DARKNESS DESCENDS
Darkness descends / Burning of Sodom / Hunger of the undead / Merciless death / Death is certain (life is not) / Black prophesies / Perish in flames
CD CDFLAG 6
Under One Flag / '89 / Pinnacle

Dark Carnival

LAST GREAT RIDE
CD SFTRI 431CD
Sympathy For The Record Industry / Jan '97 / Cargo / Greyhound / Plastic Head

Dark Comedy

SEVEN DAYS
Electic / Bar / March / Ina room / Solace / Darkness / War of the worlds / Without a sound / Paranoid / Bar
CD ELY 007CD
Elypsia / May '97 / Arabesque / Plastic Head / Vital

Dark Funeral

SECRETS OF THE BLACK ARTS
CD NFR 011CD
No Fashion / Feb '96 / Plastic Head

Dark Heresy

ABSTRACT PRINCIPLES
CD USR 020CD
Unisound / Nov '95 / Plastic Head

Dark Lantern

DARK LANTERN
CD SP 002CD
Silent Pocket / Nov '95 / ADA

Dark Side Cowboys

APOCRYPHAL, THE
CD MACDL 948
Resurrection / Nov '96 / Plastic Head

Dark Throne

GOATLORD
CD FOG 013CD
Moonfog / Nov '96 / Plastic Head

TOTAL DEATH
CD FOG 011CD
Moonfog / Mar '96 / Plastic Head

Dark Tranquility

ENTER SUICIDAL ANGELS
CD OPCD 049
Osmose / Nov '96 / Plastic Head

GALLERY, THE
CD OPCD 033L
Osmose / Apr '96 / Plastic Head
CD OPCD 033
Osmose / Jan '96 / Plastic Head

MINDS VOL.1
CD OPCDL 052
CD OPCD 052
Osmose / Apr '97 / Plastic Head

OF CHAOS AND ETERNAL LIGHT
CD SPI 023CD
Spinefarm / May '95 / Plastic Head

SKYDANCER
CD SPI 016CD
Spinefarm / Apr '96 / Plastic Head

SKYDANCER/OF CHAOS AND ETERNAL LIGHT
CD SPI 034CD
Spinefarm / Oct '96 / Plastic Head

Darkfield

DANCE ON THE GRAVE, A
CD RPS 005CD
Repulse / Jun '95 / Plastic Head

Darkman

WORLDWIDE
Who's the darkman / Brand new day (I'm no puppet) / Yabba dabba do / What's not yours / Wicked / She used to call me / Worldwide ting / What is hardcore / Lighter / Come with the funk / Flip da script / Hot and cold
CD 5294162
Wild Card / Oct '95 / PolyGram

Darkness

BROKEN HARD
CD 15389
Laserlight / Aug '91 / Target/BMG

Darko, George

HIGH LIFE IN THE AIR
CD BLDCD 522
Boulevard / Sep '96 / Grapevine/PolyGram / Total/BMG

Darkseed

ROMANTIC TALES
CD IR 010CD
Invasion / Apr '95 / Plastic Head

Darkside

MELANCHOLIA OF A DYING WORLD
CD SPV 8453552
SPV / Aug '96 / Koch / Plastic Head

Darkthrone

PANZERFAUST
CD FOG 005CD
Moonfog / May '95 / Plastic Head

Darlahood

BIG FINE THING
Grow your own / Sister dementia / Runaway clocks / De nature boy / New York City / Not again / Hey baby (Take me with you) / Rsvp / I've got pictures / Watch your mouth / Big fine thing / 99% Bulletproof
CD 9362462142
Warner Bros. / Oct '96 / Warner Music

Darling, David

CELLO
Darkwood / No place nowhere / Fables / Darkwood II / Lament / Two or three things / Indiana Indian / Totem / Psalm / Choral / Bell / In November / Darkwood III
CD 5119822
ECM / Sep '92 / New Note/Pinnacle

CYCLES
Cycle song / Cycle #1: Namaste / Fly / Ode / Cycle #2: Trio / Cycle #3: Quintet and coda / Jessica's sunwheel
CD 8431722
ECM / Nov '91 / New Note/Pinnacle

DARKWOOD
Dawn / In motion / Journey / Light / Earth / New morning / Returning / Picture / Medi-vial dance / Searching / Up side down / Be-ginning / Passage
CD 5237502
ECM / Feb '95 / New Note/Pinnacle

Darling, Erik

BORDER TOWN AT MIDNIGHT
CD FE 1417
Folk Era / Dec '94 / ADA / CM

Darlingheart

WISH YOU WERE HERE
CD DHCD 3
Fontana / Jul '93 / PolyGram

D'Arnell, Andrea

VILLERS-AUX-VENTS
CD 422498
New Rose / May '94 / ADA / Direct / Discovery

Darren, James

BEST OF JAMES DARREN, THE
Angel face / I ain't sharin' Sharon / Because they're young / Goodbye cruel world / Her royal majesty / Conscience / Gotta have love / Mary's little lamb / Life of the party / Hail to the conquering hero / Pin a medal on Joey / They should have given you the oscar / Put on a happy face / Just think of tonight / Punch and Judy
CD NEMCD 694
Sequel / Aug '94 / BMG

Darrow, Chris

FRETLESS
CD TX 2012CD
Taxim / Jan '94 / ADA

Dart

36 CENTS AN HOUR
CD CHE 39CD
Che / Mar '96 / SRD

Daryll-Ann

COME AROUND
Come around / Doll / Shamrock / Good thing / Mirror mind / Ocean girl
CD HUTDM 44
Hut / May '94 / EMI

SEABORNE WEST
Stay / Low light / Doctor and I / Sheila / Allright / Holida why / You're so vain / Birth-mark / Boy you were / Liquid / HP confirm / Soft and fat
CD CDHUT 26
Hut / Apr '95 / EMI

Das Baul

REAL SUGAR (Das Baul, Paban & Sam Mills)
Dil ki doya / Nacho kali / Porojonome / Ore poinkha / Boshondharar buke / Mon fakira / Chuncholo mon / Mon moti / Gopun pre-mer kotha
CD CDRW 65
Realworld / Mar '97 / EMI

Das Bose Ding

CLEANHAPPYDIRTY
CD BEST 1090CD
Acoustic Music / Apr '96 / ADA

Das Damen

DAS DAMEN
CD SST 040CD
SST / May '93 / Plastic Head

JUPITER EYE
CD SST 095CD
SST / May '93 / Plastic Head

MARSHMELLOW CONSPIRACY
CD SST 218CD
SST / '88 / Plastic Head

TRISKAIDEKAPHOBE
CD SST 190CD
SST / May '93 / Plastic Head

Das EFX

DEAD SERIOUS
Mic checka / Jussummen / They want efx / Looseys / Dum dums / East coast / If only / Brooklyn to T-neck / Klap ya handz / Straight out the sewer
CD 7567918272
Atlantic / May '92 / Warner Music

HOLD IT DOWN
Intro (once again) / Real hip-hop / Micro-phone master / Buck-buck / 40 a blunt / Bad news / Hardcore rap act / Comin' thru / Represent the real / Ready to rock rough rhymes / Dedicated / Hold it down / Alright / Real hip hop / Can't have nuttin' / Here it is / Here we go / No diggedy / Knockin' niggaz off
CD 7559618292
Atlantic / Sep '95 / Warner Music

STRAIGHT UP SEWASIDE
Intro / Undaground rappa / Gimme dat mi-craphone / Check it out / Interlude / Freak it / Rappaz / Interview / Baknaffek / Kaught in da ak / Wontu / Krazy wit da books / It'z lik dat / Host wit da most
CD 7567922652
Atlantic / Dec '93 / Warner Music

Das Ich

DIE PROPHETEN
CD EFA 11201
Danse Macabre / Apr '93 / SRD

SATANISCHE VERSE
CD EFA 112322
Danse Macabre / Jul '94 / SRD

STAUB
CD EFA 112362
Danse Macabre / Nov '94 / SRD

STIGMA
CD EFACD 112332
Danse Macabre / Jun '94 / SRD

Das Klown

LAUGHIN' STACK
CD EFA 122152
Poshboy / Oct '94 / RTM/Disc

Das, Partho

MUSIC OF THE SITAR
CD VICG 52222
JVC World Library / Mar '96 / ADA / CM / Direct

Das Pferd

KISSES (Das Pferd & Randy Becker)
CD ITM 1430
ITM / Jan '91 / Koch / Tradelink

Das, Puma Chandra

SONGS OF THE BAULS
CD VICG 52672
JVC World Library / Mar '96 / ADA / CM / Direct

Dash, Julian

JULIAN DASH 1950-1953
CD BMCD 1050
Blue Moon / Apr '97 / Cadillac / Discovery / Greensleeves / Jazz Music / Jet Star / TKO Magnum

Dash Rip Rock

GET YOU SOME OF ME
CD SECT2 10021
Sector 2 / Jan '96 / Cargo / Direct

Datacide

ONDAS
CD RI 040CD
Rather Interesting / Dec '96 / Plastic Head

Datblygu

LIBERTINO
CD ANKST 037CD
Ankst / Jun '93 / Shellshock/Disc

WYAU/PYST
CD ANKST 60CD
Ankst / Sep '95 / Shellshock/Disc

Dauerlutscher

DAUERLUTSCHER
CD LF 067
Lost & Found / Mar '94 / Plastic Head

Daugherty, Michael

METROPOLIS SYMPHONY/BIZARRO (Daugherty, Michael & Baltimore Symphony Orchestra)
CD 4521032
Argo / Oct '96 / PolyGram

Daughters Of Conceptual ...

DAUGHTERS OF CONCEPTUAL SEX DEATH (Daughters Of Conceptual Sex Death)
CD MUZA 06CD
Muzamuza / Jun '97 / Cargo

Daughters Of Zion

AISHA
CD NGCD 538
Twinkle / May '93 / Jet Star / Kingdom / SRD

Daun, Tom

ALL IN A GARDEN GREEN (Harp Music)
CD TUT 167
Wundertute / Oct '94 / ADA / CM / Duncans

Dauner, Wolfgang

GET UP AND DAUNER
CD 5335482
MPS Jazz / Feb '97 / PolyGram

Dave & Deke Combo

MOONSHINE MELODIES
CD NOHITCD 009
No Hit / Jan '94 / Cargo / SRD

Dave Dee, Dozy, Beaky, Mick ...

BEST OF DAVE DEE, DOZY, BEAKY, MICK & TICH (Dave Dee, Dozy, Beaky, Mick & Tich)
Legend of Xanadu / Bend it / Save me / Hold tight / Touch me, touch me / Wreck of the Antoinette / Snake in the grass / No time / My woman's man / Zabadak / Okay / You make it move / Mr. President / Don Juan / Sun goes down / Is it love / Last night in Soho / Legend of Zanadu
CD 5518232
Spectrum / Nov '95 / PolyGram

GREATEST HITS (Dave Dee, Dozy, Beaky, Mick & Tich)
Legend of Xanadu / Hideaway / Bend it / Zabadak / It's so hard to love you / Okay / Hold tight / Wreck of the Antoinette / Save me / Here's a heart / Touch me touch me / Last night in Soho
CD QED 122
Tring / Nov '96 / Tring

GREATEST HITS (Dave Dee, Dozy, Beaky, Mick & Tich)
Save me / Legend of Xanadu / Wreck of the Antoinette / Okay / Bend it / It's hard to love you / Zabadak / Last night in soho / Here's a heart / Touch me touch me / Hideaway / Hold tight
CD 300362
Hallmark / Jul '96 / Carlton

HITS (Dave Dee, Dozy, Beaky, Mick & Tich)
CD 12274
Laserlight / Apr '94 / Target/BMG

HOLD TIGHT (Dave Dee, Dozy, Beaky, Mick & Tich)
Hold tight / Hideaway / Bend it / Save me / Touch me touch me / Okay / Zabadak / Legend of Xanadu / Last night in Soho / Wreck of the Antoinette / Here's a heart / It's so hard to love you / Matthew and son / Do wah diddy diddy
CD PLATCD 205
Platinum / Feb '97 / Prism

ZABADAK (Dave Dee, Dozy, Beaky, Mick & Tich)
Legend of Xanadu / Bend it / Save me / Mr. President / My woman's man / All I want to do / Master Llewellyn / I'm on the up / If I were a carpenter / Zabadak / Okay / Don Juan / She's so good / Hands off / Help me / Hard to love you / Nose for trouble / We've got a good thing goin'
CD 5509392
Spectrum / Jan '95 / PolyGram

ZABADAK (The Best Of Dave, Dee, Dozy, Beaky, Mick & Tich)
CD MACCD 263
Autograph / Feb '97 / BMG

Davenport, Cow Cow

ACCOMPANIST, THE
CD BDCD 6040
Blues Document / May '93 / ADA / Hot Shot / Jazz Music

Davenport, Jeremy

JEREMY DAVENPORT
Was it something I did / Night we met in Paris / They can't take that away from me / I see your face before me / Why oh why / Joy Jones in the Temple of Doom / I'm old fashioned / Watch out / I'm confessin' that I love you / Lora with an O / Just in case / I'm in the mood for love
CD CD 83376
Telarc / Jul '96 / Conifer/BMG

Davern, Kenny

BREEZIN' ALONG
CD ARCD 19170
Arbors Jazz / May '97 / Cadillac

I'LL SEE YOU IN MY DREAMS
CD MM 5020
Music Masters / Oct '94 / Nimbus

I'LL SEE YOU IN MY DREAMS
Blue Lou / Sweet and lovely / Liza / Pee Wee's blues / Riverboat shuffle / Oh Miss Hanna / My melancholy baby / Royal Gar-den blues / (In my) solitude / I'll see you in my dreams
CD 8208392
Limelight / Mar '93 / PolyGram

LIVE AND SWINGING (Davern, Kenny & John Peters)
That's a plenty / Man I love / Poor butterfly / Royal Garden blues / Blue monk / Love me or leave me
CD CMJCD 001
CMJ / '88 / Jazz Music / Wellard

MY INSPIRATION (Davern, Kenny & Bob Haggart Orchestra)
My inspiration / It had to be you / Then you've never been blue / Dogtown blues / Georgia on my mind / Farewell blues / Brother can you spare a dime / Spreadin' knowledge about / What's new / She's funny that way / Should I / Summertime / I'm confessin' that I love you / Travellin' all alone / Sweet Lorraine / Embraceable you
CD 8442882
Limelight / Aug '91 / PolyGram

NEVER IN A MILLION YEARS (Davern, Kenny & Dick Wellstood)
CD ____ CHR 70019
Challenge / Jun '95 / ADA / Direct / Jazz Music / Wellard

ONE HOUR TONIGHT (Davern, Kenny & Dick Wellstood)
Elsa's dream / Pretty baby / Love is the thing / If I could be with you one hour tonight
CD ____ MM 5003
Music Masters / Oct '94 / Nimbus

SUMMIT REUNION 1992
CD ____ CRD 324
Chiaroscuro / Feb '95 / Jazz Music

Davey, Alan

CAPTURED ROTATION
Call / Never come down / Higher than before / Ancient light / Space bass / Hawkstrel / Nebula / Thunderbird / Nova dive / Spacial wave / Quirk / Pre-Med
CD ____ EBSSCD 122
Emergency Broadcast System / Nov '96 / BMG

Davey, Shaun

GRANUALI
Dubhdarra / Ripples in the rockpools / Defence of Hens Castle / Free and easy / Rescue of Hugh de Lacy / Dismissal / Hen's march / Death of Richard-an-Irainn / Sir Richard Bingham / Spanish Armada / New age
CD ____ TARACD 3017
Tara / Dec '96 / ADA / CM / Conifer/BMG / Direct

PILGRIM, THE
CD ____ TARA 3032CD
Tara / Oct '94 / ADA / CM / Conifer/BMG / Direct

RELIEF OF DERRY SYMPHONY
CD ____ TARACD 3024
Tara / Jul '92 / ADA / CM / Conifer/BMG / Direct

David

ANOTHER DAY, ANOTHER LIFETIME
CD ____ 852123
Arcade / Apr '97 / Discovery

David & David

BOOMTOWN
Boomtown / Rock for the forgotten / Welcome to the boomtown / Swallowed by the cracks / Ain't so easy / Being alone together / River's gonna rise / Swimming in the ocean / All alone in the big city / Heroes
CD ____ CDA 5134
A&M / '89 / PolyGram

David & Jonathan

VERY BEST OF DAVID & JONATHAN
Michelle / Softly whispering your name / You ought to meet my baby / This golden ring / Bye bye brown eyes / I know / Speak her name / Ten storeys high / I've got that girl on my mind / You've got your troubles / Lovers of the world unite / Laughing fit to cry / Be sure / Scarlet ribbons / Gilly gilly ossenfeffer katzenellenbogen by the sea / How bitter the taste of love / Every now and then / One born every minute / See me cry / She's leaving home
CD ____ C5CD507
See For Miles/C5 / Jul '90 / Pinnacle

David Devant & His Spirit Wife

WORK LOVELIFE MISCELLANEOUS
CD ____ KINDCD 1
Rhythm King / Jun '97 / 3mv/Pinnacle / BMG

David, Ian

I MUST JUST LEAVE A KISS
I must just leave a kiss / Sail with you only / Our room / Let me at least stay in your heart / Power behind the throne / Latin calipso / Babe / My airline hostess (coffee or tea) / Chivalry and song / Now I find
CD ____ DVDCD 1
Zonespec / Sep '89 / EMI

David J

SONGS FROM ANOTHER SEASON
I'll be your chauffeur / Fingers in the grease / Longer look / Sad side to the sandboy / New woman is an attitude / Sweet anaesthesia / On the outskirts (of a strange dream) / I'll be your chauffeur (original version) / Moon in the man / Little star / Stranded trans-atlantic hotel nearly famous blues / National anthem of nowhere / Nature boy
CD ____ BEGA 112CD
Beggars Banquet / Jul '90 / RTM/Disc / Warner Music

David, Jean

CHIR HACHIRIM - THE SONG OF SONGS
CD ____ 926282
BUDA / Jul '95 / Discovery

David, Kal

DOUBLE TUFF
CD ____ SC 880042
Lipstick / May '95 / Vital/SAM

Davidson, Fiona

FONNSHEEN
CD ____ FONOCD 13
Watercolour / Mar '96 / ADA

Davidson, Matthew

SPACE SHUFFLE & OTHER FUTURISTIC RAGS
CD ____ SOSCD 1252
Stomp Off / May '93 / Jazz Music / Wellard

Davies, Dave

DAVE DAVIES AND GLAMOUR
CD ____ MAUCD 617
Mau Mau / Sep '92 / Pinnacle

Davies, Debbie

I GOT THAT FEELING
CD ____ BPCD 5039
Blind Pig / Feb '97 / ADA / CM / Direct / Hot Shot

LOOSE TONIGHT
CD ____ BPCD 5015
Blind Pig / Dec '94 / ADA / CM / Direct / Hot Shot

PICTURE THIS
Picture this / Don't take advantage of me / Twenty four hour fool / I wonder why (you're so mean to me) / Livin' on lies / Better off with the blues / Sidetracked / Lovin' cup / Buzz me / San-Ho-Zay / How long 'til I win your love / Going back to luka
CD ____ FIENDCD 732
Demon / Jun '93 / Pinnacle

Davies, Gail

GREATEST HITS
Waiting here for you / Tell me why / Jagged edge of a broken heart / Someone is looking for someone like you / I'll be there / It's a lovely lovely world / Blue heartache / Grandma's song / Bucket to the South / I'm hungry I'm tired / You turn me on I'm a radio / Boys like you / You're a hard dog / Not a day goes by / Singing the blues / Kentucky / Unwed Fathers / What can I say / Round the clock lovin' / Mama I'm sick
CD ____ GAIL 0096
Gail Davies / Jul '97 / Direct

Davies, Ray

TEQUILA (Davies, Ray & Button Down Brass)
Tequila / This guy's in love with you / Do you know the way to San Jose / Somethin' stupid / Chitty chitty bang bang / Can't take my eyes off you / More I see you / Up up and away / Let the heartaches begin / Green grow the rushes-o / Love is blue / Bonnie and Clyde / Look of love / Delilah / By the time I get to Phoenix / MacArthur park / What a wonderful world / It's not unusual / They say it's wonderful / Young girl / Fool on the hill / Last waltz
CD ____ 5329392
Mercury / Aug '96 / PolyGram

Davies, Steve Gwyn

AN UBHAL AS AIRDE
CD ____ VITAL 02CD
Vital Spark / Nov '95 / ADA

Davis, Alvin

LET THE VIBES DECIDE
Call me baby / Rising / Money or love / Organ grinder / Mia / Need you / Guidance / Let the vibes decide / Greeting / Message from the heart / End of the day
CD ____ RIPEXD 213
Ripe / Feb '95 / Pinnacle

Davis, Anthony

EPISTEME
CD ____ GCD 79508
Gramavision / Jun '96 / Vital/SAM

GHOST FACTORY, THE
CD ____ GCD 79429
Gramavision / Sep '95 / Vital/SAM

HIDDEN VOICES (Davis, Anthony & James Newton Quartet)
CD ____ IN 1041CD
India Navigation / Jan '97 / Discovery / Impetus

LADY OF THE MIRRORS
CD ____ IN 1047CD
India Navigation / Jan '97 / Discovery / Impetus

MIDDLE PASSAGE
Behind the rock / Middle passage / Particle W / Proposition for life
CD ____ GRCD 8401
Gramavision / Feb '85 / Vital/SAM

TRIO 2 (Davis, Anthony & James Newton/Abdul Wadud)
Who's life / Thursday's child / Eclipse / Kiano / Invisible island / First movement / Second movement / Third movement / Simultaneity / Flat out
CD ____ 794 412
Gramavision / Mar '90 / Vital/SAM

Davis, Art

LIFE
CD ____ SN 1143CD
Soul Note / Sep '95 / Cadillac / Harmonia Mundi / Wellard

Davis, Betty

CRASHIN' FROM PASSION
CD ____ RAZCD 2099
Razor & Tie / May '96 / Koch

HANGIN' OUT IN HOLLYWOOD
CD ____ CPCD 8148
Charly / Mar '96 / Koch

Davis, Blind John

BLIND JOHN DAVIS 1938
I had a dream / I know the baby loves me / Hey hey Mama / Woman I love / I heard an echo / Trick's done turned on you / Don't lie to me / Harlem blues / When the blues came out to sing / Pretty blues for listening / When I've been drinking / Bartender's bounce / Penny pinching blues
CD ____ ECD 260562
Evidence / Sep '94 / ADA / Cadillac / Harmonia Mundi

FIRST RECORDING SESSIONS
CD ____ SOB 35202
Story Of The Blues / Dec '92 / ADA / Koch

Davis, Carlene

REGGAE SONGBIRD
CD ____ RRTGCD 7703
Rohit / '88 / Jet Star

SONGS OF FREEDOM
CD ____ LG 21076
Lagoon / Mar '93 / Grapevine/PolyGram

Davis, Cedell

FEEL LIKE DOIN' SOMETHING WRONG
I don't know why / Every day every way / She's got the devil in her / Boogie chillen / Baby I love you so / If you like fat women / Guitar boogie / Falling rain blues / In the evening / Sit down on my knee / Got to be moving on / So long / Murder my baby / Green onions
CD ____ FIENDCD 745
Demon / Nov '93 / Pinnacle

Davis, Charles

REFLECTIONS (Davis, Charles & Barry Harris)
CD ____ 1232472
Red / Nov '92 / ADA / Cadillac / Harmonia Mundi

Davis, Daniel

I KNOW A PLACE
I know a place / I'm not listening anymore / It's been a pleasure (not knowing you) / Better half of my heart / What I wouldn't give / Ruth Ann / My heart's not in it / Beer and money / From where I stand / Here's lookin' at you
CD ____ 5311722
A&M / Aug '96 / PolyGram

Davis, Eb

GOOD TIME BLUES (Davis, Eb Bluesband)
CD ____ BEST 1016CD
Acoustic Music / Nov '93 / ADA

Davis, Eddie 'Lockjaw'

EDDIE 'LOCKJAW' DAVIS & MICHAEL STARCH TRIO/KARL RATZER (Davis, Eddie 'Lockjaw' & Michael Starch Trio/ Karl Ratzer)
CD ____ WOLF 120588
Wolf / Jul '96 / Hot Shot / Jazz Music / Swift

EDDIE 'LOCKJAW' DAVIS/ MICHEL ATTENOUX & HIS ORCHESTRA (Davis, Eddie 'Lockjaw' / Michel Attenoux & his Orchestra)
CD ____ STCD 5009
Storyville / May '93 / Cadillac / Jazz Music / Wellard

JAW'S BLUES
CD ____ ENJACD 30972
Enja / Jan '95 / New Note/Pinnacle / Vital/ SAM

JAWS
CD ____ OJCCD 218
Original Jazz Classics / Nov '95 / Complete/Pinnacle / Jazz Music / Wellard

LIGHT AND LOVELY
CD ____ BB 883
Black & Blue / Apr '97 / Discovery / Koch / Wellard

LOCKJAW COOKBOOK VOL.1
CD ____ OJCCD 652
Original Jazz Classics / Feb '92 / Complete/Pinnacle / Jazz Music / Wellard

LOCKJAW COOKBOOK VOL.2
CD ____ OJCCD 653
Original Jazz Classics / Feb '92 / Complete/Pinnacle / Jazz Music / Wellard

SWINGIN' TIL GIRLS
CD ____ SCCD 31058
Steeplechase / Jul '88 / Discovery / Impetus

TOUGH TENORS (Davis, Eddie 'Lockjaw' & Johnny Griffin)
Again 'n' again / Tin tin deo / If I had you / Jim dawg / When we were one / Gigi
CD ____ 8212932
Milestone / Jun '86 / Cadillac / Complete/ Pinnacle / Jazz Music / Wellard

TRANE WHISTLE
Trane whistle / Whole Nelson / You are too beautiful / Stolen moment / Walk away / Jaws
CD ____ OJCCD 429
Original Jazz Classics / Apr '97 / Complete/ Pinnacle / Jazz Music / Wellard

WITH MILT (Davis, Eddie 'Lockjaw' & Sonny Stitt)
CD ____ CDC 9028
LRC / Mar '91 / Harmonia Mundi / New Note/Pinnacle

Davis, Guy

CALL DOWN THE THUNDER
CD ____ RHRCD 89
Red House / Nov '96 / ADA / Koch

STOMP DOWN RIDER
CD ____ RHRCD 80
Red House / Dec '95 / ADA / Koch

Davis, James

CHECK-OUT TIME (Davis, James 'Thunderbird')
I'm ready now / You did me wrong / Hello sundown / Check our time / What else is there to do / If I had my life to live over / Your turn to cry / Come by here / I should've known better / Case of love / Bloodshot eyes / Dark end of the street
CD ____ FIENDCD 149
Demon / Mar '92 / Pinnacle

Davis, Janet-Lee

MISSING YOU
CD ____ FADCD 30
Fashion / Apr '95 / Jet Star / SRD

Davis, Jesse

FROM WITHIN
Journey to Epiphany / Tai's tune / Portrait of Desiree / You've changed / Introspection / You never know / If I should lose you / From within / Six and four
CD ____ CCD 4727
Concord Jazz / Oct '96 / New Note/ Pinnacle

HIGH STANDARDS
Rush hour / I hear a rhapsody / Isms / Peace / Jubilation / Hues / Big push / On a misty night / Strike up the band / Just a little blues
CD ____ CCD 4624
Concord Jazz / Nov '94 / New Note/ Pinnacle

YOUNG AT ART
East of the sun and west of the moon / Brother Roj / I love Paris / Ask me now / Georgiana / Waltz for Andre / Little flowers / One for cannon / Tipsy / Fine and dandy
CD ____ CCD 4565
Concord Jazz / Aug '93 / New Note/ Pinnacle

Davis, Jesse Ed

JESSE ED DAVIS
CD ____ 7567803032
Atlantic / Jan '96 / Warner Music

Davis, John

BLUE MOUNTAINS
CD ____ SHR 90CD
Shrimper / Jan '97 / Cargo

I'LL BURN
CD ____ SHR 85CD
Shrimper / Nov '96 / Cargo

LEAVE HOME
CD ____ COMM 37CD
Communion / Dec '96 / Cargo

ROOM FOR SPACE (Davis, John & Dennis Callaci)
CD ____ SHR 74CD
Shrimper / Dec '96 / Cargo

Davis, Larry

BLUES KNIGHTS (Davis, Larry & Byther Smith)
Giving up on love: *Davis, Larry* / I tried: *Davis, Larry* / Teardrops: *Davis, Larry* / That's alright Mama: *Davis, Larry* / I don't have a mother: *Smith, Byther* / I'm a honey bee: *Smith, Byther* / What is this: *Smith, Byther* / Don't make me talk to much: *Smith, Byther* / Addressing the nation with the blues: *Smith, Byther* / I'm broke: *Smith, Byther*
CD ECD 260422
Evidence / Mar '94 / ADA / Cadillac / Harmonia Mundi

I AIN'T BEGGIN' NOBODY
CD ECD 26016
Evidence / Feb '93 / ADA / Cadillac / Harmonia Mundi

SOONER OR LATER
How could you do it to me / I'm working on it / Penitentiary blues / You'll need another favour / Help the poor / Letter from my darling / Goin' out west (part 1 and 2) / 102 St. blues / How long / Bluebird / Littlerock
CD CDBB 9511
Bullseye Blues / Sep '92 / Direct

Davis, 'Little' Sammy

I AIN'T LYIN'
I ain't lyin' / Daniel / Sammy's shuffle / Shorty / That's my girl / Someday / Devil's trail / When I leave / Bad luck blues / Somebody's fool / Hey little girl / California blues / I-man stomp / Play me for a fool
CD DE 682
Delmark / Mar '97 / ADA / Cadillac / CM / Direct / Hot Shot

Davis, Linda

SOME THINGS ARE MEANT TO BE
Some things are meant to be / Love story in the making / Walk away / Always will / Neither one of us / She doesn't ask / Cast iron heart / There isn't one / What do I know / If I could live your life
CD 07822188042
Arista / Jan '96 / BMG

Davis, Link

1948-1963
CD KKCD 06
Krazy Kat / Jul '93 / Hot Shot / Jazz Music

BIG MAMOU
Big mamou / Pretty little dedon / Mamou waltz / Hey garcon / Lonely heart / Time will tell / Gumbo ya-ya (everybody talks at once) / Falling for you / Crawfish crawl / You're little but you're cute / Mama say no / Every time I pass your door / You show up missing / Cajun love / Kajalena / Va t'cacher
CD EDCD 279
Edsel / Mar '92 / Pinnacle

Davis, Meg

CLADDAGH WALK, THE
For Ireland I'd not tell her name / Castle of Dromore / Burning West Indies / She moved through the fair / Broom o'the Cowdenknowes / Claddagh walk / Lake of Ponchartrain / If I were a blackbird / P stands for Paddy / Eileen Aroon / My Lagan love / Loch Tay boat song / Queen of May / Last Leviathan
CD LCDM 9030
Lismor / Nov '90 / ADA / Direct / Duncans / Lismor

Davis, Michael

MIDNIGHT CROSSING
CD LIP 890352
Lipstick / Dec '95 / Vital/SAM

Davis, Miles

'58 SESSIONS
On Green Dolphin Street / Fran dance / Stella by starlight / Love for sale / Straight no chaser / My funny valentine / Oleo
CD 4679182
Columbia / Apr '92 / Sony

AGHARTA
Prelude / Maiysha / Interlude / Theme from Jack Johnson
CD 4678972
Columbia / Sep '93 / Sony

AMANDLA
Catembe / Big time / Jo Jo / Jilli / Cobra / Hannibal / Amandla / Mr. Pastorius
CD K 9258732
WEA / May '89 / Warner Music

AND MODERN JAZZ GIANTS
CD OJCCD 347
Original Jazz Classics / Feb '92 / Complete/Pinnacle / Jazz Music / Wellard

ASCENSEUR POUR L'ECHAFAUD (Lift To The Scaffold/Original 1957 Soundtrack)
Nuit sur Les Champs-Elysee / Assassinat / Motel / Final / Le petit bal / Sequence voiture / Generique / L'assassinat de Carala / Sur l'autoroute / Julien dans l'ascenseur / Florence dans l'ascenseur / Florence sur Les Champs-Elysee / Diner au motel / Evasion de Julien / Visite du vigile / Au bar du petit bac / Chez le photographe du motel
CD 8363052
Fontana / Mar '94 / PolyGram

AT CARNEGIE HALL (2CD Set)
So what / Spring is here / No blues / Oleo / Someday my prince will come / Meaning of the blues / Lament / New rhumba / Concierto de Aranjuez (part 1) / Concierto de Aranjuez (part 2) / Teo / Walkin' / I thought about you
CD Set 4723572
Sony Jazz / Apr '96 / Sony

AT FILLMORE (2CD Set)
CD 4769092
Columbia / Oct '94 / Sony

AT LAST (Davis, Miles & The Lighthouse All Stars)
Infinity promenade / 'Round midnight / Night in Tunisia / Drum conversation / At last
CD OJCCD 480
Original Jazz Classics / Feb '92 / Complete/Pinnacle / Jazz Music / Wellard

AT THE ROYAL ROOST 1948 & BIRDLAND 1950-53
52nd street / Half Nelson / You go to my head / Chasin' the Bird / Hot house / Wee / Tempus fugit / Evance (out of the blue) / Move / Tenderly / Night in Tunisia / Dig
CD LEJAZZCD 45
Le Jazz / Jun '95 / Cadillac / Koch

AUDIO ARCHIVE
Out of nowhere / Night in Tunisia / Yardbird suite / Scrapple the apple / Ornithology / Don't blame me / Moose the mooche / Bird of paradise / Embraceable you / My old flame / Bird's nest: *Davis, Miles & Charlie Parker* / Tweet bop: *Davis, Miles & Charlie Parker* / Slam blam blues: *Davis, Miles & Charlie Parker* / Cool head blues: *Davis, Miles & Charlie Parker* / Riff raff: *Davis, Miles & Charlie Parker*
CD CDAA 027
Tring / Jun '92 / Tring

AURA
Intro / White / Yellow / Orange / Red / Green / Blue / Electric red / Indigo / Violet
CD 4633512
Columbia / Oct '89 / Sony

BALLADS
Baby, won't you please come home / I fall in love too easily / Bye bye blackbird / Basin Street blues / Once upon a summertime / Song no.2 / Wait till you see her / Corcovado
CD 4610992
Columbia / Apr '89 / Sony

BALLADS AND BLUES
I waited for you / Yesterdays / One for Daddy-O / Moon dreams / How deep is the ocean / Weirdo / Enigma / It never entered my mind / Autumn leaves
CD CDP 8366332
Blue Note / Apr '96 / EMI

BEST OF MILES DAVIS
CD DLCD 4023
Dixie Live / Mar '95 / TKO Magnum

BEST OF MILES DAVIS, THE
Move / Godchild / Budo / Dear old Stockholm / Donna / Yesterdays / Tempus fugit / Enigma / CTA / Well you needn't / It never entered my mind / Weirdo / Something else / Autumn leaves
CD BNZ 286
Blue Note / Feb '92 / EMI

BIRDLAND DAYS
CD FSCD 124
Fresh Sound / Jan '91 / Discovery / Jazz Music

BIRDLAND SESSIONS
CD LEJAZZCD 23
Le Jazz / Feb '94 / Cadillac / Koch

BIRTH OF THE COOL
Move / Jeru / Moon dreams / Venus De Milo / Budo / Deception / Darn that dream / Godchild / Boplicity / Rocker / Israel / Rouge
CD CDP 7928622
Capitol / Sep '92 / EMI

BIRTH OF THE COOL/MILES DAVIS VOL.1/MILES DAVIS VOL.2 (The Originals/3CD Set)
Move / Jeru / Moon dreams / Venus de Milo / Budo / Deception / Godchild / Boplicity / Rocker / Israel / Rouge / Tempus fugit / Kelo / Enigma / Ray's idea / How deep is the ocean / CTA / Dear old Stockholm / Chance it / Yesterdays / Donna / CTA / Wouldn't you / Take off / Weirdo / Would'n you / I waited for you / Ray's idea / Donna / Well you needn't / Leap / Lazy Susan / Tempus fugit / It never entered my mind
CD Set CDOMB 007
Blue Note / Mar '97 / EMI

BITCHES BREW
Pharaoh's dance / Bitches brew / Spanish key / John McLaughlin / Miles runs the voodoo down / Sanctuary
CD Set 4606022
Columbia / Oct '91 / Sony

BITCHES BREW LIVE
CD JZCD 373
Suisa / Nov '92 / Jazz Music / THE

BLACK BEAUTY (Live at Filmore West)
Directions / Miles runs the voodoo down / Willie Nelson / I fall in love too easily / Sanctuary / It's about that time / Bitches brew / Masqualero / Spanish key
CD 65138
Sony Jazz / Aug '97 / Sony

BLUE HAZE
CD CDSGP 042
Prestige / Mar '93 / Else / Total/BMG

BLUE MOODS
CD OJCCD 432
Original Jazz Classics / Oct '93 / Complete/Pinnacle / Jazz Music / Wellard

BLUING (Miles Davis Plays The Blues)
Bluing / Blue 'n' boogie / Bag's groove / Green haze / Dr. Jackle / No line / Vierd blues / Trane's blues / Blues by five
CD PRCD 11004
Prestige / Jun '97 / Cadillac / Complete/Pinnacle

BOPPING THE BLUES
Don't sing me the blues / I've always got the blues / Don't explain to me baby / Baby, won't you make up your mind
CD BLCD 760102
Black Lion / Jun '88 / Cadillac / Jazz Music / Koch / Wellard

BYE BYE BLACKBIRD
CD CDSGP 0264
Prestige / Jan '97 / Else / Total/BMG

CBS YEARS 1955-85 (4CD Set)
Generique / All blues / Eighty one / Blues for Pablo / Summertime / Straight no chaser / Footprints / Florence sur les Champs Elysees / I thought about you / Someday my Prince will come / Bye bye blackbird / My funny valentine / Love for sale / Budo / Miles / Files de Kilimanjaro / Fran dance / Seven steps to heaven / Flamenco sketches / So what / Water babies / Saeta / Masqualero / Pinocchio / Summer night / Fall / It's about that time / Sivad / What it is / Ms. Morrisine / Shout / Honky Tonk / Star on Cicely / Thinkin' one thing and doin' another / Miles runs the voodoo down
CD 4632462
Columbia / Jan '95 / Sony

CHRONICLE: THE COMPLETE PRESTIGE RECORDINGS (8CD Set)
Ahmad's blues / Airegin / Bag's groove / Bemsha swing / Bitty ditty / Blue haze / Blue 'n' boogie / Blue room / Blues by five / Bluing / But not for me / Changes / Compulsion / Conception / Denial / Diane / Dig / Dr. Jackle / Down / Doxy / Ezz-thetic / Floppy / For adults only / Four / Gal in Calico / Green haze / Half nelson / Hibeck / How am I to know / I could write a book / I know / I didn't / I see your face before me / I'll remember April / If I were a bell / In your own sweet way / It could happen to you / It never entered my mind / It's only a paper moon / Just squeeze me / Love me or leave me / Man I love / Miles ahead / Minor march / Morpheus / My funny valentine / My old flame / Night in Tunisia / No line / Odjenar / Old devil moon / Oleo / Out of the blue / 'Round midnight / Salt peanuts / Serpent's tooth / Smooch / Solar / Something I dreamed last night / S'posin' / Stablemates / Surrey with the fringe on top / Swing spring / Tasty pudding / Theme / There is no greater love / Trane's blues / Tune up / Vierd blues / Walkin' / Well you needn't / When I fall in love / When lights are low / Whispering / Will you still be mine / Willie the wailer / Wouldn't you / Yesterdays / You don't know what love is / You're my everything
CD Set 8 PCD 012
Prestige / Apr '92 / Cadillac / Complete/Pinnacle

CIRCLE IN THE ROUND
Circle in the round / Two bass hit / Love for sale / Blues No. 2 / Teo's bag / Side car / Splash sanctuary / Guinevere
CD Set 4679892
Columbia / Sep '93 / Sony

COLLECTORS ITEM
Compulsion / Serpent's tooth / 'Round midnight / In your own sweet way / Vierd blues / No line / My old flame / Nature boy / There's no you / Easy living / Alone together
CD OJCCD 71
Original Jazz Classics / Feb '92 / Complete/Pinnacle / Jazz Music / Wellard

COMPLETE COLUMBIA STUDIO RECORDINGS (6CD Set) (Davis, Miles & Gil Evans)
CD Set CXK 67397
Sony Jazz / Sep '96 / Sony

COMPLETE CONCERT 1964, THE (My Funny Valentine & Four More)
Introduction by Mort Fega / My funny valentine / All of you / Go go (Theme and re-introduction) / Stella by starlight / All blues / I thought about you / So what / Walkin' / Joshua / Go go (Theme and announcement) / Four / Seven steps to heaven / There is no greater love / Do go
CD Set 4712462
Columbia / May '93 / Sony

COMPLETE PRESTIGE RECORDINGS, THE (Chronicle 1951-1965/8CD Set)
Morpheus / Down / Blue room / Whispering / I know / Odjenar / Ezz-thetic / Hibeck / Yesterdays / Conception / Out of the blue / Denial / Bluing / Dig / My old flame / It's only a paper moon / Compulsion / Serpent's tooth / 'Round midnight / Tasty pudding / Willie the wailer / Floppy / For adults only / When lights are low / Tune up / Miles ahead / Smooch / Four / Old devil moon / Blue haze / Solar / You don't know what love is / Love me or leave me / I'll remember April / Blue 'n' boogie / Walkin' / Airegin / Oleo / But not for me / Doxy / Bag's groove / Bemsha / Swing swing Spring / Man I love / I didn't / Will you still be mine / Green haze / I see your face before me / Night in Tunisia / Gal in Calico / Dr. Jackle / Bitty ditty / Minor march / Changes / No line / Vierd blues / Stablemates / How am I to know / Just squeeze me / There is no greater love / Theme / In your own sweet way / S'posin' / In your own sweet way / Diane / Trane's blues / Something I dreamed last night / It could happen to you / Woody 'n' you / Ahmad's blues / Surrey with the fringe on top / It never entered my mind / When I fall in love / Salt peanuts / Four / Theme / If I were a bell / Well, you needn't / Round midnight / Half Nelson / You're my everything / I could write a book / Oleo / Airegin / Tune up / When lights are low / Blues by five / My funny valentine
CD Set PCD 0122
Prestige / Nov '96 / Cadillac / Complete/Pinnacle

CONCIERTO DE ARANJUEZ
CD CD 14543
Jazz Portraits / Jan '94 / Jazz Music

COOKIN' AND RELAXIN' (Davis, Miles Quintet)
Cookin' - My funny valentine / Blues by five / Airegin / Tune up / When the lights are low / Relaxin' / You're my everything / I could write a book / Oleo / It could happen to you / Woody 'n' you
CD CDJZD 003
Prestige / Jan '91 / Cadillac / Complete/Pinnacle

COOKIN', WALKIN', WORKIN', STEAMIN' (4CD Set)
It never entered my mind / Four / In your own sweet way / Theme / Trane's blues / Ahmad's blues / Half Nelson / Theme / Surrey with the fringe on top / Salt peanuts / Something I dreamed last night / Diane / Well you needn't / When I fall in love / My funny valentine / Blues by five / Airegin / Tune up/When lights are low / Walkin' / Blue 'n' boogie / Solar / You don't know what love is / Love me or leave me
CD Set 4PRCD 8805
Prestige / Nov '96 / Cadillac / Complete/Pinnacle

COOL
If I were a bell / You're my everything / I could write a book / Oleo / It could happen to you / Woody 'n' you
CD MSCD 19
Music De-Luxe / Nov '95 / TKO Magnum

COOL JAZZ CLASSICS
I'll remember April / Compulsion / Serpent's tooth / Max is making wax / That old black magic / Whispering / Bird of paradise / Conception / Miles ahead / Morpheus / Ray's idea / When lights are low / 'Round midnight / Ornithology / Yardbird suite / Embraceable you / Don't blame me
CD BN 008
Blue Nite / Nov '96 / Target/BMG

COTE BLUES
CD JMY 10102
JMY / Aug '93 / Harmonia Mundi

DARK MAGUS
Moja / Moja / Wili / Wili / Tatu / Tatu / Nne / Nne
CD 65137
Sony Jazz / Aug '97 / Sony

DAVISIANA (Davis, Miles Quintet)
CD MCD 0332
Moon / Jan '92 / Cadillac / Harmonia Mundi

DECOY
Decoy / Robot 415 / Code MD / Freaky deaky / What is it / That's right / That's what happened
CD CD 25951
Columbia / Sep '93 / Sony

DIG (Davis, Miles & Sonny Rollins)
CD OJCCD 5
Original Jazz Classics / Feb '92 / Complete/Pinnacle / Jazz Music / Wellard

DOO BOP
Mystery / Doo bop song / Chocolate chip / High speed chase / Blow / Sonya / Fantasy / Duke booty / Mystery (reprise)
CD 7599269382
WEA / Mar '94 / Warner Music

ESP
ESP / Eighty one / Little one / RJ / Agitation / Iris / Mood

CD 4678992
Columbia / Oct '91 / Sony

ESSENTIAL MILES DAVIS, THE
'Round midnight / My funny valentine / Cencierto De aranjuez / Summertime / All blues / Milestones / Wallkin
CD 4671442
Columbia / Aug '92 / Sony

FESTIVAL INTERNATIONAL DE JAZZ PARIS 1949 (Davis, Miles & Tadd Dameron Quintet)
Rifftide / Good bait / Don't blame me / Lady bird / Wah hoo / Allen's alley / Embraceable you / Ornithology / All the things you are
CD 4852572
Sony Jazz / Sep '96 / Sony

FILLES DE KILIMANJARO
Frelon brun (brown hornet) / Tout de suit / Petits machins (little stuff) / Filles de Kilimanjaro (girls of Kilimanjaro) / Mademoiselle Mabry
CD 4670882
Columbia / Oct '91 / Sony

FRIDAY NIGHT AT THE BLACK HAWK, SAN FRANCISCO VOL.1
CD 4633342
Columbia / Jan '95 / Sony

GET UP WITH IT
He loved him madly / Maiysha / Honky tonk / Rated X / Calypso frelimo / Red China blues / Mtume / Billy Preston
CD LICD 9211552
Line / Nov '96 / CM / Direct
CD 4852562
Sony Jazz / Sep '96 / Sony

GREAT JAZZ PERFORMANCES (2CD Set)
Whispering / I'll remember April / Compulsion / Serpent's tooth / Blue haze / Smooch / Down / Night in Tunisia / Embraceable you / Moose the mooch / Ornithology / Yardbird suite / 'Round midnight / Autumn leaves / That old devil moon / Four / Miles ahead / Blue room / Morpheus / When lights are low / Bird of paradise / Don't blame me / My old flame / Out of nowhere / Scrapple the apple / So what / All of you
CD Set TNC 96211
Natural Collection / Aug '96 / Target/BMG

GREEN DOLPHIN STREET (Davis, Miles Quintet)
CD NI 4002
Natasha / Jun '93 / ADA / Cadillac / CM / Direct / Jazz Music

HIGHLIGHTS FROM THE PLUGGED NICKEL
Milestones / Yesterdays / So what / Stella by starlight / Walkin' / 'Round midnight
CD 4814342
Sony Jazz / Nov '95 / Sony

IN A SILENT WAY
Ssh peaceful / In a silent way / It's about that time
CD 4509822
Columbia / Oct '93 / Sony

IN CONCERT
CD 4769102
Columbia / Oct '94 / Sony

JAZZ AT THE PLAZA VOL.1
CD 4715102
Columbia / Jan '95 / Sony

JAZZ PORTRAITS
Now's the time / Night in Tunisia / Donna Lee / Cheryl / Milestones / Half nelson / Marmaduke / Jeru / Boplicity / Rocker / Ezz-thetic / Yesterdays / Compulsion / Tempus fugit / Tune up / It never entered my mind / Old devil moon / I'll remember April
CD CD 14503
Jazz Portraits / May '94 / Jazz Music

KIND OF BLUE
So what / Freddie Freeloader / Blue in green / Al blues / Flamenco sketches / Flamenco sketches
CD 4804102
Mastersound / Jul '95 / Sony
CD CK 64935
Sony Jazz / Apr '97 / Sony

KIND OF BLUE/MILESTONES/STELLA BY STARLIGHT
CD Set 4722742
Columbia / Oct '92 / Sony

LEGENDARY STOCKHOLM CONCERT (Davis, Miles & John Coltrane)
CD NI 4011
Natasha / Jan '93 / ADA / Cadillac / CM / Direct / Jazz Music

LIVE (2CD Set)
Intruders / New blues / One phone call / Street scenes / Perfect way / Senate / Me and you / Tutu / Movie stars / Splatch / Time after time / Wayne's tune / Full Nelson
CD Set 24327
Laserlight / Mar '96 / Target/BMG

LIVE AROUND THE WORLD
CD 9362460322
Warner Bros. / Jul '96 / Warner Music

LIVE AT MONTREUX (Davis, Miles & Quincy Jones)
Introduction by Claude Nobs and Quincy Jones / Boplicity / Introduction to Miles ahead medley / Springsville / Maids of cadiz / Duke / My ship / Miles ahead / Blues for pablo / Introduction to Porgy and Bess medley / Orgone / Gone gone gone / Summertime / Here come de honey man / Pan piper / Solea
CD 93624522142
Warner Bros. / Sep '93 / Warner Music

LIVE AT NEWPORT 1958 & 1963 (2CD Set) (Davis, Miles & Thelonious Monk)
Introduction: *Davis, Miles* / Ah-leu-cha: *Davis, Miles* / Straight no chaser: *Davis, Miles* / Fran dance: *Davis, Miles* / Two bass hit: *Davis, Miles* / Bye bye blackbird: *Davis, Miles* / Theme: *Davis, Miles* / Introduction: *Monk, Thelonious* / Criss cross: *Monk, Thelonious* / Light blue: *Monk, Thelonious* / Nutty: *Monk, Thelonious* / Blue monk: *Monk, Thelonious* / Epistrophy: *Monk, Thelonious*
CD Set C2K 53585
Columbia / Oct '94 / Sony

LIVE AT THE PLUGGED NICKEL 1965 (8CD Set)
If I were a bell / Stella by starlight / Walkin' / I fall in love too easily / Theme / My funny valentine / Four / When I fall in love / Agitation / 'Round midnight / Milestones / All of you / Oleo / No blues / I thought about you / On green dolphin street / So what / Autumn leaves / All blues / Yesterdays
CD Set CXK 66955
Sony Jazz / Jul '95 / Sony

LIVE EVIL
Sivad / Little church / Gemini/Double image / What I say / Nem um talev / Selim / Funky tonk / Inamorata
CD 4852552
Sony Jazz / Sep '96 / Sony

LIVE IN 1958-59 (Davis, Miles All Stars)
CD EBCD 21012
Flyright / Dec '90 / Hot Shot / Jazz Music / Wellard

LIVE IN SINDELFINGEN 1964 (Davis, Miles Quintet)
CD JZCD 372
Suisa / Nov '92 / Jazz Music / THE

LIVE IN ST LOUIS & PARIS 1963 (Davis, Miles Quintet)
CD JZCD 371
Suisa / Nov '92 / Jazz Music / THE

LIVE IN STOCKHOLM 1960 COMPLETE (Davis, Miles & John Coltrane/Sonny Stitt)
CD DRCD 228
Dragon / Sep '89 / ADA / Cadillac / CM / Roots / Wellard

LIVE TUTU (Davis, Miles Band)
CD JZCD 375
Suisa / Nov '92 / Jazz Music / THE

LIVE/EVIL
Sivad / Little church / Medley / Nem um talvez / Selim / Funky tonk / Inamorata and norration
CD 65135
Sony Jazz / Aug '97 / Sony

MAN WITH THE HORN (Davis, Miles & John Coltrane)
Fat time / Backseat Betty / Shout Aida / Man with the horn / Ursula
CD 4687012
Columbia / Sep '93 / Sony

MELLOW MILES
Miles / Summertime / So what / Time after time / Miles ahead / Freddie freeloader / Bye bye blackbird / Pfrancing / 'Round midnight / It ain't necessarily so / Human nature
CD 4694402
Columbia / Dec '91 / Sony

MILES AHEAD
Springsville / Maids of Cadiz / Duke / My ship / Miles ahead / Blues for Pablo / New rhumba / Meaning of the blues / Lament / I don't wanna be kissed
CD 4743702
Columbia / Jan '95 / Sony

MILES AHEAD
CD CD 14540
Jazz Portraits / Jan '94 / Jazz Music

MILES AHEAD 1956-58
CD CD 56038
Jazz Roots / Jul '95 / Target/BMG

MILES AND COLTRANE (Davis, Miles & John Coltrane)
CD 4608242
Columbia / Oct '93 / Sony

MILES AND HORNS
CD OJCCD 53
Original Jazz Classics / Feb '92 / Complete/Pinnacle / Jazz Music / Wellard

MILES DAVIS
That old devil moon / Four / Ladybird / Woody 'n' you / Squirrel / Blue room / Confirmation / Down / Out of the blue / Move / Smooch / Moose the Mooch / My old flame / Out of nowhere / Scrapple the apple / Night in Tunisia

CD BN 009
Blue Nite / Feb '97 / Target/BMG

MILES DAVIS
I'll remember April / Tempus Fugit / It never entered my mind / Walkin' / Compulsion / Old devil moon / Tune up / Jeru / Ezzthetic / Rocker / Boplicity / Now's the time / Milestones
CD 399548
Koch Presents / Jun '97 / Koch

MILES DAVIS & KEITH JARRETT LIVE (Davis, Miles Band)
CD JZCD 374
Suisa / Nov '92 / Jazz Music / THE

MILES DAVIS & LENNIE TRISTANO (Davis, Miles & Lennie Tristano)
CD NI 4015
Natasha / Aug '93 / ADA / Cadillac / CM / Direct / Jazz Music

MILES DAVIS & MILT JACKSON (Davis, Miles & Milt Jackson)
CD OJCCD 12
Original Jazz Classics / Feb '92 / Complete/Pinnacle / Jazz Music / Wellard

MILES DAVIS & THE JAZZ GIANTS
CD FCD 60015
Fantasy / Oct '93 / Jazz Music / Pinnacle / Wellard

MILES DAVIS AT FILLMORE
Wednesday miles / Thursday miles / Friday miles / Saturday miles
CD 65139
Sony Jazz / Aug '97 / Sony

MILES DAVIS COLLECTION
CD COL 035
Collection / Jun '95 / Target/BMG

MILES DAVIS GOLD (2CD Set)
CD Set D2CD 4022
Deja Vu / Jun '95 / THE

MILES DAVIS IN CONCERT
CD Set 710455
RTE / Apr '95 / ADA / Koch

MILES DAVIS IN CONCERT (Live at the Philarmonic Hall)
Foot fooler in concert / Rated x / Honky tonk / Thene from Jack Johnson / Black satin / Slickaphonics in concert / Ife / Right off/The Theme
CD 65140
Sony Jazz / Aug '97 / Sony

MILES IN ANTIBES
CD 4629602
Columbia / Jan '95 / Sony

MILES IN BERLIN
CD CD 62976
Columbia / Jan '95 / Sony

MILES IN THE SKY
Stuff / Paraphernalia / Black comedy / Country son
CD 4772092
Columbia / Sep '93 / Sony

MILES SMILES
Orbits / Circle / Footprints / Dolores / Freedom jazz dance / Gingerbread boy
CD 4710042
Columbia / Apr '92 / Sony

MILESTONES
CD 4608272
Columbia / Oct '93 / Sony

MILESTONES 1945-54
CD CD 56009
Jazz Roots / Aug '94 / Target/BMG

MISCELLANEOUS DAVIS
Hackensack / 'Round midnight / Now's the time / Four / Walkin' / Oh lady be good / All of you / Four
CD JUCD 2050
Jazz Unlimited / Nov '94 / Cadillac / Jazz Music / Wellard

MOSTLY MILES (Newport Jazz Festival July 3rd/6th 1958)
CD NCD 8813
Phontastic / '93 / Cadillac / Jazz Music / Wellard

MUSINGS OF MILES, THE
I didn't / Will you still be mine / Green haze / I see your face before me / Night in Tunisia / Gal in Calico
CD OJCCD 4
Original Jazz Classics / Feb '92 / Complete/Pinnacle / Jazz Music / Wellard

NEFERTITI
Nefertiti / Fall / Hand jive / Madness / Riot / Pinocchio
CD 4670892
Columbia / Oct '91 / Sony

NEW MILES DAVIS QUINTET
CD OJCCD 6
Original Jazz Classics / Feb '92 / Complete/Pinnacle / Jazz Music / Wellard

ON THE CORNER
On the corner / New York girl / Thinkin' one thing and doin' another / Vote for Miles / Black satin / One and one / Helen Butte / Mr. Freedom X
CD 4743712
Columbia / Feb '94 / Sony

PANGAEA (2CD Set)
Zimbabwe / Gondwana
CD 4670872
Columbia / Sep '93 / Sony

PARAPHERNALIA
CD JMY 10132
JMY / Aug '92 / Harmonia Mundi

PARIS CONCERT
CD JZCD 341
Suisa / Jan '93 / Jazz Music / THE

PORGY AND BESS (Davis, Miles & Gil Evans Orchestra)
Buzzard song / Bess you is my woman now / Gone gone gone / Summertime / Bess, oh where's my Bess / Prayer / O Doctor Jesus / Fisherman / Strawberry and devil crab / My man's gone now / It ain't necessarily so / Here come de honey man / I loves you Porgy / There's a boat that's leavin' soon for New York / I loves you Porgy / Gone
CD CK 65141
Sony Jazz / Apr '97 / Sony

QUIET NIGHTS
CD CD 85556
Columbia / Jan '95 / Sony

RARITIES AND PRIVATE COLLECTIONS 1956-59
CD JZCD 314
Suisa / Feb '91 / Jazz Music / THE

REAL BIRTH OF THE COOL - RARE AND LIVE
CD JZCD 313
Suisa / Feb '91 / Jazz Music / THE

REAL BIRTH OF THE COOL, THE
CD BS 18005
Bandstand / Jul '96 / Swift

ROUND ABOUT MIDNIGHT
'Round midnight / Ah leu cha / All of you / Bye bye blackbird / Tadd's delight / Dear old Stockholm
CD 4606052
Columbia / Oct '91 / Sony

ROUND MIDNIGHT
CD CD 53045
Giants Of Jazz / Mar '92 / Cadillac / Jazz Music / Target/BMG

SATURDAY NIGHT AT THE BLACK HAWK, SAN FRANCISCO VOL.2
CD 4651912
Columbia / '88 / Sony

SEVEN STEPS TO HEAVEN
Basin Street blues / Seven steps to heaven / I fall in love too easily / So near, so far / Baby, won't you please come home / Joshua
CD 4669702
Columbia / Apr '92 / Sony

SKETCHES OF SPAIN
Concierto de Aranjuez / Amor brujo / Pan piper / Saeta / Solea
CD 4606042
Columbia / Oct '91 / Sony

SOME DAY MY PRINCE WILL COME
Someday my Prince will come / Old folks / Drad-dog / Teo / I thought about you / Pfancing
CD 4663122
Columbia / Jan '95 / Sony

SORCERER
Prince of Darkness / Vonetta / Limbo / Masqualero / Pee Wee / Sorcerer
CD 4743692
Columbia / Sep '93 / Sony

STAR PEOPLE
Come get it / It gets better / Speak / Star people / U'un I / Star on Cicely
CD CD 25395
Columbia / Sep '93 / Sony

STEAMIN' WITH THE MILES DAVIS QUINTET
CD OJCCD 391
Original Jazz Classics / Feb '92 / Complete/Pinnacle / Jazz Music / Wellard

STOCKHOLM 1960
CD TAXCD 3716
Tax / Aug '95 / Cadillac / Jazz Music / Wellard

THEIR GREATEST CONCERT (Davis, Miles & John Coltrane)
CD JZCD 315
Suisa / Feb '91 / Jazz Music / THE

THIS IS JAZZ
'Round midnight / Stella by starlight / Springsville / Summertime / So what / Someday my prince will come / Seven steps to heaven / Walkin' / ESP
CD CK 64616
Sony Jazz / May '96 / Sony

THIS IS JAZZ
Circle / My ship / Old folks / Mood / Dear old Stockholm / I loves you Porgy / Basin street blues / Time after time / Flamenco sketches
CD CK 65038
Sony Jazz / May '97 / Sony

TRANSITION
CD MRCD 125
Magnetic / Sep '91 / TKO Magnum

TRIBUTE TO JACK JOHNSON
Right off / Yesternow
CD _______ 4710032
Columbia / Sep '93 / Sony

TUNE UP (Davis, Miles & Stan Getz)
CD _______ NI 4008
Natasha / Jun '93 / ADA / Cadillac / CM / Direct / Jazz Music

TUTU
Tutu / Tomaas / Portia / Splatch / Backyard ritual / Perfect way / Don't lose your mind / Full nelson
CD _______ 9254902
WEA / Oct '86 / Warner Music

VERY BEST OF MILES DAVIS, THE
Time after time / Summertime / Bye bye blackbird / It ain't necessariy so / Once upon a summertime / Concierto de Aranjuez / 'Round midnight / I don't wanna be kissed (by anyone but you) / So what / Jean Pierre / Human nature / Shout / Miles
CD _______ SONYTV 17CD
Sony TV / Sep '96 / Sony

WALKIN'
Walkin': *Davis, Miles All Stars* / Blue 'n' boogie: *Davis, Miles All Stars* / Solar: *Davis, Miles All Stars* / You don't know what love is: *Davis, Miles All Stars* / Love me or leave me: *Davis, Miles All Stars*
CD _______ OJCCD 213
Original Jazz Classics / Feb '92 / Complete/ Pinnacle / Jazz Music / Wellard

WALKIN'
CD _______ CD 14537
Jazz Portraits / Jan '94 / Jazz Music

WE WANT MILES
Jean Pierre / Backseat Betty / Fast track / My man's gone now / Kix
CD _______ 4699022
Columbia / Sep '93 / Sony

WHAT I SAY VOL.1
CD _______ JMY 10152
JMY / Apr '94 / Harmonia Mundi

WHAT I SAY VOL.2
CD _______ JMY 10162
JMY / Apr '94 / Harmonia Mundi

WORKIN' (Davis, Miles Quintet)
CD _______ OJCCD 296
Original Jazz Classics / Feb '92 / Complete/Pinnacle / Jazz Music / Wellard

YOU'RE UNDER ARREST
One phone call / Street scenes / Human nature / Ms. Morrisine / Katia (prelude) / Time after time / You're under arrest / Then there were none / Something's on your mind
CD _______ 4687032
Columbia / Sep '93 / Sony

Davis, Morgan

MORGAN DAVIS
CD _______ SP 1148CD
Stony Plain / Oct '93 / ADA / CM / Direct

Davis, Rev. Gary

COMPLETE EARLY RECORDINGS, THE
CD _______ YAZCD 2011
Yazoo / Oct '94 / ADA / CM / Koch

FROM BLUES TO GOSPEL
CD _______ BCD 124
Biograph / '92 / ADA / Cadillac / Direct / Hot Shot / Jazz Music / Wellard

GOSPEL BLUES & STREET SONGS (Davis, Rev. Gary & Pink Anderson)
John Henry / Everyday in the week / Ship / Titanic / Greasy greens / Wreck of ol' 97 / I've got mine / He's in the jailhouse now / Blow Gabriel / Twelve gates to the city / Samson and Delilah / Oh Lord / Search my heart / Get right church / You got to go down / Keep your lamp trimmed and burning / There was a time that I was blind
CD _______ OBCCD 524
Original Blues Classics / Nov '92 / Complete/Pinnacle / Wellard

HARLEM STREET SINGER
Samson and Delilah / Let us get together right down here / I belong to the band / Pure religion / Great change since I been born / Death don't have no mercy / Twelve gates to the city / Goin' to sit down on the banks of the river / Tryin' to get home / Lo I be with you always / I am the light of this world / Lord I feel just like goin' on
CD _______ OBCCD 547
Original Blues Classics / Nov '92 / Complete/Pinnacle / Wellard

I AM A TRUE VINE (1962-1963)
I am a true vine / Lord stand by me / Won't you hush / Mean ol' world / Moon is goin' down / Sportin' life blues / Get right church / Blow Gabriel / Slippin' til my gal comes in partner / Wall hollow blues / Blues in E / Piece without words / Whoopin' blues / I want to be saved
CD _______ HTCD 07
Heritage / '91 / ADA / Direct / Hot Shot / Jazz Music / Swift / Wellard

O GLORY
CD _______ EDCD 482
Edsel / Jun '96 / Pinnacle

PURE RELIGION AND BAD COMPANY
CD _______ SFWCD 40035
Smithsonian Folkways / Oct '94 / ADA / Cadillac / CM / Direct / Koch

REVEREND BLIND GARY DAVIS
I'm going to sit down on the banks of the river / Twelve gates to the city / I heard the angels singing / Twelve sticks / Make believe stunt / Waltz time candyman / C rag / Walking dog blues
CD _______ HTCD 02
Heritage / Oct '89 / ADA / Direct / Hot Shot / Jazz Music / Swift / Wellard

SAY NO TO THE DEVIL
Say no to the devil / Time is drawing near / Hold to God's unchanging hand / Bad company brought me here / I decided to go down / Lord I looked down the road / Little Bitty baby / No one can do me like Jesus / Boy in the wilderness / Trying to get to heaven in due time
CD _______ OBCCD 519
Original Blues Classics / Nov '92 / Complete/Pinnacle / Wellard

SIGN OF THE SUN
Sun is going down / When the train comes along / If I had my way / Twelve gates / God's gonna separate / Get right Church / Saints / God don't work like a natural man / There's destruction in this land
CD _______ HTCD 03
Heritage / Oct '90 / ADA / Direct / Hot Shot / Jazz Music / Swift / Wellard

Davis, Richard

NOW'S THE TIME
CD _______ MCD 6005
Muse / Sep '92 / New Note/Pinnacle

Davis, Sammy Jr.

COLLECTION, THE
After today / Candy man / Fabulous places / Where are the words / All that jazz / I'm always chasing rainbows / Lonely is the name / We'll be together again / Every time we say goodbye / Going's great / If my friends could see me now / I'm a brass band / All the good things in life / People tree / Good life / Please don't take your time / Come back to me / I've gotta be me / She believes in me / At the crossroads
CD _______ CCSCD 225
Castle / May '89 / BMG

GREAT, THE
That old black magic / Hey there / Something's gotta give / Stan' up an' fight (until you hear de bell) / Someone to watch over me / I'll know / Frankie and Johnny / Sit down you're rockin' the boat / because of you / Back track / Glad to be unhappy / Lonesome road / Lady is a tramp / Song and dance man / Circus / Adelaide / New York's my home / Love me or leave me / Easy to love / All of you
CD _______ CDMFP 6055
Music For Pleasure / Mar '89 / EMI

Davis, Sara

TUNDRA
CD _______ CAKECD 14
Soundcakes / Jun '94 / 3mv/Sony

Davis Sisters

MEMORIES
I forgot more than you'll ever know / Sorrow and pain / Rock-a-bye boogie (master) / You're gone / Sorrow and pain (fast version) / You're gone (swinging version) / Heartbreak ahead / Jealous love / Kaw-Liga / Rag mop / Your cheatin' heart / Crying steel guitar waltz / Just when I needed you / It wasn't God who made honky tonk angels / Tomorrow's just another day to cry / Tomorrow I'll cry / Jambalaya / Takin' time out for tears / Rock-a-bye boogie (alt.) / Gotta git a goin' / You weren't ashamed to kiss me last night / Foggy mountain top / Just like me / Don't take him for granted / I've closed the door / Medley / She loves him and he loves me / Single girl / Show me / Christmas boogie / Fiddle diddle boogie / Everlovin' / Come back to me / Tomorrow I'll cry over you / When I stop lovin' you / I'll get him back / It's the girl who gets the blame / Toodle-ooh (to you) / Baby be mine / Blues for company / Lonely and blue / Let's go steady / Lying brown eyes / Everywhere he went / Take my hand, precious Lord / Dig a little deeper in God's love
CD _______ BCD 15722
Bear Family / Jul '93 / Direct / Rollercoaster / Swift

Davis, Skeeter

END OF THE WORLD, THE
End of the world / Silver threads and golden needles / Mine is a lonely life / Once upon a time / Why I'm walkin' / Don't let me cross over / My colouring book / Where nobody knows me / Keep your hands off my baby / Something precious / Longing to hold you again / He called me baby
CD _______ TC 017
That's Country / Mar '94 / BMG

ESSENTIAL SKEETER DAVIS, THE
I forgot more than you'll ever know / Set him free / Am I that easy to forget / One you slip around with / (I can't help you) I'm falling too / No, never / My last date (with you) / Optimistic / End of the world / Gonna get along without ya now / Where I ought to be / I can't stay mad at you / I'm saving my love / Silver threads and golden needles / Mine is a lonely life / Let me get close to you / Fuel to the flame / What does it take (to keep a man like you satisfied) / I'm a lover (not a fighter) / Bus fare to Kennedy
CD _______ 74321665362
RCA / Feb '96 / BMG

SHE SINGS THEY PLAY (Davis, Skeeter & NRBQ)
Things to you / Everybody wants a cowboy / I can't stop loving you now / Heart to heart / Ain't nice to talk like that / Everybody's clown / Someday my Prince will come / How many tears / You don't know what you got till you lose it / Roses on my shoulder / Temporarily out of order / May you never be alone
CD _______ ROUCD 3092
Rounder / '88 / ADA / CM / Direct

Davis, Spencer

24 HOURS - LIVE IN GERMANY (Davis, Spencer Band)
CD _______ INAK 859
In Akustik / Mar '95 / Direct / TKO Magnum

8 GIGS A WEEK (2CD Set) (Davis, Spencer Group)
Dimples / I can't stand it / Jump back / Here right now / Searchin' / Midnight train / It's gonna work out fine / My babe / Kansas City / Every little bit hurts / Sittin' and thinkin' / I'm blue / She put the hurt on me / I'll drown in my own tears / I'm getting better / Goodbye Stevie / Strong love / Georgia on my mind / It hurts me so / Oh pretty woman / Look away / This hammer / Please do something / Let me down easy / Somebody help me / Watch your step / Nobody knows you (When you're down and out) / Midnight special / When I come home / High time baby / Hey darling / I washed my hands in muddy water / You must believe me / Trampoline / Since I met you baby / Mean woman blues / Dust my broom / When a man loves a woman / Neighbour neighbour / On the green light / Stevie's blues / Take this hurt off me / Stevie's groove / I can't get enough of it / Waltz for Lumumba / Together till the end of time / Gimme some lovin' / Back into my life again / I'm a man / Blues in F
CD Set _______ CRNCD 5
Island / Mar '96 / PolyGram

CATCH YOU ON THE REBOP (Live '73) (Davis, Spencer Group)
Let's have a party / Catch you on the rebop / I'm a man / Man jam / Gimme some lovin' / Living in a back street / Today, gluggo, tomorrow the world / Lega eagle shuffle / Fastest thing on / One night / Trouble in mind / Tumble down tenament row / Hanging around / Mr. Operator
CD _______ RPM 150
RPM / Jun '95 / Pinnacle

FUNKY (Davis, Spencer Group)
CD _______ OW 34529
One Way / Jun '97 / ADA / Direct / Greyhound

GIMME SOME LOVIN'
Gimme some lovin' / Crossfire / Such a good woman / Somebody help me / It must be love / Mistakes / Keep on running / I'm a man / No other baby / Love is on a roll / Blood runs hot / Don't want you no more / Private number: *Davis, Spencer & Dusty Springfield*
CD _______ 304312
Hallmark / Jun '97 / Carlton

KEEP ON KEEPING ON
Keep on running / Somebody help me / I'm a man / Gimme some loving / Blood runs hot / Don't want you no more / Love is on a roll / Crossfire / Private number / No other baby / Mistakes / It must be love / Such a good woman
CD _______ MSCD 4
Music De-Luxe / Apr '94 / TKO Magnum

LIVE TOGETHER
CD _______ INAK 8410
In Akustik / Sep '95 / Direct / TKO Magnum

SPOTLIGHT ON SPENCER DAVIS
Love is on a roll / Keep on running / It must be love / Somebody help me / Don't want you no more / Crossfire / I'm a man / Private number / Such a good woman / Gimme some lovin' / No other baby / Blood runs hot / Mistakes
CD _______ HADCD 123
Javelin / Feb '94 / Henry Hadaway / THE

TAKING OUT TIME 1967-69 (Davis, Spencer Group)
CD _______ RPMCD 127
RPM / May '94 / Pinnacle

Davis, Thornetta

SUNDAY MORNING MUSIC
CD _______ SPCD 324
Sub Pop / Oct '96 / Cargo / Greyhound / Shellshock/Disc

Davis, Tyrone

BEST OF THE FUTURE YEARS, THE
CD _______ ICH 1153CD
Ichiban / Feb '94 / Direct / Koch

I'LL ALWAYS LOVE YOU
I'll always love you / Prove my love / Talk to you / Let me love you / Do U still love me / Can I change my mind / Woman needs to be loved / Mom's apple pie
CD _______ ICH 1103CD
Ichiban / Oct '93 / Direct / Koch

SOMETHING'S MIGHTY WRONG
CD _______ ICH 1135CD
Ichiban / Apr '94 / Direct / Koch

YOU STAY ON MY MIND
You stay on my mind / Let me be your pacifier / I found myself when I lost you / All because of your love / You can win if you want / I won't let go / Something good about a woman / You're my heart / You're my soul
CD _______ ICH 1170CD
Ichiban / May '94 / Direct / Koch

Davis, Walter

ENGINEER'S BLUES
CD _______ ALB 1012CD
Aldabra / Aug '92 / CM / RTM/Disc

Davison, 'Wild' Bill

'S WONDERFUL (Davison, 'Wild' Bill & His New Yorkers)
CD _______ JCD 181
Jazzology / '92 / Jazz Music

'WILD' BILL DAVISON & PAPA BUE'S VIKING JAZZ BAND (Davison, 'Wild' Bill & Papa Bue Viking Jazz Band)
CD _______ STCD 5523
Storyville / May '97 / Cadillac / Jazz Music / Wellard

AFTER HOURS
CD _______ JCD 22
Jazzology / '92 / Jazz Music

COMMODORE MASTER TAKES
That's a plenty / Panama / River boat shuffle / Muskrat ramble / Clarinet marmalade / Original Dixieland one step / At the Jazz band ball / Baby, won't you please come... / I don't stand a ghost of a chance with you / Jazz me blues / Little girl / Squeeze me / Monday day / I'm confessin' that I love you / Big butter and egg man / I wish I could shimmy like my... / Sensation rag / Who's sorry now / On the Alomo / Someday sweetheart / High society / Wrap your troubles in dreams / I'm coming Virginia / Wabash blues
CD _______ CMD 14052
Commodore Jazz / Feb '97 / New Note/ BMG

JAZZ ON A SATURDAY AFTERNOON VOL.1
CD _______ JCD 37
Jazzology / '92 / Jazz Music

JAZZ ON A SATURDAY AFTERNOON VOL.2
CD _______ JCD 38
Jazzology / '92 / Jazz Music

JUST A GIG
CD _______ JCD 191
Jazzology / '91 / Jazz Music

LADY OF THE EVENING
CD _______ JCD 143
Jazzology / '92 / Jazz Music

RUNNING WILD
Blue room / I surrender dear / Monday date / Am I blue / You took advantage of me / If I had you / I never knew / (Back home again in) Indiana / When it's sleepy time down South / I want to be happy / Sunny side of the street / Running wild
CD _______ JSPCD 1044
JSP / Oct '90 / ADA / Cadillac / Direct / Hot Shot / Target/BMG

SHOWCASE
CD _______ JCD 83
Jazzology / '92 / Jazz Music

SOLO FLIGHT
CD _______ JCD 114
Jazzology / '92 / Jazz Music

STARS OF JAZZ (Davison, 'Wild' Bill/ Freddy Randall Band)
CD _______ JCD 62
Jazzology / Oct '91 / Jazz Music

STARS OF JAZZ VOL.2 (Davison, 'Wild' Bill/Freddy Randall Band)
CD _______ JCD 63
Jazzology / Oct '91 / Jazz Music

SWEET AND LOVELY (Davison, 'Wild' Bill & Strings)
CD STCD 4060
Storyville / Feb '90 / Cadillac / Jazz Music / Wellard

THIS IS JAZZ VOL.1
CD JCD 42
Jazzology / '92 / Jazz Music

TOGETHER AGAIN (Davison, 'Wild' Bill & Ralph Sutton)
Limehouse blues / Am I blue / Grandpa's spells / Three little words / Reunion blues / Back in your own backyard / I've got the world on a string / Rockin' chair
CD CMJCD 003
CMJ / Apr '89 / Jazz Music / Wellard
CD STCD 8216
Storyville / Dec '95 / Cadillac / Jazz Music / Wellard

WILD BILL AT BULL RUN
CD JCD 30
Jazzology / Nov '96 / Jazz Music

WILD BILL DAVISON & HIS FAMOUS JAZZ BAND (Davison, 'Wild' Bill & His Famous Jazz Band)
CD JCD 103
Jazzology / '92 / Jazz Music

WILD BILL IN DENMARK VOL.2
CD STCD 5524
Storyville / May '97 / Cadillac / Jazz Music / Wellard

Daweh Congo

MILITANCY
CD RN 0050
Runnetherlands / Jul '97 / Jet Star

Dawkins, Jimmy

ALL FOR BUSINESS
All for business / Cotton country / Moon man / Down so long / Welfare blues / Having such a hard time / Sweet home Chicago / Born in poverty / Jammin' with Otis / Hippies playground / Moon man
CD DD 634
Delmark / Mar '97 / ADA / Cadillac / CM / Direct / Hot Shot

B PHUR REAL
CD DOG 9110CD
Wild Dog / Aug '95 / Koch

BLISTERSTRING (Dawkins, Jimmy Band)
Feel so bad / Blue Monday / Chitlins con carne / She got the blues too / If you're ready / Blues with a feeling / Ode to Billie Joe / Welfare line / Shufflin' the blues / People will talk / Sea of luv
CD DE 641
Delmark / Nov '96 / ADA / Cadillac / CM / Direct / Hot Shot

BLUES AND PAIN
CD DOG 9108CD
Wild Dog / Jun '94 / Koch

BLUES FROM ICELAND (Dawkins, Jimmy/Chicago Beau/Blue Ice Bragason)
Welfare line / That's alright / You don't love me / Feel so bad / Too much alcohol / Sometimes I have a heartache / Nightlife / One room country shack / Help me / Tin pan alley
CD ECD 26064
Evidence / Mar '95 / ADA / Cadillac / Harmonia Mundi

FEEL THE BLUES
(If you got to) Love somebody / Highway man / So good to be me / Last days / Feel the blues / Christmas time blues / Have a little mercy / We got to go / So good to me
CD JSPCD 282
JSP / Jan '97 / ADA / Cadillac / Direct / Hot Shot / Target/BMG

HOT WIRE 81
You just a baby child / Ruff times / Welfare line / Kold actions / Roc-kin-sole / Peeper's music / My way
CD ECD 260432
Evidence / Mar '94 / ADA / Cadillac / Harmonia Mundi

TRIBUTE TO ORANGE (Dawkins, Jimmy & Gatemouth Brown/Otis Rush)
All for business / You've got to keep on trying / Ain't never had nothing / Born in poverty / Marcelle Morgantini's Cassoulet / Your love / Tribute to orange / Mississippi bound / Life is a mean mistreater / Mean Atlantic ocean / Serves you right to suffer / Marcelle, Jacques et Luc / Ode to Billy Joe
CD ECD 260312
Evidence / Feb '93 / ADA / Cadillac / Harmonia Mundi

Dawn

CANDIDA
CD RE 21192
Razor & Tie / Dec '96 / Koch

TIE A YELLOW RIBBON
CD BR 1452
BR Music / Jun '94 / Target/BMG

TIE A YELLOW RIBBON (The Very Best Of Dawn/Tony Orlando)
Tie a yellow ribbon / Knock three times / Up on the roof / Rainy day man / Candida / Jolie / Let's run away girl / Carolina in my mind / What are you doing Sunday / Personality / Did you ever think she'd run away from you / You're a lady / Vaya con dios / Steppin' out gonna boogie tonight / Home / All in the game / Who's in the strawberry patch with Sally / Country / She can't hold a candle to you / Sweet gypsy rose
CD 74321454762
Camden / Feb '97 / BMG

Dawn

5 DAYS WISER
Feel like living / Five days wiser / Sister mystery / Mesmerize / Make it right / Good luck
CD R 4062
Rough Trade / Aug '97 / Pinnacle

NIER SOLEN GAR NIFER FUR EVUGHER
CD NR 006CD
Necropolis / Apr '95 / Plastic Head

SORGH PA SVARTE VINGAR FLOGH
CD NR 6664CD
Necropolis / Oct '96 / Plastic Head

Dawn, Dolly

MEMORIES OF YOU
CD ACD 201
Audiophile / Feb '91 / Jazz Music

Dawson

CHEESE MARKET
CD GRUFF 11CD
Gruff Wit / Nov '95 / SRD

Dawson, Dana

BLACK BUTTERFLY
Interlude - Black butterfly / 3 is family / Got to give me love / Show me / Dignified / Interlude - Visions / You are my baby / So good together / How I wanna be loved / All of these things / Nothing in this world / Interlude - Love me / Baby do right by me / Stop yourself / Intentions / Touch me / Interlude - Proverbs / Sad sad songs / Interlude - Home / Salvation / Interlude - Angel
CD CDEMC 3749
EMI / May '96 / EMI

Dawson, Julian

LIVE ON THE RADIO
CD WM 1003
Watermelon / Jun '93 / ADA / Direct

LOST ALBUM, THE
CD HYCD 296161
Hypertension / Mar '96 / ADA / CM / Direct / Total/BMG

MOVE OVER DARLING
If I neede rain / Move over darling / Every tear's a weapon / Waiting for the moon / It came from Memphis / All the King's horses / Ghost of his own name / Locked out of paradise / Never take a fall / It's not time now / Pilgrims / Action man / There's more to love
CD FLED 3012
Fledg'ling / Jun '97 / ADA / CM / Direct

TRAVEL ON
Uneasy rider / Never alone / Just can't say no / Sigh heart don't break / New Columbus / You're listening now / Hosanna / Queen of the bayou / My own damn bed / Brando's perfect girl / Gabriel's hill
CD HYCD 296160
Hypertension / Feb '97 / ADA / CM / Direct / Total/BMG

Dawson, Peter

PETER DAWSON
Floral dance / Drake goes west / Glorious Devon / Up from Somerset / When the Sergeant Major's on parade / Vulcan's song / Non piu'andrai / Largo al factotum / Toreador's song (Bizet 'Carmen') / Bachelor gay / Smuggler's song / Yeomen of England / Old father Thames / Phil the fluter's ball / Waltzing Matilda / Ol' man river / Waiata poi / Drum major / I am a roamer
CD GEMMCD 9336
Pearl / '90 / Harmonia Mundi

PETER DAWSON
I travel the road / Old Father Thames / Smuggler's song / Boots / Soldier's dream / When the Sergeant Major's on parade / Danny Deever / Old comrades - the boys of the old brigade / Yeoman of England / Drake goes West / Glorious Devon / Fishermen of England / Friend o' mine / Floral dance / Drake's drum / Phil the flutter's ball / Cobbler's song / Bachelor gay / Whalin' up the Lochlan / Admiral's broom / By the side of the road / Gentleman Jim / Joggin' along the highway
CD CDMFP 6351
Music For Pleasure / Jun '97 / EMI

SCOTTISH AND IRISH SONGS
Auld sangs o'hame / Auld hoose / O sing to me an Irish song / Mountains of Mourne / Star o' Rabbie Burns / Jug of punch / Border ballad / Off to Philadelphia / There far far awa' / Away in Athlone / Paddy's wedding / Father O'Flynn / Molly of Donegal / Pride of Tipperary / Turn ye tae me / She is far from the land / With my shillelagh under me arm / Fiddler of Dooney / Kerry dance / Phil the fluter's ball
CD MIDCD 008
Moidart / Jul '95 / Conifer/BMG

SINGS THE YEOMAN OF ENGLAND
CD PASTCD 7007
Flapper / Jun '93 / Pinnacle

SOMEWHERE A VOICE IS CALLING
El Abanico / Banjo song / Boots / Cobbler's song / Down among the dead men / Drum major / Fishermen of England / Fleet's not in port very long / Floral dance / Friend o' mine / Give me the rolling sea / Glorious Devon / If those lips could only speak / In a monastery garden / Jerusalem / Love and wine / Man who brings the sunshine / Mountains o' Mourne / Snowbird / Somewhere a voice is calling / Tomorrow is another day / Waiata poi / Waltzing Matilda / We saw the sea / Winding road
CD CDAJA 5114
Living Era / Sep '93 / Select

SONGS OF THE SEA
Drake's drum / Outward bound / Old superb / Devon, O Devon / Homeward bound / Sons of the sea / Shipmates o'mine / Admiral Broom / At Santa Barbara / Cargoes / Rocked in the cradle of the deep / Tune the bosun played / Jolly Roger / Anchored / Rolling down to Rio / Little Admiral
CD GEMMCD 9381
Pearl / '90 / Harmonia Mundi

Dawson, Ronnie

JUST ROCKIN' AND ROLLIN'
Just rockin' and rollin' / You got a long way to go / Veronica / Fish out of water / Home cookin' / Club wig wam / You're humbuggin' me / Mexigo / It wouldn't do no good / She's a bad un / High on love / Sucker for a cheap guitar / Hoodlum / Tired of travellin' / No dice / Party town
CD NOHIT 019CD
No Hit / May '97 / Cargo / SRD

MONKEY BEAT
CD NOHITCD 008
No Hit / Jan '94 / Cargo / SRD

ROCKIN' BONES
Rockin' bones / Congratulations to me / Do do do / Who's been here / Action packed / Tied down / I make the love / Riders in the sky / Jump and run / Tired of waitin' / I'm on your wagon / Who put the cat out / Reelin' and rockin' / Straight skirts / Searchin' for my baby / Everybody clap your hands
CD NOHITCD 001
No Hit / Jan '94 / Cargo / SRD

Dax, Danielle

COMATOSE NON-REACTION (2CD Set)
CD Set BOT131 06CD
Biter Of Thorpe / Oct '96 / World Serpent

INKY BLOATERS
CD BOT131 04CD
Biter Of Thorpe / Oct '96 / World Serpent

POP EYES
Here come the harvest buns / Bed caves / Tower of lies / Numb companions / Everyone squeaks quietly
CD BOT131 01CD
Biter Of Thorpe / Oct '96 / World Serpent

Day Behaviour

ADORED
Carouse / Cinematic / Shortness of breath / Hello / Il sogno / Clown / Beginning of something else / Movie / Momentary laughter / Remarkable rocket / Gullible / Treno notturno
CD NONS 352
Nons / Mar '97 / Pinnacle

Day Blindness

DAY BLINDNESS
CD FLASH 42
Flash / Jul '97 / Greyhound

Day, Bobby

ROCKIN' ROBIN
Rockin' Robin / Bluebird, the buzzard and the oriole / Over and over / Come seven / Honeysuckle baby / My blue Heaven / I don't want to / When the swallows come back to Capistrano / Beep beep beep / Ain't gonna cry no more / Little bitty pretty one / Life can be beautiful / That's all I want / Mr. and Mrs. rock 'n' roll / Sweet little thing / Three young rebs from Georgia
CD CDCH 200
Ace / May '91 / Pinnacle

Day, Dennis

AMERICA'S FAVOURITE IRISH TENOR
CD CDSG 402
Starline / Aug '89 / Jazz Music

Day, Doris

'S WONDERFUL
CD HCD 226
Hindsight / Mar '95 / Jazz Music / Target/BMG

'S WONDERFUL
'S wonderful / My blue Heaven / You oughta be in pictures / Hundred years from today / September in the rain / I'm a big girl now / Don't worry 'bout me / Just you, just me / I gotta sing away these blues / Sentimental journey / I can't give you anything but love / Light your lamp / Singin' in the rain / Blues skies / I got it bad and that ain't good / Be anything but mine / Crying my heart out for you / Let's be buddies / While the music plays on / Dig it
CD SUMCD 4008
Summit / Nov '96 / Sound & Media

16 MOST REQUESTED SONGS
Sentimental journey / My dreams are getting bigger all the time / It's magic / Love somebody / Again / Bewitched, bothered and bewildered / Would I love you (love you, love you) / Why did I tell you I was going to Shanghai / Starbust / Guy is a guy / When I fall in love / Secret love / If I give my heart to you / I'll never stop loving you / Whatever will be will be (Que sera sera) / Everybody loves a lover
CD 4721952
Columbia / May '95 / Sony

BEST OF DORIS DAY, THE
CD MATCD 315
Castle / Dec '94 / BMG

BEST OF DORIS DAY, THE
Move over darling / Love me or leave me / Sentimental journey / Whatever will be will be (Que sera sera) / Secret love / Everybody loves a lover / Softly as I leave you / It had to be you / Singin' in the rain / Make somebody happy / Very thought of you / Fly me to the moon / Bewitched, bothered and bewildered / April in Paris / When I fall in love / I'll never stop loving you
CD 4837222
Columbia / Feb '96 / Sony

BEST OF DORIS DAY, THE
Sentimental journey / September in the rain / 'S wonderful / You brought a new kind of love to me / Stardust / Blue skies / I've gotta sing away these blues / I can't give you anything but love / My blue heaven / I could write a book / Hundred years from today / I'm a big girl now / S'posin' / You oughta be in pictures / I'm in the mood for love / Be anything, but be mine / I got it bad and that ain't good / Light your lamp / Singin' in the rain / Just you, just me / Don't worry 'bout me / Crying my heart out for you
CD CD 6056
Music / Jan '97 / Target/BMG

BLUE SKIES
CD PLSCD 213
Pulse / Apr '97 / BMG

BLUE SKIES
Stardust / I could write a book / Don't worry 'bout me / You oughta be in pictures / Sentimental journey / Singin' in the rain / I got it bad and that ain't good / Blue skies / Light your lamp / You bought a new kind of love to me / I'm in the mood for love / I'm a big girl now / I can't give you anything but love / My blue heaven / Just you, just me / Hundred years from today / 'S wonderful / I gotta sing away the blues / S'posin' / September song
CD 306472
Hallmark / Jun '97 / Carlton

COLLECTION, THE
CD COL 071
Collection / Mar '95 / Target/BMG

CUTTIN' CAPERS/BRIGHT AND SHINY (2CD Set)
Cuttin' capers / Steppin' out with my baby / Makin' whoopee / Lady's in love with you / Why don't we do this more often / Let's take a walk around the block / I'm sitting on top of the world / Get out and get under the moon / Fit as a fiddle / Me too / I feel like a feather in the breeze / Let's fly away / Bright and shiny / I want to be happy / Keep smilin', keep laughin', be happy / Singin' in the rain / Gotta feelin' / Happy talk / Make someone happy / Riding high / On the sunny side of the street / Clap yo' hands / Stay with the happy people
CD 4775932
Columbia / Oct '94 / Sony

DAY BY DAY/DAY BY NIGHT (2CD Set)
Song is you / Hello my lover, goodbye / Goodbye / But not for me / I remember you / I hadn't anyone till you / But beautiful / Autumn leaves / Don't take your love from me / There will never be another you / Gone with the wind / Gypsy in my soul / Day by day / I see your face before me / Close your eyes / Night we called it a day / Dream a little dream of me / Under a blanket of blue / You do something to me / Stars fell on Alabama / Moon song / Wrap your troubles in dreams (and dream your troubles away) / Soft as the starlight / Moonglow / Lamp is low
CD 4757492
Columbia / Feb '94 / Sony

DAY BY DAY/LATIN FOR LOVERS/ SHOWTIME (3CD Set)
Song is you / Hello my lover, goodbye / But not for me / I remember you / I hadn't anyone till you / But beautiful / Autumn leaves / Don't take your love from me / There will never be another you / Gone with the wind / Gypsy in my soul / Day by day, night by night / I see your face before me / Close your eyes / Night we called it a day / Dream a little dream of me / Under a blanket of blue / You do something to me / Stars fell on Alabama / Moon song / Wrap your troubles in dreams (and dream your troubles away) / Soft as the starlight / Moonglow / Lamp is low / Quiet nights of quiet stars / Fly me to the moon / Meditation / Dansero / Summer has gone / How insensitive / Slightly out of tune / Our day will come / Be true to me / Latin for lovers / Perhaps, perhaps, perhaps / Be mine tonight / Love him more / Can't help falling in love / Since I fell for you / Losing you / (Now and then there's) A fool such as I / As long as he needs me / Night life / Funny / Softly as I leave you / Lollipops and roses / Love him / Moonlight lover / Whisper away / Showtime part 1 / I got the sun in the morning / Ohio / I love Paris / When I'm not near the boy I love / People will say we're in love / I've grown accustomed to his face / Surrey with the fringe on top / They say it's wonderful / Wonderful guy / On the street where you live / Sound of music / Showtime part 2 / Tea for two / Lullaby of broadway / Cuddle up a little closer / I may be wrong / Makin' whoopee / Be my little baby bumble bee / Secret love / Till we meet again / Ain't we got fun / Just one of those things / It had to be you / Love me or leave me
CD Set 4853132
Columbia / Oct '96 / Sony

DAYDREAMING (The Very Best Of Doris Day)
Move over darling / Secret love / Whatever will be will be (Que sera sera) / Lullaby of broadway / Love me or leave me / It's magic / Everybody loves a lover / Dream a little dream of me / Pillow talk / Cheek to cheek / Fly me to the moon / Close your eyes / Quiet night of quiet stars / Night and day / Let's face the music and dance / Pennies from heaven / Over the rainbow / I'll never stop loving you / If I give my heart to you / Bewitched / Very precious love / Black hills of Dakota / Teacher's pet / Makin' whoopee / Ready, willing and able / Sentimental journey
CD 4873612
Columbia / Apr '97 / Sony

DORIS DAY COLLECTOR'S EDITION
CD DVGH 7032
Deja Vu / Apr '95 / THE

DORIS DAY SINGS SONGS FROM CALAMITY JANE/PAJAMA GAME
CD 4676102
Columbia / Jul '93 / Sony

DORIS DAY/PEGGY LEE ESSENTIALS (Day, Doris & Peggy Lee)
CD LECDD 633
Wisepack / Aug '95 / Conifer/BMG / THE

GIRL NEXT DOOR, THE
CD ENTCD 223
Entertainers / Nov '87 / Target/BMG

GREAT VOCALIST, THE
CD CDSR 050
Telstar / Nov '94 / BMG

HOORAY FOR HOLLYWOOD VOL.1 & 2
Hooray for Hollywood / Cheek to cheek / It's easy to remember / Way you look tonight / I'll remember April / Blues in the night / Over the rainbow / Love is here to stay / In the still of the night / Night and day / Easy to love / I had the craziest dream / I've got my love to keep me warm / Soon / That old black magic / You'll never know / Foggy day / It's magic / It might as well be spring / Nice work if you can get it / Three coins in the fountain / Let's face the music and dance / Pennies from heaven / Oh, but I do
CD 4871892
Columbia / Mar '97 / Sony

I HAVE DREAMED/LISTEN TODAY
I have dreamed / I believe in dreams / I'll buy that dream / My ship / All I do is dream of you / When I grow too old to dream / We'll love again / Periwinkle blues / Someday I'll find you / You stepped out of a dream / Oh what a beautiful dream / Time to say goodnight / Listen today / Pillow talk / Heart full of love / Anyway the wind blows / Oh what a lover you'll be / No / Love me in the daytime / I enjoy being a girl / Tunnel of love / He's so married / Roly Poly / Possess me / Inspiration
CD 4840312
Columbia / Jun '96 / Sony

IT'S MAGIC
It takes time / Pete / My young and foolish heart / Tell me, dream face (What am I to you) / I'm still sitting under the apple tree / Just an old love of mine / That's the way he does it / Why she we both be lonely / Papa, won't you dance with me / Say something nice about me baby / It's magic / Just imagine / Pretty baby / Confess / Love somebody / Tacos, Enchilados and Beans / No moon at all / Put 'em in a box / Imagination / It's the sentimental thing to do / I've only myself to blame / Thoughtless / It's a quiet town (In Crossbone county) / Someone like you / My dream is yours / I'm in love / It's you or no one / My darling, My darling (With orchestra) / That certain party / His fraternity pin / If you will marry me / You was / I'll string along with you / Powder your face with sunshine / Don't gamble with romance / I'm beginning to miss you / That old feeling / When your lover has gone / You go to my head / How it lies, how it lies, how it lies / If I could be with you one hour tonight / Everywhere you go / Again (Where are you) Now that I need you / Blame my absent minded heart / Let's take an old fashioned walk / You're my thrill / Bewitched, bothered and bewildered / At the cafe rendezvous / It's a great feeling / It's better to conceal than reveal / You can have him / Sometimes, I'm happy / Land of love (come my love and live with me) / I didn't know what time it was / I'm confessin' that I love you / Last mile home / Canadian capers (Cuttin' capers) / Here comes Santa Claus / Ol' St Nicholas / It's on the tip of my tongue / River Seine (La Seine) / (It happened at the) festival of roses / Three rivers, The (The Allegheny, Susquehanna and the Old Mo / (There's a) Bluebird on your windowsill / Crocodile tears / Game of broken hearts / Quicksilver / I'll never slip around again / I don't wanna be kissed by anyone but you / With you anywhere you are / Save a little sunbeam (For a rainy, rainy day) / Mama what'll I do / I said my pyjamas / Enjoy yourself / I may be wrong, but I think you're wonderful / Very thought of you / Too marvellous for words / With a song in my heart / Spesh'lly you / Marriage ties / Before I loved you / I went a wooing / I didn't slip, I wasn't pushed, I fell / Hoop dee doo / I can't get over a boy like you (Loving a girl like me) / I've forgotten you / I'll be around / Darn that dream / Here in my arms / Tea for two / I only have eyes for you / Do do do / Crazy rhythm / I know that you know / Oh me, oh my / I want to be happy / He's such a gentleman / Load of hay / I love the way you say goodnight / Orange coloured sky / Comb and paper polka / Pumpernickel / You are my sunshine / Everlasting arms / David's Psalm / Christmas story / I've never been in love before / Bushel and a peck / You love me / Best thing for you / If I were a bell / Silver bells / It's a lovely day today / From this moment on / I am loved / Nobody's chasing me / Ten thousand four hundred thirty-two sheep / You're getting to be a habit with me / Somebody loves me / Please don't talk about me when I'm gone / Just one of those things / Lullaby of Broadway / I love the way you say good night / (In) a shanty in old Shanty Town / Fine and dandy / Would I love you (Love you, love you) / Say something nice about me baby / It's magic / Pretty baby, / Thoughtless, / It's you or no one / My darling, my darling (With piano) / His fraternity pin / Let's take an old fashioned walk, / You're my thrill / Do do do
CD Set BCD 15609
Bear Family / Mar '93 / Direct / Rollercoaster / Swift

LATIN FOR LOVERS/LOVE HIM
Quiet nights of quiet stars / Fly me to the moon / Meditation / Dansero / Summer has gone / How insensitive / Slightly out of tune / Our day will come / Be true to me / Latin for lovers / Perhaps, perhaps, perhaps / Be mine tonight / Can't help falling in love / Since I fell for you / Losing you / Fool such as I / As long as he needs me / Whisper away / Moonlight lover / Love him / Lollipops and roses / Softly as I leave you / Funny / Night life
CD 4810182
Columbia / Aug '95 / Sony

LEGENDS IN MUSIC
CD LECD 091
Wisepack / Sep '94 / Conifer/BMG / THE

LES BROWN & HIS ORCHESTRA WITH DORIS DAY
CD HCD 103
Hindsight / Nov '94 / Jazz Music / Target/ BMG

MOVE OVER DARLING 1960-1968 (8CD Set)
What does a woman do / Please don't eat the daisies / Falling / Blue train / Daffa down dilly / Here we go again / On the street where you live / When I'm not near the boy I love / I love Paris / Surrey with the fringe on top / Ohio / I've grown accustomed to his face / They say it's wonderful / Wonderful guy / Show time / People will say we're in love / I got the sun in the morning / Happy talk / Ridin' high / Stay with the happy people / Clap yo' hands / Singin' in the rain / I want to be happy / Make someone happy / On the sunny side of the street / Twinkle and shine / Bright and shiny / Gotta feelin' / Keep smilin' keep laughin' be happy / Oh what a beautiful dream / I'll buy that dream / Time to say goodnight / All I do is dream of you / My ship / We'll love gain / I believe in dreams / Periwinkle blue / Let no walls divide / Look all around / In the secret place / As a child / Someday I'll find you / You stepped out of a dream / I have dreamed / Let no walls divide / When I grow too old to dream / Who knows what might have been / Should I surrender / Lover come back / Close your eyes / Fools rush in / Remind me / Yes / Control yourself / Day dreaming / You're good for me / Nobody's heart / Wait till you see him / Give me time / Who are we to stay / Day dreaming / Close your eyes / My one and only love / In love in vain / Falling in love again / Nearer my God to thee / I need thee every hour / Abide with me / Lord's prayer / Walk with Him / In the garden / Prodigal son / If I can help somebody / Scarlet ribbons / Bless this house / You'll never walk alone/ Be still and know/Let the little gir / Let the little girl limbo / Move over darling / Twinkle lullaby / More / Lollipops and roses / Can't help falling in love / Softly as I leave you / As long as he needs me / Losing you / Since I fell for you / Love him / Night life / Fool such as I / Funny / Moonlight lover / Send me no flowers / Rainbow's end / Oowee baby / Have yourself a merry little Christmas / Toyland / Christmas song / Winter wonderland / Silver bells / White Christmas / Be a child at Christmas time / Snowfall / Let it snow, let it snow, let it snow / Christmas waltz / I'll be home for Christmas / Christmas present / Getting to know you / Sleepy baby / With a smile and a song / Whatever will be will be (Que sera sera) / Zip-a-dee-doo-dah / Give a little whistle / Inch worm / Swinging on a star / Lilac tree / Children's marching song / Do re mi / High hopes / Send me no flowers / I remember you / Sentimental journey / It could happen to you / At last / I'll never smile again / Serenade in blue / It's beeen a long, long time / More I see you / I'm beginning to see the light / I had the craziest dream / Come to baby do / Slightly out of tune / Quiet night for quiet stars / Meditations / Summer has gone / Fly me to the moon / Perhaps, perhaps, perhaps / Our day will come / Be true to me / Dansero / Por favor / How insensitive / Be mine tonight / Catch the bouquet / Another go around / Whisper away / Do not disturb / Au revoir is goodbye with a smile / There they are / Every now and then (you come around) / Glass bottom boat / Sorry / Caprice / For all we know / Snuggled on your shoulder / Are you lonesome tonight / Wonderful one / Street of dreams / Oh how I miss you tonight / Life is just a bowl of cherries / All alone / Faded summer love / Sleepy lagoon / If I had my life to live over / Blue train / Daffa down dilly / Let the little girl limbo / Catch the bouquet / Another go around / Do not disturb / Glass bottom boat / Circus is on parade: *Day, Doris & Martha Raye/Jimmy Durante* / Over and over again / Why can't I: *Day, Doris & Martha Raye* / This can't be love / Most beautiful girl in the world: *Day, Doris & Stephen Boyd* / My romance / Most beautiful girl in the world: *Day, Doris & Jimmy Durante* / Little girl blue / Sawdust, spangles and dreams: *Day, Doris & Stephen Boyd/ Martha Raye/Jimmy Durante* / Overture / Colonel Buffalo Bill: *Day, Doris & Leonard Stokes* / I'm a bad, bad man: *Day, Doris & Robert Goulet* / Doin' what comes naturally / Girl that I marry: *Day, Doris & Robert Goulet* / You can't get a man with a gun / They say it's wonderful: *Day, Doris & Robert Goulet* / My defences are down: *Day, Doris & Robert Goulet* / Moonshine lullaby / I'm an Indian too / I got lost in his arms / Who do you love I hope: *Day, Doris & Kelly Brown/Renee Winters* / I got the sun in the morning / Anything you can do: *Day, Doris & Robert Goulet* / There's no business like show business: *Day, Doris & Ensemble*
CD Set BCD 15800
Bear Family / Apr '97 / Direct / Rollercoaster / Swift

PERSONAL CHRISTMAS COLLECTION
Christmas song / Silver bells / Here comes Santa Claus / Ol' Saint Nicholas / Christmas story / Have yourself a merry little Christmas / Be a child at Christmas time / Toyland / Christmas present / Christmas waltz / Winter wonderland / Snowfall / White Christmas / Let it snow, let it snow, let it snow
CD 4777712
Columbia / Nov '96 / Sony

QUE SERA SERA (5CD Set)
Whatever will be will be (Que sera sera) / Somebody somewhere / We'll love again / Julie / Love in a home / Gone with the wind / Song is you / Don't take your love from me / Gypsy in my soul / Autumn leaves / I remember you / Hello, my lover, goodbye / Day by day / But beautiful / There will never be another you / But not for me / I hadn't anyone till you / Today, will be yesterday tomorrow / Party's over / Nothing in the world / Whad'ja put in that kiss / Man who invented love / Twelve O'clock / Tonight / Rickety rackety rendevous / Through the eyes of love / I'm not at all in love / Once a year day / Small talk / There once was a man / Seven and a half cents / Under a blanket of blue / I see your face before me / Moon song / Dream a little dream of me / You do something to me / Wrap your troubles in dreams / Close your eyes / Wrap your toubles in dreams / Let's face the music and dance / I've got my love to keep me warm / Nice work if you can get it / Cheek to cheek / Moonglow / Lamp is low / Soft as the starlight / Night we called it a day / Stars fell in Alabama / It's easy to remember / It might as well be spring / I'll remember April / Three coins in the fountain / In the still of the night / Soon / Foggy day / Our love is here to stay / Run away, skidaddle skidoo / Teacher's pet / Walk a chalk line / You'll never know / I had the craziest dream / Over the rainbow / Oh, but I do / Easy to love / That old black magic / Pennies from heaven / Way you look tonight / Night and day / Hooray for Hollywood / Very precious love / Blues in the night / Everybody loves a lover / Tunnel of love / Instant love / Posses me / Kissin' my honey / That Jane from Maine / Steppin' out with my baby / Lady's in love with you / I enjoy being a girl / Let's fly away / Why don't we do this more often / Fit as a fiddle (and ready for love) / Let's take a walk around the block / Makin' whoopee / You're driving my crazy / Get out and under the moon / I feel like a feather in the breeze / I'm sitting on top of the world / Cuttin' capers / Me too (ho-ho-ha-ha) / Love me in the daytime / Anyway the wind blows / Be prepared / Perfect understanding / It happend to Jane / He's so married / Deck the halls with boughs of holly / Inspiration / Posess me / What does a woman do / Pillow talk / Roly poly / Heart full of love / Sound of music / Oh what a lover you'll be / No / Fellow needs a girl / What every girl should know / Mood indigo / What's the use of wonderin' / My kinda lover / When you're smiling / You can't have everything / Hundred years from today / Everlasting arms / Something wonderful / Not only should you love him
CD Set BCD 15797
Bear Family / Feb '96 / Direct / Rollercoaster / Swift

SECRET LOVE
It's so laughable / Something wonderful / We kiss in a shadow / Very good advice / Tell me (why nights are lonely) / Till we meet again / Moonlight baby / My life's desire / I'm forever blowing bubbles / Every little moment / Love ya / Cuddle up a little closer / Why did I tell you I was going to Shanghai / Lonesome and sorry / Ask me (because I'm so in love) / Kiss me goodbye love / Got him off my hands / Baby doll / Oops / If that doesn't do it / Domino / Makin' whoopee / It had to be you / My buddy / One I love / Moonlight bay / I'll see you in my dreams / I wish I had a girl / Ain't we got fun / Nobody's sweetheart / How lovely cooks the meat / Sugarbush / Guy is a guy / Little kiss goodnight / Gently Johnny / Who who who / Take me in your arms / Make it soon / My love and devotion / It's magic / When I fall in love / Cherries / April in Paris / No two people / You can't lose me / I know a place / That's what makes Paris Paree / I'm gonna ring the bell tonight / Second star to the right / Your Mother and mine / Mr. Tip toe / Ma says, Pa says / Full time job / Beautiful music to love you by / You have my sympathy / Let's walk that way / Candy lips / Be my little baby / King Chanticleer / If you were the only girl in the world / Your eyes have told me so / Just one girl / By the light of the silvery moon / When the red, red robin comes bob, bob, bobbin' along / Purple cow / Kiss me again stranger / Black hills of Dakota / 'Tis Harry I'm planning to marry / Just blew in from the windy city / This too shall pass away / Woman's touch / Choo choo train / Secret love / I can do without you / Deadwood stage / Love you Dearly / Lost in loveliness / I speak to the stars / What every girl should know / Blue bells of broadway / Kay Muleta / Anyone can fall in love / Jimmy unknown someone / Else's roses / If I give my heart to you / There's a rising moon for every falling star / You, my love / Hold me in your arms / Till my love comes to me / Ready, willing and able / Two hearts, two kisses (make one love) / Foolishly yours / I'll never stop loving you / Love's little island / Ooh bang jiggly jang let it ring / I've gotta sing away these blues / Live it up / I'm a big girl now / When I'm happy / Love's little island / It all depends on you / You made me love you / Stay on the right side / Mean to me / Everybody loves my baby / Sam the old accordion man / Shaking the blues away / Ten cents a dance / Never look back / At sundown / Love me or leave me / Overture / You made me love you (I didn't want to do it)
CD Set BCD 15746
Bear Family / Mar '95 / Direct / Rollercoaster / Swift

SENTIMENTAL JOURNEY
Blue skies / Sentimental journey / I can't give you anything but love / Everything I have is yours / I got it bad and that ain't good / Day by day / In the moon mist / Kiss to remember / There's good blues tonight / Moon on my pillow / I'm making believe / While the music plays on / Beau night in hotchkiss corner / Easy as pie / Booglie wooglie piggy / Let's be buddies / Barbara Allen / Dig it
CD BSTCD 9115
Best Compact Discs / Apr '94 / Complete/ Pinnacle

SENTIMENTAL JOURNEY
CD HCD 200
Hindsight / Nov '94 / Jazz Music / Target/ BMG

SENTIMENTAL JOURNEY
My blue heaven / September in the rain / 'S wonderful / You brought a new kind of love to me / Stardust / Blue skies / I've gotta sing away these blues / I can't give you anything but love / Sentimental journey / I could write a book / Singin' in the rain / I'm a big girl now / S'posin' / You ought to be in pictures / I'm in the mood for love / Be anything, but be mine / I got it bad and that ain't good / Light your lamp / Hundred years from today / Just you, just me / Don't worry 'bout me / Crying my heart out for you
CD TRTCD 164
TrueTrax / Dec '94 / THE

SENTIMENTAL JOURNEY
Singin' in the rain / I've got it bad, and that ain't good / Blue skies / Crying my heart out for you / I'm in the mood for love / s'posin' / My blue heaven / Stardust / I gotta sing away these blues / I'm a big girl now / September in the rain / You brought a new kind of love to me / Hundred years from today / Be anything, but be mine / Light up your lamp / Don't worry 'bout me / Sentimental journey
CD MUCD 9015
Musketeer / Apr '95 / Disc

SHOW TIME/DAY IN HOLLYWOOD (2CD Set)
Showtime (part one) / I got the sun in the morning / Ohio / I love Paris / When I'm not near the boy I love / People will say we're in love / I've grown accustomed to his face / Surrey with the fringe on top / They say it's wonderful / Wonderful guy / On the street where you live / Showtime (part two) / Tea for two / Lullaby of Broadway / Cuddle up a little closer / I may be wrong, but I think you're wonderful / Makin' whoopee / Be my little baby bumble bee / Secret love / Till we meet again / Ain't we got fun / Just one of those things / It had to be you / Love me or leave me
CD 4757502
Columbia / Feb '94 / Sony

SOUNDTRACKS FROM DORIS DAY (I'll See You In My Dreams/Tea For Two/On Moonlight Bay)
I'll see you in my dreams / Ain't we got fun / One I love / I wish I had a girl / Nobody's sweetheart / My buddy / Makin' whoopee / Crazy rhythm / Here in my arms / I know that you know / I want to be happy / Do do do / I only have eyes for you / Oh me oh my / Tea for two / Moonlight Bay / Till we meet again / Love ya / Christmas story / I'm forever blowing bubbles / Cuddle up a little closer / Every little moment / Tell me
CD CD 342
Entertainers / Mar '96 / Target/BMG

Day, Jimmy

STEEL & STRINGS (Golden Steel Guitar Hits)
Panhandle rag / Roadside rag / Texas playboy rag / Remington ride / Coconut grove / Boot hill drag / Bud's bounce / B Bowman's hop / Georgia steel guitar / Steelin' the blues / Indian love call / Please help me, I'm falling / I love you because / Am I that easy to forget / Fallen star / She thinks I still care / Making believe / I love you so much it hurts / Wild side of life / Release me / Funny how time slips away / I can't stop loving you / I fall to pieces
CD BCD 15583
Bear Family / Apr '92 / Direct / Rollercoaster / Swift

Day One

HALLOWED GROUND
CD BV 131182
Black Vinyl / Nov '96 / Cargo

Dayglo Abortions

CORPORATE WHORES
CD AR 62112
A&R International / Mar '97 / Cargo

LITTLE MAN IN THE CANOE
CD AR 1105CD
A&R International / Mar '97 / Cargo

Dayjah

URBAN JUNGLE (Dayjah & The Disciples)
CD TEMCD 3
Third Eye / Aug '97 / SRD

Dayne, Taylor

GREATEST HITS
Say a prayer / Tell it to my heart / I'll always love you / Can't get enough of your love / With every beat of my heart / Love will lead you back / Don't rush me / Prove your love / I'll be your shelter / Heart of stone / Send me a lover / I'll wait
CD 7822187742
Arista / Jan '96 / BMG

SOUL DANCING
I'll wait / Send me a lover / Can't get enough of your love / Say a prayer / Dance with a stranger / I could be good for you / Soul dancing / Door to your heart / Someone like you / Memories / If you were mine / Let's spend the night together
CD 74321154212
Arista / Jul '96 / BMG

TELL IT TO MY HEART
Tell it to my heart / In the darkness / Don't rush me / I'll always love you / Prove your love / Do you want it right now / Carry your heart / Want ads / Where does that boy hang out / Upon the journey's end
CD 258898
Arista / Jan '93 / BMG

Dayspring

DREAMSTATE
CD NA 023CD
New Age / Jul '96 / Plastic Head

Dayton Family

FBI
79th and Halstead / Hand that rocks the cradle / FBI / Real with this / Player haters / Eyes closed / What's on my mind / Killer G's / Posse is Dayton ave / Blood bath / Mewspaper / Stick and move / Ghetto
CD 4867342
Relativity / Nov '96 / Sony

Daytona

CHICANE
CD ZULU 010CD
Zulu / Oct '95 / Plastic Head

Dazzie Dee

REBIRTH (Dazzie Dee & Coolio/Ice Cube)
CD 50545
Raging Bull / Jun '97 / Prime / Total/BMG

Dazzling Killmen

FACE OF COLLAPSE
CD GR 12CD
Skingraft / Apr '94 / SRD

RECUERDA
CD GR 36CD
Skingraft / Jul '96 / SRD

DBF

NOT BOUND BY THE RULES
You deceive yourself / Election's just a farce / Suicide Billy / Make it a lie / Too wide apart / Narrow-minded / Not bound to rules / Nothing to prove / Rape your mind / Too much wasn't said / Am I too weak / Religion / Blank minds / No personality
CD 853881
SPV / Jul '89 / Koch / Plastic Head

dBh

UNWILLING TO EXPLAIN
Sense of hatred / White God sent / My great country / Out of control / Face / Reduced / Assimilation / Misogynist / No coalesce / Shooter / Obedience / Two people
CD DEDCD 028S
Dedicated / May '97 / BMG / Vital

DB's

PARIS AVENUE
CD MON 6122
Monkey Hill / Jan '95 / Direct / Koch

RIDE THE WILD TOM TOM
We should be in bed / Everytime anytime / Let's live for today / Little hands / You got it wrong / Tell me two times / Nothing is wrong / Purple hose / Ash / I read New York Rocker / Walking the ceiling (it's good to be alive) / Baby talk / Dynamite (original demo) / Soul kiss (part one) / Bad reputation / Modern boys and girls / What about that cat / What's the matter with me / Fight / She's green, I'm blue / If and when / Soul kiss (part two) / Death of rock / Purple hose (slight return) / Hardcore Judy / Spy in the house of love
CD RSACD 805
Sequel / Dec '94 / BMG

DC 3

VIDA
CD SST 156CD
SST / Jul '89 / Plastic Head

DC Talk

FREE AT LAST
Luv is a verb / That kinda girl / Jesus is just alright / Say the words / Socially acceptable / Free at last / Time is... / Hard way / Lean on me / I don't want it / Word 2 the Father
CD FFD 3002
Alliance Music / Jul '95 / EMI

D'Cruze

CONTROL
CD SUBBASECD 2
Suburban Base / Oct '95 / Pinnacle / Prime

DCS

BHANGRA'S GONNA GET YOU
CD DMUT 1086
Multitone / Jul '89 / BMG

DDC

PLATE FULLA FUNK
CD GT 0230
Grapetree / May '96 / Else

De Almaden, Escudero & ...

FLAMENCO DE TRIANA (De Almaden, Escudero & Ramos)
CD TCD 1041
Tradition / Mar '97 / ADA / Vital

De Alvear, Maria

EN AMOR DURO
CD ARTCD 6112
Hat Art / Jan '93 / Cadillac / Harmonia Mundi

De Boignard, Faubourg

LA RAVINE
CD 495012
Acousteak / Mar '96 / ADA / Discovery

De Bora, Naomi

PRIVATE EYES
CD BRAM 1991282
Brambus / Nov '93 / ADA

De Buddelschipper

SHANTIES AND SEEMANNSLIEDER
CD EUCD 1178
ARC / '91 / ADA / ARC Music

De Burgh, Chris

AT THE END OF A PERFECT DAY
Broken wings / Round and round / I will / Summer rain / Discovery / Brazil / In a country churchyard / Rainy night in Paris / If you really love her let her go / Perfect day
CD CDMID 112
A&M / Oct '92 / PolyGram

BEAUTIFUL DREAMS
Missing you / Carry me (Like a fire in your heart) / Discovery / Snows of New York / In love forever / Shine on / Lady in red / In dreams / I'm not crying over you / Always on my mind / Say goodbye to it all / One more mile to go
CD 5404322
A&M / Oct '95 / PolyGram

BEST MOVES
Every drop of rain / In a country churchyard / Patricia the stripper / Satin green shutters / Spanish train / Waiting for the hurricane / Broken wings / Lonely sky / Spaceman came travelling / Crusader / Traveller
CD 3950832
A&M / Apr '95 / PolyGram

CRUSADER
Carry on / I had the love in my eyes / Something else again / Girl with April in her eyes / Just in time / Devil's eyes / It's such a long way home / Old fashioned people / Quiet moments / Crusader / You and me
CD CDMID 113
A&M / Oct '92 / PolyGram

EASTERN WIND
Traveller / Record company bash / Tonight / Wall of silence / Flying home / Shadows and light / Some things never change / Tourist attraction / Eastern wind
CD CDMID 167
A&M / Aug '91 / PolyGram

FAR BEYOND THESE CASTLE WALLS
Hold on / Key / Windy night / Sin City / New moon / Watching the world / Lonesome cowboy / Satin green shutters / Turning around / Goodnight
CD CDMID 110
A&M / Oct '92 / PolyGram

FLYING COLOURS
Sailing away / Carry me (like a fire in your heart) / Tender hands / Night on the river / Leather on my shoes / Suddenly love / Missing you / I'm not scared anymore / Don't look back / Just a word away / Risen Lord / Last time I cried / Simple truth (a child is born)
CD 3952242
A&M / Apr '95 / PolyGram

GETAWAY, THE
Don't pay the ferryman / Living on the island / Crying and laughing / I'm counting on you / Getaway / Ship to shore / Borderline / Where peaceful waters flow / Revolution / Light a fire / Liberty
CD 3949292
A&M / Apr '95 / PolyGram

HIGH ON EMOTION - LIVE FROM DUBLIN
Last night / Sailing away / Revolution / I'm not scared anymore / Spanish train / Borderline / Risen Lord / Last time I cried / Lady in red / Spaceman came travelling / Patricia the stripper / Missing you / Say goodbye to it all / Don't pay the ferryman / High on emotion
CD 3970862
A&M / Apr '95 / PolyGram

HITS OF CHRIS DE BURGH, THE (David, Ron Orchestra)
Don't pay the ferryman / Getaway / Spaceman came travelling / Sailing away / Diamond in the dark / High on emotion / Lady in red / Borderline / Missing you / Tender hands / Ship to shore
CD QED 217
Tring / Nov '96 / Tring

INTO THE LIGHT
One word straight to the heart / For Rosanna / Leader / Vision / What about me / Last night / Fire on the water / Ballroom of romance / Lady in red / Say goodbye to it all / Spirit of man / Fatal hesitation
CD 3951212
A&M / Apr '95 / PolyGram

INTO THE LIGHT/ FLYING COLOURS (2CD Set)
Last night / Ballroom of romance / Say goodbye to it all / Fata hesitation / For Rosanna / What about me / Carry me / Night on the river / Suddenly love / Fire on the water / Lady in red / Spirit of man / One word / Leader / Sailing away / Tender hands / Leather on my shoes
CD CDA 24116
A&M / Jul '92 / PolyGram

MAN ON THE LINE
Ecstasy of flight (I love the night) / Sight and touch / Taking it to the top / Head and the heart / Sound of a gun / High on emotion / Much more than this / Man on the line / Moonlight and vodka / Transmission ends
CD CDMID 188
A&M / Jul '93 / PolyGram

POWER OF TEN
Where will we be going / By my side / Heart of darkness / In your eyes / Separate tables / Talk to me / Brother John / Connemara coast / Shine on / Celebration / She means everything to me / Making the perfect man
CD 3971882
A&M / Apr '95 / PolyGram

SPANISH TRAIN AND OTHER STORIES
Spanish train / Lonely sky / This song for you / Patricia the stripper / Spaceman came travelling / I'm going home / Painter / Old friend / Tower / Just another poor boy
CD CDMID 111
A&M / Oct '92 / PolyGram

SPARK TO A FLAME
This waiting heart / Don't pay the ferryman / Much more than this / Sailing away / Lady in red / Borderline / Say goodbye to it all / Ship to shore / Missing you / Diamond in the dark / Tender hands / Spaceman came travelling / Where peaceful waters flow / High on emotion / Spanish train / Fatal hesitation
CD CDBCD 100
A&M / Oct '89 / PolyGram

THIS WAY UP
This silent world / This is love / This weight on me / Here is your paradise / Oh my brave hearts / Blonde hair, blue jeans / Son and the father / Up here in heaven / You are the reason / Love's got a hold on me / Snows of New York
CD 5402332
A&M / May '94 / PolyGram

De Cadiz, Beni

GREAT FIGURES OF FLAMENCO VOL.17
CD LDX 274992
La Chant Du Monde / Jun '94 / ADA / Harmonia Mundi

De Cana, Flor

MUEVETE (MOVE IT)
CD FF 70463
Flying Fish / Jul '89 / ADA / CM / Direct / Roots

De Carlo, Julio

TODO CORAZON 1924-1928
CD EBCD 83
El Bandoneon / Jan '97 / Discovery

De Courson, Hughes

CHARLEMAGNE
CD 669412
Melodie / Mar '96 / ADA / Discovery / Grapevine/PolyGram / Greensleeves / Jet Star

De Dakar, Etoile

VOL.2 (Phiapathioloy)
Thiapathioly / Dokhama say ne ne / Diandioli / Dounyan / Defal gnou guess / Dagotte
CD STCD 3006
Stern's / Mar '94 / ADA / CM / Stern's

De Danann

ANTHEM
Wren's nest / Let it be / Johnstone hornpipe / Connie from Constantinople / Johnny I hardly knew you / Ril and Spideal / Anthem for Ireland / Jimmy Byrnes and Dinkies / Diglake fields / Duo in G / Paddy's lamentation
CD _____ DARCD 013
Dara / Sep '93 / ADA / CM / Direct / Else / Grapevine/PolyGram

BALLROOM
CD _____ GLCD 3040
Green Linnet / Feb '95 / ADA / CM / Direct / Highlander / Roots

DE DANANN
Cuckoo's nest medley / Come back again to me Mavourneen / Conlon's jig/Padraig O'Keefe's head of cabbage/Boys of Malin / My Irish Molly-O / Hey Jude / Maggie / Coleraine jig/Derrane's/John Stenson's / Kitty's wedding/The rambler / Teetotlar/St. Anne's / Then you'll remember me / Morrison's/The tailor's thimble/Wellington's / I'm leaving Tipperary
CD _____ KCD 430
Celtic Collections / Jan '97 / Target/BMG

HIBERNIAN RHAPSODY
CD _____ PED 9601
Bee's Knees / Dec '96 / ADA / CM / Roots

JACKET OF BATTERIES, A
CD _____ CMCD 066
Celtic Music / Oct '94 / CM

MIST COVERED MOUNTAINS, THE
Mac's fancy/Mist covered mountain / Cameronian reel/Doon reel / Seamaisin / Mulvihill's reel/Dawn / Banks of the Nile / Johnny Leary's polka/O'Keefe's polka/ Johnny do I miss you / Mr. O'Connor / Henry Joy / Cottage in the grove/Sean Ryan's reel / Maire Mhor / Langstrom's pony/Tap room/Lord Ramsey's reel
CD _____ CEFCD 087
Gael Linn / Jan '94 / ADA / CM / Direct / Grapevine/PolyGram / Roots

STAR SPANGLED MOLLY, THE
CD _____ TFCB 5006CD
Third Floor / Oct '94 / ADA / Direct / Total/ BMG

De Fabriek

PWZ
CD _____ EFA 015622
Apocalyptic Vision / Sep '95 / Cargo / Plastic Head / SRD

De Forest, Carmaig

DEATHGROOVELOVEPARTY
CD _____ KFWCD 145
Knitting Factory / Feb '95 / Cargo / Plastic Head

De France, Jean Michel

FEELINGS (Music Of The Pan Flute)
Woman in love / Man and a woman / La mer / My heart in my hands / About the clouds / Love serenade / Dolannes melodie / Guernica / We are the world / Feelings / Autumn leaves / Adagio / Song for Anna / Liebestraum / L for love / Ave Maria / Summer love affair / El condor pasa
CD _____ PWK 130
Carlton / May '90 / Carlton

De Franco, Buddy

BORN TO SWING
CD _____ HCD 701
Hindsight / Nov '94 / Jazz Music / Target/ BMG

BUDDY DE FRANCO QUARTET, THE (De Franco, Buddy Quartet)
Titoro / Bright one / Lover man / Jack the fieldstalker / Mine / Deep purple / Yesterdays / Cable car / If I should lose you / Now's the time / Laura / I'll remember April / Foggy day / What can I say dear / Gerry's tune
CD _____ CD 53227
Giants Of Jazz / Oct '96 / Cadillac / Jazz Music / Target/BMG

BUENOS AIRES CONCERTS, THE
Billie's bounce / Triste / Ja da / Yesterdays / Mood indigo / Scrapple from the apple / Street of dreams / Song is you
CD _____ HEPCD 2014
Hep / Nov '95 / Cadillac / Jazz Music / New Note/Pinnacle / Wellard

FIVE NOTES OF BLUES
CD _____ 500302
Musidisc / Nov '93 / Discovery

FREE FALL
Free fall / Please send me someone to love / Free sail / Yesterdays / Threat of freedom / Free fall / Free sail
CD _____ CHCD 71008
Candid / Mar '97 / Cadillac / Direct / Jazz Music / Koch / Wellard

HARK (De Franco, Buddy & Oscar Peterson Quartet)
All too soon / Summer me, Winter me / Llovisna (Light rain) / By myself / Joy spring / This is all I ask / Hark / Why am I
CD _____ OJCCD 867
Original Jazz Classics / Nov '95 / Complete/ Pinnacle / Jazz Music / Wellard

MR. LUCKY (2CD Set)
In a mellow tone / Lamp is low / Mood indigo / Scrapple from the apple / Mar descancado / You do something to me / Mr. Lucky / In a sentimental mood / Billie's bounce / Meditation
CD Set _____ JLR 103610
Live At EJ's / Apr '97 / Target/BMG

De Goal, Charles

DOUBLE FACE
CD _____ ROSE 96CD
New Rose / Dec '86 / ADA / Direct / Discovery

De Gonzaga, Luizinho

GONZAGUINHA
Baiao / Guardo / Humanos / Respeita januario / Asa branca / Gonazaga / Uma vez por semana / Borboleta prateda / Avassaladora / Olha pro ceu / A vida do viajante
CD _____ 68951
Tropical / Apr '97 / Discovery

De Graaf, Dick

NEW YORK STRAIGHT AHEAD (De Graaf, Dick & Tony Lakatos Trio)
CD _____ CHR 70033
Challenge / Sep '96 / ADA / Direct / Jazz Music / Wellard

SAILING
CD _____ CHR 70024
Challenge / Sep '95 / ADA / Direct / Jazz Music / Wellard

De Grassi, Alex

BEYOND THE NIGHT SKY
Rain is pouring / Beyond the night sky / Bells of London / Boo maramba / Mama Papa / When my soul embraces you / Sleepytime / A La Nanita Nan / As you drift away / Swedish lullaby / Waters of time / Brahms lullaby
CD _____ R 272537
Earthbeat / Nov '96 / ADA / Direct

WORLD'S GETTING..., THE
CD _____ 01934111312
Windham Hill / Sep '95 / BMG

De Johnette, Jack

ALBUM ALBUM (Special Edition)
Festival / New Orleans strut / Zoot suite / Ahmad the terrible / Monk's mood / Third world anthem
CD _____ 8234672
ECM / Jan '89 / New Note/Pinnacle

DANCING WITH NATURE SPIRITS
Dancing with nature spirits / Anatolia / Healing song for Mother earth / Amanations / Time warps
CD _____ ECM 55310242
ECM / Jun '96 / New Note/Pinnacle

DEJOHNETTE COMPLEX, THE
Equipoise / Major general / Miles' mode / Requiem / Mirror image / Papp-Daddy and me / Brown, warm and wintry / Requiem
CD _____ OJCCD 617
Original Jazz Classics / Jun '96 / Complete/ Pinnacle / Jazz Music / Wellard

NEW DIRECTIONS
CD _____ 8293742
ECM / Jan '89 / New Note/Pinnacle

NEW DIRECTIONS IN EUROPE
Salsa for Eddie / Bayou fever / Where or Wayne / Multo spillagio
CD _____ 8291582
ECM / '88 / New Note/Pinnacle

PIANO ALBUM, THE
CD _____ LCD 15042
Landmark / Aug '88 / New Note/Pinnacle

PICTURES
Picture 1 / Picture 2 / Picture 3 / Picture 4 / Picture 5 / Picture 6
CD _____ 5192842
ECM / Jun '93 / New Note/Pinnacle

SPECIAL EDITION (De Johnette, Jack Special Edition)
One for Eric / Zoot suite / Central Park West / India / Journey to the twin planet
CD _____ 8276942
ECM / Jan '89 / New Note/Pinnacle

TIN CAN ALLEY (De Johnette, Jack Special Edition)
Tin can alley / Pastel rhapsody / Riff raff / Gri gri man / I know
CD _____ 51775422
ECM / Nov '93 / New Note/Pinnacle

WORKS: JACK DEJOHNETTE
Bayou fever / Gri gri man / To be continued / One for Eric / Unshielded desire / Blue
CD _____ 8254272
ECM / Jun '89 / New Note/Pinnacle

De Jong, Tracie

LONGEST DAY, THE
CD _____ CDMANU 1440
Manu / Dec '93 / ADA / Discovery

De Jonge, Henk

JUMPING SHARK
CD _____ BVHAASTCD 9103
Bvhaast / Nov '90 / Cadillac

De Jorge, Juan

SONGS FROM THE SOUL (De Jorge, Juan Group)
Cascabeles de oro / Camino sin horizonte / Margarita por tu amor / Querer o amar / Bajan los comechingones / Hermano / Indio soy de Tucuman / Por que te ame / Galopando voy / Buscando la paz / Sabes mi amor / El humahuaqueno / Quisiera volver a verte / La donosa
CD _____ PS 65186
PlayaSound / Jun '97 / ADA / Harmonia Mundi

De La Isla, Camaron

GRAND FIGURES OF FLAMENCO VOL.15
CD _____ LDX 274957
La Chant Du Monde / May '94 / ADA / Harmonia Mundi

De La Matrona, Pepe

GREAT SINGERS OF FLAMENCO VOL.2
CD _____ LDC 274 829
La Chant Du Monde / '88 / ADA / Harmonia Mundi

De La Rosa, Tony

ATOTONILCO
CD _____ ARHCD 362
Arhoolie / Apr '95 / ADA / Cadillac / Direct

ES MI DERECHO
CD _____ ROUCD 6066
Rounder / Jun '95 / ADA / CM / Direct

De La Soul

3 FEET HIGH AND RISING
Intro / Magic number / Change in speak / Cool breeze on the rocks / Can U keep a secret / Jenifa (taught me) / Ghetto thang / Transmitting live from Mars / Eye know / Take it off / Little bit of soap / Tread water / Say no go / Do as De La does / Plug tunin' / De La orgee / Buddy / Description / Me, myself and I / This is a recording 4 living in a fulltime era / I can do anything / DAISY age / Plug tunin' (12" mix) / Potholes in my lawn
CD _____ TBCD 1019
Tommy Boy / Jun '97 / RTM/Disc

STAKES IS HIGH
CD _____ TBCD 1149
Tommy Boy / Feb '97 / RTM/Disc

De Lay, Paul

OCEAN OF TEARS
Bottom line / Don't shame me / Ocean of tears / Maybe our luck will change / Hopefully / If she is / Slip, stumble, fall / What went wrong / Stop your groanin' / I win
CD _____ ECD 260792
Evidence / Oct '96 / ADA / Cadillac / Harmonia Mundi

TAKE IT FROM THE TURNAROUND
Merry way / Ain't that right / Other one / Great round world / Chalk and roll / Silly smile / Why can't you love me / Every woman I get / Oat bran / Worn out shoe / Second hand smoke / I can't quit you no / No use worryin' / What's the big idea / I missed you bad / Don't feel nothin' / Lou's blues / Just this one / Prisoner's song
CD _____ ECD 260762
Evidence / Apr '96 / ADA / Cadillac / Harmonia Mundi

De Lone, Austin

DE LONE AT LAST
Blithe'd ale boogie / Deeper well / Little bitty record / Big big fun / Visions of Johanna / No money / Done doin' good / Beaver strut / Louise / My baby, my baby / Put your wig back on / For Lesley
CD _____ FIENDCD 706
Demon / Oct '91 / Pinnacle

De Lucia, Paco

ANTOLOGIA
Almoraima / Cancion de amor / Gloria al Nino Ricardo / Solo quiero caminar / Punta umbria / Rio ancho / Danza ritual del fuego / Compadres / Fuente y caudal / Casilda / Cepa Andaluza / Rumba improvisada
CD _____ 5284212
Mercury / Apr '96 / PolyGram

LIVE IN AMERICA (De Lucia, Paco Sextet)
Mi nino curro / La barrosa / Alcazar de Sevilla / Peroche / Tio sabas / Soniquete / Zyryab / Buana buana King Kong
CD _____ 5188092
Philips / Mar '93 / PolyGram

ZYRYAB
CD _____ 8467072
Phonogram / Jan '93 / PolyGram

De Lucie, Autour

AUTOUR DE LUCIE
CD _____ 067003010429
Nettwerk / Oct '96 / Greyhound / Pinnacle / Vital

De Marcos, Juan

A TODA CUBA LE GUSTA (De Marcos, Juan Afro Cuban All Stars)
Amor verdadero / Alto songo / Habana del este / A toda cuba le gusta / Fiesta de la rumba / Los sitio' asere / Pio mentiroso / Maria Caracoles / Clasiqueando con Ruben / Elube chango
CD _____ WCD 047
World Circuit / Mar '97 / ADA / Cadillac / Direct / New Note/Pinnacle

De Mbanga, Labiro

NDINGA MAN CONTRE-ATTAQUE : NA WOU GO PAY (Protest Songs From Cameroon)
CD _____ LBLC 2506
Indigo / Jan '93 / New Note/Pinnacle

De Melo, Armenio

SPIRIT OF FADO, A (De Melo, Armenio & Jose Maria Nobrega)
CD _____ PS 65705
PlayaSound / Feb '93 / ADA / Harmonia Mundi

De Moron, Bernabe

FLAMENCO ESPANOLA
CD _____ TCD 1020
Tradition / May '96 / ADA / Vital

De Norte A Sur

FOLKSONGS FROM VENEZUELA
CD _____ EUCD 1149
ARC / '91 / ADA / ARC Music

INSPIRATION MEXICANA - SONGS & DANCES FROM MEXICO (De Norte A Sur & Friends)
CD _____ EUCD 1196
ARC / Sep '93 / ADA / ARC Music

De Palma, Victor

BEGUINE/BOSSA NOVA/RUMBA (De Palma, Victor Orquesta)
CD _____ 9163
Divucsa / Oct '96 / Discovery

CHA CHA CHA/CALYPSO/MAMBO (De Palma, Victor Orquesta)
CD _____ 9161
Divucsa / Oct '96 / Discovery

COME DANCING (De Palma, Victor & His Orchestra)
CD _____ CDSGP 060
Prestige / Oct '93 / Else / Total/BMG

SAMBA (De Palma, Victor Orquesta)
CD _____ 9166
Divucsa / Oct '96 / Discovery

SLOW/SWING/FOXTROT (De Palma, Victor Orquesta)
CD _____ 9162
Divucsa / Oct '96 / Discovery

De Paris, Wilbur

DOCTOR JAZZ VOL.7 (De Paris, Wilbur & His Rampart Street Ramblers)
CD _____ STCD 6047
Storyville / Jul '96 / Cadillac / Jazz Music / Wellard

De Paul, Lynsey

BEST OF LYNSEY DE PAUL, THE
Sugar me / Rock bottom / Won't somebody dance with me / All night / Getting a drag / If I don't get you the next one will / Brandy / Storm in a teacup / Rockadile / Just visiting / Sleeping blue nights / Way it goes / Blind leading the blind / Water / So good to you / Fur immer
CD _____ 12842
Laserlight / Nov '96 / Target/BMG

JUST A LITTLE TIME
Sugar me / Getting a drag / Words don't mean a thing / We got love / Storm in a teacup / Dancing on a Sunday night / Just a little time / Instant love / Now and then / Won't somebody dance with me / Sugar me (club mix) / Getting a drag (club mix)
CD _____ MSCD 9
Magnum Music / Oct '94 / TKO Magnum

LYNSEY DE PAUL
Sugar me / Getting a drag / Words don't mean a thing / We got love / Storm in a teacup / (Dancing) on a Saturday night / Just a little time / Instant love / Now and then / Won't somebody dance with me / Sugar me / Getting a drag

CD ______ QED 128
Tring / Nov '96 / Tring

De Ridder, Willem

SNUFF (De Ridder, Willem & Hafler Trio)
CD ______ SPL 2
Touch / Oct '95 / Kudos / Pinnacle

De Shannon, Jackie

YOU'RE THE ONLY DANCER/QUICK TOUCHES
CD ______ EDCD 420
Edsel / May '95 / Pinnacle

De Trebert, Irene

MADEMOISELLE SWING 1938-1946 (2CD Set)
CD Set ______ FA 056
Fremeaux / Jan '97 / ADA / Discovery

De Utrera, Pitine

GUITARRA FLAMENCA
CD ______ ARN 64237
Arion / Jun '93 / ADA / Discovery

De Ville, Willy

BEST OF WILLY DE VILLE, THE
CD ______ 3018902
Wotre Music / Jan '97 / Discovery / New Note/Pinnacle

BIG EASY FANTASY
CD ______ 122151
Wotre Music / Jan '96 / Discovery / New Note/Pinnacle

MIRACLE
Due to gun control / Could you would you / Heart and soul / Assassin of love / Spanish Jack / Storybook love / Southern politician / Angel eyes / Miracle
CD ______ RVCD 41
Raven / Nov '94 / ADA / Direct

VICTORY MIXTURE
Hello my lover / It do me good / Key to my heart / Beating like a tom tom / Every dog has its day / Big blue diamonds / Teasin' you / Ruler of my heart / Who shot the la la / Junkers blues
CD ______ 652304
New Rose / Mar '95 / ADA / Direct / Discovery

De Vit, Tony

FANTAZIA PRESENTS THE REMIXES (Various Artists)
CD ______ FRX 1CD
Fantazia / Apr '96 / 3mv/Sony / Prime

De Wilde, Laurent

BACK BURNER, THE
Yesterdays / Basame mucho / Late bloomer / What is this thing called love / Lost / Gallop's gallop / You've changed / Ba-Lue Bolivar Ba-Lues-Are
CD ______ 4807842
Sony Jazz / Apr '96 / Sony

SPOON-A-RHYTHM
Edward K / Relaxin' at Camarillo / Fathers / 'Round midnight / Spoon-a-rhythm / Invitation / Tune for T / Totem / Live and Dyrek / So long Barney
CD ______ 4872532
Sony Jazz / May '97 / Sony

De Zes, Winden

SAX SEXTET - MAN MET MUTS
CD ______ BVHAASTCD 9004
Bvhaast / Dec '87 / Cadillac

Deacon Blue

OUR TOWN (Greatest Hits Of Deacon Blue)
Dignity / Wages day / Real gone kid / Your swaying arms / Fergus sings the blues / I was right and you were wrong / Chocolate girl / I'll never fall in love again / When will you (make my telephone ring) / Twist and shout / Your town / Queen of the new year / Only tender love / Cover from the sky / Love and regret / Beautiful stranger / Will we be lovers / Loaded / Bound to love / Still in the mood
CD ______ 4766422
Columbia / Apr '94 / Sony

RAINTOWN
Born in a storm / Raintown / Ragman / He looks like Spencer Tracy now / Loaded / When will you (make my telephone ring) / Chocolate girl / Dignity / Very thing / Love's great fears / Town to be blamed / Riches / Kings of the Western world / Shifting sands / Suffering / Ribbons and bows / Angeliou / Just like boys
CD ______ 4505492
CBS / Feb '88 / Sony

RAINTOWN/WHEN THE WORLD KNOWS YOUR NAME (2CD Set)
Born in a storm / Raintown / Ragman / He looks like Spencer Tracy now / Loaded / When will you (make my telephone ring) / Chocolate girl / Dignity / Very thing / Love's great fears / Town to be blamed / Riches / Kings of the Western world / Queen of the New Year / Wages day / Real gone kid / Love and regret / Circus lights / This changing light / Sad love girl / Fergus sings the blues / World is lit by lightning / Silhouette / Hundred things / Your constant heart / Orphans
CD Set ______ 466532
CBS / Feb '90 / Sony

RICHES AND MORE
Which side are you on / Kings of the western world / Angeliou / Just like boys / Riches / Church / Shifting sand / Suffering / Ribbons and bows / Dignity / I'll never fall in love again / Look of love / Are you there (with another girl) / Message to Michael
CD ______ 4871472
Columbia / Feb '97 / Sony

WHEN THE WORLD KNOWS YOUR NAME
Queen of the New Year / Real gone kid / Circus lights / Sad loved girl / Hundred things / Silhouette / Wages day / Love and regret / This changing light / Fergus sings the blues / Orphans / World is lit by lightning
CD ______ 4633212
Columbia / Oct '95 / Sony

Dead And Gone

GOD LOVES EVERYONE BUT YOU
CD ______ VIRUS 191CD
Alternative Tentacles / Jan '97 / Cargo / Greyhound / Pinnacle

Dead Beat

FILE UNDER FUCK
CD ______ LF 134MCD
Lost & Found / May '95 / Plastic Head

Dead Boys

NIGHT OF THE LIVING DEAD BOYS
CD ______ BCD 4017
Bomp / Mar '94 / Cargo / Greyhound / RTM/Disc / Shellshock/Disc

YOUNGER, LOUDER AND SNOTTIER
CD ______ BCD 4064
Bomp / Jun '97 / Cargo / Greyhound / RTM/Disc / Shellshock/Disc

Dead C

REPENT
CD ______ SB 66
Siltbreeze / Feb '97 / Cargo / Vital

TRAPDOOR FUCKING EXIT
Heaven / Hell is now love / Mighty / Power / Bury / Bury (refutation, omnium, haeresium) / Sky / Bone / Krossed / Calling slowly / Helen said this / Acoustico
CD ______ SB 021
Siltbreeze / Feb '97 / Cargo / Vital

WHITE HOUSE, THE
Voodoo spell / New snow / Your hand / (PROCHAM) / Bitcher / Outside
CD ______ SB 402
Matador / Aug '95 / Vital

Dead Can Dance

AION
Arrival and the reunion / Mephisto / Fortune presents gifts not according / End of words / Wilderness / Garden of Zephirus / Saltarello / Song of Sibyl / As the bell rings the Maypole sign / Black sun / Promised womb / Radharc
CD ______ CAD 0007CD
4AD / Apr '90 / RTM/Disc

DEAD CAN DANCE
Fatal impact / Trial / Frontier / Fortune / Ocean / East of Eden / Threshold / Passage in time / Wild in the woods / Musica eternal
CD ______ CAD 404 CD
4AD / Feb '87 / RTM/Disc

INTO THE LABRYNTH
CD ______ CAD 3013CD
4AD / Jun '93 / RTM/Disc

PASSAGE IN TIME, A
CD ______ CAD 1010CD
4AD / Oct '91 / RTM/Disc

SERPENTS EGG, THE
Host of Seraphim / Orbis de ignis / Severance / Writing on my father's hand / In the kingdom of the blind / Chant of the paladin / Song of Sophia / Echolalia / Mother tongue / Ulysses
CD ______ CAD 808CD
4AD / Oct '88 / RTM/Disc

SPIRITCHASER
Nierika / Song of the stars / Indus / Song of the dispossessed / Dedicace outo / Snake and the moon / Song of the nile / Devorzhum
CD ______ CAD 6008CD
4AD / Jun '96 / RTM/Disc

SPLEEN AND IDEAL
This tide / De profundis / Ascension / Circumradiant dawn / Cardinal sin / Mesmerism / Enigma of the absolute / Advent / Abatar / Indoctrination / Out of the depth of sorrow / Design for living
CD ______ CAD 512CD
4AD / Jan '86 / RTM/Disc

TOWARD THE WITHIN
CD ______ DAD 4015CD
4AD / Oct '94 / RTM/Disc

WITHIN THE REALM OF A DYING SUN
Anywhere out of the world / Windfall / In the wake of adversity / Xavier / Dawn of the iconoclast / Cantara / Summoning up the muse / Persphone (the gathering of flowers)
CD ______ CAD 705CD
4AD / Jul '87 / RTM/Disc

Dead Famous People

ALL HAIL THE DAFFODIL
CD ______ LADIDA 016CD
La-Di-Da / Jul '94 / Vital

ARRIVING LATE IN TORN AND FILTHY JEANS
CD ______ UTIL 007 CD
Utility / Jul '89 / Grapevine/PolyGram

Dead Flowers

ALTERED STATE CIRCUS
Elephant's eye was eerie / Altered state circus / Warm within - chemical binolculas / Slough factor 9 / Full fist / Free the weed / Vodaphone in Oz
CD ______ DELECCD 022
Delerium / Oct '94 / Cargo / Pinnacle / Vital

SMELL THE FRAGRANCE
Absolution / Drowning / Jesus toy / Piece of sky / So far gone / Can't understand / Swimming around / Manic depression / Third eye shades / Crack down / Our tabs
CD ______ CDRUNE 002
Mystic Stones / Oct '93 / Vital

Dead Fly Boy

DEAD FLY BOY
CD ______ SECT2 1001
Sector 2 / Jul '95 / Cargo / Direct

Dead Fucking Last

GRATEFUL
Alien/We are the dead / 300lb mushroom / Leave me alone / Grateful song / You and me / Live 4 today / Short breath / Retribution / All in your head / Four twenty / You can't make me / Help wanted / Ought to be a law / 14 acre mosh / Camel toe / Powerless / Alcohol/Autumn's fall
CD ______ 64932
Epitaph / Apr '97 / Pinnacle / Plastic Head

PROUD TO BE
CD ______ 864532
Epitaph / Aug '95 / Pinnacle / Plastic Head

Dead Kennedys

BEDTIME FOR DEMOCRACY
CD ______ VIRUS 50CD
Alternative Tentacles / Jan '92 / Cargo / Greyhound / Pinnacle

FRANKENCHRIST
CD ______ VIRUS 45CD
Alternative Tentacles / Feb '92 / Cargo / Greyhound / Pinnacle

FRESH FRUIT FOR ROTTING VEGETABLES
Kill the poor / Forward to death / When ya get drafted / Let's lynch the landlord / Drug me / Your emotions / Chemical warfare / California uber alles / I kill children / Stealing people's mail / Funland at the beach / Ill in the head / Holiday in Cambodia / Viva Las Vegas
CD ______ VIRUS 1CD
Alternative Tentacles / '88 / Cargo / Greyhound / Pinnacle
CD ______ CDBRED 10
Cherry Red / Mar '95 / Pinnacle

GIVE ME CONVENIENCE OR GIVE ME DEATH
CD ______ VIRUS 57CD
Alternative Tentacles / Sep '87 / Cargo / Greyhound / Pinnacle

PLASTIC SURGERY DISASTERS
Government flu / Terminal preppie / Trust your mechanic / Well paid scientist / Buzzbomb / Forest fire / Halloween / Winnebago warrior / Riot / Bleed for me / I am the owl / Dead end / Moon over marin / In God we trust
CD ______ VIRUS 27CD
Alternative Tentacles / Mar '92 / Cargo / Greyhound / Pinnacle

VIRUS 100 (Dead Kennedy's Cover Versions Album) (Various Artists)
Ill in the head: *Victim's Family* / Saturday night holocaust: *Neurosis* / Police truck: *Didjits* / Winnebago warrior: *Nixon, Mojo* / Too drunk to fuck: *Johns, Evan* / California uber alles: *Disposable Heroes Of Hiphoprisy* / Forward to death: *No Means No* / Halloween: *Alice Donut*
CD ______ VIRUS 100CD
Alternative Tentacles / Mar '92 / Cargo / Greyhound / Pinnacle

Dead Moon

HARD WIRED IN LJUBLJANA (CD/CD-Rom Set)
CD ______ MMCD 067
CD Set ______ MMCD 06768
Music Maniac / Jul '97 / Cargo

Dead Mould

POLYMOG
Hit / Almost natural / Drape / Screwball / Second half / Through the lungs / What it takes / Tall / Big muff / Diggin' a hole
CD ______ SPV 08545872
SPV / Jan '97 / Koch / Plastic Head

Dead On

ALL FOR YOU
CD ______ 36700053
Mausoleum / Oct '91 / Grapevine/ PolyGram

Dead Or Alive

MAD, BAD AND DANGEROUS TO KNOW
Brand new lover / I'll save you all my kisses / Son of a gun / Then there was you / Come inside / Something in my house / Hooked on love / I want you / Special star
CD ______ 4655742
Epic / Mar '97 / Sony

YOUTHQUAKE
You spin me round (like a record) / I wanna be a toy / DJ hit that button / In too deep / Big daddy of the rhythm / Cake and eat it / Lover come back to me / My heart goes bang / It's been a long time / Lover come back to me (extended mix)
CD ______ 4778532
Epic / Oct '94 / Sony

Dead Orchestra

SOUNDS LIKE TIME TASTES
CD ______ MASSCD 064
Massacre / Aug '95 / Plastic Head

Dead Reckoners

NIGHT OF RECKONING, A
Intro / I desire fire / Cryin' for nothing / You tell me / Rocky road / Workin' on it / Always will / Waiting for the assassin / Pearl earrings / Too much love / When we're gone, long gone / Outro
CD ______ DR 00072
Avid / Mar '97 / Avid/BMG / Koch / THE

Dead Ringer Band

HOME FIRES
Home fires / More about love / Always be me / Australian son / Honky tonk from hell / I'd go home if I had one / Why / Family man / Burning flame / Just wanted to see you so bad / Sin city / Guitar talk / Gypsy bound
CD ______ FIENDCD 798
Demon / Aug '97 / Pinnacle

RED DESERT SKY
CD ______ LARRCD 302
Larrikin / Nov '94 / ADA / CM / Direct / Roots

Dead World

MACHINE, THE
CD ______ NB 0892
Nuclear Blast / Jan '94 / Plastic Head

Dead Youth

INTENSE BRUTALITY
CD ______ GCI 9800
Plastic Head / Jun '92 / Plastic Head

Deadbolt

TIJUANA HIT SQUAD
CD ______ HED 059
Headhunter / Oct '96 / Cargo

Deadcats

BUCKET O' LOVE
CD ______ FLY 1001
Flying Saucer / Jun '96 / Nervous

Deadguy

FIXATION ON A CO WORKER
CD ______ VR 030
Victory Europe / Jan '96 / Plastic Head

Deadline

DOWN BY LAW
CD ______ CPCD 8192
Charly / Jun '96 / Koch

Deadly Nighshades

DEADLY NIGHTSHADES, THE
Totally female / Monster / Love blackmailer / James / That song / Vampire / Train / Who's that living next door / Nocturnal / Stray cats / Red turns to brown / Twilight
CD ______ HOT 1051
Hot / Feb '96 / Hot Records

Deadspot

ADIOS DUDE
Addiction / Right through you / Inside / Deadspot / Friday night in hell / This means war / Power tool / Another day / My death / Jesus is my best friend
CD **HMRXD 149**
Heavy Metal / May '90 / Revolver / Sony

BUILT IN PAIN
CD **CZ 032CD**
C/Z / Oct '91 / Plastic Head

Deadstar

DEADSTAR
CD **CORDD 008**
Discordant / Aug '97 / RTM/Disc

Deadstock

DEADSTOCK
Monophonic man / Suite 303 / Oedipus sucks / Nobody / Fold unfold fold / Six sided something
CD **TRUCD 12**
Internal / Nov '96 / Pinnacle / PolyGram

Deaf School

SECOND COMING
What a way to end it all / Shake some action / Hi Jo hi / Nearly moonlight night motel / Taxi / Ronnie Zamora / Thunder and lightning / Blue velvet / Princess princess / I wanna be your boy / Lines / Capaldis cafe / Second honeymoon / Final act
CD **FIENDCD 135**
Demon / Oct '88 / Pinnacle

Deaf Shepherd

SPARK O' NATURES FIRE, A
Gie's a drink / Waltzes / Minister's set / Logan braes / New Pa / Finbarr / Ah surely / Peggy Gordon / Double pipe set / Lost for words at sea / Foreign set
CD **CDTRAX 104**
Greentrax / Mar '96 / ADA / Direct / Duncans / Highlander

Deal, Bill

BEST OF BILL DEAL AND THE RHONDELS (Deal, Bill & The Rhondells)
I've been hurt / What kind of fool do you think I am / May I / Are you ready for this / Can I change my mind / Words / Touch me / I've gotta be me / Soulful strut / It's too late / Everybody's got something to hide / Nothing succeeds like success / Swinging tight / I'm gonna make you love me / I've got my needs / Harlem shuffle / River deep, mountain high / Hooked on a feeling / Hey bulldog / Tuck's theme / So what if it rains / I live in the night
CD **NEMCD 644**
Sequel / Apr '94 / BMG

Dean Brothers

CHANCE TO DANCE, A
CD **MTNCD 003**
Milltown / Jan '97 / Grapevine/PolyGram / PolyGram

ON THE RIGHT TRACKS
CD **MTNCD 002**
Milltown / Sep '96 / Grapevine/PolyGram / PolyGram

SAME TRAIN DIFFERENT TRACK
CD **DVCD 002**
Deansville / Jun '97 / CM

Dean Close School Chapel ...

MICHAELMAS TO WHITSUNTIDE (Dean Close School Chapel Choir)
Sing lullaby / And there were shepherds / Break forth / Lo now we count them blessed / Miserere mei / Three kings / When to the temple Mary went / Spirit of the Lord / Little road to Bethlehem / Crucifixus / I waited for the Lord / Ascendit Deus / Tibi Christe / Beata nobis gaudia / Haec dies / Caelos ascendit hodie / Wash me throughly / Alleluia, a new work / Strife is o'er
CD **CDPS 405**
Alpha / '91 / Abbey Recording

Dean, Elton

ALL THE TRADITION (Dean, Elton & Howard Riley Quartet)
Darn that dream / Longest day / Crescent / Convivial convocation / I remember Clifford
CD **SLAMCD 201**
Slam / Apr '91 / Cadillac

ELTON DEAN & HIS UNLIMITED SAXOPHONE COMPANY
CD **OGCD 002**
Ogun / Oct '92 / Cadillac / Jazz Music / Wellard

RUMOURS OF AN INCIDENT (Dean, Elton Quartet & Roswell Rudd)
CD **SLAMCD 223**
Slam / May '97 / Cadillac

TWO'S AND THREE'S
He who dares / PR Department / Uprising / Reconciliation / KT / Riolity / Duke
CD **BP 167CD**
Blueprint / Jul '97 / Pinnacle

VORTEX TAPES, THE
Second thoughts / First impressions / Going fourth / Third time lucky / Taking the fifth
CD **SLAMCD 203**
Slam / Oct '96 / Cadillac

Dean, Graham

GRAHAM DEAN QUARTET, THE
CD **GFD 001**
Scorpio / Jun '94 / Complete/Pinnacle

Dean, Hazell

GREATEST HITS
Searchin' / Whatever I do (wherever I go) / Evergreen / Jealous love / Back in my arms once again / They say it's gonna rain / Turn it into love / You're too good to be true / Who's leaving who / Maybe (we should call it a day) / No fool (for love) / Ain't nothing like the real thing: *Dean, Hazell & Daryl Pandy* / Searchin'/Whatever I do/Stand up / Who's leaving who (Bobs tambourine mix)
CD **CDGOLD 1023**
EMI Gold / May '96 / EMI

Dean, Jimmy

BIG BAD JOHN
Big bad John / I won't go huntin' with you Jake / Smoke, smoke, smoke / Dear Ivan / To a sleeping beauty / Cajun Queen / PT 109 / Walk on boy / Little bitty big John / Steel man / Little black book / Please pass the biscuits / Gonna raise a ruckus tonight / Day that changed the world / Gotta travel on / Sixteen tons / Oklahoma Bill / Night train to Memphis / Make the waterwheel roll / Lonesome road / Grasshopper MacClean / Old Pappy's new banjo / You're nobody 'til somebody loves you / Cajun Joe / Nobody / Kentucky means paradise
CD **BCD 15723**
Bear Family / Jul '93 / Direct / Rollercoaster / Swift

Dean, Kevin

KEVIN'S HEAVEN
Make me a present of you / Big wood / Sincerely / Retournez SVP / Ill wind / Mock's nest / You are my sunshine / How deep is the ocean / This is new
CD **DTRCD 103**
Double Time / Nov '96 / Express Jazz

Dean/Riley

DECREASING CIRCLES
CD **BP 221CD**
Blueprint / Oct '96 / Pinnacle

Deanta

DEANTA
CD **GLCD 1126**
Green Linnet / May '93 / ADA / CM / Direct / Highlander / Roots

READY FOR THE STORM
CD **GL 1147CD**
Green Linnet / Oct '94 / ADA / CM / Direct / Highlander / Roots

WHISPER OF A SECRET
Two days to go / Willie and Mary / Usual suspects / Paddy and the bandit / Lone shanakyle / Waltz of the white lilies / At the crossroads / Blacksmith / Cogair ruin / Druid's mountain / Where are you / Scarta Glen road
CD **GLCD 1173**
Green Linnet / Jun '97 / ADA / CM / Direct / Highlander / Roots

Dear Janes

NO SKIN
CD **TRACD 107**
Transatlantic / Apr '96 / Pinnacle

SOMETIMES I
Girl of your dreams / Niagara tears / Brides of the cross / Dear Jane / Air traffic / Sometimes I / Outside my window / My guilty hand / Some small corner / Jesus put me down / I'm heading home / PMP
CD **TRACD 104**
Transatlantic / Feb '95 / Pinnacle

Dearie, Blossom

BLOSSOM DEARIE - VOCAL CLASSICS
'Deed I do / Lover man / Everything I've got / Comment allez vous / More than you know / Thou swell / It might as well be Spring / Tout doucement / You for me / Now at last / I hear music / Wait till you see her / I won't dance / Fine Spring morning / They say it's Spring / Johnny one note / Blossom's blues
CD **8379342**
Verve / Feb '93 / PolyGram

CHRISTMAS SPICE, IT'S SO NICE
CD **CHECD 00103**
Master Mix / '91 / Jazz Music / New Note/ Pinnacle / Wellard

ET TU BRUCE
Bruce / Hey John / Someone's been sending me flowers / You have lived in autumn / Alice in Wonderland / Satin doll / Riviera / Inside a silent tear
CD **CDCHE 5**
Master Mix / Aug '89 / Jazz Music / New Note/Pinnacle / Wellard

JAZZ MASTERS
CD **5299062**
Verve / Apr '96 / PolyGram

NEEDLEPOINT MAGIC
Ballad of the shape of things / Lush life / When the world was young / I'm hip / Baby, it's cold outside / I like you, you're nice / Sweet surprise / I'm shadowing you / Sweet Georgie fame / Peel me a grape / Two sleepy people
CD **CDCHE 3**
Master Mix / Oct '91 / Jazz Music / New Note/Pinnacle / Wellard

ONCE UPON A SUMMERTIME
Tea for two / Surrey with the fringe on top / Moonlight saving time / It amazes me / If I were a bell / We're together / Teach me tonight / Once upon a summertime / Down with love / Manhattan / Doop doo de doop / Our love is here to stay
CD **5172232**
Verve / Feb '93 / PolyGram

SONGS OF CHELSEA
My attorney Bernie / Everything I've got / C'est Le Printemps / When in Rome / Let the flower grow / My new celebrity is you / What time is it now / You fascinate me so / There ought to be moonlight saving time / Chelsea Aire
CD **CDCHE 2**
Master Mix / Jan '90 / Jazz Music / New Note/Pinnacle / Wellard

TWEEDLE DUM AND TWEEDLE DEE (Dearie, Blossom & Mike Renzi)
CD **CHECD 00101**
Master Mix / '91 / Jazz Music / New Note/ Pinnacle / Wellard

WINCHESTER IN APPLE BLOSSOM TIME
Spring can really hang you up the most / Sunday afternoon / Wonderful guy / To touch the hand of love / Wheelers and dealers / Jazz musician / Surrey with the fringe on top / Love is an elusive celebration / Lucky to be me / You're for loving / Summer is gone / Sammy / It amazes me / If I were a bell
CD **CHECD 8**
Master Mix / '89 / Jazz Music / New Note/ Pinnacle / Wellard

Dearly Beheaded

TEMPTATION
CD **CDMFN 203**
CD **CDMFNX 203**
Music For Nations / Jun '96 / Pinnacle

Deason, Sean

RAZORBACK
CD **K7R 008CD**
Studio K7 / Oct '96 / Prime / RTM/Disc

Death

SYMBOLIC
CD **RR 89572**
Roadrunner / Sep '96 / PolyGram

Death Angel

FROLIC THROUGH THE PARK
Third floor / Road mutants / Why you do this / Bored / Confused / Guilty of innocence / Open up / Shores of sin / Cold gin / Mind rape
CD **7725492**
Restless / Jul '94 / Vital

ULTRA-VIOLENCE
Thrashers / Evil priest / Voracious souls / Kill as one / Ultra violence / Mistress of pain / Final death / IPFS
CD **7725482**
Restless / Jul '94 / Vital

Death In June

93 DEAD SUNWHEELS
CD **BADVCCD 93**
New European / Oct '96 / World Serpent

BLACK WHOLE OF LOVE BOX SET
CD Set **BADVC 39**
New European / Oct '96 / World Serpent

BURIAL
CD **UBADVCCD 4**
New European / Oct '96 / World Serpent

BUT WHAT ENDS...
CD **BADVCCD 36**
New European / Oct '96 / World Serpent

CATHEDRAL OF TEARS, THE
CD **BADVCCD 34**
New European / Oct '96 / World Serpent

CORN YEARS, THE
CD **BADVCCD 7**
New European / Feb '89 / World Serpent

DEATH IN JUNE PRESENT OCCIDENTAL MARTYR
CD **NERO 8CD**
Twilight Command / Oct '96 / World Serpent

DEATH IN JUNE PRESENTS KAPO
CD **NERO 13CD**
Twilight Command / Jan '97 / World Serpent

GUILTY HAVE NO PAST, THE
CD **BADVCCD 3**
New European / Jan '90 / World Serpent

NADA
CD **BADVCCD 13**
New European / Jan '90 / World Serpent

OSTENBRAUN
CD **SD 01**
New European / Oct '96 / World Serpent

PARADISE RISING
CD **BADVCCD 63**
New European / Oct '96 / World Serpent

ROSE CLOUDS OF HOLOCAUST
CD **BADVCCD 38**
New European / Oct '96 / World Serpent

SCORPION WIND - HEAVEN SENT
CD **NERO 39CD**
Twilight Command / Oct '96 / World Serpent

WALL OF SACRIFICES, THE
CD **BADVCCD 88**
New European / Jan '90 / World Serpent

Death In Vegas

DEAD ELVIS
CD **HARD 22LPCD**
Concrete / Jun '97 / 3mv/Pinnacle / Prime / RTM/Disc / Total/BMG

Death Of Samantha

WHERE THE WOMEN WEAR THE GLORY
CD **HMS 121CD**
Homestead / Nov '88 / Cargo / SRD

Death SS

HEAVY DEMONS
CD **BABEDISCCD 002**
Plastic Head / Jul '92 / Plastic Head

Deathcore

SPONTANEOUS
CD **842976**
Nuclear Blast / Sep '90 / Plastic Head

SPONTANEOUS UNDERGROUND
CD **NB 034CD**
Nuclear Blast / Oct '92 / Plastic Head

Deathfolk

DEATHFOLK
CD **NAR 047CD**
New Alliance / May '93 / Plastic Head

DEATHFOLK VOL.2
CD **NAR 076CD**
New Alliance / May '93 / Plastic Head

Deathless

ANHEDONIA
CD **EL 104**
Electrip / Nov '92 / Plastic Head

NONDEATHLESS
CD **EL 105CD**
Electrip / Sep '93 / Plastic Head

Deathline International

ARASHI SYNDROME
CD **COPCD 029**
Cop International / May '97 / Cargo

Deathprod

TREETOP DRIVE
CD **MAD 004CD**
Mad / Mar '95 / Plastic Head

Deaville, Gillman

WAYS TO FLY
CD **FF 70636**
Flying Fish / Nov '94 / ADA / CM / Direct / Roots

DeBarge, El

HEART, MIND & SOUL
Where you are / Can't get enough / Where is my love / You got the love I want / It's got to be real / Slide / I'll be there / Special lady / Starlight, moonlight, candlight / You are my dream / Heart, mind and soul
CD **9362453752**
Warner Bros. / Jun '94 / Warner Music

Debriano, Santi

OBEAH
CD **FRLCD 008**
Freelance / Oct '92 / Cadillac / Koch

PANAMANIACS (Debriano, Santi Group)
CD FRLCD 019
Freelance / Nov '93 / Cadillac / Koch

SOLDIERS OF FORTUNE
CD FRLCD 012
Freelance / Oct '92 / Cadillac / Koch

Debustrol

NEUROPATOLOG
CD MONITOR 2
Monitor / Jan '92 / CM

Decameron

THIRD LIGHT/TOMORROW'S PANTOMIME
Rock and roll away / All the best wishes / Strawman / Saturday / Wide as the years / Journey's end / Road to the sea / Trapeze / Ungodly / Morning glory / Deal / Fallen over / Ask me tomorrow / Tomorrow's pantomime / Shadows on the stairs / So this is God's country / Peace with honour
CD ESMCD 568
Essential / Jul '97 / BMG

Decameron

MY SHADOW
CD NFR 013CD
No Fashion / Jun '96 / Plastic Head

Decan, Chen

CHINESE FOLK MUSIC (Decan, Chen Chinese Ensemble)
CD EUCD 1167
ARC / '91 / ADA / ARC Music

Deceased

BLUEPRINTS
CD RR 6920CD
Nuclear Blast / Dec '96 / Plastic Head

FEARLESS UNDEAD MACHINES
Silent creature / Contamination / Fearless undead machines / From the ground they came / Night of the deceased / Graphic repulsion / Mysterious research / Beyound science / Unhuman drama / Psychic / Destiny
CD RR 69572
Relapse / Aug '97 / Pinnacle / Plastic Head

December Band

MOOSE LODGE HALL VOL.1 1965
CD BCD 197
GHB / Mar '97 / Jazz Music

December Moon

SOURCE OF ORIGIN
CD SP 1032CD
Spinefarm / May '96 / Plastic Head

Decimator

CARNAGE CITY STATE MOSH PATROL
Raider / Mutoids / F H Blood Island / CCSMP / Devil's bridge / Rogue decimator / Dustbowl / Stealer of souls
CD NEAT 1047D
Neat / '89 / Pinnacle

DIRTY, HOT & HUNGRY
CD NEATCD 1052
Neat / Nov '92 / Pinnacle

Decollation

CURSED LANDS
CD POSH 0004
Listenable / Oct '93 / Plastic Head

Decomposed

FUNERAL OBSESSION
CD CYBERCD 2
Cybersound / May '92 / Vital

HOPE FINALLY DIED
CD CANDLE 003CD
Candlelight / Jan '94 / Plastic Head

Deconstruction

DECONSTRUCTION
LA Song / Single / Get at 'em / Iris / Dirge / Fire in the hole / Son / Big sur / Hope / One / America / Sleepyhead / Wait for history / That is all / Kilo
CD 74321248522
American / Aug '95 / BMG

Decoryah

BREATHING THE BLUE
CD 398414130CD
Metal Blade / Jun '97 / Pinnacle / Plastic Head

FALL DARK WATERS
CD 398414111CD
Metal Blade / Jun '96 / Pinnacle / Plastic Head

Decree

WAKE OF DEVASTATION
CD 08543432
Westcom / Mar '97 / Koch / Pinnacle

Decry

COMPLETE DECRY (2CD Set)
CD Set CLP 9908
Cleopatra / Feb '97 / Cargo / Greyhound / Plastic Head / RTM/Disc / SRD

Dedale

CHRONIQUES URBAINES
CD DP 93009CD
Mustradem / Apr '94 / ADA

LE MAITRE DHU
CD DP 91007CD
Mustradem / Apr '94 / ADA

NO PAST
CD DP 9501CD
Mustradem / Aug '95 / ADA

OBSESSION
CD DP 92008CD
Mustradem / Apr '94 / ADA

Dede, Amayke

OKYENA SESEE
CD KO 3
Kotoko / Jan '97 / Stern's

Dedeyan, Garo

GIFT OF THE GODS
CD WAV 1004
Wave / Apr '97 / Else

Dedication Orchestra

IXESHA
CD Set OGCD 102/103
Ogun / Dec '94 / Cadillac / Jazz Music / Wellard

Dee, Brian

CLIMB EVERY MOUNTAIN
I have dreamed / I should care / Your song / Pete Kelly's blues / Nuages / Koo / Instep / Day by day / You are the sunshine of my life / Uncle's friend / Triple play / I surrender Dear / How insensitive / Dream / To the shores of Tripoli / Unforgettable / Homebase / Climb every mountain
CD SPJCD 552
Spotlite / May '95 / Cadillac / Jazz Music / New Note/Pinnacle / Swift

SECOND SIGHT (Dee, Brian Trio)
Bruised blues / Certain smile / Dream dancing / Elba mel delba / Second sight / Seven steps to heaven / In your own sweet way / Hermitage / Promised land / More bruised blues
CD SPJCD 543
Spotlite / May '93 / Cadillac / Jazz Music / New Note/Pinnacle / Swift

Dee, David

GOIN' FISHIN'
Heatin' me up / Rainy night in Georgia / If I knew then / Special way of making love / Part time love / Goin' fishin' / Workin' this dream overtime / Lead me on / Thought my lovin' was over
CD ICH 1114CD
Ichiban / Oct '93 / Direct / Koch

Dee, Joey

HEY, LET'S TWIST (The Best Of Joey Dee & The Starliters) (Dee, Joey & The Starlighters)
Peppermint twist (part 1) / Peppermint twist (part 2) / Hey, let's twist / Roly poly / Joey's blues / Shout / Irresistible you / Crazy love / Everytime (I think about you) - part I / What kind of love is this / I lost my baby / Keep your mind on what you're doing / Help me pick up the pieces / Baby, you're driving me crazy / Hot pastrami / Dance, dance, dance / Ya ya / Fannie Mae
CD CDROU 5010
Roulette / Aug '90 / EMI

Dee, Johnny

LOVE COMPILATION
Theme for Johnny Dee / When my heart goes wild / Goodbye flip flap guitar / Why I like Max Eider (Part 1) / Blue girl from north town / Day in Waterloo / Hey gentle girl / Bachelor kisses / So what / Why I like Max Eider (Part 3)
CD MASKCD 038
Vinyl Japan / Mar '94 / Plastic Head / Vinyl Japan

Dee, Kiki

ALMOST NAKED
CD TB 01
Tickety Boo / Oct '95 / Grapevine/ PolyGram

AMOUREUSE
Amoureuse / I got the music in me / Loving and free / (You don't know) How glad I am / Chicago / First thing in the morning / One jump ahead of the storm / Dark side of your soul / Stay with me baby / Why don't I run away from you / Runnin' out of fools / You hold me too tight / Can't take my eyes off you / On a magic carpet ride / Step by step / You need help / One step / Talk to me
CD 5521162
Spectrum / Mar '96 / PolyGram

Dee, Sonny

CHICAGO - THAT'S JAZZ VOL.2 (Dee, Sonny Allstars)
Who's sorry now / My cutie's due at two to two / You're in kentucky sure as you're born / Trouble in mind / Mandy, make up your mind / Is it true what they say about Dixie / When / Mama's gone goodbye / Goodbye / Do you know what it means to miss New Orleans / Moonglow / Who cares / It's been so long / Lady's in love with you / Blue and broken hearted / Miss Annabelle Lee / Since my best gal turned me down
CD LACD 26
Lake / Mar '93 / ADA / Cadillac / Direct / Jazz Music / Target/BMG

Deebank, Maurice

INNER THOUGHT ZONE
Watery song / Four corners of the earth / Study No.1 / Golden hills / Silver fountain of Paradise Square / So Serene / Dance Of Deliverance / Pavanne / Tale from Scriabins lonely trail / Maestoso Con Anima
CD CDMRED 61
Cherry Red / Nov '92 / Pinnacle

Deee-Lite

DEW DROPS IN THE GARDEN
Bring me your love / Party happening people / Say ahhh / Picnic in the summertime / River of freedom / When you told me you loved me / Call me / Sampladelic / DMT (Dance music trance) / Apple juice kissing / What is this music / Music selector is the soul reflector / Stay in bed forget the rest / Somebody / Bittersweet loving / Mind melt
CD 7559615262
Elektra / Jul '94 / Warner Music

REMIX ALBUM, THE
CD 7559618722
Elektra / Feb '97 / Warner Music

WORLD CLIQUE
Good beat / Power of love / Try me on...I'm very you / Smile on / What is love / World clique / ESP / Groove is in the heart / Who was that / Deep ending w/gloop / Deee-lite theme / Build the bridge
CD 7559609572
Elektra / Sep '90 / Warner Music

Deele

BEST OF THE DEELE, THE
Two occasions / Shoot 'em up movies / Body talk / I surrender / Just my luck / Sexy love / You're all I've ever known / Suspicious / Material thangz / I'll send you roses / Sweet November / Let no one separate us / Can-U-dance / Dry your eyes / Crazy 'bout cha / Eyes of stranger
CD DEEPM 001
Deep Beats / Nov '96 / BMG

Deems, Barrett

DEEMUS
Deed I do / New Orleans / Shine / After you've gone / Seven come eleven / Six appeal / I love Paris / Get happy
CD DD 492
Delmark / Jul '97 / ADA / Cadillac / CM / Direct / Hot Shot

HOW D'YOU LIKE IT SO FAR
CD DE 472
Delmark / Dec '95 / ADA / Cadillac / CM / Direct / Hot Shot

Deene, Carol

JOHNNY GET ANGRY
Sad movies / Don't forget / Norman / On the outside looking in / Johnny get angry / Somebody's smiling / Some people / Kissin' / James (hold the ladder steady) / It happened last night / Let me do it my way / Growin' up / Want to stay here / Oh oh oh Willie / Who's been sleeping in my bed / Love is wonderful / Hard to say goodnight / Very first kiss / I can't forget someone like you / Most people do / He just don't know / Up in the penthouse / Dancing in your eyes / Please don't be unfaithful again / Time / Love not have I
CD GEMCD 005
Diamond / Jan '97 / Pinnacle

Deep Blue Something

HOME
Gammer Gerten's needle / Breakfast at Tiffany's / Halo / Josey / Water prayer / Done / Song to make love to / Kadinski Prince / Home / Red light / I can wait / Wouldn't change a thing
CD IND 90002
Interscope / Sep '96 / BMG

Deep Dish

CREAM SEPARATES VOL.1 (Mixed By Deep Dish) (Various Artists)
Never tell you: *Rhythm & Sound/Tikiman* / Rise: *Rivera, Sandy & Kings Of Tomorrow Presents* / Flirt: *Horn* / Glide by shooting: *Two Lone Swordsmen* / Fade II black: *Kot* / Love revolution: *Mysterious People* / Fly life: *Basement Jaxx* / Untitled: *Listenin' Parlour* / Gosp: *LWS* / Summer madness: *Daemyon, Jerald* / Twenty minutes of disco glory: *DJ Garth & ETI* / Tick tock: *Chia Pet* / Don't ever stop: *Dubbing Double* / Theme from the Blue Cucaracha: *Innocent* / Samba magic: *Summer Daze* / In your soul: *Latino Circus*
CD 74321462002
De-Construction / Mar '97 / BMG

DJ'S TAKE CONTROL VOL.1 (Mixed By Deep Dish - 2CD Set) (Various Artists)
CD Set ORCD 028
One / May '96 / Total/BMG

Deep Forest

BOHEME
Anathasia / Marta's song / Gathering / Lament / Bulgarian melody / Deep folk song / Freedom cry / Twosome / Cafe europa / Katharina / Boheme
CD 4786232
Columbia / May '95 / Sony

DEEP FOREST
Deep forest / Sweet lullaby / Hunting / Night bird / First twilight / Savannah dance / Desert walk / White whisper / Second twilight / Sweet lullaby (mix) / Forest hymn
CD 4741782
Columbia / Feb '94 / Sony

Deep Freeze Mice

I LOVE YOU LITTLE BOBO WITH YOUR DELICATE GOLDEN LIONS (2CD Set)
CD Set JAR 011
Jarmusic / Jul '97 / Cargo

Deep Freeze Productions

IF THEY MOVE KILL 'EM
Who the hell / Inda soupe / 5th dimension / Burnt sienna / Let sleeping dogs lie / Instant mayhem / Inda soupe / Beat the hell
CD SSRCD 002
Sureshot / Apr '97 / Prime / RTM/Disc / Vital

Deep Purple

24 CARAT PURPLE
Woman from Tokyo / Fireball / Strange kind of woman / Never before / Black night / Speed king / Smoke on the water / Child in time
CD CDFA 3132
Fame / Oct '87 / EMI

ANTHOLOGY (2CD Set)
Hush / Mandrake root / Shield / Wring that neck / Bird has flown / Bloodsucker / Speed king / Black night / Child in time / Fireball / Strange kind of woman / Highway star / Smoke on the water / Pictures of home / Woman from Tokyo / Smooth dancer / Sail away / Lay down stay down / Burn / Stormbringer / Hold on / Gypsy / Mistreated / Gettin' tighter / Love child / You keep on moving / No one came
CD Set CDEM 1374
EMI / Mar '91 / EMI

BATTLE RAGES ON, THE
Battle rages on / Lick it up / Anya / Talk about love / Time to kill / Ramshackle man / Twist in the tale / Nasty piece of work / Solitaire / One man's meat
CD 74321154202
RCA / Aug '95 / BMG

BOOK OF TALIESYN, THE
Listen, learn, read on / Wring that neck / Kentucky woman / Exposition / We can work it out / Shield / Anthem / River deep, mountain high
CD CZ 171
Premier/EMI / Feb '96 / EMI

BOOK OF TALIESYN, THE/SHADES OF DEEP PURPLE/DEEP PURPLE (The Originals Vol.1/3CD Set)
Listen, learn, read on / Wring that neck / Kentucky woman / Exposition / We can work it out / Shield / Anthem / River deep, mountain high / And the address / Hush / One more rainy day / Prelude / Happiness / I'm so glad / Mandrake / Root / Help / Love help me / Hey Joe / Chasing shadows / Blind / Lalena / Fault line / Painter / Why didn't Rosemary / Bird has flown / April
CD Set CDOMB 002
EMI / Mar '97 / EMI

BURN
Burn / Might just take your life / Lay down stay down / Sail away / You fool no one / What's goin' on here / Mistreated / A-Zoo
CD CZ 203
EMI / Jul '89 / EMI

CALIFORNIA JAMMING
Burn / Might just take your life / Mistreated / Smoke on the water / Your fool no-one/ The mule / Space truckin'
CD PRMUCD 2
Premier/EMI / May '96 / EMI

CHILD IN TIME
Nobody's home / Mean streak / Wasted sunsets / Hungry daze / Unwritten law / Mad dog / Spanish archer / Mitzi dupree / Woman from Tokyo (live) / Child in time (live)

/ Strange kind of woman (live) / Highway star (live)
CD ______ 5513392
Spectrum / Aug '95 / PolyGram

COLLECTION, THE
Mandrake root / Wring that neck / Living wreck / Black night / Smoke on the water / Demon's eye / Lady double dealer / Comin' home / Never before
CD ______ CDGOLD 1080
EMI Gold / Feb '97 / EMI

COLLECTION, THE
Mandrake root / Wring that neck / Living wreck / Black night / Smoke on the water / Demon's eye / Lady double dealer / Comin' home / Never before
CD ______ DC 878642
Disky / Mar '97 / Disky / THE

COME HELL OR HIGH WATER
Highway star / Black night / Twist in the tale / Perfect strangers / Anyone's daughter / Child in time / Anya / Speed king / Smoke on the water
CD ______ 74321234162
RCA / Feb '97 / BMG

COME TASTE THE BAND
Comin' home / Lady Luck / Gettin' tighter / Dealer / I need love / Drifter / Love child / This time around / Owed to 'G' / You keep on moving
CD ______ CDFA 3318
Fame / Jul '95 / EMI

CONCERTO FOR GROUP AND ORCHESTRA
Wring that neck / Child in time / Moderato - allegro: First movement / Andante: Second movement / Vivace - presto: Third movement
CD ______ CZ 342
EMI / Jul '90 / EMI

DEEP PURPLE
Chasing shadows / Blind / Lalena / Fault line / Painter / Why didn't Rosemary / Bird has flown / April part 1
CD ______ CDFA 3317
Fame / Apr '95 / EMI

DEEP PURPLE FAMILY ALBUM, THE (Various Artists)
If you've gotta pick a baby: *Collins, Glenda & The Outlaws* / You'll never stop me loving you: *MI5* / I take what I want: *Artwoods* / I can see through you: *Episode Six* / Hush: *Deep Purple* / Snowbound: *Mouson, Alphonse* / Black night: *Deep Purple* / Into the fire: *Deep Purple* / Burn: *Deep Purple* / Love is all: *Glover, Roger & Guests* / You keep on moving: *Deep Purple* / Kill the king: *Rainbow* / Arabella: *Paice, Ashton, Lord* / Northwinds: *Whitesnake* / LA cutoff: *Hughes, Glenn* / Stallion: *Simper, Nick* / Nervous: *Gillan* / Clouds and rain: *Gillan & Glover* / Perfect strangers: *Deep Purple*
CD ______ VSOPCD 187
Connoisseur Collection / May '93 / Pinnacle

DEEP PURPLE IN CONCERT
Speed king / Wring that neck / Child in time / Mandrake root / Highway star / Strange kind of woman / Lazy / Never before / Space truckin' / Lucille / Smoke on the water
CD Set ______ CDEM 1434
EMI / Feb '92 / EMI

DEEPEST PURPLE
Black night / Speed king / Fireball / Strange kind of woman / Child in time / Woman from Tokyo / Highway star / Space truckin' / Burn / Demon's eye / Stormbringer / Smoke on the water
CD ______ CDFA 3239
Fame / Jul '90 / EMI

FINAL CONCERTS, THE (Deep Purple Mark 3 - 2CD Set)
CD Set ______ DPVSOPCD 230
Connoisseur Collection / Jul '96 / Pinnacle

FIREBALL
Fireball / No, no, no / Demon's eye / Mule / Fools / No one came / Anyone's daughter
CD ______ CZ 30
EMI / Jan '88 / EMI

FIREBALL (25th Anniversary Edition)
Fireball / No no no / Demon's eye / Anyone's daughter / Mule / Fools / No one came / Strange kind of woman / I'm alone / Freedom / Slow train / Demon's eye / Midnight in Moscow / Robin Hood / William Tell / Fireball (take 1) / Piano insert / No one came
CD ______ CDDEEPP 2
EMI / Sep '96 / EMI

GEMINI SUITE-LIVE
Guitar/Voice / Organ/Bass / Drums/Finale
CD ______ RPM 114
RPM / Jul '93 / Pinnacle

GREEN BULLFROG SESSIONS, THE (Green Bullfrog)
My baby left me / Makin' time / Lawdy Miss Clawdy / Bullfrog / I want you / I'm a free man / Walk a mile in my shoes / Lovin' you is good for me baby / Who do you love / Ain't nobody home / Louisiana man
CD ______ NSPCD 503
Connoisseur Collection / Nov '91 / Pinnacle

HOUSE OF BLUE LIGHT
Bad attitude / Unwritten law / Call of the wild / Mad dog / Black and white / Hard lovin' woman / Spanish archer / Strangeways / Mitzi dupree / Dead or alive
CD ______ 8313182
Polydor / Jan '87 / PolyGram

IN ROCK (25th Anniversary Edition)
Speed king / Blood sucker / Child in time / Flight of the rat / Into the fire / Living wreck / Hard lovin' man / Black night / Studio chat 1 / Speed king / Studio chat 2 / Cry free / Studio chat 3 / Jam stew / Studio chat 4 / Flight of the rat / Studio chat 5 / Woffle and speed king / Studio chat 6 / Black night
CD ______ CDDEEPP 1
Harvest / Jun '95 / EMI

IN THE ABSENCE OF PINK (Knebworth 1985 - 2CD Set)
Highway star / Nobody's home / Strange kind of woman / Gypsy's kiss / Perfect strangers / Lazy / Knocking at your back door / Space truckin' / Difficult to cure / Speed king / Black night / Smoke on the water
CD Set ______ DPVSOPCD 163
Connoisseur Collection / Jun '91 / Pinnacle

INTERVIEW PICTURE DISC
CD ______ CBAK 4054
Baktabak / Apr '92 / Arabesque

KNOCKING AT YOUR BACK DOOR
Knocking at your back door / Bad attitude / Son of Aleric / Nobody's home / Black night / Perfect strangers / Unwritten law / Call of the wild / Hush / Smoke on the water / Space trucking
CD ______ 5114382
Polydor / Mar '92 / PolyGram

LIVE AT THE OLYMPIA (2CD Set)
Fireball / Maybe I'm a leo / Ted the mechanic / Pictures of home / Black night / Cascades / I'm not your lover / Sometimes I feel like screaming / Woman from Tokyo / No one came / Purpendicular walls / Rosa's cantina / Smoke on the water / When blind man cries / Speed king / Perfect strangers / Hey cisco / Highway star
CD Set ______ CDEM 1615
EMI / Jun '97 / EMI

LIVE IN JAPAN (3CD Set)
Highway star / Child in time / Mule / Strange kind of woman / Lazy / Space truckin' / Black night / Speed king
CD Set ______ CDEM 1510
EMI / Nov '93 / EMI

MACHINE HEAD
Highway star / Maybe I'm a leo / Pictures of home / Never before / Smoke on the water / Lazy / Space truckin'
CD ______ CDFA 3158
Fame / May '89 / EMI

MADE IN EUROPE (Live)
Burn / Mistreated / Lady double dealer / You fool no one / Stormbringer
CD ______ CZ 344
EMI / Jul '90 / EMI

MADE IN JAPAN
Highway star / Child in time / Smoke on the water / Mule / Strange kind of woman / Lazy / Space truckin'
CD ______ CDFA 3268
Fame / Oct '92 / EMI

NOBODY'S PERFECT - LIVE
Highway star / Strange kind of woman / Perfect strangers / Hard lovin' woman / Bad attitude / Knocking at your back door / Child in time / Lazy / Black night / Woman from Tokyo / Smoke on the water / Space truckin'
CD ______ 8358972
Polydor / Jun '88 / PolyGram

ON THE WINGS OF A RUSSIAN FOXBAT (Live In California 1976/2CD Set)
Burn / Lady Luck / Getting tighter / Love child / Smoke on the water / Lazy / Grind / This time around / Stormbringer / Highway star / Going down
CD Set ______ DPVSOPCD 217
Connoisseur Collection / May '95 / Pinnacle

PERFECT STRANGERS
Knocking at your back door / Under the gun / Nobody's home / Mean streak / Perfect strangers / Gypsy's kiss / Wasted sunsets / Hungry daze / Not responsible
CD ______ 8237772
Polydor / Mar '91 / PolyGram

PROGRESSION
Perfect strangers / Under the gun / Knocking at your back door / Gypsy's kiss / Not responsible / Black night / Smoke on the water / Hush / Bad attitude / Dead or alive / Hard lovin' woman / Call of the wild
CD ______ 5500272
Spectrum / May '93 / PolyGram

PURPENDICULAR
Vavoom Ted the mechanic / Loosen my strings / Soon forgotten / Sometimes I feel like screaming / Cascades - I'm not your lover / Aviator / Rosa's cantina / Castle full of rascals / Touch away / Hey Cisco / Somebody stole my guitar / Purpendicular waltz
CD ______ 74321338022
RCA / Jan '96 / BMG

PURPLE RAINBOWS
Black night / Speed king / Child in time / Strange kind of woman / Fireball / Smoke on the water / Highway star / Woman from Tokyo / Perfect strangers / Hush / Since you been gone: *Rainbow* / I surrender: *Rainbow* / Fool for your loving: *Whitesnake* / Here I go again: *Whitesnake* / Night games: *Bonnet, Graham* / Rock 'n' roll children: *Dio*
CD ______ 8455342
PolyGram TV / Apr '94 / PolyGram

SCANDINAVIAN NIGHTS (2CD Set)
Wring that neck / Speed king / Into the fire / Paint it black / Mandrake root / Child in time / Black night
CD Set ______ DPVSOPCD 125
Connoisseur Collection / Oct '88 / Pinnacle

SHADES OF DEEP PURPLE
And the address / Hush / One more rainy day / Prelude: happiness / I'm so glad / Mandrake root / Help / Love help me / Hey Joe
CD ______ CDFA 3314
Fame / Apr '97 / EMI

SINGLES A'S AND B'S
Hush / One more rainy day / Emmaretta / Wring that neck / Hallelujah / April, part 1 / Black night / Speed king / Strange kind of woman / I'm alone / Demon's eye / Fireball / Kentucky woman / Bird has flown / Never before / When a blind man cries / Smoke on the water / Black night (live) / Might just take your life / Coronarias redig / You keep on moving / Lovechild
CD ______ CDP 7810092
EMI / Apr '97 / EMI

SLAVES AND MASTERS
King of dreams / Cut runs deep / Fire in the basement / Truth hurts / Breakfast in bed / Love conquers all / Fortune teller / Too much is not enough / Wicked ways
CD ______ 74321187192
RCA / Apr '94 / BMG

SMOKE ON THE WATER (Various Artists)
CD ______ RR 89672
Roadrunner / Nov '94 / PolyGram

STORMBRINGER
Stormbringer / Love don't mean a thing / Holy man / Hold on / Lady double dealer / You can't do it right / High ball shooter / Gypsy / Soldier of fortune
CD ______ CZ 142
EMI / Oct '88 / EMI

STORMBRINGER/WHO DO WE THINK WE ARE/COME TASTE THE BAND (The Originals Vol.2/3CD Set)
Stormbringer / Love don't mean a thing / Holy man / Hold on / Lady Double Dealer / You can't do it right / High ball shooter / Gypsy / Soldier of fortune / Woman from Tokyo / Mary Long / Super trouper / Smooth dancer / Rat bat blue / Place in line / Our lady / Comin' home / Lady Luck / Gettin' tighter / Dealer / I need love / Drifter / Love child / This time around / Owed to 'G' / You keep on moving
CD Set ______ CDOMB 017
EMI / Mar '97 / EMI

THIRD ALBUM
Chasing shadows / Blind / Lalena / Painter / Why didn't Rosemary / Bird has flown / April
CD ______ CZ 172
Harvest / Mar '89 / EMI

WHO DO WE THINK WE ARE
Woman from Tokyo / Mary Long / Super trouper / Smooth dancer / Rat bat blue / Place in line / Our lady
CD ______ CDFA 3311
Fame / Dec '94 / EMI

Deep Space Network

DSN & HIA (Deep Space Network & Higher Intelligence Agency)
CD ______ EFA 006242
Source / Feb '97 / SRD / Vital

Deep Throat

VERSION 3.0
CD ______ CDDVN 20
Devotion / Jun '93 / Pinnacle

Deepika

I ALT SLAGS LYS
CD ______ FXCD 118
Kirkelig Kulturverksted / Jul '93 / ADA

Deerheart

QUEEN, WORKER, DRONE
CD ______ GR 044CD
Goldenrod / Oct '96 / Cargo

Dees, Sam

SECOND TO NONE
We always come back strong / Tag / Your love is like a boomerang / Number one, second to none / Home wreckers / Your fool or your man / World don't owe you nothing / I like to party / I'm gonna give you just enough rope (To hang yourself) / Cry to me / Who are you gonna love (Your woman or your wife) / Good guys don't always win / Vanishing love / Nothing comes to a sleeper but a dream / I wish that I could be him / False alarm / You've been doing wrong for so long / Win or lose / Run to me / Help me my Lord / Touch me with your love / Just my alibi / Worn out broken heart
CD ______ CDKEND 125
Kent / Jun '95 / Pinnacle

Def Leppard

ADRENALIZE
Let's get rocked / Heaven is / Make love like a man / Tonight / White lightning / Stand up (kick love into motion) / Personal property / Have you ever / I wanna touch you / Tear it down
CD ______ 5109782
Bludgeon Riffola / Mar '92 / PolyGram

CONVERSATIONALIZE
CD ______ CBAK 4029
Baktabak / Feb '94 / Arabesque

HIGH 'N' DRY
High 'n' dry (Saturday night) / You got me runnin' / Let it go / Another hit and run / Lady strange / On through the night / Mirror mirror (look into my eyes) / No, no, no / Bringin' on the heartbreak / Switch 625
CD ______ 8188362
Bludgeon Riffola / Jan '89 / PolyGram

HYSTERIA
Women / Rocket / Animal / Love bites / Pour some sugar on me / Armageddon it / Gods of war / Don't shoot shotgun / Run riot / Hysteria / Excitable / Love and affection
CD ______ 8306752
Bludgeon Riffola / '87 / PolyGram

INTERVIEW DISC
CD ______ SAM 7020
Sound & Media / Nov '96 / Sound & Media

ON THROUGH THE NIGHT
Answer to the master / Hello America / It could be you / It don't matter / Overture / Rock brigade / Rocks off / Satellite / Sorrow is a woman / When the walls came tumblin' down
CD ______ 8225332
Bludgeon Riffola / Jan '89 / PolyGram

PYROMANIA
Rock rock (til you drop) / Photograph / Stagefright / Too late for love / Die hard the hunter / Foolin' / Rock of ages / Comin' under fire / Action not words / Billy's got a gun
CD ______ 8103082
Bludgeon Riffola / '88 / PolyGram

RETRO ACTIVE
CD ______ 5183052
Bludgeon Riffola / Oct '93 / PolyGram

SLANG
Truth / Turn to dust / Slang / All I want is everything / Breathe a sigh / Deliver me / Gift of flesh / Blood runs cold / Where does love go when it dies / Pearl of Euphoria
CD ______ 5324862
Bludgeon Riffola / May '96 / PolyGram

SLANG
Truth / Turn to dust / Slang / All I want is everything / Work it out / Breathe a sigh / Deliver me / Gift of flesh / Blood runs cold / Where does love go when it dies / Pearl of Euphoria / Armageddon it / Two steps behind / From the inside / Animal / When love and hate collide / Pour some sugar on me
CD Set ______ 5324932
Bludgeon Riffola / May '96 / PolyGram

TELLTALES (Interview Disc)
CD ______ TELL 11
Network / Jun '97 / Total/BMG

VAULT
Pour some sugar on me / Photograph / Love bites / Let's get rocked / Two steps behind / Animal / Heaven is / Rocket / When love and hate collide / Action / Make love like a man / Armageddon it / Have you ever needed someone so bad / Rock of ages / Hysteria / Bringin' on the heartbreak
CD ______ 5286562
CD Set ______ 5286572
Bludgeon Riffola / Oct '95 / PolyGram

Defecation

PURITY DILUTION
CD ______ NB 018CD
Nuclear Blast / Nov '92 / Plastic Head

Defects

DEFECTIVE BREAKDOWN
CD ______ AHOY 29
Captain Oi / Dec '94 / Plastic Head

Definition Of Sound

EXPERIENCE
Boom boom / Pass the vibes / Lucy / Will you love me / Experience / Here comes the sun / Feels like heaven / Child / Take me on / Mama's not coming home / Wishes in the wind
CD ______ 5287402
Fontana / Feb '96 / PolyGram

LICK, THE
Looking good / Can I get over / What are you under / Together / Move your body / She hangs out / Sunshine and rain / Too young to know / Travelling man / Cry
CD CIRCD 24
Circa / Sep '92 / EMI

LOVE AND LIFE
When a lion awakens / Now is tomorrow / Passion and pain / Wear you love like heaven / Reality / Rise like the sun / What's going on / Dream girl / Change / Blues / Moira Jane's cafe / Won / City lights / Time is running out
CD CIRCD 14
Circa / Jun '91 / EMI

Defleshed

MA BELLE SCALPELLE
CD IR 009CD
Invasion / Apr '95 / Plastic Head

DeFrancesco, Joey

STREET OF DREAMS, THE
CD BIGMO 20252E
Big Mo / Nov '95 / ADA / Direct

Defunkt

AVOID THE FUNK (Defunkt Anthology)
CD HNCD 1320
Hannibal / May '89 / ADA / Vital

CRISIS
CD EMY 1352
Enemy / Mar '92 / Grapevine/PolyGram

CUM FUNKY
CD EMY 1402
CD Set EMY 1442
Enemy / Nov '94 / Grapevine/PolyGram

DEFUNKT SPECIAL EDITION (Live Tribute To Muddy Waters & Jimi Hendrix)
CD EMY 1482
Enemy / Nov '94 / Grapevine/PolyGram

LIVE AND REUNIFIED
CD EMY 1452
Enemy / Nov '94 / Grapevine/PolyGram

LIVE AT THE KNITTING FACTORY
CD KFWCD 104
Knitting Factory / Nov '94 / Cargo / Plastic Head

LIVE AT THE KNITTING FACTORY, NYC
CD Set EMY 122
Enemy / Sep '91 / Grapevine/PolyGram

Deiana, Gesuino

PINTADERAS (Made In Sardinia)
Tutu tutu / Ateras ninnas / Arvekes et tenores / Abu et Mont' Arbu / Sole de Oriente / Istorias de intro et fora / Andhendhe a benalonga / Arbeskidas / Sonos a de notte / Pintaderas / Zocculas de prata / Terra de 'entos / Carignos de luna / Biddh' 'e babois / Uas / Cuccos et arteros sonos / Froredillu / Turulu 'e monachus / In sa rena et in su mar-ea
CD WSCD 007
Womad Select / May '97 / ADA / Direct

Deicide

AMON : FEASTING THE BEAST
Lunatic of God's creation / Sacrificial suicide / Crucifixation / Carnage in the temple of the damned / Dead by dawn / Blasphereion / Feasting the beast / Day of darkness / Oblivious to nothing
CD RR 91112
Roadrunner / Feb '93 / PolyGram

DEICIDE
Lunatic of God's creation / Oblivious to evil / Blasphereion / Carnage in the temple of the damned / Day of darkness / Sacrificial suicide / Dead by dawn / Deicide / Mephistopheles / Crucifixion
CD RO 93812
Roadracer / Mar '96 / PolyGram

LEGION
CD RC 91922
Roadrunner / Mar '96 / PolyGram

ONCE UPON THE CROSS
CD RR 89492
Roadrunner / May '95 / PolyGram

Deighton Family

ROLLING HOME
I love you because / I can see clearly now / Save the last dance for me / Road to Newcastle / Green rolling hills of West Virginia / Reuben's train / Under the Boardwalk / I forgot to remember to forget / When I get home / Leather britches / Rollin' home / Has he got a friend / Gilbert Clancy's reel
CD GLCD 1116
Green Linnet / '92 / ADA / CM / Direct / Highlander / Roots

Deighton, Matt

VILLAGER
CD FOCUSCD 1
Focus / Jun '95 / Pinnacle

Deine Lakaien

ACOUSTIC
CD EFA 155882
Gymnastic / Sep '95 / SRD

DARK STAR TOUR '92
CD EFA 15567
Gymnastic / Apr '93 / SRD

WINTER FISH TESTOSTERONE
CD EFA 155952
Gymnastic / Mar '96 / SRD

Deinonychus

SILENCE OF DECEMBER, THE
Black sun / I, ruler of paradise in black / Silencer of December / Final affliction of Xafan / Shining blaze over darkland / Under the autumn tree / Here lies my kingdom / My travels through the midnight sky / Red is my blood, cold is my heart / Bizarre landscape
CD NIHIL 5CD
Cacophonous / Jun '97 / Plastic Head / RTM/Disc

WEEPING OF A THOUSAND YEARS
CD NIHIL 13CD
Cacophonous / Jul '96 / Plastic Head / RTM/Disc

Deiseal

LONG LONG NOTE, THE
Shores of loch Ghamhna / Si beag si mor / Raindrops/The first of May / My love I miss her so / Long (long) note / Soporific/The rights of man / Mna na hEireann / Stranger at the gate/Boston blues / Lord inchiquin / Lakeside
CD SCD 193
Starc / Jan '94 / ADA / Direct

SUNSHINE DANCE
CD SCCD 596
Starc / Jun '96 / ADA / Direct

Deity Guns

100M
CD RIK 001CD
Semantic / Feb '94 / Plastic Head

TRANS LINES APPOINTMENT
CD ABBCD 047
Big Cat / May '93 / 3mv/Pinnacle

Dekker, Desmond

ACTION (Dekker, Desmond & The Aces)
Mother pepper / Don't blame me / Unity / 007 / You're got your troubles / Personal posession / It pays / Your generation / Mother long tongue / Sabotage / Unforgettable / Mother young gal / Keep a cool head / Jump a ting a ling / Gimme gimme / Fu manchu
CD HSCD 1001
Hot Shot / Oct '96 / Grapevine/PolyGram / Jet Star / THE / TKO Magnum
CD 444012
Beverly / Mar '97 / Jet Star

BLACK & DEKKER
Israelites / Lickin' stick / It mek / Please don't bend / Many rivers to cross / Hippo / 007 / Workout / Problems / Rude boy train / Pickney girl / Why fight
CD STIFFCD 11
Disky / Jan '94 / Disky / THE

BLACK & DEKKER/COMPASS POINT
Israelites / Lickin' stick / It mek / Please don't bend / Many rivers to cross / Hippo / 007 / Workout / Problems / Rude boy train / Pickney gal / Why fight / I'll get by / Moving on / We can and shall / Hurt so bad / Isabella / Come back to me / Cindy / I do believe/My destiny / Big headed / That's my woman / Allamanna
CD DOJOCD 77
Dojo / Feb '94 / Disc

CRUCIAL CUTS - BEST OF DESMOND DEKKER
CD MCCD 115
Music Club / Jun '93 / Disc / THE

DESMOND DEKKER ARCHIVE
007 / Please don't bend / Go tell my people / Shing a ling / Mother nature / Yaketty yak / When I'm cold / First time for a long time / It pays / Israelites / It mek / Life, hope and faith / Where did it go / What will you gain / Look what they're doing to me / You can get it if you really want / Trample / Little darling / Warlock / Baby come back
CD RMCD 208
Rialto / Sep '96 / Disc / Total/BMG

FIRST TIME FOR A LONG TIME
Hanging tree / Fu man chu / Generosity / Pickney gal / Hippopotamus / Licking stick / Perserverance / Where did it go (the song we used to sing) / Get up little Suzie / It gotta be so / First time for a long time / What will you gain / Little darling / My reward / Please don't bend / Stop the wedding / Go and tell my people / Look what you're doing to me / Life, hope and faith / Trample / Reggae recipe / Mother nature / Father Noah / Life of opportunity / When I'm cold / Yakety yak
CD CDTRL 379
Trojan / May '97 / Direct / Jet Star

GREATEST HITS
You can get it if you really want it / Archie wah wah / Mother nature / Where did it go / More you live / What will you gain / Look what they're doing to me / Israelites / Reggae recipe / Licking stick / Pickney gal / It mek / Life of opportunity / I believe / My reward / 007
CD QED 123
Tring / Nov '96 / Tring

INTENSIFIED (Dekker, Desmond & The Aces)
CD 0444022
Rhino / Mar '97 / Grapevine/PolyGram / Jet Star

ISRAELITES
Israelites / Beware / Everybody join hands / It mek / Sing a little song / Busted lad / My world is blue / Mother nature / Money and friends / No place like home
CD CDTRO 9104
Trojan / Aug '92 / Direct / Jet Star

ISRAELITES
CD 12361
Laserlight / May '94 / Target/BMG

ISRAELITES, THE
CD MACCD 233
Autograph / Aug '96 / BMG

KING OF KINGS (Dekker, Desmond & The Specials)
CD CDTRL 324
Trojan / Mar '94 / Direct / Jet Star

KING OF SKA
CD CDTRL 292
Trojan / Mar '94 / Direct / Jet Star

MOVING ON
CD CDTRL 369
Trojan / Aug '96 / Direct / Jet Star

MUSIC LIKE DIRT
King of Ska / It's a shame / Rudie got soul / Rude boy train / Mother's young gal / Sweet music / You've got your troubles / Keep a cool head / Mother long tongue / Personal possession / Bongo gal / Don't blame me / Hey Grandma / Music like dirt / Nincompoop / It mek / Problems / Coconut water
CD CDTRL 301
Trojan / Mar '94 / Direct / Jet Star

OFFICIAL LIVE AND RARE (Dekker, Desmond & The Aces)
CD Set CDTRD 404
Trojan / Nov '89 / Direct / Jet Star

ORIGINAL REGGAE HITSOUND, THE (Dekker, Desmond & The Aces)
007 / Get up, Edina / Beautiful and dangerous / Shing a ling / Pretty Africa / Wise man / Sabotage / Unity / It pays / Israelites / It mek / Warlock / Archie wah wah / Pickney girl / Reggae recipe / You can get it if you really want / Hippopotamus song / Lickin' stick / More you live
CD CDTRL 226
Trojan / Mar '94 / Direct / Jet Star

VOICE OF SKA (Dekker, Desmond & The Aces)
007 / Wise man / Pickney gal / It mek / Unity / Music like dirt / Mother long tongue / Warlock / Licking stick / Sweet music / Personal possession / Hippopotamus / Beautiful and dangerous / Get up Edina / Sabotage / Rude boy train
CD EMPRCD 594
Emporio / Oct '95 / Disc

Del Amitri

CHANGE EVERYTHING
CD 3953852
A&M / Jun '92 / PolyGram

DEL AMITRI
Heard through a wall / Hammering heart / Former owner / Sticks and stones girl / Deceive yourself (in ignorant heaven) / I was here / Crows in a wheatfield / Keepers / Ceasefire / Breaking bread
CD CCD 1499
Chrysalis / Dec '90 / EMI

SOME OTHER SUCKER'S PARADE
Not where it's at / Some other sucker's parade / Won't make it better / What I think she sees / Medicine / High times / Mother nature's writing / No family man / Cruel light of day / Funny way to win / Through all that nothing / Life is full / Lucky guy / Make it always be too late
CD 5407052
A&M / Jun '97 / PolyGram

TWISTED
Food for songs / Start with me / Here and now / One thing left to do / Tell her this / Being somebody else / Roll to me / Crashing down / It might as well be you / Never enough / It's never too late to be alone / Driving with the brakes on
CD 5403962
A&M / Aug '95 / PolyGram

WAKING HOURS
Kiss this thing goodbye / Opposite view / Move away Jimmy Blue / Stone cold sober / You're gone / When I want you / This side of the morning / Empty / Hatful of rain / Nothing ever happens
CD 3970102
A&M / Apr '95 / PolyGram

Del Ferro, Mike

LIVE (Del Ferro, Mike & Frank Vaganee Group)
To John / Feels like summer / I don't know why / Sal's delight / Waltz three / Jump'n joy / Seven dwarfs / Due duel / Mooch / Little thing / Lanotas circle
CD AL 73057
A / Nov '96 / Cadillac / Direct

Del Gastor, Paco

FLAMENCO DE LA FRONTERA
CD NI 5352
Nimbus / Oct '94 / Nimbus

Del Monte, Dino

ENTRE LOS TIEMPOS
CD 21096CD
Sonifolk / Nov '96 / ADA / CM

Del Rey, Teisco

MANY MOODS OF TEISCO DEL REY
CD UPSTART 007
Upstart / Jul '94 / ADA / Direct

PLAY MUSIC FOR LOVERS
CD UPSTART 030
Upstart / Feb '96 / ADA / Direct

Del Tha Funky Homosapien

I WISH MY BROTHER GEORGE WAS HERE
What is a booty / Mistadobalina / Wacky world of rapid transit / Pissin' on your steps / Dark skin girls / Money for sex / Ahonetwo, ahonetwo / Prelude / Dr. Bombay / Sunny meadowz / Sleepin' on my couch / Hoodz come in dozens / Same old thing / Ya lil crumbsnatchers
CD 7559611332
Elektra / Dec '91 / Warner Music

Del-Vikings

BEST OF THE DEL-VIKINGS, THE (The Mercury Years)
Cool shake / Jitterbug Mary / Come along with me / Somewhere over the rainbow / Voodoo man / Can't wait / Sunday / Kind of love / I'm sitting on top of the world / Oh baby (I need your kisses) / Big beat / I'm spinning / When I come home / Nobody's kisses but yours / Meeting of the eyes / Friendly eyes / Oh tonight / That's why (I love you so) / You are invited / Bells / Heaven on Earth / Flat tyre
CD 5527532
Spectrum / Feb '97 / PolyGram

COME GO WITH ME
Come go with me / Don't be a fool / In the still of the night / Yours / I'm spinning / Over the rainbow / White cliffs of Dover
CD FLYCD 34
Flyright / Apr '91 / Hot Shot / Jazz Music / Wellard

DEL-VIKINGS VOL.2
CD FLYCD 53
Flyright / Nov '92 / Hot Shot / Jazz Music / Wellard

Delafose, Geno

FRENCH ROCKIN' BOOGIE
CD ROUCD 2131
Rounder / Aug '94 / ADA / CM / Direct

Delafose, John

BLUES STAY AWAY FROM ME (Delafose, John & The Eunice Playboys)
CD ROUCD 2121
Rounder / Jan '94 / ADA / CM / Direct

JOE PETE GOT TWO WOMEN
CD ARHCD 335
Arhoolie / Apr '95 / ADA / Cadillac / Direct

LIVE AT RICHARD'S ZYDECO DANCE HALL VOL.2 (Delafose, John & The Eunice Playboys)
CD ROUCD 2070
Rounder / '88 / ADA / CM / Direct

Delagado, Luis

AL ANDALUS
CD 21042CD
Sonifolk / Jun '94 / ADA / CM

Delakian, Michel

BIARRITZ
CD BBRC 9107
Big Blue / Dec '91 / Harmonia Mundi

Delaney & Bonnie

ACCEPT NO SUBSTITUTE
Get ourselves together / Someday / Ghetto / When the battle is over / Dirty old man / Love me a little bit longer / I can't take it much longer / Do right woman, do right man / Soldiers of the cross / Gift of love
CD CDTB 050
Thunderbolt / Feb '88 / TKO Magnum

ON TOUR WITH ERIC CLAPTON (Delaney & Bonnie/Friends)
Things get better / Poor Elijah / Only you know and I know / I don't want to discuss it / That's what my man is for / Where there's a will / Comin' home / Little Richard medley: *Clapton, Eric*
CD _______________ 7567903972
Atlantic / Feb '92 / Warner Music

Delano, Peter

BITE OF THE APPLE
Spontaneous / Heartfelt / Distant stage / Reflected spirit / Sweetest sounds / Sunrise remembered / Improvisation #2 blues / On the spot / Demonic disorder / Castellaras
CD _______________ 5218692
Verve / Jul '94 / PolyGram

PETER DELANO
Elephants in the sky / Experiencing change / Gesticulations / Entranced / Miles' mode / Piano improvisation / I remember Clifford / Say Uncle / Central Park waltz / Anicca / Autumn leaves / Reminiscence
CD _______________ 5196022
Verve / Mar '94 / PolyGram

Delavier, Katrien

IRISH HARP, THE
CD _______________ PS 65095
PlayaSound / Sep '92 / ADA / Harmonia Mundi

Delerium

FACES FORMS AND ILLUSIONS
CD _______________ DCD 9008
Dossier / May '89 / Cargo / SRD

KARMA (2CD Set)
CD _______________ 067003011327
CD Set _______________ 067003011421
Delerium / Apr '97 / Cargo / Pinnacle / Vital

MORPHEUS
CD _______________ DCD 9010
Dossier / '89 / Cargo / SRD

SEMANTIC SPACES
CD _______________ W 230092
Nettwerk / Apr '95 / Greyhound / Pinnacle / Vital

SPHERE
CD _______________ EFA 084532
Dossier / Feb '94 / Cargo / SRD

SPHERES VOL.2
CD _______________ EFA 08460 2
Dossier / Sep '94 / Cargo / SRD

SYROPHENIKAN
CD _______________ DCD 9015
Dossier / '89 / Cargo / SRD

Delevantes

LONG ABOUT THAT TIME
CD _______________ ROUCD 9041
Rounder / May '95 / ADA / CM / Direct
CD _______________ CRCDM 6
CRS / Sep '96 / ADA / Direct / Jet Star

Delgado, Andre

ESSENTIAL PANPIPES
CD _______________ SPLCD 003
Sloane / Apr '96 / Grapevine/PolyGram

Delgado, Isaac

CON GANAS
CD _______________ 74321342772
Milan / Jun '96 / Conifer/BMG / Silva Screen

EL CHEVERE DE LA SALAS/EL CABELLERO DEL SON (Delgado, Isaac & Adalberto Alvarez)
CD _______________ 74321331192
Milan / May '96 / Conifer/BMG / Silva Screen

Delgado, Junior

DANCE A DUB
Dance a dub / Hooligan stew / Mr. Dub / Crack a dub / Kidnapped on a subway / Ups / Downs / Enter / Torture / Herb eye
CD _______________ ABB 133CD
Big Cat / Jun '97 / 3mv/Pinnacle

FREEDOM HAS IT'S PRICE
CD _______________ IMCD 0016
Incredible Music / Apr '97 / Jet Star / SRD

MR. FIXIT
CD _______________ RNCD 2055
Rhino / May '94 / Grapevine/PolyGram / Jet Star

SISTERS AND BROTHERS
Row fisherman row / Caution / Warning / Effort / Hold me tighter / She's gonna marry me / Easy girl / Live like a hermit / My miss world / Sisters and brothers
CD _______________ CDBM 027
Blue Moon / Nov '96 / Cadillac / Discovery / Greensleeves / Jazz Music / Jet Star / TKO Magnum

TREASURE FOUND VOL.1
CD _______________ IMCD 001
Incredible Music / Mar '95 / Jet Star / SRD

TREASURE FOUND VOL.2 (More Treasure Found)
CD _______________ IMCD 0014
Incredible Music / Apr '97 / Jet Star / SRD

Delgados

DOMESTIQUES
CD _______________ CHEM 10CD
Chemikal Underground / Nov '96 / SRD

Delicatessen

HUSTLE INTO BED
CD _______________ STFCD 2
Starfish / Aug '96 / Pinnacle

SKIN TOUCHING WATER
I'm just alive / CF Kane / Zebra/Monkey/Liar / Red, blue and green / Watercress / Classic adventure / Appeased / Chomsky / You cut my throat, I'll cut yours / Sick of flying saucers / Smiling you're stupid / Inviting both sisters out to dinner / Advice / Love's liquid / Froth / If she was anybody else
CD _______________ STFCD 001X
Starfish / May '95 / Pinnacle

Delico, Stephane

AQUARELLES
CD _______________ ED 13024CD
L'Empreinte Digitale / Jul '95 / ADA / Harmonia Mundi

Delinquent Habits

DELINQUENT HABITS
Tres delinquentes / Lower Eastside / Juvy / What it be like / I'm addicted / Realm / SALT (shit ain't like that) / Good times / Break 'em off / What's real iz real / If you want some / Another fix / Underground connection / When the stakes are high
CD _______________ 07863669292
Loud / Nov '96 / BMG

Delirious

KING OF FOOLS
Sanctify / Deeper / Revival town / All the way / August 30th / Promise / King or cripple / Hands of kindness / White ribbon day / King of fools / History maker / What a friend I've found
CD _______________ FURYCD 1
Furious / Jun '97 / Total/Pinnacle

Dello, Pete

INTO YOUR EARS...PLUS (Dello, Pete & Friends)
It's what you've got / There's nothing that I can do for you / I'm a gambler / Harry the earwig / Do I still figure in your life / Uptight Basil / Taking the heart out of love / Here me only / On a time said Sylvie / Good song / It's the way / Go away / Arise Sir Henry / Madam Chairman (of the committee)
CD _______________ SEECD 257
See For Miles/C5 / Sep '89 / Pinnacle

Dells

ON THEIR CORNER
Oh what a night / Wear it on our face / Love is so simple / I can sing a rainbow/Love is blue / O-O, I love you / There is / Nadine / Love we had / Run for cover / Stay in my corner / Give your baby a standing ovation / Always together / Open up my heart / I miss you / Since I found you / My pretending days are over / Learning to love you was easy / I wish it was me you loved
CD _______________ MCD 09333
Chess/MCA / Apr '97 / BMG / New Note/ BMG

Delmar, Elaine

'S WONDERFUL
Some of my best friends / Touch of your lips / In a sentimental mood / 'S Wonderful / Stardust / I did it all for you / Little girl blue / Carioca / They can't take that away from me / We could be flying / They say it's wonderful / Ol' man river / There's a small hotel / Joy / My foolish heart / Like a lover / Love for sale
CD _______________ JHRCD 027
Ronnie Scott's Jazz House / Sep '91 / Cadillac / Jazz Music / New Note/Pinnacle / TKO Magnum

Delmonas

DELMONAS/DELMONAS 5
Dr. Goldfoot / Heard about him / Why don't you smile now / Black elk speaks / Hound dog / Delmona / I feel like giving in / Keep your big mouth shut / When I want you / Black Ludella / Your love / Don't fall in love (every single time) / Jealousy / Jealousy (French version) / That boy of mine / Can't sit down / Kiss me honey / I've got everything I need / Uncle Willy / Farmer John / You did him wrong / Dangerous charms / Long drop / I feel alright
CD _______________ ASKCD 032
Vinyl Japan / Oct '93 / Plastic Head / Vinyl Japan

Delmore Brothers

FREIGHT TRAIN BOOGIE
Blues stay away from me / Freight train boogie / Trouble ain't nothin' but the blues / Boogie woogie baby / Rounder's blues / Mobile boogie / Used car blues / Pan American blues / Pan American boogie / Field hand man / Brown's ferry blues / Peach tree street boogie / Blues you never lose / Steamboat boogie / Muddy water / Sand mountain blues / Hillbilly boogie / You can't do wrong and get by / Kentucky Mountain / Weary day / Take it to the Captain
CD _______________ CDCHD 455
Ace / Aug '93 / Pinnacle

Delphines

DELPHINES
CD _______________ DEL 100CD
Abstract / Jun '97 / Cargo / Pinnacle / Total/BMG

Delphium

HOW CAN YOU HIDE FROM WHAT NEVER GOES AWAY
CD _______________ OUT 003CD
Outsider / Jul '97 / Cargo / Shellshock/ Disc

Delray, Leon

I'M STILL WAITIN'
All the lonely girls / Please don't ask me why / Macho man / I'm not in love / My love for you / Day by day / Good mornin' / I wanna be free / Unfree / I'm still waiting (for your call) / I wonder will we ever learn / I wanna be free (reprise)
CD _______________ 101S 8770572
101 South / Nov '93 / New Note/Pinnacle

Delta 72

R & B OF MEMBERSHIP, THE
CD _______________ TG 172CD
Touch & Go / Jul '96 / SRD

SOUL OF A NEW MACHINE, THE
CD _______________ TG 182CD
Touch & Go / Aug '97 / SRD

Delta 9

ALPHA DECAY
CD _______________ VC 109CD
Vinyl Communication / Mar '97 / Cargo / Greyhound / Plastic Head

DISCO INFERNO
Welcome to hell / Drox / In the void / Watch yer back / Son of a bitch / Headstrong / Oblivion / Atomizer / Yellow fever / Abomination / Only way out / Trained to hate and destroy / Real hardcore / 246 / Sine / Headstrong / Infidel / Mortified
CD _______________ MOSH 165CD
Earache / Jan '97 / Vital

NO BLUFF
CD _______________ 503632
Declic / Apr '95 / Jet Star

Delta Accordion Band

50 PARTY FAVOURITES
It's a sin to tell a lie / Ain't she sweet / I want to be happy / Baby face / My blue heaven / Your cheatin' heart / From a Jack to a King / Walk on by / I love you because / Take these chains from my heart / You are my sunshine / Blackpool belle / She'll be coming round the mountain / Down by the riverside / When the saints go marching in / Whiskey in the jar / Muirsheen Durkin / Holy ground / Mountain dew / I'll tell me Ma / She's a lassie from Lancashire / I belong to Glasgow / On top of Old Smokey / In my Liverpool home / Wild colonial boy / Yellow rose of Texas / Little brown jug / Happy wanderer / Marie's wedding / Scotland the brave / Kiss me goodnight Sergeant Major / We're gonna hang out the washing on the Siegfried Line / Run rabbit run / Oh Johnny, oh Johnny oh / Hey little hen / Daisy bell / Home on the range / Cockles and mussels / Goodnight Irene / My Bonnie lies over the ocean / Rothesay / Campbeltown Loch / Campbells are coming / Coming through the rye / Road to the Isles / Lily of Laguna / By the light of the silvery moon / Barefoot days / Maybe it's because I'm a Londoner / Roll me over
CD _______________ CD 6058
Music / Feb '97 / Target/BMG

Delta Four

MEMORIES OF NEW ORLEANS 1991-1992
CD _______________ PKCD 014
PEK / Jul '96 / Cadillac / Jazz Music / Wellard

Delta Of Venus

NEUTRAL A
CD _______________ SR 1006
Scout / Jan '96 / Koch

Delta Plan

INDELIBLE
CD _______________ NZCD 055
Nova Zembla / Jun '96 / Plastic Head

Delta Rhythm Boys

DRY BONES
CD _______________ MCCD 028
Magnum America / Nov '96 / TKO Magnum

Deltas

BOOGIE DISEASE
CD _______________ NERDCD 002
Nervous / Jun '95 / Nervous / TKO Magnum

LIVE
Raging sea / You can't judge a book by the cover / As you like it / Tuffer than tuff / Boogie disease / Gimme the drugs / Cigarette / Cool off baby / Teenage ball / Long black train / Honky tonk women / Nine below zero / I got you / How come you do me / Kokomo
CD _______________ JE 256
Visionary/Jettisoundz / Mar '93 / Cargo / Pinnacle / RTM/Disc / THE

TUFFER THAN TUFF LIVE
CD _______________ LOMACD 34
Loma / Nov '94 / BMG

Deltones

NANA CHOC CHOC IN PARIS
CD _______________ PHZCD 31
Unicorn / Jan '89 / Plastic Head

Deluigi, Silvana

TANGOS
CD _______________ SM 16132
Wergo / Jan '96 / ADA / Cadillac / Harmonia Mundi

TANGUERA - WOMAN IN TANGO
CD _______________ SM 15032
Wergo / Nov '92 / ADA / Cadillac / Harmonia Mundi

Demasse, Seleshe

SONGS FROM ETHIOPIA
CD _______________ SM 15162
Wergo / Nov '93 / ADA / Cadillac / Harmonia Mundi

Dembo, Konte

BAATOTO
CD _______________ WWCD 05
World / Dec '88 / Grapevine/PolyGram

DeMent, Iris

INFAMOUS ANGEL
Let the mystery be / These hills / Hotter than mojave in my heart / When love was young / Our town / Fifty miles of elbow room / Infamous angel / Sweet forgivness / After you've gone / Mama's opry / Higher ground
CD _______________ 9362452382
Warner Bros. / May '93 / Warner Music

MY LIFE
Sweet is the melody / You've done nothing wrong / Calling for you / Childhood memories / No time to cry / Troublesome waters / Mom and Dad's waltz / Easy's getting harder every day / Shores of Jordan / My life
CD _______________ 9362454932
Warner Bros. / Mar '94 / Warner Music

WAY I SHOULD, THE
CD _______________ 9362461882
Warner Bros. / Oct '96 / Warner Music

Demented Are Go

BEST OF DEMENTED ARE GO, THE
Pervy in the park / Busty hymen / Holy hack jack / Pickled and preserved / Transvestite blues / PVC chair / Nuke mutants / Satan's rejects / Cripple in the woods / Call of the wired / Surf ride to oblivion / Shadow crypt / Human slug / Sick spasmoid / Country woman / One shrp knife / Brain damaged chile / Flight 103
CD _______________ DOJOCD 125
Dojo / May '93 / Disc

IN SICKNESS AND IN HEALTH/KICKED OUT OF HELL
Be bop a lula / Pervy in the park / (I was born on a) Busted hymen / Holy hack Jack / Frenzied beat / Pickled and preserved / Crazy horses / Transvestite blues / Rubber buccaneer / Vibrate / Rubber love / Nuke mutants / PVC chair / Don't go into the woods / Satan's rejects / Human slug / Cripple in the woods / Decomposition / Cast iron arm / Call of the wired / Rubber plimsoles / Shadow crypt / Surf ride to oblivion / Old black Joe / Sick spasmoid / Vietnam / Jet tune boogie
CD _______________ LOMACD 15
Loma / Feb '94 / BMG

LIVE AT THE KLUB FOOT APRIL '87
CD _______ DOJOCD 23
Dojo / Jun '94 / Disc

TANGENITAL MADNESS
CD _______ DAGCD 1
Fury / Apr '95 / Nervous / TKO Magnum

WHO PUT GRANDMA UNDER THE STAIRS
CD _______ RRCD 218
Receiver / May '96 / Grapevine/PolyGram

Demented Ted

PROMISE IMPURE
Existance lies beneath / Despair / Psychopathology / Incisions / Liquid remains / Geneticide / Between two eternities / Forgotten
CD _______ CDVEST 2
Bulletproof / Mar '94 / Pinnacle

Demolition 23

DEMOLITION 23
CD _______ CDMFN 176
Music For Nations / Oct '94 / Pinnacle

Demolition Doll Rods

TASTY
CD _______ ITR 048CD
In The Red / Jun '97 / Cargo / Greyhound

Demolition Hammer

EPIDEMIC OF VIOLENCE
CD _______ CM 97282
Century Media / Sep '94 / Plastic Head

TIMEBOMB
CD _______ CM 770712
Century Media / Aug '94 / Plastic Head

TORTURED EXISTENCE
CD _______ 0897132
Century Media / Sep '90 / Plastic Head

Demon

BLOW OUT
CD _______ SONICCD 11
Sonic / May '92 / Total/BMG

BRITISH STANDARD APPROVED
CD _______ SONICCD 4
Sonic / Sep '90 / Total/BMG

ONE HELLUVA NIGHT (Live In West Germany)
CD Set _______ DEMONCD 1
Sonic / Aug '90 / Total/BMG

PLAGUE, THE
Plague / Nowhere to run / Fever in the city / Blackheath / Writings on the wall / Only sane man / Step to far
CD _______ HTDCD 36
HTD / Jul '95 / CM / Pinnacle

TAKING THE WORLD BY STORM
Commercial dynamite / Taking the world by storm / Life brigade / Remembrance day / What do you think about hell / Blue skies in Red Square / Time has come
CD _______ HTDCD 32
HTD / Mar '95 / CM / Pinnacle

Demone, Gitane

DEMONIX (Demone, Gitane & Marc Ickx)
CD _______ CLP 9816
Cleopatra / Oct '96 / Cargo / Greyhound / Plastic Head / RTM/Disc / SRD

LOVE FOR SALE
CD _______ CD 004
Dark Vinyl / Jan '94 / Plastic Head / World Serpent

Demoniac

PREPARE FOR WAR
CD _______ EOR 003CD
Osmose / Apr '95 / Plastic Head

STORMBLADE
CD _______ EOR 005CD
Evil Omen / May '97 / Plastic Head

Dempsey, Little Jimmy

GUITAR MUSIC
CD _______ CNCD 5937
Disky / Jun '92 / Disky / THE

Dempsey, Peter

LOVE'S GARDEN OF ROSES
It's only a tiny garden / Zinetta / Go lovely Rose / E'en as a lovely flower / Ah, may the red rose live alway / In the garden of your heart / Vucchella / English rose / Child's song / Roses of Picardy / Raindrop kissed a rose / Yearning / Thank God for a garden / Now sleeps the crimson petal / To a wild rose / Old flagged path / Mighty like a rose / Love sends a little gift of roses / Thora / Do you know my garden / Rose of Tralee / There's a bower of roses by Bendemmer's stream / Garden in the rain / Rose still blooms in Picardy / Love's garden of roses
CD _______ MDMCD 005
Moidart / May '96 / Conifer/BMG

Den Fule

LUGUMLEIK
Tuss ola / Nordafjells / Pal karls vals / Raddascottis / Lugumleik / Dickapolskan / Langdans / Vallat / Tre strommingar / Slangpolska / Kopmanpolska / Modus mats / Pslam / Nordic wolf
CD _______ XOUCD 104
Xource / May '97 / ADA / Direct

SKALV
Skalv / Snail / Skagget / Fly med mig / Gammel husin / Den bla slatten / Ormsla / Det ar jag / Munnharpevals / Offerklippans sang / Koptespakte / Jagaren och algen / Rammeslatten / Paki / Storebackepolskan / Vinge
CD _______ XOUCD 109
Xource / May '97 / ADA / Direct

Denayer, Oscar

ACCORDION FAVOURITES
CD _______ HRCD 8056
Disky / Sep '94 / Disky / THE

Denim

DENIM ON ICE
Great pub rock revival / It fell off the back of a lorry / Romeo Jones is in love again / Bumburger / Supermodels / Shut up Sidney / Mrs. Mills / Best song in the world / Synthesizers in the rain / Job centre / Council house / Glue and smack / Jane Suck died in 77 / Grandad's false teeth / Silly rabbit / Don't bite too much out of the apple / Myriad of hoops / Denim on ice
CD _______ ECHCD 008
Echo / Feb '96 / EMI / Vital

NOVELTY ROCK
New potatoes / On a chicory tip / Robin's nest / Internet curtains / Snake bite / Ape hangers / Great grape ape hangers / Ankle tattoos / Tampax advert / Supermarket / Running in the city / I will cry at Christmas
CD _______ ADISCCD 001
Premier/EMI / Jan '97 / EMI

Dênio, Amy

BIRTHING CHAIR BLUES
CD _______ KFWCD 111
Knitting Factory / Nov '94 / Cargo / Plastic Head

Denison/Kimball Trio

NEUTRONS
CD _______ QS 48CD
Quarter Stick / Aug '97 / Cargo / SRD

SOUL MACHINE
CD _______ GR 22CD
Skingraft / May '95 / SRD

WALLS IN THE CITY
CD _______ GR 16CD
Skingraft / Oct '94 / SRD

Deniz Tek

BAD ROAD
CD _______ CITCD 917
Citadel / Jul '97 / Greyhound

Denman, John

ENGLAND - NEW ENGLAND (Denman, John & Paula Fan)
CD _______ BML 002
British Music / Jan '96 / Forties Recording Company

SPLENDID BRITISH CLARINET WORKS (Denman, John & Paula Fan)
CD _______ BML 009
British Music / Jan '96 / Forties Recording Company

Dennehy, Tim

WINTER'S TEAR, A (Traditional & Original Songs Of Love, Loss & Longing)
CD _______ CICD 087
Clo Iar-Chonnachta / Dec '93 / CM

Dennerlein, Barbara

BARBARA DENNERLEIN
CD _______ CD 250964
Bebab / Nov '91 / Cadillac / Harmonia Mundi

LIVE ON TOUR (Dennerlein, Barbara, Oscar Klein & Charly Antolini)
CD _______ CD 250965
Bebab / Nov '91 / Cadillac / Harmonia Mundi

Dennis, Cathy

AM I THE KIND OF GIRL
West End pad / Fickle / When dreams turn to dust / Stupid fool / Am I the kinda girl / Homing the rocket / That is why you love me / Waterloo sunset / Don't take my heaven / Date / Crazy ones
CD _______ 5331512
Polydor / Mar '97 / PolyGram

Dennis, Denny

I SING YOU A THOUSAND LOVE SONGS
May I have the next romance with you / I stumbled over love / Time on my hands / Hurry home / Rosita / Sweet is the word for you / I have eyes / If I should fall in love again / Will you remember / Goodnight my love / Sweet someone / Pretty little quaker girl / Thru the courtesy of love / Deep purple / I let a song go out of my heart / Blue Hawaii / South of the border (Down Mexico way) / Always and always / Dearest love / Where are the songs we sung
CD _______ PAR 2026
Parade / Jul '94 / Disc

TRIBUTE, A
Angels never leave heaven / Bird on the wing / Blue skies are just around the corner / Did you ever see a dream walking / Glory of love / Goodbye to summer / Hear my song Violetta / I fall in love with you every day / I was lucky / I wished on the moon / I'll string along with you / If you please / In the middle of a kiss / In the mission by the sea / Just one more chance / Let's call the whole thing off / Let's face the music and dance / Louise / Mexicali Rose / South of the border (Down Mexico way) / Stardust / Two sleepy people: *Dennis, Denny & Vera Lynn* / Way you look tonight / Whispers in the dark / Would you
CD _______ CDAJA 5127
Living Era / '94 / Select

Denny & Dunipace Pipe Band

PLAY SCOTLANDS BEST
Scotland the brave / Rowan tree / Bonnie Galloway / Old rustic bridge / Black Watch polka / Mull of Kintyre / Green hills / When the battle is over / Lynn Shannon's wedding / Dunipace / Danish knife grinder's spring song / Crossing the Minch / AA Cameron's strathspey / Miller of Drone / Donald's wedding / McFarlane's reel / John Wilson / Muckin' o' Geordie's byre / Glendaurel highlanders / Bonnie Dundee / Amazing grace / Day thou gavest Lord is ended / Flower of Scotland / MacKay's farewell to the 71st / Rose among the heather / Fiddlers' joy / De'il among the tailors / Pigeon on the gate / Kate Dalrymple / Going home / Mist covered mountains of home / Morag of Dunvegan / Skye boat song / Dark island / Highland wedding / Susan Macleod / Kate Robertson / Barren rocks of Aden / Highland laddie / Mhairi's wedding / Black bear / Flowers of the forest / Drum salute
CD _______ CD ITV 385
Scotdisc / May '87 / Conifer/BMG / Duncans / Ross

Denny, Martin

EXOTIC SOUNDS OF MARTIN DENNY, THE
CD _______ CREV 039CD
Rev-Ola / Jul '95 / 3mv/Vital

HYPNOTIQUE/EXOTICA 3
CD _______ SCP 9713
Scamp / Mar '97 / Cargo / Greyhound

Denny, Sandy

ATTIC ATTACKS 1972-1984, THE
CD _______ SPDCD 1052
Special Delivery / Jun '95 / ADA / CM / Direct

BEST OF SANDY DENNY, THE
Listen listen / Lady / One way donkey ride / It'll take a long time / Farewell, farewell / Tam Lin / Pond in the stream / Late November / Solo / Sea / Banks of the Nile / Next time around / For shame of doing wrong / Stranger to himself / I'm a dreamer / Who knows where the time goes
CD _______ IMCD 217
Island / Mar '96 / PolyGram

NORTH STAR GRASSMAN AND THE RAVENS
Late November / Blackwater side / Sea Captain / Down in the flood / John the gun / Next time around / Optimist / Let's jump the broomstick / Wretched Wilbur / North star grassman and the ravens / Crazy lady blues
CD _______ IMCD 133
Island / Jun '91 / PolyGram

RENDEZVOUS
I wish I was a fool for you / Gold dust / Candle in the wind / Take me away / One way donkey ride / I'm a dreamer / All our days / Silver threads and golden needles / No more sad refrains
CD _______ HNCD 4423
Hannibal / Jan '87 / ADA / Vital

SANDY
CD _______ IMCD 132
Island / Jun '91 / PolyGram

SANDY AND THE STRAWBS (Denny, Sandy & The Strawbs)
Nothing else will do / Who knows where the time goes / How everyone but Sam was a hypocrite / Sail away to the sea / And you need me / Poor Jimmy Wilson / All I need is you / Tell me what you see in me / I've been my own worst friend / Two weeks last summer / Always on my mind / Stay a while with me / On my way
CD _______ HNCD 1361
Hannibal / Jul '91 / ADA / Vital

WHO KNOWS WHERE THE TIME GOES (3CD Set)
Lady / Nothing more / Memphis Tennessee / Solo / John the gun / Knockin' on Heaven's door / Who knows where the time goes / Music weaver / Take away the load / Sweet Rosemary / Now and then / By the time it gets dark / What is true / Sail away to the sea / Farewell, farewell / Quiet joys of brotherhood / Tamlin / You never wanted me / Autopsy / One more chance / Stranger to himself / Pond and the stream / Banks of the Nile / Two weeks last summer / Late November / Gypsy Davey / Winter winds / Sea / When will I be loved / Listen listen / Next time around / Tomorrow is a long time / One way donkey ride / Burton Town / Blackwater side / It'll take a long time / Walking the floor over you / Friends / For shame of doing wrong / I'm a dreamer / Full moon
CD Set _______ HNCD 5301
Hannibal / Jun '96 / ADA / Vital

Denson, Karl

BABY FOOD
CD _______ MM 801048
Minor Music / May '95 / Vital/SAM

CHUNKY PECAN PIE
Waltz for Leslie / Is it a bell / Fried bananas / Heart of the wanderer / Blue eyed peas / Banana boy / In order to form a more perfect union
CD _______ MM 801041
Minor Music / Jun '94 / Vital/SAM

D STANDS FOR DIESEL
CD _______ GB 002CD
Greyboy / Jul '96 / Timewarp

Dent De Lion

LES BEAUX YEAUX BLEUS
CD _______ MINCD 795
Minuit / Mar '96 / ADA

Dentists

BEHIND THE DOOR I KEEP THE UNIVERSE
This is not my flag / Space man / Sorry is not enough / In orbit / Faces on stone / Smile like oil on water / Tremendous Many / Gas / Brittle sin and flowers / Apple beast / Water for a man on fire / Waiter
CD _______ 7567922882
WEA / Mar '94 / Warner Music

DRESSED
CD _______ ME 2001
Metwo / Aug '92 / Pinnacle

POWDERED LOBSTER FIASCO
Pocket of silver / Charms and the girls / Outside your inside / Box of Sun / Beautiful day / I can see your house from up here / We thought we'd gone to Heaven / Leave me alive / All coming down / Snapdragon
CD _______ SHED 002 CD
Creation / Jun '93 / 3mv/Vital

Denver, John

BEST OF JOHN DENVER LIVE, THE
Rocky mountain high / Country road / Back home again / I guess he'd rather be in Colorado / Matthew / Sunshine on my shoulders / Darcy Farrow / Wild montana skies / Medley / Bet on the blues / I think I'd rather be a cowboy / Fly away / I'm sorry / Annie's song / Poems / Prayers and promises / Calypso
CD _______ 4873902
Epic / Jul '97 / Sony

COLLECTION, THE
CD _______ 280729
Column / Nov '96 / Total/BMG

DIFFERENT DIRECTIONS
CD _______ MCCD 237
Music Club / Mar '96 / Disc / THE

EARTH SONGS
Windsong / Rocky mountain suite / Rocky mountain high / Sunshine on my shoulders / Eagle and the hawk / Eclipse / Flower that shattered the stone / Raven's child / Children of the universe / To the wild country / American child / Calypso / Islands / Earth day every day (celebrate)
CD _______ MCCD 035
Music Club / Sep '91 / Disc / THE

FLOWER THAT SHATTERED THE STONE, THE
Thanks to you / Postcard from Paris / High, wide and handsome / Eagles and horses / Little further north / Raven's child / Ancient rhymes / Gift you are / I watch you sleeping / Stonehaven sunset / Flower that shattered the stone
CD _______ MCCD 154
Music Club / Feb '94 / Disc / THE

HIGHER GROUND
CD _______ MCCD 197
Music Club / Mar '95 / Disc / THE

ROCKY MOUNTAIN COLLECTION, THE (2CD Set)
Leaving on a jet plane / Rhymes and reasons / Follow me / Aspenglow sunshine on my shoulders / My sweet lady / Take me home country roads / Poems, prayers and promises / Eagle and the hawk / Starwood in Aspen / Friends with you / Goodbye again / Rocky mountain high / I'd rather be a cowboy / Farewell Andromeda / Back home again / Annie's song / Thank God I'm a country boy / Sweet surrender / This old guitar / Fly away / Looking for space / Windsong / Calypso / I'm sorry / Like a sad song / Come and let me look in your eyes / How can I leave you again / Thirsty boots / It amazes me / I want to live / Autograph / Some days are diamonds / Seasons of the heart / Shanghai breezes / Perhaps love: *Denver, John & Placido Domingo* / Wild Montana skies: *Denver, John & Emmylou Harris* / Love again / Flying for me
CD Set ______ **07863668372**
RCA / Mar '97 / BMG

TAKE ME HOME
Take me home, country roads / Back home again / Thank God I'm a country boy / I'm sorry / Grandma's feather bed / Eagle and the hawk / Children of the universe / Potter's wheel / Tenderly calling / Windsong / Rocky mountain suite (Cold nights in Canada) / Bread and roses / Alaska and me / Home grown tomatoes / Never a doubt / Country girl in Paris
CD ______ **CTS 55434**
Country Stars / Apr '96 / Target/BMG

TWO DIFFERENT DIRECTIONS (2CD Set)
CD Set ______ **DBP 102008**
Double Platinum / Oct '95 / Target/BMG

WILDLIFE CONSERVATION SOCIETY CONCERT
Rocky mountain high / Rhymes and reasons / Country roads / Back home again / I guess he'd rather be in Colorado / Matthew / Sunshine on my shoulders / You say the battle is over / Eagles and horses / Darcy Farrow / Whispering Jesse / Me and my uncle / Wild mountain skies / Leaving on a jet plane/Goodbye again / Bet on the blues / Harder they fall / Shanghai breeze / Fly away / Song for all lovers / Dreamland express / For you / Is it love / Falling out of love / Annie's song / Poems prayers and promises / Calypso / Amazon / This old guitar
CD ______ **4806942**
Columbia / Aug '95 / Sony

Denver, Karl

JUST LOVING YOU
From a Jack to a King / Garden party / I can't stop loving you / San Fernando / King of the road / Just loving you / Song for Maria / Walk on by / Won't give up / Runaway / Voices of the Highlands / Little bitty tear / Travelling light / Answer to everything / Story of my life
CD ______ **PZA 004CD**
Plaza / Oct '93 / Pinnacle

Denzil

PUB
Fat loose and fancies me / Running this family / Rake around the grave / Useless / Sunday service Hengistbury Head / Too scared to be true / Bastard son of Elvis / Funny moon / Shame / Who made you so cynical about me / Autistic / If only Alan won the pools / Seven years in these boots / Your sister song / Cutie / Goodnight darling
CD ______ **74321189662**
RCA / Jan '95 / BMG

Deodato, Eumir

OS CATEDRATICOS 73
CD ______ **100001CD**
Rare Brazil / Apr '97 / Cargo

PRELUDE/DEODATO VOL.2
CD ______ **4505582**
CBS / Jan '94 / Sony

Depeche Mode

101
Pimpf / Behind the wheel / Strangelove / Sacred / Something to do / Blasphemous rumours / Stripped / Somebody / Things you said / Black celebration / Shake the disease / Nothing / Pleasure little treasure / People are people / Question of time / Never let me down again / Question of lust / Master and servant / Just can't get enough / Everything counts
CD ______ **CDSTUMM 101**
Mute / Jan '89 / RTM/Disc

BLACK CELEBRATION
Black celebration / Fly on the windscreen (Final) / Question of lust / Sometimes / It doesn't matter / Question of time / Stripped / Here is the house / World full of nothing / Dressed in black / New dress / But not tonight / Breathing in fumes / Black day
CD ______ **CDSTUMM 26**
Mute / Jan '86 / RTM/Disc

BROKEN FRAME, A
CD ______ **CDSTUMM 9**
Mute / RTM/Disc

CONSTRUCTION TIME AGAIN
CD ______ **CDSTUMM 13**
Mute / Jan '86 / RTM/Disc

MUSIC FOR THE MASSES
Things you said / Strangelove / Sacred / Little 15 / Behind the wheel / I want you now / To have and to hold / Nothing / Pimpf / Agent Orange / Never let me down again / To have and to hold (Spanish taster) / Pleasure little treasure
CD ______ **CDSTUMM 47**
Mute / Sep '87 / RTM/Disc

SINGLES '81-'85
People are people / Master and servant / It's called a heart / Just can't get enough / See you / Shake the disease / Everything counts / New life / Blasphemous rumours / Leave in silence / Get the balance right / Love in itself / Dreaming of me
CD ______ **CDMUTEL 1**
Mute / '85 / RTM/Disc

SOME GREAT REWARD
If you want to / Master and servant / Lie to me / Something to do / Blasphemous rumours / Somebody / People are people / It don't matter / Stories of old / Pipeline / Everything counts / Two minute warning
CD ______ **CDSTUMM 19**
Mute / '84 / RTM/Disc

SONGS OF FAITH AND DEVOTION
I feel you / Walking in my shoes / Condemnation / Mercy in you / In your room / Get right with me / Rush / One caress / Higher love / Judas
CD ______ **CDSTUMM 106**
Mute / Apr '93 / RTM/Disc

SONGS OF FAITH AND DEVOTION - LIVE
CD ______ **LCDSTUMM 106**
Mute / Dec '93 / RTM/Disc

SPEAK AND SPELL
New life / Just can't get enough / I sometimes wish I was dead / Puppets / Boys say go / No disco / What's your name / Photographic / Tora tora tora / Big muff / Any second now
CD ______ **CDSTUMM 5**
Mute / Jun '88 / RTM/Disc

SPEAKING ONLY (Interview Disc)
CD ______ **3D 011**
Network / Dec '96 / Total/BMG

ULTRA
Barrel of a gun / Love thieves / Home / It's no good / Uselink / Useless / Sister of night / Jazz thieves / Freestate / Bottom line / Insight
CD ______ **CDSTUMM 148**
Mute / Apr '97 / RTM/Disc

VIOLATOR
World in my eyes / Sweetest perfection / Personal Jesus / Halo / Waiting for the night / Enjoy the silence / Policy of truth / Blue dress / Clean
CD ______ **CDSTUMM 64**
Mute / Mar '90 / RTM/Disc

Depravity

SILENCE OF THE CENTURIES
CD ______ **CDAR 017**
Adipocre / May '94 / Plastic Head

Depth Charge

NINE DEADLY VENOMS
CD ______ **STEAM 100CD**
Vinyl Solution / Nov '94 / RTM/Disc

Der Dritte Raum

DER DRITTE RAUM
CD ______ **HHCD 008**
Harthouse / Nov '94 / Mo's Music Machine / Prime / Vital

WELLANBAD
Wellenbad / Narkose / Vier megahertz / Trommelmaschchine / Raupe / Alienoid / Unterwasser / Wind / Geister / Uberreichweite
CD ______ **EYEUKCD 008**
Eye Q / Apr '96 / Vital

Deranged

ARCHITECTS OF PERVERSIONS
CD ______ **RPS 002MCD**
Repulse / Apr '95 / Plastic Head

RATED X (2CD Set)
CD Set ______ **RPS 010CD**
Repulse / May '96 / Plastic Head

Derek & The Dominoes

DEREK AND THE DOMINOES IN CONCERT (2CD Set)
Why does love got to be so sad / Got to get better in a little while / Let it rain / Presence of the Lord / Tell the truth / Bottle of red wine / Roll it over / Blues power / Have you ever loved a woman
CD Set ______ **8314162**
Polydor / Jan '94 / PolyGram

LAYLA REMASTERED - 20TH ANNIVERSARY EDITION (2CD Set)
CD Set ______ **8470832**
Polydor / Oct '90 / PolyGram

LIVE AT THE FILLMORE
Got to get better in a little while / Why does love got to be so sad / Key to the highway / Blues power / Have you ever loved a woman / Bottle of red wine / Tell the truth / Nobody knows you when you're down and out / Roll it over / OPresence of the Lord / Little wing / Let it rain / Crossroads
CD Set ______ **5216822**
Polydor / Apr '96 / PolyGram

Deris, Andi

COME IN FROM THE RAIN
House of pleasure / Come in from the rain / Think higher / Good bye Jenny / King of 7 eyes / Foreign rainbow / Somewhere, someday, someway / They wait / Now that I know this ain't love / Could I leave forever / 1000 Years away
CD ______ **SRECD 701**
Reef / May '97 / Pinnacle

Derise, Joe

HOUSE OF FLOWERS
CD ______ **ACD 153**
Audiophile / Apr '93 / Jazz Music

SINGS & PLAYS THE JIMMY VAN HEUSEN ANTHOLOGY
CD ______ **ACD 234**
Audiophile / Oct '92 / Jazz Music

Derome, Jean

CONFITURES DE GAGAKU
CD ______ **VICTOCD 05**
Victo / Oct '94 / Harmonia Mundi / ReR Megacorp

Derrane, Joe

GIVE US ANOTHER
CD ______ **GLCD 1149**
Green Linnet / Jun '95 / ADA / CM / Direct / Highlander / Roots

IRISH ACCORDION MASTERS
CD ______ **COPCD 5009**
Copley / Feb '96 / ADA

IRISH ACCORDION, THE
CD ______ **COP 5008CD**
Cop / Mar '94 / ADA

RETURN TO INIS MOR (Derrane, Joe & Carl Hession)
CD ______ **GLCD 1163**
Green Linnet / Jun '96 / ADA / CM / Direct / Highlander / Roots

Derrero

DERRERO
CD ______ **BNR 102CD**
Big Noise / Jun '97 / Shellshock/Disc

Derriere Le Miroir

ALIBI
CD ______ **EFA 119022**
Apollyon / Jan '94 / SRD

PREGNANT
CD ______ **EFA 119312**
Derriere / Mar '94 / SRD

Derringer, Rick

BACK TO THE BLUES
Trouble in paradise / Blue suede blues / Mean town blues / Sorry for your heartache / Sink or swim / Diamond / Cry baby / Unsolved mystery / Blue velvet
CD ______ **RR 90482**
Roadrunner / Sep '96 / PolyGram

ELECTRA BLUES
CD ______ **RR 89682**
Roadrunner / Sep '94 / PolyGram

TEND THE FIRE
CD ______ **0630153412**
East West / Aug '96 / Warner Music

Dervish

AT THE END OF THE DAY
Touching cloth / Ar eirinn ni neosfainn ee hi / Jim Coleman's set / An spailpin fanach / Packie Duignan's / Lone shanakyle / Drag her round the road / Peata beag / Trip to Sligo / Sheila Nee lyer / Kilavill set / I courted a wee girl / Josefin's waltz / Thirty seconds / Eileen McMahon
CD ______ **WHRL 003**
Whirling Discs / Sep '96 / ADA / Direct

BOYS OF SLIGO, THE
Donegal set / Dolphin / Clapton jigs / Thos Byrnes / Man of Arran / Jackson's / Cliffs of Glencolumbkille / Silgo set / Martin Wynne's / Lad O'Beirne's / McDermotts / Raphoe reel / Chestnut tree / Boys of silgo / Montaghan twig / World's end set / Eddie Kelly's jigs / Return from Camden Town / Key of the Convent / Tommie people's reel / Dancing bear / Oreaga / Walsh's fancy / Congress / Spoil the dance
CD ______ **SUNCD 1**
Sound / Sep '94 / ADA

HARMONY HILL
CD ______ **WHRL 001CD**
Whirling Discs / Aug '93 / ADA / Direct

PLAYING WITH FIRE
CD ______ **WHRL 002**
Whirling Discs / Apr '95 / ADA / Direct

Des, Henri

DES NO.5
CD ______ **MCD 237 684**
Accord / '88 / Cadillac / Discovery

Des Plantes, Ted

CHRISTMAS NIGHT IN HARLEM STRIDE STYLE
CD ______ **SACD 125**
Solo Art / Jan '97 / Jazz Music

TED DES PLANTES
CD ______ **JCD 225**
Jazzology / Oct '93 / Jazz Music

Desanto, Sugar Pie

DOWN IN THE BASEMENT (The Chess Years)
In the basement / I want to know / Mama didn't raise no fools / There's gonna be trouble / I don't feel sorry / Maybe you'll be there / Do I make myself clear / Use what you got / Can't let you go / Soulful dress / I don't wanna fuss / Going back to where I belong / It won't be long / She's got everything / Wish you were mine / Slip-in mules
CD ______ **MCD 09275**
Chess/MCA / Apr '97 / BMG / New Note/BMG

Descendents

ALL
CD ______ **SST 112CD**
SST / May '93 / Plastic Head

BONUS FAT
Bonus fat
CD ______ **SST 144CD**
SST / May '93 / Plastic Head

ENJOY
CD ______ **SST 242CD**
SST / Sep '90 / Plastic Head

EVERYTHING SUCKS
CD ______ **64812**
Epitaph / Sep '96 / Pinnacle / Plastic Head

HALLRAKER
CD ______ **SST 205CD**
SST / May '93 / Plastic Head

I DON'T WANT TO GROW UP
CD ______ **SST 143CD**
SST / Feb '88 / Plastic Head

LIVEAGE
All / I'm not a loser / Silly girl / I wanna be a bear / Coolidge / Weinerschnitel / I don't want to grow up / Kids / Wendy / Get the time / Descendents / All-o-gistics / Myage / My dad sucks / Van / Surburban home / Hope / Clean sheets
CD ______ **SST 163CD**
SST / Jan '88 / Plastic Head

MILO GOES TO COLLEGE
CD ______ **SST 142CD**
SST / May '93 / Plastic Head

SOMERY
CD ______ **SST 259CD**
SST / May '93 / Plastic Head

TWO THINGS AT ONCE
CD ______ **SST 145CD**
SST / May '93 / Plastic Head

Desert Rose Band

LIFE GOES ON
CD ______ **4748692**
Curb / Dec '93 / Grapevine/PolyGram

Desford Colliery Band

ANDREW LLOYD WEBBER IN BRASS (Desford Colliery Caterpillar Band)
CD ______ **340472**
Koch / Dec '94 / Koch

GREGSON (Desford Colliery Caterpillar Band)
Dances and arias / Concerto for french horn and brass band / Connotations / Of men and mountains
CD ______ **DOYCD 017**
Doyen / Nov '92 / Conifer/BMG

MAKING TRACKS (Desford Colliery Caterpillar Band)
Westward go / London overture / Little red bird / Russky percusky / River city serenade / Impromptu for tuba / Mountain song / Folks who live on the hill / Poinciana / Pantomime / Trumpet blues and cantabile / Make believe / Oceans
CD ______ **QPRL 045D**
Polyphonic / Jun '90 / Complete/Pinnacle

Designer

GOIN' DE DISTANCE
CD _____ JW 057CD
Soca / Feb '94 / Jet Star

Desmond, Johnny

ONCE UPON A TIME/BLUE SMOKE
All the things you are / My heart stood still / Night and day / Where or when / Symphony / Together / I'll be seeing you / I'll walk alone / I'll remember April / Sweet Lorraine / Amor / Time on my hands / I'm through with love / No-one ever tells you / Party's over / I gotta right to sing the blues / It's a lonesome old town / Blue smoke / Last night when we were young / Why shouldn't I / Imagination / That old feeling / You go to my head / I'm glad there is you / Bluesmoke
CD _____ 4810162
Columbia / Aug '95 / Sony

Desmond, Paul

BEST OF PAUL DESMOND, THE
Song to a seagull / Take ten / Romance de amor / Was a sunny day / Summer song/ Summertime / Squeeze me / I'm old fashioned / Nuages / You'd be so nice to come home to / Autumn leaves / Skylark / Vocalise
CD _____ ZK 45484
Sony Jazz / Feb '96 / Sony

DESMOND BLUE
My funny Valentine / Desmond blue / Then I'll be tired of you / I've got you under my skin / Late lament / I should care / Like someone in love / Ill wind / Body and soul / Advise and consent / Autumn leaves / Imagination
CD _____ 09026687082
RCA Victor / Feb '97 / BMG

FEELING BLUE
When Joanna loved me / Alone together / Here's that rainy day / Body and soul / Samba d'Orpheu / Polka dots and moonbeams / Bewitched / That old feeling / I've got you under my skin / I've grown accustomed to her face / One I love (belongs to someone else) / Easy living / Embarcadero / All the things you are
CD _____ 74321400552
Camden / Sep '96 / BMG

LIKE SOMEONE IN LOVE
Just squeeze me / Tangerine / Meditation / Nuages / Like someone in love / Things ain't what they used to be
CD _____ CD 83319
Telarc / Nov '92 / Conifer/BMG

PAUL DESMOND & THE MJQ (Desmond, Paul & The MJQ)
CD _____ 4749842
Sony Jazz / May '94 / Sony

PAUL DESMOND QUARTET AND JIM HALL (Desmond, Paul & Jim Hall)
CD _____ CD 53224
Giants Of Jazz / Nov '95 / Cadillac / Jazz Music / Target/BMG

POLKA DOTS AND MOON BEAMS
When Joanna loved me / Polka dots and moonbeams / Here's that rainy day / Easy living / I've grown accustomed to your face / Bewitched, bothered and bewildered
CD _____ ND 90637
Bluebird / Apr '92 / BMG

PURE DESMOND
Squeeze me / I'm old fashioned / Nuages / Why shouldn't I / Everything I love / Warm valley / Till the clouds roll by / Mean to me / Song from MASH / Wave
CD _____ ZK 40806
Sony Jazz / Feb '96 / Sony
CD _____ ZK 64767
Mastersound / Jan '96 / Sony

SKYLARK
Take ten / Romance de amor / Was a sunny day / Music for a while / Skylark / Indian summer
CD _____ ZK 44170
Sony Jazz / Feb '96 / Sony

TAKE TEN
Take ten / El prince / Alone together / Embarcadero / Black orpheus / Nancy / Samba d'Orpheus / One I love
CD _____ 07863661462
Bluebird / Apr '93 / BMG

TRIBUTE TO PAUL DESMOND, A (Various Artists)
CD _____ JD 156
Chesky / May '97 / Discovery / Goldring

TWO OF A MIND (Desmond, Paul & Gerry Mulligan)
All the things you are / Stardust / Two of a mind / Blight of the fumble bee / Way you look tonight / Out of nowhere
CD _____ 09026685132
RCA Victor / Oct '96 / BMG

Desmond, Trudy

MAKE ME RAINBOWS
CD _____ 378032
Koch Jazz / May '96 / Koch

TAILOR MADE
Day by day / Goody goody / I see your face before me / Lucky to be me / I'm shadowing you / By myself / Anyone can whistle / I thought about you / Make someone happy / Guess I'll hang my tears out to dry / People will say we're in love / I'll never be the same
CD _____ TJA 10015
Jazz Alliance / Oct '92 / New Note/Pinnacle

Desotos

CRUISIN' WITH THE DESOTOS
CD _____ WCD 9026
Wilson Audiophile / Sep '91 / Quantum Audio

Despair

DECAY OF HUMANITY
Decay of humanity / Delusion / Distant territory / Radiated / Cry for liberty / Victims of vanity / Silent screaming / Satantic verses
CD _____ 8497122
Century Media / Aug '90 / Plastic Head

Desperadoes Steel Orchestra

JAMMER, THE
Jammer / No pan / Ah goin an party tonight / Moliendo cafe / Africa / Rebecca / Symphony in G / Musical volcano
CD _____ DE 4023
Delos / Jan '94 / Nimbus

Des'ree

I AIN'T MOVIN'
Herald the day / Crazy maze / You gotta be / Little child / Strong enough / Trip on love / I ain't movin' / Living in the city / In my dreams / Love is here / I ain't movin' (Percussion reprise)
CD _____ 4758432
Sony Soho2 / May '94 / Sony

MIND ADVENTURES
Average man / Feel so high / Sun of '79 / Why should I love you / Stand on my own ground / Competitive world / Mind adventures / Laughter / Save me / Momma, please don't cry
CD _____ 4712632
Sony Soho2 / Mar '96 / Sony

Destination

AEOA
CD _____ FX 168
Kirkelig Kultuverksted / Aug '96 / ADA

Destinations

HERE WE ARE
CD _____ LI 1001
Little Italy / Oct '96 / Nervous

Destiny

NOTHING LEFT TO FEAR
CD _____ CDATV 18
Active / May '91 / Pinnacle

Destroy All Monsters

BORED
You're gonna die / November 22nd 1963 / Meet the creeper / Nobody knows / What do I get / Goin' to lose / Bored
CD _____ CDMRED 94
Cherry Red / Apr '97 / Pinnacle

SILVER WEDDING
CD _____ SFTRI 444
Sympathy For The Record Industry / Oct '96 / Cargo / Greyhound / Plastic Head

Destroyer 666

UNCHAIN THE WOLVES
CD _____ MIM 7325CD
Modern Invasion / Jun '97 / Plastic Head

VIOLENCE IS THE PRINCE OF THIS WORLD
CD _____ MIM 7320CD
Modern Invasion / Jan '96 / Plastic Head

Destruction

BEST OF DESTRUCTION, THE (2CD Set)
CD Set _____ SPV 08476482
SPV / Mar '97 / Koch / Plastic Head

DESTRUCTION
CD _____ UAM 0447
UAM / Oct '95 / Plastic Head

INFERNAL OVERKILL/SENTENCE OF DEATH
CD _____ 857529
Steamhammer / '89 / Pinnacle / Plastic Head

LIVE WITHOUT SENSE
CD _____ CDNUK 126
Noise / Feb '89 / Koch

MAD BUTCHER/ETERNAL DEVASTATION
CD _____ 851860
SPV / '89 / Koch / Plastic Head

Desultory

BITTERNESS
CD _____ CDZORRO 77
Metal Blade / Jun '94 / Pinnacle / Plastic Head

SWALLOW THE SNAKE
CD _____ 398414109CD
Metal Blade / Sep '96 / Pinnacle / Plastic Head

Det Hedenske Folk

DET HEDENSKE FOLK/ABYSSIC HATE (United By Heathen Blood) (Det Hedenske Folk/Abyssic Hate)
CD _____ BLCR 7002CD
Bloodless Creations / Jun '97 / Plastic Head

Det-Ri-Mental

XENOPHOBIA
Bhangra attack / Informer / Total revolution / Richmans world (suffering pt 2) / Children of a rat race (aye man) / Sista India / Bank robber / Babylon / Living on the edge / Unkown identity (Inn-a-England)
CD _____ DEBTCD 003
Debt / Oct '95 / Vital

Detective

DETECTIVE
Recognition / Got enough love / Grim reaper / Nightingale / Detective man / Ain't none of your business / Deep down / Wild hot summer / One more heartache
CD _____ 7567914152
Atlantic / Jan '96 / Warner Music

IT TAKES ONE TO KNOW ONE
Help me up / Competition / Are you talkin' to me / Dynamite / Something beautiful / Warm love / Betcha won't dance / Fever / Tear jerker
CD _____ 7567804032
Atlantic / Jan '96 / Warner Music

Deteriorate

SENECTUOS ENTRANCE, THE
CD _____ RRS 952CD
Die Hard/Progress / Sep '96 / Plastic Head

Detest

DORVAL
CD _____ NB 104
Nuclear Blast / Mar '94 / Plastic Head

Dethmuffen, Miles

CLUTTER
CD _____ QTZ 012
Quartz / Apr '94 / SRD

Dethrone

LET THE DAY BEGIN
CD _____ CDFLAG 41
Under One Flag / Sep '90 / Pinnacle

Detour

HONKY TONKIN' TIL IT HURTS
CD _____ 15377
Laserlight / Aug '91 / Target/BMG

Detroit

GET OUT THE VOTE (Detroit & Mitch Ryder)
CD _____ NER 3010CD
Total Energy / May '97 / Cargo / Greyhound

Detroit Emeralds

DO ME RIGHT/YOU WANT IT YOU GOT IT
Do me right / Wear this ring (With love) / Long live the king / What you gonna do about me / You can't take this love for you, from me / Just now and then / Lee / If I lose your love / And I love her / I can't see myself (Doing without you) / Holding on / Admit your love is gone / You want it, you got it / There's love for me somewhere / I'll never sail the sea again / Take my love / Feel the need / I've got to move / Baby let me take you (in my arms) / I bet you get the one you love / Till you decide to come home / Radio promo medley:
CD _____ CDSEWD 067
Westbound / Apr '93 / Pinnacle

I'M IN LOVE WITH YOU
Shake your head / You're getting a little too smart / What'cha gonna wear tomorrow / My dreams have got the best of me / So long / I think of you / Heaven couldn't be like this/Without you baby
CD _____ CDSEW 006
Westbound / Jun '89 / Pinnacle

I'M IN LOVE WITH YOU/FEEL THE NEED IN ME
Shake your head / So long / You're getting too smart / I think of you / What'cha gonna wear tomorrow / Heaven couldn't be like this/Without you baby / My dreams have got the best of you / Set it out / Take it or leave it / Feel the need in me / Wednesday / Love for you / Look what has happened to our love / Sexy ways / Love has come to me
CD _____ CDSEWD 068
Westbound / Nov '93 / Pinnacle

Detroit Escalator Co.

SOUNDTRACK (313)
Gratiot / Abstract forward motion (as a mission) / Force / Inverted man (falling) / Tai Chi and traffic lights / Gathering memory / Shifting gears / Untitled triangle
CD _____ FERCD 002
Ferox / Oct '96 / Prime / SRD / Vital

Detroit Spinners

DANCIN' AND LOVIN'
Disco ride / Body language / Let's boogie, let's dance / Medley: Working my way back to you / Forgive me girl / With my eyes / 1122 Boogie Woogie Avenue
CD _____ 8122711152
Atlantic / Jan '96 / Warner Music

LOVE TRIPPIN'
Love trippin' / Heavy on the sunshine / Medley: Cupid / I've loved you for a long time / I just want to be with you / Street wise / Working my way back to you / I just want to fall in love / Now that you're mine again / Split decision / I'm takin' you back / Pipe dream / Body language
CD _____ 7567803782
Atlantic / Jan '96 / Warner Music

Detroit, Marcella

FEELER
CD _____ AAACD 1
AAA / Jan '97 / Total/BMG

Detroiters

OLD TIME RELIGION (Detroiters & Golden Echoes)
He walks with me / Mother on the train take 2 / Mother on the train take 3 / Angels watching over me / I trust in Jesus / Ride on king Jesus / Mother, don't cry about your child / Let Jesus lead you / Mother, I need your prayer / Old time religion / Sometimes / Body and soul / Shady green pastures / Where shall I be / Down on my knees / My life is in his hands / When the saints go marching in (take 2) / When the saints go marching in / When I lay my burden down / I'm so happy in the service of the lord / Waiting and watching / Yield not to temptation take 1 / Yield not to temptation take 2 / Yield not to temptation take 3
CD _____ CDCHD 467
Ace / Mar '93 / Pinnacle

Deuce

ON THE LOOSE
Call it love / Talk to me / What you wanna be / Rumours / Let's call it a day / I need you / Boyfriend girlfriend / I'll be there for you / I was wrong / Kiss it
CD _____ 8286642
London / Aug '95 / PolyGram

dEUS

IN A BAR UNDER THE SEA
I don't mind whatever happens / Fell off the floor man / Opening night / Theme from turnpike / Little arithmetics / Gimme the heat / Serpentine / Shocking lack thereof / Supermarketsong / Memory of a festival / Guilty pleasures / Nine threads / Disappointed in the sun / Roses / Wake me up before I sleep
CD _____ CID 8052
Island / Oct '96 / PolyGram

MY SISTER IS MY CLOCK
Middlewave / Almost white / Health insurance / Little ghost / How to row a cat / Only a colour to her / Sick sugar / Sweetness / Horror party jokes / Void / Sans titre pour sira / Glovesong / Lorre in the forest
CD _____ IMCD 8031
Island / Jan '95 / PolyGram

WORST CASE SCENARIO
Intro / Suds and soda / WCS (1st draft) / Jigsaw you / Morticiachair / Via / Right as rain / Mute / Let's get lost / Hotellounge (be the death of me) / Shake your hip / Great American nude / Secret hell / Divebomb djingle
CD _____ CID 8028
Island / Aug '94 / PolyGram

Deuter-D

CALL OF THE UNKNOWN-SELECTED PIECES 1972-1986
Starchild / Peru le Peru / Call of the unknown / Sky beyond clouds / Cathedral / From here to here / High road / Alchemy / Pacifica / Silence is the answer / Haleakala mystery / Album / Solitary bird / Echo of the beast / Back to a planet / La Illaha il allah
CD Set _____ CDKUCK 076/077
Kuckuck / Feb '87 / ADA / CM

CICADA
From here to here / Light / Cicada / Sun on my face / From here to here (reprise) / Sky

beyond clouds / Haiku / Alchemy / Between two breaths
CD CDKUCK 056
Kuckuck / Feb '87 / ADA / CM

HENON
Nada / Sha / Ebony / Basho / Ari / Gentle darkness / Terra Linda / Indian girl / Fjaril / Rainmoon / Chicken itza
CD CDKUCK 11099
Kuckuck / Jul '92 / ADA / CM

LAND OF ENCHANTMENT
Pierrot / Maui morning / Silver air / Waves and dolphins / Santa Fe / Celestial harmony / Peru le Peru / Petite fleur / Wind of dawn
CD CDKUCK 081
Kuckuck / Jan '88 / ADA / CM

NIRVANA ROAD
CD CDKUCK 068
Kuckuck / Jul '84 / ADA / CM

SANDS OF TIME
CD CDKUCK 120902
Kuckuck / Feb '91 / ADA / CM

Deutsch, Alex

PINK INC. (Deutsch, Alex, George Garzone & Jammaladeen Tacuma)
CD DIW 852
DIW / Nov '91 / Cadillac / Harmonia Mundi

Deutscher, Drafi

DIE DECCA JAHRE 1963-68
Teeny / Shu-bi-do the slop / Grun, grun ist Tennessee / Kleine Peggy Lou / Shake hands / Come on let's go / Cinderella baby / Es ist besser, wenn du gebst / Keep smiling / Es war einmal / Hast du alles vergessen / Heute male ich dein Bild, Cindy Lou / Mr. Tambourine man / Keiner weiss, wie es morgen sein wird / Nimm mich so wie ich bin / Ich geh' durch's Feuer fur dich / Marmor, Stein und Eisen bricht / Das sind die einsamen jahre / Honey bee / Hello little girl / Ich hab' den mond in meiner tasche / An deiner seite / Old old Germany / Mit schirm, Frack und Melone / Mit schirm, charme und melone / Die goldene zeit: *Deutscher, Drafi & Manuela* / Take it easy: *Deutscher, Drafi & Manuela* / Was sind sie ohne Regen: *Deutscher, Drafi & Manuela* / Sweet dreams for you my love / Darlin' / Der hauptmann von Kopenick / Zwei fremde augen / Rock 'n' roll lady / Alice im Wunderland / Marble breaks, iron bends / Wanna take you home / Summertime / Bachelor boy / Trouble / Amanda / Wake up / Crying in the morning / Bleib, oh bleib / Junge leute brauchen liebe / Shake your hands / Good golly Miss Molly / Memphis, Tennessee / Roll over Beethoven / What'd I say / What's the matter baby / Mit siebzehn fangt das Leben erst an / Komm zu mir / Zip a dee doo dah / Lion sleeps tonight / Hippy hippy shake / Shakin' all over / Ready Teddy / Marnor, stein und eisen bricht / Wunder / I don't need that kind of lovin' / Language of love / Tranen der liebe / Ich will frei sein / Welche farbe had die welt / He's got the whole world in his hands / Noah's arche / Waterloo / Denn da waren wir beide noch kinder / Liebe, gluck und treue / Bring grusse zu Mary
CD Set BCD 15416
Bear Family / Dec '87 / Direct / Rollercoaster / Swift

Deutschmark Bob

BAD WITH WIMMIN (Deutschmark Bob & The Deficits)
CD CD 12878
Crypt / Apr '97 / Shellshock/Disc

BUSH HOG'N MAN
CD EFA 12894CD
Crypt / Jul '97 / Shellshock/Disc

Deux Filles

SILENCE AND WISDOM
CD BAH 1
Humbug / Feb '93 / Total/Pinnacle

Devan

RAGGAFUNKIN'
CD WCCD 001
Wild Cherry / Sep '96 / Koch / Scratch/BMG

Devas

EMBODIED
CD MSECD 016
Mouse / Oct '95 / Grapevine/PolyGram

DeVaughan, William

BE THANKFUL FOR WHAT YOU GOT/ FIGURES CAN'T CALCULATE
Give the little man a great big hand / Something's being done / Blood is thicker than water / Kiss and make up / You gave me a brand new start / Be thankful for what you got / Sing a love song / You can do it / We are his children / Be thankful for what you've got / Hold on to love / Boogie Dan / Figures can't calculate (the love I have for you) / Love comes so easy with you / You send me / I've never found a girl
CD NEMCD 700
Sequel / Nov '94 / BMG

Devi, Girija

GIRIJA DEVI IN CONCERT
CD C 560056
Ocora / Oct '95 / ADA / Harmonia Mundi

Deviant Electronics

BRAINWASHING IS CHILD'S PLAY
CD HEXCD 2
Helix / Mar '97 / Cargo

Deviants

DEVIANTS VOL.3
CD CTCD 061
Captain Trip / Jul '97 / Greyhound

DISPOSABLE
CD CTCD 042
Captain Trip / Jul '97 / Greyhound

Deviants

PARTIAL RECALL
Billy the monster / Trouble coming every day / Broken statue / Whole things starts / But Charlie it's still moving / Observe the ravens / Society of the horseman / Summertime blues / Don't talk to me Mary / You can't move me / In my window box / Epitaph can point the way / Mona the whole trip / People call me crazy / Half price drinks / Death of a dream machine
CD DOCD 1989
Drop Out / Sep '92 / Pinnacle

PTOOFF
CD DOCD 1988
Drop Out / Nov '92 / Pinnacle

Deviate

CRISIS OF CONFIDENCE
CD MASSCD 042
Massacre / Oct '94 / Plastic Head

THORN OF THE LIVING
CD IS 889890CD
I Scream Music / Jun '97 / Plastic Head

Deviated Instinct

RE-OPENING OLD WOUNDS
CD DAR 011CD
Desperate Attempt / Nov '94 / SRD

Devil Dogs

30 SIZZLING SLABS
CD EFA 11561 CD
Crypt / Jun '93 / Shellshock/Disc

CHAOS BLAST
CD MTR 218CD
Empty / Sep '95 / Cargo / Greyhound / Plastic Head / SRD

CHOAD BLAST
CD EFA 123572
Empty / Mar '94 / Cargo / Greyhound / Plastic Head / SRD

SATURDAY NIGHT FEVER
CD EFA 115362
Crypt / Jan '97 / Shellshock/Disc

Devine, Ian

CARDIFFIANS (Devine, Ian & Alison Statton)
CD TWI 9062
Les Disques Du Crepuscule / Oct '96 / Discovery

Devine, Sydney

50 COUNTRY WINNERS
Country roads / Early morning rain / Gentle on my mind / Hello Mary Lou / Oh lonesome me / Sea of heartbreak / Lonesome number one / Blue blue day / Four walls / He'll have to go / You're free to go / Sweet dreams / Send me the pillow that you dream on / Satin sheets / Wild side of life / This song is just for you / Blackboard of my heart / Married by the bible, divorced by the law / Crying time / Together again / I can't stop loving you / Take these chains from my heart / Dear God / Where could I go but to the Lord / House of gold / You'll never walk alone / Blanket on the ground / Old flames / Blowin' in the wind / Sing me / Tiny bubbles / Early shells / Stand beside me / Gypsy woman / You're my best friend / Till the rivers all run dry / Please help me, I'm falling / Fraulein / I fall to pieces / It keeps right on a-hurtin' / Eighteen yellow roses / Ramblin' rose / Red roses for a blue lady / Irene / Lucille / Amanda / Lovesick blues / Singin' the blues / Knee deep in the blues / Long gone lonesome blues
CD Set PLATCD 18
Platinum / Oct '87 / Prism

CRYING TIME
Crying time / Broken engagement / My son calls another man daddy / Long black limousine / Two little orphans / Eighteen yellow roses / Old Shep / Letter edged in black / Nobody's child / I ain't crying, mister / Gentle mother / Come home rolling stone
CD EMPRCD 505
Emporio / Apr '94 / Disc

GREEN GRASS OF HOME, THE
CD CDITV 530
Scotdisc / Dec '90 / Conifer/BMG / Duncans / Ross

NORFOLK COUNTRY
CD CDITV 598
Scotdisc / Nov '94 / Conifer/BMG / Duncans / Ross

VERY BEST OF SYDNEY DEVINE, THE
I can't stop loving you / Blackboard of my heart / Lovesick blues / Two little orphans / Bye bye love / Take these chains from my heart / Ain't that a shame/Blueberry hill / Corrine corrina / I ain't cryin' mister / Room full of roses / Crying time / Help me make it through the night / May the bird of paradise fly up your nose / Donna / Send me the pillow that you dream on / You're sixteen / It keeps right on hurtin' / She wears my ring / Rose Marie / Maggie
CD MCVD 30011
Emerald Gem / Nov '96 / BMG

Devo

DEVO LIVE
Gates of steel / Be stiff / Planet Earth / Freedom of choice / Whip it / Girl U want
CD CDV 2106
Virgin / May '93 / EMI

DUTY NOW FOR THE FUTURE
Devo corporate anthem / Clockout / Timing x / Wiggly world / Block head / Strange pursuits / SIB (swelling itching brain) / Triumph of the will / Day my baby gave me a surprise / Pink pussycat / Secret agent man / Smart patrol / Redeye express / Mr. DNA
CD CDV 2125
Virgin / May '93 / EMI

DUTY NOW FOR THE FUTURE/OH NO IT'S DEVO/ARE WE NOT MEN (3CD Set)
CD Set TPAK 38
Virgin / Oct '94 / EMI

FREEDOM OF CHOICE
Girl u want / It's not right / Snowball / Ton o' lov / Freedom of choice / Gates of steel / Cold war / Don't you know / That's pep / Mr. B's ballroom / Planet Earth
CD CDV 2241
Virgin / May '93 / EMI

HARD CORE DEVO
CD 422105
New Rose / May '94 / ADA / Direct / Discovery

HARDCORE VOL.2
CD RCD 20208
Rykodisc / Sep '91 / ADA / Vital

HOT POTATOES: THE BEST OF DEVO
Jocko Homo / Mogoloid / Satisfaction / Whip it / Girl u want / Freedom of choice / Peek-a-boo / Through being cool / That's good / Working in a coalmine / Devo corporate anthem / Be stiff / Gates of steel / Come back Jonee / Secret agent man / Day my baby gave me a surprise / Beautiful world / Big mess / Whip it (remix)
CD CDVM 9016
Virgin / Aug '93 / EMI

LIVE MONGALOID YEARS
CD RCD 20209
Rykodisc / Oct '92 / ADA / Vital

NEW TRADITIONALISTS
Through being cool / Jerkin' back 'n' forth / Pity you / Soft things / Race of doom / Going under / Love without anger / Super thing / Beautiful world / Enough said
CD CDV 2125
Virgin / May '93 / EMI

NOW IT CAN BE TOLD
CD 727552
Restless / Feb '95 / Vital

OH NO IT'S DEVO
Time out for fun / Peek-a-boo / Out of sync / Explosions / That's good / Patterns / Big mess / Speed racer / What I must / I desire / Deep sleep
CD CDV 2241
Virgin / May '93 / EMI

Q. ARE WE NOT MEN (A. We Are Devo)
Uncontrollable urge / Satisfaction / Praying hands / Space junk / Monogoloid / Jocko homo / Too much paranoias / Gut feeling / Slap your mammy / Sloppy (I saw my baby gettin') / Shrivel up / Come back Jonee
CD CDV 2106
Virgin / May '93 / EMI

SMOOTH NOODLE MAPS
Stuck in a loop / Post post-modern man / When we do it / Spin the wheel / Morning dew / Chance is gonna cum / Big picture / Pink jazz trancers / Jimmy / Devo has feelings too / Dawghaus
CD 727572
Restless / Feb '95 / Vital

TOTAL DEVO
Baby doll / Disco dancer / Some things never change / Plain truth / Happy guy / Shadow / I'd cry if you died / Agitated / Man turned inside out / Blow up
CD 727562
Restless / Feb '95 / Vital

Dew Scented

IMMORTELLE
CD SPV 08518262
SPV / Mar '96 / Koch / Plastic Head

Dexy's Midnight Runners

BECAUSE OF YOU
Celtic soul brothers / Show me / Liars A to E / This is what she's like / Let's make this precious / Soon / Reminisce (Part 1) / Because of you / Let's get this straight / Old / All in all / One of those things / Dubious / Occasional flicker
CD 5500032
Spectrum / May '93 / PolyGram

DON'T STAND ME DOWN
CD CRECD 154
Creation / Jun '97 / 3mv/Vital

IT WAS LIKE THIS
Breakin' down the walls of heartache / Tell me when my light turns green / Teams that meet in Caffs / Dance stance / Geno / I'm just looking / Thankfully not living in Yorkshire it doesn't apply / Seven days too long / I couldn't help it if I tried / Respect / Horse / Keep it / Love part 1 / There there my dear / Keep it part 2 (Inferiority part 1) / One way love / Plan B / Soul finger
CD PRMUCD 1
Premier/EMI / May '96 / EMI

SEARCHING FOR THE YOUNG SOUL REBELS
Burn it down / Tell me when my light turns to green / Teams that meet in the caffs / I'm just looking / Geno / Seven days too long / I couldn't help it if I tried / Thankfully not living in Yorkshire it doesn't apply / Keep it / Love part one / There there my dear
CD CZ 31
EMI / Jan '88 / EMI

TOO RYE AYE (Remastered)
Celtic soul brothers / Let's make this precious / All in all (this one last wild waltz) / Jackie Wilson said (I'm in heaven when you smile) / Old / Plan B / I'll show you / Liars A to E / Until I believe in my soul / Come on Eileen
CD 5148392
Mercury / Mar '96 / PolyGram

TOO RYE AYE/DON'T STAND ME DOWN (2CD Set)
Celtic soul brothers / Let's make this precious / All in all (this one last wild waltz) / Jackie Wilson said (I'm in heaven when you smile) / Old / Plan B / I'll show you / Liars A to E / Until I believe in my soul / Come on Eileen / Occasional flicker / This is what she's like / Knowledge of beauty / One of those things / Reminisce part 2 / Listen to this / Waltz
CD Set 5286082
Mercury / Aug '95 / PolyGram

VERY BEST OF DEXY'S MIDNIGHT RUNNERS, THE
Come on Eileen / Jackie Wilson said (I'm in heaven when you smile) / Let's get this straight / Because of you / Show me / Celtic soul brothers / Liars A to E / One way love / Old / Geno / There there my dear / Breakin' down the walls of heartache / Dance stance / Plan B / Keep it / I'm just looking / Soon / This is what she's like / Soul finger
CD 8464602
Mercury / May '91 / PolyGram

Deyess

LITTLE GODDESS
CD STCD 1040
Stern's / Oct '92 / ADA / CM / Stern's

DFA

OM23
Empire / Oo su kushi / Heckmondwike / Jewels and calories / Dark matter / OM23 / Sonic soul surfer / Departure / Mondo cahoona / Heaven's inferno
CD CDKTB 97
Dreamtime / May '97 / Kudos / Pinnacle

DFL

MY CRAZY LIFE
CD GR 002CD
Grand Royal / Apr '97 / EMI

D'Gary

MALAGASY GUITAR
CD SHCD 65009
Shanachie / May '93 / ADA / Greensleeves / Koch

MBO LOZA
Gofo libre / Atahora fabiby / Mibaby diavolana / Mare rano / Lehibeny / Te-beheloky / Ragnandria / Kinanga / Mbo loza / Asmine / Manoro
CD LBLC 2535
Indigo / Apr '97 / New Note/Pinnacle

Dhar, Sheila

VOYAGE INTERIEUR
CD C 560017/18
Ocora / Jan '93 / ADA / Harmonia Mundi

Dhomont, Francis

ACOUSMATRIX 8/9
CD BVHAASTCD 9107/8
Bvhaast / Oct '93 / Cadillac

FORET PROFONDE
CD IMED 9634
Diffunzioni Musicali / Jun '97 / ReR Megacorp

SOUS LE REGARD D'UN SOLEIL NOIR
CD IMED 9633
Diffunzioni Musicali / Jun '97 / ReR Megacorp

DI

STATE OF SHOCK
Hated / Clownhouse / What is life / Runaround / Colors and blood / It's not right / Paranoid's demise / Dream / Better than expected / Martyr man / Lexicon devil
CD CDVEST 14
Bulletproof / May '94 / Pinnacle

TRAGEDY AGAIN
Tragedy again / Chiva / Nick the whip / Manhole / Sasha / Diablo I / Blue velvet / Backseat driver / Love to me is a sin / On our way / Diablo II
CD EM 94262
Roadrunner / Dec '89 / PolyGram

Di Bart, Tony

FALLING FOR YOU
Falling for you / Real thing / Secrecy / Turn your love around / Do it / Father / Why did ya / What am I gonna do / We got the love / Stay a little while
CD CLECD 555
Cleveland City / Oct '96 / 3mv/Sony / Grapevine/PolyGram

Di Franco, Ani

ANI DI FRANCO
Both hands / Talk to me now / Slant / Work your way out / Dog coffee / Lost woman song / Pale purple / Rush hour / Fire door / Story / Every angle / Out of habit / Letting the telephone ring / Egos like hairdos
CD RBR 001CD
Righteous Babe / Jul '95 / ADA
CD COOKCD 112
Cooking Vinyl / Jan '97 / Vital

DILATE
Untouchable face / Outta me, onto you / Superhero / Dilate / Amazing grace / Napoleon / Shameless / Done wrong / Going down / Adam and eve / Joyful girl
CD COOKCD 103
Cooking Vinyl / Jul '96 / Vital
CD RBR 8
Righteous Babe / May '96 / ADA

IMPERFECTLY
CD RBR 003CD
Righteous Babe / Jul '95 / ADA

LIKE I SAID - SONGS 1990-91
CD RBR 005CD
Righteous Babe / Jul '95 / ADA

LIVING IN CLIP (2CD Set)
Whatever / wherever / Gravel / Willing to fight / Shy / Joyful girl / Hide and seek / Napoleon / I'm no heroine / Amazing Grace / Anticipate / Tiptoe / Sorry I am / Diner/ Slant / 32 Flavours / Out of range / Untouchable face / Shameless / Distracted / Adam and Eve / Fire door / Both hands / Out of habit / Every state line / Not so soft / Travel tips / Wrong with me / In or out / We're all gonna blow / Letter to a John / Overleaf
CD Set COOKCD 122
Cooking Vinyl / Jun '97 / Vital

MORE JOY LESS SHAME
Joyful girl / Shameless / Both hands
CD COOKCD 119
Cooking Vinyl / Dec '96 / Vital

NOT A PRETTY GIRL
Worthy / Tiptoe / Cradle and all / Shy / Sorry I am / Light of some kind / Not a pretty girl / Million you never made / Hour follows hour / 32 flavors / Asking too much / This bouquet / Crime for crime
CD RBR 007CD
Righteous Babe / Nov '95 / ADA
CD COOKCD 113
Cooking Vinyl / Jan '97 / Vital

NOT SO SOFT
CD RBR 002CD
Righteous Babe / Jul '95 / ADA

OUT OF RANGE
CD HAVENCD 3
Haven / Jan '95 / Pinnacle / Shellshock/ Disc

PUDDLE DIVE
CD HAVENCD 2
Haven / Jan '95 / Pinnacle / Shellshock/ Disc

WOMEN IN (E)MOTION FESTIVAL
CD T&M 105
Tradition & Moderne / Nov '94 / ADA / Direct

Di Gojim

NOCH A SJOH
CD SYNCD 161
Syncoop / Jun '94 / ADA / Direct

Di Meola, Al

BEST OF AL DI MEOLA
July / Traces of a tear / Maraba / Song to the Pharoah Kings / Etude / Rhapsody of fire / Coral / Beijing demons / Ballad
CD BNZ 305
Blue Note / Feb '93 / EMI

CASINO
Egyptian danza / Chasin' the voodoo / Dark eye tango / Senor mouse / Fantasia suite for two guitars / Viva la danzarina / Guitars of the exotic isle / Rhapsody Italia / Bravoto fantasia / Casino
CD 4682152
Sony Jazz / Jan '95 / Sony

COLLECTION, THE
CD CCSCD 310
Castle / Sep '91 / BMG

ELECTRIC RENDEZVOUS
God bird / Change / Electric rendezvous / Passion, grace and fire / Cruisin' / Black cat shuffle / Ritmo de la noche / Somalia / Jewel inside a dream
CD 4682162
Columbia / Nov '93 / Sony

ELEGANT GYPSY
Flight over Rio / Midnight tango / Mediterranean sundance / Race with devil on Spanish highway / Lady of Rome / Sister of Brazil / Elegant gypsy suite
CD 4682132
Sony Jazz / Jan '95 / Sony

HEART OF THE IMMIGRANTS
Nightclub 1960 / Vistaero / Carousel requiem / Tango II / Under a dark moon / Bordel 1900 / Indigo / Heru mertar/Don't go so far away / Parranda / Someday my Prince will come / Cafe 1930 / They love me from fifteen feet away / Milonga del angel
CD RZ 79052
Tomato / May '93 / Vital

KISS MY AXE
South bound traveller / Embrace / Kiss my axe / Morocco / Gigi's playtime rhyme (interlude No. 1) / One night last June / Phantom / Erotic interlude (interlude No. 2) / Global safari / Interlude 3 / Purple orchids / Prophet (interlude No.4) / Oriana (September 24, 1988)
CD 700782
Tomato / Jul '92 / Vital

LAND OF THE MIDNIGHT SUN
Wizard / Sarabande from violin sonata in B minor / Pictures of the sea (love theme) / Land of the midnight sun / Golden dawn suite (morning fire) / Calmer of the tempests / From ocean to the clouds / Short tales of the Black Forest
CD 4682142
Sony Jazz / Jan '95 / Sony

LIVE - FRIDAY NIGHT IN SAN FRANCISCO (Di Meola, Al & John McLaughlin/Paco De Lucia)
Mediterranean sundance / Rio Ancho / Short tales of the Black Forest / Frevo rasgado / Fantasia suite for two guitars / Guardian angel
CD 8000472
Philips / Mar '88 / PolyGram

ORANGE & BLUE
CD 5237242
PolyGram Jazz / Oct '94 / PolyGram

SCENARIO
CD CK 38944
Sony Jazz / Aug '97 / Sony

SPLENDIDO HOTEL
CD 4670902
Sony Jazz / Jan '95 / Sony

THIS IS JAZZ
Race with the devil on Spanish highway / Ritmo de la noche / Short tales of the black forest / Nena / Fantasia suite for two guitars / Viva la danzarina / Guitars of the exotic isle / Rhapsody italia / Bravoto fantasia / African night / Cruisin / Spanish eyes / Passion / Grace and fire / Silent story in her eyes / Sarabande
CD CK 65047
Sony Jazz / May '97 / Sony

TOUR DE FORCE
CD 4682172
Sony Jazz / Jan '95 / Sony

Di Novi, Gene

LIVE AT THE MONTREAL BISTRO TORONTO (Di Novi, Gene Trio)
Introduction / TNT / Happy harvest / Things we did last summer/Indian summer / Terry's little tune / Nieves / Tune for Mac / AB's blues / It happened in Monterey / You better go now / Coffee time / Tiny's blues
CD CCD 79726
Candid / Jan '97 / Cadillac / Direct / Jazz Music / Koch / Wellard

RENAISSANCE OF A JAZZ MASTER
Cockeyed optimist / Springsville / Till the clouds roll by / Right as the rain / Bill / It never entered my mind / Budding memories / Elegy / My old flame / Have a heart / Speak low
CD CCD 79708
Candid / Feb '97 / Cadillac / Direct / Jazz Music / Koch / Wellard

Di Sarli, Carlos

A LA GRAN MUNECA
CD BMT 003
Blue Moon / Feb '97 / Cadillac / Jazz Music / Greensleeves / Jazz Music / Jet Star / TKO Magnum

Diabate, Abdoulaye

DJIRIYO
CD STCD 1066
Stern's / Mar '96 / ADA / CM / Stern's

Diabate, Djanke

SABOU SABOU
CD SMCD 1169
Sonima / Jan '97 / Stern's

Diabate, Mama

N'NA NIWALE
CD PAMOA 205
PAM / Mar '95 / ADA / Direct

Diabate, Sekou Bembeya

DIAMOND FINGERS
CD 2002849
Dakar Sound / Jan '97 / Stern's

Diabate, Sekouba

LE DESTIN
CD OA 202
PAM / Feb '94 / ADA / Direct

Diabate, Sona

KANKELE TI
CD PAM 401
PAM / Feb '94 / ADA / Direct

Diabate, Toumani

DJELIKA
Djelika / Mankoman djan / Cheik oumar bah / Marielle / Kandjoura / Aminata santoro / Tony vander / Sankoun djabi
CD HNCD 1380
Hannibal / Sep '95 / ADA / Vital

KAIRA
CD HNCD 1338
Hannibal / May '89 / ADA / Vital

Diablos Rising

666
CD CD 023
Osmose / Oct '94 / Plastic Head

BLOOD, VAMPIRISM AND SADISM
CD KRONH 02CD
Osmose / Feb '96 / Plastic Head

Diabolical Masquerade

PHANTOM LODGE, THE
CD CDAR 039
Adipocre / May '97 / Plastic Head

RAVENDUSK IN MY HEART
CD CDAR 036
Adipocre / Dec '96 / Plastic Head

Diaboliks

DANGER
CD ID 123341CD
Dionysus / Nov '96 / Cargo / Greyhound / Plastic Head

Diabolique

WEDDING THE GROTESQUE
CD BS 011CD
Burning Sun / Mar '97 / Plastic Head

Diagne, Boubacar

TABALA WOLOF (Sufi Drumming From Senegal)
CD VPU 1002CD
Village Pulse / May '97 / ADA

Diamond Accordion Band

COUNTRY CRAZY (45 Great Country Hits)
Blanket on the ground / Top of the world / Take me home country roads / Hey good lookin' / Old faithfull / Don't fence me in / Spanish eyes / Yellow bird / South of the border / Tie a yellow button / Are you lonesome tonight / Adios amigo / Yellow rose of texas / You're cheatin heart / San antonio rose / Cryin' time / Only you / Crazy / Sweet dreams / I fall to pieces / She's got you / Oh lonesome me / Sea of heartbreak / Hello Mary Lou / Things / One day at a time / King of the road / From a jack to a king / Walk on by / Lil 'ole wine drinker me / Blueberry hill / Who's sorry now / You're my best freind / Paper roses / Roses of picardy / Red roses for a blue lady / Ramblin' rose / Wolverton mountain / Jambalaya / Pretty brwon eyes / Welcome to my world / Distant drums / Ten guitars / Beautiful sunday / Is this the way to Amarillo / Stand by your man / You're cheatin' heart / Send me the pillow you dream on
CD MCVD 30007
Emerald Gem / Nov '96 / BMG

PLAY COUNTRY GREATS
CD EMPRCD 510
Emporio / Apr '94 / Disc

SINGALONG PARTY
Robert E Lee / California here I come / Baby face / I'm looking over a four leaf clover / Carolina in the morning / Pretty baby / My mammy / Toot toot tootsie / Chinatown my chinatown / Ma he's making eyes at me / April showers / Rock bye baby / Don't dilly dally / Goodbye Dolly Gray / Run rabbit run / Wish me luck / Swanee / You made me love / Maybe it's because I'm a Londoner / Underneath the arches / Whatever will be will be (Que sera sera) / Liverpool Lou / How much is that doggie / After the ball is over / Happy wanderer / Roll out the barrel / It's a long way to Tipperary / Pack up your troubles / By the light of the silvery moon / If you were the only girl in the world / Lily of laguna / Mocking bird hill / Oh dear what can the matter be / Two lovely black eyes / Two little girls in blue
CD EMPRCD 591
Emporio / Oct '95 / Disc

WALTZES
Annie's song / Tulips from Amsterdam / By the side of Zuder Zee / Miller's daughter / Carnival of Venice / Tippi-tippi-tin / Softly softly, good luck, good health, god bless you / Old rockin' chair / There goes my everything / My Florence / We will make love / Delilah / Lady of Spain / Cruisin' down the river / Windmill song / Under the bridges of Paris / Gordon for me / Northern lights of Aberdeen / These are my mountains / Home on the range / Carolina moon / When I grow too old to dream / I wonder whose kissing her now / Far away places / Ramona / Where the blue of the night / Whiffenspoof song / It's sin to tell a lie / Four in the morning / Morning has broken / Oh what a beautiful morning / Three o'clock in the morning / Anniversary waltz / Now is the hour / Beautiful dreamer / Moon river / Plaisir d'amour / Edelweiss / Somewhere my love / Loveliest night of the year / Reine de musette / You take the high road / I belong to glasgow / Flower of Scotland / Auld lang syne / Twelfth of never / Are you lonesome tonight / Eternally / Daisy bell / Irene goodnight / My bonnie lies over the ocean / On top of old smokey / Anna Marie / When the girl in your arms / You're the only good thing that's happened to me / I'll be with you in apple blossom time / Always / Let me call you sweetheart
CD MCVD 30009
Emerald Gem / Nov '96 / BMG

Diamond Head

AM I EVIL
Am I evil / Heat of the night / Don't you ever leave me / Borrowed time / To Heaven from Hell / Dead reckoning / Lightning to the nations / Sucking my love
CD WKFMXD 92
FM / Sep '94 / Revolver / Sony

BEHOLD THE BEGINNING
It's electric / Prince / Sweet and innocent / Sucking my love / Streets of gold / Play it loud / Shoot out the lights / Waited too long / Helpless
CD HMRXD 165
Heavy Metal / May '91 / Revolver / Sony

DEATH & PROGRESS
Starcrossed (lovers of the night) / Truckin' / Calling your name (the light) / I can't help myself / Paradise / Dust run / Wild on the streets / Damnation street / Home
CD ESMCD 387
Essential / Jul '96 / BMG

DIAMOND HEAD
CD HMRXD 92
Heavy Metal / May '87 / Revolver / Sony

DIAMOND HEAD - IN THE BEGINNING
CD WKFMCD 165
FM / Feb '91 / Revolver / Sony

EVIL LIVE
CD Set ESDCD 219
Essential / Sep '94 / BMG

Diamond Rio

CLOSE TO THE EDGE
Oh me, oh my, sweet baby / In a week or two / It does get better than this / Sawmill road / Calling all hearts (Come back home) / This Romeo ain't got Julie yet / I was meant to be with you / Old weakness (Coming on strong) / Demons and angels / Nothing in this world / Close to the edge
CD 07822186562
Arista / Oct '93 / BMG

FOUR IV
Holdin' / Walkin' away / That's what I get for loving you / She misses him on Sunday the most / She sure did like to run / It's all in your head / Who am I / Love takes you there / Is that askin' too much / Just another heart / Big
CD ____ 07822188122
Arista / Apr '96 / BMG

GREATEST HITS
How your love makes you feel / Meet me in the middle / Mirror mirror / Mama don't you forget to pray for me / Norma Jean Riley / In a week or two / Love a little stronger / Night is fallin' in my heart / Bubba Hyde / Walkin' away / It's all in your head / Holdin' / She misses him on Sunday the most / Imagine that
CD ____ 07822188442
Arista / Jul '97 / BMG

LITTLE STRONGER, A
CD ____ 07822187452
Arista / Aug '94 / BMG

Diamond Wookie

FOXBURY RULES, THE
Avenue du bois / Hand me downs / Back to the flat / Oscar / Unglamorous madness / To Monte Carlo Mr Noyes / Dance of the dibnah
CD ____ IBCD 7
Internal Bass / Apr '97 / Prime / Timewarp / Total/BMG

Diamond, Jim

JIM DIAMOND
I won't let you down / I should have known better / Hi ho silver / Not man enough / Our love / I still love you / We dance the night away / It's true what they say / If you're gonna break my heart / Devil in my eyes / Child's heart / Goodnight tonight
CD ____ 8438472
PolyGram TV / May '93 / PolyGram

Diamond, Neil

12 GREATEST HITS VOL.2
Beautiful noise / Hello again / Forever in blue jeans / September morn / Desiree / You don't bring me flowers / America / Be / Longfellow serenade / If you know what I mean / Yesterday's songs / Love on the rocks
CD ____ CD 85844
CBS / May '87 / Sony

20 GOLDEN GREATS: NEIL DIAMOND
CD ____ MCD 11452
MCA / May '96 / BMG

BEAUTIFUL NOISE
Beautiful noise / Stargazer / Lady oh / Don't think / Feel / Surviving the life / If you know what I mean / Street life / Home is a wonderful heart / Jungletime / Signs / Dry your eyes
CD ____ 4504522
CBS / Mar '91 / Sony

CHRISTMAS ALBUM, THE
O come o come Emmanuel/We three kings of Orient are / Silent night / Little drummer boy / Santa Claus is coming to town / Christmas song / Morning has broken / Happy Christmas (war is over) / White Christmas / God rest ye merry gentlemen / Jingle bell rock / Hark the herald angels sing / Silver bells / You make it feel like Christmas / Holy night
CD ____ 4724102
Columbia / Nov '96 / Sony

CHRISTMAS ALBUM, THE VOL.2
Joy to the world / Mary's boy child / Deck the halls/We wish you a merry Christmas / Winter wonderland / Have yourself a merry little Christmas / I'll be home for Christmas / Rudolph the red nosed reindeer / Sleigh ride / Candlelight carol / Away in a manger / O come all ye faithful (Adeste Fidelis) / O little town of Bethlehem / Angels we have heard on high / First Noel / Hallelujah chorus
CD ____ 4775982
Columbia / Nov '94 / Sony

CLASSICS (The Early Years)
Kentucky woman / Cherry, Cherry / Solitary man / You got to me / I got the feelin' (oh no no) / Thank the Lord for the night time / I'm a believer / Girl, you'll be a woman soon / Shilo / Do it / Red red wine / Boat that I row
CD ____ CD 32349
CBS / Apr '89 / Sony

DIAMOND SYMPHONIES, THE (London Philharmonic Orchestra)
Overture / Holly Holy / Cracklin' Rosie / Brother love's travelling / Salvation show / Play me / Forever in blue jeans / Sweet Caroline / September morn / I am...I said / Beautiful noise / You don't bring me flowers / Song sung blue / Shilo / Kentucky woman / Song sung blue reprise
CD ____ QED 053
Tring / Nov '96 / Tring

DIAMOND SYMPHONIES, THE (The Music Of Neil Diamond) (London Philharmonic Orchestra)
Overture / Holly holy / Medley / Play me / Forever in blue jeans / Sweet Caroline / September morn / I am...I said / Beautiful noise / You don't bring me flowers / Medley
CD ____ ECD 3300
K-Tel / Feb '97 / K-Tel

GREATEST HITS (1966-1992)
Solitary man / Cherry, Cherry / I got the feelin' (oh no no) / Thank the Lord for the night time / Girl, you'll be a woman soon / Kentucky woman / Shilo / You got to me / Brooklyn roads / Red red wine / I'm a believer / Sweet caroline / Soolaimon / Cracklin' rosie / Song sung blue / Play me / Holly holy / Morning side / Crunchy granola suite / Brother love's travelling salvation show / I am...I said / Longfellow serenade / Beautiful noise / If you know what I mean / Desiree / September morn / You don't bring me flowers / Forever in blue jeans / Hello again / America / Love on the rocks / Yesterday's songs / Heartlight / Headed for the future / Heartbreak hotel: *Diamond, Neil & Kim Carnes* / All I really need is you
CD Set ____ 4715022
Columbia / Jun '92 / Sony

HOT AUGUST NIGHT
Prologue / Crunchy granola suite / Done too soon / Dialogue / Solitary man / Cherry, Cherry / Sweet Caroline / Porcupine pie / You're so sweet / Red red wine / Soggy pretzels / And the grass won't pay no mind / Shilo / Girl, you'll be a woman soon / Play me / Canta libre / Morningside / Song sung blue / Cracklin' Rosie / Holly holy / I am...I said / Walk off / Soolaimon / Brother Love's travelling salvation show / Encore
CD Set ____ MCLDD 19042
MCA / Apr '92 / BMG

HOT AUGUST NIGHTS VOL.2
Song of the whales / Headed for the future / September morn / Thank the Lord for the night time / Cherry, Cherry / Sweet Caroline / Hello again / Love on the rocks / America / Forever in blue jeans / You don't bring me flowers / I dreamed a dream / Back in LA / Song sung blue / Cracklin' Rosie / I am...I said / Holly holy / Soolaimon / Brother Love's travelling salvation show / Heartlight
CD ____ 4604082
CBS / Nov '87 / Sony

IN MY LIFETIME (3CD Set)
In my lifetime / Hear them bells / Blue destiny / Million miles away / Good kind of lonely / What will I do / At night / Clown town / Flame / Straw in the wind / Solitary man / Cherry, Cherry / I got the feelin' (oh no no) / I'm a believer / Kentucky woman / Boat that I row / Girl, you'll be a woman soon / You got to me / Thank the Lord for the night time / Red red wine / Shilo / Brooklyn roads / And the grass won't pay no mind / Sweet Caroline / Holly holy / Brother love's travelling salvation show / Cracklin' Rosie / Done too soon / Morningside / Soolaimon / He ain't heavy, he's my brother / Crunchy Granola suite / Play me / I am...I said / Song sung blue / Jonathan Livingston Seagull suite / Prologue / Lonely looking sky / Skybird / Dear father / Be / I've been this way before / Longfellow serenade / Beautiful noise / If you know what I mean / Dry your eyes / Desire / September morn / Forever in blue jeans / You don't bring me flowers: *Diamond, Neil & Barbra Streisand* / America / Love on the rocks / Scotch on the rocks / Hello again / Yesterday's songs / I'm alive / Heaven can wait / Heartlight / Just need to love you more / You make it feel like Christmas / Falling / Dancing to the party next door / Story of my life / I'm sayin' I'm sorry / If there were no dreams / Headed for the future / Hooked on the memory of you / Angel above my head / Everybody
CD Set ____ C3K 65013
Columbia / Oct '96 / Sony

LIVE IN AMERICA (2CD Set)
America / Hello again / Kentucky woman / You got me / Cherry, Cherry / I'm a believer / Sweet Caroline / Love on the rocks / Hooked on the memory of you / Lady oh / Beautiful noise / Play me / Up on the roof / You've lost that lovin' feelin' / River deep, mountain high / I who have nothing / Missa / Soolaimon / Holly holy / Grass won't pay no mind / You don't bring me flowers / September morn / Hava nagila / Solitary man / Red red wine / Song sung blue / Forever in blue jeans / Heartlight / Cracklin' Rosie / I am...I said / Crunchy granola suite / Brother Love's travelling salvation show
CD Set ____ 4772112
Columbia / Jun '97 / Sony

LOVE AT THE GREEK
Kentucky woman / Sweet Caroline / Last Picasso / Longfellow serenade / Beautiful noise / Lady oh / Stargazer / If you know what I mean / Surviving the life / Glory road / Song sung blue / Holly Holy / Brother Love's travelling salvation show / Jonathan Livingstone Seagull / I've been this way before / Be / Dear father / Lonely looking sky / Sanctus / Skybird / Be (encore)
CD ____ CD 95001
CBS / Mar '87 / Sony

LOVE SONGS
Theme / If you go away / Last thing on my mind / Coldwater morning / Juliet / Both sides now / Play me / Hurtin' you don't come easy / Husbands and wives / Until it's time for you to go / And the grass won't pay no mind / Modern day version of love / Suzanne
CD ____ MCBD 19525
MCA / Apr '97 / BMG

LOVESCAPE
If there were no dreams / Mountains of love / Someone who believes in you / When you miss your love / Fortunes of the night / One hand, one heart / Hooked on the memory of you / Wish everything was alright / Way / Sweet LA days / All I really need is you / Lonely lady no.17 / I feel you / Common ground
CD ____ 4688902
Columbia / Oct '91 / Sony

MOODS
Song sung blue / Porcupine pie / High rolling man / Canta Libre / Captain sunshine / Play me / Gitchy goomy / Walk on water / Theme / Prelude in E Major / Morningside
CD ____ MCLD 19043
MCA / Apr '92 / BMG

NEIL DIAMOND SONGBOOK (Various Artists)
CD ____ VSOPCD 172
Connoisseur Collection / Jun '92 / Pinnacle

SEPTEMBER MORN
September morn / Mama don't know / That kind / Jazz time / Good Lord loves you / Dancing in the street / Shelter of your arms / I'm a believer / Sun ain't gonna shine anymore / Stagger Lee
CD ____ 4844552
Columbia / Feb '97 / Sony

SERENADE
I've been this way before / Rosemary's wine / Lady Magdelene / Last Picasso / Longfellow serenade / Yes I will / Reggae strut / Gift of song
CD ____ 4650122
Columbia / Dec '95 / Sony

STONES
I am...I said / Last thing on my mind / Husbands and wives / Chelsea morning / Crunchy Granola Suite / Stones / If you go away / Suzanne / I think it's going to rain today
CD ____ MCLD 19118
MCA / Apr '92 / BMG

SWEET CAROLINE/MOODS (2CD Set)
Brother love's travelling salvation show / Dig in / River runs, newgrown plums / Juliet / Long gone / And the grass won't pay no mind / Glory road / Deep in the morning / If I never knew your name / Memphis streets / You're so sweet / Horseflies keep hangin' round your face / Hurtin' you don't come easy / Sweet Caroline / Song sung blue / Porcupine pie / High rolling man / Canta libre / Captain Sunshine / Play me / Gitchy goomy / Walk on water / Theme / Prelude in E major / Morningside
CD Set ____ MCD 33005
MCA / Jul '96 / BMG

TAP ROOT MANUSCRIPT
Cracklin' Rosie / Free life / Coldwater morning / Done too soon / He ain't heavy, he's my brother / African trilogy / I am the lion / Madrigal / Soolaimon / Missa / African suite / Child's song
CD ____ MCLD 19119
MCA / Aug '92 / BMG

TENNESSEE MOON (The Nashville Collection)
Tennessee moon / One good love / Shame / Matter of love / Marry me / Deep inside of you / Gold don't rust / Like you do / Can anybody hear me / Win the world / No limit / Reminisce for a while / Kentucky woman / If I lost my way / Everybody / Talking optimist blues (good day today) / Blue highway
CD ____ 4813782
Columbia / Feb '96 / Sony

ULTIMATE COLLECTION, THE
Sweet Caroline / Song sung blue / Cracklin Rosie / Love on the rocks / Beautiful noise / Forever in blue jeans / Hello again / Red, red wine / Everybody's talkin' / Girl, you'll be a woman soon / I'm a believer / Heartlight / Up on the roof / Desiree / If you know what I mean / Longfellow serenade / Play me / You got to me / I (who have nothing) / I am...I said / Solitary man / He ain't heavy, he's my brother / Cherry, Cherry / Walk on water / Soolaimon / Sun ain't gonna shine anymore / Stones / You've lost that loving feelin': *Diamond, Neil & Dolly Parton* / Morning has broken / Chelsea morning / Mr. Bojangles / Yesterdays songs / Thank the lord for the night time / Brother Love's travelling salvation show / September morn / Kentucky woman / I got the feelin' (oh no, no) / America / Holly Holy / You don't bring me flowers: *Diamond, Neil & Barbra Streisand*
CD ____ MOODCD 45
Sony Music / Aug '96 / Sony

UP ON THE ROOF (Songs From The Brill Building)
You've lost that lovin' feelin' / Up on the roof / Love potion no.9 / Will you still love me tomorrow / Don't be cruel / Do wah diddy diddy / I who have nothing / Do you know the way to San Jose / River deep, mountain high / Groovy kind of love / Spanish Harlem / Sweets for my sweet / Happy birthday sweet sixteen / Ten lonely guys / Save the last dance for me
CD ____ 4743562
Columbia / Oct '93 / Sony

VELVET GLOVES AND SPIT (2CD Set)
Two bit manchild / Modern day version of love / Honeydrippin' times / Pot smoker's song / Brooklyn roads / Shilo / Sunday sun / Holiday Inn blues / Practically newborn / Knackelflerg / Merry go round
CD ____ MCLD 19044
MCA / Apr '92 / BMG

VERY BEST OF NEIL DIAMOND
Sweet Caroline / Girl, you'll be a woman soon / Walk on water / Soolaimon / Morningside / Cracklin' Rosie / Play me / Holly holy / Stones / Song sung blue / Brooklyn roads / I am...I said
CD ____ PWKS 510
Carlton / Feb '96 / Carlton

Diamonds

BEST OF THE DIAMONDS, THE (The Mercury Years)
Why do fools fall in love / Church bells may ring / Cool baby cool / Ka ding dong / My judge and my jury / Every minute of the day / Little darlin' / Zip zip / Don't say goodbye / Words of love / Dance with me / Daddy cool / Silhouettes / Stroll / Walking along / High sign / She say (oom dooby doom) / Batman, Wolfman, Frankenstein or Dracula / Oh Carol / Believe me / Chimes in my heart / One summer night
CD ____ 5527592
Spectrum / Feb '97 / PolyGram

Di'Anno, Paul

HARD AS IRON (Di'Anno, Paul & Dennis Stratton)
CD ____ CDTB 176
Thunderbolt / Jun '96 / TKO Magnum

HEARTUSER
Heartuser / Tales of the unexpected / Antigue
CD ____ WKFMPD 1
FM / Aug '84 / Revolver / Sony

IRON MEN, THE
CD ____ ASBCD 004
Scratch / Jul '95 / Koch / Scratch/BMG

ORIGINAL IRON MAN, THE
CD ____ ASBCD 008
Scratch / Dec '96 / Koch / Scratch/BMG

SOUTH AMERICAN ASSAULT
CD ____ SPV 08438952
SPV / Aug '94 / Koch / Plastic Head

Diary Of Dreams

END OF FLOWERS
CD ____ EFA 036012
Accession / Mar '96 / SRD

Dias, Jose Barrense

ESCULTOR DE IMAGEM
CD ____ KAR 973
Kardum / Sep '93 / Discovery

Dias, Sergio

MIND OVER MATTER
CD ____ EXPALCD 8
Expression / Aug '91 / Pinnacle

Diatribe

DIATRIBE
CD ____ REC 007
Re-Constriction / Nov '96 / Cargo

Diaz, Alirio

ART OF SPANISH GUITAR, THE
CD ____ 14129
Laserlight / Jun '94 / Target/BMG

Diaz, Daniel

YEARS ALONE, THE
CD ____ XENO 4031CD
Xenophile / Mar '96 / ADA / Direct

Diaz, Diomedes

CANTANDO (Diaz, Diomedes & Nicholas Colacho Mendoza)
Esperanza / Cantando / Te necesito / Myriam / Cardon guarjiro / El medallon / Por amor a dios / Paisana mia / Siempre contigo / Las cosas del amor
CD ____ CDORB 055
Globestyle / Mar '90 / Pinnacle

Diaz, Hugo

20 BEST OF CLASSICAL "TANGO ARGENTINO" (Diaz, Hugo Trio)

CD EUCD 1094
ARC / '91 / ADA / ARC Music

TANGO ARGENTINO (Diaz, Hugo Trio)
CD EUCD 1327
ARC / Nov '95 / ADA / ARC Music

Diaz, Joaquin

AFFINITES
CD CD 001CD
Caskabel / Nov '95 / ADA

Diaz, Servando

POSTALES DE MI TIERRA 1940-1942 (Diaz, Servando Trio)
CD TCD 081
Tumbao Cuban Classics / Jul '96 / Discovery

Dibango, Manu

AFRIJAZZY
Masa lemba / Bushman promenade / Gombo sauce / Soir au village / Makossa / Kango / Doula serenade / Abelley sphere
CD EMY 1372
Enemy / Oct '92 / Grapevine/PolyGram

BAO BAO
Makossa rock / Afro beat / Boat people / Big blow / Bao Bao / Chapo-So jam
CD MPG 74035
Movieplay Gold / Jan '97 / Target/BMG

ELECTRIC AFRICA
CD CPCD 8152
Celluloid / Nov '95 / Discovery / Koch

LAMASTABASTANI
CD 859062
Melodie / Apr '96 / ADA / Discovery / Grapevine/PolyGram / Greensleeves / Jet Star

LES INOUBLIABLES DE...
CD 592137
Flarenasch / Feb '97 / Discovery

NEGROPOLITAINES
CD 859052
Melodie / Nov '92 / ADA / Discovery / Grapevine/PolyGram / Greensleeves / Jet Star

PAPA GROOVE
CD 382025
Wotre Music / Jul '96 / Discovery / New Note/Pinnacle

POLYSONIK
Senga Abele lion roar / Yeke Tenge lion line / Soma Loba / Polysonik / Mincalor lion feeling / Kwala Kwala / Negriers / Jazzeries / Polysonik / Mincalor
CD EXVP 7CD
Expression / Feb '97 / Pinnacle

SOUL MAKOSSA
Soul makossa / Rencontre / Taoumba / Moni / New bell 'hard pulsation' / O Boso / Kata kata / Soukouss / Pepe soup / Essimo / Nights in Zeralda
CD 139 215
Musidisc / Aug '90 / Discovery

WAKAFRIKA
Soul Makossa / Biko / Wakafrika / Emma / Homeless / Lady / Hi-life / Wimoweh / Am oh / Jingo / Pata pata / Diarabi / Ca va chouia
CD BLM 001CD
Blue Music / Jun '94 / ADA / CM / Pinnacle

Diblo

MONDO RY
CD 410082
Melodie / '91 / ADA / Discovery / Grapevine/PolyGram / Greensleeves / Jet Star

Dicabor

DICABOR
CD EFA 004102
Space Teddy / Feb '95 / SRD

LIVE AT THE INTERFERENCE FESTIVAL (Dicabor & Dr. Motte)
CD EFA 004122
Space Teddy / Feb '96 / SRD

Dick Nixons

PAINT THE WHITE HOUSE BLACK
CD 422106
New Rose / Jun '94 / ADA / Direct / Discovery

Dick, Robert

THIRD STONE FROM THE SUN
CD 804352
New World / Sep '93 / ADA / Cadillac / Harmonia Mundi

Dickens, Hazel

FEW OLD MEMORIES, A
CD ROUCD 11529
Rounder / '88 / ADA / CM / Direct

HAZEL & ALICE (Dickens, Hazel & Alice Gerrard)
Mining camp blues / Hello stranger / Green rolling hills of West Virginia / Few more years shall roll / Two soldiers / Sweetest gift, a mother's smile / Tomorrow I'll be gone / My better years / Custom made woman blues / Don't put her down, you helped put her there / You gave me a song / Pretty bird / Gallop to Kansas
CD ROUCD 0027
Rounder / May '95 / ADA / CM / Direct

PIONEERING WOMEN OF BLUEGRASS (Dickens, Hazel & Alice Gerrard)
CD SFWCD 40065
Smithsonian Folkways / Jun '96 / ADA / Cadillac / CM / Direct / Koch

Dickens, Little Jimmy

I'M LITTLE BUT I'M LOUD (The Little Jimmy Dickens Collection)
CD RE 21072
Razor & Tie / Jul '96 / Koch

Dickenson, Vic

BREAKS, BLUES AND BOOGIES
My favourite blues / Downtown cafe boogie / Uptown cafe blues / Breaks / I can't believe that you're in love with me / Blues mizz / Victory stride / Joy-mentin' / After you've gone / Just you, just me / Ygon mili jam session / I'm through with love / My blue Heaven / DB blues / Lester blows again / Jammin' with Lester / GUMPEY / Sugar / Blues in the South / Blues for yesterday / I want a little girl
CD TPZ 1065
Topaz Jazz / Jul '97 / Cadillac / Pinnacle

Dickie, Neville

CHARLESTON MAD AND OTHER SONGS OF THE 1920'S
CD SOSCD 1324
Stomp Off / May '97 / Jazz Music / Wellard

HARLEM STRUT
CD SOSCD 1302
Stomp Off / Jul '96 / Jazz Music / Wellard

OH PLAY THAT THING
CD SOSCD 1309
Stomp Off / Jul '96 / Jazz Music / Wellard

Dickies

IDJIT SAVANT
CD CDHOLE 002
Golf / May '95 / Plastic Head

WE AREN'T THE WORLD
CD RE 140CD
ROIR / Nov '94 / Plastic Head / Shellshock/Disc

Dickinson, Bruce

ACCIDENT OF BIRTH
CD RAWCD 124
Raw Power / May '97 / Pinnacle

ALIVE IN STUDIO A (2CD Set)
CD Set RAWDD 102
Raw Power / Apr '96 / Pinnacle

SKUNKWORKS
CD RAWCD 106
Raw Power / Apr '96 / Pinnacle

Dickinson, Jim

THOUSAND FOOTPRINTS IN THE SAND, A (Dickinson, Jim & Chuck Prophet)
CD 3018392
Last Call / Apr '97 / Cargo / Direct / Discovery

Dickinson, Rev. Emmett

REV. EMMETT DICKINSON VOL.1 1929-1930
CD DOCD 5441
Document / May '96 / ADA / Hot Shot / Jazz Music

Dicks

DICKS 1980-1986
CD VIRUS 200CD
Alternative Tentacles / Apr '97 / Cargo / Greyhound / Pinnacle

Dickson, Barbara

AFTER DARK
Right moment / Same sky / Only a dream in Rio / Lush life / I don't believe in you / Caravan / Fortress around your heart / I think it's going to rain today / It's money that I love / Pride (in the name of love) / No milk today / I know him so well
CD CLACD 302
Castle / Aug '92 / BMG

BEST OF BARBARA DICKSON, THE
Caravan song / January February / In the night / Crying game / Run like the wind / Tonight / With a little help from my friends / Answer me / Can't get by without you / Will you love me tomorrow / Stop in the name of love / As time goes by / Stardust / It's really you / I don't believe in miracles / Now I don't know / Tell me it's not true / I believe in you
CD 4837962
Columbia / Feb '96 / Sony

DARK END OF THE STREET
CD TRACD 117
Transatlantic / Apr '96 / Pinnacle

DON'T THINK TWICE IT'S ALL RIGHT
Don't think twice, it's alright / With God on our side / When the ship comes in / Maggie's farm / Tears of rage / Oxford town / You ain't goin' nowhere / When I paint my masterpiece / Times they are a changin' / Ring them bells / Hard rain's gonna fall / Blowin' in the wind
CD MOODCD 25
Columbia / Mar '96 / Sony

GOLD
I know him so well / Missing you / Another good day for goodbye / Touch touch / Anyone who had a heart / Day in the life / You send me / What is love
CD CLACD 297
Castle / '92 / BMG

NOW AND THEN
Follow you follow me / Fine partly cloudy / I think it's going to rain today / Friend in need / It might be you / Fortress around your heart / If you go away / Same sky / September song / If you're right / How long / Peter / West coast of Clare / Tenderly / I don't believe in you / Angie baby / Who are you anyway / Caravans / No milk today / Day in the life / Thousands are sailing / Dream of you / It's raining again today / Every now and then
CD VSOPCD 166
Connoisseur Collection / Jul '91 / Pinnacle

PARCEL OF ROGUES, A
Van Diemen's land / My lagan love / My Johnny was a shoemaker / Fine flowers in the valley / I once loved a lad / Jock O'Hazeldean / Sule skerry / Farewell to whisky / Lovely Joan / Donald Og / Geordie / Oh dear me / Parcel o' rogues
CD CTVCD 126
Castle / Feb '94 / BMG

RIGHT MOMENT, THE
Right moment / Tenderly / She moved through the fair / Time after time / Follow you, follow me / It's raining again today / Wouldn't it be good / Boulder to Birmingham / Who are you anyway / Vanishing days of love / Angie baby / Making history / Fine partly cloudy / If you go away
CD CLACD 310
Castle / Sep '92 / BMG

WORLD OF BARBARA DICKSON, THE
Answer me / Here comes the sun / Lover's serenade / Morning comes quickly / Deep into my soul / High tide / Who was it stole your heart away / Give me space / Drift away / People get ready / From now on / When you touch me this way / I could fall / There's a party in my heart / Stolen love / It makes me feel good / Lean on me / Long and winding road
CD 5520122
Spectrum / May '96 / PolyGram

Dictators

FUCK 'EM IF THEY CAN'T TAKE A JOKE
CD DANCD 052
Danceteria / Nov '94 / ADA / Plastic Head / Shellshock/Disc

Diddley, Bo

20TH ANNIVERSARY OF ROCK 'N' ROLL, THE
Ride the water (part 1) / Not fade away / Kill my body / Drag on / Ride on the water (part 2) / Bo Diddley jam - I'm a man / Hey Bo Diddley / Who do you love / Bo Diddley's a gun slinger / I'm a man
CD EDCD 318
Edsel / '91 / Pinnacle

AIN'T IT GOOD TO BE FREE
Ain't it good to be free / Bo Diddley put the rock in rock 'n' roll / Gotta be a change / I don't want your welfare / Mona, where's your sister / Stabilize yourself / I don't know where I've been / I ain't gonna force it on you / Evil woman / Let the fox talk
CD 422107
New Rose / May '94 / ADA / Direct / Discovery

BO DIDDLEY - THE CHESS YEARS (12CD Set)
I'm a man / Little girl / Bo Diddley / You don't love me (You don't care) / Diddley daddy / She's fine, she's mine / Pretty thing / Heart o-matic love / Bring it to Jerome / Spanish guitar / Dancing girl / Diddy wah diddy / I'm looking for a woman / I'm bad / Who do you love / Cops and robbers / Down home special / Hey Bo Diddley / Mona (I need you baby) / Say boss man / Before you accuse me / Say man / Hush your mouth / Bo's guitar / Clock strikes twelve / Dearest Darling / Willie and Lillie / Bo meets the monster / Crackin' up / Don't let it go / I'm sorry / Oh yeah / Blues blues / Great Grandfather / Mamma mia / Bucket / What do you know about love / Lazy woman / Come on baby / Nursery rhyme (Puttentang) / Mumblin' guitar / I love you so / Story of Bo Diddley / She's alright / Limber / Say man back again / Run Diddley Daddy / Roadrunner / Spend my life with you / Love you baby / Diddlin' / Cadillac / Limbo / Look at my baby / You know I love you / Let me in / Signifying blues / Live my life / Scuttle bug / Love me / Deed and deed I do / Walkin' and talkin' / Travellin' west / Crawdad / Ride on Josephine / No more lovin' / Do what I say / Doing the crawdaddy / Whoa / Mule (shine) / Cheyenne / Sixteen tons / Working man / Gunslinger / Somwhere / Sick and tired / Huckleberry bush / All together / Mess around / Shank / Twister / Bo Diddley is a lover / Love is a secret / Bo diddley is loose / Congo / Aztec / Call me / Bo's vacation / Hong Kong / Mississippi / Quick draw / You're looking good / Back home / Not guilty / Moon baby / Untitled instrumental / My babe / Detour / Stay sharp / Pills (love's labours lost) / Bo's bounce / I want my baby / Two flies / Background / Please Mr. Engineer / Doin' the jaguar / I know, I'm alright / For the love of Mike / Mr. Khrushchev / You all green / Bo's twist / I can tell / You can't judge a book by the cover / Sad sack / Rock 'n' roll / Mama don't allow no twistin' / Give me a break / Babes in the woods / Who may your lover be / Here 'tis / Bo's a lumberjack / (Extra read all about) Ben / Help out / Gimme gimme / Same old thing / Diana / Met you on a Saturday / Put the shoes on willie / Pretty girl / Ol' man river / Surfer's love call / Cookie headed Diddley / Greatest lover in the world / Surf sink or swim / Low tide / Africa speaks / Memphis / Old smokey / Bo Diddley's dog / I'm alright / Mr. Custer / Bo's waltz / What's buggin' you / Monkey Diddle / Hey good lookin' / Mama keep your big mouth shut / Jo-Ann / When the saints go marching in / Mush mouth Millie / London stomp / Rooster stew / Mummy walk / La la la / Yeah yeah yeah / Rain man / I wonder why (people don't like me) / Brother bear / Bo Diddley's hoot'nanny / Let's walk awhile / You ain't bad / Somebody beat me / Greasy spoon / Let me pass / Tonight is ours / Soul food / Let the kids dance / Hey red riding hood / He's so mad / Stop my monkey / Root hoot / Stinkey / Cornbread / Fireball / 500% more man / We're gonna get married / Easy / Do the frog / Yakky doodle / Ooh baby / Back to school / Juke / Long distance call / I just want to make love to you / Sad hours / Wrecking my love life / Boo-ga-loo before you go / Little red rooster / Sweet little angel / Goin' down slow / Spoonful / I'm high again / Another sugar Daddy / Bo Diddley 1969 / Soul train / Elephant man / I've got a feeling / If the bible's right / Power house / Funky sly / Shut up woman / Back soul / You Bo Diddley / I don't like you / Hot buttered blues / Bo's beat / Chuck's beat / I love you more than you'll ever know / Shape I'm in / Pollution / Bad moon rising / Down on the corner / I said shutup woman / Bad side of the moon / Lodi / Go for broke / Look at granma / Woman / Hey Jerome / Take it all off / I've had it hard / Bad trip / Good thing / Infatuation / Bo Diddley-itis / I hear you knocking / Make a hit record / Do the robot / Get out of my life / Don't want no lyin' woman / Bo-jam / Husband in law / Sneakers on a rooster / Going down / I've been workin' / Hit or miss / He's got all the whisky / Bite you / Evelee / Stop the pusher / You've got a lot of nerve / I'm sweet on you baby / You got to love me baby / Rollercoaster / I got to go / Billy's blues / Billy's blues / She's alright (unedited) / Signifying blues (extended version) / Pretty baby / You can shimmy / I'm hungry / Oh yes / Watusi bounce / Soup maker / Hey, go go
CD Set CDREDBOX 8
Charly / Feb '94 / Koch

BO DIDDLEY IS A LOVER
Not guilty / Hong Kong, Mississippi / You're looking good / Bo's vacation / Congo / Bo Diddley is a lover / Aztec / Back home / Bo Diddley is loose / Love is a secret / Quick draw / Two flies / Help out / Diana / Mamma mia / What do you know about love / My babe
CD SEECD 391
See For Miles/C5 / Dec '93 / Pinnacle

BO'S BLUES
Down home special / You don't love me (you don't care) / Blues blues / 500% more man / Live my life / She's fine, she's mine / Heart-o-matic love / Bring it to Jerome / Pretty thing / You can't judge a book by the cover / Clock strikes twelve / Cops and robbers / Run diddley daddy / Before you accuse me / Diddy wah diddy / Bo's blues / Little girl / I'm a man / I'm bad / Who do you love / I'm looking for a woman / Two flies
CD CDCHD 396
Ace / Aug '93 / Pinnacle

CHESS MASTERS
I'm a man / Diddley daddy / Pretty thing / Bring it to Jerome / Diddy wah diddy / Who do you love / Hey Bo Diddley / Mona / Say boss man / Before you accuse me / Day man / Hush your mouth / Dearest darling / Crackin' up / I'm sorry / Mumblin' guitar / Roadrunner / Sixteen tons / Ride on Josephine / You can't judge a book by the cover

CD ____________ **CDMF 077**
Magnum Force / '90 / TKO Magnum

COLLECTION, THE
CD ____________ **CCSCD 417**
Castle / Jun '96 / BMG

EP COLLECTION, THE
Little girl / Put the shoes on Willie / Run Diddley daddy / Bo Diddley / I'm a man / Bring it on Jerome / Pretty thing / Greatest lover in the world / She's fine, she's mine / Hey good lookin' / Deed and deed I do / I'm sorry / Dearest darling / Bo meets the monster / Rooster stew / Bo's a lumberjack / Let me in / Hong Kong, Mississippi / Hey Bo Diddley / Before you accuse me / Story of Bo Diddley / You're looking good / I'm looking for a woman / Hush your mouth
CD ____________ **SEECD 321**
See For Miles/C5 / Jul '91 / Pinnacle

HEY BO DIDDLEY
Bo Diddley / Hey Bo Diddley / I'm a man / Bring it to Jerome / Diddley daddy / Before you accuse me / Pretty thing / Who do you love / Dearest darling / You can't judge a book by the cover / Say, mam / I'm looking for a woman / Roadrunner / Mona / Cops and robbers / Story of Bo Diddley / Say bossman / Hush your mouth / Nursery rhyme / I'm sorry / Live my life
CD ____________ **CDRB 1**
Charly / Apr '94 / Koch

HEY BO DIDDLEY/BO DIDDLEY
Hey Bo Diddley / I'm a man / Detour / Before you accuse me / Bo Diddley / Hush your mouth / My babe / Roadrunner / Shank / I know / Here 'tis / I'm looking for a woman / I can tell / Mr. Khrushchev / Diddlin' / Give me a break / Who may your lover be / Bo's bounce / You can't judge a book by the cover / Babes in the woods / Sad sack / Mama don't allow no twistin' / You all green / Bo's twist
CD ____________ **BGOCD 287**
Beat Goes On / Jul '95 / Pinnacle

HIS BEST
CD ____________ **MCD 09373**
Chess/MCA / Aug '97 / BMG / New Note/ BMG

IN CONCERT WITH MAINSQUEEZE
CD ____________ **AIM 1023CD**
Aim / Oct '93 / ADA / Direct / Jazz Music

LET ME PASS...PLUS
Let me pass / Stop my monkey / Greasy spoon / Tonight is ours / Root toot / Slinkey / Hey red riding hood / Let the kids dance / He's so mad / Soul food / Cornbread / Somebody beat me / 500% more man / Mama keep your big mouth shut / We're gonna get married / Easy
CD ____________ **SEECD 392**
See For Miles/C5 / Jan '94 / Pinnacle

LIVING LEGEND
CD ____________ **ROSE 188CD**
New Rose / Sep '89 / ADA / Direct / Discovery

MAN AMONGST MEN, A
CD ____________ **0630148172**
Code Blue / May '96 / Warner Music

MIGHTY BO DIDDLEY, THE
CD ____________ **TX 51161CD**
Triple X / Sep '95 / Plastic Head

RARE AND WELL DONE
She's alright / Heart-o-matic love / I'm a man / Little girl / She's fine, she's mine / Bo meets the monster / I'm bad / Blues blues / Rock 'n' roll / No more lovin' / Cookie headed Diddley / Moon baby / Please Mr. Engineer / We're gonna get married / I'm high again
CD ____________ **MCD 09331**
Chess/MCA / Apr '97 / BMG / New Note/ BMG

STORY OF BO DIDDLEY
CD ____________ **3001062**
Scratch / Jul '95 / Koch / Scratch/BMG

Diddley, Sir Bald

PIE GO-MANIA (Diddley, Sir Bald & His Wig-Outs)
CD ____________ **PIECD 001**
Alopecia / Feb '96 / Plastic Head

WHAT'S IN YOUR FRIDGE
CD ____________ **WIGLP 003**
Alopecia / May '95 / Plastic Head

Die Art

BUT
CD ____________ **RTD 19519042**
Our Choice / Nov '94 / Pinnacle

Die Cheerleader

FILTH BY ASSOCIATION
CD ____________ **ABT 097CD**
Abstract / Oct '93 / Cargo / Pinnacle / Total/BMG

Die Drei Travellers

EINE TUTE LUFT AUS BERLIN
Manana/Fridericus-Rex-marsch/Helenenmarsch / Berlin ist auch 'ne schone stadt genau wie Bonn / Wenn ich minister war / Eine tute luft aus Berlin / Es geht wieder los / Neubau swing / Der neue hut / 3D song (ich mochte dich gern plastisch sehn) / Bella Ida / Wann darf ich sie besuchen / Tina Marie / Ein kleiner Eskimo traumt von melonen / 08/15 cocktail / Fraulein/Ich kusse ihre hand, Madame/Schoner / Gigolo/Heut liegt was in der luft / Rechts um / Das schonste am tag ist der morgen / Mich hat's erwischt / Hatschi-boogie / Sieben kleine spatzen / Musikanten tango / Ja, ja die sachsen / Janz weit weg von Berlin / Ich hab' so'n appetit uff'ne bulette / Rosalinde / Sind sie ringer, sind sie boxer / August / Komm herab von deinem esel, schone Gina / Ach kunigunde / Katja polka
CD ____________ **BCD 16014**
Bear Family / Apr '97 / Direct / Rollercoaster / Swift

ICH TRAUME NUR VON BERLIN
Hol' dir 'ne braut aus Berlin / Ich traume nur von Berlin / Tina Marie / Parodie / Benny's bierbar / Ich will keine sauren gurken / Das alte boot am Havelstrand / Barbier mambo / Klapperstorch song / Noch ein tor / Blau weisse hertha / Bleib nicht gleich schiessen / Fahren sie langsam / Heimweh nach dem kurfurstendamm / Die duften madchen von Berlin / 0-3-1-1 Berlin Berlin: *Oldorp, Fred* / Orchestra Italiana: *Oldorp, Fred* / Wer mal am kurfurstendamm seinen kaffee trank: *Oldorp, Fred* / Lucky aus Texas: *Oldorp, Fred* / Die polizei die regelt den verkehr: *Oldorp, Fred* / Ein fensterplatz im himmel: *Oldorp, Fred* / Kleiner bar von Berlin: *Oldorp, Fred* / Ich hab' nach einen koffer in Berlin: *Oldorp, Fred* / Afrika: *Oldorp, Fred* / Au revoir: *Oldorp, Fred* / Nim kein bier mit nach Munchen: *Oldorp, Fred* / Im endeffekt da hast du ja nach mich: *Oldorp, Fred* / Der Berliner liebt musike: *Oldorp, Fred* / Ich bin een Berliner junge: *Oldorp, Fred* / Zu vaters zeiten: *Oldorp, Fred*
CD ____________ **BCD 16026**
Bear Family / May '97 / Direct / Rollercoaster / Swift

Die Hard

LOOKING OUT FOR...
CD ____________ **CR 007CD**
Conversion / Jul '96 / Plastic Head

Die Haut

HEAD ON
CD ____________ **INDIGO 29222**
What's So Funny About / Oct '96 / Cargo

SWEAT (Die Haut Live)
CD ____________ **INDIGO 29402**
What's So Funny About / Oct '96 / Cargo

Die Kreuzen

CENTURY DAYS
CD ____________ **TGLP 30CD**
Touch & Go / Aug '88 / SRD

Die Krupps

FINAL REMIXES, THE
To the hilt / Paradise of sin / Language of reality / Fatherland / Worst case scenario / Shellshocked / Crossfire / Bloodsuckers / Iron man / Inside out / New temptation / Dawning of doom / Ministry of fear / Hi tech low life / Metal machine music / Rings of steel
CD ____________ **ATLASCDD 006**
Equator / Sep '94 / Pinnacle

FOUNDATION
CD ____________ **CTCD 057**
Captain Trip / Jul '97 / Greyhound

METALLE MASCHINEN MUSIK
CD ____________ **KRUPPS 1CD**
The Grey Area / Aug '91 / RTM/Disc

METAMORPHOSIS 1981-1992
CD ____________ **CLP 9812**
Cleopatra / Oct '96 / Cargo / Greyhound / Plastic Head / RTM/Disc / SRD

ODYSSEY OF THE MIND
Last flood / Scent / Metalmorphasis / Isolation / Final option / Alive / Odyssey / LCD / Eggshell / Jekyll or Hyde
CD ____________ **CDXMFN 187**
CD ____________ **CDMFN 187**
Music For Nations / Jul '95 / Pinnacle

PARADISE NOW
Moving beyond / Gods of void / Paradise now / Black beauty / Reconstruction / Behind taste of taboo / Rise up / Fire / Full circle / Vortex / 30 Seconds / Society treaty
CD ____________ **CDMFN 218**
Music For Nations / May '97 / Pinnacle

Die Laughing

GLAMOUR AND SUICIDE
CD ____________ **FEATSHIH 13CD**
Grave News / Apr '96 / Plastic Head

HEAVEN IN DECLINE
CD ____________ **FETISH 15CD**
Grave News / Jun '96 / Plastic Head

Die Lustigen Junggesellen

EDELWEISS
CD ____________ **CNCD 5996**
Disky / Jul '94 / Disky / THE

Die Monster Die

CHROME MOLLY
CD ____________ **JBM 1 CD**
Johnson Brothers Music / Mar '93 / SRD

Die Sonne Satan

SIGILLO
CD ____________ **SMCD 1**
Cacophonous / Sep '96 / Plastic Head / RTM/Disc

Die Toten Hosen

LEARNING ENGLISH VOL.1
CD ____________ **CDVIR 11**
Virgin / Mar '92 / EMI

LOVE, PEACE AND MONEY
Return of Alex / Year 2000 / All for the sake of love / Love song / Sexual / Diary of a lover / Put your money where your mouth is (Buy me) / Love is here / More and more / My land / Wunsch dir was / Wasted years / Perfect criminal / Love machine / Chaos bros
CD ____________ **CDVIR 27**
Virgin / Dec '94 / EMI

Died Pretty

DOUGHBOY HOLLOW
Doused / DC / Sweetheart / Godless / Satisfied / Stop myself / Battle of Stanmore / Love song / Disaster / Out in the rain / Turn your head
CD ____________ **BEGA 121CD**
Beggars Banquet / '92 / RTM/Disc / Warner Music

EVERY BRILLIANT EYE
Sight unseen / Underbelly / Herr godiva / Face toward the sun / Prayer / Ture fools fall / Whitlam Square / Rue for the day / From the dark
CD ____________ **BEGA 108CD**
Beggars Banquet / Apr '90 / RTM/Disc / Warner Music

LOST
Lost / As must have / Winterland / Crawls away / Towers of strength / Out of my hands / Springenfall / Caesar's cold / One day / Free dirt
CD ____________ **BEGA 101CD**
Beggars Banquet / Apr '89 / RTM/Disc / Warner Music

Dieform

ARCHIVES AND DOCUMENTS
CD ____________ **NORMAL 95CD**
Normal / '89 / ADA / Direct

ARCHIVES AND DOCUMENTS
Face against ground / Bondage / New York / Serenade / Serial clones / Deadline 2 / North valley / Necron x / Third generation / Shaved girls / Was / Nostalgia / Tomorrow / Crash in the sky / Eternal language / Reflex 3 / Criminal passion / Sing song / Dance msuic / Maldoror / Es lebe der tod 3 / Murder /projection / Tote kinder aus deutschland / Ataxia / Uns kill / Psychotrope / Dog handler / Purple rain / Newel/ light / Crypt / Song of parlysis / Oltre / Fleshwounds / Post mortem / Sad memory
CD Set ____________ **TUECD 9202**
Tuesday / Mar '95 / Vital

DIE PUPPE
CD ____________ **NORMAL 81CD**
Normal / '89 / ADA / Direct

PHOTOGRAMMES
CD ____________ **NORMAL 106CD**
Normal / '89 / ADA / Direct

POUPEE MECHANIQUE
CD ____________ **NORMAL 83CD**
Normal / '89 / ADA / Direct

SOME EXPERIENCES WITH SHOCK
CD ____________ **NORMAL 82CD**
Normal / '89 / ADA / Direct

TEARS OF EROS
CD ____________ **HY 39100632**
Hyperium / Jul '93 / Cargo / Plastic Head

Dieheim, Susan

DESERT EQUATIONS (Dieheim, Susan & Richard Horowitz)
Ishtar / Got away / I'm a man / Tear / Azax attra / Jum jum / Armour / Desert equations
CD ____________ **MTM 8CD**
Made To Measure / May '96 / New Note/ Pinnacle

Diesel Boy

COCK ROCK
CD ____________ **DON 001CD**
Honest Don's / Jan '97 / Greyhound / Plastic Head

Diesel Park West

LEFT HAND BAND (The Very Best Of Diesel Park West)
All the myths on Sunday / Here I stand / Jackie's still sad / When the hoodoo comes / Fall to love / Boy on top of the news / Bell of hope / I want no mystery / Fine Lily fine / Girl with the name / Like Princes do / King fluid / Let's talk American / Heathen a go go / Above these things / While the world cries decency
CD ____________ **CDCHRM 105**
Chrysalis / Feb '97 / EMI

VERSUS THE CORPORATE WALTZ
CD ____________ **FIENDCD 747**
Demon / May '93 / Pinnacle

Dietrich, Marlene

COLLECTION, THE
CD ____________ **COL 054**
Collection / Mar '95 / Target/BMG

ESSENTIAL MARLENE DIETRICH, THE
Ich bin von kopf bis fuss auf liebe eingestellt / Quand l'amour meurt / Give me the man / Leben ohne liebe kannst du nicht / Mein blondes baby / Allein in einer grossen stadt / Peter / Lola / Wer wird den weinen / Johnny wenn du geburtstag hast / Lili Marlene / Dejeuner du matin / Ou vont les fleurs / Wenn die soldaten / In den kasernen / Und wenn er wiederkommt / Wenn der sommer wieder einzieht / Blowin' in the wind / Der welt war jung / Where have all the flowers gone / Ich werde dich lieben / Der trommelmann / Auf der mundharmonika
CD ____________ **CDEMS 1399**
EMI / May '91 / EMI

FALLING IN LOVE AGAIN
Falling in love again / You do something to me / Ich bin die fesche Lola / You go to my head / Blonde woman / Peter / Boys in the back room / Hot voodoo / Wo ist der man / I've been in love before / Johnny / Give me the man / Mol, je Mennuie / You've got that look / Assez / I gotta get a man
CD ____________ **HADCD 217**
Spotlight On / Jun '97 / Henry Hadaway

FOR THE BOYS IN THE BACKROOM
Lili Marlene / Black market / Johnny / Boys in the backroom / You've got that look / This world of ours / You do something to me
CD ____________ **BSTCD 9109**
Best Compact Discs / May '92 / Complete/ Pinnacle

HIGHLIGHTS AND EVERGREENS (Marlene Dietrich On Radio 1930-1947)
Lili Marlene / Johnny / Quand l'amour / Meurt / Black market / Falling in love again / Illusions / Ich bin die fesche / Lola / Peter / You go to my head / Give me the man
CD ____________ **RY 89**
Radio Years / Aug '97 / Complete/Pinnacle

LILI MARLENE
Lili Marlene / Symphonie / You do something to me / Falling in love again / You go to my head / I've been in love before / You've got that look (that leaves me weak) / Boys in the backroom / Nmm dich unacht vor blonden frauen / Wenn ich mir was wunschen durfte / Ich bin die fesche Lola / Quand l'amour meurt / Give me the man / Kinder, heut abend, da such ich mir was aus / Leben ohne liebe / Wenn die beste freudin / Es liegt in der luft
CD ____________ **CD 393**
Entertainers / Jun '96 / Target/BMG

MARLENE
Kinder, heute'abend / Leben ohne liebe kannst du nicht / Falling in love again / Ich bin die fesche Lola / Quand l'amour meurt / Johnny / Mein blondes baby / Wenn die beste freundin / Wenn ich mir'was wunschen durfte / Allein in einer grossen stadt / Ich bin von kopf bis fuss auf liebe eingestellt / Es liegt in der luft/potpourri / Nimm dich in acht vor blonden frauen / Give me the man
CD ____________ **CDAJA 5039**
Living Era / Oct '88 / Select

MARLENE DIETRICH
CD ____________ **LCD 6006/7**
Fresh Sound / Jan '93 / Discovery / Jazz Music

MARLENE DIETRICH
CD ____________ **16058**
Laserlight / May '94 / Target/BMG

MARLENE DIETRICH
Lili Marlene / La vie en rose / Lola / Boys in the backroom / I may never go home anymore / Another Spring, another love / Go away from my window / Honeysuckle rose / Such trying times / Near you / Allein / Johnny / I can't give you anything but love / Laziest gal in town / Frag nicht warum ich gehe / I wish you love / I'll come back again (maybe I'll come back) / Illusions / Falling in love again / Shir hatan / You go to my head
CD ____________ **399536**
Koch Presents / May '97 / Koch

MARLENE DIETRICH COLLECTOR'S EDITION
CD ____________ **DVGH 7012**
Deja Vu / Apr '95 / THE

MARLENE DIETRICH IN LONDON
I can't give you anything but love / Laziest girl in town / Shir Hatan / La vie en rose / Jonny / Go away from my window / Allein in einer grossen stadt / Lili Marlene / Das lied ist aus / Lola / I wish you love
CD _____ CDSBL 13110
DRG / Nov '92 / Discovery / New Note/ Pinnacle

MARLENE DIETRICH LIVE AT THE CAFE DE PARIS
CD _____ CD 47254
Sony Classical / Nov '91 / Sony

SEI LIEB ZU MIR
CD _____ RMB 75056
Remember / Aug '93 / Total/BMG

Diez Brothers

CLOSE UP
CD _____ ISCD 114
Intersound / Oct '91 / Jazz Music

Diez, Stefan

BAY SONGS (Diez, Stefan Group)
CD _____ ISCD 158
Intersound / Sep '96 / Jazz Music

Dif Juz

EXTRACTIONS
Crosswinds / Starting point / Love insane / Twin and earth
CD _____ CAD 505 CD
4AD / Feb '87 / RTM/Disc

Difference Engine

BREADMAKER
Five listens / Simon's day / Never pull / Tsunami / Flat / Bugpowder / Epiphany
CD _____ LADIDA 034
La-Di-Da / Jul '94 / Vital

Different Trains

ON THE RIGHT TRACK
Birth / This is life / Bits of dust / Dust in the wind / Market place / In my house / Sweet children / Class / To be continued / Workmen / Work / Rain / Tired tide / Swim against the tide / Cruel trick
CD _____ GEPCD 1008
Giant Electric Pea / Apr '94 / Pinnacle

Diga Rhythm Band

DIGA
Sweet sixteen / Magnificent sevens / Happiness is drumming / Razooli / Tal mala
CD _____ RCD 10101
Rykodisc / Sep '91 / ADA / Vital

Digable Planets

BLOWOUT COMB
May 4th movement / Black ego / Dog it / Jettin' / Borough check / Highing fly / Dial 7 (Axiomos of creamy spices) / Art of easing / KB's Alley (mood dudes groove) / Graffiti / Blowing down / Ninth Wonder (Blackitolism) / For corners
CD _____ CDCHR 6087
Cooltempo / Oct '94 / EMI

REACHIN' (A NEW REFUTATION OF TIME AND SPACE)
It's good to be here / Pacifics / Where I'm from / What cool breezes do / Time and space / Rebirth of slick / Last of the spiddyocks / Jimi diggin' cats / La femme fetal / Escapism / Appointment at the fat clinic / Nickel bags / Swoon units / Examination of what
CD _____ CDCHR 6064
Cooltempo / Jan '94 / EMI

Digance, Richard

BEST OF THE TRANSATLANTIC YEARS, THE
England's green and pleasant land / My friend upon the road / Migration memoirs / Natural gas / As the crow flies / Mr. Jailer / How the west was lost / Drag queen blues / Working class millionaire / Dear River Thames / Edward Sayer's brass band / Show me the door / I hear the press gang / Midnight windmill / Money machine / Will we ever see them again / Red lights of Antwerp / Rosemary McLaren of The Strand / Final bow
CD _____ ESMCD 497
Essential / Apr '97 / BMG

LIVE AT THE QEH/COMMERCIAL ROAD
Dear Diana / Summertime day in Stratford / Down petticoat lane / Drinking with Rosie / Journey of the salmon / Up on the seventh floor / Drag queen blues (nearly) / Right back where I started / Taken my lifetime away / I want to be there when you make it / Suicide Sam / Jungle cup final / East end ding dong / Think of me / Jumping Jack frog / Nightingale sang in Berkeley Square / Beauty Queen / Goodbye my friend, goodbye / Heavyweight Albert / Back Street international / Jimmy Greaves
CD _____ BGOCD 304
Beat Goes On / Nov '95 / Pinnacle

Diggers

MOUNT EVEREST
CD _____ CRECD 193
Creation / Mar '97 / 3mv/Vital

Diggle, Steve

HERE'S ONE I MADE EARLIER
CD _____ AXSO 2CD
AX-S / Aug '96 / SRD

Digi Dub

5 YEARS OF DIGI DUB
CD _____ DDCD 002
Digi Dub / Mar '97 / Kudos / Pinnacle / Vital

Digital Orgasm

COME DANCIN'
Another world / Startouchers / Time to believe / Switch the mood / Magick / Running out of time (remix) / Moog eruption / Keep on flying / This generation / Reality / Running out of time / Moog eruption (remix)
CD _____ 4509905022
Dead Dead Good / Aug '92 / Pinnacle

Digital Poodle

DIVISION
Division / Forward march / Totalitarian / Head of Lenin / Left/right / Binary / Elektronic espionage / Reform / Crack / Red star / Rifle
CD _____ LUDDITECD 222
Death Of Vinyl / Mar '94 / Vital

Digital Sun

SPIRAL OF POWER
CD _____ PR 0016CD
Polytox / Jun '97 / Shellshock/Disc

Digital Underground

FUTURE RHYTHM
CD _____ 0097782RAP
Edel / Jul '97 / Pinnacle

SONS OF THE P
DFLO shuffle / Heartbeat props / No nose job / Sons of the P / Flowin' on the D-line / Kiss you back / Tales of the funky / Higher heights of spirituality / Family of the underground / D-flowstrumental / Good thing we're rappin'
CD _____ BLRCD 12
Big Life / Oct '91 / Mo's Music Machine / Pinnacle / Prime

Digits

LITTLE MISCARRIAGE
CD _____ TG 103CD
Touch & Go / Oct '92 / SRD

Digweed, John

JOURNEYS BY DJ VOL.4
CD _____ JDJCD 4
JDJ / Feb '94 / 3mv/Pinnacle / SRD

Dillard & Clark

FANTASTIC EXPEDITION OF DILLARD & CLARK (Dillard, Doug & Gene Clark)
Out on the side / She darked the sun / Don't come rollin' / Train leaves here this morning / Radio song / Git it on brother (git in line brother) / In the plan / Something's wrong / Why not your baby / Lyin' down the middle / Don't be cruel
CD _____ EDCD 192
Edsel / Jun '90 / Pinnacle

THROUGH THE MORNING, THROUGH THE NIGHT (Dillard, Doug & Gene Clark)
No longer a sweetheart of mine / Through the morning, through the night / Rocky top / So sad / Corner street bar / I bowed my head and cried holy / Kansas City Southern / Four walls / Polly / Rollin' in my sweet baby's arms / Don't let me down
CD _____ EDCD 195
Edsel / Feb '91 / Pinnacle

Dillard, Rodney

LET THE ROUGH SIDE DRAG
CD _____ FF 537CD
Flying Fish / Jul '92 / ADA / CM / Direct / Roots

Dillard, Varetta

GOT YOU ON MY MIND
Square dance rock / If (you want to be my baby) / Got you on my mind / Mama don't want (what papa don't want) / One more time / I'm gonna tell my Daddy on you / Skinny Jimmy / Darling listen to the words of this song / Leave a happy fool alone / CC rider / That's why I cry / I got a lot of love / Undecided / Pray for me mother / I miss you Jimmy / Star of fortune / Rules of love / Falling / Old fashioned / Honey / What'll I do / Just multiply / Give me the right / Time was / I can't help myself / That old feeling / Cherry blossom / Pennies from Heaven / Night is never long enough
CD _____ BCD 15431
Bear Family / Jul '89 / Direct / Rollercoaster / Swift

LOVIN' BIRD, THE
(Twee twee twee) the lovin' bird / Teaser / Good to me / Mercy Mr. Percy / Whole lot of lip / What can I say / I don't know what it is but I like it / Hey sweet love / You don't know what you're missing / Little bitty tear / Positive love / You ain't foolin' nobody / You better come home / You know I'm too good for you / Wondering where you are / Scorched / Good gravy baby / One more time / Star of fortune / Rules of love / Old fashioned
CD _____ BCD 15432
Bear Family / Jul '89 / Direct / Rollercoaster / Swift

Dillard-Hartford-Dillard

GLITTER GRASS/PERMANENT WAVE
Don't come rollin' / Cross the borderline / Two hits and the joint turned brown / Don't lead me on / Bear Creek hop / No end love / Biggest whatever / Lost in a world / High dad in the morning / California is nicer than you / Artificial limitations / Get no better / Break it to me gently / That'll be the day / Blue morning / Same thing / Yakety yak / Something's wrong / Boogie on reggae woman / Country boy rock and roll / No beer in heaven
CD _____ FF 036CD
Flying Fish / Feb '93 / ADA / CM / Direct / Roots

Dillards

HOMECOMING AND FAMILY REUNION
Old bald eagle / Hop high ladies / Cripple Creek / Whole world round / Ground hog / High dad in the morning / Douglas and I used to sit around and play / Old Joe Clark / Tennessee breakdown / Ebo Walker / Old man at the mill / Listen to the sound / Daddy was a mover / Banjo signal / Interview fragment
CD _____ FF 70215
Flying Fish / Sep '96 / ADA / CM / Direct / Roots

MOUNTAIN ROCK
Caney Creek / Don't you cry / Reason to believe / Big bayou / Walkin' in Jerusalem / I've just seen a face / High sierra / Never see my home again / Somebody touched me / Fields have turned brown / Orange blossom special
CD _____ 15295
Laserlight / Aug '91 / Target/BMG

TAKE ME ALONG FOR THE RIDE
Someone's throwing stones / In my life / Like a hurricane / Take me along for the ride / Against the grain / Hearts overflowing / Bed of clover / Banks of the rouge bayou / Move on (life of the common man) / Food on the table / Wide wide Dixie highway / Great connection
CD _____ VCD 79464
Vanguard / Jan '97 / ADA / Pinnacle

TRIBUTE TO THE AMERICAN DUCK/ ROOTS & BRANCHES
CD _____ BGOCD 306
Beat Goes On / Mar '96 / Pinnacle

Dilleshaw, John

COMPLETE RECORDED WORKS 1929-1930
CD _____ DOCD 8002
Document / Jan '97 / ADA / Hot Shot / Jazz Music

Dillinger

CB 200
CB 200 / No chuck it / Cokane in my brain / General / Power bank / Plantation heights / Race day / Natty kick like lightning / Buckingham Palace / Crankface
CD _____ RRCD 30
Reggae Refreshers / Sep '91 / PolyGram / Vital

COCAINE
Cocaine in my brain / Jah love / Funkey punk / Mickey Mouse crab louse / I thurst / Loving pauper / Flat foot hustlin' / Crabs in my pants / Marijuana in my brain / Cocaine (remix)
CD _____ CPCD 8020
Charly / Feb '94 / Koch

DILLINGER
CD _____ EXP 012
Experience / May '97 / TKO Magnum

FUNKY PUNK
CD _____ LG 21061
Lagoon / Nov '92 / Grapevine/PolyGram

I NEED A WOMAN
CD _____ RB 3004
Reggae Best / May '94 / Grapevine/ PolyGram

MARIJUANA IN MY BRAIN
Marijuana in my brain / Addis Ababbaithiopia / Bouncing ball / Step it in Ethiopia / Stop stealing in the name of Jah / Come praise Jah Jah / Hard being Thomas / Rasta vibration / African roots reggae
CD _____ CDBS 559
Burning Sounds / Jul '97 / Grapevine/ PolyGram / Jet Star / Total/BMG

SAY NO TO DRUGS
CD _____ LG 21003
Lagoon / Jun '93 / Grapevine/PolyGram

THREE PIECE SUIT
CD _____ LG 21081
Lagoon / Aug '93 / Grapevine/PolyGram

TOP RANKING
CD _____ RNCD 2129
Rhino / Nov '95 / Grapevine/PolyGram / Jet Star

Dillingham, Todd

ART INTO DUST
Little visions / Girl of the scene / You don't mind / Art into dust / Celebration bonfire / It really matters / Never want to see / Fading (just for you) / Fine time no time / African device / Fly / Crabs advancing / Luminous glow / Green pears / Am I alone / Interstellar overdrive
CD _____ VP 121CD
Voiceprint / Jan '93 / Pinnacle

SGT. KIPPER
CD _____ WO 25CD
Woronzow / Jul '95 / Pinnacle

VAST EMPTY SPACES
Vast empty spaces / Shiny girl / Myriad girl-paintings / Rely on me / Dollis broof / Millero / Wonderland / Mullardo / Tranquil water / Nine you dont' want to / Up the ass of a swan / Animal bizarre / Where is the brave
CD _____ VP 153CD
Voiceprint / Aug '94 / Pinnacle

VOICEPRINT RADIO SESSION
CD _____ VPR 002CD
Voiceprint / Oct '94 / Pinnacle

Dillon, Cheralee

CITRON
CD _____ GRCD 380
Glitterhouse / Dec '95 / Avid/BMG

POOL
CD _____ GRCD 310
Glitterhouse / Feb '94 / Avid/BMG

Dillon Fence

OUTSIDE IN
CD _____ MR 0492
Mammoth / Jun '93 / Vital

ROSEMARY
CD _____ MR 00332
Mammoth / Nov '92 / Vital

Dillon, Leonard

ONE STEP FORWARD
CD _____ PRCDSP 400
Prestige / Jun '92 / Else / Total/BMG

Dillon, Phyllis

LOVE WAS ALL I HAD
CD _____ RNCD 2088
Rhino / Dec '94 / Grapevine/PolyGram / Jet Star

ONE LIFE TO LIVE
CD _____ TICD 15004
Studio One / Mar '95 / Jet Star

Dillon, Sandy

DANCING ON THE FREEWAY
CD _____ GY 004
NMC / Mar '94 / Total/Pinnacle

Dils

I HATE THE RICH
CD _____ DAMGOOD 008
Damaged Goods / Jul '92 / Shellshock/ Disc

Dim Dim

NECTARINE (Book/CD Set)
CD _____ BRCD 057
Brinkman / Apr '97 / Cargo

Dim Stars

DIM STARS
CD _____ PAPCD 014
Paperhouse / Apr '92 / RTM/Disc

Dim Sum Clip Job

HARMOLODIC JEOPARDY
CD _____ AVAN 051
Avant / Oct '96 / Cadillac / Harmonia Mundi

Dime Bag

DIME BAG
CD _____ HB 10
Heatblast / Mar '93 / SRD

Dime Store Prophets

FANTASTIC DISTRACTION
CD _____ 246654
Sara Bellum / May '97 / Greyhound

Dimension 5

TRANSDIMENSIONAL
CD INTALCD 001
Intastella / Jun '97 / Arabesque / Flying UK / Prime

Dimitri From Paris

MONSIEUR DIMITRI'S DE-LUXE HOUSE OF FUNK (Various Artists)
Free ton style: *Dimitri From Paris* / Free lovin': *Morning Kids* / You love my music: *Switchblade Sisters* / Number one: *Sir Mang, Raymond* / May the funk be with you: *Second Crusade* / Captain dobbey: *Teddy G* / Visions of paradise: *Sinclair, Bob* / High priestess: *Karma* / Vibe PM: *Mondo Grosso* / Ola-Le: *Takada* / Spy's spice: *UFO* / N'ssi n'ssi: *Khaled, Cheb* / Sometimes: *Brand New Heavies* / Isobel: *Bjork*
CD MMLCD 024
Mixmag Live / Aug '97 / Pinnacle

SACRE BLEU
Prologue / Sacre francais / Monsieur Dimitri joue du stylophone / Nothing to lose / Un termede / Reveries / Attente musicale / Dirty Larry / Free ton style / Un terlude / Une very stylish fille / Un woman's paradis / La rythme et le cadence / Le moogy reggae / Encore un terlude / Un world myteriouse / Par un chemin different / Nothing to lose (lounge instrumentale) / Epilogue
CD YP 011ACD
Yellow / Nov '96 / Timewarp
CD 0630178322
East West / Apr '97 / Warner Music

Dimmu Borgir

DEVIL'S PATH
CD SHAGRATH 006CD
Hot / Oct '96 / Plastic Head

ENTHRONE DARKNESS TRIUMPHANT
CD NB 247CD
Nuclear Blast / Jun '97 / Plastic Head

STORMBLAST
Alt lys er svunnet hen / Broderskapets ring / Nar sjelen hentes til helvete / Sorgens kammer / Da den kristne satte livet til / Stormblast / Dodsferd / Antikrist / Vinder fra en ensom grav / Guds fortapelse - apenbaring av dommedag
CD NIHIL 12CD
Cacophonous / Jun '97 / Plastic Head / RTM/Disc

Dimple Minds

LIVE IN ALZHEIM
CD SPV 08476932
SPV / May '95 / Koch / Plastic Head

Din

FANTASTIC PLANET
CD HY 39100162CD
Hyperium / Nov '92 / Cargo / Plastic Head

Dingle

RED DOG
Hot dingle wood / Haemorrhage / Birdy num num / Xylocheese / Fred Lane / Fleas / Ouise / Vodka tonic / Sailing / Journey on a davenport / Ba da da da / Without hot water / Still going / Still going (instrumental) / Soliloquy / Drinking song / 2-Note / Nuevo imperial / Celine / Mambo samba / Java
CD NAR 110CD
New Alliance / May '94 / Plastic Head

Dinosaur Jr.

BUG
CD BFFP 31 CD
Blast First / Oct '88 / RTM/Disc

FOSSILS
CD SST 275CD
SST / Oct '96 / Plastic Head

GREEN MIND
Wagon / Puke and cry / Flying cloud / How'd you pin that one on me / Water / Muck / Thumb / Green mind / Blowing it/I live for that look
CD 9031734482
Blanco Y Negro / Feb '91 / Warner Music

HAND IT OVER
I don't think / Never bought it / Nothin's goin' on / I'm insane / Can't we move this alone / Sure not over you / Loaded / Mick / I know yer insane / Gettin' rough / Gotta know
CD 0630183122
Blanco Y Negro / Mar '97 / Warner Music

WHERE HAVE YOU BEEN
Out there / Start choppin' / What else is new / On the way / Not the same / Get me / Drawerings / Hide / Goin' home / I ain't sayin'
CD 4509916272
Blanco Y Negro / Feb '93 / Warner Music

WITHOUT A SOUND
Feel the pain / I don't think so / Yeah right / Outta hand / Grab it / Even you / Mind glow / Get out of this / On the brink / Seemed like the thing to do / Over your shoulder
CD 4509969332
Warner Bros. / Aug '94 / Warner Music

YOU'RE LIVING ALL OVER ME
CD SST 1330CD
SST / May '93 / Plastic Head

Dio

ANGRY MACHINES
CD 08518292
SPV / Nov '96 / Koch / Plastic Head

DIAMONDS (The Best Of Dio)
Holy diver / Rainbow in the dark / Don't talk to strangers / We rock / Last in line / Evil eyes / Rock 'n' roll children / Sacred heart / Hungry for heaven / Hide in the rainbow / Dream evil / Wild one / Lock up the wolves
CD 5122062
Vertigo / Jun '92 / PolyGram

ELF ALBUMS, THE (Carolina County Ball/Trying To Burn The Sun) (Elf)
Carolina county ball / LA 59 / Ain't it all amusing / Happy / Annie New Orleans / Rocking chair rock 'n' roll blues / Rainbow / Do the same thing / Blanche / Black swampy water / Prentice wood / When she smiles / Good time music / Liberty road / Shotgun boogie / Wonderworld / Street walker
CD VSOPCD 167
Connoisseur Collection / Sep '91 / Pinnacle

HOLY DIVER
Stand up and shout / Holy diver / Gypsy / Caught in the middle / Don't talk to strangers / Straight through the heart / Invisible / Rainbow in the dark / Shame on the night
CD 8110212
Vertigo / Mar '88 / PolyGram

Dion

BEST OF DION & THE BELMONTS (Dion & The Belmonts)
Teenager in love / I wonder why / Where or when / Every little thing I do / Lover's prayer / No one knows / That's my desire / Don't pity me / In the still of the night / Will you love me still / Run around Sue / Lonely teenager / Sandy / Lovers who wander / Runaway girl / Queen of the hop / Lonely world / King without a Queen / Kissin' game / Tonight, tonight / Wanderer
CD CDMFP 6218
Music For Pleasure / Apr '96 / EMI

BEST OF THE GOSPEL YEARS, THE
Centre of my life / Still in the spirit / I put away my idols / Truth will set you free / New Jersy wife / New breed of man / Sweet surrender / Healing / Train for glory / I believe (sweet Lord Jesus) / Hymn to him / Come to the cross / He's the one / Simple ironies / Daddy / Golden sun, silver moon / You need a love / Day of the Lord
CD CDCHD 644
Ace / Apr '97 / Pinnacle

DREAM ON FIRE
CD VR 3327
Vision / Oct '92 / Pinnacle

LAURIE, SABINA & UNITED ARTISTS SIDES VOL.1, THE (Belmonts)
Come on little angel / Tell me why / Smoke from your cigarette / That background sound / How about me / My love is real / Searching for a new love / I don't know how to cry / I need someone / Hombre / Don't get around much anymore / Why / You're like a mystery / Today my love has gone away / I got a feeling / I don't know why / We belong together / Such a long way / Come take a walk with me / Ann-Marie / Diddle-dee-dum / I confess / Summertime time / Walk on boy / Now it's all over / Not responsible / Time to dream / Dancin' girl / Have you heard / (I've got) More important things to do / Tell my why
CD CDCHD 58C
Ace / Aug '95 / Pinnacle

PRESENTING DION & THE BELMONTS (Dion & The Belmonts)
I wonder why / Teen angel / Where or when / You better not do that / Just you / I got the blues / Don't pity me / Teenager in love / Wonderful girl / Funny feeling / I've cried before / That's my desire / No one knows / I can't go on
CD CDCHM 107
Ace / Jul '89 / Pinnacle

RETURN OF THE WANDERER/FIRE IN THE NIGHT
Looking for the heart of Saturday night / You've awakened something in me / Pattern of my lifeline / Street heart theme / Spanish Harlem incident / Fire in the night / Hollywood / Street mama / You are my star / Midtown American main street gang / Guitar queen / (I used to be a) Brooklyn dodger / Power of love within / Do you believe in magic / We don't talk anymore / Midnight lover / All quiet on 34th Street / Poor boy
CD CDCHD 936
Ace / Jun '90 / Pinnacle

ROAD I'M ON, THE (A Retrospective/ 2CD Set)
Can't we be sweethearts / Ruby baby / Will love ever come my way / This little girl of mine / Sunday kind of love / Gonna make it alone / This little girl / Fever / Donna the prima donna / Drip drop / Baby please don't go / 900 miles / Work song / Chicago blues / Road I'm on (Gloria) / Ruby baby / Donna the prima donna / Too much monkey business / I'm the hoochie koochie man / Katie May / You can't judge a book by its cover / Johnny B Goode / Spoonful / Kickin' child / Drop down baby / It's all over now, baby blue / Knowing I won't go back there / My love / Tomorrow won't bring the rain / Time in my heart for you / All I want to do is live my life / I can't help but wonder where I'm bound / Two ton feather / Born to cry / You move me
CD Set 4868232
Legacy / Feb '97 / Sony

RUNAROUND SUE
Runaround Sue / Somebody nobody wants / Dream lover / Life is but a dream / Wanderer / Runaway girl / I'm gonna make it somehow / Majestic / Could somebody take my place tonight / Little star / Lonely world / In the still of the night / Kansas City / Take good care of my baby
CD CDCHM 148
Ace / Aug '89 / Pinnacle

Dion, Celine

C'EST POUR VIVRE
CD NTRCD 076
Nectar / Mar '97 / Pinnacle

C'EST POUR VIVRE
Mon ami m'a quittee / La dodo la do / Hymne a L'amitie / Je ne veux pas / C'est pour vivre / En amour / Ne me plaignez pas / Les chemins de ma maison / Hello Mister Sam / Trois heures vingt / Trop jeune a dix sept ans / Paul et Virginie / La voix du bon dieu / Benjamin
CD BX 5122
BR Music / Mar '97 / Target/BMG

CELINE DION
Introduction / Love can move mountains / Show your emotion / If you asked me to / If you could see me now / Halfway to heaven / Beauty and the beast / With this tear / Did you give enough love / If I were you / I love you, goodbye / Little bit of love / Water from the moon / Nothing broken but my heart / Where does my heart beat now
CD 4715089
Epic / Nov '92 / Sony

CELINE DION/UNISON
Love can move mountains / Show some emotions / If you asked me to / If you could see me now / Halfway to heaven / Did you give enough love / If I were you / Beauty and the beast / I love you, goodbye / Little bit of love / Water from the moon / With this tear / Nothing broken but my heart / (If there was) Any other way / If love is out of the question / Where does my heart beat now / Last to know / I'm loving every moment with you / Love by another name / Unison / I feel too much / If we could start over / Have a heart
CD Set DIONCD 2
Epic / May '95 / Sony

COLLECTION 1982-1988, THE (2CD Set)
Ne partez pas sans moi / D'amour ou d'amitie / Visa pour les beaux jours / Les oiseaux du bonheur / Tellement j'ai d'amour pour toi / La religieuse / C'est pour toi / Avec toi / Mon reve de toujours / Du soleil au couer / A quatre pas d'ici / Un amour pour moi / Billy / Comment t'aimer / Mon ami m'a quittee / La dodo la do / Hymne a l'amitie / Je ne veux pas / C'est pour vivre / En amour / Ne me plaignez pas / Les chemins de ma maison / Hello Mister Sam / Trois heures vingt / Trop juene a dix sept ans / Paul et Virginie / La voix du bon dieu / Benjamin
CD Set BS 81012
BR Music / May '97 / Target/BMG

COLOUR OF MY LOVE, THE
Power of love / Misled / Think twice / Only one road / Everybody's talkin' my baby down / Next plane out / Real emotion / When I fall in love / Love doesn't ask why / Refuse to dance / I remember LA / No living without loving you / Lovin' proof / Just walk away / Colour of my love
CD 4747432
Epic / Feb '94 / Sony

D'EUX
Pour que tu maimes encore / Le ballet / Regarde moi / Je seia pas / La moire d'abraham destin / Les derniers seront les premiers / Mrai ou tu iras / J'attendais / Priere paienne / Vole
CD 4802862
Epic / Sep '95 / Sony

FALLING INTO YOU
It's all coming back to me now / Because you loved me / Falling into you / Make you happy / Seduces me / All by myself / Declaration of love / (You make me feel like) A natural woman / Dreaming of you / I love you / If that's what it takes / I don't know / River deep, mountain high / Your light / Call the man / Fly
CD 4837922
Epic / Mar '96 / Sony

FOR YOU
CD DSHLCD 7021
D-Sharp / Jan '96 / Pinnacle

LES PREMIERES ANNEES
D'amour ou d'amitic / Visa pour les beaux jours / En amour / Les oiseaux du bonheur / Tellement j'ai d'amour pour toi / La religieuse / C'est pour toi / Ne partez pas sans moi / Mon ami m'a quitce / Avec toi / Mon reve de toujours / Du soleil au coeur / A quatre pas d'ici / Un amour pour moi / Billy / Comment t'aimer / Je ne veux pas / C'est pour vivre
CD 4881042
Epic / Jun '97 / Sony

LIVE A PARIS
J'attendais / Destin / Power of love / Regarde, moi / River deep mountain high / Ziggy les derniers seront les premiers / J'irai ou tu iras / Je sais pas / Le ballet priere paienne / Pour que tu m'aimes encore / Quand on n'a que l'amour / Vole / To love you more
CD 4866062
Epic / Oct '96 / Sony

NE PARTEZ PAS SANS MOI
Ne partez pas sans moi / D'amour ou d'amitle / Visa pour les beaux jours / Les oiseaux du bonheur / Teliment j'al d'amour pour tol / La religeuse / C'est pour toi / Avec toi / Mon reve de tourjours / Du soileil au coeur / A quatre pas d'icl / U amour pour moi / Billy / Comment t'aimer
CD CD 2005
BR Music / Jun '96 / Target/BMG

UNISON
(If there was) any other way / If love is out of the question / Where does my heart beat now / Last to know / I'm loving every moment with you / Love by another name / Unison / I feel too much / If we could start over / Have a heart
CD 4672032
Epic / Sep '94 / Sony

Diop, Mapathe

SABAR WOLOF (Dance Drumming Of Senegal)
CD VPU 1003CD
Village Pulse / May '97 / ADA

Diop, Wasis

NO SANT
African dream / Di na wo / Hoaal du Baah / TGV / Ma na / Dames electriques / NOP / No sant / Issa thiaw / La danse des Maures / Den ma ba / SB-LE voyager
CD 5265652
Mercury Black Vinyl / Jan '96 / PolyGram

Diorio, Joe

DOUBLE TAKE
CD RMCD 4502
Ram / Sep '93 / Cadillac / Harmonia Mundi

MORE THAN FRIENDS
CD RMCD 4514
Ram / Apr '94 / Cadillac / Harmonia Mundi

WE WILL MEET AGAIN
CD RMCD 4501
Ram / Sep '93 / Cadillac / Harmonia Mundi

Dioubate, Oumou

LANCEY
CD STCD 1046
Stern's / Oct '93 / ADA / CM / Stern's

Dioulasso, Bob

BALAFONS, PERCUSSIONS, ETC
CD 824812
BUDA / Nov '90 / Discovery

Dip Tse Chok Ling Monks

SACRED CEREMONIES VOL.1 (Tantric Hymns & Music Of Tibetan Buddhism)
CD 170742
Celestial Harmonies / Jan '95 / ADA / Select

SACRED CEREMONIES VOL.2 (Tantric Hymns & Music Of Tibetan Buddhism)
CD 170792
Celestial Harmonies / Jan '95 / ADA / Select

SACRED CEREMONIES VOL.3 (Ritual Music Of Tibetan Buddhism)
CD 131323
Celestial Harmonies / Oct '96 / ADA / Select

Diplomats

DON'T FAKE THE JAZZ
Just another day / Elegant evening / Don't fake the jazz / Old Jack swang / Iva's groove / Last chance / It's you / Jean Pierre / 6 AM
CD RIPEXD 197
Ripe / Nov '95 / Pinnacle

Dir Han Tan

CHANTS TRADITIONAL DU PAYS VANNETAIS
CD ARN 64364
Arion / Feb '97 / ADA / Discovery

Dire Straits

ALCHEMY - LIVE
Once upon a time in the west / Expresso love / Private investigations / Sultans of swing / Two young lovers / Telegraph Road / Solid rock / Going home / Romeo and Juliet
CD 8182432
Vertigo / Jun '96 / PolyGram

BROTHERS IN ARMS
So far away / Money for nothing / Walk of life / Your latest trick / Why worry / Ride across the river / Man's too strong / One world / Brothers in arms
CD 8244992
Vertigo / Jun '96 / PolyGram

COMMUNIQUE
Angel of mercy / Follow me home / Lady writer / News / Once upon a time in the West / Communique / Portobello belle / Single headed sailor / Where do you think you're going / So far away / Money for nothing / Walk of life / Your latest trick / Why worry / Ride across the river / Man's too strong / One world / Brothers in arms
CD 8000522
Vertigo / Jun '96 / PolyGram

DIRE STRAITS
Down to the waterline / Water of love / Setting me up / Six blade knife / Southbound again / Sultans of swing / In the gallery
CD 8000512
Vertigo / Jun '96 / PolyGram

LIVE AT THE BBC
Down to the waterline / Six blade knife / Water of love / Wild West End / Sultans of swing / Lions / What's the matter baby / Tunnel of love
CD WINCD 072
CD WINCD 072X
Windsong / Jun '95 / Pinnacle

LOVE OVER GOLD
Telegraph Road / Private investigations / Industrial disease / It never rains / Love over gold
CD 8000882
Vertigo / Jun '96 / PolyGram

MAKING MOVIES
Tunnel of love / Romeo and Juliet / Skateaway / Expresso love / Les boys / Hand in hand / Solid rock / Down to the waterline / Water of love / Setting me up / Six blade knife / Southbound again / Sultans of swing / In the gallery / Wild West End / Lions
CD 8000502
Vertigo / Jun '96 / PolyGram

MONEY FOR NOTHING
Sultans of swing / Down to the waterline / Portobello belle / Twisting by the pool / Romeo and Juliet / Where do you think you're going / Walk of life / Private investigations / Money for nothing / Tunnel of love / Brothers in arms / Telegraph Road
CD 8364192
Vertigo / Jun '96 / PolyGram

ON EVERY STREET
Calling Elvis / On every street / When it comes to you / Fade to black / Bug / You and your friend / Heavy fuel / Iron hand / Ticket to heaven / My parties / Planet of New Orleans / How long
CD 5101602
Vertigo / Jun '96 / PolyGram

ON THE NIGHT
Calling Elvis / Walk of life / Heavy fuel / Romeo and Juliet / Private investigations / Your latest trick / On every street / You and your friend / Money for nothing / Brothers in arms
CD 5147662
Vertigo / Jun '96 / PolyGram

Direct Hits

MAGIC ATTIC
CD TANGCD 9
Tangerine / Oct '94 / RTM/Disc

Directions In Groove

DIG DEEPER
Two way dreamtime / Medium rare / Favourite / DNA / Pythonicity / Shelflife / Hip replacement / Suffer the children / Gil / Big theme / Den / Terrified from dizzy heights / Re-invent yourself / Inner blue funk
CD 5186092
Verve / Dec '93 / PolyGram

DIRECTIONS IN GROOVE
Re-invent yourself / Sweet thing / Taylor's cube / Heaven on Earth / Freezerville
CD 5184362
Mercury / Dec '93 / PolyGram

SPEAKEASY
CD 5285392
Verve / May '96 / PolyGram

Dirt

BLACK AND WHITE (2CD Set)
CD Set SKULD 027CD
Skuld / May '97 / Cargo

Dirtcoldfight

HYMNAL
CD CSR 017CD
Cavity Search / Oct '95 / Plastic Head

Dirtsman

ACID
CD VYDCD 011
Vine Yard / Jul '96 / Grapevine/PolyGram

Dirty 3

DIRTY 3
CD ABB 93CD
Big Cat / Aug '95 / 3mv/Pinnacle

HORSE STORIES
CD ABB 115CD
Big Cat / Sep '96 / 3mv/Pinnacle

SAD AND DANGEROUS
CD ABB 107CD
Big Cat / Apr '96 / 3mv/Pinnacle

Dirty Beatniks

ONE ONE SEVEN IN THE SHADE
CD WALLCD 011
Wall Of Sound / Nov '96 / Prime / Soul Trader / Vital

Dirty Dogs

FREE LUNCH
CD DDCD 4401
Dog's Dinner / Apr '97 / Timewarp

Dirty Dozen

EARS TO THE WALL
Funky nuts / Blackbird special / My feet can't fail me now / Gettin' in the cut / Reprieve / I hold the key / Five aquariums / L'acenceur / Flow on / In the meantime
CD MR 1422
Mammoth / Jul '96 / Vital

Dirty Dozen Brass Band

LIVE (Mardi Gras In Montreux)
CD ROUCD 2052
Rounder / '88 / ADA / CM / Direct

THIS IS JAZZ
Charlie dozen / It's all over now / Georgia swing / Voodoo / Don't you feel my leg / Lost souls (of Southern Louisiana) / Cortege / Do I have to go / Mourning march / Memoirs / Inquest / Shout / Moose the mooche / Monkey / Gemini rising / Open up (Whatcha gonna do for the rest of your life) / Remember when / New Orleans blues / When I'm walking (Let me walk) / Old rugged cross
CD CK 65046
Sony Jazz / May '97 / Sony

Dirty Hands

LETTERS FOR KINGS
CD BNVCD 10
Black & Noir / Jan '92 / Plastic Head

Dirty Looks

ONE BAD LEG
CD CDMFN 178
Music For Nations / Jan '95 / Pinnacle

Dirty Old Man River

DIRTY OLD MAN RIVER
CD RDL 102
Radial / May '97 / Cargo / Vital

Dis Bonjour A La Dame

DIS BONJOUR A LA DAME
CD 0630104362
East West / Jul '95 / Warner Music

Disappear Fear

DEEP SOUL DIVER
CD CDPH 1173
Philo / May '95 / ADA / CM / Direct

DISAPPEAR FEAR
CD CDPH 1171
Philo / Aug '95 / ADA / CM / Direct

LIVE AT THE BOTTOM LINE
CD CDPH 1172
Philo / Jun '95 / ADA / CM / Direct

SEED IN THE USA
CD CDPH 1180
Philo / Jun '96 / ADA / CM / Direct

Disbelief

DISBELIEF
CD CRS 046CD
Nuclear Blast / Jun '97 / Plastic Head

Discard

FOUR MINUTES PAST MIDNIGHT
CD RIP 001
Ripping / Sep '94 / Plastic Head

Discepolo, Enrique S.

HOMENAJE A LOS POETAS DEL TANGO
CD EBCD 76
El Bandoneon / Jul '96 / Discovery

Discharge

DISCHARGED (A Tribute To Discharge) (Various Artists)
CD PREACH 001CD
Rhythm Vicar / Jun '92 / Plastic Head

PROTEST AND SURVIVE (2CD Set)
Realities of war / Fight back / War's no fairytale / Decontrol / It's no TV sketch / Warning / Anger burning / Hear nothing, see nothing, say nothing / Nightmare continues / Protest and survive / I won't subscribe / Blood runs red / Never again / Too monstrous nuclear stockpiles / Why / Ain't no feeble bastard / Visions of war / Does this system work / Look at tomorrow / Massacre of innocents / State violence, state control / Price of silence / Born to die in the gutter / More I see / Ignorance / Where there is a will / Anger burning / In defence of our future / Hell on earth / Cries of help / Final bloodbath / Drunk with power / City of fear / Kiss tomorrow goodbye / Terror police / Exiled in hell / Psycho active / Shootin' up the world
CD Set SMDCD 131
Snapper / May '97 / Pinnacle

SEEING, FEELING, BLEEDING
CD NB 085
Nuclear Blast / Dec '93 / Plastic Head

WHY
Vision of war / Look at tomorrow / Maimed and slaughtered / Ain't no feeble bastard / Massacre of innocence / Doomsday / Does this system work / Why / Mania for conquest / Is this to be / State violence / State control
CD PLATE 002CD
Clay / Apr '93 / Cargo

Disciples

FOR THOSE WHO UNDERSTAND
CD BSL 101CD
Boomshakalacka / Nov '95 / Jet Star / SRD

INFINITE DESTINY OF DUB
CD DBHD 004CD
Dubhead / Oct '96 / SRD

REBIRTH (Disciples & Rootsman)
CD TEMCD 007
Third Eye / Aug '97 / SRD

RESONATIONS
Eastern fire / Wild fire / From Genesis to revelation / Root of creation / Mabrak / Thunder and lightning / Fire burn / Faithful man / Inner spirit / Iyaman say / After the battle / Tribute to Don / Salute to the brave
CD NLX 5004CD
Cloak & Dagger / May '95 / Vital

Disciplin A Kitschne

I THINK I SEE MYSELF ON CCTV
CD BABACDL 1
The Record Label / Sep '96 / Pinnacle

Disco Inferno

DI GO POP
In sharky water / New clothes for the new world / Starbound : All burnt out and nowhere to go / Crash at every speed / Even the sea sides against us / Next year / Whole wide world ahead / Footprints in snow
CD R 3072
Rough Trade / Feb '94 / Pinnacle

IN DEBT
Entertainment / Arc in round / Broken / Emigre / Interference / Leisure time / Set sail / Hope to God / Freethought / Bleed clean / Next in line / Incentives / Waking up / Glancing away / Fallen down the wire / No edge no end
CD CHE 4CD
Che / Sep '95 / SRD

TECHNICOLOUR
CD R 4102
Rough Trade / Jul '96 / Pinnacle

Discount

ATAXIA'S ALLRIGHT TONIGHT
CD LM 16
Liquid Meat / Jun '97 / Cargo

Disembowelment

TRANSCENDENCE INTO THE PERIPHERAL
CD NB 0962
Nuclear Blast / Jan '94 / Plastic Head

Disfear

BRUTAL SIGHT OF WAR, A
CD LF 060CD
Lost & Found / Aug '93 / Plastic Head

Disgrace

SUPERHUMAN DOME
CD SPV 08412652
SPV / Mar '96 / Koch / Plastic Head

Disgust

BRUTALITY OF WAR
Intro / Mother earth / Millions suffer and die / Horrific end / Thrown into oblivion / Civilisation decoys / Relentless slaughter / And still... / Light of death / What kind of mind / You have no right / Sea of tears / Anguished cry / Heaps of flesh / Outro
CD MOSH 104CD
Earache / Nov '93 / Vital

WORLD OF NO BEAUTY, A
CD NB 232CD
Nuclear Blast / Mar '97 / Plastic Head

Disgusting

SHAPESHIFTERBIRTHBLUES
CD HNF 011CD
Head Not Found / Nov '95 / Plastic Head

Disharmonic Orchestra

EXPOSITIONSPROPHYLAXE
CD 8429812
Nuclear Blast / Dec '90 / Plastic Head

PLEASURE DOME
CD SPV 08476772
SPV / Jun '94 / Koch / Plastic Head

Dishrags

LOVE IS SHIT
CD OPM 2112CD
Other People's Music / Feb '97 / Greyhound / Plastic Head

Dishwalla

PET YOUR FRIENDS
Pretty babies / Haze / Counting blue cars / Explode / Charlie Brown's parents / Give / Miss Emma Peel / Moisture / Feeder / All she can see / Only for so long / Date wih Sarah / It's gonna to take some time
CD 5403432
A&M / Oct '96 / PolyGram

Disinformation

R&D
CD ASH 29CD
Ash International / Apr '96 / Kudos / Pinnacle

Disjam

MONEY
CD YO 40242
Yo Mama / May '97 / Cargo / Plastic Head

Disjecta

CLEAN PIT AND LID
CD WARPCD 41
Warp / Apr '96 / Prime / RTM/Disc

Disley, Diz

DIZ DISLEY & HIS STRING QUARTET AT THE WHITE BEAR
CD JCD 212
Jazzology / Mar '95 / Jazz Music

Dismember

CASKET GARDEN
CD NB 1302
Nuclear Blast / Mar '95 / Plastic Head

INDECENT AND OBSCENE
CD NB 077CD
Nuclear Blast / Jul '93 / Plastic Head

LIKE AN EVER FLOWING STREAM
CD NB 163CD
Nuclear Blast / Jun '96 / Plastic Head

MASSIVE KILLING CAPACITY
CD NB 123CD
Nuclear Blast / Sep '95 / Plastic Head

MISANTHROPIC
CD NB 254CD
Nuclear Blast / Jun '97 / Plastic Head

PIECES
CD NB 060CD
Nuclear Blast / Apr '92 / Plastic Head

Disorder

COMPLETE DISORDER
Today's war / Violent crime / Complete disorder / Insane youth / You've got to be someone / More than fights / Daily life / Rampton song / Provocated war / Bullshit everyone / Three blind mice / Buy I gurt pint / Stagnation / Life / Out of order / Condemned / Media / Suicide children / Preachers / Remembrance day

CD _______________ CDPUNK 46
Anagram / Oct '96 / Cargo / Pinnacle

LIVE IN OSLO/VIOLENT WORLD
Complete disorder / Daily life / More than fights / Remembrance day / Maternal obsession / Bent edge / Provocated wars / God nose / Education / Driller killer / Prisoner of conscience / Stagnation / Life / Rampton / After 16 / Fuck your nationality / Out of order / Rhino song / Intro 21 / Ate seconds 22 / Another fight another gig / Gods are born in the USA / I don't like war / Joleen 26 / Fur else / Health hazard / Todays world / Violent world / Dope not Pope / Distortion til U vomit / Take what you need
CD _______________ CDPUNK 39
Anagram / Oct '94 / Cargo / Pinnacle

MASTERS OF THE GLUENIVERSE (Disorder/Mushroom Attack)
CD _______________ DAR 010CD
Desperate Attempt / Nov '94 / SRD

REST HOME FOR SENILE OLD PUNKS
CD _______________ CDPUNK 88
Anagram / Feb '97 / Cargo / Pinnacle

UNDER THE SCALPEL BLADE
Driller killer / Education / Security guard / Go-song / Transparency / Victim of the NHS / Bent edge / Rhino song / God nose / Overproduction / Other side of the fence / Fuck your nationality / Men make frontiers / Prisoner of conscience / After / Double standards / Be bad be glad / Marriage story / Love and flowers / Togetherness and unity
CD _______________ CDPUNK 19
Anagram / Apr '96 / Cargo / Pinnacle

Disposable Heroes Of ...

HYPOCRISY IS THE GREATEST LUXURY (Disposable Heroes Of Hiphoprisy)
Satanic reverses / Famous and dandy (like Amos 'n' Andy) / Television (the drug of a nation) / Language of violence / Winter of the long hot summer / Hypocrisy is the greatest luxury / Everyday life has become a health risk / INS Greencard A-19 191 500 / Socio-genetic experiment / Music and politics / Financial leprosy / California uber alles / Water pistol man
CD _______________ BRCD 584
4th & Broadway / Apr '92 / PolyGram
CD _______________ IMCD 250
Island / Mar '97 / PolyGram

Disrupt

UNREST
CD _______________ RR 69062
Nuclear Blast / Dec '94 / Plastic Head

Dissect

SWALLOW SWOUMING MASS
CD _______________ CYBERCD 5
Cyber / Sep '93 / Amato Disco / Arabesque / Plastic Head

Dissecting Table

HUMAN BREEDING
Least mean square algorithm for personality alteration / Man in the black box / Behind the ethereal thorns / Human breeding market
CD _______________ RR 69542
Relapse / May '97 / Pinnacle / Plastic Head

ULTIMATE PSYCHOLOGICAL
CD _______________ DVLR 3
Dark Vinyl / Aug '94 / Plastic Head / World Serpent

ZIGOKU
CD _______________ DVO 16CD
Dark Vinyl / Sep '93 / Plastic Head / World Serpent

Dissection

SOMBERLAIN
CD _______________ NFR 006
No Fashion / Jan '95 / Plastic Head

STORM OF THE LIGHTS BANE
CD _______________ NB 129CD
Nuclear Blast / Jan '96 / Plastic Head

WHERE DEAD ANGELS LIE
CD _______________ NB 167CD
Nuclear Blast / May '96 / Plastic Head

Dissidenten

INSTINCTIVE TRAVELLER
Taste of melon / Instinctive traveller / Broken moon / Dreamcatcher / Blue world / Seek to sigh / Lobster song / Shine on me / Live and experience / Never say no / World is like a mirror
CD _______________ EXIL 55352
Exil / Jul '97 / Direct

MIXED UP JUNGLE
CD _______________ EXIL 55312
Exil / Jun '97 / Direct

Dissober

SOBER LIFE
CD _______________ DISTCD 6
Distortion / Jun '94 / Plastic Head

Dissolve

THAT THAT IS...IS (NOT)
CD _______________ KRANK 005CD
Kranky / Mar '97 / Cargo / Greyhound

THIRD ALBUM FROM THE SUN
CD _______________ KRANK 018CD
Kranky / Jul '97 / Cargo / Greyhound

Distant Cousins

DISTANT COUSINS
CD _______________ GHETTCD 002
Ghetto / Mar '89 / Sony

DISTANT COUSINS (Remix)
CD _______________ GHETTD 2X
Ghetto / Apr '90 / Sony

Distorted Pony

INSTANT WINNER
CD _______________ TR 22CD
Trance / Apr '94 / SRD

District Singers

TWELFTH PARTY SINGALONG
Green grassy slopes / South down militia / Enniskillen dragoons / Ducks of Magheralin / Sash / Aughalee heroes / My Aunt Jane / Lily O / Ould Lammas fair / B for Barney / I'll tell me ma / Auld orange flute / My bonnie lies over the ocean / Northern lights of old Aberdeen / End of the road / Orange and blue / Black velvet band / Old mud cabin on the hill / Sprigs of Kilkrea / Wild rover / Love is teasin' / Muirsheen durkin / Home boys home / No surrender / Derry's walls / When you and I were young Maggie / Mountains of Mourne / Battle of Garvagh / Star of County Down / Courtin' in the kitchen / Protestant boys / Scottish soldier / Roamin' in the gloamin' / Old rustic bridge / London lights / Twenty one years
CD _______________ CDUCD 11
Ulster Music / Apr '97 / ADA / CM / Direct / Duncans / Koch / Ross

District Six

IMGOMA YABANTWANA
CD _______________ D6 002
D6 / Mar '90 / New Note/Pinnacle

Disturbed Company

CABIN FEVER
CD _______________ IND 049CD
Incentive / Jun '96 / Plastic Head

Ditch Croaker

CHIMPFACTOR
CD _______________ SYM 0072
Symbiotic / May '97 / Cargo

Ditch Witch

EVERYWHERE, NOWHERE
CD _______________ GROW 122
Grass / Apr '94 / Pinnacle / SRD

Dive

CONCRETE JUNGLE
CD _______________ MHCD 018
Minus Habens / May '94 / Plastic Head

Diverse Interpreten

CLASSIC REFERENCE
CD _______________ BLR 84 008
L&R / May '91 / New Note/Pinnacle

REFERENCE
CD _______________ BLR 84 001
L&R / May '91 / New Note/Pinnacle

REFERENCE VOL.2
CD _______________ BLR 84 020
L&R / May '91 / New Note/Pinnacle

REHEARSAL
CD _______________ BLR 84 010
L&R / May '91 / New Note/Pinnacle

Diversion

JAM TOMORROW
CD _______________ TOAD 3CD
Newt / May '94 / Plastic Head

Divine

BORN TO BE CHEAP
Gang bang / Alphabet rap / Native love / Shake it up / Shoot your shot / Love reaction
CD _______________ CDMGRAM 84
Anagram / Aug '94 / Cargo / Pinnacle

CREAM OF DIVINE
CD _______________ PWKS 4228
Carlton / Nov '94 / Carlton

ORIGINALS
CD _______________ AVEXCD 30
Avex / Apr '96 / 3mv/Pinnacle

ORIGINALS/REMIXES (2CD Set)
CD Set _______________ AVEXCD 33X
Avex / Apr '96 / 3mv/Pinnacle

REMIXES
CD _______________ AVEXCD 29
Avex / Apr '96 / 3mv/Pinnacle

YOU THINK YOU'RE A MAN
Divine's theme / You think you're a man / Give it up / I'm so beautiful / Show me around / Walk like a man / Twistin' the night away / Good time / Hard magic / Little baby / Hey you / Divine reprise
CD _______________ QED 226
Tring / Nov '96 / Tring

Divine Comedy

CASANOVA
Something for the weekend / Becoming more like Alfie / Middle class heroes / In and out of Paris and London / Charge / Songs of love / Frog Princess / Woman of the world / Dogs and the horses / Theme from Casanova / Through a long and sleepless night
CD _______________ SETCD 025
Setanta / Apr '96 / Vital

FANFARE FOR THE COMIC MUSE
CD _______________ SETCDM 002
Setanta / Aug '90 / Vital

LIBERATION
Festive Road / Death of a supernaturalist / Bernice bobs her hair / I was born yesterday / Your Daddy's car / Europop / Timewatching / Popsinger's fear of the pollen count / Queen of the South / Victoria falls / Three sisters / Europe by train / Lucy
CD _______________ SETCD 011
Setanta / Aug '97 / Vital

PROMENADE
Bath / Going downhill fast / Booklovers / Seafood song / Geronimo / When the lights go out all over Europe / Summerhouse / Neptune's daughter / Drinking song / Ten seconds to midnight / Tonight we fly
CD _______________ SETCD 013
Setanta / Aug '97 / Vital

SHORT ALBUM ABOUT LOVE, A
In pursuit of happiness / Everybody knows (except you) / Someone / Timewatching / If / If I were you (I'd be through me) / I'm all you need
CD _______________ SETCD 036
Setanta / Feb '97 / Vital

Divine Horsemen

DEVIL'S RIVER
CD _______________ ROSE 102CD
New Rose / Dec '86 / ADA / Direct / Discovery

SNAKE HANDLER
CD _______________ SST 140CD
SST / May '93 / Plastic Head

Divine Soma Experience

WELCOME TO THE LAND OF DRAGONS
Ravi Shankar's bizarre sitar (dub) / Somae / Music is magic / Impossible possibilities / Chillout and chill'um / Icaro (Magical curing song)
CD _______________ DIVINE 001CD
Divine / Sep '94 / Vital

Divine Works

DIVINE WORKS
Divine works I / Ancient person of my heart / O' Ecclesia / Interlude I / Divine works II / Father of eternal life / Gloria deo patri / Graces naked danced / Tranquility / Interlude II / Da nobis indicio / Divine
CD _______________ VTCD 119
Virgin / Jul '97 / EMI

Divisia

WIFEBEATER
CD _______________ T 62CD
Theologian / Jun '97 / Cargo / Plastic Head

Dixie Cups

BEST OF DIXIE CUPS, THE
Chapel of love / Girls can tell / I'm gonna get you yet / All grown up / Ain't that nice / Gee baby gee / Iko iko / Another boy like mine / Poeple say / Thank you mama, thank you papa / Gee the moon is shining bright / Little bell / Wrong direction / True true love / You should have seen the way he looked at me
CD _______________ 12659
Laserlight / May '97 / Target/BMG

HIT SINGLE COLLECTABLES
CD _______________ DISK 4511
Disky / Apr '94 / Disky / THE

Dixie Hummingbirds

DIXIE HUMMINGBIRDS 1939-1947
CD _______________ DOCD 5491
Document / Nov '96 / ADA / Hot Shot / Jazz Music

Dixie Jubilee Singers

DIXIE JUBILEE SINGERS 1924-1928
CD _______________ DOCD 5438
Document / May '96 / ADA / Hot Shot / Jazz Music

Dixie Stompers

AIN'T GONNA TELL NOBODY
CD _______________ DD 224
Delmark / Aug '94 / ADA / Cadillac / CM / Direct / Hot Shot

Dixie Waste

START THE MADNESS
CD _______________ VIRION 104
Sound Virus / Sep '94 / Plastic Head

Dixon, Bill

VADE MECUM VOL.1
CD _______________ SN 1212082
Soul Note / Oct '94 / Cadillac / Harmonia Mundi / Wellard

VADE MECUM VOL.2
CD _______________ 1212112
Soul Note / Jul '97 / Cadillac / Harmonia Mundi / Wellard

Dixon, Don

IF I'M A HAM WELL YOU'RE A SAUSAGE
Don Dixon (aged 8) and his sister Anne / Praying mantis / Southside girl / Just rites / Girls LTD / Borrowed time / Your sister told me / Heart in a box / Renaissance eyes / Teenage suicide / Million angels sigh / Oh cheap chatter / I can hear the river / Gimme little sign / Calling out for love / Bad reputation / Sweet surrender / Don Dixon (age 8) and his sister Susan
CD _______________ MAUCD 616
Mau Mau / Feb '92 / Pinnacle

MOST OF THE GIRLS LIKE TO DANCE
Praying Mantis / (You're a) big girl now / Swallowing pride / Wake up / Talk to me / Pocket / Skin deep / Eyes on fire / Girls LTD / Just rites / Ice on the river / Renaissance eyes / Fighting for my life / Southside girl
CD _______________ FIENDCD 60
Demon / Jan '86 / Pinnacle

ROMANTIC DEPRESSIVE
CD _______________ SHCD 5501
Sugar Hill / Apr '95 / ADA / CM / Direct / Koch / Roots

Dixon, Errol

MISTER BOOGIE WOOGIE
CD _______________ DM 10015
DMA Jazz / Jul '96 / Jazz Music

Dixon, Floyd

MARSHALL TEXAS IS MY HOME
Hard living alone / Please don't go / Old memories / Hole in the wall / Time brings about a change / Me quieras / Call operator 210 / Ooh eee ooh eee / Chicken growing / Carlos / Nose trouble / Reap what you sow / Judgement day / Instrumental shuffle / Hey bartender / Never can tell when a woman changes her mind / Oh baby / What is life without a home / Rita / I'll always love you / Oooh little girl
CD _______________ CDCHD 361
Ace / Nov '93 / Pinnacle

MR. MAGNIFICANT HITS AGAIN
CD _______________ IMP 706
IMP / Sep '95 / ADA / Discovery

WAKE UP AND LIVE
CD _______________ ALCD 4841
Alligator / May '96 / ADA / CM / Direct

Dixon, Reginald

AT THE BLACKPOOL TOWER WURLITZER
Blackpool song mixture medleys 7 and 8: *Dixon, Reginald & Cavan O'Connor* / Canadian capers / Dixon hits medleys 3 and 7 / Dixonland medley 2 / Dixontime medleys 1, 2, 3, 9 and 10 / Dixon request medley / Fifty years of song medley / Goodnight: *Dixon, Reginald & Cavan O'Connor* / In a Persian market / It's time to sing Sweet Adeline again: *Dixon, Reginald & Cavan O'Connor* / Parade of the tin soldiers / Sanctuary of the heart / Sunrise serenade / Tauber memories medley / Waltz memories medley / Was love a dream
CD _______________ CDAJA 5134
Living Era / Jul '94 / Select

MAGIC OF REGINALD DIXON, THE
Over the waves / Whatever will be will be (Que sera sera) / My resistance is low / At sundown / Dancing with tears in my eyes / Pasadena / Bewitched, bothered and bewildered / Pretty girl is like a melody / Is it true what they say about Dixie / Sweet and lovely / Broadway melody / I can't give you anything but love / Peg o' my heart / Red roses for a blue lady / Sunshine of your smile / Second hand rose / There, I've said it again / Yes sir that's my baby / This is my lovely day / Shine / You can't stop me from dreaming / When you wore a tulip / Guilty / If you knew Susie like I know Susie / Happy days and lonely nights / On a slow boat to China / Nobody's sweetheart / Shepherd of

the hills / Alice blue gown / Bill Bailey, won't you please come home / Am I wasting my time on you / My sweetie went away / Oh johnny oh johnny oh / Glad rag doll / Time on my hands / Jeepers creepers / Amazing grace / Old rugged cross / I do like to be beside the seaside / Pigalle / Lullaby of Broadway / Carolina moon / Toot toot tootsie / Dream of Olwen / South of the border (Down Mexico way) / Stein song / Wistful waltz / Storm at sea / Life on the ocean wave / Jack's the lad / Drunken sailor / Anchors aweigh / Skye boat song / Fingal's cave / Imperial echoes / Whispering / Beer barrel polka / Charmaine / Harry Lime theme / Minuet / At the Darktown strutter's ball / Anniversary waltz / MacNamara's band / I kiss your hand, Madame / Happy days are here again / When the saints go marching in
CD CDDL 1060
EMI / Apr '93 / EMI

MUSIC MAESTRO PLEASE (The Early Years)
You can't stop me dreaming / Little old lady / Whispers in the dark / Horsey horsey / Afraid to dream / Goodnight to you all / Music goes 'round and around / Lights out / Take me back to my boots and saddle / When the poppies bloom again / I dream of San Marino / I'm in a dancing mood / In the chapel in the moonlight / Way you look tonight / When a lady meets a gentleman down South / When I'm with you / Fine romance / Sing baby sing / Did your mother come from Ireland / When did you leave Heaven / Oh my goodness / It looks like rain in Cherry Blossom lane / Greatest mistake of my life / Wake up and live / Is it true what they say about Dixie / Sweetheart let's grow old together / Touch of your lips / Bells across the meadow / Music maestro please / Little lady make believe / Lost / Lovely lady / Glory of love / Sally / Love is everywhere / Looking on the bright side / Smile when you say goodbye / When I grow too old to dream / Sing as we go / Desert song / Deep in my heart dear / Dream lover / Laughing Irish eyes / It's a sin to tell a lie / On the beach at Bali-bali / At the cafe continental / Empty saddles / Pretty girl is like a melody / You're here, you're there / Ten pretty girls / Love is good for anything that ails you / Martial moments / Martial moments
CD GRCD 44
Grasmere / '91 / Highlander / Savoy / Target/BMG

REGINALD DIXON AT THE BLACKPOOL TOWER
Medley / St. Louis blues/Limehouse blues/ Jealousy / My blue heaven/Star dust/Goodnight sweetheart / Bolero / I hate myself/Isle of Capri/My song for you / I won't dance/ Lovely to look at/Smoke gets in your eyes / Rustle of spring / With my eyes open I'm dreaming/If/I never had a chance / Harlemania/Ain't misbehavin'/My sweetie went away / Ma, he's making eyes at me/Alexander's ragtime band / Medley / I'll walk beside you / Dream lover/Nobody's using it now/March of the Grenadiers/Lo / Skater's waltz / Why do I love you/You are my love/ Ol' man river / Somebody stole my gal / Love makes the world go round/Change partners / Sweet music/Ev'ryday/Fare thee well Annabelle / Sunrise serenade / When Mother Nature sings her lullaby / Bugle call rag / Medley
CD PASTCD 7039
Flapper / May '94 / Pinnacle

TOWER BALLROOM FAVOURITES
Tiger rag / Autumn leaves / Moonlight serenade / These foolish things / Dardanella / Elizabethan serenade / La paloma / Russian rag / Peanut vendor / Wedding of the painted doll / Temptation rag / Czardas / Sabre dance / Sweet and lovely / Canadian capers / Continental / Jealous··· / 12th Street rag / Deep purple / Cherokee / Toy trumpet / Stardust
CD CC 255
Music For Pleasure / May '90 / EMI

Dixon, Willie

CHESS BOX, THE (2CD Set) (Various Artists)
My babe: *Little Walter* / Violent love: *Big Three* / Third degree: *Boyd, Eddie* / Seventh son: *Mabon, Willie* / Crazy for my baby: *Dixon, Willie* / Pain in my heart: *Dixon, Willie* / Hoochie coochie man: *Waters, Muddy* / Evil: *Howlin' Wolf* / Mellow down easy: *Little Walter* / When the lights go out: *Witherspoon, Jimmy* / Young fashioned ways: *Waters, Muddy* / Pretty thing: *Diddley, Bo* / I'm ready: *Waters, Muddy* / Do me right: *Fulson, Lowell* / I just want to make love to you: *Waters, Muddy* / Tollin' blues: *Fulson, Lowell* / 29 ways: *Dixon, Willie* / Walkin' the blues: *Dixon, Willie* / Spoonful: *Howlin' Wolf* / You know my love: *Rush, Otis* / You can't judge a book by its cover: *Diddley, Bo* / I ain't superstitious: *Howlin' Wolf* / You need love: *Waters, Muddy* / Little red rooster: *Howlin' Wolf* / Back door man: *Howlin' Wolf* / Dead presidents: *Little Walter* / Hidden charms: *Howlin' Wolf* / You shook me: *Waters, Muddy* / Bring it on home: *Williamson, Sonny Boy* / 300 pounds of joy: *Howlin' Wolf* / Weak brain, narrow mind: *Dixon, Willie* / Wang dang doodle: *Taylor, Koko* / Same thing: *Waters, Muddy* / Built for comfort: *Howlin' Wolf* / I can't quit you baby: *Little Milton* / Insane asylum: *Taylor, Koko*
CD Set MCD 16500
Chess/MCA / Apr '97 / BMG / New Note/ BMG

CRYIN' THE BLUES (Live At Liberty Hall) (Dixon, Willie & Johnny Winter)
Sittin' and cryin' the blues / Spoonful / I just want to make love to you / Chicago here I come / Tore down / You know it ain't right / Mean mistreater/Baby what you want me to do / Roach stew / Killing floor
CD CDTB 166
Thunderbolt / Mar '95 / TKO Magnum

HIDDEN CHARMS
CD ORECD 515
Silvertone / Mar '94 / Pinnacle

I'M THE BLUES
Pain in my heart / My babe / Walking the blues / (Back home again in) Indiana / Hoochie coochie man / Little red rooster / Spoonful
CD CD 52026
Blues Encore / Mar '93 / Target/BMG

WILLIE'S BLUES (Dixon, Willie & Memphis Slim)
Nervous / Good understanding / That's my baby / Slim's thing / That's all I want baby / Don't you tell nobody / Youth to you / Sittin' and cryin' the blues / Bluit for comfort / I got a razor / Go easy / Move me
CD CDCHD 349
Ace / Jun '92 / Pinnacle
CD OBCCD 501
Original Blues Classics / Nov '92 / Complete/Pinnacle / Wellard

DIY

STRICTLY FOR GROOVERS (Various Artists)
Orange is orange: *Firenze* / Elevator: *Victor Dynagroove Ensemble* / Up there out there: *Essa* / Be still: *Overview* / Thelma: *Sandmen* / Cassiopeia: *Nail* / Eve's theme: *Serve Chilled*
CD WARPCD 18
Warp / Dec '93 / Prime / RTM/Disc

Diyici, Senem

TAKALAR (Diyici, Senem Sextet)
CD CDLLL 17
La Lichere / Aug '93 / ADA / Discovery

Dizrhythmia

DIZRHYTHMIA
CD RES 117CD
Resurgence / Nov '96 / Pinnacle

DJ 7

TECHNODROME (DJ 7 & The Sound Generators)
Back in the UK / I wanna be a hippie / Inside out / Forever young / There is a star / Endless summer / Tears don't lie / Stars / I kiss your lips / Come take my hand / Move your ass / Spaceman / Hardcore vibes / Knockin' / Texas cowboys / Power rangers
CD 12840
Laserlight / May '96 / Target/BMG

DJ Cam

DJ CAM (2CD Set)
CD Set SDW 010CD
Shadow / Feb '97 / Cargo / Plastic Head

MAD BLUNTED JAZZ (2CD Set)
CD Set SDW 0102
Shadow / Nov '96 / Cargo / Plastic Head

SUBSTANCES
Intro:friends and enemies / Essence part one / Meera / Essence part two / Sound system children / Alexandra's interlude / Innervisions / Essence part three / Hip hop pioneer / Essence part four / Lost kingdom / Essence part five / Angel dust / Essence part six / Twilight zone / Outro
CD 4854052
Columbia / Mar '97 / Sony

UNDERGROUND LIVE ACT
CD IRCD 1
Inflammable / Jul '96 / Timewarp

UNDERGROUND VIBES
Intro / Gansta shit / Mad blunted jazz / Suckers never play that / Sang lien / Underground vibes / Romanic love / Return of the Jedi / Other aspect / Dieu reconnaitra les siens / Free your tunrtable and your scratch will follow / Dieu reconnaitra les siens minux 8
CD CAMCD 004
Street Jazz / Jul '96 / Timewarp
CD 4877142
Epic / Aug '97 / Sony

DJ Cyclone

BEST OF MY BOX, THE (Various Artists)
CD MDMA 9704CD
Acid Fever / May '97 / Cargo / Prime

DJ Dimitri

JOURNEYS BY DJ VOL.3
CD JDJ 13CD
JDJ / Mar '95 / 3mv/Pinnacle / SRD

DJ Duke

JOURNEYS BY DJ VOL.2 (Various Artists)
CD JDJ 12CD
JDJ / Jan '95 / 3mv/Pinnacle / SRD

DJ Erick Morillo

DJ ERICK MORILLO LIVE AND MORE (Various Artists)
CD SR 323CD
Strictly Rhythm / Nov '95 / Prime / RTM/ Disc / SRD / Vital

DJ Flavours

THROW YOUR HANDS UP
Throw your hands up
CD ROWTCD 96008
Ruff On Wax / Apr '97 / Mo's Music Machine

DJ Food

RECIPE FOR DISASTER, A
Dark river / Inosan / Scratch yer head / Brass neck / Fungle junk / Half step / Dusk / Bass city roller / Spiral / Scratch yer butt / Akaire / Little samba / Scientific youth / SE 1 / Hipslop
CD ZENCD 020
Ninja Tune / Oct '95 / Kudos / Pinnacle / Prime / Vital

REFRIED FOOD VOL.1
Strange taste / Spiral dub / Freedom / Sexy bits / Scratch yer head / Mella / Half step / Turtle soup / Spiral / Dark lady / Dark river / Dark blood / Consciousness
CD ZENCD 021
Ninja Tune / Feb '96 / Kudos / Pinnacle / Prime / Vital

DJ Hell

X-MIX VOL.5 (Wildstyle) (Various Artists)
CD K7 039CD
Studio K7 / Nov '95 / Prime / RTM/Disc

DJ Hixxy

BONKERS VOL.1 (Mixed By DJ Hixxy & MC Sharkey) (Various Artists)
Toytown: *DJ Hixxy & MC Sharkey* / Steam train: *Hopscotch* / Love of my life: *DJ Dougal* / A-ha ha ha: *DJ Hixxy* / Together forever: *DJ Hixxy & Banana Man* / Let the music: *Eruption* / Party Time: *DJ Dougal & Eruption* / Funfair: *Force & Styles* / Airhead: *DJ Brisk* / Now is the time: *Brown, Scott* / Calypso summer: *DJ Vinylgroover & DJ Quatro* / Hold me now: *Highlander* / Like a dream: *Bass D & King Matthew* / Bust a new jam: *Seduction & Eruption* / Step to the side: *DJ Seduction* / On top: *Sense Of Summer* / Thumper: *DJ Hixxy* / Wantin' to get high: *DJ Hixxy & Ikon* / Frantik: *Druid & Sharkey* / Rocket to the moon: *Druid & Sharkey* / Tweedledum: *Druid & Bananaman* / Rainbow islands: *Seb* / Is there anybody there: *DJ Ham* / Techno round the world: *Sense Of Summer* / On and on: *Brisk* / Wonder land: *Force & Styles* / All systems go: *Force & Styles* / Teknostorm: *Vampire* / Outside world: *Bunter, Billy & D'Zyne/Supreme* / Revolution: *MC Sharkey* / Truth: *Smith, Marc & Sharkey* / Bonkers anthem: *Druid & Sharkey* / Pumpin: *Druid & Sharkey* / Feel the heat: *Sy & Sharkey* / Burns this joint: *Terrible twins*
CD REACTCD 083
React / Jul '96 / Arabesque / Prime / Vital

BONKERS VOL.2 (Mixed By DJ Hixxy & MC Sharkey - 2CD Set) (Various Artists)
Rave station: *Ramos & Supreme/UFO* / Tekniq: *Ramos & Supreme/UFO* / Future dimensions: *Druid & DJ Energy* / Body slam: *Bang The Future* / Twister: *GSI* / Whores in the house: *DJ Darryl* / Rock 'n' roll: *DJ Quatiro* / E-motion: *Druid & Trixxy* / Inside beat: *Rapido* / Boom 'n' pow: *Smith, Marc* / Droppin' bombs: *DJ Fury* / Genesis: *Trixxy & Sharkey* / UR Everything: *Helix* / Living dream: *Evolve* / Ultraworld 5: *DJ Eclipse* / See the stars trixxy: *DJ Eclipse* / Revolution part 1: *Sharkey* / Therapy: *Trixxy & Sharkey* / My way: *Antisocial* / On top: *Sense Of Summer* / Now you've got: *Antisocial* / Forever young: *Antisocial* / Whistle: *Antisocial* / People's party: *DJ Hixxy & Sunset Regime* / Critical heights: *Unkown Project* / Paradise and dreams: *Force & Styles* / Scream: *Antisocial* / 24-7: *Antisocial* / Big up the bass: *Blitz, Blaze & Revolution* / Sugar & spice: *Evolve* / Your mind: *DJ Demo* / Antisocial: *Antisocial* / Dream surprise: *Dougal & Micky Skeedale* / Is this love: *DJ Fade & Melody* / Wham bam: *DJ Vinylgroover*
CD Set REACTCD 101
React / Apr '97 / Arabesque / Prime / Vital

DJ Honda

DJ HONDA
Dat's my word / DJ battle (round 1) / Game of death / Cold blooded / What did you expect / Freestyle '95 / Zulu shout out / Bread and Jerry / Earth 'till it's down / DJ battle (round 3) / What it look like / Out for the cash (5 deadly venoms) / Old school jam
CD 4852332
Epic / Oct '96 / Sony

DJ Hurricane

HURRA, THE
Now you do / Elbow room / Four fly guys / Can we all get along / Stick em up / Pat your foot / Get blind / Comin' off / What's really going on / Where's my niggas at / Hurra / Pass me the gun / Feel the blast
CD WIJ 043CD
Wiiija / Feb '95 / RTM/Disc

DJ Jazzy Jeff

CODE RED (DJ Jazzy Jeff & The Fresh Prince)
Somethin' like dis / I'm looking for the one to be with me / Boom, shake the room / Can't wait to be with you / Twinkle twinkle (I'm not a star) / Code red / Shadow dreams / Just kickin' it / Ain't no place like home / I wanna rock / Scream / Boom shake the room
CD CHIP 140
Jive / Mar '97 / Pinnacle

HOME BASE (DJ Jazzy Jeff & The Fresh Prince)
I'm all that / Summertime / Things that U do / This boy is smooth / Ring my bell / Dog is a dog / Caught in the middle / Trapprd on the dancefloor / Who stole the DJ / You saw my blinker / Dumb dancin' / Summertime
CD CHIP 116
Jive / Mar '97 / Pinnacle

DJ Keoki

JOURNEYS BY DJ INTERNATIONAL (Keoki)
CD JDJIL 50202
JDJ / Aug '94 / 3mv/Pinnacle / SRD

MIXING IT UP WITH
CD MM 800352
Moonshine / Jul '95 / Mo's Music Machine / Prime / RTM/Disc

WE ARE ONE
CD SUB 4D
Subversive / Oct '95 / 3mv/Sony / Amato Disco / Mo's Music Machine / Prime / Vital
CD ADR 90003
Mic Mac / Mar '96 / Vital/SAM

DJ Kool

LET ME CLEAR MY THROAT
I'm not from Philly / Let me clear my throat / I got dat feelin' / Put the hump (in your back) / Music ain't loud enuff / Twenty minute workout / Let me clear my throat / I'm done
CD 74321421152
Loud / Feb '97 / BMG

DJ Krush

DJ KRUSH
CD SDW 0042
Shadow / May '97 / Cargo / Plastic Head

MEISO
Only the strong survive / Anticipation / What's behind the darkness / Meiso / By path 1 / Blank / Ground / By path 2 / Most wanted man / By path 3 / 3rd eye / Oce 9504 / Duality / By path - would you take it
CD MW 039CD
Mo Wax / Sep '95 / PolyGram / Vital

MILIGHT
Intro / Shin sekkai / Jikan no hashi I / Real / Listen / Supanova / Jikan no hashi II / Le temps / Hitotsu no mirai / Shinjiro / Light (can you see it) / Mind games / Skin against skin / Jugoya / Jikan no hashi III / To-u-kyo
CD MW 077CD
Mo Wax / Aug '97 / PolyGram / Vital

STRICTLY TURNTABILIZED
Intro / Lunation / Fucked up pendulum / Kemuri / Loop / Silent ungah / Interlude / Dig this vibe / Yeah / To the infinity / Nightmare of ungah (sandro in effect)
CD MW 025CD
Mo Wax / Apr '96 / PolyGram / Vital

DJ Loops

BEATS TO SAMPLE
Evil / Bone / Slip / Light up / Stuffed / Moved / Pumped / Middle / Fatso / Tooty / Tooty 11 / So bad / Mash up / Holey / Buzz / Baz / Batty / Slam
CD BRCD 608
4th & Broadway / Feb '94 / PolyGram

DJ Nemesis

JAMM ATTACK RAVE BEATS
CD STARMIX 3CD
Music Of Life / Feb '92 / Grapevine/ PolyGram

DJ Quik

QUIK IS THE NAME
CD FILERCD 402
Profile / Apr '91 / Pinnacle

SAFE & SOUND
CD ______ FILECD 462
Profile / Feb '95 / Pinnacle

DJ Rap

INTELLIGENCE (DJ Rap & Voyager)
Mad up / Abyss / Losing control / Burning love / Spiritual aura / Two loves / Drum / Roughest gunark / See the future / Baby don't keep me waiting
CD ______ PTCD 001
Proper Talent / Sep '95 / Vital

JOURNEY INTO DRUM BASS
CD ______ JDJDB 1CD
JDJ / Mar '95 / 3mv/Pinnacle / SRD

DJ Red Alert

SLAMMIN' VINYL (DJ Red Alert & Mike Slammer)
CD ______ GUMH 011
Gumh / Nov '94 / SRD

DJ Seduction

HARDCORE N-R-G (2CD Set) (Various Artists)
Tekno harmony remix: *Sy & Unknown* / Remix: *Cheddar* / Remix: *Cheddar* / Take it from the groove remix: *Vinyl Groover* / Anthem remix: *Elation* / In effect remix: *Slammer, Mike* / Tearin' my love apart: *Vinyl Junkie* / Jump to this: *Go Mental* / We're flying: *Stu J & UFO* / Now is the time remix: *Brown, Scott* / Here I am: *DJ Ham & DJ Demo/Justin Time* / Let it lift you: *Bunter, Billy* / Pure space: *Supreme & UFO* / Sample mania remix: *DJ Seduction* / Music so wonderful: *DJ Vibes* / Down to love: *Force & Styles* / Hallelujah: *DJ Seduction* / DJs mixing: *Edit V* / Hop on the dancefloor: *Seduction & Bunter* / Touch the magic: *Stripey J* / Bust the new jam: *Seduction & Eruption* / Partytime remix: *Dougal & Eruption* / Hardcore fever: *DJ Energy* / Big spill: *DJ Ham & DJ Demo/Justin Time* / Higher love: *JDS* / Tonight's the night: *Vinyl Groover* / Feel the power: *DJ Codene* / Popcorn: *Ravers choice 4* / Fire: *Doe, John* / Don't go away: *Maurizio*
CD Set ______ SOLIDSCD 003
Solid State / Sep '96 / Prime / Vital

DJ Seeq

INSTRUMENTAL BREAKBEAT
CD ______ 3020262
Jimmy Jay / Jul '97 / Cargo

DJ Shadow

ENDTRODUCING...
Best foot forward / Building steam with a grain of salt / Number song / Changeling / Transmission / What does your soul look like / Untitled / Stem/Long stem / Transmission / Mutual slump / Organ donor / Why hip hop sucks in '96 / Midnight in a perfect world / Napalm brain/Scatter brain / What does your soul look like / Transmission
CD ______ MW 059CD
Mo Wax / Sep '96 / PolyGram / Vital

DJ Slipmatt

HELTER SKELTER (2CD Set)
CD Set ______ CDHSR 096
Helter Skelter / Nov '96 / Pinnacle / Plastic Head / SRD

DJ Smurf

VERSASTYLES
CD ______ WRA 81452
Wrap / Mar '95 / Koch

DJ Sneak

BLUE FUNK FILES
Computer games / Grinder / Sneak attack / Grace of tracks / Sounds in my head / For the love of house / Jugglin' thoughts / Who's knockin' / Psychic bounty killaz / Futuristic cipher / Junglist steelos
CD ______ ULTRA 2002
Ultra / Jun '97 / Mo's Music Machine / Prime / RTM/Disc

BUGGIN' DA BEATS (Various Artists)
Ride: *Ailey, Vince* / Cassio's theme: *Groove Box* / Sunrise: *Fiasco, Johnny* / Strong enough: *Manhattan People* / It's you: *Chandler, Kerri* / Stress free: *Juice & Co.* / Zombie dawn: *Tranquil Elephantizer* / Holding on to your love: *Cooke, Stephanie* / Earthshaker EP: *Republic* / Gimme some horns: *Essentials* / Kindred spirits: *Special Agents* / Trouble: *Roach Motel Presents 2 Stupid Dogz* / Way: *Global Communication* / Special K: *DJ Sneak* / Life is changing: *Castelli, Cricco*
CD ______ MM 800672
Moonshine / May '97 / Mo's Music Machine / Prime / RTM/Disc

KINKY TRAX COLLECTION, THE (DJ Sneak/Princess Julliana - 2CD Set) (Various Artists)
Moist womanly needs: *Weebles & Princess Julia* / Do it your way: *Mood II Swing* / Deeper go deeper: *Juice Company* / Love love love: *Those Guys* / Version 10: *Swag* / I'm the baddest bitch: *Bell, Norma Jean* / I'm ready: *Donald O* / Get hi: *Roger S* / So in love: *Wild Pursuit* / Stand up: *Jones, Nick* / Night: *Roach Motel* / Yeah yeah: *Dixon, Daniel* / Find your way: *Crosby, B.J.* / If Madonna calls: *Vasquez, Junior* / Get lost: *Alan X* / Stickin' to my groove: *Chunky Kutz* / Transaxual: *Armando* / Mack Daddy shoot: *Kenlou* / Something I feel: *Alias* / Love potion: *Baby Pop* / Let's go disco: *Southern Comfort & Nolan Epps* / Only 4 U: *Cajmere* / Latin Seoul: *DJ Sneak* / Pain in my brain: *Outsider* / Free: *Morel, Nasty* / Play it again: *DJ Sneak* / Disco breaks: *DJ Sneak* / Ooh: *Mood II Swing* / Psychic bounty killaz: *DJ Sneak & Armand Van Helden* / It's a damn shame: *Long, Wyndell* / Salsa break: *G-Dubs & Ben Starr* / Check this out: *Fisher, Cevin* / What I want: *Groove Source* / Fly away: *Edwards, Todd* / Day & night: *Baby Pop*
CD Set ______ REACTCD 091
React / Oct '96 / Arabesque / Prime / Vital

DJ Soulslinger

DON'T BELIEVE
CD ______ JS 120CD
Jungle Sky / Jun '97 / Cargo

DJ Soup

SOUPER LOOPS
CD ______ TKCD 62
2 Kool / May '97 / Pinnacle / SRD

DJ Spike

GLOBAL 2000
CD ______ BLCCD 9
Blanc / Feb '95 / Pinnacle / Shellshock/Disc

TASTELESS CUTS
Baby bye / Gaps in space / Mr. President / Spike part one / MPB 105 / German / Designer drugs / Stick out
CD ______ BL 001 CD
Blanc / Apr '92 / Pinnacle / Shellshock/Disc

DJ Spooky

NECROPOLIS (The Dialogic Project)
CD ______ KFWCD 185
Knitting Factory / Oct '96 / Cargo / Plastic Head

SONGS OF A DEAD DREAMER
CD ______ EFA 709612
Asphodel / Sep '96 / Cargo / SRD

DJ SS

ROLLERS CONVENTION
CD ______ FORM 4CD
Formation / Nov '94 / SRD

DJ Supreme

STOLEN BEATS & RIPPED OFF SCRATCHES
Superstition Revisited / Incorporated Beat / Hammonds drummer / Big soul / Kool's return / Radio break / Impeach - the sequel / Buddy's solo / Hard 'n' horny / Love break / Dead ringer / Jungle vibes / Forty Scratch vibes
CD ______ STARMIX 4CD
Music Of Life / Oct '92 / Grapevine/ PolyGram

DJ Toolz

BREAKBEATS 'N' GROOVES VOL.1
Takin 1 back / Slots / Funky donkey / To the beat y'all / Eight ins for Rita / Drummer / Thirteenth break / Flute of the groove / Col' favor / Smoove B / Bus stop / Gimmi gimmi / Twenty dollars / Biz beat / Congo soul / Texas B boy
CD ______ TOOLCD 001
Ninja Tune / Jul '93 / Kudos / Pinnacle / Prime / Vital

DJ Triple

JUNGLE BREAKS & BEATS (DJ Triple & Bassman)
CD ______ MOLCD 38
Music Of Life / Mar '95 / Grapevine/ PolyGram

DJ Vadim

USSR REPERTOIRE
Intro / Relax with Pep pt.6 / Headz ain't ready / Next shit / Lounge vibes / Live in Paris / Lord forgive me / Relax with Pep pt.5 / Suckas wearing tainted sunglasses / Aural prostitution / Knowledge be born / This goes out / Buggin' out / Melodies in Hinge Creek / Times are hard / Schematics / Call me / Bloke 1 / Who the hell am I / Relax with Pep pt.2 / Abstractions / Mental gymnastics / Foundation / USSR Repetoire / Help me / Melodies in vertical theory / Reality (who is the realist) / Nuisance caller / Level test / Variations in chair creek and cradle / Lounge shiznits / Live from Paris / Morning prayer / Knowledge vs wisdom / Heads still ain't ready
CD ______ ZENCD 025
Ninja Tune / Oct '96 / Kudos / Pinnacle / Prime / Vital

DJ Wally

DJ WALLY'S GENETIC FLAW
Japaneez wine / Possi purple / Fractured beaker / Feelin' groovy / Mr. Beaver saves the day / Space people / Ricco's love / At war / Last chance to comprehend / Mustard plaster / Ridiculous sound / Bitchley's kow korn
CD ______ HE 117CD
Home Entertainment / Feb '97 / Cargo

Djalti

CHARMING RAI
CD ______ 829272
BUDA / Sep '96 / Discovery

Djiboudjep

PARFUM D'EPICES ET GOUT DE SEL
CD ______ 869CD
Escalibur / May '97 / ADA / Discovery / Roots

Djip

SOUMBAYO
CD ______ 3020302
Arcade / Jun '97 / Discovery

Djole, Africa

LIVE - THE CONCERT IN BERLIN 1978
CD ______ FMPCD 01
FMP / Feb '86 / Cadillac

Djur Djura

VOICES OF SILENCE (Adventures In Afropea 2)
CD ______ 9362452112
Luaka Bop / May '94 / Warner Music

Djwahl Khul

SCHLACHTUNGSKIND
CD ______ EFA 121632
Apollyon / Aug '95 / SRD

DM Bob & The Deficits

BAD WITH WIMMEN
CD ______ EFA 128782
Crypt / Jul '96 / Shellshock/Disc

DM3

GARAGE SALE
CD ______ CITCD 533
Citadel / Jul '97 / Greyhound

DMX Krew

FFRESSSHH
Introduction / You can't hide your love / Bonkers goes back to school / Radio DMX / Body rock / Sound of the DMX / We are gonna make you move / I'm all alone / Space pirate / Europa / Ready to roll / Black music / Acknowledgement
CD ______ CAT 053CD
Rephlex / Jul '97 / Prime / RTM/Disc

SOUND OF THE STREET
CD ______ CAT 029CD
Rephlex / Sep '96 / Prime / RTM/Disc

DMZ

WHEN I GET OFF
CD ______ VOXXCD 2004
Voxx / Jul '93 / Else / RTM/Disc

DNA

DNA
CD ______ AVAN 006
Avant / Sep '93 / Cadillac / Harmonia Mundi

DNS

BOMBS AND CLOUDS
CD ______ MA352
Machinery / Dec '93 / Koch

Do Bandolim, Jacob

MANDOLIN MASTER OF BRAZIL
CD ______ ACD 3
Acoustic Disc / Jul '97 / ADA / Koch

Do Carmo, Lucilia

PORTUGAL - A SPIRIT OF FADO VOL.4
CD ______ PS 65704
PlayaSound / Oct '92 / ADA / Harmonia Mundi

Do'A

ANCIENT BEAUTY (Do'A World Music Ensemble)
CD ______ CDPH 9004
Philo / Dec '86 / ADA / CM / Direct

COMPANIONS OF THE CRIMSON COLOURED ARK (Do'A World Music Ensemble)
CD ______ CDPH 9009
Philo / Dec '86 / ADA / CM / Direct

EARLY YEARS, THE (Do'A World Music Ensemble)
CD ______ ROUCD 11539
Rounder / '88 / ADA / CM / Direct

DOA

BLACK SPOT, THE
CD ______ 352992
Frantic / Dec '96 / Cargo

GREATEST SHITS
CD ______ QQP 019CD
QQP / Nov '92 / Plastic Head

LOGGERHEADS
CD ______ VIRUS 130CD
Alternative Tentacles / Sep '93 / Cargo / Greyhound / Pinnacle

MURDER
CD ______ 723762
Restless / Feb '95 / Vital

NEW YORK CITY SPEEDCORE
Total annihilation / Ya mutha / Brooklyn mob / NYC speedcore / Wanna be a gangsta / Zu leiten / Uncle Bill's message / Pound down on your brain / Kill / Uncle Bill's message / Minute madness / Extreme gangsta / Our father / Ya mutha III / Noize core / I'll give you hard / Ya mutha II / You're dead / This is DOA
CD ______ MOSH 164CD
Earache / Jan '97 / Vital

TALK - ACTION = 0
CD ______ 725062
Restless / Feb '95 / Vital

THIRTEEN FLAVOURS OF DOOM
CD ______ VIRUS 117CD
Alternative Tentacles / Oct '92 / Cargo / Greyhound / Pinnacle

Dob

LA LU LA ROO
CD ______ BUNG 0102
City Slang / Jan '97 / RTM/Disc

Dobkins, Carl Jr.

MY HEART IS AN OPEN BOOK
My heart is an open book / If you don't want my lovin' / Love is everything / My pledge to you / Lucky devil / Fool such as I / Promise me / Take time out / Chance to belong / In my heart / Ask me no questions / Sawdust Dolly / Pretty little girl in the yellow dress / Open up your arms / I'm sorry / Three little piggies / Class ring / Exclusively yours / For your love / True love / Raining in my heart / Sue / That's what I call true love / One little girl / Genie / Different kind of love / Lovelight / That's all I need to know
CD ______ BCD 15546
Bear Family / Feb '91 / Direct / Rollercoaster / Swift

Dobrogosz, Steve

FINAL TOUCH, THE
CD ______ DRAGONCD 195
Dragon / May '86 / ADA / Cadillac / CM / Roots / Wellard

JADE
CD ______ DRCD 203
Dragon / Jul '87 / ADA / Cadillac / CM / Roots / Wellard

TRIO
CD ______ 1232
Caprice / Dec '87 / ADA / Cadillac / CM / Complete/Pinnacle

Dobson, Dobby

AT LAST
CD ______ ANGCD 22
Angella / Jul '94 / Jet Star

GREATEST HITS
CD ______ SONCD 0072
Sonic Sounds / Nov '94 / Jet Star

IF I ONLY HAD TIME
CD ______ ANGCD 018
Angella / Jun '97 / Jet Star

NOTHING BUT LOVE VOL.3
CD ______ PILCD 303
Pioneer / Feb '96 / RTM/Disc / THE

SWEET DREAMS
CD ______ PKCD 32993
K&K / Jul '93 / Jet Star

SWEET DREAMS AGAIN VOL.2
CD ______ PILCD 301
Pioneer / Feb '96 / Jet Star

Dobson, Richard

HEARTS & RIVERS (Dobson, Richard & State Of The Heart)
CD ______ BRAM 1990142
Brambus / Nov '93 / ADA

ONE BAR TOWN
CD ______ 199568CD
Brambus / Jul '95 / ADA

RICHARD DOBSON SINGS TOWNES VAN ZANDT
CD ______ BRAMBUS 1994502
Brambus / Jul '94 / ADA

DOC

HELTER SKELTER
Return of da livin' dead / From Ruthless to Death Row / Secret plan / Komurshell / For my dawgs / 45 Automatic / Sonz o'light / Bitches / Da hereafter / Erotix shit / Welcome to the new world / Killa instinct / Brand new formula / Crazy bitches
CD 74321288282
RCA / Jan '96 / BMG

Doc Holliday

SON OF THE MORNING SUN
CD CDIRS 972190
Intercord / Aug '93 / Plastic Head

Doc Houlind

TRIBUTE TO GEORGE LEWIS, A (Doc Houlind Copenhagen Ragtime Band)
CD MECCACD 1037
Music Mecca / Nov '94 / Cadillac / Jazz Music / Wellard

Doc Ice

RELY ON SELPH
CD WRA 8127CD
Wrap / Jun '94 / Koch

Doc Martin

UNITED DJ'S OF AMERICA VOL.4/LOS ANGELES (Various Artists)
CD UNDJACD 4
Stress / Jul '96 / Mo's Music Machine / Pinnacle / Prime

Doc Tahri

EINSTEIN WAS A BULLFIGHTER
CD EFA 12363
Musical Tragedies / Jul '97 / SRD

Doc Wor Mirran

GARAGE PRETENSIONS
CD EFA 113642
Musical Tragedies / Jan '94 / SRD

Doctor Bison

BLOATED VEGAS YEARS, THE
Clean the air / Sweet embrace / Place for us / Sense / Kentucky red hair / Make me yours / Come around / Ocean of dreams / Cut down / Baptism of vodka / Right about you
CD PLAYCD 20
Workers Playtime / Apr '97 / Pinnacle

Dodd, Ken

GREATEST HITS (An Hour Of Hits)
Happiness / Love is like a violin / Somewhere my love / River / Eight by ten / They didn't believe me / As time goes by / I wish you love / More than ever / So deep is the night / Tears / Still / Broken hearted / She / Old fashioned way / For all we know / What a wonderful world / Happy days and lonely nights / Just out of reach / Let me cry on your shoulder / Promises
CD CC 202
Music For Pleasure / May '88 / EMI

Dodds, Baby

BILL RUSSELL'S HISTORIC RECORDINGS
CD AMCD 17
American Music / Feb '95 / Jazz Music

Dodds, Johnny

BLUE CLARINET STOMP (1926-1928)
Weary blues / New Orleans Stomp / Wild man blues / Melancholy / Come on and stomp, stomp, stomp / After you've gone / Joe Turner blues / When Erastus plays his old kazoo / Blue clarinet stomp / Blue piano stomp / Bucktown stomp / Weary city / Bull fiddle blues / Blue washboard stomp / Sweet Lorraine / Pencil papa / My little Isabel-A / Heah' me talkin' / Goober dance / Too tight-A
CD DGF 3
Frog / Oct '94 / Cadillac / Jazz Music / Wellard

CLASSICS 1926
CD CLASSICS 589
Classics / Aug '91 / Discovery / Jazz Music

CLASSICS 1927
CD CLASSICS 603
Classics / Sep '91 / Discovery / Jazz Music

CLASSICS 1927-1928
CD CLASSICS 617
Classics / Sep '92 / Discovery / Jazz Music

CLASSICS 1928-1940
CD CLASSICS 635
Classics / Nov '92 / Discovery / Jazz Music

INTRODUCTION TO JOHNNY DODDS 1923-1940, AN
CD 4014
Best Of Jazz / Apr '95 / Discovery

JOHNNY DODDS (1926-1928)
Perdido street blues / Gatemouth / Too tight / Papa dip / Mixed salad / I can't say / Flatfoot / Mad dog / Ballin' the Jack / Grandma's ball / My baby / Oriental man / Get 'em again blues / Brush stomp / My girl / Sweep 'em clean / Lady love / Brown bottom Bess
CD JSPCD 319
JSP / Apr '92 / ADA / Cadillac / Direct / Hot Shot / Target/BMG

JOHNNY DODDS & JELLY ROLL MORTON (Dodds, Johnny & Jelly Roll Morton)
CD DGF 9
Frog / Nov '96 / Cadillac / Jazz Music / Wellard

JOHNNY DODDS & JIMMY BLYTHE (Dodds, Johnny & Jimmy Blythe)
Little bits / Your folks / Struggling / Easy come, easy go blues / Struggling (2nd take) / Blues stampede / Bohunkus blues / I'm goin' huntin' / Buddy Barton's jazz / If you want to be my sugar Papa / Messin' around / Messin' around (2nd take) / Weary way blues / Adam's apple / Poutin' Papa / Idle hour special / Hot stuff / 47th Street stomp / My baby / Oriental man / Ape man
CD CBC 1015
Chris Barber Collection / Nov '93 / Cadillac / New Note/Pinnacle

JOHNNY DODDS 1926-1940 (3CD Set)
What a man / Who's gonna do your lovin' / Nobody else will do / Bohunkus blues / Buddy Burton's jazz / Little bits / Struggling / Perdido street blues / Gatemouth / Too tight / Papa did / Mixed salad / I can't say / Flat foot floogie / Mad dog / Messin' around / Adam's apple / East coast trot / Chicago buzz / Idle hour special / 47th street stomp / Someday sweetheart / Stock yards strut / Salty dog / Ape man / Yours folks / House rent rag / Memphis shake / Carpet alley breakdown / Hen party blues / Stomp time blues / It must be the blues / Oh daddy / Loveless love / 19th street blues / San / Oh Lizzie (A lovers lament) / New St. Louis blues / Clarinet wobble / Easy come, easy go blues / Blues stampede / I'm goin' huntin' / If you want to be my sugar papa / Weary blues / New Orleans stomp / Wild man blues / Melancholy / Wolverine blues / Mr. Jelly Lord / There'll come a day / Weary way blues / Cootie stomp / Poutin' papa / Hot stuff / Have mercy
CD Set CDAFS 10233
Affinity / Jan '93 / Cadillac / Jazz Music / Koch

JOHNNY DODDS 1926-40
CD CD 14559
Jazz Portraits / Jul '94 / Jazz Music

JOHNNY DODDS STORY 1923-1929
CD 158412
Jazz Archives / Feb '96 / Discovery

JOHNNY DODDS VOL.1
CD VILCD 0022
Village Jazz / Sep '92 / Jazz Music / Target/BMG

JOHNNY DODDS VOL.2
CD VILCD 0172
Village Jazz / Aug '92 / Jazz Music / Target/BMG

KING OF THE NEW ORLEANS CLARINET (1926-1938)
CD BLE 592352
Black & Blue / Dec '92 / Discovery / Koch / Wellard

MYTH OF NEW ORLEANS, THE (1926-1940)
CD CD 53077
Giants Of Jazz / Mar '92 / Cadillac / Jazz Music / Target/BMG

OH DADDY
Riverside blues / Jackass blues / Frog tongue stomp / East coast stomp / Chicago buzz / In the alley blues / Someday sweetheart / Oh Daddy / Loveless love / 19th Street blues / New Orleans stomp / Wild man blues / Potato head blues / Melancholy blues / Beale Street blues / Wolverine blues / Mr. Jelly Lord / There'll come a day / Come on and stomp stomp stomp / After you've gone / Joe Turner's blues / When Erastus plays his old kazoo / Oriental man / Piggly wiggly
CD TPZ 1060
Topaz Jazz / Jan '97 / Cadillac / Pinnacle

Dodge, Arthur

ARTHUR DODGE & THE HORSEFEATHERS (Dodge, Arthur & The Horsefeathers)
CD BIR 045
Barber's Itch / Feb '97 / Cargo

Dodge City Productions

STEPPIN' UP AND OUT
CD BRCD 587
4th & Broadway / May '93 / PolyGram

Dodgeball

HOORAY FOR EVERYTHING
CD GR 58
Goldenrod / Jun '97 / Cargo

Dodgy

DODGY ALBUM, THE
CD 5400822
A&M / Jun '93 / PolyGram

FREE PEACE SWEET
Intro / In a room / Trust in me / You've gotta look up / If you're thinking of me / Good enough / Ain't no longer asking / Found you / One of those rivers / Prey for drinking / Jack the lad / Long life / UKRIP / Homegrown
CD 5405732
A&M / Jun '96 / PolyGram

HOMEGROWN
Staying out for the summer / Melodies haunt you / So let me go far / Crossroads / One day / We are together / Whole lot easier / Making the most of / Waiting for the day / What have I done wrong / Grassman
CD 5402822
A&M / Oct '94 / PolyGram

Doernberg, Ferdy

JUST A PIANO AND A HANDFUL OF DREAMS
CD 08412112
SPV / Jan '96 / Koch / Plastic Head

Dog Boy Jones

OUT FOR KICKS
Train / I'm going walking / Spin your partner / Hey na na / Dear Jane / Out for kicks / Blue dress / Cross the river / Almost gone / Louisiana bayou / Billy and Rebecca / Boys in the rodeo / White lies / Let it rain
CD LCD 80009
Lizard / May '97 / Direct / RTM/Disc

Dog Eat Dog

ALL BORO KINGS
CD RR 90208
Roadrunner / Feb '96 / PolyGram

PLAY GAMES
Bulletproof / Isms / Hi lo / Rocky / Step right in / Rise above / Games / Getting live / Buggin' / Numb / Sore loser / Games / Getting live / Rocky
CD RR 88762
CD RR 88765
Roadrunner / Aug '97 / PolyGram

WARRANT
It's like that / Dog eat dog / World keeps spinnin' / In the dog house / Psychorama / In the dog house (remix)
CD RR 90712
Roadrunner / Jun '93 / PolyGram

Dog Faced Hermans

BUMP AND SWING
CD K 153CD
Konkurrel / Jun '94 / SRD

HUM OF LIFE
CD K147D
Konkurrel / Mar '93 / SRD

THOSE DEEP BUDS
CD K 155C
Konkurrel / Oct '94 / SRD

Dog, Tim

PENCILLIN IN WAX
Intro / Low down / Nigga / Robbin Harris shit / Fuck compton / DJ quick beat down / Step to me / Phone conversation w/reporter / Bronx nigga / You ain't shit / I ain't takin' no shorts / NFL shit / I'll wax anybody / Michel'le conversation / Can't fuck around / Dog's gonna getcha / Goin' wild in the Penile / Get off the dick / I ain't havin' it / Patriotic pimp / Secret fantasies
CD 4693492
Ruff House / Feb '92 / Sony

Dog Town Balladeers

ANTIQUE WINE AND ROSES
CD RE 10034
Relative / Mar '97 / Cargo

Dogfeet

DOGFEET
CD CA 36002
Kissing Spell / Jun '97 / Greyhound

Doggett, Bill

14 HITS (Doggett, Bill Combo)
CD KCD 5009
King / Apr '97 / Avid/BMG

DOGGETT BEAT FOR DANCING FEET, THE
Soft / And the angels sing / Ding dong / Honey / Easy / Hammerhead / Ram-bunk-shush / Chloe / Hot ginger / King Bee / What a difference a day makes / Shinding
CD KCD 557
King / Mar '90 / Avid/BMG

LEAPS AND BOUNDS
Bo-do rock / Honky tonk / Rainbow riot / Blue largo / Big boy / You ain't no good / Big dog / Hippy dippy / Backwards / Shindig / After hours / Peacock alley / In the wee hours / Leaps and bounds / Your kind of woman / Yocky dock / Wild oats
CD CDCHARLY 281
Charly / Sep '91 / Koch

Dogheimsgard

KRONET TIL KONGE
CD MR 006CD
Malicious / Oct '95 / Plastic Head

Dogpile

LIVE BUTT PLUGGED
CD EL 109
Electrip / Dec '93 / Plastic Head

Dogs D'Amour

DOG'S HITS AND THE BOOTLEG ALBUM
CD WOLCD 1020
China / Aug '91 / Pinnacle

ERROL FLYNN
Drunk like me / Hurricane / Errol Flynn / Princess valium / Trail of tears / Prettiest girl in the world / Goddess from the gutter / Satellite kid / Planetary pied piper / Dog's hair / Ballad of Jack / Girl behind the glass
CD 8397002
China / Sep '89 / Pinnacle

GRAVEYARD OF EMPTY BOTTLES, A
CD WOLCD 1005
China / Mar '91 / Pinnacle

MORE UNCHARTERED HEIGHTS OF DISGRACE
CD WOLCD 1032
China / Apr '93 / Pinnacle

SKELETONS (The Very Best Of Dogs D'Amour)
How come it never rains / Kid from Kensington / Heroine / Satellite kid / I don't want to go / Victims of success / Lady Nicotine / Johnny Silvers / Empty world / I think it's love again / Billy two rivers / Last bandit / Trail of tears / All or nothing / Pretty pretty once
CD NTRCD 082
Nectar / Jul '97 / Pinnacle

STRAIGHT
CD WOLCD 1007
China / Mar '91 / Pinnacle

Dogstar

ILLUMINATE FABRICATI
CD LALACD 3
La La Land / Apr '94 / RTM/Disc

Doherty, John

BUNDLE AND GO
Hudie Gallagher's march / Black mare of Fanad / March of the meena toiten bull / Kiss the maid behind the bier/The bargain is over / 21 Highland / Paps o' Glencoe / Hare in the corn / Knights of St. Patrick / Dispute at the crossroads / Roaring Mary / Miss Patterson's slippers / Cat that kittled in Jamie's wig / Welcome home royal Charlie / Darby Gallagher / Teelin highland / Heathery breeze / Monaghan switch / Black haired lass / Paddy's rambles through the park
CD OSS 17CD
Ossian / Jan '94 / ADA / CM / Direct / Highlander

FLOATING BOW, THE (Traditional Folk Music From Donegal)
Spirits of wine/Madame Bonaparte / Further in the deeper / An chuilfhionn/The flogging reel / Drops of brandy / Miss Patterson's slipper / Day I listed/Fantastic reel / Willie McLennan's / Lancer's jig/Gusty's frolics / Tom Tailor's / Scots Mary / Sligo maid's lament/Hand me down the tackle / Enniskillen Dragoons/Nora Crionna/Piobaire an cheideadh / Cameronian / Dulaman na binne bui / Within a mile of Dublin/Old Simon's hornpipe / Glenconwell's hornpipe / Mint in the corn / Highlanders/The wind that shakes the barley / Sean sa cheo / King George IV / Lancer's jig/The silver slipper / Mountain road / Braes of Maas / Bonnie Kate / Maidin fhomhair/Miss McLeod
CD CCF 31CD
Claddagh / Nov '96 / ADA / CM / Direct

TAISCE (The Celebrated Recordings)
CD CEFCD 072
Gael Linn / Jul '97 / ADA / CM / Direct / Grapevine/PolyGram / Roots

Doherty, Sally

SALLY DOHERTY
CD DDE 3932
Scout / May '96 / Koch

Doherty, Tom

TAKE THE BULL BY THE HORNS
Three sisters reels / Donegal reel/The maid I daren't tell / Cathy Jones/The keel row / Road to the Isles/Auld Rigadoo / Maggie

pickie / I've a polkie trimmed with blue/The gallope / Liverpool/Derry / Connaught man's rambles / Sally gardens/Cooley's / Humours of whiskey / Take the bull by the horns / Primrose lass / Corn rigs / Bridge O'Leary's / Paddy McGinty's goat/Green grow the rushes-o / Sweet cup of tea/ Drowsy Maggie / Miss Drummond of Perth/ Mollymusk / Silver spear/Mountain road/ Maid behind the bar / Queen of the fair/Off she goes
CD _______________ GLCD 1131
Green Linnet / Jul '93 / ADA / CM / Direct / Highlander / Roots

Dokken

ONE NIGHT LIVE
Into the fire / Unchain the night / Maze / Nothing left to say / From the beginning / Tooth and nail / Just got lucky / I will remember / Alone again / In my dreams / Nowhere man / It's not love
CD _______________ 06076862062
CMC / Apr '97 / BMG

Dokken, Don

UP FROM THE ASHES
CD _______________ GED 24301
Geffen / Jun '97 / BMG

Dol-Lop

CRYPTIC AUDIO
Shadow / Bluehouse / Doum / Hybrid / Phase / Qoke / Stem
CD _______________ VWM 16
Swim / Jun '97 / Kudos / RTM/Disc / SRD

Dolan, Joe

BEST OF JOE DOLAN
CD _______________ MATCD 277
Castle / Sep '93 / BMG

GREATEST HITS VOL.1
CD _______________ CDC 001
Ceol / Feb '97 / CM

GREATEST HITS VOL.2
CD _______________ CDC 002
Ceol / Feb '97 / CM

LOVE SONG COLLECTION
CD _______________ DHCD 721
Outlet / Jan '95 / ADA / CM / Direct / Duncans / Koch / Ross

MAKE ME AN ISLAND (The Best Of Joe Dolan)
CD _______________ PLSCD 201
Pulse / Apr '97 / BMG

MORE & MORE
CD _______________ RITZSCD 416
Ritz / Apr '93 / Pinnacle

MUSIC OF JOE DOLAN, THE
Sixteen brothers / You're such a good looking woman / You belong to me baby / Hypnotise / Frozen rivers / Sister Mary / More and more / Lady in blue / Maybe someday my love / Disco crazy / Most wanted man in the USA / Hush hush Maria
CD _______________ 12644
Laserlight / Apr '96 / Target/BMG

Dolan, Michael

TRIBUTE TO MICHAEL DOLAN, A (Various Artists)
CD _______________ GLCD 3097
Green Linnet / Jan '95 / ADA / CM / Direct / Highlander / Roots

Dolan, Packie

FORGOTTEN FIDDLE PLAYER OF THE 1920'S, THE
CD _______________ VVCD 1
Viva Voce / Jul '94 / ADA / Direct

PACKIE DOLAN
CD _______________ VIVAVOCE 006CD
Viva Voce / Nov '94 / ADA / Direct

Dolby, Thomas

ASTRONAUTS AND HERETICS
I love you, goodbye / Cruel / Silk pyjamas / I live in a suitcase / Eastern block (the sequel) / Close but no cigar / That's why people fall in love / Neon sister / Beauty of a dream
CD _______________ CDV 2701
Virgin / Jul '92 / EMI

FLAT EARTH, THE
Flat earth / Screen kiss / Mulu the rain forest / I scare myself / Hyperactive / White City / Dissidents
CD _______________ CDP 746 028 2
Parlophone / Jul '84 / EMI

GATE TO THE MIND, THE
CD _______________ 74321233862
RCA / Mar '95 / BMG

GOLDEN AGE OF WIRELESS, THE
She blinded me with science / Radio silence / Airwaves / Flying north / Weightless / Europa and the pirate twins / Windpower / Commercial break-up / One of our submarines is missing / Cloudburst at Shingle Street
CD _______________ CDFA 3319
Fame / Apr '95 / EMI

RETROSPECTACLE - THE BEST OF THOMAS DOLBY
Europa and the pirate twins / Urges / Leipzig / Windpower / Airwaves / She blinded me with science / One of our submarines is missing / Screen kiss / Hyperactive / I scare myself / Flat earth / Pulp culture / Budapest by Blimp / Cruel / Close but no cigar / I love you, goodbye
CD _______________ CDEMC 3659
EMI / Sep '96 / EMI

Doldinger, Klaus

DOLDINGER'S BEST
Blues for George / Two getting together / Minor kick / Quartenwalzer / Guachi guaro / Viva Brasilia / Fiesta / Raga up and down / Saragossa / Waltz of the jive cats / Comin' home baby / I feel free / Stormy Monday blues / Compared to what
CD _______________ 92242
Act / Feb '96 / New Note/Pinnacle

Doldrums

ACUPUNCTURE
CD _______________ KRANK 016
Kranky / Feb '97 / Cargo / Greyhound

Dole, Gerard

CO CO COLINDA (15 Original Songs)
CD _______________ PS 65086
PlayaSound / Apr '92 / ADA / Harmonia Mundi

Dollar

BEST OF DOLLAR, THE
Mirror, mirror (mon amour) / I wanna hold your hand / Love's gotta hold on me / Shooting star / Who were you with in the moonlight / We walked in love / Takin' a chance on you / Hand held in black and white / Oh l'amour / Videotheque / Kiss / Outta my head, outta my heart / It's nature's way (no problem) / I don't want our love thing to die / She said she said / Give me some kind of magic
CD _______________ ECD 3370
K-Tel / Jun '97 / K-Tel

DOLLAR
Shooting star / We walked in love / Ring ring / Who were you with in the moonlight / Kiss / Love's gotta hold on me / Takin' a chance on you / Outta my head outta my head / I wanna hold your hand / It's nature's way / Oh l'amour / No dull moments / She said, she said / Addicted to love / I don't want our love thing to die / Give me some kind of magic / Give me some kind of kind
CD _______________ 306142
Hallmark / Jan '97 / Carlton

Dollface

GIANT
CD _______________ KCCD 3
Kill City / Jul '95 / Total/Pinnacle

Dollis, Bo

1313 HOODOO STREET (Dollis, Bo & The Wild Magnolias)
I been hoodood / Run Joe / Angola bound / Might mighty chief / Hey hey / Louisiana / Walk on gilded spiders / Voodoo / Quitters never win / I know you Mardi Gras / Injuns here they come / Indian red
CD _______________ AIMA 3CD
Aim / Nov '96 / ADA / Direct / Jazz Music

Dolly Mixture

DEMONSTRATION TAPES
Dream come true / Ernie Ball / He's so frisky / Didn't song / Will he kiss me tonight / Miss Candy Twist / Shonay shonay / How come you're such a hit with the boys, Jane / Side street walker / Treasure hunt / Never let it go / Angel treads / Welcome to the perfect day / Step close now / Stareaway / In your eyes / Understanding / Never mind Sundays / Spend your wishes / Day by day / Wave away / Sorry to leave you / Winter seems fine / Grass is greener / Round the corner / Remember this / Whistling in the dark
CD _______________ RM 001CD
Royal Mint / Mar '96 / Vital

Dolphino, Jim

IRON LEGS (The Fun Runners' Ballad)
Iron legs / Wind / Very special place / Goldfish song / Walking on air / I've got a great big hole in my shoe / Seasons of my love / Little boy / Looking for nuts / As I sit and watch the rain / Kiss me, my amore / Wise old man
CD _______________ MYSCD 001
Myson / Jul '97 / Myson Music / Scratch/ BMG

Dolphy, Eric

1958-1961
CD _______________ CD 53164
Giants Of Jazz / Nov '95 / Cadillac / Jazz Music / Target/BMG

AT THE FIVE SPOT VOL.1
CD _______________ OJCCD 133
Original Jazz Classics / Feb '92 / Complete/Pinnacle / Jazz Music / Wellard

BERLIN CONCERTS
CD _______________ ENJACD 300792
Enja / Nov '94 / New Note/Pinnacle / Vital/ SAM

CANDID DOLPHY
Reincarnation of a love bird / Stormy weather / African lady / Quiet please / Moods in free time / Hazy hues / It ain't nobody's business if I do / Body and soul
CD _______________ CCD 79033
Candid / Feb '97 / Cadillac / Direct / Jazz Music / Koch / Wellard

CARIBE
Caribe / Blues in 6-8 / First bass line / Mambo Ricci / Spring is here / Sunday go meetin'
CD _______________ OJCCD 819
Original Jazz Classics / Jun '96 / Complete/ Pinnacle / Jazz Music / Wellard

COMPLETE PRESTIGE RECORDINGS, THE (9CD Set)
GW / On Green Dolphin Street / Les / 245 / Glad to be unhappy / Miss Toni / April fool / GW / 245 / Screamin' the blues / March on, march on / Drive / Meetin' / Three seconds / Alto-itis / Lautir / Curtsy / Geo's tune / They all laughed / Head shakin' / Dianna / Out there / Serene / Baron / Eclipse / 17 West / Sketch of melba / Feather / Caribe / Blues in 6/8 / First bass line / Mambo ricci / Spring is here / Sunday go meetin' / Trane whistle / Whole Nelson / You are too beautiful / Stolen moment / Walk away / Jaws / Mrs. Parker of K.C. / Ode to Charlie Parker / Far cry / Miss Ann / Left alone / Tenderly / It's magic / Serene / Images / Six and four / Mama Lou / Ralph's new blues / Straight ahead / III-44 / Rally / Bass duet / Softly as in a morning sunrise / Where / Yes indeed / Saucer eyes / Status seeking / Duquility / Thirteen / We diddit / Warm canto / Warp and woof / Fire waltz / Like someone in love / God bless the child / Aggression / Like someone in love / Fire waltz / Bee vamp / Prophet / Booker's waltz / Status seeking / Number eight / Bee vamp / Don't blame me / When lights are low / Don't blame me / Les / Way you look tonight / Woody 'n' you / Laura / Glad to be unhappy / God bless the child / In the blues / Hi-fly / Oleo
CD Set _______________ 9PRCD 44182
Prestige / Nov '96 / Cadillac / Complete/ Pinnacle

ERIC DOLPHY 1961
CD _______________ CD 14553
Jazz Portraits / Jul '94 / Jazz Music

ERIC DOLPHY IN EUROPE VOL.2
CD _______________ OJCCD 414
Original Jazz Classics / Mar '93 / Complete/Pinnacle / Jazz Music / Wellard

ESSENTIAL, THE
GW / Les / Meetin' / Feathers / Eclipse / Ode to Charlie Parker / Bird's mother / Ralph's new blues / Status seeking
CD _______________ FCD 60022
Fantasy / Apr '94 / Jazz Music / Pinnacle / Wellard

FAR CRY (Dolphy, Eric & Booker Little)
CD _______________ OJCCD 4002
Original Jazz Classics / Mar '93 / Complete/Pinnacle / Jazz Music / Wellard

HOT, COOL AND LATIN
CD _______________ BMCD 3057
Blue Moon / Jul '97 / Cadillac / Discovery / Greensleeves / Jazz Music / Jet Star / TKO Magnum

IN EUROPE VOL.1
Hi fly / Glad to be unhappy / God bless the child / Oleo
CD _______________ OJCCD 413
Original Jazz Classics / Apr '93 / Complete/ Pinnacle / Jazz Music / Wellard

IN EUROPE VOL.3
Woody 'n' you / When lights are low / In the blues
CD _______________ OJCCD 416
Original Jazz Classics / Apr '93 / Complete/ Pinnacle / Jazz Music / Wellard

IRON MAN
Iron man / Mandrake / Come Sunday / Burning spear / Ode to the CP
CD _______________ CDGR 147
Charly / May '97 / Koch

LAST DATE
Epistrophy / South Street exit / Madrig speaks, the panther walks / Hypochristmutreefuzz / You don't know what love is
CD _______________ 5101242
EmArCy / Sep '92 / PolyGram

MEMORIAL ALBUM (Dolphy, Eric & Booker Little)
CD _______________ OJCCD 353
Original Jazz Classics / May '93 / Complete/Pinnacle / Jazz Music / Wellard

MUSIC MATADOR
Jitterbug waltz / Music matador / Alone together / Love me
CD _______________ LEJAZZCD 14
Le Jazz / Jun '93 / Cadillac / Koch

OUT THERE
CD _______________ OJCCD 23
Original Jazz Classics / May '93 / Complete/Pinnacle / Jazz Music / Wellard

OUT TO LUNCH
Hat and beard / Something sweet, something tender / Gazzellioni / Out to lunch / Straight up and down
CD _______________ CDP 7465242
Blue Note / Mar '95 / EMI

OUTWARD BOUND
CD _______________ OJCCD 222
Original Jazz Classics / Feb '91 / Complete/Pinnacle / Jazz Music / Wellard

Dom Um Romao

SAUDADES
CD _______________ WLACS 16CD
Waterlilly Acoustics / Nov '95 / ADA

Domaci Kapela

JEDNE NOCI SNIL
CD _______________ R 0010
Rachot / Jun '97 / ReR Megacorp

Domain

CRACK IN THE WALL
CD _______________ FT 30016CD
Flametrader / Jan '92 / Plastic Head

Domancich, Sophia

L'ANNEE DES TREIZE LUNES
CD _______________ A 15
Seventh / Oct '95 / Cadillac / Harmonia Mundi / ReR Megacorp

Dome

DOME VOL.1 & 2
CD _______________ DOME 12CD
The Grey Area / Aug '92 / RTM/Disc

DOME VOL.3 & 4
CD _______________ DOME 34CD
The Grey Area / Aug '92 / RTM/Disc

Dominator

FORBIDDEN PLEASURES
CD _______________ SHWL 304CD
World Serpent / Oct '96 / World Serpent

Domingo, Enrico

STRICTLY DANCING: MAMBO (Domingo, Enrico & His Big Band)
CD _______________ 15335
Laserlight / May '94 / Target/BMG

Domingo, Placido

AT THE NEW YORK STATE THEATRE
CD _______________ MSCD 2
Magnum Music / May '94 / TKO Magnum

FROM MY LATIN SOUL
CD _______________ CDC 7548782
Premier/EMI / Jul '96 / EMI

FROM MY LATIN SOUL VOL.2
Sabra dios / Un minuto de amor / Sabor a mi / La paloma / Capullito de aleli / Cuando calienta el sol / Guantanamera / Que daria / Alma latino / Volver, volver / El rey / Perdon / Obsession / Maria Elena / Corazon, corazon / Fina / Estampa / Bahia / Copacabana / Princesita / Ay, ay, ay
CD _______________ 724355636928
EMI / May '97 / EMI

GOLDEN VOICE, THE
CD _______________ MU 5041
Musketeer / Oct '92 / Disc

PURE DOMINGO
Somewhere over the rainbow / Recondita armonia / Softly, so softly / Amor, vida de mi vida / Somewhere my love / Donna non vida mai / Girls where made to love and kiss / Love story / Vienna, city of my dreams / Be my love / Un 'aura amorosa / You are my heart's delight / Spanish eyes / Mi aidea / È lucevan le stelle / Do not ask me / Flor roja / Celeste aida
CD _______________ CDC 5556162
Premier/EMI / Jul '96 / EMI

Dominic Sonic

COLD TEARS
CD _______________ CRAMCD 065
Southern / Nov '89 / SRD

Dominion

INTERFACE
CD _______________ CDVILE 63
Peaceville / Aug '96 / Pinnacle

Dominique, Lisa

ROCK 'N' ROLL LADY
Rock 'n' roll lady / All fall down / Gamble / Somebody special / Holding on to your love

/ Time bomb / Jealous heart / Slow down / One foot back in your door / Trouble
CD _______________ WKFMXD 117
FM / May '89 / Revolver / Sony

Dominique, Natty

NATTY DOMINIQUE 1953
CD _______________ AMCD 18
American Music / Aug '94 / Jazz Music

Domino

DOMINO
Diggady Domino / Ghetto jam / AFD / Do you qualify / Jam / Money is everything / Sweet potato pie / Raincoat / Long beach thang / That's real
CD _______________ 4757592
Columbia / Feb '94 / Sony

Domino, Anna

ANNA DOMINO
CD _______________ TWICD 600
Les Disques Du Crepuscule / Oct '96 / Discovery

COLOURING THE EDGE AND OUTLINE
CD _______________ TWI 8652
Les Disques Du Crepuscule / Oct '96 / Discovery

MYSTERIES OF AMERICA
CD _______________ TWI 8882
Les Disques Du Crepuscule / Oct '96 / Discovery

THIS TIME
CD _______________ TWI 7772
Les Disques Du Crepuscule / Oct '96 / Discovery

Domino, Fats

50 GREATEST HITS
CD Set _______________ DBP 102006
Double Platinum / Feb '95 / Target/BMG

AUDIO ARCHIVE
CD _______________ CDAA 048
Tring / Jun '92 / Tring

BEST OF FATS DOMINO, THE
Blueberry Hill / Whole lotta lovin' / Fat man / Blue Monday / I'm walkin' / I'm in love again / Be my guest / When my dreamboat comes home / Let the four winds blow / I'm gonna be a wheel someday / Walking to New Orleans / Ain't that a shame / I want to walk you home / My blue Heaven / Valley of tears
CD _______________ CDMFP 6026
Music For Pleasure / Apr '88 / EMI

BEST OF FATS DOMINO, THE
Blueberry Hill / Ain't that a shame / Please don't leave me / Blue Monday / Fat man / I'm in love again / I'm walkin' / I'm ready / I'm gonna be a wheel someday / I want to walk you home / Whole lotta lovin' / Be my guest / My girl Josephine / Walking to New Orleans / Let the four winds blow / Jambalaya
CD _______________ CDP 7902942
EMI / Jul '88 / EMI

BEST OF FATS DOMINO, THE (My Blue Heaven)
My blue heaven / Fat man / Please don't leave me / Ain't that a shame / I'm in love again / When my dreamboat comes home / Blueberry Hill / Blue Monday / I'm walkin' / Valley of tears / Big beat / Yes my darling / Whole lotta lovin' / I'm ready / I'm gonna be a wheel someday / I want to walk you home / Be my guest / Walking to New Orleans / Let the four winds blow / What a party
CD _______________ CZ 368
Liberty / Nov '90 / EMI

BEST OF FATS DOMINO, THE
When the saints go marching in / Blueberry Hill / So long / Whole lotta loving / Walking to New Orleans / Heartbreak Hill / Jambalaya / Blue Monday / Ballin' the jack / Kansas City / My blue Heaven / I'm walking
CD _______________ 399232
Koch Presents / May '97 / Koch

BEST OF FATS DOMINO, THE
CD _______________ MATCD 325
Castle / Feb '95 / BMG

BEST OF FATS DOMINO, THE
CD _______________ MACCD 148
Autograph / Aug '96 / BMG

BLUEBERRY HILL
CD _______________ PWK 021
Carlton / '88 / Carlton

BLUEBERRY HILL
CD _______________ KWEST 5400
Kenwest / Oct '94 / THE

EP COLLECTION VOL.2, THE
You said you love me / Rose Mary / Baby please / Where did you stay / Love me / Don't you hear me calling you / Don't you know / I can't go on / When my dream boat comes home / What's the reason (I'm not pleasing you) / Honey chile / What will I tell my heart / My happiness / Rooster song / It's you I love / Valley of tears / Wait and see / Big beat / When I see you / I still love you / I want you to know / Country boy / Be my guest / Won't you come on back / What a party / My real name
CD _______________ SEECD 455
See For Miles/C5 / Oct '96 / Pinnacle

EP COLLECTION, THE
Ain't that a shame / All by myself / My blue heaven / Bo weevil / Coquette / Tired of crying / It must be love / Sick and tired / Telling lies / Please don't leave me / Margie / Blueberry Hill / I want to walk you home / I'm ready / I'm in the mood for love / So long / Walking to New Orleans / Don't come knocking / Let the four winds blow / I'm in love again / Poor me / Don't blame it on me / Blue Monday / Fat man
CD _______________ SEECD 416
See For Miles/C5 / Nov '94 / Pinnacle

FAT MAN SINGS, THE
Ain't that a shame / All by myself / Blueberry Hill / Margie / I hear you knocking / Don't blame it on me / You always hurt the one you love / Walking to New Orleans / Honey Chile / My happiness / Sick and tired / Country boy / Your cheatin' heart / You win again / One night / It keeps rainin' / Trouble blues / Nothing new (Same old thing) / My blue heaven / Fat man
CD _______________ CDMFP 5938
Music For Pleasure / Apr '92 / EMI

FAT MAN, THE (3CD Set)
When I'm walking (let me walk): *Humperdinck, Engelbert* / I got a right / There goes my heart again / Just a lonely man / Red sails in the sunset / Bye baby bye bye / Forever forever / I'm livin' right / Can't go on without you / Land of a 1000 dances / Song for Rosemary / Tell me the truth baby / I don't want to set the world on fire / You know I miss you / Fats on fire / Land of make believe / Old man trouble / Love me / Mary, oh Mary / Gotta get a job / Fat man / Valley of tears / Fats' shuffle / I'm a fool to care / When my dreamboat comes home / Wigs / Trouble on mind / Man that's all / Kansas city / Reelin' and rockin' / Slowboat to China / Monkey business / Heartbreak hill / (I met) the girl I'm gonna marry / Why don't you do right / Ballin' the Jack / Lazy lady / Goodnight sweetheart / Let me call you sweetheart / That certain someone / Nobody needs you like me / Who cares / Something you got baby / If you don't know what love is / Packin' up / (All of my life) for you / Sally was a good old girl / Whole lot of trouble / If I get rich / My old time used to be / Any old time / Shame on you / Sleeping on the job / Girl I love / After hours/ I almost lost my mind / Just can't get New Orleans (off my mind) / Move with the groove / Something about you baby / If I get rich / I'm walkin' / Blueberry hill, 1990
CD Set _______________ SA 872622
Disky / Sep '96 / Disky / THE

FATS DOMINO
CD _______________ LECD 047
Dynamite / May '94 / THE

FATS DOMINO IN CONCERT
CD _______________ CDSGP 0162
Prestige / Aug '95 / Else / Total/BMG

FATS DOMINO LIVE
Introduction / Blueberry Hill / Please don't leave me / Domino twist / Let the four winds blow / Whole lotta lovin' / Blue Monday / You win again / I'm walkin' / I'm gonna be a wheel someday / I'm in the mood for love / Jambalaya / O what a price / Ain't that a shame / So long / When the saints go marching in / Deep in the heart of Texas
CD _______________ 15071
Laserlight / Aug '91 / Target/BMG

GREATEST HITS
CD _______________ MU 5015
Musketeer / Oct '92 / Disc

HITS ALIVE (2CD Set)
CD Set _______________ CPCD 82912
Charly / Jul '97 / Koch

IMPERIAL SINGLES VOL.1 1950-1952, THE
Fat man / Detroit city blues / Boogie woogie baby / Little bee / Hide away blues / She's my baby / Brand new baby / Hey La Bas boogie / Every night about this time / Korea blues / Tired of crying / What's the matter baby / Don't lie to me / Sometimes I wonder / No no baby / Right from wrong / Careless love / Rockin' chair / You know I miss you / I'll be gone / Goin' home / Reelin' & rockin' / Trust in me / Poor poor me / Dreaming / How long / Cheatin' / Nobody loves me / Fat man's hop / Hey fat man
CD _______________ CDCHD 597
Ace / Jun '96 / Pinnacle

IMPERIAL SINGLES VOL.2 1953-1956, THE
Going to the river / Mardi Gras in New Orleans / Please don't leave me / Girl I love / You said you love me / Rose Mary / Don't leave me this way / Something's wrong / Little school girl / You done me wrong / Baby please / Where did you stay / You can pack your suitcase / I lived my life / Don't you hear me calling you / Love me / I know / Thinking of you / Don't you know / Helping hand / Ain't that a shame / La la / All by myself / Troubles of my own / Poor me / I can't go on (Rosalie) / Bo weevil / Don't blame it on me / Swanee river hop / If you need me
CD _______________ CDCHD 649
Ace / Apr '97 / Pinnacle

IN CONCERT
Blueberry Hill / I'm ready / Ain't that a shame / I'm walking / Domino twist / My toot toot / My girl Josephine / Jambalaya (on the bayou) / Fat man / So long/CC Rider / Walking to New Orleans / Whole lotta loving / I want to walk you home / Blue Monday / Going to the river / Let the four winds blow / I'm in love again / I'm gonna be a wheel someday
CD _______________ 100392
CMC / May '97 / BMG

JAMBALAYA
Jambalaya / Ain't that a shame (live) / Let the four winds blow / Blue Monday / I'm walkin' / When the Saints go marching in / Blueberry Hill / Walking to New Orleans / My blue heaven / I left my heart in San Francisco / You win again / I done got over it / Mardi Gras in New Orleans
CD _______________ 5501792
Spectrum / Mar '94 / PolyGram

MAGIC OF FATS DOMINO IN CONCERT
Blueberry hill / I'm ready / Ain't that a shame / My girl Josephine (hello Josephine) / Blue Monday / Jambalaya / What a price / I'm in the mood for love / Let the four winds blow / I want to walk you home / I'm gonna be a wheel someday / Whole lotta loving / Dance with Mr Domino (Domino twist) / Fat man / Please don't leave me / I'm in love again / Be my guest / Red sails in the sunset / Goin' home
CD _______________ QED 060
Tring / Nov '96 / Tring

ROLLIN'
CD _______________ 2696632
Tomato / Apr '90 / Vital

SPOTLIGHT ON FATS DOMINO
Ain't that a shame / Blueberry hill / Lawdy Miss Clawdy / Fat man / When the saints go marching in / Blue Monday / Domino twist / I'm in the mood for love / I'm in love again / Jambalaya / Lady Madonna / There goes my heart again / Honest papa's love their mama's / Oh what a price / Whole lotta lovin' / Be my guest
CD _______________ HADCD 133
Javelin / Feb '94 / Henry Hadaway / THE

THAT'S FATS
Sally was a good old girl / Reelin' and rockin' / Fat man / Blueberry Hill / If you don't know what love is / When my dreamboat comes home / Why don't you do right / On a slow boat to China / Trouble in my mind / Monkey business / Heartbreak Hill / I'm gonna be a wheel today / Be my guest / Ballin' the jack / Wigs / Man that's all
CD _______________ 12661
Laserlight / Sep '96 / Target/BMG

VERY BEST OF FATS DOMINO, THE
I'm walkin' / Blueberry Hill / I'm ready / Going to the river / My girlfriend Josephine / I want to walk you home / Let the four winds blow / Ain't that a shame / Jambalaya / I'm gonna be a wheel some day / Blue Monday / I'm in love again / Walking to New Orleans / Whole lotta loving / My toot toot / When the saints go marching in
CD _______________ PLATCD 128
Platinum / Feb '97 / Prism

WALKING TO NEW ORLEANS
Detroit City blues / Fat man / Hide away blues / She's my baby / Brand new baby / Little Bee / Boogie woogie baby / Hey la bas boogie / Korea blues / Every night about this time / Careless love / Hey fat man / Tired of crying / Tired of crying / What's the matter baby / I've got eyes for you / Stay away / Don't you lie to me / My baby's gone / Rockin' chair / Sometimes I wonder / Right from wrong / You know I'll miss you / I'll be gone / No, no baby / Reelin' and rockin' / Goin' home / Fat man's hop / How long / How long / Long lonesome journey / Long lonesome journey / Poor, poor me / Poor, poor me / Trust in me / Cheatin' / Mardi Gras in New Orleans / I guess I'll be on my way / Nobody loves me / Dreaming / Going to the river / I love her / Second line jump / Goodbye / Swanee river hop / Rosemary / Please don't leave me / Domino stomp / You said you love me / Rosemary / Fats Domino blues / Ain't it good / Girl I love / Don't leave me this way / Something's wrong / Fats' frenzy / Goin' back home / You left me / You left me / 44 / Barrell house / Little school girl / If you need me / You done me wrong / Thinking of you / Baby please / Where did you stay / You can pack your stay / I lived my life / Little Mama / I know / Love me / Don't you hear me calling you / Don't you know / Helping hand / Help me / All by myself / Ain't it a shame / Oh ba-a-aby / La la / Blue Monday / Troubles of my own / What's wrong / Poor me / I can't go on / I'm in love / Bo Weevil / Don't blame it on me / Howdy podner / So long / I can't go on this way / My blue heaven / Don't know what's wrong / Ida Jane / When my dreamboat comes home / What's the reason / Twist set me free / Blueberry Hill / Honey chile / I'm walkin' / What will I tell my heart / I'm in the mood for love / Would you / My happiness / Don't deceive me / Rooster song / Telling lies / As time goes by / Town talk / Twistin' the spots / It's you I love / Valley of tears / Valley of tears / Wait and see / True confession / Sailor boy / It must be love / Big beat / Little Mary / Stack and Billy / When I see you / Oh whee / I still love you / My love for her / I want you to know / Yes my darling / Don't you know I love you / Sick and tired / No, no / Prisoner's song / One of these days / (I'll be glad when you're dead) you rascal you / Young school girl / I'm gonna be a wheel someday / How can I be happy / Lazy woman / Isle of Capri / Coquette / Once in a while / Sheikh of Araby / Whole lotta lovin' / I miss you so / Margie / I'll always be in love with you / HAnds across the table / If you need me / So glad / At the Darktown strutter's ball / Margie / Sheikh of Araby / My heart is bleeding / I hear you knocking / Li'l Liza Jane / Every night / When the saints go marching in / Country boy / I'm ready / I'm ready / I want to walk you home / When I was young / When I was young / Easter Parade / I've been around / Be my guest / Tell me that you love me / Before I grow too old / Walking to New Orleans / Walking to New Orleans / Don't come knockin' / Don't come knockin' / La la / Put your arms around me honey / Three nights a week / Shu Rah / Rising Sun / My girl Josephine / You always hurt the one you love / Magic Isles / Natural born lover / Am I blue / It's the talk of the town / It keeps rainin' / What a price / Ain't that just like a woman / Fell in love on Monday / Fell in love on Monday / Trouble in mind / Hold hands / Bad luck and trouble / I've been calling / I just cry / Ain't gonna do it / Won't you come on back / I can't give you anything but love / I'm alone because I love you / Good hearted man / (In) a shanty in old Shanty Town / Along the Navajo trail / One night / Let the four winds blow / Trouble blues / You win again / Your cheatin' heart / Let the four winds blow / What a party / Rockin' bicycle / Did you ever see a dream walking / Birds and the bees / Wishing ring / Jambalaya / Do you know what it means to miss New Orleans / South of the border (Down Mexico way) / Teenage love / Stop the clock / Goin' home / My real name / Hum diddy doo / Those eyes / I want to go home / Dance with Mr. Domino / Nothing new (same old thing)
CD Set _______________ BCD 15541
Bear Family / Oct '93 / Direct / Rollercoaster / Swift

WHEN I'M WALKING
CD _______________ 12362
Laserlight / May '94 / Target/BMG

Dominoes

14 HITS (Dominoes & Jackie Wilson)
CD _______________ KCD 5007
King / Apr '97 / Avid/BMG

18 HITS (Dominoes & Clyde McPhatter)
CD _______________ KCD 5006
King / Apr '97 / Avid/BMG

DOMINOES MEET THE RAVENS (Dominoes & Ravens)
Take me back to heaven: *Dominoes* / Green eyes: *Ravens* / On Chapel Hill: *Ravens* / Stop you're sending me: *Dominoes* / Happy go lucky baby: *Ravens* / Bells of San Raquel: *Ravens* / We'll raise a ruckus tonight: *Ravens* / Gimme gimme gimme: *Dominoes* / Rockin' at the record hop: *Ravens* / She's fine, she's mine: *Ravens* / Take me back to heaven (Faster version): *Dominoes* / Boots and saddles: *Ravens* / Ashamed: *Ravens* / Come to me baby: *Dominoes* / Same sweet wonderful one: *Ravens* / Sweethearts on parade: *Dominoes* / I'll always be in love with you: *Ravens* / Unbeliever: *Ravens* / Take me back to heaven (Unreleased version): *Dominoes* / Bye bye baby blues: *Ravens*
CD _______________ NEMCD 716
Sequel / Mar '95 / BMG

Dominus

FIRST 9
CD _______________ POD 030
Progress / Nov '96 / Cargo / Plastic Head

VIEW TO THE DIM
CD _______________ RRS 942CD
Lost & Found / Sep '95 / Plastic Head

Domnerus, Arne

ANTIPHONE BLUES
CD _______________ PCD 7744
Proprius / Dec '95 / Jazz Music / May Audio

ARNE DOMNERUS
CD _______________ NCD 8831
Phontastic / Aug '94 / Cadillac / Jazz Music / Wellard

ARNE DOMNERUS SEXTET (Domnerus, Arne Sextet)
CD _______________ PHONTCD 9303
Phontastic / Feb '95 / Cadillac / Jazz Music / Wellard

DOMPAN AT THE SAVOY
Rombacksbotten / Morning glory / Nearness of you / Solitude / Honeysuckle rose / Take the train
CD _______________ NCD 8806

Phontastic / '93 / Cadillac / Jazz Music / Wellard

DOWNTOWN MEETING (Domnerus, Arne & Bengt Hallberg)
Gone with the wind: *Domnerus, Arne* / Embraceable you: *Domnerus, Arne* / On the sunny side of the street: *Domnerus, Arne* / I cover the waterfront: *Domnerus, Arne* / Song from Utanmyra: *Domnerus, Arne*
CD ______ **PHONT CD 7518**
Phontastic / Apr '88 / Cadillac / Jazz Music / Wellard

JAZZ AT THE PAWNSHOP
CD ______ **PCD 7778**
Proprius / Dec '95 / Jazz Music / May Audio

JAZZ AT THE PAWNSHOP VOL.2
CD ______ **PCD 9044**
Proprius / Dec '95 / Jazz Music / May Audio

JAZZ AT THE PAWNSHOP VOL.3
CD ______ **PCD 9058**
Proprius / Dec '95 / Jazz Music / May Audio

SKETCHES OF STANDARDS
CD ______ **PCD 9036**
Proprius / Dec '95 / Jazz Music / May Audio

Don & Dewey

JUNGLE HOP
Jungle hop / Little love / Hey Thelma / Baby gotta party / Miss Sue / Good morning / Leavin' it all up to you / Jelly bean / Sweet talk / Farmer John / Just a little lovin' / Letter / When the sun has begun to shine / Bim bam / Day by day / Koko Joe / Justine / Little Sally Walker / Kill me / Big boy Pete / Pink champagne / Jump awhile / Mammer-jammer / Get your hat
CD ______ **CDCHD 358**
Ace / Nov '91 / Pinnacle

Don Caballero

DON CABALLERO VOL.2
CD ______ **TG 143CD**
Touch & Go / Sep '95 / SRD

Don Carlos

DAY TO DAY LIVING
Hog and goat / I like it / Dice cups / Roots man party / Hey Mr. Babylon / Street life / English woman / I'm not crazy / At the bus stop
CD ______ **GRELCD 45**
Greensleeves / Sep '89 / Jet Star / SRD

DEEPLY CONCERNED
Deeply concerned / Cool Johnny cool / Ruff we ruff / Jah people unite / Black station white station / Satan control them / Money lover / Night rider / Crazy girl
CD ______ **RASCD 3029**
Ras / Apr '89 / Direct / Greensleeves / Jet Star / SRD

EASE UP (Don Carlos & Gold)
CD ______ **RASCD 3150**
Ras / Jun '94 / Direct / Greensleeves / Jet Star / SRD

HARVEST TIME
Fuss fuss / I Love Jah / Harvest time / In pieces / White squall / Magic man / Young girl / Music crave / Hail the roots
CD ______ **CDBM 066**
Blue Moon / Jul '93 / Cadillac / Discovery / Greensleeves / Jazz Music / Jet Star / TKO Magnum

PLANTATION
Plantation / Promise to be true / Teardrops / Declaration of rights / Ain't too proud to beg / Pretty baby / Nice time (late night blues) / get up / Unity is strength / Leggo me shirt gate man
CD ______ **TWCD 1062**
Tamoki Wambesi / Nov '95 / Greensleeves / Jet Star / Roots Collective / SRD
CD ______ **CPCD 8188**
Charly / Sep '96 / Koch

PROPHECY
Gimme gimme your love / Crucial situation / Version / Working everyday / Live in harmony / Prophecy / Jah hear my plea
CD ______ **CDBM 054**
Blue Moon / Nov '88 / Cadillac / Discovery / Greensleeves / Jazz Music / Jet Star / TKO Magnum

RAS PORTRAITS
Jah Jah hear my plea / Just a passing glance / Deeply concerned / Harvest time / Johnny big mouth / Springheel skanking / Prophecy / Cool Johnny cool / Laser beam / Ease up the pressure / Jah people unite / Christine / You are my sunshine
CD ______ **RAS 3307**
Ras / Jun '97 / Direct / Greensleeves / Jet Star / SRD

RAVING TONIGHT (Don Carlos & Gold)
CD ______ **RASCD 3005**
Ras / Nov '92 / Direct / Greensleeves / Jet Star / SRD

THEM NEVER KNOW NATTY DREAD HAVE HIM CREDENTIAL (Don Carlos & Gold)
CD ______ **78249700084**
Channel One / Jun '96 / Jet Star

TIME IS THE MASTER
CD ______ **RASCD 3217**
Ras / Nov '92 / Direct / Greensleeves / Jet Star / SRD

Don-E

UNBREAKABLE
Intro / Welcome to my world / Oh my gosh / Love makes the world go round / Unbreakable / Someday somehow / Interlude / Undercover lover / Stop what you're doing / Me oh my / Emancipate our love / Peace in the world / Never ever / So fine / U don't have 2 cry
CD ______ **BRCD 586**
4th & Broadway / Jul '92 / PolyGram

Donahue, Jerry

BRIEF ENCOUNTERS (Donahue, Jerry & Doug Morter)
CD ______ **ARIS 883510CD**
Hypertension / Sep '93 / ADA / CM / Direct / Total/BMG

NECK OF THE WOOD
CD ______ **RGFCD 011**
Road Goes On Forever / Mar '91 / Direct

TELECASTING
CD ______ **CMML 88001CD**
Music Maker / Jul '94 / ADA / Grapevine/ PolyGram

Donahue, Sam

CONVOY 1945 VOL.1
Convoy / Deep night / I've found a new baby / Moten swing / Homeward bound / Lonesome nights / Saxophone Sam / Without a song / Bugle call rag / You was right, baby / Just you, just me / Out of this world / Take me in your arms / C jam blues / Gypsy love song / On the sunny side of the street / My silent love / Please get us out
CD ______ **HEPCD 2**
Hep / Jun '94 / Cadillac / Jazz Music / New Note/Pinnacle / Wellard

LST PARTY - 1945 VOL.2
World is waiting for the sunrise / Dinah / I can't give you anything but love / Play fiddle play / Cocktails for two / Mean to me / Minor de luxe / C jam blues / C jam blues (Breakdown) / Liza / My heart stood still / LST Party / St. Louis blues / Moten swing / Convoy take / Paradise / Dear Al / My melancholy baby / Bugle call rag
CD ______ **HEPCD 5**
Hep / Oct '94 / Cadillac / Jazz Music / New Note/Pinnacle / Wellard

Donahue, Tim

VOICES IN THE WIND
CD ______ **44030**
Eclipse / Jun '97 / Greyhound

Donaldson, Eric

KEEP ON RIDING
CD ______ **3021452**
Arcade / Jun '97 / Discovery
CD ______ **RN 7017**
Rhino / May '97 / Grapevine/PolyGram / Jet Star

KENT VILLAGE PLUS
CD ______ **RNCD 2119**
Rhino / Sep '95 / Grapevine/PolyGram / Jet Star

LOVE OF COMMON PEOPLE
CD ______ **JMC 200116**
Jamaican Gold / Jun '95 / Grapevine/ PolyGram / Jet Star

VERY BEST OF ERIC DONALDSON
CD ______ **RNCD 2054**
Rhino / May '94 / Grapevine/PolyGram / Jet Star

Donaldson, John

MEETING IN BROOKLYN
CD ______ **BDV 9405**
Babel / Mar '95 / ADA / Cadillac / Diverse / Harmonia Mundi
CD ______ **378082**
Koch Jazz / May '96 / Koch

SING THE LINE (Donaldson, John & Andrew Cleyndert/Dave Mattacks)
Sing the line / Ladies in Mercedes / Wedding / Unrelated incident / Sad to say / Fruit / Chanterelle / Only child / Wild mountain thyme / Compensation
CD ______ **RD 00123**
Red Dot / Jan '97 / New Note/Pinnacle
CD ______ **378422**
Koch Jazz / Jun '97 / Koch

Donaldson, Lou

BEST OF LOU DONALDSON VOL.1, THE
CD ______ **CDARC 509**
Charly / Apr '94 / Koch

BEST OF LOU DONALDSON VOL.2, THE
Peepin' / Midnight creeper / Caravan / Summertime / Brother soul / Turtle walk / Everything I do gonh be funky / Minor bash / Pot belly
CD ______ **CDP 8377452**
Blue Note / Aug '96 / EMI

BIRDSEED
Cherry / Walkin' again / Pennies from heaven / Red top / Blue bossa / Black door blues / Dorothy / Bird seed
CD ______ **MCD 91982**
Milestone / Apr '94 / Cadillac / Complete/ Pinnacle / Jazz Music / Wellard

CARACUS
Hot dog / Just a dream / Ornithology / I don't know why (I just do) / Night train / I be blue / Caracus / Li'l darlin'
CD ______ **MCD 92172**
Milestone / Jul '94 / Cadillac / Complete/ Pinnacle / Jazz Music / Wellard

FORGOTTEN MAN (Donaldson, Lou Quartet)
CD ______ **CDSJP 153**
Timeless Jazz / Jan '88 / New Note/ Pinnacle

GOOD GRACIOUS
Bad John / Holy ghost / Cherry / Caracas / Good gracious / Don't worry 'bout me
CD ______ **CDP 8543252**
Blue Note / Feb '97 / EMI

GRAVY TRAIN
Gravy train / South of the border / Polka dots and moonbeams / Avalon / Candy / Twist time / Glory of love / Gravy train / Glory of love
CD ______ **CDP 8533572**
Blue Note / Nov '96 / EMI

MR. SHING-A-LING
Ode to Billy Joe / Humpback / Shadow of your smile / Peepin' / Kid
CD ______ **CDP 7842712**
Blue Note / Jan '97 / EMI

QUARTET, QUINTET AND SEXTET
If I love again / Down home / Best things in life are free / Lou's blues / Cheek to cheek / Sweet ice / Stroller / Roccus / Caracas / Moe's bluff / Roccus / Cheek to cheek / Lou's blues / Things we did last summer / After you've gone
CD ______ **CDP 7815372**
Blue Note / May '96 / EMI

RIGHTEOUS REED - BEST OF LOU DONALDSON
Alligator boogaloo / Reverend Moses / Peepin' / Midnight creeper / Say it loud, I'm black and I'm proud / Snake bone / Turtle walk / Everything I do gonh be funky / Hamp's hump / (Don't worry) If there's a hell below, we're all gonna go / Sassy soul strut / Gravy train / Crosstown shuffle / Who's making love / Caterpillar
CD ______ **CDP 8307212**
Blue Note / Sep '94 / EMI

SUNNY SIDE UP
Blues for JP / Man I love / Politely / It's you or no one / Truth / Goose grease / Softly as in a morning sunrise
CD ______ **CDP 8320952**
Blue Note / Aug '95 / EMI

Donaldson, Walter

YES SIR, THAT'S MY BABY (The Songs Of Walter Donaldson) (Various Artists)
How ya gonna keep 'em down on the farm: *Cantor, Eddie & Victor Young Orchestra* / My mammy: *Jolson, Al* / Carolina in the morning: *Whiteman, Paul & His Orchestra* / That certain party: *Lewis, Ted & His Band* / I wonder where my baby is tonight: *Hylton, Jack & His Orchestra* / Yes sir, that's my baby: *Cantor, Eddie* / When you're in love: *Schipa, Tito & Rosario Bourdon Orchestra* / Where'd you get those eyes: *Lewis, Ted & His Band* / My blue heaven: *Austin, Gene & Nat Shilkret Orchestra* / Sam the old accordion man: *Etting, Ruth* / At sundown: *Spanier, Muggsy Ragtime Band* / Just like a melody out of the sky: *Edwards, Cliff* / Because my baby don't mean maybe now: *Whiteman, Paul & His Orchestra* / Love me or leave me: *Etting, Ruth* / Makin' whoopee: *Cantor, Eddie & Orchestra* / Hello beautiful: *Chevalier, Mauice & Leonard Joy Orchestra* / My baby just cares for me: *Payne, Jack & His Band* / Little white lies: *Hanshaw, Annette* / You're driving me crazy: *Armstrong, Louis Orchestra* / That's what I like about you: *Teagarden, Jack & His Orchestra* / An evening in Caroline: *Boswell Sisters & Dorsey Brothers Orchestra* / Sleepy head: *Mills Brothers* / I've had my moments: *Quintet De Hot Club Du France* / It's been so long: *Fox, Roy & His Orchestra* / Did I remember: *Holiday, Billie & Her Orchestra* / Mr. Meadowlark: *Crosby, Bing & Johnny Mercer/Victor Young Orchestra*
CD ______ **CDAJA 5206**
Living Era / Nov '96 / Select

Donatto, L.C.

TEXAS ZYDECO
CD ______ **CD 52038**
Blues Encore / Oct '95 / Target/BMG

Done Lying Down

JOHN AUSTIN RUTLEDGE
CD ______ **ABT 0992**
Abstract / Oct '94 / Cargo / Pinnacle / Total/BMG

Doneda, Michel

OGOOUE OGOWAY (Live At Banlieu Blues Festival 1994)
CD ______ **TE 003**
BUDA / Jul '95 / Discovery

Donegan, Dorothy

DOROTHY DONEGAN
CD ______ **ACD 281**
Audiophile / Aug '95 / Jazz Music

EXPLOSIVE, THE
CD ______ **ACD 209**
Audiophile / May '95 / Jazz Music

LIVE AT THE 1991 FLOATING JAZZ FESTIVAL
CD ______ **CRD 318**
Chiaroscuro / Mar '96 / Jazz Music

LIVE AT THE 1992 FLOATING JAZZ FESTIVAL
CD ______ **CRD 323**
Chiaroscuro / Mar '96 / Jazz Music

LIVE AT THE WIDDER BAR
Lover / Tea for two / Autumn in New York / Makin' whoopee / Take the 'A' train / Prelude to a kiss / Like someone in love
CD ______ **CDSJP 247**
Timeless Jazz / Aug '90 / New Note/ Pinnacle

MAKIN' WHOOPEE
Here's that rainy day / Lullaby in rhythm / Am I blue / These foolish things / All of me / Makin' whoopee / I can't get started (with you) / Poor butterfly
CD ______ **BLE 591462**
Black & Blue / Dec '90 / Discovery / Koch / Wellard

Donegan, Lonnie

BEST OF LONNIE DONEGAN
CD ______ **KAZCD 21**
Kaz / Jul '92 / BMG

BEST OF LONNIE DONEGAN, THE
CD ______ **GOLD 213**
Disky / May '94 / Disky / THE

COLLECTION, THE
Rock Island line / Lost John / Nobody's child / Bring a little water Sylvie / Frankie and Johnny / Cumberland gap / Mule skinner blues / Puttin' on the style / My Dixie darling / Ham 'n' eggs / Grand coulee dam / Times are getting hard boys / Long summer day / Does your chewing gum lose its flavour on the bedpost... / Whoa Buck / Battle of New Orleans / Fancy talking tinker / Miss Otis regrets / Talking guitar blues / My old man's a dustman / Have a drink on me / Keep on the sunny side / Pick a bale of cotton / This train
CD ______ **CCSCD 223**
Castle / Feb '93 / BMG

EP COLLECTION VOL.2, THE
Midnight special / Worried man blues / Railroad Bill / Ballad of Jesse James / Mule skinner blues / On a monday / Bewildered / It is no secret / Corine Corina / Nobody understands me / No hiding place / Lorelei / Party's over / New burying ground / When the sun goes down / Stagger Lee / Ol' Riley / Old Hannah / Glory / Kevin Barry / My laggan love / Junko partner / Sorry, but I'm gonna have to pass / Pick a bale of cotton / Losing by a hair
CD ______ **SEECD 382**
See For Miles/C5 / Oct '93 / Pinnacle

EP COLLECTION, THE
Lost John / Stewball / Railroad Bill / Ballad of Jesse James / Little water, Sylvie / Dead or alive / Don't you rock me daddy-o / Cumberland Gap / Puttin' on the style / Gamblin' man / My dixie darling / Jack O'Diamonds / Grand coulee dam / Sally, don't you grieve / Betty, Betty, Betty / Tom Dooley / Does your chewing gum lose its flavour on the bedpost... / Fort Worth jail / Battle of New Orleans / Sal's got a sugar lip / My old man's a dustman / I wanna go home / Have a drink on me / Michael, row the boat ashore / Lumbered
CD ______ **SEECD 346**
See For Miles/C5 / Oct '96 / Pinnacle

FAVOURITE FLAVOURS
Cumberland gap / Battle of New Orleans / Pick a bale of cotton / Michael, row the boat ashore / Bring a little water Sylvie / Sorry, but I'm gonna have to pass / Comancheros / Frankie and Johnny / Lorelei / Nobody's child / Have a drink on me / Joshua Fit De Battle Of Jericho / Tom Dooley / Aunt Rhody (The old grey goose) / Mule skinner blues / Nobody knows the trouble I've seen / Miss Otis regrets / 500 miles away from home / Corine Corina / Does your chewing gum lose its flavour on the bedpost...
CD ______ **5507612**
Spectrum / Mar '95 / PolyGram

KING OF SKIFFLE
CD ____ MACCD 165
Autograph / Aug '96 / BMG

LONNIE DONEGAN
CD ____ CDMFP 5917
Music For Pleasure / '91 / EMI

MORE THAN 'PYE IN THE SKY
Rock Island line / John Henry / Nobody's child / Wabash cannonball / Hard time blues / You don't know my mind / Midnight special / Precious Lord lead me on / Passing stranger / On a christmas day / Take my hand, precious Lord / When the sun goes down / New burying ground / Worried man blues / Harmonica blues / Ballad of Jesse James / Ol' Riley / Railroad Bill / Lost John / Stewball / Stagger Lee / Bring a little water Sylvie / Dead or alive / Frankie and Johnny / How long blues / I'm a ramblin' man / I'm Alabamy bound / Wreck of ol' 97 / Nobody's child / I shall not be moved / Don't you rock me Daddy-o / Cumberland Gap / Love is strange / Light fingers / Gamblin' man / Puttin' on the style / My Dixie darling / I'm just a rolling stone / Jack O'Diamonds / Grand coulee dam / Hard travellin' / Ham 'n' eggs / Nobody loves like an Irishman / Sally don't you grieve / Ain't you glad you got religion / Lonesome traveller / Light from the lighthouse / I've got rocks in my bed / I've got rocks in my bed (alt.) / Long summer day / Sunshine of his love / Times are getting hard boys / Ain't no more cane on the Brazos / Lazy John / Betty, Betty, Betty / Whoa Buck / Shorty George / Baby don't you know that's love / Lonnie with Alan Freeman / Lonnie's skiffle party / Lonnie's skiffle party (part 2) / Darling Corey / Bewildered / It is no secret / My Lagan love / Rock of my soul / Aunt Rhody (the old grey goose) / Tom Dooley / Does your chewing gum lose its flavour on the bedpost... / Kevin Barry / My only son was killed in Dublin / Chesapeake Bay / Ace in the hole / Fortworth Jail / Battle of New Orleans / Sal's got a sugar lip / Just a closer walk with thee / Ice cream / Fancy talking tinker / Gloryland / Gold rush is over / House of the rising sun / Miss Otis regrets / Take this hammer / San Miguel / Jimmie Brown the newsboy / John Hardy / John Hardy (alt.) / Mr. Froggie / You pass me by / Talking guitar blues (American version) / Talking guitar blues (British version) / Golden vanity / My old man's a dustman / I wanna go home / I wanna go home (alt.) / Corine Corina / In all my wildest dreams / Beyond the sunset / Nobody understands me / Junco partner / Lorelei / Wreck of the John B / Sorry, but I'm gonna have to pass / Lively / Black cat (crossed my path today) / Banana split for my baby / Leave my woman alone / Bury me beneath the willow / When I was young / Virgin Mary / Just a wearyin' for you / Ramblin' round / Have a drink on me / Seven daffodils / Keep on the sunny side / Tiger rag / Michael, row the boat ashore / Lumbered / Michael, row the boat ashore (stereo) / Red berets / Comancheros / Party's over / Over the rainbow / I'll never fall in love again / It was a very good year / I'll never smile again / I'll never fall in love again (alt.) / His eye is on the sparrow / Nobody knows the trouble I've seen / Steal away / Good news, chariot's a-comin' / Born in Bethlehem / Joshua fit de battle of Jericho / No hiding place / Noah found grace in the eyes of the Lord / Sing hallelujah / This train / We shall walk through the valley / Pick a bale of cotton / Market song / Tit bits / Losing by a hair / Trumpet sounds / Rise up / I've got a girl so fine / It's a long road to travel / Lemon tree / 500 miles away from home / Cajun Joe (the bully of the bayou) / Fisherman's luck / Louisiana man / Interstate 40 / Bad news / There's a big wheel / Diamonds of dew / Nothing to gain / Lovey told me goodbye / Beans in my ears / Get out of my life / Blistered / Bound for Zion / Where in this world are we going / Doctor's daughter / Reverend Mr. Black / Farewell (fare thee well) / Wedding bells / Won't you tell me / My sweet Marie / After taxes / I'm gonna be a bachelor / She was a T-bone talking woman / World Cup Willie / Ding ding / Leaving blues / Auntie Maggie's remedy / Over in the new buryin' ground / Leavin' blues / Bury my body / Diggin' my potatoes / When I move to the sky / On a Monday / In the evening / Old Hannah (go down old Hannah) / Mule skinner blues / Precious memories / Brother Moses smote the water / Ella speed / Glory (false start) / Black girl / Glory
CD ____ BCD 15700
Bear Family / Oct '93 / Direct / Rollercoaster / Swift

ORIGINALS
CD ____ SEECD 331
See For Miles/C5 / Sep '91 / Pinnacle

PUTTING ON THE STYLE
CD Set ____ NXTCD 233
Sequel / Nov '92 / BMG

ROCK MY SOUL
Rock Island line / Bring a little water Sylvie / Have a drink on me / Does your chewing gum loose its flavour / My old man's a dustman / Don't you rock me daddy o / Pick a bale of cotton / Battle of New Orleans / Cumberland gap / Midnight special / Stewball / San Miguel / Wreck of the old '97 / Rock my soul / Joshua fit the battle of Jericho / Michael row the boat ashore
CD ____ 21040
Laserlight / Jul '97 / Target/BMG

Donn, Larry

THAT'S WHAT I CALL A BALL
CD ____ CLCD 4429
Collector/White Label / Aug '96 / TKO Magnum

Donna

MY HAPPINESS
CD ____ SPCD 12
Spindle / Nov '95 / Else / Jet Star

Donna Maria

REGGAE LOVE MUSIC VOL.4
CD ____ PILCD 204
Pioneer / Nov '94 / Jet Star

Donnelly, Des

REMEMBER
CD ____ DDCD 001
Des Donnelly / Dec '94 / CM

WELCOME
CD ____ MMRCD 1005
Magnetic / Mar '96 / ADA

Donnelly, Martin

STONE AND LIGHT
CD ____ RTMCD 72
Round Tower / Feb '96 / Avid/BMG

Donner, Ral

COMPLETE RAL DONNER 1959-1962, THE
CD Set ____ NEDCD 190
Sequel / Feb '92 / BMG

Donohoe, Martin

FREE SPIRIT (Donohoe, Martin & Phil Cunningham)
CD ____ CICD 089
Clo Iar-Chonnachta / Mar '96 / CM

Donovan

CATCH THE WIND
CD ____ PLSCD 130
Pulse / Jul '96 / BMG

COLOURS - LIVE
Jennifer juniper / Catch the wind / Hurdy gurdy / Sunshine superman / Sadness / Universal soldier / Cosmic wheels / Atlantis / Wear our love like heaven / To Susan on the west coast waiting / Colours / Young girls blues / Young but growing / Stealing / Sailing homeward / Love will find a way / Lalena / Make up your mind to be happy
CD ____ MDCD 6
Magnum Music / May '94 / TKO Magnum

COSMIC WHEELS
Cosmic wheels / Earth sign man / Sleep / Maria Magenta / Wild witch lady / Music makers / Intergalactic laxative / I like you / Only the blues / Appearance
CD ____ 4773782
Epic / Aug '94 / Sony

DONOVAN
Atlantis / Sunshine Superman / Jennifer Juniper / Hurdy gurdy man / Universal soldier / Catch the wind / To Susan on the west coast / Lalena / Sailing homeward / Love will find a way / Make up your mind be happy / Wear your love like heaven / Young but growing / Cosmic wheels / Sadness / Stealing / Young girl blues
CD ____ EXP 013
Experience / May '97 / TKO Magnum

DONOVAN IN CONCERT
Isle of Islay / Young girl blues / There is a mountain / Poor cow / Celeste / Fat angel / Guinevere / Widow with a shawl / Preachin' love / Lullaby of Spring / Writer in the sun / Pebble and the man / Rules and regulations / Mellow yellow
CD ____ BGOCD 90
Beat Goes On / Dec '90 / Pinnacle

DONOVAN LIVE IN CONCERT
Jennifer Juniper / Catch the wind / Hurdy gurdy man / Sunshine superman / Sadness / Universal soldier / Cosmic wheels / Atlantis / Wear your love like heaven / To Susan on the west coast waiting / Colours / Young girl blues / Young but growing / Stealing / Sailing homeward / Love will find a way / Lalena
CD ____ QED 063
Tring / Nov '96 / Tring

EP COLLECTION, THE
CD ____ SEECD 300
See For Miles/C5 / '90 / Pinnacle

FAIRYTALE
Colours / I'll try for the sun / Sunny Goodge Street / Oh deed I do / Circus of sour / Summer day reflection song / Candy man / Jersey Thursday / Belated of a crystal man / Little tin soldier / Ballad of Geraldine
CD ____ CLACD 226
Castle / Feb '91 / BMG

GIFT FROM A FLOWER TO A GARDEN, A
Song of the naturalist's wife / Enchanted gypsy / Isle of Islay / Mandolin man and his secret / Lay of the last tinker / Tinker and the crab / Widow with shawl portrait / Lullaby of spring / Magpie / Starfish on the toast / Epistle to Derroll / Voyage into the golden screen / Wear your love like heaven / Mad John's escape / Skip-a-long Sam / Sun / There was a time / Oh gosh / Little boy in corduroy / Under the greenwood tree / Land of doesn't have to be / Someone's singing
CD ____ BGOCD 194
Beat Goes On / Apr '97 / Pinnacle

GREATEST HITS AND MORE
Sunshine superman / Wear your love like heaven / Jennifer Juniper / Barabajagal / Hurdy gurdy man / Epistle to dippy / To Susan on the west coast waiting / Catch the wind / Mellow yellow / There is a mountain / Happiness runs / Season of the witch / Colours / Superlungs My supergirl / Lalena / Atlantis / Preachin' love / Poor cow / Teen angel / Aye my love
CD ____ CZ 193
EMI / Oct '89 / EMI

INTROSPECTIVE: DONOVAN
CD ____ CINT 5007
Baktabak / Feb '92 / Arabesque

MELLOW (2CD Set)
CD Set ____ SMDCD 158
Snapper / Jul '97 / Pinnacle

ORIGINALS
Sunshine superman / Legend of a girl child Linda / Three King Fishers / Ferris wheel / Bert's blues / Season of the witch / Trip / Guinevere / Fat angel / Celeste / Mellow yellow / Writer in the sun / Sand and foam / Observation / Bleak City woman / House of Jansch / Young girl blues / Museum / Hampstead incident / Sunny South Kensington / Hurdy gurdy man / Peregrine / Entertaining of a shy girl / As I recall it / Get thy bearings / Hi it's been a long time / West Indian lady / Jennifer Juniper / River song / Tangier / Sunny day / Sun is a very magic fellow / Teas / Barabajagal / Superlungs my supergirl / Where is she / Happiness runs / I love my shirt / Love song / To Susan on the West Coast waiting / Atlantis / Trudi / Pamela Jo
CD Set ____ DONOVAN 1
EMI / Oct '94 / EMI

SUNSHINE SUPERMAN
CD ____ BGOCD 68
Beat Goes On / Feb '91 / Pinnacle
CD ____ HADCD 197
Javelin / Nov '95 / Henry Hadaway / THE

SUNSHINE SUPERMAN
CD ____ RMB 75059
Remember / Sep '93 / Total/BMG

SUNSHINE SUPERMAN
Sunshine superman / Legend of a girl child Linda / Three king fishers / Ferris wheel / Bert's blues / Season of the witch / Trip / Guiney ere / Fat angel / Celeste
CD ____ CDGOLD 1066
EMI Gold / Oct '96 / EMI

SUNSHINE SUPERMAN
Lady of stars / I love you baby / Bye bye girl / Every reason / Season of the witch / For every boy there is a girl / Local boy chops wood / Sunshine superman / Living for the lovelight in your eyes / Till I see you again
CD ____ 100082
CMC / May '97 / BMG

SUNSHINE TROUBADOR
Season of the witch / For every boy there is a girl / Every reason / Till I see you again / Bye bye girl / Lady of the stars / Living for the love light in your eyes / I love you baby / Local boy chops wood / Sunshine superman
CD ____ 305012
Hallmark / Jul '97 / Carlton

SUTRAS
Please don't bend / Give it all up / Sleep / Everlasting sea / High your love / Clear-browed one / Way / Deep peace / Nirvana / Eldorado / Be mine / Lady of the lamp / Evernow / Universe am I
CD ____ 74321397432
RCA / Oct '96 / BMG

UNIVERSAL SOLDIER
Colours / Catch the wind / Ballad of a crystal man / Josie / Do you hear me now / Candy man / Belated forgiveness plea / Tangerine puppet / Ballad of Geraldine / Universal soldier / Turquoise / I'll try for the sun / Summer day reflection song / Why do you treat me like you do / Hey gyp (Dig the slowness) / To sing for you / You're gonna need somebody on your bond / Little tin soldier
CD ____ 5507212
Spectrum / Jan '95 / PolyGram

VERY BEST OF DONOVAN, THE
CD ____ ARTFULCD 5
Artful / Mar '97 / Pinnacle / Total/BMG

Donovan, Jason

BETWEEN THE LINES
CD ____ HFCD 14
PWL / May '90 / Warner Music

GREATEST HITS
CD ____ HFCD 20
PWL / Sep '91 / Warner Music

TEN GOOD REASONS
Too many broken hearts / Nothing can divide us / Every day (I love you more) / You can depend on me / Time heals / Sealed with a kiss / Question of pride / If I don't have you / Change your mind / Too late to say goodbye / Especially for you: *Donovan, Jason & Kylie Minogue*
CD ____ HFCD 7
PWL / May '89 / Warner Music

Donuts

SLAM DUNKIN' GOOD TUNES
CD ____ BLSCD 1
Ruf / Feb '97 / Pinnacle

Doo Rag

CHUNCKED AND MUDDLED
CD ____ BLT 10048
Bloat / Dec '96 / Cargo

Doobie Brothers

BROTHERHOOD
Something you said / Is love enough / Dangerous / Our love / Divided highway / Under the spell / Excited / This train I'm on / Showdown / Rollin' on
CD ____ CDEST 2141
Capitol / Apr '91 / EMI

CAPTAIN AND ME, THE
Natural thing / Long train runnin' / China grove / Dark eyed Cajun woman / Clear as the driven snow / Without you / South City midnight lady / Evil woman / Busted down around O'Connelly Corners / Ukiah / Captain and me
CD ____ K 246217
Warner Bros. / Feb '95 / Warner Music

DOOBIE BROTHERS
Nobody / Slippery St. Paul / Greenwood Creek / It won't be right / Travellin' man / Feeling down farther / Master / Growin' a little each day / Beehive state / Closer every day / Chicago
CD ____ 7599262152
Warner Bros. / May '95 / Warner Music

DOOBIE BROTHERS, THE
Quicksilver princess / I'll keep on givin' / Runaround ways / Make it easy / Coke can changes / Excitement / On our way up / Song to JC / Another way / Paupers diary / Blue Jay / By yourself / Tilted park crud munchery
CD ____ EXP 014
Experience / May '97 / TKO Magnum

EARLY YEARS, THE
CD ____ KLMCD 055
BAM / Sep '96 / Koch / Scratch/BMG

LISTEN TO THE MUSIC (The Very Best Of The Doobie Brothers)
Long train runnin' / China grove / Listen to the music / Takin' it to the streets / Black water / Jesus is just alright / Rockin' down the highway / Take me in your arms / Without you / South city midnight lady / It keeps you runnin' / Little darlin' / You belong to me / Minute by minute / Here to love you / Real love / What a fool believes / Long train runnin' (mix)
CD ____ 9548328032
Warner Bros. / May '94 / Warner Music

LIVIN' ON THE FAULT LINE
Nothin' but a heartache / Little darlin' / Livin' on the fault line / Larry the logger two-step / Need a lady / You're made that way / Chinatown / There's a light / You belong to me / Echoes of love
CD ____ K 9273152
Warner Bros. / Jun '89 / Warner Music

MINUTE BY MINUTE
Here to love you / What a fool believes / Minute by minute / Dependin' on you / Don't stop to watch the wheels / Open your eyes / Sweet feelin' / Streamer lane breakdown / You never change / How do fools survive
CD ____ 256486
Warner Bros. / '88 / Warner Music

ROCKIN' DOWN THE HIGHWAY - THE WILDLIFE CONCERT
China grove / What a fool believes / Dangerous / Jesus is just alright / Rockin' down the highway / Dependin' on you / Eyes of silver / Another park another Sunday / Slack key sequel rag (instrumental) / South city midnight lady / Clear as the driven snow / Black water / Wild ride / Slow burn / Doctor / Take me in your arms (rock me) / Long train runnin' / Without you / Excited / Dark eyed Cajun woman / Neal's fandango / Listen to the music / Minute by minute / Takin' it to the streets
CD ____ 4844522
Columbia / Aug '96 / Sony

TOULOUSE STREET
Listen to the music / Rockin' down the highway / Mamaloi / Toulouse Street / Cotton mouth / Don't start me talkin' / Jesus is just alright / White sun / Disciple / Snakeman
CD 7599272632
Warner Bros. / May '93 / Warner Music

WHAT WERE ONCE VICES ARE NOW HABITS
Another park another Sunday / Black water / Daughters of the sea / Down in the track / Eyes of silver / Flying cloud / Pursuit on 53rd street / Road angel / Song to see you through / Spirit / Tell me what you want (and I'll give you what you need) / You just can't stop it
CD 759927802
Warner Bros. / Jul '93 / Warner Music

Doof

LET'S TURN ON
CD TIPCD 10
Tip / Nov '96 / Arabesque / Mo's Music Machine / Pinnacle / Prime

Doom

DOOMED FROM THE START
CD DISCCD 5
Discipline / Sep '96 / Plastic Head

FUCK PEACEVILLE
CD EXIST 024CD
Profane Existence / Apr '97 / Cargo

GREATEST INVENTION, THE
CD DISCCD 10
Discipline / Aug '93 / Pinnacle

PEEL SESSIONS, THE (29.5.79)
Symptom of the universe / Multinationals / Expoitation / Circles / No religion / Relief / Sold out / War crimes / Means to an end / Dream to come true / Natural abuse / Days go by / Life lock / Bury the debt / Life in freedom / Money drug / Fear of the future
CD SFPMCD 203
Strange Fruit / '89 / Pinnacle

RUSH HOUR OF THE GODS
CD FE 021CD
Flat Earth / Mar '97 / Cargo

Doomstone

THOSE WHO SATAN HATH JOINED
CD NOSF 002CD
Nosferatu / Jan '95 / Plastic Head

Doonan Family

FENWICK'S WINDOW
CD FSCD 12
Folksound / Jan '91 / CM / Roots

Doonican, Val

50 YEARS OF LOVE SONGS
Way we were / Where is love / Secret love / Groovy kind of love / On the wings of love / Somewhere / Unforgettable / You needed me / Can't help falling in love / All my loving / Unchained melody / We've only just begun / Sometimes when we touch / Hello young lovers / Our love is here to stay / Alomost like being in love / Mind if I make love to you / April love / When I fall in love / Save the best for last
CD 3036000152
Carlton / May '96 / Carlton

CHRISTMAS ALBUM
CD PWKS 4218
Carlton / Oct '95 / Carlton

VERY BEST OF VAL DOONICAN, THE
Special years / Elusive butterfly / If the whole world stopped loving / Morning / For the good times / First time ever I saw your face / Heaven is my woman's love / Now / Paddy McGinty's goat / Walk tall / If I knew then what I know now / What would I be / O'Rafferty's motor car / Marvellous toy / Song sung blue / King of the road / Two streets / I'm just a country boy / Delaney's donkey
CD MCCD 008
Music Club / Feb '91 / Disc / THE

Doors

AMERICAN PRAYER, AN (Music By The Doors) (Morrison, Jim/Doors)
Awake / To come of age / Poet's dreams / World on fire / American prayer
CD 7559618122
Elektra / May '95 / Warner Music

BEST OF THE DOORS, THE
Break on through / Light my fire / Crystal ship / People are strange / Strange days / Love me two times / Five to one / Waiting for the sun / Spanish caravan / When the music's over / Hello I love you / Roadhouse blues / LA Woman / Riders on the storm / Touch me / Love her madly / Unknown soldier / End
CD 9603452
Elektra / Nov '85 / Warner Music

CEREMONY CONTINUES, THE
CD CBAK 4052
Baktabak / Mar '92 / Arabesque

DOORS
Break on through / Soul kitchen / Crystal ship / Twentieth Century Fox / Alabama song / Light my fire / Back door man / I looked at you / End of the night / Take it as it comes / End
CD 9740072
Elektra / Feb '89 / Warner Music

DOORS IN CONCERT, THE
House announcer / Who do you love / Medley / Alabama song / Backdoor man / Love hides / Five to one / Build me a woman / When the music's over / Universal mind / Petition the Lord with prayers / Dead cats / Dead rats / Break on through / Celebration of the lizard / Soul kitchen / Roadhouse blues / Gloria / Light my fire / You make me real / Texas radio and the big beat / End / Unkown soldier / Close to you / Moonlight drive / Little red rooster / Love me two times
CD 7559610822
Elektra / May '91 / Warner Music

DOORS LIVE, THE
Soul kitchen / Alabama song / Five to one / Love hides / Build me a woman / Who do you love / Break on through no.2 / Dead cats dead rats / Petition the lord with prayers / House announcer / Hill dwellers / Wake up / Universal mind / Close to you / Palace of exile / Names of the kingdom / Little game / Lions in the street / Not to touch the earth / When the music's over / Backdoor man
CD 7559619722
Elektra / Nov '96 / Warner Music

GREATEST HITS
Light my fire / Break on through / Roadhouse blues / People are strange / End / Touch me / Hello I love you / LA woman / Love her madly / Ghost song / Riders on the storm / Love me two times
CD 7559618602
Elektra / Nov '95 / Warner Music

INTERVIEW DISC
CD DISSCD 2
Wax / Apr '96 / RTM/Disc / Total/BMG

LA WOMAN
Changeling / Love her madly / Cars hiss by my window / LA woman / L'America / Hyacinth house / Crawlin' kingsnake / Wasp / Riders on the storm
CD 9750112
Elektra / Feb '89 / Warner Music

MORRISON HOTEL
Roadhouse blues / Waiting for the sun / You make me real / Peace frog / Blue Sunday / Ship of fools / Land ho / Spy / Queen of the highway / Indian summer / Maggie McGill
CD 9750072
Elektra / Feb '89 / Warner Music

OPENING THE DOORS OF PERCEPTION - INTERVIEWS
CD RVCD 33
Raven / May '94 / ADA / Direct

SOFT PARADE
Tell all the people / Touch me / Shaman's blues / Do it / Easy rider / Wild child / Running blue / Wishful sin / Soft parade
CD 9750052
Elektra / Feb '89 / Warner Music

STONED BUT ARTICULATE (Pronouncements Of Jim Morrison 1968) (Morrison, Jim)
CD OZITCD 0020
Ozit / Mar '97 / Cargo / Direct

STRANGE DAYS
Strange days / You're lost / Little girl / Love me two times / Unhappy girl / Horse latitudes / Moonlight drive / People are strange / My eyes have seen you / I can't see your face in my mind / When the music's over
CD 9740142
Elektra / '89 / Warner Music

ULTIMATE COLLECTED SPOKEN WORDS 1967-1970 (Interview Disc/2CD Set) (Morrison, Jim)
CD Set OZITCD 0025
Ozit / May '97 / Cargo / Direct

WAITING FOR THE SUN
Hello I love you / Love street / Not to touch / Earth / Summer's almost gone / Winter time love / Unknown soldier / Spanish caravan / My wild love / We could be so good together / Yes the river knows / Five to one
CD 9740242
Elektra / '89 / Warner Music

DOP

MUSICIANS OF THE MIND
DOP Chant / Oh yeah / Take me / Groovy beat (part 1) / Dance spirit / Future le funk / Let's party / Get out on this dancefloor / Dancefloor / Oh no / Don't stop the music / Ric / Groovy beat
CD GRCD 003
Guerilla / Jul '94 / Pinnacle

MUSICIANS OF THE MIND VOL.2
Come to me / Together / String vest / Lion / Party rockin' / Satisfy / Here I go / Ooh la la / Electronic funk / Lust / Catwalk
CD GRCD 010
Guerilla / Jul '94 / Pinnacle

Dope Fiends

HELTER SKELTER
CD SEVE 007CD
7 / Jun '96 / Pinnacle / Warner Music

Doran, Christy

WHAT A BAND
CD ARTCD 6105
Hat Art / May '92 / Cadillac / Harmonia Mundi

Dorau, Andreas

ARGER MIT DER UNSTERBLICHKEIT
CD EFA 037532
Atatak / Apr '95 / SRD

ERNTE
CD EFA 037642
Atatak / Apr '95 / SRD

Dordan

IRISH TRADITIONAL & BAROQUE
CD CEFCD 150
Gael Linn / Jan '94 / ADA / CM / Direct / Grapevine/PolyGram / Roots

JIGS TO THE MOON
CD CEFCD 168
Gael Linn / Oct '94 / ADA / CM / Direct / Grapevine/PolyGram / Roots

Dore, Charlie

THINGS CHANGE
CD BICD 1
Black Ink / Aug '95 / Grapevine/PolyGram

Dorge, Christian

LYCIA
CD DW 100
Isol / Feb '95 / Plastic Head

Dorge, Pierre

BALLAD ROUND THE LEFT CORNER
CD SCCD 31132
Steeplechase / Jul '88 / Discovery / Impetus

Dorham, Kenny

ARRIVAL OF KENNY DORHAM, THE
CD FSRCD 200
Fresh Sound / Dec '92 / Discovery / Jazz Music

BEST OF KENNY DORHAM, THE
Minor's holiday / Lotus flower / Mexico city / Philly twist / Blue bossa / Short story / Una mas / Fox
CD CDP 8536482
Blue Note / Jan '97 / EMI

JAZZ CONTRASTS
CD OJCCD 28
Original Jazz Classics / Oct '92 / Complete/Pinnacle / Jazz Music / Wellard

NEW YORK 1953-1956
CD LS 2918
Landscape / Feb '93 / THE

OSMOSIS
CD BLCD 760146
Black Lion / May '91 / Cadillac / Jazz Music / Koch / Wellard

QUIET KENNY
CD OJCCD 250
Original Jazz Classics / Sep '93 / Complete/Pinnacle / Jazz Music / Wellard

ROUND ABOUT MIDNIGHT AT THE CAFE BOHEMIA VOL.2
Royal roost / My heart stood still / Prophet / KD's Blues / Riffin' / Who cares / Monaco / NY (theme)
CD BNZ 26
Blue Note / May '87 / EMI

UNA MAS
Una mas / Straight ahead / Sao Paulo / If ever I would leave you
CD BNZ 27
Blue Note / May '87 / EMI

WEST 42ND STREET
CD BLCD 760119
Black Lion / Oct '92 / Cadillac / Jazz Music / Koch / Wellard

Doriz, Dany

THIS ONE'S FOR BASIE
CD BB 8602
Black & Blue / Apr '96 / Discovery / Koch / Wellard

Doro

ANGELS NEVER DIE
CD 5143092
Vertigo / Mar '93 / PolyGram

Dorough, Bob

CLANKIN ON TIN PAN ALLEY
CD BL 005
Bloomdido / Oct '93 / Cadillac

DEVIL MAY CARE (Bethlehem Jazz Classics)
Old devil moon / It could happen to you / I had the craziest dream / You're the dangerous type / Ow / Polka dots and moonbeams / Yardbird suite / Baltimore Oriole / Midnight sun / Johnny one note / I don't mind / Devil may care / Yardbird suite
CD CDGR 138
Charly / Apr '97 / Koch

JUST ABOUT EVERYTHING
Don't think twice, it's alright / Baltimore Oriole / I've got just about everything / Message / Crawdad song / Better than anything / But for now / 'Tis autumn / Baby, you should know it / Lazy afternoon
CD ECD 220942
Evidence / Jul '94 / ADA / Cadillac / Harmonia Mundi

MEMORIAL CHARLIE PARKER (Dorough, Bob & Bill Takas)
CD 214 W242
Philology / Aug '91 / Cadillac / Harmonia Mundi

Dorset, Ray

COLD BLUE EXCURSION
Got to be free / Cold blue excursion / With me / Have pity on me / Time is now / Livin' ain't easy / Help your friends / I need it / Because I want you / Nightime / Maybe that's the way / Always on my mind
CD BGOCD 282
Beat Goes On / Oct '96 / Pinnacle

Dorsey Brothers

BEST OF THE BIG BANDS, THE
Somebody stole Gabriel's horn / Mood Hollywood / Sing (it's good for ya) / By heck / My dog loves your dog / Old man Harlem / She reminds me of you / Shim sham shimmy / She's funny that way / Blue room / But I can't make a man / Judy / Nasty man / Annie's cousin Fanny / I'm getting sentimental over you
CD 4716492
Columbia / Jun '92 / Sony

DORSEY BROTHERS 1955
CD JUCD 2026
Jazz Unlimited / Jul '96 / Cadillac / Jazz Music / Wellard

DORSEY BROTHERS VOL.1 NEW YORK 1928
CD BDW 8004
Jazz Oracle / May '97 / Jazz Music

DORSEY BROTHERS VOL.2 NEW YORK 1929-1930
CD BDW 8005
Jazz Oracle / May '97 / Jazz Music

HARLEM LULLABY
Somebody stole Gabriel's horn / Stay on the right side of the road / Here is my heart / Stormy weather / Love is the thing / Don't blame me / Shadows on the Swanee / I like a guy what takes his time / Easy rider / You've got me crying again / I gotta right to sing the blues / Is that religion / Harlem lullaby / There's a cabin in the Pines / Lazybones / Shoutin' in the Amen Corner / Snowball / Give me Liberty or give me love / Doin' the uptown lowdown
CD HEPCD 1006
Hep / Dec '91 / Cadillac / Jazz Music / New Note/Pinnacle / Wellard

LIVE IN THE MEADOWBROOK, 28 OCTOBER 1955 (Dorsey Brothers Orchestra)
CD JH 1003
Jazz Hour / Feb '91 / Cadillac / Jazz Music / Target/BMG

MOOD HOLLYWOOD
I'm getting sentimental over you / It don't mean a thing / Shim sham shimmy / Blue room / It's the talk of the town / Dinah / Mood Hollywood / By heck / Dr. Heck / Dr. Heckle and Mr. Jibe / Mean to me
CD HEPCD 1005
Hep / Apr '96 / Cadillac / Jazz Music / New Note/Pinnacle / Wellard

Dorsey, Don

BACH BUSTERS
CD CD 80123
Telarc / '87 / Conifer/BMG

Dorsey, Jimmy

1939-40 (Dorsey, Jimmy Orchestra)
CD CCD 30
Circle / May '93 / Jazz Music / Swift / Wellard

1940 (Dorsey, Jimmy Orchestra)
CD CCD 46
Circle / May '93 / Jazz Music / Swift / Wellard

22 ORIGINAL BIG BAND RECORDINGS
CD HCD 415
Hindsight / Sep '92 / Jazz Music / Target/BMG

DON'T BE THAT WAY 1935-1940 (Dorsey, Jimmy Orchestra)
CD _____ RACD 7120
Aerospace / May '96 / Jazz Music / Montpellier

GREAT JIMMY DORSEY, THE
Contrasts / Imagination / Just for a thrill / Perfidia / Fools rush in / I'm steppin' out with a memory tonight / Blueberry hill / You, you darling / Green eyes / In a little Spanish town / Tangerine / Nearness of you
CD _____ HCD 333
Hindsight / Apr '96 / Jazz Music / Target/BMG

I REMEMBER YOU
Tangerine / Keep a knockin' / Dixieland dectour / Begone / Cherokee / I remember you / Green eyes / Always in my heart / Tropical magic / Time was / You make me love you / Holiday for strings / My ideal / They're either too young or too old / Besame mucho / Amapola / Maria elena / Yours / Brazil / At the crossroads
CD _____ RAJCD 852
Empress / May '95 / Koch

JIMMY DORSEY
CD _____ 15759
Laserlight / Aug '92 / Target/BMG

JIMMY DORSEY 1939-1940
Contrasts / Shine on harvest moon / Imagination / Blue Lou / Just for a thrill / Fools rush in / Carolina in the morning / At least you could say hello / Moonlight on the river / I'm stepping out with a memory tonight / Julia / Nearness of you / Shoot the meatballs to me Dominick boy / You, you darlin' / Blueberry hill / Flight of the jitterbug
CD _____ HCD 101
Hindsight / Jul '96 / Jazz Music / Target/BMG

JIMMY DORSEY AT THE 400 RESTAURANT 1946 (Dorsey, Jimmy Orchestra)
All the things you ain't / Grand Central getaway / Sunset Strip / Together / Opus no.1 / I've got a crush on you / Outer drive / Come to baby do / Town hall tonight / Lover / It's the talk of the town / Super chief / Lover man / King Porter stomp / Here I go again / I can't believe that you're in love with me / Man with the horn / This can't be love / Contrasts
CD _____ HEPCD 41
Hep / Dec '91 / Cadillac / Jazz Music / New Note/Pinnacle / Wellard

PENNIES FROM HEAVEN
It's the natural thing to do / Slap that bass / Love bug will bite you / Dorsey Dervish / Pick yourself up / Moon got in my eyes / In a sentimental mood / Rap tap on wood / I love to sing / All you want to do is dance / They can't take that away from me / Serenade to nobody in particular / Let's call a heart a heart / Swingin' the jinx away / Stompin' at the Savoy / After you / Listen to the mockingbird / Pennies from Heaven
CD _____ CDAJA 5052
Living Era / May '88 / Select

PERFIDIA (Dorsey, Jimmy Orchestra)
CD _____ 15768
Laserlight / Jul '92 / Target/BMG

SHINE ON HARVEST MOON
I've got rhythm / Grand Central getaway / Sowing wild oats / Just you, just me / Sophisticated swing / Together hit the note / (I would do) anything for you / Three little words / Shine on harvest moon / Imagination / I'm stepping out with a memory tonight / Carolina in the morning / Nearness of you / Moonlight on the river / Someday sweetheart / Fools rush in / Begin the beguine / Sunset strip
CD _____ GRF 067
Tring / '93 / Tring

THEN AND NOW (Dorsey, Jimmy Orchestra)
CD _____ 7567818012
Atlantic / Jul '93 / Warner Music

Dorsey, Lee

FREEDOM FOR THE FUNK
CD _____ CPCD 8068
Charly / Nov '94 / Koch

GREAT GOOGA MOOGA
Lottie mo / Ya ya / Do re mi / Hoodlum Joe / You're breaking me up / Messed around (and fell in love) / Ay aa ay / Great googa mooga / People sure act funny / Ride your pony / Can you hear me / Get out of my life woman / Confusion / Working in a coalmine / Holy cow / My old car / Go go girl / Love lots of lovin' / Four corners (part 1) / Lover was born
CD _____ CDNEV 3
Charly / Sep '91 / Koch

WORKING IN A COALMINE
CD _____ RMB 75055
Remember / Nov '93 / Total/BMG

WORKING IN A COALMINE
CD _____ QSCD 6007
Charly / Jan '95 / Koch

Dorsey, Tommy

1944- ALL TIME HIT PARADE
On the sunny side of the Street / April in Paris / What is this thing called love / I may be wrong, but I think you're wonderful / East of the sun and west of the moon / Embraceable you / Cheek to cheek / I'll be seeing you / Dancing in the dark / I can't give you anything but love / I'll walk alone / South of the border (Down Mexico way) / Summertime / If you are but a dream / Amor / Lover come back to me / Top hat, white tie and tails / Lamp is low / Boogie woogie / I'll never smile again / Song of India / As time goes by / Hawaiian war chant
CD _____ HEPCD 39
Hep / Apr '90 / Cadillac / Jazz Music / New Note/Pinnacle / Wellard

AT THE FAT MAN'S
Blue skies / Dawn on the desert / At the Fat Man's / Bingo, bango, boffo / Marie / Chloe / Well git it / At sundown / Opus one / Candy / Continental / Call you sweetheart / Feels so good / Pussy Willow / Broadcasts from 1945-1948
CD _____ HEPCD 43
Hep / Jun '93 / Cadillac / Jazz Music / New Note/Pinnacle / Wellard

BEST OF TOMMY DORSEY
Maria / Stardust / Little white lies / I'll never smile again / Yes indeed / Boogie woogie / Opus one / Song of India / Who / Royal Garden blues / Once in a while / I'm getting sentimental over you
CD _____ ND 90587
Bluebird / Aug '92 / BMG
CD _____ DCD 5330
Disky / Dec '93 / Disky / THE

BEST OF TOMMY DORSEY
CD _____ DLCD 4010
Dixie Live / Mar '95 / TKO Magnum

BIG BAND BASH (Dorsey, Tommy Orchestra)
Opus one / On the sunny side of the street / I'm getting sentimental over you / Boogie woogie / Blue skies / Royal garden blues / Chicago / Stardust / Sheel of Araby / Song of India / Swing low, sweet chariot / There are such things / Well git it / Marie / What is this thing called love / Imagination / Weary blues / Yes indeed / Liebestraum / East of the sun and west of the moon / Hawaiian war chant / Whispering / Mendelssohn's spring song
CD _____ CD 53082
Giants Of Jazz / Mar '90 / Cadillac / Jazz Music / Target/BMG

CARNEGIE HALL V-DISC SESSION APRIL 1944, THE (Dorsey, Tommy Orchestra)
Minor goes muggin' / I dream of you / Milkman keep those bottles quiet / I never knew / Song of India / Tess's torch song / Irresistible you / Losers weepers / Wagon wheels / Paramount on parade / TD chant / Then I'll be happy / Small fry / Pennies from heaven / Somebody loves me / Indian summer / I'm in the mood to be loved / Sweet and lovely / Chicago / Lady in red / For all we know / I'm nobody's baby / Three little words
CD _____ HEPCD 40
Hep / Dec '90 / Cadillac / Jazz Music / New Note/Pinnacle / Wellard

CLASSICS 1928-1935
CD _____ CLASSICS 833
Classics / Sep '95 / Discovery / Jazz Music

CLASSICS 1935-1936
CD _____ CLASSICS 854
Classics / Feb '96 / Discovery / Jazz Music

CLASSICS 1936
CD _____ CLASSICS 878
Classics / Apr '96 / Discovery / Jazz Music

CLASSICS 1936-1937
CD _____ CLASSICS 916
Classics / Jan '97 / Discovery / Jazz Music

COMPLETE RECORDINGS 1940-1942, THE (4CD Set) (Dorsey, Tommy & Frank Sinatra)
CD Set _____ 852137
New Rose / May '94 / ADA / Direct / Discovery

DANCE WITH DORSEY
Opus One / Lamp Is Low / You grow sweeter as the years go by / How Am I To Know / All I remember is you / Well alright / Big Dipper / Tin Roof Blues / Sweet Sue, Just You / Copenhagen / Panama / Chinatown, my Chinatown / When the midnight choo choo leaves for Alabam' / Big Apple / Hawaiian War Chant / Song Of India / Chicago / Marie
CD _____ PAR 2068
Parade / Jul '94 / Disc

ESSENTIAL V-DISCS, THE
CD _____ JZCD 334
Suisa / Jan '93 / Jazz Music / THE

GO THEIR SEPARATE WAYS (Dorsey, Tommy & Jimmy)
Sinner kissed an angel / Blue skies / What'cha know Joe / East of the sun and west of the moon / Too romantic / How about you / Lady is a tramp / Fools rush in / Hawaiian war chant / Be careful it's my heart / Night in Sudan / Six lessons from Madame La Zonga / Bogg it / Arthur Murray taught me dancing in a hurry / Not mine / If you build a better mousetrap / Whispering grass / Dolimite / Aurora / I can't resist you / So do I / Contrasts
CD _____ RAJCD 817
Empress / Mar '97 / Koch

GREAT TOMMY DORSEY, THE
Music maestro please / Stardust / Who / Marie / Song of India / Hawaiian war chant / East of the sun and west of the moon / Night in Sudan / That's a plenty / Night and day / Smoke gets in your eyes / Tea for two / Beale Street blues / Lonesome road / Turn off the moon / After you've gone / Lady is a tramp / Call of the canyon / After I say I'm sorry / Polka dots and moonbeams / Too romantic
CD _____ PASTCD 9740
Flapper / Mar '91 / Pinnacle

INTRODUCTION TO TOMMY DORSEY 1928-1942, AN
CD _____ 4029
Best Of Jazz / Feb '96 / Discovery

MASTERPIECES VOL.15 1935-44
CD _____ 158342
Masterpieces / Mar '95 / BMG

MOONLIGHT IN VERMONT
Marie / You're my everything / Song of India / Love for sale / Taking a chance on love / This love of mine / Opus one / Swanee river / I'm getting sentimental over you / Boogie woogie / Melancholy serenade / Autumn in New York / I should care / Oo do do / It started all over again / I dream of you / Moonlight in Vermont / There are such things / High and mighty / Who / In a little Spanish town / Little girl / Granada
CD _____ GRF 068
Tring / '93 / Tring

MUSIC MAESTRO PLEASE (Dorsey, Tommy & His Orchestra)
Shine on harvest moon / Milenberg joys (parts 1 & 2) / Tea for two / Stomp it off / March of the toys / Chloe (song of the swamp) / Come rain or come shine / Keepin' out of mischief now / Satan takes a holiday / Smoke gets in your eyes / I hadn't anyone till you / Music maestro please / I'll see you in my dreams / Washboard blues / Lamp is low / Loose lid special / Rhythm saved the world / Is this gonna be my lucky summer / Josephine / You're a sweetheart
CD _____ CD 430
Entertainers / Mar '97 / Target/BMG

OPUS ONE (Dorsey, Tommy Orchestra & Frank Sinatra)
CD _____ CD 14526
Jazz Portraits / Jan '94 / Jazz Music

PORTRAIT OF TOMMY DORSEY, A
CD _____ GALE 404
Gallerie / May '97 / Disc / THE

POST-WAR ERA, THE
Come rain or come shine / Then I'll be happy / Song is you / Hollywood hat / Bingo, bango, bofo / Tom Foolery / Fresh money / Rest stop / At sundown / How are things in Glocca Morra / Trombonology / Puddle wump / Continental / Drumology / Pussy willow / Hucklebuck / I'm in the mood for love / Summertime / I get a kick out of you / Picalili Dilly / Comin' thro' the rye / Birmingham bounce
CD _____ 07863661562
Bluebird / Apr '93 / BMG

RADIO DAYS VOL.1
CD _____ CDSG 405
Starline / Aug '89 / Jazz Music

SONG OF INDIA (Dorsey, Tommy Orchestra)
They didn't believe me / Cheek to cheek / Opus one / Tico-tico / Blue skies / I'll never smile again / Begin the beguine / There's no you / Midriff / Cuttin' out / Pussy willow / Hollywood hat / Then I'll be happy / Lovely weather for ducks / And the angels sing / Somebody loves me / Boogie woogie / Song of India / On the sunny side of the street / Non drastic / Swanee river
CD _____ DBCD 08
Dance Band Days / Jul '87 / Prism

STOP, LOOK AND LISTEN
After you've gone / Beale Street blues / Boogie woogie / Chinatown, my Chinatown / Davenport blues / Easy does it / He's a gypsy from Poughkeepsie / Liebestraum / Lonesome road / Mandy, make up your mind / Maple leaf rag / Marie / Night and day / Royal Garden blues / Sheikh of araby / Song of India / Stomp it off / Stop, look and listen / Swanee river / Symphony in riffs / Tin roof blues / Twilight in Turkey / Weary blues
CD _____ CDAJA 5105
Living Era / May '93 / Select

SWEET & HOT (Meadowbrook Broadcast 24/2/40)
CD _____ TAX 37052
Tax / Aug '94 / Cadillac / Jazz Music / Wellard

TOMMY DORSEY
CD _____ 22709
Music / Nov '95 / Target/BMG

TOMMY DORSEY & HIS ORCHESTRA 1935-47 (Dorsey, Tommy Orchestra)
CD _____ TAXS 42
Tax / Aug '94 / Cadillac / Jazz Music / Wellard

TOMMY DORSEY & HIS ORCHESTRA 1940-43
CD _____ JH 1035
Jazz Hour / Oct '93 / Cadillac / Jazz Music / Target/BMG

TOMMY DORSEY 1942 (Dorsey, Tommy Orchestra)
CD _____ JH 1013
Jazz Hour / Feb '92 / Cadillac / Jazz Music / Target/BMG

TOMMY DORSEY AND HIS CLAMBAKE SEVEN 1936-1938 (Dorsey, Tommy & His Clambake Seven)
At the codfish ball / Milkman's matinee / Twilight in Turkey / He's a gypsy from Poughkeepsie / Alibi baby / Is this gonna be my lucky summer / Who'll be the one this summer / Posin' / All you want to do is dance / Having wonderful time (wish you were here) / After you / Stardust on the moon / Big apple / Lady is a tramp / Tears in my heart / Josephine / If the man in the moon / Nice work if you can get it / You're a sweetheart / When the midnight choo choo leaves for Alabam' / Everybody's doing it
CD _____ RTR 79012
Retrieval / Jul '97 / Cadillac / Direct / Jazz Music / Swift / Wellard

TOMMY DORSEY AND HIS GREATEST BAND
Boogie woogie / Amor / But she's my buddy's chick / Swing high / Like a leaf in the wind / Marie / Opus No.1 / Wagon wheels / Clarinet cascades / Land of dreams / Song of India / Swanee river / Losers weepers / There is no breeze to cool the flames / Minor goes muggin' / We'll git it / On the sunny side of the street / Rest stop / I'm in love with someone / That's my home / I'm getting sentimental over you
CD _____ JASMCD 2537
Jasmine / Nov '94 / Conifer/BMG / Hot Shot / TKO Magnum

TOMMY DORSEY ORCHESTRA/DAVID ROSE STRING ORCHESTRA (Dorsey, Tommy Orchestra & Dave Rose)
CD _____ 15777
Laserlight / Jul '93 / Target/BMG

TOMMY DORSEY VOL.1
CD _____ 15755
Laserlight / Aug '92 / Target/BMG

TOMMY DORSEY WITH FRANK SINATRA
Marie / Too romantic / Polka dots and moonbeams / This is the beginning of the end / Hear my song / i haven't time to be a millionaire / Head on my pillow / I'll never smile again / One I love / Call of the canyon / Shadows on the sand / Do you know why / Yearning / Not so long ago / Stardust / How am I to know / Oh look at me now / You lucky people you / Without a song / Everything happens to me / Let's get away from it all / Love me as I am / Love of mine / Blue skies / How do you do without me / Violets for your furs / How about you / My melancholy baby / Dig down deep / It started all over again / I'll take Tallulah / Song is you
CD _____ 7432115182
Jazz Tribune / Jun '94 / BMG

TOMMY DORSEY WITH FRANK SINATRA
CD _____ CD 56004
Jazz Roots / Aug '94 / Target/BMG

WELL, GIT IT (Dorsey, Tommy Orchestra)
CD _____ JASSCD 14
Jass / Oct '91 / ADA / Cadillac / CM / Direct / Jazz Music

Dos

UNO CON DOS
CD _____ NAR 061CD
New Alliance / May '93 / Plastic Head

Dos Of Soul

COME AROUND
CD _____ 5318422
Mercury / Sep '96 / PolyGram

Dos Santos, Jovino

CABO VERDE NHA TERRA
CD _____ PS 65174
PlayaSound / Nov '96 / ADA / Harmonia Mundi

MORNAS & COLADERAS FROM CAPE VERDE
CD PS 65127
PlayaSound / May '94 / ADA / Harmonia Mundi

Dosta Crew

ALL TOGETHER
We got wayz... / Right on time / Daddy's girl / I need a cheetah / Gotta good thing / All together / Ya gotta have bones / Two of a kind / Koko's kandy shop / That body / Suckers will scatter
CD WRA 8103 CD
Wrap / Nov '91 / Koch

Dotsero

JUBILEE
CD NOVA 9136
Nova / Jan '93 / New Note/Pinnacle

OFF THE BEATEN PATH
CD NOVA 9023
Nova / Jan '93 / New Note/Pinnacle

Double Exposure

BEST OF DOUBLE EXPOSURE, THE
CD CDGR 149
Charly / Jul '97 / Koch

TEN PERCENT
Ten percent / Gonna give my love away / Everyman / Baby I need your loving / Just can't say hello / My love is free / Pick me
CD CPCD 8062
Charly / Nov '94 / Koch

Double Muffled Dolphin

LIONS ARE GROWING
CD APR 011CD
April / Aug '96 / Plastic Head / Shellshock/ Disc

MY LEFT SIDE IS OUT OF SYNC
CD APR 004CD
April / Jan '95 / Plastic Head / Shellshock/ Disc

Double Nelson

CEUX QUI L'ONT FAIT
CD 760255
Cobalt / Nov '90 / Grapevine/PolyGram

LE GRAND CORNET
CD RM 002
Room Tone / Feb '97 / Cargo

Double Trio

GREEN DOLPHY SUITE (Arcado String Trio/Trio De Clarinettes)
Green Dolphy Street / Cold water music / Clic / Bosnia / Muhu / Suite domestique
CD ENJ 90112
Enja / Jul '95 / New Note/Pinnacle / Vital/ SAM

Double U

ABSURD FJORD
CD COMM 041CD
Communion / Dec '96 / Cargo

Double Vision

DOUBLE VISION
Conscience / Somebody / Trouble / Torn to pieces / Time / Ain't never giving up / Should I stay / Shades / Dawning / Kickstart / Summer never ending
CD JAZIDCD 104
Acid Jazz / Aug '94 / Disc

UNSAFE BUILDING
CD HV 295012
Happy Vibes / Dec '96 / ZYX

Doubt

PROFIT
CD CD 7913003
Progress Red / Jun '93 / Plastic Head

Doucet, David

QUAND J'AI PARTI
T'en as eu / Balfa waltz / Zydeco sont pas sales / J'ai passe / Bee la manche / Ton papa / French blues (Je m'endors) / J'etais au bal / Les bons temps rouler / Pacquent d'epingles / Coulee rodair / J'ai fait la tour / La valse des cajuns
CD ROUCD 6040
Rounder / '91 / ADA / CM / Direct

Doucet, Michael

BEAU SOLO
CD ARHCD 321
Arhoolie / Apr '95 / ADA / Cadillac / Direct

GREAT CAJUN (Doucet, Michael & Cajun Brew)
CD ROUCD 6017
Rounder / Apr '93 / ADA / CM / Direct

MAD REEL, THE (Doucet, Michael & Beausoleil)
CD ARHCD 397
Arhoolie / Apr '95 / ADA / Cadillac / Direct

MICHAEL DOUCET & CAJUN BREW (Doucet, Michael & Cajun Brew)
Wooly bully / Bayou pom pom / Un autre soir ennuyant / Hey good lookin' / Last Wednesday night / Louie louie / Woman or a man / Pauline / Zydeco boogaloo / Like a real cajun / J'ai passe devant ta porte / Do you want to dance
CD ROUCD 6017
Rounder / May '93 / ADA / CM / Direct

Dougal

DJ DOUGAL TAKES CONTROL (DJ Dougal)
CD KICKCD 39
Kickin' / Jun '96 / Prime / SRD

Doughboys

HAPPY ACCIDENTS
Countdown / Sorry wrong number / Deep end / Intravenus DeMilo / Happy home / Sunflower honey / Far away / Happy sad day / Wait and see / Every bit of nothing / Dream day / Apprenticeship of Lenny Kravitz / Tupperware party
CD LC 9336 2
Restless / Nov '90 / Vital

WHEN UP TURNS TO DOWN
CD EM 92442
Roadrunner / Nov '91 / PolyGram

Doughnuts

AGE OF CIRCLE
CD VR 025CD
Victory / Nov '95 / Plastic Head

Doughten, John

TIME FOR LOVE, A
CD SSC 1073D
Sunnyside / Feb '97 / Discovery

Douglas, Blair

BENEATH THE BERET
CD SKYECD 02
Macmeanma / Jan '92 / ADA / CM / Duncans / Highlander

SUMMER IN SKYE, A
CD SKYECD 09
Macmeanma / Oct '96 / ADA / CM / Duncans / Highlander

Douglas, Carl

KUNG FU FIGHTING
Kung fu fighting / Witchfinder general / When you got love / Changing times / I want to give you everything / Dance the kung fu / Never had this dream before / I don't care what people say / Blue eyed soul / Blue eyed soul / Shanhaid / Honest woman / Loving you / Kung fu fighting
CD 21023
Laserlight / Jul '97 / Target/BMG

Douglas, Craig

BEST OF THE EMI YEARS, THE
Teenager in love / My first love affair / Come softly to me / Dream lover / Riddle of love / Only sixteen / Thirty nine steps / Battle of New Orleans / Heart of a teenage girl / My hour of love / Where's the girl (I never met) / Oh what a day / New boy pretty blue eyes / After all / Change of heart / Girl next door / Hundred pounds of clay / Hundred pounds of clay (revised lyrics) / Hello spring / Another you / There is no greater love / Time / Ring-a-ding / When my little girl is smiling / Our favourite melodies / Rainbows / Painted smile / It all depends on you / Five foot two, eyes of blue / Walkin' my baby back home / Row row row
CD CDEMS 1494
EMI / May '93 / EMI

ONLY SIXTEEN
Our favourite melodies / Time / Hundred pounds of clay / Change of heart / Rainbows / Riddle of love / When my little girl is smiling / Pretty blue eyes / There is no greater love / Girl next door / Wish it were me / Sandy / Hello spring / Another you / Teenager in love / Only sixteen / Oh what a day / Dream lover / Ring-a-ding doo
CD SEECD 34
See For Miles/C5 / Feb '90 / Pinnacle

Douglas, Dave

CONSTELLATIONS (Douglas, Dave Tiny Bell Trio)
CD ARTCD 6175
Hat Art / Oct '95 / Cadillac / Harmonia Mundi

PARALLEL WORLDS
CD 1212262
Soul Note / Jan '94 / Cadillac / Harmonia Mundi / Wellard

Douglas, Jerry

EVERYTHING'S GONNA WORK OUT FINE
CD ROU 11535
Rounder / '89 / ADA / CM / Direct

SKIP, HOP AND WOBBLE (Douglas, Jerry & Russ Barenberg/Edgar Meyer)
CD SHCD 3817
Sugar Hill / Sep '96 / ADA / CM / Direct / Koch / Roots

SLIDE RULE
Ride the wild turkey / Pearlie Mae / When papa played the dobro / We hide and seek / Shoulder to shoulder / Uncle Sam / It's a beautiful life / I don't believe you've met my baby / Rain on Oliviatown / Hey Joe / New day medley / Shenandoah breakdown
CD SHCD 3797
Sugar Hill / Jul '92 / ADA / CM / Direct / Koch / Roots

UNDER THE WIRE
TOB / Dhaka rock / Time gone by / Monroe's hornpipe / Before the blues / Trip to Kilkerrin / Grant's corner / Redhill / Two friends / New day
CD SHCD 3831
Sugar Hill / Apr '95 / ADA / CM / Direct / Koch / Roots

YONDER (Douglas, Jerry & Peter Rowan)
CD SHCD 3847
Sugar Hill / Dec '96 / ADA / CM / Direct / Koch / Roots

Douglas, Johnny

IT'S MAGIC (Douglas, Johnny Strings)
All the things you are / Only love / Music of the night / It's magic / At this time of year / Sleepy shores / Warsaw concerto / Dulcima / Secret love / Dream of Olwen / Birthday waltz / Time / Quiet nights and quiet stars / Moonlight serenade / Windows of Paris / I can tell by the look in your eye
CD DLCD 115
Dulcima / Apr '95 / Savoy / THE

MORE ROMANCE WITH THE CLASSICS (Douglas, Johnny Strings)
Swan / Eighteenth variation from a Rhapsody on a theme of Paganini / Serenade / Piano concerto no.2 / Adagio / Romance no. 2 / Dreaming / Intermezzo from Cavaleria Rusticana / Swan lake / Spring song / Requiem for a love affair / Moonlight sonata / Symphony No. 5 / Romeo and Juliet / Sonata in D
CD DLCD 105
Dulcima / Sep '88 / Savoy / THE

ON SCREEN (Douglas, Johnny Strings)
Days of wine and roses / Gigi / Call me irresponsible / Summer knows / Laura / Dungeons and dragons / Like someone in love / Affair to remember / Smile / Young at heart / Railway children / As time goes by / Dulcima / Somewhere in time / Way we were
CD DLCD 110
Dulcima / May '91 / Savoy / THE

ON STAGE (Douglas, Johnny Strings)
I could write a book / Bali Ha'i / Tap your troubles away / Hey there / All I ask of you / Ascot Gavotte / If I loved you / Sweetest sounds / I won't send roses / Stranger in paradise / Where or when / Heather on the hill / I have dreamed / Try to remember / Love changes everything
CD DLCD 109
Dulcima / Oct '90 / Savoy / THE

ROMANCING WITH THE CLASSICS
CD DLCD 103
Dulcima / May '94 / Savoy / THE

Douglas, K.C.

BIG ROAD BLUES
Big road blues / Buck dance / Tore your playhouse down / Whisky headed woman / Catfish blues / Howlin' blues / Kansas City blues / Bottle up and go / KC blues / Key to the highway
CD OBCCD 569
Original Blues Classics / Oct '95 / Complete/Pinnacle / Wellard

KC'S BLUES
CD OBCCD 533
Original Blues Classics / Nov '92 / Complete/Pinnacle / Wellard

Douglass, Greg

MAELSTROM
CD TX 2007CD
Taxim / Jan '94 / ADA

Doumbia, Mamadou

YAFA (Doumbia, Mamadou & Mandinka)
CD JCD 90132
JVC / May '97 / Direct / New Note/ Pinnacle / Vital/SAM

Dour, Yann

JOB DAOULAS
CD CAR 013CD
Diffusion Breizh / Apr '95 / ADA

Dove

WRECKING BALL
CD LF 041CD
Lost & Found / Nov '92 / Plastic Head

Dove Shack

THIS IS THE SHACK
CD 5279332
RAL / Oct '95 / PolyGram

Dover, Connie

IF EVER I RETURN
CD TPM 301CD
Taylor Park / May '97 / ADA

SOMEBODY
CD TPMD 0101CD
Taylor Park / '92 / ADA

WISHING WELL
CD TPMD 21CD
Taylor Park / Apr '94 / ADA

Dowling, Leslie Rae

UNBOUNDED WATERS
CD 4509971082
Warner Bros. / Aug '94 / Warner Music

Dowling, Mike

BEATS WORKIN'
Police dog blues / Train that carried my girl from town / Beats workin' / DW Washburn / Ace in the hole / Jan's song / Louis Collins / Lonely at the bottom / Jitterbug waltz / Bottleneck march / Nothin' could be better / Jump children
CD SCR 46
Strictly Country / Feb '97 / ADA / Direct

SWAMP DOG BLUES
CD SCR 39
Strictly Country / Sep '95 / ADA / Direct

Down By Law

BLUE
CD E 864192
Epitaph / Nov '92 / Pinnacle / Plastic Head

DOWN BY LAW/GIGANTOR (Down By Law/Gigantor)
CD LF 064CD
Lost & Found / Aug '93 / Plastic Head

LAST OF THE SHARPSHOOTERS
USA today / No equalizer / Call to arms / Gun of '96 / Get out / Burning heart / Question marks and periods / Urban napalm / DJG / Concrete times / No one gets away / Last goodbye / Factory day / Cool crowd / Self destruction
CD 65012
Epitaph / Aug '97 / Pinnacle / Plastic Head

PUNKROCKACADEMYFIGHTSONG
CD E 864312
Epitaph / Jun '94 / Pinnacle / Plastic Head

Down Home Jazzband

PADDLE WHEELIN' ALONG
CD SOSCD 1300
Stomp Off / Jul '96 / Jazz Music / Wellard

Down To Reality

PERVERT INHUMANITY
CD LF 270CD
Lost & Found / May '97 / Plastic Head

Down To The Bone

FROM MANHATTAN TO STATEN
CD IBCD 3
Internal Bass / Nov '96 / Prime / Timewarp / Total/BMG

Down Town Jazzband

DOWN TOWN HIGHLIGHTS (2CD Set)
Tears / Bird of Bleekerstreet / Knock out stomp / On the street where you live / Jada / Song of the islands / Saint Louis blues / Muskrat ramble / Third little girl / Cheerin' rag / You must have been a beautiful baby / Eurovision blues / Down town blues / 1919 Rag / I'm coming Virginia / I've got what it takes / Royal garden blues / Mame / Thinking blues / Mabel's dream / As long as I live / Change / Buddy's habbits / Kenia blues / Pearls / Wouldn't it be lovely / Jazz me blues / New Orleans function / Little bird / Lonesome road / Psychotechnical change / High society / Basin Street blues / Wolga song / St James infirmary / Baboon rag / Jamie's blues / Potato head blues / Do you know what it means to Miss New Orleans / New Orleans stomp / John's boogie / King Porter stomp
CD Set CDTTD 606
Timeless Jazz / Apr '96 / New Note/ Pinnacle

Downchild

GONE FISHING
CD SP 1139CD
Stony Plain / Oct '93 / ADA / CM / Direct

Downes, David

PAVILION
CD WCL 11006
White Cloud / May '94 / Select

RUSTED WHEEL OF THINGS, THE
CD WCL 110112
White Cloud / May '95 / Select

Downes, Geoffrey

EVOLUTION
CD BP 215CD
Blueprint / Jun '96 / Pinnacle

LIGHT PROGRAM, THE
Ethnic dance / East West / Urbanology / Symphonie electronique / Oceania electronique
CD BP 216CD
Blueprint / Mar '96 / Pinnacle

VOX HUMANA
Tears / Video killed the radio star / Roads of destiny / Plastic age / Ave Maria / Network / All of the time / Concerto / Satellite blues / England / Moon under the water / White car / Adagio
CD BP 214CD
Blueprint / Oct '95 / Pinnacle

Downes, Paul

OVERDUE
CD HTDCD 55
HTD / Mar '96 / CM / Pinnacle

Downey, Morton

IRISH NIGHTINGALE, THE
CD CDAJA 5173
Living Era / May '96 / Select

Downing, Will

COME TOGETHER AS ONE
Come together as one / Sake of love / Sometimes I cry / Love call / Love we share / Too soon / I'll wait / Rules of love / Test of time / Closer to you / Wishing on a star
CD BRCD 538
4th & Broadway / Oct '89 / PolyGram

DREAM FULFILLED, A
She / I'll wait / Giving my all to you / I try / For all we know / Something's going on / Don't make me wait / I go crazy / No love intended / World is a ghetto
CD IMCD 212
4th & Broadway / Mar '96 / PolyGram

LOVE'S THE PLACE TO BE
CD IMCD 218
4th & Broadway / Mar '96 / PolyGram

MOODS
CD BRCD 612
4th & Broadway / Nov '95 / PolyGram

WILL DOWNING
In my dreams / Do you / Free / Love supreme / Security / Set me free / Sending out an SOS / Dancing in the moonlight / Do you remember love
CD IMCD 190
Island / Mar '94 / PolyGram

Downliners Sect

BIRTH OF SUAVE, THE
CD HOG2
Hangman's Daughter / Sep '94 / Shellshock/Disc / SRD

SAVAGE RETURN
Bad girls looking for fun / Piccadilly run / Ain't I got you / Hard case / Midnight call / Pan American boogie / Eel pie memories / Down the road apiece / Talking 'bout you / Studio 51 / Bad penny / Who do you love / Cadillac / Bye bye Johnny / Just like I treat you / Before you accuse me
CD CDKVL 9033
Kingdom / May '94 / Kingdom

SINGLES A'S AND B'S
Cadillac / Roll over Beethoven / Beautiful Delilah / Shame, shame, shame / Green onions / Nursery rhymes / Baby what's wrong / Be a sect maniac / Little Egypt / Sect appeal / Find out what's happening / Insecticide / Wreck of ol' 97 / Leader of the sect / I want my baby back / Midnight hour / Now she's dead / I got mine / Waiting in heaven somewhere / Bad storm coming / Lonely and blue / All night worker / He was a square / Glendora / I'll find out / Cost of living / Everything I've got to give / I can't get away from you / Roses
CD SEECD 398
See For Miles/C5 / May '97 / Pinnacle

Download

EYES OF STANLEY PAIN
CD 8522502
Westcom / May '96 / Koch / Pinnacle

SIDEWINDER
CD 07322472
Westcom / May '96 / Koch / Pinnacle

Downset

DO WE SPEAK A DEAD LANGUAGE
Intro / Empower / Eyes shut tight / Keep on breathing / Hurl a stone / Fire / Touch / Against the spirits / Sickness / Pocket full of fatcaps / Sangre de mis manos / Horrifying / Permanent days unmoving / Ashes in hand / Sickness (Reprise)
CD 5324162
Talkin' Loud / Jun '96 / PolyGram

Dowsett, Janet

ENCORE
CD CDGRS 1280
Grosvenor / Aug '95 / Grosvenor

KALEIDOSCOPE
I could have danced all night / Groovy kind of love / Tea for two / Water fountain / Splanky / Pavanne / Elizabethan serenade / Disney medley / Dizzy fingers / Aranjuez mon amour / Walking in the sunshine / Adagio for organ and strings in G minor / Hello Dolly/Mame / West Side story medley / Prelude in classic style / Forgotten dreams
CD CDGRS 1259
Grosvenor / Feb '95 / Grosvenor

Doy, Carl

PIANO BY CANDLELIGHT VOL.1
CD NELCD 101
Timbuktu / Aug '93 / Pinnacle

PIANO BY CANDLELIGHT VOL.2
CD NELCD 102
Timbuktu / Aug '93 / Pinnacle

PIANO BY CANDLELIGHT VOL.3
CD NELCD 103
Timbuktu / Aug '93 / Pinnacle

Doyle, Matthew

LYREBIRD
CD 150232
Celestial Harmonies / Aug '96 / ADA / Select

Doyle, Roger

BABEL VOL.1
CD SIDO 001CD
Silver Door / Oct '96 / World Serpent

BABEL VOL.2
Entry level 1 / Mr. Brady's room / Temple music (Earth to Earth) / Yunnus / Entry level 2 / Dressing room / Concert music - pagoda charm / Mansard / Squat
CD SIDO 002CD
Silver Door / Jul '97 / World Serpent

Dp-Sol

LIVE IN OSLO
CD TSF 9006
Play It Again Sam / Apr '95 / Discovery / Plastic Head / Vital

DR Base

BATTERED AND CRISPIED (Fish Tails Vol.1/The DR Base Album)
Beaufort 8 / Barracuda: *DR Base & Karim* / Manta / Freedom: *Fierce Base* / NWA: *DR Base & Karim* / Beat the system / Blue oyster / New improved shit: *Fierce Base* / Specialist '95 / Dream within '96 / Anacoda: *DR Base & Karim* / Captain Tinrib's back again: *Ganesh* / Breakdown: *Incisions*
CD RIBCD 2001
Tinrib / Mar '97 / Mo's Music Machine / Prime / RTM/Disc

Dr. & The Crippens

RAPHANADOSIS
Garden centre murders / Braindead / Epic / I'm so dumb / Henenlotter / Kid with the removable face / Skintight / Jimmy goes to Egypt / Extreme noise T / Bench / Zombies in Disneyland / Elvis shroud / My brother is a headcase / Anti-christ on button moon / Greenfinger / Eight years in office / Podbreath / Nightmare on Sesame Street
CD ACHE 18CD
Manic Ears / May '89 / Target/BMG

Dr. & The Medics

INSTANT HEAVEN
CD MAMA 005
Madman / May '96 / Pinnacle

Dr. Alban

HELLO AFRIKA
No coke / Groove machine II / Sweet reggae mujsic / China man / Alban prelude / Hello Afrika / Proud (to be Afrikan) / Our father / U and Mi / Thank you
CD 261391
Arista / Aug '95 / BMG

LOOK WHO'S TALKING
Hard pan di drums / Look who's talking / Free up Soweto / Away from home / Gimme dat loven / Let the beat go on / Fire / Home sweet home / Go see the dentist / Sweet little girl / Plastic smile / Awillawillawillaey / Stone radio
CD 74321201532
Arista / Aug '94 / BMG

SECOND EDITION
CD 74321135652
Arista / Apr '93 / BMG

Dr. Alimantado

BEST DRESSED CHICKEN IN TOWN
Gimme mi gun / Plead I cause / Poison flour / Ride on / Just the other day / Best dressed chicken in town / Unitone skank / I killed the barber / Ital galore / I am the greatest says Muhammed Ali / Johnny was a baker / Tribute to the dark / Can't conquer natty dreadlock / I shall fear no evil
CD KMCD 1
Keyman / May '97 / Greensleeves / Jet Star / SRD

BORN FOR A PURPOSE
Chant to Jah / Return of Muhammed Ali / Sons of thunder / Dreadlocks dread / Call on Jah / Born for a purpose / Careless Ethiopians repent / Oil crisis / Sitting in the park / Marriage licence
CD GRELCD 22
Greensleeves / Jul '87 / Jet Star / SRD

IN THE MIX
CD KMCD 003
Keyman / Oct '88 / Greensleeves / Jet Star / SRD

KING'S BREAD
CD ISDACD 5000
Keyman / Apr '94 / Greensleeves / Jet Star / SRD

LOVE IS
CD KMCD 1001
Keyman / Nov '83 / Greensleeves / Jet Star / SRD

PRIVILEGED FEW
CD KMCD 009
Keyman / Nov '94 / Greensleeves / Jet Star / SRD

REGGAE REVUE VOL.1
CD KMCD 002
Keyman / Oct '88 / Greensleeves / Jet Star / SRD

Dr. Didg

OUT OF THE WOODS
Street music / Devon / Easy / King tut / Ever increasing circles / Brolga / Suntan / Rave on / Say what you like / Under the influence
CD HNCD 1384
Hannibal / Apr '95 / ADA / Vital

Dr. Dixie

BEST OF DOCTOR DIXIE JAZZ BAND (Dr. Dixie Jazz Band)
CD CDTTD 521
Timeless Traditional / Jan '88 / Jazz Music / New Note/Pinnacle

Dr. Dre

AFTERMATH (Various Artists)
Aftermath (intro) / East coast, west coast killas: *Group Therapy* / Sh'tin' on the world: *Mel Man* / Blunt time: *RBX* / Been there done that: *Dr. Dre* / Choices: *Summerson, Kim* / As the world keeps turning: *Miscellaneous* / STR-8 gone: *King T* / Please: *Wilcher, Maurice* / Do 4 love: *Lockhart, Jheryl* / Sexy dance: *RC* / No second chance: *Whoz Who* / Lyrical assault weapon: *Sharief* / Nationowl: *Nowl* / Fame: *RC*
CD IND 90044
Interscope / Dec '96 / BMG

CHRONIC, THE
Chronic / Fuck wit Dre day (and everybody's celebratin') / Let me ride / Day the niggaz took over / Nuthin' but a G thang / Deeez nuuuts / Li'l ghetto boy / Nigga witta gun / Rat-tat-tat-tat / Twenty dollar sack pyramid / Lyrical gangbang / High powered / Doctor's office / Stranded on death row / Roach (the chronic outro)
CD IND 57128
Interscope / Feb '97 / BMG

Dr. Feelgood

25 YEARS OF DR. FEELGOOD (2CD Set)
She does it right / I don't mind / All through the city / Keep it out of sight / Roxette / I can tell / Sneakin' suspicion / Back in the night / Going back home / Riot in cell block No.9 / She's a wind up / That's it, I quit / Nighttime / Milk and alcohol / Put him out of your mind / Shotgun blues / No mo do yakamo / Jumping from love to love / Violent love / Rat race / Crazy 'bout girls / Dangerous / Mad man blues / Dimples / Hunting shooting fishing / See you later alligator / King for a day / Baby Jane / Sugar turns to alcohol / Down by the jetty blues / Double crossed / Wolfman callin' / One step forward / Roadrunner / Down at the doctors / Heart of the city / World keeps turning / Instinct to survive / Going out west / You got me
CD Set GRAND 20
Grand / May '97 / ADA / Direct / Vital

AS IT HAPPENS
Take a tip / Every kind of vice / Down at the doctors / Baby Jane / Sugar shaker / Things get better / She's a windup / Ninety nine and a half (won't do) / Buddy Buddy friends / Milk and alcohol / Matchbox / As long as the price is right / Night time / Riot in cell block 9 / Blues had a baby and they named it rock 'n' roll
CD GRANDCD 15
Grand / Sep '95 / ADA / Direct / Vital

BE SEEING YOU
Ninety nine and a half (won't do) / She's a wind up / I thought I had it made / I don't wanna know / That's it I quit / As long as the price is right / Hi rise / My buddy buddy friends / Blues had a baby and they named it rock 'n' roll / Looking back / Sixty minutes
CD GRANDCD 14
Grand / Sep '95 / ADA / Direct / Vital

BRILLEAUX
I love you so you're mine / You've got my number / Big enough / Don't wait up / Get rhythm / Where is the next one / Play dirty / Grow too old / Rough ride / I'm a real man / Come over here / Take what you can get
CD GRANDCD 04
Grand / Sep '95 / ADA / Direct / Vital

CASE HISTORY (The Best Of Dr. Feelgood)
Going back home / Back in the night / Roxette / She does it right / Sneakin' suspicion / No mo do yakamo / She's a wind up / As long as the price is right / Down at the doctors / Milk and alcohol / Violent love / Jumping from love to love / Best in the world / Rat race / Close but no cigar / Play dirty / Don't wait up / See you later alligator
CD CDP 7467112
Liberty / Apr '83 / EMI

CASE OF THE SHAKES, A
Jumping from love to love / Going some place else / Best in the world / Punch drunk / King for a day / Violent love / No mo do yakamo / Love hound / Coming to you / Who's winning / Drives me wild / Case of the shakes
CD GRANDCD 10
Grand / Sep '95 / ADA / Direct / Vital

CLASSIC
Hunting shooting fishing / Break these chains / Heartbeat / (I wanna) make love to you / Hurricane / Quit while you're behind / Nothing like it / Spy Vs. spy / Highway 61 / Crack me up
CD GRANDCD 11
Grand / Sep '95 / ADA / Direct / Vital

DOCTOR'S ORDERS
Close but no cigar / So long / You don't love me / My way / Neighbour, neighbour / Talk of the devil / Hit, git and split / I can't be satisfied / Saturday night fish fry / Drivin' wheel / It ain't right / I don't worry about a thing / She's in the middle / Dangerous
CD GRANDCD 06
Grand / Sep '95 / ADA / Direct / Vital

DOWN AT THE DOCTORS
If my baby quit me / Styrofoam / Tanqueray / Roadrunner / Wolfman callin' / Double crossed / One step forward / Mojo workin' / Milk and alcohol / Down at the doctors / Freddie's footsteps / Heart of the city
CD GRANDCD 18
Grand / Sep '95 / ADA / Direct / Vital

DOWN BY THE JETTY
She does it right / Boom boom / More I give / One weekend / I don't mind / Twenty yards behind / Keep it out of sight / All through the city / Cheque book / Oyeh / Bony Moronie / Tequila
CD GRANDCD 05
Grand / Sep '95 / ADA / Direct / Vital

FAST WOMEN AND SLOW HORSES
She's the one / Sweet sweet lovin' (gone sour on me) / Trying to live my life without you / Rat race / Baby jump / Crazy about girls / Sugar bowl / Educated fool / Bum's rush / Baby why do you treat me this way / Beautiful Delilah / Monkey
CD GRANDCD 03
Grand / Sep '95 / ADA / Direct / Vital

FEELGOOD FACTOR, THE
Feelgood factor / Tanqueray / Tell me no lies / Styrofoam / I'm in the mood for you / Double crossed / Lying about the blues / She moves me / Wolfman callin' / One step forward / One to ten / Fool for you
CD GRANDCD 17
Grand / Sep '95 / ADA / Direct / Vital

LET IT ROLL
Java blues / Feels good / Put him out of your mind / Bend your ear / Hong Kong money / Keeka smeeka / Shotgun / Pretty face / Ridin' on the L and N / Drop everything and run
CD GRANDCD 07
Grand / Sep '95 / ADA / Direct / Vital

LIVE IN LONDON
King for a day / As long as the price is right / Baby Jane / See you later alligator / You upset me / She does it right / Back in the night
CD GRANDCD 08
Grand / Sep '95 / ADA / Direct / Vital

LOOKING BACK (5CD Set)
Roxette / All through the city / Cheque book / 20 yards behind / She does it right / Bonie moronie/Tequila / Going back home / You shouldn't call the doctor (if you can't afford the pills / I can tell / Back in the night / I'm a man / I don't mind / I'm a hog for you baby / Checkin' up on my baby / Stupidity

/ Johnny B Goode / Lights out / You'll be mine / Walking on the edge / Hey Mama keep your big mouth shut / Nothin' shakin' (but the leaves on the trees) / Sneakin' suspicion / She's a windup / Looking back / 99 & a half won't do / Baby Jane / As long as the price is right / Down at the doctors / Take a tip / Every kind of vice / Milk and alcohol / Sugar shaker / Night time / Riot in cell block 9 / My buddy buddy friends / Great balls of fire / Pretty face / Put him out of your mind / Java blue / Hong Kong money / No mo do Yakamo / Jumping from love to love / Violent love / Shotgun blues / Waiting for Saturday night / Trying to live my life without love / She's the one / Crazy about girls / Monkey / Rat race / You don't love me / She's in the middle / Dangerous / I can't be satisfied / Close but no cigar / My way / Rock me baby / Tore down / Dust my broom / I love you so you're mine / Don't wait up / Come over here / Get rhythm / I'm a real man / See you later alligator / Quit while you're behind / Hunting shooting fishing / (I wanna) Make love to you / Mad man blues / King for a day / Primo blues / Standing at the crossroads again / Two times nine / Down by the jetty blues / No time / Wolfman calling / Feelgood factor / If my baby quits me / Roadrunner / One step forward / Mojo workin' / Heart of the city / Route 66 / Keep it out of sight / Homeward / You upset me baby / Down at the (other) doctor's / Love hound / Don't take but a few minutes / Eileen / Touch of class / She's got her eyes on you / Solitary blues / Looking at you
CD Set ACDFEEL 195
Liberty / Oct '95 / EMI

MAD MAN BLUES
Dust my broom / Something you got / Dimples / Living on the highway / Tore down / Madman blues / I've got news for you / My babe / Can't find the lady / Rock me baby
CD GRANDCD 02
Grand / Sep '95 / ADA / Direct / Vital

MALPRACTICE
I can tell / Going back home / Back in the night / Another man / Rollin' and tumblin' / Don't let your daddy know / Watch your step / Don't you just know it / Riot in cell block 9 / Because you're mine / You shouldn't call the doctor
CD GRANDCD 09
Grand / Sep '95 / ADA / Direct / Vital

ON THE JOB
Drives me wild / Java blues / Jumping from love to love / Pretty face / Nomo do yakamo / Love hound / Best in the world / Who's winning / Ridin' on the L 'n' N / Case of the shakes / Shotgun blues / Goodnight Vienna
CD GRANDCD 16
Grand / Sep '95 / ADA / Direct / Vital

ON THE ROAD AGAIN
Wine, women and whisky / Sweet Louise / World keeps turning / On the road again / Instinct to survive / Mellow down easy / Going out West / Cheap at half the price / Second opinion / What am I to believe / Repo man / You got me
CD GRAND 19
Grand / Aug '96 / ADA / Direct / Vital

PRIMO
Heart of the city / My sugar turns to alcohol / Going down / No time / World in a jug / If my baby quit me / Primo blues / Standing at the crossroads again / Been down so long / Don't worry baby / Down by the jetty blues / Two times nine
CD GRANDCD 12
Grand / Sep '95 / ADA / Direct / Vital

PRIVATE PRACTICE
Down at the doctors / Every kind of vice / Things get better / Milk and alcohol / Night time / Let's have a party / Take a tip / It wasn't me / Greaseball / Sugar shaker
CD GRANDCD 01
Grand / Sep '95 / ADA / Direct / Vital

SINGLES - THE UA YEARS
Roxette / She does it right / Back in the night / Ging back home / Riot in cell block 9 / Sneakin' suspicion / She's a wind up / Baby Jane / Down at the doctors / Milk and alcohol / As long as the price is right / Put him out of your mind / Hong Kong money / No mo do yakamo / Jumping from love to love / Violent love / Waiting for Saturday night / Monkey / Trying to live my life without you / Crazy about girls / My way / Madman blues / See you later alligator / Hunting shooting fishing / Don't wait up / Milk and alcohol (New recipe)
CD CDEM 1332
Liberty / May '89 / EMI

SNEAKIN' SUSPICION
Sneakin' suspicion / Paradise / Nothin' shakin' (but the leaves on the trees) / Time and the devil / Lights out / Lucky seven / All my love / You'll be mine / Walking on the edge / Hey mama keep your mouth shut
CD GRANDCD 13
Grand / Sep '95 / ADA / Direct / Vital

STUPIDITY PLUS (Live 1976-1990)
I'm talking about you / Twenty yards behind / Stupidity / All through the city / I'm a man / Walking the dog / She does it right / Going back home / I don't mind / Back in the night / I'm a hog for you / Checkin' up on my baby / Roxette / Riot in cell block 9 / Johnny B Goode / Take a trip / Every kind of vice / She's a wind up / No mo do yakamo / Love hound / Shotgun blues / King for a day / Milk and alcohol / Down at the doctors
CD CDP 795 934 2
Liberty / Mar '91 / EMI

Dr. Fink

I'M IN THE MOOD FOR THE BEATLES (Dr. Fink & The Mystery Band)
CD LPCD 1024
Disky / Apr '94 / Disky / THE

Dr. Hook

COMPLETELY HOOKED (The Best Of Dr. Hook)
Sylvia's mother / Cover of the Rolling Stone / Everybody's makin' it big but me / You make my pants want to get up and dance / Sleeping late / Only sixteen / Walk right in / Millionaire / More like the movies / When you're in love with a beautiful woman / Sexy eyes / If not you / Little bit more / Sharing the night together / I don't want to be alone tonight / Better love next time / In over my head / Years from now / Sweetest of all / Couple more years
CD CDESTV 2
Capitol / May '92 / EMI

DR. HOOK (Dr. Hook & The Medicine Show)
Sylvia's mother / Marie Lavauz / Sing me a rainbow / Hey Lady Godiva / Four years older than me / Kiss it away / Making it natural / I call that true love / When she cries / Judy / Mama I'll sing one song for you
CD 4805222
Columbia / May '95 / Sony

MAKING LOVE AND MUSIC - THE 1976-79 RECORDINGS
When you're in love with a beautiful woman / Little bit more / If not you / Up on the mountain / Bad eye Bill / Who dat / Let the loose end drag / I'm a lamb / Making love and music / Radio / Everybody loves me / Oh Jesse / Jungle in the zoo / More like the movies / I don't feel much like smilin' / Mountain Mary / Leviate / Dooley Jones / Sexy energy / Love monster
CD CDMFP 5979
Music For Pleasure / Apr '93 / EMI

PLEASURE AND PAIN (The History Of Dr. Hook/3CD Set)
Sylvia's mother / Cover of the 'Rolling Stone' / Ballad of Lucy Jordon / Levitate / Only sixteen / I got stoned and missed it / Millionaire / Everybody's makin' it big but me / Cooky and Lila / Everybody loves me / More like the movies / Little bit more / If not you / Radio / Jungle to the zoo / What about you / I need the high / Couple more years / Making love and music / Lay too low too long / Sleeping late / Walk right in / Let the loose end drag / I'm a lamb / Sharing the night together / Sweetest of all / Storms never last / I don't want to be alone tonight / Knowing she's there / Clyde / When you're in love with a beautiful woman / I gave her comfort / You make my pants want to get up and dance / Better love next time / In over my head / Sexy eyes / Oh Jessie / Years from now / I don't feel much like smilin' / What do you want / Love monster / Mountain Mary / Girls can get it / Baby makes her blue jeans talk / Feels good / I couldn't believe / Rings of grass / Stuck on the wrong side of love / That plane / Lonely man / I never got to know her / You can't take it with you / I've been him / Bread upon the water / Here comes the blues again / Stagolee / Shadow knows / #1 Rock radio station / Pleasure and pain / There's a light / Walkin' my cat named dog / Carry me Carrie / Oo poo pa doo
CD Set HOOKBOX 1
Capitol / Oct '96 / EMI

SHARING THE NIGHT TOGETHER
Better love next time / Sharing the night together / Sexy eyes / When you're in love with a beautiful woman / If not you / Little bit more / Oh Jesse / Years from now / Sweetest of all / In over my head / I don't feel much like smilin' / I don't wanna be alone tonight / Only sixteen / All the time in the world / Everybody is making it big but me / Storms never last / More like the movies / What about you / Couple more years / Makin' love and music
CD CDGOLD 1051
EMI Gold / Jul '96 / EMI

VERY BEST OF DR. HOOK, THE
CD 10302
CMC / Jun '97 / BMG

Dr. Israel

7 TALES OF ISRAEL
CD WSCD 009
Word Sound Recordings / Aug '96 / Cargo / SRD

Dr. John

AFTERGLOW
I know what I've got / Gee baby ain't I good to you / I'm just a lucky so and so / Blue skies / So long / New York City blues / Tell me you'll wait for me / There must be a better world somewhere / I still think about you / I'm confessin' that I love you
CD GRB 70002
GRP / Jun '95 / New Note/BMG

BABYLON
Babylon / Glowin' / Black widow spider / Barefoot lady / Twilight zone / Patriotic flag waver / Lonesome guitar strangler
CD 7567804382
Atco / Feb '92 / Warner Music

BRIGHTEST SMILE IN TOWN, THE
Saddled the cow / Boxcar boogie / Brightest smile in town / Waiting for a train / Monkey puzzle / Average kind of guy / Pretty Libby / Marie Le Veau / Come rain or come shine / Suite home New Orleans
CD FIENDCD 9
Demon / Oct '90 / Pinnacle

CRAWFISH SAUCE
Crawfish soiree (bring your own) / Tipitina / In the night / Woman is the root of all evil / Time had come / Shoo raa / Zu zu man / Baldhead / Mean cheatin' woman / Make your own bed well / Little closer to my home / Della
CD AIMA 4CD
Aim / May '97 / ADA / Direct / Jazz Music

CUT ME WHILE I'M HOT
CD CDTB 158
Thunderbolt / Mar '95 / TKO Magnum

DESITIVELY BONNAROO
Quitters never win / Stealin' / What comes around (goes around) / Me, you, loneliness / Mos' scocious / (Everybody wanna get rich) Rite away / Let's make a better world / R U 4 Real / Sing along song / Can't git enough / Go tell the people / Destitively bonnaroo
CD 7567804412
Atco / Dec '93 / Warner Music

DOCTOR JOHN PLAYS MAC REBENNACK
Dorothy / Mac's boogie / Memories of Professor Longhair / Nearness of you / Delicado / Honey dripper / Big Mac / New island midnight / Saints / Pinetop / Silent night / Dance a la negres / Wade in the water
CD FIENDCD 1
Demon / '88 / Pinnacle

DR. JOHN
CD GRP 7002
GRP / Jun '95 / New Note/BMG

GOIN' BACK TO NEW ORLEANS
Litanie des saints / Careless love / My indian red / Milneburg joys / I thought I heard Buddy Bolden say / Basin Street blues / Didn't he ramble / Do you call that a buddy / How come my dog don't bark / Goodnight Irene / Fess up / Since I fell for you / (I'll be glad when you're dead) you rascal you / Cabbagehead / Goin' home tomorrow / Blue Monday / Scald dog medley / I can't go on / Goin' back to New Orleans
CD 7599269402
Atco / Mar '94 / Warner Music

GRIS GRIS
Gris gris gumbo ya ya / Danse Kalinda ba doom / Mama roux / Danse fambeaux / Croker courtbullion / Jump sturdy / Walk on gilded splinters
CD 7567804372
Atlantic / Jan '95 / Warner Music

GUMBO
Iko Iko / Blow wind blow / Big chief / Somebody changed the lock / Mess around / Let the good times roll / Junko partner / Stagger Lee / Tipitina / Those lonely lonely nights / Huey Smith medley / Little Liza Jane
CD 7567803982
Atco / Mar '93 / Warner Music

HOLLYWOOD BE THY NAME
New Island soiree / Reggae doctor / Way you do the things you do / Swanee river boogie / Yesterday / Babylon / Back by the river / Medley / Hollywood be thy name / I wanna rock
CD BGOCD 62
Beat Goes On / Oct '89 / Pinnacle

IN A SENTIMENTAL MOOD
Makin' whoopee / Candy / Accentuate the positive / My buddy / In a sentimental mood / Black night / Don't let the sun catch you crying / Love for sale / More than you know
CD K 9258892
Atco / Apr '89 / Warner Music

IN THE RIGHT PLACE
Right place wrong time / Same old same old / Just the same / Qualified / Travelling mood / Peace brother peace / Life / Such a night / Shoo fly marches on / I been hoodood / Cold cold cold
CD 7567803602
Atco / Mar '93 / Warner Music

LOSER FOR YOU, BABY
Time had come / Loser for you baby / Ear is on strike / Little closer to my home / I pulled the cover off you two lovers / New Orleans / Go ahead on / Just like a mirror / Bring your love / Bald head / Make your own
CD CDTB 066
Thunderbolt / Nov '88 / TKO Magnum

MOS'SCOCIOUS (Dr. John Anthology)
Bad neighborhood / Morgus the magnificent / Storm warning / Sahara / Down the road / Gris gris gumbo ya ya / Mama Roux / Jump sturdy / I walk on guilded splinters / Black widow spider / Lop garoo / Wash Mama wash / Mardi gras day / Familiar reality / Opening / Zu zu mamou / Mess around / Somebody changed the lock / Iko iko / Junko partner / Tipitina / Huey Smith medley / Right place wrong time / Travelling mood / Life / Such a night / I been hoodood / Cold cold cold / Quitters never win / What comes around (goes around) / Mos' scocious / Let's make a better world / Back by the river / I wanna rock / Memories of Professor Longhair / Honey dripper / Pretty libby / Makin' whoopee / Accentuate the positive / More than you know
CD Set 8122714502
Atco / Feb '94 / Warner Music

REMEDIES
Loop garoo / What goes around / Wash Mama wash / Chippy, chippy / Mardi gras day / Angola anthem
CD 7567804392
Atco / Feb '91 / Warner Music

SUN, MOON AND HERBS, THE
Black John the conqueror / Where ya at mule / Craney crow / Familiar reality / Opening / Pots on fiyo (file gumbo) / Who I got to fall on / Zu zu mamou / Familiar reality (reprise)
CD 7567804402
Atco / Jan '89 / Warner Music

TELEVISION
Television / Lissen / Limbo / Witchy red / Only the shadow knows / Shut D Fonk up / Spaceship relationship / Hold it / Money / U lie too much / Same day service
CD GRM 40252
GRP / Jun '95 / New Note/BMG

VERY BEST OF DR. JOHN, THE
CD 9548335532
Atco / May '95 / Warner Music

VOODOO BLUES
Zu zu man / One late night / Mean cheatin' woman / Woman is the root of all evil / She's just a square / In the night / Tiptina / Shoo-ra / Bald headed / Trader John / Helpin' hand / Cat and mouse game
CD 305982
Hallmark / Jan '97 / Carlton

ZU ZU MAN
In the night / Tipitina / Grass is greener / Did she mention my name / Shoo ra / Zu zu man / One night late / She's just a square / Mean cheatin' woman / Helpin' hand
CD CDTB 069
Thunderbolt / May '89 / TKO Magnum

Dr. K's Blues Band

ROCK THE JOINT
I can't lose / Walkin' / Key to the highway / Crippled Clarence / Pet cream man / Feel so bad / Messin' with kid / Don't quit the man you love, for me / Rolty's banjo shuffle / Strobe lemming's lament / Lond distance call
CD SEECD 361
See For Miles/C5 / Oct '92 / Pinnacle

Dr. Magic

SAMPLE THIS (EVERYTHING YOU NEED)
CD WIZZD 29
Wizz / Mar '96 / Grapevine/PolyGram

Dr. Mastermind

DOCTOR MASTERMIND
Domination / Right way / Man of the year / We want the world / Control / Abuser / Black leather maniac / I don't wanna die
CD RR 9605 2
Roadrunner / Dec '87 / PolyGram

Dr. Nerve

ARMED OBSERVATION/OUT OF BOMB FRESH
CD RUNE 38X
Cuneiform / Apr '86 / ReR Megacorp

EVERY SCREAMING EAR
CD RUNE 88
Cuneiform / Jun '97 / ReR Megacorp

Dr. Numa

DR. NUMA
CD RA 012CD
Radikal Ambience / Oct '96 / Plastic Head

Dr. Octagon

DR. OCTAGON
Into / 3000 / I got to tell you / Earth people / No awareness / Technical difficulties / General hospital / Blue flowers / Visit to the gynaecologist / Bear witness / Dr. Octagon / Girl let me touch you / I'm destructive / Wild and crazy / Elective surgery / On production / Biology 101 / Waiting list
CD MW 046CD
Mo Wax / Apr '96 / PolyGram / Vital

INSTRUMENTALYST
Blue flowers / Girl let me touch you / 3000 / Mosebumps / Tricknology 101 / I'm destructive / No awareness / Waiting list / On production / Technical difficulties / Catapillar / Wild 'n' crazy / Earth people / Dr. Octagon
CD ______ **MW 064CD**
Mo Wax / Nov '96 / PolyGram / Vital

Dr. Phibes

HYPNOTWISTER (Dr. Phibes & The House Of Wax Equations)
Deadpan control freak / Real world / Anticlockwise / Moment of time / Misdiagnosedive / Hazy lazy hologram / Jugular junkie / Bearhug / Hypnotwister / Burning cross
CD ______ **CDDRP 1**
Quigley/Offside / May '93 / PolyGram

Dr. Rain

KNIFE RAN AWAY WITH THE SPOON, THE
Suzanne / Turn your head around / It hurts to see you smiling / Go for your gun / Ratlin' blue / Heaven and hell / Wasted on you / Party girl / Wonderful lowlife / Between the Devil and the deep blue sea / What's your name
CD ______ **72787210032**
RCA / Nov '92 / BMG

Dr. Robert

OTHER FOLK
CD ______ **ROOTCD 1**
Art Bus / May '97 / 3mv/Pinnacle

Dr. Rockitt

MUSIC OF SOUND
CD ______ **CLR 424CD**
Clear / Oct '96 / Prime / RTM/Disc

Dr. Space Toad Experience

DR. SPACE TOAD EXPERIENCE WITH CAP
CD ______ **BP 222CD**
Blueprint / Sep '96 / Pinnacle

Dr. Strangely Strange

KIP OF THE SERENES
Strangely strange but oddly normal / Dr. Dim and Dr. Strange / Roy Rogers / Dark haired lady / On the West Cork hack / Tale of two orphanages / Strings in the earth and air / Ship of fools / Frosty mornings / Donnybrook fair
CD ______ **3DCID1004**
Island / Jul '92 / PolyGram

Dracul

DIE HAND GOTTES
CD ______ **DW 078CD**
Deathwish / Dec '96 / Plastic Head

Dragon

FALLEN ANGEL
CD ______ **CDFLAG 48**
Under One Flag / Oct '90 / Pinnacle

Dragonfly

DRAGONFLY
CD ______ **842970**
EVA / May '94 / ADA / Direct

Dragonsfire

ROYAL ARRAY, A
Sumer is y-cumen in / Earl of Salisbury's Pavan and Galliard / Boar's head carol / Courtly capers: English dance tunes / Greensleeves / Come again - Sweet love doth now invite / Agincourt song / Woods so wilde / Now is the month of Maying / Blame not my lute / Ampleforth / Green grow'th the holly
CD ______ **URCD 102**
Upbeat / Jul '90 / Cadillac / Target/BMG

Drags

DRAGSPLOITATION
CD ______ **ES 110CD**
Estrus / Nov '95 / Cargo / Greyhound / Plastic Head

Drain

HORROR WRESTLING
CD ______ **0630137742**
East West / Apr '96 / Warner Music

OFFSPEED AND IN THERE
CD ______ **TR 49CD**
Trance / Apr '96 / SRD

Drain Bramaged

HAPPY DRUNX
CD ______ **KNR 117**
Know / Jun '97 / Cargo / Greyhound

Draiocht

DRUID & THE DREAMER, THE
CD ______ **CBM 006CD**
Cross Border Media / Oct '93 / ADA / Direct / Grapevine/PolyGram

Drake, Bob

LITTLE BLACK TRAIN
Charge / No title / Conductor / Leach field coyote / Dust bowl / Haunted land / Unlit galaxies / Outside influences / Graveyard variations / Unattended funeral / Shed, cans / Glory / Ends of time / Same old story / Little nameless Sonata
CD ______ **CTA 6**
Crumbling Tomes Archive / Jun '97 / ReR Megacorp / RTM/Disc

Drake, Nick

BRYTER LAYTER
Introduction / Hazey Jane / At the chime of the city clock / One of these things first / Hazey Jane / Bryter layter / Fly / Poor boy / Northern sky / Sunday
CD ______ **IMCD 71**
Island / '89 / PolyGram

FIVE LEAVES LEFT
Time has told me / River man / Three hours / Day is done / Way to blue / Cello song / Thoughts of Mary Jane / Man in a shed / Fruit tree / Saturday Sun
CD ______ **IMCD 8**
Island / '89 / PolyGram

FRUIT TREE (4CD Set)
CD Set ______ **HNCD 5402**
Hannibal / Jun '96 / ADA / Vital

PINK MOON
Pink moon / Place to be / Road / Which will / Horn / Things behind the sun / Know / Parasite / Ride / Harvest breed / From the morning
CD ______ **IMCD 94**
Island / Feb '90 / PolyGram

TIME OF NO REPLY
Joey / Clothes of sand / May fair / I was made to love magic / Strange meetings II / Been smoking too long
CD ______ **HNCD 1318**
Hannibal / May '89 / ADA / Vital

WAY TO BLUE (An Introduction To Nick Drake)
Cello song / Hazey Jane / Way to blue / Things behind the sun / River man / Poor boy / Time of no reply / From the morning / One of these things first / Northern sky / Which will / Time has told me / Pink moon / Black eyed dog / Fruit tree
CD ______ **IMCD 196**
Island / May '94 / PolyGram

Drake, Tony

TEXTURE
Birth of love / These lips of gold / This is how much I love you / Cherish / Strangest dream / One / Haunting / In the hearts of angels / Night descends / Moisture/After the moment / These moments fade / Love's release / Texture
CD ______ **ELECTM 30CD**
New Electronica / Nov '96 / Beechwood/ BMG / Plastic Head

Dramarama

10 FROM 5
Work for food / What are we gonna do / Last cigarette / Haven't got a clue / Shadowless heart / Some crazy dame / Would you like / Memo to Turner / It's still warm / Work for food (acoustic version)
CD ______ **3705615842**
Chameleon / Sep '93 / Warner Music

BOX OFFICE BOMB
Steve and Edie / New dream / Whenever I'm with her / Spare change / 400 blows / Pumpin (my heart) / It's still warm / Out in the rain / Baby rhino's eye / Worse than being by myself / Modesty personified
CD ______ **ROSE 138CD**
New Rose / Jan '88 / ADA / Direct / Discovery

CINEMA VERITE
CD ______ **ROSE 74CD**
New Rose / Nov '85 / ADA / Direct / Discovery

Dramatics

ABC YEARS 1974-1980
CD ______ **SCL 2108**
Ichiban Soul Classics / Dec '95 / Koch

BEST OF THE DRAMATICS, THE
Get up and get down / Thank you for your love / Whatcha see is whatcha get / In the rain / (Gimme some) good soul music / Fall in love, lady love / Devil is dope / You could become the very heart of me / Fell for you / Hey you get off my mountain / Beware the man with the candy in his hand / And I panicked / I dedicate my life to you / I made myself lonely / Highway to heaven / Toast to the fool
CD ______ **CDSXD 115**
Stax / Jul '97 / Pinnacle

WHATCHA SEE IS WHATCHA GET/ DRAMATIC EXPERIENCE, A
Get up and get down / Thank you for your love / Hot pants in the summertime / What'cha see is what'cha get / In the rain / Good soul music / Fall in love, lady love / Mary don't cha wanna / Devil is dope / You could become the very heart of me / Now you got me loving you / Fell for you / Jim, what's wrong with him / Hey you get off my mountain / Beautiful people / Beware of the man (with the candy in his hand)
CD ______ **CDSXD 963**
Stax / Jan '91 / Pinnacle

Drambuie Kirkliston Pipe Band

LINK WITH THE '45
King has landed in Moidart / Glenfinnan highland gathering / March of the Cameron men / Johnny Cope / Southward bound / Wae's me for Prince Charlie / Forty five revolution / Link with the '45 / Young pretender / White rose of Culloden / Skye boat song / Fugitive / Tribute to the lost souls / Will ye no' come back again
CD ______ **CDTRAX 084**
Greentrax / Apr '95 / ADA / Direct / Duncans / Highlander

Drame, Adama

30 YEARS OF DJEMBE
CD ______ **PS 65177**
PlayaSound / Dec '96 / ADA / Harmonia Mundi

MANDINGO DRUMS
CD ______ **PS 65085**
PlayaSound / Apr '92 / ADA / Harmonia Mundi

MANDINGO DRUMS VOL.2 (Drame, Adama & Foliba)
CD ______ **PS 65122**
PlayaSound / Feb '94 / ADA / Harmonia Mundi

Dranes, Arizona

ARIZONA DRANES 1926-1929
CD ______ **DOCD 5186**
Document / Oct '93 / ADA / Hot Shot / Jazz Music

Dransfield

FIDDLER'S DREAM
Up to now / Blacksmith / Alchemist and the pedlar / It's dark in here / Handsome meadow boy / Fool's song / Ballad of Dickie Lubber / Blacksmith / What will we tell them / Violin
CD ______ **ESMCD 462**
Transatlantic / Jan '97 / Pinnacle

Dransfield, Barry

BE YOUR OWN MAN
I once was a fisherman / John Barleycorn / Jezebel waltz / Farewell to Hong Kong/Mrs Wong's / Bonny boy / Grey funnel line / Be your own man / Derby ram / Water is wide / La fete de fancy / One for Jo / You can't change me now / Gossip Joan / Festus Burke / Bonny bunch of roses / Lily Bulero / Friendship reel/Welly reel / Daddy fox
CD ______ **RHYD 5003**
Rhiannon / Oct '94 / ADA / Direct / Vital

WINGS OF THE SPHINX
Byker hill / Bunch of keys / Paddy of the Turnpike / Recruited collier / Gypsy Davey / Wings of the sphinx / Irish session / Queen of hearts / Cat and the fiddler / Perfect earth / Favourite quick march / Italian dance / Week before easter / Thousands or more / Lament for a passing / Angel / Mermaid / Sheebeg sheemore
CD ______ **RHYD 5010**
Rhiannon / Jul '96 / ADA / Direct / Vital

Dransfield, Robin

UP TO NOW (A History Of Robin & Barry Dransfield/2CD Set) (Dransfield, Robin & Barry)
Rout of the blues / Trees they do grow high / Morpeth rant/Nancy / Lord of all I behold / Bold Nelson's praise/Princess Royal/Saddle the pony / Werewolf / Girl of dances / Cuckoo's nest / Up to now / Blacksmith / Alchemist and the pedlar / It's dark in here / Handsome meadow boy / Fool's song / Ballad of Dickie Lubber / What will we tell them / Violin / You can't change me now / Talcahuano girls / Conscript's farewell / Bogie's bonnie belle / Sligo fancy/Coleman's two halves / Seeds of love / Peggy Gordon / Banks of the sweet Dundee / Holmfirth anthem / Two ravens / Good ale for my money / Doctor Slime / Too much to do / Catch the morning dew / Fiddler's progress / O'Carolan's concerto / Tidewave / Spencer the rover / Be your own man / Daddy fox / Week before Easter / Irish session
CD Set ______ **FRDCD 18**
Free Reed / Jun '97 / ADA / CM / Direct

Drax

TALES FROM THE MENTAL PLANE
CD ______ **TROPE 013**
Trope / May '95 / Plastic Head / Vital

Drayton, Luce

SUICIDAL ANGEL
Dreamer / I said hey / Drown in you / Holding on alone / What about sky / Bitter blisters / La la la / All in vain / To be loved / Tears of our youth / Kiss the blues goodbye
CD ______ **0097984WHE**
What So Ever / Jul '97 / Total/BMG

Dread & Fred

IRON WORKS VOL.3
CD ______ **SHAKA 937CD**
Jah Shaka / Mar '94 / Jet Star / SRD

Dread Flimstone

FROM THE GHETTO (Dread Flimstone & Modern Tone Age Family)
From the ghetto / Into u / Sitting / Knowledge / Tribute / fantasy / Justice / Roots / Slackness / Police
CD ______ **5108702**
Acid Jazz/FFRR / Nov '91 / PolyGram

Dread Knight

ELECTRONIC BAND
CD ______ **TASTE 60CD**
Taste / Aug '95 / Plastic Head / SRD

Dread Zone

360 DEGREES
CD ______ **CRECD 162**
Creation / Oct '93 / 3mv/Vital

PERFORMANCE DEADZONE...LIVE
CD ______ **TTPCD 002**
Totem / Oct '94 / Grapevine/PolyGram / THE

Dreadful Shadows

BURIED AGAIN
CD ______ **DW 27631**
Deathwish / Apr '97 / Plastic Head

ESTRANGEMENT
CD ______ **SPV 08423612**
SPV / Jul '94 / Koch / Plastic Head

Dreadful Snakes

SNAKES ALIVE
CD ______ **ROUCD 177**
Rounder / Jun '95 / ADA / CM / Direct

Dreadline

BRAVEDANCES
CD ______ **CDSGP 0212**
Prestige / Sep '96 / Else / Total/BMG

Dreadzone

BIOLOGICAL RADIO
Biological radio / Moving on / Third wave / Lost tribe / Earth angel / Messengers / Heat the pot / Alli Baba / Dream within a dream
CD ______ **CDV 2808**
Virgin / Jul '97 / EMI

SECOND LIGHT
Life, love and unity / Little Britain / Canterbury tale / Captain Dread / Cave of angels / Zion youth / One way / Shining path / Out of heaven
CD ______ **CDV 2778**
Virgin / May '95 / EMI

Dream

DREAM, THE
CD ______ **REVXD 143**
Black / Apr '90 / Revolver / Sony

Dream Academy

DREAM ACADEMY
Life in a northern town / Edge of forever / Johnny new light / In places on the run / This world / Bound to be / Moving on / Love parade / Party / One dream
CD ______ **7599252652**
Blanco Y Negro / Jan '96 / Warner Music

Dream City Film Club

DREAM CITY FILM CLUB
Night of nights / Shit tinted shades / Pissboy / Because you wanted it / Filth dealer / Mama / Porno Paradiso / Situation desperate / Perfect piece of trash / Vague / If I die / 'Til the end of the world
CD ______ **BBQCD 191**
Beggars Banquet / Jun '97 / RTM/Disc / Warner Music

Dream Disciples

CURE FOR PAIN, A
CD ______ **CR 00303CD**
Resurrection / Oct '96 / Plastic Head

VEIL OF TEARS
CD ______ **0020CR001**
Carrion / Sep '96 / Pinnacle / Plastic Head

Dream Machine

STEPS
CD ______ **MSECD 013**
Mouse / Jun '95 / Grapevine/PolyGram

Dream Sequence

ENDLESS REFLECTION (Dream Sequence & Blake Baxter)
CD ________ EFA 017802
Tresor / Jun '95 / 3mv/BMG / Prime / SRD

Dream State

CLOCKWORK MANNEQUIN
Mannequin man / Alive in the rain / Innocence / Highway / Spirit in you / Rampage / My friend / Operator
CD ________ ZUCD 1
Zukris / Mar '97 / Else

Dream Syndicate

3 & 1/2
CD ________ NORM 156CD
Normal / Nov '93 / ADA / Direct

DAY BEFORE WINE AND ROSES, THE
CD ________ NORMAL 176CD
Normal / Dec '94 / ADA / Direct

DREAM SYNDICATE
Sure thing / That's what you always say / When you smile / Some kinda itch
CD ________ VEXCD 10
Demon / Jul '92 / Pinnacle

GHOST STORIES
Side I'll never show / Loving the sinner, hating the sin / Weathered and torn / I have faith / Black / My old haunts / Whatever you please / See that my grave is kept clean / Someplace better than this / When the curtain falls
CD ________ 727582
Restless / Sep '95 / Vital

LIVE AT RAJI'S
Still holding on to you / Forest for the trees / Until lately / That's what you always say / Burn / Merrittville / Days of wine and roses / Medicine show / Halloween / Boston / John Coltrane stereo blues
CD ________ FIENDCD 176
Demon / Apr '90 / Pinnacle

LOST TAPES 1985-88, THE
CD ________ NORMAL 156CD
Normal / Mar '94 / ADA / Direct

OUT OF THE GREY
Out of the grey / Forest for the trees / 50 in a 25 zone / Boston / Blood money / Slide away / Dying embers / Now I ride alone / Drinking problem / Dancing blind / You can't forget / Let it rain / Cinnamon girl / Ballad of Dwight Frye / Shake your hips / I won't forget / Lonely bull
CD ________ NORMAL 184CD
Normal / Jul '97 / ADA / Direct

Dream Team

DRUM 'N' BASS WORLD SERIES, THE
12 am / Suka DJ / Time / Check the tekniq / Switch / Dedicated / Rollin' raw / Survival of the fit / Mad / Insane / Click
CD ________ JOK 25CD
Joker / Feb '97 / SRD

Dream Theater

AWAKE
Lie / 6:00 / Erotomania / Silent man / Lifting shadows off a dream / Scarred / Innocence faded / Mirror / Voices / Caught in a web / Space-dye vest
CD ________ 7567901262
Atlantic / Oct '94 / Warner Music

CHANGE OF SEASON, A
CD ________ 7559618422
Atlantic / Sep '95 / Warner Music

IMAGES AND WORDS
Pull me under / Another day / Take the time / Surrounded / Metropolis / Miracle and the sleeper / Under a glass moon / Wait for sleep / Learning to live
CD ________ 7567921482
Atlantic / Feb '92 / Warner Music

LIVE AT THE MARQUEE
Metropolis / Miracle and the sleeper / Fortune in lies / Bombay vindaloo / Surrounded / Pull me under / Killing hand / Another hand
CD ________ 7567922862
Atlantic / Feb '92 / Warner Music

Dream Warriors

AND NOW THE LEGACY BEGINS
Mr. Bibbinut spills his guts / My definition of a boombastic jazz style / Follow me not / Ludi / U never know a good thing till u lose it / And the legacy begins / Tune from the missing channel / Wash your face in my sink / Voyage through the multiverse / U could get arrested / Journey on / Face in the basin / Do not feed the alligators / Twelve sided dance / Maximum 60 lost in a dream
CD ________ IMCD 204
Island / Apr '95 / PolyGram

MASTER PLAN, THE
Fear none / Era of 'stay real' / Here today gone tomorrow / Sound clash / Master plan / Float on / What do you want 'ladies' / From the beginning / Test of purity / Luvz history lesson / Dem no ready / Who's the crook / First ya live / Times are changing / Sound clash
CD ________ CTCD 56
Cooltempo / Jan '97 / EMI

Dreamcatcher

DREAMCATCHER
CD ________ CIDM 1118
Mango / May '97 / PolyGram / Vital

Dreamfish

DREAMFISH
CD ________ RSNCD 9
Rising High / Sep '93 / 3mv/Sony

Dreamgrinder

AGENTS OF THE MIND
CD ________ CDBLEED 15
Bleeding Hearts / Nov '95 / Pinnacle

Dreamlovers

BEST OF THE DREAMLOVERS, THE
CD ________ NEMCD 673
Sequel / May '94 / BMG

Dreams Of Ireland

22 SONGS OF HOME
CD ________ PLATCD 3930
Platinum / May '94 / Prism

Dreamside

APAIKA
CD ________ DW 098CD
Deathwish / Apr '96 / Plastic Head

PALE BLUE LIGHTS
CD ________ DW 0732
Deathwish / Jan '95 / Plastic Head

Dremmwel

HEOL LOAR
CD ________ 862CD
Escalibur / Nov '96 / ADA / Discovery / Roots

Dresher, Paul

OPPOSITES ATTRACT
CD ________ 804112
New World / Aug '92 / ADA / Cadillac / Harmonia Mundi

Dresser, Mark

CABINET OF DR. CALIGARI
CD ________ KFWCD 155
Knitting Factory / Feb '95 / Cargo / Plastic Head

FORCE GREEN
CD ________ 1212732
Soul Note / Jan '96 / Cadillac / Harmonia Mundi / Wellard

INVOCATION
CD ________ KFWCD 173
Knitting Factory / Oct '96 / Cargo / Plastic Head

Drever, Ivan

FOUR WALLS
Ballad of Jimmy Fry / Catching the dream / Timmer the Tartar / Colonel Sir Neil Macrae of Howden end / How far / Called to fire / Christy Jane Drever / We sometimes hurt too / Kinnairdie's awa wi' the geese / John Boocock's reel / Brave souls / Braes O'Gleniffer
CD ________ IRCD 037
Iona / Jul '96 / ADA / Direct / Duncans

Drew, Kenny

AND FAR AWAY (Drew, Kenny Quartet)
CD ________ SNCD 1081
Soul Note / Jan '86 / Cadillac / Harmonia Mundi / Wellard

KENNY DREW & NIELS-HENNING ORSTED PEDERSON (Drew, Kenny & Niels-Henning Orsted Pederson)
CD ________ STCD 8274
Storyville / May '96 / Cadillac / Jazz Music / Wellard

KENNY DREW TRIO (Drew, Kenny Trio)
CD ________ OJCCD 65
Original Jazz Classics / Nov '95 / Complete/Pinnacle / Jazz Music / Wellard

MORNING
CD ________ SCCD 31048
Steeplechase / Jul '88 / Discovery / Impetus

TALKIN' AND WALKIN'
CD ________ CDP 7844392
Blue Note / Feb '97 / EMI

YOUR SOFT EYES (Drew, Kenny Trio)
CD ________ SNCD 1031
Soul Note / Jan '86 / Cadillac / Harmonia Mundi / Wellard

Drew, Kenny Jr.

LIVE AT MAYBECK RECITAL HALL VOL.39
Stella by starlight / Peace / After you / Ugly beauty / Well you needn't / Coral sea / Images / Straight no chaser / Waitin' for my dearie / Autumn leaves
CD ________ CCD 4653
Concord Jazz / Jul '95 / New Note/Pinnacle

LOOK INSIDE, A
CD ________ 5142112
Antilles/New Directions / Feb '94 / PolyGram

Drew, Ronnie

COLLECTION, THE
CD ________ CHCD 1053
Chyme / Feb '95 / ADA / CM / Direct / Koch

IRISH ROVER, THE
CD ________ CDRONNIE 001
Outlet / Mar '97 / ADA / CM / Direct / Duncans / Koch / Ross

DRI

4 OF A KIND
CD ________ 398417012CD
Metal Blade / May '96 / Pinnacle / Plastic Head

CROSSOVER
CD ________ ROTCD 2092
Rotten / Nov '95 / Plastic Head

DEALING WITH IT
Snap / Marriage / Counter attack / Nursing home blues / Give my taxes back / Equal people / Bail out / Evil minds / I'd rather be sleeping / Yes ma'am / God is broke / I don't need society / Explorer / On my way home / Argument the war / Slit my wrists
CD ________ ROTCD 2091
Rotten / Nov '95 / Plastic Head

DEFINITION
CD ________ ROTCD 2093
Rotten / Nov '95 / Plastic Head

DIRTY ROTTEN
CD ________ ROTCD 001
Rotten / Nov '95 / Plastic Head

FOUR OF A KIND
All for nothing / Manifest destiny / Gone too long / Do the dream / Shut up / Modern world / Think for yourself / Slumlord / Dead in a ditch / Suit and the guy / Man unkind
CD ________ CDMZORRO 46
Metal Blade / Aug '92 / Pinnacle / Plastic Head

FULL SPEED AHEAD
CD ________ ROTCD 2099
Rotten / Nov '95 / Plastic Head

THRASH ZONE
CD ________ 398147002CD
Metal Blade / Oct '95 / Pinnacle / Plastic Head

Dribbling Darts

PRESENT PERFECT
CD ________ FNCD 247
Flying Nun / Jul '94 / RTM/Disc

Drift Pioneer

METAL ELF BOY
CD ________ TEQM 95004
TEQ / Jun '97 / Cargo / Plastic Head

Drifters

70'S CLASSICS
Kissin' in the back row of the movies / You're more than a number in my little black book / Hello happiness / Like sister and brother / There goes my first love / Sweet Caroline / Harlem child / Like a movie I've seen before / Songs we used to sing / Love games / Down on the beach tonight / Every night's a Saturday night with you / Can I take you home little girl / Anothe lonely weekend / Summer in the city / Midnight cowboy
CD ________ MCCD 100
Music Club / Mar '93 / Disc / THE

BEST OF THE DRIFTERS, THE
CD ________ 74321265062
RCA / Aug '95 / BMG

BOOGIE WOOGIE ROLL (Greatest Hits 1953-1958)
CD ________ 7567819272
Atlantic / Mar '95 / Warner Music

CLYDE MCPHATTER & THE DRIFTERS (McPhatter, Clyde & The Drifters)
Honey love / Money honey / Someday (you'll want me to want you) / Such a night / Bells of St. Mary's / Warm your heart / Whatcha gonna do / White Christmas / Lucille / Way I feel / Gone / Let the boogie woogie roll / Don't dog me / Bip bam / If I didn't love you like I do / There you go / Try try baby / Everyone's laughing / Hot ziggety / Three thirty three
CD ________ RSACD 803
Sequel / Sep '96 / BMG

COLLECTION, THE
CD ________ 74321292762
RCA / Jul '95 / BMG

DRIFTERS COLLECTION, THE
CD ________ COL 011
Collection / Jun '95 / Target/BMG

DRIFTERS COLLECTION, THE
Under the boardwalk / I count the tears / Up on the roof / Please stay / On Broadway / When my little girl is smiling / (If you cry) True love true love / There goes my baby / This magic moment / Some kind of wonderful / Dance with me / Save the last dance for me / Sweets for my sweet / Saturday night at the movies / Stand by me: *King, Ben E.* / Spanish Harlem: *King, Ben E.*
CD ________ PLATCD 175
Platinum / Mar '96 / Prism

DRIFTERS, THE
CD ________ LECD 039
Dynamite / May '94 / THE

DRIFTERS, THE
On Broadway / Save the last dance for me / Dance with me / There goes my baby / Up on the roof / Under the boardwalk / This magic moment / Please stay / Sweets for my sweet / Some kind of wonderful / Third rate romance / Night moves / Another Saturday night / I can help / Cupid / Any day now / Wonderful world / Bring it on home to me / Stand by me / Short people
CD ________ QED 039
Tring / Nov '96 / Tring

ESSENTIAL COLLECTION, THE
CD Set ________ LECD 620
Wisepack / Apr '95 / Conifer/BMG / THE

GOOD LIFE WITH THE DRIFTERS, THE
What kind of fool am I / I wish you love / More / Tonight / On the street where you live / Who can I turn to / Quando quando quando / Desafinado / As long as she needs me / Good life / Temptation / Christmas song / I remember Christmas / In the park / Looking through the eyes of love
CD ________ RSACD 835
Sequel / Sep '96 / BMG

GREATEST
Hello happiness / Kissin' in the back row of the movies / Always something there to remind me / Every night / Sweet Caroline / If it feels good do it / Save the last dance for me / There goes my first love / Like sister and brother / I can't live without you / Harlem child / You've got your troubles / Love games / Down on the beach tonight
CD ________ CDMFP 5734
Music For Pleasure / Oct '91 / EMI

GREATEST HITS
CD ________ CDSGP 0153
Prestige / Apr '95 / Else / Total/BMG

GREATEST HITS
Save the last dance for me / Dance with me / Sweets for my sweet / Three times a lady / There goes my baby / This magic moment / Under the boardwalk / Some kind of wonderful / On Broadway / Medley / Up on the roof / Saturday night at the movies / Stand by me / My way / Spanish Harlem / I do believe I'm falling in love / Plain, simple but sweet / Feelings
CD ________ 100382
CMC / May '97 / BMG

GREATEST HITS AND MORE 1959-1965
There goes my baby / Oh my love / Baltimore / Hey senorita / Dance with me / (If you cry) True love, true love / This magic moment / Lonely winds / Nobody but me / Save the last dance for me / I count the tears / Sometimes I wonder / Please stay / Room full of tears / Sweets for my sweet / Some kind of wonderful / Loneliness of happiness / Mexican divorce / Somebody new dancing with you / Jackpot / She never talked to me that way / When my little girl is smiling / Stranger on the shore / What to do / Up on the roof / Another night with the boys / I feel good all over / Let the music play / On Broadway / I'll take you home / If you don't come back / Didn't it / One way love / He's just a playboy / Under the Boardwalk / I don't want to go on without you / I've got sand in my shoes / Saturday night at the movies / At the club / Come on over to my place
CD ________ 7567819312
Atlantic / Jul '93 / Warner Music

I'LL TAKE YOU WHERE THE MUSIC'S PLAYING
I'll take you where the music's playing / Nylon stockings / We gotta sing / Up in the streets of Harlem / Memories are made of this / You can't love them all / My islands in the sun / Aretha / Baby what I mean / Ain't it the truth / Up jumped the devil / Still burning in my heart / I need you now / Country to the city / Your best friend / Steal away / Black silk / You've got to pay your dues / Rose by any other name / Be my lady / It takes a good woman
CD ________ RSACD 836
Sequel / Nov '96 / BMG

ON BROADWAY
CD ________ 15074
Laserlight / Aug '92 / Target/BMG

PACKET OF THREE VOL.1 (3CD Set) (Drifters/James Brown/Bob Marley & The Wailers)
Under the Boardwalk: *Drifters* / True love: *Drifters* / My girl: *Drifters* / Up on the roof: *Drifters* / Save the last dance for me: *Drifters* / There goes my baby: *Drifters* / Please stay: *Drifters* / This magic moment: *Drifters* / Another Saturday night: *Drifters* / Sweets for my sweet: *Drifters* / Unchained melody: *Drifters* / Saturday night at the movies: *Drifters* / Cupid: *Drifters* / On Broadway: *Drifters* / Third rate romance: *Drifters* / Summertime: *Drifters* / Night moves: *Drifters* / I can help: *Drifters* / Dance with me: *Drifters* / Short people: *Drifters* / Give it up or turn it loose: *Brown, James* / It's too funky in here: *Brown, James* / Try me: *Brown, James* / (Get up I feel like being a) sex machine: *Brown, James* / Get on the good foot: *Brown, James* / Georgia on my mind: *Brown, James* / Hot pants: *Brown, James* / I got the feeling: *Brown, James* / It's a man's man's man's world: *Brown, James* / Cold sweat: *Brown, James* / I can't stand myself: *Brown, James* / Papa's got a brand new bag: *Brown, James* / I got you (I feel good): *Brown, James* / Please please please: *Brown, James* / Body heat: *Brown, James* / Jam: *Brown, James* / Soul rebel: *Marley, Bob & The Wailers* / Try me: *Marley, Bob & The Wailers* / It's alright: *Marley, Bob & The Wailers* / My cup: *Marley, Bob & The Wailers* / Corner stone: *Marley, Bob & The Wailers* / No water: *Marley, Bob & The Wailers* / There she goes: *Marley, Bob & The Wailers* / Mellow wood: *Marley, Bob & The Wailers* / Treat you right: *Marley, Bob & The Wailers* / Caution: *Marley, Bob & The Wailers* / Mr. Brown: *Marley, Bob & The Wailers* / Duppy conqueror: *Marley, Bob & The Wailers* / Small axe: *Marley, Bob & The Wailers* / Rebel's hop: *Marley, Bob & The Wailers* / African herbsman: *Marley, Bob & The Wailers* / Sun is shining: *Marley, Bob & The Wailers* / Brain washing: *Marley, Bob & The Wailers* / All in one: *Marley, Bob & The Wailers* / Stand alone: *Marley, Bob & The Wailers*
CD Set ____ **KLMCD 301**
BAM / Nov '96 / Koch / Scratch/BMG

PEARLS FROM THE PAST
CD ____ **KLMCD 008**
BAM / Nov '93 / Koch / Scratch/BMG

ROCKIN' AND DRIFTIN'
Moonlight bay / Ruby baby / Drip drop / I got to get myself a woman / Fools fall in love / Hypnotized / Yodee Yakee / I know / Soldier of fortune / Drifting away from you / Your promise to be mine / It was a tear / Adorable / Steamboat / Honey bee / I should have done right / No sweet lovin' / Honky tonk / Sadie my lady / Souvenirs / Suddenly there's a valley / On bended knee: *Pinkney Flyers* / My only desires: *Pinkney Flyers*
CD ____ **RSACD 815**
Sequel / Nov '96 / BMG

SAVE THE LAST DANCE FOR ME
CD ____ **AVC 511**
Avid / Dec '92 / Avid/BMG / Koch / THE

SAVE THE LAST DANCE FOR ME
CD ____ **MACCD 156**
Autograph / Aug '96 / BMG

SAVE THE LAST DANCE FOR ME
Dance with me / Baltimore / Hey Senorita / Lonely winds / Oh my love / There goes my baby / This magic moment / (If you cry) true love, true love / Sometimes I wonder / I count the tears / I feel good all over / Save the last dance for me / Nobody but me / Roomfull of tears / Sweets for my sweet / When my little girl is smiling / Night shift / Lonely winds
CD ____ **RSACD 817**
Sequel / Sep '96 / BMG

SPOTLIGHT ON DRIFTERS
Under the boardwalk / I count the tears / Up on the roof / Please stay / On Broadway / When my little girl is smiling / (If you cry) true love, true love / There goes my baby / This magic moment / Some kind of wonderful / Dance with me / Save the last dance for me / Sweets for my sweet / Saturday night at the movies
CD ____ **HADCD 122**
Javelin / Feb '94 / Henry Hadaway / THE

UNDER THE BOARDWALK
Under the boardwalk / Please stay / Twist / Some kinda wonderful / My girl / Sand in my shoes / This magic moment / I count the tears / Money honey / True, true love / Honey love / When my little girl is smiling / On broadway / Dance with me / Lonely winds / There goes my baby / Sweets for my sweet / Save the last dance for me
CD ____ **MUCD 9016**
Musketeer / Apr '95 / Disc

UNDER THE BOARDWALK
If you don't come back / I'll take you home / Didn't I / One way love / Under the boardwalk / He's just a playboy / I don't want to go without you / I've got sand in my shoes / Saturday night at the movies / Under the boardwalk / On Broadway / There goes my baby / Spanish lace / At the club / Answer the phone / Saturday night at the movies / Under the boardwalk / Follow me / Chains of love / Far from the maddening crowd / Come on over to my place / Outside place
CD ____ **RSACD 834**
Sequel / Nov '96 / BMG

UP ON THE ROOF
Please stay / Some kind of wonderful / Loneliness or happiness / Mexican divorce / Somebody new dancing with you / Jackpot / She never talked to me that way / Stranger on the shore / What to do / Another night with the boys / Up on the roof / Let the music play / On Broadway / I don't want nobody: *Lewis, Rudy* / Baby I dig love: *Lewis, Rudy* / Only in America / Rat race / In the land of make believe / Beautiful music / Vaya con dios
CD ____ **RSACD 833**
Sequel / Sep '96 / BMG

VERY BEST OF THE DRIFTERS
CD ____ **8122712112**
Atlantic / Jun '93 / Warner Music

VERY BEST OF THE DRIFTERS, THE
Save the last dance for me / There goes my first love / Kissin' in the back row of the movies / Down on the beach tonight / Like sister and brother / Can I take you home little girl / You're more than a number in my little red book / Every night's a Saturday night with you / Sweet Caroline / Love games / Harlem child / Summer in the city / Songs we used to sing / Something tells me (something's gonna happen tonight) / If only I could start again / Another lonely weekend / Midnight cowboy / Always something there to remind me / Don't cry on the weekend / Hello happiness
CD ____ **74321446742**
Camden / Feb '97 / BMG

Driftwood, Jimmie

AMERICANA
Unfortunate man / Fair Rosamund's bower / Soldier's joy / Country boy / I'm too young to marry / Pretty Mary / Sailor man / Zelma Lee / Rattlesnake song / Old Joe Clark / Tennesee stud / Razor back steak / First covered wagon / Maid of Argenta / Bunker Hill / Song of the cowboys / Peter Francisco / Four little girls in Boston / Slack your rope, hangman / Run Johnny run / Arkansas traveller / Damn Yankee lad / Chalamette / Battle of New Orleans / Land where the bluegrass grows / Widders of Bowling green / Get along boys / Sweet Betsy from pike / Shoot the buffalo / Song of the pioneer / I'm leavin' on the wagon train / Jordan am a hard road to travel / Marshall of Silver City / Wilderness road / Pony express / Mooshatonio / Shanty in the holler / Big river man / Big John Davy / On top of Pikes peak / Fi di diddle um-a-dazey / Song of creation / Battle of San Juan hill / Banjer pickin' man / Tucumcari / St. Brendan's Isle / He had a long chain on / Big Hoss / Sal's got a sugar lip / Ox driving song / General Custer / What was your name in the States / Billy the kid / Jesse James / Billy Yank and Johnny Reb / Won't you come along and go / Rock of Chickamauga / How do you like the army / Git along little yearlings / Oh Florie / I'm a poor rebel soldier / My black bird has gone / Goodbye Reb, you'all come / On top of Shiloh's hill / When I swim the Golden River / Giant of the Thunderhead / Shanghai'd / Santy Anny O-Roe / Bullies Row / Land of the Amazon / What could I do / Driftwood at sea / In a cotton shirt and a pair of dungarees / Davy Jones (Song of a dead soldier) / Sailor, sailor marry me / Diver boy / Ship that never returned / Sailing away on the ocean / John Paul Jones / Bear flew over the ocean
CD Set ____ **BCD 15465**
Bear Family / Apr '92 / Direct / Rollercoaster / Swift

Drill

PAROXYSM
CD ____ **BLOODCD 002**
Retribution / Oct '94 / Plastic Head

SKIN DOWN
CD ____ **ABT 092 CD**
Abstract / May '91 / Cargo / Pinnacle / Total/BMG

Driller Killer

BRUTALIZED
CD ____ **DISTCD 8**
Distortion / Jun '94 / Plastic Head

FUCK THE WORLD
CD ____ **KRONH 006CD**
Osmose / Apr '97 / Plastic Head

LIFE
CD ____ **DISTEP 20**
Distortion / Nov '95 / Plastic Head

Drink Small

BLUES DOCTOR, THE
Tittie man / Little red rooster / So bad / Something in the milk ain't clean / Rub my belly / Baby leave your panties home / Stormy Monday blues / I'm gonna move to the outskirts of town / John Henry Ford
CD ____ **ICH 1062CD**
Ichiban / Oct '93 / Direct / Koch

ROUND TWO
DUI / Steal away / Thank you, pretty baby / Don't let nobody know / Widow woman / I'm tired now / Honky tonk / They can't make me hate you / Bishopville women / Can I come over tonight
CD ____ **ICH 9009CD**
Ichiban / Jun '94 / Direct / Koch

Driscoll, Julie

1969
CD ____ **OW 30013**
One Way / Sep '94 / ADA / Direct / Greyhound

Driscoll, Phil

CLASSIC HYMNS
CD ____ **MHD 001**
Nelson Word / Jan '89 / Nelson Word

Drisket

CELTIC HARP
Plangstigh Ewen / Dainty davie / Dime ramo verdi / Iona / Sun and shadow / Vincenta / Enezen du / Plantxy / George brabazon / Vieux chateau sous la lune / Boulavogue / King william's march / Dafydd y garreg wen / Pardon sant fiakr / Piljadur ha displijadur
CD ____ **ANT 016**
Tring / Nov '96 / Tring

Drive Like Jehu

YANK CRIME
CD ____ **ELM 22CD**
Elemental / May '94 / RTM/Disc

Drive, She Said

DRIVE SHE SAID
If this is love / Don't you know / Love has no pride / Hold on / I close my eyes / Hard way home / But for you / Maybe it's love / If I told you / As she touches me
CD ____ **CDMFN 100**
Music For Nations / Apr '90 / Pinnacle

DRIVIN' SHE SAID
CD ____ **CDMFN 118**
Music For Nations / Sep '91 / Pinnacle

EXCELLERATOR
CD ____ **CDMFN 149**
Music For Nations / Oct '93 / Pinnacle

Driver, Betty

GIRL FROM THE STREET, THE
I'll take romance / I fall in love with you every day / Moon remembered / I'm getting sentimental over you / What goes on here in my heart / With you / So little time / Red maple leaves / Sweetest song in the world / Twitterpated / World will sing again / Sailor with the navy blue eyes/It's spring again/ Potato Pete / Swing bugler / We mustn't miss the last bus home / What more can I say/Booglie wooglie piggy/Rose O'Day / Red silken stockings / Dreamer's holiday / Leprechaun lullaby / Bullfrog (samba)
CD ____ **CDMFP 6209**
Music For Pleasure / Feb '96 / EMI

D'Rivera, Paquito

LA HABANA
CD ____ **MES 158202**
Messidor / Nov '92 / ADA / Koch

REUNION (D'Rivera, Paquito & Arturo Sandoval)
Mambo influenciado / Reunion / Tanga / Claudia / Friday morning / Part I, II, III / Body and soul / Caprichosos de la habana
CD ____ **158052**
Messidor / Feb '91 / ADA / Koch

WHO'S SMOKING (D'Rivera, Paquito & James Moody)
Who's smoking / Giant steps / Irremediablemente solo (incurably alone) / Linda's moody / Desert storm / Nuestro bolero / I mean you / You got it, diz / Out of nowhere
CD ____ **CCD 79523**
Candid / Feb '97 / Cadillac / Direct / Jazz Music / Koch / Wellard

Drivin' N' Cryin'

FLY ME COURAGEOUS
CD ____ **CID 9991**
Island / Mar '92 / PolyGram

Droge, Pete

FIND A DOOR (Droge, Pete & The Sinners)
Mr. Jade / Wolfgang / Don't have to be that way / Dear Dianne / Brakeman / You should be running / That ain't right / Find a door / Out with you / Sooner or later / Lord is busy
CD ____ **743213745022**
American / Sep '96 / BMG

NECKTIE SECOND
If you don't love me (I'll kill myself) / Northern bound train / Strayin street / Faith in you / Two steppin' monkey / Sunspot stopwatch / Hardest thing to do / So I am over you / Dog on a chain / Hampton Inn Room 306
CD ____ **74321242302**
American / Apr '95 / BMG

Drolma, Choying

CHO (Drolma, Choying & Steve Tibbetts)
Ngakso / Kyema mimin / Kyamdro semkye / Ngani troma pt 1 / Ngani troma pt 2 / Cho chendren / Kangyi tengi / Ney ogmin choying podrang / Shengshik pema jungney / Om oana phem / Leymon tendrel 2 / Nubchok dechen / SSenge wangchuk / Dechen monlam / Tal
CD ____ **HNCD 1404**
Hannibal / Jan '97 / ADA / Vital

Drome

FINAL CORPORATE COLONIZATION OF THE UNCONSCIOUS
Age of the affordable retina / Hinterland, Kassler Kessel / Down at heels / Hoax what did you get / Steel lung, bye one / Nuzzling / Wonderland / Squirrel / Marathon/Texas / Party in the woods 4
CD ____ **ZENCD 011**
Ninja Tune / Feb '94 / Kudos / Pinnacle / Prime / Vital

Drone

DRONE
CD ____ **FFR 024**
Freek / Dec '96 / RTM/Disc / SRD

FAT CONTROLLER, THE
CD ____ **QDKCD 007**
Normal / Mar '94 / ADA / Direct

Drone Summit

DRONE SUMMIT
CD ____ **DR 005CD**
Drug Racer / Jul '97 / Cargo

Drones

FURTHER TEMPTATIONS
Persecution complex / Bone idol / Movement / Be my baby / Corgi crap / Sad so sad / Change / Lookalikes / Underdog / No more time / City drones / Just want to be myself / Lift off the bans / Lookalikes / Corgi crap / Hard on me / You'll lose / Just want to be myself / Bone idol / I can't see / Fooled today
CD ____ **CDPUNK 20**
Anagram / Oct '93 / Cargo / Pinnacle

TAPES FROM THE ATTIC
CD ____ **OVER 60CD**
Overground / Apr '97 / Shellshock/Disc / SRD

Drones

GIANT BONSAI
CD ____ **DRO 1996CD**
Drones / Aug '96 / ADA

Droney, Chris

FERTILE ROCK, THE
CD ____ **CICD 110**
CICD / Jul '95 / ADA

Drop

WITHIN BEYOND
CD ____ **CHAPMCD 061**
Chapter 22 / Nov '91 / Vital

Drop 19's

DELAWARE
CD ____ **HUTCD 004**
Hut / Aug '92 / EMI

NATIONAL COMA
Limp / All swimmers are brothers / Skull / Cuban / Rot winter / Martini love / 7/8 / Franco inferno / My hotel deb / Moses brown / Superfeed / Dead / Royal
CD ____ **CDHUT 14**
Hut / Sep '93 / EMI

Drop Acid

MAKING GOD SMILE
CD ____ **LS 92502**
Roadrunner / Nov '91 / PolyGram

Droste, Silvia

AUDIOPHILE VOICINGS
CD ____ **BLR 84 004**
L&R / May '91 / New Note/Pinnacle

Drovers

TIGHTROPE TOWN
CD ____ **TX 2010CD**
Taxim / Jan '94 / ADA

Drovers Old Time Medicine ...

SUNDAY IN PETERS CREEK (Drovers Old Time Medicine Show)
CD ____ **HYMN 6**
Fundamental / Aug '97 / Cargo / Plastic Head / Shellshock/Disc

Dru Hill

DRU HILL
Anthem / Nothing to prove / Tell me / Do U believe / Whatever U want / Satisfied / April showers / All alone / Never make a promise / So special / In my bed / Love's train / Share my world / 5 steps
CD _______ 5243062
4th & Broadway / Dec '96 / PolyGram

Drug Free America

NARCOTICA
CD _______ CBKTB 21
Dreamtime / Jul '95 / Kudos / Pinnacle

TRIP
Detroit walkabout / One Alien/Nation / Out on the blue horizon / Orient pearl and cherry blue / Drop zone (reprise,live) / Cygni X-1
CD _______ CYBERCD 001
Cybersound / Oct '92 / Vital

TRIP - THE DREAMTIME REMIXES
Cyberspace / Detroit walkabout / One alien nation under a groove / Out on the blue / Horizon / Orient pearl and cherry blue / Can you feel / Drop zone / Cygni X-1 / Drop zone (free Yibet)
CD _______ CDKTB 14
Dreamtime / Apr '95 / Kudos / Pinnacle

Drugstore

DRUGSTORE
Speaker 12 / Favourite sinner / Alive / Solitary party groover / If / Devil / Saturday sunset / Fader / Super glider / Baby Astrolab / Gravity / Nectarine / Accelerate
CD _______ 8285562
Honey / Mar '95 / RTM/Disc

Druid

TOWARD THE SUN/FLUID DRUID
Voices / Remembering / Theme / Toward the sun / Red carpet for an evening / Dawn of evening / Shangri la / Razor truth / Painters clouds / FM 145 / Crusade / Nothing but morning / Barnaby / Kestrel / Left to find / Fisherman's friend
CD _______ BGOCD 285
Beat Goes On / Aug '95 / Pinnacle

Druidspear

...SLOW
CD _______ ANEWCD 1
Anew / Jun '97 / Greyhound

Drukpa Tibetan Monks

TIBETAN BUDDHIST RITES FROM BHUTAN MONASTRIES BOX SET
CD Set _______ LYRCD 9001
Lyrichord / May '94 / ADA / CM / Roots

TIBETAN BUDDHIST RITES FROM BHUTAN MONASTRIES VOL.1
CD _______ LYRCD 7255
Lyrichord / Feb '94 / ADA / CM / Roots

TIBETAN BUDDHIST RITES FROM BHUTAN MONASTRIES VOL.2 (Drukpa & Nyingmapa Tibetan Monks)
CD _______ LYRCD 7256
Lyrichord / Feb '94 / ADA / CM / Roots

TIBETAN BUDDHIST RITES FROM BHUTAN MONASTRIES VOL.3
CD _______ LYRCD 7257
Lyrichord / May '94 / ADA / CM / Roots

TIBETAN BUDDHIST RITES FROM BHUTAN MONASTRIES VOL.4
CD _______ LYRCD 7258
Lyrichord / May '94 / ADA / CM / Roots

Drum Club

LIVE IN ICELAND
Oscillate and infiltrate / Bug / Follow the sun / Reefer / Crystal express / De-lushed / Plateau of wolves / U make me feel so good
CD _______ SBR 003
Sabres Of Paradise / Aug '95 / Vital

Drumhead

DANGEROUS DUB VOL.2 (Drumhead & Ninja Shark)
CD _______ COPCD 4
Copasetic / Mar '96 / BMG / Grapevine/ PolyGram / Jet Star / Pinnacle

Drummers Of Burundi

DRUMMERS OF BURUNDI
CD _______ RWMCD 1
Realworld / Mar '92 / EMI

Drummond, Bill

MAN, THE
CD _______ CRECD 14
Creation / May '94 / 3mv/Vital

Drummond, Billy

GIFT, THE (Drummond, Billy Quartet)
CD _______ CRISS 1083CD
Criss Cross / May '94 / Cadillac / Direct / Vital/SAM

NATIVE COLOURS (Drummond, Billy Quintet)
CD _______ CRISS 1057CD
Criss Cross / May '92 / Cadillac / Direct / Vital/SAM

Drummond, Don

BEST OF DON DRUMMOND, THE
CD _______ SOCD 9008
Studio One / Mar '95 / Jet Star

GREATEST HITS
Corner stone / Musical communion / Mesopotamia / Cool smoke / Burning torch / Alipang / Don memorial / Stampede / Thorough fare
CD _______ TICD 004
Treasure Isle / May '89 / Jet Star / SRD

MEMORIAL
CD _______ LG 21023
Lagoon / Jul '93 / Grapevine/PolyGram

Drummond, Ray

CAMERA IN A BAG (Drummond, Ray Quintet)
CD _______ CRISS 1040CD
Criss Cross / Nov '90 / Cadillac / Direct / Vital/SAM

CONTINUUM
Blues from the sketchpad / Some serious steppin' / Intimacy of the blues / Sakura / Blues in the closet / Equipoise / Gloria's step / Sail away / Sophisticated lady
CD _______ AJ 0111
Arabesque / Aug '94 / New Note/Pinnacle

EXCURSION
Susanita / Penta-major / Prelude / Quads / Invitation / Well you needn't / Andei / Blues African / Exscursion
CD _______ AJ 0106
Arabesque / Jun '93 / New Note/Pinnacle

VIGNETTES
Susanita-like / Ballade poetique / Dance to the lady / Dedication (to John Hicks) / 1-95 / Poor butterly / Eleanor Rigby / Ballade poetique
CD _______ AJ 0122
Arabesque / Jun '96 / New Note/Pinnacle

Drumpact

NEW MUSIC
CD _______ EPC 886
European Music Production / Oct '92 / Harmonia Mundi

Drunk

DERBY SPIRITUAL, A
CD _______ JAG 02
Jagjaguwar / May '97 / Cargo

Drunk In Punk

TAPPED
CD _______ FO 25CD
Fearless / Apr '97 / Cargo / Plastic Head

Drunken Boat

DRUNKEN BOAT
Tragic hands / New pop / Accidents / Home skull crusher / Pony / Jubilee / Lisa's dream / Shit suit / Uniform gold / Stacko / Spin around / What's going on
CD _______ EFACD 6185
House In Motion / Oct '92 / SRD

Drunken State

KILT BY DEATH
CD _______ HMRXD 151
Heavy Metal / May '90 / Revolver / Sony

Drusky, Roy

18 ORIGINAL COUNTRY CLASSICS
El Paso / Crystal chandeliers / Honey come back / Ring of fire / End of the world / (I'd be a) legend in my time / Take good care of her / Battle ofNew Orleans / Abilene / Early morning rain / Together again / Talk back trembling lips / Lonely street / Waitin' for a train / Cryin' time / Sunday morning coming down / Almost persuaded / When two worlds collide
CD _______ 5525562
Spectrum / Sep '96 / PolyGram

Dry Branch Fire Squad

FERTILE GROUND
Devil, take the farmer / Darling Nellie across the sea / Where we'll never die / Turkey in the straw / There's nothing between us / Love has bought me to dispair / Honest farmer / Great Titanic / Golden morning / Do you ever dream of me / Old time way / Bonaparte's crossing the Rhine
CD _______ ROUCD 0258
Rounder / '89 / ADA / CM / Direct

JUST FOR THE RECORD
CD _______ ROUCD 306
Rounder / Jan '94 / ADA / CM / Direct

LIVE AT LAST
Late last night / True historia / Aragon Mill / Economical talk / John Henry / Pitiful thing / Cowboy song / Housework is my life / Red rocking chair / Cultural exchange / Someone play Dixie for me / Hambone/Balo's song / Testosterone poisoning / Midnight on the stormy deep / Banjo jokes / Bluegrass breakdown / World's greatest folk singer / Hard times / Goin' up the mountain / Walk the streets of glory
CD _______ ROUCD 0339
Rounder / Oct '96 / ADA / CM / Direct

TRIED AND TRUE
CD _______ ROUCD 11519
Rounder / '88 / ADA / CM / Direct

Dry Throat Fellows

DO SOMETHING
CD _______ SOSCD 1226
Stomp Off / '92 / Jazz Music / Wellard

Dschinn

DSCHINN
CD _______ SB 037
Second Battle / Jun '97 / Greyhound

D'Semble

D'SEMBLE
CD _______ BBCD 4001
Blue Black / Oct '93 / Cadillac

Dub Doctor

ZULU DUB
CD _______ ROTCD 011
Reggae On Top / Sep '96 / Jet Star / SRD

Dub Funk Association

SPIRITS UNDER PRESSURE
CD _______ TNTYCD 003
Tanty / Oct '96 / Fat Shadow / Jet Star / Total/BMG

Dub Ghecko

LOVE TO THE POWER OF EACH
CD _______ DBHD 003CD
Dubhead / Oct '96 / SRD

Dub Judah

BETTER TO BE GOOD
CD _______ DJCD 004
Dub Jockey / Aug '94 / Jet Star / SRD

DUB FACTOR 3 IN CAPTIVITY DUB CHRONICLES
Wipe away the tears / Warning / Burn the wicked one / Conscious man / In captivity / Rise up / Remember / Jah people come / Love your freedom / Driving on / Stand firm / Repatriation dub / Good, the dub and the free / Young pool
CD _______ NRCD 011
Nubian / Mar '95 / Jet Star / Vital

Dub Mix Specialists

DUB MIX SPECIALISTS VOL.1
CD _______ DMSCD 101
DMS / Sep '96 / SRD

Dub Narcotic

BOOT PARTY
CD _______ KLP 40CD
K / Jun '96 / Cargo / Greyhound / SRD

INDUSTRIAL BREAKDOWN
CD _______ SOUL 8CD
Soul Static Sound / Jul '95 / SRD

RIDING SHOTGUN
CD _______ KCD 50
K / Nov '95 / Cargo / Greyhound / SRD

SHIP TO SHORE
CD _______ KLP 60CD
K / Oct '96 / Cargo / Greyhound / SRD

Dub Specialists

17 DUB SHOTS
CD _______ CDHB 142
Heartbeat / Aug '95 / ADA / Direct / Greensleeves / Jet Star

DUB TO DUB VOL.1 (Break To Break)
CD _______ CP 001CD
Crispy / May '95 / SRD

DUB TO DUB VOL.2 (Beat To Beat)
CD _______ CP 002CD
Crispy / Jun '96 / SRD

DUB TO DUB, BREAK TO BREAK
CD _______ CP 001CD
Crispy / Apr '97 / SRD

Dub Syndicate

CLASSIC SELECTION VOL.1
CD _______ ONUCD 5
On-U Sound / Jul '89 / Jet Star / SRD

CLASSIC SELECTION VOL.3
CD _______ ONUCD 69
On-U Sound / Jul '94 / Jet Star / SRD

ECHOMANIA
CD _______ ONUCD 24
On-U Sound / Sep '93 / Jet Star / SRD

ITAL BREAKFAST
CD _______ ONUCD 84
On-U Sound / Mar '96 / Jet Star / SRD

LIVE
CD _______ ONUCD 19
On-U Sound / Mar '93 / Jet Star / SRD

ONE WAY SYSTEM
CD _______ DANCD 115
Danceteria / Nov '94 / ADA / Plastic Head / Shellshock/Disc

RESEARCH AND DEVELOPMENT
CD _______ ONUCD 85
On-U Sound / Oct '96 / Jet Star / SRD

STONED IMMACULATE
CD _______ ONUCD 15
On-U Sound / '93 / Jet Star / SRD

TUNES FROM THE MISSING CHANNEL
Ravi Shankar / Show is coming / Must be dreaming / Overboard / Forever more / Geoffrey Boycott / Wellie / Jolly / Out and about
CD _______ ONUCD 18638
On-U Sound / Aug '97 / Jet Star / SRD

Dub Tractor

EVENING WITH DUB TRACTOR, AN
CD _______ CDADA 1001
Additive / Feb '97 / Mo's Music Machine / RTM/Disc

Dub War

DUB WARNING
CD _______ WOWCD 37
Words Of Warning / '94 / SRD / Total/ BMG

PAIN
CD _______ GMOSH 121CD
Earache / Feb '95 / Vital
CD _______ MOSH 121CD
Earache / Sep '97 / Vital

WORDS OF DUB WARNING
CD _______ WOWCD 47
Words Of Warning / Dec '95 / SRD / Total/BMG

WRONG SIDE OF BEAUTIFUL
Control / Armchair thriller / Greedee / Baseball bat / One chill / Enemy maker / Million dollar love / Silencer / Cry dignity / Can't stop / Prisoner / Love is / Mission / Universal jam
CD _______ MOSH 159CD
Earache / Sep '96 / Vital

XTRA PAIN
Why / Mental / Nar say a ting / Mad zone / Strike it / Respected / Pain / Nations / Gorrit / Spiritual warfare / Fool's gold / Over now / Psycho system / Words of warning / Original murder
CD _______ MOSH 121CDF
Earache / Aug '95 / Vital

Dubadelic

2001: A BASS ODYSSEY
CD _______ WSCD 007
Word Sound Recordings / Apr '96 / Cargo / SRD

Dubas, Marie

INTEGRAL 1927-1945 (2CD Set)
CD _______ FA 053
Fremeaux / Oct '96 / ADA / Discovery

Dubber, Goff

CLARINET MARMALADE (Dubber, Goff & The Neville Dickie Trio)
Clarinet marmalade / Lonesome (si tu vois ma mere) / South side strut / Memphis blues / Black bottom stomp / Indian summer / Shreveport stomp / Saturday night out / Memories of you / Louisiana and me / I hear ya talkin' / Lou-easy-an-i-a / Gone but not forgotten (my inspiration) / Your folks / Wrap up your troubles in dreams / At the jazz band ball
CD _______ LACD 78
Lake / May '97 / ADA / Cadillac / Direct / Jazz Music / Target/BMG

Dube, Lucky

HOUSE OF EXILE
CD _______ SHCD 43094
Shanachie / Apr '92 / ADA / Greensleeves / Koch

Dublin City Ramblers

BEST OF THE DUBLIN CITY RAMBLERS
Ferryman / Rare ould times / Paddy lie back / O'Carolan's draught / Green hills of Kerry / Mary's song / John O'Dreams / Punch and Judy man / Town of Ballybay / Nancy Spain / Belfast mill / Slievenamon / My green valleys / Crack was ninety in the Isle of Man
CD _______ DOCDX 9005
Dolphin / Jul '96 / CM / Else / Grapevine/ PolyGram / Koch

CRACK WAS 90, THE
CD _______ CDIRLSH 022
Outlet / Jul '97 / ADA / CM / Direct / Duncans / Koch / Ross

CRAIC AND THE PORTER BLACK, THE (The Best Of Irish Pub Songs)
CD _______________ DOCDK 107
Dolphin / Nov '95 / CM / Else / Grapevine/ PolyGram / Koch

FLIGHT OF THE EARLS
CD _______________ DOCD 9015
Delmark / Nov '93 / ADA / Cadillac / CM / Direct / Hot Shot

FROM IRELAND - WHISKEY IN THE JAR (Dublin City Ramblers/Spailpin)
Sweet Betsy from Pike: *Dublin City Ramblers* / Foggy dew: *Dublin City Ramblers* / Rising of the moon: *Spailpin* / Scarce o' tatties: *Spailpin* / Gentleman soldier: *Dublin City Ramblers* / Nightingale: *Spailpin* / Loch Lomond: *Dublin City Ramblers* / White, orange and green: *Spailpin* / Greensleeves: *Dublin City Ramblers* / Fiddler's green: *Spailpin* / Feilims' little boat Phelims: *Spailpin* / Night visiting sun: *Dublin City Ramblers* / Beggar man: *Spailpin* / Gartan mother's lullaby: *Dublin City Ramblers* / Ramblin' Irishman: *Spailpin* / Lord Randall: *Dublin City Ramblers* / Port Lairge: *Spailpin* / Turtle dove: *Dublin City Ramblers* / Arthur McBride: *Spailpin*
CD _______________ 15160
Laserlight / '91 / Target/BMG

HERE'S TO THE IRISH
CD _______________ SOW 90143
Sounds Of The World / Apr '95 / Target/ BMG

HOME AND AWAY (20 Collected Irish Ballads)
CD _______________ DOCD 101
Dolphin / Aug '96 / CM / Else / Grapevine/ PolyGram / Koch

Dublin Concert Orchestra

SHAMROCK FAVOURITES (Dublin Concert Orchestra/Alan Loraine Orchestra)
Wearing of the green / Believe me if all those endearing young charms / Harp that once thro' Tara's halls / Kerry dance / Ould orange flute / Minstrel boy / Londonderry air / Galway piper / Down went McGinty / Rose of Tralee / Cockles and mussels / Kitty of Coleraine / Daughters of Erin / Dear little Shamrock / Tis the last rose of Summer / Irish washerwoman / Teetotaler's reel / I know where I'm going / Bendemeer's stream / Rakes of mallow / Fairy dance / Patrician theme / Happy Colleen / Spring theme / Farmer's frolic / Postman's knock / Killarney / Low back'd car / Erin is my home / Aileen aroon / Rory O'Moore / Fisher's hornpipe / Kathleen Mavoureen / I'm sitting by the stile / Mary / Sprig of shillelagh / Rakes of Kildare / Shamus O'Brien / Pretty girl milking her cow / St. Patrick was a gentleman / St. Patrick's day / Come back to Erin / Barndoor / Miss McLeod's / Silent oh Moyle / Off to Philadelphia / I'll take you home again Kathleen / Nursery song / Balladeer / Pastorale / Fairy builder / Industrial theme / Merry theme
CD _______________ SUMCD 4075
Summit / Nov '96 / Sound & Media

Dubliners

15 YEARS ON
Wild rover / Ploughboy lads / Three sea captains / Bunclody / Seven drunken nights / Belfast hornpipe / Black Velvet Band / Carrickfergus / Last night's fun/Congress reel / Bank of the sweet primroses / Weila weila weila / Four green fields / Town I loved so well / Salamanca / Spancil Hill / McAlpine's fusiliers / Boulavogue / Old triangle / Spanish lady / O'Carolans devotion / Thirty foot trailer / Down by the glenside / Fiddlers green / Molly Malone
CD _______________ CHCD 1025
Chyme / Jan '95 / ADA / CM / Direct / Koch

20 GREATEST HITS
CD _______________ CD 11
Sound / Jan '89 / ADA

20 ORIGINAL GREATEST HITS VOL.1
CD _______________ CHCD 1028
Chyme / Dec '88 / ADA / CM / Direct / Koch

20 ORIGINAL GREATEST HITS VOL.2
Monto / Black Velvet Band / Johnston's motorcar / Drops of brandy/Lady Carberry / Button pusher / Old triangle / Downfall of Paris / Johnny McGory / Spanish lady / Killieburne brae / Molly Malone / God save Ireland / Spancil Hill / Peat bog soldiers / Joe Hill / Molly Maguires / Hand me down me bible / Musical priest/Blackthorn stick / Schoolday's over / Wild Rover
CD _______________ CHCD 1014
Chyme / Jul '93 / ADA / CM / Direct / Koch

20 ORIGINAL GREATEST HITS VOL.3
Kimmage / Biddy Mulligan / Waltzing Matilda / Lord Inchquinn / All for me grog / Lifeboat Mona / Lark in the morning / Mero / Down by the Glenside / McAlpine's fusiliers / Dublin in the rare oul times / Weile weile waile / Acrobat/Village bells / Scorn not his simplicity / Smith of Bristol / Parcel of rogues / Barney's banjo selection / Parting glass
CD _______________ CHCD 1015
Chyme / Jun '96 / ADA / CM / Direct / Koch

25TH ANNIVERSARY (2CD Set)
Rose of Allendale / Salonika / Reels / Now I'm easy: *Dubliners & Stockton's Wing* / Sally Wheatley / Oro se do bheatha bhaile / Irish rover: *Dubliners & Pogues* / Molly Malone / Protect and survive / Planxty Irwin / Three score and ten / Don't get married / Luke - a tribute / Ballad of St. Anne's reel / Cil chais / Cunla: *Dubliners & Stockton's Wing* / Clavalitos / Jigs / Leaving Nancy / O'Connell's steam engine / Rambling rover / Last of the great whales / Mountain dew: *Dubliners & Pogues* / Red roses for me: *Dubliners & Finbar Furey* / Marino waltz / Cod liver oil / I loved the ground she walked on / Love is pleasing / Sick note
CD Set _______________ ESDCD 422
Essential / Aug '96 / BMG

30 YEARS A-GREYING
Rose / Eileen oge / Three jigs / Death of the bear / Galway shawl / Auld triangle / Will the circle be unbroken / Sands of Sudan / Manchester rambler / Drag that fiddle / Call and the answer / Boots of Spanish leather / Two hornpipes / I'll tell me Ma / Sweet Thames flow softly / Whiskey in the jar / Deportees / Nora / Three reels / Liverpool Lou / What will we tell the children / Man you don't meet every day
CD _______________ ESDCD 423
Essential / Aug '96 / BMG

40 TRADITIONAL IRISH TUNES
CD _______________ CHCD 1052
Chyme / Dec '94 / ADA / CM / Direct / Koch

AT HOME WITH THE DUBLINERS
CD _______________ EUCD 1093
ARC / '89 / ADA / ARC Music

AT THEIR BEST
CD _______________ PLSCD 161
Pulse / Feb '97 / BMG

BEST OF THE DUBLINERS, THE
Off to Dublin in the green / Sunshine hornpipe/The mountain road / Will you come to the bower / Peggy Lettermore / Donegal reel/Longford collector / Roddy McCorley / I'll tell my Ma / Mason's apron / Foggy dew / Old orange flute / Roisin dubh / Holy ground
CD _______________ HILLCD 4
Wooded Hill / Sep '96 / Direct / World Serpent

BEST OF THE DUBLINERS, THE
CD _______________ TRTCD 205
TrueTrax / Feb '96 / THE

COLLECTION VOL.2, THE
Roddy McCorley / Twwang man / Sligo maid/Colonel Rodney / Woman from Wexford / Roisin Dubh / Air fa la la la lo / Peggy Lettermore / Easy and slow / Kerry recruit / Donegal reel / Longford collector / Tramps and hawkers / Home boys home / Sunshine hornpipe / Mountain road / Will you come to the bower / I'll tell me ma / Mason's apron / Holy ground / Boulavogue / Master McGrath / Walking in the dew / Nightingale / Sea shanty
CD _______________ CCSCD 270
Castle / Sep '90 / BMG

COLLECTION, THE
Wild rover / Chief O'Neill's favourite / Glendalough Saint / Off to Dublin in the green / Love is pleasing / Nelson's farewell / Monto / Dublin fusiliers / Rocky road to Dublin / Leaving of Liverpool / Old orange flute / Jar of porter / Prefad san ol / High reel / Patriot game / Swallow tail reel / McAlpine's fusiliers / Hot asphalt / Within a mile of Dublin / Finnegan's wake / Banks of the roses / My love is in America / Foggy dew / Sea around us
CD _______________ CCSCD 164
Castle / Sep '87 / BMG

COMPLETE DUBLINERS (2CD Set)
CD Set _______________ SMDCD 150
Snapper / Jul '97 / Pinnacle

DEFINITIVE TRANSATLANTIC COLLECTION, THE
Wild rover / Ragman's ball / Holy ground / Tramps and hawkers / Rocky road to Dublin / Banks of the roses / Swallow tail reel / Sligo maid/Colonel Rodney / Woman from Wexford / Patriot game / Roisin dubh / Fa la la lo / My love is in America / Kerry recruit / Leaving of Liverpool / Finnegan's wake / Sea around us / McAlpine's fusiliers / Hot asphalt / Glendalough saint / Within a mile of Dublin / Will you come to the bower / Boulavogue / Walking in the dew
CD _______________ ESMCD 518
Essential / Jul '97 / BMG

DUBLIN
Finnegan's wake / Raglan Road / Zoo / Logical Gardens / Sez she
CD _______________ CLACD 337
Castle / Aug '93 / BMG

DUBLINERS COLLECTION VOL.1, THE (2CD Set)
Biddy Mulligan / Springhill disaster / Doherty's reel/Down the broom/The honeymoon reel / Foggy dew / Weila weila weila / Kimmage / Donegal Danny / Queen of the fair/Tongs by the fire / Louse house in Kilkenny / Home boys home / High Germany / Whiskey in the jar / Champion at keeping them rolling / Scholar/Teetotaler / Joe Hill / Free the people / Sun is burning / Monto / Johnston's motorcar / Musical priest/Blackthorn stick / Battle of the Somme / Smith of Bristol / Button pusher / Molly Maguires / Kid on the mountain / Parcel o' rogues / School day's over / Jail of Claun Meala / Skibereen / Ojos negros / Killieburne brae / Saxon shilling / Lowlands of Holland / Holy ground
CD Set _______________ CHCD 1011
Chyme / Jul '93 / ADA / CM / Direct / Koch

DUBLINERS COLLECTION VOL.2, THE (2CD Set)
Black velvet band / Hey Johnny McGory / Night visiting song / Drops of brandy/Lady Carberry / Farewell to Carlingford / Bunch of red roses / Lord of the dande / Rebel/ Padraig Pearse / Ploughboy lads / Irish rover / Avondale / Downfall of Paris / Spancil Hill / Fiddler's green / Gentleman soldier / Dicey Reilly / God save Ireland / Song for Ireland / Master Magrath / Building up and tearing England down / Three sea Captains / Sam Hall / Town I love so well / Lark in the morning / I knew Danny Farrell / All for me grog / Humpty dumpty / Gartan Mother's lullaby / Home boys home / Maid behind the bar/Toss the feathers / On Raglan Road / Cuanla / Dublin in the rare ol' times / Molly Malone / Farewell to Ireland
CD Set _______________ CHCD 1094
Chyme / Aug '96 / ADA / CM / Direct / Koch

DUBLINERS LIVE
Fairmoyle lassies/Sporting Paddy / Black velvet band / Whiskey in the jar / All for me grog / Belfast hornpipe/Tim Maloney / Four poster bed/Colonel Rodney / Finnegan's wake / McAlpine's fusiliers / Waterford boys/Humours of Scariff/Flannel jacket / Galway races / Btuilding up and tearing England down / Sick note-Murphy and the bricks / Seven drunken nights / Scholar/ Teetotaller/High reel / Home boys home / Dirty old town / Blue mountain rag / Wild rover / Wealia waile / Holy ground
CD _______________ CHCD 1006
Chyme / Jun '96 / ADA / CM / Direct / Koch

DUBLINERS LIVE
CD _______________ CC 8235
Music For Pleasure / Jan '92 / EMI

DUBLINERS, THE
Seven drunken nights / Galway races / Irish navvy / I wish I were back in Liverpool / Zoological gardens / Rising of the moon / Whiskey on a Sunday / Dundee weaver / Seven deadly sins / Leaving of Liverpool / Maids, when you're young never wed an old man / Dirty old town / Donkey reel / Black velvet band / Pub with no beer / Peggy Gordon / Net hauling song / Nancy Whisky / Paddy's gone to France / Skylark / Tibby Dunbar / Go to sea no more
CD _______________ CC 227
Music For Pleasure / Sep '88 / EMI

DUBLINERS, THE
Wild rover / Ragman's ball / Preab san ol / High reel / Holy ground / Tramps and hawkers / Home boys home / Rocky road to Dublin / Banks of the roses / I'll tell my ma / Swallow's tail reel / Jar of porter / Love is pleasing / Nightingale
CD _______________ HILLCD 12
Wooded Hill / Feb '97 / Direct / World Serpent

ESSENTIAL COLLECTION, THE
CD _______________ CDMFP 6345
Music For Pleasure / May '97 / EMI

FURTHER ALONG
CD _______________ TRACD 243
Transatlantic / Jun '96 / Pinnacle

GREATEST HITS
Wild rover / Lark in the morning / Lifeboat Mona / Weila weila waile / Down by the glenside / Lord of the dance / Danny Farrell / Seven drunken nights / Mero / Champion at keepin' them rolling / Free the people / Dirty old town / Skibbereen / Louse house at Kilkenny / Gentleman soldier / Monto / Band played waltzing Matilda / Springheel disaster / Joe Hill / Whiskey in the jar
CD _______________ CDIRISH 007
Outlet / Mar '97 / ADA / CM / Direct / Duncans / Koch / Ross

INSTRUMENTAL
CD _______________ CH 1052CD
Outlet / Sep '94 / ADA / CM / Direct / Duncans / Koch / Ross

IRISH PUB SONGS
CD _______________ CDPUB 027
Outlet / Oct '95 / ADA / CM / Direct / Duncans / Koch / Ross

IRISH REBEL BALLADS
Johnston's motorcar / Ould triangle / Four green fields / God save Ireland / Charles Stewart Parnell / Town I loved so well / Free the people / Down by the glenside / Boulavogue / Take it down from the mast / Rebel / Wrap the green flag 'round me / West's awake / Nation once again
CD _______________ CHCD 1055
Chyme / Oct '95 / ADA / CM / Direct / Koch

LIVE AT THE ROYAL ALBERT HALL
Black velvet band / McAlpine's fusiliers / Peggy Gordon / Wella walla / Monto / Cork hornpipe / Leaving of Liverpool / Whisky on a Sunday / I wish I were back in Liverpool / Flop eared mule (Donkey Reel) / Navvy boots / Whiskey in the jar / Maids, when you're young never wed an old man / Seven drunken nights
CD _______________ CDMFP 6127
Music For Pleasure / May '97 / EMI

LIVE IN CARRE, AMSTERDAM
Sweets of May / Dicey Reilley / Song for Ireland / Building up and tearing England down / Dunphy's hornpipe / Leitrim fancy / Down the broom / Dirty old town / Old triangle / Whiskey in the jar / Humours of Scariff / Flannel jacket / Galway races / Prodigal son / Sick note / Wild rover / Seven drunken nights
CD _______________ 5509292
Spectrum / Jul '95 / PolyGram

MILESTONES
CD _______________ TRACD 110
Transatlantic / Apr '96 / Pinnacle

OFF TO DUBLIN GREEN
CD _______________ MATCD 211
Castle / May '93 / BMG

ORIGINAL DUBLINERS
Seven drunken nights / Galway races / Old alarm clock / Colonel Fraser and O'Rourke's reel / Rising of the moon / McCafferty / I'm a rover / Weila waila / Travelling people / Limerick rake / Zoological gardens / Fairmoye lasses and sporting Paddy / Black velvet band / Poor Paddy on the railway / Seven deadly sins / Net hauling song / Nancy Whiskey / Many young men of twenty / Paddy's gone to France/Skylark / Molly Bawn / Dundee weaver / Irish navvy / Tibby Dunbar / Inniskillen Dragoons / I wish I were back in Liverpool / Go to sea no more / Instrumental medley / Darby O'Leary / Cork hornpipe / Peggy Gordon / Maid of the sweet brown knowe / Quare bungle rye / Flop eared mule (Donkey reel) / Poor old Dicey Riley / Whiskey on a Sunday / Gentleman soldier / Navvy boots / Maids, when you're young never wed an old man / Rattlin' roarin' Willie / Mrs. McGrath / Carolan concerto / Partin' glass / Muirsheen durkin / Nation once again / Whiskey in the jar / Old triangle / Pub with no beer / Kelly, the boy from Killane / Croppy boy / Sullivan's John / Come and join the British Army / Shoals of herring / Mormon braes / Drink it up men / Maloney wants a drink
CD Set _______________ CDEM 1480
EMI / Mar '93 / EMI

PARCEL OF ROGUES, A
Spanish lady / Foggy dew / Kid on the mountain / Avondale / Acrobats / Village bells / Blantyre explosion / False hearted lover / Thirty foot trailer / Boulavogue / Doherty's reel / Down the broom / Honeymoon reel / Killieburne brae
CD _______________ EUCD 1061
ARC / '89 / ADA / ARC Music

REVOLUTION
CD _______________ CHCD 1002
Chyme / Jan '95 / ADA / CM / Direct / Koch

SEVEN DRUNKEN NIGHTS
Seven Drunken nights / Finnegan's wake / Monto / Auld triangle / Dirty old town / Sam Hall / Holy ground / Black velvet ground / Whiskey in the jar / McAlpine's fusileers / All for me grog / Wild rover / Weila wallia / Home boys home
CD _______________ CHCD 1032
Chyme / '88 / ADA / CM / Direct / Koch

SONGS FROM IRELAND
CD _______________ SOW 90108
Sounds Of The World / Oct '95 / Target/ BMG

SONGS OF DUBLIN
CD _______________ CHCD 1054
Chyme / Oct '95 / ADA / CM / Direct / Koch

ULTIMATE IRISH FOLK ALBUM, THE
Monto / Town I loved so well / Raglan Road / Wild rover / Spring Hill disaster / Seven drunken nights / Whiskey in the jar / Dirty old town / Auld triangle / Dublin in the rare old times / Finnegan's wake / Song for Ireland
CD _______________ KCD 445
Celtic Collections / Jan '97 / Target/BMG

WHISKEY IN THE JAR (3CD Set)
Whiskey in the jar / Galway races / Old alarm clock / Rising of the moon / Poor paddy on the railway / Nancy Whiskey / Darby O'leary / Maid of the sweet brown knowe / Quare bungle rye / Poor old Dicey Riley / Mursheen Durkin / McCafferty / Travelling people / Molly bawn / Seven drunken nights / Weila waila / Limerick rake / Net hauling song / Whiskey on a Sunday / Mrs McGrath / Partin' grass / (The Bonny) shoals of herring / Mormon braes / Dundee weaver / I wish I were back in Liverpool / Go to sea no more / All for me grog / Gentleman soldier / I'm a rover / Fairmoye lasses and sporting paddy / Black velvet band / Seven deadly sins / Many young men of twenty / Maloney wants a drink /

Croppy boy / Come and join the British army / Maids when you're young never wed an old man / Tibby Dunbar / Inniskillen dragoons / Peggy Gordon / Kelly, the boy from Killan / Nation once again
CD Set ______ SA 872862
Disky / Sep '96 / Disky / THE

WILD ROVER, THE
CD ______ 295943
Ariola / Oct '94 / BMG

WILD ROVER, THE
CD ______ PDSCD 535
Pulse / Aug '96 / BMG

Dubmerge

WAKE UP
CD ______ BUD 1
Bud Urge / May '96 / Jet Star

Dubplate Vibe Crew

VOICE OF DUB
CD ______ SOLDCD 003
Solardub / May '97 / Jet Star / SRD

Dubrovniks

AUDIO SONIC LOVE AFFAIR
CD ______ NORMAL 127
Normal / May '94 / ADA / Direct

DUBROVNIK BLUES
CD ______ NORMAL 117
Normal / May '94 / ADA / Direct

MEDICINE WHEEL
CD ______ NORMAL 167CD
Normal / Dec '94 / ADA / Direct

Dubstar

DISGRACEFUL
Stars / Anywhere / Just a girl she said / Elevator song / Day I see you again / Week in week out / Not so manic now / Popdorian / Not once, not ever / St. Swithin's day / Disgraceful
CD ______ FOODCD 13
Food / Oct '95 / EMI

DISGRACEFUL: REPACKAGED & REMIXED (2CD Set)
Stars / Anywhere / Just a girl she said / Elevator song / Day I see you again / Week in week out / Not so manic now / Popdorian / Not once, not ever / St. Swithin's day / Disgraceful / Stars (Mother Dub mix) / Elevator song (Biff & Memphis mix) / Anywhere (Crunch chill) / Not once, not ever / Not so manic now (Way out West mix) / Stars (Way out West mix) / Not so manic now (Mother's whole dub) / Disgraceful (Steve Hillier mix)
CD Set ______ FOODCOR 13
Food / Jul '96 / EMI

Duchaine, Kent

JUST ME AND MY GUITAR
CD ______ CAD 01CD
Cadillac / Jun '94 / ADA

LOOKIN' BACK
CD ______ CAD 1313CD
Cadillac / Jun '94 / ADA

TAKE A LITTLE RIDE WITH ME
CD ______ CAD 1414CD
Cadillac / Apr '95 / ADA

Duchesne, Andre

L' OU 'L
CD ______ VICTOCD 010
Victo / Nov '94 / Harmonia Mundi / ReR Megacorp

Duchin, Eddie

EDDIE DUCHIN STORY, THE (Original Mono Recordings 1933-1938) (Duchin, Eddie Orchestra)
I cover the waterfront / Let's fall in love / Ill wind / She reminds me of you / Riptide / Easy come, easy go / I only have eyes for you / Learning / One night of love / Lovely to look at / I won't dance / Isn't this a lovely day / Moon over Miami / I'm an old cowhand / Follow your heart / Love will tell / It's de-lovely / Moonlight and shadows / Someone to care for me / Too marvellous for words / Merry-go-round broke down / Star is born / 10 o'clock town / Get out of town
CD ______ CDAJA 5205
Living Era / Oct '96 / Select

Ducks Deluxe

ALL TOO MUCH
CD ______ 622402
Skydog / Mar '96 / Discovery

TAXI TO THE TERMINAL ZONE
Coast to coast / Nervous breakdown / Daddy put the bomp / I got you / Please please please / Fireball / Don't mind rockin' tonite / Heart's on my sleeve / Falling on my sleeve / Falling for tha woman / West Texas trucking board / It's all over now / Cherry pie / It don't matter tonite / I'm crying / Love's melody / Teenage head / Rio Grande / My my music / Rainy night in Kilburn / Paris 9

CD ______ MAUCD 610
Mau Mau / Oct '91 / Pinnacle

Ducret, Marc

NEWS FROM THE FRONT
Pour Agnes / Can I call you wren / News from the front / Fanfare / Wren is such a strange name / Silver rain / Golden wren
CD ______ 8491482
jMT / Feb '92 / PolyGram

Dudley, Anne

ANCIENT AND MODERN
Canticles of the sun and the moon / Veni sanct spiritus / Communion / Veni veni emmanuel / Tallis canon / Holly and the ivy / Coventry carol / Prelude / Vater unser im himmerlreich
CD ______ ECHCD 003
Echo / Feb '95 / EMI / Vital

SONGS FROM THE VICTORIOUS CITY (Dudley, Anne & Jaz Coleman)
Awakening / Endless festival / Minarets and memories / Force and fire / Habebe / Ziggarats and Cinnamon / Hannah / Conqueror / Survivor's tale / In a timeless place
CD ______ WOLCD 1009
China / Apr '91 / Pinnacle

Dudley-Smith, Timothy

TELL OUT, MY SOUL (Dudley-Smith, Timothy & All Souls Church Orchestra/ Choir)
When the Lord in glory comes / As water to the thirsty / Born by the Holy Spirit's breath / Christ is risen as He said / Christ is the one who calls / Fill your hearts with joy and gladness / Holy child / How still you lie / I lift my eyes / Lighten our darkness / Lord, for the years / Name of all Majesty / Safe in the shadow of the Lord / We come as guests invited
CD ______ KMCD 936
Kingsway / Aug '96 / Complete/Pinnacle

Due Nueva America

FIESTA LATINA - LATIN AMERICAN SONGS
Maria Paleta / Pampa Lirima / Brasileirinho / Patricia / El condor pasa / Delicado / LA llorona / Candombe mulato / Seleccion san juanitos / Del caribe a los Andes / Senora tentacion / Camino real / La partida / Flor de cacao / Aptao
CD ______ EUCD 1203
ARC / Sep '93 / ADA / ARC Music

Duellists

ENGLISH HURDY GURDY MUSIC
Starters, Alfriston / Force and fire / Miserden, indigo / Duellists / Doyenne / Capriole, drystone / Kate at the gate / Magog, monkey puzzle / Bluesaussis, biscuit shuffle / Baba yaga's cat / Poolside
CD ______ PATCCD 20397D
Panic ATC / May '97 / ADA / CM / Direct

Duet Emmo

OR SO IT SEEMS
CD ______ CDSTUMM 11
Mute / Aug '92 / RTM/Disc

Duff, Mary

COLLECTION, THE
CD ______ RITZRCD 550
Ritz / Oct '95 / Pinnacle

JUST LOVING YOU
She broke her promise / End of the world / Moonlighter / What do they know / More than I can say / Power of love / Secret love / When you're not a dream / If anything should happen to you / What the eyes don't see / Tonight we might fall in love again / Cliffs of Dooneen / Strangers / Just loving you
CD ______ CD 0075
Ritz / Jun '95 / Pinnacle

LOVE SOMEONE LIKE ME
Love someone like me / She's got you / Are you teasing me / Crazy / Forever and ever Amen / It's not over (if I'm not over you) / Daddy's hands / Pick me up on your way down / Dear God / Chicken every Sunday / There won't be any patches in heaven / Do me with love
CD ______ RITZCD 503
Ritz / '91 / Pinnacle

SHADES OF BLUE
Road to Eden / Wounded heart / Face in the crowd / Just like yesterday / I just knew / Michael / Suffering in silence / I don't blame you / I'd just as soon go / No one's living here / Love lines / Isle of hope / Dark island
CD ______ RITZCD 0082
Ritz / Apr '97 / Pinnacle

SILVER AND GOLD
Your one and only / Picture of me (without you) / Walk the way the wind blows / Deep water / Silver and gold / Mama was a working man / Sunshine and rain / Homeland / One you slip around with / Where would that leave me / I'll be your San Antone rose / Fields of Athenry / Beautiful meath / Down by the Sally gardens
CD ______ RITZCD 0066
Ritz / May '92 / Pinnacle

WINNING WAYS
Goin' gone / Yellow roses / Eighteen wheels and a dozen roses / Can I sleep in your arms / Once a day / Does Fort Worth ever cross your mind / One bird on a wing / Just out of reach / Heartaches by the number / I'm not that lonely yet / Come on in / Maggie
CD ______ RITZCD 506
Ritz / '91 / Pinnacle

Duffy, Stephen

UPS AND DOWNS, THE (Duffy, Stephen 'Tin Tin')
Kiss me / She makes me quiver / Masterpiece / But is it art / Wednesday Jones / Icing on the cake / Darkest blues / Be there / Believe in me / World at large alone
CD ______ DIXCD 5
10 / Apr '85 / EMI

Dufourcet, Marie

DUETS FOR ORGAN AND PIANO (Dufourcet, Marie Bernadette & Francoise Dechico Cartier)
CD ______ PRCD 347
Priory / Sep '92 / Priory

Dug Dug's

DUG DUG'S
CD ______ PECD 472
Ciruela El / Jun '97 / Greyhound

Duggan Family

DUGGAN'S TRAD, THE
CD ______ CICD 090
Clo Iar-Chonnachta / Dec '93 / CM

Duggan, John

MISSION, THE
Memories of the mission / Night the telly blinked / Country boy / Michael mor agus city Sue / Radioholic / Cigarettes / Barmaid I met in Kinsale
CD ______ SUNCD 9
Sound / '93 / ADA

Duh

BLOWHARD
CD ______ TUPCD 032
Tupelo / Feb '92 / RTM/Disc

UNHOLY HAND JOB, THE
CD ______ K 163C
Konkurrel / Nov '95 / SRD

Duhan, Johnny

FAMILY ALBUM
Room / Ordinary town / Trying to get the balanace right / Young mothers / Couple of kids / Corner stone / Well knit family / We had our trouble then / Storm is passed / Voyage
CD ______ RTMCD 16
Round Tower / Jul '90 / Avid/BMG

Duignan, Eoin

COUMINEOL
CD ______ CEFCD 163
Gael Linn / Jan '94 / ADA / CM / Direct / Grapevine/PolyGram / Roots

Duisit, Lorraine

FEATHER RIVER (Duisit, Lorraine & Tom Espinola)
CD ______ CDPH 9012
Philo / '88 / ADA / CM / Direct

Duke

RETURN OF THE DREAD VOL.1
CD ______ DUKE 2 CD
Music Of Life / Sep '91 / Grapevine/ PolyGram

Duke, George

BRAZILIAN LOVE AFFAIR
Brazilian love affair / Summer breezin' / Cravo E Canela / Alone / 6 a.m. / Brazilian sugar / Sugar loaf mountain / Love reborn / Up from the sea it arose and ate Rio in one / I need you now / Ao que vai Nascer
CD ______ 4712832
Sony Jazz / Jan '95 / Sony

COLLECTION, THE
Reach for it / Dukey stick / Party down / Say that you will / Festival / I want you for myself / Brazilian love affair / Up from the sea it arose and ate Rio in one swift bite / Sweet baby / Shine on / Son of reach for it (the funky dream) / Born to love you / Heroes / Better ways / Mothership connection / Finger prints
CD ______ CCSCD 298
Castle / Oct '91 / BMG

DON'T LET GO
CD ______ EK 35366
Sony Jazz / Aug '97 / Sony

DREAM ON
CD ______ EK 37532
Sony Jazz / Aug '97 / Sony

GUARDIAN OF THE LIGHT
Overture / Light / Shane / Born to love you / Silly fightin' / You / War fugue interlude / Reach out / Give me your love / Stand / Soon / Celebrate / Fly away
CD ______ 4738982
Sony Jazz / Jul '95 / Sony

I LOVE THE BLUES SHE HEARD ME CRY/AURA WILL PREVAIL/LIBERATE (Three Orginals/2CD Set)
Chariot / Look into her eyes / Sister Serene / That's what she said / Mashavu / Rokkinrowl / Prepare yourself / Great child within us - ego / Someday / I love the blues, she heard me cry / Dawn / For love / Foosh / Floop de loop / Malibu fools / Echidna's arf / Uncle Remus / Aura / Don't be shy / Seeing you / Back to where we never left / What the... / Tryin' and cryin' / I c'n hear that / After the love / Tzina / Liberated fantasies
CD Set ______ 5191982
MPS Jazz / Apr '93 / PolyGram

ILLUSIONS
CD ______ 9362457552
Elektra / Dec '96 / Warner Music

RENDEZVOUS
CD ______ EK 39262
Sony Jazz / Jul '95 / Sony

SNAPSHOT
From the void (intro) / History (I remember) / Snapshot / No rhyme, no reason / Six o'clock / Ooh baby / Fame / Geneva / Speak low / Keeping love alive / Until sunrise / Bus tours / In the meantime / Morning after
CD ______ 9362450262
Elektra / Oct '92 / Warner Music

Dukes Of Dixieland

DIXIE ON PARADE (2CD Set)
Sweet Georgia Brown / Basin street blues / South Rampart street parade / Washington and Lee swing / My blue heaven / Sheik of Araby / Waiting for the Robert E Lee / Toot toot tootsie / Tailgate ramble / High society / Clarinet marmalade / When my sugar walks down the street / (There'll be a) Hot time on the old town tonight / Darktown strutters ball / Mama don't allow it / Limehouse blues / Missisippi mud / Milenberg joys / Down by the old mill stream / Ol'man river / St. Louis blues / Tiger rag / Original Dixieland one-step / Wolverine blues / Slide, frog, slide / Dill pickles rag / After you've gone / Riverside blues / Lazy river / Dear old southland / Down by the riverside / Ain't she sweet / Twelfth street rag / Johnson rag / Bugle call rag / Swanee river / St. James infirmary / Copenhagen / San / When it's sleepy time down south / Beale Street blues
CD Set ______ DBG 53051
Double Gold / Aug '96 / Target/BMG

Dukes Of Stratospehar

CHIPS FROM THE CHOCOLATE FIREBALL
Twenty five o'clock / Bike ride to the moon / My love explodes / What in the world... / Your gold dress / Mole from the ministry / Vanishing girl / Have you seen Jackie / Little lighthouse / You're a good man Albert Brown (curse you red barrel) / Collideascope / You're my drug / Shiny cage / Brainiac's daughter / Affiliated / Pale and precious
CD ______ COMCD 11
Virgin / Aug '87 / EMI

Dukowski, Chuck

UNITED GANG MEMBERS (Dukowski & Cutler)
CD ______ NAR 094CD
New Alliance / May '94 / Plastic Head

Dulcimer

DULCIMER
Sonnet to the fall / Pilgrim from the city / Morman's casket / Ghost of the wandering minstrel boy / Gloucester City / Starlight / Caravan / Lisa's song / Time in my life / Fruit of the musical tree / While it lasted / Suzanne
CD ______ SEECD 266
See For Miles/C5 / Sep '89 / Pinnacle

INTO THE LIGHT
Blessing / Robbie / Guardian angel / Confession (do it again) / Christmas song / Dreams of art nouveau / Ship of fools / See if you can find me / Footnote / Dance of the Chinese horsemen / Bridge of seven wonders / Statues
CD ______ PCOM 1148
President / Mar '97 / Grapevine/PolyGram / President / Target/BMG

ROB'S GARDEN
Rob's garden / Across the fields / Silver on white / Smoke / Mean old girl / Creation (poet and the firebird) / Indiana Jones / Army boy / Martin Hussingtree / Come the day / Shining way / Ghost of England
CD ______ PCOM 1144

President / Oct '95 / Grapevine/PolyGram / President / Target/BMG

ROOM FOR THOUGHT
CD ____ HBG 122/6
Background / Apr '94 / Background / Greyhound

Dulfer, Candy

SAX-A-GO-GO
CD ____ 74321111812
RCA / Mar '93 / BMG

SAXUALITY
Pee wee / Saxuality / So what / Jazzid / Heavenly city / Donja / There goes the neighborhood / Mr. Lee / Get the funk / House is not a home
CD ____ 260696
RCA / Aug '95 / BMG

Dulfer, Hans

EXPRESS DELAYED (Dulfer, Hans & Herbert Noord)
Home is not a house / Troubleshooter / Take it away babe / Carrow / Meeting the six / Troubleshooter 2
CD ____ MCD 0041
Limetree / Apr '96 / New Note/Pinnacle

Dull Knife

ELECTRIC INDIAN
CD ____ SB 026
Second Battle / Jun '97 / Greyhound

Dulzaineros Del Vilorio

SIERTERIA
CD ____ 20084
Sonifolk / Aug '96 / ADA / CM

Dumb

THIRSTY
CD ____ UP 040
Up / Jan '97 / Cargo / Greyhound

Dumisani Ras

MISTER MUSIC
CD ____ 505322
Declic / Oct '96 / Jet Star

Dumitrescu, Iancu

A PRIORI
A priori / 5 implosions / Mythos de sacrae / Lamentationem / Icarus
CD ____ EDMN 1006
Editions Modern / Oct '95 / ReR Megacorp

AU DELA DE MOVEMUR
Au dela de mouvemur / Monades / Ekagrata / Signum gemini / Zodiaque
CD ____ EDMN 1003
Editions Modern / Oct '95 / ReR Megacorp

GALAXY
Galaxy / Movemur / Reliefs / Memorial / Basoreliefs
CD ____ EDMN 1005
Editions Modern / Oct '95 / ReR Megacorp

IANCU DUMITRESCU & ANA-MARIA AVRAM (Dumitrescu, Iancu & Ana-Maria Avram)
CD ____ EDMN 1008
Editions Modern / Jun '97 / ReR Megacorp

MEDIUM III
Medium III / Cogito / Trompe l'oeil / Aulodie moiritica / Apogeum / Perspectives
CD ____ EDMN 1001
Editions Modern / Oct '95 / ReR Megacorp

MUISIQUE DE PAROLES
Muisique de paroles / Astalos
CD ____ EDMN 1004
Editions Modern / Oct '95 / ReR Megacorp

SACREES
Sacrees / Harryphones (alpha and epsilon) / Grande ourse
CD ____ EDMN 1002
Editions Modern / Oct '95 / ReR Megacorp

Dummer, John

CABAL...PLUS (Dummer, John Blues Band)
I need love / Just a feeling / No chance with you / Young fashioned ways / Sitting and thinking / Low down Santa Fe / When you got a good friend / Welfare blues / Hound dog / Blue guitar / After hours / Daddy please don't cry / Doblee doooblee jubilee / Monkey speaks his mind / Travelling man / 40 days / Nine by nine / Going in the out / Medicine weasel / Endgame
CD ____ SEECD 456
See For Miles/C5 / Oct '96 / Pinnacle

NINE BY NINE
World's in a tangle / Soulful dress / Let me love you baby / Screaming and crying / Big feeling blues / New skin game / No chance now / Reconsider baby / Down home girl / I can't be satisfied / Nine by nine / I love you honey / Riding in the moonlight / Walkin' blues / Lovin' man / Statesboro' blues / Monkey speaks his mind / Young blood / Be careful what you do / Shame, shame, shame / Walking the dog
CD ____ IGOCD 2021
Indigo / May '95 / ADA / Direct

Dumpster Juice

GET THAT OUT OF YOUR MOUTH
Clown midget / DDS / Hud / Bowl / Stockton / Pound / Chisel you weasel / Farmer gatherer / Living dead / Gerald / Mommy's sobbin' / Kwan tu
CD ____ 892712
Spanish Fly / May '94 / Vital

Dunaj

LA LA LA
CD ____ R 0009
Rachot / Jun '97 / ReR Megacorp

Dunbar, Aynsley

AYNSLEY DUNBAR RETALIATION, THE (Dunbar, Aynsley Retaliation)
CD ____ MCAD 22101
One Way / May '94 / ADA / Direct / Greyhound

BLUE WHALE
Willing to fight / Willie the pimp / It's your turn / Days / Going home
CD ____ 14814
Spalax / May '96 / ADA / Cargo / Direct / Discovery / Greyhound

DOCTOR DUNBAR'S PRESCRIPTION (Dunbar, Aynsley Retaliation)
CD ____ MCAD 22102
One Way / May '94 / ADA / Direct / Greyhound

TO MUM FROM AYNSLEY AND THE BOYS (Dunbar, Aynsley Retaliation)
CD ____ MCAD 22069
One Way / May '94 / ADA / Direct / Greyhound

Dunbar, Sly

SLY, WICKED AND SLICK
Rasta fiesta / Sesame Street / Lover's bop / Senegal market / Mr. Music / Queen of the minstrels / Dirty Harry / Oriental taxis
CD ____ CDFL 9018
Virgin / Jun '91 / EMI

Dunbar, Valerie

BEST OF VALERIE DUNBAR, THE
Always Argyll / Mull of Kintyre / How great thou art / Medley / Loch Lomond / Old rugged cross / Scotland again / Bonnie Gallowa' / Annie Laurie / Medley / Lochingar / Scotland forever / Dumbartons drums / Lovely Argyll / Mingulay boat song / Flower of Scotland / Medley / Medley
CD ____ CDLOC 1099
Lochshore / Nov '96 / ADA / Direct / Duncans

SCARLET RIBBONS
CD ____ CDKLP 69
Klub / Sep '90 / ADA / CM / Direct / Duncans / Ross

Duncan, Gordon

CIRCULAR BREATH, THE
Macdonald's / High drive / Jolly tinker / Clan meets tribe / Contradiction / Herring in salt / Circular breath / Shepherd's crook / Blow my chanter / MacFadden's / MacDougall's / Gathering
CD ____ CDTRAX 122
Greentrax / Mar '97 / ADA / Direct / Duncans / Highlander

JUST FOR SEAMUS
CD ____ CDTRAX 075
Greentrax / Aug '94 / ADA / Direct / Duncans / Highlander

Duncan, Hugo

IRISH COLLECTION, THE
CD ____ CDIRISH 005
Outlet / Oct '95 / ADA / CM / Direct / Duncans / Koch / Ross

Duncan, Jock

YE SHINE WHAR YE STAN
Gruel / Rhynie / Lothian hairst/Hairsters' reel / Cruel mother / Hash O' Benagoak / Bogie's bonnie belle / Glenlogie / Bonnie Udny / Bonnie lass O' Fyvie / Sleepytoon / Mormond braes / Hairst O' Rettie / Macfarlan O' the Sprotts / Plouboy lads / Drumdelgie / Battle of Harlaw/Desperate battle / Banks of Inverurie / Barnyards O' Delgaty
CD ____ SPRCD 1039
Springthyme / Feb '97 / ADA / CM / Direct / Duncans / Highlander / Roots

Duncan, John

SEND
CD ____ TO 20
Touch / Oct '95 / Kudos / Pinnacle

Duncan, Johnny

LAST TRAIN TO SAN FERNANDO (4CD Set) (Duncan, Johnny Bluegrass Boys)
Last train to San Fernando / Rockabilly baby / Footprints in the snow / Blue blue heartache / Jig along home / If you love me baby / Goodnight Irene / Freight train blues / Press on / Johnny's blue yodel / Out of business / Get along home Cindy / Old Blue / Calamity Mose / Just a little lovin' / Which way did he go / More and more / Just a closer walk with thee / Travellin' blues / St. James Infirmary / Mind your own business / Kaw-Liga / Ella speed / Doin' my time / Where could I go / Can't you line 'em / Gypsy Davy / Blue yodel / Old dusty road / Itching for my baby / I heard the bluebirds sing / Railroad, steamboat, rivers and canals / More and more / Geisha girl / All the monkeys ain't in the zoo / This train / Rosalie / Hey good lookin' / Wedding bells / Moanin' the blues / Cold cold heart / Jambalaya / Your cheatin' heart / Long gone lonesome blues / Half as much / May you never be alone / Salute to Hank Williams / My son calls another man Daddy / My lucky love / Any time / Kansas City / That's alright darlin' / Yellow yellow moon / Rockabilly medley / Waltz medley / Railroad medley / Gospel medley / Sleepy eyed John / Tobacco Road / Legend of Gunga Din / Hannah / Waitin' for the sandman / Long time gone / Will you be mine / She's my baby / You shouldn't have cried / Baby we're really in love / Bluebird Island / Ballad of Jed Clampett / Dang me / Which way did he go / My little baby / I thank my lucky stars / Beyond the sunset / Just a little walk with Jesus / Amazing grace / Where could I go to but to the Lord / Just a closer walk with thee / Walking in Jerusalem just like John / Precious Lord hold my hand / No hiding place down there / I've just told Mama goodbye / In the garden / Press on / When God dips his pen of love in my heart / Last train to San Fernando / Little things / I fought the law / Out of business / I wonder where you are tonight / Someone stole my steel guitar / Joe and Mabel's 12th Street Bar and Grill / Margie's at Lincoln's Park Inn / Footprints in the snow / Kaw-Liga / I ain't buyin' / Mustang prang / Life can be beautiful / Hello heartache / If it feels good, do it / Wild side of life / Just for what I am / Salty dog blues / Just a little lovin' / Footprints in the snow / Blue blue heartaches / Someone to give my love to / Hank Williams medley / Smoke smoke smoke (that cigarette) / Tom Dooley / Last train to San Fernando / Mustang prang
CD Set ____ BCD 15947
Bear Family / Dec '96 / Direct / Rollercoaster / Swift

Duncan, Sammy

SAMMY DUNCAN & HIS HOT SOUTH JAZZ BAND
CD ____ JCD 264
Jazzology / Jun '96 / Jazz Music

Duncan, Stuart

STUART DUNCAN
Bushy fork of John Creek/Mason's apron / G Forces / Thai clips / Passing / Miles to go / Lee highway blues / Lonely moon / Whistling Rufus / Summer of my dreams / My dixie home / Two o'clock in the morning
CD ____ ROUCD 0263
Rounder / '92 / ADA / CM / Direct

Duncan, Tommy

BENEATH A NEON STAR IN A HONKY TONK
Gossip song / California waltz / Got a letter from my kid today / Jesus is mine / Take your burden to the Lord / Nancy Jane / Relax and take it easy / Move a little closer / I was just walking out the door / I've turned a gadabout / I hit the jackpot / I don't want to hurt you / Excuse me, I gotta go / Tomato can / Who drank my beer / Where oh where has my little... / It may take a long long time / Grits and gravy blues / Beneath a neon star in a honky tonk / Stars over San Antone / I reckon in a Texan / I guess you were right / Tennessee church bells / Hound dog / That certain feeling / San Antonio rose / Daddyo loves Mammyo / Crazy mixed up kid
CD ____ BCD 15957
Bear Family / Dec '96 / Direct / Rollercoaster / Swift

TEXAS MOON
I'm thru wastin' time on you / Take me back to Tulsa / Worried over you / Time changes everything / September / Gamblin' polka dot blues / You put me on my feet / Just a plain old country boy / In the jailhouse now / Chattanooga shoe shine boy / I don't believe you're mine / Never no mo' blues / Texas moon / Just a little bit jealous / We got good business / Please come back home / High country / All star boogie / There's not a cow in Texas / See who's sorry now / Sick, sober and sorry / Mississippi river blues / Wrong road home blues / Sweet Mama hurry home or... / My sweet wildflower / I'm swing you
CD ____ BCD 15907
Bear Family / Dec '96 / Direct / Rollercoaster / Swift

Dundee Strathspey & Reel ...

FIDDLE ME JIG (Dundee Strathspey & Reel Society)
CD ____ LCOM 9047
Lismor / Aug '91 / ADA / Direct / Duncans / Lismor

Dunham Jazz & Jubilee ...

DUNHAM JAZZ & JUBILEE SINGERS 1927-1931 (Dunham Jazz & Jubilee Singers)
CD ____ DOCD 5498
Document / Nov '96 / ADA / Hot Shot / Jazz Music

Dunham, Sonny

SONNY DUNHAM
CD ____ CCD 085
Circle / Oct '93 / Jazz Music / Swift / Wellard

Dunkelziffer

DUNKELZIFFER III
CD ____ FUNFUNDVIERZ 23
Funfundvierz / Jun '97 / Cargo / Greyhound

IN THE NIGHT
CD ____ FUNFUNDVIERZ 2
Funfundvierz / Jun '97 / Cargo / Greyhound

LIVE
CD ____ CTCD 058
Captain Trip / Jun '97 / Greyhound

Dunkley, Errol

EARLY YEARS, THE
CD ____ RNCD 2104
Rhino / May '95 / Grapevine/PolyGram / Jet Star

ERROL AGAIN
CD ____ SCHCD 01
Schema / Jul '97 / Jet Star

OK FRED (Dunkley, Errol & Sly & Robbie)
CD ____ RNCD 2017
Rhino / Jul '93 / Grapevine/PolyGram / Jet Star

PLEASE STOP YOUR LYING
CD ____ RGCD 0041
Rocky One / Apr '97 / Jet Star

PROFILE
CD ____ 665432
Melodie / Jul '97 / ADA / Discovery / Grapevine/PolyGram / Greensleeves / Jet Star

Dunlap, Slim

OLD NEW ME
Rockin' here tonight / Just for the hell of it / Isn't it / Partners in crime / Taken on the chin / From the git go / Busted up / Ain't exactly good / King and Queen / Ballad of the opening band / Love lost
CD ____ 892312
Medium Cool / Nov '93 / Vital

TIMES LIKE THIS
CD ____ 892772
Restless / Nov '96 / Vital

Dunmall, Paul

FOLKS (Dunmall, Paul & Paul Rogers)
Dingle at Leigh / Malvern Hills / S-round / Pete's reel / Himalayan balsam / Lament 4 / Nan / Grandad / Francis Thompson / St. Edburga / Alfrick's swan / Hornpipe / Cruck barn / Lucky Oscar / Lament 1 & 2 / Hairy fox / Grassnake / Nu / Nibly point / Bank Farm / Two dogs at Pigeon House
CD ____ SLAMCD 212
Slam / Oct '96 / Cadillac

QUARTET, SEXTET AND BABU TRIO (2CD Set)
Dubunni / Moths and spiders / In the haddock / Devil's chair / Lert / Trickly hausen / Shun fat / Separate balls
CD Set ____ SLAMCD 207
Slam / Oct '96 / Cadillac

SOLILOQUY - 1986
CD ____ MR 15
Matchless / '90 / Cadillac / ReR Megacorp

Dunn, Holly

GETTING IT DUNN
CD ____ 7599269492
WEA / Sep '92 / Warner Music

LIFE, LOVE AND ALL THE STAGES
CD ____ 5141611402
River North / Mar '96 / Direct

Dunn, Johnny

JOHNNY DUNN VOL.1 (1921-1922)
CD ____ JPCD 1522
Jazz Perspectives / Jul '96 / Hot Shot / Jazz Music

JOHNNY DUNN VOL.2 (1922-1928)
CD ______ **JPCD 1523**
Jazz Perspectives / Jul '96 / Hot Shot / Jazz Music

Dunn, Larry

LOVER'S SILHOUETTE (Dunn, Larry Orchestra)
Lover's silhouette / 2000 SKY-5 / Don't it make you wanna cry / Italian lady (A song for Mama) / Heaven sent (Michael's song) / Where's the love / Between 7 and earth / Pure faith (guitar interlude) / Maybe in my dreams / Jahap / Enchanted
CD ______ **101S 870712**
101 South / Nov '93 / New Note/Pinnacle

Dunn, Roy

KNOW'D THEM ALL
She cooked cornbread for her husband / Further on down the line / Everything I get a hold to / CC rider / You're worrying me / Lost lover blues / Stranger's blues / Move to Kansas city / Red cross store / Don't tear my clothes / I changed the lock / Pearl Harbour blues / Mr. Charlie / Bachelor's blues / Roy's matchbox blues
CD ______ **TRIX 3312**
Trix / Nov '93 / New Note/Pinnacle

Dunn, Willie

AKWESASNE NOTES
CD ______ **TRIK 032**
Trikont / Oct '94 / ADA / Direct

PACIFIC
CD ______ **TRIK 075**
Trikont / Oct '94 / ADA / Direct

Dunn-Packer Band

LOVE AGAINST THE WALL
CD ______ **TRCD 9905**
Tramp / Nov '93 / ADA / CM / Direct

Dunne, Mickey

LIMERICK LASSIES
CD ______ **SD 001CD**
SD Recordings / Apr '94 / ADA

Dunne, Pecker

TRAVELLIN' PEOPLE (Dunne, Pecker & Margaret Barry)
Dirty old town / Come back Paddy Reilly / Last of the travellin' people / She moved through the fair / Ballybunion by the sea / Down by the broom / Portlaoise jail / Cottage with the horseshoe / Wexford / Her mantle so green / Whiskey in the jar / Leprachaun / Tinker's lullaby / If you ever go o'er to Ireland / Down by the Liffeyside / Half door / Ould Morris van / Blarney stone / McAlpines fusiliers / Lovely Derry on the banks of the Foyle / Roisin dubh
CD ______ **MCVD 30012**
Emerald Gem / Nov '96 / BMG

Dunnery, Francis

ONE NIGHT IN SAUCHIEHALL STREET
CD ______ **COTINDCD 2**
Cottage Industry / May '95 / Total/BMG

TALL BLOND HELICOPTER
48 hours / Too much saturn / In my dreams / Johnny Podell song / Because I can / Immaculate / Father and Son
CD ______ **7567828252**
Atlantic / Apr '96 / Warner Music

Dunphy, Sean

IRELAND TO REMEMBER
CD ______ **DOCDX 9014**
Dolphin / Jul '96 / CM / Else / Grapevine/ PolyGram / Koch

Dunvant Male Choir

WELSH CELEBRATION
CD ______ **BNA 5057**
Bandleader / Sep '91 / Conifer/BMG

Duo Bertrand

DUO BERTRAND
CD ______ **AVPL 12CD**
Diffusion Breizh / Apr '94 / ADA

Duo Dre

TRE
Ouverture - strange new world / Vogel tut noot / Waltz in the woods / Veteran's day / Plan / Sushi moto / Unseren lieben frauen
CD ______ **8379502**
Amadeo / Oct '94 / PolyGram

Duo Peylet-Cunilot

MUSIQUE DES KLEZMORIM
CD ______ **925672**
BUDA / Jun '93 / Discovery

MUSIQUE KLEZMER
CD ______ **925682**
BUDA / Jun '93 / Discovery

Dupa, Sangwa

BUDDHIST TANTRAS OF GYUTO
CD ______ **7559791982**
Nonesuch / Jan '95 / Warner Music

Dupree, 'Champion' Jack

1945-53
CD ______ **KKCD 08**
Krazy Kat / Nov '92 / Hot Shot / Jazz Music

BIGTOWN PLAYBOYS BURNLEY FESTIVAL
CD ______ **JSPCD 231**
JSP / Oct '89 / ADA / Cadillac / Direct / Hot Shot / Target/BMG

BLUES FOR EVERYBODY
Heartbreaking women / Watchin' my stuff / Ain't no meat on de bone / Blues got me rockin' / Tongue tied blues / Please tell me baby / Harelip blues / Two below zero / Let the doorbell ring / Blues for everybody / That's my pa / She cooks me cabbage / Failing health blues / Stumbling block / Mail order woman / Silent partner / House rent party / Rub a little boogie / Walking the blues / Daybreak rock
CD ______ **CD 52029**
Blues Encore / Mar '93 / Target/BMG

BLUES FROM THE GUTTER
Strollin' / TB Blues / Can't kick the habit / Evil woman / Nasty boogie / Junkers blues / Bad blood / Goin' down slow / Frankie and Johnny / Stack-o-lee
CD ______ **7567824342**
Atlantic / Jul '93 / Warner Music

BLUES OF CHAMPION JACK DUPREE VOL.1, THE
CD ______ **STCD 8019**
Storyville / Jul '96 / Cadillac / Jazz Music / Wellard

BLUES OF CHAMPION JACK DUPREE VOL.2, THE
CD ______ **STCD 8020**
Storyville / Jul '96 / Cadillac / Jazz Music / Wellard

CHAMPION JACK DUPREE
CD ______ **DOCD 5444**
Document / May '96 / ADA / Hot Shot / Jazz Music

CHAMPION JACK DUPREE 1945-1946 (The Joe Davis Sessions)
Rum cola blues / She makes good jelly / Johnson street boogie / I'm a doctor for women / Wet neck mama / Love strike blues / Gin Mill Sal / Fisherman's blues / FDR blues
CD ______ **FLYCD 22**
Flyright / Sep '90 / Hot Shot / Jazz Music / Wellard

CHAMPION JACK DUPREE 1977-1983
CD ______ **157712**
Blues Collection / Feb '93 / Discovery

HOME (Charly Blues - Masterworks Vol. 40)
My baby's coming home / (I'll be glad when you're dead) you rascal you / No tomorrow / Heart of the blues is sound / Japanese special / Hard feeling / Blues from 1921 / Don't mistreat your woman
CD ______ **CDBM 40**
Charly / Jan '93 / Koch

JACK DUPREE, JIMMY RUSHING & MUDDY WATERS (Dupree, Jack & Jimmy Rushing/Muddy Waters)
Get some more you fool / Way I feel / In the moonlight / She's mine, she's yours / Somebody's been spoiling these woman / Harelip blues / Everybody blues / Walking the blues / Silent partner / Overhead blues / Sugar sweet / All aboard / I'm ready / Forty days and forty nights
CD ______ **17062**
Laserlight / Jul '96 / Target/BMG

NEW ORLEANS BARRELHOUSE 1960
CD ______ **PYCD 53**
Magpie / Oct '93 / Hot Shot / Jazz Music

NEW ORLEANS BARRELHOUSE BOOGIE
Gamblin' man blues / Warehouse man blues / Chain gang blues / New low down dog / Black woman swing / Cabbage greens No.1 / Cabbage greens no.2 / Angola blues / My cabin inn / Bad health blues / That's alright Mama / Gibing blues / Dupree shake dance / My baby's gone / Wee head woman / Junkers blues / Oh red / All alone blues / Big time Mama / Shady lane / Hurry down sunshine / Jackie P blues / Heavy heart blues / Morning tea / Black cow blues
CD ______ **4721922**
Columbia / May '93 / Sony

ONE LAST TIME
CD ______ **BB 9522CD**
Bullseye Blues / Aug '93 / Direct

WON'T BE A FOOL NO MORE
Third degree / TV mama / He knows the rules / Ain't it a shame / Ooh-la-la / Big leg Emmas / Won't be a fool no more / Calcutta blues / Take it slow and easy / She's all in my life / Poor, poor me / Twenty four hours / Pigfoot and a bottle of beer / Down in the valley / Too early in the morning / Shim-sham-shimmy
CD ______ **SEECD 388**
See For Miles/C5 / Oct '93 / Pinnacle

Dupree, Cornell

CAN'T GET THROUGH
Can't get through / Southern comfort / Double clutch / Sweet thing / Slippin' in / Let the sun shine on me again / Duck soup / Could it be
CD ______ **CDMT 020**
Meteor / Mar '93 / TKO Magnum

CHILD'S PLAY
Bumpin' / Short stuff / Putt's pub / For blues sake / Child's play / Smooth sailin' / Ramona / Just what you need / Mr. Bojangles
CD ______ **CDMT 024**
Meteor / Jan '94 / TKO Magnum

Dupree, Simon

KITES (Dupree, Simon & The Big Sound)
Kites / Like the sun like the fire / Sleep / For whom the bell tolls / Broken hearted pirates / Sixty minutes of your love / Lot of love / Love / Get off my Bach / There's a little picture playhouse / Daytime, nightime / I see the light / What is soul / Amen / Who cares / She gave me the sun / Thinking about my life / It is finished / I've seen it all before / You need a man / Reservations
CD ______ **SEECD 368**
See For Miles/C5 / May '97 / Pinnacle

Duprees

BEST OF THE DUPREES, THE
You belong to me / Why don't you believe me / Check yourself / Save your heart for me / Carousel / Two different worlds / Hope / Goodnight my love / Sky's the limit / People / My own true love / Have you heard / Delicious / Groovin' is easy / My love, my love / Ring of love / One in a million / Beautiful / My special angel / Delicious (Disco version)
CD ______ **NEMCD 674**
Sequel / Apr '94 / BMG

THEIR COMPLETE COED MASTERS
You belong to me / Unbelievable / I gotta tell her now / Ginny / I wish I could believe you / Please let her know / Have you heard / September in the rain / These foolish things / So little time / Exodus / Where are you / I'm yours / Try to remember / My own true love / So many have told me / It isn't fair / Sand and the sea / My dearest one / As time goes by / Sunset to sunrise / Take me as I am / Why don't you believe me / Gone with the wind / Wishing ring / Things I love / It's no sin / Yours / Love eyes / I'd rather be in your arms / Let's make love again
CD ______ **CDCHD 617**
Ace / Feb '96 / Pinnacle

Dura Delinquent

DURA DELINQUENT
CD ______ **K 173**
Konkurrent / May '97 / SRD

Duran Duran

BIG THING
Big thing / I don't want your love / All she wants is / Too late Marlene / Drug (It's just a state of mind) / Do you believe in shame / Palomino / Interlude one / Land / Flute interlude / Edge of America / Lake shore driving / Drug (It's just a state of mind)
CD ______ **DC 881642**
Disky / Aug '97 / Disky / THE
CD ______ **CDPRG 1007**
Parlophone / Jun '97 / EMI

DECADE
Planet Earth / Girls on film / Hungry like the wolf / Rio / Save a prayer / Is there something I should know / Union of the snake / Reflex / Wild boys / View to a kill / Notorious / Skin trade / I don't want your love / All she wants is
CD ______ **CDDDX 10**
Parlophone / Nov '89 / EMI

DURAN DURAN
Girls on film / Planet Earth / Anyone out there / To the shore / Careless memories / Night boat / Sound of thunder / Friends of mine / Tel Aviv
CD ______ **CDPRG 1003**
Parlophone / Aug '95 / EMI

LIBERTY
Violence of summer / Liberty / Hothead / Serious / All along the water / My Antarctica / First impressions / Read my lips / Can you deal with it / Venice drowning / Downtown
CD ______ **CDPRG 1009**
Parlophone / Aug '93 / EMI

NOTORIOUS
Notorious / American science / Skin trade / Hold me / Vertigo (do the demolition) / So misled / Meet el presidente / Winter marches on / Proposition / Matter of feeling
CD ______ **CDPRG 1006**
Parlophone / Aug '93 / EMI

RIO
Rio / My own way / Lonely in your nightmare / Hungry like the wolf / Hold back the rain / New religion / Last chance on the stairway / Save a prayer / Chauffeur
CD ______ **CDPRG 1004**
Parlophone / Aug '93 / EMI

SEVEN AND THE RAGGED TIGER
Reflex / New moon on Monday / I'm looking for cracks in the pavement / I take the dice / Of crime and passion / Union of the snake / Shadows on your side / Tiger tiger / Seventh stranger
CD ______ **CDPRG 1005**
Parlophone / Aug '93 / EMI

THANK YOU
White lines (don't don't do it) / I want to take you higher / Perfect day / Watching the detectives / Lay lady lay / 911 is a joke / Success / Crystal ship / Ball of confusion / Thank you / Drive-by / I want to take you higher again
CD ______ **CDDDB 36**
Parlophone / Mar '95 / EMI

WEDDING ALBUM, THE
Too much information / Ordinary world / Love voodoo / Drowning man / Shotgun / Stop dead / Breath after breath / UMF / None of the above / Time for temptation / Shelter / To whom it may concern / Sin of the city
CD ______ **CDDDB 34**
Parlophone / Feb '93 / EMI

Duran, Hilario

KILLER TUMBAO
Homage to Chano Pozo / Alfredo's mood / Longina / Song for Yemaya / Brasiliangada / Three for one / Los Tres Golpes / Killer Tumbao / Timba Mabo
CD ______ **JUST 1012**
Justin Time / Aug '97 / Cadillac / New Note/ Pinnacle

Durant, Jon

THREE IF BY AIR
Pale and crystal / Was there something out there / Shadows beginning to fade / Escalator / Sombrero fallout / Final frontiers / Alien communication technique
CD ______ **ALCD 1005**
Alchemy / Aug '97 / Pinnacle

Durante, Jimmy

AS TIME GOES BY (The Best Of Jimmy Durante)
As time goes by / If I had you / Smile / Hi lili hi lo / Make someone happy / Young at heart / Hello, young lovers / Try a little tenderness / Glory of love / I'll be seeing you / September song / I'll see you in my dreams
CD ______ **9362454562**
WEA / Nov '96 / Warner Music

I SAY IT WITH MUSIC
CD ______ **VN 169**
Viper's Nest / Aug '95 / ADA / Cadillac / Direct / Jazz Music

SEPTEMBER SONG
CD ______ **NI 4026**
Natasha / Feb '94 / ADA / Cadillac / CM / Direct / Jazz Music

Durao, Eduardo

TIMBILA
Ngono utane vuna kudima / Walamba kudja mundino / Haguma nguma tekenha / Eduardo Durao mauaia / Magueleguele / Nhantumbuane / Unichenguile
CD ______ **CDORBD 065**
Globestyle / Jan '91 / Pinnacle

Durbin, Deanna

BEST OF DEANNA DURBIN
It's raining sunbeams / My own / Spring in my heart / One fine day / Love is all / Perhaps / Last rose of summer / Can't help singing / Blue Danube dream / californ-i-ay / Because / Turntable song / Spring will be a little late this year / Home sweet home / Waltzing in the clouds / Ave Maria
CD ______ **MCLD 19183**
MCA / May '93 / BMG

CAN'T HELP SINGING
CD ______ **JASCD 101**
Jasmine / Nov '95 / Conifer/BMG / Hot Shot / TKO Magnum

FAN CLUB, THE
Amapola / Because / When April sings / Waltzing in the clouds / My own / Brindisi / Beneath the lights of home / Spring in my heart / It's raining sunbeams / Musetta's waltz song / Love is all / Perhaps / One fine day / Home sweet home / Last rose of summer / Il bacio / Ave Maria / Loch Lomond / Alleluia
CD ______ **PASTCD 9781**
Flapper / May '92 / Pinnacle

ULTIMATE COLLECTION, THE (24 Greatest Hits)
It's foolish but it's fun / Waltzing in the clouds / Beneath the lights of home / Spring in my heart / Estrellita / Il bacio / Because / Cielito lindo / When April sings / Spring will

be a little late this year / Always / It's raining sunbeams / My hero / When the roses bloom again / Brindisi / Ave Maria / Amapola / Love's old sweet song / Poor butterfly / Les filles de Cadiz / Musetta's waltz song / Last rose of summer / Perhaps / Can't help singing
CD PLATCD 143
Platinum / Mar '96 / Prism

WITH A SONG IN MY HEART
Waltzing in the clouds / My own / Brindisi / It's raining sunbeams / Beneath the lights of home / Love is all / Les filles de cadiz / Perhaps / One fine day / Spring in my heart / Amapola / Estrellita / When April sings / Musetta's waltz song / Because / Blue Danube dream / Poor butterfly / Last rose of summer / It's foolish but it's fun / Home sweet home
CD PLCD 534
President / Mar '93 / Grapevine/PolyGram / President / Target/BMG

Durham Constabulary Brass ...

GENTLE TOUCH, THE (Durham Constabulary Brass Band)
CD BNA 5079
Bandleader / Mar '93 / Conifer/BMG

Durham, Judith

MONA LISA
Catch the wind / Love song / Someone out there / Heart on my sleeve / Turn turn turn / Adios amor / Saltwater / Northern lights / Put a little love in your heart / Morning has broken / Mona Lisas and Mad Hatters / You've got a friend / End of the world
CD CDJDTV 1
EMI TV / Feb '97 / EMI

Durham, Mike

BOUNCING AROUND (West Jesmond Rhythm Kings)
CD BCD 352
GHB / Nov '96 / Jazz Music

CHICAGO BUZZ (West Jesmond Rhythm Kings)
Mama's gonna slow you down / Big boy / Anywhere Sweetie goes / Sweet Emmalina / 2.19 blues / Down among the sugar cane / Chicago buzz / Breeze / Brownskin Mama / Candy lips / One I love just can't be bothered with me / Oh sister, ain't that hot / That's my stuff / Shout 'em Aunt Tillie / Magnolia's wedding day / Angry / Sweet substitute / Wa wa wa
CD LACD 74
Lake / Mar '97 / ADA / Cadillac / Direct / Jazz Music / Target/BMG

SHAKE 'EM LOOSE
CD LACD 45
Lake / Feb '95 / ADA / Cadillac / Direct / Jazz Music / Target/BMG

Durham School Chapel Choir

FLOREAT DUNELMIA
CD CDCA 929
SCS Music / Nov '93 / Conifer/BMG

Durrant, Richard

RICHARD DURRANT'S DUELLIN' BANJOS
Duellin' banjos / Old Joe Clarke / Bill Cheetham / Dance of the Welsh vicar / Stoney creek / Jerusalem ridge / Frosty morning / Foggy mountain breakdown / Billy in the low ground / Wild wood flower / Mason's apron / Salamanca / Byrne's hornpipe / Nine points of roguery / Star of Munster / Loch Neagh / Czardas / Down in the swamp / Speed the plough / Swing low, sweet chariot
CD QED 172
Tring / Nov '96 / Tring

Durutti Column

BREAD AND CIRCUSES
Pauline / Tomorrow / Dance 11 / Hilary / Street fight / Royal infirmary / Black horses / Dance 1 / Blind elevator girl / Osaka
CD TWI 9882
Les Disques Du Crepuscule / Nov '93 / Discovery

FIDELITY
CD TWI 9762
Les Disques Du Crepuscule / Apr '96 / Discovery

GUITAR AND OTHER MACHINES, THE
Arpeggiator / Waht is it to me (woman) / Red shoes / Jongleur grey / When the world / USP / Bordeaux sequence / Pol in B / English landscape tradition / Miss Haymes / Don't you think you're funny / LFO mod / Dream topping / 28 oldham street / Otis / ELT / Finding the sea / Bordeaux
CD 8288282
Factory Too / Dec '96 / Pinnacle / PolyGram

LC
Sketch for dawn / Portrait for Fraser / Jacqueline / Messidor / Sketch for dawn / Never known / Act committed / Detail for Paul / Missing boy / Sweet cheat gone / For Mimi / Belgian friends / Self portrait / One christmas for your thoughts / Danny / Enigma
CD 8288272
Factory Too / Dec '96 / Pinnacle / PolyGram

LIPS THAT WOULD KISS
CD FBN 2CD
Les Disques Du Crepuscule / Nov '96 / Discovery

LIVE AT THE BOTTOM LINE
CD RE 512CD
ROIR / Nov '94 / Plastic Head / Shellshock/Disc

RETURN OF THE DURUTTI COLUMN
Sketch for summer / Requiem for a father / Katherine / Conduct / Beginning / Jazz / Sketch for winter / Collete / In d
CD 8288292
Factory Too / Dec '96 / Pinnacle / PolyGram

SEX & DEATH
Anthony / Rest of my life / For Colette / Next time / Beautiful lies / My irascible friend / Believe in me / Fermina / Where should I be / Fado / Madre mio / Blue period
CD FACD 201
Factory Too / Nov '94 / Pinnacle / PolyGram

VINI REILLY
Love no more / Poling / Opera I / People's pleasure park / Red square / Finding the sea / Otis / William B / They work every day / Opera II / Homage to the Catalonea / Requiem again / My country / Paradise passage road / Les preger's tune / Bhuddist prayer / Misere / Real drums - real drummer / Pathway / Rob Grey's elegy / Shirt no.7
CD 8188262
Factory Too / Dec '96 / Pinnacle / PolyGram

Dury, Ian

BEST OF IAN DURY, THE
CD DC 869752
Disky / Aug '96 / Disky / THE

BUS DRIVER'S PRAYER & OTHER STORIES, THE
That's enough of that / Bill Haley's last words / Poor Joey / Quick quick slow / Fly in the ointment / O'Donegal / Poo poo in the prawn / Have a word / London talking / D'orine the cow / Your horoscope / No such thing as love / Two old dogs without a name / Bus driver's prayer
CD FIENDCD 702
Demon / Nov '92 / Pinnacle

IAN DURY
CD Set IAN 1
Demon / Aug '91 / Pinnacle

IAN DURY AND THE BLOCKHEADS
Intro / Wake up and make love with me / Clevor Trever / If I was with a woman / Billericay dickie / Quiet / My old man / Spasticus autisticus / Plaistow Patricia / There ain't half been some clever bastards / Sweet Gene Vincent / What a waste / Hit me with your rhythm stick / Blockheads
CD FIENDCD 777
Demon / Aug '91 / Pinnacle

Dusk

DUSK
CD CYBERCD 15
Cyber / Feb '95 / Amato Disco / Arabesque / Plastic Head

Duskin, 'Big' Joe

CINCINNATI STOMP
CD ARHCD 422
Arhoolie / Sep '95 / ADA / Cadillac / Direct

DON'T MESS WITH THE BOOGIE MAN
Don't mess with the boogie man / Down on my bended knees / Big Joe's boogie prayer / Oodle adle / Mean and evil / Dirty rat swing / Cuban sugar mill / Call my job / Keep it to yourself / Low down dog / CC rider / So long / Boogie woogie on St. Louis blues / Ida B / Yancey special
CD IGOCD 2062
Indigo / May '97 / ADA / Direct

DOWN THE ROAD APIECE
CD WOLF 120713
Wolf / Jul '96 / Hot Shot / Jazz Music / Swift

Dust In My Head

WIND IN MY HEART
CD PARCD 019
Parasol / Oct '96 / Cargo

Dusty, Slim

GOLDEN ANNIVERSARY ALBUM, THE
Country revival / Leave him in the long yard / Pub with no beer / Walk a country mile / Camooweal / Indian Pacific / Highway fever / Man from Snowy River / Lights on the hill / Three Rivers hotel / Beat of the government stroke / I don't sleep at night / When the rain tumbles down in July / Angel of Goulburn Hill / Kelly's offsider / Things I see around me / Biggest disappointment / Duncan: *Dusty, Slim & Rolf Harris*
CD PRMCD 13
Premier/EMI / Sep '96 / EMI

Dutch Jazz Orchestra

PORTRAIT OF A SILK THREAD
Blue star / Bagatelle / Love has passed me by again / La sacre supreme / Portrait of a silk thread / Tonk / Wounded love / Cashmere cutie / Lana Turner / Pentonsilic / Lament for an orchid
CD KOKO 1310
Kokopelli / Aug '96 / New Note/Pinnacle

Dutch Swing College Band

40 YEARS AT ITS BEST 1945-85
CD CDTTD 516
Timeless Traditional / Sep '86 / Jazz Music / New Note/Pinnacle

BACK IN TIME (1990-1945)
Way down yonder in New Orleans / (Back home again) In Indiana / Coal black shine / Gatemouth / Everybody loves my baby / Exactly like you / Dear old Southland / On the sunny side of the street / You're driving me crazy / Clarinet marmalade / Royal Garden blues / Freeze and melt / Buddy's habits / Knee drops / Weary blues / Froggie moore rag / That's a plenty / Willie the weeper / Hodge podge
CD 8420452
Philips / Mar '93 / PolyGram

COLLECTORS ITEMS (Previously Unreleased Material/First-Time Srereo Versions)
Oh baby / New Orleans / Millenberg joys / Muskrat ramble / Rockin' chair / St. Louis blues / Mandy, make up your mind / Aunt Hagar's blues / I've found a new baby / Big city blues / Stomp meeting / East St. Louis toodle-oo / From Monday on / Beu mir bist du schon / Flying East / Chinatown, my Chinatown / Blues for Pete / Fly me to the moon / Desiree / Flying home
CD 5141002
Philips / Mar '93 / PolyGram

DIGITAL ANNIVERSARY
Bourbon Street parade / Wabash blues / Caribbean parade / Is it true what they say about Dixie / Clarinet games / Saturday night is the loneliest night of the week / Coal black shine / Third Street blues / Gladiolus rag / Columbus Stockade blues / Devil in the moon / Original Dixieland one-step / Rose room / Swing 36 / Sunday
CD 8245852
Philips / Jan '92 / PolyGram

DIGITAL DIXIE (Live At North Sea Jazz Festival 1981, The Hague)
Way down yonder in New Orleans / Knee drops / West End blues / At a Georgia camp meeting / I want a little girl / China boy / Creole belles / Sugar the kazoos / Down home rag / On Green Dolphin Street
CD 8000652
Philips / Jan '92 / PolyGram

DIGITAL DUTCH
West Side stomp / Buddy Bolden's blues / Papa Dip / Sidewalk blues / Clarinet case / Louisiana / My gal Sal / Coney Island washboard / Perdido street blues / Tailspin / Gatemouth / Perdido / Do you know what it means to miss New Orleans / Chicago / Drum blues
CD 8140682
Philips / Jan '92 / PolyGram

DIGITAL JUBILEE (Live At Congresgebouw, The Hague 18/5/1990)
Way down yonder in New Orleans / Hindustan / St. Louis blues / Take the 'A' train / Wild man blues / It's only a paper moon / Black bottom stomp / Altotude / Bo Bo's boogie / At the banks of the Wabash / Japanese sandman / Temptation rag / Ain't misbehavin' / Strike up the band / Absent minder blues / 1919 rag
CD 8450902
Philips / Mar '93 / PolyGram

DUTCH SAMBA
Corro / Velas blancas / Girl from Ipanema / Samba de Orfeu / Menina flor meditacao / Manana / Corcovado / Poinciana / Samba de Quena / Eso es el amor / La adelita
CD CDTTD 552
Timeless Traditional / Jun '89 / Jazz Music / New Note/Pinnacle

DUTCH SWING COLLEGE BAND & TEDDY WILSON (Dutch Swing College Band & Teddy Wilson)
Limehouse blues / Riverboat shuffle / Undecided / Rhythm king / Sweet Georgia Brown / China boy / Runnin' wild / How come you do me like you do / You must have been a beautiful baby / Paradise island / Happy days are here again
CD CDTTD 525
Timeless Traditional / Oct '96 / Jazz Music / New Note/Pinnacle

DUTCH SWING COLLEGE BAND WITH GUESTS VOL.1
Mandy, make up your mind / I gotta right to sing the blues / Blues / I wanny be happy / Keepin' out of mischief now / I got rhythm / Lotus blossom / Swing that music / Poor butterfly / As long as I live / Nobody knows you (when you're down and out) / Shimmeshawabble / Wild dog
CD 8307712
Philips / Jan '91 / PolyGram

JOINT IS JUMPIN', THE
Milenberg joys / Grandpa's spells / Squeeze me / Bugle call rag / Peg o' my heart / King Porter stomp / Ballin' the Jack / Clarinet marmalade / Drop me off in Harlem / Freeze and melt / Snowy morning blues / Limehouse blues / Keepin' out of mischief now / Joint is jumpin'
CD CDTTD 594
Timeless Jazz / Jul '95 / New Note/Pinnacle

LIVE IN 1960 (Best Of Dixieland)
Way down in yonder in New Orleans / South Rampart Street parade / Apex blues / Ory's creole underground / Mood indigo / King of the zulus / Opus 5 / Tin roof blues / Freeze and melt / Please don't talk about me when I'm gone / Out of the gallion / Carry me back to old Virginny / Jazz me blues / Waery blues / Way down yonder in New Orleans
CD 8387652
Philips / May '90 / PolyGram

LIVE IN CONCERT 1974
Way down yonder in New Orleans / Charleston hound / Apex blues / Shiny stockings / Muskrat ramble / Jump the rabbit / At the jazz band ball / I'm coming Virginia / Bag O'Blues / My inspiration / Runnin' wild / De bas van drakestein / Chimes blues / That's a plenty / Face to face / I surrender dear / Original Dixieland one step
CD AL 73080
Challenge / Mar '97 / ADA / Direct / Jazz Music / Wellard

OLD FASHIONED WAY, THE
CD JHR 73566
Jazz Hour / Nov '93 / Cadillac / Jazz Music / Target/BMG

STOMPIN' THE HITS
CD 15137
Laserlight / May '94 / Target/BMG

SWINGING STUDIO SESSIONS
At the Jazz Band Ball / Savoy blues / Fidgety feet / CC rider / Royal Garden blues / Some of these days / Tiger rag / Just a closer walk with thee / March of the Indians / Mood indigo / I wish I could shimmy like my sister Kate / I've been working on the railroad / East St. Louis toodle-oo / Cornet chop suey / When it's sleepy time down South / Dippermouth blues / Davenport blues / Shake it and break it
CD 8242562
Philips / May '85 / PolyGram

Duterte, Jean-Francois

TRADITIONAL FRENCH SONGS
CD 926662
BUDA / Feb '97 / Discovery

Dutronc

DUTRONC
CD DAMGOOD 70CD
Damaged Goods / Jan '96 / Shellshock/ Disc

Duvall, Huelyn

THREE MONTHS TO KILL
CD CLCD 4415
Collector/White Label / Oct '96 / TKO Magnum

Dwarves

HORROR STORIES
CD VOXXCD 2037
Voxx / Aug '88 / Else / RTM/Disc

SUGAR FIX
Anybody out there / Evil primeval / Reputation / Lies / Saturday night / New Orleans / Action man / Smack city / Cain novacaine / Underworld / Wish that I was dead
CD SPCD 76/243
Sub Pop / Jul '93 / Cargo / Greyhound / Shellshock/Disc

TOOLIN' FOR LUCIFER'S CRANK
CD RECESS 32CD
Recess / Feb '97 / Cargo

Dwyer, Finbarr

PURE TRADITIONAL IRISH ACCORDIAN
CD PTICD 1004
Pure Traditional Irish / Apr '94 / ADA / CM / Direct / Ross

Dyer, Johnny

JUKIN
CD BP 5028CD
Blind Pig / Feb '96 / ADA / CM / Direct / Hot Shot

LISTEN UP
CD BT 1101CD
Black Top / Apr '94 / ADA / CM / Direct

SHAKE IT
CD BT 1114CD
Black Top / Apr '95 / ADA / CM / Direct

Dyewitness

BATTLE FOR YOUR MIND
CD MMCD 1003

Mo's Music Machine / Feb '97 / Mo's Music Machine / Pinnacle

Dying Fetus

PURIFICATION THROUGH VIOLENCE
CD RRS 960CD
Progress / Mar '97 / Cargo / Plastic Head

Dyke & The Blazers

SO SHARP
Funky Broadway (part 1) / Funky Broadway (part 2) / Uhh (part 1) / Runaway people / We got more soul / It's your thing / Shot gun Slim / So sharp / Let a woman be a woman - let a man be a man / You are my sunshine / Funky walk (part 2) / Wrong house / Don't bug me / City dump / My sisters and my brothers / Funky walk (part 1) / Uhh part 2 / Broadway combination / Stuff / Funky bull part 1 / Funky bull part 2 / Wobble / Uhh (edit) / I'm so all alone
CD CDKEND 004
Kent / Aug '91 / Pinnacle

Dykes, Omar

MUDDY SPRINGS ROAD
CD PRD 70602
Provogue / Mar '94 / Pinnacle

Dylan, Bob

30TH ANNIVERSARY CONCERT CELEBRATION (2CD Set) (Various Artists)
Like a rolling stone: *Mellencamp, John Cougar* / Leopardskin pillbox hat: *Mellencamp, John Cougar* / Introduction: *Kristofferson, Kris* / Blowin' in the wind: *Wonder, Stevie* / Masters of war: *Vedder, Eddie/Mike McCready* / Foot of pride: *Reed, Lou* / Times they are a changin': *Chapman, Tracy* / It ain't me babe: *Carter, June/Johnny Cash* / What was it you wanted: *Nelson, Willie* / I'll be your baby tonight: *Kristofferson, Kris* / Seven days: *Winter, Johnny* / Highway 61: *Winter, Johnny* / Just like a woman: *Havens, Richie* / Just like Tom Thumb's blues: *Young, Neil* / All along the watchtower: *Young, Neil* / When the ship comes in: *Clancy Brothers & Tommy Makem* / I shall be released: *Hynde, Chrissie* / Don't think twice, it's alright: *Clapton, Eric* / Emotionally yours: *O'Jays* / You ain't goin' nowhere: *Cash, Rosanne & Mary Chapin-Carpenter/Shawn Colvin* / Absolutely sweet Marie: *Harrison, George* / Licence to kill: *Petty, Tom & The Heartbreakers* / Rainy day women 12 & 35: *Petty, Tom & The Heartbreakers* / Mr. Tambourine man: *McGuinn, Roger* / It's alright Ma (I'm only bleeding): *Dylan, Bob* / My back pages: *Dylan, Bob* / Girl from the North Country: *Dylan, Bob* / Knockin' on Heaven's door: *Dylan, Bob*
CD Set 4740002
Columbia / Jun '97 / Sony

ANOTHER SIDE OF BOB DYLAN
All I really want to do / Black crow blues / Spanish Harlem incident / Chimes of freedom / I shall be free / To Ramona / Motorpsycho nightmare / My back pages / I don't believe you (she acts like we never have met) / Ballads in plain D / It ain't me babe
CD CD 32034
CBS / Nov '89 / Sony

BASEMENT TAPES (Dylan, Bob & The Band)
Odds and ends: *Dylan, Bob* / Orange juice blues (blues for breakfast): *Dylan, Bob* / Million dollar bash: *Dylan, Bob* / Yaroo Street scandal: *Dylan, Bob* / Goin' to Acapulco: *Dylan, Bob* / Kate's been gone: *Dylan, Bob* / You ain't goin' nowhere: *Dylan, Bob* / Don't ya tell Henry: *Dylan, Bob* / Nothing was delivered: *Dylan, Bob* / Open the door, Homer: *Dylan, Bob* / Long distance operator: *Dylan, Bob* / This wheel's on fire: *Dylan, Bob* / Lo and behold: *Dylan, Bob* / Bessie Smith: *Dylan, Bob* / Clothes line saga: *Dylan, Bob* / Apple suckling tree: *Dylan, Bob* / Mrs. Henry: *Dylan, Bob* / Tears of rage: *Dylan, Bob* / Too much of nothing: *Dylan, Bob* / Yea, heavy and a bottle of bread: *Dylan, Bob* / Ain't no more cane: *Dylan, Bob* / Crash on the levee (down in the flood): *Dylan, Bob* / Ruben Remus: *Dylan, Bob* / Tiny Montgomery: *Dylan, Bob*
CD 4661372
CBS / Nov '89 / Sony

BASEMENT TAPES, THE (2CD Set)
Odds and ends / Orange juice blues (blues for breakfast) / Million dollar bash / Yazoo street scandal / Goin' to Acapulco / Katie's been gone / You ain't goin' nowhere / Don't ya tell Henry / Nothing was delivered / Open the door / Homer / Long distance operator / Wheel's on fire / Lo and behold / Bessie Smith / Clothes line saga / Apple sucking tree / Please / Mrs. Henry / Tears of rage / Too much of nothing / Heavy and a bottle of bread / Ain't no more cane / Crash on the levee (down in the flood) / Reben Remus / Tiny Montgomery / This wheel's on fire
CD Set 4678502
Columbia / Jun '96 / Sony

BEFORE THE FLOOD (2CD Set) (Dylan, Bob & The Band)
Most likely you'll go your way and I'll go mine / Lay lady lay / Rainy day women 12 & 35 / Knockin' on Heaven's door / It ain't me babe / Ballad of a thin man / Up on Cripple Creek / I shall be released / Endless highway / Night they drove old Dixie down / Stagefright / Don't think twice, it's alright / Just like a woman / It's alright Ma (I'm only bleeding) / Shape I'm in / When you awake / Weight / All along the watchtower / Highway 61 revisited / Like a rolling stone / Blowin' in the wind
CD Set CD 22137
CBS / Jun '96 / Sony

BEST OF BOB DYLAN, THE (2CD Set)
Blowin' in the wind / Times they are a-changin' / Don't think twice, it's alright / Mr. Tambourine man / Like a rolling stone / Just like a woman / All along the watchtower / Lay lady lay / If not for you / Knockin' on Heaven's door / Forever young / Tangled up in blue / Shelter from the storm / I shall be released / Oh sister / Gotta serve somebody / Jokerman / Everything is broken
CD Set SONYTV 28CD
Sony TV / Jun '97 / Sony

BIOGRAPH (3CD Set)
Lay lady lay / If not for you / Times they are a changin' / Blowin' in the wind / Masters of war / Percy's song / Like a rolling stone / Subterranean homesick blues / Mr. Tambourine man / It ain't me babe / Million dollar bash / It's all over now baby blue / Positively 4th Street / Heart of mine / I believe in you / Time passes slowly / Forever young / Baby let me follow you down / I'll be your baby tonight / I'll keep it with mine / Lonesome death of Hattie Carroll / Mixed-up confusion / Tombstone blues / Groom's still waiting at the altar / Most likely you'll go your way and I'll go mine / Jet pilot / Lay down your weary tune / I don't believe you (she acts like we never have met) / Visions of Johanna / Every grain of sand / Quinn the Eskimo / Dear landlord / You angel you / To Ramona / You're a big girl now / Abandoned love / Tangled up in blue / Can you please crawl out of your window / Isis / Caribbean wind / Up to me / Baby I'm in the mood for you / I wanna be your lover / I want you / On a night like this / Just like a woman / Romance in Durango / Senor (tales of Yankee power) / Gotta serve somebody / I shall be released / Knockin' on Heaven's door / All along the watchtower / Solid rock
CD Set CD 66509
CBS / Jan '86 / Sony

BLONDE ON BLONDE
Rainy day women 12 & 35 / Pledging my time / Visions of Johanna / One of us must know / I want you / Stuck inside a mobile with the Memphis blues again / Leopardskin pillbox hat / Just like a woman / Most likely you'll go your way and I'll go mine / Temporarily like Achilles / Absolutely sweet Marie / Fourth time around / Obviously five believers / Sad eyed lady of the Lowlands
CD Set CK 64411
Columbia / Feb '95 / Sony
CD 4804172
Columbia / Jul '95 / Sony

BLOOD ON THE TRACKS
Tangled up in blue / Simple twist of fate / You're a big girl now / Idiot wind / You're gonna make me lonesome when you go / Meet me in the morning / Lily Rosemary and the jack of hearts / If you see her / Say hello / Shelter from the storm / Buckets of rain
CD 4678422
Columbia / Sep '93 / Sony

BOB DYLAN
She's no good / Talkin' New York blues / In my time of dying / Man of constant sorrow / Fixing to die blues / Pretty Peggy-O / Highway 51 blues / Gospel plow / Baby let me follow you down / House of the rising sun / Freight train blues / Song to Woody / See that my grave is kept clean
CD CD 32001
CBS / Nov '89 / Sony

BOB DYLAN SONGBOOK, THE (Various Artists)
All I really want to do: *Cher* / Girl on the North Country: *Stewart, Rod* / Si tu dois partir: *Fairport Convention* / You ain't goin' nowhere: *Byrds* / Wanted man: *Cash, Johnny* / Absolutely sweet Marie: *Flamin' Groovies* / Outlaw blues: *Edmunds, Dave* / To Ramona: *Price, Alan* / I pity the poor immigrant: *Collins, Judy* / Tears of rage: *Band* / Love minus zero: *Walker Brothers* / Blowin' in the wind: *Darin, Bobby* / Tomorrow is a long time: *Stewart, Rod* / Too much of nothing: *Fotheringay* / Knockin' on heaven's door: *Campbell, Stan* / Wicked messenger: *Faces* / Ballad of Hollis Brown: *Simone, Nina* / You angel you: *Manfred Mann's Earthband* / This wheel's on fire: *Driscoll, Julie & Brian Auger* / Mighty quinn: *Puckett, Gary & The Union Gap* / Nothing was delivered: *Byrds* / When the ship comes in: *Hollies* / Highway 61 revisited: *Winter, Johnny* / Maggie's farm: *Burke, Solomon*
CD VSOPCD 158
Connoisseur Collection / Apr '91 / Pinnacle

BOOTLEG SERIES VOL.1-3, THE (Rare & Unreleased 1961-1991/3CD Set)
Hard times in New York Town / He was a friend of mine / Man on the street / No more auction block / House carpenter / Talkin' Bear Mountain picnic massacre blues / Let me die in my footsteps / Rambling gambling Willie / Talkin' Hava negeilah blues / Quit your low down ways / Worried blues / Kingsport Town / Walkin' down the line / Walls of red wing / Paths of victory / Talkin' John Birch paranoid blues / Who killed Davey Moore / Only a hobo / Moonshiner / When the ship comes in / Time they are a changin' / Last thoughts on Woody Guthrie / Seven curses / Eternal circle / Suze (The cough song) / Mama you been on my mind / Farewell, Angelina / Subterranean homesick blues / If you gotta go, go now / Sitting on a barbed wire fence / Like a rolling stone / It takes a lot to laugh, it takes a train to cry / I'll keep it with mine / She's your lover now / I shall be released / Santa Fe / If not for you / Wallflower / Nobody 'cept you / Tangled up in blue / Call letter blues / Idiot wind / If you see her / Golden loom / Catfish / Seven days / Ye shall be changed / Every grain of sand / You changed my life / Need a woman / Angelina / Someone's got a hold of my heart / Tell me / Lord protect my child / Foot of pride / Blind Willie McTell / When the night comes falling from the sky / Series of dreams
CD Set 4680862
Columbia / Apr '91 / Sony

BRINGING IT ALL BACK HOME
Subterranean homesick blues / She belongs to me / Maggie's farm / Love minus zero / Outlaw blues / On the road again / Bob Dylan's 15th dream / Mr. Tambourine man / Gates of Eden / It's alright Ma (I'm only bleeding) / It's all over now baby blue
CD CD 32344
CBS / Jun '89 / Sony

DESIRE
Hurricane / Isis / Mozambique / One more cup of coffee / Oh sister / Joey / Romance in Durango / Black Diamond Bay / Sara
CD CD 32570
Columbia / Jan '95 / Sony

DOWN IN THE GROOVE
Let's stick together / When did you leave Heaven / Sally Sue Brown / Death is not the end / Had a dream about you, baby / Ugliest girl in the world / Silvio / Ninety miles an hour (down a dead end street) / Shenandoah / Rank strangers to me
CD 4602672
CBS / Jun '88 / Sony

DYLAN (A Fool Such As I)
Lily of the west / Can't help falling in love / Sarah Jane / Ballad of Ira Hayes / Mr. Bojangles / Mary Ann / Big yellow taxi / Fool such as I / Spanish is the loving tongue
CD CD 32286
Columbia / Feb '91 / Sony

DYLAN AND THE DEAD (Dylan, Bob & Grateful Dead)
Slow train / I want you / Gotta serve somebody / Queen Jane approximately / Joey / All along the watchtower / Knockin' on Heaven's door
CD 4633812
CBS / Apr '94 / Sony

EMPIRE BURLESQUE
Tight connection to my heart (has anybody seen my love?) / Seeing the real you at last / I'll remember you / Clean cut kid / Emotionally yours / Dark eyes / Something's burning baby / Never gonna be the same again / Trust yourself / When the night comes / Falling from the sky
CD 4678402
Columbia / Feb '91 / Sony

FREEWHEELIN' BOB DYLAN, THE
Blowin' in the wind / Girl from the North Country / Masters of war / Down the highway / Bob Dylan's blues / Hard rain's gonna fall / Don't think twice, it's alright / Bob Dylan's dream / Oxford Town / Talking World War III blues / Corine Corina / Honey just allow me one more chance / I shall be free
CD CDCBS 32390
CBS / Nov '89 / Sony

FREEWHEELIN'/ANOTHER SIDE OF BOB DYLAN/TIMES THEY ARE A... (3CD Set)
CD Set 4673902
CBS / Dec '90 / Sony

GOOD AS I'VE BEEN TO YOU
Frankie and Albert / Jim Jones / Blackjack Davy / Canadee-I-O / Sittin' on top of the world / Little Maggie / Hard times / Step it up / Tomorrow night / Arthur McBride / You're gonna quit me / Diamond Joe / Froggie went a-courtin'
CD 4727102
Columbia / Feb '97 / Sony

GOOD AS I'VE BEEN TO YOU/ GREATEST HITS
CD Set 4727102D
Columbia / Feb '93 / Sony

GREATEST HITS
Blowin' in the wind / It ain't me babe / Times they are a changin' / Mr. Tambourine man / She belongs to me / It's all over now baby blue / Subterranean homesick blues / One of us must know / Like a rolling stone / Just like a woman / Rainy day women 12 & 35 / I want you
CD 4609079
Columbia / Apr '97 / Sony

GREATEST HITS VOL.2
CD 4712432
Columbia / Jul '93 / Sony

GREATEST HITS VOL.3
Tangled up in blue / Changing the guards / Groom's still waiting at the alter / Hurricane / Forever young / Jokerman / Dignity / Silvio / Ring them bells / Gotta serve somebody / Series of dreams / Brownsville girl / Under the red sky / Knockin' on heaven's door
CD 4778052
Columbia / Nov '94 / Sony

HARD RAIN'S A-GONNA FALL, A
Maggie's farm / One too many mornings / Stuck inside a mobile with the Memphis blues again / Oh sister / Lay lady lay / Shelter from the storm / You're a big girl now / I threw it all away / Idiot wind
CD CD 32308
CBS / Nov '89 / Sony

HIGHWAY '61 REVISITED
Like a rolling stone / Tombstone blues / It takes a lot to laugh, it takes a train to cry / From a Buick 6 / Ballad of a thin man / Queen Jane approximately / Highway 61 revisited / Just like Tom Thumb's blues / Desolation Row
CD 4609532
CBS / Nov '89 / Sony

HIGHWAY '61 REVISITED/JOHN WESLEY HARDING (2CD Set)
Like a rolling stone / Tombstone blues / It takes a lot to laugh, it takes a train to cry / From a Buick 6 / Ballad of a thin man / Queen Jane approximately / Highway 61 revisited / Just like Tom Thumb's blues / Desolation row / John Wesley Harding / As I went out one morning / I dreamed I saw St. Augustine / All along the watchtower / Ballad of Frankie Lee and Judas Priest / Drifter's escape / Dear landlord / I'm a lonesome hobo / I pity the poor immigrant / Wicked messenger / Down along the cove / I'll be your baby tonight
CD Set 4668312
Columbia / Jul '92 / Sony

INFIDELS
Jokerman / Sweetheart like you / Neighbourhood bully / Licence to kill / Man of peace / Union sundown / I and I / Don't fall apart on me tonight
CD 4607272
CBS / Nov '89 / Sony

JOHN WESLEY HARDING
John Wesley Harding / As I went out one morning / I dreamed I saw St. Augustine / Drifter's escape / All along the watchtower / I am a lonesome hobo / Ballad of Frankie Lee and Judas Priest / Dear landlord / I pity the poor immigrant / Wicked messenger / Down along cove / I'll be your baby tonight
CD 4633592
CBS / Nov '89 / Sony

KNOCKED OUT LOADED
You wanna ramble / They killed him / Drifting too far from the shore / Precious memories / Maybe someday / Brownsville girl / Got my mind made up / Under your spell
CD 4670402
Columbia / Feb '91 / Sony

LIVE AT THE BUDOKAN
Mr. Tambourine Man / Shelter from the storm / Love minus zero / No limit / Ballad of a thin man / Don't think twice, it's alright / Once more cup of coffee (valley below) / Like a rolling stone / I shall be released / Is your love in vain / Blowin' in the wind / Just like a woman / Oh sister / Simple twist of fate / All along the watchtower / I want you / All I really want to do / Knockin' on Heaven's door / It's alright ma (I'm only bleeding) / Forever young / Times they are a changin'
CD CD 96004
CBS / Jul '87 / Sony

MORE GREATEST HITS (2CD Set)
Watching the river flow / Don't think twice, it's alright / Lay lady lay / Stuck inside a mobile with the Memphis blues again / I'll be your baby tonight / All I really want to do / My back pages / Maggie's farm / Tonight I'll be staying here with you / Positively 4th Street / All along the watchtower / Mighty Quinn / Just like Tom Thumb's blues / Hard rain's gonna fall / If not for you / New morning / Tomorrow is a long time / When I paint my masterpiece / I shall be released / You ain't goin' nowhere / Down in the flood
CD Set 4678512
Columbia / Jun '96 / Sony

NASHVILLE SKYLINE
Girl from the North Country / Nashville skyline rag / To be alone with you / I threw it all away / Peggy Day / Lay lady lay / One more night / Tell me that it isn't true / Country pie / Tonight I'll be staying here with you
CD CD 63601
CBS / Jan '86 / Sony

NEW MORNING
If not for you / Day of the locusts / Time passes slowly / Went to see the gypsy / Winterlude / If dogs run free / New morning

/ Sign in the window / One more weekend / Man in me / Three angels / Father of night
CD _______________ CD 32267
Columbia / Feb '94 / Sony

OH MERCY
Political world / Where teardrops fall / Ring them bells / Man in the long black coat / Most of the time / What good am I / Disease of conceit / What was it you wanted / Shooting star
CD _______________ 4658002
CBS / Sep '89 / Sony

PLANET WAVES
On a night like this / Going going gone / Tough mama / Hazel / Something there is about you / Forever young / Dirge / You angel you / Never say goodbye / Wedding song
CD _______________ CD 32154
CBS / Nov '89 / Sony

SAVED
Satisfied mind / Saved / Covenant woman / What can I do for you / Solid rock / Pressing on / In the garden / Saving grace / Are you ready
CD _______________ CD 32742
Columbia / Feb '91 / Sony

SELF PORTRAIT
All the tired horses / Alberta no.1 / I've forgotten more than you'll ever know / Days of 49 / Early morning rain / In search of little Sadie / Let it be me / Woogie boogie / Belle Isle / Living the blues / Like a rolling stone / Copper kettle / Gotta travel on / Blue moon / Boxer / Mighty Quinn / Take me as I am / It hurts me too / Minstrel boy / She belongs to me / Wigwam / Alberta no.2
CD _______________ 4601122
Columbia / Feb '91 / Sony

SHOT OF LOVE
Shot of love / Heart of mine / Property of Jesus / Lenny Bruce / Watered-down love / Dead man dead man / In the Summertime / Trouble / Every grain of sand
CD _______________ 4746892
Columbia / Feb '97 / Sony

SLOW TRAIN COMING
Gotta serve somebody / Precious angel when you gonna wake me up / I believe in you / Slow train / Gonna change my way of thinkin' / Do right to me baby / When he returns / Man gave names to all the animals / Changing of the guard / New pony / No time to think / Baby stop crying / Is your love in vain / Senor / True love tends to forget / We better talk this over / Where are you tonight / Journey through dark heat
CD _______________ CD 32524
CBS / Apr '89 / Sony

STREET LEGAL
Changing of the guard / New pony / No time to think / Baby stop crying / Is your love in vain / Senor (tales of Yankee power) / True love tends to forget / We better talk this over / Where are you tonight / Journey through dark heat
CD _______________ CD 32389
Columbia / Apr '95 / Sony

SUBTERRANEAN/HIGHWAY 61/ NASHVILLE SKYLINE (3CD Set)
CD Set _______________ 4673912
CBS / Dec '90 / Sony

TIMES THEY ARE A-CHANGIN', THE
Times they are a changin' / Ballad of Hollis Brown / With God on our side / One too many mornings / North Country blues / Only a pawn in their game / Boots of Spanish leather / When the ship comes in / Lonesome death of Hattie Carroll / Restless farewell
CD _______________ CD 32021
CBS / Nov '89 / Sony

UNDER THE RED SKY
Wiggle wiggle wiggle / Under the red sky / Unbelievable / Born in time / TV talkin' song / 10,000 men / Two times two / God knows / Handy Dandy / Cat's in the well
CD _______________ 4671882
CBS / Sep '90 / Sony

UNPLUGGED
Tombstone blues / Shooting star / All along the watchtower / Times they are a-changin' / John Brown / Desolation row / Rainy day women 12 & 35 / Dignity / Love minus zero / No limit / Knockin' on heaven's door / Like a rolling stone / With God on our side
CD _______________ 4783742
Columbia / Mar '95 / Sony

WORLD GONE WRONG
World gone wrong / Love Henry / Ragged and dirty / Blood in my eyes / Broke down engine / Delia / Stagger Lee / Two soldiers / Jackaroe / Lone pilgrim
CD _______________ 4748572
Columbia / Nov '93 / Sony

Dylans

SPIRIT FINGER
CD _______________ BBQCD 144
Beggars Banquet / Apr '94 / RTM/Disc / Warner Music

Dynamic Blues Band

ONE MORE KISS AND ONE MORE BEER
CD _______________ STINGCD 039
Blue Sting / Jul '97 / CM / Hot Shot / Jazz Music / Swift

Dynamics

WHAT A SHAME
What a shame / She's for real (Bless you) / Let me be your friend / You'll never find a man like me / Woe is me / Voyage through the mind / You're the only one funkey key / Count your chips / Shucks I love you / We're gonna be together / Show the world (we can do it) / Sweet games of love / Let's start all over / Baby, baby I love you / I've been blessed / I'm thinking / Beautiful music (makes you dance) / Get myself high
CD _______________ NEMCD 720
Sequel / Feb '95 / BMG

Dynasty

BEST OF DYNASTY, THE
I don' want to be a freak (but I can't help myself) / I've just begun to love you / Do me right / Adventures in the land of music / Love in the fast lane / Check it out / Questions / Your piece of the rock / Satisfied / Something to remember / Groove control / Here I am / Strokin' / Does that ring a bell / Only one
CD _______________ NEMCD 679
Sequel / Oct '94 / BMG

Dyoxen

FIRST AMONG EQUALS
CD _______________ CDATV 17
Active / Jul '92 / Pinnacle

DYS

FIRE AND ICE
CD _______________ TG 2981CD
Taang / Jul '91 / Cargo

Dysart & Dundonald Pipe Band

IN CONCERT, BALLYMENA 1983
CD _______________ COMD 2053
Temple / Jan '94 / ADA / CM / Direct / Duncans / Highlander

PIPE BANDS OF DISTINCTION
CD _______________ CDMON 803
Monarch / Dec '89 / ADA / CM / Direct / Duncans

Dysney Moon

RUNAWAY
CD _______________ WHALE 101CD
Christine / Aug '93 / Friendly Overtures

Dyson, Ronnie

SOUL SESSION
Let the love begin / Constantly / Tender loving care / Waiting for you / I gave you all of me / Are we so far apart / My fantasy / It's all over your face / Don't need you now / You better be fierce
CD _______________ 303072
Hallmark / Jun '97 / Carlton

Dystopia

HUMAN GARBAGE
CD _______________ EFA 124032
Common Cause / Dec '94 / Plastic Head / SRD

Dystrophy

SPIEGEL MEINER KALTE
CD _______________ SR 0003CD
Serenades / Nov '95 / Plastic Head

Dzintars

SONGS OF AMBER
Blow wind blow / Breaking flax / Sun moves quickly / Sleep my child / Song of the wind / Autumn landscape / Tomtit's message / Where have you been, brother / Orphan girl in white / Di raike / Christmas masquerade / Oi hanuke / So silent is the Ukranian night / Forest shook from dancing
CD _______________ RCD 10130
Rykodisc / Sep '91 / ADA / Vital

E

E-40

HALL OF GAME
CD CHIP 174
Jive / Mar '97 / Pinnacle

E-De-Cologne

SYNTHETIC OVERDOSE
CD EFA 008782
Shockwave / Sep '96 / SRD

E-Z Rollers

DIMENSIONS OF SOUND
CD ASHADOW 5CD
Moving Shadow / Jul '96 / SRD

Each Dawn I Die

NOTES FROM A ...
CD DVLR 009CD
Dark Vinyl / Nov '95 / Plastic Head / World Serpent

Eagle Brass Band

LAST OF THE LINE, THE
CD BCD 170
GHB / Jul '96 / Jazz Music

Eagles

BEST OF THE EAGLES, THE (Vienna Classic Rock Orchestra)
CD 323834
Koch International / May '97 / Koch

COMMON THREAD (The Songs Of The Eagles) (Various Artists)
Take it easy / Peaceful easy feeling / Desperado / Heartache tonight / Tequila sunrise / Take it to the limit / I can't tell you why / Lyin' eyes / New kid in town / Saturday night / Already gone / Best of my love / Sad cafe
CD 74321166772
Giant / Oct '93 / BMG

DESPERADO
Doolin Dalton / Twenty one / Out of control / Tequila sunrise / Desperado / Certain kind of fool / Outlaw man / Saturday night / Bitter Creek
CD K 253008
Asylum / '89 / Warner Music

EAGLES
Take it easy / Witchy woman / Chug all night / Most of us are sad / Nightingale / Train leaves here this morning / Take the devil / Earlybird / Peaceful easy feeling / Trying / Doolin Dalton / Twenty one / Out of control / Tequila sunrise / Desperado / Certain kind of fool / Outlaw man / Saturday night / Bitter creek
CD 2530092
Asylum / Feb '87 / Warner Music

EAGLES LIVE
Hotel California / Heartache tonight / I can't tell you why / Long run / New kid in town / Life's been good / Seven Bridges Road / Wasted time / Take it to the limit / Doolin Dalton / Desperado / Saturday night / All night long / Life in the fast lane / Take it easy
CD 7559605912
Asylum / Feb '92 / Warner Music

HELL FREEZES OVER
Get over it / Love will keep us alive / Girl from yesterday / Learn to be still / Tequila sunrise / Hotel California / Wasted time / Pretty maids all in a row / I can't tell you why / New York minute / Last resort / Take it easy / In the city / Life in the fast lane / Desperado
CD GED 24725
Geffen / Nov '94 / BMG

HOTEL CALIFORNIA
Hotel California / New kid in town / Life in the fast lane / Wasted time / Wasted time (reprise) / Pretty maids all in a row / Try and love again / Last resort / Victim of love
CD 253051
Asylum / May '87 / Warner Music

LONG RUN, THE
Long run / I can't tell you why / In the city / Disco strangler / King of Hollywood / Heartache tonight / Those shoes / Teenage jail / Greeks don't want no freaks / Sad cafe
CD 252181
Asylum / '86 / Warner Music

ON THE BORDER
Already gone / You never cry like a lover / Midnight flyer / My man (mon homme) / On the border / James Dean / 01 55 / Is it true / Good day in hell / Best of my love
CD 243005
Asylum / Jun '83 / Warner Music

ONE OF THESE NIGHTS
One of these nights / Too many hands / Hollywood waltz / Journey of the sorcerer / Lyin' eyes / Take it to the limit / Visions / After the thrill is gone / I wish you peace
CD K253014
Asylum / '89 / Warner Music

TELLTALES (Interview Disc)
CD TELL 13
Network / Jun '97 / Total/BMG

VERY BEST OF THE EAGLES, THE
Take it easy / Witchy woman / Peaceful easy feeling / Doolin dalton / Desperado / Tequila sunrise / Best of my love / James Dean / I can't tell you why / Lyin' eyes / Take it to the limit / One of these nights / Hotel California / New kid in town / Life in the fast lane / Hertache tonight / Long run
CD 9548323752
Asylum / Jul '94 / Warner Music

Eagles

SMASH HITS...PLUS
March of the Eagles / Dance on / Lonely bull / Desperados / Scarlett O'Hara / Stranger on the shore / Al di la / Exodus / Johnny's tune / Bristol express / Pipeline / Some people / Old Ned (theme from Steptoe and son) / Maigret / Happy Joe / Special agent / Hava nagila / Sukiyaki / Desafinado / Theme from Station Six Sahara / Wishin' and hopin' / Come on baby (to the Floral Dance) / Moonstruck / Andorra / Theme to Oliver Twist / Telstar
CD SEECD 277
See For Miles/C5 / '89 / Pinnacle

Eaglesmith, Fred

DRIVE-IN MOVIE
CD CDVER 42182
Ichiban / Apr '96 / Direct / Koch

Eaglin, Snooks

BABY YOU CAN GET YOUR GUN
You give me nothing but the blues / Oh sweetness / Lavinia / Baby you can get your gun / Drop the bomb / That certain door / Mary Joe / Nobody knows / Pretty girls everywhere
CD FIENDCD 96
Demon / Mar '92 / Pinnacle

COUNTRY BOY DOWN IN NEW ORLEANS
CD ARHCD 348
Arhoolie / Apr '95 / ADA / Cadillac / Direct

LIVE IN JAPAN
Quaker city / I went to the Mardi Gras / Soul train / Don't take it so hard / Josephine / Down yonder (we go ballin) / Lillie Mae / Nine pound steel / It's your thing / Yours truly / (Boogie on) Reggae woman / Black night / Traveling mood / Reprise
CD CDBT 1137
Black Top / Mar '97 / ADA / CM / Direct

NEW ORLEANS STREET SINGER
Alberta / That's alright / Malaguena / When they ring the golden bells / Remember me / Fly right back baby / I don't know / Mean ol' world / I must see Jesus / She's one black rat / Don't you lie to me / Well I had my fun / Brown skin woman / Mama don't you tear my clothes / Who's been foolin' you / When shadows fall / One more drink / I got a woman / Come back baby / Trouble in mind / I got my questionaire / Drifter
CD STCD 8023
Storyville / Dec '94 / Cadillac / Jazz Music / Wellard

OUT OF NOWHERE
Oh lawdy, my baby / Lipstick traces / Young girl / Out of nowhere / You're so fine / Mailman blues / Well-a, well-a, baby-la / Kiss of fire / It's your thing / Playgirl / West side baby / Cheetah
CD JJCD 13
Black Top / Apr '90 / ADA / CM / Direct

SOUL'S EDGE
Josephine / Show me the way back home / Ling ting tong / Aw'some funk / I'm not ashamed / Nine pound steel / Answer now / Skinny minnie / Thrill on the hill / You and me / I went to the mardi gras / Talk to me / Mama and papa / God will take care
CD BT 1112CD
Black Top / Apr '95 / ADA / CM / Direct

TEASIN' YOU
CD BT 1072CD
Black Top / '92 / ADA / CM / Direct

THAT'S ALL RIGHT (Eaglin, Blind Snooks)
CD OBCCD 568
Original Blues Classics / Jul '95 / Complete/Pinnacle / Wellard

Ealey, Robert

I LIKE MUSIC WHEN I PARTY
Shake your butt / See about me / Don't I love you / Is your bathroom clean / Too many ways / Cristena / Elloise / Shoo-be-doo / Graveyard blues / When the lights go out (let's push it) / Picture on the wall / Wild wild west
CD CDBT 1138
Black Top / May '97 / ADA / CM / Direct

IF YOU NEED ME (Texas Blues Legend)
CD IMP 705
Iris Music / Jul '95 / Discovery

Ealey, Theodis

IF YOU LEAVE ME, I'M GOING WHI CHA
CD ICH 1164CD
Ichiban / Jan '94 / Direct / Koch

STUCK BETWEEN RHYTHM AND BLUES
CD ICH 1185CD
Ichiban / Dec '95 / Direct / Koch

Eamonn, Harvey

PRICE OF STONE, THE
CD CDRPM 0015
RP Media / Apr '97 / Essential/BMG

EAR

BEYOND THE PALE
CD ABB 96CD
Big Cat / Jun '96 / 3mv/Pinnacle

PHENOMENA 256
CD ORBIT 005CD
Space Age / Sep '96 / Plastic Head

Earl 16

NOT FOR SALE
CD NXXCD 01
Next Step / Dec '93 / Jet Star / SRD

ROOTSMAN
CD RNCD 2038
Rhino / Jan '94 / Grapevine/PolyGram / Jet Star

Earl Brutus

YOUR MAJESTY, WE ARE HERE
Navyhead / I'm new / Male milk / On me not in me / Don't leave me behind mate / Thelmex / Black speedway / Motorola / Shrunken head / Curtsy / Blind date / Life's too long / Karl Brutus / Single seater Xmas
CD BLUFF 036CD
Deceptive / Sep '96 / Vital

Earl, Jimmy

JIMMY EARL
CD EFA 120672
Hotwire / May '95 / SRD

Earl, Johnny

AMERICAN DREAM, THE
CD F 3020 P
Fury / Nov '91 / Nervous / TKO Magnum

BURNING THE FLOOR
CD PCM 001
Pollytone / Apr '97 / Nervous / Pollytone

GIVE ME THE RIGHT (Earl, Johnny & The Jordonaires)
CD WCPCD 1007
West Coast / Sep '92 / Koch / Scratch/ BMG

PRESLEY STYLE OF..., THE
CD ROCKCD 9115
Rockhouse / Oct '91 / Nervous

SINGER MAN, THE
CD CDRPM 008
JEM / Feb '97 / Nervous

Earl, Ronnie

BLUES & FORGIVENESS (Earl, Ronnie & The Broadcasters)
CD CCD 11042
Crosscut / Jun '94 / ADA / CM / Direct

BLUES UNION (Earl, Ronnie & Joe Beard)
Lay for me sometime / Just to be with you / I count the days you're gone / Sinners prayer / Sally Mae / Please don't light the flame / Feets out in the hall / Think / Telling it like it is / Don't know why / Late in the evening
CD AQCD 1039
Audioquest / Apr '96 / ADA / New Note/ Pinnacle

COLOUR OF LOVE (Earl, Ronnie & The Broadcasters)
CD 5375622
Verve / Jul '97 / PolyGram

DEEP BLUES (Earl, Ronnie & The Broadcasters)
CD CD 1033
Black Top / '88 / ADA / CM / Direct

GRATEFUL HEART - BLUES & BALLADS (Earl, Ronnie & The Broadcasters)
CD CDBB 9565
Bullseye Blues / Mar '96 / Direct

I LIKE IT WHEN IT RAINS
CD ANTCD 0002
Antones / Jan '93 / ADA / Hot Shot

LANGUAGE OF THE SOUL (Earl, Ronnie & The Broadcasters)
Eddie's gospel groove / Beautiful child / Indigo burell / Blues for Martin Luther King / Harvard square stomp / Barcelona morning / I am with you / Green light / Through floods and storms / Blue guitar / Bill's blues
CD BBCD 9554
Bullseye Blues / Nov '94 / Direct

PEACE OF MIND (Earl, Ronnie & The Broadcasters)
I want to shout about it / I wish you could see me now / Peace of mind / T-Bone boogie / Wayne's blues / Bonehead too / More than I deserve / Can't keep from cryin' / I cried my eyes out / No use crying / Stickin' / Wayward angel
CD FIENDCD 169
Demon / Jun '90 / Pinnacle

PLAYS BIG BLUES
CD CDBTEL 7002
Black Top / Mar '97 / ADA / CM / Direct

SOUL SEARCHIN' (Earl, Ronnie & The Broadcasters)
CD CD 1042
Black Top / '88 / ADA / CM / Direct

Earland, Charles

BLACK TALK
CD OJCCD 335
Original Jazz Classics / Nov '95 / Complete/Pinnacle / Jazz Music / Wellard

BLACK TALK/BLACK DROPS
Black talk / Mighty burner / Here comes Charlie / Aquarius / More today than yesterday / Sing a simple song / Don't say goodbye / Lazybird / Letha / Raindrops keep falling on my head / Buck green
CD CDBGPD 093
Beat Goes Public / Apr '95 / Pinnacle

LEAVING THIS PLANET
Leaving this planet / Red clay / Warp factor 8 / Brown eyes / Asteroid / Mason's galaxy / No me esqueca (Don't forget me) / Tyner / Van jay / Never ending melody
CD PRCD 660022
Prestige / Jan '94 / Cadillac / Complete/ Pinnacle

WHIP APPEAL
CD MCD 5409
Muse / Nov '91 / New Note/Pinnacle

Earle, Steve

ANGRY YOUNG MAN (The Very Best Of Steve Earle)
Copperhead Road / Devil's right hand / Johnny come lately / Waiting on you / Angry young man / I ain't never satisfied / It's all up to you / No. 29 / Nowhere Road / San Antonio girl / Rain came down / Fearless heart / Guitar town / My old friend the blues / Someday / Other kind
CD NTMCD 532
Nectar / Aug '96 / Pinnacle

COPPERHEAD ROAD
Copperhead Road / Snake oil / Back to the wall / Devil's right hand / Johnny come lately / Even when I'm blue / You belong to me / Waiting on you / Once you love / Nothing but a child
CD MCLD 19213
MCA / Sep '93 / BMG

ESSENTIAL STEVE EARLE, THE
Guitar town / Hillbilly highway / Devil's right hand / Goodbye's all we got left to say / Six days on the road / Someday / Good ol' boy (gettin' tough) / Copperhead road / Rain came down / I ain't ever satisfied / Nowhere road / Week of living dangerously / Continental trailways blues
CD MCLD 19325
MCA / Sep '96 / BMG

EXIT O
Nowhere road / Sweet little '66 / No. 29 / Angry young man / San Antonio girl / Rain came down / I ain't ever satisfied / Week of

living dangerously / I love you too much / It's all up to you
CD MCLD 19070
MCA / Oct '92 / BMG

I FEEL ALRIGHT
I feel alright / Hard-core troubadour / More than I can do / Hurtin' me, hurtin' you / Now, she's gone / Poor boy / Valentine's day / Unrepentant / CCKMP / Billy and Bonnie / South Nashville blues / You're still standin' there
CD TRACD 227
Transatlantic / Apr '96 / Pinnacle

SHUT UP AND DIE LIKE AN AVIATOR (Live)
Good ol' boy (gettin' tough) / Devil's right hand / I ain't ever satisfied / Someday / West Nashville boogie / Snake oil / Blue yodel / Other kind / Billy Austin / Copperhead road / Fearless heart / Guitar town / I love you too much / She's about a mover / Rain came down / Dead flowers
CD MCLD 19326
MCA / Sep '96 / BMG

TRAIN A COMIN'
CD TRACD 111
Transatlantic / Apr '96 / Pinnacle

Earls

REMEMBER THEN (The Best Of The Earls)
Remember then / Life is but a dream / Eyes / Out in the cold again / Looking for my baby / Remember me baby / Never / Lookin' my way / All through our teens / Don't forget / Cry cry cry / Without you / Amor / Let's waddle / I believe / Oh what a time / Cross my heart / Kissing / Ol' man river / Never (alt take) / Ask anybody / Our day will come / I keep a tellin' you
CD CDCHD 366
Ace / May '92 / Pinnacle

Earls, Jack

HEY SLIM, LET'S BOP (His Complete Sun Recordings)
CD CPCD 8197
Charly / Jun '96 / Koch

Earls Of Suave

BASEMENT BAR AT THE HEARTBREAK HOTEL, THE
Ain't that lovin' you baby / Cheat / Fool such as I / Ring of fire / Sea of love / She's my witch / Mondo moodo / Stranger in my own hometown / Nothing takes the place of you / Somebody buy me a drink / Really gone this time / You can call (But I won't answer) / Cheap wine / Yabba dabba doo (So are you) / One more beer / Little ole wine drinker me / Nobody knows
CD ASKCD 042
Vinyl Japan / Jul '94 / Plastic Head / Vinyl Japan

Earth

CAPSULAR EXTRACTION
CD 8P123B
Sub Pop / Feb '94 / Cargo / Greyhound / Shellshock/Disc

EARTH VOL.2
CD SPCD 65/222
Sub Pop / Feb '93 / Cargo / Greyhound / Shellshock/Disc

PENTASTAR: IN THE STYLE OF DEMONS
CD SPCD 361
Sub Pop / Jul '96 / Cargo / Greyhound / Shellshock/Disc

Earth Crisis

ALL OUT WAR
CD VR 203
Victory / May '95 / Plastic Head

DESTROY THE MACHINES
CD VE 022CD
Victory / Aug '95 / Plastic Head

FIRESTORM
CD VR 122
Victory / Apr '94 / Plastic Head

GOMORRAH'S SEASON ENDS
CD VR 044CD
Victory / Dec '96 / Plastic Head

LIVE CALIFORNIA TAKEOVER (Earth Crisis/Snapcase/Strife)
CD VR 042CD
Victory / Sep '96 / Plastic Head

Earth Nation

LIVE
Liquid desert / Artificial dream / Chilled dreams / Outburts / Falling tears / Transfiguration / Lay in / Alienated
CD EYEUKCD 009
Eye Q / Jun '96 / Vital

TERRA INCOGNITA
CD EYEUKCD 005
Eye Q / Sep '95 / Vital

THOUGHTS IN PAST FUTURE
Lord giveth / Falling tears / Revelation / In your mind / World in blue / Chilled dreams / Claim for passion / Alienated / Isolation / In retrospect / Lord taketh
CD 4509955572
Eye Q / May '94 / Vital

Earth Water Air Fire

AVALON
Hydroscope / Red fish / Miditation / Nautical dream / Cumana / Thunderdome / Earthbound / Gemini / Moontribe / Stereogen / Nautical mix / Gothama
CD SSR 128
SSR / Nov '93 / Amato Disco / Grapevine/ PolyGram / Prime / RTM/Disc

Earth, Wind & Fire

BEST OF EARTH, WIND AND FIRE VOL.1, THE
Got to get you into my life / Fantasy / Saturday night / Love music / Getaway / That's the way of the world / September / Shining star / Reasons / Sing a song
CD CD 32536
Columbia / Jun '89 / Sony

BEST OF EARTH, WIND AND FIRE VOL.2, THE
Turn on (the beat box) / Let's groove / After the love has gone / Fantasy / Devotion / Serpentine fire / Love's holiday / Boogie wonderland / Saturday nite / Mighty mighty
CD 4632002
Columbia / May '91 / Sony

BOOGIE WONDERLAND (The Best Of Earth, Wind & Fire)
Boogie wonderland / Let's groove / September / Fantasy / Got to get you into my life / Saturday nite / In the stone / Mighty mighty / I've had enough / Love's holiday / Star / Reasons / Getaway / System of survival / Spread your love / Let me talk / After the love has gone / Let your feelings show
CD TCD 2879
Telstar / Aug '96 / BMG

EARTH, WIND & FIRE
Help somebody / Moment of truth / Love is life / Fan the fire / C'mon children / World today / Bad tune
CD 7599268612
Warner Bros. / Jan '96 / Warner Music

ETERNAL DANCE, THE (3CD Set)
Fan the fire / Love is life / I think about lovin' you / Interlude / Time is on your side / Where have all the flowers gone / Power / Keep your head to the sky / Mighty mighty / Feelin' blue / Hey girl / Open our eyes / Shining star / That's the way of the world / Kalimba story/Sing a message to you (live) / Head to the sky/Devotion / Sun goddess (live) / Mighty mighty (Live) / Can't hide love / Sing a song / Sunshine / Getaway / Saturday nite spirit / Ponta de areia / Fantasy / Saturday night spirit / Ponta de Ariea 'Brazilian rhyme' / Serpentine fire / I'll write a song for you / Be ever wonderful / Beijo / Got to get you into my life / September / Boogie wonderland / After the love has gone / In the stone / Dirty / Let me talk / And love goes on / Pride demo / Let's groove / Wanna be with you / Little girl / Night dreamin' / Fall in love with me / Magnetic / System of survival / Thinking of you / Gotta find out
CD Set 4726142
Columbia / Jan '93 / Sony

FACES
Let me talk / Turn it into something good / Pride / You / Sparkle / Back on the road / Song in my heart / You went away / Love goes on / Sailaway / Take it to the sky / Win or lose / Share your love / In time / Faces
CD 4746792
Columbia / Feb '97 / Sony

IN THE NAME OF LOVE
CD EAGCD 002
Eagle / Jul '97 / BMG

LET'S GROOVE (The Best Of Earth, Wind & Fire)
Let's groove / Boogie wonderland / Saturday nite / In the stone / I've had enough / Can't let go / Fall in love with me / Star / September / Jupiter / Got to get you into my life / Fantasy / Evil / That's the way of the world / You can't hide love / Reasons / After the love has gone
CD 4865112
Columbia / Apr '97 / Sony

LIVE AND UNPLUGGED
CD AVEXCD 20
Avex / Nov '95 / 3mv/Pinnacle

LOVE SONGS, THE
After the love has gone / I'm in love / You / Reasons / Sailaway / Fantasy / Could it be right / All about love / Be ever wonderful / We're living in our own time / Daydreamin' / I'll write a song for you / Wait / That's the way of the world / You can't hide love / Miracles
CD 4677682
Columbia / Oct '95 / Sony

MILLENNIUM, YESTERDAY, TODAY
Even if you wonder / Sunday morning / Blood brothers / Kalimba interlude / Spend the night / Divine / Two hearts / Honor the magic / Love is the greatest story / L word / Just another lonely night / Super hero / Wouldn't change a thing about you / Love across the wire / Chicago (Chi-town) blues / Kalimba blues
CD Set 9362452742
WEA / Sep '93 / Warner Music

POWER LIGHT/ELECTRIC UNIVERSE/ SPIRIT (3CD Set)
CD Set 4688042
Columbia / Jul '94 / Sony

SWEET SWEETBACK'S BAADASSS SONG (Original Soundtrack)
Sweetback losing his cherry / Sweetback getting it so hard... / Come on feet / Sweetback's theme / Hoppin' John/Voices/Mojo woman/Voices / Sanra Z/Voices / Reggin hanging on in there as best they can/Voices / Won't bleed me / Man tries running his usual game...
CD CDSXE 103
Stax / Mar '97 / Pinnacle

THAT'S THE WAY OF THE WORLD
Shining star / That's the way of the world / Happy feelin' / All about love / Yearnin' learnin' / Reasons / Africano / See the light
CD 4844672
Columbia / Feb '97 / Sony

Earthling

RADAR
First Transmission / Ananada's theme / Nefisa / I still love Albert Einstein / Accident at injured strings / Soup or no soup / God's interlude / Echo on my mind / Infinite M / Planet of the apes / By means of beams / Freak, freak / I could just die
CD CTCD 44
Cooltempo / Sep '97 / EMI

Earthmen

FALL AND RISE OF MY FAVORITE SIXTIES GIRL
Figure 8 / Brittle / Fall and rise of my favorite sixties girl / Things that worry grown-ups / Tell the women we're going / Language of you and me
CD 958882
Seed / Jul '94 / Vital

TEEN SENSATIONS
Cool chick / Stacey's cupboard / Blonde / Momentum / Encouragement kiss / Roll / Too far down / In the south / Flyby / Elephant
CD 142412
Seed / Nov '93 / Vital

Earthrise

DEEPER THAN SPACE
CD SR 9344
Silent / Mar '94 / Cargo / Plastic Head

Earwig

UNDER MY SKIN I AM LAUGHING
CD LADIDA 024CD
La-Di-Da / Jul '94 / Vital

Easley, Bill

WIND INVENTIONS
CD SSC 1022CD
Sunnyside / Sep '96 / Discovery

East 17

AROUND THE WORLD - THE JOURNEY SO FAR (The Hit Singles)
Stay another day / Around the world / Let it rain / Deep / Thunder / It's alright / Do U still / Steam / Hey child / Hold my body tight / House of love / If you ever: *East 17 & Gabrielle* / Someone to love / Slow it down / Gold / West End girls
CD 8288502
London / Nov '96 / PolyGram

AROUND THE WORLD - THE JOURNEY SO FAR (The Hit Singles/Limited Edition 2CD Set)
House of love / Deep / It's alright / Stay another day / Steam / Let it rain / Slow it down / I you ever: *East 17 & Gabrielle* / West End girl / Around the world / Thunder / Gold / Do u still / Someone to love / Hey child / Hold my body tight / Stay another day / Let it rain / Hold my body tight / House of love / Deep / Gold / Do u still / Steam / Deep / Let it rain / Slow it down
CD Set 8288522
London / Nov '96 / PolyGram

STEAM
Steam / Let it all go / Hold my body tight / Stay another day / Around the world / Let it rain / Be there / MF Power / Generation XTC
CD 8285422
London / Oct '94 / PolyGram

UP ALL NIGHT
Innocent erotic / Thunder / I remember / Do U still / Gotta keep on / Ghetto / It's all over / Someone to love / Right here with you / Free your mind / Don't you feel so good / Best days / Looking for
CD 8286992
London / Oct '95 / PolyGram

WALTHAMSTOW
House of love / Deep / Gold / Love is more than a feeling / I disagree / Gotta do something / Slow it down / I want it / It's alright / Feel what u can't c / West End girls
CD 8284262
London / Jul '93 / PolyGram

East Down Septet

CHANNEL SURFING
East 9th street / Which Ralph are you / Knock knock / Mist flower / Abeyance / Once upon a time in the west / Downside / Tell me when / Joke's on me / Take it home
CD HEPCD 2069
Hep / Mar '97 / Cadillac / Jazz Music / New Note/Pinnacle / Wellard

OUT OF GRIDLOCK
Claudia's car / Three views of a secret / Mothers of the veil / Suite from Taxi Driver / It smells good / Knew rhythm / Black Monday / Gray whale / Cowboy song / Dedication
CD HEPCD 2063
Hep / Jun '95 / Cadillac / Jazz Music / New Note/Pinnacle / Wellard

East London Chorus

ESSENTIALLY CHRISTMAS
CD 053030
Koch / Nov '92 / Koch

East Meets West

DUBOLOGY PRESENTS MEGADUB
CD DOR 100CD
Dubology / Sep '95 / Jet Star / SRD

MEGADUB
CD DOR 001CD
Dubology / Apr '97 / Jet Star / SRD

East Of Java

IMP AND THE ANGEL, THE
CD PLASCD 018
Plastic Head / Jan '90 / Plastic Head

East River Pipe

EVEN THE SUN WAS AFRAID
Here we go / Marty / Sleeping with tallboy / Hide my life away from you / Fan the flame / When the ground walks away / Powerful man / Fan the flames
CD SARAH 407CD
Sarah / May '95 / Vital

GOODBYE CALIFORNIA
Firing room / Silhouette town / Dogman / When will your friends all disappear / Bernie Shaw / Psychic whore / Forty miles / Make a deal with the city
CD SARAH 405CD
Sarah / Mar '95 / Vital

MEL
CD SHINKANSEN 7CD
Shinkansen / Dec '96 / SRD

POOR FRICKY
Bring on the loser / Ah dictaphone / Crawl away / Metal detector / Put down / Superstar in France / Keep all your windows tight tonight / Make it real / Hey, where's your girl / Walking the dog / Million trillion
CD SARAH 621CD
Sarah / Nov '94 / Vital

East Village

DROPOUT
Silver train / Shipwrecked / Here it comes / Freeze out / Circles / When I wake tomorrow / Way back home / What kind of friend of this / Black autumn / Everybody knows
CD HVNLP 003CD
Heavenly / Nov '93 / 3mv/Pinnacle / BMG / Vital

East West Ensemble

ZURNA
CD ITM 001478
ITM / Nov '92 / Koch / Tradelink

East Yorkshire Brass Band

FACE THE MUSIC
CD EYBCD 1
LWA / May '96 / THE

Eastern Rebellion

MOSAIC
Sunflower / John's blues / I'll let you know / Mosaic / One for Kel / My old flame / I've grown accustomed to her face / Shoulders / My one and only love / Bittersweet
CD 8208502
Limelight / Aug '92 / PolyGram

SIMPLE PLEASURE
In the kitchen / Roni's decision / Dear Ruth / Simple pleasure / Sixth Avenue / My ideal / All the things you are / My man's gone now / Theme for Ernie
CD 5180142
Limelight / Mar '93 / PolyGram

Eastley, Max

NEW AND REDISCOVERED MUSICAL INSTRUMENTS (Eastley, Max & David Toop)
Hydrophone / Metallophone / Elastic aerophone / Centriphone / Do the bathosphere / Divination of the bowhead whale / Chairs story
CD ____ CDOVD 478
EG / Jun '97 / EMI

Easton, Sheena

GOLD COLLECTION, THE
Morning train (9 to 5) / Moody (my love) / Modern girl / Paradox / For your eyes only / One man woman / Summer's over / Take my time / Calm before the storm / Just another broken heart / Savoir faire / Are you man enough / Back in the city / Letters from the road / I don't need your word / So we say goodbye
CD ____ CDGOLD 1008
EMI Gold / Mar '96 / EMI

WORLD OF SHEENA EASTON, THE - THE SINGLES COLLECTION
Morning Train (nine to five) / Modern girl / For your eyes only / You could've been with me / When he shines / Machinery / I wouldn't beg for water / We've got tonight / Telefone (Long distance love affair) / Almost over you / Devil in a fast car / Strut / Sugar walls / Swear / Do it for love / Jimmy Mack / Magic of love / So far, so good / Eternity
CD ____ CDEMS 1495
EMI / Jun '93 / EMI

Easton, Ted

KIDNEY STEW (Easton, Ted & His Band)
CD ____ DD 631
Delmark / Nov '93 / ADA / Cadillac / CM / Direct / Hot Shot

Easy Club

ESSENTIAL
Easy club reel - Janine's reel / Dirty old town / Diamond / Euphemia / Train journey north / Black is the colour of my true love's hair / Little cascade / Quiet man / Fause, fause hae ye been / Skirlie beat / Auld toon shuffle / Road to Gerenish / Innocent railway / Auchengeich / North sea chinaman / Desert march / This for that / Murdo Mackensie of Torridon / Collier's 8 hour day / Arnish light / Eyemouth disaster / Easy club reel
CD ____ ECLCD 9103
Eclectic / Jan '96 / ADA / New Note/ Pinnacle

Easy Riders

MARIANNE (2CD Set)
What'cha gonna do / So true blues / Marianne / US Adam / Rollin' home / Everybody loves Saturday night / Lonesome rider / Goodbye Chiquita / Champagne wine / South coast / Hot crawfish / Red sundown / Yermo's nightmare and Yermo red / Sky is high / Send for the captain / Don't hurry worry me / True love and tender care / Tina / Sweet sugar cane / I won't tell / Strollin' blues / Fare thee well / Weary travellin' blues / Blues ain't nothin' / Times / Man about town / Shorty Joe / Green fields / Blue mountain / Windjammer / Kari waits for me / Delia / (I heard that) Lonesome whistle / Wanderin' blues / Eddystone light / Drill ye tarriers drill / East Virginia / I ride an old paint / Mayfield mountain / Ravin' gambler / Gambler's blues / John Henry / Six wheel driver / I'm gonna leave you now / Saturday's child / Love is a golden ring / Ride away / Vaquero / Take off your old coat / Il fait si beau / Glory glory / My pretty quadron / Forever new / Poor boy / Lights of town / Cry of the wild goose / Young in love / Ballad of the Alamo / Green leaves of summer / Remember the Alamo / Laredo / Green grow the lilacs / Long lean Deliah / Leina / Plain old plainsmen / Girl I left behind / Here's to the ladies / Tennessee babe / Mi amor, mi corazon / Haven't we met before / Silver and gold / Go tell her for me / Brother Simon and sister Mary / Ten men from Tennessee / Deerfoot Dan / Sam Hall/Nellie / Maggie Gonzales / Along comes me / 900 Miles / Bachelor's boy / Jeb Jone's daughter / See all the people / Bill goat hill / Ta pedia tou pirea (never on a sunday) / Marianne P / Pajarillo barranquero / Toro / Wabash cannon ball / Run come see Jerusalem / Adieu Cherie / Dead eye Sam / Devil cat / Speak a word of love (I wish, I wish) / Lady from Laramie / Little King / Oh Brandy leave me alone / Boll weevil / Black eyed Susie / Story of creation / Cotton eyed Joe / Billy boy / Roving gambler / Jennie Jenkins / Black is the colour / I know where I'm going / Ev'ryone's crazy ceptin me / Running away / Secret / Nellie Lou / Last freight / Solitary singer / Mr. Buzzard / Tick tock song / Across the wild Missouri / Girl in the wood / Fast freight / Hoofbeat serenade / Stay a while / Rollin' stone / World belongs to me / Three jolly rogues of Lynne / Charmin' bells / Nine hundred miles / Greensleeves / John Hardy / Fond affection / Box of rosewood / Man you don't meet every day / Tom Jack / Wait by the willow / Golden minute / Mackerel feet / Sparrow grass and brown bread / Gypsy Davey / Tall timber / Come home Zelda / Ride away Vaquero / Quit kicking my dog around / Man of the sky / Christopher Columbus
CD Set ____ BCD 15780
Bear Family / Aug '95 / Direct / Rollercoaster / Swift

Easybeats

FRIDAY ON MY MIND
CD ____ 422126
New Rose / May '94 / ADA / Direct / Discovery

LIVE - STUDIO AND STAGE
CD ____ RVCD 40
Raven / Oct '95 / ADA / Direct

VERY BEST OF THE EASYBEATS
CD ____ BRCD 118
BR Music / Jan '95 / Target/BMG

Eat Static

ABDUCTION
CD ____ BARKCD 001
Ultimate / Jul '94 / Pinnacle

IMPLANT
CD ____ BARKCD 005
Ultimate / May '94 / Pinnacle

Eater

COMPLETE EATER, THE
You / Public toys / Room for one / Lock it up / Sweet Jane / I don't need it / Ann / Get raped / Space dreaming / Queen Bitch / My business / Waiting for the man / Fifteen / No more / No brains / Peace and love (H-Bomb) / Outside view / Thinking of the USA / Michael's monetary system / She's wearing green / Notebook / Jeepster / Debutante's ball / Holland / What she wants she needs / Reach for the sky / Point of view / Typewriter babes
CD ____ CDPUNK 10
Anagram / Apr '93 / Cargo / Pinnacle

Eatman, Heather

MASCARA FALLS
Goodbye Betty-Jean / Barbs / Miss Liberty / City of your heart / Amelia waltz / Halfway hotel / Lucky you / Sheila / Big bass drum / Used car / Greyhound
CD ____ OBR 014
Oh Boy / May '97 / ADA / CM / Direct

Eaton, John

INDIANA ON OUR MINDS
CD ____ CRD 304
Chiaroscuro / Mar '96 / Jazz Music

MADE IN AMERICA
CD ____ CRD 333
Chiaroscuro / Jan '97 / Jazz Music

Eaton, Nigel

MUSIC OF THE HURDY-GURDY, THE
Il Pastor Fido (Vivaldi) / Les Amusements d'une heure (Baton) / Crocodile bourree / Lady Diamond/New Jig / Satins blanc / Malashevska / Laride / Queen Adelaide
CD ____ CDSDL 374
Saydisc / Mar '94 / ADA / Direct / Harmonia Mundi

Eazy E

EAZY-DUZ IT
CD ____ IMCD 124
4th & Broadway / Apr '91 / PolyGram

ETERNAL E
Boyz-n-the-hood / 8 ball: *NWA* / Eazy duz it / Eazy-er said than dunn / No more questions: *NWA* / We want Eazy / Nobody move / Radio / Only if you want it / Neighborhood sniper / I'd rather fuck you: *NWA* / Automobile: *NWA* / Niggaz my height don't fight / Eazy Street
CD ____ CDPTY 122
Priority/Virgin / Jan '96 / EMI

STR8 OFF THA STREETZ OF MUTHAPHUKKIN COMPTON
First power / Old school shit / Sorry Louis / Just tah let U know / Sippin' on a 40 / Nutz on ya chin / Tha muthaphukkin real / Lickin', suckin', phukkin' / Hit the hooker / My baby's mama / Creep n' oh crawl / Wut would you do / Gangsta beat for the street / Eternal E
CD ____ 4835762
Ruthless / Jan '96 / Sony

Ebbage, Len

SAY IT WITH MUSIC (Ebbage, Len Band)
CD ____ CDTS 054
Maestro / Dec '95 / Savoy

Eberhardt, Cliff

MONA LISA CAFE
CD ____ SHCD 8017
Shanachie / Oct '95 / ADA / Greensleeves / Koch

NOW YOU ARE MY HOME
CD ____ SHAN 8008CD
Shanachie / Dec '93 / ADA / Greensleeves / Koch

Eberle, Ray

GLENN MILLER'S MEN 1943-1947 (Eberle, Ray & His Orchestra)
CD ____ JH 1011
Jazz Hour / '91 / Cadillac / Jazz Music / Target/BMG

Ebi

TEN
CD ____ EFA 004132
Space Teddy / Feb '96 / SRD

ZEN
CD ____ EFA 117572
Space Teddy / May '94 / SRD

Ebogo, Ange

EXPLOSION
CD ____ DTC 027
Stern's / Jan '91 / ADA / CM / Stern's

Ebony Band

MUSIC FROM THE SPANISH CIVIL WAR
CD ____ BVHAASTCD 9203
Bvhaast / Jan '86 / Cadillac

Ebrel, Annie

TRE HO TI HA MA HINI
CD ____ GWP 012
Gwerz / May '96 / ADA / Discovery

(EC) Nudes

VANISHING POINT
Opening / Delta / Axis / It might be better / 1003rd tale of Sheherezade / Salvatore / Crystal palace / Objects / Yippee / Radio / O pastor / Qu'est que tu fais / Afterture
CD ____ RERN 1
ReR/Recommended / Jun '97 / ReR Megacorp / RTM/Disc

EC8OR

EC8TOR
Cocain duck / You will never find / Think about / Pick the best one / Victim / Overload / Discriminate / We are pissed / Lichterloh / Plastic creatures / Intro / Speed erection / Short circuit / Iche suche nichts / Cheap drops
CD ____ DHRCD 003
Digital Hardcore / Nov '95 / Vital

SPEX IS A FAT BITCH
Spex is a fat bitch / I don't wanna be a part of this / One track minded fuckhead / Notorious 30's / Need / All of us can be rich
CD ____ DHRMCD 009
Digital Hardcore / Nov '96 / Vital

Echo & The Bunnymen

BALLYHOO (The Best Of Echo & The Bunnymen)
Rescue / Do it clean / Villiers terrace / All that jazz / Over the wall / Promise / Disease / Back of love / Cutter / Never stop / Killing moon / Silver / Seven seas / Bring on the dancing horses / People are strange / Game / Lips like sugar / Bedbugs and ballyhoo
CD ____ 0630191032
WEA / Jun '97 / Warner Music

EVERGREEN
Don't let it get you down / In my time / I want to be there (when you come) / Evergreen / I'll fly tonight / Nothing lasts forever / Baseball Bill / Altamont / Just a touch away / Empire state halo / Too young to kneel / Forgiven
CD ____ 8289052
London / Jul '97 / PolyGram

Echo Art

COREOGRAFIE
CD ____ NT 6712
Robi Droli / Jan '94 / ADA / Direct

Echo City

SONIC SPORT 1983-88
Shirtful of ice / Tour tuns / Singaraja bemo ride / Night strike / On tarr catch / In the field / In aluminium / Red red red / Spiv / Song for the black economy / Engineer and more
CD ____ GR 001CD
Voiceprint / Mar '95 / Pinnacle

Echo Park

RETURN TO HEAR
CD ____ HE 2
Helium / Nov '96 / Cargo

Echo System

HEADLAND
Bosphoressence / Jahan (The vast world) / Ish / Modulator / Chant 96 (The dome of light) / Mystic ships / Hydrophonics / Shimmer / Drum fish
CD ____ DVNT 009CD
Deviant / Jun '96 / Prime / Vital

Echobelly

EVERYONE'S GOT ONE
CD ____ FAUV 3CD
Fauve / Jun '96 / 3mv/Vital

ON
CD ____ FAUV 6CD
Fauve / Sep '95 / 3mv/Vital

Echolyn

AS THE WORLD
All ways the same / As the world / Uncle / How long have I waited / Best regards / Cheese stands alone / Prose / Short essay / My dear wormwood / Entry 11/19/93 / One for the show / Wiblet / Audio verite / Settled land / Habit worth forming / Never the same
CD ____ CYCL 025
Cyclops / May '95 / Pinnacle

WHEN THE SWEET TURNS
CD ____ CYCL 036
Cyclops / Jun '96 / Pinnacle

Eckert, Rinde

FINDING MY WAY HOME
CD ____ DIW 859
DIW / Jun '92 / Cadillac / Harmonia Mundi

Ecklund, Peter

IN ELKHART
CD ____ JCD 246
Jazzology / Aug '95 / Jazz Music

Eckstine, Billy

AT BASIN STREET EAST (Eckstine, Billy & Quincy Jones)
Alright, OK you win / Caravan / Don't get around much anymore / I'm just a lucky so and so / Sophisticated lady / In the still of the night / Ma, she's making eyes at me / Everything I have is yours / Fool that I am / I'm falling for you / Work song
CD ____ 8325922
EmArCy / Feb '94 / PolyGram

BEST OF THE MGM YEARS, THE (2CD Set)
CD Set ____ 8194422
Verve / May '94 / PolyGram

BILLY ECKSTINE
CD ____ CD 325
Entertainers / Feb '95 / Target/BMG

BILLY ECKSTINE
I got a date with the rhythm man / I stay in the mood for you / Good jelly blues / If that's the way you feel / I want to talk about you / Blowing the blues away / Opus X / I'll wait and pray / Real thing happend to me / Cottage for sale / I apologize / I hear a rhapsody / I'm beginning to see the light / That old black magic / Misty
CD ____ 17070
Laserlight / Aug '96 / Target/BMG

BILLY ECKSTINE SINGS WITH BENNY CARTER (Eckstine, Billy & Benny Carter)
You'd be so nice to come home to: *Eckstine, Billy & Benny Carter/Helen Merrill* / My funny valentine / Here's that rainy day / Summertime / Kiss from you / Memories of you / I've got the world on a string / Now that I need you / Over the rainbow / September song / Autumn leaves / Didn't we: *Eckstine, Billy & Benny Carter/Helen Merrill*
CD ____ 8320112
EmArCy / Jan '93 / PolyGram

BILLY'S BEST
CD ____ 5264402
PolyGram Jazz / Feb '95 / PolyGram

CLASSICS 1944-1945
CD ____ CLASSICS 914
Classics / Jan '97 / Discovery / Jazz Music

IMAGINATION
It was so beautiful / I gotta right to sing the blues / Love is just around the corner / I don't stand a ghost of a chance with you / Faded summer love / What a little moonlight can do / Imagination / Lullaby of the leaves / I cover the waterfront / I wished on the moon / That's all
CD ____ 8481622
EmArCy / Mar '94 / PolyGram

JAZZ MASTERS
I left my hat in Haiti / My foolish heart / Imagination / Kiss of fire / Now it can be told / I apologize once / I lost my sugar in Salt Lake City / So far / Jealousy / Everything I have is yours / Strange sensation / Because you're mine / Sitting by the window / Have a good time / Passing strangers
CD ____ 5166932
Verve / Feb '94 / PolyGram

MAGNIFICENT MR. B
CD ____ PASTCD 7086
Flapper / Feb '96 / Pinnacle

MR. B & THE BE BOP BAND
Blowing the blues away / I stay in the mood for you / Good jelly blues / I got a date with rhythm / If that's the way you feel / Opus x

/ Real thing happened to me / I want to talk about you / Without a song / Mean to me / Mr. Chips / Don't blame me / Air mail special / Love me or leave me / Lonesome lover blues / A cottage for sale / I love the rhythm in a riff / Last night / Prisoner of love / I'm in the mood for love / You call it madness but I call it love / All I sing is blues / Long long journey / It ain't like that no more
CD _______________ PLCD 545
President / Aug '96 / Grapevine/PolyGram / President / Target/BMG

Eclipse First

ECLIPSE FIRST
CD _______________ IRCD 012
Iona / Oct '90 / ADA / Direct / Duncans

NAMES AND PLACES (Eclipse First & Scotrail Vale Of Atholl Pipe Band)
Landing at roscoff / West wind / Isle de groix / La grande nuit du port de peche / Games / Road to copshie / Oban inn / Victoria bar / Craigdarroch arms
CD _______________ IRCD 133
Iona / Sep '91 / ADA / Direct / Duncans

Ecllerzie

MUSIQUES A DANSER
CD _______________ CDUP 68
Diffusion Breizh / May '93 / ADA

Economist

NEW BUILT GHETTO
CD _______________ MASSCD 030
Massacre / Jun '94 / Plastic Head

ECP

STRAIGHT LACE PLAYAZ
CD _______________ WRA 8143
Wrap / Nov '95 / Koch

Ecstasy Of St. Theresa

FREE D
CD _______________ CDFRE 4
Free / Feb '94 / RTM/Disc

Ectogram

I CAN'T BELIEVE IT'S NOT REGGAE
CD _______________ ANKST 069CD
Ankst / Oct '96 / Shellshock/Disc

Ecume

ECUME
CD _______________ CDLLL 127
La Lichere / Aug '93 / ADA / Discovery

Eddie & The Hot Rods

DOING ANYTHING THEY WANNA DO...
Get out of Denver / Horseplay / All I need is money / Writing on the wall / Wooly bully / Been so long / Get across to you / Double checkin' woman / GLORIA / At night / I got mine / I see the light / Teenage depression / Do anything you wanna do / Quit this town / Telephone girl / Moon tears / You better run
CD _______________ CDMGRAM 108
Anagram / Oct '96 / Cargo / Pinnacle

END OF THE BEGINNING, THE (The Best Of Eddie & The Hot Rods)
Anything you wanna do / Quit this town / Telephone girl / Teenage depression / Kids are alright / Get out of Denver / Till the night is gone let's rock / Schoolgirl love / Hard drivin' man / On the run / Power and the glory / Ignore them still life / Life on the line / Circles / Take it or leave it / Echoes / We sing the cross / Beginning of the end / Gloria / Satisfaction
CD _______________ IMCD 156
Island / Jul '94 / PolyGram

GASOLINE DAYS
CD _______________ CMCD 008
Creative Man / Apr '96 / Total/Pinnacle

GET YOUR BALLS OFF
CD _______________ 622412
Skydog / Mar '96 / Discovery

LIVE AND RARE
CD _______________ RRCD 177
Receiver / Aug '93 / Grapevine/PolyGram

Eddy, Duane

20 TWANGY HITS
CD _______________ CDSR 049
Telstar / May '94 / BMG

BECAUSE THEY'RE YOUNG
CD _______________ BR 1492
BR Music / May '94 / Target/BMG

BEST OF DUANE EDDY, THE
(Dance with) The guitar man / Peter Gunn theme / Because they're young / Some kinda earthquake / Theme from Dixie / Shazam / Kommotion / Trambone / Bonnie came back / Detour / Rebel rouser / Play me like you play your guitar / Lonely one / Movin' and groovin' / Cannonball / Yep / Ramrod / Ring of fire / Ragbone / Forty miles of bad road
CD _______________ ECD 3314
K-Tel / Mar '97 / K-Tel

ESPECIALLY FOR YOU/GIRLS, GIRLS, GIRLS
Peter Gunn / Only child / Lover / Fuzz / Yep / Along the Navajo trail / Just because / Quiniela / Trouble in mind / Tuxedo junction (stereo) / Hard times / Along came Linda / Tuxedo junction (mono) / I want to be wanted / That's all you got / I'm sorry / Sioux City Sue / Tammy / Big Liza / Mary Ann / Annette / Tuesday / Sweet Cindy / Patricia / Mona Lisa / Connie / Carol
CD _______________ BCD 15799
Bear Family / Apr '94 / Direct / Rollercoaster / Swift

GHOSTRIDER
CD _______________ CURCD 032
Hit / Nov '96 / Grapevine/PolyGram

HIS TWANGY GUITAR AND THE REBELS
Kicking asphalt / Rockestra theme / Theme for something really important / Spies / Blue city / Trembler / Los Companeros / Lost innocence / Rockabilly holiday / Last look back
CD _______________ SEECD 417
See For Miles/C5 / Oct '96 / Pinnacle

RCA YEARS, THE
CD _______________ 74321127012
RCA / Jun '96 / BMG

SHAZAM
Guitar man / Peter Gunn / Because they're young / Some kinda earthquake / Dixie / Shazam / Kommotion / Trambone / Bonnie come back / Detour / Rebel rouser / Play me like you play your guitar / Lonely one, (The) / Movin' and groovin' / Cannonball / Yep / Ramrod / Ring of fire / Ragbone / Forty miles of bad road
CD _______________ CD 6010
Music / Apr '96 / Target/BMG

THAT CLASSIC TWANG
Rebel rouser / Moovin 'n' groovin / Ramrod / Cannonball / Mason Dixon lion / Lonely one / 3.30 blues / Yep / Peter Gunn / Forty miles of bad road / Quiet three / Some kinda earthquake / Bonnie come back / First love, first tears / Shazam / Because they're young / Kommotion / Pete / Theme from Dixie / Ring of fire / Drivin' home / Gidget goes Hawaiian / Avenger / Shazam
CD _______________ BCD 15702
Bear Family / Apr '94 / Direct / Rollercoaster / Swift

TWANG'S THE THANG/SONGS OF OUR HERITAGE
My blue heaven / Tiger love and turnip greens / Last minute of innocence / Route 1 / You are my sunshine / St. Louis blues / Night train to Memphis / Battle / Trambone / Blueberry hill / Rebel walk / Easy / Cripple creek / Riddle song / John Henry / Streets of Laredo / Prisoner's song / In the pines / Ole Joe Clark / Wayfaring stranger / On top of old smokey / Mule train / Scarlet ribbons
CD _______________ BCD 15807
Bear Family / Apr '94 / Direct / Rollercoaster / Swift

TWANGIN' FROM PHOENIX TO LA (The Jamie Years/7CD Set)
I want some lovin' baby / Soda fountain girl / Ramrod (ford, version) / Caravan (ford version) / Up and down / Moovin 'n' groovin / Pretty jane / Want me / Rebel rouser / Stalkin' / Have love will travel / Look at me / Doo waddie / Dear 53310761 / Walker / Lonely one / Cannonball / Mason Dixon lion / Lonesome road / I almost lost my mind / Loving you / Anytime / Three 30 blues / Yep (take 7) / Dixie, part 1 / Dixie, part 2 / Yep (master) / Raid / Quiet three (basic track) / Peter Gunn / Lover / Along the Navajo trail / First love, first tears / Quiet three (master) / Forty miles of bad road / Some kinda earthquake / Some kind of earthquake (UK version) / Route 1 / Tiger love and turnip greens / Trambone / My blue heaven / Secret seven / You are my sunshine / Last minute of innocence / Rebel walk (without overdub) / Blueberry hill / Battle (without overdub) / St. Louis blues / Nightrain to Memphis / Bonnie came back / Lost island (master) / Kommotion / Rebel walk (master) / Battle (master) / Easy / Lost island (lost flute version) / Cripple creek / Riddle song / John Henry / Streets of Laredo / Prisoner's song / In the pines / Old Joe Clark / Old Joe Clark (take 27 master) / Wayfaring stranger / Top of old smokey / Mule train / Scarlet ribbons / Shazam / Kommotion / Kommotion / Because they're young / Theme for moon children (take 1) / Because they're young (take 27 master) / Theme for moon children (take 4, master) / Back porch, part 1 / Back porch, part 2 / Words mean nothing / Girl on death row / Pepe / Lost friend / Runaway pony / Drivin' home / I want to be wanted / That's all you gotta do / I'm sorry / Mary Ann / Sioux City Sue / Sweet Cindy / Tuesday / Jo Ann / Big Liza / Mona Lisa / Patricia / Connie / Carol / Dixie / Gidget goes Hawaiian / Ring of fire / Bobbie / Avenger / Londonderry air / Just because / Caravan part 1 / Caravan part 2 / Stalkin / Along came Linda / Back porch / Battle / Trouble in mind
CD Set _______________ BCD 15778
Bear Family / Nov '94 / Direct / Rollercoaster / Swift

Eddy, Nelson

16 CLASSIC PERFORMANCES
CD _______________ CWNCD 2025
Javelin / Jul '96 / Henry Hadaway / THE

16 MOST REQUESTED SONGS (Eddy, Nelson & Jeanette MacDonald)
Ah sweet mystery of life / I'm falling in love with someone / Tramp, tramp, tramp along the highway / Italian street song / When I grow too old to dream / Mounties / Rose Marie / Indian love call / Farewell to dreams / Will you remember / Lover come back to me / One kiss / Softly as in a morning sunrise / Stouthearted men / At the balalaika / Toreador's song
CD _______________ CWNCD 2042
Crown / Jun '97 / Henry Hadaway

AH, SWEET MYSTERY OF LIFE (Eddy, Nelson & Jeanette MacDonald)
Indian love call / Who are we to say (obey your heart) / Isn't it romantic / Hills of home / Auf wiedersehen / Ah sweet mystery of life / Rose Marie / Lover come back to me / Mounties / 'Neath the southern moon / Beyond the blue horizon / When I grow too old to dream / Italian street song / Song of love / Sylvia / Senorita / Farewell to dreams / I'm falling in love with someone / Goodnight / Trees / One kiss / Will you remember
CD _______________ PASTCD 7026
Flapper / Nov '93 / Pinnacle

IN THE STILL OF THE NIGHT
That great come and get it day / In the still of the night / You and the night and the music / Rosalie / It ain't necessarily so / Bess you is my woman now / Stout hearted men / June is bustin' out all over / Shortnin' bread / It's a grand day for singing / Beyond the blue horizon / Shadrack
CD _______________ 12597
Laserlight / May '97 / Target/BMG

LOVE'S OLD SWEET SONG
When I grow too old to dream / Rose Marie / 'Neath the southern moon / Deep river / Perfect day / Rosary / Thy beaming eyes / Sylvia / Dusty road / Auf wiedersehen / Smilin' through / Ah sweet mystery of life / Love's old sweet song / At dawning / Oh promise me / Hills of home / Mounties / Trees / Dream / Through the years
CD _______________ CDHD 150
Happy Days / '89 / Conifer/BMG

ROSE MARIE
CD _______________ CD 23111
All Star / Sep '93 / BMG

SMILIN' THROUGH
Great day / Without a song / Song of the Volga boatmen / At the balalaika / Magic of your love / Dear little cafe / Call of life/If you could come with me / Tokay / I'll see you again / I'm falling in love with someone / Sympathy / My hero / Chocolate soldier / At dawning / Trees / Smilin' through / Perfect day / Waterboy / Shortnin' bread / None but the lonely heart / Pilgrim's song / Chanson du torleador / Vision fugitive
CD _______________ CDMOIR 436
Memoir / Oct '96 / Jazz Music / Target/BMG

Eddy, Samuel

STRANGERS ON THE RUN
CD _______________ SPV 08589422
SPV / Jan '96 / Koch / Plastic Head

Edegran Orchestra

SHIM SHAM SHIMMY (Edegran Orchestra & New Orleans Jazz Ladies)
CD _______________ BCD 323
GHB / Mar '95 / Jazz Music

Edelman, Judith

PERFECT WORLD
CD _______________ FIENDCD 787
Demon / Sep '96 / Pinnacle

Eden 224

HOLOCAUSTIC SODA
CD _______________ TOPYCD 075
Temple / May '94 / Pinnacle / Plastic Head

Eden's Children

EDEN'S CHILDREN/SURE LOOKS REAL
CD _______________ 3797
Head / Jun '97 / Greyhound

Edge Of Sanity

NOTHING BY DEATH REMAINS
CD _______________ BMCD 10
Black Mark / '92 / Plastic Head

PURGATORY AFTERFLOW
CD _______________ BMCD 061
Black Mark / Oct '94 / Plastic Head

SPECTRAL SORROWS, THE
CD _______________ BMCD 37
Black Mark / Nov '93 / Plastic Head

UNORTHODOX
Unorthodox / Enigma / Incipience to the butchery / In the veins/Darker than black / Human aberration / Everlasting / After afterlife / Beyond the unknown / Nocturnal / Curfew for the damned / Cold sun / Day of maturity / Requiscon by page / Dead but dreaming / When all is said
CD _______________ BMCD 018
Black Mark / Jun '92 / Plastic Head

Edgewise

EDGEWISE
Angel face / In my hands / Crime pays / In the past / Orange / Virgo / Lost in space / Cardinal / Piss and vinegar
CD _______________ GG 009CD
Gain Ground / Mar '97 / Cargo

Edison, Harry

COPENHAGEN STUDIO SESSION 1976 (Edison, Harry 'Sweets' & Eddie 'Lockjaw' Davis)
CD _______________ STCD 8225
Storyville / May '97 / Cadillac / Jazz Music / Wellard

EDISONS LIGHTS (Edison, Harry 'Sweets')
CD _______________ OJCCD 804
Original Jazz Classics / Jun '95 / Complete/Pinnacle / Jazz Music / Wellard

HARRY 'SWEETS' EDISON (Edison, Harry 'Sweets')
CD _______________ CD 53174
Giants Of Jazz / May '95 / Cadillac / Jazz Music / Target/BMG

SWING SUMMIT (Live At Birdland 1990) (Edison, Harry 'Sweets' & Buddy Tate)
Centrepiece / S'wonderful / Out of nowhere / Bags groove / Just friends / Blue creek / Idaho
CD _______________ CCD 79050
Candid / Feb '97 / Cadillac / Direct / Jazz Music / Koch / Wellard

WHISPERING (2CD Set) (Edison, Harry 'Sweets' & Eddie 'Lockjaw' Davis)
What is this thing called love / My funny valentine / I'll remember April / But beautiful / Just squeeze me / Shiny stockings / Whispering / Ain't misbehavin' / Out of nowhere / Corcovado / Meet the flintstones / Satin doll
CD Set _______________ JLR 103612
Live At EJ's / Apr '97 / Target/BMG

Edith Strategy

EDITH STRATEGY
CD _______________ ABB 19 CD
Big Cat / Jul '90 / 3mv/Pinnacle

Edmunds, Dave

BEST OF DAVE EDMUNDS, THE
Deborah / Girls talk / I knew the bride / A1 on the jukebox / Race is on / I hear you knocking / Almost saturday night / Sabre dance / Queen of hearts / Crawling from the wreckage / Here comes the weekend / Trouble boys / Ju ju man / Singin' the blues / Born to be with you
CD _______________ 7567903382
Warner Bros. / Mar '97 / Warner Music

BEST OF DAVE EDMUNDS, THE
Something about you / I hear you knocking / Deep in the heart of Texas / Information / Breaking out / From small things, big things come / Shape I'm in / Some other guy / Bail you out / SOS / Slippin' away / Generation rumble / Your true love / Steel claw / Queen of hearts / How could I be so wrong
CD _______________ 74321125402
Arista / Sep '93 / BMG

CHRONICLES
Sabre dance: *Love Sculpture* / You can't catch me: *Love Sculpture* / I hear you knocking / Down down down / Baby I love you / Born to be with you / Warmed over kisses (leftover love) / From small things, big things come / Slippin' away / Something about you / Get out of Denver / I knew the bride / Trouble boys / Girls talk / Queen of hearts / Crawling from the wreckage / Singin' the blues / Almost Saturday night / Race is on / Baby ride easy
CD _______________ VSOPCD 209
Connoisseur Collection / Nov '94 / Pinnacle

COLLECTION, THE
I hear you knockin' / You can't catch me / Stumble / Sabre dance / In the land of the few / Blues helping / Down down down / Farandole / Wang dang doodle / (I am) a lover not a fighter / Egg or the hen / 3 o'clock blues / So unkind / Promised land / Dance dance dance / Outlaw blues / Sweet little rock 'n' roller / Don't answer the door
CD _______________ DC 878622
Disky / Mar '97 / Disky / THE

COMPLETE EARLY EDMUNDS, THE
Morning dew / It's a wonder / Brand new woman / Stumble / Three o'clock blues / I believe to my soul / So unkind / Summertime / On the road again / Don't answer the door / Wang dang doodle / Come back baby / Shake your hips / Blues helping / In the land of the few / Seagull / Nobody's talking / Farandole / You can't catch me / Mars / Sabre dance / Sabre dance / Why / People, people / Think of love / Down down down / I hear you knocking / Hell of a pain

/ It ain't easy / Promised land / dance, dance, dance / I'm a lover not a fighter / Egg or the hen / Sweet little rock 'n' roller / Outlaw blues / Black Bill / Country roll / I'm comin' home / Blue Monday / I'll get along
CD Set CDEM 1406
EMI / Jul '91 / EMI

I HEAR YOU KNOCKING
You can't catch me / Stumble / Sabre dance / In the land of the few / Blues helping / Down, down, down / I hear you knocking / Farandole / Wang-dang-doodle / (I am) a lover not a fighter / Egg or the hen / 3 o'clock blues / So unkind / Promised land / Dance, dance, dance / Outlaw blues / Sweet little rock 'n' roller / Don't answer the door
CD CDGOLD 1083
EMI Gold / Feb '97 / EMI

ROCKIN' (The Best Of Dave Edmunds)
From small things / Slipping away / Don't you doublecross me / Shape I'm in / Information / Bail you out / Feel so right / Don't call me tonight / Louisiana man / Warmed over kisses / Deep in the heart / Steel claw / SOS / Can't get enough / Something about you / Girls talk / Here comes the weekend / Queen of hearts / Wanderer / Crawlin' from the wreckage / I hear you knocking / I knew the bride (when she used to rock 'n' roll)
CD 74321451922
Camden / Feb '97 / BMG

Edsel

EDSEL EP
CD DIS 1145CD
CD 1145
Radiopaque / Mar '97 / Cargo

Edsel Auctioneer

GOOD TIME MUSIC OF, THE
Summer hit / Simple / Filled / Stuntman / What's the use / Instrumental 2-1 / Hangover / Faces 1 / Haircut / Country song / Short changed / Just can't believe it
CD A 078D
Alias / Apr '95 / Vital

Edsels

EVERLASTING BEST CO
CD GROW 122
Grass / Apr '94 / Pinnacle / SRD

Edu Lobo

MISSA BREVE
CD MOFB 3748CD
Rare Brazil / Apr '97 / Cargo

Edward II

TWO STEPS TO HEAVEN (Edward II & The Red Hot Polkas/Mad Professor)
Bjorn again polka / Swing easy / Untitled polka / Steamboats / Lover's two step / Pomp and pride / Queen's jig / Cliffhanger / Staffordshire hornpipe / Jenny Lind / Stack of wheat / Brimfield hornpipe / Swedish polka / Two step to heaven
CD COOKCD 019
Cooking Vinyl / Jul '96 / Vital

ZEST
CD OCKCD 0042
Ock / Oct '96 / ADA / Direct

Edward, John

BLUE RIDGE (Edward, John & The Seldom Scene)
Don't that road look rough and rocky / How long have I been waiting for you / Blue ridge / Seven daffodils / Sunshine / Only a hobo / God gave you to me / Little hands / I don't believe I'll stay here anymore / Don't crawfish me baby
CD SHCD 3747
Sugar Hill / Mar '89 / ADA / CM / Direct / Koch / Roots

Edwards, Clarence

I LOOKED DOWN THAT RAILROAD
CD 7422508
WMD / Jan '97 / Discovery

SWAMPIN'
CD 422398
Last Call / Feb '97 / Cargo / Direct / Discovery

Edwards, Cliff

SINGING IN THE RAIN
CD ACD 17
Audiophile / Jun '95 / Jazz Music

Edwards, Don

WEST OF YESTERDAY
Habit / Bad half hour / Gypsy Davey / Rose of old pawnee / Run along lttle dogies / Jim I wore a tie / I wanted to die in the desert / Freedom song / At the end of a long lonely day / Blue bonnet lane / West of yesterday / Texas plains
CD 9461872
Warner Western / Nov '96 / Warner Music

Edwards, Honeyboy

DELTA BLUESMAN
Roamin' and ramblin' blues / You got to roll / Water Coast blues / Stagolee / Just a spoonful / Spread my raincoat down / Hellatakin' blues / Wind howlin' blues / Worried life blues / Tear it down rag / Army blues / Big Katie Allen / Black cat / Number 12 at the station / Rocks in my pillow / Decoration Day / Who may your regular be / Eye full of tears / Bad whiskey and cocaine
CD IGOCD 2003
Indigo / Jun '95 / ADA / Direct

I'VE BEEN AROUND
Pony blues / Sad and lonesome / Ham bone blues / Ride with me tonight / I'm a country man / Banty rooster / Take me in your arms / You're gonna miss me / I feel so good today / Things have changed / Big fat Mama / Eyes full of tears / Woman I'm loving / Big road blues
CD TRIX 3319
Trix / Mar '95 / New Note/Pinnacle

WHITE WINDOWS
West Helena blues / Don't say I don't love you / Build myself a cave / Don't you lie to me / 61 Highway / Drop down Mama / It's been so long since I laughed and talked with you / Shake 'em on down / Take a walk with me / War is over / Roll and tumble / Goin' down slow / Lay my burden down
CD ECD 260392
Evidence / Sep '93 / ADA / Cadillac / Harmonia Mundi

Edwards, Jackie

20 SUPER HITS
CD SONCD 0026
Sonic Sounds / Apr '92 / Jet Star

DO IT SWEET
CD CSDSGP 074
Prestige / Apr '95 / Else / Total/BMG

IN PARADISE
CD CDTR 344
Trojan / Jun '94 / Direct / Jet Star

MEMORIAL
CD RNCD 2026
Rhino / Jan '94 / Grapevine/PolyGram / Jet Star

SINGING HITS FROM STUDIO ONE AND MORE
Sad news / Love I can feel / Mean girl / I'm still waiting / OK Fred (my name is Fred) / Mr. Fix It (do it sweet) / Sugar plum / Welcome you back home / Dearest you're nearest to my heart / Vow (I'll be your very own king of the ghetto) / You're mine / I'm a peaceful man / Money in your pocket / Ali Baba / Never never / Further you look / Before the next teardrop / Last farewell / Pretty star
CD RN 7014
Rhino / Apr '97 / Grapevine/PolyGram / Jet Star
CD 3020762
Arcade / Jul '97 / Discovery

Edwards, John

CAREFUL MAN
Cold hearted woman / How can I make it without you / Vanishing love / Tin man / Look on your face / It's those little things that count / It's got to be the real thing this time / Ain't that good enough / Time / We always come back strong / I had a love / Everybody don't get a second chance / Way we were / Stop this merry go round / Spread the news / Careful man / Claim jumpin / I'll be your puppet / You we're made for love / You're messing up a good thing / It's a groove / Exercise my love / Danny Boy
CD CDKEND 127
Kent / Jan '96 / Pinnacle

Edwards, Rupie

DUB BASKET
CD RNCD 2014
Rhino / Jun '93 / Grapevine/PolyGram / Jet Star

IRIE FEELINGS
Wanderer / Dub master / Rasta Dreadlocks / Free the wind / Wandering dub / Feeling horn / Dub master special / Spangy / Rasta Dreadlocks dub / What can I do / Feeling time / Ten dread commandment
CD CDTRL 281
Trojan / May '90 / Direct / Jet Star

LET THERE BE VERSION
CD CDTRL 280
Trojan / May '90 / Direct / Jet Star

SWEET GOSPEL VOL.4
CD RECD 06
Rupie Edwards / Oct '94 / Jet Star

Edwards, Scott

DISTANT HORIZONS
CD CD 0001
Out Of Orbit / Jul '94 / Plastic Head / SRD

Edwards, Teddy

BLUE SAXOPHONE
Prelude / Blue saxophone / Lennox lady / No name number one / Ballad for Susan / Brazilian skies / Hot tamale Joe / Them dirty old blues / Glass of water / Serenade in blue / Hymn for the homeless / Going home
CD 5172982
Verve / Jan '93 / PolyGram

MISSISSIPPI LAD
Little man / Safari walk / Blue sombrero / Mississippi lad / Three base hit / I'm not your fool anymore / Symphony on Central / Ballad for a bronze beauty / Call of love
CD 5111112
Verve / Apr '91 / PolyGram

Edwards, Teddy

BIG BOY TEDDY EDWARDS 1930-1936 (Edwards, 'Big Boy' Teddy)
CD DOCD 5440
Document / May '96 / ADA / Hot Shot / Jazz Music

Edwards, Terry

DORA SUAREZ (Edwards, Terry & James Johnston)
Dora / Empire Gate / Voice / Mourning / College Hill / Season of storms
CD HUNKACDL 006
Clawfist / Nov '93 / Cargo / Vital

I DIDN'T GET WHERE I AM TODAY (Edwards, Terry & The Scapegoats)
King of the cheap thing / Boots off / I like my low-life low / Asthma / Lurch / Ditch / Good-time-strange-thing / Out of the clear / Evening falls / Tallis's canon / Dog food / I didn't get where I am today
CD WIJCD 1061
Wiiija / Jun '97 / RTM/Disc

MY WIFE DOESN'T UNDERSTAND ME
CD STIM 7CD
Stim / Sep '95 / SRD

NO FISH IS TOO WEIRD FOR HER AQUARIUM
CD STIM 005
Stim / Jul '94 / SRD

PLAYS, SALUTES AND EXECUTES
CD STIM 4
Stim / Oct '93 / SRD

Edwards, Willie

EVERLASTIN' TEARS
Everlastin' tears / Dollar in / Been a long time / Read between the lines / Helpless, hopeless feeling / True what they say / Heart of deception / Can't create desire / Won't be back / Bottom's falling out / Company store / 90's blues
CD JSPCD 281
JSP / Jan '97 / ADA / Cadillac / Direct / Hot Shot / Target/BMG

Eek-A-Mouse

MOUSE-A-MANIA
CD RASCD 30616
Ras / '88 / Direct / Greensleeves / Jet Star / SRD

RAS PORTRAITS
Freak / Penni walli / I like them all / Oh me oh my / Do me / Gun shot a cry / Assasinator / Macho man / What me ago do / De di doo / Night before Christmas
CD RAS 3308
Ras / Jun '97 / Direct / Greensleeves / Jet Star / SRD

SKIDIP
Sensee party / Looking sexy / Modelling queen / You na love reggae music / Always on my mind / Do you remember / Skidip / Na make mi girl go away / Fat and slim / Where is my baby
CD GRELCD 41
Greensleeves / Sep '89 / Jet Star / SRD

U-NEEK
CD CIDM 1092
Island / Jul '93 / PolyGram

VERY BEST OF EEK-A-MOUSE, THE
Anarexol / Star daily news or cleaner / Noah's ark / Terrorists in the city / Peeni walli / Wild like a tiger / Wa-do-dem / Assassinator / Christmas a come
CD GRELCD 105
Greensleeves / Aug '87 / Jet Star / SRD

WA DO DEM
Ganja smuggling / Long time ago / Operation eradication / There's a girl in my life / Slowly but surely / Wa-do-dem / Lonesome journey / I will never leave my love / Noahs ark / Too young to understand
CD GRELCD 31
Greensleeves / May '87 / Jet Star / SRD

Eel Grinders

AQUAMARINE
CD EEL 001CD
Sargasso Sounds / Aug '96 / ADA

Eels

BEAUTIFUL FREAK
Novocaine for the soul / Susan's house / Rags to rags / Beautiful freak / Not ready yet / My beloved monster / Flower / Guest list / Mental / Spunky / Your lucky day in hell / Manchild
CD DRD 50001
Dreamworks / Feb '97 / BMG

Eerk & Jerk

DEAD BROKE
CD PCD 1409
Profile / Nov '91 / Pinnacle

Effective Force

BACK AND TO THE LEFT (2CD Set)
In the beginning / Reality labyrinth / Make me forget / Back and to the left / Big surprise / Left hand, right hand / Fish / Ultimate flower / Trouble and desire / So / My time is yours (Past, present and future) / Diamond bullet will to power / Illuminate the planet world in order / Time zero / Complete mental breakdown / My time is yours the end amen / Illumination / Everglade (Effective force remix) / Punishing the atoms / Super illuminated
CD Set DVNT 011CD
Deviant / Jun '96 / Prime / Vital

Effigies

REMAINS NONVIEWABLE
CD TG 135CD
Touch & Go / Oct '95 / SRD

Eg

TURN ME ON, I'M A ROCKET MAN
CD 0630132962
WEA / Feb '96 / Warner Music

Eg & Alice

24 YEARS OF HUNGER
Rockets / In a cold way / Mystery man / I have seen myself / So high, so low / New year's eve / Indian / Doesn't mean that much to me / Crosstown / IOU / I wish
CD 9031753882
WEA / Aug '91 / Warner Music

Egan, Mark

MOSAIC
CD EFA 034512
Wavetone / Nov '95 / SRD

Egan, Seamus

TRADITIONAL MUSIC FROM IRELAND
CD SHCD 34015
Shanachie / Dec '95 / ADA / Greensleeves / Koch

WHEN JUNIPERS SLEEP
CD SHCD 79097
Shanachie / Jan '96 / ADA / Greensleeves / Koch

Egdom, Emiel Van

HYBRID GROOVE
You're in my heart / Modal mood / Elegance d'etiquette / Gentle giant Aussi / Hybrid groove / Sad nostalgia / These things do happen / Star of the sea / Dig this / NY dream / Emmelage / How's my heart
CD AL 73081
Nefertiti / Jul '97 / Direct

Ege Bam Yasi

HOW TO BOIL AN EGG
CD UGTCD 001
UGT / Oct '95 / Plastic Head

Egebjer, Boo

BOO EGEBJER AND STEVE DOBROGOSZ/MARGARETA ANDERSSON (Egebjer, Boo & Steve Dobrogosz/Margareta Andersson)
CD LW 9601
Supreme / Jan '97 / Cadillac / Jazz Music

Egg

ALBUMEN
Fat boy goes to the cinema / Time to enjoy / Get some money to get her / Bend / Jam together / Big duck / Sunglasses / Roche (don't you ever stop) / Shopping / Shoplifting / 284 windows and a door
CD ZEN 011CD
CD ZEN 011CDM
Indochina / Jul '96 / Pinnacle

Eggman

FIRST FRUITS
CD CRECD 201
Creation / May '96 / 3mv/Vital

Eggs

BRUISER
CD TEENBEAT 76CD
Teenbeat / Sep '94 / Cargo / SRD / Vital

HOW DO YOU LIKE YOUR LOBSTER
CD ______ TB 156CD
Teenbeat / Jul '95 / Cargo / SRD / Vital

Egmose, Willy

PA GYNGENDE GRUND (Egmose, Willy Trio & Asger Rosenberg)
CD ______ MECCACD 2023
Music Mecca / May '97 / Cadillac / Jazz Music / Wellard

Egmose, Willy Trio

BARE DET SWINGER
CD ______ MECCACD 1046
Music Mecca / Nov '94 / Cadillac / Jazz Music / Wellard

Egypt

PRESERVING THE DEAD
Baby, please don't go / Coal train union / Egypt / Khartoom / Legend of the lighthouse / Ecccentric man / Pearl of the orient / Lady luck
CD ______ HTDCD 21
HTD / Sep '96 / CM / Pinnacle

Ehrlich, Marty

CAN YOU HEAR A MOTION
Black hat / Welcome / Pictures in a glass house / North star / Ode to Charlie Parker / Reading the river / One for Robin / Comme il faut
CD ______ ENJ 80522
Enja / May '94 / New Note/Pinnacle / Vital/ SAM

EMERGENCY PEACE (Ehrlich, Marty Dark Woods Ensemble)
Emergency peace / Dusk / Painter / Tucked sleave of a one-armed boy / Unison / Double dance / Circle the heart / Charlie in the Parker / Tribute
CD ______ 804092
New World / Jun '91 / ADA / Cadillac / Harmonia Mundi

JUST BEFORE THE DAWN (Ehrlich, Marty Dark Woods Ensemble)
CD ______ 804742
New World / Aug '95 / ADA / Cadillac / Harmonia Mundi

LIVE WOOD (2CD Set) (Ehrlich, Marty Dark Woods Ensemble)
CD Set ______ CD 986
Music & Arts / Aug '97 / Cadillac / Harmonia Mundi

NEW YORK CHILD
New York child / Generosity / Georgia blue / Tell me this / Elvin's exit / Prelude / Time and the wild words / Untitled / Turn again
CD ______ ENJ 90252
Enja / Aug '96 / New Note/Pinnacle / Vital/ SAM

PLIANT PLIANT
CD ______ ENJA 506548
Enja / Jul '88 / New Note/Pinnacle / Vital/ SAM

Ehrling, Thore

JAZZ HIGHLIGHTS
CD ______ DRCD 236
Dragon / Sep '87 / ADA / Cadillac / CM / Roots / Wellard

SWEDISH SWING (1945 & 1947)
CD ______ ANC 9503
Ancha / Jun '95 / Cadillac / Jazz Music / Wellard

Eide, Khalifa Ould

MOORISH MUSIC FROM MAURITANIA (Eide, Khalifa Ould & Dimi Mint Abba)
CD ______ WCD 019
World Circuit / Oct '90 / ADA / Cadillac / Direct / New Note/Pinnacle

Eightball & MJG

COMIN' OUT HARD
CD ______ RAP 60142
Rapture / Oct '94 / Plastic Head

ON THE OUTSIDE
CD ______ RAP 60152
Rapture / Nov '94 / Plastic Head

Eighth Wonder

FEARLESS
Cross my heart / When the phone stops ringing / Baby baby / Will you remember / Wild love / I'm not scared / Use me / Anything at all / My baby's heartbeat / Dress / Stay with me
CD ______ 4884082
Epic / Jun '97 / Sony

Eikas, Sigmund

JOLSTRING
CD ______ HCD 7101
Musikk Distribujson / Apr '95 / ADA

Eiliff

EILIFF
CD ______ SPMWWRCD 0067
SPM / Jul '97 / Greyhound

GIRLRLS
CD ______ SPMWWRCD 0068
SPM / Jul '97 / Greyhound

Eimerman, Herb

FROM YOUR WINDOW
CD ______ DLS 123782
Black Vinyl / Nov '96 / Cargo

STORY IN YOUR EYES
CD ______ DLS 102750
Black Vinyl / Nov '96 / Cargo

Einherjer

AURORA BOREALIS
CD ______ NR 6662
Necropolis / Sep '96 / Plastic Head

Einhorn, Andreas

OCEAN BLUE (Einhorn, Andreas & Wilhelm Magnus)
CD ______ ISCD 157
Intersound / Sep '96 / Jazz Music

Einniu

EINNIU
CD ______ CICD 086
Clo Iar-Chonnachta / Dec '93 / CM

Einstein

THEORY OF EMCEES SQUARED, THE
CD ______ STEIN 1 CD
Music Of Life / Jun '90 / Grapevine/ PolyGram

Einsturzende Neubauten

ENDE NEU
CD ______ BETON 504CD
CD ______ BETON 504CDX
Mute / Aug '96 / RTM/Disc

ENDE NEU REMIXED
CD ______ BETON 602CD
Mute / Sep '97 / RTM/Disc

FAUSTMUSIK
CD ______ EG 0501
Mute / Feb '96 / RTM/Disc

KOLLAPS
CD ______ INDIGO 25172
Zick Zack / Oct '96 / Cargo / SRD

MALADICTION
CD ______ BETON 206CD
Mute / Mar '93 / RTM/Disc

STRATEGIES AGAINST ARCHITECTURE
CD ______ CDSTUMM 14
Mute / Apr '88 / RTM/Disc

TABULA RASA
CD ______ BETON 106CD
Mute / Jan '93 / RTM/Disc

Eisenvater

EISENVATER VOL.2
CD ______ WB 1012CD
We Bite / Aug '93 / Plastic Head

III
CD ______ WB 1132CD
We Bite / Jul '95 / Plastic Head

Either/Orchestra

ACROSS THE OMNIVERSE (10 Years In The Life Of A Band/2CD Set)
CD Set ______ AC 3272
Accurate / May '97 / Direct

DIAL E
Doxy / Nicole is always in Tokyo / 17 December / Lady's blues
CD ______ AC 2222
Accurate / May '97 / Direct

Eitzel, Mark

60 WATT SILVER LINING
There is no easy way down / Sacred heart / Always turn away / Saved / Cleopatra Jones / When my plane finally goes down / Mission rock / Wild sea / Aspirin / Some bartenders have the gift of pardon / South-end on sea / Everything is beautiful
CD ______ CDV 2798
Virgin / Mar '96 / EMI

SONGS OF LOVE
Firefly / Channel No. 5 / Western sky / Blue and grey shirt / Gary's song / Outside this bar / Room above the club / Last harbour / Kathleen / Crabwalk / Jenny / Take courage / Nothing can bring me down
CD ______ FIENDCD 213
Demon / Apr '91 / Pinnacle

WEST
If you have to ask / Free of harm / Helium / Stunned and frozen / Then it really happens / In your life / Lower Eastside tourist / Three inches of wall / Move myself ahead / Old photographs / Fresh screwdriver / Live or die
CD ______ 9362466022
Warner Bros. / Jun '97 / Warner Music

El Amin, Muhamed

VOICE OF SUDAN
CD ______ SM 15232
Wergo / Feb '97 / ADA / Cadillac / Harmonia Mundi

El Bad

BAD MOTHERFUCKERS
CD ______ SST 330CD
SST / Jun '96 / Plastic Head

El Chino

VIEJA LETANIA
CD ______ B 6836
Auvidis/Ethnic / Dec '96 / ADA / Harmonia Mundi

El Din, Hamza

AVAILABLE SOUND
Er'rasoul / Saqiat darius / Ashranda / Nabra / Shortunga / El aanqa / Shams esh'shamusa
CD ______ LR 9621
Lotus / Nov '96 / Impetus / Stern's

ECLIPSE
CD ______ RCD 10103
Rykodisc / Nov '91 / ADA / Vital

LILY OF THE NILE
CD ______ WLAAS 11CD
Waterlilly Acoustics / Nov '95 / ADA

MUWASHSHAH
CD ______ VICG 5416
JVC World Library / Jul '96 / ADA / CM / Direct

SONGS OF THE NILE
CD ______ VICG 50072
JVC World Library / Mar '96 / ADA / CM / Direct

El Flaco

THUB
CD ______ SECT2 10016
Sector 2 / Aug '95 / Cargo / Direct

El Gato's Rhythm Orchestra

STRICTLY DANCING: CHA CHA
CD ______ 15336
Laserlight / May '94 / Target/BMG

El Ghiwan, Nass

CHANSONS DE NASS EL GHIWAN
CD ______ 824672
BUDA / Nov '90 / Discovery

CHANTS GNAWA DU MAROC
CD ______ 824682
BUDA / Nov '90 / Discovery

El Gran Encuentro

DEL COMBO SHOW
El gran encuentro / Si mi merenguito pega / Odio y amor / Talento de TV / Canto a la guira / Consejo a las casadas / Diez anos de amores / Marcela la peligrosa
CD ______ 66058074
RMM / Nov '95 / New Note/Pinnacle

El Malo

STARSHIP IN WORSHIP
CD ______ 99 2126
Ninetynine / Jul '96 / Timewarp

WORST UNIVERSAL JET SET, THE
CD ______ 99 2142
Ninetynine / Jul '96 / Timewarp

El Masry, Hussein

ARABIAN EMOTIONS
CD ______ 12455
Laserlight / Jul '95 / Target/BMG

NOMADE
CD ______ KAR 994
Kardum / Jun '97 / Discovery

ZAGAL
CD ______ AUB 006781
Auvidis/Ethnic / Aug '93 / ADA / Harmonia Mundi

El Medioni, Maurice

CAFE ORAN (El Medioni, Maurice Et Son Pianoriental)
CD ______ CDPIR 1045
Piranha / Jan '97 / Direct / Stern's

El Mondao

FLAMENCO NUEVO
CD ______ EUCD 1116
ARC / '91 / ADA / ARC Music

FLAMENCO TOTAL
CD ______ EUCD 1089
ARC / '89 / ADA / ARC Music

El Mubarak, Abdel Aziz

ABDEL AZIZ EL MUBARAK
Tahrimni minnak / Ahla eyyoun / Ah'laa jarah / Tarig ash-shoag / Bitgooli la
CD ______ CDORB 023
Globestyle / Jan '89 / Pinnacle

El Nino De Almaden

GREAT SINGERS OF FLAMENCO VOL.1
CD ______ LDC 274 830
La Chant Du Monde / '88 / ADA / Harmonia Mundi

El Nino De Marchena

ART OF FLAMENCO VOL.15, THE (The Bloom Of Decadence)
CD ______ MAN 4898
Mandala / May '97 / ADA / Harmonia Mundi / Mandala

ARTE FLAMENCO VOL.15
Soleares / Fandango de Galarosa / Canto de la roda de Sevilla / Punto del Platanal / Fandangos de Marchena / Columbiana / Punto Cubano / Tarantas de Linares / Petenera / Guajira / Buleras por Solea / Fandangos / Aire de la sierra de Cordoba / Columbiana
CD ______ HMCD 78
Harmonia Mundi / May '97 / Cadillac / Harmonia Mundi

El Rumbero

EL RUMBERO
CD ______ CDGRUB 23
Food For Thought / Sep '92 / Pinnacle

El Sonido De La Ciudad

GRAND TANGO, THE
CD ______ MVCD 1079
CBC / Jul '95 / Kingdom

El Tachuela, Rafa

GIPSY FLAMENCO GUITARRAS
CD ______ EUCD 1330
ARC / Nov '95 / ADA / ARC Music

Elanara

MOSAIC D'ESPANA (Spanish And Sephardic Songs)
CD ______ CDE 84334
Meridian / Jul '97 / Nimbus

Elastic Band

EXPANSIONS ON LIFE
CD ______ CDP 1001DD
Pseudonym / Jun '97 / Greyhound

Elastic Purejoy

ELASTIC PUREJOY
If Samuel Beckett had met Lenny Bruce / Soul and fire / Unchain my sister / Element of doubt / Stiff / Suburban yoke / You are my perfect PFM / Claxton vs the Fourth Estate / Monkey bone-walker / Witness
CD ______ WDOM 010CD
World Domination / Jun '94 / Pinnacle / RTM/Disc

Elastica

ELASTICA
Line up / Annie / Connection / Car song / Smile / Hold me now / SOFT / Indian / Blue / All-nighter / Waking up / Two to one / Vaseline / Never here / Stutter / Cleopatra
CD ______ BLUFF 014CD
Deceptive / Mar '95 / Vital

Elbert, Donnie

LITTLE PIECE OF LEATHER, A
Run little girl / Who's it gonna be / Little piece of leather / Memphis / Do whatcha wanna / Your red wagon / Down home blues / Never again / That funky ol' feeling / Lilly Lou
CD ______ TKOCD 021
TKO / Apr '92 / TKO

R & B MAVERICK (2CD Set)
Get ready / Time hangs on my mind / Along came pride / Baby please come home / Without you / Can't get over losing you / If I can't have you / Will you ever be mine / Little piece of leather / One thousand, nine hundred and seventy years / Where did our love go / What can I do / Get myself together / Sweet baby / That's if you love me / This feeling of losing you / Love is strange / You're gonna cry when I'm gone / (In between the heartaches) another tear will take its place / Come see me / Free / Love of your own / You don't have to be a star (to be in my show) / What a difference a day made / Back in my arms again / Will you still love me tomorrow / What do you do / Reachin' for a dream / Cry cry cry / Mr. Peanut in the White House / You should be dancing
CD Set ______ NEDCD 288
Sequel / Jul '97 / BMG

Elcka

LIKE STALLIONS
CD ______ CID 8057
Island / Aug '97 / PolyGram

ELD

CARVED
CD ______ DISC 026
Discordia / Oct '96 / Cargo

Elders, Betty

CRAYONS
CD ______ FF 642CD
Flying Fish / Nov '95 / ADA / CM / Direct / Roots

Eldopa

1332
CD ______ EBM 006CD
East Bay Menace / Jun '97 / Cargo

Eldridge, Roy

1935-1941
CD ______ CD 56066
Jazz Roots / Jul '95 / Target/BMG

BIG SOUND OF LITTLE JAZZ
CD ______ TPZ 1021
Topaz Jazz / May '95 / Cadillac / Pinnacle

CLASSICS 1935-1940
CD ______ CLASSICS 725
Classics / Dec '93 / Discovery / Jazz Music

CLASSICS 1943-1944
CD ______ CLASSICS 920
Classics / Apr '97 / Discovery / Jazz Music

FIESTA IN JAZZ
Sittin' in / Sittin' in no.2 / Stardust / Body and soul / 46 West 52 / 46 West 52 no.2 / Gasser / Jump through the wind / Minor jive / Don't be that way / I want to be happy / Fiesta in brass / Fiesta in brass / St. Louis blues / I can't get started (With you) / After you've gone / Fish market / Twilight time
CD ______ LEJAZZCD 46
Le Jazz / Oct '95 / Cadillac / Koch

FRENCHIE ROY
CD ______ VGCD 655009
Vogue / Jan '93 / BMG

HECKLERS HOP
I hope Gabriel likes my music / Mutiny in the parlour / I'm gonna clap my hands / Swing is here / Wabash stomp / Florida stomp / Heckler's hop / Where the lazy river goes by / That thing / After you've gone / Sittin' in / Stardust / Body and soul / Forty six, west fifty two / It's my turn now / You're a lucky guy / Pluckin' the bass / I'm gettin' sentimental over you / High society / Muskrat ramble / Who told you I cared / Does your heart beat for me
CD ______ HEPCD 1030
Hep / Mar '91 / Cadillac / Jazz Music / New Note/Pinnacle / Wellard

LITTLE JAZZ (1950-1960)
CD ______ CD 53187
Giants Of Jazz / May '95 / Cadillac / Jazz Music / Target/BMG

LITTLE JAZZ
CD ______ 158362
Jazz Archives / Jul '95 / Discovery

LIVE IN 1959 (Eldridge, Roy & Coleman Hawkins)
CD ______ STCD 531
Stash / Feb '91 / ADA / Cadillac / CM / Direct / Jazz Music

MONTREUX 1977
Between the Devil and the deep blue sea / Go for / I surrender Dear / Joie De Roy / Perdido / Bye bye blackbird
CD ______ OJCCD 373
Original Jazz Classics / Apr '93 / Complete/Pinnacle / Jazz Music / Wellard

NIFTY CAT, THE
Jolly Hollis / Cotton / 5400 North / Ball of fire / Wineola / Nifty cat
CD ______ 803492
New World / Jan '96 / ADA / Cadillac / Harmonia Mundi

ROY & DIZ (Eldridge, Roy & Dizzy Gillespie)
Sometimes I'm happy / Algo bueno / Trumpet blues / I'm through with love / Can't we be friends / Don't you think I don't know why / If I had you / Blue moon / I've found a new baby / Pretty-eyed baby / I can't get started (With you) / Limehouse blues
CD ______ 5216472
Verve / Jul '94 / PolyGram

ROY ELDRIDGE (1935-1941)
CD ______ CD 14571
Jazz Portraits / May '95 / Jazz Music

ROY ELDRIDGE AND VIC DICKENSON (Eldridge, Roy & Vic Dickenson)
CD ______ STCD 8239
Storyville / Jan '97 / Cadillac / Jazz Music / Wellard

Electra, Carmen

CARMEN ELECTRA
Go go dancer / Good Judy girlfriend / Go on (Witcha bad self) / Step to the mic / ST / Fantasia erotica / Everybody get on up / Segue / Fun / Just a little lovin' / Segue / All that / Segue / This is my house
CD ______ 7599253382
Paisley Park / Apr '93 / Warner Music

Electrafixion

BURNED
CD ______ 0630112482
WEA / Sep '95 / Warner Music

Electric Band

VOLTAGE
CD ______ 92624
Oberoi / May '94 / Jet Star

Electric Bluebirds

BACK ON THE TRAIN
Back on the train / Trouble with me / Alligator man / Tell it like it is / I don't need you / City limits / La Vie Malheureuse (Cajun Belle) / Stranger's just a friend / When the money's all gone / Dixieland rock / Dark hollow / Un Majoda sin licencia / Rocki-n'n'rollin' with Granmaw / Sad memory / Delia live / Colinda (Queen Ida's tune) / Careless love / Bluebird two-step / You don't miss your water / Allons y Lafayette / Madame Etienne / Square dancin' Mama / Los amores del Flaco / Waltz across Texas
CD ______ GEMCD 001
Diamond / Oct '96 / Pinnacle

Electric Boys

FREEWHEELIN'
CD ______ 5217222
Polydor / Mar '94 / PolyGram

Electric Family

MARIOPAINT
CD ______ 55IRDCOM 3CD
Irdial / Oct '95 / RTM/Disc

Electric Flag

GROOVIN' IS EASY
Spotlight: *Electric Chairs* / I was robbed last night / I found out / Never be lonely again / Losing game / My baby wants to test me / I should have left her / You don't realise / Groovin' is easy
CD ______ CDTB 1006
Thunderbolt / Nov '88 / TKO Magnum

Electric Frankenstein

ACTION HIGH
CD ______ LOUDEST 24
One Louder / Jun '97 / Mo's Music Machine / Shellshock/Disc / SRD

ELECTRIC FRANKENSTEIN CONQUERS THE WORLD
CD ______ 198192
Nesak / Jun '97 / Greyhound

SICK SONGS
CD ______ 198292
Kado / Jun '97 / Greyhound

TIME IS NOW
CD ______ NITR 005
Demolition Derby / Jan '97 / Greyhound / Nervous

Electric Groove Temple

SEQUENCE ME
CD ______ TCNCD 4
Trichone / Sep '96 / SRD

Electric Hellfire Club

BURN, BABY, BURN
CD ______ CLEO 72692
Cleopatra / Mar '94 / Cargo / Greyhound / Plastic Head / RTM/Disc / SRD

CALLING DR. LUV
CD ______ CLP 9797
Cleopatra / Oct '96 / Cargo / Greyhound / Plastic Head / RTM/Disc / SRD

KISS THE GOAT
CD ______ CLEO 95502
Cleopatra / Aug '95 / Cargo / Greyhound / Plastic Head / RTM/Disc / SRD

Electric Kings

NOT FOR SALE
CD ______ MWCD 2017
Music & Words / Dec '95 / ADA / Direct

Electric Love Hogs

ELECTRIC LOVE HOGS
CD ______ 8283052
London / Jul '93 / PolyGram

Electric Orange

CYBERDELIC
Cyberdelic/Unaffected fruit / Vaporized dance / Funny in the bathroom / Kirschen / Sweet absurd / B-movie / Steal no egg / Mothers cake / Tartisma zemini / She-wah / More end/Cyberdelic
CD ______ DELECCD 041
Delerium / Apr '97 / Cargo / Pinnacle / Vital

ORANGE COMMUTATION
Electripity chapter 99 / Journey through weird scenes featuring cows in space / Return of Eugene, be careful / Back in a strange world / Reflections of 2072 and everywhere
CD ______ DELECCDS 036
Delerium / Mar '96 / Cargo / Pinnacle / Vital

Electric Prunes

STOCKHOLM 1967
CD ______ CDHB 67
Heartbeat / May '97 / ADA / Direct / Greensleeves / Jet Star

Electric Skychurch

KNOWONENESS
CD ______ MM 800322
Moonshine / Apr '96 / Mo's Music Machine / Prime / RTM/Disc

Electric Universe

STARDIVER
Alien encounter (part 2) / From the heart / Radio SPACE / Rising sun / Online information / Luna overdrive / Technologic / Astral voyage / Sunset skyline / Stardiver / Alien encounter (part 1)
CD ______ SUB 48412
Distance / Jun '97 / 3mv/Sony / Prime

Electric Wizard

ELECTRIC WIZARD
CD ______ RISE 009CD
Rise Above / Jan '96 / Plastic Head / Vital

Electro Assassin

BIOCULTURE
CD ______ HY 39100692
Hyperium / Nov '93 / Cargo / Plastic Head

DIVINE INVASION
CD ______ SPV 08461252
SPV / Jun '96 / Koch / Plastic Head

Electrocution

INSIDE THE UNREAL
CD ______ BABECD 6
Rosemary's Baby / Sep '93 / Plastic Head

Electroids

ELEKTRO WORLD
CD ______ WARPCD 35
Warp / Aug '95 / Prime / RTM/Disc

Electronic

ELECTRONIC
CD ______ CDPRG 1012
EMI / Feb '94 / EMI

RAISE THE PRESSURE
Forbidden city / For you / Dark angel / One day / Until the end / Second nature / If you've got love / Out of my league / Interlude / Freefall / Visit me / How long / Time can tell
CD ______ CDPCS 7382
Parlophone / Jul '96 / EMI

Electronic Eye

IDEA OF JUSTICE, THE
CD ______ RBADCD 14
Beyond / Oct '95 / Kudos / Pinnacle

Elegy

LABYRINTH OF DREAMS
CD ______ TT 00052
T&T / Apr '97 / Koch

LOST
CD ______ TT 00172
T&T / Apr '97 / Koch

PRIMAL INSTINCT
Take my love / Labyrinth of dreams / Always with you / Spirits / Erase me
CD ______ TT 00253
T&T / Sep '96 / Koch

STATE OF MIND
Equinox / Visual vortex / Trust / Beyond / Shadow dancer / Aladdin's cave / State of mind / Destiny calling / Resurrection / Losers game / Suppression
CD ______ TT 00302
T&T / Jun '97 / Koch

SUPREMACY
CD ______ TT 00092
T&T / Apr '97 / Koch

Elektraws

SHOCK ROCK
CD ______ NERCD 083
Nervous / Jan '96 / Nervous / TKO Magnum

Elektric Music

ESPERANTO
TV / Showbusiness / Kissing the machine / Lifestyle / Crosstalk / Information / Esperanto / Overdrive
CD ______ 4509929992
East West / Jun '93 / Warner Music

Element

HOLD MY BREATH
CD ______ LF 238CD
Lost & Found / Sep '96 / Plastic Head

Elementales

AL BANO MARIA
CD ______ 21060CD
Sonifolk / Apr '95 / ADA / CM

ELEMENTALES
CD ______ J 1030CD
Sonifolk / Jun '94 / ADA / CM

Elements

FAR EAST
CD ______ LIP 890162
Lipstick / Feb '95 / Vital/SAM

FAR EAST VOL.2
CD ______ EFA 034522
Wavetone / Nov '95 / SRD

Elements Of Life

MOLECULAR DREAMS
CD ______ OMWCD 001
Oxygen / Jul '97 / RTM/Disc

Elend

LECONS DE TENEBRES
CD ______ HOLY 8CD
Holy / Nov '94 / Plastic Head

LES TENEBRES DU DEHORS
CD ______ HOLY 017CD
Holy / Apr '96 / Plastic Head

WEEPING NIGHTS
CD ______ HOLY 026CD
Elend / Jun '97 / Plastic Head

Elephant

ELEPHANT
CD ______ HB0162
Heatblast / Feb '94 / SRD

Elephant Talk

IN A BIG SEA
CD ______ INFRACD 0001
Knock On Wood / Apr '97 / Discovery

Elevate

ARCHITECT, THE
CD ______ FLOWCD 002
Flower Shop / Mar '96 / SRD

BRONZEE
CD ______ FLOWCD 001
Flower Shop / Oct '94 / SRD

Eleven Pictures

INTIALS
CD ______ M 7022CD
Mascot / Feb '97 / Plastic Head

Eleven Years From Yesterday

ELEVEN YEARS FROM YESTERDAY
CD ______ BEADCD 1
Bead / May '90 / Cadillac

Eleventh Dream Day

EIGHTH
For a King / Writes a letter home / Two smart cookies / Insomnia / View from the rim / April / Motion sickness / Last call
CD ______ EFA 049892
City Slang / Feb '97 / RTM/Disc

EL MOODIO
Makin' like a rug / Figure it out / After this time is gone / Murder / Honeyslide / That's the point / Motherland / Raft / Bend bridge / Rubber band
CD ______ 7567824802
East West / Mar '93 / Warner Music

LIVED TO TELL
Rose of jericho / Dream of a sleeping sheep / I could be lost / It's not my world / You know what it is / Frozen mile / Strung up and/or out / North of wasteland / It's all a game / Trouble / There's this thing / Daedalus / Angels spread your wings
CD ______ 7567821792
East West / Jun '91 / Warner Music

PRAIRIE SCHOOL FREAKOUT
CD ______ 422128
New Rose / May '94 / ADA / Direct / Discovery

URSA MAJOR
CD ______ EFA 049432
City Slang / Jan '95 / RTM/Disc

Elgart, Charlie

BALANCE
On the breeze of a shadow / My sentiments exactly / Balance / Bryanna / Sight unseen / Goodbye my friend / Sundance
CD _______ **PD 83068**
Novus / Dec '89 / BMG

SIGNS OF LIFE
Float / Sojourn / This thing we share / Signs of life / I cry for you / When I'm with Stu / Summer dusk
CD _______ **PD 83045**
RCA / Mar '89 / BMG

Elgart, Larry

SENSATIONAL SWING (Six Medleys Of Timeless Swing Favourites) (Elgart, Larry & His Manhattan Swing Orchestra)
Switched on swing / Switched on big bands / Switched on a star / Switched on Astaire / Switched on the blues / Switched on Broadway
CD _______ **ECD 3042**
K-Tel / Jan '95 / K-Tel

Elharrachi, Dahmane

DAHMANE ELHARRACHI
CD _______ **AAA 142**
Club Du Disque Arabe / Dec '96 / ADA / Harmonia Mundi

Eli, Billy

SOMETHING'S GOING ON (Eli, Billy & Lost In America)
CD _______ **MRCD 1295**
Club De Musique / Jun '96 / Direct

Elias, Elaine

LONG STORY, A
Back it time / Long story / Horizonte / Just kidding / Avida continua (life goes on) / Nile / Get it / Just for you / Karamura / Let me go (vida real)
CD _______ **CDP 7954762**
Blue Note / Oct '91 / EMI

SOLOS AND DUETS
Autumn leaves / Masquerade is over / Interlude / Way you look tonight: *Elias, Elaine & Herbie Hancock* / All the things you are / Joy spring / Have you met Miss Jones / Just enough: *Elias, Elaine & Herbie Hancock* / Messages: *Elias, Elaine & Herbie Hancock* / Asa branca
CD _______ **CDP 8320732**
Blue Note / Oct '95 / EMI

THREE AMERICANS, THE
Up dawn / Time is now / Caipora / Chorango / Chega de saudade / Crystal and lace / Brigas nunca mais / Introduction to Guarani / O Guarani / Jungle journey / Missing you / Jumping fox
CD _______ **CDP 8533282**
Blue Note / Jun '97 / EMI

Elias Hulk

UNCHAINED
Anthology of dreams / Nightmare / Been around too long / Yesterday's trip / We can fly / Free / Delhi blues / Ain't got you
CD _______ **SEECD 286**
See For Miles/C5 / Jan '90 / Pinnacle

Elijah's Mantle

ANGELS OF PEVERSITY
CD _______ **DNDC 001CD**
De Nova Da Capo / Oct '96 / World Serpent

BETRAYALS AND ECSTASIES
CD _______ **DNDC 006CD**
De Nova Da Capo / Oct '96 / World Serpent

POETS AND VISIONARIES
Preface / Hymn to beauty / Windows / Spleen / Vampire / Ophelia / Night in hell / Adieu
CD _______ **DNDC 009**
De Nova Da Capo / Jan '97 / World Serpent

REMEDIES IN HERESIES
CD _______ **DNDC 002CD**
De Nova Da Capo / Oct '96 / World Serpent

SORROWS OF SOPHIA
CD _______ **DNDC 003CD**
De Nova Da Capo / Oct '96 / World Serpent

Elite Syncopators

RAGTIME SPECIAL
CD _______ **SOSCD 1286**
Stomp Off / Mar '95 / Jazz Music / Wellard

Elkanger Bjorsvik Musikklag

VIKINGS, THE
CD _______ **DOYCD 023**
Doyen / Feb '93 / Conifer/BMG

Elkin, A.P.

ARNHEM LAND
CD _______ **LARRCD 288**
Larrikin / Jun '94 / ADA / CM / Direct / Roots

Elkins-Payne Jubilee Singers

ELKINS-PAYNE JUBILEE SINGERS (1923-1929)
CD _______ **DOCD 5356**
Document / Jun '95 / ADA / Hot Shot / Jazz Music

Ellefson, Art

AS IF TO SAY
CD _______ **SKCD 22030**
Sackville / Jun '93 / Cadillac / Jazz Music / Swift

Ellen Jamesians

IN SEARCH OF
CD _______ **BIRD 089**
Birdnest / Jun '97 / Cargo / Plastic Head

Elles

AALLE KREKAJENTE
CD _______ **ELLES 9401CD**
Musikk Distribujson / Dec '94 / ADA

Elliman, Yvonne

FOOD OF LOVE
Casserole me over / More than one, less than five / I want to make you laugh / Muesli dreams / I can't explain / Sunshine / Hawaii / I don't know how to love him blues / Moon struck one / Happy ending / Love's bringing me down
CD _______ **CSAPCD 124**
Connoisseur Collection / Nov '96 / Pinnacle

Elling, Kurt

MESSENGER
Nature boy / April in Paris / Suite / Beauty of all things / Dance / Prayer for Mr. Davis / Endless / It's just a thing / Ginger bread boy / Prelude to a kiss / Time of the season
CD _______ **CDP 8527272**
Parlophone / Apr '97 / EMI

Ellington, Duke

1952 SEATTLE CONCERT, THE
Skin deep / How could you do a thing like that to me / Sophisticated lady / Perfido / Caravan / Harlem suite / Hawk talks / Don't get around much anymore / In a sentimental mood / Mood indigo / I'm beginning to see the light / Prelude to a kiss / It don't mean a thing if it ain't got that swing / Solitude / Let a song go out of my heart / Jam with Sam
CD _______ **07863665312**
Bluebird / Apr '95 / BMG

20 JAZZ CLASSICS
Thing's ain't what they used to be / Satin doll / Flamingo / Liza / In a sentimental mood / My old flame / If I give my heart to you / Caravan / Stardust / Harlem air shaft / Band call / Bakiff / In the mood / One-o'clock jump / Flying home / Warm valley / C jam blues / Black and tan fantasy / Reflections in D / Rockin' in rhythm
CD _______ **CDMFP 6161**
Music For Pleasure / May '95 / EMI

22 ORIGINAL BIG BAND RECORDINGS
CD _______ **HCD 410**
Hindsight / Sep '92 / Jazz Music / Target/ BMG

70TH BIRTHDAY CONCERT (2CD Set)
Rockin' in rhythm / BP / Take the 'A' train / Tootie for Cootie / 4.30 blues / El Gato / Black butterfly / Things ain't what they used to be / Laying on mellow / Satin doll / Azure / In triplicate / Perdido / Fifi / Prelude to a kiss/I'm just a lucky so and so / I let a song go out of my heart / Prelude to a kiss / I'm just a lucky so and so / Do nothin' 'til you hear from me / Just squeeze me / Don't get around much anymore / Mood indigo / Sophisticated lady / Caravan / Black swan / Final Ellington speech
CD Set _______ **CDP 8327462**
Blue Note / Sep '95 / EMI

AFRO-EURASIAN ECLIPSE, THE
CD _______ **OJCCD 645**
Original Jazz Classics / Mar '93 / Complete/Pinnacle / Jazz Music / Wellard

ANATOMY OF A MURDER
CD _______ **4691372**
Sony Jazz / Jan '95 / Sony

AT NEWPORT (Ellington, Duke & Buck Clayton)
Take the 'A' train: *Ellington, Duke Orchestra* / Sophisticated lady: *Ellington, Duke Orchestra* / I got it bad and that ain't good: *Ellington, Duke Orchestra* / Skin deep: *Ellington, Duke Orchestra* / You can depend on me: *Clayton, Buck All Stars* / Newport jump: *Clayton, Buck All Stars* / In a mellow tone: *Clayton, Buck All Stars*
CD _______ **4773202**
Columbia / Nov '94 / Sony

AT THE GREEK 1966 (Ellington, Duke & Ella Fitzgerald)
CD _______ **DSTS 1013**
Status / '94 / Harmonia Mundi / Jazz Music / Wellard

AUDIO ARCHIVE
Mooche / Honeysuckle rose / Take the 'A' train / Mood indigo / Sophisticated lady / Crosstown / Caravan / Tea for two / Frustration / Perdido / One O'clock jump / Colatura / 920 special / Love you madly / Moon mist / Rose of the Rio Grande / Just squeeze me / Jam with Sam / Black and tan fantasy / Primin' at the prom
CD _______ **CDAA 014**
Tring / Jun '92 / Tring

BACK TO BACK (Duke Ellington & Johnny Hodges Play The Blues) (Ellington, Duke & Johnny Hodges)
Weary blues / St. Louis Blues / Loveless love / Royal Garden blues / Wabash blues / Basin Street blues / Beale Street blues
CD _______ **8236372**
Verve / Jan '88 / PolyGram

BEST OF DUKE ELLINGTON, THE
CD _______ **DLCD 4009**
Dixie Live / Mar '95 / TKO Magnum

BEST OF EARLY ELLINGTON, THE
East St. Louis toodle-oo / Birmingham breakdown / Black and tan fantasy / Take it easy / Jubilee stomp / Black beauty / Yellow dog blues / Tishomingo blues / Awful sad / Mooche / Doin' the voom voom / Rent part blues / Harlem flat blues / Jolly wog / Jazz convulsions / Sweet Mama / Cotton club stomp (take B) / Mood indigo / Rockin' in rhythm / Creole rhapsody parts 1 and 2
CD _______ **GRP 16602**
American Decca / Aug '96 / New Note/BMG

BEST OF THE FORTIES VOL.1 (1940-1942)
CD _______ **BMCD 3019**
Blue Moon / Sep '95 / Cadillac / Discovery / Greensleeves / Jazz Music / Jet Star / TKO Magnum

BLACK, BROWN AND BEIGE
CD _______ **ND 86641**
Bluebird / Oct '95 / BMG

BLACK, BROWN AND BEIGE
Part I / Part II / Part III / Part IV (Come Sunday) / Part V (Come Sunday interlude) / Part VI (23rd psalm)
CD _______ **CK 64274**
Mastersound / Nov '95 / Sony

BLANTON-WEBSTER YEARS, THE
You, you darlin' / Jack the bear / Koko / Morning glory / So far, so good / Conga brava / Do nothin' 'til you hear from me / Me and you / Cotton tail / Never no lament / Dusk / Bojangles / Portrait of Bert Williams / Blue goose / Harlem air shaft / At a Dixie roadside diner / All too soon / Rumpus in Richmond / My greatest mistake / Sepia panorama / There shall be no night / In a mellow tone / Five o'clock whistle / Warm valley / Flaming sword / Jumpin' punkins / Across the track blues / John Hardy's wife / Blue Serge / After all / Chloe / Bakiff / Are you sticking / I never felt this way before / Just a sittin' and a rockin' / Giddybug gallop / Sidewalks of New York / Chocolate shake / Flamingo / I got it bad and that ain't good / Clementine / Brown skin gal / Girl in my dreams tries to look like you / Jump for joy / Moon over Cuba / Take the 'A' train / Five o'clock drag / Rocks in my bed / Blip blip / Chelsea Bridge / Raincheck / What good would it do / I don't know what kind of blues I got / Perdido / C jam blues / Moon mist / What am I here for / I don't mind / Someone / My little brown book / Main stem / Johnny come lately / Hayfoot strawfoot / Sentimental lady / Slip of the lip (can sink a ship) / Sherman shuffle
CD Set _______ **74321131812**
Bluebird / Mar '93 / BMG

BLUE FEELING
Black and tan fantasy / Creole love call / Harlem twist / Black Beauty / Swampy river / Cotton club stomp / Shout 'em Aunt Tillie / Ring dem bells / Echoes of the jungle / Blue Harlem / Drop me off at Harlem / Bundle of blues / Harlem speaks / Hyde Park / Blue feeling / Merry go round / Clarinet lament / I'm slapping Seventh Avenue with the sole of my shoe / Riding on a blue note / I let a song go out of my heart / Blue light / Koko / Conga Brava / Jack the Bear
CD _______ **PPCD 78103**
Past Perfect / Feb '95 / Glass Gramophone Co.

BLUES IN ORBIT
Blues in orbit / Track 360 / Villes ville is the place, man / Brown penny / Three J's blues / Smada / Pie eye's blues / C jam blues / Sweet and pungent / In a mellow tone / Sentimental lady / Blues in blueprint / Swingers get the blues too / Singer's jump
CD _______ **4608232**
Sony Jazz / Jan '95 / Sony

BRUNSWICK SESSIONS VOL.1 1932-1935, THE
CD _______ **RBD 3001**
Mr. R&B / Oct '91 / CM / Swift / Wellard

BRUNSWICK SESSIONS VOL.2, THE (Ellington, Duke Orchestra)
Clouds in my heart / Blue mood / Ducky wucky / Jazz cocktail / Raisin' the rent / Happy as the day is long / Drop me off in Harlem / Blackbirds melody / Swing low, sweet chariot
CD _______ **RBD 3002**
Mr. R&B / Oct '91 / CM / Swift / Wellard

CARNEGIE HALL 1948 (Ellington, Duke Orchestra)
CD Set _______ **VJC 1024/252**
Vintage Jazz Classics / '91 / ADA / Cadillac / CM / Direct

CHEEK TO CHEEK 1935
CD _______ **PHONTCD 7657**
Phontastic / Apr '94 / Cadillac / Jazz Music / Wellard

CLASSIC DUKE ELLINGTON, THE (2CD Set)
Rockin' in rhythm / I let a song go out of my heart / Concerto for Cootie / Tonight I shall sleep / I got it bad and that ain't good / Misty mornin' / Jump for joy / East St. Louis toodle-oo / Ring dem bells / Mood to be wooed / Perdido / Black & tan fantasy / Solitude / Main stem / Chelsea Bridge / Three little words / Jack the bear / Azure / Cotton club stomp / Mood indigo / Drop me off in Harlem / Mooche / Moonglow / Take the 'A' train / Creole love call / Sophisticated lady / Harlem air shaft / All too soon / In a sentimental mood / Sepia panorama / Echoes of Harlem / Gal from Joe's / Bojangles / Prelude to a kiss / Black beauty / Things ain't what they used to be / I'm beginning to see the light / Ko Ko / It don't mean a thing (if it ain't got that swing) / Caravan / Black, brown and beige suite
CD Set _______ **CPCD 82592**
Charly / Jan '97 / Koch

CLASSICS 1924-1927
CD _______ **CLASSICS 539**
Classics / Dec '90 / Discovery / Jazz Music

CLASSICS 1927-1928
CD _______ **CLASSICS 542**
Classics / Dec '90 / Discovery / Jazz Music

CLASSICS 1928
CD _______ **CLASSICS 550**
Classics / Dec '90 / Discovery / Jazz Music

CLASSICS 1928-1929
CD _______ **CLASSICS 559**
Classics / Oct '91 / Discovery / Jazz Music

CLASSICS 1929
CD _______ **CLASSICS 569**
Classics / Oct '91 / Discovery / Jazz Music

CLASSICS 1929-1930
CD _______ **CLASSICS 577**
Classics / Oct '91 / Discovery / Jazz Music

CLASSICS 1930 VOL.1
CD _______ **CLASSICS 586**
Classics / Aug '91 / Discovery / Jazz Music

CLASSICS 1930 VOL.2
CD _______ **CLASSICS 596**
Classics / Sep '91 / Discovery / Jazz Music

CLASSICS 1930-1931 (Ellington, Duke Orchestra)
CD _______ **CLASSICS 605**
Classics / Oct '92 / Discovery / Jazz Music

CLASSICS 1931-1932 (Ellington, Duke Orchestra)
CD _______ **CLASSICS 616**
Classics / Sep '92 / Discovery / Jazz Music

CLASSICS 1932-1933 (Ellington, Duke Orchestra)
CD _______ **CLASSICS 626**
Classics / Sep '92 / Discovery / Jazz Music

CLASSICS 1933
CD _______ **CLASSICS 637**
Classics / Nov '92 / Discovery / Jazz Music

CLASSICS 1933-1935
CD _______ **CLASSICS 646**
Classics / Nov '92 / Discovery / Jazz Music

CLASSICS 1935-1936
CD _______ **CLASSICS 659**
Classics / Nov '92 / Discovery / Jazz Music

CLASSICS 1936-1937
CD _______ **CLASSICS 666**
Classics / Nov '92 / Discovery / Jazz Music

CLASSICS 1937 VOL.1
CD _______ **CLASSICS 675**
Classics / Mar '93 / Discovery / Jazz Music

CLASSICS 1937 VOL.2 (Ellington, Duke Orchestra)
CD _______________ CLASSICS 687
Classics / Mar '93 / Discovery / Jazz Music

CLASSICS 1938 VOL.1 (Ellington, Duke Orchestra)
CD _______________ CLASSICS 700
Classics / Jul '93 / Discovery / Jazz Music

CLASSICS 1938 VOL.2
CD _______________ CLASSICS 717
Classics / Jul '93 / Discovery / Jazz Music

CLASSICS 1938 VOL.3
CD _______________ CLASSICS 726
Classics / Dec '93 / Discovery / Jazz Music

CLASSICS 1938-1939
CD _______________ CLASSICS 747
Classics / Aug '94 / Discovery / Jazz Music

CLASSICS 1939 VOL.1
CD _______________ CLASSICS 765
Classics / Aug '94 / Discovery / Jazz Music

CLASSICS 1939 VOL.2
CD _______________ CLASSICS 780
Classics / Nov '94 / Discovery / Jazz Music

CLASSICS 1939-1940
CD _______________ CLASSICS 790
Classics / Jan '95 / Discovery / Jazz Music

CLASSICS 1940 VOL.1
CD _______________ CLASSICS 805
Classics / Mar '95 / Discovery / Jazz Music

CLASSICS 1940 VOL.2
CD _______________ CLASSICS 820
Classics / Jul '95 / Discovery / Jazz Music

CLASSICS 1940-1941
CD _______________ CLASSICS 837
Classics / Sep '95 / Discovery / Jazz Music

CLASSICS 1941
CD _______________ CLASSICS 851
Classics / Feb '96 / Discovery / Jazz Music

CLASSICS 1942-1944
CD _______________ CLASSICS 867
Classics / Mar '96 / Discovery / Jazz Music

CLASSICS 1944-1945
CD _______________ CLASSICS 881
Classics / Jul '96 / Discovery / Jazz Music

CLASSICS 1945
CD _______________ CLASSICS 915
Classics / Jan '97 / Discovery / Jazz Music

COLLECTION, THE
CD _______________ HBCD 501
Hindsight / Sep '92 / Jazz Music / Target/BMG

COMPLETE DUKE ELLINGTON VOL.1
CD _______________ KAZCD 501
Kaz / May '96 / BMG

COMPLETE DUKE ELLINGTON VOL.10
CD _______________ KAZCD 510
Kaz / May '96 / BMG

COMPLETE DUKE ELLINGTON VOL.2
CD _______________ KAZCD 502
Kaz / May '96 / BMG

COMPLETE DUKE ELLINGTON VOL.3
CD _______________ KAZCD 503
Kaz / May '96 / BMG

COMPLETE DUKE ELLINGTON VOL.4
CD _______________ KAZCD 504
Kaz / May '96 / BMG

COMPLETE DUKE ELLINGTON VOL.5
CD _______________ KAZCD 505
Kaz / May '96 / BMG

COMPLETE DUKE ELLINGTON VOL.6
CD _______________ KAZCD 506
Kaz / May '96 / BMG

COMPLETE DUKE ELLINGTON VOL.7
CD _______________ KAZCD 507
Kaz / May '96 / BMG

COMPLETE DUKE ELLINGTON VOL.8
CD _______________ KAZCD 508
Kaz / May '96 / BMG

COMPLETE DUKE ELLINGTON VOL.9
CD _______________ KAZCD 509
Kaz / May '96 / BMG

CONCERT OF SACRED MUSIC
CD _______________ DSTS 1015
Status / Jul '97 / Harmonia Mundi / Jazz Music / Wellard

CONNECTICUT JAZZ FESTIVAL
CD _______________ IAJRCCD 1005
IAJRC / Jun '94 / Jazz Music / Wellard

COOL ROCK (Ellington, Duke Orchestra)
CD _______________ 15782
Laserlight / Aug '92 / Target/BMG

CORNELL UNIVERSITY CONCERT (2CD Set)
CD Set _______________ MM 65114
Music Masters / Oct '96 / Nimbus

COTTON CLUB DAYS - LEGENDARY LIVE BROADCASTS
CD _______________ JZCD 335
Suisa / Jan '93 / Jazz Music / THE

COTTON CLUB STOMP (Ellington, Duke Orchestra)
CD _______________ CD 14544
Jazz Portraits / Jan '94 / Jazz Music

COTTON CLUB STOMP 1927-1931
CD _______________ CD 56051
Jazz Roots / Mar '95 / Target/BMG

COUNT MEETS THE DUKE, THE (Ellington, Duke Orchestra & Count Basie Orchestra)
CD _______________ 4505092
Sony Jazz / Jan '95 / Sony

CRYSTAL BALLROOM, FARGO VOL.1 1940
CD _______________ TAX 37202
Tax / Aug '94 / Cadillac / Jazz Music / Wellard

CRYSTAL BALLROOM, FARGO VOL.2 1940
CD _______________ TAX 37212
Tax / Aug '94 / Cadillac / Jazz Music / Wellard

DRUM IS A WOMAN, A
CD _______________ 4713202
Sony Jazz / Jan '95 / Sony

DUKE ELLINGTON (2CD Set)
CD Set _______________ R2CD 4019
Deja Vu / Jan '96 / THE

DUKE ELLINGTON
CD _______________ 22710
Music / Feb '96 / Target/BMG

DUKE ELLINGTON & HIS GREAT VOCALISTS
It don't mean a thing if it ain't got that swing / St. Louis blues / I can't give you anything but love / Diga diga doo / I must have that man / Solitude / Woman'll get you / Don't get around much anymore / Take love easy / On a turquoise cloud / Love you madley / Take the 'A' train / Sophisticated lady / Autumn leaves / Love (my everything)
CD _______________ CK 66372
Columbia / Jul '95 / Sony

DUKE ELLINGTON & HIS ORCHESTRA 1963
CD _______________ CD 14564
Jazz Portraits / May '95 / Jazz Music

DUKE ELLINGTON 1927-1934
Creole love call / Black beauty / Got everything but you / Duke steps out / Jungle nights in Harlem / Blue feeling
CD _______________ HRM 6001
Hermes / Jan '89 / Nimbus

DUKE ELLINGTON 1927-1941 (Ellington, Duke Orchestra)
East St. Louis toodle-oo / Blues I love to sing / Black and tan fantasy / Washington wobble / Creole love call / Black beauty / Mooche / Misty mornin' / Hot and bothered / Jubilee stomp / Take it easy / Cotton club stomp / Tiger rag / Ring dem bells / Old man blues / Mood indigo / Dicty glide / Doing the voom voom / Hop head / Wall Street wail / Saratoga swing / Echoes of the jungle / Rockin' in rhythm / Take the 'A' train / Don't get around much anymore / Cotton tail / I got it bad and that ain't good / Conga brava / Do nothin' 'til you hear from me / Portrait of Bert Williams / Warm valley / Solitude / Country gal / Prelude to a kiss / I let a song go out of my heart / Diminuedno in blue / Crescendo in Ibue / Echoes of Harlem / Caravan / Clarinet lament / Merry go round / In a sentimental mood / Live and love tonight / Sophisticated lady / Harlem speaks / Slippery horn / In a mellow tone / Koko / Jack the bear / Harlem air shaft / Just a sittin' and a rockin' / Sepia panorama / Jumpin' punkins / Mr. J.B. blues / Body and soul / Bojangles / Sidewalks of New York / Pitter panther patter / Across the track blues / Plucked again / Blues / Chloe / C Blues / Weely / Junior hop / Dusk / Blue Serge / Morning glory
CD Set _______________ CDB 1201
Giants Of Jazz / '92 / Cadillac / Jazz Music / Target/BMG

DUKE ELLINGTON 1931-1932 (Ellington, Duke Orchestra)
CD _______________ CD 53046
Giants Of Jazz / Mar '90 / Cadillac / Jazz Music / Target/BMG

DUKE ELLINGTON 1941
CD _______________ UCD 19003
Forlane / Jul '88 / Target/BMG

DUKE ELLINGTON AND HIS ORCHESTRA 1927-1931 (Ellington, Duke Orchestra)
CD _______________ CD 53030
Giants Of Jazz / Aug '88 / Cadillac / Jazz Music / Target/BMG

DUKE ELLINGTON AND HIS ORCHESTRA 1941-1951 (Ellington, Duke Orchestra)
CD _______________ CD 53057
Giants Of Jazz / Mar '92 / Cadillac / Jazz Music / Target/BMG

DUKE ELLINGTON AND HIS ORCHESTRA VOL.2 1930 (Ellington, Duke Orchestra)
CD _______________ CD 596
Classic Jazz Masters / Sep '91 / Wellard

DUKE ELLINGTON AND JOHN COLTRANE (Ellington, Duke & John Coltrane)
In a sentimental mood / Take the Coltrane / Big Nick / Stevie / My little brown book / Angelica / Feeling of jazz
CD _______________ IMP 11662
Impulse Jazz / Oct '95 / New Note/BMG

DUKE ELLINGTON AND THE SMALL GROUPS 1936-1950
CD _______________ CD 53070
Giants Of Jazz / May '92 / Cadillac / Jazz Music / Target/BMG

DUKE ELLINGTON COLLECTORS' EDITION
CD _______________ DVX 08042
Deja Vu / Apr '95 / THE

DUKE ELLINGTON GOLD (2CD Set)
CD _______________ D2CD 4019
Deja Vu / Jun '95 / THE

DUKE ELLINGTON IN CONCERT
CD Set _______________ RTE 15032
RTE / Apr '95 / ADA / Koch

DUKE ELLINGTON PRESENTS THE SOLOISTS 1951-1958
In a mellotone / East St. Louis toodle-oo / Koko / Sophisticated lady / Cotton tail / Mooche / Bensonality / Prelude to a kiss / Satin doll / Mood indigo / Just a-settin' and a-rockin' / I got it bad and that ain't good / Harlem air shaft / Blues in orbit / Hawk talks / Jeep's blues / El Gato / Theme for Trambean / Smada / Take the 'A' train
CD _______________ CD 53066
Giants Of Jazz / Mar '92 / Cadillac / Jazz Music / Target/BMG

DUKE ELLINGTON PRESENTS... (Big Band Bounce & Boogie) (Ellington, Duke Orchestra)
Summertime / Laura / I can't get started (with you) / My funny Valentine / Everything but you / Frustration / Cotton tail / Daydream / Deep purple / Indian summer / Blues
CD _______________ CDGR 123
Charly / Mar '97 / Koch

DUKE ELLINGTON VOL.1
CD _______________ 15710
Laserlight / Apr '94 / Target/BMG

DUKE ELLINGTON VOL.1 1927-1931
CD _______________ KJ 144FS
King Jazz / Oct '93 / Cadillac / Discovery / Jazz Music

DUKE ELLINGTON VOL.10 (Rockin' In Rhythm 1930-1931)
CD _______________ 152312
Hot 'n' Sweet / May '95 / Discovery

DUKE ELLINGTON VOL.12 (Echoes Of The Jungle 1931-1932)
CD _______________ 152332
Hot 'n' Sweet / Mar '96 / Discovery

DUKE ELLINGTON VOL.2 (Creole Rhapsody)
CD _______________ 152322
Hot 'n' Sweet / Feb '95 / Discovery

DUKE ELLINGTON VOL.2
CD _______________ 15753
Laserlight / Apr '94 / Target/BMG

DUKE ELLINGTON VOL.2 1931-1938
CD _______________ KJ 145FS
King Jazz / Oct '93 / Cadillac / Discovery / Jazz Music

DUKE ELLINGTON VOL.7 (Wall Street Wail 1929)
CD _______________ 152232
Hot 'n' Sweet / Dec '93 / Discovery

DUKE ELLINGTON VOL.8 (Jungle Blues 1929-1930)
CD _______________ 152242
Hot 'n' Sweet / Dec '93 / Discovery

DUKE ELLINGTON VOL.9 (Mood Indigo 1930)
CD _______________ 152252
Hot 'n' Sweet / May '94 / Discovery

DUKE PLAYS ELLINGTON
CD _______________ TPZ 1020
Topaz Jazz / May '95 / Cadillac / Pinnacle

DUKE'S BIG FOUR (Ellington, Duke Quartet)
Cotton tail / Blues / Hawk talks / Prelude to a kiss / Love you madly / Just squeeze me / Everything but you
CD _______________ CD 2310703
Pablo / Nov '95 / Cadillac / Complete/ Pinnacle

ECHOES OF HARLEM
CD _______________ MACCD 276
Autograph / Aug '96 / BMG

ELLINGTON (Never-Before Released Recordings 1965-1972) (Ellington, Duke Orchestra)
Old circus train / Swamp goo / Trombone buster / Bourbon street / Jingles jollies / Mellow ditty / To know you is to love you / Naidni remmus / Prowling cat / Madiera / Thanks for the beautiful land / Charpoy / Portrait of Louis Armstrong / Girdle hurdle / Sans snyphelle / Woods
CD _______________ 8208352
Limelight / May '91 / PolyGram

ELLINGTON '56
East St. Louis toodle-oo / Creole love call / Stompy Jones / Jeep is jumpin' / Jack the bear / In a mellow tone / Koko / Midriff / Stomp, look and listen / Unbooted character / Lonesome lullaby / Upper Manhattan medical group / Cotton tail / Daydream / Deep purple / Indian summer / Laura / Blues
CD _______________ LEJAZZCD 27
Le Jazz / Aug '94 / Cadillac / Koch

ELLINGTON AT NEWPORT (Ellington, Duke Orchestra)
CD _______________ 4509862
Sony Jazz / Jan '95 / Sony

ELLINGTON INDIGOS
Solitude / Where or when / Mood indigo / Night and day / Prelude to a kiss / All the things you are / Willow weep / For me / Tenderly / Dancing in the dark / Autumn leaves / Sky fell down
CD _______________ 4723642
Sony Jazz / Jun '96 / Sony

ELLINGTON MEETS HAWKINS (Ellington, Duke & Coleman Hawkins)
Limbo jazz / Mood indigo / Ray Charles' place / Wanderlust / You dirty dog / Self portrait (of the bean) / Jeep is jumpin' / Ricitic / Solitude
CD _______________ IMP 11622
Impulse Jazz / Oct '95 / New Note/BMG

ELLINGTON SUITES, THE
Queen's suite / Goutelas suite / Uwis suite
CD _______________ OJCCD 446
Original Jazz Classics / Feb '92 / Complete/ Pinnacle / Jazz Music / Wellard

ESSENTIAL DUKE ELLINGTON, THE (4CD Set)
CD _______________ CDDIG 13
Charly / Apr '95 / Koch

ESSENTIAL RECORDINGS, THE
CD _______________ LEJAZZCD 2
Le Jazz / Mar '93 / Cadillac / Koch

ESSENTIAL V-DISCS, THE
CD _______________ JZCD 301
Suisa / Feb '91 / Jazz Music / THE

ETERNAL DUKE ELLINGTON
CD _______________ PHONTCD 7666
Phontastic / Apr '94 / Cadillac / Jazz Music / Wellard

FAR EAST SUITE - SPECIAL MIX, THE
Tourist point of view / Bluebird of Delhi / Ifashan / Depk / Mount Harissa / Blue pepper (Far East of the blues) / Agra / Amad / Ad lib on Nippon / Tourist point of view (Alt. Take) / Bluebird of Delhi (Alt. Take) / Isfahan / Amad (Alt. Take)
CD _______________ 07863665512
Bluebird / Jun '95 / BMG

FARGO, NORTH DAKOTA 1940 (Ellington, Duke Orchestra)
CD Set _______________ VJC 1019/20 2
Vintage Jazz Classics / Oct '91 / ADA / Cadillac / CM / Direct

FEELING OF JAZZ, THE
CD _______________ BLCD 760123
Black Lion / Feb '89 / Cadillac / Jazz Music / Koch / Wellard

FOUR SYMPHONIC WORKS
Harlem / Three black kings / New world a comin' / Black, brown and beige
CD _______________ MM 65096
Music Masters / Oct '96 / Nimbus

GENEROSITY OF MOOD, A
Mood Indigo / It don't mean a thing if it ain't got that swing / East St. Louis toodle-oo / Black and tan fantasy / Rockin' in rhythm / Mooche / Solitude / Caravan / Wall Street wail / When your smiling / Cotton Club Stomp / Running wild / Wang wang blues / Twelfth street rag / Creole rhapsody / Is that religion / Hot and bothered / Old man blues / Ring dem bells
CD _______________ PAR 2036
Parade / Oct '94 / Disc

GITANES - JAZZ 'ROUND MIDNIGHT (Ellington, Duke & Billy Strayhorn)
CD _______________ 5107072
Polydor / Oct '91 / PolyGram

GREAT CHICAGO CONCERTS, THE (The Travelog Edition/Unreleased Masters/2CD Set)
Ring dem bells / Jumpin' punkins / Beale Street blues / Memphis blues / Golden feather / Air conditioned jungle / Very unbooted character / Sultry sunset / Magnolias just dripping with molasses / Hearsay / There was nobody looking / Happy go lucky local / Things ain't what they used to be / Hiawatha / Ride Red ride / Blues riff / Improvisation / Honeysuckle rose / Blue skies

/ Star spangled banner / In a mellotone / Solid old man / Come Sunday/Work song / Rugged Romeo / Circe / Dancers in love / Coloratura / Frankie and Johnny / Caravan / Take the 'A' train / Mellow ditty / Fugue / Jam a ditty / Magenta haze / Pitter panther patter / Suburbanite
CD Set 8444012
Limelight / Jun '94 / PolyGram
CD Set MM 65110
Music Masters / Oct '96 / Nimbus

GREAT DUKE ELLINGTON
Take the 'A' train / Just you, just me / Come rain or come shine / Blue Lou / Tea for two / How high the moon / One o'clock jump / Crosstown / Pretty woman / 9.20 Special / On the Alamo / Perdido
CD HCD 335
Hindsight / Mar '96 / Jazz Music / Target/BMG

GREAT ELLINGTON UNITS, THE
Daydream / Good Queen Bess / That's the blues, old man / Junior hop / Without a song / My Sunday gal / Mobile bay / Linger awhile / Charlie the chulo / Lament for Javanette / Lull at dawn / Ready Eddy / Some Saturday / Subtle slough / Menelik, the lion of Judah / Poor bubber / Squatty roo / Passion flower / Things ain't what they used to be / Going out the back way / Brown suede / C jam blues
CD ND 86751
Bluebird / Nov '88 / BMG

GREAT JAZZ VOCALISTS SING ELLINGTON AND STRAYHORN (Various Artists)
I got it bad (and that ain't good): *Reeves, Dianne* / I ain't got nothin' but the blues: *Rawls, Lou* / Prelude to a kiss: *Wilson, Nancy* / Do nothin' 'til you hear from me: *Lincoln, Abbey* / Lush life: *Wilson, Nancy* / Something to live for: *Horne, Lena* / Just a sittin' and a rockin': *Nance, Ray* / Warm valley: *Lincoln, Abbey* / It don't mean a thing (if it ain't got that swing): *Ross, Annie & Gerry Mulligan* / I didn't know about you: *Christy, June* / Jump for joy: *Vaughan, Sarah* / Sophisticated lady: *Vaughan, Sarah* / Medley:prelude to a kiss/I'm beginning to see the light: *Vaughan, Sarah* / Drop me off in Harlem: *Armstrong, Louis* / I'm just a lucky so and so: *Armstrong, Louis* / Day dream: *Christy, June* / It's kind of lonesome out tonight: *Cole, Nat 'King' Trio* / Come Sunday: *Williams, Joe*
CD CDP 8552212
Blue Note / Mar '97 / EMI

GREAT LONDON CONCERTS, THE (The Travelog Edition/Unreleased Masters)
Take the 'A' train / Intro / Perdido / Caravan / Isfahan / Opener / Harlem / Take the 'A' train / Mood indigo / C jam blues / Don't get around much anymore / Diminuendo and crescendo in blue / Single petal of a rose / Kinda Dukish / Rockin' in rhythm
CD 5184462
Limelight / Jun '94 / PolyGram
CD MM 65106
Music Masters / Oct '96 / Nimbus

GREAT PARIS CONCERT, THE
Kinda dukish / Rockin' in rhythm / On the sunny side of the street / Star crossed lovers / All of me / Asphalt jungle / Do nothin' 'til you hear from me / Tutti for cootie / Suite Thursday / Perdido / Eighth veil / Rose of the Rio Grande / Cop out / Bula / Jam with Sam / Happy go lucky local / Tone parallel to Harlem / Don't get around much anymore / Black and tan fantasy / Creole love call / Mooch / Things ain't what they used to be / Pyramid / Blues (from black brown and beige) / Echoes of Harlem / Satin doll
CD 7567813032
Atlantic / Feb '92 / Warner Music

GREAT TIMES (Ellington, Duke & Billy Strayhorn)
Cotton tail / C jam blues / Flamingo / Bang-up blues / Tonk / Johnny come lately / In a blue summer garden / Great times / Perdido / Take the 'A' train / Oscarlypso / Blues for blanton
CD OJCCD 108
Original Jazz Classics / Sep '93 / Complete/ Pinnacle / Jazz Music / Wellard

GREATEST HITS
Take the 'A' train / Sophisticated lady / Perdido / Prelude to a kiss / C jam blues / Mood indigo / Mooche / Satin doll / Solitude / What am I here for / I got it bad and that ain't good / Skin deep
CD 4629592
Sony Jazz / Oct '93 / Sony

GREATEST JAZZ BAND IN THE WORLD...EVER, THE (2CD Set)
Take the 'A' train / Sophisticated lady / Harlem speaks / I let a song go out of my heart / Merry go round / Echoes of Harlem / Country gal / Caravan / Don't get around much anymore / Cotton tail / In a sentimental mood / Crescendo in blue / I got it bad and that ain't good / Concerto for Cootie (do nothing till you hear from me) / Prelude to a kiss / Hyde park / Diminuendo in blue / Solitude / Drop me in Harlem / Mooche / Showboat shuffle / Harmony in Harlem / Creole rhapsody pts. 1 & 2 / Slippery horn / Steppin' into swing society / Warm valley / It don't mean a thing (if it ain't got that swing) / In a jam / East St. Louis toodle-oo / Clarinet lament (Barney's concerto) / Gal from Joe's / Black & tan fantasy / Doin the voom voom / Stompy Jones / Ring dem bells / Merry go round 2
CD Set 330222
Hallmark / Jul '96 / Carlton

HAPPY BIRTHDAY DUKE (5CD Set)
CD Set 15965
Laserlight / Oct '95 / Target/BMG

HAPPY BIRTHDAY DUKE VOL.2 (Ellington, Duke Orchestra)
CD 15784
Laserlight / Jul '92 / Target/BMG

HAPPY BIRTHDAY DUKE VOL.3 (Ellington, Duke Orchestra)
CD 15785
Laserlight / Jul '92 / Target/BMG

HAPPY BIRTHDAY DUKE VOL.4 (Ellington, Duke Orchestra)
CD 15786
Laserlight / Aug '92 / Target/BMG

HAPPY BIRTHDAY DUKE VOL.5 (Ellington, Duke Orchestra)
CD 15787
Laserlight / Aug '92 / Target/BMG

HAPPY-GO-LUCKY LOCAL (Ellington, Duke Orchestra)
CD MVSCD 52
Musicraft / Jul '88 / Warner Music

HARLEM (Ellington, Duke Orchestra)
Blow by blow / Caravan / Satin doll / Harlem: *Ellington, Duke Orchestra & Johnny Hodges* / Things ain't what they used to be / All of me / Prowling cat / Opera / Happy reunion / Tutti for cootie
CD CD 2308245
Pablo / Oct '92 / Cadillac / Complete/ Pinnacle

HIS ORCHESTRA AND HIS SMALL GROUPS
C Jam blues / Perdido / Sultry sunset / Blue skies (trumpet no end) / It don't mean a thing if it ain't got that swing / Magenta haze / Things ain't what they used to be (times's-a-wastin') / I'm beginning to see the light / Moonmist / Chelsea bridge / Jump for joy / Main stem / What am I here for / Johnny come lately / Do nothin' 'til you hear from me / Snibor / On a turquoise cloud / Park at 106th / In a sentimental mood / Black and tan fantasy / Caravan / Creole love call / Great times / Brown Betty / Dancers in love / Clothed man / Charlie the chulo / Chasin' chippies / Rent party blues / Tonk / Tip toe topic / Frankie and Johnny / Subtle slough / Without a song / Blues for blanton / Dooji wooji / Oscarlypso / Jeep's blues / Things ain't what they used to be / Good Queen Bess / Squaty roo / Menelik, the Lion of Judah / Lull at dawn / Goin' out the back way / Who knows / In a mellow tone / East St. Louis toodle-oo / Koko / Sophisticated lady / Cotton tail / Mooche / Bensonality / Prelude to a kiss / Satin doll / Mood indigo / Just a sittin' and a rockin' / I got it bad and that ain't good / Harlem air shaft / Blues in orbit / Hawk talks / El gato / Trambean (Theme from) / Smada / Take the 'A' train
CD Set CDB 1211
Giants Of Jazz / '92 / Cadillac / Jazz Music / Target/BMG

HOLLYWOOD HANGOVER
CD MCCD 019
Magnum America / Nov '96 / TKO Magnum

IN CONCERT AT THE PLEYEL PARIS
CD DAWE 39
Magic / Oct '92 / Cadillac / Harmonia Mundi / Jazz Music / Swift / Wellard

IN CONCERT AT THE PLEYEL PARIS VOL.2 1958
El Gato / Take the 'A' train / MB blue / VIP boogie / Jam with Sam / Stompy Jones / Hi fi fo fun / Medley / Hawkes talks
CD DAWE 40
Magic / May '90 / Cadillac / Harmonia Mundi / Jazz Music / Swift / Wellard

IN THE UNCOMMON MARKET
Bula / Silk lace / Asphalt jungle / Star crossed lovers / Getting sentimental over you / ESP (extra sensory perception) / Paris blues / Shepherd / Kinda Dukish
CD CD 2308247
Pablo / Apr '94 / Cadillac / Complete/ Pinnacle

INCOMPARABLE, THE (Ellington, Duke Orchestra)
Rockin' in rhythm / Such sweet thunder / Newport up / St. Louis blues / Walkin' and singin' the blues / Anatomy of a murder / El gato / Hank cinq (hank sank) / Jam with Sam / Things ain't what they used to be / Don't get around much anymore / Do nothin' 'til you hear from me / I've got it bad, and that ain't good / I'm beginning to see the light / Caravan / I let a song go out of my heart
CD DBCD 11
Dance Band Days / Dec '88 / Prism

INDISPENSABLE DUKE ELLINGTON VOL.5 & 6, THE
Koko / Bojangles (II) / Pitter panther patter (II) / Body and soul (take 2) / Sophisticated lady (II) / Jack the bear / Koko / Morning glory / Conga brava / Do nothin' 'til you hear from me / Bojangles / Cotton tail / Never no lament / Dusk / Portrait of Bert Williams / Blue goose / Harlem air shaft / At a Dixie roadside diner / All too soon / Rumpus in Richmond / Sepia panorama / In a mellow tone / Five o'clock whistle / Warm valley / Across the track blues / Chloe / Sidewalks of New York / Pitter panther patter / Body and soul / Sophisticated lady / Mr. J.B. Blues
CD Set ND 89750
Jazz Tribune / May '94 / BMG

INDISPENSABLE DUKE ELLINGTON VOL.7 & 8, THE
Take the 'A' train / Jumpin' punkins / John Hardy's wife / Blue serge / After all / Are you sticking / Just a sittin' and a rockin' / Giddybug gallop / Chocolate shake / I got it bad and that ain't good / Clementine / Brown skin gal / Jump for you / Five o'clock drag / Rocks in my bed / Bli-blip / Raincheck / I don't know what kind of blues I got / Chelsea bridge / Perdido / C jam blues / Moon mist / What am I here for / I don't mind / Someone / My little brown book / Main stem / Johnny come lately / Hayfoot strawfoot / Sentimental lady / Slip of the lip (can sink a ship) / Sherman shuffle
CD 74321155242
Jazz Tribune / Jun '94 / BMG

INDISPENSABLE DUKE ELLINGTON VOL.9 & 10, THE (The Small Groups)
Daydream / Good Queen Bess / That's the blues, old man / Junior hop / Without a song / My Sunday gal / Mobile Bay / Linger awhile / Charlie the Chulo / Lament for Javanette / Lull at dawn / Ready Eddy / Dear old Southland / Solitude / Some Saturday / Subtle slough / Menelik, the Lion of Judah / Poor bubber / Squattyroo / Passion flower / Things ain't what they used to be / Going out the back way / Brown suede / Noir blue / C jam blues / June / Frankie and Johnny / Jumpin' room only / Tonk / Drawing room blues
CD Set 74321115232
RCA / Mar '94 / BMG

INDISPENSABLE DUKE ELLINGTON, THE
CD 74321155252
RCA / Apr '94 / BMG

INTIMACY OF THE BLUES, THE (Ellington, Duke Small Bands)
Intimacy of the blues / Out south / Tell me 'bout my baby / Kentucky Avenue / Near North / Soul country / Noon morning / Rockochet / Tippy-toeing through the jungle garden / Just a sittin' and a rockin' / All too soon
CD OJCCD 624
Original Jazz Classics / Jun '96 / Complete/ Pinnacle / Jazz Music / Wellard

INTRODUCTION TO DUKE ELLINGTON 1927-1941, AN
CD 4024
Best Of Jazz / Sep '95 / Discovery

JACK THE BEAR
CD AMSC 573
Avid / Jun '96 / Avid/BMG / Koch / THE

JAZZ COCKTAIL (Ellington, Duke Orchestra)
Stevedore stomp / Creole love call / It don't mean a thing if it ain't got that swing / Hot and bothered / Rose room / Old man blues / Jungle nights in Harlem / Tiger Bay / Sweet jazz o'mine / Mood indigo / Sing you sinners / Limehouse blues / Double check stomp / Swing low, sweet chariot / Jazz cocktail / Creole rhapsody
CD CDAJA 5024
Living Era / Oct '88 / Select

JAZZ MASTERS
Take the 'A' train / La plus belle / Africaine / Flirtibird / Diminuendo in blue/Blow by blow / Loveless love / Going up / St. Louis blues / Stompy Jones / Caravan / Total jazz / Perdido / Jam with Sam / Rockin' in rhythm
CD 5163382
Verve / Feb '94 / PolyGram

JAZZ MASTERS
CD CDMFP 6298
Music For Pleasure / Mar '97 / EMI

JAZZ PARTY
CD 4600592
Sony Jazz / Jan '95 / Sony

JAZZ PORTRAITS (Ellington, Duke Orchestra)
Take the 'A' train / Don't get around much anymore / Cotton tail / I got it bad and that ain't good / Conga brava / Do nothin' 'til you hear from me / Portrait of Bert Williams / Solitude / I let a song go out of my heart / Prelude to a kiss / Caravan / Merry go round / In a sentimental mood / In a mellow tone / Sophisticated lady / Koko / Harlem air shaft / Just a sittin' and a rockin'
CD CD 14505
Jazz Portraits / May '94 / Jazz Music

JAZZ PROFILE
Satin doll / Star dust / One o'clock jump / Stormy weather / Take the 'A' train / 4.30 blues / In triplicate / Chile bowl / Janet / Happy reunion / Caravan / Wig wise
CD CDP 8549002
Blue Note / May '97 / EMI

JUMP FOR JOY (The Genius Of Duke Ellington)
CD CECD 8
Collector's Edition / Jul '96 / TKO Magnum

JUMP FOR JOY VOL.2
CD JHR 73544
Jazz Hour / May '93 / Cadillac / Jazz Music / Target/BMG

KEEP IT MOVIN'
Dick's boogie / Skirts / Between some place goin' no place / Sittin' on a tree top / Venetian sunset / J for Johnny / Accentuate the positive / Stringin' the blues / Mexican bandit / Rooftop / Like dig / Wilt the stilt / Savoy non-stop / Dedicated to the Duke / Coffee mornin' / Keep it movin'
CD CDMT 015
Meteor / Oct '96 / TKO Magnum

LATIN AMERICAN SUITE (Ellington, Duke Orchestra)
CD OJCCD 469
Original Jazz Classics / Mar '93 / Complete/Pinnacle / Jazz Music / Wellard

LIVE AT MONTEREY 1960 (The Unheard Recordings Part 1) (Ellington, Duke Orchestra)
Deep river/Take the 'A' train / Perdido / Overture: Nutcracker suite / Half the fun / Jeep's blues / Newport up / Sophisticated lady / Suite Thursday / Dance of the floreadores / Jam with Sam / Jones
CD DSTS 1008
Status / May '95 / Harmonia Mundi / Jazz Music / Wellard

LIVE AT MONTEREY 1960 (The Unheard Recordings Part 2) (Ellington, Duke Orchestra & Cannonball Adderley Quintet)
Big P / Blue Daniel / Chant / Old country / Dis here / Sunny side of the street / Goin' to Chicago / Sent for you yesterday / You can't run around / Red carpet
CD DSTS 1009
Status / May '95 / Harmonia Mundi / Jazz Music / Wellard

LIVE AT NEWPORT 1958 (2CD Set) (Ellington, Duke Orchestra)
Introduction / Take the 'A' train / Princess blue / Duke's place / Just scratchin' the surface / Happy reunion / Junie flip / Mr. Gentle and Mr. Cool / Jazz festival jazz / Feet bone / Hi fi fo fum / I got it bad and that ain't good / Bill Bailey, Won't you please come home / Won't you please come home / Prima bara dubla / El gato / Multicoloured blue / Introduction to Mahalia Jackson / Come Sunday / Keep your hands on the plow / Take the 'A' train / Jones
CD Set C2K 53584
Columbia / Oct '94 / Sony

LIVE AT THE BLUE NOTE
Take the 'A' train / Newport up / Haupe (Polly's theme) / Flirtibird / Pie Eye's blues / Almost cried / Dual fuel (dual filter) / Sophisticated lady / Mr. Gentle and Mr. Cool / El Gato / C Jam blues / Tenderly / Honeysuckle rose / Drawing room blues / Tonk / In a mellow tone / All of me / Things ain't what they used to be / Jeep's blues / Mood indigo / Perdido / Satin doll / A disarming visit / Medley
CD CDS 8286372
Roulette / Feb '94 / EMI

LIVE AT THE NEWPORT JAZZ FESTIVAL 1959
Take the 'A' train / Idiom '59 / Rockin' in rhythm / Flirtibird / Perdido / Cop out / VIP boogie / Jam with Sam / Skin deep / Things ain't what they used to be / Jones
CD 8420712
EmArCy / Jan '93 / PolyGram

LIVE AT THE RAINBOW GRILL (Ellington, Duke Octet)
CD MCD 0492
Moon / Nov '93 / Cadillac / Harmonia Mundi

LIVE AT THE SALLE PLEYEL
CD JMY 10112
JMY / Aug '91 / Harmonia Mundi

LIVE AT THE WHITNEY
Black and tan fantasy / Prelude to a kiss / Do nothin' 'til you hear from me / Caravan / Meditation / Mural from two perspectives / Sophisticated lady / Solitude / Soda fountain rag / New world a-coming / Amour, amour / Soul soothing beach / Lotus blossom / Flamingo / Le sucrier velors / Night shepherd / C jam blues / Mood indigo / I'm beginning to see the light / Dancers in love / Kixx / Satin doll
CD IMP 11732
Impulse Jazz / Oct '95 / New Note/BMG

LIVE IN PARIS 1959
Black and tan fantasy / Creole love call / Mooche / Newport up / Sonet in search of amour / Kinda duckish/Rockin in rhythm / El gato / All of me / Won't you come home, Bill Bailey / Walkin' and singin' the blues / VIP boogie / Jam with Sam / Skin deep / Ellington medley
CD CDAFF 777

Affinity / Sep '91 / Cadillac / Jazz Music / Koch

MASTERPIECES BY ELLINGTON
CD _______________ 4694072
Sony Jazz / Jan '95 / Sony

MASTERS OF JAZZ VOL.6 (Ellington, Duke Orchestra)
CD _______________ STCD 4106
Storyville / Feb '89 / Cadillac / Jazz Music / Wellard

MELLOW
Do nothin' 'til you hear from me / Mood indigo / Chelsea bridge / Morning glory / Sophisticated lady / Blue serge / Black and tan fantasy / Perdido / 'A' train / In a mellotone / Moon mist / I got it bad and that ain't good / Solitude / Creole love call / Prelude to a kiss / Dusk / Midriff / Across the track blues / Sentimental lady / Esquire Swank / In a sentimental mood / Dusk
CD _______________ 74321487312
Camden / May '97 / BMG

MONEY JUNGLE
Money jungle / Fleurette Africaine (the African flower) / Very special / Warm valley / REM blues / Little Max / Wig wise / Switchblade / Caravan / Backward country boy blues / Solitude
CD _______________ CDP 7463982
Blue Note / Mar '95 / EMI

MOOD INDIGO
CD _______________ CDSGP 087
Prestige / Sep '94 / Else / Total/BMG

MOOD INDIGO (The Best Of Duke Ellington)
CD _______________ TRTCD 194
TrueTrax / Jun '95 / THE

MOOD INDIGO
CD _______________ HADCD 193
Javelin / Nov '95 / Henry Hadaway / THE

MUSIC IS MY MISTRESS (Classics In Jazz) (Ellington, Duke Orchestra)
C jam blues / All of me / Black and tan fantasy / Danish eyes / Queenie pie reggae / Azure / Jack the bear / Sweet Georgia Brown / Flower is a lovesome thing / Music is my mistress / Duke's suite
CD _______________ 8208012
Limelight / Nov '89 / PolyGram

MY PEOPLE (Ellington, Duke Orchestra)
Ain't but the one / Will you be there / Come Sunday / David danced before the Lord with all his might / My mother and my father / Montage / My people / Blues ain't / Workin' blues / My man sends me / Jail blues / Lovin' lover / King fit the battle of Alabam' / What colour is virtue
CD _______________ 4722042
Sony Jazz / Nov '92 / Sony

NEW ORLEANS SUITE
Blues for New Orleans / Bourbon Street jingling jollies / Portrait of Louis Armstrong / Thanks for the beautiful land on the delta / Portrait of Wellman Braud / Second line / Portrait of Sidney Bechet / Aristocracy of Jean Lafitte / Portrait of Mahalia Jackson
CD _______________ 7567813762
Atlantic / Mar '93 / Warner Music

NEW YORK CONCERTS, THE
CD _______________ MM 65122
Music Masters / Oct '96 / Nimbus

NEWPORT 1958
CD _______________ 4684362
Sony Jazz / Jan '95 / Sony

PASSION FLOWER
CD _______________ MCD 0742
Moon / Aug '95 / Cadillac / Harmonia Mundi

PIANIST, THE
Don Juan / Slow blues / Looking glass / Shepherd / Tap dancer's blues / Sam Woodyard's blues / Duck amok / Never stop remembering Bill / Fat mess
CD _______________ OJCCD 717
Original Jazz Classics / Aug '96 / Complete/ Pinnacle / Jazz Music / Wellard

PIANO IN THE BACKGROUND (Ellington, Duke Orchestra)
CD _______________ 4684042
Sony Jazz / Jan '95 / Sony

PIANO IN THE FOREGROUND (Ellington, Duke Orchestra)
CD _______________ 4749302
Sony Jazz / Jan '95 / Sony

PLAYING THE BLUES 1927-1939
CD _______________ BLE 592322
Black & Blue / Nov '92 / Discovery / Koch / Wellard

POPULAR DUKE ELLINGTON, THE
Take the 'A' train / I got it bad and that ain't good / Perdido / Mood indigo / Black and tan fantasy / Twitch / Solitude / Do nothin' 'til you hear from me / Mooche / Sophisticated lady / Creole love call
CD _______________ 09026687052
RCA Victor / Mar '97 / BMG

PORTRAIT OF DUKE ELLINGTON, A
CD _______________ GALE 405
Gallerie / May '97 / Disc / THE

PRELUDE TO A KISS (Ellington, Duke & Dee Dee Bridgewater/Hollywood Bowl Orch.)
Mood indigo / Daydream / Come Sunday / Bli blip / Solitude / Fleurette Africaine / Midnight indigo / I'm beginning to see the light / Prelude to a kiss / Caravan / Night creature
CD _______________ 4467172
Philips / Nov '96 / PolyGram

PRICELESS JAZZ
Jeep is jumpin' / Mood indigo / Limbo jazz / Wanderlust / In a sentimental mood / Stevie / My little brown book / C jam blues / Lotus blossom / Medley / Satin doll
CD _______________ GRP 98752
GRP / Jul '97 / New Note/BMG

PRIVATE COLLECTION VOL.1 (Studio Sessions Chicago 1956)
March 19th blues / Feet bone / In a sentimental mood / Discontented / Jump for joy / Just scratchin' the surface / Prelude to a kiss / Miss Lucy / Uncontrived / Satin doll / Do not disturb / Love you madly / Short sheet cluster / Moon mist / Long time blues
CD _______________ MSCD 22
Music De-Luxe / Jul '95 / TKO Magnum

QUINTESSENCE, THE (1926-1941/2CD Set)
CD Set _______________ FA 204
Fremeaux / Oct '96 / ADA / Discovery

RECOLLECTIONS OF THE BIG BAND ERA
Minnie the moocher / For dancers only / It's a lonesome old town / Cherokee / Midnight sun will never set / Let's get together / I'm getting sentimental over you / Chant of the weed / Ciribiribin / Contrasts / Christopher Columbus / Auld lang syne / Tuxedo junction / Smoke rings / Artistry in rhythm / Waltz you saved for me / Woodchopper's ball / Sentimental journey / When it's sleepy time down South / One o'clock jump / Goodbye / Sleep, sleep, sleep / Rhapsody in blue
CD _______________ 7567900432
Atlantic / Feb '94 / Warner Music

REMEMBERING DUKE ELLINGTON (RTE Concert Orchestra)
CD _______________ 8990053
Naxos / Oct '95 / Select

RING DEM BELLS
Mooche / Ring dem bells / Frustration / Colortura / Rose of the Rio Grande / Love you madly / Harlem speaks / Caravan / Primpin' at the prom / Jam with Sam / One O'Clock jump / Take the 'A' train / Crosstown / Perdido / Pretty woman / 920 special / Moon mist / Just squeeze me / Prelude to a kiss (medley) / Tootie for cootie
CD _______________ GRF 039
Tring / Jun '92 / Tring

ROCKIN' IN RHYTHM
CD _______________ JHR 73504
Jazz Hour / May '93 / Cadillac / Jazz Music / Target/BMG

ROCKIN' IN RHYTHM VOL.1 (Ellington, Duke Orchestra)
Shoe shine boy / Trumpet in spades / Solitude / Happy as the day is long / Cootie's concerto / In a jam / Uptown beat / Yearning for love / Love is like a cigarette / Exposition swing / Showboat shuffle / Barney's concerto / It was a sad night in Harlem / East St. Louis toodle-oo / Mooche / It don't mean a thing if it ain't got that swing / Rockin' in rhythm / Black and tan fantasy
CD _______________ CDAJA 5057
Living Era / Nov '88 / Select

ROCKIN' IN RONNIE'S (Echoes Of Ellington)
CD _______________ JHCD 050
Ronnie Scott's Jazz House / Mar '97 / Cadillac / Jazz Music / New Note/Pinnacle / TKO Magnum

SARATOGA SWING (Ellington, Duke Cotton Club Orchestra)
Take the 'A' train / Perdido / Five o'clock whistle / Sidewalks of New York / At a Dixie roadside diner / Sophisticated lady / Harlem air shaft / Me and you / Concerto for Cootie / My greatest mistake / Johnny come lately / Sepia panorama / Cotton tail / Don't get around much anymore / Blue goose / C jam blues / Pitter panther patter / Raincheck / Hayfoot strawfoot / Moon mist / Morning glory / Saratoga swing
CD _______________ RAJCD 842
Empress / Jan '97 / Koch

SECOND SACRED CONCERT
CD _______________ PCD 24045
Prestige / Nov '95 / Cadillac / Complete/ Pinnacle

SIDE BY SIDE (Ellington, Duke & Johnny Hodges)
Stompy Jones / Squeeze me / Big shoe / Going up / Just a memory / Let's fall in love / Ruin / Bend one / You need go rock
CD _______________ 8215782
Verve / Sep '93 / PolyGram

SONNY LESTER COLLECTION
CD _______________ CDC 9066
LRC / Nov '93 / Harmonia Mundi / New Note/Pinnacle

SOPHISTICATED LADY
Take the 'A' train / I got it bad and that ain't good / Chelsea Bridge / Perdido / C Jam blues / Caravan / Mood indigo / It don't mean a thing if it ain't got that swing / Sophisticated lady / Things ain't what they used to be (time's a wasting) / Just squeeze me / Concerto for Cootie / Never no lament / Just a-settin' and a-rockin' / Prelude to a kiss / In a sentimental mood / I let a song go out of my heart / Solitude / St. Louis blues
CD _______________ 09026685162
RCA Victor / Oct '96 / BMG

SOPHISTICATED LADY (Ellington, Duke Orchestra)
CD _______________ ENTCD 251
Entertainers / Mar '92 / Target/BMG

SOPHISTICATED LADY
CD _______________ 9026685162
RCA / Jul '96 / BMG

STEREO REFLECTIONS
CD _______________ NI 4016
Natasha / Jul '93 / ADA / Cadillac / CM / Direct / Jazz Music

SUCH SWEET THUNDER
CD _______________ 4691402
Sony Jazz / Jan '95 / Sony

TAKE THE 'A' TRAIN
Taffy twist / Flirtibird / Smada / What am I here for / Take the 'A' train / I'm gonna go fishin' / Boo-dah / Black and tan fantasy / Feeling of jazz / Jump for joy / I let a song out of my heart / Don't get around much anymore
CD _______________ EMPRCD 565
Emporio / May '95 / Disc

TAKE THE 'A' TRAIN
Taffy twist
CD _______________ MU 5035
Musketeer / Oct '92 / Disc

TAKE THE 'A' TRAIN
CD _______________ VJC 10032
Victorious Discs / Aug '90 / Jazz Music

TAKE THE 'A' TRAIN
Mooche / Ring dem bells / Frustration / Colorotura / Rose of the Rio Grande / Love you madly / Caravan / Primpin' at the prom / Jam with Sam / One o'clock jump / Take the 'A' train / Crosstown / Perdido / Pretty woman / 9.20 special / Moon mist / Just squeeze me / Medley / Do nothin' 'til you hear from me / Tootie for cootie
CD _______________ QED 070
Tring / Nov '96 / Tring

TAKE THE 'A' TRAIN 1933-1941 (Ellington, Duke Orchestra)
CD _______________ CD 56012
Jazz Roots / Aug '94 / Target/BMG

THIS IS JAZZ
East St. Louis toodle-oo / In a sentimental mood / Stompy Jones / Prelude to a kiss / C jam blues / Sentimental lady / Take the 'A' train / Satin doll / In a mellotone / Solitude / Mood indigo / Diminuendo and crescendo in blue
CD _______________ CK 64617
Sony Jazz / May '96 / Sony

TIMON OF ATHENS
CD _______________ VSD 5466
Varese Sarabande / Mar '94 / Pinnacle

TRIBUTE TO DUKE ELLINGTON (Live At The Montreux Jazz Festival) (Various Artists)
CD _______________ BLCD 760208
Black Lion / Nov '95 / Cadillac / Jazz Music / Koch / Wellard

TRIBUTE TO DUKE ELLINGTON VOL.1, A (Various Artists)
Take the 'A' train / Satin doll / I'm beginning to see the light / It don't mean a thing / In my solitude / Don't get around much anymore / Satin doll / Jeep is jumpin' / Blue light / Sophisticated lady
CD _______________ 8747012
DA Music / Jul '96 / Conifer/BMG

TRIBUTE TO DUKE ELLINGTON, A (Hendricks, Barbara & Monty Alexander Trio)
CD _______________ CDC 5553462
EMI Classics / Nov '96 / EMI

TWO GREAT CONCERTS IN EUROPE
Take the 'A' train / Caravan / Do nothin' 'til you hear from me / Fancy dance / Hawk talks / Swamp drum / Main stem / Tattooed bride / Threesome / Take the 'A' train (version) / Satin doll/Sophisticated lady / Meow, shorted encore / I got it bad and that ain't good / Harmong in Harlem / Things ain't what they used to be / Perdido / New concerto for Cootie / Carolina shout
CD _______________ 302284
Accord / Dec '89 / Cadillac / Discovery

TWO ON ONE (Ellington, Duke & Count Basie)
CD _______________ CDTT 7
Charly / Apr '94 / Koch

UNKNOWN SESSION
Everything but you / Black beauty / All too soon / Something to live for / Mood indigo / Creole blues / Don't you know I care (or don't you care to) / Flower is a lovesome thing / Mighty like the blues / Tonight I shall sleep / Dual highway / Blues
CD _______________ 4720842
Columbia / Nov '93 / Sony

VINTAGE PERFORMANCES (Jazz Recollections) (Ellington, Duke Orchestra)
Black Beauty / Stormy weather / Get yourself a new broom / Anytime anyday anywhere / Rockin' in rhythm / Bundle of blues / Jazz cocktail / East St. Louis toodle-oo / 12th Street rag / Best wishes / Blue Harlem / Sumpin' about rhythm / I'm satisfied / Lightnin' / Awful sad / Black and tan fantasy
CD _______________ 8205922
Limelight / Jan '88 / PolyGram

YALE CONCERT
CD _______________ OJCCD 664
Original Jazz Classics / Feb '92 / Complete/Pinnacle / Jazz Music / Wellard

YOUNG DUKE 1927-1940, THE (Ellington, Duke Orchestra)
Jazz cocktail / Drop me off in Harlem / Slippery horn / Blue ramble / Merry go round / In the shade of the old apple tree / Raisin' the rent / Blue tune / Kissin' my baby goodnight / Bundle of blues / Stompy Jones / Baby, when you ain't there / Blue feeling / Rockin' chair / East St. Louis Toodle-oo / Rockin' in rhythm / Awful sad / Jazz convulsions / Dusk / Blue goose / Girl in my dreams tries to look like you / Flamingo
CD _______________ PASTCD 9771
Flapper / Jan '92 / Pinnacle

Elliot, Jack

SOUTH COAST (Elliott, Ramblin' Jack)
CD _______________ RHRCD 59
Red House / Jul '95 / ADA / Koch

Elliot, Missy

SUPA DUPA FLY (Elliot, Missy 'Misdemeanor')
Busta's intro / Hit 'em wit da he / Sock it 2 me / Rain (Supa dupa fly) / Beep me 911 / They don't wanna fuck wit me / Pass da blunt / Bite our style / Friendly skys / Best friends / Don't be comin' / Izzy izzy ahh / Why you hurt me / I'm talkin' (the biz) / Gettaway / Busta's outro / Missy's finale
CD _______________ 7559620622
East West / Jul '97 / Warner Music

Elliot, Richard

CITY SPEAK
City speak / Walk the walk / Unspoken words / Amazon / I'll make love to you / Scotland / Sweet surrender / Down hill run / When the lights go out / All I need / That's all she wrote
CD _______________ CDP 8326202
Blue Note / Apr '96 / EMI

Elliot, Tim

TIM ELLIOT & THE TROUBLEMAKERS (Elliot, Tim & Troublemakers)
CD _______________ TRCD 9918
Tramp / Nov '93 / ADA / CM / Direct

Elliott, Bern

BEAT YEARS, THE (Elliott, Bern & The Fenmen)
Money / Nobody but me / New Orleans / Chills / I can tell / Do the mashed potato / Please Mr. Postman / Shake sherry shake / Talking about you / Everybody needs a little love / Shop around / Little Egypt / Good times: *Elliott, Bern & The Klan* / What do you want with my baby: *Elliott, Bern & The Klan* / Guess who: *Elliott, Bern* / Make it easy on yourself: *Elliott, Bern* / Forget her: *Elliott, Bern* / Voodoo woman: *Elliott, Bern* / Lipstick traces: *Elliott, Bern* / Be my girl: *Fenmen* / Rag doll: *Fenmen* / I've got everything you need babe: *Fenmen* / Every little day now: *Fenmen*
CD _______________ SEECD 239
See For Miles/C5 / Oct '93 / Pinnacle

Elliott, G.H.

GOLDEN AGE OF MUSIC HALL, THE
I'se a-waiting for yer Josie / If the man on the moon were a coon / There's a little cupid in the moon / Lou, Sue, Mary, Dinah / Chocolate Major / Hello Susie Green / On the Mississippi / She has such dreamy eyes / My southern maid / Waiting / Way down yonder / My picture girl / You'd never know that old home town of mine / When the sun goes down in dixie / Give her a great big kiss for me / My Michaelmas daisy / If you're going back to dixie / Mississippi honeymoon / In Carolina / Tickle the keys of your silvery saxophone / Maybe it's the moon / My gal's given me the go-bye / That's just like heaven to me / Sue, Sue, Sue / I used to sigh for the silvery moon
CD _______________ PASTCD 7033
Flapper / Jan '94 / Pinnacle

Elliott, Jack

HARD TRAVELLIN' (Songs By Woody Guthrie & Others)
Hard travellin' / Grand coulee dam / New York Town / Tom Joad / Howdido / Dust

bowl blues / This land is your land / Pretty Boy Floyd / Philadelphia lawyer / Talking Columbia blues / Dust storm disaster / Riding in my car / 1913 massacre / So long (it's been good to know yuh) / Sadie Brown / East Virginia blues / I belong to glasgow / Cuckoo / Rollin' in my sweet baby's arms / South coast / San Francisco Bay blues / Last letter / Candy man / Tramp on the street / Railroad Bill
CD _______ CDWIK 952
Big Beat / Aug '90 / Pinnacle

KEROUAC'S LAST DREAM (Elliott, Ramblin' Jack)
CD _______ TUT 72163
Wundertute / Jan '94 / ADA / CM / Duncans

ME AND BOBBY MCGEE
CD _______ ROUCD 0368
Rounder / Nov '95 / ADA / CM / Direct

RAMBLIN' JACK
CD _______ TSCD 477
Topic / Feb '96 / ADA / CM / Direct

Elliott, Paul & Glen

APRIL PAVES THE WAY
April paves the way / Ballybay / Red Rose cafe / Peat bog soldiers / Monto / Tarry Flynn / Murshin Durkin / Tipperary / Between us both / Banks of the roses / Shoals of herring / Patrick was a gentleman / Happy go lucky / Blarney roses / Song about nothing / Wild colonial boy / Galway races / Tell me ma / Walk on talk on / Stop giving out / Roots
CD _______ FSCD 44
Folksound / Jun '97 / CM / Roots

Ellis, Alton

BEST OF ALTON ELLIS
CD _______ SOCD 8019
Studio One / Mar '95 / Jet Star

CRY TOUGH
CD _______ CDHB 106
Heartbeat / May '93 / ADA / Direct / Greensleeves / Jet Star

DUKE REID COLLECTION
CD _______ RNCD 2083
Rhino / Dec '94 / Grapevine/PolyGram / Jet Star

LEGENDARY ALTON ELLIS, THE
CD _______ ATCD 012
All Tone / Dec '93 / Jet Star

SOUL GROOVER
Dance crasher / Girl I've got a date / Rocksteady / Duke of Earl / All my tears (come rolling) / Ain't that loving you / Why birds follow spring / Oowee baby(Baby I love you) / How can I / Willow tree / My time is the right time / Message / Trying to reach my goal / If I had the right / Give me your love / Breaking up / Personality / Diana / Remember that Sunday / What does it take to win your love / You've made me so very happy / I'll be waiting / Soul groover / Lord deliver us / You are mine / All that we need is love
CD _______ CDTRL 385
Trojan / Jul '97 / Direct / Jet Star

STILL IN LOVE
Still in love / Rock steady / Change of plan / Breaking up / Play it cool / Reggae with you
CD _______ CDHR 708
Horse / May '96 / Jet Star / Total/BMG

SUNDAY COMING
CD _______ CDHB 3511
Heartbeat / Feb '95 / ADA / Direct / Greensleeves / Jet Star

VALLEY OF DECISION
CD _______ CDSGP 071
Prestige / Sep '94 / Else / Total/BMG

Ellis, Brad

CHICAGO AND ALL THAT JAZZ (Ellis, Brad Group)
CD _______ VSD 5798
Varese Sarabande / Mar '97 / Pinnacle

Ellis, Don

DON ELLIS
I'll remember April / Sweet and lovely / Out of nowhere / All things you are / You stepped out of a dream / My funny valentine / I love you / Just one of those things / Johnny come lately / Angel eyes / Lover / Form / Sallie / How time passes / Simplex one
CD _______ CD 53262
Giants Of Jazz / Jan '96 / Cadillac / Jazz Music / Target/BMG

HOW TIME PASSES
How time passes / Sally / Simplex one / Waste / Improvisational suite
CD _______ CCD 9004
Candid / Feb '97 / Cadillac / Direct / Jazz Music / Koch / Wellard

OUT OF NOWHERE
Sweet and lovely / My funny valentine / I love you / I'll remember April / Just one of those things / You stepped out of a dream / All the things you are / Out of nowhere / Just one of those things / I love you
CD _______ CCD 9032
Candid / Feb '97 / Cadillac / Direct / Jazz Music / Koch / Wellard

Ellis, Herb

DOGGIN' AROUND (Ellis, Herb & Red Mitchell)
CD _______ CCD 4372
Concord Jazz / Apr '89 / New Note/ Pinnacle

JAZZ MASTERS, THE (Ellis, Herb/Ray Brown/Serge Ermoll)
CD _______ AIM 1039CD
Aim / Jun '95 / ADA / Direct / Jazz Music

SOFT WINDS 1946-1996 (Ellis, Herb & Lou Carter/Johnny Frigo)
CD _______ CRD 342
Chiaroscuro / May '97 / Jazz Music

TEXAS SWINGS
CD _______ JR 10022
Justice / Apr '94 / Koch

TOGETHER (Ellis, Herb & Stuff Smith)
CD _______ 378052
Koch / Jan '96 / Koch

TWO FOR THE ROAD (Ellis, Herb & Joe Pass)
Love for sale / Am I blue / Seven come eleven / Guitar blues / Oh lady be good / Cherokee (concept 1) / Cherokee (concept 2) / Gee baby ain't I good to you / Try a little tenderness / I found a new baby / Angel eyes
CD _______ OJCCD 726
Original Jazz Classics / Jun '94 / Complete/ Pinnacle / Jazz Music / Wellard

WINDFLOWER (Ellis, Herb & Remo Palmier)
CD _______ CCD 4056
Concord Jazz / Jul '96 / New Note/ Pinnacle

Ellis, John

ACRYLIC
CD _______ OPT 0041CD
Optic Nerve / Apr '97 / Plastic Head

DANCIN' WI' CLAYMORES (Ellis, John & His Highland Country Band)
Twa bonnie reels / Pipe jig and march / GS Manclennan selection / Folk waltz / Grand march / Eva three step / Slow air and march / Strip the willow / Mackay's music medley / Pipe march / Locl Leven castle (Reel set) / March, strathspey and reel / Gaelic waltzes / Polka / Highland fair (jig set) / Highland hornpipes / Gay gordons / Braes of breadalbane / Queens bridge (reel set)
CD _______ LCOM 5210
Lismor / Mar '92 / ADA / Direct / Duncans / Lismor

FIRE IN THE KILT (Ellis, John & His Highland Country Band)
Grand march / Pipe march / Strip the willow / Waltz, strathspey and pipe reel / Fiddle hornpipes / Fife hunt / Gaelic waltzes / Two pipe marches / Pipe hornpipe / Highland lass / Orcadian polkas / Old fashioned waltz / Two step-Canadian jigs / Hornpipe and pipe reel / Scottish waltz / March, strathspey and reel / Gay Gordons
CD _______ LCOM 5158
Lismor / Feb '97 / ADA / Direct / Duncans / Lismor

REEL KICK, A (Ellis, John & His Highland Country Band)
Gates of Edinburgh / Quaker jig / Gaelic waltz / Polka / Eight men of Moidart / March, strathspey and reel / Highland Schottische / Pipe tunes / Hornpipes / Pipe marches
CD _______ LCOM 5120
Lismor / Oct '96 / ADA / Direct / Duncans / Lismor

Ellis, Lisle

ELEVATIONS
CD _______ VICTOCD 027
Victo / Oct '94 / Harmonia Mundi / ReR Megacorp

Ellis, Osian

CLYMAU CYTGERDD/DIVERSIONS
Caneuon plant / Tri darn byrfyfyr / Clymau cytgerdd i ddwy delyn / Consierto i'r delyn / Canu penillion / Gavotte / Caniadau llanelwy / Sonata yn f leiaf / Caneuon atgof
CD _______ SCD 4038
Sain / Jun '89 / ADA / Direct / Greyhound

Ellis, Paul

CARNIVAL OF VOICES, A
CD _______ CDPH 1191
Philo / Aug '96 / ADA / CM / Direct

STORIES
CD _______ CDPH 1181
Philo / Oct '95 / ADA / CM / Direct

Ellis, Pee Wee

NEW SHIFT
CD _______ MM 801060
Minor Music / Oct '96 / Vital/SAM

SEPIA TONALITY
What are you doing the rest of your life / I should care / Stardust / Sepia tonality / Cleaning windows / Cherry red / Body and soul / Prayer of love / Why not / Come rain or come shine
CD _______ MM 801040
Minor Music / Jun '94 / Vital/SAM

YELLIN BLUE
CD _______ MM 801049
Minor Music / May '95 / Vital/SAM

Ellis, Steve

LOVE THAT'S EVERYTHING
CD _______ HADCD 210
Javelin / Jul '96 / Henry Hadaway / THE

Ellis, Tinsley

COOL ON IT (Ellis, Tinsley & Heartfixers)
Drivin' woman / Cool on it / Hong Kong Mississippi / Second thoughts / Sailor's grave on the prairie / Greenwood chainsaw boogie / Tulane / Time to quit / Sugaree / Wild weekend
CD _______ ALCD 3905
Alligator / May '93 / ADA / CM / Direct

FANNING THE FLAMES
Leavin' here / Pawnbroker / Loneliness is here to stay / Put me where you want me / Born in Georgia / Fender blender / Deaf, dumb, crippled and blind / So many tears / Must be the devil / Dangling by a thread / Mr. night time
CD _______ ALCD 4778
Alligator / May '93 / ADA / CM / Direct

FIRE IT UP
Diggin' my own grave / Just dropped in / Standing on the edge of love / Soulful / Are you sorry / I walk alone / Change your mind / Break my rule / One sunny day / If that's how he loves you / Look what you done / Everyday
CD _______ ALCD 4852
Alligator / May '97 / ADA / CM / Direct

GEORGIA BLUE
Can't you lie / You picked a good time / Crime of passion / Double eyed whammy / Look ka py py / Free manwells / Texas stomp / I've made nights by myself / Hot potato / She wants to sell my monkey / As the years go passing by / Lucky lot
CD _______ ALCD 4765
Alligator / Apr '93 / ADA / CM / Direct

STORM WARNING
To the devil for a dime / Cut you loose / Quitter never wins / Panhead / Next miss wrong / Early in the morning / When I howl / Side tracked / Wanted man / Sun is shining / Bush doctor / Mercy mercy mercy
CD _______ ALCD 4823
Alligator / Oct '94 / ADA / CM / Direct

TROUBLE TIME
Highway man / Hey hey baby / Sign of the blues / What have I done wrong / Big chicken / Axe / Come morning / Restless heart / Bad dream No.108 / Hulk / Now I'm gone / Red dress
CD _______ ALCD 4805
Alligator / May '93 / ADA / CM / Direct

Ellis, Tony

DIXIE BANNER
CD _______ FF 444CD
Flying Fish / Apr '94 / ADA / CM / Direct / Roots

FAREWELL MY HOME (Ellis, Tony & Bill)
Rain on the water / Merrywang / T-model Ford / Hartford's waltz / Farewell my home / Montana march / Wild fox / Cherry blossom waltz / Red dog / Kate bride of Matt / Snow camp / Wind chimes and nursery rhymes / Going to the country fair / Straw dolls / Wade's dixieliner special railroad blues no.9 / My Mama loves me / Uncle Shorty / Johnny come-a-running / Trail of tears / Dawson George / One horned goat / Hangman's song / Come thy fount of every blessing
CD _______ FF 70620
Flying Fish / Jul '97 / ADA / CM / Direct / Roots

Ellison, Lorraine

STAY WITH ME (The Best Of Lorraine Ellison)
Stay with me / Good love / I've got my baby back / I'm over you / No matter how it all turns out / I want to be loved / Heart be still / Try (just a little bit harder) / In my tomorrow / I'm gonna cry 'til my tears run dry / Only your love / You don't know nothing about love / Time is on my side / Doin' me dirty / Caravan / I'll be home / Many rivers to cross / Road I took to you / Walk around heaven / Stormy weather / No better than you're doin' / I'll fly away / No relief
CD _______ SCL 2106
Ichiban Soul Classics / Nov '95 / Koch

Ellwood, William

NATURAL SELECTIONS
Half moon / First love / Laughing earth / Summer words / Elysain fields / Simpatico / Barefoot dance / Blue period / Night calling / Spirit river / Cotton wood / Gymnopedie No.1
CD _______ ND 61049
Narada / Aug '95 / ADA / New Note/ Pinnacle

Elman, Ziggy

CLASSICS 1938-1939
CD _______ CLASSICS 900
Classics / Nov '96 / Discovery / Jazz Music

ZIGGY ELMAN AND FRIENDS - 1947 (Elman, Ziggy & His Orchestra)
CD _______ CCD 70
Circle / '92 / Jazz Music / Swift / Wellard

Elmerhassel

BILLYOUS
Dehydration / Nearing home / Business as usual / Calm and collected / Bare back / Pert host / Safeish / Simian / Almost at one / Exposure / Common flowers
CD _______ DPROMCD 18
Dirter Promotions / Mar '94 / Cargo / Pinnacle / World Serpent

ELO

AFTERGLOW (3CD Set)
10538 Overture / Mr. Radio / Kuiama / In old England town (Boogie no.2) / Mama / Roll over beethoven / Bluebird is dead / Ma-ma-ma belle / Showdown / Can't get it out of my head / Boy blue / One summer dream / Evil woman / Tightrope / Strange magic / Do ya / Nightrider / Waterfall / Roackarial / Telephone line / So fine / Livin' thing / Mr. Blue Sky / Sweet is the night / Turn to stone / Sweet talkin' woman / Steppin' out / Midnight blue / Don't bring me down / Twilight / Julie don't live here / Shine a little love / When time stood still / Rain is falling / Bouncer / Hello my old friend / Hold on tight / Four little diamonds / Mandalay / Buildings have eyes / So serious / Matter of fact / No way out / Getting to the point / Destination unkown / Rock 'n' roll is king
CD Set _______ CD 46090
Legacy / Jul '94 / Sony

ALL TIME GREATEST
Standing in the rain / Evil woman / Showdown / Can't get it out of my head / Livin' things / Mr. Blue Sky / Telephone line / Strange magic / Sweet talking woman / Confusion / Do ya / Rockaria / Roll over Beethoven / Hold on tight / Turn to stone / Rock and roll is king / Don't bring me down
CD _______ RM 1546
BR Music / Jun '97 / Target/BMG

BALANCE OF POWER
Heaven only knows / So serious / Getting to the point / Secret lives / Is it alright / Sorrow about to fall / Without someone / Calling America / Endless lies / Send it
CD _______ 4685762
Epic / Jun '91 / Sony

BEST OF ELO II LIVE, THE (ELO II)
Standing in the rain / Evil woman / Can't get it out of my head / Do ya / Rockaria / Mr Blue Sky / Telephone line / Strange magic / Sweet talkin' woman / Roll over Beethoven / Livin' thing / Last train to London / Rock and roll is King / Turn to stone / Hold on tight / Showdown
CD _______ 3036000722
Carlton / Apr '97 / Carlton

DISCOVERY
Shine a little love / Confusion / Need her love / Diary of Horace Wimp / Last train to London / Midnight blue / On the run / Wishing / Don't bring me down
CD _______ 4500832
Epic / Jun '91 / Sony

DISCOVERY/OUT OF THE BLUE/TIME (3CD Set)
Shine a little love / Confusion / Need her love / Diary of Horace Wimp / Last train to London / Midnight blue / On the run / Wishing / Don't bring me down / Turn to stone / It's over / Sweet talkin' woman / Across the border / Night in the city / Starlight / Believe me now / Steppin' out / Whale / Standin' in the rain / Big wheels / Summer and lightning / Mr. Blue Sky / Sweet is the night / Birmingham blues / Wild West hero / Jungle / Prlogue / Twilight / Yours truly 2095 / Ticket to the moon / Way life's meant to be / Another heart breaks / Rain is falling / From the end of the world / Lights go down / Hear is the news / 21st century man / Hold on tight / Epilogue
CD Set _______ 4853402
Epic / Oct '96 / Sony

EARLY ELO 1971-1973
10538 overture / Look at me now / Nellie takes her bow / Battle of Marston Moor / First movement / Mr. Radio / Manhattan rumble (49th street massacre) / Queen of the hours / Whispers in the night / Roll over Beethoven / In old England town (Boogie no.2) / Momma / From the sun to the world

/ Kuiama / Showdown / Baby I apologize / Auntie / Ma Ma belle / Bev's trousers
CD Set ______ **CDEM 1419**
EMI / Aug '91 / EMI

ELDORADO
Eldorado overture / Can't get it out of my head / Boy blue / Laredo tornado / Poorboy (The Greenwood) / Mr. Kingdom / Nobody's child / Illusions in G Major / Eldorado / Eldorado (finale)
CD ______ **4768312**
Epic / May '94 / Sony

ELDORADO/NEW WORLD RECORD/ OUT OF THE BLUE (3CD Set)
CD Set ______ **4722672**
Epic / Oct '92 / Sony

GOLD COLLECTION, THE
10538 Overture / Mr. Radio / All over the world / Look at me now / Manhattan rumble / In old England town (boogie no.2) / Ma ma belle / Roll over Beethoven / Battle of Marston Moor / Queen of the hours / Showdown / First movement (Jumping biz) / Whisper in the night / Momma
CD ______ **CDGOLD 1002**
EMI Gold / Mar '96 / EMI

GREATEST HITS VOL.1
Telephone line / Evil woman / Livin' thing / Can't get it out of my head / Showdown / Turn to stone / Rockaria / Sweet talkin' woman / Ma-ma-ma belle / Strange magic / Mr. Blue sky
CD ______ **4503572**
Epic / Jun '91 / Sony

GREATEST HITS VOL.2
Rock 'n' roll is King / Hold on tight / All over the world / Wild West hero / Diary of Horace Wimp / Shine a little love / Confusion / Ticket to the moon / Don't bring me down / I'm alive / Last to train / Don't walk away / Here is the news / Calling America / Twilight / Secret messages
CD ______ **4719562**
Epic / Jul '93 / Sony

ONE NIGHT (Live In Australia/2CD Set) (ELO II)
Standing in the rain / Evil woman / Don't wanna / Showdown / Can't get you out of my head / Whiskey girl / Livin' thing / One more tomorrow / Mr. Blue Sky / Telephone line / Ain't necessarily so / Fox / Strange magic / Sweet talking woman / Confusion / Rockaria / Roll over Beethoven / All fall down / Witness / 1000 eyes / Hold on tight / Turn to stone / Rock 'n' roll is king / Last train to London / Don't bring me down
CD Set ______ **SPV 08944072**
SPV / Sep '96 / Koch / Plastic Head

OUT OF THE BLUE
Turn to stone / It's over / Sweet talkin' woman / Across the border / Night in the city / Starlight / Jungle / Believe me now / Steppin' out / Standing in the rain / Summer and lightning / Mr. Blue sky / Sweet is the night / Whale / Wild West hero
CD ______ **4508852**
Epic / Jun '91 / Sony

POWER OF A MILLION LIGHTS (ELO II)
CD ______ **96125 ULT**
Ultra Pop / Aug '94 / Grapevine/PolyGram / THE

SECRET MESSAGES
Secret messages / Loser gone wild / Take me on and on / Bluebird / Four little diamonds / Stranger / Danger ahead / Letter from Spain / Train of gold / Rock 'n' roll is king
CD ______ **4624872**
Epic / Jun '91 / Sony

TIME
Prologue / Twilight / Yours truly 2095 / Ticket to the moon / Way life's meant to be / Another heart breaks / Rain is falling / From the end of the world / Lights go down / Here is the news / 21st century man / Hold on tight / Epilogue
CD ______ **4602122**
Epic / Jun '91 / Sony

TIME/SECRET MESSAGE/DISCOVERY (3CD Set)
Prologue / twilight / Yours truly / Ticket to the moon / 2095 / Way life's meant to be / Another heart breaks / Rain is falling / From the end of the world / Lights go down / Here is the news / 21st Century man / Hold on tight / Epilogue / Secret messages / Loser gone wild / Bluebird / Take me on and on / Four little diamonds / Stranger / Danger ahead / Letter from Spain / Train of gold / Rock 'n' roll is king / Shine a little love / Confusion / Need her love / Diary of Horace Wimp / Last train to London / Midnight blue / On the run / Wishing / Don't bring me down
CD Set ______ **4775262**
Epic / Oct '94 / Sony

Eloy

CHRONICLES VOL.1
CD ______ **SPV 08448182**
SPV / Feb '97 / Koch / Plastic Head

CHRONICLES VOL.2
CD ______ **SPV 08448192**
SPV / Feb '97 / Koch / Plastic Head

DESTINATION
CD ______ **SPV 08448082**
SPV / Dec '96 / Koch / Plastic Head

METROMANIA
CD ______ **HMIXD 21**
Heavy Metal / Sep '84 / Revolver / Sony

RA
CD ______ **REVXD 120**
Revolver / Aug '89 / Revolver / Sony
CD ______ **SPV 0854802**
SPV / Dec '96 / Koch / Plastic Head

TIDES RETURN FOREVER
CD ______ **SPV 08448202**
SPV / Dec '96 / Koch / Plastic Head

Els Cosins Del Sac

AL FINAL DELL BALL T'ESPERO
CD ______ **20057CD**
Sonifolk / Dec '94 / ADA / CM

Els Trobadors

ET ADES SERA L'ALBA
CD ______ **F 1016CD**
Sonifolk / Jun '94 / ADA / CM

Elsdon, Alan

JAZZ JOURNEYMEN
Lord Randal / Saturday afternoon blues / Diga diga doo / There's yes yes in your eyes / Panama rag / Four or five times / Two deuces / Come back sweet Papa / Lovely Rita, meter maid / Satisfaction
CD ______ **BLCD 760519**
Black Lion / Apr '96 / Cadillac / Jazz Music / Koch / Wellard

KEEPERS OF THE FLAME
CD ______ **PARCD 504**
Parrot / Dec '94 / BMG / Jazz Music / THE / Wellard

Elsdon, Tracy

RELATIVELY SPEAKING
Half the moon / Relatively speaking / Only a woman's heart / Somewhere under the sun / Heaven / You were my lover / Lonely street / One careful owner / Just when I needed you most / Water is wide / Dream a little dream of me / Loving arms / Golden years / I'll walk beside you
CD ______ **RCD 534**
Ritz / Oct '93 / Pinnacle

Elstak, Nedley

MACHINE, THE
CD ______ **ESP 10762**
ESP / Jan '93 / Jazz Music

Elvis Hitler

HELLBILLY
CD ______ **LS 94362**
Restless / Dec '89 / Vital

Elwood, Michael

ROLLING VALENTINE (Elwood, Michael & Beth Galiger)
CD ______ **DJD 3219**
Dejadisc / Sep '95 / ADA / Direct

Ely, Brother Claude

SATAN GET BACK
I'm crying holy unto the lord / There's a leak in this old building / Send down the rain / There ain't no grave gonna hold my body down / Talk about Jesus / I'm just a stranger here / Thank you Jesus / I want to rest / You've got to move / Farther on / Jesus is the rock / Little David play your harp / There's a higher power / Holy holy holy (That's all right) / Dip your finger in the water (And cool my thumb) / Do you want to shout / Those prayers and words still guide me / My crucified one / Old fireside / Fare you well / I want to go to heaven / You took the wrong road again / Stop that train
CD ______ **CDCHD 456**
Ace / Sep '93 / Pinnacle

Ely, Joe

DIG ALL NIGHT
Settle for love / For your love / My eyes got lucky / Maybe she'll find me / Drivin' man / Dig all night / Grandfather blues / Jazz street / Rich man, poor boy / Behind the bamboo shade
CD ______ **FIENDCD 130**
Demon / Oct '88 / Pinnacle

LETTER TO LAREDO
CD ______ **TRACD 222**
Transatlantic / Apr '96 / Pinnacle

LORD OF THE HIGHWAY
Lord of the highway / (Don't put a) lock on my heart / Me and Billy The Kid / Letter to LA / No rope, Daisy-o / Thinks she's French / Everybody got hammered / Are you listening Lucky / Row of dominoes / Silver city
CD ______ **FIENDCD 101**
Demon / Sep '87 / Pinnacle

NO BAD TALK OR LOUD TALK
Honky tonk masquerade / If you were a bluebird / Dallas / Fingernails / Boxcars / Tonight I think I'm gonna go downtown / I had my hopes up high / Fools fall in love / Treat me like a Saturday night / Maria / Down on the drag / Hard livin' / Musta notta gotta lotta / Suckin' a big bottle of gin / Johnny's blues / She never spoke Spanish to me / Because of the wind / West Texas waltz
CD ______ **EDCD 418**
Edsel / Mar '95 / Pinnacle

TIME FOR TRAVELLIN'
Mardi gras waltz / Tennessee's not the state I'm in / Gambler's pride / All my love / Jericho(now all your walls must come tumbling down) / I'll be your fool / Cornbread moon / Standin' at the big hotel / Crazy lemon / Crawdad train / In another world / She leaves you where you are / Time for travellin' / Wishin for you / Hold on / I keep gettin paid the same / Road hawg / Dam of my heart / Bet me
CD ______ **EDCD 486**
Edsel / Aug '96 / Pinnacle

Elysian Fields

ADELAIN
CD ______ **USR 018CD**
Unisound / Jan '96 / Plastic Head

Elysium

DANCE FOR THE CELESTIAL BEINGS
CD ______ **NZCD 039**
Nova Zembla / Sep '95 / Plastic Head

El'Zabar, Kahil

RENAISSANCE OF THE RESISTANCE (El'Zabar, Kahil Ritual Trio)
Sweet meat / Ornette / Renaissance of the resistance / Trane in mind / Golden sea / Fatsmo / Save your love for me
CD ______ **DE 466**
Delmark / Mar '97 / ADA / Cadillac / CM / Direct / Hot Shot

EM & I

HEAVENLY
CD ______ **99 1600**
Ninetynine / Jul '96 / Timewarp

Emanuel, Carol

TOPS OF TREES
CD ______ **378022**
Koch Jazz / Sep '96 / Koch

Embale, Carlos

RUMBERO MAYOR
CD ______ **CD 0020**
Egrem / Mar '96 / Discovery

Embalmer

THERE WAS BLOOD EVERYWHERE
There was blood everywhere / Necro-philing cabinet / Bloodsucking freaks / May the wounds bleed forever / Rotten body fluids / Bone box / Morbid confessions / Cellar
CD ______ **RR 69702**
Relapse / Aug '97 / Pinnacle / Plastic Head

Emblow, Jack

ENJOY YOURSELF (Emblow, Jack & The French Collection)
CD ______ **CDTS 001**
Maestro / Aug '93 / Savoy

PICK YOURSELF UP (Emblow, Jack & The French Collection)
Pick yourself up / Hot time in the old town tonight / Boiled beef and carrots / Don't dilly dally on the way / Any old iron / I don't want to walk without you / Little on the lonely side / Dance of the hours / Guantanamera / Yes, we have no bananas / Whilst strolling in the park / Lily of laguna / Narcissus / La cucuracha / I yi yi yi yi (I like you very much) / Black orpheus samba / No strings / I'm putting all my eggs in one basket / I'm a dreamer (aren't we all) / I double dare you / Moonstruck / Bill Bailey, won't you please come home / Question and answer / Dubarry waltz / Endearing young charms / Rose of tralee / Mother McChree / Slow rhumbas / La golondrina / Indian summer / Pokarekareana / Estrellita / Too marvellous for words / Chihuahua / Opus one
CD ______ **GRCD 46**
Grasmere / '91 / Highlander / Savoy / Target/BMG

Embryo's Reise

AFGHANISTAN, PAKISTAN AND INDIA
CD ______ **30202**
Schneeball / May '97 / Cargo / Greyhound

Emerald Accordian Band

IRELAND'S DANCING DAYS
Catch me if you can / Golden jubilee / Come back Paddy Reilly / Believe me if all those endearing young charms / Come back to Erin / Westmeath bachelor / Old woman from Wexford / Rose of Killarney / Sweet slievenamon / Galway shawl / Hucklebuck / Athole highlanders / Champion / Irish washerwoman / Rose of tralee / Banks of my own lovely lee / I'll tell me ma / Marie's wedding / Forty shades of green / Mursheen durkin / Wild colonial boy / Leaving of Liverpool / Red rose cafe / Kathleen / Village where I went to school / If your Irish (come into the parlour) / Bold O'Donaghue / St Bernard waltz / Green glens of Antrim / Boys from the county Armagh / Simple Simon says / Bluebell polka / How can you buy Kilarney / My wild Irish rose / Bunch of Thyme / I'll take you home again Kathleen / Old rustic bridge
CD ______ **MCVD 30002**
Emerald Gem / Nov '96 / BMG

Emerson, Billy

MOVE BABY, MOVE (Emerson, Billy 'The Kid')
No teasing around / If lovin's believin' / Hey little girl / I'm not going home / Woodchuck / When my baby quit me / Move baby, move / When it rains it pours / Little fine healthy thing / Something for nothing / Cherry pie / Satisfied / When my baby quit me / No greater love / Red hot / Shim sham shimmy / Every woman I know (crazy 'bout automobiles) / Tomorrow never comes / Don't start me to lying / If you won't stay home / Don't be careless / Do the chicken / Somebody show me the pleasure is all mine / Do yourself a favour / You never miss the water
CD ______ **CPCD 8276**
Charly / Jan '97 / Koch

Emerson, Darren

CREAM SEPARATES VOL.2 (Mixed By Darren Emerson) (Various Artists)
Seawall: *Envoy* / Modus vivendi: *Modus Vivendi* / Paper moon: *51 Days* / Indulge: *Howard, Neal* / In a vision: *Virgo Four* / Unicorn: *Blue Maxx* / Warrior: *Oniero* / Airport martini: *Curtin, Dan* / Party: *Willpower* / Sugar: *Nimbus Quartet* / Sueno latino: *Sueno Latino* / Song for Olivia: *Cliff Hanger* / Art Lukm: *Holy Ghost Inc.* / Confusion the waitress: *Underworld*
CD ______ **74321462012**
De-Construction / Mar '97 / BMG

Emerson, Keith

CHANGING STATES
CD ______ **AMPCD 026**
AMP / Apr '95 / Cadillac / Discovery / TKO Magnum

CHRISTMAS ALBUM, THE
CD ______ **AMPCD 018**
AMP / Feb '95 / Cadillac / Discovery / TKO Magnum

Emerson, Lake & Palmer

BEST OF EMERSON, LAKE AND PALMER, THE
CD ______ **ESSCD 296**
Essential / Nov '95 / BMG

BLACK MOON
Black moon / Paper blood / Affairs of the heart / Romeo and Juliet / Farewell to arms / Changing states / Burning bridges / Close to home / Betterdays / Footprints in the snow
CD ______ **ESMCD 506**
Essential / May '97 / BMG

BRAIN SALAD SURGERY
Jerusalem / Toccata / Still you turn me on / Benny the bouncer / Karn evil 9 / First impression (part 1) / First impression / Second impression / Third impression
CD ______ **ESMCD 344**
Essential / Mar '96 / BMG

EMERSON, LAKE AND PALMER
Barbarian / Take a pebble / Knife edge / Three fates / Clotho / Lachesis / Auropos / Tank / Lucky man
CD ______ **ESMCD 340**
Essential / Mar '96 / BMG

LIVE AT THE ROYAL ALBERT HALL
CD ______ **8289332**
Victory / Jan '93 / PolyGram

LIVE AT THE ROYAL ALBERT HALL
Karn evil 9 / Tarkus (medley) / Knife edge / Paper blood / Romeo and Juliet / Creole dance / Still, you turn me on / Lucky man / Black moon / Pirates / Finale (medley)
CD ______ **ESMCD 504**
Essential / May '97 / BMG

LOVE BEACH
All I want is you / Love beach / Taste of my love / Gambler / For you / Canario / Memoirs of an officer and a gentleman / Prologue / Education of a gentleman / Love at first sight / Letters from the front / Honourable company
CD ______ **ESMCD 363**
Essential / Aug '96 / BMG

PICTURES AT AN EXHIBITION
Promenade / Gnome / Sage / Old castle / Blues variation / Hut of Baba Yaga / Curse of Baba Yaga / Great gate of Kiev / End (nutrocker)
CD ______ **ESMCD 342**
Essential / Mar '96 / BMG

RETURN OF THE MANTICORE (4CD Set)
Touch and go / Hang on to a dream / 21st Century schizoid man / Fire / Pictures at an exhibition / I believe in Father Christmas / Introductory Fanfare/Peter Gunn / Tiger in a spotlight / Toccata / Trilogy / Tank / Lucky man / Tarkus / From the beginning / Take a pebble / Knife edge / Paper blood / Hoedown / Rondo / Barbarian / Still ... you turn me on / Endless enigma / C'est la vie / Enemy God dances with the black spirits / Bo Diddley / Bitches crystal / Time and a place / Living sin / Karn evil 9 / Honky tonk train blues / Jerusalem / Fanfare for the common man / Black moon / Watching over you / Toccata con fuoco / For you / Prelude and fugue / Memoirs of an officer and a gentleman / Pirates / Affairs of the heart
CD Set ______ **8284592**
Victory / Dec '93 / PolyGram
CD Set ______ **ESFCD 421**
Essential / Nov '96 / BMG

TARKUS
Tarkus / Eruption / Stones of years / Iconoclast / Mass / Manticore / Battlefield / Aquatarkus / Jeremy Bender / Bitches crystal / Only way / Infinite space (conclusion) / Time and a place / Are you ready Eddy
CD ______ **ESMCD 341**
Essential / Mar '96 / BMG

TRILOGY
Endless enigma (part 1) / Fugue / Endless enigma (part 2) / From the beginning / Sheriff / Hoedown / Trilogy / Living sin / Abboddon's bolero
CD ______ **ESMCD 343**
Essential / Mar '96 / BMG

WELCOME BACK MY FRIENDS TO THE SHOW THAT NEVER ENDS
Hoedown / Jerusalem / Toccata / Tarkus / Take a pebble / Piano improvisations / Jeremy Bender/The Sheriff / Karn evil 9
CD ______ **ESDCD 359**
Essential / Aug '96 / BMG

WORKS LIVE
Introductory Fanfare / Peter Gunn / Tiger in a spotlight / C'est la vie / Watching over you / Maple leaf rag / Enemy God dances with the black spirits / Fanfare for the common man / Knife edge / Show me the way to go home / Abaddon's bolero / Pictures at an exhibition / Closer to believing / Piano concerto no. 1 / Tank
CD ______ **ESDCD 362**
Essential / Aug '96 / BMG

WORKS VOL.1
Piano concerto no. 1 / Lend your love to me tonight / C'est la vie / Hallowed be thy name / Nobody loves you like I do / Closer to believing / Enemy God dances with the black spirits / LA nights / New Orleans / Two part invention in D minor / Food for your soul / Tank / Fanfare for the common man / Pirates
CD ______ **ESDCD 360**
Essential / Aug '96 / BMG

WORKS VOL.2
Tiger in the spotlight / When the apple blossoms bloom in the windmills of your mind / I'll be your valentine / Bullfrogs / Brain salad surgery / Barrelhouse shake down / Watching over you / So far to fall / Maple leaf rag / I believe in Father Christmas / Close but not touching
CD ______ **ESMCD 361**
Essential / Aug '96 / BMG

Emery, James

STANDING ON A WHALE FISHING FOR MINNOWS
New water / In a secret place / Cobalt blue / Strings of thread / Texas koto blues / Crepusule with Nellie / Standing on a whale fishing for minnows / Arc into distant night / Black diamonds and pink whisper / Epicenter / Poetry in stillness
CD ______ **ENJ 93122**
Enja / Jul '97 / New Note/Pinnacle / Vital/SAM

TURBULENCE (Emery, James & Iliad Quartet)
CD ______ **KFWCD 106**
Knitting Factory / Nov '94 / Cargo / Plastic Head

Emery, Jon

IF YOU DON'T BUY THIS I'LL FIND SOMEBODY WHO WILL
She was bad / I let the freight train carry me on / I'm the fool (who told you to go) / If you don't leave me / I bought her roses / Midnight, music city USA / Rockin' Rhonda ain't rockin' no more / Fool in El Paso / I'm comin' home / Old that train / Christy-Ann / Fiddlin' John Carson / God don't never change / Chicken pickin' (break song) / Man who never lies
CD ______ **BCD 15897**
Bear Family / Aug '95 / Direct / Rollercoaster / Swift

EMF

SCHUBERT DIP
Children / Long Summer days / When you're mine / Travelling not running / I believe / Unbelievable / Girl of an age / Admit it / Lies / Long time / Live at the Bilson
CD ______ **CDPCS 7353**
Parlophone / Feb '94 / EMI

STIGMA
They're here / Arizona / It's you / Never know / Blue highs / Inside / Getting through / She bleeds / Dog / Light that burns twice as bright
CD ______ **CDPCSD 122**
Parlophone / Sep '92 / EMI

Emils

FIGHT TOGETHER
CD ______ **WB 025CD**
We Bite / Feb '88 / Plastic Head

Emler, Andy

HEAD GAMES (Emler, Andy Mega Octet)
CD ______ **LBLC 6553**
Label Bleu / Jan '93 / New Note/Pinnacle

Emmett, Rik

SPIRAL NOTEBOOK
CD ______ **IRS 993515CD**
Intercord / Jan '96 / Plastic Head

Emotions

BEST OF MY LOVE
Best of my love / Flowers / I don't wanna love your love / Feeling is / Me for you / Key to my heart / Blessed / Rejoice / Love is right on / All night, all night / Smile / Walking the line / Boogie wonderland / 'Cause I love you / Yes, I am
CD ______ **4836762**
Columbia / Jun '96 / Sony

EMOTIONS LIVE IN 1996
CD ______ **50548**
Raging Bull / Feb '97 / Prime / Total/BMG

Emperor

ANTHEMS TO THE WELKIN AT DUSK
CD ______ **CANDLE 023CD**
Candlelight / May '97 / Plastic Head

IN THE NIGHTSIDE ECLIPSE
CD ______ **CANDLE 008CD**
Candlelight / Jan '95 / Plastic Head

Emperor Sly

HEAVY ROTATION
CD ______ **ZD 6CD**
Zip Dog / Nov '95 / Grapevine/PolyGram / SRD / Vital

Emperor's New Clothes

WISDOM & LIES
Luke's idea / Mystery daydream / Missing the sea / What's gone has disappeared / Stone's throwing / Making photographs underwater / Wishing hues of green / Don't you / Nowhere / Colours make waves
CD ______ **JAZIDCD 122**
Acid Jazz / Apr '95 / Disc

Empire, Alec

DESTROYER, THE
Intro / We all die / Suicide / Bang your head / Don't lie white girl / Firebombing / I just wanna destroy / Bonus beats / Nobody gets out alive / My body cannot die / Peak / Heartbeat that isn't there / I don't care what happens / My face would crack / Pleasure is our business / Ending
CD ______ **DHRCD 004**
Digital Hardcore / Jun '96 / Vital

GENERATION STAR WARS
CD ______ **EFA 006612**
Mille Plateau / Mar '95 / SRD

LOW ON ICE
CD ______ **EFA 006882**
Mille Plateau / Oct '95 / SRD

LTD EDITIONS
CD ______ **EFA 006522**
Mille Plateau / May '94 / SRD

Empire Brass

EMPIRE BRASS ON BROADWAY
Phantom of the opera / Hello Dolly / Man of La Mancha / Macavity / Don't cry for me Argentina / Mambo / Easy Street / Till there was you / Seventy six trombones / Fugue for tinhorns / At the end of the day / Lonely goatherd / Night and day / Bali Ha'i / Put on a happy face / Big spender
CD ______ **80303**
Telarc / Jun '92 / Conifer/BMG

PASSAGE
CD ______ **CD 80355**
Telarc / Jan '95 / Conifer/BMG

Empirion

ADVANCED TECHNOLOGY
CD ______ **XLCD 117**
XL / Oct '96 / Warner Music

Empress Of Fur

HOW DOES THAT MAD BAD HAWAIIAN VOODOO GRAB YOU
CD ______ **RAUCD 011**
Raucous / Jan '95 / Nervous / RTM/Disc / TKO Magnum

Empty Set

THIN, SLIM AND NONE
CD ______ **FLIP 96100**
Flippaut / Oct '96 / Cargo

Empyria

BEHIND CLOSED DOORS
CD ______ **TT 00232**
T&T / Apr '96 / Koch

Emsland Hillbillies

ENDLICH/BAUER BARNES MUHLE
Ich weiss etwas, was keiner weiss / Liebe Mama / Country freak / Ich liebe meinen diesel / Der geburtstag / Jungs, ab morgen / Popstar / Endlich / Hey hey / Emslander / Das alte lied / Original aschendorfer countryband / Wieder auf dem sofa / Der letzte joint zum aschied / Ich ging ins casino / Radarwagen / Erika's sonnenburg der liebe / Schroder goes country / Bauer barnes muhle / Cowboy roadie / Der fremde / Iglu himmel / Die gute alte sonne / Rechts vom kanal / Der krzeste countrysong der welt / Fernfahrer harmann
CD ______ **BCD 16183**
Bear Family / May '97 / Direct / Rollercoaster / Swift

En Slave

HALF PAST HUMAN
CD ______ **WSCD 005**
World Serpent / Oct '96 / World Serpent

En Vogue

BORN TO SING
Party / Strange / Lies / Hip hop bugle boy / Hold on / Part of me / You don't have to worry / Time goes on / Just can't stay away / Don't go / Luv lines / Waitin' on you
CD ______ **7567820842**
Atlantic / Jun '90 / Warner Music

EV3
Whatever / Don't let go (love) / Right direction / Damn I want to be your lover / Too gone, too long / You're all I need / Let it flow / Sitting by heaven's door / Love makes you do thangs / What a difference a day makes / Eyes of a child / Does anybody hear me
CD ______ **7559620972**
Atlantic / Jun '97 / Warner Music

FUNKY DIVAS
This is your life / My lovin' / Hip hop lover / Free your mind / Desire / Give him something he can feel / It ain't over till the fat lady sings / Give it up, turn it loose / Yesterday / Hooked on your love / Love don't love you / What is love / Runaway love / Whatta man: *Salt n' Pepa & En Vogue*
CD ______ **7567923102**
Atlantic / Dec '96 / Warner Music

Enaid & Einalem

CELTIC NIGHTS
CD ______ **2689**
NorthSound / Aug '96 / Gallant

Enchantment

DANCE THE MARBLE NAKED
CD ______ **CM 770662**
Century Media / May '94 / Plastic Head

End

GUSTO
CD ______ **GUSTCD 1**
Expression / Aug '91 / Pinnacle

End Of Green

INFINITY
CD ______ **NB 140CD**
Nuclear Blast / Jan '96 / Plastic Head

Endemic Void

EQUATIONS
Hydrosphere / Tidal / Lionstone / Serious intent / Knight moves / Infectious / Evolution / Turn da tide / Inner daze / Confused / Intermission
CD ______ **WORDD 004**
Language / Nov '96 / Grapevine/PolyGram / Prime / Vital

Enders, Johannes

HOME GROUND
High spirits / Dolores Carla Maria / Dog house / Trixi one / Prix / Home ground / Black Nile / Trixi two / Evidence / Panta rhei
CD ______ **ENJACD 91052**
Enja / Jun '97 / New Note/Pinnacle / Vital/SAM

Endino's Earthworm

ENDINO'S EARTHWORM
CD ______ **CRZ 021CD**
Cruz / May '93 / Plastic Head

Endless

BEYOND THE ABYSS
CD ______ **DISC 1886CD**
Deathwish / Jan '96 / Plastic Head

Endpoint

AFTERTASTE
CD ______ **DOG 024CD**
Doghouse / Nov '94 / Plastic Head

LAST RECORD
CD ______ **DOG 030CD**
Doghouse / Aug '95 / Plastic Head

Endraum

IN FLIMMANDER NACHT
CD ______ **EFA 112292**
Danse Macabre / Mar '94 / SRD

Endresen, Sidsel

EXILE
Here the moon / Quest / Stages, I, II, III / Hunger / Theme I / Waiting train / Dreaming / Dust
CD ______ **5217212**
ECM / Apr '94 / New Note/Pinnacle

Endsley, Melvin

I LIKE YOUR KIND OF LOVE
I like your kind of love / Is it true / I got a feeling / Keep a lovin' me baby / Let's fall out of love / Just want to be wanted / I ain't gettin' nowhere with you / Hungry eyes / Loving on my mind / Lonely all over again / There's bound to be / Gettin' used to the blues / Bringin' the blues to my door / I'd just be fool enough
CD ______ **BCD 15595**
Bear Family / May '93 / Direct / Rollercoaster / Swift

Endura

DREAMS OF DARK WAVES
CD ______ **NACD 202**
Nature & Art / Oct '95 / Plastic Head

GREAT GOD PAN
Oriflamme / Alpha- wolf / Dark face of Eve / From sickening skies / Sucking the sour vine / Sperm of metals / Truth is a sharp knife / Saturns tree / Black dog crossed my path / Hymn to Pan / Battle song of Endura
CD ______ **SAG 5**
Elfenblut / Jul '97 / RTM/Disc

Energy Orchard

ENERGY ORCHARD
CD ______ **MNMCD 2**
M&M / Oct '95 / Total/BMG

PAIN KILLER
Surrender to the city / She's the one I adore / Wasted / D F Dogs / Shipyard song / Past is another country / Remember my name / Sight for sore eyes / Pain killer / I hate to say goodbye
CD ______ **TRACD 100**
Transatlantic / Apr '96 / Pinnacle

SHINOLA
Coming through / Madame George / Atlantic City / Stay away / Don't fail me now / In my room / Seven sisters / Star of County Down / London Fields / Big town / I'm no angel
CD ______ **TRACD 103**
Transatlantic / Feb '95 / Pinnacle

Engel, Detlef

EIN ENGEL, OHNE FLUGEL
Ein Engel, ohne flugel / Komm' zu mir darling / So klar wie die sterne / Mr. Blue / Traumen / Sugar baby / Ich such ein herz / Junges gluck / Oh I love you / War' nur nicht der and're gekommen / Isabella / Alle twens geh'n heut' tanzen / Zeig' mir bei nacht die sterne / Vier kleine schuhe / Mein herz schlagt nur fur Susie / Sweety sleepy melodie / Schenk mir doch ein bild von dir / Du du bist ja so sch'n / Wenn du nicht bei mir bist / Ist das liebe oder nicht / Was kann das sein / Ich bin nicht so, wie alle andern / Bitte gib mir einen kuss / Lass mich heute nicht allein / Oh no / Rote rosen / Das ist leicht gesagt / Goodnight / Let's go / Geh'n wir
CD ______ **BCD 16106**
Bear Family / Dec '96 / Direct / Rollercoaster / Swift

Engelstaub

IGNIS FATUUS: IRRLICHTER
CD ______ **EFA 121542**
Apollyon / Jul '94 / SRD

Engin, Esin

BELLY DANCE MUSIC
CD ______ **EUCD 1309**
ARC / Jul '95 / ADA / ARC Music

Engine

AUTOWRECK
CD SPRAYCD 304
Making Waves / Oct '93 / CM

Engine 54

54-95
CD EFA 127682
Heatwave / Sep '95 / SRD

Engine 88

CLEAN YOUR ROOM
Bottle / Funny car / Mangos / Pelican / Spinach / Des Moines / Lonely pimp / GTO / Drowning / Crackers / Baby doll / Firefly / Twenty
CD CAROL 17842
Caroline / May '96 / Cargo / Vital

SNOWMAN
Ballerina / Seconal / Stairway / Manclub / Istanbul / Snowman / Curious / Trouble / Cold-blooded / Mustard / Butchery / Killer willow / Precious
CD CAR 7588
Caroline / Mar '97 / Cargo / Vital

Engine Kid

ANGEL'S WINGS
CD REV 038CD
Revelation / May '95 / Plastic Head

Engkilde, August

BAND OF INNER URGE
CD STCD 4210
Storyville / May '97 / Cadillac / Jazz Music / Wellard

England

LAST OF THE JUBBLIES
CD MABEL 1
Vinyl Tap / Jan '96 / Cargo / Greyhound / Vinyl Tap

England, Buddy

FATE'S A FIDDLER, LIFE'S A DANCE
CD LARRCD 304
Larrikin / Nov '94 / ADA / CM / Direct / Roots

England, Ty

TWO WAYS TO FALL
It starts with L / Two ways to fall / I'll take today / Never say never / Last dance / Backslider's prayer / Irresistible you / Kick back / All of the above / Sure
CD 07863669302
RCA Nashville / Oct '96 / BMG

TY ENGLAND
Redneck son / Smoke in her eyes / Should've asked her faster / Her only bad habit is me / New faces in the fields / Swing like that / You'll find somebody new / Blues ain't news to me / It's lonesome everywhere / Is that you
CD 74321285932
RCA / Aug '95 / BMG

England's Glory

LEGENDARY LOST ALBUM
Devotion / Wide waterway / City of fun / First time I saw you / Broken arrows / Bright lights / It's been a long time / Guest / Peter and the pets / Showdown / Predictably blonde / Weekend / Trouble in the world
CD CDMGRAM 73
Anagram / Sep '96 / Cargo / Pinnacle

Englesstaub

ALLEUS MALEFICARUM
CD AP 00310593
Apollyon / Dec '93 / SRD

English Brass Ensemble

LYRIC BRASS
CD CDDCA 660
ASV / Apr '89 / Select

English Chorale

CHORAL CHRISTMAS, A
O come all ye faithful (adeste fidelis) / While shepherds watched / We three Kings / God rest ye merry gentlemen / In dulce jubilo / Silent night / Good King Wenceslas / O little town of Bethlehem / In the bleak midwinter / First Noel / Once in royal David's city / Away in a manger / Hark the herald angels sing
CD CDVIP 168
Virgin VIP / Nov '96 / EMI

English Dogs

ALL THE WORLD'S A RAGE
CD SPV 08453632
SPV / Jun '96 / Koch / Plastic Head

ALL THE WORLD'S A RAGE
CD IRC 053
Impact / Jun '97 / Cargo

BOW TO NONE
CD IRC 021
Impact / Mar '97 / Cargo

WHERE LEGEND BEGAN
CD PRAGE 003CD
Powerage / Jun '97 / Plastic Head

English Philharmonic ...

PHILHARMONIC ROCK (English Philharmonic Orchestra)
Jesus Christ Superstar selection / When I fall in love / Whiter shade of pale / Greatest love of all / Reach out I'll be there / Beatles selection / Lady in red / Bohemian rhapsody / Dream theme
CD QED 089
Tring / Nov '96 / Tring

Enid

AERIE FAERIE NONSENSE
Prelude / Mayday galliard / Ondine / Childe Roland / Fand: first movement / Fand: second movement
CD MNTLCD 6
Newt / May '94 / Plastic Head

ANARCHY ON 45 (2CD Set)
CD Set MNTLCD 13
Mantella / Jul '96 / Plastic Head

AT THE HAMMERSMITH
CD MNTLCD 10
Newt / May '94 / Plastic Head

FINAL NOISE
Childe Roland / Hall of mirrors / Song for Europe / Something wicked this way comes / Sheets of blue / Chaldean crossing / La rage / Earth born / Jerusalem
CD MNTLCD 3
Newt / May '94 / Plastic Head

IN THE REGION OF THE SUMMER STARS
Fool / Falling tower / Death the reaper / Lovers / Devil / Sun / Last judgement / In the region of the Summer stars
CD MNTLCD 7
Newt / May '94 / Plastic Head

SALOME
O Salome / Streets of blue / Change / Jack / Flames of power
CD MNTLCD 9
Newt / May '94 / Plastic Head

SEED AND THE SOWER, THE
Children crossing / Bar of shadow / La rage / Longhome / Earth born
CD MNTLCD 2
Newt / Apr '94 / Plastic Head

SIX PIECES
Sanctus / Once she was / Ring master / Punch and Judy man / Hall of mirrors / Dreamer / Joined by the heart
CD MNTLCD 4
Newt / May '94 / Plastic Head

SOMETHING WICKED THIS WAY COMES
Raindown / Jessica / And then there was none / Evensong / Bright star / Song for Europe / Something wicked this way comes
CD MNTLCD 1
Newt / May '94 / Plastic Head

SUNDIALER
CD MNTLCD 12
Mantella / Oct '95 / Plastic Head

TOUCH ME
Humoresque / Cortege / Elegy (touch me) / Gallevant / Albion fair / Joined by the heart
CD MNTLCD 5
Newt / May '94 / Plastic Head

TRIPPING THE LIGHT FANTASTIC
Ultraviolet cat / Little shiners / Gateway / Tripping the light fantastic / Freelance human / Dark hydraulic / Biscuit game
CD MNTLCD 11
Newt / Nov '94 / Plastic Head

Enigma

CROSS OF CHANGES
Second chapter / Eyes of truth / Return to innocence / I love you... I'll kill you / Silent warrior / Dream of the dolphin / Age of loneliness (Carly's song) / Out from the deep / Cross of changes / Return to innocence (mix) / Age of loneliness (mix) / Eyes of truth (mix)
CD CDVIR 20
Virgin / Jan '94 / EMI

LE ROI EST MORT, VIVE LE ROI
Le Roi est mort, vive le Roi / Morphing thru time / Third of its kind / Beyond the invisible / Why / Shadows in silence / Child in us / TNT for the brain / Almost full moon / Roundabout / Prism of life / Odyssey of the mind
CD CDVIR 60
Virgin / Nov '96 / EMI

MCMXC AD
Voice of Enigma / Principles of lust / Sadness / Find love / Sadness (reprise) / Callas went away / Mea culpa / Voice and the snake / Knocking on forbidden doors / Back to the rivers of belief / Way to eternity / Hallelujah / Rivers of belief
CD CDVIR 1
Virgin / Dec '90 / EMI

Enloe, Lyman

FIDDLE TUNES I RECALL
CD CUY 2707CD
County / Apr '96 / ADA / Direct

Ennen, Thea

ALL ABOARD (Ennen, Thea & The Algorythms)
Surfboard / Patience / Warm North / Your own prison / Mama Mama / Common sense / Ain't that something / Promised land / Lonely love / Cradle / Cream corn / Standing
CD ATM 1122
Atomic Theory / Oct '96 / ADA / Direct

Ennis, Seamus

BEST OF IRISH PIPING
CD TARACD 1002/9
Tara / Aug '95 / ADA / CM / Conifer/BMG / Direct

BONNY BUNCH OF ROSES
CD TCD 1023
Tradition / Aug '96 / ADA / Vital

PURE DROP/FOX CHASE
CD TARA 1002/9CD
Tara / Jul '95 / ADA / CM / Conifer/BMG / Direct

WANDERING MINSTREL, THE
Wandering minstrel/Jackson's morning brush / Boys of Bluehill/Dunphy's hornpipe / Glennephin cuckoo/Littlefair Cannavans / Frieze breeches / Flags of Dublin/Wind that shakes the barley / Little stack of barley/ Cronin's hornpipe / New Demesne / Blackbird / Gillan's apples / Walls of Liscarroll/ Stone in the field / Molly O'Malone / Kiss the maid behind the barrel / Happy to meet and sorry to part
CD OSS 12CD
Ossian / Mar '94 / ADA / CM / Direct / Highlander

Ennis, Skinnay

1956/57 LIVE IN STEREO
When summer is gone / Cheek to cheek / Got a date with an angel / Love for sale / You've got me crying again / I've got you under my skin / Breathless / Rhythm is our business / Whispers in the night / Scatterbrain / Josephine / I went out of my way / There ought to be a moonlight savings time / Foggy day / Untitled instrumental / Boy, a girl, and a lamplight / Girlfriend
CD JH 1027
Jazz Hour / Feb '93 / Cadillac / Jazz Music / Target/BMG

Eno, Brian

ANOTHER GREEN WORLD
Sky saw / Over Fire Island / St. Elmo's fire / In dark trees / Big ship / I'll come running / Another green world / Sombre reptiles / Little fishes / Golden hours / Becalmed / Zawinul / Lava / Everything merges with the night / Spirits drifting
CD EGCD 21
EG / May '87 / EMI

ANOTHER GREEN WORLD/BEFORE & AFTER SCIENCE/APOLLO (3CD Set)
CD Set EGBC 7
EG / Nov '89 / EMI

APOLLO (Atmospheres & Soundtracks)
Under stars / Secret place / Matta / Signals / Ending (ascent) / Under stars II / Drift / Silver morning / Deep blue day / Weightless / Always returning / Stars
CD EGCD 53
EG / Jan '87 / EMI

BEFORE & AFTER SCIENCE/WARM JETS/ANOTHER GREEN WORLD (Compact Collection/3CD Set)
No one receiving / Backwater / Kurt's rejoinder / Energy fools the magician / King's lead hat / Here he comes / Julie with... / By this river / Through hollow lands / Spider and I / Needles in the camel's eye / Paw paw negro blowtorch / Baby's on fire / Cindy tells me / Driving me backwards / On some faraway beach / Blank Frank / Dead fink's don't talk / Some of them are old / Here come the warm jets / Sky saw / Over Fire Island / St. Elmo's fire / In dark trees / Big ship / I'll come running / Another green world / Sombre reptiles / Little fishes / Golden hours / Becalmed / Zawinul / Lava / Everything merges with the night / Spirits drifting
CD Set TPAK 36
Virgin / Oct '94 / EMI

BEFORE AND AFTER SCIENCE
No one receiving / Backwater / Kurt's rejoinder / Energy fools the magician / King's lead hat / Here he comes / Julie with... / By this river / Through hollow lands / Spider and I
CD EGCD 32
EG / Jan '87 / EMI

BEGEGNUNGEN (Eno, Brian & Moebius/ Rodelius/Plank)
CD SKYCD 3090
Sky / Nov '94 / Greyhound / Koch / Vital/ SAM

BEGEGNUNGEN VOL.2 (Eno, Brian & Moebius/Rodelius/Plank)
CD SKYCD 3095
Sky / Nov '94 / Greyhound / Koch / Vital/ SAM

BRIAN ENO VOL.1 (3CD Set)
Another green world / Energy fools the magician / Dover beach / Slow water / Untitled / Chemin de fer / Empty landscape / Reactor / Secret / Don't look back / Marseilles / Two rapid formations / Sparrowfall / Sparrowfall / Sparrowfall / Events in dense fog / There is nobody / Patrolling wire borders / Measured room / Task force / M 386 / Final sunset / Dove / Roman twilight / Dawn, marshland / Always returning I / Signals / Drift study / Approaching train / Always returning II / Asian river / Theme of creation / St. Tom / Warszawa / Chemistry / Courage / Moss garden / Tension block / Strong flashes of light / More volts / Mist/rhythm / He renomo / Stream with bright fish / Her fleeting smile / Arc of doves / Stars / Index of metals (edit) / 1/1 / Ikebukero / Lost day / Thursday afternoon (edit) / Discreet music / Dunwich beach, autumn, 1960 / Neroli (edit)
CD Set ENOBX 1
Virgin / Oct '93 / EMI

BRIAN ENO VOL.2 (3CD Set)
Needle in the camel's eye / Baby's on fire / Cindy tells me / On some faraway beach / Blank Frank / Dead finks don't talk / Some of them are old / Here come the warm jets / Seven deadly finns / Burning airlines... / Back in Judy's jungle / Great pretender / Third uncle / Put a straw... / True wheel / Taking tiger mountain / Lion sleeps tonight / Sky saw / Over fire island / St. Elmo's fire / In dark trees / Big ship / I'll come running / Sombre reptiles / Golden hours / Becalmed / Zawinul/Lava / Everything merges / Spirits drifting / No one receiving / Backwater / Kurt's rejoinder / King's lead hat / Here he comes / Julie with... / By this river / Through hollow lands / Spider and I / RAF / America is waiting / Regiment / Jezebel spirit / Very very hungry / Spinning away / One word / Empty frame / River / Soul of Carmen Miranda / Belldog / I fall up / Stiff / Are they thinking of me / Some words / Under / Over
CD Set ENOBX 2
Virgin / Oct '93 / EMI

DISCREET MUSIC
Discreet music 1 and 2 / Fullness of wind (part 1) / French catalogues (part 2) / Brutal adour (part 3)
CD EEGCD 23
EG / '87 / EMI

DROP, THE
Slip, dip / But if / Belgiam drop / Cornered / Block drop / Out/out / Swanky / Coasters / Blissed / MC Organ / Boomcubist / Hazard / Rayonism / Dutch blur / Back clack / Dear world / Iced world
CD ASCD 032
All Saints / Jun '97 / Discovery / Vital

HEADCANDY
CD Set 6896400052
EG / Jan '95 / EMI

HERE COME THE WARM JETS
Needles in the camel's eye / Paw paw negro blowtorch / Baby's on fire / Cindy tells me / Driving me backwards / On some faraway beach / Blank Frank / Dead finks don't talk / Some of them are old / Here come the warm jets
CD EGCD 11
EG / Jul '93 / EMI

MORE BLANK THAN FRANK (Desert Island Selection)
Here he comes / Everything merges with the night / On some faraway beach / I'll come running (to tie your shoe) / Taking tiger mountain / Backwater / St. Elmo's fire / No one receiving / Great pretender / King's lead hat / Julie with ... / Back in Judy's jungle
CD EGCD 65
EG / Jun '87 / EMI

MUSIC FOR AIRPORTS (Ambient 1)
1/1 / 2/1 / 1/2 / 2/2
CD EEGCD 17
EG / Jan '87 / EMI

MUSIC FOR FILMS
M 386 / Aragon / From the same hill / Inland sea / Two rapid formations / Slow water / Sparrow fall 1 / Sparrow fall 2 / Sparrow fall 3 / Quartz / Events in dense fog / There is nobody / Patrolling wire borders / Task force / Strange light / Final sunset / Measured room / Alternative 3
CD EEGCD 5
EG / '87 / EMI

MUSIC FOR FILMS VOL.3 (Various Artists)
Tension block: *Lanois, Daniel & Brian Eno* / Err: *Eno, Brian & Michael Brook* / 4 minute warning: *Eno, Brian & Michael Brook* / For her atoms: *Mahlin, Misha & Lydia Kavina* / Balthus bemused by colour: *Budd, Harold* /

Theme from Creation: *Eno, Brian* / Saint Tom: *Eno, Brian* / White mustang: *Lanois, Daniel & Brian Eno* / Sirens: *Lanois, Daniel & Brian Eno* / Asian river: *Eno, Brian* / Zaragoza: *Laraaji* / Quixote: *Eno, Roger* / Fleeting smile: *Eno, Roger* / Theme for Opera: *Eno, Brian & Roger Eno* / Kalimba: *Laraaji*
CD ASCD 004
All Saints / Mar '96 / Discovery / Vital

MY LIFE IN THE BUSH OF GHOSTS (Eno, Brian & David Byrne)
America is waiting / Mea culpa / Help me somebody / Regiment / Jezebel spirit / Moonlight in glory / Come with us / Carrier / Secret life / Mountain of needles / Very very hungry
CD EGCD 48
EG / Jul '93 / EMI

NEROLI
Neroli
CD ASCD 015
All Saints / Jun '93 / Discovery / Vital

NERVE NET
Fractal zoom / Wire shock / What actually happened / Pierre and mist / My squelchy life / Decentre / Juju space jazz / Roil the choke / Ali click / Distributed being
CD 9362450332
WEA / Aug '92 / Warner Music

ON LAND (Ambient 4)
Lizard point / Lost day / Tal coat / Shadow / Lantern marsh / Unfamiliar wind (Leeks hills) / Clearing / Dunwich Beach, Autumn 1960
CD EEGCD 20
EG / Apr '82 / EMI

PLATEAUX OF MIRRORS (Ambient 2) (Eno, Brian & Harold Budd)
First light / Steal away / Plateaux of mirror / Above Chiangmai / Arc of doves / Not yet remembered / Chill air / Among fields of crystal / Wind in lonely fences / Failing light
CD EEGCD 18
EG / Jan '87 / EMI

SPINNER (Eno, Brian & Jah Wobble)
Where we lived / Like Organza / Steam / Garden recalled / Marine radio / Unusual balance / Space diary / Spinner / Transmitter and trumpet / Left where it fell
CD ASCD 023
All Saints / Oct '95 / Discovery / Vital

TAKING TIGER MOUNTAIN BY STRATEGY
Burning airlines give you so much more / Back in Judy's jungle / Fair lady of Limbourg / Mother whale eyeless / Great pretender / Third uncle / Put a straw under baby / True wheel / China my china / Taking tiger mountain
CD EGCD 17
EG / Jul '93 / EMI

THURSDAY AFTERNOON
Thursday afternoon
CD EGCD 64
EG / Jul '93 / EMI

TRIBUTE TO BRIAN ENO, A (Various Artists)
CD CLP 0016
Cleopatra / Jul '97 / Cargo / Greyhound / Plastic Head / RTM/Disc / SRD

WRONG WAY UP (Eno, Brian & John Cale)
CD ASCD 12
All Saints / Jun '92 / Discovery / Vital

Eno, Roger

BETWEEN TIDES
Out at dawn / Field of gold / Prelude for St. John / Ringinglow / Frost / One gull / Silent hours / Between tides / Winter music / While the city sleeps / Sunburst / Autumn / Almost dark
CD ASCD 01
All Saints / Feb '96 / Discovery / Vital

FAMILIAR, THE (Eno, Roger & Kate St. John)
Our man in Havana / Wonderful year / We stay still / Rain outside an open door / Song of songs / Mister bosco / Familiar / Blue sea / Lament / Heartland / I've been searching / Days of delay / In a lonely world
CD ASCD 013
All Saints / Apr '97 / Discovery / Vital

ISLANDS
CD SINE 001
Sine / Sep '95 / Grapevine/PolyGram

LOST IN TRANSLATION
CD ASCD 018
All Saints / Feb '95 / Discovery / Vital

MUSIC OF NEGLECTED ENGLISH COMPOSERS
Heavenly sarum / In a old mellow air / Zimzally bim / Tango for the new woman / Ragtime / Old winter / Telestrion / Holiday of a lifetime / Strewwlpeter / Travellen / Bright September / Hour of darkness 1 / Hour of darkness 2 / Hour of darkness 3 / Hour of darkness 4 / Petersfield / How the years turn / Ely diamond / Love affair (version 873) / Love affair (final version) / Anonymous postcard / Still day
CD RES 126CD
Resurgence / Apr '97 / Pinnacle

SWIMMING
Paddington frisk / Whole wide world / Slow river / In water / Amukidi / Swimming / Over the hils / Boatman / Little things left behind / Hewendaway / Aryis / Where the road leads to nowhere / How you shone / Parting glass / Subcircus: *Subcircus*
CD ASCD 028
All Saints / Sep '96 / Discovery / Vital

VOICES
Place in the wilderness / Day after / At the water's edge / Grey promenade / Paler sky / Through the blue / Evening tango / Recalling winter / Voices / Old dance / Reflections on IKB
CD EEGCD 42
EG / Jul '93 / EMI

Enola Gay

FOTH
CD SHARK 105CD
Shark / Jun '95 / Plastic Head

Enriquez, Bobby

WILDMAN RETURNS, THE
Pink Panther / Our love is here to stay / Groovin' high / Walkin' shoes / Starlight souvenirs / Easy living / I'm confessin' that I love you / As long as I live / Blue Hawaii / Misty
CD ECD 22059
Evidence / Oct '93 / ADA / Cadillac / Harmonia Mundi

Ensemble Bash

LAUNCH
Shiftwork / Apple blossom / Gene pool / Kumpo / Shining through / Shaken not stirred / Suite d'Lorenzo / Dash me something
CD SK 69246
Sony Classical / Feb '97 / Sony

Ensemble Berehinya

VOROTARCHILC: THE GATEKEEPER
CD PAN 7002
Pan / Feb '94 / ADA / CM / Direct

Ensemble Crai

ROMANIAN PAN PIPES
CD PS 65176
PlayaSound / Dec '96 / ADA / Harmonia Mundi

Ensemble Dede Gorgud

HEYVA GULU: DANCES & ASHUG MELODIES FROM NAKHICHEVAN (Anthology Of Azerbaijanian Music)
CD PAN 2021CD
Pan / Mar '94 / ADA / CM / Direct

Ensemble Del Doppio ...

JESUS CHRIST WAS BORN (Ensemble Del Doppio Bordonne)
CD NT 6722
Robi Droli / Jan '94 / ADA / Direct

Ensemble Folk-Art

BULGARIA - WOMEN'S CHORUS
CD PS 65102
PlayaSound / Mar '93 / ADA / Harmonia Mundi

Ensemble Galilei

FOLLOWING THE MOON
CD DIS 80139
Dorian Discovery / Feb '96 / Conifer/BMG / Select

Ensemble Kolkheti

BATONEBO
CD PAN 7004CD
Pan / Apr '96 / ADA / CM / Direct

OH BLACK EYED GIRL
CD PANCD 2006
Pan / May '93 / ADA / CM / Direct

Ensemble Kutaisi

MAKRULI: POLYPHONIC SONGS FROM GEORGIA
CD PAN 7001
Pan / Feb '94 / ADA / CM / Direct

Ensemble Morkos

CEDRE
CD ED 13067
L'Empreinte Digitale / Jan '97 / ADA / Harmonia Mundi

Ensemble Musica Criolla

MUSIQUE TRADITIONALE DU CHILI
CD 824742
BUDA / Nov '90 / Discovery

Ensemble Nihon No Oto

TRADITIONAL CHAMBER MUSIC OF JAPAN
CD AUB 6784
Auvidis/Ethnic / Feb '94 / ADA / Harmonia Mundi

Ensemble Nipponia

KABUKI AND OTHER TRADITIONAL MUSIC
CD 7559720842
Nonesuch / Jan '95 / Warner Music

TRADITIONAL VOCAL AND INSTRUMENTAL MUSIC
CD 7559720722
Nonesuch / Jan '95 / Warner Music

Ensemble Of The Bulgarian ...

HARVEST, A SHEPHERD, A BRIDE, A (Ensemble Of The Bulgarian Republic)
CD 7559720112
Nonesuch / Jan '95 / Warner Music

Ensemble Recherche

MORTON FELDMAN/SAMUEL BECKETT - WORDS & MUSIC (Ensemble Recherche & Omar Ebrahim/Stephen Lind)
CD MO 782084
Montaigne / Oct '96 / Harmonia Mundi

Ensemble Renaissance

MARCO POLO - THE JOURNEY
CD AS 20032
Al Segno / Jun '96 / Vital/SAM

Ensemble Tzigane Chiokerly

SERENADE
CD PV 785092
Disques Pierre Verany / Jul '93 / Kingdom

Enslaved

ELD
CD OPCD 053
Osmose / Mar '97 / Plastic Head

ENSLAVED
CD ANTIMOSH 008CD
Deathlike Silence / Apr '94 / Plastic Head

ENSLAVED/EMPEROR (Enslaved/ Emperor)
CD CANDLE 12CD
Candlelight / Jan '94 / Plastic Head

FROST
CD OP 025
Osmose / Nov '94 / Plastic Head

ENT

DAMAGE 381
Utopia burns / Punishment solitude / Icon off guilt / Jesus on my side / Cold world / Damage / Shallow existence / Chaos perverse / Crawl / Downside
CD MOSH 173CD
Earache / Jul '97 / Vital

Enteli

ENTELI
CD PSCD 77
Phono Suecia / Oct '94 / Cadillac / Impetus

LIVE
CD AMCD 738
Amigo / May '97 / ADA / Cadillac / CM / Wellard

Enthroned

PROPHECIES OF PAGAN
CD EORCD 004
Osmose / May '96 / Plastic Head

Entombed

CLANDESTINE
CD MOSH 037CD
Earache / Mar '97 / Vital

ENTOMBED
Out of hand / God of thunder / Black breath / Stranger aeons / Dusk / Shreds of flesh / Crawl / Forsaken / Bitter loss / Night of the vampire / State of emergency / Vandal X / Hey bitch
CD MOSH 125CD
Earache / Mar '97 / Vital

LEFT HAND PATH
Left hand path / Drowned / Revel in flesh / When life has ceased / Supposed to rot / But life goes on / Bitter loss / Morbid devourment / Deceased / Truth beyond / Carnal leftovers
CD MOSH 021CD
Earache / Mar '97 / Vital

RIDE, SHOOT STRAIGHT AND SPEAK THE TRUTH
To ride, shoot straight and speak the truth / Lights out / Wound / They / DCLXVI / Parasight / Somewhat vulgar / Put me out / Just as sad / Damn deal done / Wreckage / Like this with the devil / Boats / Mr. Uffe's horrorshow
CD CDMFN 216
CD CDMFNX 216
Music For Nations / Mar '97 / Pinnacle

WOLVERINE BLUES
Eyemaster / Rotten soil / Wolverine blues / Demon / Contempt / Full of hell / Blood song / Hollowman / Heavens die / Out of hand
CD MOSH 082CD
Earache / Sep '97 / Vital

Entwistle, John

IN CONCERT 1975
CD 880302
King Biscuit / Jul '97 / Greyhound

Enuff Z Nuff

SEVEN
Wheels / Still have tonight / Down hill / Its no good / 5 miles away / LA burning / New kind of motion / Clown on the town / U & I / On my way back home / We don't have to be / So sad to see you / Jealous guy / For you girl / I won't let you go
CD CDMFN 212
Music For Nations / Feb '97 / Pinnacle

TWEAKED
Stoned / Life is strange / If I can't have / Love song / Bullet from a gun / Without your love / Jesus closed his eyes / Mr. Jones / We're all right / Style / My dear dream / My heroin / It's 2 late
CD CDMFN 190
Music For Nations / Sep '95 / Pinnacle

Enya

CELTS, THE
Celts / Aldebaran / I want tomorrow / March of the celts / Deireadh an tuath / Sun in the stream / To go beyond / Fairytale / Epona / Triad: St. Patrick cu chulainn oisin / Portrait / Boadicea / Bard dance / Dan y dwr / To go beyond
CD 4509911672
WEA / Nov '92 / Warner Music

MEMORY OF TREES, THE
Memory of trees / Anywhere is / Pax deorum / Athair ar neamh / From where I am / China roses / Hope has a place / Tea-house moon / Once you had gold / La sonadora / On my way home
CD 0630128792
WEA / Nov '96 / Warner Music

SHEPHERD MOONS
Shepherd moons / Caribbean blue / How can I keep from singing / Ebudae / Angeles / No holly for Miss Quinn / Book of days / Evacuee / Lothlorien / Marble halls / After ventus / Smaointe
CD 9031755722
WEA / Nov '91 / Warner Music

WATERMARK
Watermark / Cursum perfico / On your shore / Storms in Africa / Exile / Miss Clare remembers / Orinoco flow / Evening falls / River / Longships / Na laetha geal m'oige / Storms in Africa (part II)
CD 2292438752
WEA / Aug '93 / Warner Music

Enzso

ENZSO
Poor boy / Message to my girl / I knew I never / Straight old line / Stuff and nonsense / My mistake / Voices / I see red / Under the wheel / Dirty creature / Stranger than fiction / Time for a change
CD 4838702
Columbia / Mar '97 / Sony

Eon

VOID DWELLER
CD STEAM 45 CD
Vinyl Solution / Oct '92 / RTM/Disc

Epic Soundtracks

DEBRIS
CD RTS 20
Return To Sender / Jan '96 / ADA / Direct

SLEEPING STAR
CD NORMAL 186CD
Normal / Aug '95 / ADA / Direct

Epidemic

DECAMERON
CD CDZORRO 50
Metal Blade / Sep '92 / Pinnacle / Plastic Head

EXIT PARADISE
CD CDZORRO 79
Metal Blade / Aug '94 / Pinnacle / Plastic Head

TRUTH OF WHAT WILL BE, THE
CD CORE 4CD
Metalcore / Oct '90 / Plastic Head

Epidemics

EPIDEMICS, THE
Never take no for an answer / What would I do without you / Situations / You don't love me anymore / Love is alright / You can be anything / No cure / Don't I know you / Give an inch / Full moon
CD ________ 8275222
ECM / May '87 / New Note/Pinnacle

Epilepsy

BAPHOMET - TAROT OF THE UNDERWORLD (CD Box With Tarot Cards & Book)
CD Set ________ KK 144CD
KK / Jan '96 / Plastic Head

ROZIS
CD ________ PA 009CD
Paragoric / Aug '95 / Cargo / Plastic Head

Epilogue

HIDE
Swords and knives / Hide / Wheel of love / Living a lie / In the city / Travelling man / No sign of life / Into the clock / Matthew / Flame
CD ________ CYCL 010
Cyclops / Aug '97 / Pinnacle

Epinette, Georges

EPINETTE & BARON (Epinette, Georges & Jean Baron)
CD ________ KMCD 57
Keltia Musique / Feb '96 / ADA / Discovery

Episode Six

COMPLETE PYE SESSIONS
CD ________ NEXCD 156
Sequel / Jul '91 / BMG

Epitaph

SEEMING SALVATION
CD ________ THRO 17CD
Thrash / Nov '94 / Plastic Head

EPMD

BUSINESS AS USUAL
I'm mad / Hardcore / Rampage / Manslaughter / Jane 3 / For my people / Mr. Bozack / Gold digger / Give the people / Rap is outta control / Brothers on my jock / Underground / Hit squad heist / Funky piano
CD ________ 5235102
Def Jam / Jan '96 / PolyGram

BUSINESS NEVER PERSONAL
Boon dox / Nobody's safe chump / Can't hear nothing but the music / Chill / Headbanger / Scratch bring it back / Crossover cummin' at cha / Play the next man / It's going down / Who killed Jane
CD ________ 4719632
Def Jam/CBS / Sep '92 / Sony

Epstein Brothers

KINGS OF FREYLEKH
CD ________ SM 16112
Wergo / Dec '95 / ADA / Cadillac / Harmonia Mundi

Equals

ALL THE HITS PLUS MORE
CD ________ CDPT 001
Prestige / Jun '92 / Else / Total/BMG

GREATEST HITS
CD ________ AHLCD 38
Hit / May '96 / Grapevine/PolyGram

GREATEST HITS
Viva Bobby Joe / Baby come back / Backstreet / Laurel and Hardy / Rub a dub dub / Michael and the slipper tree / No place to go / Black skinned blue eyed boys / Bad boy / Gimme some lovin' / Black is black / Domino / I get so excited / Softly, softly
CD ________ 399349
Koch Presents / Jun '97 / Koch

VERY BEST OF THE EQUALS, THE
Baby come back / Hold me closer / Viva Bobby Joe / Laurel and Hardy / Another sad and lonely night / Rub-a-dub dub / Softly, softly / Soul brother Clifford / I get so excited / Teardrops / You'd better tell her / I can see, but you don't know / Black skinned blue eyed boys / I won't there / I'm a poor man / Michael and his slipper tree / Cinderella / Christine / Friday night / Honey gum / No love can be sweeter / Ain't got nothing to give you / Leaving you is hard to do / Put some rock 'n' roll in your soul / Diversion
CD ________ SEECD 374
See For Miles/C5 / Jun '96 / Pinnacle

VIVA EQUALS
CD ________ MCCD 289
Music Club / Mar '97 / Disc / THE

Equation

RETURN TO ME
CD ________ 0630153422
Blanco Y Negro / Jul '96 / Warner Music

Equidad Bares

MES ESPAGNES
CD ________ Y 225049CD
Silex / Apr '95 / ADA / Harmonia Mundi

Equinox

LABYRINTH
CD ________ PRO 017
Progress / Feb '97 / Cargo / Plastic Head

Equipe 84

RACCOLTA DI SUCCESSI V2
CD ________ 182562
Ricordi / Aug '93 / Discovery

Equomanthorn

NINDINUGGA NIMSHIM
CD ________ USR 009CD
Unisound / Jan '96 / Plastic Head

Era

AMENO
CD ________ 5349812
Mercury / Aug '97 / PolyGram

Erasure

CHORUS
Chorus / Waiting for the day / Joan / Breath of life / Am I right / How I love to hate you / Turns the love to anger / Siren song / Perfect stranger / Home
CD ________ CDSTUMM 95
Mute / Oct '91 / RTM/Disc

CIRCUS, THE
It doesn't have to be / Hideaway / Don't dance / If I could / Sexuality / Victim of love / Leave me to bleed / Sometimes / Circus / Spiralling
CD ________ CDSTUMM 35
Mute / '87 / RTM/Disc

COWBOY
Rain / Worlds on fire / Reach out / In my arms / Don't say your love is killing me / Precious / Treasure / Boy / How can I say / Save me darling / Love affair
CD ________ CDSTUMM 155
Mute / Mar '97 / RTM/Disc

ERASURE
Guess I'm into feeling / Rescue me / Sono luminus / Fingers and thumbs (Cold summer's day) / Rock me gently / Grace / Stay with me / Love the way you do so / Angel / I love you / Long goodbye
CD ________ CDSTUMM 138
Mute / Oct '95 / RTM/Disc

I SAY, I SAY, I SAY
CD ________ CDSTUMM 115
Mute / May '94 / RTM/Disc

INNOCENTS, THE
Little respect / Ship of fools / Phantom bride / Chains of love / Hallowed ground / 65,000 / Heart of stone / Yahoo / Imagination / Witch in the ditch / Weight of the world
CD ________ CDSTUMM 55
Mute / Apr '88 / RTM/Disc

POP - THE FIRST 20 HITS
Who needs love like that / Heavenly action / Oh l'amour / Sometimes / It doesn't have to be / Victim of love / Circus / Ship of fools / Chains of love / Little respect / Stop / Drama / You surround me / Blue savanna / Star / Chorus / Love to hate you / Am I right / Breath of life / Take a chance on me / Who needs love like that (remix)
CD ________ CDMUTEL 2
Mute / Nov '92 / RTM/Disc

TWO RING CIRCUS
CD ________ CDSTUMM 35 R
Mute / '87 / RTM/Disc

WILD
Piano song (instrumental) / Blue Savannah / Drama / How many times / Star / La Gloria / You surround me / Brother and sister / 2000 miles / Crown of thorns / Piano song
CD ________ CDSTUMM 75
Mute / Oct '89 / RTM/Disc

WONDERLAND
Who needs love like that / Reunion / Cry so easy / Push me, shove me / Heavenly action / Say what / Love is a loser / Senseless / My heart... so blue / Oh l'amour / Pistol
CD ________ CDSTUMM 25
Mute / '86 / RTM/Disc

Erazerhead

SHELLSHOCKED - BEST OF ERAZERHEAD
CD ________ AHOY 28
Captain Oi / Dec '94 / Plastic Head

Erdegran, Lars

CRESCENT CITY CHRISTMAS
CD ________ BCD 425
GHB / Jan '97 / Jazz Music

Erdmann, Dietrich

WORKS FOR STRING ORCHESTRA
CD ________ CTH 2145
Thorofon / Jul '92 / DI Music

Ergin, Mehmet

BEYOND THE SEVEN HILLS
Sema / Beyond the seven hills / Cabuk / Rumeli / Two parts / Nine faces / Selling the aroma / Sun of tabriz / Spiral / Tiptoe dancin'
CD ________ MCD 70020
MCA / Nov '96 / BMG

Erguner Brothers

PRELUDE TO CEREMONIES OF THE WHIRLING DERVISHES
CD ________ VICG 50052
JVC World Library / Mar '96 / ADA / CM / Direct

Erguner, Kudsi

DERVISHES OF TURKEY - SUFI MUSIC
CD ________ PS 65120
PlayaSound / Feb '94 / ADA / Harmonia Mundi

PESHREV & SEMAI OF TANBURI DJEMI BEY
Seddiaraban peshrev / Taksim on tanbur / Seddiaraban saz semaisi / Muhayyer peshrev / Muhayyer saz semaisi / Taksim on oud and kanun / Ferahfeza peshrev / Taksim on the ney / Ferahfeza saz semaisi / Neva peshrev / Huseyni / Nikriz sirto
CD ________ CMPCD 3013
CMP / Oct '94 / Cargo / Grapevine/PolyGram / Vital/SAM

Eric & The Good Good Feeling

FUNKY
CD ________ EQNCD 1
Equinox / Nov '89 / Total/BMG

Eric B & Rakim

PAID IN FULL
I ain't no joke / Eric B is on the cut / My melody / I know you got soul / Move the crowd / As the rhyme goes on / Chinese arithmetic / Eric B for president / Extended beat / Paid in full
CD ________ IMCD 9
4th & Broadway / '89 / PolyGram

Erick

ESTRANGED
Progress / Terry / Anarchy / 4004 BC 9 a.m. / Beast / Martini 2000 / Egyptians in space / Half hearted Jon / 2 Ways 2 love U / Moral village / Death boll tell
CD ________ CLOD 14
Fragment / Aug '93 / Fragment Records

Erickson, Eddie

ON EASY STREET
CD ________ ARCD 19111
Arbors Jazz / Nov '94 / Cadillac

Erickson, Lenita

LENITA ERICKSON
CD ________ DCD 9628
Dream Circle / Nov '96 / Cargo / Plastic Head

Erickson, Roky

ALL THAT MAY DO MY RHYME
CD ________ TR 33CD
Trance / Feb '95 / SRD

CLICK YOUR FINGERS APPLAUDING THE PLAY
CD ________ 422130
New Rose / May '94 / ADA / Direct / Discovery

GREMLINS HAVE PICTURES
Night of the vampire / Interpreter / Song to Abe Lincoln / John Lawman / Anthem / Warning / Sweet honey pie / I am / Cold night for alligators / Heroin / I have always been here before / Before in the beginning
CD ________ FIENDCD 66
Demon / Oct '90 / Pinnacle

I THINK OF DEMONS (Erickson, Roky & The Aliens)
Two headed dog / I think of demons / I walked with a zombie / Don't shake me Lucifer / Night of the vampire / Bloody hammer / White faces / Cold night for alligators / Creature with the atom brain / Mine mine mind / Stand for the fire / Wind and more
CD ________ EDCD 528
Edsel / Jun '97 / Pinnacle

LIVE DALLAS 1979 (Erickson, Roky & The Nervebreakers)
CD ________ 422404
New Rose / May '94 / ADA / Direct / Discovery

LOVE TO SEE YOU BLEED
CD ________ SFMDCD 2
Swordfish / Feb '93 / RTM/Disc

MAD DOG
CD ________ SFMDCD 001
Swordfish / Feb '92 / RTM/Disc

WHERE THE PYRAMID MEETS THE EYE (A Tribute To Roky Erickson) (Various Artists)
Reverberation (doubt): *ZZ Top* / If you have ghosts: *Harding, John Wesley* / I had to tell you: *Poi Dog Pondering* / She lives in a time of her own: *Judybats* / Slip inside this house: *Primal Scream* / You don't love me yet: *Bongwater* / I have always been here before: *Cope, Julian* / You're gonna miss me: *Sahm, Doug & Sons* / Cold night for alligators: *Southern Pacific* / Fire engine: *Lloyd, Richard* / Bermuda: *Vibrating Egg* / I walked with a zombie: *REM* / Earthquake: *Butthole Surfers* / Don't slander me: *Barton, Lou Ann* / Red temple prayer (two headed dog): *Sister Double Happiness* / Burn the flames: *Thin White Rope* / Postures (leave your body behind): *Thomas, Chris & Tabby* / Nothing in return: *Burnett, T-Bone* / Splash 1 / We sell soul / White faces / Reverberation (doubt): *Jesus & Mary Chain*
CD ________ 7599264222
Sire / Feb '91 / Warner Music

Eric's Trip

ALBUM
CD ________ SPCD 136336
Sub Pop / Oct '94 / Cargo / Greyhound / Shellshock/Disc

LOVE TARA
CD ________ SPCD 115293
Sub Pop / Nov '93 / Cargo / Greyhound / Shellshock/Disc

PETER
CD ________ SPCD 102/274
Sub Pop / Jun '93 / Cargo / Greyhound / Shellshock/Disc

PURPLE BLUE
CD ________ SPCD 333
Sub Pop / Jan '96 / Cargo / Greyhound / Shellshock/Disc

Ericson, Rolf

STOCKHOLM SWEETNIN'
CD ________ DRCD 256
Dragon / Oct '94 / ADA / Cadillac / CM / Roots / Wellard

Ericsson, Lena

DOODLIN'
Days of wine and roses / Doodlin' / Too long at the fair / Love for sale / My second home / Cheek to cheek / Hey John / But not for me / (I'm afraid) the masquerade is over
CD ________ NCD 8808
Phontastic / Dec '94 / Cadillac / Jazz Music / Wellard

Erkose Ensemble

TURKISH TZIGANE MUSIC
CD ________ CMP CD 3010
CMP / Jul '92 / Cargo / Grapevine/ PolyGram / Vital/SAM

Eroglu, Musa

INSTRUMENTAL MUSIC FROM ANATOLIA (Eroglu, Musa & Arif Sag)
CD ________ 926202
BUDA / Jul '95 / Discovery

Erosion

DOWN
CD ________ WB 1138CD
We Bite / Feb '96 / Plastic Head

EROSION VOL.3
CD ________ WB 095CD
We Bite / Nov '92 / Plastic Head

MORTAL AGONY
CD ________ WB 036CD
We Bite / Dec '88 / Plastic Head

Erotic Dissidents

NAKED ANGEL
Introduction / Jack to the air / Sure beats are working / Right rhythm, right time / Off your ass / Mind fuck / TWAT / Body language / I wanna be loved by you / Move your ass / Shake your hips
CD ________ SD 4005 CD
SPV / Jul '89 / Koch / Plastic Head

Erotic Suicide

ABUSEMENT PARK
CD ________ 341972
No Bull / Oct '95 / Koch

Erraji, Hassan

IA DOUNIA (Erraji, Hassan & Arabesque/Sabra)
CD ________ TUGCD 002
Riverboat / Nov '90 / New Note/Pinnacle / Stern's

MUSIC FOR ARABIAN DULCIMER AND LUTE
CD ______ SDL 415CD
Saydisc / Mar '96 / ADA / Direct / Harmonia Mundi

Erskine, Peter

AS IT IS
Glebe ascending / Lady in the lake / Episode / Woodcocks / Esperanca / Touch her soft lips and part / Au contraire / For Ruth / Romeo and Juliet
CD ______ 4290852
ECM / May '96 / New Note/Pinnacle

PETER ERSKINE
Leroy Street / ESP / All's well that ends / Coyote blues / In statu nascendi / Change of mind / My ship
CD ______ OJCCD 610
Original Jazz Classics / Feb '92 / Complete/ Pinnacle / Jazz Music / Wellard

SWEET SOUL
Touch her soft lips and part / Press enter / Sweet soul / To be or not to be / Ambivalence / Angels and devils / Speak low / Scholastic / Distant blossom / But is it art / In your own sweet way
CD ______ PD 90616
Novus / May '92 / BMG

TIME BEING (Erskine, Peter & John Taylor/Palle Danielsson)
CD ______ 5217192
ECM / Sep '94 / New Note/Pinnacle

Erstrand, Lars

DREAM DANCING
CD ______ OP 9101CD
Opus 3 / Sep '91 / Direct / Jazz Music

LARS ERSTRAND
CD ______ CD 19405
Opus 3 / May '96 / Direct / Jazz Music

LARS ERSTRAND AND FOUR BROTHERS (Erstrand, Lars & Four Brothers)
CD ______ OP 8402CD
Opus 3 / Sep '91 / Direct / Jazz Music

TRIBUTE TO LIONEL HAMPTON (Erstrand, Lars & Wobbling Woodwinds)
CD ______ NCD 8835
Phontastic / Feb '95 / Cadillac / Jazz Music / Wellard

Ervin, Booker

BLUES BOOK
Blues book / Eeerie dearie / One for Mort / No booze blooze / True blue
CD ______ OJCCD 780
Original Jazz Classics / Jan '94 / Complete/ Pinnacle / Jazz Music / Wellard

SONG BOOK, THE
Lamp is low / Come Sunday / All the things you are / Just friends / Yesterdays / Our love is here to stay
CD ______ OJCCD 779
Original Jazz Classics / Apr '94 / Complete/ Pinnacle / Jazz Music / Wellard

SPACE BOOK, THE
Number two / I can't get started / Mojo / There is no greater love
CD ______ OJCCD 896
Original Jazz Classics / Oct '96 / Complete/ Pinnacle / Jazz Music / Wellard

THAT'S IT
Mojo / Uranus / Poinciana / Speak low / Booker's blues / Boo
CD ______ CCD 79014
Candid / Feb '97 / Cadillac / Direct / Jazz Music / Koch / Wellard

Eschete, Ron

CLOSER LOOK, A
Like someone in love / One for Pop / When it's sleepy time down South/Stars fell on Alabama / Do you know what it means to miss New Orleans / You stepped out of a dream / I'll be seeing you / Mona Lisa / Amazing Grace / Stardust / Coquette / My foolish heart / Manha De Carnaval / My blue heaven
CD ______ CCD 4607
Concord Jazz / Jul '94 / New Note/Pinnacle

COME RAIN OR COME SHINE
Azul serape / Some other time / Come rain or come shine / Theme for Jeff / Naima / Girl next door / Moanin' / Nuages / Loads of love / Goodbye
CD ______ CCD 4665
Concord Jazz / Sep '95 / New Note/ Pinnacle

SOFT WINDS
I'll close my eyes / Sleepwalk / 1-5 blues / Where or when / Because of you / Sweet and lovely / But beautiful / Soft winds / Rumpled silk skin / My romance
CD ______ CCD 4737
Concord Jazz / Dec '96 / New Note/ Pinnacle

Escorts

FROM THE BLUE ANGEL
Dizzy Miss Lizzy / All I want is you / One to cry / Tell me baby / I don't want to go without you / Don't forget to write / C'mon home baby / You'll get no lovin' that way / Let it be me / Mad mad world / From head to toe / Night time
CD ______ EDCD 422
Edsel / May '95 / Pinnacle

Escorts

PRISONERS OF SOUL
I'll be sweeter tomorrow / By the time I get to Phoenix / Little green apples / All we need (is another chance) / Look over your shoulder / I'm so glad I found you / Ooh baby baby / Disrespect can wreck / Let's make love (at home sometimes) / Corruption (man's self destruction) / We've come too far to end it now / Brother / I only have eyes for you / Shoo nough / La la means I love you / Within without / I can't stand to see you cry
CD ______ NEMCD 931
Sequel / Jul '97 / BMG

Escoude, Christian

GIPSY WALTZ (Escoude, Christian Gipsy Octet)
Soir de dispute / Jeannette / Bluesette / Swing valse / Django / Flambee / Montalbanaise / Carmette / Valse Catalane
CD ______ 8387722
EmArCy / Jan '90 / PolyGram

HOLIDAYS (Escoude, Christian Gipsy Trio)
Bird alone / J'aime Paris au mois de Mai / Holiday for strings / Nem um talvez / Que nadie sepa mi sufrir / La foule / Cavatina / Day I met Bill Evans / After you've gone / Lyle's song
CD ______ 5143042
EmArCy / Feb '94 / PolyGram

WITH STRINGS (Christian Escoude Plays Django Reinhardt)
Django for ever / Anouman / Diminuswing / Djangology / Belleville / Troublant bolero / Nuages / Nuits de St. Germain des pres / Sweet chorus / Manoir de mes reves / Improvisation / Swing 39 / Django for ever
CD ______ 5101322
EmArCy / Jan '93 / PolyGram

Escovedo, Alejandro

13 YEARS
CD ______ WMCD 1017
Watermelon / Sep '96 / ADA / Direct

END, THE/LOSING YOUR TOUCH
CD ______ WMCD 0017
Watermelon / Sep '96 / ADA / Direct

GRAVITY
Paradise / Broken bottle / By eleven / Bury me / Five hearts breaking / Oxford / Last to know / She doesn't live here anymore / Pyramid of tears / Gravity/Falling down again
CD ______ 422409
New Rose / May '94 / ADA / Direct / Discovery
CD ______ WMCD 1007
Watermelon / Nov '96 / ADA / Direct

WITH THESE HANDS
Put you down / Slip / Crooked frame / 2 am / Nickel and a spoon / Little bottles / Sometimes / Guilty was his name / Tired skin / With these hands / Tugboat (fro Sterling Morrison)
CD ______ RCD 10343
Rykodisc / Mar '96 / ADA / Vital

Escovedo, Pete

E STREET
Another star / Sambacu / Fantasy / Boomerang / Smile please / Like a volcano / You're my little girl / La familia / Waterfall / Lord remember me
CD ______ CCD 47482
Concord Vista / Apr '97 / New Note/ Pinnacle

FLYING SOUTH
Flying South / All this love / Cabo frio / Tiemblas / Flying easy / Still life / Esta noche / Como rien / Leyte / Canto para chango / El alma de carnival
CD ______ CCD 4684
Concord Jazz / Feb '96 / New Note/ Pinnacle

YESTERDAY'S MEMORIES - TOMORROW'S DREAMS
Charango sunrise / Moving pictures / Azteca Mozambique / Ah ah / Cueros / Modern dance / Zina's Zamba / Yesterday's memories, tomorrow's dreams / Revolt
CD ______ CCD 45002
Concord Jazz / Jul '87 / New Note/Pinnacle

Eskalte Gaeste

KUNSTSCHEISSE
CD ______ EFA 11891
EFA / Apr '93 / SRD

Eskelin, Ellery

FIGURE OF SPEECH
CD ______ 1212322
Soul Note / Apr '93 / Cadillac / Harmonia Mundi / Wellard

SUN DIED, THE
CD ______ 1212822
Soul Note / Oct '96 / Cadillac / Harmonia Mundi / Wellard

Eskenazi, Roza

REMBETISSA
Rast Gazel / Ousak Mare / Mes'tou Zambikou ton teke / Ferte Birres / Derti ke Pono Apoktisa / Yiati Foumaro Kokaini / Hariklaki / Yinome Andhras / Konialis / Dhodheka Cronon Koritsi / Barberaki / Yiannoula / Me Zournadhes Ke Daoulia / Yiannousena / Ouzo, hasis / O Xenitevmenos / Mes' to Vathi Skotadhi / Tou Psara o Tios / To Gri Gri / Ta Dhika Sou Ta Sfalmata
CD ______ ROUCD 1080
Rounder / Sep '96 / ADA / CM / Direct

REMBETISSA 1933-1936
CD ______ HTCD 35
Heritage / Jun '97 / ADA / Direct / Hot Shot / Jazz Music / Swift / Wellard

Eskens, Margot

EIN HERZ, DAS KANN MAN NICHT KAUFEN
CD ______ BCD 15952
Bear Family / Jun '96 / Direct / Rollercoaster / Swift

OB IN BOMBAY, OB IN RIO
Ob in Bombay, ob in Rio / Coeur blesse, armes herz / Mein schonster traum / Gluck und tranen / Si petite / Melodie von laramie / Oh Smoky, oh Smoky / Sole, sole / Schau' mich an / Eine reise in die vergangerheit / Ich tausche mit keinem auf der welt / Ein bisschen seligkeit / Moonlight song / Mama / Vergiss mein nicht / Serenade der liebe / Lieberlei ist leider keine liebe / Wenn die sonne hinter den dachern versinkt / Eine weisse hochzeitskutsche: *Eskens, Margot & Kurt Stelly* / Mutti, du darfst doch nicht weinen / Es kam der fruhling / Einsamer sonntag / Bald schon da sehen wir uns wieder / Sail to Bombay, sail to Rio / Mama / Si tu m'aimes tant que ca / Melancolie / Quaranta notti / Ma melodie
CD ______ BCD 16138
Bear Family / Apr '97 / Direct / Rollercoaster / Swift

Eskimos & Egypt

PERFECT DISEASE
CD ______ TPLP 37CD
One Little Indian / Sep '93 / Pinnacle

Eskovitz, Bruce

ONE FOR NEWK
Moving out / No moe / Airegin / Poor butterfly / Valse hot / Paradox / Strode rode / Pent-up house / Count your blessings / Tenor madness
CD ______ 378012
Koch Jazz / May '96 / Koch

ESP Summer

ESP SUMMER
CD ______ PER 005
Perdition Plastics / May '97 / Cargo

Espacio, Cuarto

REENCUENTRO
Tumbania / Sancho / Reencuentro / Pantera / Tranquilidad / Polka and son / Reencuentro (reprise) / Hay gritos / Momo
CD ______ INT 30602
Intuition / Nov '93 / New Note/Pinnacle

Esperanto

ESPERANTO
You're the one / Are you the best / Only a miracle / Turning point / All good things / Love affair / Don't let love pass away / Something that you said / Glad that you were mine
CD ______ SJRCD 023
Soul Jazz / Mar '95 / New Note/Pinnacle / Timewarp / Vital

Espinasse, Philippe

CAMINS (Espinasse, Philippe & J.M.)
CD ______ 173192
Musidisc / Jan '97 / Discovery

Espiritu

ANOTHER LIFE
CD ______ HVNLP 18CD
CD ______ HVNLP 18CDX
Heavenly / Aug '97 / 3mv/Pinnacle / BMG / Vital

Esplendor Geometrico

CONTOL REMOTO 1.0
CD ______ EFA 015642
Apocalyptic Vision / Feb '96 / Cargo / Plastic Head / SRD

ESPLENDOR GEOMETRICO 1980-1988
CD ______ AV 020CD
Apocalyptic Vision / Nov '96 / Cargo / Plastic Head / SRD

Esplin, Joss

SCOTLAND 'TIL I RETURN (Esplin, Joss & Sandra Wright)
CD ______ JJCD 1020
Beechwood / Jan '93 / Duncans / Ross

Esposito, Favio

NEAPOLITAN SONGS
CD ______ 926702
BUDA / Apr '97 / Discovery

Esposito, Gene

RHYTHM SECTION
CD ______ PS 004CD
P&S / Sep '95 / Discovery

Esquerita

SOCK IT TO ME BABY
Introduction by Little Richard / Sock it to me baby / Nobody want you when you're down and out / Mississippidod damn / Wig wearin' baby / I can't stand it anymore / Get along, honey, honey / I guess I'll go through life alone / Never again / Till then / At the Dewdrop Inn / (I don't want nobody gonna) steal my love from me / What's wrong with you
CD ______ BCD 15504
Bear Family / Nov '93 / Direct / Rollercoaster / Swift

Esquire

COMING HOME
CD ______ WCPCD 1011
West Coast / Sep '96 / Koch / Scratch/ BMG

Esquivel, Juan Garcia

CABARET MANANA
Mini skirt / Johnson rag / Night and day / El cable / Harlem nocturne / Mucha muchacha / Time on my hands / Malaguena / Guanacoa / Sentimental journey / Estrellita / Limehouse blues / Todavia / April in Portugal / Take the 'A' train / Question mark / It had to be you / Yeyo / Lullaby of Birdland / Flower girl from Bordeaux
CD ______ 07863666572
RCA / Aug '96 / BMG

OTHER WORLDS, OTHER SOUNDS
Granada / Begin the beguine / Night and day / Poinicana / Playfully / Adios / That old black magic / Nature boy / Magic is the moonlight / Speak low / Ballerina / It had to be you / I only have eyes for you / Anna / Frenesi
CD ______ 74321357472
RCA / Jul '96 / BMG

Essence

DANCING IN THE RAIN (The Best Of Essence)
Out of grace / Like Christ / Only for you / Cat / Everything / Drifting / Mirage / In your heart / Time / Forever in death / Waves of death / Burned in heaven / Endless lakes / Ice / U 4 life / Angelic / How to make me hate / Mirage '94 / Afterworld / Thirty second song
CD ______ CDMGRAM 82
Anagram / Aug '94 / Cargo / Pinnacle

ECSTASY/NOTHING LASTS FOREVER
Burned in Heaven / Only for you / Like Christ / Angelic / Ice / Afterworld / So gorgeously / Despair / One more wasted night / Separation / How you make me hate / September / Out of grace / Everything / Never let go / Air / Thirtysecond song / All is empty
CD ______ CDMGRAM 103
Anagram / Mar '96 / Cargo / Pinnacle

MONUMENT OF TRUST, A
Mirage / Drifting / In teats / Nothing / Waves of death / Happiness / Lollipop / Years of doubt / Fire / Death cell / Monument of trust
CD ______ CDMGRAM 96
Anagram / Sep '95 / Cargo / Pinnacle

PURITY
Last preach / Reflected dream / Cat / Blind / Never mine / Endless lakes / Forever in death / Salvation / Waving girl / Purity / Confusion / From my mouth / Swaying wind
CD ______ CDMGRAM 95
Anagram / Sep '95 / Cargo / Pinnacle

Essence All-Stars

AFRO CUBANO CHANT
CD ______ HIBD 8009
Hip Bop / Feb '96 / Koch / Silva Screen

BONGO BOP
CD ______ HIBD 8017
Hip Bop / May '97 / Koch / Silva Screen

ORGANIC GROOVES
Broadway / Luny tune / True blue / Old wine, new bottles / Smokin'
CD _____ HIBD 8010
Hip Bop / Sep '96 / Koch / Silva Screen

Essex

BEST OF THE ESSEX, THE
Easier said than done / Whenever I need my baby / Where is he / Every night / I love her / Come on to my party / Walkin' miracle / She's got everything / More than it would help / Marriage license / In my dreams / You talk too much / There's no fool like a young fool / Where there's a will / Make him feel like a man / Don't fight it baby / When somethin's hard to get / Just for the boy / I'm making it over / Everybody's got you (for their own) / Be my baby / Be sure / When the music stops / Real true lover
CD _____ NEMCD 714
Sequel / Nov '94 / BMG

Essex, David

BACK TO BACK
Africa / Father and son / Fall at your feet / Awesome story / True love ways / Love train / Singin' the blues / Never meant to hurt you / You really got me / Really nice / Won't back down / Oh Father
CD _____ 5237902
Polydor / Oct '94 / PolyGram

BEST OF DAVID ESSEX, THE
Hold me close / Gonna make you a star / If I could / Lamplight / Coming home / Cool out tonight / Bring in the sun / For Emily, whenever I might find her / Rolling stone / City lights / Stardust / Good ol' rock and roll / Turn me loose / America / On and on
CD _____ 4810362
Columbia / Dec '95 / Sony

COLLECTION, THE
Oh what a circus / Heart on my sleeve / No substitutes / Imperial wizard / Silver dream machine / Hot love / Ships that pass in the night / Me and my girl (Night-clubbing) / High flying, adored / Winter's tale / Smile / Won't change me now / Goodbye first love / Tahiti / Fishing for the moon / You're in my heart / Falling angels riding
CD _____ 5517952
Spectrum / Nov '95 / PolyGram

COVER SHOT
Everlasting love / Time after time / Waterloo sunset / First cut is the deepest / Here comes the night / Paint it black / Out of time / Horse with no name / Letter / I can't let Maggie go / New York mining disaster 1941 / Summer in the city
CD _____ 5145632
PolyGram TV / Mar '93 / PolyGram

GREATEST HITS
Rock on / Gonna make you a star / Hold me close / Winter's tale / Oh what a circus / Silver dream machine / My and my girl (nightclubbing) / Tahiti / Lamplight / Stardust / Cool out tonight / If I could / Myfanwy / Rollin' stone / You're in my heart / Sun ain't gonna shine anymore / Africa - you shine / Rock on (new version)
CD _____ 5103082
Mercury / Oct '91 / PolyGram

MISSING YOU
CD _____ 5295822
PolyGram TV / Nov '95 / PolyGram

NIGHT AT THE MOVIES, A
Girl, you'll be a woman soon / Can you feel the love tonight / Crying game / Wind beneath my wings / Stardust / Together in electric dreams / Oh what a circus / Seperate lives / St. Elmo's fire / Kiss from a rose / Somewhere out there / Silver dream machine / Sea of love / If I had words (anthem)
CD _____ 55376082
PolyGram TV / May '97 / PolyGram

SHOWSTOPPERS
Phantom of the opera / Bright eyes / Forty second street/Lullaby of Broadway / Summertime / Ghostbusters / Save the people / Out here on my own / I dreamed a dream / Corner on the sky / Tahiti
CD _____ MSCD 14
Music De-Luxe / Mar '95 / TKO Magnum

SPOTLIGHT ON DAVID ESSEX
CD _____ 8481812
Mercury / Jul '93 / PolyGram

Essig, David

REBEL FLAG
CD _____ APCD 072
Appaloosa / '92 / ADA / Direct / TKO Magnum

TREMBLE AND WEEP
CD _____ APCD 126
Appaloosa / Jun '96 / ADA / Direct / TKO Magnum

Essix, Eric

FIRST IMPRESSIONS
CD _____ NOVA 8920
Nova / Sep '92 / New Note/Pinnacle

SECOND THOUGHTS
CD _____ NOVA 9138
Nova / Sep '92 / New Note/Pinnacle

Estefan, Gloria

ABRIENDOS
Abriendo puertas / Tres deseos / Mas alla / Dulce amor / Farolita / Nuevo dia / La parranda / Milagro de amor / Lejos de ti / Felicidade
CD _____ 4809922
Epic / Oct '95 / Sony

ANYTHING FOR YOU (Estefan, Gloria & Miami Sound Machine)
Betcha say that / Let it loose / Can't stay away from you / Give it up / Surrender / Rhythm is gonna get you / Love toy / I want you so bad / 1-2-3 / Anything for you / Rhythm is gonna get you (12" mix) / Betcha say that (remix)
CD _____ 4631252
Epic / Oct '88 / Sony

ANYTHING FOR YOU/CUTS BOTH WAYS
Betcha say that / Let it loose / Can't stay away from you / Give it up / Surrender / Rhythm is gonna get you / Love toy / I want you so bad / 1-2-3 / Anything for you / Rhythm is gonna get you (12" mix) / Betcha say that (Mix) / Ay ay ay / Here we are / Say / Think about you now / Nothin' new / Oye mi canto (Hear my voice) / Don't wanna lose you / Get on your feet / Your love is bad for me / Cuts both ways
CD Set _____ 4784852
Epic / Mar '95 / Sony

ANYTHING FOR YOU/CUTS BOTH WAYS/INTO THE LIGHT (3CD Set)
Betcha say that / Let it loose / Can't stay away from you / Give it up / Surrender / Rhythm is gonna get you / Love toy / I want you so bad / 1-2-3 / Anything for you / Ay, ay / Here we are / Say / Think about you now / Nothin' new / Oye mi canto / Don't wanna lose you / Get on your feet / Your love is bad for me / Cuts both ways / Coming out of the dark / Seal our fate / What goes around / Nayib's song (I am here for you) / Remember me with love / Heart with your name on it / Sex in the 90's / Don't wanna lose you (Portugese version) / Close my eyes / Language of love / Light of love / Can't forget you / Live for loving you / Mama yo can't go / Desda la oscuridad / Words get in the way
CD Set _____ 4853152
Epic / Oct '96 / Sony

CUTS BOTH WAYS
Ay ay ay / Here we are / Say / Think about you / Nothin' oye mi canto / Don't wanna lose you / Get on your feet / Your love is bad for me / Cuts both ways
CD _____ 4651452
Epic / Sep '94 / Sony

DESTINY
Destiny / I'm giving you up / Steal your heart / Heart never learns / You'll be mine (party time) / Path of the right love / Show me the way back to your heart / Along came you (a song for Emily) / Higher / Reach
CD _____ 4839322
Epic / Jun '96 / Sony

EXITOS DE GLORIA ESTEFAN
Renacer / Conga / No sera facil / Dr. Beat / Regresa a mi / No ti olvidare / Dingue li bangue / No me vuelvoa ennamorar / Si voy a perderte / Oye mi canto (hear my voice)
CD _____ 4675202
Epic / Nov '90 / Sony

EYES OF INNOCENCE (Miami Sound Machine)
Dr. Beat / Prisoner of love / OK / Love me / Orange express / I need a man / Eyes of innocence / When someone comes into your life / I need your love / Do you want to dance
CD _____ 4746872
Epic / Feb '97 / Sony

GREATEST HITS
Dr. Beat / Can't stay away from you / Bad boy / 1-2-3 / Anything for you / Here we are / Rhythm is gonna get you / Get on your feet / Don't wanna lose you / Coming out of the dark / Christmas through your eyes / I see your smile / Go away / Always tomorrow
CD _____ 4723322
Epic / Nov '92 / Sony

HOLD ME, THRILL ME, KISS ME
Hold me, thrill me, kiss me / How can I be sure / Everlasting love / Traces / Don't let the sun catch you crying / You've made me so very happy / Turn the beat around / Breaking up is hard to do / Love on a two way street / Cherchez la femme / It's too late / Goodnight my love / Don't let the sun go down on me
CD _____ 4774162
Epic / Oct '94 / Sony

INTO THE LIGHT
Coming out of the dark / Seal our fate / What goes around / Nayib's song (I am here for you) / Remember me with love / Heart with your name on it / Sex in the '90s / Close my eyes / Language of love / Light of love / Can't forget you / Live for loving you / Mama you can't go / Desde la oscuridad
CD _____ 4677822
Epic / Apr '95 / Sony

MI TIERRA
Con los anos que me quedan / Mi Tierra / Ayer / Mi buen Amor / Tus Ojos / No hay mal Que por bien no Venga / Si senor / Volveras / Montuno / Hablemos el Mismo Idioma / Hablas de mi / Tradicion
CD _____ 4737992
Epic / Jun '93 / Sony

PRIMITIVE LOVE (Miami Sound Machine)
Body to body / Primitive love / Words get in the way / Falling in love (Uh-oh) / Conga / Mucho money / You made a fool of me / Movies / Surrender paradise
CD _____ 4634002
Epic / Feb '94 / Sony

Estes, Gene

ON THE EDGE (Estes, Gene Quartet)
CD _____ PCD 7095
Progressive / Jul '96 / Jazz Music

Estes, 'Sleepy' John

BROKE AND HUNGRY
CD _____ DD 608
Delmark / Dec '95 / ADA / Cadillac / CM / Direct / Hot Shot

BROWNSVILLE BLUES
CD _____ DD 613
Delmark / Jan '93 / ADA / Cadillac / CM / Direct / Hot Shot

ELECTRIC SLEEP
CD _____ DD 619
Delmark / Dec '88 / ADA / Cadillac / CM / Direct / Hot Shot

I AIN'T GONNA BE WORRIED NO MORE
CD _____ CD 2004
Yazoo / Sep '92 / ADA / CM / Koch

LEGEND OF SLEEPY JOHN ESTES, THE
CD _____ DD 603
Delmark / May '87 / ADA / Cadillac / CM / Direct / Hot Shot

SLEEPY JOHN ESTES 1929-1937
CD _____ DOCD 5015
Document / Aug '91 / ADA / Hot Shot / Jazz Music

SLEEPY JOHN ESTES 1935-1938
CD _____ BLE 592542
Black & Blue / Dec '92 / Discovery / Koch / Wellard

SLEEPY JOHN ESTES 1937-1941
CD _____ DOCD 5016
Document / Aug '91 / ADA / Hot Shot / Jazz Music

SOMEDAY BABY (The Essential Recordings Of 'Sleepy' John Estes)
This girl I love / She's got long curly hair / Broken hearted / Ragged and dirty too / Divin' duck blues / Milk cow blues / Poor John blues / Stack o'dollars / Stop that thing / Someday baby blues / Married woman blues / Drop down Mama / I ain't gonna be worried no more / Floating bridge / Jack and Jill blues / Everybody oughta make a change / Liquor store blues / New someday baby / Brownsville blues / Special agent / Time is drawing near / Tell me how about it / You shouldn't do that / Lawyer clerk blues
CD _____ IGOCD 2041
Indigo / Nov '96 / ADA / Direct

Estevan, Pedro

NOCTURNOS Y ALLEVOSIAS
CD _____ 21050CD
Sonifolk / Jun '94 / ADA / CM

Estragon, Vladimir

THREE QUARKS FOR MISTER MARK
CD _____ 888803
Tiptoe / Nov '89 / New Note/Pinnacle

Estrand, Lars

BEAUTIFUL FRIENDSHIP, A
CD _____ SITCD 9204
Sittel / Feb '94 / Cadillac / Jazz Music

SECOND SET: BEAUTIFUL FRIENDSHIP
Oh lady be good / Someone to watch over me / 'S wonderful / Our love is here to stay / Man I love / Tiger rag / Dream dancing / Between the devil and the deep blue sea / Things ain't what they used to be
CD _____ SITCD 9205
Sittel / Aug '94 / Cadillac / Jazz Music

Estrellas Caiman

DESCARGA IN NEW YORK
CD _____ CCD 9035
Fresh Sound / Jan '97 / Discovery / Jazz Music

Estudiantina Invasora

ESTUDIANTINA TRADITION, THE
CD _____ NI 5448
Nimbus / Nov '96 / Nimbus

Etant Donnes

ROYAUME
Royaume / Matin / Quatre / Bleu
CD _____ SPL 2
Spiral / Mar '91 / President

Etchingham Steam Band

ETCHINGHAM STEAM BAND, THE
CD _____ FLED 3002
Fledg'ling / Apr '95 / ADA / CM / Direct

Eternal

ALWAYS AND FOREVER
Stay / Crazy / Save our love / Oh baby, I / I'll be there / Sweet funky thing / Never gonna give you up / Just a step from heaven / Let's stay together / This love's for real / So good / If you need me tonight / Don't say goodbye / Amazing grace
CD _____ CDEMD 1053
EMI / Nov '93 / EMI

BEFORE THE RAIN
Don't you love me / I wanna be the only one / How many tears / Grace under pressure / Someday / Think about me / Promises / I'm still crying / All my love / What do you mean / Why am I waiting / It's never too late
CD _____ CDEMD 1103
EMI / Mar '97 / EMI

POWER OF A WOMAN
Power of a woman / I am blessed / Good thing / Telling you now / Hurry up / Redemption song / It will never end / Who are you / Secrets / Your smile / Don't make me wait / Up to you / Faith in love
CD _____ CDEMD 1090
EMI / Sep '97 / EMI

Eternal Afflict

JAHWEH KDRESH
CD _____ EFA 112642
Danse Macabre / Mar '94 / SRD

LUMINOGRAPHIC AGONY
CD _____ EFA 11252
Glasnost / Apr '93 / SRD

NOW MIND REVOLUTION
CD _____ EFA 11258
Glasnost / Apr '93 / SRD

WAR
CD _____ EFA 155762
Gymnastic / Dec '94 / SRD

Eternal Basement

NERV
CD _____ HHCD 011
Harthouse / Apr '95 / Mo's Music Machine / Prime / Vital

Eternal Dirge

KHAOS MAGICK
CD _____ SPV 08412662
SPV / Aug '96 / Koch / Plastic Head

Eterne

STILL DREAMING
CD _____ CANDLE 009CD
Candlelight / Sep '95 / Plastic Head

Ethel The Frog

ETHEL THE FROG
Eleanor Rigby / Apple of your eye / Staying on my mind / You need wheels / Bleeding heart / Fight back / Don't do it / Why don't you ask / Whatever happened to love / Fire bird
CD _____ CDMETAL 11
Anagram / Jun '97 / Cargo / Pinnacle

Ethereal

OMSANTHI
CD _____ USR 019CD
Unisound / Jan '96 / Plastic Head

Ethereal Winds

FIND THE WAY
CD _____ CYBERCD 14
Cyber / May '95 / Amato Disco / Arabesque / Plastic Head

Etheridge, John

ASH
In / Ash / Venerable bede / Ugetsu / Baiere / Your own sweet way / Chips / Infant eyes / Nardis / You don't know what love is / There is no greater love / Little wing / 81 / Out
CD _____ VP 175CD
Voiceprint / Sep '94 / Pinnacle

Etheridge, Melissa

BRAVE AND CRAZY
No souvenirs / Brave and crazy life / You used to love to dance / Angels / You can sleep while I drive / Testify / Let me go / My back door / Skin deep / Royal station 4/16
CD _____ IMCD 241
Island / Mar '97 / PolyGram

MELISSA ETHERIDGE
Similar features / Chrome plated heart / Like the way I do / Precious pain / Don't need / Late September dogs / Occasionally / Watching you / Bring me some water / I want you
CD ______ CID 9879
Island / May '88 / PolyGram

NEVER ENOUGH
2001 / It's for you / Letting go / Keep it precious / Boy feels strange / Meet me in the back / Must be crazy for me / Place your hand / Dance without sleeping / Ain't it heavy
CD ______ IMCD 214
Island / Mar '96 / PolyGram

YES I AM
I'm the only one / If I wanted to / Come to my window / Silent legacy / I will never be the same / All American girl / Yes I am / Resist / Ruins / Talking to my angel
CD ______ CID 8010
Island / Apr '94 / PolyGram

YOUR LITTLE SECRET
Your little secret / I really like you / Nowhere to go / Unusual kiss / I want to come over / All the way to heaven / I could have been you / Shriner's park / Change / War is over
CD ______ CID 8042
Island / Nov '95 / PolyGram

Ethik

INDIVIDUAL TRAFFIC (Ethik II)
CD ______ EAT 003CD
Eat Raw / Oct '95 / Cargo / Plastic Head

MUSIC FOR STOCK EXCHANGE
CD ______ DIGI 1001CD
Digitrax / Oct '95 / Plastic Head

Ethiopians

CLAP YOUR HANDS
CD ______ LG 21086
Lagoon / Sep '93 / Grapevine/PolyGram

LET'S SKA AND ROCK STEADY
CD ______ JMC 200103
Jamaican Gold / Nov '92 / Grapevine/ PolyGram / Jet Star

ORIGINAL REGGAE HIT SOUNDS
Free man / Train to Skaville / Engine 54 / Come on now / Train to glory / Whip / Everything crash / Things a get bad to worse / Well red / One / Hong Kong flu / Gun man / What a fire / Woman capture man / Feel the spirit / Drop him / Good ambition / No baptism / Selah / Pirate / Word is love
CD ______ CDTRL 228
Trojan / Mar '94 / Direct / Jet Star

OWNER FE DE YARD
CD ______ HBCD 127
Heartbeat / Apr '94 / ADA / Direct / Greensleeves / Jet Star

SIR JJ & FRIENDS
CD ______ LG 21088
Lagoon / Sep '93 / Grapevine/PolyGram

SLAVE CALL
CD ______ HBCD 56
Heartbeat / Nov '92 / ADA / Direct / Greensleeves / Jet Star

WOMAN CAPTURE MAN
CD ______ RB 3006
Reggae Best / Jul '94 / Grapevine/ PolyGram

WORLD GOES SKA, THE
I need you / Do it sweet / Stay loose mama / World goes ska / Give me your love / You get the dough / Sh-boom / Long time now / I'm not losing now / Everyday talking / Wreck it up / Hang on (don't let it go) / I'll never get burnt / So you look on it / He's not a rebel / Mothers tender care / Sad news / Rim bam bam / I need someone / Solid as a rock
CD ______ CDTRL 312
Trojan / Mar '94 / Direct / Jet Star

Ethyl Meatplow

HAPPY DAYS, SWEETHEART
Suck / Devil's johnson / Car / Queenie / Close to you / Tommy / Mustard requiem / Abazab / Ripened peach / Feed / Rise / For my sleepy lover / Sad bear / Coney island
CD ______ 3704613542
WEA / Oct '90 / Warner Music

Etnica

ALIEN PROTEIN
CD ______ BR 014CD
Blue Room Released / Apr '96 / Essential/ BMG / SRD

Etoile 2000

DAKAR SOUND VOL.1
CD ______ 2002868
Dakar Sound / Jan '97 / Stern's

Etoile De Dakar

XALIS
CD ______ ADC 303
PAM / Feb '94 / ADA / Direct

Etting, Ruth

LOVE ME OR LEAVE ME
CD ______ PASTCD 7061
Flapper / Jan '96 / Pinnacle

TEN CENTS A DANCE
Ten cents a dance / Button up your overcoat / Funny, dear, what love can do / But I do, you know I do / Mean to me / I'm yours / If I could be with you one hour tonight / Don't tell him what happened to me / Body and soul / Sam, the old accordion man / Dancing with tears in my eyes / Hello baby / What wouldn't I do for that man / Could I, certainly could / Kiss waltz / Shakin' the blues away / You're the cream in my coffee / Lonesome and sorry / Laughing at life / Love me or leave me
CD ______ CDAJA 5008
Living Era / '88 / Select

Etzel, Roy

SERENADE
CD ______ INT 860196
Interchord / '88 / CM

Eubanks, Kevin

BEST OF KEVIN EUBANKS, THE
Moments aren't momoments / Sorrir / Smile / Wave / Cookin' / Face to face / Navigator / It's all the same to me / Essence / Forbidden romance / Hope / Songhouse
CD ______ GRP 98402
GRP / Jan '96 / New Note/BMG

FACE TO FACE
Face to face / That's what friends are for / Essence / Silent waltz / Moments aren't moments / Wave / Relaxin' at Camarillo / Ebony surprise / Trick bag
CD ______ GRP 95392
GRP / Jan '93 / New Note/BMG

LIVE AT BRADLEYS
Speak low / Sometimes I feel like a Motherless child / June in January / In a sentimental mood / Alter ego / Red top / Mercy mercy mercy
CD ______ CDP 8301332
Blue Note / Oct '96 / EMI

Eubanks, Robin

DEDICATION (Eubanks, Robin & Steve Turre)
New breed / VO / Red, black and green blues / Trance dance / Perpetual groove / Especially for you / Koncepts / Victory
CD ______ 8344332
jMT / Jul '90 / PolyGram

DIFFERENT PERSPECTIVES
Midtown / Night before / Taicho / You don't know what love is / Overjoyed / Walkin' / Different perspectives
CD ______ 8344242
jMT / Feb '89 / PolyGram

KARMA
Karma / Mino / Maybe next time / Evidently (for Thelonious Monk) / Send one your love / Never give up / Yearning / Pentacourse / Resolution of love / Remember when (for Art Blakey)
CD ______ 8344462
jMT / May '91 / PolyGram

WAKE UP CALL
United / Ceora / Soliloquy / Oriental folk song / Wake up call / You are too beautiful / Scrapple from the apple / Rush hour
CD ______ SJL 1001
Sirocco / Sep '97 / New Note/Pinnacle

Eugenius

EUGENIUS
CD ______ PAPCD 011
Paperhouse / Aug '92 / RTM/Disc

MARY QUEEN OF SCOTS
CD ______ RUST 008CD
Creation / Jan '94 / 3mv/Vital

Eulogy

ESSENCE
CD ______ SPV 077140782
SPV / Sep '94 / Koch / Plastic Head

Euphone

EUPHONE
CD ______ HEFTY 06
Hefty / May '97 / Cargo

Euphoria

GIFT FROM EUPHORIA, A
Lisa / Stone river hill song / Did you get the letter / Through a window / Young Miss Pflugg / Lady Bedford / Suicide on the hillside, Sunday morning, after tea / Sweet Fanny Adams / I'll be home to you / Sunhine woman / Hollyville train / Docker's son / Something for the milkman / Too young to know
CD ______ SEECD 465
See For Miles/C5 / Oct '96 / Pinnacle

Euro Grass

MADE IN EUROPE
Headin' West / When I get to the border / Lookin' out my back door / Once upon a heartbeat / Que Rico Chacoli De Sopuerta / Ocean front property / Woodstock / You've got a crazy heart / Old Indian dream / Pure homemeade love / Cajun girl / Don't think twice, it's alright / TPPC
CD ______ SCRA 6
Strictly Country / Feb '97 / ADA / Direct

Eurogroove

IN THE GROOVE
CD ______ AVEXCD 28
CD ______ AVEXCDX 28X
CD ______ AVEXCD 29R
Avex / Apr '96 / 3mv/Pinnacle

Europa String Choir

STARVING MOON, THE
Monkey never lies / Sermon on the Mount / Waltz / Mama Tequila / Delicate little me / Carol / Saving grace / Camomilla / La pasta / Prelude / Dancing bride / Little Sinfonie / Health food frenzy / Starving moon
CD ______ DGM 9509
Discipline / Nov '95 / Pinnacle

Europe

EUROPE
In the future to come / Female / Seven doors hotel / King will return / Boyazant / Children of the time / Words of wisdom / Paradise beach / Memories
CD ______ 4777862
Columbia / Feb '97 / Sony

EUROPE 1982-1992
In the future to come / Seven doors hotel / Stormwind / Open your heart / Scream of anger / Dreamer / Final countdown / On broken wings / Rock the night / Carrie / Cherokee / Superstitious / Ready or not / Prisoners in paradise (Single edit) / I'll cry for you / Sweet love child / Yesterday's news
CD ______ 4735892
Epic / Mar '96 / Sony

FINAL COUNTDOWN, THE
Love chaser / On the loose / Heart of stone / Time has come / Final countdown / Cherokee / Ninja / Danger on the track / Rock the night / Carrie
CD ______ 4663282
Epic / Mar '90 / Sony

European Concert Orchestra

EUROPEAN FAVOURITES
European anthem / White cliffs of Dover / We'll keep a welcome / Skye boat song / La vie en rose / Luxembourg polka / Walk in the Black Forest / Granada / Portuguese washerwoman / Chanson des Scieurs de long / Tulips from Amsterdam / O sole mio / Wonderful Copenhagen / Zorba's dance / Danny boy
CD ______ CDEURO 1
Premier/MFP / Feb '92 / EMI

European Music Orchestra

GUEST
CD ______ SN 1212992
Soul Note / Oct '94 / Cadillac / Harmonia Mundi / Wellard

Eurythmics

BE YOURSELF TONIGHT
It's alright (baby's coming back) / Would I lie to you / There must be an angel (playing with my heart) / I love you like a ball and chain / Sisters are doin' it for themselves: *Eurythmics & Aretha Franklin* / Conditioned soul / Adrian / Here comes that sinking feeling / Better to have lost in love than never to have loved at all
CD ______ ND 74602
RCA / May '90 / BMG

EURYTHMICS LIVE 1983-1989 (2CD Set)
Never gonna cry again / Love is a stranger / Sweet dreams (are made of this) / This city never sleeps / Somebody told me / Who's that girl / Right by your side / Here comes the rain again / Sexcrime (1984) / I love you like a ball and chain / Would I lie to you / There must be an angel (playing with my heart) / Thorn in my side / Let's go / Missionary man / Last time / Miracle of love / I need a man / We too are one / (My my) Baby's gonna cry / Don't ask me why / Angel / I need you / You have placed a chill in my heart / Here comes the rain again (acoustic) / Would I lie to you (acoustic) / It's alright (Baby's coming back) / Right by your side (acoustic) / When tomorrow comes
CD Set ______ 74321171452
RCA / Feb '94 / BMG
CD Set ______ 74321177042
RCA / Aug '95 / BMG

GREATEST HITS
Love is a stranger / Sweet dreams (are made of this) / Who's that girl / Right by your side / Here comes the rain again / There must be an angel (playing with my heart) / Sisters are doin' it for themselves: *Eurythmics & Aretha Franklin* / It's alright (baby's coming back) / When tomorrow comes / You have placed a chill in my heart / Sexcrime (1984) / Thorn in my side / Don't ask me why / Angel / Would I lie to you / Missionary man / I need a man / Miracle of love
CD ______ PD 74856
RCA / Mar '91 / BMG

IN THE GARDEN
English summer / Belinda / Take me to your heart / She's invisible now / Your time will come / Caveman head / Never gonna cry again / All the young people (of today) / Sing, sing / Revenge
CD ______ ND 75036
RCA / Aug '91 / BMG

REVENGE
Let's go / Take your pain away / Little of you / Thorn in my side / In this town / I remember you / Missionary man / Last time / When tomorrow comes / Miracle of love
CD ______ 74321125292
RCA / Sep '93 / BMG

SAVAGE
Beethoven (I love to listen to) / I've got a lover back in Japan / Do you want to break up / You have placed a chill in my heart / Shame / Savage / I need a man / Put the blame on me / Heaven / Wide eyed girl / I need you / Brand new day
CD ______ 74321134402
RCA / May '93 / BMG

SWEET DREAMS (ARE MADE OF THIS)
Love is a stranger / I've got an angel / Wrap it up / Could give you a mirror / Walk / Sweet dreams (are made of this) / Jennifer / Somebody told me / This city never sleeps / This is the house
CD ______ ND 71471
RCA / Aug '95 / BMG

TOUCH
Here comes the rain again / Regrets / Right by your side / Cool blue / Who's that girl / First cut / Aqua / No fear, no hate, no pain (no broken hearts) / Paint a rumour
CD ______ ND 90369
RCA / Sep '89 / BMG

TOUCH DANCE
Cool blue / Paint a rumour / Regrets / First cut / Cool blue (instrumental) / Paint a rumour (instrumental)
CD ______ ND 75151
RCA / Jan '92 / BMG

WE TOO ARE ONE
We too are one / King and Queen of America / (My my) Baby's gonna cry / Don't ask me why / Angel / Revival / You hurt me (I hate you) / Sylvia / How long / When the day goes down
CD ______ 74321208982
RCA / Jun '94 / BMG

EVA

EXTRA VEHICULAR ACTIVITY
CD ______ KICKCD 26
Kickin' / Jul '95 / Prime / SRD

Eva-lution

SOUL GLIDE
CD ______ SUNFCD 001
Sunflower / Jul '95 / ADA / Direct / Vital

Evans, Adriana

ADRIANA EVANS
Love is all around / Seeing is believing / Heaven / Reality / Hey brother / Trippin' / I'll be there / Love me / Looking for your love / Swimming / Say you won't / In the sun
CD ______ 7863675092
Loud / Jul '97 / BMG
CD ______ 07863669582
Loud / Mar '97 / BMG

Evans, Bill

1960 BIRDLAND SESSIONS, THE (Evans, Bill Trio)
CD ______ C&BCD 106
Cool & Blue / Dec '92 / Discovery / Jazz Music

ALONE
Here's that rainy day / Time for love / Midnight mood / One a clear day / Never let me go / All the things you are/Midnight mood / Time for love
CD ______ 8338012
Verve / Feb '94 / PolyGram

AT SHELLY'S MANNE-HOLE (Evans, Bill Trio)
Isn't it romantic / Boy next door / Wonder why / Swedish pastry / Our love is here to stay / Blues in F / 'Round midnight / Stella by starlight
CD ______ OJCCD 263
Original Jazz Classics / Feb '92 / Complete/ Pinnacle / Jazz Music / Wellard

AT THE MONTREUX JAZZ FESTIVAL 1968
One for Helen / Sleepin' bee / Mother of earl / Nardis / I loves you Porgy / Touch of your

lips / Embraceable you / Someday my Prince will come / Walkin' up / Quiet now
CD _____ 8278442
Verve / Mar '94 / PolyGram

AT THE VILLAGE VANGUARD (Evans, Bill Trio)
My foolish heart / My romance (take 1) / Solar / Gloria's step (take 2) / My man's gone now / All of you / I loves you Porgy / Milestones / Waltz for Debby / Jade visions
CD _____ FCD 60017
Fantasy / Apr '94 / Jazz Music / Pinnacle / Wellard

AUTUMN LEAVES
Emily / There will never be another you / Stairway to the stars / Someday my Prince will come / Blue in green / 'Round midnight / Autumn leaves
CD _____ CD 53211
Giants Of Jazz / Nov '95 / Cadillac / Jazz Music / Target/BMG

BEST OF BILL EVANS LIVE 1964-1968, THE
CD _____ 5338252
Verve / Mar '97 / PolyGram

BILL EVANS ALBUM, THE
Funkallero / Two lonely people / Sugar plum / Waltz for Debby / TTTT / Re: person I knew / Comrade Conrad
CD _____ 4809892
Sony Jazz / Dec '95 / Sony

BILL EVANS ALBUM, THE
Funkallero / Two lonely people / Sugar plum / Waltz for Debby / TTT / Re: person I knew / Comrade Conrad / Waltz for Debby / Re: person I knew / Funkallero
CD _____ CK 64963
Sony Jazz / Sep '96 / Sony

BILL EVANS AT TOWN HALL VOL.1 (Live At The New York Town Hall 21/2/66)
I should care / Spring is here / Who can I turn to / Make someone happy / Solo - In memory of his Father / Beautiful love / My foolish heart / One for Helen
CD _____ 8312712
Verve / Jan '94 / PolyGram

BILL EVANS TRIO WITH SYMPHONY ORCHESTRA (Arranged/Conducted By Claus Ogerman) (Evans, Bill Trio)
Granados / Valse / Prelude / Time remembered / Pavanne / Elegie / My bells / Blue interlude
CD _____ 8219832
Verve / Mar '94 / PolyGram

BLUE IN GREEN
CD _____ MCD 9185
Milestone / Oct '93 / Cadillac / Complete/ Pinnacle / Jazz Music / Wellard

BLUE IN GREEN
Elsa / Detour ahead / Skidoo / Alfie / Peri's scope / Blue in green / Emily / Who can I turn to / Some other time / Nardis / Waltz for Debby
CD _____ LEJAZZCD 42
Le Jazz / Jun '95 / Cadillac / Koch

BRILLIANT BILL EVANS, THE
Laurie / Letter to Evans / Mornin' glory / Mash (theme from) / Up with the lark / Gary's theme / Bill's hit tune / Knit for Mary F
CD _____ CDSJP 329
Timeless Jazz / Apr '96 / New Note/ Pinnacle

BRILLIANT BILL EVANS, THE/ CONSECRATION VOL.1 & 2 (3CD Set)
Laurie / Letter to Evan / Mornin' glory / Theme from MASH / Up with the lark / Gary's theme / Bill's hit tune / Knit for Mary F / You and the night and the music / Emily / Two lonely people / I do it for your love / Re: person I knew / Polka dots and moonbeams / Knit for Mary F / Someday my Prince will come / Tiffany / My foolish heart / Days of wine and roses / Your story / Turn out the stars / Like someone in love / My romance
CD Set _____ CDSJP 009
Timeless / Oct '96 / New Note/Pinnacle

BUT BEAUTIFUL (Evans, Bill Trio & Stan Getz)
Grandfather's waltz / Stan's blues / But beautiful / Emily / Lover man / Funkallero / Peacocks / You and the night and the music / See saw / Two lonely people
CD _____ MCD 9249
Milestone / Aug '96 / Cadillac / Complete/ Pinnacle / Jazz Music / Wellard

BUT BEAUTIFUL (Live At Middelheim Jazz Festival Antwerp 1974) (Evans, Bill Trio & Stan Getz)
CD _____ JD 1208
Jazz Door / Oct '96 / Koch

COMPLETE FANTASY RECORDINGS 1973-1979, THE (9CD Set)
Mornin' glory / Up with the lark / Yesterday / I heard the rain / My romance / When Autumn comes / TTTT / Hullo Bolinas / Gloria's step / On Green Dolphin Street / Up with the lark / Quiet now / Gloria's step / When in Rome / It amazes me / Since we met / Midnight mood / See saw / Elsa / Sareen Jurer / Time remembered / Turn out the stars / But beautiful / Re: person I knew / Sugar plum / Alfie / TTT / Dolphin Dance/ Very early / 34 skidoo / Emily / Are you all the things / Invitation / Blue Serge / Showtype tune / Nature of things / Are you all the things / Face without a name / Falling grace / Hi lili hi lo / Gone with the wind / Saudade do Brasil / My foolish heart / Touch of your lips / Some other time / When in Rome / We'll be together again / Young and foolish / Waltz for Debby / But beautiful / Days of wine and roses / Elsa / Milano / Venutian rhythm dance / Django / But beautiful / Minha / Driftin' / I love you / Summer knows / In a sentimental mood / Touch of your lips / In your own sweet way / Make someone happy / All of you / What kind of fool am I / People / Since we met / But not for me/ Isn't it romantic/The opener / Sweet Dulcinea / Martina / Second time around / Child is born / Bass face / Nobody else but me / Sugar plum / Time remembered / 34 skidoo / TTTT / Turn out the stars / Someday my prince will come / Minha / All of you / Waltz for Debby / Eiderdown / Every time we say goodbye / Pensativa / Speak low / When I fall in love / Night and day / I will say goodbye / Dolphin dance / Seascape / Peau douce / Nobody else but me / I will never say goodbye / Opener / Quiet light / House is not a home / Orson's theme / Marian McPartland's piano jazz interview / Kaleidoscope / Waltz for Debby / All of you / In your own sweet way / Touch of your lips / Reflections in D / I love you / Days of wine and roses / This is all I ask / While we're young
CD Set _____ FCD 10122
Fantasy / Nov '96 / Jazz Music / Pinnacle / Wellard

COMPLETE RIVERSIDE RECORDINGS, THE (12CD Set)
I love you / Five / Conception / Easy living / Displacement / Speak low / Our delight / No cover, no minimum / No cover, no minimum / I got it bad and that ain't good / Waltz for Debby / My romance / Minority / Young and foolish / Night and day / Oleo / Tenderly / What is there to say / Peace piece / Lucky to be me / Some other time / Epilogue / You and the night and the music / How am I to know / Woody 'n' you / Woody 'n' you / My heart stood still / On Green Dolphin Street / Peri's scope / Witchcraft / Spring is here / What is this thing called love / Come rain or come shine / Blue in green / Blue in green / Blue in green / Autumn leaves / Autumn leaves / Someday my prince will come / When I fall in love / Elsa / Sweet and lovely / Beautiful love / Beautiful love / I wish I knew / Boy next door / Haunted heart / Nardis / Nardis / How deep is the ocean / Israel / Who cares / Who cares / Goodbye / Nancy / Toy / Elsa / Waltz for Debby / Venice / Know what I mean / Know what I mean / Alice in Wonderland / My foolish heart / All of you / My romance / Some other time / Solar / Gloria's step / My man's gone now / All of you / Detour ahead / Waltz for Debby / Alice in wonderland / I loves you Porgy / My romance / Milestones / Detour ahead / Gloria's step / Waltz for Debby / All of you / Jade visions / Jade visions / A few final bars / Danny boy / Like someone in love / In your own sweet way / Easy to love / How my heart sings / Summertime / If you could see me now / Waking up / Very early / Showtype tune / Re: person I used to know / 34 skidoo / Polka dots and moonbeams / I should care / I fall in love too easily / Everything I love / In love in vain / Stairway to the stars / In your own sweet way / It might as well be Spring / Wrap your troubles in dreams / When you wish upon a star / You go to my head / You and the night and the music / Interplay / I'll never smile again / I'll never smile again / Loose bloose / Loose bloose / Fudgesicle built for four / Time remembered / Funkallero / My bells / Then come you / Fun ride / What kind of fool am I / My favourite things/Easy to love/Baubles, bangles and beads / When I fall in love / Spartacus/Nardis / Everything happens to me / April in Paris / All the things you are / Santa Claus is coming to town / I loves you Porgy / What kind of fool am I / Love is here to stay / Ornithology / Autumn in New York/ How about you / How about you / All the things you are / Lover man / Love is here to stay / Stella by starlight / 'Round midnight / Boy next door / Isn't it romantic / What is this thing called love / How about you / Blues in F/five / Everything happens to me / In a sentimental mood / My heart stood still / Time remembered / Wonder why / Swedish pastry
CD Set _____ 12RCD 0182
Riverside / Nov '96 / Cadillac / Complete/ Pinnacle / Jazz Music

CONSECRATION VOL.1 (Evans, Bill Trio)
You and the night and the music / Emily / Two lonely people / I do it for your love / Re: person I knew / Polka dots and moonbeams / Knit for Mary F / Someday my Prince will come
CD _____ CDSJP 331
Timeless Jazz / Apr '96 / New Note/ Pinnacle

CONSECRATION VOL.2 (Evans, Bill Trio)
Tiffany / My foolish heart / Days of wine and roses / Your story / Turn out the stars / Like someone in love / My romance
CD _____ CDSJP 332
Timeless Jazz / Apr '96 / New Note/ Pinnacle

CONVERSATIONS WITH BILL EVANS (Thibaudet, Jean-Yves)
Song for Helen / Waltz for Debby / Turn out the stars / Noelle's theme / Reflections in D / Here's that rainy day / Hullo Bolinas / Spartacus / Since we met / Peace piece / Your story / Lucky to be me
CD _____ 4555122
Decca / May '97 / PolyGram

CONVERSATIONS WITH MYSELF
'Round midnight / How about you / Spartacus love theme / Blue monk / Stella by starlight / Hey there / NYC's no lark / Just you, just me / Bemsha swing / Sleeping blue
CD _____ 8219842
Verve / Mar '93 / PolyGram

EMPATHY/A SIMPLE MATTER OF CONVICTION
Washington twist / Danny boy / Let's go back to the waltz / With a song in my heart / Goodbye / I believe in you / Simple matter of conviction / Stella by starlight / Orbit / Laura / My melancholy baby / I'm getting sentimental over you / Star eyes / Only child / These things called changes
CD _____ 8377572
Verve / Jan '90 / PolyGram

EVERYBODY DIGS BILL EVANS
Minority / Young and foolish / Lucky to be me / Night and day / Epilogue / Tenderly / Peace piece / What is there to say / Oleo
CD _____ OJCCD 68
Original Jazz Classics / Feb '92 / Complete/ Pinnacle / Jazz Music / Wellard

EXPLORATIONS
CD _____ OJCCD 37
Original Jazz Classics / Feb '92 / Complete/Pinnacle / Jazz Music / Wellard

HOW MY HEART SINGS (Evans, Bill Trio)
CD _____ OJCCD 369
Original Jazz Classics / Feb '92 / Complete/Pinnacle / Jazz Music / Wellard

I WILL SAY GOODBYE (Evans, Bill Trio)
I will say goodbye / Dolphin dance / Seascape / Peau douce / Nobody else but me / I will say goodbye (take 2) / Opener / Quiet light / House is not a home / Orson's theme
CD _____ OJCCD 761
Original Jazz Classics / Oct '93 / Complete/ Pinnacle / Jazz Music / Wellard

INTERMODULATION (Evans, Bill & Jim Hall)
I've got you under my skin / My man's gone now / Turn out the stars / Angel face / Jazz samba / All across the city
CD _____ 8337712
Verve / Jan '93 / PolyGram

INTERPLAY (Evans, Bill & Freddie Hubbard)
CD _____ OJCCD 308
Original Jazz Classics / Feb '92 / Complete/Pinnacle / Jazz Music / Wellard

JAZZ MASTERS
Israel / Here's that rainy day / Just you, just me / Sleepin' bee / Let's go back to the waltz / Funkallero / NYC's no lark / Mother of earl / Bemsha swing / Angel face / Alfie / On Green Dolphin Street / Quiet now
CD _____ 5198212
Verve / May '94 / PolyGram

JAZZHOUSE
How deep is the ocean / How my heart sings / Goodbye / Autumn leaves / California here I come / Sleepin' bee / Polka dots and moonbeams / Stella by starlight / Five (theme)
CD _____ MCD 91512
Milestone / Apr '94 / Cadillac / Complete/ Pinnacle / Jazz Music / Wellard

LIVE IN PARIS VOL.1
CD _____ FCD 125
France's Concert / Jun '89 / BMG / Jazz Music

LIVE IN PARIS VOL.1 1972
Re: Person I knew / Gloria's step / Waltz for Debby / Turn out the stars / Two lonely people / What are you doing the rest of your life
CD _____ FCD 107
Esoldun / Jun '88 / Target/BMG

LIVE IN PARIS VOL.2
Twelve tone tune / Sugar plum / Quiet now / Very early / Autumn leaves / Time remembered / My romance / Someday my Prince will come
CD _____ FCD 114
France's Concert / Jun '88 / BMG / Jazz Music

LIVE IN STOCKHOLM 1965
CD _____ LS 2917
Landscape / Feb '93 / THE

LIVE IN SWITZERLAND
CD _____ LS 2914
Landscape / Jun '93 / THE

LIVE IN SWITZERLAND 1975
CD _____ JH 01
Jazz Helvet / Dec '90 / TKO Magnum

LIVE IN TOKYO
Mornin' glory / Up with the lark / On Green Dolphin Street / Gloria's step / Hullo bolinas / TTTT / When autumn comes / My romance / Yesterday I heard the rain
CD _____ 4812652
Sony Jazz / Dec '95 / Sony

LIVE SWITZERLAND 1975 (Evans, Bill Trio)
CD _____ 449142
Landscape / Jun '93 / THE

LOOSE BLUES
Loose bloose / Time remembered / Funkallero / My bells / There came you / Fudgesickle built for four / Fun ride
CD _____ MCD 92002
Milestone / Aug '94 / Cadillac / Complete/ Pinnacle / Jazz Music / Wellard

MIDNIGHT MOOD
CD _____ ATJCD 54969
All That's Jazz / Oct '92 / Jazz Music / THE

MODERN DAYS AND NIGHTS (The Music Of Cole Porter)
Cole Porter flat / I love you / Love for sale / What is this thing called love / Everytime we say goodbye / I've got you under my skin / Just one of those things / Night and day
CD _____ DTRCD 120
Double Time / Mar '97 / Express Jazz

MONTREUX VOL.2
Very early / Alfie / 34 Skidoo / How my heart sings / Israel / I hear a rhapsody / Peri's scope
CD _____ 4812642
Sony Jazz / Dec '95 / Sony

MONTREUX VOL.3 (Evans, Bill & Eddie Gomez)
CD _____ OJCCD 644
Original Jazz Classics / Feb '92 / Complete/Pinnacle / Jazz Music / Wellard

MOODS UNLIMITED (Evans, Bill & Hank Jones/Red Mitchell)
Yesterdays / There is no greater love / All the things you are / In a sentimental mood / Night and day
CD _____ ECD 220722
Evidence / Nov '93 / ADA / Cadillac / Harmonia Mundi

MOONBEAMS (Evans, Bill Trio)
CD _____ OJCCD 434
Original Jazz Classics / Feb '92 / Complete/Pinnacle / Jazz Music / Wellard

NEW JAZZ CONCEPTIONS
I love you / Five / I got it bad and that ain't good / Conception / Easy living / Displacement / Speak low / Waltz for Debby / Our delight / My romance / No cover, no minimum
CD _____ OJCCD 25
Original Jazz Classics / Feb '92 / Complete/ Pinnacle / Jazz Music / Wellard

PERSON I KNEW
Re: Person I knew / Sugar plum / Alfie / TTT / Excerpt from Dolphin dance / Very early / 34 skidoo / Emily / Are you all the things
CD _____ OJCCD 749
Original Jazz Classics / Apr '93 / Complete/ Pinnacle / Jazz Music / Wellard

PORTRAIT IN JAZZ
Come rain or come shine / Autumn leaves / Witchcraft / When I fall in love / Peri's scope / What is this thing called love / Spring is here / Someday my Prince will come / Blue in green
CD _____ OJCCD 88
Original Jazz Classics / Feb '92 / Complete/ Pinnacle / Jazz Music / Wellard

QUIET NOW
Very airy / Sleepin' bee / Quiet now / Turn out the stars / Autumn leaves / Nardis
CD _____ LEJAZZCD 32
Le Jazz / Sep '94 / Cadillac / Koch

RARE CONCERT RECORDINGS - 1962-65-69
CD _____ JZCD 359
Suisa / Feb '91 / Jazz Music / THE

SECRET SESSIONS, THE (8CD Set)
Very early / 'Round midnight / One for helen / Blue in green / Turn out the stars / Waltz for Debby / Time remembered / Autumn leaves / I should care / Elsa / Who can I turn to (when nobody needs me) / My foolish heart / In your own sweet way / Five (theme) / Gloria's step / Nardis / Someday my Prince will come / Who can I turn to (when nobody needs me) / Come rain or come shine / If you could see me now / Spring is here / Re: person I knew / Sleepin' bee / Emily / Alfie / Walkin' up / You're gonna hear from me / Some other time / I'll remember april / Alice in wonderland / I love you / Very early / Round midnight / Stella by starlight / My man's gone now / Turn out the stars / In a sentimental mood / When I fall in love / Nardis / Come rain or come shine / Gloria's step / Round midnight / Blue in green / Waltz for Debby / Detour ahead / On green dolphin street / My foolish heart / If you could see me now / Elsa / How deep is the ocean / Polka dots and moonbeams / I'm getting sentimental over you / I should care / Star eyes / Peri's scope /

Haunted heart / Airegin / Little lulu / Five (theme) / Turn out the stars / Nardis / California, here I come / Very early / Easy living / Wonder why / Time remembered / You and the night and the music / Beautiful love / Waltz for Debby / I fall in love too easily / My man's gone now / Who can I turn to (when nobody needs me) / Polka dots and moonbeams / Emily / Ev'rything I love / Someday my prince will come / Shadow of your smile / Sleepin' bee / Blue in green / For heaven's sake / Love is here to stay / In a sentimental mood / How my heart sings / On green dolphin street / My foolish heart / Stella by starlight / Midnight mood / What are you doing the rest of your life / I should care / Autumn leaves / Re: person I knew / Alfie / Very early / Polka dots and moonbeams / Mornin' glory / Yesterday I heard the rain / Emily / Time remembered / Who I can I turn to (when nobody needs me) / Dolphin dance / Sugar plum / Turn out the stars / Quiet now / Waltz for Debby
CD Set _____ **MCD 44212**
Milestone / Jan '97 / Cadillac / Complete/ Pinnacle / Jazz Music / Wellard

SERENITY
CD _____ **LEJAZZCD 5**
Le Jazz / Mar '93 / Cadillac / Koch

SINCE WE MET
Since we met / Midnight mood / See saw / Sareen jurer / Time remembered / Turn out the stars / But beautiful
CD _____ **OJCCD 622**
Original Jazz Classics / Aug '94 / Complete/ Pinnacle / Jazz Music / Wellard

SMALL HOTEL, A (Evans, Bill Trio)
CD _____ **FDM 365612**
Dreyfus / Jul '93 / ADA / Direct / New Note/Pinnacle

SOLO SESSIONS VOL.1
CD _____ **MCD 9170**
Milestone / Oct '93 / Cadillac / Complete/ Pinnacle / Jazz Music / Wellard

SUNDAY NIGHT AT THE VILLAGE VANGUARD
CD _____ **OJCCD 140**
Original Jazz Classics / Feb '92 / Complete/Pinnacle / Jazz Music / Wellard

TIME TO REMEMBER
CD _____ **NI 4009**
Natasha / Jun '93 / ADA / Cadillac / CM / Direct / Jazz Music

TOKYO CONCERT, THE
CD _____ **OJCCD 345**
Original Jazz Classics / Feb '92 / Complete/Pinnacle / Jazz Music / Wellard

TRIO '65 (Evans, Bill Trio)
Israel / Elsa / 'Round midnight / Our love is here to stay / How my heart sings / Who can I turn to / Come rain or come shine / If you could see me now
CD _____ **5198082**
Verve / Dec '93 / PolyGram

TURN OUT THE STARS (The Music Of Bill Evans) (Repertory Quartet)
CD _____ **MECCACD 1098**
Music Mecca / May '97 / Cadillac / Jazz Music / Wellard

YOU'RE GONNA HEAR FROM ME
You're gonna hear from me / Waltz for Debby / Time remembered / Emily / Someday my Prince will come / 'Round midnight / Nardis / Who can I turn to / Our love is here to stay
CD _____ **MCD 91642**
Milestone / Aug '94 / Cadillac / Complete/ Pinnacle / Jazz Music / Wellard

Evans, Bill

ALTERNATIVE MAN
Alternative man / Path of least resistance / Let the juice loose / Gardiners garden / Survival of the fittest / Jo Jo / Cry in her eyes / Miles away / Flight of the falcon
CD _____ **BNZ 30**
Blue Note / Jul '87 / EMI

ESCAPE
Swing hop / Escape / Reality / Sunday after / Rattletrap / Flash in dreamland / Coravilas / Easilee / Undercover / La di da / Armsakimbo / Aftermath
CD _____ **ESC 036502**
Escapade / Apr '96 / New Note/Pinnacle

LIVE IN EUROPE
How my heart sings / Time to remember / Twelve toned tune / Waltz for Debby / Stella by starlight / Someday my Prince will come / 'Round midnight
CD _____ **LIP 890292**
Lipstick / Jun '96 / Vital/SAM

PETITE BLONDE
Prize hat / Branca's hal / Millenium / Oh so hip / Daddy's long leg / Watcher / Stansfield
CD _____ **LIP 890122**
Lipstick / Jun '96 / Vital/SAM

PUSH
Push / Road to ruin / If only in your dreams / London House / Night wing / Stand up and do something / Hobo / You gotta believe / Life is dangerous / U R what U hear / Simple life / Matter of time
CD _____ **LIP 890222**
Lipstick / Jun '96 / Vital/SAM

STARFISH AND THE MOON
Something in the rose / Starfish and the moon / Little slow poke / I'll miss you / Whiskey talk / Last goodbye / Red dog / It's only history / Big blue hat / Shady lady
CD _____ **ESC 036542**
Escapade / Sep '97 / New Note/Pinnacle

Evans, Bill

NATIVE AND FINE
CD _____ **ROUCD 0295**
Rounder / Nov '95 / ADA / CM / Direct

Evans, Ceri

HIDDEN TREASURE (Evans, Ceri Sextet)
CD _____ **BLJCD 001**
Big Life Jazz / Aug '96 / Pinnacle

Evans, Dave

GOIN' ROUND THIS WORLD
CD _____ **REB 1602CD**
Rebel / Dec '96 / ADA / Direct

Evans, Delyth

DELTA
Taith ar y fferi / Pibddawns y sipsi newydd / Pibddawns y gof / Branle / Mwynder maldwyn / Merch megan / Pandeirada de nebra / Y maerdy/Pibddawns merthyr / Eleanor Plunkett / Beto o Lansanffraid / Elsie Marley / Er gwell er gwaeth / A l'rntree de l'este / Carolan's receipt for drinking / Jackson's bottle of brandy / Baltiorum / Cariad pur / Gymnopedie III / Carolan's farewell to music / Ysbryd Kilvrough
CD _____ **SAIN 4062CD**
Sain / Aug '94 / ADA / Direct / Greyhound

Evans, Doc

STOMP AND BLUES (Evans, Doc Jazzband)
CD _____ **JCD 195**
Jazzology / Oct '93 / Jazz Music

Evans, Faith

FAITH
Faith (interlude) / No other love / Fallin' in love / Ain't nobody / You are my joy / Love don't live here anymore: *Evans, Faith & Mary J. Blige* / Come over: *Evans, Faith & Mary J. Blige* / Soon as I get home: *Evans, Faith & Mary J. Blige* / All this love: *Evans, Faith & Mary J. Blige* / Thank you Lord: *Evans, Faith & Mary J. Blige* / You used to love me: *Evans, Faith & Mary J. Blige* / Give it to me: *Evans, Faith & Mary J. Blige* / You don't understand: *Evans, Faith & Mary J. Blige* / Reasons: *Evans, Faith & Mary J. Blige*
CD _____ **78612730032**
Arista / Aug '95 / BMG

Evans, Gil

BRITISH ORCHESTRA, THE
Hotel me / Friday 13th / London / Little wing
CD _____ **MOLECD 8**
Mole Jazz / May '83 / Cadillac / Impetus / Jazz Music / Wellard

BUD AND BIRD (Evans, Gil & The Monday Night Orchestra)
CD _____ **K32Y 6171**
Electric Bird / Sep '88 / New Note/ Pinnacle

COMPLETE RECORDINGS (2CD Set) (Evans, Gil & Laurent Cugny/Big Band Lumiere)
Rhythm-a-ning / London / Stone free / Charles Mingus' sound of love / La Nevada / Golden hair / Orange was the colour of her dress, then silk blue / Zee zee / C blues / Parabola / Goodbye Pork Pie Hat
CD _____ **8387942**
EmArCy / Mar '93 / PolyGram

GIL EVANS & TEN
Remember / Ella Speed / Big stuff / Nobody's heart / Just one of those things / If you could see me now / Jambangle
CD _____ **OJCCD 346**
Original Jazz Classics / Sep '93 / Complete/ Pinnacle / Jazz Music / Wellard

HONEY MAN
CD _____ **RD 5022CD**
Robi Droli / Apr '95 / ADA / Direct

INDIVIDUALISM OF GIL EVANS, THE
CD _____ **8338042**
Verve / Oct '93 / PolyGram

JAZZ MASTERS
Time of the barracudas / Greensleeves / Last night when we were young / Moon and sand / Las Vegas tango / Spoonful / Concorde / I will wait for you / Barbara song
CD _____ **5218602**
Verve / Feb '94 / PolyGram

LIVE AT THE PUBLIC THEATRE NEW YORK 1980 VOL.1
Anita's dance / Jelly roll / Alyrio / Variation on the misery / Orgone / Up from the skies
CD _____ **ECD 220892**
Evidence / Jun '94 / ADA / Cadillac / Harmonia Mundi

LIVE AT THE PUBLIC THEATRE NEW YORK 1980 VOL.2
Copenhagen sight / Zee zee / Sirhan's blues / Stone free / Orange was the colour of her dress, then silk blue
CD _____ **ECD 220902**
Evidence / Jun '94 / ADA / Cadillac / Harmonia Mundi

LUNAR ECLYPSE (Evans, Gil & His Orchestra)
CD _____ **1298067112**
Robi Droli / Jun '93 / ADA / Direct

ORCHESTRA 1957-59
CD _____ **CD 53158**
Giants Of Jazz / Sep '94 / Cadillac / Jazz Music / Target/BMG

OUT OF THE COOL
La Nevada / Where flamingos fly / Bilbao song / Stratusphunk / Sunken treasure / Sister Sadie
CD _____ **IMP 11862**
Impulse Jazz / Mar '96 / New Note/BMG

PLAYS THE MUSIC OF JIMI HENDRIX (Evans, Gil Orchestra)
Angel / Crosstown traffic / Castles made of sand / Up from the skies (take 1) / 1983 / Voodoo chile / Gypsy eyes / Little wing / Up from the skies (take 2) / Little Miss Lover
CD _____ **ND 88409**
Bluebird / Nov '88 / BMG

PRIESTESS
Priestess / Short visit / Lunar eclipse / Orange was the colour of her dress, then silk blue
CD _____ **ANCD 8717**
Antilles/New Directions / May '87 / PolyGram

RHYTHM-A-NING (Evans, Gil & Laurent Cugny/Big Band Lumiere)
Rhythm-a-ning / London / Stone free / Charles Mingus' sound of love / La Nevada
CD _____ **8364012**
EmArCy / Mar '93 / PolyGram

SVENGALI
Thoroughbred / Blues in orbit / Eleven / Cry of hunger / Summertime / Zee zee
CD _____ **92072**
Act / Apr '94 / New Note/Pinnacle

WHERE FLAMINGOS FLY
Zee zee / Nana / Love your love / Jelly rolls / Where flamingos fly / El matador
CD _____ **3908312**
A&M / Jul '94 / PolyGram

Evans, Guy

LONG HELLO VOL.4, THE
Holsworthy market place / Trick or treat / Der traum von julius / Rock of riley / Caretaker's wife / Wonderful brothers / Martha's express wishes / Hamburg station / Solo kabine / Finger points / Haben sie waffen oder funk dabei / Slow slither loop / My feet are freezing but my knees are warm
CD _____ **VP 112CD**
Voiceprint / Mar '93 / Pinnacle

UNION CHAPEL CONCERT, THE (2CD Set) (Evans, Guy & Peter Hammill)
Fireworks / Forest of pronouns / Anatol's proposal / After the show / Roger and out / Accidents / Soundbeam melody / Women of Ireland / Ship of fools / Hamburg station / Seven wonders / Barber's adagio / Red shift / Lemmings / Traintime
CD Set _____ **FIE 9115**
Fie / Mar '97 / Vital

Evans, Jenny

SHINY STOCKINGS
Shiny stockings / Good old days / Softly as in a morning sunrise / That's what zoot said / You go to my head / In a mellow tone / Caravan / Willow weep for me / Alright, ok you win / Honeysuckle rose / Song of autumn / April in Paris / All of me
CD _____ **ENJ 93172**
Enja / May '97 / New Note/Pinnacle / Vital/ SAM

Evans, Paul

FABULOUS TEENS AND BEYOND, THE
Midnite special / Hushabye little guitar / I'm in love again / Hambone rock / Over the mountain, across the sea / Tutti frutti / Butterfly / Slippin' and slidin' / Honey love / I'm walkin' / Since I met you baby / 60 Minute man / Fool / Seven little girls sitting in the back seat / Worshipping an idol / Happy go lucky me / Fish in the ocean / Brigade of broken hearts / Blind boy / Twins / After the hurricane / Just because I love you / Show folk / Why / Roses are red / Disneyland Daddy / Willie's sung with everyone (but me) / Hello, this is Joanne
CD _____ **CDCHD 551**
Ace / Nov '95 / Pinnacle

Evans, Sara

THREE CHORDS AND THE TRUTH
True lies / Shame about that / Three chords and the truth / If you ever want my lovin' / Imagine that / Even now / I don't wanna see the light / I've got a tiger by the tail / Unopened / Walk out backwards / Week the river raged
CD _____ **74321482512**
RCA / Jun '97 / BMG

Evans, Terry

BLUES FOR THOUGHT
Too many cooks / Hey Mama, keep your big mouth shut / Shakespeare didn't quote that / Natcha bone lover / That's the way love turned out for me / So fine / Get your lies straight / Live, love and friends / Honey boy / I want to be close to you, God
CD _____ **VPCD 16**
Pointblank / Jan '93 / EMI

PUTTIN' IT DOWN
Money in your pocket / Too many ups and downs / Walking in the same tracks / Down in Mississippi / In this day and time / Rooftop tomcat / Lover like you / One sided love affair / Nasty doll / Blues no more
CD _____ **AQCD 1038**
Audioquest / Nov '95 / ADA / New Note/ Pinnacle

Evans, Tony

FALLING INTO YOU
Falling into you / La piu bella del mondo / Dance away / I wanna dance with somebody / I love to love / I'm so excited / Love ain't here anymore / Dream a little dream / Amore scusami / Another time another place / Young hearts run free / That's what I am / Memory / Boom bang a bang
CD _____ **CDE 1034**
Tema / May '96 / Savoy / Target/BMG

I WON'T SEND ROSES (Evans, Tony & His Orchestra)
CD _____ **CDE 1025**
Tema / May '93 / Savoy / Target/BMG

WHERE DID YOU LEARN TO DANCE (Evans, Tony Orchestra & Singers)
Where did you learn to dance / What a little moonlight can do / Night lights / That Sunday, that summer / Dance only with me / Waltzing in the clouds / Sunset tango / Starlight tango / Words get in the way / When you tell me that you love me / Young girl / Don't cry for me Argentina / Love is in the air / Choo choo ch'boogie / Tell him / Spaniard that blighted my life
CD _____ **CDE 1035**
Tema / Mar '97 / Savoy / Target/BMG

WRAP YOUR ARMS AROUND ME (Evans, Tony & His Orchestra)
Wrap your arms around me / Portrait of my love / Let's do it / Too young / April in Portugal / You can't hurry love / Malaguana / Sweet Heaven / Let there be love / This can't be love / I love Paris / Daddy's little girl / Plaisir d'amour / Tropicana tango / Under the bridges of Paris
CD _____ **CDE 1033**
Tema / Mar '96 / Savoy / Target/BMG

EVE

IN THE BEGINNING
CD _____ **THE 4177CD**
Ichiban / Apr '94 / Direct / Koch

Evelev, Yale

CUBA CLASSICS VOL.3 (Diablo al Infierno - New Directions in Cuban Music)
Bacalao con pan / Asoyin / El baile del buey cansao / Tu no sabes de amor / Ikiri ada / Rompe saraguey / Congo yambumba / No me carezcas / Que viva chango / Homenaje / Guillermo tell / Diablo al infierno
CD _____ **9362451072**
Luaka Bop / Feb '93 / Warner Music

Even

LESS IS MORE
CD _____ **RUB 052CD**
Rubber / Jan '97 / ADA / CM / Direct / Jazz Music / Roots

Evenson, Dean

OCEAN DREAMS
CD _____ **SP 7140CD**
Soundings Of The Planet / Aug '96 / Else

WIND DANCER (Evenson, Dean & Tom Barabas)
CD _____ **SP 7149CD**
Soundings Of The Planet / Jul '96 / Else

Everclear

SPARKLE AND FADE
Electra made me blind / Heroin girl / You made me feel like a whore / Santa Monica / Summerland / Strawberry / Heartspark dollarsign / Twistinside / Her brand new skin / Nehalem / Queen of the air / Pale green stars / Chemical smile / My sexual life
CD _____ **CDEST 2257**
Capitol / Mar '96 / EMI

SPARKLE AND FADE
Electra made me blind / Heroin girl / You make me feel like a whore / Santa Monica / Summerland / Strawberry / Heartspark dollarsign / Twistinside / Her brand new

skin / Nehalem / Queen of the air / Pale green stars / Chemical smile / My sexual life / Heroin girl / Summerland / Annabella / Sparkle / Heartspark dollarsign / American girl
CD _______________ CDESTX 2257
Capitol / Oct '96 / EMI

WHITE TRASH HELL
Heroin girl / Pacific wonderland / Blondes / Detroit / 1975 / For Pete's sake / Fire maple song
CD _______________ FIREMCD 45
Fire / Mar '97 / Pinnacle / RTM/Disc

WORLD OF NOISE
CD _______________ FIRECD 46
Fire / Feb '95 / Pinnacle / RTM/Disc

Everett, Betty

LOVE RHYMES/HAPPY ENDINGS
Sweet Dan / I gotta tell somebody / I wanna be there / Be anything, but be mine / Wondering / Who will your next fool be / I'm your friend / Just a matter of time / I'm afraid of losing you / La la la / Try it you'll like it / Here's the gift / God only knows / Things I say to his shoulder / Bedroom eyes / Keep it up / Just a little piece of you / Don't let it end ('til you let it begin) / As far as we can go / Happy endings
CD _______________ CDSEWD 085
Southbound / Jul '93 / Pinnacle

Everett, Sangoma

COURAGE TO LISTEN TO YOUR HEART
Mombasa / Crossroads / Murivel / Auburn prive / Liberated / African plains
CD _______________ TCB 97202
TCB / Jun '97 / New Note/Pinnacle

Evergreen

EVERGREEN
CD _______________ HBLP 0996CD
Hi-Ball / Mar '97 / Cargo

Evergreen Classic Jazz Band

EVERGREEN CLASSIC JAZZ BAND
CD _______________ SOS 1202
Stomp Off / Oct '92 / Jazz Music / Wellard

Evergreens

IRISH ROVER, THE (20 Classics From The Emerald Isle)
Star of County Down / Do you want your old lobby washed down / Irish rover / Old folks at home / Maggie / Cumberland Road / Marie's wedding / New York girls / Gentle mother / She moved through the fair / Come back Paddy Reilly / MacNamara's band / Seven drunken nights / Your mother's eyes / Red is the rose / Cliffs of Dooneen / Water is deep / Three drunken maidens / Holy ground / Parting glass
CD _______________ EMPRCD 659
Emporio / Jun '96 / Disc

SONGS OF IRELAND
Wild rover / I'll tell me ma / Leaving of Liverpool / Black velvet band / Galway bay / Old bog road / Spanish lady / Mountains of mourne / I'll take you home again Kathleen / Danny boy / Rovin' I will go / Molly malone / Peggy Gordon / Spinning wheel / Muirsheen durkin / Bunch of thyme / Rose of tralee / Whistling gyspy rover / Whiskey in the jar / Carrickfergus
CD _______________ EMPRCD 578
Emporio / Jul '95 / Disc

Everly Brothers

ALL I HAVE TO DO IS DREAM (Original Hits & Rarities)
All I have to do is dream / Claudette / Bye bye love / Devoted to you / Hey doll baby / Roving gambler / Rip it up / When will I be loved / Bird dog / Oh true love / Wake up little Susie / Maybe tomorrow / Poor Jenny / Let it be me / Be bop a lula / Put my little shoes away / Long time gone / Love of my life / Leave my woman alone / All I have to do is dream
CD _______________ 3036000832
Carlton / Jun '97 / Carlton

BEST OF THE EVERLY BROTHERS
CD _______________ DCD 5324
Disky / Dec '93 / Disky / THE

BEST OF THE EVERLY BROTHERS, THE
CD _______________ MCCD 209
Music Club / Jul '95 / Disc / THE

BYE BYE LOVE
CD _______________ ENTCD 207
Entertainers / Sep '87 / Target/BMG

CLASSIC EVERLY BROTHERS (1955-1960)
Keep a lovin' me / Suns keeps shining / If here love isn't true / That's the life I have to live / I wonder if I care as much / Bye bye love / Should we tell him / Wake up little Susie / Hey doll baby / Maybe tomorrow / Brand new heartache / Keep a knockin' / Leave my woman alone / Rip it up / This little girl of mine / Be bop a lula / All I have to do is dream / Claudette / Devoted to you / Bird dog / Problems / Love of my life / Take a message to Mary / Poor Jenny (one o'clock version) / Poor Jenny (ten o'clock version) / Oh true love / Till I kissed you / Oh what a feeling / Let it be me / Since you broke my heart / Like strangers / When will I be loved / Roving gambler / Who's gonna shoe your pretty little feet / Rockin' alone in an old rocking chair / Put my little shoes away / Down in the willow garden / Long time gone / Lightning express / That silver haired daddy of mine / Barbara Allen / Oh so many years / I'm here to get my baby out of jail / Kentucky
CD Set _______________ BCD 15618
Bear Family / Feb '92 / Direct / Rollercoaster / Swift

EB84
CD _______________ RE 2040
Razor & Tie / Aug '96 / Koch

EP COLLECTION, THE
I'm here to get my baby out of jail / Rockin' alone in an old rockin' chair / Long time gone / (Til) I kissed you / Oh, what a feeling / Let it be me / Since you broke my heart / Bye bye love / I wonder if I care as much / Maybe tomorrow / Wake up little Susie / That silver haired daddy of mine / Devoted to you / Rip it up / Leave my woman alone / Should we tell him / Hey, doll baby / Claudette / Birddog / All I have to do is dream / Brand new heartache / This little girl of mine / Keep a knockin' / Be bop a lula / Problems / Poor Jenny
CD _______________ SEECD 482
See For Miles/C5 / Aug '97 / Pinnacle

EVERLY BROTHERS AND THE FABULOUS STYLE OF...
This little girl of mine / Maybe tomorrow / Bye bye love / Brand new heartache / Keep a knockin' / Be bop a lula / Poor Jenny / Rip it up / I wonder if I care as much / Wake up little Susie / Leave my woman alone / Should we tell him / Hey doll baby / Claudette / Like strangers / Since you broke my heart / Let it be me / Oh what a feeling / Take a message to Mary / Devoted to you / When will I be loved / Bird dog / Till I kissed you / Problems / Love of my life / Poor Jenny (2nd version) / All I have to do is dream
CD _______________ CDCH 932
Ace / Apr '90 / Pinnacle

EVERLY BROTHERS ON WARNER BROTHERS, THE (2CD Set)
Cathy's clown / So sad (to watch good love go bad) / Walk right back / Love hurts / Sleepless nights / Nashville blues / Lucille / What kind of girl are you / Made to love / Radio and tv / Stick with me baby / Always it's you / Temptation / Ebony eyes / Crying in the rain / Don't blame me / True love / That's old fashioned (that's the way love should be) / Nancy's minuet / I'm not angry / How can I meet her / Burma shave / Muskrat / Just one time / Lonely street / Sweet dreams / Price of love / Man with money / Love is strange / Give me a sweetheart / You're the one I love / You're my girl / Kiss your man goodbye / Gone, gone, gone / Don't let the whole world know / Don't forget to cry / Nothing matters but you / It's all over / Empty boxes / Bowling green / Love of the common people / (I'd be) a legend in my time / I'm movin' on / T for Texas / I wonder if I care as much / Lord of the manor / Sing me back home / Shady grove / Cuckoo bird / I'm on my way home again
CD Set _______________ 9362451642
Warner Bros. / Jul '96 / Warner Music

EVERLY BROTHERS, THE
When will I be loved / Problems / Bye bye love / Wake up little Susie / Barbara Allen / This little girl of mine / Bird dog / I'm here to get my baby out of jail / Claudette / Roving gambler / Leave my woman alone / Long time gone / Oh so many years / All I have to do is dream / Poor Jenny / Be bop a lula / Like strangers / Take a message to Mary
CD _______________ 399540
Koch Presents / May '97 / Koch

EVERLY BROTHERS, THE
CD _______________ HM 008
Harmony / Jun '97 / TKO Magnum

EVERLY COUNTRY
CD _______________ VSOPCD 237
Connoisseur Collection / Jun '97 / Pinnacle

FABULOUS EVERLY BROTHERS, THE
Bye bye love / Wake up little Susie / All I have to do is dream / Bird dog / Problems / Till I kissed you / Let it be me / When will I be loved / Take a message to Mary / Claudette / Poor Jenny / Devoted to you
CD _______________ CDFAB 006
Ace / Sep '91 / Pinnacle

GOLDEN YEARS OF THE EVERLY BROTHERS
Walk right back / Crying in the rain / Wake up little Susie / Love hurts / Claudette / Till I kissed you / Love is strange / Ebony eyes / Temptation / Let it be me / Don't blame me / Cathy's clown / All I have to do is dream / Lucille / So sad (to watch good love go bad) / Bird dog / When will I be loved / No one can make my sunshine smile / Ferris wheel / Price of love / Muskrat / Problems / How can I meet her / Bye bye love
CD _______________ 9548319922
Warner Bros. / May '93 / Warner Music

GREATEST HITS LIVE
Wake up little Susie / Bird dog / ('Till) I kissed you / Let it be me / Cathy's clown / Lucille / Crying in the rain / Love is strange / Price of love / Walk right back / Claudette / All I have to do is dream / So sad / Temptation / For the love of Barbara Allen / Bye bye love
CD _______________ RM 1528
BR Music / Jun '97 / Target/BMG

GREATEST LOVE SONGS VOL.1 (Live At The Royal Albert Hall)
Price of love / Walk right back / Claudette / Crying in the rain / Love is strange / (Take a) a message to Mary / Maybe tomorrow / I wonder if I care as much / When will I be loved / Bird dog / Devoted to you / Ebony eyes / Love hurts / For the love of Barbara Allen / Lightning express / Put my little shoes away / Long time gone / Down in the willow garden / Step it up and go
CD _______________ PLATCD 168
Platinum / Mar '96 / Prism

GREATEST LOVE SONGS VOL.2 (Live At The Royal Albert Hall)
Cathy's clown / Gone gone gone / You send me / So sad (to watch a good love go bad) / Blues stay away from me / Bye bye love / All I have to do is dream / (Till) I kissed you / Temptation / Be bop a lula / Lucille / Let it be me / Good golly Miss Molly
CD _______________ PLATCD 169
Platinum / Mar '96 / Prism

GREATEST RECORDINGS
Wake up little Susie / Problems / Take a message to Mary / I wonder if I care as much / Poor Jenny / Love of my life / Bird dog / Like strangers / Hey doll baby / Leave my woman alone / Till I kissed you / Claudette / Should we tell him / All I have to do is dream / Rip it up / When will I be loved / Bye bye love / Let it be me
CD _______________ CDCH 903
Ace / '88 / Pinnacle

HIT SINGLE COLLECTABLES
CD _______________ DISK 4502
Disky / Apr '94 / Disky / THE

MERCURY YEARS
CD _______________ 5109092
Mercury / Jul '93 / PolyGram

NICE GUYS
Trouble / What about me / Eden to Cainin / Chains / Meet me in the bottom / In the good old days / Nice guys / Stained glass morning / Dancing on my feet / Mr. Soul / Don't you even try / Kiss your man goodbye
CD _______________ CDMF 1028
Magnum Force / Nov '88 / TKO Magnum

ORIGINAL BRITISH HIT SINGLES, THE
Bye bye love / I wonder if I care as much / Wake up little Susie / Maybe tomorrow / Should we tell him / This little girl of mine / All I have to do is dream / Claudette / Bird dog / Devoted to you / Problems / Love of my life / Poor Jenny / Take a message to Mary / Till I kissed you / Oh what a feeling / Let it be me / Since you broke my heart / When will I be loved / Be bop a lula / Like strangers / Leave my woman alone
CD _______________ CDCHM 544
Ace / Nov '94 / Pinnacle

RARE SOLO CLASSICS
Let it be me / So sad (to watch a good love go bad) / Sweet southern love / Brother jukebox / Dare to dream again / Since you broke my heart / Lonely days / Yesterday just passed my way / Nighht rider / Deep water / Love at last sight / Never like this / Lettin' go / Turn the memories loose again / In your eyes / Oh, I'd like to go away / What a feeling / Love angel
CD _______________ PWKS 4259
Carlton / Mar '96 / Carlton

RE-UNION
Price of love / Walk right back / Claudette / Crying in the rain / Love is strange / (Take a) message to Mary / When will I be loved / Bird dog / Devoted to you / Ebony eyes / Love hurts / Gone gone gone / Cathy's clown / You send me / So sad (to watch good love go bad) / Bye bye love / All I have to do is dream / Wake up little Susie / Till I kissed you / Temptation / Be bop a lula / Lucille / Let it be me / Good golly Miss Molly
CD _______________ MOCD 3002
More Music / Feb '95 / Sound & Media

REUNION CONCERT (2CD Set)
Price of love / Walk right back / Claudette / Crying in the rain / Love is strange / (Take a) message to Mary / Maybe tomorrow / I wonder if I care as much / When will I be loved / Bird dog / Devoted to you / Ebony eyes / Love hurts / For the love of Barbara Allen / Lightning express / Put my little shoes away / Long time gone / Down in the willow garden / Step it up and go / Cathy's clown / Gone gone gone / You send me / So sad (to watch good love go bad) / Blues (stay away from me) / Bye bye love / All I have to do is dream / Wake up little Susie / Till I kissed you / Temptation / Be bop a lula / Lucille / Let it be me / Good golly Miss Molly
CD Set _______________ PLATCD 5901
Platinum / Oct '93 / Prism

CD Set _______________ 24316
Delta Doubles / Mar '96 / Target/BMG

REUNION CONCERT, THE
Price of love / Walk right back / Claudette / Crying in the rain / Love is strange / Take a message to Mary / When will I be loved / Bird dog / Devoted to you / Ebony eyes / Love hurts / Cathy's clown / Gone, gone, gone / You send me / Bye bye love / All I have to do is dream / Wake up little Susie / (Til) I kissed you / Temptation / Be bop a Lula / Lucille / Let it be me / Good golly miss moll
CD _______________ EMPRCD 587
Emporio / Oct '95 / Disc

REUNION CONCERT, THE (2CD Set)
CD Set _______________ CPCD 82992
Charly / May '97 / Koch

ROOTS
CD _______________ 7599269272
Warner Bros. / May '95 / Warner Music

SIMPLY THE BEST
CD _______________ WMCD 5704
Disky / Oct '94 / Disky / THE

SONGS OUR DADDY TAUGHT US
Roving gambler / Down in the willow garden / Long time gone / Lightning express / That silver haired daddy of mine / Who's gonna shoe your pretty little feet / Barbara Allen / Oh so many years / I'm here to get my baby out of jail / Rockin' alone in an old rocking chair / Kentucky / Put my little shoes away
CD _______________ CDCHM 75
Ace / Nov '90 / Pinnacle

STORIES WE COULD TELL
All I really want to do / Breakdown / Green river / Mandolin wind / Up in Mabel's room / Del Rio Dan / Ridin' high / Christmas Eve can kill you / Three armed poker playin' river rat / I'm tired of singing my song in Las Vegas / Brand new Tennessee waltz / Lay it down / Husbands and wives / Woman don't you try to tie me down / Sweet memories / Ladies love outlaws / Not fade away / Somebody nobody knows / Good hearted woman / Stories we could tell
CD _______________ 74321432552
Camden / Jan '97 / BMG

SUSIE Q
Love with your heart / How can I meet her / Nothing but the best / Sheikh of Araby / To show I love you / Suzie Q / Am abend auf der heide / Sag su wiedersehen / When snowflakes fall in the summer / Little Hollywood girl / He's got my sympathy / Silent treatment
CD _______________ CDMF 052
Magnum Force / Jun '88 / TKO Magnum

SWEET MEMORIES
CD _______________ 295 728
Ariola Express / Sep '92 / BMG

Everly, Don

BROTHER JUKE BOX
Love at last sight / So sad (to watch good love go bad) / Letting go / Since you broke my heart / Never like this / Deep water / Yesterday just passed my way again / Oh I'd like to go away / Oh what a feeling / Turn the memories loose again / Brother juke box
CD _______________ CDSD 002
Sundown / Sep '94 / TKO Magnum

Everly, Phil

LOUISE
Louise / Sweet Suzanne / She means nothing to me / Man and a woman / Who's gonna keep me warm / One way love / Sweet pretender / Better than now / Oh baby oh / God bless older ladies / Never gonna dream again / I'll mend your broken heart / When I'm dead and gone
CD _______________ CDMF 053
Magnum Force / Jan '88 / TKO Magnum

PHIL EVERLY
She means nothing to me: *Richard, Cliff & Phil Everly* / I'll mend your broken heart: *Richard, Cliff & Phil Everly* / God bless older ladies / Sweet pretender / Never gonna dream again / Better than now / Woman and a man / Louise / When I'm dead and gone / Sweet Suzanne / Oh baby oh (you're the star)
CD _______________ BGOCD 199
Beat Goes On / Feb '95 / Pinnacle

Everton Blender

LIFT UP YOUR HEAD
CD _______________ CDHB 169
Heartbeat / Jan '95 / ADA / Direct / Greensleeves / Jet Star

WORLD CORRUPTION
Coming harder / World corruption / Just wanna be / Man / Live up / Bob Marley / Piece a di Blender / Blow your nose / Blend dem / Material girl / Baa baa white sheep / When you wrong / If you want to dance: *Everton Blender & Prezident Brown* / Blow your nose: *Everton Blender & Prezident Brown*
CD _______________ GRELCD 231
Greensleeves / Oct '96 / Jet Star / SRD

Everton FC

FOREVER EVERTON (Everton FC/ Supporters)
CD _______ CDGAFFER 5
Cherry Red / Apr '96 / Pinnacle

Every New Dead Ghost

ENDLESS NIGHTMARE
CD _______ NIGHTCD 001
Plastic Head / Jul '92 / Plastic Head

NEW WORLD, A
CD _______ PLASCD 024
Plastic Head / Nov '90 / Plastic Head

RIVER OF SOULS
CD _______ APOREK 1110893
Apollyon / Feb '95 / SRD

WHO'S SANE ANYWAY
CD _______ AJE 07
Alea Jacta Est / Jun '93 / Plastic Head

Everyman Band

WITHOUT WARNING
Patterns which connect / Talking with himself / Multibluetonic blues / Celebration / Trick of the wool / Huh what he say / Al ur
CD _______ 8254052
ECM / '88 / New Note/Pinnacle

Everything But The Girl

AMPLIFIED HEART
Rollercoaster / Troubled mind / I don't understand anything / Walking to you / Get me / Missing / Two star / We walk the same line / 25th December / Disenchanted
CD _______ 4509964822
Blanco Y Negro / Jun '94 / Warner Music

BABY THE STARS SHINE BRIGHT
Come on home / Don't leave me behind / Country mile / Cross my heart / Don't let the teardrops rust your shining heart / Careless / Sugar Finney / Come hell or high water / Fighting talk / Little Hitler
CD _______ 2409662
Blanco Y Negro / Aug '86 / Warner Music

BEST OF EVERYTHING BUT THE GIRL
Missing / Driving / Old friends / One place / I don't want to talk about it / Love is strange / Only living boy in New York / Apron strings / When all's well / Another bridge / Each and every one / Rollercoaster / Better things / Protection
CD _______ 0630166372
Blanco Y Negro / Oct '96 / Warner Music

EDEN
Each and every one / Bittersweet / Tender blue / Another bridge / Spice of life / Dust bowl / Crabwalk / Even so / Frost and fire / Fascination / I must confess / Soft touch
CD _______ 2403952
Blanco Y Negro / '84 / Warner Music

HOME MOVIES (The Best of Everything But The Girl)
Driving / Each and every one / Another bridge / Fascination / Native land / Come on home / Cross my heart / Apron strings / I don't want to talk about it / Night I heard Caruso sing / Imagining America / Understanding / Twin cities / Love is strange / I didn't know I was looking for love / Only living boy in New York
CD _______ BYN 29CD
Blanco Y Negro / Apr '93 / Warner Music

IDLEWILD
Love is here where I live / These early days / Oxford Street / Night I heard Caruso sing / Goodbye Sunday / Shadow on a harvest moon / Blue moon rose / Tears all over town / Lonesome for a place I know / Apron strings / I don't want to talk about it
CD _______ K 2438402
Blanco Y Negro / Nov '94 / Warner Music

LANGUAGE OF LIFE, THE
Driving / Get back together / Meet me in the morning / Me and Bobby D / Language of life / Take me / Imagine America / Letting love go / My baby don't love me / Road
CD _______ 2462602
Blanco Y Negro / Jan '90 / Warner Music

LOVE NOT MONEY
When all's well / Ugly little dreams / Shoot me down / Are you trying to be funny / Sean / Ballad of the times / Anytown / This love (not for sale) / Trouble and strife / Angel / Heaven help me / Kid
CD _______ 2406572
Blanco Y Negro / May '85 / Warner Music

WALKING WOUNDED
Before today / Wrong / Single / Heart remains a child / Walking wounded / Flipside / Big deal / Mirrorball / Good cop bad cop
CD _______ CDV 2803
Virgin / Jun '96 / EMI

WORLDWIDE
Old friends / Understanding / You lift me up / Talk to me like the sea / British summertime / Twin cities / Frozen river / One place / Politics aside / Boxing and pop music / Feeling alright
CD _______ 9031753082
Blanco Y Negro / Oct '91 / Warner Music

Evil Dead

ANNIHILATION OF CIVILISATION
CD _______ 847603
Steamhammer / '90 / Pinnacle / Plastic Head

RISE ABOVE
CD _______ 557590
Steamhammer / '88 / Pinnacle / Plastic Head

Evil Mothers

CROSSDRESSER
CD _______ CDDVN 26
Devotion / Dec '93 / Pinnacle

PITCHFORKS & PERVERTS
CD _______ CDDVN 30
Devotion / May '94 / Pinnacle

SPIDER SEX AND CAR WRECKS
Free poison / Something wicked this way please / Spider sex and car wrecks / I like fur / You had enough / Backbiter / Give up the ghost / Loud and clear / Geek / Corpse / Last suffer / Ready set die
CD _______ VIRUS 193
Alternative Tentacles / Mar '97 / Cargo / Greyhound / Pinnacle

Evil Superstars

LOVE IS OKAY
No more people / Power of Haha / Go home for lunch / Parasol / Your dump or mine / Rocking all over / Pantomiming with her parents / Oh funlump / We need your head / 1,000,000 demons can't be wrong / Satan is in my ass / Death by summer / Miss your disease
CD _______ PDOXCD 002
Paradox / Feb '96 / PolyGram / Vital

Evil's Toy

HUMAN REFUSE
CD _______ HY 85921053
Hyperium / Jun '94 / Cargo / Plastic Head

Evol

DREAMQUEST
CD _______ CDAR 037
Fatwreck Chords / Dec '96 / Plastic Head

SAGA, THE
CD _______ CDAR 026
Adipocre / May '95 / Plastic Head

Evolution

THEORY OF EVOLUTION
CD _______ WARPCD 29
Warp / Apr '95 / Prime / RTM/Disc

Evora, Cesaria

CABO VERDE
Tchintchirote / Sabine larga'm / Partida / Sange de berona / Apocalipse / Mar e morada de sodade / Bo e di meu cretcheu / Coragem irmon / Quem bo e / Regresso / Zebra / Mae velha / Pe di boi / Ess pais
CD _______ 74321453932
RCA / Feb '97 / BMG

CESARIA EVORA
Petit pays / Xandinba / Tudo tem se limite / Consedjo / D'nhirim reforma / Rotcha 'scribida / Oriundina / Tudo dia e dia / Nha cancera ka tem medida / Areia de salamansa / Flor na paul / Doce Guerra
CD _______ 74321254192
RCA / Nov '96 / BMG

DIVA AUX PIEDS NUS
CD _______ 824532
BUDA / Jun '93 / Discovery

LIVE A L'OLYMPIA
CD _______ 795912
Melodie / Oct '96 / ADA / Discovery / Grapevine/PolyGram / Greensleeves / Jet Star

MUSIC FROM CAPE VERDE
CD _______ 824842
BUDA / Nov '90 / Discovery

Ewell, Don

DON EWELL MEETS PAMELA & LLEW HIRD
CD _______ BCD 342
GHB / Jun '95 / Jazz Music

IN JAPAN 1975 (Ewell, Don & Yoshio Toyama)
CD _______ JCD 179
Jazzology / Oct '91 / Jazz Music

IN NEW ORLEANS (Ewell, Don & Herb Hall Quartet)
CD _______ JCD 256
Jazzology / Jul '96 / Jazz Music

LIVE AT THE 100 CLUB
CD _______ SACD 89
Solo Art / Jul '93 / Jazz Music

Ex

BLUEPRINTS FOR A BLACKOUT
CD _______ EX 19D
Konkurrel / May '93 / SRD

INSTANT
CD _______ EX 063064D
Konkurrel / Nov '95 / SRD

JOGGERS AND SNOGGERS
CD _______ EX 40/41
Ex / Apr '92 / Pinnacle

SCRABBLING AT THE LOCK (Ex & Tom Cora)
CD _______ EX 051D
ReR/Recommended / Mar '92 / ReR Megacorp / RTM/Disc

SHRUG THEIR SHOULDERS (Ex & Tom Cora)
CD _______ EX 57CD
ReR/Recommended / Sep '93 / ReR Megacorp / RTM/Disc

TUMULT
CD _______ EX 14D
Konkurrel / May '93 / SRD

WEATHERMEN SHRUB
CD _______ EX 57CD
Ex / Feb '94 / Pinnacle

Ex-Cathedra

TARTAN MATERIAL
CD _______ DAMGOOD 106CD
Damaged Goods / Sep '96 / Shellshock/ Disc

Ex-Press

DEFINITIVE ARTICLE, THE
CD _______ YP 007ACD
Yellow / Jul '96 / Timewarp

Exact Life

GERONIMO
CD _______ SOH 023CD
Suburbs Of Hell / Jan '96 / Kudos / Pinnacle / Plastic Head

Excelsior Brass Band

EXCELSIOR NEW ORLEANS JAZZ BAND
CD _______ BARX 051CD
Bartrax / Nov '95 / Jazz Music

Excessive Force

CONQUER YOUR WORLD
CD _______ CDDVN 12
Devotion / Jul '92 / Pinnacle

Excidium

INNOCENT RIVER
CD _______ CDAR 034
Adipocre / Jan '96 / Plastic Head

Exciter

BETTER LIVE THAN DEAD
Stand up and fight / Heavy metal maniac / Victims of sacrifice / Under attack / Sudden impacts / Delivering to the master / I am the beast / Blackwitch / Long live the loud / Rising of the dead / Cry of the banshee / Pounding metal / Violence and force
CD _______ CDBLEED 5
Bleeding Hearts / Mar '93 / Pinnacle

KILL AFTER KILL
Rain of terror / No life no future / Cold blooded murder / Smashin' 'em down / Shadow of the cross / Dog eat dog / Anger, hate and destruction / Second coming / Born to kill
CD _______ N 01922
Noise / Apr '92 / Koch

Exciters

SOMETHING TO SHOUT ABOUT (Complete Roulette Sessions)
Something to shout about / I want you to be my boy / Stars are shining bright / Run mascara / I knew you would / Talkin' 'bout my baby / Tonight, tonight / I know, I know / Baby did you change your mind / Love, life, peace / There they go / Are you satisfied / That's how love starts / My father / Just not ready
CD _______ NEMCD 730
Sequel / May '95 / BMG

Excrement

SCORCHED
CD _______ IR 012CD
Invasion / Apr '95 / Plastic Head

Excrement Of War

CATHODE RAY COMA
CD _______ FINNREC 07CD
Finn / Jun '94 / Cadillac / Plastic Head

Excretion

VOICE OF HARMONY
CD _______ WAR 007CD
Wrong Again / Apr '96 / Plastic Head

Excruciate

PASSAGE OF LIFE
CD _______ THR 019
Thrash / Jul '93 / Plastic Head

Executive Slacks

BEST OF EXECUTIVE SLACKS
CD _______ CLEO 94632
Cleopatra / Jul '94 / Cargo / Greyhound / Plastic Head / RTM/Disc / SRD

Exeter Bramclean Boys Choir

MELODIES OF MEDITATION, THE
CD _______ CDDSC 2
Golden Sounds / Jul '94 / Grapevine/ PolyGram

Exile

LATEST AND GREATEST
CD _______ CDI 9149
Intersound / Nov '96 / Direct

Exit

SET
CD _______ IRE 2092
I / Aug '97 / SRD

Exit 13

ETHOS MUSICK
CD _______ RR 69132
Roadrunner / Dec '94 / PolyGram

SMOKING SONGS
CD _______ RR 69342
Relapse / Feb '97 / Pinnacle / Plastic Head

Exit 23

JUST A FEW MORE
CD _______ RR 6966CD
Relapse / Nov '95 / Pinnacle / Plastic Head

Exit EEE

EPIDEMIC
CD _______ NRR 0185
No Respect / Nov '93 / Arabesque / Plastic Head

Exmortem

LABYRINTHS OF HORROR
CD _______ PHONO 1001CD
Euphonious Metal / Aug '95 / Plastic Head

Exocet

CONFUSION
CD _______ MASSCD 068
Massacre / Sep '95 / Plastic Head

Exodus

ANOTHER LESSON IN VIOLENCE
CD _______ CM 77173CD
Century Media / Jun '97 / Plastic Head

Exodus Quartet

WAY OUT THERE
CD _______ EX 3372
Instinct / Nov '96 / Timewarp

Experiment Fear

ASSUMING
CD _______ MASSCD 054
Massacre / Jun '95 / Plastic Head

Experimental Audio Research

KONER EXPERIMENT, THE
CD _______ EFA 006862
Mille Plateau / Mar '97 / SRD

Experimental Flux

MODULATION RENOVATIO
CD _______ EFA 001
Clubscene / Oct '94 / Clubscene / Grapevine/PolyGram / Mo's Music Machine / Prime

Experimental Pop Band

DISCGROTESQUE
CD _______ SF 017
Swarf Finger / Jun '97 / Cargo

WOOF
CD _______ SF 009CD
Swarf Finger / Jan '97 / Cargo

Exploding White Mice

EXPLODING WHITE MICE
CD _______ NORMAL 119CD
Normal / Aug '90 / ADA / Direct

Exploited

BEAT THE BASTARDS
If you are sad / They lie / Sea of blood / I syrs / Fight back / Police TV / Law for the rich / Don't blame me / Beat the bastards /

System fucked up / Massacre of innocents / Affected by them / Serial killer
CD CDJUSTX 22
CD CDJUST 22
Rough Justice / Mar '96 / Pinnacle

DEATH BEFORE DISHONOUR
CD CDJUST 6
Rough Justice / Sep '90 / Pinnacle

LET'S START A WAR (SAID MAGGIE ONE DAY)
Let's start a war (said Maggie one day) / Insanity / Safe below / Eyes of the vulture / Should we, can't we / Rival leaders / God save the Queen / Psycho / Kidology / False hopes / Another day to go nowhere / Wankers
CD DOJOCD 183
Dojo / Feb '94 / Disc

LIVE AND LOUD
Law and order / Let's start a war (said Maggie one day) / Horror epics / Cop cars / Blown to bits / Hitler's in the charts again / Belsen was a gas / Alternative / I hate you / UK 82 / Rival leaders / Maggie / Troops of tomorrow / Sex and violence / Daily news / Crashed out / SPG / Exploited barmy army / Dead cities / I believe in anarchy
CD CDPUNK 18
Anagram / Apr '96 / Cargo / Pinnacle

MASSACRE, THE
CD CDJUST 15
Rough Justice / Sep '90 / Pinnacle

PUNK'S NOT DEAD
Punk's not dead / Mucky pup / Cop cars / Free flight / Army life / Blown to bits / Sex and violence / SPG / Royalty / Dole Q / Exploited barmy army / Ripper / Out of control / Son of a copper / I believe in anarchy / Dogs of war / What you gonna do
CD DOJOCD 106
Dojo / Mar '93 / Disc

SINGLES COLLECTION, THE
Army life / Fuck the mods / Crashed out / Exploited barmy army / I believe in anarchy / What you gonna do / Dogs of war / Blown to bits / Dead cities / Hitler's in the charts again / Class war / SPG / Cop cars / Yop / Attack / Alternative / Troops of tomorrow / Computers don't blunder / Addiction / Rival leaders / Army style / Singalongabushell
CD DOJOCD 118
Dojo / Apr '93 / Disc

SINGLES, THE
CD CLEO 5000CD
Cleopatra / Jan '94 / Cargo / Greyhound / Plastic Head / RTM/Disc / SRD

TOTALLY EXPLOITED
Punk's not dead / Army life / Fuck a mod / Barmy army / Dogs of war / Dead cities / Sex and violence / Yops / Daily news / Dole Q / Believe in anarchy / God save the queen / Psycho / Blown to bits / Insanity / SPG / Jimmy Boyle / USA / Attack / Rival leaders
CD DOJOCD 1
Dojo / Jun '86 / Disc

TROOPS OF TOMORROW
Jimmy Boyle / Daily news / Disorder / Alternative / Rapist / Troops of tomorrow / UK 82 / Sid Vicious was innocent / War / They won't stop / So tragic / Germs / USA
CD DOJOCD 107
Dojo / Mar '93 / Disc

Explorers

LIVE IN LONDON
Ship of fools / Lorelei / Crack the whip / Robert Louis Stevenson / Breath of life / It's over / Voodoo Isle / You go up in smoke / Soul fantasy / Prussian blue / Two worlds apart / Venus de Milo
CD EXVP 3CD
Expression / Feb '97 / Pinnacle

Expresion

Q'EROS
CD TUMICD 031
Tumi / '93 / Discovery / Stern's

Expulsion

MAN AGAINST
CD GOD 027CD
Godhead / Jun '97 / Plastic Head

OVERFLOW
CD GOD 011CD
Godhead / May '95 / Plastic Head

Exquisite Corpse

INNER LIGHT
CD KK 107CD
KK / Oct '93 / Plastic Head

SEIZE
CD KK 083CD
KK / Aug '92 / Plastic Head

Extra Prolific

LIKE IT SHOULD BE
Intro / Brown sugar / In front of the kids / Is this right / Sweet potato pie / Cash (cash money) / One motion / Never changing / First sermon / No what / It's alright / In 20 minutes / Go back to school / Fat outro
CD CHIP 150
Jive / Sep '94 / Pinnacle

Extrema

POSITIVE PRESSURE
CD FLY 190CD
Flying / Nov '95 / Plastic Head

TENSION AT THE SEAMS
CD BABECD 5
Rosemary's Baby / Sep '93 / Plastic Head

Extremadura

PULSES
CD WWCD 018
Universal Egg / Apr '96 / SRD

Extreme

EXTREME
Little girls / Wind me up / Kid ego / Watching waiting / Mutha (don't wanna go to school today) / Teacher's pet / Big boys don't cry / Smoke signals / Flesh and blood / Rock-a-bye bye
CD CDA 5238
A&M / Mar '89 / PolyGram

III SIDES TO EVERY STORY
CD 5400062
A&M / Sep '92 / PolyGram

PORNOGRAFFITI
Decadance dance / Li'l Jack horny / When I'm president / Get the funk out / More than words / Money (In God we trust) / It's a monster / Pornograffiti / When I first kissed you / Suzi / He-man woman hater / Song for love / Hole hearted
CD CDMID 191
A&M / May '94 / PolyGram

WAITING FOR THE PUNCHLINE
There is no God / Cynical / Tell me something I don't know / Hip today / Naked / Midnight express / Leave me alone / No respect / Evilangelist / Shadow boxing / Unconditionally / Fair-weather faith / Waiting for the punchline
CD 5403052
A&M / Jan '95 / PolyGram

Extreme Noise Terror

PEEL SESSIONS, THE (10.11.87/16.2.90)
False profit / Use your mind / Human error / Only in it for the music / Subliminal music / Punk, fact and fiction / Deceived / Another nail in the coffin / Carry on screaming / Conned thru life / Work for never / Third world genocide / I am a bloody fool / In it for life / Shock treatment
CD SFPSCD 208
Strange Fruit / Aug '90 / Pinnacle

RETROBUTION (Ten Years Of Terror)
Raping the earth / Bullshit propaganda / Love brain / Work for never / We the helpless / Invisible war / Subliminal music / Human error / Murder / Think about it / Pray to be saved / Conned thru life / Deceived / Third World genocide
CD MOSH 083CD
Earache / Jan '95 / Vital

Exxplorer

RECIPE FOR POWER, A
CD MASSCD 041
Massacre / Oct '94 / Plastic Head

Eye Hate God

DOPESICK
CD CM 77114CD
Century Media / Apr '96 / Plastic Head

TAKE AS NEEDED FOR PAIN
CD CM 770522
Century Media / Sep '93 / Plastic Head

Eyeless In Gaza

ALL UNDER THE LEAVES
CD ASCALESR 021
Ambivalent Scale / Oct '96 / World Serpent

BACK FROM THE RAINS
Between these dreams / Twilight / Back from the rains / Lie still, sleep long / Catch me / Evening music / She moved through the fair / Sweet life longer / New love here / Welcome now / Your rich sky / Flight of swallows / My last lost melody / New risen / Bright play of eyes / Scent on evening air / Drumming the beating heart
CD CDBRED 69
Cherry Red / Jul '89 / Pinnacle

BITTER APPLES
CD ASCALE 020CD
Ambivalent Scale / Oct '96 / World Serpent

CAUGHT IN FLUX
Sixth sense / Point You / Voice from the tracks / Scale Amiss / Decoration / Continual / Soul on thin ice / Rose petal knot / Skeleton framework / See red / Half light / Every which way / The eyes of the beautiful losers / Still air / Out from the day-to-day / True colour / Keynote inertia
CD CDMRED 145
Cherry Red / Sep '97 / Pinnacle

DRUMMING THE BEATING HEART/ PALE HANDS I LOVED SO WELL
Transcience blues / Ill wind blows / One by one / Picture the day / Dreaming at rain / Two / Veil like calm / Throw a shadow / Pencil sketch / At arms length / Lights of April / Before you go / Tall and white nettles / Warm breath soft and slow / Blue distance / Sheer cliffs / Falling leaf/Fading flower; Goodbye to summer / Lies of love / To Ellen / Pale Saints / Letters to she / Light sliding / Big clipper ship
CD CDMRED 127
Cherry Red / Mar '96 / Pinnacle

MYSTERY SEAS
CD ASCALE 018CD
Ambivalent Scale / Oct '96 / World Serpent

RUST RED SEPTEMBER
Changing stations / Pearl and pale / New risen / September hills / Taking steps / Only whispers / Leaves are dancing / No perfect stranger / Corner of dusk / Bright play of eyes / Stealing Autumn
CD CDMRED 111
Cherry Red / Jun '96 / Pinnacle

TRANSIENCE IN BLUE
CD IR 006CD
Integrity / Jan '90 / SRD / Vital

VOICE - THE BEST OF EYELESS IN GAZA (Recollections 1980-1986)
Kodak ghosts run amok / No noise / Seven years / From A to B / Speech rapid fire / Invisibility / Others / Rose petal knot / Out from the day today / Transcience blues / Picture the day / Two / Veil like calm / One by one / Pencil sketch / Through eastfields / Changing stations / Corner of dusk / Drumming the beating heart / New risen / Sun bursts in / Welcome now / Back from the rains / Lilt of music / Evening music / Between these dreams
CD CDBRED 104
Cherry Red / Jun '96 / Pinnacle

Eyeliners

CONFIDENTIAL
CD SFTRI 484CD
Sympathy For The Record Industry / May '97 / Cargo / Greyhound / Plastic Head

Eyephone

EVERGREENS
CD 39130092
Hypnotism / Mar '97 / Cargo

Eyes Of The Nightmare Jungle

FATE
CD SPC 08425152
SPV / Jan '94 / Koch / Plastic Head

INNOCENCE
CD SPV 08461722
SPV / May '95 / Koch / Plastic Head

Eyewitness

EYEWITNESS
CD NTHEN 17
Now & Then / Apr '95 / Plastic Head

Eyges, David

LIGHTNIN' STRIKES (Eyges, David & Byard Lancaster)
CD BLE 592212
Black & Blue / Feb '93 / Discovery / Koch / Wellard

eYT

CUBIC SPACE
CD MEYCD 12
Magick Eye / Nov '95 / Cargo / SRD

Eyuphuro

MAMA MOSAMBIKI
Samukeha (the nostalgic man) / Mwanuni (the bird) / Akakswela / We awaka (you are mine) / Kihiyeny / Nifungo (the key of the house) / Oh mama (oh mother) / Nuno maalani (single mother of a single mother
CD CDRW 10
Realworld / '90 / EMI

Ezio

BLACK BOOTS ON LATIN FEET
Saxon street / Thirty and confused / Just to talk to you again / Cancel today / Go / Steal away / Further we stretch / Tuesday night / 1000 years / Agony / Wild side / Brave man / Angel song
CD 74321240152
Arista / Jun '97 / BMG

DIESEL VANILLA
Deeper / Moon / Accordion girl / Cinderella / One more walk round the dancefloor / Maybe sometimes / Alex / Call you tomorrow / Back on your own again
CD MCD 60038
MCA / Jun '97 / BMG

F

F/I

EARTHPIPE
CD ______ POT 2
PDCD / Aug '93 / Plastic Head

Fab 5

BEST OF FAB 5, THE
CD ______ PKCD 32593
K&K / Jul '93 / Jet Star

GOOD BUDDY
CD ______ VPCD 2043
VP / Sep '96 / Greensleeves / Jet Star / Total/BMG

Fabares, Shelly

BEST OF SHELLY FABARES, THE
Johnny Angel / What did they do before rock n' roll / Johnny loves me / I'm growing up / Welcome home / Big star / Things we did last summer / I left a note to say goodbye / Telephone (Won't you ring) / Billy boy / Ronnie, call me when you get a chance / How lovely to be a woman / Bye bye birdie / Football seasons over / He don't love me
CD ______ NEMCD 695
Sequel / Aug '94 / BMG

Fabian

THIS IS FABIAN
Tiger / Turn me loose / Got the feeling / Mighty cold (to a warm warm heart) / Tomorrow / I'm a man / Hypnotised / Come on and get me / Tongue tied / Gonna get you / Steady date / King of love / Stop thief / Hound dog man / Lilly Lou / Long before / Wild party / Shivers / This friendly world / I'm gonna sit right down and write myself a letter / String along / Girl like you / About this thing called love / Kissin' and twistin' / Love that I'm giving to you / Grapevine
CD ______ CDCHD 321
Ace / Jul '91 / Pinnacle

Fabich, Rainer

BACK ON EARTH
CD ______ ISCD 161
Intersound / Sep '96 / Jazz Music

Fabre, Candido

SON DE CUBA
CD ______ TUMICD 059
Tumi / May '96 / Discovery / Stern's

Fabric

BODY OF WATER
Failure / Value / A Student baby / Stick colour / Trudgeth / Helpless / Carried away / Quilt / Instrumental / Wild place / Shake it / Truth / Freedom / March of the machines / Seven / Saturnalia / Without
CD ______ WCAR 004CD
Whole Car / Sep '94 / RTM/Disc

LIGHTBRINGER
CD ______ WCAR 005CD
Whole Car / Oct '95 / RTM/Disc

Fabulous Flee Rekkers

JOE MEEK'S FABULOUS FLEE REKKERS
Lone rider / Stage to Cimarron / Sunburst / Fireball / Shiftless Sam / Blue tango / Isle of Capri / Brer Robert / Miller like wow / Twistin' the chestnuts / Black buffalo / Fandango / Sunday date / Bitter rice / Hangover / PF & (Phil the fluter's ball)
CD ______ C5CD 564
See For Miles/C5 / May '97 / Pinnacle

Fabulous Poodles

HIS MASTERS VOICE
CD ______ NEMCD 697
Sequel / Jun '95 / BMG

Fabulous Sister Brothers

LIVE IN KEMP TOWN
Intro / Here I am / Let your love / I lift up my voice / I will comfort you / Capitol Hill / Lead me on / Glory day / That the world / Up jump shout
CD ______ FSB 01
FSB / Sep '95 / FSB

Fabulous Thunderbirds

BEST OF THE FABULOUS THUNDERBIRDS, THE
Wait on time / Scratch my back / Rock with me / Let me in / Runnin' shoes / I'm a good man (if you give me a chance) / Dirty work / I believe I'm in love / One's too many / Tell me why / Can't tear it up enuff / Diddy wah diddy / Give me all your lovin' / My babe / 'Neighbour' tend to your business / Monkey / Crawl / Roll, roll, roll / How do you spell love / You ain't nothing but fine / Sugar coated love / She's tuff
CD ______ CDCHRM 100
Chrysalis / Feb '97 / EMI

BUTT ROCKIN'/T-BIRD RHYTHM
I believe I'm in love / One's too many / Give me all your lovin' / Roll roll roll / Cherry pink and apple blossom white / I hear you knocking / Tip on in / I'm sorry / Mathilda / Tell me why / In orbit / Can't tear it up enuff / How do you spell love / You're humbuggin' me / My babe / Neighbour tend to your business / Monkey / Diddy wah diddy / Lover's crime / Poor boy / Tell me (pretty baby) / Gotta have some/Just got some
CD ______ BGOCD 193
Beat Goes On / Jun '93 / Pinnacle

FABULOUS THUNDERBIRDS, THE/ WHAT'S THE WORD
Wait on time / Scratch my back / Rich woman / Full time lover / Pocket rockets / She's tuff / Marked deck / Walkin' to my baby / Rock with me / C-boy's blues / Let me in / Running shoes / You ain't nothing but fine / Low-down woman / Extra Jimmies / Sugar coated love / Last call for alcohol / Crawl / Jumpin' bad / Learn to treat me right / I'm a good man if you treat me right / Dirty work / That's enough of that stuff / Los Fabulosos Thunderbirds
CD ______ BGOCD 192
Beat Goes On / Jun '93 / Pinnacle

HOT STUFF (The Greatest Hits)
Tuff enuff / Twist of the knife / Why get up / Got love if you want it / Rock this place / Stand back / You can't judge a book by its cover / Powerful stuff / Wrap it up / Two time my lovin / Look at that, look at that
CD ______ 4722262
Epic / Feb '97 / Sony

PORTFOLIO
Crawl / She's tuff / Scratch my back / Tip on in / That's enough of that stuff / Full time lover / Sugar coated love / Wait on time / Los Fabulosos Thunderbirds / I'm a good man if you treat me right / You ain't nothing but fine / Walkin' to my baby / Marked deck / Learn to treat me right / I believe I'm in love / How do you spell love / Mathilda / One's too many / Dirty work / Can't tear it up enuff / Cherry pink and apple blossom white / Monkey / Give me all your lovin' / Diddy wah diddy / My babe / Roll roll roll
CD ______ MPCD 1599
Chrysalis / Jun '97 / EMI

ROLL OF THE DICE
Roll of the dice / Too many irons / How do I get you back / Here comes the night / Taking it too easy / I don't want to be / Mean love / I can't win / Memory from hell / Looking forward / Do as I say / Zip a dee do dah
CD ______ 01005821032
Private Music / Sep '95 / BMG

Face Down

MINDFIELD
CD ______ RR 89022
Roadrunner / Apr '96 / PolyGram

Face To Face

DON'T TURN AWAY
CD ______ FAT 515CD
Fatwreck Chords / Mar '94 / Plastic Head

Face Value

CHOICES
CD ______ WB 2130CD
We Bite / Sep '95 / Plastic Head

FACE VALUE
CD ______ CR 012CD
Conversion / Jul '96 / Plastic Head

Faceless

ACHIEVMENT
CD ______ NBX 010
Noisebox / May '95 / RTM/Disc / Vital

Faceplate

CASUAL OBSERVATION
CD ______ RR 85201CD
Rokaroola / Jun '96 / Plastic Head

Faces

ALL SHAPES AND SIZES FAMILY ALBUM (Various Artists)
Black coffee: *Humble Pie* / Heartbreaker: *Free* / Won't get fooled again: *Who* / In a broken dream: *Python Lee Jackson* / Reason to believe: *Stewart, Rod* / Poacher: *Lane, Ronnie & Slim Chance* / Waiting for a girl like you: *Foreigner* / Can feel the fire: *Wood, Ronnie* / Cindy incidentally: *Faces* / Afterglow of your love: *Small Faces* / Whatcha gonna do about it: *Marriott, Steve* / Ready or not: *Jones, Kenny* / Looking for a love: *Small Faces* / La di da: *McLagan, Ian* / Sorry she's mine: *Winston, Jimmy*
CD ______ VSOPCD 231
Connoisseur Collection / Sep '96 / Pinnacle

FIRST STEP
Wicked messenger / Devotion / Shake shudder shiver / Stone / Around the plynth / Flying / Pinapple and the monkey / Nobody knows / Looking out the window / Three button hand me down
CD ______ 7599263762
Warner Bros. / Sep '93 / Warner Music

LONG PLAYER
Bad 'n' ruin / Tell everyone / Sweet Lady Mary / Richmond / Maybe I'm amazed / Had me a real good time / On the beach / I feel so good / Jerusalem
CD ______ 7599261912
Warner Bros. / Sep '93 / Warner Music

NOD'S AS GOOD AS A WINK TO A BLIND HORSE, A
Miss Judy's farm / You're so rude / Love lived here / Last orders please / Stay with me / Debris / Memphis / Too bad / That's all you need
CD ______ 7599259292
Warner Bros. / Sep '93 / Warner Music

OOH LA LA
Silicone grown / Cindy incidentally / Flags and banners / My fault / Borstal boys / Fly in the ointment / If I'm on the late side / Glad and sorry / Just another honky / Ooh la la
CD ______ 7599263682
Warner Bros. / Sep '93 / Warner Music

Facil

FACIL
CD ______ IAE 004
Instinct Ambient Europe / May '95 / Plastic Head

Faction

HEAVEN
CD ______ TMCD 056
Third Mind / Oct '90 / Pinnacle / Third Mind

Faction Zero

LIBERATION
CD ______ IJT 002
IJT / Feb '97 / Cargo / Greyhound

Faddis, Jon

JON AND BILLY (Faddis, Jon & Billy Harper)
Jon and Billy / Water bridge-mizu hashi san / Ballad for Jon Haddis / Two d's from Shinjyuku, dig and dug / Seventeen bar blues / This all-koredake
CD ______ ECD 22052
Evidence / Jul '93 / ADA / Cadillac / Harmonia Mundi

Fadela & Sahrawi

WALLI
Bab Wahran / Walli / Dellali (my lover) / Dance the Rai / Dawh (they took him away) / Hasni / Wayala / Mani / Dougih / Waadi (just my luck) / N'sel fik
CD ______ ROUCD 5076
Rounder / Feb '97 / ADA / CM / Direct

Fading Out

FADING OUT
CD ______ PR 12CD
Palace / Dec '96 / Cargo

Fagen, Donald

KAMAKIRIAD
Trans island skyway / Countermoon / Springtime / Snowbound / Tomorrow's girls / Florida room / On the dunes / Teahouse on the tracks
CD ______ 9362452302
Warner Bros. / Dec '96 / Warner Music

NIGHTFLY, THE
New frontier / IGY / Green Flower Street / Ruby baby / Maxine / Walk between raindrops / Goodbye look / Night fly
CD ______ 9236962
Warner Bros. / Oct '82 / Warner Music

ORIGINS OF STEELY DAN, THE (Fagen, Donald & Walter Becker)
CD ______ CDSGP 029
Prestige / Mar '94 / Else / Total/BMG

Fagin, Joe

BEST OF JOE FAGIN
Am I asking too much / Crazy in love / That's livin' alright / (Cry) for no one / Younger days / Forever now / Only love can show the way / Epitaph (for a drunk) / Why don't we spend the night / Put out the light / Get it right / Love hangs by a thread / As time goes by / So much for saying goodbye / Breaking away / She's leaving home / Annie
CD ______ CDWM 107
Westmoor / Jan '96 / Target/BMG

Fahey, John

CHRISTMAS GUITAR VOL.1
CD ______ CDVR 002
Varrick / Dec '94 / ADA / CM / Direct / Roots

COMPLETE BLIND JOE DEATH
On doing all evil deed blues / St. Louis blues / Poor boy long way from home / Uncloudy day / John Henry / In Christ there is no East or West / Desperate man blues / Sun gonna shine in my back door / Sligo river blues / On doing all evil deed blues / St. Louis blues / Poor boy long way from home / Uncloudy day / John Henry / In Christ there is no East or west / Desperate man blues / Sun gonna shine in my backdoor / Sligo river blues / I'm gonna do all I can for my Lord / Transcendental waterfall / West coast blues
CD ______ CDTAK 1002
Takoma / Apr '96 / ADA / Pinnacle

ESSENTIAL JOHN FAHEY, THE
CD ______ VCD 55
Vanguard / Nov '96 / ADA / Pinnacle

FARE FORWARD VOYAGERS
CD ______ SHANCD 99005
Shanachie / '92 / ADA / Greensleeves / Koch

LET GO
Let go / Black Mommy / Dvorak / World is waiting for the sunrise / Deep river/Old man river / Lights out / Pretty afternoon / Sunset on Prince George's country / Layla / Old country rock
CD ______ CDVR 008
Varrick / Feb '97 / ADA / CM / Direct / Roots

OLD FASHIONED LOVE
In a Persian market / Jaya shiva shankaram / Marilyn / Assassination of Stefan Grossman / Old fashioned love / Boodle am shake / Keep your lamp trimmed and burning / I saw the light shining 'round and 'round
CD ______ SHCD 99001
Shanachie / Jun '91 / ADA / Greensleeves / Koch

OLD GIRLFRIENDS AND OTHER HORRIBLE MEMORIES
CD ______ CDVR 031
Varrick / Feb '92 / ADA / CM / Direct / Roots

POPULAR SONGS OF CHRISTMAS AND NEW YEAR
CD ______ VR 012CD
Varrick / Feb '95 / ADA / CM / Direct / Roots

RAILROAD
CD ______ SHAN 99003CD
Shanachie / '92 / ADA / Greensleeves / Koch

RAIN FORESTS, OCEANS AND OTHER THEMES
CD ______ CDVR 019
Rounder / Dec '86 / ADA / CM / Direct

TRANSFIGURATION OF BLIND JOE DEATH, THE
Beautiful Linda Getchell / Orinda-moraga / I am the resurrection / On the sunny side of the ocean / Tell her to come back home / My station will be changed after a while / 101 is a hard road to travel / How green was my valley / Bicycle built for two / Death of the Clayton Peacock / Brenda's blues / Old southern medley / Come back baby / Poor boy / St. Patrick's hymn
CD ______ CDTAK 7015
Takoma / May '97 / ADA / Pinnacle

VOICE OF THE TURTLE, THE
Bottleneck blues / Bill Cheatham / Lewisdale blues / Bean vine blues / Bean vine blues / Raga called Pat part 3 / Raga called Pat part 4 / Train / Je ne me suis reveillais matin pas en May / Story of Dorothy Gooch part 1 / Nine pound hammer / Lonesome valley
CD ______ CDTAK 1019
Takoma / Jul '96 / ADA / Pinnacle

Faine Jade

INTROSPECTION: A FAINE JADE RECITAL
Tune up / Dr. Paul overture / People games play / Cold winter sun symphony in D major / I lived tomorrow yesterday / Ballad of the bad guys (1956 AD) / Piano interlude / Introspection / In a brand new groove / On the inside there's a middle / Don't hassle me / Grand finale / Stand together in the end / Dr. Paul / People games play / Don't hassle me (instrumental)
CD _______________ **CDWIKD 141**
Big Beat / Mar '95 / Pinnacle

Fair, Jad

HONEY BEE
CD _______________ **DRJIM 19**
Dr. Jim / Jul '97 / Cargo / Greyhound

I LIKE IT WHEN YOU SMILE
CD _______________ **PAPCD 009**
Paperhouse / Feb '92 / RTM/Disc

IT'S SPOOKY (Fair, Jad & Daniel Johnston)
CD _______________ **PAPCD 019**
Paperhouse / Jul '93 / RTM/Disc

Fairburn, Werly

EVERYBODY'S ROCKIN'
I'm a fool about your love / Everybody's rockin' / All the time / My heart's on fire / Speak to me baby / Telephone baby / No blues tomorrow / I'm jealous / I guess I'm crazy / That sweet love of mine / Nothin' but lovin' / Love spelled backwards is evol / Broken hearted me / Stay close to me / It's heaven / Old mem'ries come back / Good deal Lucille / Baby he's a wolf / Won't it be nice / Little bit of nothing / Prison cell of love / Spiteful heart / It's a cold weary world / I feel like cryin' / Camping with Marie / Let's live it over / Doggone that moon / Black widow spider woman / You are my sunshine
CD _______________ **BCD 15578**
Bear Family / Nov '93 / Direct / Rollercoaster / Swift

Fairclough Group

SHEPHERD WHEEL
Jacob's ladder / Shepherd wheel / Yaller belly / Saint Monda / Rattening / Stoneburst / Racing / When there's nothing left to burn
CD _______________ **ASCCD 1**
ASC / Jun '95 / Cadillac / New Note/ Pinnacle

Fairclough, Peter

WILDSILK (Fairclough, Peter & Keith Tippett)
Emerald lake / Under thunder / Wild silk / Skretch for Gary / Casting the net / Recurring dream / In the glade of the woodstone bird / Through the gate / Fountain / Humble
CD _______________ **ASCCD 8**
ASC / May '96 / Cadillac / New Note/ Pinnacle

Fairer Sax

DIVERSIONS WITH THE FAIRER SAX
Arrival of the Queen of Sheba / Sixteenth century dances / Fugue in D minor (Bach) / Aria / Moment musicale (Schubert) / Something doing
CD _______________ **CDSDL 365**
Saydisc / Oct '87 / ADA / Direct / Harmonia Mundi

Fairey Engineering Works ...

SPECTRUM (Fairey Engineering Works Band)
CD _______________ **QPRL 058D**
Polyphonic / Aug '93 / Complete/Pinnacle

TOP BRASS (Fairey Engineering Works Band)
King cotton / Perpetuum mobile / Send in the clowns / Lohengrin - intro to act 3 / Girl I left behind me / If / Round the clock / Queen of Sheba / Can can / Don't cry for me Argentina / Polly wolly doodling / Hustle / Peace / Fanfare and soliloquy
CD _______________ **SUMCD 4131**
Sound & Media / Jun '97 / Sound & Media

TRIUMPHANT RHAPSODY (Fairey Engineering Works Band)
CD _______________ **QPRL 068D**
Polyphonic / Sep '94 / Complete/Pinnacle

Fairfield Four

STANDING ON THE ROCK
Don't leave me by myself / Hope to shout in glory / I can tell you the time / My prayer / Come on to this altar / I love the name Jesus / Does Jesus care / Leave it there / Love like a river / Who is that knocking / His eye is on the sparrow / How I got over / This evening our father / Hear me when I pray / When the battle is over / Standing on the rock / Somebody touched me / On my journey now / Old time religion / Talking about Jesus / No room at the inn / When we bow / Let's go / Don't drive your children away / Packin' every burden / Poor pilgrim
CD _______________ **CDCHD 449**
Ace / Aug '93 / Pinnacle

Fairground Attraction

AY FOND KISS
Jock O'Hazeldean / Walkin' after midnight / Trying times / Winter rose / Allelujah (live) / Watching the party / Game of love / You send me / Mystery train / Do you want to know a secret / Cajun band / Ae fond kiss
CD _______________ **74321193712**
RCA / Apr '94 / BMG

COLLECTION, THE
Comedy waltz (live) / Clare / Perfect / Find my love / Walkin' after midnight / Smile in a whisper / You send me / Do you want to know a secret / Allelujah / Moon on the rain / Fairground attraction / Wind knows my name / Watching the party / Winter rose / Moon is mine / Ae fond kiss
CD _______________ **74321232512**
Arista / Feb '97 / BMG

FIRST OF A MILLION KISSES
Smile in a whisper / Perfect / Moon on the rain / Find my love / Fairground attraction / Wind knows my name / Clare / Comedy waltz / Moon is mine / Station Street / Whispers / Allelujah / Falling backwards / Mythology
CD _______________ **74321134392**
RCA / May '93 / BMG

PERFECT - THE BEST OF FAIRGROUND ATTRACTION
CD _______________ **74321292772**
RCA / Jul '95 / BMG

VERY BEST OF FAIRGROUND ATTRACTION, THE
Perfect / Find my love / Fairground attraction / Smile in a whisper / Clare / Walkin' after midnight / Do you want to know a secret / Allelujah / Moon is mine / Watching the party / Winter rose / Wind knows my name / Jock O'Hazeldean / Comedy waltz / You send me / Aye fond kiss
CD _______________ **74321446752**
Camden / Feb '97 / BMG

Fairhurst, Richard

HUNGRY ANTS
CD _______________ **BDV 9504**
Babel / Jan '96 / ADA / Cadillac / Diverse / Harmonia Mundi

Fairies Fortune

SNOWFISH
CD _______________ **EFA 155852**
Gymnastic / Aug '95 / SRD

Fairport Convention

25TH ANNIVERSARY PACK (Rosie/John Babbacombe Lee/Nine/Rising For The Moon)
CD _______________ **FCBX 1**
Island / Aug '92 / PolyGram

5 SEASONS
CD _______________ **HTCD 48**
HTD / Jan '96 / CM / Pinnacle

ANGEL DELIGHT
Lord Marlborough / Sir William Gower / Bridge over the river Ash / Wizard of the wordly game / Journeyman's grace / Angel delight / Banks of the sweet primroses / Instrumental medley / Bonnie black hare / Sickness and diseases
CD _______________ **IMCD 166**
Island / Mar '93 / PolyGram

BONNY BUNCH OF ROSES
Adieu adieu / Bonnie bunch of roses / Eynsham poacher / General Taylor / James O'Donnell's jig / Last waltz / Poor ditching boy / Royal selleccion number 13 / Run Johnny run
CD _______________ **WRCD 011**
Woodworm / Oct '88 / Pinnacle
CD _______________ **5129882**
Vertigo / Jan '92 / PolyGram

ENCORE ENCORE (Farewell Farewell Remastered)
Matty groves / Orange blossom special / John Lee / Bridge over the river Ash / Sir Patrick Spens / Mr. Lacey / Walk awhile / Bonny black hare / Journeyman's grace / Meet on the ledge / Rubber band / Hen's march/Four poster bed / Flatback caper / Dirty linen
CD _______________ **FP 001CD**
Folkprint / Jul '97 / Pinnacle

EXPLETIVE DELIGHTED
CD _______________ **TRUCKCD 16**
Terrapin Truckin' / Nov '95 / ADA / Direct / Total/BMG

FAIRPORT CONVENTION
Time will show the wiser / I don't know where I stand / Decameron / Jack O'Diamonds / Portfolio / Chelsea morning / Sun shade / Lobster / It's alright ma, it's only witchcraft / One sure thing / MI breakdown
CD _______________ **8352302**
Polydor / Oct '90 / PolyGram

FAIRPORT CONVENTION 9
Hexhamshire lass / Polly on the shore / Briliancy medley and Cherokee shuffle / To Althea from prison / Tokyo / Bring 'em down / Big William / Pleasure and pain / Possibly parsons green
CD _______________ **IMCD 154**
Island / Aug '92 / PolyGram

FAREWELL, FAREWELL
Matty groves / Orange blossom special / John Lee / Bridge over the river Ash / Sir Patrick Spens / Mr. Lacey / Walk awhile / Bonnie black hare / Journeyman's grace / Meet on the ledge
CD _______________ **SIVCD 0002**
Red Steel / May '96 / Pinnacle

FULL HOUSE
Walk awhile / Dirty linen / Sloth / Sir Patrick Spens / Flatback caper / Doctor of physick / Flowers of the forest
CD _______________ **HNCD 4417**
Hannibal / Nov '91 / ADA / Vital

GLADYS LEAP
CD _______________ **SIVCD 0003**
Red Steel / May '96 / Pinnacle

HEYDAY (BBC Radio Sessions)
CD _______________ **HNCD 1329**
Hannibal / Oct '87 / ADA / Vital

HISTORY OF FAIRPORT CONVENTION, THE
Meet on the ledge / Fotheringay / Mr. Lacey / Book song / Sailor's life / Si tu dois partir / Who knows where the time goes / Matty Groves / Crazy man Michael / Now be thankful (Medley) / Walk awhile / Sloth / Bonnie black hare / Angel delight / Bridge over the river Ash / John Lee / Breakfast in Mayfair / Hanging song / Hen's march / Four poster bed
CD _______________ **IMCD 128**
Island / Jun '91 / PolyGram

HOUSE FULL (Live In Los Angeles)
Sir Patrick Spens / Banks of the sweet primroses / Toss the feathers / Sloth / Staines morris / Matty groves / Mason's apron / Battle of the Somme
CD _______________ **HNCD 1319**
Hannibal / Jul '90 / ADA / Vital

IN REAL TIME
Reynard the fox / Widow of Westmorland's daughter / Hiring fair / Crazy man Michael / Close to the wind / Big three medley / Meet on the ledge
CD _______________ **IMCD 10**
Island / '90 / PolyGram

JEWEL IN THE CROWN
CD _______________ **WRMCD 023**
Woodworm / Jan '95 / Pinnacle

JOHN BABBACOMBE LEE
John's reflections / This was the happiest period of his life / Tragedy now strikes hard / John was hardly more than a bewildered observer / When it comes he can cannot sleep
CD _______________ **IMCD 153**
Island / Aug '92 / PolyGram

LIEGE AND LIEF
Come all ye / Reynardine / Matty groves / Farewell farewell / Deserter / Lark in the morning (medley) / Tamlin / Crazy man Michael / Rakish paddy / Foxhunters jigs / Toss the feathers
CD _______________ **IMCD 60**
Island / '89 / PolyGram

LIVE
Matty Groves / Rosie / Fiddlestix / John the gun / Something you got / Sloth / Dirty linen / Down in the flood / Sir B MacKenzie
CD _______________ **IMCD 95**
Island / Feb '90 / PolyGram

OLD, NEW, BORROWED AND BLUE
CD _______________ **WRCD 024**
Woodworm / May '96 / Pinnacle

RISING FOR THE MOON
Rising for the moon / Restless / White dress / Let it go / Stranger to himself / What is true / Iron lion / Dawn / After halloween / Night-time girl / One more chance
CD _______________ **IMCD 155**
Island / Aug '92 / PolyGram

ROSIE
Rosie / Matthew, Mark, Luke and John / Knights of the road / Peggy's pub / Plainsman / Hungarian rhapsody / My girl / Me with you / Hen's march / Furs and feathers
CD _______________ **IMCD 152**
Island / Aug '92 / PolyGram

UNHALFBRICKING
Genesis hall / Si tu dois partir / Autopsy / Cajun woman / Who knows where the time goes / Percy's song / Million dollar bash / Sailor's life
CD _______________ **IMCD 61**
Island / Nov '89 / PolyGram

WHAT WE DID ON OUR HOLIDAYS
Fotheringay / Mr. Lacey / Book song / Lord is in this place / No man's land / I'll keep it with mine / Eastern rain / Nottamun town / Tale in hard time / She moved through the fair / Meet me on the ledge / End of a holiday
CD _______________ **IMCD 97**
Island / Feb '90 / PolyGram

WHO KNOWS WHERE THE TIME GOES
John Gaudie / Sailing boat / Tom Paine / Bowman's retreat / Spanish main / Golden glove / Slipolgy / Wishful waltz / Life's a long song / Dangerous / Heard it throught the grapevine / Who knows where the time goes
CD _______________ **WRCD 025**
Woodworm / Aug '97 / Pinnacle

WOODWORM YEARS, THE
Level pegging / Hiring fair / Wat Tyler / Portmeirion / Honour and praise / Deserter / From a distance / Rosemary's sister / Red and gold / Summer before the war / Tripping up the stairs / Claudy banks / Three jigs for Jamie / Ginnie
CD _______________ **SIVCD 0005**
Red Steel / Dec '96 / Pinnacle

Fairweather, Al

MADE TO MEASURE (Fairweather, Al & Friends)
By the fireside / Music goes round and round / Sue's blues / Exactly like you / Goody goody / Easy to love / Sometimes I'm happy / Tin roof blues / I can't give you anything but love / Red for go / September in the rain / If I had you / Coe-pilot / Grapevine / Doin' the racoon
CD _______________ **LACD 75**
Lake / Mar '97 / ADA / Cadillac / Direct / Jazz Music / Target/BMG

Fairweather, Digby

PORTRAIT OF DIGBY FAIRWEATHER
CD _______________ **BLCD 760505**
Black Lion / Apr '91 / Cadillac / Jazz Music / Koch / Wellard

WITH NAT IN MIND (Fairweather, Digby & His New Georgians)
CD _______________ **JCD 247**
Jazzology / Aug '95 / Jazz Music

Faitelson, Dalia

COMMON GROUND (Faitelson, Dalia Group)
Dahab / Eye of the morning / East west / My treasure / Trail of a trail / Captain / Mustafa / Common ground / Cheek to cheek / Alone with you
CD _______________ **STCD 4196**
Storyville / Nov '94 / Cadillac / Jazz Music / Wellard

Faith & The Muse

ANNWYN, BENEATH THE WAVES
CD _______________ **EFACD 6486**
Tess / Jul '96 / SRD

Faith, Adam

ADAM
Wonderful time / Diamond ring / Summertime / Greenfinger / Piper of love / Girl like you / Turn me loose / So many ways / Singin' in the rain / Fare thee well my pretty maid / I'm a man / Hit the road to dreamland / Wonderful time / Diamond ring / Summertime / Greenfinger / Piper of love / Girl like you / Turn me loose / So many ways / Singin' in the rain / Fare thee well my pretty maid / I'm a man / Hit the road to dreamland
CD _______________ **DORIG 106**
EMI / Aug '97 / EMI

ADAM FAITH SINGLES COLLECTION (His Greatest Hits)
Got a heartsick feeling / What do you want / Poor me / Someone else's baby / When Johnny comes marching home / Made you / How about that / Who am I / Easy going me / Don't you know it / Time has come / Lonesome / As you like it / Don't that beat all / What now / First time / We are in love / Message to Martha / Someone's taken Maria away / Cheryl's goin' home
CD _______________ **CZ 260**
EMI / Jan '90 / EMI

BEST OF ADAM FAITH
What do you want / Poor me / Someone else's baby / Johnny comes marching home / Made you / How about that / Lonely pup (in a christmas shop) / This is it / Who am I / Easy going me / Don't you know it / Time has come / Lonesome / As you like it / Don't that beat all / What now / Walkin' tall / First time: *Faith, Adam & The Roulettes* / We are in love: *Faith, Adam & The Roulettes* / If he tells you: *Faith, Adam & The Roulettes* / I love being in love with you: *Faith, Adam & The Roulettes* / Message to Martha / Stop feeling sorry for yourself / Someone's taken Maria away: *Faith, Adam & The Roulettes* / Cheryl's goin' home
CD _______________ **CDMFP 6048**
Music For Pleasure / Jan '89 / EMI

BEST OF THE EMI YEARS, THE
What do you want / (Got a) Heartsick feeling / From now until forever / Ah poor little baby / Poor me / Summertime / Wonderful time / Someone else's baby / When Johnny comes marching home / Made you / Hit the road to dreamland / I'm a man / How about that / With open arms / Singin' in the rain / Fare thee well my pretty maid / Lonely pup (in a Christmas shop) / This is it / Who am I / Sho' know a lot about love / As long as

you keep loving me / I'm gonna love you too / Easy going me / Wonderin' / Watch your step / Don't you know it / Time has come / Help each other romance / Lonesome / Ballad of a broken heart / (I'm) Knockin' on wood / As you like it / Learning to forget / You 'n' me / Face to face / You can do it if you try / Don't that beat all / Mix me a person / Baby take a bow / What now / What have I got / Walkin' tall / Forget me not / First time / So long baby / Made for me / We are in love / If he tells you / Come closer / Talk to me / It's alright / I love being in love with you / Message to Martha / I've gotta see my baby / Stop feeling sorry for yourself / I'll stop at nothing / Hand me down things / Talk about love / Someone's taken Maria away / I don't need that kind of lovin' / If you ever need me / Cheryl's goin' home / What more can anyone do / Cowman milk your cow / To hell with love / Close the door / You make my life worthwhile
CD ______ CDEM 1513
EMI / Feb '94 / EMI

MIDNIGHT POSTCARDS
Body to body / Stuck in the middle / When I'm dead and gone / Once the love has gone / I'll be your baby tonight / Roxy roxy / Back on the road / Squeeze box / Why me / Promise / Not without you / All I ever need is you / Making up
CD ______ 8213982
PolyGram TV / Nov '93 / PolyGram

Faith, George

SOULFUL
CD ______ CDSGP 073
Prestige / Jul '95 / Else / Total/BMG

TO BE A LOVER (HAVE MERCY)
CD ______ RRCD 31
Reggae Refreshers / Sep '91 / PolyGram / Vital

Faith Healers

IMAGINARY FRIEND
CD ______ PURECD 027
Too Pure / Oct '93 / Vital

Faith, Michael

SUSPENDED ANIMATION
CD ______ CMMR 922
Music Maker / Oct '93 / ADA / Grapevine/ PolyGram

Faith No More

ALBUM OF THE YEAR (2CD Set)
Collision / Strip search / Last cup of sorrow / Naked in front of the computer / Helpless / Mouth to mouth / Ashes to ashes / Ahe loves me not / Got that feeling / Paths of glory / Home sick home / Pristina / Last cup of sorrow / Last cup of sorrow / Ashes to ashes / Ashes to ashes / She loves me not / Ashes to ashes
CD ______ 8289012
CD Set ______ 8288022
Slash / Jun '97 / PolyGram

ANGEL DUST
CD ______ 8284012
Slash / Jan '93 / PolyGram

INTRODUCE YOURSELF
Faster disco / Anne's song / Introduce yourself / Chinese arithmetic / Death march / We care a lot / R 'N' R / Crab song / Blood / Spirit
CD ______ 8280512
Slash / Apr '87 / PolyGram

KING FOR A DAY, FOOL FOR A LIFETIME
Get out / Ricochet / Evidence / Gentle art of making enemies / Star AD / Cuckoo for caca / Caralho voador / Ugly in the morning / Digging the grave / Take this bottle / King for a day / What a day / Last to know / Just a man
CD ______ 8285602
Slash / Mar '95 / PolyGram

LIVE AT THE BRIXTON ACADEMY
Epic / From out of nowhere / We care a lot / Falling to pieces / Real thing / Warriors / Zombie eaters / Edge of the world / Grade / Cowboy song
CD ______ 8282382
Slash / Feb '91 / PolyGram

REAL THING, THE
From out of nowhere / Epic / Falling to pieces / Surprise you're dead / Zombie eaters / Real thing / Underwater love / Morning after / Woodpecker from Mars / War pigs / Edge of the world
CD ______ 8281542
Slash / Jun '89 / PolyGram

WE CARE A LOT
We care a lot / Jungle / Mark Bowen / Jim / Why do you bother / Greed / Pills for breakfast / As the worm turns / Arabian disco / New beginnings
CD ______ 8288052
Slash / Sep '96 / PolyGram

Faith Over Reason

EYES WIDE SMILE
CD ______ ABBCD 027
Big Cat / Sep '91 / 3mv/Pinnacle

Faith, Percy

16 MOST REQUESTED SONGS
Swedish rhapsody / Moulin Rouge / Delicado / Baubles, bangles and beads / Rain in Spain / Show me / Malaguena / Summer place / I will follow you / There for young lovers / Sound of music / Tara's theme / Girl from Ipanema / Oscar / Love theme from Romeo and Juliet / MacArthur Park
CD ______ 4724172
Columbia / Nov '92 / Sony

VIVA THE MUSIC OF MEXICO/THE MUSIC OF BRAZIL
Granada / La golondrina / La cucaracha / Chiapanecas / Estrellita / El rancho grande / La paloma / Noche de ronda / Mexican hat dance / Guadalajara / Zandunga / Jesusita en chihuahua / Cuanto la gusta / Solamente una vez / Brazil / Delicado / Tu sabes / Ba-tu-ca-da / Amorada / Bandit / Baia / Tico-tico / Little dreamer / Maxixe / Atrevido / Minute samba
CD ______ 4871922
Columbia / Mar '97 / Sony

Faithful Dawn

TEMPERANCE
CD ______ NIGHTCD 014
Nightbreed / May '97 / Plastic Head

Faithfull, Marianne

20TH CENTURY BLUES
Alabama song / Want to buy some illusions / Pirate Jenny / Salomon song / Boulevard of broken dreams / Complainte de la Seine / Ballad of the soldier's wife / Intro / Mon ami, my friend / Falling in love again / Mack the knife / 20th Century blues / Don't forget me / Surabaya Johnny / Outro
CD ______ 74321386562
RCA Victor / Sep '96 / BMG

BLAZING AWAY
Les prisons du roy / Guilt / Sister Morphine / Why'd ya do it / Ballad of Lucy Jordan / Blazing away / Broken English / Strange weather / Working class hero / As tears go by / When I find my life / Times Square / She moved through the fair
CD ______ IMCD 207
Island / Apr '95 / PolyGram

BROKEN ENGLISH
Working class hero / What's the hurry / Ballad of Lucy Jordan / Why d'ya do it / Broken English / Witch's song / Guilt / Brain drain
CD ______ IMCD 11
Island / '89 / PolyGram

CHILD'S ADVENTURE, A
CD ______ IMCD 206
Island / Apr '95 / PolyGram

DANGEROUS ACQUAINTANCES
Sweetheart / Intrigue / Easy in the city / Strange one / Tenderness / For beauty's sake / So sad / Eye communication / Truth, bitter truth
CD ______ IMCD 205
Island / May '95 / PolyGram

FAITHFULL - A COLLECTION OF HER BEST SONGS
Broken english / Ballad of Lucy Jordan / Working class hero / Guilt / Why'd ya do it / Ghost dance / Trouble in mind / Times Square / Strange weather / She / As tears go by
CD ______ CID 8023
Island / Aug '94 / PolyGram

FAITHLESS
Dreamin' my dreams / Vanilla O'Lay / Wait for me down by the river / I'll be your baby tonight / Lady Madelaine / All I wanna do in life / Way you want me to be / Wrong road again / That was the day (Nashville) / This time / I'm not Lisa / Honky tonk angels
CD ______ CLACD 148
Castle / Apr '89 / BMG

SECRET LIFE, A
Prologue / Sleep / Love in the afternoon / Flaming September / She / Bored by dreams / Losing / Wedding / Stars line up / Epilogue
CD ______ IMCD 225
Island / Sep '96 / PolyGram

STRANGE WEATHER
Stranger intro / Boulevard of broken dreams / I ain't goin' down to the well no more / Yesterdays / Sing of judgement / Strange weather / Love life and money / I'll keep it with mine / Hello stranger / Penthouse serenade / As tears go by / Stranger on earth
CD ______ IMCD 12
Island / '89 / PolyGram

VERY BEST OF MARIANNE FAITHFULL
As tears go by / Come and stay with me / Scarborough Fair / Monday, Monday / Yesterday / Last thing on my mind / What have they done to the rain / This little bird / In my time of sorrow / Is this what I get for loving you / Tomorrow's calling / Reason to believe / Sister Morphine / Go away from my world / Summer nights
CD ______ 8204822
Deram / Sep '87 / PolyGram

Faithless

REVERENCE
CD ______ CHEKXCD 500
CD ______ CHEKCD 500
Cheeky / Nov '96 / 3mv/BMG / Prime

Fajt, Pavel

PAVEL FAJT & PLUTO (Fajt, Pavel & Pluto)
CD ______ MAMO 402
Indies / Jun '97 / ReR Megacorp

Falay, Maffy

HANK'S TUNE (Falay, Maffy Sextet)
CD ______ LICD 3157
Liphone / Jan '97 / Cadillac / Jazz Music

Falco, Tav

BEHIND THE MAGNOLIA CURTAIN/ BLOW YOUR TOP (Falco, Tav Panther Burns)
CD ______ 422135
New Rose / May '94 / ADA / Direct / Discovery

DISAPPEARING ANGELS (Falco, Tav Panther Burns)
CD ______ SFTRI 460CD
Sympathy For The Record Industry / Oct '96 / Cargo / Greyhound / Plastic Head

LIFE SENTENCE (Falco, Tav Panther Burns)
CD ______ 422136
New Rose / May '94 / ADA / Direct / Discovery

LOVE'S LAST WARNING (The Best Of Tav Falco's Panther Burns) (Falco, Tav Panther Burns)
CD ______ 422088
Last Call / Nov '96 / Cargo / Direct / Discovery

MIDNIGHT IN MEMPHIS (Falco, Tav Panther Burns)
CD ______ 422141
New Rose / May '94 / ADA / Direct / Discovery

RED DEVIL
CD ______ ROSE 140CD
New Rose / Feb '88 / ADA / Direct / Discovery

SHADOW ANGELS AND DISAPPEARING DANCERS
CD ______ MRCD 111
Munster / Mar '97 / Cargo / Greyhound / Plastic Head

SHADOW DANCER
CD ______ IRS 993513CD
Intercord / Feb '96 / Plastic Head
CD ______ 4222462
Last Call / Nov '96 / Cargo / Direct / Discovery

SUGAR DITCH REVISITED
CD ______ 422137
New Rose / May '94 / ADA / Direct / Discovery

UNRELEASED SESSIONS (Falco, Tav Panther Burns)
CD ______ FM 1011CD
Marilyn / Jul '92 / Pinnacle

WORLD WE KNEW, THE (Falco, Tav Panther Burns)
CD ______ 422140
New Rose / May '94 / ADA / Direct / Discovery

Falcon, Bobby

SOMETHING WONDERFUL
CD ______ EMCD 1003
Don One / May '96 / Jet Star

Falconer, Elizabeth

ISSHIN EMERGING (Koto Music)
CD ______ CD 973
Music & Arts / Jul '97 / Cadillac / Harmonia Mundi

Fall

15 WAYS TO LEAVE YOUR MAN (Live)
Chilinist / Don't call me darling / 15 ways to leave your man / DIY meat / Pearl city / Feeling numb / LA / Big new prinz / Mr. Pharmacist / Everything hurtz / Mixer / Das vaulture ans ein nutter-wain / M5 6-7pm / Return / Reckoning / Hey student
CD ______ RRCD 239
Receiver / Aug '97 / Grapevine/PolyGram

45 84 89 (The A Sides)
Oh brother / CREEP / No bulbs 3 / Rollin' dany / Couldn't get ahead / Cruiser's creek / LA / Living too late / Hit the North / Mr. Pharmacist / Hey Luciani / There's a ghost in my house / Victoria / Big new prinz / Wrong place right time / Jerusalem / Dead beat descendant
CD ______ BEGA 111CD
Beggars Banquet / Sep '90 / RTM/Disc / Warner Music

B SIDES
Oh brother / God box / CREEP / Pat-trip dispenser / Slang King 2 / Draygo's guilt / Clear off / No bulbs / Petty thief lout / Vixen / Hot aftershave bop / Living too long / Lucifer over Lancashire / Auto-tech pilot / Entitled / Shoulder pads / Sleep debt snatches / Mark'll sink us / Haf found bormann / Australians in Europe / Northerns in Europe / Hit the North part 2 / Guest informant / Tuff like boogie / Twister / Bremen nacht run out / Acid priest 2088 / Cab it up / Kurious oranj / Hit the North
CD Set ______ BEGA 116CD
Beggars Banquet / Dec '90 / RTM/Disc / Warner Music

BEND SINISTER
ROD / Dr. Faustus / Shoulder pads / Mr. Pharmacist / Gross chapel / US 80's - 60's / Terry Waite sez / Bournemouth runner / Riddler / Shoulder pads 2
CD ______ BEGA 75CD
Beggars Banquet / Jan '88 / RTM/Disc / Warner Music

CODE: SELFISH
Birmingham School Of Business / Free range / Return / Time enough at last / Everything hurtz / Immortality / Two face / Just waiting / So-called dangerous / Gentlemen's agreement / Married two kids / Crew filth
CD ______ 5121622
Cog Sinister / Mar '96 / PolyGram

COLLECTION, THE
CD ______ CCSCD 365
Castle / Mar '93 / BMG

EXTRICATE
Sing Harpy / I'm Frank / Bill is dead / Black monk theme pt.1 / Popcorn double feature / Telephone thing / Hilary / Chicago now / Littlest rebel / And therein... / Black monk theme pt.2 / Arms control poseur / British people in hot weather / Extricate
CD ______ 8422042
Cog Sinister / Mar '96 / PolyGram

FALL IN A HOLE
Impression of J Temperance / Man whose head expanded / Room to live / Hip priest / Lie dream of a casino soul / Prole art theatre / Hard life in country / Classical / Mere pseud maged / Marquis Cha - Cha / Backdrop / Fantastic life / English scheme / Joker hysterical face / No Xmas for John Quays / Solicitor in studio
CD ______ COGVP 102CD
Voiceprint / Apr '97 / Pinnacle

FALL, THE (2CD Set)
CD Set ______ SMDCD 132
Snapper / Jul '97 / Pinnacle

FIEND WITH A VIOLIN
I feel voxish / Man whose head expanded / Ed's babe / What you need / LA / Petty thief lout / Fiend with a violin / Spoilt Victorian child / Bombast / Married, two kids / Haven't found it yet / Gentleman's agreement
CD ______ RRCD 211
Receiver / Apr '96 / Grapevine/PolyGram

FRENZ EXPERIMENT
Frenz / Carry bag man / Get a hotel / Victoria / Athlete cured / In these times / Steak place / Bremen nacht / Guest informant / Oswald defence lawyer
CD ______ BEGA 91CD
Beggars Banquet / '88 / RTM/Disc / Warner Music

GROTESQUE
Pay your rates / English scheme / New face in hell / C'N'C's mithering / Container drivers / Impression of J Temperance / In the park / WMC blob 59 / Gramme Friday / NWRA
CD ______ CLACD 391
Castle / Sep '93 / BMG

HIP PRIESTS AND KAMERADS
Lie dream of a casino soul / Classical / Fortress / Look, know / Hip priest / Who makes the nazis / Just step sideways / Room to love / Mere pseud mag ed / ED / Hard life in country / I'm into CB / Fantastic life / Jawbone and the air rifle / And this day
CD ______ SITL 13CD
Lowdown/Beggars Banquet / '88 / RTM/ Disc / Warner Music

I AM KURIOUS ORANJ
Overture from 'I am kurious oranj' / Dog is life / Jerusalem / Kurious oranj / Wrong place right time / Win fall CD / Van plague / Bad news girl
CD ______ BEGA 96CD
Beggars Banquet / Nov '88 / RTM/Disc / Warner Music

LEGENDARY CHAOS TAPES, THE
Middle class rap / English scene / New face in hell / That man / An old lover / Male slags / Prole art threat / Container drivers / Jawbone & the air rifle / In the park / Leave the capital / Spectre versus rector / Pay your rates / Impression of J Temperance
CD ______ SAR 1005
Scout / Nov '96 / Koch
CD ______ COGVP 101CD
Voiceprint / Jul '97 / Pinnacle

LIGHT USER SYNDROME, THE
CD ______ JETCD 1012
Jet / May '96 / Total/Pinnacle

LIVE AT THE WITCH TRIALS
Frightened / Like to blow / Rebellious jukebox / No Xmas for John Quays / Mother sister / Industrial estate / Underground medicine / Two steps back / Live at the witch trials / Futures and pasts / Music scene
CD ______ COGVP 103CD
Voiceprint / Jun '97 / Pinnacle

LIVE IN THE CITY
CD ______ ARTFULCD 3
Artful / Jan '97 / Pinnacle / Total/BMG

OSWALD DEFENCE LAWYER
Just waiting / Oswald defence lawyer / Victoria / Frenz / Two by four / Bad news girl / Get a hotel / Guest information / Big new prinz / Bremen nacht / Crazy bag man / Bombast
CD ______ RRCD 213
Receiver / Apr '96 / Grapevine/PolyGram

OTHER SIDE OF THE FALL, THE (Sinister Waltz/Fiend With A Violin/ Oswald Defence/3CD Set)
Talk a lot of wind / Couldn't get ahead / Blood outta stone / Arid Al's dream / Knight / Devil and death / Chicago now / Birthday / Pumpkin head escapes / Wings / Dr. Faustus / Telephone thing / Black monk theme / Get out of the quantifier / Edinburgh man / I feel voxish / Man whose head expanded / Ed's babe / What you need / LA / Petty thief lout / Fiend with a violin / Spoilt Victorian child / Bombast / Married, two kids / Haven't found it yet / Gentleman's agreement / Just waiting / Oswald defence lawyer / Victoria / Frenz / Two by four / Bad news / Bad news girl / Get a hotel / Guest informant / Big new prinz / Bremen nacht / Carry big man / Bombast
CD Set ______ RRXCD 506
Receiver / Oct '96 / Grapevine/PolyGram

PERVERTED BY LANGUAGE
Eat y'self fitter / Neighbourhood of infinity / Garden / Hotel Bloedel / Smile / I feel voxish / Tempo house / Hexen definitive/Strife knot
CD ______ CLACD 392
Castle / Sep '93 / BMG

SEMINAL LIVE
Dead beat descendant / Pinball machine / HOW / Squid law / Mollusc in tyrol / Kurious oranj / Frenz / Hit the North / Two times four / Elf prefix / LA / Victoria / Pay your rates / Cruiser's creek / In these times
CD ______ BBL 102CD
Lowdown/Beggars Banquet / Jun '89 / RTM/Disc / Warner Music

SHIFT WORK
So what about it / Idiot joy showland / Edinburgh man / Pitsville direkt / Book of lies / High tension line / War against intelligence / Shiftwork / You haven't found it yet / Mixer / White lightning / Lot of wind / Rose / Sinister waltz
CD ______ 8485942
Cog Sinister / Mar '96 / PolyGram

SINISTER WALTZ
Talk a lot of wind / Couldn't get ahead / Blood outta stone / Arid Al's dream / Knight / Devil and the death / Chicago now / Birthday / Pumpkin head escapes / Wings / Dr. Faustus / Telephone thing / Black monk theme / Get out of the quantifier / Edinburgh man
CD ______ RRCD 209
Receiver / Apr '96 / Grapevine/PolyGram

THIS NATION'S SAVING GRACE
Mansion / Bombast / Barmy / What you need / Spoilt Victorian child / LA / Gut of the quantifier / My new house / Paintwork / I am Damo Suzuki / To Nkroachment : Yarbles
CD ______ BBL 67CD
Lowdown/Beggars Banquet / Feb '90 / RTM/Disc / Warner Music

TOTALES TURN
Fiery Jack / Rowche rumble / Muzorewi's daughter / In my area / Choc stock / Spector vs Rector 2 / Cary Grant's wedding / That man / New puritan / No xmas for John Quays
CD ______ DOJOCD 83
Dojo / Nov '92 / Disc

WONDERFUL AND FRIGHTENING WORLD OF THE FALL, THE
Lay of the land / Two times four / Copped it / Elves / Oh brother / Draygo's guilt / God box / Clear off / CREEP / Pat trip dispenser / Slang King / Bug day / Stephen song / Craigness / Disney's dream debased / No bulbs
CD ______ BBL 58 CD
Lowdown/Beggars Banquet / Jul '88 / RTM/Disc / Warner Music

Falla Trio

WEST SIDE STORY/PULCINELLA/JAZZ SONATA
CD ______ CCD 42013
Concord Jazz / Feb '89 / New Note/ Pinnacle

Fallen Angels

HAPPY EVER AFTER
Happy ever after / Millworker / Aililiu na gamhna / Love is a rose / Throwing doves / Sunrise sunset / Virtual strangers / Greatest gift / Tha mullad / She moved through the fair / Madam I'm a darlin' / Starfish and coffee / Fragile / That lonesome road / I saw my Jesus
CD ______ TARACD 4005
Tara / Apr '97 / ADA / CM / Conifer/BMG / Direct

Fallen Christ

ABDUCTION RITUAL
CD ______ POSH 005CD
Osmose / Nov '94 / Plastic Head

Falling Joys

PSYCHOHUM
Black bandages / Incinerator / God in a dustbin / Challenger / Dynamite / Lullaby / Parachute / Natural scene / Fortune teller / Psychohum / Winter's tale / Ending or beginning
CD ______ VOLTCD 059
Volition / Jun '92 / Pinnacle / Vital

WISH LIST
CD ______ VOLTCD 029
Volition / Jan '92 / Pinnacle / Vital

Falling Wallendas

FALLING WALLENDAS
CD ______ VAGUE 1001
Vague / Apr '97 / Pinnacle

False Virgins

INFERNAL DOLL
CD ______ OUT 1072
Brake Out / Nov '94 / Direct

SKIN JOB
CD ______ OUT 1042
Brake Out / Nov '94 / Direct

Falstaff

FALSTAFF VOL.2
CD ______ HMS 2342
Homestead / Mar '97 / Cargo / SRD

Faltskog, Agnetha

EYES OF A WOMAN
One way love / Eyes of a woman / Just one heart / I won't let you go / Angels cry / Click track / We should be together / I won't be leaving you / Save me / I keep turning off lights / We move as one
CD ______ 8256002
Polydor / Jan '93 / PolyGram

WRAP YOUR ARMS AROUND ME
Heat is on / Can't shake loose / Shame / Stay / Once burned, twice shy / Mr. Persuasion / Wrap your arms around me / To love / I wish tonight could last forever / Man / Take good care of your children / Stand by my side
CD ______ 8132422
Polydor / Jan '93 / PolyGram

Falu, Eduardo

RESOLANA
CD ______ NI 5281
Nimbus / Sep '94 / Nimbus

Fambrough, Charles

BLUES AT BRADLEY'S
Duck feathers / Blues for Bu / Andrea / Better days are coming / Steve's blues
CD ______ ESJCD 236
Essential Jazz / Oct '94 / BMG

CHARMER, THE
Charmer / Beautiful love: *Ibrahim, Abdullah* / Alycia love / Oasis / Lullaby for Shana: *Washington, Grover Jr.* / Little man / Sparks: *O'Connell, Bill*
CD ______ ESJCD 232
Essential Jazz / Oct '94 / BMG

CITY TRIBES
Canto de Guebra / Hunt / Add a lesson / Dolores / Alligators / Irish lullaby / Laura Marie / Past time / City tribes
CD ______ ECD 221492
Evidence / Apr '96 / ADA / Cadillac / Harmonia Mundi

KEEPER OF THE SPIRIT
Angels at play / Pop pop's song / Life above the means / Little this, a little that / Keeper of the spirit / Tears of romance / Save that time / Descent / Kaln / Secret hiding place
CD ______ AQCD 1033
Audioquest / Aug '95 / ADA / New Note/ Pinnacle

Fame, Georgie

20 BEAT CLASSICS
Yeh yeh / Getaway / Do re mi / My girl / Sweet things / Point of no return / Get on the right track baby / Baby / Ride your pony / Moody's mood for love / Funny how time slips away / Sunny sitting in the park / Green onions / In the meantime / Papa's got a brand new bag / Blue Monday / Pride and joy / Pink champagne / Let the sunshine in / I love the life I live, I live the life I love
CD ______ 8478102
Polydor / Jan '92 / PolyGram

BEST OF GEORGIE FAME 1967-1971, THE (2CD Set)
Ballad of Bonnie and Clyde / This guy's in love with you / Seventh son / Try my world / And I love her / Peaceful / Mellow yellow / Because I love you / By the time I get to Phoenix / Rosetta: *Fame, Georgie & Alan Price* / When I'm sixty four / Everything happens to me / Knock on wood / St. James Infirmary / Ask me nice / Hideaway / Exactly like you / Yellow man: *Fame, Georgie & Alan Price* / Blossom / Bird in a world of people
CD Set ______ 4851272
Columbia / Aug '96 / Sony

BLUES AND ME, THE
CD ______ GOJ 60052
Go Jazz / Jun '96 / Vital/SAM

COOL CAT BLUES
Cool cat blues / Every knock is a boost / You came a long way from St. Louis / Big brother / It should have been me / Yeah yeah / Moondance / Cats' eyes / I love the life I live, I live the life I love / Survival / Little pony / Rockin' chair
CD ______ GOJ 60022
Go Jazz / Jun '96 / Vital/SAM

FIRST THIRTY YEARS, THE
Do the dog / Yeh yeh / Getaway / Ballad of Bonnie and Clyde / Rosetta / Daylight / Samba (toda menina baiana) / In crowd / C'est la vie / Fully booked / That ol' rock and roll / Sitting in the park / Do re mi / Like we used to be / Sunny / Seventh son / Ali shuffle / Hurricane / Moody's mood for love / Dawn yawn / Mellow yellow / Woe is me / Funny how time slips away / Old music master
CD ______ VSOPCD 144
Connoisseur Collection / Dec '89 / Pinnacle

GEORGIE FAME & THE DANISH RADIO BIG BAND 1992-93 (Fame, Georgie & Danish Radio Big Band)
CD ______ MECCACD 1040
Music Mecca / Oct '93 / Cadillac / Jazz Music / Wellard

GEORGIE FAME LIVE AT RONNIE SCOTT'S
Was / Cool cat blues / Tell me how you feel / Zulu / Was / Vinyl / Mercy mercy/Van Lose Stairway / Blues medley
CD ______ TLW 003
TLW / Oct '96 / Vital/SAM

GET AWAY WITH
Yeh yeh / Green onions / Let the good times roll / Sitting in the park / Funny how time slips away / Shop around / Baby, please don't go / Get away / Eso beso / In the meantime / Sunny / Ride your pony / Night train / I love the life I live, I live the life I love
CD ______ 5500152
Spectrum / May '93 / PolyGram

NO WORRIES (Fame, Georgie & The Australian Blue Flames)
Oh lady be good / Ole buttermilk sky / Eros hotel / Little Samba / It ain't right / On a misty night / Cats' eyes / Parchman farm / Zulu / Saturday night fish fry / Try na get along with the blues / Yeh yeh / Get away
CD ______ FLCD 5099
Four Leaf Clover / May '88 / Cadillac / Wellard

SELECTION OF STANDARDS... (Fame, Georgie & Hoagy Carmichael/Annie Ross)
CD ______ CDSL 5197
DRG / '88 / Discovery / New Note/ Pinnacle

THREE LINE WHIP
It happened to me / Kan tsukete / Vinyl / Mercy mercy mercy/Vanlose stairway / Since I fell for you / Zavalo / You are there / Declaration of love / Will Carling / It happened to me (reprise)
CD ______ TLW 001
Three Line Whip / May '94 / New Note/ Pinnacle

Familia Valera Miranda

SON, THE
CD ______ NI 5421
Nimbus / Feb '95 / Nimbus

Family

ANYWAY
Good news bad news / Willow tree / Holding the compass / Strange band / Normans / Part of the load / Lives and ladies / Anyway
CD ______ CLACD 375
Castle / May '94 / BMG

AS & BS
CD ______ CCSCD 354
Castle / Nov '92 / BMG

BANDSTAND
Burlesque / Bolero babe / Coronation / Dark eyes / Broken nose / My friend the sun / Glove / Ready to go / Top of the hill / Rockin' R's
CD ______ ESMCD 565
Essential / Aug '97 / BMG

COLLECTION, THE
CD ______ CCSCD 374
Castle / Mar '93 / BMG

ENTERTAINMENT
Weaver's answer / Observations from a hill / Hung-up down / Summer '67 / How-hi-the-li / Second generation woman / From the past archives / Dim / Processions / Face in the crowd / Emotions
CD ______ SEECD 200
See For Miles/C5 / Oct '96 / Pinnacle

FEARLESS
Between blue and me / Sat'dy barfly / Larf and sing / Spanish tide / Save some for thee / Take your partners / Children / Crinkley grin / Blind / Burning bridges / In my own time / Seasons
CD ______ ESMCD 567
Essential / Aug '97 / BMG

IT'S ONLY A MOVIE
It's only a movie / Leroy / Buffet tea for two / Boom bang / Boots 'n' roots / Banger / Sweet desiree / Suspicion / Check out / Stop this car / Drink to you
CD ______ ESMCD 566
Essential / Aug '97 / BMG

MUSIC IN A DOLL'S HOUSE
Chase / Mellowing grey / Never like this / Me, my friend / Hey Mr. Policeman / See through windows / Variation on a theme of hey Mr. policeman / Winter / Old songs new songs / Variation on the theme of the breeze / Variation on a theme of me my friend / Peace of mind / Voyage / Breeze / Three times time
CD ______ SEECD 100
See For Miles/C5 / Apr '94 / Pinnacle

PEEL SESSIONS, THE
CD ______ DEI 83332
Dutch East India / Mar '93 / Plastic Head / SRD

SONG FOR ME, A
Drowned in wine / Some poor soul / Love is a sleeper / Stop for the traffic (through the heart of me) / Wheels / Song for sinking lovers / Hey let it rock / Cat and the rat / 93's OK J / Song for me
CD ______ CLACD 376
Castle / Nov '93 / BMG

Family Cat

MAGIC HAPPENS
Wonderful excuse / Amazing hangover / Move over I'll drive / Your secrets will stay mine / Airplane gardens / Gone so long / Hamlet for now / Golden book / Rockbreaking / Spring the atom / Blood orange / Nowhere to go but down
CD ______ 74321204662
Dedicated / May '94 / BMG / Vital

TELL 'EM WE'RE SURFING
CD ______ BCRLCD 1
Big Cat / Mar '90 / 3mv/Pinnacle

Family Dogg

WAY OF LIFE, A
CD ______ BX 4532
BR Music / Oct '95 / Target/BMG

Family Foundation

ONE BLOOD
One Blood / 10 Snide E / Tarzan / It's not over / Someday / Red hot interview
CD ______ MHFCD 1
380 / Jan '93 / Warner Music

Famous Castle Jazz Band

FAMOUS CASTLE JAZZ BAND
CD ______ GTCD 10030
Good Time Jazz / Oct '93 / Complete/ Pinnacle

Famous Five

LOST IN FISHPONDS
CD ______ UNCCD 3
Uncle / Jun '95 / Direct

Famous Monsters

SUMMERTIME EP
CD ______ BLAZE 90CD
Fire / Aug '95 / Pinnacle / RTM/Disc

Fanatik

SEISMIC ACTIVITY
Mission one / Big world / Hallucinate / Ramadan / Catacombs of conscience / Kontortion / Post millennium / Sun torture / Disk jock no.2 / Parallel / Soundscape / Produce man / Remedy / Home improvement / Subwoofer contents / Deep sleep / Chameleon, the aftershock / Home-made remedy / Q vibe / Comatose / Aftershock / Unrankable talent
CD ______ AGV 010CD
All Good Vinyl / Feb '97 / Vital

Fancy

SOMETHING TO REMEMBER/WILD THING
Wild thing / Love for sale / Move on / I don't need your love / One night / Touch me / US Surprise / Between the devil and me / I'm a woman / Feel good / Fancy / She's riding the rock machine / I was made to love him / You've been in love too long / Something to remember / Everybody's cryin' mercy / Tour song / Stop / Music maker / Bluebird
CD _____ **SRH 802**
Rock Heritage / Feb '97 / Koch

Fane, Alan

KALAMAN N'GONE/DOZON N'GONI (Fane, Alan Fote Mocoba)
CD _____ **2002850**
Dakar Sound / Jan '97 / Stern's

Fania Allstars

LATIN SOUL & JAZZ
Viva tirado / Chanchullo / Smoke / There you go / Mama guelo / El raton / Soul makossa / Congo bongo
CD _____ **CDHOT 504**
Charly / Oct '93 / Koch

Fankhauser, Merrell

BOUNTY THINGS
CD _____ **SC 6094**
Sundazed / Jun '97 / Cargo / Greyhound / Rollercoaster

Fantastic Four

ALVIN STONE (BIRTH AND DEATH OF A GANGSTER)/NIGHT PEOPLE
Alvin Stone (birth and death of a gangster) / Have a little mercy / County line / Let this moment last forever / Words / My love won't stop at nothing / Medley: Night people/Lies divided by jive / If I lose my job / Hideaway / By the river under the tree / Don't risk your happiness on foolishness / They took the show on the road
CD _____ **CDSEWD 057**
Westbound / Jan '93 / Pinnacle

GOT TO HAVE YOUR LOVE/BRING YOUR OWN FUNK
She'll be right for me / Mixed up moods and attitudes / There's fire down below / Ain't I been good to you / Cash money / I got to have your love / Disco pool blues / Give me all the love you got / Super lover / I just want to love ya baby / Shout (Let it all hang out) / Cold and windy night / Sexy lady / Realize (When you're in love) / BYOF (Bring your own funk)
CD _____ **CDSEWD 92**
Westbound / Jun '94 / Pinnacle

Fantasy Band

KISS
CD _____ **SH 5028**
Shanachie / Mar '97 / ADA / Greensleeves / Koch

Fantasyy Factoryy

TALES TO TELL
CD _____ **LC 3163**
Ohrwaschl / Jun '97 / Greyhound

Far Tulla

BEST OF IRISH BALLADS
CD _____ **CHCD 017**
Chart / May '96 / Direct / Koch

Farafina

FASO DENOU
Mama Sara / Kara mogo mousso / Dounouia / Nanore / Faso denou / Hereyo mibi / Ourodara sidiki / Lanaya / Bi mousso
CD _____ **CDRW 35**
Realworld / May '93 / EMI

Farah Dance Orchestra

TURKISH DELIGHT
CD _____ **CNCD 5957**
Disky / Jul '93 / Disky / THE

Farantouri, Maria

17 SONGS
CD _____ **68950**
Tropical / Apr '97 / Discovery

Farber, Mitch

STARCLIMBER
Starclimber / Lonely promises / Chooser / Sky dance / Monuments / Time line
CD _____ **MCD 5400**
Muse / Sep '92 / New Note/Pinnacle

Fardon, Don

INDIAN RESERVATION (The Best Of Don Fardon)
Indian reservation / Gimme gimme good lovin' / Letter / Treat her right / I'm alive / Follow your drum / Delta queen / Running bear / Belfast boy / Take a heart / Lola / It's been nice loving you / Hudson Bay / On the beach / Tobacco Road / California maiden / Coming on strong / Mr. Station Master / Miami sunset / Riverboat / I need somebody / For your love / Girl / Sunshine woman
CD _____ **C5CD 540**
See For Miles/C5 / Jun '96 / Pinnacle

NEXT CHAPTER, THE
Indian reservation / Good woman's love / Cocktail bar blues / Brown eyed and blue / Fear of losing you / Champion of the rodeo / Gone country / Who's that man / Caught in the crossfire / Belfast boy / Jodie's song / Take a heart / Do you remember / Indian reservation
CD _____ **CDSGP 0353**
Prestige / May '97 / Else / Total/BMG

Farflung

SO MANY MINDS, SO LITTLE TIME
CD _____ **CLP 0009**
Purple Pyramid / Jul '97 / Cargo

Farholt, Ann

SECRET LOVE (Farholt, Ann & Henrik Bay Duo)
CD _____ **MECCACD 1085**
Music Mecca / May '97 / Cadillac / Jazz Music / Wellard

Farian, Frank

HIT COLLECTION (The Hits Of Frank Farian) (Various Artists)
CD _____ **74321199402**
Arista / Jun '94 / BMG

Farina, Mimi

SOLO
CD _____ **CDPH 1102**
Philo / Dec '86 / ADA / CM / Direct

Farina, Richard

MEMORIES (Farina, Richard & Mimi)
Quiet joys of brotherhood / Joy 'round my brain / Lemonade lady / Downtown / Almond joy / Blood red roses / Morgan the pirate / Dopico / House of un-American blues activity dream / Shallow song / All the world has gone by / Pack up your sorrows
CD _____ **VMD 79263**
Vanguard / Oct '95 / ADA / Pinnacle

REFLECTIONS IN A CRYSTAL WIND (Farina, Richard & Mimi)
Reflections in a crystal wind / Bold marauder / Dopico / Swallow song / Chrysanthemum / Sell out agitation waltz / Hard loving loser / Mainline prosperity blues / Allen's interlude / House of un-American blues activity dream / Raven girl / Miles / Children of darkness
CD _____ **VMD 79204**
Vanguard / Oct '95 / ADA / Pinnacle

Farjami, Hossein

PLAYS SANTOOR (Folk Music From Iran)
CD _____ **EUCD 1100**
ARC / '91 / ADA / ARC Music

Farkas, Andras

FAMOUS HUNGARIAN GIPSY TUNES (Farkas, Andras & Budapest Ensemble)
CD _____ **EUCD 1133**
ARC / '91 / ADA / ARC Music

POPULAR GIPSY MELODIES (Farkas, Andras & Budapest Ensemble)
CD _____ **EUCD 1197**
ARC / Sep '93 / ADA / ARC Music

Farley & Heller

JOURNEYS BY DJ VOL.12 (2CD Set) (Various Artists)
CD Set _____ **JDJCD 12**
JDJ / Oct '96 / 3mv/Pinnacle / SRD

Farley Jackmaster Funk

REAL HOUSE ALBUM, THE
CD _____ **LIBTCD 001**
4 Liberty / May '96 / BMG / Mo's Music Machine / Pinnacle / SRD

Farlow, Billy C.

GULF COAST BLUES
CD _____ **APCD 102**
Appaloosa / Nov '95 / ADA / Direct / TKO Magnum

I AIN'T NEVER HAD TOO MUCH FUN
CD _____ **APCD 074**
Appaloosa / '92 / ADA / Direct / TKO Magnum

Farlow, Tal

CHROMATIC PALETTE
All alone / Nuages / I hear a rhapsody / If I were a bell / St Thomas / Blue art too / Stella by starlight / One for my baby (And one more for the road)
CD _____ **CCD 4154**
Concord Jazz / Mar '94 / New Note/Pinnacle

COOKIN' ON ALL BURNERS
You'd be so nice to come home to / If I should lose you / I've got the world on a string / Love letters / Lullaby of the leaves / I thought about you / I wished on the moon / Why shouldn't I / Just friends
CD _____ **CCD 4204**
Concord Jazz / Jul '96 / New Note/Pinnacle

JAZZ MASTERS
CD _____ **5273652**
Verve / Feb '95 / PolyGram

LEGENDARY TAL FARLOW, THE
You stepped out of a dream / When your lover has gone / I got it bad and that ain't good / When lights are low / Who cares / I can't get started (with you) / Prelude to a kiss / Everything happens to me
CD _____ **CJ 266 390**
Concord Jazz / '88 / New Note/Pinnacle

RETURN OF TAL FARLOW, THE/1969
CD _____ **OJCCD 356**
Original Jazz Classics / Nov '95 / Complete/Pinnacle / Jazz Music / Wellard

SIGN OF THE TIMES
Fascinating rhythm / You don't know what love is / Put a happy face / Stompin' at the Savoy / Georgia on my mind / You are too beautiful / In your own sweet way / Bayside blues
CD _____ **CCD 4026**
Concord Jazz / May '92 / New Note/Pinnacle

TAL FARLOW
Way you look tonight / Just one of those things / There will never be another you / Stella by starlight / Tenderly / Lean on me / Jordu / Strike up the band / Autumn in New York / Cherokee / Bernie's tune / Tal's blues / Night and day / It's you or no one / I like to recognize the tune / Swinging till the girls come home
CD _____ **CD 53247**
Giants Of Jazz / Feb '97 / Cadillac / Jazz Music / Target/BMG

Farlowe, Chris

AS TIME GOES BY
Bewitched / Glow / Sunday kind of love / As time goes by / Drinking again / These foolish things / At last / Blues as blues can get / You don't know me / Trust in me / I thought of you / Don't let me be lonely
CD _____ **CDEC 4**
Out Of Time / Feb '97 / Direct / Total/BMG

EXTREMELY
CD _____ **INAK 8905**
In Akustik / Sep '95 / Direct / TKO Magnum

FROM HERE TO MAMA ROSA
Travelling into make believe / Fifty years / Where do we go from here / Questions / Head in the clouds / Are you sleeping / Black sheep / Winter of my life / Mama Rosa / Put out the light
CD _____ **CDEC 6**
Out Of Time / Nov '96 / Direct / Total/BMG

HIT SINGLE COLLECTABLES
CD _____ **DISK 4509**
Disky / Apr '94 / Disky / THE

I'M THE GREATEST
Paint it black / Think / Satisfaction / Handbags and gladrags / Baby make it soon / Looking for you / My colouring book / Don't just look at me / Moanin' / It was easier to hurt her / What becomes of the broken hearted / In the midnight hour / North west south east / Out of time / Yesterdays papers / Ride on baby / My way of giving / Headlines / Don't play that song (You lied) / I just don't know what to do with myself / You're so good for me / Life is but nothing / Dawn / Reach out, I'll be there / Mr. Pitiful
CD _____ **SEECD 396**
See For Miles/C5 / Oct '96 / Pinnacle

LONESOME ROAD
CD _____ **IGOXCD 500**
Indigo / Dec '95 / ADA / Direct

OLYMPIC ROCK AND BLUES CIRCUS (Farlowe, Chris, Brian Auger & Pete York)
CD _____ **BLR 84 013**
L&R / May '91 / New Note/Pinnacle

OUT OF TIME
Try me / Rock 'n' roll soldier / Some mother's son / Hold on / Blues anthem / Waiting in the wings / Function to function / Working in a parking lot / Make it fly / On the beach / Out of time
CD _____ **JHD 054**
Tring / Jan '93 / Tring

R & B YEARS, THE
CD _____ **CDRB 5**
Charly / Apr '94 / Koch

Farm

HULLABALOO
Messiah / Shake some action / Comfort / Man who cried / Hateful / Golden vision / To the ages / All American world / Distant voices
CD _____ **9362455882**
Warner Bros. / Aug '94 / Warner Music

SPARTACUS
Hearts and minds / How long / Sweet inspiration / Groovy train / Higher and higher / Don't let me down / Family of man / Tell the story / Very emotional / All together now / Higher and higher / Very emotional / Groovy train / All together now
CD _____ **ESMCD 580**
Essential / Jul '97 / BMG

Farmer, Art

ART FARMER & LEE KONITZ/JOE CARTER
CD _____ **STCD 571**
Stash / Mar '94 / ADA / Cadillac / CM / Direct / Jazz Music

ART FARMER SEPTET (Farmer, Art Septet)
CD _____ **OJCCD 54**
Original Jazz Classics / Sep '93 / Complete/Pinnacle / Jazz Music / Wellard

EARLY ART
Soft shoe / Confab in tempo / I'll take romance / Wisteria / Autumn nocturne / I've never been in love before / Gone with the wind / Alone together / Pre amp
CD _____ **OJCCD 880**
Original Jazz Classics / Jun '96 / Complete/Pinnacle / Jazz Music / Wellard

FOOLISH
Larry's delight / Al-leu-cha / D's dilemma / In a sentimental mood / Foolish memories / Farmer's market
CD _____ **CDLR 45008**
L&R / Dec '88 / New Note/Pinnacle

IN CONCERT
Half Nelson / Darn that dream / Barbados / I'll remember April
CD _____ **ENJ 40882**
Enja / Jul '95 / New Note/Pinnacle / Vital/SAM

LIVE AT THE HALF NOTE
CD _____ **7567906662**
Atlantic / Apr '95 / Warner Music

MANHATTAN (Farmer, Art Quintet)
CD _____ **SNCD 1026**
Soul Note / '86 / Cadillac / Harmonia Mundi / Wellard

MEANING OF ART, THE
On the plane / Just the way you look tonight / Lift your spirit high / One day forever / Free verse / Home / Johnny one note
CD _____ **AJ 0118**
Arabesque / Dec '95 / New Note/Pinnacle

MEETS MULLIGAN & HALL
CD _____ **MCD 0512**
Moon / Apr '94 / Cadillac / Harmonia Mundi

MIRAGE (Farmer, Art Quintet)
CD _____ **SNCD 1046**
Soul Note / '86 / Cadillac / Harmonia Mundi / Wellard

OUT OF THE PAST
Ponsu / Lullaby of the leaves / Day after / Tonk / Blue room / Kayin' / Nobody's heart
CD _____ **GRP 18092**
GRP / Apr '96 / New Note/BMG

PHD
PhD / Affaire d'amour / Mr. Day's dream / Summary / Blue wail / Like someone in love / Rise to the occasion / Ballade art
CD _____ **CCD 140552**
Contemporary / Apr '94 / Cadillac / Complete/Pinnacle / Jazz Music / Wellard

SOMETHING TO LIVE FOR (The Music Of Billy Strayhorn)
Isfahan / Bloodcount / Johnny come lately / Something to live for / Upper Manhattan medical group / Raincheck / Daydream
CD _____ **CCD 140292**
Contemporary / Apr '94 / Cadillac / Complete/Pinnacle / Jazz Music / Wellard

TWO TRUMPETS (Farmer, Art & Donald Byrd)
CD _____ **OJCCD 18**
Original Jazz Classics / Nov '95 / Complete/Pinnacle / Jazz Music / Wellard

WARM VALLEY
Moose the mooche / And now there's you / Three little words / Eclypso / Sad to say / Upper Manhattan medical group / Warm valley
CD _____ **CCD 4212**
Concord Jazz / Mar '92 / New Note/Pinnacle

WORK OF ART, A (Farmer, Art Quartet)
She's funny that way / Love walked in / Change partners / Red cross / You know I care
CD _____ **CCD 4179**
Concord Jazz / Jul '96 / New Note/Pinnacle

YOU MAKE ME SMILE (Farmer, Art Quintet)
CD _____ **SNCD 1076**
Soul Note / '86 / Cadillac / Harmonia Mundi / Wellard

Farmer Boys

FLASH CRASH AND THUNDER
Flash crash and thunder / Cool down Mame / Yearnin' / Burning heart / Somehow, someway, someday / Flip flop / Charming Betsy / Lend a helpin' hand / It pays to advertise / Someone to love me / My baby done left me / Oh how it hurts / No one / You lied / You're a hungdinger / I'm just too lazy / Onions, onions
CD _______ BCD 15579
Bear Family / Mar '92 / Direct / Rollercoaster / Swift

Farmer's Manual

FSCK
CD _______ TRAY 2CD
Ashtray / Aug '97 / Kudos

Farmers

ROCK ANGEL
CD _______ FF 548CD
Flying Fish / '92 / ADA / CM / Direct / Roots

Farmers Market

SPEED/BALKAN/BOOGIE
CD _______ FX 148CD
Musikk Distribujson / Apr '95 / ADA

Farnham, Allen

COMMON THREAD, THE
Common thread / Hamma-ron / Nocturne / Glide / Falling grace / Interlude / How deep is the ocean / In a sentimental mood / No more blues / Very early
CD _______ CCD 4634
Concord Jazz / Mar '95 / New Note/ Pinnacle

PLAY CATION
M'kashi b'nashi / Play cation / Long ago and far away / My man's gone now / Foot prince / Alone together / Stablemates / Daydream / Cheek to Chico
CD _______ CCD 4521
Concord Jazz / Sep '92 / New Note/ Pinnacle

Farnham, John

AGE OF REASON
Age of reason / Blow by blow / Listen to the wind / Two strong hearts / Burn down the night / Beyond the call / We're no angels / Don't tell me it can't be done / Fire / Some do, some don't / When the war is over / It's a long way to the top (if you wanna rock 'n' roll)
CD _______ 74321138982
RCA / Sep '95 / BMG

CHAIN REACTION
That's freedom / In days to come / Burn for you / See the banners fall / I can do anything / All our sons and daughters / Chain reaction / In your hands / New day / Time has come / First step / Time and money
CD _______ 74321369142
RCA / Jun '96 / BMG

WHISPERING JACK
Pressure down / You're the voice / One step away / Reasons / Going going gone / No one comes close / Love to shine / Trouble / Touch of paradise / Let me out
CD _______ 74321187202
RCA / Apr '94 / BMG

Farnon, Robert

AT THE MOVIES (Farnon, Robert & His Orchestra)
Moment I saw you / Early one morning / Best things in life are free / Wouldn't it be loverly / How beautiful is night / You're the cream in my coffee / Pictures in the fire / I guess I'll have to change my plan / Great day / When I fall in love / Melody fair / Just imagine / Lady Barbara / Trolley song / Way we were / Sunny side up
CD _______ CDSIV 6111
Horatio Nelson / Jul '95 / Disc

Farr, Deitra

SEARCH IS OVER, THE
Anywhere but here / Bad company / You've got to choose / Waiting for you / I refuse to lose / How much longer / Taking the long way home / Waiting for the blues / Search is over / Must have been an angel / Stealin' your love / This I know to be free
CD _______ JSPCD 284
JSP / Jul '97 / ADA / Cadillac / Direct / Hot Shot / Target/BMG

Farrar, John

JOHN FARRAR
Reckless / Tell someone who cares / Can't hold back / Gettin' loose / Cheatin' his heart out again / Recovery / It'll be me babe / Falling / From the heart
CD _______ SEECD 484
See For Miles/C5 / Jul '97 / Pinnacle

Farrell, Eileen

EILEEN FARRELL SINGS ALEC WILDER
Lady sings the blues / Where do you go / Moon and sand / Worm has turned / Blackberry winter / I'll be around
CD _______ RR 36CD
Reference Recordings / '90 / Jazz Music / May Audio

EILEEN FARRELL SINGS HAROLD ARLEN
Let's fall in love / Out of this world / I wonder what became of me / I've got the world on a string / Like a straw in the wind / Down with love / Happiness is a thing called Joe / Woman's prerogative / Come rain or come shine / Little drops of rain / Over the rainbow / When the sun comes out / As long as I live / My shining hour / Last night when we were young
CD _______ RR 30CD
Reference Recordings / '90 / Jazz Music / May Audio

EILEEN FARRELL SINGS RODGERS AND HART
I could write a book / I wish I were in love again / Wait 'til you see him / I didn't know what time it was / Love me tonight / Nobody's heart / It never entered my mind / Mountain greenery / Sing for your supper / Can't you do a friend a favour / Lover / My heart stood still / Little girl blue / You're nearer
CD _______ RR 32CD
Reference Recordings / '90 / Jazz Music / May Audio

EILEEN FARRELL SINGS TORCH SONGS
Stormy weather / 'Round midnight / End of a love affair / Black coffee / When your lover has gone / Don't explain / This time the dream is on me / I get along without you very well / Something cool ... and more
CD _______ RR 34CD
Reference Recordings / '90 / Jazz Music / May Audio

I GOTTA RIGHT TO SING THE BLUES
CD _______ CD 47255
Sony Classical / Nov '91 / Sony

LOVE IS LETTING GO
Just in time / Why did I choose you / Love is letting go / I've never been in love before / Country boy / Where were you this afternoon / Everyday / I dream of you / Quiet thing / Time after time / My love turned me down today / I'll be tired of you / For Eileen
CD _______ DRGCD 91436
DRG / Oct '95 / Discovery / New Note/ Pinnacle

WITH THE LOONIS MCGLOHON QUARTET
CD _______ ACD 237
Audiophile / Apr '93 / Jazz Music

Farren, Mick

FRAGMENTS OF BROKEN PROBES (Farren, Mick & The Deviants)
CD _______ CTCD 046
Captain Trip / Jun '97 / Greyhound

GRINGO MADNESS (Farren, Mick & Tijuana Bible)
Leader hotel / Mark of zorro / Lone sungularity / Solitaire devil / Spider kissed / Jezebel / Long walk with the devil/Jumping Jack flash / Movement of the whores on revolution plaza / Hippie death cult / Last night the alhambra burned down / Eternity is a very long time / Memphis psychosis / Riot in cell block 9
CD _______ CDWIK 117
Big Beat / Feb '93 / Pinnacle

Farrenden, Shaun

YIDAKI
CD _______ ALUNA 001
Aluna / May '96 / ADA

YODAKI (DIDJERIDU)
CD _______ ALUNA 1995
Knock On Wood / Apr '97 / Discovery

Farreyrol, Jacqueline

REUNION ISLAND TRADITIONS
CD _______ PS 65091
PlayaSound / Jul '92 / ADA / Harmonia Mundi

Farside

RIGGED
CD _______ REVEL 033
Revelation / Aug '94 / Plastic Head

Fascinating Aida

IT WIT DON'T GIVE A SHIT GIRLS
CD _______ SCENECD 23
First Night / Sep '97 / Pinnacle

LOAD OF OLD SEQUINS, A
Boring / Radiating love / Yuppies / Shattered illusions / Songs of the homesick / Lieder / Another man / Whites blues / My dream man / All bonjour monsieur / Jealousy / Sew on a sequin / Taboo
CD _______ OCRCD 6018
First Night / Mar '96 / Pinnacle

Fascinations

OUT TO GET'CHA
Girls are out to get you / You'll be sorry / I'm so lucky (He loves me) / Such a fool / I'm in love / OK for you / I can't stay away from you / Say it isn't so (Take four) / Say it isn't so (Take eight) / Just another reason / Hold on / Trust in you / Crazy / I've been trying / If / Still trying / Don't start none / Little bird / Lucky / Foolish one / So sorry / Out to get'cha
CD _______ NEMCD 881
Sequel / Mar '97 / BMG

Fasoli, Claudio

CITIES (Fasoli, Claudio & Dalla Porta/ Elgart/Goodrick)
CD _______ RMCD 4503
Ram / Nov '93 / Cadillac / Harmonia Mundi

Fassaert, Tammy

JUST PASSIN' THROUGH
CD _______ SCR 36
Strictly Country / Nov '95 / ADA / Direct

Fast Freddie's Fingertips

NEW TOWN SOUL
CD _______ 323184
Koch / Aug '94 / Koch

WHAT'S MY NAME
CD _______ SCRCD 010
Scratch / Sep '96 / Koch / Scratch/BMG

Fastbacks

ANSWER THE PHONE DUMMY
CD _______ SPCD 259
Sub Pop / Nov '94 / Cargo / Greyhound / Shellshock/Disc

QUESTION IS NO
CD _______ SP 146B
Sub Pop / Mar '94 / Cargo / Greyhound / Shellshock/Disc

ZUCKER
CD _______ SP 231 CD
Sub Pop / Jan '93 / Cargo / Greyhound / Shellshock/Disc

Fat & Frantic

QUIRK
Too late / Last night my wife hoovered my head / Rise up / Who's your friend Eddy / I don't want to say goodbye / Africa / It's you / If I could be your milkman / Aggressive sunbathing / Senator's daughter / I'm sorry / I wish / Darling Doris / River
CD _______ 5018524 01102
I'll Call You / Aug '90 / Total/BMG

Fat

AUTOMAT HIGHLIFE
CD _______ RERFATCD
ReR/Recommended / Apr '91 / ReR Megacorp / RTM/Disc

Fat Boy Slim

BETTER LIVING THROUGH CHEMISTRY
CD _______ BRASSIC 2CD
Skint / Sep '96 / 3mv/Vital / Mo's Music Machine / Prime

Fat Larry's Band

CLOSE ENCOUNTERS OF A FUNKY KIND
Close encounters of a funky kind / Stand up / Good time / Can't keep my hands to myself / Last chance to dance / Everything is disco / Hey Pancho, it's disco / Zoom / Play with me / Boogie town / I love you so / Dirty words / Lookin' for love / You gotta help yourself
CD _______ CDSEWD 095
Southbound / Jan '95 / Pinnacle

OFF THE WALL
Sparkle / Peaceful journey / Castle of joy / Passing time / Easy / Don't you worry about tomorrow / Time / I love you so / In the pocket
CD _______ CDSXE 069
Stax / Nov '92 / Pinnacle

Fat Mattress

FAT MATTRESS VOL.1
All nightdrinker / I don't mind / Bright new way / Petrol pump assistant / Mr. Moonshine / Magic forest / She came in the morning / Everything's blue / Walking through a garden / How can I live / Little girl in white / Marguerita / Which way to go / Future days / Cold wall of stone
CD _______ NEXCD 196
Sequel / May '92 / BMG

FAT MATTRESS VOL.2
Storm / Anyway you want / Leafy lane / Naturally / Roamin' / Happy my love / Childhood dream / She / Highway / At the ball / People / Hall of kings / Long red / Words / River
CD _______ NEXCD 197
Sequel / May '92 / BMG

Fat Tony

LAST NIGHT A DJ (Various Artists)
CD _______ 21CCCD 003
21st Century Opera / Mar '96 / Total/BMG

Fat Tuesday

CALIFUNERAL
CD _______ CDZORRO 43
Metal Blade / Jul '92 / Pinnacle / Plastic Head

Fat Tulips

STARFISH
So unbelievable / World away from me / Ribs / Sweetest child / Chainsaw / I promise you / My secret place / Double decker bus / Clumsy / If God exists / Big toe / Nothing less than you deserve / Letting go / Death of me / Never
CD _______ ASKCD 034
Vinyl Japan / Jul '94 / Plastic Head / Vinyl Japan

Fatal Opera

FATAL OPERA
CD _______ MASSCD 051
Massacre / Apr '95 / Plastic Head

Fatala

GONGOMA TIMES
Timini / Yekeke / Maane / Gongoma times / Seoraba / Boke (N'yaraloum-ma) / Limbadji toko / Sohko / Soisisa
CD _______ RWMCD 4
Realworld / Jan '93 / EMI

Fatback Band

14 KARAT
Let's do it again / Angel / Backstrokin' / Concrete jungle / Without your love / Gotta get my hands on some (money) / Your love is strange / Lady groove / Chillin' out
CD _______ CDSEWM 060
Southbound / Jun '93 / Pinnacle

21 KARAT FATBACK
I found lovin' / Girl is fine / Night fever / (Are you ready) Do the bus stop / Double Dutch / King Tim III (Personality jock) / Wicky wacky / I like girls / Gotta get my hands on some (money) / Let's do it again / Master Booty / Backstrokin' / Keep on steppin' / Freak the freak the funk (rock) / Take it any way you want it / Spanish hustle / Rockin' to the beat / On the floor / Booty / Yum yum (gimme some) / Is this the future / Party time
CD _______ CDSEWD 101
Southbound / Mar '95 / Pinnacle

BRITE LITES/ BIG CITY
Freak the freak the funk (rock) / Let me do it to you / Big city / Do the boogie woogie / Hesitation / Wild dreams
CD _______ CDSEWM 045
Southbound / Jan '92 / Pinnacle

FEEL MY SOUL
Feeling mellow (Instrumental) / Meet me over my house / Three dimensional world / Sketches of life / You've got a friend / Feeling mellow / Makin' love / Why is it so hard to do (Things I wanna do) / Feel my soul
CD _______ DEEPM 018
Deep Beats / Mar '97 / BMG

FIRED UP 'N' KICKIN'
I'm fired up / Boogie freak / Get out on the dance floor / At last / I like girls / Snake / Can't you see
CD _______ CDSEW 041
Southbound / Jul '91 / Pinnacle

GIGOLO
Rockin' to the beat / Rub down / I'm so in love / Higher / Do it / Gigolo / Oh girl / Na na hey hey kiss her goodbye
CD _______ CDSEWM 081
Southbound / Nov '93 / Pinnacle

HOT BOX
Hot box / Come and get the love / Love spell / Gotta get my hands on some (money) / Backstrokin' / Street band
CD _______ CDSEWM 056
Southbound / Sep '92 / Pinnacle

IS THIS THE FUTURE
Is this the future / Double love affair / Spread love / Funky aerobics (Body movement) / Up against the wall / Finger lickin' good / Sunshine lady / Girl is fine
CD _______ CDSEWM 058
Southbound / Apr '94 / Pinnacle

KEEP ON STEPPIN'
Mr. Bass man / Stuff / New York style / Love / Can't stop the flame / Wicky wacky / Feeling / Keep on stepping / Breaking up with someone you love is hard to do
CD _______ CDSEW 001
Southbound / Jun '89 / Pinnacle

LET'S DO IT AGAIN
Street dance / Free form / Take a ride (On the soul train) / Wichita lineman / Baby I'm want you / Let's do it again / Goin' to see

my baby / Give me one more chance / Green green grass of home
CD ______ DEEPM 020
Deep Beats / Mar '97 / BMG

MAN WITH THE BAND
Man with the band / Master Booty / Funk backin' / Mile high / I gotta thing for you / Midnight freak / Zodiac man
CD ______ CDSEW 036
Southbound / Jan '91 / Pinnacle

NIGHT FEVER
Night fever / Little funky dance / If that's the way you want it / Joint (you and me) / Disco crazy / Booty / No more room on the dancefloor / December '63 (oh what a night)
CD ______ CDSEW 008
Southbound / Aug '89 / Pinnacle

NYCNYUSA
Double Dutch / Soul finger (gonna put on you) / Spank the baby / Duke walk / NYCNYUSA / Love street / Changed man / Cosmic woman
CD ______ CDSEW 030
Southbound / Jul '90 / Pinnacle

ON THE FLOOR
On the floor / UFO (Unidentified funk object) / Burn baby burn / She's my shining star / Hip so slick / Do it to me now
CD ______ CDSEWM 091
Southbound / Mar '94 / Pinnacle

PEOPLE MUSIC
Nija walk (Street walk) / Gotta have you (Day by day) / Fatbackin' / Baby doll / Clap your hands / Soul march / Soul man / To be with you / Kiba
CD ______ DEEPM 019
Deep Beats / Mar '97 / BMG

RAISING HELL
(Are you ready) do the bus stop / All day / Put your love (in my tender care) / Groovy kind of day / Spanish hustle / I can't help myself / Party time
CD ______ CDSEW 028
Southbound / Apr '90 / Pinnacle

TASTY JAM
Take it any way you want it / Wanna dance / Keep your fingers out of the jam / Kool whip / High steppin' lady / Get ready for the night
CD ______ CDSEWM 088
Southbound / Feb '94 / Pinnacle

WITH LOVE
He's a freak undercover / Rastajam / I love your body language / I found lovin' / I wanna be your lover / Please stay / Wide glide
CD ______ CDSEW 024
Southbound / Feb '90 / Pinnacle

XII
You're my candy sweet / Disco bass / Gimme that sweet, sweet lovin' / King Tim III (personality jock) / Disco queen / Love in perfect harmony
CD ______ CDSEWM 049
Southbound / Apr '92 / Pinnacle

YUM YUM
Yum yum (gimme some) / Trompin' / Let the drums speak / Put the funk on you / Feed me your love / Boogie with Fatback / Got to learn how to dance / If you could turn into me / (Hey) I feel real good
CD ______ CDSEW 016
Southbound / Nov '89 / Pinnacle

Fates Warning

CHASING TIME
CD ______ 398414085CD
Metal Blade / Apr '97 / Pinnacle / Plastic Head

INSIDE OUT
CD ______ MASSCD 037
Massacre / Jun '94 / Plastic Head

NIGHT ON BROCKEN
CD ______ 398414053CD
Metal Blade / May '96 / Pinnacle / Plastic Head

NO EXIT
CD ______ 398414047CD
Metal Blade / Apr '96 / Pinnacle / Plastic Head

PARALLELS
CD ______ CDZORRO 31
Metal Blade / Nov '91 / Pinnacle / Plastic Head

PLEASANT SHADE OF GREY
CD ______ MASSCD 125
Massacre / Jun '97 / Plastic Head

SPECTRE WITHIN
CD ______ 398414054CD
Metal Blade / May '96 / Pinnacle / Plastic Head

Father Dom

FATHER DOM
I'm fed up / Father Dom story / Hard to handle / Grand pooba... / Letter to my listeners / U don't stop / I can't stay mad (at you forever) / Everybody wants to be an MC / Now we gotcha / Keep on doin' watcha doin'
CD ______ CDWRA 8105
Wrap / Feb '92 / Koch

Father MC

THIS IS FOR THE PLAYERS
CD ______ CDMISH 3
Mission / Nov '95 / 3mv/Sony

Fatman

FATMAN VS. SHAKA (First, Second & Third Generation Of Dub) (Fatman & Jah Shaka)
CD ______ FM 001CD
Fatman / May '95 / Jet Star / SRD

SAME SONG DUB (Fatman Riddim Section)
CD ______ LG 21103
Lagoon / Apr '95 / Grapevine/PolyGram

Fattburger

ALL NATURAL INGREDIENTS
CD ______ SH 5026CD
Shanachie / Oct '96 / ADA / Greensleeves / Koch

GOOD NEWS
CD ______ 3287 2
Enigma / Oct '87 / EMI

LIVIN' LARGE
CD ______ SHCD 5012
Shanachie / Mar '95 / ADA / Greensleeves / Koch

Fatty George

FATTY'S SALON 1958
CD ______ RST 91425
RST / Oct '92 / Hot Shot / Jazz Music

Faubert, Michel

CAREME ET MARDI-GRAS
CD ______ MPCD 1095
Mille Pattes / Apr '96 / ADA

MAUDITE MEMOIRE
CD ______ MPCD 995
Mille Pattes / Apr '96 / ADA

Faucett, Dawnett

TAKING MY TIME
Slow dancing / Don't stop to count the memories / Mama never told me / Bus won't be stopping / Heart heart / Cheap perfume / Good for you / Taking my time / As far as love can throw me / Dusty road / Two empty arms / Unwanted
CD ______ SORCD 0054
D-Sharp / Oct '94 / Pinnacle

Faulk, Dan

FOCUSING IN (Faulk, Dan Quintet)
CD ______ CRISS 1076CD
Criss Cross / Nov '93 / Cadillac / Direct / Vital/SAM

Faulkner, John

KIND PROVIDENCE
Sweet Thames flow softly / Walecatchers/ Drunken landlady / Planxty gan ainm / Wild rover / Johnny Coughlin / McCaffery / Banks of Newfoundland / Forger's farewell / Road to Cashel/Jackie Daly's reel / Newry town
CD ______ GLCD 1064
Green Linnet / Feb '93 / ADA / CM / Direct / Highlander / Roots

NOMADS/FANAITHE
MacCrimmon will never come back / MacCrimmon's lament / Sucah a Parcel of Rogues in a Nation / Farewell to Scotland/ In the mist / Young Munroe / La reel du Pendu / Cape Sky waltz/Joe Tom's reels / I am a little orphan/Two step too / I loved a lass / Jolly bold robber / Flowers of Finae / Child owlet/Erskine's folly / Nomads of the road/Pristina
CD ______ CIC 071CD
Clo Iar-Chonnachta / Jan '92 / CM

Faust

71 MINUTES OF
CD ______ RERF 1CD
ReR/Recommended / Jun '96 / ReR Megacorp / RTM/Disc

FAUST
CD ______ KLANG 01
Klangbad / Nov '96 / Cargo

FAUST IV
Krautrock / Sad skinhead / Jennifer / Jus' a second / Picnic on a frozen river, Deuxieme tableux / Giggy smile / Lauft... Heist das es lauft oder es kommt bald... Lauft / It's a bit of a pain
CD ______ CD 0501
Virgin / Oct '92 / EMI

FAUST TAPES, THE
CD ______ RERF 2CD
ReR/Recommended / Jun '96 / ReR Megacorp / RTM/Disc

KIRK
CD ______ RERHCD 2
ReR/Recommended / Oct '96 / ReR Megacorp / RTM/Disc

OUTSIDE THE DREAM SYNDICATE (Faust & Tony Conrad)
CD ______ LITHIUM 3
Southern / Jan '94 / SRD

RIEN
CD ______ CHROMIUM 24
TOE / Jun '97 / Cargo

UNTITLED
CD ______ KLANG 001
Klangbad / Feb '97 / Cargo

YOU KNOW FAUST
Hurricane / Tenne laufen / C pluus / Irons / Cendre / Sixty sixty / Winds / Liebeswehen 2 / Elektron 2 / Ella / Men from the moon / Der pfad / Noizes from Pythagoras / Na sowas / L'oiseau / Huttenfreak / Teutonentango
CD ______ RERF 3CD
ReR/Recommended / Jan '97 / ReR Megacorp / RTM/Disc

Faust, Alban

BORDUNMUSIK FRAN DALSLAND
CD ______ TONART 41CD
Tonart / Nov '96 / ADA

Faux, George

TIME FOR A LAUGH AND A SONG
Birthday reel / Farewell to the building / Cultural dessert / Kellswater / Parker's fancy / Farewell to London / Artesian water / Leggett's reel - the old grey cat / Do me amma / Gallant brigantine / Dominic's march / Time for a laugh and a song
CD ______ HARCD 006
Harbour Town / Oct '93 / ADA / CM / Direct / Roots

Faver, Colin

TECHMIX VOL.1 (On The Decks With Colin Faver) (Various Artists)
CD ______ KICKCD 40
Kickin' / Aug '96 / Prime / SRD

Favre, Pierre

WINDOW STEPS
Snow / Cold nose / Lea / Girimella / En passant / Aguilar / Passage
CD ______ 5293482
ECM / Feb '96 / New Note/Pinnacle

Favreau, Eric

VIOLIN & ACCORDION (Favreau, Eric & Joaquin Diaz)
CD ______ B 6837
Auvidis/Ethnic / Nov '96 / ADA / Harmonia Mundi

Fawkes, Wally

FIDGETY FEET
CD ______ SOSCD 1248
Stomp Off / Jul '93 / Jazz Music / Wellard

Fay, Colin

DANCING ON THE CEILING
Snowbird / Walking the floor / Swanee / Please baby please / Ain't we got fun / Melody in F / Oh my Papa / Andantiono / Dancing on the ceiling / Silver threads among the gold / Rose room / Coppelia / Love theme from The Thorn Birds / Nocturne in Eb / If those lips could only speak / I'll be your sweetheart / Let the rest of the world go by / Pretty baby / Make mine love / Strollin' / Underneath the arches / Louise / Broken doll / Honeysuckle and the bee / Nola / Glory of love / Waiting at the church / Oh Mr Porter / Daddy wouldn't buy me a bowwow / On the banks of wabash / Lily of Laguna / Man who broke the bank at Monte Carlo / Let's all go down the strand / Wot'cher (Knocked 'em in the Old Kent Road) / Fall in and follow me / Light of foot / Life on the ocean wave / Stephanie Gavotte / Kind regards / Tell me pretty maiden / Ascot gavotte / Ay ay ay / La concordia / Pablo the dreamer / Creole tango
CD ______ GRCD 52
Grasmere / Aug '92 / Highlander / Savoy / Target/BMG

Fay, Rick

GLENDENA FOREVER (Fay, Rick & Jackie Coon)
CD ______ ARCD 19104
Arbors Jazz / Nov '94 / Cadillac

HELLO HORN
CD ______ ARCD 19102
Arbors Jazz / Nov '94 / Cadillac

LIVE AT LONE PINE
CD ______ ARCD 19101
Arbors Jazz / Nov '94 / Cadillac

LIVE AT THE STATE THEATRE
CD ______ ARCD 29102
Arbors Jazz / Nov '94 / Cadillac

MEMORIES OF YOU
CD ______ ARCD 19103
Arbors Jazz / Nov '94 / Cadillac

OH BABY
CD ______ ARCD 19105
Arbors Jazz / Nov '94 / Cadillac

ROLLING ON
I double dare you / Blues (my naughtie sweetie gives to me) / Somebody loves me / Tishomingo blues / Manoir de mes reves / Come back Papa
CD ______ ARCD 19108
Arbors Jazz / Nov '94 / Cadillac

SAX-O-POEM
CD ______ ARCD 19113
Arbors Jazz / Nov '94 / Cadillac

THIS IS WHERE I CAME IN
CD ______ ARCD 19106
Arbors Jazz / Nov '94 / Cadillac

Faye, Alice

ON SCREEN & RADIO 1932-1943
CD ______ VJB 1947
Vintage Jazz Band / May '96 / Cadillac / Hot Shot / Jazz Music / Wellard

Faye, Glenda

FLATPICKIN' FAVORITES
CD ______ FF 70432
Flying Fish / Oct '89 / ADA / CM / Direct / Roots

Fays, Raphael

VOYAGES
CD ______ BEST 1015CD
Acoustic Music / Nov '93 / ADA

Faze Action

PLANS AND DESIGNS
Plans and designs / Original disco motion / In and out / In the trees / Astral projection / Turn the point / Vortex
CD ______ NUX 115CD
Nuphonic / May '97 / Amato Disco / Prime / RTM/Disc

Fear

HAVE ANOTHER BEER WITH FEAR
CD ______ SECT2 10020
Sector 2 / Jan '96 / Cargo / Direct

LIVE FOR THE RECORD
CD ______ LS 92522
Roadrunner / Nov '91 / PolyGram

Fear Factory

DEMANUFACTURE
Demanufacture / Self bias resistor / Zero signal / Replica / New breed / Dog day sunrise / Body hammer / Flashpoint / H-K (Hunter killer) / Pisschrist / Therapy for pain
CD ______ RR 89562
Roadrunner / Jun '95 / PolyGram

FEAR IS THE MINDKILLER
CD ______ RR 90822
Roadrunner / Apr '93 / PolyGram

REMANUFACTURE
CD ______ RR 88342
Roadrunner / Jun '97 / PolyGram

SOUL OF A NEW MACHINE
CD ______ RR 91602
Roadrunner / Jun '96 / PolyGram

Fear Of God

TOXIC VOODOO
CD ______ CDVEST 24
Bulletproof / Jul '94 / Pinnacle

Fearing, Stephen

ASSASSIN'S APPRENTICE, THE
CD ______ CSCCD 1001
CRS / Aug '95 / ADA / Direct / Jet Star

BLUE LINE
CD ______ RUE CD 003
New Routes / Apr '90 / Pinnacle

Fearon, Phil

BEST OF PHIL FEARON & GALAXY, THE (Fearon, Phil & Galaxy)
Dancing tight / Head over heels / What do I do / Nothing is too good for you / I can prove it / Everybody's laughing / Burning my bridges / Wait until tonight (my love) / All I give to you / You don't need a reason / This kind of love / Ain't nothing but a house party / If you're gonna fall in love / Fantasy real
CD ______ MCCD 150
Music Club / Feb '94 / Disc / THE

DANCING TIGHT (Fearon, Phil & Galaxy)
Dancing tight / Wait until tonight (my love) / Head over heels / Ain't nothing but a house party / Fantasy real / This kind of love / You don't need a reason / I can prove it / Everybody's laughing / What do I do / I can prove it (edit)
CD ______ MOCD 3006
More Music / Feb '95 / Sound & Media

DANCING TIGHT - THE BEST OF GALAXY (Fearon, Phil & Galaxy)
What do I do / Dancing tight / This kind of love / Head over heels / You don't need a reason / Wait until tonight (my love) / If you're gonna fall in love / Everybody's laughing / I can prove it / All I give to you / Fantasy real / Ain't nothing but a house party / Nothing is too good for you / Anything you want
CD _____ CDCHEN 31
Ensign / Oct '92 / EMI

GREATEST HITS (Fearon, Phil & Galaxy)
Dancing tight / Wait until tonight / What do I do / This kind of love / If you're gonna fall in love / Nothing is too good for you / Fantasy real / Everybody's laughing / I can prove it / Ain't nothing but a house party / You don't need a reason / All I give to you / Anything you want / Head over heels / This kind of love (Morales mix) / Fantasy real (12" mix)
CD _____ CDGOLD 1032
EMI Gold / May '96 / EMI

Feast

HONEYSUCKLE SIPS
Crazy / Not gonna cry / For your heart / Anastasia / All over / Let you down / Still walking / Trust me / Staring out of stars / Obsession / Say we'll meet again / Above the water
CD _____ HOT 1062CD
Hot / Mar '97 / Hot Records

Feather, Leonard

CLASSICS 1937-1945
CD _____ CLASSICS 901
Classics / Nov '96 / Discovery / Jazz Music

Feathers, Charlie

CHARLIE FEATHERS
Man in love / When you come around / Pardon me mister / Fraulein / Defrost your heart / Mean woman blues / I don't care if tomorrow never comes / Cootzie coo / We can't seem to remember to forget / Long time ago / Seasons of my heart / Uh huh honey / Oklahoma hills
CD _____ 7559611472
Nonesuch / Jul '91 / Warner Music

GONE GONE GONE
Peepin' eyes / I've been deceived / Defrost your heart / Wedding gown of white / We're getting closer to being apart / Bottle to the baby / One hand loose / Can't hardly stand it / Everybody's lovin' my baby / Too much alike / When you come around / When you decide / Nobody's woman / Man in love / I forgot to remember to forget / Uh huh honey / Mound of clay / Tongue tied Jill / Gone gone gone / Two to choose / Send me the pillow that you dream on / Folsom Prison blues
CD _____ CDCHARLY 278
Charly / Sep '91 / Koch

GOOD ROCKIN' TONITE
CD _____ EDCD 355
Edsel / Sep '92 / Pinnacle

HONKY TONK MAN
CD _____ 422407
Last Call / Feb '97 / Cargo / Direct / Discovery

ROCK-A-BILLY 1954-1973 (The Definitive Collection Of Rare & Unissued Recordings)
Bottle to the baby / So ashamed / Honky tonk kind / Frankie and Johnny / Defrost your heart / Runnin' around / I've been deceived / Corine Corina / Wedding gown of white / Defrost your heart / Bottle to the baby / I can't hardly wait / One hand loose / Everybody's lovin' my baby / Dinky John / South of Chicago / I'm walking the dog / Today and tomorrow / Wild wild party / Where's she at tonight / Don't you know / Wild side of life / Long time ago / Tongue tied Jill / Folsom Prison blues / Gone gone gone
CD _____ CDZ 2011
Zu Zazz / Apr '94 / Rollercoaster

THAT ROCKABILLY CAT
Gone gone gone / Tongue tied Jill / Wild side of life / Do you know / Rock me / Wide river / Crazy heart / Uh huh honey / Cold dark night / Rain / Mama oh Mama / Cherry wine / There will be three / I'm movin' on
CD _____ EDCD 348
Edsel / Jun '92 / Pinnacle

February

EVEN THE NIGHT
CD _____ FEBCD 1
February / Oct '96 / Cargo

Feddy, Jason

FISH ON THE MOON
CD _____ REDHEDCD 1
Redhead / Nov '94 / CM

I THOUGHT THE MOON WAS MEANT FOR ME
Even the rain / No faith / All that you do to me / Ragtime to riches / Road / Anyway / I depend on you / Let it be summer / Kicking up the pavement / She's not to blame / Angels / I want holding
CD _____ TACD 2
Thin Air Music / Sep '97 / Pinnacle

Federal Music Society

COME AND TRIP IT (Hyman, Dick & Gerard Schwarz Orchestras)
Prima donna waltz / Jenny Lind polka / Minuet and gavotte / Country fiddle music / Natilie polka-mazurka / Flying cloud / Victoria gallop / Flirt polka / La sonnambula / Eliza Jane McCue / Blaze-away / Hiawatha / Sweet man
CD _____ 802932
New World / Aug '94 / ADA / Cadillac / Harmonia Mundi

Federation

EARTH LOOP
CD _____ ZEN 008CD
Indochina / Feb '96 / Pinnacle

Feds

CHICAGO BUREAU
CD _____ DSR 060CD
Dr. Strange / May '97 / Cargo / Greyhound / Plastic Head

Feed Your Head

AMBIENT COMPILATION
CD _____ BARKCD 002
Planet Dog / Jul '94 / Pinnacle

Feedback Bleep

ENGRAM
CD _____ EFA 119712
Electro Smog / Apr '95 / SRD

Feeder

POLYTHENE
Polythene girl / My perfect day / Cement / Crash / Radiation / Suffocate / Descend / Stereo world / Tangerine / Waterfall / Forgive / Twentieth century trip
CD _____ ECHCD 015
Echo / May '97 / EMI / Vital

SWIM
Sweet 16 / Stereo world / WIT / Descend / World asleep / Swim
CD _____ ECHCD 009
Echo / May '96 / EMI / Vital

Feedtime

BILLY
CD _____ ARR 72015CD
Amphetamine Reptile / Jun '96 / Plastic Head

Feelings

DEARLING DARLING
CD _____ DRL 035
Darla / Jun '97 / Cargo

Feenjon/Avram

SALUTE TO ISRAEL
CD _____ MCD 71746
Monitor / Jun '93 / CM

Feeny, Michael

MY OLD IRISH ROSE
CD _____ CNCD 5951
Disky / Jul '93 / Disky / THE

Feetpackets

LISTEN FEETPACKETS
CD _____ DISCUS 01
Discus / Feb '86 / Cadillac

Feidman, Giora

MAGIC OF THE KLEZMER, THE (Feidman, Giora & The Feidman Ensemble)
Song of rejoicing / Mr. Mzirion / Mothers in law / Happiness is a nigon / Cigarettes / With much sentiment / Frilling / Market place in jaffa / Hopkefe / Nigon / Dudele / Music for ghetto / Humoresque / Gershwin suite / Freilach
CD _____ DE 4005
Delos / Jan '94 / Nimbus

SILENCE AND BEYOND (Feidman Plays Ora Bat Chaim)
Skipping (Improv no.19) / Im waltz spirit / Grain of sand / Not for our sake / Beyond the now / In the self / In silence and joy / Love and joy / Elokim Eli Ata / Prayer / Psalm of thanks / Golem / At dawn / In freilach spirit
CD _____ 364992
Koch Schwann / Jun '97 / Koch

Feinstein, Michael

PURE IMAGINATION
Pure imagination / Swinging on a star / Teddy bears' picnic / Because we're kids / Ferdinand the bull / Not much of a dog / Lydia, the tattoed lady / Dressing song / Ugly bug ball / When you wish upon a star / Mole people / Alice in wonderland medley / Aren't you glad you're you / I like old people / Ten feet off the ground / Be kind to your parents / Jitterbug / Johnny Fedora and Alice Blue Bonnet / Angels on your pillow
CD _____ 7559610462
Elektra / Jun '92 / Warner Music

Felder, Don

AIRBORNE
Bad girls / Winners / Haywire / Who tonight / Never surrender / Asphalt jungle / Night owl / Still alive
CD _____ 7599602952
Warner Bros. / Jul '96 / Warner Music

Felder, Wilton

FOREVER ALWAYS
Lillies of the nile / For lovers only / My way / My one and only love / Rainbow visions / Forever / Goin' crazy / Asian flower / African queen / Mr. Felder
CD _____ CPCD 8141
Charly / Nov '95 / Koch

NOCTURNAL MOODS
Feel so much better / Night moves / Southern pearl / If I knew then what I know now / Sugar loaf / Love steps / Out of sight not out of mind / Since I fell for you / Music of the night
CD _____ CPCD 8124
Charly / Oct '95 / Koch

Feldman, Morton

COMPOSITIONS 1952-75
CD _____ RZCD 1010
FMP / Oct '94 / Cadillac

FOR CHRISTIAN WOLFF
CD Set _____ ARTCD 36120
Hat Art / Apr '93 / Cadillac / Harmonia Mundi

FOR PHILIP GUSTON
CD _____ ARTCD 46104
Hat Art / Jul '92 / Cadillac / Harmonia Mundi

FOR SAMUEL BECKETT
CD _____ ARTCD 6107
Hat Art / Jan '93 / Cadillac / Harmonia Mundi

PIANO AND STRING QUARTETS (Feldman, Morton & Aki Takahashi/ Kronos Quartet)
CD _____ 7559793202
Nonesuch / Jan '95 / Warner Music

TRIO
CD _____ ARTCD 6195
Hat Art / Jul '97 / Cadillac / Harmonia Mundi

Feldman, Victor

ARTFUL DODGER, THE
Limehouse blues / Haunted ballroom / Walk on the heath / Isn't she lovely / Smoke gets in your eyes / Agitation / Artful Dodger / St. Thomas
CD _____ CCD 4038
Concord Jazz / Jun '89 / New Note/ Pinnacle

FIESTA AND MORE
Fiesta / Elusive spirit / With your love / Forever / Summer games / Amigos / Viva Zapata / Heart to heart / Brazilia / Candy dance / Villa nueva / So much time
CD _____ JVC 90232
JVC / Aug '97 / Direct / New Note/Pinnacle / Vital/SAM

HIS OWN SWEET WAY
Fine romance / Alley blues / Thought about you / Autumn leaves / Swinging on a star / Azul serape / Llevestraum / Too blue / In your own sweet way / Fly me to the moon / Basin Street blues
CD _____ JHAS 605
Ronnie Scott's Jazz House / Jun '96 / Cadillac / Jazz Music / New Note/Pinnacle / TKO Magnum

TO CHOPIN WITH LOVE (Feldman, Victor Trio)
Mr. C meets Mr. T. / Star drift / Dream dance / Pola nova / Polka surprise / Night flight / Waltz for Scotty
CD _____ HCD 610
Hindsight / Jul '97 / Jazz Music / Target/ BMG

Feleus, Pali

ZIGEUNERORKEST ZIGEUNERKAPELLE (Feleus, Pali & Gipsy Band)
CD _____ SYNCOOP 5755CD
Syncoop / Feb '95 / ADA / Direct

Felice, Dee

DEE FELICE (Felice, Dee & The Sleep Cat Band)
CD _____ JCD 168
Jazzology / Feb '91 / Jazz Music

Felice, John

NOTHING PRETTY (Felice, John & The Lowdowns)
Don't be telling me / Ain't we having fun / I'll never sing that song again / Not the one / Perfect love / Nowadaze kids / Nothing pretty / Dreams / Don't make me wait / Can't play it safe
CD _____ ROSE 141CD
New Rose / Mar '88 / ADA / Direct / Discovery

Feliciano, Jose

AND I LOVE HER
And I love her / Light my fire / For my love / You're no good / Always something there to remind me / Yesterday / Don't let the sun catch you crying / I want to learn a love song / Find somebody and the sun will shine / Rain / Twilight time
CD _____ 743213394626
Camden / Jan '96 / BMG

BEST OF JOSE FELICIANO
Light my fire / California dreamin' / And the sun will shine / Windmills of your mind / Miss Otis regrets / Rain / First of May / Guantanamera / Che sara / Destiny / Suzie Q / Hi-heel sneakers / Cico and the man (theme) / Hitchcock railway / Malaguena / No dogs allowed
CD _____ ND 89561
RCA / Feb '90 / BMG

BEST OF JOSE FELICIANO, THE
CD _____ TRTCD 203
TrueTrax / Jul '96 / THE

CHE SARA
CD _____ WMCD 6544
Disky / May '94 / Disky / THE

COLLECTION, THE
Che sera sera / Light my fire / Hi-heel sneakers / La bamba / California dreamin' / Jealous guy / Samba Pati / This could be the last time / Daniel / Right here waiting / Chico (and the man) / Time after time / In my life / Angela / Volvere / Stay with me / Affirmation / Pegao / Rain / You send me
CD _____ COL 074
Collection / Apr '96 / Target/BMG

HITS COLLECTION, THE
Time after time / In my life / Light my fire / California dreamin' / You send me / Que sera / Daniel / Right here waiting / Jealous guy / Last time / La bamba / Chico and the man / Stay with me / Hi-heel sneakers / Angela / Affirmation / Rain / Pegao / Mule skinner blues / Y volere
CD _____ 100262
CMC / May '97 / BMG

JOSE FELICIANO
Bamboleo / La bamba / Che sera sera / Angela / Malaguena / Y volvere / Samba pa ti / Pegao / Daniel / Right here waiting / Affirmation / Chico and the man / La entrada de Bilbao
CD _____ CD 62110
Saludos Amigos / Oct '96 / Target/BMG

LIGHT MY FIRE
CD _____ PLSCD 101
Pulse / Apr '96 / BMG

LIGHT MY FIRE
Light my fire / Stay with me / Chico and the man / And I love her / You're no good / Don't let the sun catch you crying / Daytime dreams / Pegao / Always something there to remind me / California dreamin' / And the sun will shine / Here, then and everywhere / Essence of your love / Sunny / By the time I get to Phoenix / Yesterday / Nature boy / Rain / In my life / And the feeling's good
CD _____ 74321449252
Camden / Feb '97 / BMG

LIGHT MY FIRE
Daniel / Right here waiting / You send me / Hi-heel sneakers / Rain / Angela / Mule skinner blues / Affirmation / Chico the man / Samba pati / Che sera sera / La bamba / Light my fire / In my life / Last time / California dreamin' / Time after time / Jealous guy
CD _____ PLATCD 110
Platinum / Feb '97 / Prism

LIGHT MY FIRE
Light my fire / California dreamin' / Daniel / Jealous guy / Volvere / Pegao / Rain / In my life / You send me / Right here waiting / Stay with me / Affirmation / Mystery train / Last time / Hi-heel sneakers / Mule skinner blues / La bamba / Chico and the man / Bamboleo
CD _____ WB 870972
Disky / Mar '97 / Disky / THE

PRESENT TENSE
California dreamin' / Light my fire / Bamboleo / Right here waiting / Affirmation / Rain / Chico and the man / Daniel / Mule skinner blues / Last time / La bamba / Stay with me / You send me / Mystery train / Malaguena / Time after time / Hi heel sneakers / Jealous guy / In my life
CD _____ FR 008CD
Fragile / May '96 / Grapevine/PolyGram

PRESENT TENSE
CD _____ NTMCD 554
Nectar / Jun '97 / Pinnacle

TRIBUTE TO THE BEATLES, A
CD _______ 290810
RCA / Dec '92 / BMG

Felix

ONE
Fastslow / Fools in love / You gotta work / Stars / It's me / Don't you want me / It will make me crazy
CD _______ 74321264952
De-Construction / Jul '96 / BMG

Felix Da Housecat

THEE ALBUM - 'METROPOLIS PRESENT DAY'
Some kinda special / Marine mood / Metropolis present day / Little bloo / Trippin' on a trip / Ano.Th.A. Level / Submarine / B4 wuz then / Cycle spin / Footsteps of rage / Thee dawn / Radikal thanx
CD _______ FEAR 011CD
Radikal Fear / May '95 / Vital

Felix, Julie

EL CONDOR PASA
Amazing grace / Mr. Tambourine man / Early morning rain / San Francisco / Vincent / Where have all the flowers gone / Going to the zoo / Scarborough fair / Blowing in the wind / Let it be / Dona Dona / Soldier from the 60's / If I could / Where you are / Last thing on my mind / Man gave names to all the animals / I miss you / Bring on Lucie (free da people) / So much trouble / Changing / We better talk this over / Steal away again / My preservation kit / Big bang / Yoko (we believe)
CD _______ SCD 26
Start / Feb '97 / Disc

Fell, Simon H.

COMPILATION
CD _______ CDBF 01
Bruce's Fingers / Oct '93 / Cadillac / Discovery

COMPILATION VOL.2
CD _______ CDBF 04
Bruce's Fingers / Oct '93 / Cadillac / Discovery

Fell, Terry

TRUCK DRIVIN' MAN
Truck driving man / Caveman / Don't drop it / Play the music / I'm hot to trot / Mississippi River shuffle / Get aboard my wagon / You don't give a hang about me / He's in love with you / I believe my heart / What am I worth / Over and over / I nearly go crazy / That's the way the big ball bounces / Don't do it Joe / Consolation prize / Let's stay together till after Christmas / (We wanna see) Santa do the mambo / Wham bam hot ziggity zam / If I didn't have you / That's what I like / Fa-so-la / I can hear you cluckin' / What's good for the goose
CD _______ BCD 15762
Bear Family / Nov '93 / Direct / Rollercoaster / Swift

Fellinis, Broun

APHROKUBIST IMPROVISATIONS VOL.9
CD _______ MM 800222
Moonshine / Aug '95 / Mo's Music Machine / Prime / RTM/Disc

Fellow Travellers

FEW GOOD DUBS, A
CD _______ OKCD 33023
Okra / Dec '94 / ADA / Direct

JUST A VISITOR
CD _______ OKCD 33016
Okra / Sep '93 / ADA / Direct

LOVE SHINES BRIGHTER
CD _______ RTS 4
Return To Sender / Nov '94 / ADA / Direct

NO EASY WAY
CD _______ OKRACD 010
Okra / Mar '94 / ADA / Direct

THINGS AND TIME
CD _______ OKCD 33020
Okra / Sep '93 / ADA / ..rect

Fellows, Stephen

MOOD X
CD _______ CSA 301
RPM / Aug '97 / Pinnacle

Felony, Jayo

TAKE A RIDE
CD _______ 5282912
Island / Sep '95 / PolyGram

Felsons

ONE STEP AHEAD OF THE POSSE
CD _______ TMC 9607
Music Corporation / May '96 / Pinnacle

Felt

ABSOLUTE CLASSIC MASTERPIECES
Primitive painters / Day the rain came down / My darkest light will shine / Textile ranch / Sunlight bathed the golden glow / Crystal ball / Dismantled King is off the throne / Fortune / Dance of deliverance / Stagnant pool / Red indians / World is a soft as lace / Penelope tree / Trails of colour dissolve / Evergreen dazed / Templeroy / Something sends me to sleep / Index
CD _______ CDBRED 97
Cherry Red / Oct '96 / Pinnacle

ABSOLUTE CLASSIC MASTERPIECES VOL.2
CD Set _______ CRECD 150
Creation / Sep '93 / 3mv/Vital

BUBBLEGUM PERFUME
I will die with my head in flames / I didn't mean to hurt you / Autumn / There's no such thing as victory / Final resting place of the ark / Don't die on my doorstep / Book of swords / Gather up your wings and fly / Bitter end / Voyage to illumination / Stained glass windows / Space blues / Be still / Magellan / Sandman's on the rise again / Wave crashed on my doorstep / Declaration / Darkest ending / Rain of crystal spires / Ballad of the band
CD _______ CRECD 69
Creation / Apr '90 / 3mv/Vital

CRUMBLING THE ANTISEPTIC BEAUTY/SPLENDOUR OF FEAR, THE
Evergreen dazed / Fortune / Birdman / Cathedral / I worship the sun / Templeroy / Red Indians / World is as soft as lace / Optimist and the poet / Mexican bandits / Stagnant pool / Preacher in New England
CD _______ CDBRED 72
Cherry Red / May '96 / Pinnacle

FOREVER BREATHES THE LONELY WORD
CD _______ CRECD 011
Creation / Oct '90 / 3mv/Vital

GOLDMINE TRASH
Something sends me to sleep / Trails of colours dissolve / Dismantled King is off the throne / Penelope tree / Sunlight bathed the golden glow / Crystal ball / Day the rain came down / Fortune / Vasco da Gama / Primitive painters
CD _______ CDMRED 79
Cherry Red / Sep '87 / Pinnacle

IGNITE THE SEVEN CANNONS
My darkest night will shine / Day the rain came down / Scarlet servants / I don't know which way to turn / Primitive painters / Textile ranch / Black ship in the harbour / Elegance of an only dream / Serpent shade / Caspian see / Southern state tapestry / Roman litter / Sempiternal darkness / Spanish house / Imprint / Sunlight bathed the golden glow / Vasco da Gama / Crucifix heaven / Dismantled King is off the throne / Crystal ball / Whirlpool vision of shame
CD _______ CDBRED 65
Cherry Red / May '96 / Pinnacle

KISS YOU KIDNAPPED CHARABANC/ DEAD MEN TELL NO TALES
CD _______ CRECD 862
Creation / May '88 / 3mv/Vital

LET THE SNAKES CRINKLE THEIR HEADS TO DEATH
CD _______ CRECD 009
Creation / May '94 / 3mv/Vital

ME AND A MONKEY ON THE MOON
Can't make love / Mobile shack / Free / Budgie jacket / Cartoon sky / New day dawning / August path / Never let you go / Hey sister / Get out of my mirror
CD _______ ACME 24CD
El / Oct '96 / Pinnacle

PICTORIAL JACKSON REVIEW
CD _______ CRELP 030CD
Creation / Mar '88 / 3mv/Vital

POEM OF THE RIVER
CD _______ CRECD 017
Creation / May '94 / 3mv/Vital

POEM OF THE RIVER/FOREVER BREATHES THE LONELY WORD
CD _______ CRECD 653
Creation / May '88 / 3mv/Vital

STRANGE IDOLS PATTERN & OTHER SHORT STORIES
Roman litter / Sempiternal darkness / Spanish house / Imprint / Sunlight bathed the golden glow / Vasco da Gama / Crucifix heaven / Dismantled King is off the throne / Crystal ball / Whirlpool vision of shame
CD _______ CD BRED 65
Cherry Red / Feb '93 / Pinnacle

TRAIN ABOVE THE CITY
CD _______ CRECD 035
Creation / Oct '88 / 3mv/Vital

Felten, Eric

GRATITUDE
CD _______ 1212962
Soul Note / Sep '95 / Cadillac / Harmonia Mundi / Wellard

T-BOP (Felten, Eric & Jimmy Knepper)
CD _______ 1211962
Soul Note / Sep '93 / Cadillac / Harmonia Mundi / Wellard

Felts, Narvel

DRIFT AWAY (The Best Of Narvel Felts 1973-1979)
Drift away / Before you have to go / All in the name of love / Rockin' little angel / When your good love was mine / Fraulein / Until the end of time / She loves me like a rock / I want to stay / Wrap my arms around the world / Reconsider me / Foggy misty morning / Funny how time slips away / Blue suede shoes / Somebody hold me / Away / Lonely teardrops / Lonely kind of love / My prayer / Garden of Eden / Feeling's right / Moments to remember / To love somebody / Stirrin' up feelin's / One run for the roses / Never again / Everlasting love / End
CD _______ BCD 15690
Bear Family / May '96 / Direct / Rollercoaster / Swift

MEMPHIS DAYS
Night creature / Your true love / Blue darlin' / What you're doing to me / Sad and blue / She's in your heart to stay / Return / Welcome home / Love is gone / Tear down the wall / Four seasons of life / Come what may / Lola did a dance / Lovelight man / Mr. Pawnshop broker / Tongue tied Jill / All that heaven sent / I had a girl / Slippin' and slidin' / Larry and Joellen / You were mine / Get on the right track baby / Sweet sweet loving / Mountain of love / Private detective / One man at a table
CD _______ BCD 15515
Bear Family / Oct '90 / Direct / Rollercoaster / Swift

THIS TIME
This time / Since I met you baby / Butterfly / You're out of my reach / Chased by the dawn / No one will ever know / Endless love / Little bit of soap / Sound of the wind / All in the game / I'd trade all of my tomorrows / Greatest gift / I had to cry / Dee Dee / Eighty six Miles
CD _______ HIUKCD 123
Hi / Sep '92 / Pinnacle

Fem 2 Fem

ANIMUS
CD _______ AHLCD 33
Hit / Aug '95 / Grapevine/PolyGram

Feminine Complex

LIVIN' LOVE
CD _______ TB 196
Teenbeat / Jun '97 / Cargo / SRD / Vital

Fender, Freddy

CANCIONES DE MI BARRIO
CD _______ ARHCD 366
Arhoolie / Apr '95 / ADA / Cadillac / Direct

COLLECTION, THE
CD _______ COL 013
Collection / Oct '95 / Target/BMG

CRAZY BABY
Crazy baby / Wasted days and wasted nights / What'd I say / Something on your mind / Loving cajun / Style / Mean woman / La Bamba / Get out of my life woman / Only one / Coming home soon / Before the next teardrop falls / Since I met you baby / Wild side of life / Rains came / Mathilda / You'll lose a good thing / Just because / Black shirt / You made a fool / Coming round the mountain
CD _______ CDSB 012
Starburst / Jul '96 / TKO Magnum

FREDDY FENDER
CD _______ DS 005
Desperado / Jun '97 / TKO Magnum

GREATEST HITS
Your cheatin' heart / These arms of mine / She's about a mover / Baby I want to love you / High school dance / Talk to me / Let the good times roll / In the still of the night / Man can cry / Wasted days and wasted nights / Crazy baby / Enter my heart / La Bamba / I'm leaving it all up to you / Wild side of life / Sweet summer day / Mathilda / Silver wings / Since I met you baby / Before the next teardrop falls
CD _______ HADCD 167
Javelin / May '94 / Henry Hadaway / THE

IN HIS PRIME
Before the next teardrop falls / Wasted days and wasted nights / You'll lose a good thing / Vaya con dios / Living it down / Rains came / If you don't love me / Think about me / Walking piece of heaven / Wild side of life / Since I met you baby / I'm a fool to care / She's about a mover / It's raining / Talk to me / Tell it like it is / Just out of reach of my two open arms / I can't help it (if I'm still in love with you) / What a difference a day made / Pass me by (if you're only passing through)
CD _______ EDCD 516
Edsel / Aug '97 / Pinnacle

WASTED DAYS & WASTED NIGHTS
Wasted days and wasted nights / Rains came / You'll lose a good thing / Almost persuaded / I'm leaving it all up to you / Man can cry / Wild side of life / She's about a mover / Crazy baby / Girl who waits on tables / Before the next teardrop falls / Lovin' cajun style / But I do / Sweet summer day / Silver wings / Running back / Enter my heart / Going out with the tide / Baby I want to love you / Just because
CD _______ GRF 072
Tring / Feb '93 / Tring

Fenech, Paul

DADDY'S HAMMER
Guitar slinger / Daddy's hammer / Hear me howl / Running back to you / Scrape your sanity / Snakin' with the bad guys / Locked in a room with Betty / Cold cold baby / (We're) not like you / One fine day / (Alone) In the killing room / 1000 Guns for Pablo
CD _______ CDGRAM 87
Anagram / Mar '95 / Cargo / Pinnacle

Fenton, George

TRAILS OF LIFE
CD _______ CDSGP 030
Prestige / Oct '92 / Else / Total/BMG

Fenwick, Ray

GROUPS AND SESSIONS 1962-1976 (Various Artists)
It's for you: *Rupert & The Red Devils* / Everytime I do: *Rupert & The Red Devils* / Crawdaddy Simone: *Syndicats* / Please call me: *Tee Set* / So I came back to you: *Tee Set* / Long ago: *After Tea* / After tea: *After Tea* / After Tea: *Davis, Spencer Group* / Mr. 2nd class: *Davis, Spencer Group* / Bad boy: *Musicians Union Band* / Let the circle stay unbroken: *Fenwick, Ray* / USA: *Fenwick, Ray* / Have mercy: *Hardin & York* / Ghost town: *Guitar Orchestra* / Get out of my life: *Diddley, Bo* / Blue bird: *Fenwick, Ray* / She's riding the rock machine: *Fancy* / Catch you on the rebop: *Davis, Spencer Group* / Livin' in a black street: *Davis, Spencer Group* / Magpie: *Murgatroyd Band* / Trying to get to you: *Gillan, Ian* / Clear air turbulence: *Gillan, Ian*
CD _______ RPM 176
RPM / Jun '97 / Pinnacle

KEEP AMERICA BEAUTIFUL, GET A HAIRCUT
Stateside / Anniversary / I wanna stay here / City ride / Dream / Back USA / New Jersey turnpike
CD _______ SJPCD 013
Angel Air / Aug '97 / Pinnacle

Feon, Daniel

EVIT DANSAL (Feon, Daniel & Jil Lehart)
CD _______ 432CD
Diffusion Breizh / Jul '95 / ADA

Ferber, Mordy

MR. X
CD _______ EFA 015052
Ozone / Jul '95 / Mo's Music Machine / Pinnacle / SRD

Ferbos, Lionel

LIONEL FERBOS & LARS EDEGRAN'S NEW ORLEANS BAND (Ferbos, Lionel & Lars Edegran)
CD _______ BCD 340
GHB / Jun '96 / Jazz Music

Ferguson, Maynard

AMERICAN MUSIC HALL 1972, THE
CD _______ DSTS 1004
Status / '94 / Harmonia Mundi / Jazz Music / Wellard

BODY AND SOUL
Expresso / Body and soul / MOT / Mira Mira / Last dive / Beautiful hearts / Central Park
CD _______ TJA 10027
Jazz Alliance / Feb '96 / New Note/Pinnacle

FOOTPATH CAFE
Get it to go / Footpath cafe / Brazil / That's my desire / Crusin' for a bluesin' / Poison ya' blues / Break the ice / Hit and run
CD _______ IOR 83122
In & Out / Sep '95 / Vital/SAM

HIGH VOLTAGE
CD _______ CDENV 517
Enigma / Feb '89 / EMI

JAZZ MASTERS
CD _______ 5299052
Verve / Apr '96 / PolyGram

LIVE AT PEACOCK LANE (Ferguson, Maynard & His Orchestra)
CD _______ JH 1030
Jazz Hour / Jul '93 / Cadillac / Jazz Music / Target/BMG

LIVE AT THE GREAT AMERICAN MUSIC HALL
CD _______ DSTS 1007
Status / May '95 / Harmonia Mundi / Jazz Music / Wellard

MAYNARD FERGUSON ORCHESTRA 1967
CD ______ **JAS 9504**
Just A Memory / Dec '95 / New Note/ Pinnacle

MAYNARD FERGUSON SEXTET 1967
CD ______ **JAS 9503**
Just A Memory / Dec '95 / New Note/ Pinnacle

NEW SOUNDS OF...1964
CD ______ **FSCD 2010**
Fresh Sound / Nov '94 / Discovery / Jazz Music

ONE MORE TRIP TO BIRDLAND (Ferguson, Maynard & Big Bop Nouveau)
You got it / Manteca / Vibe / Cajun cookin' / Milestones / She was too good to me / Birdland / Blues from around here / It don't mean a thing (if it ain't got that swing)
CD ______ **CCD 4729**
Concord Jazz / Oct '96 / New Note/ Pinnacle

STORM
Admiral's horn / Jar star / Take the 'A' train / Latino lovewalk / Sesame Street / As time goes by / Go with the flo / Hit in the head
CD ______ **74321374872**
Bluebird / Feb '97 / BMG

THESE CATS CAN SWING (Ferguson, Maynard & Bip Bop)
Sugar / Caravan / I don't wanna be a hoochie coochie man no mo' / Sweet bab suite (Bai Rav) / I'll be around / He can't swing / It's the gospel truth
CD ______ **CCD 4669**
Concord Jazz / Oct '95 / New Note/ Pinnacle

THIS IS JAZZ
Birdland / Everybody loves the blues / McArthur Park / Fox hunt / Cheshire cat walk / 'Round midnight / Gospel John / Gonna fly now
CD ______ **CK 64970**
Sony Jazz / Oct '96 / Sony

Fermenting Innards

MYST
CD ______ **INV 016CD**
Invasion / Nov '95 / Plastic Head

Fernandel

ANTHOLOGIE
CD ______ **EN 522**
Fremeaux / Feb '96 / ADA / Discovery

ETOILES DE LA CHANSON
CD ______ **878152**
Music Memoria / Jun '93 / ADA / Discovery

L'IRRESISTIBLE
CD ______ **UCD 19028**
Forlane / Jun '95 / Target/BMG

Fernandez, Fernando

EL CROONER DE MEXICO
CD ______ **ALCD 026**
Alma Latina / Apr '97 / Discovery

GRANDES EXITOS VOL.1
CD ______ **ALCD 028**
Alma Latina / Apr '97 / Discovery

GRANDES EXITOS VOL.2
CD ______ **ALCD 031**
Alma Latina / Apr '97 / Discovery

Fernandez, Roberto

NEW YORK SESSIONS (Fernandez, Roberto 'Fats')
CD ______ **CDCH 564**
Milan / Feb '91 / Conifer/BMG / Silva Screen

Fernando, Alfredo

MILONGAS FROM URUGUAY
CD ______ **EUCD 1098**
ARC / '91 / ADA / ARC Music

TRIBUTE TO CARLOS GARDEL
CD ______ **EUCD 1134**
ARC / '91 / ADA / ARC Music

Fernhill

CA NOS
Ffarwel i Aberystwyth / Cowboi / Brigg fair / Gwenith gwyn / Ridees pastwn mawr / March glas / Le gabier de Terre-Neuve / Lloer dirion / Banks of the Nile / Pilons l'herbe
CD ______ **BEJOCD 14**
Beautiful Jo / Nov '96 / ADA / Direct

Ferrari, Luc

ACOUSMATRIX VOL.3
CD ______ **BVHAASTCD 9009**
Bvhaast / Oct '93 / Cadillac

Ferre, Boulou

NEW YORK NY
CD ______ **SCCD 31404**
Steeplechase / Apr '97 / Discovery / Impetus

TRINITY
CD ______ **SCCD 31171**
Steeplechase / Jul '88 / Discovery / Impetus

Ferre, Leo

PREMIERE CHANSON
CD ______ **LDX 274967**
La Chant Du Monde / Sep '93 / ADA / Harmonia Mundi

Ferrel, Frank

BOSTON FIDDLE
CD ______ **ROUCD 7018**
Rounder / Aug '96 / ADA / CM / Direct

Ferrell, Rachelle

FIRST INSTRUMENT
You send me / You don't know what love is / Bye bye blackbird / Prayer dance / Inchworm / With every breath I take / What is this thing called love / My funny valentine / Don't waste your time / Extensions / Autumn leaves
CD ______ **CDP 8728202**
Blue Note / Jun '95 / EMI

Ferrero, Medard

INOUBLIABLES DE L'ACCORDEON
CD ______ **882392**
Music Memoria / Aug '93 / ADA / Discovery

Ferrick, Melissa

MASSIVE BLUR
Honest eyes / Happy song / Hello dad / What have I got to lose / Love song / Ten friends / For once in my life / Blue sky night / Massive blur / Take me all / Wonder why / Meaning of love / In a world like this / Breaking vows
CD ______ **7567825022**
Elektra / Dec '93 / Warner Music

Ferris, Glenn

FACE LIFT
CD ______ **ENJACD 90892**
Enja / Feb '96 / New Note/Pinnacle / Vital/ SAM

FLESH AND STONE
CD ______ **ENJACD 80882**
Enja / Jan '95 / New Note/Pinnacle / Vital/ SAM

Ferron

PHANTOM CENTER
CD ______ **9425762**
Earthbeat / Jan '96 / ADA / Direct

Ferry, Bryan

ANOTHER TIME, ANOTHER PLACE
In crowd / Smoke gets in your eyes / Walk a mile in my shoes / Funny how time slips away / You are my sunshine / What a wonderful world / It ain't me babe / Finger poppin' / Help me make it through the night / Another time another place
CD ______ **EGCD 14**
EG / Sep '91 / EMI

ANOTHER TIME/THESE FOOLISH THINGS/LET'S STICK TOGETHER (Compact Collection/3CD Set)
CD ______ **TPAK 22**
Virgin / Nov '92 / EMI

BETE NOIRE
Limbo / Kiss and tell / New town / Day for night / Zamba / Right stuff / Seven deadly sins / Name of the game / Bete noire
CD ______ **CDV 2474**
Virgin / Nov '87 / EMI

BOYS AND GIRLS
Sensation / Slave to love / Don't stop the dance / Wasteland / Windswept / Chosen one / Valentine / Stone woman / Boys and girls
CD ______ **EGCD 62**
EG / Sep '91 / EMI

BRIDE STRIPPED BARE, THE
Sign of the times / Can't let go / Hold on I'm comin' / Same old blues / When she walks in the room / Take me to the river / What goes on / Carrickfergus / That's how strong my love is / This island Earth
CD ______ **EGCD 36**
EG / Sep '91 / EMI

IN YOUR MIND
This is tomorrow / All night operator / One kiss / Love me madly again / Tokyo Joe / Party doll / Rock of ages / In your mind
CD ______ **EGCD 27**
EG / Sep '91 / EMI

LET'S STICK TOGETHER
Let's stick together / Casanova / Sea breezes / Shame, shame, shame / 2HB / Price of love / Chance meeting / It's only love / You go to my head / Re-make/Re-model / Heart on my sleeve
CD ______ **EGCD 24**
EG / Jan '84 / EMI

MAMOUNA
Don't want to know / NYC / Your painted smile / Mamouna / Only face / Thirty nine steps / Which way to turn / Wild cat days / Gemini moon / Chain reaction
CD ______ **CDV 2751**
Virgin / Sep '94 / EMI

MORE THAN THIS (The Best Of Bryan Ferry & Roxy Music)
Virginia Plain: *Roxy Music* / Hard rain's gonna fall / Street life: *Roxy Music* / These foolish things / Love is the drug: *Roxy Music* / Dance away: *Roxy Music* / Let's stick together / Angel eyes: *Roxy Music* / Slave to love / Oh yeah: *Roxy Music* / Don't stop the dance / Same old scene: *Roxy Music* / Is your love strong enough / Jealous guy: *Roxy Music* / Kiss and tell / More than this: *Roxy Music* / I put a spell on you / Avalon: *Roxy Music* / Your painted smile / Smoke gets in your eyes
CD ______ **CDV 2791**
Virgin / Oct '95 / EMI

TAXI
I put a spell on you / Will you still love me tomorrow / Answer me / Just one look / Rescue me / All tomorrow's parties / Girl of my best friend / Amazing grace / Taxi / Because you're mine
CD ______ **CDV 2700**
Virgin / Mar '93 / EMI

THESE FOOLISH THINGS
Hard rain's gonna fall / River of salt / Don't ever change / Piece of my heart / Baby I don't care / It's my party / Don't worry baby / Sympathy for the devil / Tracks of my tears / You won't see me / I love how you love me / Loving you is sweeter than ever / These foolish things
CD ______ **EGCD 9**
EG / Jul '93 / EMI

Fertile Crescent

FERTILE CRESCENT
CD ______ **KFWCD 118**
Knitting Factory / Nov '92 / Cargo / Plastic Head

Fertilizer

PAINTING OF ANNOYANCE
CD ______ **IR 008CD**
Invasion / Apr '95 / Plastic Head

Fervant, Thierry

LEGENDS OF AVALON
CD ______ **QMCD 7042**
Quartz / Sep '90 / SRD

UNIVERSE
CD ______ **QMCD 7012**
Quartz / Sep '90 / SRD

Fessler, Peter

FOOT PRINTS
CD ______ **MM 801058**
Minor Music / Oct '96 / Vital/SAM

Fest, Manfredo

AMAZONAS
Secret love / Florianopolis / Amazonas / Caminhos crizados (Crossed paths) / O Pato (The Duck) / Madison Square / Over the rainbow / Guarana / Tristeza de nos dois (Sad for both of us) / Lullaby of birdland / Ela E Carioca (She's a child of Rio) / Estate (Summer)
CD ______ **CCD 47662**
Concord Picante / Apr '97 / New Note/ Pinnacle

COMECAR DE NOVO
Fetuccini Manfredo / Voce e eu / You must believe in spring / Where's montgomery / Bonita / Seresta / Lush life / Morning / How insensitive / Brazilian divertimento # 2 / Comecar de novo / Vera cruz
CD ______ **CCD 4660**
Concord Jazz / Aug '95 / New Note/ Pinnacle

FASCINATING RHYTHM
Fascinating rhythm / Berimbau / Samba do aviao / Marcia / Summertime / Samba do soho / Spring can really hang you up the most / Triste / Route 66 / Tenderly / Eyes of love / Arigo
CD ______ **CCD 4711**
Concord Picante / Jul '96 / New Note/ Pinnacle

Fester

WINTER OF SIN
CD ______ **NFR 002**
No Fashion / Oct '94 / Plastic Head

Fesu

WAR WITH NO MERCY
CD ______ **CDTURM 7**
Continuum / Jul '94 / Pinnacle

Fetisch Park

EGO EX NIHIL
CD ______ **STCD 103**
Staalplaat / Feb '96 / Vital/SAM

TROST
CD ______ **XCD 037**
Extreme / Nov '96 / Vital/SAM

Fetish 69

ANTI-BODY
CD ______ **NB 087**
Nuclear Blast / Dec '93 / Plastic Head

BRUTE FORCE
Void / Marooned / Stares to nowhere / Stomach turner / Tough center/harter ken / Hellville (pop 7,000)
CD ______ **SPASM 005CD**
Intellectual Convulsion / Jul '93 / Vital

Fever Tree

FEVER TREE/ANOTHER TIME ANOTHER PLACE
Imitation situation (tocatta and fugue) / Where do you go / San Francisco girls (return of the natives) / Ninety nine and one half / Man who paints the pictures / Filigree and shadow / Sun also rises / Day tripper/ We can work it out / Nowadays Clancy can't even sing / Unlock my door / Come with me / Man who paints the pictures (part 2) / What time did you say it was in salt lake city / Don't come crying to me girl / Fever / Grand candy young sweet / Jokes are for sad people / I've just seen evergreen / Peace of mind / Death is the dancer
CD ______ **SEECD 364**
See For Miles/C5 / Jun '97 / Pinnacle

Few Good Men

TAKE A DIP
Tonite / Walk you thru / Let's take a dip / All of my love / Please baby don't cry / Have I never / Thang for you young girl / Don't cry (behind my back) / Sexy day / Good man / 1-900-G-Man (How I say I love you)
CD ______ **73008260212**
Arista / Nov '95 / BMG

Fez Combo

FOLLOW THE SPIRIT
CD ______ **RTCD 403**
Right Tempo / Jul '96 / New Note/ Pinnacle / Timewarp

FFA Coffi Pawb

HEI VIDAL
CD ______ **AMKSTCD 036**
Ankst / Mar '93 / Shellshock/Disc

Fflaps

AMHERSAIN
CD ______ **PROBE 21C**
Probe Plus / Jul '89 / SRD

FFW

KILLER (Freaky Fukin Weirdoz)
CD ______ **EFA 15525CD**
Sub Up / Feb '92 / SRD

FFWD

FFWD
CD ______ **INTA 1CD**
Intermodo / Aug '94 / RTM/Disc

Fiahlo, Fransico

BEST OF FADO PORTUGUESE
CD ______ **EUCD 1165**
ARC / '91 / ADA / ARC Music

MEU ALENTEJO
CD ______ **EUCD 1113**
ARC / '91 / ADA / ARC Music

O FADOAL LATINO
CD ______ **EUCD 1075**
ARC / '89 / ADA / ARC Music

Fiasco, Johnny

ACID WASH VOL.2
Phantoms / Shifted / Here I cum / Darkness / Motivate / Sweet-n-sour / Psycho drums / Walk track 2 / Get up off your ass
CD ______ **TRXUKCD 002**
Trax UK / Jun '96 / Mo's Music Machine / Pinnacle / Prime

Fiction Factory

THROW THE WARPED WHEEL OUT
Feels like heaven / Heart and mind / Hanging gardens / All or nothing / Hit the mark / Ghost of love / Tales of tears / First step / Warped wheel
CD ______ **4805232**
Columbia / May '95 / Sony

Fiddle, Johnny

CAJUN GIRL
CD ______ **RPCDS 001**
Rivet Productions / Dec '94 / ADA

Fiddle Puppets

LIFT UP YOUR WINGS
CD ______ HEE 009CD
Yodel-Ay-Hee / Jun '94 / ADA

Fiddler, John

RETURN OF THE BUFFALO
CD ______ RMCCD 0197
Red Steel / May '96 / Pinnacle

Fiddler's Green

KING SHEPHERD
CD ______ EFA 127502
Deaf Shepherd / May '95 / SRD

Fiddlers Five

FIDDLE MUSIC FROM SCOTLAND
CD ______ COMD 2044
Temple / Feb '94 / ADA / CM / Direct / Duncans / Highlander

Fiedler, Arthur

POPS CHRISTMAS PARTY (Boston Pops Orchestra/Arthur Fiedler)
CD ______ 09026616852
RCA Victor / Nov '95 / BMG

Field Day

BIG WHEELS
CD ______ CARTCD 1
Car Tunes / Dec '96 / Cargo

Field Mice

FOR KEEPS
CD ______ SARAH 607CD
Sarah / Mar '95 / Vital

Field Of Blue

FIELD OF BLUE
CD ______ HUBCD 001
Hubba Dots / Nov '96 / Grapevine/ PolyGram

Fields, Brandon

OTHER PLACES
CD ______ NOVA 9025
Nova / Sep '92 / New Note/Pinnacle

OTHER SIDE OF THE STORY, THE
CD ______ NOVA 8602
Nova / Jan '93 / New Note/Pinnacle

TRAVELER
CD ______ NOVA 8811
Nova / Sep '92 / New Note/Pinnacle

Fields, Ernie

IN THE MOOD (Fields, Ernie Orchestra)
In the mood / Annie's rock / Strollin' after school / Chattanooga choo choo / Workin' out / Honky tonk / Tuxedo junction / Volare cha cha / My prayer / Knocked out / Dipsy doodle / Raunchy / Tea for two cha cha / It's all in the game / Boot / Christopher Columbus / Things ain't what they used to be / Begin the beguine / Teen flip / Honeydripper / Charleston / Castle rock / String of pearls / Ernie's tune / Hucklebuck
CD ______ CDCHD 540
Ace / Mar '96 / Pinnacle

Fields, Gracie

BEST OF GRACIE FIELDS, THE
Sally / Clatter of the clogs / Singing in the bathtub / Laugh at life / I took my harp to a party / She fought like a tiger for 'er 'onour / Will you love me when I'm mutton / Little pudden basin / Lat's all go posh / Eee by gum / Nowt about owt / Smile when you say goodbye / Biggest aspidistra in the world / She's one of those old fashioned ladies / Ring down the curtain / Pass shoot goal / Sing as we go / Dicky bird hop / You've got to be smart to be in the army / Fall in and follow the band / Wish me luck as you wave me goodbye
CD ______ CD 6057
Music / Feb '97 / Target/BMG

GRACIE FIELDS
Looking on the bright side / Isle of Capri / Painting the clouds with sunshine / Biggest aspidistra in the world / Sing as we go / Body and soul / Sally / You're more than all the world to me / Love in bloom / Stormy weather / Ring down the curtain / I give my heart / Oh mamma (The butchers boy) / Where are you / Turn 'Erbert's face to the wall mother / OLd violin / Snow White / Holy city / Now it can be told / Gracie's hit medley / Alexander's ragtime band / Love is everywhere / Melody at dawn
CD ______ PASTCD 9710
Flapper / '90 / Pinnacle

GRACIE FIELDS
Sally / Smoke gets in your eyes / Nature boy / Indian summer / Ciao ciao bambino / Young at heart / You didn't want me when you had me / Autumn leaves / Take me to your heart again / Moon river / Happy talk / September song / Jealousy / Ugly duckling / Carefree heart / My favourite things / People / Kerry dance / House is haunted / You're breaking my heart / Little donkey / Lord's prayer / Blow the wind southerly / Sing as we go
CD ______ CDMFP 6360
Music For Pleasure / Jun '97 / EMI

GRACIE FIELDS COLLECTORS EDITION
CD ______ DVX 08052
Deja Vu / Apr '95 / THE

SALLY
Sally / Sing as we go / Red sails in the sunset / One of the little orphans of the storm / There's a lovely lake in London / Isle of Capri / We've got to keep up with the Joneses / In my little bottom drawer / Roll along prairie moon / It looks like rain in Cherry Blossom Lane / Greatest mistake of my life / I never cried so much in all my life / Smile when you say goodbye / I haven't been the same girl since / You haven't altered a bit / Did your mother come from Ireland / Turn 'Erbert's face to the wall mother / When I grow too old to dream
CD ______ CDGFR 099
Tring / Jun '92 / Tring

SING AS WE GO
Sally / Oh sailor behave / Just one more chance / It isn't fair / Bargain hunter / Mary Rose / My lucky day / There's a lovely lake in London / Walter, Walter, lead me to the altar / Chapel in the moonlight / Sing as we go / It's a sin to tell a lie / I'll never say Never Again again / Pity the poor goldfish / In my little bottom drawer / Laugh at life / I took my harp to a party / Mocking bird went cuckoo / Fred Fanna / Stop and shop at the Co-op shop / We've got to keep up with the Joneses / Have you forgotten so soon / Roll along prairie moon / Goody goody / Daisy daisy / Light in the window
CD ______ RAJCD 833
Empress / Jul '94 / Koch

THAT OLD FEELING
Sweetest song in the world / Turn 'Erbert's face to the wall mother / Home / Remember me / Round the bend of the road / Will you remember / When I grow too old to dream / That old feeling / Fred Fannakapan / My first love song / Walter, Walter, lead me to the altar / Goodnight my love / Red sails in the sunset / Ah sweet mystery of life / Smilin' through / Giannina mia / There's a lovely lake in London / We've got to keep up with the Joneses / I never cried so much in all my life / First time I saw you / Fall in and follow the band / Sally
CD ______ CDAJA 5062
Living Era / Jun '89 / Select

THAT OLD FEELING
CD ______ PASTCD 7050
Flapper / Sep '94 / Pinnacle

Fields Of The Nephilim

BURNING THE FIELDS
CD ______ MOO 1CD
Jungle / Dec '93 / RTM/Disc / SRD

DAWNRAZOR
Intro / Slow kill / Volcane / Vet for the insane / Dust / Reanimator / Dawnrazor / Sequel / Power / Preacher man / Secrets / Tower
CD ______ SITL 18CD
Lowdown/Beggars Banquet / '88 / RTM/ Disc / Warner Music

EARTH INFERNO
Intro (dead but dreaming) / For her light / At the gates of silent memory (paradise regained) / Moonchild / Submission / Preacher man / Love under will / Summer land / Last exit for the lost / Psychonaut / Dawnrazor
CD ______ BEGA 120CD
Beggars Banquet / Apr '91 / RTM/Disc / Warner Music

ELIZIUM
(Dead but dreaming) for her light / At the gates of silent memory (paradise regained) / Submission / Summer land / Wail of summer.. and will your heart be also
CD ______ BEGA 115CD
Beggars Banquet / Oct '90 / RTM/Disc / Warner Music

LAURA
CD ______ CONTECD 196
Contempo / Oct '91 / Plastic Head

NEPHILIM, THE
Endemoniada / Celebrate / Watchman / Moonchild / Chords of souls / Last exit for the lost / Phobia
CD ______ SITU 22 CD
Situation 2 / Sep '88 / Pinnacle

REVELATIONS
CD ______ BEGA 137CD
Beggars Banquet / Jul '93 / RTM/Disc / Warner Music

ZOON (Nefilim)
CD ______ BEGA 172CD
Beggars Banquet / Mar '96 / RTM/Disc / Warner Music

Fields, Scott

DISASTER AT SEA (Fields, Scott Ensemble)
CD ______ CD 961
Music & Arts / Feb '97 / Cadillac / Harmonia Mundi

Fier, Anton

DREAMSPEED
CD ______ AVAN 009
Avant / Nov '93 / Cadillac / Harmonia Mundi

Fiestas

OH SO FINE
So fine / Dollar bill / That was me / Mr. Dillon, Mr. Dillon / Come on and love me / Mexico / Last night I dreamed / Lawman / Our anniversary / Railroad song / Try it one more time / Mama put the law down / Fine as wine / You can be my girlfriend / Anna / I'm your slave
CD ______ CDCHD 382
Ace / Feb '93 / Pinnacle

Fifteen

BUZZ
CD ______ GROW 152
Grass / Nov '94 / Pinnacle / SRD

Fifty Lashes

HARDER
CD ______ CDVEST 36
Bulletproof / Oct '94 / Pinnacle

Fighting Cause

PINT OF SPITE
CD ______ LRR 022
Last Resort / Oct '96 / Cargo

Figlin, Arkadi

PARTS OF A WHOLE (A Jazz Portrait)
CD ______ MK 437061
Mezhdunarodnaya Kniga / Jul '92 / Complete/Pinnacle

Figueres, Miguel

FLAMENCO
Guantanamera / La tani / Maruja limon / Carmen Carmela / Campanilleros / Javeras / Taka taka ta / Pasadoble campero / Maria Isabel / Zorongo / Martinetes / Y no te olvido / Esperanza / Triana morena / A mi me pesa / Bata de lunares / Camino verde / Fandangos de Isabel / Tangos de grana
CD ______ QED 221
Tring / Nov '96 / Tring

Fila Brazillia

BLACK MARKET GARDENING
CD ______ PORK 037
Pork / Nov '96 / Kudos / Pinnacle / Prime

LUCK BE A WEIRDO TONIGHT
CD ______ PORK 045
Pork / May '97 / Kudos / Pinnacle / Prime

MESS
CD ______ PORK 030
Pork / Apr '96 / Kudos / Pinnacle / Prime

Filarfolket

SMUGGLE
CD ______ CDAM 71
Temple / Jul '95 / ADA / CM / Direct / Duncans / Highlander

VINTERVALS
Tartan / Cowboyhalling / Polska / Polska to Ola Laingen / Rida ranka / Se makaroni / Svalan/Bosse buses marsch / Vintervalsen / Slangen / Hallingpolska / Lyckovalsen / Honsafotter and gulerotter / Gustav vasa / Potatisvalsen / Dammsugare efter bodil i / Ravmarschen / Daggvisa / Rockan / Tuffpolska
CD ______ RESCD 504
Resource / Jul '97 / ADA / Direct

File

2 LEFT FEET
CD ______ FF 507CD
Flying Fish / '92 / ADA / CM / Direct / Roots

LA VIE MARRON
CD ______ GLCD 2124
Green Linnet / Aug '96 / ADA / CM / Direct / Highlander / Roots

Filipinos

PEEL BACK THE SKIN
CD ______ TWIST 003CD
Wild / Jun '92 / Pinnacle

Filska

HARVEST HOME
CD ______ AT 044CD
Attic / May '96 / ADA / CM

Filter

SHORT BUS
CD ______ 9362458642
Warner Bros. / Apr '95 / Warner Music

Filthy Christians

MEAN
CD ______ MOSH 017CD
Earache / Apr '90 / Vital

Fimbulwinter

SERVANTS OF SORCERY
CD ______ HR 001CD
Hot / Feb '96 / Plastic Head

Fin De Siecle

END OF THE CENTURY
CD ______ TIRCD 003
Totem / Apr '96 / Grapevine/PolyGram / THE

Final 2

FINAL VOL.2
CD ______ SNTX 3001CD
Sentrax Corporation / May '96 / Plastic Head

Final Conflict

ASHES TO ASHES
CD ______ FLY 008CD
Tackle Box / Jun '97 / Cargo

REBIRTH
CD ______ FLY 005CD
Tackle Box / Feb '97 / Cargo

Final Exit

TEG
CD ______ DFR 6
Desperate Flight / Oct '96 / Cargo

UMEA
CD ______ DFR 15
Desperate Flight / Jun '97 / Cargo

Finchley Boys

EVERLASTING TRIBUTES
CD ______ 852127
EVA / Jun '94 / ADA / Direct

Fine Arts Brass Ensemble

LIGHTER SIDE OF FINE ARTS BRASS ENSEMBLE, THE
CD ______ CDSDL 381
Saydisc / Aug '90 / ADA / Direct / Harmonia Mundi

Fine Tooth Combine

BIG BIG SOUR
CD ______ FTC 003CD
FTC / Jun '96 / Plastic Head / SRD

Fine Young Cannibals

FINE YOUNG CANNIBALS
Johnny come home / Couldn't care more / Don't ask me to choose / Funny how love is / Suspicious minds / Blue / Move to work / On a promise / Time isn't kind / Life is a stranger
CD ______ 8280042
London / Jan '86 / PolyGram

FINEST
She drives me crazy / Flame / Johnny come home / Good thing / Suspicious minds / Blue / Ever fallen in love / Don't look back / Tell me what / I'm not the man I used to be / Couldn't care more / Funny how love is / Take what I can get / Since you've been gone / She drives me crazy
CD ______ 8288542
FFRR / Nov '96 / PolyGram

FINEST (2CD Limited Edition Set)
She drives me crazy / Flame / Johnny come home / Good thing / Suspicious minds / Blue / Ever fallen in love / Don't look back / Tell me what / I'm not the man I used to be / Couldn't care more / Funny how love is / Take what I can get / Since you've been gone / She drives me crazy / Motherless child / Wade in the water / Love for sale / Prick up your ears / Pull the sucker off / You never know
CD Set ______ 8288552
FFRR / Nov '96 / PolyGram

RAW AND THE COOKED, THE
She drives me crazy / Good thing / I'm not the man I used to be / I'm not satisfied / Tell me what / Don't look back / It's OK (It's alright) / Don't let it get you down / As hard as it is / Ever fallen in love
CD ______ 8280692
London / Jan '89 / PolyGram

RAW AND THE REMIX, THE
I'm not satisfied / Good thing / Johnny come home / I'm not the man I used to be / She drives me crazy / It's OK (it's alright) / Johnny takes a trip / Tired of getting pushed around / Don't look back
CD ______ 8282212
London / Nov '90 / PolyGram

Finger, Peter

BETWEEN THE LINES
CD ______ BEST 1079CD
Acoustic Music / Nov '95 / ADA

INNERLEBEN
CD _______________ BEST 1019CD
Acoustic Music / Nov '93 / ADA

NIEMANDSLAND
CD _______________ BEST 1001CD
Acoustic Music / Nov '93 / ADA

SOLO
CD _______________ BEST 1032CD
Acoustic Music / Nov '93 / ADA

Fingers, Eddie

TILL DEATH DO US DISCO (Fingers, Eddie Music)
Till death do us disco / Silicon mysteries / Long hard funky dreams / Midnight safari / Graveyard shuffle / Transilvania transcendental / Hot summer dreams / Apres minuit
CD _______________ MASSCD 022
Infinite Mass / Nov '94 / Pinnacle

Fini Tribe

GROSSING 10K
CD _______________ TPLP 24 CD
One Little Indian / Dec '89 / Pinnacle

NOISE LUST AND FUN
CD _______________ TPCD 21
One Little Indian / Nov '89 / Pinnacle

UNEXPECTED GROOVY TREAT, AN
CD _______________ TPLP 34CD
One Little Indian / Aug '92 / Pinnacle

Fink, Cathy

CATHY FINK & MARCY MARXER (Fink, Cathy & Marcy Marxer)
Last night I dreamed / Love's last chance / Frieght train blues / My prairie home / I've endured / Early / I'm not alone anymore / Names / Walking in the glory / Are you tired of me / Tune medley / Crawdad song
CD _______________ SHCD 3775
Sugar Hill / Jul '89 / ADA / CM / Direct / Koch / Roots

COLLECTION FOR KIDS, A (Fink, Cathy & Marcy Marxer)
CD _______________ ROUCD 8029
Rounder / Apr '94 / ADA / CM / Direct

DOGGONE MY TIME
Where the west begins / I'm so lonesome I could cry / Cuckoo / Sara McCutcheon / Cat's got the measles / Coal mining woman / Monkey medley / Midnight prayerlight / No tell motel / When it's darkness on the delta / Cotton patch rag / Coming home / Little Billy Wilson / Shenandoah Falls / My old Kentucky home
CD _______________ SHCD 3783
Sugar Hill / Jul '90 / ADA / CM / Direct / Koch / Roots

GRANDMA SLID DOWN THE MOUNTAIN
CD _______________ ROUCD 8010
Rounder / Oct '88 / ADA / CM / Direct

PARENTS' HOME COMPANION, A (Fink, Cathy & Marcy Marxer)
CD _______________ ROUCD 8031
Rounder / Feb '95 / ADA / CM / Direct

WHEN THE RAIN COMES DOWN
CD _______________ ROUCD 8013
Rounder / '88 / ADA / CM / Direct

Finkel, Sigi

SWEET SUE (Finkel, Sigi & John Abercrombie/Enrico Rava)
CD _______________ JL 111432
Lipstick / Feb '96 / Vital/SAM

Finlayson, Willy

VERY MUCH ALIVE
CD _______________ BRGCD 03
Music Maker / Jul '94 / ADA / Grapevine/ PolyGram

Finley, Karen

CERTAIN LEVEL OF DENIAL, A (2CD Set)
CD Set _______________ RCD 40317
Rykodisc / Feb '95 / ADA / Vital

Finn

FINN
Only talking sense / Eyes of the world / Mood swinging man / Last day of June / Suffer never / Angel's heap / Niwhai / Where is my soul / Bullets in my hairdo / Paradise (wherever you are) / Kiss the road of Raratonga
CD _______________ CDFINN 1
Parlophone / Sep '97 / EMI

Finn, Alec

BLUE SHAMROCK
CD _______________ 7567827352
Warner Bros. / Apr '95 / Warner Music

Finn, Tim

BEFORE AND AFTER
Hit the ground running / Protected / In love with it all / Persuasion / Many's the time (in Dublin) / Funny way / Can't do both / In your sway / Strangeness and charm / Always never now / Walk you home / I found it
CD _______________ CDEST 2202
Capitol / Jun '93 / EMI

Finnegan, Brian

WHEN THE PARTY'S OVER
CD _______________ ARADCD 101
Acoustic Radio / Mar '94 / CM

Finnegans

FINNEGANS, THE
CD _______________ CDMANU 1439
Manu / Dec '93 / ADA / Discovery

Finnerty, Barry

STRAIGHT AHEAD
Count up / Straight ahead / Outness / I can't make you love me / Sheer lunacy / OD / Inner urge / Elvinesque / Carnaval / Bells
CD _______________ AJ 0116
Arabesque / Jun '95 / New Note/Pinnacle

Finneus Gauge

MORE ONCE MORE
More wants more / King of the chord change / Press the flesh / Desire / Doogins (the evil spawn) / Customer service / Mess of finesse / Sidewalk sale / Calling card / Salvation / Abandon / Finding the strength
CD _______________ CYCL 055
Cyclops / Aug '97 / Pinnacle

Finnigan, Jim

IRISH HARVEST DAY
CD _______________ DHCD 722
Outlet / Jan '95 / ADA / CM / Direct / Duncans / Koch / Ross

Firat, Ozan

TURKEY: MUSIC OF THE TROUBADORS
CD _______________ AUB 006771
Auvidis/Ethnic / Jun '93 / ADA / Harmonia Mundi

Fire

MAGIC SHOEMAKER
Children of immagination / Tell you a story / Magic shoes / Reason for everything / Only a dream / Flies like a bird / Like to help you if I can / I can see the sky / Shoemaker / Happy man am I
CD _______________ SEECD 294
See For Miles/C5 / '90 / Pinnacle

Fire & Ice

GUIDED BY THE SUN
CD _______________ BADVCCD 144
New European / Oct '96 / World Serpent

HOLLOW WAYS
Lord of secrets / Militia templi / Seeker / Old grey widowmaker / Huldra's maze / Rising of the moon / Holy vehm / Ershebeth / Fetter / Svartalfar
CD _______________ FREMDCD 211
Fremdheit / Jul '97 / World Serpent

RUNA
CD _______________ FREMDCD 24
Fremdheit / Oct '96 / World Serpent

Fire Crow, Joseph

NORTHERN CHEYENNE FLUTE
CD _______________ 14995
Spalax / Jan '97 / ADA / Cargo / Direct / Discovery / Greyhound

Fire Dept.

ELPEE FOR ANOTHER TIME
CD _______________ YEPCD 3
Yep / May '96 / SRD

Fire Escape

PSYCHOTIC REACTION/RAW AND ALIVE (Fire Escape & The Seeds)
Psychotic reaction: *Fire Escape* / Talk talk: *Fire Escape* / Love special delivery: *Fire Escape* / Trip: *Fire Escape* / 96 tears: *Fire Escape* / Blood beat: *Fire Escape* / Trip maker: *Fire Escape* / Journey's end: *Fire Escape* / Pictures and designs: *Fire Escape* / Fortune teller: *Fire Escape* / No escape: *Seeds* / Satisfy you: *Seeds* / Night time girl: *Seeds* / Up in her room: *Seeds* / Gypsy plays his drums: *Seeds* / Can't seem to make you mine: *Seeds* / Mumble and bumble: *Seeds* / Forest outside your door: *Seeds* / 900 million people daily (all making love): *Seeds* / Pushin' too hard: *Seeds*
CD _______________ DOCD 1990
Drop Out / Oct '91 / Pinnacle

Fire Facts

REMAND CENTRE
CD _______________ SHCD 6016
Sky High / Jul '95 / Direct / Jet Star

Fire, Jack

DESTRUCTION OF SUARESILLE, THE
CD _______________ ESD 1213
Estrus / Sep '95 / Cargo / Greyhound / Plastic Head

Fire Merchants

IGNITION
CD _______________ MD 94352
Roadrunner / Dec '89 / PolyGram

LANDLORDS OF ATLANTIS
CD _______________ EFA 130012
Ozone / May '94 / Mo's Music Machine / Pinnacle / SRD

Fire Next Time

NORTH AND SOUTH
Fields of France / Can't forgive / Stay with me now / Supasave / We've lost too much / Too close / St. Mary's steps / Following the hearse / North and South
CD _______________ 8358552
Polydor / Oct '88 / PolyGram

Fireballs

BEST OF THE FIREBALLS, THE (The Original Norman Petty Masters)
Torquay / Bulldog / Carioca / Yacky doo / Foot patter / Dumbo / Vaquero / Long long ponytail / Gunshot / Nearly sunrise / Rik-a-tik / Quite a party / Really big time / Peg leg / Fireball / Panic button / Cry baby / Tuff-a-nuff / Find me a golden street / Blacksmith blues / Daytona drag / Kissin' / Chief whoopin' koff / El ringo / Torquay
CD _______________ CDCHD 418
Ace / Sep '92 / Pinnacle

BEST OF THE FIREBALLS, THE
Do you think / Wishing / True love ways / Call in the sheriff / Don't stop / Good good lovin' / Won't be long / Sugar shack / Ain't gonna tell anybody / Daisy petal pickin' / When my tears have dried / Look at me / I'll send for you / What kind of love / Cry baby / Bull moose / Lonesome tears / Indian giver / Red Cadillac and a black moustache / Almost eighteen / Pretend / I wonder why / Maybe baby / Everyday / Little baby / It's so easy / Bottle of wine / Come on react / Goin' away / Can't you see I'm trying
CD _______________ CDCHD 468
Ace / Oct '94 / Pinnacle

BLUE FIRE / RARITIES
Blue fire / Blues in the night / Bluesday / Wang wang blues / Birth of the blues / Blacksmith blues / Blue tinted blues / Wabash blues / Big daddy blues / Basin Street blues / Bye bye blues / St. Louis blues / Almost paradise / Sweet talk / Sneakers / I doubt it / Yacky doo / Clink clink classic / Spotnick / Power packed / Vaquero (Latino) / Vaquero / Wicked / Rik-a-tik / Teekee / Gunshot / Dooop / Tuff-a-nuff / Joshi / Don't lie to me / Torquay
CD _______________ CDCHD 472
Ace / Oct '93 / Pinnacle

FIREBALLS/VAQUERO
Torquay / Guess what / Panic button / Let there be love / Nearly sunrise / Long long ponytail / Bulldog / I wonder why / Foot patter / Blind date / Kissin' / Cry baby / Vaquero / La raspa / In a little Spanish town / Cielito lindo / La golondrina / Tequila / Spur / Spanish legend / Jesusita en chihuahua / La borachita / Gay ranchero / El rancho grande
CD _______________ CDCHD 447
Ace / Mar '93 / Pinnacle

TORQUAY/CAMPUSOLOGY
Torquay / Alone / Joey's song / Last date / Chief whoopin' koff / El ringo / Wheels / Honey / Rawhide / Tuff-a-nuff / Dumbo / Quite a party / Ahhh soul / Campusology / Daytona drag / Evermore / Peg leg / Sheezburger / In the mood / Mr. Mean / Mrs. Mean / Gently, gently / Mr. Reed / Find me a golden street
CD _______________ CDCHD 452
Ace / Apr '93 / Pinnacle

Firebirds

TAKING BY STORM
CD _______________ FBCD 101
Pollytone / Jan '95 / Nervous / Pollytone

THIS IS IT
CD _______________ PEPCD 105
Pollytone / Mar '95 / Nervous / Pollytone

TOO HOT TO HANDLE
CD _______________ PEPCD 103
Pollytone / Jan '95 / Nervous / Pollytone

Firefall

FIREFALL
It doesn't matter / Love isn't all / Livin' ain't livin' / No way out / Dolphin's lullaby / Cinderella / Sad ol' love song / You are the woman / Mexico / Do what you want
CD _______________ 8122703792
WEA / Mar '93 / Warner Music

GREATEST HITS
CD _______________ 8122710552
WEA / Jul '93 / Warner Music

Firehose

FROMOHIO
CD _______________ SST 235CD
SST / Feb '89 / Plastic Head

IF'N
Sometimes / Honey please / For the singer of REM / Anger / Hear me / Backroads / From one comes one / Making the freeway safe for the freeway / Operation solitaire / Windmilling / Me and you remembering / In memory of Elizabeth Cotton / Soon / Thunderchild
CD _______________ SST 115CD
SST / May '93 / Plastic Head

RAGIN' FULL ON
Locked in / Brave captain / Under the influence of meat puppets / Chemical wire / Another theory shot to shit on your ... / It matters / On your knees / Candle and the flame / Choose any memory / Perfect pairs / This / Caroms / Relatin' dudes to jazz / Things could turn around
CD _______________ SST 079CD
SST / May '93 / Plastic Head

Firehouse

MR. MACHINERY OPERATOR
Formal introduction / Blaze / Herded into pools / Witness / Number seven / Powerful hankerin' / Rocket sled/Fuel tank / Quicksand / Disciples of the 3-way / More famous quotes / Sincerely / Hell-hole / 4.29.92 / Cliffs thrown down
CD _______________ 4729672
Epic / Mar '93 / Sony

Firehouse Five

AT DISNEYLAND
CD _______________ GTCD 10049
Good Time Jazz / Oct '93 / Complete/ Pinnacle

DIXIELAND FAVOURITES (Firehouse Five Plus Two)
CD _______________ FCD 60008
Fantasy / May '95 / Jazz Music / Pinnacle / Wellard

GOES SOUTH
CD _______________ GTCD 12018
Good Time Jazz / Oct '93 / Complete/ Pinnacle

Fireside

DO NOT TAILGATE
Interlace / Smoke boy / Left rustle / Kilolin / Shelagh / Cement / Sucking the dust / Circular / Wheeler / Black soup / Lovecar / In place / Not in my palace
CD _______________ 74321361382
American / Sep '96 / BMG

Firewater

GET OFF THE CROSS
CD _______________ TWA 04CD
Jetset / Apr '97 / Cargo / Greyhound

Fireworks

LIT UP
CD _______________ LB 0020
Last Beat / Jun '97 / Greyhound

OFF THE AIR
CD _______________ ANDA 195
Au-Go-Go / Feb '97 / Cargo / Greyhound / Plastic Head

SET THE WORLD ON FIRE
CD _______________ EFA 115732
Crypt / Apr '94 / Shellshock/Disc

Firk, Backwards Sam

TRUE BLUES & GOSPEL
CD _______________ STCD 0002
Stella / Aug '94 / ADA

Firkins, Michael Lee

CACTUS CRUZ
CD _______________ RR 88482
Roadrunner / Oct '96 / PolyGram

CHAPTER 11
CD _______________ RR 88952
Roadrunner / Sep '96 / PolyGram

Firpo, Roberto

MILONGA ORILLERA
CD _______________ EBCD 75
El Bandoneon / Jul '96 / Discovery

First Choice

BEST OF FIRST CHOICE
Armed and extremely dangerous / Smarty pants / One step away / Newsy neighbours / This little woman / This is the house (where love is) / Love and happiness / Runnin' out of fools / Wake up to me / Player / Guilty / Love freeze / Boy named Junior / All I need is time / Guess what Mary Jones did / Hustler Bill / You took the words right out of my mouth / You've been doing wrong for so long / Don't fake it / Why can't I touch you (if you let me make love to you) / This is the house

CD _______ CDSEWD 096
Southbound / Aug '94 / Pinnacle

BEST OF FIRST CHOICE, THE
CD _______ CDGR 141
Charly / Jul '97 / Koch

DELUSIONS
CD _______ CPCD 8060
Charly / Nov '94 / Koch

HOLD YOUR HORSES
Let me down easy / Good morning midnight / Great expectations / Hold your horses / Love thang / Double cross
CD _______ CPCD 8096
Charly / Apr '95 / Koch

First Class

FIRST CLASS/SST
Beach baby / Won't someone help me / What became of me / Surfer Queen / First day of your life / Long time gone / Dreams are ten a penny / Bobby Dazzler / Disco kid / I was always a joker / I was a star / Ain't no love / Child's play / Old time love / Baby blue / Life is whatever you want it to be / Carry on singing my song / Smiles on a summer night / Seven Ten to nowhere / Autumn love / And she cried / Wake up America / Song was wrong
CD _______ SEECD 443
See For Miles/C5 / Jun '96 / Pinnacle

First Class Bluesband

FIRST CLASS BLUES
CD _______ BEST 1031CD
Acoustic Music / Nov '93 / ADA

First Down

WORLD SERVICE
CD _______ EFA 610092
Blitzvinyl / Apr '95 / SRD

First House

ERINDIRA
Day away / Innocent erendira / Journeyers to the east / Bracondale / Grammenos / Stranger than paradise / Bridge call / Doubt / Further away
CD _______ 8275212
ECM / Apr '86 / New Note/Pinnacle

Fisc

HANDLE WITH CARE
Come run riot / Won't let go / Love fight / Hold your head up / Let me leave / Live it up / Lover under attack / Handle with care / Got to beat the clock / Speed limit 55
CD _______ CDMFN 91
Music For Nations / Mar '89 / Pinnacle

Fischbacher Group

MYSTERIOUS PRINCESS (Fischbacher Group & Adam Nussbaum)
CD _______ BEST 1025
Acoustic Music / Nov '93 / ADA

Fischer, Clare

JUST ME - SOLO PIANO EXCURSIONS
Autumn leaves / Pra braden / 'Round midnight / I'm gettin' sentimental over you / I'd do anything for you / Liebesleid / After you've gone / Guajira / Ill wind / Pensativa / Topsy
CD _______ CCD 4679
Concord Jazz / Feb '96 / New Note/Pinnacle

LEMBRANCAS (REMEMBRANCES)
CP (Charlie Palmieri) / Fina / Coco B / Curumim / Endlessly / On Green Dolphin Street / Xapun / Gilda / Pan pipe dance / And miles to go / Strut
CD _______ CCD 4404
Concord Jazz / Mar '90 / New Note/Pinnacle

Fischer-Z

KAMIKAZE SHIRT
CD _______ WELFD 6
Welfare / Apr '94 / Total/BMG

STREAM
CD _______ WELFD 8
Recognition / Mar '95 / Total/BMG

Fish

ACOUSTIC SESSIONS
CD _______ DDICK 6CD
Dick Bros. / Sep '96 / Pinnacle

OUTPATIENTS 1993 (Various Artists)
Time and a word: *Fish* / Mark 13: *Dream Disciples* / One love: *One Eternal* / Don't ask me: *Joyriders* / Seeker: *Fish* / Swing your bag: *Guaranteed Pure* / Traveller's tales: *Avalon* / Out of my life: *Fish* / Best friend: *Joyriders* / Dream is dead: *Dream Disciples*
CD _______ DDICK 1CD
Dick Bros. / Sep '96 / Pinnacle

PIGPENS BIRTHDAY
CD _______ DDICK 16CD
Dick Bros. / Sep '96 / Pinnacle

SUITS
1470 / Lady let it lie / Emperor's song / Fortunes of war / Somebody special / No dummy / Pipeline / Jumpsuit city / Bandwagon / Raw meat
CD _______ DDICK 4CD
Dick Bros. / Sep '96 / Pinnacle

SUNSETS ON EMPIRE
CD _______ DDICK 26CD
CD _______ DDICK 25CD
Dick Bros. / May '97 / Pinnacle

SUSHI (2CD Set)
Fearless / Big wedge / Boston tea party / Credo / Family business / View from a hill / He knows you know / She chameleon / Kayleigh / White Russian / Company / Just good friends / Jeepster / Hold your head up / Lucky / Internal exile / Cliche / Last straw / Poets moon / Five years
CD Set _______ DDICK 2CD
Dick Bros. / Sep '96 / Pinnacle

VIGIL IN THE WILDERNESS OF MIRRORS
Vigil / Big wedge / State of mind / Company / Gentlemen's excuse me / Voyeur / Family business / View from the hill / Cliche
CD _______ CDEMD 1015
EMI / Feb '90 / EMI

YANG
Lucky / Big wedge / Lady let it lie / Lavender / Credo / Gentlemen's excuse me / Kayleigh / State of mind / Somebody special / Sugar mice / Punch and Judy / Fortunes of war / Internal exile
CD _______ DDICK 12CD
Dick Bros. / Sep '96 / Pinnacle

YIN
Incommunicado / Family business / Just good friends / Pipeline / Institution waltz / Tongues / Time and a word / Company / Incubus / Solo / Favourite stranger / Boston tea party / Raw meat
CD _______ DDICK 11CD
Dick Bros. / Sep '96 / Pinnacle

Fish Heads & Rice

SOMETHING SMELLS FISHY
CD _______ APCD 121
Appaloosa / Nov '96 / ADA / Direct / TKO Magnum

Fish Karma

SUNNYSLOPE
CD _______ 422433
New Rose / May '94 / ADA / Direct / Discovery

Fish Out Of Water

LUCKY SCARS
Just like in the movies (Part 1) / Once in a lifetime / Take it easy / Cry from the city / Belfast boy / Her old man / Parisienne prelude / Persistence of memory / MS Madness / He like a drink / Take it easy (Instrumental) / Cry from the city (Dub) / Lucky scars / Just like the movies (Part 2)
CD _______ SRCD 004
Stream / Nov '96 / Stream / Vital

Fish, R.A.

RHYTHMIC ESSENCE (The Art of the Dumbek)
CD _______ LYRCD 7411
Lyrichord / Jan '92 / ADA / CM / Roots

Fishbelly Black

FISHBELLY BLACK
CD _______ BBCD 72107
Backbeat / Jul '96 / Jet Star / Timewarp

MOVIN'
CD _______ BBCD 721172
Backbeat / Jul '96 / Jet Star / Timewarp

Fisher, Andy

MAN IN THE WOODS, A
Oh what a kiss / Mr. Cannibal / Computer no.9 / Man in the woods / Crazy bull fandango / Der babyspeck ist weg / Carnaby Street / No wine in Texas / Telephone / Heinzelmannchen's hitparade / Sleep well / Bunte papageien und ein grunes krokodil / Olympia ole / Ich will das nicht / Who really wants it / Kartoffelbeat / Walter, Walter / Mrs. Thunderbird / Monsieur controleur / Max nix / Fraulein, fraulein / Very nice day / Mademoiselle bon bon / German beer drinking song / Forgotten cafe in Berlin / Gilly, Gilly Oxenpfeffer / If they ever made me a king / General Bum Bum / Comrade Komzak / Equal goes it lose
CD _______ BCD 16163
Bear Family / Apr '97 / Direct / Rollercoaster / Swift

Fisher, Archie

SUNSET'S I'VE GALLOPED INTO... (Fisher, Archie & Garnet Rogers)
Ashfields and Brine / Yonder banks / Shipyard apprentice / Cuillins of Home / Southside blues / Silver coin / Prescence / Gunsmoke and whiskey / Bill Hosie / I wandered by a brookside / Merry England / Great North road / Eastfield / Black horse / All that you ask
CD _______ CDTRAX 020
Greentrax / Apr '92 / ADA / Direct / Duncans / Highlander

WILL YE GANG, LOVE
CD _______ GLCD 3076
Green Linnet / May '93 / ADA / CM / Direct / Highlander / Roots

Fisher, Eddie

EDDIE FISHER
CD _______ DVAD 6062
Deja Vu / May '95 / THE

Fisher, King

KING FISHER & HIS ALL-STARS
CD _______ JCD 13
Jazzology / Jul '96 / Jazz Music

Fisher, Matthew

SALTY DOG RETURNS, A
Dance band on the Titanic / Salty dog returns / Nutrocker / Whiter shadow of pale / Pilgrimage / Rathunter / Strange conversation continues / G String / Sex and violence / Green onions / Linda's theme / Downliners Sect manifesto / Peter Grump
CD _______ CDKVL 9032
Kingdom / May '94 / Kingdom

STRANGE DAYS
CD _______ BGOCD 308
Beat Goes On / Mar '96 / Pinnacle

Fisher, Natalie

NATALIE FISHER
CD _______ 4509966412
Warner Bros. / Aug '94 / Warner Music

Fisher, Ray

TRADITIONAL SONGS OF SCOTLAND (Fisher, Ray & Colin Ross/Martin Carthy/John Kirkpatrick)
Night visiting song / Wark o' the weavers / Lady Keith's lament / Gallowa' hills / Coulter's candy / Willie's fatal visit / Twa recruiting sergeants / Floo'ers o' the forest / MacGinty's meal and ale / Baron o'Brackley / Gypsy laddie / Lang biding here / Jute mill song / Hie, Jeannie hie / Johnny my man / My laddie's bedside / What can a young Lassie / Nicky Tams
CD _______ CDSDL 391
Saydisc / Mar '94 / ADA / Direct / Harmonia Mundi

Fisher-Turner, Simon

EDWARD 2 (Fisher-Turner 5)
CD _______ IONIC 8CD
Mute / Nov '91 / RTM/Disc

LIVE BLUE ROMA (The Archaeology Of Sound)
CD _______ CDMUTE 149
Mute / Jun '95 / RTM/Disc

LIVE IN JAPAN
CD _______ BAH 7
Humbug / May '93 / Total/Pinnacle

NADJA
CD _______ IONIC 16CD
Mute / Apr '96 / RTM/Disc

REVOX
Scott / I just woke up man, is it too early / Miaw / Blackouts / Sappora sky / Pop song 93 / Fall / Boxer / Luch at Great Rissington / Recover / Where are we going / Iona / Stuck inside lady / Mr. Davidson's tube / Moist
CD _______ BAH 16
Humbug / Feb '94 / Total/Pinnacle

SEX APPEAL
CD _______ MONDE 7 CD
Cherry Red / Oct '92 / Pinnacle

SIMON TURNER
CD _______ CRECD 64
Creation / May '94 / 3mv/Vital

Fisherstreet

OUT IN THE NIGHT
CD _______ CLUNCD 057
Mulligan / Feb '86 / ADA / CM

Fishtank No.9

ITSELF
CD _______ COPCD 030
Cop International / Jun '97 / Cargo

Fisk, Steve

448 DEATHLESS DAYS
CD _______ SST 159CD
SST / May '93 / Plastic Head

Fisk University Jubilee Singers

FISK UNIVERSITY JUBILEE SINGERS VOL.1 1909-1911
CD _______ DOCD 5533
Document / Apr '97 / ADA / Hot Shot / Jazz Music

FISK UNIVERSITY JUBILEE SINGERS VOL.2 1915-1920
CD _______ DOCD 5534
Document / Apr '97 / ADA / Hot Shot / Jazz Music

FISK UNIVERSITY JUBILEE SINGERS VOL.3 1924-1940
CD _______ DOCD 5535
Document / Apr '97 / ADA / Hot Shot / Jazz Music

Fitz Of Depression

LET'S GIVE IT A TWIST
CD _______ FIRECD 44
Fire / Jan '95 / Pinnacle / RTM/Disc

SWING
CD _______ KLCD 41
K / May '96 / Cargo / Greyhound / SRD

Fitzgerald, Ella

70 MINUTES OF JAZZ WITH THE UNIQUE ELLA FITZGERALD
CD _______ ENTCD 226
Entertainers / '88 / Target/BMG

75TH BIRTHDAY SALUTE
Tisket-a-tasket / Undecided / Don't worry 'bout me / Stairway to the stars / Five o'clock whistle / Cow cow boogie / Flying home / Oh Lady be good / How high the moon / My happiness / Black coffee / Dream a little dream of me / Smooth sailin' / Rough ridin' / Goody goody / Angel eyes / Preview / Blue Lou / Lullaby of birdland / If you can't sing it, you'll have to swing it (Mr. Paganini) / I wished on the moon / Until the real thing comes along / Old devil moon
CD _______ GRP 26192
GRP / Apr '93 / New Note/BMG

ALL THAT JAZZ
Dream a little dream of me / My last affair / Baby don't you quit now / Oh look at me now / Jersey bounce / When your lover has gone / That ole devil called love / All that jazz / Just when we're falling in love / Good morning heartache / Little jazz / Nearness of you
CD _______ CD 2310938
Pablo / Nov '95 / Cadillac / Complete/Pinnacle

AT THE MONTREUX JAZZ FESTIVAL 1975
Caravan / Satin doll / Teach me tonight / Wave / It's all right with me / Let's do it / How high the moon / Girl from Ipanema / Ain't nobody's business if I do
CD _______ OJCCD 789
Original Jazz Classics / May '94 / Complete/Pinnacle / Jazz Music / Wellard

AT THE OPERA HOUSE (Live In Chicago & Los Angeles 1957)
It's all right with me / Don't cha go 'way mad / Bewitched, bothered and bewildered / Stompin' at the Savoy / These foolish things / Ill wind / Goody goody / Moonlight in Vermont / Oh lady be good
CD _______ 8312692
Verve / Jan '94 / PolyGram

AUDIO ARCHIVE
Don't be that way / Fine romance / Flying home / That old black magic / Cryin' mood / If you should ever leave / Everyone's wrong but me / Cheek to cheek / Basin Street blues / Tisket-a-tasket / Starlit hour / Chewing gum / We can't go on this way / Sing song swing / Stairway to the stars / Can't we be friends / Lover come back to me / Moonlight in Vermont / Is there someone else / Who you hunchin
CD _______ CDAA 001
Tring / Jun '92 / Tring

BASIN STREET BLUES
Basin Street blues / Starlit hour / We can't go on this way / Stairway to the stars / Lover come back to me / Is there somebody else / Tisket-a-tasket / Sing song swing / That old black magic / Sugar blues / It's a blue world / Flying home / Who ya hunchin' / Chewing gum / Goin' and gettin' it / I wanna be a rug cutter / Don't be that way / Can't we be friends / Cheek to cheek / Fine romance / Moonlight in Vermont / Foggy day
CD _______ GRF 064
Tring / Jun '92 / Tring

BASIN STREET BLUES
Basin street blues / Starlit hour / We can't go on this way / Stairway to the stars / Lover come back to me / Tisket-a-tasket / Sing song swing / That old black magic / Sugar blues / It's a blue world / Flying home / Chewin' gum / Don't be that way / Can't we be friends / Cheek to cheek / Fine romance / Moonlight in Vermont / Foggy day
CD _______ QED 050
Tring / Nov '96 / Tring

BEST IS YET TO COME (Fitzgerald, Ella & Nelson Riddle)
I wonder where our love has gone / Don't be that way / God bless the child / You're driving me crazy / Goodbye / Any old time / Autumn in New York / Best is yet to come / Deep purple / Somewhere in the night
CD _______ CD 2312138
Pablo / Apr '87 / Cadillac / Complete/Pinnacle

BEST IS YET TO COME, THE (2CD Set)
I ain't got nothin' but the blues / One note samba / (I don't stand a) Ghost of a chance with you / I get a kick out of you / Something to live for / Cotton tail / Take love easy / Don't be that way / Sweet Georgia Brown / They can't take that away from me / You've got a friend / Satin doll / How high the moon / How long has this been going on / When your lover has gone / That old feeling / I've got you under my skin / Tennessee waltz / Dream dancing / Mack the knife / Fine and mellow / I'm in the mood for love / Speak low / Jersey bounce / All that jazz / Please don't talk about me when I'm gone / After you've gone / Ain't misbehavin' / Honeysuckle rose / I wonder where our love has gone / Summertime / Foggy day / How long has this been going on / Dreamer (vivo sonhando) / Best is yet to come
CD Set ______ PACD 0032
Pablo / Jan '97 / Cadillac / Complete/ Pinnacle

BEST OF ELLA FITZGERALD
Tisket-a-tasket / Stairway to the stars / Into each life some rain must fall / It's only a paper moon / Flying home / (I love you) for sentimental reasons / Oh lady be good / How high the moon / Basin Street blues / My one and only love / I've got the world on a string / Walkin' by the river / Lover come back to me / Mixed emotions / Smooth sailin' / If you can't sing it, you'll have to swing it (Mr. Paganini) / I wished on the moon / That old black magic / It's too soon to know / Tender trap
CD ______ MCBD 19521
MCA / Apr '95 / BMG

BEST OF ELLA FITZGERALD
Dreamer / Fine and mellow / Street of dreams / This love that I've found / How long has this been going on / You're blase / Honeysuckle rose / I'm walkin' / I'm getting sentimental over you / Don't be that way
CD ______ PACD 24054212
Pablo / Apr '94 / Cadillac / Complete/ Pinnacle

BEST OF ELLA FITZGERALD
CD ______ DLCD 4005
Dixie Live / Mar '95 / TKO Magnum

BEST OF ELLA FITZGERALD, THE
Undecided / Stairway to the stars / Five o'clock whistle / Cow cow boogie / Flying home / Stone cold dead in the market / You won't be satisfied until you break my heart / I'm just a lucky so and so / I didn't mean a word I said / Oh lady be good / How high the moon / My happiness / In the evening when the sun goes down / Smooth sailing / Hard hearted Hannah / Lullaby of birdland / Blue Lou / You'll have to swing it (Mr Paganini) parts 1 & 2 / Airmail special / A-tisket a-tasket
CD ______ GRP 16592
GRP / May '96 / New Note/BMG

BEST OF ELLA FITZGERALD, THE (2CD Set)
CD Set ______ MOVCDD 2
Wax / Feb '97 / RTM/Disc / Total/BMG

BEST OF THE SONGBOOKS - BALLADS, THE
Oh lady be good / I'm old fashioned / Laura / Daydream / Easy to love / It was written in the stars / How long has this been going on / Let's begin / Now it can be told / There is a small hotel / Do nothin' 'til you hear from me / Ill wind / You're laughing at me / Ship without a sail / Travellin' light / This time the dream's on me
CD ______ 5218672
Verve / Aug '94 / PolyGram

BEST OF THE SONGBOOKS, THE
Something's gotta give / Our love is here to stay / Bewitched, bothered and bewildered / I've got my love to keep me warm / Lady is a tramp / I got it bad and that ain't good / Miss Otis regrets / 'S wonderful / Between the devil and the deep blue sea / Love for sale / They can't take that away from me / Midnight sun / Hooray for love / Why was I born / Cotton tail / Every time we say goodbye
CD ______ 5198042
Verve / Dec '93 / PolyGram

BEWITCHED
Bewitched, bothered and bewildered / Puttin' on the ritz / Way you look tonight / From this moment on / I concentrate on you / Lady is a tramp / Daydream / Johnny one note / How about me / I'll be hard to handle / Why can't you behave / Always true to you in my fashion / Satin doll / Here in my arms / It never entered my mind / Ace in the hole / Have you met Miss Jones / Don't fence me in / Azure / Don't get around much anymore
CD ______ CD 377
Entertainers / Mar '96 / Target/BMG

BIG BOY BLUE
Big boy blue / Dedicated to you / You showed me the way / Cryin' mood / Love is the thing so they say / All over nothing at all / If you ever should leave / Everyone's wrong but me / Deep in the heart of the south / Just a simple melody / I got a guy / Holiday in Harlem / Rock it for me / I want to be happy / Dipsy doodle / If dreams come true / Hallelujah / Bei mir bist du schon / It's my turn now / 'S wonderful / I was doing all right / Tisket-a-tasket
CD ______ GRF 091
Tring / '93 / Tring

BLUE MOON
Blue moon / This can't be love / In the still of the night / Let yourself go / You can have him / Alexander's ragtime band / Can't help lovin' dat man / She didn't say yes / Manhattan / My funny valentine / Thou swell / Anything goes / Miss Otis Regrets / All of you / How deep is the ocean / Lazy / Let's begin / Blue room / I could write a book / Prelude to a kiss
CD ______ CD 378
Entertainers / Oct '96 / Target/BMG

BLUELLA (Ella Fitzgerald Sings The Blues)
Smooth sailing / Duke's place / St. Louis blues / C jam blues / Fine and mellow / Happy blues / Billie's bounce / I'm walkin' / Fine and mellow / St. Louis blues / Basella
CD ______ 23109602
Pablo / Feb '97 / Cadillac / Complete/ Pinnacle

CELEBRATED
Organ grinder's swing / If dreams come true / Crying my heart out for you / I'll chase the blues away / It ain' what you do / Sugar blues / Sing song swing / My heart belongs to daddy / Baby won't you please come home / Undecided / Under the spell of the blues / A-tisket a-tasket / My man / Chew chew chew / Shine / My last affair
CD ______ CDMT 029
Meteor / Nov '96 / TKO Magnum

CHEEK TO CHEEK (Fitzgerald, Ella & Louis Armstrong)
Fine romance / I can't give you anything but love: *Fitzgerald, Ella* / Foggy day / Cheek to cheek / Can't we be friends / Don't be that way / I'm puttin' all my eggs in one basket / I've got my love to keep me warm / Let's call the whole thing off / Love is here to stay / Moonlight in Vermont / Stars fell on Alabama / Tenderly / Nearness of you / They can't take that away from me / St. James Infirmary: *Armstrong, Louis* / How high the moon: *Fitzgerald, Ella* / What a wonderful world: *Armstrong, Louis*
CD ______ BN 010
Blue Nite / Nov '96 / Target/BMG

CLAP HANDS, HERE COMES CHARLIE
Night in Tunisia / You're my thrill / My reverie / Stella by starlight / 'Round midnight / Jersey bounce / Signing off / Cry me a river / This year's kisses / Good morning heartache / I was born to be blue / Clap hands, here comes Charlie / Spring can really hang you up the most / Music goes 'round and around / One I love belongs to somebody else / I got a guy / This could be the start of something big
CD ______ 8356462
Verve / Mar '90 / PolyGram

CLASSIC ELLA FITZGERALD, THE (2CD Set)
Sing, song, swing / 'S wonderful / Organ grinder's swing / Tisket-a-tasket / Sing me a swing song (and let me dance) / All over nothing at all / If you can't sing it, you'll have to swing it (Mr. Paganini) / My melancholy baby / Undecided / Darktown strutters ball / Stairway to the stars / I'll chase the blues away / Big boy blue / Goodnight, my love / Imagination / I was doing all right / Moon Ray / Dedicated to you / Baby, won't you please come home / My man (mon homme) / I'm beginning to see the light / Can't help lovin' dat man / Into each life some rain must fall / Benny's coming home on Saturday / This love of mine / He's my guy / Cow cow boogie / It's only a paper moon / Somebody nobody loves / Time alone will tell / Mama, come home / Kiss goodnight / Stone cold dead in de market / Make love to me / Jim / And her tears flowed like wine / Once too often / Cry you out of my heart / Petootie pie / Flying home
CD Set ______ CPCD 82502
Charly / Nov '96 / Koch

CLASSICS 1935-1937
CD ______ CLASSICS 500
Classics / Apr '90 / Discovery / Jazz Music

CLASSICS 1937-1938
Big boy blue / Dedicated to you / You showed me the way / Cryin' mood / Love is the thing so they say / All over nothing at all / If you ever should leave / Everyone's wrong but me / Deep in the heart of the south / Just a simple melody / I've got a guy / Holiday in Harlem / Rock it for me / I want to be happy / Dipsy doodle / If dreams came true / Hallelujah / Bei mir bist du schon / It's my turn now / 'S Wonderful / I was doing all right / Tisket-a-tasket
CD ______ CLASSICS 506
Classics / Apr '90 / Discovery / Jazz Music

CLASSICS 1938-1939
CD ______ CLASSICS 518
Classics / Apr '90 / Discovery / Jazz Music

CLASSICS 1939
CD ______ CLASSICS 525
Classics / Apr '90 / Discovery / Jazz Music

CLASSICS 1939-1940
CD ______ CLASSICS 566
Classics / Oct '91 / Discovery / Jazz Music

CLASSICS 1940-1941
CD ______ CLASSICS 644
Classics / Nov '92 / Discovery / Jazz Music

CLASSICS 1941-1944
CD ______ CLASSICS 840
Classics / Nov '95 / Discovery / Jazz Music

CLASSY PAIR, A (Fitzgerald, Ella & Count Basie)
I'm getting sentimental over you / Organ grinder swing / Just a sittin' and a rockin' / My kind of trouble is you / Ain't misbehavin' / Some other Spring / Teach me tonight / Don't worry 'bout me / Honeysuckle rose / Sweet Lorraine / Please don't talk about me when I'm gone
CD ______ CD 2312132
Complete / May '94 / Complete/Pinnacle

COLE PORTER SONGBOOK VOL.1
All through the night / Anything goes / Miss Otis regrets / Too darn hot / In the still of the night / I get a kick out of you / Do I love you / Always true to you in my fashion / Let's do it / Just one of those things / Every time we say goodbye / All of you / Begin the beguine / Get out of town / I am in love / From this moment on
CD ______ 8219892
Verve / Feb '93 / PolyGram

COLE PORTER SONGBOOK VOL.2
You do something to me / Ridin' high / Easy to love / It's alright with me / Why can't you behave / What is this thing called love / You're the top / Love for sale / It's de-lovely / Night and day / Ace in the hole / So in love / I've got you under my skin / I concentrate on you / Don't fence me in / I love Paris
CD ______ 8219902
Verve / Feb '93 / PolyGram

COLE PORTER SONGBOOKS (Parts 1 & 2/2CD Set)
All through the night / Anything goes / Miss Otis regrets / Too darn hot / In the still of the night / I get a kick out of you / Do I love you / Always true to you in my fashion / Let's do it / Just one of those things / Every time we say goodbye / All of you / Begin the beguine / Get out of town / I am in love / From this moment on / I love Paris / You do something to me / Riding high / Easy to love / It's all right with me / Why can't you behave / What is this thing called love / You're the top / Love for sale / It's de-lovely / Night and day / Ace in the hole / So in love / I've got you under my skin / I concentrate on you / Don't fence me in
CD Set ______ 8219892/9902
Verve / Mar '93 / PolyGram

COLLECTION, THE
CD ______ COL 014
Collection / Apr '95 / Target/BMG

COMPLETE ELLA FITZGERALD & LOUIS ARMSTRONG ON VERVE, THE (3CD Set) (Fitzgerald, Ella & Louis Armstrong)
CD Set ______ 5372842
Verve / May '97 / PolyGram

COMPLETE RECORDINGS 1933-40, THE (3CD Set)
I'll chase the blues away / Love and kisses / Rhythm and romance / Crying my heart out for you / Under the spell of the blues / When I get low I get high / Sing me a swing song / Little bit later on / Love you're just a laugh / Devoting my time to you / If you can't sing it, you'll have to swing it (Mr. Paganini) / Swinging on the reservation / I've got the spring fever blues / Vote for Mr. Rhythm / My melancholy baby / All my life / Goodnight my love / Oh yes take another guess / Did you mean it / My last affair / Organ grinder swing / Shine / Darktown strutters ball / Big boy blues / Dedicated to you / Wake up and live / You showed me the way / Cryin' mood / Love is the thing so they say / Just a simple melody / I got a guy / Holiday in Harlem / Rock it for me / I want to be happy / Dipsy doodle / If dreams come true / Hallelujah / Tisket-a-tasket / Heart of mine / I'm just a jitterbug / All over nothing at all / If you ever should leave / Everyone's wrong but me / Deep in the heart of the south / Bei mir bist du schon / It's my turn now / 'S Wonderful / I was doing all right / This time it's real / What do you know about love / You can't be mine (and someone else's too) / We can't go on this way / Saving myself for you / If you only knew / Strictly from Dixie / Woe is me / Pack up your sins and go to the devil / MacPherson is rehearsin' / Everybody step / Ella / Wacky dust / Gotta pebble in my shoe / I can't stop loving you / I let a tear fall in the river / FDR Jones / I love each move you make / It's foxy / I found my yellow basket / Undecided / T'ain't what you do (it's the way that you do it) / One side of me / My heart belongs to Daddy
CD Set ______ CDAFS 10203
Affinity / Oct '93 / Cadillac / Jazz Music / Koch

COMPLETE SONGBOOKS, THE
CD Set ______ 5198322
Verve / Dec '93 / PolyGram

CONCERT YEARS 1953-1983, THE (4CD Set)
On the sunny side of the street / Body and soul / Why don't you do right / Oh lady / Oh lady be good / I got it bad and that ain't good / How high the moon / My funny valentine / Smooth sailing / Frim fram sauce / Perdido / Imagine my frustration / Duke's place / Satin doll / Something to live for / So danco samba / Don't be that way / You've changed / Let's do it / On the sunny side of the street / Cotton tail / Night and day / Cole Porter medley / Ballad medley / Bossa medley / They can't take that away from me / St. Louis blues / St. Louis blues / Love / Begin the beguine / Indian summer / You've got a friend / Spring can really hang you up the most / Shiny stockings / I can't stop loving you / C jam blues / Sweet Georgia Brown / They can't take that away from me / Man I love / It don't mean a thing if it ain't got that swing / Lemon drop / Very thought of you / Happy blues / Caravan / Teach me tonight / Wave / It's all right with me / How high the moon / Ain't nobody's business if I do / Too close for comfort / I ain't got nothin' but the blues / Day by day / Ordinary fool / Billie's bounce / Please don't talk about me when I'm gone / Make me rainbows / After you've gone / 'Round midnight / You've changed / Basella / Manteca / Willow weep for me / All of me / Blue moon / Night and day / Flying home
CD Set ______ 4PACD 4414
Pablo / Nov '96 / Cadillac / Complete/ Pinnacle

DAYDREAM: THE BEST OF THE DUKE ELLINGTON SONGBOOK
CD ______ 5272232
Verve / Jun '95 / PolyGram

DEDICATED TO YOU
My heart belongs to Daddy / My last affair / Dedicated to you / If dreams come true / Goodnight my love / T'ain't what you do (it's the way that you do it) / Love and kisses / Rhythm and romance / What do you know about love / I want to be happy / Tisket-a-tasket / My melancholy baby / I've got the Spring fever blues / If you ever should leave / Devoting my time to you / I can't stop loving you
CD ______ SUMCD 4012
Summit / Nov '96 / Sound & Media

DIGITAL III AT MONTREUX (Fitzgerald, Ella & Count Basie/Joe Pass)
I can't get started (with you) / Good mileage / I don't stand a ghost of a chance with you / Flying home / I cover the waterfront / Li'l darlin' / In your own sweet way / Oleo
CD ______ CD 2308223
Pablo / May '94 / Cadillac / Complete/ Pinnacle

DREAM DANCING (Fitzgerald, Ella & Cole Porter)
Dream dancing / I've got you under my skin / I concentrate on you / My heart belongs to Daddy / Love for sale / So near and yet so far / Down in the depths / After you / Just one of those things / I get a kick out of you / All of you / Anything goes / At long last love / C'est magnifique / Without love
CD ______ CD 2310 814
Pablo / May '94 / Cadillac / Complete/ Pinnacle

DUKE ELLINGTON SONGBOOK, THE (3CD Set)
Rockin' in rhythm / Drop me off in Harlem / Daydream / Caravan / Take the 'A' train / I ain't got nothin' but the blues / Clementine / I didn't know about you / I'm beginning to see the light / Lost in meditation / Perdido / Cotton tail / Do nothin' 'til you hear from me / Just a sittin' and a rockin' / Solitude / Rocks in my bed / Satin doll / Sophisticated lady / Just squeeze me (but don't tease me) / It don't mean a thing if it ain't got that swing / Azure / I let a song go out of my heart / In a sentimental mood / Don't get around much anymore / Prelude to a kiss / Mood indigo / In a mellow tone / Love you madly / Lush life / Squatty roo / I'm just a lucky so and so / All too soon / Everything but you / I got it bad and that ain't good / Bli-blip / Chelsea Bridge / Portrait of Ella Fitzgerald / E and D blues
CD Set ______ 8370352
Verve / Apr '89 / PolyGram

EASY LIVIN' (Fitzgerald, Ella & Joe Pass)
CD ______ CD 2310921
Pablo / Oct '92 / Cadillac / Complete/ Pinnacle

ELLA & LOUIS (3CD Set) (Fitzgerald, Ella & Louis Armstrong)
Fine romance / Foggy day / Cheek to cheek / St. James Infirmary / Can't we be friends / Don't be that way / I'm puttin' all my eggs in one basket / I've got my love to keep me warm / How high the moon / Let's call the whole thing off / Love is here to stop / Moonlight in Vermont / Stars fell on Alabama / Tenderly / Nearness of you / They

can't take that away from me / I can't give you anything but love: *Fitzgerald, Ella* / What a wonderful world: *Armstrong, Louis* / Jeepers creepers: *Armstrong, Louis* / Kiss to build a dream on: *Armstrong, Louis* / When the saints go marching in: *Armstrong, Louis* / Mack the knife: *Armstrong, Louis* / C'est si bon: *Armstrong, Louis* / St. Louis blues: *Armstrong, Louis* / Black and blue: *Armstrong, Louis* / Dippermouth blues: *Armstrong, Louis* / Bye & bye: *Armstrong, Louis* / Rockin' chair: *Armstrong, Louis* / C jam blues: *Armstrong, Louis* / Stardust: *Armstrong, Louis* / Royal Garden blues: *Armstrong, Louis* / Indiana: *Armstrong, Louis* / I used to love you: *Armstrong, Louis* / Where did you sleep last night: *Armstrong, Louis* / If I could be with you: *Armstrong, Louis* / Way down yonder in New Orleans: *Armstrong, Louis* / Goody goody: *Fitzgerald, Ella* / It's only a paper moon: *Fitzgerald, Ella* / We can't go on this way: *Fitzgerald, Ella* / That old black magic: *Fitzgerald, Ella* / Tisket a-tasket: *Fitzgerald, Ella* / Sing song swing: *Fitzgerald, Ella* / Baby it's cold outside: *Fitzgerald, Ella & Sarah Vaughan* / You'll have to swing it: *Fitzgerald, Ella* / You'll never know: *Fitzgerald, Ella* / Taking a chance on love: *Fitzgerald, Ella* / Flying home: *Fitzgerald, Ella* / Oh lady be good: *Fitzgerald, Ella* / Cow cow boogie: *Fitzgerald, Ella* / Oh Johnny: *Fitzgerald, Ella* / Lover come back to me: *Fitzgerald, Ella* / Body & soul: *Fitzgerald, Ella* / I can't get it started: *Fitzgerald, Ella* / Smooth sailing: *Fitzgerald, Ella*
CD Set ______ **KBOX 359**
Collection / Nov '96 / Target/BMG / TKO Magnum

ELLA A NICE
Night and day / Get out of town / Easy to love / You do something to me / Body and soul / Man I love / Porgy / Bossa scene / Girl from Ipanema / Fly me to the moon / O nosso amor / Cielito lindo / Magdalena / Aqua de beber / Summertime / They can't take that away from me / Mood indigo / Do nothin' 'til you hear from me / It don't mean a thing if it ain't got that swing / Something / St. Louis blues / Close to you / Put a little love in your heart
CD ______ **OJCCD 442**
Original Jazz Classics / Feb '92 / Complete/ Pinnacle / Jazz Music / Wellard

ELLA ABRACA JOBIM
CD ______ **CD 2630201**
Pablo / Oct '92 / Cadillac / Complete/ Pinnacle

ELLA AND BASIE (On The Sunny Side Of The Street) (Fitzgerald, Ella & Count Basie)
Honeysuckle rose / 'Deed I do / Into each life some rain must fall / Them there eyes / Dream a little dream of me / Tea for two / Satin doll / I'm beginning to see the light / Shiny stockings / My last affair / Ain't misbehavin' / On the sunny side of the street
CD ______ **8215762**
Verve / Jan '88 / PolyGram

ELLA AND FRIENDS
Frim fram sauce / Dream a little dream of me / Can anyone explain / Would you like to take a walk / Who walks in when I walk out / Into each life some rain must fall / I'm making believe / I'm beginning to see the light / I still feel the same about you / Petootie pie / Baby, it's cold outside / Don't cry, cry baby / Ain't nobody's business but my own / I'll never be free / It's only a paper moon / Cry you out of my heart / For sentimental reason / It's a pity to say goodnight / Fairy tales / I gotta have my baby back
CD ______ **GRP 16632**
American Decca / Jul '96 / New Note/BMG

ELLA AND LOUIS (Fitzgerald, Ella & Louis Armstrong)
Can't we be friends / Isn't this a lovely day (to be caught in the rain) / Moonlight in Vermont / They can't take that away from me / Under a blanket of blue / Foggy day / Tenderly / Stars fell on Alabama / Nearness of you / April in Paris / Cheek to cheek
CD ______ **8253732**
Verve / Sep '85 / PolyGram

ELLA AND LOUIS AGAIN (Fitzgerald, Ella & Louis Armstrong)
Don't be that way / They all laughed / Autumn in New York / Stompin' at the Savoy / I won't dance / Gee baby ain't I good to you / Let's call the whole thing off / I've got my love to keep me warm / I'm putting all my eggs in one basket / Fine romance / Our love is here to stay / Learnin' the blues
CD ______ **8253742**
Verve / Feb '93 / PolyGram

ELLA AND OSCAR (Fitzgerald, Ella & Oscar Peterson)
Mean to me / How long has this been going on / When your lover has gone / More than you know / There's a lull in my life / Midnight sun / I hear music / Street of dreams / April in Paris / Hear music
CD ______ **CD 2310759**
Pablo / '94 / Cadillac / Complete/Pinnacle

ELLA AT DUKE'S PLACE (Fitzgerald, Ella & Duke Ellington Orchestra)
CD ______ **5297002**
Verve / Jun '96 / PolyGram

ELLA FITZGERALD
CD ______ **CD 109**
Timeless Treasures / Oct '94 / THE

ELLA FITZGERALD
CD ______ **22708**
Music / Nov '95 / Target/BMG

ELLA FITZGERALD
Ain't nobody's business but mine / Smooth sailing / Tisket-a-tasket / Vei mir du schoen / Airmail special / Stardust / But not for me / Flying home / Basin Street blues / How high the moon
CD ______ **MCD 33682**
MCA / Nov '95 / BMG

ELLA FITZGERALD (2CD Set)
CD Set ______ **R2CD 4018**
Deja Vu / Jan '96 / THE

ELLA FITZGERALD (4CD Set)
You showed me the way / Love is the thing so they say / If you should ever leave / Everyone's wrong but me / All or nothing at all / Big boy blue / Deep in the heart of the south / Just a simple melody / I gotta guy / Holiday in Harlem / Rock it for me / I want to be happy / Dipsy doodle / If dreams come true / Hallelujah / Dedicated to you / Cryin' mood / Bei mir bist du schoen / It's my turn now / 'S wonderful / I was doin' all right / Tisket a tasket / Basin street blues / Starlit hour / We can't go on this way / Stairway to the stars / Lover come back to me / Sing song swing / That old black magic / Little white lies / Sugar blues / Smooth sailing / Chewin' gum / Don't worry 'bout me / Don't be that way / Can't we be friends / Cheek to cheek / Fine romance / Moonlight in Vermont / Foggy day / My wubba dolly / Baby won't you please come home / Imagination / Taking a chance on love / One I love belongs to someone else / I got it bad and that ain't good / My heart belongs to daddy / What can I say after I say I'm sorry / Cabin in the sky / Three little words / Ella / FDR Jones / I must have that man / My melancholy baby / Goodnight my love / My last affair / Wake up and live / Darktown strutters ball
CD Set ______ **QUAD 009**
Tring / Nov '96 / Tring

ELLA FITZGERALD
CD ______ **15705**
Laserlight / Apr '94 / Target/BMG

ELLA FITZGERALD & HER FAMOUS ORCHESTRA
CD ______ **JZCD 332**
Suisa / Jan '93 / Jazz Music / THE

ELLA FITZGERALD & JOE PASS AGAIN (Fitzgerald, Ella & Joe Pass)
I ain't got nothin' but the blues / 'Tis autumn / My old flame / That old feeling / Rain / I didn't know about you / You took advantage of me / I've got the world on a string / All too soon / One I love (belongs to somebody else) / Solitude / Nature boy / Tennessee waltz / One note samba
CD ______ **CD 2310772**
Pablo / Oct '93 / Cadillac / Complete/ Pinnacle

ELLA FITZGERALD & THE CHICK WEBB ORCHESTRA
CD ______ **JZCD 331**
Suisa / Jan '93 / Jazz Music / THE

ELLA FITZGERALD 1957-58
CD ______ **CD 53159**
Giants Of Jazz / Jan '94 / Cadillac / Jazz Music / Target/BMG

ELLA FITZGERALD COLLECTION
Little white lies / Imagination / Taking a chance on love / Three little words / When my sugar walks down the street / Can't help lovin' dat man / Darktown strutters ball / Just a simple melody / I want to be happy / Bei mir bist du schon / Tisket-a-tasket / FDR Jones / I found my yellow basket / This love of mine / Make love to me / Cow cow boogie / Once too often / Into each life rain must fall / I'm making believe / I'm confessin' that I love you / I'm beginning to see the light / It's only a paper moon
CD ______ **PAR 2066**
Parade / Aug '96 / Disc

ELLA FITZGERALD COLLECTOR'S EDITION
CD ______ **DVAD 6032**
Deja Vu / Apr '95 / THE

ELLA FITZGERALD GOLD (2CD Set)
CD Set ______ **D2CD 4018**
Deja Vu / Jun '95 / THE

ELLA FITZGERALD SINGS CHRISTMAS
O holy night / It came upon a midnight clear / Hark the Herald Angels sing / Away in a manger / Joy to the world / First Noel / Silent night / O come all ye faithful (adeste fidelis) / Sleep my little Jesus / Angels we have heard on high / O little town of Bethlehem / We three kings / God rest ye merry gentlemen
CD ______ **CDMFP 6241**
Music For Pleasure / Oct '96 / EMI

ELLA FITZGERALD SONGBOOK, THE
Deedle-de-dum / Shake down the stars / Gulf coast blues / Five o'clock whistle / So long / Louisville, K-Y / Taking a chance on love / I'm the loneliest gal in town / Three little words / Hello ma, I done it again / One I love (belongs to somebody else) / Keep cool, fool / My man / I can't believe that you're in love with me / I must have that man / When my sugar walks down the street / I got it bad and that ain't good / Melinda the mousie / Can't help lovin' dat man / Into each life some rain must fall / Paper moon / Flying home / Stone cold dead in de market / Petootie pie / That's rich / One side of me / My heart belongs to daddy / Sugar pie / It's slumbertime along the swanee / Chew chew chew (your bubble gum) / Don't worry 'bout me / If that's what you're thinking, you're wrong / If you ever change your mind / Little white lies / Coochi coochi coo / That was my heart / Betcha nickel / Stairway to the stars / I want the waiter (with the water) / That's all, brother / Out of nowhere / My last goodbye / Billy (I always dream of Billy) / I'm not complainin' / You're gonna lose your gal / After I say I'm sorry / My wubba dolly / Sugar blues / Starlit hour / I got a guy / Holiday in Harlem / Rock it for me / I want to be happy / Dipsy doodle / Hallelujah / I was doing all right / Tisket-a-tasket / I'm just a jitterbug / This time it's real / You can't be mine (and somebody else's too) / We can't go on this way / Pack up your sins and go to the devil / Everybody step / Ella / Wacky dust / Gotta pebble in my shoe / Strictly from dixie / Woe is me / FDR Jones / I love each move you make / It's foxy / I found my yellow basket / Undecided / T'ain't what you do (it's the way that you do it) / I'll chase the blues away / Love and kisses / Rhythm and romance / My melancholy baby / Crying my heart out for you / When I get low I get high / Sing me a swing song (and let me dance) / Little bit later on / Love, you're just a laugh / Devoting my time to you / Vote for Mr rhythm / Goodnight my love / Didja mean it / Organ grinder's swing / Shine / Darktown strutters ball / Take another guess / Big boy blue / Dedicated to you / Cryin' mood / Love is the thing, so they say / If you ever should leave / Everyone's wrong but me / Somewhere deep in the heart of the south / Just a simple melody
CD Set ______ **MBSCD 451**
Castle / Dec '96 / BMG

ELLA FITZGERALD WITH THE CHICK WEBB BAND
Harlem Congo / I gotta guy / I'll chase the blues away / If you can't sing it, you'll have to swing it (Mr. Paganini) / Squeeze me / Vote for Mr. Rhythm / If dreams come true / Down home rag (sweatman) / Crying my heart out for you / Sing me a swing song / Liza / Tisket-a-tasket / Little bit later on / Strictly jive / Rock it for me / Everybody step / Sweet Sue, just you / Pack up your sins and go to the devil / When I get low I get high / Midnite in Harlem / Love you're just a laugh / Take another guess
CD ______ **PASTCD 9762**
Flapper / Aug '91 / Pinnacle

ELLA FITZGERALD WITH THE TOMMY FLANAGAN TRIO (Fitzgerald, Ella & Tommy Flanagan Trio)
I won't dance / That old black magic / Medley / Cabaret / I love you madly / Man and a woman / Alright, OK you win / People / I concentrate on you / Mr. Paganini / I'm beginning to see the light / My heart belongs to Daddy / Just one of those things / I can't give you anything but love baby
CD ______ **17109**
Laserlight / Mar '97 / Target/BMG

ELLA IN LONDON
Sweet Georgia Brown / They can't take that away from me / Every time we say goodbye / It don't mean a thing if it ain't got that swing / You've got a friend / Lemon drop / Very thought of you / Happy blues / Man I love
CD ______ **CD 2310711**
Pablo / Apr '94 / Cadillac / Complete/ Pinnacle

ELLA IN ROME 1958 (The Birthday Concert)
St. Louis blues / These foolish things / Just squeeze me / Angel eyes / That old black magic / Just one of those things / I loves you Porgy / It's alright with me / I can't give you anything but love / When you're smiling / Foggy day / Midnight sun / Lady is a tramp / Sophisticated lady / Caravan / Stompin' at the Savoy
CD ______ **8354542**
Verve / Mar '93 / PolyGram

ELLA RETURNS TO BERLIN (1961 Live)
Give me the simple love / Take the 'A' train / I'd like to get to know you on a slow boat to China / Why was I born / Can't help lovin' dat man / You're driving me crazy / Rock it for me / Witchcraft / Anything goes / Cheek to cheek / Misty / Caravan / If you can't sing it, you'll have to swing it (Mr. Paganini) / Mack the knife / Fanfare for Ella / 'Round midnight / Joe Williams' blues / Fanfare for Ella / This can't be love
CD ______ **8377582**
Verve / Apr '91 / PolyGram

ELLA SWINGS BRIGHTLY WITH NELSON (Fitzgerald, Ella & Nelson Riddle Orchestra)
When your lover has gone / Don't be that way / Love me or leave me / I hear music / What am I here for / I'm gonna go fishin' / I won't dance / I only have eyes for you / Gentleman is a dope / Mean to me / Alone together / Pick yourself up / Call me darling / Somebody loves me / Cheerful little earful
CD ______ **5193472**
Verve / Mar '93 / PolyGram

ELLA SWINGS EASY
All or nothing at all / If dreams come true / 'S wonderful / I was doing alright / A-tisket a-tasket / Undecided / T'ain't what you do (it's the way that you do it) / My heart belongs to Daddy / Little white lies / Stairway to the stars / Baby what else can I do / Sugar blues / Baby won't you please come home / Imagination / Five o'clock whistle / Taking a chance on love / Cabin in the sky / I'm the lonesomest gal in town / Three little words / One I love belongs to somebody else / When my sugar walks down the street / I got it bad and that ain't good / Can't help lovin' dat man / You don't know what love is / He's my guy
CD ______ **CDMOIR 508**
Memoir / Jan '95 / Jazz Music / Target/ BMG

ELLA SWINGS GENTLY WITH NELSON (Fitzgerald, Ella & Nelson Riddle Orchestra)
Sweet and slow / Georgia on my mind / I can't get started (With you) / Street of dreams / Imagination / Very thought of you / It's a blue world / Darn that dream / She's funny that way / I wished on the moon / It's a pity to say goodnight / My one and only love / Body and soul / Call me darling / All of me
CD ______ **5193482**
Verve / Mar '93 / PolyGram

ELLA SWINGS LIGHTLY
Little white lies / You hit the spot / What's your story Morning Glory / Just you, just me / As long as I live / Teardrops from my eyes / Gotta be this or that / Moonlight on the Ganges / My kinda love / Blues in the night / If I were a bell / You're an old smoothie / Little Jazz / You brought a new kind of love to me / Knock me a kiss / 720 in the books / Oh what a night for love / Little jazz / Dreams are made for children / Oh what a night for love
CD ______ **5175352**
Verve / Feb '93 / PolyGram

ELLA WISHES YOU A SWINGING CHRISTMAS
Jingle bells / Winter wonderland / Santa Claus is coming to town / Have yourself a merry little Christmas / What are you doing New Year's Eve / Sleigh ride / Christmas song / Good morning blues / Let it snow, let it snow, let it snow / Rudolph the red nosed reindeer / Frosty the snowman / White Christmas
CD ______ **8271502**
Verve / Mar '93 / PolyGram

ELLA WITH (1936-1937/2CD Set)
All over nothing at all / If you ever should leave / It's my turn now / Everyone's wrong but me / Bei mir bist du schon / Little bit later on / I want to be happy / Hallelujah / Crying my heart out for you / If you can't sing it, you'll have to swing it (Mr. Paganini) / Holiday in Harlem / Cryin' mood / Devoting my time to you / Rock it for me / At the Darktown strutter's ball / Sing me a swing song / Vote for Mr. Rhythm / Just a simple melody / Swinging on the reservation / Under the spell of the blues / I got the spring fever blues / Rhythm and romance / If dreams come true / Take another guess / Dipsy doodle / I've got a guy / When I get low I get high / Did you mean it / Dedicated to you / Big boy blues / Goodnight my love / Shine
CD Set ______ **CDAJD 055**
Living Era / Jul '96 / Select

ELLA, BILLIE, SARAH (Fitzgerald, Ella & Billie Holiday/Sarah Vaughan)
Oh Johnny oh Johnny oh: *Fitzgerald, Ella* / Blue Lou: *Fitzgerald, Ella* / Diga diga doo: *Fitzgerald, Ella* / I want the waiter (with the water): *Fitzgerald, Ella* / Limehouse blues: *Fitzgerald, Ella* / T'ain't what you do (it's the way that you do it): *Fitzgerald, Ella* / Traffic jam: *Fitzgerald, Ella* / I'm confessin' that I love you: *Fitzgerald, Ella* / Breakin' down: *Fitzgerald, Ella* / Swing out: *Fitzgerald, Ella* / Swing brother swing: *Holiday, Billie* / Do nothin' 'til you hear from me: *Holiday, Billie* / You're driving me crazy: *Holiday, Billie* / Lover man: *Holiday, Billie* / Ain't nobody's business if I do: *Holiday, Billie* / My man (mon homme): *Holiday, Billie* / They can't take that away from me: *Holiday, Billie* / He's funny that way: *Holiday, Billie* / Don't be late: *Holiday, Billie* / God bless the child: *Holiday, Billie* / Lover come back to me: *Holiday, Billie* / Don't explain: *Holiday, Billie* / Same old story: *Holiday, Billie* / Detour ahead: *Holiday, Billie* / Billie's blues: *Holiday, Billie* / Miss Brown top you: *Holiday, Billie* / It's you or no one: *Vaughan, Sarah* / Tenderly: *Vaughan, Sarah* / Lord's prayer: *Vaughan, Sarah* / What a difference a day makes: *Vaughan, Sarah* / Gentleman friend: *Vaughan, Sarah* / East of the sun and west of the moon: *Vaughan, Sarah* / Motherless child: *Vaughan, Sarah* / One I love belongs somebody else: *Vaughan, Sarah* / September: *Vaughan, Sarah* / Time after time:

Vaughan, Sarah / Hundred years from today: *Vaughan, Sarah* / Signing off: *Vaughan, Sarah* / I cover the waterfront: *Holiday, Billie* / Them there eyes: *Holiday, Billie* / No smokes: *Vaughan, Sarah* / What more can a woman do: *Vaughan, Sarah* / Mean to me: *Vaughan, Sarah*
CD Set ________________ **TKOCDB 026**
TKO / May '92 / TKO

FABULOUS ELLA FITZGERALD, THE (2CD Set)
T'ain't what you do (it's the way that you do it) / My heart belongs to Daddy / Don't worry 'bout me / Little white lies / I want the waiter (with the water) / Imagination / Five o'clock whistle / Taking a chance on love / Three little words / My man (mon homme) / When my sugar walks down the street / I got it bad and that ain't good / Can't help lovin' dat man / Sing me a swing song (and let me dance) / Organ grinder's swing / Darktown strutters ball / If you ever should leave / Just a simple melody / Rock it for me / I want to be happy / If dreams come true / Bei mir bist du schoen / 'S wonderful / Tisket-a-tasket / McPherson is rehearsin' (to swing) / FDR Jones / I found my yellow basket / This love of mine / Somebody nobody loves / You don't know what love is / Make love to me / My heart and I decided / He's my guy / Cow cow boogie / Once too often / Into each life some rain must fall / I'm making believe / I'm confessin' that I love you / I'm beginning to see the light / It's only a paper moon
CD Set ________________ **MUCD 9505**
Musketeer / May '96 / Disc

FINE AND MELLOW
Fine and mellow / I'm just a lucky so and so / I don't stand a ghost of a chance with you / Rockin' in rhythm / I'm in the mood for love / 'Round midnight / I can't give you anything but love / Man I love / Polka dots and moonbeams
CD ________________ **CD 2310829**
Pablo / May '94 / Cadillac / Complete/ Pinnacle

FIRST LADY OF JAZZ
Tisket-a-tasket / Darktown strutters ball / I want to be happy / Everybody step / If you can't sing it, you'll have to swing it (Mr. Paganini) / Crying my heart out for you / Little bit later on / If dreams come true / Rock it for me / All over nothing at all / Sing me a swing song / When I get low I get high / I'll chase the blues away / Holiday in Harlem / I gotta guy / Everyone's wrong but me
CD ________________ **HADCD 154**
Javelin / May '94 / Henry Hadaway / THE

FIRST LADY OF SONG (3CD Set)
Perdido / Lullaby of Birdland / Too young for the blues / Too darn hot / Miss Otis regrets / April in Paris / Undecided / Can't we be friends / Bewitched, bothered and bewildered / Just a sittin' and a rockin' / I'm just a lucky so and so / Airmail special / Tisket-a-tasket / Baby don't you go away mad / Angel eyes / I won't dance / Summertime / Oh lady be good / More than you know / Lush life / Blue skies / These foolish things / Travellin' light / You're an old smoothie / Makin' whoopee / How long has this been going on / Detour ahead / Mack the knife / How high the moon / Black coffee / Let it snow, let it snow, let it snow / Get happy / Heart and soul / If you can't sing it, you'll have to swing it (Mr. Paganini) / Night in Tunisia / I can't get started (With you) / Don't be that way / After you've gone / Hernando's hideaway / Fine romance / 'Deed I do / Hear me talkin' to ya / Can't buy me love / Day in, day out / Something to live for / You've changed / Jazz samba / It don't mean a thing if it ain't got that swing
CD Set ________________ **5178982**
Verve / Jan '93 / PolyGram

FLYING HOME
CD ________________ **CDSGP 084**
Prestige / Oct '93 / Else / Total/BMG

FOR THE LOVE OF ELLA FITZGERALD (2CD Set)
Tisket-a-tasket / Oh lady be good / Stompin' at the Savoy / How high the moon / Mr. Paganini / Sweet Georgia Brown / Mack the knife / Caravan / Night in Tunisia / Rockin' in rhythm / Honeysuckle rose / I got rhythm / Fine romance / On the sunny side of the street / Party blues / Cotton tail / Misty / Sophisticated lady / Midnight sun / Solitude / How long blues / I loves you Porgy / Summertime / Mood indigo / Laura / Stormy weather / Autumn in New York / These foolish things / I can't get started (With you) / CC rider / I love Paris / Blues in the night
CD Set ________________ **8417662**
Verve / Jan '90 / PolyGram

FOREVER ELLA
CD ________________ **5293872**
Verve / Mar '96 / PolyGram

FOREVER GOLD
CD ________________ **ST 5008**
Star Collection / Apr '95 / BMG

GEORGE & IRA GERSHWIN SONGBOOK, THE (3CD Set)
Sam and Delilah / But not for me / My one and only / Let's call the whole thing off / I've got beginner's luck / Oh lady be good / Nice work if you can get it / Things are looking up / Just another rhumba / How long has this been going on / 'S wonderful / Man I love / That certain feeling / By Strauss / Who cares / Someone to watch over me / Real American folk song / They all laughed / Looking for a boy / My cousin from Milwaukee / Somebody from somewhere / Foggy day / Clap yo' hands / For you, for me, for evermore / Stiff upper lip / Strike up the band / Soon / I've got a crush on you / Bidin' my time / Aren't you kind of glad we did / Of thee I sing / Half of it dearie blues / I was doing all right / He loves and she loves / Love is sweeping the country / Treat me rough / Our love is here to stay / Slap that bass / Isn't it a pity / Shall we dance / Love walked in / You've got what gets me / They can't take that away from me / Embraceable you / I can't be bothered now / Boy what love has done to me / Fascinating rhythm / Oh so nice / Lorelei / Let's kiss and make up / I got rhythm / Boy wanted / Funny face
CD Set ________________ **8250242**
Verve / Feb '93 / PolyGram

GITANES - JAZZ 'ROUND MIDNIGHT
Man I love / Reaching for the moon / Blue moon / Moonlight becomes you / Our love is here to stay / With a song in my heart / ow deep is the ocean / September song / Good morning heartache / 'Round midnight / I got it bad and that ain't good / One for my baby (and one more for the road) / Cry me a river / Do nothin' 'til you hear from me
CD ________________ **5100352**
Verve / Oct '91 / PolyGram

GOLDEN YEARS 1936-1945, THE (2CD Set)
CD Set ________________ **FA 973**
Fremeaux / Feb '97 / ADA / Discovery

HAROLD ARLEN SONGBOOK VOL.1 (Fitzgerald, Ella & Billy May Orchestra)
Blues in the night / Let's fall in love / Stormy weather / Sing my heart / Between the devil and the deep blue sea / My shining hour / Hooray for love / This time's the dream's on me / That old black magic / I've got the world on a string / Let's take a walk around the block / Ill wind / Accentuate the positive
CD ________________ **8175272**
Verve / Oct '88 / PolyGram

HAROLD ARLEN SONGBOOK VOL.2 (Fitzgerald, Ella & Billy May Orchestra)
When the sun comes out / Come rain or come shine / As long as I live / Happiness is a thing called Joe / It's only a paper moon / Man that got away / One for my baby (and one more for the road) / It was written in the stars / Get happy / I gotta right to sing the blues / Out of this world / Ding dong the witch is dead / Over the rainbow
CD ________________ **8175282**
Verve / Jan '97 / PolyGram

HOW HIGH THE MOON
How high the moon / Flying home / Oh Johnny / As you desire me / There's a small hotel / Robbin's nest / Diga diga doo / Blue Lou / I want the waiter with the water / Lemon drop / Sing song swing / Old Mother Hubbard / Limehouse blues / Thou swell / Mr. Paganini / Starlit hour
CD ________________ **100482**
CMC / May '97 / BMG

INCOMPARABLE ELLA, THE
Lady is a tramp / Manhattan / Very thought of you / From this moment on / I've got you under my skin / Foggy day / With a song in my heart / Cheek to cheek / I've got a crush on you / Night and day / Every time we say goodbye / It's only a paper moon / I get a kick out of you / I got rhythm / My funny valentine / That old black magic
CD ________________ **8356102**
PolyGram TV / Apr '94 / PolyGram

INTIMATE ELLA, THE
Black coffee / Angel eyes / I cried for you / I can't give you anything but love baby / Then you've never been blue / I hadn't anyone till you / My melancholy baby / Misty / September song / One for my baby (and one more for the road) / Who's sorry now / I'm getting sentimental over you / Reach for tomorrow
CD ________________ **8398382**
Verve / Mar '90 / PolyGram

IRVING BERLIN SONGBOOK VOL.1
Let's face the music and dance / You're laughing at me / Let yourself go / You can have him / Russian lullaby / Puttin' on the Ritz / Get thee behind me, Satan / Alexander's ragtime band / Top hat, white tie and tails / How about me / Cheek to cheek / I used to be colour blind / Lazy / How deep is your love / All by myself / Remember
CD ________________ **8295342**
Verve / Mar '93 / PolyGram

IRVING BERLIN SONGBOOK VOL.2
Reaching for the moon / Slumming on Park Avenue / Song is ended (but the melody lingers on) / I'm putting all my eggs in one basket / Now it can be told / Always / It's a lovely day today / Change partners / No strings / I've got my love to keep me warm / How's chances / Heatwave / You keep coming back like a song / Blue skies / Suppertime
CD ________________ **8295352**
Verve / Mar '93 / PolyGram

IT AIN'T WHAT YOU DO
CD ________________ **CWNCD 2023**
Javelin / Jul '96 / Henry Hadaway / THE

JAZZ COLLECTOR EDITION (5CD Set) (Fitzgerald, Ella & Louis Armstrong)
CD Set ________________ **15910**
Laserlight / Jan '92 / Target/BMG

JAZZ MASTERS
I hear music / I ain't got nothin' but the blues / Everything I've got / I loves you Porgy / Mack the knife / I'm putting all my eggs in one basket / Man that got away / Just you, just me / I've got the world on a string / Tisket-a-tasket / These foolish things / Heatwave / I never had a chance / How high the moon / In the evening / Signing off
CD ________________ **5198222**
Verve / Apr '93 / PolyGram

JAZZ MASTERS (Fitzgerald, Ella & Louis Armstrong)
I've got my love to keep me warm / Isn't this a lovely day (to be caught in the rain) / Learnin' the blues / I got plenty o' nuttin' / Moonlight in Vermont / Under a blanket of blue / I'm puttin' all my eggs in one basket / Our love is here to stay / April in Paris / Tenderly / Bess you is my woman now / They all laughed
CD ________________ **5218512**
Verve / Feb '94 / PolyGram

JAZZ PORTRAITS
If you can't sing it, you'll have to swing it (Mr. Paganini) / Love you're just a laugh / Swinging on the reservation / I got the spring fever blues / Rock it for me / Holiday in Harlem / Cryin' mood / Just a simple melody / Love is the thing so they say / You showed me the way / My melancholy baby / All my life / If dreams come true / Take another guess / Pack up your sins and go to the devil / I love each move you make / Sugar pie / I got a guy
CD ________________ **CD 14524**
Jazz Portraits / May '94 / Jazz Music

JAZZ SIDES, THE
CD ________________ **5276552**
Verve / Mar '96 / PolyGram

JEROME KERN SONGBOOK, THE
Let's begin / Fine romance / All the things you are / I'll be hard to handle / You couldn't be cuter / She didn't say yes / I'm old fashioned / Remind me / Way you look tonight / Yesterdays / Can't help lovin' dat man / Why was I born
CD ________________ **8256692**
Verve / Oct '92 / PolyGram

JOHNNY MERCER SONGBOOK, THE
Too marvellous for words / Early Autumn / Day in, day out / Laura / This time the dream is on me / Skylark / Single-o / Something's gotta give / Travellin' light / Midnight sun / Dream / I remember you / When a woman loves a man
CD ________________ **8232472**
Verve / Feb '92 / PolyGram

LADY TIME
I'm walkin' / All or nothing at all / I never had a chance / I cried for you / What will I tell my heart / Since I fell for you / And the angels sing / I'm confessin' that I love you / Mack the knife / That's my desire / I'm in the mood for love
CD ________________ **OJCCD 864**
Original Jazz Classics / Nov '95 / Complete/ Pinnacle / Jazz Music / Wellard

LEGENDARY DECCA RECORDINGS 1935-1955 (4CD Set)
Undecided / Stairway to the stars / Five o'clock whistle / Cow cow boogie / Flying home / Stone cold dead in the market / You won't be satisfied until you break my heart / I'm just a lucky so and so / I didn't mean a word I said / Oh lady be good / How high the moon / My happiness / In the evening / Smooth sailing / Airmail special / You'll have to swing it / Blue Lou / Lullaby of birdland / Hard hearted Hannah / Frim fram sauce / Dream a little dream of me / Can anyone explain / Would you like to take a walk / Who walks in when I walk out / Each life some rain must fall / I'm making believe / I'm beginning to see the light / I still feel the same about you / Petootie pie / Baby it's cold outside / Don't cry, cry baby / Ain't nobody's business but my own / I'll never be free / It's only paper moon / (Gonna) Cry you out of my heart / (I love you) For sentimental reasons / It's a pity to say goodnight / Fairy tales / I gotta have my baby back / Someone to watch over me / My one and only / But not for me / Looking for a boy / I've got a crush on you / Maybe / Soon / I'm glad there is you / What is there to say / People will say we're in love / Please be kind / Until the real thing comes along / Makin whoopee / Imagination / Stardust / My heart belongs to Daddy / You leave me breathless / Baby, what else can I do / Nice work if you can get it / Basin street blues / I've got the world on a string / Goody goody / Angel eyes / Gordon Jenkins / Happy talk / I'm gonna wash that man right out of my hair / Black coffee / I wished on the moon / Bob Haggart / Sunday kind of love / That's my desire / Thanks for the Memory / It might as well be spring / You'll never know / I can't get started (With you) / That old black magic / Old devil moon / Lover come back to me / Between the devil and the deep blue sea / Toots camarata / (Love is) the tender trap / My one and only love
CD Set ________________ **GRP 46482**
GRP / Nov '95 / New Note/BMG

LEGENDARY ELLA FITZGERALD, THE
My heart belongs to Daddy / 'S wonderful / Shine / T'ain't what you do (it's the way that you do it) / If you can't sing it, you'll have to swing it (Mr. Paganini) / Tisket-a-tasket / My melancholy baby / Goodnight my love / Dedicated to you / My last affair / Darktown Strutters ball / Rock it for me / All over nothing at all / If you ever should leave / It's my turn now / Saving myself for you / This time it's real / Love is the thing so they say
CD ________________ **NTMCD 553**
Nectar / Apr '97 / Pinnacle

LEGENDS IN MUSIC
CD ________________ **LECD 090**
Wisepack / Sep '94 / Conifer/BMG / THE

LET'S GET TOGETHER
CD ________________ **17003**
Laserlight / Jul '94 / Target/BMG

LIKE SOMEONE IN LOVE
There's a lull in my life / More than you know / What will I tell my heart / I never had a chance / Close your eyes / We'll be together again / Then I'll be tired of you / Like someone in love / Midnight sun / I thought about you / You're blase / Night wind / What's new / Hurry home / How long has this been going on / I'll never be the same / Lost in a fog / Everything happens to me / So rare
CD ________________ **5115242**
Verve / Sep '93 / PolyGram

LOVE & KISSES
CD ________________ **17009**
Laserlight / Aug '93 / Target/BMG

MACK THE KNIFE (The Complete Ella In Berlin - Live 1960)
That old black magic / Our love is here to stay / Gone with the wind / Misty / Lady is a tramp / Man I love / Love for sale / Just one of those things / Summertime / Too darn hot / Lorelei / Mack the knife / How high the moon
CD ________________ **5195642**
Verve / Oct '93 / PolyGram

MY HAPPINESS (Fitzgerald, Ella & Bing Crosby)
CD ________________ **PARCD 002**
Parrot / Jan '96 / BMG / Jazz Music / THE / Wellard

MY HEART BELONGS TO DADDY
CD ________________ **MU 5040**
Musketeer / Oct '92 / Disc

NEWPORT JAZZ FESTIVAL LIVE AT CARNEGIE HALL, JULY 5, 1973 (2CD Set)
I've gotta be me / Good morning heartache / Miss Otis regrets / Medley: Don't worry about me/These foolish things / Any old blues / Tisket-a-tasket / Indian summer / Smooth sailin' / You turned the tables on me / Nice work if you can get it / I've got a crush on you / Medley: I can't get started / Young man with the horn / 'Round midnight / Stardust / C Jam blues / Medley: Taking a chance on love / I'm in the mood for love / Lemon drop / Some of these days / People
CD Set ________________ **C 2K66809**
Sony Jazz / Aug '95 / Sony

NICE WORK IF YOU CAN GET IT (Fitzgerald, Ella & Andre Previn)
Let's call the whole thing off / How long has this been going on / Who cares / I've got a crush on you / Someone to watch over me / Embraceable you / They can't take that away from me / Foggy day / But not for me / Nice work if you can get it
CD ________________ **CD 2312140**
Pablo / '94 / Cadillac / Complete/Pinnacle

NIGHT AND DAY
Night and day / All the things you are / Let's face the music and dance / All through the night / Spring is here / I wish I were in love again / There's a small hotel / Everything I've got / Isn't it romantic / Begin the beguine / Fine romance / Remember / Top hat, white tie and tails / Yesterdays / Cheek to cheek / You couldn't be cuter / Ridin' high / All by myself / Sophisticated lady / It don't mean a thing
CD ________________ **CD 379**
Entertainers / Jun '96 / Target/BMG

ONE AND ONLY ELLA FITZGERALD, THE
Tisket-a-tasket / My man (mon homme) / I want to be happy / Got a pebble in my shoe / This love of mine / Once too often / Billy / Rock it for me / Hellelujah / Gulf coast blues / Undecided / I'm confessin' that I love you / I got it bad and that ain't good / Strictly from Dixie / MacPherson is rehearsin' / Wake up and live / Bei mir bist du shon / Darktown strutters ball / Ella / Taking a chance on love
CD ________________ **ECD 3302**
K-Tel / Feb '97 / K-Tel

ONE SIDE OF ME
When my sugar walks down the street / My man / Someone to watch over me / If dreams come true / I let a tear fall in the river / Dipsy doodle / Don't worry 'bout me / I was doing all right / 'S wonderful / All over nothing at all / Starlit hour / Looking for a boy / Time alone will tell / Rhythm & romance / Sugar blues
CD ______ **AMSC 565**
Avid / Aug '96 / Avid/BMG / Koch / THE

PABLO YEARS, THE (20CD Set)
CD Set ______ **PACD 0202**
Pablo / Nov '96 / Cadillac / Complete/ Pinnacle

PERFECT MATCH, A (Fitzgerald, Ella & Count Basie)
Please don't talk about me when I'm gone / Sweet Georgia Brown / Some other Spring / Make me rainbows / After you've gone / 'Round midnight / Fine and mellow / You've changed / Honeysuckle rose / St. Louis blues / Basella
CD ______ **CD 2312110**
Pablo / Apr '94 / Cadillac / Complete/ Pinnacle

PORTRAIT OF ELLA FITZGERALD, A
CD ______ **GALE 406**
Gallerie / May '97 / Disc / THE

PRICELESS JAZZ
Tisket-a-tasket / Goody, goody / Someone to watch over me / Makin' whoopee / Flying home / Nice work if you can get it / How high the moon / But not for me / If you can't sing it, you'll have to swing it (Mr. Paganini) / Oh lady be good / My heart belongs to daddy / Lullaby of Birdland / It might as well be spring / Stairway to the stars / Old devil moon / Lover come back to me
CD ______ **GRP 98702**
GRP / Jul '97 / New Note/BMG

RHYTHM AND ROMANCE
Rhythm and romance / Take another guess, oh yes / Dedicated to you / Tisket-a-tasket / Ella / Baby won't you please come home / I'm the lonesomest gal in town / I got it bad and that ain't good / My heart and I decided / Cow cow boogie / Time alone will tell / I'm confessin' / I'm beginning to see the light / That's the way it is / It's only a paper moon / Benny's coming home on Saturday / Flying home / Stone cold dead in the market / Petootie pie / You won't be satisfied / Frim fram sauce / I'm just a lucky so-and-so / I didn't mean a word I said / (I love you) for sentimental reasons / It's a pity to say goodnight
CD ______ **CDAJA 5212**
Living Era / Feb '97 / Select

RODGERS & HART SONGBOOK VOL.1
Have you met Miss Jones / You took advantage of me / Ship without a sail / This can't be love / Lady is a tramp / Manhattan / Johnny one note / I wish I were in love again / Spring is here / It never entered my mind / Where or when / Little girl blue / I've got five dollars / Dancing on the ceiling / Blue room / To keep my love alive / With a song in my heart
CD ______ **8215792**
Verve / Feb '92 / PolyGram

RODGERS & HART SONGBOOK VOL.2
Give it back to the Indians / Ten cents a dance / There's a small hotel / I didn't know what time it was / I could write a book / My funny Valentine / Bewitched, bothered and bewildered / My romance / Wait till you see her / Lover / Isn't it romantic / Blue moon / Mountain greenery / Here in my arms / Everything I've got / Thou swell / My heart stood still
CD ______ **8215802**
Verve / Feb '92 / PolyGram

ROYAL ROOST (Fitzgerald, Ella & Ray Brown)
CD ______ **C&BCD 112**
Cool & Blue / Oct '93 / Discovery / Jazz Music

SING ME A SWING SONG (Fitzgerald, Ella & Chick Webb Orchestra)
CD ______ **JHR 73512**
Jazz Hour / '91 / Cadillac / Jazz Music / Target/BMG

SING SONG SWING
CD ______ **17008**
Laserlight / Jul '93 / Target/BMG

SONGBOOKS, THE (The Silver Collection)
Oh lady be good / Nice work if you can get it / Fascinating rhythm / All the things you are / Yesterdays / Can't help lovin' dat man / Come rain or come shine / It's only a paper moon / Over the rainbow / Laura / Skylark / This time the dream is on me / Puttin' on the Ritz / Alexander's ragtime band / Cheek to cheek / My funny Valentine / Lady is a tramp / Have you met Miss Jones / Manhattan
CD ______ **8234452**
Verve / Nov '84 / PolyGram

SPEAK LOVE
Speak love / Come love / There's no you / I may be wrong, but I think you're wonderful / At last / Thrill is gone / Gone with the wind / Blue and sentimental / Girl talk / Georgia on my mind
CD ______ **CD 2310888**
Pablo / Apr '94 / Cadillac / Complete/ Pinnacle

STAIRWAY TO THE STARS
CD ______ **MACCD 163**
Autograph / Aug '96 / BMG

STOCKHOLM 1957
CD ______ **TAX 37032**
Tax / Aug '94 / Cadillac / Jazz Music / Wellard

STOCKHOLM CONCERT 1966 (Fitzgerald, Ella & Duke Ellington)
Imagine my frustration / Duke's place / Satin doll / Something to live for / Wives and lovers / So danco samba / Let's do it / Lover man / Cotton tail
CD ______ **CD 2308242**
Pablo / May '94 / Cadillac / Complete/ Pinnacle

SUNSHINE OF YOUR LOVE
Hey Jude / Sunshine of your love / This girl's in love with you / Watch what happens / Alright, OK you win / Give me the simple life / Useless landscape / Old devil moon / Don't cha go 'way mad / House is not a home / Trouble is a man / I love you madly
CD ______ **5331022**
MPS Jazz / Nov '96 / PolyGram

SWING IT
'S wonderful / Do you mean it / One I love (belongs to somebody else) / Shake down the stars / Goodnight my love / Out of nowhere / Jim / Baby won't you please come home / (What can I say) after I say I'm sorry / Melancholy baby / When my baby walks down the street / Imagination / My last affair / All my life / Oh yes, take another guess / You don't know what love is / Sing, song, swing / I was doin' alright / If you can't sing it, you'll have to swing it (Mr. Paganini) / He's my guy
CD ______ **306512**
Hallmark / Jun '97 / Carlton

SWINGS
You got me singin' the blues / Angel eyes / Lullaby of birdland / Tenderly / Do nothin' 'til you hear from me / April in Paris / I can't give you anything but love / Love for sale / Papa loves mambo / Lover come back to me / Just one of those things / Airmail special / I'm beginning to see the light / Sophisticated lady / Old mother hubbard / How high the moon
CD ______ **BSTCD 9111**
Best Compact Discs / Apr '94 / Complete/ Pinnacle

TAKE LOVE EASY (Fitzgerald, Ella & Joe Pass)
Take love easy / Once I loved / Don't be that way / You're blase / Lush life / Foggy day / Gee baby ain't I good to you / You go to my head / I want to talk about you
CD ______ **CD 2310702**
Pablo / Jan '92 / Cadillac / Complete/ Pinnacle

THESE ARE THE BLUES
Jailhouse blues / In the evening / CC rider / You don't know my mind / Trouble in mind / How long how long blues / Cherry red / Down hearted blues / St. Louis blues / Hear me talkin' to ya
CD ______ **8295362**
Verve / Nov '93 / PolyGram

TISKET-A-TASKET
You showed me the way / Love is the thing, so they say / If you ever should leave / Everyone's wrong but me / All or nothing at all / Big boy blue / Deep in the heart of the South / Just a simple melody / I gotta guy / Holiday in Harlem / Rock it for me / I want to be happy / Dipsy doodle / If dreams come true / Hallelujah / Dedicated to you / Cryin' mood / Bei mir bist du schone / It's my turn now / 'S wonderful / I was doing all right / Tisket-a-tasket
CD ______ **QED 090**
Tring / Nov '96 / Tring

UNFORGETTABLE SOUND OF ELLA FITZGERALD, THE (40 Swing Classics From The First Lady Of Jazz/2CD Set)
If you can't sing it, you'll have to swing it (Mr. Paganini) / Somebody nobody loves / Make love to me / Benny's coming home on Saturday / If it weren't for you / 'S wonderful / When my sugar walks down the street / Jim / Rock it for me / Baby, what else can I do / Imagination / Cow cow boogie: *Fitzgerald, Ella & The Ink Spots* / You won't be satisfied (until you break my heart): *Fitzgerald, Ella & Louis Armstrong* / It's only a paper moon / Goodnight, my love: *Fitzgerald, Ella & Benny Goodman Orchestra* / All my life / Dedicated to you: *Fitzgerald, Ella & The Mills Brothers* / And her tears flowed like wine / Mama, come home / Petootie pie: *Fitzgerald, Ella & Louis Jordan* / Undecided / This love of mine / Sugar blues / Out of nowhere / Sing song swing / Moonray / Shake down the stars / I was doing all right / Baby, won't you please come home / You don't know what love is / He's my guy / Tisket-a-tasket / Oh yes, take another guess / I'm beginning to see the light: *Fitzgerald, Ella & The Ink Spots* / My melancholy baby / It's a pity to say goodnight / I'm just a lucky so and so / Into each life some rain must fall / Stone cold dead in the market: *Fitzgerald, Ella & Louis Jordan* / Frim fram sauce: *Fitzgerald, Ella & Louis Armstrong*
CD ______ **330352**
Hallmark / Mar '97 / Carlton

VERY BEST OF ELLA FITZGERALD, THE
CD ______ **PLSCD 120**
Pulse / Apr '96 / BMG

WAR YEARS 1941-1947, THE
Jim / This love of mine / Somebody loves me / You don't know what love is / Make love to me / Mama come home / My heart and I decided / He's my guy / Cow cow boogie / Time alone will tell / Once too often / Into each life some rain must fall / I'm making believe / Tears flowed like wine / I'm confessin' that I love you / I'm beginning to see the light / That's the way it is / It's only a paper moon / Cry you out of my heart / Kiss goodnight / Benny's coming home on Saturday
CD ______ **GRP 26282**
GRP / Sep '94 / New Note/BMG

WITH TOMMY FLANAGAN
CD ______ **OJCCD 376**
Original Jazz Classics / Feb '92 / Complete/Pinnacle / Jazz Music / Wellard

YOUNG ELLA (4CD Set)
CD Set ______ **CDDIG 10**
Charly / Aug '96 / Koch

Fitzgerald, Patrick

SAFETY PINS STUCK IN MY HEART (The Very Best Of Patrick Fitzgerald)
Banging and shouting / Safety pin stuck in my heart / Work rest play reggae / Set we free / Optimism reject / Buy me sell me / Little dippers / Trendy / Backstreet boys / Babysitter / Irrelevant battles / Cruellest crime / Paranoid ward / Bingo crowd / Life at the top / Ragged generation for real / Live out my stars / George / All sewn up / Improve myself / Tonight 22 / Mr. and Mrs. / Animal mentality / Mr. and Mrs. 23 / Superbeing / Waiting for the final cue / Without sex / Pop star pop star
CD ______ **CDPUNK 31**
Anagram / Apr '94 / Cargo / Pinnacle

Fitzi Niceness

IMPRESSIONS OF LOVE
CD ______ **0133CD**
Fitzinicen / Jun '97 / Jet Star

Fiuczynski, David

LUNAR CRUSH
Vog / Pacifica / Gloria ascending / Pineapple / Quest / Freelance Brown / Slow blues for Fuzy's Mama / Lillies that fester / 122 St. Marks / Fima's sunrise
CD ______ **R 279498**
Gramavision / Jun '94 / Vital/SAM

Five Americans

I SEE THE LIGHT
I see the light / Losing game / Goodbye / I know they lie / Twist and shout / She's a-my-own / Train / It's a crying shame / I'm so glad / Don't blame me / Outcast / What'd I say / Train (unissued version) / Good times (unissued version)
CD ______ **CDSC 6018**
Sundazed / Apr '94 / Cargo / Greyhound / Rollercoaster

Five Blind Boys Of Alabama

DEEP RIVER (Five Blind Boys Of Alabama & Clarence Fountain)
Deep river (part one) / Don't play with God / Reminiscing / God said it / Look where he brought me from / Down on bended knees / I believe in you / I'm getting better all the time / Brother Moses / Every time I feel the spirit / Just a closer walk with thee / I've got the love of Jesus / Deep river (part two)
CD ______ **7559614412**
Nonesuch / Nov '92 / Warner Music

FIVE BLIND BOYS OF ALABAMA 1948-1951
CD ______ **FLYCD 946**
Flyright / Jul '96 / Hot Shot / Jazz Music / Wellard

I BROUGHT HIM WITH ME
Rain / He's got what I want / Do Lord / Better all the time / Listen to the lambs / If I had a hammer / No dope / Hush / King Jesus / Walking Jerusalem / Lord will make a way / Praying time / Amazing grace / Looking back
CD ______ **70010870032**
Private Music / Nov '95 / BMG

OH LORD STAND BY ME/ MARCHING UP TO ZION
Oh Lord / Stand by me / You got to move / Lord have mercy / Living for Jesus / Take my hand, precious Lord / I'll fly away / This may be the last time / Alone and motherless / Since I met Jesus / Our father's praying ground / Broken hearts of mine / Here am I / Marching up to Zion / Servant's prayer amen / Count me in / When I lost my mother / There is a fountain / I've been born again / He'll be there / Think about me / Does Jesus care / Fix it Jesus / Goodbye mother / I've got a home
CD ______ **CDCHD 341**
Ace / Nov '93 / Pinnacle

SERMON, THE
Sermon / All the way / I'll fly away / Without the help of Jesus / I'm on the battlefield / Heavenly light / Sit down servant / Standing by the bedside / When I need him most / Precious Lord / This may be the last time / Our father's praying ground / Marching up to Zion / God's promise / You got to move / Old time religion / Does Jesus care / Swingin' on the golden gate / I cried / Hallelujah / Golden bells / Heaven on my mind / I'm going through / Fix it Jesus / I've been born again / When death comes / In the garden
CD ______ **CDCHD 479**
Ace / Jul '93 / Pinnacle

SWING LOW SWEET CHARIOT
CD ______ **JEWEL 3127**
Jewel / Apr '96 / ADA

Five Blind Boys Of Mississippi

JESUS IS A ROCK
Let's have a church / I'm willing to run / Leave you in the hands of the Lord / Where there's a will / You don't know / I'm a soldier / Jesus loves me / I'm a-rolling / My robe will fit me / All over me / Somebody's mother / No need to cry / I never heard a man / Oh why / Don't forget the bridge / Waiting at the river / Jesus is a rock in a weary land / I've been weeping for a mighty long time / One talk with Jesus / I haven't been home in a mighty long time
CD ______ **CPCD 8086**
Charly / Apr '95 / Koch

MEET THE BLIND BOYS
CD ______ **JEWEL 3126**
Jewel / Apr '96 / ADA

Five Day Train

ROUGH MARMALADE
CD ______ **HBG 123/1**
Background / Apr '93 / Background / Greyhound

Five Eight

ANGRIEST MAN, THE
CD ______ **SKYCD 3101**
Sky / Sep '94 / Greyhound / Koch / Vital/ SAM

WEIRDO
CD ______ **SKYCD 3102**
Sky / May '94 / Greyhound / Koch / Vital/ SAM

Five Hand Reel

COLLECTION, THE
Bratach bana / Pinch of snuff / Man's not a man / Haughs o' Cromdale / Fond kiss / P is for Paddy / Cruel brother / Carrickfergus / My love is like a red red rose / Bonny Earl O' Mornay / Trooper and the maid / Beef can close / Knight and the shepherd's daughter / When a man's in love / Maid of Listowell / Medley
CD ______ **74321451932**
Camden / Feb '97 / BMG

Five HT

NEUROTRANSMITTER
CD ______ **HYPOXIA 003CD**
Hypoxia / Jun '96 / Plastic Head

Five Keys

DREAM ON
I burned your letter / How can I forget you / Gonna be too late / I took your love for a toy / Dancing senorita / Dream on / Your teeth and your tongue / I've always been a dreamer / You broke the only heart / When Paw was courtin' Maw / Rosetta / Ziggus / I can't escape from you / Will you / Wrapped in a dream / Do something for me / Valley of love / No say's my heart / That's what you're doing to me / Now I know I love you / Stop your crying / Girl you better stop it / I'll never stop loving you / Bimbo
CD ______ **CDCHARLY 265**
Charly / Mar '91 / Koch

Five Knuckle Chuckle

CHARLIE HORSE
CD ______ **BMCD 079**
Black Mark / Dec '95 / Plastic Head

Five Red Caps

FIVE RED CAPS 1943-1945
Boogie woogie on a Saturday night / It's got a hole in it / Mary had a little jam / Don't fool with me / Mama put your britches on / Just for you / Somebody's lyin' / I learned a lesson I'll never forget / Sugar lips / Lennox Avenue jump / Monkey & the baboon
CD ______ **FLYCD 60**
Flyright / May '96 / Hot Shot / Jazz Music / Wellard

Five Royales

REAL THINGS, THE
Baby don't do it / Come over here / Laundromat blues / All righty / I want to thank you / Send me somebody
CD ________ RBD 802
Mr. R&B / Apr '91 / CM / Swift / Wellard

Five Star

FIVE STAR
Slightest touch / System addict / Can't wait another minute / Another weekend / With every heartbeat / Stay out of my life / Rain or shine / Find the time / RSVP / Love take over / If I say yes / Let me be the one / Strong as steel / There's a brand new world / Rock my world / All fall down
CD ________ 74321183252
Ariola Express / Feb '94 / BMG

Five Star Galaxy

GALAXY STRIKES BACK VOL.2, THE (Various Artists)
Gigantesque, bizarre et magnifique: *Rollercone* / Dome: *Stade* / Final countdown: *Rollercone* / Escape: *Capitaine Nemo* / Voyage sur hypnose: *Le Gooster* / Stadium: *Stade* / Swing machine: *Les Fous Du Volant* / Greetings from Goree: *Le Gooster* / Zero gravity: *Rollercone* / Who is Mr. Stevens: *Le Gooster* / Immersion: *Rollercone* / Pendulum: *MGM* / Autostrada: *MGM & Rollercone* / Tales from the darkside: *Le Gooster*
CD ________ UR 27CD
Five Star / Mar '97 / Vital/SAM

Five-A-Slide

STRIKE UP THE BAND
CD ________ BLCD 760509
Black Lion / Oct '93 / Cadillac / Jazz Music / Koch / Wellard

Five-O

IF U R NOT PART OV DA SOLUTION
CD ________ WRA 8129CD
Wrap / Apr '94 / Koch

Fix

COLD DAYS
CD ________ LF 078
Lost & Found / Mar '94 / Plastic Head

Fixtures

DEVIL'S PLAYGROUND
CD ________ VIRUS 187CD
Alternative Tentacles / Dec '96 / Cargo / Greyhound / Pinnacle

Flack, Roberta

BEST OF ROBERTA FLACK - SOFTLY WITH THESE SONGS
First time ever I saw your face / Will you still love me tomorrow / Where is the love / Killing me softly / Feel like makin' love / Closer I get to you / More than everything / Only heaven can wait (for love) / Back together again / Making love / Tonight, I celebrate my love / Oasis / And so it goes / You know what it's like / Set the night to music / My foolish heart / Uh-uh ooh-ooh look out (here it comes)
CD ________ 7567824982
Atlantic / Feb '94 / Warner Music

BLUE LIGHTS IN THE BASEMENT
Why don't you move in with me / Closer I get to you / Fine fine day / This time I'll be sweeter / 25th of last December / After you / I'd like to be baby to you / Soul deep / Love is the healing / Where I'll find you
CD ________ 7567827912
Atlantic / Mar '93 / Warner Music

BORN TO LOVE (Flack, Roberta & Peabo Bryson)
Tonight, I celebrate my love / Blame it on me / Heaven above me / Born to love / Maybe / I just came here to dance / Comin' alive / You're lookin' like love to me / Can we find love again
CD ________ MUSCD 508
MCI Original Masters / Nov '94 / Disc / THE

CHAPTER TWO
Reverend Lee / Do what you gotta do / Just like a woman / Let it be me / Gone away / Until it's time for you to go / Impossible dream / Business goes on as usual
CD ________ 7567813732
Atlantic / Jan '96 / Warner Music

FEEL LIKE MAKIN' LOVE
Feeling that glow / I wanted it too / I can see the sun in late December / Some gospel according to Mathew / Feel like makin' love / Mr. Magic / Early every midnight / Old heart break top ten / She's not blind
CD ________ 7567803332
Atlantic / Feb '91 / Warner Music

FIRST TAKE
Compared to what / Angelitos negros / Our ages or our hearts / I told Jesus / Hey, that's no way to say goodbye / First time ever I saw your face / Tryin' times / Ballad of the sad young man
CD ________ 7567827922
Atlantic / Feb '91 / Warner Music

KILLING ME SOFTLY
Killing me softly / Jesse / No tears (In the end) / I'm the girl / River / Conversation love / When you smile / Suzanne
CD ________ 7567827932
Atlantic / Feb '91 / Warner Music

LIVE AND MORE
CD ________ 7567814112
Atlantic / Dec '96 / Warner Music

QUIET FIRE
Go up Moses / Bridge over troubled water / Sunday and Sister Jones / See you then / Will you still love me tomorrow / To love somebody / Let them talk / Sweet bitter love
CD ________ 7567813782
Atlantic / Feb '91 / Warner Music

ROBERTA
CD ________ 7567825972
Atlantic / Nov '94 / Warner Music

YOU'VE GOT A FRIEND (Flack, Roberta & Donny Hathaway)
CD ________ 7567827942
Atlantic / Feb '91 / Warner Music

Flag Of Convenience

BEST OF STEVE DIGGLE & FLAG OF CONVENIENCE (The Secret Public Years 1981-1989) (Diggle, Steve & Flag Of Convenience)
Fifty Years comparative wealth / Shut out the light / Here comes the fire brigade / Life on the telephone / Picking up on audio sound / Other mans sin / Men from the city / Who is innocent / Drift away / Change / Longest life / Arrow has come / Keep on pushing (live) / Pictures in my mind / Last train to safety / Exiles / Can't stop the world / Shot down with a gun / Tragedy in Market Street / Tomorrows sunset / Life with the lions
CD ________ CDMGRAM 74
Anagram / Feb '94 / Cargo / Pinnacle

Flag Of Democracy

EVERYTHING SUCKS
CD ________ BC 1708CD
Blitzcore / Nov '96 / Cargo

Flamin' Groovies

GROOVE IN
CD ________ 890011
New Rose / May '94 / ADA / Direct / Discovery

GROOVIES GREATEST, THE
CD ________ 7599259482
Sire / Jan '96 / Warner Music

IN PERSON
CD ________ CED 255
Norton / Jul '97 / Greyhound

LIVE 1968/1970
CD ________ 842070
EVA / May '94 / ADA / Direct

LIVE AT THE FESTIVAL OF THE SUN BARCELONA
CD ________ AIM 1051CD
Aim / Apr '95 / ADA / Direct / Jazz Music

OLDIES BUT GROOVIES (The Best Of The Flamin' Groovies)
Shake some action / Married woman / Slow death / Tallahassee lassie / Teenage head / Way over my head / Searching / She's got a hold on me / You tore me down / Money / I'm only what you want me to be / I can't hide
CD ________ AIM 2001CD
Aim / May '97 / ADA / Direct / Jazz Music

ONE NIGHT STAND
CD ________ AIM 1008CD
Aim / Oct '93 / ADA / Direct / Jazz Music

SHAKE SOME ACTION
Shake some action / Sometimes / Yes it's true / St. Louis blues / You tore me down / Please please girl / Let the boy rock 'n' roll / Don't you lie to me / She said yeah / I'll cry alone / Misery / I say her / Teenage confidential / I can't hide
CD ________ AIM 1017CD
Aim / Oct '93 / ADA / Direct / Jazz Music

SNEAKERS/ROCKFIELD SESSIONS
CD ________ COLLECT 12
Aim / Oct '93 / ADA / Direct / Jazz Music

STEP UP
CD ________ AIM 1030CD
Aim / Oct '93 / ADA / Direct / Jazz Music

SUPERSNEAKER
CD ________ SC 6077
Sundazed / Nov '96 / Cargo / Greyhound / Rollercoaster

Flaming Ember

WESTBOUND NO.9
Spinning wheel / Westbound no.9 / Mind, body and soul / Shades of green / Going in circles / Why don't you stay / Flashbacks and re-runs / This girl is a woman now / Stop the world (and let me off) / Heart on (loving you) / Where's all the joy / Empty crowded room / I'm not my brother's keeper
CD ________ HDHCD 503
HDH / Apr '92 / Pinnacle

Flaming Lips

CLOUDS TASTE METALLIC
CD ________ 9362459112
Warner Bros. / Sep '95 / Warner Music

IN A PRIEST DRIVEN AMBULANCE
Shine on sweet Jesus-Jesus song no.5 / Unconsciously screamin' / Rainin' babies / Take metamars / Five stop mother superior rain / Stand in line / God walks among us now-Jesus song no.7 / Mountain side / What a wonderful world / Lucifer rising / Let me be it
CD ________ 723592
Restless / Sep '96 / Vital

TELEPATHIC SURGERY
Drug machine / Michael time to wake up / Miracle on 42nd Street / UFO story / Shaved gorilla / Begs and achin' / Right now / Hare Krishna stomp wagon / Chrome plated suicide / Redneck school of technology / Spontaneous combustion of John / Last drop of morning dew
CD ________ CDENV 523
Enigma / Feb '89 / EMI

TRANSMISSIONS FROM THE SATELLITE HEART
Turn it on / Pilot can at the queer of God / Oh my pregnant head (Labia in the sunlight) / She don't use jelly / Chewin' the apple of your eye / Superhumans / Be my head / Moth in the incubator / #@#@@#@ (Plastic Jesus) / When yer twenty two / Slow nerve action
CD ________ 9362453342
Warner Bros. / Jun '93 / Warner Music

Flaming Stars

BRING ME THE REST OF ALFREDO GARCIA
CD ________ ASKCD 067
Vinyl Japan / Mar '97 / Plastic Head / Vinyl Japan

SONGS FROM THE BAR ROOM FLOOR
Face on the bar room floor / Forget my name / You can't lie / Who's out there / Burnt out wreck of a man / Bring me the rest of Afredo Garcia / Kiss tomorrow goodbye / Ballad of the walking wounded / Downhill without brakes / Theme from Dog Instruction / Back of my mind / Down to you / Oncoming train / Tubs twist / Like trash / 3 A.M. On the bar room floor
CD ________ ASKCD 062
Vinyl Japan / Jun '96 / Plastic Head / Vinyl Japan

Flamingos

COMPLETE CHESS MASTERS, THE
CD ________ MCD 09378
Chess/MCA / Jul '97 / BMG / New Note/ BMG

I ONLY HAVE EYES FOR YOU
CD ________ NEMCD 609
Sequel / Apr '91 / BMG

I'LL BE HOME
Someday someway / Golden teardrops / Cross over the bridge / Carried away / You ain't ready / Hurry home baby / Blues in the letter / On my merry way / Dream of a lifetime / If I could love you / I really don't want to know / I found a new baby / Kokomo / That's my baby (chicka boom) / Whispering stars / Chickie-um-bah / I'll be home / Kiss from your lips / Get with it / Nobody's love / Would I be crying / Shilly dilly / Stolen love
CD ________ CDINS 5072
Charly / Jun '93 / Koch

Flanagan & Allen

ARCHES AND UMBRELLAS
Music, maestro please / Umbrella song / Oi / Milking time in Switzerland / Nice people / New MP / Run rabbit run / (We're gonna hang out the) washing on the Siegfried Line / Sending out an SOS for you / Down and out blues / Sport of kings / Home town / If a grey-haired lady says How's yer father / Free / Digging holes / FDR Jones / Dreaming / How do you do Mr. Right / Crazy Gang at sea / Underneath the arches / Flanagan and Allen memories
CD ________ PASTCD 9720
Flapper / '90 / Pinnacle

LET'S BE BUDDIES
Are you having any fun / Round the back of the arches / Let's be buddies / Smiths and the Jones / Don't ever walk in the shadows / Why don't you fall in love with me / Down forget-me-not lane / Corn silk / We'll smile again / What more can I say / Yesterday's dreams / Down every street / I don't want to walk without you / If a grey-haired lady says How's yer father / Umbrella man / Can't we meet again / Underneath the arches / Rose o'day / I'm nobody's baby / In a little rocky valley / On the outside looking in / Miss you / Washing on siegfried line / Million years
CD ________ RAJCD 832
Empress / Jul '94 / Koch

UNDERNEATH THE ARCHES
Run rabbit run / Miss you / Smiths and the Jones / In a little rocky valley / Two very ordinary people / Down every street / Flying through the rain / FDR Jones / On the outside looking in / Roll on tomorrow / There's a boy coming home on leave / Shine on harvest moon / We'll smile again / Underneath the arches
CD Set ________ CDDL 1209
Music For Pleasure / Jun '91 / EMI

WE'LL SMILE AGAIN
Underneath the arches / Dreaming / Wanderer / Can't we meet again / Million tears / Home town / Music, maestro, please / Umbrella man / Nice people / Run, rabbit, run / We're gonna hang out the washing on the Siegfried / FDR Jones / If a grey haired lady says "How's your Father" / On the outside looking in / Yesterday's dream / Down forget me not lane / Rose O'Day (The filla-ga-dusha-song) / What more can I say / I don't want to walk without you / Miss you / We'll smile again / Round the back of the arches / Flying through the rain / Shine on, harvest moon / Two very ordinary people
CD ________ CDAJA 5194
Living Era / May '96 / Select

Flanagan Brothers

TUNES WE LIKE TO PLAY
CD ________ VV 007
Viva Voce / Aug '96 / ADA / Direct

Flanagan, Kevin

ZANZIBAR (Flanagan, Kevin & Chris Ingham Quartet)
Don't loook at me like that / Po-town / Walk between raindrops / Born to be blue / Pent-up house / Waiting for dusko / It's your dance / Gloryhound / Sleepin' bee / Zanzibar
CD ________ GBCD 2
Gray Brothers / Sep '95 / Pinnacle

Flanagan, Ralph

DANCE AGAIN
CD ________ DAWE 75
Magic / Jul '96 / Cadillac / Harmonia Mundi / Jazz Music / Swift / Wellard

HOT TODDY
CD ________ AERO 1032
Aerospace / Jul '96 / Jazz Music / Montpellier

LET'S DANCE WITH RALPH FLANAGAN (Flanagan, Ralph Orchestra)
CD ________ DAWE 74
Magic / Jan '96 / Cadillac / Harmonia Mundi / Jazz Music / Swift / Wellard

Flanagan, Tommy

3
CD ________ CD 20036
Pablo / May '86 / Cadillac / Complete/ Pinnacle

3 FOR ALL (Flanagan, Tommy & Red Mitchell/Phil Woods)
CD ________ ENJACD 308167
Enja / Jan '95 / New Note/Pinnacle / Vital/ SAM

CATS, THE (Flanagan, Tommy & John Coltrane/Kenny Burrell)
Minor mishap / How long has this been going on / Eclypso / Solacium / Tommy's time
CD ________ OJCCD 79
Original Jazz Classics / Jun '86 / Complete/ Pinnacle / Jazz Music / Wellard

JAZZ POET
Raincheck / Lament / Willow weep for me / Caravan / That tired routine called love / Glad to be happy / St. Louis blues / Mean streets
CD ________ CDSJP 301
Timeless Jazz / Nov '89 / New Note/ Pinnacle

LADY BE GOOD...FOR ELLA
Oh lady be good / Love you madly / Isn't it a pity / How high the moon / Smooth sailing / Alone too long / Angel eyes / Cherokee / Rouge ridin' / Pete Kelly's blues / Oh lady be good
CD ________ 5216172
Groovin' High / Jun '94 / PolyGram

LET'S
Let's / Mean what you say / To you / Bird song / Scratch / Thadrack / Child is born / Three in one / Quietude / Zec / Elusive
CD ________ ENJ 80402
Enja / Nov '93 / New Note/Pinnacle / Vital/ SAM

MAGNIFICENT TOMMY FLANAGAN, THE
CD ________ PCD 7059
Progressive / Oct '91 / Jazz Music

MASTER TRIO
CD ________ PRCDSP 204
Prestige / May '94 / Else / Total/BMG

MONTREUX 1977 (Flanagan, Tommy Trio)
CD _______ OJCCD 372
Original Jazz Classics / Nov '95 / Complete/Pinnacle / Jazz Music / Wellard

YOU'RE ME (Flanagan, Tommy & Red Mitchell)
You're me / Darn that dream / What am I here for / When I have you / All the things you are / Milestones / Whisper not / There'll never be another you
CD _______ PHONTCD 7528
Phontastic / Apr '94 / Cadillac / Jazz Music / Wellard

Flanders & Swann

AT THE DROP OF A HAT
Transport of delight / Song of reproduction / Gnu song / Design for living / Je suis les tenebreux / Songs for our time / Song of the weather / Reluctant cannibal / Greensleeves / Misalliance / Kokoraki / Madeira m'dear / Too many cookers / Vanessa / Tried by the centre court / Youth of the heart / Hippopotamus song / Happy song / Satellite moon / Philogical waltz
CD _______ CZ 515
EMI / Sep '92 / EMI

AT THE DROP OF ANOTHER HAT
Gas man cometh / Sounding brass / Los Olivados / In the desert / Ill wind / First and second law / All gall / Horoscope / Friendly duet / Bedstead men / By air / Slow train / Song of patriotic prejudice / Built up area / In the bath / Sea fever / Hippo encore
CD _______ CZ 517
EMI / Sep '92 / EMI

BESTIARY OF FLANDERS & SWANN, THE
Warthog / Sea horse / Chameleon / Whale / Sloth / Rhinoceros / Twosome - Kang and Jag (Kangaroo tango and jaguar) / Dead ducks / Elephant / Armadillo / Spider / Duck billed Platypus/Humming bird/Portuguese man-o'war / Wild boar / Ostrich / Wompom / Twice shy / Commonwealth fair / P**P*B****B**D****** / Paris / Ein kleine nachtmusik cha cha cha / Hundred song / Food for thought / Bed / Twenty tons of TNT / War of 14-18
CD _______ CZ 516
EMI / Sep '92 / EMI

COMPLETE FLANDERS AND SWANN
Transport of delight / Song of reproduction / Gnu song / Design for living / Je suis les tenebreux / Songs for our time / Song of the weather / Reluctant cannibal / Greensleeves / Misalliance / Kokoraki / Madeira m'dear / Too many cookers / Vanessa / Tried by the centre court / Youth of the heart / Hippopotamus song / Gas man cometh / Sounding brass / Los olivados / In the desert / Ill wind / First and second law / All gall / Horoscope / Friendly duet / Bedstead men / By air / Slow train / Song of patriotic prejudice / Built up area / In the bath / Sea fever / Hippo encore / Warthog / Sea horse / Chameleon / Whale / Sloth / Rhinoceros / Twosome - Kang and Jag / Dead ducks / Elephant / Armadillo / Spider / Threesome / Wild boar / Ostrich / Wompom / Twice shy / Commonwealth fair / Paris / Eine kleine nachtmusik cha cha cha / Hundred song / Food for thought / Bed / Twenty tons of TNT / War of 14-18
CD Set _______ CDFSB 1
EMI / Aug '91 / EMI

TRANSPORT OF DELIGHT, A (The Best Of Flanders & Swann)
CD _______ CDGO 2061
EMI / Aug '94 / EMI

Flare

GRIP
Turbinates / Cycling round / Curved flow / Clinch / Parts and wholes / Sweet katharsis / Curved sunburst / Transition / One blink / Grip
CD _______ SBLCD 5011
Sublime / Oct '96 / Vital

RE-GRIP
Turbinates / Cycling around / Curved flow / Clinch / Parts and wholes / Sweet katharsis / Curved sunburst / Transition / One blink / Grip
CD _______ SBLCD 5012
Sublime / Feb '97 / Vital

REFERENCE TO DIFFERENCE
Out of the inside / Morceau / Fading sky / Interjection / Scene one / Finite time / Non essentia / Nervewench / Into the inside
CD _______ SBLCD 5006
Sublime / Apr '96 / Vital

Flash

FLASH
CD _______ OW S2117796
One Way / Sep '94 / ADA / Direct / Greyhound

IN THE CAN
CD _______ OW S2156841
One Way / Sep '94 / ADA / Direct / Greyhound

OUT OF OUR HANDS
CD _______ OW S2117414
One Way / Sep '94 / ADA / Direct / Greyhound

Flat Duo Jets

FLAT DUO JETS
CD _______ DOG 004CD
Wild Dog / Sep '94 / Koch

GO GO HARLEM BABY
CD _______ SKYCD 5031
Sky / Sep '94 / Greyhound / Koch / Vital/ SAM

IN STEREO
CD _______ SKYCD 5023
Sky / Sep '94 / Greyhound / Koch / Vital/ SAM

WHITER TREES
CD _______ SKYCD 5033
Sky / Sep '94 / Greyhound / Koch / Vital/ SAM

Flat Earth Society

WALEECO/LOST SPACE KIDS
CD _______ AA 042
Arf Arf / Jul '97 / Greyhound

Flatlanders

MORE A LEGEND THAN A BAND
Dallas / Tonight I'm gonna go downtown / You've never seen me cry / She had everything / Rose from the mountain / One day at a time / Jolie blon / Down in my hometown / Bhagavan decreed / Heart you left behind / Keeper of the mountain / Stars in my life / One more road
CD _______ SSCD 34
Rounder / '90 / ADA / CM / Direct

Flatley, Michael

MICHAEL FLATLEY
CD _______ BUA 9501CD
BUA / Apr '95 / ADA

Flatt & Scruggs

DON'T GET ABOVE YOUR RAISIN' (Flatt, Lester & Earl Scruggs)
CD _______ SSCD 08
Rounder / Feb '94 / ADA / CM / Direct

FLATT AND SCRUGGS 1948-1959 (4CD Set) (Flatt, Lester & Earl Scruggs)
God loves his children / I'm going to make Heaven my home / We'll meet again sweetheart / My cabin in Caroline / Baby blue eyes / Bouquet in Heaven / Down the road / Why don't you tell me so / I'll never shed another tear / No mother or dad / Is it too late now / Foggy mountain breakdown / Cora is gone / Preaching, praying, singing / Pain in my heart / Rollin' in my sweet baby's arms / Back to the cross / Farewell blues / Old salty dog blues / Take me in a lifeboat / Will the roses bloom / I'll just pretend / Come back darling / I'm head over heels in love / I'm waiting to hear you call me darling / Old home town / I'll stay around / We can't be darlings anymore / Jimmie Brown the newsboy / Somehow tonight / Don't get above your raising / I'm working on a road / He took your place / I've lost you / 'Tis sweet to be remembered / I'm gonna settle down / Earl's breakdown / I'm lonesome and blue / Over the hills to the poorhouse / My darling's last goodbye / Get in line brother / Brother I'm getting ready to go / Why did you wander / Flint Hill special / Thinking about you / If I should wander back tonight / Dim lights, thick smoke / Dear old Dixie / Reunion in Heaven / Pray for the boys / I'll go stepping too / I'd rather be alone / Foggy mountain chimes / Someone took my place with you / Mother prays loud in her sleep / That old book of mine / Your love is like a flower / Be ready for tomorrow may never come / Till the end of the world rolls around / You're not a drop in the bucket / Don't that road look rough and rocky / Foggy mountain special / You can feel it on your soul / Old fashioned preacher / Before I met you / I'm gonna sleep with one eye open / Randy Lynn rag / On my mind / Blue Ridge cabin home / Some old day / It won't be long / No mother in this world / Gone home / Bubbling in my soul / Joy bells / What's good for you / No doubt about it / Who will sing for me / Give mother my crown / Six white horses / Shuckin' the corn / I'll take the blame / Don't let your deal go down / Hundred years from now / Give me the flowers while I'm living / Is there room for me / Let those brown eyes smile at me / I won't be hanging around / I don't care anymore / Big black train / Mama's and daddy's little girl / Crying alone / Million years in glory / Heaven / Building on sand / Jesus saviour pilot me / Crying my heart out over you / Ground speed / Who knows right from wrong / Iron curtain / Cabin on the hill / Someone you have forgotten / Foggy mountain rock / You put me on my feet
CD Set _______ BCD 15472
Bear Family / Jan '94 / Direct / Rollercoaster / Swift

FLATT AND SCRUGGS 1959-1963 (5CD Set) (Flatt, Lester & Earl Scruggs)
Angel band / When the angels carry me home / I'll never be lonesome again / Get on the road to glory / Take me in your lifeboat / Bubbling in my soul / Heaven / Joy bells / Give me flowers while I'm living / You can feel it in your soul / Give mother my crown / Great historical bum / I've lost you forever / Polka on a banjo / All I want is you / Shuckin' the corn / Home sweet home / Fireball mail / Cripple creek / Reuben (Instrumental) / John Henry / Cumberland gap / Lonesome road blues / Sally Goodin (instrumental) / Little darlin', pal of mine (Instrumental) / Sally Ann / Bugle call rag / I ain't gonna work tomorrow / If I should wander back tonight / Cold, cold loving / Welcome to the club / False hearted lover / Picking in the wildwood / Homestead on the farm / Foggy mountain top / You are my flower / Forsaken love / Storms are on the ocean / Gathering flowers from the hillside / Worried man blues / On the rock where Moses stood / Keep on the sunny side / Jimmie brown the newsboy / Just ain't / Where will I shelter my sheep / I saw mother with God last night / Go home / Old Joe Clark / Sally Goodin / Black mountain rag / Billy in the lowground / Twinkle little star / Old fiddler / Soldier's joy / Georgia shuffle / Golden slippers / Tennessee Wagner / Handsome Molly / Coal loadin' Johnny / Hear that whistle blow (a hundred miles) / Too old for a broken heart / Legend of the Johnson boys / All the good times are past and gone / George Alley's FFV / This land is your land / Philadelphia lawyer / Sun's gonna shine in my back door some day / Hear the wind blow / I'll be no man's wife / McKinley's gone / Nine pound hammer / Ellen Smith / Life of trouble / Hard travellin' / Wreck of ol' 97 / Ninety nine years is almost for life / Over the hills to the poorhouse / New York town / Dixie home / Pastures of plenty / Bound to ride / When I left East Virginia / Drowned in the deep blue sea / My native home / Coal miner's blues / Salty dog blues / Durham's reel / Down the road / Rainbow / Big ball in Brooklyn / Flint Hill special / Dig a hole in the meadow / I hung my head and cried / Hot corn, cold corn / Little darlin', pal of mine / Mama don't allow it / Footprints in the snow / Martha White theme / I wonder where you are tonight / Old Macdonald / He will set your fields on fire / Let the church roll on / Picking the wildwood flower / Fiddle and banjo / Old leather britches / Ballad of Jed Clampett / Yonder stands little Maggie / Reuben / Mama blues / I know what it mean to be lonesome / Foggy mountain rock / Take this hammer / Rollin' in my sweet baby's arms / Gotta travel on / Mountain dew / Pearl, Pearl, Pearl / What about you / Rambling gambler / I'm troubled / My Sarah Jane / Train that carried my girl from town / Little birdy / Po' rebel soldier
CD Set _______ BCD 15559
Bear Family / Jun '92 / Direct / Rollercoaster / Swift

FLATT AND SCRUGGS 1964-1969 (6CD Set) (Flatt, Lester & Earl Scruggs)
Petticoat junction / Have you seen my dear companion / Good things (outweigh the bad) / Working it out / Amber tresses (tied in blue) / Jimmie Brown / Newsboy / When Papa played the dobro / Fireball / Father's table grace / I'm walking with him / My wandering boy / Sally don't you grieve / Faded red ribbon / Bummin' an old freight train / Georgia Buck / Hello stranger / Please don't wake me / You're gonna miss me when I'm gone / I still miss someone / Wabash cannonball / Rose conelly / You've been fooling my baby / Will you be lonesome too / Big shoes to fill / Branded wherever I go / Starlight on the rails / Loafer's glory / I'll be on the good road some day / Confessing / Gonna have myself a ball / Rock, salt and nails / Soldier's return / Memphis / Jackson / Colours / For lovin' me / Houston / Detroit city / Foggy mountain breakdown / Kansas city / Nashville blues / Take me back to Tulsa / Last public hanging in West Virginia / Boys form Tennessee / Ten miles from Natchez / Seattle town / Green acres / I had a dream / When the saints go marching in / God gave Noah the rainbow sign / Call me on home / Stone that builders refused / Wait for the sunshine / No Mother in this world / Thank God I'm on my way / Troublesome waters / Last thing on my mind / Mama, you been on my mind / It was only the wind / Why can't I find myself with you / Southbound / I'm gonna ride the steamboat / Roust-a-bout / Nashville cats / Train number 1262 / Bringin in the Georgia mail / Going across the sea / Atlantic coastal line / East bound train / Orange blossom special / Last train to Clarksville / California up tight band / Don't think twice it's alright / Four strong winds / Blowin' in the wind / It ain't me babe / Down in the flood / Buddy don't you roll so slow / Where have all the flowers gone / This land is your land / Mr. Tambourine man / Ode to Billie Joe / Like a rolling stone / I'd like to say a word for Texas / I'll be your baby tonight / Folsom prison blues / Gentle on my mind / Times they are a-changin' / If I were a carpenter / Universal soldier / Long road to Houston / Catch the wind / Rainy day women / Frieda Florentine / Nashville skyline rag / I walk the line / Ruby, don't take your love to town / Boy named Sue / Maggie's farm / Wanted man / One more night / One too many mornings / Girl from the north country / Honey, just allow me one more chance / Tonight will be fine / Story of Bonnie and Clyde / Another ride with Clyde / Picture of Bonnie / Barrow gang will get you little man / Bang you're alive / See Bonnie die, see Cly die / Get away / Chase / Highway's end / Pick along / John Hardy was a desperate little man / Jazzing / Evelina / Tommy's song / Lonesome Ruben / Spanish two step / Careless love / Liberty / Bill Cheatham / Nothin' to it / Lost all my money / Maggie blues / Steamboat whistle blues / Paul and Silas / Cannonball blues / You are my flower / Old leather britches / Across the blue ridge mountains / Old folks / Going back to Harlan / Poor rebel soldier / No hiding place down here / Going up cripple creek / Foggy mountain special / Bile them cabbage down / Old Joe Clark / Sally goodine / Black mountain rag / Billy in the lowground / Twinkle little star / Old fiddler / Soldier's joy / Cheyenne / Down yonder / Georgia shuffle / Golden slippers / Tennessee Wagner / Chicken reel / Theme from Beverly Hillbillies / Beverly Hills / Vittles / Long talk with that boy / Jethro's a powerful man / Elly's spring song / Back home USA / Critters / What a great doctor Granny is / Lady lessons / Birds and the bees / Love or money / Close
CD Set _______ BCD 15879
Bear Family / Nov '95 / Direct / Rollercoaster / Swift

FOGGY MOUNTAIN JAMBOREE
CD _______ CUY 118CD
County / Aug '96 / ADA / Direct

GOLDEN ERA, THE (Flatt, Lester & Earl Scruggs)
Flint Hill special / Your love is like a flower / I'm waiting to hear you call me darling / I'm head over heels in love / I'm working on a road / Till the end of the world rolls around / Jimmie Brown the newsboy / Earl's breakdown / Someone took my place with you / I'm gonna sleep with one eye open / Dim lights, thick smoke / Don't that road look rough and rocky / Randy lynn rag / Old home town / Brother I'm getting ready to go
CD _______ SSCD 05
Rounder / '92 / ADA / CM / Direct

MERCURY SESSIONS VOL.1 (Flatt, Lester & Earl Scruggs)
CD _______ SSCD 18
Rounder / Dec '87 / ADA / CM / Direct

MERCURY SESSIONS VOL.2 (Flatt, Lester & Earl Scruggs)
My little girl in Tennessee / Will the roses bloom / I'll never shed another tear / Bouquet in heaven / Cabin in Caroline / I'll never love another / God loves his children / Pain in my heart / Baby blue eyes / Doing my time / Preaching, praying, singing / Why don't they tell me so / Foggy mountain breakdown / I'm going to make heaven my home
CD _______ SSCD 19
Rounder / Dec '87 / ADA / CM / Direct

Flatts, Vincent

FLATT OUT
CD _______ MYS 101CD
Mystic / May '96 / Pinnacle

Flatville Aces

CRAWFISHTROMBONES
CD _______ FLATCD 123
Flat / Apr '94 / ADA / Direct / Else

Flavin, Mick

COUNTRY ALL THE WAY
California okie / She's got a way (of makin' me forget) / Writing on the wall / I'll be there (if you ever want me) / Cotton Jenny / Family tree / In my father's house / Flowers in the snow / I met a friend of yours today / What we love to do / Lovin' understanding man / I sleep just like a baby / Old man on the porch / You beat all I've ever seen / I won't be in Atlanta anynore
CD _______ RITZRCD 564
Ritz / Jul '97 / Pinnacle

COUNTRY SOUNDS
In the echoes of my mind / You're the reason / Walk softly on the bridges / Love bug / I wish it was that easy going home / County of Fermanagh / Can you feel it / Yours to hurt tomorrow / Life's too short to be unhappy / Grand tour / Dreams of Donegal / If you remember me / Maria's heading out to California / Take my back home to Mayo
CD _______ RITZRCD 545
Ritz / Nov '94 / Pinnacle

LIGHTS OF HOME, THE
Someday you'll love me / I see an angel every day / On the wings of love / It started all over again / For a minute there / One of these days (I want to be in your nights) / I never loved you more / Little things in life / Lights of home / Connemara rose / Keeper of my heart / You done me wrong / Old home in Mayo / Table in the corner / Little

mountain church mouse / Longford on my mind
CD RITZRCD 533
Ritz / Aug '93 / Pinnacle

SWEET MEMORY
If you're gonna do me wrong (do it right) / Gonna have love / What she don't know won't hurt her / Way down deep / I took a memory to lunch / Old school yard / She's my rose / Haven't you heard / Wine flowed freely / Lady Jane / Hills of Tyrone / All I can be (is a sweet memory)
CD RITZRCD 517
Ritz / Jun '92 / Pinnacle

TRAVELLIN' LIGHT
Jennifer Johnson and me / Blue blue day / Hard times lovin' can bring / Where have all the lovers gone / Home to Donegal / Old side of town / Roads and other reasons / Travellin' light / There is no other way / Rarest flowers
CD RITZCD 507
Ritz / '91 / Pinnacle

Flavournaughts

MY INBRED PEDIGREE CHUMS
Enchantress (stone cold heartbreaker) / Shivers / Asa quebrada / Flower of the valley / Keeping the rabbie in line / Mexican rave / If you know me / Double decker / Jamie's magic ending / Bustin' outta no way street / Last drag / New dawn / Magic ending (Reprise)
CD NOZACD 005
Ninebar / May '97 / Kudos / Prime / RTM/ Disc

Fleck, Bela

DAYBREAK
CD ROUCD 11518
Rounder / '88 / ADA / CM / Direct

DEVIATION (Fleck, Bela & The New Grass Revival)
CD ROUCD 0196
Rounder / Jul '95 / ADA / CM / Direct

DOUBLE TIME
Spunk / Black forest / Double play / Lowdown / Bullfrog shuffle / Another morning / Light speed / Sweet rolls / Ladies and gentleman / Right as rain / Far away / Ready to go / Fast lane
CD ROUCD 0181
Rounder / May '97 / ADA / CM / Direct

DRIVE
Whitewater / Slipstream / Up and around the bend / Natchez trace / See rock city / Legend / Lights of home / Down in the swamp / Sanctuary / Open road
CD ROUCD 0255
Rounder / Aug '88 / ADA / CM / Direct

INROADS
Tonino / Somerset / Cecata / Four wheel drive / Ireland / Perplexed / Old country / Hudson's bay / Close to home
CD ROUCD 0219
Rounder / May '93 / ADA / CM / Direct

LIVE ART (2CD Set) (Fleck, Bela & The Flecktones)
Intro / New South Africa / Stomping grounds / Lochs of dread / Big foot / Far East medley / Flying saucer dudes / UFO tofu / Interlude - libation, the water ritual / Vix 9 / Message / Improv/Amazing grace / Shubbee's doobie / Oh darling / Blu bop / Sunset road / More law / Early reflection/ Bach/The ballad of Jed Clampett / Cheese-balls in cowtown / Sinister minister / Flight of the cosmic hippo
CD Set 9362462472
Warner Bros. / Jul '97 / Warner Music

PLACES
CD ROUCD 11522
Rounder / '88 / ADA / CM / Direct

TABULA RASA (Fleck, Bela & V.M. Batt/ Jie-Bing Chen)
CD WLACS 44CD
Waterlilly Acoustics / Aug '96 / ADA

THREE FLEW OVER THE CUCKOOS'S NEST
Vix 9 / At last we meet again / Spunky and Clorissa / Bumbershoot / Blues for Gordon / Monkey see / Message / Interlude (return of the ancient ones) / Drift / Celtic melody / Peace, be still / Longing / For now
CD 9362453282
Warner Bros. / Jun '94 / Warner Music

Flecknor, Gregory

MONKEY BOOTS (Flecknor, Gregory Quartet)
CD CLR 419CD
Clear / Oct '95 / Prime / RTM/Disc

Fleetwood Mac

25 YEARS - SELECTIONS FROM THE CHAIN (2CD Set)
Paper doll / Love shines / Love in store / Goodbye angel / Heart of stone / Silver springs / Oh Diane / Big love / Rhiannon / Crystal / Chain / Over my head / Dreams / Go your own way / Sara / Hold me / Gypsy / Make me a mask / Don't stop / Everywhere / Tusk / Not that funny / Beautiful child / Teen beat / Need your love so bad / Did you ever love me / Oh well, part 1 / I believe my time ain't long / Bermuda triangle / Why / Station man / Albatross / Black magic woman / Stop messin' around / Trinity / Heroes are hard to find / Green manalishi
CD 9362451882
WEA / Feb '93 / Warner Music

25 YEARS - THE CHAIN (4CD Set)
Paper doll / Love shines / Stand back / Crystal / Isn't it midnight / Big love / Everywhere / Affairs of the heart / Heart of stone / Sara / That's all for everyone / Over my head / Little lies / Eyes of the world / Oh Diane / In the back of my mind / Make me a mask / Save me / Goodbye angel / Silver springs / What makes you think you're the one / Think about me / Gypsy / You make loving fun / Second hand news / Love in store / Chain / Teen beat / Dreams / Only over you / I'm so afraid / Love is dangerous / Gold dust woman / Not that funny / Warm ways / Say you love me / Don't stop / Rhiannon / Walk a thin line / Storms / Go your own way / Sisters of the moon / Monday morning / Landslide / Hypnotised / Lay it all down / Angel / Beautiful child / Brown eyes / Save me a place / Tusk / Never go back again / Songbird / I believe my time ain't long / Need your love so bad / Rattlesnake shake / Oh well, part 1 / Stop messin' around / Green manalishi / Albatross / Man of the world / Love that burns / Black magic woman / Watch out / String-a-long / Station man / Did you ever love me / Sentimental lady / Come a little bit closer / Heroes are hard to find / Trinity / Why
CD Set 9362451292
WEA / Feb '93 / Warner Music

ALBATROSS (Fleetwood Mac & Christine Perfect)
Albatross / Rambling pony / I believe my time ain't long / Dr. Brown / Stop messin' around / Love that burns / Jigsaw puzzle blues / Need your love tonight / I'd rather go blind / Crazy about you baby / And that's saying a lot / I'm on my way / No road is the right road / Let me go (leave me alone) / I'm too far gone (to turn around) / When you say
CD CD 31569
Columbia / Feb '91 / Sony

BEHIND THE MASK
Skies the limit / Love is dangerous / In the back of my mind / Do you know / Save me / Affairs of the heart / When the sun goes down / Behind the mask / Stand on the rock / Hard feelings / Freedom / When it comes to love / Second time
CD 7599261112
WEA / Feb '95 / Warner Music

BEST OF FLEETWOOD MAC, THE
Albatross / Black magic woman / Doctor Brown / Long grey mare / Love that burns / Merry go round / My baby's good to me / No place to go / Ramblin' pony / World keep on turning / Watch out
CD 4837242
Columbia / Feb '96 / Sony

BLUES COLLECTION, THE
CD CCSCD 216
Castle / Apr '89 / BMG

BLUES YEARS, THE
CD MATCD 266
Castle / May '94 / BMG

BLUES YEARS, THE
CD PLSCD 198
Pulse / Apr '97 / BMG

BOSTON LIVE
Oh well / Like it this way / World in harmony / Only you / Black magic woman / Jumping at shadows / Can't hold on
CD CLACD 152
Castle / Oct '89 / BMG

CLASSIC MAC (Plays Fleetwood Mac Classics) (London Rock Orchestra)
Oh well (Part one) / Black magic woman / Future games / Green manalishi / Dragon fly / Need your love so bad / Tusk / Albatross / Jigsaw puzzle blues / Sentimental lady / Man of the world / Oh well (Part two) / Hypnotised / Don't stop
CD DCD 5368
Disky / Apr '94 / Disky / THE

DANCE, THE
Chain / Dreams / Everywhere / Rhiannon / I'm so afraid / Temporary one / Bleed to love her / Big love / Landslide / Say you love me / My little demon / Silver springs / You make loving fun / Sweet girl / Go your own way / Tusk / Don't stop
CD 9362467022
Warner Bros. / Aug '97 / Warner Music

FLEETWOOD MAC
Monday morning / Warm always / Blue letter / Rhiannon / Over my head / Crystal / Say you love me / Landslide / I'm so afraid / World turning / Sugar daddy
CD 254043
WEA / Dec '85 / Warner Music

FLEETWOOD MAC
My heart beats like a hammer / Merry go round / Long grey mare / Hellhound on my trail / Shake your moneymaker / Looking for somebody / No place to go / My baby's good to me / I loved another woman / Cold black night / World keeps on turning / Got to move
CD 4773582
Columbia / Aug '94 / Sony

FLEETWOOD MAC
Man of the world / Got to move / Bleeding heart / Buzz me / I held my baby last night / My baby's a good 'un / How blue can you get / My baby's sweet / World keeps on turning / Dream / Don't know which way to go
CD EXP 015
Experience / May '97 / TKO Magnum

FLEETWOOD MAC FAMILY ALBUM, THE (Various Artists)
Respectable: *Cheynes* / If you wanna be happy: *Peter B's Looners* / Double trouble: *Mayall, John & The Bluesbreakers* / I'd rather go blind: *Chicken Shack* / Shape I'm in: *Spencer, Jeremy* / When you say: *Perfect, Christine* / Ram Jam city: *Kirwan, Danny* / Put a record on: *Tramp* / Sentimental lady: *Welch, Bob* / Stop draggin' my heart around: *Nicks, Stevie & Tom Petty & The Heartbreakers* / Rattlesnake shake: *Fleetwood, Mick* / Now I know: *McVie, John* / Don't say no: *Burnette, Billy* / We just disagree: *Mason, Dave* / Fleetwood Mac: *Fleetwood Mac*
CD VSOPCD 222
Connoisseur Collection / Feb '96 / Pinnacle

FLEETWOOD MAC LIVE
CD SSLCD 207
Savanna / Jun '95 / THE

FLEETWOOD MAC/PIOUS BIRD OF GOOD OMEN/MR. WONDERFUL (3CD Set)
My heart beats like a hammer / Merry go round / Long grey mare / Hellbound on my trail / Shake your moneymaker / Looking for somebody / No place to go / My baby's good to me / I loved another woman / Cold black night / World keeps on turning / Got to move / Need your love so bad / Coming home / Rambling pony / Big boat: *Fleetwood Mac & Eddie Boyd* / I believe my time ain't long / Sun is shining / Albatross / Black magic woman / Just the blues: *Fleetwood Mac & Eddie Boyd* / Jigsaw puzzle blues / Looking for somebody / Stop messin' round / Stop messin' round / I've lost my baby / Rollin' man / Dust my broom / Love that burns / Doctor Brown / Need your love tonight / If you be my baby / Evenin' boogie / Lazy poker blues / Comin' home / Tryin' so hard to forget
CD Set 4853162
Columbia / Oct '96 / Sony

GREATEST HITS
Green Manalishi / Oh well / Shake your moneymaker / Need your love so bad / Rattlesnake shake / Dragonfly / Black magic woman / Albatross / Man of the world / Stop messin' around / Love that burns
CD 4607042
CBS / Apr '89 / Sony

GREATEST HITS
As long as you follow / No questions asked / Rhiannon / Don't stop / Go your own way / Hold me / Everywhere / Gypsy / Say you love me / Dreams / Little lies / Sara / Tusk / Oh Diane / Big love / You make loving fun / Seven wonders
CD 9258382
WEA / Nov '88 / Warner Music

LIVE AT THE BBC (2CD Set)
CD Set EDFCD 297
Essential / Sep '95 / BMG

LONDON LIVE '68
Got to move / I held my baby last night / My baby's sweet / My baby's a good un / Don't know which way to go / Buzz me / Dream / World keeps turning / How blue can you get / Bleeding heart
CD CDTB 11038
Thunderbolt / Mar '95 / TKO Magnum

MADISON BLUES LIVE
CD MACCD 187
Autograph / Aug '96 / BMG

MIRAGE
Love in store / Can't go back / That's alright / Book of love / Gypsy / Only over you / Empire State / Straight back / Hold me / Oh Diane / Eyes of the world / Wish you were here
CD K 256952
WEA / '89 / Warner Music

MISTER WONDERFUL
Stop messin' round / Coming home / Rollin' man / Dust my broom / Love that burns / Dr. Brown / Need your love tonight / If you be my baby / Evenin' boogie / Lazy poker blues / I've lost my baby / Trying so hard to forget
CD 4746122
Columbia / Mar '96 / Sony

ORCHESTRAL FLEETWOOD MAC (London Rock Orchestra)
Oh well (part one) / Black magic woman / Future games / Greem manalishi / Dragonfly / Need your love so bad / Tusk / Albatross / Jigsaw puzzle blues / Sentimental lady / Man of the world / Oh well (part two) / Hypnotised / Don't stop
CD EMPRCD 546
Emporio / Nov '94 / Disc

PIOUS BIRD OF GOOD OMEN, THE
Need your love so bad / Coming home / Rambling pony / Big boat / I believe my time ain't long / Sun is shining / Albatross / Black magic woman / Just the blues / Jigsaw puzzle blues / Looking for somebody / Stop messin' around
CD 4805242
Columbia / May '95 / Sony

RUMOURS
Second hand news / Dreams / Never going back again / Don't stop / Go your own way / Songbird / Chain / You make loving fun / I don't want to know / Oh daddy / Gold dust woman
CD 256344
WEA / Dec '83 / Warner Music

TANGO IN THE NIGHT
Big love / Seven wonders / Everywhere / Caroline / Tango in the night / Mystified / Little lies / Family man / Welcome to the room...Sara / Isn't it midnight / When I see you again / You and I (part 2)
CD 9254712
WEA / Apr '87 / Warner Music

THEN PLAY ON
Coming your way / Closing my eyes / Fighting for Madge / When you say / Showbiz blues / Underway / One sunny day / Although the sun is shining / Rattlesnake shake / Without you / Searching for Madge / My dream / Like crying / Before the beginning
CD 9274482
WEA / '88 / Warner Music

TIME
CD 9362459202
WEA / Oct '95 / Warner Music

TUSK
Over and over / Ledge / Think about me / Save me a place / Sara / What makes you think you're the one / Storms / That's all for everyone / Not that funny / Sisters of the moon / Angel / That's enough for me / Brown eyes / Never make me cry / I know I'm not wrong / Honey hi / Beautiful child / Walk a thin line / Tusk / Never forget
CD K2 66088
WEA / Mar '87 / Warner Music

Fleming & John

DELUSIONS OF GRANDEUR
CD REX 460122
Rex / Nov '95 / Cadillac

Flesh & Blood

BLUES FOR DAZE
CD NTHEN 037CD
Now & Then / May '97 / Plastic Head

Flesh Eaters

DRAGSTRIP RIOT
CD SST 273CD
SST / May '93 / Plastic Head

PREHISTORIC FITS
CD SST 264CD
SST / May '93 / Plastic Head

SEX DIARY OF MR. VAMPIRE
CD SST 292CD
SST / May '93 / Plastic Head

Flesh For Lulu

LONG LIVE THE NEW FLESH
Lucky day / Postcards from paradise / Hammer of love / Siamese twist / Sooner or later / Good for you / Crash / Way to go / Sleeping dogs / Dream on cowboy
CD BBL 82CD
Beggars Banquet / Feb '90 / RTM/Disc / Warner Music

PLASTIC FANTASTIC
Decline and fall / House of cards / Time and space / Every little word / Slowdown / Highwire / Slide / Day one / Choosing you / Stupid on the street / Avenue / Plastic fantastic
CD BEGA 100CD
Beggars Banquet / '88 / RTM/Disc / Warner Music

Flesh 'n' Bone

THUGS
CD 5335392
Mo Thugs/Def Jam / Dec '96 / PolyGram

Fleshcrawl

DESCEND INTO THE ABSURD
Between the shadows they crawl / Phrenetic Tendencies / Perpetual dawn / Purulent bowel erosion / Lost in a grave / Never to die again / Festering flesh / Infected subconscious / Evoke the excess
CD BMCD 027
Black Mark / Oct '92 / Plastic Head

IMPURITY
CD BMCD 48
Black Mark / Mar '94 / Plastic Head

Fleshold

PATHETIC
CD ______ MASSCD 049
Massacre / May '95 / Plastic Head

Fleshrevels

STONED AND OUT
CD ______ FINNREC 009CD
Finn / Jun '96 / Cadillac / Plastic Head

Fleshtones

BEAUTIFUL LIGHT
CD ______ NAK 61162
Naked Language / Jan '94 / Koch

BLAST OFF
CD ______ RE 107CD
ROIR / Jul '97 / Plastic Head / Shellshock/ Disc

FLESHTONES
BYOB / Critical list / Shadowline / American beat / Cara - Lin / Watch Junior go / Atom spies / Way I feel / Comin' in dead stick / Judy / Soul struttin' / Rockin' this joint / Rocket USA
CD ______ ESMCD 573
Essential / Jul '97 / BMG

LABORATORY OF SOUND
Let's go / High on drugs / Sands of our lives / Nostradamus Jr / Sweetest thing / Hold you / Accelerated emotion / Train of thought / One step less / Motor needs gas / Psychedelic swamp / Fading away / We'll never forget
CD ______ 118542
Musidisc UK / Oct '95 / Grapevine/ PolyGram

POWERSTANCE
Armed and dangerous / I'm still thirsty / Waiting for a message / Let it rip / Three fevers / Living legends / I can breathe / Mod teepee / House of rock / Irresistible / Candy ass
CD ______ NAK 6101
Naked Language / Jan '94 / Koch

Fleshy Ranks

BUSTIN' OUT
CD ______ HBCD 163
Heartbeat / Oct '94 / ADA / Direct / Greensleeves / Jet Star

Fletcher, Liz

MELLOW MANIA
Come in out of the rain / My foolish heart / Occasional man / Sunshine / Wild child / Scotch mist / Serenade in blue / Stormy weather / You stepped out of a dream / Lullaby / Since you asked me / Green / Softly as in a morning sunrise / If you ever loved (the meaning of the blues)
CD ______ BBJ 1001
Black Box Music / Sep '97 / ADA / Direct

Fleurety

MIN TID SKAL KOMME
CD ______ AMAZON 005CD
Misanthropy / Jul '95 / Plastic Head

Fleurine

MEANT TO BE
Lazay and satisfied / My souldance with you / Favourite love affair / Velejar / Meant to be / My hearts escapade / I've got just about everything / When I think of one / Escolher / It's all in the mind / Call me now / One dream gone / High in the sky
CD ______ BM 1001
Blue Music / Feb '97 / New Note/Pinnacle

Flex

STEPPIN' OUT
CD ______ OMCD 11
One Movement / Jul '96 / Timewarp

Flibbertigibbet

WHISTLING JIGS TO THE MOON
CD ______ KSCD 9510
Kissing Spell / Jun '97 / Greyhound

Flies Inside The Sun

AN AUDIENCE OF OTHERS (INCLUDING HERSELF)
CD ______ KRANK 008CD
Kranky / Mar '97 / Cargo / Greyhound

FLIES INSIDE THE SUN
CD ______ MET OO2
Metonymic / Dec '96 / Cargo

Flight Recorder

PINKERTON'S COLOURS/FLYING MACHINE (2CD Set)
Smile a little smile for me / Send my baby home again / Marie take a chance / Waiting on the shores of nowhere / Maybe we've been loving too long / There she goes / That same old feeling / Baby make it soon / Broken hearted me, evil hearted you / Thing called love / My baby's coming home / Memories of Melinda / Devil has posession of your mind / Hey little girl / Pages of your life / Yes I understand / Hanging on the edge of sadness / Flying machine / Mirror mirror / Don't stop loving me baby / Magic rocking horse / Mum and Dad / On a street car / Duke's jetty / There's nobody I'd sooner love / Kentucky woman / Behind the mirror / Look at me, look at me / People say / One man band / Lies in your eyes / Me without you / Can't break the habit / Shadows on a foggy day / If you were true / Shine a little light / St. Louis child / 4 o'clock in New York / Hard, hard year / Strawberry fool / Angel (she was born out of love)
CD Set ______ NEDCD 290
Sequel / Jul '97 / BMG

Flint, Tim

FLINTASIA
CD ______ CDGRS 1279
Grosvenor / Aug '95 / Grosvenor

SHOW TUNES - AND THEN SOME
Overture / All I need is the girl / We kiss in a shadow / I have dreamed fugue for tin horns / Anything goes / On the street where you live / This can't be love / I've never been in love before / They say that falling in love is wonderful / Once in love with Amy / Give my regards to Broadway / Bandology / La Calinda / Love walked in/Forgotten dreams / Autumn concerto / April in Paris / Thunder and lightning polka / Tritsch tratsch polka / 9.20 Special
CD ______ CDGRS 1264
Grosvenor / Sep '93 / Grosvenor

TOO MARVELLOUS FOR WORDS
Moment of truth / Where are you / Too marvellous for words / Sweet Lorraine / Shiny stockings / Somewhere along the way / Bahn frei / Rock revolution / Disney selection / When you wish upon a star / Heigh ho / Whistle while you work / Party gras / Jolly holiday / With a smile and a song / So this is love / Unbirthday song / It's a small world / Pomp and circumstance No.1
CD ______ KGRS 1242
Grosvenor / '91 / Grosvenor

Flip Flap

MORNING TRACKS VOL.1
Dawn / 4th insight: *Suger Plant & Flip Flap* / Spiritual healing: *Muses Rapt* / White light into you: *Suger Plant* / Express way to your mind: *Fractal Express* / ISP (Indian Summer Project): *Okino, Shuntaro* / Party continues: *Fractal Express* / Phenix: *Okino, Shuntaro* / Niji - morning track
CD ______ KSC 2187
Ki-Oon / Jul '97 / Sony

Flippen, Benton

OLD TIMES, NEW TIMES
CD ______ ROUCD 0326
Rounder / Oct '94 / ADA / CM / Direct

Flipper

AMERICAN GRAFISHY
CD ______ DABCD 1
Beggars Banquet/Def America / May '93 / Pinnacle

BLOW'N CHUNKS
CD ______ RE 126CD
ROIR / Nov '94 / Plastic Head / Shellshock/Disc

GENERIC FLIPPER
CD ______ DABCD 3
Beggars Banquet / Jun '93 / RTM/Disc / Warner Music

LIVE AT CBGB'S 1983
CD ______ OVER 63CD
Overground / Jul '97 / Shellshock/Disc / SRD

SEX BOMB BABY
Sex bomb / Love canal / Ha ha ha / Sacrifice / Falling / Ever get away / Earthworm / Games' got a price / Old lady who swallowed a fly / Brainwash / Lowrider / End the game
CD ______ 74321298982
Infinite Zero / Oct '95 / BMG

Flitcroft, Iain

GRANADALAND WURLITZER
Wurlitzer march / Reilly, ace of spies / Rose medley / Cavaquinho / Waltz medley / Tango Havana / Musetta's waltz song / White Horse Inn / Granada television medley / Masterpiece / Quickstep / City of Chester / Vija / Ballet Egyptien / Paris medley / Samba incognito / Medley / Buffoon / Granada connection
CD ______ OS 213
Bandleader / Aug '95 / Conifer/BMG

Floating Jazz Festival Trio

FLOATING JAZZ FESTIVAL TRIO, THE
CD ______ CRD 340
Chiaroscuro / May '97 / Jazz Music

Flock

FLOCK
Clown / I am the tall tree / Tired of waiting / Store brought / Store thought / Truth
CD ______ 4694432
Epic / Feb '95 / Sony

Flock Of Seagulls

20 CLASSICS OF THE 80'S
Tokyo / Who's that girl she's got it / DNA / How could you ever leave me / ELectrics / Remember David / Messages / Don't ask me / Traveller / Rosenmontag / 2.30 / Better and better / Euorpean I wish I was / Say so much / Telecommunication / End / Space age love song / It's not me talking / Over my head / Love on your knees
CD ______ EMPRCD 562
Emporio / Mar '95 / Disc

BEST OF A FLOCK OF SEAGULLS, THE
I ran / Space age love song / Telecommunication / More you live, the more you love / Nightmares / Wishing (if I had a photograph of you) / It's not me talking / Transfer affection / Who's that girl / DNA I ran
CD ______ CHIP 41
Jive / Jun '91 / Pinnacle

BEST OF A FLOCK OF SEAGULLS, THE
CD ______ MCCD 114
Music Club / Jun '93 / Disc / THE

BEST OF A FLOCK OF SEAGULLS, THE
I ran / Space age love song / Telecommunication / More you live, the more you love / Nightmares / Wishing (if I had a photograph of you) / (It's not me) talking / Transfer affection / Who's that girl (she's got it) / DNA / Wishing (if I had a photograph of you) / More you live, the more you love
CD ______ QED 082
Tring / Nov '96 / Tring

Floodgate

PENALTY
CD ______ RR 88902
Roadrunner / Oct '96 / PolyGram

Flook

LIVE
Branohm/Trip to Herve's / Knocknamoe jig/ Custy's/Trip to Brittany / Jizique / Brian's reel/Peter's epic journey / In another life / Blackberry blossom/The independence / History man / Dub reel
CD ______ SMALLCD 9405
Smallworld / Feb '97 / ADA / Cadillac / Direct / Total/BMG

Floors

SUPERBE
CD ______ DE 010
Dead Elvis / Nov '96 / RTM/Disc

Floppy Sounds

DOWNTIME
Actual footage / Durexx / Daisy / Since I split / Superhype / Ultrasong / Oblivion / Excursions / Deliverance / Sprawl / Weird
CD ______ SLIPCD 040
Slip 'n' Slide / Feb '96 / Amato Disco / Prime / RTM/Disc / Vital

Florence

OCCURRENCES
Dream the dream / Departure / Transit / Arrival / Jump shock / Undiscovered / Instantaneous drive / Second hand culture / Collapse of commerce / Coincidental harmony
CD ______ ELEC 32CD
New Electronica / Apr '97 / Beechwood/ BMG / Plastic Head

Florence, Bob

BOB FLORENCE & HIS BIG BAND (Florence, Bob Big Band)
Party harty / Trinity fair / BBC / Jewels / Willowcrest / Invitation / Forgetful / Samba de rollins / Collage
CD ______ HEPCD 2064
Hep / Jun '95 / Cadillac / Jazz Music / New Note/Pinnacle / Wellard

SOARING (Florence, Bob Limited Edition)
CD ______ SB 2082
Sea Breeze / Jan '97 / Jazz Music

STATE OF THE ART (Florence, Bob Limited Edition)
Just friends / Moonlight serenade / Silky / Crunch / Stella by starlight / All the things you are / Mr. Paddington / BBC / Auld lang syne
CD ______ CDPC 797
Prestige / Oct '90 / Else / Total/BMG

Flores, Caledonio E.

HOMENAJE A LOS POETAS DEL TANGO
CD ______ EBCD 73
El Bandoneon / Jul '96 / Discovery

Flores, Lola

OLE
CD ______ SCCD 995
Seeco / Mar '96 / Discovery

Flores, Pedro

1938-1942
CD ______ HQCD 49
Harlequin / May '95 / Hot Shot / Jazz Music / Swift / Wellard

PEDRO FLORES 1935-1938
CD ______ HQCD 72
Harlequin / Jun '96 / Hot Shot / Jazz Music / Swift / Wellard

Flores, Rosie

AFTER THE FARM
CD ______ HACD 8033
Hightone / Jul '94 / ADA / Koch

HONKY TONK REPRISE, A
CD ______ ROUCD 3136
Rounder / Jun '96 / ADA / CM / Direct

LITTLE BIT OF HEARTACHE, A (Flores, Rosie & Ray Campi)
This song is just for you / Seperate ways / Where honky tonk angels spread there wings / Train kept a rollin' / All I have to do is dream / I'm gonna wear the pants / Bandera highway / There ain't a cow in Texas / Little bit of heartache / Eighteen wheels / If teardrops were pennies / Joe and old merle / My baby's doin' alright / Living on love / Crazy / Let's say goodbye
CD ______ WMCD 1059
Watermelon / May '97 / ADA / Direct

ONCE MORE WITH FEELING
CD ______ HCD 8047
Hightone / Jun '94 / ADA / Koch

ROCKABILLY FILLY
CD ______ HITCD 8067
Hightone / Oct '95 / ADA / Koch

Florida

BRASS ROOTS
CD ______ FLP 003CD
Florida / Nov '95 / ADA

Flory, Chris

CITY LIFE
Alexandria, VA / Besame mucho / s'posin' / Tin tin por tin tin / Good morning heartache / JA Blues / My shining hour / So danco samba / Drafting / Come back to me / New York / Penthouse serenade / Cafe solo
CD ______ CCD 4589
Concord Jazz / Feb '94 / New Note/ Pinnacle

FOR ALL WE KNOW
Soft winds / T'ain't me / Avalon / Tenderly / Close your eyes / Lee's blues / It had to be you / For all we know / Airmail special / Ninth Avenue shuffle / Lullaby of the leaves
CD ______ CCD 4403
Concord Jazz / Jan '90 / New Note/ Pinnacle

WORD ON THE STREET
When I grow old to dream / Snibor / Comes love / Crazy he calls me / Going to meeting / Taps Miller / I'm a fool to want you / You don't know me at all / Don't you know I care / Touch of your lips
CD ______ DTRCD 119
Double Time / Nov '96 / Express Jazz

Flotsam & Jetsam

DOOMSDAY FOR THE DECEIVER
CD ______ 398414077 CD
Metal Blade / Mar '96 / Pinnacle / Plastic Head

HIGH
CD ______ 398414126CD
Metal Blade / Jun '97 / Pinnacle / Plastic Head

Flotsam & Jetsam

FLOTSAM AND JETSAM
Introduction / King Canute / Mrs. Peer Gynt / PC Lamb / Maude-Marie / Optimist and pessimist / Polonaise in the Mall / Melodrama of the mice / Only a few of us left / Businessman's love song / Simon the bootlegger / Song of the air / Move into my house / Little Betty Bouncer / Weather reports / We never know what to expect / Schubert's toy shop / Village blacksmith / Alsation and the pekinese / Modern diver / Little Joan / What was the matter with Rachmaninov / British pantomime / Ghost of old king's jester / High-brow sailor / When I grow old, dad / Postscript
CD ______ PASTCD 9723
Flapper / '90 / Pinnacle

FLOTSAM AND JETSAM VOL.2
CD ______ PASTCD 9749
Flapper / Jul '91 / Pinnacle

Flour

FOURTH AND FINAL
CD ______ TG 125CD
Touch & Go / Apr '94 / SRD

Flouride, Klaus

BECAUSE I SAY SO
CD _____ VIRUS 67CD
Alternative Tentacles / Jul '89 / Cargo / Greyhound / Pinnacle

LIGHT IS FLICKERING, THE
CD _____ VIRUS 95CD
Alternative Tentacles / '92 / Cargo / Greyhound / Pinnacle

Flowchart

IN THE SPIRIT OF KENNY G
CD _____ BBPTC 60CD
Black Bean & Placenta Tape Club / Jun '97 / Cargo

Flower

HOLOGRAM SKY
CD _____ SR 330491CD
Semaphore / Jul '91 / Plastic Head

Flowered Up

LIFE WITH BRIAN, A
Sunshine / Take it / Mr. Happy reveller / Hysterically blue / It's on / Silver plan / Phobia / Egg rush / Doris... is a little bit partial / Crackerjack
CD _____ 8282442
London / Jun '92 / PolyGram

Flowerpot Men

LET'S GO TO SAN FRANCISCO
Let's go to San Francisco / Walk in the sky / Am I losing you / You can never be wrong / Man without a woman / In a moment of madness / Young birds fly / Journey's end / Mythological Sunday / Blow away / Piccolo man / Silicon City
CD _____ C5CD 526
See For Miles/C5 / Mar '97 / Pinnacle

VERY BEST OF THE FLOWERPOT MEN, THE
Let's go to San Francisco / Walk in the sky / Am I losing you / Man without a woman / You can never be wrong / Piccolo man / Mythological Sunday / Sweet baby Jane / Journey's end / Let's go to San Francisco / Silicon city / Busy doin' nothing / White dove / Cooks of cake kindness / Gotta be free / Heaven knows when / Brave new world / Children of tomorrow / Let's go to San Francisco
CD _____ SUMCD 4111
Sound & Media / Mar '97 / Sound & Media

Flowers, Mike

GROOVY PLACE, A (Flowers, Mike Pops Orchestra)
Groovy place / Wonderwall / In crowd / Light my fire / Please release me / Venus as a boy / Crusty girl / Velvet Underground medley / Freebase / 1999
CD _____ 8287432
London / Aug '96 / PolyGram

Floyd, Eddie

CALIFORNIA GIRL/DOWN TO EARTH
California girl / Didn't I blow your mind this time / Why is the wine sweeter (on the other side) / Rainy night in Georgia / Love is you / People, get it together / Laurie / Hey there lonely girl / I feel good / Too much is too little for me / You got that kind of love / People get ready / Linda Sue Dixon / My mind was messed around at the time / When the sun goes down / Salvation / I only have eyes for you / Tears of joy / Changing love
CD _____ CDSXD 087
Stax / Jul '95 / Pinnacle

I'VE NEVER FOUND A GIRL
Bring it on home to me / Never gonna give you up / Girl I love you / Hobo / I need you woman / I've never found a girl / I'll take her / Slip away / I'm just the kind of fool / Water / Sweet things you do
CD _____ CDSXE 059
Stax / Jul '92 / Pinnacle

KNOCK ON WOOD
Knock on wood / Something you got / But it's alright / I stand accused / If you gotta make a fool of somebody / I don't want to cry / Raise your hand / Got to make a comeback / 634 5789 / I've just been feeling bad / Hi-heel sneakers / Warm and tender love
CD _____ 7567802832
Atlantic / Oct '94 / Warner Music

KNOCK ON WOOD (The Best Of Eddie Floyd)
Knock on wood / Raise your hand / Big bird / On a Saturday night / Things get better / Love is a doggone good thing / I've never found a girl / Consider me / Bring it on home to me / I've got to have your love / Blood is thicker than water / Baby, lay your head down / Too weak to fight / Oh how it rained / Why is the wine sweeter (on the other side) / Soul Street / Don't tell your mama / Girl, I love you / People, get it together / Something to write home about / Check me out / Stealing love
CD _____ CDSX 010
Stax / Mar '88 / Pinnacle

KNOCK ON WOOD (The Best Of Eddie Floyd)
California girl / Knock on wood / Bring it on home to me / Mr. Blue / When I'm with you / On a Saturday night / Got to make a comeback / I've never found a girl / I've got a reason to smile / Raise your hand
CD _____ AIM 2009CD
Aim / May '97 / ADA / Direct / Jazz Music

RARE STAMPS/I'VE NEVER FOUND A GIRL
Bring it on home to me / Never give you up / Girl I love you / Hobo / I need you woman / I've never found a girl / I'll take her / Slip away / I'm just the kind of fool / Water / Sweet things you do / Knock on wood / Raise your hand / Love's a doggone good thing / On a Saturday night / Thing's get better / Big bird / Got to make a comeback / I've just been feeling bad / This house / I've got to have your love / Consider me / Never let you go / Ain't that good / Laurie
CD _____ CDSXD 096
Stax / Jul '93 / Pinnacle

Floyd, Frank

GREAT MEDICAL MENAGERIST, THE (Floyd, 'Harmonica' Frank)
Mosquito bar britches / Blue yodel No.6 / Swanproot / Tour De Floyd / Great medical menagerist / Sweet temptation / Howlin' tomcat / Shampoo / Blue yodel No.7 / Steppin' to Covington / Movement like Elgin / Knothole blues
CD _____ EDCD 384
Edsel / Apr '97 / Pinnacle

Floyd, Gary

BROKEN ANGELS
CD _____ GRCD 367
Glitterhouse / Jun '97 / Avid/BMG

WORLD OF TROUBLE
CD _____ GRCD 316
Glitterhouse / Sep '94 / Avid/BMG

Floyd, Ruth Naomi

PARADIGMS FOR DESOLATE TIMES
CD _____ BLJCD 2
Big Life Jazz / Aug '96 / Pinnacle

Flu Thirteen

SPIN CYCLE
CD _____ ITU 001613
Interplanetary / Feb '97 / Cargo

Flue

SOMETIMES
CD _____ TORSO 12031
Torso / May '87 / SRD

Fluf

WAIKIKI
CD _____ HED 070CD
Headhunter / Jun '97 / Cargo

Fluffy

BLACK EYE
Nothing / Hypersonic / Black eye / Scream / I wanna be your lush / Crossdresser / Psychofudge / Too famous / Technicolour yawn / Cosmetic dog / Crawl / Husband / Dirty old bird / Cheap
CD _____ CDV 2817
Virgin / Oct '96 / EMI

Flugschadel

FLUGSCHADEL
CD _____ EFA 800232
Platten Meister / Mar '94 / SRD

OTHNIEL
CD _____ EFA 800312
Platten Meister / Apr '95 / SRD

Fluke

OTO
Bullet / Tosh / Cut / Freak / Wobbler / Squirt / OK / Setback
CD _____ CIRCD 31
Circa / Jul '95 / EMI

SIX WHEELS ON MY WAGON
Groovy feeling / Love letters / Glidub / Electric guitar / Top of the world / Slid / Slow motion / Spacey (catch 22 dub) / Astrosapiens / Oh yeah / Eko / Life support / Philly / Glorious / Cool hand flute / Joni / Easy peasy / Phin / Jig / Taxi / Coolest
CD _____ CIRCD 27
Circa / Oct '93 / EMI

Flush

LOCUST FUDGE
CD _____ GRCD 280
Glitterhouse / Aug '93 / Avid/BMG

Flux

PROTOPLASMIC
Patterns of traffic / Hollow spaces / Unknown codes / Light fuse / Protoplasmic / Stretched out / Airtrap / Immanence
CD _____ RR 69582
Relapse / Jul '97 / Pinnacle / Plastic Head

USCHI'S HOUSE
CD _____ MA 010
M / Jun '97 / Timewarp

Flux Of Pink Indians

FUCKING CUNTS TREAT US LIKE PRICKS
CD _____ TPCD 3
One Little Indian / Jun '88 / Pinnacle

NOT SO BRAVE
CD _____ OVER 67CD
Overground / Jul '97 / Shellshock/Disc / SRD

UNCARVED BLOCK
CD _____ TPCD 1
One Little Indian / Jun '88 / Pinnacle

Fly Ashtray

CLUMPS TAKES A RIDE
Second song / Soft pack / L'age-nt-snopee / Dolphin brain / Sink / Man who stayed in ed all day / Ssssss / Do what you can / Best boy / Hypoblast / Ignells 2 / Crows / It doesn't matter / Hoafie hoafie / Ostrich atmosphere / Bad head park (Theme from) / Anyway / Head park rev / Non-ignells
CD _____ WORD 0042
See Eye / Aug '92 / Vital

Fly Right Trio

WILD ABOUT
CD _____ TBCD 2008
Nervous / Mar '93 / Nervous / TKO Magnum

Flying Bulgar Klezmer Band

AGADA - TALES FROM OUR ANCESTORS
CD _____ DIS 80120
Dorian / Apr '96 / Conifer/BMG / Select

JEWISH ROOTS FOLK WORLD MUSIC
CD _____ DIS 80106
Dorian / Apr '96 / Conifer/BMG / Select

Flying Burrito Brothers

BACK TO THE SWEETHEART OF THE RODEO (Burrito Brothers)
Back to the sweethearts of the rodeo / Burning embers / Red shoes / Shoot for the moon / Moonlight rider / Carry me / Baby, won't you let me be the one / Gold guitar / True, true love / I'm impressed / Let's do something crazy / You're a fool to love / Mean streets / Like a shadow / I don't believe you met my baby / My heart skips a beat / Do you know Mary Lou / One man woman / Roadmaster / I've got a new heartache / You should know me by now / My shoes keep walkin' back to you / This could be the night / You're running wild / Should we tell him / Burn the midnight oil / Last call / Take a message to merry
CD Set _____ AP 054552
Appaloosa / Jun '95 / ADA / Direct / TKO Magnum
CD _____ CDSD 502
Sundown / Feb '96 / TKO Magnum

BURRITO DELUXE
Lazy days / Image of me / High fashion queen / If you gotta go, go now / Man in the fog / Farther along / Older guys / Cody, Cody / God's own singer / Down in the churchyard
CD _____ EDCD 194
Edsel / Jun '90 / Pinnacle

COLLECTION, THE
CD _____ CCSCD 366
Castle / Mar '93 / BMG

DIM LIGHTS, THICK SMOKE AND LOUD MUSIC
Train song / Close all the honky tonks / Sing me back home / Tonight the bottle let me down / Your angel steps out of heaven / Crazy arms / Together again / Honky tonk women / Green green grass of home / Bony Moronie / To love somebody / Break my mind / Dim lights, thick smoke
CD _____ EDCD 197
Edsel / Mar '87 / Pinnacle

DOUBLE BARREL (Burrito Brothers)
She's single again / New shade of blue / Price of love / Ain't love just like the rain / One more time / Sailor / No easy way out / Tonight / Hearts in my eyes / Ain't worth the powder / Late in the night / I'm confessing / Let your heart do the talking
CD _____ CDSD 079
Sundown / Nov '95 / TKO Magnum

ENCORE (Live 1990) (Burrito Brothers)
Dim lights, thick smoke / You ain't goin' nowhere / Hickory wind / White line fever / Sweet little Colette / Big bayou / Sweet Suzanna / Wild horses / Silverwings / Help wanted / Cannonball rag / When it all comes down to love / Wheels
CD _____ CDSD 069
Sundown / Nov '90 / TKO Magnum

EYE OF A HURRICANE
Wheel of love / Like a thief in the night / Bayou blues / Angry words / Rosetta knows / Heart highway / I sent your saddle home / Jukebox Saturday night / Arizona moon / Wild wild West / Eye of a hurricane / Sunset boulevard / Smile
CD _____ CDSD 075
Magnum Music / Nov '93 / TKO Magnum

EYE OF THE HURRICANE
CD _____ OW 30330
One Way / Jul '94 / ADA / Direct / Greyhound

FROM ANOTHER TIME
Diggi diggi li / Wheels / Dim lights, thick smoke / Faded love / Devil in disguise / Building fires / Bon soir blues / White line fever / Sin City / She thinks I still care / Why baby why / Close all the honky tonks
CD _____ CDSD 072
Sundown / Apr '91 / TKO Magnum

GILDED PALACE OF SIN, THE
Christine's tune / Sin City / Do right woman, do right man / Dark end of the street / My uncle / Wheels / Juanita / Hot burrito / Do you know how it feels to be lonesome / Hippie boy
CD _____ EDCD 191
Edsel / '88 / Pinnacle

GUILDED PALACE OF SIN/BURRITO DELUXE
Christine's tune / Sin city / Do right woman / Dark end of the street / My uncle / Wheels / Juanita / Hot Burrito / Hot burrito / Do you know how it feels / Hippie boy / Lazy days / Image of me / High fashion queen / If you gotta go / Man in the fog / Farther along / Older guys / Cody, cody / God's own singer / Down in the churchyard / Wild horses
CD _____ 5407042
A&M / Mar '97 / PolyGram

HOLLYWOOD NIGHTS 79-82
She belongs to everyone but me / Somewhere tonight / Baby, how'd we ever get this way / Too much honky tonkin' / My abandoned heart / She's a friend of mine / Louisiana / Why must the ending always be so sad / That's when you know it's over / She's a hell of a deal / Another shade of grey / Damned if I'll be lonely tonight / If something should come between us / Run to the night / Coast to coast / Closer to you / True love never runs dry / Tell me it ain't so
CD _____ CDSD 067
Sundown / May '90 / TKO Magnum

LIVE FROM TOKYO
Big bayou / White line fever / Dim lights, thick smoke / There'll be no teardrops tonight / Rollin' in my sweet baby's arms / Hot burrito / Colorado / Rocky top / Six days on the road / Truck drivin' man
CD _____ CDSD 025
Sundown / '86 / TKO Magnum

OUT OF THE BLUE (2CD Set)
Sing me back home / Hot burrito no.2 / Break my mind / Dark end of the street / Cody, Cody / Wheels / Hot burrito no.1 / Sin city / Do right woman / God's own singer / Older guys / Train song / Lazy days / Christine's tune / Close up the honky tonks / Do you know how it feels / High fashion queen / Man in the fog / To love somebody / My uncle / Hippie boy / Juanita / Image of me / Farther along / If you gotta go / Bony Moronie / Six days on the road / Wild horses / Down in the churchyard / Wake up little Susie / Pick me up on your way down / Just because / Lodi / Money honey / I shall be released / White line fever / Ain't that a lot of love / Don't fight it / Losing game / Tried so hard / All alone / 100 years from now
CD Set _____ 5404082
A&M / Apr '96 / PolyGram

TOO MUCH HONKY TONKIN'
She belongs to everyone but me / She's a friend of a friend / If somtehing should become between us / Closer to you / Somewhere tonight / Baby how'd we ever get this way / Too much honky tonkin' / Midnight magic woman / My abandoned heart / Louisiana / Cheating king of love / Why must the ending always be so sad / That's when you know it's over / You / I swear I son't miss her anymore / She's a hell of a deal / Damned if I'll be lonely tonight / When you're gicing yourself to a stranger / Run to the night / Coast to coast / True love never runs dry / Another shade of gray / Tell me it ain't so
CD _____ CTS 55439
Country Stars / May '96 / Target/BMG

WHEELS (A Tribute To Clarence White & Gram Parsons) (Burrito Brothers & Co.)
Six white horses / Emmy / Bugler / Promised land / Freeborn man / Games people play / Detroit city / 500 miles away from home / Four strong winds / Shame on me / Streets of Baltimore / Millers cave / Christine's tune / Wheels
CD _____ APCD 049
Appaloosa / '88 / ADA / Direct / TKO Magnum

Flying Luttenbachers

REVENGE
CD ______ **GR 37CD**
Skingraft / Sep '96 / SRD

Flying Medallions

WE LOVE EVERYBODY
CD ______ **JIZCD 1**
Big Life / Sep '94 / Mo's Music Machine / Pinnacle / Prime

Flying Neutrinos

I'D RATHER BE IN NEW ORLEANS
CD ______ **FIXCD 29**
Fiction / Jan '97 / PolyGram

Flying Nun

PILOT
Submarine / Frank / Shades / Carousel of freaks / Life on the ground
CD ______ **OLE 1512**
Matador / Sep '95 / Vital

Flying Pickets

LOST BOYS
Remember this / I heard it through the grapevine / Disco down / So close / Tears of a clown / When you're young and in love / You've lost that lovin' feelin' / Psycho killer / Wide boy / Factory / Monica engineer / Only you / Masters of war / Who's that girl
CD ______ **MTD 021**
Moving Target / Dec '93 / CM

ONLY YOU - THE BEST OF THE FLYING PICKETS
Only you / I heard it through the grapevine / Tears of a clown / You've lost that lovin' feelin' / Sealed with a kiss / Only the lonely / Space oddity / Who's that girl / When you're young and in love / Groovin' / Coral island / Buffalo soldier / I got you babe / Summer in the city / Get off my cloud / Higher and higher
CD ______ **CDVIP 115**
Virgin VIP / Mar '94 / EMI

Flying Saucer Attack

CHORUS
Feedback song / Light in the evening / Popul vuh ill / Always / Feedback song demo / Second hour / Beach red lullaby / There, but not there / February 8th / There dub
CD ______ **WIGCD 22**
Domino / Nov '95 / Vital

DISTANCE
CD ______ **WIGCD 12**
Domino / Oct '94 / Vital

FLYING SAUCER ATTACK
CD ______ **VHF 11**
VHF / Dec '96 / Cargo

FURTHER
CD ______ **WIGCD 20**
Domino / Apr '95 / Vital

Flyscreen

COUNCIL POP
CD ______ **WOWCD 42**
Words Of Warning / May '95 / SRD / Total/BMG

Flyte Reaction

CREATE A SMILE
CD ______ **SPLENCD 3**
Backs / Jun '95 / RTM/Disc

FM

APHRODISIAC
CD ______ **CDMFN 141**
Music For Nations / Oct '92 / Pinnacle

DEAD MAN'S SHOES
CD ______ **RAWCD 107**
Raw Power / Apr '96 / Pinnacle

INDISCREET
That girl / Other side of midnight / Love lies dying / I belong to the night / American girls / Hot wired / Face to face / Frozen heart / Heart of the matter
CD ______ **BGOCD 184**
Beat Goes On / Mar '93 / Pinnacle

NO ELECTRICITY REQUIRED
CD ______ **CDMFN 155**
Music For Nations / Oct '93 / Pinnacle

ONLY THE STRONG (The Best Of FM 1984-1994)
That girl / Other side of midnight / American girls / Face to face / Frozen heart / Tough it out / Don't stop / Bad luck / Burning my heart down / Let love be the leader / I heard it through the grapevine / Only the strong survive / Dangerous ground / Breathe fire / Blood and gasoline / All or nothing / Closer to heaven
CD ______ **VSOPCD 203**
Connoisseur Collection / Aug '94 / Pinnacle

TAKIN' IT TO THE STREETS
CD ______ **CDMFN 119**
Music For Nations / Oct '91 / Pinnacle

FM Sound Lab

LET'S DO LUNCH (Rave Jazz)
Let's do lunch / Say what / Transilvania / Superleggera / Planet cricklewood / Save the whales, eat a Viking / Heat seeker / Just desserts / Let's do lunch / Let's do lunch
CD ______ **VCIJD 3**
Vocal Cords / Nov '93 / Grapevine/ PolyGram

Focus

FOCUS VOL.3
Round goes the gossip / Love remembered / Sylvia / Carnival fugue / Focus III / Answers Questions Answers Questions / Anonymus II / Elspeth of Nottingham / House of the king
CD ______ **PRMCD 10**
Premier/EMI / Jun '96 / EMI

HOCUS POCUS: THE BEST OF FOCUS
Hocus pocus / Anonymus / House of the king / Focus / Janis / Focus II / Tommy / Sylvia / Focus III / Harem scarum / Mother focus / Focus IV / Bennie Helder / Glider / Red sky at night / Hocus pocus (US single version)
CD ______ **CDP 8281622**
EMI / May '94 / EMI

IN AND OUT OF FOCUS
Focus / Black Beauty / Sugar Island / Anonymus / House of the King / Happy nightmare / Why dream / Focus (instrumental)
CD ______ **PRMCD 8**
Premier/EMI / Jun '96 / EMI

MOVING WAVES
Hocus pocus / Le clochard (bread) / Janis / Moving waves / Focus II / Eruption
CD ______ **PRMCD 9**
Premier/EMI / Jun '96 / EMI

Foden Motor Works Band

WORLD OF THE BRASS BAND, THE (Foden Motor Works Band & Fairey Aviation/Morris Motors Band)
Coronation march / Shepherd's hey / Lilac time / Ruy blas overture / Perpetuum mobile / Marche Slave / Czech polka / Orpheus in the underworld / Trumpet voluntary / Elizabethan serenade / Merrie England / Swedish rhapsody / Finlandia / Chit chat polka / William Tell overture
CD ______ **4529392**
Decca / Aug '97 / PolyGram

Foetus

BOIL
CD ______ **ABB 119CD**
Big Cat / Aug '96 / 3mv/Pinnacle

GASH
CD ______ **ABB 88CD**
Big Cat / May '95 / 3mv/Pinnacle

MALE (Foetus Corruptus)
CD ______ **ABB 31/2CD**
Big Cat / Feb '92 / 3mv/Pinnacle

NAIL (Scraping Foetus Off The Wheel)
CD ______ **WOMBFIP 004CD**
Some Bizarre / Apr '86 / Pinnacle

NULL/VOID (2CD Set)
CD Set ______ **CLP 99312**
Cleopatra / Jun '97 / Cargo / Greyhound / Plastic Head / RTM/Disc / SRD

Fogelberg, Dan

INNOCENT AGE, THE (2CD Set)
Nexus / Innocent age / Sand and the foam / In the passage / Lost in the sun / Run for the roses / Leader of the band/Washington Post / March / Same auld lang syne / Stolen moments / Lion's share / Only the heart may know / Reach / Aireshire lament / Times like these / Hard to sat / Empty cages / Ghosts
CD Set ______ **4874822**
Epic / Jun '97 / Sony

Fogerty, John

BLUE MOON SWAMP
Southern streamline / Hot rod heart / Blueboy / Hundred and ten in the shade / Rattlesnake highway / Bring it down to Jelly Roll / Walking in a hurricane / Swamp river days / Rambunctions boy / Joy of my life / Blue moon nights / Bad bad boy
CD ______ **9362454262**
Warner Bros. / Jun '97 / Warner Music

BLUE RIDGE RANGERS (Blue Ridge Rangers)
Blue Ridge Mountain blues / Somewhere listening (for my name) / You're the reason / Jambalaya / She thinks I still care / California blues / Workin' on a building / Please help me, I'm falling / Have thine own way / I ain't never / Hearts of stone / Today I started loving you again
CD ______ **CDFE 506**
Fantasy / Oct '87 / Jazz Music / Pinnacle / Wellard

CENTERFIELD
Old man down the road / Rock 'n' roll girls / Big train / I saw it on TV / Mr. Greed / Searchlight / Centerfield / I can't help myself / Zanz kant danz
CD ______ **9252032**
WEA / Feb '85 / Warner Music

JOHN FOGERTY
Rockin' all over the world / (I'll be glad when you're dead) you rascal you / Wall / Travellin' high / Lonely teardrops / Almost Saturday night / Where the river flows / Sea cruise / Dream song / Flying away / Comin' down the road / Ricochet
CD ______ **CDFE 507**
Fantasy / Sep '87 / Jazz Music / Pinnacle / Wellard

Foghat

AKA ROCK & ROLL
CD ______ **8122708902**
WEA / Mar '93 / Warner Music

BEST OF FOGHAT
I just want to make love to you / Maybellene / Ride ride ride / Take it or leave it / Home in my hand / Drivin' wheel / Fool for the city / Slow ride / Stone blue / Honey hush / Night shift / Wild cherry / Third time lucky (first time I was a fool) / Easy money / Chateau lafitte '59 boogie / Eight days on the road
CD ______ **8122700882**
WEA / Jul '93 / Warner Music

BEST OF FOGHAT - VOL.2, THE
CD ______ **8122705162**
WEA / Jul '93 / Warner Music

ENERGIZED
Honey hush / Step outside / Golden arrow / Home in my hand / Wild cherry / That'll be the day / Fly by night / Nothin' I won't do
CD ______ **8122708832**
WEA / Mar '93 / Warner Music

FOGHAT LIVE
Fool for the city / Home in my hand / I just want to make love to you / Road fever / Honey hush / Slow ride
CD ______ **8122708842**
WEA / Mar '93 / Warner Music

FOGHAT VOL.1
I just want to make love to you / Trouble trouble / Leavin' again / Fools hall of fame / Sarah Lee / Highway (killing me) / Maybellene / Hole to hide in / Gotta get to know you
CD ______ **8122708872**
WEA / Mar '93 / Warner Music

FOOL FOR THE CITY
Fool for the city / My babe / Slow ride / Terraplane blues / Save your loving (for me) / Drive me home / Take it or leave it
CD ______ **8122708822**
WEA / Mar '93 / Warner Music

NIGHTSHIFT
Drivin' wheel / Don't run me down / Burning the midnight oil / Nightshift / Hot shot love / Take me to the river / I'll be standing by
CD ______ **8122708882**
WEA / Mar '93 / Warner Music

ROCK 'N' ROLL OUTLAW
CD ______ **8122708892**
WEA / Mar '93 / Warner Music

STONE BLUE
CD ______ **8122708812**
WEA / Mar '93 / Warner Music

Fohlin, Ingvar

MAGDEBURGERSPELMAN
CD ______ **AW 11CD**
Tongang / Aug '96 / ADA

Fol, Raymond

PARIS SWINGS THE 60'S (Fol, Raymond & Pierre Michelot)
Le printemps: *Fol, Raymond Big Band* / L'ete: *Fol, Raymond Big Band* / L'automne: *Fol, Raymond Big Band* / L'hiver: *Fol, Raymond Big Band* / Cherokee: *Michelot, Pierre & His Orchestra* / Gavotte: *Michelot, Pierre & His Orchestra* / Akkilino: *Michelot, Pierre & His Orchestra* / Elephant green: *Michelot, Pierre & His Orchestra* / Sous les ponts de Paris: *Michelot, Pierre & His Orchestra* / Chet: *Michelot, Pierre & His Orchestra* / Bye bye blackbird: *Michelot, Pierre & His Orchestra* / Sweet feeling: *Michelot, Pierre & His Orchestra* / Klook's shadow: *Michelot, Pierre & His Orchestra*
CD ______ **8326572**
ECM / Mar '88 / New Note/Pinnacle

Folan, Declan

SKIN AND BOW (Folan, Declan & J. Davey)
CD ______ **SUN 23CD**
Sun / Nov '96 / ADA

Folds, Ben

BEN FOLDS FIVE (Folds, Ben Five)
Jackson Cannery / Philosophy / Julianne / Where's summer B / Alice Childress / Underground / Sports and wine / Uncle Walter / Best imitation of myself / Video / Last polka / Boxing
CD ______ **CAROL 002CD**
Caroline / Apr '96 / Cargo / Vital

WHATEVER AND EVER AMEN (Folds, Ben Five)
One angry dwarf and 200 solemn / Faces / Fair / Brick / Song for the dumped / Selfless / Cold and composed / Kate / Smoke / Cigarette / Steven's last night in town / Battle of who could care less / Missing the war
CD ______ **4866982**
Epic / Mar '97 / Sony

Folds, Chuck

HITTING HIS STRIDE
CD ______ **ARCD 19117**
Arbors Jazz / Nov '94 / Cadillac

Foley, Sue

WITHOUT A WARNING
CD ______ **ANTCD 0025**
Antones / May '94 / ADA / Hot Shot

YOUNG GIRL BLUES
Queen Bee / (Me and my) Chauffeur blues / Cuban getaway / Mean old lonesome train / Gone blind / Walkin' home / But I forgive you / Off the hook / Hooked on love / Little mixed up / Time to travel
CD ______ **ANTCD 0019**
Alligator / Jun '92 / ADA / CM / Direct

Folk & Rackere

FOLK & RACKERE 1976-1985
Vanner och frander / En sjomansbrud skall blakladd ga / Harpans kraft / Nas ingars polska / Inga litimor / Major brack / Maria / Naktergalen / Aggavisan / Haugebonden / Ruben ranzo / De tva systrarna / Silibrand / Flickan gar pa golvet / Det blaser nordost
CD ______ **RES 515CD**
Resource / Jul '97 / ADA / Direct

Folk Aerobics

FOLK YOUR WAY TO FITNESS
CD ______ **HTDCD 75**
HTD / Jul '97 / CM / Pinnacle

Folk Friends

1
CD ______ **TUT 72160**
Wundertute / Jan '94 / ADA / CM / Duncans

2
CD ______ **CDTUT 72150**
Wundertute / '89 / ADA / CM / Duncans

Folk Implosion

DARE TO BE SURPRISED
CD ______ **COMM 45CD**
Communion / Jun '97 / Cargo

TAKE A LOOK
CD ______ **COMM 032CD**
Communion / Dec '96 / Cargo

Folke Rabe

WAS (WHAT)
CD ______ **DEX 12CD**
Dexter's Cigar / Jun '97 / Cargo

Folkloyuma

MUSIC FROM THE ORIENTE DE CUBA: THE RUMBA
CD ______ **NI 5425**
Nimbus / Apr '95 / Nimbus

Foly, Liane

REVE ORANGE
Au fur et a mesure / Nuit halogene / Goodbye lover / Reve orange / Blue notes / Va savoir / Be my boy / Sun / S'en balancer
CD ______ **CDVIR 7**
Virgin / Jun '91 / EMI

SWEET MYSTERY
CD ______ **CDVIR 19**
Virgin / Apr '94 / EMI

Fonsea

ET SE ANGES NOIRS
CD ______ **CNCD 5981**
Disky / Apr '94 / Disky / THE

Fonseca

MELODIES FROM PORTUGAL
CD ______ **EUCD 1087**
ARC / '89 / ADA / ARC Music

Fontana, Wayne

GAME OF LOVE (Fontana, Wayne & The Mindbenders)
Game of love / She's got the power / You don't know me / Git it / Jaguar and the thunderbirds / Certain girl / One more time / Um um um um um um / Where have you been / Keep your hands off my baby / Too many tears / Girl can't help it / Cops and robbers / I'm gonna be a wheel someday / Since you've been gone / It's just a little bit too late
CD ______ **8322602**
Mercury / May '88 / PolyGram

WORLD OF WAYNE FONTANA & THE MINDBENDERS, THE (Fontana, Wayne & The Mindbenders)
Game of love / Groovy kind of love / Pamela Pamela / Um um um um um um / Just a little bit too late / Ashes to ashes / It was easier to hurt her / Hello Josephine / Uncle Joe, the ice cream man / Words of Bartholomew / Like I did / Letter / Come on home / First taste of love / Goodbye bluebird / She needs love / (Can't live with you) can't live without you / Storybook children / Stop, look and listen / Something keeps calling me back
CD _____ 5514362
Spectrum / May '96 / PolyGram

Fontenot, Canray

LOUISIANA HOT SAUCE CREOLE STYLE
CD _____ ARHCD 381
Arhoolie / Apr '95 / ADA / Cadillac / Direct

Foo Fighters

COLOUR AND THE SHAPE, THE
Doll / Monkey wrench / Hey Johnny Park / My poor brain / Wind up / Up in arms / My hero / See you / Enough space / February stars / Everlong / Walking after you / New way home
CD _____ CDEST 2295
Roswell / May '97 / EMI

FOO FIGHTERS
This is a call / I'll stick around / Big me / Alone and easy target / Good grief / Floaty / Weenie beenie / Oh George / For all the cows / X-static / Watershed / Exhausted
CD _____ CDEST 2266
Roswell / Jul '95 / EMI

Fool Proof

NO FRICTION
CD _____ 188804 2
Gramavision / Feb '89 / Vital/SAM

For Carnation

PROMISED WORKS
CD _____ RUNT 30
Runt / Jun '97 / Cargo / Greyhound / Plastic Head

For Love Not Lisa

MERGE
Softhand / Slip slide melting / Lucifer for now / Daring to pick up / Simple line of decline / Travis Hoffman / Just a phase / Traces / Mother's faith / Swallow / More than a girl / Merge
CD _____ 7567922832
WEA / Oct '93 / Warner Music

For Real

FREE
Intro / Like I do / Good morning sunshine / Hold me / So in love / Remember / Will you love me / Saddest song I ever heard / Nothing without you / How can I get close to you / Love will be waiting at home / Free
CD _____ 75444370132
Rowdy / Jul '97 / BMG

IT'S A NATURAL THANG
Easy to love / Where did your love go / You don't wanna miss / Just a matter of time / Li'l bit / Don't wanna love you now / You don't know nothin' / With this ring (say yes) / D'yer mak'er / Harder I try / I like / Thinking of you / Prayer
CD _____ 5401562
A&M / Feb '95 / PolyGram

Forbert, Steve

AMERICAN IN ME, THE
CD _____ GED 24459
Geffen / Jun '97 / BMG

JACKRABBIT SLIM
Romeo's tune / Sweet love that you give (sure goes a long, long way) / I'm in love with you / Say goodbye to little Jo / Wait / Make it all so real / Baby / Complications / Sadly sorta like a soap opera
CD _____ 4851072
Epic / Nov '96 / Sony

MISSION OF THE CROSS
CD _____ 74321259902
RCA / Apr '95 / BMG

ROCKING HORSE HEAD
If I want you now / My time ain't long / Shaky ground / Dear Lord / Moon man (I'm waiting on you) / Don't stop / Some will rake the coals / I know what I know / Good planets are hard to find / Big new world / Open house / Dream, dream
CD _____ 74321407482
RCA / Nov '96 / BMG

STREETS OF THIS TOWN
Running on love / Don't tell me, I know / I blinked once / Mexico / As we live and breathe / On the streets of this town / Hope, faith and love / Perfect stranger / Wait a little longer / Search your heart
CD _____ GED 24194
Geffen / Jun '97 / BMG

Forbes, Roy

LOVE TURNS TO ICE
CD _____ FF 70499
Flying Fish / Jul '89 / ADA / CM / Direct / Roots

Forbidden

POINT OF NO RETURN, THE (The Best Of The Forbidden)
Chalice of blood / Out of body (out of mind) / Feel no pain / Step by step / Off the edge / One foot in hell / Through the eyes of glass / Tossed away / March into fire / Victim of changes
CD _____ CDMFLAG 73
Under One Flag / Nov '92 / Pinnacle

Force & Styles

HARDCORE EXPLOSION '97 (Remixed By Force & Styles/Hixxy & Dougal - 2CD Set) (Various Artists)
Heart of gold: *Force & Styles* / Surrender: *Eruption* / People's party: *DJ Hixxy & Sunset Regime* / Come on: *Walford Project* / Apollo 13: *Force & Styles* / Euro bounce: *Force & Styles* / Love of my life: *Dr. Who* / Stay with me: *Eruption* / I'm gonna get ya: *Eruption & Dougal* / Sunshine: *Slipmatt & Eruption* / Pacific sun: *Force & Styles* / Muzik: *Happy Rollers* / Rock dis place: *Chewy* / Wonderland: *Force & Styles* / Techno wonderland: *Ravers Choice* / Shinning down: *Force & Styles* / Set you free: *Zoom* / Fun fair: *Force & Styles* / Pretty green eyes: *Force & Styles* / Simply electric: *Force & Styles* / Let the music: *Eruption* / Party time: *Eruption & Dougal* / Poison fruit: *Walford Project* / Fantasy: *Eruption* / Party people: *Slipmatt & Eruption* / SMD 5: *SMD* / Something like dis: *Slippery Project* / Kick your leg in the air: *Elogic & DNA* / Forever together: *DJ Hixxy & Banana Man* / Frantic: *Druid & Sharkey*
CD Set _____ SUMCD 116
Supreme Underground / Feb '97 / Pinnacle

Force Dimension

DEUS EX MACHINA
CD _____ KK 049CD
KK / Aug '90 / Plastic Head

FORCE DIMENSION
CD _____ KK 020CD
KK / '90 / Plastic Head

Force Mass Motion

MOTIONS BEYOND
CD _____ CUTCD 003
Rabbit City / Oct '96 / Amato Disco / Jumpstart / Mo's Music Machine / Prime

Force Of Music

KINGS & QUEENS OF DUB
CD _____ TWCD 1017
Tamoki Wambesi / Oct '94 / Greensleeves / Jet Star / Roots Collective / SRD

Forcefield

INSTRUMENTALS
Tokyo / Talisman / Perfect world / I lose again / Secret waters / Look don't touch / Three card shuffle / Rendezvous / Osaka
CD _____ PCOM 1121
President / Jun '92 / Grapevine/PolyGram / President / Target/BMG

LET THE WILD RUN FREE (Forcefield IV)
Let the wild run free / Can't get enough of your love / Money talks / I will not go quietly / Ball of confusion / Wind cries mary / Living by numbers / In a perfect world
CD _____ PCOM 1110
President / Nov '90 / Grapevine/PolyGram / President / Target/BMG

TALISMAN, THE (Forcefield II)
Talisman / Year of the dragon / Tired of waiting for you / Heartache / Good is good / Carrie / Without your love / I lose again / Mercenary / Black night / I lose again (instrumental)
CD _____ PCOM 1095
President / Aug '88 / Grapevine/PolyGram / President / Target/BMG

TO OZ AND BACK (Forcefield III)
Hit and run / Always / Stay away / Desire / Tokyo / Who'll be the next in line / Wings on my feet / Firepower / Hold on / Rendezvous
CD _____ PCOM 1100
President / Oct '89 / Grapevine/PolyGram / President / Target/BMG

Forces Of Nature

LIVE FROM MARS VOL.1
Spanish inq / Jazz bell / Illogical voyager / Glaciers / New killer / Train of life / Deep / Hidden agendas / Somewhere out there
CD _____ CUP 025CD
Clean Up / Oct '96 / Amato Disco / Prime / Vital

Forcione, Antonio

DEDICATO
CD _____ NAIMCD 013
Naim Audio / Mar '97 / Koch

Ford, Charles

AS REAL AS IT GETS (Ford, Charles Band)
CD _____ CCD 11048
Crosscut / Feb '97 / ADA / CM / Direct

CHARLES FORD BAND, THE (Ford, Charles Band)
CD _____ ARHCD 353
Arhoolie / Apr '95 / ADA / Cadillac / Direct

REUNION - LIVE
CD _____ CCD 11043
Crosscut / Nov '94 / ADA / CM / Direct

Ford, Douglas

PIPES AND DRUMS OF SCOTLAND (Ford, Douglas & The Gordon Highlanders)
Amazing grace / My home in the hills / Conund rum / Miss Kirkwood / Scotland the brave / Reveille / Rustic bridge by the mill / Miss McLeod O'Raasey / Cock of the north / Skye boat song / Bonnie Dundee
CD _____ SOW 90149
Sounds Of The World / Jan '96 / Target/BMG

Ford, Emile

GREATEST HITS
CD _____ SSLCD 201
Savanna / Jun '95 / THE

VERY BEST OF EMILE FORD & THE CHECKMATES (Ford, Emile & The Checkmates)
What do you want to make those eyes at me for / After you've gone / Hold me, thrill me, kiss me / Keep on doin' what you're doin' / Them there eyes / Questions / Still / You'll never know what you're missing / Trouble / Lawdy Miss Clawdy / Joker / Yellow bird / Buona sera / I don't / Danny boy / That lucky old sun / Counting teardrops / Heavenly / What am I gonna do / On a slow boat to China / Don't tell me your troubles / Red sails in the sunset / Send for me / Kiss to build a dream on / Scarlet ribbons / Vaya con dios / Move along
CD _____ SEECD 309
See For Miles/C5 / Jan '91 / Pinnacle

VERY BEST OF EMILE FORD, THE
CD _____ SOW 703
Sound Waves / May '94 / Target/BMG

Ford, Jim

HARLAN COUNTY
Harlan County / I'm gonna make her love me / Changing colors / Dr. Handy's dandy candy / Love on my brain / Long road ahead / Under construction / Working my way to LA / Spoonful / To make my life beautiful
CD _____ EDCD 519
Edsel / Jun '97 / Pinnacle

Ford, Lita

BEST OF LITA FORD, THE
What do ya know about love / Kiss me deadly / Shot of poison / Hungry / Gotta let go / Larger than life / Only women bleed / Playin' with fire / Back to the cave / Lisa / Close my eyes forever
CD _____ 07863660472
RCA / Aug '92 / BMG

DANGEROUS CURVES
Larger than life / What do ya know about love / Shot of poison / Bad love / Playin' with fire / Hellbound train / Black widow / Little too early / Holy man / Tambourine dream / Little black spider
CD _____ 74321160002
RCA / Feb '94 / BMG

GREATEST HITS
CD _____ 7863660372
RCA / Aug '96 / BMG

INTERVIEW COMPACT DISC: LITA FORD
CD _____ CBAK 4020
Baktabak / Nov '89 / Arabesque

LITA
Back to the cave / Can't catch me / Blueberry / Kiss me deadly / Falling in and out of love / Fatal passion / Under the gun / Broken dreams / Close my eyes forever
CD _____ 74321138872
RCA / Feb '94 / BMG

Ford Pier

MECONIUM
CD _____ WRONG 15
Wrong / Nov '95 / SRD

Ford, Ricky

AMERICAN - AFRICAN BLUES
American - African blues / Environ / Of / Complex harmony / Descent / Mostly arco / Encore / American - African blues
CD _____ CCD 79528
Candid / Feb '97 / Cadillac / Direct / Jazz Music / Koch / Wellard

EBONY RHAPSODY
Intro / Ebony rhapsody / Mon amour / Independence blues / Mirror man / In a sentimental mood / Setting sun blues / Broadway / Red, crack and blue
CD _____ CCD 79053
Candid / Feb '97 / Cadillac / Direct / Jazz Music / Koch / Wellard

HOT BRASS
Ford variations / Banging, bashing, bowing and blowing / Night in Valencia / 11/15/91 / Cop out / Hot brass / Mood blues / Speak now / Carbon / It don't mean a thing if it ain't got that swing
CD _____ CCD 79518
Candid / Feb '97 / Cadillac / Direct / Jazz Music / Koch / Wellard

MANHATTAN BLUES
In walked Bud / Misty / Ode to crispus attacks / Bop nouveau / My little strayhorn / Manhattan blues / Half nelson / Portrait of Mingus / Land preserved
CD _____ CCD 79036
Candid / Feb '97 / Cadillac / Direct / Jazz Music / Koch / Wellard

SAXOTIC STOMP
CD _____ MCD 5349
Muse / Sep '92 / New Note/Pinnacle

Ford, Robben

BLUES COLLECTION 1971-1991, THE
Excuse my blues: *Ford, Charles Band* / Love me or leave me: *Musselwhite, Charley* / Blue Stu: *Musselwhite, Charley* / Blue and lonesome: *Ford, Charles Band* / That will never do: *Ford, Charles Band* / Cotton creeper: *Ford, Charles Band* / Still a stranger: *Musselwhite, Charley* / Take out some insurance / Help the poor / Mellow down easy: *Ford, Mark* / Going down slow: *Ford, Robben & Jimmy Witherspoon* / Pretty woman
CD _____ CCD 11054
Crosscut / Jun '97 / ADA / CM / Direct
CD _____ BRR 127CD
Blue Rock-It / May '97 / ADA

FORD AND FRIENDS (Ford Blues Band)
CD _____ BRCD 126
Blue Rock-It / Dec '96 / ADA

FORD BLUES BAND, THE (Ford Blues Band)
CD _____ CCD 11024
Crosscut / '92 / ADA / CM / Direct

FORDS AND FRIENDS (Ford Blues Band)
Tell me Mamma / Another fine day / Happy anniversary baby / I'm in love / Sign / Baby please / Sahara moon / Hey sister / Old Bill / Little baby / That happy look in your eye / Luther's lament
CD _____ CCD 11052
Crosscut / Jun '97 / ADA / CM / Direct

HANDFUL OF BLUES (Ford, Robben & The Blue Line)
Rugged road / Chevrolet / When I leave here / Strong will to live / I just want to make love to you / Think twice / Good thing / Tired of talking / Running out on me / Top of the hill / Don't let me be misunderstood / Miller's son
CD _____ BTR 70042
Blue Thumb / Aug '95 / New Note/BMG

HOTSHOTS (Ford Blues Band)
CD _____ CCD 11041
Crosscut / Nov '95 / ADA / CM / Direct

INSIDE STORY, THE
CD _____ 7559610212
Elektra / Jan '96 / Warner Music

LIVE AT THE BREMINALE '92 (Ford Blues Band)
CD _____ CCD 11038
Crosscut / Jul '93 / ADA / CM / Direct

ROBBEN FORD AND BLUE TRAIN
Brother / You cut me to the bone / Real man / My love will never die / Prisoner of love / Tell me I'm your man / Start it up / Life song
CD _____ GRS 10022
GRP / Aug '92 / New Note/BMG

TIGER WALK
In the beginning / Ghosts / Freedom / Red lady / Oasis / Just like it is / I can't stand the rain / Champ / Tiger walk / Comin' up / Don't let the sun catch you crying / Chevrolet
CD _____ BTR 70122
Blue Thumb / May '97 / New Note/BMG

Ford, Tennessee Ernie

SHOWTIME
Night train to Memphis / Catfish boogie / You gotta see Mama tonight / Cool water / Just because / My little red wagon / Do the hucklebuck / Up the lazy river
CD _____ DATOM 7
A Touch Of Magic / Apr '94 / Harmonia Mundi

SIXTEEN TONS
Milk 'em in the morning blues / Country junction / Smoky mountain boogie / Antici-

pation blues / Mule train / Cry of the wild goose / My hobby / Feed 'em in the morning blues / Shot gun boogie / Tailormade woman / You're my sugar: *Ford, Tennessee Ernie & Kay Starr* / Rock City boogie / Kissin' bug boogie / Hey good lookin': *Ford, Tennessee Ernie & Helen O'Connell* / Ham bone: *Ford, Tennessee Ernie & Bucky Tibbs* / Everybody's got a girl but me / Snow shoe Thompson / Blackberry boogie / Hey Mr. Cotton Picker / Kiss me big / Catfish boogie / Ballad of Davy Crockett / Sixteen tons / Roving gambler / Black eyed Susan Brown
CD _______________ BCD 15487
Bear Family / Feb '90 / Direct / Rollercoaster / Swift

ULTIMATE COLLECTION, THE
CD Set _______________ RE 2134
Razor & Tie / Jul '97 / Koch

Ford-Payne, Sherree

SHERREE FORD-PAYNE
CD _______________ ALMOCD 009
Almo Sounds / May '96 / Pinnacle

Fordham, Julia

FALLING FORWARD
I can't help myself / Caged bird / Falling forward / River / Blue sky / Different time, different place / Threadbare / Love and forgiveness / Honeymoon / Hope, prayer and time / Safe
CD _______________ CIRCD 28
Circa / May '94 / EMI

JULIA FORDHAM
Happy ever after / Comfort of strangers / Few too many / Invisible war / My lover's keeper / Cocooned / Where does the time go / Woman of the 80's / Other woman / Behind closed doors / Unconditional love
CD _______________ CIRCD 4
Circa / Apr '92 / EMI

PORCELAIN
Lock and key / Porcelain / Girlfriend / For you only for you / Genius / Did I happen to mention / Towerblock / Island / Your lovely face / Prince of peace
CD _______________ CIRCD 10
Circa / Sep '89 / EMI

SWEPT
CD _______________ CIRCD 18
Circa / Oct '91 / EMI

Foreheads In A Fishtank

STRIPPER
CD _______________ TOAD 5CD
Newt / Jun '94 / Plastic Head

Foreigner

AGENT PROVOCATEUR
Tooth and nail / That was yesterday / I want to know what love is / Growing up the hard way / Reaction to action / Stranger in my own house / Love in vain / Down on love / Two different worlds / She's too tough
CD _______________ 7819992
Atlantic / Jan '85 / Warner Music

CLASSIC HITS LIVE
Double vision / Cold as ice / Damage is done / Women / Dirty white boy / Fool for you anyway / Head games / Not fade away / Waiting for a girl like you / Jukebox hero / Urgent / Love maker / I want to know what love is / Feels like the first time
CD _______________ 7567825252
Atlantic / Dec '93 / Warner Music

DOUBLE VISION
Hot blooded / Blue morning, blue day / You're all I am / Back where you belong / Love has taken it's toll / Double vision / Tramontane / I have waited so long / Lonely children / Spellbinder
CD _______________ K250 476
Atlantic / Aug '83 / Warner Music

FOREIGNER
Feels like the first time / Cold as ice / Starrider / Headknocker / Damage is done / Long long way from home / Woman oh woman / At war with the world / Fool for the anyway / I need you
CD _______________ 250356
Atlantic / Apr '83 / Warner Music

FOREIGNER 4
Night life / Jukebox hero / Break it up / Waiting for a girl like you / Luanne / Urgent / I'm gonna win / Woman in black / Girl on the moon / Don't let go
CD _______________ 7567827952
Atlantic / Feb '91 / Warner Music

HEAD GAMES
Dirty white boy / Love on the telephone / Women I'll get even with you / Seventeen / Head games / Modern day / Blinded by science / Do what you like / Rev on the red line
CD _______________ 250651
Atlantic / Nov '85 / Warner Music

MR. MOONLIGHT
White lie / Rain / Until the end of time / All I need to know / Running the rise / Real world / Big dog / Hole in my soul / I keep hoping / Under the gun / Hand on my heart
CD _______________ 74321232852
Arista / Aug '96 / BMG

RECORDS
Cold as ice / Double vision / Head games / Waiting for a girl like you / Feels like the first time / Urgent / Dirty white boy / Jukebox hero / Long long way from home / Hot blooded
CD _______________ 7567828002
Atlantic / Nov '95 / Warner Music

VERY BEST OF FOREIGNER...AND BEYOND
Soul doctor / Prisoner of love / With heaven on our side / Jukebox hero / Hot blooded / Cold as ice / Head games / Waiting for a girl like you / Urgent / Double vision / I want to know what love is / Say you will / That was yesterday / I don't want to live without you / Rev on the red line / Dirty white boy / Feels like the first time
CD _______________ 7567899992
Atlantic / Dec '92 / Warner Music

Foreman, Bruce

THERE ARE TIMES (Foreman, Bruce Quartet)
CD _______________ CCD 4332
Concord Jazz / Dec '87 / New Note/ Pinnacle

Forest

FOREST/FULL CIRCLE
Bad penny / Glade somewhere / Lovemaker's ways / While you're gone / Sylvie / Fantasy you / Fading light / Do you want some smoke / Don't want to go / Nothing else will matter / Mirror of life / Rain is on my balcony / Hawk the hawker / Bluebell dance / Midnight hanging of a runaway serf / To Julie / Gypsy girl and rambleaway / Do not walk in the rain / Much ado about nothing / Graveyard / Famine song / Autumn child
CD _______________ BGOCD 236
Beat Goes On / Sep '94 / Pinnacle

Forest, Andy J.

BLUE ORLEANS
CD _______________ APCD 128
Appaloosa / Nov '96 / ADA / Direct / TKO Magnum

HOG WILD
CD _______________ APCD 036
Appaloosa / '92 / ADA / Direct / TKO Magnum

HOGSHEAD CHEESE (Forest, Andy J. & Kenny Holladay)
CD _______________ APCD 118
Appaloosa / Oct '95 / ADA / Direct / TKO Magnum

LIVE (Forest, Andy J. Band)
CD _______________ APCD 066
Appaloosa / '92 / ADA / Direct / TKO Magnum

Forest, Helen

ON THE SUNNY SIDE OF THE STREET
CD _______________ ACD 047
Audiophile / Oct '93 / Jazz Music

Forever Amber

LOVE CYCLE
CD _______________ HBG 122/7
Background / Apr '94 / Background / Greyhound

Forgodsake

BLASTHEAD
Armchair enthusiast / Wake up now / If this is what it takes / Bad sex / Half past anything / Blasthead / Strange / Negative / In front of me / Crash / This one / Not today / Sky high / Dumbtown
CD _______________ CDBLEED 3
Bleeding Hearts / Apr '93 / Pinnacle

Forgotten Rebels

PRIDE AND DISGRACE, THE
CD _______________ OPM 2105CD
Other People's Music / Oct '96 / Greyhound / Plastic Head

Forkeye

PI8
CD _______________ HCCD 001
Human Condition / Sep '93 / RTM/Disc

Forman, Bruce

PARDON ME (Forman, Bruce Quartet)
CD _______________ CCD 4368
Concord Jazz / Feb '89 / New Note/ Pinnacle

Forman, Mitchel

CHILDHOOD DREAMS
CD _______________ 1210502
Soul Note / Jan '93 / Cadillac / Harmonia Mundi / Wellard

Formanek, Michael

NATURE OF THE BEAST
Emerger / Dry season / Grand bizarre / Don't go there / Excruciation / El Nino / Lickin' center / Thick skin / Dangerous crustaceans
CD _______________ ENJ 93082
Enja / Apr '97 / New Note/Pinnacle / Vital/ SAM

Format

MEDIA CIRCUS
CD _______________ CDC 001
Christel Deesk / Sep '96 / Vital

Formby, George

AT THE FLICKS
I could make a living at that / Baby / It's in the air / They can't fool me / Goodnight, little fellow, goodnight / Pardon me / I'm making headway now / I could not let the stable down / I wish I was back on the farm / Count your blessings and smile / Oh don't the wind blow cold / Emperor of Lancashire / You're everything to me / You can't go wrong in these / I played on my Spanish guitar / I'd do it with a smile / Barmaid at the Rose & Crown / Get crackin' / Home Guard blues / Bell bottom George / Serves you right / Got to get your photo in the press / Hillbilly Willie / Unconditional surrender
CD _______________ PLCD 554
President / Nov '96 / Grapevine/PolyGram / President / Target/BMG

BELL-BOTTOM GEORGE
Bell bottom George / When the lads of the village get crackin' / When the waterworks caught fire / It serves you right / Got to get your photo in the press / If I had a girl like you / Thirty thirsty sailors / I'd do it with a smile / Home guard blues / Swim little fish / At the baby show / Hold your hats on / Mr. Wu's an air raid warden now / Bar maid at the Rose and Crown / I wish I was back on the farm / Delivering the morning milk / Grandad's flannelette nightshirt / Guarding the homes of the Home Guard / Our Sergeant Major / Baby / She's never been seen since then / Swimmin' with the wimmin'
CD _______________ PASTCD 7043
Flapper / May '94 / Pinnacle

BEST OF GEORGE FORMBY, THE
CD _______________ MU 3006
Musketeer / Oct '92 / Disc

BEST OF GEORGE FORMBY, THE
Auntie Maggie's remedy / Why don't women like me / With my little ukelele in my hand / When I'm cleaning windows (The window cleaner) / Chinese laudry blues / Leaning on a lampost / With my little stick of Blackpool rock / Swimmin' with the wimmin' / Mother what'll I do now / In my little snapshot album / Mr. Wu's a window cleaner now / Wedding of Mr Wu / Lancashire toreador / Our Sergeant Major / Madame Moscovitch / Sitting on the ice in the ice rink / I told my baby with the ukelele / It's turned out nice again / Sitting on the sands allnight / When I'm cleaning windows (The window cleaner) / Hid tiddley hi ti island / Bless em' all
CD _______________ CD 6019
Music / Apr '96 / Target/BMG

FORMBY AT WAR - LIVE
Auntie Maggie's remedy / Frank on his tank / Guarding the homes of the home guard / Chinese laundry blues / Cleaning windows / Little stick of Blackpool rock / Imagine me in the maginot line / When the lads of the village get crackin' / Thirty thirsty sailors / Out in the Middle East / Mr. Wu's an air raid warden now / It's in the air / Little ukulele / Down the old coal hole / Bless 'em all
CD _______________ CDGRS 1224
Grosvenor / '91 / Grosvenor

HIS GREATEST FAVOURITES
I'm the ukelele man / Leaning on a lamppost / Auntie Maggie's remedy / With my little stick of Blackpool rock / When I'm cleaning windows (The window cleaner) / Mr. Wu's a window cleaner now / Chinese laundry blues / Do de o do / Blue eyed blonde next door / Like the big pots do / When I'm cleaning windows (The window cleaner) / I don't like / Easy going chap / Noughts and crosses / Lancashire hot pot swingers / You can't go wrong in these / Who are you a-shoving off / I'm the husband of the wife of Mr.Wu / Hitting the high spots / Kiss your mansy pansy / I can tell it by my horoscope / I'm the emperor of Lancashire
CD _______________ PASTCD 7001
Flapper / Feb '93 / Pinnacle

I'M THE UKELELE MAN
When I'm cleaning windows (The window cleaner) / Auntie Maggie's remedy / Leaning on a lamp-post / In my little snapshot album / With my little stick of Blackpool rock / Mr. Wu's a window cleaner now / Our Sergeant Major / I'm the ukelele man / Bless 'em all / I don't like / Joo-jah tree / Chinese laundry blues / Baby / Why don't women like me / Running round the fountains in Trafalgar Square / My ukelele / De do o'do / Believe it or not / I went all hot and cold / Wedding of Mr. Woo / In a little Wigan garden / Alexander's ragtime band
CD _______________ RAJCD 801
Empress / Jul '94 / Koch

IT'S TURNED OUT NICE AGAIN
Keep your seats please / On the beat / It ain't nobody's biz'ness what I do / Goody goody / I like bananas / Sitting on the sands all night / On the Wigan Boat Express / Talking to the moon about you / Some of these days / Hard hearted Hannah / Sweet Georgia Brown / Sweet Sue, just you / Dinah / Tiger rag / Hitting the high spots / Home guard blues / Goodnight little fellow, goodnight / When I'm cleaning windows (The window cleaner) / Lad from Lancashire / Oh you have no idaea / Riding in the TT races / They can't fool me / Under the blasted oak / I always get to bed by half-past nine / Down the old coal hole / I wonder who's under her balcony now / Delivering the morning milk / Leaning on a lamp-post / It's turned out nice again
CD _______________ PPCD 78105
Past Perfect / Feb '95 / Glass Gramophone Co.

IT'S TURNED OUT NICE AGAIN
Sitiing on the ice rink / Do de oh doh / Chinese laundry blues / Madame Moskovitch / My ukelele / Fanlight Fanny / Keep fit / Biceps, buscle & brawn / Gallant Dick Turpin parts 1&2 / When we feather our nest / Our Sergeant Major / Isle of Man / Hitting the high spots now / Said the little brown hen / Trailing around in a trailor / Men of Harlech / John Peel / Heart of oak / On Ilkley Moor / Loch Lomond / Come landlord fill the flowing bowl / Auld lang syne / My old Kentucky home / Camptown races / She'll be coming round the mountain / Old folks at home (Swanee river) / Oh Suzanna / Over there / Anchors aweigh / If I had a girl like you / Ring your little bell / Under the blasted oak / Oh you have no idea / Blackpool Prom / Daring young man / I'd like a dream like that / Up in the air and down in the dumps / She's got two of everything / Old cane bottom chair / It's a grand and healthy life / With my little stick of Blackpool rock / I'm the husband of the wife of Mr. Wo / When I'm cleaning windows (The window cleaner)
CD _______________ RAJCD 878
Empress / May '96 / Koch

LEGENDARY GEORGE FORMBY, THE
Leaning on a lamp-post / Auntie Maggie's remedy / In my little snapshot album / With my little stick of Blackpool rock / When I'm cleaning windows (The window cleaner) / When I'm cleaning windows (The window cleaner) / Mr. Wu's a window cleaner now / Our Sergeant Major / Mother, what'll I do now / Grandad's flannelette nightshirt / I'm the ukelele man / Mr. Wu in the Air Force / Unconditional surrender / Home guard blues / Cook house serenade / Spotting on the top of Blackpool Tower / I wonder who's under her balcony now / It serves you right / I don't like / Bless 'em all
CD _______________ CC 8234
Music For Pleasure / Dec '93 / EMI

V FOR VICTORY
CD _______________ RKD 23
Redrock / Mar '95 / Target/BMG / THE

VERY BEST OF GEORGE FORMBY, THE (20 Great Songs)
Leaning on a lamp-post / With my little stick of Blackpool rock / Chinese laundry blues / When I'm cleaning windows (The window cleaner) / Swimmin' with the wimmin' / With my little ukelele in my hand / Why don't women like me / You can't keep a growing lad down / Mother, what'll I do now / There's nothing proud about me / In my little snapshot album / Old kitchen kettle / Isle of Man / Lancashire toreador / Our sargeant major / Believe it or not / Madame moscovitch / As the hours and the days and the months and the years roll / Sitting on the ice in the ice rink / I told my baby with the ukelele
CD _______________ PLATCD 28
Platinum / Aug '90 / Prism

WHEN I'M CLEANING WINDOWS
When I'm cleaning windows (The window cleaner) / Oh don't the wind blow cold / It's turned out nice again / With my little stick of Blackpool rock / Hi tiddly hi ti island / It's in the air / Count your blessings and smile / Easy going chap / Grandad's flannelette nightshirt / Hillbilly Willie / Hitting the high spots / I don't like / I'm a froggie / Keep your seats please / Lancashire hot pot swingers / Leaning on a lamp-post / Like the big pots do / Mr. Wu's a window cleaner now / My plus fours / Our sergeant major / Rhythm in the alphabet / Somebody's wedding day / They can't fool me / You can't stop me from dreaming
CD _______________ CDAJA 5079
Living Era / Apr '91 / Select

WHEN I'M CLEANING WINDOWS
Sitting on the ice in the ice rink / Do de o do / Chinese laundry blues / You can't stop me from dreaming / Pleasure cruise / Keep fit / Riding in the TT races / Hindoo man / It ain't nobody's biz'ness what I do / Goody goody / I like bananas / Lancashire Toreador / Farmer's boy / You can't keep a growing lad down / You're a li-a-ty / With my little stick of Blackppol rock / Trailing around in

a trailer / Why don't women like me / Dare devil Dick / Somebody's wedding day / Sitting on the sands all night / Madame Moscovitch / With my little ukelele in my hand / Fanlight Fanny / When I'm cleaning windows (The window cleaner) / Leaning on a lamp-post
CD ____ PLCD 538
President / Jul '95 / Grapevine/PolyGram / President / Target/BMG

Formell, Juan

AY DIOS AMPARAME (Formell, Juan Y Los Van Van)
CD ____ 74321401352
Milan / Sep '96 / Conifer/BMG / Silva Screen

SANDUNGUERA (Formell, Juan Y Los Van Van)
CD ____ MES 159892
Messidor / Jun '93 / ADA / Koch

Forrest, Helen

1983 STUDIO SESSIONS
I've heard that song before / I don't want to walk without you / Happiness is a thing called Joe / But not for me / I cried for you / I had the craziest dream / You made me love you / You'll never know / More than you know
CD ____ VN 1006
Viper's Nest / Nov '96 / ADA / Cadillac / Direct / Jazz Music

CREAM OF HELEN FORREST
CD ____ PASTCD 7062
Flapper / May '95 / Pinnacle

DOUBLE DATE WITH HELEN FORREST AND CHRIS CONNOR (Forrest, Helen & Chris Connor)
CD ____ STCD 14
Stash / Oct '91 / ADA / Cadillac / CM / Direct / Jazz Music

EMBRACEABLE YOU (Previously Unreleased 1949-1950)
CD ____ HCD 257
Hindsight / Jul '95 / Jazz Music / Target/BMG

I WANNA BE LOVED
CD ____ HCD 250
Hindsight / Mar '94 / Jazz Music / Target/BMG

VOICE OF THE BIG BANDS, THE
Deep in a dream: *Forrest, Helen & Artie Shaw Orchestra* / Deep purple: *Forrest, Helen & Artie Shaw Orchestra* / Comes love: *Forrest, Helen & Artie Shaw Orchestra* / Day in, day out: *Forrest, Helen & Artie Shaw Orchestra* / All the things you are: *Forrest, Helen & Artie Shaw Orchestra* / Moonray: *Forrest, Helen & Artie Shaw Orchestra* / How high the moon: *Forrest, Helen & Benny Goodman Orchestra* / Shake down the stars: *Forrest, Helen & Benny Goodman Orchestra* / It never entered my mind: *Forrest, Helen & Benny Goodman Orchestra* / I'm nobody's baby: *Forrest, Helen & Benny Goodman Orchestra* / Taking a chance on love: *Forrest, Helen & Benny Goodman Orchestra* / Yes my darling daughter: *Forrest, Helen & Benny Goodman Orchestra* / Bewitched: *Forrest, Helen & Benny Goodman Orchestra* / I found a million dollar baby: *Forrest, Helen & Benny Goodman Orchestra* / When the sun comes out: *Forrest, Helen & Benny Goodman Orchestra* / Devil sat down and cried: *Forrest, Helen & Harry James Orchestra* / I don't want to walk without you: *Forrest, Helen & Harry James Orchestra* / Skylark: *Forrest, Helen & Harry James Orchestra* / He's my guy: *Forrest, Helen & Harry James Orchestra* / I had the craziest dream: *Forrest, Helen & Harry James Orchestra* / I've heard that song before: *Forrest, Helen & Harry James Orchestra* / Close to you: *Forrest, Helen & Harry James Orchestra* / Long ago and far away: *Forrest, Helen & Dick Haymes* / It had to be you: *Forrest, Helen & Dick Haymes*
CD ____ JASMCD 2545
Jasmine / May '97 / Conifer/BMG / Hot Shot / TKO Magnum

Forrest, Jimmy

ALL THE GIN IS GONE
All the gin is gone / Laura / You go to my head / Myra / Caravan / What's new / Sunkenfoal
CD ____ DD 404
Delmark / Jul '97 / ADA / Cadillac / CM / Direct / Hot Shot

BLACK FORREST
CD ____ DD 427
Delmark / Oct '86 / ADA / Cadillac / CM / Direct / Hot Shot

FORREST FIRE
Forrest fire / Remember / Dexter's deck / Jim's jam / Bag's groove / When your love has gone / Help
CD ____ OJCCD 199
Original Jazz Classics / Jan '94 / Complete/Pinnacle / Jazz Music / Wellard

HONKERS AND BAR WALKERS VOL.1 (Forrest, Jimmy & Tab Smith)
CD ____ DD 438
Delmark / Mar '97 / ADA / Cadillac / CM / Direct / Hot Shot

MOST MUCH
CD ____ OJCCD 350
Original Jazz Classics / Jan '95 / Complete/Pinnacle / Jazz Music / Wellard

NIGHT TRAIN
CD ____ DD 435
Delmark / Apr '86 / ADA / Cadillac / CM / Direct / Hot Shot

SIT DOWN AND RELAX WITH JIMMY FORREST
Tuxedo junction / Moonglow / Rocks in my bed / Organ grinder's swing / Tin tin deo / Moon was yellow and the night was cold / That's all
CD ____ OJCCD 895
Original Jazz Classics / Oct '96 / Complete/Pinnacle / Jazz Music / Wellard

Forrester, Sharon

THIS TIME
CD ____ VPCD 1434
VP / Oct '95 / Greensleeves / Jet Star / Total/BMG

Forsen, Arne

UR HJARTANS DJUP (Forsen, Arne & Pia Olby)
CD ____ DRCD 198
Dragon / Apr '87 / ADA / Cadillac / CM / Roots / Wellard

Forsmark Tre

VASTGOTALATAR
CD ____ FMPCD 001
FMP / May '93 / Cadillac

Forster, John

ENTERING MARION
CD ____ PH 1164CD
Philo / Jan '94 / ADA / CM / Direct

HELIUM
CD ____ CDPH 1214
Philo / Aug '97 / ADA / CM / Direct

Forster, Robert

CALLING FROM A COUNTRY PHONE
CD ____ BBL 127CD
Beggars Banquet / Sep '95 / RTM/Disc / Warner Music

DANGER IN THE PAST
Baby stones / Leave here satisfied / Is this what you call change / Danger in the past / Justice / River people / Heart out to tender / Dear black dream / I've been looking for somebody
CD ____ BEGA 113CD
Beggars Banquet / Sep '90 / RTM/Disc / Warner Music

I HAD A NEW YORK GIRLFRIEND
CD ____ BBQCD 161
Beggars Banquet / Aug '94 / RTM/Disc / Warner Music

WARM NIGHTS
CD ____ BEGL 185CD
Beggars Banquet / Jul '96 / RTM/Disc / Warner Music

Forsythe, Guy

HIGH TEMPERATURE (Forsythe, Guy Band)
CD ____ LDCD 80001
Lizard / Aug '94 / Direct / RTM/Disc

Fortaleza

SOY DE SANGRE KOLLA
CD ____ FF 529CD
Flying Fish / '92 / ADA / CM / Direct / Roots

Forte

DIVISION
CD ____ MASSCD 035
Massacre / Jun '94 / Plastic Head

Forthcoming Fire

ILLUMINATION
CD ____ HY 39100702
Hyperium / Jan '94 / Cargo / Plastic Head

Fortran 5

BAD HEAD PARK
CD ____ CDSTUMM 104
Mute / Jun '93 / RTM/Disc

BLUES, THE
CD ____ CDSTUMM 79
Mute / Sep '91 / RTM/Disc

Fortunairs Barber Shop ...

SWEET ADELINE (Fortunairs Barber Shop Quartet)
Sweet Adeline / Alabama jubilee/Down yonder / Heart of my heart / Auctioneer / Danny boy / Ride the chariot / In the evening by the moonlight / If the good Lord's willing and the creek don't rise / You made me love you/It had to be you / Sunny side up / No more sorrows / Wedding ball rag / Roses of Picardy / Start off each day with a song / Wonderful day like today / When day is done / California here I come / April showers / Gonna build a mountain / When somebody thinks you're wonderful / I'm looking over a four leaf clover / I'll take you home again Kathleen / How could Little Red Riding Hood
CD ____ GRCD 77
Grasmere / Oct '96 / Highlander / Savoy / Target/BMG

Fortune, Jesse

FORTUNE TELLIN' MAN
Dark is the night / Fortune tellin' man / Get mad at my money / Sandu / Too many cooks / Lovingest woman in town / Specter's walk / Gambler's blues / Be careful with a fool / Ain't about money / Losing hand
CD ____ DD 658
Delmark / Mar '97 / ADA / Cadillac / CM / Direct / Hot Shot

Fortune, Johnny

LIFE GOES ON
CD ____ Z 501
Zorch / Apr '97 / Nervous

Fortune, Sonny

MONK'S MOOD
Little rootie tootie / Mysterioso / Nutty / I mean you / Monk's wood / Ruby my dear / In walked bud / Off minor
CD ____ KCD 5048
Konnex / Nov '93 / SRD

Fortunes

FORTUNES
CD ____ GRF 186
Tring / Jan '93 / Tring

SPOTLIGHT ON FORTUNES
You've got your troubles / Here comes that rainy day feeling again / Caroline / Seasons in the sun / Don't throw your love away / When your heart speaks to you / Anna Maria / Storm in a teacup / Mumba Sarah / Half way to paradise / It's a beautiful dream / Funny how love can be
CD ____ HADCD 113
Javelin / Feb '94 / Henry Hadaway / THE

STORM IN A TEACUP/HERE COMES THAT RAINY DAY FEELING AGAIN
Storm in a teacup / Man is a man / Red Clay county line / Whether you like it or not / Today I killed a man / Freedom come, freedom go / Someone is standing outside / Four and twenty hours / Excuse me friend / There's a man / Here comes that rainy day feeling again / Night started to cry / I gotta dream / Just a line to let you know / All my calender is you / Hear the band / Oh babe / Eye for the main chance / Thoughts / Noises (in my head)
CD ____ BGOCD 310
Beat Goes On / Jun '96 / Pinnacle

WORLD OF THE FORTUNES, THE
Caroline / You've got your troubles / Looking through the eyes of love / Here it comes again / All cried out / Maria / Won't you give him (one more chance) / Truly yours / Coloured lights / I'll have my tears to remind me / This golden ring / Our love has gone / Am I losing my touch / This empty place / Laughing fit to cry / Look homeward angel / You can have her / You gave me somebody to love / Silent street / Time to be going
CD ____ 5520232
Spectrum / May '96 / PolyGram

Foskett, Jeffrey

OTHER TAKES, THE
CD ____ NC 961011
New Surf / Jul '97 / Greyhound

THRU MY WINDOW
CD ____ NC 961007
New Surf / Jul '97 / Greyhound

Foster & Allen

100 GOLDEN GREATS
CD Set ____ TCD 2791
Telstar / Oct '95 / BMG

100 GOLDEN LOVE SONGS (2CD Set)
CD Set ____ STAC 2846
Telstar / Oct '96 / BMG

AFTER ALL THESE YEARS
Old Dungarvan oak / When I dream / Bluebell polka / Do you think you could love again / Leaving of Liverpool / Rose of Allendale / I still love you / Cottage by the sea / Old Ardboe / Scots polka / Rose of Mooncoin / Six foot seven woman / When my blue moon turns gold again / After all these years
CD ____ RITZSCD 420
Ritz / Jun '92 / Pinnacle

BUNCH OF THYME
Bunch of thyme / Fiddler / Come back Paddy Reilly / Drink up the cider / Green willow / Living here London / Blacksmith / Alice Benbolt / Benbulben of Sligo / Wise maid / Cooley's reel / Foster's fancy / Nancy Miles / Courtin' in the kitchen
CD ____ RITZSCD 408
Ritz / Apr '93 / Pinnacle

BY REQUEST
CD ____ TCD 2670
Telstar / Oct '93 / BMG

CHRISTMAS ALBUM
CD ____ TCD 2459
Telstar / Nov '90 / BMG

FOSTER & ALLEN SELECTION, THE
Blind / Green willow / Jacqueline waltz / Cocky farmer / Polkas / Fagins wake / Sligo maid / Nancy Myles / Old flames / Oslo waltz / Salonika / Boys of Bluehill / Bally James Duff / Green groves of Erin / Gentle Annie / Sweets of May
CD ____ RITZSCD 409
Ritz / Apr '93 / Pinnacle

I WILL LOVE YOU ALL OF MY LIFE
I will love you all my life / Whiskey on a Sunday / Birdie song / Mull of Kintyre / Swedish rhapsody / Forever and ever / I'll take you home again Kathleen / Cock o' the North / If those lips could only speak / Mountains of Mourne / Happy hour / When I grow too old to dream
CD ____ RITZSCD 419
Ritz / Jun '92 / Pinnacle

MAGGIE
Maggie / Old rustic bridge by the mill / Harvest moon / Isle of Innisfree / Mist upon the morning / Hornpipes / Sweethearts in the spring / Blue eyes cryin' in the rain / Molly my lovely Molly / Seasons of my heart / Reels / Nell Flaherty's drake / Farewell to Derry / Johnny Brown
CD ____ RITZSCD 418
Ritz / Jun '92 / Pinnacle

MEMORIES
CD ____ CDSR 037
Telstar / Oct '93 / BMG

OLD LOVES NEVER DIE (2CD Set)
CD Set ____ CDSR 085
Telstar / May '97 / BMG

SHADES OF GREEN
CD ____ TCD 2899
Telstar / Apr '97 / BMG

SOUVENIRS
CD ____ CDSR 075
Telstar / May '96 / BMG

VERY BEST OF FOSTER & ALLEN, THE
Bunch of thyme / Old flames / Maggie / I will love you all my life / Blacksmith / Oslo waltz / Place in the choir / Just for old times sake / Job of journeywork / Spinning wheel / We will make love / Maid behind the bar / My love is in America / Molly darling / Before I met you / Gentle mother
CD ____ RITZRCD 523
Ritz / Apr '93 / Pinnacle

VERY BEST OF THE LOVE SONGS VOL.2
CD ____ RITZRCD 524
Ritz / Apr '93 / Pinnacle

WORLD OF FOSTER & ALLEN, THE
CD ____ TCD 2478
Telstar / Apr '91 / BMG

Foster, David

CHRISTMAS ALBUM, THE
Carol of the bells / Blue Christmas / First Noel / It's the most wonderful time of the year / Grown up Christmas list / O holy night / Go tell it on the mountain / Mary had a baby, yes Lord / I'll be home for Christmas / Mary's boy child / Christmas song / Away in a manger / White Christmas
CD ____ 6544922952
Atlantic / Feb '93 / Warner Music

Foster, Frank

FRANKLY SPEAKING (Foster, Frank & Frank Weiss)
When did you leave Heaven / Up and coming / One morning in May / Two Franks / This is all I ask / Blues backstage / An' all such stuff as'dat / Summer knows
CD ____ CCD 4276
Concord Jazz / Sep '86 / New Note/Pinnacle

LEO RISING
You're only as old as you look / Simone / Gray Thursday / Cidde alto / Leo rising / When April comes again / Last night when we were young / Derricksterity
CD ____ AJ 0124
Arabesque / Apr '97 / New Note/Pinnacle

Foster, Gary

MAKE YOUR OWN FUN
Alone together / Peacocks / Warne-ing / Nica's dream / What a life / I concentrate on you / Some other Spring / Teef / I'll close my eyes / Easy living / Sweet lips
CD ____ CCD 4459

Concord Jazz / May '91 / New Note/ Pinnacle

Foster, John

ESSENCE OF TIME, THE (Foster, John Band)
CD _____ QPRL 047D
Polyphonic / Sep '91 / Complete/Pinnacle

Foster, Mo

BEL ASSIS (Foster, Mo & Gary Moore)
Light in your eyes / Walk in the country / Gaia / Crete re-visited / So far away / Analytical engine / Pump II / Jaco / Bel assis / And then there were ten / Nomad
CD _____ INAK 11003CD
In Akustik / Jul '97 / Direct / TKO Magnum

SOUTHERN REUNION (Foster, Mo & Gary Moore)
Gil / Blue / Achill island / Waves / Tricotism / National anthem / Southern reunion / Grand unified boogie / Fractal landscape / Shin kan sen
CD _____ INAK 11006CD
In Akustik / Jul '97 / Direct / TKO Magnum

Foster, Radney

DEL RIO, TX 1959
Just call me lonesome / Don't say goodbye / Easier said than done / Fine line / Went for a ride / Nobody wins / Louisiana blue / Closing time / Hammer and nails / Old silver
CD _____ 07822187132
Arista / Jun '94 / BMG

LABOR OF LOVE
Willing to talk / Labor of love / My whole wide world / Never say die / Jesse's soul / Everybody gets the blues / If it were me / Broke down / Precious pearl / Last chance for love / Fine line / Nobody wins / Making it up as I go along / Walkin' talkin' woman
CD _____ 74321229842
Arista / Apr '95 / BMG

Fotheringay

FOTHERINGAY (Fotheringay & Sandy Denny)
Nothing more / Sea / Ballad of Ned Kelly / Winter winds / Peace in the end / Way I feel / Pond and the stream / Too much of nothing / Banks of the Nile
CD _____ HNCD 4426
Hannibal / May '89 / ADA / Vital

Foulplay

SUSPECTED
CD _____ ASHADOW 2CD
Moving Shadow / Oct '95 / SRD

Foundations

ALL THE HITS PLUS MORE
Every one's a winner / Born to live and born to die / If there were no music / Baby now that I've found you / Same sad feeling / Bring back / In the bad, bad old days / Tender touch / Any old time / It's a burning love / Everyday / Back on my feet again / Let's make this love last forever / Build me up buttercup
CD _____ CDSGP 0244
Prestige / Apr '97 / Else / Total/BMG

BRITISH 60'S, THE (Foundations/Equals)
Baby come back: *Equals* / Viva Bobby Joe: *Equals* / Black skin blue eyed boys: *Equals* / Michael and the slipper tree: *Equals* / Laurel and Hardy: *Equals* / Rub a dub dub: *Equals* / I get so excited: *Equals* / Softly softly: *Equals* / Get back: *Equals* / Hey baby: *Equals* / Baby now that I found you: *Foundations* / Build me up buttercup: *Foundations* / Dock of the bay: *Foundations* / Any old time you're sad and lonely: *Foundations* / Back on my feet again: *Foundations* / Born to live and born to die: *Foundations* / In the bad old days: *Foundations* / Keep loving you: *Foundations* / Knock on wood: *Foundations* / Together flowers: *Foundations*
CD _____ PLATCD 202
Platinum / Feb '97 / Prism

FOUNDATIONS, THE
CD _____ KLMCD 032
BAM / Nov '94 / Koch / Scratch/BMG

THAT SAME OLD FEELING
Baby now that I've found you / Back on my feet again / Tomorrow / Harlem shuffle / Mr. Personality man / I can take or leave your lovin' / Let the heartaches begin / Am I groovin' you / We are happy people / That same old feeling / Any old time / Build me up buttercup / Born to live, born to die / Waiting on the shores of nowhere / Come on back to me / In the bad, bad old days
CD _____ 21041
Laserlight / Jul '97 / Target/BMG

Foundland

EVERYBODY'S NEIGHBOUR
CD _____ XOUCD 112
Xource / Mar '96 / ADA / Direct

Foundry Bar Band

ROLLING HOME
Conundrum / Rollin' home / Murdo's wedding / Weaver / Braes of Castlegrant / Come by the hills / Dashing white sergeant / Muckin' O' Geordie's byre / Row her in ma plaide / Barren rocks of Aden / Aince upon a time / Skye gathering / Angus MacLeod / All for me grog / Scotland the brave
CD _____ SPRCD 1026
Springthyme / Dec '88 / ADA / CM / Direct / Duncans / Highlander / Roots

Fountain, Pete

BEST OF PETE FOUNTAIN, THE
While we dance at the Mardi Gras / Closer walk / Columbus stockade blues / Do you know what it mean to New Orleans / Fascination medley (4 Parts) / China boy (Go sleep) / Bye bye Bill Baily / Lazy river / Yes indeed / High society / Stranger on the shore / Over the waves / Oh lady be good / You're nobody 'til somebody loves you / somebody loves you / My blue heaven / Put on your old grey bonnet / For Pete's sake / When the saints come marching in march / St. Louis Blues / When my baby smiles at me
CD _____ GRP 16652
American Decca / Aug '96 / New Note/BMG

DO YOU KNOW WHAT IT MEANS TO MISS NEW ORLEANS
CD _____ BCD 300
GHB / Aug '94 / Jazz Music

DO YOU KNOW WHAT IT MEANS TO MISS NEW ORLEANS (Playing Dixieland/Louis Armstrong Favourites - 2CD Set)
Do you what it means to miss New Orleans / When the saints go marching in / Just a closer walk with thee / Sweethearts on parade / When it's sleepy time down south / Tin roof blues / Wabash blues / St Louis blues / Wing wang blues / I've found a new baby / Ja da / Tiger rag / Someday sweetheart / Birth of the blues / Dear old southland / That da da strain / At the jazz band ball / Jazz me blues / St James infirmary / Panama / Of all the wrongs you've done to me / Milenberg joys / I wish I could shimmy like my sister Kate / Struttin' with some barbecue / Bourbon street parade / Ballin' with Jack / Rockin' chair / South Rampart Street parade / Farewell blues / Careless love / Basin Street blues / (What did I do to be so) Black and blue / That's a plenty / Sheik of Araby / Dippermouth blues / Washboard blues / Muskrat ramble / I gotta right to sing the blues
CD _____ GRP 26582
American Decca / Apr '96 / New Note/BMG

HIGH SOCIETY
High society / Farewell blues / At the Darktown strutter's ball / Ballin' the Jack / Muskrat ramble / Twelth street rag / Tin roof blues / Won't you come home, Bill Bailey
CD _____ 07863660712
Bluebird / Oct '92 / BMG

NEW ORLEANS ALL-STARS
CD _____ TCD 1047
Tradition / May '97 / ADA / Vital

PETE FOUNTAIN
Waiting for the Robert E Lee / South Rampart Street Parade / Angry / Bonaparte's retreat / Original dixieland one-step / Land of dreams / Mahogany Hall Stomp / Royal Garden blues / Sailing down the Chesepeake Bay / Up a lazy river / Milenburg joys / Margie / High society / I'm going home / Farewell blues
CD _____ 504CD 16
504 / Aug '94 / Cadillac / Jazz Music / Target/BMG / Wellard

PETE FOUNTAIN AT PIPER'S OPERA HOUSE
CD _____ JCD 217
Jazzology / Aug '94 / Jazz Music

Fountainhead

DRAIN
CD _____ DOG 021
Doghouse / Nov '94 / Plastic Head

Fountains Of Wayne

FOUNTAINS OF WAYNE
Radiation vibe / Sink to the bottom / Joe Rey / She's got a problem / Survival car / Barbara H / Sick day / I've got a flair / Leave the biker / You curse at girls / Please don't rock me tonight / Everything's ruined
CD _____ 7567927252
Atlantic / May '97 / Warner Music

FOUR

ORDER
Going to extremes / Sweetest surrender / New York Jamaica London Ethiopia / SMILE / Non-stop traffic / Wait until tonight / Lay of the land / Hold me like china / Little more love / Four reasons unknown
CD _____ CDKUFF 1
Kuff / Sep '96 / EMI

Four 80 East

FOUR 80 EAST
CD _____ BOOM 1
Boom Tang / Jun '97 / Timewarp

Four Aces

FOUR ACES
CD _____ CD 113
Timeless Treasures / Oct '94 / THE

GREATEST HITS
CD _____ CD 338
Entertainers / Feb '95 / Target/BMG

LOVE IS A MANY SPLENDOURED THING
CD _____ RMB 75060
Remember / Aug '92 / Total/BMG

Four Bitchin' Babies

BUY ME, BRING ME, TAKE ME
CD _____ PHCD 1150
Philo / May '93 / ADA / CM / Direct

Four Brothers

MAKOROKOTO
Makorokoto / Rugare / Wapenga nayo bonus / Ndakatadzeiko / Sara Tasangana / Pamusoroi / Nhaka yemusiiranwa / Uchandifunga / Guhwa uri mwana waani / Ndakatambura / Vimbayi / Rumbidzai / Rudo imoto / Pasi pano pane zviedzo / Maishoko ababa namai / Siya zviriko
CD _____ BAKECD 004
Cooking Vinyl / May '90 / Vital

TOGETHER AGAIN
Four and one moore / So blue / Swinging door / Four in hand / Quick one / Four brothers / Ten years later / Pretty one / Aged in wood / Here we go again
CD _____ 74321130402
RCA / Sep '93 / BMG

Four Champions

IRISH TRADITIONAL ACCORDION
Hill 60 / Spring well / Jackie Coleman's / Reel of Rio / McGuires / Maud Millar's / Molly's / Return from Camden Town / Tom Moyland's frolic / Paddy Ryan's dream / Farewell to Cailroe / Miller's maid / Skylark / Josie McDermott / Bunch of green rushes / Richard Dwyer's / Paddy Kelly's / Concert flute / Upstairs in a tent / Mason's apron / Pigeon on the gate / Drunken tinker / Fahy's / Finbar Dwyer's No.2 / Meadow / Ballinasloe fair / Bunch of Keys / Lady Montgomery / Farrell Garret / Dillan Brown's / Sonny McDonagh's
CD _____ PHCD 1027
Outlet / Mar '97 / ADA / CM / Direct / Duncans / Koch / Ross

Four Courts

TRADITIONAL IRISH MUSIC AND SONG FROM COUNTY CLARE
CD _____ TRADCD 001
GTD / Feb '91 / ADA / Else

Four Freshmen

DAY BY DAY
CD _____ HCD 604
Hindsight / Feb '95 / Jazz Music / Target/ BMG

EASY STREET (Live On The Ray Anthony TV Show 1958)
Day by day / You're so far above me / Love is just around the corner / You stepped out of a dream / Charmaine / Get a date with an angel / Easy Street / After you've gone / Somebody loves me / He who loves and runs away / Crazy bones / Day isn't long enough / How do you like your eggs in the morning / Someone like you / We'll be together again / This can't be love / Graduation day / Frosty the snowman / Love turns Winter to Spring / There'll never be another you / It's a blue world
CD _____ RACD 1023
Aerospace / Jun '97 / Jazz Music / Montpellier

GRADUATION DAY
CD _____ 12120
Laserlight / Jan '94 / Target/BMG

IT'S A BLUE WORLD
CD _____ VN 170
Viper's Nest / Mar '96 / ADA / Cadillac / Direct / Jazz Music

LIVE AT BUTLER UNIVERSITY (Four Freshmen & Stan Kenton Orchestra)
There will never be another you / After you / Byrd Avenue / Surfer girl / Girl talk / When the feeling hit you / Walk on by / What are you doing the rest of your life / Brand new key / Teach me tonight / Beautiful friendship / Summer has gone / Hymn to her / Come back to me / It's not unusual / Coming round the mountain / Walk softly / Artistry in rhythm
CD _____ GNPD 1059
GNP Crescendo / Aug '95 / ZYX

VOICES IN STANDARDS
Come fly with me / Young at heart / I've got you under my skin / Nearness of you / You'd be so nice to come home to / All the way / Embraceable you / I'm a fool to want you / All or nothing at all / In the wee small hours / Witchcraft / Time after time / How insensitive / Nancy / Nice 'n' easy / Put your dreams away
CD _____ HCD 801
Hindsight / Jul '96 / Jazz Music / Target/ BMG

Four Horsemen

GETTIN' PRETTY GOOD AT BARELY GETTIN' BY
CD _____ 4701440252
SPV / Apr '96 / Koch / Plastic Head

Four Lovers

JOYRIDE
What is a thing called love / Joyride / Such a night / Girl in my dreams / Diddilly diddilly baby / Shake a hand / Please don't leave me / You're the apple of my eye / Stranger / White Christmas / It's too soon to know / San Antonio rose / Night train / Cimarron / Lawdy Miss Clawdy / This is my story / (I love you) for sentimental reasons / I want a girl - just like the girl that married dear old Dad / Memories of you / Jambalaya / Be lovey lovey / Love sweet love / Happy am I / Never never / Honey love / (I love you) for sentimental reasons / White Christmas / Girl in my dreams / Diddilly diddilly baby / Such a night / Honey love
CD _____ BCD 15424
Bear Family / Apr '89 / Direct / Rollercoaster / Swift

Four Men & A Dog

BARKING MAD
Hidden love/Sheila Coyles / Wee Johnny set / Wrap it up / Foxhunters / Waltzing for dreamers / Reel / Polkas / Swing set / Short fat Fanny / Jigs / Cruel father / High on a mountain / McFadden's reels
CD _____ CBMMCCD 001
Special Delivery / Sep '91 / ADA / CM / Direct

DR. A'S SECRET REMEDIES
Papa Genes Tree / Bertha / Last month of Summer / Mother of mercy / Punch in the dark / Take it on back / Samba / Hollow time / Last nite / Woodstock set / Heading West / Hector the hero
CD _____ TRACD 106
Transatlantic / Apr '96 / Pinnacle

LONG ROADS
CD _____ TRACD 223
Transatlantic / Jun '96 / Pinnacle

SHIFTING GRAVEL
CD _____ SPDCD 1047
Special Delivery / May '93 / ADA / CM / Direct

Four Pennies

TWO SIDES OF FOUR PENNIES/MIXED BAG
Da doo ron ron / Sweeter than you / Claudette / If you love me / Do you want me to / Love's journey / You went away / Will you love me tomorrow / Now we are through / Pony time / Come to me / Why do you cry / Cryin' inside / Look down / I'm on my own / She didn't say yes / It is no secret / Iko Iko / Without love / Try to find another man / Maracabama / Stewball / All my sorrows / Someday soon / Wild goose / Let it be me
CD _____ BGOCD 346
Beat Goes On / Mar '97 / Pinnacle

WORLD OF THE FOUR PENNIES, THE
Juliet / Black girl / Keep the freeway open / I found out the hard way / Tell me girl / Till another day / If you love me / Miss bad Daddy / You went away / Running scared / Love's journey / No sad songs for me / Square peg / Sweeter than you / Way out love / Trouble is my middle name / Now we are through / San Francisco Bay / Do you want me to / Until it's time for you to go
CD _____ 5511012
Spectrum / May '96 / PolyGram

Four Preps

THREE GOLDEN GROUPS IN ONE
Hello again / Big man / Summer place / Church bells may ring / Can't take my eyes off you / Got a girl / Graduation day / Hurt so bad / I'll sing for you / MacArthur Park / I heard it through the grapevine / You've lost that lovin' feelin' / Hard habit to break / Why do fools fall in love / When I fall in love / Stroll / Little darlin' / Put your head on my shoulder / Ride like the wind / Stand by me / Love love love / Down by the station / Going out of my head / Lazy summer night / Silhouettes / Twenty six miles (Santa Catalina) / Shangri la / Over the rainbow / I'll still be loving you / Somewhere
CD _____ C5MCD 588
See For Miles/C5 / Aug '92 / Pinnacle

Four Sides

SQUARE ONE
CD _____ SQUARE 1
Square 1 / Mar '97 / Jet Star

Four Tops

ANTHOLOGY
Baby I need your loving / Without the one you love / Ask the lonely / I can't help myself / It's the same old song / Something about you / Shake me, wake me / Loving you is sweeter than ever / Reach out, I'll be there / Standing in the shadows of love / I got a feeling / Bernadette / Seven rooms of gloom / (You keep) running away / Walk away Renee / If I were a carpenter / Yesterdays dreams / I'm in a different world / Can't seem to get you out of my mind / It's all in the game / Still water / River deep, mountain high / Just seven numbers / In these changing times / I can't quit your love / Nature planned it / You gotta have love in your heart / What is a man / Do what you gotta do / MacArthur Park part 2 / Simple game / So deep within you / Hey man / We gotta get you a woman
CD Set ____ 5301902
Motown / Jan '92 / PolyGram

FOUR TOPS SINGLES COLLECTION
Reach out, I'll be there / Standing in the shadows of love / Bernadette / Walk away Renee / If I were a carpenter / Simple game / Seven rooms of gloom / Loving you is sweeter than ever / You keep running away / Yesterday's dreams / I'm in a different world / What is a man / Loco in Acapulco / Indestructible / When she was my girl / It's all in the game / Still water (love) / I can't help myself / Do what you gotta do / Keeper of the castle / Don't walk away
CD ____ 5157102
Motown / Sep '92 / PolyGram

MOTOWN EARLY CLASSICS
Reach out I'll be there / Love feels like fire / I can't help myself / I'm grateful / It's the same old song / Just as long as you need me / Baby I need your loving / Call on me / Where did you go / Your love is amazing / Tea house in Chinatown / Ask the lonely / Sad souvenirs / Don't turn away / Love has gone / Is there anything that I can do / Darling, I hum our song / Helpless
CD ____ 5521192
Spectrum / Jul '96 / PolyGram

MOTOWN'S GREATEST HITS: FOUR TOPS
CD ____ 5300162
Motown / Jan '92 / PolyGram

UNTIL YOU LOVE SOMEONE - MORE BEST OF THE FOUR TOPS (1965-1970)
Teahouse in your kitchen / Your love is amazing / Since you've been gone / Helpless / Love feels like fire / I like everything about you / Stay in my lonely arms / Darling I hum our song / I got a feeling / Brenda / Until you love someone / You can't hurry love / Wonderful baby / What else is there to do (but think about you) / What is a man / Nothing / LA (My town) / Reflections
CD ____ 8122711832
WEA / Jun '93 / Warner Music

WITH LOVE
Don't walk away / Sweet understanding love / When she was my girl / I believe in you and me / Tonight I'm gonna love you all over / Ain't no woman (like the one I've got) / One more mountain to climb / Keeper of the castle / Let me set you free / Sad hearts / Are you man enough / Seven lonely nights / Catfish / We all gotta stick together
CD ____ 5501352
Spectrum / Oct '93 / PolyGram

Fourmost

FIRST AND FOURMOST
Till you say you'll be mine / Yakety yak / Girls, girls, girls / My block / So fine / Some kind of wonderful / Girl can't help it / Today I'm in love / In crowd / Baby sittin' boogie / Heebie jeebies / Sure to fall (in love with you) / Bound to lose my heart / Something's got a hold on me / Till you say you'll be mine / Yakety yak / Girls, girls, girls / My block / So fine / Some kind of wonderful / Girl can't help it / Today I'm in love / In crowd / Baby sittin' boogie / Heebie jeebies / Sure to fall (in love with you) / Bound to lose my heart / Something's got a hold on me
CD ____ DORIG 116
EMI / Aug '97 / EMI

Fourplay

BEST OF FOURPLAY, THE
Max-o-man / 101 Eastbound / Higher ground: *Fourplay & Take 6* / Fourplay and pleasure / Chant / After the dance: *Fourplay & El Debarge* / Bali run / Play lady play / Between the sheets: *Fourplay & Chaka Khan* / Amorose / Any time of day / Why can't it wait till morning: *Fourplay & Phil Collins*
CD ____ 9362466612
Warner Bros. / Jul '97 / Warner Music

BETWEEN THE SHEETS
Chant / Monterrey / Between the sheets / Li'l darlin' / Flying east / One in the AM / Gulliver / Amoroso / Summer child / Anthem / Song for Somalia
CD ____ 9362452402
WEA / Aug '93 / Warner Music

FOURPLAY
Bali run / 101 eastbound / Foreplay / Moonjogger / Max-o-man / After the dance / Quadrille / Midnight stroll / October morning / Wish you were here / Rainforest
CD ____ 7599266562
WEA / Mar '94 / Warner Music

Fourth Way

FOURTH WAY, THE
CD ____ COD 022
Jazz View / Aug '92 / Harmonia Mundi

Fourth World

ENCOUNTERS OF THE FOURTH WORLD
Burning money / What you see / Canja na cavaca / Pandeiro solo/Seven seeds / Yara/ Firewalk / Scorpio rising / Final celebration
CD ____ BW 045
B&W / Nov '96 / New Note/Pinnacle / SRD / Vital/SAM

FOURTH WORLD
Esperanza / River Sao Francisco / Starfish / Povo da Lira / Africa / Earthquake / Lua / Seven steps / Firewater - Jive talk / Santa Anita
CD ____ BW 030
B&W / Nov '96 / New Note/Pinnacle / SRD / Vital/SAM

FOURTH WORLD
CD ____ JHCD 026
Ronnie Scott's Jazz House / Jan '94 / Cadillac / Jazz Music / New Note/Pinnacle / TKO Magnum

LIVE IN SOUTH AFRICA 1993
Lua flora / Jive talk / Rain thing berimbau / Toque de quica / Seven steps / Treme terra
CD ____ BNETCD 003
Bootleg.Net / Feb '97 / Vital/SAM

Fowler, Lemuel

LEM FOWLER (1923-1927) (Fowler, Lem & Helen Baxter/H. McDonald)
CD ____ JPCD 1520
Jazz Perspectives / May '95 / Hot Shot / Jazz Music

Fowley, Kim

ANIMAL GOD OF THE STREET
CD ____ 622482
Skydog / Apr '97 / Discovery

DAY THE EARTH STOOD STILL, THE
CD ____ 14260
Spalax / Jan '97 / ADA / Cargo / Direct / Discovery / Greyhound

HIDDEN AGENDA AT THE 13TH NOTE (Fowley, Kim & The BMX Bandits)
Jaded / Ugly dream / Crabmeat / Ballad of a suicidal teenager / Medicine girl / Secret and sometimes cunning exploits of a Glaswegian mortua / Volcano / Sleep / Alice Cooper's roadie's lovechild / Dancing with death on the lilac / Super highway / Tokyo summertime love affair number 69 / Susan was bleeding / Do you want to dance / It's my party / Peaches / Vampire scarecrow / Kimotronix / Sight surfing
CD ____ RRCD 231
Receiver / Mar '97 / Grapevine/PolyGram

KINGS OF SATURDAY NIGHT (Fowley, Kim & Ben Vaughn)
CD ____ SECT2 1002
Sector 2 / Jul '95 / Cargo / Direct

MONDO HOLLYWOOD
CD ____ CREV 036CD
Rev-Ola / Nov '95 / 3mv/Vital

OUTRAGEOUS/GOOD CLEAN FUN
CD ____ CREV 033CD
Rev-Ola / Feb '95 / 3mv/Vital

WHITE NEGROES IN DEUTSCHLAND
CD ____ USMCD 1021
Marilyn / Jul '93 / Pinnacle

Fowlkes, Eddie

BLACK TECHNOSOUL (Fowlkes, Eddie 'Flashin')
CD ____ EFA 017952
Tresor / Jun '96 / 3mv/BMG / Prime / SRD

IN DA MIX (Fowlkes, Eddie 'Flashin')
CD ____ OL 1
On The Lid / Apr '97 / Prime

TECHNOSOUL (Fowlkes, Eddie 'Flashin' & 3MB)
My soul / Computee / Move me / Tribal joy / Hoodlum child / Golden apple / Image-a-nation
CD ____ TRESOR 8CD
Tresor / Apr '93 / 3mv/BMG / Prime / SRD

Fox

FOR FOX SAKE
CD ____ FLASH 34
Flash / May '97 / Greyhound

Fox, Bob

HOW ARE YOU OFF FOR COALS (Songs Of The Mining Communities Of North East England) (Fox, Bob & Benny Graham/Celebrated Working Men)
Celebrated working man/Oakey's strike evictions / Funny names at Tanfield / South Medomsley strike / I wish pay Friday wad come / Old miner / Trimdon Grange explosion / Geordie Black / Have a game for the crack / Little chance / Wor Nanny's a maizor / Going to the mine / Big hewer / When it's ours / Blackleg mining man / Farewell Johnny miner / Miner's lifeguard
CD ____ FECD 111
Fellside / Feb '97 / ADA / Direct / Target/ BMG

Fox, Donal

UGLY BEAUTY (Fox, Donal & David Murray)
Ugly beauty / Vamping with TT / 'Round midnight / Hope scope / Song for Murray / Icarus / Becca's ballad / Picasso / Golden ladders / Hope scope (Live)
CD ____ ECD 221312
Evidence / Dec '95 / ADA / Cadillac / Harmonia Mundi

Fox, Mandy

FIRST TIME EVER (Fox, Mandy & HARA)
Invocation / Missing / Here it comes / You / Flight of the eagle / First time ever / Zoodat / She moved through the fair / Let me go soldier / Bliss / Prayer / Soukhous by night / Call
CD ____ SLAMCD 220
Slam / Oct '96 / Cadillac

Fox, Paul

TRIBULATION DUB VOL.1
CD ____ WSPCD 002
WSP / Nov '93 / Jet Star

Fox, Robert

GATHERING OF SPIRITS, A
CD ____ FXCD 4
FX / Aug '96 / Else

Fox, Roy

ROY FOX
CD ____ PASTCD 9745
Flapper / Aug '91 / Pinnacle

Fox, Samantha

GREATEST HITS
CD ____ CHIP 122
Jive / Sep '92 / Pinnacle

GREATEST HITS
Touch me (I want your body) / Do ya do ya (wanna please me) / Nothing's gonna stop me now / I only wanna be with you / I surrender (to the spirit of the night) / I wanna have some fun / Hold on tight / Just one night / Naughty girls (need love too) / I promise you (get ready) / (I can't get no) satisfaction / Love house / Another woman / Spirit of America / Hot lovin' / Giving me a hard time / Even in the darkest hours
CD ____ 100032
CMC / May '97 / BMG

GREATEST HITS OF SAMANTHA FOX, THE
Touch me touch me (I want your body) / Do ya do ya (wanna please me) / Nothing's gonna stop me now / I only wanna be with you / I surrender (to the spirit of the night) / I wanna have some fun / Hold on tight / Just one night / Naughty girls (need love too) / I promise you (get ready) / Satisfaction / Love house / Another woman (too many people) / Spirit of America / Hot lovin' / Giving me a hard time / Even in the darkest hours
CD ____ QED 046
Tring / Nov '96 / Tring

HITS ALBUM, THE
Touch me (I want your body) / Nothing's gonna stop me now / I only wanna be with you / Do ya do ya (wanna please me) / Love house / Satisfaction / I wanna have some fun / Hot for you / More more more / Love to love you baby / Naughty girls (need love too) / Hurt me hurt me / But the pants stay on / Hot lovin' / Even in the darkest hours / Just one night / Another woman (too many people) / Pleasure zone / Spirit of America / I surrender (to the spirit of the night)
CD ____ EMPRCD 557
Emporio / Mar '95 / Disc

INTERVIEW COMPACT DISC: SAM FOX
CD ____ CBAK 4023
Baktabak / Nov '89 / Arabesque

SAM
Nothing's gonna stop me now / Want you to want to / Tonight's the night / Best is yet to come / Ready for this / Dream city / Satisfaction / Do ya do ya (wanna please me) / I promise you / Lovehouse / Hold on tight / Suzie don't leave me with your boyfriend / One in a million / Never gonna fall in love again
CD ____ 5501162
Spectrum / Oct '93 / PolyGram

Foxley, Ray

PROFESSOR FOXLEY'S SPORTING HOUSE MUSIC
CD ____ BLR 84 021
L&R / May '91 / New Note/Pinnacle

RAY FOXLEY & BLACK EAGLE JAZZBAND (Foxley, Ray & Black Eagle Jazzband)
CD ____ SOSCD 1257
Stomp Off / Oct '93 / Jazz Music / Wellard

Foxx, Inez & Charlie

COUNT THE DAYS
CD ____ CDRB 26
Charly / Aug '95 / Koch

Foxx, John

ASSEMBLY
CD ____ CDVM 9002
Virgin / Jun '92 / EMI

CATHEDRAL OCEANS
Cathedral oceans / City as memory / Through Summer rooms / Geometry and coincidence / If only... / Shifting perspective / Floating islands / Infinite in all directions / Avenham collanade / Sunset rising / Invisible architecture
CD ____ META 001
Metamatic / Mar '97 / Pinnacle

GARDEN, THE
Europe after the rain / Systems of romance / When I was a man and you were a woman / Dancing like a gun / Pater Noster / Night suit / You were there / Fusion / Walk away / Garden / Fission
CD ____ CDV 2194
Virgin / Jul '93 / EMI

METAMATIC
Plaza / He's a liquid / Underpass / Metal beat / No-one driving / New kind of man / Blurred girl / 030 / Tidal wave / Touch and girl
CD ____ CDV 2146
Virgin / Jul '93 / EMI

SHIFTING CITY (Foxx, John & Louis Gordon)
Crash / Noise / Here we go / Shadow man / Through my sleeping / Forgotten years / Everyone / Shifting city / Concrete / Bulletproof / Invisible / Ocean we can breathe
CD ____ META 002
Metamatic / Mar '97 / Pinnacle

Foyer Des Arts

DIE UNFAEHIGKETT ZU FRUEHSTUECKEN
CD ____ EFA 4522 CD
Funfundvierz / Jun '89 / Cargo / Greyhound

Fracasso, Michael

LOVE AND TRUST
CD ____ DJD 3205
Dejadisc / May '94 / ADA / Direct

WHEN I LIVED IN THE WILD
CD ____ BOHB 003
Bohemia Beat / Feb '95 / ADA / CM / Direct

Fraction

MOON BLOOD
CD ____ ANT 2411
Anthology / May '97 / Cargo / Greyhound

Fracture

KILLERNET
CD ____ SPV 0822462
SPV / Oct '96 / Koch / Plastic Head

Fracus, Dimitru

IMPROVISATIONS ON FAMOUS ROMANIAN THEMES (Fracus, Dimitru & Marcel Cellier)
Marie Polale ciurate / Cinrec de unstrainare / Quand dieu crea les montagnes / Les moutons, les bergers / Dooina prieteniei / Doina Cind eram copil d-un an / Bruil lui cepzan / Doina Cresta frunza / Entre ciel et terre / Appels des sommets et danse du berger / Doina lui constantin gherghina / Poarga din pomezau / Doina au sommet de la collins / Suite: Un soir en transylvanie / Doina: Les plaines du banat / Duex danses dominicales / Oh montagnes aux sapins majesteux / Ardalean de la zarvesti / Cind s a pierduit ciobanul oile
CD ____ PV 750003
Disques Pierre Verany / Jul '94 / Kingdom

Fradon, Amy

TAKE ME HOME (Fradon, Amy & Leslie Ritter)
CD ____ SHCD 8013
Shanachie / Dec '94 / ADA / Greensleeves / Koch

Fraley, J.P.

MAYSVILLE (Fraley, J.P. & Annadeene)
CD ____ ROUCD 0351
Rounder / Nov '95 / ADA / CM / Direct

Frames

FITZCARRALDO (Frames DC)
CD 0630128452
ZTT / Jul '96 / Warner Music

Frampton Hill

WELCOME TO FRAMPTON HILL
CD 0630179842
East West / May '97 / Warner Music

Frampton, Peter

FRAMPTON COMES ALIVE
(Baby) Something's happening / Doobie wah / Show me the way / It's a plain shame / All I want to be (is by your side) / Wind of change / Baby, I love your way / I wanna go to the sun / Penny for your thoughts / (I'll give you) money / Shine on / Jumpin' Jack Flash / Lines on my face / Do you feel like we do
CD 5407162
A&M / Mar '97 / PolyGram

FRAMPTON COMES ALIVE VOL.2
Day in the sun / Lying / For now / Most of all / You / Waiting for your love / I'm in you / Talk to me / Hang on to a dream / Can't take that away / More ways than one / Almost said goodbye / Off the hook / Show me the way / Baby I love your way / Lines on my face / Do you feel like we do
CD EIRSCD 1074
CD Set EIRSCDX 1074
IRS/EMI / Oct '95 / EMI

LOVE TAKER
CD HADCD 199
Javelin / Nov '95 / Henry Hadaway / THE

MOON'S TRAIN
CD INAK 11004
In Akustik / Oct '96 / Direct / TKO Magnum

PACIFIC FREIGHT
CD CDSGP 0243
Prestige / Feb '96 / Else / Total/BMG

SHINE ON
CD CDMID 174
A&M / Oct '92 / PolyGram

SHOWS THE WAY
Friday on my mind / Roadrunner / Signed, sealed, delivered (I'm yours) / Baby, I love your way / I can't stand it no more / You don't know like I know / Wind of change / Show me the way / We've just begun / (I'll give you) money / Breaking all the rules / All night long / Jumpin' Jack Flash
CD 5501032
Spectrum / Mar '94 / PolyGram

Fran, Carol

SEE THERE (Fran, Carol & Clarence Holliman)
CD BT 1100CD
Black Top / Apr '94 / ADA / CM / Direct

SOUL SENSATION (Fran, Carol & Clarence Holliman)
CD BT 1071CD
Black Top / Feb '92 / ADA / CM / Direct

France, Marie

MARIE FRANCE
CD 3014632
Last Call / Feb '97 / Cargo / Direct / Discovery

Francis, Connie

24 GREATEST HITS
Where the boys are / If I didn't care / Hurt / Vacation / Are you lonesome tonight / Together among my souvenirs / Everybody's somebody's fool / Old time rock 'n' roll / My heart has a mind of its own / Crying time / My happiness / Lipstick on your collar / Who's sorry now / Stupid cupid / Misty blue / Torn between two lovers / Breakin' in a brand new broken heart / Many tears ago / Don't break the heart that loves you / Cry / Frankie / Second hand love / Something stupid
CD PLATCD 3910
Platinum / Nov '90 / Prism

24 GREATEST HITS
CD RMB 75069
Remember / Jan '94 / Total/BMG

COLLECTION, THE
Stupid Cupid / Lipstick on your collar / Don't break the heart that loves you / Jealous heart / Where the boys are / Breakin' in a brand new broken heart / Plenty good lovin' / Singin' the blues / Valentino / You always hurt the one you love / My heart has a mind of its own / Heartaches by the number / Bye bye love / Your cheatin' heart / I can't stop loving you / Walk on by / Among my souvenirs / My happiness
CD 5518222
Spectrum / Nov '95 / PolyGram

CONNIE FRANCIS
You made me love you / I'm walkin' / Ain't that a shame / Tweedle dee / Too young / How deep is the ocean / I'll get by / Love eyes / Young at heart / Temptation / April love / Singin' the blues / Tennessee waltz / Come rain or come shine / If you love me tonight / Jalousie / Tango delle rose / Quiereme mucho / Besame mucho / These foolish things remind me of you / Don't be cruel / Because of you
CD CD 365
Entertainers / Jun '96 / Target/BMG

KISSIN', TWISTIN', GOIN' WHERE THE BOYS ARE (The Early Sixties/5CD Set)
Teddy / It would be worth it / No one / No one / My dream / Cashin' in / Valentino / Valentino / Yes indeed / Amen / Accentuate the positive / Lonesome Road / I think of you / Millionaire / Jealous of you / Robot man / Everybody's somebody's fool / I think of you / Robot man / My heart has a mind of it's own / My heart has a mind of it's own / My heart has a mind of it's own / I've got reason to worry / My heart has a mind of it's own / My heart has a mind of it's own / Love is where you find it / Swanee / My love, my love / Angel eyes / I got lost in his arms / Gone with the wind / How long has this been going on / It might as well be Spring / Ol' man Mose / Dat's love / Taboo / You're nobody 'til somebody loves you / Where the boys are / On the outside lookin' in / Many tears ago / Happy New Year baby / Breakin' in a brand new broken heart / No one / Without your love / Auf wiederseh'n / Baby Roo / One tear too many / Let the rest of the world go by / Someone else's boy / It's time to say goodnight / Too many rules / You love / Your love / Together / Together / O Suzanna / On top of Old Smokey / Every night (when the sun goes in) / Boll weevil / Clementine / She'll be comin' round the mountain / Come on Jerry / Careless love / True love, true love / Aura Lee / Red River valley / Beautiful brown eyes / High noon / Love is a many splendored thing / Three coins in the fountain / Around the world / Tammy / April love / Anna / Where is your heart / Love me tender / Young at heart / Never on Sunday / Moonglow / Pretty little baby / (He's my) Dreamboat / He's just a scientist / Hollywood / Sing along / You tell me your dream / In the good old summertime / I love you truly / Home on the range / And the band played on / My wild Irish rose / Auld lang syne / Tavern in the town / Down in the valley / When the boy in your arms / I'm falling in love with yiou / Baby's first Christmas / Don't break the heart that loves you / White cliffs of Dover / White cliffs of Dover / Mr. Twister / Mr. Twister / Ain't that better baby / Don't cry on my shoulder / Love bird / Does ol' Broadway ever sleep / Gonna git that man / Johnny darlin' / Teach me how to twist / Kiss 'n' twist / Cha cha twist / Lovey dovey twist / Telephone lover / Drop it Joe / Hey ring a ding / Mommy your daughter's fallin' in love / I won't be home to you / My real happiness / Little bit of heaven / Mother Machree / How can you buy Killarney / Danny Boy / How are things in Glocca Morra / My wild Irish rose / When Irish eyes are smiling / Too-ra-loo-ra-loo-ral / It's a great day for the Irish / Great day for the Irish / Dear old Donegal / MacNamara's band / Did your mother come from Ireland / I'm so alone / It happened last night / No one ever sends me roses / I was such a fool / Second hand love / Second hand love / You'll never know / Lullaby of Broadway / Zip-a-dee-doo-dah / Moon river / Whatever will be will be (Que sera sera) / (Somewhere) Over the rainbow / Secret love / When you wish upon a star / Buttons & bows / High hopes / Last time I saw Paris / All the way / Way you look tonight / It's time to say goodnight
CD Set BCD 15826
Bear Family / Jun '96 / Direct / Rollercoaster / Swift

SING GREAT COUNTRY FAVORITES (Francis, Connie & Hank Williams Jr.)
Bye bye love / Send me the pillow that you dream on / Wolverton mountain / No letter today / Please help me, I'm falling / Singin' the blues / Walk on by / If you've got the money, I've got the time / Mule skinner blues / Making believe / Blue blue day / No letter today (alt) / Wabash cannonball / Mule skinner blues (Alt.take)
CD BCD 15737
Bear Family / Aug '93 / Direct / Rollercoaster / Swift

SINGLES COLLECTION, THE
Lipstick on your collar / Everybody's somebody's fool / I'm sorry I made you cry / I'm gonna be warm this winter / Together / V-A-C-A-T-I-O-N / I'll get by / Frankie / Many tears ago / Mama/Robot man / Fallin' / Among my souvenirs / In the valley of love / Who's sorry now / Stupid cupid/Carolina moon / Breakin' in a brand new broken heart / Plenty good lovin' / Baby's first Christmas / You always hurt the one you love / Don't break the heart that loves you / My happiness / Valentino / Where the boys are/Baby Roo / My heart has a mind of its own / Senza fine / Jealous heart / My child
CD 5191312
PolyGram TV / Apr '93 / PolyGram

SOUVENIRS (2CD Set)
CD Set 5333822
Polydor / Nov '96 / PolyGram

SWINGING CONNIE, THE (Francis, Connie & Joe Mazzu Orchestra)
CD ACD 286
Audiophile / Nov '96 / Jazz Music

ULTIMATE
CD MAR 043
Marginal / Jun '97 / Greyhound

WHITE SOX, PINK LIPSTICK AND STUPID CUPID (5CD Set)
Didn't I love you enough / Freddy / (Oh please) Make him jealous / Goody goodbye / Are you satisfied / My treasure / My first real love / Believe in me / Forgetting / Send for my baby / I never had a sweetheart / Little blue wren / Everyone needs someone / My sailor boy / No other one / I leaned on a man / Faded orchid / Eighteen / My sisters clothes / Majesty of love / You my darling you / Who's sorry now / You were only fooling (while I was falling in love) / I'm beginning to see the light / Rudolph the red nosed reindeer / Wheel of fortune / How can I make you believe in me / You belong to me / Daddy's little girl / I'm sorry I made you cry / I cried for you / You always hurt the one you love / I'll get by / Lock up your heart / Heartaches / I'm nobody's baby / My melancholy baby / I miss you so / It's the talk of the town / If I had you / How deep is the ocean / Carolina moon / Stupid Cupid / Happy days and lonely nights / Fallin' / You're my everything / My happiness / Don't speak of love / Love eyes / Never before / In the valley of love / Time after time / Blame it on my youth / How did he look / That's all / Toward the end of the day / I really don't want to know / No-one to cry to / If I didn't care / If you love me tonight / Come rain or come shine / All by myself / Hold me, thrill me, kiss me / Song is ended (but the melody lingers on) / There will never be another you / Melancholy serenade / Rock-a-bye your baby with a Dixie melody / Hallelujah, I love him so / My thanks to you / Bells of St. Mary's / Good luck, good health, God bless you / Garden in the rain / Try a little tenderness / Goodnight sweetheart / Cruising down the river / I'll close my eyes / Very thought of you / These foolish things / Tree in the meadow / Gypsy / Now is the hour / You're gonna miss me / Frankie / Lipstick on your collar / Oh, Frankie / I almost lost my mind / I'm walkin' / Just a dream / Heartbreak hotel / I hear you knocking / Tweedle dee / Ain't that a shame / It's only make believe / Sincerely / Don't be cruel / Bye bye love / Earth angel / Hearts of stone / Silhouettes / Plenty good lovin' / Singin' the blues / My special angel / Tennessee waltz / Let me go, lover / Young love / Half as much / Anytime / Your cheatin' heart / Cold cold heart / Peace in the valley / Too young / Temptation / You made me love you / Prisoner of love / Young at heart / It's not for me to say / Thinking of you / That's my desire / Because of you / Where the blue of the night meets the gold of the day / April love / Cry / God bless America / Among my souvenirs / Snapdragon / No one / Tiger and the mouse / Forgetting (take 10) / Lock up your heart (slow version) / My melancholy baby (take 2) / No one (take 2) / Tiger and the mouse, The (take 4)
CD Set BCD 15616
Bear Family / Jul '93 / Direct / Rollercoaster / Swift

WITH LOVE TO BUDDY
Heart beat / Maybe baby / That'll be the day / It doesn't matter anymore / Love made a fool out of you / Not fade away / Bo Diddley / It's so easy / Love is strange / Oh boy / Well alright / Everyday / Peggy Sue / Raining in my heart / Think it over / You've got love / Early in the morning / Rave on
CD 3036000412
Carlton / May '96 / Carlton

WORLD OF CONNIE FRANCIS, THE
Look of love / What kind of fool am I / Hold me, thrill me, kiss me / White cliffs of Dover / True love / Strangers in the night / Moon river / Young at heart / Tammy / Three coins in the fountain / Love me tender / Love is a many splendoured thing / Stardust / Last waltz / My foolish heart / Am I blue / My heart cries for you / I wish I had a wooden heart / Wayward wind / Trains, boats and planes
CD 5513092
Spectrum / May '96 / PolyGram

Francis, Dean

THIS GROOVE'S FOR YOU
This groove's for you / Just funkin' around / Without guns / I got the hots / It's okay / Got a funky disposition / Dancefloor jazz / In the rain / Know when to leave it alone
CD ME 000332
Soulciety/Bassism / Sep '95 / EWM

Francis, Panama

GETTIN' IN THE GROOVE (Francis, Panama & The Savoy Sultans)
Song of the Islands / Stitches / Rhythm Dr Man / Freezy / Chequered had / Second balcony jump / Nuages / Little John special
CD BLE 233320
Black & Blue / Dec '90 / Discovery / Koch / Wellard

Francis, W.J.

RAGGA LOVE
CD MRCD 002
Metronome / Dec '92 / Jet Star

Francis, Winston

SWEET ROCK STEADY
CD LKJCD 017
LKJ / Jun '97 / Grapevine/PolyGram / Jet Star

Franck, Albert

UN PARISIEN A PARIS
CD ROSE 236CD
New Rose / Feb '91 / ADA / Direct / Discovery

Franck, Thomas

THOMAS FRANCK IN NEW YORK (Franck, Thomas Quartet)
CD CRISS 1052CD
Criss Cross / Nov '91 / Cadillac / Direct / Vital/SAM

Franco, Gian

SEA, THE (Franco, Gian Reverberi)
CD CDPM 6001
Prestige / Mar '90 / Else / Total/BMG

Frank & Walters

GRAND PARADE, THE
Colours / Indian ocean / Little dolls / Russian ship / I suppose / Saturday night / How can I exist / Mrs. Xavier / Have you ever / Tony Cochran / Landslide / Lately
CD SETCD 054
Setanta / Jun '97 / Vital

TRAINS AND BOATS AND PLANES
CD 8284022
Go Discs / Jul '93 / PolyGram

Frank Chickens

YUKASITA UNDERFLOOR
CD CMCD 009
Creative Man / Jun '96 / Total/Pinnacle

Frank, Ed

NEW NEW ORLEANS MUSIC VOL.1 (Frank, Ed Quintet)
CD ROUCD 2065
Rounder / '88 / ADA / CM / Direct

Frank, Erik

NOVELTY ACCORDION 1936-1968
CD DRCD 310
Dragon / May '97 / ADA / Cadillac / CM / Roots / Wellard

Frank, Jackson C.

BLUES RUN THE GAME
CD CRESTCD 021
Mooncrest / Jun '96 / ADA / Direct

Franke, Bob

HEART OF THE FLOWER, THE
CD DARINGCD 3016
Daring / Oct '95 / ADA / CM / Direct

Franke, Christopher

KLEMANIA
Scattered thoughts of a canyon flight / Inside a morphing space / Silent waves
CD SI 85042
Sonic Images / Sep '95 / Pinnacle

Frankel, Judy

SEPHARDIC SONGS OF LOVE & HOPE
CD GVMCD 157
Global Village / May '93 / ADA / Direct

Frankfurt Jazz Ensemble

ATMOSPHERIC CONDITIONS PERMITTING (2CD Set)
CD Set 5173542
ECM / Dec '95 / New Note/Pinnacle

Frankie Goes To Hollywood

BANG (Greatest Hits)
Relax / Two tribes / War / Ferry 'cross the Mersey / Warriors of the wasteland / For heaven's sake / World is my oyster / Welcome to the pleasure dome / Watching the wildlife / Born to run / Rage hard / Power of love / Bang
CD 4509939122
ZTT / Oct '93 / Warner Music

LIVERPOOL
Warriors of the wasteland / Rage hard / Kill the pain / Maximum joy / Watching the wildlife / Lunar bay / For heaven's sake / Is anybody out there
CD 4509947442
ZTT / Mar '94 / Warner Music

WELCOME TO THE PLEASURE DOME
World is my oyster / Welcome to the pleasure dome / Relax / War / Two tribes / Happy

hi / Born to run / Wish the lads were here (inc ballad of '32) / Krisco kisses / Black night white light / Only star in heaven / Power of love / Bang....
CD 4509947452
ZTT / Feb '95 / Warner Music

WHOLE TWELVE INCHES, THE
Relax / Two tribes / Welcome to the pleasure dome / Rage hard / Warriors of the wasteland
CD 4509952922
ZTT / Dec '96 / Warner Music

Franklin, Aretha

30 GREATEST HITS
I never loved a man (the way I love you) / Respect / Do right woman, do right man / Dr. Feelgood / Save me / Baby I love you / (You make me feel like) a natural woman / Chain of fools / Since you've been gone / Ain't no way / Think / I say a little prayer / House that Jack built / See saw / Weight / Share your love with me / Eleanor Rigby / Call me / Spirit in the dark / Don't play that song (You lied) / You're all I need to get by / Bridge over troubled water / Spanish harlem / Rock steady / Oh me oh my (I'm a fool for you baby) / Daydreaming / Wholly holy / Angel / Until you come back to me / I'm in love
CD 7567816682
Atlantic / Mar '93 / Warner Music

AMAZING GRACE
Mary don't you weep / Precious Lord, take my hand / You've got a friend / Old landmark / Give yourself to Jesus / How I got over / What a friend we have in Jesus / Amazing grace / Precious memories / Climbing higher mountains / God will take care of you / Wholly Holy / You'll never walk alone / Never grow old
CD 7567813242
Atlantic / Jun '93 / Warner Music

ARETHA ARRIVES
Satisfaction / You are my sunshine / Never let me go / 96 tears / Prove it / Night life / That's life / Ronettes / Ain't nobody / Going down slow / Baby I love you
CD 8122712742
Atlantic / Jan '93 / Warner Music

ARETHA FRANKLIN
Respect / Think / Chain of fools / I say a little prayer / (You make me feel like) A natural woman / I never loved a man (the way I loved you) / Don't play that song (You lied) / Call me / Share your love with me / Jesus on the main line / He's all right / He will wash you white as snow / Power / While the blood runs warm / Yield not to temptation / This little light of mine / Day is past and gone
CD EXP 016
Experience / May '97 / TKO Magnum

ARETHA GOSPEL
There is a fountain filled with blood / Precious Lord (take my hand) / Precious Lord (take my hand) / You grow closer / Never grow old / Day is past and gone / He will wash you white as snow / While the blood runs warm / Yield not to temptation
CD MCD 91521
Chess/MCA / Apr '97 / BMG / New Note/ BMG

ARETHA IN PARIS
Satisfaction / Don't let me lose this dream / Soul serenade / Night life / Baby I love you / Groovin' / Natural woman / Come back baby / Dr. Feelgood / Respect / Since you've been gone / I never loved a man (the way I love you) / Chain of fools
CD 8122718522
Atlantic / Dec '94 / Warner Music

ARETHA NOW
Think / I say a little prayer / See saw / Night time is the right time / You send me / You're a sweet sweet man / I take what I want / Hello sunshine / Change / I can't see myself leaving you
CD 8122712732
Atlantic / Feb '93 / Warner Music

ARETHA'S GOLD
I never loved a man (the way I love you) / Do right woman, do right man / Respect / Dr. Feelgood / Baby I love you / (You make me feel like) a natural woman / Chain of fools / Since you've been gone / Ain't no way / Think / You send me / House that Jack built / I say a little prayer / See saw
CD 7567814452
Atlantic / Jun '93 / Warner Music

ARETHA'S JAZZ
Ramblin' / Today I sing the blues / Pitiful / Crazy he calls me / Bring it on home to me / Somewhere / Moody's mood for love (Moody's love) / Just right tonight
CD 7567812302
Atlantic / Mar '93 / Warner Music

COLLECTION, THE
Walk on by / It ain't necessarily so / What a difference a day makes / Once in a lifetime / Over the rainbow / You made me love you / Say it isn't so / Unforgettable / My guy / Exactly like you / Try a little tenderness / I'm sitting on top of the world / Skylark / Solitude / Where are you / Love for sale / Swanee / I surrender dear / Look for the silver lining / Lover come back to me / Make someone happy / Ol' man river / I apologise
CD CCSCD 152
Castle / Jul '87 / BMG

EARLY YEARS, THE
This bitter Earth / Without the one you love / Cry like a baby / Trouble in mind / Muddy water / Walk on by / Skylark / Drinking again / Evil gal blues / Laughing on the outside / God bless the child / Take a look / Nobody knows the way I feel this morning / I wonder (where are you tonight)
CD 4868192
Columbia / May '97 / Sony

GREATEST HITS
Spanish Harlem / Chain of fools / Don't play that song (You lied) / I say a little prayer / Dr. Feelgood / Let it be / Do right woman, do right man / Bridge over troubled water / Respect / Baby I love you / (You make me feel like) a natural woman / I never loved a man (the way I love you) / You're all I need to get by / Call me
CD 7567814512
Atlantic / Jun '93 / Warner Music

GREATEST HITS 1980-1994
CD 74321162022
Arista / Feb '96 / BMG

HEY NOW HEY (The Other Side Of The Sky)
CD 8122718532
Atlantic / Dec '94 / Warner Music

I NEVER LOVED A MAN THE WAY I LOVE YOU
Respect / Drown in my own tears / I never loved a man (the way I love you) / Soul serenade / Don't let me lose this dream / Baby baby baby / Dr. Feelgood / Good times / Do right woman, do right man / Save me / Change is gonna come
CD 7567814392
Atlantic / Mar '93 / Warner Music

JAZZ TO SOUL (2CD Set)
Today I sing the blues / (Blue) by myself / Maybe I'm a fool / All night long / Blue holiday / Nobody like you / Sweet lover / Just for a thrill / If ever I would leave you / Once in a while / This bitter Earth / God bless the child / Skylark / Muddy water / Drinking again / What a difference a day makes / Unforgettable / Love for sale / Misty / Impossible / This could be the start of something / Won't be long / Operation heartbreak / Soulville / Runnin' out of fools / Trouble in mind / Walk on by / Every little bit hurts / Mockingbird / You'll lose a good thing / Cry like a baby / Take it like you give it / Land of dreams / Can't you just see me / (No no) I'm losing you / Bit of soul / Why was I born / Until you were gone / Lee cross
CD Set CD 48515
Legacy / Nov '93 / Sony
CD Set 4772342
Columbia / Jun '96 / Sony

LADY SOUL
Chain of fools / Money won't change you / People get ready / Niki Hoeky / Natural woman / Since you've been gone / Good to me as I am to you / Come back baby / Groovin' / Ain't no way
CD 7567818182
Atlantic / Mar '93 / Warner Music

LET ME IN YOUR LIFE
Let me into your life / Every natural thing / Ain't nothing like the real thing / I'm in love / Until you come back to me / (I'm afraid) the masquerade is over / With pen in hand / Oh baby / Eight days on the road / If you don't think / Song for you
CD 8122718542
Atlantic / Dec '94 / Warner Music

LIVE AT FILLMORE WEST
Respect / Love the one you're with / Bridge over troubled water / Eleanor Rigby / Make it with you / Don't play that song (You lied) / Dr. Feelgood / Spirit in the dark / Reach out and touch
CD 8122715262
Atlantic / Feb '94 / Warner Music

LOVE SONGS
Baby I love you / I say a little prayer for you / You send me / You make me feel like a natural woman / Day dreaming / You and me / Call me / Oh me oh my (I'm a fool for you baby) / I'm in love / Look into your heart / Crazy he calls me / Something he can feel / This girl's in love with you / Brand new me / If you don't think / Ain't nothing like the real thing
CD 8122725762
Rhino / Mar '97 / Warner Music

QUEEN OF SOUL
I never loved a man (the way I love you) / Do right woman, do right man / Dr. Feelgood / Baby I love you / (You make me feel like) A natural woman / Chain of fools / Since you've been gone / Ain't no way / Save me / House that Jack built / Think / I say a little prayer / See saw / Daydreaming / Call me / Don't play that song (You lied) / Border song (Holy Moses) / You're all I need to get by / I'm in love / Spanish Harlem / Rock steady / Angel / Until you come back to me
CD 7567806062
Atlantic / Oct '94 / Warner Music

QUEEN OF SOUL - THE ATLANTIC RECORDINGS (4CD Set)
CD Set 8122710632
Atlantic / Nov '92 / Warner Music

SOUL '69
Ramblin' / Today I sing the blues / River's invitation / Pitiful / Crazy he calls me / Bring it on home to me / Tracks of my tears / If you gotta make a fool of somebody / Gentle on my mind / So long / I'll never be free / Elusive butterfly
CD 8122715232
Atlantic / Feb '94 / Warner Music

SPIRIT IN THE DARK
Don't play that song (You lied) / Thrill is gone / Pullin' / You and me / Honest I do / Spirit in the dark / When the battle is over / One way ticket / Try Matty's / That's all I want from you / Oh no, not my baby / Why I sing the blues
CD 8122715252
Atlantic / Feb '94 / Warner Music

THIS GIRL'S IN LOVE WITH YOU
Son of a preacher man / Share your love with me / Dark end of the street / Let it be / Eleanor Rigby / This girl's in love with you / It ain't fair / Weight / Call me / Sit down and cry
CD 8122715242
Atlantic / Feb '93 / Warner Music

UNFORGETABLE (A Tribute To Dinah Washington)
Unforgettable / Cold cold heart / What a difference a day makes / Drinking again / Nobody knows the way I feel this morning / Evil gal blues / Don't say you're sorry again / This bitter Earth / If I should lose you / Soulville / Lee cross
CD 4805082
Columbia / May '95 / Sony

WHO'S ZOOMIN' WHO
Freeway of love / Another night / Sweet bitter love / Who's zoomin' who / Sisters are doin' it for themselves: *Eurythmics & Aretha Franklin* / Until you say you love me / Push / Ain't nobody ever loved you / Integrity
CD 259053
Arista / Aug '88 / BMG

YOUNG, GIFTED AND BLACK
Oh me oh my / Daydreaming / Rock steady / Young, gifted and black / All the king's horses / Brand new me / April fools / I've been loving you too long / First snow in Kokomo / Long and winding road / Didn't I / Border song
CD 8122715272
Atlantic / Feb '94 / Warner Music

Franklin, Kirk

KIRK FRANKLIN AND FAMILY (Franklin, Kirk & The Family)
Why we sing / He's able / Silver and gold / Call on the lord / Real love / He can handle it / Letter from my friend / Family worship / Speak to me / Till we meet again
CD GCD 2119
Alliance Music / Jun '95 / EMI

WHATYA LOOKIN' 4 (Franklin, Kirk & The Family)
Saviour more than life / Whatcha lookin' 4 / Melodies from heaven / Conquerors / Don't take your joy away / When I think about Jesus / Mama's song / Jeus paid it all / I love you Jesus / Washed away / Where the spirit is / Let me touch you / Anything
CD GCD 2127
Alliance Music / Oct '96 / EMI

Franko, Mladen

FUN AND ROMANCE (Franko, Mladen & Norman Candler)
CD ISCD 123
Intersound / '91 / Jazz Music

Franks, Michael

ART OF TEA
Nightmoves / Egg plant / Monkey see, Monkey do / St. Elmo's fire / Don't know why I'm so happy I'm sad / Jive / Popsicle toes / Mr. Blue / Sometimes I just forget to smile
CD 7599272242
WEA / Aug '81 / Warner Music

DRAGONFLY SUMMER
Coming to life / Soul mate / Dragonfly summer / Monk's new tune / Learning what love means / I love Lucy / Practice makes perfect / String of pearls / Keeping my eye on you / Dream / You were meant for me / How I remember you
CD 9362452272
Warner Bros. / May '93 / Warner Music

OBJECTS OF DESIRE
Jealousy / Ladies night / No deposit love / Laughing gas / Wonderland / Tahitian moon / Flirtation / Love duet / No one but you
CD 7599236482
Warner Bros. / May '94 / Warner Music

Franks, Nick

DARK ANDROMEDA
Dark andromeda / Girl by the lough / Land of the rising moon / Gone to Texas / Love will find a way / Sugar loaf / Stone mountain breakdown / Long time ago
CD WMMSCD 1003
Warner Sisters / Apr '97 / Pinnacle

Franks, Rebecca

ALL OF A SUDDEN (Franks, Rebecca Coupe)
CD JR 009022
Justice / Sep '92 / Koch

SUIT OF ARMOUR (Franks, Rebecca Coupe)
CD JR 009012
Justice / Nov '92 / Koch

Frantic

CONCEPTION
CD FLASH 31
Flash / Jul '97 / Greyhound

Frantic Flintstones

ENJOY YOURSELF
Enjoy yourself / Cradle baby / Black Caddi / I gotta baby / You don't love me anymore / Tip of my tongue / Ain't got a / Draw your breaks / She done me wrong / Mummy's boy / Sunset of my tears / Up your nose / Crazy Clems dream / Chop one up Chuck
CD CDGRAM 86
Anagram / Sep '94 / Cargo / Pinnacle

JAMBOREE
Detroit dirt box / Love for a nutter / Your time is up / Mean mean woman / Diablo / Saty with me / Sweet Georgia Brown / Lunatics (are raving) / Busted / Mindkill / (To the Devil) a son / Oh 898 / Candy man / He's waiting / Sad 'n' lonely / Suspended / Chop chop splash splash / Honeychild / Hey Chuck / Detroit blood box
CD CDMPSYCH 015
Anagram / Aug '97 / Cargo / Pinnacle

MY WOMAN IS...
CD TBCD 2006
Nervous / Mar '93 / Nervous / TKO Magnum

ROCKIN' OUT/NOT CHRISTMAS ALBUM
Rockin' out / What the hell / One night stand / Hot head baby / Chuck blows a fuse / Rockin' bones / Let's go somewhere / No one stays / Frantic / Wider road to hell / Honey maker / Necro blues / Oh little town of Bedrock / Gone gone well gone / Alone again / 'Round midnight / Just because / Santa Claus bring my baby back to me / Santa Claus is back in town / Blue Christmas / Ole black joe
CD CDMPSYCHO 6
Anagram / Jun '95 / Cargo / Pinnacle

Fraser, Alasdair

DAWN DANCE
CD CUL 106CD
Culburnie / Jul '95 / ADA / CM / Direct / Duncans / Highlander / Ross

DRIVEN BOW, THE (Fraser, Alasdair & Jody Stretcher)
CD CUL 102CD
Culburnie / Jul '95 / ADA / CM / Direct / Duncans / Highlander / Ross

PORTRAIT OF A SCOTTISH FIDDLER
CD CUL 009CD
Culburnie / Jul '96 / ADA / CM / Direct / Duncans / Highlander / Ross

SKYEDANCE (Fraser, Alasdair & Paul Machlis)
CD CUL 101CD
Culburnie / Oct '95 / ADA / CM / Direct / Duncans / Highlander / Ross

Fraser, Dean

BIG UP
Dick Tracy / None a jah jah children no cry / Big up/Armageddon time / Shine eye gal / Place called Africa / Queen of the minstrels / Natty never get weary / Bank of the river / Have mercy / African elation / It's me again Jah
CD IJCD 4003
Island Jamaica Jazz / May '97 / PolyGram

CLASSICS
CD RNCD 2080
Rhino / Dec '94 / Grapevine/PolyGram / Jet Star

DEAN PLAYS BOB VOL.1
CD RASCD 3127
Ras / Jun '96 / Direct / Greensleeves / Jet Star / SRD

DEAN PLAYS BOB VOL.2
CD RASCD 3186
Ras / Feb '96 / Direct / Greensleeves / Jet Star / SRD

JESUS LOVES ME
CD SONCD 0091
Sonic Sounds / Jul '97 / Jet Star

PUMPIN' AIR
Redemption song / Rent a car / I'll always love you / Moody's mood for love / Stop, look, listen (To your heart) / For the love of

you / To Sir with love / His house and me / Always and forever
CD RRCD 38
Island / Jul '92 / PolyGram

RAS PORTRAITS
Roots rock raggae / Johnny was / One drop / Africa unite / Zimbabwe / Ram dancehall / Bad card / Crazy baldheads / Rastaman chant / Chant down babylon / Unforgettable / Just because
CD RAS 3325
Ras / Jul '97 / Direct / Greensleeves / Jet Star / SRD

RAW SAX
CD GRELCD 129
Greensleeves / Sep '89 / Jet Star / SRD

SINGS AND BLOWS
Falling in love / Jamaican lady / Girlfriend / Magnet and steel / Voyage to Atlantis
CD GRELCD 113
Greensleeves / Jun '88 / Jet Star / SRD

TAKING CHANCES
CD RASCD 3106
Ras / Jun '93 / Direct / Greensleeves / Jet Star / SRD

Fraser, Donald

WORLD ANTHEMS (Fraser, Donald & English Chamber Orchestra)
Olympic theme / Marcha real / Advance Australia fair / Jeszche Polska / Patra amada, Brasil / King Christian / Ee mungu nguvu ye tu / O Canada / God save the Queen / Ch'i lai / La brabanconne / Maamme laulu / Isten aldd meg a Magyard / Ja vi elsker dette landet / Einigkeit und recht und freiheit / Kde domov kuj / Star spangled banner / Segnorees apo tin kopsi / Wilhelmus Van Nassouwe / Peaceful reign / Hatikvah / Walla zaman algunud / La Marseillaise / Sean eternos los laurales / Du camla, du fria / Mexicanos al grito de guerra / Ethiopia / Land der berge / Lietuva / Inno di mameli
CD 09026613442
RCA / Jul '92 / BMG

Fraser Highlanders

LIVE IN CONCERT IN IRELAND
Lord Lovat's lament / Beverley's wedding / Ishabel T MacDonald / Catrina Baker / Gordon MacRae's favourite / Cliffs of Dooneen / Brig Gen Ronald Cheape of Tiroran / Laggan love song / Lament for the children / Up to the line / John MacColl's farewell to the Scottish / Farewell to Erin / Journey to Skye / Mason's apron / Fair maid of Barra
CD Set LCDM 8003
Lismor / '89 / ADA / Direct / Duncans / Lismor

MEGANTIC OUTLAW CONCERT, THE
4/4 marches / Medley / Solo piping: *Black Hairy Tongue* / Drum fanfare / Waulking songs / Hornpipes / Megantic outlaw / Piping duet: *Branch, Billy & The Sons Of Blues* / Airs / Jigs
CD LCOM 8014
Lismor / Sep '92 / ADA / Direct / Duncans / Lismor

Fraser, Iain

NORTHLINS
Old fincastle / Northlins / Pride of the north / Blue bonnets / Devil in the kitchen / Golden mile / Walnut grove / Valparaiso / Loup / Tummelside / Drummossie moor / North wall / Farewell to whiskey / Am balachan siubhlach / Merry making / Last light
CD IRCD 027
Iona / Aug '94 / ADA / Direct / Duncans

Fraser, Simon

ALIVE IN AMERICA (Fraser, Simon University Pipe Band)
Trad II / 6/8 Marches / Hornpipes and jigs / Set / Scotstoun medley / Do mo chara maith / Slow air and reels / Compound II / Medley / Calleach an dudain / Drops / Hornpipes / Drums
CD LDDC 8017
Lismor / Jul '96 / ADA / Direct / Duncans / Lismor

DO MO CHARA MAITH (Fraser, Simon University Pipe Band)
Iochanside / McPhedran's Strathspey / AA Cameron's Strathspey / Lexy McAskill / Blackberry bush / Our ain fireside / MacLeod medley / Compound / 420 Byng Street / Buskin' / Flowers of Edinburgh / Drops / Highland Set / Maestro and the minions / Sorcerer Set / Three Fours / Boys / Do mo chara maith / Three stripes / Caileach an Dudain
CD LCOM 5236
Lismor / Jul '94 / ADA / Direct / Duncans / Lismor

Fraser-Myers Band

FAST JAZZ, FAST WOMEN AND ASTONS
Sweet lullaby / Miss Mayhew / Zagato / Lunch at Langan's / Say what / Project 215 / Volante / DB 2 Mark 3 / Salvadori / Superleggera
CD VCTMD 4
Vocal Cords / Aug '94 / Grapevine/ PolyGram

Fraternity Of Man

FRATERNITY OF MAN
CD EDCD 437
Edsel / Oct '95 / Pinnacle

GET IT ON
CD EDCD 438
Edsel / Oct '95 / Pinnacle

Fraunhofer Saitenmusik

VOLSMUSIK
CD TRIK 0107
Trikont / Oct '94 / ADA / Direct

Frazier Chorus

SUE
Dream kitchen / Forty winks / Sloppy heart / Sugar high / Typical / Little chef / Storm / Ha ha happiness / Living room / Forgetful / Shi-head
CD CDV 2578
Virgin / Dec '88 / EMI

Freak Of Nature

FREAK OF NATURE
CD CDMFN 146
Music For Nations / Mar '93 / Pinnacle

GATHERING OF FREAKS
CD CDMFN 169
Music For Nations / Sep '94 / Pinnacle

Freakniks

UNDER THE SUN
CD SCCD 001
Scenario / Oct '96 / Essential/BMG

Freakpower

DRIVE-THRU BOOTY
Moonbeam woman / Turn on tune in cop out / Get in touch / Freak power / Running away / Change my mind / What it is / Waiting for the story to end / Rush / Big time / Whip
CD BRCD 606
4th & Broadway / Apr '95 / PolyGram

MORE OF EVERYTHING FOR EVERYBODY
CD BRCD 619
4th & Broadway / Jun '96 / PolyGram

Freaks Of Desire

INTOXICATED
CD 0630139852
Anxious / Mar '96 / Warner Music

Freakwater

DANCING UNDER WATER
CD THRILL 040CD
Thrill Jockey / May '97 / Cargo / Greyhound

OLD PAINT
CD EFA 049652
City Slang / Oct '95 / RTM/Disc

Freaky Chakra

FREAKY CHAKRA & SINGLE CELL ORCHESTRA (Freaky Chakra & Single Cell Orchestra)
Intro / Lurking / Piledriver / Trepidations in love / I want to fall / Wishfullness / Trying to find you / Anthem of the forgotten / Way
CD ASW 6166
Astralwerks / Sep '96 / Cargo / Vital

Freaky Realistic

FREALISM
Frealism / Something new/Cosmic love vibes / Koochie ryder / Love that loves / Leonard Nimoy / Reach / Salvate spacial / Trickle in / Imaginary pavillions / Make it happen / Sooner / Most / This is freaky realistic / Reprise/Frealism
CD 5179192
Polydor / Oct '93 / PolyGram

Fred, John

AGNES ENGLISH/PERMANENTLY STATED (Fred, John & The Playboys)
CD 528872
Magic / Jul '97 / Greyhound

Fred Locks

BLACK STAR LINER
CD STCD 001
Starlight / Nov '94 / Jet Star
CD VPCD 2037
VP / Sep '95 / Greensleeves / Jet Star / Total/BMG

CULTURALLY
CD TYCD 008
Tan Yah / Jan '96 / Jet Star
CD SDCD 918
Starlight / May '96 / Jet Star

LOVE & ONLY LOVE
CD TMCD 2
Tribesman / Nov '94 / Jet Star / SRD

Fred, Maguy

SUCCES ET RARETES 1930-1933
CD 701642
Chansophone / Nov '96 / Discovery

Freddie & The Dreamers

EP COLLECTION, THE
CD SEECD 299
See For Miles/C5 / '90 / Pinnacle

VERY BEST OF FREDDIE & THE DREAMERS, THE
If you gotta make a fool of somebody / I understand / It doesn't matter anymore / Jailer bring me water / I think of you / If you've got a minute, baby / Feel so blue / Do the Freddie / Thou shalt not steal / See you later alligator / I'm telling you now / I don't love you anymore / Viper / You were made for me / Over you / Money (that's what I want) / Tell me when / Playboy / Don't make me cry / Little you
CD CDSL 8261
Music For Pleasure / Jul '95 / EMI

Freddie Fresh

ACCIDENTALLY CLASSIC
Flow / Gimme / Barogue / Dilema / Hey / Chupacabbra / Fat beat / Bum bum / Cherrish electronique / Open spaces / Ah / Represent / Flava / Portion / Menagerie
CD HHCD 23
Harthouse / Mar '97 / Mo's Music Machine / Prime / Vital

Freddy K

RAGE OF AGE
CD ACVCD 8
ACV / Jun '95 / Plastic Head / SRD

Frederic

PHASES AND FACES 1967-1969
CD AA 061
Arf Arf / Jul '97 / Greyhound

Frederick The Great

BROADWAY USA
CD HIICD 804
Hard Hat / Oct '94 / Else

Frederiksen/Phillips

FREDERIKSEN/PHILLIPS
CD ERCD 1021
Now & Then / Jul '95 / Plastic Head

Fredrix, Dee

GRACE
Dirty money / And so I will wait for you / Whatever it takes / Hold on to what we've got / How can this be wrong / There but for the grace / If I could relive your love / Don't get in my way / Buried treasure / Look my way
CD 4509917882
East West / Mar '93 / Warner Music

Free

ALL RIGHT NOW
Wishing well / All right now / Little bit of love / Come together in the morning / Stealer / Sail on / Mr. Big / My brother Jake / The hunter / Be my friend / Travellin' in style / Fire and water / Travelling man / Don't say you love me
CD CIDTV 2
Island / Feb '91 / PolyGram

FIRE & WATER/ HEARTBREAKER
CD Set ITSCD 3
Island / Nov '92 / PolyGram

FIRE AND WATER
Oh I wept / Remember / Heavy load / Fire and water / Mr. Big / Don't say you love me / All right now
CD IMCD 80
Island / Apr '90 / PolyGram

FREE
I'll be creepin' / Songs of yesterday / Lying in the sunshine / Trouble on double time / Mouthful of grass / Woman / Free me / Broad daylight / Mourning sad mourning
CD IMCD 64
Island / '89 / PolyGram

FREE AT LAST
Catch a train / Soldier boy / Magic ship / Sail on / Travelling man / Little bit of love / Guardian of the Universe / Child / Goodbye
CD IMCD 82
Island / Feb '90 / PolyGram

FREE LIVE
All right now / I'm a mover / Be my friend / Fire and water / Ride on pony / Mr. Big / Hunter / Get where I belong
CD IMCD 73
Island / '89 / PolyGram

FREE STORY, THE
I'm a mover / I'll be creepin' / Mourning sad morning / All right now / Heavy load / Fire and water / Be my friend / Stealer / Soon I will be gone / Mr. Big / Hunter / Get where I belong / Travelling man / Just for the box / Lady / My brother Jake / Little bit of love / Sail on / Come together in the morning
CD IMCD 226
Island / Sep '96 / PolyGram

FREE THE FREE
I'll be creepin' / Songs of yesterday / Lying in the sunshine / Trouble on double time / Mouthfull of grass / Woman / Free me / Broad daylight / Mourning sad morning
CD 8427822
Island / Sep '89 / PolyGram

HEARTBREAKER
Wishing well / Come together in the morning / Travellin' in style / Heartbreaker / Muddy water / Common mortal man / Easy on my soul / Seven angels
CD IMCD 81
Island / Feb '90 / PolyGram

HIGHWAY
Highway song / Stealer / On my way / Be my friend / Sunny day / Ride on pony / Love you so / Bodies / Soon I will be gone
CD IMCD 63
Island / '89 / PolyGram

MOLTEN GOLD
I'm a mover / Hunter / Walk in my shadow / I'll be creepin' / Songs of yesterday / Woman / Broad daylight / Mouthful of grass / All right now / Oh I wept / Heavy load / Don't say you love me / Stealer / Highway song / Be my friend / Soon I will be gone / My brother Jake / Fire and water / Ride on pony / Mr. Big / Time away / Molten gold / Catch a train / Travelling man / Little bit of love / Sail on / Wishing well / Come together in the morning / Travellin' in style / Heartbreaker
CD CRNCD 2
Island / May '94 / PolyGram

TONS OF SOBS
Over the green hills (part 1) / Worry / Walk in my shadow / Wild Indian woman / Going down slow / I'm a mover / Hunter / Moonshine sweet tooth / Over the green hills (Part 2)
CD IMCD 62
Island / '89 / PolyGram

Free Flow

FREE FLOW
CD RR 103CD
Roots / Jul '96 / Timewarp

Free Hot Lunch

EAT THIS
CD FF 540CD
Flying Fish / '92 / ADA / CM / Direct / Roots

Free Jazz Quartet

PREMONITIONS - 1989
CD MR 18
Matchless / '90 / Cadillac / ReR Megacorp

Free Kitten

NICE ASS
Harvest spoon / Rock of ages / Proper band / What's fair / Kissing well / Call back / Blindfold test / Greener pastures / Revlon liberation orchestra / Boasta / Scratch tha DJ / Secret sex friend / Royal flush / Feelin' / Alan Licked has ruined music for an entire generation
CD WIJ 041CD
Wiiija / Jan '95 / RTM/Disc

UNBOXED
Skinny butt / Platinumb / Smack / Falling backwards / Oneness / Dick / Yoshimi Vs. Mascis / Oh bondage up yours / 1-2-3 / Party with me punker / John stark blues / Guilty pleasure / Sex boy / Cleopatra / Loose lips / Oh baby
CD WIJ 036CD
Wiiija / Jun '94 / RTM/Disc

Free The Spirit

PAN PIPE MOODS
I will always love you / Everything I do (I do it for you) / Holding back the years / Love theme from Bladerunner / Sacrifice/Nikita / From a distance / Wonderful tonight / Without you / Circle of life / Love is all around / Can you feel the love tonight / Mission / Careless whisper / Cockeye's song / Wonderful life / It must have been love / Evergreen / World in union
CD 5271972
PolyGram TV / Jan '95 / PolyGram

Freed Unit

FIELD REPORTS FROM OUT THERE
CD SRCD 002
Sorted / May '97 / Cargo

Freeez

FREEEZ FRAME (The Best Of Freeez)
CD MCCD 131
Music Club / Sep '93 / Disc / THE

Freeform

HETERARCHY
CD WISE 01
Worm Interface / Jun '97 / Kudos / Pinnacle / Plastic Head

Freelon, Nnenna

SHAKING FREE
Out of this world / Black is the colour of my true love's hair / I live to love you / Shaking free / Stories we hold / Birk's works / My shining hour / Visions / I thought about you / What am I here for / Nature boy / Blue daughter
CD CCD 4714
Concord Jazz / Aug '96 / New Note/ Pinnacle

Freeman

ROUGH ROADS
CD NAR 116CD
New Alliance / Dec '94 / Plastic Head

Freeman, Bud

CHICAGO/AUSTIN HIGH SCHOOL JAZZ IN HI-FI (Freeman, Bud Summa Cum Laude)
China boy / Sugar / Liza / Nobody's sweetheart / Chicago / At sundown / Prince of wails / Jack hits the road / Forty seventh and state / There'll be some changes made / At the jazz band ball
CD 74321130312
RCA / Sep '93 / BMG

CLASSICS 1928-1938
CD CLASSICS 781
Classics / Nov '94 / Discovery / Jazz Music

CLASSICS 1939-1940
CD CLASSICS 811
Classics / May '95 / Discovery / Jazz Music

CLASSICS 1945-1946
CD CLASSICS 942
Classics / Jun '97 / Discovery / Jazz Music

SOMETHING TO REMEMBER YOU BY
CD BLCD 760153
Black Lion / Jul '91 / Cadillac / Jazz Music / Koch / Wellard

Freeman, Chico

CHICO
CD IN 1031CD
India Navigation / Jan '97 / Discovery / Impetus

DESTINY'S DANCE
CD OJCCD 799
Original Jazz Classics / Nov '95 / Complete/Pinnacle / Jazz Music / Wellard

FOCUS (Freeman, Chico Quintet)
Bemsha swing / Blackfoot / Ah, George, we hardly knew ya / To hear a tear drop in the rain / Playpen / Peacemaker / Rhythm-a-ning
CD CCD 140732
Contemporary / Jan '97 / Cadillac / Complete/Pinnacle / Jazz Music / Wellard

FREEMAN AND FREEMAN (Freeman, Chico & Von Freeman)
CD IN 1070CD
India Navigation / Jan '97 / Discovery / Impetus

GROOVIN' LATE (Live At Ronnie Scott's)
Going places / Groovin' late / Free association / In a sentimental mood / What if / Traveller
CD CLACD 336
Castle / '93 / BMG

LUMINOUS (Freeman, Chico & Arthur Blythe)
Footprints / Luminous / Naima's love song / Avotja / You are too beautiful
CD JHCD 010
Ronnie Scott's Jazz House / Jan '94 / Cadillac / Jazz Music / New Note/Pinnacle / TKO Magnum

MYSTICAL DREAMER (Freeman, Chico & Brainstorm)
Footprints / Did I say anything (prelude) / On the Nile / Sojourn / Mystical dreamer / I'll be there / Did I say anything
CD 70062
In & Out / Jan '90 / Vital/SAM

NO TIME LEFT (Freeman, Chico Quartet)
CD BSR 0036CD
Black Saint / '86 / Cadillac / Harmonia Mundi

OUTSIDE WITHIN, THE
CD IN 1042CD
India Navigation / Jan '97 / Discovery / Impetus

SPIRIT SENSITIVE
CD IN 1045CD
India Navigation / Jan '97 / Discovery / Impetus

STILL SENSITIVE
CD IN 1071CD
India Navigation / Jan '97 / Discovery / Impetus

SWEET EXPLOSION (Freeman, Chico & Brainstorm)
Peaceful heart / Exotic places / Afro tang / My heart / Pacifica 1 / Pacifica 2 / Pacifica 3 / Read the signs / On the Nile
CD 70102
In & Out / Dec '90 / Vital/SAM

THRESHOLD
Trespasser / Duet / Mist / Subway / blues for Miles / Chejudo / Oleo / Chant / Lena's lullaby / Awakening
CD IOR 70222
In & Out / Sep '95 / Vital/SAM

UNSPOKEN WORD, THE (Freeman, Chico Quintet)
Unspoken word: *Freeman, Chico* / Gano club: *Freeman, Chico* / Playpen: *Freeman, Chico* / Infant eyes: *Freeman, Chico* / Peace maker: *Freeman, Chico* / Misty: *Freeman, Chico* / Rhythm-a-ning: *Freeman, Chico*
CD JHCD 030
Ronnie Scott's Jazz House / Aug '94 / Cadillac / Jazz Music / New Note/Pinnacle / TKO Magnum

UP AND DOWN (Freeman, Chico & Mal Waldron)
CD 1201362
Black Saint / Sep '92 / Cadillac / Harmonia Mundi

Freeman, Ernie

RAUNCHY
CD CDCHD 659
Ace / Aug '97 / Pinnacle

Freeman, George

BIRTH SIGN
Mama, papa, brother / Cough it up / My scenery / Must be, must be / Birth sign / Hoss / My ship
CD DD 424
Delmark / Mar '97 / ADA / Cadillac / CM / Direct / Hot Shot

Freeman, Ken

TRIPODS
CD GERCD 1
GR Forrester / Nov '95 / Pinnacle

Freeman, Louise

LISTEN TO MY HEART
When push comes to shove / Save your love / Nothin's gonna win me (but love) / Love is gone / Back in stride / I don't want to talk about it / Fever / Unchained melody
CD ICH 1111CD
Ichiban / Oct '93 / Direct / Koch

Freeman, Russ

BRAVE NEW WORLD (Freeman, Russ & The Rippingtons)
Brave new world / Urban wanderer / Key to the Forbidden City / Hideaway / Caravan of love / Faith / First time I saw her / Cicada / While my guitar gently weeps / Ain't no stoppin' us now / Virtual reality
CD GRP 98352
GRP / Mar '96 / New Note/BMG

SAHARA (Freeman, Russ & The Rippingtons)
Native sons of a distant land / True companion / I'll be around / Principles of desire / Sahara / Till we're together again / Best is yet to come / Journey's end / Girl with the indigo eyes / Porscha
CD GRP 97812
GRP / Sep '94 / New Note/BMG

Freeman, Von

SERENADE AND BLUES
Serenade in blue / After dark / Time after time / Von Freeman's blues / I'll close my eyes
CD CHIEFCD 3
Chief / Jun '89 / Cadillac

Freestyle Fellowship

INTERCITY GRIOTS
Blood / Bullies of the block / Everything's everything / Shammy's / Heat mizer / Six tray / Danger / Inner city boundaries / Bomb zombies / Cornbread / Way cool / Hot potato / Mary / Park bench people
CD BRCD 595
4th & Broadway / Apr '93 / PolyGram

Freestyle Files

FREESTYLE FILES VOL.2 (2CD Set)
CD Set K7 053CD
Studio K7 / Mar '97 / Prime / RTM/Disc

FUTURISTIC ELECTRONICS (2CD Set)
CD Set K7 048CD
Studio K7 / Sep '96 / Prime / RTM/Disc

Freewheelers

WAITIN' FOR GEORGE
Best be on your way / What's the matter Ruth / Mother nature lady / Ghost of Tchoupitulas Street / My little friend / (Chico's sellin') Maps to the stars / Crime pays / Walkin' funny / About Marie / Kiss her for the punk / Elevator man / Blame / Let the music bring a smile
CD 74321279682
American / Mar '96 / BMG

Freewill

ALMOST AGAIN
CD LF 181CD
Lost & Found / Dec '96 / Plastic Head

Freeze

CRAWLING BLIND
CD LF 075
Lost & Found / Mar '94 / Plastic Head

FIVE WAY FURY
CD LF 032CD
Lost & Found / Apr '92 / Plastic Head

FREAKSHOW
CD LF 198CD
Lost & Found / Jan '96 / Plastic Head

FREEZE/KILLRAYS (Split CD) (Freeze/ Killrays)
CD LF 143MCD
Lost & Found / Jul '95 / Plastic Head

TOKEN BONES
CD DSR 062CD
Dr. Strange / Jun '97 / Cargo / Greyhound / Plastic Head

Frehel

CHANSOPHONE 1933-1939
CD 701252
Chansophone / Jun '93 / Discovery

Frehley, Ace

12 PICKS
Into the night / Words are not enough / Insane / Hide your heart / Trouble walkin' / Rock soldiers / Rip it out / Breakout / Cold gin / Shock me / Rocket ride / Deuce
CD SPV 08518712
Steamhammer / May '97 / Pinnacle / Plastic Head

FREHLEY'S COMET (Frehley's Comet)
Rock soldiers / Breakout / Into the night / Something moved / We got your rock / Love me right / Calling to you / Dolls / Stranger in a strange land / Fractured too
CD 7567817492
Atlantic / Jan '96 / Warner Music

LIVE PLUS ONE (Frehley's Comet)
Rip it out / Breakout / Something moved / Rocket ride / Words are not enough
CD 7567818262
Atlantic / Jan '96 / Warner Music

SECOND SIGHTING (Frehley's Comet)
Insane / Time ain't runnin' out / Dancin' with danger / It's over now / Loser in a fight / Juvenile delinquent / Fallen angel / Separate / New kind of lover / Acorn is spinning
CD 7567818622
Atlantic / Jan '96 / Warner Music

TROUBLE WALKING (Frehley's Comet)
Shot full of rock / Do ya / Five card stud / Hide your heart / Lost in limbo / Trouble walkin' / 2 young 2 die / Back to school / Remember me / Fractured III
CD 7567820422
Atlantic / Jan '96 / Warner Music

Freight Hoppers

WHERE'D YOU COME FROM, WHERE'D YOU GO
Sandy river / Cotton eyed Joe / Mississippi Joe / Little Sadie / Texas gals / Johnson boys / Logan County blues / Gray cat on a Tennessee Farm / Four cent cotton / Cornbread, molasses and sassafras / Dark hollow blues / Elzick's farewell / Pretty little girl / How many biscuits can you eat this morning / Kentucky whiskey / Bright morning stars
CD ROUCD 0403
Rounder / Nov '96 / ADA / CM / Direct

Frejlechs

YIDDISH KLEZMER MUSIC
CD EUCD 1185
ARC / Apr '92 / ADA / ARC Music

Frej's Jazz

NORDLYD
CD MECCACD 1039
Music Mecca / Nov '94 / Cadillac / Jazz Music / Wellard

French Alligators

SOUS LA GALLERIE
CD FA 003CD
French Alligator / Jan '95 / ADA

French Charleston Orchestra

STRICTLY DANCING: CHARLESTON
CD 15339
Laserlight / May '94 / Target/BMG

French, Frank

BUCKTOWN (French, Frank & Scott Kirby)
CD SOSCD 1306
Stomp Off / Jul '96 / Jazz Music / Wellard

French, John

INVISIBLE MEANS (French, Frith, Kaiser & Thompson)
Peppermint rock / To the rain / Lizard's tail / March of the cosmetic surgeons / Suzanne / Quick sign / Invisible means / Book of lost dreams
CD FIENDCD 199
Demon / Oct '90 / Pinnacle

LIVE, LOVE, LARF, LOAF (French, Frith, Kaiser & Thompson)
Wings a la mode / Killerman gold posse / Where's the money / Hai sai oji-san / Drowned dog black night / Surfin' USA / Blind step away / Second time / Tir-nan darag / Disposable thoughts / Bird in god's garden/Lost and found
CD FIENDCD 102
Demon / '88 / Pinnacle

WAITING ON THE FLAME
CD FIENDCD 759
Demon / Oct '94 / Pinnacle

French, Robert

ROBERT FRENCH, HEAVY D & FRIENDS (French, Robert & Heavy D)
CD RASCD 3148
Ras / Aug '95 / Direct / Greensleeves / Jet Star / SRD

Frente

MARVIN THE ALBUM
CD TVD 93367
Mushroom / May '94 / 3mv/Pinnacle

SHAPE
CD D 93429
Mushroom / Oct '96 / 3mv/Pinnacle

Frenzy

(IT'S A) MAD, MAD WORLD
(It's a) mad mad world / So far away / Part of me / CC rider / Pressure / Hot rod satellite / Rock hard / Brand new gun / Crunch / I can't tell you / Ready or not / Show me the way / This is the fire / Can't stop thinkin' about you / Reward / Scandalous / Forever young / Wild night / Ready or not (mix)
CD RAGECD 111
Rage / Mar '93 / Nervous / TKO Magnum

BEST OF FRENZY
Hall OF Mirrors / Robot Riot / Misdemeanour / Clockwork Toy / I See Red / Schitzophrenic / Emotions / Hot Rod Satellite / Gotta Go / Cry Or Die / Long Gone / Sweet Money / Wound up / Aftermath / Ain't nobody's business if I do / Don't Give Up / House On Fire / Hunt / Howard Hughes / Can't Stop Thinking About You
CD RAGECD 107
Rage / Nov '90 / Nervous / TKO Magnum

CLOCKWORK TOY
CD NERCD 065
Nervous / '91 / Nervous / TKO Magnum

HALL OF MIRRORS
One last chance / Schizophrenic emotions / Choice / Hall of mirrors / frenzy / Asylum moves / Skeleton rock / Sweet money / Ghost train / Long gone / Surfin' bird / Was it me / Wound up / Frustration
CD NERDCD 016
Nervous / Jul '90 / Nervous / TKO Magnum

THIS IS THE FIRE
Ready Or Not / Robot Riot / This Is The Fire / Come back my love / Wild night / Can't Stop Thinking About You / Another Day / I Want Your Lovin': *Scandalous* / Scandalous / Forever Young / Reward
CD RAGECD 101
Rage / Aug '92 / Nervous / TKO Magnum

Freq

HEAVEN
Xirtam / Darkness / Fury / Dreamscape / Xirtam 3 / Untitled / Dolphin dreams / Phoenix
CD SUB 48422
Distance / Jun '97 / 3mv/Sony / Prime

Fresh Claim

BROKEN
Broken man / Pillar sways / Morning ashtray blues / Wayfaring stranger / Driving through the rain / Defiled / Slow burning candle / Broken jam
CD PCDN 146
Plankton / Nov '95 / Plankton

ROCK COMMUNION, THE
What a friend we have in Jesus / Peruvian Gloria / Father hear the prayer we offer / Sanctus (Holy, holy, holy) / Blessed is he /

Christ has died / Agnus dei (Lamb of God) / Purple robe / Broken by / Jesus light of the world / Eternal love / Father on high / Swing low, sweet chariot / Oh sacred head / Crown him with many crown
CD ______ PCN 142
Plankton / Aug '94 / Plankton

Fresh, Doug E

PLAY
Where's da party at / It's on / Take 'em up-town / I-ight / Original old school / Freaks / Freak it out / It's really goin' on here / Who's got all the money / Get da money / Hands in the air / Doug E got it going on / Keep it going / Breath of fresh air
CD ______ GEECD 17
Gee Street / Oct '95 / PolyGram

Freshies

VERY VERY BEST OF THE FRESHIES, THE
CD ______ CDMRED 129
Cherry Red / Apr '96 / Pinnacle

Fresu, Paolo

WANDERLUST (Fresu, Paolo Quartet)
Trunca peltunta / Favole / Wanderlust / Geremeas variazione quattro / Children of 10,000 years / Appuntamento sol treno / Soul eyes / Seven up / Hush / In quelle sere d'autunno / Simplicity / Touch her soft lips and parts
CD ______ 74321464352
RCA Victor / Aug '97 / BMG

Fretblanket

JUNK FUEL
CD ______ 5219972
Polydor / Aug '94 / PolyGram

Fretless AZM

ASTRAL CINEMA
Framed in funk / Rhythm in bass / Thought for food / Air conditioning / Swamp thing swing / Steppin' on the cracks / Rake island / Big wheel butterflies / Streets of old / Out house
CD ______ HOLCD 27
Holistic / May '97 / Kudos / Pinnacle / Plastic Head / Prime

DISTANT EARTH
Manipulation / Jam sandwich / Brass lines and basses / Descend / Electronic arms / Distant earth
CD ______ HOLCD 26
Holistic / Jun '97 / Kudos / Pinnacle / Plastic Head / Prime

FROM MARZ WITH LOVE
CD ______ HOLCD 24
Holistic / Aug '96 / Kudos / Pinnacle / Plastic Head / Prime

Frey, Glenn

ALLNIGHTER, THE
Allnighter / Sexy girl / I got love / Somebody else / Lover's moon / Smuggler's blues / Let's go home / Better in the USA / Living in darkness / New love
CD ______ MCLD 19009
MCA / Apr '92 / BMG

LIVE
Peaceful easy feeling / New kid in town / One you love / Wild mountain thyme / Strange weather / I've got mine / Lyin' eyes/ take it easy / River of dreams / True love / Love in the 21st century / Smugglers blues / Heat is on / Heartache tonight / Desperado
CD ______ MCLD 19343
MCA / Oct '96 / BMG

SOLO CONNECTION
This way to happiness / Who's been sleeping in my bed / Common ground / Call on me / One you love / Sexy girl / Smuggler's blues / Heat is on / You belong to the city / True love / Soul searchin' / Part of me, part of you / I've got mine / River of dreams / Rising high / Brave new world
CD ______ MCD 11227
MCA / Apr '95 / BMG

SOUL SEARCHING/STRANGE WEATHER (2CD Set)
Livin' right / True love / I did it for your love / Working man / Two hearts / Some kind of blue / Can't put out this fire / Let's pretend we're still in love / Soul searching / It's your life / Silent spring / Long hot summer / Agua tranquillo / Love in the 21st century / He took advantage / River of dreams / Before the ship goes down / I've got mine / Rising sun / Brave new world / Delicious / Walk in the dark / Big life / Part of me, part of you
CD Set ______ MCD 33727
MCA / Jul '96 / BMG

STRANGE WEATHER
Silent spring / Long hot summer / Strange weather / Agua tranquillo / Love in the 21st century / He took advantage / River of dreams / Before the ship goes down / I've got mine / Rising sun / Brave new world / Delicious / Walk in the dark / Big life / Part of me, part of you
CD ______ MCAD 10599
MCA / Jul '92 / BMG

Freya, Jo

LUSH (Freya, Jo & Kathryn Locke)
CD ______ NMCD 5
No Master's Voice / Feb '96 / ADA / Direct

TRADITIONAL SONGS OF ENGLAND
All things are quite silent / As I set off to Turkey / As Sylvie was walking / General Wolfe / Though I live not where I love / Sailor's life / Rounding the Horn / Lord Franklin / Unquiet grave / Broomfield wager / There was a lady all skin and bone / Geordie / Maids, when you're young never wed an old man / Bold William Taylor / Lovely Joan / Blacksmith courted me / Carnal and the crane / Green Cockade / Fourpence a day / Streams of lovely Nancy / Sweet England
CD ______ CDSDL 402
Saydisc / Mar '94 / ADA / Direct / Harmonia Mundi

Freyda

GLOBALULLABIES
CD ______ 9425712
Music For Little People / Jan '96 / Direct

Freyja

FREYJA
Entradilla / Freylech / Csardas / Le moulin des deux roues / Snieder danz/reelin' over the rooftops / Krummshots / Rossignolet / Lost papers / Setalos kopogos tusszentos csardas / Vecinos
CD ______ OSMOCD 006
Osmosys / Jul '96 / Direct

Friction

REPLICANT WALK
CD ______ EMY 1092
Enemy / Jan '90 / Grapevine/PolyGram

Frida

SHINE
Shine / One little lie / Face / Twist in the dark / Slowly / Heart of the country / Come to me / Chemistry tonight / Don't do it / Comfort me
CD ______ 8235802
Polydor / Jan '93 / PolyGram

SOMETHING'S GOING ON
Tell me it's over / I see red / I got something / Strangers / To turn the stone / I know there's something going on / Threnody / Baby don't you cry no more / Way you do / You know what I mean / Here we'll stay
CD ______ 8001022
Polydor / Jan '93 / PolyGram

Friday, Gavin

ADAM 'N' EVE
I want to live / Falling off the edge of the world / King of trash / Why say goodbye / Saint divine / Melancholy baby / Fun and experience / Big no no / Where in the world / Wind and rain / Eden
CD ______ CID 9984
Island / Mar '92 / PolyGram

EACH MAN KILLS THE THING HE LOVES
Each man kills the thing he loves / He got what he wanted / Tell tale heart / Man of misfortune / Apologia / Rags to riches / Dazzle and delight / Next thing to murder / Next / Love is just a word / You take away the sun / Another blow on the bruise / Death is not the end
CD ______ IMCD 175
Island / Jul '93 / PolyGram

SHAG TOBACCO
CD ______ IMCD 227
Island / Sep '96 / PolyGram

Fridge

CEEFAX
EDM / Helicopter / Tricity / More eh4-800 / Jazz loop / Robots in disguise / EDM 2 / Oracle / EDM 3 / Zed ex ay-ti-wan
CD ______ OPR 6CD
Output / Mar '97 / RTM/Disc

Friedlander, Erik

CHIMERA
CD ______ AVAN 057
Avant / Jan '96 / Cadillac / Harmonia Mundi

Friedman, Dean

DEAN FRIEDMAN / WELL WELL SAID THE ROCKING CHAIR
Company / Ariel / Solitaire / Woman of mine / Song for my mother / Letter / I may be young / Humor me / Funny papers / Love is not enough / Rocking chair / I've had enough / Lucky stars / Shopping bag ladies / Don't you ever dare / Deli song (corned beef on wry) / Lydia / S and M / Let down your hair
CD ______ CDWIKD 98
Chiswick / Apr '91 / Pinnacle

RUMPLED ROMEO
First date / McDonald's girl / Are you ready yet / Hey Larry / Love is real / Buy my baby a car / Special effects / I depend on you, Jesus / Marginal middle class / I will never leave you
CD ______ CDWIK 106
Chiswick / May '92 / Pinnacle

VERY BEST OF DEAN FRIEDMAN
Lucky stars / Company / Solitaire / Letter / Humor me / Love is not enough / Woman of mine / Lydia / Ariel / Rocking chair / I've had enough / Shopping bag ladies / Deli song (corned beef on wry) / S and M / Funny papers / I may be young
CD ______ MCCD 036
Music Club / Sep '91 / Disc / THE

Friedman, Don

DAYS OF WINE AND ROSES (Friedman, Don Trio)
CD ______ 1212722
Soul Note / Feb '97 / Cadillac / Harmonia Mundi / Wellard

FRIEDMAN/PEPPER/KNEPPER (Friedman, Don/Pepper Adams/Jimmy Knepper)
CD ______ PCD 7036
Progressive / Jun '93 / Jazz Music

I HEAR A RHAPSODY
CD ______ ST 577
Stash / Jul '94 / ADA / Cadillac / CM / Direct / Jazz Music

LIVE AT MAYBECK RECITAL HALL VOL.33
In your own sweet way / Alone together / Prelude to a kiss / Invitation / Memory for Scotty / I concentrate on you / How deep is the ocean / Sea's breeze
CD ______ CCD 4608
Concord Jazz / Aug '94 / New Note/ Pinnacle

MY ROMANCE
CD ______ SCCD 31403
Steeplechase / Apr '97 / Discovery / Impetus

OPUS D'AMOUR (Friedman, Don & Don Thompson)
CD ______ SKCD 3058
Sackville / Jul '96 / Cadillac / Jazz Music / Swift

Friedman, Maria

MARIA FRIEDMAN
I happen to like New York / Man with the child in his eyes / Golden days / If you go away / I'm gorgeous / My romance / In the sky / Paris in the rain / Toby's song / Man that got away / Guess who I saw today / Play the song again / Finishing the hat / Now and then / Broadway baby
CD ______ 3036000012
Carlton / Oct '95 / Carlton

Friedman, Marty

DRAGON'S KISS
CD ______ RR 9529 2
Roadrunner / '89 / PolyGram

INTRODUCTION
Arrival / Bittersweet / Be / Escapism / Luna / Mama / Loneliness / Siberia
CD ______ RR 8950 2
Roadrunner / Dec '94 / PolyGram

SCENES
Tibet / Angel / Valley of enternity / Night / Realm of the senses / West / Trance / Triumph
CD ______ RR 91042
Roadrunner / Sep '96 / PolyGram

TRUE OBSESSIONS
CD ______ 398414219CD
Metal Blade / Oct '96 / Pinnacle / Plastic Head

Friedmann

INDIAN SUMMER
CD ______ BIBERCD 66301
In Akustik / '88 / Direct / TKO Magnum

LEGENDS OF LIGHT
Fairies of sternsea / Mount belenos / Joy of Beltane / Seven silver stars / Spring has come to wiesental / Sunday in Alsace / Memories of Lugnasad / Black cherries, white wine / Lament of the white goddess / Sun at midnight
CD ______ ND 63033
Narada / Oct '95 / ADA / New Note/ Pinnacle

VOYAGER IN EXPANSE
CD ______ INAK 860 CD
In Akustik / '88 / Direct / TKO Magnum

Friedmann, Bernd

LEISURE ZONES
CD ______ ASH 25
Ash International / Jan '96 / Kudos / Pinnacle

Friends From Rio

FRIENDS FROM RIO
Batacuda com mongo / Casa forte / Para Lennon E McCartney / Fransisco cat / Maracatudo / Os grilos (The crickets) / Bebe / Batunk / Aquila coisas todas
CD ______ F 007CD
Far Out / Jul '96 / Timewarp

MISTURADA VOL.1 (Friends From Rio Remixes) (Various Artists)
Francisco cat: *Pressure Drop* / Casa forte: *Natural Element* / Os grilos: *Takemura, Nobukazu* / Batacuda com mingo: *Mighty Black Forest* / Batunk: *DJ First Klas* / Maracatudo: *Wax Doctor* / Bebe: *Hightower Set* / Aquilas coisas todas: *APE* / Para Lennon and McCartney: *Da Lata* / Bebe: *Takemura, Nobukazu*
CD ______ FARO 010CD
Far Out / Oct '96 / Amato Disco / New Note/ Pinnacle

Friends Of Dean Martinez

SHADOW OF YOUR SMILE, THE
CD ______ SPCD 306
Sub Pop / Sep '95 / Cargo / Greyhound / Shellshock/Disc

Friesen, David

1,2,3 (Friesen, David Trio)
My funny valentine / Come rain or come shine / Getting sentimental over you / How deep is the ocean / Only trust your heart / Sarabande / Dark sky / Going forth
CD ______ BCD 00172
Burnside / May '96 / Koch

LONG TRIP HOME
CD ______ ITM 970073
ITM / Sep '92 / Koch / Tradelink

OTHER TIMES, OTHER PLACES
Festival dance / Tyrone's dedication / Song for my daughter / Father's delight / Song for my family / Our 25th year / Childhood walk / Years through time
CD ______ 66052001
Global Pacific / Feb '91 / Pinnacle

RETURNING (Friesen, David & Glen Moore)
CD ______ BCD 00132
Burnside / Jul '96 / Koch

THREE TO GET READY
CD ______ ITMP 970084
ITM / Oct '95 / Koch / Tradelink

TWO FOR THE SHOW
CD ______ ITM 960079
ITM / Oct '95 / Koch / Tradelink

UPON THE SWING
CD ______ SHAM 1020CD
Shamrock / Nov '95 / ADA / Wellard

Frifot

JARVEN
CD ______ CAP 21551CD
Caprice / Nov '96 / ADA / Cadillac / CM / Complete/Pinnacle

Fringe

IT'S TIME FOR THE FRINGE
CD ______ 1212052
Soul Note / Sep '93 / Cadillac / Harmonia Mundi / Wellard

Fripp, Robert

1995 SOUNDSCAPES VOL.1
CD ______ DGM 9505
Discipline / Mar '96 / Pinnacle

BLESSING OF TEARS, A (1995 Soundscape)
Cathederal of tears / First light / Midnight blue / Reflection 1 / Second light / Blessing of tears / Returning 1 / Returning 2
CD ______ DGM 9506
Discipline / Aug '95 / Pinnacle

BRIDGE BETWEEN
Kan-non power / Yamanashi blues / Hope / Chromatic fantasy / Contrapunctus / Bicycling to Afghanistan / Blue / Blockhead / Passacaglia / Therenody for souls in torment
CD ______ DGM 9303
Discipline / Sep '94 / Pinnacle

CHEERFUL INSANITY (Giles, Giles & Fripp)
Saga of Rodney Toady / North meadow / Newly weds / One in a million / Call tomorrow / Digging my lawn / Little children / Crukster / Thursday morning / Just George / How do they know / Elephant song / Sun is shining / Suite No.1 / Erudite eyes
CD ______ 8209652
London / Jul '93 / PolyGram

ESSENTIAL FRIPP & ENO, THE (Fripp, Robert & Brian Eno)
Heavenly music corporation / Swastika girls / Wind on water / Evening star / Healthy colours
CD ______ CDVE 920
Venture / Apr '94 / EMI

EVENING STAR (Fripp, Robert & Brian Eno)
Wind on water / Evening star / Evensong / Wind on wind / Index of metals
CD ____ EEGCD 3
EG / '87 / EMI

EXPOSURE
Breathless / Chicago / Disengage / Exposure / First inaugural address to the IACE Sherbourne House / Here comes the flood / I may not have had enough of me but I've had enough of you / Mary / North star / NY3 / Urban landscape / Water music 1 / You burn me up I'm a cigarette / Preface / Postscript / Haaden two / Water music 2
CD ____ EGCD 41
EG / Jan '87 / EMI

GOD SAVE THE KING
God save the King / Under heavy manners / Heptaparaparshinokh / Inductive resonance / Cognitive dissonance / Dislocated / HG Wells / Eye needles / Trap
CD ____ EEGCD 9
EG / Jun '85 / EMI

INTERGALACTIC BOOGIE EXPRESS LIVE
Connecticut yankee in the court of King Arthur / Rhythm of the universes / Lark's thrak / Circulation I / Intergalactic boogie express / G Force / Eye of the needle / Corrente / Driving force / Groove penetration / Flying home / Circulation II / Fireplace / Fragments of skylab / Asturias / Prelude circulation / Cheeseballs / Prelude in C minor / Wabash cannonball
CD ____ DGM 9502
Discipline / Sep '95 / Pinnacle

LET THE POWER FALL (An Album Of Frippertronics)
1984 / 1985 / 1986 / 1987 / 1988 / 1989
CD ____ EEGCD 10
EG / '87 / EMI

NO PUSSY FOOTING (Fripp, Robert & Brian Eno)
Heavenly music corporation / Swastika girls
CD ____ EEGCD 2
EG / Jan '87 / EMI

ROBERT FRIPP AND THE LEAGUE OF CRAFTY GUITARISTS - LIVE
Guitar craft theme 1: Invocation / Tight muscle party at love beach / Chords that bind / Guitar craft theme 3: Eye of the needle / All or nothing / Crafty march / Guitar craft theme 2: Aspiration / All or nothing / Circulation / Fearful symmetry / New world
CD ____ EEGCD 43
EG / Nov '86 / EMI

SHOW OF HANDS (Fripp, Robert & The League Of Crafty Guitarists)
CD ____ EEG 21022
EG / Jul '93 / EMI

THAT WHICH PASSES
On acceptance / On the approach of doubt / Leap / Worm in paradise / New worlds / On triumph / On awe / This too shall pass / Fear of light / Time to die
CD ____ DGM 9507
Discipline / Sep '96 / Pinnacle

Frisco Syncopators

SAN FRANCISCO BOUND
CD ____ SOSCD 1211
Stomp Off / Oct '92 / Jazz Music / Wellard

Frisell, Bill

BEFORE WE WERE BORN
Before we were born / Pip squeak / Hard plains drifter / Steady girl / Some song and dance / Goodbye / Lone ranger
CD ____ 7559608432
Nonesuch / Jan '94 / Warner Music

HAVE A LITTLE FAITH
CD ____ 7559793012
Nonesuch / Jan '94 / Warner Music

IN LINE
Start / Throughout / Two arms / Shorts / Smile on you / Beach / In line / Three / Godson song
CD ____ 8370192
ECM / Jul '91 / New Note/Pinnacle

IS THAT YOU
CD ____ 7559609562
Nonesuch / Jan '94 / Warner Music

LIVE
CD ____ GCD 79504
Gramavision / Oct '95 / Vital/SAM

LOOKOUT FOR HOPE (Frisell, Bill Band)
Lookout for hope / Little brother Bobby / Hangdog / Remedios / Beauty / Lonesome / Melody for Jack / Hackensack / Little bigger / Animal race / Alien prints (for D Sharpe)
CD ____ 8334952
ECM / Feb '88 / New Note/Pinnacle

QUARTET
CD ____ 7559794012
Nonesuch / May '96 / Warner Music

RAMBLER
Tone / Music I heard / Rambler / When we go / Resistor / Strange meeting / Wizard of odds
CD ____ 8252342
ECM / May '85 / New Note/Pinnacle

SAFETY BY NUMBERS - AMERICAN BLOOD (Frisell, Bill & Victor Godsey)
CD ____ VBR 20642
Vera Bra / Oct '94 / New Note/Pinnacle / Pinnacle

THIS LAND
CD ____ 7559793162
Nonesuch / Jun '94 / Warner Music

WHERE IN THE WORLD
CD ____ 7559611812
Nonesuch / Jan '94 / Warner Music

WORKS: BILL FRISELL
Monica Jane / Beach / When we go throughout / Black is the colour of my true love's hair / Wizard of odds / Conception vessel / Etude
CD ____ 8372732
ECM / Jun '89 / New Note/Pinnacle

Frishberg, Dave

DOUBLE PLAY (Frishberg, Dave & Jim Goodwin)
CD ____ ARCD 19118
Arbors Jazz / Nov '94 / Cadillac

GETTING SOME FUN OUT OF LIFE
CD ____ CCD 4037
Concord Jazz / Jul '96 / New Note/ Pinnacle

LET'S EAT HOME
Brenda Starr / Let's eat home / Mr. George / Matty / Mooche / I was ready / Strange music / Ship without a sail / Lookin' good / Underdog
CD ____ CCD 4402
Concord Jazz / Jan '90 / New Note/ Pinnacle

WHERE YOU AT
CD ____ BL 010
Bloomdido / Oct '93 / Cadillac

Frith, Fred

DROPERA
CD ____ RECDEC 32
Rec Rec / Oct '95 / Cadillac / Plastic Head / ReR Megacorp / SRD

EYE TO EAR
CD ____ TZA 7503
Tzadik / Feb '97 / Cargo

IMPROVISATIONS (Frith, Fred & J.P. Drouet)
CD ____ TE 012
EPM / Jul '97 / ADA / Discovery

NOUS AUTRES (Frith, Fred & Rene Luiser)
CD ____ VICTOCD 01
Victo / Nov '94 / Harmonia Mundi / ReR Megacorp

STEP ACROSS THE BORDER
CD ____ RECDEC 30
Rec Rec / May '93 / Cadillac / Plastic Head / ReR Megacorp / SRD

TECHNOLOGY OF TEARS
CD ____ RECDEC 20
Rec Rec / Apr '88 / Cadillac / Plastic Head / ReR Megacorp / SRD
CD ____ SST 172CD
SST / May '93 / Plastic Head

TOP OF HIS HEAD, THE
Title theme / Driving to the train / Wheels within / Hold on hold / Lucy leaves a note / Gus escapes / Gravity's a rule / Channel change / Orbit / Fall to call / Underwater dream / This old earth / Donuts / Long drive / Lucy / Premonition / Questions and answers / Performance / Title theme (conclusion) / Way you look tonight
CD ____ MTM 21
Made To Measure / Apr '96 / New Note/ Pinnacle

WITH ENEMIES LIKE THESE, WHO NEEDS FRIENDS (Frith & Kaiser)
CD ____ SST 147CD
SST / May '93 / Plastic Head

Frizzell, Lefty

LIFE'S LIKE POETRY (12CD Set)
I love you a thousand ways / If you've got the money, I've got the time / Shine, shave shower / Cold feet / Don't think it ain't been fun dear / When payday comes around / My baby's just like money / Look what thoughts will do / You want everything but me / I want to be with you always / Give me more more more (of your kisses) / How long will it take (to stop loving you) / Always late (with your kisses) / Mom and dad's waltz / You can go on your way now / Treasure untold / Blue yodel / Travellin' blues / My old pal / Lullaby yodel / Breakman's blues / My rough and rowdy ways / I love you (Though you're no good) / It's just you (I could love always) / (Darling now) you're here so everything's alright / I've got reasons to hate you / Don't stay away / If you can spare the time (I won't miss the money) / King without a Queen / Forever (and always) / I know you're lonesome (while waiting for me) / Lost love blues / That's me without you / Send her here to be mine / I won' good for nothin' / If I lose you (I'll lose my world) / I'm an old old man (Tryin' to love while I can) / You're just mine (Only in my dreams) / I'll try / Bring your sweet self back / Time changes things / All of me (loves all of you) / California blues / Never no' mo' blues / We crucified our Jesus / When it comes to measuring love / Sleep, baby, sleep / (I'm) Lonely and blue / Before you go, make sure you know / Two friends of mine in love / Hopeless love / Then I'll come back to you / Tragic letter (The letter that you left) / You can always count on me / I've been away way too long / Run 'em off / Darkest moment (is just before the light of da / You're too late / My little her and him / I love you mostly / You're there, I'm ere / Let it be so / Mama / Making believe / Moonlight, Darling and you / I'll sit alone and cry / Forest fire (Is in your heart) / Sweet lies / Your tomorrows will never come / It gets late so early / I'm lost between right and wrong / Promises (promises, promises) / My love and baby's gone / Today is that tomorrow (I dreamed of yesterday) / First to have a second chance / These hands / You can't divorce my heart / Treat her right / Heart's highway / I'm a boy left alone / Just can't live that fast (anymore) / Waltz of the angels / Lullaby waltz / Glad I found you / Now that you are gone / From an angel to a devil / Lover by appointment / Sick, sober and sorry / No one to talk to (but the blues) / Is it only that you're lonely / Mailman bring me no more blues / You've still got it / Tell me dear / To stop loving you (means cry) / Torch within my heart / Time out for the blues / (Darling) let's turn back the years / You win again / Why should I be lonely / Signed, sealed, delivered (I'm yours) / Nobody knows but me / If you're ever lonely darling / Silence / Release me / Our love's no bluff / You're humbuggin' me / She's gone / Cigarettes and coffee blues / I need your love / My bucket's got a hole in it / Sin will be the chaser for the wine / Knock again, true love / Long black veil / One has been to another / Farther than my eyes can see / My blues will pass / Ballad of the blue and grey / That's all I can remember / So what, let it rain / What you gonna do, Leroy / I feel sorry for me / Heaven's plan / Looking for you / Stranger / Few steps away / Forbidden lovers / Just passing through / That reminds me of me / Don't let her see me cry / Through the eyes of a fool / James river / Preview of coming attractions / Lonely heart / What good did you get (out of breaking my heart) / When it rains the blues / I'm not the man I'm supposed to be / Saginaw Michigan / There's no food in this house / Rider / Nester / I was coming home to you / Hello to him (goodbye to me) / I can tell / Make that one for the road a cup of coffee / Gator hollow / It costs too much to die / She's gone, gone, gone / Confused / How far down can I go / It's bad (when it's that way) / I don't trust you anymore / Little unfair / Woman let me sing you a song / Preparations to be blue / Love looks good on you / It's hard to please you / You don't want me to get well / Writing on the wall / I just couldn't see the forest (for the trees) / I'm not guilty / It couldn't happen to a nicer guy / Everything keeps coming back (but you) / Heart (don't love her anymore) / You don't have to be present to win / My feet are getting cold / Is there anything I can do / Old gang's gone / Song from a lonely heart / You gotta me puttin' me on / There in the mirror / Get this stranger out of me / Money tree / Hobo's pride / When the rooster leaves the yard / Anything you can spare / Only way to fly / Only way to fly (Laughing version) / Prayer on your lips is like freedon in your hands / Little ole wine drinker me / Word or two to Mary / Almost persuaded / Have you ever been untrue / When the grass grows green again / Marriage bit / I'll remember you / Wasted way of live / Blind street singer / Honky tonk hill / My baby is a tramp / She brought love sweet love / Watermelon time in Georgia / I must be getting over you / Out of you / It's raining all over the world / There's something lonley in this house / Three cheers for the good guys / Article from life / Honky tonk hill (without overdub) / Honky tonk stardust cowboy / What am I gonna do / Give me more, more, more (of your kisses) / You babe / This just ain't a good day for leavin' / Down by the railroad track / Let me give her the flowers / If I had half the sense (A fool was born with) / Somebody's words / Lucky arms / True love needs to be in touch / My house is your honky tonk / I buy the wine / If she just helps me to get over you / Falling / Railroad lady / I can't get over you to save my life / I never go around mirrors / That's the way love goes / She found the key / I wonder who's building the bridge / My wishing room / I'm gonna hang out my mind today / Sittin' and thinkin' / I'm not that good at goodbye / Yesterday just passed my way again / Life's like poetry / Darling I'm missing you / I'll never cry over you / My confession / I hope you're not lonely when I'm gone / My baby and my wife / It's all over now / Worried mind / Maiden's prayer / I'm wasting my life away / You nearly lose your mind / Just can't live that fast (anymore) / Just can't live that fast (anymore) / Honey baby, you were wrong / Please me mine, dear blue eyes / I'm yours if you want me / I'll be a bachelor till I die / Yesterday's mail / Shine, shave and shower / I want to be with you / Always / Ida red / Always late / Theme and If you've got the money / Make the one for the road a cup of coffee / Darling let's turn back the years / Things / At the woodchoppers' ball / Stay all night / Somebody's pushing / Mona Lisa: *Frizzell, David* / Sunday down in Tennessee: *Frizzell, David* / I'll make it up to you / Too much love / My abandoned heart / Wait till I'm asleep / Not this time / Why didn't you tell me our love was wrong / Forever and always / Please don't stay away so long / Please don't stay away so long / You have never known to be wrong / Reason why my heart's in misery / Just little things like that / I love you so / Fool's advice / When me and my baby go steppin' out / When me and my baby go steppin' out / Brakeman's blues
CD Set ____ BCD 15550
Bear Family / Feb '92 / Direct / Rollercoaster / Swift

Froboess, Conny

DIE SINGLES 1958-59
Diana / Teenager Susan / I love you baby / Schicke schicke schuh / Auch du hast dein schicksal in der hand / Glockergiesser rock / Blue jean boy / Sunshine / Hey boys, how do you do / Jolly joker / Teenager melodie: *Froboess, Conny & Will Brandes* / Ich mocht mit dir traumen: *Froboess, Conny & Will Brandes* / Holiday in Honolulu: *Froboess, Conny & Will Brandes* / Ob 15 ob 16 ob 17 jahre alt / Mr. Music / Wenn das mein grosser bruder wusste / Kleine Lucienne / Such das gluck des lebens / Little girl / Ein madchen mit sechzehn / Lieber disc jockey / Billy, Jack and Joe / Een meisje ven zestien / Liefde als zonneschijn
CD ____ BCD 15410
Bear Family / Dec '87 / Direct / Rollercoaster / Swift

DIE SINGLES 1960-62
Yes my darling: *Froboess, Conny & Rex Gildo* / Lippenstift am jacket / Midi midinette / Wer wird der erste sein / Lago maggiore / Junge mach musik / Sag mir was du denkst: *Froboess, Conny & Peter Kraus* / Das geht di leute gar nichts an: *Froboess, Conny & Rex Gildo* / Papa liebt mama / Nicht so schuchtern, junger mann / Ich bin fur die liebe nicht zu jung / Mein vater war ein cowboy / Firulin: *Froboess, Conny & Rex Gildo* / Oky doky: *Froboess, Conny & Rex Gildo* / Mariandl / Nur ein kleines medaillon / Einen kuss und noch einen kuss / Tanz noch einmal mit mir / Zwei kleine Italiener / Hallo, hallo, hallo / Das tu' ich alles nur fur dich (Italian) / Un bacio al' Italiano (Italian) / Hallo, hallo, hallo (Italian) / Twe kleine Italianen (Dutch) / Hallo, hallo, hallo (Dutch)
CD ____ BCD 15411
Bear Family / Dec '87 / Direct / Rollercoaster / Swift

DIE SINGLES 1962-64
CD ____ BCD 15452
Bear Family / Feb '90 / Direct / Rollercoaster / Swift

DIE SINGLES 1964-1967
Diese nacht hat viele lichter / Ist es wahr / Meine hochzeitsreise mach'ich auf den mond / Schone manner sind nicht sehr gefahrlich / Gestern um dreiviertel zehn / Es muss nicht dies sein / Ich geh' durch den regen / Tausend und noch ein paar traume / Der sommer geht / Und das leben geht weiter / Schreib' es in den sand / So ist das leben / Ich komme nie mehr los von dir / Oh Gloria / Georgy girl / Frage und antwort / Adios, adios / Arme kleine sterne / Mein herz schlagt daba daba dab / Liverpool waltz / Die sommerballade von der armen Louise / Folg dem sonnenschein / Um die welt geht die reise / L'amourette / Dis moi si tu veux / Les yeux de Paris / On peux bien dire / Jolly Joker / Hey boys / How do you do
CD ____ BCD 15491
Bear Family / Aug '91 / Direct / Rollercoaster / Swift

Froese, Edgar

AGES
Metropolis / Era of the slaves / Tropic of Capricorn / Nights of automatic women / Icarus / Children's deeper study / Ode to Granny A / Pizarro and Atahualpa / Golgatha and the circle closes
CD ____ CDOVD 480
Virgin / Jun '97 / EMI

AQUA
Upland / Panorphelia / NGC / Aqua
CD ____ CDV 2016
Virgin / Jun '87 / EMI

AQUA/BLACKOUTS/TIMEWIND (Froese, Edgar & Ashra Tempel/Klaus Schulze)
CD Set ____ TPAK 12
Virgin / Oct '90 / EMI

BEYOND THE STORM
Heatwave city / Dome of yellow turtles / One fine day in Siberia / Magic lantern / Walkabout / Genesta in the afternoon glow / Moonlight on a crawler lane / Scarlet score for Mescalero / Upland / Santa Elena Mar-

isal / Macula transfer / Drunken Mozart in the desert / Descent like a hawk / Carneol / Light cone / Detroit snackbar dreamer / Epsilon in Malaysian pale / Tierra del fuego / Bobcats in the sun / Metropolis / Year of the falcon / Juniper mascara / Shores of Guam / Pinnacles / Stuntman / Days of camouflage / Tropic of Capricorn / Vault of the heaven
CD ___ AMBT 5
Virgin / Jun '95 / EMI

PINNACLES
Specific gravity of smile / Light cone / Walkabout / Pinnacles
CD ___ CDV 2277
Virgin / May '88 / EMI

STUNTMAN
Stuntman / It would be like Samoa / Detroit snackbar dreamer / Drunken Mozart in the desert / Dali-esque sleep fuse / Scarlet score for Mescalero
CD ___ CDV 2139
Virgin / '87 / EMI

Froggatt, Raymond

COLLECTION, THE
CD ___ RBMCD 0017
Red Balloon / May '97 / Koch

SOMEDAY
CD ___ RBMCD 0016
Red Balloon / Oct '95 / Koch

Frogs

MY DAUGHTER THE BROAD
CD ___ OLE 1552
Matador / Jun '96 / Vital

Frohmader, Peter

GATES
CD ___ EFA 127612
Atonal / Sep '95 / SRD

From The Fire

30 DAYS & DIRTY NIGHTS
CD ___ CDATV 22
Active / Jul '92 / Pinnacle

Fromenteau, Michele

L'ART DE LA VIELLE A ROUE VOL.1
CD ___ ARN 60355
Arion / Feb '97 / ADA / Discovery

Frongia, Enrico

ARGIA (Frongia, Enrico & Alberto Balia)
CD ___ NT 6713
Robi Droli / Jan '94 / ADA / Direct

Front 242

LIVE CODE 5413356424225
Der verfluchte engel / Motion / Masterhit / Flag / Tragedy for you / Im rhythmus bleiben / Skin / Headhunter / Welcome to paradise / Crapage / Soul manager / Punish your machine / Religion
CD ___ BIAS 242CD
Play It Again Sam / Oct '94 / Discovery / Plastic Head / Vital

LIVE TARGET
Rhythm of time / Soul manager / Don't crash / Im rhythmus bleiben / DSM 123 and Moldavia / No shuffle / Gripped by fear / Never stop / Headhunter / Tragedy for you / Welcome to paradise / Punish your machine / Intro/Circling overland
CD ___ GUZZ 1888
Guzzi / Dec '92 / Vital

MUT@GE MIX@GE
Rhythm of time / Happiness / Gripped by fear / Mixed by fear / Crapage / Junkdrome / Religion / Break me / Dancesoundtrackmusic
CD ___ RRE 020CD
Play It Again Sam / Feb '96 / Discovery / Plastic Head / Vital

NO COMMENT (1984-1985)
Commando mix / S fr nomenklatura pt 1/2 / Deceit / Lovely day / No shuffle / Special forces / See the future (live) / In November / Body to body
CD ___ MK 002CD
Mask / Jun '92 / Vital

Front Page Review

MYSTIC SOLDIERS
Prophecies/Morning blue / Prism fawn / One eyed minor / Feels like love / Silver children / Valley of eyes / Without you / For the best offer
CD ___ CDWIKD 166
Big Beat / Feb '97 / Pinnacle

Front Range

BACK TO RED RIVER
CD ___ SHCD 3811
Sugar Hill / Jan '94 / ADA / CM / Direct / Koch / Roots

NEW FRONTIER, THE
Waiting for the real thing / Chains of darkness / Down in Caroline / Without you / Why don't you leave me baby / Lonesome night / When I still needed you / So far away / Burning the breakfast / Shady river / Building on the rock / Happy after all
CD ___ SHCD 3801
Sugar Hill / Jul '92 / ADA / CM / Direct / Koch / Roots

ONE BEAUTIFUL DAY
CD ___ SHCD 3830
Sugar Hill / Mar '95 / ADA / CM / Direct / Koch / Roots

RAMBLIN' ON MY MIND
CD ___ SHCD 3861
Sugar Hill / Feb '97 / ADA / CM / Direct / Koch / Roots

Frontier

FRONTIER
Frontier
CD ___ 103 FR
Humbolt Pie / Nov '96 / Cargo

HEATER
CD ___ TOW 004
Tug O' War / May '97 / SRD

Frontline Assembly

BLADE, THE
CD ___ TM 91192
Roadrunner / Sep '92 / PolyGram

CAUSTIC GRIP
CD ___ TM 91162
Roadrunner / Sep '96 / PolyGram

CORRODED DISORDER
CD ___ 08422332CD
Westcom / Jan '96 / Koch / Pinnacle

GASHED SENSES AND CROSSFIRE
No limit / Hypocrisy / Prayer / Big money / Sedation / Anti-social / Shut down / Digital tension dementia / Fools game
CD ___ TM 91152
Roadrunner / Sep '96 / PolyGram

HARD WIRED
CD ___ 08622290CD
Westcom / Nov '95 / Koch / Pinnacle
CD ___ 08522292CD
Westcom / May '96 / Koch / Pinnacle

INITIAL COMMAND
Initial command
CD ___ KK 006CD
KK / '88 / Plastic Head

LIVE WIRED (2CD Set)
CD Set ___ 08843262
Westcom / Sep '96 / Koch / Pinnacle

MILLENNIUM
CD ___ RR 90192
Roadrunner / Sep '96 / PolyGram

STATE OF MIND
CD ___ DCD 9005
Dossier / Aug '88 / Cargo / SRD

TACTICAL NEURAL IMPLANT
CD ___ TM 91882
Third Mind / Sep '96 / Pinnacle / Third Mind

TOTAL TERROR VOL.1
CD ___ EFA 08451CD
Dossier / Nov '93 / Cargo / SRD

TOTAL TERROR VOL.2
CD ___ EFA 08452CD
Dossier / Nov '93 / Cargo / SRD

Frost

FROST MUSIC
CD ___ VMD 6520
Vanguard / Oct '96 / ADA / Pinnacle

ROCK 'N' ROLL MUSIC
CD ___ VMD 6541
Vanguard / Oct '96 / ADA / Pinnacle

Frost, Edith

CALLING OVER TIME
CD ___ DC 89CD
Drag City / Jun '97 / Cargo / Greyhound

Frost, Frank

JELLY ROLL KING
CD ___ CDCHARLY 223
Charly / Jul '90 / Koch

JELLY ROLL KING (Charly Blues - Masterworks Vol. 36)
Everything's alright / Lucky to be living / Jelly roll king / Bay you're so kind / Gonna make you mine / Now twist / Big boss man / Jack's jump / So tired of living by myself / Now what you gonna do / Pocket full of shells / Just come on home / Crawlback / My back scratcher / Things you do / Ride with your daddy tonight / Pocket full of money / Didn't mean no harm
CD ___ CDBM 36
Charly / Jan '93 / Koch

KEEP YOURSELF TOGETHER (Frost, Frank & Sam Carr)
Keep yourself together / Frank's boogie woogie / Tired of living by myself / You're so kind / Going to Chicago / Just a feeling / Cotton needs pickin' / Come on home / All my life / Everything's gonna be alright / My soul lover
CD ___ ECD 260772
Evidence / Apr '96 / ADA / Cadillac / Harmonia Mundi

Frostbite

SECOND COMING
CD ___ TPLP 666CD
One Little Indian / Aug '93 / Pinnacle

SECRET ADMIRER
CD ___ USCD 011
Underground Symphony / Nov '96 / Cargo

Frozen Brass

ASIA
CD ___ PANCD 2020
Pan / May '93 / ADA / CM / Direct

Frozen Doberman

BONZAI
CD ___ FD 019CD
Modern Invasion / Jul '95 / Plastic Head

Frozen Sun

UNSPOKEN
CD ___ DSFA 1003CD
DSFA / Jun '96 / Plastic Head

Frugivore

BIONAUT, THE
CD ___ DIGI 1002CD
Digitrax / Oct '95 / Plastic Head

Fruitcake

ROOM FOR SURPRISE
CD ___ CYCL 032
Cyclops / May '96 / Pinnacle

Fruminous Bandersnatch

YOUNG MAN'S SONG
You gotta believe / Chain reaction / Rosemary's baby / What is a Bandersnatch / Woodrose syrup / Now that you've gone / 45 Cents / Pulpit huff / Paper / Cheshire / Black box / Can-a-bliss
CD ___ CDWIKD 169
Big Beat / Jun '96 / Pinnacle

Fruscella, Tony

TONY'S BLUES
CD ___ C&BCD 107
Cool & Blue / Dec '92 / Discovery / Jazz Music

Frusciante, John

NIANDRA LADES AND USUALLY JUST A T-SHIRT
CD ___ 74321236792
American / Nov '95 / BMG

Frustrated

ANTHOLOGY OF EXPERIMENTAL MUSIC
CD ___ DIS 011CD
Disturbance / Jun '94 / Plastic Head / Prime

Fruupp

FUTURE LEGENDS/SEVEN SECRETS
Future legends / Decision / As day breaks with dawn / Garveyard epistle / Lord of the incubus / Olde tyme future / Song for a thought / Wise as wisdom / White eyes / Garden lady / Three spires / Elizabeth / Seventh secret
CD ___ C5HCD 645
See For Miles/C5 / Aug '96 / Pinnacle

PRINCE OF HEAVEN'S EYES/MODERN MASQUERADES
It's all up now / Prince of Darkness / Jaunting car / Annie Austere / Knowing you / Crystal Brook / Seaward sunset / Perfect wish / Misty morning way / Masquerading with Dawn / Mystery might / Why / Janet Planet / Sheba's song
CD ___ C5HCD 646
See For Miles/C5 / Jul '96 / Pinnacle

Fry, Albert

THIAR I DTIR CHONAILL
CD ___ CIC 081CD
Clo Iar-Chonnachta / Nov '93 / CM

Frye, Howard

GYPSY MANDOLIN
CD ___ MCD 71463
Monitor / Jun '93 / CM

FSK

INTERNATIONAL
CD ___ EFA 155482
Sub Up / Mar '96 / SRD

PEEL SESSIONS, THE (3.8.86/21.5.87)
I wish I could sprechen sie Deutch / Die musik finik findet immer nach haus / Dr. Arnold Fanck / Am tafelberg von kepstadt / Komm gib mir deine hand / Girl / Birthday / Don't pass me by
CD ___ SFPMCD 204
Strange Fruit / '89 / Pinnacle

Fu Manchu

DAREDEVIL
CD ___ BL 19
Bongload / Feb '97 / Cargo / Greyhound / Plastic Head

EARLY RECORDINGS
CD ___ ELS 014
Elastic / May '97 / Cargo / Plastic Head

IN SEARCH OF...
Lazy magician / Missing link / Asphalt risin' / Neptune's convoy / Redline / Cyclone launch / Strat-o-streak / Solid hex / Falcon has landed / Sea hag / Bargain / Supershooter
CD ___ MR 1342
Mammoth / Mar '96 / Vital

NO ONE RIDES FOR FREE
CD ___ BL 10
Bongload / Feb '97 / Cargo / Greyhound / Plastic Head

Fu-Schnickens

NERVOUS BREAKDOWN
Breakdown / Sum dum monkey / Visions (20/20) / Watch ya back door / Aaahh ooohhh / Sneakin' up on ya / Got it covered / Who stole the pebble / Hi Lo / What's up doc (Can we rock): *Fu-Schnickens & Shaquille O'Neal* / Breakdown (remix)
CD ___ CHIP 153
Jive / Oct '94 / Pinnacle

Fuchs, Wolfgang

BITS AND PIECES
CD ___ OWN 90004
FMP / May '97 / Cadillac

FINKFARKER (Fuchs, Wolfgang & George Katzer)
CD ___ FMPCD 26
FMP / Nov '86 / Cadillac

Fuck

BABY LOVES A FUNNY BUNNY
Boy meets girl / Swinger / Love me 2 / Flight of the mongeese / Tired / 22 no / Nice burg lettuce / Talent or / Ballet high / Part of me / Rococo / Like you / Loosened mind / Crush a butterfly / Whimper and cry
CD ___ NORMAL 204CD
Normal / Feb '97 / ADA / Direct
CD ___ WLR 2229
Walt Rhesus Lamplighter / Jun '97 / Cargo

PARDON MY FRENCH
L'il Hilda / Fuck Motel / Le serpent / Bestest friend / Compromise / One lb of In / La Jolla / For Lori / Raggy rag / Tether / Dirty brunette / To my gurl / Thoroughfare / Sometimes / Am I losin' / Scribble dribble
CD ___ OLE 2612
Matador / Jun '97 / Vital

PRETTY...SLOW
CD ___ WALT 008
Walt Rhesus Lamplighter / May '97 / Cargo

Fudge

FEROCIOUS RHYTHM OF PRECISE LAZINESS, THE
Oreo dust / Jr high blur / Peanut butter / Mystery machine / Mull / Wayside / Pez / Astronaut / 20-Nothing dub / Drive / Snowblind
CD ___ QUIGD 2
Quigley / Mar '93 / EMI

Fudge Tunnel

COMPLICATED FUTILITY OF IGNORANCE, THE
Random acts of cruelty / Joy of irony / Backed down / Cover up / Six eight / Long day / Excuse / Find your fortune / Suffering makes great stories / Circle of friends, circle of trends / Rudge with A G
CD ___ MOSH 119CD
Earache / Sep '94 / Vital

CREEP DIETS
Grey / Tipper Gore / Ten percent / Face down / Grit / Don't have time for you / Good kicking / Hot salad / Creep diets / Stuck / Always
CD ___ MOSH 064CD
Earache / Apr '93 / Vital

HATE SONGS IN E
CD ___ MOSH 036CD
Earache / Jan '93 / Vital

IN A WORD
Sex mammoth / Bed crumbs / Boston baby / Sweet meat / Grey / Spanish fly / Ten percent / Good kicking / Stuck / Tipper Gore / Gut rot / SRT / Kitchen belt / For madmen only / Changes
CD ___ MOSH 099CD
Earache / Jun '95 / Vital

Fugain, Michel

DIAMOND COLLECTION, THE
CD 3009412
Arcade / Feb '97 / Discovery

SES MEILLEURS MOMENTS (2CD Set)
CD Set 3018532
Flarenasch / Feb '97 / Discovery

Fugazi

FUGAZI
Waiting room / Bulldog front / Bad mouth / Burning / Give me the cure / Suggestion / Glue man
CD DIS 30CD
Dischord / Dec '88 / SRD

IN ON THE KILLTAKER
Facet squad / Public witness programme / Returning the screw / Smallpox champion / Rend it / Twenty three beats off / Sweet and low / Cassavetes / Great cop / Walken's syndrome / Instrument / Last chance for a slow dance
CD DIS 70D
Dischord / Jun '93 / SRD

MARGIN WALKER
Margin walker / And the same / Burning too / Provisional / Lockdown / Promises
CD DIS 35CD
Dischord / Jul '89 / SRD

RED MEDICINE
Do you like me / Bed for the scraping / Latest disgrace / Birthday pony / Forensic scene / Combination lock / Fell, destroyed / By you / Version / Target / Back to base / Downed city / Long distance runner
CD DIS 90CD
Dischord / May '95 / SRD

REPEATER
Turnover / Repeater / Brendan No.1 / Merchandise / Blueprint / Sieve-fisted find / Greed / Two beats off / Styrofoam / Reprovisional / Shut the door
CD DIS 44CD
Dischord / Mar '90 / SRD

STEADY DIET OF NOTHING
Exit only / Reclamation / Nice new outfit / Stacks / Latin roots / Steady diet of nothing / Long division / Runaway return / Polish / Dear justice letter / KYEO
CD DISCHORD 60CD
Dischord / Sep '91 / SRD

Fugees

BLUNTED ON REALITY
Introduction / Nappy heads / Blunted interlude / Recharge / Free-style interlude / Vocab / Special new bulletin interlude / Boof baf / Temple / How hard is it / Harlem chit chat interlude / Some seek stardom / Giggles / Da kid from Haiti interlude / Refugees on the mic / Living like there ain't no tomorrow / Shouts out from the block
CD 4747132
Ruff House / Jul '96 / Sony

SCORE, THE (Refugee Camp)
Red intro / How many mics / Ready or not / Zealots / Beast / Fu-gee-la / Family business / Killing me softly / Score / Mask / Cowboys / No woman no cry / Manifesto/ Outro
CD 4835492
Ruff House / Feb '96 / Sony

SCORE, THE (The Bootleg Versions)
Ready or not / Nappy heads / Don't cry, dry your eyes / Vocab / Killing me softly / No woman no cry
CD 4868242
Ruff House / Nov '96 / Sony

Fugs

FIRST ALBUM
Slum Goddess / Ah sunflower weary of time / Supergirl / Swinburne stomp / I couldn't get high / How sweet I roamed / Carpe diem / My baby done left me / Boobs a lot / Nothing / We're the fugs / Defeated / Ten commandments / CIA man / In the middle of their first recording session The Fugs sign / I saw the best minds of my generation rock / Spontaneous salute at Andy Warhol / War kills babies / Fugs national anthem / Fugs spaghetti death / Rhapsody of Tuli
CD CDWIKD 119
Fugs/Big Beat / Jun '93 / Pinnacle

FUGS LIVE FROM THE 60'S
Doin' alright / Swedish nada / Homage to Catherine and William Blake / I couldn't / Johnny pissoff and the red angel / JOB / My baby done left me / Garden is open / Exorcism of the grave of Senator Joseph McCarthy / Yodeling yippie / Ten commandments / Swinburne stomp
CD CDWIKD 125
Fugs/Big Beat / May '94 / Pinnacle

NO MORE SLAVERY
No more slavery / Cold war / Dreams of sexual gratification / South Africa / Dover beach / Smoking gun / Working for the yankee dollar / Just like a jail / Here come the levellers / What would Tom Paine do / Technology is going to set us free / Hymn to America / Days of auld lang hippie / Ballad of the League Of Militant Agnostics / You can't go into the same river twice
CD CDWIKD 145
Big Beat / Sep '96 / Pinnacle

REAL WOODSTOCK FESTIVAL, THE (Byrdcliffe Barn, Woodstock NY - 14th August 1994/2CD Set) (Fugs & Allen Ginsberg/Friends)
Nova slum goddess / Poe job / Cia man / Crystal liason / Golden age / Rock 'n' roll hall of fame / Frenzy / Sonnet 29: Fortune and men's eyes / Postmodern nothing / Ramses the II is dead, my love / When the mode of the music changes / Ten commandments, together with the ten amendments / Woodstock nation / Augries of innocence / They're closing up the loopholes of life / Einstein never wore socks / Shadows of paradise / I want to know / Song for Janis Joplin / Cave 64 / Down by the Salley Gardens / Coming down / Wide wide river / How sweet I roamed from field to field / Morning morning / Nurse's song (and all the hills echoed)
CD Set CDWIK2 160
Fugs/Big Beat / Sep '95 / Pinnacle

REFUSE TO BE BURNT-OUT (Live In The 1980's)
Five feet / If you want to be President / Nova slum goddess / Nicaragua / Fingers of the sun / Wide wide river / How sweet I roamed / Refuse to be burnt-out / Country punk / CIA man / Ban the bomb / Keeping the issues alive / Dreams of sexual perfection / Summer of love
CD CDWIKD 139
Fugs/Big Beat / Mar '95 / Pinnacle

SECOND ALBUM
Frenzy / I want to know / Skin flowers / Group grope / Coming down / Dirty old man / Kill for peace / Morning morning / Doin' alright / Virgin forest / Mutant stomp / Carpe diem / Wide wide river / Nameless voices crying for kindness
CD CDWIKD 121
Fugs/Big Beat / Sep '93 / Pinnacle

STAR PEACE
CD ROSE 115CD
New Rose / Jun '87 / ADA / Direct / Discovery

Fuji Dub

LAGOS-BROOKLYN-BRIXTON
CD TRECD 116
Triple Earth / Jun '97 / Grapevine/ PolyGram / Stern's

Fukushima, Kazuo

WORKS FOR FLUTE AND PIANO
CD ARTCD 6114
Hat Art / Oct '92 / Cadillac / Harmonia Mundi

Fulham FC

VIVA EL FULHAM (Fulham FC/ Supporters)
Fulham stomp / Viva el Fulham: *Rees, Tony & The Cottagers* / Julie Brown loves Captain Cook: *Barrett, Les* / Love me: *Barrett, Les & Paul* / Maybe it's because I'm a Londoner: *Mullery, Alan & Friends* / Sugar sugar: *Moore, Bobby & Friends* / You lucky people / These boots are made for walking: *Fulham Flurries* / Interview with Johnny Haynes / Victory / You and me and Fulham: *Bay, Tony* / Interview with George Cohen / Interview with Jimmy Hill / Going up: *Stevenage Road Boys*
CD CDGAFFER 17
Cherry Red / Apr '97 / Pinnacle

Full House

SPACIOUSLY DECEPTIVE
CD 101REC 3CD
101 / Feb '96 / ADA

Full Monte

SPARK IN THE PARK
Bubbling marsh / Spark in the dark / Mogadonic tonic / Lift life / Grand Hotel ascenseur / Spiritual cleavage / Wind dance
CD SLAMCD 209
Slam / Oct '96 / Cadillac

Full Moon

EUPHORIA
CD DMCD 1031
Demi-Monde / Feb '92 / RTM/Disc / TKO Magnum

Full Moon Scientists

MEN IN WHITE COATS
CD HANDCD 1
Hard Hands / Oct '94 / Prime / RTM/Disc / Sony

Fuller, 'Blind' Boy

1935-1940
Baby you gotta change your mind / Baby I don't have to worry / Looking for my woman / Precious lord / Jesus is a holy man / Bye bye baby / You got to have your dollar / Shake that shimmy / Truckin' my blues away
CD TMCD 01
Travellin' Man / Apr '90 / Hot Shot / Jazz Music / Wellard

BLIND BOY FULLER VOL.1 1935-1936
CD DOCD 5091
Document / '92 / ADA / Hot Shot / Jazz Music

BLIND BOY FULLER VOL.2 1937
CD DOCD 5092
Document / '92 / ADA / Hot Shot / Jazz Music

BLIND BOY FULLER VOL.3 1937
CD DOCD 5093
Document / '92 / ADA / Hot Shot / Jazz Music

BLIND BOY FULLER VOL.4 1937-1938
CD DOCD 5094
Document / '92 / ADA / Hot Shot / Jazz Music

BLIND BOY FULLER VOL.5 1938-1940
CD DOCD 5095
Document / '92 / ADA / Hot Shot / Jazz Music

BLIND BOY FULLER VOL.6 1940
CD DOCD 5096
Document / '92 / ADA / Hot Shot / Jazz Music

BULL CITY BLUES
CD ALB 1010CD
Aldabra / Mar '94 / CM / RTM/Disc

EAST COAST PIEDMONT BLUES
Rag mama rag / Baby you gotta change your mind / My brownskin sugar plum / I'm a rattlesnakin' daddy / I'm climbin' on top of the hill / Baby I don't have to worry / Looking for my woman / Ain't it a cryin' shame / Walking my troubles away / Sweet honey hole / Somebody's been playing with that thing / Log cabin blues / Keep away from my woman / Cat man blues / Untrue blues / Black and tan fantasy / Big leg woman gets my pay / You've got something there / I'm a stranger here / Evil hearted woman
CD 4679232
Columbia / May '91 / Sony

HARMONICA & GUITAR 1937-1945 (Fuller, Blind Boy & Sonny Terry)
CD 158562
Blues Collection / Oct '96 / Discovery

TRUCKIN' MY BLUES AWAY
CD YAZCD 1060
Yazoo / Apr '91 / ADA / CM / Koch

Fuller, Bobby

BEST OF THE BOBBY FULLER FOUR (Fuller, Bobby Four)
I fought the law / Love's made a fool of you / Another sad and lonely night / She's my girl / New shade of blue / My true love / Pamela / Let her dance / Never to be forgotten / Thunder reef / Baby my heart / Fool of love / Only when I dream / Don't ever let me know / King of the wheels / Think it over / Magic touch / Keep a knockin'
CD CDCHM 388
Ace / Mar '92 / Pinnacle

I FOUGHT THE LAW (Fuller, Bobby Four)
CD 842614
EVA / May '94 / ADA / Direct

I FOUGHT THE LAW/THE KRLA KING OF THE WHEELS (Fuller, Bobby Four)
Thunder reef / Wolfman / She's my girl / King of the wheels / Lonely dragster / Phantom dragster / KRLA top eliminator / Let her dance / Julie / New shade of blue / Only when I dream / You kiss me / Little Annie Lou / I fought the law / Another sad and lonely night / Saturday night / Take my word / Fool of love / Never to be forgotten / Love's made a fool of you / Don't ever let me know / My true love / Magic touch / I'm a lucky guy
CD CDCHD 956
Ace / Nov '90 / Pinnacle

LIVE AT PJ'S PLUS (Fuller, Bobby Four)
Anytime at all / Wooly bully / Gloria / Oh boy / Think it over / Thunder reef / Hi-heel sneakers / Slow down / I fought the law / New shade of blue / Let her dance / CC rider / My babe / Keep a knockin' / Long tall Sally / Baby my heart / Pamela / My true love / Our favourite Martian / Never to be forgotten
CD CDCHD 314
Ace / Jul '91 / Pinnacle

SHAKEDOWN (The Texas Tapes Revisited/2CD Set)
CD Set DFBX 2902
Del-Fi / Nov '96 / Cargo / Koch

Fuller, Curtis

BOSS OF THE SOUL STREAM TROMBONE, THE
CD FSRCD 209
Fresh Sound / Oct '96 / Discovery / Jazz Music

NEW TROMBONE
Vonce / Transportation blues / Namely you / What is this thing called love / Blue Lawson / Alicia
CD OJCCD 77
Original Jazz Classics / Aug '96 / Complete/ Pinnacle / Jazz Music / Wellard

Fuller, Jesse

FRISCO BOUND
CD ARHCD 360
Arhoolie / Apr '95 / ADA / Cadillac / Direct

FULLER'S FAVOURITES
Red river blues / How long blues / You can't keep a good man down / Key to the highway / Tickling the strings / Midnight special / Stranger blues / Fables aren't nothing but doggone lies / Brown skin gal I got my eyes on you / Cincinnati blues / Hump in your back / Trouble if I don't use my head
CD OBCCD 528
Original Blues Classics / Nov '92 / Complete/Pinnacle / Wellard

JAZZ, FOLK SONGS, SPIRITUALS & BLUES
CD OBCCD 564
Original Blues Classics / Jan '94 / Complete/Pinnacle / Wellard

LONE CAT, THE
Leavin' Memphis, Frisco bound / Take it slow and easy / Monkey and the engineer / New Corrine / Guitar blues / Running wild / Hey hey / In that great land / Way you treat me / Down home waltz / Beat it on down the line / Buck and wing
CD OBCCD 526
Original Blues Classics / Nov '92 / Complete/Pinnacle / Wellard

RAILROAD WORKSONG
Move on down the line / Stealing / Ninety nine years and one dark day / Animal fair / Sleeping in the midnight cold / Stagolee / Bill Bailey, Won't you please come home / San Francisco Bay blues / Crazy waltz / Railroad worksong / Meet my loving mother / I love my baby / Tune (Creole love call) / Running wild / Stranger blues / Hanging around a skin game / Monkey and the engineer / Buck dancer's jump
CD LACD 24
Lake / Jan '93 / ADA / Cadillac / Direct / Jazz Music / Target/BMG

SAN FRANCISCO BAY BLUES
San Francisco Bay blues / Jesse's new midnight special / Morning blues / Little black train / Midnight cold / Whoa mule / John Henry / I got a mind to ramble / Crazy about a woman / Where could I go but to the Lord / Stealin' back to my old time used to be / Brown skin gal
CD OBCCD 537
Original Blues Classics / Nov '92 / Complete/Pinnacle / Wellard

Fuller, Johnny

FULLER'S BLUES
CD DDCD 4311
Diving Duck / '88 / CM / Duncans / Impetus

Fuller, Robert

AM FUSS DER BLAUEN BERGE
Riding / Fighting (Am fuss der blauen berge) / Uberall auf der Welt / Schone madchen sind wie blumen / My only friend / Margerita (einmal ist die Reise aus) / Hang my hat out in the prairie / My blue mountains / Adios Mexicana / Baby come home / Beide heissen Jenny / Horse and no saddle / Ein einsamer cowboy
CD BCD 15963
Bear Family / May '96 / Direct / Rollercoaster / Swift

Fully

NEW BEGINNING, A (Fully/Lady Luck)
CD IJT 004
IJT / Jun '97 / Cargo / Greyhound

Fulson, Lowell

FIRST RECORDINGS
CD ARHCD 443
Arhoolie / May '97 / ADA / Cadillac / Direct

HOLD ON
CD BBCD 9525
Bullseye Blues / Jan '93 / Direct

IT'S A GOOD DAY
CD ROUCD 2088
Rounder / '88 / ADA / CM / Direct

OL' BLUES SINGER, THE
Do you love me / Step at a time / Name of the game / Walk on / Old blues singer / Monday morning blues / Cloudy day / Just a kiss / Kansas city bound / Something's wrong
CD IGOCD 2022
Indigo / May '95 / ADA / Direct

ONE MORE BLUES
CD BLE 597242
Black & Blue / Dec '90 / Discovery / Koch / Wellard

SAN FRANCISCO BLUES
CD BLC 760176
Black Lion / Dec '92 / Cadillac / Jazz Music / Koch / Wellard

THEM UPDATE BLUES
What's the matter baby / Think about it / Don't lie / My secret love / Sun going down / Get on down (them update blues) / Lonely man / Forty four / Too soon to tell / Not a dime / L & L special
CD CDBB 9558
Bullseye Blues / Aug '95 / Direct

THINK TWICE BEFORE YOU SPEAK
Parachute woman / I'm tough / Think twice before you speak / Well oh well / One room country shack / Meet me in the bottom / Come on / You're gonna miss me / Lowell's jump / Come back baby / Sinner's prayer
CD JSPCD 290
JSP / Jul '97 / ADA / Cadillac / Direct / Hot Shot / Target/BMG

TRAMP/ SOUL
Tramp / I'm sinking / Get your game up tight / Back door key / Two way wishing / Lonely day / Black nights / Year of 29 / No hard feelings / Hustlers game / Goin' home / Pico / Talkin' woman / Shattered dreams / Sittin' here thinkin' / Little angel / Change your ways / Blues around midnight / Everytime it rains / Just one more time / Ask at any door in town / Too many drivers / My aching back
CD CDCHD 339
Ace / Nov '93 / Pinnacle

Fun Boy Three

BEST OF FUN BOY THREE, THE
CD DC 864262
Disky / Mar '96 / Disky / THE

FUN BOY THREE
Sanctuary / Way on down / Lunatics (have taken over the asylum) / Life in general (Lewe in Algemeen) / Faith hope and charity / Funrama 2 / Best of luck mate / T'ain't what you do (it's the way that you do it) / Telephone always rings / I don't believe it / Alone
CD CDGOLD 1013
EMI Gold / Mar '96 / EMI

REALLY SAYING SOMETHING (The Best Of The Fun Boy Three)
Lunatics (have taken over the asylum) / 'Tain't what you do it's the way that you do it: *Fun Boy Three & Bananarama* / Really saying something: *Fun Boy Three & Bananarama* / Summertime / Summer of '82 / Funrama theme: *Fun Boy Three & Bananarama* / Lunacy legacy / Tunnel of love / Our lips are sealed / Faith, hope and charity / More I see (the less I believe) / Telephone always rings / Alibi / Farmyard connection / Going home / We're having all the fun / Pressure of life (takes weight off the body) / Things we do / Well fancy that
CD CDCHRM 102
Chrysalis / Feb '97 / EMI

SINGLES, THE (Fun Boy Three/ Colourfield)
CD VSOPCD 196
Connoisseur Collection / Apr '94 / Pinnacle

WAITING
Murder, she said / More I see (the less I believe) / Going home / We're having all the fun / Farmyard connection / Tunnel of love / Our lips are sealed / Pressure of life / Things we do / Well fancy that
CD CDGOLD 1048
EMI Gold / Jul '96 / EMI

Fun Factory

ALL THEIR BEST
CD 0042172REG
Edel / Jul '97 / Pinnacle

NONSTOP
CD 0041062REG
Edel / Jul '97 / Pinnacle

Fun Horns

LIVE IN SOUTH AMERICA
CD KR 30060
Babel / Feb '96 / ADA / Cadillac / Diverse / Harmonia Mundi

Fun Lovin' Criminals

COME FIND YOURSELF
Fun lovin' criminal / Passive/Aggressive / Grave and the constant / Scooby snacks / Smoke 'em / Bombin' the L / I can't get with that / King of New York / We have all the time in the world / Bear hug / Come find yourself / Crime and punishment / Mathadonia / I can't get with that (smoove) / Coney Island girl
CD CDCHR 6113
Chrysalis / Jun '97 / EMI

Fun Republic

HAPPY PEOPLE AND MORE REALITY TV
CD EFA 046212
Pork Pie / Oct '95 / SRD

Fun With Atoms

NORTHERN DISTORTION
CD BV 162962
Black Vinyl / Nov '96 / Cargo

Fun-Da-Mental

SEIZE THE TIME
CD NATCD 33
Nation / May '94 / RTM/Disc

WITH INTENT TO PERVERT THE COURSE OF JUSTICE
CD NATCD 56
Nation / Jul '95 / RTM/Disc

Funbug

SPUNKIER
CD CDHOLE 006
Golf / Oct '95 / Plastic Head

Funderburgh, Anson

ANSON FUNDEBURGH AND THE ROCKETS (Funderburgh, Anson & The Rockets)
CD CD 1038
Black Top / '88 / ADA / CM / Direct

BLACK TOP BLUES-A-RAMA VOL.1 (Live At Tipitina's) (Funderburgh, Anson & The Rockets)
CD CD 1044
Black Top / '88 / ADA / CM / Direct

HARPOON MAN
CD APCD 117
Appaloosa / Oct '95 / ADA / Direct / TKO Magnum

LIVE AT THE GRAND
CD BT 1111CD
Black Top / Apr '95 / ADA / CM / Direct

LIVE AT THE GRAND EMPORIUM (Funderburgh, Anson & The Rockets)
CD BT 1111CD
Black Top / Feb '95 / ADA / CM / Direct

RACK 'EM UP
Tell me what I have done wrong / Since we've been together / Rack 'em up / Mama and poppa / Twenty miles / Hold that train, conductor / I'm your professor / I'll keep on trying / All your love / Are you out there / Lemonade / Meanstreak
CD FIENDCD 147
Demon / Oct '89 / Pinnacle

SINS (Funderburgh, Anson & The Rockets)
Man needs his loving / I'll be true / Don't want no leftovers / Walked all night / My kind of baby / Changing neighbourhoods / I can't stop loving you / Chill out / My heart / Trying to make you mine / Sleeping in the ground / Hard hearted woman
CD DIAB 804
Diabolo / Feb '94 / Pinnacle

THAT'S WHAT THEY WANT (Funderburgh, Anson & Sam Myers)
Lookin' the world over / Oh-oh / Last time around / Monkey around / That's what they want / Dew is falling / Mudslide / I don't play / I don't want you cutting off your hair / Don't quit the one you love for me / I've been dogged by women / Meanest woman / I'm shakin'
CD CDBT 1140
Black Top / May '97 / ADA / CM / Direct

Funeral Oration

BELIEVER
CD HR 616CD
Hopeless / Jan '97 / Plastic Head

FUNERAL ORATION
CD HR 606CD
Hopeless / Nov '95 / Plastic Head

SURSUM LUNA
CD AV 017
Avant Garde / Aug '96 / Plastic Head / RTM/Disc

Funhouse

GENERATION GENERATOR
CD HMAXD 160
Heavy Metal / Oct '90 / Revolver / Sony

NEVER AGAIN
CD NACDL 949
Resurrection / Oct '96 / Plastic Head

Funk D'Void

TECHNOIR
Light / Martian love dance / Herbie on rhodes / Fewshun / Bad coffee / Dope lullaby / Angelic upstart / Lucky strike / Soundtrack / Snakebite / V-Ger / Thank you
CD SOMACD 8
Soma / Jun '97 / RTM/Disc

Funk Inc.

ACID INC - THE BEST OF FUNK INC
Chicken lickin' / Sister Jane / Jung bongo / Where are we going / Smokin' at Tiffany's / Kool's back again / Give me your love / Let's make love and stop the war / Better half / Bowlegs
CD CDBGP 1011
Beat Goes Public / Oct '91 / Pinnacle

FUNK INC./CHICKEN LICKIN'
Kool is back / Bowlegs / Sister Janie / Thrill is gone / Whipper / Chicken lickin' / Running away / They trying to get me / Better half / Let's make peace and stop the war / Jung bongo
CD CDBGPD 040
Beat Goes Public / Sep '92 / Pinnacle

HANGIN' OUT/SUPERFUNK
Smokin' at Tiffany's / Give me your love / We can be friends / Dirty red / I can see clearly now / I'll be around / Message from the Meters / Goodbye so long / Hill where the lord hides / Honey, I love you / Just don't mean a thing / I'm gonna love you just a little bit more baby
CD CDBGPD 058
Beat Goes Public / Feb '93 / Pinnacle

PRICED TO SELL
It's not the spotlight / Priced to sell / God only knows / Where are we going / Gimme some lovin' / Somewhere in my mind / Girl of my dreams
CD CDBGPM 075
Beat Goes Public / Jun '93 / Pinnacle

URBAN RENEWAL
Ants in yo pants / Urban renewal / Spasms / Sneaky / Thang / Days and nights in St. Ignace / Still called the blues / Get some more / 6th Street stroll / Memphis underground
CD CDBGPD 104
Beat Goes Public / Apr '96 / Pinnacle

Funkadelic

AMERICA EATS ITS YOUNG
You hit the nail on the head / If you don't like the effects, don't produce the cause / Everybody is going to make it this time / Joyful process / We hurt too / Loose booty / Philmore / I call my baby pussycat / America eats its young / Biological speculation / That was my girl / Balance / Miss Lucifer's love / Wake up
CD CDSEWD 029
Westbound / Jul '90 / Pinnacle

BEST OF FUNKADELIC 1976-1981, THE
One nation under a groove / Cholly (funk getting ready to roll) / Who says a funk band can't play rock / Coming round the mountain / Smoky / Cosmic slop / Electric spanking of war babies / Funk gets stronger / Uncle Jam / Icka prick / (Not just) knee deep
CD CDGR 104
Charly / Aug '96 / Koch

ELECTRIC SPANKING OF WAR BABIES
Electric spanking of war babies / Electrocuties / Funk gets stronger / Brettino's bounce / She loves you / Shockwaves / Oh, I / Icka prick
CD CDGR 102
Charly / Jun '93 / Koch

FINEST
I'll bet you / I got a thing, you got a thing, everybody got a thing / Funky dollar bill / I wanna know if it's good to you / Hit it and quit it / You and your folks, me and my folks / Joyful process / Loose booty / You can't miss what you can't measure / Cosmic slop / Red hot Mama / Standing on the verge of getting it on / Let's take it to the stage / Get off your ass and jam / Undisco kidd / Maggot brain / Maggot brain / Maggot brain
CD CDSEWD 115
Westbound / Jul '97 / Pinnacle

FUNKADELIC LIVE
Funkentelechy / Cosmic slop / Maggot brain / Bop gun / Funk gettin' ready to roll / It ain't legal / Flashlight / Mothership connection / Give up the funk / Let's take it to the stage / Do that stuff / Undisco kidd / Children of production / Atomic dog / Maceo, not Charlie / Red hot Mama / Into you / Standing on the verge of getting it on / One nation under a groove / Coming round the mountain / Won't you dance / Quickie / Aquaboogie / I wanna know if it's good to you / Up for the down stroke / Hit it and quit it / Gamin' on ya / Put your hands together / Dog you out / P-funk / You do me / Nickel bag o'solos / Dope dog / I call my baby pussycat / Lampin / Microphone fiend underground angel / Yank my doodle sum'else / I got a thing, you got a thing, everybody got a thing / All your goodies are gone / Lifted
CD Set NEFCD 273
Sequel / Oct '94 / BMG

FUNKADELIC LIVE (Live At Meadowbrook, Rochester, Michigan 12/ 9/71)
Alice in my fantasies / Maggot brain / I call my baby pussycat / I call my baby pussycat / Good old music / I got a thing, you got a thing, everybody got a thing / All your goodies are gone (The loser's seat) / I'll bet you / You and your folks, me and my folks / Free your mind and your ass will follow
CD CDSEWD 108
Westbound / Apr '96 / Pinnacle

FUNKADELIC PICTURE DISC BOX SET
CD Set WBOXPD 1
Westbound / Aug '90 / Pinnacle

FUNKADELIC PICTURE DISC BOX SET VOL.2 (Cosmic slop/Tales of.../Let's take it.../Standing on...)
CD Set WBOXPD 5
Westbound / Feb '94 / Pinnacle

HARDCORE FUNK JAM
CD CPCD 8064
Charly / Nov '94 / Koch

HARDCORE JOLLIES
Osmosis phase one / Coming round the mountain / Smoky / If you got funk, you got style / Hardcore jollies / Terribitus phase two / Soul mate / Cosmic slop / You scared the lovin outta me / Adolescent funk
CD CDGR 101
Charly / Jun '93 / Koch

MUSIC FOR YOUR MOTHER (Funkadelic 45's - 2CD Set)
Music for my mother / Music for my mother (instrumental) / Can't shake it loose / As good as I can feel / I'll bet you / Qualify and satisfy / Open our eyes / I got a thing, you got a thing, everybody got a thing / Fish, chips and sweat / I wanna know if it's good to you / You and your folks, me and my folks / Funky dollar bill / Can you get to that / Back in our minds / I miss my baby / Baby I owe you something good / Hit it and quit it / Whole lot of BS / Loose booty / Joyful process / Cosmic slop / If you don't like the effects, don't produce the cause / Standing on the verge of getting it on / Jimmy's got a little bit of bitch in him / Red hot Mama / Vital juices / Better by the pound / Stuffs and things / Let's take it to the stage / How do yeaw view you
CD Set CDSEW 2055
Westbound / Oct '92 / Pinnacle

ONE NATION UNDER A GROOVE
One nation under a groove / Groovallegiance / Who says a funk band can't play rock / Promentalshitbackwashipsychosisenema squad / Into you / Cholly (funk getting ready to roll) / Lunchmeataphobia / PE squad / Doodoo chasers / Maggot brain
CD CDGR 100
Charly / Jul '93 / Koch

UNCLE JAM WANTS YOU
Freak of the week / (Not just) knee deep / Uncle Jam / Field manoeuvers / Holly wants to go to California / Foot soldiers
CD CDGR 103
Charly / Jun '93 / Koch

Funkdoobiest

BROTHERS DOOBIE
This it it (interlude) / Rock on / What the deal / Lost in thought / Dedicated / Ka sera sera / Pussy ain't shit / XXX Funk / It ain't going down / You're dummin' / Tomahawk bang / Super hoes / Who ra ra
CD 4783812
Epic / Jul '95 / Sony

Funki Porcini

HED PHONE SEX
Word of vice / B Monkey / Dubble / King ashabanapal part 1 / Deep / King Ashabanapal part 2 / Michael's little friend / White slave / Poseathon / Wicked, cruel, nasty and bad / Pork alumen / Softest thing in the world (motorway accident) / Tiny kangeroo dolphin (from hell) / Long road / Mushroom head / Pork kiss head
CD ZENCD 017
Ninja Tune / May '95 / Kudos / Pinnacle / Prime / Vital

LOVE, PUSSYCATS & CAR WRECKS
Purrfect / Groover / Last song / Snip & lick / Car wreck / Afterlife / 12 points off your licence / Venus / Hyde Park / Theme music for nothing / I'm such a small thing / Going down
CD ZENCD 023
Ninja Tune / Jun '96 / Kudos / Pinnacle / Prime / Vital

Funkmaster Flex

60 MINS OF FUNK VOL.1
CD 7863674722
RCA / Feb '97 / BMG

MIX TAPE VOL.1 - 60 MINUTES OF FUNK
CD 07863668052
RCA / Nov '95 / BMG

Funky Aztecs

DAY OF THE DEAD
CD 50502
Raging Bull / Apr '97 / Prime / Total/BMG

Funky Company

TENDENCY OF LOVE
CD FARCD 402
Family Affair / Jul '96 / Timewarp

Funky DL

CLASSIC WAS THE DAY
CD ALMCD 17
Almost / Jul '97 / Pinnacle

Funky Green Dogs

GET FIRED UP
Way / Firedup / Noticiasuno / Somekindoflove / Untiltheday / Noticiasdos / Sogood / Why / Pigsty / Noticiastres / Icametostomp / Ride / Nightofthefunkygreendogsfromouterspace
CD _______ TWCD 90001
Twisted UK / Apr '97 / Amato Disco / BMG / Prime / RTM/Disc / Vital

Funky New Orleans Jazz Band

FUNKY NEW ORLEANS JAZZ BAND
CD _______ MMRC CD 5
Merry Makers / Feb '94 / Jazz Music

Funny Farm

AMPUTATE
CD _______ PRO 026
Progress / May '97 / Cargo / Plastic Head

BITING THE HAND
CD _______ 33842
Progress / Feb '97 / Cargo / Plastic Head

Funny Hill

COWBOY BOOTS
CD _______ BRAM 1989062
Brambus / Nov '93 / ADA

LIVE IN NASHVILLE
CD _______ BRAM 1990152
Brambus / Nov '93 / ADA

Fur

FUR
Beautiful wreck / Brazil / They say / Ocelot / Beauty and speed / Devil to the lamb / I'm not coming / James Brown / X-offender / Sex drive
CD _______ BLK 026ECD
Blackout / Dec '95 / Plastic Head / Vital

Furbowl

AUTUMN YEARS
CD _______ BMCD 47
Black Mark / Mar '94 / Plastic Head

Furey, Finbar

BEST OF FINBAR & EDDIE FUREY, THE (Furey, Finbar & Eddie)
Rakish Paddy / Curragh of Kildare / Lonesome boatman / Bogy's bonny belle / Blackbird / Her Father didn't like me anyway / Drops of brandy / Planxty Davy / Eamonn an chnuic / Farewell to Tarwathy / Eddie's fancy / My Lagan love / Fox chase / Prickly bush / Coppers and brass / Reynardine / Bonny bunch of roses / Sliabh na mban / This town is not your own / Dawning of the day
CD _______ MCCD 293
Music Club / Jun '97 / Disc / THE

DAWNING OF THE DAY
CD _______ BGOCD 291
Beat Goes On / Oct '95 / Pinnacle

FINBAR & EDDIE FUREY/THE LONESOME BOATMAN (Furey, Finbar & Eddie)
Spanish cloak / Come by the hills / Sliabh na mban / Dainty Davy / Tattered Jack Welch / Flowers in the valley / Pigeon on the gate / Graham's flat / Leezy Lindsay / Piper in the meadow straying / Curragh of Kildaire / Eamonn an Chnuic / This town is not your own / Rocking the baby / Bill Hart's favourite / Dance around the spinning wheel / Let me go to the mountains / McShane / Colonel Fraser / Lonesome boatman / Carron Lough bay / Prickly bush / Bogy's bonny belle / Fox chase
CD _______ ESMCD 524
Essential / Apr '97 / BMG

TRADITIONAL IRISH PIPE MUSIC
Rakish Paddy / Hag with the money / Castle terrace / Madam Bonaparte / Young girl milking the cow / Fin's favourite / Peter Byrnes fancy / O'Rouke's reel / Roy's hands / Planxty Davy / Bonny bunch of roses / Eddie's fancy / Silver spear / Spanish cloak / Sliabh na mban (mountain of the women) / Piper in the meadow straying (set dance) / Rocking the baby (jig)
CD _______ HILLCD 13
Wooded Hill / Feb '97 / Direct / World Serpent

WIND AND THE RAIN, THE
Aran girl / Ocean / Anac cuan / Gypsy goboy / You enter my soul / My song of emigration / Roy's tribute / Journey's of love / Wind and the rain / Amandan / Travelling lady / Takes two / Garrickfergus / Mrs. A
CD _______ ECD 3371
K-Tel / Jun '97 / K-Tel

Fureys

7 CLADDAGH ROAD
Sound of thunder / Donegal / Mary Skeffington / Liffey walls / Roy's tribute / Living on the edge of your town / America cried / 6000 lonely miles / I remember Mary / Amadan / Cross me heart / Mo Chuileann
CD _______ CDDPR 132
Premier/MFP / Jan '95 / EMI

BEST OF THE FUREYS
Spanish cloak / dainty Davie / Castle Terrace / Roy's hands / Dance around the spinning wheel / Let me go to the mountains / McShane / Colonel Fraser / Carron Lough Bay / Prickly bush / Fox chase / Bill Hart's favourite / Silver spear / Tattered Jack Welch / Pigeon on the gate / Fin's favourite / Peter Byrne's fancy / Bonny bunch of roses / Eddie's fancy / O'Rourke's reel
CD _______ TRTCD 137
TrueTrax / Dec '94 / THE

BEST OF THE FUREYS AND DAVEY ARTHUR (Fureys & Davey Arthur)
When you were sweet sixteen / Maggie / Morning has broken / Twelfth of never / Annie's song / I'll take you home again Kathleen / Love is pleasin' / Beautiful dreamer / Bonnie Mary of Argyle / Just a song at twilight / Bless this house / I'll be your sweetheart / Last rose of summer / If I had my life to live over / Wait till the clouds roll by / Scarlet ribbons / Perfect day / When I grow too old to dream / Come by the hills / Anniversary waltz
CD _______ MCCD 010
Music Club / Feb '91 / Disc / THE

COLLECTION, THE (Fureys & Davey Arthur)
Paddy in Paris / Reason I left Mullingar / Mountains of Mourne / Irish eyes / Who do you think you are / Lovers / Ted Furey's selection / Evening falls / Night Ferry / Portland town / Ned of the hill / October song / Leaving Nancy / Garrett Barry's jig / Sitting alone / Big ships / From where I stand / Morning cloud
New copperplate etc / Dreaming my dreams / Lament / I'll be there / First leaves of Autumn
CD _______ CCSCD 231
Castle / Oct '89 / BMG

FINEST (Fureys & Davey Arthur)
When you were sweet sixteen: *Fureys* / Dublin: *Fureys* / When I leave behind Neidin: *Fureys* / Green fields of France: *Fureys* / Lonesome boatman: *Fureys* / I will love you ev'ry time: *Fureys* / Stealaway: *Fureys* / Red rose cafe: *Fureys* / Maggie: *Fureys*
CD _______ CLACD 319
Castle / '92 / BMG

FOUR GREEN FIELDS (Furey, Finbar & Eddie)
CD _______ TUT 72166
Wundertute / Jan '94 / ADA / CM / Duncans

FUREYS & DAVEY ARTHUR,THE (Fureys & Davey Arthur)
When you were sweet sixteen / Alchoholidays / Steals away / Poem to the lonesome boatman / Lonesome boatman / Silver threads among the gold / Green fields of France / Siege of a nation / I will love you every time / Gallipoli / Old man / She came to me
CD _______ EMPRCD 518
Emporio / Jul '94 / Disc

FUREYS, THE (The Ultimate Irish Love Songs Experience)
When you were sweet sixteen / Leezy Lindsay / Grand affair / Steal away / I will love you / My love is like a red red rose / Lonesome boatman / I'll take you home again Kathleen / Red Rose Cafe / Maggie / Yesterday's people / Old man / Old Joe / Siege of a nation / Anniversary waltz / Green fields of France
CD _______ KCD 425
Celtic Collections / Jan '97 / Target/BMG

MAY WE ALL MEET AGAIN
CD _______ CDC 008
Ceol / Feb '97 / CM

SOUND OF THE FUREYS & DAVEY ARTHUR, THE (Fureys & Davey Arthur)
Green fields of France / Gypsy Davey / Reason I left Mullinger / Clare to here / Ask me father / Finbar Dwyers / Old oak tree / Lark on the strand / Her father didn't like me anyway / Shipyard slips / Leaving Nancy / O'Carolans tribute / Roster / Night ferry / Lament / Beer, beer, beer / Lonesome boatman
CD _______ RGCD 11
Polydor / '88 / PolyGram

SPANISH CLOAK, THE
CD _______ PLSCD 106
Pulse / Apr '96 / BMG

WHEN YOU WERE SWEET SIXTEEN (Fureys & Davey Arthur)
Green fields of France / When you were sweet sixteen / My love is like a red red rose / Anniversary song / I will love you ev'ry time / Yesterdays people / Lonesome boatman / Old man / Oh Babushka / Belfast mill / Siege of a nation / Yesterdays men
CD _______ CLACD 171
Castle / Feb '90 / BMG

WINDS OF CHANGE
Oro oro / It's good to see you / Sweet and gentle love / Old george / Didn't It rain / North by north / Mary and me / Campfire in the dark / Travelling lady / If I don't bring you flowers / Cry of the celts / Man of our times / Noraleen / Song for the fox / Goodbye booze
CD _______ RITZLCD0069
Ritz / Oct '92 / Pinnacle

Furic, Stephane

STEPHANE FURIC
CD _______ 1212152
Soul Note / May '91 / Cadillac / Harmonia Mundi / Wellard

Furioso

FURIOSO
CD _______ CDGRUB 24
Food For Thought / Sep '92 / Pinnacle

Furnaceface

UNSAFE AT ANYSPEED
CD _______ FURCD 1
Cargo / Dec '96 / Cargo

Furniture

FURNITURE SCRAPBOOK, THE
CD _______ SURCD 013
Survival / Sep '91 / ADA / Pinnacle

Furtado, Tony

FULL CIRCLE
CD _______ ROUCD 0323
Rounder / Oct '94 / ADA / CM / Direct

ROLL MY BLUES AWAY
Waterslide / Ghost of Blind Willie Johnson / Stark raven / Can you hear the rain / Willow tree / Knave's bane / Song for Early / Boat's up the river / Bolinas / Mudville / Sundin / Crow Canyon
CD _______ ROUCD 0343
Rounder / Feb '97 / ADA / CM / Direct

WITHIN REACH
Ralph Trischka / St. John's fire / I will / Waiting for Guiteau/President Garfield's Hornpipe / Queen Anne's lace / Sao Miguel / Julia Dealaney/The Drunken landlady / Drake's bay / Magpie on the gallows / Duskus
CD _______ ROUCD 0290
Rounder / '92 / ADA / CM / Direct

Further

5 FURTHER JOURNEYS
CD _______ FUR 100CD
Abstract / Sep '94 / Cargo / Pinnacle / Total/BMG

SUPER GRIP TAPE
CD _______ SHED 003CD
Creation / Aug '93 / 3mv/Vital

Furudate, Tetsuo

AUTREMENT QU'ETRE
CD _______ DSA 54040
Les Disques Du Soleil / Dec '95 / Harmonia Mundi

Fury, Billy

ALL THE BEST
I will / Like I've never been gone / Last night was made for love / I'm lost without you / When will you say I love you / Run to my lovin' arms / It's only make believe / Maybe tomorrow / In thoughts of you / Give me your word / That's love / Once upon a dream / Colette / Wonderous place / Thousand stars / I'll never find another you / Fools errand (Do you really love me) / Jealousy / Someone else's girl / Halfway to paradise
CD _______ ECD 3041
K-Tel / Jan '95 / K-Tel

AM I BLUE
Wondrous place / That's enough / Tell me how you feel / Am I blue / What am I living for / Baby, what you want me to do / This diamond ring / Away from you / Give me your word / I'll never quite get over you / Didn't see the real thing come along / Letter full of tears / Last night was made for love / I'm hurting all over / Somebody else's girl / I will / Don't jump / Don't walk away / (Here I am) Broken hearted / I'm lost without you
CD _______ 8289022
London / Jul '93 / PolyGram

BILLY FURY HIT PARADE, THE
Maybe tomorrow / Colette / That's love / Thousand stars / Halfway to paradise / Jealousy / I'd never find another you / Last night was made for love / Once upon a dream / Because of love / Like I've never been gone / When will you say I love you / In summer / Somebody else's girl / Do you really love me too / I will / It's only make believe / Lost without you / In thoughts of you / Run to my lovin' arms
CD _______ 8205032
London / Jan '87 / PolyGram

HALFWAY TO PARADISE
Halfway to paradise / Don't worry / You're having the last dance with me / Push push / Fury's tune / Talkin' in my sleep / Stick around / Thousand stars / Cross my heart / Comin' up in the world / He will break your heart / Would you stand by me
CD _______ 8209242
London / Aug '90 / PolyGram

HALFWAY TO PARADISE (The Greatest Hits)
Colette / That's love / Thousand stars / Fools errand (do you really love me) / I'd never find another you / I will / Like I've never been gone / I'm lost without you / Jealousy / Halfway to paradise / Last night was made for love / When will you say I love you / It's only make believe / In thoughts of you / Once upon a dream / Maybe tomorrow
CD _______ PLATCD 49
Platinum / Feb '97 / Prism

LEGENDS IN MUSIC
CD _______ LECD 086
Wisepack / Sep '94 / Conifer/BMG / THE

ONE AND ONLY, THE
Be mine tonight / No trespassers / Love or money / Love sweet love / Let me go lover / Devil or angel / Don't tell me lies / Deborah / This little girl of mine / I'm telling you / Someday
CD _______ 5298612
Polydor / Mar '96 / PolyGram

OTHER SIDE OF BILLY FURY
Cross my heart / King for tonight / What do you think you're doing of / All I wanna do is cry / I'll never fall in love again / Didn't you see the real thing come along / If I lose you / Alright goodbye / Where do you run / Away from you / She's so far out she's in / Baby, what you want me to do / Talkin in my sleep / Running around / You don't know / Last kiss / What am I gonna do / Gonna type a letter / Don't knock upon my door / Nothin' shakin' / Go ahead and ask her / Glad all over
CD _______ SEECD 383
See For Miles/C5 / Oct '93 / Pinnacle

PARADISE
Halfway to paradise / It's only make believe / Last night was made for love / I will / Wonderous place / Don't worry / We were meant for each other / Our day will come / I'll never fall in love again / Forget him / Love or money / Begin the beguine / Be mine tonight / Don't leave me this way
CD _______ 5500112
Spectrum / May '93 / PolyGram

ROCKIN' AND BOPPIN'
CD _______ MAR 018
Marginal / Jun '97 / Greyhound

ROUGH DIAMONDS AND PURE GEMS
Sticks 'n' stones / Things are changing / Loving you / I'll go along with it / Suzanne in the mirror / Phone box / Any morning now / Lady / Certain things / All the way to the USA / Well alright / Baby get yourself together / Driving nicely / Your words / Maybe baby / Sheila / Lazy life / I'm gonna love you too / In my room / I love you / Lyanna / Going back to Germany / Come outside and play / Easy living / Day by day / Dreaming of St. Louis
CD _______ CDMF 072
Magnum Force / Apr '91 / TKO Magnum

SOUND OF FURY + 10
That's love / My advice / Phone call / You don't know / Turn my back on you / Don't say it's over / Since you've been gone / It's you I need / Alright, goodbye / Don't leave me this way / Gonna type a letter / Margo / Don't knock upon my door / Time has come / Angel face / Last kiss / My Christmas prayer / Baby how I cried / I got someone / Don't jump
CD _______ 8206272
London / Jul '93 / PolyGram

VERY BEST OF BILLY FURY
CD _______ SOW 709
Sound Waves / Jul '93 / Target/BMG

WE WANT BILLY/BILLY
Sweet little sixteen / Wedding bells / I'm movin' on / I'd never find another you / Like I've never been gone / How many nights, how many days / She cried / Our day will come / One kiss / Baby come on / Sticks and stones / Just because / Once upon a dream / When will you say I love you / Willow weep for me / Let me know / Million miles from nowhere / All my hopes / Hard times / That's alright / Unchain my heart / Halfway to paradise / Last night was made for love / We were meant for each other / Bumble bee / Chapel on the hill / I'll show you / One step from heaven / (Here I am) Broken hearted
CD _______ BGOCD 258
Beat Goes On / Feb '95 / Pinnacle

Fury Of Five

NO REASON TO SMILE
CD _______ GAIN 007CD
Gain Ground / Dec '96 / Cargo

Fury Things

BIG SATURDAY ILLUSION, THE
CD _______ TR 43CD
Trance / Apr '96 / SRD

FU's

ORIGIN OF, THE
CD _______ LF 020CD
Lost & Found / Apr '92 / Plastic Head

REVENGE
CD _______ LF 037CD
Lost & Found / Jun '92 / Plastic Head

Fusco, Andy

BIG MAN'S BLUES
Embraceable you / Stablemates / Big man's blues / Love letters / Airegin / My old flame / Pensativa / Scooter / Little melonae / Con-ruthsion
CD ____ **DTRCD 116**
Double Time / Dec '96 / Express Jazz

Fuse

DIMENSION INTRUSION
CD ____ **WARPCD 12**
Warp / May '93 / Prime / RTM/Disc

Fusion

BEST OF BRITISH, THE (2CD Set)
CD Set ____ **FUSCD 002**
Future Vinyl / Nov '96 / Total/BMG

Fuster, Francis

NINKIRIBI - LISTEN EVERYBODY
CD ____ **FMFD 0193**
4th & Broadway / Sep '93 / PolyGram

Future

1998
CD ____ **RRCD 1998**
Receiver / May '90 / Grapevine/PolyGram

Future 3

WE ARE THE FUTURE
CD ____ **APR 010CD**
April / Aug '96 / Plastic Head / Shellshock/ Disc

Future Funk

FUTURE FUNK - THE ALBUM
CD ____ **DAN 487243**
Dance Pool / Jun '97 / Intergroove

Future Homosapiens

MOONROCK
Rocktasm / Bleep one / 4th dimension blues / Brain of Helmut Zaccariah / Driving deep south / Something in my food / Disco hell / Keep on rolling / Bleep two / Future Homosapiens / Bleep three / Little chef
CD ____ **NASA 7CD**
Galactic Disco / Jun '97 / Prime / RTM/Disc / Vital

Future Loop Foundation

TIME AND BASS
CD ____ **BARKCD 020**
Planet Dog / Jul '96 / Pinnacle

Future Sound Of London

DEAD CITIES
Herd killing / Dead cities / Her face forms in summertime / We have explosive / Everyone in the world is doing something without me / My kingdom / Max / Antique toy / Quagmire / In a state of permanent abyss / Glass / Yage / Vit drowning / Through your gills I breathe / First death in the family
CD ____ **CDV 2814**
CD ____ **CDVX 2814**
Virgin / Oct '96 / EMI

ISDN
Just a fuckin' idiot / Far out son of lung and the ramblings of a madman / Appendage / Slider / Smokin' Japanese babe / You're creeping me out / Eyes pop - skin explodes - everybody dead / It's my mind that works / Dirty shadows / Tired / Egypt / Are they fighting us / Kai / Amoeba / Study of six guitars / Snake hips
CD ____ **CDV 2755**
Virgin / Dec '94 / EMI
CD ____ **CDVX 2755**
Virgin / Jun '95 / EMI

LIFEFORMS
Cascade / Ill flower / Flak / Bird wings / Dead skin cells / Lifeforms / Eggshell / Among myselves / Domain / Spineless jelly / Interstat / Vertical pig / Cerebral / Life Form Ends / Vit / Omnipresence / Room 208 / Elaborate burn / Little brother
CD ____ **CDV 2722**
Virgin / May '94 / EMI

Futuresound

BEST OF FUTURESOUND, THE
CD ____ **CAT 025CD**
Rephlex / Jan '96 / Prime / RTM/Disc

Fuxa

3 FIELD ROTATION
CD ____ **IRE 1012**
I / Sep '96 / SRD

VERY WELL ORGANISED
CD ____ **IRE 1062**
Che / Mar '97 / SRD

Fuzzbird

WELCOME TO SANTA'S SEX SHOP
CD ____ **MKCD 06**
Mook / Apr '97 / SRD

Fuzztones

IN HEAT
In heat / Chedenne rider / Black box / It came in the mail / Heathen set / What you don't know / Nine months later / Everything you got / Shame on you / Me Tarzan, you Jane / Hurt on hold / Charlotte's remains
CD ____ **SITUCD 23**
Situation 2 / Jun '89 / Pinnacle

Fuzzy

FUZZY
Flashlight / Bill / Postcard / Now I know / Four Wheel friend / Almond / Lemon ring / Rock song / Intro / Sports / Severe / Got it / Surfing / Girlfriend
CD ____ **142542**
Seed / Jul '94 / Vital

Fuzzy Mountain String Band

FUZZY MOUNTAIN STRING BAND
CD ____ **ROUCD 11571**
Rounder / Jul '95 / ADA / CM / Direct

Fyffe, Will

WILL FYFFE (Legendary Scottish Singer Performs His Best Songs)
It isn't the hen that cackles the most / Spirit of a man from Aberdeen / Wedding of Mary Maclean / I'm the landlord at the inn at Aberfoyle / He's been on the bottle since a baby / She was the belle of the ball / Railway guard / Train that's taking you home / Twelve and a tanner a bottle / Will Fyffe's war-time sketch: Clyde built / I belong to Glasgow / I'm 94 today
CD ____ **LCOM 5234**
Lismor / May '94 / ADA / Direct / Duncans / Lismor

Fygi, Laura

BEWITCHED
Dream a little dream / It's crazy / Good morning heartache / Let there be love / I only have eyes for you / Bewitched / End of a love affair / Love you for sentimental reasons / Just one of those things / Girl talk / I wish you love / Willow weep for me
CD ____ **5147242**
Verve / Sep '94 / PolyGram

INTRODUCING/BEWITCHED (2CD Set)
CD Set ____ **5329792**
Verve / Jan '97 / PolyGram

LADY WANTS, THE
CD ____ **5189242**
PolyGram Jazz / Nov '94 / PolyGram

WATCH WHAT HAPPENS WHEN (Laura Fygi Meets Michel Legrand)
CD ____ **5345982**
Mercury / May '97 / PolyGram

G

G&K Ceili Band

SONGS JIGS AND REELS
CD ____ PLSCD 168
Pulse / Apr '97 / BMG

G-Love & Special Sauce

COAST TO COAST MOTEL
Sweet sugar Mama / Leaving the city / Nancy / Kiss and tell / Chains no.3 / Sometimes / Everybody / Soda pop / Bye bye baby / Tomorrow night / Small fish / Coming home
CD ____ 4809792
Okeh/Epic / Jan '96 / Sony

G-LOVE & SPECIAL SAUCE
Things I used to do / Blues music / Garbage man / Eyes have miles / Baby's got sauce / Rhyme for the summertime / Cold beverage / Fatman / This ain't living / Walk to slide / Shooting hoops / Some peoples like that / Town to town / I love you
CD ____ 4766322
Okeh/Epic / Jul '94 / Sony

G-Man

KUSHTI
CD ____ WM 9
Swim / May '96 / Kudos / RTM/Disc / SRD

G-Squad

G-SQUAD
CD ____ YUMECD 001
MC Projects / Oct '96 / Pinnacle / Prime

Gaar, Burton

ONE HUNDRED POUNDS OF TROUBLE
One hundred pounds of trouble / Real good woman / No / I won't cry / It's still raining / Bim bam thank you Mam / Step out lady / Tear it up / Short red dress / Face down on the bottom / Because of you / I be gone / Where the girl is
CD ____ CCD 11053
Crosscut / Jun '97 / ADA / CM / Direct

Gaard Quintet

GAARD QUINTET
CD ____ MECCACD 1036
Music Mecca / Nov '94 / Cadillac / Jazz Music / Wellard

Gaberlunzie

FOR AULD LANG SYNE
CD ____ CDLDL 1224
Lochshore / Oct '95 / ADA / Direct / Duncans

HIGHLAND LINES
CD ____ CDLOC 1056
Lochshore / Jul '90 / ADA / Direct / Duncans

TWA CORBIES
Twa corbies / Loch Tay boat song / Flower in the snow / Born beyond the border / Slow goin' easy / MacPherson's rant / Wallace / Old Balgedie road / Margaret's waltz medley / Jute mill song / Lonely in the bothy
CD ____ CDLDL 1260
Lochshore / May '97 / ADA / Direct / Duncans

Gabin, Jean

JEAN GABIN ANTHOLOGY
CD ____ EN 525
Encyclopaedia / Sep '96 / Discovery

LA COMPILATION
CD ____ UCD 19033
Forlane / Jun '95 / Target/BMG

Gable, Bill

THERE WERE SIGNS
Go ahead and run / Who becomes the slave / All the posters come down / Three levels of Nigeria / Cape Horn / High trapeze / There were signs / Letting the jungle in / Leaving Venice to the rain
CD ____ 259759
Private Music / Apr '89 / BMG

Gable, Tony

SEVEN HILLS
CD ____ INAK 3031
In Akustik / Oct '96 / Direct / TKO Magnum

TONY GABLE & 206
Slip / Tailwind / Island lady / Bus song / Camano island / Pockets / Lake Union / Homeport / Futon fun
CD ____ 101S 71462
101 South / Nov '93 / New Note/Pinnacle

Gabrels, Reeves

SECRET SQUALL OF NOW, THE
CD ____ UPSTART 020
Upstart / Sep '95 / ADA / Direct

Gabriel, Peter

PASSION SOURCES (Various Artists)
Shamus ud doja / Call to prayer / Sankarabaranam pancha nadai pallavi / Ulvi / Fallahi / Sabahiva / Atejbeit / Prelude in tchahargah / Wedding song / Magdelene's house / Yoky / Nass el ghiwane / Song of complaint
CD ____ RWCD 2
Virgin / Jun '89 / EMI

PETER GABRIEL 1/2/3 (Compact Collection/3CD Set)
CD Set ____ TPAK 9
Virgin / Oct '90 / EMI

PETER GABRIEL 3/DEUTSCHES ALBUM
Eindringling / Keine selbstkontrolle / Frag mich nicht immer / Schnappshub (ein familienfoto) / Und durch den draht / Spiel ohne grenzen / Du bist nicht wie wir / Ein normales leben / Biko
CD ____ XCDSD 4019
Virgin / '88 / EMI

PETER GABRIEL VOL.1
Moribund the burgermeister / Solsbury Hill / Modern love / Excuse me / Humdrum / Slowburn / Waiting for the big one / Down the dolce vita / Here comes the flood
CD ____ PGCD 1
Charisma / May '87 / EMI

PETER GABRIEL VOL.2
On the air / DIY / Mother of violence / Wonderful day in a one way world / White shadow / Indigo / Animal magic / Exposure / Flotsam and jetsam / Perspective / Home sweet home
CD ____ PGCD 2
Charisma / May '87 / EMI

PETER GABRIEL VOL.3
Intruder / No self control / I don't remember / Family snapshot / And through the wire / Games without frontiers / Not one of us / Lead a normal life / Biko
CD ____ PGCD 3
Charisma / May '87 / EMI

PETER GABRIEL VOL.4
Rhythm of the heat / San Jacinto / I have the touch / Family and the fishing net / Shock the monkey / Lay your hands on me / Wallflower / Kiss of life
CD ____ PGCD 4
Charisma / '86 / EMI

PETER GABRIEL VOL.4 (German)
Der rythmus der hitze / Das fischernetz / Kontakt / San Jacinto / Schock den affen / Handauflegen / Nicht die erde hat dich verschluckt / Mundzumundeatmung
CD ____ XPGCD 4
Virgin / Apr '88 / EMI

PLAYS LIVE (2CD Set)
San Jacinto / Solsbury Hill / No self control / Shock the monkey / I don't remember / Humdrum / On the air / Biko / Rhythm of the heat / I have the touch / Not one of us / Family snapshot / DIY / Family and the fishing net / Intruder / I go swimming
CD Set ____ CDPGD 100
Virgin / '88 / EMI

SECRET WORLD LIVE
Come talk to me / Steam / Across the river / Slow marimbas / Shaking the tree / Red rain / Blood of Eden / Kiss that frog / Washing of the water / Solsbury Hill / Digging in the dirt / Sledgehammer / Secret world / Don't give up / In your eyes
CD Set ____ PGDCD 8
Virgin / Aug '94 / EMI

SHAKING THE TREE
Solsbury Hill / I don't remember / Sledgehammer / Family snapshot / Mercy Street / Shaking the tree / Don't give up: *Gabriel, Peter & Kate Bush* / Here comes the flood / Games without frontiers / Shock the monkey / Big time / Biko / San Jacinto / Zaar / Red rain / I have the touch
CD ____ PGTVD 6
Virgin / Nov '90 / EMI

SO
Red rain / Sledgehammer / Don't give up / That voice again / In your eyes / Mercy street / Big time / We do what we're told (Milgram's 37) / This is the picture (excellent birds)
CD ____ PGCD 5
Charisma / '86 / EMI

US
Come talk to me / Love to be loved / Blood of Eden / Steam / Only us / Washing of the water / Digging in the dirt / Fourteen black paintings / Kiss that frog / Secret world
CD ____ PGCD 7
Virgin / Sep '92 / EMI

Gabriela

DETRAS DEL SOL
Verano en la pampa / Sueno transparente / Noches de Tilcara / Tren de la medianoche/ Rambler / Luz del mundo / Estos son mis dias / Estrella austral / Cuando me vaya / Hermana Maria / Duerme
CD ____ INT 35062
Intuition / Aug '97 / New Note/Pinnacle

Gabrielle

FIND YOUR WAY
Going nowhere / Who could love you / Find your way / I wanna know / Dreams / I wish / We don't talk / Second chance / Say what you gotta say / Because of you / Inside your head
CD ____ 8284412
Go Beat / Oct '93 / PolyGram

GABRIELLE
Forget about the world / People may come / I live in hope / Baby I've changed / Give me a little more time / If you really cared / There she goes / Our love is over / If I could / Alone / Have you ever wondered / So glad / Miracle / If you ever: *Gabrielle & East 17* / Walk on by / Forget about the world
CD ____ 8288582
Go Beat / Nov '96 / PolyGram

Gad, Pablo

BEST OF PABLO GAD
CD ____ ROTCD 1
Reggae On Top / Nov '93 / Jet Star / SRD

EPISTLES OF DUB VOL.1 (Gad, Pablo & Conscious Sounds)
CD ____ ROTCD 002
Reggae On Top / Nov '94 / Jet Star / SRD

LIFE WITHOUT DEATH
CD ____ ROTCD 005
Reggae On Top / Jul '95 / Jet Star / SRD

Gadd, Eric

DO YOU BELIEVE IN GADD
CD ____ 4509967772
East West / Oct '94 / Warner Music

Gade, Jacob

TANGO JALOUSIE
CD ____ MECCACD 1005
Music Mecca / Nov '94 / Cadillac / Jazz Music / Wellard

Gadgets

BLUE ALBUM, THE
CD ____ PLASCD 16
Plastic Head / May '89 / Plastic Head

GADGETREE
CD ____ PLASCD 013
Plastic Head / May '89 / Plastic Head

INFANTREE/FRUITS OF AKELDAMA
CD ____ PLASCD 012
Plastic Head / Jul '89 / Plastic Head

LOVE, CURIOSITY, FRECKLES AND DOUBT
CD ____ PLASCD 014
Plastic Head / Jul '89 / Plastic Head

Gadzouk

GADZOUK
CD ____ REVCC 013
Revco / Jul '96 / Grapevine/PolyGram / Timewarp

Gaelforce Orchestra

ABIDE WITH ME
Lord's my shepherd / By cool siloam's shady rill / There is a green hill faraway / When I survey the wondrous cross / O worship the king (all glorious above) / Lead kindly light / Praise my soul the king of heaven / Day thou gavest Lord is ended / O for a closer walk with God / O God of Bethel by whose hand / I to the hills will lift mine eyes / All people that on earth do dwell / Behold the mountain to the lord / Holy holy holy, Lord God almighty / Child in a manger
CD ____ LCOM 5230
Lismor / Oct '93 / ADA / Direct / Duncans / Lismor

FROM HIGHLANDS TO LOWLANDS
Maciain of Glencoe / Dream Angus / Ca' the yowes / Crimond / Green grow the rushes-o / Mingulay boat song / Aye waukin' o / Queen's Maries / Mo mathair (my mother) / Bluebells of Scotland / Jock O'Hazeldean / Cradle song / Proud lion rampant / Old Scots songs
CD ____ LCDM 9025
Lismor / '90 / ADA / Direct / Duncans / Lismor

FROM THE GREEN ISLAND TO THE LAND OF THE EAGLE
Green Island / Pat Murphy's meadow / Meeting of the waters / After all these years / Rose of Tralee / My cavan girl / Danny boy / Song for Ireland / Boolavogue / Flight of Earls / Little grey home in the West / Banks of my own lovely Lee / Green glens of Antrim / shores of Amerikay
CD ____ LCDM 9029
Lismor / '90 / ADA / Direct / Duncans / Lismor

SCOTLAND AGAIN
Skye boat song / Loch Lomond / Westering home / Red red rose / Glencoe / Flowers of the forest / Mull of Kintyre / Bonnie lass O'Ballochmyle / Scotland again / Star o' Rabbie Burns / Annie Laurie / Man's a man for a' that / Auld lang syne
CD ____ LCOM 5169
Lismor / May '96 / ADA / Direct / Duncans / Lismor

SCOTLAND FOREVER
Scotland forever / Loch tay boat song / Calling me home / Scotland for me / Ae fond kiss / Culloden / John Anderson, my Jo / Highland cathedral / Mull of the cool bens / Bonnie Galloway / Scotland my home / Flower o' the Quern / Land for all seasons / Scotland yet
CD ____ LCOM 5179
Lismor / May '96 / ADA / Direct / Duncans / Lismor

SKYE HIGH
Of a' the airts / Abide with me / Northern lights of old Aberdeen / Afton water / Skye high / Bonnie wee thing / Durisdeer / Annie McKelvie / Cuillin / Fair maid of Barra / Broom o'the cowdenknowes / Isle of Mull / Clearcall a'chuain / Amazing grace
CD ____ LCOM 5215
Lismor / Oct '91 / ADA / Direct / Duncans / Lismor

STOIRM (Gaelforce)
CD ____ GH 002CD
Goatshed / Oct '94 / ADA

Gaffney, Chris

LOSER'S PARADISE
CD ____ HCD 8062
Hightone / Aug '95 / ADA / Koch

Gaida Orchestra

BAGPIPE MUSIC FROM THE RHODOPE MOUNTAINS
CD ____ VICG 52242
JVC World Library / Mar '96 / ADA / CM / Direct

Gaillard, Slim

ANYTIME, ANYPLACE, ANYWHERE
How high the moon / Anytime anyplace anywhere / I can't get started (with you) / Slim's jam No.2 / Everything's OK in the UK / Music goes 'round and around / Satin doll / Honeysuckle rose
CD ____ HEPCD 2020
Hep / Mar '96 / Cadillac / Jazz Music / New Note/Pinnacle / Wellard

AT BIRDLAND 1951
Flat foot floogie, no 1 / Cement mixer / Laughin' in rhythm / Imagination / Oh lady be good / Sabroso / Flat foot flogie, No.2 / Fine and dandy / Srenade in sulfur 8 / Sound off / Serenade in vout / Ya ha ha
CD ____ HEPCD 21
Hep / Jan '96 / Cadillac / Jazz Music / New Note/Pinnacle / Wellard

CEMENT MIXER PUTTI PUTTI
Cement mixer / Vout Orenee / Please wait for me / Slim Gaillard's boogie / Harlem hunch / Tutti frutti / Travellin' blues / Laguna / Boogin' at Berg's / Dunkin' bagel / Novachord boogie / Tee say Malee / Atomic cocktail / Yep roc heresay / Penicilin boogie / Jumpin' at the record shop / Minuet in vout / Dreisix cents / Early mornin' boogie / That ain't right baby / Riff city / Mean Mama blues / Chicken rhythm / Santa Monica jump / Mean pretty Mama / School kids' hop
CD ____ PLCD 558
President / Mar '97 / Grapevine/PolyGram / President / Target/BMG

CLASSICS 1937-1938
CD ____ CLASSICS 705
Classics / Jul '93 / Discovery / Jazz Music

CLASSICS 1939-1940
CD CLASSICS 724
Classics / Dec '93 / Discovery / Jazz Music

CLASSICS 1940-1942
CD CLASSICS 753
Classics / May '94 / Discovery / Jazz Music

CLASSICS 1945 VOL.1
CD CLASSICS 864
Classics / Mar '96 / Discovery / Jazz Music

CLASSICS 1945 VOL.2
CD CLASSICS 911
Classics / Jan '97 / Discovery / Jazz Music

GROOVE JUICE SPECIAL, THE (Gaillard, Slim & Slam Stewart)
Flat foot floogie / Chinatown, my Chinatown / Oh lady be good / Ti-pi-tin / Vol vistu gaily star / Dopey Joe / Sweet Safronia / Chicken rhythm / Matzoh balls / Chittlin switch blues / Swingin' in the key of C / Boot-ta-la-za / Bongo / Lookin' for a place to park / Tip on the numbers / B19 / African jive / Palm springs jump / Ra-da-da-da / Groove juice special
CD 4851002
Sony Jazz / Nov '96 / Sony

LAUGHING IN RHYTHM (The Best Of The Verve Years 1946-1954)
Opera in vout / Arabian boogie / Boip boip / Bartender's just like my Mother / Serenade to a poodle / Soony roony / Laughing in rhythm / Genius / Babalu / Oh lady be good / Yo yo yo / Federation blues / Chicken rhythm / Yip roc heresy / Make it do / You goofed / Gomen nasai / Potato chips / Mishugana mambo / Tip light
CD 5216512
Verve / Aug '94 / PolyGram

LEGENDARY MCVOUTIE
Voutoreene / Operatic aria / Hey stop that dancing up there / Chicken rhythm / Yep roc heresi / Gaillard special / Matzoh balls / Advocado seed soup symphony / Sonny boy / Cement mixer / Fried chicken o routie / African jive / Ya ha ha / Advocado seed soup symphony (part 2)
CD HEPCD 6
Hep / Jul '90 / Cadillac / Jazz Music / New Note/Pinnacle / Wellard

SHUCKIN' & JIVIN'
Vout orenee / Please wait for me / Sighing boogie / Voot boogie / Nightmare boogie / Slim Gaillard's boogie / Harlem hunch / Tutti frutti / Travellin' blues / Sightseeing boogie / Central avenue boogie / Boogie / Slim's cement boogie / Still wailin' / Shuckin' and jivin' / House rent party / She's just right for me / Be bop Santa Claus / Watch them resolutions
CD CDCHARLY 279
Charly / Nov '92 / Koch

SIBONEY
Siboney / Cocinero / Voodoo / Midnight congas / Havana / La comparsa / Lecumi / 10,000 congas / Nanjigo / Carnival / Memories of Maria
CD IGOCD 2066
Indigo / Jun '97 / ADA / Direct

SLIM & SLAM - COMPLETE RECORDINGS 1938-1942 (3CD Set) (Gaillard, Slim & Slam Stewart)
Flat foot floogie / Chinatown, my Chinatown / That's what you call romance / Ti-pi-tin / Eight, nine and ten / Dancing on the beach / Oh Lady be good / Ferdinand the bull / Tutti frutti / Look-a-there / Humpty dumpty / Dark eyes / Bei mir bist due schoen / Jump session / Laughin' in rhythm / Vol vistu gailey star / Dopey Joe / Sweet Safronia / It's gettin' kinda chilly / Buck dance rhythm / I got rhythm / Lady's in love with you / Caprice paganini / That's a bringer / A-well-a-take-um-a-Joe / Chicken rhythm / Swingin' in C / Boot-ta-la-za / It's you, only you / Beatin' the board / Look out / Matzoh balls / Early in the morning / Chitlin' switch blues / Huh uh-huh / Windy city hop / Baby be mine / Sploghm / Fitzwater Street / Don't let us say goodbye / Rhythm mad / Bongo / Broadway jump / Put your arms around me / Baby / Lookin' for a place to park / Hit that mess / Hey chef / Ah now / Tip on the numbers / Slim slam boogie / Bassology / Bingie-bingie-scootie / B-19 / Champagne lullaby / African jive / Palm springs jump / Groove juice special-1 / Ra-da-da-da
CD Set CDAFS 10343
Affinity / Jun '93 / Cadillac / Jazz Music / Koch

SLIM & SLAM 1938 (Gaillard, Slim & Slam Stewart)
CD TAXS 12
Tax / Aug '94 / Cadillac / Jazz Music / Wellard

SLIM & SLAM 1938-39 (Gaillard, Slim & Slam Stewart)
CD TAXS 22
Tax / Aug '94 / Cadillac / Jazz Music / Wellard

SLIM & SLAM 1940-42 (Gaillard, Slim & Slam Stewart)
CD TAXS 72
Tax / Aug '94 / Cadillac / Jazz Music / Wellard

SLIM AND SLAM (Gaillard, Slim & Slam Stewart)
Flat foot floogie / Chinatown, my Chinatown / That's what you call romance / Ti-pi-tin / 8,9 and 10 / Dancing on the beach / Oh lady be good / Ferdinand the bull / Tutti frutti / Look-a there / Humpty Dumpty / Jump session / Laughin' in rhythm / Vol vist du gaily star / Dopey Joe / Sweet Safronia / It's gettin' kinda chilly / Buck dance rhythm / Dark eyes / Bei mir bist du schoen / I got rhythm / Lady's in love with you / Caprice paganini
CD CD 53270
Giants Of Jazz / Jun '96 / Cadillac / Jazz Music / Target/BMG

SLIM'S JAM
8, 9 and 10: *Gaillard, Slim & Slam Stewart* / Ferdinand's the bull: *Gaillard, Slim & Slam Stewart* / Tutti frutti: *Gaillard, Slim & Slam Stewart* / Jump session: *Gaillard, Slim & Slam Stewart* / Laughin' in rhythm: *Gaillard, Slim & Slam Stewart* / Sweet safronia: *Gaillard, Slim & Slam Stewart* / Vout orenee: *Gaillard, Slim Orchestra* / Sighing boogie: *Gaillard, Slim Trio* / Harlem hunch: *Gaillard, Slim Orchestra* / Travelling blues: *Gaillard, Slim Orchestra* / Scotchin' with the soda: *Gaillard, Slim Trio* / Cement mixer: *Gaillard, Slim Trio* / Cuban rhumbarini: *Gaillard, Slim Trio* / Dizzy boogie: *Gaillard, Slim Orchestra* / Flat foot floogie: *Gaillard, Slim Orchestra* / Poppity pop: *Gaillard, Slim Orchestra* / Slim's jam: *Gaillard, Slim Orchestra* / Jumpin' at the record shop: *Gaillard, Slim Quartet* / Drel six cents: *Gaillard, Slim Quartet* / Laguna: *Gaillard, Slim Quartet* / Dunkin' bagel: *Gaillard, Slim Quartet* / Buck dance rhythm: *Gaillard, Slim Quartet* / Chicken rhythm: *Gaillard, Slim Orchestra*
CD TPZ 1068
Topaz Jazz / May '97 / Cadillac / Pinnacle

Gailmor, Jon

GENERATIONS
CD GLCD 1082
Green Linnet / Jul '88 / ADA / CM / Direct / Highlander / Roots

Gaines, Earl

I BELIEVE IN YOUR LOVE
CD APCD 119
Appaloosa / Oct '95 / ADA / Direct / TKO Magnum

Gaines, Grady

FULL GAIN (Gaines, Grady & The Texas Upsetters)
Mr. Blues in the sky / I've been out there / If I don't get involved / Full gain / Shaggy dog / Soul twist / If I loved you a little less / Your girlfriend / Stealing love / There is something on your mind / Gangster of the blues / Miss Lucy Brown
CD FIENDCD 148
Demon / '88 / Pinnacle

HORN OF PLENTY (Gaines, Grady & The Texas Upsetters)
CD BT 1084CD
Black Top / Jan '93 / ADA / CM / Direct

Gaines, Rosie

CLOSER THAN CLOSE
CD 5305782
Polydor / Aug '97 / PolyGram

Gaines, Steve

ONE IN THE SUN
Give it to get it / It's alright / Black jack David / On the road / One in the sun / Talkin' about love / Nothin' is now / Take my time / Summertime's here
CD WKFMXD 136
FM / Nov '89 / Revolver / Sony

Gainsbourg, Serge

COULEUR CAFE
Cha cha cha du loup / Mambo miam miam / L'anthracite / Laissez-moi tranquille / Leau a la bouche / Les amours perdues / Erotico tico / Ces petits riens / Baudelaire / Couleur cafe / Pauver Lola / Les cigarillos / New York / Tatou Jeremie / Ce grand merchant vous / Labas c'est naturel / Joanna / Marabout / L'ami caouette
CD 5289492
Philips / Oct '96 / PolyGram

DU JAZZ DANS LE RAVIN
Angoisse / Du jazz dans le ravin / Requiem pour un twisteur / Chez les ye ye / Black march / Black trombone / Ce mortel ennui / Generique / Coco and co / Intoxicated man / Elaeudania teitia / Le talkie-walkie / Some small chance / Quand tu t'y mets / La fille au rasoir / Quand mon / Me fair les yeux deux / Fugue / Machins choses / Negative blues / Wake me at five
CD 5226292
Philips / Oct '96 / PolyGram

Gaither, Bill

BILL GAITHER VOL.1 1935-1941
CD DOCD 5251
Document / May '94 / ADA / Hot Shot / Jazz Music

BILL GAITHER VOL.2 1935-1941
CD DOCD 5252
Document / May '94 / ADA / Hot Shot / Jazz Music

BILL GAITHER VOL.3 1935-1941
CD DOCD 5253
Document / May '94 / ADA / Hot Shot / Jazz Music

BILL GAITHER VOL.4 1935-1941
CD DOCD 5254
Document / May '94 / ADA / Hot Shot / Jazz Music

BILL GAITHER VOL.5 1940-1941
CD DOCD 5255
Document / Dec '94 / ADA / Hot Shot / Jazz Music

Galactic Cowboys

FEEL THE RAGE
CD 398414117CD
Metal Blade / Oct '96 / Pinnacle / Plastic Head

HORSE THAT BUD BOUGHT, THE
CD 3984144127CD
Metal Blade / Jun '97 / Pinnacle / Plastic Head

MACHINE FISH
CD 3984114105CD
Metal Blade / Jan '96 / Pinnacle / Plastic Head

Galahad

CLASSIC ROCK LIVE
CD GHCRS 1
Blueprint / Jul '96 / Pinnacle

OTHER CRIMES AND MISDEMEANOURS VOL.2
Dreaming from the inside / Opiate / Reach in to the flames / Dreams of tomorrow / GSX / Truth of you / Aqua nimue / Painted lady / Pretty in the sun / There must be a way / Rollercoaster / Suffering in silence
CD GHCD 5
Avalon / Jul '97 / Pinnacle

SLEEPERS
Sleepers / Julie Anne / Live and learn / Dentist song / Picture of bliss / Before, after and beyond / Exorcising demons / Middle-ground / Amaranth
CD GHCD 4
Avalon / Aug '95 / Pinnacle

VOICEPRINT RADIO SESSION
CD VPR 018CD
Voiceprint / Oct '94 / Pinnacle

Galahad Acoustic Quintet

NOT ALL THERE
Sir Galahad / Mother mercy / Club 18-30 / Dreaming from the inside / Melt / White lily / Through the looking glass / Looking up at the apple trees / Shrine / Legless in Gaza / Iceberg / Where there's all or nothing
CD GAQ 001CD
Avalon / Jan '95 / Pinnacle

Galas, Diamanda

LITANIES OF SATAN
CD CDIS 001
Mute / Apr '89 / RTM/Disc

MASQUE OF THE RED DEATH
CD GALAS 001
Mute / Dec '88 / RTM/Disc

SAINT OF THE PIT/DIVINE PUNISHMENT
La treizieme revient / E-eaoyme / L'heautontimoroumenos / Artemis / Cris d'aveugle
CD CDSTUMM 33
Mute / Apr '88 / RTM/Disc

SCHREI X LIVE/SCHREI 27
CD CDSTUMM 146
Mute / Sep '96 / RTM/Disc

SINGER, THE
CD CDSTUMM 103
Mute / Apr '92 / RTM/Disc

SPORTING LIFE (Galas, Diamanda & John Paul Jones)
CD CDSTUMM 127
Mute / Sep '94 / RTM/Disc

VENA CAVA
CD CDSTUMM 119
Mute / Sep '93 / RTM/Disc

YOU MUST BE CERTAIN OF THE DEVIL
Swing low, sweet chariot / Let's not chat about despair / You must be certain of the devil / Malediction / Double barrel prayer / Birds of death / Let my people go / Lord's my shepherd
CD CDSTUMM 46
Mute / Jun '88 / RTM/Disc

Galaxie 500

COPENHAGEN
Decomposing trees / Fourth of July / Summertime / Sorry / When will you come home / Spook / Listen, the snow is falling / Here she comes now / Don't let our youth go to waste
CD RCD 10363
Rykodisc / Apr '97 / ADA / Vital

GALAXIE 500 BOX SET (4CD Set)
Flowers / Pictures / 3.23 / Parking lot / Don't let our youth go to waste / Temperature's rising / Oblivious / It's getting late / Instrumental / Tugboat / 3.53 / King of Spain / Blue thunder / Tell me / Snowstorm / Strange / When will you come home / Decomposing trees / Another day / Leave the planet / 2.40 / Plastic bird / Isn't it a pity / Victory garden / Ceremony / Cold night / Fourth of July / Hearing voices / Spook / Summertime / Way up high / Listen, the snow is falling / Sorry / Melt away / King of Spain (part 2) / Here she comes now / Cheese & onions / Them / Final day / Blue thunder (with sax) / Maracas song / Crazy / Jerome / Song in 3 / Oblivious (alternate) / I can't believe it's me / Walking song / Other side / On the floor / Rain/Don't let our youth go to waste
CD Set RCD 10355
Rykodisc / Sep '96 / ADA / Vital

ON FIRE
CD RCD 10357
Rykodisc / Apr '97 / ADA / Vital

THIS IS OUR MUSIC
Fourth of July / Hearing voices / Spook / Summertime / Way up high / Listen, the snow is falling / Sorry / Melt away / King of Spain, part two
CD RCD 10358
Rykodisc / Apr '97 / ADA / Vital

TODAY
Flowers / Pictures / Parking lot / Don't let our youth go to waist / Temperature's rising / Oblivious / It's getting late / Instrumental / Tugboat / King of Spain / Crazy
CD RCD 10356
Rykodisc / Apr '97 / ADA / Vital

Galaxy P

OLD FRIENDS
CD CRCD 23
Charm / Sep '93 / Jet Star

Galaxy Trio

IN THE HAREM
CD ES 107CD
Estrus / Jun '95 / Cargo / Greyhound / Plastic Head

Galbraith, Alastair

MORSE AND GAUDY LIGHT
CD EJ 08CD
Emperor Jones / Sep '96 / SRD

Gales Brothers

LEFT HAND BRAND
Fight this power / Hand me down / Somethin's got a hold on me / House of blues / Worried man / You don't love me / Talking in your sleep / Rockin' horse ride / Talk is cheap / Somebody / Sign of the times / Deck is stacked / Guitar man
CD HBSCD 87005
House Of Blues / Apr '96 / ADA / BMG
CD 70010870052
House Of Blues / Jun '96 / ADA / BMG

Gales, Larry

MESSAGE FROM MONK, A (Gales, Larry Sextet)
Straight no chaser / 'Round midnight / Off minor / Ruby my dear / Let's call this / Message from the high priest
CD CCD 79503
Candid / Feb '97 / Cadillac / Direct / Jazz Music / Koch / Wellard

Gall, Gunter

TIVOLI
CD BEST 1007CD
Acoustic Music / Nov '93 / ADA

Gallagher & Lyle

BEST OF GALLAGHER & LYLE, THE
Heart on my sleeve / I wanna stay with you / Showdown / You're the one / Song and dance man / I believe in you / Wilie / Mhairu / Love on the airwaves / Runaway / Breakaway / Heartbreaker / All grown up / I'm amazed / Country morning / Never give up on love / Hurts to learn / We / Sittin' down music / Every little teardrop
CD 5518302
Spectrum / Nov '95 / PolyGram

HEART ON MY SLEEVE - VERY BEST OF GALLAGHER & LYLE
Breakaway / I wanna stay with you / Every little teardrop / Heart on my sleeve / Stay young / Fifteen summers / Heart in New York / You put the heart back in the city / When I'm dead and gone / Malt and barley

blues / Willie / Layna / We / Keep the candle burning / Runaway / I believe in you
CD CDMID 172
A&M / Oct '92 / PolyGram

Gallagher, Bridie

GIRL FROM DONEGAL, THE
Girl from Donegal / At the close of an Irish day / Boys from the coArmagh / Cottage by the Lee / My lovely Irish rose / When will you marry me Johnny / Tumble down shack in Athlone / Road by the river / Killarney and you / My mother's last goodbye / Noreen Brown / Lovely Derry on the banks of the Foyle / Irish jaunting car / Faithful sailor boy / Hills of Donegal / I'll forgive but I'll never forget / Two little orphans / Heart of Donegal / Rose of Kilkenny / Cutting the corn in Cresslough
CD MCVD 30010
Emerald Gem / Nov '96 / BMG

Gallagher, Eve

WOMAN CAN HAVE IT ALL
Heaven has to wait / You can have it all / Love come down / Good enough / Change your mind / Master of disguise / Love don't slip away / Crimes of the heart / Last night / Amazing grace
CD CLECD 444
Cleveland City / Mar '97 / 3mv/Sony / Grapevine/PolyGram

Gallagher, Rory

DEFENDER
Kick back city / Loan shark blues / Continental op / I ain't no saint / Failsafe day / Road to hell / Doin' time / Smear campaign / Don't start me talkin' / Seven days / Seems to me / No peace for the wicked
CD FIENDCD 98
Demon / Jul '87 / Pinnacle

LIVE IN EUROPE
Messin' with the kid / Laundromat / I could've had religion / Pistol slapper blues / Going to my home town / In your town / Bullfrog blues
CD CLACD 406
Castle / '95 / BMG

STAGE STRUCK
Shin kicker / Wayward child / Brute force and ignorance / Moonchild / Follow me / Bought and sold / Last of the independents / Shadow play
CD CLACD 407
Castle / '95 / BMG

TOP PRIORITY
Follow me / Philby / Wayward child / Keychain / At the depot / Bad penny / Just hit town / Off the handle / Public enemy no.1
CD FIENDCD 123
Demon / May '88 / Pinnacle

Gallant, Joe

BLUES FOR ALLAH PROJECT, THE (Gallant, Joe & Illuminati)
CD KFWCD 188
Knitting Factory / Oct '96 / Cargo / Plastic Head

Gallery

WIND THAT SHAKES THE BARLEY
CD KSCD 9503
Kissing Spell / Jun '97 / Greyhound

Galli, Sandro

SPECTRUM
CD ACVCD 9
ACV / Oct '95 / Plastic Head / SRD

Galli-Curci, Amelita

LO HERE AND THE GENTLE LARK (25 Songs And Arias)
Una voce poca fa / Ah talor del tuo pensiero / Love's old sweet song / My old Kentucky home / Comin' thro' the rye / Russian nightingale song / Estrellita / Clavelitos / La paloma / Al pensar en el dueno de mis amores / Parla / La serenata / No te vayas, te lo pido / Dreamin' time / Sometime / Say a little prayer for me / Kiss me again / Kiss in the dark / Pretty mocking bird / Lo here the gentle lark / Deh, torna, mio bene / Sevillana / Dov'e l'indiana bruna / Nella calma
CD AJA 5201
ASV / Jun '96 / Select

Galliano

4OUR
Who ate the fly / Ease your mind / Slack hands / Roofing tiles / Slighty frayed / Best lives of our days / Thunderhead / Freefall/ Anyone else / Some came / Funny how / Western front / Who's in charge / Battles are brewing
CD 5328112
Talkin' Loud / Sep '96 / PolyGram

IN PURSUIT OF THE 13TH NOTE
Leg in the sea of history / Welcome to the story / Coming on strong / Sweet you like your favourite gears / Cemetary of drums (Theme from Buhaina) / Five sons of the Mother / Storm clouds gather / Nothing has changed / Fifty seventh minute of the twenty third hour / Power and glory / Stoned again / Reviewing the situation / Little ghetto boy / Me, my Mike, my lyrics / Love bomb / Welcome to the story (summer breeze)
CD 8484932
Talkin' Loud / Apr '91 / PolyGram

JOYFUL NOISE UNTO THE CREATOR, A
Grounation part 1 / Jus' reach / Skunk funk / Earth boots / Phantom / Jazz / New world order / So much confusion / Totally together / Golden flower / Prince of peace / Grounation part 2
CD 8480802
Talkin' Loud / Jun '92 / PolyGram

LIVE AT THE LIQUID ROOM
Intro/Slack hands / Jus' reach / Freefall / Twyford Down / Roofing tiles / Prince of peace / Storm clouds / Jazz / Thunderhead / Long time gone/Outro
CD 5360272
Talkin' Loud / Jul '97 / PolyGram

PLOT THICKENS, THE
Was this the time / Blood lines / Rise and fall / Travels the road / Twyford down / Little one / Down in the gulley / Long time gone / Believe / Do you hear them / Better all the time / What colour our flag / Cold wind
CD 5224502
Talkin' Loud / May '94 / PolyGram

THICKER PLOT, A (Remixes)
Long time gone (mix) / Bloodlines / Believe / Skunk funk / Travels the road / Long time gone / Twyford down / Rise and fall / Better all the time
CD 5264262
Talkin' Loud / Oct '94 / PolyGram

Galliano, Richard

NEW MUSETTE (Galliano, Richard Quartet)
CD LBLC 6547
Label Bleu / Jan '92 / New Note/Pinnacle

NEW YORK TANGO
Vuelvo al sur / Soleil / New York tango / Ten years ago / Fou rire / Sertao / A l'encre rouge / Blue day / Perle / To Django / Three views of a secret
CD FDM 365812
Dreyfus / Oct '96 / ADA / Direct / New Note/ Pinnacle

PANAMANHATTAN
Summer in Central Park / Spleen / Doom / Allee des brouillards / Small ballad / Portrait of Jenny / Ballade pour Marion / Little waltz / Des voiliers
CD FDM 365142
Dreyfus / Aug '96 / ADA / Direct / New Note/ Pinnacle

VIAGGIO
Waltz for Nicky / Java indigo / Viaggio / Billie / Tango pour claude / Christopher's bossa / Coloriage / Romance / Little muse / La liberte est une fleur
CD FDM 365622
Dreyfus / Mar '94 / ADA / Direct / New Note/ Pinnacle

Galliard Brass Ensemble

CAROLS FOR BRASS
Joy to the world / Rejoice and be merry / It came upon a midnight clear / O come, all ye faithful / Once in Royal David's City / Deck the halls with boughs of holly / Wexford carol / Ding dong merrily on high / Hosanna to the Son of David / Rejoice in the Lord always / Queum vidistis pastores / Boston and Judea / Puer natus in Bethlehem / Hodie Christus natus est / In dulci jubilo
CD CD QS 6035
Quicksilva / Oct '89 / Koch

Galliards

STRANGE NEWS
CD HOP 941CD
Grasshopper / Apr '95 / ADA

Gallinger, Karen

LIVE AT THE JAZZ BAKERY
CD SBCD 3016
Sea Breeze / Jun '96 / Jazz Music

Gallivan, Joe

ORIGIN OF MAN, THE (Gallivan, Joe & Brian Cuomo/Elton Dean)
CD NB 102
No Budget / May '97 / Cadillac

Gallon Drunk

IN THE LONG STILL NIGHT
CD EFA 049822
City Slang / Sep '96 / RTM/Disc

Galloway, Jim

KANSAS CITY NIGHTS
CD SKCD 3057
Sackville / Jul '96 / Cadillac / Jazz Music / Swift

Gallucio, Lo

BEING VISITED
CD KFWCD 186
Knitting Factory / Jun '97 / Cargo / Plastic Head

Galper, Hal

LIVE AT PORT TOWNSEND '91
Hey there / I remember April / Introduction / Giant steps / Tune walking / What is this thing called love / Tune talking / Balcony rock
CD DTRCD 105
Double Time / Nov '96 / Express Jazz

PORTRAIT: HAL GALPER TRIO (Galper, Hal Trio)
After you've gone / Giant steps / In your own sweet way / I'll be seeing you / What is this thing called love / I didn't care / I should care
CD CCD 4383
Concord Jazz / Jun '89 / New Note/ Pinnacle

REBOP
All the things you aren't / Laura / It's magic / Jackie-ing / I don't stand a ghost of a chance with you / Take the Coltrane
CD ENJ 90292
Enja / Oct '95 / New Note/Pinnacle / Vital/ SAM

Galvin, Mick

AT HOME IN IRELAND
CD FRCD 031
Foam / Oct '94 / CM

Galway, James

CELTIC MINSTREL, THE
Over the sea to Skye / I dreamt I dwelt in marble halls / Cath chiem an fhia / Shoheen Sholyoh / I'll take you home again Kathleen / Dark Island / Minstrel boy / She moved through the fair / Slievenamon / When you & I were young, Maggie / Carrickfergus / Last rose of summer / Down by the Salley Gardens / Fields of Athenry / Danny boy
CD 74321383502
RCA Victor / Jul '96 / BMG

ENCHANTED FOREST, THE (Melodies Of Japan)
Enchanted forest / Lyrical shortpiece / Nakasendo (The old road) / Zui zui zukkorobashi (Children's play song) / Star children / Song of the deep forest (Improvisation) / Tokuyama lullaby / Hietsuki bushi (Love song) / Usuhiki uta (Song of the mill) / Love song / Echoes / Song of clay / Harukoma (Spring horse-dance) / Sakura / Romantic world
CD RD 87893
RCA / Sep '90 / BMG

GALWAY AT THE MOVIES
CD 0926613262
RCA / Sep '93 / BMG

GREATEST HITS VOL.1
Annie's song / Thorn birds / Memory / Danny boy / Perhaps / Kanon in D / Pink panther / Sabre dance / Clair de Lune
CD RD 87778
RCA / Jul '88 / BMG

I WILL ALWAYS LOVE YOU
Wind of change / I will always love you / Here, there and everywhere / Tears in heaven / Whole new world / Dreamlover / Belle-ile-en-mer / Holding back the years / When a man loves a woman / Last song / Golden slumbers / Little Jeannie / Always on my mind / If you leave me now / Caruso / Can't help falling in love / I just called to say I love you / Tu
CD 74321262212
RCA Victor / Feb '95 / BMG

IN THE PINK (Galway, James & Henry Mancini)
Pink panther / Thorn birds / Breakfast at Tiffany's / Penny whistle jig / Crazy world / Pie in the face polka / Baby elephant walk / Two for the road / Speedy Gonzalez / Molly McGuires / Cameo for flute / Days of wine and roses / Roses / Charade / Moon River
CD RD 85315
RCA / Jan '85 / BMG

JAMES GALWAY CHRISTMAS COLLECTION, THE (2CD Set)
Silent night / Shepherd's pipe carol / Air from Suite No.3 in D / I saw three ships / Greensleeves / Zither carol / Holy boy / Patapan / Past three o'clock / Sinfonia from the Christmas oratorio / Ave Maria / Chorale from the Christmas Oratorio / I wonder as I wander / Sheep may safely graze / Jesus Christ the apple tree / We wish you a merry Christmas / In dulci jubilo / Il est ne, le divin enfant / Es ist ein Ros' entsprungen / Messiah - pastoral symphony / Kling Glockchen, Klingeling / O Jesulein suss / Adagio / Ein kindlein in der wiegen / O tannenbaum / O come all ye faithful (adeste fidelis) / Ave Maria / Zu Bethlehem geboren / Still, still, still / Canon / In dulci jubilo / O du frohliche / Jesu, joy of man's desiring / Silent night
CD Set 74321411972
RCA Victor / Oct '96 / BMG

LARK IN THE CLEAR AIR
CD 09026619552
RCA / Apr '94 / BMG

LEGENDS (Galway, James & Phil Coulter)
Riverdance / Harry's game / Believe me if all those endearing young charms / Mna na h-Eireann / Battle of Kinsale / Thornbirds / Lannigan's ball/The Kerry dances / Ddanny boy / Music for a found harmonium / Lament for the wild geese / My Lagan love / Ashokan farewell / An Cailin Fionn / Hoedown
CD 09026687762
RCA Victor / May '97 / BMG

WIND BENEATH MY WINGS, THE
CD RD 60862
RCA / Oct '91 / BMG

Gambale, Frank

GREAT EXPLORERS, THE
Frankly speaking / Final frontier / Jaguar / Great explorers / Duet tuet / She knows me well / Thunder current / Dawn over the Nullarbor / Cruising altitude / Naughty business
CD JVC 20202
JVC / Jun '93 / Direct / New Note/Pinnacle / Vital/SAM

PASSAGES
Little charmer / 6.8 shaker / Passages / White room / D-Day / Nuncios near / Free spirit / One with everything / Romania / Ulura / Another alternative
CD JVC 20362
JVC / Aug '94 / Direct / New Note/Pinnacle / Vital/SAM

THINKING OUT LOUD
Magritte / Bondi beach / No-neck Louie / Gaudi / Felicidade / Dali / Infinity / Lover's night / Avengers suite / My little viper
CD JVC 20452
JVC / Oct '95 / Direct / New Note/Pinnacle / Vital/SAM

THUNDER FROM DOWN UNDER
Humid being / Faster than an arrow / Samba di somewhere / Kuranda / Obsessed for life / Leave ozone alone / Land of wonder / Obrigado fukuoka / Robo roo / Forgotten but not gone / Mambo jambo / One not two
CD JVC 20242
JVC / Apr '94 / Direct / New Note/Pinnacle / Vital/SAM

Gambetta, Beppe

DIALOGS
CD BRAM 1991222
Brambus / Nov '93 / ADA

GOOD NEWS FROM HOME
CD GLCD 2117
Green Linnet / Mar '95 / ADA / CM / Direct / Highlander / Roots

Gambit Jazzmen

GAMBIT JAZZMEN AND FRIENDS
CD RSC 658
Raymer / Mar '97 / Jazz Music

KING OF THE MARDI GRAS
CD LACD 54
Lake / Oct '95 / ADA / Cadillac / Direct / Jazz Music / Target/BMG

Game Theory

BIG SHOT CHRONICLES
Here it is tomorrow / Where you going northern / I've tried subtlety / Erica's world / Make any vows / Regenisraen / Crash into June / Book of millionaires / Only lesson learned / Too closely / Never mind / Like a girl Jesus / Girl with a guitar / Come home with me / Seattle / Linus and Lucy / Faithless
CD A 046D
Alias / Feb '94 / Vital

DISTORTION OF GLORY
Something to show / Tin scarecrow / White blues / Date with an angel / Mary Magdalene / Young drug / Bad year at UCLA / All I want is everything / Stupid heart / Sleeping through heaven / It gives me chills / TGARTG / Dead center / Penny, things won't / Metal and glass exact / Selfish again / Life in July / Shark pretty / Nine lives to rigel five / Red baron / Kid convenience / Too late for tears
CD A 048D
Alias / Feb '94 / Vital

REAL NIGHTIME
Here comes everybody / Twenty four / Waltz the halls always / I mean it this time / Friend of the family / If and when it all falls apart / Curse of the frontierland / Rayon drive / She'll be a verb / Real nightime / You can't have me / I turned her away / Any other hand / I want to hold your hand / Couldn't I just tell you
CD A 047D
Alias / Feb '94 / Vital

TWO STEPS FROM THE MIDDLE AGES
Room for one more, honey / What the whole world wants / Picture of agreeability / Amelia have you lost / Rolling with the moody girls / Wyoming / In a delorean / You

drive / Leilian / Wish I could stand or have / Don't entertain me twice / Throwing the election / Initiations week
CD CDENV 507
Enigma / Oct '88 / EMI

Gameface

GOOD
CD NS 005CD
Network Sound / Jul '96 / Plastic Head

THREE TO GET READY
CD DSR 038CD
Dr. Strange / Jun '97 / Cargo / Greyhound / Plastic Head

Gamez, Celia

LA GRAN ESTRELLA DE MADRID VOL.1
CD 20082
Sonifolk / Aug '96 / ADA / CM

LA GRAN ESTRELLA DE MADRID VOL.2
CD 20083
Sonifolk / Aug '96 / ADA / CM

Gamil, Soliman

ANKH
CD TO 14CD
Touch / Apr '90 / Kudos / Pinnacle

EGYPTIAN MUSIC
CD TO 7
Touch / Oct '95 / Kudos / Pinnacle

L'ART DU QUANUN EGYPTIEN
CD ARN 60273
Arion / Feb '97 / ADA / Discovery

Gamma Ray

ALIVE 1995
Land of the free / Man on a mission / Rebellion in dreamland / Space eater / Fairytale / Tribute to the past / Heal me / Saviour / Abyss of the void / Ride the sky / Future world / Heavy metal mania
CD N 02652
Noise / Jun '96 / Koch

FUTURE MADHOUSE
CD N 02033
Noise / Jun '93 / Koch

INSANITY AND GENIUS
Tribute to the past / No return / Last before the storm / Cave principle / Future madhouse / Gamma ray (edited version) / Insanity and genius / Eighteen years / Your torn is over / Heal me / Brothers
CD N 02032
Noise / Jun '93 / Koch

LAND OF THE FREE
CD N 02272
Noise / May '95 / Koch

SIGN NO MORE
CD N 01782
Noise / Oct '91 / Koch

Ganc, David

BALADAS BRASILIERAS
CD 829282
BUDA / Jul '96 / Discovery

Gandalf

COLOURS OF THE EARTH
CD SKV 080CD
Sattva Art / Jul '95 / THE

GANDALF
Golden earrings / Hang on to a dream / Never to far / Scarlet ribbons / You upset the grace of living / Can you travel alone / Nature boy / Tiffany rings / Me about you / I watch the moon
CD SEECD 326
See For Miles/C5 / Jun '97 / Pinnacle

Gandy, Bruce

COMPOSERS SERIES VOL.2
CD LCOM 5242
Lismor / Aug '95 / ADA / Direct / Duncans / Lismor

Ganelin Trio

ENCORES
CD CDLR 106
Leo / Oct '94 / Cadillac / Impetus / Wellard

OPUSES
CD CDLR 171
Leo / '90 / Cadillac / Impetus / Wellard

POCO A POCO
CD CDLR 101
Leo / Feb '89 / Cadillac / Impetus / Wellard

Gang Green

ANOTHER WASTED NIGHT
Another wasted night / Skate to hell / Last chance / Alcohol / Have fun / Nineteenth hole / Skate hate / Let's drink some beer / Protect and serve / Another bomb / Voices carry / Sold out Alabama
CD TAANG 131CD
Taang / Nov '92 / Cargo

KING OF BANDS
CD RR 92542
Roadrunner / Nov '91 / PolyGram

YOU GOT IT
CD RR 349591
Roadrunner / '89 / PolyGram

Gang Of Four

BRIEF HISTORY OF THE 20TH CENTURY (The EMI Compilation)
At home he's a tourist / Damaged goods / Ntur's not in it / Not great men / Anthrax / Return the gift / It's her factory / What we all want / Paralysed / Hole in the wallet / Cheeseburger / To hell with poverty / Capital (it fails us now) / Call me up (If I'm home) / I will be a good boy / History of the world / I love a man in a uniform / Is it love / Woman town / We live as we dream, alone
CD CDEMC 3583
EMI / Oct '90 / EMI

ENTERTAINMENT
Ether / Naturals not in it / Damaged goods / Return the gift / Guns before butter / I found that essence rare / Glass / Contract / At home he's a tourist / 5-45 / Love like anthrax / Not great men / Outside the trains don't run on time / He'd send in the army / It's her factory
CD CZ 541
EMI / Jan '95 / EMI

SHRINKWRAPPED
CD WENCD 003
When / Oct '95 / Pinnacle

SOLID GOLD
Paralysed / What we all want / If I could keep it for myself / Outside the trains don't run on time / Why theory / Cheeseburger / Republic / In the ditch / Hole in the wallet / He'd send in the army / To hell with poverty / Capital (it fails us now) / History's bunk / Cheeseburgher / What we all want (live)
CD CZ 561
Premier/EMI / Feb '96 / EMI

Gang Starr

DAILY OPERATION
Daily operation (intro) / Place where we dwell / Flip the script / Ex girl to next girl / Solioquy of chaos / I'm the man / 92 interlude / Take it personal / 2 deep / 24-7-365 / No shame in my game / Conspiracy / Illest brother / Hardcore composer / BYS / Much too much (Mack A Mil) / Take two and pass / Stay tuned
CD CCD 1910
Cooltempo / May '92 / EMI

HARD TO EARN
Intro (the first steps) / Alongwaytogo / Code of the streets / Brainstorm / Tonz 'o' gunz / Planet / Aiiight chill... / Speak ya clout / Dwyck / Words from the Nutcracker / Mass appeal / Blowin' up the spot / Suckas need bodyguards / Now you're mine / Mostly the voice / FALA / Comin' for the datazz
CD CTCD 38
Cooltempo / Feb '94 / EMI

STEP IN THE ARENA
Name tag (Premier and The Guru) / Step in the arena / Form of intellect / Execution of a chump (No more Mr. Nice Guy Pt. 2) / Who's gonna take the weight / Beyond comprehension / Check the technique / Lovesick / Here today, gone tomorrow / Game plan / Take a rest / What you want this time / Street ministry / Just to get a rep / Say your prayers / As I read my S-A / Precisely the right rhymes / Meaning of the name
CD CCD 1798
Cooltempo / Jan '91 / EMI

Ganger

FORE
Hollywood loaf / Missile that back-fired / Drummers arms and bionic thumbs / Smorgasbord / Fore / Jellyneck / Anomovieshot / Prisoner of my eyeball
CD WIGCD 30
Domino / Apr '97 / Vital

Gangsta Tribe

GOTTA COME UP
CD CON 45022
Ichiban / May '96 / Direct / Koch

Ganguly, Rita

THUMRI AND DADRA (Vocal Art Of Hindustan)
CD VICG 53472
JVC World Library / Mar '96 / ADA / CM / Direct

Gangwar

STREET FIGHTING
CD 622582
Skydog / Apr '97 / Discovery

Ganksta C

STEPCHILD
CD FILECD 455
Profile / Jan '95 / Pinnacle

Gant, Cecil

CECIL GANT
Cecil boogie / Hit that jive Jack / Hogan's alley / I gotta girl / Boogie blues / Sloppy Joe / Playing myself the blues / Time will tell / Cecil's mop top / Train time blues
CD KKCD 03
Krazy Kat / Apr '90 / Hot Shot / Jazz Music

Gantry, Elmer

VERY BEST OF ELMER GANTRY/ VELVET OPERA, THE (Gantry, Elmer & Velvet Opera)
Mother writes / Long nights of summer / Mary Jane / Air / Looking for a happy life / Reactions of a young man / Flames (single version) / Dreamy / Talk of the devil / And I remember / To be with you / Painter / Volcano / Raga / Eleanor Rigby / Money by / Raise the light / Warm day in July / Black Jack Davy / Anna Dance square / Statesboro blues / There's a hole in my pocket
CD SEECD 437
See For Miles/C5 / May '97 / Pinnacle

Ganxsta Rid

OCCUPATION HAZARDOUS
If I die, let me roll / Chilling on the west side / One life, last breath / Happy feelings / Karson makes u bounce / Gs from the otha side / Born May 1st / Occupation hazardous / Rid is coming / Operation green light / Tell em who sent yo ass / Once upon a mossburg
CD CDVEST 65
Bulletproof / Nov '95 / Pinnacle

Ganzie, Terry

TEAM UP
CD VYDCD 012
Vine Yard / Jul '96 / Grapevine/PolyGram

Gap Band

AIN'T NOTHIN' BUT A PARTY
CD 50532
Raging Bull / Feb '97 / Prime / Total/BMG

BEST OF THE GAP BAND, THE
Early in the morning / Shake / Outstanding / Why you wann hurt me / Yearning / Open your mind / You dropped a bomb on me / You can always count on me / I don't believe you want to get up and dance / Steppin' out / Humping around / Boys are back in town / Party train
CD 5224572
Mercury / Jun '94 / PolyGram

LIVE AND WELL
Intro / Gap Band party / Wide / Oops upside your head / Outstanding / Humpin' / No hiding place / Burn rubber / Gotta get up / Early in the morning / Party train / Drop the bomb / Yearning for your love / Yearning - reprise / Mega mix
CD ESMCD 442
Essential / Oct '96 / BMG

OOPS UPSIDE YOUR HEAD
Oops upside your head / Outstanding / Burn rubber on me (why you wanna hurt me) / Party lights / Jammin' in America / You dropped a bomb on me / Boys are back in Town / Baby baba boogie / Steppin' (out) / Humpin' (edit version) / When I look in your eyes / Yearning for your love / Sweet Caroline / You can count on me / Open your mind (wide) / I don't believe you want to get up and dance (oops)
CD 5511722
Spectrum / Aug '95 / PolyGram

Garbage

GARBAGE
Super vixen / Queer / Only happy when it rains / As Heaven is wide / Not my idea / Stroke of luck / Vow / Stupid girl / Dog new tricks / My lover's box / Fix me now / Milk
CD D 31450
Mushroom / Oct '95 / 3mv/Pinnacle

INTERVIEW DISC
CD GAR 1CD
Wax / Jan '97 / RTM/Disc / Total/BMG

Garbage Collectors

GARBAGE COLLECTORS
CD PER 029
Semantic / Feb '94 / Plastic Head

Garbarek, Jan

AFTENLAND
CD 8393042
ECM / Nov '89 / New Note/Pinnacle

ALL THOSE BORN WITH WINGS
Last clown / Yellow fever / Soulful Bill / La divetta / Cool train / Loop
CD 8313942
ECM / Feb '87 / New Note/Pinnacle

DANSERE
CD 8291932
ECM / Oct '86 / New Note/Pinnacle

DIS
Vandrere / Krusning / Viddene / Skygger / YR / Dis
CD 8274082
ECM / Feb '86 / New Note/Pinnacle

ESOTERIC CIRCLE (Garbarek, Jan & Terje Rypdal)
Traneflight / Rabalder / Esoteric circle / VIPs / SAS 644 / Nefertiti / Gee / Karin's mode / Breeze ending
CD FCD 41031
Freedom / Aug '96 / Cadillac / Jazz Music / Koch / Wellard

EVENTYR
CD 8293842
ECM / Aug '88 / New Note/Pinnacle

GRAY VOICE, THE
CD 8254062
ECM / Aug '88 / New Note/Pinnacle

I TOOK UP THE RUNES
Gula gula / Molde canticle (parts 1-5) / His eyes were suns / I took up the runes / Buena hora, buenos vientos
CD 8438502
ECM / Nov '90 / New Note/Pinnacle

LEGENDS OF THE SEVEN DREAMS
He comes from the North / Aichuri, the song man / Tongue of secrets / Brother wind / It's name is secret road / Send word / Voy cantando / Mirror store
CD 8373442
ECM / Oct '88 / New Note/Pinnacle

OFFICIUM (Garbarek, Jan & The Hilliard Ensemble)
CD 4453692
ECM / Sep '94 / New Note/Pinnacle

PHOTO WITH BLUE SKY (Garbarek, Jan Group)
Blue sky / White cloud / Windows / Red roof / Wives / Picture
CD 843 168 2
ECM / Oct '90 / New Note/Pinnacle

PLACES
CD 8291952
ECM / Oct '86 / New Note/Pinnacle

ROSENSFOLE (Garbarek, Jan & Maria Buen-Garnas)
CD 8392932
ECM / Jun '89 / New Note/Pinnacle

STAR
Star / Jumper / Lamenting / Anthem / Roses for you / Clouds in the mountain / Snowman / Music of my people
CD 8496492
ECM / Oct '91 / New Note/Pinnacle

TRIPTYKON
Rim / Selji / JEV / Sang / Triptykon / Etu hei / Bruremarsi
CD 8473212
ECM / Jun '92 / New Note/Pinnacle

TWELVE MOONS
Twelve moons / Psalm / Brother wind march / There were swallows / Tall tear trees / Arietta / Gautes-Margjit / Darvanan / Huhai / Witch-tai-to
CD 5195002
ECM / May '93 / New Note/Pinnacle

USTAD SHAUKAT HUSSAIN-MADAR (Garbarek, Jan & Anouar Brahem)
Sull lull / Madar / Sebika / Bahia / Ramy / Jaw / Joron / Qaws / Epilogue
CD 5190752
ECM / Feb '94 / New Note/Pinnacle

VISIBLE WORLD
Red wind / Creek / Survivor / Healing smoke / Visible world (Chiaro) / Desolate mountains I / Desolatae mountains II / Visible world (Scuro) / Giulietta / Desolate mountains III / Pygmy lullaby / Quest / Arrow / Scythe / Evening land
CD 5290862
ECM / Apr '96 / New Note/Pinnacle

WAYFARER
Gesture / Wayfarer / Gentle / Pendulum / Spor / Singsong
CD 8119682
ECM / Aug '86 / New Note/Pinnacle

WITCHI-TAI-TO
AIR / Kukka / Hasta siempre / Witchi-tai-to / Desireless
CD 8333302
ECM / Mar '88 / New Note/Pinnacle

WORKS: JAN GARBAREK
Folk songs / Skirk and hyl / Passing / Selje / Viddene / Snipp, snapp, snute / Beast of Kommodo / Svevende
CD 8232662
ECM / Jun '89 / New Note/Pinnacle

Garber, Jan

22 ORIGINAL BIG BAND RECORDINGS (Garber, Jan & His Orchestra)
CD HCD 403
Hindsight / Oct '92 / Jazz Music / Target/ BMG

GREAT JAN GARBER, THE
My dear / S'wonderful / More than you know / Maria Elena / Star dust / It's a wonderful world / Lovely to look at / Oh lady be good / It's only a paper moon / Birth of the blues / I'll see you in my dreams / Things we did last summer
CD HCD 331

Hindsight / Apr '96 / Jazz Music / Target/ BMG

Garbo, Chuck

DRAWERS TROUBLE
CD ROUCD 2123
Rounder / Aug '93 / ADA / CM / Direct

Garbutt, Vin

BANDALIZED
CD HROCD 9
Home Roots / Apr '96 / ADA

BYPASS SYNDROME, THE
CD HROCD 8
Home Roots / Apr '96 / ADA

PLUGGED
CD HROCD 11
Home Roots / Apr '96 / ADA

Garcia, Carlos

TANGO VOL.2 (Garcia, Carlos & The Tango Allstars)
CD VICG 53432
JVC World Library / Mar '96 / ADA / CM / Direct

Garcia, Chris

CHUTNEY BUCCHANAL
CD JMC 1120
JMC / May '96 / Jet Star

Garcia, Jerry

ALMOST ACOUSTIC (Garcia, Jerry Acoustic Band)
Swing low, sweet chariot / Blue yodel no. 9 (Standing on the corner) / I'm troubled / Oh babe, it ain't no lie / Casey Jones / Ripple / Deep elem blues / I'm here to get my baby out of jail / Girl at the crossroads bar / Diamond Joe / Spike diver blues / I've been all around this world / Oh the wind and the rain / Gone home
CD GDCD 4005
Grateful Dead / Feb '89 / Pinnacle

COMPLIMENTS OF GARCIA
Let it rock / That's what love will make us do / Turn on the bright lights / What goes around / Mississippi moon / Hunter gets captured by the game / Russian lullaby / He ain't give you none / Let's spend the night together / Midnight town
CD GDCD 4011
Grateful Dead / Mar '89 / Pinnacle

HOOTEROLL (Garcia, Jerry & Howard Wales)
CD RCD 10052
Rykodisc / Oct '87 / ADA / Vital

HOW SWEET IT IS... (Garcia, Jerry Band)
How sweet it is / Tough Mama / That's what love will make you do / Someday baby / Cats under the stairs / Tears of rage / Think / Gomorrah / Tore up over you / Like a road
CD GDCD 4051
Grateful Dead / Jun '97 / Pinnacle

JERRY GARCIA AND DAVID GRISMAN (Garcia, Jerry & David Grisman)
CD ACD 2
Acoustic Disc / Jun '97 / ADA / Koch

OLD AND IN THE WAY (Garcia, Jerry & David Grisman/Peter Rowan)
Pig in a pen / Midnight moonlight / Old and in the way / Knockin' on your door / Hobo song / Panama red / Wild horses / Kissimmee kid / White dove / Land of the Navajo
CD SHCD 3746
Sugar Hill / Feb '85 / ADA / CM / Direct / Koch / Roots

REFLECTIONS
Might as well / Mission in the rain / They love each other / I'll take a melody / It must have been the roses / Tore up (over you) / Catfish John / Comes a-time
CD GDCD 4008
Grateful Dead / May '89 / Pinnacle

SHADY GROVE (Garcia, Jerry & David Grisman)
CD AC 21CD
Acoustic Disc / Apr '97 / ADA / Koch

WHEEL, THE
Deal / Sugaree / Late for supper / Eep hour / Odd little place, An / Bird song / Loser / Spidergawd / To lay me down / Wheel
CD GDCD 4003
Grateful Dead / Feb '89 / Pinnacle

Garcia-Fons, Renaud

ALBOREA
Al Cameron / Alborea / Natgo / Secret zambra / Eosine / Gus's smile / Amadu / Sacre coeur / Tropea / Fort apache / Rue de buci
CD ENJ 90572
Enja / Feb '96 / New Note/Pinnacle / Vital/ SAM

LEGENDS
Funambule / Aube / Sesame / Inanga / Moreno / Like someone in love / Procession / Fille des sables / La guitare a King Kong / Legendes / Elle / Mi saeta
CD ENJ 93142
Enja / Feb '97 / New Note/Pinnacle / Vital/ SAM

Garcons

DIVORCE
French boy / Critics / 25th Street / French boy reprise / French boy / Critics / 25th Street / French boy reprise / Encore l'amour
CD THECD 107
Other / Jun '97 / Mo's Music Machine / Pinnacle

Gardel, Carlos

CARLOS GARDEL
Tomo y obligo / Almagro / Viejo rincon / Silencio / Rencor / Secreto / Volvio una noche / La cancion de Buenos Aires / Juventud / Volver / Senda florida / Bandoneon arrabalero / Lo han visto con otra / Cuesta abajo / Muneca brava / Tango Argentino / Palomita blanca / Dandy / La garconniere / Milonga sentimental / Viejo smocking / Tortazos / Sueno de juventud / El dia que me quieras / Silbando / Mi Buenos Aries querido / Paseo de Julio / Farolito de papel / Por una cabeza / Caprichosa / Parlez moi d'amour / Mi noche triste / Medianoche / Pompas / Vieja recova / Tu vieja ventana / Lejana tierra mia / La cumparsita
CD FA 054
Fremeaux / Oct '96 / ADA / Discovery

LA CUMPARSITA
La cumparasita / Mano a mano / Tomo y obligo / Milonga sentimental / Chorra / Compadron / Lo han visto con otra / Bandoneon arrabalero / Mi noche triste / Barrio reo / Rencor / Viejo smoking / Dandy / Muneca / Senda Florida / Carnaval / Malevaje / Melodia de arrabal
CD CD 62128
Saludos Amigos / Jul '97 / Target/BMG

MANO A MANO
CD BM 506CD
Blue Moon / Jul '96 / Cadillac / Discovery / Greensleeves / Jazz Music / Jet Star / TKO Magnum

ORATORIO CARLOS GARDEL (Various Artists)
CD 873086
Milan Sur / Feb '97 / Conifer/BMG

PASSION OF THE TANGO, THE
CD 74321447942
Milan Sur / Feb '97 / Conifer/BMG

POR UNA CABEZA
CD BM 507CD
Blue Moon / Jul '96 / Cadillac / Discovery / Greensleeves / Jazz Music / Jet Star / TKO Magnum

TANGO
CD CD 62027
Saludos Amigos / Oct '93 / Target/BMG

TANGO ARGENTINO
Mano a mano / Lo han visto con orta / La cumparsita / Me da penda confesarlo / La cancion de beunos aires / Yra yra / Misa de once / A la luz del candil / Caminot / Alma, en pena / Desden / Adios muchachos / Melodia de arrabal / Guitarra mia / Tomo y obligo / Tango Argentino
CD CD 12527
Music Of The World / Jun '96 / ADA / Target/BMG

Garden, Bill

BILL GARDEN'S HIGHLAND FIDDLE ORCHESTRA (Garden, Bill & His Highland Fiddle Orchestra)
French Canadian special / Stings to the bow (reels and jigs) / De'il among the tailors / Blackthorn stick / Roaring jelly / Brumley brae / Slow air, strathspey and reel / Hornpipes / Reel of Tulloch / Robert Burns waltz / March, strathspey and reel / Scots and Irish (reels and jigs) / Polka / Country hoedown / Intercity waltz / Schottische reel / Sir Harry Lauder selection
CD CD ITV 423
Scotdisc / Dec '86 / Conifer/BMG / Duncans / Ross

IOLAIRE (Garden, Bill Fiddle Orchestra)
CD CDITV 514
Scotdisc / Jul '90 / Conifer/BMG / Duncans / Ross

TRAVEL THE LAKES (Garden, Bill Fiddle Orchestra)
CD CDITV 577
Scotdisc / Sep '94 / Conifer/BMG / Duncans / Ross

Gardiner, Bobby

MASTER'S CHOICE, THE
Fermoy lassies, Doon reel, concertina reel / Paul Halfpenny, Mulvihills / Reel of Rio, the ash plant / Shoe the donkey, Sonnys / Cathaoir an phiobaire, Chorus jig / Blind Mary / Tailor's thimble, Lilies in the field, Take your choice / McDermotts, Humours of Lissadell / Colleys delight / Banbridge town, Mr. McGuire, Pride of the Bronx / Jack Gorman's favourite showjumper drinking whiskey / Road to Ballymac/Silver birch / Johnson's / Kilty town, The lobster / Gentian waltz / Sporting nell/Earl's chair
CD OSS 86CD
Ossian / Aug '93 / ADA / CM / Direct / Highlander

MEMORIES OF CLARE
CD COPCD 5010
Copley / Feb '96 / ADA

Gardiner, Boris

IT'S WHAT'S HAPPENING
CD RNCD 2125
Rhino / Nov '95 / Grapevine/PolyGram / Jet Star

REGGAE HAPPENING
CD JMC 200110
Jamaican Gold / Sep '93 / Grapevine/ PolyGram / Jet Star

THIS IS BORIS GARDINER
CD RNCD 2006
Rhino / May '93 / Grapevine/PolyGram / Jet Star

Gardiner, Paula

TALES OF INCLINATION
CD SCDC 2103
Sain / Nov '95 / ADA / Direct / Greyhound

Gardiner, Ronnie

MY SWEDISH HEART
CD SITCD 9225
Sittel / Aug '95 / Cadillac / Jazz Music

Gardner, Dave

EMPTY DREAMS
CD PLAN 006CD
Planet / Jul '95 / Direct

Gardner, Freddy

VALAIDA VOL.1 1935-1937
CD HQCD 12
Harlequin / '92 / Hot Shot / Jazz Music / Swift / Wellard

VALAIDA VOL.2
CD HQCD 18
Harlequin / Feb '94 / Hot Shot / Jazz Music / Swift / Wellard

Gardner, Jeff

SKY DANCE
CD 500332
Musidisc / Nov '93 / Discovery

SPIRIT CALL
CD 087142
Ulysse / Mar '96 / Discovery

Gardner, Joanna

JOANNA GARDNER
I never thought / We can make it / Special feelings / Friday night / Watching you / I could never love another like you / Pick up the pieces / Spooky
CD EXCDM 1
Expansion / Sep '96 / 3mv/Sony

Gardony, Laszlo

BREAKOUT
CD 74321378872
RCA / May '96 / BMG

Garfunkel, Art

ACROSS AMERICA (The Very Best Of Art Garfunkel)
Heart in New York / Crying in the rain / Scarborough Fair / Poem on the underground wall / I only have eyes for you / Homeward bound / All I know / Bright eyes / El Condor Pasa / Bridge over troubled water / Mrs. Robinson / 59th Street Bridge song (Feelin' groovy) / I will / April come she will / Sound of silence / Grateful / Goodnight, my love
CD VTCD 113
Virgin / Dec '96 / EMI

ART GARFUNKEL ALBUM, THE
Bright eyes / Breakaway / Heart in New York / I shall sing / Ninety nine miles from LA / All I know / I only have eyes for you / Watermark / Sometimes when I'm dreaming / Travellin' boy / Same old tears on a new background / What a wonderful world / I believe / Scissors cut
CD 4663332
CBS / Oct '90 / Sony

BREAKAWAY
I believe / Rag doll / Breakaway / Disney girls / My little town / Waters of March / I only have eyes for you / Looking for the right one / Ninety nine miles from LA / Same old tears on a new background
CD 4688732
Epic / Feb '97 / Sony

FATE FOR BREAKFAST
In a little while / Since I don't have you / I know / Sail on a rainbow / Miss you nights / Bright eyes / Finally found a reason / Beyond the tears / Oh how happy / When someone doesn't want you / Take me away
CD 4879462
Columbia / Jul '97 / Sony

Garibian, Ludwig

ARMENIA (Garibian, Ludwig Trio & Folk Lab)
CD MWCD 9303
Music & Words / Jul '93 / ADA / Direct

Garioch Fiddlers

AT HAME
CD CDR 038
Donside / Mar '96 / Ross

Garland, Hank

HANK GARLAND AND HIS SUGAR FOOTERS
Sugarfoot rag / Third man theme / Flying eagle polka / Sugarfoot boogie / Hillbilly express / Seventh and union / Lowdown Billy / Sentimental journey / Doll dance / Chic, No. 1 / Chic, No. 2 / E string rag / Guitar shuffle / I'm movin' on / This cold war with you / I'll never slip around again / Some other world / I'm crying
CD BCD 15551
Bear Family / Apr '92 / Direct / Rollercoaster / Swift

Garland, Judy

25 GREATEST HITS
CD ENTCD 271
Entertainers / Mar '92 / Target/BMG

ALL THE THINGS YOU ARE
CD VJCD 1043
Vintage Jazz Classics / May '93 / ADA / Cadillac / CM / Direct

ALWAYS CHASING RAINBOWS (The Young Judy Garland)
All God's chillun got rhythm / Buds won't bud / Cry baby cry / Embraceable you / End of the rainbow / Everybody sing / FDR Jones / I'm always chasing rainbows / I'm just wild about Harry / I'm nobody's baby / In between / It never rains but it pours / Oceans apart / Our love affair / Over the rainbow / Sleep my baby sleep / Stompin' at the Savoy / Sweet sixteen / Swing Mister Charlie / Ten pins in the sky / You can't have everything / Zing went the strings of my heart
CD CDAJA 5093
Living Era / Jul '92 / Select

BEST OF JUDY GARLAND
On the Atchison, Topeka and The Santa Fe / I'm always chasing rainbows / But not for me / Meet me in St. Louis / For me and my gal / In between / Dear Mr. Gable / FDR Jones / Embraceable you / Trolley song / I got rhythm / Boy next door / Zing went the strings of my heart / When you wore a tulip / I'm nobody's baby / Over the rainbow
CD DCD 5332
Disky / Dec '93 / Disky / THE

BEST OF JUDY GARLAND, THE
That's entertainment / More / Come rain or come shine / It's yourself / Lucky day / I could go on singin' (till the cows come home) / Day in, day out / Foggy day / Almost like being in love/This can't be love / Fly me to the moon / Battle Hymn of the Republic / Zing went the strings of my heart / You'll never walk alone / Old devil moon / Maggie May / You made me love you/For me and my girl/The trolley song / Man that got away / Rock-a-bye your baby with a Dixie melody / As long as he needs me / Over the rainbow
CD CDSL 8258
Music For Pleasure / Sep '95 / EMI

CAPITOL YEARS, THE
That's entertainment / You made me love you / For me and my girl / Trolley song / Man that got away / Lucky day / I can't give you anything but love / Zing went the strings of my heart / I hadn't anyone till you / Come rain or come shine / Shine on harvest moon / Some of these days / My man (mon homme) / I don't care / Do I love you / If I love again / Old devil moon / This is it / Do it again / Who cares / Over the rainbow
CD CZ 247
Capitol / Nov '89 / EMI

CHASING RAINBOWS
I never knew / Oceans apart / Love / But not for me / Embraceable you / Over the rainbow / Blues in the night / How about you / Poor little rich girl / No lover no nothing / For me and my gal / Trolley song / This heart of mine / You made me love you
CD RMB 75007
Remember / Nov '93 / Total/BMG

COLLECTOR'S GEMS FROM THE MGM FILMS
Waltz with a swing / Americana, opera vs jazz / Everbody sing / Yours and mine / Your broadway and my broadway / Got a pair of new shoes / Sun showers / Down on melody farm / Why, because / Ever since the world began / Shall I sing a melody / In between / It never rains, but what it pours / Bei mir bist du schoen / Meet the beat of my heart / Zing went the strings of my heart / On the bumpy road to love / Ten pins in the sky / I'm nobody's baby / All I do is dream of you / Alone / It's a great day for the Irish / Danny boy / Pretty girl milking her cow / Singin' in the rain / Easy to love / We

must have music / I'm always chasing rainbows / Minnie from Trinidad / Every little moment has a meaning of its own / Tom, Tom, the piper's son / When I look at you / Paging Mr. Greenback / Where there's music / Joint is really jumping at Carnegie hall / D'ya love me / Mack the black / Love of my life / Voodoo / You can't get a man with a gun / There's no business like show business / They say it's wonderful / Girl that I marry / I've got the sun in the morning / Let's go west, again / Anything you can do / There's no business like show business
CD Set __________ **CDODEON 22**
EMI / Jan '97 / EMI

EARLY YEARS, THE
CD __________ **AVC 536**
Avid / May '94 / Avid/BMG / Koch / THE

JUDY AT CARNEGIE HALL
When you're smiling / Almost like being in love (medley) / Who cares / Puttin' on the Ritz / How long has this been going on / Just you, just me / Man that got away / San Francisco / That's entertainment / Come rain or come shine / You're nearer / Foggy day / If love were all / Zing went the strings of my heart / Stormy weather / You made me love you (medley) / Rock-a-bye your baby with a Dixie melody / Over the rainbow / Swanee / After you've gone / Chicago / Trolley song, The (overture) / Over the rainbow (overture) / Man that got away / This can't be love (medley) / Do it again / You go to my head / Alone together / I can't give you anything but love
CD __________ **CZ 76**
Capitol / Jun '87 / EMI

JUDY GARLAND
CD __________ **DVGH 7062**
Deja Vu / May '95 / THE

JUDY GARLAND ON RADIO (2CD Set)
Balboa / Feelin' like a million / They can't take that away from me / Thanks for the memory / Could you pass in love / Sweet sixteen / FDR Jones / Comes love / All the things you are / Don't get around much anymore / But not for me / I lost my sugar in Salt Lake City / Taking a chance on love / Over the rainbow / I may be wrong / Program introduction / Trolley song / Have yourself a merry little Christmas / Judy's spoken tribute to Jerome Kern / I won't dance / Can't help lovin' dat man / Why do I love you / Look for the silver lining
CD Set __________ **JZCL 5006**
Jazz Classics / Nov '96 / Cadillac / Direct / Jazz Music

JUDY GARLAND SHOW, THE (5CD Set)
CD Set __________ **15942**
Laserlight / Oct '95 / Target/BMG

JUDY GARLAND SHOWS, THE
Introdustion / Just in time / When you're smiling (the whole world smiles with you) / You do something to me / Too marvellous for words: *Sinatra, Frank* / You do something to me: *Garland, Judy & Dean Martin* / You must have been a beautiful baby: *Martin, Dean* / You do something to me (reprise): *Garland, Judy & Frank Sinatra/ Dean Martin* / One I love belongs to someone else: *Sinatra, Frank & Dean Martin* / I can't give you anything but love / You're nobody 'til somebody loves you: *Garland, Judy & Frank Sinatra/Dean Martin* / You made me love you / Rock-a-bye your baby with a Dixie melody / Swanee / I never will forget / San Francisco / Fly me to the moon / Old soft shoe: *Garland, Judy & Donald O'Connor* / Chicago (that toddling town) / Closing theme
CD __________ **OTA 101911**
On The Air / Feb '97 / Target/BMG

LEGENDARY AMSTERDAM CONCERT 1960, THE (2CD Set)
When you're smiling (The whole world smiles with you) / Almost like in love / This can't be love / Do it again / You go to my head / Alone together / Who cares (As long as you care for me) / Puttin' in the ritz / How long has this been going on / Just you, just me / Man that got away / San Francisco / That's entertainment / I can't give you anything but love / Come rain or come shine / You're nearer / If love were all / Foggy day (In London town) / Zing went the strings of my heart / Stormy weather / You made me love you (I didn't want to do it) / For me and my gal / Trolley song / Rock-a-bye your baby with a Dixie melody / Swanee / It's a great day for the Irish / After you've gone / San Francisco (Reprise) / Sail away / Something's coming / Just in time / Get me to the church on time / Joey, Joey, Joey / Never will I marry / Hey, look me over / Party's over / Some people
CD Set __________ **DBG 53044**
Double Gold / Jul '96 / Target/BMG

LEGENDS IN MUSIC
CD __________ **LECD 094**
Wisepack / Sep '94 / Conifer/BMG / THE

MAIL CALL (Garland, Judy & Bing Crosby)
CD __________ **15413**
Laserlight / Jan '93 / Target/BMG

MISS SHOWBUSINESS
Zing went the strings of my heart / Stompin' at the savoy / All God's chillun got rhythm / Everybody sing / You made me love you / Over the rainbow / Sweet sixteen / Embraceable you / (Can this be) The end of the rainbow / I'm nobody's baby / Pretty girl milking her cow / It's a great day for the Irish / Sunny side of the street / For me and my gal / That old black magic / When you wore a tulip
CD __________ **HADCD 156**
Javelin / May '94 / Henry Hadaway / THE

ON THE RADIO 1936-1944
CD __________ **VJC 1043**
Vintage Jazz Classics / Feb '93 / ADA / Cadillac / CM / Direct

ONE AND ONLY, THE
This is the time of evening / While we were young / Carolina in the morning / Danny boy / Pretty girl milking her cow / Last night when we were young / April showers / Dirty hands, dirty face / Memories of you / Be myself / Me and my shadow / Little girl blue / I get the blues when it rains / Zing went the strings of my heart / I hadn't anyone till you / More than you know / That's entertainment / Down with love / Old devil moon / I've confessed to the breeze (I love you) / Hello bluebird / I could go on singing / Trolley song / Over the rainbow / Man that got away / When you're smiling / Day in, day out / I can't give you anything but love / When the sun comes out / Who cares (as long as you care for me) / Puttin' on the Ritz / How long has this been going on / Just you, just me / Hey look me over / Joey Joey Joey / Party's over / I wish you love / As long as he needs me / More / Battle hymn of the Republic / Maybe I'll come back (I will come back) / We could make such beautiful music / Bob White / Don't rain on my parade / Smile / Just in time / Make someone happy / Once in a lifetime / Lucky day / Judy at the palace / Shine on harvest moon / Some of these days / My man (mon homme) / I don't care / Stormy weather / You go to my head / Come rain or come shine / San Francisco / Swanee / Rock-a-bye your baby with a dixie melody / Happiness is a thing called Joe / It's a great day for the Irish / You'll never walk alone / I happen to like New York / You made me love you / For me and my gal / Why was I born / Do it again / Chicago / After you've gone
CD __________ **CDGFR 017**
Tring / Jun '92 / Tring

OVER THE RAINBOW
Over the rainbow / Stompin' at the Savoy / Swing Mr. Charlie / Zing went the strings of my heart / All God's chillun got rhythm / Everybody sing / You made me love you / It never rains but it pours / In between / Sweet sixteen / Embraceable you / (Can this be) the end of the rainbow / I'm nobody's baby / Wearing of the green / Friendship / I'm always chasing rainbows / Pretty girl milking her cow / It's a gret day for the Irish
CD __________ **CD 406**
Entertainers / Oct '96 / Target/BMG

OVER THE RAINBOW
Do it again / Too late now / When you're smiling / Rock-a-bye your baby / Johnny one note / Friendly star / They can't take that away from me / You belong to me / It's all for me / I'd like to hate myself in the morning / Give my regards to Broadway / Alexander's ragtime band / You go to my head / Over the rainbow
CD __________ **100732**
CMC / May '97 / BMG

PORTRAIT OF JUDY GARLAND, A
CD __________ **GALE 407**
Gallerie / May '97 / Disc / THE

SONGS FROM THE MOVIES
Somewhere over the rainbow / Come rain or come shine / Give my regards to Broadway / Carolina in the morning / Rock-a-bye baby
CD __________ **BSTCD 9110**
Best Compact Discs / May '92 / Complete/ Pinnacle

SWEET SIXTEEN
CD __________ **CD 23123**
All Star / Sep '92 / BMG

WHEN YOU'RE SMILING (Garland, Judy & Bing Crosby)
CD __________ **PARCD 003**
Parrot / Jan '96 / BMG / Jazz Music / THE / Wellard

YOU MADE ME LOVE YOU
Fascinating rhythm / (Can this be) the end of the rainbow / Buds won't bud / In between / Swing Mr. Charlie / How about you / Our love affair / Friendship / I'm just wild about Harry / Nobody's baby / I'm always chasing rainbows / Swanee / Dear Mr. Gable, you made me love you / All God's chillun got rhythm / FDR Jones / Cry baby cry / Sweet sixteen / Embraceable you / Zing went the strings of my heart / Over the rainbow
CD __________ **304592**
Hallmark / Jul '97 / Carlton

YOUNG JUDY GARLAND
Swanee / Friendship / Embraceable you / Pretty girl milking her cow / It's a great day for the Irish / Zing went the strings of my heart / Oceans apart / FDR Jones / I'm just wild about Harry / How about you / In between / Figaro / Sweet sixteen / Jitterbug / Over the rainbow / Dear Mr. Gable / You can't have everything / It never rains but it pours / Ten pins in the sky / Buds won't bud / Our love affair / I'm always chasing rainbows / Everybody sing / All God's chillun got rhythm / I'm nobody's baby
CD __________ **PASTCD 7014**
Flapper / Jun '93 / Pinnacle

ZING WENT THE STRINGS OF MY HEART
Trolley song / Boy next door / For me and my gal / Jitterbug / Pins in the sky / I'm just wild about Harry / I'm always chasing rainbows / Figaro / Zing went the strings of my heart / You've got me where you want me / It never rains but what it pours / Oceans apart / Buds won't bud / I'm nobody's baby / When you wore a tulip / Over the rainbow / Friendship / Embraceable you / Our love affair / Can this be the end of the rainbow / Meet me in St. Louis, Louis / Yah-ta-ta, yah-ta-ta
CD __________ **RAJCD 873**
Empress / Apr '96 / Koch

Garland, Peter

NANA & VICTORIO
CD __________ **AVAN 012**
Avant / Nov '92 / Cadillac / Harmonia Mundi

Garland, Red

ALL MORNIN' LONG (Garland, Red Trio)
CD __________ **OJCCD 293**
Original Jazz Classics / Feb '92 / Complete/Pinnacle / Jazz Music / Wellard

CAN'T SEE FOR LOOKIN'
I can't see for lookin' / Soon / Blackout / Castle rock
CD __________ **OJCCD 918**
Original Jazz Classics / May '97 / Complete/ Pinnacle / Jazz Music / Wellard

GROOVY (Garland, Red Trio)
CD __________ **OJCCD 61**
Original Jazz Classics / Nov '95 / Complete/Pinnacle / Jazz Music / Wellard

MANTECA (Garland, Red Trio)
Manteca / S'wonderful / Lady be good / Exactly like you / Mort's report / Portrait of Jenny
CD __________ **OJCCD 428**
Original Jazz Classics / May '97 / Complete/ Pinnacle / Jazz Music / Wellard

PC BLUES, THE
Ahmad's blues / Lost April / Why was I born / Tweedle dee dee / PC blues
CD __________ **OJCCD 898**
Original Jazz Classics / Sep '96 / Complete/ Pinnacle / Jazz Music / Wellard

RED GARLAND TRIO & EDDIE 'LOCKJAW' DAVIS (Garland, Red Trio & Eddie 'Lockjaw' Davis)
CD __________ **OJCCD 360**
Original Jazz Classics / Nov '95 / Complete/Pinnacle / Jazz Music / Wellard

RED IN BLUESVILLE
CD __________ **OJCCD 295**
Original Jazz Classics / Sep '93 / Complete/Pinnacle / Jazz Music / Wellard

ROJO (Red Garland Trio & Ray Barretto)
Rojo / We kiss in a shadow / Darling je vous aime beaucoup / Ralph J Gleason blues / You better go now / Mr. Wonderful
CD __________ **OJCCD 772**
Original Jazz Classics / Jun '94 / Complete/ Pinnacle / Jazz Music / Wellard

SOUL BURNIN'
On Green Dolphin Street / If you could see me now / Rocks in my bed / Soul burnin' / Blues in the night / Little bit of Basie
CD __________ **OJCCD 921**
Original Jazz Classics / Jun '97 / Complete/ Pinnacle / Jazz Music / Wellard

SOUL JUNCTION (Garland, Red Quintet & John Coltrane)
CD __________ **OJCCD 481**
Original Jazz Classics / Jun '95 / Complete/Pinnacle / Jazz Music / Wellard

Garland, Terry

ONE TO BLAME, THE
Good time blues / 'Round midnight / Stagger Lee / Phonograph blues / Nasty boogie woogie / Closer walk with thee / Rollin' and tumblin' / Going down slow / It'll be me / When a brother dies / All aboard
CD __________ **FIENDCD 775**
Demon / Feb '96 / Pinnacle

Garland, Tim

PLAYING TO THE MOON (Garland, Tim Quartet)
CD __________ **JHCD 047**
Ronnie Scott's Jazz House / Oct '96 / Cadillac / Jazz Music / New Note/Pinnacle / TKO Magnum

POINTS ON THE CURVE - NORTH SHIP SUITE
CD __________ **FMRCD 01**
Future / Oct '87 / ADA / Harmonia Mundi

TALES FROM THE SUN
CD __________ **EFZ 1014**
EFZ / Sep '95 / Vital/SAM

Garlaza, Faustino

MARIMBA DE GUATEMALA
Me lo dijo adela / Quien sera / Corazon de melon / Aquarla do Brasil (Brazil) / Tico tico / Adios / Besame mucho / Cachito / Quando calienta el sol / Solamente una vez / Noches de ronda / Perfida / Frenesi / Cielito lindo / Guadalajara / Vereda tropical / Maria Elena / Grandada / Autumn leaves (Las hojas muertas)
CD __________ **CD 12531**
Music Of The World / Jun '96 / ADA / Target/BMG

Garling, Tom

MAYNARD FERGUSON PRESENTS
Shrimp tales / Trinology / Bill Evans / I'm getting sentimental over you / Forging behind / Rainer's dream / How my heart sings / Ilene's dance / Here's that rainy day
CD __________ **CCD 47522**
Concord Jazz / May '97 / New Note/ Pinnacle

Garmarna

GARMARNA
CD __________ **MASS 54CD**
Mass Productions / Jul '95 / ADA

GUDS SPELEMAN
Herr mannelig / Vanner och Frander / Hailing fran Makedonien / Min man / Hilla lilla / Drew drusnaar/Idar som igar / Njaalkeme / Herr holger / Guds speleman
CD __________ **MASSCD 69**
Mass Productions / Mar '96 / ADA
CD __________ **XOUCD 113**
Xource / May '97 / ADA / Direct

LE MYSTERE DES CHANTS VIKINGS
CD __________ **7992107**
Arcade / Jul '97 / Discovery

VITTRAD
CD __________ **MASS 61CD**
Mass Productions / Jul '94 / ADA

Garner, Erroll

1950-1951
CD __________ **CD 53216**
Giants Of Jazz / Nov '95 / Cadillac / Jazz Music / Target/BMG

BODY AND SOUL
Way you look tonight / Body and soul / (Back home again in) Indiana / Honeysuckle rose / I'm in the mood for love / I can't get started (with you) / Play piano play / Undecided / You're blase / Sophisticated lady / Ain't she sweet / I didn't know / Fine and dandy / Robbin's nest / Please don't talk about me when I'm gone / It's the talk of the town / You're driving me crazy / Ja da / Summertime / I never knew
CD __________ **4679162**
Sony Music / '91 / Sony

CLASSICS 1940-1945
CD __________ **CLASSICS 873**
Classics / Apr '96 / Discovery / Jazz Music

CLASSICS 1944 VOL.1
CD __________ **CLASSICS 802**
Classics / Mar '95 / Discovery / Jazz Music

CLASSICS 1944 VOL.2
CD __________ **CLASSICS 818**
Classics / May '95 / Discovery / Jazz Music

CLASSICS 1944 VOL.3
CD __________ **CLASSICS 850**
Classics / Feb '96 / Discovery / Jazz Music

CLASSICS 1945-1946
CD __________ **CLASSICS 924**
Classics / Apr '97 / Discovery / Jazz Music

CLOSEUP IN SWING/A NEW KIND OF LOVE
Something to me / My silent love / All of me / St. Louis blues / Some of these days / I'm i the mood for love / El Papa Grande / Best things in life are free / Back in your own backyard / You've brought a new kind of love to me / Louise / Fashion interlude / Steve's song / Paris mist / Mimi / Theme from a new kind of love / In the park in Paree / Paris mist (waltz swing) / Tease
CD __________ **CD 83383**
Telarc Archive / Sep '97 / Conifer/BMG

CONCERT BY THE SEA
I'll remember April / Teach me tonight / Mambo Carmel / It's all right with me / Red top / April in Paris / They can't take that away from me / Where or when / Erroll's theme
CD __________ **4510422**
CBS / Oct '93 / Sony

DREAMSTREET/ONE WORLD CONCERT
Just one of those things / I'm gettin' sentimental over you / Blue Lou / Come rain or come shine / Lady is a tramp / Sweet Lorraine / Dreamstreet / Mambo Gotham / Oklahoma medley / Way you look tonight / Happiness is a thing called Joe / Sweet and lovely / Mack the knife / Lover come back / Misty / Dancing tambourine / Thanks for the memory
CD CD 83350
Telarc / Feb '96 / Conifer/BMG

ENCORES IN HI FI
Moonglow / Sophisticated Lady / Robbin's nest / Creme De Menthe / Humoresque / How high the moon / Fancy / Groovy day / Man I love
CD 4677072
Sony Jazz / Jan '95 / Sony

ERROLL GARNER (Garner, Erroll & Friends)
CD CD 53103
Giants Of Jazz / Mar '92 / Cadillac / Jazz Music / Target/BMG

ERROLL GARNER COLLECTION VOL.1 (Easy To Love)
Somebody stole my gal / September song / My blue heaven / For all we know / Easy to love / Somebody loves me / I hadn't anyone till you / Lover come back to me / As time goes by / Out of nowhere / Taking a chance on love
CD 8329942
EmArCy / Oct '93 / PolyGram

ERROLL GARNER COLLECTION VOL.2 (Dancing On The Ceiling)
It had to be you / Crazy rhythm / Our love is here to stay / Don't blame me / Dancing on the ceiling / Whispering / After you've gone / There will never be another you / Like home / What is this thing called love / Ain't misbehavin'
CD 8349352
EmArCy / Mar '93 / PolyGram

ERROLL GARNER COLLECTION VOL.3
Cecilia / Idaho / Margie / Stars fell on Alabama / Way down yonder in New Orleans / Louise / Peg o' my heart / Heart / Kittin on the keys / Ramona / My gal Sal / I've got the world on a string / Dinah / Too marvellous for words / California here I come
CD 8424192
EmArCy / Mar '93 / PolyGram

ERROLL GARNER COLLECTION VOL.4 & 5 (Solo Time/2CD Set)
Liza / It might as well be Spring / If I could be with you / Flamingo / In a little Spanish town / I'll never smile again / That old black magic / Slow boat to China / Indian summer / These foolish things / Man I love / Ol' man river / I'll get by / April in Paris / Last time I saw Paris / Sleepy lagoon / Cottage for sale / Coquette / I only have eyes for you / I want to be loved / World is waiting / For the sunrise / Our waltz / I can't escape from you / Thanks for the memory
CD Set 5118212
EmArCy / Oct '93 / PolyGram

ERROLL GARNER PLAYS GERSHWIN AND KERN
Strike up the band / Love walked in / I got rhythm / Someone to watch over me / Foggy day / Nice work if you can get it / Lovely to look at / Can't help lovin' dat man / Only make believe / Ol' man river / Dearly beloved / Why do I love you / Fine romance
CD 8262242
EmArCy / Feb '93 / PolyGram

GITANES - JAZZ 'ROUND MIDNIGHT
I've got you under my skin / Don't blame me / I can't get started (With you) / No moon / I let a song go out of my heart / Again / Memories of you / Jitterbug waltz / Misty / I've got the world on a string / Exactly like you / All my loves are you / Don't worry 'bout me / Part time blues / There's a small hotel / Over the rainbow
CD 8461912
Verve / Mar '93 / PolyGram

HUMORESQUE 1953-1956
Humoresque / Moonglow / In a mellow tone / Don't worry 'bout me / Exactly like you / Cremy de menthe (Dreamy) / Oh lady be good / I've got the world on a string / Rosalie / There's a small hotel / Mean to me / Easy to love / All of a sudden / You are my sunshine / Part time blues / I wanna be a rug cutter / 7-11 Jump / Alexander's ragtime band
CD CD 53226
Giants Of Jazz / Jun '96 / Cadillac / Jazz Music / Target/BMG

JAZZ MASTERS
I wanna be a rug cutter / Misty / Smooth one / Love in bloom / (All of a sudden) My heart sings / Don't be that way / Jump / St. James infirmary / Don't worry 'bout me / Is you is or is you ain't my baby / Part time blues / Yesterdays / Oh lady be good / Fandango / I've got the world on a string
CD 5181972
Verve / Feb '94 / PolyGram

JAZZ PORTRAITS
Misty / Play piano play / Pastel / Trio / Turquoise / Frankie and Johnny Fantasy / Impressions / This can't be love / Moonglow / I can't give you anything but love / Blue and sentimental / Way you look tonight / She's funny that way / I can't believe that you're in love with me / Cool blues / Bird's nest / Frantonality / Man I love
CD CD 14508
Jazz Portraits / May '94 / Jazz Music

LIVE AT CARMEL, CALIFORNIA SEPT. 1955
CD CD 53034
Giants Of Jazz / Jan '89 / Cadillac / Jazz Music / Target/BMG

LIVE IN LA
CD DM 15006
DMA Jazz / Jul '96 / Jazz Music

LONG AGO AND FAR AWAY
When Johnny comes marching home / It could happen to you / I don't know why / It could happen to you / My heart stood still / When you're smiling / Long ago and far away / Poor butterfly / Spring is here / Petite waltz / Petite waltz bounce / Lover / How high the moon / People will say we're in love / Laura / I cover the waterfront / Penthouse serenade
CD 4606142
Sony Jazz / Jan '95 / Sony

MAGICIAN & GERSHWIN & KERN
Close to you / It gets better every time / Someone to watch over me / Nightwind / One good turn / Watch what happens / Yesterdays / I only have eyes for you / Muncho gusto / Strike up the band / Love walked in / I got rhythm / Foggy day / Nice work if you can get it / Lovely to look at / Can't help lovin' dat man / Only make believe / Ol' man river / Dearly beloved / Why do I love you / Fine romance
CD CD 83337
Telarc / Apr '95 / Conifer/BMG

MAMBO MOVES GARNER
Mambo Garner / Night and day / Mambo blues / Old black magic Cherokee / Sweet and lovely / Russian lullaby / Begin the beguine / Mambo nights / Sweet Sue / Imagination
CD 8349092
Mercury / Oct '93 / PolyGram

MISTY
Misty / Very thought of you / It might as well be spring / Dreamy / I didn't know what time it was / Moment's delight / On the street where you live / Other voices / This is always / Solitaire / St. Louis blues / Summertime / 'S wonderful / Easy to love / Way you look tonight / I'm in the mood for love
CD CD 56019
Jazz Roots / Aug '94 / Target/BMG

MOONGLOW
CD CDSGP 098
Prestige / May '94 / Else / Total/BMG
CD TCD 1010
Tradition / Feb '96 / ADA / Vital

NOW PLAYING - A NIGHT AT THE MOVIES/UP IN ERROLL'S ROOM
You made me love you / As time goes by / Sonny boy / Charmaine / I found a million dollar baby / I'll get by / Three o'clock in the morning / Stella by starlight / Jeannine I dream of lilac time / Just a gigolo / How deep is the ocean / It's only a paper moon / Newsreel tag / Watermelon man / It's the talk of the town / Groovin' high / Girl from Ipanema / Coffee song / Cheek to cheek / Up in Erroll's room / Lot of living to do / I got rhythm
CD CD 83378
Telarc Archive / Sep '96 / Conifer/BMG

ORIGINAL MISTY, THE
Misty / I've got the world on a string / 7-11 jump / Don't worry 'bout me / You are my sunshine / Part time blues / All of a sudden / In a mellow tone / There's a small hotel / I wanna be a rug cutter / Exactly like you / Oh lady be good
CD 8349102
Mercury / Feb '94 / PolyGram

OVERTURE TO DAWN
CD LEJAZZCD 49
Le Jazz / Nov '95 / Cadillac / Koch

PARIS IMPRESSIONS
CD 4756242
Sony Jazz / Jan '95 / Sony

PLAY PIANO PLAY 1950-1953 (Garner, Erroll Trio)
Way you look tonight / Sophisticated lady / Fine and Dandy / Petite waltz bounce / Body and soul / I never knew / Please don't talk about me when I'm gone / Play, piano, play / Ain't she sweet / Groovy day / Frenesi / Robbin's nest / St. Louis blues / S'wonderful / You're driving me crazy / Summertime / Undecided / It's the talk of the town / You're blase / I didn't know / Ja-da
CD CD 53221
Giants Of Jazz / May '97 / Cadillac / Jazz Music / Target/BMG

PLAYS GERSHWIN AND KERN
Strike up the band / Love walked in / I got rhythm / Someone to watch over me / Foggy day / Nice work if you can get it / Lovely to look at / Can't help lovin' dat man / Only make believe / Ol' man river / Dearly beloved / Why do I love you / Fine romance
CD 8262242
Mercury / Jun '86 / PolyGram

SOLILOQUY - AT THE PIANO
Caravan / There is no greater love / Avalon / Lullaby of Birdland / Memories of you / Will you still be mine / You'd be so nice to come home to / You's be so nice to come home to / No more time / I surrender dear / If I had you / Don't take your love from me
CD 4656312
Sony Jazz / Jan '95 / Sony

SOLITAIRE
I'll never smile again / Then you've never been blue / It's the talk of the town / Solitaire / Cottage for sale / That old feeling / Over the rainbow / Yesterdays / Who / When a gypsy makes his violin cry / Salud segovia
CD 5182792
Mercury / May '94 / PolyGram

THAT'S MY KICK/GEMINI
That's my kick / Shadow of your smile / Like it is / It ain't necessarily so / Autumn leaves / Blue moon / More / Gaslight / Nervous waltz / Passing through / Afinidad / How high the moon / It could happen to you / Gemini / When a gypsy makes his violin cry / Tea for two / Something / Eldorado / These foolish things
CD CD 83332
Telarc / Sep '94 / Conifer/BMG

THIS IS JAZZ
Lover / It's the talk of the town / When you're smiling / Laura / Dancing in the dark / How high the moon / Easy to love / Moonglow / Lullabye of Birdland / Poor butterfly / If I had you / My heart stood still / Love for sale / Dreamy / St. Louis blues
CD CK 64968
Sony Jazz / Oct '96 / Sony

Garner, Larry

DOUBLE DUES
Scared of you / No free rides / Buster / Shut it down / Dreaming again / Taxman / Broke bluesman / Tale spreaders / California sister / Past 23
CD JSPCD 273
JSP / Jan '97 / ADA / Cadillac / Direct / Hot Shot / Target/BMG

TOO BLUES
CD JSP 249CD
JSP / May '93 / ADA / Cadillac / Direct / Hot Shot / Target/BMG

Garner, Lynn

KEEP THE CIRCLE TURNING
CD DLD 1063
Dance & Listen / Dec '95 / Savoy / Target/BMG

Garnet Silk

GARNET SILK & THE DJ'S RULE THING
CD RNCD 2035
Rhino / Oct '93 / Grapevine/PolyGram / Jet Star

GARNET SILK GOLD
CD CRCD 20
Charm / Aug '93 / Jet Star

IT'S GROWING
CD NWSCD 1
New Sound / Mar '93 / Jet Star
CD VYDCD 4
Vine Yard / Sep '95 / Grapevine/PolyGram

LORD WATCH OVER OUR SHOULDERS
CD GRELCD 219
Greensleeves / Aug '95 / Jet Star / SRD

LOVE IS THE ANSWER
CD SCCD 3
Steely & Cleevie / Nov '94 / Jet Star

NOTHING CAN DIVIDE US
CD CRCD 38
Charm / Apr '95 / Jet Star

REGGAE MAX
CD JSRNCD 4
Jet Star / Jun '96 / Jet Star

Garnett, Carlos

BLACK LOVE
Black love / Ebonesque / Banks of the Nile / Mother of the future / Taurus Woman
CD MCD 5040
Muse / Aug '96 / New Note/Pinnacle

FUEGO EN MI ALMA (FIRE IN MY SOUL)
Fuego en mi alma / Catch me if you can / Eternal justice / Fuego en mi alma / Little sunflower / Urd14me / Love thy neighbor / Mystic moon / Shalome
CD HCD 7001
High Note / Apr '97 / New Note/Pinnacle

Garnier, Laurent

30
Deep sea diving / Sweet mellow d / Crispy bacon / Formax / Hoe / Mid summer night / Kall it / La minute du repondeur le plus casse-couilles / Theme from Larry's dub / Feel the fire / Flashback / I funk up / Asterix question mark asterix / Le voyage de Simone / Last winter in Alaska
CD F 063CD
CD F 063CDLTD
F-Communications / Mar '97 / Prime / Vital

LABORATOIRE MIX (2CD Set) (Various Artists)
Jungle: *Jungle Wonz* / Moon Walk: *Funky People* / Help me: *Green Velvet* / People everyday (we just wanna be free): *Holmes, Braxton* / Basemental: *AJ Sound* / Ruhrschnellweg: *Broccoli Brothers* / Sides of iron: *Chaser* / Tomorrow is the first day: *6K* / You gotta believe: *FRD* / Takks: *Landstrumm, Neal* / House-O-matic: *DJ Deeon* / Ambulance: *Armani, Robert* / Speaker: *Speaker* / Gas mask: *Brown, Steven* / Bleu: *Scan X* / Flash: *Kosmic Messenger* / XTC: *K-Hand* / Bytes accapellas: *Aux 88* / Amazon: *World 2 World* / Force: *Garnier, Laurent* / Die Kosmischen Kuriere: *3MB & Juan Atkins* / Let it go: *Tyree* / Wipe: *Teste* / All the way in: *Big Foot Part 2* / Conflexx: *Ratio* / Mind control music: *Club MCM* / Reverting: *Purpose Maker* / Te qua: *Timeblind* / Man-Me: *DJ Shufflemaster* / Essit musique: *Essit Musique* / Nervous acid: *Konders, Bobby* / Acid Eiffel: *Choice* / Beyond the dance: *Rhythim Is Rhythim* / Icct Hedral: *Aphex Twin*
CD Set REACTCD 087
React / Oct '96 / Arabesque / Prime / Vital

SHOT IN THE DARK
Shapes under water / Astral dreams / Bouncing metal / Rising spirit / Harmonic grooves / Force / Geometric world / 022 / Rex attitude / Raw cut / Track for Mike / Silver string
CD F 014CD
F-Communications / Oct '94 / Prime / Vital

Garrett, Amos

AMOSBEHAVIN'
CD SP 1189CD
Stony Plain / Oct '93 / ADA / CM / Direct

BURIED ALIVE IN THE BLUES
Home in my shoes / Move on down the line / Don't tell me / Smack dab in the middle / Ha ha in the daytime / Stanley Street / Hair of the dog / Too many rivers / Buried alive in the blues / What a fool I was / Lost love / All my money / Bert's boogie / Got to get you off my mind
CD VDCD 110
Voodoo / Jun '96 / Direct

I MAKE MY HOME IN MY SHOES
CD SP 1132CD
Stony Plain / Oct '93 / ADA / CM / Direct

LIVE IN JAPAN (Garrett, Amos & Doug Sahm)
CD FM 1008CD
Marilyn / Jul '92 / Pinnacle

OFF THE FLOOR LIVE
CD VDCD 113
Voodoo / Jun '96 / Direct

RETURN OF THE FORMERLY BROTHERS, THE (Garrett, Amos/Doug Sahm/Gene Taylor)
Smack dab in the middle: *Formerly Brothers* / Big mamou: *Formerly Brothers* / Teardrops on your letter: *Formerly Brothers* / Drunk: *Formerly Brothers* / Don't tell me: *Formerly Brothers* / Coming back home: *Formerly Brothers* / Sure is a good thing: *Formerly Brothers* / Amarillo highway: *Formerly Brothers* / Banks of the old Ponchartrain: *Formerly Brothers* / Just like a woman: *Formerly Brothers* / Gene's boogie: *Formerly Brothers* / Queen of the Okanagan: *Formerly Brothers*
CD RCD 10127
Rykodisc / Aug '92 / ADA / Vital

THIRD MAN IN
CD SP 1179CD
Stony Plain / Oct '93 / ADA / CM / Direct

Garrett, Vernon

CAUGHT IN THE CROSSFIRE
Lonely, lonely nights / Bottom line / Drifting apart / Love me right / If you can't help me baby / Somebody done messed up / Don't make me pay for his mistakes / Walkin' the back streets and crying / Caught in the crossfire
CD ICH 1128CD
Ichiban / Oct '93 / Direct / Koch

TOO HIP TO BE HAPPY
Are you the one / You just call me / You don't know nothin' about love / Too hip to be happy / Doors of my heart / Special kind of lady / She's a burgular / I'll be doggone / Gonna have to use my head / Li'l black woman
CD ICH 1169CD
Ichiban / May '94 / Direct / Koch

Garrick, David

ALL THE HITS PLUS MORE
CD CDSGP 0261
Prestige / May '96 / Else / Total/BMG

Garrick, Michael

FOR LOVE OF DUKE AND RONNIE
Webster's mood / Samba changes / Swallows on the water / StormFor love of Duke / Two trumpets / Kyrie / Salvation march / Water patterns / Blue dusk girl / Trick of the light or grandma's spells / Shadowplay / And Ronnie; The open question
CD ______ **JAZA 4**
Jazz Academy / Jul '97 / Cadillac

LADY IN WAITING, A (Garrick, Michael Trio)
CD ______ **JAZA 1**
Jazz Academy / Oct '94 / Cadillac

METEORS CLOSE AT HAND (2CD Set)
CD ______ **JAZA 2**
Jazz Academy / Dec '95 / Cadillac

Garrido, David

EL SONIDO DEL TIEMPO
CD ______ **20051CD**
Sonifolk / Dec '94 / ADA / CM

Garrido, Lolita

LA VOL DEL BOLERO EN ESPANA VOL.1
CD ______ **ALCD 041**
Alma Latina / Jul '97 / Discovery

LA VOL DEL BOLERO EN ESPANA VOL.2
CD ______ **ALCD 043**
Alma Latina / Jul '97 / Discovery

Garside, Melanie

FOSSIL
Big white room / Broken fingers / She knows / Has and to do / Stay / Sick on words / Hide / Learn to learn / Smile / Besides / Centered sideways
CD ______ **ECHCD 006**
Echo / May '96 / EMI / Vital

Garside, Robin

RAGMAN'S TRUMPET, THE
CD ______ **GET 2CD**
Get / Aug '94 / ADA

Garson, Michael

GERSHWIN FANTASIA, A
CD ______ **RR 84CD**
Reference Recordings / May '96 / Jazz Music / May Audio

OXFORD SESSIONS VOL.1
CD ______ **RR 37CD**
Reference Recordings / May '96 / Jazz Music / May Audio

OXFORD SESSIONS VOL.2
CD ______ **RR 53CD**
Reference Recordings / May '96 / Jazz Music / May Audio

REFLECTIONS (Garson, Michael & Jim Walker)
Portrait of a friend / Love / First song / Waltz of the Arts / Ethereal / Yearnings / Syrinx / Pied Piper / Park / Magic spell / Homecoming / You're one of a kind / Reflections / Reason / Admiration
CD ______ **RR 18CD**
Reference Recordings / May '96 / Jazz Music / May Audio

SERENDIPITY
Serendipity / Lady / Autumn leaves / I should care / Spirit of play / Trio blues / My romance / Promise / Tam's jam / Searching / My one and only love
CD ______ **RR 20CD**
Reference Recordings / May '96 / Jazz Music / May Audio

Gary D

D TRANCE VOL.3 (3CD Set) (Various Artists)
CD Set ______ **PIAS 55600526**
DJ's Present / Oct '96 / Plastic Head

D TRANCE VOL.4 (3CD Set) (Various Artists)
CD Set ______ **PIAS 556200925**
DJ's Present / Dec '96 / Plastic Head

D-TRANCE VOL.5 (3CD Set)
CD Set ______ **PIAS 556201325**
DJ's Present / Apr '97 / Plastic Head

Gary, John

SINGS COLE PORTER
CD ______ **ACD 274**
Audiophile / Apr '95 / Jazz Music

Gary, Thomas

KOLD KAGE, THE
Threshold / Gate of faces / Intellect / Infernal machine / Divide / Peace of the korridor / First strike / Beyond the fall of night / Kold kage / Kulture bandits
CD ______ **8491512**
jMT / Oct '91 / PolyGram

Garzon, Armando

BOLEROS (Garzon, Armando & Quinteto Oriente)
Dos gardenias / Pensamiento / Sublime ilusion / Reclamo mistico / Quiereme mucho / Si llego a besarte / Mienteme mas / Y tu que has hecho / Contigo en la distancia / La puerta / Juramento / Chan chan / Se te olvida / Si me pudieras querer
CD ______ **CORA 131**
Corason / Oct '96 / ADA / CM / Direct

Garzone, George

FOUR'S & TWO'S
Four's and two's / Have you met Miss Jones / In memory of Lauren Nichols / One time / To my papa / Snow place like home / Mingus that I knew / Tutti Italiani / Hey open up / In a sentimental mood
CD ______ **NYC 60242**
NYC / Sep '96 / New Note/Pinnacle

Gas 0095

EMIT 0095
CD ______ **EMIT 0095**
Time Recordings / Feb '95 / Pinnacle

Gas Huffer

BEER DRINKING
CD ______ **EFA 11396D**
Musical Tragedies / Apr '93 / SRD

INHUMAN ORDEAL OF SPECIAL AGENT GAS HUFFER, THE
CD ______ **864592**
Epitaph / Feb '96 / Pinnacle / Plastic Head

INTERGRITY TECHNOLOGY AND SERVICE
CD ______ **MT 181CD**
Burning Heart / Sep '95 / Plastic Head

MTI
CD ______ **E 11373 CD**
Musical Tragedies / Jan '93 / SRD

ONE INCH MASTERS
CD ______ **E 864392**
Epitaph / Aug '94 / Pinnacle / Plastic Head

Gas Mark 5

GUIZERS
CD ______ **REGULO 3**
Regulo / Oct '94 / ADA

JUMP
CD ______ **REGULO 2**
Regulo / Oct '94 / ADA

Gascoyne, Geoff

VOICES OF SPRING
Breakfast with Jr / Pao de acucar / John Brown's body / Pass the pepper / Voices of Spring / Black Nile / On the street where you live / Spring break / To itch his own / Tyrone / If it's magic
CD ______ **JITCD 9605**
Jazzizit / Sep '96 / New Note/Pinnacle

Gaskin

END OF THE WORLD/NO WAY OUT
CD ______ **CDMETAL 6**
British Steel / Feb '97 / Cargo / Pinnacle / Plastic Head

Gaskins, Ray

CAN'T STOP
Can't stop / Summertime / Feel the fire / Crystal clear / Beans on toast / Love changes / Who's been getting your love / Weak / Tell me
CD ______ **LIP 89462**
Lipstick / Oct '96 / Vital/SAM

REACH
Reach / Down home / Lovin' factor / Never say die / Knee deep / Lullabye / Blues "R" gonna' get you / Song for my son / No one has wanted more / I want to talk about God
CD ______ **MTCD 1006**
MT / Apr '96 / Grapevine/PolyGram / New Note/Pinnacle

SHADY LANE
Just imagine me / Who's right, who's wrong / Outstanding / Yo funky Mama / Chilli funk / We had to say goodbye / Shady lane / Mo' chicken / Again and again / Spain (I can recall) / PY / Mo chicken
CD ______ **LIPHOT 89532**
Lipstick Hot / May '97 / New Note/BMG

SOUL CRUSADE
Come back to me / London strut / Soul crusade / Fall / About the music / Ain't easy / I know it's you / Kissing you / All about love / Easy sax
CD ______ **MTCD 1002**
MT / May '96 / Grapevine/PolyGram / New Note/Pinnacle

Gaslini, Giorgio

AYLER'S WINGS
CD ______ **1212702**
Soul Note / Apr '91 / Cadillac / Harmonia Mundi / Wellard

GASLINI PLAYS MONK
CD ______ **1210202**
Soul Note / May '92 / Cadillac / Harmonia Mundi / Wellard

LAMPI (LIGHTNINGS)
CD ______ **1212902**
Soul Note / May '94 / Cadillac / Harmonia Mundi / Wellard

SCHUMANN REFLECTIONS
Von fremden landern und menschen / Kuriose geschichte / Hasche-mann / Schmann reflections / Bittendes kind / Gluckes genius / Wichtige begebenheit / Traumerei / Am kamin / Ritter vom steckenpferd / Fast zu ernst / Furchtenmachen / Kind im einschlummern / De ditcher spricht
CD ______ **1211202**
Soul Note / May '92 / Cadillac / Harmonia Mundi / Wellard

Gasparyan, Djivan

I WILL NOT BE SAD IN THIS WORLD
Cool wind is blowing / Brother hunter / Look here, my dear / I will not be sad in this world / Little flower garden / Your strong mind / Ploughman / Dle Yaman
CD ______ **ASCD 06**
All Saints / Mar '96 / Discovery / Vital

MOON SHINES AT NIGHT
Lovely spring / Sayat nova / 7th December 1988 / Don't make me cry / You have to come back to me / Tonight / They took my love away / Moon shines at night / Apricot tree / Mother of mine
CD ______ **ASCD 016**
All Saints / Sep '93 / Discovery / Vital

Gaster, Marvin

UNCLE HENRY'S FAVORITES
CD ______ **ROUCD 382**
Rounder / May '96 / ADA / CM / Direct

Gastr Del Sol

CROOKT, CRACKT OR FLY
CD ______ **DC 43CD**
Drag City / Dec '96 / Cargo / Greyhound

SERPENTINE SIMILAR
CD ______ **DEX 13CD**
Dexter's Cigar / Jun '97 / Cargo

UPGRADE AND AFTERLIFE
CD ______ **DC 90CD**
Drag City / Dec '96 / Cargo / Greyhound

Gate

MONOLAKE
CD ______ **KRYPTON 36**
Table Of The Elements / Mar '97 / Cargo

Gatecrashers

TWENTY GOOD REASONS
CD ______ **PT 603001**
Part / Jun '96 / Nervous

Gates, David

FIRST ALBUM
CD ______ **7559609102**
Elektra / Jan '96 / Warner Music

GOODBYE GIRL
Goodbye girl / Took the last train / Overnight sensation / California lady / Ann / Drifter / He don't know how to love you / Clouds suite / Lorilee / Part time love / Sunday rider / Never let her go
CD ______ **7559611722**
Elektra / Jan '96 / Warner Music

Gates Of Ishtar

BLOODRED PATH
CD ______ **SP 1031CD**
Spinefarm / Jun '96 / Plastic Head

DAWN OF FLAMES, THE
CD ______ **IR 027CD**
Cyclone Empire / May '97 / Plastic Head

Gates, Rev. J.M.

REV. J.M. GATES VOL.2 1926
CD ______ **DOCD 5432**
Document / Jul '96 / ADA / Hot Shot / Jazz Music

REV. J.M. GATES VOL.3 1926
CD ______ **DOCD 5433**
Document / Jul '96 / ADA / Hot Shot / Jazz Music

REV. J.M. GATES VOL.4 1926
CD ______ **DOCD 5442**
Document / May '96 / ADA / Hot Shot / Jazz Music

REV. J.M. GATES VOL.5 1927
CD ______ **DOCD 5449**
Document / May '96 / ADA / Hot Shot / Jazz Music

REV. J.M. GATES VOL.6 1928-1929
CD ______ **DOCD 5457**
Document / Jun '96 / ADA / Hot Shot / Jazz Music

REV. J.M. GATES VOL.7 1929-1930
CD ______ **DOCD 5469**
Document / Jul '96 / ADA / Hot Shot / Jazz Music

REV. J.M. GATES VOL.8 1930-1934
CD ______ **DOCD 5483**
Document / Nov '96 / ADA / Hot Shot / Jazz Music

REV. J.M. GATES VOL.9 1934-1941
CD ______ **DOCD 5484**
Document / Nov '96 / ADA / Hot Shot / Jazz Music

Gateway Jazz Band

IN THE MOMENT
CD ______ **5293462**
ECM / Sep '96 / New Note/Pinnacle

Gateway Trio

HOMECOMING
Homecoming / Waltz new / Modern times / Calypso falto / Short cut / How's never / In your arms / 7th D / Oneness
CD ______ **5276372**
ECM / Oct '95 / New Note/Pinnacle

Gathering

ADRENALINE
CD ______ **CM 77135CD**
Century Media / May '96 / Plastic Head

ALMOST A DANCE
CD ______ **FDN 2008CD**
Foundation 2000 / Dec '93 / Plastic Head

ALWAYS
CD ______ **FDN 2004CD**
Foundation 2000 / Jul '92 / Plastic Head

MANDYLION
CD ______ **CM 77098**
Century Media / Sep '95 / Plastic Head

NIGHT TIME BIRDS
CD ______ **CM 77168CD**
Century Media / Jun '97 / Plastic Head

Gatica, Lucho

HISTORIA DE UN AMOR
CD ______ **CD 62035**
Saludos Amigos / Apr '94 / Target/BMG

Gattis, Keith

KEITH GATTIS
CD ______ **07863668342**
RCA / Jun '96 / BMG

Gatto, Roberto

ASK (Gatto, Roberto & John Scofield)
Ask / There will never be another you / 100 flowers waltz / Tango's time / Blue Christmas / Of what
CD ______ **INAK 8802CD**
In Akustik / Jul '97 / Direct / TKO Magnum

NOTES (Gatto, Roberto & Michael Brecker)
Steggae / Town Street / Green ice blue eyes / Can you make it / Long step / First blues / Pedals / La coda del Gatto
CD ______ **INAK 8805CD**
In Akustik / Jul '97 / Direct / TKO Magnum

Gatton, Danny

RELENTLESS (Gatton, Danny & Joey DeFrancesco)
CD ______ **BIGMO 2023**
Big Mo / Aug '94 / ADA / Direct

Gaudreau, Jimmy

LIVE IN HOLLAND (Gaudreau, Jimmy Bluegrass Unit)
CD ______ **SCR 21**
Strictly Country / Jul '95 / ADA / Direct

Gaughan, Dick

COPPERS AND BRASS (Scots & Irish Dance Music On Guitar)
Coppers and brass / Gander in the pratie hole / O'Keefe's / Foxhunter's / Flowing tide / Fairies hornpipe / Oak tree / Music in the glen / Planxty Johnson / Gurty's frolics / Spey in spate / Hurricane / Alan MacPherson of Mosspark / Jig of slurs / Thrush in the storm / Flogging reel pipes / Ask my father / Lads of Laois / Connaught heifers / Bird in the bush / Boy in the gap / MacMahon's reel / Strike the gay harp / Shores of Lough Gowna / Jack broke da prison door / Donald blue / Wha'll dance wi' wattie
CD ______ **GLCD 3064**
Green Linnet / Oct '93 / ADA / CM / Direct / Highlander / Roots

GAUGHAN
Bonnie Jeannie O'Bethelnie / Bonnie lass among the heather / Crooked Jack / Recruited colliers / Pound a week rise / My Donald / Willie o' Winsbury / Such a parcel of rogues in a nation / Gillie Mor
CD ______ **TSCD 384**
Topic / Nov '90 / ADA / CM / Direct

PARALLEL LINES (Gaughan, Dick & Andy Irvine)
CD _______ CDTUT 724007
Wundertute / Oct '89 / ADA / CM / Duncans

SAIL ON
Land of the North Wind / Son of man / Ruby Tuesday / Waist deep in the big muddy / No cause for alarm / 51st (Highland) Division's farewell to Sicily / No gods and precious few heroes / Geronimo's cadillac / 1952 Vincent black lightning / Sail on / Freedom come all ye
CD _______ CDTRAX 109
Greentrax / Jun '96 / ADA / Direct / Duncans / Highlander

SONGS OF EWAN MACCOLL, THE (Gaughan, Dick & Dave Burland/Tony Capstick)
Ballad of accounting / Moving on song / Jamie Foyers / Freeborn man / Manchester rambler / Schooldays end / Thirty foot trailer / Big hewer / First time ever I saw your face
CD _______ CROCD 215
Black Crow / Jul '97 / CM / Roots

WOODY LIVES
Hard travellin' / Vigilante man / deportees / Do re mi / Tom Joad / This land is your land / Pretty boy Floyd / Philadelphia lawyer / Pastures of plenty / Will you miss me
CD _______ CROCD 217
Black Crow / Jun '88 / CM / Roots

Gaunt

I CAN SEE YOUR MOM FROM HERE
CD _______ EFACD 115872
Crypt / Nov '94 / Shellshock/Disc

YEAH, ME TOO
CD _______ ARRCD 66009
Amphetamine Reptile / Dec '95 / Plastic Head

Gauthe, Jacques

CASSOULET STOMP (Gauthe, Jacques & His Creole Rice Jazzband)
CD _______ SOSCD 1170
Stomp Off / Feb '89 / Jazz Music / Wellard

CLARINET SERENADERS (Gauthe, Jacques & Alain Marquet Clarinet Serenaders)
CD _______ SOSCD 1216
Stomp Off / Oct '92 / Jazz Music / Wellard

JACQUES GAUTHE & CREOLE RICE YERBA BUENA JAZZBAND
CD _______ SOSCD 1256
Stomp Off / Apr '94 / Jazz Music / Wellard

JACQUES GAUTHE & HIS CREOLE RICE JAZZ BAND OF NEW ORLEANS
CD _______ BCD 331
GHB / Jun '96 / Jazz Music

Gauty, Lys

1932-33
CD _______ 122
Chansophone / Nov '92 / Discovery

Gauze

COLLECTION, THE
CD _______ JPC 02
Japan Punk Collection / Nov '96 / Cargo

Gavin, Frankie

BEST OF FRANKIE GAVIN, THE
CD _______ RTE 187CD
RTE / Dec '95 / ADA / Koch

FRANKIE GAVIN & ALEC FINN (Gavin, Frankie & Alec Finn)
CD _______ SHANCD 34009
Shanachie / Jan '95 / ADA / Greensleeves / Koch

FRANKIE GOES TO TOWN
CD _______ GLCD 3051
Green Linnet / Oct '93 / ADA / CM / Direct / Highlander / Roots

IRELAND
CD _______ C 570400
Ocora / Mar '97 / ADA / Harmonia Mundi

IRISH CHRISTMAS
CD _______ BK 003CD
Bee's Knees / Jan '94 / ADA / CM / Roots

IRLANDE (Gavin, Frankie & Arty McGlynn)
CD _______ C 560021CD
Oscora / Apr '94 / ADA

TRIBUTE TO JOE COOLEY (Gavin, Frankie & Paul Brock)
CD _______ CEFCD 115
Gael Linn / Jan '94 / ADA / CM / Direct / Grapevine/PolyGram / Roots

UP AND AWAY
CD _______ CEFCD 103
Gael Linn / Jan '94 / ADA / CM / Direct / Grapevine/PolyGram / Roots

Gavioli Fair Organ

TWELFTH STREET RAG
CD _______ GRCD 63
Grasmere / May '94 / Highlander / Savoy / Target/BMG

Gay Gordon

ULTIMATE PARTY ALBUM (Gay Gordon & The Mince Pies)
Happy Birthday to you / 21 today / Celebration / Congratulations / Happy birthday / Birthday medley / Wedding / Wedding march / Wedding march / Conga / Knees up Mother Brown / Hokey cokey / Charleston / Glenn Miller megamix / Essential wally party medley / Anniversary waltz / Last waltz / Agadoo / Can can / Birdie song / Simple Simon says / Big Ben strikes 12 / Auld lang syne / National anthem
CD _______ XMAS 007
Tring / Nov '96 / Tring

Gay, Noel

SONGS OF NOEL GAY, THE
CD _______ PASTCD 7035
Flapper / Jan '95 / Pinnacle

Gayden, Mac

NIRVANA BLUES
CD _______ WH 3305CD
Winter Harvest / Apr '96 / ADA / Direct

Gaye, Marvin

ANTHOLOGY
CD _______ 5301812
Motown / Jan '92 / PolyGram

BEST OF MARVIN GAYE
CD _______ 5302922
Motown / Mar '94 / PolyGram

DIANA & MARVIN (Gaye, Marvin & Diana Ross)
You are everything / Love twins / Don't knock my love / You're a special part of me / Pledging my love / Just say just say / Stop, look, listen (to your heart) / I'm falling in love with you / My mistake (was to love you) / Include me in your life
CD _______ 5300482
Motown / Jan '93 / PolyGram

DISTANT LOVER
Third World girl / I heard it through the grapevine / Come get to this / Let's get it on / God is my friend / What's going on / Inner city blues / Joy / Ain't nothing like the real thing / Heaven must have sent you / If this world were mine / Rockin' after midnight / Distant lover / Sexual healing
CD _______ MU 3003
Musketeer / Oct '92 / Disc

DISTANT LOVER
CD _______ HADCD 165
Javelin / May '94 / Henry Hadaway / THE

FOR THE VERY LAST TIME
I heard it through the grapevine / Come get to this / Let's get it on / God is love / What's going on / Inner city blues / Joy / Ain't nothing like the real thing / Your precious love / If this world were mine / Rockin' after midnight / Distant lover / Percussian suite / Sexual healing
CD _______ MDCD 1
MMG Video / Jan '94 / TKO Magnum

HERE, MY DEAR
Here my dear / I met a little girl / When did you stop loving me, when did I stop loving you / Anger / Funky space reincarnation / You can leave but it's goin' to cost you / Falling in love again / Is that enough / Everybody needs love / Time to get it together / Sparrow / Anna's song
CD _______ 5302532
Motown / Mar '96 / PolyGram

I WANT YOU
I want you / Come live with me angel / Angel / After the dance / Feel all my love inside / I wanna be where you are / All the way round / Since I had you / Soon I'll be loving you again / I want you (intro jam) / After the dance (plus instrumental)
CD _______ 5300212
Motown / Jul '94 / PolyGram

IN CONCERT
I heard it through the grapevine / Come get to this / Let's get it on / God is love / What's going on / Inner city blues (make me wanna holler) / Joy / Medley / Rockin' after midnight / Distant lover / Sexual healing
CD _______ CDSGPO 152
Prestige / Dec '96 / Else / Total/BMG

IN CONCERT
I heard it through the grapevine / Sexual healing / Let's get it on / Medley / Come get to this / Distant lover / God is love / Inner city blues / Intermission/Percussion interlude / What's going on / Joy
CD _______ 100302
CMC / May '97 / BMG

INNER CITY BLUES (A Tribute To Marvin Gaye) (Various Artists)
Save the children: *Bono* / Let's get it on: *Boyz II Men* / Trouble man: *Cherry, Neneh* / You're the man: *Digable Planets* / Inner city blues: *Gaye, Nona* / I want you: *Madonna & Massive Attack* / God is love/Mercy mercy me: *Sounds Of Blackness* / What's going on: *Speech* / Just to keep you satisfied: *Stansfield, Lisa* / Stubborn kind of fellow: *Wonder, Stevie*
CD _______ 5304522
Motown / Sep '95 / PolyGram

LEGENDARY MARVIN GAYE, THE (2CD Set)
CD Set _______ ALPCD 102
Alpha Entertainments / Sep '97 / Pinnacle

LET'S GET IT ON
Let's get it on / Please don't stay (once you go away) / If I should die tonight / Keep gettin' it on / Distant lover / You sure love to ball / Just to keep you satisfied / Come get to this
CD _______ 5300552
Motown / Jul '92 / PolyGram

MARVIN GAYE LIVE
CD _______ STACD 082
Wisepack / Jul '93 / Conifer/BMG / THE

MARVIN GAYE LIVE
CD _______ 1120072
Vono Disc / Sep '96 / Koch

MASTER 1961 - 1984, THE (4CD Box Set)
CD Set _______ 5304922
Motown / May '95 / PolyGram

MIDNIGHT LOVE
Joy / My love is waiting / Midnight lady / Sexual healing / Rockin' after midnight / Till tomorrow / Turn on some music / Third world girl
CD _______ CD 85977
Columbia / Jul '94 / Sony

MIDNIGHT LOVER, THE (Live In Concert)
I heard it through the grapevine / Come get to this / Let's get it on / God is love / What's going on / Inner city blues / Joy / Ain't nothing like the real thing / Heaven must have sent you / If this world were mine / Rockin' after midnight / Distant lover / Sexual healing
CD _______ SUMCD 4043
Summit / Nov '96 / Sound & Media

MOTOWN EARLY CLASSICS
How sweet it is (to be loved by you) / No good without you / I'll take care of you / You've been a long time coming / Lucky lucky me / Little darling (I need you) / Stubborn kind of fellow / Never let you go (shalu-bop) / I'm yours, you're mine / Wherever I lay my hat (that's my home) / One of these days / Got to get my hands on some lovin' / She's got to be real / Can I get a witness / Now that you've won me / You're a wonderful one / Stepping closer to your heart / Need somebody
CD _______ 5521182
Spectrum / Jul '96 / PolyGram

MOTOWN'S GREATEST HITS: MARVIN GAYE
I heard it through the grapevine / Let's get it on / Too busy thinking about my baby / How sweet it is (to be loved by you) / You're all I need to get by: *Gaye, Marvin & Tammi Terrell* / Got to give it up: *Gaye, Marvin & Tammi Terrell* / That's the way love is / You are everything: *Gaye, Marvin & Diana Ross* / Can I get a witness / I'll be doggone / What's going on / Abraham, Martin and John / It takes two: *Gaye, Marvin & Kim Weston* / Stop, look, listen (to your heart): *Gaye, Marvin & Diana Ross* / Chained / Trouble man / I want you / You ain't livin' till you're livin': *Gaye, Marvin & Tammi Terrell* / Onion song: *Gaye, Marvin & Tammi Terrell* / Wherever I lay my hat (that's my home)
CD _______ 5300122
Motown / Jan '92 / PolyGram

MPG
Too busy thinking about my baby / This magic moment / That's the way love is / End of our road / Seek and you shall find / Memories / Only a lonely man would know / It's a bitter pill to swallow / More than a heart can stand / Try my true love / I got to get to California / It don't take much to keep me
CD _______ 5302102
Motown / Aug '93 / PolyGram

ROMANTICALLY YOURS
More / Why did I choose you / Maria / Shadow of your smile / Fly me to the moon / I won't cry anymore / Just like / Walking in the rain / I live for you / Stranger in my life / Happy go lucky
CD _______ 4631582
Columbia / Dec '95 / Sony

SEEK AND YOU SHALL FIND - MORE BEST OF MARVIN GAYE (1963-1981)
Wherever I lay my hat (that's my home) / Get my hands on some lovin' / No good without you / You've been a long time coming / When I had your love / You're what's happening (in the world today) / Loving you is sweeter than ever / It's a bitter pill to swallow / Seek and you shall find / Gonna keep on tryin' till I win your love / Gonna give her all the love I've got / I wish it would rain / Abraham, Martin and John / Save the children / You sure love to ball / Ego tripping out / Praise / Heavy love affair
CD _______ 8122711822
WEA / Jun '93 / Warner Music

SEXUAL HEALING (Live In Indianapolis)
Third world girl / Heard it through the grapevine / Come get to this / Let's get it on / God is my friend / What's going on / Inner city blues (makes me wanna holler) / Joy / Ain't nothing like the real thing / Heaven must have sent your precious love / If this world were mine / Rockin' after midnight / Distant lover / Sexual healing
CD _______ CD 6047
Music / Oct '96 / Target/BMG

THAT'S THE WAY LOVE IS
Gonna give her all the love I've got / Yesterday / Groovin' / I wish it would rain / That's the way love is / How can I forget / Abraham, Martin and John / Gonna keep on tryin' till I win your love / No time for tears / Cloud 9 / Don't you miss me a little bit baby / So long
CD _______ 5302142
Motown / Aug '93 / PolyGram

TRIBUTE TO THE GREAT NAT KING COLE, A
Nature boy / Ramblin' rose / Too young / Pretend / Straighten up and fly right / Mona Lisa / Unforgettable / To the ends of the earth / Sweet Lorraine / It's only a paper moon / Send for me / Calypso blues
CD _______ 5300542
Motown / Jul '92 / PolyGram

TROUBLE MAN
Trouble man main theme / T plays it cool / Poor Abbey Walsh / Break in (police shoot big) / Cleo's apartment / Trouble man / Trouble man, Theme from / T stands for trouble / Trouble man main theme / Life is a gamble / Deep in it / Don't mess with Mr. T / There goes mister 'T'
CD _______ 5300972
Motown / Jan '92 / PolyGram

VULNERABLE
CD _______ 5307862
Polydor / Aug '97 / PolyGram

WHAT'S GOING ON
What's going on / What's happening brother / Flyin' high / Save the children / God is love / Mercy mercy me / Right on / Wholly holy / Inner city blues
CD _______ 5300222
Motown / Jul '94 / PolyGram

Gaylads

AFTER STUDIO ONE
CD _______ MRCD 001
Metronome / Apr '97 / Jet Star

FIRE AND RAIN
CD _______ HSCD 1004
Hot Shot / Oct '96 / Grapevine/PolyGram / Jet Star / THE / TKO Magnum

OVER THE RAINBOW'S END
CD _______ CDTRL 351
Trojan / Apr '95 / Direct / Jet Star

SOUL BEAT
CD _______ SOCD 001
Studio One / Mar '95 / Jet Star

Gayle, Charles

CONSECRATION
CD _______ 1201382
Black Saint / Nov '93 / Cadillac / Harmonia Mundi

DELIVERED (Gayle, Charles Quartet)
Yes God is real / Lord's prayer / Sought me / AMAZING GRACE / Go down Moses / Motherless child / Come out / Receive / These things / Delivered
CD _______ 213CD 024
2.13.61 / Jun '97 / Pinnacle

KINGDOM COME (Gayle, Charles Trio)
CD _______ KFWCD 157
Knitting Factory / Feb '95 / Cargo / Plastic Head

MORE LIVE AT THE KNITTING FACTORY (Gayle, Charles Quartet)
CD _______ KFWCD 137
Knitting Factory / Feb '95 / Cargo / Plastic Head

RAINING FIRE
CD _______ SHCD 137
Silkheart / Oct '94 / Cadillac / CM / Jazz Music / Wellard

REPENT
CD _______ KFWCD 122
Knitting Factory / Nov '94 / Cargo / Plastic Head

TESTAMENTS
CD _______ KFWCD 174
Knitting Factory / Oct '96 / Cargo / Plastic Head

TOUCHIN' ON TRANE
CD _______ FMPCD 48
FMP / Oct '86 / Cadillac

TRANSLATION VOL.1
CD ______ SHCD 134
Silkheart / Oct '94 / Cadillac / CM / Jazz Music / Wellard

Gayle, Crystal

BEST ALWAYS
Ready for the times to get better / Crazy / For the good times / Silver threads and golden needles / When I dream / Talkin' in your sleep / Oh Lonesome me / I fall to pieces / Beyond you / Don't it make my brown eyes blue / Break my mind
CD ______ RITZRCD 530
Ritz / Jun '93 / Pinnacle

BEST OF CRYSTAL GAYLE, THE
Cry / Turning away / Baby what about you / Straight to the heart / Till I gain control again / Only love can save me now / Long and lasting love / Our love is on the faultline / I don't wanna lose your love / Sound of goodbye
CD ______ 7599256222
Warner Bros. / May '94 / Warner Music

BEST OF CRYSTAL GAYLE, THE
CD ______ PLSCD 122
Pulse / Jun '96 / BMG

BEST OF CRYSTAL GAYLE, THE
CD ______ TRTCD 168
TrueTrax / Jul '96 / THE

COUNTRY CLASSICS
Somebody loves you / Don't it make my brown eyes blue / Ready for times to get better / You never miss a real good thing / You / Trouble with me is you / River road / Wrong road again / Talking in your sleep / Why have you left the one you left me for / Green door / Wayward wind / High time / Sweet baby on my mind / Never ending story of love
CD ______ CDMFP 6324
Music For Pleasure / Apr '97 / EMI

COUNTRY GIRL
Why have you left the one you left me for / Wrong road again / When I dream / They come out at night / Wayward wind / You never miss a real good thing ('til he says goodbye) / Forgettin' 'bout you / I'll do it all over again / Someday soon / Ready for the times to get better / I still miss someone / Sweet baby on my mind / Somebody loves you / We should be together / River road / This is my year for Mexico
CD ______ CDMFP 6037
Music For Pleasure / Nov '88 / EMI

EMI COUNTRY MASTERS
Somebody loves you / High time / I'll get over you / Woman's heart (is a handy place to be) / Restless / You / Wrong road again / Beyond you / Hands / Counterfeit love / This is my year for Mexico / Dreaming my dreams with you / One more time (Karneval) / Oh my soul / Come home Daddy / You never miss a real good thing ('Til he says goodbye) / I'll do it all over again / It's all right with me / Going down slow / Make a dream come true / Funny / We must believe in magic / Cry me a river / Wayward wind / Why have you left the one you left me for / Don't it make my brown eyes blue / Ready for the times to get better / Someday soon / I still miss someone / Talking in your sleep / Green door / Paintin' this old town blue / All I wanna do in life / When I dream / Time will prove I'm right / Your kisses will / Your old cold shoulder / Too deep for tears / We should be together / River road / I wanna come back to you / Heart mender / Everybody's reaching out for someone / Just an old love / Never ending song of love / Once in a very blue moon / Trouble with me is you / Love to, can't do / 99% Of the time / Faithless love
CD ______ CDEM 1499
EMI / May '93 / EMI

HOLLYWOOD TENNESSEE/TRUE LOVE
Keepin' power / Woman in me / Ain't no sunshine / You never gave up on me / Hollywood / Lovin' in these troubled times / Love crazy love / Lean on me / Crying in the rain / Tennessee / Our love is on the faultline / Deeper in the fire / 'Til I gain control again / Baby what about you / You bring out the lover in me / Take me to the dance / True love / Everything I own / Let your feelings show / Easier said than done / He is beautiful to me
CD ______ ESMCD 549
Essential / Jun '97 / BMG

LOVE SONGS
Hello I love you / Cry me a river / Dreaming my dreams with you / Someday soon / I'll do it all over again / I wanna come back to you / Somebody loves you / It's all right with me / Coming closer / Don't it make my brown eyes blue / When I dream / I'll get over you / Heart mender / Funny / I still miss someone / Talking in your sleep / Right in the palm of your hand / Beyond you / Going down is slow / Woman's heart (is a handy place to be)
CD ______ CDMFP 5629
Music For Pleasure / Aug '96 / EMI

MISS THE MISSISSIPPI/THESE DAYS
Half the way / Other side of me / Room for one more / Don't go my love / Dancing the night away / It's like we never said goodbye / Blue side / Little bit of the rain / Danger zone / Miss the Mississippi and you / Too many lovers / If you ever change your mind / Ain't no love in the heart of the city / Same old story (same old song) / Help yourselves to each other / Take it easy / I just can't leave your love alone / You've almost got me believin' / Lover man / What a little moonlight can do
CD ______ ESMCD 520
Essential / Jun '97 / BMG

SINGLES ALBUM
Somebody loves you / Wrong road again / I'll get over you / High time / Ready for the times to get better / You never miss a real good thing ('Til he says goodbye) / River road / Don't it make my brown eyes blue / When I dream / Talking in your sleep / Why have you left the one you left me for / All I wanna do in life / We should be together / Too deep for tears
CD ______ CZ 204
Liberty / Jul '89 / EMI

SOMEDAY
Anchor deep / Diamonds from dust / My old friend / He'll be there / I saw / Medley / Medley
CD ______ RITZCD 0083
Ritz / Apr '97 / Pinnacle

SONGBIRD/NOBODY WANTS TO BE ALONE
Sound of goodbye / I don't wanna lose your love / Me against the night / Cage the songbird / Turning away / Come back (when you can stay forever) / Victim or a fool / You made a fool of me / On our way to love / Take me home / Long and lasting love / Tonight, tonight / Nobody wants to be alone / Love does that to fools / Coming to the dance / You were there for me / Touch and go / Someone like you / New way to say I love you / God bless the child
CD ______ ESMCD 553
Essential / Jul '97 / BMG

STRAIGHT TO THE HEART/NOBODY'S ANGEL
Straight to the heart / Cry / Take this heart / Little bit closer / Do I have to say goodbye / Deep down / Crazy in the heart / Only love can save me now / Nobody should have to love this way / Lonely girl / Nobody's angel / Prove me wrong / Old habits die hard / Tennessee nights / When love is new / Hopeless romantic / Love may find you / Love found me / Heat / After the best
CD ______ ESMCD 554
Essential / Jul '97 / BMG

Gayle, Michelle

MICHELLE GAYLE
Get off my back / Happy just to be with you / Walk with pride / Looking up / Girlfriend / Freedom / Personality / It doesn't matter / Your love / Sweetness / One day / Say what's on your mind / Rise up / Baby don't go / All night long
CD ______ 74321234122
RCA / Dec '95 / BMG

SENSATIONAL
Fly away / Do you know / Sensational / Working overtime / Don't keep me waiting / No place like home / It's a high / Yesterday / Talk it over / Fakin' it / Fly away / Happy just to be with you
CD ______ 74321419322
RCA / Apr '97 / BMG

Gaynor, Gloria

ALL THE BEST
Heat is on / Everybody wants to rule the world / What a wonderful world / Every breath you take / Suddenly / Every time you go away / Don't you dare call it love / I will survive / Never can say goodbye / Reach out (I'll be there) / I am what I am / I want to know what love is / Broken wings / Careless whisper / He's out of my life / Top shelf / Eye of the tiger / Power of love / Feel so real
CD ______ 305922
Hallmark / Jan '97 / Carlton

CARELESS WHISPER
Eye of the tiger / Every breath you take / Broken wings / What a wonderful world / I want to know what love is / Feel so real / He's out of my life / Every time you go away / Everybody wants to rule the world / Careless whisper / Heat is on / Suddenly / Power of love / I will survive / Never can say goodbye / Reach out (I'll be there) / I am what I am / Don't you dare call it love / Top shelf
CD ______ MU 5075CD
Start / Apr '97 / Disc

COLLECTION, THE
I will survive / Reach out, I'll be there / How high the moon / Let me know (I have a right) / All I need is your sweet lovin' / Don't stop us / Substitute / Goin' out of my head / Anybody wanna party / (If you want it) Do it yourself / Can't fight the feeling / One number 1 / I've got you under my skin / Tonight / Honey bee / This love affair / We can start all over again / Walk on by / I am what I am
CD ______ 5518392
Spectrum / Mar '96 / PolyGram

GLORIA GAYNOR - THE HITS
CD ______ OVCCD 003
Satellite Music / Mar '94 / THE

GREATEST HITS
CD ______ 13885992
Galaxy / Jun '97 / ZYX

HITS OF GLORIA GAYNOR, THE
Stop in the name of love / I will survive / Runaround love / For you, my love / Mack side / Love me real / Tease me / America / Even a fool would let go
CD ______ 12665
Laserlight / Apr '96 / Target/BMG

I AM WHAT I AM
CD ______ MU 5045
Musketeer / Oct '92 / Disc

I WILL SURVIVE
CD ______ LMCD 001
Wisepack / Sep '93 / Conifer/BMG / THE

I WILL SURVIVE
I will survive / Reach out, I'll be there / (If you want it) do it yourself / I am what I am / Reason for the season / Can't take my eyes off you / How high the moon / Never can say goodbye / Feelings / Mama San
CD ______ QED 026
Tring / Nov '96 / Tring

I WILL SURVIVE
I will survive / Mack-side / Runaround love / Even a fool would let go / Stop in the name of love / America / For you, my love / Love me real / Tease me / I will survive
CD ______ 100042
CMC / May '97 / BMG

I WILL SURVIVE - THE BEST OF GLORIA GAYNOR
I will survive / Honey bee / Never can say goodbye / Reach out, I'll be there / Let me know (I have a right) / How high the moon / Casanova Brown / (If you want it) Do it yourself / I am what I am / All I need is your sweet lovin / Walk on by / We can start all over again / Let's mend what's been broken / I will survive (Classic 12" mix)
CD ______ 5196652
Polydor / Mar '96 / PolyGram

POWER OF LOVE, THE
Everytime you go away / Don't you dare call it love / Everybody wants to rule the world / What a wonderful world / Broken wings / Top shelf / Hits medley (I will survive, never can say goodbye, reach ou / Power of love / Eye of the tiger / Heat is on / Feel so real / Suddenly / He's out of my life / Every breath you take / I want to know what love is
CD ______ ECD 3098
K-Tel / Jan '95 / K-Tel

GBH

ATTACK AND REVENGE
CD ______ RR 349678
Roadrunner / '89 / PolyGram

CHURCH OF THE TRULY WARPED
Pure greed / Not enough / Leather coffin / Candy man / Lords of discipline / Where the wild things are / Church of the truly warped / Back / I need energy / Evil Evar / All for the cause
CD ______ PRAGE 008CD
Powerage / Oct '96 / Plastic Head

FRIDGE TOO FAR, A
Go home / Twenty floors below / Checking out / Needle inna haystack / See you bleed / Pass the axe / Crossfire / Captain Chaos / Fist of regret / Nocturnal journal
CD ______ CDJUST 13
Rough Justice / Oct '89 / Pinnacle

FROM HERE TO REALITY
CD ______ PRAGE 007CD
Powerage / Oct '96 / Plastic Head

LIVE IN LOS ANGELES
CD ______ CDPUNK 82
Anagram / Sep '96 / Cargo / Pinnacle

MIDNIGHT MADNESS AND BEYOND
CD ______ CDJUST 2
Rough Justice / Aug '87 / Pinnacle

NO NEED TO PANIC
CD ______ CDJUST 7
Rough Justice / '89 / Pinnacle

PUNK JUNKIES
CD ______ WB 1151CD
We Bite / Sep '96 / Plastic Head

Gean, Ralph

STAR UNBORN, A
Homicidal me / Hey Doctor Casey / Japanese rain song / Planet of the rain / Granny's grave / You're drivin' me crazy / Asshole song / Bobbit song / Star trekkin' rock 'n' roll cowboy / Hard to be a killer / Godess of love / Experimental love / Guitar pickin' teabag / Wearin' that loved on look
CD ______ HH 3307CD
Hierarchy / Jul '97 / World Serpent

Gear

BED AND BREAKFAST
CD ______ HAIR 7
Hair / Feb '96 / SRD

Geballe, Tony

NATIVE OF THE RAIN
CD ______ DGM 9703
Discipline / Sep '97 / Pinnacle

Geckoes

ART GECKO
CD ______ OCK 003CD
Ock / Jul '95 / ADA / Direct

Gee, Jonathan

CLOSER TO (Gee, Jonathan Trio)
Lifecycle / Prayer to love / Bye bye blackbird / In a sentimental mood / Serious red / Why / Everybody's song but my own / Closer to
CD ______ ASCCD 14
ASC / Mar '97 / Cadillac / New Note/ Pinnacle

Gee, Peter

VISION OF ANGELS, A
CD ______ PEND 8CD
Pendragon/Toff / Apr '97 / Pinnacle

Geers, Didier

IT AIN'T THE MEAT, IT'S THE MOTION (Geers, Didier Group)
CD ______ MECCACD 1072
Music Mecca / May '97 / Cadillac / Jazz Music / Wellard

Geesin, Ron

HYSTERY - THE RON GEESIN STORY
Ron's address to a notion / Parallel bar / Mental passage / Coughsemble / Whistling heart / Go / Fore-teases / Twisted pair / Big imp / Morecambe bay / Sit down, Mamma / T'mith / Throb thencewards thrill / Chromatic essence and smoked hips (the time dance) / Frenzy / Animal autos / Where daffodils do thrive / Vocal chords / Upon composition / Can't you stop that thing / Syncopot / Song of the wire / Affections for string quartet / With a smile up his nose they entered / Three vignettes / Certainly random / Raise of eyebrows / No.8 Scalpel incision
CD ______ CDBRED 110
Cherry Red / Dec '93 / Pinnacle

LAND OF MIST
CD ______ CLEO 95602
Cleopatra / Apr '96 / Cargo / Greyhound / Plastic Head / RTM/Disc / SRD

RAISE OF EYEBROWS/AS HE STANDS
Raise of eyebrows / Freedom for four voices and me / Psychedelia / Positives / It's all very new, you know / Female / Certainly random / Eye that nearly saw / Two fifteen string guitars for nice poeple / From an electric train / World of too much sound / Another female / We're all going to Liverpool / Ha ha but reasonable / Can't stop that thing / Looming view / Rise up Sebastian / Concrete line up / Upon composition / Mr. Peugeot's trot / To Roger Waters wherever you are / Cymbal and much electronics / Up above my heart / Twist and knit for two guitars / Wrap a keyboard round a plant / Middle of whose night / Waiting for life / On-through-out-up
CD ______ SEECD 433
See For Miles/C5 / Aug '95 / Pinnacle

Geet

NO PROBLEM
CD ______ CDSR 012
Star / May '90 / Pinnacle / Stern's

Geezer

BLACK SCIENCE
CD ______ EAGCD 001
Eagle / Jul '97 / BMG
CD ______ TVT 60202
TVT / Jun '97 / Cargo / Greyhound

Geezer Lake

KING FROST PARADE
CD ______ THK 040
Thick / Feb '97 / Cargo

Gege & The Mother Tongue

MOTHER TONGUE
CD ______ GOJ 60182
Go Jazz / Jun '96 / Vital/SAM

Gehenna

FIRST SPELL
CD ______ HNF 003CD
Head Not Found / Jun '96 / Plastic Head

MALICE
CD ______ NIHIL 16CD
Cacophonous / Sep '96 / Plastic Head / RTM/Disc

SEEN THROUGH THE VEILS OF DARKNESS (The Second Spell)
Lord of flies / Shairak Kinnummh / Vinterriket / Witch is born / Through the veils of darkness / Mystical play of shadows / Eves of the sun / Myth / Dark poems author

CD NIHIL 9CD
Cacophonous / Jun '97 / Plastic Head / RTM/Disc

Gehhenah

KING OF THE SIDEWALK
CD OPCD 046
Osmose / Nov '96 / Plastic Head

Gehrman, Shura

ENGLISH SONGS
Songs of travel / Shropshire lad / Selected songs
CD NI 5033
Nimbus / '88 / Nimbus

FOLKSONGS OF THE BRITISH ISLES
CD NI 5082
Nimbus / '88 / Nimbus

Geils, J. Band

BEST OF THE J. GEILS BAND, THE
Southside shuffle / Give it to me / Where did our love go / Ain't nothing but a house party / Detroit breakdown / Whammer jammer / I do / Must of got lost / Looking for a love
CD 7567815572
WEA / Feb '84 / Warner Music

CENTREFOLD
Sanctuary / One last kiss / Take it back / Come back / Love stinks / Til the walls come tumbling down / Just can't wait / Centrefold / Flamethrower / Freeze-frame / Piss on the wall / Angel in blue / I do / Land of 1,000 dances / Concealed weapons / You're getting even while I'm getting odd
CD VSOPCD 234
Connoisseur Collection / Mar '97 / Pinnacle

FREEZE FRAME
Freeze frame / Rage in the cage / Centrefold / Do you remember when / Insane, insane again / Flamethrower / River blindness / Angel in blue / Piss on the wall
CD BGOCD 196
Beat Goes On / Jul '93 / Pinnacle

LADIES INVITED
Chimes / Did you no wrong / Diddyboppin' / I can't go on / Lady makes demands / Lay your good thing down / My baby don't love me / No doubt about it / Take a chance (on romance) / That's why I'm thinking of you
CD 7567814312
Atlantic / Feb '95 / Warner Music

LOVE STINKS
Just can't wait / Come back / Takin' you down / Night time / No anchovies, please / Love stinks / Tryin' not to think about it / Desire / Till the walls come tumblin' down
CD BGOCD 254
Beat Goes On / Dec '94 / Pinnacle

SANCTUARY
I could hurt you / One last kiss / Take it back / Sanctuary / Teresa / Wild man / I can't believe you / I don't hang around much anymore / Jus' can't stop me
CD BGOCD 262
Beat Goes On / May '95 / Pinnacle

SHOWTIME
Jus' can't stop me / Just can't wait / Till the walls come tumblin' down / Sanctuary / I'm falling / Love rap / Love stinks / Stoop down 39 / I do / Centrefold / Land of 1000 dances
CD BGOCD 264
Beat Goes On / Nov '95 / Pinnacle

Geins't Nait

FRIGO
CD PPP 109
PDCD / Sep '93 / Plastic Head

Gelato, Ray

FULL FLAVOUR, THE (Gelato, Ray's Giants Of Jive)
CD AKD 034
Linn / Mar '95 / PolyGram

GELATO ALL'ITALIANA
CD NDCD 209
Durium / May '97 / Nervous

GELKATO ESPRESSO
CD NDCD 203
Durium / May '97 / Nervous

Geldof, Bob

LOUD MOUTH (The Best Of Bob Geldof/ Boomtown Rats)
I don't like Mondays: *Boomtown Rats* / This is the world calling / Rat trap: *Boomtown Rats* / Great song of indifference / Love or something / Banana republic: *Boomtown Rats* / Crazy / Elephant's graveyard: *Boomtown Rats* / Someone's looking at you: *Boomtown Rats* / She's so modern: *Boomtown Rats* / House on fire: *Boomtown Rats* / Beat of the night / Diamond smiles: *Boomtown Rats* / Like clockwork: *Boomtown Rats* / Room 19 (Sha la la la lee) / Mary of the 4th form: *Boomtown Rats* / Looking after no. 1: *Boomtown Rats*
CD 5222832
Vertigo / Apr '94 / PolyGram

Geller, Herb

HERB GELLER PLAYS AL COHN
Mr. George / Danielle / Mr. Music / Halley's comet / Pensive / Flugelbird / High on you / You 'n me / Woody's lament / El cajon / Underdog / Tasty pudding / T'ain't no use / Infinity
CD HEPCD 2066
Hep / Mar '96 / Cadillac / Jazz Music / New Note/Pinnacle / Wellard

JAZZ SONG BOOK, A
CD 60062
Tiptoe / Nov '89 / New Note/Pinnacle

THAT GELLER FELLER
CD FSRCD 091
Fresh Sound / Jul '92 / Discovery / Jazz Music

Gema Y Pavel

COSA DE BROMA
La caminadora / Jurame / Aixa / Ay del amor / Longina / Mayeya / Noche de ronda / El zun zun / Te amo / Girl / 'Hacia donde / Oshe
CD INT 31812
Intuition / Sep '96 / New Note/Pinnacle

TRAMPAS DEL TIEMPO
Domingo AM / El bobo / Lo feo / Habana, devorando claridad / Trampas del tiempo / Parar de fumar / Ay, Maria / La capital / Marginal DS / Huella del azar / Helado sobre ruedas / La carretera, fuera de tiempo / Bajo la luna / Al bord de la locura / Guajira a la Algeria / Parar de fumar
CD INT 31792
Intuition / Dec '96 / New Note/Pinnacle

Gemini Gemini

FLAVOURS OF THELONIUS MONK, THE
CD ITMP 970082
ITM / Oct '95 / Koch / Tradelink

GEMINI GEMINI
CD ITMP 970063
ITM / Oct '95 / Koch / Tradelink

Genaro, Tano

PIONNIER DU TANGO ARGENTIN
CD 883142
Music Memoria / Aug '93 / ADA / Discovery

Genaside II

NEW LIFE 4 THE HUNTED (2CD Set)
New life 4 the hunted / Distant noises: *Genaside II & Rose Windross* / Waistline firecracker: *Genaside II & Killerman Archer* / Come to the fools: *Genaside II & Sharon Williams* / Just as rough: *Genaside II & Eek-A-Mouse* / Narra mine: *Genaside II & Sharon Williams* / Choose ya weapon: *Genaside II & Killerman Archer/Otherized FAM* / Blacker shade: *Genaside II & Rose Windross* / Why you watching me: *Genaside II & Rose Windross* / Basic killer instinct: *Genaside II & Killerman Archer/Otherized FAM/ Cappadonna* / Under the bridge: *Genaside II & Rose Windross* / Blue precious metal / New life II the hunted: *Genaside II & Rose Windross* / Waistline firecracker: *Genaside II & Killerman Archer* / Distant noises: *Genaside II & Rose Windross* / Blue precious metal / Why you watching me: *Genaside II & Rose Windross*
CD TRUCD 14
CD Set TRUDC 14
Internal / Sep '96 / Pinnacle / PolyGram

Gencturk, Vedad

ART OF THE TURKISH UD, THE
CD ARN 60265
Arion / Sep '96 / ADA / Discovery

GENE

DIVING DREAMS
CD 720155
Magnum Music / Oct '92 / TKO Magnum

KATCHINA
CD 720143
Magnum Music / Feb '93 / TKO Magnum

Gene

DRAWN TO THE DEEP END
CD GENEC 3
CD GENED 3
Polydor / Feb '97 / PolyGram

OLYMPIAN
Haunted by you / Your love, it lies / Truth, rest your head / Car that sped / Lefthanded / London, can you wait / To the city / Still can't find the phone / Sleep well tonight / Olympian / We'll find our own way
CD 5274462
Costermonger / Feb '97 / PolyGram / Vital

TO SEE THE LIGHTS
Be my light, be my guide / Sick, sober and sorry / Her fifteen years / Haunted by you / I can't decide if she really loves me / Car that sped / For the dead (version) / Sleep well tonight / How much for love / London, can you wait / I can't help myself / Child's body / Don't let me down / I say a little prayer / Do you want to hear it from me / This is not my crime / Olympian / For the dead
CD 5298072
Costermonger / Feb '97 / PolyGram / Vital

Gene Loves Jezebel

DISCOVER
Heartache / Over the rooftops / Kicks / White horse / Wait and see / Desire / Beyond doubt / Sweetest thing / Maid of Sker / Brand new moon
CD BEGA 73CD
Beggars Banquet / Oct '86 / RTM/Disc / Warner Music

HEAVENLY BODIES
CD 74785502102
Arista / Jun '93 / BMG

HOUSE OF DOLLS, THE
Gorgeous / Motion of love / Set me free / Suspicion / Every door / Twenty killer hurts / Treasure / Message / Drowning crazy / Up there
CD BEGA 87CD
Beggars Banquet / Oct '87 / RTM/Disc / Warner Music

IN THE AFTERGLOW (2CD Set)
CD Set PINKGCD 1
Pink Gun / Oct '95 / RTM/Disc / Total/ BMG

KISS OF LIFE
Jealous / Kiss of life / Szyzygy / Tangled up in you / Evening star / It'll end in tears / Why can't I / Walk away / Two shadows / I die for you
CD BEGA 109CD
Beggars Banquet / Aug '90 / RTM/Disc / Warner Music

General Degree

GENERAL DEGREE
CD VPCD 1491
VP / May '97 / Greensleeves / Jet Star / Total/BMG

General Echo

12" OF PLEASURE
Lorna she love young boy banana / It's my desire to set your crutches on fire / Me know everything about she pum pum / Old man love young gal vegie / This are the cockie tribulation / Bathroom sex / This a loves corner / Love me waist don't bother me face / Love bump / She have a pair of headlamp breast
CD GRELCD 15
Greensleeves / Mar '97 / Jet Star / SRD

General Lafayette

JESTER
Oh my beloved Father / Power of music / Love in the eyes of a child / Blow the trumpet at the new moon / Trumpet on fire / Going back to Scotland / Jester / Gentle to the soul / Lizzie's song (Is on the radio) / Sentimental value / Jupiter / Burn's theme / Silent anguish / Country barn dance
CD PZA 003CD
Plaza / Mar '93 / Pinnacle

KING OF THE BROKEN HEARTS
CD PZA 007CD
Plaza / Nov '89 / Pinnacle

LOVE IS A RHAPSODY
Angel in blue / For the girl who couldn't find love / Melody for you / Florence serenade / Love is a rhapsody / Life is for loving / Lonely trumpet / Love you love me Aloha
CD PZA 001CD
Plaza / Jul '88 / Pinnacle

PIERROT
CD PZA 009CD
Plaza / Apr '91 / Pinnacle

General Levy

RUMBLE IN THE JUNGLE VOL.1 (General Levy & Top Cat)
CD JFCD 001
Fashion / Jan '95 / Jet Star / SRD

WICKEDER GENERAL, THE
CD FADCD 024
Fashion / Dec '92 / Jet Star / SRD

General Pecos

BACK WITH A VENGEANCE
CD WRCD 010
World / Jun '97 / Jet Star / TKO Magnum

TALK BOUT GUN
CD GRELCD 185
Greensleeves / Jun '93 / Jet Star / SRD

General Public

RUB IT BETTER
Tough / Rainy days / Hold it deep / Big bed / Punk / Friends again / It's weird / Never not alone / Handgun / Blowhard / Warm love / Rub it better
CD 4783582
Epic / Oct '95 / Sony

General TK

I SPY
I spy
CD GRELCD 183
Greensleeves / Mar '93 / Jet Star / SRD

General Trees

RAGGA RAGGA RAGAMUFFIN
CD RRTGCD 7702
Rohit / Aug '88 / Jet Star

Generation

BRUTAL REALITY
CD CDZORRO 82
Metal Blade / Nov '94 / Pinnacle / Plastic Head

Generation X

GENERATION X
Hundred punks / Listen / Ready steady go / Kleenex / Promises, promises / Day by day / Invisible man / Kiss me deadly / Too personal / Valley of the dolls / Running with the boss sound / Night of the cadillacs / Friday's angels / King rocker / Wild youth / Dancing with myself / Triumph / Revenge / Youth youth youth / From the heart
CD CDGOLD 1039
EMI Gold / Jul '96 / EMI

Genesis

ABACAB
No reply at all / Me and Sarah Jane / Keep it dark / Dodo / Lurker / Man on the corner / Who dunnit / Like it or not / Another record / Abacab
CD CBRCDX 102
Charisma / Oct '94 / EMI

AND THEN THERE WERE THREE
Scenes from a night's dream / Snowbound / Ballad of big / Burning rope / Deep in the motherlode / Down and out / Follow you follow me / Lady lies / Many too many / Say it's alright Joe / Undertow
CD CDSCDX 4010
Charisma / Oct '94 / EMI

DUKE
Behind the lines / Duchess / Guide vocal / Man of our times / Misunderstanding / Heathaze / Turn it on again / Alone tonight / Cul-de-sac / Please don't ask / Duke's end / Duke's travels
CD CBRCDX 101
Charisma / Oct '94 / EMI

FOXTROT
Watcher of the skies / Time table / Get 'em out by Friday / Can-utility and the coastliners / Horizon / Supper's ready
CD CASCDX 1058
Charisma / Aug '94 / EMI

GENESIS
Mama / Illegal alien / That's all / Taking it all too hard / Just a job to do / Home by the sea / Second home by the sea / It's gonna get better / Silver rainbow
CD GENCD 1
Charisma / Dec '83 / EMI

GENESIS LIVE
Watcher of the skies / Get 'em out by friday / Knife / Return of the giant hogweed / Musical box
CD CLACDX 1
Charisma / Aug '94 / EMI

INTERVIEW COMPACT DISC
CD CBAK 4028
Baktabak / Sep '90 / Arabesque

INVISIBLE TOUCH
Invisible touch / Tonight tonight tonight / Land of confusion / In too deep / Anything she does / Domino / Throwing it all away / Brazilian
CD GENCD 2
Charisma / Dec '86 / EMI

LAMB LIES DOWN ON BROADWAY, THE
Lamb lies down on Broadway / Riding the scree / In the rapids / It / Fly on a windshield / Broadway melody of 1974 / Cuckoo cocoon / In the cage / Grand parade of lifeless packaging / Back in NYC / Hairless heart / Counting out time / Carpet crawlers / Chamber of 32 doors / Lilywhite lilith / Waiting room / Anyway / Here comes the supernatural anaesthetist / Lamia / Silent sorrow in empty boats / Colony of slippermen (The arrival) / Colony of slippermen (A visit to the doctor) / Colony of slippermen (The-Raven) / Ravine / Light dies down on Broadway
CD CGSCDX 1
Charisma / Aug '94 / EMI

NURSERY CRYME
Musical box / For absent friends / Return of the giant hogweed / Seven stones / Harold the barrel / Harlequin / Fountain of Salmacis
CD CASCDX 1052
Charisma / Aug '94 / EMI

SECONDS OUT
Squonk / Carpet crawlers / Robbery, assault and battery / Afterglow / Firth of fifth / I know what I like (in your wardrobe) / Lamb lies down on Broadway / Musical box

(closing section) / Supper's ready / Cinema show / Dance on a volcano / Los Endos
CD Set _______ GECDX 2001
Virgin / Sep '94 / EMI

SELLING ENGLAND BY THE POUND
Dancing with the moonlit knight / I know what I like (in your wardrobe) / Firth of fifth / More fool me / Battle of Epping Forest / After the ordeal / Cinema show / Aisle of plenty
CD _______ CASCDX 1074
Charisma / Aug '94 / EMI

SELLING ENGLAND BY THE POUND/ THE LAMB LIES DOWN ON BROADWAY (3CD Set)
CD Set _______ TPAK 17
Virgin / Nov '91 / EMI

SUPPER'S READY (A Tribute To Genesis) (Various Artists)
CD _______ RR 89122
Roadrunner / Nov '95 / PolyGram

THREE SIDES LIVE
Behind the lines / Duchess / Me and Sarah Jane / Follow you follow me / One for the vine / Fountain of Salmacis / Watcher of the skies / Turn it on again / Dodo / Abacab / Misunderstanding / In the cage / Afterglow / Paperlate / You might recall / Me and Virgil / Evidence of autumn / Open door
CD Set _______ GECDX 2002
Virgin / Oct '94 / EMI

TRESPASS
Looking for someone / White mountain / Visions of angels / Stagnation / Dusk / Knife
CD _______ CASCDX 1020
Charisma / Aug '94 / EMI

TRESPASS/NURSERY CRYME/ FOXTROT (3CD Set)
CD Set _______ TPAK 1
Virgin / Oct '90 / EMI

TRICK OF THE TAIL, A
Dance on a volcano / Entangled / Squonk / Madman moon / Robbery, assault and battery / Ripples / Trick of the tail / Los Endos
CD _______ CDSCDX 4001
Charisma / Oct '94 / EMI

WAY WE WALK, THE (The Shorts)
Land of confusion / No son of mine / Jesus he knows me / Throwing it all away / I can't dance / Mama / Hold on my heart / That's all / In too deep / Tonight tonight tonight / Invisible touch
CD _______ GENCD 4
Virgin / Nov '92 / EMI

WAY WE WALK, THE (The Longs)
Drum duet / Dance on a volcano / Lamb lies down on broadway / Musical box / Firth of fifth / I know what I like (in your wardrobe) / Driving the last spike / Domino / Fading lights / Home by the sea / Second home by the sea
CD _______ GENCD 5
Virgin / Jan '93 / EMI

WE CAN'T DANCE
No son of mine / Jesus he knows me / Driving the last spike / I can't dance / Never a time / Dreaming while you sleep / Tell me why / Living forever / Hold on my heart / Way of the world / Since I lost you / Fading lights
CD _______ GENCD 3
Virgin / Nov '91 / EMI

WE KNOW WHAT WE LIKE (The Music Of Genesis) (London Symphony Orchestra/David Palmer)
CD _______ 07863562422
RCA Victor / Jul '95 / BMG

WIND AND WUTHERING
Eleventh Earl of Mar / One for the vine / Your own special way / Wot gorilla / All in a mouse's night / Blood on the rooftops / Unquiet slumbers for the sleepers / In that quiet earth / Afterglow
CD _______ CDSCDX 4005
Charisma / Oct '94 / EMI

Genest, Michel

ANGELS IN OUR MIDST (Genest, Michel & Anton Mizerak)
Metamorphosis / Magical iridescene / Crystal fantasy / Angel presence / Island of paradise / Land of enchantment / Open door / Ancient a'bode / Samsara / Radiant rainbow prism / Angel of Samsara / Sun-ra / Angels of paradisse / Metamorphosis (Reprise)
CD _______ CD 257
Narada / Aug '96 / ADA / New Note/ Pinnacle

Genetic Control

FIRST IMPRESSIONS
First impressions
CD _______ LF 069
Lost & Found / Jan '94 / Plastic Head

Genetik System

INITIATIK
CD _______ DI 432
Distance / Feb '97 / 3mv/Sony / Prime

Geneva

FURTHER
CD _______ NUDE 7CD
Nude / Jun '97 / 3mv/Vital

Genf

IMPORT/EXPORT
CD _______ COMPOST 035
Compost / Jun '97 / Plastic Head / SRD / Timewarp

Genie

ONE WORLD EXPERIENCE
Rhythm talking / One world / Who killed Jesus / Rhythm talking / Attitude / Attitude / Some people / Black rock / Attitude / Utopia / Wild friends / One world / Mary's freedom train / Comet hopper / Some people / City life / Lonely world / Acid tribe
CD _______ JUMPCD 1
Strobe / Jun '97 / Else

Genitorturers

120 DAYS OF GENITORTURE
CD _______ CDFLAG 81
Under One Flag / Oct '93 / Pinnacle

Genius/GZA

LIQUID SWORDS
Liquid swords / Duel of the iron mic / Living in the world today / Gold / Cold world / Labels / 4th Chamber / Shadowboxin' / Hell's wind staff / Killah hills 10304 / Investigate reports / Swordsman / I gotcha back / Basic instructions / Before leaving earth: *Genius At Work*
CD _______ GED 24813
Geffen / Nov '95 / BMG

Gentle Giant

ACQUIRING THE TASTE
Pentagruel's nativity / Edge of twilight / House the street the room / Acquiring the taste / Wreck / Moon is down / Black cat / Plain truth
CD _______ 8429172
Vertigo / Feb '97 / PolyGram

EDGE OF TWILIGHT (2CD Set)
Advent of panurge / Funny ways / Peel the paint / Acquiring the taste / Cogs in cogs / House, the street, the moon / Boys in the band / Schooldays / Raconteur troubadour / Wreck / Nothing at all / Why not / Playing the game / Mister class and quality / Three friends / Proclamation / Cry for everyone / Isn't it quiet and cold / Plain truth / Knots / Alucard / Aspirations / Pantagruel's nativity / River / Face / Moon is down / Edge of twilight / No God's a man / So sincere / Think of me with kindness / Valedictory
CD Set _______ 5341012
Vertigo / Oct '96 / PolyGram

GENTLE GIANT
Alucard / Funny ways / Giant / Isn't it quiet and cold / Nothing at all / Queen / Why not
CD _______ 8426242
Vertigo / Feb '97 / PolyGram

LAST STEPS (Live 1980)
CD _______ RMCCD 0205
Red Steel / Nov '96 / Pinnacle

LAST TIME - LIVE 1980, THE
CD _______ TRUCKCD 1010
Terrapin Truckin' / Apr '94 / ADA / Direct / Total/BMG

LIVE - PLAYING THE FOOL
Just the song / Proclamation / On reflection / Excerpts from Octopus / Funny ways / Runaway / Experience / So sincere / Freehand / Breakdown in Brussels / Peel the paint / I lost my head
CD _______ TRUCKCD 1009
Terrapin Truckin' / Dec '94 / ADA / Direct / Total/BMG

LIVE AT THE BBC
CD _______ BOJCD 018
Strange Fruit / Jul '96 / Pinnacle

LIVE IN CONCERT
Two weeks in Spain / Free hand / On reflection / Just the same / Playing the game / Memories of old days / Betcha thought we couldn't do it / I'm turning around / For nobody / Mark time
CD _______ WINCD 066
Windsong / Oct '94 / Pinnacle

OCTOPUS
Advent of panurge / Raconter troubadour / Cry for everyone / Knots / Boys in the band / Dog's life / Think of me with kindness / River
CD _______ 8426942
Vertigo / Feb '97 / PolyGram

Gentle People

SOUNDTRACKS FOR LIVING
CD _______ CAT 045CD
Rephlex / Jan '97 / Prime / RTM/Disc

Gentlemen Of Jazz

10 YEARS ANNIVERSARY
CD _______ MECCACD 1067
Music Mecca / May '97 / Cadillac / Jazz Music / Wellard

THIRD TIME ROUND
CD _______ MECCACD 130591
Music Mecca / Nov '94 / Cadillac / Jazz Music / Wellard

WE'LL MEET AGAIN
CD _______ MECCACD 1026
Music Mecca / Nov '94 / Cadillac / Jazz Music / Wellard

Gentry, Bobbie

BEST OF BOBBIE GENTRY, THE
Ode to Billie Joe / All I have to do is dream / I'll never fall in love again / Raindrops keep falling on my head / Mississippi delta / Little green apples / Natural to be gone / Son of a preacher man / Season come, seasons go / Gentle on my mind / Touch 'em with love / Where's the playground Johnny / My elusive dreams / Grey hound goin' somewhere / You've made me so very happy / Mornin' glory / I wouldn't be surprised / Ace insurance man / Glory hallelujah, how they'll sing / Let it be me
CD _______ CDMFP 6115
Music For Pleasure / Mar '94 / EMI

TOUCH 'EM WITH LOVE
CD _______ CREV 038CD
Rev-Ola / Nov '95 / 3mv/Vital

Genty, Alain

LA COULEUR DU MILIEU
CD _______ GWP 006CD
Gwerz / Jul '94 / ADA / Discovery

Geordie

VERY BEST OF BRIAN JOHNSON AND GEORDIE, THE
All because of you / Black cat woman / House of the Rising Sun / Electric lady / Natural born loser / Geordie stomp / I cried today / We're all right now / Francis was a rocker / Going to the city / Rock 'n' roll fever / You do this to me
CD _______ 100632
CMC / May '97 / BMG

George Banton

BEST OF GEORGE BANTON, THE
CD _______ LDRCD 022
Londisc / Apr '97 / Jet Star

JESUS IS EVERYTHING 2 ME
CD _______ CRCD 57
Charm / Jan '97 / Jet Star

YOU'RE ALL I NEED
CD _______ CRCD 58
Charm / Jul '97 / Jet Star

George, Lowell

THANKS I'LL EAT IT HERE
What do you want the girl to do / Honest man / Two trains / Can't stand the rain / Cheek to cheek / Easy money / Twenty million things / Find a river / Himmler's ring
CD _______ 7599267552
WEA / Jul '93 / Warner Music

George, Siwsann

CANEUON TRADDODIADOL CYMRU (Traditional Songs Of Wales)
Adar man y mynydd / Y gwcw fach / Can Merthyr / Miner's life / Blodau'r flwyddyn / Hen ferchetan / Hiraeth / Can y Cardi / Cainc yr aradwr / Titrwm tatrwm / Yr hen wr mwyn / Yr eneth gadd ei gwrthod / Bachgen bach o dincer / Mae'r ddaear yn glasu / Ar fore Dydd Nadolig / Clywch clywch / Llangollen market / Can y bugail / Lisa lan / Marwnad yr ehedydd / Llongau Caernarfon / Yr insiwrans agent / Rhybudd i'r carwr
CD _______ CDSDL 406
Saydisc / Sep '94 / ADA / Direct / Harmonia Mundi

George, Sophia

LATEST SLANG
CD _______ RNCD 2004
Rhino / May '93 / Grapevine/PolyGram / Jet Star

Georgia Melodians

GEORGIA MELODIANS 1924-1926
Why did you do it / Red hot Mamma / Charley, my boy / San / Everybody loves my baby / Doo wac a doo (A 'wow-wow') / I'm satisfied (Beside that sweetie o'mine) / I'm bound for Tennessee / My Mammy's blues / Give us the charleston / Yes, Sir, that's my baby / She's drivin' me wild / Red hot Henry Brown / Spanish shawl / Charleston ball / I've found a new baby / Hangin' around / Rhythm of the day / Ev'ry body's charleston crazy / I can't get the one I want
CD _______ CBC 1031
Timeless Jazz / Aug '96 / New Note/ Pinnacle

Georgia Satellites

GEORGIA SATELLITES
Keep your hands to yourself / Railroad steel / Battleship chains / Red lights / Myth of love / I can't stand the pain / Golden lights / Over and over / Nights of mystery / Every picture tells a story
CD _______ 7559604962
Elektra / Jan '93 / Warner Music

LET IT ROCK (The Best Of Georgia Satellites)
Don't pass me by / Keep your hands to yourself / Battleship chains / Myth of love / Can't stand the pain / Nights of mystery / Let it rock / Open all night / Sheila / Mon cheri / Down and down / Saddle up / Hippy hippy shake / I dunno / All over but the crying / Six years gone / Hard luck boy / Almost Saturday night/Rockin' all over the world / Dan takes five / Another chance
CD _______ 7559613362
Elektra / Feb '93 / Warner Music

VERY BEST OF THE GEORGIA SATELLITES, THE
CD _______ 10322
CMC / Jun '97 / BMG

Georgians

GEORGIANS 1922-1923, THE
I wish I could shimmy like my sister Kate / Chicago (that toddling town) / Way down yonder in New Orleans / Nothing but / Loose feet / Aggravatin' Papa / You tell her, I stutter / You've got to see Mama every night / Farewell blues / Snakes hips / Old King Tut / Barney Google / Henpecked blues / Long lost Mama / Land of cotton blues / Mamma loves Papa / Mamma goes where Papa goes / Somebody's wrong / I'm sitting pretty in a pretty little city / Learn to do the strut / Home town blues / You maybe fast but Your Mamma's gonna slow you down / Shake your feet / Old fashioned love
CD _______ RTR 79003
Retrieval / Nov '96 / Cadillac / Direct / Jazz Music / Swift / Wellard

Geraci, Little Anthony

TAKE IT FROM ME (Geraci, Little Anthony & Sugar Ray Norcia)
CD _______ CDTC 1149
Tonecool / Nov '94 / ADA / Direct

Geraldine Fibbers

GERALDINE FIBBERS, THE
Marmalade / Get thee gone / Grand tour / Outside of town / They suck / Fancy / Blue cross
CD _______ DGHUTM 22
Hut / Jan '95 / EMI

LOST SOMEWHERE BETWEEN THE EARTH AND MY HOME
Lily Belle / Small song / Marmalade / Dragon lady / Song about walls / House is falling / Outside of town / French song / Dusted / Richard / Blast of baby / Get thee gone
CD _______ CDHUT 28
Hut / Jul '95 / EMI

Geraldo

DANCING IN THE BLITZ
Good morning / I'm nobody's baby / Whose little what is it are you / I've got my eyes on you / Where or when / When night is through / Don't worry bout me / Sierra Sue / Singing hills / I can't love you anymore / Let's top the clock / Ferryboat serenade / Sweetheart it's you / Don't you ever cry / Love stay in my heart / World is waiting for the sunrise / Blue orchids / We'll go smiling along / Nightingale sang in berkely square / Goodnight again
CD _______ PAR 2009
Parade / Apr '95 / Disc

GERALDO
All of me / C'est si bon / Carnival time / That's you / Russian lullaby no.4 / Can't you read between the lines / Box 155 / Old master painter / Orange coloured sky / I still love you / Medley / I do, I do, I do / We all have a song in our hearts / Taps Miller / Patience and fortitude / Music, music, music / Jungle fantasy / Undecided / I never loved anyone / In Charlie's footsteps / Slow coach / Two moods / I only have eyes for you / Sometimes / Medley
CD _______ CDMFP 6359
Music For Pleasure / Jun '97 / EMI

GERALDO AND HIS ORCHESTRA
CD _______ PASTCD 7070
Flapper / Jul '95 / Pinnacle

JOURNEY TO A STAR, A (Geraldo & His Orchestra)
Sweet Sue, just you / Goodnight again / World is waiting for the sunrise / I can't love you anymore / Singing hills / Don't you ever cry / Breathless / Elmer's tune / Hey Mabel / Jim / Jingle jangle jingle / My devotion / Canzonetta / Russian rose / Waiter and the porter and the upstairs maid / Humpty dumpty heart / Frenes / Ain't it a shame about mame / Blue in the night / What is

this thing called love / Journey to a star / Don't ask me why
CD RAJCD 811
Empress / May '97 / Koch

TIP-TOP TUNES
In a little Spanish town: *Geraldo Strings* / Nearness of you: *Geraldo & His Concert Orchestra* / Top hat, white tie and tails: *Geraldo & His Dance Orchestra* / Autumn concerto: *Geraldo & His Concert Orchestra* / Hallelujah: *Geraldo & His Dance Orchestra* / Signature tune: *Geraldo & His Concert Orchestra* / My heart stood still: *Geraldo & His Concert Orchestra* / There's a small hotel: *Geraldo & His Concert Orchestra* / Heather on the hill: *Geraldo & His Concert Orchestra* / Rockin' through Dixie: *Geraldo & His Dance Orchestra* / Nature boy: *Geraldo Strings* / What is this thing called love: *Geraldo & His Concert Orchestra* / I'm on a seesaw: *Geraldo & His Concert Orchestra* / So many times I have cried over you: *Geraldo Strings* / When Johnny comes marching home: *Geraldo & His Dance Orchestra* / Begin the beguine: *Geraldo & His Concert Orchestra* / Isle of Innisfree: *Geraldo Strings* / Arkansas traveller: *Geraldo & His Dance Orchestra*
CD CDHD 135
Happy Days / '89 / Conifer/BMG

TOP HAT, WHITE TIE AND TAILS (Geraldo & His Orchestra)
Top hat, white tie and tails / Lullaby of Broadway / My foolish heart / Somebody loves me / Night and day / Great day / Hallelujah / I get a kick out of you / Stardust / Strike up the band / Embraceable you / Continental / Pavanne / Time after time / Folks who live on the hill / Trombonology / Ding dong, the witch is dead / Trolley song / Without a song
CD 302942
Hallmark / Jun '97 / Carlton

Gerd

THIS TOUCH IS GREATER THAN MOODS
First crisium appearance / Nautiloidea / Qare scent spangled arcanum / Vulcan Princess / Carxan 71 / Carxan 72 / Century city / Trendor vualda / Austaris solalia / Osiris' starshaft
CD EVOGD 03CD
Universal Language / May '97 / Prime / RTM/Disc

Geremia, Paul

GAMBLIN' WOMAN BLUES
CD RHRCD 54
Red House / Dec '96 / ADA / Koch

REALLY DON'T MIND/MY KIND OF PLACE
CD FF 395CD
Flying Fish / May '93 / ADA / CM / Direct / Roots

SELF PORTRAIT IN BLUES
CD SHAM 1024CD
Shamrock / Apr '95 / ADA / Wellard
CD RHRCD 77
Red House / Dec '96 / ADA / Koch

Germ

GONE
CD GPRCD 6
GPR / Aug '94 / 3mv/Vital

Germano, Lisa

EXCERPTS FROM A LOVE CIRCUS
Baby on a plane / Beautiful schizophrenic / Bruises / I love a snot / Forget it, it's a mystery / Victoria's secret / Small heads / We suck / Lovesick / Singing to the birds / Messages from Sophia / Big big world
CD CAD 6012CD
4AD / Sep '96 / RTM/Disc

GEEK THE GIRL
CD CAD 4017CD
4AD / Oct '94 / RTM/Disc

HAPPINESS
CD CAD 4005CD
4AD / Apr '94 / RTM/Disc

Germs

GERMICIDE: LIVE AT THE WHISKEY
CD RE 108CD
ROIR / Nov '94 / Plastic Head / Shellshock/Disc

MEDIA BLITZ
CD CLEO 3736CD
Cleopatra / Jan '94 / Cargo / Greyhound / Plastic Head / RTM/Disc / SRD

Geronimo

PEACE TO THE CHIEF
CD TRP 002CD
Trechoma / Sep '95 / Plastic Head

Gerrard, Alice

PIECES OF MY HEART
CD COP 134CD
Copper Creek / May '97 / ADA

Gerrard, Lisa

MIRROR POOL, THE
Violina: The last embrace / La bas: Song of the drowned / Persian love song : The silver gun / Sanvean: I am your shadow / Rite / Ajhon / Glorafin / Majhnavea's music box / Largo / Werd / Laurelei / Celon / Ventelas / Swans / Nilleshna / Gloradin
CD CAD 5009CD
4AD / Aug '95 / RTM/Disc

Gerry & The Pacemakers

BEST OF GERRY & THE PACEMAKERS, THE
CD PLSCD 129
Pulse / Apr '96 / BMG

EMI YEARS, THE
How do you do it / Maybellene / I like it / Chills / Pretend / Jambalaya / You're the reason / Hello little girl / You'll never walk alone / Shot of rhythm and blues / Slow down / It's alright / I'm the one / Don't let the sun catch you crying / You've got what I like / It's just because / You, you, you / It's gonna be alright / Ferry 'cross the Mersey / I'll wait for you / Hallelujah, I love her so / Reelin' and rockin' / Why oh why / Baby you're so good to me / Walk hand in hand / Dreams / Give all your love to me / I'll be there / La la la / Fool to myself / Girl on a swing
CD CDEMS 1443
EMI / May '92 / EMI

EP COLLECTION, THE
How do you do it / Away from you / I like it / Chills / You'll never walk alone / Shot of rhythm and blues / You've got what I like / I'm the one / Don't let the sun catch you crying / Where have you been all my life / Maybellene / You're the reason / It's gonna be alright / I'll wait for you / Ferry 'cross the Mersey / You win again / Reelin' and rockin' / Whole lotta shakin' goin' on / Skinny Lizzie / My babe / What'd I say
CD SEECD 95
See For Miles/C5 / Mar '95 / Pinnacle

FERRY CROSS THE MERSEY (Remastered)
It's gonna be all right / Why oh why / Fall in love / Think about love / I love you too: *Fourmost* / All quiet on the Mersey front: *Martin, George Orchestra* / This thing called love / Baby you're so good to me / I'll wait for you / She's the only girl for me / Is it love: *Black, Cilla* / Ferry cross the Mersey / It's gonna be alright / I love you too: *Fourmost* / All quiet on the Mersey front: *Martin, George Orchestra* / This thing called love / Baby you're so good to me / I'll wait for you / She's the only girl for me / Is it love: *Black, Cilla* / Ferry cross the Mersey / Why oh why / Fall in love / Think about love
CD DORIG 114
EMI / Jul '97 / EMI

GERRY & THE PACEMAKERS
CD GRF 191
Tring / Jan '93 / Tring

NON-STOP PARTY ALBUM, THE
Party medley / 60's medley / Light's down low medley / 70's medley / Roll 'n' roll medley / You'll never walk alone
CD EMPRCD 658
Emporio / Jun '96 / Disc

VERY BEST OF GERRY & THE PACEMAKERS
How do you do it / I like it / It's gonna be alright / I'll be there / Girl on a swing / Come back to me / When, oh when / Don't let the sun catch you crying / You'll never walk alone / I'm the one / Walk hand in hand / La la la / It's alright / Give all your love to me / Hallelujah, I love her so / Ferry 'cross the Mersey
CD CDMFP 5654
Music For Pleasure / Mar '93 / EMI

YOU'LL NEVER WALK ALONE
CD MSCD 033
Music De-Luxe / Jun '96 / TKO Magnum

Gershwin, Frances

FOR GEORGE & IRA 1928-1938
CD ACD 116
Audiophile / Mar '97 / Jazz Music

Gershwin, George

'S MARVELLOUS (Gershwin, George & Ira)
CD 5216582
Verve / Feb '94 / PolyGram

'S WONDERFUL
CD 5139282
Verve / Apr '92 / PolyGram

20 INTRUMENTAL GREATS
But not for me / Embraceable you / Fascinating rhythm / Foggy day / I got rhythm / It ain't necessarily so / Let's call the whole thing off / Liza / Man I love / Nice work if you can get it / Shall we dance / Someone to watch over me / 'S wonderful / They can't take that away from me / Who cares / Long ago and far away / Summertime / There's a boat that's leavin' soon for New York / Oh I can't sit down / Somebody loves me
CD GRF 108
Tring / '93 / Tring

CRAZY FOR GERSHWIN (Various Artists)
CD VN 165
Viper's Nest / Mar '96 / ADA / Cadillac / Direct / Jazz Music

CRAZY FOR GERSHWIN (Lythgoe, Clive)
Fascinating rhythm / Man I love / I'll build a stairway to paradise / Somebody loves me / Strike up the band / Clap yo' hands / Oh lady be good / Liza / Do it again / 'S wonderful / Who cares / My one and only / Do do do / That certain feeling / Sweet and low down / I got rhythm
CD EMPRCD 558
Emporio / May '95 / Disc

FOREVER GEORGE GERSHWIN (Various Artists)
S'Wonderful: *London, Julie* / Bidin' my time: *Cole, Nat 'King'* / An American in Paris: *Brown, Les* / Do it again: *Garland, Judy* / I got rhythm: *Darin, Bobby* / Fascinating rhythm: *Damone, Vic* / Gershwin - king of rhythm: *Adler, Larry* / How long has this been going on: *Christy, June* / Embraceable you: *Cole, Nat 'King' Trio* / I'll build you a stairway to paradise: *Minnelli, Liza* / It ain't necessarily so: *MacKintosh, Ken* / Nice work if you can get it: *Southern, Jeri* / Love walked in: *Haymes, Dick* / Rhapsody in blue: *Adler, Larry* / Slip that bass: *Roy, Harry & His Band* / Someone to watch over me: *Wilson, Nancy* / Strike up the band: *Getz, Stan* / Summertime: *Rawls, Lou* / Our love is here to stay: *Shore, Dinah* / Man I love: *Lee, Peggy*
CD CDMFP 6261
Music For Pleasure / Nov '96 / EMI

GENIUS OF GEORGE GERSHWIN, THE (Starlight Orchestra)
But not for me / Embraceable you / Fascinating rhythm / Foggy day / I got rhythm / It ain't necessarily so / Lets call the whole thing off / Liza / Man I love / Nice work if you can get it / Shall we dance / Someone to watch over me / 'S wonderful / They can't take that away from me / Who cares / Long ago and far away / Summertime / There's a boat that leaving soon for new york / Oh I can't sit down / Somebody loves me
CD QED 109
Tring / Nov '96 / Tring

GEORGE GERSHWIN PLAYS GEORGE GERSHWIN
Rhapsody in blue / Hang on to me / Fascinating rhythm / Half of it dearie blues / I'd rather charleston / Sweet and low down / That certain feeling / Looking for a boy / Then do we dance / Do do do / Someone to watch over me / Clap yo' hands / Maybe / My one and only / Three preludes / Andante / 'S wonderful/Funny face / Rhapsody in blue / American in Paris / It ain't necessarily so / Buzzard song / Summertime / Bess you is my woman now / My man's gone now / Concerto in F (Third movement) / I got rhythm/Of thee I sing
CD Set GEMMCDS 9483
Pearl / Mar '91 / Harmonia Mundi

GEORGE GERSHWIN PLAYS GERSHWIN
Rhapsody in blue / American in Paris / It ain't necessaruly so / Buzzard song / Summertime/Crapgame/A woman is a sometime thing / Bess you is my woman now / I got plenty o' nuthin' / Where is my Bess / Summertime / My man's gone now / Concerto in F / I got rhythm/Of thee I sing
CD CD 48035
Magic Talent / Oct '96 / Target/BMG

GERSHWIN PERFORMS GERSHWIN (Rare Recordings 1931-1935)
Signature / Of thee I sing / Man I love / I got rhythm / Swanee / Mine / Love is sweeping the country / Wintergreen for President / Facinating rhythm/Liza / Second prelude / Woman is a sometime thing: *Gershwin, George & Edward Matthews* / My man's gone now: *Gershwin, George & Ruby Elzy* / Bess you is my woman now: *Gershwin, George & Todd Duncan/Anne Brown*
CD 8208422
Limelight / Jun '91 / PolyGram

GERSHWIN PLAYS GERSHWIN: THE PIANO ROLLS VOL.1
CD 7559792872
Nonesuch / Jul '94 / Warner Music

GERSHWIN PLAYS GERSHWIN: THE PIANO ROLLS VOL.2
CD 7559793702
Nonesuch / Nov '95 / Warner Music

GERSHWIN STORY (Amsterdam Saxophone Quartet)
CD I 9611502
Masters Music / Dec '96 / ZYX

GREAT MELODIES, THE (Gershwin, George/Cole Porter)
An American in Paris / Man I love / Our love is here to stay / Someone to watch over me / Foggy day / Strike up the band / They can't take that away from me / From me / Medley (Gershwin, a portrait) / Another openin' another show / I love you Samantha / Begin the beguine / I've got you under my skin / Let's do it / Love for sale / So in love / Anything goes
CD 300582
Hallmark / Jul '96 / Carlton

ONE AND ONLY GEORGE GERSHWIN, THE (Various Artists)
When do we dance: *Gershwin, George* / I got plenty o' nuttin': *Crosby, Bing* / Embraceable you: *Garland, Judy* / Half of it dearie blues: *Astaire, Fred* / 'S Wonderful: *Goodman, Benny* / Man I love: *Welch, Elisabeth & Benny Carter* / Swanee: *Jolson, Al* / I'll build a stairway to paradise: *Whiteman, Paul* / I was doing all right: *Fitzgerald, Ella* / I got rhythm: *Waller, Fats & his Rhythm Orchestra* / Someone to watch over me: *Lawrence, Gertrude* / Liza: *Wilson, Teddy* / Love walked in: *Armstrong, Louis* / Nice work if you can get it: *Andrews Sisters* / They can't take that away from me: *Holiday, Billie* / Oh Lady be good: *Lee, Buddy* / But not for me: *Forrest, Helen* / Let's call the whole thing off: *Astaire, Fred* / Summertime: *Crosby, Bing* / Somebody loves me: *Teagarden, Jack* / Andante: *Gershwin, George*
CD PAR 2033
Parade / Sep '94 / Disc

RHAPSODY IN BLUE
Rhapsody in blue / American in Paris / Swanee / Walking the dog / Let's call the whole thing off / Somebody loves me / Our love is here to stay / 'S Wonderful / Embraceable you / Oh Lady be good
CD BCD 106
Biograph / Jul '91 / ADA / Cadillac / Direct / Hot Shot / Jazz Music / Wellard

SELF PORTRAIT
Rhapsody in blue / That certain feeling / Left all again blues / Grieving for you / I'm a lonesome little raindrop / Just snap your fingers at care / Make believe / Land where the good songs go / Some Sunday morning / American in Paris / Rhapsody in blue
CD SUMCD 4051
Summit / Nov '96 / Sound & Media

STARS SALUTE GEORGE GERSHWIN, THE (Various Artists)
They all laughed: *Astaire, Fred* / But not for me: *Garland, Judy* / I was doing alright: *Fitzgerald, Ella* / Somebody loves me: *Carter, Benny Orchestra* / Swanee: *Jolson, Al* / They can't take that away from me: *McCrae, Carmen* / Summertime: *Holiday, Billie* / Swonderful: *Day, Doris* / Someone to watch over me: *Wiley, Lee* / Man I love: *Forrest, Helen* / I got rhythm: *Waller, Fats Orchestra* / Liza: *Webb, Chick Orchestra* / Fascinating rhythm: *Lee, Buddy* / Love walked in: *Armstrong, Louis* / Shall we dance: *Astaire, Fred* / Nice work if you can get it: *Dorsey, Tommy* / Oh lady be good: *Shaw, Artie* / Foggy day: *Grantham, Cyril & Geraldo Orchestra* / Embraceable you: *Garland, Judy* / How long has this been going on: *Lee, Peggy*
CD 300352
Hallmark / Jul '96 / Carlton

SUMMERTIME (Various Artists)
CD MACCD 257
Autograph / Aug '96 / BMG

TRIBUTE TO GERSHWIN, A (Various Artists)
'S wonderful / Summertime / Fascinating rhythm / Oh lady be good / Man I love / Summertime / Man I love / I can't get started / But not for me / 'S wonderful/Summertime/But not for me/I got rhythm / Man I love
CD 8747072
DA Music / Jul '96 / Conifer/BMG

TWO SIDES OF GEORGE GERSHWIN, THE
Rhapsody in blue / Three piano preludes / Andante / American in Paris / Sweet and low down / That certain feeling / Looking for a boy / When do we dance / Do do do / Someone to watch over me / Clap yo' hands / Maybe / My one and only / 'S wonderful / Funny face
CD DHDL 101
Halcyon / Oct '91 / Cadillac / Harmonia Mundi / Jazz Music / Swift / Wellard

Gershwin, Ira

'S WONDERFUL (Various Artists)
Our love is here to stay: *Clooney, Rosemary* / Soon: *Sloane, Carol* / Liza: *Torme, Mel* / Fascinating rhythm: *McCorkle, Susannah* / Long ago and far away: *Clooney, Rosemary* / Love walked in: *Anderson, Ernestine* / I can't get started: *Sheldon, Jack* / 'S Wonderful: *Allyson, Karrin* / Things are looking up: *Stallings, Mary* / Embraceable you: *Maria, Tania* / He loves and she loves: *Sloane, Carol* / Isn't it a pity: *Torme, Mel & Cleo Laine* / But not for me: *Stallings, Mary* / Foggy day: *Clooney, Rosemary*
CD CCD 4741
Concord Jazz / Nov '96 / New Note/ Pinnacle

Gertz, Bruce

BLUEPRINT (Gertz, Bruce Quartet)
Proton / Neves / It should / Otto's motto / While you were out / Cryptic current / Other you / Backspace / Red yellow green / Blueprint / Proton II

CD FRLCD 017
Freelance / Nov '92 / Cadillac / Koch
CD ECD 22196
Evidence / Aug '97 / ADA / Cadillac / Harmonia Mundi

Gessinger, Nils

SCRATCH BLUE
Roll / Stranger / What a fool believes / Scratch blue / What's new / Brood / Until morning / Sunstroke / Winter breeze / Moving / Maple clouds / Can't stop naggin' / Downside day / Ducks 'n' cookies
CD GRP 98502
GRP / Nov '96 / New Note/BMG

Gessle, Per

WORLD ACCORDING TO GESSLE
(You make me feel so) stupid / Do you wanna be my baby / Saturday / Elvis in Germany / I want you to know / Reporter / B any 1 U wanna B / Wish you the best / Kix / T-t-take it / It'll be alright / There is my baby / Lay down your arms
CD CDEMD 1105
EMI / May '97 / EMI

Getaway Cruiser

INSTRUMENTALS
CD ME 012CD
Mind Expansion / Mar '97 / Cargo

PHONES CALLING
CD SKL 201
Skillet / Mar '97 / Cargo

Geto Boys

RESURRECTION, THE
Ghetto prisoner / Still / World is a ghetto / Open minded / Killer for scratch / Hold it down / Blind leading the blind / First light of day / Time taker / Geto boys and girls / Geto fantasy / I just wanna die / Niggas and flies / Visit with Larry Hoover / Point of no return
CD CDVUS 103
Virgin / Apr '96 / EMI

Gettel, Michael

ART OF NATURE, THE
Light of the land / When all is quiet (she dreams if horses) / Watershed / Shelter / Fire from the sky / Solace / Where eagles soar / Midsummer / Crosswind
CD ND 63032
Narada / Jul '95 / ADA / New Note/Pinnacle

KEY, THE
Waiting / Turning of a key / Breaking the silence / When hearts collide / Search / Glimmer of hope / Broken / Light of a candle / Letting go / Awakening / Through the doorway
CD ND 63027
Narada / Jun '94 / ADA / New Note/Pinnacle

SAN JUAN SUITE VOL.2 (Piano Passages)
Calling / Safe passage / Every shade of green / Sundance / Whisper on the tide / Wind and water / Sea of glass / Tale of the whales / Moonrise over Orcas
CD ND 62806
Narada / Feb '97 / ADA / New Note/Pinnacle

SKYWATCHING
Anasazi Roads / Skywatching / Windows and walls / Prelude / Sacred side (in ruins) / Wellspring / Prelude: Kiva / Sipapu / Tekohananae (to the morning) / Prelude: Stillness / Scent of rain / Where the road meets the sky
CD ND 63025
Narada / May '93 / ADA / New Note/Pinnacle

Getz, Stan

'ROUND MIDNIGHT
CD JD 1266
Koch / Nov '94 / Koch

'ROUND MIDNIGHT
CD JHR 73542
Jazz Hour / May '93 / Cadillac / Jazz Music / Target/BMG

'ROUND MIDNIGHT IN PARIS
CD BS 18001
Bandstand / Jul '96 / Swift

ACADEMY OF JAZZ (Getz, Stan & Bob Brookmeyer)
CD COD 024
Jazz View / Mar '92 / Harmonia Mundi

ANNIVERSARY (Live At The Montmartre Club, Copenhagen)
El Cahon / I can't get started (with you) / Stella by starlight / Stan's blues / I thought about you / What is this thing called love / Blood count
CD 8387692
EmArCy / Jul '90 / PolyGram

APASIONADO
Apasionado / Coba / Waltz for Stan / Espanola / Madrugada / Amorous cat / Midnight ride / Lonely Lady
CD 3952972
A&M / Aug '90 / PolyGram

AT LARGE VOL.1
CD JUCD 2001
Jazz Unlimited / Jan '89 / Cadillac / Jazz Music / Wellard

AT LARGE VOL.2
CD JUCD 2002
Jazz Unlimited / Dec '91 / Cadillac / Jazz Music / Wellard

AT THE OPERA HOUSE (Live In Chicago & Los Angeles 1957) (Getz, Stan & J.J. Johnson)
Billie's bounce / My funny valentine / Crazy rhythm / Blues in the closet / Yesterdays / It never entered my mind
CD 8312722
Verve / Jan '93 / PolyGram

AUDIO ARCHIVE
Autumn leaves / Billie's bounce / Heart place / Kali-au / Chappaqua
CD CDAA 028
Tring / Jun '92 / Tring

AUTUMN LEAVES
CD WWCD 2046
West Wind / Apr '90 / Koch

BEST OF TWO WORLDS, THE
CD 4715112
Sony Jazz / Jan '95 / Sony

BIG BAND BOSSA NOVA
Manha de carnaval / Balanco no samba / Melancolico / Entre amigos / Chega de saudade / Noite triste / Samba de uma nota so / Bim bom
CD 8257712
Verve / Jan '93 / PolyGram

BILLY HIGHSTREET SAMBA
Hospitality creek / Anytime tomorrow / Be there than / Billy highstreet samba / Dirge / Page two / Body and soul / Tuesday next
CD 8387712
EmArCy / Jul '90 / PolyGram

BIRDLAND SESSIONS 1952 (Getz, Stan Quintet)
CD FSRCD 149
Fresh Sound / Dec '90 / Discovery / Jazz Music

BLUE SKIES
Spring is here / Antigny / Easy living / There we go / Blue skies / How long has this been going on
CD CCD 4676
Concord Jazz / Dec '95 / New Note/Pinnacle

BROTHERS, THE
CD OJCCD 8
Original Jazz Classics / Apr '87 / Complete/Pinnacle / Jazz Music / Wellard

CAPTAIN MARVEL
CD 4684122
Sony Jazz / Jan '95 / Sony

DOLPHIN,THE (Getz, Stan Quartet)
Time for love / Joy Spring / Dolphin / Close enough for love
CD CCD 4158
Concord Jazz / Jul '87 / New Note/Pinnacle

DYNASTY (Live At Ronnie Scott's 1971/ 2CD Set)
Dum dum dum / Ballad for Leo / Our kind of Sabi / Mona / Theme for Emmanuel / Invitation / Ballad for my dad / Song for Martine / Dynasty / I remember Clifford
CD Set 8391172
Verve / Jan '93 / PolyGram

EARLY STAN
Motion / Lee / Michelle / T and S / Signal / 'Round midnight / Terry's tune (original, alternate and alternate two) / Cuddles (Speedway)
CD OJCCD 654
Original Jazz Classics / Apr '93 / Complete/Pinnacle / Jazz Music / Wellard

ESSENTIAL STAN GETZ, THE
Ligia / Lester left town / Blue Serge / Hopscotch / Anna / Captain Marvel / What am I here for / Lush life / Double rainbow / Peacocks / La Fiesta
CD 4715182
Columbia / Jul '93 / Sony

FOCUS
I'm late / Her / Pan / I remember when / Night rider / Once upon a time / Summer afternoon
CD 8219822
Verve / Oct '93 / PolyGram

FOR MUSICIANS ONLY (Getz, Stan & Sonny Stitt/Dizzy Gillespie)
Be bop / Dark eyes / Wee / Lover come back to me / Dark eyes
CD 8374352
Verve / Aug '89 / PolyGram

GETZ AU GO GO (Getz, Stan Quartet & Astrud Gilberto)
Singing song / Telephone song / One note samba / Only trust your heart / Corcovado / It might as well be Spring / Eu e voce / Summertime / Six nix pix flix / Here's that rainy day
CD 8217252
Verve / Jan '93 / PolyGram

GETZ MEETS MULLIGAN IN HI-FI (Getz, Stan & Gerry Mulligan)
Let's fall in love / Anything goes / Too close for comfort / That old feeling / This can't be love / Ballad / Scrapple from the apple / I didn't know what time it was
CD 8493922
Verve / Mar '91 / PolyGram

GETZ/GILBERTO VOL.1 (Getz, Stan & Joao Gilberto/Antonio Carlos Jobim)
Girl from Ipanema / Doralice / Para machuchar meu coracao / Desafinado / Corcovado / So danco samba / O grande amor / Dreamer
CD 8100482
Verve / Dec '83 / PolyGram

GETZ/GILBERTO VOL.2 (Live At Carnegie Hall) (Getz, Stan & Joao Gilberto)
Grandfather's waltz / Tonight I shall sleep with a smile on my face / Stan's blues / Here's that rainy day / Samba da minha terra / Rosa morena / Um braco no bronfa / Bim bom / Meditation / O pato / It might as well be Spring / Only trust your heart / Corcovado / Girl from Ipanema / Eu e voce
CD 5198002
Verve / Dec '93 / PolyGram

GIRL FROM IPANEMA, THE (The Bossa Nova Years/4CD Set)
Desafinado / Samba dees days / O pato / Samba triste / Samba de uma nota so / E luxo so / Baia / Manha de carnival / Balanco no samba / Melancolico / Entre amigos / Chega de saudade / Noite triste / Samba de uma nota so / Bim bom / Sambalero / So danco samba / How insensitive / O morro nao tem vez / Samba de duas notas / Menina flor / Mania de Maria / Saudade vem correndo / Um abraco no Getz / Ebony samba / Ebony samba / Tribute to Stan / Girl from Ipanema / Doralice / Para machuchar mew coracao / Desafinado / Corcovado / So danco samba / O grande amor / Dreamer / Corcovado / It might as well be Spring / Eu e voce / Only trust your heart / Telephone song / Samba de uma nota so / Corcovado / Menina moca / Once again / Winter moon / Do what you do / Samba da Sahra / Maracatu - too / Eu e voce / Corcovado / Girl from Ipanema
CD Set 8236112
Verve / Jan '90 / PolyGram

GITANES - JAZZ 'ROUND MIDNIGHT (Getz, Stan & Joao Gilberto/Astrud Gilberto)
Girl from Ipanema: *Getz, Stan & Astrud Gilberto* / Once upon a Summertime: *Gilberto, Astrud* / Once again: *Getz, Stan & Laurindo Almeida* / Thanks for the memory: *Getz, Stan* / I haven't got anything better to do: *Gilberto, Astrud* / How insensitive: *Getz, Stan & Luiz Bonfa* / Corcovado: *Gilberto, Astrud & Joao Gilberto* / Manha de carnaval: *Gilberto, Astrud* / Desafinado: *Getz, Stan & Charlie Byrd* / Avarandado: *Gilberto, Joao* / Look to the rainbow: *Gilberto, Astrud* / Sambalero: *Getz, Stan & Luiz Bonfa* / It might as well be Spring: *Getz, Stan & Astrud Gilberto* / Shadow of your smile: *Gilberto, Astrud* / Bronx blues: *Getz, Stan & Oscar Peterson*
CD 8414452
Verve / Oct '92 / PolyGram

HIGHLIGHTS VOL.1 (The Best Of The Verve Years/2CD Set)
Stella by starlight / Exactly like you / It don't mean a thing if it ain't got that swing / Handful of stars / Wee / Ballad / You're blase / My funny valentine / 'Round midnight / Desafinado / Manha de carnaval / Girl from Ipanema / Corcovado / Melinda / Cool mix / With the wind and the rain / Night in Tunisia / Over the rainbow / Sniles / Blues for Herky / Gold rush / Goodbye / I'm late I'm late / I didn't know what it was / Sweet rain / I remember Clifford / Communication 72
CD Set 8474302
Verve / May '91 / PolyGram

HIGHLIGHTS VOL.2 (The Best Of The Verve Years/2CD Set)
Thanks for the memory / Rustic hop / Round up time / Cherokee / East of the sun and West of the moon / Serenade in blue / Dark eyes / Where or when / Billie's bounce / Blues for junior / Honeysuckle rose / All the things you are / Folks who live on the hill / Airegin / Who could care / Chega de saudade / Corcovado / Maria Moca / My heart stood still / When the world was young / Litha / I remember Clifford
CD Set 5173302
Verve / Jan '93 / PolyGram

IMMORTAL CONCERTS (Stan Getz meets Joao & Astrud Gilberto) (Getz, Stan & Joao Gilberto/Astrud Gilberto)
Corcovado / O Pato / It might as well be Spring / Samba da minha terra / One note samba / Tonight I shall sleep / Bim bom / Singing song / Telephone song / Here's that rainy day / Eu e voce / Rosa moreno / Grandfather's waltz / Only trust your heart / Um abraco no bonfa / Stan's blues / Meditation / Summertime / Six mix pix flix
CD CD 53021
Giants Of Jazz / Jun '88 / Cadillac / Jazz Music / Target/BMG

IN CONCERT (Getz, Stan & Joe Farrell/ Paul Horn/Michael Garson)
Heartplace / Kali-au / Chappaqua / Nature boy / 500 miles high / Lady Day / Autumn leaves / Billie's bounce
CD CDGATE 7022
Kingdom Jazz / '89 / Kingdom

IN CONCERT
CD DM 15009
DMA Jazz / Jul '96 / Jazz Music

JAZZ MASTERS
Desafinado / Shine / Body and soul / Gladys / It never entered my mind / Jordu / Windows / Dynsty / Her / Girl from Ipanema
CD 5198232
Verve / May '94 / PolyGram

JAZZ MASTERS (Getz, Stan & Dizzy Gillespie)
Dark eyes / Be bop / It's the talk of the town / Mooche / Way you look tonight / It don't mean a thing if it ain't got that swing
CD 5218522
Verve / Feb '94 / PolyGram

JAZZ MASTERS (Bossa Nova 1962-1967)
CD 5299042
Verve / Apr '96 / PolyGram

JAZZ PORTRAITS (Getz, Stan & Joao Gilberto/Astrud Gilberto)
Corcovado / It might as well be spring / Eu e voce / Girl from Ipanema / O pato (the duck) / Um abraco no bonfa / Meditation / Here's that rainy day / Samba de minha terra / One note samba / Telephone song / Only trust your heart / Stan's blues / Bim bom / Rosa morena / Singing song
CD CD 14514
Jazz Portraits / May '94 / Jazz Music

JAZZ SAMBA (Getz, Stan & Charlie Byrd)
Desafinado / Samba dees days / O Pato / Samba triste / Samba de uma nota so / E luxo so / Baia
CD 8100612
Verve / Apr '89 / PolyGram

JAZZ SAMBA ENCORE (Getz, Stan & Luiz Bonfa)
Sambalero / So danco samba / O morro noa tem vez / How insensitive / Samba de duas notas / Mania de Maria suadade vem correndo / Um abraco no Getz / Ebony samba / Menina flor
CD 8236132
Verve / Mar '93 / PolyGram

LIVE AT MONTMARTRE VOL.1
CD SCCD 31073
Steeplechase / '90 / Discovery / Impetus

LIVE AT MONTMARTRE VOL.2
CD SCCD 31074
Steeplechase / '90 / Discovery / Impetus

LIVE FROM 1952-1955
CD LS 2911
Landscape / Nov '92 / THE

LIVE IN EUROPE
CD Set JWD 102304
JWD / Nov '94 / Target/BMG

LIVE IN PARIS
Un grand amor / Blood count / Airegin / Blue skies / On the up and up / I wanted to say / Tempus fugit
CD FDM 365772
Dreyfus / Apr '96 / ADA / Direct / New Note/Pinnacle

LYRICAL STAN GETZ, THE
Willow weep for me / La fiesta / Captain Marvel / Ligia / Misty / Lover man
CD 4608192
Sony Jazz / Jan '95 / Sony

MOVE
CD NI 4005
Natasha / Jun '93 / ADA / Cadillac / CM / Direct / Jazz Music

NATURE BOY VOL.2
CD JHR 73554
Jazz Hour / Jan '93 / Cadillac / Jazz Music / Target/BMG

NOBODY ELSE BUT ME
CD 5216602
Verve / Nov '94 / PolyGram

PEOPLE TIME (2CD Set) (Getz, Stan & Kenny Barron)
East of the sun and west of the moon / Night and day / I'm okay / Like someone in love / Stablemates / I remember Clifford / Gone with the wind / First song / There is no greater love / Surrey with the fringe on top / People time / Softly as in a morning sunrise / Hush-a-bye / Soul eyes
CD Set 5101342
Verve / Mar '92 / PolyGram

PURE GETZ (Getz, Stan Quartet)
On the up and up / Blood count / Very early / Sippin' at bells / I wish I knew / Come rain or come shine / Tempus fugit
CD CCD 4188
Concord Jazz / Dec '86 / New Note/Pinnacle

QUARTETS
CD _______________ OJCCD 121
Original Jazz Classics / Feb '93 / Complete/Pinnacle / Jazz Music / Wellard

RARE DAWN SESSIONS
CD _______________ BCD 132
Biograph / Oct '94 / ADA / Cadillac / Direct / Hot Shot / Jazz Music / Wellard

RARE RECORDINGS AND COLLECTIBLES (The Golden Age of Jazz)
CD _______________ JZCD 363
Suisa / May '92 / Jazz Music / THE

ROOST YEARS, THE (The Best Of Stan Getz)
Gone with the wind / Yesterdays / Hershey Bar / Imagination / Split kick / It might as well be Spring / Parker '51 / Signal / Everything happens to me / Budo / Potter's luck / Wild wood / Autumn leaves / Lullaby of Birdland / Moonlight in Vermont / Sometimes I'm happy
CD _______________ CDROU 1047
Roulette / Oct '91 / EMI

SERENITY (Live At The Cafe Montmartre Copenhagen 1987)
On green dolphin street / Voyage / Falling in love / I remember you / I love you
CD _______________ 8387702
EmArCy / May '91 / PolyGram

SILVER COLLECTION, THE (Getz, Stan & Oscar Peterson)
I want to be happy / Pennies from heaven / Bewitched, bothered and bewildered / I don't know why I just do / How long has this been going on / I can't get started (With you) / Polka dots and moonbeams / I'm glad there is you / Tour's end / I was doing all right / Bronx blues / Three little words / Detour ahead / Sunday / Blues for Henry
CD _______________ 8278262
Verve / Oct '86 / PolyGram

SONG IS YOU, THE
Song is you / O grande amor / For Jane / Dane's chant / Major General / Folk tune for bass / Tonight I shall sleep/Desafinado / All the things you are / Summer night / One night samba
CD _______________ 17078
Laserlight / Jan '97 / Target/BMG

SPRING IS HERE
How about you / You're blase / Easy living / Sweet Lorraine / Old devil moon / I'm old fashioned / Spring is here
CD _______________ CCD 4500
Concord Jazz / Mar '92 / New Note/ Pinnacle

STAN & CHET (Getz, Stan & Chet Baker)
CD _______________ 8374362
Verve / Mar '96 / PolyGram

STAN GETZ (Getz, Stan & Jimmy Raney/Al Haig/Teddy Kotick)
CD _______________ CD 53113
Giants Of Jazz / Jun '92 / Cadillac / Jazz Music / Target/BMG

STAN GETZ & BILL EVANS (Getz, Stan & Bill Evans)
Night and day / But beautiful / Funkallero / My heart stood still / Melinda / Grandfather's waltz / Carpetbagger's theme / WNEW / My heart stood still / Grandfather's waltz / Night and day
CD _______________ 8338022
Verve / Jan '93 / PolyGram

STAN GETZ AT THE SHRINE (Live In Los Angeles 1954)
Flamingo / Lover man / Pernod / Tasty pudding / I'll remember April / Polka dots and moonbeams / Open country / It don't mean a thing if it ain't got that swing / We'll be together again / Feather merchant
CD _______________ 5137532
Verve / Jan '93 / PolyGram

STAN GETZ PLAYS
Stella by starlight / Time on my hands / 'Tis Autumn / Way you look tonight / Lover come back to me / Body and soul / Stars fell on Alabama / You turned the tables on me / Thanks for the memory / Hymn of the Orient / These foolish things / How deep is the ocean / Nobody else but me / Down by the sycamore tree / I hadn't anyone till you / With the wind and the rain in your hair
CD _______________ 8335352
Verve / Sep '93 / PolyGram

STAN GETZ QUARTET & QUINTET (1950-1952)
CD _______________ CD 53137
Giants Of Jazz / Nov '92 / Cadillac / Jazz Music / Target/BMG

STAN GETZ WITH LAURINDO ALMEIDA (Getz, Stan & Laurindo Almeida)
Menina moca / Once again / Winter moon / Do what you do / Samba da Sahra / Maracatu - too / Corcovado
CD _______________ 8231492
Verve / Jan '93 / PolyGram

SWEET RAIN
Litha / O grande amor / Sweet rain / Con Alma / Windows / There will never be another you
CD _______________ 8150542
Verve / Jan '93 / PolyGram

THIS IS JAZZ
La fiesta / Who cares / Ligia / Misty / Aguas de marco / Lester left / Town / Blue serge / Captain Marvel / Peacocks / Count Basie / This is jazz / One o'clock jump / Lester leaps in / 9:20 special / Oh lady be good / Goin' to Chicago blues / Red bank boogie / Dickie's dream / Miss thing / Tickle toe / How long blues / Broadway / Rock-a-bye Basie / Blow top / Let me see / Taxi wardance / Moten swing jumpin' at the Woodside
CD _______________ CK 64969
Sony Jazz / Oct '96 / Sony

WEST COAST SESSIONS, THE (3CD Set)
CD Set _______________ 5319352
Verve / Dec '96 / PolyGram

WEST COAST SESSIONS, THE (Highlights)
CD _______________ 5370842
Verve / May '97 / PolyGram

WITH CAL TJADER SEXTET (Getz, Stan Sextet)
CD _______________ OJCCD 275
Original Jazz Classics / Feb '92 / Complete/Pinnacle / Jazz Music / Wellard

WITH EUROPEAN FRIENDS
All God's chillun got rhythm / Broadway / Ladybird / Dear old Stockholm / East of the sun and west of the moon / They all fall in love / Theme for Manuel / Our kind of sabi
CD _______________ 17079
Laserlight / May '97 / Target/BMG

YOURS AND MINE
You'd be so nice to come home to / Joanne Julia / Yours and mine / Con alma / People time / What is this thing called love / Yesterdays
CD _______________ CCD 4740
Concord Jazz / Dec '96 / New Note/ Pinnacle

GGFH

HALLOWEEN
Little Missy / Blood is thicker / Chainsaw / She comes to you / Curiosity killed the cat / Thorns / Night stalker / As I touch you / Plaster Christ '88 / Ireland / Fetal infection / Dread / Missy '84 / Go away / Missy's revenge
CD _______________ KTB 012
Dreamtime / Oct '94 / Kudos / Pinnacle

Ghanaian Inspiration

RIVER PRA
CD _______________ MECCACD 1092
Music Mecca / May '97 / Cadillac / Jazz Music / Wellard

Ghetto Mafia

DRAW THE LINE
CD _______________ FTR 4184CD
Ichiban / May '94 / Direct / Koch

Ghiglioni, Tiziana

CANTA LUIGI TENCO
CD _______________ W 602
Philology / Apr '94 / Cadillac / Harmonia Mundi

I'LL BE AROUND (Ghiglioni, Tiziana, Enrico Rava & Mal Waldron)
CD _______________ 1212562
Soul Note / Jun '91 / Cadillac / Harmonia Mundi / Wellard

SOUNDS OF LOVE
Beautiful singing / My old flame / All of me / Ruby my dear / Naima / Sound of love / I remember you / My funny valentine / Straight no chaser
CD _______________ 1210562
Soul Note / Nov '90 / Cadillac / Harmonia Mundi / Wellard

Ghillies

NINETIES COLLECTION VOL.2
Hornpipes / Reels / Slow air / Marches / Slow air / Strathspey and reels / Jigs and reels / Hornpipes / Marches / Slow air / Jigs / Slow air / Strathspey and reels / Slow air and reels
CD _______________ CDTRAX 5006
Greentrax / Feb '97 / ADA / Direct / Duncans / Highlander

Ghorwane

MAJURUGENTA
Muthimba / Majurugenta / Matarlatanta / Xai-xai / Mavabwyi / Sathuma / Buluku / Terehuma / Akuhanha
CD _______________ CDRW 29
Realworld / Jul '93 / EMI

Ghost

ICH MACHINE
CD _______________ INDIGO 29152
What's So Funny About / Dec '96 / Cargo

LAMA RABI RABI
CD _______________ DCD 113
Drag City / Jan '97 / Cargo / Greyhound

SECOND TIME AROUND
CD _______________ INDIGO 11752
Strange Ways / Dec '96 / Cargo / Pinnacle

TEMPLE STONE
CD _______________ INDIGO 11782
Strange Ways / Dec '96 / Cargo / Pinnacle

Ghost

OTHER SIDE, THE
CD _______________ NTHEN 020CD
Now & Then / Mar '96 / Plastic Head

Ghostface Killah

IRON MAIDEN
Iron maiden / Wildflower / Faster blade / 260 / Assassination day / Poisonous darts / Winter warz / Box in hand / Fish / Camay / Daytona 500 / Motherless child / Black Jesus / After the smoke is clear / All that I got is you / Soul controller / Marvel
CD _______________ 4853892
Razor Sharp/Epic / Oct '96 / Sony

Ghostings

LIPS LIKE RED
CD _______________ SPV 08561772
SPV / Aug '95 / Koch / Plastic Head

Ghosts

FULL FRONTAL DUBLOTOMY
CD _______________ CDZM 2
Zanders / Apr '96 / SRD

Ghoststorm

FROZEN IN FIRE
CD _______________ BMCD 65
Black Mark / May '95 / Plastic Head

Ghriallais, Nora

NATIVE CONNEMARA IRISH SINGING
CD _______________ NGCD 001
Claddagh / May '94 / ADA / CM / Direct

Giammarco, Maurizio

HORNITHOLOGY (Giammarco, Maurizio Quartet)
Old home / Sky walker / End of a bop affair / No Spanish night / Arboreal code / Unexpected flight / Voce vai ver
CD _______________ CDSGP 040
Prestige / Feb '93 / Else / Total/BMG

INSIDE (Giammarco, Maurizio Quartet)
CD _______________ 1212542
Soul Note / Jan '94 / Cadillac / Harmonia Mundi / Wellard

Gianelli, Fred

TELEPATHIC ROMANCE
CD _______________ EFA 501112
Sahko / Aug '96 / Plastic Head / SRD

TELEPATHIC WISDOM VOL.1
Acid diji 3 / Salacious / Fox hunt / Precognition / Eloquence / Clairvoyance / Fingered / Kooky scientist / Painkiller / EOD / Excelsior / Sleeps with the foxes / Acid diji 2
CD _______________ SUPER 2025CD
Superstition / Feb '95 / Plastic Head / SRD / Vital

TELEPATHIC WISDOM VOL.2
CD _______________ SUPER 2062
Superstition / Sep '96 / Plastic Head / SRD / Vital

Giant

LAST OF THE RUNAWAYS
I'm a believer / Innocent days / I can't get close enough / I'll see you in my dreams / No way out / Shake me up / It takes two / Stranger to me / Hold back the night / Love welcome home / Big pitch
CD _______________ CDA 5272
A&M / Apr '90 / PolyGram

Giant Sand

BACKYARD BARBECUE BROADCAST
CD _______________ OUT 1262
Brake Out / Aug '96 / Direct
CD _______________ 379142
Koch International / Jan '96 / Koch

BEST OF GIANT SAND VOL.2, THE
Can't find love / Get to leave / Town with a little or no pity / Dreamville New Mexico / October anywhere / Almost the politicians wife / Badlands / Christmas Day (maybe it'll help) / Sucker in a cage / Who am I / Death dying and channel 5 / Sandman / Sisters and brothers / Sage advice / Love like a train / Trickle down system
CD _______________ GSCD 2
Demon / Jul '95 / Pinnacle

BUILD YOUR OWN NIGHT, IT'S EASY (Official Bootleg Series Vol.1)
No name guitars / Sled / Elevator music / Spit / Corridor of love / Mason card / Hank's rap city / Less the lie / Scorcher / Bed of nails / Crumb / TW's forgotten chorus / Smokey Joe's deep blue pancakes
CD _______________ GSFANCD 1
Epiphany / Feb '97 / Cargo

CENTRE OF THE UNIVERSE
CD _______________ OUT 1092
Brake Out / Nov '92 / Direct

GIANT SONGS (The Best Of Giant Sand)
Down on town / Valley of rain / Thin line man / Body of water / Moon over Memphis / Uneven light of day / Big rock / One man's woman, no man's land / Mountain of love / Curse of a thousand flames / Barrio / Graveyard / Heartland / Underground train / Bigger than that / Wearing the robes of bible black / Fingernail moon, barracuda and me
CD _______________ GSCD 1
Demon / Jul '89 / Pinnacle

GOODS & SERVICES
CD _______________ OUT 1222
Brake Out / Aug '96 / Direct

LONG STEM RANT
Unfinished love / Sandman / Bloodstone / Searchlight / Smash jazz / Sucker in a cage / Patsy does Dylan / It's long 'bout now / Lag craw / Loving cup / Paved road to Berlin / Anthem / Picture shows / Drum and guitar / Get to leave / Searchlight cha cha / Return of the big red guitar / Stuck dog / Real gone blue guitar / Jig is up
CD _______________ HMS 148 2
Homestead / May '93 / Cargo / SRD

LOVE SONGS
CD _______________ FIENDCD 129
Demon / Sep '90 / Pinnacle

PURGE & SLOUCH
CD _______________ OUT 1152
Brake Out / Nov '94 / Direct

RAMP
CD _______________ R 2762
Rough Trade / Oct '91 / Pinnacle

STORM
Town where no town belongs / Back to black and grey / Bigger than that / Right makes right / Three sixes / Replacement / Storm / Was is a big word / Town with little or no pity / Weight
CD _______________ FIENDCD 115
Demon / Sep '90 / Pinnacle

STROMAUSFALL
CD _______________ RTS 7
Return To Sender / Nov '94 / ADA / Direct

SWERVE
Trickle down system / Dream stay / Former versions of ourselves / Angels at night / Can't find love / Swerver / Sisters and brothers / Swerving / Every grain of sand / Some kind of / Swervette / Final swerve
CD _______________ FIENDCD 204
Demon / Oct '90 / Pinnacle

VALLEY OF RAIN/BALLAD OF A THIN LINE MAN
Down on town (love's no answer) / Black venetian blind / Curse of a thousand flames / Artists / Man of want / Valley of rain / Tumble and tear / October anywhere / Death, dying and channel 5 / Torture of love / Thin line man / All along the watchtower / Graveyard / Body of water / You can't put your arms around a memory / Hard man to get to know / Who am I / Desperate man
CD _______________ DIAB 831
Demon / Jun '97 / Pinnacle

Giants Causeway

IS THERE ANYWAY
CD _______________ MASSCD 070
Massacre / Aug '95 / Plastic Head

Giants Chair

PURITY AND CONTROL
CD _______________ CR 022CD
Caulfield / Nov '96 / Cargo

Gibb, Andy

GREATEST HITS
I just want to be your everything / Thicker than water / Shadow dancing / Everlasting love / Don't throw it all away / Time is time / Me / Will you still love me tomorrow / After dark / Desire
CD _______________ 5115852
Polydor / Jul '94 / PolyGram

Gibb, Robin

HOW OLD ARE YOU
Juliet / How old are you / In and out of love / Kathy's gone / Don't stop the night / Another lonely night in New York / Danger / He can't love you / Hearts on fire / I believe in miracles
CD _______________ 8108962
Polydor / Apr '94 / PolyGram

SECRET AGENT
Boys (do fall in love) / In your diary / Rebecca / Secret agent / Living in another world / X-ray eyes / King of fools / Diamonds
CD _______________ 8217972
Polydor / Jul '84 / PolyGram

Gibbons, Carroll

CALLS THE TUNES
FDR Jones / My heart belongs to Daddy / Apple for the teacher / Wish me luck / Moon love / They can't black out the moon / In an 18th Century drawing room / It's a lovely day tomorrow / Scatterbrain / It's a hap hap happy day / Faithful forever / Let the people sing / Midnight in Mayfair / Oh Johnny / When you wish upon a star / Walkin' thru' Mockin' Bird Lane / Over the rainbow / Little rain must fall / My Capri serenade / Nightingale sang in Berkeley Square / I've got my eyes on you / Shake down the stars / Indian summer / Woodpecker song / Fools rush in / Let's put out the lights / When that man is dead and gone / Give me something to remembr you by / Goodnight / Good luck and carry on / Weep no more / One look at you / We three / South American way / I hear a rhapsody / Dolores / Boa noite / You and your kiss / I yi yi yi yi / You are too beautiful / When the blackbird says bye bye / Imagination / All the things you are / Blueberry hill / Sleepy lagoon / Never took a lesson in my life / You're as pretty as a picture / My own / Be a good scout / I wanna go back to Bali / Daydreaming / Latin quarter / You never looked so beautiful / I've got a pocketful of dreams / Change partners / Blue skies are round the corner / Two sleepy people / Penny Serenade
CD ______ RAJCD 863
Empress / Apr '96 / Koch

CARROLL GIBBONS
Grandma said / Ten little miles from town / They say / Say it's my heart / I have eyes / Remember me / Nice work if you can get it / Five o'clock whistle / You walk by / Breathless / Old black magic / You leave me breathless / Accentuate the positive / If I had a wishing ring / Mary Lou / We talk about you ev'ry night / Five minutes more / It's a beautiful day / As long as I live / To bed early / Prisoner of love / Saturday night / Pablo the dreamer / So ends my search for a dream / Let's take the long way home
CD ______ CDMFP 6354
Music For Pleasure / Jun '97 / EMI

CARROLL GIBBONS WITH THE SAVOY HOTEL ORPHEANS
On the air / Sweet as a song / With thee I swing / Let me give my happiness to you / Three wishes / I need you / Certain age / Moonbeam dance / When anybody plays or sings / Every woman thinks / Cabin in the cotton / Living in dreams / Oo - that kiss / Gay imposters / Isn't it romantic / Remember (Carroll Gibbons medley) / Any broken hearts to mend / Tomorrow is another day / Bubbling over / Goodbye to summer / Shall we dance
CD ______ PASTCD 9734
Flapper / Mar '91 / Pinnacle

ON THE AIR
Black coffee / Body and soul / By the fireside / Carroll calls the tunes / Everything I have is yours / Fascinating rhythm / Flamingo / For me, for you: *Gibbons, Carroll & Hildegarde* / Garden in the rain: *Gibbons, Carroll & George Metaxa* / Happy go lucky / Heaven can wait / I need some cooling off/ My heart stood still / I'm just beginning to care / Life is just a bowl of cherries / Linda: *Gibbons, Carroll & Al Bowlly* / Lovely to look at / Moonbeam dance / On the air / Smoke gets in your eyes / Summer rain / Sweet and lovely: *Gibbons, Carroll & Al Bowlly* / Under a blanket of blue / When day is done / Whispers in the dark / With thee I swing
CD ______ CDAJA 5142
Living Era / Oct '94 / Select

TIME WAS
On the air / Always in my heart / Old Uncle Bud / Yankee doodle boy / Madelaine / Turn your money in your pocket / Tropical magic / Elmer's tune / Tomorrow's sunrise / Moonlight cocktail / Miss you / Concerto for two / Sinner kissed an angel / Darling / I walked into a dream without knocking / As time goes by / I don't want anybody at all / Tell me the truth / Put your arms around me honey / Amodola / I should have known years ago / Time
CD ______ RAJCD 823
Empress / Mar '94 / Koch

Gibbons, Leroy

FOUR SEASON LOVER
CD ______ FMCD 004
Fatman / Jan '97 / Jet Star / SRD

Gibbons, Steve

BIRMINGHAM TO MEMPHIS
CD ______ AKD 019
Linn / Apr '93 / PolyGram

ON THE LOOSE (Gibbons, Steve Band)
Down the road apiece / Chuck in my car / absolutely gone / Love part one / Trucker / On the loose / To be alone with you / Love 'n' peace / Like a rolling stone
CD ______ CDMF 041
Magnum Force / May '92 / TKO Magnum

STEVE GIBBONS- LIVE
CD ______ 848829
SPV / Sep '90 / Koch / Plastic Head

Gibbs, Georgia

GEORGIA GIBBS
'Deed I do / I get a kick out of you / Let's do it / One I love belongs to somebody else / On the sunny side of the street / Comes love / You've got to see Mama every night / Lonesome road / I got it bad and that ain't good / Wrap your troubles in dreams / Seven lonely days / Man that got away / I'll be seeing you / How did he look / Baby, won't you please come home / After you've gone / It's the talk of the town / He's funny that way / Say it isn't so / If I had you / I'll always be in love with you / Somebody loves me / I love in Paris
CD ______ CD 382
Entertainers / Mar '96 / Target/BMG

Gibbs, Joe

EXPLOSIVE ROCKSTEADY (Joe Gibbs Amalgamated 1967-1973) (Various Artists)
CD ______ CDHB 72
Heartbeat / May '92 / ADA / Direct / Greensleeves / Jet Star

JOE GIBBS RARE GROOVES (Various Artists)
CD ______ RGCD 014
Rocky One / Nov '94 / Jet Star

MIGHTY TWO, THE (Gibbs, Joe & Errol Thompson)
CD ______ HBCD 73
Heartbeat / Nov '92 / ADA / Direct / Greensleeves / Jet Star

REGGAE TRAIN, THE (1968-1971) (Gibbs, Joe & Friends)
CD ______ CDTRL 261
Trojan / Sep '94 / Direct / Jet Star

STATE OF EMERGENCY
CD ______ RGCD 037
Rocky One / Apr '96 / Jet Star

Gibbs, Michael

CENTURY/CLOSE MY EYE
CD ______ IONIC 10CD
Mute / Jan '94 / RTM/Disc

HARDBOILED
CD ______ IONIC 11CD
Mute / Jul '93 / RTM/Disc

IRON AND SILK
CD ______ IONIC 7CD
Mute / Nov '91 / RTM/Disc

Gibbs, Mike

BIG MUSIC (Gibbs, Mike Orchestra)
Wall to wall / Pride aside / Kosasa / Almost ev'ry day / Watershed / Mopsus / Adult / Pride outside
CD ______ CDVE 27
Venture / Oct '88 / EMI
CD ______ 92312
Act / May '96 / New Note/Pinnacle

BY THE WAY (Gibbs, Mike Orchestra)
Beauteous being / Blueprint / To Lady Mac: In sympathy / Something similar / World without / Rain before it falls / Jeunesse / Roses are red / Turn of the century / Out of the question / Just a head/Fanfare
CD ______ AHUM 016
Ah-Um / Nov '93 / Cadillac / New Note/ Pinnacle

EUROPEANA - JAZZPHONY NO.1 (Gibbs, Mike & Joachim Kuhn)
Castle in heaven / Black is the colour of my true love's hair / Shepherd of Breton / Ingrian rune song / Groom's sister / Norwegian psalm / Three angels / Heaven has created / She moved through the fair / Crebe de chet / Midnight sun / Londonderry air / Otra jazzpana
CD ______ 92202
Act / Mar '95 / New Note/Pinnacle

ONLY CHROME WATER FALL ORCHESTRA (Gibbs, Mike Orchestra)
To Lady Mac: In retrospect / Nairam / Blackgang / Antique / Undergrowth / Tunnel of love / Unfinished sympathy
CD ______ BGOCD 273
Beat Goes On / May '95 / Pinnacle

Gibbs, Terry

DREAM BAND
CD ______ CCD 7647
Contemporary / Jun '95 / Cadillac / Complete/Pinnacle / Jazz Music / Wellard

DREAM BAND VOL.2 (The Sundown Sessions)
CD ______ CCD 7652
Contemporary / Jun '95 / Cadillac / Complete/Pinnacle / Jazz Music / Wellard

DREAM BAND VOL.3 (Flying Home)
CD ______ CCD 7654
Contemporary / Jun '95 / Cadillac / Complete/Pinnacle / Jazz Music / Wellard

DREAM BAND VOL.4 (The Main Stem)
CD ______ CCD 7656
Contemporary / Jun '95 / Cadillac / Complete/Pinnacle / Jazz Music / Wellard

DREAM BAND VOL.5 (The Big Cat)
CD ______ CCD 7657
Contemporary / Nov '95 / Cadillac / Complete/Pinnacle / Jazz Music / Wellard

KINGS OF SWING (Gibbs, Terry & Buddy De Franco/Herb Ellis)
Seven come eleven / Soft winds / Man I love / Undecided / Body and soul / Just one of those things / Stompin' at the savoy / These foolish things / Airmail special
CD ______ CCD 140672
Pablo / Jan '94 / Cadillac / Complete/ Pinnacle

MEMORIES OF YOU (Gibbs, Terry & Buddy De Franco/Herb Ellis)
Flying home / Rose room / I surrender dear / Dizzy spells / Don't be that way / Poor butterfly / Avalon / Memories of you / After you've gone
CD ______ CCD 14066
Contemporary / Apr '94 / Cadillac / Complete/Pinnacle / Jazz Music / Wellard

PLAY THAT SONG (Gibbs, Terry Quartet)
CD ______ CRD 337
Chiaroscuro / Jun '96 / Jazz Music

Gibert, Allain

CHARIOT D'OR
CD ______ Y 225051CD
Silex / Aug '96 / ADA / Harmonia Mundi

Gibney, David

SHAMAN JOURNEY
CD ______ DD 101CD
Subspace / May '96 / Else

Gibson, Anthony T.

COMPLETE ANTHONY T. GIBSON, THE
Aint no way / Say it isn't so / Special kinda woman / My heart is in your hands / Sitting in the park / I want a lover / If you need someone / Girl on the sidelines / Is it for real / Take the money and run / At this moment / Searching for romance
CD ______ AT CD016
ATR / Apr '93 / Beechwood/BMG

Gibson Brothers

HITS
CD ______ KWEST 5408
Kenwest / Feb '93 / THE

Gibson, Banv

JAZZ BABY (Gibson, Banv & NOR Hot Jazz)
CD ______ SOSCD 1073
Stomp Off / Aug '90 / Jazz Music / Wellard

Gibson, Bob

REVISITED (Gibson, Bob & Hamilton Camp)
CD ______ FE 1413
Folk Era / Dec '94 / ADA / CM

Gibson, Clifford

BEAT YOU DOING IT
CD ______ YAZCD 1027
Yazoo / Mar '92 / ADA / CM / Koch

Gibson, Debbie

ANYTHING IS POSSIBLE
Another brick falls / Anything is possible / Reverse psychology / One step ahead / It must've been my boy / Lead them home my dreams / One hand, one heart / Sure / Negative energy / Mood swings / Where have you been / (This so called) Miracle / Stand your ground / Deep down / Try / In his mind
CD ______ 7567821627
Atlantic / Mar '91 / Warner Music

BODY MIND SOUL
Love or money / Do you have it in your heart / Free me / Shock your mama / Losin' myself / How can this be / When I say no / Little birdy / Kisses 4 one / Tear down these walls / Goodbye
CD ______ 7567824512
Atlantic / Apr '93 / Warner Music

OUT OF THE BLUE
Out of the blue / Staying together / Only in my dreams / Foolish beat / Red hot / Wake up to love / Shake your love / Fallen angel / Play the field / Between the lines
CD ______ K 781 780 2
Atlantic / Sep '87 / Warner Music

Gibson, Don

BEST OF DON GIBSON
CD ______ 74321218482
Arista / Jun '94 / BMG

COLLECTION, THE
Oh lonesome me / Snap your fingers / Just one time / Take these chains from my heart / Sweet dreams / Release me / Blue blue day / Funny familiar forgotten feelings / Kaw-liga / There goes my everything / Touch the morning / Too soon to know / Cold cold heart / I'm all wrapped up in you / You've still got a place in my heart / Sweet sensuous sensation / Why you been gone so long / I can't stop loving you / Lonesome number one / You win again / Mansion on the hill / Legend in my time / Yesterday just passed my way again / Fan the flame feed the fire
CD ______ CCSCD 158
Castle / Feb '93 / BMG

COUNTRY CLASSICS
Oh lonesome me / Blue blue day / Give myself a party / I can't stop loving me / Who cares / Just one time / Sweet dreams / Sea of heartbreak / Lonesome number one / I need thee every hour / Bring back your love to me / One day at a time / Touch the morning / Woman (sensuous woman) / Country green / I can mend your broken heart
CD ______ CD 6075
Music / Apr '97 / Target/BMG

DON GIBSON THE SINGER, THE SONGWRITER (1949-1960)
I lost my love / Why am I so lonely / Automatic mamma / Cloudy skies / I love no one but you / Carolina breakdown / Roses are red / Wiggle wag / Dark future / Just let me love you / Blue million tears / Red lips, white lies and blue hours / Sample kisses / No shoulder to cry on / Let me stay in your arms / We're stepping out tonight / Waitin' down the road / Walkin' in the moonlight / I just love the way you tell a lie / You cast me out (forevermore) / Symptoms of love / Selfish with your kisses / Ice cold heart / Many times I've waited / Road of life alone / Run boy / Sweet dreams / I must forget you / Taller than trees / Satisfied / Wait for the light to shine / Cannan's land / Faith unlocks the door / Evening prayer / Lord I'm coming home / Climbing up the mountain / Where no one stands alone / Known only to him / My God is real / That lonesome valley / Who cares (for me) / When will this ever end / Sweet sweet girl / Stranger to me / Won't cha come back to me / Stranger to me / As much / Who cares (for me) / I wish it had been a dream / Ages and ages ago / Even tho' / Didn't work out did it / It's my way / Almost / Do you think / Foggy river / Midnight / Lonesome old house / Ah-ha / It happens every time / I ain't gonna waste my time / I ain't a-studyin' you baby / I'm gonna fool everybody / I believed in you / What a fool I was for you / You're the only one for me / I love you still / Everything turns out for the best / I can't leave / Sittin' here cryin' / Too soon to know / Pretty rainbow / Blue blue day / Tell it like it is / Oh lonesome me / I can't stop loving you / It has to be / Give myself a party / Look who's blue / Bad bad day / Take me as I am / Heartbreak Avenue / We could / If you don't know it / Blues in my heart / Give myself a party / Don't tell me your troubles / I couldn't care less / Don't tell me your troubles / Heartbreak Avenue / Big hearted me / Maybe tomorrow / Everybody but me / I'm movin' on / Just one time / I may never get to heaven / Lonely Street / On the banks of the old Ponchartrain / Why don't you love me / If I can stay away / Never love again / Streets of Laredo / My love for you / My hands are tied / It only hurts for a little while / Legend in my time / Far far away / Foolish me / My tears don't show / World is waiting for the sunrise / What about me / Next voice you hear / Hurtin' inside / Time hurts (as well as it heals) / What's the reason I'm not pleasin' you / Sweet dreams / Same street
CD Set ______ BCD 15475
Bear Family / Jan '92 / Direct / Rollercoaster / Swift

LEGEND IN MY TIME, A
Sittin' here cryin' / Blue blue day / Oh lonesome me / I can't stop loving you / Look who's blue / If you don't know it / Bad bad day / Sweet sweet girl / Give myself a party / Who cares / Didn't work out did it / Lonesome old house / Don't tell me your troubles / I couldn't care less / Just one time / Legend in my time / Far far away / Sweet dreams / Sea of heartbreak / I sat back and let it happen / Lonesome number one / I can mend your broken heart / If you knew me / If you don't know the sorrow / Think of me / I'm crying inside
CD ______ BCD 15401
Bear Family / Nov '87 / Direct / Rollercoaster / Swift

SINGER SONGWRITER 1961 - 1966
Sweet dreams / I think it's best (To forget me) / That's how it goes / Sea of heartbreak / No one will ever know / Born to lose / Beautiful dreamer / Camptown races / Fireball mail / Last letter / White silver sands / Driftwood on the river / Lonesome road / Above and beyond / I sat back and let it happen / I know the score / Same old trouble / So how come (no one loves me) / Lonesome number one / Let's fall out of love (Tonight) / I let her get lonely / I can mend your broken heart / For a little while / It makes no difference now / Settin' the woods on fire / Baby we're really in love / I love you so much it hurts / It's a sin / I'm sorry for you my friend / This cold war with you / Where is your heart tonight / Blue dream / How's the world treating you / May you never be alone / We live in two different worlds / Old ship of zion / Then I met the master / I'd rather have Jesus / Be ready / Can't see myself / For old time's sake / It

was worth it all / Head over heels in love with you / I can't stop loving you / Legend in my time / Give myself a party / Oh lonesome me / Don't tell me your troubles / Love has come my way / Blue blue day / Just one time / Oh such a stranger / After the heartache / Anything new gets old (Except my love for you) / God walks these hills / Do you know my Jesus / Hide me rock of ages / Where else would I want to be / If I can help somebody / He's everywhere / You don't knock / When they ring the golden bells / There she goes (Let her go) / If you knew me / If you don't know the sorrow / Mixed up love / There she goes / Think of me / 'Cause I believe in you / Then I'll be free / Love that can't be / Waltz of regret / When your house is not a home / Watch where you're going / You're going away / Again / Too much hurt / Born loser / Wound time can't erase / Around the town / I'm crying inside / Dark as a dungeon / Right away / Lovin' lies / All the world is lonely now / Worried mind / There's a big wheel / Take these chains from my heart / Singin' the blues / With your love on my mind / Address unknown / My adobe hacienda / Lonely street / Cryin' heart blues / I can't tell my heart that / (Yes) I'm hurting / My whole world is hurt / You can't laugh (At a fool) / My tomorrows (They don't come easy) / Don't you ever get tired of hurting me / Once a day / My friends are gonna be strangers / Vaya con dios / Just call me lonesome / With love on my mind / Stranger to me / Maria Elena / Blues in my mind / Making believe / Somebody loves you darlin' / I'd just be fool enough / Lost highway / Let's fall out of love / I thought I heard you calling my name / Don't touch me / How do you tell someone / Just out of reach / When I stop dreaming / Cute little girls
CD Set ____ BCD 15664
Bear Family / Nov '93 / Direct / Rollercoaster / Swift

VERY BEST OF DON GIBSON, THE
Oh lonesome me / Blue blue day / Give myself a party / I can't stop loving you / Who cares / Just one time / Sweet dreams / Sea of heartbreak / Lonesome number one / I can mend your broken heart / Country green / Woman (sensuous woman) / Touch the morning / One day at a time / Bring back your love to me / I need thee every hour
CD ____ PLATCD 217
Platinum / Feb '97 / Prism

Gibson, Harry

WHO PUT THE BENZEDRINE IN MRS. MURPHY'S OVALTINE (Gibson, Harry 'The Hipster')
Hey man, you just made my day / Get hip to Shirley MacLaine / I flipped my wig in San Francisco / Back in the days of Dixieland and Bop / Boogity woogity blues / Thanks for the use of the hall / Get hip to Shirley MacLaine / They call him Harry The Hipster / Me and Max / Who put the benzedrine in Mrs Murphy's ovaltine / Lowdown slowdown inflationary blues / Maple Leaf rag and a little bit of The Entertainer / Ragtime raggedy Ann
CD ____ DE 687
Delmark / Nov '96 / ADA / Cadillac / CM / Direct / Hot Shot

Gibson, Lacy

CRYING FOR MY BABY
You'd better be sure / Easy woman / Crying for my baby / Chicago women / Blackjack / CB blues / Pleading for love / Take my love (I want to give it all to you) / My love is real / Dirty old man / Shake it baby
CD ____ DE 689
Delmark / Jun '97 / ADA / Cadillac / CM / Direct / Hot Shot

Gibson, Lee

NEARNESS OF YOU, THE
Time after time / Never let me go / They can't take that away from me / Good morning heartache / Here's that rainy day / Nice 'n' easy / Lady is a tramp / Foggy day / Please don't talk about me when I've gone / Nearness of you / Teach me tonight / I only have eyes for you
CD ____ ZECD 3
Zephyr / Mar '96 / Cadillac / Jazz Music / New Note/Pinnacle

Gibson, Steve

BOOGIE WOOGIE ON A SATURDAY NIGHT (Gibson, Steve & The Red Caps)
Sidewalk shuffle / Bobbin' / Would I mind / Always / Freehearted / How I cry / Three dollars and ninety nine cents / D'ya eat yet, Joe / Boogie woogie on a Saturday night / I went to your wedding / My tzatskele (my little darling) / Feeling kinda happy / Nuff of that stuff / Win or lose / Two little kisses / I may hate myself in the morning / Wait / Big game hunter / Shame / Do I, do I, do I / Why don't you love me / Truthfully / When you come to me / Fussing and fighting (unissued) / Thing / Am I to blame / I'm to blame / Sleepy little cowboy
CD ____ BCD 15490
Bear Family / Jul '90 / Direct / Rollercoaster / Swift

Gidea Park

ENDLESS SUMMER DAYS
Surf is up / Surfer's paradise / Have you seen that girl / Lai lo la limbo / Party beach / American girls / And your dreams come true / I got rhythm / Bring back those surfin' days / Lazin' on the beach / Back in '65 / Don't look back / Summertime city / Endless summer days / Stay healthy
CD ____ 304432
Hallmark / Jul '97 / Carlton

Gieco, Leon

DESENCHUFADO
CD ____ 68977
Tropical / Apr '97 / Discovery

MENSAJES DE ALMA
CD ____ 68964
Tropical / Apr '97 / Discovery

Gift

MULTUM IN PARVA
Little deranged puppet Pt.1 / Sinking ship / OK this is the pops / Don't need a reason / Restless spirit / Little deranged puppet Pt.2 / Never too young / Social cleansing / Date with failure / Bayond the tears / Kelly K / Jezebel / Little deranged puppet Pt.3
CD ____ TK 93CD068
T/K / Oct '94 / Pinnacle

Gigantic

ANSWER
CD ____ HB 12CD
Heatblast / Mar '93 / SRD

Gigantor

ATOMIC
CD ____ LF 186CD
Lost & Found / Nov '95 / Plastic Head

GIGANTOR/BASEBALL ANNIE (Gigantor/Baseball Annie)
CD ____ LF 240CD
Lost & Found / Sep '96 / Plastic Head

MAGIC BOZO SPIN
CD ____ LF 074CD
Lost & Found / May '94 / Plastic Head

SINGLES AND MORE, THE
CD ____ LF 129CD
Lost & Found / Jan '95 / Plastic Head

Giger, Paul

SCHATTENWELT
CD ____ 4377762
ECM / Jun '93 / New Note/Pinnacle

Gigolo Aunts

FLIPPIN' OUT
CD ____ FIRECD 35
Fire / May '95 / Pinnacle / RTM/Disc

WHERE I FIND MY HEAVEN
CD ____ NTMCD 549
Nectar / Jun '97 / Pinnacle

Gil, Gilberto

GILBERTO EM CONCERTO
CD ____ WWCD 2200
West Wind Latina / Apr '92 / Koch

PARABOLICAMARA
Madalena / Parabolicamara / Un sonho / Buda nago / Serafim / Quero ser teu funk / Neve na bahia / Ya olokum / O fim da historia / De onde vem o baiao / Falso toureiro / Sina
CD ____ 9031762922
Warner Bros. / Mar '92 / Warner Music

QUANTA
Quanta / Ciencia e arte / Estrela / Danca de Shiva / Vendedor de caranguejo / Chiquinho azevedo / Pilula de alho / Opachoro / Graca divina / Pela internet / Guerra santa / Atimo de po / Fogo liquido / Pop wu wei / O lugar do nosso amor / De ouro e marfim / Sala do som / Un abraco no Joao / O mar e o lago / La lune de goree
CD ____ 0630189192
Warner Bros. / Jun '97 / Warner Music

SOUNDS OF BRAZIL
CD ____ SOW 90121
Sounds Of The World / Jun '94 / Target/BMG

Gilbert & Lewis

8 TIME
CD ____ CAD 16 CD
4AD / May '88 / RTM/Disc

Gilbert, Bruce

AB OVO
CD ____ CDSTUMM 117
Mute / Jan '96 / RTM/Disc

SONGS FOR FRUIT
CD ____ CDSTUMM 77
Mute / Sep '91 / RTM/Disc

THIS WAY TO THE SHIVERING MAN
Work for 'do you me? I did' / Hommage / Shivering man / Here visit / Epitaph for Henran Brenlar / Angelfood
CD ____ STUMM 18 CD
Mute / Aug '84 / RTM/Disc

Gilbert, Vance

EDGEWISE
CD ____ PH 1156CD
Philo / Mar '94 / ADA / CM / Direct

FUGITIVES
CD ____ CDPH 1186
Philo / Aug '95 / ADA / CM / Direct

Gilberto, Astrud

BEACH SAMBA
Stay / Misty roses / Face I love / Banda / Oba oba / Canoeiro / I had the craziest dream / Bossa na prai / My foolish heart / Dia das rosas / You didn't have to be so nice / Nao bate o corocoa / Goodbye sadness / Call me / Here's that rainy day / Tu meu delirio / It's a lovely day today
CD ____ 5198012
Verve / Apr '93 / PolyGram

GIRL FROM IPANEMA, THE
Girl from Ipanema / Black magic / Love for sale / Meu piao / Far away: *Gilberto, Astrud & Chet Baker* / Mamae eu quero/Chica chica boom chic / All I've got / Puppy song / Wanting you / We'll make today last night again
CD ____ 307672
Hallmark / Jul '97 / Carlton

JAZZ MASTERS
Dreamer / Girl from Ipanema / Once upon a summertime / Felicidade / Certain sadness / Agua de beber / Frevo / Corcovado / Dindi / Look to the rainbow / Day by day / Shadow of your smile / Aruanda / Gentle rain / Tristeza / Berimbau
CD ____ 5198242
Verve / Apr '93 / PolyGram

LOOK TO THE RAINBOW
Berimbau / Once upon a summertime / Felicidade / I will wait for you / Frevo / Maria Moita / Look at the rainbow / Bim bom / Lugar bonito / El preciso aprender a ser so / She's a carioca / Certain smile / Certain sadness / Nega do cabelo duro / So nice / Voce ja foi a Bahia / Portuguese washerwoman
CD ____ 8215562
Verve / Sep '93 / PolyGram

MUSIC FOR THE MILLIONS
Once I loved / Auga de beber / Meditation / And roses and roses / How insensitive / O morro / Dindi / Photograph / Dreamer / So tinha de ser com voce / All that's left is to say goodbye
CD ____ 8234512
Verve / Feb '92 / PolyGram

THIS IS...ASTRUD GILBERTO
Girl from Ipanema / How insensitive / Beach samba / Fly me to the moon / Without him / Face I love / It's a lovely day today / Parade (A banda) / Bim bom / Shadow of your smile / I haven't got anything better to do / Look at the rainbow / Agua de beber / Aruanda
CD ____ 8250642
Verve / Sep '92 / PolyGram

Gilberto, Joao

DESAFINADO
CD ____ CD 62024
Saludos Amigos / Jan '93 / Target/BMG

Gilchrist, Hector

LEA RIG, THE (Gilchrist, Hector & Liz Thomson)
CD ____ WGS 274CD
Wild Goose / May '96 / ADA

Gildo, Rex

REX GILDO
CD ____ 16010
Laserlight / Aug '91 / Target/BMG

Giles, Angie

SURFACE
CD ____ CID 9986
Island / Apr '92 / PolyGram

Gilgamesh

GILGAMESH
One end more / Phil's little dance / Worlds of Zin / Lady and friend / Notwithstanding / Arriving twice / Island of Rhodes / Paper boat / As if your eyes were open / For absent friends / We are all / Someone else's food / Jamo and other boating disasters / 5 just C
CD ____ CACD 2007
Virgin / Jun '97 / EMI

Gill, John

CAROLINA SHOUT
CD ____ RQCD 1403
Request / Mar '94 / Jazz Music / Wellard

DOWN HOME FIVE
CD ____ SDSCD 1264
Stomp Off / Jun '94 / Jazz Music / Wellard

JOHN GILL & HIS NOVELTY ORCHESTRA OF NEW ORLEANS
CD ____ SOSCD 1270
Stomp Off / Apr '94 / Jazz Music / Wellard

MIDNIGHT CAKEWALK
CD ____ SOSCD 1304
Stomp Off / Jul '96 / Jazz Music / Wellard

RAGTIME DYNASTY, THE
Original rags / Charleston rag / Sensation rag / Pork and beans / Evergreen rag / Pearls / Wildcat blues / Jingles / Keep your temple / Hobson Street blues / Root beer rag / Heliotrope bouquet / Grace and beauty / Silver swan rag / Reindeer rag / Chicago breakdown / Echo of spring / Crave / Piccadilly / Eubie's classical rag
CD ____ RQCD 1405
Request / Nov '96 / Jazz Music / Wellard

Gill, Johnny

LET'S GET THE MOOD RIGHT
CD ____ 5307492
Motown / Oct '96 / PolyGram

Gill, Vince

ESSENTIAL VINCE GILL, THE
Victim of life's circumstances / Oh Carolina / I've been hearing things about you / Turn me loose / Radio / Livin' the way I do / Midnight train / True love / Ain't it always that way / Oklahoma borderline / With you / Way back home / Losing your love / Everybody's sweetheart / Don't say that you love me / Something's missing / Colder than winter / Cinderella / Let's do something / I never knew lonely
CD ____ 74321665352
RCA / Feb '96 / BMG

HIGH LONESOME SOUND, THE
One dance with you / High lonesome sound / Pretty little Adriana / Little more love / Down to New Orleans / Tell me lover / Given more time / You and you alone / Worlds apart / Jenny dreamed of trains
CD ____ MCD 11422
MCA / Jun '96 / BMG

I STILL BELIEVE IN YOU
Don't let our love start slippin' away / No future in the past / Nothin' like a woman / Tryin' to get over you / Say hello / One more last chance / Under these conditions / Pretty words / Love never broke anyone's heart / I still believe in you
CD ____ MCLD 19352
MCA / Apr '97 / BMG

POCKET FULL OF GOLD
I quit / Look at us / Take your memory with you / Pocket full of gold / Strings that tie you down / Liza Jane / If I didn't have you in my world / Little left over / What's a man to do / Sparkle
CD ____ MCLD 19321
MCA / Sep '96 / BMG

SOUVENIRS
CD ____ MCD 11394
MCA / Dec '95 / BMG

WHEN I CALL YOUR NAME
CD ____ MCAD 42321
MCA / Mar '94 / BMG

WHEN LOVE FINDS YOU
Whenever you come around / You better think twice / Real lady's man / What the cowgirls do / When love finds you / If there's anything I can do / South side of Dixie / Maybe tonight / Which bridge to cross (which bridge to burn) / If I had my way / Go rest high on that mountain / Ain't nothing like the real thing / I can't tell you why
CD ____ MCD 11078
MCA / May '94 / BMG

Gillan, Ian

ACCIDENTALLY ON PURPOSE (Gillan & Glover)
Clouds and rain / Evil eye / She took my breath away / Dislocated / Via Miami / I can't dance to that / Can't believe you wanna leave / Lonely Avenue / Telephone box / I thought no / Cayman Island / Purple people eater / Chet
CD ____ CDV 2498
Virgin / Feb '88 / EMI

CHERKAZOO AND OTHER STORIES
CD ____ RPM 104
RPM / Jul '93 / Pinnacle

CHILD IN TIME (Gillan)
Lay me down / You make me feel so good / Shame / My baby loves me / Down the road / Child in time / Let it slide
CD ____ CDVM 2606
Virgin / Apr '90 / EMI

DOUBLE TROUBLE (Gillan)
I'll rip your spine out / Restless / Men of war / Sunbeam / Nightmare / Hadely bop bop / Life goes on / Born to kill / No laughing in Heaven / No easy way / Trouble / Mutually assured destruction / If you believe me / New Orleans

CD CDVM 3506
Virgin / Nov '89 / EMI

FUTURE SHOCK (Gillan)
Future shock / Night ride out of Phoenix / Ballad of the Lucitania Express / No laughing in Heaven / Sacre bleu / New Orleans / Bite the bullet / If I sing softly / Don't want the truth / For your dreams / One for the road / Bad news / Take a hold of yourself / MAD / Maelstrom / Trouble / Your sister's on my list / Handles on her hips / Higher and higher / I might as well go home (mystic)
CD CDVIP 131
Virgin VIP / Apr '95 / EMI

GILLAN TAPES VOL.1
CD SJPCD 004
Blueprint / Jan '97 / Pinnacle

GLORY ROAD (Gillan)
Unchain your brain / Are you sure / Time and again / No easy way / Sleeping on the job / On the rocks / If you believe me / Running white face city boy / Nervous / Your mother was right / Red watch / Abbey of Thelema / Trying to get to you / Come tomorrow / Dragon's tongue / Post-fade brain damage
CD CDVM 2171
Virgin / Nov '89 / EMI

IAN GILLAN'S GARTH ROCKETT & THE MOONSHINERS STORY (Rockett, Garth & The Moonshiners)
CD ROHACD 3
EMI / Feb '90 / EMI

JAPANESE ALBUM (Gillan)
CD RPM 113
RPM / Jul '93 / Pinnacle

MAGIC (Gillan)
What's the matter / Bluesy blue sea / Caught in a trap / Long gone / Driving me wild / Demon driver / Living a lie / You're so right / Living for the city / Demon driver (reprise) / Breaking chains / Fiji / Purple sky / South Africa: *Gillan, Ian* / John / Helter skelter / Smokestack lightnin'
CD CDVM 2238
Virgin / Nov '89 / EMI

MR. UNIVERSE (Gillan)
Mr. Universe / Second sight / Secret of the dance / She tears me down / Roller / Vengeance / Puget sound / Dead of night / Message in a bottle / Fighting man / On the rocks / Bite the bullet / Mr. Universe (version) / Smoke on the water / Lucille
CD CDVM 2589
Virgin / Mar '83 / EMI

ROCK PROFILE (Various Artists)
Can I get a witness: *Gillan, Ian & The Javelins* / Little one: *Episode Six* / Driving me wild: *Gillan* / Strange kind of woman: *Deep Purple* / Temple / You make me feel so good: *Gillan, Ian Band* / Secret of the dance: *Gillan* / Roller: *Gillan* / Nervous: *Gillan* / Trouble: *Gillan* / MAD: *Gillan* / If I sing softly: *Gillan* / Bluesy blue sea: *Gillan* / Clouds and rain: *Gillan & Glover* / South Africa: *Gillan, Ian* / No more cane on the Brazos: *Gillan, Ian* / Dancing nylon shirt: *Gillan, Ian*
CD VSOPCD 214
Connoisseur Collection / Jul '95 / Pinnacle

ROCKFIELD MIXES, THE (Gillan, Ian Band)
Over the hill / Clear air turbulence / Fire moons / Money lender / Angelo manchenio / This is the way / Goodhand Liza
CD SPJCD 007
Angel Air / Mar '97 / Pinnacle

SOLE AGENCY & REPRESENTATION (Gillan, Ian & The Javelins)
Too much monkey business / It'll be me / You really got a hold on me / It's only make believe / Can I get a witness / Poison Ivy / Rave on / Blue Monday / You better move on / Something else / Money / Love potion no.9 / Let's dance / Roll over Beethoven
CD RPM 132
RPM / Aug '94 / Pinnacle

TOOL BOX
Hang me out to dry / Tool box / Dirty dog / Candy horizon / Don't hold me back / Pictures of hell / Dancing nylon shirt / Bed of nails / Gassed up / Everything I need
CD GILVP 102CD
Resurgence / Jul '97 / Pinnacle

TROUBLE - THE BEST OF GILLAN (Gillan)
Trouble / New Orleans / Fighting man / Living for the city / Helter skelter / Mr. Universe / Telephone box / Dislocated / Sleeping on the job / MAD (Mutually Assured Destruction) / No laughing in heaven / Nightmare / Restless / Purple sky / Born to kill / Smoke on the water
CD CDVIP 108
Virgin VIP / Nov '93 / EMI

VERY BEST OF GILLAN (Gillan)
Sleeping on the job / Secret of the dance / Time and again / Vengeance / Roller / MAD / Dead of night / Nightmare / Don't want the truth / If you believe me / Trouble / New Orleans / Living for the city / Restless / No laughing in heaven / Smoke on the water
CD MCCD 032
Music Club / Sep '91 / Disc / THE

Gillespie, Dana

ANDY WARHOL
CD GY 001
NMC / Mar '94 / Total/Pinnacle

BLUES IT UP
Lotta what you got / My man stands out / Fat Sam from Birmingham / Sweet meat / Ugly papa / Sweets / King size papa / One hour mama / 300 pounds of joy / Don't you make me high / Big ten inch record / Below the belt / Long lean baby / Tongue in cheek / Meat balls / Wasn't that good / Joe's joint / Organ grinder / Come on (if you're coming) / Nosey Joe / It ain't the meat / Sixty minute man / Snatch and grab it
CD CDCHD 950
Ace / Aug '90 / Pinnacle

HAVE I GOT NEWS FOR YOU
CD WCD 120942
Wolf / Oct '96 / Hot Shot / Jazz Music / Swift

HOT STUFF
Lovin' machine / Pencil thin Papa / Easy does it / Meat on their bones / Raise a little hell / Empty bed blues / Play with your poodle / Big fat Mamas are back in style again / Too many drivers / Sailor's delight / Built for comfort / Fat meat is good meat / Hot stuff / Tall skinny Papa / Big car / Spoonful / Diggin' my potatoes / Mainline baby / Pint size Papa / Horizontal boogie
CD CDCHD 605
Ace / Nov '95 / Pinnacle

Gillespie, Dizzy

'S WONDERFUL
CD VGCD 670508
Vogue / Jan '93 / BMG

20TH/30TH ANNIVERSARY
CD 5335502
MPS Jazz / Dec '96 / PolyGram

AFRO-CUBAN JAZZ MOODS (Gillespie, Dizzy & Machito)
Oro, incienso y mirra / Calidoscopico / Pensativo / Exuberante
CD OJCCD 447
Original Jazz Classics / Oct '92 / Complete/ Pinnacle / Jazz Music / Wellard

AT MONTREUX '75 (Gillespie, Dizzy Big Seven)
CD OJCCD 739
Original Jazz Classics / May '93 / Complete/Pinnacle / Jazz Music / Wellard

AUDIO ARCHIVE
Long long summer / All these things you are / Ray's idea / Dizzy atmosphere / Oop bop sh'bam / Emanon / Lorraine / Things to love / Rumbop concerto/Study in soulphony / Groovin' high / Desafinado / Hot house / Good dues blues / Blue 'n' boogie / Oop-bop-a-da / Our delight / Three hearts in a tangle
CD CDAA 022
Tring / Oct '91 / Tring

BAHIANA
Carnival / Samba / Barcelona / In the land of the living dead / Behind the moonbeam / Truth / Pele / Olinga
CD 2625708
Pablo / Jun '96 / Cadillac / Complete/ Pinnacle

BE BOP
Kush / Be bop / Swing low, sweet chariot / Brother K / Minor walk / Emanon / Two bass hit / Things to come / Oop-pop-a-dah
CD 17126
Laserlight / May '97 / Target/BMG

BEBOP & BEYOND PLAYS DIZZY GILLESPIE (Gillespie, Dizzy & Benny Carter)
Wheatleigh Hall / Manteca / I waited for you / Ray's idea / That's Earl, brother / Con Alma / Diddy wah diddy / Father time / Rhythm man
CD R2 79170
Bluemoon / Feb '92 / New Note/Pinnacle

BEST OF DIZZY GILLESPIE
Unicorn / Free ride / Pensavito / Exuberante / Behind the moonbeam / Shim-sham-shimmy
CD CD 2405411
Pablo / Apr '94 / Cadillac / Complete/ Pinnacle

BEST OF DIZZY GILLESPIE
CD DLCD 4019
Dixie Live / Mar '95 / TKO Magnum

BIRK'S WORKS (The Music Of Dizzy Gillespie) (Various Artists)
Birk's works: *Burrell, Kenny* / Groovin' high: *Fuller, Gil & The Monterey Jazz orchestra* / Be bop: *Clark, Sonny* / I waited for you: *Davis, Miles* / Manteca: *Evans, Gil* / Champ: *Smith, Jimmy* / Groovin high: *Parker, Charlie* / Night in Tunisia: *Rollins, Sonny* / Anthropology: *Jordan, Clifford* / Leap here: *Metronome All Stars*
CD BNZ 310
Blue Note / Mar '93 / EMI

CLASSICS 1945
CD CLASSICS 888
Classics / Jul '96 / Discovery / Jazz Music

CLASSICS 1945-1946
CD CLASSICS 935
Classics / Jun '97 / Discovery / Jazz Music

COMPLETE DIAL SESSIONS 1946-1948 (Gillespie, Dizzy & Sonny Berman/Fats Navarro)
Diggin' Diz / Confirmation / Diggin' for Diz / Dynamo / When I grow too old to dream / 'Round midnight / Curbstone souffle / Nocturne / Woodchopper's holiday / Somebody loves me / Blue Serge / Guilty / Yardbird suite / Stranger in town / As time goes by / Move
CD SPJCD 132
Spotlite / Oct '96 / Cadillac / Jazz Music / New Note/Pinnacle / Swift

COMPLETE RCA VICTOR RECORDINGS 1947-1949, THE
Manteca / Anthropology / King Porter stomp / Yours and mine / Blue rhythm fantasy / Hot mallets / 52nd Street / Night in Tunisia / Ol' man rebop / Ow / Oop-bop-a-da / Stay on it / Algo bueno / Cool breeze / Cubana be, cubana bop / Ool-ya-koo / Minor walk / Good bait / Guarachi guaro / Duff capers / Lover come back to me / I'm beboppin' too / Swedish suite / St. Louis blues / I should care / That old black magic / You go to my head / Jump di-le ba / Dizzier and dizzier / Hey Pete / Let's eat more meat / Jumpin' and symphony Sid / If love is trouble / In the land of oo-bla-dee / Overtime / Victory ball
CD 0786366528
Bluebird / Apr '95 / BMG

COOL WORLD, THE/DIZZY GOES HOLLYWOOD (Original Soundtrack)
CD 5312302
Verve / Jul '96 / PolyGram

DEEGEE DAYS (Savoy Sessions)
Tin tin deo / Birk's works / We love to boogie / Oh lady be good / Champ / I'm in a mess / School days / Swing low, sweet cadillac / Bopsie's blues / I couldn't beat the rap / Caravan / Nobody knows / Bluest blues / On the sunny side of the street / Stardust / Time on my hands / Blue skies / Umbrella man / Confessin' / Ooh-shoo-be-doo-bee / They can't take that away from me
CD VGCD 650101
Vogue / Jan '93 / BMG

DIGITAL AT MONTREUX
Christopher Columbus / I'm sitting on top of the world / Manteca / Get the booty / Kisses
CD CD 2308226
Pablo / Oct '92 / Cadillac / Complete/ Pinnacle

DIZ 'N' BIRD AT CARNEGIE HALL (Gillespie, Dizzy & Charlie Parker)
Night in Tunisia / Dizzy atmosphere / Groovin' high / Confirmation / Koko / Cool breeze / Relazin' at Camarillo / One bass hit / Nearness / Salt peanuts / Cubano-be, cubano-bop / Hot house / Toccata for trumpet / Oop-pop-a-da / Things to come
CD CDP 8570612
Blue Note / Jun '97 / EMI

DIZ AND GETZ (Gillespie, Dizzy & Stan Getz)
It don't mean a thing if it ain't got that swing: *Getz, Stan & Dizzy Gillespie* / I let a song go out of my heart: *Getz, Stan & Dizzy Gillespie* / Exactly like you: *Getz, Stan & Dizzy Gillespie* / It's the talk of the town: *Getz, Stan & Dizzy Gillespie* / Impromptu: *Getz, Stan & Dizzy Gillespie* / One alone: *Getz, Stan & Dizzy Gillespie* / Girl of my dreams: *Getz, Stan & Dizzy Gillespie* / Siboney: *Getz, Stan & Dizzy Gillespie*
CD 8335592
Verve / Aug '90 / PolyGram

DIZ MEETS STITT (Gillespie, Dizzy & Sonny Stitt)
CD MCD 0362
Moon / Aug '92 / Cadillac / Harmonia Mundi

DIZZIER AND DIZZIER
52nd Street theme / Night in Tunisia / Anthropology / Two bass hit / Cool breeze / Cubana be / Minor walk / Good bait / Lover come back to me / I'm be boppin' too / St. Louis blues / That old black magic / You go to my head / Dizzier and dizzier / Hey Pete, let's eat more meat / Jumpin' with Symphony Sid / In the land of oo-bla-dee
CD 09026685172
RCA Victor / Oct '96 / BMG

DIZZY (Gillespie, Dizzy Big Seven)
CD CD 20038
Pablo / May '86 / Cadillac / Complete/ Pinnacle

DIZZY FOR PRESIDENT
Dizzy atmosphere / Morning of the carnival / Cup bearers / I'm in the mood for love / Desfinado / Gee baby ain't I good to you / No more blues / Vote Dizzy (Salt peanuts)
CD ADC 1
Douglas Music / May '97 / Cadillac / New Note/Pinnacle

DIZZY GILLESPIE
CD CD 14554
Jazz Portraits / Jul '94 / Jazz Music

DIZZY GILLESPIE
Blue 'n boogie / Groovin' high / All the things you are / Dizzy atmosphere / Hot house / Oop bop sh'bam / That's earl brother / Our delight / Good dues blues / Ray's idea / Things to come / Emanon / Relaxin' at Camarillo / Guarachi guarro / Soulphony in three hearts / Ooh-poo-pah-doo / Ool-ya-koo / I'm be-boppin' too
CD 17071
Laserlight / Aug '96 / Target/BMG

DIZZY GILLESPIE & HIS ORCHESTRA 1928-49
CD CD 53119
Giants Of Jazz / Jan '94 / Cadillac / Jazz Music / Target/BMG

DIZZY GILLESPIE & THE DOUBLE SIX OF PARIS
Emanon / Anthropology / Tin tin deo / One bass hit / Two bass hit / Groovin' high / Ooh-shoo-be-doo-bee / Hot house / Con alma / Blue 'n' boogie / Champ / Ow
CD 8302242
Philips / Mar '93 / PolyGram

DIZZY GILLESPIE 1940-1946
CD 158812
Jazz Archives / Feb '97 / Discovery

DIZZY GILLESPIE 1946-1949
Manteca / Good bait / Ool-ya-koo / 52nd Street / Night in Tunisia / Ol' man rebop / Anthropology / Owl / Oop-bop-a-da / Cool breeze / Cubana be, Cubana bop / Minor walk / Guarachi guaro / Duff capers / Lover come back to me / I'm beboppin' too / Overtime / Victory ball / Swedish suite / St. Louis blues / Katy mo' meat / Jumpin' with Symphony Sid / In the land of oo-bla-dee
CD Set ND 89763
Jazz Tribune / May '94 / BMG

DIZZY GILLESPIE MEETS PHIL WOODS QUARTET
CD CDSJP 250
Timeless Jazz / Jan '88 / New Note/ Pinnacle

DIZZY GILLESPIE SEXTET (Gillespie, Dizzy Sextet)
CD CD 53099
Giants Of Jazz / Mar '92 / Cadillac / Jazz Music / Target/BMG

DIZZY'S DIAMONDS (The Best Of The Verve Years 1954-1964/3CD Set)
Prelude / 'Bout to wail / Umbrella man / Chains / Birk's works / Stella by starlight / Dizzy's business / Autumn leaves / Dizzy's blues / Flamingo / Jordu / Evening sound / Take the 'A' train / Blue 'n' boogie / Bonnie's blues / Ool-ya-koo / Blues after dark / Heat's on / Leap frog / Where's Adam / There's no greater love / Just one of those things / I know that you know / Swing low, sweet Cadillac / Dizzy atmosphere / Manteca / Fiesta mojo / Night in Tunisia / And then she stopped / Tin tin deo / Desafinado / Africana / Pergunte ao Joao / Caravan / This lovely feeling / Ungawa / Begin the beguine / Con alma / Rio Pakistan / Jambo
CD Set 5138752
Verve / Apr '92 / PolyGram

DUETS (Gillespie, Dizzy & Sonny Rollins/Sonny Stitt)
Wheatleigh Hall / Sumphin' / Con alma / Anythin' / Haute mon
CD 8352532
Verve / Mar '93 / PolyGram

FREE RIDE
Unicorn / Incantation / Wrong number / Free ride / Ozone madness / Love poem for Donna / Last stroke of midnight
CD OJCCD 784
Original Jazz Classics / Jun '94 / Complete/ Pinnacle / Jazz Music / Wellard

GIANT, THE
CD 139 217
Accord / '86 / Cadillac / Discovery

GILLESPIANA/CARNEGIE HALL CONCERT 1961
Prelude / Blues / Panamericana / Africana / Manteca / This is the way / Ool-ya-koo / Kush / Tunisian fantasy
CD 5198092
Verve / Dec '93 / PolyGram

GITANES - JAZZ 'ROUND MIDNIGHT
Don't try to keep up with the Joneses / Poor Joe / And then we stopped / Barbados carnival / Jambo / Lorraine / Rumbola / Tangorine / Confusion / I can't get started (with you) / Whisper not / There is no greater love / Constantinople / Sea breeze
CD 5100882
Verve / Oct '91 / PolyGram

IN CONCERT (Gillespie, Dizzy Quintet)
CD RTE 710465
RTE / May '95 / ADA / Koch

IT DON'T MEAN A THING
It don't mean a thing if it ain't got that swing / I let a song go out of my heart / It's the talk of the town / Impromptu / Siboney / Exactly like you / Girl of my dreams
CD CDSGP 062
Prestige / May '93 / Else / Total/BMG

JAM AT MONTREUX '77
CD OJCCD 381
Original Jazz Classics / Feb '92 / Complete/Pinnacle / Jazz Music / Wellard

JAZZ MASTERS
Manteca / November afternoon / Night in Tunisia / Tour de force / Trumpet blues / Con alma / I can't get started (with you) / 'Round midnight / Africana / Birk's works / Desafinado / Leap frog / Swing low, sweet Cadillac
CD 5163192
Verve / Apr '93 / PolyGram

JAZZ MATURITY...WHERE IT'S COMING FROM (Gillespie, Dizzy & Roy Eldridge)
CD OJCCD 807
Original Jazz Classics / Oct '95 / Complete/Pinnacle / Jazz Music / Wellard

JIVIN' IN BEBOP
CD MCD 0452
Moon / Nov '93 / Cadillac / Harmonia Mundi

LIVE AT CHESTER (Gillespie, Dizzy Big Band)
CD JH 1029
Jazz Hour / Jul '93 / Cadillac / Jazz Music / Target/BMG

LIVE AT THE 1986 FLOATING JAZZ FESTIVAL (Gillespie, Dizzy & Buddy Rich/Clark Terry)
CD CRD 300
Chiaroscuro / Mar '96 / Jazz Music

MANTECA
CD CD 14575
Complete / Nov '95 / THE

MEMORIAL ALBUM
CD NI 4018
Natasha / May '93 / ADA / Cadillac / CM / Direct / Jazz Music

MOST IMPORTANT RECORDINGS
CD CD OFF 830562
Ogun / Mar '90 / Cadillac / Jazz Music / Wellard

NIGHT IN TUNISIA
Night in Tunisia / Emanon / Chga de Saudade / Con Alma / This is the way / Kush
CD 17108
Laserlight / Mar '97 / Target/BMG

NIGHT IN TUNISIA, A
CD CD 53122
Giants Of Jazz / Nov '92 / Cadillac / Jazz Music / Target/BMG

ON THE SUNNY SIDE OF THE STREET
CD MCD 077
Moon / Dec '95 / Cadillac / Harmonia Mundi

OO BOP
CD TCD 1027
Tradition / Aug '96 / ADA / Vital

PLEYEL CONCERT 1948/PLEYEL CONCERT 1949 (Original Vogue Masters) (Gillespie, Dizzy & Max Roach Quintet)
Ooh-poo-pah-doo / Round about midnight / Algo bueno / I can't get started / Two bass hit / Good bait / Afro-Cuban drum suite / Ool-ya-koo / Things to come / Prince Albert / Baby sis / Tomorrow / Maximum
CD 74321409412
Vogue / May '97 / BMG

PLEYEL CONCERT 1953 (Original Vogue Masters) (Gillespie, Dizzy Quintet)
Intro / Champ / Good bait / Swing low, sweet Cadillac / Oh lady be good / Mon homme / Bluest blues / Birk's works / Ooh-shoo-be-doo-bee / They can't take that away from me / Play fiddle play / I can't get started (with you) / Embraceable you / Tin tin deo / On the sunny side of the street / School days
CD 74321429212
Vogue / Apr '97 / BMG

PROFESSOR BOP
Blue 'n' boogie / Groovin' high / Dizzy atmosphere / All the things you are / Hot house / Oop bop sh'bam / Our delight / Things to come / Ray's idea / Emanon / Good dues blues
CD LEJAZZCD 25
Le Jazz / Feb '94 / Cadillac / Koch

QUINTET, THE
CD OJCCD 44
Original Jazz Classics / Feb '92 / Complete/Pinnacle / Jazz Music / Wellard

SMALL GROUPS 1945-1946
CD CD 56055
Jazz Roots / Mar '95 / Target/BMG

SONNY SIDE UP (Gillespie, Dizzy & Sonny Rollins/Sonny Stitt)
On the sunny side of the street / Eternal triangle / After hours / I know that you know
CD 8256742
Verve / Feb '87 / PolyGram

SOUL TIME
CD MACCD 274
Autograph / Aug '96 / BMG

SUMMERTIME (Gillespie, Dizzy & Mongo Santamaria)
Virtue / Afro blue / Summertime / Mambo Mongo
CD OJCCD 6266
Original Jazz Classics / Feb '92 / Complete/ Pinnacle / Jazz Music / Wellard

SWING LOW SWEET CADILLAC
Swing low, sweet cadillac / Mas que nada / Something in your smile / Kush / Bye
CD IMP 11782
Impulse Jazz / Feb '96 / New Note/BMG

SYMPHONY SESSIONS, THE
Manteca / Con alma / Lorraine / Brother K / Tin tin deo / Fiesta mojo / Night in Tunisia
CD SION 18110
Sion / Jul '97 / Direct

TALKIN' VERVE
CD 5338462
Verve / Mar '97 / PolyGram

THINGS TO COME
Things to come / Ray's idea / Montego / Milan is love / N'Bani / Something in your smile / Yesterdays
CD 17107
Laserlight / Jan '97 / Target/BMG

TO BIRD WITH LOVE
Billie's bounce / Be bop / Ornithology / Anthropology / Oo pa pa da / Diamond jubilee blues / Theme
CD CD 83316
Telarc / Nov '92 / Conifer/BMG

TO DIZ, WITH LOVE (Diamond Jubilee recordings)
Billie's bounce / Confirmation / Mood indigo / Straight no chaser / Night in Tunisia
CD 83307
Telarc / May '92 / Conifer/BMG

TRUMPET ROYALTY (25 Unreleased Tracks)
CD VJC 10092
Victorious Discs / Aug '90 / Jazz Music

Gillespie, Hugh

CLASSIC
CD GLCD 3066
Green Linnet / Jun '92 / ADA / CM / Direct / Highlander / Roots

Gillet & Greitez

TERRACOTA
CD BEST 1056
Acoustic Music / Oct '94 / ADA

Gillette, Steve

LIVE IN CONCERT (Gillette, Steve & Cindy Mangsen)
CD BRAMBUS 199231
Brambus / Oct '94 / ADA

Gilley, Mickey

MICKEY GILLEY
Still care about you / Keepin' on / That's how it's going to be / I miss you so / Just out of reach / Grapevine / Fraulein / No greater love / Boy who didn't pass / Ain't goin' home / Black Mountain rag / Turn around / Rocky top / CC Rider
CD PRACD 4004
Prairie / Jun '97 / Henry Hadaway

THAT HEART BELONGS TO ME
I'm to blame / Night after night / Suzie Q / I'll make it all up to you / Breathless / Is it wrong / Lonely wine / Forgive / My babe / Turn around and look at me / She's still got a hold on you / Running out of reasons / World of our own / That heart belongs to me / I'm gonna put my love in the want ads / Without you / It's just a matter of making up my mind / New way to live / There's no one like you / You can count me missing / Still care about you / Grapevine / That's how it's gotta be / Boy who didn't pass / Fraulein / I miss you so / Just out of reach / Keepin' on / Watching the way
CD GRF 074
Tring / Feb '93 / Tring

Gillies, Alasdair

AMONG MY SOUVENIRS
Take me home / I dream of Jeannie with the light brown hair / Among my souvenirs / I will love you all my life / Tak a dram / Scarlet ribbons / Scotland my home / Banners of Scotland / Bonnie Mary of Argyle / Say you'll stay until tomorrow / Beautiful dreamer / More than yesterday / Maggie / Messin' about on the river
CD CD ITV 416
Scotdisc / Dec '86 / Conifer/BMG / Duncans / Ross

WORLD'S GREATEST PIPERS VOL.12, THE
2/4 Marches / Strathspey and Reel / Gaelic airs and hornpipes / 6/8 Marches / March, Strathspey and Reel / Gaelic Air and Jigs / Strathspeys and Reels / 2/4 Marches / Jigs / Gaelic Airs, Strathspeys and Reels
CD LCOM 5231
Lismor / Jul '94 / ADA / Direct / Duncans / Lismor

Gillies, Anne Lorne

HILLS OF LORNE
CD CDLOC 1008
Lochshore / May '97 / ADA / Direct / Duncans

OH MY LAND
Sad am I far from my home / Lullaby for Donald gorm of Sleat / Great song of Macleod / Alasdair son of Great Colla / I'm asleep don't wake me / Silver whistle / My fair young love / Farewell to the lovely tartan / Oh my land / When I was young / Say goodbye for me/Young Alasdair son of the son of Nicol / Mavis comes in spring / Isle of joy / Surge of the sea / Freedom
CD RCD 052
Iona / May '97 / ADA / Direct / Duncans

SONGS OF THE GAELS, THE
Am buachaille ban / Ho ro chall eile / Na h-uain air an tulaich / Cumha iain ghairbh ratharsair / Allt an t-siucair / Griogal cridhe / Coille'n fhasaich / Gur moch rinn mi dusgagh / Mo dhomhnallan fhin / Nach gorach mi'gad chaoinead / Orain luaidh / Iain glinn cuaich / A fhleasgaich a'chuil dualaich / A'chuairt shamhraidh
CD CDLOC 1014
Lochshore / May '97 / ADA / Direct / Duncans

Gillis, Brad

GILROCK RANCH
Gilrock ranch / Lions, tigers and bears / Honest to god / Slow blow / Monster breath / Shades of pomposity / Gospel / Opus winfrus / Afterthought / If looks could kill
CD CDGRUB 27
Food For Thought / Jan '93 / Pinnacle

Gillman, Jane

ONE LOOK BACK
Howlin' at the moon / Song on the radio / Song of Baltimore / Ready for the time to come / Open up / Three quarters / Falling in place / One look back / What tomorrow finds / Tell the rooster / Listen to the thunder / Elsa's tune
CD GLCD 2101
Green Linnet / Oct '93 / ADA / CM / Direct / Highlander / Roots

PICK IT UP
CD GLCD 1068
Green Linnet / Feb '92 / ADA / CM / Direct / Highlander / Roots

Gillum, Bill 'Jazz'

BLUEBIRD RECORDINGS 1934-1938, THE
Early in the morning / Harmonica stomp / Sarah Jane / I want you by my side / Jockey blues / Don't scandalize my name / My old Lizzie / Alberta blues / My old suitcase / Birmingham blues / Just like Jessie James / Reefer head woman / Gillum's windy blues / New 'Sail on little girl' / Sweet sweet woman / Boar hog blues / Worried and bothered / I'm that man down in the mine / Uncertain blues / Good old 61 highway / You're laughing now / I'm gonna get it
CD 07863667172
Bluebird / Feb '97 / BMG

HARMONICA & WASHBOARD BLUES (1937-1940) (Gillum, Bill 'Jazz' & Washboard Sam)
CD BLE 592522
Black & Blue / Dec '92 / Discovery / Koch / Wellard

JAZZ GILLUM VOL.1 - 1936-38
CD DOCD 5197
Document / Oct '93 / ADA / Hot Shot / Jazz Music

JAZZ GILLUM VOL.2 - 1938-41
CD DOCD 5198
Document / Oct '93 / ADA / Hot Shot / Jazz Music

JAZZ GILLUM VOL.3 - 1941-46
CD DOCD 5199
Document / Oct '93 / ADA / Hot Shot / Jazz Music

JAZZ GILLUM VOL.4 - 1946-49
CD DOCD 5200
Document / Oct '93 / ADA / Hot Shot / Jazz Music

KEY TO THE HIGHWAY 1935-1942
CD 158402
Blues Collection / Sep '95 / Discovery

Gilmer, Jimmy

SUGAR SHACK/BUDDY'S BUDDY (Gilmer, Jimmy & The Fireballs)
Sugar shack / Let's talk / Linda Lu / Lonesome tears / Let the good times roll / Red Cadillac and a black moustache / Won't be long / Little baby / I wonder why / Suzie Q / Pretend / Almost eighteen / Look at me: *Gilmer, Jimmy* / Wishing: *Gilmer, Jimmy* / I'm gonna love you too: *Gilmer, Jimmy* / Think it over: *Gilmer, Jimmy* / Lonesome tears: *Gilmer, Jimmy* / Maybe baby: *Gilmer, Jimmy* / Listen to me: *Gilmer, Jimmy* / Everyday: *Gilmer, Jimmy* / Words of love: *Gilmer, Jimmy* / It's so easy: *Gilmer, Jimmy* / Little baby: *Gilmer, Jimmy* / Oh boy: *Gilmer, Jimmy*
CD CDCHD 646
Ace / Apr '97 / Pinnacle

Gilmore, Jimmie Dale

AFTER AWHILE
Tonight I think I'm gonna go downtown / My mind's got a mind of its own / Treat me like a Saturday night / Chase the wind / Go to sleep alone / After a while / Number 16 / Don't be a stranger to your heart / Blue moon waltz / These blues / Midnight train / Story of you
CD 7559611482
Nonesuch / Sep '91 / Warner Music

BRAVER NEW WORLD
CD 7559618362
Warner Bros. / Jul '96 / Warner Music

SPINNING AROUND THE SUN
Where are you going / Santa fe thief / So I'll run / I'm so lonesome I could cry / Mobile line (France blues) / Nothing of the kind / Just a wave, reunion: *Gilmore, Jimmie Dale & Lucinda Williams* / I'm gonna love you / Another colorado / Thinking about you
CD 7559615022
Elektra / Sep '93 / Warner Music

Gilmour, David

ABOUT FACE
Until we sleep / Murder / Love on the air / Blue light / Out of the blue / You know I'm right / Cruise / Let's get metaphysical / Near the end / All lovers are deranged
CD CDP 7460312
Harvest / Aug '84 / EMI

Giltrap, Gordon

GORDON GILTRAP/PORTRAIT
Gospel song / Fast approaching / Don't you feel good / Birth of spring / Won't you stay awhile Suzanne / Wilderness / Adolescent years / Saturday girl / Don't you hear your mother's voice / Ives horizon / Blyth Hill / Willow pattern / Portrait / Thoughts in the rain / Never ending solitude / Tuxedo / All characters ficticious / Lucifer's cage / Careful as you go / Free for all / William Taplin / Hands of fate / Confusion / Young love
CD TDEM 15
Trandem / Apr '94 / ADA / CM / Pinnacle

GUITARIST
CD CMML 88006CD
Music Maker / Jul '94 / ADA / Grapevine/ PolyGram

MATTER OF TIME, A (Giltrap, Gordon & Martin Taylor)
CD CDSGP 007
Prestige / Aug '91 / Else / Total/BMG

MUSIC FOR THE SMALL SCREEN
CD MRCD 1
Munchkin / May '95 / Grapevine/PolyGram

ON A SUMMER'S NIGHT
CD CMMR 924CD
Music Maker / Jul '94 / ADA / Grapevine/ PolyGram

ONE TO ONE
CD NP 002CD
Nico Polo / Sep '89 / ADA / Direct / Roots

SOLO ALBUM
CD CDSGP 021
Prestige / Jul '96 / Else / Total/BMG

Gin Blossoms

CONGRATULATIONS, I'M SORRY
Day job / Highwire / Follow you down / Not only numb / As long as it matters / Perfectly still / My car / Virginia / Whitewash / I can't figure you out / Memphis time / Competition smile / Til I hear it from you
CD 5404702
A&M / Feb '96 / PolyGram

NEW MISERABLE EXPERIENCE
Lost horizons / Hey jealousy / Mrs. Rita / Until I fall away / Hold me down / Cajun song / Hands are tied / Found out about you / Allison road / Twenty nine / Pieces of the night / Cheatin'
CD 3954032
Fontana / Feb '96 / PolyGram

Gin On The Rocks

COOLEST GROOVE
CD 847025
Steamhammer / Dec '90 / Pinnacle / Plastic Head

Gina G

FRESH
Just a little bit / Fresh / Ti amo / Every time I fall / Follow the light / Gimme some love / Rhythm of my life / Missin' you like crazy / I belong to you / Higher than love / It doesn't mean goodbye
CD 0630178402
Eternal / Mar '97 / Warner Music

Ginger

FAR OUT
CD W 230096
Nettwerk / May '97 / Greyhound / Pinnacle / Vital

GINGER
CD W 26320
Nettwerk / Jul '97 / Greyhound / Pinnacle / Vital

Gingrich, Brian

WHITE RIM OF HEAVEN, THE
Knotted cord / Slowing in motion / White rim stories / Batterie of last resort / Fading days / Heavenly reception / Reversal of plans
CD ALCD 1008
Alchemy / Aug '97 / Pinnacle

Ginn, Greg

DICK
Never change, baby / I want to believe / You wanted it / I won't give in / Creeps / Strong violent type / Don't tell me / You dirty rat / Disgusting reference / Walking away / Ignorant order / Slow fuse / You're going to get it
CD CRZ 032CD
Cruz / Sep '93 / Plastic Head

GETTING EVEN
CD CRZ 029CD
Cruz / May '93 / Plastic Head

LET IT BURN BECAUSE
CD CRZ 036CD
Cruz / Jul '94 / Plastic Head

PAYDAY
CD CRZ 028CD
Cruz / May '93 / Plastic Head

Ginsberg, Allen

LION FOR REAL, THE
Scribble / Christmas gift / Lion for real / Shrouded stranger / Cleveland, the flats / Stanzas written at night in radio city / Hum bom / Guru / C'mon Jack / Gregory Corso's story / End / Sunset / Krai majales / Ode to failure
CD 5349082
Mercury / Jun '97 / PolyGram

Ginuwine

BATCHELOR, THE
Intro / Pony / Tell me do U wanna / Holler / Hello / Lonely daze / Ginuwine 4 Ur mind / Only when Ur lonely / I'll so anything/I'm sorry / World is so cold / When doves cry / G thang / 550 what
CD 4853912
Epic / Oct '96 / Sony

Giordand, Vince

QUALITY SHOUT
CD SOSCD 1260
Stomp Off / Apr '94 / Jazz Music / Wellard

Gipsy Fire

GIPSY FIRE
CD INT 845149
Interchord / Feb '91 / CM

Gipsy Kings

ALLEGRIA
Tena tinita / La dona / Sueno / Un amor / Pharoan / Recuerdo / Allegria / Solituda / Papa, no pega la mama / Tristessa / Pena Penita / Djobi djoba / Papa / No pega la mama / Pharaon
CD 4667622
Columbia / Jul '93 / Sony

ESTRELLAS
La rumba / A ti a ti / Siempre acaba tu vida / Forever / Mujer / Campesino / Cata luna igual se entonces / Pararito / Tierra gitana / A tu vera / Mi carazon / Estrellas
CD 4813452
Columbia / Nov '95 / Sony

GIPSY KINGS
Tu quieres volver / Moorea / Bem bem Maria / Un amor / Inspiration / Mi minera / Djobi djoba / Faena / Quiero saber / Amor amor / Duende / Bamboleo
CD 4691232
Columbia / Jul '93 / Sony

GIPSY KINGS/MOSAIQUE/ESTE MUNDO (3CD Set)
Bamboleo / Tu quieres volver / Moorea / Bem, bem, Maria / Un amor / Inspiration / A mi manera (comme d'habitude) / Djobi djoba / Faena / Quiero saber / Amor, amor / Duende / Caminando por la calle / Viento del arena / Mosaique / Carmino / Passion / Soy / Volare (nel blu di pinto di blu) / Trista pena / Liberte / Serana / Bossamba / Vamos a bailar / Baila me / Sin Ella / Habla me / Lagrimas / Oy / Mi vada / El manuro / No volvere / Furia / Oh mai / Ternuras / Este mundo
CD Set 4853172
Columbia / Oct '96 / Sony

GREATEST HITS
Djobi djoba / Baila me / Bamboleo / Pida me la / Bem bem Maria / Voalre (Nel blu di pinto di blue) / Moorea / A mi manera (Comme d'habitude) / Un amor / Galaxia / Escucha me / Tu quieres volver / Soy / La quiero / Allegria / Vamos a bailar / La Dona / Djobi dojoba
CD 4772422
Columbia / Jul '96 / Sony

LIVE
Intro / Allegria / La dona / El mauro / Bem bem Maria / Trista pena / Odeon / Sin ella / Quiero saber / Habla me / Galaxia / Fandango / Tu quieres volver / Oh mai / Djobi djoba / Bamboleo
CD 4726482
Columbia / Feb '97 / Sony

LIVE/ESTE MUNDO
CD Set 4726482D
Columbia / Feb '93 / Sony

LOVE & LIBERTE
Escucha me / Montana / Michael / Pedir a tu Corazon / Queda te aqui / Guitarra negra / Non vivire / Madre mia / Ritmo de la noche / Navidad / Campana / Love and liberte / La quiero
CD 4749502
Columbia / Nov '93 / Sony

LOVE SONGS
Un amor / Gitano soy / A mi manera / No volvere / Love and liberte / Quiero saber / Mi corazon / Caminando por al calle / Madre mia / Passion / Habla me / Tu quieres volver / Mujer / Trista pena / Inspiration
CD 4843952
Columbia / Jul '96 / Sony

LUNA DE FUEGO
Amor d'un dia / Luna de fuego / Calaverada / Galaxia / Ruptura / Gypsy rock / Viento del arean / Princessa / Olvidado / Ciento
CD 4667632
Columbia / Feb '91 / Sony

MOSAIQUE
Caminando por la calle / Viento del arena / Mosaique / Camino / Passion / Soy / Volare / Trista pena / Liberte / Serana / Bossamba / Vamos a Bailar
CD 4662132
Columbia / Jul '93 / Sony

Girault, Martine

REVIVAL
Intro interlude / Bring back our love / Good love / Been thinking 'bout you / Love to love you baby / These are the best days / Don't dog me / Revival / We've got tomorrow / Special / I wish / Soulfully yours / Outro interlude / Revival
CD 74321432172
RCA / Feb '97 / BMG

Girl

BLOOD, WOMEN, ROSES
CD PRODCD 4
Product Inc. / May '87 / Vital

SHEER GREED
Hollywood tease / Things you say / Lovely Lorraine / Strawberries / Little Miss Ann / Doctor doctor / Do you love me / Take me dancing / What's up / Passing clouds / My number / Heartbreak America
CD JETCD 1009
Jet / Sep '94 / Total/Pinnacle

WASTED YOUTH
Thru the twilight / Old dogs / Ice in the blood / Wasted youth / Standard romance / Nice 'n' nasty / McKitty's back / Nineteen / Overnight angels / Sweet kids
CD JETCD 1010
Jet / Oct '94 / Total/Pinnacle

Girl

FIRED UP
CD EBCD 29
Eightball / Jan '95 / Vital

Girl Trouble

GIRL TROUBLE LIVE
CD EFA 123552
Empty / Jan '94 / Cargo / Greyhound / Plastic Head / SRD

NEW AMERICAN SHAME
CD EFA 11390CD
Musical Tragedies / Jun '93 / SRD

Girlandia

CELTIC HEIR
CD BRAM 1993462
Brambus / Mar '94 / ADA

Girlfriend

MAKE IT COME TRUE
CD 74321152172
Arista / May '93 / BMG

Girls Against Boys

8 ROUNDS (Girls Against Boys/Guided By Voices)
CD RR 13CD
Radiopaque / Mar '97 / Cargo

CRUISE YOURSELF
CD TG 134CD
Touch & Go / Oct '94 / SRD

HOUSE OF GVSB
CD TG 149CD
Touch & Go / Mar '96 / SRD

NINETIES VS. EIGHTIES
CD AS 3CD
Touch & Go / '93 / SRD

TROPIC OF SCORPIO
CD AS 4CD
Touch & Go / '94 / SRD

VENUS LUXURE NO.1 BABY
CD TG 117CD
Touch & Go / '94 / SRD

Girls At Our Best

PLEASURE
Getting nowhere fast / Warm girls / Politics / It's fashion / Go for gold / Pleasure / Too big for your boots / I'm beautiful now / Waterbed babies / Fun city teenagers / 600,000 / Heaven / China blue / Fast boyfriends / She flipped / Goodbye to that jazz / This train
CD ASKCD 047
Vinyl Japan / Oct '94 / Plastic Head / Vinyl Japan

Girlschool

GIRLSCHOOL
CD CMGCD 006
Communique / Nov '92 / Plastic Head

IN CONCERT 1984
CD 880322
King Biscuit / Jul '97 / Greyhound

LIVE
CD CMGCD 013
Communique / Nov '95 / Plastic Head

Gisbert, Greg

HARCOLOGY (Gisbert, Greg Quintet)
CD CRISS 1084CD
Criss Cross / May '94 / Cadillac / Direct / Vital/SAM

Gismonti, Egberto

ACADEMIA DE DANCAS
CD 5112022
Carmo / Feb '92 / New Note/Pinnacle

ALMA
Baiao Malandro / Palhaco / Loro / Maracuta / Karate / Agua & Vinho / Frevo / Cigana / Ruth / Sanfona / Fala de Peixao / Realejo / 7 Aneis
CD 5291232
Carmo / Oct '96 / New Note/Pinnacle

AMAZONIA
Dois Curumins na floresta / O senhor dos caminhos / Trenzinho amazonico / Forro na beira da mata / Os deuses da selva 1 / O baile dos caraibas / O coracao das trevas / Danca das amazonas / Todos os fogos O fogo / Ciranda no ceu / Os deuses da selva II / Sertao/Forrobodo / Ao redor da fogueira / Turma do mercado / Fuga and destruicao / Floresta (Amazonia) / Forro Amazonico / Ruth / No coracao dos homens
CD 5177162
Carmo / Jun '93 / New Note/Pinnacle

ARVORE
Luzes da ribalta / Memoria e fado / Academic de danca / Tango / Encontro no bar / Adagio / Variacoes sombre um tema de leo brouwer / Salvador
CD 8490762
Carmo / May '91 / New Note/Pinnacle

CIRCENSE
Karate / Cego aderaldo / Magico / Palhaco / Ta boa, santa / Equilibrista / Ciranda / Mais que a paixao
CD 8490772
Carmo / May '91 / New Note/Pinnacle

DANCA DOS ESCARVOS
CD 8377532
ECM / Nov '89 / New Note/Pinnacle

DUAS VOZES (Gismonti, Egberto & Nana Vasconcelos)
Rio De Janeiro / Tomarapeba / Dancando / Fogueira / Bianca / Don Quixote / O dia / A noite
CD 8236402
ECM / Apr '86 / New Note/Pinnacle

INFANCIA
CD 8478892
ECM / Sep '91 / New Note/Pinnacle

KUARUP
Senhores da Terra / Ossuario / Valsa de Francisca / Anta / Urucum / A Forca da Floresta / A Danca da Floresta / Aguas / Sonia / A Morte da Floresta / Valsa de Francisca / O Som da Floresta / Jogos da Floresta 1 / Jogos da Floresta 2 / Mutacao
CD 8431992
Carmo / May '91 / New Note/Pinnacle

MEETING POINT
Strawa zzabumba / Strawa maxixe / Musica para cordas / Frevo / A pedriha cai / Eterna / Musica de sobrevivencia
CD 5336812
ECM / May '97 / New Note/Pinnacle

NO CAIPIRA
Saudacoes / No caipira and zambumba / Noca and Garrafas / Pira and Bambuzal / Palacio de pinturas / Maracatu, sapo, queimada and Grilo / Frevo / Esquenta muie and banda de pffanos / Frevo rasgado / Sertao Brasiliero / Selva Amazonica / Uana Lua and Kalimbas / Cancao da espera / Danca das sombras
CD 5177152
Carmo / Jun '93 / New Note/Pinnacle

SANFONA
CD 8293912
ECM / Aug '88 / New Note/Pinnacle

SOL DO MEIO DIA
Palacio de pinturas / Raga / Kalimba / Coracao / Cafe / Sapain / Dance solitaria No.2 / Baiao Malandro
CD 8291172
ECM / Jun '86 / New Note/Pinnacle

SOLO
Selva Amazonica / Pau Rolou / And zero / Frevo / Salvador / Ciranda Nordestina
CD 8271352
ECM / Dec '85 / New Note/Pinnacle

TREM CAIPIRA
Trenzinho do Caipira / Dansa / Bachianas brasileiras No.5 / Desejo / Cantiga / Cancao de Carreiro / Preludio / Pobre cega
CD 8417752
Carmo / Feb '92 / New Note/Pinnacle

WORKS: EGBERTO GISMONTI
Loro / Gismonti / Mauro senise / Zeca assumpcao / Nene raga / Vasconcelos / Colin Walcott / Ciranda nordestina / Magico / Garbarek / Charlie Haden / Maracutu / Nene salvador
CD 8232692
ECM / Jun '89 / New Note/Pinnacle

ZIG ZAG (Gismonti, Egberto Trio)
Mestico & Cabocio / Orixas / Carta de Amor / Um anjo / Forrobodo
CD 5293492
ECM / Feb '96 / New Note/Pinnacle

Gitbox

TOUCH WOOD
Engagement / Wedlock / Sipho / Les bouche du monde / Elfwalk / Springscape / Journey / Oceanscape / Be longing / Morman X and the Major's cheque / Icescape / Neither a candle for the angel nor a poker for the devil / Autumnscape / In vocation / Rajasthani heart / Panda miracle / Touch wood
CD DGM 9511
Discipline / Nov '95 / Pinnacle

Gits

FRENCHING THE BULLY
CD CZ 051CD
C/Z / Dec '92 / Plastic Head

Giuffre, Jimmy

CARLA
Carla / Whirrr / Cry, want / Emphasis / Jesus Maria / Sonic / Trudgin' / Gamut / Venture / Stretching out / In the mornings out there
CD CD 53257
Giants Of Jazz / Jun '96 / Cadillac / Jazz Music / Target/BMG

FLIGHT, BREMEN 1961
CD ARTCD 6071
Hat Art / Oct '92 / Cadillac / Harmonia Mundi

FREE FALL
Propulsion / Threewe / Ornothoids / Dichotomy / Man alone / Spasmodic / Yggdrasill / Divided man / Primordial call / Five ways
CD 44807082
Sony Jazz / Dec '95 / Sony

JIMMY GIUFFRE 3, 1961 (Giuffre, Jimmy Trio)
Jesus Maria / Emphasis / In the mornings out there / Scootin' about / Cry want / Brief hesitation / Venture / Afternoon / Trudgin' / Ictus / Carla / Sonic / Whirrr / That's true, that's true / Goodbye / Flight / Gamut / Me too / Temporarily / Herb and Ictus
CD Set 8496442
ECM / Mar '92 / New Note/Pinnacle

JIMMY GIUFFRE THREE, THE
CD 7567909812
Atlantic / Apr '95 / Warner Music

LIQUID DANCERS
CD 1211582
Soul Note / Apr '91 / Cadillac / Harmonia Mundi / Wellard

RIVER STATION (Giuffre, Jimmy & Andre Jaume)
CD CELPC 26
CELP / Nov '93 / Cadillac / Harmonia Mundi

TRAIN AND THE RIVER, THE
Train and the river / Elephant / Tibetan sun / Listening / River chant / Tide is in / Tree people / Om / Celebration

CD ______ CHCD 71011
Candid / Mar '97 / Cadillac / Direct / Jazz Music / Koch / Wellard

TRIO AND QUARTET
Song is you / Gotta dance / Train and the river / Train and river / Two kinds of of blues / Voodoo / Crazy she calls me / That's the way it is / My all / Crawdad suite / Green country (New England mood) / Little melody / Careful / Crab / Four brothers
CD ______ CD 53252
Giants Of Jazz / Jan '96 / Cadillac / Jazz Music / Target/BMG

Gizavo, Regis

MIKEA
Mpembe / Siniko / Tsikaholy / Malaso / Zeombanao / Misoholo / Mafy / Mikea / Mahavatse / Taligne
CD ______ LBLC 2529
Indigo / Jun '96 / New Note/Pinnacle

Glacial Fear

ATLASPHERE
CD ______ NOSFVS 007
Nosferatu / Nov '95 / Plastic Head

Glackin, Kevin

NORTHERN LIGHTS (Na Saighneain) (Glackin, Kevin & Seamus)
CD ______ CEFCD 140
Gael Linn / Jan '94 / ADA / CM / Direct / Grapevine/PolyGram / Roots

Glackin, Paddy

IN FULL SPATE
CD ______ CEFCD 153
Gael Linn / Jan '94 / ADA / CM / Direct / Grapevine/PolyGram / Roots

SEIDEAN SI
CD ______ CEFCD 171
Gael Linn / Aug '95 / ADA / CM / Direct / Grapevine/PolyGram / Roots

WHIRLWIND, THE (Glackin, Paddy & Robbie Hannon)
CD ______ SHCD 79093
Shanachie / Oct '95 / ADA / Greensleeves / Koch

Gladiators

CASH, THE
CD ______ 087962
Melodie / Jan '97 / ADA / Discovery / Grapevine/PolyGram / Greensleeves / Jet Star

DREADLOCKS THE TIME IS NOW
Mix up / Bellyfull / Looks is deceiving / Chatty chatty mouth / Soul rebel / Eli Eli / Hearsay / Rude boy ska / Dreadlocks the time is now / Jah works / Pocket money / Get ready / Stick a bush / Write to me / Naturality / Struggle / Day we go / Sweet so till / Hello Carol
CD ______ CDFL 9001
Frontline / Jul '90 / EMI / Jet Star

STORM, THE
Lovin' you / Cuss cuss / Community / Fools rush in / Reggae music / Storm / Hello my love / Love got the power / Rewind / Sun comes out
CD ______ 111222
Musidisc UK / Jul '95 / Grapevine/ PolyGram

TRUE RASTAMAN, A
No rice and peas / Let's face it / Think twice (A wise saying) / Sea breeze / Hearts on fire / South Africa / True Rastaman / Giddie head / Every moment / One way ticket
CD ______ 109632
Musidisc / Feb '94 / Discovery

Glam Rock Allstars

NON STOP GLAM ROCK (35 All Time Glam Smash Hits Megamix)
Yeah glisten / Rock 'n' roll pt.1 / Do you wanna touch me (oh yeah) / Can the can / Devil gate drive / 48 crash / My coo ca choo / Jealous mind / Blockbuster / Hot love / Metal guru / Get it on / Sugar baby love / Dynamite / Angel face / Goodbye my love / Cum on feel the noize / Mama weer all crazee now / Gudbuy 't Jane / Son of my father / Jean Genie / Waterloo / Mamma mia / SOS / Glass of champagne / (Dancing) on a Saturday night / Do you wanna dance / Tiger feet / John I'm only dancing / Ballroom blitz / Hell raiser / Fox on the run / I can do it / Tell him / Hello hello I'm back again / I'm the leader of the gang (I am)
CD ______ 305452
Hallmark / Oct '96 / Carlton

Glamorous Hooligan

WASTED YOUTH CLUB CLASSICS
Hooli cool downbeat / Billy Liar does De Niro / Stoned Island Estate / Lazy bomb / New age pension / Pure fiction / Tokyo heartwash / Next steppas / Naked beatbox / Charlie don't cybersurf
CD ______ MOBCD 007
Mass Of Black / Apr '96 / Vital

Glandien, Lutz

SCENES FROM NO MARRIAGE
CD ______ RERLG 1
ReR/Recommended / Oct '96 / ReR Megacorp / RTM/Disc

Glands Of External Secretion

NOSEJOB
CD ______ STAR 4CD
Starlight / Dec '96 / Cargo

Glaser, Tompall

OUTLAW, THE
It never crossed my mind / Bad times / What are we doing with our lives / How I love them old songs / On second thought / Drinkin' them beers / My mother was a lady / Duncan and Brady / Easy on my mind / Wonder of it all / You can have her / Release me / Tennessee blues / Come back Shane / It'll be her / It ain't fair / Sweethearts or strangers / Late nite show / I just want to hear the music / Storms never last
CD ______ BCD 15605
Bear Family / Jun '92 / Direct / Rollercoaster / Swift

ROGUE, THE
Rogue / Tears on my pillow / Forever and ever / Shackles and chains / My pretty quadron / Lean on me / I'll hold you in my heart / True love / Open arms / I love you so much it hurts / Chattanooga shoe shine boy / You can't borrow back any time / Like an old country song / Sad country songs / What a town / Don't think you're too good for country music / Unwanted outlaw / Man you think you see / When I dream / Burn Georgia burn / Billy Tyler / Carry me on
CD ______ BCD 15596
Bear Family / Apr '92 / Direct / Rollercoaster / Swift

Glasgow Celtic FC

GLASGOW CELTIC FC SUPPORTERS SONGS (2CD Set) (Various Artists)
Why I follow Celtic / I'll follow Celtic / 25th of May / Johnny Thompson we remember / Gemmell the great / Our famous Celtic team / Celtic is the name / O'Donnell Abu / We sing our Celtic songs / Men of the west / Flags are out for Celtic / Wrap the green flag / Choice / Celtic 4, Rangers 0 / Celtic and proud of it / Bold Celtic men / Old fenian gun / Celtic crazy / Johnny Thompson was his name / God save Ireland / Big Jock manager of Celtic / Wearing of the green / Three cheers for Tommy Gemmell / Celtic are the boys / Celtic story / When the Celts go marching in / Here to cheer the famous Glasgow Celtic / Celtic vocal waltz / Legend of Jimmy McCrory / After the game melody / Charlie Tully - Celtic's famous boy / Parkhead men / Wee Jimmy / Sir Robert Kelly / Big Jock Stein / Famous Glasgow Celtic / Nation once again / Sean South / Joe McDonnell / Glory Glory Glasgow Celtic / Bye bye rangers / Coatbridge shamrock / Celtic 7, Rangers 1 / I'm coming home Glasgow Celtic / On the one road / McAlpine's fusiliers / Boys of the old brigade / Fields of Athenry / Soldier's song
CD Set ______ TSCD 1888
Outlet / Apr '97 / ADA / CM / Direct / Duncans / Koch / Ross

HAIL HAIL CELTIC (Various Artists)
CD ______ CDGAFFER 12
Cherry Red / Nov '96 / Pinnacle

Glasgow Gaelic Musical ...

CENTENARY SELECTION, A (Glasgow Gaelic Musical Association)
CD ______ LCOM 5220
Lismor / Jun '93 / ADA / Direct / Duncans / Lismor

GAELIC GALORE (Glasgow Gaelic Musical Association)
Tuireadh nan treun / 'S olc a dh' fhag an uiridh mi / O hi ri ri, tha e tighinn / Maighdeanan na h-airidh / Tir an airm / Seoladh dhachaidh / An aitireachd ard / Allt an t-siucair / An ubhal as airde / Nuair bha mi og / Strathspeys and reels / O righ nan dul / 'S cian bho dh'fhag mi leodhas / An t-Iarla diurach / Cathair a chulchinn / Cearcall a' chuain / Oran an lennaibh og / Och nan och, tha mi fo mhulad / Caberfeidh
CD ______ LCOM 9037
Lismor / Oct '90 / ADA / Direct / Duncans / Lismor

Glasgow Islay Gaelic Choir

TRIBUTE TO RUNRIG
CD ______ CDLOC 1094
Lochshore / Jun '96 / ADA / Direct / Duncans

Glasgow Orpheus Choir

20 CLASSIC RECORDINGS
All in the April evening / Belmont peat / Fire smoothing prayer / Bonnie Dundee Orlington / Eriskay love lilt / Lilt / Ca' the Yowes / Crimond / Hark, hark the echo falling / Bluebird / Ellan Vannin / Jesu joy of man's desiring / Cloud capp'd towers / Faery song / Campbells are coming / Far away / Iona boat song / Cradle song / Sea sorrow / All through the night
CD ______ MOICD 007
Moidart / Nov '92 / Conifer/BMG

O LIGHT OF LIFE
O light of life / Kendron / O can ye sew cushions / Far away/old woman / Herdmaiden's song / In silent night / I live not where I love / Ae fond kiss / White waves on the water / Dashing white sergeant / Scots wha hae / Laird of cockpen / Haste thee nymph / Come kindly death / Dumbarton's drum / Deep river / All creatures now are merry minded / Mice and men / Go lovely rose / Gretna green / Isle of Mull / To take the air (a bonny lass was walking) / Strathcathro / Shower
CD ______ MOICD 012
Moidart / Dec '96 / Conifer/BMG

Glasgow Phoenix Choir

FEEL GOOD
CD ______ CDLOC 1080
Lochshore / Jul '94 / ADA / Direct / Duncans

WITH VOICES RISING
Scots wha hae / In the Wheatfield / When the saints go marching in / Annie Laurie / Time for man go home / Brother James' air / Shenandoah / John Anderson, my Jo / Tumbalalaika / Little cherry tree / Corn rigs / Dream angus / Death o' death oh me lawd / Loch Lomond / Campbells are coming / All my trials / Lament of Mary Queen Of Scots / Battle of the republic
CD ______ LCDM 9024
Lismor / Aug '90 / ADA / Direct / Duncans / Lismor

Glasgow Police Pipe Band

PIPES ARE CALLING, THE
CD ______ EMPRCD 703
Emporio / Mar '97 / Disc

Glasgow Rangers FC

FAMOUS GLASGOW RANGERS (Various Artists)
CD ______ CDGAFFER 11
Cherry Red / Nov '96 / Pinnacle

GLASGOW RANGERS FC SUPPORTERS SONGS (2CD Set) (Various Artists)
Paisley (Town of) / Rangers ABC / Johnston king of the ball / Rangers in shirts of blue / Rangers our greatest pride / I'll follow rangers / Best team in the land / Stars of Ibbrox / March on to victory / Gers go marching on / Follow follow / Men of Ibrox / Rangers true and blue / Bonnie Rangers / Scottish nonsense song / Call them Glasgow rangers / Maggie McDonald / We are the people / Aye ready / Wonders of the world / Red, white and blue / King Kai / March on Glasgow rangers / Blue flag / No surrender / Green grassy slopes of the Boyne / Sash / Le reve passe - the Rangers story / We shall not be moved / Rangers over here / Every other Saturday / Old mud cabin / Glory glory / Scarf / Lambeg drums / Cry is Glasgow Rangers / My dear old Belfast town / Land of no surrender / Legend of Willie Woodburn / It's Rangers for me / Sandy Sandy / I'm off to join the orange walk / Ranger story / Flower of Scotland / Men of Harlech / God save the Queen
CD Set ______ TSCD 300
Outlet / Apr '97 / ADA / CM / Direct / Duncans / Koch / Ross

Glasgow, Deborahe

DEBORAHE GLASGOW
CD ______ GRELCD 135
Greensleeves / Dec '89 / Jet Star / SRD

GIMME YOUR LOVE
CD ______ WRCD 011
World / Jun '97 / Jet Star / TKO Magnum

Glass House

CRUMBS OFF THE TABLE
Crumbs off the table / If it ain't love (it don't matter) / Touch me Jesus / I surrendered / You ain't livin' (unless you're lovin') / Stealing moments (from another woman's life) / Let it flow / Giving up the flow / Thanks I needed that / I don't see me in your eyes anymore / Hotel / I can't be you, you can't be me / He's in my life / VIP / Look what we've done to love / Heaven is there to guide us / Don't go looking for something (you don't want to see)
CD ______ HDHCD 505
HDH / Apr '92 / Pinnacle

Glass, Philip

1000 AIRPLANES ON THE ROOF
1000 airplanes on the roof / City walk / Girlfriend / My building disappeared / Screens of memory / What time is grey / Labyrinth / Return to the hive / Three truths / Encounter / Grey cloud over New York / Where have you been as the doctor / Normal man running
CD ______ CDVE 39
Venture / Feb '89 / EMI

AKHNATEN (2CD Set)
CD Set ______ M2K 42457
Sony Classical / Feb '88 / Sony

EINSTEIN ON THE BEACH
CD ______ 7559793232
Nonesuch / Jan '95 / Warner Music

ESSENTIAL PHILIP GLASS, THE
CD ______ SK 64133
Sony Music / Dec '93 / Sony

GLASSMASTERS (3CD Set)
Window of appearances / III/The dam / Vow / Open the kingdom / Attack and fall / Confrontation and rescue / Funeral of Amenhotep III / Floe / Dance No.5 / Spaceship / Photographer act III / Building/Train / Knee play 3 / Facades / Akhnaten Act III4 epilogue / Freezing / Akhnanten's hymn to the aten / Satyagraha Act III3 evening song / Knee play 5 / Mad rush
CD Set ______ SM3K 62960
Sony Classical / Apr '97 / Sony

HEROES SYMPHONY, THE (The Music Of David Bowie/Brian Eno)
CD ______ 4543082
Point Music / Mar '97 / PolyGram

HYDROGEN JUKEBOX (Glass, Philip & Allen Ginsberg)
CD ______ 7559792862
Nonesuch / Jan '95 / Warner Music

ITAIPU
CD ______ SK 46352
Sony Classical / Nov '93 / Sony

LOW SYMPHONY, THE (From Music By David Bowie & Brian Eno)
CD ______ 4381502
Philips / Mar '93 / PolyGram

MUSIC IN 12 PARTS (3CD Set) (Glass, Philip Ensemble)
CD Set ______ 7559793242
Nonesuch / Oct '96 / Warner Music

NORTH STAR
Etoile polaire (North star) / Victor's lament / River run / Mon pere, mon pere / Are years what? (for Marianne Moore) / Lady Day / Ange des orages / Ave / Ik-ook / Montage
CD ______ CDV 2085
Virgin / Jun '88 / EMI

PASSAGES (Glass, Philip & Ravi Shankar)
Offering / Channels and winds / Meetings along the edge / Sadhanipa / Ragas in minor scale / Prashanti
CD ______ 260947
Private Music / Sep '90 / BMG

SATYAGRAHA (3CD Set)
CD Set ______ M3K 39672
Sony Classical / Jan '94 / Sony

SOLO PIANO
CD ______ SMK 45576
Sony Classical / Jan '96 / Sony

Glasse, Paul

ROAD TO HOME, THE
CD ______ DOSCD 7004
Dos / May '94 / ADA / CM / Direct

Glaz

AR GEST
CD ______ 504362
Declic / Mar '96 / ADA

GLAZ
CD ______ CD 848
Escalibur / Aug '93 / ADA / Discovery / Roots

Gleason, Jackie

HOW SWEET IT IS (The Jackie Gleason Velvet Brass Collection)
CD ______ RE 21112
Razor & Tie / Jul '96 / Koch

JACKIE GLEASON
There'll be some changes made / How about you / Crazy rhythm / Petite waltz / Don't blame me / You can't pull the wool over my eyes / Soon / My blue heaven / Lady is a tramp / Most beautiful girl in the world / Who cares / I've got my eyes on you / Best things in life are free / I never knew / World is waiting for the sunrise / Love nest / Man I love / But not for me / Am I blue / What's new / September song / Out of nowhere / Take the 'A' train
CD ______ CD 390
Entertainers / Mar '96 / Target/BMG

Gledhill, Simon

SHALL WE DANCE
Shall we dance / Fleurette / El relicario / These foolish things / Garland of Judy / Canyon caballero / No matter what happens / Veradero / Dancing in the dark / Autumn crocus / June night on marlow reach / Swing time / My silent love / Themes from: Skyscraper fantasy / Haunted ballroom
CD ______ OS 205
OS Digital / Jul '94 / Conifer/BMG

Glee Club

MINE
Need / Blame / No reason / Bad child's dolly / Already there / Free to believe / Drives you away / Remember the years / All the promises / Take you there / Icy blue
CD _____ SETCD 012
Setanta / Jan '94 / Vital

Gleeson, Barry

PATH ACROSS THE OCEAN
Path across the ocean / Mulligar recruit / Roy Roger um / Sleeveless charms / What will we do when we have no money / This is Macaronic / Irish jubilee / Sweet daffodil Mulligan / Sheila Nee Iyer (sile ni ghaidhre) / False false fly / Calf meal in Roscrea / Slip jigs and reels / Shrieken artaner / Cuppid's visitation to Mick Dwyer
CD _____ CD 001
Wavelength / Sep '94 / ADA / CM / Direct
CD _____ TERRCD 001
Terra Nova / Nov '96 / Direct

Gleeson, Patrick

FOUR SEASONS
Spring / Summer / Autumn / Winter
CD _____ VCD 47212
Varese Sarabande / '87 / Pinnacle

Glenfiddle

NEVERTHELESS
CD _____ EFA 800392
Twah / Dec '95 / SRD

Glenn, Glen

GLEN GLENN STORY/EVERYBODY'S MOVIN' AGAIN
If I had me a woman / One cup of coffee / Hold me baby / Baby let's play house / Laurie Ann / Be bop a lula / Kitty Kat / Everybody's movin' / Shake, rattle and roll / Treat me nice / Blue jeans and a boy's shirt / I got a woman / Kathleen / Would ja' / I'm glad my baby's gone away / Down the line / Come on / Flip flop and fly / Jack and Jill boogie / I sure do love you baby / Bony Moronie / Mean woman blues / Rock 'n' roll Ruby / Sick and tired / Rockin' around the mountain / Why don't you love me / Ugly and slouchy / You win again / Everybody's movin' again
CD _____ CDCHD 403
Ace / Jun '92 / Pinnacle

Glenn Underground

ATMOSFEAR
Isralee night fails / Entercourse of the new age / Rising son / May datroit / Colouration / Dance slam / Sound struck / Midnight groove
CD _____ PF 043CD
Peacefrog / Apr '96 / Mo's Music Machine / Prime / RTM/Disc / Vital

JERUSALEM EP'S, THE
Black slaves = Israel / Sun, moon and 12 stars / Keep the hidden treasures / Servants jazz house / H-Dance / Negro city / To the King Ol / There is a time
CD _____ PF 066CD
Peacefrog / May '97 / Mo's Music Machine / Prime / RTM/Disc / Vital

PARABLES
CD _____ DFDCD 003
Defender / Jul '96 / Essential/BMG / Prime / SRD

Glennie, Evelyn

GREATEST HITS (2CD Set)
Entrances / Halasana / Sorbet no.1 / Rhythm song / My spine / Slaughter on 10th Avenue / Sorbet no.5 / Little prayer / Eldorado / Sorbet no.7 / Black key study / Divertimento / Taps in tempo / Born to be wild / Michi for marimba / Sorbet no.4 / Light in darkness / Anvil chorus / Rhapsody / Swan / Sorbet no.3
CD Set _____ 74321476292
RCA Victor / May '97 / BMG

Glide

SPACE AGE FREAK OUT
CD _____ OCH 001L
Ochre / Jul '97 / SRD

Glinn, Lillian

LAST SESSION 1929 (Glinn, Lillian & Mae Glover)
CD _____ SOB 035372
Story Of The Blues / Oct '92 / ADA / Koch

LILLIAN GLINN 1927-1933
CD _____ DOCD 5184
Document / Oct '93 / ADA / Hot Shot / Jazz Music

Glitter Band

VERY BEST OF THE GLITTER BAND, THE
Angel face / Painted lady / Makes you blind / My first mistake / Let's get together again / Tell him / Love street / Sweet baby blue / Tears I cried / Rock on / People like you and people like me / Almost American / Let me love you / Gotta get a message back to you / Just for you / Write me a letter / Tuna biscuit / Love in the sun / Where have you been / Goodbye my love
CD _____ 3036400062
Essential Gold / May '96 / Carlton

Glitter, Gary

GARY GLITTER
CD _____ GRF 200
Tring / Jan '93 / Tring

GARY GLITTER'S GANGSHOW
Rock 'n' roll (part 2) / I didn't know I loved you (till I saw you rock 'n' roll) / When I'm on / Do you wanna touch me (Oh yeah) / Alright with the boys / Hello hello I'm back again / Shake it up / Always yours / Frontiers of style / Only way to survive / Rock 'n' roll (part 1) / Good rockin' tonight / Baby let's play house / Be bop a lula / Another rock'n'roll Christmas / I love you love me love / Leader of the gang
CD _____ CCSCD 234
Castle / Nov '89 / BMG

GLITTER
Rock 'n' roll / Baby please don't go / Wanderer / I didn't know I loved you (till I saw you rock 'n' roll) / Ain't that a shame / School day (ring ring goes the bell) / Rock on / Donna / Famous instigator / Clapping song / Shaky sue / Rock 'n' roll part 2 / I am the leader of the gang (I am) / It's not a lot / Just fancy that / Thank you baby for myself
CD _____ DOJOCD 100
Dojo / Jul '96 / Disc

LEADER VOL.2
Ready to rock / Tonight / Why do you do it / Wild women / (The only way to) survive / Let's go party / Are you hard enough / Shake it up / It's enough / Am I losing you
CD _____ CCSCD 443
Castle / Oct '96 / BMG

LEADER, THE
CD Set _____ TFP 026
Tring / Nov '92 / Tring

MANY HAPPY RETURNS - THE HITS
Rock 'n' roll (part 1) / Rock 'n' roll (part 2) / I didn't know I loved you (till I saw you rock 'n' roll) / Ready to rock / Rock on / Doing alright with the boys / I'm the leader of the gang (I am) / Wanderer / Do you wanna touch me (Oh yeah) / Hello hello I'm back again / I love you love me love / You belong to me / It takes all night long / Oh yes, you're beautiful / Love like you and me / Little boogie woogie (in the back of my mind) / Dance me up / Through the years / Always yours / Remember me this way / And the leader rocks on / Another rock and roll Christmas
CD _____ CDFA 3303
Fame / Jan '94 / EMI

GLO

EVEN AS WE
Deiea / I'm in your gravity / Travellers stargate / Crystal world / Doom ghosts / And / Pagli herbus / Spirit lover / Walk the streets / Goddesses love oranges / Let's GLO / Back to the sea
CD _____ GLISSCD 002
GAS / Jul '97 / Pinnacle

Glo Worm

GLIMMER
CD _____ KLP 54CD
K / May '96 / Cargo / Greyhound / SRD

Global

GIG NA GIG
CD _____ GLISSCD 003
GAS / Jul '97 / Pinnacle

Global Communication

76.14
CD _____ DEDCD 014
Dedicated / Jul '94 / BMG / Vital

REMOTION
CD _____ DEDCD 021
Dedicated / Nov '95 / BMG / Vital

Global Goon

GLOBAL GOON
CD _____ CAT 0038CD
Rephlex / Dec '96 / Prime / RTM/Disc

Global Noise Attack

SEIZURE
CD _____ TCD 001
Tumult Productions / Dec '96 / Cargo

Globe Unity Orchestra

20TH ANNIVERSARY
CD _____ FMPCD 45
FMP / Nov '89 / Cadillac

RUMBLING - 1975
CD _____ FMPCD 40
FMP / Dec '89 / Cadillac

Glod

GLOD
CD _____ EEE 22CD
Audioglobe / Sep '94 / Plastic Head

Glommin Geek

DIG A HOLE IN THE SKY
CD _____ WD 014CD
Wide / Aug '92 / Plastic Head / SRD

Gloria

20 SONGS
CD _____ PHCD 535
Outlet / Jan '95 / ADA / CM / Direct / Duncans / Koch / Ross

Glory

CRISIS VS. CRISIS
CD _____ DCD 9622
Dream Circle / Mar '97 / Cargo / Plastic Head

Glory Box

BEGIN
CD _____ CCD 512651
Celebration / Feb '97 / Shellshock/Disc

Gloucester Cathedral Choir

CHRISTMAS CAROLS
As with gladness men of old / We three Kings / Personent hodie / Infant King / Quem pastores Laudavere / In dulci jubilo / Sussex carol / Adam lay y bounden / Whence is that goodly fragrance / Of the Father's heart begotten / In the bleak midwinter / Cherry tree carol / Tomorrow shall be my dancing day / Virgin most pure / O come, O come, Emmanuel / Joys seven / Twelve days of Christmas / See amid the winter's snow / Past three o'clock / Jingle bells / King Jesus hath a garden / Shepherd's pipe carol / Christmas is coming / Sans day carol / Torches / Great and mighty wonder / Angels from the realms of glory / Jeus Christ the apple tree
CD _____ XMAS 002
Tring / Nov '96 / Tring

MUSIC FOR CHRISTMAS
There is no rose / O little one sweet / See amid the winter's snow / I sing of a maiden / Three mummers / Sing lullaby / Carol of praise / New Year carol / Hymn of the Nativity / Carol for today / Tomorrow shall be my dancing day / Lamb / O little town of Bethlehem / Silent night / Blessed be that maid Mary / Whence is that goodly fragrance / Ding dong merrily on high / It came upon a midnight clear / Once in Royal David's City
CD _____ CDCA 917
Alpha / Nov '91 / Abbey Recording

Glove

BLUE SUNSHINE
Like an animal / Looking glass girl / Sex-eye-make-up / Blues in drag / Mr. Alphabet says / Punish me with kisses / This green city / Orgy / Perfect murder / Relax
CD _____ 8150192
Polydor / Aug '90 / PolyGram

Glover, May

MAY GLOVER 1927-1931
CD _____ DOCD 5185
Document / Oct '93 / ADA / Hot Shot / Jazz Music

Glover, Roger

BUTTERFLY BALL, THE/WIZARD'S CONVENTION (Various Artists)
Dawn / Get ready / Saffron Dormouse and Lizzy Bee / Harlequin hare / Old blind mole / Magician moth / No solution / Behind the smile / Fly away / Aranea / Sitting in a dream / Waiting / Sir Maximus Mouse / Dreams of Sir Bedivere / Together again / Watch out for the bat / Little chalk blue / Feast / Love is all / Homeward / Craig song / When the sun stops shining / Loose ends / Money to burn / Who's counting on me / Make it soon / Until tomorrow / Light of my life / She's a woman / Swanks and swells
CD _____ VSOPCD 139
Connoisseur Collection / Oct '89 / Pinnacle

ELEMENTS/THE MASK
First a ring of clay / Next a ring of fire / Third ring's watery flow / Fourth ring's with the wind / Finale / Divided world / Getting stranger / Mask / Fake it / Dancin' again / (You're so) Remote / Hip level / Don't look down
CD _____ VSOPCD 183
Connoisseur Collection / Apr '93 / Pinnacle

Glu Gun

JUST GLU IT
CD _____ EFA 113892
Poshboy / May '94 / RTM/Disc

Glue

MACHINE KEEP ME WARM
CD _____ FAN 1012
Fantastick / Jun '94 / SRD

Glue Gun

SCENE IS NOT FOR SALE, THE
CD _____ FO 10CD
Fearless / Apr '97 / Cargo / Plastic Head

Gluecifer

RIDIN' THE TIGER
CD _____ JAZZ 005CD
White Jazz / Jun '97 / Plastic Head

GMT

WAR GAMES
CD _____ 36700043
Mausoleum / Oct '91 / Grapevine/ PolyGram

Gnaoua, Jilala

MOROCCAN TRANCE MUSIC VOL.1
CD _____ SUBCD 01336
Sub Rosa / Jul '97 / Direct / RTM/Disc / SRD / Vital

Go To Blazes

ANY TIME
CD _____ GRCD 374
Glitterhouse / Aug '95 / Avid/BMG

Go West

ACES AND KINGS (The Best Of Go West)
We close our eyes / King of wishful thinking / Tracks of my tears / Call me / Faithful / Don't look down (the sequel) / One way street / What you won't do for love / From Baltimore to Paris / Goodbye girl / I want to hear it from you / Tell me / King is dead
CD _____ CDCHR 6050
Chrysalis / Oct '93 / EMI

BANGS AND CRASHES
We close our eyes / Man in my mirror / Goodbye girl / SOS / Eye to eye / Ball of confusion / Call me / Haunted / Missing person / Don't look down / One way street / Innocence
CD _____ CCD 1536
Chrysalis / Jun '97 / EMI

GO WEST
We close our eyes / Don't look down / Call me / Eye to eye / Haunted / SOS / Goodbye girl / Innocence / Missing persons
CD _____ CDGOLD 1014
EMI Gold / Mar '96 / EMI

Go-Betweens

16 LOVERS LANE
Love goes on / Quiet heart / Love is a sign / You can't say no forever / Dive for your memory / Devil's eye / Streets of your town / Clouds / Was there anything I could do / I'm alright
CD _____ BBL 2006CD
Beggars Banquet / Mar '96 / RTM/Disc / Warner Music

1978-1990
Karen / Eight pictures / Hammer the hammer / I need two heads / Cattle and cane / When people are dead / Man o'sand to girl o'sea / Sound of the rain / Bachelor kisses / People say / Draining the pool for you / World weary / Spring rain / Rock 'n' roll friend / Wrong road / Dusty in here / Clarke sisters / King in mirrors / Right here / Second hand furniture / Bye bye pride / girl, black girl / House that Jack Kerouac built / Don't call me gone / Streets of your town / Mexican postcard / Love is a sign / You won't find it again
CD _____ BEGA 104CD
Beggars Banquet / Mar '90 / RTM/Disc / Warner Music

BEFORE HOLLYWOOD
Bad debt follows you / Two steps step out / Before Hollywood / Dusty in here / Ask / Cattle and cane / By chance / As long as that / On my block / That way
CD _____ BBL 2002CD
Beggars Banquet / Mar '96 / RTM/Disc / Warner Music

LIBERTY BELLE AND THE BLACK DIAMOND EXPRESS
Spring rain / Ghost and the black hat / Wrong road / To reach me / Twin layers of lightning / In the core of a flame / Head full of steam / Bow down / Palm down / Apology accepted
CD _____ BBL 2004CD
Beggars Banquet / Mar '96 / RTM/Disc / Warner Music

SEND ME A LULLABY
CD _____ BBL 2001CD
Beggars Banquet / Mar '96 / RTM/Disc / Warner Music

SPRING HILL FAIR
Bachelor kisses / Five words / Old way out / You've never lived / Part company / Slow slow music / Draining the pool for you /

River of money / Unkind and unwise / Man o'sand to girl o'sea
CD BBL 2003CD
Beggars Banquet / Mar '96 / RTM/Disc / Warner Music

TALLULAH
Right here / You tell me / Someone else's wife / I just get caught out / Cut it out / House that Jack Kerouac built / Bye bye pride / Spirit of a vampyre / Clarke sisters / Hope then strife
CD BBL 2005CD
Beggars Banquet / Mar '96 / RTM/Disc / Warner Music

Go-Getters

REAL GONE
CD PT 601001
Part / Jun '96 / Nervous

Go-Go's

RETURN TO THE VALLEY OF THE GO-GO'S
Living at the Canterbury/Party pose / Fashion seekers / He's so strange / London boys / Beatnik beach / Cool jerk / We got the beat / Our lips are sealed / Surfing and spying / Vacation / Speeding / Good for gone / Head over heels / Can't stop the world / Mercenary / Good girl / Beautiful / Whole world lost its head
CD EIRSCD 1071
IRS/EMI / Mar '95 / EMI

Goa Gil

KOSMOKRATOR (Deck Wizards Series) (Various Artists)
Phosphorescence: *Infinity Project* / Thunderstorm: *Kuro* / Between the nothing: *Shakta & Ping Pong* / Option paralysis: *Sephalopod* / Oxygen cult: *Deviant Electronics* / Rollercoaster: *Growling Mad Scientists* / Po tolo: *Nommos* / Alternate dimension: *MFG* / Iron sun: *Dimension 5* / Lepton head: *Shakta*
CD PDCD 005
Phantasm/Psychic Deli / Feb '97 / Vital/ SAM

Goat

AS YOU LIKE
Don't cry / Fallen over you / Mother / Zombie break out / D'ya like it / How long
CD BBL 110CD
Beggars Banquet / Sep '90 / RTM/Disc / Warner Music

MEDICATION TIME
Sexman / Everybody wants to be there / Good times / Bug / Falling / Lying in the flowers / Something wrong / In the fields / Is this me / I want you back / Beneath the skin
CD BEGACD 119
Beggars Banquet / Jun '91 / RTM/Disc / Warner Music

SACRED PILGRIM
CD RRS 950CD
Die Hard/Progress / Sep '96 / Plastic Head

Goats Don't Shave

OUT IN THE OPEN
Coming home / Help / Children of the highway / Rose street / Arranmore / This world / She's leaving / Song for Fionula / War / Let it go / Lock it in
CD COOKCD 075
Cooking Vinyl / Sep '94 / Vital

RUSTY RAZOR
Let the world keep on turning / Las Vegas (In the hills of Donegal) / Eyes / John Cherokee / Evictions / Biddy from Sligo/Connaught man's rambles / Ranger / Mary Mary / Closing time / What she means to me / Crooked Jack / When you're dead
CD COOKCD 074
Cooking Vinyl / Jul '97 / Vital

Goblins

GOBLIN PRIDE
CD ALP 304
CD TRUCK 04CD
Truckstop / Jun '97 / SRD

God & Texas

CRIMINAL ELEMENT
Incoming / Bury magnets / D 2 / Cold bringer / Chromalox / Breach / Drive time / In the blast furnace / Flat black wide / Cruel andunusual
CD 729002
Restless / Nov '93 / Vital

DOUBLE SHOT
Confidential scrape / Codename: Soul albino / In the flesh again / Lower / Meet me at the inversion layer / Zappatos del diablo / Red room / Back on the downside / Profiteerings / Goodbye blacksheep / Chevalier / Outro
CD 729022
Restless / Sep '94 / Vital

God

APPEAL TO HUMAN GREED
CD ABB 79XCD
Big Cat / Jun '95 / 3mv/Pinnacle

GOD
CD PPP 106
PDCD / Jan '94 / Plastic Head

POSSESSION
Pretty / Fucked / Return to hell / Soul fire / Hate meditation / Lord I'm on my way / Love / Black Jesus
CD CDOVD 485
Virgin / Jun '97 / EMI

God Bullies

KILL THE KING
CD VIRUS 152CD
Alternative Tentacles / Oct '94 / Cargo / Greyhound / Pinnacle

God Forsaken

DREAMS OF DESOLATION
CD CDAR 08
Adipocre / Feb '94 / Plastic Head

TIDE HAS TURNED
CD CDAR 025
Adipocre / May '95 / Plastic Head

God Is My Co-Pilot

BEST OF GOD IS MY CO-PILOT, THE
CD ALP 82CD
Atavistic / Nov '96 / Cargo / SRD

CHILDREN CAN BE SO CRUEL
CD MIGUEL 1
Miguel / May '97 / Cargo

PEEL SESSIONS, THE
CD SFRSCD 004
Strange Fruit / Jan '97 / Pinnacle

PUSS 02
CD DSA 54041
Les Disques Du Soleil / Dec '95 / Harmonia Mundi

TIGHT LIKE FIST
CD KFWCD 148
Knitting Factory / Feb '95 / Cargo / Plastic Head

God Lives Underwater

EMPTY
Still / All wrong / Empty / Don't know how to be / No more love / 23 / We were wrong / Weaken / Tortoise / Scared / Lonely again / Nothing / Try / Waste of time / Drag me down
CD 74321295182
American / Oct '95 / BMG

God Machine

ONE LAST LAUGH IN A PLACE OF DYING
Tremelo song / Mama / Alone / In bad dreams / Painless / Love song / Life song / Devil song / Hunter / Evol / Train song / Flower song / Boy by the roadside / Sunday song
CD FIXCD 27
Fiction / Oct '94 / PolyGram

SCENES FROM A 2ND STOREY
Dream machine / She said / Blind man / I've seen the man / Desert song / Home / It's all over / Temptation / Out / Ego / Seven / Purity / Piano song
CD 5171562
Fiction / Jan '93 / PolyGram

Godard, Michel

ABORIGENE
CD HOP 200002
Label Hopi / May '94 / Harmonia Mundi

LE CHANT DU SERPENT
CD CDLLL 37
La Lichere / Oct '93 / ADA / Discovery

LOOSE WIRES
Chanson pour Lise / Stara pesma / Monster / It's still quite dark but there are some signs of light / Bakija / Les enfants qui s'aiment / Emilio / Spiritual / Locusts have returned and they are bigger than ever / Down home where the blowfish roam / Immaculate conception
CD ENJ 90712
Enja / May '97 / New Note/Pinnacle / Vital/ SAM

Godard, Vic

END OF THE SURREY PEOPLE
Imbalance / Johnny Thunders / Water was bad / Malicious love / On the shore / Nullify my reputation (I'm gonna) / Won't turn back / Talent to follow / Same mistakes / Pain barrier / I can't stop you / End of the Surrey people
CD DUBH 936CD
Postcard / Jun '93 / Vital

WHAT'S THE MATTER BOY (Godard, Vic & The Subway Sect)
Birth and death / Stand back / Watching the devil / Enclave / Out of touch / Vertical integration / Split up the money / Stool pigeon / Double negative / Exit no return / Empty shell / Make me sad / View
CD MAUCD 645
Mau Mau / Apr '96 / Pinnacle

Godchildren Of Soul

GODCHILDREN OF SOUL, THE
CD TOTCD 4
Total / Sep '95 / Total/BMG

Goddess

SEXUAL ALBUM, THE
Sexual / Lingerie / X-rated / Cleopatra / Erotic / In my bed / Boyz / Je t'aime / She's wild / Sexual (safe sex version)
CD 4724882
Epic / Nov '92 / Sony

Godfathers

AFTERLIFE
CD IRS 845255CD
Intercord / Feb '96 / Plastic Head

BIRTH, SCHOOL, WORK, DEATH (The Best Of The Godfathers)
Birth, school, work, death / She gives me love / Unreal world / Just because you're not paranoid / Cause I said so / Angela / Walking talking Johnny Cash blues / Miss that girl / This is war / If only I had time / Love is dead / Another you / Gone to Texas / Don't let me down / Lonely man / When am I coming down / Cold turkey / Birth, school, work, death (remix)
CD 4784232
Epic / Jul '96 / Sony

GOLDEN DELICIOUS/THE GODFATHERS
CD IRS 988574CD
Intercord / May '96 / Plastic Head

ORANGE
CD 986974
Intercord / Oct '93 / Plastic Head

Godflesh

GODFLESH
CD MOSH 020CD
Earache / Feb '94 / Vital

LOVE AND HATE IN DUB
Circle of shit / Wake / Almost heaven / Gift from heaven (breakbeat) / Frail (now broken) / Sterile prophet / Kingdom come / Time, death wastefulness in dub / Sterile prophet(in dub) / Domain / Gift from heaven
CD MOSH 178CD
Earache / Jul '97 / Vital

PURE
CD MOSH 032CD
Earache / Sep '94 / Vital

SELFLESS
Xnoybis / Bigot / Black bored angel / Anything is mine / Empyreal / Crush my soul / Body dome light / Toll / Heartless / Mantra / Go spread your wings
CD MOSH 085CD
Earache / Sep '94 / Vital

SONGS OF LOVE AND HATE
Wake / Sterile prophet / Circle of shit / Hunter / Gift from heaven / Amoral / Angel domain / Kingdom come / Time death and wastefulness / Frail / Almost heaven
CD MOSH 157CD
Earache / Sep '97 / Vital

STREETCLEANER
CD MOSH 015CD
Earache / Sep '94 / Vital

Godheads

ORDINARY SWOON
CD CDZOT 181
Zoth Ommog / Jul '97 / Cargo / Plastic Head

Godheadsilo

SKYWARD IN TRIUMPH
CD SPCD 347
Sub Pop / Apr '96 / Cargo / Greyhound / Shellshock/Disc

Godley & Creme

IMAGES
Englishman in New York / Get well soon / Wedding bells / Power behind the throne / Out in the cold / My body the car / Bits of blue sky / Cry / Little piece of heaven / Save a mountain for me / Wide boy / Party / Submarine / Last weekend
CD 5500072
Spectrum / May '93 / PolyGram

Godplow

RED GIANT JUDAS
CD GROW 0472
Grass / May '95 / Pinnacle / SRD

Godrays

SONGS FOR TV STARS
Comforting Joe / Songs for TV stars / Vampires suck / Darling / Careless / Both your names (Janus' creepy girlfriend) / Still just a night thing / 30 second song / Crummy / Boyscout thriller / Crack you up / Bother (the blushes) / Crazy / Carkeys, ponytail and gum
CD YARDCD 017
Vernon Yard / Oct '96 / Vital

Godsend

AS THE SHADOWS FALL
CD HOLY 3CD
Holy / May '94 / Plastic Head

Godspeed

RIDE
Ride / Not enough / Hate / Abstract life / Stubborn ass / Downtown / Born and raised / Houston St. / Mind blaster / Christ / My brother
CD 7567825732
WEA / Mar '94 / Warner Music

Godstar

SLEEPER
CD TAANG 79CD
Taang / Dec '93 / Cargo

Godzilla

VOLUME
CD TOPYCD 073
Temple / May '94 / Pinnacle / Plastic Head

Godzuki

FREE WADE
CD GS 003
Time Stereo/Go Sonic / Mar '97 / Cargo

Goebbels, Heiner

DISASTROUS LANDING
CD 5279302
ECM / Dec '95 / New Note/Pinnacle

HORSTUCKE
CD 5133682
ECM / Jun '94 / New Note/Pinnacle

LIVE A VICTORIAVILLE (Goebbels, Heiner & Alfred Harth)
CD VICTOCD 04
Victo / Nov '94 / Harmonia Mundi / ReR Megacorp

MAN IN THE ELEVATOR, THE (Goebbels, Heiner & Heiner Muller)
CD 8371102
ECM / Nov '88 / New Note/Pinnacle

Goforth, Gene

EMMINENCE BREAKDOWN
Dialog / Charleston no.1 / Dialog / Dink's Dusty Miller / Dialog / Quail is a pretty bird / Black river / Wolves a'howlin' / Roy Wooliver's money musk / Jawbone / Hamilton ironworks / Uncle Dink / Say old man / Fiddler's hornpipe / Emminence breakdown / Prettiest little girl in the county / Devil's hornpipe / Sally Goodin / Knockin' at your door / White river / Gettin' out the way of the Federalds / Little brown jug / Grandmammy look at Uncle Sam / Dialog / Rocky road to Denver / Comin' down from Denver / Hop skip squirrel
CD ROUCD 0388
Rounder / Feb '97 / ADA / CM / Direct

Gogh Van Go

GOGH VAN GO
Bed where we hide / Say you will / Vinyl / Long shory short / Tunnel of trees / Call it romance / 97 / Have a whirl / Instant karma / Kiss the ground / Say you will
CD ATLASCD 005
Equator / Apr '94 / Pinnacle

Goins, Herbie

SOULTIME (Goins, Herbie & The Nightimers)
Outside of heaven / Look at Granny run run / I don't mind / Pucker up buttercup / Coming home to you / No. 1 in your heart / Satisfaction / Good good lovin' / Cruisin' / Knock on wood / 36-22-36 / Turn on your love light / Coming home to you (Live)
CD SEECD 362
See For Miles/C5 / Oct '92 / Pinnacle

Gol

SENSATIONS OF TONE
CD WOLCD 1065
China / Mar '96 / Pinnacle

Gola, Andy

LIVE IN HAVANA
CD TUMICD 060
Tumi / Sep '96 / Discovery / Stern's

Gold, Andrew

HALLOWEEN HOWLS
CD R 272532
Music For Little People / Nov '96 / Direct

Gold Blade

HOME TURF
Strictly hardcore / Soul power / Genius is pain / Soul on fire / Hail the people / Canal street / Breakdown / Saddest song / Black Elvis / Not even Jesus / Feel my disease / Down town / Jacknife / Meet thy saviour / Fastest man alive / True believers
CD ______ TOPPCDX 058
CD ______ TOPPCD 058
Ultimate / Apr '97 / Pinnacle

Gold, Brian

BULLSEYE (Gold, Brian & Tony)
CD ______ VPCD 1435
VP / Oct '95 / Greensleeves / Jet Star / Total/BMG

Gold, Graham

CLUB CUTS '97 (Mixed By Graham Gold - 2CD Set) (Various Artists)
Fly life: *Basement Jaxx* / In the head: *Gat Decor* / Scared: *Slacker* / Encore une fois: *Sash* / I love you...stop: *Red 5* / Sound of Eden: *Casino* / Get into the music: *DJ's Rule & Karen Brown* / Killin' time: *Cousins, Tina* / Underwater love: *Smoke City* / You got the love: *Source & Candi Staton* / Ready or not: *Course* / Get up (everybody): *Stingily, Byron* / Fired up: *Funky Green Dogs* / Spin spin sugar: *Sneaker Pimps* / Show me love: *Robin S* / Where can I find love: *Livin' Joy* / Drive me crazy: *Partizan* / Up to no good: *Porn Kings* / Tha wildstyle: *DJ Supreme* / Just playin': *JT Playaz* / I have peace: *Strike* / So in love with you: *Duke* / Gotta love for you: *Serial Diva* / Driving south: *Future Homosapiens* / Funk phenomena: *Van Helden, Armand* / If Madonna calls: *Vasquez, Junior* / Morning light: *Team Deep* / Offshore: *Chicane* / Footprint: *Disco Citizens* / Comin' up: *Chemical Heaven* / Come with me: *Qattara* / Galaxia: *Moonman* / Going out of my head: *Fatboy Slim* / Remember me: *Blueboy*
CD Set ______ TCD 2898
Telstar / May '97 / BMG

Gold Tooth Display

MONSTERPIECE
CD ______ 69012
Immigrant / May '97 / Cargo

Goldberg, Barry

REUNION
CD ______ OW 24833
One Way / Jul '94 / ADA / Direct / Greyhound

TWO JEWS BLUES
CD ______ OW 27672
One Way / Jul '94 / ADA / Direct / Greyhound

Goldberg, Ben

BEN GOLDBERG & TREVOR DUNN/ JOHN SCOTT/KENNY WOLLESEN PROJECT
CD ______ KFWCD 160
Knitting Factory / Feb '95 / Cargo / Plastic Head

Goldberg, Stu

FANCY GLANCE
CD ______ INAK 8614 CD
In Akustik / Dec '87 / Direct / TKO Magnum

Golden Bough

BEST OF GOLDEN BOUGH
CD ______ EUCD 1145
ARC / '91 / ADA / ARC Music

BEYOND THE SHADOWS
CD ______ EUCD 1092
ARC / '89 / ADA / ARC Music

BOATMAN'S DAUGHTER
CD ______ EUCD 1037
ARC / '89 / ADA / ARC Music

FAR FROM HOME
CD ______ EUCD 1065
ARC / '89 / ADA / ARC Music

FLIGHT OF FANTASY
CD ______ EUCD 1045
ARC / '89 / ADA / ARC Music

GOLDEN BOUGH
CD ______ EUCD 1123
ARC / '91 / ADA / ARC Music

WINDING ROAD
CD ______ EUCD 1051
ARC / '89 / ADA / ARC Music

WINTER'S DANCE
CD ______ EUCD 1046
ARC / '89 / ADA / ARC Music

Golden Claw Music

ALL BLUE REVIEW
CD ______ INFECT 7CD
Infectious / Jul '94 / RTM/Disc

Golden Dawn

POWER PLANT
Evolution / This way please / Starvation / I'll be around / Seeing is believing / My time / Nice surprise / Everyday / Tell me why / Reaching out to you
CD ______ 842969
EVA / May '94 / ADA / Direct

Golden Eagle Jazz Band

MOROCCO BLUES
CD ______ SOSCD 1192
Stomp Off / Aug '90 / Jazz Music / Wellard

Golden Eagles

LIGHTNING AND THUNDER (Golden Eagles & Monk Boudreaux)
CD ______ ROUCD 2073
Rounder / '88 / ADA / CM / Direct

Golden Gate Quartet

FROM SPIRITUALS TO SWING VOL.2
CD ______ 7805732
Jazztime / Aug '93 / Discovery

GOLDEN GATE QUARTET 1937-1941
Massa' in the cold cold ground / Siants go marching in / Golden gate gospel train / Gabriel blows his horn / Lead me on and on / Sweet Adeline / Preacher and the bear / Noah / Take your burdens to God / Travellin' shoes / Packing up / Getting ready to go / Born ten thousand years ago / Jonah in the whale / I looked down the road and wondered / Everytime I feel the spirit / My walking sticks / Daniel saw the stones / Whoa babe
CD ______ FA 057
Fremeaux / Apr '97 / ADA / Discovery

GOLDEN GATE QUARTET VOL.1 1937-1938
CD ______ DOCD 5472
Document / Sep '96 / ADA / Hot Shot / Jazz Music

GOLDEN GATE QUARTET VOL.2 1938-1939
CD ______ DOCD 5473
Document / Sep '96 / ADA / Hot Shot / Jazz Music

GOLDEN GATE QUARTET VOL.3 1939
CD ______ DOCD 5474
Document / Sep '96 / ADA / Hot Shot / Jazz Music

GOLDEN GATE QUARTET VOL.4 1939-1943
CD ______ DOCD 5475
Document / Sep '96 / ADA / Hot Shot / Jazz Music

GOSPEL TRAIN (Golden Gate Jubilee Quartet)
CD ______ JSPCD 602
JSP / Jul '93 / ADA / Cadillac / Direct / Hot Shot / Target/BMG

GREATEST HITS 1946-1950
CD ______ BMCD 3016
Blue Moon / Sep '95 / Cadillac / Discovery / Greensleeves / Jazz Music / Jet Star / TKO Magnum

NEGRO SPIRITUALS VOL.1 (My Walking Stick)
My walking stick / Ol'man Mose / Stormy weather / Dipsy doodle / Motherless child / To the rock / Hide me in thy bosom / Golden gate gospel train / Bedside of a neighbor / Job / Travelin' shoes / Lead me on and on / Sampson / Take your burdens to God / Bye and bye little children / God almighty said / Let that liar alone / I heard Zion moan
CD ______ CD 12537
Music Of The World / Jun '96 / ADA / Target/BMG

NEGRO SPIRITUALS VOL.2 (When The Saints Go Marching Home)
When the saints go marching home / Massas in the cold cold ground / Packing up getting ready to go / If I had my way / I looked down the road and I wondered / Way down in Egypt land / I'm a pilgrim / Every time that I feel the spirit / John the revelator / You'd better mind / Sweet Adeline / Bonnet / Timber / Our Father / Rock my soul / Cheer the weary traveller
CD ______ CD 12541
Music Of The World / Jun '96 / ADA / Target/BMG

RADIO TRANSCRIPTIONS 1941-1944
CD ______ DOCD 5502
Document / Nov '96 / ADA / Hot Shot / Jazz Music

THEIR EARLY YEARS 1937-1939
CD ______ BMCD 3015
Blue Moon / Sep '95 / Cadillac / Discovery / Greensleeves / Jazz Music / Jet Star / TKO Magnum

TRAVELIN' SHOES
Golden gate gospel train / Beside of a neighbor / Job / Motherless child / Travellin' shoes / Dipsy doodle / Lead me on and on / Sampson / Take your burdens to God / Bye and bye little children / God almighty said / Let that liar alone / To the rock / Cheer the weary traveler / I heard Zion moan / Packing up, getting ready to go / Noah / Ol' man Mose / Hide me in thy bosom / If i had my way / I looked down the road and i wondered / Way down in Egypt land / I'm a pilgrim / Stormy weather / My walking stick
CD ______ 07863660632
Bluebird / Oct '92 / BMG

Golden Palominos

BLAST OF SILENCE
CD ______ CPCD 8225
Charly / Mar '97 / Koch

DEAD HORSE, A
CD ______ CPCD 8185
Charly / Jun '96 / Koch

DEAD INSIDE
Victim / Belfast / Ride / Ambitions are / Drown / Holy / You are never ready / Metal eye / Thirst / Curses
CD ______ 729072
Restless / Oct '96 / Vital

GOLDEN PALOMINOS, THE
Clean plate / Hot seat / Under the cap / Monday night / Cookout / ID / Two sided fist
CD ______ CPCD 8198
Charly / Dec '96 / Koch

HISTORY OF THE GOLDEN PALAMINOS VOL.2 (1986-1989)
CD ______ MAUCD 626
Mau Mau / Aug '92 / Pinnacle

NO THOUGHT, NO BREATH, NO EYES, NO HEART
Heaven (you have to be in hell to see heaven) / No skin (tempting fate) / Gun/Little suicides (brown stainwalls, red jelly corners) / No skin (cold spells) / No skin (aural circumcision) / No skin (funky hornsey)
CD ______ 727902
Restless / Mar '95 / Vital

PURE
Little suicides / Heaven / Anything / Wings / Pure / No skin / Gun / Break in the road / Touch you
CD ______ 7727612
Restless / Oct '94 / Vital

THIS IS HOW IT FEELS
Sleepwalk / Prison of the rhythm / I'm not sorry / This is how it feels / To a stranger / Wonder / Breakdown / These days / Rain holds / Twist the knife / Bird flying / Divine kiss
CD ______ 727352
Restless / Nov '93 / Vital

VISIONS OF EXCESS
CD ______ CPCD 8151
Celluloid / Nov '95 / Discovery / Koch

Golden Smog

DOWN BY THE OLD MAINSTREAM
V / Ill-fated / Pecan pie / Yesterday I cried / Glad and sorry / Won't be coming home / He's a dick / Walk where he walked / Nowhere bound / Friend / She don't have to see you / Red headed stepchild / Williamton angel / Radio King
CD ______ RCD 10325
Rykodisc / Mar '97 / ADA / Vital

Golden Star

DHOOTAKADA BAI DHOOTAKADA
CD ______ CDSR 019
Star / Aug '90 / Pinnacle / Stern's

Goldfinger

GOLDFINGER
Mind's eye / Stay / Here in your bedroom / Only a day / King for a day / Anxiety / Answers / Anything / Mable / City with twp faces / My girlfriends shower sucks / Miles away / Nothing to prove / Pictures
CD ______ UND 53007
Universal / Nov '96 / BMG

Goldie

TIMELESS
Timeless / Saint Angel / State of mind / This is a bad / Sea of tears / Jah the seventh seal / Sense of rage / Still life / Angel / Adrift / Kemistry / You and me
CD ______ 8286462
FFRR / Sep '95 / PolyGram

Goldie, Don

DON GOLDIE & HIS DANGEROUS JAZZ BAND
CD ______ JCD 135
Jazzology / Jul '96 / Jazz Music

Golding, Peter

STRETCHING THE BLUES
Good rockin' tonight / Stretching the blues / Thanks to the blues / Fashion designer blues / Burglar jump / Treasure of the blues / Stumble / Crucify me / Living in a memory / Chatanoogie shoe shine boy / Pete's bop / Blues in the night/train / Good rockin' tonight
CD ______ IGOCD 2063
Indigo / May '97 / ADA / Direct

Goldings, Larry

CAMINHOS CRUZADOS
So danco samba / Caminhos cruzados / Ho-ba-la-la / O amor en paz / Where or when / Manine / Avarandado / Serenata / Menina-moca / Words / Una mas
CD ______ 01241631842
Novus / Jun '95 / BMG

Goldmine

CARTWHEELS AND HANDSPRINGS
CD ______ ADPTCD 3
Adept / Mar '97 / 3mv/Pinnacle

Goldsboro, Bobby

HONEY (22 Greatest Hits)
See the funny little clown / Whenever he holds you / Me japanese boy, I love you / Summer (the first time) / Brand new kind of love / Watching scotty grow / Can you feel it / I'm a drifter / Glad she's a woman / Straight life / Autumn of my life / Honey / Blue autumn / It hurts me / It's too late / Broomstick cowboy / It breaks my heart / If you've got a heart / If you wait for love / Voodoo woman / Little things / I don't know you anymore
CD ______ RMB 75084
Remember / Jan '96 / Total/BMG

HONEY - THE BEST OF BOBBY GOLSBORO
See the funny little clown / Hello loser / Whenever he holds you / My Japanese boy, I love you / I don't know you anymore / Little things / Voodoo woman / It breaks my heart / If you wait for love / If you've got a heart / Broomstick cowboy / It's too late / It hurts me / Blue Autumn / Honey / Autumn of my life / Straight life / Glad she's a woman / I'm a drifter / Can you feel it / Watching Scotty grow / Brand new kind of love / Summer (the first time)
CD ______ 295898
RCA / Jul '93 / BMG

VERY BEST OF BOBBY GOLDSBORO, THE
Honey / Straight life / With pen in hand / Muddy Mississippi line / Blue Autumn / Little things / Summer (the first time) / Watchin' Scotty grow / See the funny little clown / Cowboy and the lady / Broomstick cowboy / It's too late / Autumn of my life / Hello summertime / I'm a drifter / Love divine / Payin' for the good times / Street dancin'
CD ______ C5CD534
See For Miles/C5 / Dec '89 / Pinnacle

Goldsby, John

TALE OF THE FINGERS (Goldsby, John Quartet)
Op / Terrace / Three short stories for contrabass and piano / Tale of the fingers / Twilight time / Tricotism / Time and again / Beautiful / Seven minds / Pitter, panther, patter
CD ______ CCD 4632
Concord Jazz / Feb '95 / New Note/ Pinnacle

Goldschmidt, Per

FRAME, THE
Blues for Trane / Snowgirl / Frame / Loneliness / Bermuda triangle
CD ______ CDSJP 290
Timeless Jazz / Aug '90 / New Note/ Pinnacle

FRANKLY (A Tribute To Frank Sinatra)
You and the night and the music / It happend in Monterey / Theme for Eve / Forever Frank / Frankly speaking / Man alone / Too marvellous for words / Fly me to the moon / Come fly with me / You make me feel so young / Second to none
CD ______ MCD 92242
Milestone / Mar '97 / Cadillac / Complete/ Pinnacle / Jazz Music / Wellard

Goldsmith, Jerry

AIR FORCE ONE
CD ______ CDVSD 5825
Colosseum / Aug '97 / Pinnacle

Goldy, Craig

HIDDEN IN PLAIN SIGHT (Craig Goldy's Ritual)
CD ______ CDMFN 125
Music For Nations / Mar '92 / Pinnacle

Golgotha

MELANCHOLY
CD ______ RPS 011CD
Repulse / Jan '96 / Plastic Head

SYMPHONY IN EXTREMIS
CD ______ CMGCD 009
Communique / Jul '93 / Plastic Head

UNMAKER OF WORLDS
CD ______ CMGCD 003
Communique / Nov '90 / Plastic Head

Golia, Vinny

HAUNTING THE SPIRITS INSIDE THEM (Golia, Vinny & Joelle Leandre/Ken Filiano)
CD ______ CD 893
Music & Arts / Jan '96 / Cadillac / Harmonia Mundi

REGARDS FROM NORMAN DESMOND
CD ______ FSNT 008CD
Fresh Sound / Mar '95 / Discovery / Jazz Music

Golson, Benny

BENNY GOLSON IN PARIS
CD ______ CDSW 8418
DRG / Jan '89 / Discovery / New Note/ Pinnacle

BENNY GOLSON QUARTET
Up jump spring / Voyage / Beautiful love / Gypsy jingle-jangle / Stable mates
CD ______ 17076
Laserlight / Mar '97 / Target/BMG

GONE WITH GOLSON
CD ______ OJCCD 1850
Original Jazz Classics / Jul '94 / Complete/Pinnacle / Jazz Music / Wellard

GROOVIN' WITH GOLSON
CD ______ OJCCD 226
Original Jazz Classics / Sep '93 / Complete/Pinnacle / Jazz Music / Wellard

THIS IS FOR YOU JOHN
Jam the avenue / Greensleeves / Origin / Change of heart / Times past (this is for you, John) / Page 12 / Vilia
CD ______ CDSJP 235
Timeless Jazz / Jan '88 / New Note/ Pinnacle

THREE LITTLE WORDS
CD ______ JHAS 609
Ronnie Scott's Jazz House / Apr '97 / Cadillac / Jazz Music / New Note/Pinnacle / TKO Magnum

TIME SPEAKS
I'll remember April / Time speaks / No dancin' / Jordu / Blues for Duane / Theme for Maxine
CD ______ CDSJP 187
Timeless Jazz / Jan '87 / New Note/ Pinnacle

Golub, Jeff

UNSPOKEN WORDS
CD ______ 1390082
Gaia / May '89 / New Note/Pinnacle

Gomes, Carmen

CALLIN' FROM KC (Gomes, Carmen Inc.)
Dig dis / Freewheel blues / Big city / MMM, come on in my kitchen / And what if I don't / Matter of truth / It's about time / Sidekick / Topaz / I've grown accustomed to his face / Callin' from KC / What a little moonlight can do / Case of blues
CD ______ BY 951018
Byton World Series / Oct '96 / New Note/ Pinnacle

Gomez, Alice

WHILE THE EAGLE SLEEPS
CD ______ TTCD 130
Talking Taco / Mar '96 / ADA

Gomez, Claudia

TIERRADENTRO
CD ______ XEPCD 4039
Xenophile / Mar '96 / ADA / Direct

Gomez, Eddie

NEXT FUTURE
Next future / Intro and body / Dreaming of you / North Moore St. / Lost tango (for Astor Piazzolla) / Tenderly / Cheeks (dedicated to Dizzy Gillespie) / Love letter (to my father) / Basic trane-ing / Walter (pigeon)
CD ______ SCD 90052
Stretch / Mar '97 / New Note/Pinnacle

STREET SMART
Street smart / Lorenzo / I'caramba / It was you all along / Blues period / Double entendre / Carmen's song / Bella horizonte / Besame mucho
CD ______ 4662252
Epic / Apr '90 / Sony

Gomez, Jill

CABARET CLASSICS (Gomez, Jill & John Constable)
CD ______ DKPCD 9055
Unicorn-Kanchana / Aug '88 / Harmonia Mundi

Gomorrah

REFLECTIONS OF AN INANIMATE MATTER
CD ______ BMCD 067
Black Mark / Aug '95 / Plastic Head

TRAUMA
CD ______ 14509
Spalax / Feb '97 / ADA / Cargo / Direct / Discovery / Greyhound

Gonashvili, Hamlet

HAMLET GONASHVILI
CD ______ 8557772
Origins / Jul '97 / Discovery

Gone

ALL THE DIRT THAT'S FIT TO PRINT
CD ______ SST 306CD
SST / Sep '94 / Plastic Head

CRIMINAL MIND
CD ______ SST 300CD
SST / Jan '94 / Plastic Head

GONE II, BUT NEVER TOO GONE
CD ______ SST 086CD
SST / May '93 / Plastic Head

LET'S GET REAL, REAL GONE FOR A CHANGE
CD ______ SST 061CD
SST / May '93 / Plastic Head

Gonella, Nat

CRAZY VALVES (Gonella, Nat & His Georgians)
How'm I doin / Capri caprice / Skeleton in the cupboard / I can't dance / Crazy valves / Bessie couldn't help it / Take another guess / Nagasaki / Just a crazy song / Sheikh of Araby / Tiger rag / Copper coloured gal / Ol' man mose / Trumpetuous / I'm gonna clap my hands / Makin' a fool of myself / Bill Tell / Georgia on my mind
CD ______ CDAJA 5055
Living Era / Sep '88 / Select

CREAM OF NAT GONELLA, THE
CD ______ PASTCD 9750
Flapper / Aug '91 / Pinnacle

JAZZ SIDE, THE
I ain't got nobody / Stormy weather / Nobody's sweetheart / (I'll be glad when you're dead) you rascal you / How'm I doin' / Continental / Troublesome trumpet / Black coffee / I heard / That's my home / E flat blues / Wabash blues / Harlem hokum blues / Mama don't allow it / Get hot / Way down yonder in New orleans / Crazy valves / Cocktail swing / Bill tell / Jeepers creepers / Georgia on my mind / For no reason at all / Seven days leave / Hot malletts
CD ______ RAJCD 882
Empress / Aug '96 / Koch

NAT GONELLA
Nagasaki / Mayor of Alabam / When you're smiling / Medley / Bessie couldn't help it / You rascal you / Just a crazy song / I'd like to see Somoa of Samoa / Junk man's blues / Down t'Uncle Bill's / Crazy values / On the sunny side of the street / Twilight in Turkey / His old cornet / Tiger rag / Get hot / Some of these days / T'ain't what you do (it's the way that you do it) / Ain't misbehavin' / Ciribiribin / Flat foot floogie / Makin' a fool of myself / Swing and sway / Bill Tell / Medley
CD ______ CDMFP 6350
Music For Pleasure / Jun '97 / EMI

NATURALLY GONELLA
Yeah man / Truckin' / Hot lips / Sheikh of Araby / Black coffee / Blow Gabriel blow / Capri caprice / Oh Peter (you're so nice) / Georgia rockin' chair / Lazy river / Sweet and hot / Pidgin English hula / Squareface / Japanese sandman / Ghost of Dinah / Jig time / Gonna wed that gal o' mine / Peanut vendor / Sophisticated lady / Georgia on my mind / Tuxedo Junction / Big noise from Winnetka / I understand / At the woodchoppers' ball / South with the boarder / Hep hep the jumpin' jive / Johnson rag / If you were the only girl in the world / Beat me Daddy, eight to the bar / In the mood / Ay ay ay / No Mama no / I haven't time to be a millionaire / Vox poppin' / Oh Buddy I'm in love / It's a pair of wings for me / Eep ipe wanna piece of pie / Sunrise serenade / Yes my darling daughter / Plucking on the golden harp
CD ______ RAJCD 804
Empress / Oct '93 / Koch

Gong

25TH BIRTHDAY PARTY (Gong Live October 8/9th 1994 At The Forum/2CD Set)
Thom intro / Floating into a birthday gig / You can't kill me / Radio gnome 25 / I am you pussy / Pot head pixies / Never glid before / Eat that phonebook / Gnomic address / Flute salad / Oily way
CD Set ______ VPGAS 101CD
GAS / Mar '97 / Pinnacle

ABOUT TIME (El Alien's New Wave Dispensation) (New York Gong)
Preface / Much too old / Black September / Materialism / Strong woman / I'm a Freud / O my photograph / Jungle windo / Hours gone
CD ______ CDCRH 118
Charly / Feb '97 / Koch

ANGEL'S EGG (Radio Gnome Invisible Vol.2)
Other side of the sky / Sold to the highest Buddha / Castle in the clouds / Prostitute poem / Givin' my luv to you / Selene / Flute salad / Oily way / Outer temple / Inner temple / Love is how you make it / I never gild before / Eat that phonebook code
CD ______ CDV 2007
Virgin / Jun '90 / EMI
CD ______ 14833
Spalax / Oct '96 / ADA / Cargo / Direct / Discovery / Greyhound
CD ______ CDCRH 119
Charly / Feb '97 / Koch

BEST OF GONG, THE
Wet cheese delirum / Tropical fish / Seline / Flying teapot / Pot head Pixies / Outer temple / Eat the phone book coda / Magick mother invocation / Master builder / Mister long shanks / O Mother I am your fantasy / Squeezing sponges over policemen's heads / Octave doctors and the crystal machine / Zero the hero and the witches spell / Castle in the clouds / Inner temple / Sprinkling of clouds / Much too old
CD ______ NTMCD 517
Nectar / Oct '95 / Pinnacle

BEST OF GONG, THE
CD ______ 3015912
Mantra / Nov '96 / Cargo / Direct / Discovery

BEST OF GONG, THE
CD ______ 1119611
Tumult Productions / Dec '96 / Cargo

BREAKTHROUGH
CD ______ EUCD 1053
ARC / '89 / ADA / ARC Music

CAMEMBERT ELECTIQUE (Not What You Think...Unreleased Studio Tracks)
Cafe Montelieu demos / Garcon ou fille / Dynamite/Goldilocks / Rock 'n' roll angel/ Nightmare of Mr. Respectable / Hyp hypnotise you / Haunted chateau rehersals / Big city energy / Gongwash indelible
CD ______ AGASCD 001
GAS / Mar '97 / Pinnacle

CAMEMBERT ELECTRIQUE
Radio gnome predection / You can't kill me / I've bin stone before / Mr. Long Shanks: O Mother I am your fantasy / Dynamite: I am your animal / Wet cheese delirium / Squeezing sponges over policemen's heads / Fohat digs holes in space / And you tried so hard / Tropical fish: Selene / Gnome the second
CD ______ 14826
Spalax / Oct '96 / ADA / Cargo / Direct / Discovery / Greyhound
CD ______ CDCRH 111
Charly / Feb '97 / Koch

CONTINENTAL CIRCUS
CD ______ 642089
Mantra / May '96 / Cargo / Direct / Discovery

EXPRESSO VOL.2
Heavy tune / Golden dilemma / Sleepy / Soli / Boring / Three blind mice
CD ______ CDV 2099
Virgin / Jun '90 / EMI

EYE (Mother Gong)
Fanfare / She's the mother of / Sunday / Beds / Time is a hurrying dog / Ancient / Zen / Quantum / Spirit canoe / What if we were gods and goddesses / Auction / Little boy / Magic stories / Excuses / Sax canoe / Fairy laughter / Virtual reality
CD ______ VP 176CD
Voiceprint / Sep '94 / Pinnacle

FLOATING ANARCHY 1977 (Planet Gong)
Psychological overture / Floating anarchy / Stone innoc Frankenstein / New age transformation try / No more sages / Opium for the people / Allez Ali Baba black sheep have you any bullshit / Mama maya mantram
CD ______ 14829
Spalax / Oct '96 / ADA / Cargo / Direct / Discovery / Greyhound
CD ______ CDCRH 115
Charly / Feb '97 / Koch

FLYING TEAPOT (Radio Gnome Invisible Vol.1)
Radio gnome invisible / Pot head pixies / Octave doctors and the crystal machine / Zero the hero and the witches spell / Witches song I am your pussy
CD ______ 14828
Spalax / Oct '96 / ADA / Cargo / Direct / Discovery / Greyhound
CD ______ CDCRH 114
Charly / Feb '97 / Koch

GAZEUSE
Expresso / Night illusion / Percolations (part 1) / Percolations (part 2) / Shadows of / Mireille / Esnuria
CD ______ CDV 2074
Virgin / Jun '90 / EMI

GLASTONBURY 1989 (Gong Maison)
CD ______ AGASCD 004
GAS / Sep '96 / Pinnacle

GONG MAISON (Gong Maison)
CD ______ DMCD 1022
Demi-Monde / Feb '90 / RTM/Disc / TKO Magnum

HISTORY AND THE MYSTERY OF THE PLANET GONG, THE
Concert intro / Captain Shaw and Mr. Gilbert / Love makes sweet music / DLTinterview / Riot 1968 / Dreaming it / I feel so lazy / And I tried so hard / Radio gnome pre-mix / Pot head pixies / Majick brother / Line up / Clarence in Wonderland / Breakthrough interview / Where have all the hours gone / Gong poem / Dey a Goddess / Opium for the people / Red alert / 13/8 / Gliss-u-well / Future / Dream / Chernobyl rain / Let me be one
CD ______ CDTB 116
Thunderbolt / '91 / TKO Magnum

HOW TO NUKE THE EIFFEL TOWER
Away away / Nuclear mega waste / Chernobyl rain
CD ______ VPGAS 102CD
GAS / Oct '96 / Pinnacle

LIVE 1990
CD ______ NINETY 1
Demon / Mar '93 / Pinnacle

LIVE AT SHEFFIELD 1974
CD ______ 890042
Mantra / May '96 / Cargo / Direct / Discovery

LIVE AU BATACLAN 1973
CD ______ 890025
Mantra / May '96 / Cargo / Direct / Discovery

LIVE ETC
You can't kill me / Zero the hero and the witches spell / Flying teapot / Dynamite: I am your animal / 6/8 / Est-ce que je suis / Ooby-scooby doomsday or the D-day DJ's got the / Radio gnome invisible / Oily way / Outer temple / Inner temple / Where have all the flowers gone / Isle of everywhere / Get it inner / Master Builder / Flying teapot (reprise)
CD ______ CDVM 3501
Virgin / '90 / EMI

MAGICK BROTHER
Mystic sister: Magick brother / Magick brother / Glad to say to say / Rational anthem / Chainstore chant: pretty Miss Titty / Pretty miss titty / Fable of a Fredfish / Hope you feel OK / Ego / Gong song / Princess dreaming / Five and twenty schoolgirls / 'Cos you got green hair
CD ______ 14812
Spalax / Oct '96 / ADA / Cargo / Direct / Discovery / Greyhound

MYSTERY AND HISTORY OF GONG, THE (Gong Rarities 1971-1972)
CD ______ 14518
Spalax / Jun '97 / ADA / Cargo / Direct / Discovery / Greyhound

OWL AND THE TREE, THE
I am a tree: *Allen, Daevid & Gong* / Lament for the future of the forest: *Allen, Daevid & Gong* / Hands: *Allen, Daevid & Gong* / Unseen ally: *Allen, Daevid & Gong* / La dea madri: *Allen, Daevid & Gong* / Owly song: *Allen, Daevid & Gong* / I am my own lover: *Allen, Daevid & Gong* / Tudor love poem: *Allen, Daevid & Gong*
CD ______ CDTB 118
Thunderbolt / Feb '92 / TKO Magnum

PARAGONG LIVE 1973 (Paragong)
Camembert psilocybin flashback / Pourquoi dormons nous
CD ______ AGASCD 002
GAS / Oct '96 / Pinnacle

PRE MODERNIST WIRELESS ON RADIO
Magick brother / Clarence in wonderland / Tropical fish / Selene / You can't kill me / Radio gnome direct broadcast / Crystal machine / Zero the hero and the orgasm witch / Captain capricorns dream saloon / Radio gnome invisible / Oily way / Sleepy
CD ______ SFRCD 137
Strange Fruit / Dec '95 / Pinnacle

SHAMAL
Wingful of eyes / Chandra / Bambooji / Cat in Clark's shoes / Mandrake / Shamal
CD ______ CDV 2046
Virgin / Jun '90 / EMI

SHE MADE THE WORLD MAGENTA
Magenta / Water / She made the world / Weather / Malicious sausage / Sea horse / Spirit calling / Tattered jacket / Warn / When the show is over / I am a witch / Spirit of the bush / Blessed be
CD ______ VP 134CD
Voiceprint / May '93 / Pinnacle

SUFFER (Gongzilla)
Gongzilla / Bad habits / Sing / Gongzilla's dilemma / Mr. Sinister Minister / Almost you / Mezzanine / Hip hopnosis / Allan Qui / Senna / Camel
CD ______ LOLO 0032
Blueprint / Dec '96 / Pinnacle

VERY BEST OF GONG, THE
Dynamite I am your animal / Radio Gnome / Invisible / Zero the hero and the witches spell / Flute salad / Oily way / Outer temple, inner temple / I never glid before / Isle of

Everywhere / You'll never blow yer trip forever / Eat that phonebook coda / Stone innocent Frankenstein
CD _____ SUMCD 4117
Sound & Media / May '97 / Sound & Media

VOICEPRINT RADIO SESSION (Mother Gong)
CD _____ VPR 007CD
Voiceprint / Oct '94 / Pinnacle

WILD CHILD (Mother Gong)
CD _____ DMCD 1026
Demi-Monde / Jul '94 / RTM/Disc / TKO Magnum

WINGFUL OF EYES, A
Heavy tune / Cat in Clark's shoes / Night illusion / Golden dilemma / Wingful of eyes / Three blind mice / Expresso / Soli / Shadows of / Mandrake / Bambouji
CD _____ CDOVD 462
Virgin / Jan '96 / EMI

YOU (Radio Gnome Invisible Vol.3)
APHP's advice / Thoughts for nought / Magick mother invocation / Master builder / Sprinkling of clouds / Perfect mystery / Isle of everywhere / You never blow your trip forever
CD _____ CDV 2019
Virgin / Jun '90 / EMI
CD _____ 14834
Spalax / Oct '96 / ADA / Cargo / Direct / Discovery / Greyhound
CD _____ CDCRH 120
Charly / Feb '97 / Koch

YOU (Remixes/2CD Set)
CD Set _____ GLISSCD 001
GAS / Jul '97 / Pinnacle

Gonnella, Ron

RON GONNELLA'S INTERNATIONAL FRIENDSHIP FIDDLE
BBC echoes / Cape Breton ceudh / Hector MacAndrews favourites / Congratulations all round / Sounds of Strathearn / Touch of Gaelic / Bonnie Dundee / Boston tea party / Jimmy Shand special / Strathspey king and friends / Scottish dance music corner / Canadian connection / Fiddlers two / My friend Adam Rennie / New York, New York / Music of William Marshall
CD _____ CDITV 453
Scotdisc / Aug '88 / Conifer/BMG / Duncans / Ross

Gonsalves, Paul

GETTIN' TOGETHER
CD _____ OJCCD 203
Original Jazz Classics / Feb '92 / Complete/Pinnacle / Jazz Music / Wellard

JAZZ TILL MIDNIGHT (Gonsalves, Paul & Eddie 'Lockjaw' Davis)
CD _____ STCD 4123
Storyville / Feb '90 / Cadillac / Jazz Music / Wellard

JUST A-SITTIN' AND A-ROCKIN' (Gonsalves, Paul & Ray Nance)
BP blues / Lotus blossom / Don't blame me / Just a sittin' and a rockin' / Hi ya, Sue / Angel eyes / I'm in the market for you / Tea for two
CD _____ BLCD 760148
Black Lion / May '91 / Cadillac / Jazz Music / Koch / Wellard

PAUL GONSALVES MEETS EARL HINES (Gonsalves, Paul & Earl Hines)
CD _____ BLCD 760177
Black Lion / Mar '93 / Cadillac / Jazz Music / Koch / Wellard

Gonzalez, Celina

FIESTA GUAJIRA
Yo soy el punto Cubana / Muero de olivdo / Santa Barbara / Oye mi le lo ley / Guajiro Guarachero / Paisajes naturales / El refran se te Olivido / Aguacero aguacerito / Mi tierra es asi
CD _____ WC 34CD
World Circuit / Oct '93 / ADA / Cadillac / Direct / New Note/Pinnacle

QUE VIVA CHANGO
Santa Barbara / Oye mi le lo lei / El refran se te olivido / Aurora / Mi terra es asi / El reto / Yo soy el punto Cubana / Camina y ven / Aguacero aguacerito / Guateque campesino / Paisajes / El hijo del sibony
CD _____ PSCCD 1002
Pure Sounds From Cuba / Feb '95 / Henry Hadaway / THE

RICH HARVEST
Yo soy el punto Cubano / Rezo a oya / Mi son es un misterio / Tambores Africanos / Asi quiero vivir / Alla voy / San Lazaro / Que se yo / La verdad de mi verdad / Sin penas ni glorias / A la patrona de Cuba / Herencia paterna / Los soneros de mi Cuba / Rezo a oya / La casa de yagua / Popurri Cubano
CD _____ TUMICD 066
Tumi / Sep '96 / Discovery / Stern's

SANTA BARBARA
CD _____ CD 0042
Egrem / Mar '96 / Discovery

Gonzalez, Dennis

DEBENGE DEBENGE
CD _____ SHCD 112
Silkheart / May '89 / Cadillac / CM / Jazz Music / Wellard

NAMESAKE (Gonzalez, Dennis New Dallas Quartet)
CD _____ SHCD 106
Silkheart / May '88 / Cadillac / CM / Jazz Music / Wellard

WELCOME TO US
CD _____ 378232
Koch Jazz / Nov '96 / Koch

Gonzalez, Jerry

CROSSROADS (Gonzalez, Jerry & The Fort Apache Band)
Malandro / Rumba Columbia I / Vonce / Thelingus / Guaguanco I / Ezekiel / Saw the wheel / Rumba Columbia II / Viva cepeda / Lament / Guaguanco II / Fort apache / Elegua
CD _____ MCD 92252
Milestone / Mar '97 / Cadillac / Complete/ Pinnacle / Jazz Music / Wellard

EARTH DANCE (Gonzalez, Jerry & The Fort Apache Band)
CD _____ SSC 1050D
Sunnyside / May '91 / Discovery

FIRE DANCE (Gonzalez, Jerry & The Fort Apache Band)
Isabel / Liberator / Elegua / Today's nights / Verdad amarga / Let's call this / Ugly beauty
CD _____ MCD 92582
Milestone / Nov '96 / Cadillac / Complete/ Pinnacle / Jazz Music / Wellard

PENSATIVO (Gonzalez, Jerry & The Fort Apache Band)
CD _____ MCD 92422
Milestone / Feb '96 / Cadillac / Complete/ Pinnacle / Jazz Music / Wellard

RIVER IS DEEP, THE (Gonzalez, Jerry & The Fort Apache Band)
CD _____ 40402
Enja / Apr '91 / New Note/Pinnacle / Vital/ SAM

Gonzalez, Ruben

INTRODUCING
La enganadora / Cumbanchero / Tres lindas Cubanas / Melodia del rio / Mandinga / Siboney / Almendra / Tumbao / Como siento yo
CD _____ WCD 049
World Circuit / May '97 / ADA / Cadillac / Direct / New Note/Pinnacle

Goo Goo Dolls

BOY NAMED GOO, A
CD _____ 9362457502
Warner Bros. / Apr '95 / Warner Music

GOO GOO DOLLS
CD _____ 140792
Metal Blade / Oct '95 / Pinnacle / Plastic Head

HOLD ME UP
CD _____ 398417018CD
Metal Blade / May '96 / Pinnacle / Plastic Head

JED
Out of sight / No way out / Down on the corner / Road to Salinas / Misfortune / Gimme shelter / Up yours / Sex maggot / Had enough / Em elbmuh / Artie / James Dean
CD _____ 398414035CD
Metal Blade / Jun '97 / Pinnacle / Plastic Head

Goober Patrol

VACATION
CD _____ GOOD 002CD
3rd Stone / Apr '96 / Plastic Head / Vital

Gooch, Jon

VELVET PIANO, THE
Music of the night/Memory / Chopin E' nocturne / Tea for two / Wind beneath my wings / Misty / West on sunset / Eddy Duchin medley / My one and only love / Up a lazy river / Daytona drift / All the things you are / Moonsway / As time goes by / Without you/All by myself / Stardust / Everything I do (I do it for you) / Vocal medley / Meditation - thais
CD _____ AZJG 14CD
Tinkling Ivories / Jul '97 / Azurre Music / Bridport Record Centre

Good Fellas

GOOD FELLAS
Rap city / Witches / Head and out / Candy / Almost always / Secret love / Bossami / Cherokee / Taxi driver
CD _____ ECD 22050
Evidence / Jul '93 / ADA / Cadillac / Harmonia Mundi

GOOD FELLAS VOL.2
Look out / Dr. Jamie / It's you or no one / In the dream / Anti-calypso / I'll miss you / Welcome / Pop gun / Quick way / Breezilee
CD _____ ECD 220772
Evidence / Mar '94 / ADA / Cadillac / Harmonia Mundi

Good Morning Blues

NEVER MAKE A MOVE TO SOON
CD _____ SITCD 9201
Sittel / Aug '94 / Cadillac / Jazz Music

Good Ol' Persons

GOOD 'N' LIVE
CD _____ SHCD 2208
Sugar Hill / Jan '96 / ADA / CM / Direct / Koch / Roots

PART OF A STORY
Broken hearted lover / Easy substitute / My my my / I don't hurt anymore / It's gonna rain / You're a flower / Crossing the Cumberlands / It seems there's nothing I can do / This young boy / Part of a story
CD _____ FR 104
Flat Rock / May '97 / ADA / Direct

Good Pants

ALL TALK, NO PANTS
Duelling banjos / Shady grove / I like likker / Grandma's feather bed / It takes no time / Rueben's train / Don't take your guns to town / Bitter creek / Oozlin' Daddy / Windy mountain / Hey Joe / One last match / Naughty little poem / Blues stay away from me / Girl I left behind me / Happy wanderer / Arkansas traveller
CD _____ CRAW 001
Crawdaddy / May '97 / CM / Direct

Good Riddance

COMPREHENSIVE GUIDE TO MODERN REBELLION, A
CD _____ FATCD 539
Fatwreck Chords / Jun '96 / Plastic Head

FOR GOD AND COUNTRY
CD _____ FAT 23
Fatwreck Chords / Mar '95 / Plastic Head

Good Rockin' Tonight

THERE'S NO ONE ELSE
CD _____ GRT 3
GRT / Jan '97 / Nervous

Good Sons

SINGING THE GLORY DOWN
Help me to find / Leaving time / When the night comes / Gospel Hall / Riding the range / You are everything / God's other son / Tower of strength / Watch my dreamboat sail / Day to day / My own prayers / When I turn out the light
CD _____ GRCD 379
Glitterhouse / Nov '96 / Avid/BMG

Goodbye Harry

FOOD STAMP BBQ
CD _____ CRZ 037CD
Cruz / Jan '95 / Plastic Head

I CAN SMOKE
CD _____ CRZ 038CD
Cruz / Sep '96 / Plastic Head

Goodbye Mr. Mackenzie

FIVE
CD _____ BLOKCD 002
Blokshok / Mar '96 / Pinnacle

JEZEBEL
CD _____ BLOKCD 004
Blokshok / Jul '95 / Pinnacle

LIVE ON THE DAY OF STORMS
Goodwill city / Blacker than black / Face to face / Diamonds / Pleasure search / Sick baby / Goodbye Mr. Mackenzie / Dust
CD _____ BLOKCD 001
Blokshok / Apr '96 / Pinnacle

Goodchilde

STRAIGHT OUT THE FRIDGE
CD _____ LZ 127
Backs / Mar '96 / RTM/Disc

Goode, B.

SHOCK OF THE NEW
Tribute to Clifford & Sonny / Old folks / You don't know what love is / Hermit / Winter's song / Stew's blues / Clock radio / New blues
CD _____ DD 440
Delmark / Mar '97 / ADA / Cadillac / CM / Direct / Hot Shot

Goodfellaz

GOODFELLAZ
Sugar honey ice tea / Why you wanna flip on me / If you walk away / Hey / Show and prove / Backslidin' / Nothing at all / Anytime will do / For better or worse / No matter / Pour your love down / If you walk away
CD _____ 5333962
Polydor / May '97 / PolyGram

Goodhouse, Sissy

THIRD CIRCLE, THE
CD _____ 14936
Spalax / Jan '97 / ADA / Cargo / Direct / Discovery / Greyhound

Goodies

YUM YUM
Goodies theme / Funky gibbon / Inbetweenies / Please let us play / Custard pie / Black pudding Bertha / Cricklewood / Good old country music / Nappy love / Baby Samba / Wild thing / Rock with a policeman / Crickelwood shakedown / Panic / I'm a teapot / Working the line / Sick man blues / Last chance dance / Father Christmas do not touch me / Make a daft noise for Christmas
CD _____ MCCD 294
Music Club / May '97 / Disc / THE

Gooding, Cuba

MEANT TO BE IN LOVE
CD _____ TRI 4162CD
Ichiban / Feb '94 / Direct / Koch

Goodman, Benny

16 MOST REQUESTED SONGS
Let's dance / Don't be that way / Avalon / Flying home / Memories of you / Somebody stole my gal / Clarinet a la King / Jersey bounce / Why don't you do right / After you've gone / Stompin' at the Savoy / Sing sing sing / Symphony / Liza / How am I to know / Goodbye
CD _____ 4743962
Columbia / Feb '94 / Sony

1928-31 (Goodman, Benny Orchestra)
CD _____ CLASSICS 693
Classics / May '93 / Discovery / Jazz Music

1935-1938
CD _____ CD 56060
Jazz Roots / Mar '95 / Target/BMG

AIR CHECKS 1937-1938
Let's dance / Moten swing / Vibraphone blues / Peckin' / Nagasaki / St. Louis blues / Sugarfoot stomp / I'm a ding dong daddy from Dumas / Bumble Bee stomp / Naughty waltz / Vieni vieni / Roll 'em / Have you met Miss Jones / Shine / When Buddha smiles / Laughing at life / You turned the tables / My gal Sal / Mama that moon is here again / Time on my hands / In the shadow of the old apple tree / Benny sent me / Moonlight on the highway / Killer diller / Someday sweetheart / Goodbye / Riding high / Nice work if you can get it / Sheikh of Araby / Sunny disposish / Whispers in the dark / Life goes to a party / Moonglow / I hadn't anyone till you / Down south camp meeting / Sweet leilani / Sometimes I'm happy / King Porter stomp / Limehouse blues / Minnie The Moocher's wedding day / Running wild / At the Darktown strutter's ball / Bugle call rag / Clarinet marmalade / Stardust / Everybody loves my baby / Josephine / Caravan
CD Set _____ 4729902
Columbia / Oct '93 / Sony

ALL THE CATS JOIN IN VOL.1
Clarinade / All the cats join in / Mad boogie / Remember / Somebody stole my gal / At the Darktown strutter's ball / Lucky / Rattle and roll / Body and soul / Oh lady be good
CD _____ TKOCD 015
TKO / '92 / TKO

AUDIO ARCHIVE
Stompin' at the Savoy / Jumpin' at the woodside / Jersey bounce / Let's dance / Christopher Columbus / Down South camp meeting / South of the border (down Mexico way) / I'm gonna sit right down and write myself a letter / Sing sing sing / Somebody stole my gal / You turned the tables on me / You bought a new kind of love to me / When Buddha smiles / When I grow too old to dream / What can I say after I'm sorry / King Porter stomp / You're a sweetheart / Bugle call rag / Fascinating rhythm / Big John special
CD _____ CDAA 012
Tring / Oct '91 / Tring

AVALON - THE SMALL BANDS (Goodman, Benny Quartet)
Avalon / Handful of keys / Man I love / Smiles / Liza / Where or when: *Goodman, Benny Trio* / Vieni vieni / I'm a ding dong daddy from Dumas / Sweet Lorraine: *Goodman, Benny Trio* / Blues in your flat / Sugar / Dizzy spells / Opus 1/2 / I must have that man: *Goodman, Benny Trio* / Sweet Georgia Brown / 'S wonderful / Pick-a-rib (part 1): *Goodman, Benny Quintet* / Pick-a-rib (part 2): *Goodman, Benny Quintet* / I cried for you: *Goodman, Benny Quintet* / I know that you know / Opus 3/4
CD _____ ND 82273
Bluebird / Oct '90 / BMG

BANGKOK 1956
Let's dance / Don't be that way / King Porter stomp / Trigger fantasy / Roll'em / One o'clock jump / Down South camp meeeting / Yarm yen/In the evening / Sugar foot stomp / Big John special / Flying home / World is waiting for the sunrise / Oh lady be good / Sai fon/Falling rain / Stompin' at the Savoy / Thai Royal anthem
CD _____ **TCB 43042**
TCB / Jun '97 / New Note/Pinnacle

BASEL 1959
Let's dance / Airmail special / Rachel's dream / Memories of you / Slipped disc / Get happy / Tenbone / Go, Margot, go / Marchin' and swingin' / Breakfast feud / Body and soul / I want to be happy
CD _____ **TCB 43032**
TCB / Dec '96 / New Note/Pinnacle

BENNY & THE SINGERS (Goodman, Benny & His Orchestra)
CD _____ **CDMOIR 516**
Memoir / Aug '96 / Jazz Music / Target/BMG

BENNY GOODMAN
CD _____ **295715**
Ariola / Apr '93 / BMG

BENNY GOODMAN
CD _____ **CWNCD 2006**
Javelin / Jun '95 / Henry Hadaway / THE

BENNY GOODMAN
CD _____ **22703**
Music / Feb '96 / Target/BMG

BENNY GOODMAN (Goodman, Benny & Arturo Toscanini/Bela Bartok)
Clarinet Quintet in A major KV 581: *Goodman, Benny & Budapest String Quartet* / Contrasts: *Goodman, Benny & Joseph Szigeti/Bela Bartok* / Rhapsody in blue: *Goodman, Benny & Arturo Toscanini/Earl Wild*
CD _____ **CD 48047**
Magic Talent / Oct '96 / Target/BMG

BENNY GOODMAN
CD _____ **15703**
Laserlight / Apr '94 / Target/BMG

BENNY GOODMAN & HIS GREAT VOCALISTS
Riffin' the scotch / Blue moon / Gal in Calico / Blue skies / Symphony / It's only a paper moon / Gotta this or that / Close a pages in a book / Every time we say goodbye / Serenade in blue / Somebody else is taking my place / I got it bad and that ain't good / Taking a chance on love / Peace, brother / There'll be some changes made / Loch Lomond
CD _____ **CK 66198**
Columbia / Jul '95 / Sony

BENNY GOODMAN 1934
CD _____ **CCD 111**
Circle / Oct '91 / Jazz Music / Swift / Wellard

BENNY GOODMAN AND HIS ORCHESTRA (Goodman, Benny Orchestra)
CD _____ **11042**
Laserlight / '86 / Target/BMG

BENNY GOODMAN AND HIS ORCHESTRA 1935 - 1939 (Goodman, Benny Orchestra)
CD _____ **CD 53042**
Giants Of Jazz / Jan '89 / Cadillac / Jazz Music / Target/BMG

BENNY GOODMAN AND HIS ORCHESTRA 1935-1939 (Goodman, Benny Orchestra)
Don't be that way / King Porter stomp / Roll 'em / Down south camp meeting / Goodbye / Christopher Columbus / One o'clock jump / Bugle call rag / Sing sing sing / I want to be happy / Smoke house rhythm / Stompin' at the Savoy / Topsy / Sugarfoot stomp / Kingdom of swing / Bach goes to town / Sent for you yesterday / Sing me a swing song
CD _____ **CD 56005**
Jazz Roots / Aug '94 / Target/BMG

BENNY GOODMAN CLASSICS 1935-1941
CD _____ **NEOVOX 879**
Neovox / Oct '93 / Wellard

BENNY GOODMAN IN STOCKHOLM (1959) (Goodman, Benny & Flip Phillips)
CD _____ **PHONTCD 8801**
Phontastic / '88 / Cadillac / Jazz Music / Wellard

BENNY GOODMAN ORCHESTRA & SEXTET (Goodman, Benny Orchestra)
CD _____ **CD 14562**
Jazz Portraits / May '95 / Jazz Music

BENNY GOODMAN ORCHESTRA/TRIO/ QUARTET (6CD Set)
CD Set _____ **NCD 8841-8846**
Phontastic / Jan '97 / Cadillac / Jazz Music / Wellard

BENNY GOODMAN PLAYS EDDIE SAUTER
Love never went to college / Darn that dream / Faithful forever / Fable of the rose / Shake down the stars / Cocoanut grove / Hour of parting / Who cares / Nostalgia / Man I love / Benny rides again / These things you left me / Superman / More than you know / Time on my hands / Intermezzo / Something new / When the sun comes out / Birth of the blues / Clarinet a la king / Let's give love a chance / Tangerine / Moonlight on the Ganges
CD _____ **HEPCD 1053**
Hep / Jan '97 / Cadillac / Jazz Music / New Note/Pinnacle / Wellard

BENNY GOODMAN PLAYS FLETCHER HENDERSON
Japanese sandman / Get rhythm in your feet / Blue skies / Sometimes I'm happy / King Porter stomp / Devil and the deep blue sea / Sandman / Basin Street blues / If I could be with you one hour tonight / When Buddha smiles / Christopher Columbus / Down south camp meeting / St. Louis blues / Alexander's ragtime band / I want to be happy / Chloe (song of the swamp) / Rosetta / Can't we be friends / Sugarfoot stomp / Wrappin' it up / Bumble bee stomp / Rose of Washington square
CD _____ **HEPCD 1038**
Hep / Nov '93 / Cadillac / Jazz Music / New Note/Pinnacle / Wellard

BENNY GOODMAN SEXTET & CHARLIE CHRISTIAN 1939-1941
CD _____ **4656792**
Sony Jazz / Jan '95 / Sony

BENNY GOODMAN STORY, THE
Down South camp meetin' / And the angels sing / Goodbye / Sing sing sing / Shine / One o'clock jump / Bugle call rag / King Porter stomp / Let's dance / Don't be that way / It's been so long / Sometimes I'm happy / Goody goody / Avalon / Moonglow / Alicia's blues / Memories of you / China boy / Seven come eleven
CD _____ **CDP 8335692**
Capitol Jazz / Nov '95 / EMI

BENNY GOODMAN SWINGS AGAIN
CD _____ **4756252**
Sony Jazz / Jan '95 / Sony

BENNY GOODMAN TRIO AND QUARTET SESSIONS VOL.1 (Goodman, Benny Trio & Quartet)
After you've gone / Body and soul / Who / Someday, sweetheart / China boy / More than you know / All my life / Oh lady be good / Nobody's sweetheart / Too good to be true / Moonglow / Dinah / Exactly like you / Vibraphone blues / Sweet Sue, just you / My melancholy baby / Tiger rag / Stompin' at the Savoy / Whispering / Ida / Tea for two / Running wild
CD _____ **ND 85631**
Bluebird / Apr '88 / BMG

BENNY GOODMAN VOL.3 & 4
Smiles / Liza / Where or when / Silhouetted in the moonlight / Vieni vieni / I'm a ding dong daddy from Dumas / Bei mir bist du schon / Sweet Lorraine / Blues in your flat / Sugar / Dizzy spells / Opus onen half / I must have that man / Sweet Georgia Brown / 'S wonderful / Pick-a-rib / I cried for you / I know that you know and you know that I know
CD _____ **ND 89754**
Jazz Tribune / Jun '94 / BMG

BENNY RIDES AGAIN (2CD Set)
CD Set _____ **CPCD 82632**
Charly / Jan '97 / Koch

BENNY'S BOP
Mary's idea / Bye bye blues bop / There's a small hotel / Blue views / I can't give you anything but love / You took advantage of me / Where oh where has my little dog gone / Pepper (Patsy's idea) / String of pearls / I'll see you in my dreams / Undercurrent blues
CD _____ **HEPCD 36**
Hep / Oct '93 / Cadillac / Jazz Music / New Note/Pinnacle / Wellard

BERLIN 1980
Oh lady be good / Here's that rainy day / Hary Pepl's blues / Avalon / Poor butterfly / Airmail special / You must meet my wife / Don't be that way/Stompin' at the Savoy / If I had you / World is waiting for the sunrise / Stompin' at the Savoy / Bei mir bist du schon / Sing sing sing / Good-bye
CD _____ **TCB 43022**
TCB / Nov '96 / New Note/Pinnacle

BEST OF BENNY GOODMAN, THE
Don't be that way / Sing sing sing / And the angels sing / Loch Lomond / King Porter stomp / Stompin' at the Savoy / One o'clock jump / After you've gone / Goodnight my love / Goodbye
CD _____ **DCD 5331**
Disky / Dec '93 / Disky / THE

BEST OF BENNY GOODMAN, THE
CD _____ **DLCD 4011**
Dixie Live / Mar '95 / TKO Magnum

BIRTH OF SWING (1935-1936), THE
Hunkadola / I'm livin' in a great big way / Hooray for love / Dixieland band / Japanese sandman / You're a heavenly thing / Restless / Always / Get rhythm in your feet / Ballad in blue / Blue skies / Dear old Southland / Sometimes I'm happy / King Porter stomp / Devil and the deep blue sea / Jingle bells / Santa Claus came in the spring / Goodbye / Madhouse (take 1) / Madhouse (take 2) / Sandman / Yankee Doodle never went to town / No other one / Eeny meeny miney mo / Basin Street blues / If I could be with you one hour tonight / When Buddha smiles / It's been so long / Stompin' at the Savoy / Goody goody / Breakin' in a pair of shoes / Get happy / Christopher Columbus / I know that you know / Stardust / You can't pull the wool over my eyes / Glory of love / Remember / Walk Jennie walk / House hop / Sing me a swing song / (I would do) anything for you / In a sentimental mood / I've found a new baby / Swingtime in the Rockies / These foolish things / There's a small hotel / You turned the tables on me / Here's love in your eyes / Pick yourself up / Down South camp meeting / St. Louis blues / Bugle call rag (take 1) / When a lady meets a gentleman down South / You're giving me a song and a dance / Organ grinder swing / Peter Piper / Riffin' at the Ritz / Alexander's ragtime band / Somebody loves me / T'ain't no use / Bugle call rag (take 2) / Jam session / Goodnight my love / Take another guess / Did you mean it
CD Set _____ **ND 90601(3)**
Bluebird / Jan '92 / BMG

BREAKFAST BALL
CD _____ **TQ 201**
Happy Days / Jun '93 / Conifer/BMG

CAMEL CARAVAN BROADCASTS 1939 VOL.1
Jeepers creepers / Hold tight / I cried for you / Undecided / Angels sing / Basin Street blues / Roll 'em
CD _____ **NCD 8817**
Phontastic / '93 / Cadillac / Jazz Music / Wellard

CAMEL CARAVAN BROADCASTS 1939 VOL.2
CD _____ **NCD 8818**
Phontastic / '93 / Cadillac / Jazz Music / Wellard

CAMEL CARAVAN BROADCASTS VOL.3 (Goodman, Benny Orchestra)
CD _____ **NCD 8819**
Phontastic / '93 / Cadillac / Jazz Music / Wellard

CARNEGIE HALL CONCERTS VOL.1 1938
Don't be that way / One o'clock jump / Shine / Honeysuckle rose / Body and soul / Avalon
CD _____ **CD 53101**
Giants Of Jazz / May '92 / Cadillac / Jazz Music / Target/BMG

CARNEGIE HALL CONCERTS VOL.2 1938-1939
Loch Lomond / Stompin' at the Savoy / Dizzy spells / Don't be that way / Stardust
CD _____ **CD 53102**
Giants Of Jazz / May '92 / Cadillac / Jazz Music / Target/BMG

CLASSIC YEARS, THE
CD _____ **CDSGP 0175**
Prestige / Feb '96 / Else / Total/BMG

CLASSICS 1931-1933
CD _____ **CLASSICS 719**
Classics / Jul '93 / Discovery / Jazz Music

CLASSICS 1934-1935
CD _____ **CLASSICS 744**
Classics / Feb '94 / Discovery / Jazz Music

CLASSICS 1935
CD _____ **CLASSICS 769**
Classics / Aug '94 / Discovery / Jazz Music

CLASSICS 1935-1936
CD _____ **CLASSICS 789**
Classics / Nov '94 / Discovery / Jazz Music

CLASSICS 1936 VOL.1
CD _____ **CLASSICS 817**
Classics / May '95 / Discovery / Jazz Music

CLASSICS 1936 VOL.2
CD _____ **CLASSICS 836**
Classics / Sep '95 / Discovery / Jazz Music

CLASSICS 1936-1937
CD _____ **CLASSICS 858**
Classics / Feb '96 / Discovery / Jazz Music

CLASSICS 1937
CD _____ **CLASSICS 879**
Classics / Apr '96 / Discovery / Jazz Music

CLASSICS 1937-1938
CD _____ **CLASSICS 899**
Classics / Oct '96 / Discovery / Jazz Music

CLASSICS 1938
CD _____ **CLASSICS 925**
Classics / Apr '97 / Discovery / Jazz Music

COMPLETE CAMEL CARAVAN SHOWS 20 & 28/9/1938
CD _____ **JH 1025**
Jazz Hour / Feb '93 / Cadillac / Jazz Music / Target/BMG

COMPLETE VAMEL CARAVAN SHOWS 1938 (Goodman, Benny Orchestra)
CD _____ **JH 1038**
Jazz Hour / Feb '95 / Cadillac / Jazz Music / Target/BMG

CREAM SERIES, THE
Stompin' at the Savoy / Sing sing sing / My melancholy baby / Louise / 'S Wonderful / Avalon / Who / Make believe / When a lady meets a gentleman down South / Chloe / Bach goes to town / Handful of keys / Take another guess / Dear old Southland / Sandman / Goodnight my love / Nobody's sweetheart / He ain't got rhythm / Japanese sandman / Vibraphone blues / Did you mean it
CD _____ **PASTCD 9743**
Flapper / Sep '91 / Pinnacle

DIFFERENT VERSION VOL.1 (1939-1942)
CD _____ **NCD 8821**
Phontastic / Apr '94 / Cadillac / Jazz Music / Wellard

DIFFERENT VERSION VOL.2
CD _____ **NCD 8822**
Phontastic / Jun '94 / Cadillac / Jazz Music / Wellard

DIFFERENT VERSION VOL.3
CD _____ **NCD 8823**
Phontastic / Jun '94 / Cadillac / Jazz Music / Wellard

DIFFERENT VERSION VOL.4 (1942-1945)
CD _____ **NCD 8824**
Phontastic / Apr '94 / Cadillac / Jazz Music / Wellard

DIFFERENT VERSION VOL.5
CD _____ **NCD 8825**
Phontastic / Jun '94 / Cadillac / Jazz Music / Wellard

DON'T BE THAT WAY (Goodman, Benny Orchestra)
CD _____ **CD 14527**
Jazz Portraits / Jan '94 / Jazz Music

EARLY YEARS
Old man Harlem / Keep on doin' what you're doin' / Nobody's sweetheart now / Ain't cha glad / Dr. Heckle and Mr. Jibe / Georgia jubilee / Texas tea party / Honeysuckle rose / Sweet Sue, just you / Hundred years from today / Riffin' the scotch / Your mother's son-in-law / Love me or leave me / I can't give you anything but love / Baby / I gotta right to sing the blues
CD _____ **BCD 109**
Biograph / Jul '91 / ADA / Cadillac / Direct / Hot Shot / Jazz Music / Wellard

ESSENTIAL BENNY GOODMAN, THE
Let's dance / Flying home / Good enough to keep / Sm-o-o-oth one / Scarecrow / Clarinet a la King / Jersey bounce / Mission to Moscow / Body and soul / After you've gone / Liza / King Porter stomp / Down South camp meeting / South of the border (Down Mexico way) / Wrappin' it up
CD _____ **4671512**
Columbia / Jul '93 / Sony

ESSENTIAL V-DISCS, THE
CD _____ **JZCD 304**
Suisa / Feb '91 / Jazz Music / THE

GREAT JAZZ ORCHESTRAS (5CD Set) (Goodman, Benny/Duke Ellington/Glenn Miller/Artie Shaw)
Blue skies: *Goodman, Benny* / Dear old Southland: *Goodman, Benny* / Sometimes I'm happy: *Goodman, Benny* / King Porter stomp: *Goodman, Benny* / Goodbye: *Goodman, Benny* / When buddha smiles: *Goodman, Benny* / Goody goody: *Goodman, Benny* / Get happy: *Goodman, Benny* / Christopher Columbus: *Goodman, Benny* / I know that you know: *Goodman, Benny* / Stardust: *Goodman, Benny* / I've found a new baby: *Goodman, Benny* / Swingtime in the Rockies: *Goodman, Benny* / Somebody loves me: *Goodman, Benny* / Bugle call rag: *Goodman, Benny* / Sophisticated lady: *Ellington, Duke* / Harlem speaks: *Ellington, Duke* / In a sentimental mood: *Ellington, Duke* / Merry go round: *Ellington, Duke* / Echoes of harlem: *Ellington, Duke* / Caravan: *Ellington, Duke* / Dominuendo in blue: *Ellington, Duke* / Crescendo in blue: *Ellington, Duke* / I let a song go out of my heart: *Ellington, Duke* / Prelude to a kiss: *Ellington, Duke* / Solitude: *Ellington, Duke* / Do nothin' 'til you hear from me: *Ellington, Duke* / Cotton tail: *Ellington, Duke* / I got it bad and that ain't good: *Ellington, Duke* / Take the 'A' train: *Ellington, Duke* / Wishing (will make it so): *Miller, Glenn* / Stairway to the stars: *Miller, Glenn* / Moon love: *Miller, Glenn* / Over the rainbow: *Miller, Glenn* / In the mood: *Miller, Glenn* / Careless: *Miller, Glenn* / Tuxedo junction: *Miller, Glenn* / When you wish upon a star: *Miller, Glenn* / Imagination: *Miller, Glenn* / Fools rush in: *Miller, Glenn* / Song of the Volga boatmen: *Miller, Glenn* / You and I: *Miller, Glenn* / Chattanooga choo choo: *Miller, Glenn* / Elmer's tune: *Miller, Glenn* / String of pearls: *Miller, Glenn* / Moonlight cocktail: *Miller, Glenn* / Begin the beguine: *Shaw, Artie* / Back bay shuffle: *Shaw, Artie* / Indian love call: *Shaw, Artie* / Nightmare: *Shaw, Artie* / What is this thing called love: *Shaw, Artie* / Deep purple: *Shaw, Artie* / Traffic jam: *Shaw, Artie* / Comes love: *Shaw, Artie* / Ser-

enade to savage: *Shaw, Artie* / Oh lady be good: *Shaw, Artie* / Frenesi: *Shaw, Artie* / Special delivery stomp: *Shaw, Artie* / Summit ridge drive: *Shaw, Artie* / Temptation: *Shaw, Artie* / Moonglow: *Shaw, Artie* / Swinging at the Daisy Chain: *Shaw, Artie* / Honeysuckle rose: *Shaw, Artie* / Roseland shuffle: *Shaw, Artie* / One o'clock jump: *Shaw, Artie* / John's idea: *Shaw, Artie* / Time out: *Shaw, Artie* / Topsy: *Shaw, Artie* / Swingin' the blues: *Shaw, Artie* / Blue and sentimental: *Shaw, Artie* / Texas shuffle: *Shaw, Artie* / Jumpin' the woodside: *Shaw, Artie* / Pannasie stomp: *Shaw, Artie* / Cherokee (parts 1and2): *Shaw, Artie* / You can depend on me: *Shaw, Artie* / Jive at five: *Shaw, Artie* / Oh Lady be good: *Shaw, Artie*
CD Set __________ **CDPAK 4**
Charly / Jan '93 / Koch

HAPPY SESSION (Goodman, Benny Orchestra)
CD __________ **4765232**
Sony Jazz / May '94 / Sony

HARRY JAMES YEARS VOL.1
I want to be happy / Chloe / Rosetta / Peckin' / Can't we be friends / Sing sing sing / Roll 'em / When it's sleepy time down South / Changes / Sugarfoot stomp / I can't give you anything but love / Minnie the moocher's wedding day / Camel hop - Take 1/2 / Life goes to a party / Don't be that way
CD __________ **07863661552**
Bluebird / Apr '93 / BMG

I'M NOT COMPLAININ' (Goodman, Benny & His Band)
Clarinet a la King / My old flame / Cornsilk / Birds of a feather / I'm not complainin' / Time on my hands / I can't give you anything but love / Gilly / Yes my darling daughter / I'm always chasing rainbows / Let the door knob hitcha / Good evenin' good lookin' / Something new / I found a million dollar baby / When the sun comes out / Smoke gets in your eyes / I hear a rhapsody / It's always you / Tuesday at ten / Elmer's tune / Down down down / Cherry
CD __________ **RAJCD 813**
Empress / May '97 / Koch

IN MOSCOW 1962
CD __________ **CD 53195**
Giants Of Jazz / Nov '95 / Cadillac / Jazz Music / Target/BMG

IN STOCKHOLM 1958
CD __________ **NCD 8801**
Phontastic / Apr '94 / Cadillac / Jazz Music / Wellard

INDISPENSABLE BENNY GOODMAN VOL.1 & 2 1935-1936, THE (Goodman, Benny Orchestra)
Blue skies / Dear old Southland / Sometimes I'm happy / King Porter stomp / Between the Devil and the deep blue sea / Mad house / If I could be with you one hour tonight / When Buddha smiles / Stompin' at the Savoy / Breakin' in a pair of shoes / I hope Gabriel likes my music / Mutiny in the parlour / I'm gonna clap my hands / Swing is here / Get happy / Christopher Columbus / I know that you know / Stardust / You forgot to remember / House hop / (I would do) anything for you / I've found a new baby / Swingtime in the Rockies / Pick yourself up / Down south camp meeting / St. Louis blues / Love me or leave me / Bugle call rag / Organ grinder swing / Riffin' at the Ritz / Somebody loves me
CD Set __________ **74321155212**
RCA / Mar '94 / BMG

INTRODUCTION TO BENNY GOODMAN 1928-1941, AN
CD __________ **4007**
Best Of Jazz / May '94 / Discovery

JAZZ MASTERS
CD __________ **8444102**
Verve / Feb '95 / PolyGram

JAZZ MASTERS
CD __________ **CDMFP 6304**
Music For Pleasure / Mar '97 / EMI

JAZZ PORTRAIT
CD __________ **CD 14573**
Complete / Nov '95 / THE

JAZZ PORTRAITS (Goodman, Benny Trio & Quartet)
Dinah / Sweet Sue, just you / Moonglow / After you've gone / Body and soul / Who / Exactly like you / Tiger rag / Stompin' at the Savoy / Whispering / China boy / Oh lady be good / Nobody's sweetheart / Tea for two / Running wild / Avalon / Sugar / Blues in my flat
CD __________ **CD 14520**
Jazz Portraits / May '94 / Jazz Music

KING OF SWING (36 Joyful Jazz Masterpieces/2CD Set) (Goodman, Benny Orchestra)
Bugle call rag / I've found a new baby / I know that you know / Blue skies / Dear old southland / When Buddha smiles / Somebody loves me / Swingtime in the rockies / Get happy / Christopher Columbus / Sometimes I'm happy / Goodbye / Goody goody / King porter stomp / Stardust / Airmail special / Bewitched / Earl / Superman / Henderson stomp / How long has this been going on / Peace brother / Clarinet a la king / Zaggin' with zig / Cherry / Solo flight / All the cats join in / Tangerine / How deep is the ocean / It never entered my mind / When the sun comes out / My old flame / Pound ridge / Honeysuckle rose / Beyond the moon
CD Set __________ **330362**
Hallmark / Mar '97 / Carlton

KING OF SWING 1935-1955, THE
Don't be that way / King Porter stomp / Roll 'em / Down South camp meeting / Goodbye / Christopher Columbus / One o'clock jump / If I could be with you one hour tonight / Bugle call rag / Goody goody / Sing sing sing / I want to be happy / Smoke house rhythm / Stompin' at the Savoy / Topsy / Sugarfoot stomp / Kingdom of swing / Bach goes to town / St. Louis blues / Sent for you yesterday / He ain't got rhythm / Sing me a swing song / After you've gone / Body and soul / Who / China boy / Oh Lady be good / Nobody's sweetheart / Moonglow / Dinah / Exactly like you / Sweet Sue, just you / Just you / Tiger rag / Whispering / Tea for two / Running wild / Avalon / Sugar / Blues in my flat / Pick a rib / Shivers / Rose room / Boy meet god / On the Alamo / Let's dance / Jumpin' at the woodside / Get happy / Blue Lou / Seven come eleven / Memories of you / Somebody stole my gal / Rock Rimmon / And the angels sing / Airmail special / Jersey bounce / Lullaby of the leaves / What can I say after I say I'm sorry / East of the sun and west of the moon / Temptation rag / You brought a new kind of love to me / Four or five times / Big John special / I got rhythm / Loved walked in / Stealin' apples / Undercurrent blues / Clarinet a la King
CD Set __________ **CDB 1206**
Giants Of Jazz / '92 / Cadillac / Jazz Music / Target/BMG

KING OF SWING, THE
CD __________ **300154**
Accord / Dec '89 / Cadillac / Discovery

KING OF SWING, THE
CD __________ **PWK 027**
Carlton / '88 / Carlton

KING OF SWING, THE
Don't be that way / Stompin' at the Savoy / One o'clock jump / Bach goes to town / Bugle call rag / St. Louis blues / Kingdom of swing
CD __________ **BSTCD 9106**
Best Compact Discs / May '92 / Complete/Pinnacle

KING PORTER STOMP
Someday, sweetheart / Mad house / Sandman / If I could be with you one hour tonight / When Buddha smiles / Hunkadola / I'm living in a great big way / Dixieland band / Japanese Sandman / You're a heavenly thing / Restless / Always / Ballad in Blue / Dear old Southland / Sometimes I'm happy / King Porter stomp / Between the Devil and the deep blue sea / After you've gone / Body and soul
CD __________ **CDSVL 176**
Saville / Oct '87 / Conifer/BMG

KING PORTER STOMP
King Porter stomp / Clarinade / And the angels sing / All the cats join in / Mad boogie / One o'clock jump / Clarinet a la King / 'S Wonderful / Jealousy / Rattle and roll / I want to be loved / Remember / Somebody stole my gal / Don't be that way / Tattle tale / Blue skies / Mahzel / Moon-faced and starry eyed / Old buttermilk / Oh baby / Theme (goodbye)
CD __________ **DBCD 02**
Dance Band Days / Jun '86 / Prism

KING SWINGS, THE
CD __________ **SLCD 9007**
Starline / Jun '94 / Jazz Music

LET'S DANCE
CD __________ **15780**
Laserlight / Jan '93 / Target/BMG

LIVE 1937
Whispers in the dark / Avalon / Roses in December / I'm a ding dong daddy (from Dumas) / Body and soul / Sweet Sue-just you / Where or when / Nagasaki / Handful of keys / Oh, lady be good / Everybody loves my baby / More than you know / Vieni, vieni / Who / Limehouse blues / Where or when / Dinah / Can't help lovin' that man / Avalon
CD __________ **VN 1009**
Viper's Nest / Nov '96 / ADA / Cadillac / Direct / Jazz Music

LIVE AT CARNEGIE HALL (40th Anniversary Concert/2CD Set)
Let's dance / I've found a new baby / Send in the clowns / Loch Lomond / Stardust / I love a piano / Roll 'em / King Porter stomp / Rocky raccoon / Yesterday / That's a plenty / How high the moon / Moonglow / Oh lady be good / Jersey bounce / Someone to watch over me / Please don't talk about me when I'm gone / Medley / Sing sing sing / Goodbye / Seven come eleven / Christopher Columbus
CD Set __________ **8203492**
London / Mar '93 / PolyGram

LIVE AT CARNEGIE HALL (2CD Set)
Don't be that way / One o'clock jump / Sensation rag / I'm coming Virginia / When my baby smiles at me / Shine / Blue reverie / Life goes to a party / Honeysuckle rose / Body and soul / Avalon / Man I love / I got rhythm / Blue skies / Loch Lomond / Blue room / Swingtime in the Rockies / Bei mir bist du schon / China boy / Stompin' at the Savoy / Dizzy spells / Sing sing sing / Big John's special
CD Set __________ **4509832**
Sony Jazz / Oct '93 / Sony

LIVE AT THE CARNEGIE HALL 6 OCTOBER 1939 (Goodman, Benny & Glenn Miller)
CD __________ **EBCD 21032**
Flyright / Dec '90 / Hot Shot / Jazz Music / Wellard

LIVE AT THE INTERNATIONAL WORLD EXHIBITION (Brussels 1958: Unissued Recordings) (Goodman, Benny Orchestra)
Let's dance / When you're smiling / Sent for you yesterday / Pennies from Heaven / Goin' to Chicago / Soon / Who cares / 'Deed I do / I hadn't anyone till you / I've got you under my skin / There's no fool like an old fool / Sometimes I'm happy / Oh boy I'm lucky / Song is ended (but the melody lingers on) / I'm coming Virginia / Fine romance / Harvard blues / If I had you / Goodbye theme
CD __________ **DAWE 36**
Magic / Sep '93 / Cadillac / Harmonia Mundi / Jazz Music / Swift / Wellard

LIVE DOWN UNDER 1973 (Goodman, Benny Sextet)
CD __________ **TMCD 21302**
Jazzband / Jul '97 / Cadillac / Hot Shot / Jazz Music / Wellard

MANHATTAN ROOM VOL.1 1937 (Satan Takes A Ride)
CD __________ **VN 171**
Viper's Nest / Aug '95 / ADA / Cadillac / Direct / Jazz Music

MANHATTAN ROOM VOL.1-6 1937 (6CD Set)
CD Set __________ **VN 177**
Viper's Nest / Mar '96 / ADA / Cadillac / Direct / Jazz Music

MANHATTAN ROOM VOL.2 1937 (One O'Clock Jump)
CD __________ **VN 172**
Viper's Nest / Aug '95 / ADA / Cadillac / Direct / Jazz Music

MANHATTAN ROOM VOL.3 1937 (Jam Session)
CD __________ **VN 173**
Viper's Nest / Aug '95 / ADA / Cadillac / Direct / Jazz Music

MANHATTAN ROOM VOL.4 1937
CD __________ **VN 174**
Viper's Nest / Mar '96 / ADA / Cadillac / Direct / Jazz Music

MANHATTAN ROOM VOL.5 1937
CD __________ **VN 175**
Viper's Nest / Mar '96 / ADA / Cadillac / Direct / Jazz Music

MANHATTAN ROOM VOL.6 1937
CD __________ **VN 176**
Viper's Nest / Mar '96 / ADA / Cadillac / Direct / Jazz Music

MASTERPIECES 1935-42
CD __________ **158172**
Masterpieces / Mar '94 / BMG

MASTERPIECES OF BENNY GOODMAN, THE
CD __________ **393322**
Music Memoria / Jul '96 / ADA / Discovery

ON RADIO WITH ARTURO TOSCANINI/ BUDAPEST STRING QUARTET (Goodman, Benny & Arturo Toscanini)
Clarinet quintet in A major KV 581 / Rhapsody in blue / American in Paris
CD __________ **RY 60**
Radio Years / Jun '96 / Complete/Pinnacle

PERMANENT GOODMAN VOL.1 1926-1938
CD __________ **PHONTCD 7659**
Phontastic / Feb '89 / Cadillac / Jazz Music / Wellard

PERMANENT GOODMAN VOL.2 1939-1945
CD __________ **PHONTCD 7660**
Phontastic / Apr '94 / Cadillac / Jazz Music / Wellard

PLAYS JIMMY MUNDY
Mad house / You can't pull the wool over my eyes / House hop / Sing me a swing song / In a sentimental mood / Swingtime in the rockies / These foolish things / There's a small hotel / Bugle call rag / Jam session / Did you mean it / When you and I were young / Swing low, sweet chariot / He ain't got rhythm / Sing sing sing / I'm like a fish out of water / Sweet stranger / Margie / Farewell blues / Roll' em / Camel hop
CD __________ **HEPCD 1039**
Hep / Feb '94 / Cadillac / Jazz Music / New Note/Pinnacle / Wellard

PORTRAIT OF BENNY GOODMAN, A
CD __________ **GALE 408**
Gallerie / May '97 / Disc / THE

RADIO TRANSCRIPTS VOL.1 1935 (Goodman, Benny & His Rhythm Makers)
Makin' whoopee / Poor butterfly / Between the Devil and the deep blue sea / Farewell blues / I would do almost anything for you / Bugle call rag
CD __________ **TAX 37082**
Tax / Aug '94 / Cadillac / Jazz Music / Wellard

RADIO TRANSCRIPTS VOL.2 1935 (Goodman, Benny & His Rhythm Makers)
Royal Garden blues / Down South camp meeting / Lovely to look at / Stardust / Sugarfoot stomp / Wrappin' it up
CD __________ **GRV 74602**
Gramavision / Sep '91 / Vital/SAM
CD __________ **TAX 37192**
Tax / Aug '94 / Cadillac / Jazz Music / Wellard

RARE RECORDINGS FROM YALE UNIVERSITY MUSIC LIBRARY VOL.1-5 (Swing Swing Swing/6CD Set)
Sweet Georgia Brown / Macedonia lullaby / Soft lights and sweet music / Broadway / Marching in rhythm / Marching and swinging / Batunga train / Cherokee / Slipped disc / Diga diga doo / Lullaby in rhythm / Don't blame me / Blue room / Let's dance / Honeysuckle rose / Running wild / Mean to me / Memories of you / Stompin' at the Savoy / Blue and sentimental / One o'clock jump / I found a new baby / Stairway to the stars / Body and soul / Airmail special / Nice work if you can get it / Sing sing sing / Goodbye / Bugle call rag / On the sunny side of the street / 'Deed I do / Who cares / Blue skies / I want a little girl / Sometimes I'm happy / Fine romance / Harvard blues / I'm coming Virginia / Soon / Medley / Pennies from heaven / Stompin' at the Savoy / Flying home / This is my lucky day / Roll 'em / Brussels blues / When you're smiling / Happy session blues / Autumn nocturne / Oh baby / What a difference a day makes / Oh gee, oh joy / Earl / More than you know / You couldn't be cuter / I've grown accustomed to her face / Swift as the wind / Them there eyes / Room without windows / People / Benny rides again / Let's dance / No way to stop it / Memories of you / Medley / I want to be happy / Gotta be this or that / Between the devil and the deep blue sea / Body and soul / Don't get around much anymore / Sweet and lovely / After you've gone / Ten bone / St. James Infirmary / Airmail special / My baby done tol' me / Medley / Lazy afternoon / St. Louis blues / Rachel's dream / Easy living / I found a new baby / Breakfast feud / No way to stop / Sleep
CD Set __________ **8443122**
Limelight / Aug '92 / PolyGram
CD Set __________ **MM 65095**
Music Masters / Jan '95 / Nimbus

RARE RECORDINGS FROM YALE UNIVERSITY MUSIC LIBRARY VOL.6-10 (The King Of Swing - 5CD Set)
CD Set __________ **MM 65130**
Music Masters / Oct '96 / Nimbus

ROLL 'EM (Goodman, Benny & Sid Catlett)
CD __________ **VJC 10322**
Vintage Jazz Classics / Oct '92 / ADA / Cadillac / CM / Direct

RUNNIN' WILD (Goodman, Benny Quartet)
CD __________ **CDSGP 099**
Prestige / Mar '94 / Else / Total/BMG

SMALL COMBOS 1935-1941
CD __________ **CD 53039**
Giants Of Jazz / Mar '92 / Cadillac / Jazz Music / Target/BMG

SMALL GROUPS, THE
After you've gone / Avalon / Exactly like you / Flying home / Gone with "what" wind / Good enough to keep / Limehouse blues / Moon glow / More than you know / Oh Lady be good / On the Alamo / On the sunny side of the street: *Goodman, Benny & Peggy Lee* / Opus 1/2 / Opus 3/4 / Pick-a-rib / Running wild / Sheikh of araby / Smo-o-o-oth one / Someday sweetheart / Stardust / Sweet Georgia Brown / Wang wang blues / Wholly cats / World is waiting for the sunrise
CD __________ **CDAJA 5144**
Living Era / Dec '94 / Select

STOMPIN' AT THE SAVOY
King Porter stomp / Goodbye / Goody goody / Stompin' at the Savoy / These foolish things / Bugle call rag / Goodnight my love / Don't be that way / One o'clock jump / Sing sing sing
CD __________ **JHR 73518**
Jazz Hour / Oct '92 / Cadillac / Jazz Music / Target/BMG

SWING KING
Let's dance / Don't be that way / When Buddha smiles / Down south camp meeting / You turned the tables on me / King Porter stomp / Sometimes I'm happy / Blue skies / Sugarfoot stomp / I know that you know / Why don't you do right / Perfidia / Smoke gets in your eyes / Stardust / Clarinet a la King / After you've gone / Someday sweetheart / Big John special

CD ______ PAR 2029
Parade / Sep '94 / Disc

SWING SESSIONS - PREMIERE RELEASE
CD ______ HCD 254
Hindsight / Sep '94 / Jazz Music / Target/ BMG

THIS IS JAZZ
Sing sing sing (with a swing) / Flying home / Wang wang blues / Don't be that way / Running wild / King Porter stomp / Limehouse blues / Mission to Moscow / You turned the tables on me / Avalon / Memories of you
CD ______ CK 64620
Sony Jazz / May '96 / Sony

TOGETHER AGAIN (Goodman, Benny Quartet)
Who cares / Dearest / Seven come eleven / I've found a new baby / Somebody loves me / I'll get by / Say it isn't so / Running wild / I got it bad and that ain't good / Four once more
CD ______ 09026685932
RCA Victor / Oct '96 / BMG

TRIBUTE TO BENNY GOODMAN (Various Artists)
CD ______ NHCD 025
Nagel Heyer / Jul '96 / Jazz Music

UNDERCURRENT BLUES
Lonely moments / Whistle blues / Shirley steps out / Stealin' apples / Undercurrent blues / Shishkabop / Huckle buck / Bop hop / Trees / Dreazag / Bedlam / In the land of oo-bla-dee / Blue Lou / Fiesta time / Egg head
CD ______ CDP 8320862
Capitol Jazz / Aug '95 / EMI

WAY DOWN YONDER (V-Discs)
CD ______ VJC 10012
Victorious Discs / Aug '90 / Jazz Music

WHEN BUDDHA SMILES
Music Hall rag / Always / Blue skies / Down home rag / Ballad in blue / Devil and the deep blue sea / Mad house / Down South Camp meeting / Can't we be friends / Sugarfoot stomp / Big John special / Jumpin' at the woodside / Night and day / Board meeting / When Buddha smiles / Take another guess / Roll 'em / Don't be that way / Wrappin' it up / Stealin' apples / Honeysuckle rose / Zaggin' with Zig
CD ______ CDAJA 5071
Living Era / May '90 / Select

WORLD WIDE
CD Set ______ TCB 43012
TCB / Jan '94 / New Note/Pinnacle

WRAPPIN' IT UP
CD ______ AMSC 608
Avid / Jul '97 / Avid/BMG / Koch / THE

YALE ARCHIVES VOL.1 (Classics In Jazz)
Sweet Georgia Brown / Macedonia lullaby / Soft lights and sweet music / Broadway / Marching and swinging / Batunga train / Cherokee / Slipped disc / Diga diga doo / Lullaby in rhythm / Blue room
CD ______ 8208022
Limelight / Mar '93 / PolyGram

YALE ARCHIVES VOL.1-5 (6CD Set)
CD Set ______ 650952
Music Masters / May '95 / Nimbus

YALE ARCHIVES VOL.2 (Classics In Jazz/Live At The Basin Street)
Let's dance / Honeysuckle Rose / Running wild / Mean to me / Memories of you / Stompin' at the Savoy / Blue and sentimental / One o'clock jump / I've found a new baby / Stairway to the stars / Body and soul / Airmail special / Nice work if you can get it / Sing sing sing / Goodbye
CD ______ 8208032
Limelight / Mar '93 / PolyGram

YALE ARCHIVES VOL.3 (Big Band In Europe)
Let's dance / Bugle call rag / On the sunny side of the street / 'Deed I do / Who cares / Blue skies / I want a little girl / Sometimes I'm happy / Fine romance / Harvard blues / Brussels blues / I'm coming Virginia / Soon / Pennies from Heaven / Stompin' at the Savoy / Flying home / This is my lucky day / Roll 'em / When you're smiling / Medley
CD ______ 8208142
Limelight / Mar '93 / PolyGram

YALE ARCHIVES VOL.4 (Big Band Recordings)
Happy session blues / Autumn nocturne / Oh baby / What a difference a day makes / Oh gee, oh joy / Earl / More than you know / You couldn't be cuter / I've grown accustomed to her face / Swift as the wind / Them there eyes / Room without windows / People / Benny rides again
CD ______ 8208202
Limelight / Mar '93 / PolyGram

YALE ARCHIVES VOL.5 (2CD Set)
Let's dance / No way to stop it / Memories of you / Sleep / I want to be happy / Gotta be this or that / Between the Devil and the deep blue sea / Don't get around much anymore / Sweet and lovely / After you've gone / Ten bone / Breakfast feud / St. James Infirmary / Airmail special / My baby done tol' me / Lazy afternoon / St. Louis blues / Rachel's dream / Easy living / I found a new baby / Body and soul / Medley / Medley
CD Set ______ 8208272
Limelight / Mar '93 / PolyGram

YALE ARCHIVES VOL.6 (Live At The Rainbow Grill, New York 1966-1967)
Between the devil and the deep blue sea / I guess I'll have to change my plans / There is no greater love / Don't be that way / Oh lady be good / Come rain or come shine / St. Louis blues / All the things you are / I've found a new baby / Avalon / Enbraceable you / Sweet Georgia Brown / Look for the silver lining / By myself / Honeysuckle rose
CD ______ 5186762
Limelight / Mar '93 / PolyGram

YALE ARCHIVES VOL.7 (Florida Sessions)
Sleep / Sometimes I'm happy / Rosetta / Dark shadows / Tea for two / Deacon and the elder / I want to be happy / Someone to watch over me / Ten bone / Sweet Miss / Time on my hands / Splanky / Best thing for you
CD ______ 5186772
Limelight / Mar '93 / PolyGram

Goodman, Dave

LIVE 1996
Let it go / Little Jimi / Santa Fe / My only friend / Down the line / Hard, sad & lonely time
CD ______ BCD 17009
Bear Family / Nov '96 / Direct / Rollercoaster / Swift

Goodman, Gabrielle

TRAVELLIN' LIGHT
Travellin' light / Cherokee / Over the rainbow / Manilla / Never too late / Someone to watch over me / Blues walk / My funny valentine / Use me / Don't explain
CD ______ 5140062
jMT / Dec '93 / PolyGram

UNTIL WE LOVE
CD ______ 5140152
jMT / Dec '94 / PolyGram

Goodman, Steve

AFFORDABLE ART
If Jethro were here / Vegematic / Old smoothies / Talk backwards / How much tequila (did I drink last night) / When my rowboat comes in / Souvenirs / Take me out to the ballgame / Dying cub fan's last request / California promises / Watchin' Joey glow / Grand canyon song
CD ______ RPJ 002CD
Red Pajamas / May '97 / ADA / Direct

ARTISTIC HAIR
East St. Louis tweed / Let's give a party / Winter wonderland / Elvis imitators / Tico tico / Water is wide / Red red robin / Chicken cordon bleus / Old fashioned / City of New Orleans / Three legged man / You never even call me by my name
CD ______ RPJ 001CD
Red Pajamas / May '97 / ADA / Direct

BEST OF THE ASYLUM YEARS VOL.1, THE
Between the lines / Jessie's jig (Rob's romp, Beth's bounce) / Hand it to you / Death of a salesman / Still trying to care / Twentieth century is almost over / Banana republics / Two lovers / I'm attracted to you / One bite of the apple / One that got away
CD ______ RPJ 006CD
Red Pajamas / May '97 / ADA / Direct

BEST OF THE ASYLUM YEARS VOL.2, THE
This hotel room / Bobby don't stop / Men who love women who love men / That's what friends are for / Just lucky I guess / My old man / Video tape / Danger / Door number three / I can't sleep / You can turn to me / Spoon river
CD ______ RPJ 007CD
Red Pajamas / May '97 / ADA / Direct

EASTER TAPES, THE
Introduction / Red red robin / I don't know where I'm going... / Blue skies / This hotel room / I can't sleep / Banana republics / City of New Orleans / Chicken cordon bleus / It's a sin to tell a lie / Easter parade / Video tape / Big iron / Somebody else's troubles / Don't fence me in / 18 yellow roses / Splish splash / Rudolph the red nosed (Easter) reindeer / Runaway
CD ______ RPJ 009CD
Red Pajamas / May '97 / ADA / Direct

NO BIG SURPRISE (The Steve Goodman Anthology/2CD Set)
Between the lines / Take me out to the ballgame / Go cubs go / City of New Orleans / Would you like to learn to dance / Souvenirs / Red ball jets / One that got away / Talk backwards / If she were you / Danger / You better get out while you can (The ballad of Carl Martin) / Yellow coat / Bannan republics / California promises / Bobby don't stop / My old man / This hotel room / Where's the party / I just keep falling in love / Watchin' Joey glow / Dutchman / In real life / Chicken cordon blues / I don't know where I'm goin', but I'm goin' nowhere in a hur / Is it true what they say about Dixie / Turnpike Tom / Elvis imitators / Lincoln park pirates / Wonderful world of sex / Vegematic / Dying cub fan's last request / Men who love women who love men / Auctioneer / Broken string song / Just lucky I guess / I'll fly away / It's a sin to tell a lie / Born to be wild / Teen angel / Tell Laura I love her / (Laurie) Strange things happen / You never even call me by my name / Don't let the stars get in your eyes / As time goes by
CD Set ______ RPJ 008CD
Red Pajamas / May '97 / ADA / Direct

SANTA ANA WINDS
Face on the cutting room floor / Telephone answering tape / One that got away / Queen of the road / Fourteen days / Hot tub refugee / I just keep falling in love / Big rock candy mountain / Santa Ana winds / You better get it while you can
CD ______ RPJ 003CD
Red Pajamas / May '97 / ADA / Direct

SOMEBODY ELSE'S TROUBLES
Dutchman / Six hours ahead of the sun / Song for David / Chicken Gordon blues / Somebody else's troubles / Loving of the game / I ain't heard you play no blues / Don't do me any favours anymore / Vegetable song / Lincoln Park pirates / Ballad of Penny Evans / Election year rag
CD ______ OW 28560
One Way / May '94 / ADA / Direct / Greyhound

STEVE GOODMAN
I don't know where I'm going / Rainbow road / Donald and Lydia / You never even called me by my name / Mind your own business / Eight ball blues / City of New Orleans / Turnpike Tom / Yellow coat / So fine / Jazzman / Would you like to learn to dance
CD ______ OW 28559
One Way / May '94 / ADA / Direct / Greyhound

TRIBUTE TO STEVE GOODMAN, A (Various Artists)
Souvenirs: *Prine, John* / Blues that Steve taught me: *Holstein, Ed* / Face on the cutting room floor: *Nitty Gritty Dirt Band* / Gentle on my mind: *Hartford, John* / I will not be your fool: *Bromberg, David* / Lady is a tramp: *Burns, Jethro* / I can't sleep: *Koloc, Bonnie* / California promises: *Lincoln Park Pirates & Jim Rothermel* / All over the world: *Guthrie, Arlo* / City of New Orleans: *Guthrie, Arlo* / Thanksgiving song: *Holstein, Fred* / Satisfied mmind: *Bowers, Bryan* / Angel from Montgomery: *Raitt, Bonnie & John Prine* / My old man: *Prine, John* / I don't wanna know: *Havens, Richie* / Water is wide: *Amram, David* / Cochroaches on parade: *Waller, Harry* / Dutchman: *Smith, Michael* / Please don't bury me: *Prine, John*
CD ______ RPJ 004CD
Red Pajamas / May '97 / ADA / Direct

UNFINISHED BUSINESS
Whispering man / Mind over matter / God bless our mobile home / Millie make some chillli / In real life / Now and then there's a fool such as I / Don't get sand in it / Dutchman / Colorado Christmas / My funny valentine
CD ______ RPJ 005CD
Red Pajamas / May '97 / ADA / Direct

Goodrich, Andy

MOTHERLESS CHILD
Natch'l natch'l / You must believe in Spring / Quasimodo / Reminiscing / Stranger in paradise / Serenade in black / Stablemates / Motherless child
CD ______ DE 495
Delmark / Jul '97 / ADA / Cadillac / CM / Direct / Hot Shot

Goodrick, Mick

IN PAS(S)ING
Feebles, fables and ferns / In the tavern of ruin / Summer band camp / Pedal pusher / In passing
CD ______ 8473272
ECM / Mar '92 / New Note/Pinnacle

RARE BIRDS (Goodrick, Mick & Joe Diorio)
CD ______ RMCD 4505
Ram / Nov '93 / Cadillac / Harmonia Mundi

SUNSCREAMS (Goodrick, Mick Quartet)
CD ______ RMCD 4507
Ram / Apr '94 / Cadillac / Harmonia Mundi

Goodson, Sadie

SADIE GOODSON & SAMMY RIMMINGTON (Goodson, Sadie & Sammy Rimmington)
CD ______ BCD 298
GHB / Nov '96 / Jazz Music

Goodwin, Bill

NO METHOD (Goodwin, Bill/ Hal Galper/ Billy Peterson)
CD ______ FSRCD 136
Fresh Sound / Dec '90 / Discovery / Jazz Music

Goodwin, Ron

MY KIND OF MUSIC (Goodwin, Ron & Bournemouth Symphony Orchestra)
Trap, The (London marathon theme) / Here where you are / Kojak / Hill Street Blues / Star Trek / Dynasty / Dallas / Here's that rainy day / Tribute to Miklos Rosza / Ben Hur / Red house / Four feathers / Parade of the Charioteers / Trolley song / Zip a dee doo dah / Someday my Prince will come / I wanna be like you / Little April showers / When you wish upon a star / Caravan - the girl from Corsica / Stephen Foster tribute / Oh Susanna / Swanee River / Beautiful dreamer / Camptown races / Drake 400 suite / Battle finale
CD ______ CHAN 8797
Chandos / '89 / Chandos

Goofus Five

1926-27
Poor Papa (he's got nothin' at all) / I wonder what's become of Joe / Ya gotta know how to love / Where'd you get those eyes / Mary Lou / Someone is losin' Susan / Crazy quilt / Sadie Green the vamp of New Orleans / Heebie jeebies / Tuck in Kentucky and smile / I need lovin' / I've got the girl / Farewell blues / I wish I could shimmy like my sister Kate / Muddy water / Wang wang blues / Whisper song / Arkansas blues / Lazy weather / Vo-do-do-de-o blues / Ain't that a grand and glorious feeling / Clementine / Nothin' doe-does like it used to do-do-do / I left my sugar standing in the rain (and she melted away)
CD ______ CBC 1017
Timeless Historical / Aug '94 / New Note/ Pinnacle

Goombay Dance Band

HITS COLLECTION VOL.1
CD ______ 10082
CMC / Jun '97 / BMG

HITS COLLECTION VOL.2
CD ______ 10102
CMC / Jun '97 / BMG

Goops

GOOPS, THE
Dead/Alive / I don't care / Day I met Iggy / City slang / Use no hooks / Nobodys goes to waste / Never live it down / Island earth / Booze cabana / I am legend
CD ______ BLK 018ECD
Blackout / Oct '95 / Plastic Head / Vital

Gopalakrishan, Parur

RAGA BHOOP (Gopalakrishan, Parur & Ustad Sultan Khan)
CD ______ NRCD 0065
Navras / Nov '96 / New Note/Pinnacle

Gopalakrishnan, K.S.

CARNATIC FLUTE
CD ______ SM 15022
Wergo / Nov '91 / ADA / Cadillac / Harmonia Mundi

Gor Jus Wrex

FATHER LIAM'S IRISH MIST
Irish rover / Bucks of Oranmore / Dirty old town / Sally Gardens / Ordinary man / Ag Fas Fos / Langstrom's pony / Hard station / Ride on / From Clare to here / Homes of Donegal / Rainy night in Soho / Blackbird
CD ______ CDMFP 6349
Music For Pleasure / May '97 / EMI

Gordon, Bobby

DON'T LET IT END
CD ______ ARCD 19112
Arbors Jazz / Nov '94 / Cadillac

PLAYS BING (A Tribute To Bing Crosby)
CD ______ ARCD 19172
Arbors Jazz / May '97 / Cadillac

Gordon, Dexter

AFTER HOURS
CD ______ SCCD 31224
Steeplechase / '88 / Discovery / Impetus

BACKSTAIRS (2CD Set)
Tangerine / I told you so / Skylark / Backstairs / It's you or no one / Tanya / As time goes by / Jumpin' blues
CD Set ______ JLR 103603
Live At EJ's / May '96 / Target/BMG

BALLADS
Darn that dream / Don't explain / I'm a fool to want you / Ernie's tune / You've changed / Willow weep for me / Guess I'll hang my tears out to dry / Body and soul
CD ______ BNZ 275
Blue Note / Sep '92 / EMI

BEST OF DEXTER GORDON (Blue Note Years)
It's you or no one / Society red / Smile / Cheesecake / Three o'clock in the morning / Soy califa / Don't explain / Tanya
CD ______ BNZ 142
Blue Note / Sep '92 / EMI

BLUE DEX (Dexter Gordon Plays The Blues)
Sticky wicket / Panther / Blue Monk / Lonesome lover blues / Jumpin' blues / Oh Karen / Gingerbread boy
CD _____ PRCD 11003
Prestige / Jun '97 / Cadillac / Complete/ Pinnacle

BODY AND SOUL
CD _____ BLCD 760118
Black Lion / Feb '89 / Cadillac / Jazz Music / Koch / Wellard

BOTH SIDES OF MIDNIGHT
CD _____ BLCD 760103
Black Lion / Dec '88 / Cadillac / Jazz Music / Koch / Wellard

CHASE, THE
Chase / Mischievous lady / Lullaby in rhythm / Horning in / Chromatic aberration / Talk of the town / Blues bikini / I don't stand a ghost of a chance with you / Sweet and lovely / Duel
CD _____ CD 53064
Giants Of Jazz / Mar '90 / Cadillac / Jazz Music / Target/BMG

CHASE, THE
CD _____ STB 613
Stash / Aug '95 / ADA / Cadillac / CM / Direct / Jazz Music

CLUBHOUSE
Hanky panky / I'm a fool to want you / Devilette / Clubhouse / Jody / Lady Iris B
CD _____ CDP 7844452
EMI / Sep '92 / EMI

COME RAIN OR COME SHINE
CD _____ JHR 73508
Jazz Hour / May '93 / Cadillac / Jazz Music / Target/BMG

COMPLETE BLUE NOTE SIXTIES SESSIONS (6CD Set)
I was doing alright / I want more / You've changed / Society red / For regulars only / It's you or no one / For regular's only / Landslide / Modal mood / Clear the dex / Boy saxophonist / Soul sister / Smile / Ernie's tune / I want more / End of a love affair / Serenade in blue / You said it / Love locked out / Blue Gardenia / Second balcony jump / Where are you / Six bits bite / Oh lady be good / On be bop / Three o'clock in the morning / Second balcony jump / Cheese cake / I guess I'll hang my tears out to dry / Love for sale / McSpliens / Backbone / Soy Califa / Until the real thing comes along / You stepped out of a dream / Don't explain / Our love is here to stay / Broadway / Stairway to the stars / Night in Tunisia / Willow weep for me / Scrapple from the apple / Coppin' the haven / Tanya / It all began / Kong Neptune / Darn that dream / Hanky panky / Devilette / Clubhouse / Jodi / I'm a fool to want you / Lady Iris B / Le coiffeur / Manha de Carnaval / Flick of a trick / Everybody's somebody's fool / Very saxily yours / Shiny stockings / Who can I turn to / Heartaches / Dexter on Bird
CD Set _____ CDP 8342002
Blue Note / Nov '96 / EMI

COMPLETE SESSIONS ON DIAL, THE
Mischievious lady / Lullaby in rhythm / Chase / Chromatic abberation / It's the talk of the town / Blue bikini / I don't stand a ghost of a chance with you / Sweet and lovely / Horning in / Duel / Blues in Teddy's flat
CD _____ SPJCD 130
Spotlite / Apr '95 / Cadillac / Jazz Music / New Note/Pinnacle / Swift

DADDY PLAYS THE HORN
Daddy plays the horn / Confirmation / Number four / Darn that dream / Autumn in New York / You can depend on me
CD _____ CDGR 121
Charly / Mar '97 / Koch

DEXTER BLOWS HOT AND COOL
Silver plated / Cry me a river / Rhythm mad / Don't worry 'bout me / I hear music / Bonna Rue / I should care / Blowin' for Dootsie / Tenderly
CD _____ CDBOP 006
Boplicity / Feb '89 / Pinnacle

DEXTER GORDON 1943-1946
CD _____ 158792
Jazz Archives / Feb '97 / Discovery

DEXTER GORDON QUARTET (1955-1967) (Gordon, Dexter Quartet)
CD _____ CD 53065
Giants Of Jazz / Mar '92 / Cadillac / Jazz Music / Target/BMG

DEXTERITY - NEW YORK 1977 & COPENHAGEN 1967
CD Set _____ JWD 102303
JWD / Oct '94 / Target/BMG

GO
Cheesecake / Guess I'll hang my tears out to dry / Second balcony jump / Love for sale / Where are you / Three o'clock in the morning
CD _____ CDP 7460942
EMI / Mar '95 / EMI

JUMPIN' BLUES
Evergreenish / (I love you) for sentimental reasons / Star eyes / Rhythm-a-ning / If you could see me now / Jumpin' blues
CD _____ OJCCD 899
Original Jazz Classics / Sep '96 / Complete/ Pinnacle / Jazz Music / Wellard

LIVE AT THE AMSTERDAM PARADISO
Fried bananas / What's new / Good bait / Rhythm-a-ning / Willow weep for me / Junior / Scrapple from the apple / Closing announcement / Introduction
CD _____ LEJAZZCD 28
Le Jazz / Aug '94 / Cadillac / Koch

LONG TALL DEXTER
Blow Mr. Dexter / Dexter's deck / Dexter's cuttin' out / Dexter's minor mad / Long tall Dexter / Dexter rides again / I can't escape from you / Dexter digs in / Settin' the pace / So easy so easy / Dexter's riff / Dexter's mood / Dextrose index / Dextivity / Wee dot / Lion roars / After hours bop
CD _____ VGCD 650117
Vogue / Oct '93 / BMG

LULLABY OF BIRDLAND
CD _____ JHR 73556
Jazz Hour / Jan '93 / Cadillac / Jazz Music / Target/BMG

MORE THAN YOU KNOW
CD _____ SCCD 31030
Steeplechase / Jul '88 / Discovery / Impetus

OUR MAN IN PARIS
Scrapple from the apple / Willow weep for me / Stairway to the stars / Night in Tunisia / Our love is here to stay / Like someone to love / Broadway
CD _____ BNZ 34
Blue Note / Jun '87 / EMI

REVELATION (Gordon, Dexter & Benny Bailey)
CD _____ SCCD 31373
Steeplechase / May '96 / Discovery / Impetus

SOMETHING DIFFERENT
CD _____ SCCD 31136
Steeplechase / Jul '88 / Discovery / Impetus

STABLE MABLE (Gordon, Dexter Quartet)
CD _____ SCCD 31040
Steeplechase / Oct '90 / Discovery / Impetus

TAKE THE 'A' TRAIN
But not for me / Take the 'A' train / For all we know / Blues walk / I guess I'll hang my tears out to dry / Love for sale
CD _____ BLC 760133
Black Lion / Oct '94 / Cadillac / Jazz Music / Koch / Wellard

TOWER OF POWER
Montmartre / Rainbow people / Stanley the steamer / Those were the days
CD _____ OJCCD 299
Original Jazz Classics / Sep '93 / Complete/ Pinnacle / Jazz Music / Wellard

TOWER OF POWER AND MORE POWER, THE
Tower of power / Rainbow people / Stanley the steamer / Those were the days / More power / Ladybird / Meditation / Fried bananas / Boston Bernie / Sticky wicket
CD _____ CDJZD 004
Fantasy / Jan '91 / Jazz Music / Pinnacle / Wellard

WE THREE (Gordon, Dexter & Zoot Sims/Al Cohn)
CD _____ BCD 137
Biograph / Aug '95 / ADA / Cadillac / Direct / Hot Shot / Jazz Music / Wellard

Gordon, Frank

CLARION ECHOES
CD _____ SNCD 1096
Soul Note / '86 / Cadillac / Harmonia Mundi / Wellard

Gordon Highlanders

BAGPIPES AND DRUMS OF SCOTLAND, THE
CD _____ 15159
Laserlight / May '94 / Target/BMG

COCK 'O' THE NORTH
CD _____ BNA 5077
Bandleader / Jan '93 / Conifer/BMG

HOUR OF THE GORDON HIGHLANDERS, A
CD _____ CC 294
EMI / May '93 / EMI

MARCHES ECOSSAISES
CD _____ 824922
BUDA / Nov '90 / Discovery

Gordon, Jimmie

MISSISSIPPI MUDDER 1934-1941
CD _____ SOB 035182
Story Of The Blues / Feb '93 / ADA / Koch

Gordon, Joe

GORDON FAMILY, THE (Gordon, Joe & Sally Logan)
Rose of Allendale / Craigieburn woods / Band boys / Holy City / Wee toon clerk / Faraway land / Jig selection / Dark lochnagar / Medley of reels / Hunting tower / Bonnio gallows / Charness waltz / My ain folk / Dantesque / Darvol dam
CD _____ CDGR 142
Ross / Oct '92 / CM / Duncans / Highlander / Ross

JOE GORDON & SCOTT LA FARO (Gordon, Joe & Scott La Faro)
CD _____ FSCD 1030
Fresh Sound / Jan '93 / Discovery / Jazz Music

Gordon, Jon

JON GORDON QUARTET, THE (Gordon, Jon Quartet)
CD _____ CRD 316
Chiaroscuro / Mar '96 / Jazz Music

SPARK
CD _____ CRD 330
Chiaroscuro / Mar '96 / Jazz Music

Gordon, Michael

TRANCE
CD _____ 4524182
Argo / Nov '96 / PolyGram

YO SHAKESPEARE
CD _____ 4432142
Argo / Jan '95 / PolyGram

Gordon, Rob

COMPLETE CALEDONIAN BALL (Gordon, Rob & His Band)
Circassian circle / Brisk young lad / Byron strathspey / Saltire society reel / Hebridean weaving lilt / Johnnie Walker / Crammond Bridge / Silver star / Cumberland reel / New Scotia quadrille / Dundee whaler / Bannetstane / Lomond waltz / Angus reel / Belle of Bon Accord / Rab the ranter / C'est l'amour / Wind on Loch Fyne / Seton's ceilidh band / New petronella / Bonnie lass o'Bon Accord / Bank Street reel / Joe McDiarmid's jig / Broon's reel / Rothesay rant
CD Set _____ LCDM 8005
Lismor / Dec '88 / ADA / Direct / Duncans / Lismor

OLD TIME AND SEQUENCE BALL
Quadrilles (patience) / Flirtation / Chrysanthemum waltz / Silver wedding waltz / Mississippi dip / Dinkie one step / Ideal schottische / Ken and Cathy Jamieson Barn dance / Marine four step / Southern two step / Stanley and Vera Carson's polka / Swedish masquerade / Foxtrots and saunters / Moonlight saunter / Heather mixture polka / Waltz cotillion (half figure) / Lancers / Waltzmaree / Honeysuckle waltz
CD _____ LCDM 9014
Lismor / '89 / ADA / Direct / Duncans / Lismor

Gordon, Robert

ALL FOR THE LOVE OF ROCK 'N' ROLL
CD _____ 422506
New Rose / Mar '95 / ADA / Direct / Discovery

BLACK SLACKS
Summertime blues / I just found out / Boppin' the blues / Picture of you / I just met a memory / Am I blue / Walk on by / Blue Christmas / Fire / Twenty flight rock / But, but / Sea cruise / Bad boy / Red cadillac and a black moustache / Uptown / Five days, five days / Are you gonna be the one / Standing on the outside of her door / Loverboy / Take me back / Too fast to live, too young to die / Born to lose / Is it wrong / Torture / Black slacks (live)
CD _____ BCD 15489
Bear Family / Apr '90 / Direct / Rollercoaster / Swift

GREETINGS FROM NY CITY
CD _____ 422155
New Rose / Feb '97 / ADA / Direct / Discovery

LIVE AT THE LONE STAR
CD _____ 422156
New Rose / Feb '97 / ADA / Direct / Discovery

ROBERT GORDON IS RED HOT
Red hot / Fool / I sure miss you / Flyin' saucer rock 'n' roll / Way I walk / Lonesome train (on a lonesome track) / I want to be free / Rockabilly boogie / All by myself / Catman / Wheel of fortune / Love baby / It's only make believe / Crazy man crazy / Woryin' kind / Nervous / Sweet love on my mind / Need you / Someday, someway / Look who's blue / Drivin' wheel / Something's gonna happen / Fire / Black slacks
CD _____ BCD 15446
Bear Family / Apr '89 / Direct / Rollercoaster / Swift

ROBERT GORDON WITH LINK WRAY/ FRESH FISH SPECIAL (Gordon, Robert & Link Wray)
Red hot / I sure miss you / Summertime blues / Boppin' the blues / Sweet surrender / Flying saucers rock 'n' roll / Fool / It's in the bottle / Woman (you're my woman) / Is this the way / May I walk / Red cadillac and a black moustache / If this is wrong / Five days, five days / Fire / I want to be free / Twenty flight rock / Sea cruise / Lonesome train (on a lonesome track) / Blue eyes / Rock Billy boogie / Black slacks / Love my baby / All by myself / Nervous / Sweet love on my mind / Drivin' wheel / Someday someway / Fire (Live)
CD _____ RVCD 57
Raven / Mar '97 / ADA / Direct

ROBERT GORDON WITH LINK WRAY/ FRESH FISH SPECIAL (Gordon, Robert & Link Wray)
Red hot / I sure miss you / Summertime blues / Boppin' the blues / Sweet surrender / Flyin' saucer rock 'n' roll / Fool / It's in the bottle / Woman (you're my woman) / Is this the way / Way I walk / Red Cadillac and a black moustache / If this is wrong / Five days five days / Fire / I want to be free / Twenty flight rock / Sea cruise / Lonesome train (on a lonesome track) / Blue eyes (don't run away) / Endless sleep
CD _____ CDCHD 656
Ace / Jun '97 / Pinnacle

TOO FAST TO LIVE...TOO YOUNG TO DIE
Too fast to live...too young to die / Red hot / Are you gonna be the one / Black slacks / Crazy man / Born to lose / Way I walk / Love my baby / Uptown / Rock billy boogie / Red Cadillac / Woman / Am I blue / Drivin' wheel / All by myself / Sweet love on my mind / Bad boy / Fire / Twenty flight rock / Summertime blues / Lonesome train / Sea cruise / Boppin' the blues / Flying saucer rock 'n' roll / Fool / If this is wrong
CD _____ 74321500222
Camden / Jun '97 / BMG

Gordon, Rosco

ROSCO'S RHYTHM
T-model boogie / Decorate the counter / I wade through muddy water (dream on baby) / I love you better than I love myself / Just love me baby / Weeping blues / Do the chicken (dance with you) / Love for you baby / That's what you do to me / I found a new love / I don't like it / Hard headed woman / Shoobie oobie / Cheese and crackers / Real pretty Mama / Sally Jo / Torro / Do the bop / Nineteen years / Tired of living / If you don't love me baby / Love with me baby / Hey little girl / New Orleans LA
CD _____ CPCD 8273
Charly / Apr '97 / Koch

Gordon, Roxy

SMALLER CIRCLES
Smaller circles / Andrew Gray and the ghost / Long gone Texas woman / Murder / Indians / Gods / I dreamed I saw Joe Hill last night / Willie / Santa Fe freight / Bead Mountain, Valera / Texas eagle
CD _____ RGF/WOWCD 031
Road Goes On Forever / May '97 / Direct

Gordons

FIRST ALBUM AND FUTURE SHOCK
CD _____ FNE 16 CD
Flying Nun / '88 / RTM/Disc

Gore

CRUEL PLACE, THE
Breeding / Cruel place / Garden of evil / Death has come
CD _____ MD 7905CD
Megadisc / Apr '89 / Vital

LIFELONG DEADLINE
CD _____ MM1
Barooni / Mar '93 / Plastic Head / SRD

MEST/694'3
CD _____ MBMCD 07
Messback / Feb '97 / Cargo

Gore, Lesley

IT'S MY PARTY
Hello, young lovers / Something wonderful / It's my party / Danny / Party's over / Judy's turn to cry / Just let me cry / Misty / Cry me a river / I would / No more tears / Cry and you cry alone / I understand / Cry / Sunshine, lollipops, and rainbows / What kind of fool am I / If that's the way you want it / She's a fool / I'll make it up to you / Old crowd / I struck a match / Consolation prize / Run Bobby run / Young and foolsih / Fools rush in / My foolish heart / That's the way the ball bounces / After he takes me home (1 Voice) / After he takes me home (2 Voices) / You don't own me (Mono) / You don't own me (Stereo) / Time to go / You name it / That's the way boys are / Boys / I'm coolin', no foolin' / Don't deny it / I don't wanna be a loser / It's gotta be you / Leave me alone / Don't call me / Look of love / Wonder boy / Secret love / Maybe / Live and learn / Sometimes I wish I were a boy

/ Hey now / Died inside / Movin' away / It's about that time / Little girl go home / Say goodbye / You've come back / I just don't know if I can / That's the boy / All of my life / What's a girl supposed to do / Before and after / I cannot hope for anyone / I don't care / You didn't look around / Baby that's me / No matter what you do / Sunshine and lollipops / What am I gonna do with you / Girl in love / Just another fool / My town, my guy and me / Let me dream / Things we did last summer / Start the party again / I can tell / I won't love you anymore / I just can't get enough of you / Only last night / Any other girl / To know him is to love him / Young love / Too young / Will you still love me tomorrow / We know we're in love / Yeah yeah yeah that boy of mine / That's what I'll do / Lilacs and violets / Off and running / Happiness is just around the corner / Hold me tight / Cry like a baby / Treat me like a lady / Maybe now / Bubble broke / California nights / I'm going out the same way I came in / Bad / Love goes on forever / Summer and Sandy / I'm falling down / Brink of disaster / On a day like today / Where can I go / You sent me silver bells / He won't see the light / Magic colours / How can I be sure / To Sir with love / It's a happening world / Small talk / Say what you see / He gives me love (La la la) / Brand new me / I can't make it without you / Look the other way / Take good care (Of my heart) / I'll be standing by / Ride a tall white horse / 98.6 / Summer symphony / All cried out / One by one / Wedding bell blues / Got to get you into my life / Goodbye Tony (You don't own me) / Musikant (Time to go) / So sind die boys alle / Nur du allein / Hab ich das verdient / Der erste tanz / Little little liebling / Sieben girls / Tu t'en vas / Je ne sais plus / Je n'ose pas / Si ton coeur le desire / Je sais qu'en jour / C'est trop tard / Eh non / Te voila / Judy's turn to cry (Italian) / You don't own me (Italian) / Lazy day
CD Set ____ **BCD 15742**
Bear Family / Jun '94 / Direct / Rollercoaster / Swift

IT'S MY PARTY (The Mercury Anthology)
Hello young lover / It's my party / Judy's turn to cry / Judy let me cry / Sunshine, lollipops and rainbows / If that's the way you want it / She's a fool / Old crowd / Consolation prize / Run Bobby run / That's the way the ball bounces / After he takes me home / You don't own me / That's the way boys are / I'm coolin', no foolin' / I don't wanna be a loser / Don't call me, I'll call you / Look of love / Wonder boy / Maybe I know / Sometimes I wish I were a boy / Hey now / Movin' away / Little girl go home / I just don't know if I can / All of my life
CD ____ **5325172**
Mercury / Oct '96 / PolyGram

START THE PARTY AGAIN
CD ____ **RVCD 31**
Raven / Jan '94 / ADA / Direct

Gore, Martin L

COUNTERFEIT
Compulsion / In a manner of speaking / Smile in the crowd / Gone / Never turn your back on mother earth / Motherless child
CD ____ **CDSTUMM 67**
Mute / Apr '89 / RTM/Disc

Gore Slut

THESE DAYS ARE THE QUIET KIND
CD ____ **PSYCHOBABBLE 008**
Stickman / Jun '97 / Cargo / Pinnacle

Gorefest

EINDHOVEN INSANITY
CD ____ **NB 091**
Nuclear Blast / Aug '93 / Plastic Head

ERASE
CD ____ **NB 231CD**
Nuclear Blast / Apr '97 / Plastic Head

MINDLOSS
CD ____ **NB 086**
Nuclear Blast / Aug '93 / Plastic Head

SOUL SURVIVOR
CD ____ **NB 143CD**
Nuclear Blast / Apr '96 / Plastic Head

Gorgoroth

ANTICHRIST
CD ____ **MR 008CD**
Malicious / May '96 / Plastic Head

PENTAGRAM
CD ____ **TE 001CD**
Embassy / Oct '94 / Plastic Head
CD ____ **MR 007CD**
Malicious / Apr '96 / Plastic Head

Gories

HOUSEROCKIN
CD ____ **EFA 11577 2**
Crypt / Sep '94 / Shellshock/Disc

Gorilla Biscuits

START TODAY
New direction / Degradation / Forgotten / Start today / First failure / Time flies / Stand still / Good intentions / Things we say / Two sides / Competition / Cats and dogs
CD ____ **WB 054CD**
We Bite / Nov '89 / Plastic Head

Gorillas

MESSAGE TO THE WORLD
CD ____ **DAMGOOD 49**
Damaged Goods / Nov '94 / Shellshock/ Disc

Gorka, John

I KNOW
CD ____ **RHRCD 18**
Red House / Jul '95 / ADA / Koch

OUT OF THE VALLEY
Good noise / That's why / Carnival knowledge / Talk about love / Big time lonesome / Furniture / Mystery to me / Out of the valley / Thoughtless behaviour / Always going home / Flying red horse / Up until then
CD ____ **72902103252**
High Street / Aug '94 / BMG

TEMPORARY ROAD
CD ____ **72902103152**
High Street / Jan '95 / BMG

Gorky's Zygotic Mynci

BARAFUNDLE
Diamond dew / Barafundle bumbler / Starmoonsun / Patio song / Better rooms / Heywood lane / Pen gwag glas / Bola bola / Cursed, coined and crucified / Sometimes the father is the son / Meirion wyllt / Wizard and the lizard / Miniature kingdoms / Dark night / Hwyl fawr I pawb / Wordless song
CD ____ **5347692**
Fontana / Apr '97 / PolyGram

BWYD TIME
CD ____ **ANKST 059CD**
Ankst / Apr '97 / Shellshock/Disc

INTRODUCING
CD ____ **5328162**
Fontana / Sep '96 / PolyGram

MERCHED
CD ____ **ANKST 048CD**
Ankst / Apr '97 / Shellshock/Disc

PATIO
CD ____ **ANKSTCD 055**
Ankst / Apr '97 / Shellshock/Disc

TATAY
CD ____ **ANKST 47CD**
Ankst / Apr '97 / Shellshock/Disc

Gorl, Robert

ELEKTRO (Gorl, Robert & Pete Namlock)
CD ____ **PK 08109**
Fax / Mar '96 / Plastic Head

WATCH THE REAL COPYCAT
CD ____ **EFA 122922**
Disko B / Sep '96 / SRD

Gorman, Skip

GREENER PRAIRIE, A
CD ____ **ROUCD 0329**
Rounder / Oct '94 / ADA / CM / Direct

LONESOME PRAIRIE LOVE
CD ____ **ROUCD 359**
Rounder / May '96 / ADA / CM / Direct

Gorme, Eydie

20 LOVE SONGS
CD ____ **RMB 75025**
Remember / Jan '92 / Total/BMG

EYDIE GORME COLLECTOR'S EDITION
CD ____ **DVAD 6052**
Deja Vu / Apr '95 / THE

Y LOS PANCHOS
Sabras que te quiero / Dime / Esta tarde vi lover / Eres tu / Nosotros / Piel canela / Y... / Sabor a mi / Quiereme mucho / Noche de ronda / Caminito / Since I fell for you / Breaking up is hard to do / You're nobody till somebody loves you
CD ____ **CD 62101**
Saludos Amigos / Oct '96 / Target/BMG

Gospel Hummingbirds

TAKING FLIGHT
CD ____ **BPCD 5023**
Blind Pig / Dec '95 / ADA / CM / Direct / Hot Shot

Gospel Messengers

YOU CAN LEAN ON ME
CD ____ **INAK 9040**
In Akustik / Feb '97 / Direct / TKO Magnum

Gospel Of The Horns

SATANISTS DREAM
CD ____ **ENSTD 001MCD**
Polyphemus / Jul '96 / Plastic Head

Gospel Voices

MAGIC GOSPEL
Wi se Lanmou (Oh happy day) / Operator / Gat away Jordan / This little light of mine / Lord I want to be a Christian / Joshua fit the battle of Jericho / Louez-Le / Freedom / Praise him / I want to be ready / Thank you Lord / When the saints
CD ____ **19136**
Forlane / Jan '97 / Target/BMG

Gospellers

WE'VE GOT THE POWER
CD ____ **VSCD 100**
Vision UK / Dec '95 / Jet Star

Goss, Kieran

BRAND NEW STAR
CD ____ **DARA 3047**
Dara / Aug '97 / ADA / CM / Direct / Else / Grapevine/PolyGram

NEW DAY
CD ____ **DARA 3064**
Dara / Aug '97 / ADA / CM / Direct / Else / Grapevine/PolyGram

Gostanzo, Sonny

SONNY'S ON THE MONEY
CD ____ **STCD 555**
Stash / Jan '93 / ADA / Cadillac / CM / Direct / Jazz Music

Gota

IT'S SO DIFFERENT HERE
CD ____ **EX 3472**
Instinct / Feb '97 / Cargo

Gotham Gospel

BEST OF GOTHAM GOSPEL
Harmonizing four / Dixie hummingbird / Echo gospel singers / Edna Gallmon Cook / Zion harmonizers / Harmony kings / Rugged cross singers
CD ____ **HTCD 04**
Heritage / Oct '90 / ADA / Direct / Hot Shot / Jazz Music / Swift / Wellard

Gottlieb, Danny

NEW AGE OF CHRISTMAS
CD ____ **7567820542**
Atlantic / Jul '93 / Warner Music

Gottsching, Manuel

E2 E4
CD ____ **14241**
Spalax / Oct '96 / ADA / Cargo / Direct / Discovery / Greyhound

Goubert, Simon

HAITI
CD ____ **A 7**
Seventh / Apr '93 / Cadillac / Harmonia Mundi / ReR Megacorp

L'ENCIERRO
CD ____ **A XVIII**
Seventh / Dec '95 / Cadillac / Harmonia Mundi / ReR Megacorp

Goudreau, Barry

BARRY GOUDREAU
Hard luck / Nothin' to lose / What's a fella to do / Mean woman blues / Leavin' tonight / Dreams / Life is what you make it / Sailin' away / Cold cold wind
CD ____ **RE 21042**
Razor & Tie / Jul '96 / Koch

Gouds Thumb

GOUDS THUMB
Together / 29 / Tangerine / Beautiful local / Chemicals / Trophies / Piss pool / Apnea / El Campeon Macizo / Bottom feeder / Manny / Jesus arms / Anea electric
CD ____ **RR 88062**
Roadrunner / Jul '97 / PolyGram

Gough, Orlando

MESSAGE FROM THE BORDER
Saeta / Late / Currulao
CD ____ **09026683322**
Catalyst / Oct '96 / BMG

Goulder, Dave

STONE, STEAM AND STARLINGS
Clearing place / Carter / Stone on stone / These dry stone walls / Go from my window / Proper little gent / Colours / Seven summers / Friar in the well / Sally gardens / Follower / I will go with my father / Footplate cuisine
CD ____ **HARCD 017**
Harbour Town / Oct '93 / ADA / CM / Direct / Roots

Gouldman, Graham

GRAHAM GOULDMAN THING, THE
CD ____ **EDCD 346**
Edsel / Apr '92 / Pinnacle

Goulesco, Lido

CHANTS FOLKLORIQUES TZIGANES
CD ____ **824412**
BUDA / Nov '90 / Discovery

Goulet, Robert

ROBERT GOULET
CD ____ **DVAD 6102**
Deja Vu / May '95 / THE

Gourds

DEM'S GOOD BEEBIE
Piss and moan blues / Caledonia / Dying of the pines / Jenny Brown / Clear night / Sweet Lil / When wine was cheap / Money honey / Honduras / Ringing dark and true / Pine tar ramparts / Makes me roll / Trampled by the sun / Web before you walk into it / I come up / All the labour
CD ____ **MUSA 501**
Munich / Feb '97 / ADA / CM / Direct / Greensleeves

Gourlay, James

GOURLAY PLAYS TUBA (Gourlay, James & The Britannia Building Society Band)
CD ____ **DOYCD 028**
Doyen / Apr '94 / Conifer/BMG

Gourley, Jimmy

GOOD NEWS
CD ____ **BL 007**
Bloomdido / Oct '93 / Cadillac

Gouzil, Denis

LE P'TIT GROUILLOT QUI DANSE (Gouzil, Denis Groupe)
CD ____ **EPC 885**
European Music Production / Feb '92 / Harmonia Mundi

Government Issue

CRASH
CD ____ **WB 042CD**
We Bite / Dec '88 / Plastic Head

FINALE
CD ____ **LF 012CD**
Lost & Found / Apr '92 / Plastic Head

MAKE AN EFFORT
CD ____ **LF 114CD**
Lost & Found / Oct '94 / Plastic Head

YOU
CD ____ **WB 3041CD**
We Bite / Sep '93 / Plastic Head

Gowen, Alan

IMPROVISATIONS (Gowen, Alan & Hugh Hopper)
Floating path / Now what exactly / Zaparoshti / Ranova / Al'Quest / Winged trilby / Six cream bombs from Beaune / Rubber daze
CD ____ **BP 186CD**
Blueprint / Jul '97 / Pinnacle

Gowen, Miller & Sinclair

BEFORE A WORD IS SAID
Above and below / Reflexes in the margin / Nowadays a silhouette / Silver star / Fourfold / Before a word is said / Umbrellas / Fleeting glance
CD ____ **BP 130CD**
Blueprint / Sep '96 / Pinnacle

Goya Dress

ROOMS
CD ____ **NUDE 5CD**
Nude / May '96 / 3mv/Vital

Goyeneche, Roberto

TANGOS DEL SUR (Goyeneche, Roberto & Nestor Marconi)
CD ____ **883289**
Milan Sur / Feb '97 / Conifer/BMG

Goykovich, Dusko

BALKAN BLUE (2CD Set)
Simona / Yardbird suite / Medium rare / Adriatica / You've changed / Miss Bo / Nights of Skopje / Snap shot / You'd be so nice / Balkan dance / Bosna calling / Pannonia / East of Montenegro / Macedonia / Schumakya / Haze on the Danube / Ohrid / Finale
CD Set ____ **ENJ 932022**
Enja / Sep '97 / New Note/Pinnacle / Vital/ SAM

BALKAN CONNECTION
Doboy / You're my everything / Bopper / Manhattan mood / Balkan blue / You don't know what love is / Handful of soul / Why not you / Nights of skopje / Nella

CD ENJ 90472
Enja / Aug '96 / New Note/Pinnacle / Vital/ SAM

BEBOP CITY
Sunrise in St. Petersburg / In the sign of Libra / Be bop city / Lament / Bop town / No love without tears / One for klook / Day by day / Brooklyn blues
CD ENJ 90152
Enja / Jul '95 / New Note/Pinnacle / Vital/ SAM

BELGRADE BLUES
CD HHCD 1008
Hot House / Jan '91 / Cadillac / Harmonia Mundi / Wellard

SOUL CONNECTION
Soul connection / Ballad for miles / Inga / I'll close my eyes / Blues time / Adriatica / NYC / Blues valse / Teamwork song
CD ENJ 80442
Enja / Mar '94 / New Note/Pinnacle / Vital/ SAM

Goz Of Kermeur

IRONDELLES
CD CDRECDE 61
ReR/Recommended / Apr '94 / ReR Megacorp / RTM/Disc

Gozategi

GOZATEGI
CD KDCD 405
Elkar / May '97 / ADA

GP's

SATURDAY ROLLING AROUND
CD HTDCD 53
HTD / Mar '96 / CM / Pinnacle

Graae, Jason

YOU'RE NEVER FULLY DRESSED WITHOUT A SMILE
CD VSD 5711
Varese Sarabande / Oct '96 / Pinnacle

Grabbers

HAND YOU'RE DEALT, THE
CD F 021CD
Fearless / Apr '97 / Cargo / Plastic Head

Grabham, Mick

MICK THE LAD
Sweet blossom woman / Scraunchy / You'll think of me / I won't be there / Waitin' round on you / There's ben a few since then / Let it all down / Two fifteen / Saga / On fire for you baby / Diamonds / Hit and miss / Wanderer
CD SJPCD 012
Angel Air / Jul '97 / Pinnacle

Grable, Betty

PIN UP GIRL, THE (2CD Set)
Cowboy number / Snake dance / Let's k-nock k-nees / Music in my heart / Boys will be boys / What goes on here in my heart / Down Argentine way / Two dreams met / Hawaii-A / Sheik of Araby / You started something / Loveliness and love / Kindergarten conga / Hi ya love / Another little dream wouldn't do us any harm / Are you kidding / I'm still crazy for you / I heard the birdies sing / Sing me a song of the islands / Down on Ami Ami Oni Oni Isle / O'Brien has gone Hawaiian / Run little raindrop run / Pan American jubilee / Cuddle up a little closer / Pretty baby / Miss Lulu from Louisville / Take it from there / Beautiful Coney Island / There's danger in a dance / Waiting at the church / My heart tells me / Sweet Rosie O'Grady / Going to the County Fair / You're my little pin up girl / Don't carry tales out of school / Once too often / Song of the very merry widow / Welcome to the Diamond Horseshoe / In Acapulco / Medley / Cooking up a show/The more I see you / Vamp / We have been around/Carolina in the morning / Powder, lipstick and rouge / I'm always chasing rainbows / Darktown strutter's ball / I can't begin to tell you
CD Set JASCD 1034
Jasmine / Apr '97 / Conifer/BMG / Hot Shot / TKO Magnum

Grace

IF I COULD FLY
Not over yet / Down to earth / If I could fly / One day / You don't know / Orange / Love songs / You're not mine / Mineral / Skin on skin / I want to live
CD 0630149472
Perfecto/East West / Jul '97 / Warner Music

Grace

POPPY
CD CYCL 044
Cyclops / Nov '96 / Pinnacle

PULLING STRINGS & SHINY THINGS
Fool / Lean on me / Earth bites back / Every cloud has a silver lining / Architecht of war / Hanging Rock / Gift
CD CYCL 002
Cyclops / Feb '94 / Pinnacle

Grace, Teddy

TEDDY GRACE 1937-40
I've taken a fancy to you / Oh Daddy blues / I'll never let you cry / You don't know my mind / Goodbye Jonah / Low down blues / Ears in my heart / Graveyard blues / Love me or leave me / Hey lawdy Papa / Crazy blues / Mama doo-shee (blues) / Monday morning / Gee but I hate to go home alone / Betty and Dupree / Sing (It's good for ya) / Arkansas blues / See what the boys in the backroom will have / Down home blues / Gulf coast blues / I'm the lonesomest gal in town
CD CBC 1016
Chris Barber Collection / Nov '93 / Cadillac / New Note/Pinnacle

TURN ON THAT RED HOT HEAT
Rockin' chair swing / Turn off the moon / I want a new romance / I'm losing my mind over you / Over the rainbow / I've got rain in my eyes / Turn on that red hot heat / Rock it for me / I'm so in love / I thought about you
CD HEPCD 1054
Hep / Jun '97 / Cadillac / Jazz Music / New Note/Pinnacle / Wellard

Gracenotes

DOWN FALLS THE DAY
CD GN 001CD
Gracenotes / Jan '94 / ADA

Gracie, Charlie

IT'S FABULOUS
CD CTCD 2
Stomper Time / May '95 / TKO Magnum

Graciela

CON MACHITO Y SU ORQUESTA
CD ALCD 020
Alma Latina / Jul '96 / Discovery

Gracious

ECHO
Echo / Winter / Homecoming / Cynic's gate / Autumn / Mangroove / Summer / Faith / Spring / Oil pressure
CD CENCD 015
Centaur / Mar '96 / Pinnacle

GRACIOUS/THIS IS GRACIOUS
Introduction / Hell / Dream / Blood red sun / Prepare to meet thy maker / What's come to be / Hold me down / Heaven / Fugue in D minor / Supernova / Arrival of the traveller / Say goodbye to love / CBS / Blue skies and alibis
CD BGOCD 256
Beat Goes On / Feb '95 / Pinnacle

Grady Cain

FACES OF CAIN
CD INF 80005CD
Infinity / Nov '96 / Plastic Head

Graewe, Georg

1995 SAN FRANCISCO CONCERT, THE
10.38 / 4.30 / 5.00 / 4.05 / 7.20 / 4.50 / 3.00
CD CD 968
Music & Arts / Jun '97 / Cadillac / Harmonia Mundi

SATURN CYCLE
CD CD 958
Music & Arts / Dec '96 / Cadillac / Harmonia Mundi

Graf, Bob

BOB GRAF AT WESTMINSTER
Bernie's tune / Street of dreams / Dear old Stockholm / Funky ride / Four
CD DE 401
Delmark / Mar '97 / ADA / Cadillac / CM / Direct / Hot Shot

Graff, Randy

DOING SOMETHING RIGHT
CD VSD 5652
Varese Sarabande / Aug '96 / Pinnacle

Graham Central Station

AIN'T NO BOUT A DOUBT IT
Jam / Your love / It's alright / I can't stand the rain / Ain't nothing but a Warner Brothers party / Ole Smokey / Easy rider / Water luckiest people
CD 7599263462
WEA / Jan '96 / Warner Music

GRAHAM CENTRAL STATION
We've been waiting / It ain't no fun to me / Hair / We be's getting down / Tell me what it is / Can you handle it / People / Why / Ghetto
CD 7599263392
WEA / Jan '96 / Warner Music

MIRROR
Entrow / Save me / Mirror / Do yah / Love / Forever / I got a reason / Priscilla
CD 7599263472
Warner Bros. / Jan '96 / Warner Music

RELEASE YOURSELF
GCS / Release yourself / Got to go through it to get to it / 'Tis your kind of music / Feel the need (in me) / Hey Mr. Writer / Today / I believe in you
CD 7599263522
Warner Bros. / Jan '96 / Warner Music

Graham, Davey

FOLK BLUES AND ALL POINTS IN BETWEEN
Leaving blues / Cocaine / Rock me baby / Moanin' / Skillet / Ain't nobody's business if I do / Maajun / I can't keep from crying sometimes / Going down slow / Better git it in your soul / Freight train blues / Both sides now / No preacher blues / Bad boy blues / I'm ready / Hoochie coochie man / Blue raga
CD SEECD 48
See For Miles/C5 / May '90 / Pinnacle

GUITAR PLAYER...PLUS, THE
Don't stop the carnival / Sermonette / Take five / How long blues / Sunset eyes / Cry me a river / Angie / 3/4 AD / Ruby and the pearl / Buffalo / Exodus / Yellow bird / Blues for Betty / Hallelujah, I love her so / Davy's train blues
CD SEECD 351
See For Miles/C5 / Jun '92 / Pinnacle

Graham, David

VERY THOUGHT OF YOU, THE
West side story / Jumpin' Charlie / Slow foxtrot / Bossa nova / Let it be me / Quickstep / Love changes everything / Tango Havana / Miranda's theme / Swingin' shepherd blues / Ave Maria
CD OS 216
OS Digital / Nov '95 / Conifer/BMG

Graham, Larry

BEST OF LARRY GRAHAM & GRAHAM CENTRAL STATION
CD 9362460432
WEA / Apr '96 / Warner Music

Graham, Len

DO ME JUSTICE
CD CC 37CD
Claddagh / Dec '94 / ADA / CM / Direct

YE LOVERS ALL
CD CC 41CD
Claddagh / Dec '94 / ADA / CM / Direct

Graham, Tammy

TAMMY GRAHAM
CD 7822188422
MCA / Jul '97 / BMG

Graham-White, Susan

NOT AFRAID TO FLY
CD BLX 10029CD
Blix Street / Aug '96 / ADA

Grainger, Porter

PORTER GRAINGER 1923-1929
CD JPCD 1521
Jazz Perspectives / Jul '96 / Hot Shot / Jazz Music

Grainger, Richard

THUNDERWOOD
Silent spring / Old Whitby town / Golden Grove/Mallaig moorings / Northern town bay / Foxhunting song / Streets of Kings Cross / Mermaid / Polly on the shore / Glasgow wedding/Far from home / Grove fisherman / Ghost of Old Solem / From Mulgrave to Eskside / Thunderwood
CD FSCD 27
Folksound / Aug '94 / CM / Roots

Gramm, Lou

FOREIGNER IN A STRANGE LAND
Won't somebody take her home / Don't you know me, my friend / Better know your heart / I can't make it alone / How do you tell someone / Society's child / I wish today was yesterday / My baby / Headin' home / Watch you walk away
CD CDTB 065
Thunderbolt / '88 / TKO Magnum

Grampian Police Pipe Band

PIPES AND DRUMS
CD EUCD 1261
ARC / Mar '94 / ADA / ARC Music

Grand Dominion Jazz Band

GRAND DOMINION JAZZBAND VOL.2
CD SOSCD 1268
Stomp Off / Oct '93 / Jazz Music / Wellard

Grand Luxe

GRAND LUXE
CD 3031732
Village Vert / Jul '97 / Cargo

Grand, Otis

ALWAYS HOT (Grand, Otis & The Dance Kings)
CD SPCD 1019
Special Delivery / Oct '88 / ADA / CM / Direct

ALWAYS HOT (Grand, Otis & The Dance Kings)
Love at first sight / Woke up this morning / Fix our love / Always hot / Shame shame shame / Whole lotta lovin' / Rebecca / Don't know why / Let's party / No alibi
CD IGOXCD 505
Indigo / Feb '97 / ADA / Direct

HE KNOWS THE BLUES
Things are getting harder to do / You hurt me / Jumpin' for Jimmy / Grand style / Real gone lover / SRV (My mood too) / Leave that girl / Ham / Your love pulls no punches / Swing turn / Teach me how to love you / He knows the blues
CD NEX CD 219
Sequel / Jul '92 / BMG

NOTHING ELSE MATTERS
CD NEXCD 272
Sequel / Sep '94 / BMG

PERFUME & GRIME
Six ways (Pam's tune) / How come / Don't ask why / Magic mood / Knock knock / Between heaven & hell / Perfume & grime / Just one more time / 100 years / She's got my dog / When my heart beats like a hammer / It took a long time / Has been husband / Grime time
CD NEGCD 282
Sequel / Aug '96 / BMG

Grand Puba

2000
Very special / I like it (I wanna be where you are) / Keep on / Little of this / Amazing / Play it cool / Change gonna come / Playin' the game / Don't waste my time / 2000 / Back stabbers
CD 7559616192
Elektra / Jun '95 / Warner Music

REEL TO REEL
Check tha resume / 360 degrees (what goes around) / That's how we move it / Check it out / Big kids don't play / Honey don't front / Lick shot / Ya know how it goes / Reel to reel / Soul controller / Proper education / Back it up / Baby what's your name
CD 7559613142
Elektra / Dec '96 / Warner Music

Grand Theft

HIKING INTO ETERNITY
CD EPI 004
Epilogue / May '97 / Greyhound

Grandjean, Etienne

ACCORDEON DIATONIQUE AND VIOLON
CD GRI 190822
Griffe / Sep '96 / ADA / Discovery

CIRCUS VALSE
CD CD 842
Diffusion Breizh / May '93 / ADA

LA BELLE SOCIETE
CD BPCD 9391
Boucherie Productions / May '97 / ADA

Grandmaster Flash

GRANDMASTER FLASH VS. THE SUGARHILL GANG (2CD Set) (Grandmaster Flash & The Sugarhill Gang)
CD Set SMDCD 164
Snapper / Jul '97 / Pinnacle

GREATEST HITS (Grandmaster Flash & Melle Mel)
White lines (don't don't do it) / Step off / Pump me up / Jesse / Beat street / Vice / Freedom / Birthday party / Flash to the beat / It's nasty (genius of love) / Message / Scorpio / Message II (survival) / New York, New York
CD NEMCD 622
Sequel / May '92 / BMG

MORE HITS (Grandmaster Flash & The Furious Five)
Adventures of Grandmaster Flash on the wheels of steel / Message / Showdown / She's fresh / It's a shame / White lines / World war III / Hustlers convention / King of the streets / Super rappin' no.1 / New adventures of Grandmaster
CD DEEPM 004
Deep Beats / Nov '96 / BMG

ON THE STRENGTH (Grandmaster Flash & The Furious Five)
Gold / Cold in effect / Yo baby / On the strength / King / Fly girl / Magic carpet ride / Leave here / This is where you got it from / Boy is dope / Back in the old days of hip-hop
CD 7559607692
Elektra / Jan '97 / Warner Music

Grandmothers

DREAMS IN LONG PLAY
CD ______ CD 986970
Intercord / Aug '93 / Plastic Head

DREAMS ON LONGPLAY
CD ______ EFAO 34032
Muffin / Apr '95 / SRD

WHO COULD IMAGINE
CD ______ NETCD 53
Network / Nov '94 / Direct / Greensleeves / SRD

Granelli, Jerry

BROKEN CIRCLE
Sign 'o' the times / Red and blue days / Washing of the water / From far away / Boogie stop shuffle / Lonnie's lament/Song of a good name / Crazy Horse's dream / Holy road / Broken circle / Dream horse leaving / Wounded knee / Crazy Horse's dream (reprise)
CD ______ INT 35012
Intuition / Sep '96 / New Note/Pinnacle

FORCES OF FLIGHT
CD ______ ITMP 970061
ITM / Apr '93 / Koch / Tradelink

KOPUTAI
Koputai / Pillars / Haiku / I could see forever / Julia's child / In the moment
CD ______ ITMP 970058
ITM / Jan '94 / Koch / Tradelink

Graney, Dave

MY LIFE ON THE PLAINS
CD ______ FIRE 33020
Fire / Oct '91 / Pinnacle / RTM/Disc

NIGHT OF THE WOLVERINE
CD ______ 5321292
This Way Up / May '96 / PolyGram / SRD

SOFT 'N' SEXY SOUND, THE
CD ______ 5284162
This Way Up / Sep '96 / PolyGram / SRD

SOFT 'N' SEXY SOUND/1001 AUSTRALIAN NIGHTS (2CD Set)
Birds and the goats / I'm gonna live in my own big world / Apollo 69 / I'm not afraid to be heavy / Deep inside a song / Pre-revolutionary scene / Rock 'n' roll is where I hide / Salty girls / Outward bound / Scorched earth love affair / Morrison floorshow / Dandies are never unbuttoned / Night of the wolverine / You wanna be loved / You're just too hip, baby / I'm gonna live in my own big world / Birds and the goats / I'm not afraid to be heavy / Deep inside a song / Scorched earth love affair / Rock 'n' roll is where I hide
CD Set ______ 5340592
This Way Up / Sep '96 / PolyGram / SRD

Granger

UNDERWATER HUM
CD ______ SH 5712
Shanachie / Oct '96 / ADA / Greensleeves / Koch

Grant, Amy

AGE TO AGE
In a little while / I have decided / I love a lonely day / Don't run away / Fat baby / Sing your praises to the Lord / El-Shaddai / Raining on the inside / Got to let it go / Arms of love
CD ______ MYRCD 6697
Myrrh / '88 / Nelson Word

AMY GRANT
CD ______ MYRCD 6586
Myrrh / '88 / Nelson Word

AMY GRANT IN CONCERT VOL.1
CD ______ MYRCD 6668
Myrrh / '88 / Nelson Word

AMY GRANT IN CONCERT VOL.2
CD ______ MYRCD 6677
Myrrh / '88 / Nelson Word

BEHIND THE EYES
CD ______ 5407602
A&M / Sep '97 / PolyGram

CHRISTMAS ALBUM, A
Tennessee Christmas / Hark the herald angels sing / Preiset dem Konig (Praise the King) / Emmanuel / Little town / Christmas hymn / Love has come / Sleigh ride / Christmas song / Heirlooms / Mighty fortress / Angels we have heard on high
CD ______ MYRCD 6768
Myrrh / '88 / Nelson Word

FATHER'S EYES
CD ______ MYRCD 6625
Myrrh / '88 / Nelson Word

HEART IN MOTION
Good for me / Baby baby / Every heartbeat / That's the way love is / Ask me / Galileo / You're not alone / Hats / I will remember you / How can we see that far / Hopes set high
CD ______ 3953212
A&M / Apr '91 / PolyGram

HEART IN MOTION/LEAD ME ON (2CD Set)
CD Set ______ CDA 24123
A&M / Jul '94 / PolyGram

HOME FOR CHRISTMAS
Have yourself a merry little Christmas / It's the most wonderful time of the year / Joy to the world / Breath of heaven (Mary's song) / O'come all ye faithful / Grown up Christmas list / Rockin' around the Christmas tree / Winter wonderland / I'll be home for Christmas / Night before Christmas / Emmanuel, God with us / Jesu joy of man's desiring
CD ______ 5400012
A&M / Nov '95 / PolyGram

HOUSE OF LOVE
Lucky one / Say you'll be mine / Whatever it takes / House of love / Power / Oh how the years go by / Big yellow taxi / Helping hand / Politics of kissing / Love has a hold on me / Our love / Children of the world
CD ______ 5402882
A&M / Jul '95 / PolyGram

NEVER ALONE
Look what has happened to me / So glad / Walking away with you / Family / Don't give up on me / That's the day / If I have to die / All I ever have to be / It's a miracle / Too late / First love / Say once more
CD ______ MYRCD 6645
Myrrh / '88 / Nelson Word

STRAIGHT AHEAD
CD ______ MYRCD 6757
Myrrh / '88 / Nelson Word

UNGUARDED
Love of another kind / Find a way / Everywhere I go / I love you / Stepping in your shoes / Fight / Wise up / Who to listen to / Sharayah / Prodigal
CD ______ MYRCD 6806
Myrrh / '88 / Nelson Word

Grant, Darrell

BLACK ART
CD ______ CRISS 1987CD
Criss Cross / Sep '95 / Cadillac / Direct / Vital/SAM

NEW BOP, THE
CD ______ CRISS 1106
Criss Cross / Dec '95 / Cadillac / Direct / Vital/SAM

Grant, David

VERY BEST OF DAVID GRANT & JAKI GRAHAM, THE (Grant, David & Jaki Graham)
Could it be I'm falling in love / Round and around / Set me free / Turn around / Rock the midnight / So excited / Love me tonight / Heaven knows / Mated / Watching you watching me / Love will find a way / Step right up / Facts of love / Stop and go / Breaking away / Where our love begins
CD ______ CDGOLD 1033
EMI Gold / May '96 / EMI

Grant, Della

BLACK ROSE
CD ______ RG 5803
Twinkle / Feb '95 / Jet Star / Kingdom / SRD

DAWTA OF THE DUST
CD ______ RGCD 5804
Twinkle / Oct '95 / Jet Star / Kingdom / SRD

ROOTICALLY YOURS
CD ______ NGCD 542
Twinkle / Feb '94 / Jet Star / Kingdom / SRD

Grant, Eddy

BEST OF EDDY GRANT, THE
I don't wanna dance / Gimme hope Jo'anna / Electric Avenue / Walking on sunshine / Do you feel my love / Symphony for Michael opus 2 / Living on the front line / Front line symphony / Can't get enough of you / Neighbour, neighbour / I love you, yes I love you / It's our time / Romancing the stone / Till I can't take love no more / War party / Say I love you
CD ______ CDMFP 6203
Music For Pleasure / Nov '95 / EMI

BEST OF EDDY GRANT, THE
CD ______ DC 866122
Disky / Mar '96 / Disky / THE

FILE UNDER ROCK
Harmless piece of fun / Don't talk to strangers / Hostile country / Win or lose / Gimme hope Jo'Anna / Another riot / Say hello to Fidel / Chuck (is the king) / Long as I'm wanted by you / Put a hold on it
CD ______ CDFA 3232
Fame / Aug '89 / EMI

GOING FOR BROKE
Romancing the stone / Boys in the street / Come on let me know / Till I can't take love no more / Political bassa bassa / Telepathy / Only heaven knows / Irie Harry / Rock you good / Blue wave
CD ______ 920412
Ice / Jun '92 / Jet Star / Pinnacle

GREATEST HITS
I don't wanna dance / Gimme hope Joanna / Electric Avenue / Walking on sunshine / Do you feel my love / Symphony for Michael Opus / Living on the front line / Front line symphony / I can't get enough of you / Neighbour, neighbour / I love you, yes I love you / It's our time / Romancing the stone / Till I can't take love no more / War party / Say I love you
CD ______ CDGOLD 1061
EMI Gold / Oct '96 / EMI

PAINTINGS OF THE SOUL
CD ______ 90202
Ice / Mar '92 / Jet Star / Pinnacle

Grant, Gogi

SUDDENLY THERE'S...
CD ______ PS 014CD
P&S / Feb '97 / Discovery

Grant, Isla

LIFE'S STORYBOOK COVER
Listen to the childern / It's been a long time / Mothers chair / God please forgive me / Mother / Keeper of my heart / Life's storybook cover / Ghosts of Culloden / There's nothing new - I'm missing you / Like leaves in the wind / Cottage in the country / Dark, deep, rolling water / Scotland you are in my heart forever / Precious Lord - please lead me / Till the day that he met you / My homeland
CD ______ CDELM 4100
ELM / Nov '96 / Duncans

Grant, Julie

YOU CAN COUNT ON ME
Somebody tell him / Every letter you write / So many ways / Unimportant things / When you're smiling / Lonely sixteen / Up on the roof / When you ask about love / Count on me / Then only then / That's how heartaches are made / Cruel world / Don't ever let me down / Somebody cares / Hello love / It's alright / Every day I have to cry / What what you do with my baby / You're nobody 'til somebody loves you / I only care about you / Come to me / Can't get you out of my mind / Baby baby / My world is empty without you / Giving up / 'Cause I believe in you / Lonely without you / As long as I know he's mine / Stop / When the loving ends
CD ______ RPM 133
RPM / Aug '94 / Pinnacle

Grant Lee Buffalo

COPPEROPOLIS
Homespun / Bridge / Arousing thunder / Even the oxen / Crackdown / Armchair / Bethlehem steel / All that I have / Two and two / Better for us / Hyperion and sunset / Comes to blows / Only way down
CD ______ 8287602
Slash / Jun '96 / PolyGram

FUZZY
Shining hour / Jupiter and Teardrop / Fuzzy / Wish you well / Hook / Soft wolf tread / Stars 'n' stripes / Dixie drugstore / America snoring / Grace / You just have to be crazy
CD ______ 8283892
Slash / Jun '93 / PolyGram

MIGHTY JOE MOON
Lone star song / Mockingbirds / It's the life / Sing along / Mighty Joe Moon / Demon called deception / Lady Godiva and me / Drag / Last days of Tecumseh / Happiness / Honey don't think / Side by side / Rock of ages
CD ______ 8285412
Slash / Aug '94 / PolyGram

Grant Street String Band

GRANT STREET STRING BAND
Things in life / Bear song / Old crossroads / I cried again / Cash on the barrelhead / Fiddle medley / My sweet love ain't around / Say old man can you play the fiddle / Seasons of the heart / In my dear old Southern home / Once a day / Crossing the Cumberlands / Prairie lullaby
CD ______ FR 103
Flat Rock / May '97 / ADA / Direct

Grant, Tom

HAVE YOURSELF A MERRY LITTLE CHRISTMAS
CD ______ SH 5025
Shanachie / Nov '96 / ADA / Greensleeves / Koch

IN MY WILDEST DREAMS
Monkey magic / Mambo to the moon / Show me the way / In my wildest dreams / I've just begun to love you / Time traveller / Squeeze and please / Love on ice / Heidi's song
CD ______ 8495302
Verve / Mar '93 / PolyGram

INSTINCT
CD ______ SHCD 5015
Shanachie / Oct '95 / ADA / Greensleeves / Koch

VIEW FROM HERE, THE
Night falls on the Casbah / Dance walker / Hang time / Next life / Your tender touch / Your look says it all / Lucky dog / Journey within / Clear thoughts / Everytime you go away / Water spirits / Some of the old
CD ______ 5176572
Verve / Mar '93 / PolyGram

Grapow, Roland

FOUR SEASONS OF LIFE
Prelude No.1/Presto / Winner / No more disguise / Show me the way / I remember / Dedicated to... / Bread of charity / 4 seasons of life / Finale de souvenir
CD ______ SRECD 702
Reef / Jun '97 / Pinnacle

Grappelli, Stephane

85 AND STILL SWINGING
CD ______ CDC 7549182
Angel / Jun '94 / EMI

AT THE WINERY VOL.1
You took advantage of me / So danco samba / Sheikh of Araby / Straighten up and fly right / Just in time / Talk of the town / Body and soul
CD ______ CCD 4131
Concord Jazz / Sep '86 / New Note/ Pinnacle

AT THE WINERY VOL.2
You are the sunshine of my life / Love for sale / Angel's camp / Willow weep for me / Chicago / Talking a chance on love / Minor swing / Let's fall in love / Just you, just me
CD ______ CCD 4139
Concord Jazz / Jul '87 / New Note/Pinnacle

AUDIO ARCHIVE
You took advantage of me / Star eyes / Anything goes / Don't blame me / Moonlight in Vermont / Caravan / It might as well be spring / Have you met Miss Jones / Love song / Sing hallelujah
CD ______ CDAA 026
Tring / Jan '91 / Tring

BLUE SKIES (Grappelli, Stephane & Eddy Louiss)
CD ______ 500552
Musidisc / Jan '94 / Discovery

COLLECTION, THE
CD ______ CCSCD 274
Castle / Oct '90 / BMG

CRAZY RHYTHM
CD ______ MATCD 232
Castle / Dec '92 / BMG

CRAZY RHYTHM
CD ______ PLSCD 177
Pulse / Apr '97 / BMG

EMOTION
CD ______ ATJCD 5960
All That's Jazz / Jun '92 / Jazz Music / THE

FEELING + FINESSE = JAZZ
Django / Nuages / Alabamy bound / You better go now / Daphne / Le tien / Minor swing / Makin' whoopee / How about you / Soft winds
CD ______ 7567901402
Atlantic / Jul '93 / Warner Music

FLAMINGO (Grappelli, Stephane & Michel Petrucciani)
These foolish things / Little peace in C for U / Flamingo / Sweet Georgia Brown / I can't get started / I got rhythm / I love New York in June / Misty / I remember April / Lover man / There will never be another you / Valse du passa
CD ______ FDM 365802
Dreyfus / Aug '96 / ADA / Direct / New Note/ Pinnacle

GRAPPELLI STORY (Les Enregistrements Historiques de 1938 a 1992 - 2CD Set))
Stompin' at Decca / My sweet / It had to be you / Nocturne / Alexander's ragtime band / Blue ribbon rag / Oh lady be good / Stephane tune / Tiger rag / Stephane's blues / Jive bomber / Body and soul / Liza / Folks who live on the hill / Weep no more / Nuages / Nearness of you / 'S wonderful / Fascinating rhythm / Just one of those things / Lady is a tramp / I want to be happy / Dans la vie / It's only a paper moon / Flower is a lovesome thing / Minor swing / Daphne / Makin' whoopee / Pent-up house / Django / Darling Je vous aime beaucoup / Willow weep for me / How high the moon / More / Lonely street / Time after time / Misty / Shine / Lover man / I'm coming Virginia / La chanson des rues / Sweet chorus / Mon homme
CD ______ 5158072
Verve / May '94 / PolyGram

GRAPPELLI, WOODS & BELLSON (Grappelli, Stephane & Phil Woods/Louie Bellson)
CD ______ DM 15014
DMA Jazz / Jul '96 / Jazz Music

HOT 'N' SWEET
CD ______ TRTCD 179
TrueTrax / Jun '95 / THE

I GOT RHYTHM
I saw stars / Continental / Avalon / Some of these days / After you've gone / Body and soul / Mystery Pacific / Alabamy bound / Viper's dream / Oh lady be good / Daphne / My serenade / Dinah / Noel brings the swing / I never knew / Tiger rag / Minor swing / I found a new baby
CD CD 6049
Music / Feb '97 / Target/BMG

I HEAR MUSIC
I hear music / All God's chillun got rhythm / Honeysuckle rose / Do you know what it means to miss New Orleans / It's you or no one / If I were a bell / Chicago / Nuages - Daphne / La chanson des rues / Fascinating rhythm / Them their eyes / You are the sunshine of my life / I won't dance / Ol' man river / Someone to watch over me / I got rhythm / How high the moon
CD JHR 73586
Jazz Hour / Apr '95 / Cadillac / Jazz Music / Target/BMG

IN CONCERT (Grappelli, Stephane & McCoy Turner)
CD GATE 7025
Kingdom Jazz / Sep '95 / Kingdom

IT MIGHT AS WELL BE SWING
CD JWD 102216
JWD / Jul '95 / Target/BMG

JAZZ MASTERS
Pennies from Heaven / Solitude / Ain't misbehavin' / Star eyes / Insensiblement / Folks who live on the hill / Nuages / Manoir de mes Reves/Daphne / Are you in the mood / Tears / Djangology / Shine / Nightingale sang in Berkeley Square / Someone to watch over me / I got rhythm
CD 5167582
Verve / Apr '93 / PolyGram

JOUE GEORGE GERSHWIN ET COLE PORTER (Plays Gershwin & Porter)
CD MCD 139 004
Accord / '88 / Cadillac / Discovery

JUST ONE OF THOSE THINGS
Cheek to cheek / Are you in the mood / Just one of those things / There's a small hotel / Pent-up house / I'll remember April / Surrey with the fringe on top / I get a kick out of you / Blue moon / Them there eyes / I can't give you anything but love / How high the moon / Waltz du passe / My one and only love
CD CDM 769 172 2
EMI / Feb '88 / EMI

JUST ONE OF THOSE THINGS (Live At The Montreux Festival 1973)
CD BLCD 760180
Black Lion / Apr '93 / Cadillac / Jazz Music / Koch / Wellard

LA GRANDE REUNION (Grappelli, Stephane & Baden Powell)
CD 557322
Accord / Nov '93 / Cadillac / Discovery

LE JAZZ HOT (Quintette Du Hot Club De France/Grappelli's Hot Four)
I can't give you anything but love / Them there eyes / Honeysuckle rose / I've found a new baby / Night and day / Stomping at Decca / In the still of the night / China boy / My sweet / Oriental shuffle / Billets doux / Sweet chorus / Georgia on my mind / Black and white / Three little words / Limehouse blues / Swing guitars / After you've gone / Sweet georgia brown / Daphne / Nagasaki / Shine / Swing from paris / Souvenirs
CD 300162
Hallmark / Jul '96 / Carlton

LIVE 1992 (Live In Colombes)
Minor swing / Galerie des Princes / Ballade / Tears / Blues for Django and Stephane / Stella by starlight / Sweet chorus / Oh lady be good / Someone to watch over me / I got rhythm
CD 5173922
Birdology / Mar '93 / PolyGram

LIVE AT THE BLUE NOTE
All God's chillun got rhythm / Night and day / I get a kick out of you / It's you or no one / I let a song go out of my heart / Honeysuckle rose / Medley / Nuages / Daphne / Blue moon / Do you know what it means to miss New Orleans / Oh lady be good / Medley / Sweet Georgia Brown
CD CD 83397
Telarc / May '96 / Conifer/BMG

LIVE IN COPENHAGEN (Grappelli, Stephane & Joe Pass)
CD J33J 20041
Pablo / Aug '86 / Cadillac / Complete/ Pinnacle

LIVE IN LONDON
This can't be love / Flamingo / Them there eyes / After you've gone / Nuages / Tea for two
CD BLCD 760139
Black Lion / Oct '90 / Cadillac / Jazz Music / Koch / Wellard

MASTER OF VIOLIN
All of me / Star eyes / Anything goes / Caravan / Don't blame me / Moonlight in Vermont / It might as well be spring / Have you met Miss Jones
CD 722010
Scorpio / Sep '92 / Complete/Pinnacle

NUAGES (Grappelli, Stephane & Django Reinhardt)
Billets doux / Nuages / Exactly like you / China boy / Swing '39 / Them there eyes / St. Louis blues / Appel direct / I've found a new baby / Ultrafox / Twelfth year / Japanese sandman / I wonder where my baby is tonight / Chasing shadows / Djangology / Oh lady be good / Charleston / I'll see you in my dreams
CD TRTCD 148
TrueTrax / Oct '94 / THE

ONE AND ONE
CD MCD 9181
Milestone / Oct '93 / Cadillac / Complete/ Pinnacle / Jazz Music / Wellard

PARISIAN THOROUGHFARE
Love for sale / Perugia / Two cute / Parisian thoroughfare / Improvisation on prelude in E minor / Wave / Hallelujah
CD BLCD 760132
Black Lion / Oct '94 / Cadillac / Jazz Music / Koch / Wellard

PARISIAN THOROUGHFARE
After you've gone / Out of nowhere / It's only a paper moon / What a difference a day made / How high the moon / Parisian thoroughfare / I would do anything for you / 'Deed I do / As time goes by / You are the cream in my coffee / Sysmo / You're driving me crazy / It had to be you / My blue heaven / Flonville
CD 17125
Laserlight / May '97 / Target/BMG

PORTRAIT OF STEPHANE GRAPPELLI, THE
Nearness of you / Tournesol / Stardust / I saw stars / There will never be another you / Memories of you / Star eyes / Paradise / Nice work if you can get it / I got rhythm / Honeysuckle rose / Honeysuckle rosew / Them there eyes
CD EMPRCD 567
Emporio / May '95 / Disc

REUNION (Grappelli, Stephane & Martin Taylor)
Jive at five / Willow weep for me / Drop me off in Harlem / Miraval / Jenna / Reunion / Emily / Hotel splendid / La dame du lac / I thought about you / It's only a paper moon
CD AKD 022
Linn / Oct '93 / PolyGram

SATIN DOLL
CD 440162CD
Musidisc / Jul '94 / Discovery

SHADES OF DJANGO
Lover come back to me / Sweet Lorraine / Shine / Solitude / Ain't misbehavin' / Souvenir de Villingen / Hot lips / My heart stood still / Nearness of you / Joy / Nightingale sang in Berkeley Square / Cherokee / Lover man
CD 8259552
MPS Jazz / Mar '93 / PolyGram

SPECIAL STEPHANE GRAPPELLI (1947-1961)
Qui, pour vous revoir: *Grappelli, Stephane Hot Four* / Tea for two / Pennies from Heaven: *Grappelli, Stephane & Jack Dieval* / Can't help lovin' dat man: *Grappelli, Stephane & Jack Dieval* / Girl in Calico: *Grappelli, Stephane & Jack Dieval* / World is waiting for the sunrise: *Grappelli, Stephane & Jack Dieval* / I can't recognize the tune: *Grappelli, Stephane & Jack Dieval* / You took advantage of me: *Grappelli, Stephane & Jack Dieval* / Folks who live on the hill: *Grappelli, Stephane & Jack Dieval* / Looking at you: *Grappelli, Stephane & Jack Dieval* / Swing '39: *Grappelli, Stephane Quartet* / Belleville: *Grappelli, Stephane Quartet* / Manoir de mes reves: *Grappelli, Stephane Quartet* / Djangology: *Grappelli, Stephane Quartet* / Have you met Miss Jones: *Grappelli, Stephane Quartet* / This can't be love: *Grappelli, Stephane Quartet* / Alemberts: *Grappelli, Stephane Quartet* / Marno: *Grappelli, Stephane Quartet* / Blue moon / Foggy day
CD CZ 317
EMI / Jun '90 / EMI

STARDUST
CD BLC 760117
Black Lion / Apr '91 / Cadillac / Jazz Music / Koch / Wellard

STEFF AND SLAM (Grappelli, Stephane Trio & Slam Stewart)
CD BB 8632
Black & Blue / Feb '96 / Discovery / Koch / Wellard

STEPHANE GRAPPELLI
Just one of those things / Misty / More / Them there eyes / I remember Django / Little star / Tournesol / Two cute / This can't be love / Sweet Georgia Brown / It don't mean a thing (if it ain't got that swing)
CD 8747172
DA Music / Jul '96 / Conifer/BMG

STEPHANE GRAPPELLI & JEAN-LUC PONTY (Grappelli, Stephane & Jean-Luc Ponty)
CD 556552
Accord / Mar '96 / Cadillac / Discovery

STEPHANE GRAPPELLI 1935-40
CD CLASSICS 708
Classics / Jul '93 / Discovery / Jazz Music

STEPHANE GRAPPELLI 1941-43
CD CLASSICS 779
Classics / Mar '95 / Discovery / Jazz Music

STEPHANE GRAPPELLI AND FRIENDS IN PARIS (2CD Set)
CD Set 500762
Musidisc / Sep '96 / Discovery

STEPHANE GRAPPELLI MEETS BARNEY KESSEL (Grappelli, Stephane & Barney Kessel)
CD BLC 760150
Black Lion / Apr '91 / Cadillac / Jazz Music / Koch / Wellard

STEPHANE GRAPPELLI MEETS EARL HINES
CD BLCD 760168
Black Lion / Oct '93 / Cadillac / Jazz Music / Koch / Wellard

STEPHANE GRAPPELLI WITH JEAN LUC PONTY (Grappelli, Stephane & Jean-Luc Ponty)
CD MCD 139 139
Accord / '88 / Cadillac / Discovery

STEPHANE GRAPPELLI/JEAN-LUC PONTY VOL.2 (Grappelli, Stephane & Jean-Luc Ponty)
CD 139 210
Accord / '86 / Cadillac / Discovery

STEPHANE'S TUNE 1937-1944
CD 158582
Jazz Archives / Jul '96 / Discovery

STEPHANOVA
Tune up / Thou swell / Norwegian dance / Fulton Street samba / My foolish heart / Lover / Way you look tonight / Stephanova / Smoke rings and wine / Tangerine / Waltz for Queenie / Sonny boy
CD 292E 6033
Concord Jazz / Jan '90 / New Note/ Pinnacle

TOGETHER AT LAST (Grappelli, Stephane & Vassar Clements)
CD FF 70421
Flying Fish / Oct '89 / ADA / CM / Direct / Roots

VENUPELLI BLUES (Grappelli, Stephane & Joe Venuti)
I can't give you anything but love / My one and only love / Undecided / Venupelli blues / I'll never be the same / Tea for two
CD LEJAZZCD 18
Le Jazz / Jun '93 / Cadillac / Koch

VINTAGE 1981
If I had you / I can't get started (with you) / Blue moon / But not for me / It's only a paper moon / Jamie / I'm coming Virginia / Do you know what it means to miss New Orleans / Isn't she lovely / Swing '42 / Honeysuckle rose
CD CCD 4169
Concord Jazz / Nov '92 / New Note/ Pinnacle

Grass Is Greener

WOLVES A'HOWLIN'
CD REB 1730CD
Rebel / Apr '96 / ADA / Direct

Grass Roots

WHERE WERE YOU WHEN I NEEDED YOU
CD VSD 5511
Varese Sarabande / Jul '95 / Pinnacle

Grass Show

SOMETHING SMELLS GOOD IN STINKVILLE
Freak show / 1962 / Out of the void / Unreal world / Cavemankind / All that she wants / Talk talk talk / Make love not war / Losing touch / Love 180 / Alice / Getting you out of my head
CD FOODCD 20
Food / Jun '97 / EMI

Grassy Knoll

GRASSY KNOLL
Culture of complaint / March eighteenth / Unbelievable truth / Altering the gates of the mind / Conversations with Julian Dexter / Floating above the earth / Less than one / Low / Evolution / Beauty within / Illusions of peace
CD NET 059CD
Nettwerk / Oct '94 / Greyhound / Pinnacle / Vital

Grateful Dead

AMERICAN BEAUTY
Box of rain / Friend of the Devil / Operator / Sugar magnolia / Ripple / Brokedown palace / Till the morning comes / Attic of my life / Truckin
CD K2 46074
WEA / Oct '89 / Warner Music

ANTHEM OF THE SUN
That's it for the other one / Cryptical envelopment / Quadlibet / For tender feet / Faster we go, the rounder we get / We leave the castle / Alligator / Caution (do not stop on the tracks)
CD 7599271732
WEA / Feb '94 / Warner Music

ARISTA YEARS 1977-1995, THE (2CD Set)
Estimated prophet / Passenger / Samson & Delilah / Terapin station / Good lovin' / Shakedown street / Fire on the mountain / I need a miracle / Alabama getaway / Far from me / Saint of circumstance / Dire wolf / Cassidy / Feel like a stranger / Franklin's tower / Touch of grey / Hell in a bucket / West LA fa- away / Throwing stones / Black muddy river / Foolish heart / Built to last / Just a little light / Picasso moon / Standing on the moon / Eyes of the world
CD Set 078221893428
Arista / Oct '96 / BMG

BLUES FOR ALLAH
Help on the way / Slipknot / Franklin's tower / King Solomon's marbles / Music never stopped / Crazy fingers / Sage and spirit / Blues for Allah / Sand castles and glass camels / Unusual occurrences in the desert
CD GDCD 4001
Grateful Dead / Feb '89 / Pinnacle

DICK'S PICKS VOL.1 (Tampa, Florida 19/12/73 - 2CD Set)
Here comes the sunshine / Big river / Mississippi half step / Weather report suite / Big railroad blues / Playing in the band / He's gone / Truckin' / Nobody's fault but mine / Jam / Other one / Jam / Stella blue / Around and around
CD Set GDCD2 4019
Grateful Dead / Jan '96 / Pinnacle

DICK'S PICKS VOL.2 (Columbus, Ohio 31/10/71)
Dark star/Jam / Sugar magnolia / St. Stephen / Not fade away / Going down the road feeling bad / Not fade away
CD GDCD 4020
Grateful Dead / Feb '96 / Pinnacle

DICK'S PICKS VOL.3 (Pembroke Pines, Florida 22/5/77 - 2CD Set)
Funiculi funicula / Music never stopped / Sugaree / Lazy lightning / Supplication / Dancin' in the streets / Help on the way / Slipknot / Franklin's tower / Samson and Delilah / Sunrise / Estimated prophet / Eyes of the world / Wharf rat / Terrapin station / (Walk me out in the) Morning dew
CD Set GDCD2 4022
Grateful Dead / Dec '95 / Pinnacle

DICK'S PICKS VOL.4 (Fillmore East 13-14/2/70 - 3CD Set)
CD Set GDCD3 4023
Grateful Dead / Dec '96 / Pinnacle

DICK'S PICKS VOL.5 (Oakland Auditorium Arena 26/12/79 - 3CD Set)
CD Set GDCD3 4025
Grateful Dead / Dec '96 / Pinnacle

DICK'S PICKS VOL.6 (Hartford Civic Center 14/10/83 - 3CD Set)
Hell in a bucket / Dupree's diamond blues / Just a little light / Walkin' blues / Jack-a-roe / Never trust a woman / When I paint my masterpiece / Row Jimmy / Blow away / Playing in the band / Uncle John's band / Lady with a fan / Terrapin station / Mud love buddy jam / Drums / Space / Wheel / All along the watchtower / Stella blue / Not fade away / And we bid you goodnight / I will take you home / Goin' down the road feelin' bad / Black Peter / Around and around / Brokedown palace
CD Set GDCD3 4026
Grateful Dead / Dec '96 / Pinnacle

DICK'S PICKS VOL.7 (Alexandra Palace 9-11/9/1974 - 3CD Set)
Scarlet begonias / Mexicali blues / Row Jimmy / Black throated wind / Mississippi half step uptown toodeloo / Beat it down the line / Tennessee Jed / Playing in the band / Weather report suite / Stella blue / Jack Straw / Brown-eyed women / Big river / Truckin' / Wood Green jam / Wharf rat / Me and my uncle / Not fade away / Dark star / Spam jam / Morning dew / US blues
CD Set GDCD3 4027
Grateful Dead / Apr '97 / Pinnacle

DOZIN' AT THE KNICK (3CD Set)
Alabama getaway / Greatest story ever told / They love each other / Mama tried / Big river / Althea / CC rider / Tennesee Jed / Hell in a bucket / Keep your day job / Scarlet begonias / Fire on the mountain / Estimated prophet / Eyes of the world / Drums / Spinach jam / Other one / Stella blue / Sugar magnolia / US blues
CD Set GDCD3 4024
Grateful Dead / Dec '96 / Pinnacle

EUROPE '72
Cumberland blues / He's gone / One more saturday night / Jack straw / You can win again / China cat sunflower / Sunflower / I know you rider / Brown eyed woman / Hurts me too / Ramblin' rose / Sugar magnolia / Mr. Charlie / Tennessee Jed / Truckin' / Epilogue / Prelude
CD 7599272652
Warner Bros. / Nov '94 / Warner Music

FALLOUT FROM THE PHIL ZONE (2CD Set)
Dancin' in the streets / New speedway boogie / Viola lee blues / Easy wind / Mason's children / Hard to handle (yes I am) / Music never stopped / Jack-a-roe / In the midnight hour / Visions of Johanna / Box of rain
CD Set GDCD2 4052
Grateful Dead / Jun '97 / Pinnacle

FURTHER (Various Artists)
CD 20012
Hybrid / May '97 / Greyhound

GRATEFUL DEAD, THE
Bertha / Mama tried / Big railroad blues / Playing in the band / Other one / Me and my uncle / Big boss man / Me and Bobby McGee / Johnny B Goode / Wharf rat / Not fade away / Goin' down the road / Feelin' bad
CD 7599271922
WEA / Feb '93 / Warner Music

GRATEFUL DEAD: INTERVIEW PICTURE DISC
CD CBAK 4039
Baktabak / Apr '90 / Arabesque

GRAYFOLDED
CD SA 1969
Swell Artifact / Jun '97 / Greyhound

HEARTBITS VOL.2 (Mickey & The Heartbeats)
CD ANT 2912
Anthology / Jun '97 / Cargo / Greyhound

HUNDRED YEAR HALL
Bertha / Me and my uncle / Next time you see me / China cat sunflower / I know you rider / Jack straw / Big railroad / Playing in the band / Turn on your lovelight / Going down the road feeling bad / One more Saturday night
CD Set GDCD2 4021
Grateful Dead / Oct '95 / Pinnacle

IN THE DARK
Touch of grey / Hell in a bucket / When push comes to shove / West LA fadeaway / Tons of steel / Throwing stones / Black muddy river
CD 261145
Arista / Jul '96 / BMG

INFRARED ROSES
Crowd sculpture / Parallelogram / Little Nemo in Nightland / Riverside rhapsody / Post-modern highrise table top stomp / Infrared roses / Silver apples of the moon / Speaking in swords / Magnesium night light / Sparrow hawk row / River of nine sorrows / Apollo at the Ritz
CD GDCD 4016
Grateful Dead / Jan '92 / Pinnacle

INTERVIEW DISC
CD TELL 06
Network / Dec '96 / Total/BMG

LIVE DEAD
Dark star / Death don't have no mercy / Feedback / And we bid you goodnight / St. Stephen / Eleven / Turn on your love / Light
CD K 9271812
WEA / Jun '89 / Warner Music

MUSIC NEVER STOPPED, THE (The Roots Of The Grateful Dead) (Various Artists)
CD SHCD 6014
Shanachie / Oct '95 / ADA / Greensleeves / Koch

NIGHT OF THE GRATEFUL DEAD (Interview Disc)
CD OTR 1100024
Metro Independent / Apr '97 / Essential/BMG

ONE FROM THE VAULT
Introduction / Help on the way / Franklin's tower / Music never stopped / It must have been the roses / Eyes of the world / King Solomon's marbles / Around and around / Sugaree / Big river / Crazy fingers / Other one / Sage and spirit / Goin' down the road feeling bad / US blues / Blues For Allah
CD Set GDCD2 4015
Grateful Dead / May '91 / Pinnacle

RELIX BAY ROCK SHOP (Tribute To Jerry Garcia) (Various Artists)
CD RBRS 00098
Relix / Jul '97 / ADA / Greyhound

RISEN FROM THE VAULTS
CD DILCD 1001
Dare International / Jan '94 / Total/BMG

SHAKEDOWN STREET
Good lovin' / France / Shakedown Street / Serengeti / Fire on the mountain / I need a miracle / From the heart of me / Stagger Lee / All new minglewood blues / If I had the world to give
CD 251133
Arista / Jun '91 / BMG

SKELETONS FROM THE CLOSET
Golden road (to unlimited devotion) / Truckin' / Rosemary / Sugar magnolia / St. Stephen / Uncle John's band / Casey Jones / Mexicali blues / Turn on your love light / One more Saturday night / Friend of the devil / Don't fall in love (rock 'n' roll) / Do you believe / Creeper / Wednesday / Remember (walkin' in the sand) / Call your name / Take you home / Halloween / Rollercoaster / Blizzard / On the run
CD CDTB 018
Thunderbolt / '87 / TKO Magnum

STEAL YOUR FACE
Promised land / Cold rain and snow / Around and around / Stella blue / Mississippi half step uptown toodeloo / Ship of fools / Beat it on down the line / Big river / Black throated wind / US blues / El Paso / Sugaree / It must have been the roses / Casey Jones
CD Set GDCD2 4006
Grateful Dead / Mar '89 / Pinnacle

TERRAPIN STATION
Estimated prophet / Dancing in the street / Passenger / Samson and Delilah / Sunrise / Lady with the fan / Terrapin station / Terrapin / Terrapin transit / At a siding / Terrapin fever / Refrain
CD 260175
Arista / Nov '90 / BMG

TWO FROM THE VAULT
CD Set GDCD2 4018
Grateful Dead / Apr '92 / Pinnacle

WAKE OF THE FLOOD
Mississippi half step uptown toodeloo / Row Jimmy / Here comes sunshine / Weather report / Let me sing your blues away / Stella blue / Eyes of the world
CD GDCD 4002
Grateful Dead / Nov '87 / Pinnacle

WORKINGMAN'S DEAD
Uncle John's band / High time / Dire wolf / New speedway boogie / Cumberland blues / Black Peter / Easy wind / Casey Jones
CD K 246049
WEA / Jun '89 / Warner Music

Gratz, Wayne

BLUE RIDGE
Blue ridge part 1 / Blue ridge part 2 / Heart in the clouds / Sacred river / Dancing lights / Waterfall / Trail of tears / Fields are burning / Scenes of reflection / Past time / Peaks of otter / Pathway to waterrock / White on white / Endless mountains
CD ND 61047
Narada / May '95 / ADA / New Note/ Pinnacle

FROM ME TO YOU
Here, there and everywhere / And I love her / From me to you / Michelle / In my life / If I fell / You've got to hide your love away / Girl / Do you want to know a secret / Yesterday / Norwegian wood / Long and winding road / All my loving / PS I love you / Hey Jude
CD ND 62811
Narada / Aug '97 / ADA / New Note/ Pinnacle

GIFT OF THE SEA, A
Gift of the sea / At sunrise / Oceanus / Steps in the sand / Two solitudes / Ships / Island / Spanish galleon / Tidal dance / By the sea / Soaring / Shells
CD ND 61054
Narada / Jul '96 / ADA / New Note/Pinnacle

MUSIC OF THE NIGHT
Think of me / With one look / Don't cry for me Argentina / As if we never said goodbye / Music of the night / Memory / Love changes everything / I don't know how to love him / Pie Jesu / Another suitcase in another hall / All I ask of you
CD ND 62810
Narada / Aug '97 / ADA / New Note/ Pinnacle

Grave

AND HERE I DIE
CD MC 770622
Century Media / Feb '94 / Plastic Head

DEVOLUTION
CD PRO 006CD
Prophet / Nov '92 / Pinnacle

HATING LIFE
CD CM 77105CD
Century Media / Apr '96 / Plastic Head

INTO THE GRAVE
CD CM 97212
Century Media / Sep '94 / Plastic Head

SOULLESS
CD CM 770702
Century Media / Jun '94 / Plastic Head

Gravediggaz

NIGGAMORTIS
Just when you thought it was over (intro) / Constant elevation / Nowhere to run, nowhere to hide / Defective trip (trippin') / Two cups of blood / Blood brothers / 360 questions / 1-800 suicide / Diary of a madman / Mommy what's a gravedigga / Bang yo head / Here comes the Gravediggaz / Graveyard chamber / Death trap / Six feet deep / Rest in peace (outro)
CD GEECD 14
Gee Street / Jun '94 / PolyGram

PICK THE SHOVEL AND THE SICKLE
CD GEE 1000562
Gee Street / Aug '97 / 3mv/Pinnacle

Gravedigger

TUNES OF WAR
CD GUN 102CD
Gun / Oct '96 / Plastic Head

WITCH HUNT
CD NCD 002
Noise / '88 / Koch

Gravedigger V

ALL BLACK & HAIRY/THE MIRROR CRACKED
CD VOXXCD 2025
Voxx / Oct '94 / Else / RTM/Disc

Graveland

1000 SWORDS
CD A 101CD
Embassy / Jun '96 / Plastic Head

Gravenites, Nick

DON'T FEED THE ANIMALS (Gravenites, Nick & Animal Mind)
CD TX 1020CD
Taxim / Dec '96 / ADA

Graverobbers

SOUL PARKING
CD FM 02
Fundamental / Nov '96 / Cargo / Plastic Head / Shellshock/Disc

Graves, Blind Roosevelt

1929-36
CD DOCD 5105
Document / Nov '93 / ADA / Hot Shot / Jazz Music

Graveyard Rodeo

ON THE VERGE
CD CM 770692
Century Media / Aug '94 / Plastic Head

Gravity Kills

GRAVITY KILLS
Foward / Guilty / Blame / Down / Here / Enough / Inside / Goodbye / Never / Last / Hold
CD CDV 2819
Virgin / Feb '97 / EMI

MANIPULATED
CD TVT 59162
TVT / Jun '97 / Cargo / Greyhound

Gravity Wax

LOW ENERGY PARTICULATE
CD ME 013
Mind Expansion / May '97 / Cargo

Gravity's Pull

RADIO STATION WAGON
CD SH 5706
Shanachie / Mar '96 / ADA / Greensleeves / Koch

Gray, David

CENTURY ENDS, A
Shine / Century ends / Debauchery / Let the truth sing / Gathering dust / Wisdom / Lead me upstairs / Living room / Birds without wings / It's all over
CD CDHUT 9
Hut / Apr '93 / EMI

FLESH
What are you / Light / Coming down / Falling free / Made up my mind / Mystery of love / Lullaby / New horizons / Love's old song / Flesh
CD CDHUT 17
Hut / Sep '94 / EMI

Gray, Dobie

DRIFT AWAY
CD CDCOT 106
Cottage / Jan '94 / Koch / THE

DRIFT AWAY (The Very Best Of Dobie Gray)
CD RE 21122
Razor & Tie / Aug '96 / Koch

VERY BEST OF DOBIE GRAY, THE
Drift away / I can see clearly now / Cupid / Loving arms / If I ever needed you / Slip away / In crowd / Ain't that good news / We had it all / I'm only speaking my heart / Lean on me / I can live with that / It's not because we didn't try / It's over
CD 306162
Hallmark / Jan '97 / Carlton

Gray, Glen

CONTINENTAL, THE
CD HCD 261
Hindsight / Oct '95 / Jazz Music / Target/ BMG

MOONGLOW 1930-1936 (Gray, Glen & Orchestra)
CD RACD 7126
Aerospace / May '96 / Jazz Music / Montpellier

UNCOLLECTED 1939-1940, THE (Gray, Glen & The Casa Loma Orchestra)
CD HCD 104
Hindsight / Jan '95 / Jazz Music / Target/ BMG

Gray, Henry

DON'T START THAT STUFF (Gray, Henry & Short Fuse)
CD 7422468
WMD / Jan '97 / Discovery

Gray, Kellye

STANDARDS
CD JR 001012
Justice / Sep '92 / Koch

Gray Matter

THOG
CD DIS 68VCD
Dischord / Sep '92 / SRD

Gray, Owen

CALL ON ME
CD WRCD 0020
Techniques / Nov '95 / Jet Star

LET'S GO STEADY
CD FECD 21
First Edition / Dec '95 / Jet Star

MISS WIRE WAIST
CD PICD 209
Body Music / Jun '95 / Jet Star

ON TOP
CD RNCD 2073
Rhino / Oct '94 / Grapevine/PolyGram / Jet Star

OUT IN THE OPEN
CD VPCD 2045
VP / Feb '96 / Greensleeves / Jet Star / Total/BMG

Gray, Russell

SOLO
From the shores of the mighty pacific / Traumerei / Chablis / Caro nome / Fantasia on themes from Carmen / Salut d'amour / Concerto for cornet and brass bands / Bess you is my woman now / Sunshine of your smile / Aye waukin' o / Una furtiva lagrima / Song and dance / Londonderry air
CD QPRL 070D
Polyphonic / Jan '95 / Complete/Pinnacle

Gray, Simon

VANISHING POINT
CD KLB 30012
Extreme / Nov '94 / Vital/SAM

Gray, Wardell

HOW HIGH THE MOON
CD MCD 076
Moon / Dec '95 / Cadillac / Harmonia Mundi

MEMORIAL VOL.1
CD OJCCD 50
Original Jazz Classics / Nov '95 / Complete/Pinnacle / Jazz Music / Wellard

ONE FOR PREZ
CD BLCD 760106
Black Lion / Feb '89 / Cadillac / Jazz Music / Koch / Wellard

WAY OUT WARDELL
Blue Lou / Sweet Georgia Brown / Tenderly / Just you, just me / One o'clock jump
CD CDBOP 014
Boplicity / Jul '91 / Pinnacle

Grayon, James Clare

NICE WORK
CD SRCD 002
Stream / Nov '96 / Stream / Vital

Greaney, Con

ROAD TO ATHEA
CD CIC 082CD
Clo Iar-Chonnachta / Nov '93 / CM

Great Big Sea

UP
Run runaway / Going up / Fast as I can / Mari-mac / Dancing with Mrs. White / Something to it / Buying time / Lukey / Old black rum / Chemical worker's song / Wave over wave / Billy peddle / Nothing out of nothing / Jolly butcher / Rant and roar
CD COOKCD 130
Cooking Vinyl / Jun '97 / Vital

Great British Jazz Band

BRITISH JAZZ ODYSSEY, A
Riff up them stairs / KC blues / Very thought of you / Sizzle / Badger / Duke's joke / Nightingale sang in Berkeley Square / Jump / Serenade to a wealthy widow / Blues for Welshie / We fell out of love / Go Ghana / Tidy / Gypsy / Limehouse blues
CD ____ CCD 79740
Candid / Feb '97 / Cadillac / Direct / Jazz Music / Koch / Wellard

JUBILEE
Jubilee / Jazz me blues / Original Dixieland one-step / Washboard blues / Prelude to a kiss / Idaho / Imagination / Beautiful friendship / Petite fleur / Someday sweetheart / Apex blues / All I do is dream of you / Chelsea bridge / Tiger rag
CD ____ CCD 79720
Candid / Feb '97 / Cadillac / Direct / Jazz Music / Koch / Wellard

Great Circle Saxophone ...

CHILD KING DICTATOR FOOL (Great Circle Saxophone Quartet)
Stay fresh baggies / Falling from grace / Black shag / Red and green / Emma's nemesis / Hole in the sky / Now what / Thing turning (for Janet) / Blood indigo / Son of splorb / Snake tectonics / Stay fresh baggies
CD ____ 805162
New World / Jun '97 / ADA / Cadillac / Harmonia Mundi

Great Guitars

RETURN OF THE GREAT GUITARS, THE
Things ain't what they used to be / When lights are low / Smooth one / My funny valentine / Lady in red / Soft winds / Bernie's tune / I remember you / Waltz for Wes / Seven, come eleven / Billy Bean / Nigh Roby get-a-way / On the trail
CD ____ CCD 4715
Concord Jazz / Aug '96 / New Note/ Pinnacle

STRAIGHT TRACKS
I'm putting all my eggs in one basket / Clouds / Gravy waltz / Um abraco no bonfa / Little rock getaway / It might as well be Spring / Kingston cutie / Favela
CD ____ CCD 4421
Concord Jazz / Nov '90 / New Note/ Pinnacle

Great Jazz Trio

STANDARD COLLECTION VOL.1
After you've gone / Summertime / Days of wine and roses / As time goes by / You'd be so nice to come home to / Summer knows / Georgia on my mind / Prelude to a kiss / St. Louis blues / Danny boy
CD ____ MCD 0031
Limetree / Dec '95 / New Note/Pinnacle

STANDARD COLLECTION VOL.2
Angel eyes / Autumn leaves / Black orpheus / Gone with the wind / Over the rainbow / Softly as in a morning sunrise / Misty / On Green Dolphin Street / Alone together / Dark eyes
CD ____ MCD 0032
Limetree / Dec '95 / New Note/Pinnacle

Great Scots

GREAT LOST GREAT SCOTS ALBUM
CD ____ SC 11048
Sundazed / May '97 / Cargo / Greyhound / Rollercoaster

Great Speckled Bird

GREAT SPECKLED BIRD
CD ____ SPCD 1200
Stony Plain / Dec '94 / ADA / CM / Direct

Great Unravelling

GREAT UNRAVELLING
CD ____ KRS 277CD
Kill Rock Stars / Feb '97 / Cargo / Greyhound / Plastic Head

Great White

ONCE BITTEN
Lady red light / Gonna getcha / Rock me / All over now / Fast road / What do you do / Face the day / Gimme some lovin'
CD ____ NSPCD 515
Connoisseur Collection / Jun '95 / Pinnacle

SAIL AWAY
Short overture / Mothers eyes / Cryin' / Momma don't stop / Alone / All right / Sail away / Gone with the wind / Livin' in the USA / If I ever saw a good thing / Call it rock 'n' roll / All over now / Love is a lie / Old rose motel / Babe I'm gonna leave you / Rock me / Once biten twice shy
CD Set ____ 72445110802
Zoo Entertainment / Aug '94 / BMG

SHOT IN THE DARK
CD ____ RE 21102
Razor & Tie / Jul '96 / Koch

Greater Than One

G-FORCE
CD ____ TORSOCD 149
Torso / Jun '89 / SRD

Greatest Show On Earth

HORIZONS/THE GOING'S EASY
Sunflower morning / Angelina / Skylight man / 1 Day of the lady / Real cool world / I fought for love / Horizons / Again and again / Borderline / Magic woman touch / Storytimes and nursery rhymes / Leader / Love magnet / Tell the story
CD ____ SEECD 473
See For Miles/C5 / Feb '97 / Pinnacle

Greaves, John

ACCIDENT
Photography / Salt / Accident / Milk / Irma / Sad emission / Wax / Ruby / Rose sob / Silence / For bearings
CD ____ BP 234CD
Blueprint / Sep '97 / Pinnacle

LITTLE BOTTLE OF LAUNDRY
Solitary / World tonight / Deck of the moon / Old antiquity / Rose C"est la vie / Lullaby / Almost perfect lovers / Le garcon vert / Let her go / Dedans
CD ____ BP 232CD
Blueprint / Jun '97 / Pinnacle

SONGS
Old kinderhook / Song / Swelling valley / Green fuse / KewRhone / Eccentric waters silence / Price we pay / L'aise aux ex-sans trique / Back where we began / Gegenstand
CD ____ RES 112CD
Resurgence / Apr '97 / Pinnacle

Greco, Buddy

16 MOST REQUESTED SONGS
Lady is a tramp / Like young / Something's gotta give / This could be the start of something / I love being here with you / Around the world / Roses of Picardy / Teach me tonight / My kind of girl / At long last love / Mr. Lonely / Most beautiful girl in the world / Call me irresponsible / She loves me / You win again / It had better be tonight
CD ____ 4744002
Columbia / Feb '94 / Sony

BUDDY AND SOUL/SOFT AND GENTLE
Come rain or come shine / How long has this been going on / I'm in love / After the lights go down low / People will say we're in love / I didn't know what time it was / I'm gonna laugh you out of my life / Let me love you / But beautiful / Fly me to the moon / Just walk away / Round midnight soft and gentle / I love you love / What kind of fool am I / Nancy / My funny valentine / Then I'll be tired of you / Gigi / Angel eyes / Passing pastels / Bewitched / Moonlight in Vermont / I left my heart in San Francisco / Easy way
CD ____ 4840322
Columbia / Jun '96 / Sony

BUDDY GRECO
CD ____ DVAD 6082
Deja Vu / May '95 / THE

IN STYLE
Movin' on / Me and Mrs. Jones / Hungry years / Lady is a tramp / Love won't let me wait / My funny valentine / Baubles, bangles and beads / Touch me in the morning / More I see you / She loves me / You better go now / Bewitched, bothered and bewildered / Satin doll / This is all I ask / Girl talk / Teach me tonight / Legacy / Passing pastels / Neither one of us / Ready for your love / Around the world / When I fall in love
CD ____ 74321431582
Camden / Oct '96 / BMG

IT'S MY LIFE/MOVING ON
It's gonna take some time / October 4th 1971 / If / Power and the glory / You've got a friend / Without you / Your song / As long as she will stay / Song for you / It's my life / Macarthur park / Movin' on / Touch me in the morning / Maggi / Baby lean on me / I know where I belong / What's going on / Beautiful friendship / Neither one of us (wants to be first to say go) / If I could live my life again / I could be the one / Cardboard California
CD ____ C5CD 634
See For Miles/C5 / Oct '95 / Pinnacle

MACARTHUR PARK
Around the world / Bewitched, bothered and bewildered / This is all I ask / She loves me / You better go now / Me and Mrs. Jones / Georgia road / Baubles, bangles and beads / Satin doll / Like young / My funny valentine / Girl talk / Lady is a tramp / Touch me in the morning / Legacy / Hungry years / Neither one of us / Passing pastels / Macarthur park
CD ____ CYCD 71911
Celebrity / Feb '97 / Cadillac / Direct / Wellard

ROUTE 66: TRIBUTE TO NAT 'KING' COLE
Gee baby ain't I good to you / Route 66 / Nature boy / I'm lost / Sweet Lorraine / Straighten up and fly right / What is this thing called love / Lush life / Smile / It's only a paper moon / Walkin' my baby back home / That's all / Moonlight in Vermont / Sweet Georgia Brown / But not for me / When I fall in love / LOVE
CD ____ CYCD 1901
Celebrity / Feb '97 / Cadillac / Direct / Wellard

Greedsville

CASINO ROYALE COLLECTION
Disco queen / Casino / Simple moonshine / Du cats / Jazz the spanish fly / Caller 38 / Stroll by the sea / It's a gas / Splash
CD ____ CDBLEED 9
Bleeding Hearts / Mar '94 / Pinnacle

Green, Al

AL
Tired of being alone / Call me / I'm still in love with you / Here I am (come and take me) / Let's stay together / Sha la la (make me happy) / LOVE Love / Look what you done for me / Love and happiness / Take me to the river / I can't get next to you / How can you mend a broken heart / I tried to tell myself / I've never found a girl / Oh me, oh my (Dreams in my arms) / You ought to be with me
CD ____ AGREECD 1
Beechwood / Oct '92 / Beechwood/BMG / Pinnacle

CALL ME/I'M STILL IN LOVE WITH YOU
CD ____ HIUKCD 111
Hi / Mar '91 / Pinnacle

CHRISTMAS ALBUM PLUS
CD ____ HILOCD 21
Hi / Oct '95 / Pinnacle

CHRISTMAS ALBUM/CHRISTMAS CHEERS (Green, Al & Ace Cannon)
White Christmas: *Green, Al* / Christmas song: *Green, Al* / Winter wonderland: *Green, Al* / I'll be home for Christmas: *Green, Al* / Jingle bells: *Green, Al* / What Christmas means to me: *Green, Al* / Oh holy night: *Green, Al* / Silent night: *Green, Al* / Feels like Christmas: *Green, Al* / Santa Claus is coming to town: *Cannon, Ace* / Rudolph the red nosed reindeer: *Cannon, Ace* / Here comes Santa Claus: *Cannon, Ace* / Frosty the snowman: *Cannon, Ace* / Blue Christmas: *Cannon, Ace* / I saw Mommy kissing Santa Claus: *Cannon, Ace* / Let it snow, let it snow, let it snow: *Cannon, Ace* / Jingle bell rock: *Cannon, Ace* / Rockin' around the Christmas tree: *Cannon, Ace*
CD ____ HIUKCD 126
Hi / Oct '91 / Pinnacle

COVER ME GREEN
I want to hold your hand / My girl / Letter / Light my fire / I say a little prayer / Summertime / Get back / For the good times / Oh pretty woman / I'm so lonesome I could cry / Lean on me / Unchained melody / Ain't no mountain high enough / People get ready / Amazing grace
CD ____ HIUKCD 107
Hi / Apr '91 / Pinnacle

DEEP SHADE OF GREEN, A (3CD Set)
What am I going to do with myself / One woman / Are you lonely for me baby / True love / God is standing / Tired of being alone / Let's stay together / Old time lovin' / I've never found a girl / How can you mend a broken heart / Judy / Look what you have done for me / What a wonderful thing love is / Simply beautiful / For the good times / One of these good old days / You ought to be with me / Call me / Here I am / Have you been making out OK / I'm so lonely I could cry / Funny how time slips away / So good to be here / Home again / Free at last / Unchained melody / Sha-la-la / God blessed our love / I'm hooked you / LOVE / I wish you were here / Strong as death / Could I be the one / There is love / Love sermon / I didn't know / There's no way / Together again / I'd fly away / Soon as I got home / Something / Have a good time / Nothing takes the place of you / Belle / Feels like summer / Dream / To sir with love / Up above my head / I'll be standing by / Eli's game / Silent night / People get ready / Spirit might come / On and on
CD Set ____ HIBOOK 12
Hi / Feb '97 / Pinnacle

DON'T LOOK BACK
Best love / Love is a beautiful thing / Waiting on you / What does it take / Keep on pushing love / You are my everything / One love / People in the world / Give it everything / Your love / Fountain of love / Don't look back / Love in motion
CD ____ 74321163102
RCA / Feb '97 / BMG

EXPLORES YOUR MIND
Sha la la / Take me to the river / God blessed our love / City / One night stand / I'm hooked on you / Stay with me forever / Hangin' on / School days
CD ____ HIUKCD 413
Hi / Sep '86 / Pinnacle

FLIPSIDE OF AL GREEN, THE
CD ____ HIUKCD 141
Hi / May '93 / Pinnacle

GREATEST HITS
Let's stay together / I can't get next to you / You ought to be with me / Look what you done for me / Let's get married / Tired of being alone / Call me / I'm still in love with you / Here I am (come and take me) / How can you mend a broken heart
CD ____ HIUKCD 425
Hi / Feb '87 / Pinnacle

GREATEST HITS VOL.2 (Take Me To The River)
Drivin' wheel / I've never found a girl / Love and happiness / Living for you / Sha la la / LOVE Love / One woman / Take me to the river / Rhymes / Oh me, oh my (dreams in my arms) / Glory glory / Full of fire / Keep me cryin' / Belle
CD ____ HIUKCD 438
Hi / Oct '87 / Pinnacle

GREEN IS BLUES/AL GREEN GETS NEXT TO YOU
One woman / Talk to me / My girl / Letter / I stand accused / Gotta find a new world / What am I gonna do with myself / Tomorrow's dream / Get back baby / Get back / Summertime / I can't get next to you / Are you lonely for me baby / God is standing by / Tired of being alone / I'm a ram / Drivin' wheel / Light my fire / You say it / Right now, right now / All because
CD ____ HIUKCD 106
Hi / Aug '90 / Pinnacle

HAVE A GOOD TIME/THE BELLE ALBUM
CD ____ HIUKCD 119
Hi / Sep '91 / Pinnacle

IS LOVE / FULL OF FIRE
LOVE Love / Rhymes / Love sermon / There is love / Could I be the one / Love ritual / I didn't know / Oh me, oh my (dreams in my arms) / I gotta be more (take me higher) / I wish you were here / Glory glory / That's the way it is / Always / There's no way / I'd fly away / Full of fire / Together again / Soon as I get home / Let it shine
CD ____ HIUKCD 114
Hi / May '91 / Pinnacle

LET'S STAY TOGETHER
Let's stay together / I've never found a girl / So you're leaving / It ain't no fun to me / Talk to me, talk to me / Old time lovin / Judy / What is this feelin / Tomorrow's dream / How can you mend a broken heart / La la for you
CD ____ HIUKCD 405
Hi / Jul '86 / Pinnacle

LIVIN' FOR YOU / EXPLORES YOUR MIND
Livin' for you / Home again / Free at last / Let's get married / So good to be here / Sweet sixteen / Unchanged malady / My God is real / Beware / Sha la la / Take me to the river / God blessed our love / City / One nite stand / I'm hooked on you / Stay with me forever / Hangin' on / School days
CD ____ HIUKCD 113
Hi / May '91 / Pinnacle

LOVE IS REALITY
Just can't let you go / I can feel it / Love is reality / Positive attitude / Again / Sure feels good / I like it / You don't know me / Long time / Why
CD ____ 701927160X
Nelson Word / Apr '92 / Nelson Word

LOVE RITUAL (Rare & Previously Unreleased 1968-1972)
Love ritual / So good to be here / Ride Sally ride / Surprise attack / Love is real / I think it's for the feeling / Up above my head / Strong as death / Mimi / I want to hold your hand
CD ____ HIUKCD 443
Hi / '89 / Pinnacle

SUPREME AL GREEN, THE
Tired of being alone / I can't get next to you / Let's stay together / How can you mend a broken heart / Love and happiness / I'm still in love with you / Simply beautiful / What a wonderful thing love is / Call me / My God is real / Let's get married / Sha la la (make me happy) / Take me to the river / Love ritual / LOVE Love / I didn't know / Full of fire / Belle
CD ____ HIUKCD 130
Hi / Apr '92 / Pinnacle

TOKYO - LIVE
LOVE Love / Tired of being alone / Let's stay together / How can you mend a broken heart / All 'n' all / God blessed our love / You ought to be with me / For the good times / Belle / Sha la la / Let's get married / Dream / I feel good / Love and happiness
CD ____ HIUKCD 104
Hi / Apr '90 / Pinnacle

TRUST IN GOD
Don't it make you wanna go home / No not one / Trust in God / Lean on me / Ain't no mountain high enough / Up the ladder to the roof / Never met nobody like you / Holy spirit / All we need is a little more love
CD ____ HIUKCD 423
Hi / Jul '86 / Pinnacle

YOU SAY IT
You say it / I'll be standing by / True love / Right now, right now / Memphis, Tennessee / I'm a ram / Listen / Baby what's wrong

with you / Ride Sally ride / Eli's game / Sweet song / Everything to me / Starting all over again
CD HIUKCD 444
Hi / Jun '90 / Pinnacle

Green, Bennie

BENNIE GREEN WITH ART FARMER (Green, Bennie & Art Farmer)
CD OJCCD 1800
Original Jazz Classics / Jan '94 / Complete/Pinnacle / Jazz Music / Wellard

BLOWS HIS HORN
CD OJCCD 1728
Original Jazz Classics / Jan '94 / Complete/Pinnacle / Jazz Music / Wellard

WALKING DOWN
CD OJCCD 175
Original Jazz Classics / Jan '93 / Complete/Pinnacle / Jazz Music / Wellard

Green, Benny

ELLINGTON LEGACY, THE (Green, Benny & Joe Van Enkhuizen)
Blues at sundown / Do not disturb / Jeeps blues / Isfahan / Take it easy / In the stands / Country gal / Gypsy without a song / Blue light / I'm just a lucky so and so / Timon of Athens / Fontainebleau forest
CD CD 5115
September / Feb '94 / Cadillac / Kingdom

KALEIDOSCOPE
Kaleidoscope / Thursday's lullaby / Sexy mexy / Patience / Central park south / My girl Bill / Apricot / You're my melody / Kaleidoscope
CD CDP 8520372
Blue Note / Feb '97 / EMI

Green Day

1039/SMOOTHED OUT SLAPPY HOURS
At the library / Don't leave me / I was there / Disappearing boy / Green day / Going to Pasalacqua / Road to acceptance / Rest / Judges daughter / Paper lanterns / Why do you want him / 409 in your coffee maker / Knowledge / 1,000 hours / Dry ice / Only of you / The one I want / I want to be alone
CD 65222
Epitaph / Aug '97 / Pinnacle / Plastic Head

DOOKIE
Burnout / Having a blast / Chump / Longview / Welcome to paradise / Pulling teeth / Basket case / She / Sassafras roots / When I come around / Coming clean / Emenius sleepus / In the end / FOD
CD 9362455292
Reprise / Feb '94 / Warner Music

INSOMNIAC
Armatage shanks / Brat / Stuck with me / Geek stink breath / Stuart and the ave / 86 / Panic song / No pride / Brain stew / Jaded / Westbound sign / Tight wad hill / Walking contradiction / Bab's uvula
CD 9362460462
Reprise / Oct '95 / Warner Music

INTERVIEW DISC
CD SAM 7026
Sound & Media / Jan '97 / Sound & Media

KERPLUNK
2000 light years away / One for the razorbacks / Welcome to paradise / Christie road / Private ale / Dominated love slave / One of my lies / 80 / Android / No one knows / Who wrote holden caulfield / Words I might have ate / Sweet children / Best thing in town / Strangeland / My generation
CD LOOKOUT 46CD
Lookout / Dec '96 / Cargo / Greyhound / Shellshock/Disc
CD 65172
Epitaph / Aug '97 / Pinnacle / Plastic Head

SMOOTH
CD LOOKOUT 22CD
Lookout / Dec '96 / Cargo / Greyhound / Shellshock/Disc

Green, Earl

FEEL THE FIRE
Leaving this town / You'll never change her / Turn my world around / I just got some / Borderline / Take my advice / She's sweet to me / Down home girl / Laughing to keep from crying / Feel the fire / Living without her / Sick and tired / Beauty of the night / Turn my world around (Version 2) / Nothing but heartaches / Dark days
CD ABACACD 002
Abacabe / Jul '96 / Direct / Hot Shot

Green, Freddie

KING OF RHYTHM SESSION
Lil' Darlin / Kid from Red Bank / Port of Rico / Kansas city side / Woolafunt's lament / Up in the blues / Learnin' the blues / 9:20 Special / Swinging back / Doggin' around / It had to be you / This year's kisses / Freddie's tune / Babe's blues / Duet
CD CD 53254
Giants Of Jazz / Jun '96 / Cadillac / Jazz Music / Target/BMG

Green, Grant

BEST OF GRANT GREEN VOL.1, THE (Street Funk & Jazz Grooves)
Grantstand / Lazy afternoon / Sookie sookie / Talkin' about JC / Jean de Fleur / Windjammer / Walk in the night / I don't want nobody / Cease the bombing / Final comedown / In the middle / Wives and lovers / My favourite things / Ain't it funky now
CD BNZ 317
Blue Note / Jun '93 / EMI

BEST OF GRANT GREEN VOL.2, THE
Back out / Cease the bombing / Ain't it funky now / Sookie sookie / Cantaloupe woman / California green / Final connection / Windjammer
CD CDP 8377412
Blue Note / Aug '96 / EMI

CARRYIN' ON
Ease back / Hurt so bad / I don't want nobody to give me nothing / Upshot / Cease the bombing
CD CDP 8312472
Blue Note / Mar '95 / EMI

COMPLETE QUARTETS WITH SONNY CLARK, THE (2CD Set)
Airegin / It ain't necessarily so / I concentrate on you / Things we did last summer / Song is you / Nancy with the laughing face / Airegin / On Green Dolphin Street / Shadrack / What is this thing called love / Moon river / Gooden's corner / Two for one / Oleo / Little girl blue / Tune up / Hip funk / My favorite things / Oleo
CD Set CDP 8571942
Blue Note / Aug '97 / EMI

GRANT GREEN
Reaching out / Our Miss Brooks / Flick of a prick / One for Blena / Baby, you should know it / Falling in love with love
CD BLCD 760129
Black Lion / May '90 / Cadillac / Jazz Music / Koch / Wellard

LATIN BIT, THE
Mambo Inn / Besame mucho / Mama Inez / Brazil / Tico tico / My little suede shoes / Blues for Juanita / Grenada / Hey there
CD CDP 8376452
Blue Note / Jun '96 / EMI

Green Hornets

GET THE BUZZ
CD WIGCD 008
Alopecia / Jul '96 / Plastic Head

Green Jelly

333
Carnage rules / Orange krunch / Pinata head / Fixation / Bear song / Fight / Super elastic / Jump jerk / Anthem / Slave boy
CD 74321235362
Zoo Entertainment / May '95 / BMG

CEREAL KILLER
Obey the cowgod / Three little pigs / Ugly truth / Cereal killer / Rock 'n' roll pumpkin / Anarchy in the UK / Electric harley house (of love) / Trippin' on XTC / Mis-adventures of Shit man / House me teenage rave / Fight of the Skajaquada / Green Jelly theme song
CD 72445110382
Zoo Entertainment / Jun '93 / BMG

Green, Jesse

LIFT OFF
CD CRD 319
Chiaroscuro / Mar '96 / Jazz Music

ROUND TRIP
CD BHCD 00032
Bad Habits / Jul '95 / BMG

SEA JOURNEY (Green, Jesse Trio)
CD CRD 328
Chiaroscuro / Nov '95 / Jazz Music

Green, Lee

LEE GREEN VOL.1 - 1929-1930
CD DOCD 5187
Document / Oct '93 / ADA / Hot Shot / Jazz Music

LEE GREEN VOL.2 - 1930-1937
CD DOCD 5188
Document / Oct '93 / ADA / Hot Shot / Jazz Music

Green, Lloyd

STEELS THE HITS
Misty moonlight / Ruby, don't take your love to town / My elusive dream / Crazy arms / Too much of you / There goes my everything / Take these chains from my heart / Moody river / No another time / Moon river / Feelings / My love / Little bit more / You and me / Amie / Desperado / Kiss the moonlight / Edgewater beach / Stainless steel
CD PLATCD 33
Platinum / Jul '92 / Prism

Green On Red

BEST OF GREEN ON RED
CD WOLCD 1047
China / Jun '94 / Pinnacle

GAS FOOD LODGING
That's what dreams / Black river / Hair of the dog / This I know / Fading away / Easy way out / Sixteen ways / Drifter / Sea of Cortez / We shall overcome
CD MAUCD 612
Mau Mau / Jun '92 / Pinnacle

HERE COME THE SNAKES
Keith can't read / Morning blue / Broken radio / Tenderloin / DT blues / Rock 'n' roll disease / Zombie for love / Change / Way back home
CD WOLCD 1013
China / Mar '91 / Pinnacle

LITTLE THINGS IN LIFE (1987-91)
Gold in the graveyard / Shed a tear (for the lonesome) / Broken radio / Rock 'n' roll disease / Good patient woman / Little things in life / Quarter / Pills and booze / We had it all / Hector's out / Zombie for love / Sixteen ways / Change / Fading away / Are you sure Hank done it this way / Hair of the dog
CD MCCD 037
Music Club / Sep '91 / Disc / THE

NO FREE LUNCH
CD OW 30015
One Way / Sep '94 / ADA / Direct / Greyhound

SCAPEGOATS
CD WOLCD 1001
China / Apr '91 / Pinnacle

THIS TIME AROUND
This time around / Cool million / Reverend Luther / Good patient woman / You couldn't get arrested / Quarter / Foot / Hold the line / Pills and booze / We're all waiting
CD WOLCD 1019
China / Jul '91 / Pinnacle

Green Pajamas

GHOSTS OF LOVE
CD BCD 4033
Bomp / Jul '90 / Cargo / Greyhound / RTM/Disc / Shellshock/Disc

Green, Peter

BANDIT
Proud Pinto / Clown / In the skies / Rubbing my eyes / Bandit / Promised land / Last train to San Antone / Lost my love / Momma don't cha cry / One woman love / Tribal dance / Just for you / Black womaan / Funky jam
CD 74321474642
Milan / Apr '97 / Conifer/BMG / Silva Screen

BLUE GUITAR
Gotta see her tonight / Last train to San Antone / Woman don't / What'cha gonna do / Walkin' the road / Apostle / Fool no more / Loser two times / Slabo day / Crying won't bring you back
CD RNCD 1003
Rhino / Jun '96 / Grapevine/PolyGram / Jet Star

END OF THE GAME, THE
Bottoms up / Timeless time / Descending scale / Burnt foot / Hidden depth / End of the game
CD 7599267582
Reprise / Jan '96 / Warner Music

GREEN AND GUITAR (The Best Of Peter Green)
CD MCCD 244
Music Club / Jun '96 / Disc / THE

IN THE SKIES
In the skies / Slabo day / Fool no more / Funky chunk / Tribal dance / Seven stars / Just for you / Proud pinto / Apostle
CD RNCD 1001
Rhino / Jun '96 / Grapevine/PolyGram / Jet Star

KATMANDU
Dust my broom / One more night with you / Crane's train boogie / Boogie all the way / Zulu gone West / Blowing all my troubles away / Stranger's blues / Sweet sixteen / Who's that knocking / Case
CD 100642
CMC / May '97 / BMG

LAST TRAIN TO SAN ANTONE
Proud pinto / Clown / In the skies / Rubbing my eyes / Bandit / Funky jam / Black woman / Just for you / Tribal dance / One woman love / Momma don't cha cry / Lost my love / Last train to San Antone / Promised land
CD FG 2801
Frog / Apr '96 / Total/BMG

LEGEND
CD RNCD 1009
Rhino / Nov '96 / Grapevine/PolyGram / Jet Star

LITTLE DREAMER
Loser two times / Momma don't cha cry / Born under a bad sign / I could not ask for more / Baby when the sun goes down / Walkin' the road / One woman love / Cryin' won't bring you back / Little dreamer
CD RNCD 1002
Rhino / Jun '96 / Grapevine/PolyGram / Jet Star

ONE WOMAN LOVE
CD PACD 7013
Disky / Feb '93 / Disky / THE

RARITIES
CD APCD 052
Appaloosa / Jun '97 / ADA / Direct / TKO Magnum

RATTLESNAKE GUITAR (The Music Of Peter Green/2CD Set) (Various Artists)
CD Set CTC 0205
Coast To Coast / Mar '96 / Grapevine/ PolyGram

SPLINTER GROUP
Hitch hiking woman / Travelling riverside blues / Look on yonder wall / Homework / Stumble / Help me / Watch your step / From 4 till late / Steady rolling man / It takes time / Dark end of the street / Going down
CD SARCD 101
Snapper / May '97 / Pinnacle

TWO GREENS MAKE A BLUES (Green, Peter & Mick)
CD CLACD 426
Castle / Mar '97 / BMG

WHITE SKY
Time for me to go / Shining star / Clown / White sky (love that evil woman) / It's gonna be me / Born on the wild side / Falling apart / Indian lover / Just another guy
CD RNCD 1004
Rhino / Jun '96 / Grapevine/PolyGram / Jet Star

Green River

COME ON DOWN
CD HMS 0312
Homestead / May '94 / Cargo / SRD

DRY AS A BONE/REHAB DOLL
This town / PCC / Ozzie / Unwind / Baby takes / Searchin' / Ain't nothing to do / Queen bitch / Forever means / Rehab doll / Swallow my pride / Together we'll never / Smilin' and dyin' / Porkfist / Take a dive / One more stitch
CD SPCD 72
Sub Pop / May '94 / Cargo / Greyhound / Shellshock/Disc

Green, Urbie

SEA JAM BLUES (Green, Urbie Quintet)
CD CRD 338
Chiaroscuro / May '97 / Jazz Music

Greenbaum, Norman

SPIRIT IN THE SKY/BACK HOME AGAIN
Junior Cadillac / Spirit in the sky / Jubilee / Alice Bodine / Tars of India / Power / Good lookin' woman / Milk cow / Marcy / Back home again / Rhode Island Red / Canned ham / Titfield thunder / Miss Fancy / Lucille got stealed / Circulate / Hook and ladder / Damper / I J Foxx
CD EDCD 470
Edsel / Feb '96 / Pinnacle

Greenberg, Rowland

HOW ABOUT YOU
Seven up / I don't stand a ghost of a chance with you / Have you met Miss Jones / Georgia on my mind / Stella by starlight / Gone with the wind / Basin Street blues / Strike up the band / On the sunny side of the street / Taps Miller / Sweet and lovely
CD GECD 155
Gemini / Jan '88 / Cadillac

Greenberry Woods

RAPPLE DAPPLE
Trampoline / No 37 (Feels so strange) / Sentimental role / I'll send a message / Oh Christine / I knew you would / Waiting for dawn / That's what she said / Sympathy song / Adieu / Busted / More and more / Nowhere to go / Hold on
CD 9362454952
WEA / May '94 / Warner Music

Greene, Burton

BURTON GREENE TRIO ON TOUR
CD ESP 10742
ESP / Jan '93 / Jazz Music

Greene, Jack

JOLLY GREEN GIANT, THE
Ever since my baby went away / There goes my everything / All the time / What locks the door / You are my treasure / Love takes care of me / Statue of a fool / Back in the arms of love / Wish I didn't have to miss you / Whole world comes to me / If this is love / Something unseen / There's a whole lot about a woman / Makin' up his mind / Much obliged / What in the world has gone wrong with our love / Satisfaction / I need somebody bad / It's time to cross that bridge / He little thing'd her out of my arms

CD EDCD 515
Edsel / Mar '97 / Pinnacle

Greene, Richard

SALES TAX TODDLE
Drunken man's dream / Along about daybreak / Sales tax toddle / With body and soul / Done gone waltz / My little Georgia rose / I'll be sixteen next Sunday / Close by / 16 days in Georgia / Last ride / No one but my darlin' / Little rabbit
CD REBCD 1737
Rebel / Jul '97 / ADA / Direct

Greenfields

HOBO BY MY SIDE, A
Stay away / Broken heart / Who's that guy called Tom T Hall / Riverboat queen / Moonlight rider / San Bernardino / Come home with me tonight / Baby's gone / Rolling down / What a wonderful world / Hobo blues
CD BCD 15698
Bear Family / Jul '93 / Direct / Rollercoaster / Swift

Greenfields Of America

LIVE IN CONCERT
CD GLCD 1096
Green Linnet / Aug '92 / ADA / CM / Direct / Highlander / Roots

Greengate

METAPHYSICAL VIBRATION
CD FUZ 006
Fuzzy Box / Mar '97 / Cargo

Greenslade

BEDSIDE MANNERS ARE EXTRA
Bedside manners are extra / Pilgrims progress / Time to dream / Drum folk / Sunkissed you're not / Chalkhill
CD 7599268662
WEA / Jan '96 / Warner Music

GREENSLADE
Feathered friends / English western / Drowning man / Temple song / Melange / What are you doin' to me / Sundance
CD 7599268122
WEA / Jan '96 / Warner Music

SHADES OF GREEN 1972-1975
CD EMCD 9701
Earcotic / Jul '97 / Greyhound

SPYGLASS GUEST
Spirit of the dance / Little red fry up / Rainbow / Siam seesaw / Joie de vivre / Red light / Melancholic race / Theme for an imaginary western
CD 7599268672
WEA / Jan '96 / Warner Music

TIME AND TIDE
Animal farm / Newsworth / Time / Tide / Catalan / Flatery stakes / Waltz for a fallen idol / Ass's ears / Doldrums / Gangsters
CD 7599268682
WEA / Jan '96 / Warner Music

Greenslade, Dave

PENTATEUCH OF THE COSMOLOGY, THE
Intriot / Moondance / Beltempest / Glass / Three brides / Birds and bats and dragonflies / Nursery hymn / Minstrel / Fresco / Kashrinn / Barcarolle / Dry land / Forest kingdom / Vivat regina / Scream but not heard / Mischief / War / Lament for the sea / Miasma generator / Exile / Jubilate / Tiger the dove
CD BGOCD 170
Beat Goes On / Jul '94 / Pinnacle

Greenwich, Sonny

LIVE AT SWEET BASIL
CD JUST 262
Justin Time / Jul '92 / Cadillac / New Note/Pinnacle

Greer, Big John

BIG JOHN'S ROCKIN' (3CD Set)
CD Set BCD 15554
Bear Family / Feb '92 / Direct / Rollercoaster / Swift

Greeson, Ron

BLUEFUSE
CD HEDC 002
Headscope / Jun '93 / TKO Magnum

Gregory, Michael

WHAT TO WHERE
Jubilee / One / Still waiting / Heart of happiness / Superstitious game / Last home at / Where / What / Falling down / Fan the flame / Slow burn (there's more) / Elan
CD PD 83023
Novus / Dec '88 / BMG

Gregory, Steve

BUSHFIRE
CD LJKCD 011
LKJ / Mar '95 / Grapevine/PolyGram / Jet Star

Gregson & Collister

LOVE IS A STRANGE HOTEL
For a dancer / Move away Jimmy Blue / How men are / Love is a strange hotel / Even a fool would let go / One step up / Things we do for love / (I heard that) Lonesome whistle / Same situation / Always better with you / Today I started loving you again / Most beguiling eyes
CD SPCD 1035
Special Delivery / Oct '90 / ADA / CM / Direct

MISCHIEF
CD SPCD 1010
Special Delivery / Sep '87 / ADA / CM / Direct

Gregson, Clive

CAROUSEL OF NOISE (Live/Unreleased Tracks)
CD CGCD 9401
Gregsongs / May '95 / ADA / Direct

I LOVE THIS TOWN
CD FIENDCD 786
Demon / Sep '96 / Pinnacle

PEOPLE AND PLACES
CD FIENDCD 764
Demon / Apr '95 / Pinnacle

STRANGE PERSUASIONS
Summer rain / Jewel in your crown / I still see her face / Home is where the heart is / Play the fool / Poor relation / This town / Safety net / American car / I fell apart
CD FIENDCD 45
Demon / Jan '90 / Pinnacle

Grekis, Paraskevas

BOUZOUKIS
CD PS 65173
PlayaSound / Nov '96 / ADA / Harmonia Mundi

Grenadier Guards Band

BRITISH GRENADIERS, THE
British Grenadiers / Scipio / First battalion bugle call / Queens company / Second battalion bugle call / Nilmegen / Third battalion bugle call / Inkerman / Rule Brittania / Grenadiers march / Duke of York / Duke of Gloster's march / Belle isle / Portsmouth / Wargramer grenadier march / Last post / Grenadiers return / Reveille / Musick marziale
CD BNA 5015
Bandleader / Oct '87 / Conifer/BMG

DRUMS AND FIFES (The 1st & 2nd Battalion Of Grenadier Guards)
British Grenadiers / Girl I left behind me / Goodbye Dolly Gray / Garry Owen / Pack up your troubles in your old kit bag / Lilliburlero / Great escape / Hazlemere / Old grey mare / Brazil / See the conquering hero comes / Scipio / Red cloak / Army and Marine / Bugle calls / Marching down the years / Potpourri / Regimental music of the 18th century / First battalion bugle call / Parade flute call / Second battalion bugle call / Drummer's call / Third battalion bugle call / Ye British Grenadiers / Flag and empire / Prussia's glory / Eton boating song / Attention / Belle Isle march / Prince Rupert's march / Duke of York / Captain Money's march / Fanfare
CD BNA 5003
Bandleader / Nov '86 / Conifer/BMG

MARCH SPECTULAR (Bands Of The Grenadier, Coldstream & Irish Guards)
British Grenadiers / Scipio / Grenadiers march / Milanollo / Gigaro / St. Patrick's day / Let erin remember / Through bolts and bars / Army and marine / Furchtlos und treu / Red men's march / Nijmegen / Dunedin / Badenviller / Carry on / Bond of friendship / Independentia / King's troop / Luftwaffe March / Imperial echoes / Admiral of the air / Trafalgar / Frensham / Pioneer spirit / quis separabit / Wellington / San Lorenzo / Sons of the brave / Star of St Patrick
CD BNA 5040
Bandleader / '91 / Conifer/BMG

MARCHING WITH THE GRENADIER GUARDS
British Grenadiers / Tour of duty / Imperial echoes / Zapfenstreich nr1 / Old comrades / Scipio march / Blaze away / Troop 'Les Huguenots' / Hands across the sea / Colonel Bogey / Grenadiers slow march / Liberty bell / Purple pageant / Radetzky march / Duke of York / Europe united / Coronation bells / New colonial march
CD CDGUARDS 1
Premier/MFP / Oct '90 / EMI

ON STAGE
Fanfare - stage presence / Full speed ahead / Grenadiers waltz / Overture on themes of Offenbach / Love changes everything / Carnival of Venice / Debutante / Prelude to romance / Send in the clowns / Portrait in time / Me and my girl / March and dance of the comedians / Les miserables / Spanish rhapsody fiesta / March: Atlantis / Three bavarian dances
CD BNA 5032
Bandleader / Aug '89 / Conifer/BMG

SOUSA MARCHES/STIRRING MARCHES OF THE USA SERVICES (Grenadier Guards Band/Major Rodney Bashford)
Stars and stripes forever / El capitan / High school cadets / Washington post / Picadore / Invincible eagle / Semper fidelis / Manhattan beach / Liberty bell / Thunderer / King Cotton / Hands across the sea / Anchors aweigh / Samper paratus / She wore a yellow ribbon / West Point march / Ballad of the Green Berets / Caissons go rolling along / Marine Corps hymn / Air Corps / Commando march / Guadalcanal march / Thru' the years 1776-1969 medley
CD 4489572
Phase 4 / Aug '96 / PolyGram

WHEN THE GUARDS ARE ON PARADE
British grenadiers / Scorpio / Duke of York / Grenadiers return / Queen's company / Inkerman / Royal salute / Army and marine / Glorious victory / Army of the nile / Great little army / Royal standard / Steadfast and true / King's guard / National emblem / Birdcake walk / Old grenadier / Namur / Belgian gendarmes / Mareth / Line / When the guards are on parade / Bravest of the brave / On the square / Contemptibles
CD BNA 5104
Bandleader / Mar '94 / Conifer/BMG

WORLD OF THE MILITARY BAND, THE
Imperial march / March militaire / March / March / March with honour crowned / Coronation march: crown imperial / Entry of the Boyards / Turkish march / Hungarian march / Procession of the sirdar / Radetzky march / Grand march / Grand march / March / Coronation march / March militaire / Pomp and circumstance march no.1
CD 4529382
Decca / Aug '97 / PolyGram

Grenadine

NOPALITOS
CD SMR 23CD
Simple Machines / Oct '94 / SRD

Grenfell, Joyce

BEST OF JOYCE GRENFELL
I'm going to see you today / Nursery school (flowers) / Learn to loosen / Visitor / Old tyme dancing (stately as a galleon) / I wouldn't go back / Committee / Green summer / Wedding is on Saturday / Narcissus (the laughing record) / Old girls school reunion / Wrong songs for wrong singers (or songs to make you sick) / Shirley's girlfriend / Dear Francois / Nicodemus / Drifting / Nursery school (sing song time) / Ballad / Hostess / Artist's room / Lullaby / Opening numbers / Oh Mr. Du Maurier / Nursery school (free activity period) / I like life / Terrible worrier / Hymn / Writer of children's books / Picture postcard (keepsake) / Boat train / Duet / Ethel / Opera interval / Three brothers / Nursery school (story time) / Slow down / Two character studies / American mother / Unsuitable / One is one and all alone / It's almost tomorrow / Encores / Nursery school (Nativity play) / Woman on the bus / Fan / Time / First flight / There's nothing new to tell you / I don't 'arf love you: *Grenfell, Joyce & Norman Wisdom* / Telephone call / Bring back the silence / Life and literature / Maud / Eng Lit 1 / Joyful noise / Life story / Ferry boats of Sydney / Nursery school (going home time) / London Scottish / Useful and acceptable gifts
CD JOYCE 1
Premier/EMI / Mar '96 / EMI

Gretschen Hofner

MARIA CALLOUS
CD OPIUMCD 2
Poppy / Jun '97 / 3mv/Vital

Gretsy, Alan

BOBCATS RECAPTURED
CD JCD 258
Jazzology / Dec '95 / Jazz Music

Grey, Al

CENTER PIECE - LIVE AT THE BLUE NOTE
Diz related / South side / I wish I knew / Homage to Norman / Nascimento / SWB Blues / Lester leaps in / Bewitched, bothered and bewildered / Center piece
CD CD 83379
Telarc / Sep '95 / Conifer/BMG

CHRISTMAS STOCKIN' STUFFER
CD 74039
Capri / Nov '93 / Cadillac / Wellard

FAB
CD 74038
Capri / Nov '93 / Cadillac / Wellard

LIVE AT THE 1990 FLOATING JAZZ FESTIVAL
CD CRD 313
Chiaroscuro / Mar '96 / Jazz Music

NEW AL GREY QUINTET, THE
Bluish grey / Sonny's tune / Don't blame me / Syrup and bisquits / T'ain't no use / Al's rose / Night and day / Call it whatchawanna / Underdog / Stompin' at the Savoy / Al's blues / Rue prevail / Soap gets in your eyes
CD CRD 305
Chiaroscuro / Oct '91 / Jazz Music

TRULY WONDERFUL (Grey, Al & Jimmy Forrest)
CD STCD 552
Stash / '92 / ADA / Cadillac / CM / Direct / Jazz Music

Grey, Carola

GIRLS CAN'T HIT
Bits and pieces / Aspects of eve / Golden boy greets Buddah / Search for Taco / 3/3/3/5/5/5/4/4 / Girls can't hit / It's all good / Don't play it again Sam / Room 201
CD LIP 89452
Lipstick / Feb '97 / Vital/SAM

Grey, Jerry

SOUND OFF
CD DAWE 73
Magic / Oct '95 / Cadillac / Harmonia Mundi / Jazz Music / Swift / Wellard

Grey Lady Down

CRIME
12.02 / All join hands / Thrill of it all / Ballad of Billy Grey / Circus of thieves / Annabez / Fugitive / I believe
CD CYCL 001
Cyclops / Feb '94 / Pinnacle

FEAR
And finally / Roller coaster / Modern day cavalier / Final decree / Sliding / Usurper / Paper chains
CD CYCL 053
Cyclops / Jul '97 / Pinnacle

FORCES
Paradise lost / Battlefields of counterpane / Without a trace / Cold stage / I believe / Flyer
CD CYCL 020
Cyclops / Jun '95 / Pinnacle

Grey, Michael

COMPOSERS SERIES VOL.1
CD LCOM 5217
Lismor / Sep '94 / ADA / Direct / Duncans / Lismor

Greyboy

FREESTYLIN'
CD URCD 003
Ubiquity / Jul '96 / Cargo / Timewarp

LAND OF THE LOST
CD URCD 012
Ubiquity / Jul '96 / Cargo / Timewarp

TOWN CALLED EARTH, A
CD GBR 005
Greyboy / Jun '97 / Timewarp

Greyboy Allstars

WEST COAST BOOGALOO
CD GB 001CD
Greyboy / Jul '96 / Timewarp

Greyhound

BLACK AND WHITE
Black and white / Dream lover / Stand for our rights / Jamaica rum / Sky high / Wily / Only love can win / Mango rock / Unchained melody / Hold on to your happiness / Wappadusa / Some dark city
CD C5CD 539
See For Miles/C5 / Oct '92 / Pinnacle

Grid

456
Face the sun / Ice machine / Crystal clear / Aquarium / Instrument / Heartbeat / Oh six one / Figure of eight / Boom / Leave your body / Fire engine red
CD CDV 2696
Virgin / Oct '92 / EMI

ELECTRIC HEAD
One giant step / Interference / Are you receiving / Islamatron / Traffic / Driving instructor / Beat called love / Friend of the devil / Sugar magnolia / Operator / Candy man / Ripple / Brokedown palace / Till the morning comes / Attics of my life / Truckin' / Floatation / Strange electric sun / Typical Waterloo sunset / Dr. Celine / Machine delay / This must be heaven / Beautiful and profound / Intergalactica / Central locking / First stroke
CD 9031715572
East West / Sep '90 / Warner Music

EVOLVER
Wake up / Rollercoaster / Swamp thing / Throb / Rise / Shades of sleep / Higher peaks / Texas cowboys / Spin cycle / Golden dawn
CD 74321227182
De-Construction / Aug '96 / BMG

MUSIC FOR DANCING
Floatation / Crystal clear / Boom / Figure of 8 / Rollercoaster / Texas cowboys / Swamp thing / Crystal clear (remix) / Figure of 8 (remix) / Diablo / Rollercoaster (remix)
CD _______ 74321276702
De-Construction / Sep '95 / BMG

Grief

AU DELA
CD _______ DANCD 023
Danceteria / Jan '90 / ADA / Plastic Head / Shellshock/Disc

KITTYSTRA QUATRE
CD _______ DANCD 014
Danceteria / Jan '90 / ADA / Plastic Head / Shellshock/Disc

Grief

COME TO GRIEF
CD _______ CM 77087
Century Media / Jan '95 / Plastic Head

Grief Society

HOW WE USED TO LIVE
CD _______ GIEXCD 001
Gentlemen In Exile / Nov '96 / Else

Grier, David

FREEWHEELING
Wheeling / Shadowbrook / Old hotel rag / Angeline the baker / Bluegrass itch / Alabama jubilee / Blue midnite star / Roanoke / If I knew her name / Gold rush / Fog rolling over the Glen / New soldier's joy
CD _______ ROUCD 0250
Rounder / '91 / ADA / CM / Direct

LONE SOLDIER
CD _______ ROUCD 0309
Rounder / Apr '95 / ADA / CM / Direct

Grievous Angels

NEW CITY OF SIN
CD _______ BS 020CD
Bloodshot / Jun '97 / Cargo

ONE JOB TOWN
CD _______ SP 1162CD
Stony Plain / Oct '93 / ADA / CM / Direct

Griffin, Buck

LET'S ELOPE BABY
Pretty Lou / Girl in 1209 / You'll never come back / Stutterin' Papa / Watchin' the 7:10 roll by / Broken heart with alimony / Jessie Lee / Bow my back / Old bee tree / Every night / Party / Little Dan / Neither do I / Cochise / Go-stop-go / Bawlin' and squalin' / Let's elope baby / It don't make no never mind / Meadow lark boogie / Rollin' tears / One day after payday / Going home all alone / Twenty six steps / First man to stand on the moon / Sorry I never knew you / Lord give me strength / Next to mine / Lookin' for the green
CD _______ BCD 15811
Bear Family / Jun '95 / Direct / Rollercoaster / Swift

Griffin, Della

I'LL GET BY
If you were the only boy in the world / But beautiful / I'm gettin' sentimental over you / Fools rush in / You and me (against the world) / I'll get by / Two different worlds / East of the Sun and West of the moon
CD _______ MCD 5568
Muse / Sep '96 / New Note/Pinnacle

TRAVELIN' LIGHT
Smile / Travellin' light / Out of nowhere / Some other Spring / Second time around / Easy living / Trouble in mind / Trust in me / Blue gardenia
CD _______ MCD 5496
Muse / Jul '94 / New Note/Pinnacle

Griffin, Johnny

BIG SOUL-BAND, THE (Griffin, Johnny Orchestra)
Wade in the water / Panic room blues / Nobody knows the trouble I've seen / Meditation / Holla / So tired / Deep river / Jubilation
CD _______ OJCCD 485
Original Jazz Classics / Oct '96 / Complete/ Pinnacle / Jazz Music / Wellard

DANCE OF PASSION
CD _______ 5126042
Antilles/New Directions / Jan '93 / PolyGram

LITTLE GIANT, THE
Catharsis / What's new / Hot sausage / Woody 'n' you / Where's your overcoat boy / Little John / 63rd Street theme / Playmates / Message / Kerry dancers / Black is the colour of my true love's hair / Green grow the rushes-o / Londonderry air
CD _______ OJCCD 136
Original Jazz Classics / Jun '96 / Complete/ Pinnacle / Jazz Music / Wellard

MAN I LOVE, THE
Man I love / Hush-a-bye / Blues for Harvey / (I'm afraid) the masquerade is over / Sophisticated lady / Wee / I'll get by / Mean to me / I'll never be the same / Easy living / Foolin' myself / Without your love / Me, myself and I / Sailboat in the moonlight / Travellin' all alone / She's funny that way / Getting some fun out of life / I can't believe that you're in love with me / Back in your own backyard / You can't be mine (and someone else's too) / Say it with a kiss
CD _______ BLCD 760107
Black Lion / Jun '88 / Cadillac / Jazz Music / Koch / Wellard

WAY OUT
CD _______ OJCCD 1855
Original Jazz Classics / Jul '94 / Complete/Pinnacle / Jazz Music / Wellard

WOE IS ME
CD _______ JHR 73559
Jazz Hour / Oct '92 / Cadillac / Jazz Music / Target/BMG

Griffin, Rex

LAST LETTER, THE (3CD Set)
Why should I care if you're blue / Blue eyes lullaby / Just for old times sake / Love call yodel / I don't love anybody but you / Trail to home sweet home / Let me call you sweetheart again / Mean woman blues / Dixieland sweetheart / Down in old Alabama / Everybody's tryin' to be my baby / If you call that gone goodbye / Yodelling cowboy's last song / I love you Nellie / I'm just passing through / I'm ready to reform / Walkin' blues / Old faded photograph / Sittin' on the old setee / Sweet Mama hurry home / Would you leave me alone little darling / Last love call yodel / Last letter / Over the river / Answer to the last letter / My hillbilly baby / I think I'll give up (it's all over now) / Beyond the last mile / Just partners / Lovesick blues / I love you as before / I'll never tell you that I love you / Nobody wants to be my baby / Maybe you'll think about me / You got to go to work / Old rose and a curl / Everybody's tryin' to be my baby / I'm just passin' through / I don't love anybody but you / Let me call you sweetheart / Just for old time's sake / I'm ready to reform / Walkin' blues / Old faded photograph / Trail to home sweet home / Nobody wants to be my baby / Mean woman blues / Why should I care if you're blue / I love you Nellie / Yum yum blues / Toodle-oo sweet Mama / Too good to be true / That old sweetheart of mine / Blue eyes lullaby / Yodelling cowboy's last song / Love call yodel / How can I be sure / I'm crying inside / I don't mean to mean / Thousand times or more / I'm free as the breeze / I lost again / Misery: *Griffin, Buddy* / Same tear twice: *Griffin, Buddy* / Last letter: *Griffin, Buddy* / No love, no heartaches: *Griffin, Buddy* / If you call that gone goodbye: *Griffin, Buddy* / You got to go to work: *Griffin, Buddy* / Gods of love: *Griffin, Buddy* / Shuckin' corn: *Griffin, Buddy* / High and dry: *Griffin, Buddy* / Don't talk about you love: *Griffin, Buddy* / Don't hold your breath: *Griffin, Buddy* / My Carolina mountain home: *Griffin, Buddy* / Let me walk along beside you: *Griffin, Buddy* / Just wait and see: *Griffin, Buddy* / Bartender's girl: *Griffin, Buddy* / Red rose, a bouquet or a roomful: *Griffin, Buddy*
CD Set _______ BCD 15911
Bear Family / Dec '96 / Direct / Rollercoaster / Swift

Griffin, Sid

LITTLE VICTORIES
When I'm out walking with you / Jimmy Reed / Good times tomorrow, hard times today / Rate of exchange / I wish I was a mountain / Distant trains / Sailers and soldiers / Man who invented the blues / Monk's mood / Flak jacket / Alma Mater / Jerusalem Road
CD _______ SID 007
Prima / May '97 / Direct

Griffith, Grace

GRACE GRIFFITH
CD _______ BLX 10028CD
Blix Street / Apr '96 / ADA

Griffith, Nanci

BEST OF NANCI GRIFFITH
Trouble in the fields / From a distance / Speed of the sound of loneliness / Love at the five and dime / Listen to the radio / Gulf coast highway / I wish it would rain / Ford Econoline / If wishes were changes / Wing and the wheel / Late night Grand hotel / From Clare to here / It's just another morning here / Tumble and fall / There's a light beyond these woods (Mary Margaret) / Outbound plane / Lone star state of mind / It's a hard life wherever you go / Road to Aberdeen
CD _______ MCD 10966
MCA / Oct '93 / BMG

BLUE ROSES FROM THE MOONS
Everything's comin' up roses / Two for the road / Wouldn't that be fine / Battlefield / Saint Teresa of Avila / Gulf Coast highway / I fought the law / Not my way home / Is this all there is / Maybe tomorrow / Waiting for love / I'll move along / Morning train / She ain't goin' nowhere
CD _______ 75599620152
Warner Bros. / Mar '97 / Warner Music

FLYER
Flyer / Nobody's angel / Say it isn't so / Southbound train / These days in a open book / Time of inconvenience / Don't forget about me / Always will / Going back to Georgia / Talk to me while I'm listening / Fragile / On Grafton street / Anything you need but me / Goodnight to a Mothers dream / This heart
CD _______ MCD 11155
MCA / Sep '94 / BMG

LAST OF THE TRUE BELIEVERS, THE
Last of the true believers / Love at the five and dime / St. Olav's gate / More than a whisper / Banks of the old Pontchartrain / Looking for the time / Goin' gone / One of these days / Love's found a shoulder / Fly by night / Wing and the wheel
CD _______ CDPH 1109
Philo / Nov '96 / ADA / CM / Direct

LATE NIGHT GRANDE HOTEL
CD _______ MCLD 19304
MCA / Oct '95 / BMG

LITTLE LOVE AFFAIRS
Anyone can be somebody's fool / I knew love / Never mind / Love wore a halo / So long ago / Gulf coast highway / Little love affairs / I wish it would rain / Outbound plane / I would change my life / Sweet dreams will come
CD _______ MCLD 19211
MCA / Aug '93 / BMG

LONE STAR STATE OF MIND
Lone star state of mind / Cold hearts, closed minds / From a distance / Beacon Street / Nickel dreams / Sing one for sister / Ford econoline / Trouble in the fields / Love in a memory / Let it shine on me / There's a light beyond these woods (Mary Margaret)
CD _______ MCLD 19176
MCA / Nov '92 / BMG

OTHER VOICES, OTHER ROOMS
Across the great divide / Woman of the phoenix / Tecumseh valley / Three fights up / Boots of spanish leather / Speed of the sound of loneliness / From Clare to here / I can't help but wonder where I'm bound / Do re mi / This old town / Comin' down in the rain / Ten degrees and getting colder / Morning song to Sally / Night rider's lament / Are you tired of me darling / Turn around / Wimoweh
CD _______ MCD 10796
MCA / Mar '93 / BMG

POET IN MY WINDOW
CD _______ MCLD 1911
MCA / Oct '91 / BMG

Griffiths, Albert

WHOLE HEAP, A (Griffiths, Albert & The Gladiators)
CD _______ HBCD 11554
Heartbeat / '88 / ADA / Direct / Greensleeves / Jet Star

Griffiths, Marcia

AT STUDIO ONE
CD _______ SOCD 1126
Studio One / Mar '96 / Jet Star

DREAMLAND
Dreamland / Tell me now / Truly / Mark my word / Stay / Feel like jumping / Lonesome feeling / Survival / Melody life / I've got to go back home
CD _______ CDSGP 0148
Prestige / Oct '95 / Else / Total/BMG

INDOMITABLE
CD _______ PHCD 26
Penthouse / Sep '93 / Jet Star

LAND OF LOVE, THE
CD _______ PHCD 2045
Penthouse / Jan '97 / Jet Star

MARCIA
CD _______ DGCD 7
Germaine / Apr '89 / Jet Star

MARCIA GRIFFITHS AND FRIENDS
CD _______ RNCD 2040
Rhino / Jan '94 / Grapevine/PolyGram / Jet Star

PUT A LITTLE LOVE IN YOUR HEART (The Best Of Marcia Griffiths)
Toil (my ambition) / Don't let me down / Put a little love in your heart / Young, gifted and black / We've got to get ourselves together / Private number / Band of gold / Pied piper / But I do / Your love / I don't care / You're mine / Help me up / First time ever I saw your face / Play me / There's no me without you / I just don't want to be lonely / Gypsy man / Sweet bitter love / When will I see you again
CD _______ CDTRL 325
Trojan / Mar '94 / Direct / Jet Star

STEPPIN'
CD _______ SHCD 44007
Shanachie / Jun '91 / ADA / Greensleeves / Koch

Grifters

CRAPPIN YOU NEGATIVE
CD _______ 185192
Southern / May '94 / SRD

EYES FULL OF GOLD
CD _______ SPCD 327
Sub Pop / Feb '96 / Cargo / Greyhound / Shellshock/Disc

ONE SOCK MISSING
CD _______ 185112
Southern / Jun '93 / SRD

Grill

LIGHT
CD _______ CDPPP 111
PDCD / Feb '94 / Plastic Head

Grillo, Alex

VIBRAPHONE ALONE
CD _______ CELPC 24
CELP / Nov '93 / Cadillac / Harmonia Mundi

Grimes, Carol

ALIVE AT RONNIE SCOTT'S
Solitude / Never say never / Give me liberty / Wild women / Lush life / Who do you want / Where are you / Life is dangerous / Your shoes are hot / We said yes
CD _______ JHCD 034
Ronnie Scott's Jazz House / '91 / Cadillac / Jazz Music / New Note/Pinnacle / TKO Magnum

LAZY BLUE EYES (Grimes, Carol & Ian Shaw)
I got it bad and that ain't good / You always miss the water (when the well runs dry) / I'm scared / Don't explain / Lush life / In a sentimental mood / Lover man / I ain't got nothin' but the blues / I cover the waterfront / I love you / Spring can really hang you up the most / Lazy blue eyes / Snake / Misty / Body and soul
CD _______ CDWIK 93
Big Beat / Oct '90 / Pinnacle

Grimes, Tiny

COMPLETE TINY GRIMES VOL.1 1944-1946, THE
CD _______ BMCD 6005
Blue Moon / Jul '96 / Cadillac / Discovery / Greensleeves / Jazz Music / Jet Star / TKO Magnum

COMPLETE TINY GRIMES VOL.2 1944-1950, THE
CD _______ BMCD 6006
Blue Moon / Jul '96 / Cadillac / Discovery / Greensleeves / Jazz Music / Jet Star / TKO Magnum

COMPLETE TINY GRIMES VOL.3 1950, THE
CD _______ BMCD 6007
Blue Moon / Jan '97 / Cadillac / Discovery / Greensleeves / Jazz Music / Jet Star / TKO Magnum

COMPLETE TINY GRIMES VOL.4 1950-1953, THE
CD _______ BMCD 6008
Blue Moon / Jan '97 / Cadillac / Discovery / Greensleeves / Jazz Music / Jet Star / TKO Magnum

COMPLETE TINY GRIMES VOL.5 1953-1954, THE
CD _______ BMCD 6009
Blue Moon / Jan '97 / Cadillac / Discovery / Greensleeves / Jazz Music / Jet Star / TKO Magnum

SOME GROOVY FOURS
Tiny's boogie woogie / Everyday I have the blues / Swinging Mama / Some groovy fours / I found a new baby / Tee mine sy / Lester leaps in / Sid West End blues / Li'l darlin' / Swinging Mama / Frankie and Johnny / Food for thought / Morgantini with mine
CD _______ BB 8742
Black & Blue / Jan '97 / Discovery / Koch / Wellard

TINY GRIMES AND THE ROCKIN' HIGHLANDERS (Grimes, Tiny & His Rockin' Highlanders)
Call of the wild / St. Louis blues / Tiny's jump / Howlin' blues / Frankie and Johnny boogie / My baby's cool / Pert skirt / Hey Mr. J.B. / Drinking beer / Marie
CD _______ KKCD 01
Krazy Kat / Apr '89 / Hot Shot / Jazz Music

Grimethorpe Colliery Band

CLASSIC BRASS
Florentiner march / William Tell overture / Sweet Georgia Brown / Serenade / Sugar blues / Mr. Jums / Valdres march / MacArthur Park / Gymnopedie No.1 / Mr. Lear's carnival / Misty / Procession to the Minster

/ Irish tune from County Derry / Finale from Faust
CD _____ CDMFP 6058
Music For Pleasure / May '89 / EMI

FIREBIRD (Conducted By Ray Farr)
Midnight sleighride / On with the motley / Songs of the quay / In a sentimental mood / Pictures at an exhibition / Festive prelude / Scherzo / Berne patrol / Why did I choose you / Firebird
CD _____ QPRL 010
Polyphonic / May '94 / Complete/Pinnacle

GRIMETHORPE
CD _____ CHAN 4545
Chandos / Mar '97 / Chandos

GRIMETHORPE COLLIERY BAND
Red sky at night / Hogarth's hoe down / I dream of Jeannie with the light brown hair / Barney's tune / Cornet concerto / Chinese takeaway / Parade / Paris le soir / Mosaic / Stars and stripes forever / Moorside suite / Severn suite
CD _____ 4500232
Decca / Aug '93 / PolyGram

OLD RUGGED CROSS, THE
CD _____ PLSCD 194
Pulse / Apr '97 / BMG

PAGANINI VARIATIONS FOR BRASS BAND
Raven's wood / Journey into freedom / Queen of the night's aria / Ruby Tuesday / Buster strikes back / Finale from organ symphony No. 3 / President / Girl with the flaxen hair / Blue John / Blue rondo a la Turk / Panagini variations
CD _____ DOYCD 015
Doyen / May '92 / Conifer/BMG

POPULAR HYMNS
CD _____ MATCD 268
Castle / Apr '93 / BMG

WAGNER
CD _____ DOYCD 033
Doyen / Jan '96 / Conifer/BMG

WILBY
CD _____ DOYCD 029
Doyen / Mar '94 / Conifer/BMG

YOUR 20 FAVOURITE HYMNS
CD _____ PWKS 4248
Carlton / May '97 / Carlton

Grimetime

SPIRIT OF DISGUST
CD _____ KCCD 1
Kill City / Jun '94 / Total/Pinnacle

Grimms

ROCKING DUCK
Interruption at the Opera House / Three times corner / Sex maniac / Galatic love poem / Chairman Shankly / Italian job / Albatross ramble / Humanoid boogie / Short blues / Summer with the Monarch / Twyfords vitromant / Following you / Newly pressed suit / Eleventh hour / Conservative government figures / Brown paper carrier bag / Soul song / Rockin' duck / Songs of the stars / Right mask / Policeman's lot / Question of habit / Take it while you can / Poetic license / Masked poet / Hiss and boo / Gruesome / FX / Blab blab blab / Backwards thru space / Do chuck a mao mao
CD _____ EDCD 370
Edsel / Jun '93 / Pinnacle

Grin

GONE CRAZY
You're the weight / Boy and girl / What about me / One more time / True thrill / Beggar's day / Nightmare / Believe / Ain't for free
CD _____ 5407062
A&M / Mar '97 / PolyGram

Grip Inc.

NEMESIS
CD _____ SPV 08518322
SPV / Feb '97 / Koch / Plastic Head

POWER OF INNER STRENGTH
CD _____ SPV 08576922
SPV / Mar '96 / Koch / Plastic Head

Grisman, David

ACOUSTIC CHRISTMAS
CD _____ ROUCD 0190
Rounder / '88 / ADA / CM / Direct

DAVID GRISMAN ROUNDER ALBUM
Hello / Sawing on the strings / Waiting on Vasser / I ain't broke but I'm badly bent / Op 38 / Hold to God's unchanging hand / Boston boy / Cheyenne / Till the end of the world rolls around / You'll find her name written there / On and on / Bob's Brewin / So long
CD _____ ROUCD 0069
Rounder / '88 / ADA / CM / Direct

DAWG '90
CD _____ ACD 1
Acoustic Disc / May '97 / ADA / Koch

DAWGANOVA (Grisman, David Quintet)
Dawganova / April's wedding bossa / Barkley's bug / Caliente / Brazilian breeze / Tico Tico / El Cumbanchero / Manha de Carnaval / Nature boy
CD _____ ACD 17
Acoustic Disc / Jun '97 / ADA / Koch

DAWGWOOD (Grisman, David Quintet)
CD _____ ACD 7
Acoustic Disc / Jul '97 / ADA / Koch

DGQ 20 (3CD Set) (Grisman, David Quintet)
CD Set _____ ACD 20
Acoustic Disc / Jun '97 / ADA / Koch

EARLY DAWG
CD _____ SHCD 3713
Sugar Hill / Jan '94 / ADA / CM / Direct / Koch / Roots

HERE TODAY (Grisman, David & Various Artists)
I'll love nobody but you / Once more / Foggy mountain chimes / Children are cryin' / Hot corn / Cold corn / Lonesome river / My walking shoes / Love and wealth / Billy in the lowground / Making plans / Sweet little Miss blue eyes / Going up home to live in green pastures
CD _____ ROUCD 0169
Rounder / Aug '93 / ADA / CM / Direct

HOME IS WHERE THE HEART IS
True life blues / Down in the willow garden / My long journey home / Little Willie / Highway of sorrow / Sophronie / My aching heart / Close by / Feast here tonight / Leavin' home / Little cabin home on the hill / I'm comin' back / But I don't know when / Salty Dawg blues / If I lose / Sad and lonesome day / My little Georgia rose / Foggy mountain top / I'm my own grandpa / Pretty Polly / Home is where the heart is / Nine pound hammer / Memories of mother and day / Teardrops in my eyes / House of gold
CD Set _____ ROUCD 0251/2
Rounder / Aug '88 / ADA / CM / Direct

NOT FOR KIDS ONLY (Grisman, David & Jerry Garcia)
CD _____ ACD 9
Acoustic Disc / Jul '97 / ADA / Koch

TONE POEMS VOL.2 (The Sounds Of The Great Jazz Guitars & Mandolins) (Grisman, David & Martin Taylor)
CD _____ AC 018CD
Acoustic Disc / Apr '97 / ADA / Koch

Griswalds

ALL THE WAY DOWN
All the way down / Can't break away / Footstompin' / Let go / Big Daddy Cool / Aunt Nancey's bull / My love don't mean a thing / Lil' Bonnie Blue / What the fool made me do / Good, the bad, the ugly / What I say is right
CD _____ JSPCD 280
JSP / Jan '97 / ADA / Cadillac / Direct / Hot Shot / Target/BMG

Grits

RARE BIRDS
CD _____ CUNEIFORM 55912
Cuneiform / Jun '97 / ReR Megacorp

Grodes

LET'S TALK ABOUT GIRLS (Grodes/ Dearly Beloved)
CD _____ BA 0010
Bacchus Archives / Feb '97 / Cargo / Plastic Head

Grolnick, Don

BLUE NOTE SESSIONS, THE (2CD Set)
Nothing personal / Tagliono / Weaver of dreams / His Majesty the baby / I want to be happy / Persimmons / Or come fog / Five bars / Heart of darkness / What is this thing called love / One bird, one stone / Nighttown Genie / Spot that man / Cost of living / Blues for pop
CD Set _____ CDP 8571972
Blue Note / Aug '97 / EMI

Gronemeyer, Herbert

CHAOS
Chaos / Promise my love / Lead me home / Hard heads / Greenland / I've had enough / Puss in boots / Hole in my head / No guarantee / Wave
CD _____ CDEMC 3758
EMI / Sep '96 / EMI

Groon

REFUSAL TO COMPLY
CD _____ DIS 002
FMR/Dissenter / Oct '95 / Cadillac / Harmonia Mundi

Groove & The Gang

MR. BOOGALOO
CD _____ CS 8517
Mic Mac / Mar '96 / Vital/SAM

Groove Collective

GROOVE COLLECTIVE
Restrike / Balimka / Nerd / Rahsaanasong / Ms. Grier / Whatugot / El golpe avisa / Genji monogatari / Buddha head / Saturday afternoon
CD _____ 9362455412
WEA / Mar '94 / Warner Music

WE THE PEOPLE
Jay Wrestles the Bari Constrictor / Loisaida / Lift off / Everybody (We the people) / Fly / Sneakey / I am / Caterpillar / Hide it / Anthem / Sedate / Jay wrestles the Bari Constrictor, 2 / She's so heavy (I want you) / Where are your white shoes
CD _____ IMP 11632
Impulse Jazz / May '96 / New Note/BMG

Groove Corporation

CO-OPERATION
CD _____ CORPCD 1
Network / Sep '95 / 3mv/Sony / Pinnacle

Groove Juice Special

GROOVE JUICE SPECIAL & SWEET SUBSTITUTE (Groove Juice Special & Sweet Sunstitute/Al Fairweather)
Fat and greasy / My new celebrity is you / Mama bought a chicken / Rockabye Basie / Porgy / 5 guys named Moe / Lucky Jim / Twisted / Hucklebuck / King size papa / Smoke rings / Nagasaki / Hotel Noel
CD _____ LACD 83
Lake / Jul '97 / ADA / Cadillac / Direct / Jazz Music / Target/BMG

Groove Theory

GROOVE THEORY
10 minute high / Time flies / Ride / Come home / Baby love / Tell me / Hey you / Hello it's me / Good 2 me / Angel / Keep tryin' / You're not the one / Didja know / Boy at the window
CD _____ 4783822
Epic / Nov '95 / Sony

Groove Thing

ADVENTURE, THE
CD _____ EBCD 21
Eightball / Jan '95 / Vital

Groove Tunnel

LIVEN UP
CD _____ DRCD 008
Detour / Mar '96 / Detour / Greyhound

Grooverider

GROOVERIDER PRESENTS THE PROTOTYPE YEARS (2CD Set) (Various Artists)
Subway: *Ed Rush* / Dreams of heaven: *Codename John & Grooverider* / Threshold: *Cybotron & Dillinja* / Secrets: *John B* / Grey odyssey: *Optical* / Mute: *Matrix* / Silver blade: *Dillinja* / Deep inside: *Codename John & Grooverider* / Locust: *Ed Rush & Fierce* / Going gets tuff: *Lemon D* / Warned: *Codename John & Grooverider* / Still: *Boymerang*
CD Set _____ 4872192
Higherground / Mar '97 / Sony

GROOVERIDER'S HARDSTEP SELECTION VOL.1 (Various Artists)
CD _____ KICKCD 15
Kickin' / Nov '94 / Prime / SRD

GROOVERIDER'S HARDSTEP SELECTION VOL.2 (Various Artists)
CD _____ KICKCD 24
Kickin' / Jul '95 / Prime / SRD

Groovezilla

GROOVEZILLA
CD _____ 9040232
Mausoleum / Mar '95 / Grapevine/ PolyGram

Groovie Ghoulies

APPETITE FOR ADRENOCHROME
CD _____ LOOKOUT 148CD
Lookout / Sep '96 / Cargo / Greyhound / Shellshock/Disc

BORN IN THE BASEMENT
CD _____ LOOKOUT 149CD
Lookout / Sep '96 / Cargo / Greyhound / Shellshock/Disc

WORLD CONTACT DAY
CD _____ LOOKOUT 151CD
Lookout / Jun '96 / Cargo / Greyhound / Shellshock/Disc

Groovy

GROOVY
CD _____ XCD 033
Extreme / Dec '95 / Vital/SAM

Grope

PRIMATES
CD _____ RRS 941CD
Lost & Found / Sep '95 / Plastic Head

SOUL PIECES
CD _____ PCD 026MCD
Progress / Apr '96 / Cargo / Plastic Head

Gross, Helen

HELEN GROSS 1924-1925
CD _____ DOCD 5477
Document / Sep '96 / ADA / Hot Shot / Jazz Music

Gross, Henry

RELEASE/SHOW ME TO THE STAGE
CD _____ CDWIKD 104
Chiswick / Apr '92 / Pinnacle

Grossman, Stefan

BEST OF THE TRANSATLANTIC YEARS, THE
Hot dogs / Cincinnati flow rag / New York City rag / Roll and tumble blues / Shake sugaree / Candyman / Morning comes / Take a whiff on me / Blues for Mr Sam / Vestapol/That's no way to get along / Those lazy blues / Blues jumped the rabbit / Teddy Roosevelt / Those pleasant days / Hi dum diddle / Bo's rag / So they say / Sound techniques recording blues / Alibi / Waterfalls / Fat man / Kokomo / Belzona blues / Orphan Sunday / Little Sally Walker
CD _____ ESMCD 437
Essential / Oct '96 / BMG

Grossman, Steve

BOUNCING WITH MR. AT
Afternoon in Paris / Soultrane / Why don't I / Whims of chambers / Exemporaneous / My little suede shoes / Soul eyes / CTA
CD _____ FDM 365792
Dreyfus / Apr '96 / ADA / Direct / New Note/ Pinnacle

HOLD THE LINE (Grossman, Steve Quartet)
CD _____ DIW 912
DIW / Oct '96 / Cadillac / Harmonia Mundi

MY SECOND PRIME
CD _____ 1232462
Red / Nov '91 / ADA / Cadillac / Harmonia Mundi

REFLECTIONS (Grossman, Steve & Alby Cullaz/Simon Goubert)
CD _____ 500212
Musidisc / Nov '93 / Discovery

SOME SHAPES TO COME
CD _____ OW 30329
One Way / Sep '94 / ADA / Direct / Greyhound

TIME TO SMILE
415 Central Park West / Circus / I'm confessin' that I love you / Extemporaneous / This time the dreams on me / Time to smile / Till there was you / EJ's blues
CD _____ FDM 365662
Dreyfus / Dec '94 / ADA / Direct / New Note/ Pinnacle

WAY OUT EAST VOL.1
CD _____ 1231762
Red / Apr '93 / ADA / Cadillac / Harmonia Mundi

WAY OUT EAST VOL.2
CD _____ 1231832
Red / Apr '93 / ADA / Cadillac / Harmonia Mundi

Grosvener, Luther

FLOODGATES
CD _____ RBCD 10072
Ruf / Oct '96 / Pinnacle

Grosz, Marty

LIVE AT THE LA CLASSIC (Grosz, Marty & His Orphan Newsboys)
CD _____ JCD 230
Jazzology / Jan '94 / Jazz Music

MARTY GROSZ & HIS ORPHAN NEWSBOYS
CD _____ SOSCD 1225
Stomp Off / Oct '92 / Jazz Music / Wellard

MARTY GROSZ & HIS SWINGING FOOLS
CD _____ CD 022
Nagel Heyer / May '96 / Jazz Music

MARTY GROSZ & KEITH INGHAM (Grosz, Marty & Keith Ingham & Their Paswonky Serenaders)
CD _____ SOSCD 1214
Stomp Off / Oct '92 / Jazz Music / Wellard

ON REVIVAL DAY (Grosz, Marty & His Sugar Daddies)
CD _____ JCD 260
Jazzology / Jul '96 / Jazz Music

SINGS OF LOVE (Grosz, Marty & Tiny Signa)
CD _____ JCD 210
Jazzology / Oct '93 / Jazz Music

SWING IT (Grosz, Marty & Destiny's Tots)
Let's swing it / Skeleton in the closet / Emaline / Old man harlem / Love dropped in for

tea / Little girl / Sunrise serenade / I've got a feeling / You're foolin' / What's the use / Eye opener / Sun will shine tonight / It's been so long / I surrender dear / It's the last time / Sonny boy / High hat, a piccolo and a cane
CD JCD 180
Jazzology / Apr '89 / Jazz Music

THANKS
CD J&MCD 502
J&M / Oct '93 / Cadillac / Discovery / Jazz Music / Wellard

Grotesque

IN THE EMBRACE OF EVIL
CD BS 007CD
Burning Sun / Nov '96 / Plastic Head

Grotus

MASS
That's entertainment / Bad itch / White trash blues / Ebola reston / Hand to mouth / Ain't nobody's business if I do / Sick / Collect 'em all / Wild Bill / Bottom line / Back in the day
CD 8286042
London / Mar '96 / PolyGram

SLOW MOTION APOCALYPSE
Up rose the mountain / Good evening / Same old sauce / Hourglass / Shivayanama / Complications / Kali yuga / Clean / Sleep-walking / Medicine / Slow motion apocalypse
CD VIRUS 118CD
Alternative Tentacles / Mar '93 / Cargo / Greyhound / Pinnacle

Ground Zero

GROUND ZERO
CD DSA 54047
CDSA / Dec '96 / Harmonia Mundi / ReR Megacorp

REVOLUTIONARY PEKING OPERA
CD RERGZ 1
ReR/Recommended / Jul '96 / ReR Megacorp / RTM/Disc

Groundhogs

BACK AGAINST THE WALL
Back against the wall / No to submission / Blue boar blues / Waiting in the shadows / Ain't no slaver / Stick to your grass / In the meantime / 54156
CD CDTB 111
Thunderbolt / '91 / TKO Magnum

BEST OF THE GROUNDHOGS, THE
Cherry red / Split / Mistreated / Still a fool / Split / Times / Groundhog / BDD / Strange town / You had a lesson / Rich man, poor man / Earth is not room enough / Eccentric man / Split / Amazing Grace
CD CDGOLD 1074
EMI Gold / Feb '97 / EMI

BLACK DIAMOND/CROSSCUT SAW
CD BGOCD 131
Beat Goes On / Feb '92 / Pinnacle

BLUES OBITUARY
BDD / Daze of the weak / Times / Mistreated / Express man / Natchez burning / Light was the day
CD BGOCD 6
Beat Goes On / Jan '89 / Pinnacle

FOUR GROUNDHOGS ORIGINALS (Scratching/Blues Obituary/Thank Christ/Split - 4CD Set)
Rocking chair / Early in the morning / Waking blues / Married men / No more doggin' / Man trouble / Come back baby / You don't love me / Still a fool / BDD / Daze of the weak / Times / Mistreated / Express man / Natchez burning / Light was the day / Strange town / Darkness is no friend / Soldier / Thank Christ for the bomb / Ship on the ocean / Garden / Status people / Rich man, poor man / Eccentric man / Split / Cherry red / Year in the life / Junkman / Groundhog
CD Set CDHOGS 1
Premier/EMI / Feb '96 / EMI

GROUNDHOG NIGHT
Shake for me / No more doggin' / Eccentric man / 3744 James Road / I want you to love me / Garden / Split part 1 / Split part 2 / Still a fool / I love you misogyny / Thank Christ for the bomb / Soldier / Mistreated / Me and the devil / Cherry red / Ground hog blues / Been there, done that / Down in the bottom
CD HTDCD 12
HTD / Jun '93 / CM / Pinnacle

GROUNDHOGS
CD CSAPCD 112
Connoisseur Collection / Oct '92 / Pinnacle

GROUNDHOGS BEST 1969-1972
Ground hog / Strange town / Bog roll blues / You had a lesson / Eccentric man / Earth is not room enough / BDD / Split part 1 / Cherry red / Mistreated / 3744 James Road / Soldier / Sad is the hunter / Garden / Split part 4
CD CZ 282
EMI / Mar '90 / EMI

HOG WASH
CD BGOCD 44
Beat Goes On / '89 / Pinnacle

HOGS ON THE ROAD
Ground hogs / Hogs in the road / Express man / Strange town / Eccentric man / 3744 James Road / I want you to love me / Split IV / Soldier / Back against the wall / Garden / Split / Waiting in the shadows / Light my light / Me and the devil / Mistreated / Ground hogs blues / Cherry red
CD CDTB 114
Thunderbolt / '91 / TKO Magnum

NO SURRENDER
Razor's edge / 3744 James Road / Superseded / Light my light / One more chance / Garden / Split Pt. 2 / Eccentric man / Strange town / Cherry red
CD HTDCD 2
HTD / Dec '90 / CM / Pinnacle

RAZOR'S EDGE
Razor's edge / I confess / Born to be with you / One more chance / Protector / Superseded / Moving fast standing still / I want you to love me
CD BUT CD 005
Hound Dog / Oct '92 / Street link

SCRATCHING THE SURFACE
Rocking chair / Early in the morning / Waking blues / Married men / No more doggin' / Man trouble / Come back baby / You don't love me / Still a fool / Oh death / Gasoline / Rock me / Don't pass the hat around
CD BGOCD 15
Beat Goes On / Jul '89 / Pinnacle

SOLID
CD CLACD 266
Castle / Jun '92 / BMG

SPLIT
Split / Cherry red / Year in the life / Junk man groundhog / Split (pts 2-4)
CD BGOCD 76
Beat Goes On / Dec '89 / Pinnacle

THANK CHRIST FOR THE BOMB
Strange town / Darkness is no friend / Soldier / Thank Christ for the bomb / Ship on the ocean / Garden / Status people / Rich man, poor man / Eccentric man
CD BGOCD 67
Beat Goes On / '89 / Pinnacle

WHO WILL SAVE THE WORLD
CD BGOCD 77
Beat Goes On / Apr '91 / Pinnacle

Group Called Smith

SMITH
CD VSD 5489
Varese Sarabande / Mar '95 / Pinnacle

Group Home

LIVIN' PROOF
Intro / Inna citi life / Livin' proof / Serious rap shit / Suspended in time / Sacrifice / Up against the wall / 4 give my sins / Baby paw / 2 thousand / Supa star / Realness
CD 8287252
Payday / Mar '96 / PolyGram / Vital

Groupa Batuque Percussion ...

SAMBA DE RUA (Groupa Batuque Percussion Project)
Wilson's intro / Jandaia / Parou al / Tabla samba / Onda leve / Mama samba / Aoyama san / Percussao livre
CD FARO 017CD
Far Out / Aug '97 / Amato Disco / New Note/Pinnacle

Groupe Kalyi Jag

GYPSY SONGS OF HUNGARY
CD PS 65112
PlayaSound / Nov '93 / ADA / Harmonia Mundi

Growing Movement

CIRCLE OF TORTURE
CD WB 1107CD
We Bite / Apr '94 / Plastic Head

Growling Mad Scientists

CHAOS LABORATORY
CD HADSHCD 01
Hadshot Haheizart / Jun '97 / Shellshock/ Disc

GRP All Star Big Band

ALL BLUES
Cookin' at the continental / Stormy Monday blues / All blues / Birk's works / Goodbye Pork Pie Hat / Senor blues / Blue miles / Mysterioso/Ba-lue bolivar ba-lues-are / Some other blues / Aunt Hagar's blues
CD GRP 98002
GRP / Feb '95 / New Note/BMG

Grubbs, David

BANANA CABBAGE
CD ZINC 30
Table Of The Elements / Mar '97 / Cargo

Gruberova, Edita

CHILDREN'S SONGS OF THE WORLD
Poesje mauw / D'esos caballos / Si toutes les filles / Che baccan / Es klappert die muhle / Spi mladjenec / Miala kasienka / Numi numi / Tancuj tancuj / Una flor de la cantuta / Three blind mice / Aa aa alin lasta / Haragszik / Pridi ty suhajko / Yuyake koyake / Heidschi bumbeidschi / Pera ston pera kambo / L'inverno e passato / Mi jachol lassim / Sakura / Dolina dolina / Humpty dumpty / Kumbaya / Nana mara haath / Katten og killingen / Ciobanas / Schyau / Joli tambour / Ba ba vita lamm / Itsy bitsy spider / Tala al-badru 'alaina / Alle voglein
CD NC 706602
Nightingale Classics / Feb '94 / Complete/ Pinnacle / Koch

Gruntz, George

HAPPENING NOW (Gruntz, George Concert Jazz Band '87)
CD ARTCD 6008
Hat Art / '88 / Cadillac / Harmonia Mundi

MOCK-LO-MOTION
Mock-lo-motion / You should know by now / One for kids / Annalisa / Giuseppi's blues / Vodka-pentatonic
CD TCB 95552
TCB / Feb '96 / New Note/Pinnacle

MPS JAZZ YEARS, THE
CD 5335522
MPS Jazz / Dec '96 / PolyGram

SINS'N'WINS'N'FUNS (Gruntz, George Concert Jazz Band)
Leave on yr shoes / Reggae / Kinda Gruntzy / Rockin' in rhythm / Preacher / Trombone man / Berlin tango / Room 608 / Dimple / Yellow rose of Texas / C jam blues / Plainsong / GG Deconne
CD TCB 96602
TCB / Nov '96 / New Note/Pinnacle

Grupo ABC

AMOR DE MACARADA
Grupo ABC / Que lastima / Amore de mascarada / No quiero problema / Macario / Que he de hacer / Mesie bombe / Princelda de amor
CD 66058086
RMM / Feb '96 / New Note/Pinnacle

Grupo Belen De Tarma

CHICHA
CD TUMICD 045
Tumi / '94 / Discovery / Stern's

Grupo Caneo

FASE IV
La rutina / Te recuerdo iqual que ayer / Sacala a bailar / Con el corazon en la mano / Mujeres divinas / Negrita / No te vayas a marchar / Aunque to amo
CD 66058041
RMM / Jul '94 / New Note/Pinnacle

Grupo Chicontepec

MEXICAN LANDSCAPES VOL.2
CD PS 65902
PlayaSound / Jan '92 / ADA / Harmonia Mundi

Grupo De Capoeira Angola ...

CAPOEIRA ANGOLA FROM SALVADOR, BRAZIL (Grupo De Capoeira Angola Pelourinho)
CD SFWCD 40465
Smithsonian Folkways / Mar '96 / ADA / Cadillac / CM / Direct / Koch

Grupo Folklorico

CONCEPTS IN UNITY (Grupo Folklorico & Experimental Nuevoyorquino)
CD CDGR 153
Charly / May '97 / Koch

Grupo Los Pinos

MUSICA CAMPESINA
CD TUMICD 056
Tumi / Mar '96 / Discovery / Stern's

Grupo Mandarina

DISPUESTAS A TODO
La boquita / Cada vez / Lo quiero a morir / El hueso / El falsante / Tu jeego se acabo / Me nacio del alma / Mandarina navidena / Pena solo pena
CD 66058073
RMM / Oct '95 / New Note/Pinnacle

Grupo Mantaza

MAMBORAMA
CD UCD 19076
Forlane / Jul '95 / Target/BMG

Grupo Merecumbe

MUSIC FROM COLOMBIA, CUMBIA, MERENGUE...
CD EUCD 1253
ARC / Mar '94 / ADA / ARC Music

Grupo Raison

TE PARACES AL AMOR
CD CD 0097
Egrem / Mar '96 / Discovery

Grupo Sierra Maestra

CON SALSA A CUBA
CD CD 0084
Egrem / Mar '96 / Discovery

Grupo Tierra De Barros

POR SAN MARCOS
CD 20088
Sonifolk / Aug '96 / ADA / CM

Grushecky, Joe

END OF THE CENTURY
CD PLR 0092
PLR / Feb '97 / Pinnacle

Grusin, Dave

GRUSIN COLLECTION, THE
CD GRP 95792
GRP / Aug '91 / New Note/BMG

HAVANA
Main title / Night walk / Cuba libre / Santa Clara suite / Los rumberos de Belen / Love theme / Hurricane country / Lost in a sweet place / Mambo lido / El conuco / Adios habana / La academia
CD GRP 20032
GRP / Jan '93 / New Note/BMG

MIGRATION
Punta del soul / Southwest passage / First time love / Western women / Dancing in the township / Old bones / In the middle of the night / TKO / Polina / Suite from the Milagro beanfield war / Lupita / Coyote angel / Pistolero / Milagro / Fiesta
CD GRP 95922
GRP / Sep '89 / New Note/BMG

ORCHESTRAL ALBUM, THE
Cuba libre / Santa Clara suite (Four movements) / Three cowboy songs (Three movements) / Medley: Bess you is my woman/I loves you Porgy / Suite from the Milagro Beanfield War (Five movements) / Heart is a lonely hunter / Summer sketches / Condor / On Golden Pond
CD GRP 97972
GRP / Oct '94 / New Note/BMG

TWO FOR THE ROAD (A Tribute To Henry Mancini)
Peter Gunn / Dreamsville / Mr. Lucky / Moment to moment / Baby elephant walk / Two for the road / Days of wine and roses / Hatari / Whistling away the dark / Soldier in the rain
CD GRP 98652
GRP / Apr '97 / New Note/BMG

Grusin, Don

DON GRUSIN
Number eight / Hot / Shuffle city / Cuidado / Nice going / Cowboy reggae / Kona / What a friend we have in Jesus
CD JMI 20102
JVC / Nov '93 / Direct / New Note/Pinnacle / Vital/SAM

IOK-LA
Majesty / Good lookin' / Danger / Electric man / Julie Ann / Mongolia / Reggie de american babies / One more soldier / Dance / Sadie
CD JVC 20112
JVC / Aug '96 / Direct / New Note/Pinnacle / Vital/SAM

Gryphon

COLLECTION VOL.2, THE
CD ITEMCD 3
Curio / May '95 / ADA / Plastic Head

COLLECTION, THE
CD ITEMCD 1
Progress / Jul '92 / Vital

GRYPHON
CD ITEMCD 4
Curio / May '95 / ADA / Plastic Head

GRYPHON/MIDNIGHT MUSHRUMPS
Kemp's jig / Sir Gavin Grimbold / Touch and go / Three jolly butchers / Pastime with good company / Unquiet grave / Estampie / Astrologer / Tea wrecks / Juniper suite / Devil and the farmer's wife / Midnight mushrumps / Ploughboy's dream / Last flash of Gaberdine Tailor / Gulland Rock / Dubbel Dutch / Ethelion
CD ESMCD 356
Essential / Jan '96 / BMG

MIDNIGHT MUSHRUMPS
Midnight mushrumps / Ploughboys dream / Last flash of gaberdine tailor / Gulland rock / Dubbel dutch / Ethelion
CD ITEMCD 5
Curio / May '95 / ADA / Plastic Head

RAINDANCE
CD ITEMCD 7
Curio / May '95 / ADA / Plastic Head

RED QUEEN TO GRYPHON THREE
CD ITEMCD 6
Curio / May '95 / ADA / Plastic Head

RED QUEEN TO GRYPHON THREE/ RAINDANCE
Opening move / Second spasm / Lament / Checkmate / Down the dog / Raindance / Mother nature's son / Le cambriouleur est dans le mouchoir / Ormolu / Fontinental version / Wallbanger / Don't say go / (Ein klein) heldenleben
CD ESMCD 460
Essential / Jan '97 / BMG

TREASON
Spring song / Flash in the pantry / Snakes and ladders / Major disaster / Round and round / Falero lady / Fall of the leaf
CD C5CD 602
See For Miles/C5 / Mar '97 / Pinnacle

GTS

TRACKS FROM THE DUSTSHELF
CD GTR 001CD
GT / Feb '96 / Plastic Head

Guacaran, Mario

LLANOS HARP
CD PS 65163
PlayaSound / May '96 / ADA / Harmonia Mundi

Guadalquivir

FLAMENCO INSTRUMENTAL
CD PS 65100
PlayaSound / Feb '93 / ADA / Harmonia Mundi

Guana Batz

HELD DOWN AT LAST/LOAN SHARK
Down on the line / Get no money / Can't take the pressure / Nightwatch / Lady bacon / King rat / You're my baby / Nightmare fantasy / Please give me something / Bust out / Pile driver boogie / My way / Slippin' in / Tiny minds / Radio sweetheart / Life's a beech / Loan shark / Shake your moneymaker / I'm weird / Hippy hippy shake / Live for the day / No particular place to go / I'm on fire
CD LOMCD 13
Loma / Feb '94 / BMG

ROUGH EDGES/ELECTRA GLIDE IN BLUE
Street wise / Open your mouth / One night / Good news / Rocking on creek road / Fight back / Spy catcher / Love generator / Bring my cadillac back / Rocking with ollie vee / Two shadows / You can run / Electra glide in blue / Green eyes / Texas eyes / No matter how / Wonderous place / Katherine / Sylin / Spector love / Self made prison / Who needs it / Lover man / Take a rocket
CD LOMCD 14
Loma / Feb '94 / BMG

UNDER COVER
You're my baby / Please give me something / Bust out / My way / Slippin' in / Radio sweetheart / Shake your moneymaker / Hippy hippy shake / No particular place to go / I'm on fire / Baby blue eyes / Batman / One night / Bring my cadillac back / Rock around with Ollie Vee / Wonderous place / Lights out / Johnny B Goode / Joe 90 / Train kept a rollin' / Devils guitar (live) / Rockin' in the graveyard / Rocky road blues / Dynamite (live) / Rock this town / Endless sleep (live)
CD CDMPSYCHO 7
Anagram / Sep '95 / Cargo / Pinnacle

Guapo

TOWERS OPEN FIRE
CD PTOOL 005
Power Tool / Jun '97 / Shellshock/Disc / SRD

Guaraldi, Vince

BOY NAMED CHARLIE BROWN, A (Guaraldi, Vince Trio)
Oh good grief / Pebble beach / Happiness is / Schroeder / Charlie Brown theme / Linus and Lucy / Blue Charlie Brown / Baseball theme / Freda / Fly me to the moon
CD FCD 8430
Fantasy / Jun '96 / Jazz Music / Pinnacle / Wellard

CHARLIE BROWN CHRISTMAS, A
CD FCD 8431
Fantasy / Nov '95 / Jazz Music / Pinnacle / Wellard

JAZZ IMPRESSIONS OF BLACK ORPHEUS (Guaraldi, Vince Trio)
CD OJCCD 437
Original Jazz Classics / Nov '95 / Complete/Pinnacle / Jazz Music / Wellard

VINCE GUARALDI TRIO
Django / Fenwyck's farfel / Never never land / Chelsea bridge / Fascinating rhythm / Lady's in love with you / Sweet and lovely / Ossobucco / Three coins in a fountain / It's de-lovely
CD OJCCD 149
Original Jazz Classics / Apr '96 / Complete/ Pinnacle / Jazz Music / Wellard

Guardiola, Jose

RECORDANDO LOS ANOS 60
CD 5043
Divucsa / Oct '96 / Discovery

Guards Division

BANDS OF PARADE (Massed Bands Of Guards Division)
CD BNA 5063
Bandleader / Jun '91 / Conifer/BMG

SCARLET AND GOLD (Massed Bands Of Guards Division)
National anthem / Duke of Cambridge / Me and my girl / Slave's chorus / Radetzky march / Strauss garland / Universal judgement / Procession of the nobles / Anvil chorus / American patrol / William Tell overture / Il silenzio / Trombones to the fore / March to the scaffold / Cockles and mussels / Crown imperial
CD BNA 5016
Bandleader / Apr '88 / Conifer/BMG

Guedon, Henri

RETROSPECTIVE (2CD Set)
CD Set FA 048
Fremeaux / May '96 / ADA / Discovery

Guem

DANSE-PERCUSSIONS
CD LDX 274968
La Chant Du Monde / Sep '93 / ADA / Harmonia Mundi

Guerin, Erica

GET REAL
CD KS 034CD
Kingsnake / Jul '97 / Hot Shot

Guerouabi, Hachemi

LE CHAABI
CD AAA 119
Club Du Disque Arabe / Oct '95 / ADA / Harmonia Mundi

Guerra, Juan Luis

BACHATA ROSA (Guerra, Juan Luis & 4.40)
Rosalia / Como abeja al panal / Carta de amor / Estrellitas y duendes / Pedir su mano / La bilirrubina burbujas de amor / Bachata rosa / Reforestame / Acompaneme civil
CD 261 927
Ariola / Nov '91 / BMG

Guerrero, Tony

ANOTHER DAY, ANOTHER DREAM
CD NOVA 9137
Nova / Jan '93 / New Note/Pinnacle

Guerroumi, Habib

ARABO-ANDALUSIAN MUSIC VOL.2
CD PS 65162CD
PlayaSound / Apr '96 / ADA / Harmonia Mundi

Guesch Patti

BLONDE
CD 132044
XIII Bis / Jan '97 / Discovery

NOMADE
L'homme au tablier vert -(Fleurs carnivores) / Dans l'enfer / Comment dire / Il va loin le malheur / Et meme / Nomade / J'veux pas m'en meler / Opera / Raler / Piege de lumiere / Libido / Encore / Merci
CD CDEMC 3575
EMI / May '90 / EMI

Guesnon, George

GEORGE GUESNON
CD AMCD 87
American Music / Jul '96 / Jazz Music

Guess Who

RETROSPECTIVE, A
These eyes / Laughing / Undun / No time / American woman / No sugar tonight / New mother nature / Hand me down world / Share the land / Albert Flasher / Broken / Rain dance / Sour suite / Guns, guns, guns / Running back to Saskatoon / Follow your daughter home / Star baby / Clap for the wolfman / Dancing fool
CD 74321133612
RCA / Jun '97 / BMG

Guests

BOTTLE GREEN
CD MSECD 015
Mouse / Oct '95 / Grapevine/PolyGram

Guetary, Georges

GEORGES GUETARY IN PARIS
CD CDXP 605
DRG / Jan '89 / Discovery / New Note/ Pinnacle

Guianko

ILLAMAME "YANKO"
Temes / El amor no miente / Dime / Busco un amor / Caminaria / Y me acusas / Te quiero asi / Los ojos de ana
CD 66058058
RMM / Jul '95 / New Note/Pinnacle

Guided By Voices

ALIEN LANES
Salty salute / Evil speakers / Watch me jumpstart / They're not witches / As we go up we go down / (I wanna be a) Dumbcharger / Game of pricks / Ugly vision / Good flying bird / Cigaretter tricks / Pimple zoo / Big chief chines restaurant / Closer you are / Auditorium / Motor away / Hit / My valuable hunting knife / Gold hick / King and Caroline / Striped white jets / Ex-supermodel / Blimps go 90 / Straw dogs / Chicken blows / Little whirl / My son cool / Always crush me / Alright
CD OLE 1232
Matador / Apr '95 / Vital

BEE THOUSAND
Hardcore UFO's / Buzzards and dreadful crows / Tractor rape chain / Golden heart mountain top queen directory / Hot freaks / Smothered in hugs / Yours to keep / Echos myron / Awful bliss / Mincer Ray / Big fan of pigeon / Queen of cans and jars / Her psychology today / Kicker of elves / Ester's day / Demons are real / I am a scientist / Peep-Hole / You're not an airplane
CD OLE 0842
Matador / Jul '94 / Vital

BOX
CD Set SCT 0402
Scat / Feb '95 / Vital

MAG EARWHIG
Can't hear the revolution / Sad if I lost it / I am a tree / Old grunt / Bulldog skin / Are you faster / I am produced / Knock 'em flying / Not behind the fighter jet / Choking Tara / Hollow cheek / Portable men's society / Little lines / Learning to hunt / Finest joke is upon us / Mag earwhig / Now to war / Jane of the waking universe / Colossus crawls West / Mute in the bee-hive
CD OLE 2412
Matador / May '97 / Vital

UNDER THE BUSHES, UNDER THE STARS
Man called aerodynamics / Life in finer clothing / Rhine jive click / Burning flag birthday suit / Officail ironmen rally song / Not in my airforce / System crash / Worrying song / Plantations of pale pink / Postal blowfish / Applehead / He's the uncle / Bender's bluffing muscles / Delayed reaction brats / Key losers / Catfood on the earwig / Uprooted before seeding / Don't stop now / Cooler jocks / Office of hearts / Take it to the sky / Redman and their wives / Sheetkickers / Drag days / It's like / Big boring wedding
CD OLE 1612
Matador / Mar '96 / Vital

VAMPIRE ON TITUS/PROPELLER
Wished I was a giant / No.2 In the model home / Expecting brainchild / Superior sector janitor / Donkey school / Dusted / Marches in orange / Sot / World of fun / Jar of cardinals / Unstable journey / E 5 / Cool off kid kiolowatt / Gleemer / Wondering boy poet / What about it / Perhaps now the vultures
CD OLE 0832
Matador / Oct '94 / Vital

Guignolee

RETOUR
CD GUI 1327CD
Guignolee / Apr '96 / ADA

Guilbert, Yvette

LE FIACRE
Le fiacre / Madame Arthur / Ecoute dans le jardin / Enfance / Les caquets de la couchee / L'hotel de numero trois / Les ingenues / Les quatz etudiants / La soularde / A grenelle / Je suis pocharde / La pierreuse / I want yer, ma honey / Keys of heaven / A la villette / Pourquoi me bat, mon mari / Dites moi si je suis belle / Elle etait tres bien / Je m'embrouille / Le voyage a Bethlehem
CD PASTCD 9773
Flapper / Nov '91 / Pinnacle

Guild Of Ancient Fifes & ...

BY BEAT OF DRUM (Guild Of Ancient Fifes & Drums)
Drummer's call / Drum demonstration / English march / 1775 medley / Chester Castle / Downfall of Paris / To danton me / Rogue's march / Grenadiers march / See the conquering hero comes / Toledo / It's a long way to Tipperary / San Lorenzo / Wondermarsch / Basle drum and fife display / Der morgenstreich / Sans Gene / Come lasses and lads / Glopfgaisht / Stenlemmer / Windschi / Dtitt vars / Arabi / Guards / Der vaudois / S'laggerli
CD BNA 5013
Bandleader / Feb '88 / Conifer/BMG

Guildford Cathedral Choir

EVENING AT GUILDFORD CATHEDRAL, AN
CD WSTCD 9705
Nelson Word / Nov '89 / Nelson Word

Guillory, Isaac

EASY...
CD PRCD 003
Personal / Feb '95 / CM / Duncans / Jazz Music / Ross

Guillot, Olga

LA MEJER CANCIONERA DE CUBA
CD CCD 802
Caney / Jul '96 / ADA / Discovery

Guilt

BARDSTWON UGLY BOX
CD VR 029CD
Victory Europe / Jan '96 / Plastic Head

Guinness Choir

CLASSIC IRISH SONGS
CD CHCD 1096
Chyme / Oct '95 / ADA / CM / Direct / Koch

Guitar, Bonnie

DARK MOON
Mr. Fire eyes / Dark moon / Open the door / Half your heart / If you see my heart dancing / Johnny Vagabond / Making believe / Down where the tradewinds blow / Letter from Jenny / There's a new moon over my shoulder / Moonlight and shadows / Carolina moon / By the light of the silvery moon / Shine on harvest moon / Moon is low / Get out and get under the moon / Moonlight on the Colorado / Moonlight and roses / It's only a paper moon / Prairie moon / Roll along Kentucky moon / Love is over / Love is done / Stand there mountain / I found you out / Love by the jukebox light / Big Mike / Very precious love / If you'll be the teacher
CD Set BCD 15531
Bear Family / Feb '92 / Direct / Rollercoaster / Swift

Guitar Corporation

ULTIMATE GUITAR COLLECTION (3CD Set)
CD Set COLBX 003
Focus / Feb '97 / Koch

Guitar Crusher

MESSAGE TO MAN (Guitar Crusher & Alvin Lee)
Heartfixing man / Long green folding friend / Message to man / Stealing a little love / Darling I miss you / Day by day / You know how to hurt a man / Do it well / Trying to fool the whole town / I wanna be with you / I can't stop loving you / Time to throw down
CD INAK 9034CD
In Akustik / Jul '97 / Direct / TKO Magnum

Guitar Gangsters

POWER CHORDS FOR ENGLAND
Little Miss mystery / City of the damned / Bittersweet but true / Strange kind of love / All over the world / Innocent eyes / She's my kind / Radio authority / Boy like me / Playing games again / In my world / When guitars ruled the earth
CD CDPUNK 96
Anagram / May '97 / Cargo / Pinnacle

Guitar Johnny

GUITAR JOHNNY & THE RHYTHM ROCKERS (Guitar Johnny & The Rhythm Rockers)
CD 422397
Last Call / Feb '97 / Cargo / Direct / Discovery

Guitar Junior

CRAWL, THE (Charly Blues - Masterworks Vol.1)
Crawl / Family rules (Angel Child) / I got it made (when I marry Shirley Mae) / Tell me baby / Now you know / Roll roll roll / Roll roll roll (ait take) / Broken hearted rollin' tears / Please / Pick me up on your way down / Love me love me / Knocks me out fine, fine, fine / Love me love Mary Ann / Oo wee baby
CD CD BM 1
Charly / Apr '92 / Koch

Guitar Orchestra

GUITAR ORCHESTRA
Pomp and circumstance / Stewing my wine / Fresh air / Misguided woman / Lost week-

end / Ghost town / Stella / Livewire / Last chicken in the shop / Camp town / Solomon's seal
CD SJPCD 002
Angel Air / Jan '97 / Pinnacle

GUITAR ORCHESTRA, THE
Really / Pernod for the bamboo man (aperitif) / First kiss / Closer to the heart / Ocean / Pernod for the bamboo man
CD PRKCD 6
Park / Jun '91 / Pinnacle

INTERPRETATIONS
Africa / Fool on the hill / Space oddity / Strawberry fields forever / (Don't fear) the reaper / Stranger on the shore / Don't give up / Do it again / I am the walrus / Day in the life
CD PRKCD 18
Park / May '94 / Pinnacle

Guitar Shorty

GET WISE TO YOURSELF
CD CDBT 1126
Black Top / Feb '96 / ADA / CM / Direct

TOPSY TURVY
CD BT 1094CD
Black Top / Oct '93 / ADA / CM / Direct

Guitar Slim

THINGS THAT I USED TO DO, THE
Well I done got over it / Trouble don't last / Guitar Slim / Story of my life / Letter to my girlfriend / Reap what you sow / Later for you baby / Things that I used to do / Quicksand / Bad luck blues / Think it over / Our only child / I got sumpin' for you / Sufferin' mind / Twenty five lies / Something to remember you by
CD CD 52033
Blues Encore / May '94 / Target/BMG

Guitar Wolf

MISSILE ME
Missile me / Hurricane rock / Kung fu ramone culmination tactic / Can nana fever / Midnight violence rock 'n' roll / Link Wray man / Guitar star / Racing rock / Jet rock 'n' roll / Devil stomp / Jet blues / Venus Drive
CD OLE 2192
Matador / Nov '96 / Vital

Guitaresque

GUITARESQUE
CD HCRCD 81
Hot Club / Oct '94 / Cadillac

Gulabi Sapera

MUSIQUE DU RAJASTHAN
CD Y 225213CD
Silex / Jul '95 / ADA / Harmonia Mundi

Gulieva, Gandab

AZERBAIJAN MUGAM ANTHOLOGY VOL.8
Mugam chargah / Mugam rahab / Mugam dilkash
CD W 260077
Inedit / Aug '97 / ADA / Discovery / Harmonia Mundi

Gullin, Lars

LARS GULLIN & CHET BAKER
CD DRAGONCD 224
Dragon / Feb '89 / ADA / Cadillac / CM / Roots / Wellard

LATE SUMMER
CD DRCD 244
Dragon / Nov '94 / ADA / Cadillac / CM / Roots / Wellard

MODERN SOUNDS
CD DRCD 234
Dragon / Nov '94 / ADA / Cadillac / CM / Roots / Wellard

Gullin, Peter

TENDERNESS
CD DRAGONCD 222
Dragon / Jul '87 / ADA / Cadillac / CM / Roots / Wellard

TRANSFORMED EVERGREEN (Gullin, Peter Trio)
CD DRCD 266
Dragon / Oct '94 / ADA / Cadillac / CM / Roots / Wellard

Gum-Nyon, Song

MUSIC OF THE KAYAGUM
CD VICG 50182
JVC World Library / Mar '96 / ADA / CM / Direct

Gumede, Sipho

DOWN FREEDOM AVENUE
Down freedom avenue / Godfather special / Ngiyabonga / Song for Johnny Dyani / Please don't dance / Nozipho the dancer / Nlabelela / Village lullaby / African wedding / Country side

CD BW 051
B&W / Nov '96 / New Note/Pinnacle / SRD / Vital/SAM

Gun

0141 632 6326
Rescue you / Crazy you / Seventeen / All my love / My sweet Jane / Come a long way / All I ever wanted / I don't mind / Going down / Alway's friends
CD 5407232
CD 5407222
A&M / May '97 / PolyGram

GALLUS
Steal your fire / Money to burn / Long road / Welcome to the real world / Higher ground / Borrowed time / Freedom / Won't back down / Reach out for love / Watching the world go by
CD 3953832
A&M / Mar '95 / PolyGram

SWAGGER
Stand in line / Find my way / Word up / Don't say it's over / Only one / Something worthwhile / Seems like I'm losing you / Crying over you / One reason / Vicious heart
CD 5402542
A&M / Jul '94 / PolyGram

TAKING ON THE WORLD
Better days / Feeling within / Inside out / Money (Everybody loves her) / Taking on the world / Shame on you / Can't get any lower / Something to believe in / Girls in love / I will be waiting
CD 3970072
A&M / Mar '95 / PolyGram

Gun Club

AHMED'S WILD DREAM
Masterplan / Walkin' with the beast / I hear your heart singin' / Another country's song / Sexbeat / Lupita screams / Go tell the mountain / Preachin' the blues / Stranger in town / Port of souls / Black hole / Little wing / Yellow eyes
CD 527500220
Solid / Jun '93 / Plastic Head / Vital

DEATH PARTY
CD 890012
New Rose / May '94 / ADA / Direct / Discovery

DIVINITY
CD 527900920
Solid / Jun '93 / Plastic Head / Vital

EARLY WARNING (2CD Set)
CD Set SFTRI 478
Sympathy For The Record Industry / Mar '97 / Cargo / Greyhound / Plastic Head

FIRE OF LOVE
Sex beat / Preachin' the blues / Promise me / She's like heroin to me / For the love of Ivy / Fire spirit / Ghost on the highway / Jack on fire / Black train / Cool drink of water / Goodbye Johnny / Walking with the beast
CD 422162
New Rose / May '94 / ADA / Direct / Discovery

MOTHER JUNO
Bill Bailey, won't you please come home / Thunderhead / Lupita screams / Yellow eyes / Breaking hands / Araby / Hearts / My cousin Kim / Ports of souls
CD 527500420
Solid / Nov '92 / Plastic Head / Vital

PASTORAL HIDE AND SEEK
CD 527900020
Solid / Jun '93 / Plastic Head / Vital

Gunjah

HEREDITY
CD N 02082
Noise / Feb '93 / Koch

POLITICALLY CORRECT
CD N 02552
Noise / May '95 / Koch

Gunk

FOR GOD'S SAKE
CD CDBLEED 17
Bleeding Hearts / Feb '96 / Pinnacle

Gunn, Andy

STEAMROLL
CD PRD 71012
Provogue / Apr '97 / Pinnacle

Gunn, Douglas

O'CAROLAN'S FEAST (Gunn, Douglas Ensemble)
Carolan's welcome / Planxty Connor / Cupan ui eaghra / John Kelly / Sir Arthur Shaen / Madam Cole / Plearaca na ruarcach / Carolan's receipt for drinking / Madam Maxwell / Cait Ni Bhriain / Turlough Og MacDonach / Seoirse Brabston / Charles O'Connor / Thomas O'Burke / Lament for Charles MacCabe / John Nugent / Dr. Sean O'Hairt / O'Rourke's feast
CD CDOSS 69
Ossian / Apr '93 / ADA / CM / Direct / Highlander

Gunn, Russell

GUNN FU
Gunn fun / John Wicks / Solar / Invitation / Search / Why wonder why / Minor sweet / Bern / Final call
CD HCD 7003
High Note / Apr '97 / New Note/Pinnacle

YOUNG GUNN
East St Louis / Fly me to the moon / Wade in the water / DJ / You don't know what love is / Concept / Message / There is no greater love / Blue Gene / Pannonica
CD MCD 5539
Muse / Dec '95 / New Note/Pinnacle

Gunn, Trey

3RD STAR
CD DGM 9606
Discipline / Aug '96 / Pinnacle

ONE THOUSAND YEARS
Night air / Screen door and the flower girl / Killing for London / Real life / Into the wood / Gift / Take this wish / 1000 years
CD DGM 9302
Discipline / Sep '94 / Pinnacle

Gunness, Lee

LEE GUNNESS & THE ECLIPSE ALLEY HEAVENLY SINGERS
CD BCD 354
GHB / Jul '96 / Jazz Music

LEE GUNNESS SINGS THE BLUES
CD BCD 314
GHB / Oct '93 / Jazz Music

Guns n' Roses

APPETITE FOR DESTRUCTION
Welcome to the jungle / It's so easy / Nightrain / Out ta get me / Mr. Brownstone / Paradise city / My Michelle / Think about you / Sweet child o' mine / You're crazy / Anything goes / Rocket queen
CD GFLD 19286
Geffen / Oct '95 / BMG

GN'R LIES
Reckless life / Patience / Nice boys / Used to love her / Move to the city / You're crazy / Mama kin / One in a million
CD GFLD 19287
Geffen / Oct '95 / BMG

INTERVIEW COMPACT DISC: GUNS 'N' ROSES
CD CBAK 4015
Baktabak / Nov '89 / Arabesque

INTERVIEW DISC
CD SAM 7016
Sound & Media / Nov '96 / Sound & Media

SPAGHETTI INCIDENT, THE
Since I don't have you / New Rose / Down on the farm / Human being / Raw power / Ain't it fun / Buick Mckane / Hair of the dog / Attitude / Black leather / You can't put your arms around a memory / I don't care about you / Look at your game girl
CD GFLD 19317
Geffen / Jul '96 / BMG

TRUTH OR LIES THE INTERVIEW
CD CBAK 4077
Baktabak / Feb '94 / Arabesque

USE YOUR ILLUSION VOL.1
Right next door to hell / Dust and bones / Live and let die / Don't cry / Perfect crime / You ain't the first / Bad obsession / Back off bitch / Double talkin' jive / November rain / Garden / Garden of Eden / Don't damn me / Bad apple / Dead horse / Coma
CD GEFD 24415
Geffen / Sep '91 / BMG

USE YOUR ILLUSION VOL.2
Civil war / Fourteen years / Yesterdays / Knockin' on heaven's door / Get in the ring / Shotgun blues / Breakdown / Pretty tied up / Locomotive / So fine / Estranged / You could be mine / Don't cry / My world
CD GEFD 24420
Geffen / Sep '91 / BMG

Gunshot

PATRIOT GAMES
CD STEAM 43CD
Vinyl Solution / Jun '93 / RTM/Disc

SINGLES, THE
CD STEAM 92CD
Vinyl Solution / Nov '94 / RTM/Disc

TWILIGHTS LAST GLEAMING
Intro / Maths and stats / Millenium / Mask of the phantasm / GS vibe / Ghetto heartbeat / Roots and reality / Die hard / True fist / Gunshot forever / Silkmaker / Return of The Gunshot / Kingpin / Untouchable / Inner space / Outro
CD WOWCD 51
Words Of Warning / May '97 / SRD / Total/ BMG

Gunter, Arthur

BABY LET'S PLAY HOUSE (The Best Of Arthur Gunter)
Baby let's play house / Blues after hours / Ludella / No naggin' no draggin' / Mind your own business babe / Honey babe / No happy home / Workin' for my baby / Baby can't you see / Little blue jeans woman / You're always on my mind / Baby you better listen / I want her back / Crazy me / Don't leave me now / Letter to my baby / Pigmeat / Falling in love / (Just another day) working for my baby / Story of Jesse James / She's mine, all mine / I've got a feeling something is wrong / Who will ever move you from me / Just take it easy / My baby's taking a day off / My heart's always lonesome
CD EXCD 3011
Ace / Dec '96 / Pinnacle

Gunter, Bernhard

UN PEU DE NEIGE
CD 31-GALLIUM
Table Of The Elements / Dec '96 / Cargo

Gunter, Hardrock

GONNA ROCK 'N' ROLL, GONNA DANCE ALL NIGHT
Birmingham bounce / Lonesome blues / Gonna dance all night / How can I believe you love me / My bucket's been fixed / Rifle belt and bayonet / Maybe baby / Birmingham bounce / Boppin' to Grandfather's clock / Beggars can't be choosers / It can't be right / Rock-a-bop baby / Whoo, I mean whee / We three / Jukebox help me find my baby / Fiddle bop / Hardrock rocks the moon (How high the moon) / Bloodshot eyes / Take away your rosy lips / Right key but the wrong keyhole / Mountain dew / I'll go chasin' women / Spring has sprung / Tico tico / Go low boogie / Bonaparte's retreat / Chattanooga sunshine boy / Dad gave my hog away / Guitar on the moon / Fallen angel / Gonna dance all night
CD RCCD 3031
Rollercoaster / Jul '95 / Rollercoaster / Swift

Gunther, John

BIG LUNAGE (Gunther, John & Greg Gisbert)
CD 740352
Capri / Oct '94 / Cadillac / Wellard

QUINTET (Gunther, John & Greg Gisbert)
CD 74035
Capri / Nov '93 / Cadillac / Wellard

Guo Ye

RED RIBBON
CD TUG 1010CD
Tugboat / Feb '95 / ADA

Gupta, Buddhadev Das

RAGA JAIJAIVANTI
CD NI 5314
Nimbus / Sep '94 / Nimbus

Gurd

ADDICTED
CD CC 035016CD
Major / Jan '96 / Plastic Head

GURD
CD CC 026053CD
Shark / Jun '95 / Plastic Head

Gurov, Andre

REVELATIONS OF WRATH
CD JFR 006CD
Jazz Fudge / Mar '97 / Pinnacle

Gurtu, Trilok

BELIEVE
CD CMPCD 67
CMP / Jan '95 / Cargo / Grapevine/ PolyGram / Vital/SAM

CRAZY SAINTS
Manini / Tillana / Ballad for 2 musicians / Other tune / Blessing in disguise / Crazy saints / No discrimination
CD CMPCD 66
CMP / Mar '96 / Cargo / Grapevine/ PolyGram / Vital/SAM

LIVING MAGIC
Baba / Once I wished a tree upside down / From scratch / TMNOK / Living magic / Transition / Tac, et demi
CD CMPCD 50
CMP / Jun '93 / Cargo / Grapevine/PolyGram / Vital/SAM

Guru

GURU PRESENTS THE ILL KID CLASSICS (Payday Sampler) (Various Artists)
Ill kid intro: *Bald Head Slick* / Wordplay: *Bahamadia* / Life: *Guru* / Do what pays ya: *Big Shug* / Victim of society: *Baybe* / Come clean: *Jeru The Damaja* / Who's the truest: *True Master* / Rotten apple: *Operation Rat-*

ification / Hi energy: *Fabidden* / Momentum: *Guru & Big Shug* / Attack: *Stikken Moov* / So called friends: *Group Home* / Cup of life: *Fabidden*
CD 8287292
Payday / Mar '96 / PolyGram / Vital

JAZZMATAZZ VOL.1
Intro / Loungin' / When you're near / Transit ride / No time to play / Down the backstreets / Respectful dedications / Take a look at yourself / Trust me / Slicker than most / Le bien, le mal / Sights in the city
CD CTCD 34
Cooltempo / Jun '93 / EMI

JAZZMATAZZ VOL.2
Intro (into the light) / Jazzalude I / New reality style / Lifesaver / Living in this world / Looking through darkness / Skit A (Interview) / Watch what you say / Jazzalude II / Defining purpose / For you / Insert A (Mental relaxation) / Medicine / Lost souls / Insert B (Mental relaxation) / Nobody knows / Jazzalude III / Hip hop as a way of life / Respect the artitect / Feel the music / Young ladies / Traveller / Jazzalude IV / Count your blessings / Choice of weapons / Something in the past / Skit B (A lot on my mind) / Revelation
CD CTCD 47
Cooltempo / Jul '95 / EMI

Guru Guru

LIVE
CD EFA 035012
Think Progressive / Jan '96 / Greyhound / SRD

LIVE 1972/CONNY'S SESSION 1974 (Guru Guru & Uli Trepte)
CD 14998
Spalax / Oct '96 / ADA / Cargo / Direct / Discovery / Greyhound

MOSHI MOSHI
CD EFA 035372
Think Progressive / Jul '97 / Greyhound / SRD

TANGO FANGO
CD EFA 035362
Think Progressive / Jul '97 / Greyhound / SRD

UFO
CD 14296
Spalax / Oct '96 / ADA / Cargo / Direct / Discovery / Greyhound

ULI TREPTE - LIVE 1972/CONNY PLANK'S SESSION 1974
CD SPA 14998
Spalax / Oct '96 / ADA / Cargo / Direct / Discovery / Greyhound

WAH WAH
CD EFA 035002
Think Progressive / Dec '95 / Greyhound / SRD

Gus

GUS
CD ALMCD 12
Almo Sounds / Nov '96 / Pinnacle

PROGRESSIVE SCIENCE OF BREEDING IDIOTS FOR A DUMB SOCIETY
CD WRONG 14CD
Wrong / Jun '95 / SRD

Gus Gus

POLYDISTORTION
Oh / Gun / Believe / Polyesterday / Barry / Cold breath '79 / Why / Rememberance / Is Jesus your pal / Purple
CD DADD 7005CD
4AD / Apr '97 / RTM/Disc

Gush

FROM SOUNDS TO THINGS
CD DRCD 204
Dragon / Apr '87 / ADA / Cadillac / CM / Roots / Wellard

Gustafson, John

GOOSE GREASE
Boogie woogie / Precious heart / Poem about a gnome / Don't care / Money dance / What's your game / Freshness / Cheap astrakhan / Goose grease
CD SJPCD 008
Angel Air / May '97 / Pinnacle

Gustafsson, Mats

PARROT FISH EYE
CD OD 12006
Okka Disk / Aug '95 / Cadillac / Harmonia Mundi

Gustavson, Jukka

KADONNUT HAVIAMATTOMLIN
CD BECD 4032
Beta / May '95 / Direct

Guthrie, Arlo

BEST OF ARLO GUTHRIE
Alice's restaurant massacre / Gabriel's mother's highway ballad / Sixteen blues / Coopers lament / Motor cycle song / Coming into Los Angeles / Last train / City of New Orleans / Darkest hour / Last to leave
CD 7599273402
WEA / Jan '93 / Warner Music

MORE TOGETHER AGAIN (Guthrie, Arlo & Pete Seeger)
CD RSR 0007/8
Rising Sun / Oct '94 / ADA

Guthrie, Jack

OKLAHOMA HILLS
Oklahoma hills / When the cactus is in bloom / Next to the soil / Shame on you / I'm branding my darlin' / With my heart / Careless darlin' / Oakie boogie / In the shadows of my heart / For Oklahoma / I'm yearning / No need to knock on my door / Shut that gate / I'm tellin' you / Chained to a memory / Look out for the crossing / Dallas darlin' / Colorado blues / Welcome home stranger / I still love you as I did in yesterday / Oklahoma's calling / Clouds rain trouble down / Answer to Moonlight / Please, oh please / I loved you once but I can't trust you now / Out of sight / I'm building a stairway to heaven / Ida Red / I told you once / San Antonio rose / You laughed and I cried
CD BCD 15580
Bear Family / Nov '91 / Direct / Rollercoaster / Swift

Guthrie, Woody

ASCH RECORDINGS VOL.1, THE (This Land Is Your Land)
CD SFWCD 40100
Smithsonian Folkways / May '97 / ADA / Cadillac / CM / Direct / Koch

BALLADS OF SACCO & VANZETTI
CD SFWCD 40060
Smithsonian Folkways / Apr '96 / ADA / Cadillac / CM / Direct / Koch

COLUMBIA RIVER COLLECTION
CD ROUCD 1036
Rounder / Aug '88 / ADA / CM / Direct

DUST BOWL BALLADS
CD ROUCD 1040
Rounder / '88 / ADA / CM / Direct

EARLY MASTERS
CD TCD 1017
Tradition / May '96 / ADA / Vital

GREATEST SONGS OF WOODY GUTHRIE VOL.1 (Various Artists)
CD VMD 73105
Vanguard / Jan '96 / ADA / Pinnacle

LEGENDARY PERFORMER, A
Great dust storm / I ain't got no home / Talking dust bowl blues / Vigilante man / Dust can't kill me / Dust pneumonia blues / Pretty boy Floyd / Blowin' down this road / Tom Joad / Dust bowl refugee / Do re mi / Dust bowl blues / Dusty old dust (so long it's been good to know)
CD 74321317742
RCA / Feb '96 / BMG

LIBRARY OF CONGRESS RECORDINGS VOL.1
CD ROUCD 1041
Rounder / '88 / ADA / CM / Direct

LIBRARY OF CONGRESS RECORDINGS VOL.2
CD ROUCD 1042
Rounder / '88 / ADA / CM / Direct

LIBRARY OF CONGRESS RECORDINGS VOL.3
CD ROUCD 1043
Rounder / '88 / ADA / CM / Direct

LONG WAYS TO TRAVEL (Unreleased Folkways Masters 1944-1949)
CD SFWCD 40046
Smithsonian Folkways / Jun '94 / ADA / Cadillac / CM / Direct / Koch

NURSERY DAYS
CD SFWCD 45036
Smithsonian Folkways / Dec '94 / ADA / Cadillac / CM / Direct / Koch

PASTURES OF PLENTY - WOODY GUTHRIE TRIBUTE (Various Artists)
CD DJD 3207
Dejadisc / May '94 / ADA / Direct

SONGS TO GROW ON FOR MOTHER & CHILD
CD SFWCD 45035
Smithsonian Folkways / Mar '95 / ADA / Cadillac / CM / Direct / Koch

THIS LAND IS YOUR LAND (Guthrie, Woody & Arlo)
Howdi do / Riding in my car / Along home / Mail myself to you / This land is your land / Bling-blang / All work together / Grassey grass grass / So long, it's been good to know yuh / This land is your land / All work together
CD ROUCD 8050
Rounder / May '97 / ADA / CM / Direct

VERY BEST OF WOODY GUTHRIE, THE
This land is your land / Pastures of plenty / Pretty boy Floyd / Take a whiff on me / Do re mi / Put my little shoes away / Hard travellin' / Jesus Christ / Whoopee ti yi yo / Grand coulee dam / Picture from life's other side / Talkin' hard luck blues / Philadelphia lawyer / I ain't got no home / Wreck of ol' 97 / Keep your skillet good and greasy / Dust pneumonia blues / Going down that road feeling bad / Goodnight little arlo (Goodnight little darlin') / So long (it's been good to know yuh)
CD MCCD 067
Music Club / Jun '92 / Disc / THE

WE AIN'T DOWN YET - WOODY GUTHRIE'S FRIENDS (Various Artists)
CD DIAB 812
Diabolo / Aug '94 / Pinnacle

WOODY GUTHRIE
CD DVBC 92102
Deja Vu / May '95 / THE

Gutierrez, Alfredo

EL PALITO
CD TUMICD 021
Tumi / '92 / Discovery / Stern's

FIESTA
CD 12454
Laserlight / Jul '95 / Target/BMG

Gutterball

GUTTERBALL
Trial seperation blues / Top of the hill / Lester Young / Motorcycle boy / One by one / When you make up your mind / Think it over / Falling from the sky / Please don't hold back / Preacher and the prostitute / Patent leather shoes / Blessing in disguise
CD OUT 1132
Brake Out / Jan '94 / Direct

TURNYOR HEDINKOV
CD RTS 17
Return To Sender / Aug '95 / ADA / Direct

WEASEL
CD OUT 1192
Brake Out / Aug '96 / Direct

Guttermouth

FRIENDLY PEOPLE
CD 158012
Nitro / Oct '96 / Pinnacle / Plastic Head

MUSICAL MONKEY
CD 158122
Nitro / Jul '97 / Pinnacle / Plastic Head

PUKE BALLS
CD DSR 09CD
Dr. Strange / Sep '95 / Cargo / Greyhound / Plastic Head

RECORD FORMERLY KNOWN AS...
CD 158072
Nitro / Sep '96 / Pinnacle / Plastic Head

TERI YAKIMOTO
CD 158042
Nitro / Sep '96 / Pinnacle / Plastic Head

Guv'ner

HARD FOR MEASY FOR YOU
No big deal / Red velvet chair / Little bitch on the phone / Bridge under water / Almond roca / Making headlines / Go to sleep / Wild couple / Touch wood / Amplituden / I will get you / Thespian girl / She dog stop
CD WIJ 039CD
Wiiija / Nov '94 / RTM/Disc

HUNT, THE
CD WIJCD 1057
Wiiija / Aug '96 / RTM/Disc

IN THE FISHTANK
CD FISHNO 2CD
Konkurrent / Jun '97 / SRD

Guy

FUTURE, THE
Her / Wanna get with U / Do me right / Teddy's jam 2 / Let's chill / Tease me tonite / Dog me out / Total control / Gotta be a leader / Future / Let's saty together / Where did the love go / Yearning for your love / Smile / Long gone / Wanna get with you
CD MCLD 19334
MCA / Oct '96 / BMG

Guy, Barry

AFTER THE RAIN
CD NMCD 013
Maya / Oct '94 / Complete/Pinnacle

PORTRAITS
CD INTAKTCD 035
Intakt / Oct '94 / Cadillac

STUDY-WITCH GONE GAME (Guy, Barry & Now Orchestra)
CD MCD 9402
Maya / Oct '94 / Complete/Pinnacle

Guy, Buddy

ALONE AND ACOUSTIC (Guy, Buddy & Junior Wells)
CD ALCD 4802
Alligator / May '93 / ADA / CM / Direct

BLUES GIANT
CD BLE 599002
Black & Blue / Jan '90 / Discovery / Koch / Wellard

BREAKING OUT
Have you ever been lonesome / You can make it if you try / Break out all over you / She winked her eye / I didn't know my mother had a son like me / Boogie family style / You called me in my dream / Me and my guitar / Ice around my heart
CD JSPCD 272
JSP / Oct '96 / ADA / Cadillac / Direct / Hot Shot / Target/BMG

BUDDY GUY & JUNIOR WELLS (Guy, Buddy & Junior Wells)
CD MACCD 194
Autograph / Aug '96 / BMG

BUDDY GUY AND FRIENDS
CD PDSCD 546
Pulse / Aug '96 / BMG

BUDDY'S BLUES
CD MCD 09374
Chess/MCA / Jul '97 / BMG / New Note/ BMG

COMPLETE CHESS STUDIO RECORDINGS, THE (2CD Set)
First time I met the blues / Stop around / I got my eyes on you / Brokened hearted blues / Let me love you baby / I got a strange feeling / Gully hully / Ten years ago / Watch yourself / Stone crazy / Skippin' / I found true love / Hard but it's fair / Baby (baby, baby, baby) / When my left eye jumps / That's it / Treasure untold / American bandstand / No lie / 100$ bill / My love is real / Buddy's boogie / Worried mind / Untitled instrumental / Moanin' / I dig your wig / My time after awhile / Night flight / Crazy love (crazy music) / Every girl I see / Too many ways / Leave my girl alone / Got to use your head / Keep it to myself / My mother / She suits me too a tee / Mother - in-law blues / Buddy's grove / Going to school / I cry and sing the blues / Goin' home / I suffer with the blues / Lip lap Louie / My time after a while / Too many ways / Keep it to myself / I didn't know my mother
CD Set MCD 09337
Chess/MCA / Apr '97 / BMG / New Note/ BMG

DJ PLAY MY BLUES
Good news / Blues at my babies house / She suits me to a T / Just teasin' / All your love / DJ play my blues
CD JSPCD 256
JSP / Feb '95 / ADA / Cadillac / Direct / Hot Shot / Target/BMG

DRINKIN' TNT 'N' SMOKIN' DYNAMITE (Guy, Buddy/Junior Wells & others)
Ah'w baby / Everything gonna be alright / How can one woman be so mean / Checking on my baby / When you see the little tears from my eyes / My younger days
CD NEMCD 687
Sequel / Apr '94 / BMG

FEELS LIKE RAIN
CD ORECD 525
Silvertone / Mar '93 / Pinnacle

FIRST TIME I MET THE BLUES
First time I met the blues / Slop around / Let me love you baby / Got to use your head / I dig your wig / My time after a while / Stick around / No lie / Night flight / My mother / Ten years ago / Don't know which way to go / Gully hully / I got a hully / I got a strange feeling / This is the end / Broken heart / Ed blues / You sure can't do / Try to quit you baby / I got my eyes on you / Sit and cry / Untitled instrumental / Drinking muddy water
CD CD 52015
Blues Encore / '92 / Target/BMG

HOLD THAT PLANE
Watermelon man / I'm ready / You don't love me / Hello San Francisco / Hold that plane / My time after a while / Come see about me
CD VMD 79323
Vanguard / Oct '95 / ADA / Pinnacle

LIVE AT THE CHECKERBOARD LOUNGE, CHICAGO 1979
Buddy's blues (parts 1 and 2) / I've got a right to love my woman / Tell me what's inside of you (2 versions) / Done gone over you / Things I used to do / You don't know how I feel / Dollar done sell / Don't answer the door
CD JSPCD 262
JSP / Oct '95 / ADA / Cadillac / Direct / Hot Shot / Target/BMG

LIVE IN MONTREUX (Guy, Buddy & Junior Wells)
CD ECD 200022
Everybody's / Jan '92 / Wellard

ORIGINAL BLUES BROTHERS - LIVE (Guy, Buddy & Junior Wells)
Buddy's blues / Blue Monday / Everyday I have the blues / Woman blues / Satisfaction / Messin' with the kid / No use cryin' / Just to be with you / Junior's shuffle / Out of sight

CD CDBM 007
Blue Moon / Feb '89 / Cadillac / Discovery / Greensleeves / Jazz Music / Jet Star / TKO Magnum

PLAY THE BLUES (Guy, Buddy & Junior Wells)
Man of many words / My baby left me / Come on in this house / Have mercy baby / T-bone shuffle / Poor man's plea / Messin' with the kid / This old fool / I don't know / Bad bad whiskey / Honeydripper
CD 8122702992
WEA / Mar '93 / Warner Music

REAL DEAL, THE (Buddy Guy Live)
CD ORECD 538
Silvertone / Mar '97 / Pinnacle

SLIPPIN' IN
CD ORECD 533
Silvertone / Mar '97 / Pinnacle

STONE CRAZY
Slop around / Broken hearted blues / I got my eyes on you / First time I met the blues / Let me love you baby / I got a strange feeling / Hully gully / Ten years ago / Watch yourself / Stone crazy / Hard but fair / Baby (baby, baby) / When my left eye jumps / That's it no lie / Every girl I see / Leave my girl alone / She suits me to a tee / Mother in law blues / Going home / I suffer with the blues
CD ALCD 4723
Alligator / May '93 / ADA / CM / Direct

TREASURE UNTOLD, THE (Charly Blues - Masterworks Vol.2)
I found a true love / Skippin' / Treasure untold / American bandstand / Don't know which way to go / Buddy's boogie / Worried blues / Moanin' / I dig your wig / My time after awhile / Night flight / You got to use your head / Keep it to yourself / My mother
CD CD BM 11
Charly / Apr '92 / Koch

Guy Called Gerald

BLACK SECRET TECHNOLOGY
CD JBCD 25
Juice Box / Mar '95 / PolyGram / SRD

Guy, Charles Lee

PRISONER'S DREAMS, THE
There goes a lonely man / This ole dog / You just don't know your man / Rich man's gold / Unhappy people / Prisoner's dream / Shackles and chains / They're all goin' home but one / Wall / Twenty one years / Folsom prison blues / Prisoner's song "Cigarettes, whisky and will" / Send a picture of Mother / Cold gray bars / Wishin' she was here (instead of me) / Doin' my time
CD BCD 15581
Bear Family / Apr '92 / Direct / Rollercoaster / Swift

Guy, Phil

BREAKING OUT ON TOP
CD JSPCD 260
JSP / Oct '95 / ADA / Cadillac / Direct / Hot Shot / Target/BMG

TINA NU
CD JSPCD 226
JSP / Apr '89 / ADA / Cadillac / Direct / Hot Shot / Target/BMG

Guys & Dolls

GUYS & DOLLS
CD HM 010
Harmony / Jun '97 / TKO Magnum

THERE'S A WHOLE LOT OF LOVING
There's a whole lot of loving / You don't have to say you love me / Here I go again / Our song / Love lost in a day / All the money in the world / Starship of love / Broken dreams / I got the fire in me / I heard it on the radio / Let's all get together / Guy's 'n' Dolls / Give a little love / Love matters / Always laughing / We're all in the same boat / She's leaving home / I get around / Barbara Ann / River deep mountain high / Don't wake me while I'm sleeping
CD BX 4272
BR Music / Jun '96 / Target/BMG

Guzman, Pedro

JIBARO JAZZ (The New Swing From Puerto Rico)
De aqui pa'alla / Mario brothers / Maria teina una ovejita / Mapeye montuno / Seis comerio / Guireando / Bayuya sambada / Fantasia del cuatro / Mi bella genio / Sesi antillano / Descarga machuca / Verde luz / Counting blues / Sonando con puerto rico
CD 68949
Tropical / Apr '97 / Discovery

Guzzard

ALIENATION INDEX SURVEY, THE
CD ARRCD 76019
Amphetamine Reptile / Dec '96 / Plastic Head

QUICK, FAST, IN A HURRY
CD AMREP 037CD
Amphetamine Reptile / Mar '95 / Plastic Head

Gwalarn

A-HED AN AMZER
CD KMCD 10
Keltia Musique / '91 / ADA / Discovery

GWAR

AMERICA MUST BE DESTROYED
CD CDZORRO 37
Metal Blade / Mar '92 / Pinnacle / Plastic Head
CD 398417016CD
Metal Blade / Jun '96 / Pinnacle / Plastic Head

CARNIVAL OF SOULS
CD 39841425CD
Metal Blade / Apr '97 / Pinnacle / Plastic Head

HELL-O
Time for death / Americanized / Slutman city / War toy / Pure as the artic snow / Gwar theme / Ollie North / U ain't shit / Black and huge / AEIOU / I'm in love with a dead dog / World o' filth / Captain crunch / Je m'appelle J Cousteau / Bone meal / Techno's song / Rock 'n' roll party theme
CD 398414004CD
Metal Blade / May '96 / Pinnacle / Plastic Head

RAG NA ROCK
CD 170012
Metal Blade / Oct '95 / Pinnacle / Plastic Head

ROAD BEHIND, THE
CD 398414004CD
Metal Blade / Nov '95 / Pinnacle / Plastic Head

SCUMDOGS OF THE UNIVERSE
CD 398417003CD
Metal Blade / Sep '95 / Pinnacle / Plastic Head

THIS TOILET EARTH
CD CDZORRO 63
Metal Blade / Mar '94 / Pinnacle / Plastic Head

Gwendal

GLEN RIVER
CD 345002
Melodie / Jul '96 / ADA / Discovery / Grapevine/PolyGram / Greensleeves / Jet Star

GWENDAL
CD 345012
Melodie / Mar '96 / ADA / Discovery / Grapevine/PolyGram / Greensleeves / Jet Star

Gwerinos

DI-DIDL-LAN
CD SCD 2075
Sain / Jun '95 / ADA / Direct / Greyhound

Gwernig, Youenn

JUST A TRAVELLER
CD KM 49
Keltia Musique / Sep '94 / ADA / Discovery

Gwerz

AUDELA
CD BUR CD 821
Escalibur / '88 / ADA / Discovery / Roots

LIVE
CD GWP 001CD
Gwerz / Aug '93 / ADA / Discovery

Gygafo

LEGEND OF THE KINGFISHER
CD HBG 122/2
Background / Jun '97 / Background / Greyhound

Gypsy

BE YOURSELF
CD MRSCD 9643
JW / Jan '96 / Jet Star

Gypsy

SOUNDTRACKS
CD LIMB 37CD
Limbo / Oct '94 / Amato Disco / Pinnacle / Prime

Gypsy Kyss

WHEN PASSION MURDERED INNOCENCE
CD 972210
FM / May '91 / Revolver / Sony

Gypsy Orchestra

JEWISH WEDDING
CD RCD 10105
Rykodisc / Nov '91 / ADA / Vital

Gyres

FIRST
Sly / Hi-fi driving / Break / Million miles / Hooligan / Are you ready / Falling down / On a roll / I'm alright / Pop cop / Downtime
CD SUGA 16CD
Sugar / Jul '97 / RTM/Disc

Gysin, Brion

SELF PORTRAIT JUMPING
Kick / Junk / Stop smoking / Sham pain / V V V / Baboon / All those years / Dreamachine / Page 3 / Flies / I am that I am / Off the ground / Initiate / Somebody special / Door
CD MTM 33
Made To Measure / Apr '96 / New Note/ Pinnacle

Gyuto Monks Of Bomdile

BUDDHIST CHANT VOL.2
CD VICG 5040
JVC World Library / Jun '96 / ADA / CM / Direct

FREEDOM CHANTS FROM THE ROOF OF THE WORLD
Yamantaka / Mahakala / Number 2 for Gaia
CD RCD 20113
Rykodisc / Sep '91 / ADA / Vital

GZR

PLASTIC PLANET
CD RAWCD 105
Raw Power / Apr '96 / Pinnacle

H

ICE CREAM GENIUS
CD ______ **WENCD 016**
When / Feb '97 / Pinnacle

H-Oilers

INNOCENT CATHOLIC COMBAT WALTZ, THE
CD ______ **EFA 119682**
Crippled Dick Hot Wax / Nov '94 / SRD

H-Blockx

DISCOVER MY SOUL
Try me one more time / Gimme more / Discover my soul / How do you feel / Heaven / Step back / I can't rely on you / I heard him cry / This is not America / Rainman / Duality of mind / Gotta find a way / Life is feeling dizzy / Prelude
CD ______ **74321402912**
RCA / Oct '96 / BMG

TIME TO MOVE
Pour me a glass / Revolution / Say baby / Move / Fight the force / Little girl / Risin' high / H-Blockx / Real love / Do what you wanna do (Dave don't like it) / Go freaky / Fuck the facts / Time to fight
CD ______ **74321187512**
RCA / Jan '96 / BMG

H-Town

BEGGIN' AFTER DARK
H-Town intro '94 / Sex bowl / One night gigolo / Prelude to emotion / Emotions / Cruisin' fo' honeys / Full time / 1-9800 Call GI / Tumble and rumble / Much feeling (and it tastes great) / Beggin' after dark / Indo love / Back seat (wit no sheets) / Buss one / Baby I love ya / Rockit steady / Last record
CD ______ **116312**
Musidisc / Jan '95 / Discovery

FEVER FOR DA FLAVOR
Introduction / Can't fade da H / Treat U right / Fever for da flavor / Sex me / H-town bounce / Keepin' my composure / Interlude / Lick U up / Knockin' da boots / Won't U come back / Baby I wanna
CD ______ **110702**
Musidisc / May '95 / Discovery

H2O

H20
5 Yr plan / Scene report / Spirit of '84 / I know why / Gen-eric / Surrounded / Here today/Gone tomorrow / Family tree / Hi-low / My curse / My love is real
CD ______ **BLK 030ECD**
Blackout / Sep '96 / Plastic Head / Vital

Habermann, Robert

SALUTE TO FRANK SINATRA, A
My kind of town / All or nothing at all / I'll never smile again / Oh look at me now / Night and day / Saturday night is the lonliest night of the week / Nancy / Coffee song / Put your dreams away / Song is you / Moon was yellow / One I love belongs to somebody else / All of me / Guess I'll hang my tears out to dry / I'm a fool to want you / Birth of the blues / Lean baby / You make me feel so young / Young at heart / Look to your heart / In the wee small hours of the morning / One for my baby / Strangers in the night / Let me try again / My way
CD ______ **SCATCD 2**
Sophisticat / Jun '96 / New Note/Pinnacle

Habichuela, Pepe

A MANDELI
Resuene / Al aire / El dron / Guadiana / Del cerro / Mi tierra / Boabdil / A mandeli / Mandeli
CD ______ **HNCD 1315**
Hannibal / May '89 / ADA / Vital

Hachig, Kazarian

ARMENIA ARMENIA
CD ______ **MCD 61452**
Monitor / Jun '93 / CM

Hacienda

SUNDAY AFTERNOON
CD ______ **HHCD 20**
Harthouse / Oct '96 / Mo's Music Machine / Prime / Vital

Hackberry Ramblers

CAJUN BOOGIE
CD ______ **FF 629CD**
Flying Fish / Dec '93 / ADA / CM / Direct / Roots

JOLIE BLONDE
CD ______ **ARHCD 399**
Arhoolie / Apr '95 / ADA / Cadillac / Direct

Hackett, Bobby

BOBBY HACKETT AND HIS BAND 1952 (Hackett, Bobby Band)
CD ______ **STCD 6050**
Storyville / Jan '97 / Cadillac / Jazz Music / Wellard

CLASSICS 1938-1940
CD ______ **CLASSICS 890**
Classics / Sep '96 / Discovery / Jazz Music

LIVE AT THE ROOSEVELT GRILL VOL.1
CD ______ **CRD 105**
Chiaroscuro / Mar '96 / Jazz Music

LIVE AT THE ROOSEVELT GRILL VOL.2
CD ______ **CRD 138**
Chiaroscuro / Jan '97 / Jazz Music

MILTON JAZZ CONCERT 1963 (Hackett, Bobby & Vic Dickenson/Maxine Sullivan)
CD ______ **IAJRCD 1004**
IAJRC / Jun '94 / Jazz Music / Wellard

OFF MINOR (Hackett, Bobby & Jack Teagarden)
CD ______ **VN 162**
Viper's Nest / May '95 / ADA / Cadillac / Direct / Jazz Music

STRING OF PEARLS, A
Carnegie jump / Ja da / You, you and especially you / You're a sweetheart / Please be kind / Jammin' the waltz / Clementine / Don't be that way / Jungle love / Memories of you / What's the use / I don't stand a ghost of a chance with you / Ain't misbehavin' / Sunrise serenade / Embraceable you / Clarinet marmalade / Singin' the blues / String of pearls / I must have that man / At sundown / New Orleans / Skeleton jangle / When day is done
CD ______ **TPZ 1053**
Topaz Jazz / Sep '96 / Cadillac / Pinnacle

Hackett, Steve

CURED
Hope I don't wake / Picture postcard / Can't let go / Air-conditioned nightmare / Funny feeling / Cradle of swans / Overnight sleeper / Turn back time
CD ______ **CDSCD 4021**
Virgin / Apr '89 / EMI

DEFECTOR
Steppes / Time to get out / Slogans / Leaving / Two vamps as guests / Jacuzzi / Hammer in the sand / Toast / Show / Sentimental
CD ______ **CDSCD 4018**
Virgin / '89 / EMI

HIGHLY STRUNG
Casino royale / Cell 151 / Always somewhere else / Walking through walls / Give it away / Weightless / Group therapy / India rubber man / Hackett to pieces
CD ______ **HAKCD 1**
Virgin / Apr '89 / EMI

PLEASE DON'T TOUCH
Narnia / Carry on up the vicarage / Racing in A / Kim / How can I / Icarus ascending / Hoping love will last / Land of 1000 autumns / Please don't touch / Voice of Necam
CD ______ **CDSCD 4012**
Charisma / '89 / EMI

SPECTRAL MORNINGS
Everyday / Virgin and the gypsy / Red flower of Tachai blooms everywhere / Clocks - The angel of Mons / Ballad of the decomposing man / Lost time in Cordoba / Tigermoth / Spectral mornings
CD ______ **CDSCD 4017**
Charisma / '87 / EMI

UNAUTHORISED BIOGRAPHY
Narnia / Hackett to pieces / Don't fall away from me / Spectral mornings / Steppes / Virgin and the gypsy: *Air Conditioned Nightmare* / Cell 151 / Slogans / Icarus ascending / Prayers and dreams / Star of Sirius / Hammer in the sand / Ace of wands / Hoping love will last
CD ______ **CDVM 9014**
Charisma / Oct '92 / EMI

VOYAGE OF THE ACOLYTE
Ace of wands / Hands of the priestess-part 1 / Tower struck down / Hands of the priestess-part 2 / Hermit / Star of Sirius / Lovers / Shadow of the Hierophant
CD ______ **CASCD 1111**
Charisma / '87 / EMI

Hacks-Harney, Richard

SWEETMAN
CD ______ **EDCD 483**
Edsel / Sep '96 / Pinnacle

Haco

HACO
CD ______ **HACO 1**
ReR/Recommended / Jun '97 / ReR Megacorp / RTM/Disc

Hada To Hada

MY GERMAN LOVER
CD ______ **SCD 294CD**
Starc / Apr '94 / ADA / Direct

Hadad, Astrid

AYI (Hadad, Astrid & Los Tarzanes)
CD ______ **ROUCD 5066**
Rounder / Nov '95 / ADA / CM / Direct

Haddaway

ALBUM, THE
CD ______ **74321183202**
Arista / Aug '95 / BMG

DRIVE, THE
Fly away / Breakaway / Lover by thy name / Waiting for a better world / Give it up / Catch a fire / Desert prayer / First cut is the deepest / Baby don't go / Another day without you
CD ______ **74321306662**
Arista / Sep '95 / BMG

Haddix, Travis

BIG OLE GOODUN, A
CD ______ **ICH 1168CD**
Ichiban / Jan '94 / Direct / Koch

WHAT I KNOW RIGHT NOW
CD ______ **ICH 1132CD**
Ichiban / Oct '93 / Direct / Koch

WINNERS NEVER QUIT
Homeslice / Bag lady / She's not the kind of girl / Better than nothing / Winners never quit / Something in the milk ain't clean / Beggin' business / Abused / Someone to love / I'm mean
CD ______ **ICH 1101CD**
Ichiban / Oct '93 / Direct / Koch

Haden, Charlie

ALWAYS SAY GOODBYE (Haden, Charlie Quartet West)
Introduction / Always say goodbye / Nice eyes / Relaxin' at Camarillo / Sunset afternoon / My love and I / Alone together / Our Spanish love song / Background music / Ou es-tu mon amour / Avenue of stars / Low key lightly / Celia / Everything happens to me / Ending
CD ______ **5215012**
Verve / Jul '94 / PolyGram

AS LONG AS THERE'S MUSIC (Haden, Charlie & Hampton Hawes)
Irene / Rainforest / Turnaround / As long as there's music / This is called love / Hello / Goodbye / Irene / Turnaround / As long as there's music
CD ______ **5135342**
Verve / Mar '94 / PolyGram

BALLAD OF THE FALLEN
El Segardors / If you want to write me / Ballad of the fallen / Grandola vila morena / Introduction to people / People united will never be defeated / Silence / Too late / La pasionaria / La santa espina
CD ______ **8115462**
ECM / Sep '84 / New Note/Pinnacle

BEYOND THE MISSOURI SKY (Haden, Charlie & Pat Metheny)
CD ______ **5371302**
Verve / Feb '97 / PolyGram

CLOSENESS DUETS
Ellen David / OC / For Turiya / For a free Portugal
CD ______ **3970002**
A&M / Mar '94 / PolyGram

DIALOGUES (Haden, Charlie & Carlos Paredes)
Asas sobre o mundo / Nas asas da saudade / Danca dos camponeses / Canto de trabalho / Marionetas / Song for Che / Balada da coimbra / Divertimento / Variacoes sobre o fado de Artur Paredes i Concalo Paredes / Verde anos
CD ______ **8434452**
Verve / Mar '93 / PolyGram

DREAM KEEPER (Haden, Charlie & The Liberation Music Orchestra)
Dream keeper / Rabo de nube / Nkosi sikelel 'I Afrika / Sandino / Spiritual / Feliciano ama / Canto del pilon / Hymn of the Anarchist women's movement
CD ______ **DIW 844**
DIW / Jan '92 / Cadillac / Harmonia Mundi
CD ______ **8478762**
Verve / Mar '93 / PolyGram

GOLDEN NUMBER, THE
Out of focus / Shepp's way / Turnaround / Golden number
CD ______ **3908252**
A&M / Feb '94 / PolyGram

HAUNTED HEART (Haden, Charlie Quartet West)
Introduction / Hello my lovely / Haunted heart / Dance of the infidels / Long goodbye / Lennie's pennies / Every time we say goodbye / Lady in the lake / Segment / Bad and the beautiful / Deep song
CD ______ **5130782**
Verve / Mar '92 / PolyGram

IN ANGEL CITY (Haden, Charlie Quartet West)
Sunday at the Hillcrest / First song / Red wind / Blue in green / Alpha / Live your dreams / Child's play / Fortune's fame / Tarantella / Lonely woman
CD ______ **8370312**
Verve / Jul '89 / PolyGram

LIBERATION MUSIC ORCHESTRA
Introduction / Song of the united front / El quinto regimento / Los cuatro generals (the four generals) / Ending of the first side / Song for Che / War orphans / Interlude / Circus / We shall overcome
CD ______ **IMP 11882**
Impulse Jazz / Mar '96 / New Note/BMG

MAGICO (Haden, Charlie & Jan Garbarek/Egberto Gismonti)
CD ______ **8234742**
ECM / '88 / New Note/Pinnacle

QUARTET WEST
Hermitage / Body and soul / Good life / In the moment / Bay city / My foolsih heart / Passport / Taney county / Blessing / Passion flower
CD ______ **8316732**
Verve / Aug '87 / PolyGram

STEAL AWAY (Haden, Charlie & Hank Jones)
CD ______ **5272492**
Verve / Sep '95 / PolyGram

Hades

AGAIN SHALL BE FREE
CD ______ **FMP 002**
Misanthropy / Mar '95 / Plastic Head

IF AT FIRST YOU DON'T SUCCEED
CD ______ **RR 95332**
Roadrunner / Oct '88 / PolyGram

Hadidjah, Idhah

TONGGERET
Tonggert / Bayu bayu / Mahoni / Hiji / Catetan / Arum / Bandung / Daun / Pulus / Keser / Bojong / Serat / Sahara
CD ______ **7559791732**
Nonesuch / Jan '95 / Warner Music

Hadley, Jerry

SONG OF NAPLES
Dicitencello vuie / Marechiare / Passione / Manella mia / Fenesta che lucive / Vurria / A Tazza e Cafe / A Vuchella / Core ngrato / O sole mio / Pecche / Silenzio cantatore / Ciove / Napule ca se ne va / Piscatore e Pusilleco / L'te vurria vasa / Maria, mari / Torna a Surriento / Addio, mia bella Napoli
CD ______ **09026683502**
RCA Victor / Nov '96 / BMG

Haerter, Harold

MOSTLY LIVE (Haerter, Harold & Dewey Redman)
Misterioso / Interlude / Cosmic / Dewey's tune / Mute / Interlude 2 / Children song / Walls bridges / I still love you / Spur of the moment / Interlude 3 / Variation on mute
CD ______ **8888252**
Tiptoe / Oct '96 / New Note/Pinnacle

Hafer, Dick

IN A SENTIMENTAL MOOD (Hafer, Dick Quartet)
CD ______ **PCD 7094**
Progressive / Jul '96 / Jazz Music

Hafler Trio

ALL THAT RISES MUST CONVERGE
CD ______ **KUT 5**
The Grey Area / May '93 / RTM/Disc

BANG - AN OPEN LETTER
CD KUT 1CD
The Grey Area / Jun '94 / RTM/Disc

BOOTLEG
CD ASH 13CD
Ash International / Jan '95 / Kudos / Pinnacle

FOUR WAYS OF SAYING FIVE
CD KUT 4
The Grey Area / Oct '93 / RTM/Disc

FUCK
CD TONE 3
Touch / Oct '95 / Kudos / Pinnacle

HOW TO REFORM MANKIND
CD TO 24
Touch / Oct '95 / Kudos / Pinnacle

INPOUTOF
CD KK 008CD
KK / '88 / Plastic Head

MASTERY OF MONEY
CD TO 18
Touch / Mar '91 / Kudos / Pinnacle

RESURRECTION (Hafler Trio & The Sons Of God)
CD TO 22
Touch / Oct '95 / Kudos / Pinnacle

SEVEN HOURS SLEEP
CD KUT 3CD
The Grey Area / Jun '94 / RTM/Disc

THIRSTY FISH, A
CD KUT 6
The Grey Area / May '93 / RTM/Disc

WALK GENTLY THROUGH
CD KUT 2CD
The Grey Area / Jun '94 / RTM/Disc

Hagar, Sammy

ANTHOLOGY
CD VSOPCD 207
Connoisseur Collection / Oct '94 / Pinnacle

BEST OF SAMMY HAGAR, THE
Red / (Sittin' on the) dock of the bay / I've done everything for you / Rock 'n' roll weekend / Cruisin' and boozin' / Turn up the music / Reckless / Trans am (highway wonderland) / Love or money / This planet's on fire / Plain Jane / Bad reputation / Bad motor scooter / You make me crazy
CD CPD 7802622
EMI Gold / Jun '97 / EMI

BEST OF SAMMY HAGAR, THE
CD CDGOLD 1069
EMI Gold / Oct '96 / EMI

DANGER ZONE
Love or money / Twentieth century man / Miles from boredom / Mommy says / In the night / Iceman / Bad reputation / Heartbeat / Run for your life / Danger zone
CD BGOCD 281
Beat Goes On / Jul '95 / Pinnacle

LOUD 'N' CLEAR
Rock 'n' roll weekend / Make it last / Reckless / Turn up the music / I've done everything for you / Young girl blues / Bad motor scooter / Space station no. 5
CD BGOCD 149
Beat Goes On / Aug '92 / Pinnacle

MARCHING TO MARS
Little white lie / Salvation on Sand Hill / Who has the right / Would you do it for free / Leaving the warmth of the womb / Kama / On the other hand / Both sides now / Yogi's so high (I'm stoned) / Amnesty is granted / Marching to Mars
CD TRD 11627
Track Factory / May '97 / BMG

MUSICAL CHAIRS
Turn up the music / It's gonna be alright kid / You make me crazy / Reckless / Try / Don't stop me now / Straight from the hip kid / Hey boys / Someone out there / Crack in the world
CD BGOCD 201
Beat Goes On / May '94 / Pinnacle

NINE ON A TEN SCALE
Keep on rockin' / Urban guerilla / Flamingos fly / China / Silver lights / All American / Confession (please come back) / Young girl blues / Rock 'n' roll Romeo
CD BGOCD 182
Beat Goes On / Apr '93 / Pinnacle

RED
Red / Catch the wind / Cruisin' and boozin' / Free money / Rock 'n' roll weekend / Fillmore shuffle / Hungry / Pits / Love has found me / Little star/Eclipse
CD BGOCD 181
Beat Goes On / Apr '93 / Pinnacle

STREET MACHINE
Never say die / This planet's on fire / Wounded in love / Falling in love / Growing pains / Child to man / Trans am (Highway wonderland) / Feels like love / Plain Jane
CD BGOCD 150
Beat Goes On / Oct '92 / Pinnacle

THROUGH THE FIRE (Hagar, Sammy/ Neil Schon/Kenny Aaronson/Michael Shrieve)
Top of the rock / Missing you / Animation / Valley of the kings / Giza / Whiter shade of pale / Hot and dirty / He will understand / My home town
CD RETRO 50059CD
Retroactive / Jan '96 / Plastic Head

Hagen, Nina

NINA HAGEN
Move over / Super freak family / Love heart attack / Hold me / Las Vegas / Live on Mars / Dope sucks / Only seventeen / Where's the party / Ave Maria
CD ACTIVCD 6
Activ / Feb '96 / Total/BMG

REVOLUTION BALLROOM
So bad / Revolution room / Right on time / Pollution pirates / King of hearts / L'amore / Pillow talk / Berlin / I'm gonna live the life / Gypsy love / Omhaidakhandi
CD ACTIVCD 3
Activ / Oct '95 / Total/BMG

STREET
Blumen fur die damen / Divine love, sex and romance / Ruler of my heart / Nina 4 president / Keep it live / Berlin / In my world / Gretchen / Erfurt and Gera / All 4 franckie
CD ACTIVCD 4
Activ / Feb '96 / Total/BMG

Hagfish

ROCK YOUR LAME ASS
Happiness / Stamp / Flat / Bullet / Crater / Minite maid / White food / Disappointed / Plain / Buster / Trixi / Did you notice / Gertrude / Hose / Teenage kicks
CD 8286842
London / Sep '95 / PolyGram

Haggard, Merle

20 COUNTRY NO.1'S
Okie from Muskogee / I'm a lonesome fugitive / Branded man / Sing me back home / Legend of Bonnie and Clyde / Mama tired / Hungry eyes / Workin' man blues / Always wanting you / It's not love (but it's not bad) / Old man from the mountain / Everybody's had the blues / Movin' on / Roots of my raising / Fightin' side of me / Carolyn / I wonder if they ever think of me / Daddy Frank (the guitar man) / Grandma Harp / Kentucky gambler
CD CDMFP 6114
Music For Pleasure / Mar '94 / EMI

ALL NIGHT LONG
All night long: *Haggard, Merle & Randy Travis* / Honky tonk / Night-time man / I'm a white boy / Holding things together / Uncle Lem / Farmer's daughter / Man's got to give up a lot / I've done it all / Goodbye lefty / If you've got time (to say goodbye) / September in Miami / Bar in Bakersfield
CD D277410
Curb / '91 / Grapevine/PolyGram

CAPITOL COLLECTORS SERIES: MERLE HAGGARD
Swinging doors / Tonight the bottle let me down / I'm a lonesome fugitive / Sing me back home / I take a lot of pride in what I am / Hungry eyes / Workin' man blues / Okie from Muskogee / Fightin' side of me / Soldier's last letter / Daddy Frank / I wonder if they ever think of me / Emptiest arms in the world / Things aren't funny anymore / Old man from the mountain
CD CZ 301
Capitol / Apr '90 / EMI

COUNTRY LEGEND
Twinkle twinkle lucky star / If you want to be my woman / Workin' man blues / Always late / TB blues / Fulsom prison blues / Footlights / Big city / Mama tried / Brain Cloudy blues / Milk cow blues / Begging to you / Tonight the bottle let me down / What am I gonna do (with the rest of my life) / Ida Red / San Antonio rose / Corine Corina / Take me back to Tulsa / Faded love: *Haggard, Merle & Bonnie Owens* / Maiden's prayer / Fiddle breakdown / Right or wrong / Ramblin' fever / That's the way love goes / Today I started loving you again / Okie from Muskogee / Fightin' side of me
CD PLATCD 358
Platinum / May '91 / Prism

HITS & MORE, THE
Okie from Muskogee / If you want to be my woman / Games people play / Workin' man blues / Corine Corina / Tonight the bottle let me down / What am I gonna do / Mama tried / That's the way love goes / San Antonio rose / Ramblin' fever / Take me back to Tulsa / Ida Red / Begging to you / Always late / Big city / Folsom prison blues / Medley / Footlights / Today I started loving you again
CD HADCD 168
Javelin / May '94 / Henry Hadaway / THE

I'M A LONESOME FUGITIVE/MAMA TRIED
I'm a lonesome fugitive / All of me belongs to you / House of memories / Life in prison / Whatever happened to me / Drink up and be somebody / Someone told my story / If you want to be my woman / Mary's mine / Skid row / My rough and rowdy ways / Mixed up mess of a heart / Mama tried / Green green grass of home / Little ole wine drinker me / In the good old days (when times were bad) / I could have gone right / I'll always know / Sunny side of my life / Teach me to forget / Folsom Prison blues / Run 'em off / You'll never love me now / Too many bridges to cross over
CD BGOCD 328
Beat Goes On / Mar '97 / Pinnacle

MERLE HAGGARD
CD DS 006
Desperado / Jun '97 / TKO Magnum

OKIE FROM MUSKOGEE (23 Great Songs Live At Church Street Station, Florida)
Twinkle twinkle lucky star / If you want to be my woman / Workin' man blues / Always late with your kisses / TB blues / Folsom Prison blues / Footlights / Big city / Mama tried / Brain cloudy blues/Milk cow blues / Begging to you / Tonight the bottle let me down / What am I gonna do with the rest of my life / Ida red / San Antonio rose / Corrine Corrina / Take me back to Tulsa / Faded love / Fiddle breakdown / Right or wrong / Ramblin' fever / That's the way love goes / Today I started loving you again / Okie from Muskogee / Fightin' side of me
CD PLATCD 170
Platinum / Mar '96 / Prism

OKIE FROM MUSKOGEE
Mama tried / When times were good / Today I started loving you again / Chill factor / Ida Red / Okie from Muskogee / Bill Cheatum / Mama's hungry eyes / Fightin' side of me / I think I'll just stay here and drink / Honky tonk night time man / Footlights / If I could only fly / Kern River / I knew the moment I lost you / This mornin' this evenin' so soon
CD CD 6054
Music / Jan '97 / Target/BMG

POET OF THE COMMON MAN
CD CURCD 040
Curb / Apr '97 / Grapevine/PolyGram

SAME TRAIN, A DIFFERENT TIME
California blues / Waiting for a train / Train whistle blues / Why should I be lonely / Blue yodel No. 6 / Miss the Mississippi and you / Mule skinner blues / Frankie and Johnny / Hobo Bill's last ride / Travellin' blues / Peach pickin' time in Georgia / No hard times / Down the old road to home / Jimmie Rodgers' last blue yodel / Jimmie the kid / My rough and rowdy ways / Hobo's meditation / Mother, the Queen of my heart / My Carolina sunshine girl / My old pal / Nobody knows but me / Delta blues / Mississippi delta blues / Gambling polka dot blues
CD BCD 15740
Bear Family / Oct '93 / Direct / Rollercoaster / Swift

SAME TRAIN, A DIFFERENT TIME
CD 340512
Koch / Jul '95 / Koch

SING ME BACK HOME
CD 340542
Koch International / Nov '95 / Koch

STARS OVER BAKERSFIELD (Haggard, Merle & Buck Owens)
CD CTS 55418
Country Stars / Jun '94 / Target/BMG

STRANGERS
CD 340532
Koch International / Nov '95 / Koch

SWINGING DOORS/THE BOTTLE LET ME DOWN
CD 340522
Koch International / Nov '95 / Koch

TRIBUTE TO THE BEST DAMN FIDDLE PLAYER IN THE WORLD (My Salute To Bob Wills)
Brown skin gal / Right or wrong / Brain cloudy blues / Stay a little longer / Misery / Time changes everything / San Antonio rose / I knew the moment I lost you / Roly poly / Old fashioned love / Corine Corina / Take me back to Tulsa
CD 379002
Koch / Aug '95 / Koch

TULARE DUST - THE SONGS OF MERLE HAGGARD (Various Artists)
CD HCD 8058
Hightone / Dec '94 / ADA / Koch

UNTAMED HAWK
Sing a sad song / You don't even try / Life in prison (false start) / Life in prison / You don't have far to go / Sam Hill / Please Mr. DJ / I'd trade all of my tomorrows / Strangers / Slowly but surely / Just between the two of us / Falling for you / I wanta live again / House without love / Walking the floor over you / Worst is yet to come / Piedras negras (go home) / Singin' my heart out / Skid row / If I had left it up to you / I'm gonna break every heart I can / Stranger in my arms / If I could be him / Shade tree (fix it man) / This town's not big enough / I'll take a chance / Our hearts are holding hands / Too used to being with you / That makes two of us / Forever and ever / Wait a little longer, please Jesus / Swinging doors / Girl turned ripe / I threw away the rose / Fugitive / Loneliness is eating me alive / Someone told my story / Hang up my gloves / Longer you wait / Tonight the bottle let me down / I can't stand me / Someone else you've known / High on a hilltop / I'll look over you / No more you and me / Mixed up mess of a heart / I'm a lonesome fugitive / House of memories / All of me belongs to you / Mary's mine / If you want to be my woman / Whatever happened to me / Drink up and be somebody / Gone crazy / Some of us never learn / Branded man / You don't have very far to go / Wine take me away / If you see my baby / Somewhere between / Don't get married / My hands are tied / I made the prison band / Look over me / Long black limousine / I'll leave the bottle on the bar / Sing me back home / Son of Hickory Holler's tramp / Seeing eye dog / Will you visit me on Sundays / Home is where a kid grows up / Where does the good times go / Good times / News break / My past is present / Mom and Dad's waltz / My Ramona / Because you can't be mine / Train never stops / You still have a place in my heart / Money tree / Picture from two sides of life / Legend of Bonnie and Clyde / I started loving you again / Love has a mind of it's own / Fool's castle / Is this the beginning of the end / Sunny side of my life / Run em off / I'll always know / You'll never love me now / Mama tried / In the good old days / Little ole wine drinker me / Teach me to forget / Lookin' for my mind / Green green grass of home / I could have gone right / Day the rains came / I think we're living in the good old days / Somewhere on Skid Row / Who do I know in Dallas / Folsom prison blues / You're not home yet / Too many bridges to cross over / I take a lot of pride in what I am / I just want to look at you one more time / I'm bringin' home good news / Keep me from cryin' today / I can't hold myself in line / I'm free / It meant goodbye to me when you said hello / Who'll buy the wine / She thinks I still care / What's wrong with stayin' home / When no flowers grow / Every fool has a rainbow / Hungry eyes / Silver wings
CD Set BCD 15744
Bear Family / Mar '95 / Direct / Rollercoaster / Swift

VERY BEST OF MERLE HAGGARD, THE
I take a lot of pride in what I am / I'm a lonesome fugitive / Mama tried / Daddy Frank (the guitarman) / Sing me back home / Workin' man blues / Kentucky gambler / Holding things together / Branded man / Legend of Bonnie and Clyde / Mama's hungry eyes / Swingin' doors / Carolyn / Strangers / Bottle let me down / I think I'll just stay here and drink / Fightin' side of me / Okie from Muskogee
CD ECD 3099
K-Tel / Jan '95 / K-Tel

Haggart, Bob

WORLD'S GREATEST JAZZBAND (Haggart, Bob & Yank Lawson)
CD CDTTD 533
Timeless Traditional / Jul '94 / Jazz Music / New Note/Pinnacle

Haghighi, Mohammad

MOHAMMAD HAGHIGI ROKSHAT-E-TABIDAN
CD AS 20122
Al Segno / Jun '96 / Vital/SAM

WAVE ON THE MOOR
CD AS 20022
Al Segno / Jun '96 / Vital/SAM

Hagiopian, Richard

ARMENIAN MUSIC THROUGH THE AGES
CD SFCD 40414
Smithsonian Folkways / Jun '93 / ADA / Cadillac / CM / Direct / Koch

BEST OF ARMENIAN FOLK MUSIC
CD EUCD 1222
ARC / Sep '93 / ADA / ARC Music

Hahn, Jerry

TIME CHANGES
Time changes / 245 / Method / Quiet now / Blues for allyson / Oregon / Goodbye Pork Pie Hat / Hannah bear / Stolen moments / Chelsea rose
CD ENJ 90072
Enja / May '95 / New Note/Pinnacle / Vital/SAM

Hahn, John

OUT OF THE SHADOWS
Rhino stomp / Captain Courageous / Outward bound / Looking glass / Warm summer rain / Cut to the chase / Let it ride / Deadly spell / Pickin' your seat / Second sight / Heat of the night / Inherit the wind
CD KILCD 1004
Killerwatt / Oct '93 / Kingdom

Haig, Al

ORNITHOLOGY
CD _____ **PCD 7024**
Progressive / Oct '91 / Jazz Music

Hail

TURN OF THE SCREW
Another day / Honey smothered / Good luck / Sicko God / Tape hiss / Rusty old ring / Take me back / Burlesque egg / Racer hero / Tar pits / Suspended / Down the road / Star in the sky / Fifteen seconds of silence / My friend / Did you listen to this
CD _____ **RERHCD**
ReR/Recommended / Apr '91 / ReR Megacorp / RTM/Disc

Haine Et Ses Amours

HAINE ET SES AMOURS
CD _____ **760486**
Eurobon / Nov '90 / Triple Earth

Haines, Nathan

SHIFT LEFT
CD _____ **5271502**
Verve / Nov '96 / PolyGram

Haines, Paul

DARN IT
Threats that matter / There aren't these things / Curtsy / Les paramedicaux erotiques / What is going to supposed to mean / Jubilee / On the way to here and elsewhere / Funny bird song / Inexplicably / Outside the city / Poem for Gretchen Ruth / Art in heaven / Rawilpindi blues / Sticks in the mud
CD _____ **AMCL 10142**
American Clave / Nov '93 / ADA / Direct / New Note/Pinnacle

Haino, Keiji

21ST CENTURY HARDY-GUIDE-Y MAN, THE
CD _____ **PSFD 68**
PSF / Jan '96 / Harmonia Mundi

DEATH NEVER TO BE COMPLETE, A (Fushitsusha)
Just as I told you / Though it went so well / That which is becoming to me / Continuing to be / Death to be complete / Hermitage
CD _____ **TKCF 77014**
Tokuma / Jun '97 / Harmonia Mundi

DRAWING CLOSE, ATTUNING... (Haino, Keiji & Derek Bailey)
CD _____ **TKCD 77017**
Tokuma / Jun '97 / Harmonia Mundi

I SAID, THIS IS THE SON OF NIHILISM
CD _____ **ARGON 18**
TOE / Jun '97 / Cargo

KEEPING ON BREATHING
Where is it / My shadow / There / Wafting / Here / A code / You
CD _____ **TKCD 77016**
Tokuma / Jun '97 / Harmonia Mundi

SO, BLACK IS MYSELF
CD _____ **ALIENCD 3**
Alien8 / Jun '97 / Cargo / Harmonia Mundi

TIME IS NIGH, THE (Fushitsusha)
Just before / My precious thing / Black cluster / Time is nigh
CD _____ **TKCD 77015**
Tokuma / Jun '97 / Harmonia Mundi

VOL.2 (Haino, Keiji & Loren Mazzacane Connors)
CD _____ **MPK 7005CD**
Menlo Park / May '97 / Cargo

Hair & Skin Trading Company

JO IN NINE G HELL
CD _____ **SITU 40 CD**
Situation 2 / Apr '92 / Pinnacle

OVER VALANCE
CD _____ **BBQCD 141**
Beggars Banquet / Sep '93 / RTM/Disc / Warner Music

PSYCHEDLISCHE MUSIQUE
CD _____ **FRR 11CD**
Freek / May '95 / RTM/Disc / SRD

Hair

HAIR PIECE
CD _____ **FLASH 002**
Flashback / Jun '97 / Greyhound

Haircut 100

PELICAN WEST PLUS
Favourite shirts (boy meets girl) / Love plus one / Lemon firebrigade / Marine boy / Milk film / King size / Fantastic day / Baked beans / Snow girl / Love's got me in triangles / Surprise me again / Calling Captain Autumn / Boat party / Ski club / Nobody's fool / October is orange
CD _____ **74321100782**
Arista / Oct '92 / BMG

Hairy Chapter

CAN'T GET THROUGH/EYES
CD _____ **SB 038**
Second Battle / Jun '97 / Greyhound

Haiti Cherie

CREOLE - TRADITIONAL & VOODOO SONGS
CD _____ **995342**
EPM / Aug '93 / ADA / Discovery

Hajra Gipsy Orchestra

EVENING OF GIPSY SONGS, AN
CD _____ **SOW 90129**
Sounds Of The World / Sep '94 / Target/BMG

Hakansson, Kenny

SPELAR SPRINGLEKAR
CD _____ **SRS 3620CD**
Silence / Jul '95 / ADA / Direct

Hakim, Sadik

LADYBIRD
CD _____ **STCD 4156**
Storyville / Feb '90 / Cadillac / Jazz Music / Wellard

Hakmoun, Hassan

FIRE WITHIN, THE
CD _____ **CDT 135CD**
Music Of The World / Nov '95 / ADA / Target/BMG

TRANCE (Hakmoun, Hassan & Zahar)
Bania / Only one god (Maaboud alah) / Soudan minitara (Bum bastic mix) / Challaban / Soutanbi / Soulalahoalith / Alal wahya alal (Trance mix) / Sun is gone / Soudan minitara
CD _____ **CDRW 38**
Realworld / Aug '93 / EMI

Hal

GORILLA CONSPIRATION
CD _____ **PPP 121CD**
We Bite / Jun '97 / Plastic Head

Hal Al Shedad

HAL AL SHEDAD
CD _____ **TMU 017CD**
Troubleman / Feb '97 / Cargo

Halcox, Pat

SONGS FROM TIN PAN ALLEY (Halcox, Pat & Friends)
CD _____ **JCD 186**
Jazzology / Oct '91 / Jazz Music

Hale, Terry Lee

FRONTIER MODEL
CD _____ **GRCD 311**
Glitterhouse / Apr '94 / Avid/BMG

LEAVING WEST
CD _____ **GRCD 399**
Glitterhouse / Dec '96 / Avid/BMG

OH WHAT A WORLD
CD _____ **NORMAL 152CD**
Normal / Mar '94 / ADA / Direct

TORNADO ALLEY
CD _____ **GRCD 359**
Glitterhouse / May '97 / Avid/BMG

Hale, Willie

VERY BEST OF LITTLE BEAVER, THE (Little Beaver)
Party down / Get into the party life / We three / Money vibrations / Listen to my heartbeat / I can dig it baby / When was the last time / Let's stick together / Wish I had a little girl like you / Groove on / Let the good times roll / Little girl blue / Joey / Party times / I feel like crying / I really love you
CD _____ **NEMCD 919**
Sequel / Nov '96 / BMG

Haley, Bill

BEST OF BILL HALEY (Haley, Bill & The Comets)
CD _____ **MACCD 231**
Autograph / Aug '96 / BMG

BILL HALEY
CD _____ **LECD 034**
Dynamite / May '94 / THE

BILL HALEY & THE COMETS (Haley, Bill & The Comets)
CD _____ **ENTCD 283**
Entertainers / Mar '92 / Target/BMG

BILL HALEY & THE COMETS (Haley, Bill & The Comets)
CD _____ **CD 114**
Timeless Treasures / Oct '94 / THE

BILL HALEY & THE COMETS (Haley, Bill & The Comets)
CD _____ **12396**
Laserlight / Mar '95 / Target/BMG

BILL HALEY & THE COMETS (Haley, Bill & The Comets)
Rock around the clock / Flip, flop and fly / Skinny Minnie / Love letters in the sand / Ling ting tong / See you later alligator / Rock the joint / Saints rock 'n' roll / Shake, rattle and roll / Rock-a-beatin' boogie
CD _____ **399234**
Koch Presents / Jun '97 / Koch

ESSENTIALS (Haley, Bill & Little Richard)
CD _____ **LECDD 624**
Wisepack / Aug '95 / Conifer/BMG / THE

HITS COLLECTION, THE (Haley, Bill & The Comets)
Saints rock 'n' roll / Rip it up / Don't mess around with my love / Wobble / ABC boogie / Rock around the clock / Shake, rattle and roll / See you later alligator / Razzle dazzle / Panic / Helena / This is goodbye, goodbye / I've got news for you / Train of sin / Altar of love / Blue comet blues / Skokiaan a go go / Whole lotta shakin' goin' on / How many
CD _____ **100592**
CMC / May '97 / BMG

RIP IT UP, ROCK'N'ROLL (Haley, Bill & The Comets)
(We're gonna) Rock around the clock / Saints rock 'n' roll / You hit the wrong note Billy Goat / Goofin' around / Thirteen women (and only one man in town) / Caldonia / Shake, rattle and roll / Choo choo ch' boogie / Burn that candle / Happy baby / Hook, line and sinker / Rock Lomond / See you later alligator / Mambo rock / Dim, dim the lights / Lean Jean / Tonight's the night / Calling all Comets / Rip it up / Hide and seek / Mary Lou / Teenage mothers / Move it on over / Vive la rock 'n' roll
CD _____ **VSOPCD 116**
Connoisseur Collection / '88 / Pinnacle

ROCK AROUND THE CLOCK (Haley, Bill & The Comets)
Shake, rattle and roll / ROCK / Calling all comets / See you later alligator / Saints rock 'n' roll / Razzle dazzle / ABC Boogie / Don't knock the rock / Rip it up / Rockin' thru the rye / Birth of the boogie / Rock-a-beatin' boogie / Dim, dim the lights / Mambo rock / Rudy's rock / Skinny Minnie / Thirteen women / Corine Corina / Forty cups of coffee / (We're gonna) rock around the clock
CD _____ **MOCD 3015**
More Music / Feb '95 / Sound & Media

ROCK THE JOINT (Haley, Bill & The Comets)
Rocket 88 / Tearstains on my heart / Green tree boogie / Jukebox cannonball / Sundown boogie / Icy heart / Rock the joint / Dance with a dolly / Rockin' chair on the moon / Stop beatin' around the mulberry bush / Real rock drive / Crazy man crazy / What'cha gonna do / Pat-a-cake / Fractured / Live it up / Farewell, so long, goodbye / I'll be true / Ten little Indians / Chattanooga choo choo / Straight jacket / Yes indeed
CD _____ **RCCD 3001**
Rollercoaster / Aug '90 / Rollercoaster / Swift

ROCKIN' AND ROLLIN' (Haley, Bill & The Comets)
Shake, rattle and roll / Skinny Minnie / Rip it up / See you later alligator / (We're gonna) Rock around the clock / Razzle dazzle / Crying time / Saints rock 'n' roll / Rock-a-beatin' boogie / Rock the joint / I'm walkin' / Hi-heel sneakers / Blue suede shoes / CC rider / Lawdy Miss Clawdy / Personality / Hail hail rock 'n' roll / Let the good times roll again / Battle of New Orleans / Heartaches by the number
CD _____ **5509552**
Spectrum / Mar '95 / PolyGram

ROCKIN' ROLLIN' HALEY (Haley, Bill & The Comets)
(We're gonna) Rock around the clock / Thirteen women / Shake, rattle and roll / ABC Boogie / Happy baby / Dim, dim the lights / Birth of the boogie / Mambo rock / Two hound dogs / Razzle dazzle / ROCK / Rock-a-beatin' boogie / Saints rock 'n' roll / Burn that candle / See you later alligator / Paper boy / Goofin' around / Rudy's rock / Hide and seek / Hey then, there now / Tonight's the night / Hook, line and sinker / Blue comet blues / Calling all comets / Choo choo ch' boogie / Rocking little tune / Hot dog buddy buddy / Rockin' through the rye / Teenager's mother / Rip it up / Don't knock the rock / Forty cups of coffee / Miss you / You hit the wrong note Billy Goat / Rockin' rollin' rover / Please don't talk about me when I'm gone / You can't stop me from dreaming / I'm gonna sit right down and write myself a letter / Rock Lomond / Is it true what they say about Dixie / Carolina in the morning / Dipsy doodle / Ain't misbehavin' / Beak speaks / Moon over Miami / One sweet letter from you / I'll be with you in apple blossom time / Somebody else is taking my place / How many / Move it on over / Rock the joint / Me rock a hula / Rockin' Rita / Jamaica DJ / Piccadilly rock / Pretty alouette / Rockin' rollin' schnitzlebank / Rockin' Matilda / Vive la rock 'n' roll / It's a sin / Mary Mary Lou / El rocko / Come rock with me / Oriental rock / Woodenshoe rock / Walkin' beat / Skinny Minnie / Sway with me / Lean Jean / Don't nobody move / Joey's song / Chiquita Linda / Dinah / Ida, sweet as apple cider / Whoa Mabel / Marie / Eloise / Corine Corina / BB Betty / Sweet Sue, just you / Charmaine / Dragon rock / AC rock / Catwalk / I got a woman / Fool such as I / By by me / Where did you go last night / Caldonia / Shaky / Ooh, look-a-there ain't she pretty / Summer souvenir / Puerto Rican peddler / Music music music / Skokiaan / Drowsy waters / Two shadows / In a little Spanish town / Strictly instrumental / Mack The Knife / Green door / Yeah, she's evil
CD Set _____ **BCD 15506**
Bear Family / Oct '90 / Direct / Rollercoaster / Swift

SEE YOU LATER ALLIGATOR (Haley, Bill & The Comets)
CD _____ **301374**
Accord / Dec '89 / Cadillac / Discovery

VERY BEST OF BILL HALEY & THE COMETS (Haley, Bill & The Comets)
(We're gonna) Rock around the clock / Shake, rattle and roll / See you later alligator / Saints rock 'n' roll / Rock-a-beatin' boogie / Rockin' thru the Rye / Rip it up / Don't knock the rock / Mambo rock / Rudy's rock / Razzle dazzle / Skinny Minnie / ROCK / Thirteen women / ABC boogie / Birth of the boogie / Forty cups of coffee / Two hound dogs / Burn that candle / Calling all comets
CD _____ **MCCD 068**
Music Club / Jun '92 / Disc / THE

Half Hour To Go

ITEMS FOR THE FULL OUTFIT
CD _____ **GROW 0572**
Grass / Aug '95 / Pinnacle / SRD

Half Japanese

BAND THAT WOULD BE KING, THE
CD _____ **PAPCD 018**
Paperhouse / Jul '93 / RTM/Disc

BONE HEAD
CD _____ **VIRUS 197CD**
Alternative Tentacles / Mar '97 / Cargo / Greyhound / Pinnacle

CHARMED LIFE
CD _____ **PAPCD 016**
Paperhouse / Jul '93 / RTM/Disc

FIRE IN THE SKY
CD _____ **PAPCD 010**
Paperhouse / Mar '92 / RTM/Disc

GREATEST HITS (2CD Set)
CD Set _____ **SH 21182**
Safe House / Nov '96 / Cargo

HOT
CD _____ **FIRECD 047**
Fire / Jun '95 / Pinnacle / RTM/Disc

MUSIC TO STRIP BY
CD _____ **PAPCD 017**
Paperhouse / Jul '93 / RTM/Disc

Half Man Half Biscuit

ACD
Best things in life / D'ye ken ted moult / Reasons to be miserable - part 10 / Rod Hull is alive - why / Dickie Davies eyes / Bastard son of Dean Friedman / I was a teenage armchair honved fan / Arthur's farm / Carry on cremating / Albert Hammond bootleg / Reflections in a flat / Sealclubbing / Architecture and morality Ted and Alice / Fuckin' 'ell it's Fred Titmus / Time flies by (when you're the driver of the train) / All I want for Christmas is a Dukla Prague away kit / Trumpton riots
CD _____ **PROBE 008CD**
Probe Plus / Apr '94 / SRD

BACK AGAIN IN THE DHSS
Best things in life are free / D'ye Ken Ted Moult / Reasons to be miserable - part 10 / Rod Hull is alive - Why / Dickie Davies eyes / Bastard son of Dean Friedman / I was a teenage armchair Honved fan / Fan / Arthur's farm / All I want for Christmas is a Dukla Prague away kit / Trumpton riots
CD _____ **PROBE 8CD**
Probe Plus / Nov '88 / SRD

BACK IN THE DHSS/THE TRUMPTON RIOTS EP
Busy little market town / God gave us life / Fuckin' 'ell it's Fred Titmus / Sealclubbing / 99% of gargoyles look like Bob Todd / Time flies by (when you're the driver of a train) / I hate Nerys Hughes / Len Ganley stance / Venus in flares / I love you because (you look like Jim Reeves) / Reflections in a flat / I left my heart in Papworth General / Trumpton riots / Architecture and morality Ted and Alice / 1966 and all that / Albert Hammond Bootleg / All I want for Christmas is a Dukla Prague away kit
CD _____ **PROBE 004CD**
Probe Plus / Apr '94 / SRD

MCINTYRE, TREADMORE & DAVITT
Outbreak of vitas gerulaitas / Prag vec at the Melkweg / Christian rock concert / Let's not / Yipps (my baby got the) / Hedley verityesque / Lilac Harry Quinn / Our tune / Girlfriend's finished / With him / Everything's AOR

CD PROBE 030CD
Probe Plus / Apr '94 / SRD

SOME CALL IT GODCORE
Sensitive outsider / Fretwork homework / Faithlift / Song for Europe / Even men with steel hearts / 24.99 from Argos / Sponsoring the Mospits / Fear my wraith / Styx gig (Seen by my mates coming out of a) / Friday night and the gates are low / I, trog / Tour jacket with detachable sleeves
CD PROBE 041CD
Probe Plus / Jan '97 / SRD

THIS LEADEN PALL
M 6ster / 4AD 3D CD / Running order squabble fest / Whiteness thy name is meltonian / This leaden pall / Turned up clocked on laid off / Improv workshop mimeshow gobshite / Thirteen Eurogoths floating in the dead sea / Whit week malarkey / Doreen / Quality janitor / Floreat inertia / Malayan jelutong / Numanoid hang glide / Footprints
CD PROBE 036CD
Probe Plus / Oct '93 / SRD

VOYAGE TO THE BOTTOM OF THE ROAD
Shropshire lad / Bad review / Eno collaboration / Dead men don't need season tickets / Deep house victims minibus appeal / CAMRA man / PRS yearbook (Quick the drawbridge) / Tonight Matthew I'm going to be with Jesus / Song of encouragement for the orme ascent / Monmore hares running / Itma / He who would valium take / See that my bike's kept clean / Paintball coming home
CD PROBE 45CD
Probe Plus / Jun '97 / SRD

Half Pint

20 SUPER HITS
CD SONCD 0001
Sonic Sounds / Oct '90 / Jet Star

CLASSICS
CD HCD 7009
Hightone / Aug '94 / ADA / Koch

CLASSICS IN DUB
CD HCD 7014
Hightone / Mar '95 / ADA / Koch

ONE IN A MILLION
One in a million / One big ghetto / You lick me first / What more can I really do / Milky way / Mr. Landlord / Roots man / Pick your choice / Puchie Lou / Tell me little girl
CD GRELCD 74
Greensleeves / Sep '89 / Jet Star / SRD

VICTORY
Victory / Level the vibes / Come alive / Night life lady / She's mine / Desperate lover / Cost of living / When one gone / Mama / She's gone
CD RASCD 3031
Ras / Feb '88 / Direct / Greensleeves / Jet Star / SRD

Halfway House Orchestra

HALFWAY HOUSE ORCHESTRA (New Orleans 1925-1928)
CD BDW 8001
Jazz Oracle / Jun '95 / Jazz Music

Halibuts

CHUMMING
CD UPST 009
Upstart / Oct '94 / ADA / Direct

LIFE ON THE BOTTOM
Hammerhead / Caldera / Stinky / Life on the bottom / Ta-hu-wa-hu-wai / Noodles / Hombre de Palabra / Madcap / Hula scuba / Suicide Bay / Night crawler / Duck dive / Fire one / Istanbul / Summertime
CD UPSTART 033
Upstart / Aug '96 / ADA / Direct

Hall & Oates

ABANDONED LUNCHEONETTE
When the morning comes / Had I known you better then / Las Vegas turnaround / Stewardess song / She's gone / I'm just a kid (Don't make me feel like a man) / Abandoned luncheonette / Lady rain / Laughing boy / Everytime I look at you
CD 7567815372
Atlantic / Mar '93 / Warner Music

ATLANTIC COLLECTION - THE BEST OF HALL & OATES
CD 8122722052
Atlantic / Jul '96 / Warner Music

EARLY YEARS, THE
Per Kiomen / Past times behind / Lot of changes coming / In honour of a lady / Deep river blues / If that's what makes you happy / Provider / They needed each other / Angelina / I'll be by / Seventy
CD 100742
CMC / May '97 / BMG

ESSENTIALS (Hall & Oates/Herman's Hermits)
CD LECDD 632
Wisepack / Aug '95 / Conifer/BMG / THE

H20
Maneater / Crime pays / Art of heartbreak / One on one / Open all night / Family man / Italian girls / Guessing games / Delayed reaction / At tension / Go solo
CD ND 90080
Arista / Jan '89 / BMG

LEGENDS IN MUSIC
CD LECD 084
Wisepack / Sep '94 / Conifer/BMG / THE

LIVE AT THE APOLLO
Get ready / Ain't too proud to beg / Way you do the things you do / When something is wrong with my baby / Every time you go away / I can't go for that (no can do) / One by one / Possession obsession / Adult education
CD 74321160032
RCA / Sep '93 / BMG

LOOKING BACK (The Best Of Daryl Hall And John Oates)
She's gone / Sara smile / Rich girl / You've lost that lovin' feelin' / Kiss on my list / Every time you go away / Private eyes / I can't go for that (no can do) / Maneater / One on one / Family man / Adult education / Out of touch / Method of modern love / Starting all over again / Back together again / So close / Everything your heart desires
CD PD 90388
RCA / Oct '91 / BMG

LOT OF CHANGES COMIN'
CD CDSGP 0128
Prestige / Dec '94 / Else / Total/BMG

NO GOODBYES
It's uncanny / I want to know you / For a long time / Can't stop the music / Love you like a brother / Las Vegas turnaround / She's gone / Lilly (Are you happy) / When the morning comes / Beanie G and the rose tattoo / 70's scenario
CD 7567804302
Atlantic / Jul '96 / Warner Music

REALLY SMOKIN'
Past times behind / Everyday's a lovely day / Rose come home / Flo gene / Seventy / I'm really smokin' / Christine / Over the mountain / Lemon road / Truly good song
CD CDTB 122
Thunderbolt / Jul '93 / TKO Magnum

ROCK 'N' SOUL VOL.1
Sara smile / She's gone / Rich girl / Kiss in my list / You make my dreams / Private eyes / I can't go for that (no can do) / Maneater / One on one / Wait for me / Say it isn't so / Adult education
CD 74321289832
RCA / Aug '95 / BMG

SPOTLIGHT ON HALL & OATES
Lot of changes comin' / Drying in the sun / I'll be by / Perkiomen / Fall in Philadelphia / They need each other / Provider / Back in love again / Past times behind / Deep river blues / Goodnight and good morning / In honour of a lady / Angelina / Months, weeks, days / If that's what makes you happy
CD HADCD 107
Javelin / Feb '94 / Henry Hadaway / THE

WAR BABIES
Can't stop the music / He played it much too long / Is it a star / Beanie G and the rose tattoo / You're much too soon / 70's scenario / War baby son of Zorro / I'm watching you / Better watch your back / Screaming through December / Johnny Gore and the C eaters
CD 7567814892
Atlantic / Jul '96 / Warner Music

WHOLE OATS
I'm sorry / All our love / Georgie / Fall in Philadelphia / Waterwheel / Lazy man / Goodnight and good morning / They needed each other / Southeast city window / Thank you for... / Lilly (are you happy)
CD 7567814232
Atlantic / Jan '93 / Warner Music

Hall, Aaron

TRUTH, THE
Prologue / Do anything / Open up / Get a little freaky with me / Pick up the phone / Don't be afraid / Until I found you / You keep me crying (interlude) / Let's make love / When you need me / I miss you / Until the end of time / Epilogue
CD MCLD 19340
MCA / Oct '96 / BMG

Hall, Adelaide

ADELAIDE HALL (Live At The Riverside Studios)
CD CDVIR 8312
TER / Aug '90 / Koch

HALL OF FAME
Ain't it a shame about Mame / Baby mine / Begin the beguine / Creole love call / Doin' as I please / Don't worry 'bout me / Drop me off at Harlem / I can't give you anything but love / I get along without you very well / I got rhythm / I have eyes / I hear a rhapsody / I poured my heart into a song / Mississippi mamma / Moon love / No souvenirs / Rhapsody in love / Shake down the stars / T'ain't what you do (it's the way that you do it) / That old feeling / Transatlantic lullaby / Who told you I cared
CD CDAJA 5098
Living Era / Nov '92 / Select

HALL OF MEMORIES (1927-39)
CD CDHD 169
Happy Days / Aug '90 / Conifer/BMG

RED HOT FROM HARLEM
This time it's love / You gave me everything but love / Rhapsody in love / Baby mine / I'll never be the same / I must have that man / Minnie the moocher / Too darn fickle / I'm red hot from Harlem / Doin' what I please / I got rhythm / Strange as it seems / Chlo-e / Solitude / Say you're mine / I get along without you very well / Don't worry 'bout me / T'ain't what you do (it's the way that you do it) / Shake down the stars / Who told you I cared / No souvenirs / This can't be love
CD PASTCD 7029
Flapper / Jan '94 / Pinnacle

Hall, Ben

COUNTRY WAYS AND ROCKIN' DAYS (Hall, Ben & The Ramblers/Weldon Myrick)
Blue days black nights / Even tho' / Hangin' around / Crying on my shoulder / Make believe / Sleepless nights / Gunfighter's fame / Late hours / Don't ask me why / I'd give anything / All from loving you / Rose of Monterey / Drifting along with the wind / Driftwood on the river / Stormy skies / Season for love / Only 17 / That's the way dreams go / I don't wanna go home / You're here in my mind / Weeping willow / Before you begin / Johnny Law / Hiding alone / So close / Won't you be mine / I'll never be the same / I'll still be hanging around
CD RCCD 3004
Rollercoaster / Oct '93 / Rollercoaster / Swift

Hall, Bob

ALONE WITH THE BLUES (Hall, Bob & Tom McGuinness)
CD LACD 44
Lake / Mar '95 / ADA / Cadillac / Direct / Jazz Music / Target/BMG

DOWN THE ROAD APIECE/ROLL AND SLIDE (Hall, Bob & Dave Peabody)
CD APCD 044
Appaloosa / Mar '97 / ADA / Direct / TKO Magnum

Hall, Daryl

SOUL ALONE
Power of seduction / This time / Love revelation / I'm in a Philly mood / Borderline / Stop loving me, stop loving you / Help me find a way to your heart / Send me / Wildlife / Money changes everything / Written in stone
CD 4739212
Epic / Feb '94 / Sony

Hall, Edmond

1941-57
CD CD 53199
Giants Of Jazz / Jan '95 / Cadillac / Jazz Music / Target/BMG

CLASSICS 1937-1944
CD CLASSICS 830
Classics / Sep '95 / Discovery / Jazz Music

CLASSICS 1944-1945
CD CLASSICS 872
Classics / Apr '96 / Discovery / Jazz Music

EDMOND HALL & PAPA BUE'S VIKING JAZZBAND (Hall, Edmond & Papa Bue Viking Jazz Band)
CD STCD 6022
Storyville / Jan '97 / Cadillac / Jazz Music / Wellard

EDMOND HALL/ALAN ELSDON BAND 1966 (Hall, Edmond & Alan Elsdon)
CD JCD 240
Jazzology / Mar '95 / Jazz Music

HIS LAST CONCERT
CD JCD 223
Jazzology / Nov '96 / Jazz Music

JAZZ PORTRAIT
CD CD 14578
Complete / Nov '95 / THE

Hall, G.P.

FIGMENTS OF IMAGINATION
CD FMRCD 31
Future / Mar '97 / ADA / Harmonia Mundi

Hall, Gary

TWELVE STRINGS AND TALL STORIES
CD RTMCD 78
Round Tower / Feb '96 / Avid/BMG

Hall, Glen

BOOK OF THE HEART, THE
CD 378172
Koch Jazz / Feb '97 / Koch

MOTHER OF THE BOOK, THE (Hall, Glen & Gil Evans)
CD 378162
Koch Jazz / Aug '96 / Koch

Hall, Henry

HENRY HALL & THE BBC DANCE ORCHESTRA (Hall, Henry & The BBC Dance Orchestra)
Come ye back to bonnie Scotland: *Hall, Henry & His Gleneagles Hotel Band* / Mrs. Henry Hall: *Waters, Elsie & Doris* / It's just the time for dancing / Songs that are old live forever / Love / Moon country / Curly head / Phantom of a song / Rusticanella / Little Dutch mill / Viennese memories of Lehar / By the sycamore tree / OLd violin / Red sails in the sunset / Sidewalks of Cuba / Dreaming / Someday we'll meet again / Samum / I bought myself a bottle of ink / Hits of the day / Here's to the next time
CD PASTCD 9725
Flapper / '90 / Pinnacle

HENRY HALL AND HIS ORCHESTRA (Hall, Henry & His Orchestra)
Teacher's pet / Proud of you / Goona Goo / One, two button your shoe / Blue moon / It's a sin to tell a lie / Honey coloured moon / Anything goes / Seeing is believing / My dance / Clouds will soon roll by / I paid for the lie that I told you / Lullaby of the leaves / Love makes the world go round / Big ship / It's the talk of the town / Leave the pretty girls alone / Making conversation / Broken record / Saddle your blues to a wild mustang / If ever a heart was in the right place / Who's afraid of the big bad wolf / Whistling Rufus / Hush, hush, hush here comes the bogey man / Teddy Bear's picnic
CD CDMFP 6356
Music For Pleasure / Jun '97 / EMI

THIS IS HENRY HALL (24 Tracks 1932-1939) (Hall, Henry & The BBC Orchestra)
It's just the time for dancing / Sun has got his hat on / Bahama mama, that tropical charmer / Underneath the arches / Teddy bear's picnic / Just an echo in the valley / Song is you / Night and day / April in Paris / Play to me, Gypsy / Wagon wheels / Radio times / Smoke gets in your eyes / Learning / Hands across the table / Man on the flying trapeze / Easter parade / Honey coloured moon / Take me back to my boots and saddle / Music goes 'round and around / One, two, button your shoe / South of the border / It's time to say 'goodnight' / Here's to the next time
CD CDAJA 5222
Living Era / Jun '97 / Select

Hall, Herb

OLD TYME MODERN (Hall, Herb Quartet)
Old-fashioned love / All of me / Buddy Bolden's blues / Crying my heart out for you / Swinging down Shaw's Hall / Beale Street blues / How come you do me like you do / Willow weep for me / Do you know what it means to miss New Orleans / Sweet Georgia Brown
CD SKCD 23003
Sackville / Jun '93 / Cadillac / Jazz Music / Swift

Hall, Jim

ALL ACROSS THE CITY (Hall, Jim Quartet)
Beija fior / Young one (for Debra) / All across the city / Something tells me / Prelude to a kiss / How deep is the ocean / Bemsha swing / REM State / Drop shot / Big blues / Jane
CD CCD 4384
Concord Jazz / Sep '89 / New Note/ Pinnacle

CIRCLES
(All of a sudden) My heart sings / Love letters / Down from Antigua / Echo / I can't get started (with you) / TC Blues / Circles / Aruba
CD CCD 4161
Concord Jazz / Nov '92 / New Note/ Pinnacle

CONCIERTO
Two's blues / Answer is yes / Concierto de Aranjuez / You'd be so nice to come home to / Rock skippin'
CD ZK 40807
Sony Jazz / Feb '96 / Sony

DEDICATIONS & INSPIRATIONS
Whistle stop / Hawk / Canto nostalgico / Why not dance / Joao / Seseragi / All the things you are / Bluesography / Miro / Money / Matisse / In a sentimental mood / Street dance
CD CD 83365
Telarc / May '94 / Conifer/BMG

JIM HALL
Stella by starlight / Stompin' at the Savoy / Things ain't what they used to be / Thanks for the memory / I'm getting sentimental over you / My funny valentine / Time after time / Polka dots and moonbeams / Tangerine / Romain / Seven come eleven / When you wish upon a star / Funkallero / Off center / Time enough / Abstraction
CD CD 53218

Giants Of Jazz / Jan '96 / Cadillac / Jazz Music / Target/BMG

JIM HALL'S THREE (Hall, Jim Trio)
Hide and seek / Skylark / Bottlenose blues / And I do / All the things you are / Poor butterfly / Three
CD _ CCD 4298
Concord Jazz / Mar '87 / New Note/ Pinnacle

LIVE AT TOWN HALL VOL.1 (Hall, Jim & Friends)
Alone together / St. Thomas / Skylark / Begin the beguine / All the things you are / Prelude to a kiss / 1953 thesis / Abstract and dreams / Laura's dream
CD _ 8208312
Limelight / Mar '91 / PolyGram

LIVE AT TOWN HALL VOL.2 (Hall, Jim & Friends)
Hide and seek / How deep is the ocean / Sancticity / My funny valentine / Careful
CD _ 8208432
Limelight / Oct '91 / PolyGram

SOMETHING SPECIAL
Something special / Somewhere / Down from Antigua / Steps / Deep in a dream / Where little girls play / Three / Lucky thing / Up for air / Consequently
CD _ 5184452
Limelight / May '94 / PolyGram

SUBSEQUENTLY
Subsequently / Mister Blues / Pancho / Answer is yes / Waiting to dance / I'm in the mood for love / What's it like to love / Waltz for Sonny / More than you know
CD _ 8442782
Limelight / Mar '93 / PolyGram

TEXTURES
Fanfare / Ragman / Reflections / Quadrologue / Passacaglia / Sazanami / Circus dance
CD _ 83402
Telarc Jazz / Jun '97 / Conifer/BMG

Hall, John S.

BODY HAS A HEAD
CD _ BOB 104
Bob's Airport / Nov '96 / Cargo

Hall, Juanita

GLORY OF LOVE, THE
CD _ ACD 053
Audiophile / Jul '96 / Jazz Music

Hall, Michael

ADEQUATE DESIRE
CD _ DJD 3212
Dejadisc / Dec '94 / ADA / Direct

DAY
CD _ DJD 3225
Dejadisc / Feb '96 / ADA / Direct

Hall, Pam

MAGIC
CD _ VPCD 14922
VP / Jul '97 / Greensleeves / Jet Star / Total/BMG

MISSING YOU BABY
CD _ JFRCD 002
Joe Frazier / Jul '95 / Jet Star

Hall, Rob

OPEN UP
CD _ UGCD 010697
Future / Aug '97 / ADA / Harmonia Mundi

Hall, Sandra

SHOWIN' OFF
CD _ ICH 1179CD
Ichiban / Mar '95 / Direct / Koch

Hall, Sister Pat

MARC BOLAN PRESENTS SISTER PAT HALL
CD _ EDCD 449
Edsel / Jun '96 / Pinnacle

Hall, Terry

HOME
Forever J / You / Sense / I drew a lemon / Moon on your dress / No no no / What's wrong with me / Grief disguised as joy / First attack the love / I don't got you
CD _ 0630121232
Anxious / Dec '96 / Warner Music

TERRY HALL - THE COLLECTION
Gangsters / Nite club / Ghost town / Friday night, Saturday morning / Lunatics (Have taken over the asylum) / T'ain't what you do (it's the way that you do it) / Summertime / Tunnel of love / Our lips are sealed / Colourfield / Take / Thinking of you / Castles in the air / From dawn to distraction / She / Ultra modern nursery rhymes / Missing / Beautiful people
CD _ CDCHR 1974
Chrysalis / Nov '92 / EMI

Hall, Tom T.

BALLADS OF FORTY DOLLARS/ HOMECOMING
That's how I got to Memphis / Cloudy day / Shame on the rain / Highways / Forbidden flowers / Ain't got the time / Ballad of forty dollars / I washed my face in the morning dew / Picture of your mother / World the way I want it / Over and over again / Beauty is a fading flower / Week in the country jail / Strawberry farms / Shoe shine man / Kentucky in the morning / Nashville is a groovy little town / Margie's at the Lincoln Park Inn / Homecoming / Carter boys / Flat-footin' it / George (and the Northwoods) / I miss a lot of trains
CD _ BCD 15631
Bear Family / Jul '93 / Direct / Rollercoaster / Swift

I WITNESS LIFE/ 100 CHILDREN
Salute to a switchblade / Thankyou Connersville, Indiana / Do it to someone you love / Ballad of Bill Crump / All you want when you please / Chattanooga dog / Girls in Saigon city / Hang them all / Coming to the party / America the ugly / That'll be alright with me / Hundred children / I can't dance / I want to see the parade / Sing a little baby to sleep / Mama bake a pie (Papa kill a chicken) / Ode to half a pound of ground round / Pinto the wonder horse is dead / I hope it rains at my funeral / I took a memory to lunch / Hitch hiker / Old enough to want you
CD _ BCD 15658
Bear Family / Jul '93 / Direct / Rollercoaster / Swift

Hall, Tony

MR. UNIVERSE
American tunes / Mr. Universe / Scotland / Slow air / Slow hornpipe / Blacksmith / Stitches in the britches / Local hero / Lovely Joan / Humphrey Lyttleton / Round the horn / Jack tar / Elizabethan medley
CD _ OSMOCD 003
Osmosys / Nov '95 / Direct

Hallberg, Bengt

HALLBERG TOUCH, THE
You do something to me / Little white lies / When lights are low / Oh lady be good / Coquette / Fascinating rhythm / Sometimes I'm happy / Sonny boy / In a little Spanish town / You and the night and the music / Charleston / You brought a new kind of love to me
CD _ PHONTCD 7525
Phontastic / '93 / Cadillac / Jazz Music / Wellard

HALLBERG TREASURE CHEST, THE
CD _ PHONTNCD 8828
Phontastic / '93 / Cadillac / Jazz Music / Wellard

HALLBERG'S HAPPINESS
CD _ PHONTCD 7544
Phontastic / May '95 / Cadillac / Jazz Music / Wellard

HALLBERG'S HOT ACCORDION (In The Foreground)
Tiger rag / Bye bye blues / Farewell blues / St. Louis blues / Limehouse blues / Tva solroda segel / How high the moon / Sweet Sue, just you / Blue moon / Some of these days
CD _ PHONTCD 7532
Phontastic / '93 / Cadillac / Jazz Music / Wellard

HALLBERG'S SURPRISE
CD _ PHONT CD 7581
Phontastic / Apr '88 / Cadillac / Jazz Music / Wellard

HALLBERG'S YELLOW BLUES
CD _ PHONTCD 7583
Phontastic / '88 / Cadillac / Jazz Music / Wellard

POWERHOUSE-KRAFTVERK (Hallberg, Bengt & Arne Dommerus)
CD _ PHONTCD 7553
Phontastic / '93 / Cadillac / Jazz Music / Wellard

TREASURE CHEST
CD _ NCD 8828
Phontastic / Apr '94 / Cadillac / Jazz Music / Wellard

TWO OF A KIND (Hallberg, Bengt & Karin Krog)
My man (mon homme) / Jeepers creepers / You must believe in spring / Touch of your lips / End of the day song / I ain't here / Like that / Hallelujah, I love him so / Spring in Manhattan / Love walk right in / Dear Bix / I'm coming Virginia / Ain't nobody's business if I do
CD _ CDMR 1
Meantime / Jun '96 / New Note/Pinnacle

Halle Brass

HALLE BRASS PLAY GREAGSON
CD _ DOYCD 038
Doyen / Feb '96 / Conifer/BMG

Hallett, Sylvia

LET'S FALL OUT
CD _ MASHCD 003
Mash / Oct '94 / Cadillac

Halley, David

BROKEN SPELL
CD _ DOSCD 7003
Dos / Nov '93 / ADA / CM / Direct

STRAY DOG TALK
Live and learn / Rain just falls / Opportunity knockin' / If ever you need me / Tonight / Darlene / When it comes to you / Further / Walk the line / Dream life
CD _ FIENDCD 187
Demon / Jun '90 / Pinnacle

Halliday, Lin

DELAYED EXPOSURE
Woody 'n you / How deep is the ocean / Darn that dream / Dog ear blues / My romance / Man I love / Alone together / Serpent's tooth
CD _ DD 449
Delmark / Mar '97 / ADA / Cadillac / CM / Direct / Hot Shot

EAST OF THE SUN
All the things you are / East of the sun / I found a new baby / Indian summer / My foolish heart / Corcovado / Paradox / Ira's blues / Will you still be mine
CD _ DE 458
Delmark / Mar '97 / ADA / Cadillac / CM / Direct / Hot Shot

LIN HALLIDAY WITH IRA SULLIVAN (Halliday, Lin & Ira Sullivan)
Street of dreams / My shining hour / Sophisticated lady / Dear old Stockholm / Where or when / Over the rainbow / More I see of you / Pent-up house
CD _ DE 468
Delmark / Mar '97 / ADA / Cadillac / CM / Direct / Hot Shot

Hallow's Eve

DEATH AND INSANITY
CD _ 398414059CD
Metal Blade / Nov '96 / Pinnacle / Plastic Head

MONUMENT
CD _ 398414056CD
Metal Blade / Nov '96 / Pinnacle / Plastic Head

TALES OF TERROR
CD _ 398414060CD
Metal Blade / Nov '96 / Pinnacle / Plastic Head

Hallucination Generation

BLACK HOLE & BABY UNIVERSES
CD _ THPCD 98
Thunderpussy / Feb '94 / SRD

Hallucinogen

TWISTED
CD _ BFLCD 15
Big Life / Oct '95 / Mo's Music Machine / Pinnacle / Prime

Hallyday, Johnny

NASHVILLE SESSIONS VOL.2
Hey baby / Tout bas, tout bas, tout bas / Shout / Quitte moi doucement / Oui, je veux / Ce n'est pas just apres tout / Les bras en croix / C'est une fille comme toil / Qui aurait dit ca / Pas cette chanson
CD _ BCD 15497
Bear Family / Oct '90 / Direct / Rollercoaster / Swift

TRIFT DIE RATTLES
Mein leben fangt erst richtig an / Lass die leute doch reden (Keep searching) / Wilde boys / House of the rising sun / Ma guitare / Ja der elefant (wap dou wap) / It's monkey time / Vieleicht bist du fur mich noch night die / J'ai un probleme
CD _ BCD 15492
Bear Family / Feb '90 / Direct / Rollercoaster / Swift

Halo Benders

DON'T TELL ME NOW
CD _ KLP 46CD
K / Jan '96 / Cargo / Greyhound / SRD

GOD DON'T MAKE NO JUNK
CD _ FIRECD 43
Fire / Jan '95 / Pinnacle / RTM/Disc

Halpin, Kieran

MISSION STREET
Refugee from heaven / Foreigners / Mission street / Berlin calling / China rose / Heart and soul / Nothing to show for it all / Celtic myth / Salt into the wound / Farewell to pride / Chase the dragon / Rolling the dice / Child bearing child
CD _ RTMCD 31
Round Tower / Jul '91 / Avid/BMG

Ham

BUFFALO VIRGIN
CD _ TP016CD
One Little Indian / Sep '89 / Pinnacle

Ham, Pete

7 PARK AVENUE
Catherine cares / Coppertone blues / It really doesn't matter / Live love all of your days / Would you deny / Dear father / Matted spam / No matter what / Leaving on a midnight train / Weep baby / Hand in hand / Sille veb / I know that you should / Island / Just look inside the cover / Just how lucky we are / No more / Ringside
CD _ RCD 10349
Rykodisc / Apr '97 / ADA / Vital

Hamburg Rock Band

BEST EVER ROCK COVERS, THE
Cover me / Brown sugar / You ain't seen nothing yet / Summer of '69 / Final countdown / Livin' on a prayer / Say you will / Sledgehammer / Love is a battlefield / Centrefold / Bed of roses / We will rock you / Radar love / Layla / Dirty white boy / Legs / War / 2-4-6-8 motorway
CD _ QED 224
Tring / Nov '96 / Tring

Hamburger, Neil

AMERICA'S FUNNYMAN
CD _ DC 97CD
Drag City / Dec '96 / Cargo / Greyhound

Hamel, Peter Michael

LET IT PLAY (Selected Pieces 1979-1983)
CD _ CDKUCK 078
Kuckuck / Sep '87 / ADA / CM

Hamill, Claire

LOVE IN THE AFTERNOON
CD _ NAGE 18CD
Art Of Landscape / May '88 / Sony

OCTOBER
Island / To the stars / Please stay tonight / Wall to wall carpeting / Speedbreaker / I don't get any older / Warrior of the water / Artist / Sidney gorgeous / Crying under the bedclothes / Peaceful
CD _ BP 238CD
Blueprint / Mar '97 / Pinnacle

ONE HOUSE LEFT STANDING
When I was a child / Man who cannot see tomorrow's sunshine / Consummation / River / Where are your smiles at / Baseball blues / Urge for going / Flowers for grandma / Phoenix / Smile your blues away
CD _ BP 239CD
Blueprint / Jul '97 / Pinnacle

VOICES
CD _ NAGE 8 CD
Art Of Landscape / Apr '86 / Sony

Hamilton, Andy

JAMAICA BY NIGHT
Give me the highlife / Nobody knows / Port Antonio / Mango time / Every day / Jamaica by night / Otrum / Come back girl
CD _ WCD 039
World Circuit / Sep '94 / ADA / Cadillac / Direct / New Note/Pinnacle

SILVERSHINE (Hamilton, Andy & The Blue Notes)
I can't get started (with you) / Body and soul / Old folks / You are too beautiful / Andy's blues / Uncle Joe / Silvershine
CD _ WCD 025
World Circuit / Oct '91 / ADA / Cadillac / Direct / New Note/Pinnacle

Hamilton, Chico

EUPHORIA
CD _ CHECD 7
Master Mix / Sep '89 / Jazz Music / New Note/Pinnacle / Wellard

MASTER, THE
One day five months ago / Feels good / Fancy / Stu / Gengis / Conquistadores '74 / Stacy / I can hear the grass grow
CD _ CDSXE 071
Stax / Nov '92 / Pinnacle

MY PANAMANIAN FRIEND (Hamilton, Chico & Euphoria)
CD _ 1212652
Soul Note / May '94 / Cadillac / Harmonia Mundi / Wellard

TRIO
CD _ 1212462
Soul Note / Apr '93 / Cadillac / Harmonia Mundi / Wellard

Hamilton, Claire

CELTIC HARP MOODS
Londonderry air / Riverdance / Have I told you lately / Lo, how a rose e'er blooming / Down in the Sally Gardens / Robin the hooded man / Wild mountain thyme / Flower of Scotland / Star of County Down /

On your shore / An ubhal as airde / Celtic carol / Theme from Harry's Game / Patapan / Skye boat song / Carrickfergus / Shepherd moons / Noul Nouvelet / Loch Lomond / Women of Ireland / Only a woman's heart / Danny boy
CD ____ 3036000822
Carlton / Mar '97 / Carlton

LOVE IS ALL AROUND (The Celtic Harp Of Claire Hamilton)
Love is all around / Lady in red / Tears in Heaven / Everything I do (I do it for you) / In the air tonight / On your shore / Killing me softly / Harry's game / Wonderful tonight / I will always love you / Take my breath away / Against all odds / LOve changes everything / Falling / Shepherd moon / Robin the hooded man / Think twice
CD ____ 12862
Laserlight / Dec '96 / Target/BMG

Hamilton, Colbert

COLBERT HAMILTON & THE HELL RAZORS (Hamilton, Colbert & the Hell Razors)
Wow / Mystery train / Half hearted love / Woman love / Rock therapy / Long blonde hair / Ice cold / Long black shiny car / Nervous breakdown / Love me (the way that I love you) / I'm so high / Good rockin' tonight / I'll never let you go / Don't knock upon my door / Love me
CD ____ NERCD 071
Nervous / Mar '93 / Nervous / TKO Magnum

WILD AT HEART (Hamilton, Colbert & The Nitros)
Lucille / Wild at heart / Still rockin' after all these beers / Bad reputation / Too late / Boom boom / Do you wanna rock / Abused by you / High-flyin' cat / Boogaville / Pass the bottle to the baby / Boys are back in town / Big in the world / Ninety nine girls
CD ____ NERCD 076
Nervous / Mar '94 / Nervous / TKO Magnum

Hamilton, Dirk

GO DOWN SWINGIN
CD ____ APCD 071
Appaloosa / '92 / ADA / Direct / TKO Magnum

TOO TIRED TO SLEEP
CD ____ APCD 061
Appaloosa / '92 / ADA / Direct / TKO Magnum

YEP
CD ____ APCD 107
Appaloosa / Jun '94 / ADA / Direct / TKO Magnum

Hamilton, Ed

PLANET JAZZ
Planet jazz / 4am blues / Better days ahead / Gray day / What time is it now / South of Monterey / Life on the edge / Curtis blues / Life dreams / Race against the wind / Lullabye / Say what
CD ____ CD 83387
Telarc / Apr '96 / Conifer/BMG

Hamilton, George IV

AMERICAN COUNTRY GOTHIC
If I never see midnight again / My hometown / This is our love / Little country county fairs / Farmer's dream ploughed under / Never mind / I will be your friend / More about love / Heaven knows / Back up grinnin' again / Carolina sky / I believe in you
CD ____ CDRR 304
Request / Jan '90 / Jazz Music / Wellard

COUNTRY BOY (The Best Of George Hamilton IV)
Abilene / Break my mind / Early morning rain / Steel rail blues / Urge for going / Canadian pacific / Second cup of coffee / Anyway / I'm, gonna be a country boy again / Both sides now / My novia scotia home / Travelin' light / 10 degrees and getting colder / Streets of london / Everything is beautiful / Carolina on my mind / She's a little bit country / West texas highway / Together alone / Rose and a baby ruth / Crystal chandeliers / Country music in my soul
CD ____ 74321393402
Camden / Sep '96 / BMG

COUNTRY CHRISTMAS, A
I wonder as I wander / C-H-R-I-S-T-M-A-S / Christmas in the trenches / See amid the winter's snow / Friendly beast / Joy to the world / Little Grave / Silent night / Away in a manger / Natividad / Morning star / In the bleak midwinter
CD ____ WSTCD 9707
Nelson Word / Sep '93 / Nelson Word

GEORGE HAMILTON IV 1954-1965 (6CD Set)
Beer, wine and whiskey / Sleeping at the foot of the bed / Caribbean / Satisfaction guaranteed / Satisfied mind / Out behind the barn / Serenader's swing / It's my way / I'll always remember you / Jalopy Jane / Driftin' / Daniel Boone / Driftin' / I've got a secret / Verdict / Sam / Jamaica farewell / He's movin' on / Rose and a baby Ruth / I've got a secret / It was me / If you don't know, I ain't gonna tell you / Everybody's body / I've got a secret / Sam / Rose and a baby Ruth / If you don't, I ain't gonna tell you / If I possessed a printing press / Only one love / Everybody's body / High school romance / Everybody's body / Why don't they understand / Little Tom / Even tho' / You tell me your dream / Carolina moon / Let me call you sweetheart / When I grow too old to dream / Tell me why / Aura Lee / Girl of my dreams / Drink to me only with thine eyes / Love's old sweet song / Auld lang syne / Ivy Rose / Clementine / One heart / May I / Now and for always / House of gold / I can't help it / How can you refuse him now / Your cheatin' heart / Half as much / I could never be ashamed of you / I'm so lonesome I could cry / Cold, cold heart / (I heard that) Lonesome whistle / Wedding bells / Who's taking you to the prom / I know where I'm goin' / You win again / Take these chains from my heart / So soon / When will I know / Lucy, Lucy / House a car and a wedding ring / Two of us / Steady game / Last night we fell in love / Can you blame us / Love has come to our house / Gee / One little acre / I know your sweetheart / Tremble / Why I'm walkin' / Loneliness is all around me / Before this day ends / Wrong side of the tracks / It's just the idea / Walk on the wild side of life / That's how it goes / Can't let her see me cry / To you and yours (from me and mine) / Three steps to the phone (millions of miles) / Ballad of Widder Jones / I want a girl / Those brown eyes / Where did the sunshine go / Baby blue eyes / Life's railway to heaven / East Virginia / Wall / If you don't, somebody else will / Rainbow / I will miss you when you go / Life is too short / China doll / Tender hearted baby / Commerce street and sixth avenue north / If you don't know I ain't gonna tell you / (I want to go) Where nobody knows me / Roving gambler / Oh so many years / Jimmy Brown the newsboy / Little lunch box / Come on home boy / Everglades / You are my sunshine / Last letter / If you want me to / Linda with the lonely eyes / In this very same room / Abilene / Mine / Oh so many years / Remember M, remember E, remember me / There's more pretty girls than one / You're easy to love / Fort Worth, Dallas or Houston / Fair and tender ladies / Kentucky / Candy apple red / Tag along / Little grave / Texarkana, Pecos or Houston / Truck driving man / Rose and a baby Ruth / Roll muddy river / That's alright Mama / Driftwood on the river / Let's say goodbye like we said hello / Rainbow at midnight / It's been so long darlin' / Letters have no arms / Walking the floor over you / I will miss you when you go / Half a mind / You nearly lose your mind / Fortunes in memories / Soldier's last letter / Thanks a lot / Nice place to visit / Twist of the wrist / Nice place to visit / (You don't love me) Anymore / Late Mister Jones / Write me a picture / Something special to me / I've got a secret / Slightly used / Under your spell again / Above and beyond / Excuse me (I think I've got a heartache) / Wishful thinking / I don't believe I'll fall in love today / Foolin' around / Another day, another dollar / Keep those cards and letters coming in / Under the influence of love / Big, big love / You better not do that / Long black limousine / Together again / Abilene / Three steps to the phone (millions of miles) / Rose and a baby Ruth / Fort Worth, Dallas or Houston / Before this day ends / Truck driving man / Walking the floor over you / Write me a picture / If you don't know, I ain't gonna tell
CD Set ____ BCD 15773
Bear Family / Nov '95 / Direct / Rollercoaster / Swift

Hamilton, George V

GHOST TOWN (Hamilton, George V & Nashvegas Noma)
CD ____ DFGCD 8450
Dixie Frog / Oct '96 / Direct / TKO Magnum

Hamilton, Jeff

DYNAVIBES (Hamilton, Jeff Trio & Frits Landesbergen)
Killer Joe / Just like SD / Cherokee / Long ago and far away / Sweet Lorraine / Close enough for love / Happy kick / Midnight sun / Tudo / Blues for Milt
CD ____ MR 874794
Mons / Jun '97 / Montpellier

JEFF HAMILTON TRIO, THE (Hamilton, Jeff Trio)
But not for me / Apple honey / Time passes on / Beshma swing / 52nd Street swing / Well you needn't / Night in Tunisia / Yesterdays / SKJ
CD ____ MR 874777
Mons / Jun '97 / Montpellier

Hamilton, Johnny

SWING LOW SWEET CHARIOT
CD ____ FSRCD 211
Fresh Sound / Oct '96 / Discovery / Jazz Music

Hamilton, Scott

AFTER HOURS
Beyond the bluebird / Woody 'n' you / Blues in my heart / Bye bye blues / What's new / You're not kind / Black velvet (Don cha go way mad) / How am I to know / Some other spring / Steeplechase
CD ____ CCD 47552
Concord Jazz / May '97 / New Note/ Pinnacle

CLOSE UP
All of you / I remember you / Mad about you / Robbin's nest / Was I to blame for falling in love with you / Blue City / Mr. Big and Mr. Modern / Portrait of Jennie / Soft
CD ____ CCD 4197
Concord Jazz / Jun '91 / New Note/ Pinnacle

EAST OF THE SUN
Autumn leaves / Stardust / It could happen to you / Bernie's tune / East of the sun and west of the moon / Time after time / Setagaya serenade / That's all / All the things you are / (Back home again in) Indiana
CD ____ CCD 4583
Concord Jazz / Dec '93 / New Note/ Pinnacle

GROOVIN' HIGH (Hamilton, Scott/ Ken Peplowski/ Spike Robinson)
Blues up and down / You brought a new kind of love to me / That ole devil called love / Shine / Goof and I / What's new / I'll see you in my dreams / Groovin' high / Body and soul / Jeep is jumpin'
CD ____ CCD 4509
Concord Jazz / Jun '92 / New Note/ Pinnacle

IS A GOOD WIND WHO IS BLOWING US NO ILL
CD ____ CDD 4042
Concord Jazz / Jul '92 / New Note/ Pinnacle

LIVE AT BRECON JAZZ FESTIVAL
Way down yonder in New Orleans / I can't give you anything but love / My old flame / Ow / But beautiful / Fascinatin' rhythm / Nightingale sang in Berkley Square / Come rain or come shine / Blue wales
CD ____ CCD 4649
Concord Jazz / Jun '95 / New Note/ Pinnacle

MAJOR LEAGUE (Hamilton, Scott, Jake Hanna, Dave McKenna)
Swinging at the Copper Rail / Pretty girl is like a melody / Cocktails for two / I'm through with love / Linger awhile / September in the rain / This is all I ask / It all depends on you / April in Paris
CD ____ CCD 4305
Concord Jazz / '86 / New Note/Pinnacle

MY ROMANCE
Abundance / Blue caper / Swingin' till the girls come home / My romance / Lullaby in rhythm / Will you still be mine / Poor butterfly / Sugarchile / Jan / Just a gigolo
CD ____ CCD 4710
Concord Jazz / Jul '96 / New Note/Pinnacle

ORGANIC DUKE
Jump for joy / Blue hodge / Moon mist / Paris blues / Castle rock / Just a sittin' and a rockin' / Rockin' in rhythm / Isfahan / Love you madly / Old circus train turn around blues
CD ____ CCD 4623
Concord Jazz / Nov '94 / New Note/ Pinnacle

RACE POINT
Groove yard / Chelsea Bridge / Race point / Close enough for love / Oh, look at me now / Alone together / I've just seen her / Limehouse blues / You're my thrill / You say you care / Song is you
CD ____ CCD 4492
Concord Jazz / Jan '92 / New Note/ Pinnacle

RADIO CITY
Apple honey / Yesterdays / I'll be around / Touch of your lips / Cherokee / Tonight I shall sleep with a smile on my face / Radio city / My ideal / Wig's blues / Remember
CD ____ CCD 4428
Concord Jazz / Aug '90 / New Note/ Pinnacle

RIGHT TIME, THE (Hamilton, Scott Quintet)
Just in time / If I love again / Sleep / Eventide / All through the night / Skylark / Stealing port / Dropsy
CD ____ CCD 4311
Concord Jazz / Jul '87 / New Note/Pinnacle

SCOTT HAMILTON & WARREN VACHE (Hamilton, Scott & Warren Vache)
CD ____ CCD 4070
Concord Jazz / Jul '96 / New Note/ Pinnacle

SCOTT HAMILTON PLAYS BALLADS
CD ____ CCD 4386
Concord Jazz / Sep '89 / New Note/ Pinnacle

SCOTT HAMILTON QUINTET IN CONCERT, THE (Hamilton, Scott Quintet)
I can't believe that you're in love with me / Wrap your troubles in dreams (and dream your troubles away) / I've found a new baby / When I fall in love / Whispering / Sultry serenade / Stardust / One o'clock jump
CD ____ CCD 4233
Concord Jazz / Feb '91 / New Note/ Pinnacle

SCOTT HAMILTON VOL.2
East of the sun and west of the moon / There is no greater love / Rough ridin' / These foolish things / I want to be happy / Everything happens to me / Love me or leave me / Blues for the players / Very thought of you / It could happen to you
CD ____ CCD 4061
Concord Jazz / Jun '94 / New Note/ Pinnacle

SECOND SET (Hamilton, Scott Quintet)
All the things you are / Time after time / Taps Miller / All too soon / How insensitive / I never knew / For all we know / Jumpin' the blues
CD ____ CCD 4254
Concord Jazz / May '85 / New Note/ Pinnacle

TENOR SHOES
I should care / Falling in love with love / Shadow of your smile / Nearness of you / How high the moon / Our delight / My foolish heart / OK
CD ____ CCD 4127
Concord Jazz / Apr '90 / New Note/ Pinnacle

Hamkin, Larry

POEMS AND STORIES
CD ____ NAR 114CD
New Alliance / Jul '95 / Plastic Head

Hamm, Stuart

KINGS OF SLEEP
Black ice / Surely the best / Call of the wild / Terminal beach / Count zero / I want to know / Prelude in C / Kings of sleep
CD ____ CDGRUB 13
Food For Thought / Oct '89 / Pinnacle

Hammer

TERROR
CD ____ SHARK 028
Shark / Jul '92 / Plastic Head

Hammer, Artle

JOY SPRING
CD ____ GECD 149
Gemini / Jan '89 / Cadillac

Hammer, Jan

ESCAPE FROM TELEVISION
Crockett's theme / Theresa / Colombia / Rum cay / Trial and the search / Tubbs and Valerie / Forever tonight / Last flight / Rico's blues / Before the storm / Night talk / Miami vice
CD ____ MCLD 19133
MCA / Oct '92 / BMG

Hammerbox

HAMMERBOX
CD ____ CZ 029CD
C/Z / Oct '91 / Plastic Head

Hammerhead

DUH, THE BIG CITY
CD ____ ARRCD 69012
Amphetamine Reptile / Mar '96 / Plastic Head

ETHEREAL KILLER
CD ____ ARRCD 36/266
Amphetamine Reptile / Feb '93 / Plastic Head

EVIL TWIN
CD ____ ARRCD 47 306
Amphetamine Reptile / Nov '93 / Plastic Head

INTO THE VORTEX
CD ____ ARR 50/323CD
Amphetamine Reptile / Mar '94 / Plastic Head

Hammill, Peter

AFTER THE SHOW
Ophelia / Shell / After the show / Stranger still / You hit me where I live / Sitting targets / Spirit / Porton down / Ain't nobody's business if I do / Sunshine / Lost and found / Sign / Just good friends / If I could
CD ____ CDOVD 460
Virgin / Jan '96 / EMI

AND CLOSE AS THIS
Too many of my yesterdays / Faith / Empire of delight / Silver / Beside the one you love / Other old cliches / Confidente / Sleep now
CD ____ CDV 2409
Virgin / Nov '88 / EMI

BLACK BOX
Golden promises / Losing faith in words / Jargon king / Fogwalking / Spirit / In slow time / Wipe / Flight
CD ____ CDOVD 140
Virgin / Nov '88 / EMI

CALM (AFTER THE STORM), THE
Shell / Not for Keith / Birds / Rain 3 AM / Just good friends / (On Tuesdays she used to do) yoga / Shingle song / Faith / Dropping the torch / After the show / Stranger still / If I could / Wilhelmina / Again / Been alone so long / Ophelia / Autumn / Sleep now
CD _______ CDVM 9017
Virgin / Jul '93 / EMI

CHAMELEON IN THE SHADOW OF NIGHT
German overalls / Slender threads / Rock and role / In the end / What's it worth / Easy to slip away / Dropping the torch / (In the) black room / Tower
CD _______ CASCD 1067
Charisma / '89 / EMI

ENTER K
Paradox Drive / Unconscious life / Accidents / Great experiments / Don't tell me / She wraps it up / Happy hour / Seven wonders
CD _______ FIE 9101
Fie / Apr '92 / Vital

FIRESHIPS
I will find you / Curtains / His best girl / Oasis / Incomplete surrender / Fireship / Given time / Reprise / Gaia
CD _______ FIE 9103
Fie / Mar '92 / Vital

FOOLS MATE
Imperial zeppelin / Candle / Happy / Solitude / Vision / Reawakening / Sunshine / Child / Summer song (in the Autumn) / Viking / Birds / I once wrote some poems
CD _______ CASCD 1037
Charisma / Oct '88 / EMI

FUTURE NOW, THE
Pushing thirty / Second hand / Trappings / Mousetrap (caught in) / Energy vampires / If I could / Future now / Still in the dark / Mediaevil / Motor-bike in Afrika / Cut / Palinurus (castaway)
CD _______ CASCD 1137
Charisma / Nov '88 / EMI

IN A FOREIGN TOWN
Hemlock / Invisible ink / Sci finance (revisited) / This book / Time to burn / Auto / Vote brand X / Play's the thing / Under cover names / Smile / Time to burn (instrumental)
CD _______ FIE 9108
Fire / Mar '93 / Pinnacle / RTM/Disc

IN CAMERA
Ferret and featherbed / (No more) the submariner / Tapeworm / Again / Faint heart and the sermon / Comet, the course, the tail / Gog magog (in bromine chambers)
CD _______ CASCD 1089
Charisma / Nov '88 / EMI

LOOPS & REELS
Ritual speak / Critical mass / Moebius loop / Endless breath / In slow time / My pulse / Bells, The Bells
CD _______ FIE 9105
Fie / Nov '93 / Vital

LOVE SONGS
Just good friends / My favourite / Been alone so long / Ophelia / Again / If I could / Vision / Don't tell me / Birds / (This side of) the looking glass
CD _______ CASCD 1166
Charisma / Nov '88 / EMI

MARGIN, THE (LIVE)
Future now / Porton down / Stranger still / Sign / Jargon king / Empress's clothes / Sphinx in the face / Labour of love / Sitting targets / Patient / Flight
CD _______ CDOVD 345
Virgin / Jun '91 / EMI

NADIR'S BIG CHANCE
Nadir's big chance / Institute of mental health / Open your eyes / Ain't nobody's business if I do / Been alone so long / Pompeii / Shingle / Airport / People you were going to / Birthday special / Two or three spectres / Burning
CD _______ CASCD 1099
Charisma / Nov '88 / EMI

NOISE, THE
Kick to kill the kiss / Like a shot, The entertainer / Noise / Celebrity kissing / Where the mouth is / Great european department store / Planet coventry / Primo on the parapet
CD _______ FIE 9104
Fie / Mar '93 / Vital

OFFENSICHTLICH GOLDFISCH
Offensichtlich goldfisch / Dich zu finden / Die Kalte killt den kuss / Favorit / Kaufhaus Europa / Der larm / Oase / Die prominenz kusst sich / Die tinte verlischt / Auto / Gaia / Schlaft nun
CD _______ GH 70112
Golden Hind / Jan '95 / Pinnacle

OUT OF WATER
Evidently goldfish / Not the man / No moon in the water / Our oyster / Something about Ysabel's dance / Green fingers / On the surface / Way out
CD _______ FIE 9109
Fire / Mar '93 / Pinnacle / RTM/Disc

OVER
Crying wolf / Autumn / Time heals / Alice (letting go) / This side of the looking glass / Betrayed / (On Tuesdays she used to do) Yoga / Lost and found
CD _______ CASCD 1125
Charisma / Jun '91 / EMI

PAST GO - COLLECTED
Kick to kill the kiss / I will find you / Accidents / His best girl / Sharply unclear / Patient / Planet Coventry / Ritual mask / Noise / Gift of fire / Train time / Gaia / Your tall ship
CD _______ FIE 9112
Fie / Sep '96 / Vital

PATIENCE
Labour of love / Film noir / Just good friends / Juenesse Doree / Traintime / Now more than ever / Comfortable / Patient
CD _______ FIE 9102
Fie / Apr '92 / Vital

PH7
My favourite / Careering / Porton down / Mirror images / Handicap / Equality / Not for Keith / Old school tie / Time for a change / Imperial walls / Mr. X gets tense / Faculty X
CD _______ CASCD 1146
Charisma / Apr '89 / EMI

ROARING FORTIES
Sharply unclear / Gift of fire / You can't want what you always get / Headlong stretch / Your tall ship
CD _______ FIE 9107
Fie / Sep '94 / Vital

ROOM TEMPERATURE LIVE
Wave / Just good friends / Vision / Time to burn / Four pails / Comet, the course, the tail / Ophelia / Happy hour / If I could / Something about Ysabel's dance / Patient / Cat's eye, yellow fever (running) / Running / Skin / Hemlock / Our oyster / Unconscious life / After the snow / Way out / Future now / Traintime / Modern
CD _______ FIE 9110
Fie / Jun '95 / Vital

SILENT CORNER AND THE EMPTY STAGE, THE
Modern / Wilhelmina / Lie (Bernini's Saint Theresa) / Forsaken gardens / Red shift / Rubicon / Louse is not a home
CD _______ CASCD 1083
Charisma / Nov '88 / EMI

SITTING TARGETS
Breakthrough / My experience / Ophelia / Empress's clothes / Glue / Hesitation / Sitting targets / Stranger still / Sign / What I did for love / Central hotel
CD _______ CDV 2203
Virgin / Oct '88 / EMI

SKIN
Skin / After the show / Painting by numbers / Shill / All said and done / Perfect date / Four pails / Now lover
CD _______ CDOVD 344
Virgin / '89 / EMI

SONIX
Emmene-moi bare theme / Walk in the dark / In the Polish house / Dark matter / Hospital silence / Four to the floor / Exercise for Louis / Labyrinthe dreams / Emmene-moi full theme
CD _______ FIE 9114
Fie / Nov '96 / Vital

SPUR OF THE MOMENT (Hammill, Peter & Guy Evans)
Sweating it out / Surprise / Little did he know / Without a glitch / Anatol's proposal / Multiman / Deprogramming Archie / Always so polite / Imagined brother / Bounced / Roger and out
CD _______ CDR 102
Red Hot / Mar '94 / THE

STORM (BEFORE THE CALM), THE
Nadir's big chance / Golden promises / Perfect date / Spirit / Sitting targets / Tapeworm / Ain't nobody's business if I do / Crying wolf / You hit me where I live / My experience / Breakthrough / Skin / Energy vampires / Porton down / Birthday special / Lost and found / Central hotel
CD _______ CDVM 9018
Virgin / Jul '93 / EMI

THERE GOES THE DAYLIGHT
Sci finance (revisited) / Habit of a broken heart / Sign / I will find you / Lost and found / Planet Coventry / Empress's clothes / Cat's eye, yellow fever (running) / Primo on the parapet / Central hotel
CD _______ FIE 9106
Fie / Nov '93 / Vital

TIDES
CD _______ SIN 006
Sine / Sep '96 / Grapevine/PolyGram

X MY HEART
Better time / Amnesiac / Ram origami / Forest of pronouns / Earthbound / Narcissus (Bar & Grill) / Material possession / Come clean
CD _______ FIE 9111
Fie / Mar '96 / Vital

Hammond, Albert

GREATEST HITS
Free electric band / Peacemaker / Down by the river / When I need you / Rebecca / 99 Miles from LA / It never rains in southern California / Everything I want to do / We're running out / If you gotta break another heart / Moonlight lady / These are the good old days / I'm a train / New York city here I come / Half a million miles from home / Air that I breathe
CD _______ 4631852
Columbia / Oct '95 / Sony

Hammond, Beres

BERES HAMMOND
CD _______ CRCD 1
Charm / Jul '97 / Jet Star

EXPRESSION
CD _______ CBHB 166
Heartbeat / Jun '95 / ADA / Direct / Greensleeves / Jet Star

FROM MY HEART WITH LOVE
CD _______ RGCD 026
Rocky One / Mar '94 / Jet Star

FULL ATTENTION
CD _______ CRCD 17
Charm / Apr '93 / Jet Star

IRIE AND MELLOW
CD _______ RNCD 2025
Rhino / Aug '93 / Grapevine/PolyGram / Jet Star

LIFETIME GUARANTEE
Try if you want / Where were you / Come again / Touch and go situation / It takes you / Take a tip / Fight to defend / Left me crying / Walk away from love / Love gets stronger / Way it is / Single girl / False preacher / Come back home
CD _______ GRELCD 232
Greensleeves / Apr '97 / Jet Star / SRD

LOVE AFFAIR, A
CD _______ PHCD 14
Penthouse / Jun '97 / Jet Star

LOVE FROM A DISTANCE
CD _______ VPCD 1480
VP / Mar '97 / Greensleeves / Jet Star / Total/BMG

MEET IN JAMAICA (Hammond, Beres & Mikey Zappow)
CD _______ RNCD 2115
Rhino / Jul '95 / Grapevine/PolyGram / Jet Star

PUTTING UP RESISTANCE
CD _______ RASCD 3230
Ras / Aug '96 / Direct / Greensleeves / Jet Star / SRD

REGGAE MAX
CD _______ JSRNCD 8
Jet Star / Mar '97 / Jet Star

Hammond, David

I AM THE WEE FALORIE MAN (Folk Songs Of Ireland)
CD _______ TCD 1052
Tradition / Jul '97 / ADA / Vital

Hammond, Doug

SPACES
CD _______ DIW 359
DIW / Jul '92 / Cadillac / Harmonia Mundi

Hammond, John

BIG CITY BLUES
CD _______ VMD 79153
Vanguard / Apr '97 / ADA / Pinnacle

FOUND TRUE LOVE
Found love / I hate to see you go / Fore day rider blues / Warm it up to me / Howlin' for my Darling / Hello stranger / You had too much / My mind is ramblin' / First time I met the blues / I've got to find my baby / Evolution blues / Someday baby blues
CD _______ VPBCD 26
Pointblank / Mar '96 / EMI

FROGS FOR SNAKES
You don't love me / Got to find my baby / Step it up and go / Fattenin' frogs for snakes / Gypsy woman / Key to the highway / My baby left me / Louisiana blues / Mellow down easy / Your funeral and my trial / Mellow peaches / Gone so long
CD _______ ROUCD 3060
Rounder / Aug '94 / ADA / CM / Direct

GOT LOVE IF YOU WANT IT
Got love if you want it / Driftin' blues / Dreamy eyed girl / Mattie Mae / You don't love me / Nadine / No one can forgive me but my baby / You're so fine / No place to go / Preachin' blues
CD _______ VPBCD 7
Pointblank / Mar '92 / EMI

HOT TRACKS
CD _______ VCD 79424
Vanguard / Oct '96 / ADA / Pinnacle

JOHN HAMMOND LIVE
CD _______ ROUCD 3074
Rounder / Feb '92 / ADA / CM / Direct

MILEAGE
My babe / Standing around crying / Riding in the moonlight / Big 45 / Seventh son / Red hot kisses / Help me / It hurts me too / 32-20 blues / You'll miss me / Hot tamales / Diddley daddy
CD _______ ROUCD 3042
Rounder / Aug '95 / ADA / CM / Direct

NOBODY BUT YOU
Ride till I die / Sail on / Diddley daddy / Memphis town / Lost lover blues / Nobody but you / Papa wants a cookie / If I get lucky / Cuttin' out / Killing me on my feet / Mother in law blues
CD _______ FF 502CD
Flying Fish / May '93 / ADA / CM / Direct / Roots

SO MANY ROADS
Down in the bottom / Long distance call / Who do you love / I want you to love me / Judgement day / So many roads, so many trains / Rambling blues / Oh yeah / You can't judge a book by the cover / Gambling blues / Baby please don't go / Big boss man
CD _______ VMD 79178
Vanguard / Oct '95 / ADA / Pinnacle

TROUBLE NO MORE
Just your fool / Who will be next / I'll change my style / Too tired / That nasty swing / Trouble blues / Love changin' blues / It's too late brother / Wild man on the loose / Homely girl / Baby how long / Fool's paradise
CD _______ VPBCD 15
Pointblank / Jul '93 / EMI

YOU CAN'T JUDGE A BOOK BY THE COVER
You can't judge a book by the cover / I can't be satisfied / Midnight hour blues / I hate to see you go / My babe / Shake for me / Long distance call / My starter won't start / Southbound blues / I'm leavin' you / I live the life I love / Help me / Gambling blues
CD _______ VCD 79472
Vanguard / Oct '95 / ADA / Pinnacle

Hammond, Jon

LATE RENT
CD _______ EFA 128232
Hot Wire / Feb '96 / SRD

Hamon/Le Buhe ...

GWERZIOU ET CHANTS DE HAUTE VOIX (Hamon/Le Buhe/Marie/Vassallo)
CD _______ KMRS 211CD
Keltia Musique / Feb '94 / ADA / Discovery

Hampel, Gunter

8TH OF JULY 1969, THE
CD _______ BIRTHCD 001
Birth / Oct '93 / Cadillac

CELESTIAL GLORY
CD _______ BIRTHCD 040
Birth / Oct '93 / Cadillac

DIALOG
CD _______ BIRTHCD 041
Birth / Oct '93 / Cadillac

JUBILATION
CD _______ BIRTHCD 038
Birth / Oct '93 / Cadillac

MUSIC FROM EUROPE
CD _______ ESP 10422
ESP / Jan '93 / Jazz Music

TIME IS NOW
CD _______ BIRTHCD 042
Birth / Oct '93 / Cadillac

Hampton Callaway, Ann

ANN HAMPTON CALLAWAY
Lush life / Gaze in your eyes / Perfect / I live to love you / My romance / My foolish heart / But beautiful / Like someone I love / How deep is the ocean / Here's that rainy day / All the things you are / Time for love / I've got the world on a string / Our love is here to stay / Too late now / I've got just about everything
CD _______ DRGCD 91411
DRG / Aug '92 / Discovery / New Note/ Pinnacle

BRING BACK ROMANCE
Music / How long has this been going on / This might be forever / My one and only / Affair to remember / Bring back romance / You can't rush spring / Out of this world / Quiet thing / There will never be another you / Where does love go / You go to my head / It could happen to you / My shining hour/ I'll be seeing you
CD _______ DRGCD 91417
DRG / Sep '94 / Discovery / New Note/ Pinnacle

SIBLING REVELRY (Hampton Callaway, Ann & Liz Callaway)
It's today / Sweetest sound I can see / Rhythm in my nursery rhymes / My Buddy, old friend / Friendship / Meadowlark / My heart is so full of you / Nanny named Fran / Huge medley / Our time / You must be-

lieve in spring / There's a boat that's leavin' soon for New York
CD _______ DRGCD 91443
DRG / Apr '96 / Discovery / New Note/ Pinnacle

Hampton, Lionel

77 VINTAGE
CD _______ BB 8702
Black & Blue / Sep '96 / Discovery / Koch / Wellard

ANTHOLOGY 1937-1944
CD _______ EN 516
Encyclopaedia / Sep '95 / Discovery

AT MALIBU BEACH
Flying home / Malibu swing / Autumn / Stellar PM / Breathless vibes / Short of breath
CD _______ JASMCD 2535
Jasmine / Jul '95 / Conifer/BMG / Hot Shot / TKO Magnum

AT NEWPORT '78 (Hampton, Lionel All Stars)
Stompin' at the Savoy / Hamp's the champ / Flying home / On the sunny side of the street / Carnegie hall blues
CD _______ CDSJP 142
Timeless Jazz / Jun '89 / New Note/ Pinnacle

AUDIO ARCHIVE
12th street rag / I'm in the mood for swing / Johnny get your horn and blow it / Don't be that way / It don't mean a thing if it ain't got that swing / Jumpin' jive / I can give you love / High society / Memories of you / Fiddle diddle / Stand by for further announcements / Rock hill special / If it's good (then I want it) / Down home jump / Shoe shiner's drag / Wizzin' the wizz / Muskrat ramble / Shufflin' at the Hollywood / Anytime at all / Sweethearts on parade
CD _______ CDAA 025
Tring / Jan '91 / Tring

BASIN STREET BLUES
CD _______ DM 15011
DMA Jazz / Jul '96 / Jazz Music

BEULAH'S SISTER (1942-1949) (Hampton, Lionel Big Band)
CD _______ CD 14565
Jazz Portraits / May '95 / Jazz Music

CLASSICS 1937-1938
CD _______ CLASSICS 524
Classics / Apr '90 / Discovery / Jazz Music

CLASSICS 1938-1939
CD _______ CLASSICS 534
Classics / Dec '90 / Discovery / Jazz Music

CLASSICS 1939-1940
CD _______ CLASSICS 562
Classics / Oct '91 / Discovery / Jazz Music

CLASSICS 1945-1946
CD _______ CLASSICS 922
Classics / Apr '97 / Discovery / Jazz Music

EARLY HAMP
Ramble / Moonlight blues / Charlie's idea / Over night blues / Quality shout / Stuff / Harlem / Cuttin' up / New kinda blues / California swing / Burmah girl / Gettin' ready blues / To you, sweetheart / Alboa / On a cocoanut island / You came to my rescue / Here's love in your eyes / You turned the tables on me / Sing baby sing / Sunday / California here I come
CD _______ CDAFS 1011
Affinity / Oct '93 / Cadillac / Jazz Music / Koch

FLYING HOME
Hammo's jive / On the sunny side of the street / Summertime / Blue boy / Swanee River / Flying home / Stardust / How high the moon / I only have eyes for you / Oh lady be good
CD _______ JW 77027
JWD / Nov '93 / Target/BMG

FLYING HOME
Hot mallets / Shufflin' at the Hollywood / Central avenue breakdown / Save it pretty Mama / Dinah / Four of five times / Twelfth street rag / Chasin' with chase / Rhythm, rhythm / China stomp / Blue / Pig foot sonata / Three quarter boogie / Bouncing at the Beacon / Aint'cha comin' home / Munson street breakdown / When the lights are low / Shoe shiners drag / Ring dem bells / I've found a new baby / Singin' the blues / Flying home
CD _______ RAJCD 858
Empress / Mar '97 / Koch

FOR THE LOVE OF MUSIC
Flying home / Gates groove / Gossamer wings / Don't you worry 'bout a thing / Time after time / Jazz me / Take the 'A' train / Sweet Lorraine / Another part of me / Mojazz / What a wonderful world
CD _______ 5305542
MoJazz / Oct '95 / PolyGram

HAMP & GETZ (Hampton, Lionel & Stan Getz)
Cherokee / Tenderly / Autumn in New York / East of the sun and West of the moon / I can't get started (With you) / Louise / Jumpin' at the woodside / Gladys / Headache
CD _______ 8316722
Verve / May '89 / PolyGram

HAMP - THE LEGENDARY DECCA RECORDINGS (2CD Set)
Flying home / Hamp's boogie woogie / Million dollar smile / Red cross / Hamp's blues / Evil gal blues / Stardust / Ribs and hot sauce / Blow top blues / Hey ba-ba-re bop / Rockin' in rhythm, parts 1 and 2 / Limehouse blues / Tempo's blues / Jack the fox boogie / How high the moon / Three minutes in 52nd street / Red top / Mingus fingers / Midnight sun / Chicken shack boogie / Central Avenue breakdown / Drinkin' wine spo-dee-o-dee / Moonglow / Hucklebuck / Lavender coffin / Rag mop / I wish I knew / There will never be another you / Pink champagne / Memories of you / Time on my hands / Easy to love / Twentieth century boogie / Dancing on the ceiling
CD Set _______ GRD 2652
American Decca / Feb '96 / New Note/BMG

HAMP IN HARLEM (Hampton, Lionel & His Jazz Giants)
CD _______ CDSLP 168
Timeless Jazz / Jan '88 / New Note/ Pinnacle

HAMP'S BLUES
Airmail special / EG / Psychedelic Sally / Raunchy Rita / Fum / Ham hock blues / Ring them bells / Lion's den / Here's that rainy day / Killer Joe
CD _______ 17090
Laserlight / Mar '97 / Target/BMG

HAMP'S BOOGIE WOOGIE
CD _______ CD 56014
Jazz Roots / Aug '94 / Target/BMG

I'M IN THE MOOD FOR SWING
Buzzin' round with the bees / China stomp / Everybody loves my baby / For swing / Hampton stomp / I can't get started (with you) / I'm in the mood / Jivin' the vibes / Liza / Man I love / Memories of you / My last affair / New kinda blues / Object of my affection / On the sunny side of the street / Rhythm rhythm / Ring dem bells / Running wild / Sing baby sing / Stompology / Sweet Sue, just you / Vibraphone blues / Whoa babe / You turned the tables on me
CD _______ CDAJA 5090
Living Era / Feb '92 / Select

IN VIENNA 1954 VOL.1
CD _______ RST 91423
RST / Oct '92 / Hot Shot / Jazz Music

JAZZ MASTERS (Hampton, Lionel & Oscar Peterson)
Jam blues / Always / Soft winds / Stardust / Je ne sais pas / Tenderly / Hallelujah / Sweethearts on parade / Date with Oscar
CD _______ 5218532
Verve / Feb '94 / PolyGram

JAZZ MASTERS
CD _______ CDMFP 6307
Music For Pleasure / Mar '97 / EMI

JAZZ PORTRAITS
Ring dem bells / I know that you know / On the sunny side of the street / Dinah / Sheikh of Araby / Shoe shiner's drag / House of morgan / Singin' the blues / Memories of you / Dough re mi / I've found a new baby / Jivin' with Jarvis / Twelfth street rag / After you've gone / Muskrat ramble / High society / It don't mean a thing if it ain't got that swing / Drum stomp
CD _______ CD 14519
Jazz Portraits / May '94 / Jazz Music

JIVIN' THE VIBES (Hampton, Lionel & His Orchestra)
CD _______ JHR 73537
Jazz Hour / May '93 / Cadillac / Jazz Music / Target/BMG

JIVIN' THE VIBES
CD _______ LEJAZZCD 1
Le Jazz / May '93 / Cadillac / Koch

JUST JAZZ - LIVE AT THE BLUE NOTE (Hampton, Lionel & The Golden Men Of Jazz)
CD _______ CD 83313
Telarc / Jan '93 / Conifer/BMG

LIONEL HAMPTON
CD _______ 22707
Music / Feb '96 / Target/BMG

LIONEL HAMPTON
Songs of the Negev / Exodus / Railroad no.1 / Wild Bill / Juice / More Juice / McGhee / Playboy theme / Hava Nagila / Lonesome nights / Wine song / How high the moon / Flying home / Mr. John / Mr. J
CD _______ 17068
Laserlight / Jul '96 / Target/BMG

LIONEL HAMPTON & HIS ORCHESTRA 1942-44
CD _______ CLASSICS 803
Classics / Mar '95 / Discovery / Jazz Music

LIONEL HAMPTON & LARS ERSTRAND
CD _______ NCD 8807
Phontastic / Apr '94 / Cadillac / Jazz Music / Wellard

LIONEL HAMPTON 1937-1940
CD _______ 15734
Laserlight / Apr '94 / Target/BMG

LIONEL HAMPTON 1940-41 (Hampton, Lionel & His Orchestra)
CD _______ CLASSICS 624
Classics / Nov '92 / Discovery / Jazz Music

LIONEL HAMPTON AND HIS JAZZ GIANTS (Hampton, Lionel & His Jazz Giants)
CD _______ BLE 591072
Black & Blue / Apr '91 / Discovery / Koch / Wellard

LIONEL HAMPTON AND HIS ORCHESTRA (Hampton, Lionel & His Orchestra)
Stompology / Ring dem bells / Shufflin' at the Hollywood / Hot mallets / I just couldn't take it baby / Rhythm rhythm / I can't get started (with you) / I surrender dear / Handful of keys / Make believe / China stomp / 12th Street rag / Ain't cha comin' home / Four of five times / I've found a new baby / Moonglow / Running wild / On the sunny side of the street / Shoe shiner's drag / Jivin' the vibes / Gin for christmas
CD _______ PASTCD 9789
Flapper / May '92 / Pinnacle

LIONEL HAMPTON IN PARIS
CD _______ CDSW 8415
DRG / '88 / Discovery / New Note/ Pinnacle

LIONEL HAMPTON PRESENTS GERRY MULLIGAN (Hampton, Lionel & Gerry Mulligan)
Apple core / Song for Johnny Hodges / Blight of the fumble bee / Gerry meets Hamp / Blues for Gerry / Line for Lyons / Walking shoes / Limelight
CD _______ CDGATE 7014
Kingdom Jazz / Jun '87 / Kingdom

LIVE AT MUZEVAL (Hampton, Lionel Big Band)
CD _______ CDSJP 120
Timeless Jazz / Mar '90 / New Note/ Pinnacle

LIVE AT THE BLUE NOTE (Hampton, Lionel & His Orchestra)
CD _______ CD 83308
Telarc / Oct '91 / Conifer/BMG

LIVE AT THE METROPOLE CAFE
CD _______ HCD 242
Hindsight / Feb '95 / Jazz Music / Target/ BMG

LIVE IN CANNES
CD _______ JHR 73584
Jazz Hour / Dec '94 / Cadillac / Jazz Music / Target/BMG

LIVE IN SWEDEN
CD _______ NI 4010
Natasha / Jun '93 / ADA / Cadillac / CM / Direct / Jazz Music

MADE IN JAPAN
Airmail special / Advent / Stardust / Mess is here / Interpretations, opus 5 / Minor thesis / Jodo / Valve job
CD _______ CDSJP 175
Timeless Jazz / Mar '91 / New Note/ Pinnacle

MOSTLY BALLADS
I'll be seeing you / It might as well be spring / I know why and so do you / Toot toot / Lover man / Autumn leaves / Danny boy / PS I love you / Dynamic duo / Fools rush in / Pinch me / But beautiful
CD _______ 8208342
Limelight / Sep '91 / PolyGram

MOSTLY BLUES (Classics In Jazz)
Bye bye blues / Someday my Prince will come / Take the 'A' train / Blues for jazz beaux / Walkin' uptown / Honeysuckle rose / Mostly blues / Limehouse blues / Gone with the wind
CD _______ 8208052
Limelight / Nov '89 / PolyGram

MUSKRAT RAMBLE
Muskrat ramble / Fiddle diddle / Shoe shiner's drag / Johnny get your horn and blow it / Sweethearts on parade / Stand by for further announcements / Ain't cha comin' home / Denison swing / Jumpin' jive / 12th Street rag / Down home jump / Anytime at all / Wizzin' the wiz / If it's good (then I want it) / Shufflin' at the Hollywood / Don't be that way / I'm in the mood for swing / Big wig in the wigwam / I can give you love / It don't mean a thing if it ain't got that swing / High society / Rock hill special / Memories of you
CD _______ GRF 090
Tring / '93 / Tring

QUINTESSENCE, THE (1930-1944/2CD Set)
CD Set _______ FA 211
Fremeaux / Oct '96 / ADA / Discovery

SENTIMENTAL JOURNEY
CD _______ 7567816442
Atlantic / Jun '93 / Warner Music

SMALL COMBOS 1937-1940
CD _______ CD 56058
Jazz Roots / Mar '95 / Target/BMG

SMALL COMBOS 1937-40 (Hampton, Lionel & Friends)
CD _______ CD 53050
Giants Of Jazz / Mar '92 / Cadillac / Jazz Music / Target/BMG

SONNY LESTER COLLECTION
CD _______ CDC 9068
LRC / Nov '93 / Harmonia Mundi / New Note/Pinnacle

TEMPO AND SWING
Munson Street breakdown / I've found a new baby / I can't get started (with you) / Four or five times / Gin for Christmas / Dinah / My buddy / Swingin' the blues / Shades of jade / Till Tom special / Flying home / Save it pretty Mama / Tempo and swing / House of Morgan / I'd be lost without you: *Hampton, Lionel & Helen Forrest* / Central Avenue breakdown / Jack the bellboy / Dough re mi / Jivin' with Jarvis / Blue because of you / Martin on every block / Pig foot sonata
CD _______ 74321101612
Bluebird / Mar '97 / BMG

TORRID STUFF 1944-1946, THE
CD _______ 158902
Jazz Archives / Jun '97 / Discovery

TRIBUTE TO LOUIS ARMSTRONG
Cabaret / Hello Dolly / Do you know what it means to miss New Orleans / Someday you'll be sorry / Mack the knife / Louis dream / Black and blue / Jeepers creepers / Short ribs / When it's sleepy time down South / (Back home again in) Indiana
CD _______ JWD 102215
JWD / Apr '95 / Target/BMG

VINTAGE HAMPTON
CD _______ CD 83321
Telarc / Jan '94 / Conifer/BMG

Hampton, Slide

DEDICATED TO DIZ (Hampton, Slide & The Jazz Masters)
CD _______ CD 83323
Telarc / Jun '93 / Conifer/BMG

MELLOW-DY
CD _______ CDC 9053
LRC / Nov '92 / Harmonia Mundi / New Note/Pinnacle

SLIDE (Hampton, Slide Octet)
CD _______ FSRCD 206
Fresh Sound / Jul '96 / Discovery / Jazz Music

WORLD OF TROMBONES
CD _______ BLCD 760113
Black Lion / Oct '90 / Cadillac / Jazz Music / Koch / Wellard

Hamptons

BA BA BA BA BA
CD _______ LMCD 001
Scratch / Jan '97 / Koch / Scratch/BMG

Hamsters

HAMSTER JAM
CD _______ HAMSTERCD 7
Hamsters / Jul '93 / Pinnacle

HAMSTERS
CD _______ HAMSTERCD 8
Hamsters / Jul '93 / Pinnacle

JIMI HENDRIX MEMORIAL CONCERTS VOL.1
CD _______ HAMSTERCD 10
Hamsters / Jul '96 / Pinnacle

JIMI HENDRIX MEMORIAL CONCERTS VOL.2
CD _______ HAMSTERSCD 11
Hamsters / May '96 / Pinnacle

PURPLE HAZE
CD _______ 12372
Laserlight / Aug '94 / Target/BMG

ROUTE 666
CD _______ HAMSTERCD 9
Hamsters / Feb '95 / Pinnacle

Hanatarash

4-AIDSADELIC
CD _______ PBCD 3
Public Bath / Jun '97 / Greyhound

Hancock, Butch

EATS AWAY THE NIGHT
To each his own / Moanin' of the midnight train / Eileen / One kiss / Pumpkin eater / If you were a bluebird / Junkyard in the sun / Boxcars / Baby be mine / Welcome to the real world
CD _______ GRCD 341
Glitterhouse / Nov '96 / Avid/BMG
CD _______ SHCD 1048
Sugar Hill / Jan '97 / ADA / CM / Direct / Koch / Roots

JUNKYARD IN THE SUN
CD _______ GR 341
Glitterhouse / Oct '94 / Avid/BMG

OWN AND OWN
Dry land farm / Wind's dominion / Diamond hill / 1981 - A spare odyssey / Fire water / West Texas waltz / Horseflies / If you were a bluebird / Own and own / Leo and Leona / Fools fall in love / Split and slide / Yellow rose / Like a kiss on the mouth / Ghost of Give and Take Avenue / Tell me what you want to know / Just a storm / Just tell me that / When will you hold me again
CD FIENDCD 150
Demon / Oct '89 / Pinnacle
CD SHCD 1036
Sugar Hill / Aug '96 / ADA / CM / Direct / Koch / Roots
CD GRCD 364
Glitterhouse / Nov '96 / Avid/BMG

OWN THE WAY OVER HERE
Talkin' about this Panama Canal / Only born / Smokin' in the rain / Corona del mar / Like the light at dawn / Gift horse of mercy / Neon wind / Perfection in the mud / Only makes me love you more / Already gone / Away from the mountain
CD SHCD 1038
Sugar Hill / May '93 / ADA / CM / Direct / Koch / Roots

Hancock, Herbie

BEST OF HERBIE HANCOCK - THE BLUE NOTE YEARS
Watermelon man / Driftin' / Maiden voyage / Dolphin dance / One finger snap / Cantaloupe island / Riot / Speak like a child / King cobra
CD BNZ 143
Blue Note / Dec '88 / EMI

CANTALOUPE ISLAND
Cantaloupe island / Watermelon man / Driftin' / Blind man / What it I don't / Maiden voyage
CD CDP 8293312
Blue Note / Jul '94 / EMI

CANTALOUPE ISLAND
CD MSCD 020
Music De-Luxe / Jan '96 / TKO Magnum

COMPLETE WARNER RECORDINGS, THE
CD 2457322
Warner Bros. / Feb '95 / Warner Music

DIS IS DA DRUM
CD 5281852
Mercury / Jun '95 / PolyGram

EVENING WITH HERBIE HANCOCK AND CHICK COREA, AN (2CD Set) (Hancock, Herbie & Chick Corea)
Someday my Prince will come / Liza / Button up / February moments / Maiden voyage / La fiesta
CD Set 4772962
Columbia / Nov '94 / Sony

EVENING WITH HERBIE HANCOCK AND CHICK COREA, AN (Hancock, Herbie & Chick Corea)
Homecoming / Ostinato / Hook / Bouquet / Maiden voyage / La fiesta
CD 8356802
Polydor / Mar '93 / PolyGram

FEETS DON'T FAIL ME NOW
You bet your love / Trust me / Tell everybody / Ready or not / Honey from the jar / Knee deep
CD CK 35764
Sony Jazz / Aug '97 / Sony

FUTURE SHOCK
Rockit / Future shock / TFS / Earthbeat / Autodrive / Rough
CD 4712372
Sony Jazz / Jan '95 / Sony

HEADHUNTERS
Chameleon / Watermelon man / Sly / Vein melter
CD CK 65123
Sony Jazz / Apr '97 / Sony

JAZZ COLLECTION, A
Liza / I fall in love too easily / Nefertiti / Someday my Prince will come / 'Round midnight / Well you needn't / Parade / Eye of the hurricane / Maiden voyage
CD 4679012
Columbia / Nov '93 / Sony

JAZZ PROFILE
Empty pockets / Jack Rabbit / Yams / Eye of the hurricane / Cantaloupe Island / Sorceror / I have a dream
CD CDP 8549042
Blue Note / May '97 / EMI

MAIDEN VOYAGE
Maiden voyage / Eye of the hurricane / Little one / Survival of the fittest / Dolphin dance
CD CDP 7463392
Blue Note / Mar '95 / EMI

MANCHILD
CD 4712352
Sony Jazz / Jan '95 / Sony

MR. HANDS
Spiralling prism / Calypso / Just around the corner / 4 a.m. / Shifless shuffle / Textures
CD 4712402
Sony Jazz / Jan '95 / Sony

NEW STANDARD, THE
CD 5277152
Verve / Mar '96 / PolyGram

PIANO GENIUS
Jammin' with Herbie / Herbie's blues / Rock your soul / TCB with Herbie / Soul power / Cat call
CD QED 076
Tring / Nov '96 / Tring

QUARTET WITH WYNTON MARSALIS
Well you needn't / 'Round midnight / Clear ways / Quick sketch / Eye of the hurricane / Parade / Sorcerer / Pee wee / I fall in love too easily
CD 4656262
Columbia / Nov '93 / Sony

SECRETS
CD CK 34280
Sony Jazz / Aug '97 / Sony

TAKIN' OFF
Watermelon man / Three bags full / Empty pockets / Maze / Driftin' / Alone and I
CD CDP 8376432
Blue Note / Jun '96 / EMI

TAKIN' OFF/INVENTIONS AND DIMENSIONS/EMPRYEAN ISLES (3CD Set)
Watermelon man / Three bags full / Empty pockets / Maze / Driftin' / Alone & I / Succotash / Triangle / Jack rabbit / Mimosa / Jump ahead / One finger snap / Oliloqui valley / Cantaloupe Island / Egg
CD Set CDOMB 009
Blue Note / Oct '95 / EMI

Hancock, Keith

MADHOUSE
CD HY 200107CD
Hypertension / Feb '95 / ADA / CM / Direct / Total/BMG

Hancock, Wayne

THUNDERSTORMS AND NEON LIGHTS
CD DJD 3221
Dejadisc / Nov '95 / ADA / Direct

Hand, Frederic

HEART'S SONG
CD MM 5018
Music Masters / Oct '94 / Nimbus

JAZZANTIQUA
Cantigas de Santa Maria / Rose Liz / Bachiaras / Tourdion / Lady Carey's fantasy / Chaconne / Toby and Lynn
CD MM 65150
Music Masters / Nov '96 / Nimbus

Handbell Ringers Of Great ...

CHRISTMAS HANDBELLS (Handbell Ringers Of Great Britain)
Silent night / Jingle bells / Good King Wenceslas / We three Kings / Ave Maria / Hark what mean/Christians awake / Hail smiling morn / Hark the herald angels sing / O little town of Bethlehem / O come all ye faithful (adeste fidelis) / I saw three ships / Born today is the child divine / Ding dong merrily on high / Away in a manger / Once in Royal David's city / Coventry carol / Christmas bells / Christmas is coming/Wassail song / Christmas candles / Zither carol / Stars watch high / Masters in the hall / Cowboy carol / Three Kings / Le jeux Noel de Robin et Marion / Hallelujah chorus / Puer nobis
CD 4610762
Belart / Nov '96 / PolyGram

Handfullaflowers

CAN'T STAND THE WEIGHT OF THE WORLD
CD SPV 08480822
SPV / May '96 / Koch / Plastic Head

Handraizer UK

IN THE MIX WITH TALL PAUL
CD MM 800152
Moonshine / Oct '94 / Mo's Music Machine / Prime / RTM/Disc

Hands

HANDS
CD SP 96001
Shroom / Jul '97 / Greyhound

Handsome

HANDSOME
Needles / Ride down / Going to panic / Left of Heaven / Thrown away / Dim the lights / Lead bellied / My mind's eye / Waiting / Quiet liar / Eden complex / Swimming
CD 4867682
Epic / Jun '97 / Sony

Handsome Beasts

BEAST WITHIN, THE
Mr. Mescalito / Hairy legs / Way I am / Chain gang / Beast within / Rough justice / Don't hold on / Sixth day / Let it go
CD HMRXD 132
Heavy Metal / Feb '90 / Revolver / Sony

BESTIALITY
CD CDMETAL 5
British Steel / Feb '97 / Cargo / Pinnacle / Plastic Head

Handsome Family

MILK AND SCISSORS
CD SR 1011
Scout / Sep '96 / Koch

ODESSA
CD SR 1004
Scout / Jan '96 / Koch

Handy, Captain John

CAPT. JOHN HANDY & EASY RIDERS JAZZBAND
CD BCD 325
GHB / Apr '94 / Jazz Music

CAPT. JOHN HANDY & HIS NEW ORLEANS STOMPERS VOL.1
CD BCD 41
GHB / Aug '94 / Jazz Music

CAPT. JOHN HANDY & HIS NEW ORLEANS STOMPERS VOL.2 (Handy, Captain John & His New Orleans Stompers)
CD BCD 42
GHB / Aug '94 / Jazz Music

VERY FIRST RECORDINGS
CD AMCD 51
American Music / Apr '94 / Jazz Music

Handy, John

CENTERPIECE
CD MCD 9173
Milestone / Jan '95 / Cadillac / Complete/ Pinnacle / Jazz Music / Wellard

HANDY DANDY MAN
Play the musik / Lady lady / Disco samba / Everything you touch / I gotta let her know / I can tell / Handy dandy man / You live, you learn / Sing to me
CD INAK 8618
In Akustik / Jul '97 / Direct / TKO Magnum

JOHN HANDY QUINTET
CD BCD 261
GHB / Jul '96 / Jazz Music

LIVE AT THE MONTEREY JAZZ FESTIVAL
CD 378202
Koch Jazz / Jun '96 / Koch

NEW VIEW (Handy, John New Quintet)
CD CD 378112
Koch Jazz / Jul '97 / Koch

NIGHT AT YOSHI'S NIGHTSPOT
CD BLDCD 531
Boulevard / Sep '96 / Grapevine/PolyGram / Total/BMG

WHERE GO THE BOATS (Handy, John & Lee Ritenour)
Right there right there / Moogie woogie / Where go the boats / Go for yourself / Hissing of summer / She just won't boogie with me / Erica / Salud to Sonny
CD INAK 861CD
In Akustik / Jul '97 / Direct / TKO Magnum

Handy, W.C.

FATHER OF THE BLUES
St. Louis blues / Beale Street blues / Memphis blues / Aunt Hagar's blues / Yellow dog blues / Oh, didn't he ramble / Chantezles bas / Friendless blues / Joe Turner's blues / Long gone / Loveless love / Hesitating blues / Careless love / Boogie woogie on St. Louis blues / Atlanta blues
CD CD 53223
Giants Of Jazz / Jul '97 / Cadillac / Jazz Music / Target/BMG

FATHER OF THE BLUES
CD CD 14581
Complete / Nov '95 / THE

Hanford, Jan

VESPERS
Landlocked / Delirious / Intimate / Theoria / Human response / Angels / Total truth / Denial / If I can believe what I see / Ambien II, of the five / Vespers / Dancing (moog archive 1)
CD AD 12CD
AD / Dec '96 / Disc

Hangal, Gangubai

VOICE OF TRADITION, THE
CD SM 15012
Wergo / Jan '91 / ADA / Cadillac / Harmonia Mundi

Hankansson, Kenny

2117M ABOVE SEA LEVEL
CD SRS 4731
Silence / Mar '96 / ADA / Direct

Hanly, Mick

HAPPY LIKE THIS
CD RTM 61CD
Round Tower / Jan '94 / Avid/BMG

WARTS AND ALL
Nothing in the can / What's his name / Don't try to cushion the blow / Fabulous thunderbirds / On vocals and guitar / Wherever you go / Joan / Warts and all / Let's not fight / Words and the bottle / Uncle John / Art and reality / My body and me / Happy to be here
CD RTMCD 32
Round Tower / Sep '91 / Avid/BMG

Hanna, Fred

BALLROOM CLASSICS
CD PHCD 541
Outlet / Jul '97 / ADA / CM / Direct / Duncans / Koch / Ross

IRISH PARTY FAVOURITES
CD PHCD 543
Outlet / Jul '97 / ADA / CM / Direct / Duncans / Koch / Ross

Hanna, Roland

DUKE ELLINGTON PIANO SOLOS
In my solitude / Something to live for / In a sentimental mood / Portrait of Bert Williams / Warm valley / Isfahan / Single petal of a rose / I got it bad and that ain't good / Reflections in D / Come Sunday / Caravan
CD MM 5045
Music Masters / Oct '94 / Nimbus

GLOVE
CD STCD 4148
Storyville / Feb '90 / Cadillac / Jazz Music / Wellard

IMPRESSIONS
CD BB 880
Black & Blue / Apr '97 / Discovery / Koch / Wellard

LIVE AT MAYBECK RECITAL HALL VOL.32
Love walked in / They can't take that away from me / Softly as in a morning sunrise / Gershwin medley: Fascinating rhythm/Man I love / Let's call the whole thing off / How long has this been going on / Oleo / Lush life / This can't be love
CD CCD 4604
Concord Jazz / Jul '94 / New Note/Pinnacle

PERUGIA
Take the 'A' train / I got it bad and that ain't good / Time dust gathered / Perugia / Child is born / Wistful moment
CD FCD 41010
Freedom / Sep '87 / Cadillac / Jazz Music / Koch / Wellard

REMEMBERING CHARLIE PARKER
CD PCD 7031
Progressive / Oct '91 / Jazz Music

THIS TIME IT'S REAL
CD STCD 4145
Storyville / Feb '90 / Cadillac / Jazz Music / Wellard

Hannah, Marcus

WEEDS AND LILIES
CD RTS 10
Return To Sender / Nov '94 / ADA / Direct

Hannan, Robert

TRADITIONAL IRISH MUSIC PLAYED ON UILLEANN PIPES
Flood on the Holm/Miss Monahan reel / Amhran an Tae / Liz King's jig / Stay another while/College groves / Derry hornpipe / Do you want anymore/Gallowglass / Rainy day/Shaskeen / Dark woman of the Glen / Boys of Tanderagee / Jackson's morning brush / Jenny picking cockles/My love is in America / Darby Gallagher's/An Buachaillin bui / Salamanca/Jenny's welcome to Charlie / Dark Lochnagar / Rambles of Kitty/ When sick is it tea you want / Curragh races/Trim the velvet / Chief O'Neill/Plains of Boyle / Pipe on the hob / Merry Blacksmith/Bonnie Kate/Gorman's reel
CD CC 53CD
Claddagh / Jan '91 / ADA / CM / Direct

Hanoi Rocks

BACK TO MYSTERY CITY
Strange boys play weird openings / Mental beat / Until I get you / Lick summer lover / Ice cream summer / Malibu beach nightmare / Tooting Bec wreck / Sailing down the years / Beating gets faster / Back to Mystery City
CD ESMCD 272
Essential / Mar '95 / BMG

BANGKOK SHOCKS SAIGON SHAKES
Tradegy / Stop cryin' / Lost in the city / Pretender / 11th Street kidz / First timer / Don't never leave me / Village girl / Walking with my angel / Cheyenne
CD ESMCD 273
Essential / Mar '95 / BMG

LEAN ON ME
Tragedy / Oriental beat / Motorvatin' / Taxi driver / Back to mystery city / Malibu beach nightmare / Life's been hard / Heart attack / Menaced by nightingales / Fast car / Shame, shame, shame / Rock 'n' roll / Lean on me

CD ESMCD 282
Essential / Apr '95 / BMG

ORIENTAL BEAT
Motorvatin' / Visitor / Sweet home suburbia / No law or order / Devil woman / Fallen star / Don't follow me / Teenage outsiders / M C Baby / Oriental beat / Bar blues
CD ESMCD 274
Essential / Mar '95 / BMG

SELF DESTRUCTION BLUES
Love's an injection / Dead by Xmas / Desperados / Whispers in the dark / Self destruction blues / Nothing blues / Cafe avenue / Kill city / Beer and a cigarette / Taxi driver / Problem child / I want you / Nothing new
CD ESMCD 271
Essential / Mar '95 / BMG

Hanrahan, Kip

ALL ROADS ARE MADE OF THE FLESH
CD AMCL 10292
American Clave / Aug '95 / ADA / Direct / New Note/Pinnacle

ANTHOLOGY
CD AMCL 10202
American Clave / Nov '93 / ADA / Direct / New Note/Pinnacle

DESIRE DEVELOPS AN EDGE
CD AMCL 1009/8
American Clave / Aug '94 / ADA / Direct / New Note/Pinnacle

THOUSAND NIGHTS & A NIGHT, A
Shahrazade / Sitt Al Milla/Zumurrud / Jewish doctor's tale / Aziz & Azizah / Diente De Oro / Aziz & Azizah (continued) / Al-Mummum & the Arab girl by the well / Lost Prince / Princess Dunya & Taj Al-Muluk / Princess Dunya's nocturnal realization / Yemen merchant & the three different coloured woman / Jinniya who envied human suffering / Hasheater's tale / Angel Charles & the caravan of Jinns / Shahrazade & the closing of the first night of stories
CD AMCL 10362
American Clave / Nov '96 / ADA / Direct / New Note/Pinnacle

Hanrahan, Mike

MIKE HANRAHAN
CD TUT 168
Wundertute / Oct '94 / ADA / CM / Duncans

Hanselmann, David

LET THE MUSIC CARRY ON
CD 845158
FM / May '91 / Revolver / Sony

Hansen, Ole Kock

PA EN GREN BAKKETOP
CD MECCACD 1002
Music Mecca / Nov '94 / Cadillac / Jazz Music / Wellard

Hansen, Randy

TRIBUTE TO JIMI HENDRIX, A
CD 1890692
NMC / Nov '92 / Total/Pinnacle

Hanshaw, Annette

LOVABLE AND SWEET
Black bottom / Six feet of Papa / Falling in love with you / Do, do, do / Everything's made for love / Ain't he sweet / Here or there / Nuthin' / You wouldn't fool me, would you / That's you, baby / Big city blues / Pagan love song / Ua like no a like (sweet constancy) / Lovable and sweet / Right kind of me / Telling it to the daisies / Little white lies / Body and soul / Would you like to take a walk / Walkin' my baby back home / Ho hum / Fit as a fiddle / Moon song / We just couldn't say goodbye / Let's fall in love
CD CDAJA 5220
Living Era / Apr '97 / Select

TWENTIES SWEETHEART, THE
Black bottom / Six feet of Papa / Don't take that bottom away / Here or there / I gotta get somebody to love / Wistful and blue / What do I care / Nuthin' / I'm somebody's somebody now / I like what you like / Ain't that a grand and glorious feeling / Who-oo you-oo, that's who / Under the moon / It was only a sun shower / Who's that knocking at my door / We love it / Get out and get under the moon / There must be somebody else / Mine all mine / Thinking of you / Song is ended (but the melody lingers on)
CD JASMCD 2542
Jasmine / May '95 / Conifer/BMG / Hot Shot / TKO Magnum

Hanson

MIDDLE OF NOWHERE, THE
Thinking of you / Mmmbop / Weird / Speechless / Where's the love / Yearbook song / Look at you / Lucy / I will come to you / Minute wthout you / Madeline / With you in my dreams / Man from Milwaukee
CD 5346152
Mercury / Jun '97 / PolyGram

Hanson Brothers

GROSS MISCONDUCT
CD VIRUS 116CD
Alternative Tentacles / Nov '92 / Cargo / Greyhound / Pinnacle

SUDDEN DEATH
CD K 176CD
Konkurrent / May '97 / SRD

Hanson, Mick

DO YOU HAVE A NAME
Here's that rainy day / What's next / Vera cruz / I thought about you / My one and only love / My romance / Foggy day / Alfredo / There with you / Old folks / Pause for thought / Hanson is as Hanson does / Do you have a name
CD SPJCD 555
Spotlite / May '96 / Cadillac / Jazz Music / New Note/Pinnacle / Swift

Hansson, Bo

ATTIC THOUGHTS
CD SRS 3625CD
Silence / Jul '95 / ADA / Direct

LORD OF THE RINGS
Leaving shire / Old forest/Tom Bombadil / Fog on the barrow downs / Black riders/ Flight to the ford / At the house of Elrond/ The ring goes South / Journey in the dark / Lothlorien / Shadowfax / Horns of Rohan/ The Battle of Pelennor Fields / Dreams in the house of healing / Homeward bound/ The scouring of the shire / Grey havens
CD EDCD 493
Edsel / Jun '96 / Pinnacle
CD RESCD 508
Resource / Jul '97 / ADA / Direct

MAGICIAN'S HAT
Big city / Divided reality / Elidor / Fylke / Before the rain / Findhorn's song / Playing downhill into the downs / Awakening / Wandering song / Sun (Parallel or 90 degrees) / Excursion with complications
CD RESCD 509
Resource / Jul '97 / ADA / Direct

Happy Family

MAN ON YOUR STREET
CD CAD 214CD
4AD / Nov '92 / RTM/Disc

Happy Flowers

OOF
CD HMS 136 2
Homestead / May '89 / Cargo / SRD

Happy Mondays

BUMMED
Country song / Moving in with / Mad Cyril / Fat lady wrestlers / Performance / Brain dead / Wrote for luck / Bring a friend / Do it better / Lazyitis
CD 5200132
Factory Too / Jul '95 / Pinnacle / PolyGram

LOADS
Step on / Wrote for luck / Kinky Afro / Hallelujah / Mad Cyril / Lazyitis / Tokoloshe man / Loose fit / Bob's yer uncle / Judge Fudge / Stinkin' thinkin' / Sunshine and love / Angel / Tart tart / Kuff dam / 24 hour party people
CD 5200362
Factory Too / Jul '95 / Pinnacle / PolyGram

PILLS 'N' THRILLS AND BELLYACHES
Kinky afro / God's cop / Donovan / Grandbag's funeral / Dennis and Lois / Bob's yer Uncle / Step on / Holiday / Harmony
CD 8282232
Factory Too / Jul '95 / Pinnacle / PolyGram

SQUIRREL AND G-MAN
Kuff dam / Tart tart / 'Enry / Russell / Olive oil / Weekend 5 / Little matchstick Owen / Oasis / 24 hour party people / Cob 20
CD 5200122
Factory Too / Jul '95 / Pinnacle / PolyGram

UP ALL NIGHT
CD CBAK 4046
Baktabak / Apr '91 / Arabesque

YES PLEASE
Stinkin' thinkin' / Monkey in the family / Sunshine and love / Dustman / Angel / Cut 'em loose Bruce / Theme from Netto / Love child / Total ringo / Cowboy Dave
CD 5200262
Factory Too / Jul '95 / Pinnacle / PolyGram

Har-Ell

PAGAN MOON CHILD
CD EFA 009512
Nephilim / Aug '95 / SRD

Haran, Mary Cleere

FUNNY WORLD (Mary Cleere Hart Sings Lyrics By Hart)
CD VSD 5584
Varese Sarabande / Jul '95 / Pinnacle

Harare Dread

DZIDZO
CD PVCD 05
Paxvision / May '96 / Jet Star

Harbour Kings

SUMMERCOLTS
Tattoo / Grassfires / Roads to freedom / Forsyth C / Rosemary Road / Sleepers / Searchlight / Flood dream
CD FIRE 33025
Fire / Oct '91 / Pinnacle / RTM/Disc

Hard Rain

HARD RAIN
CD 50580422
Semaphore / May '97 / Plastic Head

Hard Skin

HARD SKIN
CD HSPCD 2000
Almanac / Jan '94 / Jet Star

Hard Trance

UNDISCOVERED
CD EVCD 4
Evolution / Nov '96 / Alphamagic

Hard-Ons

YUMMY
CD SOL 26CD
Vinyl Solution / Feb '91 / RTM/Disc

Hardcastle, Paul

FIRST LIGHT
Inner changes / Sancitity / Tribal call / Source / Celestial rhythm / First light part 1 / Forest dawn / Forever dreaming / Kingdom of dreams / Nomad's flight / First light part 2 / Rush hour / Bridge / Horizons / Eden
CD NSPCD 516
Connoisseur Collection / Jun '97 / Pinnacle

JAZZ MASTERS, THE
Do you remember / Wonderland / Walkin' to freedom / Summer rain / Smooth groove / Good lovin' / Slomotion / Just can't understand / Time to move on / So much in love / Inner changes / Can you hear me
CD GRP 98582
GRP / Nov '96 / New Note/BMG

PAUL HARDCASTLE PRESENTS JAZZMASTERS
CD SPOOKCD 002
Fantom / Sep '96 / Grapevine/PolyGram / Koch / Scratch/BMG

VERY BEST OF PAUL HARDCASTLE, THE
Nineteen / Don't waste my time / Just for the money / Eat your heart out / Wizzard / Foolin' yourself / Walk in the night / 40 years / Central Park / Moonhopper / Better / Earth from space / On the run / Voices of the world
CD CDGOLD 1040
EMI Gold / Jul '96 / EMI

Hardcores

EEDENIN POLTTAJA
CD AA 026
AA / Jul '97 / Cargo / Greyhound

SANANSAATTAJAT
CD AA 029
AA / Jul '97 / Cargo / Greyhound

Hardelin

UNION (Hardelin, Thore & Oline)
CD CCD 10005CD
Musikk Distribujson / Apr '95 / ADA

Hardeman, Rick

ALL STAR RHYTHM
CD JCD 263
Jazzology / Jun '96 / Jazz Music

Hardfloor

BEST OF HARDFLOOR, THE (2CD Set)
Once again back / Into the nature / Mahogany roots / Dub dope / Fish 'n' chips / Ain't nuttin' but a format thing / Lost in the silver box / Yimtrop / Confuss / Acperience / Fever called love: *Rising High Collective* / Circus bells: *Armani, Robert* / Is there anybody out there: *Bassheads* / Beavis at bat / Strikeout / Blue Monday: *New Order* / It's no good: *Depeche Mode* / Kangaroos and bubbles / Yeke yeke: *Mori Kante*
CD Set EYEUKCD 015
Eye Q / Sep '97 / Vital

HOME RUN
CD HHCD 19S
CD HHCD 19
Harthouse / Jun '96 / Mo's Music Machine / Prime / Vital

RESPECT
CD HHCD 010
Harthouse / Dec '94 / Mo's Music Machine / Prime / Vital

TB RESUSCITATION
CD HARTUKCD 1
Harthouse / Jun '93 / Mo's Music Machine / Prime / Vital

Hardie, Alastair

COMPLIMENTS TO THE KING
CD HPMCD 002
Hardie Press / Jan '95 / ADA

Hardie, Ian

BREATH OF FRESHER AIRS, A
Mrs. Elspeth Hardie / Goat in the boat / Fiona's jig / New 19th / Mellerstain House / Knock of Braemoray / Andrew James Hardie / Cawdor wood / Palpitation reel / Mrs. Willie Wastle / Compose yourself waltz / Segs hornpipe / Macbeths of Tulloch Castle / Invernairn two-step / Lochindorb / Lochdhu waltz / Grand slam / Horsbrugh Castle / Vivianae / Helsinki Harbour / Lethen bar / White in the heather / Suitor's waltz / Bonnie lass o'wark / Lights of balintore / Liathach / Dulsie bridge / Locked bucket / Shifting sands / Esther Stephenson of Embleton / Chatterin' teeth / Nigg rigs jig / Oystercatcher / Drumochter sun / Crown knot / Snow on the ben / Up an' doon reel / Lost village of Culbin / Tarbat ness light / Drummossie muir
CD CDTRAX 049
Greentrax / Jan '92 / ADA / Direct / Duncans / Highlander

Hardie, Jonny

UP IN THE AIR (Hardie, Jonny & Gavin Marwick)
CD LDLCD 1226
Lochshore / Jan '95 / ADA / Direct / Duncans

Hardin & York

LIVE AT THE MARQUEE VOL.3
CD RPM 135
RPM / Aug '94 / Pinnacle

STILL A FEW PAGES LEFT
CD CSA 106
Thunderbird / Oct '95 / Pinnacle

Hardin, Andrew

CONEY ISLAND MOON
CD RTMCD 76
Round Tower / Jun '96 / Avid/BMG

Hardin, Eddie

DAWN TIL DUSK
CD NAGE 9 CD
Art Of Landscape / Jul '86 / Sony

SURVIVAL
Innocent victims / Lost childhood / Seeds of suspicion / Schools of thought / Perfect survivor / Lessons to learn / Where do we go from here / Slice of paradise / Never again / Rules we can't ignore
CD NAGE 19CD
Art Of Landscape / Sep '88 / Sony

WHEN WE WERE YOUNG
CD INAK 11005
In Akustik / May '97 / Direct / TKO Magnum

WIZARD'S CONVENTION VOL.2
Hot head of steam / Zermatitus blues / Happening all the time / Here I go again / Someone sings / Talking ain't cheap / Try a little tenderness / Sultana / Brickmaker blues / Can't let you go / I think it's gonna rain today / As long as I still have you / Before we say goodbye / Lucille / What a way to spend a day
CD SJPCD 009
Angel Air / Jun '97 / Pinnacle

Hardin, Tim

HANG ON TO A DREAM (The Verve Recordings/2CD Set)
Don't make promises / Green rocky road / Smugglin' man / How long / While you're on your way / It'll never happen again / Reason to believe / Never too far / Part of the wind / Ain't gonna do without / Misty roses / How can we hang on to a dream / If I were a carpenter / Red balloon / Black sheep boy / Lady came from Baltimore / Baby close it's eyes / You upset the grace of living when you lie / Speak like a child / See where you are and get out / It's hard to believe in love for long / Tribute to Hank Williams / While you're on your way / It'll never happen again / Airmobile / Whiskey, whiskey / Seventh son / Danville dame / House of the rising sun / Bo Diddley / I can't slow down / Hello baby / Rolling stone / You get a reparation / Keep your hands off her / Nobody knows you (when you're down and out) / Hoochie koochie man / So glad you're mine / You can't judge a book by its cover / She ain't home / You say you love me / How time flies / You can ruin a man / If I knew / She's up to something new / Who'll be the man / First love song
CD Set 5215832
Polydor / Feb '97 / PolyGram

NINE
Shiloh town / Rags and old iron / Person to person / Blues on my ceiling / Fire and rain / Judge and jury / Never too far / Look our love over / Darling girl / Is there no rest for the weary / While you're on your way
CD ____ **SEECD 335**
See For Miles/C5 / Feb '97 / Pinnacle

SIMPLE SONGS OF FREEDOM (The Tim Hardin Collection)
Simple song of freedom / Shiloh town / Turn the page / Playing cards/The magician / First love song / Last sweet moments / If I knew / Hoboin' / Andre Johray / Southern butterfly / Bird on a wire / Midnight caller / Yankee lady / Till we meet again / I'll be home / If I knew / Thanks to Gideon
CD ____ **4851082**
Columbia / Nov '96 / Sony

TOMORROW TODAY
CD ____ **RPMCD 128**
RPM / May '94 / Pinnacle

WORLD'S SMALLEST BIG BAND
CD ____ **RPMCD 129**
RPM / May '94 / Pinnacle

Harding, John Wesley

IT HAPPENED ONE NIGHT
Headful of something / Devil in me / Who you really are / Famous man / July 13th 1985 / One night only / Affairs of the heart / Humankind / Night he took her to the fairground / Careers service / Biggest monument / Roy Orbison knows (the best man's song) / You and your career / Bastard son
CD ____ **LFIENDCD 137**
Demon / Dec '88 / Pinnacle

NEW DEAL
CD ____ **JWHCD 1**
Kingfisher / Jan '97 / Grapevine/PolyGram

WHY WE FIGHT
Kill the messenger / Ordinary weekend / Truth / Dead centre of town / Into the wind / Hitler's tears / Get back down / Me against me / Original Miss Jesus / Where the bodies are / Millionaire's dream / Come gather round
CD ____ **9362450322**
WEA / Apr '93 / Warner Music

Harding, Mike

PLUTONIUM ALLEY
CD ____ **MOOCD 9**
Moonraker / Mar '94 / ADA

Hardkiss

DELUSIONS OF GRANDEUR
Out of body experience / 3 Nudes in a purple garden / Raincry / Pacific coastal highway / Daylight / Phoenix / Someday my plane will crash
CD ____ **5283862**
L'Attitude / Aug '95 / PolyGram / Vital

Hardship Post

SOMEBODY SPOKE
CD ____ **SPCD 289**
Sub Pop / Jul '95 / Cargo / Greyhound / Shellshock/Disc

Hardskin

HARD NUTS AND HARD CUNTS
CD ____ **HOO 31CD**
Helen Of Oi / May '97 / Cargo

Hardware

RACE, RELIGION AND HATE
CD ____ **CDMVEST 75**
Bulletproof / Aug '96 / Pinnacle

THIRD EYE OPEN
Got a feeling / Waiting on you / What's goin' down / Love obsession / Hard look / Shake it / Walls came down / 500 Years / Tell me / Leakin'
CD ____ **RCD 10304**
Black Arc / Jun '94 / Vital

Hardway, James

DEEPER, WIDER SMOOTHER SHIT
CD ____ **HEMP 3L**
CD ____ **HEMP 3CD**
Recordings Of Substance / Jul '96 / 3mv/ Vital / Kudos / Prime

Hardy, Francoise

COLLECTION, THE
Tous les garcons les filles / Oh oh cheri / Ton mellileur ami / J'suis d'accord / Va pas prendre un tambour / Le temps de l'amour / Je n'attend plus personne / Ce petit coeur / Je veux qu'il revienne / Le temps des souvenirs / Je changerais d'avis (se telefonado) / Il est des choses / Comme / Je ne suis la pour personne / Ma jeunesse fout le camp / Il n'ya pas d'amour hereux
CD ____ **74321145202**
Vogue / Apr '94 / BMG

GREATEST RECORDINGS
Tous le garcons et les filles / Le temps de l'amour / Le premier bonheur du jour / Mon amie la rose / All over the world / L'amitie / Ce petit coeur / Je ne suis la pour personne / Il est des chose / La maison ou j'ai grand / Comme / Voila
CD ____ **74321203912**
Vogue / May '95 / BMG

IN VOGUE VOL.2
CD ____ **VGCD 600145**
Vogue / Oct '93 / BMG

LE DANGER
CD ____ **CDVIR 51**
Virgin / Jun '96 / EMI

LES CHANSONS D'AMOUR
CD ____ **472478**
Flarenasch / Sep '96 / Discovery

LES CHANSONS D'AMOUR
Ce petite coeur / Il n'y a pas d'amour heureux / Mon amie la rose / Tout les garcons et les filles / L'amitie / La maison ou j'ai grandi / La temps da l'amour / Il est des choses / Ma jeunesse fout le camp / Ton meilleur ami / Voila / Parlami di te / J'ai jete mon coeur / Autumn rendez-vous / La tua mano / C'est a l'amour auquel je pense / Je ne suis pas la pour personne / Le premier bonheur du jour / Comme / Find me boy / This little heart / All over the world
CD ____ **74321415022**
Camden / Oct '96 / BMG

LES INOUBLIABLES DE...
CD ____ **472297**
Flarenasch / Feb '97 / Discovery

TOUS LES GARCONS ET LES FILLES
CD ____ **CD 352060**
Duchesse / May '93 / Pinnacle

YEH-YEH GIRL FROM PARIS
Tous les garcons et les filles / Ca a rate / La fille avec toi / Oh oh cheri / Le temps de l'amour / Il est tout pour moi / On se plait / Ton meilleur ami / J'ai jete mon coeur / Il est parti un jour / J'suis d'accord / C'est a la amour auquel je pense
CD ____ **74321264702**
Vogue / May '95 / BMG

Hardy, Hagood

MOROCCO (Hardy, Hagood Sextet)
CD ____ **SKCD 22018**
Sackville / Jun '93 / Cadillac / Jazz Music / Swift

Hardy, Jack

RETROSPECTIVE
CD ____ **BRAM 1989072**
Brambus / Nov '93 / ADA

THROUGH
CD ____ **BRAM 1990122**
Brambus / Nov '93 / ADA

TWO OF SWORDS
CD ____ **422166**
New Rose / May '94 / ADA / Direct / Discovery

Hare

PROUD TO BE LOUD
Love me to the bone / Crawling / Sorrow / Lies / Different ways / Blind / Otaku / Misery / Slum / Ready / Show me / Ice
CD ____ **CDMFN 215**
Music For Nations / Feb '97 / Pinnacle

Hare, Colin

MARCH HARE...PLUS
Get up the road / Bloodshot eyes / For where have you been / Find me / Underground girl / To my maker / Grannie, grannie / Alice / Nothing to write home about / New day / Cowboy Joe (saga) / Just like me / Charlie Brown's time / Fighting for peace
CD ____ **SEECD 261**
See For Miles/C5 / Sep '89 / Pinnacle

Hargrove, Roy

APPROACHING STANDARDS
Easy to remember / Ruby my dear / Whisper not / What's new / September in the rain / You don't know what love is / End of a love affair / Things we did last summer / Everything I have is yours / Dedicated to you / My shining hour
CD ____ **01241631782**
Novus / Oct '94 / BMG

OF KINDRED SOULS
CD ____ **01241631542**
Novus / Jul '93 / BMG

PARKER'S MOOD (Hargrove, Roy & Christian McBride/Stephen Scott Trio)
Klactoveesedstein / Parker's mood / Marmaduke / Steeplechase / Laura / Dexterity / Yardbird suite / Red cross / Repetition / Laird baird / Dewey Square / Cardboard / April in Paris / Chasin' the bird / Bongo beep / Star eyes
CD ____ **5279072**
Verve / Mar '96 / PolyGram

PUBLIC EYE
Public eye / Spiritual companion / September in the rain / Lada / Once in awhile / Heartbreaker / End of a love affair / Night watch / You don't know what love is / Little Bennie / What's new
CD ____ **PD 83113**
Novus / Jun '91 / BMG

VIBE, THE
Vibe / Caryisms / Where were you / Alter ego / Thang / Pinocchio / Milestones / Things we did last summer / Blues for booty greens / Running out of time
CD ____ **PD 90668**
Novus / Jun '92 / BMG

WITH THE TENORS OF OUR TIME (Hargrove, Roy Quintet)
Soppin' the biscuit / When we were one / Valse hot / Once forgotten / Shade of jade / Greens at the chicken shack / Never let me / Serenity / Across the pond / Wild is love / Mental phrasing / April's fool
CD ____ **5230192**
Verve / Jun '94 / PolyGram

Haricots Rouges

SANS FIL
CD ____ **BB 282**
Black & Blue / Oct '96 / Discovery / Koch / Wellard

Hariharan, A.

DIVINE UNION
CD ____ **NRCD 0068**
Navras / Feb '97 / New Note/Pinnacle

Harket, Morten

WILD SEED
CD ____ **9362459122**
Warner Bros. / Sep '95 / Warner Music

Harlan Cage

HARLAN CAGE
CD ____ **19965**
MTM / Oct '96 / Cargo

Harle, John

SHADOW OF THE DUKE, THE
CD ____ **CDC 754 298 2**
Blue Note / Sep '90 / EMI

TERROR AND MAGNIFICENCE
Mistress mine / Three ravens / Hunting the hare / Rosie-blood / Terror and magnificence
CD ____ **4526052**
Argo / Oct '96 / PolyGram

Harlem Gospel Singers

HARLEM GOSPEL SINGERS
CD ____ **0028702**
Edel / Apr '95 / Pinnacle

Harlem Hamfats

HAMFAT SWING 1936-1938
CD ____ **158932**
Blues Collection / Apr '97 / Discovery

HARLEM HAMFATS VOL.1 1936
CD ____ **DOCD 5271**
Document / Aug '94 / ADA / Hot Shot / Jazz Music

HARLEM HAMFATS VOL.2 1936-1937
CD ____ **DOCD 5272**
Document / Aug '94 / ADA / Hot Shot / Jazz Music

HARLEM HAMFATS VOL.3 1936-1938
CD ____ **DOCD 5273**
Document / Aug '94 / ADA / Hot Shot / Jazz Music

HARLEM HAMFATS VOL.4 1938-1939
CD ____ **DOCD 5274**
Document / Aug '94 / ADA / Hot Shot / Jazz Music

Harlem Jazz Camels

BLUE INTERLUDE
CD ____ **NCD 8851**
Phontastic / Nov '96 / Cadillac / Jazz Music / Wellard

DROP ME OFF IN HARLEM
CD ____ **NCD 8832**
Phontastic / Mar '94 / Cadillac / Jazz Music / Wellard

Harlem Spirit

FUSION
CD ____ **FUCD 001**
Fusion / May '97 / Jet Star

Harlem Underground

HARLEM UNDERGROUND
Cheeba cheeba / Fed up / Finger in it / Ain't no sunshine / Fed up
CD ____ **HUBCD 5**
Hubbub / Feb '96 / Beechwood/BMG / SRD / Timewarp

Harley, Steve

BEST YEARS OF OUR LIVES (Harley, Steve & Cockney Rebel)
Introducing 'The Best Years' / Mad mad moonlight / Mr. Raffles (man it was mean) / It wasn't me / Panorama / Make me smile (come up and see me) / Back to the farm / 49th parallel / Best years of our lives / Another journey / Sebastian
CD ____ **CZ 385**
EMI / Feb '91 / EMI

LIVE AND UNLEASHED (Harley, Steve & Cockney Rebel)
Make me smile (come up and see me) / Mr. Soft / Mr. Raffles (man it was mean) / When I'm with you / Star for a week / Riding the waves / Lighthouse / Best years of our lives / Psychomodo / Sling it / Sebastian / Love's a prima donna
CD ____ **QED 134**
Tring / Nov '96 / Tring

MAKE ME SMILE (The Best Of Steve Harley & Cockney Rebel - 2CD Set) (Harley, Steve & Cockney Rebel)
Mr. Soft / Riding the waves (for Virginia Woolf) / Irresistible / Mr. Raffles (man it was mean) / Freedom's prisoner / Hideaway / Judy Teen / Best years of our lives (live) / Make me smile (come up and see me) / If this is love (give me more) / Here comes the sun / Sebastian / Roll the dice / Understand / I believe (love's a prima donna) / Tumbling down
CD Set ____ **CDGO 2036**
EMI / Jan '97 / EMI

MAKE ME SMILE (Live 1989)
Dancing on the telephone / Mr. Soft / When I'm with you / Star for a week / Riding the waves (for Virginia Woolf) / Lighthouse / Best years of our lives / Sweet dreams / Pychomodo / Swing it / Sebastian / Make me smile (come up and see me) / Love's a prima Donna
CD ____ **MDCD 5**
Magnum Music / May '94 / TKO Magnum

POETIC JUSTICE
That's my life / What becomes of the broken hearted / Two damn'd lies / Loveless / Strange communications / All in a life's work / Love minus zero-no limit / Safe / Last time I saw you / Crazy love / Riding the waves
CD ____ **TRACD 242**
Transatlantic / Aug '96 / Pinnacle

STEVE HARLEY
CD ____ **GFS 072**
Going For A Song / Jul '97 / Else / TKO Magnum

STEVE HARLEY AND COCKNEY REBEL
Make me smile (come up and see me) / Sebastian / Mr. Raffles (man it was mean) / Love's a prima donna / Mr. Soft / Best years of our lives / Sweet dreams / When I'm with you / Star for a week / Riding the waves (for Virginia Woolf) / Psychomodo / Lighthouse / Sling it
CD ____ **EXP 017**
Experience / May '97 / TKO Magnum

YES YOU CAN
CD ____ **08431802**
CTE / Dec '95 / Koch

Harman, James

BLACK AND WHITE
CD ____ **BT 1118CD**
Black Top / Aug '95 / ADA / CM / Direct

CARDS ON THE TABLE (Harman, James Band)
CD ____ **BT 1104CD**
Black Top / Jul '94 / ADA / CM / Direct

ICEPICK'S STORY
Dirt road / Stranger blues / Leavin' for Memphis / Three way party / Got news / Drive-in life / Hollywood girls / Temporary blues / Phonebill blues / Sparks (start flyin') / Tall skinny Mama (Icepick's story) / Second voyage of Noah's ark / Walk the streets (cold and lonely) / I'm gone
CD ____ **MMBCD 702**
Me & My Blues / May '97 / CM / Direct

TWO SIDES TO EVERY STORY (Harman, James Band)
CD ____ **BT 1091CD**
Topic / Jul '93 / ADA / CM / Direct

Harmar, Jeff

BECAUSE OF YOU
CD ____ **VDS 5831**
Varese Sarabande / Jul '97 / Pinnacle

Harmful

HARMFUL
CD ____ **EFA 127902**
Blu Noise / Dec '95 / SRD

Harmonia

EVENTS LINE
CD ____ **1295700862**
Materiali Sonori / Jan '97 / Cargo / Greyhound / New Note/Pinnacle

Harmonizing Four

1950-1955
CD ____ **HTCD 29**
Heritage / May '95 / ADA / Direct / Hot Shot / Jazz Music / Swift / Wellard

I SHALL NOT BE MOVED
All things are possible / Farther along / Motherless child / Where would I go / But to the Lord / I shall not be moved / Lived and he loved me / His eye is on the sparrow / When I've done my best / Go down / Moses / Will he welcome me / I love to call his name / Pass me not / Close to thee / God will take care of you / Mary don't you weep / Faith of our fathers / My Lord what a morning / Live like Jesus / Lord's prayer
CD ________ CPCD 8112
Charly / Jul '95 / Koch

Harmony Rockets

PARALYZED MIND OF THE ARCHANGEL
CD ________ ABB 90CD
Big Cat / Oct '95 / 3mv/Pinnacle

Harp, Everette

WHAT'S GOING ON
What's going on / What's happening brother / Flying high / Save the children / God is love / Mercy mercy me / Right on / Wholy holy / Inner city blues / Inner city (reprise)
CD ________ CDP 8530682
Blue Note / Mar '97 / EMI

Harper Brothers

HARPER BROTHERS, THE
Mogie / Elocin / Haitian march / Easy to love / Sonny boy / Pentagram / Portrait of Jennie / Real boys / Quiet as it's kept
CD ________ 8370332
Verve / Mar '93 / PolyGram

YOU CAN HIDE INSIDE THE MUSIC
Segment / She's got the blues for sale / 'Round midnight / For my children Quamara and Scott / Since I fell for you / Kahlil / I wish I knew / I ain't got nothin' but the blues / You can hide inside the music / That's the question / PS I love you / H D H Jr (Big Brother)
CD ________ 5118202
Verve / Jan '93 / PolyGram

Harper, Ben

FIGHT FOR YOUR MIND
Opression / Ground on down / Another lonely day / Please me like you want to / Gold to me / Burn one down / Excuse me Mr / People lead / Fight for your mind / Give a man a home / By my side / Power of the gospel / God fearing man / One road to freedom
CD ________ CDVUS 93
Virgin / Jul '95 / EMI

WELCOME TO THE CRUEL WORLD
CD ________ CDVUS 69
Virgin / Jul '94 / EMI

WILL TO LIVE, THE
Faded / Homeless child / Number three / Roses from my friends / Jah work / I want to be ready / Will to live / Ashes / Widow of a living man / Glory and consequence / Mama's trippin' / I shall not walk alone
CD ________ CDVUS 128
Virgin / May '97 / EMI

Harper, Billy

BILLY HARPER QUINTET ON TOUR VOL.3
CD ________ SCCD 31366
Steeplechase / Feb '96 / Discovery / Impetus

SOMALIA
Somalia / Thy will be done / Quest / Light within / Quest in 3
CD ________ ECD 221332
Evidence / Dec '95 / ADA / Cadillac / Harmonia Mundi

Harper, Don

SYDNEY SUNDAY
St. Thomas / Polka dots and moonbeams / Honeysuckle Rose / Falling in love with love / Greensleeves / Sydney Sunday / Afternoon in the art gallery / Sunday morning / Them there eyes / Air on a G string / Softly as in a morning sunrise
CD ________ CLGCD 024
Calligraph / Jun '92 / Cadillac / Jazz Music / New Note/Pinnacle / Wellard

Harper, Nick

LIGHT AT THE END OF THE KENNEL
Hundred things / Is this really me / Shadowlands / Flying dog / Headless / Riverside
CD ________ SG 094CD
Sangraal / Dec '94 / ADA / Grapevine/ PolyGram
CD ________ TERRCD 003
Terra Nova / Nov '96 / Direct

SEED
CD ________ SRCD 095
Sangraal / Jun '96 / ADA / Grapevine/ PolyGram

Harper, Roy

BORN IN CAPTIVITY/WORK OF HEART
Stan / Drawn to the flames / Come to bed eyes / No woman is safe / I am a child / Elizabeth / No one ever gets out alive / Two lovers in the moon / We are the people / All of us children / We are the people (reprise)
CD ________ HUCD 008
Science Friction / Jan '97 / Pinnacle

BULLINAMINGVASE
CD ________ HUCD 021
Science Friction / Nov '96 / Pinnacle

BURN THE WORLD
CD ________ HUCD 013
Science Friction / Mar '97 / Pinnacle

COME OUT FIGHTING GHENGIS SMITH
Freak street / You don't need money / Ageing raver / In a beautiful rambling mess / All you need is what you have / Circle / Highgate cemetary / Come out fighting Ghengis Smith / Zaney Janey / Ballad of songwriter / Midspring dithering / Zenjam / It's tomorrow and today is yesterday / Francesca / She's the one
CD ________ HUCD 006
Science Friction / Jan '97 / Pinnacle

COMMERCIAL BREAKS
My little girl / I'm in love with you / Ten years ago / Sail away / I wanna be part of the news / Cora / Come up and see me / Fly catcher / Too many movies / Square boxes / Burn the world (part 1) / Playing prisons
CD ________ HUCD 016
Science Friction / Jan '97 / Pinnacle

DEATH OR GLORY
Death or glory / War came home / Tonight duty / Waiting for Godot / Part zed next to me / Man kind / Tallest tree / Miles remains / Fourth world / Why / Cardboard city / One more tomorrow / Plough / On summer day / If I can
CD ________ HUCD 012
Science Friction / Oct '96 / Pinnacle

FLASHES FROM THE ARCHIVES OF OBLIVION
Commune / Don't you grieve / Twelve hours of sunset / Kangaroo blues / All Ireland / Me and my woman / South Africa / Highway blues / One man rock 'n' roll band / Another day / MCP blues
CD ________ HUCD 010
Science Friction / Jan '97 / Pinnacle

FLAT, BAROQUE AND BERSERK
Don't you grieve / I hate the white man / Feeling all the Saturday / How does it feel / Goodbye / Another day / Davey / East of the sun and west of the moon / Tom Tiddler's ground / Francesca / Song of the ages / Hell's angels
CD ________ HUCD 3
Science Friction / Oct '94 / Pinnacle

FOLKJOKEOPUS
Sgt. Sunshine / She's the one / In the time of water / Composer of life / One for all / Exercising some / Control / McGoohan's blues / Manana
CD ________ HUCD 009
Science Friction / Jan '97 / Pinnacle

GARDEN OF URANIUM (Descendants Of Smith)
Laughing inside / Garden of uranium / Still life / Pinches of salt / Desert island / Government surplus / Surplus liquorice / Liquorice alltime / Maile Lei / Same shoes / Descendants of Smith / Laughing inside (Demo version)
CD ________ HUCD 014
Science Friction / Mar '97 / Pinnacle

HQ
Game (parts I-V) / Game / Spirit lives / Grown ups are just silly children / Referendum / Forget me not / Hallucinating light / When an old cricketer leaves the crease
CD ________ HUCD 019
Science Friction / Apr '97 / Pinnacle

IN BETWEEN EVERY LINE
One of those days in England / Short and sweet / Referendum / Highway blues / True story / Game / One man rock 'n' roll band / Hangman
CD ________ HUCD 018
Science Friction / Mar '97 / Pinnacle

INTERVIEW DISC VOL.1
CD ________ HUCD 099A
Science Friction / Feb '97 / Pinnacle

INTERVIEW DISC VOL.2
CD ________ HUCD 099B
Science Friction / Mar '97 / Pinnacle

INTERVIEW DISC VOL.3
CD ________ HUCD 099C
Science Friction / Mar '97 / Pinnacle

INTRODUCTION TO ROY HARPER, AN
Legend / She's the one / Tom tiddler's ground / Highway blues / Che / Hallucinating light / One of those days in England / You / Nineteen forty-eightish / Pinches of salt / Ghost dance / Tallest tree / Miles remains
CD ________ HUCD 017
Science Friction / Oct '96 / Pinnacle

LEGEND
CD ________ JHD 064CD
JHD / Oct '94 / ADA

LIFEMASK
Highway blues / All Ireland / Little lady / Bank of the dead / South Africa / Lord's prayer / Ballad of songwriter / Zaney Janey / Midspring dithering / Zenjam
CD ________ HUCD 005
Science Friction / Jan '97 / Pinnacle

LIVE AT LES COUSINS 1969
CD ________ BP 220CD
Blueprint / May '96 / Pinnacle

LIVE AT THE BBC VOL.1
Hey Francesca / Hell's angels / She's the one / I hate the white man / It's today and today is yesterday / Don't you grieve / North country girl / Hors d'oeuvres / One man rock 'n' roll band / Same old rock / South Africa / Kangeroo blues / Forever / Twelve hours of sunset / Little lady / All Ireland
CD ________ HUCD 022
Science Friction / Apr '97 / Pinnacle

LIVE AT THE BBC VOL.2
Too many movies / MCP Blues / Forever / South Africa / Highway blues / I'll see you again / Commune / Another day / North country / Twelve hours of sunset / Me and my woman
CD ________ HUCD 023
Science Friction / Apr '97 / Pinnacle

LIVE AT THE BBC VOL.3 (John Peel/ Bob Harris)
Commune / Forever / Highway blues / I'll see you again / North country / Too many movies / Forever / North country / Twelve hours of sunset / One man rock 'n' roll band / Too many movies
CD ________ HUCD 024
Science Friction / Jun '97 / Pinnacle

LIVE AT THE BBC VOL.4
Hallucinating light / Referendum / Highway blues / Too many movies / Spirit lives / Home / Game / Grown ups are just silly children
CD ________ HUCD 025
Science Friction / Jun '97 / Pinnacle

LIVE AT THE BBC VOL.5
Hallucinating light / Spirit lives / Referendum / Another day / Cherishing the lonesome / These last days / Grown ups are just silly children / Forget me not / Same old rock / I hate the white man
CD ________ HUCD 026
Science Friction / Jul '97 / Pinnacle

LIVE AT THE BBC VOL.6
Forget me not / One of those days in England / I hate the white man / Same old rock / Twelve hours of sunset / Highway blues
CD ________ HUCD 027
Science Friction / Jul '97 / Pinnacle

LOONY ON THE BUS
No change / Playing prisons / I wanna be part of the news / Burn the world / Casualty / Cora / Loony on the bus / Come up and see me / Flycatcher / Square boxes
CD ________ AWCD 1011
Awareness / Nov '88 / ADA

ONCE
Once / Once in the middle of nowhere / Nowhere to run to / Black cloud of Islam / If / Winds of change / Berliners / Sleeping at the wheel / For longer than it takes / Ghost dance
CD ________ HUCD 011
Science Friction / Mar '97 / Pinnacle

SOPHISTICATED BEGGAR
Goldfish bowl / Sophisticated beggar / Big fat silver aeroplane / Legend / Girlie / October 12th / Black clouds / Mr. Station Master / My friend / China girl
CD ________ HUCD 007
Science Friction / Jan '97 / Pinnacle

STORMCOCK
Hors d'oeuvres / One man rock 'n' roll band / Same old rock / Me and my woman
CD ________ HUCD 004
Science Friction / Apr '97 / Pinnacle

UNHINGED
Descendants of Smith / Legend / North Country / When an old cricketer leaves the crease / Three hundred words / Hope / Naked flame / Commune / South Africa / Back to the stones / Frozen moment / Highway blues / Same old rock
CD ________ HUCD 020
Science Friction / Mar '97 / Pinnacle

VALENTINE
Forbidden fruit / Male chauvinist pig blues / I'll see you again / Twelve hours of sunset / Acapulco gold / Commune / Magic woman / Che / North country / Forever / Home (studio) / Too many movies / Home
CD ________ HUCD 015
Science Friction / Jan '97 / Pinnacle

WHATEVER HAPPENED TO JUGULA (Harper, Roy & Jimmy Page)
Nineteen forty-eightish / Hangman / Elizabeth / Advertisement / Bad speech / Hope / Twentieth century man
CD ________ BBL 60 CD
Lowdown/Beggars Banquet / Aug '88 / RTM/Disc / Warner Music

Harper, Winard

BE YOURSELF
Night watch / Li'l Willie / My shell / Trane stop / Last dance / Hi fly / Quiet as it's kept / Lonesome head / You're looking at me / Toku-do / Poon
CD ________ 4781972
Epicure / Feb '95 / Sony

Harpo, Slim

BEST OF SLIM HARPO, THE
Baby scratch my back / Got love if you want it / I'm a king bee / Little queen bee (got a brand new king) / Shake your hips / Te-ni-nee-ni-nu / Buzz me baby / Buzzin' / Raining in my heart / Still rainin' in my heart / Late last night / Tip on in, Part 1 / Bobby sox baby / Don't start cryin' now / I need money (keep your alibis) / Strange love / Rock me baby / Blues hangover
CD ________ CDCHM 410
Ace / Jul '92 / Pinnacle

I'M A KING BEE
I'm a king bee / I love the life I'm livin' / Moody blues / Buzzin' / Dream girl / Got love if you want it / Wonderin' and worryin' / Strange love / You'll be sorry one day / One more day / Bobby sox baby / Late last night / Buzz me baby / Yeah yeah baby / What a dream / Don't start cryin' now / Blues hangover / My home is a prison / Please don't turn me down / Snoopin' around / raining in my heart / That's alright baby / Lover's confession / Boogie chillun
CD ________ CDCHD 510
Ace / Oct '93 / Pinnacle

RAININ' IN MY HEART
Raining in my heart / Blues hangover / Bobby sox baby / Got love if you want it / Snoopin' around / Buzz me baby / I'm a King Bee / What a dream / Don't start cryin' now / Moody blues / My home is a prison / Dream girl / Wonderin' and worryin' / Strange love / You'll be sorry one day / One more day / Late last night / Still rainin' in my heart
CD ________ ELDIABLO 8037
El Diablo / Mar '94 / Vital

SHAKE YOUR HIPS
Shake your hips / Little queen bee (got a brand new king) / Still rainin' in my heart / I need money (keep your alibis) / What's goin' on baby / Harpo's blues / Sittin' here wonderin' / We're two of a kind / I'm gonna miss you (like the devil) / Baby scratch my back / I don't want no-one (to take me away from you) / Midnight blues / Lovin' you (the way I do) / Baby you got what I want / Your love for me is gone / I'm your bread maker, baby / Stop working blues / I'm waiting on you baby / You'll never find a love as true as mine / Little Sally Walker / I gotta stop lovin' you / Blueberry Hill / Something inside of me / Tonite I'm lonely / Man is crying / Still rainin' in my heart
CD ________ CDCHD 558
Ace / Mar '95 / Pinnacle

TIP ON IN
Tip on in (part 1) / Tip on in (part 2) / I'm gonna keep what I've got / I've got to be with you tonight / Mailbox blues / Te-ni-nee-ni-nu / Mohair Sam / I just can't leave you / That's why I love you / Just for you / My baby she's got it / I've been your good thing for you / Hey little Lee / Stick your chest out baby / Folsom prison blues / Mutual friend / I've got my finger on your trigger / Price is too high / Jody man / Music's hot / You can't make it / Hippy song / Dynamite / Rock me baby / Baby please come home
CD ________ CDCHD 606
Ace / Jun '96 / Pinnacle

Harpy

HARPY
CD ________ EFA 084772
Dossier / Apr '97 / Cargo / SRD

Harrell, Tom

FORM
Vista / Brazilian song / Scene / January spring / Rhythm form / For heaven's sake
CD ________ CCD 14059
Contemporary / Oct '93 / Cadillac / Complete/Pinnacle / Jazz Music / Wellard

LABYRINTH
Samba mate / Marimba song / Cheetah / Blue in one / Hot licks on the sidewalk / Majesty / Sun cycle / Darn that dream / Bear that in mind / Labyrinth
CD ________ 09026685122
RCA Victor / Oct '96 / BMG

SAIL AWAY
Eons / Glass mystery / Dream in June / Sail away / Buffalo wings / It always is / Dancing trees / Hope Street
CD ________ CCD 14054
Contemporary / Oct '93 / Cadillac / Complete/Pinnacle / Jazz Music / Wellard

STORIES
Rapture / Song flower / Mountain / Waters edge / Story / Viable blues / Touchstone
CD ________ CCD 14043

Contemporary / Oct '93 / Cadillac / Complete/Pinnacle / Jazz Music / Wellard

Harries, Mike

DR. ROOTS GUMBO KINGS
CD _______________ CJC 008CD
CJC / Apr '94 / Jazz Music

Harriet

WOMAN TO MAN
Temple of love / Magic bed / Takes a little time / Only the lonely/Good girl / Woman to man / Fool am I / Wish
CD _______________ 9031721102
WEA / Oct '90 / Warner Music

Harrington, Gerry

SCEAL EILE (Harrington, Gerry & Eoin O'Sullivan)
CD _______________ LUN 059CD
Mulligan / Jan '94 / ADA / CM

Harrington, Jan

MY GOD IS REAL
CD _______________ MECCACD 1042
Music Mecca / Feb '94 / Cadillac / Jazz Music / Wellard

Harrington, Tim

MASTER FREQUENCY
CD _______________ TX 51217CD
Triple X / Mar '96 / Plastic Head

Harriott, Derrick

16 ROCKSTEADY HITS
CD _______________ JMC 200214
Jamaican Gold / Jul '94 / Grapevine/PolyGram / Jet Star

DANCEHALL TRAIN
CD _______________ CRCD 1016
Crystal / Mar '97 / Jet Star

DONKEY YEARS, THE
CD _______________ JMC 20012
Jamaican Gold / Apr '94 / Grapevine/PolyGram / Jet Star

RIDING THE MUSICAL CHARIOT
CD _______________ CDHB 58
Heartbeat / May '93 / ADA / Direct / Greensleeves / Jet Star

SINGS ROCKSTEADY
CD _______________ JMC 200213
Jamaican Gold / May '94 / Grapevine/PolyGram / Jet Star

SONGS FOR MIDNIGHT LOVERS
Eighteen with a bullet / Born to love you / Message from a black man / Groovy situation / Loser
CD _______________ CDTRL 198
Trojan / May '90 / Direct / Jet Star

Harris, Anita

EVERY DAY VALENTINE
Look of love / This girl's in love with you / Always something there to remind me / 24 hours from Tulsa / Whoever you are / I just don't know what to do with myself / I say a little prayer / House is not a home / Anyone who had a heart / Wives and lovers / Wishin' and hopin' / My Japanese boy / What the world needs now is love / Alfie / Walk on by / Make it easy on yourself / I'll never fall in love again / Long after tonight is over / River deep mountain high / You've lost that lovin' feelin' / Loving you / Just loving you / Anniversary waltz
CD _______________ 4841052
Columbia / May '96 / Sony

Harris, Barry

CONFIRMATION (Harris, Barry & Kenny Barron Quartet)
Confirmation / On Green Dolphin Street / Tenderly / Embraceable you / All God's chillun' got rhythm / Body and soul / East of the sun / Oleo / Nascimento
CD _______________ CCD 79519
Black & Blue / Jan '97 / Discovery / Koch / Wellard

LIVE AT DUG 1995
Luminescence / Somebody loves me / No name blues / Oblivion / It could happen to you / Cherokee / On Green Dolphin Street / I got rhythm / East of the sun / Nascimento
CD _______________ ENJACD 90972
Enja / Oct '96 / New Note/Pinnacle / Vital/SAM

LIVE AT MAYBECK RECITAL HALL VOL.12
It could happen to you / All God's chillun got rhythm / I'll keep loving you / She / Cherokee / Gone again / Lucky day / It never entered my mind / Meet the flintstones / I love Lucy / Parker's mood / Would you like to take a walk
CD _______________ CCD 4476
Concord Jazz / Aug '91 / New Note/Pinnacle

Harris, Beaver

BEAUTIFUL AFRICA
CD _______________ 1210022
Soul Note / May '92 / Cadillac / Harmonia Mundi / Wellard

Harris, Bill

FUNKY SITAR MAN (Harris, Bill 'Ravi' & The Prophets)
Path of the blazing sarong / Gimme some more/Hot pants / Soul makossa / I dream of Jeannie / Ravi's thing / Cissy strut / Look-a-py-py / Lost dragon of the Sahara / Pass the peas/Sex machine / Funky sitar man / Same beat
CD _______________ BBECD 002
Barely Breaking Even / Mar '97 / Beechwood/BMG

Harris, Corey

BETWEEN MIDNIGHT AND DAY
CD _______________ ALCD 4837
Alligator / Nov '95 / ADA / CM / Direct

FISH AIN'T BITING
High fever blues / Frankie and Johnny / Berry Owens' blues / Take me back / Fish ain't biting / Preaching blues / Bumble bee blues / God don't ever change / 5-0 blues / Mama got worried / Worried life blues / High fever blues / Jack O'Diamonds / If you leave me / Moosemilk blues / You got to move / Clean rag
CD _______________ ALCD 4580
Alligator / May '97 / ADA / CM / Direct

Harris, Craig

BLACKOUT IN THE SQUARE ROOT OF SOUL (Harris, Craig & Tailgater's Tales)
Blackout in the square root of soul (phase 1 and 2) / Generations / Free 1 / Love joy / Blue dues / Dingo / Awakening ancestors
CD _______________ 8344152
jMT / May '91 / PolyGram

Harris, Eddie

BEST OF EDDIE HARRIS, THE
Shadow of your smile / Freedom jazz dance / Sham time / Theme in search of a movie / Listen here / Live right now / 1974 Blues / Movin' on out / Boogie woogie / Bosa nova / Child is born / Is it in
CD _______________ 7567813702
Atlantic / Jun '93 / Warner Music

DANCING BY A RAINBOW
CD _______________ ENJACD 90812
Enja / Oct '95 / New Note/Pinnacle / Vital/SAM

EDDIE HARRIS ANTHOLOGY, THE
Exodus / Listen here / Cold duck time / Shadow of your smile / Theme in search of a movie / Sham time / Boogie woogie bosa nova / Is it in / Get on down / Funkaroma / It's alright now / 1974 Blues / Live right now / Freedom jazz dance / Yeah yeah yeah / Hey wado / Free speech / Cryin' blues / Giant steps / Without you / Mean greens / Recess / Steps up / Love for sale
CD _______________ 8122715142
Atlantic / Mar '94 / Warner Music

LAST CONCERT, THE
Sidewinder / Moanin' / Wade in the water / Freedom jazz dance / Work song / When a man loves a woman / Gimme some lovin' / You stole my heart
CD _______________ 92492
Act / Mar '97 / New Note/Pinnacle

LISTEN HERE
Funkaroma / I need some money / Listen here / People get funny when they get a little money / Is it in / How can I find some way to show you / Walkin' the walk / Fusion jazz dance
CD _______________ ENJACD 70792
Enja / Jun '93 / New Note/Pinnacle / Vital/SAM

LISTEN HERE (2CD Set)
I love you / Body and soul / God bless the child / Love for sale / Listen here / Theme in search of a movie / Exodus / Sonnymoon for two / Lover man (Oh, where can you be) / Cherokee / Ballad (for my love) / Three quarter miles / Now's the time / Straight, no chaser
CD Set _______________ R 103611
Live At EJ's / Apr '97 / Target/BMG

LIVE IN BERLIN
CD _______________ CDSJP 289
Timeless Jazz / May '89 / New Note/Pinnacle

SWISS MOVEMENT (Harris, Eddie & Les McCann)
Compared to what / Cold duck time / Kathleen's theme / You got it in your soulness / Generation gap
CD _______________ 7567813652
Atlantic / Apr '94 / Warner Music

YEAH, YOU RIGHT
CD _______________ LAKE 2023
Lakeside / Aug '95 / TKO Magnum

Harris, Emmylou

AT THE RYMAN
Guitar town / Half as much / Cattle call / Guess things happen that way / Hard times / Mansion on the hill / Scotland / Montana cowgirl / Like strangers / Lodi / Calling my children home / If I could be there / Walls of time / Get up John / It's a hard life wherever you go/Abraham, Martin and John / Smoke along the track
CD _______________ 7599266642
Reprise / Feb '95 / Warner Music

BALLAD OF SALLY ROSE
Ballad of Sally Rose / Rhythm guitar / I think I love him / You are my flower heart to heart / Woman walk the line / Bad news / Timberline / Long tall Sally Rose / Whitle line / Diamond in my crown / Sweetheart of the Rodeo / K-S-O-S (Instrumental medly) / Ring of fire / Wildwood flower / Six days on the road / Swing low, sweet chariot
CD _______________ 7599252052
Reprise / Jan '96 / Warner Music

BLUE KENTUCKY GIRL
Sister's coming home / Beneath still waters / Rough and rocky / Hickory wind / Save the last dance for me / Sorrow in the wind / They'll never take his love from me / Every time you leave / Blue Kentucky girl / Even cowgirls get the blues
CD _______________ 7599293922
WEA / Jan '93 / Warner Music

BRAND NEW DANCE
Wheels of love / In his world / Easy for you to stay / Better off without you / Brand new dance / Tougher than the rest / Sweet dreams of you / Rollin' and ramblin' / Never be anyone else but you / Red red rose
CD _______________ 7599263092
WEA / Oct '90 / Warner Music

COWGIRL'S PRAYER
Ways to go / Light / High powered love / You don't know me / Prayer in open D / Crescent city / Lovin' you again / Jerusalem again / Thanks to you / I hear a call / Ballad of a runaway horse
CD _______________ GRA 101CD
Grapevine / Aug '94 / Grapevine/PolyGram

DUETS
Price I pay / Love hurts / Thing about you / That lovin' feelin' again / We believe in happy endings / Star of Bethlehem / All fall down / Wild Montana skies / Green pastures / Gulf Coast highway / If I needed you / Evangeline
CD _______________ 7599257912
WEA / Aug '90 / Warner Music

ELITE HOTEL
Amarillo / Together again / Feeling single / Seeing double / Sin City / One of these days / Till I gain control again / Here, there and everywhere / Ooh Las Vegas / Sweet dreams / Jambalaya / Satan's jewelled crown / Wheels
CD _______________ K 254060
WEA / '88 / Warner Music

LUXURY LINER
Luxury liner / Pancho and Lefty / Making believe / You're supposed to be feeling good / I'll be your San Antone Rose / C'est la vie / When I stop dreaming / Hello stranger / She / Tulsa queen
CD _______________ 9273382
WEA / Jun '89 / Warner Music

PIECES OF THE SKY
Bluebird wine / Too far gone / If I could only win your love / Boulder to Birmingham / Before believing / Tonight the bottle let me down / Sleepless nights / Coat of many colours / For no one / Queen of the silver dollar
CD _______________ 7599272442
WEA / Feb '89 / Warner Music

PORTRAIT (3CD Set)
CD Set _______________ 9362453082
Reprise / Dec '96 / Warner Music

PROFILE: EMMYLOU HARRIS (The Best Of Emmylou Harris)
One of these days / Sweet dreams / To daddy / C'est la vie / Making believe / Easy from now on / Together again / If I could only win your love / Too far gone / Two more bottles of wine / Boulder to Birmingham / Hello stranger / You never can tell
CD _______________ 256570
WEA / Jun '84 / Warner Music

PROFILE: EMMYLOU HARRIS VOL.2 (The Best Of Emmylou Harris)
Blue Kentucky girl / Wayfaring stranger / Beneath still waters / Born to run / Someone like you / Mister Sandman / Pledging my love / I'm moving on / (Lost his love) On our last date / Save the last dance for me
CD _______________ 7599251612
WEA / Feb '94 / Warner Music

QUARTER MOON IN A TEN CENT TOWN
Easy from now on / Two more bottles of wine / To Daddy / My songbird / Leaving Louisiana in the broad daylight / Defying / Gravity / I ain't living long like this / One paper kid / Green rolling hills / Burn that candle
CD _______________ 9273452
WEA / Jun '89 / Warner Music

WHITE SHOES
Drivin' wheel / Pledging my love / In my dreams / White shoes / On the radio / It's only rock 'n' roll / Diamonds are a girl's best friend / Good news / Baby, better start turning 'em down / Like an old fashioned waltz
CD _______________ 7599239612
Reprise / Jan '96 / Warner Music

WRECKING BALL
Where will I be / Goodbye / All my tears / Wrecking ball / Goin' back to Harlan / Deeper well / Every grain of sand / Sweet old world / May this be love / Orphan girl / Blackhawk / Waltz across Texas tonight
CD _______________ GRACD 102
Grapevine / Sep '95 / Grapevine/PolyGram

Harris, Gene

AT LAST (Harris, Gene & Scott Hamilton Quintet)
You are my sunshine / It never entered my mind / After you've gone / Lamp is low / At last / Blues for Gene / I fall in love too easily / Some of these days / Stairway to the stars / Sittin' in the sandtrap
CD _______________ CCD 4434
Concord Jazz / Nov '90 / New Note/Pinnacle

BLACK AND BLUE (Harris, Gene Quartet)
Another star / Black and blue / CC rider / Hot toddy / Best things in life are free / Nobody knows you (when you're down and out) / It might as well be Spring / Blue bossa / Song is you / Will you still be mine
CD _______________ CCD 4482
Concord Jazz / Oct '91 / New Note/Pinnacle

BROTHERHOOD
I remember you / For once in my life / Brotherhood of man / When you wish upon a star / Sidewinder / I told you so / September song / This little light of mine / Beautiful friendship
CD _______________ CCD 4640
Concord Jazz / May '95 / New Note/Pinnacle

FUNKY GENE'S
Blues for Basie / Trouble with hello is goodbye / Old funky Gene's / Everything happens to me / Nice 'n' easy / Ahmad's blues / Bye bye blues / Children of Sanchez / Blues in Hoss's flat
CD _______________ CCD 4609
Concord Jazz / Sep '94 / New Note/Pinnacle

GENE HARRIS & THE PHILIP MORRIS SUPERBAND (Harris, Gene & The Philip Morris Superband)
Surrey with the fringe on top / Creme de menthe / When it's sleepy time down South / Our love is here to stay / I'm just a lucky so and so / Serious grease / Like a lover / Ol' man river / Do you know what it means to miss New Orleans / Porgy and Bess (medley) / You're my everything / There is no greater love / Things ain't what they used to be
CD _______________ CCD 4397
Concord Jazz / Nov '89 / New Note/Pinnacle

GENE HARRIS TRIO PLUS ONE, THE
Gene's lament / Uptown sop / Things ain't what they used to be / Yours is my heart alone / Battle hymn of the Republic
CD _______________ CCD 4303
Concord Jazz / Sep '90 / New Note/Pinnacle

IN HIS HANDS
Lean on me / Battle hymn of the republic / Will the circle be unbroken / Everyhting must change / Amazing grace / Lord I've tried / (Jesus keeps me) Near the cross / This little light of mine / Operator / His eye is on the sparrow / (He's got the) whole world in his hands / Granpa's hands
CD _______________ CCD 475582
Concord Jazz / Jun '97 / New Note/Pinnacle

IT'S THE REAL SOUL
Summertime / You don't know me / Oh lady be good / Straight, no chaser / Manage a bleu / My funny valentine / Estoril soul / That's all
CD _______________ CCD 4692
Concord Jazz / May '96 / New Note/Pinnacle

LIKE A LOVER (Harris, Gene Quartet)
Like a lover / Misterioso / Strollin' / Until the real thing comes along / Jeannie / I can't stop loving you / You make me feel so young / Oh, look at me now / Wrap your troubles in dreams (and dream your troubles away)
CD _______________ CCD 4526
Concord Jazz / Oct '92 / New Note/Pinnacle

LISTEN HERE (Harris, Gene Quartet)
His masquerade / I've got a feeling I'm falling in love / Blues for Jezebel / Lullaby / This can't be love / Don't be that way / Listen here / Sweet and lovely / Song is ended (but the melody lingers on) / To you
CD _______________ CCD 4385

Concord Jazz / Sep '90 / New Note/ Pinnacle

LITTLE PIECE OF HEAVEN, A (Harris, Gene Quartet)
Blues in baxter's pad / Scotch and soda / Take the 'A' train / My little suede shoes / Blues for ste chapelle / Ma, he's making eyes at me / Pensativa / How long has this been going on / Old dog blues / Ode to Billy Joe / Sentimental journey
CD _______ CCD 4578
Concord Jazz / Nov '93 / New Note/ Pinnacle

LIVE AT THE IT CLUB
Funku pullett / I'm still sad / On Green Dolphin Street / Baby man / Love for sale / Sittin' duck / Tammy's breeze / John Brown's body
CD _______ CDP 8353382
Blue Note / Mar '96 / EMI

TRIBUTE TO COUNT BASIE (Harris, Gene All Star Big Band)
Captain Bill / Night mist blues / Swingin' the blues / When did you leave Heaven / Blue and sentimental / Riled up / (I'm afraid) the masquerade is over / Dejection blues
CD _______ CCD 4337
Concord Jazz / May '88 / New Note/ Pinnacle

WORLD TOUR 1990 (Harris, Gene & The Philip Morris Superband)
Airmail special / Lonely bottles / Child is born / Buhaina Buhaina / Don't get around much anymore / Lover / In the wee small hours of the morning / Tricrotism / Centerpiece / Dear blues / Nica's dream / Girl talk / Battle royal / Warm valley
CD _______ CCD 4443
Concord Jazz / Feb '91 / New Note/ Pinnacle

Harris, Greg

ELECTRIC
CD _______ APCD 024
Appaloosa / Jun '94 / ADA / Direct / TKO Magnum

ELECTRO-ACUSTIC
CD _______ APCD 125
Appaloosa / Mar '97 / ADA / Direct / TKO Magnum

THINGS CHANGE
CD _______ APCD 047
Appaloosa / '92 / ADA / Direct / TKO Magnum

Harris, Jerome

IN PASSING
CD _______ MCD 5386
Muse / Sep '92 / New Note/Pinnacle

Harris, Jet

ANNIVERSARY ALBUM : JET HARRIS
CD _______ CDMM 1038
Q / '88 / BMG / Pinnacle

BEYOND A SHADOW OF A DOUBT (Harris, Jet & Alan Jones/Tangent)
Beyond a shadow of a doubt / Sometimes / Thunderhawk / Uncharted island / Theme for a new day / Foot tappin' / Stormin' Norman (parts 1, 2 & 3) / Jet meets General Custer / El warthog / Twilight shadows / New world / Truckin' truckers trot / Theme from a big film / Lads / Everyone for tennis / Moonlight miraval / Wonderful landscapes / Tandoorie boogie / Sleepless walk at midnight / Khan
CD _______ TANCD 002
Tangent / Nov '96 / Pinnacle

LIVE OVER ENGLAND (Harris, Jet & Tangent)
CD _______ ZRCD 1212
Beat Goes On / Dec '96 / Pinnacle

STUDIO SESSIONS (Harris, Jet & Tangent)
Warm turn (part 1) / Stingray / FBI / Jet meets General Custer '94 / Walk don't run / Diamonds / Love me tender / Tres bon / Truckin' truckers trot / Apache / Danny boy / Warm turn (part 2)
CD _______ TANCD 003
Tangent / Nov '96 / Pinnacle

TRIBUTES AND RARITIES (Harris, Jet & Alan Jones/Tangent)
Riders in the sky / Clifton lights / It's a dog's life / Apache / Theme for a new day / Crockett's theme / Stingray / Sleepless walk at midnight / Stratosfear / Warm turn / Lady in red / Equinox V / Elmer's theme
CD _______ TANCD 004
Tangent / Nov '96 / Pinnacle

Harris, Kim

IN THE HEAT OF THE SUMMER (Harris, Kim & Reggie)
CD _______ FE 1412
Folk Era / Nov '94 / ADA / CM

Harris, Lafayette Jr.

HAPPY TOGETHER
Happy together / I'm smilin' / In the wee small hours of the morning / Getaway / You've changed / He could be perfect for me / Achern / Solace / Lady sings the blues / Sun is / Where am I / Hat's on blues
CD _______ MCD 5541
Muse / Aug '96 / New Note/Pinnacle

Harris, Larnelle

CHRISTMAS
CD _______ CD 02474
Nelson Word / Dec '88 / Nelson Word

I CAN BEGIN AGAIN
Mighty Spirit
CD _______ CD 02506
Nelson Word / Nov '89 / Nelson Word

Harris, M.J.

M.J. HARRIS/BILL LASWELL (Harris, M.J. & Bill Laswell)
CD _______ SNT 2080
Sentrax Corporation / Oct '95 / Plastic Head

MURDER BALLADS (Harris, M.J. & Martyn Bates)
CD _______ EEE 36
Musica Maxima Magnetica / Mar '97 / Cargo / Plastic Head

Harris, Marion

VOL.4 1922-1933
Dixie highway / Carolina in the morning / Homesick / Hot lips / Aggravatin' papa / Who cares / Mississippi choo-choo / I gave you up just before you threw me down / Rose of the rio grande / St. Louis blues / I ain't got nobody / Running wild / You've got to see mama ev'ry night / Dearest / Beside a babbling brook / Two time Dan / That red-head gal / Who's sorry now
CD _______ NEO 957
Neovox / Mar '94 / Wellard

Harris, Michael

WIDOR TRADITION, THE (French Organ Music From Canterbury Cathedral)
Marche Pontificale / Suite bretonne / Berceuse / Fileuse / Les cloches de perros-guirec / Suite Francaise / Variations sur un Noel Angevin / Variations sur un theme de Clement Jannequin / Prelude et Danse Fuguee
CD _______ YORK CD 112
York Ambisonic / Oct '91 / Complete/ Pinnacle

Harris, Michael

DEFENSE MECHANIZMS
CD _______ BD 051CD
Black Dragon / Dec '91 / Else

Harris, Mick

OVERLOAD LADY
CD _______ SR 124CD
Sub Rosa / Apr '97 / Direct / RTM/Disc / SRD / Vital

Harris, Phil

THING ABOUT PHIL HARRIS, THE (The Voice Of Baloo The Bear 1931-1950)
Between the devil and the deep blue sea / Brother can you spare a dime / Buds won't bud / Darktown poker club / Darktown strutters ball / How's about it: *Harris, Phil & Leah Ray* / I got the ritz about the one I love / I wanna be a brat / Jelly bean / My kind of country / Now you've got me doing it / Old man of the mountain / One-zy two-zy / Pink elephants / River stay 'way from my door / Rose room / Some little bug / That's what I like about the South / Thing / What have we got to lose / What's the matter with Dixie / You can tell she comes from Dixie
CD _______ CDAJA 5191
Living Era / Mar '96 / Select

Harris, R.H.

SHINE ON ME (Harris, R.H. & The Soul Stirrers)
By and by / I'm still living on mother's prayer / Feel like my time ain't long / Today / I have a right to the tree of life / In that awful hour / Jesus hits like the atom bomb / Shine on me / Faith and grace / Everybody ought to love their soul / Blessed by the name of the Lord / My loved ones are waiting for me (waiting and watching) / How long / Who'll be the one / Lord's my shepherd / Christ is all / By and by Pts. 1 - 3
CD _______ CDCHD 415
Ace / Nov '93 / Pinnacle

Harris, Rhonda

RHONDA HARRIS
CD _______ RAIN 014CD
Cloudland / Nov '95 / Plastic Head / SRD

Harris, Richard

MACARTHUR PARK
CD _______ HMNCD 002
Half Moon / Jun '97 / BMG

WEBB SESSIONS 1968-1969, THE
CD _______ RVCD 52
Raven / Mar '96 / ADA / Direct

Harris, Rolf

ANIMAL MAGIC
Tie me kangaroo down sport / Maximillian mouse / Mud mud / Cat came back / Three blind mice / How much is that doggie in the window / Tit willow / Bid dog / Clock of life / Groundhog song / Six white boomers / Persian pussy cat / Wild rover / Sheepman / Kangaroo catchers / Bull dust / Dry country / Leafy Gully's shade
CD _______ CDMFP 6277
Music For Pleasure / Nov '96 / EMI

DIDGEREELY-DOO ALL THAT (The Best Of Rolf Harris)
Tie me kangaroo down sport / Sun arise / I've lost my Mummy / Carra barra wirra canna / Nick Teen and Al KHall / Maximillian mouse / Court of King Caractacus / Six white boomers / Jake the peg / Bid dog / Fijian girl / Hurry home / Two little boys / Jindabyne / She'll be right / Come and see my land (Jimmy my boy) / Lazy day / Yarrabangee / Northern territorian / Bargin' down the Thames / Pavlova / Raining on the rock / Stairway to heaven
CD _______ CDGO 2062
EMI / May '94 / EMI

Harris, Simon

BEATS, BREAKS AND SCRATCHES VOL.1 & 2
CD Set _______ MOMIX 1/2CD
Music Of Life / '89 / Grapevine/PolyGram

BEATS, BREAKS AND SCRATCHES VOL.10
CD _______ MOLCD 027
Music Of Life / Mar '93 / Grapevine/ PolyGram

BEATS, BREAKS AND SCRATCHES VOL.11
CD _______ MOLCD 31
Music Of Life / Oct '93 / Grapevine/ PolyGram

BEATS, BREAKS AND SCRATCHES VOL.12
CD _______ MOLCD 37
Music Of Life / Sep '95 / Grapevine/ PolyGram

BEATS, BREAKS AND SCRATCHES VOL.3 & 4
CD Set _______ MOMIX 3/4CD
Music Of Life / '89 / Grapevine/PolyGram

BEATS, BREAKS AND SCRATCHES VOL.7
CD _______ MOMIX 7CD
Music Of Life / Jun '91 / Grapevine/ PolyGram

BEATS, BREAKS AND SCRATCHES VOL.8
CD _______ MOMIX 8CD
Music Of Life / Nov '91 / Grapevine/ PolyGram

BEST OF BEATS, BREAKS AND SCRATCHES
CD _______ MOBEST 1CD
Music Of Life / Jun '92 / Grapevine/ PolyGram

DISTURBING THE PEACE
Theme from disturbing the peace / Time / Rock right now / Ragga house (All night long) / This is serious / Don't stop the music / Shock the house / Right here, right now / Twilight / Runaway love / Ragga house
CD _______ DISTURB 1CD
Living Beat / Nov '90 / Grapevine/PolyGram

FOR YOUR EARS ONLY
CD _______ MOLCD 39
Music Of Life / Jan '96 / Grapevine/ PolyGram

Harris, Wynonie

EVERYBODY BOOGIE
Wynonie's blues / Here comes the blues / Baby look at you / Somebody changed the lock on my door / Gone with the wind / That's the stuff you gotta watch / Straighten him out / Young man's blues / I got a lyin' woman / Everybody boogie / Time to change your tune / Rebecca's blues / Playful baby / Young and wild / Papa tree top / Take me out of the rain / I got a lyin' woman / Everybody boogie
CD _______ DE 683
Delmark / Nov '96 / ADA / Cadillac / CM / Direct / Hot Shot

GOOD ROCKING TONIGHT
Good rockin' tonight / She just won't sell no more / Blow your brains out / I want my Fanny Brown / All she wants to do is rock / Lollipop mama / Baby, shame on you / I like my baby's pudding / Wynonie's boogie / Sittin' on it all the time / Good morning judge / I feel that old age coming on / Lovin' machine / Mr. Blues is coming to town / Quiet whiskey / Rock Mr. Blues / Bloodshot eyes / Luscious woman / Down boy down / Keep on churnin' (till the butter comes)
CD _______ CDCHARLY 244
Charly / Apr '91 / Koch

HERE COMES THE BLUES (The Roots Of Rock 'n' Roll vol.4)
Around the clock part 1 / Around the clock part 2 / Cock-a-doodle-doo / Yonder goes my baby / Wynonie's blues / Here comes the blues / Young man's blues / Baby look at you / She's gone with the wind / Somebody changed the lock on my door / That's the stuff you gotta watch / I gotta lyin' woman / Rebecca's blues / Everybody's boogie / Time to change your town / Playful baby / Take me out of the rain / Papa tree top / Young and wild / Good morning Corinne / Hey ba-ba-re-bop / Hey ba-ba-re-bop / In the evening / Mr. Blues jumped the rabbit / Rugged road / Come back baby / Whiskey and Jelly Roll blues
CD _______ PLCD 559
President / Mar '97 / Grapevine/PolyGram / President / Target/BMG

WEST COAST JIVE
CD _______ DD 657
Delmark / Jul '93 / ADA / Cadillac / CM / Direct / Hot Shot

WOMEN, WHISKEY AND FISH TAILS
Greyhound / Deacon don't like it / Christina / Shake that thing / Don't take my whiskey away / Drinkin' sherry wine / Fish tail blues / Big old country fool / Shotgun wedding / Wine wine sweet wine / Git to gittin' baby / Mr. Dollar / Bad news baby (There'll be no rockin' tonite) / Bring it back / I don't know where to go / Man's best friend / Keep a talking / Please Louise / I get a thrill / There's no substitute for love / Mama your daughter done lied to me
CD _______ CDCHD 457
Ace / Sep '93 / Pinnacle

Harrison, Bobby

SOLID SILVER
It's over / Hunter / Icelandic rock and roll / Overload / Nothing stays the same / Hot stuff / Guiding light / Highway / Victim of love / Shape I am in / Get on the right track / After the storm / Oh pretty woman
CD _______ SJPCD 011
Angel Air / Jun '97 / Pinnacle

Harrison, Donald

FOR ART'S SAKE (Harrison, Donald Quintet)
So what / Nut / Softly, as in a morning sunrise / In a sentimental mood / For art's sake / Oleo / Let's go off
CD _______ CCD 79501
Candid / Feb '97 / Cadillac / Direct / Jazz Music / Koch / Wellard

FULL CIRCLE
Force / My little suede shoes / Call me / Bye bye blackbird / Nature boy / Hold it right there / Good morning heartache / Evidence of things not seen / Infinite heart / Let's go off
CD _______ 66055003
Sweet Basil / Jul '91 / New Note/Pinnacle

INDIAN BLUES
Hu-ta-nay / Indian blues / Shallow water / Ja-ki-mo-fi-na-hay / Indian red / Two way pocky way / Cherokee / Hiko hiko / Uptown ruler / Big chief / Walkin' home / Shave 'em dry: *Harrison, Donald & Dr. John*
CD _______ CCD 79514
Candid / Feb '97 / Cadillac / Direct / Jazz Music / Koch / Wellard

NOUVEAU SWING
Nouveau swing / Bob Marley / Come back Jack / Little flowers / 81 / Sincerely your / Septembro / Cold duck / New hope / Christopher Jr / South side people / Dance hall / Duck's groove / Amazing grace
CD _______ IMP 12092
Impulse Jazz / May '97 / New Note/BMG

POWER OF COOL, THE
Tropic of cool / Wind cries Mary / Shadowbrook / All I want is you / Till U comeback / Close the door / Power of cool / Too fast / Ceora / Four
CD _______ ESJCD 238
Essential Jazz / Oct '94 / BMG

Harrison, George

ALL THINGS MUST PASS
I'd have you anytime / My sweet Lord / Wah wah / Isn't it a pity / What is life / If not for you / Behind that locked door / Let it down / Run of the mill / Beware of darkness / Apple scruffs / Ballad of Sir Frankie Crisp (Let it roll) / Awaiting on you all / All things must pass / I dig love / Art of dying / Hear me Lord / Out of the blue / It's Johnny's birthday / Plug me in / I remember jeep / Thanks for the pepperoni
CD Set _______ CDS 746 688 8
EMI / May '87 / EMI

BEST OF DARK HORSE 1976-1989
Poor little girl / Blow away / That's the way it goes / Cockamamie business / Wake up my love / Life itself / Got my mind set on you / Crackerbox palace / Cloud 9 / Here comes the moon / Gone troppo / When we was fab / Love comes to everyone / All those years ago / Cheer down
CD _______ 9257262
Dark Horse / Oct '89 / Warner Music

BEST OF GEORGE HARRISON
Something / If I needed someone / Here comes the sun / Taxman / Think for yourself / For you blue / While my guitar gently weeps / My sweet Lord / Give me love (give me peace on earth) / You / Bangladesh / Dark horse / What is life
CD CDP 746 682 2
Parlophone / May '87 / EMI

CLOUD NINE
Cloud 9 / That's what it takes / Fish on the sand / Just for today / This is love / When we was fab / Devil's radio / Someplace else / Wreck of the Hesperus / Breath away from heaven / Got my mind set on you
CD 9256432
Dark Horse / Sep '87 / Warner Music

DARK HORSE
Hari's on tour / Simply shady / So sad / Bye bye love / May a love / Ding dong ding dong / Dark horse / Far east man / Is it he (Jai Sri Krishna)
CD CDPAS 10008
Parlophone / Oct '91 / EMI

ELECTRONIC SOUNDS
Under the Mersey wall / No time or space
CD CDZAPPLE 02
Apple / Oct '96 / EMI

EXTRA TEXTURE (READ ALL ABOUT IT)
You / Answer's at the end / This guitar (can't keep from crying) / Ooh baby (you know that I love you) / World of stone / Bit more of you / Can't stop thinking about you / Tired of midnight blue / Grey cloudy lies / His name is legs
CD CDPAS 10009
Parlophone / Oct '91 / EMI

LIVE IN JAPAN
I want to tell you / Old brown shoe / Taxman / Give me love (give me peace on earth) / If I needed someone / Something / What is life / Dark horse / Piggies / Got my mind set on you / Cloud 9 / Here comes the sun / My sweet lord / All those years ago / Cheer down / Devil's radio / Isn't it a pity / While my guitar gently weeps / Roll over Beethoven
CD 7599269642
Dark Horse / Jul '92 / Warner Music

LIVING IN THE MATERIAL WORLD
Give me love (give me peace on Earth) / Sue me, sue you blues / Light that has lighted the world / Don't let me wait too long / Who can see it / Living in the material world / Lord loves the one (that loves the Lord) / Be here now / Try some buy some / Day the world gets 'round / That's all
CD CDPAS 10006
Parlophone / Oct '91 / EMI

WONDERWALL MUSIC
Microbes / Red lady too / Table and Pakavaj / In the park / Drilling a home / Guru vandana / Greasy legs / Ski-ing / Gat kirwani / Dream scene / Party seacombe / Love scene / Crying / Cowboy music / Fantasy sequins / On the bed / Glass box / Wonderwall to be here / Singing om
CD CDSAPCOR 1
Apple / Jun '92 / EMI

Harrison, Joel

RANGE OF MOTION (Harrison, Joel Octet)
CD 378412
Koch Jazz / Jun '97 / Koch

Harrison, Lou

MUSIC OF LOU HARRISON, THE
CD CRICD 13
CRI / Jun '97 / ReR Megacorp

Harrison, Michael A.

MOMENTS IN PASSION
CD 101S 70782
101 South / Nov '92 / New Note/Pinnacle

Harrow

PYLON OF INSANITY
CD N 02452
Noise / Aug '94 / Koch

Harrow, Nancy

ANYTHING GOES
CD ACD 142
Audiophile / '91 / Jazz Music

LOST LADY
CD SN 1212632
Soul Note / Oct '94 / Cadillac / Harmonia Mundi / Wellard

SECRETS
CD 1212332
Soul Note / Jan '92 / Cadillac / Harmonia Mundi / Wellard

WILD WOMEN DON'T HAVE THE BLUES
Take me back baby / All too soon / Can't we be friends / On the sunny side of the street / Wild women don't get the blues / I've got the world on a string / I don't know what kind of blues I got / Blues for yesterday
CD CCD 79008
Candid / Feb '97 / Cadillac / Direct / Jazz Music / Koch / Wellard

Harrup, Albie

PRAISE HIM ON THE GUITAR
I just want to praise you / In moments like these / Jesus all for Jesus / Father I adore you / More love, more power / You are my God / Sing hallelujah to the Lord / When I feel the touch / Jesus shall take the highest honour / When I look into your Holiness / Meekness and majesty / Send the rain
CD SOPD 2051
Spirit Of Praise / Apr '92 / Nelson Word

Harry Crews

NAKED IN GARDEN HILLS
About the author / Distopia / Gospel singer / (She's in a) bad mood / Bring me down / SOS / Man hates a man / You're it / Knock-out artist / Way out / Car / Orphans
CD ABBCD 21
Big Cat / Apr '90 / 3mv/Pinnacle

Harry J All Stars

RETURN OF THE LIQUIDATOR
CD CDTRD 412
Trojan / Mar '94 / Direct / Jet Star

Harry Pussy

RIDE A DOVE
CD SB 60CD
Matador / Feb '97 / Vital

WHAT WAS MUSIC
CD SB 0602
Matador / May '96 / Vital

Hart, Antonio

HERE I STAND
Community / True friends / Flamingos / Brother nasheet / Ven devorane otra vez / Riots the voice of the unhead / Millenium / Like my own / Words don't fit in my mouth
CD IMP 12082
Impulse Jazz / Mar '97 / New Note/BMG

IT'S ALL GOOD
91st miracle / Great Grandmother's song / Puerto Rico / Through the clouds / Bartzology / Sounds in the street / Lunch time again / Uptown traveller / Forever in love / Cappuccini / Missin' Miles
CD 01241631832
Novus / Jun '95 / BMG

Hart, Billy

OSHUMARE
CD GCD 79506
Gramavision / Jun '96 / Vital/SAM

RAH
Motional / Naaj / Renedap / Dreams / Reflections / Breakup / Reminder / Jungu
CD 1888022
Gramavision / Dec '88 / Vital/SAM

Hart, Grant

ECCE HOMO
Ballad number 19 / 2541 / Evergreen memorial drive / Come come / Pink turns to blue / She floated away / Girl who lives on Heaven Hill / Admiral of the sea / Back somewhere / Last days of Pompeii / Old empire / Never talking to you again / Please don't ask / Main
CD RTD 15730962
World Service / Nov '95 / Vital

Hart, John

BRIDGES
Under the influence / Private eyes / Rite of passion / It might as well be Spring / Urban Appalachia / Rabbit's foot / Summer wishes, Winter dreams / Dealin' and wheelin' / Zingaro / Bridges
CD CCD 47462
Concord Jazz / Mar '97 / New Note/Pinnacle

HIGH DRAMA
Paradox / High drama / Blood count / I'll never be the same / Ozone / Waiting for Samuel / Luiza / Minor poet / Isfahan / Who killed Mr. Lucky
CD CCD 4688
Concord Jazz / Feb '96 / New Note/Pinnacle

Hart, Kathy

TONIGHT I WANT IT ALL (Hart, Kathy & The Bluestars)
Tonight I want it all / Blue reverie / Get in / Get the money and get out / Two plays for a quarter / Good rockin' daddy / It seemed like such a good idea / Monkey ain't made outa gold
CD BCD 119
Biograph / Jul '91 / ADA / Cadillac / Direct / Hot Shot / Jazz Music / Wellard

Hart, Mickey

AT THE EDGE
Four for Garcia / Sky water / Slow sailing / Lonesome hero / Fast sailing / Cougar run / Eliminators / Brainstorm / Pigs in space
CD RCD 10124
Rykodisc / Mar '97 / ADA / Vital

DAFOS (Hart, Mickey & Flora Purim/ Airto Moreira)
CD RCD 10108
Rykodisc / Dec '94 / ADA / Vital

MICKEY HART'S MYSTERY BOX
Where love goes (sito) / Full steam ahead / Down the road / Sandman / Next step / Look away / Only the strange remain / Sangre De Christos / Last song / John Cage is dead
CD RCD 10338
Rykodisc / Jun '96 / ADA / Vital

MUSIC TO BE BORN BY
CD RCD 0112
Rykodisc / Nov '91 / ADA / Vital

PLANET DRUM
CD RCD 80206
Rykodisc / Dec '94 / ADA / Vital

Hart, Mike

MIKE HART BLEEDS/BASHER, CHALKY, PONGO & ME
Yawny morning song / Ring song / Arty's wife / Aberfan / Almost Liverpool 6 / Intro / Interlude / Pocket full of dough / Bitchin' on a train / Sing song / Jousters / Epilogue / Shelter song / Please bring back the birch for the milkman / Disbelief blues / Dance Mr. Morning Man / Joke / Nell's song / Dear Bathseeba Everdene / Influences / I have been a rover / Christmas / War, violence, heroism and such like stupidity
CD SEECD 419
See For Miles/C5 / May '95 / Pinnacle

ROLLING THUNDER
Rolling thunder / Shoshone invocation / Fletcher carnaby / Blind John / Deep, wide and frequent / Granma's cookies / Main ten / Chase / Young man / Pump song / Hangin' on
CD GDCD 4009
Grateful Dead / Mar '89 / Pinnacle

Hart Rouge

INCONDITIONNEL
CD HYCD 200143
Hypertension / Mar '95 / ADA / CM / Direct / Total/BMG

Hart, Tim

SUMMER SOLSTICE (Hart, Tim & Maddy Prior)
False knight on the road / Bring us in good ale / Of all the birds / I live not where I love / Ploughboy and the cockney / Westron wynde / Sorry the day I was married / Dancing at Whitsun / Fly up my cock / Cannily cannily / Adam catched Eve / Three drunken maidens / Serving girls holiday
CD CRESTCD 023
Mooncrest / Nov '96 / ADA / Direct

TIM HART
Keep on travelling / Tuesday afternoon / Hillman Avenger / Lovely lady / Come to my window / Nothing to hide / Overseas / Time after time / As I go my way
CD BGOCD 305
Beat Goes On / Oct '95 / Pinnacle

Harter Attack

HUMAN HELL
Death bells of the apocalypse / Last temptation / Slaves of conformity / Message from God / Nuclear attack / Human hell / Culture decay / Thugs against drugs / Symbol of hate / Let the sleeping dogs die
CD CORE 1CD
Metalcore / Jul '89 / Plastic Head

Hartford, John

DOWN ON THE RIVER
Here I am again in love / Bring your clothes back home / Wish I had our time again / All I got is gone away / Delta queen waltz / Old time river man / Men all want to be hobos / Right in the middle of falling for you / There'll never be another you / Little boy / General Jackson
CD FF 70514
Flying Fish / '88 / ADA / CM / Direct / Roots

HARTFORD & HARTFORD
CD FF 566CD
Flying Fish / Jun '94 / ADA / CM / Direct / Roots

MARK TWANG
Skippin' in the Mississippi dew / Long hot summer days / Let him go on Mama / Don't leave your records in the sun / Tater Tate and Allen Mundy / Julia Belle Swain / Little cabin home on the hill Waugh Waugh / Austin minor sympathy / Lowest pair / Tryin' to do something to get your attention
CD FF 70020
Flying Fish / Oct '89 / ADA / CM / Direct / Roots

ME OH MY, HOW TIME DOES FLY
CD FF 440CD
Flying Fish / Jun '94 / ADA / CM / Direct / Roots

MORNING BUGLE
CD ROUCD 03656
Rounder / Aug '95 / ADA / CM / Direct

NOBODY KNOWS WHAT YOU DO
You don't have to do that / Don't want to be forgotten / In tall buildings / John McLaughlin / Granny wont'cha smoke some marijuana / False hearted tenor waltz / Joseph's dream / Down / Golden globe award / Sly feel / Somewhere my love / We'll meet again sweetheart / Nobody knows what you do
CD FF 70028
Flying Fish / Sep '96 / ADA / CM / Direct / Roots

WILD HOG IN THE RED BRUSH
Squirrel hunters / Birdie / Grandmammy look at Uncle Sam / Old Virginia reel / Flanery's dream / Down at the mouth of old Stinson / Girl with the blue dress on / Wild hog in the red brush / Over the road to Maysville / Bumble bee in a jug / Bostony / Shelvin' rock / Molly put the kettle on / West Fork gals / Portsmouth airs / Coquette / Jimmy in the swamp / Lady of the lake / Natchez under the hill
CD ROUCD 0392
Rounder / Oct '96 / ADA / CM / Direct

Hartley, Pete

CLASSICS
Ave Maria / Danny boy / Killing me softly / Jesu joy of man's desiring / Lately / Air on a G string / Georgia / Nimrod / Moon dance / Bridge over troubled water / Walking in the air / And I love her / Way we were / Cavatina
CD CDGRS 1226
Grosvenor / '91 / Grosvenor

JAZZ PROJECT, THE
Autumn leaves / One note samba / Body and soul / Yardbird suite / Shoddy bop / Take the 'A' train / Gypsy with spots / Mr. PC / Ninth floor taxman / Night and day / Ornithology / Night in Tunisia / Birdland / Pent-up house / Spain
CD CDGRS 1236
Grosvenor / '91 / Grosvenor

MORE CLASSICS
We've only just begun / Goodbye to love / Chi mai / Lyin' eyes / Midnight train to Georgia / Aria / I shot the sheriff / Desperado / Deacon blues / Laughter in the rain / Stairway to heaven / Just the two of us / Wedding of Kevin and Claire / Nessun Dorma / Gymnopedie No.1 / Oye como va / Everything I do (I do it for you)
CD CDGRS 1251
Grosvenor / '91 / Grosvenor

Hartley, Trevor

HARTICAL
CD JOVECD 2
Love Music / May '94 / Jet Star

Hartman, Dan

KEEP THE FIRE BURNIN'
Keep the fire burnin' / Love in your eyes / Living in America / I can dream about you / Name of the game / We are the young / Free ride / Vertigo / Relight my fire / Instant reply / Countdown / This is it
CD 4777592
Columbia / Sep '96 / Sony

Hartman, Johnny

ALL OF ME (Bethlehem Jazz Classics)
Blue skies / I could make you care / Tenderly / Lamp is low / While you were young / Birth of the blues / I'll follow you / I concentrate on you / Stella by starlight / I get a kick out of you / End of a love affair / All of me / Blue skies / I get a kick out of you / Birth of the blues / All of me
CD CDGR 137
Charly / Apr '97 / Koch

AND I THOUGHT ABOUT YOU
Mamselle / To each his own / Alone / Long ago and far away / I should care / Little girl blue / But beautiful / After you've gone / There's a lull in my life / How long has this been going on / I thought about you
CD CDP 8574562
Roulette / Jul '97 / EMI

I JUST DROPPED BY TO SAY HELLO
Charade / Our time / In the wee small hours of the morning / Sleepin' bee / Don't you know I care / Kiss and run / If I'm lucky / I just dropped by to say hello / Stairway to the stars / Don't call it love / How sweet it is to be in love
CD IMP 11762
Impulse Jazz / Oct '95 / New Note/BMG

PRICELESS JAZZ
They say it's wonderful / Dedicated to you / Lush life / You are too beautiful / In the wee small hours of the morning / Don't you know I care / If I'm lucky / I just dropped by to say hello / How sweet it is to be in love / My ship / More I see you / These foolish things / Let me love you

CD GRP 98732
GRP / Jul '97 / New Note/BMG

SONGS FROM THE HEART (Bethlehem Jazz Classics)
CD CDGR 130
Charly / Apr '97 / Koch

THIS ONE'S FOR TED
CD ACD 181
Audiophile / Feb '91 / Jazz Music

UNFORGETTABLE
Almost like being in love / Once in a while / Isn't it romantic / Our love is here to stay / More I see you / What do I owe you / Bidin' my time / Down in the depths / Fools rush in / Very thought of you / Unforgettable / Ain't misbehavin' / Today I love everybody / T'ain't no need / For the want of a kiss / Girl talk / That old black magic
CD IMP 11522
GRP / Aug '95 / New Note/BMG

VOICE THAT IS
My ship / More I see you / These foolish things / Waltz for Debby / It never entered my mind / Day the world stopped turning / Slow hot wind / Funny world / Joey Joey Joey / Let me love you / Sunrise sunset
CD GRP 11442
GRP / Nov '95 / New Note/BMG

Hartsman, Johnny

MADE IN GERMANY (Hartsman, Johnny & The Blues Company)
Intro / That's alright / Flute juice / Cold cold feeling / I don't want no woman / Let me love you / Ain't no sunshine / Sweet Frisco blues / Flip flop and fly
CD INAK 9025
In Akustik / Jul '97 / Direct / TKO Magnum

Hartz, Hans

GNADENIOB
CD 8107272
Mercury / '88 / PolyGram

MORGENGRAUEN
CD 8183522
Mercury / '88 / PolyGram

Harvest Ministers

FEELING MISSION, THE
That won't wash / I've a mind / Drowning man / Temple to love / Dealing with a kid / Cleaning out the store / Only seat of power / Innopportune girl / She's buried / Modernising the new you / Mental charge / Secret way / Out of costume / Happy to abort
CD SETCD 019
Setanta / Apr '95 / Vital

ORBIT
Think about me more / I never raised my voice to you / Feeling mission / Stop doubting mission / Reluctant volunteer / Object of your affection / Orbit / Ballad of Lady Yarmouth / Our destines are intertwined / Don't give a cent (to the charities of hope)
CD SETCD 033
Setanta / Jan '97 / Vital

Harvest Theory

HARVEST THEORY
CD SBR 0072
Spring Box / Aug '95 / SRD

Harvesters

PEARLS BEFORE WINE
CD FSCD 41
Folksound / Jun '97 / CM / Roots

Harvey, Alex

ALL SENSATIONS (Harvey, Alex Sensational Band)
Midnight moses / Action strasse / Delilah / St. Anthony / Sgt. Fury / Next / Give my compliments to the chef / Gang bang / Framed / Faith healer / Vambo marble eye / Anthem
CD 5122012
Vertigo / Jun '92 / PolyGram

BEST OF THE SENSATIONAL ALEX HARVEY BAND, THE (Harvey, Alex Sensational Band)
Delilah / Cheek to cheek / Jungle rubout / Man in the jar / Weights made of lead / Sgt. Fury / Boston tea party / Next / Gamblin' bar room blues / Tomorrow belongs to me / Snakebite / School's out / Love story / Faith healer / Framed
CD MCCD 001
Music Club / Feb '91 / Disc / THE

DELILAH (Harvey, Alex Sensational Band)
Delilah / Money honey / Impossible dream / Last of the teenage idols / Shake that thing / Framed / Anthem / Gamblin' bar room blues / Tomorrow belongs to me / There's no lights on the Christmas tree Mother / Cheek to cheek / Runaway / School's out / Faith healer
CD 5506332
Spectrum / Aug '94 / PolyGram

LIVE IN GLASGOW 1993 (Harvey, Alex Band)
Faithhealer / St. Anthony / Framed / Gang bang / Amos moses / Boston tea party / Midnight moses / Vambo marble eye / Armed and ready / Delilah
CD JIMBO 001
Grapevine / Apr '94 / Grapevine/PolyGram

MAFIA STOLE MY GUITAR (Harvey, Alex New Band)
Don's delight / Back in the depot / Wait for me Mama / Mafia stole my guitar / Shakin' all over / Whalers / Oh spartacus / Just a gigolo / I ain't got nobody
CD MAUCD 608
Mau Mau / Sep '91 / Pinnacle

SENSATIONAL ALEX HARVEY BAND, THE (Harvey, Alex Sensational Band)
Faith healer / Delilah / Framed / Tomahawk kid / School's out / Vambo / Boston tea party / Gang bang / Gambling bar room blues / Tomorrow belongs to me / Mrs. Blackhouse / Dogs of war / Anthem / To be continued
CD 3036001162
Carlton / Jul '97 / Carlton

Harvey, Bobby

CEILIDH DANCES (Harvey, Bobby & His Ceilidh Band)
CD CDLOC 1058
Lochshore / Dec '90 / ADA / Direct / Duncans

Harvey, Chris

WHITE SAIL, THE
Biomorph / Allegiance / Paris / Secret of the screen / Liber null / Liber null / Elation sedation / Plasmate / Pixelate / Jorg / White sail
CD AD 15CD
AD / Dec '96 / Disc

Harvey, Jonathan

IMAGININGS
CD CHILLCD 007
Chillout / May '96 / Kudos / Pinnacle / RTM/Disc

Harvey, Kike

LA ISLA BONITA
CD TUMICD 048
Tumi / '95 / Discovery / Stern's

SALSA PACHANGA Y AMOR
CD TUMICD 039
Tumi / Jun '93 / Discovery / Stern's

Harvey, Maxine

DON'T YOU BREAK MY HEART
Don't you break my heart / Right stuff / Jut a little / That's enough / Can't hide feelings / I need your love forever / Crazy for you / I'm sorry / Get on it / Get on it
CD WRCD 017
World / Jun '97 / Jet Star / TKO Magnum

Harvey, Mick

INTOXICATED MAN
CD CDSTUMM 144
Mute / Oct '95 / RTM/Disc

Harvison, Jon

LONELY AS THE MOON
CD D 001CD
Drive On / Jul '95 / ADA

Haryou Percussion Group

HARYOU PERCUSSION GROUP
CD CBCD 002
Cubop / Jul '96 / Timewarp

Hash

BASH
Twilight ball / Ghetto / Mr. Hello / I forgot my blanket / Operation herve / 4.30 a.m. hikes / Kit and kaboodle / In the grass / Mary I wanna / Orchard moons / Travelling / I'm down / American chorus / My icy death
CD 7559615132
Elektra / Nov '93 / Warner Music

Hash Jar Tempo

WELL OILED
CD DFR 24
Drunken Fish / Apr '97 / Cargo

Hashim, Michael

BLUE STREAK, A
CD STCD 546
Stash / '92 / ADA / Cadillac / CM / Direct / Jazz Music

GUYS AND DOLLS
CD STCD 558
Stash / Jan '93 / ADA / Cadillac / CM / Direct / Jazz Music

KEEP A SONG IN YOUR SOUL
Keep a song in your soul / Get some cash for your trash / Two sleepy people / Jitterbug waltz / What did I do to be so black & blue / Fats Waller's original E flat blues / Blue turning grey over you / Prisoner of love / Honeysuckle rose
CD HEPCD 2068
Hep / Nov '96 / Cadillac / Jazz Music / New Note/Pinnacle / Wellard

TRANSATLANTIC AIRS
Have you met Miss Jones / Love song from threepenny opera / Speak low / Corn squeezin's / Charade / Play the notes you like the loudest / My ship / Pleasures and regrets / Do everything / Born to be blue / Tickle toe
CD 33JAZZ 023
33 Jazz / Jul '95 / Cadillac / New Note/ Pinnacle

Hasidic New Wave

JEWS AND THE ABSTRACT TRUTH
CD KFWCD 192
Knitting Factory / Jun '97 / Cargo / Plastic Head

Haskell, Gordon

IT IS AND IT ISN'T
CD 7567805522
Atlantic / Jan '96 / Warner Music

IT'S JUST A PLOT TO DRIVE YOU CRAZY
CD BP 118CD
Blueprint / Jul '96 / Pinnacle

IT'S JUST ANOTHER PLOT TO DRIVE YOU CRAZY
CD VP 118CD
Voiceprint / Jan '93 / Pinnacle

SAILING IN MY BOAT
Boat trip / Born to be together / Flying home together / Lawbreaker / All since you went away / Oo la di doo da day / Time only knows / Better by far / Some other day / Zanzibar / Slow boat
CD VP 197CD
Voiceprint / Sep '97 / Pinnacle

VOICEPRINT RADIO SESSION
CD VPR 001CD
Voiceprint / Oct '94 / Pinnacle

Haskett, Chris

LANGUAGE
CD 213CD 002
2.13.61 / Jun '96 / Pinnacle

NON FICTION (Haskett, Chris & Brandon Finley)
Lucy in the sky with dog food / L-shape / Lizzard errands / Tribute / Sly Larry's wanna b-side / Doubt of the benefit / Drill / Wheel chair waltz / Viva voice / Twin / Zadit / Neighbors say he was a quiet man / Truth is stranger / Respistory / Maybe elephants walk / Playing in Papa's clothes / Four legs in the morning / Two legs at noon / Three legs in the evening
CD 213CD 022
2.13.61 / Apr '97 / Pinnacle

Haskins, Fuzzy

WHOLE NOTHER/RADIO ACTIVE THANG
Tangerine green / Cookie jar / Mr. Junk man / I can see myself in you / Fuz and da boog / Which way do I disco / Love's now is forever / Sometimes I rock and roll / I'll be loving you / Right back where I started from / Not yet / I think I got my thang together / This situation called love / Gimme back (Some of the love you got from me) / Things we used to do / Woman / Sinderella / Silent day
CD CDSEWD 093
Westbound / Sep '94 / Pinnacle

Haslam, Annie

ANNIE IN WONDERLAND
Introlise / If I were made of music / I never believed in love / If I loved you / Hunioco / Rockalise / Nature boy / Inside my life / Going home
CD 7599265152
WEA / Jan '96 / Warner Music

SONGS FROM RENAISSANCE DAYS (Haslam, Annie & Mike Dunford)
Africa / Dreamaker / Northern lights / No beginning no end / Only when I laugh / Body machine / Writers wronged / Island of Avalon / America / You
CD HTDCD 73
HTD / Apr '97 / CM / Pinnacle

Haslam, George

ARGENTINE ADVENTURES VOL.1
Tinto dreams / Ritmo catulo Castillo / Vidala para mi sombra / Los muchachos de Buenos Aires / Vidala para mi sombra / Welcome George / Las quenas de Barragan / Bailando con los raices / Affirmation
CD SLAMCD 304
Slam / Oct '96 / Cadillac

ARGENTINE ADVENTURES VOL.2
Tango libre / El subsuelo / Blues for Argentina / Monito / Kool / Blues no.9 for la plata / Incompleta
CD SLAMCD 307
Slam / Jan '97 / Cadillac

LEVEL TWO
Pastures now / Fells sunrise / Crossfield / Corner meadow / Fylde away / Moss house / In memory / Last load
CD SLAMCD 303
Slam / Oct '96 / Cadillac

Haslinger

FUTURE PRIMITIVE
CD WLD 9211
Varese Sarabande / Apr '95 / Pinnacle

Hasni, Cheb

CHEB HASNI
CD CDSB 107
Club Du Disque Arabe / Sep '95 / ADA / Harmonia Mundi

LATBKICHE
CD CDSB 103
Club Du Disque Arabe / Sep '95 / ADA / Harmonia Mundi

LOVER'S RAI
May God help me / That forlorn person / You ask for separation / I don't know why you are crying / Don't cry this is my destiny / My suffering was long / I know you now / I want a beautiful woman / I still have the souvenir / You the healer
CD ROUCD 5078
Rounder / Feb '97 / ADA / CM / Direct

TALGHIYABEK YA GHOZAZI
CD CDSB 102
Club Du Disque Arabe / Sep '95 / ADA / Harmonia Mundi

Hassan, Chalf

SONGS AND DANCES FROM MOROCCO
CD EUCD 1170
ARC / '91 / ADA / ARC Music

Hassan, Mehdi

HARPAL
CD IMUT 1022
Multitone / Mar '96 / BMG

HITS OF MEHDI HASSAN, THE
CD PMUT 019
Multitone / Aug '96 / BMG

LIVE IN LONDON
CD DMUT 1183
Multitone / Mar '96 / BMG

LIVE IN LONDON VOL.2
CD DMUT 1184
Multitone / Mar '96 / BMG

Hassan, Nazia

HOT LINE
CD DMUT 1043
Multitone / Mar '88 / BMG

Hassan, Umar Bin

BE BOP OR BE DEAD
Niggers are scared of revolution / AM / Bum rush / Malcolm / Pop / Love / 40 Deuce Street / Personal things / This is madness
CD 5180482
Axiom / Nov '93 / PolyGram / Vital

Hasselgard, Ake 'Stan'

PERMANENT HASSELGARD, THE
Hallelujah / All the things you are / Am I blue / Lullaby in rhythm / Swedish pastry / Mel's idea
CD NCD 8802
Phontastic / '93 / Cadillac / Jazz Music / Wellard

PERMANENT STAN HASSELGARD WITH THE AMERICANS (1945-1948)
CD PHONTCD 8802
Phontastic / '88 / Cadillac / Jazz Music / Wellard

Hasselhoff, David

NIGHT ROCKER
CD WMCD 5673
Woodford Music / Feb '93 / THE

Hassell, Jon

AKA/DARBARI/JAVA (Magic Realism)
Empire / Darbari extension
CD EEGCD 31
EG / Feb '91 / EMI

CITY: WORKS OF FICTION
Voiceprint / Mombasa / In the city of red dust / Ba ya d / Out of Adedara / Pagan / Tikal / Rain / Warriors
CD ASCD 11
All Saints / Apr '96 / Discovery / Vital

DREAM THEORY IN MALAYA
Chor moire / Courage / Dream theory / Datu bintung at jelong / Malay / These times / Gift of fire
CD EEGCD 13
EG / Feb '91 / EMI

DRESSING FOR PLEASURE
CD 9362455232
Warner Bros. / Nov '94 / Warner Music

EARTHQUAKE ISLAND
CD 269 612 2
Tomato / Mar '90 / Vital

FLASH OF THE SPIRIT (Hassell, Jon & Farafina)
Flash of the spirit (laughter) / Night moves (fear) / Air Afrique (wind) / Out pours (kongo) / Blue (prayer) / Taboo (play) / Like warriors everywhere (courage) / Dreamworld (dance) / Tales of the near future (clairvoyance) / Vampire dances / Masque
CD INT 30092
Intuition / May '91 / New Note/Pinnacle

FOURTH WORLD MUSIC (Hassell, Jon & Brian Eno)
Chemistry / Delta rain dream / Griot (over Contagious Magic) / Ba-benzele / Rising thermal / Charm
CD EEGCD 7
EG / Jan '87 / EMI

JON HASSEL VS. 808 STATE (Hassell, Jon & 808 State)
CD ASCD 17
All Saints / Apr '96 / Discovery / Vital

POWER SPOT (Hassell, Jon & Brian Eno)
Power spot / Passage D E / Solaire / Miracle steps / Wing melodies / Elephant and the orchid / Air
CD 8294662
ECM / Oct '86 / New Note/Pinnacle

SURGEON OF THE NIGHTSKY, THE
Ravinia/Vancouver / Paris 1 / Hamburg / Brussels / Paris 2
CD INT 30042
Intuition / May '91 / New Note/Pinnacle

Hatch, Tony

EASY PROJECT VOL.3, THE (The Very Best Of The Tony Hatch Orchestra) (Hatch, Tony Orchestra)
CD NEMCD 920
Sequel / Jan '97 / BMG

TONY HATCH SONGBOOK, THE (Hatch, Tony & Jackie Trent)
Downtown / Look for a star / Where are you now / Forget him / Other man's grass is always greener / Two of us / I know a place / Joanna / Call me / What would I be / Don't sleep in the subway / Sign of the times / My love / Thank you for loving me / I couldn't live without your love / Who am I / Colour my world / Opposite your smile / You're everything / Let's do it again
CD 306632
Hallmark / Jun '97 / Carlton

Hatchard, Mike

HAND-GLIDER HAS LANDED
CD EJL 021
Ensemble Jazz / Jan '96 / Forties Recording Company

Hatcher, Roger

ROGER HATCHER COLLECTION, THE (Expansion Collector Series)
Stormy love affair / Heaven is missing an angel / Sugar Daddy / Your love is a masterpiece / All my love belongs to you / Gonna make love to somebody's old lady / I dedicate my life to you / Sweetest girl in the world / I'm gonna dedicate my song to you / Warm and tender love / Gonna rock you like a baby / She's all I got / That's when I'll stop loving you / I cried like a baby / Let your love shine on me / Caught making love
CD EXCDG 1
Expansion / May '96 / 3mv/Sony

Hatchett's Swingtette

HATCHETT'S SWINGTETTE FEATURING STEPHANE GRAPELLI (Hatchett's Swingtette & Stephane Grapelli)
Alexander's ragtime band / Ting a ling / Beat me Daddy, eight to the bar / Playmates / Oh Johnny, Oh Johnny, Oh / Sweet potato piper / Sheikh of Araby / Oh how he misses his missus / I hear bluebirds / Wrap yourself in cotton wool / Scrub me Mama with a boogie beat / Blue ribbon rag / Twelfth Street rag / She had those dark and dreamy eyes / Scatterbrain / In the mood / I got rhythm / It's a hap-hap-happy day / Papa's in bed with his breeches on / Mind the Handel's hot / Ma, he's making eyes at me / Bluebirds in the moonlight
CD PASTCD 9785
Flapper / Mar '92 / Pinnacle

Hate Bombs

HERE COMES TREBLE
CD 36T 0004CD
360 Twist / Jul '97 / Greyhound

Hate Squad

PZYCHOI
CD GUN 129CD
Gun / Jun '97 / Plastic Head

Haters

MIND THE GAP
CD VC 107
Vinyl Communication / Jan '97 / Cargo / Greyhound / Plastic Head

Hatfield & The North

HATFIELD AND THE NORTH
Stubbs effect / Big jobs (poo poo extract) / Going up to people and tinkling / Calyx / Son of "There's no place like Homerton" / Aigrette / Rifferama / Fol de rol / Shaving is boring / Licks for the ladies / Bossa nochance / Big jobs No.2 / Lobster in cleavage probe / Gigantic land crabs in Earth takeover bid / Other Stubbs effect / Let's eat (real soon) / Fitter Stoke has a bath
CD CDV 2008
Virgin / Jul '87 / EMI

LIVE
CD NINETY 6
Demon / Feb '93 / Pinnacle

ROTTERS CLUB, THE
Share it / Lounging there trying / (Big) John Wayne socks psychology on the jaw / Chaos at the greasy spoon / Yes no interlude / Fitter Stoke has a bath / Didn't matter anyway / Underdub / Mumps (Your Majesty is like a cream donut-quiet) / Mumps (lumps) / Mumps (prenut) / Mumps (your majesty is like a cream donut-loud) / Halfway between heaven and earth / Oh Len's nature / Lying and gracing
CD CDV 2030
Virgin / Jun '88 / EMI

Hatfield, Juliana

BECOME WHAT YOU ARE
Supermodel / My sister / This is the sound / For the birds / Mabel / Dame with a rod / Addicted / Feelin' Massachusetts / Spin the bottle / President Garfield / Little pieces / I got no idols
CD 4509935292
East West / Dec '96 / Warner Music

ONLY EVERYTHING
CD 4509998862
East West / Dec '96 / Warner Music

Hathaway, Donny

DONNY HATHAWAY COLLECTION, A
Song for you / I love you more than you'll ever know / You were meant for me / Back together again / Where is the love / For all we know / Someday we'll all be free / Giving up / Closer I get to you / You are my heaven / What's going on / Ghetto / Young, gifted and black / You've got a friend / This Christmas
CD 7567820922
Atlantic / Apr '93 / Warner Music

DONNY HATHAWAY IN PERFORMANCE
CD 7567815692
Atlantic / Jan '96 / Warner Music

EVERYTHING IS EVERYTHING
Voices inside / Je vous aime / I believe to my soul / Misty / Sugar Lee / Tryin' times / Thank you master / Ghetto / Young, gifted and black
CD 8122722162
Atlantic / Jul '96 / Warner Music

Hato De Foces

CANTAR DE CAMINO
CD J 1017CD
Sonifolk / Jun '94 / ADA / CM

Hatoba, Omoide

KINSEI
Kinsei / Alternative funkaholic / Gion / Amen / We are hello / Mashroom airline / Sweet pea / Rock noodle / Oyaji / Touch / Theme from the ghost mountains / Good by Submarine / Japan dissolution / Human tornado / Satelite groove / Go
CD EN 003
Earthnoise / Feb '96 / Vital

Hatrix

COLLISIONCOURSSE
CD MASSCD 040
Massacre / Nov '94 / Plastic Head

Haubenstock-Ramati, Roman

FOR PIANO (2CD Set)
CD Set ARTCD 6196
Hat Hut / Mar '97 / Harmonia Mundi

Haujobb

FRAMES
CD CD 07622382
SPV / Dec '96 / Koch / Plastic Head

FREEZE FRAME FACILITY
CD SPV 08422192
SPV / May '95 / Koch / Plastic Head

MATRIX
CD Set 08543472
Westcom / May '97 / Koch / Pinnacle

SOLUTIONS FOR A SMALL PLANET
CD 08543282
Humbug / Feb '97 / Total/Pinnacle

Haunted

HAUNTED, THE
CD VOXXCD 2011
Voxx / Aug '95 / Else / RTM/Disc

Haunted Garage

POSSESSION PARK
CD CDZORRO 27
Metal Blade / Aug '91 / Pinnacle / Plastic Head

Hause, Alfred

STRICTLY DANCING: TANGO (Hause, Alfred & Big Tango Orchestra)
CD 15340
Laserlight / May '94 / Target/BMG

Have Mercy

HAVE MERCY
CD CCD 11039
Crosscut / Jan '94 / ADA / CM / Direct

Havel, Vaclav

TWO PRESIDENTS JAM SESSION (Havel, Vaclav & Bill Clinton)
CD CR 00012
Czech Radio / Nov '95 / Czech Music Enterprises

Haven, Alan

ORGAN SPECTRUM
Watch what happens / Shenandoah / One I love belongs to somebody else / How insensitive / Image / Spellbound / Tenderly / Meditation / Trust in me / Quiet nights of quiet stars / Get back / Pavanne pour une infante defunte / Flying free / Greensleeves / Exactly like you
CD OS 224
OS Digital / Dec '96 / Conifer/BMG

Haven, Will

WILL HAVEN
CD LS 001CD
Landspeed / Oct '96 / Plastic Head

Havens, Bob

IN NEW ORLEANS
CD BCD 126
GHB / Jun '95 / Jazz Music

Havens, Richie

CUTS TO THE CHASE
They dance alone / Times they are a' changin / Lives in the balance / Hawk / Old love / At a glance / My father's shoes / Darkness darkness / Young boy / Fade to blue / How the nights can fly / Comin' back to me / Don't pass it up
CD ESMCD 397
Essential / Sep '96 / BMG

RICHIE HAVENS SINGS BEATLES AND DYLAN
CD RCD 20035
Rykodisc / May '92 / ADA / Vital

Havoc & Prodeje

PRELUDE TO THE MOBB
On a mission / G'z on da move / What 'r' gonna do / We ain't nuttin but / Gonna getcha / Block to block / Kickin game / All I'm c'z iz g'z / Endo glide / Guess-a-dad / Everybody wanna G-sta / That's the way it'z goin down / Only the lonely homie / C u when u get out / To g r not to g / G'z only
CD NTMCD 542
Nectar / Feb '97 / Pinnacle

Havoc Mass

KILLING THE FUTURE
CD MASSCD 019
Massacre / Dec '93 / Plastic Head

Havohej

DETHRONE THE SON OF GOD
CD CANDLE 004CD
Candlelight / Oct '93 / Plastic Head

Hawes, Hampton

AT THE PIANO
Killing me softly with his song / Soul sign eight / Sunny morning / Blue in green / When I grow too old to dream
CD OJCCD 877
Original Jazz Classics / Aug '96 / Complete/Pinnacle / Jazz Music / Wellard

BLUES FOR BUD (1968)
Blues enough / Sonora / They say it's wonderful / Black forest / Spanish steps / My romance / Dangerous / Blues for Bud
CD BLCD 760126
Black Lion / '92 / Cadillac / Jazz Music / Koch / Wellard

FOUR
Four / Yardbird suite / There will never be another you / Bow jest / Sweet Sue, just you / Up blues / Like someone in love / Love is just around the corner / Thou swell / Awful truth
CD OJCCD 165
Original Jazz Classics / May '93 / Complete/Pinnacle / Jazz Music / Wellard

HAMPTON HAWES TRIO VOL.1
CD OJCCD 316
Original Jazz Classics / Nov '95 / Complete/Pinnacle / Jazz Music / Wellard

HIGH IN THE SKY
CD FSCD 59
Fresh Sound / Oct '90 / Discovery / Jazz Music

LIVE AT MEMORY LANE 1970 (Hawes, Hampton Allstars)
CD FSCD 1043
Fresh Sound / Jan '97 / Discovery / Jazz Music

MONTREUX 1971 (Hawes, Hampton Trio)
CD FSCD 133
Fresh Sound / Jan '91 / Discovery / Jazz Music

Hawker, Sue

WORD IS OUT (Hawker, Sue & Rob Koral)
How deep is the ocean / I can dream / Teach me tonight / Feel so good / On the town / Empty rooms / Cheek to cheek / Hold me tight / Travelling blues / Heroes / Traffic jam / Will you still love me tomorrow / Word is out / Tell me why
CD 33JAZZ 030
33 Jazz / Jan '97 / Cadillac / New Note/ Pinnacle

Hawkes, Chesney

GET THE PICTURE
Tell me something I don't know / What's wrong with this picture / Help me to help myself / Sometimes / Black or white people / Missing you already / One of those days / Fairweather Christian / Family way / Every little tear
CD CDCHR 6011
Chrysalis / Jun '93 / EMI

Hawkins, Coleman

ALIVE AT THE VILLAGE GATE (Hawkins, Coleman & Roy Eldridge/Johnny Hodges)
Satin doll / Perdido / Rabbit in jazz / Mack the knife / It's the talk of the town / Bean and the boys / Caravan
CD 5137552
Verve / Apr '92 / PolyGram

APRIL IN PARIS
Body and soul / When day is done / Bouncing with Bean / April in Paris / Angel face / I love you / There will never be another you / Little girl blue / Bean stalks again / Have you met Miss Jones
CD ND 90636
Bluebird / Apr '92 / BMG

AT EASE WITH COLEMAN HAWKINS
CD OJCCD 181
Original Jazz Classics / Nov '95 / Complete/Pinnacle / Jazz Music / Wellard

AT THE OPERA HOUSE (Hawkins, Coleman & Roy Eldridge)
Bean stalkin' / Nearness of you / Time on my hands / Walker / Tea for two / Blue moon / Cocktails for two / Kerry / Bean stalkin' / I can't get started / Walker / Stuffy
CD 5216412
Verve / Oct '94 / PolyGram

BEAN AND BEN 1944-1945 (Hawkins, Coleman & Ben Webster)
In the hush of the night / Out to lunch / Every man for himself / Look out, Jack / On the bean / Recollections / Flyin' Hawk / Drifting on a reed / Broke but happy / Blues on the bayou / Jumpin' with Judy / Blues on the delta / Bottle's empty / Save it pretty Mama / For lovers only / Peach Tree Street blues
CD HQCD 04
Harlequin / Oct '90 / Hot Shot / Jazz Music / Swift / Wellard

BEAN AND THE BOYS
In the hush of the night / Out to lunch / Every man for himself / Look out Jack / On the bean / Recollections / Flyin' hawk / Drifting on a reed / I mean you / Bean and the boys / Bean and the boys (take 2) / Cocktails for two / You go to my head / Stasch / Trust in me / Roll 'em Pete / Skrouk / Since I fell for you / My babe
CD LEJAZZCD 12
Le Jazz / Jun '93 / Cadillac / Koch

BEAN AND THE BOYS
CD PRCD 24124
Prestige / Oct '93 / Cadillac / Complete/ Pinnacle

BEAN STALKIN' (Hawkins, Coleman & Friends)
Bean stalkin' / Stompin' at the Savoy / Take the 'A' train / Indian summer / Crazy rhythm / (Back home again in) Indiana
CD _______ CD 2310933
Pablo / Jun '93 / Cadillac / Complete/ Pinnacle

BEAN, THE
CD _______ CD 53168
Giants Of Jazz / Jan '94 / Cadillac / Jazz Music / Target/BMG

BLUES WAIL (Coleman Hawkins Plays The Blues)
Juicy fruit / Blues for tomorrow / Blues wail / Soul blues / Skronk / Stealin' the bean / Foot pattin' / Blues for Ron / Pedallin'
CD _______ PRCD 11006
Prestige / Jun '97 / Cadillac / Complete/ Pinnacle

BODY AND SOUL
Meet Dr. Foo / Fine dinner / She's funny that way / Body and soul / When day is done / Sheikh of Araby / My blue Heaven / Bouncing with Bean / Say it isn't so / Spotlite / April in Paris / How strange / Half step down please / Angel face / Body and soul / I love Paris / There will never be another you / Under Paris skies / Bean stalks again
CD _______ 09026685152
RCA Victor / Oct '96 / BMG

BODY AND SOUL
Rifftide / Man I love / Body and soul / Caravan / Love for sale / Love come back to me
CD _______ WWCD 2018
West Wind / Mar '89 / Koch

BODY AND SOUL
CD _______ TPZ 1022
Topaz Jazz / Jun '95 / Cadillac / Pinnacle

CLASSICS 1943-1944
CD _______ CLASSICS 807
Classics / Mar '95 / Discovery / Jazz Music

CLASSICS 1944
CD _______ CLASSICS 842
Classics / Nov '95 / Discovery / Jazz Music

CLASSICS 1944-1945
CD _______ CLASSICS 863
Classics / Mar '96 / Discovery / Jazz Music

CLASSICS 1945
CD _______ CLASSICS 926
Classics / Apr '97 / Discovery / Jazz Music

COLEMAN HAWKINS
CD _______ CD 14560
Jazz Portraits / Jul '94 / Jazz Music

COLEMAN HAWKINS 1929-34
CD _______ CLASSICS 587
Classics / Aug '91 / Discovery / Jazz Music

COLEMAN HAWKINS 1934-37
CD _______ CLASSICS 602
Classics / Sep '91 / Discovery / Jazz Music

COLEMAN HAWKINS 1937-39
CD _______ CLASSICS 613
Classics / Feb '92 / Discovery / Jazz Music

COLEMAN HAWKINS 1939-40
CD _______ CLASSICS 634
Classics / Nov '92 / Discovery / Jazz Music

COLEMAN HAWKINS 1959-62 (Hawkins, Coleman, Roy Eldridge & Mickey Baker)
CD _______ STCD 538
Stash / '91 / ADA / Cadillac / CM / Direct / Jazz Music

COLEMAN HAWKINS AND BENNY CARTER (Hawkins, Coleman & Benny Carter)
CD _______ UCD 19011
Forlane / Jun '95 / Target/BMG

COLEMAN HAWKINS ENCOUNTERS BEN WEBSTER (Hawkins, Coleman & Ben Webster)
Blues for Yolande / It never entered my mind / La Rosita / You'd be so nice to come home to / Prisoner of love / Tangerine / Shine on harvest moon
CD _______ 8231202
Verve / Nov '93 / PolyGram

COLEMAN HAWKINS WITH THE SECTION
CD _______ VG 650134
Vogue / Oct '92 / BMG

COMPLETE RECORDINGS 1929-1940, THE (6CD Set)
Hello Lola / One hour (If I could be with you one hour tonight) / Dismal Dan / Down Georgia way / Girls like you were meant for boys like me / Georgia on my mind / I can't believe that you're in love with me / Darktown strutters ball / (I'll be glad when you're dead) you rascal you / Someday sweetheart / I wish I could shimmy like my sister Kate / River's takin' care of me / Ain't cha got music / Stringin' along on a shoe string / Shadows on the Swanee / Day you came along / Jamaica shout / Heartbreak blues / Blues rhapsody / Happy feet / I'm rhythm crazy now / Ol' man river / Minnie the moocher's wedding day / Ain't cha glad / I've got to sing a torch song / Hush my mouth / You're gonna lose your gal / Dark clouds / My Galveston gal / Georgia jubilee / Junk man / Ol' pappy / Emaline / I ain't got nobody / It sends me / On the sunny side of the street / Lullaby / Oh lady be good / Lost in a fog / I wish I were twins / I only have eyes for you / After you've gone / Some of these days / Honeysuckle rose / Hands across the table / Blue moon / Avalon / What a difference a day makes / Stardust / Chicago / Meditation / What Harlem is to me / Netcha's dream / Love cries / Sorrow / Tiger rag / It may not be true / I'm in the mood for love / I wanna go back to Harlem / Consolation / Strange fact / Original Dixieland one-step / Smiles / Something is gonna give me away / Crazy rhythm / Out of nowhere / Sweet Georgia brown / Lamentation / Devotion / Somebody loves me / Mighty like the blues / Pardon me pretty baby / My buddy / Well alright then / Blues evermore / Dear old Southland / Way down yonder in New Orleans / I know that you know / When buddha smiles / Swinging in the groove / My melancholy baby / Meet Dr. Foo / Fine dinner / She's funny that way / Body and soul / When day is done / Sheikh of araby / My blue heaven / Bouncing with Bean / Smack / I surrender dear / Dedication / Passin' it around / Serenade to a sleeping beauty / Rocky comfort / Forgive a fool / Bugle call rag / One o'clock jump / 9-20 special / Feedin' the bean
CD Set _______ CDAFS 10266
Affinity / Sep '92 / Cadillac / Jazz Music / Koch

DESAFINADO (Hawkins, Coleman Sextet)
Desafinado / I'm looking over a four leaf clover / Samba para bean / I remember you / One-note samba / O pato / Un abraco no bonfa / Stumpy bossa nova
CD _______ MCAD 33118
Impulse Jazz / Apr '90 / New Note/BMG
CD _______ IMP 12272
Impulse Jazz / Apr '97 / New Note/BMG

EARLY YEARS, THE
CD _______ CDSGP 0158
Prestige / Sep '95 / Else / Total/BMG

GENIUS OF COLEMAN HAWKINS, THE
I'll never be the same / You're blase / I wished on the moon / How long has this been going on / Like someone in love / My Melancholy baby / Ill wind / In a mellow tone / There's no you / World is waiting for the sunrise / Somebody loves me / Blues for Rene
CD _______ 8256732
Verve / Jan '86 / PolyGram

GENTLE HAWK
There will never be another you / How strange / Sih sah / I love you / Angel face / I love Paris / Body and soul / It's only a paper moon / April in Paris / I surrender dear / Mon homme / Mimi / Little girl blue / Under Paris skies / Sophisticated lady / La mer / Dinner for one / Please James / Mademoiselle de Paris / Have you met Miss Jones / Body and soul
CD _______ 74321431592
Camden / Oct '96 / BMG

HAWK EYES
CD _______ OJCCD 294
Original Jazz Classics / Feb '92 / Complete/Pinnacle / Jazz Music / Wellard

HAWK FLIES HIGH, THE
Chant / Juicy fruit / Think deep / Laura / Blue lights / Sanctity
CD _______ OJCCD 27
Original Jazz Classics / Oct '92 / Complete/ Pinnacle / Jazz Music / Wellard

HAWK IN EUROPE, THE (1934-1937)
Lullaby / Lost in a fog / Oh lady be good / Avalon / What a difference a day makes / Stardust / Meditation / Netcha's dream / Strange fact / Crazy rhythm / Honeysuckle rose / Out of nowhere / Sweet Georgia Brown / Mighty like the blues / Pardon me pretty baby / Somebody loves me / My buddy / Well alright then
CD _______ CDAJA 5054
Living Era / Jul '88 / Select

HAWK IN PARIS, THE
CD _______ 07863510592
Bluebird / Jul '93 / BMG

HAWK SWINGS, THE
Cloudy / Almost dawn / Stake out / Crosstown / Shadows
CD _______ CDBOP 015
Boplicity / Jul '91 / Pinnacle

HAWK TALKS
Lucky duck / I can't get started (with you) / Foolin' around / Man I love / Trust in me / Where is your heart / Wishing / Carioca / If I could be with you one hour tonight / Ruby / Sin / Midnight sun / And so to sleep again / Lonely wine
CD _______ FSCD 130
Fresh Sound / Jan '91 / Discovery / Jazz Music

HAWK TAWK
CD _______ TCD 1007
Tradition / Feb '96 / ADA / Vital

HIGH AND MIGHTY HAWK, THE (Jazz Recollections)
Get set / You've changed / Ooh-wee, Miss GP / Vignette / My one and only love / Bird of prey blues
CD _______ 8206002
London / May '88 / PolyGram

IN A MELLOW TONE
You blew out the flame in my heart / I want to be loved / In a mellow tone / Greensleeves / Through for the night / Until the real thing comes along / Sweetest sounds / Then I'll be tired of you / Jammin' in swingville
CD _______ OJCCD 6001
Original Jazz Classics / Apr '93 / Complete/ Pinnacle / Jazz Music / Wellard

IN CONCERT
CD _______ BS 18003
Bandstand / Jul '96 / Swift

IN EUROPE VOL.1-3 1934-1939
CD _______ CBC 1006
Bellaphon / Jun '93 / New Note/Pinnacle

JAZZ MASTERS
CD _______ 5218562
Verve / Apr '94 / PolyGram

LADY BE GOOD
Lullaby / Oh lady be good / Lost in a fog / Honeysuckle rose / Some of these days / After you've gone / After you've gone (alternative take) / I only have eyes for you / I only have eyes for you (alternative take) / I wish I were twins / I wish I were twins (alternative takes) / Hands across the table / Hands across the tables (alternate take) / Blue moon / Avalon / What a difference a day makes / Stardust / Chicago / Chicago (alternate take) / Meditation / What Harlem is to me / What Harlem is to me (alternate take) / Netcha's dream
CD _______ GRF 093
Tring / '93 / Tring

LIVE FROM THE LONDON HOUSE (Chicago 1963) (Hawkins, Coleman Quartet)
CD _______ JASMCD 2521
Jasmine / Nov '93 / Conifer/BMG / Hot Shot / TKO Magnum

MASTER, THE
I only have eyes for you / 'S wonderful / I'm in the mood for love / Bean at the met / Flame thrower / Imagination / Night and day / Cattin' at the Keynote / On the sunny side of the street / Three little words / Battle of the saxes / Louise / Make believe / Don't blame me / Just one of those things / Hallelujah / I'm yours / Under a blanket of blue / Beyond the blue horizon / (In) a shanty in old Shanty Town
CD _______ LEJAZZCD 37
Le Jazz / May '95 / Cadillac / Koch

MASTERPIECES
CD _______ 158712
Jazz Archives / Apr '97 / Discovery

MASTERS OF JAZZ VOL.12
CD _______ STCD 4112
Storyville / Feb '89 / Cadillac / Jazz Music / Wellard

PASSIN' IT AROUND
CD _______ JHR 73515
Jazz Hour / '91 / Cadillac / Jazz Music / Target/BMG

PICASSO
CD _______ CD 53117
Giants Of Jazz / Nov '92 / Cadillac / Jazz Music / Target/BMG

QUINTESSENCE, THE (1926-1944/2CD Set)
CD Set _______ FA 213
Fremeaux / Nov '95 / ADA / Discovery

RAINBOW MIST
CD _______ DDCD 459
Delmark / Aug '93 / ADA / Cadillac / CM / Direct / Hot Shot

RARE RECORDINGS AND SOUNDTRACKS (The Golden Age of Jazz)
CD _______ JZCD 362
Suisa / May '92 / Jazz Music / THE

SAVOY BROADCASTS 1940 (Hawkins, Coleman & Erskine Hawkins)
Tuxedo junction / I'll be faithful / Whispering grass / Gin mill blues / Junction blues / Gabriel meets the Duke / Leanin' on the old top rail / Midnight stroll / Body and soul / Chant of the groove / Forgive a fool / Asleep in the deep / Can't get Indiana off my mind / Passin' it around / When a congresman meets a senator down South / I can't believe that you're in love with me
CD _______ TAX 37072
Tax / Aug '94 / Cadillac / Jazz Music / Wellard

SIRIUS
Man I love / Don't blame me / Just a gigolo / One I love / Time on my hands / Sweet and lovely / Exactly like you / Street of dreams / Sugar
CD _______ OJCCD 861
Original Jazz Classics / Nov '95 / Complete/ Pinnacle / Jazz Music / Wellard

SONG OF THE HAWK
Rhythm crazy / Oh lady be good / It sends me / Ol' man river / Heartbreak blues / Day you came along / When day is done / Sweet Georgia Brown / Out of nowhere / Passin' it around / Rocky comfort / My blue heaven / Meet Dr. Foo / Blue moon / What a difference a day makes / Bouncing with bean / He's funny that way / Fine dinner / Stardust / Love cries / I ain't got nobody
CD _______ PASTCD 7032
Flapper / Jan '94 / Pinnacle

SOUL
CD _______ OJCCD 96
Original Jazz Classics / Oct '92 / Complete/Pinnacle / Jazz Music / Wellard

STANDARDS AND WARHORSES (Hawkins, Coleman & Red Allen)
CD _______ JASSCD 2
Jass / Oct '91 / ADA / Cadillac / CM / Direct / Jazz Music

SUPREME
Lover come back to me / Body and soul / In walked bud / Quintessence / Fine and dandy / Ow
CD _______ ENJ 90092
Enja / Apr '95 / New Note/Pinnacle / Vital/ SAM

SWINGVILLE 2001 (Hawkins, Coleman & the Red Garland Trio)
It's a blue world / I want to be loved / Red beans and rice / Bean's blues / Blues for Ron
CD _______ OJCCD 418
Original Jazz Classics / Apr '93 / Complete/ Pinnacle / Jazz Music / Wellard

SWINGVILLE 2005 (Hawkins, Coleman All Stars)
You blew out the flame in my heart / More bounce to the vonce / I'm beginning to see the light / Cool blue / Some stretching
CD _______ OJCCD 225
Original Jazz Classics / Feb '97 / Complete/ Pinnacle / Jazz Music / Wellard

TENOR FOR ALL SEASONS, THE (2CD Set)
Battle hymn of the republic: *Hawkins, Coleman & Red Allen* / Frankie and Johnny: *Hawkins, Coleman & Red Allen* / When the saints go marchin' in: *Hawkins, Coleman & Red Allen* / South: *Hawkins, Coleman & Red Allen* / Won't you come home Bill Bailey: *Hawkins, Coleman & Red Allen* / Blues: *Hawkins, Coleman & Red Allen* / Maryland my Maryland: *Hawkins, Coleman & Red Allen* / Stormy weather: *Hawkins, Coleman & Red Allen* / Mean to me: *Hawkins, Coleman & Red Allen* / Lonesome road: *Hawkins, Coleman & Red Allen* / Sleepy time gal: *Hawkins, Coleman & Red Allen* / Summertime: *Hawkins, Coleman & Red Allen* / All of me: *Hawkins, Coleman & Red Allen* / Tea for two: *Hawkins, Coleman & Red Allen* / Blue Lou: *Hawkins, Coleman & Roy Eldridge* / Basin Street blues: *Hawkins, Coleman & Roy Eldridge* / Just you just me: *Hawkins, Coleman & Roy Eldridge* / Rifftide: *Hawkins, Coleman & Roy Eldridge* / I can't get started/These foolish things: *Hawkins, Coleman & Roy Eldridge* / Undecided: *Hawkins, Coleman & Roy Eldridge* / Honeysuckle rose: *Hawkins, Coleman & Roy Eldridge* / Oh lady be good: *Hawkins, Coleman & Roy Eldridge* / How high the moon/Ornithology: *Hawkins, Coleman & Roy Eldridge*
CD Set _______ JZCL 5017
Jazz Classics / Jul '97 / Cadillac / Direct / Jazz Music

TODAY AND NOW (Hawkins, Coleman Quartet)
Go Li'l Liza / Quintessence / Don't love me / Love song from Apache / Put on your old grey bonnet / Swingin' Scotch / Don't sit under the apple tree
CD _______ IMP 11842
Impulse Jazz / Sep '96 / New Note/BMG

WITH HENRY RED ALLEN & HORACE HENDERSON 1933/34 (Hawkins, Coleman/Henry Allen/Horace Henderson)
Someday sweetheart / I wish I could shimmy like my sister Kate / River's takin' care of me / Ain'tcha got music / Stringin' along on a shoe string / Shadows on the Swanee / Day you come along / Jamaica shout / Heartbreak blues / Hush my mouth / You're gonna lose your gal / Dark clouds / My galveston gal / Happy feet / I'm rhythm crazy now / Ol' man river / Minnie the moocher's wedding day / Ain't cha glad / I've got to sing a torch song
CD _______ HEPCD 1028
Hep / Apr '90 / Cadillac / Jazz Music / New Note/Pinnacle / Wellard

Hawkins, Dale

LET'S ALL TWIST
CD _______ EDCD 385
Edsel / Aug '94 / Pinnacle

Hawkins, Edwin

OH HAPPY DAY (The Best Of Edwin Hawkins) (Hawkins, Edwin Singers)
Oh happy day / To my father's house / Lord don't move that mountain / Children get together / I heard the voice of Jesus say / Precious memories / Joy joy / He's a friend of mine / I'm going through / Footprints of Jesus / All you need / Jesus / I shall be free / Mine all mine / My Lord is coming back
CD NEMCD 636
Sequel / Jun '93 / BMG

OH HAPPY DAY (Hawkins, Edwin Singers)
CD TRTCD 169
TrueTrax / Jun '95 / THE

Hawkins, Erskine

CLASSICS 1936-1938
CD CLASSICS 653
Classics / Nov '92 / Discovery / Jazz Music

CLASSICS 1939-1940
CD CLASSICS 678
Classics / Mar '93 / Discovery / Jazz Music

CLASSICS 1941-1945
CD CLASSICS 868
Classics / Mar '96 / Discovery / Jazz Music

ERSKINE HAWKINS 1940-1941 (Hawkins, Erskine & His Orchestra)
CD CLASSICS 701
Classics / Jul '93 / Discovery / Jazz Music

Hawkins, George Jr.

EVERY DOG
CD IRS 993169
Edge Of Fluke / Mar '97 / Cargo

Hawkins, Hawkshaw

HAWK 1953-1961 (3CD Set)
I'll trade yours for mine / Heap of lovin' / Mark round your finger / Long way / When you say yes / I'll take a chance with you / I'll never close my heart to you / Why don't you leave this town / Rebound / One white rose / I wanna be hugged to death by you / Why didn't I hear from you / Flashing lights / Waitin' for my baby / Kokomo / Ling ting tong / Pedro Gonzales Tennessee Lopez / How could anything so pretty / Car hoppin' mama / Love you steal / Oh how I cried / Borrowing / If it ain't on the menu / I gotta have you / Standing at the end of the world / I've got it again / Sunny side of the mountain / You just stood there / Dark moon / I'll get even with you / Guilty of dreaming / Are you happy / She was here / Freedom / It's easier said than done / Sensation / Ring on your finger / It would be a doggone lie / My fate is in your hands / I'll be gone / Best of company / Action / You can't find happiness that way / I don't apologise for loving you / With this pen / Thank you for thinking of me / Twenty miles from shore / Big ole heartache / Big red benson / Soldier's joy / Patanio, the pride of the plains / Alaska Lil and Texas Bill / Darkness on the face of the earth / Put a nickel in the jukebox / I can't seem to say goodbye / No love for me / You know me much too well / My story / Love I have for you / Your conscience
CD Set BCD 15539
Bear Family / Aug '91 / Direct / Rollercoaster / Swift

Hawkins, Ronnie

FOLK BALLADS OF RONNIE HAWKINS
Summertime / Sometimes I feel like a Motherless child / I gave my love a cherry / Brave man / Poor wayfaring stranger / Virginia bride / Mister and Mississippi / John Henry / Fare thee well / Out of a hundred / Death of Floyd Collins / Love from afar
CD EDCD 386
Edsel / Aug '94 / Pinnacle

HELLO AGAIN, MARY LOU (Hawkins, Ronnie & The Hawks)
CD PRD 70242
Provogue / Feb '91 / Pinnacle

ROULETTE YEARS, THE
Ruby baby / Forty days / Horace / One of these days / What'cha gonna do when the creek runs dry / Wild little Willie / Mary Lou / Oh sugar / Odessa need your lovin' / My girl is red hot / Dizzy Miss Lizzy / Hayride / C riff rock / Baby Jean / Southern love / Someone like you / Hey Boba Lou / Love me like you can / You cheated, you lied / Dreams do come true / Lonely hours / Clara / Honey don't / Sick and tired / Ballad of Caryl Chessman / Summertime / You know I love you / Sexy ways / Come come / Searchin' / Honey love / I feel good / Suzie Q / Matchbox / What a party / Bo Diddley / Who do you love / Bossman / High blood pressure / There's a screw loose / Arkansas / Mojo man / Further on up the road / Nineteen years old / Cathy Jean / Mojo man take 1 / Hayride No.1 / Light in your window / My heart cries / Look for me / Love it up / Your love is what I need / Kansas City / Going to Moscow
CD Set NEDCD 266
Sequel / Oct '94 / BMG

SINGS THE SONGS OF HANK WILLIAMS
CD EDCD 387
Edsel / Aug '94 / Pinnacle

Hawkins, Screamin' Jay

BLACK MUSIC FOR WHITE PEOPLE
Is you is or is you ain't my baby / I feel alright / I put a spell on you / I hear you knocking / Heart attack and vine / Ignant and shit / Swamp gas / Voodoo priestess / Ice cream man / I want your body / Ol' man river / Strokin'
CD FIENDCD 211
Demon / Mar '91 / Pinnacle
CD BP 401022
Manifesto / Feb '97 / Vital

COW FINGERS AND MOSQUITO PIE
Little demon / You ain't fooling me / I put a spell on you / You made me love you / Yellow coat / Hong Kong / There's something wrong with you / I love Paris / Orange coloured sky / Alligator wine / Darling please forgive me / Take me back to my boots and saddle / Temptation / Frenzy / Person to person / Little demon / I put a spell on you / There's something wrong with you / Alligator wine
CD 4712702
Legacy / Mar '92 / Sony

I PUT A SPELL ON YOU
Portrait of a man / Itty bitty pretty one / Don't deceive me / What's gonna happen on the 8th day / Ashes / We love / It's only make believe / Please don't leave me / I put a spell on you / I don't know / Guess who / What good is it
CD CPCD 8221
Charly / Jun '96 / Koch

I SHAKE MY STICK AT YOU
CD AIM 1031CD
Aim / Oct '93 / ADA / Direct / Jazz Music

LIVE AND CRAZY
CD ECD 260032
Evidence / Jan '92 / ADA / Cadillac / Harmonia Mundi

PORTRAIT OF A MAN
CD EDCD 414
Edsel / Jan '95 / Pinnacle

REAL LIFE
Deep in love / Get down France / Serving time / Feast of the Mau-Mau / Poor folks / Constipation blues / Your kind of love / All night / Alligator wine / I feel alright / Mountain jive
CD CDCHARLY 163
Charly / Feb '89 / Koch

REAL LIFE-1983
CD 157552
Blues Collection / Feb '93 / Discovery

SCREAMIN' JAY HAWKINS 1952-1955 (The Complete Gotham & Grand Recordings)
I put a spell on you / 10,000 Lincoln continental / Why did you waste my time / No hug no kiss / Take me back / Coronation jump
CD SJHCD 71829
Screamin' Jay Hawkins / Oct '91 / Hot Shot / Jazz Music / Wellard

SOMETHIN' FUNNY GOIN' ON
Somethin' funny goin' on / I am the cool / Whistlin' past the graveyard / Rock the house / Scream the blues / Brujo / You make me sick / Give it a break / When you walked out the door / Fourteen wives
CD FIENDCD 750
Demon / Feb '94 / Pinnacle

SPELLBOUND 1955-1974
Voodoo / You put a spell on me / Makaha waves / There's too many teardrops / Two can play this game / Shattered / You're an exception to the rule / I'm not made of clay / All night / Mountain jive (unissued) / I'll be there / You're all of my life to me / Well I tried / Even though / Talk about me / In my front room / This is all / What that is (unissued) / She put the whamee on me / I put a spell on you / Two can play this game (unissued) / Shattered (unissued) / You're an exception to the rule (unissued) / What that is / Feast of the Mau-Mau / Do you really love me / Stone crazy / I love you / Constipation blues / I'm lonely / Thing called woman / Dig / I'm your man / Ask him / Reprise / Please don't leave me / I want to know / I need you / My Marion / Bit it / Move me / Goodnight my love / Our love is not for three / Ain't nobody's business if I do / Take me back / Trying to reach my goal / So long
CD Set BCD 15530
Bear Family / Oct '90 / Direct / Rollercoaster / Swift

Hawkins, Sophie B.

TONGUES AND TAILS
Damn, I wish I was your lover / California here I come / Mysteries we understand / Saviour child / Carry me / I want you / Before I walk on fire / We are one body / Listen / Live and let love / Don't stop swaying
CD 4688232
Columbia / Sep '94 / Sony

WHALER
Right beside you / Did we not choose each other / Don't don't tell me no / As I lay me down / Swing from limb to limb (my home is in your jungle) / True romance / Let me love you up / Ballad of sleeping beauty / I need nothing else / Sometimes I see / Mr. Tugboat Hello
CD 4765122
Columbia / Aug '94 / Sony

Hawkins, Ted

BEST OF THE VENICE BEACH TAPES, THE
I got what I wanted / Ladder of success / Gypsy woman / He will break your heart / There stands a glass / Country roads / (Sittin' on the) dock of the bay / Crystal chandeliers / Don't ever leave me / Let the good times roll / Chain gang / San Francisco / Bring it on home to me / Green green grass of home / Part time love / North to Alaska / Quiet place / Your cheatin' heart / Too busy thinking about my baby / Blowin' in the wind / Searchin' for my baby / Just my imagination / I love you most of all
CD UACD 101
Unamerican Activities / Jan '97 / Hot Shot

HAPPY HOUR
CD ROUCD 2033
Rounder / Jul '94 / ADA / CM / Direct

NEXT HUNDRED YEARS
Strange conversation / Big things / There stands the glass / Biloxi / Groovy little things / Good and the bad / Afraid / Green-eyed girl / Ladder of success / Long as I can see the light
CD GED 24627
Geffen / Apr '94 / BMG

WATCH YOUR STEP
Watch your step / Bring it home Daddy / If you love me / Don't lose your cool / Lost ones / Who got my natural comb / Peace and Happiness / Sweet baby / Stop your crying / Put in a cross / Sorry you're sick / Watch your step / TWA / I gave up all I had / Stay close to me
CD ROUCD 2024
Rounder / Jul '94 / ADA / CM / Direct

Hawkins, Tramaine

ALL MY BEST TO YOU
Praise the name of Jesus / Potter's house / What shall I do / Goin' up yonder / All things are possible / Changed / Coming home / Highway / He loves me / Who is he / We're all in the same boat together
CD SPD 1429
Alliance Music / Aug '95 / EMI

Hawkshaw, Alan

GIRL IN A SPORTS CAR
Girl in a sports car / Scooter girl / Sunflower / Warm hearts / Bluebird / Midnight rhapsody / Happy rainbow / Amour / Blue note / Grange Hill / Brush off / Playmate / Flapjack / Man alone / Sky train / Man of means / Love at first sight / Beauty spot / Moody / Sheer elegance / Blue haze / Piccadilly night ride / Beat boutique / Dave Allen at large / Destination venus
CD HF 53CD
Coliseum / Jun '97 / Warner Music

Hawkwind

ACID DAZE
CD Set RRCD 1X
Receiver / May '90 / Grapevine/PolyGram

ALIEN
CD EBSCD 118
Emergency Broadcast System / Dec '96 / BMG

ANTHOLOGY
CD Set ESBCD 168
Essential / Mar '92 / BMG

BEST OF FRIENDS AND FAMILY, THE
CD EMPRCD 547
Emporio / Nov '94 / Disc

BEST OF FRIENDS AND RELATIONS
CD SHARP 1724CD
Flicknife / Nov '88 / Pinnacle

BRING ME THE HEAD OF YURI GAGARIN (Live At The Empire Pool - 1973)
Ga ga / Egg / Orgone accumulator / Wage war / Urban guerilla / Masters of the universe / Welcome to the future / Sonic attack / Silver machine
CD CDTB 101
Thunderbolt / Dec '92 / TKO Magnum
CD 14846
CD CDCRH 108
Charly / Feb '97 / Koch

BUSINESS TRIP, THE
Altair / Quark, strangeness and charm / LSD / Camera that could lie / Green finned demon / Do that / Day a wall came down / Berlin axis / Void of golden light / Right stuff / Wastelands / Dream goes on / Right to decide / Dream has ended / Future / Terra mystica
CD EBSCD 111
Emergency Broadcast System / Sep '94 / BMG

CHRONICLE OF THE BLACK SWORD
Song of the swords / Shade gate / Sea king / Pulsing cavern / Elric the enchanter / Needle gun / Zarzinia / Demise / Sleep of a thousand tears / Chaos army / Horn of destiny
CD DOJOCD 72
Dojo / Feb '94 / Disc

CHURCH OF HAWKWIND
Angel voices / Nuclear drive / Star cannibal / Phenomeno of luminosity / Fall of Earth City / Church / Joker at the gate / Some people never die / Light specific data / Experiment with destiny / Last Messiah / Looking in the future
CD DOJOCD 86
Dojo / Jun '94 / Disc

DOREMI FASOL LATIDO
Brainstorm / Space is deep / One change / Lord of the light / Down through the night / Time we left this world today / Watcher / Urban guerilla / Brainbox pollution / Lord of light / Ejection
CD HAWKS 3
EMI / Mar '96 / EMI

EARLY DAZE BEST OF
Hurry on sundown / Dreaming / Masters of the universe / In the egg / Orgone accumulator / Sonic attack / Silver machine
CD CDTB 044
Thunderbolt / Jun '88 / TKO Magnum

EMERGENCY BROADCAST SYSTEM SAMPLES (Various Artists)
Camera that could lie: *Hawkwind* / Green finned demon: *Hawkwind* / Coded language: *Hawkwind* / Angels of death: *Hawkwind* / Journey: *Hawkwind* / Xenomorph: *Hawkwind* / Sonic destruction: *Hawkwind* / Rizz's radio song: *Captain Rizz* / Frenzzy: *Psychedelic Warriors* / Yassasim: *Simon House* / White zone: *Brock, Dave* / Morbius: *Spaceheads* / Brain machine: *Spaceheads* / Higher than before: *Davey, Alan*
CD EBSCD 119
Emergency Broadcast System / Nov '96 / BMG

FUTURE RECONSTRUCTIONS
Sonic attack / Forge of Vulcan / Masters of the universe / Spirit of the age / You shouldn't do that / Sonic destruction / Damnation alley / Uncle Sam's on Mars / Silver machine / Needle gun
CD EBSSCD 117
Emergency Broadcast System / Nov '96 / BMG

HALL OF THE MOUNTAIN GRILL
Psychedelic warlords (disappear in smoke) / Wind of change / D rider / Webb weaver / You'd better believe it / Hall of the mountain grill / Lost Johnny / Goat willow / Paradox / It's so easy
CD HAWKS 5
EMI / Mar '96 / EMI

HAWKWIND
Hurry on sundown / Reason is / Be yourself / Paranoia part 1 / Paranoia part 2 / Seeing it as you really are / Mirror of illusion / Bring it on home / Hurry on sundown / Kiss of the velvet whip / Cymbaline
CD HAWKS 1
EMI / Mar '96 / EMI

IN AND OUTTAKE
CD DOJOCD 153
Dojo / Nov '94 / Disc

IN SEARCH OF SPACE
You shouldn't do that / You know you're only dreaming / Masters of the universe / We took the wrong step years ago / Adjust me / Children of the sun / Silver machine / Seven by seven / Born to go
CD HAWKS 2
EMI / Mar '96 / EMI

INDEPENDENT DAYS VOL.1 & 2
Night of the hawks / Motorway city / Motorhead / Angels of death / Who's gonna win the war / Watching the grass grow / Over the top / Hurry on sundown / Kiss of the velvet whip / Kings of speed / Social alliance / Dream dancers / Dragons and fables
CD CDMGRAM 94
Anagram / Sep '95 / Cargo / Pinnacle

IT'S THE BUSINESS OF THE FUTURE TO BE DANGEROUS
It's the business of the future to be dangerous / Space is their (palestine) / Tibet is not China (part 1) / Tibet is not China (part 2) / Let barking dogs lie / Wave upon wave / Letting in the past / Camera that could lie / 3 or 4 Erections in the course of a night / Techno tropic zone exists / Gimme shelter / Avante
CD ESMCD 390
Essential / Aug '96 / BMG

LEVITATION
Levitation / Motorway city / Psychosis / World of tiers / Prelude / Who's gonna win the war / Space chase / Fifth second of forever / Dust of time
CD CLACD 129
Castle / Jul '87 / BMG

LIVE 1979
Shotdown in the night / Motorway city / Spirit of the age / Brainstorm / Lighthouse / Masters of the universe / Silver machine
CD ______ CLACD 243
Castle / Jul '94 / BMG

LIVE COLLECTION
Song of the sword / Dragons and fables / Narration / Sea king / Angels of death / Choose your masques / Flight sequence / Needle gun / Zarozinia / Lords of chaos / Dark Lords / Wizard of Pan Tang / Shade gate / Rocky paths / Pulsing cavern / Masters of the universe / Dreaming city / Moonglum (Friend without a cause) / Elric the enchanter / Conjuration of magnu / Magnu dust of time / Horn of fate
CD ______ CCSCD 321
Castle / Apr '92 / BMG

LOVE IN SPACE (2CD Set)
Abducted / Deathtrap / Wastelands / Are you losing your mind / Photo encounter / Blue skin / Robot / Alien / Sputnik Stan / Xenomorph / Vega / Love in space / Kapal / Elfin / Silver machine / Welcome / Assassins of Allah
CD Set ______ EBSSCD 120
Emergency Broadcast System / Nov '96 / BMG

MASTERS OF THE UNIVERSE
Masters of the universe / Brainstorm / Sonic attack / Orgone accumulator / It's so easy / Lost Johnny
CD ______ CDFA 3220
Fame / May '89 / EMI
CD ______ 14972
Spalax / Apr '97 / ADA / Cargo / Direct / Discovery / Greyhound

MASTERS OF THE UNIVERSE
CD ______ PLSCD 207
Pulse / Apr '97 / BMG

MIGHTY HAWKWIND CLASSICS 1980-85
Hurry on sundown / Sweet mistress of pain / King of speed (live) / Motorhead / Valium ten / Night of the hawks / Green finned demon / Dream dancers / Dragons and fables / Over the top / Free fall / Death trap
CD ______ CDMGRAM 86
Anagram / Apr '92 / Cargo / Pinnacle

ONWARD FLIES THE BIRD (Live & Rare)
CD ______ EMPRCD 710
Emporio / Mar '97 / Disc

OUT AND INTAKE
Turning point / Waiting for tomorrow / Cajun jinx / Solitary mind games / Starflight / Ejection / Assassins of Allah / Flight to Maputo / Confrontation / Five to four / Ghost dance
CD ______ SHARP 040CD
Flicknife / Apr '87 / Pinnacle

PALACE SPRINGS
Back in the box / Treadmill / Void of golden light / Lives of great men / Time we left / Heads / Acid test / Damnation alley
CD ______ CLACD 303
Castle / '92 / BMG

PSYCHEDELIC WARLORDS
CD ______ CLEO 57412
Cleopatra / Oct '94 / Cargo / Greyhound / Plastic Head / RTM/Disc / SRD

RARITIES (Hawkwind & Friends/Relations)
Aimless fight: *Underground Zero* / Psychedelia lives: *Hawkwind* / Working time: *Lloyd-Langton, Huw Group* / Rainbow warrior: *Underground Zero* / Brothel in Rosenstrasse: *Moorcock, Michael Deep Fix* / Toad on the run: *Mulo, Alman Band* / Earth calling: *Hawkwind* / Changing: *Bainbridge, Harvey* / Widow song: *Calvert, Robert* / Starcruiser: *Moorcock, Michael Deep Fix* / ICU: *Inner City Unit* / I see you: *Lloyd-Langton, Huw Group* / Human beings: *Inner City Unit* / Atom bomb: *Atom God* / Phone home Elliot: *Turner, Nik*
CD ______ CDMGRAM 91
Anagram / Mar '95 / Cargo / Pinnacle

SILVER MACHINE
Prelude / Silver machine / Shot down in the night / Dust of time / Psychosis / Ghost dance / You shouldn't do that / Urban guerilla / Who's gonna win the war / Fifth second of forever / Nuclear toy / Levitation / Space chase / Motorway city
CD ______ 5507642
Spectrum / Mar '95 / PolyGram

SPACE BANDITS
Images / Black Elk speaks / Wings / Out of the shadow / Realms / Ship of dreams / TV suicide
CD ______ CLACD 282
Castle / Jul '92 / BMG

SPACE RITUAL
Earth calling / Born to go / Down through the night / Awakening / Lord of Light / Black corridor / Space is deep / Electronic no.1 / Orgone accumulator / Upside down / Ten seconds of forever / Brainstorm / Seven by seven / Sonic attack / Time we left this world today / Masters of the universe / Welcome to the future / You shouldn't do that / Masters of the Universe
CD ______ HAWKS 4
EMI / Mar '96 / EMI

SPACE RITUAL VOL.2
Space / Accumulator / Upside down sonic attack / Time we left / Ten seconds of forever / Brainstorm / Seven by seven / Masters of the universe / Welcome to the future
CD ______ CDTB 099
Thunderbolt / Jan '91 / TKO Magnum
CD ______ 14520
Spalax / Jul '97 / ADA / Cargo / Direct / Discovery / Greyhound

STASIS (The UA Years 1971-1975)
Urban guerilla / Psychedelic warlords (disappear in smoke) / Brainbox pollution / Seven by seven / Paradox / Silver machine / You'd better believe it / Lord of light / Black corridor / Space is deep / Earth calling / Born to go / Down through the night / Awakening / You shouldn't do that
CD ______ CDFA 3267
Fame / Apr '92 / EMI

TEXT OF FESTIVAL, THE (Hawkwind Live 1970-1972)
Masters of the universe / Dreaming / You shouldn't do that / Hurry on sundown / Paranoia / See it as you really are / I do it / Came home / Sound shouldn't / Improvise / Improvise...compromise / Reprise
CD ______ CDTB 068
Thunderbolt / Mar '97 / TKO Magnum

THIS IS HAWKWIND... DO NOT PANIC
PSY power / Levitation / Circles / Space chase / Death trap / Angel of death / Show down in the night / Stonehenge decoded / Watching the grass grow
CD ______ CDMGRAM 54
Anagram / Jun '92 / Cargo / Pinnacle

TRAVELLERS AID TRUST, THE
CD ______ SHARP 2045CD
Flicknife / Dec '88 / Pinnacle

UNDISCLOSED FILES - ADDENDUM
Orctone accumulator / Ghost dance / Sonic attack / Watching the grass grow / Coded language / Damned by the curse of man / Ejection / Motorway city / Dragons and fables / Heads / Angels of death
CD ______ EBSCD 114
Emergency Broadcast System / Nov '96 / BMG

XENON CODEX, THE
War I survived / Wastelands of sleep / Neon skyline / Lost chronicles / Tides / Heads / Mutation zone / EMC / Sword of the East / Good evening
CD ______ CLACD 281
Castle / Mar '93 / BMG

ZONES
Zones / Dangerous vision / Running through the back brain / Island / Motorway city / Utopia 84 / Sociat alliance / Sonic attack / Dream worker / Brainstorm
CD ______ CDMGRAM 57
Anagram / Jun '88 / Cargo / Pinnacle

ZONES/STONEHENGE
CD ______ SHARP 1422CD
Flicknife / Nov '88 / Pinnacle

Hawley, Jane

AS WE WALK ON THIN ICE
CD ______ TX 3004CD
Taxim / Jan '94 / ADA

Haworth, Bryn

LIVE (Haworth, Bryn Band)
CD ______ KMCD 683
Kingsway / Oct '94 / Complete/Pinnacle

Hawthorne-Nelson, Vaughan

EMERGENCE
Times are a changing / Tale of tomorrow / Warrior's way / Other ways of knowing / Emergence / Forgotten silence / Inner journey / Visions of the self / Place called home / Song for the ancestors
CD ______ TML 001
TML / Sep '96 / New Note/Pinnacle / Vital/SAM

Hay, Colin James

PEAKS AND VALLEYS
Into the cornfields / She keeps me dreaming / Can't take this town / Walk amongst his ruins / Hold onto my hand / Keep on walking / Dream on / Boy boy / Conversation / Melbourne song / Sometimes I wish / Go ask an old man / Sea dogs
CD ______ HYCD 296166
Hypertension / Feb '97 / ADA / CM / Direct / Total/BMG

TOPANGA
CD ______ LICD 901304
Line / Jan '96 / CM / Direct

Hayden

MOVING CAREFUL
CD ______ SUNCD 032
Sonic Unyon / Dec '96 / Cargo

Hayden, Cathal

CATHAL HAYDEN
CD ______ CBM 012CD
Cross Border Media / Mar '94 / ADA / Direct / Grapevine/PolyGram

Hayes, Clancy

OH BY JINGO
Oh by jingo / Rose of Washington Square / Oriental strut / I'm comin' Virginia / Wise guy / Beale Street blues / Cakewalking babies / Tin roof blues / King Chanticleer / Michigan water blues / New Orleans stomp / My little bimbo / Tin roof blues / Rose of Washington Square / King Chanticleer / Michigan water blues / I'm comin' Virginia / New Orleans stomp
CD ______ DE 210
Delmark / Jun '97 / ADA / Cadillac / CM / Direct / Hot Shot

Hayes, Clifford

CLIFFORD HAYES & THE DIXIELAND JUG BLOWERS (Hayes, Clifford & The Dixieland Jug Blowers)
CD ______ YAZCD 1054
Yazoo / Apr '91 / ADA / CM / Koch

CLIFFORD HAYES & THE LOUISVILLE JUG BANDS VOL.1 1924-26 (Hayes, Clifford & The Louisville Jug Bands)
CD ______ JPCD 15012
Jazz Perspectives / May '94 / Hot Shot / Jazz Music

CLIFFORD HAYES & THE LOUISVILLE JUG BANDS VOL.2 1926-27 (Hayes, Clifford & The Louisville Jug Bands)
CD ______ JPCD 15022
Jazz Perspectives / May '94 / Hot Shot / Jazz Music

CLIFFORD HAYES & THE LOUISVILLE JUG BANDS VOL.3 1927-29 (Hayes, Clifford & The Louisville Jug Bands)
CD ______ JPCD 15032
Jazz Perspectives / May '94 / Hot Shot / Jazz Music

CLIFFORD HAYES & THE LOUISVILLE JUG BANDS VOL.4 1929-31 (Hayes, Clifford & The Louisville Jug Bands)
CD ______ JPCD 15042
Jazz Perspectives / May '94 / Hot Shot / Jazz Music

FROG HOP (Hayes, Clifford Louisville Stompers)
CD ______ DGF 10
Frog / Jan '97 / Cadillac / Jazz Music / Wellard

Hayes, Edgar

EDGAR HAYES 1937-38
CD ______ CLASSICS 730
Classics / Jan '94 / Discovery / Jazz Music

Hayes, Isaac

BRANDED
Ike's plea / Life's mood / Fragile / Life's mood II / Summer in the city / Let me love you / I'll do anything (to turn you on) / Thanks to the fool / Branded / Soulsville / Hyperbolicsyllabicsesquedalymistic
CD ______ VPBCD 24
Pointblank / May '95 / EMI

COLLECTION, THE
Shaft / Joy / Never can say goodbye / Walk on by / I stand accused / (If loving you is wrong) I don't want to be right / I just don't know what to do with myself / By the time I get to Phoenix
CD ______ VSOPCD 210
Connoisseur Collection / Feb '95 / Pinnacle

HOT BUTTERED SOUL
Walk on by / Hyperbolicsyllabicsesquedalymistic / One woman / By the time I get to Phoenix
CD ______ CDSXE 005
Stax / May '91 / Pinnacle

HOTBED
Use me / I'm gonna have to tell her / Ten commandments of love / Feel like makin' love / Hobosac and me
CD ______ CDSXE 105
Stax / Jul '94 / Pinnacle

ISAAC'S MOODS
Ike's mood / Soulsville / Joy / (If loving you is wrong) I don't want to be right / Never can say goodbye / Shaft / Ike's rap IV / Brand new me / Do your thing / Walk on by / I stand accused / Ike's rap I / Hyperbolicsyllabicsesquedalymistic / Ike's rap III / Ike's rap II
CD ______ CDSX 011
Stax / Apr '88 / Pinnacle

JOY
Joy / I love you that's all / Man will be a man / Feeling keeps on coming / I'm gonna make it (without you)
CD ______ CDSXE 047
Stax / May '92 / Pinnacle

LIVE AT THE SAHARA TAHOE
Shaft / Come on / Light my fire / Ike's rap / Never can say goodbye / Windows of the world / Look of love / Ellie's love theme / Use me / Do your thing / Men / It's too late / Rock me baby / Stormy Monday blues / Type thang / First time ever I saw your face / Ike's rap VI / Ain't no sunshine / Feelin' alright
CD Set ______ CDSXE 2053
Stax / Jul '92 / Pinnacle

PRESENTING ISAAC HAYES
Precious precious / When I fall in love / I just wamt to make love to you / Rock me baby / Going to Chicago Blues / Misty / You don't know like I know
CD ______ SCD 8596
Stax / Jan '96 / Pinnacle

RAW AND REFINED
Birth of Shaft / Urban nights / Funkalicious / Tahoe Spring / Night before / Memphis trax / Soul fiddle / Funky junky / You make me live / Making love at the ocean / Southern breeze / Didn't know love was so good / 405
CD ______ VPBCD 25
Pointblank / Jul '95 / EMI

TO BE CONTINUED
Ike's rap 1 / Our day will come / Look of love / Ike's mood / You've lost that lovin' feelin' / Runnin' out of fools
CD ______ CDSXE 030
Stax / Feb '91 / Pinnacle

WONDERFUL
Ain't no sunshine / Rolling down a mountainside / I can't help it (if I'm still in love with you) / Wonderful / Someone made you for me / Ain't that loving you (for more reasons than one) / Baby I'm a want you / Mistletoe and me / Winter snow
CD ______ CDSXE 112
Stax / Jul '97 / Pinnacle

Hayes, Louis

CRAWL, THE (Hayes, Louis Sextet)
Escape velocity / Crawl / Yesterdays / Run before the sun / Autumn in New York / Blues in five dimensions / Bushman song
CD ______ CCD 79045
Candid / Feb '97 / Cadillac / Direct / Jazz Music / Koch / Wellard

LAUSANNE, 1977 (Hayes, Louis & Woody Shaw Quintet)
In case you haven't heard / Moontrane / Contemplation / Jean-Marie / Bilad as Sudan
CD ______ TCB 02052
TCB / Nov '96 / New Note/Pinnacle

SUPER QUARTET, THE (Hayes, Louis & Company)
Bolivia / Song is you / Up jumped spring / On your own sweet way / Chelsea Bridge / Epistrophy / Blue Lou / Fee fi fo fum
CD ______ CDSJP 424
Timeless Jazz / Feb '95 / New Note/Pinnacle

Hayes, Martin

MARTIN HAYES
Morning star/The Caoilte mountains / Paddy Fahy's jig/Sean Ryan's jig / Whistler from Rosslea/Connor Dunn's / Golden castle / Star of munster / Colliers/Johnny's wedding / Brown coffin/Good natured man / Green gowned lass / I buried my wife and danced on her grave / Rooms of Doogh / Mist covered mountain / Britches / Tommy Coen's reel/The swallow
CD ______ GLCD 1127
Green Linnet / Jul '93 / ADA / CM / Direct / Highlander / Roots

THAT LONESOME TOUCH (Hayes, Martin & Dennis Cahill)
Paddy Fahy's reel / Kerfunken jig / Paul Ha-'penny/Garden of butterflies/Broken pledge / Mother and child reel/Toss the feathers / John Naughton's reel/Another Paddy Fahy reel / Cat in the corner/John Naughton's jig / Old bush/The reel with the Burl / Lament for Limerick / My love is in America / Tell her I am/Gallagher's frolics / Rolling in the barrel/The morning dew / Bucks of Oranmore/Eileen Curran/Jimmy on the moor / Peggy's waltz
CD ______ GLCD 1181
Green Linnet / Jun '97 / ADA / CM / Direct / Highlander / Roots

UNDER THE MOON
CD ______ GL 1155CD
Green Linnet / Jul '95 / ADA / CM / Direct / Highlander / Roots

Hayes, Tommy

AN RAS
CD ______ LUNCD 055
Mulligan / Jan '95 / ADA / CM

Hayes, Tubby

200% PROOF
CD ______ CHECD 00105
Master Mix / Jul '92 / Jazz Music / New Note/Pinnacle / Wellard

FOR MEMBERS ONLY (Live 1967) (Hayes, Tubby Quartet)
Dear Johnny B / This is all I ask / Dolphin dance / Mexican green / Finky minky / For members only / You know I care / Conversations at dawn / Nobody else but me / Dedication to Joy / Off the wagon / Second city steamer

CD CDCHE 10
Master Mix / Jan '91 / Jazz Music / New Note/Pinnacle / Wellard

JAZZ TETE A TETE (Hayes, Tubby & Tony Coe)
CD PCD 7079
Progressive / Jan '94 / Jazz Music

NIGHT AND DAY
Half a sawbuck / Spring can really hang you up the most / Simple waltz / I'm old fahioned / Night and day
CD JHAS 602
Ronnie Scott's Jazz House / Oct '95 / Cadillac / Jazz Music / New Note/Pinnacle / TKO Magnum

TUBBY HAYES LIVE 1969 (Hayes, Tubby Quartet)
Introduction / Off the wagon / For Heaven's sake / Vierd blues / Walkin' / Where am I going / Mainly for the Don / Grits, beans and greens
CD HQCD 05
Harlequin / Oct '91 / Hot Shot / Jazz Music / Swift / Wellard

Haymes, Dick

CAPITOL YEARS, THE
It might as well be spring / More I see you / Very thought of you / You'll never know / If there is someone lovelier than you / How deep is the ocean / Nearness of you / Where or when / Little white lies / Our love is here to stay / Love walked in / Come rain or come shine / If I should lose you / You don't know what love is / Imagination / Skylark / Isn't this a lovely day (to be caught in the rain) / What's new / Way you look tonight / Then I'll be tired of you / I like the likes of you / Moonlight becomes you / Between the Devil and the deep blue sea / When I fall in love
CD CDEMS 1364
Capitol / Jun '90 / EMI

COMPLETE DUETS, THE (Haymes, Dick & Helen Forrest)
Long ago (and far away) / Look for the silver lining / It had to be you / Together / I'll buy that dream / Some Sunday morning / I'm always chasing rainbows / Tomorrow is forever / Oh what it seemed to be / You stole my heart / Gimme a little kiss, will ya, huh / 'Til we meet again / In love in vain / All through the day / Something to remember you by / Come rain or come shine / Why does it get late so early / Something old, something new
CD MCCD 208
Music Club / Jul '95 / Disc / THE

FOR YOU, FOR ME, FOR EVERMORE
CD ACD 130
Audiophile / May '95 / Jazz Music

HOW HIGH THE MOON (Haymes, Dick & Harry James & his Orchestra)
Cherry / My silent love / All or nothing at all / Fools rush in / Maybe / Skylark / Daydreaming / Mr. Meadowlark / Things I love / Yes indeed / How high the moon / He's my guy / Montevideo / Dolores / Walkin' by the river / Spring will be so sad / Ol' man river / You've got me out on a limb / I don't want to walk without you / Maria Elena / I've got a gal in Kalamazoo / Aurora / Sinner kissed an angel / You've changed
CD CDMOIR 510
Memoir / May '94 / Jazz Music / Target/ BMG

IT HAD TO BE YOU
I'll never smile again / Take me / Together / You'll never know / How many times do I have to tell you / Put your arms around me honey / Where or when / Indiana / How blue the night / Long ago and far away / Amado mio / Button up your overcoat / Our waltz / Let the rest of the world go by / It can't be wrong / Minka / I never mention your name / Janie / By the old corral / In my arms / If you were the only girl in the world / I don't want to love you / It had to be you
CD CDMOIR 512
Memoir / Nov '95 / Jazz Music / Target/ BMG

IT'S A GRAND NIGHT FOR SINGING
How high the moon / Fools rush in / Here comes the night / Braggin' / I'll get by / Aurora / Cherry / All or nothing at all / A sinner kissed an angel / You've changed / I've got a gal in Kalamazoo / Serenade in blue / It can't be wrong / You'll never know / Long ago (& far away) / How blue the night / Let the rest of the world go by / More I see you / I wish I knew / Love letters / Isn't it kinda fun / It might as well be Spring / That's for me / It's a grand night for singing
CD PLCD 546
President / Aug '96 / Grapevine/PolyGram / President / Target/BMG

KEEP IT SIMPLE (Haymes, Dick & Loonis McGlohon Trio)
More I see / I get along without you very well / Little white lies / Almost like being in love / Stella by starlight / Very thought of you / I'll remember April / That's for me / It might as well be spring / Who cares / Our love is here to stay / Love walked in / You'll never know / There will never be another you

CD ACD 200
Audiophile / Mar '95 / Jazz Music

SOFT LIGHTS AND SWEET MUSIC
I could write a book / There's a small hotel / Soft lights and sweet music / Penthouse serenade / Imagination / I love you / Stardust / But not for me / You're driving me crazy / You're blase / Time on my hands / Love me or leave me / I surrender dear / I never knew / Yearning / These foolish things
CD HCD 265
Hindsight / May '97 / Jazz Music / Target/ BMG

STAR EYES
Star eyes / Where or when / How sweet you are / All or nothing at all / Trolley song / Over the rainbow / When I grow too old to dream / Evelina / Day by day / More I see you / I wish I knew / Dream / I love you too much / Night and day / When the red red robbin comes bob-bob-bobin' along / It might as well be spring / My foolish heart / It's magic / Lazy / Thinking of you / Nevertheless / Twenty four hours of sunshine / Best things in life are free / That lucky old sun / All the things you are / Maybe / Lovely to look at / Gypsy in my soul / They say it's wonderful / Blue skies / September song
CD JCD 633
Jass / Dec '89 / ADA / Cadillac / CM / Direct / Jazz Music
CD JZCL 6004
Jazz Classics / Feb '97 / Cadillac / Direct / Jazz Music

SWINGIN' SESSION
CD CDSG 404
Starline / Aug '89 / Jazz Music

Haynes, Graham

GRIOT'S FOOTSTEPS, THE
CD 5232622
Verve / Jan '95 / PolyGram

TRANSITION
CD 5290392
Verve / Dec '95 / PolyGram

Haynes, Roy

HOMECOMING
Evidence / Green chimneys / You're blase / Bud Powell / Star eyes / Anniversary song
CD ECD 220922
Evidence / Jul '94 / ADA / Cadillac / Harmonia Mundi

MY SHINING HOUR (Haynes, Roy & Thomas Clausen's Jazzparticipants)
My shining hour / I fall in love too easily / Bessie's blues / All blues / Skylark / Rhythm-a-ning / A la blues / Bright
CD STCD 4199
Storyville / Mar '95 / Cadillac / Jazz Music / Wellard

OUT OF THE AFTERNOON (Haynes, Roy Quartet)
Moon ray / Fly me to the moon / Raoul / Snap crackle / If I should lose you / Long wharf / Some other Spring
CD IMP 11802
Impulse Jazz / Jan '96 / New Note/BMG

TE-VOU
Like this / If I could / Blues M45 / Trinkle twinkle / Trigonometry / Good for the soul
CD FDM 365692
Dreyfus / Nov '94 / ADA / Direct / New Note/Pinnacle

TRUE OR FALSE
CD FRLCD 007
Freelance / Oct '92 / Cadillac / Koch

Haynes, Victor

OPTIMISTIC
Don't want nobody else / This is love / Turn out the light / Breakin' my heart / Respect / Optimistic / Tell me where you are / Don't stop / Do you regret / First time / Tonight / Stand up
CD EXCDP 7
Expansion / Nov '94 / 3mv/Sony

Haywains

GET HAPPY WITH...
Bythesea Road / Tobe's gone west / Fisherman's friends / Summer madness / I'm not really as foolish as you think / Billy Corkhill's better / Side / Kicked in the teeth / Now I've got one up on you / Emily's shop / Really (Bee) / Last pancake / Surfin' in my sleep / I wouldn't want that / Forget me not / Please don't let me get hurt / Rosanna / Boy called Burden / You laughing at me laughing at you / Boy racers a go-go
CD ASKCD 024
Vinyl Japan / Sep '93 / Plastic Head / Vinyl Japan

NEVER MIND MANCHESTER, HERE'S ...THE HAYWAINS
Kill karaoke / Dusty Springfield / I hate to disappoint you / New kids on the block / Your point of view doesn't count / Money-go-round / Now I've got one up on you / I'm still waiting / Always the same / Somebody loves you / Why did I ever turn you down / Bythesea road / Hold on me / Time bomb baby / Forget me not
CD ASKCD 014
Vinyl Japan / Mar '93 / Plastic Head / Vinyl Japan

Hayward, Charles

SUB ROSA SESSIONS, BARI OCTOBER 1996 (Hayward, Charles & David Shea/ Nus)
CD QUANTUM 204
Sub Rosa / Mar '97 / Direct / RTM/Disc / SRD / Vital

Hayward, Dennis

50'S IN SEQUENCE
CD CDTS 037
Maestro / Aug '93 / Savoy

DANCING FOR PLEASURE
Bless 'em all / And the band played on / Hello hello, who's your lady friend / Ship ahoy (all the nice girls love a soldier) / My bonnie lies over the ocean / Jolly good company / Darling buds of May / Forever green / Dying swan / Jupiter / Love theme from Spartacus / Morning: Peer Gynt / One fine day / Mr. Wonderful / On a clear day (You can see forever) / Misty / Can't smile without you / I don't want to walk without you / Man I love / Can't help lovin' dat man / Nellie Dean / K-K-Katy / All by yourself in the moonlight / Dickie bird hop / Tchip tchip (birdie song) / Tonight / Lara's theme / Spanish eyes / Spanish harlem / Czardas / Sandie's shawl / Raindrops keep falling on my head / Raining in my heart / I'm confessin' that I love you / When somebody thinks you're wonderful
CD CDTS 034
Maestro / Aug '93 / Savoy

DENNIS HAYWARD'S PARTY DANCES (2CD Set)
Barn dance / Paul Jones / Blackpool belle / Blame it on the Bossa Nova / Chanson d'amour / Island of dreams / Knees up Mother Brown / Clap clap sound / Alley cat / Agadoo / Hands up / Atmophere / Y viva Espana / I just called to say I love you / Conga / Simon says / Birdie song / Brown girl in the ring / Rivers of Babylon / It's a holi holiday / Let's twist again / Loco-motion / Pal of my cradle days / Cokey cokey / Sailing / You'll never walk alone / We'll meet again / Fiona's polka / Lambeth walk / St. Bernard's waltz / Virginia reel / Farmer's wife / Have a drink on me / (Hands knees and) Bomps a daisy / Charleston and the black bottom / I am the music man / Chestnut tree / Sons of the sea / Match of the day / Hip hip hip hooray / Zorba's dance / Fanfare #1/2 / March of the mods / This is your life #1/2 / Sand dance / Slosh / Harry Lime / Teddy bear's picnic / Gay Gordons / Havah nagilah / Mod rock barn dance / Chord
CD Set SAV 220CD
Savoy / Dec '95 / Savoy / THE / TKO Magnum

HAPPY DANCING FOR CHRISTMAS (2CD Set)
Santa Claus is coming to town / God rest ye merry gentlemen / We wish you a merry Christmas / Twelve days of Christmas / Deck the halls with boughs of holly / Good King Wenceslas / Christmas song / Have yourself a merry little Christmas / Winter wonderland / White Christmas / When a child is born / Mary's boy child / Little donkey / Do you hear what I hear / Little boy that Santa Claus forgot / Let it snow, let it snow, let it snow / I'm sending a letter to Santa Claus / Sleigh ride / Jingle bells / Midnight sleigh ride / Ding dong merrily on high / Silver bells / Away in a manger / We three kings / Silnet night / Holiday for bells / Snow coach / Snowy white and jingle bells / Here comes Santa Claus / Where did my snowman go / On Christmas island / Once upon a wintertime / I'll be home for Christmas / Fairy on the Christmas tree / Frosty the snowman / Rudolph the red nosed reindeer / O little town of Bethlehem / Jingle bell rock / Rockin' around the Christmas tree / I heard the bells on Christmas day / In the bleak mid-Winter / Christmas awake / Salute the happy morn / Angels from the realms of glory / CHRISTMAS / Caroling caroling / Santa Natale / Scarlet ribbons / Miners dream of home / Auld lang syne
CD Set SAV 199CD
Savoy / Dec '95 / Savoy / THE / TKO Magnum

HAPPY DANCING VOL.1 (Hayward, Dennis Organisation)
Every little while / Dancing with my shadow / Broken doll / Glad rag doll / Peg o' my heart / She's funny that way / I don't know why / Don't blame me / White cliffs of Dover / Love is the sweetest thing / It's a sin to tell a lie / Sally / Girl of my dreams / It happened in Monterey / Where the blue of the night meets the gold of the day / I'll see you again / Chinatown, my Chinatown / Waiting for the Robert E Lee / I'm looking over a four leaf clover / Alabamy bound / Yankee doodle boy / Swanee / Can't help lovin' dat man / By the fireside / Seems to me, I've heard that song before / Two sleepy people / What more can I say / Play to me Gipsy / Goodnight Vienna / Alabama Jubilee / Is it true what they say about Dixie / California here I come / Sittin' on top of the world / Give my regards to Broadway / When the midnight choo choo leaves for Alabam' / As time goes by / It's the talk of the town / It had to be you / These foolish things / Blue room / Amapola / Marta / Mairzy doats and dozy doats / Give me five minutes more / Heart of my heart / Arm in arm together / We'll meet again / I'm a dreamer (aren't we all) / All I do is dream of you / Little on the lonely side / If I had my life to live over / Falling in love again / Carolina moon / Let the rest of the world go by / Let bygones be bygones
CD SAV 132CD
Savoy / Mar '92 / Savoy / THE / TKO Magnum

HAPPY DANCING VOL.3
CD SAV 189CD
Savoy / May '93 / Savoy / THE / TKO Magnum

IT'S SEQUENCE TIME
Hello dolly/Miss Anna Belle Lee/Don't bring LuLu / Keep your sunny side up/You are my sunshine / Spread a little happiness/Smoke gets in your eyes / You are my heart's delight / Waltzing in the clouds / Sindy / All I ask of you / Always there / Tango melodica / Perhaps, perhaps, perhaps / Unforgettable/Never say goodbye / With a song in my heart/Be careful it's my heart / South of the border (Down Mexico way) / Ay ay ay / Hernando's hideaway / Whatever Lola wants (Lola gets) / Let's put out the lights and go to sleep / Shine through my dreams/My heart and I / Roses from the south / Les patineurs (skaters waltz)
CD SAV 177CD
Savoy / Jul '92 / Savoy / THE / TKO Magnum

LET'S DANCE (Hayward, Dennis & The Savoy Orchestra)
CD SAV 128CD
Savoy / Feb '92 / Savoy / THE / TKO Magnum

MUSIC FOR CELEBRATION AND SPECIAL OCCASIONS
Fanfare / Happy birthday / Barn dance medley / Congratulations / St. Bernard waltz / Wedding march / Get me to the church / My old Dutch / Anniversary waltz / Mayfair quickstep / Balmoral blues / Modern waltz / Saunter together / Saunter medley / Tango serida / Lilac waltz medley / Stripper / Can can / Four hand star / Conga / Virginia reel / Chimes of Big Ben / Auld lang syne / Gay Gordons / Easter parade / Wish me luck / Rule Britannia / Land of hope and glory / God save the Queen
CD SAV 152CD
Savoy / Dec '95 / Savoy / THE / TKO Magnum

RECALL
If I were a bell/This can't be love / There will never be another you / How am I to know/ Time was / All or nothing at all / Beautiful lady in blue / Dream lover/I'll follow my secret heart / My boy lolipop / He's a tramp / Something stupid / Cherry pink and apple blossom white / Strangers on the shore / Strangers in the night/Tonight / Women in love / Falling in love with love / Mr. Sandman/Lady be good/Baby face / Good old bad old days/Some of these days / Softly, softly/At the end of the day / Who's taking you home tonight / September in the rain/ Pennies from heaven / Embraceable you/ How about you
CD SAV 178CD
Savoy / Jul '92 / Savoy / THE / TKO Magnum

SEQUENCE TIME VOL.2
CD SAV 185CD
Savoy / May '93 / Savoy / THE / TKO Magnum

SHALL WE DANCE VOL.2 (Hayward, Dennis & His Orchestra)
On a little street in Singapore / New York, New York / Lover / Just the way you look tonight / London by night / Hi Lili hi lo / And I love you so/How soon / Yesterday/My way / Isle of Capri / What a difference a day makes / Ecstacy / Serenata / Lover come back / Dream / Indian summer/Stormy weather / Have you ever been lonely / If ever I would leave you / Stranger in Paradise / La cucaracha / Carioca / Copacabana / Tico-tico
CD SAV 174CD
Savoy / Jun '92 / Savoy / THE / TKO Magnum

SHOWTIME
CD SAV 239CD
Savoy / Dec '95 / Savoy / THE / TKO Magnum

STEP BY STEP
CD CDTS 036
Maestro / Aug '93 / Savoy

TEA DANCE VOL.2
Jeepers creepers / Be mir bist do schoen / Goody goody / Tisket-a-tasket / Don't sit under the apple tree / Undecided / Dance in the old-fashioned way / Didn't we / You'd be so nice to come home to / Wrong (it must be right) / Romanesca / Italian fiesta /

Nocturn in eb / Gymnopedie No.1 / Swan / Oh my beloved daddy / Cavatina / How wonderful to know / Hey there / Yours / I won't send roses / Portrait of my love / Magic moments / Finger of suspicion / Love and marriage / I ain't got nobody / Little bit independant / Birth of the blues / My blue heaven / Room with a view / I should care / But not for me / Tango erotique / Song of the rose / Charmaine / Edelweiss / Bless you / Linger awhile / Small fry / Brother can you spare a dime / You'll never walk alone / Sleepy shores
CD _____ SAV 170CD
Savoy / Mar '92 / Savoy / THE / TKO Magnum

Hayward, Justin

BLUE JAYS (Hayward, Justin & John Lodge)
This morning / Remember me (my friend) / My brother / You / Nights winters years / Saved by the music / I dreamed last night / Who are you now / Maybe / When you wake up
CD _____ 8204912
London / '88 / PolyGram

CLASSIC BLUE
Tracks of my tears / Blackbird / MacArthur Park / Vincent / God only knows / Bright eyes / Whiter shade of pale / Scarborough Fair / Railway hotel / Man of the world / Forever autumn / As long as the moon can shine / Stairway to Heaven
CD _____ CLACD 385
Castle / '93 / BMG

VIEW FROM THE HILL
I heard it / Broken dream / Promised land / It's not too late / Something to believe in / Way of the world / Sometimes less is more / Troubadour / Shame / Billy / Children of paradise
CD _____ 06076862022
CMC / Nov '96 / BMG

Haywire

PRIVATE SPELL
CD _____ WB 067CD
We Bite / Jul '90 / Plastic Head

Hayworth, Rita

RITA HAYWORTH
CD _____ LCD 6002/3
Fresh Sound / Jan '93 / Discovery / Jazz Music

RITA HAYWORTH COLLECTOR'S EDITION
CD _____ DVGH 7052
Deja Vu / Apr '95 / THE

Haza, Ofra

KIRYA
Kirya / Innocent-a requiem for refugees / Daw da hiya / Mystery, fate and love / Horashoot - the bridge / Don't foresake me / Barefoot / Trains of no return / Take 7/8
CD _____ 9031761272
East West / Apr '92 / Warner Music

YEMENITE SONGS
Im nin' alu / Yachilvi veyachail / A salk / Galbi / Ode le 'eli / Lefelach / Ayelet chen
CD _____ CDORB 006
Globestyle / May '87 / Pinnacle

Haze

C'EST LA VIE
Roger's revenge / Don't leave me here / Fallen leaves / Load / Mairage / For whom / Hum / Gabadon
CD _____ CYCL 041
Cyclops / Nov '96 / Pinnacle

WORLD TURTLE
Ember / See her face / Ship of fools / Edge of heaven / Don't leave me here / Epitaph / Under my skin / New dark ages / Safe harbour / Autumn / Another country / Straw house / Wooden house / Stone house
CD _____ CYCL 008
Cyclops / Jul '97 / Pinnacle

Haze

HAZECOLOUR-DIA
CD _____ SB 039
Second Battle / Jun '97 / Greyhound

Hazel

AIRIANA
CD _____ CAR 22CD
Candy Ass / Jun '97 / Cargo

ARE YOU GOING TO EAT THAT
CD _____ SPCD 144358
Sub Pop / Feb '95 / Cargo / Greyhound / Shellshock/Disc

TOREADOR OF LOVE
CD _____ SPCD 284
Sub Pop / Aug '93 / Cargo / Greyhound / Shellshock/Disc

Hazel, Monk

BENEFIT NIGHT VOL.1
CD _____ BCD 142
GHB / Jun '96 / Jazz Music

BENEFIT NIGHT VOL.2
CD _____ BCD 143
GHB / Jun '96 / Jazz Music

Hazelby, Brian

ON THE SUNNY SIDE
Strauss medley / War years medley / La danza / Chi mai / Theatre organ tribute / Badinerie / This can't be love / Intermezzo karelia suite / Nimrod / Root beer rag / Sweet Georgia Brown / Speak low / Georgia / Sunny side of the street / Nat King Cole medley / Misty / When you wish upon a star / St. Louis blues / Devils gallop
CD _____ CDGRS 1283
Grosvenor / Nov '95 / Grosvenor

Hazeldine

HOW BEES FLY
CD _____ GRCD 416
Glitterhouse / Jul '97 / Avid/BMG

He Said

HAIL
CD _____ CDSTUMM 29
Mute / Nov '86 / RTM/Disc

TAKE CARE
CD _____ CDSTUMM 57
Mute / Sep '88 / RTM/Disc

Head

HEAD
CD _____ VOXXCD 2061
Voxx / Jan '93 / Else / RTM/Disc

INTOXICATOR
Walk like an angel / Stalemate / Ice cream skin / All the boyz / Party's over / Under the influence of books / Two or three things / Soakin' my pillow / Ships in the night / B'goode or be gone / You're so vain
CD _____ CDV 2595
Virgin / Jul '89 / EMI

SNOG ON THE ROCKS, A
Out of the natch / Sex cattle man / Captain, the sailor and the dirty heartbreaker / I can't stop / Crackers (fer yer knackers) / I am the king / Don't wash your hair about it / Crazy racecourse crowd / Let's snog / Me and Mrs. Jones
CD _____ DIAB 822
Diabolo / Sep '96 / Pinnacle

Head & Hares

HEAD & HARES
CD _____ GH 1037CD
Get Hip / Jul '97 / Cargo / Greyhound

Head, Jowe

UNHINGED
CD _____ OVER 35CD
Overground / Oct '94 / Shellshock/Disc / SRD

Head Like A Hole

13
CD _____ N 02162
Noise / Aug '94 / Koch

FLIK Y'SELF OFF Y'SELF
Chalkface / Spanish goat dancer / Oily rag / Kissy kissy / Faster hooves / One pound two pound / Raw sock / Dirt eater / Pops pox 'n' vox / Spitbag / Rabbit / Nosferatoo / Theme to Nincomjool / Velvet kushin
CD _____ N 02252
Noise / Feb '95 / Koch

Head, Murray

BETWEEN US
CD _____ 951922
Pomme / Feb '97 / Discovery

SAY IT ISN'T SO
Say it ain't so Joe / Boats away / Someone's rocking my dreamboat / Never even thought / Don't forget me now / Boy on the bridge / When I'm yours / She's such a drag / Silence is a strong reply / You're so taste
CD _____ IMCD 83
Island / Feb '90 / PolyGram

SHADE
Peace of mind / Corporation corridors / (All we can do is) hold on / Not your problem / Joey's on fire / Maman / Grace / Dragonfly / Shades of the prison house
CD _____ 951942
Pomme / Feb '97 / Discovery

VOICES
CD _____ 951932
Pomme / Feb '97 / Discovery

WHEN YOU'RE IN LOVE
CD _____ 951242
Pomme / Mar '96 / Discovery

Head Of David

DUSTBOWL
CD _____ BFFP 18CD
Blast First / Apr '88 / RTM/Disc

Head Or Tales

ETERNITY BECOMES A LIE
CD _____ BMCD 069
Black Mark / Sep '95 / Plastic Head

Head Space

OF STAR AND TIME
CD _____ EBSCD 121
Emergency Broadcast System / Nov '96 / BMG

Headbutt

PISSING DOWN
Sandyard / Duffle bag / Through the slides / Adding insult.... / Always scraping shit / Barbie skin
CD _____ OINK 031 CD
Pigboy / Jan '93 / Vital

SHOWER CURTAIN
CD _____ TIRCD 001
Totem / Apr '96 / Grapevine/PolyGram / THE

TIDDLES
CD _____ DPROMCD 25
Dirter Promotions / Oct '94 / Cargo / Pinnacle / World Serpent

Headcleaner

AUFOU
CD _____ EVRCD 15
Eve / Oct '92 / Grapevine/PolyGram

NO OFFENCE MEANT, PLENTY TAKEN
Aperetif / Oscar / Understanding / Quirk / Downer / Comet / Half life / Jack / Ampallang / Big D / Mix
CD _____ 118612
Musidisc UK / Nov '95 / Grapevine/ PolyGram

Headcrash

HEADCRASH
CD _____ 4509955402
Warner Bros. / Oct '94 / Warner Music

Headhunter

REBIRTH
CD _____ CC 025050
Major / May '95 / Plastic Head

Headless Chickens

HEADLESS CHICKENS EP
CD _____ D 19853
Mushroom / Oct '94 / 3mv/Pinnacle

Headlock

IT FOUND ME
CD _____ CDVEST 31
Bulletproof / Sep '94 / Pinnacle

Headman

PHILADELPHIA EXPERIENCE, THE
CD _____ MILL 007CD
Millenium / Oct '94 / Plastic Head / Prime / SRD

Headrillaz

COLDHARBOUR ROCKS
Screaming headz / Weird planet / Spacefuck / Trepanning / Hot 'n' bovvud / If I let you live / Get yourself organised / Buggin' and breakin'
CD _____ PUSSYCDLP 006
Pussy Foot / Jun '97 / RTM/Disc

Headrush

FIVE
Easy / Crazy religion / Some people / Mountsorrel to venus / Trainer boy
CD _____ STAY 005CD
Stay Free / Aug '94 / Vital

Heads

RELAXING WITH THE HEADS
CD _____ HUK 001CD
Headhunter / Oct '96 / Cargo

Heads, Hands & Feet

HEADS, HANDS & FEET
I'm in need of your help / Send me a wire / Look at the world it's changing/Because you know me / Green liquor / Country boy / Tryin' to put me on / I wish you knew me / Devil's elbow / Pete might spook the horses / Everybody's hustlin'/Hang me dang me / Delaware / More you get, the more you want / Song for Suzie / Tirabad / Little bit lonely
CD _____ SEECD 458
See For Miles/C5 / Oct '96 / Pinnacle

HOME FROM HOME
Bring it all back home / Ain't gonna let it get me down / How does it feel to be right all the time / Achmed / Precious stone / Friend of a friend / Windy and warm / Who turned off the dark / Can you see me / Home from home / Make me feel much better
CD _____ C5CD 633
See For Miles/C5 / Oct '95 / Pinnacle

TRACKS
Let's get this show on the road / Safety in numbers / Road show / Harlequin / Dancer / Hot property / Jack Daniels / Rhyme and time / Paper chase / Song and dance
CD _____ SEECD 459
See For Miles/C5 / Oct '96 / Pinnacle

Heads Up

DUKE
CD _____ EM 93192
Roadrunner / Mar '91 / PolyGram

Headstone

STILL LOOKING
CD _____ ANT 4111
Anthology / May '97 / Cargo / Greyhound

Healey, Jeff

COVER TO COVER (Healey, Jeff Band)
Shapes of things / Freedom / Yer blues / Stop breakin' down / Angel / Evil / Stuck in the middle with you / I got the line on you / Run through the jungle / As the years go passing by / I'm ready / Communication breakdown / Me and my crazy self / Badge
CD _____ 74321238882
Arista / Mar '95 / BMG

FEEL THIS (Healey, Jeff Band)
Cruel little number / Leave the light on / Baby's lookin' hot / Lost in your eyes / House that love built / Evil and here to stay / Feel this / My kinda lover / It could all get blown away / You're coming home / Heart of an angel / Live and love / Joined at the heart / Dreams of love
CD _____ 74321120872
Arista / Aug '95 / BMG

HELL TO PAY (Healey, Jeff Band)
Full circle / I think I love you too much / I can't get my hands on you / How long can a man be strong / Let it all go / Hell to pay / While my guitar gently weeps / Something to hold on to / How much / Highway of dreams / Life beyond the sky
CD _____ 260815
Arista / Aug '96 / BMG

SEE THE LIGHT (Healey, Jeff Band)
Confidence man / River of no return / Don't let your chance go by / Angel eyes / Nice problem to have / Someday, someway / I need to be loved / Blue jean blues / That's what they say / Hideaway / See the light
CD _____ 259441
Arista / Aug '95 / BMG

Healy, Linda

PLANT Y MOR
CD _____ SCD 2072
Sain / Feb '95 / ADA / Direct / Greyhound

Heaney, Joe

COME ALL YE GALLANT IRISHMEN
CD _____ CIC 020CD
Clo Iar-Chonnachta / Jan '90 / CM

JOE HEANEY
CD _____ OSS 22CD
Ossian / Dec '93 / ADA / CM / Direct / Highlander

SAY A SONG
CD _____ NWARCD 001
Northwest / May '97 / ADA

Heap, Jimmy

RELEASE ME (Heap, Jimmy & The Melody Mastg)
Release me / Love in the valley / Just to be with you / Then I'll be happy / Heartbreaker / You're in love with you / Just for tonight / Girl with a past / Lifetime of shame / You don't kiss me 'cause you love me / One that I won / Ethyl in my gas tank (no gal in my arms) / My first love affair / Love can move mountains / Conscience / I'm guilty / This song is just for you / You ought to know / I told you so / Butternut / Long John / Mingling / Heap of boogie / You're nothin' but a nothin' / That's all I want from you / I'll follow the crowd / It takes a heap of lovin' / Cry cry darlin' / You didn't have time / Let's do it just once / This night won't last forever
CD _____ BCD 15617
Bear Family / Apr '92 / Direct / Rollercoaster / Swift

Heard, Larry

ALIEN
Faint object detection / Dance of Planet X / Micro-gravity / Flight of the comet / Dna-Rna / Galactic travels suite / Constituents of the universe / Lost echosphere / Protolife / Mysterious celestial objects / Cosmology myth / Journey to Deimos / Journey to Phoibos / Beauty of Celeste
CD _____ BMICD 031

Black Market International / Apr '96 / Prime / Soul Trader / Vital

Heart

BAD ANIMALS
Who will you run to / Alone / There's the girl / I want you so bad / Wait for an answer / Bad animals / You ain't so tough / Strangers of the heart / Easy target / RSVP
CD ______ CDEST 2032
Capitol / Jul '94 / EMI

BRIGADE
Wild child / All I wanna do is make love to you / Secret / Tall, dark handsome stranger / I didn't want to need you / Night / Fallen from grace / Under the sky / Cruel nights / Stranded / Call of the wild / I want your world to turn / I love you
CD ______ CDESTU 2121
Capitol / Feb '94 / EMI

DESIRE WALKS ON
Desire / Black on black II / Back to Avalon / Woman in me / Rage / In walks the night / My crazy head / Ring them bells / Will you be there (in the morning) / Voodoo doll / Anything is possible / Avalon / Desire walks on / La mujer que hay en mi / Te quedaras (en la manana)
CD ______ CDEST 2216
Capitol / Nov '93 / EMI

GREATEST HITS
Tell it like it is / Barracuda / Straight on / Dog and butterfly / Even it up / Bebe le strange / Sweet darlin' / I'm down/Long tall Sally / Unchained melody / Rock 'n' roll
CD ______ 4601742
CBS / Apr '94 / Sony

GREATEST HITS
Crazy on you / All I wanna do is make love to you / If looks could kill / Never / Alone / Who will you run to / Straight on / Magic man / What about love / Dreamboat Annie / Dog and butterfly / Nothin' at all / Heartless / Stranded / Will you be there in the morning / These dreams / Barracuda (live)
CD ______ CDEMC 3765
EMI / Apr '97 / EMI

HEART
If looks could kill / What about love / Never / These dreams / Wolf / All eyes / Nobody home / Nothin' at all / What he don't know / Shellshock
CD ______ CDLOVE 1
Capitol / Feb '86 / EMI

INTERVIEW, THE
CD ______ CBAK 4073
Baktabak / Feb '94 / Arabesque

LITTLE QUEEN
Little queen / Treat me well / Say hello / Cry to me / Go on cry / Barracuda / Love alive / Sylvan song / Dream of the archer / Kick it out
CD ______ 4746782
Columbia / Feb '97 / Sony

ROAD HOME, THE
Dreamboat Annie (Fantasy child) / Dog and butterfly / (Up on) Cherry Blossom Road / Back to Avalon / Alone / These dreams / Love hurts / Straight on / All I wanna do is make love to you / Crazy on you / Seasons / River / Barracuda / Dream of the archer
CD ______ CDEST 2258
Capitol / Sep '97 / EMI

ROCK THE HOUSE "LIVE"
Wild child / Fallen from grace / Call of the wild / How can I refuse / Shell shock / Love alive / Under the sky / Night / Tall, dark handsome stranger / If looks could kill / Who will you run to / You're the voice / Way back machine / Barracuda
CD ______ CDESTU 2154
Capitol / Aug '91 / EMI

Heart Throbs

CLEOPATRA GRIP
CD ______ TPLP 23CD
One Little Indian / Jun '90 / Pinnacle

JUBILEE GRIP
CD ______ TPLP 33CD
One Little Indian / Apr '92 / Pinnacle

VERTICAL SMILE
CD ______ TPLP 43CD
One Little Indian / May '93 / Pinnacle

Heartbeats

SPINNING WORLD
Ocean / Hollywood dream / All I want to do / Living in Babylon / Black mountain rag / Blue diamond mines / Signs of rain / Another day / Nine mile view of / Spinning world / They don't know you / Hand of man / Cotton eyed Joe / Power to run / Whole bunch of keys
CD ______ GLCD 2111
Green Linnet / Jul '93 / ADA / CM / Direct / Highlander / Roots

Heartdrops

THIS IS
CD ______ MLT 006
Melted / Jun '97 / Greyhound

Heartland

BRIDGE OF FOOLS
CD ______ ESM 011
Escape / Mar '97 / Cargo

WIDE OPEN
CD ______ PM 010092
Long Island / Mar '97 / Cargo

Hearts & Flowers

NOW IS THE TIME/OF HORSES, KIDS AND FORGOTTEN WOMEN
Now is the time / Save some time / Try for the sun / Rain rain / View from ward 3 / Rock 'n' roll gypsies / Reason to believe / Please / 1-2-3 Rhyme in Carnivour thyme / I'm a lonesome fugitive / Road to nowhere / 10,000 Sunsets / Now is the time for hearts and flowers / Highway in the wind / Second hand sundown queen / She sang hyms out of tune / Ode to a tin angel / When I was a cowboy / Legend of Ol' Tenbrookes / Colour your daytime / Two little boys / Extra extra
CD ______ EDCD 428
Edsel / Jul '95 / Pinnacle

Heartsman, Johnny

TOUCH, THE
Serpent's touch / Paint my mailbox blue / You're so fine / Tongue / Attitude / Got to find my baby / Butler did it / Please don't be scared of my love / Oops / Walkin' blues / Let me love you baby / Heartburn / Endless
CD ______ ALCD 4800
Alligator / May '93 / ADA / CM / Direct

Heat

GOLDFINGER
CD ______ A2Z 85008CD
A2Z / Sep '96 / Plastic Head

Heat Exchange

ONE STEP AHEAD
You're gonna love this / Shake down / Love is the reason / One step ahead / Check it out / Lost on you
CD ______ C5CD 609
See For Miles/C5 / Feb '94 / Pinnacle

Heath Brothers

AS WE WERE SAYING
Newest one / Bop agin / For seven's sake / South filthy / I'm glad there is you / Dave's haze / Daydream / Nostalgia / This is what it is
CD ______ CCD 47772
Concord Jazz / Sep '97 / New Note/ Pinnacle

Heath, Jimmy

LITTLE MAN BIG BAND
Trane connections / Two friends / Voice of the saxophone / Forever Sonny / CTA / Ellington's strayhorn / Gingerbread boy / Without you, no me
CD ______ 5139562
Verve / Apr '92 / PolyGram

REALLY BIG
Big 'P' / Old fashioned fun / Mona's mood / Dat dere / Nails / On Green Dolphin Street / My ideal / Picture of Heath
CD ______ OJCCD 1799
Original Jazz Classics / Dec '96 / Complete/ Pinnacle / Jazz Music / Wellard

Heath, Ted

AT CARNEGIE HALL/FIRST AMERICAN TOUR 1956-1957
CD ______ 8209502
Limelight / Apr '96 / PolyGram

FROM MOIRA WITH LOVE
Folks who live on the hill / Melody in F / Clair de Lune / Our love / Liebestraum / Song of India / Look for the silver lining / Procession / Skylark / Retrospect / Bill / Nearness of you / Fourth dimension / Thou swell / September song / Memories of you / Birth of the blues / Sixteen going on seventeen / Hot toddy / Georgia on my mind / Harlem nocturne / Someone to watch over me / St. Louis blues / How high the moon / Tonight / Faithful Hussar / Blues for moderns / Our waltz / Obsession / Lush slide / Eloquence / Rhapsody for drums
CD ______ CDSIV 6106
Horatio Nelson / Jul '95 / Disc

GOLDEN AGE OF TED HEATH VOL.1, THE
Opus one / Somebody loves me / Swingin' shepherd blues / My favourite things / Maria / Lullaby of Broadway / Holiday for strings / Flying home / I get a kick out of you / Jumpin' at the woodside / Man I love / Hawaiian war chant / At last / Cherokee / We'll git it / 'S Wonderful / You stepped out of a dream / Sabre dance / Blues in the night / Royal Garden blues / Moonlight in Vermont / Apple honey / Fly me to the moon / Listen to my music / Pick yourself up / Hawk talks / And the angels sing / Champ
CD ______ CDSIV 6102
Horatio Nelson / Apr '93 / Disc

GOLDEN AGE OF TED HEATH VOL.2, THE
9.20 special / East of the sun and west of the moon / Intermission riff / Ad lib frolic / Girl talk / South Rampart street parade / American patrol / That lovely weekend / Swanee river / Artistry in rhythm / Nightingale sang in Berkeley Square / Bakerloo non stop / In the mood / I had the craziest dream / Soon amapola / I can't get started (with you) / Perdido / C jam blues / Sophisticated lady / First jump / Night and day / Poor little rich girl / Swing low, sweet chariot
CD ______ CDSIV 6121
Horatio Nelson / Jul '95 / Disc

GOLDEN AGE OF TED HEATH VOL.3, THE
Let's dance / Chattanooga choo choo / Swingin' the blues / My guy's come back / Touch of your lips / Chicago / Skyliner / Nightmare / Lush slide / Serenade in blue / At the woodchoppers' ball / I've got a gal in Kalamazoo / On the sunny side of the street / I got it bad and that ain't good / Sidewalks of Cuba / After you've gone / Big John special / Chloe / Jersey bounce / Contrasts / Cotton tail / Fascinating rhythm / Snowfall / Headin' north
CD ______ CDSIV 6135
Horatio Nelson / Jul '95 / Disc

GOLDEN AGE OF TED HEATH VOL.4, THE
CD ______ CDSIV 6137
Horatio Nelson / Jul '95 / Disc

LISTEN TO MY MUSIC
CD ______ HEPCD 52
Hep / Jan '97 / Cadillac / Jazz Music / New Note/Pinnacle / Wellard

LISTEN TO MY MUSIC
East of the sun / Not so quiet please / Day by day / Twilight time / Getting nowhere / My heart goes crazy / Bakerloo non-stop / My fickle eye / Wot cher / To bed early / Any old iron / Kiss goodnight / You keep coming back like a song / So would I / My heart goes crazy / I fall in love too easily / Bells of St. Mary's / Ring dem bells / Opus one / Lullaby of Broadway / Skyliner / On the Archeson / Topeka and the Santa Fe
CD ______ RAJCD 877
Empress / Apr '97 / Koch

TED HEATH 1935-1945
Darktown strutters ball / I want to be happy / Limehouse blues / Temptation rag / Chanson Hindooe (song of India) / Bwanga / My paradise / Stage coach / 'Deed I do / Blue champagne / You rhyme with everything that's beautiful / I've got a gal in Kalamazoo / At last / Never a day goes by / How sweet you are / First jump / Opus one / Very thought of you / Cossack patrol / My guy's come back / Twilight time
CD ______ RAJCD 868
Empress / Aug '96 / Koch

VERY BEST OF TED HEATH
Listen to my music / Tail end Charlie / East of the sun / Swinging shepherd blues / Ad lib frolic / Chelsea / When the world was young / Fine romance / Deep night / Baby blue / On with the Don / Lullaby of Birdland / I'm gonna love that girl / Hawaiian war chant / Walkin' shoes / Sheila's theme / Hot toddy / That lovely weekend / Obsession / All the time and everywhere / Opus 1 / Lady bird
CD ______ CDSIV 6150
Horatio Nelson / Jul '95 / Disc

Heathen

BREAKING THE SILENCE
Death by hanging / Goblins blade / Open the grave / Pray for death / Set me free / Breaking the silence / World's end / Save the skull
CD ______ CDMFN 75
Music For Nations / Aug '89 / Pinnacle

Heatmiser

MIC CITY SONS
Get lucky / Plainclothes man / Low flying jets / Rest my head against the wall / Fix is in / Eagle eye / Cruel reminder / You gotta move / Pop in G / Blue highway / See you later
CD ______ CAR 75402
Caroline / Oct '96 / Cargo / Vital

Heatwave

ALWAYS AND FOREVER (The Best Of Heatwave)
Boogie nights / Always and forever / Groove line / Look after love / Mind blowing decisions / Razzle dazzle / Gangsters of the groove / Jitterbuggin' / Naturally / Too hot to handle / Lettin' it loose / Posin' til closin' / Sho'nuff must be love / Hold on to the one / Mind what you find / Big guns
CD ______ 4840482
Epic / May '96 / Sony

BEST OF HEATWAVE, THE
Always and forever / Boogie nights / Too hot to handle / Groove line / Look after love / Lettin' it loose / Where did I go wrong / Gangsters of the groove / Eyeballin' / Central heating / Happiness togetherness / Ain't no half steppin' / Mind blowing decisions
CD ______ EK 64914
Columbia / May '97 / Sony

BOOGIE NIGHTS
CD ______ JHD 028
Tring / Jun '92 / Tring

Heave

SCARAMANGA
CD ______ SCANCD 17
Radarscope / Apr '96 / Pinnacle

Heaven 17

BEST OF HEAVEN 17
(We don't need this) fascist groove thang / I'm your money / Height of the fighting (he-la-hu) / Play to win / Penthouse and pavement / Let me go / Trouble / Come live with me / Crushed by the wheels of industry / Sunset now / Flame down / This is mine / Foolish thing to do / Contenders / And that's no lie / Temptation
CD ______ CDVIP 110
Virgin VIP / Dec '93 / EMI

HIGHER AND HIGHER - THE BEST OF HEAVEN 17
(We don't need this) fascist groove thang (remix) / Let me go / Come live with me / This is mine / I'm your money / Play to win / And that's no lie / Contenders / We live so fast / Sunset now / Trouble / Height of the fighting (He-la-hu) / Penthouse and pavement / Crushed by the wheels if industry / (We don't need this) fascist groove thang / Temptation
CD ______ CDV 2717
Virgin / Mar '93 / EMI

HOW MEN ARE
Five minutes to midnight / Sunset now / This is mine / Fuse / Shame is on the rocks / Skin I'm in / Flamedown / Reputation / And that's no lie
CD ______ CDV 2326
Virgin / Jul '87 / EMI

LUXURY GAP
Crushed by the wheels of industry / Who'll stop the rain / Let me go / Key to the world / Temptation / Come live with me / Lady Ice and Mr. Hex / We live so fast / Best kept secret
CD ______ CDV 2253
Virgin / '83 / EMI

PENTHOUSE AND PAVEMENT
(We don't need this) fascist groove thang / Penthouse and pavement / Soul warfare / Geisha boys and temple girls / Let's all make a bomb / Height of the fighting (he-la-hu) / Song with no name / Play to win / We're going to live for a very long time
CD ______ CDV 2208
Virgin / Jul '87 / EMI

REMIX COLLECTION, THE
Tempation / Facist groove thang / That's no lie / Crushed by the wheels of industry / Train of love in motion / This is mine / Foolsih things to do / Play to win / Let me go / Penthouse and pavement / All come live with me
CD ______ CDVIP 133
Virgin VIP / Apr '95 / EMI

Heaven Deconstruction

HEAVEN DECONSTRUCTION
December / AOAcU / Acid starngel / Improper / Drun / Riversky / F / Borea / Scories / Landing / Message / Nano pata / Lova / Light residues / Under / Numiere / Windklang
CD ______ BIAS 309CD
Play It Again Sam / Jan '97 / Discovery / Plastic Head / Vital

Heavenly

DECLINE AND FALL OF HEAVENLY, THE
Me and my madness / Modestic / Skipjack / Itchy chin / Sacramento / Three star compartment / Sperm meets egg, so what / She and me
CD ______ SARAH 623CD
Sarah / Sep '94 / Vital

OPERATION HEAVENLY
CD ______ WIJCD 105
Wiiija / Oct '96 / RTM/Disc

THIS IS HEAVENLY
CD ______ ER 1010
Elefant / Jul '97 / Greyhound / SRD

Heavenly Bodies

CELESTIAL
Rains on me / Obsession / Time stands still / Con / Stars collide / Road to Maralinga / Shades of love / Cavatina / Senderoluminoso
CD ______ TMCD 27
Third Mind / Jun '89 / Pinnacle / Third Mind

Heavenly Gospel Singers

HEAVENLY GOSPEL SINGERS VOL.1 1935-1936
CD ______ DOCD 5452
Document / Jun '96 / ADA / Hot Shot / Jazz Music

HEAVENLY GOSPEL SINGERS VOL.2 1936-1937
CD DOCD 5453
Document / Jun '96 / ADA / Hot Shot / Jazz Music

HEAVENLY GOSPEL SINGERS VOL.3 1938-1939
CD DOCD 5454
Document / Jun '96 / ADA / Hot Shot / Jazz Music

HEAVENLY GOSPEL SINGERS VOL.4 1939-1941
CD DOCD 5455
Document / Jun '96 / ADA / Hot Shot / Jazz Music

Heavenly Music Corporation

CONSCIOUSNESS
CD SR 9458
Silent / Oct '94 / Cargo / Plastic Head

IN A GARDEN OF EDEN
CD SR 9335
Silent / Mar '94 / Cargo / Plastic Head

LUNAR PHASE
CD SR 9571
Silent / Feb '95 / Cargo / Plastic Head

Heaven's Gate

LIVE FOR SALE
CD SPV 07776742
SPV / Apr '94 / Koch / Plastic Head

LIVIN' IN HYSTERIA
CD 0876312
Steamhammer / May '91 / Pinnacle / Plastic Head

PLANET E
Terminated world / Planet earth / Back from the dawn / On the edge / Children play / Rebel yell / Black religion / Animal / Noah's dream / This town ain't big enough for both of us
CD SPV 08518312
SPV / Feb '97 / Koch / Plastic Head

Heavenwood

DIVA
CD MASSCD 106
Massacre / Jan '97 / Plastic Head

Heavy D

WATERBED HEV
Big Daddy / Keep it comin' / You can get it / Waterbed hev / Shake it / I'll do anything / Don't be afraid / Justa' interlude / Can you handle it / Wanna be a player / Get fresh hev / Big Daddy
CD UPTD 53033
Uptown / Apr '97 / BMG

Heavy Load

METAL ANGELS IN LEATHER
CD 15215
Laserlight / Aug '91 / Target/BMG

Heavy Pettin'

BIG BANG
CD WKFMXD 130
FM / Nov '89 / Revolver / Sony

Heavy Shift

LAST PICTURE SHOW
Double feature / Swamp monster / Rear view, earthbound / Come alive / LA nights / Steppin' out / Tango bolognese / Last picture show
CD ZEN 010CD
Indochina / Jun '96 / Pinnacle

UNCHAIN YOUR MIND/LIVE...
CD Set WOLCDL 1050
China / Feb '95 / Pinnacle

Heavy Stereo

DEJA VOODOO
CD CRECD 185
Creation / Sep '96 / 3mv/Vital

Hecate Enthroned

SLAUGHTER OF INNOCENCE/REQUIEM FOR THE DYING
CD BLACK 004CD
Blackend / Apr '97 / Plastic Head

UPON PROMETHEAN SHORES
CD BLACK 002CD
Blackend / Jun '96 / Plastic Head

Heckle

COMPLICATED FUTILITY OF IGNORANCE, THE
CD HR 621CD
Hopeless / Jun '97 / Cargo / Greyhound

Heckman, Thomas

SPECTRAL EMOTIONS
CD DBMLABCD 4
Labworks / Oct '95 / RTM/Disc / SRD

Heckstall-Smith, Dick

BIRD IN WIDNES (Heckstall-Smith, Dick & John Stevens)
CD EFA 084302
Konnex / Jul '95 / SRD

CELTIC STEPPES
CD 33JAZZ 027
33 Jazz / Mar '96 / Cadillac / New Note/ Pinnacle

DICK HECKSTALL-SMITH QUARTET
Venerable Bede / Woza nasu / Moongoose / Baiere
CD CDLR 45028
L&R / May '91 / New Note/Pinnacle

STORY ENDED, A
Future song / Crabs / Moses in the bullrushourses / What the morning was after / Pirate's dream / Same old thing / Moses in the bullrushourses (Live) / Pirates dream (Live) / No amount of loving (Live)
CD NEMCD 641
Sequel / Mar '93 / BMG

WOZA NASU
CD AUCD 737
Aura / Jan '91 / Cadillac

Hedgehog

MERCURY RED
CD VOW 37C
Voices Of Wonder / Apr '94 / Plastic Head

PRIMAL GUTTER
CD VOW 034C
Voices Of Wonder / Dec '93 / Plastic Head

THORN CHORD WONDER
CD VOW 044CD
Voices Of Wonder / Jun '95 / Plastic Head

Hedges, Chuck

NO GREATER LOVE
There is no greater love / My old flame / Samba dees days / I'll be seeing you / I'm getting sentimental over you / Magnolia rag / I thought about you / Jitterbug waltz / I remember you / I love you / Cheek to cheek
CD ARCD 19121
Arbors Jazz / Nov '94 / Cadillac

SKYLARK
When you're smiling / Here's that rainy day / Autumn leaves / 'Round midnight / Have you met Miss Jones / Jitterbug Waltz / There will never be another you / Skylark / I found a new baby
CD DD 483
Delmark / Jun '97 / ADA / Cadillac / CM / Direct / Hot Shot

SWINGTET LIVE AT ANDY'S
Softly as in a morning sunrise / New Orleans / Cheek to cheek / Nuage / It's alright with me / Gambler's waltz / Breakfast feud / I don't wanna be kissed / Liza / She's funny that way / Autumn leaves / Blues (my naughty sweetie gives me)
CD DE 465
Delmark / Mar '97 / ADA / Cadillac / CM / Direct / Hot Shot

Hedges, Michael

AERIAL BOUNDARIES
Aerial boundaries / Bensusan / Rickover's dream / Raggamuffin / After the goldrush / Hot type / Spare change / Menage a trois / Magic farmer
CD 01934110322
Windham Hill / Jan '95 / BMG

ROAD TO RETURN, THE
CD 72902103292
High Street / Jan '95 / BMG

Hedges, Ray

TUBULAR BELLS VOL.1
CD GRF 216
Tring / Mar '93 / Tring

TUBULAR BELLS VOL.2
CD GRF 217
Tring / Mar '93 / Tring

Hedningarna

HEDNINGARNA
CD ALICD 009
Alice / Dec '93 / ADA / Cadillac

HIPPJOKK
Hoglorfen / Navdi/fasa / Drafur och gildur / Dolkaren / Bierdna / Kina / Forshyttan / Dufwa / Vals i fel dur / Skane / Graucholorfen
CD SRSCD 4737
Silence / May '97 / ADA / Direct

KAKSI
Joupolle joutunut / Kruspolska / Vottikaalina / Chicago / Viktorin / Aivoton / Ful-valsen / Pal Karl / Kaivonkansi / Skamgreppet / Grodan/Widergrenen / Omas Ludvig / Kings Selma
CD XOUCD 101
Xource / Oct '93 / ADA / Direct
CD SRS 4717
Silence / May '97 / ADA / Direct

TRA
Tass on nainen / Min skog / Vargtimmen / Gorrlaus / Skrautval / Pornopolka / Raven / Saglaten / Tuuli / Tappmarschen / Tina Vieri
CD MWCD 4011
Music & Words / Dec '95 / ADA / Direct
CD SRS 4712
Silence / May '97 / ADA / Direct

Hedonist

HEAD
CD BLUE 16CD
Blue / Oct '95 / Plastic Head

Heffern, Gary

PAINFUL DAYS
CD GRCD 362
Glitterhouse / May '97 / Avid/BMG

Hegarty, Dermot

CONNEMARA ROSE
Red is the rose / Whistling thief / Ballad of Patrick Furey / Connemara by the lake / If those lips could only speak / Paddy's navy / Song to remember / Boys of Barna Sraide / Shore of Lough Bran / James Connelly / Love is teasing / Danny Farrell / Avondale / Sleive na mban / Sweet Alice Ben Bolt / Dear old Donegal / Hi for the beggarman / Lakes of coolfin / Connemara Rose / I've been everywhere
CD 3036001012
Carlton / Apr '97 / Carlton

Heights Of Abraham

ELECTRIC HUSH
Cleric / Boogie heights / High time / Dolphins / What's the number / Olive branching / EVA / 700 channels / Sunyatta / Make love
CD PORK 028
Pork / Jan '96 / Kudos / Pinnacle / Prime
CD 0630187482
CD 0630187489
Warner Bros. / Jul '97 / Warner Music

Heino

SINGLE HITS (1966-1968)
CD 16007
Laserlight / Aug '91 / Target/BMG

Heinz

TRIBUTE TO EDDIE
Tribute to Eddie / Hush-a-bye / I ran all the way home / Country boy / Don't you knock at my door / Summertime blues / Don't keep picking on me / Cut across shorty / Three steps to heaven / Come on and dance / Twenty flight rock / Look for a star / My dreams / I remember / Been invited to a party / Rumble in the night / I get up in the morning / Just like Eddie
CD RCCD 3008
Rollercoaster / Jan '94 / Rollercoaster / Swift

Heldon

ALLEZ TEIA
CD 14235
Spalax / Jan '97 / ADA / Cargo / Direct / Discovery / Greyhound

Helen Love

RADIO HITS VOL.1
CD DAMGOOD 51CD
Damaged Goods / Oct '94 / Shellshock/ Disc

RADIO HITS VOL.2
CD DAMGOOD 117CD
Damaged Goods / Mar '97 / Shellshock/ Disc

Helian, Jacques

JACQUES HELIAN & STAN KENTON 1938-54 (Helian, Jacques & Stan Kenton)
CD 8274172
Jazztime / Jan '95 / Discovery

Helias, Mark

LOOPIN' THE COOL
Munchkins / Loop the cool / One time only / Sector 51 / Seventh sign / Penta houve / Thumbs up / Hung over easy / El baz / Pacific rim
CD ENJ 90492
Enja / Feb '96 / New Note/Pinnacle / Vital/ SAM

Helicon

HELICON
CD N 02132
Noise / Mar '93 / Koch

Helios Creed

BURSTING THROUGH THE VAN ALLAN BELT
CD CLEO 94652
Cleopatra / Jun '94 / Cargo / Greyhound / Plastic Head / RTM/Disc / SRD

HELIOS CREED LIVE
CD YCLS 018CD
Your Choice / Jun '94 / Plastic Head

KISS TO THE BRAIN
CD ARR 223CD
Amphetamine Reptile / Nov '92 / Plastic Head

PLANET X
CD ARRCD 56353
Amphetamine Reptile / Oct '94 / Plastic Head

X RATED FAIRYTALES/SUPER CATHOLIC FINGER
CD CLEO 94902
Cleopatra / Sep '94 / Cargo / Greyhound / Plastic Head / RTM/Disc / SRD

Helium

DIRT OF LUCK, THE
Pat's trick / Trizie's star / Silver angel / Baby's goin' underground / Medusa / Comet / Skeleton / Superball / Heaven / Oh the wind and rain / Honeycomb / Latin song
CD OLE 1242
Matador / Apr '95 / Vital

PIRATE PRUDE
Baby vampire made me / Wanna be a vampire too, baby / XXX / OOO / I'll get you, I mean it / Love $$$
CD OLE 0782
Matador / May '94 / Vital

Helivator

GASOLINE T SHIRT
CD ORGAN 7 CD
Lungcast / Mar '93 / SRD

Helix

IT'S BUSINESS DOING PLEASURE
CD CDIRS 986969
Intercord / Aug '93 / Plastic Head

Hell, Richard

DESTINY STREET (Hell, Richard & The Voidoids)
Kid with the replaceable head / You gotta / Going going gone / Lowest common denominator / Downtown at dawn / Time / I can only give you everything / Ignore that door / Staring in her eyes / Destiny Street
CD ESMCD 574
Essential / Jul '97 / BMG

GO NOW
CD CODE 3CD
Overground / Apr '95 / Shellshock/Disc / SRD

Hellacopters

SUPERSHITTY TO THE MAX
CD JAZZ 001CD
White Jazz / Jan '97 / Plastic Head

Hellberg Duo

IHRE GROBTEN ERFOLGE
CD 16019
Laserlight / Nov '91 / Target/BMG

Hellbilly's

TORTURE GARDEN
CD RNR 005CD
Ransom Note / Oct '95 / Plastic Head

Hellborg, Jonas

AXIS
Touch my soul / Definer of out / Roman / Liquid sunshine / What can I say / Money talk / You want me / Tomorrow / No 5 / Trombone
CD DEMCD 006
Day Eight Music / Jun '93 / New Note/ Pinnacle

ELEGANT PUNK
Drone / Little wing / Glad to be back from Paris / Rosa / It's the pits, slight return / Cafe ariman / Blue in green / Hm / Reebop / Jan Johansson / Kader, the Algerian / Elegant punk for guitars / Wal / White women / Northpole English
CD DEMCD 004
Day Eight Music / Jun '93 / New Note/ Pinnacle

WORD, THE
Akasha / Zat / Saut e sarmad / Two rivers / Be and all became / Poets / Black rite / Cherokee mist / Miklagaard / Path over clouds
CD AXCD 3009
Axiom / Oct '91 / PolyGram / Vital

Hellcats

HOODOO TRAIN
Where the hell is Memphis / Crazy about you baby / Baby, please don't go / I did my part / When you walk in the room / Black door slam / Wall of death / I don't need / I've been a good thing (for you) / Hoodoo train / Don't fight it / Antartica / Shine / Silly whim / Love is dying / Hard time killin' floor

blues / What'cha doing in the woods / Where the sirens cry
CD ROSE 197CD
New Rose / Aug '90 / ADA / Direct / Discovery

Hellemny, Joel

LIP SERVICE
CD ARCD 19161
Arbors Jazz / May '97 / Cadillac

Heller, Jana

LAUGHING IN CRIME
Laughing in crime / Hunger / Mirror / See mystery / Mad waltzing / Innocent ways / (You could be) Somebody to love / Love is a temporary thing / Your heart can sing / Let it ride / Promise land / Light the lamp babe
CD CYCLECD 003
Cycle / Feb '96 / CM / Direct

Hellion

BLACK BOOK, THE
CD CDMFN 108
Music For Nations / Oct '90 / Pinnacle

Hellkrusher

BUILDINGS FOR THE RICH
Buildings for the rich / Third world exploitation / War, who needs it / Full of shit / Path to destruction / Chase is on / Sick / Conform / Dying for who / Smash the trash / Destined to die / System dictates / Threat of war / Burn a rock star / Who's system / War games / Clear the debt / Scared of change / Dead zone / Hellkrusher
CD CASE 004CD
SMR / Feb '93 / Vital

Hello

NEW YORK GROOVE...THE BEST OF HELLO
CD MCCD 112
Music Club / Jun '93 / Disc / THE

Helloween

BEST, THE REST, THE RARE, THE (The Collection 1984-1988)
CD N 01762
Noise / Jan '92 / Koch

CHAMELEON
First time / When the sinner / I don't wanna cry no more / Crazy cat / Giants / Windmill / Revolution now/San Francisco / In the night / Music / Step out of hell / I believe / Longing
CD CDFA 3308
Fame / Nov '94 / EMI

CHAMELEON
CD ESMCD 412
Essential / Aug '96 / BMG

LIVE
We burn / Wake up the mountain / Sole survivor / Chance / Why / Eagle fly free / Time of the oath / Future world / Dr. Stein / Before the war / Mr. Ego / Power / Where the rain grows / In the middle of a heartbeat / Perfect gentleman / Steel tormentor
CD RAWCD 116
Raw Power / Sep '96 / Pinnacle

MASTER OF THE RINGS
Irritation / Sole survivor / Where the rain grows / Why / Mr. Ego / Perfect gentleman / Game is on / Secret alibi / Take me home / In the middle of a heartbeat / Still we go
CD RAWCD 101
Raw Power / Apr '96 / Pinnacle

PINK BUBBLES GO APE
Pink bubbles go ape / Kids of the century / Back on the streets / Number one / Heavy metal hamsters / Going home / Someone's crying / Mankind / I'm doin' fine - crazy man / Chance / Your turn
CD ESMCD 411
Essential / Aug '96 / BMG

TIME OF THE OATH
CD RAWCD 109
Raw Power / Apr '96 / Pinnacle

Hellwitch

TERRAASYMMETRY
CD LMCD 1111
Lethal / Nov '93 / Plastic Head

Helm, Bob

BOB HELM & HIS JAZZ BAND
CD SOSCD 1310
Stomp Off / Nov '96 / Jazz Music / Wellard

Helm, Levon

AMERICAN SON
Watermelon time in Georgia / Dance me down easy / Violet eyes / Stay with me / America's farm / Hurricane / China girl / Nashville wimmin / Blue house of broken hearts / Sweet peach Georgia wine
CD EDCD 526
Edsel / Jun '97 / Pinnacle

LEVON HELM AND THE RCO ALL STARS (Helm, Levon & The RCO All-Stars)
Washer woman / Tie that binds / You got me / Blues so bad / Sing sing sing (let's make a better world) / Milk cow boogie / Rain down tears / Mood I was in / Havana moon / That's my home
CD EDCD 494
Edsel / Jul '96 / Pinnacle

Helmet

AFTERTASTE
Pure / Renovation / Exactly what you wanted / Like I care / Driving nowhere / Birth defect / Broadcast emotion / It's easy to get bored / Diet aftertaste / Harmless / (High) visibility / Insatiable / Crisis king
CD IND 90073
Interscope / Apr '97 / BMG

BETTY
Wilma's rainbow / I know / Biscuits for smut / Milquestoast / Tic / Rollo / Street crab / Clean / Vaccination / Beautiful love / Speechless / Silver Hawaiian / Overrated / Sam Hell
CD IND 92404
Interscope / Aug '96 / BMG

BORN ANNOYING
CD ARRCD 60003
Amphetamine Reptile / Apr '95 / Plastic Head

MEANTIME
In the meantime / Ironhead / Give it / Unsung / Turned out / He feels bad / Better / You borrowed / FBLA II / Role model
CD IND 92162
Interscope / Aug '96 / BMG

STRAP IT ON
Repitition / Rude / Bad mood / Sinatra / FBLA / Blacktop / Distracted / Make room / Murder
CD IND 92235
Interscope / Jul '96 / BMG

Helms, Bobby

FRAULEIN (His Decca Recordings/2CD Set)
Tennessee rock 'n' roll / I need to know how / I don't owe you nothing / Sowin' teardrops / (Got a) heartsick feeling / Far away heart / Just a little lonesome / Fool such as I / I'm leaving now (long gone daddy) / Tonight's the night / Jingle bell rock / Captain Santa Claus / No other baby / Standing at the end of my world / My shoes keep walking back to you / New river train / Hundred hearts / Hurry baby / Sad eyed baby / Someone was already there / To my sorrow / Lonely River Rhine / Then came you / Just between old sweethearts / I can't take it like you can / My greatest weakness / Yesterday's champagne / One deep love / Once in a lifetime / Fraulein / Most of the time / My special angel / just a little lonesome / Magic song / Sugar moon / Schoolboy crush / If I only knew / Love my lady / Plaything / Jacqueline / Living in the shadows of the past / Forget about him / I guess I'll miss the prom / Miss memory / Soon it can be told / Fool and the angel / Someone for everyone / Yesterday's champagne / Lonely River Rhine / How can you divide a little child / Borrowed dreams / You're no longer mine / My lucky day / Let me be the one / Guess we thought the world would end / Teach me
CD Set BCD 15594
Bear Family / Mar '92 / Direct / Rollercoaster / Swift

Helsinki Mandoliners

HELSINKI MANDOLINERS
CD KICD 38
Kansanmusiikki Instituutti / Nov '95 / ADA / Direct

Helstar

DISTANT THUNDER, A
King is dead / Bitter end / Abandon ship / Tyrannicide / Scorcher / Genius of insanity / Whore of Babylon / Winds of love / He's a woman, she's a man
CD RR 95242
Roadrunner / Aug '88 / PolyGram

MULTIPLES IN BLACK
CD MASSCD 053
Massacre / May '95 / Plastic Head

Heltah Skeltah

NOCTURNAL
CD CDPTY 133
Priority/Virgin / Aug '96 / EMI

Heltir

NEUE SACHLICHKEIT
CD DV 024CD
Dark Vinyl / Sep '95 / Plastic Head / World Serpent

Hemingway, Gerry

DEMON CHASER (Hemingway, Gerry Quintet)
CD ARTCD 6137
Hat Art / Jan '94 / Cadillac / Harmonia Mundi

SPECIAL DETAILS (Hemingway, Gerry Quintet)
CD ARTCD 6084
Hat Art / Jul '91 / Cadillac / Harmonia Mundi

Hemlock

GIVE KIDS CANDY
CD LM 015
Liquid Meat / Jun '97 / Cargo

Hemphill, Julius

FAT MAN & THE HARD BLUES (Hemphill, Julius Sextet)
CD 1201152
Black Saint / Mar '92 / Cadillac / Harmonia Mundi

FIVE CHORD STUD (Hemphill, Julius Sextet)
CD 1201402
Black Saint / Oct '94 / Cadillac / Harmonia Mundi

FLAT OUT JUMP SUITE (Hemphill, Julius Quartet)
CD 1200402
Black Saint / May '92 / Cadillac / Harmonia Mundi

LIVE FROM THE NEW MUSIC CAFE (Hemphill, Julius Trio)
CD CD 731
Music & Arts / Sep '92 / Cadillac / Harmonia Mundi

LIVE IN NEW YORK (Hemphill, Julius & Abdul Wadud)
CD 1231382
Red / Apr '95 / ADA / Cadillac / Harmonia Mundi

OAKLAND DUETS (Hemphill, Julius & Abdul Wadud)
CD CD 791
Music & Arts / Jan '94 / Cadillac / Harmonia Mundi

Henderson, Allan

TUNING PHRASES (Henderson, Allan Trio)
6/8 marches / Strathspeys and reels / An t-eilean muileach / Bush set / 2/4 marches / Pipe set / Oran arisaig / Waltzes / Tuning phrase / Tam lin / Reels / Slow air and reel
CD HYCD 297170
Hypertension / Feb '97 / ADA / CM / Direct / Total/BMG

Henderson, Bill

BILL HENDERSON & THE OSCAR PETERSON TRIO (Henderson, Bill & Oscar Peterson Trio)
You are my sunshine / Lamp is low / All or nothing at all / I wish you love / Gravy waltz / Lot of livin' to do / I see your face before me / I've got a crush on you / At long last love / Folks who live on the hill / Baby mine / Wild is love / Where are you / Charmaine / Young and foolish / Stranger on the shore
CD 8379372
Verve / Mar '93 / PolyGram

Henderson, Bugs

AT LAST
CD TX 1002CD
Taxim / Jan '94 / ADA

FOUR TENS STRIKE AGAIN
CD FC 105CD
Flat Canyon / Aug '96 / ADA

THAT'S THE TRUTH
CD TX 1013CD
Taxim / Jul '95 / ADA

YEARS IN THE JUNGLE
CD TX 1011CD
Taxim / Dec '93 / ADA

Henderson, Chick

BEGIN THE BEGUINE (1937-1940) (Henderson, Chick & The Joe Loss Band)
While a cigarette was burning / I still love to kiss you goodnight / On a little dream ranch / My prayer / Begin the beguine / By an old pagoda / Girl in the Alice Blue gown / I know now / I shall be waiting / I'll remember / It looks like rain in Cherry Blossom Lane / It's a lovely day tomorrow / May I have the next romance with you / Music maestro please / On the sentimental side / Remember me / September in the rain / Seventeen candles
CD CDAJA 5083
Living Era / Apr '91 / Select

REMEMBER ME
Till the lights of London shine again / Serenade in blue / We'll go smiling along / Somewhere in France with you / My prayer / Black out stroll / Sweet little sweetheart / Shabby old cabby / Wish me luck as you wave me goodbye / Begin the beguine / You can't stop me from dreaming / That old feeling / You're an education / Thanks for everything / Let the curtain come down / Music maestro please / I still love to kiss you goodnight / I know how / Remember me / Small cafe by Notre Dame
CD PAR 2025
Parade / Jul '94 / Disc

Henderson, Di

BY ANY OTHER NAME
CD DHC 001
Deeaitch / Dec '93 / Friendly Overtures

Henderson, Duke

GET YOUR KICKS
CD DD 668
Delmark / Dec '94 / ADA / Cadillac / CM / Direct / Hot Shot

Henderson, Eddie

DARK SHADOWS
El gaucho / 19th street / Goodbye / Cerulean blue / Dark shadows / Punjab / Certain vibe / Lament for Booker / Dawning dance / Water is wide
CD MCD 92542
Milestone / Feb '97 / Cadillac / Complete/ Pinnacle / Jazz Music / Wellard

THINK OF ME (Henderson, Eddie Quintet)
CD SCCD 31264
Steeplechase / Oct '90 / Discovery / Impetus

Henderson, Fletcher

1921-1923 VOL.1
CD DOCD 5342
Document / May '95 / ADA / Hot Shot / Jazz Music

1923-1924 VOL.2
CD DOCD 5343
Document / May '95 / ADA / Hot Shot / Jazz Music

1924-1938
CD CD 53179
Giants Of Jazz / Nov '95 / Cadillac / Jazz Music / Target/BMG

CLASSICS 1921-1923
CD CLASSICS 794
Classics / Jan '95 / Discovery / Jazz Music

CLASSICS 1923-1924 (Henderson, Fletcher Orchestra)
CD CLASSICS 683
Classics / Mar '93 / Discovery / Jazz Music

CLASSICS 1924 VOL.1
CD CLASSICS 647
Classics / Nov '92 / Discovery / Jazz Music

CLASSICS 1924 VOL.2
CD CLASSICS 657
Classics / Nov '92 / Discovery / Jazz Music

CLASSICS 1924 VOL.3
CD CLASSICS 673
Classics / Nov '92 / Discovery / Jazz Music

CLASSICS 1926-1927
CD CLASSICS 597
Classics / Sep '91 / Discovery / Jazz Music

CLASSICS 1927-1931
CD CLASSICS 572
Classics / Oct '91 / Discovery / Jazz Music

CLASSICS 1931
CD CLASSICS 555
Classics / Dec '90 / Discovery / Jazz Music

CLASSICS 1931-1932
CD CLASSICS 546
Classics / Dec '90 / Discovery / Jazz Music

CLASSICS 1932-1934
CD CLASSICS 535
Classics / Dec '90 / Discovery / Jazz Music

CLASSICS 1934-1937
CD CLASSICS 527
Classics / Apr '90 / Discovery / Jazz Music

CLASSICS 1937-1938
CD CLASSICS 519
Classics / Apr '90 / Discovery / Jazz Music

FLETCHER HENDERSON (1937-1938)
CD TPZ 1004
Topaz Jazz / Jul '94 / Cadillac / Pinnacle

FLETCHER HENDERSON & HIS ORCHESTRA (Henderson, Fletcher Orchestra)
Back in your own backyard / Rose room / Stampede / Chris and his gang / All God's chillun got rhythm / Posin' / Let 'er go / Great Caesar's ghost / If you should ever leave / Worried over you / Rhythm of the

tambourine / Slumming on Park Avenue / It's wearin' me down / Trees / If it's the last thing I do / You're in love with love / Don't let the rhythm go to your head / There's rain in my eyes / Saving myself for you / What do you hear from the mob in Scotland / It's the little things that count / Moten stomp / Stealin' apples / Sing you sinners / What's your story (what's your jive)
CD ____ GRF 088
Tring / '93 / Tring

FLETCHER HENDERSON 1923 (Henderson, Fletcher Orchestra)
CD ____ CLASSICS 697
Classics / Jul '93 / Discovery / Jazz Music

FLETCHER HENDERSON 1924-25 (Henderson, Fletcher Orchestra)
CD ____ CLASSICS 633
Classics / Nov '92 / Discovery / Jazz Music

FLETCHER HENDERSON 1925-26 (Henderson, Fletcher Orchestra)
CD ____ CLASSICS 610
Classics / Feb '92 / Discovery / Jazz Music

FLETCHER HENDERSON AND HIS ORCHESTRA - 1927 (Henderson, Fletcher Orchestra)
CD ____ CLASSICS 580
Classics / Oct '91 / Discovery / Jazz Music

FLETCHER HENDERSON AND HIS ORCHESTRA - 1936-27 (Henderson, Fletcher Orchestra)
CD ____ CD 597
Classic Jazz Masters / Sep '91 / Wellard

FLETCHER HENDERSON AND HIS ORCHESTRA VOL.2 (Henderson, Fletcher Orchestra)
CD ____ VILCD 0202
Village Jazz / Sep '92 / Jazz Music / Target/BMG

FLETCHER HENDERSON SEXTET 1950
CD ____ RST 91537
RST / Mar '95 / Hot Shot / Jazz Music

INTRODUCTION TO FLETCHER HENDERSON 1921-1941, AN
CD ____ 4019
Best Of Jazz / Mar '95 / Discovery

JAZZ PORTRAITS
Moten stomp / Sing you sinners / Back in your own backyard / Rhythm of the tambourine / Christopher Columbus / Yeah man / Clarinet marmalade / Wang wang blues / I'm coming Virginia / What'cha call 'em blues / Teapot dome blues / Stampede / Big John special / Singin' the blues / Shanghai shuffle / Chinatown, my Chinatown / New King Porter stomp / Sugarfoot stomp
CD ____ CD 14522
Jazz Portraits / May '94 / Jazz Music

QUINTESSENCE, THE (1924-1936/2CD Set)
CD Set ____ FA 219
Fremeaux / Oct '96 / ADA / Discovery

RARE RECORDINGS (The Golden Age of Jazz)
CD ____ JZCD 366
Suisa / Jun '92 / Jazz Music / THE

STUDY IN FRUSTRATION, A (The Fletcher Henderson Story/3CD Set)
CD Set ____ C3K 57596
Columbia / Oct '94 / Sony

UNDER THE HARLEM MOON
Honeysuckle Rose / New King Porter stomp / Underneath the Harlem moon / Queer notions / Night life / Nagasaki / Rhythm crazy now / Ain't cha glad / Hocus pocus / Tidal wave / Christopher Columbus / Blue Lou / Stealin' apples / Jangled nerves / Grand Terrace rhythm / Riffin' / Shoe shine boy / Sing sing sing / Jimtown blues / Rhythm of the tambourine / Back in your own backyard / Chris and his gang
CD ____ CDAJA 5067
Living Era / Mar '90 / Select

WILD PARTY (Henderson, Fletcher Orchestra)
Hocus pocus / Phantom fantasie / Harlem madness / Tidal wave / Limehouse blues / Shanghai shuffle / Big John Special / Happy as the day is long / Down South camp meeting / Wrappin' it up / Memphis blues / Wild party / Rug cutters' swing / Hotter than 'Ell / Liza
CD ____ HEPCD 1009
Hep / Aug '94 / Cadillac / Jazz Music / New Note/Pinnacle / Wellard

Henderson, Horace

CLASSICS 1940-1941 (Henderson, Horace & Fletcher)
CD ____ CLASSICS 648
Classics / Nov '92 / Discovery / Jazz Music

Henderson, Ingrid

LIGHT OF THE MOUNTAIN (Henderson, Ingrid & Allan)
Highland Road / Sound of Sleat / Air for Alex Henderson / Heights of Casino / Parson's farewell / Donnie Caolis of Burnbank / Strop the razor / Oran America / Solus a Bheinne / Irish jigs
CD ____ CDLDL 1204
Lochshore / Nov '96 / ADA / Direct / Duncans

PERPETUAL HORSESHOE (Henderson, Ingrid & Allan)
CD ____ LDL 1216CD
Lochshore / Jun '94 / ADA / Direct / Duncans

Henderson, Joe

BALLADS AND BLUES
Lazy afternoon / La mesha / Out of the night / You know I care / Ask me now / Soulville / Portrait
CD ____ CDP 8566922
Blue Note / Jul '97 / EMI

BARCELONA
Barcelona / Barcelona (contd) / Mediterranean sun / Y yo la quiero (and I love her)
CD ____ ENJACD 30372
Enja / Jun '93 / New Note/Pinnacle / Vital/SAM

DOUBLE RAINBOW
CD ____ 5272222
Verve / Mar '95 / PolyGram

ELEMENTS (Henderson, Joe & Alice Coltrane)
Fire / Air / Water / Earth
CD ____ OJCCD 913
Original Jazz Classics / May '97 / Complete/Pinnacle / Jazz Music / Wellard

FOUR
CD ____ 5236572
Verve / Jan '95 / PolyGram

JOE HENDERSON BIG BAND, THE (Henderson, Joe Big Band)
CD ____ 5334512
Verve / Oct '96 / PolyGram

KICKER, THE
CD ____ OJCCD 465
Original Jazz Classics / Nov '95 / Complete/Pinnacle / Jazz Music / Wellard

LUSH LIFE (The Music Of Billy Strayhorn)
Isfahan / Johnny come lately / Blood count / Raincheck / Lotus blossom / Flower is a lovesome thing / Take the 'A' train / Drawing room blues / Upper Manhattan medical group (UMMG) / Lush life
CD ____ 5117792
Verve / Sep '92 / PolyGram

MILESTONE YEARS 1967-1977, THE (8CD Set)
Mamacita / Kicker / Chelsea Bridge / If / Nardis / Without a song / Mo' Joe / O amor em paz / Tetragon / First trip / I've got you under my skin / Invitation / RJ / Waltz for Zweetie / Bead game / You don't know what love is / Unilateral / Scavenger / But not for me / Power to the people / Afrocentric / Black narcissus / Isotope / Opus one point five / Lazy afternoon / Foresight and afterthought / Caribbean fire dance / Recorda-me / Shade of jade / Isotope / 'Round midnight / Mode for Joe / If you're not part of the solution (you're part of the probl / Blue bossa / Closing theme / Gazelle / Invitation / Mind over matter / No me esqueca / Shade of jade / Round midnight / Out 'n' in / Blue bossa / Junk blues / Terra firma / Viz a viz / Foregone conclusion / Black is the colour of my true love's mind / Current events / Tress-cun-deo-la / Turned around / Song for sinners / Me among others / Bwaata / Tres palabras / All things considered / Canyon lady / Las Palmas / In the beginning there was Africa... / Air / Water / Fire / Earth / Butterfly dreams / Light as a feather / Love reborn / Summer night / Black narcissus / Hindsight and forethought / Power to the people / Other side of right / Good morning / Heartache / Amoeba / Gazelle / My cherie amour / Old slippers / Immaculate deception / Solution / Black miracle / Black narcissus / What can I say / Windows
CD Set ____ 8MCD 44132
Milestone / Nov '96 / Cadillac / Complete/Pinnacle / Jazz Music / Wellard

MIRROR MIRROR
Mirror mirror / Candlelight / Keystone / Joe's bolero / What's new / Blues for liebestraum
CD ____ 5190922
MPS Jazz / Apr '93 / PolyGram

RELAXIN' AT CAMARILLO
CD ____ OJCCD 776
Original Jazz Classics / Sep '93 / Complete/Pinnacle / Jazz Music / Wellard

SO NEAR, SO FAR (Musings For Miles)
Miles ahead / Joshua / Pfrancing / Flamenco sketches / Milestones / Teo / Swing Spring / Teo / Swing Spring / Circle / Side car / So near, so far
CD ____ 5176742
Verve / Jan '92 / PolyGram

STANDARD JOE, THE
CD ____ 1232482
Red / May '92 / ADA / Cadillac / Harmonia Mundi

STATE OF THE TENOR VOL.1 & 2
Beatrice / Friday the 13th / happy reunion / Loose change / Ask me now / Isotope / Stella by starlight / Boo Boo's birthday / Cheryl / Y ya la quiero / Soulville / Portrait / Bead game / All the things you are
CD ____ CDP 8288792
Blue Note / May '94 / EMI

STRAIGHT NO CHASER
CD ____ 5315612
Verve / Jun '96 / PolyGram

TETRAGON/IN PURSUIT OF BLACKNESS
Invitation / RJ / Bead game / Tetragon / Waltz for sweetie / First trip / I've got you under my skin / No me esqueca / Shade of jade / Gazelle / Mind over matter
CD ____ CDBGPD 084
Beat Goes Public / Mar '94 / Pinnacle

Henderson, Michael

BEST OF MICHAEL HENDERSON
Be my girl / I can't help it / In the night time / To be loved / (We are here) to geek you up / You are my starship / Make me feel better / Let me love you / You haven't made it to the top / Take me I'm yours / Do it all / Wide reciever / Valentine love / Reach out for me / Am I special
CD ____ NEXCD 117
Sequel / May '90 / BMG

Henderson, Mike

FIRST BLOOD (Henderson, Mike & The Bluebloods)
When I get drunk / So sad to be lonesome / Hip shakin' / Pony blues / Bloody murder / Pay Bo Diddley / When the welfare turns it's back on you / Give me back my wig / How many more years / Mean mistreater
CD ____ DR 00062
Dead Reckoning / Mar '97 / Avid/BMG

Henderson, Murray

WORLD'S GREATEST PIPERS VOL.4, THE
6/8 marches / Strathspeys and reels / Hornpipes / 3/4 marches / Air hornpipe and jig / 2/4 marches / Jigs / Piobaireachd / 2/4 marches / 9/8 marches / Strathspeys and reels
CD ____ LCOM 5159
Lismor / May '96 / ADA / Direct / Duncans / Lismor

Henderson, Ray

BEST THINGS IN LIFE ARE FREE, THE (The Songs Of Ray Henderson) (Various Artists)
Here I am: *Austin, Gene* / Five foot two, eyes of blue: *California Ramblers* / Birth of the blues: *Crosby, Bing & Jack Teagarden* / I'm sitting on top of the world: *Crumit, Frank* / My dog loves your dog: *Edwards, Cliff 'Ukelele Ike'* / Button up your overcoat: *Etting, Ruth* / You're the cream in my coffee: *Etting, Ruth* / Don't bring Lulu: *Glantz, Nathan & Chick Straun* / Sunny side up: *Hamps, Johnny & His Kentucky Serenaders* / Black bottom: *Hanshaw, Annette* / Together: *Haymes, Dick & Helen Forrest* / I'm a dreamer, aren't we all: *High Hatters* / Let's call it a day: *Hutch & Harry Roy* / Life is just a bowl of cherries: *Hutch* / Best things in life are free: *Hylton, Jack* / If I had a talking picture of you: *Hylton, Jack & Sam Browne* / Sonny boy: *Jolson, Al* / Lucky day: *Lanin, Howard & Irving Kaufman* / Bye, bye blackbird: *Layton & Johnstone* / Magnolia: *Marvin, Johnny* / Varsity drag: *O'Neal, Zelma* / That's why darkies were born: *Robeson, Paul* / Animal crackers in my soup: *Temple, Shirley* / My song: *Vallee, Rudy* / Thrill is gone: *Vallee, Rudy*
CD ____ CDAJA 5207
Living Era / Mar '97 / Select

Henderson, Scott

ILLICIT (Henderson, Scott & Tribal Tech)
Big waves / Stoopid / Black cherry / Torque / Slidin into charlisa / Root food / Riot / Paha-sapa / Babylon / Passion dance / Just because
CD ____ R27 91802
Bluemoon / Oct '92 / New Note/Pinnacle

Henderson, Wayne

RUGBY GUITAR
CD ____ FF 542CD
Flying Fish / '92 / ADA / CM / Direct / Roots

SKETCHES OF LIFE (Henderson, Wayne & The Next Crusade)
Strange love / We're gonna rock your sock off / Men cry too / I'll take you there / Color of love / Just because its jazz, (Don't mean ya can't dance) / Portrait of a dream / Ancestral chant / For old time's sake / Survival / I can't get started with you / Just because it's jazz (don't mean ya can't dance)
CD ____ CPCD 8125
Charly / Oct '95 / Koch

Hendon Citadel Band

MARCHING WITH THE SALVATION ARMY
Starlake / Torchbearers / Bravest of the Brave / Wellingtonian / Cairo red shield / Crown of conquest / In the King's service / Roll call / Salute to America / To regions fair / Joyful news / On the news / On the king's highway / Fighting for the Lord / Fount / Victors acclaimed / Southall 100
CD ____ BNA 5041
Bandleader / '91 / Conifer/BMG

Hendricks, Jon

LOVE (Hendricks, Jon & Co)
Royal Garden blues / Bright moments / Willie's tune / Good ol' lady / Li'l darlin' / I'll die happy / Love (Berkshire blues) / Tell me the truth / Swinging groove merchant(groove merchant) / Angel eyes / In a Harlem airshaft
CD ____ MCD 5258
Muse / Sep '92 / New Note/Pinnacle

Hendricks, Michele

CARRYIN' ON
CD ____ MCD 5336
Muse / Sep '92 / New Note/Pinnacle

KEEPIN' ME SATISFIED
CD ____ MCD 5363
Muse / Sep '92 / New Note/Pinnacle

Hendriks, Karl

BUICK ELECTRA (Hendriks, Karl Trio)
CD ____ GROW 382
Grass / Feb '95 / Pinnacle / SRD

MISERY & WOMEN (Hendriks, Karl Trio)
CD ____ FIRECD 39
Fire / Jun '94 / Pinnacle / RTM/Disc

Hendrix, Jimi

ARE YOU EXPERIENCED
Foxy lady / Manic depression / Red house / Can you see me / Love or confusion / I don't live today / May this be love / Fire / Third stone from the sun / Remember / Are you experienced / Purple haze / Hey Joe / Wind cries Mary
CD ____ 5210362
Polydor / Oct '93 / PolyGram

ARE YOU EXPERIENCED
Foxy lady / Manic depression / Red house / Can you see me / Love or confusion / I don't live today / May this be love / Fire / Third stone from the sun / Remember / Are you experienced / Hey Joe / Stone free / Purple haze / 51st anniversary / Wind cries Mary / Highway chile
CD ____ MCD 11608
MCA / Apr '97 / BMG

AUTHENTIC PPX STUDIO RECORDINGS VOL.1 (Get That Feeling)
Get that feeling / How would you feel / Hush now / No business / Simon says / Gotta have a new dress / Strange things / Welcome home
CD ____ SPV 08544222
SPV / Jul '96 / Koch / Plastic Head

AUTHENTIC PPX STUDIO RECORDINGS VOL.2 (Flashing)
Love, love / Day tripper / Gloomy Monday / Fool for you, baby / Don't accuse me / Hornet's nest / Flashing / Odd ball / Happy birthday
CD ____ SPV 08544212
SPV / Jul '96 / Koch / Plastic Head

AUTHENTIC PPX STUDIO RECORDINGS VOL.3 (Ballad Of Jimi)
CD ____ SPV 08544682
SPV / Feb '97 / Koch / Plastic Head

AUTHENTIC PPX STUDIO RECORDINGS VOL.4 (Live At George's Club)
CD ____ SPV 08544692
SPV / Feb '97 / Koch / Plastic Head

AXIS BOLD AS LOVE
Experience / Up from the skies / Spanish castle magic / Wait until tomorrow / Ain't no tellin' / Little wing / If six was nine / You've got me floating / Castles made of sand / She's so fine / One rainy wish / Little Miss Lover / Bold as love
CD ____ 8472432
Polydor / Oct '93 / PolyGram
CD ____ MCD 11601
MCA / Apr '97 / BMG

BAND OF GYPSIES
Who knows / Machine gun / Changes / Power to love / Message to love / We gotta live together
CD ____ MCD 11607
MCA / Apr '97 / BMG

BLUES
Hear my train a comin' / Born under a bad sign / Red house / Catfish blues / Voodoo chile blues / Mannish boy / Once I had a woman / Bleeding heart / Jelly 292 / Electric Church Red house
CD ____ 5210372
Polydor / Apr '94 / PolyGram

COLLECTION, THE
CD _____ COL 017
Collection / Jan '95 / Target/BMG

CORNERSTONES 1967-1970
Hey Joe / Purple haze / Wind cries Mary / Foxy lady / Crosstown traffic / All along the watchtower / Voodoo chile / Have you ever been (to Electric Ladyland) / Star spangled banner / Stepping stone / Room full of mirrors / Ezy ryder / Freedom / Drifting / In from the storm / Angel / Fire / Stone free
CD _____ 8472312
Polydor / Jan '93 / PolyGram

CROSSTOWN CONVERSATION
CD _____ CBAK 4082
Baktabak / Feb '94 / Arabesque

DIAMOND COLLECTION, THE
CD _____ 3004552
Arcade / Feb '97 / Discovery

EARLY YEARS, THE
Red house / Woke up this morning and found myself dead / Peoples people / Morrison's lament / Tomorrow never knows / Uranus rock / Outside woman blues / Sunshine of your love / Goodbye Bessie Mae / Soul food
CD _____ DA 430052
Blueprint / Nov '96 / Pinnacle

ELECTRIC LADYLAND
And the gods made love / Have you ever been (to Electric Ladyland) / Voodoo Chile / Crosstown traffic / Still raining, still dreaming / House burning down / All along the watchtower / Long hot summer night / Little Miss Strange / Come on (let the good times roll) / Gypsy eyes / Burning of the midnight lamp / Rainy day, dream away / 1983...(A Merman I should turn to be) / Moon, turn the tides...gently gently away
CD _____ MCD 11600
MCA / Apr '97 / BMG

EXPERIENCE
CD _____ NTRCD 036
Nectar / Mar '95 / Pinnacle

FIRST RAYS OF THE NEW RISING SUN
Freedom / Izabella / Night bird flying / Angel / Room full of mirrors / Dolly Dagger / Ezy ryder / Drifting / Beginnings / Stepping stone / My friend / Straight ahead / Hey baby (new rising sun) / Earth blues / Astro man / In from the storm / Belly button window
CD _____ MCD 11599
MCA / Apr '97 / BMG

FOOTPRINTS (Isle Of Wight/Band Of Gypsys/At Winterland/Plays Monterey)
CD Set _____ 8472352
Polydor / Mar '91 / PolyGram

FREE SPIRIT
Good times / Voices / Suspicious / Whipper / Bessie Mae / Soul food / Voice in the wind / Free spirit
CD _____ CDTB 094
Thunderbolt / Jan '91 / TKO Magnum

GOLD COLLECTION, THE
CD _____ D2CD 03
Deja Vu / Dec '92 / THE

IN FROM THE STORM (The Music Of Jimi Hendrix) (Various Artists)
And the gods made love / Have you ever been (to Electric Ladyland) / Rainy day, dream away / Wind cries Mary / Spanish castle magic / Little wing / In from the storm / Drifting / Bold as love / Burning of the midnight lamp / Purple haze / One rainy wish
CD _____ 74321315502
RCA Victor / Nov '95 / BMG

IN WORDS AND MUSIC (2CD Set)
CD Set _____ OTR 1100030
Metro Independent / Jun '97 / Essential/BMG

INTERVIEW DISC
CD _____ SAM 7006
Sound & Media / Nov '96 / Sound & Media

INTERVIEWS
CD _____ 8122707712
WEA / Jul '93 / Warner Music

INTROSPECTIVE: JIMI HENDRIX
Red house / Wake up this morning and find yourself dead / Interview part one / Bleeding heart / Interview part two
CD _____ CINT 5006
Baktabak / Apr '91 / Arabesque

JIMI HENDRIX (2CD Set)
CD Set _____ R2CD 4003
Deja Vu / Jan '96 / THE

JIMI HENDRIX (3CD Set)
Little wing / Voodoo chile / Purple haze / Sunshine of your love / Bleeding heart / Woke up this morning and found myself dead / Tomorrow never knows / Fire / Wild thing / Morrison's lament / Red house / Good times / Voices / Voice in the wind / Two and one goes / Let me go / Uranus rock / Outside woman blues / Room full of mirrors / Blues blues / Free spirit / Psycho / Wipe the sweat / Groove maker / Hot trigger / Night life / You got it / Suspicious / Goodbye Bessie Mae / She's a fox / Freedom & you / She's so fine / Sweet thing
CD Set _____ KBOX 360
Collection / Nov '96 / Target/BMG / TKO Magnum

JIMI HENDRIX (CD/CD Rom Set)
CD Set _____ WWCDR 006
Magnum Music / Apr '97 / TKO Magnum

JIMI HENDRIX AT THE MONTEREY POP FESTIVAL 1967
CD _____ ITM 960008
ITM / Sep '93 / Koch / Tradelink

JIMI HENDRIX AT WOODSTOCK
Introduction / Fire / Izabella / Hear my train a comin' / Red house / Jam back at the house (Beginnings) / Voodoo chile / Star spangled banner / Purple haze / Woodstock improvisation / Villanova Junction / Farewell
CD _____ 5233842
Polydor / Aug '94 / PolyGram

JIMI HENDRIX BOX SET
CD Set _____ JH 1
UFO / Oct '92 / Pinnacle

JIMI HENDRIX COLLECTOR'S EDITION
CD _____ DVBC 9032
Deja Vu / Apr '95 / THE

JIMI HENDRIX EXPERIENCE IN 1967 (Hendrix, Jimi Experience)
CD Set _____ JH 001
Revolver / Jul '92 / Revolver / Sony

JIMI HENDRIX GOLD (2CD Set)
CD Set _____ D2CD 4003
Deja Vu / Jun '95 / THE

JIMI HENDRIX VOL.1
Red house / Voodoo chile (slight return) / Little wing / Wild thing / Bleeding heart / Night life / Fire / Room full of mirrors / Psycho / Hot trigger / Free spirit / Groove maker / Voice in the wind / Suspicious / She's a fox / Two and one goes
CD _____ EXP 018
Experience / May '97 / TKO Magnum

JIMI HENDRIX VOL.2
CD _____ EXP 019
Experience / May '97 / TKO Magnum

JIMI PLAYS MONTEREY
Killing floor / Foxy lady / Like a rolling stone / Rock me baby / Hey Joe / Can you see me / Wind cries Mary / Purple Haze / Wild thing
CD _____ 8472442
Polydor / Jun '91 / PolyGram

LAST EXPERIENCE, THE
CD _____ CD 101
Timeless Treasures / Oct '94 / THE

LAST EXPERIENCE, THE
CD _____ SRCD 115
Strawberry / Jul '95 / TKO Magnum

LIVE AT THE ISLE OF WIGHT
Midnight lightning / Foxy lady / Lover man / Freedom / All along the watchtower / In from the storm / Intro (God save the Queen) / Message to love / Voodoo Chile / Machine gun / Dolly dagger / Red house / New rising sun
CD _____ 8472362
Polydor / Jan '93 / PolyGram

LIVE AT WINTERLAND
Prologue / Fire / Manic depression / Sunshine of your love / Spanish castle magic / Red house / Killing floor / Tax free / Foxy lady / Hey Joe / Purple haze / Wild thing / Epilogue
CD _____ 8472382
Polydor / Jun '91 / PolyGram

LIVE IN NEW YORK
CD _____ MU 5018
Musketeer / Oct '92 / Disc

NIGHT LIFE
Good feeling / Hot trigger / Psycho / Come on baby (part 1) / Come on baby (part 2) / Night life / You got it / Woke up this morning / Lime line / Peoples people / Whoa eeh
CD _____ CDTB 075
Thunderbolt / May '95 / TKO Magnum

PSYCHO
Good feeling / Hot tigger / Psycho / Come on baby / Come on baby / Night life / You got it / Woke up in the morning / Lime time / People's people / Whoa'eeh
CD _____ RM 1536
BR Music / Jun '97 / Target/BMG

PURPLE HAZE IN WOODSTOCK
CD _____ ITM 960004
ITM / Feb '94 / Koch / Tradelink

RARE HENDRIX (Hendrix, Jimi & Lonnie Youngblood Band)
Go go shoes / Red house / Wipe the sweat / People peoples / Blue's blues / Lime lime / Whoa ehh / She's a fox
CD _____ 100272
CMC / May '97 / BMG

REAL ROCK STANDARDS (2CD Set)
Little wing / Voodoo chile (slight return) / Purple haze / Sunshine of your love / Bleeding heart: *Hendrix, Jimi & Jim Morrison* / Woke up this morning and found myself dead / Tomorrow never knows: *Hendrix, Jimi & Jim Morrison* / Fire / Wild thing / Morrison's lament: *Hendrix, Jimi & Jim Morrison* / Red house / Good times / Voices / Voice in the wind / Two and one goes / Let me go / Uranus rock / Outside woman blues / Room full of mirrors
CD Set _____ TNC 96205
Natural Collection / Aug '96 / Target/BMG

REVENGE (A Tribute To Jimi Hendrix) (Various Artists)
Foxy lady: *Iggy Pop* / Up from the skies: *Jones, Rickie Lee* / Electric ladyland: *Bourelly, Jean-Paul* / Remember: *Harper, Ben* / Fire: *Red Hot Chili Peppers* / Purple haze: *Shamen* / Burning of the midnight lamp: *Living Color* / Voodoo chile: *Vaughan, Stevie Ray* / Hey Joe dub: *Kente, Ras & The Take No Prisoner Posse* / Red house: *Hooker, John Lee* / Angel: *Stewart, Rod* / Crosstown traffic: *Evans, Gil & His Orchestra* / Little Miss Lover: *Evans, Gil & His Orchestra* / Message to love: *Triad*
CD _____ 682550
Gravity / May '95 / New Note/Pinnacle

STONE FREE (A Tribute To Jimi Hendrix) (Various Artists)
Purple haze: *Cure* / Stone free: *Clapton, Eric* / Spanish castle magic: *Spin Doctors* / Red house: *Guy, Buddy* / Hey Joe: *Body Count* / Manic depression: *Seal & Jeff Beck* / Fire: *Kennedy, Nigel* / Bold as love: *Pretenders* / You got me floatin': *PM Dawn* / I don't live today: *Slash, Paul Rodgers & Band Of Gypsies* / Are you experienced: *Belly* / Crosstown traffic: *Living Color* / Third stone from the sun: *Metheny, Pat* / Hey baby (Land of the new rising sun): *MACC*
CD _____ 9362454382
WEA / Oct '93 / Warner Music

SUPERSESSION
Red house / Woke up this morning and found myself dead / Peoples peoples aka bleeding heart / Morrison's lament / Tomorrow never knows / Vranus rock / Outside woman blues / Sunshine of your love / Goodbye Bessie Mae / Soul food
CD _____ CD 8442002
Voiceprint / Jul '95 / Pinnacle

TALK (Interview)
CD _____ DISSCD 3
Wax / Apr '96 / RTM/Disc / Total/BMG

TOMORROW NEVER KNOWS
Red house / Wake up this morning and find yourself dead / Bleeding heart / Morrison's lament / Tomorrow never knows / Uranus rock / Outside woman blues / Sunshine of your love
CD _____ CDRIA 1000
Rialto / Sep '96 / Disc / Total/BMG

ULTIMATE EXPERIENCE, THE
All along the watchtower / Purple haze / Hey Joe / Wind cries Mary / Angel / Voodoo chile / Foxy lady / Burning of the midnight lamp / Highway chile / Crosstown traffic / Castles made of sand / Long hot summer night / Red house / Manic depression / Gypsy eyes / Little wing / Fire / Wait until tomorrow / Star spangled banner / Wild thing
CD _____ 5172352
Polydor / Sep '95 / PolyGram

VOODOO SOUP
CD _____ 5275202
Polydor / May '95 / PolyGram

Henke, Robert

FLOATING POINT (Henke, Robert & Gerhard Behles)
CD _____ EFA 204602
Imbalance / Jul '97 / SRD

Henley, Don

ACTUAL MILES (Greatest Hits)
Dirty laundry / Boys of summer / All she wants to do is dance / Not enough love in the world / Sunset grill / End of innocence / Last worthless evening / New York minute / I will not go quietly / Heart of the matter / Garden of Allah / You don't know me at all
CD _____ GED 24834
Geffen / Nov '95 / BMG

BUILDING THE PERFECT BEAST
Boys of Summer / You can't make love / Man with a mission / You're not drinking enough / Not enough love in the world / Building the perfect beast / All she wants to do is dance / Sunset grill / Drivin' with your eyes closed / Land of the living
CD _____ GFLD 19267
Geffen / Feb '95 / BMG

END OF THE INNOCENCE, THE
End of the innocence / How bad do you want it / I will not go quietly / Last worthless evening / New York minute / Shangri la / Little tin god / Gimme what you got / If dirt were dollars / Heart of the matter
CD _____ GFLD 19285
Geffen / Oct '95 / BMG

I CAN'T STAND STILL
I can't stand still / You better hang up / Long way home / Ain't nobody's business if I do / Talking to the moon / Dirty laundry / Johnny can't read / Them and us / La elite / Lilah / Unclouded day
CD _____ K 9600482
WEA / Jun '89 / Warner Music

Hennessey, Mike

SHADES OF CHAS BURCHELL
Shades / High on you / Blues on my mind / Days of wine and roses / Dreamstepper / Dig it / Gaby / Just friends / Soft shoe / Hanging loose / Westwood walk / Fair weather / You've changed
CD _____ IOR 70252
In & Out / Sep '95 / Vital/SAM

Hennessy, Christie

BOX, THE
CD _____ 0630146022
Celtic Heartbeat / Jul '96 / BMG

LORD OF YOUR EYES
CD _____ 4509975862
WEA / Dec '96 / Warner Music

YEAR IN THE LIFE, A
Quest / Lonely boy / Remember me / If you were to fall (and I was to fall in love with you) / Pain / Norfolk square / Vision / You can go far (if you know where you're going) / Sheila Doran / By bye love
CD _____ 4509919632
WEA / Dec '96 / Warner Music

Hennessy, Frank

THOUGHTS AND MEMORIES
Brother eagle / Jenkin's history / Keeper / Newfoundland / Valley lights / Old men and children / Mickey's song / Start and end with you / Sun's last rays / Old Camarhten oak / Fading away / Hearts on fire
CD _____ SAIN 8084CD
Sain / Aug '94 / ADA / Direct / Greyhound

Hennessys

EARLY SONGS, THE
CD _____ SCD 2044
Sain / Feb '95 / ADA / Direct / Greyhound

Henry, Clarence

BUT I DO (Henry, Clarence 'Frogman')
Ain't got no home / It won't be long / I found a home / Baby baby please / Never never / Oh Mickey / But I do / Just my baby and me / Live it right / I want to be a movie star / Steady date / Oh why / Little Susie / You always hurt the one you love / I love you, yes I do / Lonely street / Your picture / I wish I could say the same / Standing in the need of love / Little too much / On bended knees / Jealous kind / Dream myself a sweetheart / Lost without you / Takes two to Tango / Long lost and worried / Looking back
CD _____ CPCD 8007
Charly / Feb '94 / Koch

Henry Cow

IN PRAISE OF LEARNING
Living in the heart of the beast / War / Beginning / Long march / Beautiful as the moon / Terrible as an army with banners / Morning star
CD _____ ESD 80502
ReR/Recommended / Sep '93 / ReR Megacorp / RTM/Disc

LEGEND
CD _____ ESD 80482
ReR/Recommended / Nov '93 / ReR Megacorp / RTM/Disc

UNREST
Bitter storm over Ulm / Half asleep / Half awake / Ruins / Solemn music / Linguaphonie / Upon entering the Hotel Adlon / Arcades / Deluge
CD _____ ESD 80492
ReR/Recommended / Sep '93 / ReR Megacorp / RTM/Disc

VIRGIN YEARS, THE (3CD Set)
CD Set _____ RERCSB 1
ReR/Recommended / Dec '92 / ReR Megacorp / RTM/Disc

WESTERN CULTURE
CD _____ BCD
ReR/Recommended / Dec '92 / ReR Megacorp / RTM/Disc

Henry, Joe

KINDNESS OF THE WORLD
One day when the weather is warm / Fireman's wedding / She always goes / This close to you / Kindness of the world / Third reel / Dead to the world / I flew over our house last night / Some champions / Buckdancer's choice / Who would know
CD _____ MR 0572
Mammoth / Sep '93 / Vital

TRAMPOLINE
CD _____ 7567926862
Atlantic / Apr '96 / Warner Music

Henry, Pauline

DO OVER
Happy / Be thankful for what you got / Love hangover / Never knew love like this / Groove with you / Fools paradise / Save the overtime for me / When love calls / Sugar free / Happy (Dancehall)

CD 4840589
Sony Soho2 / May '96 / Sony

Henry, Vincent

VINCENT
CD CHIP 101
Jive / Jul '90 / Pinnacle

Henrys

CHASING GRACE
CD FIENDCD 784
Demon / Sep '96 / Pinnacle

PUERTO ANGEL
CD FIENDCD 769
Demon / Apr '96 / Pinnacle

Henry's Dress

BUST 'EM GREEN
CD SLR 054CD
Slumberland / Dec '96 / Cargo

Hensley, Ken

FROM TIME TO TIME
CD RMCCD 0195
Red Steel / May '96 / Pinnacle

Heptones

20 GOLDEN HITS
CD SONCD 0021
Sonic Sounds / Apr '92 / Jet Star

BETTER DAYS
CD RRTGCD 7715
Rohit / Jan '89 / Jet Star

FATTIE FATTIE
CD SOCD 9002
Studio One / Mar '95 / Jet Star

GOOD VIBES
CD CDSGP 048
Prestige / Jun '93 / Else / Total/BMG

NIGHT FOOD
Country boy / I've got the handle / Sweet talkin' / Book of rules / Mama say / Deceivers / Love won't come easy / Fatty fatty / Baby I need your lovin' / In the groove
CD RRCD 19
Reggae Refreshers / Nov '90 / PolyGram / Vital

OBSERVER STYLE
CD CC 2713
Crocodisc / Sep '94 / Grapevine/PolyGram

ON TOP
CD SOCD 0016
Studio One / Mar '95 / Jet Star

PARTY TIME
CD RRCD 14
Reggae Refreshers / Sep '90 / PolyGram / Vital

PRESSURE
CD RASCD 3164
Ras / Oct '95 / Direct / Greensleeves / Jet Star / SRD

RAINBOW VALLEY
CD CDSGP 0132
Prestige / Aug '94 / Else / Total/BMG

SEA OF LOVE
Be a man / Stick man / Sea of love / Tea for two / Choice of colour / Young, gifted and black / Ting-a-ling / Please be true / Get in the groove / Learn / I shall be released / Nine pounds of steel / Love won't come easy / Love me with all of your heart / You've lost that loving feeling / Joy joy
CD CDHB 128
Heartbeat / Mar '97 / ADA / Direct / Greensleeves / Jet Star

SWING LOW
Heaven / Promise to be true / What it is / So long / I'm proud / Book of rules / Down comes the rain / Swing low, sweet chariot / You decorated my life / Pack your things
CD CDBS 565
Burning Sounds / Mar '97 / Grapevine/ PolyGram / Jet Star / Total/BMG

VOL.1 & 2
CD CDTRL 357
Trojan / Jul '95 / Direct / Jet Star

WONDERFUL WORLD
CD RNCD 2045
Rhino / Mar '94 / Grapevine/PolyGram / Jet Star

Herawi, Aziz

MASTER OF AFGHANI LUTES
CD ARHCD 387
Arhoolie / Apr '95 / ADA / Cadillac / Direct

Herb

ON DUB
CD EBCD 002
Early Bird / Mar '97 / Essential/BMG / Jet Star

Herbal Mixture

PLEASE LEAVE MY MIND
Rock me baby / Shake it / Someone to love / Hallalujah / I'll never fall in love again / Over you baby / Please leave my mind / Love that died / Something's happening / Tailor made / Over you baby / Machines / Please leave my mind / Tailor made / Love that died / Love that died
CD BP 251CD
Blueprint / Sep '97 / Pinnacle

Herbaliser

BLOW YOUR HEADPHONES
Opening credits / Bring it / Another mother / More styles / Ginger jumps the fence / Put it on tape / Saturday night / Intermission / Shocker zulu / Blend / Shorty's judgement / Theme from control centre / Hardcore / Mr. Chombee has the flaw / End credits / Excuse me / New and improved / Mr. Chombee has the floor / Mother (for your mind)
CD ZENCD 028
Ninja Tune / Mar '97 / Kudos / Pinnacle / Prime / Vital

REMEDIES
Intro / Scratchy noise / Blomp / Styles / Interloodle / Bust a nut / Herbalize it / Wrong place / Little groove / Da trax / Up / Get downs / K-doing / Chill / Real killer / Repetitive loop
CD ZENCD 018
Ninja Tune / Sep '95 / Kudos / Pinnacle / Prime / Vital

Herbeck, Ray

RAY HERBECK & HIS MUSIC 1940
CD CCD 041
Circle / Jun '96 / Jazz Music / Swift / Wellard

Herbert

PARTS 1-3
CD PHONOCD 1
Phono / Apr '96 / Prime / RTM/Disc

Herbert, John Dale

CAJUN PICKIN' (Hebert, John Dale & Tim Broussard)
Hells on fire / Little black eyes / Big Mamou / LA Blues / Last waltz / Accordion players waltz / Big wheel / Oh bye bye / Let's two step / Weekend special
CD SOC 90253
Cajun Sound / Jul '96 / Target/BMG

Herborn, Peter

ACUTE INSIGHT
Free, forward and ahead / All along the sunstream / Beauty is... / Love in tune / Life force / Living yet
CD 8344172
jMT / May '91 / PolyGram

SOMETHING PERSONAL
Last objection / Tell me your secrets / Rush hour / All along the watchtower / Music for forgotten lovers / Evidence / Blue monochrome / Falling water
CD 8491562
jMT / Mar '94 / PolyGram

TRACES OF TRANE
My favourite things / Impressions / Naima / Acknowledgement / Love / To be / Drum thing / Resolution
CD 5140022
jMT / Apr '92 / PolyGram

Herd

FROM THE UNDERWORLD
CD BX 4512
BR Music / Oct '95 / Target/BMG

Herdman, Priscilla

FOREVER & ALWAYS
CD FF 70637
Flying Fish / Feb '95 / ADA / CM / Direct / Roots

WATER LILY, THE
CD CDPH 1014
Philo / Aug '95 / ADA / CM / Direct

Here & Now

I CAN DELIVER
Are you ready / Ten times the power / Here and now sound / I can deliver / Let's start over again / Tastin' love again / Come home / I am that I am / She loves me (not) / Hip-hop-jazz-religion
CD 7567922382
WEA / Jun '93 / Warner Music

Here Kitty Kitty

KISS ME YOU FOOL
CD IT 5CD
Iteration / Nov '94 / SRD

Heresy

VOICE OF FEAR
CD LF 191CD
Lost & Found / Oct '96 / Plastic Head

VOICE YOUR OPINION
CD LF 042CD
Lost & Found / Nov '92 / Plastic Head

Heretic

YAYOI DREAM (2CD Set)
CD Set BELLE 96032
Belle Antique / Jun '97 / ReR Megacorp

Hereticks

GODS AND GANGSTERS
CD CID 9954
Island / Mar '90 / PolyGram

Heretix

ADVENTURES OF SUPER DEVIL, THE
CD CH 228912
Cherrydisc / Oct '94 / Plastic Head

Heritage

TELL TAE ME
CD COMD 2051
Temple / Feb '94 / ADA / CM / Direct / Duncans / Highlander

Heritage

REMORSE CODE
CD CDMETAL 4
British Steel / Feb '97 / Cargo / Pinnacle / Plastic Head

Heritage Hall Jazz Band

COOKIN'
CD BCD 287
GHB / Jul '93 / Jazz Music

Heritage, Morgan

PROTECT US JAH
CD VPCD 1485
VP / Apr '97 / Greensleeves / Jet Star / Total/BMG
CD ANACD 002
Anansi / Jul '97 / Pinnacle

Herman, Jerry

EVENING WITH JERRY HERMAN, AN
CD CDSL 5173
DRG / Jan '93 / Discovery / New Note/ Pinnacle

Herman, Woody

16 CLASSIC PERFORMANCES
Golden wedding / Woodchopper's ball / Blues in the night / Las Chiapanecas / Down under / Four or five times / Woodsheddin' with Woody / Blue prelude / Yardbird shuffle / Blue frame / Fan it / Sheik of Araby / It's a blue world / Blues on parade / Blues downstairs / Amen yeah man
CD CWNCD 2031
Crown / Jun '97 / Henry Hadaway

1981 - CHICAGO (Herman, Woody & His Orchestra)
Four brothers / Come rain or come shine / Theme in search of a movie / Bijou / What are you doing the rest of your life / Sonny boy / Greasy sack blues / After hours / Take the 'A' train / As time goes by / Mood indigo / Blue flame / Woody's whistle
CD STATUSCD 105
Status / Nov '90 / Cadillac

AMEN 1937-1942 (Herman, Woody & His Orchestra)
CD RACD 7108
Aerospace / May '96 / Jazz Music / Montpellier

ANTIBES 1965 (Herman, Woody & His Orchestra)
CD CD 53110
Giants Of Jazz / Jan '95 / Cadillac / Jazz Music / Target/BMG

AT THE WOODCHOPPERS' BALL
At the woodchoppers' ball / Better get off your high horse / Blue flame / Blues downstairs / Blues in the night / Blues upstairs / Boogie woogie bugle boy / Bounce me brother with a solid four / Careless / Deep in a dream: *Herman, Woody & Connie Boswell* / Dr. Jazz / Dream valley / Fine and dandy / Frenesi / G'bye now / I'm thinking tonight of my blue eyes: *Herman, Woody & Bing Crosby* / Rumboogie / Rosetta / Sheikh of araby / Skylark / Sleepy serenade / Someone's rocking my dreamboat / String of pearls / They say: *Herman, Woody & Connie Boswell* / Whistler's mother-in-law: *Herman, Woody, Bing Crosby & Muriel Lane*
CD CDAJA 5143
Living Era / Nov '94 / Select

BEST OF WOODY HERMAN
CD DLCD 4017
Dixie Live / Mar '95 / TKO Magnum

BLUE FLAMES
Theme: Blue flame / I say a little prayer / At the woodchoppers' ball
CD CDC 9049
LRC / Nov '92 / Harmonia Mundi / New Note/Pinnacle

BLUES ON PARADE 1937-1941 (Herman, Woody & His Orchestra)
CD RACD 7122
Aerospace / May '96 / Jazz Music / Montpellier

BODY AND SOUL (Herman, Woody & Lionel Hampton)
CD DM 15019
DMA Jazz / Jul '96 / Jazz Music

CONCORD YEARS, THE
Things ain't what they used to be / Four brothers / 'Round midnight / It don't mean a thing if it ain't got that swing / Dolphin / Woody 'n' you / Blues for red / Perdido / Central Parkwest / Lemon drop / What are you doing the rest of your life / Battle royal
CD CCD 4557
Concord Jazz / Jun '93 / New Note/ Pinnacle

CREAM OF EARLY WOODY HERMAN, THE
Blues downstairs / Changing world / Herman at the Sherman / Jumpin' blues / East side kick / Big wig in the wigwam / It's a blue world / Paleface / Give a little whistle / Blues upstairs / Big morning / Jukin' / Blue ink / Farewell blues / Blues on parade / Blue prelude / Fan it / Sheikh of Araby / Blue flame / Indian boogie woogie / Dupree blues / At the woodchoppers' ball
CD PASTCD 9780
Flapper / Apr '92 / Pinnacle

CROWN ROYAL
CD 15775
Laserlight / Aug '93 / Target/BMG

FIRST HERD, THE
CD LEJAZZCD 53
Le Jazz / Jan '96 / Cadillac / Koch

GIANT STEPS
CD FCD 6099432
Fantasy / Nov '86 / Jazz Music / Pinnacle / Wellard

HERD RIDES AGAIN, THE
CD ECD 220102
Evidence / Jul '92 / ADA / Cadillac / Harmonia Mundi

HERMAN'S HEAT AND PUENTE'S BEAT (Herman, Woody & Tito Puente)
CD ECD 220082
Evidence / Jul '92 / ADA / Cadillac / Harmonia Mundi

HOLLYWOOD PALLADIUM (Herman, Woody & His Orchestra)
CD RST 915362
RST / Jun '93 / Hot Shot / Jazz Music

JANTZEN BEACH OREGON 1954
Prez conference / What is there to say / One o'clock jump / Cohn's alley / Mulligantawney / Why not / Would he / Offshore / Stardust / Hitting the bottle / Embraceable you / It happens to be me / Moten stomp / Strange / That old feeling
CD DSTS 1020
Status / Sep '96 / Harmonia Mundi / Jazz Music / Wellard

JAZZ COLLECTOR EDITION (5CD Set) (Herman, Woody/Duke Ellington/Artie Shaw)
CD Set 15911
Laserlight / Jan '92 / Target/BMG

JAZZ MASTERS
CD 5299032
Verve / Apr '96 / PolyGram

JAZZ PORTRAIT
CD CD 14574
Complete / Nov '95 / THE

LAKE COMPOUNCE & JANTZEN BEACH
CD DSTS 1021
Status / Oct '96 / Harmonia Mundi / Jazz Music / Wellard

LIVE 1957 VOL.1 (Herman, Woody & Bill Harris)
Stairway to the stars / Wailing in the woodshed / Midnight sun / Pennies from heaven / Barfly blues / At the woodchoppers' ball / Let's talk / Sleepy serenade / Preacher / Comes love / Our love is here to stay / G string strut / Trouble in mind / Pimlico
CD STATUSCD 107
Status / Nov '90 / Cadillac

LIVE 1957 VOL.2 (Herman, Woody & Bill Harris)
Would he / Body and soul / Why you / Ronettes / Square circle / Move my way / Four brothers / Stardust
CD STATUSCD 111
Status / Oct '91 / Cadillac

LIVE AT MONTEREY
CD 7567900442
Atlantic / Jul '93 / Warner Music

LIVE AT NEWPORT 1966
CD ____ EBCD 21182
JSP / Oct '90 / ADA / Cadillac / Direct / Hot Shot / Target/BMG

LIVE AT THE PEACOCK LANE 1958
CD ____ FSCD 2011
Fresh Sound / Oct '96 / Discovery / Jazz Music

LIVE IN ANTIBES 1965
CD ____ FCD 117
France's Concert / May '89 / BMG / Jazz Music

LIVE IN STEREO - 1963 (Herman, Woody & The Fourth Herd)
CD ____ JH 1006
Jazz Hour / Oct '91 / Cadillac / Jazz Music / Target/BMG

NORTHWEST PASSAGE VOL.2 (Herman, Woody & The First Herd)
CD ____ JASSCD 625
Jass / '91 / ADA / Cadillac / CM / Direct / Jazz Music

PRESENTS A CONCORD JAM VOL.1
At the woodchoppers' ball / Rose room / Just friends / Nancy with the laughing face / Body and soul / Someday you'll be sorry / My melancholy baby / Apple honey
CD ____ CCD 4142
Concord Jazz / Aug '90 / New Note/ Pinnacle

RAVEN SPEAKS, THE
Fat mama / Alone again (naturally) / Watermelon man / It's too late / Raven speaks / Summer of '42 / Reunion at Newport / Bill's blues
CD ____ OJCCD 663
Original Jazz Classics / Jun '94 / Complete/ Pinnacle / Jazz Music / Wellard

READY, GET SET, JUMP
CD ____ JHR 73527
Jazz Hour / May '93 / Cadillac / Jazz Music / Target/BMG

THIS IS JAZZ
Woodchopper's ball / Northwest passae / 23 Red / I've got news for you / Bijou (Rhumba a la jazz) / Greasy sack blues / Goof and I / Happiness is a thing called Joe / Early autumn (Summer sequence part 4) / My favourite things / Caladonia (What makes your big head so hard) / Four brothers / Everywhere / Keen and peachy / Northwest passage
CD ____ CK 65040
Sony Jazz / May '97 / Sony

THUNDERING HERD 1944, THE
CD ____ JCD 621
Jass / Feb '91 / ADA / Cadillac / CM / Direct / Jazz Music

THUNDERING HERD 1945, THE
CD ____ JCD 625
Jass / Feb '91 / ADA / Cadillac / CM / Direct / Jazz Music

V DISC YEARS VOL.1 & 2 1944-1946, THE (Herman, Woody & His Orchestra)
Flying home / It must be jelly, 'cause jam don't shake like that / Dancing in the dawn / Happiness is a thing called Joe / Red top / Jones beachead / I can't put my arms around a memory / There are no wings on a foxhole / Apple honey / Time waits for no one / Billy Bauer's tune / Golden wedding / I've got the world on a string / Yeah man (Amen) / He's funny that way / Lover man / Your father's moustache / Don't worry 'bout that mule / 125th Street prophet / I can't put my arms around a memory / Somebody loves me / John Hardy's wife / Meshugah / He's funny that way / Secunda / Jones Beachead / Caledonia / Jackson fiddles while Ralph burns / Happiness is a thing called Joe / Mean to me / Blowin' up a storm / C Jam blues/Reprise
CD Set ____ HEPCD 34/35
Hep / Nov '92 / Cadillac / Jazz Music / New Note/Pinnacle / Wellard

V DISC YEARS, THE
CD ____ HEPCD 2
Hep / Jun '87 / Cadillac / Jazz Music / New Note/Pinnacle / Wellard

WILDROOT
CD ____ TCD 1009
Tradition / Feb '96 / ADA / Vital

WOODCHOPPER'S BALL
Pillar to post / Sweet Lorraine / Blues on parade / Woodchopper's ball / Early Autumn / Stompin' at the Savoy / Linger in my arms a little longer / Surrender / Mabel Mabel / Steps / Four men on a horse / Igor / Fan it / Nero's conception / Heads up / Wild root / Tito meets Woody / Cha cha chick / Carioca / Summer sequence / Latin flight / New cha cha / Mambo hero / Blue stations
CD ____ GRF 069
Tring / '93 / Tring

WOODCHOPPER'S BALL
Blues in the night / Herman at The Sherman / Woodsheddin' with Woody / Yardbird shuffle / Get your boots laced Papa / 'Tis autumn / Pick-a-rib / Blue upstairs / Big wig in the wigwam / Blues downstairs / At the Woodchopper's ball / Bishop's blues / Golden wedding / Hot chesnuts / Blue flame / Fur trappers ball / Down under / Blue prelude / String of pearls / Dallas blues
CD ____ 306682
Hallmark / Jun '97 / Carlton

WOODCHOPPERS' BALL
CD ____ JASSCD 621
Jass / Aug '90 / ADA / Cadillac / CM / Direct / Jazz Music

WOODSHEDDIN' WITH WOODY
Blue ink / Careless / Herman at the Sherman / Get your boots laced Papa / Jukin' / It's a blue world / East side kick / Who's dat up dere / Indian boogie woogie / Woodsheddin' with Woody / Fan it / South / Too late / Four or five times / Fort Worth jail / Blues downstairs / Blues on parade / Golden wedding / Yardbird shuffle / At the woodchoppers' ball
CD ____ RAJCD 838
Empress / Mar '97 / Koch

WOODY AND FRIENDS
Caravan / I got it bad and that ain't good / Count down / Better git it in your soul / Woody 'n' you / What are you doing the rest of your life / Manteca
CD ____ CCD 4170
Concord Jazz / Jan '92 / New Note/ Pinnacle

WOODY HERMAN
CD ____ 22706
Music / Feb '96 / Target/BMG

WOODY HERMAN & HIS ORCHESTRA VOL.1 (Herman, Woody & His Orchestra)
CD ____ JH 1014
Jazz Hour / '92 / Cadillac / Jazz Music / Target/BMG

WOODY HERMAN & HIS ORCHESTRA VOL.2 (Herman, Woody & His Orchestra)
CD ____ JH 1015
Jazz Hour / '92 / Cadillac / Jazz Music / Target/BMG

WOODY HERMAN & HIS THUNDERING HERD (Herman, Woody & His Herd)
CD ____ 15774
Laserlight / Jul '93 / Target/BMG

WOODY HERMAN & ORCHESTRA 1937
CD ____ CCD 95
Circle / Apr '94 / Jazz Music / Swift / Wellard

WOODY HERMAN AND HIS ORCHESTRA 1945-1947 (Herman, Woody & His Orchestra)
CD ____ 11087
Laserlight / '88 / Target/BMG

WOODY HERMAN FEATURING STAN GETZ (Herman, Woody & Stan Getz)
Four brothers / Sweet and lovely / Early autumn / Cousins / Fanfare for the common man / Blues in the night / Blue serge / Blue Getz blues / Caldonia (what makes your big head so hard)
CD ____ 09026687022
RCA Victor / Mar '97 / BMG

WOODY HERMAN PRESENTS A GREAT AMERICAN EVENING VOL.3
I've got the world on a string / I cover the waterfront / Leopardskin pillbox hat / Avalon / Beautiful friendship / Pennies from Heaven / Wave / Caldonia
CD ____ CCD 4220
Concord Jazz / Jul '96 / New Note/Pinnacle

WOODY HERMAN VOL.1 1938-1945
CD ____ 158542
Jazz Archives / Sep '96 / Discovery

WOODY'S GOLD STAR (Herman, Woody Big Band)
Battle royal / Woody's gold star / Mambo rockland / 'Round midnight / Great escape / Dig / Rose room / In a mellow tone / Watermelon man / Samba song
CD ____ CCD 4330
Concord Jazz / Oct '87 / New Note/ Pinnacle

Hermann, Judd

HOMELESS IN THE HEART
CD ____ ATD 1115
Atomic Theory / Aug '96 / ADA / Direct

Herman's Hermits

ALL THE HITS PLUS MORE
Sunshine girl / Wonderful world / Can't you hear my heartbeat / No milk today / Mrs. Brown you've got a lovely daughter / Just a little bit better / End of the world / I can take and leave your loving / I'm Henry the VIII / Sea cruise / There's a kind of hush / Something's happening / Dandy / Listen people / I'm into something good / Must to avoid / Leaning on a lamp post / I understand just how you feel / Silhouettes / Don't go out into the rain, you're going to melt / Hold on
CD ____ CDSGP 0217
Prestige / Apr '97 / Else / Total/BMG

BEST OF HERMAN'S HERMITS
I'm into something good / Silhouettes / Wonderful world / No milk to day / There's a kind of hush / Sunshine girl / Something is happening / My sentimental friend / Can't you hear my heartbeat / Your hand in mine / I know why / Dream on / My lady / Take love, give love / Smile please / Museum / Man with the cigar / Listen people / For love / My reservations been confirmed / What is wrong - what is right / Gaslite Street / Moonshine man / Just one girl / Sleepy Joe / East West
CD ____ CC 251
Music For Pleasure / Sep '89 / EMI

BEST OF THE EMI YEARS VOL.1 1964-1966, THE
I'm into something good / I'm Henery the Eighth (I am) / Silhouettes / Show me girl / Can't you hear my heartbeat / Take love, give love / Wonderful world / Mrs. Brown you've got a lovely daughter / Just a little bit better / Must to avoid / You won't be leaving / Listen people / Hold on / This door swings both ways / Leaning on a lamp-post / All the things I do for you / Little boy sad / Dial my number / George and the dragon / East west / Dandy / No milk today
CD ____ CDEMS 1415
EMI / Sep '91 / EMI

BEST OF THE EMI YEARS VOL.2 1967-1971, THE
There's a kind of hush / Green Street green / Little Miss Sorrow, child of tomorrow / One little packet of cigarettes / Don't go out into the rain (you're going to melt) / Jezebel / Busy line / Museum / Rattler / I can take or leave your loving / It's nice to be out in the morning / Ooh, she's done it again / Sleepy Joe / Sunshine girl / Most beautiful thing in my life / Something is happening / My sentimental friend / Here comes the star / Years may come years may go / Bet your life I do / Lady Barbara / Oh you pretty thing
CD ____ CDEMS 1416
EMI / Feb '92 / EMI

EP COLLECTION, THE
Sea cruise / Mother in law / I understand / Mrs. Brown you've got a lovely daughter / Show me girl / Silhouettes / Wonderful world / Can't you hear my heartbeat / I'm into something good / Must to avoid / I'm Henery the Eighth (I am) / Just a little bit better / Walkin' with my angel / Where were you when I needed you / Hold on / George and the dragon / All the things I do for you / Wild love / Dandy / No milk today / For love
CD ____ SEECD 284
See For Miles/C5 / Jan '90 / Pinnacle

I'M INTO SOMETHING GOOD
CD ____ HADCD 207
Javelin / Jul '96 / Henry Hadaway / THE

I'M INTO SOMETHING GOOD
I'm into something good / Wonderful world / Listen people / Dandy / Must to avoid / No milk today / Steady Eddie / God knows / Leaning on the lamp post / Silhouettes / Don't say it (if you don't) / Needles and pins / Little bit bitter / End of the world / Jezebel / Mrs. Brown you've got a lovely daughter / I'm Henry the VIII, I am / Kind of hush
CD ____ PLATCD 204
Platinum / Feb '97 / Prism

LEGENDS IN MUSIC
CD ____ LECD 103
Wisepack / Nov '94 / Conifer/BMG / THE

NO MILK TODAY
CD ____ 15078
Laserlight / Aug '91 / Target/BMG

VERY BEST OF HERMAN'S HERMITS, THE
No milk today / I'm into something good / Show me girl / Silhouettes / Wonderful world / Just a little bit better / Must to avoid / You won't be leaving / This door swings both ways / East West / Dandy / I'm Henry The VIII I am / End of the world / Mrs. Brown you've got a lovely daughter
CD ____ 16152
Laserlight / Apr '96 / Target/BMG

YEARS MAY COME
Years may come, years may go / I can't take or leave your lovin' / This door swings both ways / Mrs. Brown you've got a lovely daughter / Leaning on a lampost / Must to avoid / Sleepy Joe / Something's happening / Sunshine girl / My sentimental friend / Can't you hear my heartbeat / There's a kind of hush / I'm into something good / Silhouettes / No milk today / East west / Oh you pretty things / Meet me on the corner down at Joe's cafe
CD ____ BR 1352
BR Music / Dec '95 / Target/BMG

Hermans, Ruud

BLUE HORIZON
CD ____ MWCD 1004
Music & Words / Aug '94 / ADA / Direct

Hermetic

BROTHERHOOD
CD ____ 36700062
Mausoleum / Oct '91 / Grapevine/ PolyGram

Hernandez, Nilo

NILO HERNANDEZ 1934-1938
CD ____ HQCD 84
Harlequin / Jun '97 / Hot Shot / Jazz Music / Swift / Wellard

Hernandez, Rafael

RAFAEL HERNANDEZ 1932-1939
CD ____ HQCD 68
Harlequin / Jun '96 / Hot Shot / Jazz Music / Swift / Wellard

Hernon, Marcus

BEAL A'MHURLAIGH (Hernon, Marcus & P.J.)
CD ____ CEFCD 141
Gael Linn / Jan '94 / ADA / CM / Direct / Grapevine/PolyGram / Roots

Heroin

DESTINATION
CD ____ GRAVITY 20
Gravity / Jan '97 / Cargo / Greyhound / Plastic Head

SHOWING A LUMINOUS BALL
CD ____ USR 001CD
Cold Spring / Aug '95 / Plastic Head / RTM/Disc

Herold, Ted

DIE SINGLES 1958-1960
Ich brauch' keinen ring / Lover doll / So schon ist nur die allererste liebe / Wunderbar wie du heut' wieder kusst / Hula rock / Dixieland rock / Dein kleiner bruder / Texas baby / Ich bin ein mann / Carolin / Hey baby / Kuss mich / Isabell / Crazy boy / Moonlight / 1:0 / Sunshine baby / Hast du funf minuten zeit / Auch du wirst gehn' / Hey little girl / Lonely / Oh so sweet / Nur sie / Wunderland
CD ____ BCD 15404
Bear Family / Jul '87 / Direct / Rollercoaster / Swift

DIE SINGLES 1961-62
CD ____ BCD 15592
Bear Family / Apr '92 / Direct / Rollercoaster / Swift

Heron

BEST OF HERON
Only a hobo / Lord and master / Sally Goodin / Yellow roses / Little angel / Car crash / Little boy / Goodbye / For you / John Brown / Wanderer / Great dust storm / Minstrel and a king / Winter harlequin / Smiling ladies / Love 13 (lone) / Big A / Miss Kiss / Upon reflection
CD ____ SEECD 242
See For Miles/C5 / Nov '88 / Pinnacle

Heron, Mike

MIKE HERON'S REPUTATION
Down on my knees (after Memphis) / Easy street / Evie / Residential boy / Without love / Born to be gone / Angels in disguise / Wine of his song / Meanwhile the rain / One of the finest / Singing the dolphin
CD ____ UGCD 5606
Unique Gravity / Jul '97 / ADA / Pinnacle

SMILING MEN WITH BAD REPUTATIONS
Call me diamond / Flowers of the forest / Audrey / Brindaban / Feast of Stephen / Spirit beautiful / Warm heart pastry / Beautiful stranger / No turning back / Make no mistake / Lady no wonder
CD ____ IMCD 129
Island / Jun '91 / PolyGram

WHERE THE MYSTICS SWIM
CD ____ FIENDCD 776
Demon / Feb '96 / Pinnacle

Herrera, Eddy

LOS HOMBRES CALIENTES
CD ____ 74321442102
Milan / Mar '97 / Conifer/BMG / Silva Screen

Herring Boys

LUCKY NUMBER SEVEN
CD ____ SPURCD 002
Spur / Feb '97 / Cargo

Herring, Vincent

DAWNBIRD
Sound check / August afternoon / Almost always / Toku do / Dr. Jamie / Who's kidding who / Dark side of dewey
CD ____ LCDI 5332
Landmark / Nov '93 / New Note/Pinnacle

FOLKLORE (Live At The Village Vanguard)
Folklore / Theme for Dolores / Girl next door / Romantic journey / Fountainhead / Window of opportunity / This I dig of you / Mo's theme
CD ____ 5224302
Limelight / Mar '94 / PolyGram

SCENE ONE
Elation / Roused about / What is this thing called love / Almost / Running from the cookie monster / Never forget / Where or Wayne
CD ____ ECD 221702
Evidence / Mar '97 / ADA / Cadillac / Harmonia Mundi

SECRET LOVE
Have you met Miss Jones / Skating in Central Park / Secret love / If you never / Autumn leaves / My foolish heart / Solar / Chelsea Bridge / And then again
CD 8443242
Limelight / Jan '95 / PolyGram

Herron, Paul

DIFFERENT WORLDS
Voiceless millions / Spanish point / Connemara awakes / Summer sunsets / Lonely at the station / You've got me / Blue skies / In a song / Donegal dreams / Just down the road / Feeling great / When darkness falls / Last chance
CD CDTRAX 055
Greentrax / Aug '92 / ADA / Direct / Duncans / Highlander

Hersch, Fred

LIVE AT MAYBECK RECITAL HALL VOL.31
Embraceable you / Haunted heart / In walked Bud / You don't know what love is / If I loved you / Heartsong / Everything I love / Sarabande / Song is you / Ramblin' / Body and soul
CD CCD 4596
Concord Jazz / May '94 / New Note/ Pinnacle

POINT IN TIME
Point in time / You don't know what love is / As long as there's music / Spring is here / Peacocks / Infant eyes / Cat's paws / Too soon / Evidence / Drew's blues
CD ENJ 90352
Enja / Oct '95 / New Note/Pinnacle / Vital/ SAM

RODGERS & HAMMERSTEIN
CD 7559794142
Nonesuch / Mar '97 / Warner Music

Hersh, Kristin

HIPS AND MAKERS
Your ghost / Beestung / Teeth / Sundrops / Sparky / Houdini blues / Loon / Velvet days / Close your eyes / Me and my charms / Tuesday night / Letter / Lurch / Cuckoo / Hips and makers
CD CAD 4002CD
4AD / Jan '94 / RTM/Disc

Hertfordshire Chorus

FOLLOW THAT STAR (Hertfordshire Chorus & Roger Sayer)
CD CD 340152
Koch / Nov '93 / Koch

Hertz

TALES
CD ACVCD 12
ACV / Jan '96 / Plastic Head / SRD

Hervieux, Gilbert

ARZOUSTAFF (Hervieux, Gilbert & Jacques Beauchamp)
CD EOG 101CD
EOG / Nov '96 / ADA

Herwig, Conrad

LATIN SIDE OF JOHN COLTRANE, THE
Blessing / Love supreme / Blue train / Afro-blue / Naima / Satellite / Africa / After the rain / Impressions / India / Drum thing / Blessing (reprise)
CD TCD 4003
Astor Place / Nov '96 / New Note/Pinnacle

NEW YORK BREED
Code mode / Search for peace / Cousin Mary / For Heaven's sake / Gatekeeper / 40 Bars / Deluge / In the wee small hours / New breed / I'll take romance
CD DTRCD 108
Double Time / Dec '96 / Express Jazz

NEW YORK HARD BALL (Herwig, Conrad Quartet)
Hardball / Vendetta / Zal / Code blue / I'm getting sentimental over you / Master's image / Hey, new day / Out of darkness, into light
CD 66056002
Ken Music / Jan '92 / New Note/Pinnacle

Hesitations

SOUL SUPERMAN
She won't come back / You'll never know / You can't bypass love / I believe to my soul / That's what love is / Soul superman / Soul kind of love / I'm not built that way / I'll be right there / Wait a minute / Soul superman No.2 / Clap your hands
CD SSCD 002
Goldmine / Dec '96 / Vital

Hesperus

EARLY AMERICAN ROOTS
CD MMCD 216
Maggie's Music / May '97 / ADA / CM

Hess, Fred

SWEET THUNDER
CD 74032
Capri / Nov '93 / Cadillac / Wellard

Hess, Johnny

ETOILES DE LA CHANSON
CD 8415952
Music Memoria / Jul '96 / ADA / Discovery

Hess, Nigel

WIND BAND MUSIC, THE
CD FLYCD 105
Fly / Oct '92 / Total/BMG

Hession, Carl

OLD TIME NEW TIME
CD CEFCD 173
Gael Linn / Aug '95 / ADA / CM / Direct / Grapevine/PolyGram / Roots

TRA
CD CEFCD 177
Dara / Aug '97 / ADA / CM / Direct / Else / Grapevine/PolyGram

Hester, Carolyn

AT TOWN HALL (The Complete Concert)
Come on back / Come on in / 2.10 train / Captain, my captain / Water is wide / Carry it on / High flying bird / Three young men / Outward bound / Weaving song / Sing hallelujah / That's my song / Summertime / It takes so long / Ain't that rain / Buckeye Jim / Will you send your love / Jute mill song / What's that I hear / Where did my little boy go / Sidewalk city / I saw her / Bad girl / Playboys and playgirls
CD BCD 15520
Bear Family / Jul '90 / Direct / Rollercoaster / Swift

DEAR COMPANION (2CD Set)
Swing and turn jubilee / Come back baby / I'll fly away / Dear companion / Los bibilicos / Once I had a sweetheart / Galway shawl / When Jesus lived in Galilee / Dink's song / Pobre de mi / Yarrow / Virgin Mary / My love is a rider / Gregorio cortez / Simple gits / Brave wolfe / Sally free and easy / I loved a lass / This life I'm living / Pera Stous / Tumbando cana / Coo-coo / Praties they grow small / East Virginia / Come O my love / I want Jesus / That's my song / Stay not late / Amapola / Ain't that rain / Momma's tough little soldier / Lonesome tears / Evertime / Can't help but wonder where I'm bound / Ten thousand candles / Times I've had / Jute mill song / Rivers of Texas / Earl morning / Don't ask questions / Reason to believe / Blues run the game / I love my dog / Bye bye brown eyes / One in a million sunshine girl / Majhires / Outside the window / Hello you tomorrows / Penny Lane / Blues run the game / Come back baby / Los bibilicos / I'll fly away / Virgin Mary / Lonesome tears / Summertime / I want Jesus / Lonesome tears / Outside the window / Lonesome tears
CD Set BCD 15701
Bear Family / Oct '95 / Direct / Rollercoaster / Swift

FROM THESE HILLS
CD RGFCD 033
Road Goes On Forever / Aug '96 / Direct

TEXAS SONGBIRD (Warriors Of The Rainbow/Music Medicine)
CD RGFCD 019
Road Goes On Forever / Aug '94 / Direct

TRADITIONAL ALBUM, THE
CD RGFCD 025
Road Goes On Forever / Dec '95 / Direct

Hetsheads

WE HAIL THE POSSESSED
CD RPS 003CD
Repulse / Apr '95 / Plastic Head

Heuser, Andreas

CONTINUUM
CD BEST 1086CD
Acoustic Music / May '96 / ADA

Hewerdine, Boo

BAPTIST HOSPITAL
CD 0630120452
Blanco Y Negro / Jan '96 / Warner Music

EVIDENCE (Hewerdine, Boo & Darden Smith)
All I want is everything / Reminds me (a little of you) / These chains / Out of this world / Evidence / Who, what, when, where and why / Under the darkest moon / South by South West / First chill of Winter / Love is a strange hotel / Oil on the water / Town called blue
CD HAVENCD 6
Haven / Nov '95 / Pinnacle / Shellshock/ Disc

Hewett, Howard

IT'S TIME
Crystal clear / This love is forever / Your body needs healin' / For the lover in you / I wanna know you / Say goodbye / How do I know I love you / Love of your own / Just to keep you satisfied / On and on / Call his name
CD EXCDP 9
Expansion / Dec '94 / 3mv/Sony

Hewitt, Ben

SPIRIT OF ROCK'N'ROLL, THE
Border City callgirl / Hobnobbin' with the goblins / I wanna love you tonight / Little elfin jive / Ophelia / Because I love you / Call Mama (on the phone) / Somebody wants to love you baby / Shirley Vee / Good times and some mighty fine rock'n'roll / Florida rain / Way down on your knees / Paying for your love (with my heart) / Buster Brown's got the blues / Bundle of love / Good times and some mighty fine rock'n'roll
CD BCD 16200
Bear Family / Jun '97 / Direct / Rollercoaster / Swift

Hex

BIG BANG THEORY
CD LABEL1CD 42
Label One / Nov '96 / Jazz Music

HEX
Diviner / Hermaphrodite / Ethereal message / Mercury towers / Out of the pink / Fire Island / In the net / Silvermine / Elizabeth Green / Arrangement
CD FIENDCD 156
Demon / Feb '90 / Pinnacle

Hexenhaus

AWAKENING
CD CDATV 19
Active / Aug '91 / Pinnacle

EDGE OF ETERNITY
CD CDATV 13
Active / May '90 / Pinnacle

Heymann, Ann

HARPERS LAND, THE (Heymann, Ann & Alison Kinnaird)
CD COMD 2012
Temple / Feb '94 / ADA / CM / Direct / Duncans / Highlander

QUEEN OF HARPS
CD COMD 2057
Temple / Oct '94 / ADA / CM / Direct / Duncans / Highlander

Heyward, Nick

BEST OF NICK HEYWARD AND HAIRCUT 100
Favourite shirts (boy meets girl): *Haircut 100* / Take that situation / Fantastic day: *Haircut 100* / Laura / Marine boy: *Haircut 100* / Blue hat for a blue day / Whistle down the wind / Love plus one: *Haircut 100* / Warning sign / Baked beans: *Haircut 100* / Love all day / Snow girl: *Haircut 100* / Over the weekend / Nobody's fool: *Haircut 100*
CD 260366
Ariola / Dec '89 / BMG

GREATEST HITS OF NICK HEYWARD AND HAIRCUT 100, THE (Heyward, Nick & Haircut 100)
Favourite shirt (boy meets girl): *Haircut 100* / Love plus one: *Haircut 100* / Fantastic day: *Haircut 100* / Nobody's fool: *Haircut 100* / Calling Captain Autumn: *Haircut 100* / Whistle down the wind: *Heyward, Nick* / Take that situation: *Heyward, Nick* / Blue hat for a blue day: *Heyward, Nick* / On a Sunday: *Heyward, Nick* / Love all day (and night): *Heyward, Nick* / Warning sign: *Heyward, Nick* / Over the weekend: *Heyward, Nick* / Laura: *Heyward, Nick* / Kick of love: *Heyward, Nick* / Goodbye yesterday: *Heyward, Nick* / Day it rained forever: *Heyward, Nick*
CD 74321446772
Camden / Feb '97 / BMG

TANGLED
Kill another day / Blinded / Backdated / She says she knows / World / Carry on loving / I love the things you know I don't know / Can't explain / Believe in me / Rollerblade / Breadwinner / London / She's another girl / 1961
CD 4811732
Epic / Oct '95 / Sony

Heywood, Heather

BY YON CASTLE WA'
Sands of the shore / Far over the forth / For a new baby / False, false hae ye been / I hae but son / Wandering piper / Jamie / Wife of Usher's well / Mistress Heywood's fancy / Dowie dens of yarrow / Some people cry / MacCrimmon's sweetheart / Corncrake among the whinnie knows / Aye waukin' o / Young watters / Paul's song / MacCrimmon's lament
CD CDTRAX 054
Greentrax / Dec '92 / ADA / Direct / Duncans / Highlander

SOME KIND OF LOVE
Sally gardens / Lord Lovat / Song for Ireland / Some kind of love / Let no man steal your thyme / Bonnie laddie ye gang by me / My bonnie moorhen / Cruel mother / Wid ye gang love
CD CDTRAX 010
Greentrax / Oct '94 / ADA / Direct / Duncans / Highlander

Heywood, Phil

LOCAL JOE
CD ATM 1118
Atomic Theory / Aug '96 / ADA / Direct

Hi-Fi

FEAR CITY (Hi-Fi & Roadrunners)
CD VE 17CD
Victory / Mar '95 / Plastic Head

Hi-Five

FAITHFUL
CD CHIP 145
Jive / Jan '94 / Pinnacle

GREATEST HITS
I like the way (The kissing game) / She's playing hard to get / I can't wait another minute / I just can't handle it / Quality time / Never should've let you go / What can I say to you (to justify my love) / Unconditional love / Birthday girl / What are you doin' tonight / What was then, this is now / She said
CD CHIP 155
Jive / Mar '97 / Pinnacle

KEEP IT GOIN' ON
CD CHIP 131
Jive / Nov '92 / Pinnacle

Hi-Fives

AND A WHOLE LOTTA YOU
CD LOOKOUT 135CD
Lookout / Jan '97 / Cargo / Greyhound / Shellshock/Disc

Hi-Lo's

BEST OF THE COLUMBIA YEARS, THE
CD 379262
Koch / Feb '97 / Koch

CHERRIES AND OTHER DELIGHTS
CD HCD 603
Hindsight / Mar '94 / Jazz Music / Target/ BMG

Hi-Ryze

SODIUM
CD GPRCD 10
GPR / Mar '95 / 3mv/Vital

Hi-Speed

EROIKA CON ANIMAC PLENETICO
CD CMDD 00022
Creative Man / Jun '97 / ReR Megacorp

Hi-Standard

GROWING UP
CD FAT 534CD
Fatwreck Chords / Jan '96 / Plastic Head

Hi-Tech Roots Dynamics

TOKYO DUB/BERLIN DUB
CD TBXCD 006
Top Beat / Jun '96 / Jet Star / SRD

Hiatt, John

HIATT COMES ALIVE AT BUDOKAN
Through your hands / Real fine love / Memphis in the meantime / Icy blue heart / Paper thin / Angel eyes / Your Dad did / Have a little faith in me / Drive South / Thing called love / Perfectly good guitar / Feels like rain / Tennessee plates / Lipstick sunset / Slow turning
CD 5402842
A&M / Nov '94 / PolyGram

LITTLE HEAD
Little head / Pirate radio / My sweet girl / Feelin' again / Graduated / Sure Pinocchio / Runaway / Woman sawwed in half / Far as we go / After all this time
CD CDEST 2296
Parlophone / Jun '97 / EMI

PERFECTLY GOOD GUITAR
Something wild / Straight outta time / Perfectly good guitar / Buffalo river home / Angel / Blue telescope / Cross my finger / Old habits / Wreck of the Barbie Ferrari / When you old me tight / Permanent hurt / Loving a hurricane / I'll never get over you
CD 5401302
A&M / Sep '93 / PolyGram

SLOW TURNING
Drive south / Trudy and Dave / Tennessee plates / Icy blue heart / Sometime other than now / Georgia Rae / Ride along / Slow turning / It'll come to you / Is anybody there / Paper thin / Feels like rain

CD CDA 5206
A&M / Aug '88 / PolyGram

SLUG LINE/TWO BIT MONSTERS
CD BGOCD 176
Beat Goes On / Jun '93 / Pinnacle

STOLEN MOMENTS
Real fine love / Seven little indians / Child in the wild blue yonder / Back of my mind / Stolen moments / Bring back your love to me / Rest of the dream / Thirty years of tears / Rock back Billy / Listening to old voices / Through your hands / One kiss
CD 3953102
A&M / Apr '95 / PolyGram

WALK ON
Cry love / You must go on / Walk on / Good as she could be / River knows your name / Native son / Dust down a country road / Ethylene / I can't wait / Shredding the document / Wrote it down and burned it / Your love is my rest / Friend of mine / Mile high
CD CDP 8334162
Capitol / Oct '95 / EMI

Hiatus

FROM RESIGNATION...TO REVOLT
CD POLLUTE 12
Sound Pollution / Mar '94 / Plastic Head

Hibbler, Al

AFTER THE LIGHTS GO DOWN LOW
CD 7567820442
Atlantic / Jun '95 / Warner Music

STARRING AL HIBBLER/HERE'S HIBBLER
After the lights go down low / I don't stand a ghost of a chance with you / You'll never know / Night and day / Pennies from Heaven / Shanghai Lil / Stella by starlight / September in the rain / Where are you / Count every star / There are such things / Where or when / Trees / Sweet slumber / Do nothin' 'til you hear from me / Very thought of you / On a slow boat to China / Because of you / What would people say / Just a kid named Joe / I hadn't anyone till you / I'll get along somehow / It's been a long long time / Town crier
CD JASCD 605
Jasmine / Aug '96 / Conifer/BMG / Hot Shot / TKO Magnum

Hicken, David

SHADOW OF YOUTH
CD CDSGP 9022
Prestige / Jun '95 / Else / Total/BMG

Hickey, Ersel

BLUEBIRDS OVER THE MOUNTAINS
Bluebirds over the mountain (US Version) / Hangin' around / You never can tell / Wedding / Lover's land / Goin' down that road / Love in bloom / Another wasted day / You threw a dart / Shame on me / What do you want / Due time (Incomplete) / Mighty square love affair / Teardrops at dawn / Magical love / I guess you could call it love / Lips of roses / What have I done to me / Stardust brought me you / Roll on little river (Unknown) / Don't be afraid of love / People gotta talk / I can't love another / Bluebirds over the mountain (Can version)
CD BCD 15676
Bear Family / May '93 / Direct / Rollercoaster / Swift

Hickman, John

DON'T MEAN MAYBE
Don't mean maybe / Salt river / Turkey knob / Birmingham fling / Sweet Dixie / Sally Goodin / Train 405 / Banjo signal / Ghost dance / Pike county breakdown / Goin' to town / Dixie breakdown
CD ROUCD 0101
Rounder / Feb '95 / ADA / CM / Direct

Hickman, Sara

MISFITS
CD SHCD 8026
Shanachie / Apr '97 / ADA / Greensleeves / Koch

Hickoids

HICKOID HEAVEN
CD EFA 11340CD
Musical Tragedies / Sep '93 / SRD

Hicks, Dan

VERY BEST OF DAN HICKS (Hicks, Dan & His Hot Licks)
CD SEECD 65
See For Miles/C5 / Aug '91 / Pinnacle

Hicks, Edna

EDNA HICKS VOL.1
CD DOCD 5428
Document / Jul '96 / ADA / Hot Shot / Jazz Music

Hicks, Joe

SOMETHING SPECIAL (Hicks, Joe & Jimmy Hughes)
Team: *Hicks, Joe* / Nobody knows you (when you're down and out): *Hicks, Joe* / Train of thought: *Hicks, Joe* / Rock me baby: *Hicks, Joe* / Could it be love: *Hicks, Joe* / Rusty old halo: *Hicks, Joe* / All in: *Hicks, Joe* / Water water: *Hicks, Joe* / Ruby Dean: *Hicks, Joe* / I like everything about you: *Hughes, Jimmy* / Let 'em down baby: *Hughes, Jimmy* / I'm so glad: *Hughes, Jimmy* / Lay it on the line: *Hughes, Jimmy* / Sweet things you do: *Hughes, Jimmy* / Chains of love: *Hughes, Jimmy* / I'm not ashamed to beg or plead: *Hughes, Jimmy* / It's all up to you: *Hughes, Jimmy* / Lock me up: *Hughes, Jimmy* / What side of the door: *Hughes, Jimmy* / Peeped around yonder's bend: *Hughes, Jimmy* / Just ain't as strong as I used to be: *Hughes, Jimmy* / Did you forget: *Hughes, Jimmy*
CD CDSXD 098
Stax / Jul '93 / Pinnacle

Hicks, John

BEYOND EXPECTATIONS
CD RSRCD 130
Reservoir Music / Oct '94 / Cadillac

CRAZY FOR YOU
CD 4722052
Sony Jazz / Nov '92 / Sony

GENTLE RAIN
CD SSCD 8062
Sound Hills / Jan '96 / Cadillac / Harmonia Mundi

IN CONCERT
Some other time/Some other spring / Paul's pal / Pas de trois (Dance for three) / Say it (over and over again) / Soul eyes / Take the coltrane / Oblivion
CD ECD 22048
Evidence / Mar '93 / ADA / Cadillac / Harmonia Mundi

LUMINOUS (Hicks, John & Elise Wood)
CD ECD 220332
Evidence / Sep '92 / ADA / Cadillac / Harmonia Mundi

SOME OTHER TIME
Naima's love song / Mind wine / Peanut butter in the desert / Ghost of yesterday / Some other time / With malice towards none / Dark side, light side / Night journey / After the morning / Epistrophy
CD ECD 220972
Evidence / Jul '94 / ADA / Cadillac / Harmonia Mundi

TWO OF A KIND (Hicks, John & Ray Drummond)
I'll be around / Take the Coltrane / Very early / Getting sentimental over you / For Heaven's sake / Come rain or come shine / Rose without a thorn / Without a song
CD ECD 220172
Evidence / Jul '92 / ADA / Cadillac / Harmonia Mundi

Hicksville Bombers

HICKSVILLE BOMBERS, THE
CD RAUCD 021
Raucous / Oct '96 / Nervous / RTM/Disc / TKO Magnum

Hidalgo, Giovanni

VILLA HIDALGO
CD MES 158172
Messidor / Nov '92 / ADA / Koch

Hideaway

UNABLE TO LABEL
CD BSCD 037
Blue Sting / Jan '97 / CM / Hot Shot / Jazz Music / Swift

Hideki, Kato

HOPE AND DESPAIR
CD XCD 036
Extreme / Jun '96 / Vital/SAM

Higginbotham, J.C.

INTRODUCTION TO J.C. HIGGINBOTHAM 1929-1940, AN
CD 4037
Best Of Jazz / Mar '95 / Discovery

Higgins, Billy

MR. BILLY HIGGINS
Dance of the clones / John Coltrane / Morning awakening / Humility / East side stomp
CD ECD 220612
Evidence / Nov '93 / ADA / Cadillac / Harmonia Mundi

SOWETO
CD 1231412
Red / Apr '94 / ADA / Cadillac / Harmonia Mundi

Higgins, Chuck

PACHUKO HOP
Pachuko hop / Motor head baby / Blues and mambo / Long long time / Chuck's fever / Iron pipe / Big fat Mama / Real gone hound dog / Boyle heights / Papa Charlie / Rooster / Duck walk / Stormy / Just won't treat me rite
CD CDCHD 394
Ace / Mar '92 / Pinnacle

Higgins, Eddie

BY REQUEST
CD SACD 104
Solo Art / Oct '93 / Jazz Music

IN CHICAGO
CD SACD 124
Solo Art / Aug '95 / Jazz Music

PORTRAIT IN BLACK AND WHITE
CD SSC 1072D
Sunnyside / Feb '97 / Discovery

PRELUDE TO A KISS
CD PS 010CD
P&S / Sep '95 / Discovery

THOSE QUIET DAYS
CD SSC 1052D
Sunnyside / Jun '91 / Discovery

Higgs, Joe

FAMILY
CD SHANCD 43053
Shanachie / '88 / ADA / Greensleeves / Koch

TRIUMPH
CD ALCS 8313
Alligator / Aug '92 / ADA / CM / Direct

High

HYPE
Better left untold / Healer / Sweet liberty / This is your life / Let nothing come between us / Goodbye girl / Keep on coming / Slowly happens here / Can I be / Lost and found
CD 8283542
London / Jan '93 / PolyGram

SOMEWHERE SOON
Box set go / Take your time / This is my world / Rather be Marsanne / So I can see / Minor turn / Dream of dinesh / Up and down / PWA / Somewhere soon
CD 8282242
London / Oct '90 / PolyGram

High Back Chairs

CURIOUSITY AND RELIEF
CD DIS 75CD
Dischord / Nov '92 / SRD

High Level Ranters

BONNY PIT LADDIE, THE
Hewer / Doon the waggonway / Miner's life / I wish pay Friday would come / Augengeich disaster / Collier's rant / Farewell to the Monty / Putter / Little chance / My gaffer's bait / Coal owner and the pitman's wife / Blackleg miner / Miners' lockout / South Medomsley strike / Durham lockout / Aa'm glad the strike's done / Colliers pay week / I'll have a collier / Instrumental selection / I'll make her fain to follow me / Joyful days are coming / Get her bo / Stoneman's song / Hartley calamity / Bonnie Woodha' / Banks of the Dee / Bonnie pit laddie, The (instrumental) / Bonnie pit laddie, The (vocal)
CD TSCD 486
Topic / Jul '97 / ADA / CM / Direct

NORTHUMBERLAND FOREVER
Shew's the way to Wallington / Peacock followed the hen / Sandgate girl's lament / Elsie Marley / Bellingham boat / Lamb skinnet / Adam Buckham / Meggy's foot / Lads of North Tyne / Redesdale hornpipe / Hexhamshire lass / Breakdown / Blanchland races / Lads of Alnwick / Lamshaw's fancy / Byker hill / Whinham's reel / Nancy / Because he was a bonny lad / Salmon tails up the water / Sweet Hesleyside / Dance to your daddy / Billy boy / Nae guid luck aboot the house / Mi laddie sits ower late up / Keel row / Kafoozalum / Washing day
CD TSCD 483
Topic / Jul '97 / ADA / CM / Direct

High Llamas

HAWAII
CD CDWOOL 2
Alpaca Park / Mar '96 / 3mv/Sony

High Noon

GLORY BOUND
Train of misery / Midnight shift / Rockin' wildcat / Glory bound / Too much trouble / Baby let's play house / Hold me baby / All night long / Late train / Mona Lisa / Your new flame / Who was that cat / Crazy fever / Don't have a heart left to break / Rocks me right / Feelin' no pain / Branded outlaw / Hannah Lee / Don't have a heart left to break (alt.take) / Beaumont boogie / Ain't it wrong / Havin' a whole lotta fun
CD GRCD 6039
Goofin' / Mar '97 / Nervous / TKO Magnum

LIVE IN TEXAS AND JAPAN
Rattlesnake man / Branded outlaw / I'm not blue / When she's good / Tears keep fallin' / Rockin' wildcat / My ex is why / Devil woman / My heart cries yes / Flatland saturday night / Rock too slow / Ain't it wrong / Glory bound / Who was that cat / Stranger things / How come it / Mona Lisa
CD WMCD 1063
Watermelon / May '97 / ADA / Direct

STRANGER THINGS
CD GRCD 6060
Goofin' / Nov '96 / Nervous / TKO Magnum

High Society

HIGH SOCIETY
Gotta get out of this rut / I never go out in the rain / Talk with your father / Late late train / Dancing in the moonlight / Top hat and tails / Mama said / Paper cup / Madge / I shouldn't fall in love with you / I can sing high / Walking down the strand / Private eye / Beautiful evening / All my life I gave you nothing / Powder blue / Dance till dawn
CD CYBVP 002CD
Cyberdisk / Jul '97 / Pinnacle

High Tea

NEW ST. GEORGE, THE
CD FE 1415
Folk Era / Nov '94 / ADA / CM

High Tension

LEATHER BEAUTY
CD 15198
Laserlight / Aug '91 / Target/BMG

High Tide

SEA SHANTIES/HIGH TIDE
Futilist's lament / Death warmed up / Pushed, but not forgotten / Walking down their outlook / Missing out / Nowhere / Blankman cries again / Joke / Saneonymous
CD CZ 530
EMI / Aug '94 / EMI

Higham, Darrel

MOBILE CORROSION
Like a brand new man / If you can live with it / Long lonely road / Deep in the heart of Texas / I like me just fine / Second hand information / In my heart / No will will grieve / Reverse man / Country Lila Rhue / You were right I was wrong / I've been gone a long time / Don't bug me baby / Amanda's song / Travis pickin' / Life goes on / Rockin' band blues
CD NERCD 082
Nervous / Oct '95 / Nervous / TKO Magnum

Higher Heights

TWINKLE IN A POLISH STYLEE
CD NGCD 537
Twinkle / Jan '93 / Jet Star / Kingdom / SRD

Higher Intelligence Agency

FREE FLOATER
Elapse / Hubble / Fleagle / Thirteen / Skank / Tortoise / Ting / Pinkgreen / UHI / Taz
CD RBADCD 13
Beyond / Sep '95 / Kudos / Pinnacle

POLAR SEQUENCES (Higher Intelligence Agency & Biosphere)
CD RBADCD 17
Beyond / Aug '96 / Kudos / Pinnacle

Higher Than God

DELIRIO CALDO
CD EFA 123322
Sideburn / Jul '97 / SRD

Highland Connection

GAINING GROUND
Carn na caillich / Knockdhu reel / Helsinki harbour / My tocher's the jewel / Mrs. Major L. Stewart of the island / Of java and c / Haud yer tongue Dear Sally / Campbell's roup / Seven seas hornpipe / Losing ground
CD CDTRAX 087
Greentrax / Jan '95 / ADA / Direct / Duncans / Highlander

Highlander

BORN TO BE A WARRIOR
Born to be a warrior / Journey South / Into battle / First time / I heard them cry / Run like the wind / Only one road / Homecoming / 1328 / Homeland
CD CDLDL 1201
Lochshore / Feb '97 / ADA / Direct / Duncans

Hightower Brothers

BEST OF THE HIGHTOWN BROTHERS, THE

CD NASH 4004
Nashboro / Feb '96 / Pinnacle

Highway 101

101 SQUARED
CD 9257422
Curb / Sep '88 / Grapevine/PolyGram

COUNTRY CLASSICS
You baby you / Home on the range / Tell me more / No chance to dance / Who's gonna love you / Last frontier / Fastest healin' broken heart / Love walks / You are what you do / I wonder where the love goes
CD CDMFP 6329
Music For Pleasure / Apr '97 / EMI

REUNITED (Highway 101 & Paulette Carlson)
Where'd you get your cheatin' from / Bed you made for me / Holdin' on / Hearts on the run / Setting me up / She don't have the heart to love you / Texas girl / All the reasons why / Walkin',talkin',cryin', barely beatin' broken heart / I've got your number / It must be love
CD NC 0101
Nashville Connection / Nov '96 / Direct

Highway QC's

COUNT YOUR BLESSINGS
CD CPCD 8113
Charly / Jul '95 / Koch

Highwaymen

ROAD GOES ON FOREVER, THE
Devil's right hand / Live forever / Everybody gets crazy / It is what it is / I do believe / End to understanding / True love travels a gravel road / Death and hell / Waiting for a long time / Here comes that rainbow again / Road goes on forever
CD CDEST 2253
Liberty / Apr '95 / EMI

Highwoods String Band

FEED YOUR BABIES ONIONS
CD ROUCD 11569
Rounder / Feb '95 / ADA / CM / Direct

Higsons

ATTACK OF THE CANNIBAL ZOMBIE BUSINESS MEN, THE
CD SORT 3CD
Mixture / Apr '92 / Pinnacle

CURSE OF THE HIGSONS
CD SORT 2CD
Mixture / Apr '92 / Pinnacle

Hijack

HORNS OF JERICHO, THE
Intro (Phantom of the opera) / Syndicate outta jail / Daddy rich / Back to Brixton / Airwave hijack / Hijack the terrorist group / Badman is robbin' / I had to serve you / Don't go with strangers / Brother versus brother / Paranoid schizophrenic with homicidal tendencies / Contract
CD 7599263862
WEA / Oct '91 / Warner Music

Hildegarde

DARLING, JE VOUS AIME BEAUCOUP
CD PASTCD 7066
Flapper / Jul '95 / Pinnacle

DARLING, JE VOUS AIME BEAUCOUP
Darling Je vous aime beaucoup / Honey coloured moon / I believe in miracles / Listen to the german band / For me, for you / Gloomy Sunday / Isn't this a lovely day (to be caught in the rain) / Cheek to cheek / Glory of love / Hildegarde look back (Medley) / Pretty girl is like a melody / Love walked in / It's the natural thing to do / Will you remember / There's a small hotel / This year's kisses / Pennies from heaven / (I love you) for sentimental reasons / Room with a view / my ship / Saga of Jenny Pts. 1 and 2 / Lili Marlene / Goodnight angel
CD CDAJA 5161
Living Era / May '95 / Select

Hill & Wiltchinsky

LATIN NIGHTS
Girl from Ipanema / One note samba / Volare / Spanish eyes / Begin the beguine / Latin nights / Guantanamera / Spanish Harlem / Amor / On a clear day / Light my fire / Brasilia / Breeze from Rio / Perfidia / Lambada / Copacabana / La bamba / Summer samba
CD ECD 3281
K-Tel / Jan '97 / K-Tel

ROMANTIC GUITARS
When I fall in love / Gymnopedie / Way we were / Cavatina / Lady in red / Mona Lisa / Ave Maria / Memory / Annie's song / Romanza / Adagio Rodriguez / Music of the night / Barcarolle / I know him so well / Here, there and everywhere / If / Hello / Love story / Greatest love of all / For the love of Annie
CD CDSR 024
Telstar / Sep '93 / BMG

ROMANTIC GUITARS (4CD Set)
Nights in white satin / If / Walk on by / Annie's song / When I fall in love / Autumn leaves / So deep is the night / And I love her so / Girl / Faerie queen / While my guitar gently weeps / Air on a g string / Dreams / Mountains of Mourne / Melodia / This boy / Hello / First time I ever saw your face / Way we were / And I love her / Cavatina / Music of the night / Love story / Michelle / Londonderry air (Danny boy) / El noi de la mare / Fool on the hill / Romance in d / Because / As I roved out / Elvira Madigan / Romanza / Three times a lady / I know him so well / Sound of silence / Long and winding road / Walking on air / Memory / Barcarolle / I'll take you home again Kathleen / Fur Elise / Norwegian wood (this bird has flown) / Feelings / Without you / Waves / Step inside love / Minstral boy / Ave maria / Lady in red / Groovy kind of love / Greatest love of all / Windmills of your mind / Sweet sixteen / Mona Lisa / Adagio Rodrigo / For the love of Annie / Something / Here there and everywhere / You've got a friend / My love's an arbutus / Jesu joy of man's desire / Songs without words / If I fell in love with you / Gymnopedie
CD Set QUAD 012
Tring / Nov '96 / Tring

Hill, Andrew

ETERNAL SPIRIT
Pinnacle / Golden sunset / Samba rasta / Tail feather / Spiritual lover 45 / Bobby's tune / Pinnacle (alt. take) / Golden sunset (alt. take) / Spiritual lover (alt. take)
CD CDP 7920512
Blue Note / Feb '97 / EMI

FACES OF HOPE
CD 1210102
Soul Note / Oct '90 / Cadillac / Harmonia Mundi / Wellard

LIVE AT MONTREUX
Snake hip waltz / Nefertisis / Come Sunday / Relativity
CD FCD 41023
Freedom / Dec '87 / Cadillac / Jazz Music / Koch / Wellard

SHADES
CD 1211132
Soul Note / Jan '91 / Cadillac / Harmonia Mundi / Wellard

SPIRAL
Tomorrow / Laverne / Message / Invitation / Today / Spiral / Quiet dawn
CD FCD 41007
Freedom / Sep '87 / Cadillac / Jazz Music / Koch / Wellard

STRANGER SERENADE (Hill, Andrew Trio)
CD 1210132
Soul Note / Aug '91 / Cadillac / Harmonia Mundi / Wellard

Hill, Bertha

COMPLETE RECORDED WORKS 1925-29 (Hill, Bertha 'Chippie')
CD DOCD 5330
Document / Mar '95 / ADA / Hot Shot / Jazz Music

Hill, Buck

CAPITAL HILL
CD MCD 5384
Muse / Sep '92 / New Note/Pinnacle

Hill, Dan

GREATEST HITS AND MORE
CD 341852
Koch International / Nov '95 / Koch

I'M DOING FINE
CD 332192
Koch International / Dec '96 / Koch

Hill, Faith

IT MATTERS TO ME
CD 9362458722
Warner Bros. / Aug '95 / Warner Music

TAKE ME AS I AM
Take me as I am / Wild one / Just about now / Piece of my heart / I've got this friend / Life's too short to love like that / But I will / Just around the eyes / Go the distance / I would be stronger than that
CD 9362453892
Warner Bros. / Jun '94 / Warner Music

Hill, Joe

DON'T MOURN - ORGANISE (Songs Of Labour Songwriter Joe Hill) (Various Artists)
CD SFCD 40026
Smithsonian Folkways / Nov '94 / ADA / Cadillac / CM / Direct / Koch

Hill, Jordan

JORDAN HILL
CD 7567828492
Atlantic / Sep '96 / Warner Music

Hill, Michael

BLOODLINES (Hill, Michael Blues Mob)
CD AL 4821
Alligator / Jul '94 / ADA / CM / Direct

HAVE MERCY (Hill, Michael Blues Mob)
CD ALCD 4845
Alligator / Oct '96 / ADA / CM / Direct

Hill, Noel

HILL & LINNANE (Hill, Noel & Tony Linnane)
Humours of Ballyconnell / Drunken landlady / Ryan's reel / Geese in the bog / Joe Cooley's hornpipe / Miss Monaghan / Skylark / Foxhunter / Reevey's reel / Golden keyboard / Killoran's reel / Mountain road / Anderson's reel / Carthy's / Sweeney's dream / Johnny Cope / Scotsman over the border / Tom Billy's jig / Pigeon on the gate / Daniel O'Connell / Home ruler / Kitty's wedding / Lady Ann Montgomery / Cooley's reel
CD TARACD 2006
Tara / Jan '96 / ADA / CM / Conifer/BMG / Direct

IRISH CONCERTINA, THE
Last night's fun/Trip to Durrow / Boy in the bush / Kiss the maid behind the barrel/ Dublin reel / Laird of Drumblair / Pigeon on the gate/Sean sa cheo / Farewell to Ireland / Old goman's reel / Wind that shakes the barley / Taimse I'm chodladh / Wise maid/ Bells of Tipperary / Gold ring/Larks in the morning / Salamanca reel / Over the moor to Maggie / Chicago reel / An draigheann / Thrush in the morning / Drunken sailor / Moving clouds/Devanny's goat/McDermott's reel
CD CCF 21CD
Claddagh / Oct '88 / ADA / CM / Direct

Hill Smith, Marilyn

IS IT REALLY ME
CD CDVIR 8314
TER / Sep '91 / Koch

Hill, Teddy

CLASSICS 1935-1937
CD CLASSICS 645
Classics / Nov '92 / Discovery / Jazz Music

UPTOWN RHAPSODY
Lookie lookie here comes Cookie / Got me doin' things / When the robin sings her song again / When love knocks on your heart / Uptown rhapsody / At the rug cutter's ball / Blue rhythm fantasy / Passionette / Love bug will bite you / Would you like to buy a dream / Big boy blue / Where is the sun / Harlem, twister / Marie / I know now / Lady who couldn't be kissed / You and me that used to be / Study in brown / Twilight in Turkey / China boy / San Anton / I'm happy darling, dancing with you / Yours and mine / I'm feelin' like a million / King Porter stomp
CD HEPCD 1033
Hep / Mar '92 / Cadillac / Jazz Music / New Note/Pinnacle / Wellard

Hill, Tiny

TINY HILL & HIS HILLTOPPERS 1943-44
CD CCD 55
Circle / Jan '94 / Jazz Music / Swift / Wellard

Hill, Tommy

GET READY BABY
Ain't nothing like loving / In the middle of the morning / Can't help / Life begins at four o'clock / Oh get ready, Baby / Love words / Do me a favour / Have a little faith in me / O get ready baby / In the middle of the morning
CD BCD 15709
Bear Family / Mar '93 / Direct / Rollercoaster / Swift

Hill, Vince

GREATEST HITS (An Hour Of Hits)
Take me to your heart again / Importance of your love / Little bluebird / Somewhere my love / Love letters in the sand / Doesn't anybody know my name / Here, there and everywhere / Wives and lovers / Girl talk / Merci cherie / Heartaches / Roses of Picardy / Moonlight and roses / Look around / Love story / Close to you / Danny boy / You're my world / Time for us / Spanish eyes
CD CC 201
Music For Pleasure / May '88 / EMI

I WILL ALWAYS LOVE YOU
I will always love you / Desperado / Love dies hard / Crying in the wind / Sweet dreams / Pray for love / When you walk through life / I want to know you / Sweet music man / Loving arms / It's not supposed to be that way / Sea of heartbreak / Always on my mind
CD GRCD 24
Grasmere / Feb '89 / Highlander / Savoy / Target/BMG

LOVE SONGS
I will always love you / Desperado / Love dies hard / Crying in the wind / Sweet dreams / Pray for love / When you walk through life / I want to know you / Sweet music man / Loving arms / It's not supposed to be that way / Sea of heartbreak / Always on my mind
CD PWKM 4074
Carlton / Feb '96 / Carlton

THAT LOVING FEELING
CD PRCD 142
President / May '93 / Grapevine/PolyGram / President / Target/BMG

VERY BEST OF VINCE HILL, THE
Very thought of you / I only have eyes for you / Sentimental journey / Love me tender / After you've gone / Folks who live on the hill / Among my souvenirs / Old feeling / Nevertheless / I'll get by / September song / Catch a falling star / Somewhere my love / All the things you are / Roses of Picardy / Look around (and I'll find you there) / Edelweiss / Where do I begin / Close to you / I will wait for you / Spanish eyes
CD CDMFP 6249
Music For Pleasure / Aug '96 / EMI

Hill, Warren

SHELTER
CD 1046770432
Warner Bros. / May '97 / Warner Music

Hill, Z.Z.

BRAND NEW Z.Z. HILL, THE
It ain't no use / Ha ha (laughing song) / Second chance / Our love is getting better / Faithful and true / Chockin' kind / Hold back (one man at a time) / Man needs a woman (woman needs a man) / Early in the morning / I think I'd do it / She's all I got / Raining on a sunny day / Sweeter than sweetness / Sidewalks, fences and walls / I did the woman wrong / Yours love / Laid back and easy / You and me together forever / Ain't nothin' in the news (but the blues) / Did I come back to soon (or stay away too long) / Wy whole world has ended (without you) / Cuss the wind
CD CDCHD 532
Ace / Jun '94 / Pinnacle

DOWN HOME SOUL OF Z.Z. HILL, THE
Baby I'm sorry / I need someone (to love me) / Have mercy someone / Kind of love I want / Hey little girl / I found love / No more doggin' / You can't hide a heartache / That's it / Happiness is all I need / Everybody has to cry / Nothing can change this love / Set your sights higher / Steal away / You're gonna need my loving / You're gonna make me cry / Oh darling / If I could do it all over / You don't love me / You won't hurt no more / What more / You got what I need
CD CDKEN 099
Kent / Sep '92 / Pinnacle

LOVE IS SO GOOD WHEN YOU'RE STEALING IT
CD SCL 21122
Ichiban Soul Classics / Jun '96 / Koch

MAN NEEDS A WOMAN, A
Chokin' kind / Hold back / Man needs a woman / Early in the morning / I think I'd do it / Ha ha (laughing song) / It ain't no use / Second chance / Our love is getting better / Faithful and true
CD AIM 2007CD
Aim / May '97 / ADA / Direct / Jazz Music

Hillage, Steve

FISH RISING
Fish / Meditation of the snake / Solar musick suite / Salmon song / Aftaglid
CD CDV 2031
Virgin / Jun '87 / EMI

FOR TO NEXT - AND NOT OR
These uncharted lands / Kamikaze eyes / Alone / Anthems for the blind / Bright future / Frame by frame / Waiting / Glory
CD CDV 2244
Virgin / Jul '90 / EMI

GREEN
Sea nature / Ether ships / Musick of the trees / Palm trees (love guitar) / Unidentified (flying being) / UFO over Paris / Leylines to Glassdom / Crystal City / Activation meditation / Glorious OM riff
CD CDV 2098
Virgin / Jun '90 / EMI

L
Hurdy gurdy man / Hurdy gurdy glissando / Elecktrick Gypsies / Om nama shivaya / Lunar musick suite / It's all too much
CD CDVIP 184
Virgin VIP / Apr '97 / EMI

LIVE HERALD
Salmon song / Dervish riff / Castle in the clouds / Light in the sky / Searching for the spark / Electric gypsies / Radiom / It's all too much / Talking to the sun / 1988 aktivator / New age synthesis (unzipping the zype) / Healing feeling / Lunar musick suite / Meditation of the dragon / Golden vibe
CD CDVM 3502
Virgin / Jun '90 / EMI

MOTIVATION RADIO
Hello dawn / Motivation / Light in the sky / Radio / Wait one moment / Saucer surfing / Searching for the spark / Octave doctors and the crystal machine / Not fade away (glide forever)
CD _______ CDV 2777
Virgin / Jun '88 / EMI

OPEN
Day after day / Getting in tune / Open / Definite activity / Don't dither do it / Fire inside / Earthrise
CD _______ CDV 2135
Virgin / Jun '90 / EMI

RAINBOW DOME MUSICK
Garden of paradise / Four ever rainbow
CD _______ CDVR 1
Virgin / Jun '88 / EMI

Hille, Sid

DUNJIN'S DANCE
Dunjin's dance / Searching the quiet place / Notes from a traveller / Temple of Geha / Mombassa afrique / Little mountain / Last moment / Don't lose that number
CD _______ AL 73022
A / Nov '96 / Cadillac / Direct

Hille, Veda

WOMEN IN (E)MOTION FESTIVAL
Driven / Precious heart / Slumber Queen / Instructions / Strange sad / With no caring / Old song / 26 years / '79 rose / Stupid polka / And birds / Driven
CD _______ T&M 111
Tradition & Moderne / Nov '96 / ADA / Direct

Hiller, Holger

AS IS
CD _______ CDSTUMM 60
Mute / Sep '91 / RTM/Disc

OBEN IM ECK
CD _______ CDSTUMM 38
Mute / Nov '86 / RTM/Disc

Hilliard Ensemble

17TH/18TH CENTURY SONGS & CATCHES
By a bank as I lay / Tho' I am young / Lost is my quiet / We be three poor mariners / Sweeter than roses / I spy Celia / Since time so kind to us does prove / Orpheus and Euridice / Here's that will challenge all the fair / Which is the properest day to drink / Chloe found Amyntas / Here lies a woman / On thy banks gentle Stour / So well Corinna likes the joy / My man John, a riddle / Street intrigue / When the cock begins to crow
CD _______ EC 33222
Saga Classics / Nov '96 / Complete/ Pinnacle

CODEX SPECIALNIK
CD _______ 4478072
ECM / Apr '95 / New Note/Pinnacle

HILLIARD SONGBOOK, THE
CD _______ 4532592
ECM / Oct '96 / New Note/Pinnacle

PEROTIN
CD _______ 8377512
ECM / Jan '90 / New Note/Pinnacle

Hillier, Paul

PROENSA
CD _______ 8373602
ECM / Apr '89 / New Note/Pinnacle

Hillman, Chris

BAKERSFIELD BOUND (Hillman, Chris & Herb Pedersen)
CD _______ SHCD 3850
Sugar Hill / Dec '96 / ADA / CM / Direct / Koch / Roots

CLEAR SAILING
Nothing gets through / Fallen favourite / Quits / Hot dusty roads / Heartbreaker / Playing the fool / Lucky in love / Rollin' and tumblin' / Ain't that peculiar / Clear sailing
CD _______ 7559611632
Elektra / Jan '97 / Warner Music

DESERT ROSE
Why you been gone so long / Somebody's back in town / Wall around your heart / Rough and rowdy ways / Desert rose / Running the roadblocks / I can't keep you in love with me / Treasure of love / Ashes of love / Turn your radio on
CD _______ SHCD 3743
Sugar Hill / Jun '97 / ADA / CM / Direct / Koch / Roots

HILLMEN, THE (Hillmen)
Brown mountain light / Ranger's command / Sangeree / Bluegrass choppere / Barbara Allen / Fair and tender ladies / Goin' up / When the ship comes in / Fare thee well / Winsborough Cotton Mill blues / Prisoner's plea / Back road fever / Rollon muddy river
CD _______ SHCD 3719
Sugar Hill / Jun '97 / ADA / CM / Direct / Koch / Roots

MORNING SKY
Tomorrow is a long time / Taker / Here today and gone tomorrow / Morning sky / Ripple / Good time Charlie's got the blues / Don't let your sweet love die / Mexico / It's happening to you / Hickory wind
CD _______ SHCD 3729
Sugar Hill / Jun '97 / ADA / CM / Direct / Koch / Roots

OUT OF THE WOODWORK (Hillman, Chris & Tony Rice/Larry Rice/Herb Pederson)
Hard times / Lord won't you help me / Somewhere on the road tonight / No one else / Street corner stranger / So begins the task / Dimming of the day / Just me and you / Do right woman / Change coming down / Story of love / Only passing through
CD _______ ROUCD 0390
Rounder / Feb '97 / ADA / CM / Direct

SLIPPIN' AWAY
Step on out / Slippin' away / Falling again / Take it on the run / Blue morning / Witching hour / Down in the churchyard / Love is the sweetest amnesty / Midnight again / (Take me in your) lifeboat
CD _______ 7559611622
Elektra / Mar '97 / Warner Music

THREE BYRDS LAND IN LONDON (2CD Set) (Hillman, Chris & Roger McGuin/ Gene Clark)
CD Set _______ SFRSCD 001
Strange Fruit / Feb '97 / Pinnacle

Hillman, Steve

MATRIX
Overdrive / Matrix pt.1 / Interchange / Ascendant / Sphinx dancer / Into space / Now or never / Sequent 7 / Matrix pt.2 / Dawning light / Into the blue / Tritone
CD _______ CYCL 011
Cyclops / Jun '97 / Pinnacle

RIDING THE STORM
CD _______ CYCL 035
Cyclops / May '96 / Pinnacle

Hills, Anne

ANGEL OF LIGHT
CD _______ FF 648CD
Flying Fish / Nov '95 / ADA / CM / Direct / Roots

DON'T PANIC
CD _______ FF 608CD
Flying Fish / Apr '94 / ADA / CM / Direct / Roots

NEVER GROW OLD (Hills, Anne & Cindy Mangsen)
CD _______ FF 70638
Flying Fish / Feb '95 / ADA / CM / Direct / Roots

Hilmarsson, Hilmar Orn

CHILDREN OF NATURE
CD _______ T 3314
Touch / Feb '96 / Kudos / Pinnacle

Hilton, Ronnie

RONNIE HILTON
I still believe / No other love / Veni vidi vici / Around the world / Magic moments / Blossom fell / Stars shine in your eyes / Yellow rose of Texas / Woman in love / Wonderful, wonderful / I may never pass this way again / Miracle of love / World outside / Don't let the rain come down / As I love you / One blade of grass (in a meadow) / On the street where you live / She / Marching along to the blues / Her hair was yellow / Day the rains came / Do I love you / Gift / Beautiful bossa nova
CD _______ CC 258
Music For Pleasure / Oct '90 / EMI

VERY BEST OF RONNIE HILTON, THE
Magic moments / Young and foolish / Who are we / Two different worlds / Wonder of you / Windmill in old Amsterdam / I still believe / No other love / Veni vidi vici / Around the world / Blossom fell / Stars shine in your eyes / Yellow rose of Texas / Women in love / Wonderful wonderful / I may never pass this way again / Miracle of love / World outside / Don't let the rain come down / As I love you / One blade of grass in a meadow / On the street where you live / She / Marching along to the blues / Her hair was yellow
CD _______ CDMFP 6250
Music For Pleasure / Aug '96 / EMI

Him

EGG
CD _______ 185362
Southern / Apr '96 / SRD

HIM/THE DYLAN GROUP (Him/The Dylan Group)
CD _______ BC 013
Bubblecore / Apr '97 / SRD

INTERPRETIVE BELIEF SYSTEM
CD _______ EFA 012202
Word Sound Recordings / Aug '97 / Cargo / SRD

Him Kerosene

RECORDER
CD _______ ASR 3
Ampersand / Jun '97 / Cargo

Himber, Richard

RICHARD HIMBER & HIS ORCHESTRA 1938-40
CD _______ CCD 7
Circle / Jan '94 / Jazz Music / Swift / Wellard

Hinchcliffe, Keith

CAROLAN'S DREAM
CD _______ KH 001CD
Ranmoor / Mar '94 / ADA

Hinds, Donna

GONE TOO FAR
CD _______ FECD 18
First Edition / Jun '97 / Jet Star

Hinds, Justin

SKA UPRISING (Hinds, Justin & The Dominoes)
CD _______ CDTRL 314
Trojan / Mar '94 / Direct / Jet Star

THIS CARRY GO BRING HOME (Hinds, Justin & The Dominoes)
CD _______ RNCD 2044
Rhino / Feb '94 / Grapevine/PolyGram / Jet Star

Hines, Earl 'Fatha'

1928-1932
CD _______ CLASSICS 545
Classics / Dec '90 / Discovery / Jazz Music

AALBORG, DENMARK 1965
Medley: Monday date/Blues in thirds/You can depend on me / Tea for two / Medley / Shiny stockings / Perdido / Black coffee / Medley / Boogie woogie on St. Louis blues
CD _______ STCD 8222
Storyville / Aug '94 / Cadillac / Jazz Music / Wellard

AT HOME
You are too beautiful / Love at night is out of sight / It happens to be me / Minor nothing / Moon mare / You'll never know / Cannery walk
CD _______ DD 212
Delmark / Jun '97 / ADA / Cadillac / CM / Direct / Hot Shot

AT SUNDOWN
CD _______ BB 8682
Black & Blue / Apr '96 / Discovery / Koch / Wellard

BACK ON THE STREET (Hines, Earl 'Fatha' & Jonah Jones)
CD _______ CRD 118
Chiaroscuro / Nov '95 / Jazz Music

BASIN STREET BLUES
CD _______ CDCH 560
Milan / Feb '91 / Conifer/BMG / Silva Screen

BLUES AND THINGS (Hines, Earl 'Fatha' & Jimmy Rushing)
CD _______ 804652
New World / Oct '96 / ADA / Cadillac / Harmonia Mundi

BLUES SO LOW - 1966
Oh Lady be good / It had to be you / Black and blue / Two sleepy people / Ain't misbehavin' / Jitterbug waltz / Squeeze me / Honeysuckle rose / Epinal blues / Birth of the blues / Memphis blues / Basin Street blues / Tin roof blues / Rhapsody in blue / Shiny stockings / Sweet Lorraine / Boogie woogie on St. Louis blues / I wish you love / It's a pity to say goodnight
CD _______ STCD 537
Stash / '91 / ADA / Cadillac / CM / Direct / Jazz Music

CLASSICS 1932-1934
CD _______ CLASSICS 514
Classics / Apr '90 / Discovery / Jazz Music

CLASSICS 1934-1937
CD _______ CLASSICS 528
Classics / Apr '90 / Discovery / Jazz Music

CLASSICS 1937-1939
CD _______ CLASSICS 538
Classics / Dec '90 / Discovery / Jazz Music

CLASSICS 1939-1940
CD _______ CLASSICS 567
Classics / Oct '91 / Discovery / Jazz Music

CLASSICS 1942-1945
CD _______ CLASSICS 876
Classics / Apr '96 / Discovery / Jazz Music

EARL HINES & THE DUKE'S MEN
CD _______ DD 470
Delmark / Dec '94 / ADA / Cadillac / CM / Direct / Hot Shot

EARL HINES, 1941 (Hines, Earl 'Fatha' Orchestra)
CD _______ CLASSICS 621
Classics / Nov '92 / Discovery / Jazz Music

FATHA
CD _______ CD 14556
Jazz Portraits / Jul '94 / Jazz Music

FATHA
CD _______ TPZ 1006
Topaz Jazz / Aug '94 / Cadillac / Pinnacle

FATHA JUMPS 1940-1942 (Hines, Earl 'Fatha' Orchestra)
CD _______ RACD 7115
Aerospace / May '96 / Jazz Music / Montpellier

FATHA'S BLUES
CD _______ TCD 1028
Tradition / Aug '96 / ADA / Vital

FATHER STEPS IN
GT stomp / Jezebel / Dominick swing / Grand terrace shuffle / Father steps in / Piano man / Father's getaway / Me and Columbus / Please be kind / Goodnight, sweet dreams, goodnight / Tippin' at the terrace / XYZ / Gator swing / After all I've been to you / Mellow bit of rhythm / Ridin' a riff / Solid mama / Jack climbed a beanstalk / Ridin' and jivin' / (Back home again in) Indiana / Reminiscing at Blue Note / Riff medley
CD _______ GRF 092
Tring / '93 / Tring

HINE'S TUNE (Paris 1965)
Hine's tune / One I love (belongs to someone else) / Bag's Groove / Blue turning grey over you / Don's blues / Tenderly / Boogie woogie on St. Louis blues / These foolish things / I'm a little brown bird / Que reste t'il de nos amours / Little girl blue / You are the cream in my coffee / I can't get started (with you) / Petite laitue / Cherry / Sweet lorraine / I've got the world on a string / Body and soul / Clopin clopant / C'est si bon
CD _______ FCD 101
Esoldun / '88 / Target/BMG

HINES '74
CD _______ 233073
Black & Blue / May '87 / Discovery / Koch / Wellard

HINES SHINES
CD _______ 17030
Laserlight / May '94 / Target/BMG

HINES SHINES
CD _______ DM 15003
DMA Jazz / Jul '96 / Jazz Music

IN NEW ORLEANS
Someday, sweetheart / Playing with fire / Elephant stomp / Do you know what it means to miss New Orleans / Bouncing for panassie / Blues my naughty sweetie gives to me / Sugar babe / If I could be with you one hour tonight / Someday you'll be sorry / Moonglow
CD _______ CRD 200
Chiaroscuro / Jan '97 / Jazz Music

IN PARIS
CD _______ 500562
Musidisc / May '94 / Discovery

INDISPENSABLE EARL HINES VOL.5 & 6 1944-1966, THE
My fate is in your hands / I've got a feeling I'm falling in love / Honeysuckle rose / Squeeze me / Undecided / I've found a new baby / Fatha's blues / Sunday kind of love / Tosca's dance / Jim / Black coffee / You always hurt the one you love / Save it pretty Mama / Bye bye baby / Smoke rings / Shoe shine boy / Stanley steamer / Bernard's tune / Dream of you
CD _______ ND 896182
Jazz Tribune / Jun '94 / BMG

INTRODUCTION TO EARL HINES, AN
CD _______ 4047
Best Of Jazz / Jul '97 / Discovery

JUST FRIENDS
CD _______ JHR 73506
Jazz Hour / May '93 / Cadillac / Jazz Music / Target/BMG

LIVE AT SARALEE'S
CD _______ 15790
Laserlight / Aug '92 / Target/BMG

LIVE AT THE NEW SCHOOL
CD _______ CRD 157
Chiaroscuro / Mar '96 / Jazz Music

MASTERPIECES VOL.14 1934-1942
CD _______ MASTER 158332
Masterpieces / Mar '95 / BMG

MASTERS OF JAZZ VOL.2
CD _______ STCD 4102
Storyville / '89 / Cadillac / Jazz Music / Wellard

ONE FOR MY BABY
CD ______ BLCD 760198
Koch / Nov '94 / Koch

PIANO MAN
Blues in thirds / Boogie woogie on St. Louis blues / Cavernism / Chicago rhythm / Chimes blues / Comin' in home / Earl / Every evening / Father's getaway / Fifty seven varieties / Fireworks / Harlem lament / Honeysuckle rose / Love me tonight / Monday date / Piano man / Ridin' a riff / Rosetta / Save it pretty Mama / Skip the gutter / Smokehouse blues / Solid mama / Stowaway / Two deuces / Weatherbird
CD ______ CDAJA 5131
Living Era / Oct '94 / Select

PIANO MAN 1928-1955
CD ______ CD 53118
Giants Of Jazz / Jan '94 / Cadillac / Jazz Music / Target/BMG

PLAYS DUKE ELLINGTON
CD ______ NW 361/362
New World / Aug '92 / ADA / Cadillac / Harmonia Mundi

PLAYS GEORGE GERSHWIN
CD ______ 500522
Musidisc / Jan '94 / Discovery

REUNION IN BRUSSELS
CD ______ 4722072
Sony Jazz / Nov '92 / Sony

SWINGIN' AWAY
Bright attitude / Blue lion blues / Le bijou / Don't take your love from me / Senator Sam / You can depend on me / Rosetta
CD ______ BLCD 760210
Black Lion / Apr '96 / Cadillac / Jazz Music / Koch / Wellard

TOUR DE FORCE
When your lover has gone / Indian summer / Mack the knife / I never knew (I could love anyone like I'm loving you) / Say it isn't so / Lonesome road
CD ______ BLCD 760140
Black Lion / May '90 / Cadillac / Jazz Music / Koch / Wellard

TOUR DE FORCE ENCORE
CD ______ BLCD 760157
Black Lion / '91 / Cadillac / Jazz Music / Koch / Wellard

WAY DOWN YONDER IN NEW ORLEANS
My Monday date / Song of the Islands / There'll be some changes made / Jelly Roll / Tishomingo blues / One I love (belongs to somebody else) / Rosetta / Way down yonder in New Orleans / Do you know what it means to miss New Orleans / Bouncin' for panassie / If I could be with you one hour tonight / Moonglow
CD ______ BCD 108
Biograph / Jul '91 / ADA / Cadillac / Direct / Hot Shot / Jazz Music / Wellard

WEST SIDE STORY
West Side story medley / Close to you / Why do I love you / In my solitude / Don't get around much anymore
CD ______ BLCD 760186
Black Lion / Jul '93 / Cadillac / Jazz Music / Koch / Wellard

Hinge

ACCIDENTAL MEETING OF MINDS
Pyramid club / Roar / Form / Rest / Quirky / Basilisk / Major 7th / Ransom / Rising man
CD ______ CDVEST 34
Bulletproof / Oct '94 / Pinnacle

Hinnies

DEAD FOUR
CD ______ BGRL 015 CD
Bad Girl / Sep '92 / Pinnacle

Hino, Mtohiko

IT'S THERE
CD ______ ENJACD 80302
Enja / Sep '95 / New Note/Pinnacle / Vital/SAM

Hinojosa, Tish

AQUELLA NOCHE
Tu que puedas, vuelvete / Cumbia, pola y mas / Manos, hueso y sangre / Reloj / La llorona / Azul cristal / Aquella noche / Historia de un amor / Una noche mas / Carlos dominguez / Samba san pedro / Malaguena salerosa / Estrellita
CD ______ MRCD 156
Munich / '91 / ADA / CM / Direct / Greensleeves

BEST OF THE SANDIA, THE (Watermelon 1991-1992)
Toas to Tennessee / Prairie moon / Highway calls / Crazy winds and flashing yellows / Always / Aquella noche / Samba san pedro / Anos meses y dias / Una noche mas / Cumbia polka y mas / Manos huesos y sangre / De colores / Ere tu / Gracias a la vida / Building no.9 / Everything you wish / Arbolito / By the Rio Grande
CD ______ WMCD 1062
Watermelon / May '97 / ADA / Direct

DESTINY'S GATE
Destiny's gate / Saying you will / What more can you say in a song / Esperate (wait for me) / Looking for my love in the pouring rain / I'm not through loving you yet / Love of mine / I want to see you again / Noche sin estrellas (night without stars) / Yesterday's paper / Baby believe
CD ______ 9362455662
Warner Bros. / Jul '94 / Warner Music

DREAMING FROM THE LABYRINTH
When it rains (cuando llueve) / Whisper goodbye (luego se va) / Edge of a dream (orilla de un sonar) / Laughing river running (riendo el rio corre) / Atlantico / Beyond the battle of men (batalla de hombre no habra) / Prisonary life (vida prisionera) / This song (esta cancion) / God's own open road / Sacrifices (sacrificios)
CD ______ 9362462032
Warner Bros. / Mar '97 / Warner Music

EVERY CHILD
CD ______ ROUCD 8032
Rounder / Feb '96 / ADA / CM / Direct

FRONTEJAS
Pajarillo barranquero / Malhaya la cocina / Poquita fe / Farolito / Las golondrinas / Otro vasito / Djearme Llorar / Buen amor / Polka fronterrestril / Las marias / Con su pluma en su mano / Solo tus ojos
CD ______ ROUCD 3132
Rounder / Apr '95 / ADA / CM / Direct

MEMORABILIA NAVIDENA
Abolito (little Christmas tree) / Milagro / Building / A la nantia nana / Arbolita (in English) / Cada nino/Every child / Everything you wish / Memorabilia (Honky tonker's christmas)
CD ______ WMCD 1006
Watermelon / Jun '93 / ADA / Direct

TAOS TO TENNESSEE
Midnight moonlight / Prairie song / According to my heart / Taos to Tennessee / River / Amanecer / Please be with me / Crazy wind and flashing yellows / Highway calls / Who showed you the way to my heart / Let me remember / Always
CD ______ MRCD 164
Munich / '92 / ADA / CM / Direct / Greensleeves

Hinton, Eddie

LETTERS FROM MISSISSIPPI
My searching is over / Sad and lonesome / Everybody needs love / Letters from Mississippi / Everybody meets Mr.Blue / Uncloudy day / I want a woman / Ting a ling ling / Wet weather man / I will always love you / It's alright / I'll come running (back to you)
CD ______ ZNCD 1001
Zane / Oct '95 / Pinnacle

VERY BLUE HIGHWAY
I love someone / Rock of my soul / Poor Ol' me / Sad Carol / Very blue highway / Call a blues physician / Good love is hard to find / Just don't know / Let it roll / How you goin' to Georgia / Standin' in / Hey Justine / Nobody but you
CD ______ ZNCD 1005
Zane / Oct '95 / Pinnacle

Hinton, Milt

BACK TO BASS-ICS (Hinton, Milt Trio)
CD ______ PCD 7084
Progressive / Jun '93 / Jazz Music

OLD MAN TIME (2CD Set)
CD Set ______ CRD 310
Chiaroscuro / Dec '95 / Jazz Music

Hip Young Things

DEFLOWERED
CD ______ GRCD 244
Glitterhouse / Apr '93 / Avid/BMG

ROOT 'N' VARIES
CD ______ GRCD 281
Glitterhouse / Aug '93 / Avid/BMG

SHRUG
CD ______ GRCD 347
Glitterhouse / Dec '94 / Avid/BMG

Hipsway

HIPSWAY
Honey thief / Ask the Lord / Bad thing longing / Upon a thread / Long white car / Broken years / Tinder / Forbidden / Set this day apart
CD ______ 8268212
Mercury / Sep '92 / PolyGram

Hird Family

HIRD FAMILY IN NEW ORLEANS
CD ______ BCD 332
GHB / Mar '95 / Jazz Music

Hird, Karl

KARL HIRD TRIOS
CD ______ SPR 59
Australian Jazz / Nov '96 / Jazz Music

Hiroko

MOMENTS
Night in Capri / Listen to my heartbeat / Englishman in New York / Piazza in the rain / Someday in paradise / Lady moonlight / Metropolis / Hitch hiker / Blue mosque / My heart's with you / Passarada / Gone / Moment we share / Alone again
CD ______ JVC 20542
JVC / Apr '96 / Direct / New Note/Pinnacle / Vital/SAM

Hirota, Joji

RAIN FOREST DREAM
Ubiquity / Purple spring / Celebration of harvest / Malaysian image / Satellite express / Rainforest dream / Demon dance / Pacific samba
CD ______ CDSDL 384
Saydisc / Mar '94 / ADA / Direct / Harmonia Mundi

Hirsch & Weinstein

HAIKU LINGO
CD ______ RERE 139CD
No Man's Land / Oct '95 / ReR Megacorp

Hirst, Clare

TOUGH AND TENDER
Heavy hipsters / Tough and tender / Salsita / Beautiful(ish) / Little steps / Strollin' / Just an emotion / Rudie's blues / Mi cancion / Gallicia
CD ______ 33JAZZ 025
33 Jazz / Dec '95 / Cadillac / New Note/ Pinnacle

Hirt, Al

BRASSMAN'S HOLIDAY
Royal garden blues / Yellow dog blues / I can't get started / South Rampart Street parade / Brassman's holiday / Second chance / Tin roof blues / Just a closer walk with thee / Birth of the blues / Begin the beguine / Blues in the night / Dear old Southland / Frankie and Johnny / Cornet chop suey / New Orleans / Battle hymn of the republic
CD ______ HCD 608
Hindsight / Jun '96 / Jazz Music / Target/ BMG

MASTER OF JAZZ
Tuxedo Junction / Break my mind / Deep river / Hello Dolly / I'm so lonesome I could cry / Look down that lonesome road / Stardust / When my blue moon turns to gold again / Night in Tunisia / Cotton candy / Cherry pink and apple blossom white / Moonglow / Orange blossom special / Shine / Poor butterfly / Blue eyes crying in the rain
CD ______ CWNCD 2034
Crown / Jun '97 / Henry Hadaway

Hirt, Erhard

GUTE UND SCHLECHTE ZEITEN
CD ______ EMPCD 9003
FMP / Oct '94 / Cadillac

Hirte, Marc

SECOND NATURE
CD ______ BLDCD 533
Boulevard / Sep '96 / Grapevine/PolyGram / Total/BMG

His Hero Is Gone

15 COUNTS OF ARSON
CD ______ PRANK 013CD
Prank / Feb '97 / Cargo / Plastic Head

His Name Is Alive

HOME IS IN YOUR HEAD
CD ______ CADCD 1013
4AD / Sep '91 / RTM/Disc

LIVONIA
CD ______ CAD 0008CD
4AD / Jun '90 / RTM/Disc

MOUTH TO MOUTH
CD ______ CAD 3006CD
4AD / Apr '93 / RTM/Disc

STARS ON ESP
Dub love letter / This world is not my home / Bad luck girl / What are you wearing tomorrow / Bees / What else is new list / Wall of speed / Universal frequencies / Sand that holds the lake in place / I can't live in this world anymore / Answer to rainbow at midnight / Famous goodbye king / Across the street / Movie / Last one
CD ______ CAD 6010CD
4AD / Jun '96 / RTM/Disc

Hislop, Joseph

SONGS OF SCOTLAND
Prelude to the loves of Robert Burns / Bonnie banks of Loch Lomond / Ye banks and braes o' bonnie Doon / Bonnie Mary of Argyle / Annie Laurie / Afton water / Land of the leal / Ariskay love lift / Island herdsmaid / Lea rig / MacGregor's gathering / Rigs O' Barley / My love is like a red red rose / Bonnie wee thing / Jessie the flower O' Dunblane / My love she's but a lassie yet / O my love's bonnie / Herding song / Island shieling song / Turn ye tae me
CD ______ MIDCD 003
Moidart / Jan '95 / Conifer/BMG

Hissanol

47TH AND BACK
CD ______ VIRUS 160CD
Alternative Tentacles / Apr '95 / Cargo / Greyhound / Pinnacle

Hit Parade

SOUND OF THE HIT PARADE, THE
On the road to Beaconsfield / As I lay dying / Grace darling / Hello Hannah hello / Walk away boy / Farewell my lido / Fool / House of Sarah / She won't come back / Crying / She's lost everything / So this is London
CD ______ SARAH 622CD
Sarah / Jul '94 / Vital

Hitchcock, Nicola

BOWL OF CHALK, A
Pick up your coat / My mistake / Surf on shingle / Saddest day / Writings I hide / Down to the station / What you see is what you get / How do you feel / Strange times / Queen of the blues / Where are you now / Maire
CD ______ XXCD 23
Demon / May '93 / Pinnacle

Hitchcock, Robyn

BLACK SNAKE DIAMOND ROLE
Man who invented himself / Brenda's iron sledge / Lizard / Meat / Do policemen sing / Acid bird / I watch the cars / Out of the picture / City of shame / Love / Dancing on God's thumb / Happy the golden prince / Kingdom of love / It was the night
CD ______ RSACD 819
Sequel / Feb '95 / BMG

ELEMENT OF LIGHT
If you were a priest / Winchester / Somewhere apart / Ted, Woody and Junior / President / Raymond Chandler evening / Bass / Airscape / Element of light / Never stop bleeding / Lady Waters and the hooded one / Black crow knows / Crawling / Leopard / Tell me about your drugs / Can opener / Raymond Chandler evening (demo) / President (demo) / If you were a priest (demo) / Airscape (demo) / Leopard (demo)
CD ______ RSACD 824
Sequel / Mar '95 / BMG

EYE
Cynthia Mask / Certainly clickot / Queen Elvis / Flesh cartoons / Chinese water python / Executioner / Linctus house / Sweet ghost of light / College of ice / Transparent lover / Beautiful girl / Raining twilight coast / Clean Steve / Agony of pleasure / Glass hotel / Satellite / Aquarium / Queen Elvis II / Clean Steve / Agony of pleasure / Ghost ship
CD ______ RSACD 826
Sequel / Mar '95 / BMG

FEGMANIA
Egyptian cream / Another bubble / I'm only you / My wife and my dead wife / Goodnight I say / Man with the lightbulb head / Insect mother / Strawberry mind / Glass / Fly / Heaven / Bells of Rhymney / Dwarfbeat / Somebody / Egyptian cream (demo) / Heaven (live) / Insect mother (demo) / Pit of Souls (parts I-IV)
CD ______ RSACD 822
Sequel / Mar '95 / BMG

GOTTA LET THIS HEN OUT (Hitchcock, Robyn & The Egyptians)
Listening to the Higsons / Fly / Kingdom of love / Leppo and the fly / Man with the lightbulb head / Cars she used to drive / Sounds great when you're dead / Only the stones remain / America / Heaven / My wife and my dead wife / I often dream of trains / Surgery / Brenda's iron sledge
CD ______ RSACD 823
Sequel / Mar '95 / BMG

GROOVY DECAY
Night ride to Trinidad / Fifty two stations / Young people scream / Rain / America / How do you work this thing / Cars she used to drive / Grooving on an inner plane / St. Petersburg / When I was a kid / Midnight fish / It was the night / Nightride to Trinidad (disco mix) / Midnight fish (mix)
CD ______ RSACD 820
Sequel / Feb '95 / BMG

I OFTEN DREAM OF TRAINS (Hitchcock, Robyn & The Egyptians)
Nocturne / Sometimes I wish I was a pretty girl / Cathedral / Uncorrected personality traits / Sounds great when you're dead / Flavour of night / Sleeping knights of Jesus / Mellow together / Winter love / Bones in the ground / My favourite buildings / I used to say I love you / This could be the day / Trams of old London / Furry green atom bowl / Heart full of leaves / Autumn is your last chance / I often dream of trains
CD ______ RSACD 821
Sequel / Feb '95 / BMG

INVISIBLE HITCHCOCK (Hitchcock, Robyn & The Egyptians)
All I wanna do is fall in love / Give me a spanner Ralph / Skull, a suitcase and a long red bottle of wine / It's a mystic trip / My favourite buildings / Falling leaves / Eaten by her own dinner / Pit of souls / Trash / Mr. Deadly / Star of hairs / Messages of dark / Vegetable friends / I got a message for you / Abandoned brain / Point it at Gran / Let there be more darkness / Blues in A
CD ____ RSACD 825
Sequel / Mar '95 / BMG

RESPECT (Hitchcock, Robyn & The Egyptians)
Yip song / Arms of love / Moon inside / Railway shoes / When I was dead / Wreck of the Arthur Lee / Driving aloud (radio storm) / Serpent at the gates of wisdom / Then you're dust / Wafflehead
CD ____ RHECD 1
RHE / Oct '96 / Direct

YOU AND OBLIVION
You've got / Don't you / Bird's head / She reached for a light / Victorian squid / Captain Dry / Mr. Rock 'n' Roll / August hair / Take your knife out of my back / Surgery / Dust / Polly on the shore / Aether / Fiend before the shrine / Nothing / Into it / Stranded in the future / Keeping still / September cones / Ghost ship / You and me / If I could look
CD ____ RSACD 827
Sequel / Mar '95 / BMG

Hitchers

IT'S ALL FUN AND GAMES 'TIL SOMEONE LOSES AN EYE
Sooner die / You can only love someone so much / Big mug / Killed it with my bare hands / Kimwildesongtitle / Wizard prang / U can du / Strachan / On and on / Someday we'll all grow old and die / Looking back at us / Aryan beach party / At the seaside
CD ____ MURCD 002
Murgatroid / Jul '97 / Vital

Hitchin Post

DEATH VALLEY JUNCTION
CD ____ GRCD 313
Glitterhouse / Apr '94 / Avid/BMG

Hitmen DTK

SURFIN' IN ANOTHER DIRECTION
CD ____ 842618
New Rose / May '94 / ADA / Direct / Discovery

Hitsville House Band

12 O'CLOCK STEREO
CD ____ BAH 27
Humbug / Jul '96 / Total/Pinnacle

Hittman

HITTMAN
CD ____ 857568
Steamhammer / '88 / Pinnacle / Plastic Head

hKippers

GUTTED
CD ____ ECCD 002
Eccentric / Dec '96 / Harmonia Mundi

Ho, Fred

MONKEY VOL.1 (Ho, Fred & Cindy Zuoxin Wang/Monkey Orchestra)
CD ____ 378152
Koch Jazz / Oct '96 / Koch

Hoax

SOUND LIKE THIS
CD ____ 4509979642
Warner Bros. / Dec '96 / Warner Music

UNPOSSIBLE
CD ____ 0630166392
East West / Nov '96 / Warner Music

Hobbs Angel Of Death

HOBBS ANGEL OF DEATH
CD ____ 857525
Steamhammer / '89 / Pinnacle / Plastic Head

Hobbs, Steve

CULTURAL DIVERSITY
Missing Carolina / On the run / Blame it on my youth / Sea breeze / Bag's groove / Coreaaah / Jane / DA / Astrud / Bernie's tune
CD ____ CDSJP 375
Timeless Jazz / Mar '92 / New Note/ Pinnacle

LOWER EAST SIDE, THE
CD ____ CACD 797042
Candid / Dec '95 / Cadillac / Direct / Jazz Music / Koch / Wellard

ON THE LOWER EAST SIDE
Amazing grace / Around and around / Sweet and lovely / Song is you / Pedra bonita / Thinking of Chet / Au privave / 18-35 (together again) / Pentachronic / But beautiful / What is this thing called love
CD ____ CCD 79704
Candid / Feb '97 / Cadillac / Direct / Jazz Music / Koch / Wellard

Hobex

PAYBACK EP
CD ____ SYM 044
Symbiotic / Jan '97 / Cargo

Hoch Und Deutschmeister

25 JAHRE ORIGINAL HOCH UND DEUTSCHMEISTER
CD ____ 340012
Koch / Apr '92 / Koch

Hochman, I.J.

FUN DER KHUPE
CD ____ GVCD 114
Global Village / Mar '95 / ADA / Direct

Hock, Paul

FRESH FRUIT
Fresh fruit / Barricade / Voir un ami pleurer / Sneeky / Samba for Johan Cruyff / Yvette in wonderland / Missing keys / Estate
CD ____ CDSJP 343
Timeless Jazz / Oct '91 / New Note/ Pinnacle

Hodes, Art

APEX BLUES
CD ____ JCD 104
Jazzology / Nov '96 / Jazz Music

ART HODES & THE MAGNOLIA JAZZ BAND VOL.1 & 2
CD ____ BCD 171/172
GHB / Oct '93 / Jazz Music

FINAL SESSIONS, THE
CD ____ CD 782
Music & Arts / May '94 / Cadillac / Harmonia Mundi

HODES' ART
CD ____ DD 213
Delmark / Dec '94 / ADA / Cadillac / CM / Direct / Hot Shot

KEEPIN' OUT OF MISCHIEF NOW
Tennessee waltz / When your lover has gone / I'm gonna sit right down (and write myself a letter) / Saturday night function / I'm a salty dog / Makin' whoopee / Four or five times / Love for sale / CC rider / Do you know what it means / Struttin' with some barbecue / Basin street blues / Keepin' out of mischief now / Just a closer walk with thee / Preacher
CD ____ CCD 79537
Candid / Feb '97 / Cadillac / Direct / Jazz Music / Koch / Wellard

PAGIN' MR. JELLY
Grandpa's spells / Mamie's blues / High society / Mr. Jelly lord / Buddy Bolden's blues / Pagin' Mr. Jelly / Wolverine blues / Ballin' the Jack / Pearls / Gone Jelly blues / Dr. Jazz / Oh didn't he ramble / Winnin' boy blues / Beale Street blues
CD ____ CCD 79037
Candid / Feb '97 / Cadillac / Direct / Jazz Music / Koch / Wellard

SENSATION (Hodes, Art & John Petters Hot Three)
Clarinet marmalade / Lazybones / Mama's gone goodbye / Lonesome blues / Jackass blues / Cake walkin' babies from home / Sensation / Jeep's blues / Ballin' the Jack / Snowball / Dear old Southland / Wolverine blues
CD ____ CMJCD 007
CMJ / Apr '90 / Jazz Music / Wellard

SESSIONS AT BLUE NOTE
Maple leaf rag / Yellow dog blues / Slow 'em down blues / Dr. Jazz / Shoe shiner's drag / There'll be some changes made / Jug head boogie / Back room blues / Sweet Georgia Brown / Squeeze me / Bugle call rag / Gut bucket blues / Apex blues / Shake that thing / That eccentric rag / KMH drag / Blues 'n' booze / Mr. Jelly Lord / Willie the weeper / Jack Daily blues
CD ____ DMI CDX 04
Dormouse / Dec '91 / Jazz Music / Target/ BMG

UP IN VOLLY'S ROOM
CD ____ DD 217
Delmark / Jan '93 / ADA / Cadillac / CM / Direct / Hot Shot

Hodges, Johnny

AT THE SPORTPALAST, BERLIN (2CD Set)
Take the 'A' train / In the kitchen / Mood indigo / Solitude / Satin doll / I got it bad and that ain't good / Rockin' in rhythm / Autumn leaves / Stompy Jones / C jam blues / Jeep is jumpin' / Good Queen Bess / Things ain't what they used to be / I'll get by / I let a song go out of my heart / Don't get around much anymore / Just squeeze me / Do nothin' 'til you hear from me / Rose of the Rio Grande / All of me / On the sunny side of the street / Blue moon / Perdido
CD Set ____ PACD 2620102
Pablo / Aug '96 / Cadillac / Complete/ Pinnacle

CARAVAN (Hodges, Johnny & Duke Ellington/Billy Strayhorn Allstars)
Frisky: *Hodges, Johnny Allstars* / Longhorn blues: *Hodges, Johnny Allstars* / Flower is a lovesome thing: *Hodges, Johnny Allstars* / Far away blues: *Hodges, Johnny Allstars* / How could it happen to a dream: *Hodges, Johnny Allstars* / Who struck John: *Hodges, Johnny Allstars* / June's jumpin': *Hodges, Johnny Allstars* / Lotus blossom: *Hodges, Johnny Allstars* / Violet blue: *Hodges, Johnny Allstars* / Searsy's blues: *Hodges, Johnny Allstars* / Taste: *Hodges, Johnny Allstars* / Let the zoomer's drool: *Hodges, Johnny Allstars* / Night walk: *Strayhorn, Billy Allstars* / She: *Strayhorn, Billy Allstars* / Happening: *Strayhorn, Billy Allstars* / Sultry serenade: *Strayhorn, Billy Allstars* / Moonlight fiesta: *Strayhorn, Billy Allstars* / Britt and butter blues: *Strayhorn, Billy Allstars* / Indian summer: *Strayhorn, Billy Allstars* / Swamp drum: *Strayhorn, Billy Allstars* / Caravan: *Ellington, Duke/Billy Strayhorn Allstars* / Hoppin' John: *Ellington, Duke Allstars* / Jumpin' with symphony Sid: *Ellington, Duke Allstars*
CD ____ PCD 24103
Prestige / Aug '96 / Cadillac / Complete/ Pinnacle

CLASSIC SOLOS 1928-42
CD ____ TPZ 1008
Topaz Jazz / Oct '94 / Cadillac / Pinnacle

COMPLETE SMALL GROUP SESSIONS VOL.1 1937-1938
CD ____ BMCD 1019
Blue Moon / Sep '95 / Cadillac / Discovery / Greensleeves / Jazz Music / Jet Star / TKO Magnum

COMPLETE SMALL GROUP SESSIONS VOL.2 1939-1940
CD ____ BMCD 1020
Blue Moon / Sep '95 / Cadillac / Discovery / Greensleeves / Jazz Music / Jet Star / TKO Magnum

EVERYBODY KNOWS JOHNNY HODGES
Everybody knows / Flower is a lovesome thing / Papa knows / 310 blues / Jeep is jumpin' / Main stem / I let a song go out of my heart / Don't get around much anymore / Open mike / Stompy Jones / Mood indigo / Good Queen Bess / Little brother / Jeep's blues / Do nothin' 'til you hear from me / Ruint / Sassy cue
CD ____ GRP 11162
Impulse Jazz / Jul '92 / New Note/BMG

HODGE PODGE
CD ____ EK 66972
Sony Jazz / Jan '95 / Sony

IN A MELLOW TONE (Hodges, Johnny & 'Wild' Bill Davis)
Just squeeze me / It's only a paper moon / Taffy / Good Queen Bess / LB blues / In a mellow tone / Rockville / I'll always love you / It don't mean a thing if it ain't got that swing / Belle of Belmont
CD ____ 09026685972
Bluebird / May '97 / BMG

INTRODUCTION TO JOHNNY HODGES 1928-1941, AN
CD ____ 4010
Best Of Jazz / Mar '95 / Discovery

JOHNNY HODGES AND WILD BILL DAVIS, 1965 - 1966 (Hodges, Johnny & 'Wild' Bill Davis)
On the sunny side of the street / On Green Dolphin Street / Li'l darlin' / Con sould and sax / Jeep is jumpin' / I'm beginning to see the light / Sophisticated lady / Drop me off in Harlem / No one / Johnny come lately / It's only a paper moon / Taffy / Good Queen Bess / LB blues / In a mellow tone / Rockville / I'll always love you / It don't mean a thing if it ain't got that swing / Belle of the Belmont
CD Set ____ ND 89765
Jazz Tribune / May '94 / BMG

JOHNNY HODGES PLAYS BILLY STRAYHORN
CD ____ 5218572
Verve / Apr '94 / PolyGram

MASTERS OF JAZZ VOL.9
Cambridge blue / Brute's roots / Bouncing with Ben / One for the duke / Walkin' the frog / Rabbit pie / On the sunny side / Good Queen Bess / Jeep is jumpin' / Things ain't what they used to be
CD ____ STCD 4109
Storyville / May '89 / Cadillac / Jazz Music / Wellard

PASSION FLOWER
Daydream / Good queen Bess (takes 1 and 2) / That's the blues / Old man / Junior hop / Squaty roo / Passion flower / Thing's ain't what they used to be / Goin' out the back way / Never no lamet / Blue goose / In a mellow tone / Warm valley / After all / Giddybug gallop / I got it bad and that ain't good / Clementine / Moon mist / Sentimental lady / Come Sunday / Mood to be wooed / Rock-a-bye river
CD ____ 07863666162
Bluebird / Aug '95 / BMG

PASSION FLOWER 1950-60
CD ____ CD 53171
Giants Of Jazz / Sep '94 / Cadillac / Jazz Music / Target/BMG

QUINTESSENCE, THE (2CD Set)
CD Set ____ FA 216
Fremeaux / Feb '96 / ADA / Discovery

RARITIES AND PRIVATE RECORDINGS (The Golden Age of Jazz)
CD ____ JZCD 361
Suisa / May '92 / Jazz Music / THE

TRIPLE PLAY
Take 'em off / Nearness of you / Monkey on a limb / Tiny bit of blues / For jammers only / On the way up / Big boy blues / Very thought of you / Fur piece / Sir John / Figurine / C jam blues
CD ____ 09026685922
RCA Victor / Oct '96 / BMG

USED TO BE DUKE (Hodges, Johnny Orchestra)
Used to be Duke / On the sunny side of the street / Sweet as bear meat / Madam Butterfly / Warm valley / Autumn in New York / Sweet Lorraine / Time on my hands / Smoke gets in your eyes / If you were mine / Poor butterfly / All of me / Burgundy walk / Skokiaan
CD ____ 8493942
Verve / Mar '91 / PolyGram

Hodgson, Roger

RITES OF PASSAGE
Every trick in the book / In jeopardy / Showdown / Don't you want to get high / Take the long way home / Red lake / Melancholic / Time waits for no one / No colours / Logical song / Smelly feet / Give a little bit
CD ____ UNIVP 001CD
Blueprint / Apr '97 / Pinnacle

Hoehn, Tommy

TURNING DANCE, THE
CD ____ FR 0071
Frankenstein / Jul '97 / Greyhound

Hoenig, Michael

DEPARTURE FROM THE NORTHERN WASTELAND
Departure from the northern wasteland / Hanging garden transfer / Voices of where / Sun and moon
CD ____ CDKUCK 079
Kuckuck / Sep '87 / ADA / CM

EARLY WATER (Hoenig, Michael & Manuel Gottsching)
CD ____ 14536
Spalax / Jun '97 / ADA / Cargo / Direct / Discovery / Greyhound

Hoest, Julie

WHERE I'M STANDING
CD ____ RER 322CD
Resounding / Dec '96 / ADA

Hoffner, Helen

WILD ABOUT NOTHING
Wild about nothing / Summer of love / Sacrifice / Holy river / Is there anybody out there / Perfect day / Lovers come, lovers go / Whispers in the wind / Papa's car / Say a prayer / This is the last time / Edge of a dream
CD ____ 4509923992
Magnet / Apr '93 / Warner Music

Hoffs, Susanna

SUSANNA HOFFS
CD ____ 8288412
London / Oct '96 / PolyGram

Hofgesindt

WENN'S DIE ZEIT ERLAUBT
CD ____ LZ 2072
Lowenzahn / Oct '96 / ADA

Hofmann, Holly

FURTHER ADVENTURE
CD ____ 74022
Capri / Nov '93 / Cadillac / Wellard

TAKE NOTE
CD ____ 74011
Capri / Nov '93 / Cadillac / Wellard

Hofseth, Bendik

PLANETS, RIVERS &...IKEA
CD ____ 5312342
Verve / Jun '96 / PolyGram

Hogan, John

HUMBLE MAN
Don't fight the feeling / Still got a crush on you / Walkin' in the sun / She's more to be pitied / Picture / Wreck of old no.9 / China doll / Let it be you / Humble man / I'll be gone / Something's wrong / Down by the river / Follow me / Please don't forget me
CD ____ RITZCD 0062
Ritz / Nov '91 / Pinnacle

IRISH HARVEST DAY, AN
Irish harvest day / I'll buy her roses
CD RITZCD 248
Ritz / Sep '92 / Pinnacle

LOVING YOU
CD RITZCD 558
Ritz / May '96 / Pinnacle

NASHVILLE ALBUM
Till the mountains disappear / Walk through this world with me / Baby I'm lovin' you now / Morning sun and memories / I'll give my heart to you / Stepping stone / Back home again / Far away heart / I can't help it (If I'm still in love with you) / You can't take it with you when you go / Blue moon of Kentucky / Battle hymn of love / My guitar / Fallen angel
CD RITZRCD 531
Ritz / Aug '93 / Pinnacle

VERY BEST OF JOHN HOGAN, THE
Thank God I'm a country boy / Walk through this world with me / Irish harvest day / Cottage in the country / Your cheatin' heart / China doll / My feelings for you / Wreck of old no.9 / Turn back the years / Red river valley / Back home again / My guitar / I'll buy her roses / Brown eyes / Stepping stone / Please don't forget me / Still got a crush on you / Moonlight in Mayo / I know that you know (that I love you) / Battle hymn of love
CD RCD 552
Ritz / Jul '95 / Pinnacle

Hogan, Silas

SO LONG BLUES
I'm gonna quit you pretty baby / Trouble at home blues / You're too late baby / Airport blues / Go on pretty baby / Here they are again / Lonesome la la / Roamin' woman blues / I'm goin' in the valley / Everybody needs somebody / Just give me a chance / Dark clouds rollin' / Early one morning / I'm in love with you baby / More trouble at home / Sittin' here wonderin' / So glad / Every Saturday night / Baby please come back to me / If I ever need you baby / Out and down blues / So long blues
CD CDCHD 523
Ace / May '94 / Pinnacle

Hogg, Smokey

ANGELS IN HARLEM
I want a roller / Nobody treats me right / Evil mind blues / I'm through with you / What's on your mind / You better watch that jive / Goin' back to Texas / I want my baby for Christmas / Gonna leave town / I ain't gonna put you down / Every mornin' at sunrise / If it hadn't been for you / Boogie all night long / Worryin' my life away / Angels in Harlem / Born on the 13th / Crawdad / Size 4 shoe / Little fine girl / Good mornin' baby / Sure nuff
CD CDCHD 419
Ace / Sep '92 / Pinnacle

Hoggard, Jay

OVERVIEW
CD MCD 5383
Muse / Sep '92 / New Note/Pinnacle

SOLO VIBRAPHONE
CD IN 1040CD
India Navigation / Jan '97 / Discovery / Impetus

Hogia'r Wyddfa

GOREUON
Safwn yn y bwlch / Pentre bach llanber / Y gwanwyn / TYlluanod / Ddoi di gyda mi / Titw tomos las / Llanc ifanc o lyn / Teifi / Bysus bach y wlad / Tecel / Varu cymru / Wil tatw's trwy' crwyn / Ynys yr hud / Olwen / Gwaun cwm brwynog / Hwiangerddi / Hen wr ar bont y bala / Ti a dy ddoniau / Pan fyddo'r nos yn hir / Mae nhwyr y dydd
CD SCD 4094
Sain / Jun '88 / ADA / Direct / Greyhound

Hogman, John

GOOD NIGHT SISTER
CD SITCD 9202
Sittel / Aug '94 / Cadillac / Jazz Music

Hoj, Kirsten

SPEAK LOW (Hoj, Kirsten & Soren Norbo)
CD MECCACD 1093
Music Mecca / May '97 / Cadillac / Jazz Music / Wellard

Hokum Boys

FAMOUS HOKUM BOYS VOL.2 1930-1931, THE
CD WBCD 012
Wolf / Jul '96 / Hot Shot / Jazz Music / Swift

HOKUM BOYS & BOB ROBINSON 1935-1937 (Hokum Boys & Bob Robinson)
CD DOCD 5237
Document / May '94 / ADA / Hot Shot / Jazz Music

HOKUM BOYS 1929
CD DOCD 5236
Document / May '94 / ADA / Hot Shot / Jazz Music

Holcomb, Robin

LITTLE THREE
CD 7559793662
Nonesuch / May '96 / Warner Music

Hold True

FADE
CD LF 144CD
Lost & Found / Feb '96 / Plastic Head

Holden, Lorenzo

CRY OF THE WOUNDED JUKEBOX
CD SCD 26
Southland / Oct '93 / Jazz Music

Holden, Randy

EARLY WORKS 1964-1966
CD CTCD 056
Captain Trip / Jun '97 / Greyhound

GUITAR GOD
CD CTCD 028
Captain Trip / Jul '97 / Greyhound

POPULATION II
CD FLASH 007
Flashback / Jun '97 / Greyhound

Holder, Nick

ONE NIGHT IN THE DISCO
Get up / Don't go away / Greatest dancer / Love has come / Scenic route / Zone days / Feel mighty real / Do it / Get away
CD K7R 009CD
Studio K7 / Jan '97 / Prime / RTM/Disc

Holderlin Express

ELECTRIC FLIES
CD AD 3028CD
Music Contact/Akku Disc / Nov '96 / ADA

HOLDERLIN EXPRESS
CD ADCD 3025
Music Contact/Akku Disc / Jul '94 / ADA

Holdsworth, Allan

ATAVACHRON
Non-brewed condiment / Funnels / Dominant plague / Atavachron / Looking glass / Mr. Berwell / All our yesterdays
CD JMS 186432
JMS / Feb '96 / New Note/BMG

HARD HAT AREA
Prelude / Ruhkukah / Low levels, high stakes / Hard hat area / Tullio / House of mirrors / Postlude
CD JMS 186342
JMS / Feb '96 / New Note/BMG

IOU
Things you see (When you haven't got your gun) / Where is one / Checking out / Letters of marque / Out from under / Temporary fault / Shallow sea / White line
CD JMS 186412
JMS / Feb '96 / New Note/BMG

IOU BAND LIVE (Holdsworth, Allan & Paul Williams)
Road games / White line / Panic station / Letter of Marque / Material real / Metal fatigue / Where is one / Things you see / Was there something
CD CLP 9970
Cleopatra / Apr '97 / Cargo / Greyhound / Plastic Head / RTM/Disc / SRD
CD OM 1003CD
Outer Music / Jun '97 / Pinnacle

METAL FATIGUE
Metal fatigue / Home / Devil take the hindmost / Panic station / In-merry go-round / In the mystery
CD JMS 186422
JMS / Feb '96 / New Note/BMG

NONE TOO SOON
Countdown / Nuages / How deep is the ocean / Isotope / None too soon part 1 / Interlude / None too soon part 2 / Norwegian wood / Very early / San Marcos / Inner urge
CD JMS 186872
Cream / Aug '96 / New Note/Pinnacle

SAND
Sand / Distance versus desire / Pud wud / Clown / 4.15 Bradford executive / Mac man
CD JMS 186442
JMS / Feb '96 / New Note/BMG

SECRETS
City nights / 54 Duncan Terrace / Spokes / Perila premonition / Secrets / Joshua / Maid Marion / Endomorph
CD JMS 186452
JMS / Feb '96 / New Note/BMG

THINGS YOU SEE, THE (Holdsworth, Allan & Gordon Beck)
CD JMS 186512
JMS / Feb '96 / New Note/BMG

WARDENCLYFFE TOWER, THE
Five to five / Sphere of innocence / Wardenclyffe tower / Dodgy boat / Oneipic moor / Zarabeth / Against the clock / Questions
CD JMS 186322
JMS / Feb '96 / New Note/BMG

WITH A HEART IN MY SONG (Holdsworth, Allan & Gordon Beck)
CD JMS 186642
JMS / Feb '96 / New Note/BMG

Hole

LIVE THROUGH THIS
Violet / Miss World / Plump / Asking for it / Jennifers body / Doll parts / Credit in the straight world / Softer, softest / She walks on me / I think that I would die / Gutless / Rock star
CD EFA 49352
City Slang / Apr '94 / RTM/Disc
CD GED 24631
Geffen / Jan '95 / BMG

PRETTY ON THE INSIDE
Baby doll / Garbage man / Sassy / Good sister bad sister / Mrs. Jones / Berry / Loaded / Star belly / Pretty on the inside / Clouds / Teenage whore
CD EFA 040712
City Slang / Aug '95 / RTM/Disc

Hole, Dave

PLUMBER
CD PRD 70462
Provogue / Mar '93 / Pinnacle

SHORT FUSE BLUES
CD ALCD 4807
Alligator / May '93 / ADA / CM / Direct

STEEL ON STEEL
CD PRD 70782
Provogue / Jul '95 / Pinnacle

TICKET TO CHICAGO
CD PRD 71022
Provogue / Mar '97 / Pinnacle
CD ALCD 4847
Alligator / May '97 / ADA / CM / Direct

WHOLE LOTTA BLUES
Nobody hears me crying / Short fuse blues / Quicksand / I found love / Tore down / Key to the highway / I can't be satisfied / Going down / Plumber / Berwick Road / Keep your motor runnin' / Up all night thinking / Crazy kind of woman / Blues will call your name / Counting my regrets / Travelling riverside blues
CD PRD 70932
Provogue / Sep '96 / Pinnacle

WORKING OVERTIME
CD PRD 70562
Provogue / May '94 / Pinnacle

Hole In One

TALES FROM THE PLANET ONCHET
CD 700021
Essential Dance / Aug '96 / RTM/Disc

Holi

UNDER THE MONKEY PUZZLE TREE
Under the monkey puzzle tree / Right place / Five years / Meera's sigh / I need you / First impression / Lonely swan / Chandrika / Losin' my head / Green and blue
CD RES 105CD
Resurgence / Apr '97 / Pinnacle

Holiday, Billie

16 MOST REQUESTED SONGS
Miss Brown to you / If you were mine / These foolish things / Way you look tonight / Pennies from heaven / I can't give you anything but love / I've got my love to keep me warm / Why was I born / Carelessly / Easy living / My man / I'm gonna lock my heart (and throw away the key) / Body and soul / Gloomy Sunday / God bless the child / I'm a fool to want you
CD 4744012
Columbia / Feb '94 / Sony

1939-40 (Holiday, Billie & Her Orchestra)
CD CLASSICS 601
Classics / Sep '91 / Discovery / Jazz Music

40 GREATEST SONGS (2CD Set)
St. Louis blues / Loveless love / Let's do it / Georgia on my mind / Romance in the dark / All of me / God bless the child / Am I blue / Solitude / Jim / I cover the waterfront / Love me or leave me / Gloomy Sunday / It's a sin to tell a lie / Until the real thing comes along / Trav'lin light / Let's call the whole thing off / They can't take that away from me / Mean to me / Easy livin' / Nice work if you can get it / Can't help lovin' dat man / Back in your own back yard / You got to my head / Very thought of you / What a little moonlight can do / These foolish things / Summertime / Fine romance / Pennies from heaven / I can't give you anything but love / This is my last affair / Strange fruit / Fine and mellow / I gotta right to sing the blues / Them there eyes / Swing, brother, swing / Night and day / Man I love / Body and soul
CD Set MUCD 9507
Musketeer / May '96 / Disc

AS TIME GOES BY
CD CD 53092
Giants Of Jazz / Nov '92 / Cadillac / Jazz Music / Target/BMG

AT CARNEGIE HALL
CD 5277772
Verve / Oct '95 / PolyGram

AT STORYVILLE
I cover the waterfront / Too marvellous for words / I loves you Porgy / Them there eyes / Willow weep for me / I only have eyes for you / You go to my head / He's funny that way / Billie's blues / Miss Brown to you / Lover come back to me / Ain't nobody's business if I do / You're driving me crazy
CD BLC 760921
Black Lion / Apr '91 / Cadillac / Jazz Music / Koch / Wellard

AUDIO ARCHIVE
Night and day / Hello my darling / What a little moonlight can do / I'll never fail you / Miss Brown to you / I wish I had you / Twenty four hours a day / Let's dream in the moonlight / Yankee Doodle never went to town / You're so desirable / If you were mine / Georgia on my mind / You're gonna see a lot of me / Loveless love / These 'n' that 'n' those / Please keep me in your dreams / What is this going to get us / Let's call a heart a heart / More than you know / Spreadin' rhythm around
CD CDAA 033
Tring / Jun '92 / Tring

BACK TO BACK (Holiday, Billie & Sarah Vaughan)
My man (mon homme): *Holiday, Billie* / Lover man: *Holiday, Billie* / I cover the waterfront: *Holiday, Billie* / Don't explain: *Holiday, Billie* / Them there eyes: *Holiday, Billie* / East of the sun and west of the moon: *Vaughan, Sarah* / Signing off: *Vaughan, Sarah* / No smoke blues: *Vaughan, Sarah* / What more can a woman do: *Vaughan, Sarah* / Mean to me: *Vaughan, Sarah*
CD TKOCD 023
TKO / May '92 / TKO

BEST OF BILLIE HOLIDAY
CD 4670292
Sony Jazz / Jan '95 / Sony

BEST OF BILLY HOLIDAY
CD DLCD 4015
Dixie Live / Mar '95 / TKO Magnum

BILLIE HOLIDAY
CD CD 105
Timeless Treasures / Oct '94 / THE

BILLIE HOLIDAY
CD DVX 08072
Deja Vu / May '95 / THE

BILLIE HOLIDAY (2CD Set)
CD Set R2CD 4006
Deja Vu / Jan '96 / THE

BILLIE HOLIDAY (3CD Set)
Summertime / Carelessly / Stormy weather / I'm gonna lock my heart / I've got my love to keep me warm / Fine romance / Who loves you / These foolish things / If you were mine / Let's call a heart to heart / Twenty four hours a day / Mean to me / Autumn in New York / East of the sun / I only have eyes for you / I loves you Porgy / He's funny that way / Lover man / I can't give you anything but love / That's life I guess / Gettin' some fun out of life / This is my last affair / Tenderly / Moonlight in Vermont / I got it bad and that ain't good / How deep is the ocean / It's so easy to remember / Blue moon / Sailboat in the moonlight / Do nothin' 'til you hear from me / Fine & mellow / Lover come back to me / Pennies from heaven / They can't take that away from me / My man / You let me down / Love for sale / Mood that I'm in / Me, myself & I / You go to my head / How could you / Trav'lin all alone / I don't stand a ghost of a chance with you / Detour ahead / God bless the child / It's like reaching for the moon / This year's kisses / What a little moonlight can do / Willow weep for me / Easy living / I cover the waterfront / Nice work if you can get it / No regrets / Ain't nobody's business if I do
CD Set KBOX 361
Collection / Nov '96 / Target/BMG / TKO Magnum

BILLIE HOLIDAY & HER ORCHESTRA
Lover come back to me / You go to my head / East of the sun and west of the moon / Blue moon / Solitude / I only have eyes for you / Autumn in New York / Tenderly / These foolish things / Remember / I can't face the music / I cried for you / Love me or leave me / Please don't talk about me when I'm gone / It had to be you / PS I love you
CD CD 53089
Giants Of Jazz / May '92 / Cadillac / Jazz Music / Target/BMG

BILLIE HOLIDAY 1940-1942
CD CLASSICS 680
Classics / Mar '93 / Discovery / Jazz Music

BILLIE HOLIDAY AND HER ORCHESTRA 1933-37 (Holiday, Billie & Her Orchestra)
CD _______________ CLASSICS 582
Classics / Oct '91 / Discovery / Jazz Music

BILLIE HOLIDAY AND HER ORCHESTRA 1937-39 (Holiday, Billie & Her Orchestra)
CD _______________ CD 592
Classic Jazz Masters / Sep '91 / Wellard

BILLIE HOLIDAY AND TONY SCOTT (Holiday, Billie & Tony Scott Orchestra)
CD _______________ CD 53074
Giants Of Jazz / Mar '92 / Cadillac / Jazz Music / Target/BMG

BILLIE HOLIDAY GOLD (2CD Set)
CD Set _______________ D2CD 4006
Deja Vu / Jun '95 / THE

BILLIE HOLIDAY SINGS STANDARDS
CD _______________ 5276502
Verve / Mar '96 / PolyGram

BILLIE HOLIDAY SONGBOOK, THE
Good morning heartache / My man / Billie's blues / Don't explain / Lady sings the blues / Lover man / God bless the child / Fine and mellow / Strange fruit / Stormy blues / Travellin' light / What a little moonlight can do / I cried for you / I cover the waterfront
CD _______________ 8232462
Verve / Apr '86 / PolyGram

BILLIE HOLIDAY VOL.1 1940-1941
CD _______________ JUCD 2014
Jazz Unlimited / Mar '97 / Cadillac / Jazz Music / Wellard

BILLIE HOLIDAY VOL.2 1941-1942
CD _______________ JUCD 2015
Jazz Unlimited / Mar '97 / Cadillac / Jazz Music / Wellard

BILLIE HOLIDAY WITH BARNEY KESSEL (Holiday, Billie & Orchestra/ Barney Kessel)
CD _______________ CD 53038
Giants Of Jazz / Mar '90 / Cadillac / Jazz Music / Target/BMG

BILLIE HOLIDAY/ELLA FITZGERALD ESSENTIALS (Holiday, Billie & Ella Fitzgerald)
CD _______________ LECDD 629
Wisepack / Aug '95 / Conifer/BMG / THE

BILLIE'S BEST (Selections From 'The Complete Billie Holiday On Verve')
What a little moonlight can do / Foggy day / Come rain or come shine / Comes love / He's funny that way / Stars fell on Alabama / Gone with the wind / They can't take that away from me / East of the Sun and West of the moon / Everything I have is yours / Stormy blues / Speak low / April in Paris / I've got my love to keep me warm / Some other Spring / All the way
CD _______________ 5139432
Verve / May '92 / PolyGram

BILLIE'S BLUES
1-2 Button your shoe / Let's call a heart a heart / Billie's blues / No regrets / I can't give you anything but love / This year's kisses / He ain't rhythm / Let's call the whole thing off / They can't take that away from me / Sentimental and melancholy / Way you look tonight / I'll get by / Summertime / Who wants love / He's funny that way / Now they call it swing / Nice work if you can get it / Things are looking up
CD _______________ MUCD 9002
Musketeer / Apr '95 / Disc

BILLIE'S BLUES
CD _______________ AMSC 572
Avid / Aug '96 / Avid/BMG / Koch / THE

BILLIE'S BLUES
CD _______________ WJSCD 1005
Wolf / Jul '96 / Hot Shot / Jazz Music / Swift

BILLIE'S BLUES
Wherever you are / Georgia on my mind / Until the real thing comes / Keeps on raining / What a little moonlight can do / My man / Strange fruit / Twenty four hours a day / You're gonna see a lot of me / Let's dream in the moonlight / Let's call a heart a heart / Please keep me in your dreams / These foolish things / That's life I guess / I wish I had you / Billie's blues
CD _______________ CDMT 027
Meteor / Oct '96 / TKO Magnum

BROADCAST PERFORMANCES VOL.1
CD _______________ ESP 30022
ESP / Jan '93 / Jazz Music

BROADCAST PERFORMANCES VOL.2
CD _______________ ESP 30032
ESP / Jan '93 / Jazz Music

BROADCAST PERFORMANCES VOL.3
CD _______________ ESP 30052
ESP / Jan '93 / Jazz Music

BROADCAST PERFORMANCES VOL.4
CD _______________ ESP 30062
ESP / Jan '93 / Jazz Music

CLASSICS 1937-1939
CD _______________ CLASSICS 592
Classics / Sep '91 / Discovery / Jazz Music

CLASSICS 1944
CD _______________ CLASSICS 806
Classics / Mar '95 / Discovery / Jazz Music

COLLECTION, THE
CD _______________ CCSCD 381
Castle / Oct '93 / BMG

COLLECTION, THE
CD _______________ COL 018
Collection / Apr '95 / Target/BMG

COMPLETE BILLIE HOLIDAY ON VERVE 1945-1959, THE (10CD Set)
Body and soul / Strange fruit / I cried for you / Fine and mellow / He's funny that way / Man I love / Gee baby ain't I good to you / All of me / Billie's blues / Travellin' light / He's funny that way / You better go now / You're driving me crazy / There is no greater love / I cover the waterfront / East of the Sun and West of the moon / Blue moon / You go to my head / You turned the tables on me / Easy to love / These foolish things / I only have eyes for you / Solitude / Everything I have is yours / Love for sale / Moonglow / Tenderly / If the moon turns green / Remember / Autumn in New York / My man / Lover come back to me / Stormy weather / Yesterdays / He's funny that way / I can't face the music / Blue moon / All of me / My man / Them there arms / I cried for you / What a little moonlight can do / I cover the waterfront / Billie's blues / Lover come back to me / How deep is the ocean / What a little moonlight can do / I cried for you / Love me or leave me / PS I love you / Too marvellous for words / Softly / I thought about you / Willow weep for me / Stormy blues / Say it isn't so / I've got my love to keep me warm / I wished on the moon / Always / Everything happens to me / Do nothin' 'til you hear from me / Ain't misbehavin' / Nice work if you can get it / Mandy is two / Prelude to a kiss / I must have that man / Jeepers creepers / Please don't talk about me when I'm gone / Moonlight in Vermont / Everything happens to me / When you are away dear / It had to be you / Mood that I'm in / Gone with the wind / I got it bad and that ain't good / Sun bonnet blue / I don't stand a ghost of a chance with you / I'm walkin' through Heaven with you / Just friends / Nearness of you / It's too hot for words / They say / I won't believe it / I don't want to cry anymore / Prelude to a kiss / I don't stand a ghost of a chance with you / When your lover has gone / Gone with the wind / Please don't talk about me when I'm gone / It had to be you / Nice work if you can get it / Come rain or come shine / I gotta right to sing the blues / What's new / Fine romance / I hadn't anyone till you / I get a kick out of you / Everything I have is yours / Isn't this a lovely day / Misery / Strange fruit / God bless the child / One never knows, does one / Beer barrel polka / Some of these days / My Yiddishe Momme / Lady's back in town / One never knows, does one / Travellin' light / I must have that man / Some other Spring / Lady sings the blues / Strange fruit / God bless the child / Good morning heartache / No good man / Do nothin' 'til you hear from me / Cheek to cheek / Ill wind / Speak low / We'll be together again / All or nothing at all / Sophisticated lady / April in Paris / Lady sings the blues / Ain't nobody's business if I do / Travellin' light / Billie's blues / Body and soul / Don't explain / Yesterdays / Please don't talk about me when I'm gone / I'll be seeing you / My man / I cried for you / Fine and mellow / I cover the waterfront / What a little moonlight can do / I wished on the moon / Moonlight in Vermont / Foggy day / I didn't know what time it was / Just one of those things / Comes love / Day in, day out / Darn that dream / But not for me / Body and soul / Just friends / Stars fell on Alabama / Say it isn't so / Our love is here to stay / One for my baby (and one more for the road) / They can't take that away from me / Embraceable you / Let's call the whole thing off / Gee baby ain't I good to you / Oh Lady be good / Nice work if you can get it / Willow weep for me / My man / Lover come back to me / Lady sings the blues / What a little moonlight can do / Oh lady be good / I wished on the moon / Lover man / All the way / It's not for me to say / I'll never smile again / Just one more chance / When it's sleepy time down South / Don't worry 'bout me / Sometimes I'm happy / You took advantage of me / There'll be some changes made / 'Deed I do / All of you / Baby, won't you please come home
CD Set _______________ 5176582
Verve / Jun '93 / PolyGram

COMPLETE COMMODORE RECORDINGS, THE (2CD Set)
Strange fruit / Yesterdays / Fine and mellow / I gotta right to sing the blues / How am I to know / My old flame / I'll get by / I cover the waterfront / I'll be seeing you / I'm yours / Embraceable you / As time goes by / He's funny that way / Lover come back to me / Billie's blues / On the sunny side of the street
CD Set _______________ CMD 24012
Commodore Jazz / Feb '97 / New Note/ BMG

COMPLETE RECORDINGS 1933-1940, THE (8CD Set)
Your mother's son-in-law / Riffin' the scotch / I wished on the moon / What a little moonlight can do / Miss Brown to you / Sun bonnet blue / What a night / What a moon, what a girl / I'm painting the town red / It's too hot for words / Yankee Doodle never went to town / Eeny meeny miney mo / If you were mine / These 'n' that 'n' those / You let me down / Spreadin' rhythm around / Life begins when you're in love / It's like reaching for the moon / These foolish things / I cried for you / Guess who / Did I remember / No regrets / Summertime / Billie's blues / Fine romance / I can't pretend / 1-2 Button your shoe / Let's call a heart a heart / Easy to love / With thee I swing / Way you look tonight / Who loves you / Pennies from heaven / That's life I guess / I can't give you anything but love / One never knows, does one / I've got my love to keep me warm / If my heart could only talk / Please keep me in your dreams / He ain't got rhythm / This year's kisses / Why was I born / I must have that man / Twenty four hours a day / Mood that I'm in / You showed me the way / Sentimental and melancholy / My last affair / Carelessly / How could you / Moanin' low / Where is the sun / Let's call the whole thing off / They can't take that away from me / Don't know if I'm coming or going / Sun showers / Yours and mine / I'll get by / Mean to me / Foolin' myself / Easy living / I'll never be the same / Me, myself and I / Sailboat in the moonlight / Born to love / Without your love / Getting some fun out of life / Who wants love / Travellin' all alone / He's funny that way / Nice work if you can get it / Things are looking up / My man / Can't help lovin' dat man / My first impression of you / When you're smiling / I can't believe that you're in love with me / If dreams come true / Now they call it swing / On the sentimental side / Back in your own backyard / When a woman loves a man / You go to my head / Man looks down and laughs / If I were you / Forget if you can / Having myself a time / Says my heart / I wish I had you / I'm gonna lock my heart (and throw away the key) / Any old time / Very thought of you / I can't get started (with you) / I've got a date with a dream / You can't be mine (and someone else's too) / Everybody's laughing / Here it is tomorrow again / Say it with a kiss / April in my heart / I'll never fail you / They say / You're so desirable / You're gonna see a lot of me / Hello my darling / Let's dream in the moonlight / That's all I ask of you / Dream of life / What shall I say / It's easy to blame the weather / More than you know / Sugar / You're too lovely to last / Under a blue jungle moon / Everything happens for the best / Why did I always depend on you / Long gone blues / Strange fruit / Yesterdays / Fine and mellow / I gotta right to sing the blues / Some other Spring / Night and day / Man I love / You're just a no account / You're a lucky guy / Ghost of yesterdays / Body and soul / What is this thing going to get us / Falling in love again / I'm pulling through / Tell me more / Laughing at life / Time on my hands / I'm all for you / I hear music / It's the same old story / Practice makes perfect / St. Louis blues / Loveless love
CD Set _______________ CDAFS 10198
Affinity / Jun '93 / Cadillac / Jazz Music / Koch

COMPLETE STORYVILLE CLUB SESSION, THE
CD _______________ FSRCD 151
Fresh Sound / Dec '90 / Discovery / Jazz Music

DEFINITIVE EDITION VOL.1 1936-1938, THE
CD _______________ BMCD 1021
Blue Moon / Jul '96 / Cadillac / Discovery / Greensleeves / Jazz Music / Jet Star / TKO Magnum

DEFINITIVE EDITION VOL.2 1936-1937, THE
CD _______________ BMCD 1022
Blue Moon / Jul '96 / Cadillac / Discovery / Greensleeves / Jazz Music / Jet Star / TKO Magnum

DEFINITIVE EDITION VOL.3 1937-1938, THE
CD _______________ BMCD 1023
Blue Moon / Jul '96 / Cadillac / Discovery / Greensleeves / Jazz Music / Jet Star / TKO Magnum

DEFINITIVE EDITION VOL.4 1938, THE
CD _______________ BMCD 1024
Blue Moon / Jul '96 / Cadillac / Discovery / Greensleeves / Jazz Music / Jet Star / TKO Magnum

DEFINITIVE EDITION VOL.5 1938-1939, THE
CD _______________ BMCD 1025
Blue Moon / Jul '96 / Cadillac / Discovery / Greensleeves / Jazz Music / Jet Star / TKO Magnum

DEFINITIVE EDITION VOL.6 1939-1941, THE
CD _______________ BMCD 1026
Blue Moon / Jul '96 / Cadillac / Discovery / Greensleeves / Jazz Music / Jet Star / TKO Magnum

DEFINITIVE EDITION VOL.7 1941-1944, THE
CD _______________ BMCD 1027
Blue Moon / Jul '96 / Cadillac / Discovery / Greensleeves / Jazz Music / Jet Star / TKO Magnum

EARLY CLASSICS, THE
Summertime / Sentimental and melancholy / Who loves you / Pennies from heaven / That's life, I guess / Billie's blues / When you're smiling / Carelessly / If dreams come true / Fine romance / Mood that I'm in / Let's call a heart a heart / Where is the sun / Don't know if I'm coming or going / I can't believe that you're in love with me / He's funny that way / Now they call it swing / Miss Brown to you
CD _______________ PASTCD 9756
Flapper / Aug '91 / Pinnacle

ESSENTIAL BILLIE HOLIDAY CARNEGIE HALL CONCERT, THE
Narration / Lady sings the blues / Ain't nobody's business if I do / Narration / I'll be seeing you / I love my man / Body and soul / Narration / Don't explain / Yesterdays / Narration / My man / I cried for you / Fine and mellow / I cover the waterfront / What a little moonlight can do
CD _______________ 8337672
Verve / Mar '93 / PolyGram

ESSENTIAL BILLIE HOLIDAY, THE
St. Louis blues / Solitude / Man I love / Georgia on my mind / I've got my love to keep me warm / My last affair / I'll never be the same / If dreams come true / Summertime / Billie's blues / I cried for you / Mean to me / He's funny that way / My man (mon homme) / Nice work if you can get it / Night and day
CD _______________ 4671492
Columbia / Jul '93 / Sony

ESSENTIAL LADY DAY, THE (2CD Set)
I wished on the moon / These foolish things / Easy to love / Way you look tonight / I can't give you anything but love / I've got my love to keep me warm / This year's kisses / Why was I born / I must have that man / I'll get by / Mean to me / Foolin' myself / Easy livin' / I'll never be the same / He's funny that way / Nice work if you can get it / I can't believe that you're in love with me / If dreams come true / You go to my head / Very thought of you / I can't get started / Say it with a kiss / More than you know / Sugar / Strange fruit / Yesterdays / Fine and mellow / Some other spring / Them there eyes / Night and day / Man I love / You're a lucky guy / Body and soul / Laughing at life / I hear music / Let's do it / Georgia on my mind / God bless the child / Jim / I cover the waterfront / Love me or leave me / Until the real thing comes along / Trav'lin light / My old flame / I'll be seeing you / On the sunny side of the street / Loverman / That old Devil called love / Don't explain / Lover come back to me
CD Set _______________ CPCD 82642
Charly / Dec '96 / Koch

ESSENTIAL RECORDINGS, THE
That ole devil called love / Keeps on a rainin' / Porgy / No good man / God bless the child / What is this thing called love / My man (mon homme) / Easy living / Lover man / Good morning heartache / Ain't nobody's business if I do / You're my thrill / Solitude / There is no greater love / You better go now / Weep no more
CD _______________ MCCD 095
Music Club / Mar '93 / Disc / THE

FEEL THE BLUES
Body and soul / Travellin' all alone / Billie's blues / Let's call the whole thing off / Sentimental and melancholy / Without your love / Under a blue jungle moon / If my heart could only talk / If you were mine / Night and day / God bless the child / These foolish things / St. Louis blues / Yesterday / I gotta right to sing the blues / Summertime
CD _______________ SUMCD 4005
Summit / Nov '96 / Sound & Media

FINE AND MELLOW 1936-1941
CD _______________ IGOCD 2034
Indigo / Oct '95 / ADA / Direct

FINE AND MELLOW 1939-1944
Strange fruit / Yesterdays / Fine and mellow / I gotta right to sing the blues / How am I to know / My old flame / I'll get by / I cover the waterfront
CD _______________ CDSGP 046
Prestige / May '94 / Else / Total/BMG

FINE ROMANCE, A (Billie Holiday At Her Best)
CD _______________ PLSCD 204
Pulse / Apr '97 / BMG

FIRST ISSUE (The Great American Songbook/2CD Set)
Blue moon / Nice work if you can get it / Yesterdays / Easy to love / Prelude to a kiss / Day in, day out / I've got my love to keep

me warm / Embraceable you / Our love is here to stay / Too marvellous for words / Cheek to cheek / Come rain or come shine / Let's call the whole thing off / I thought about you / Fine romance / PS I love you / Always / Do nothin' 'til you hear from me / I get a kick out of you / Say it isn't so / How deep is the ocean / Travellin' light / Remember / Stormy weather / One for my baby (and one more for the road) / But not for me / Solitude / I gotta right to sing the blues / Just one of those things / Love for sale / Foggy day / All of you / Sophisticated lady / They can't take that away from me
CD Set 5230032
Verve / Aug '94 / PolyGram

GITANES - JAZZ 'ROUND MIDNIGHT
Sophisticated lady / God bless the child / Everything happens to me / Embraceable you / You go to my head / My man / These foolish things / Good morning heartache / I don't stand a ghost of a chance with you / Solitude / I must have that man / I don't want to cry anymore / Travellin' light / One for my baby (and one more for the road) / We'll be together again
CD 8414442
Verve / Jan '92 / PolyGram

GOD BLESS THE CHILD
CD 17013
Laserlight / Jul '94 / Target/BMG

GOLD COLLECTION, THE
CD D2CD 06
Deja Vu / Dec '92 / THE

GOLDEN GREATS
CD MCLD 19096
Chess/MCA / Nov '91 / BMG / New Note/ BMG

IMMORTAL, THE
Swing brother swing / They can't take that away from me / Do nothin' 'til you hear from me / I'll get by / I love my man / I cover the waterfront / Do you know what it means to miss New Orleans / Don't explain / Keeps on a rainin' / Lover come back to me
CD CDBH 1
CBS / May '87 / Sony

INTRODUCTION TO BILLIE HOLIDAY 1935-1942, AN
CD 4003
Best Of Jazz / Dec '93 / Discovery

JAZZ AT THE PHILHARMONIC
Body and soul / Strange fruit / I cried for you / Fine and mellow / He's funny that way / Man I love / Gee baby ain't I good to you / All of me / Billie's blue / Travellin' light / He's funny that way / You better go now / You're driving me crazy / There is no greater love / I cover the waterfront / Nice work if you can get it / Willow weep for me / My man / Lover come back to me / Lady sings the blues / What a little moonlight can do / I wished on the moon / Lover man
CD 5216422
Verve / Jan '94 / PolyGram

JAZZ MASTERS
What a little moonlight can do / PS I love you / Blue moon / Remember / God bless the child / Yesterdays / Lover come back to me / Some other Spring / Nice work if you can get it / Willow weep for me / All or nothing at all / Autumn in New York / Fine romance / Good morning heartache / Please don't talk about me when I'm gone / Speak low
CD 5198252
Verve / Feb '94 / PolyGram

JAZZ PORTRAITS
Your mother's son-in-law / Sun showers / They can't take that away from me / They say / Sugar / More that you know / I gotta right to sing the blues / Fine and mellow / Strange fruit / Yesterdays / St. Louis blues / Georgia on my mind / All of me / Let's do it / Romance in the dark / Love me or leave me / I cover the waterfront / It's a sin to tell a lie
CD CD 14512
Jazz Portraits / May '94 / Jazz Music

LADY DAY 1934-1948 (4CD Set)
Lost my man blues (aka saddest tale) / What a little moonlight can do / Miss Brown to you / Twenty four hours a day / Yankee Doodle never went to town / If you were mine / These, that and those / You let me down / Spreadin' rhythm around / It's like reaching for the moon / These foolish things / I cried for you / Guess who / Let's call a heart a heart / Easy to love / With thee I swing / Way you look tonight / Who loves you / Pennies from heaven / That's life I guess / I can't give you anything but love / Please keep me in your dreams / Carelessly / How could you / Moanin' low / Sun showers / Mean to me / Swing brother swing / I wish I had you / I'll never fail you / You're so desirable / You're gonna see a lot of me / Hello my darling / Let's dream in the moonlight / More than you know / I gotta right to swing / I gotta right to swing the blues / Yesterdays / Strange fruit / Fine and mellow / Night and day / What is this going to get us / I'm all for you / I hear music / It's the same old story / Practise makes perfect / St Louis blues / Loveless love / Let's do it / Georgia / Romance in the dark / All of me / God bless the child / Jim / Wherever you are / Until the real thing comes along / Do nothin' 'til you hear from me / I'll get by / My old flame / I cover the waterfront / How am I to know / Embraceable you / I'm yours / I'll be seeing you / As time goes by / I love my man (aka Billies blues) / He's funny that way / Lover come back to me / Don't explain / You better go now / Baby, I don't cry over you / My man
CD Set FBB 905
Ember / Nov '96 / TKO Magnum

LADY DAY AND PREZ 1937-1941 (Holiday, Billie & Lester Young)
This year's kisses / Without your love / All of me / Me, myself and I / I'll get by / Mean to me / Sailboat in the moonlight / I'll never be the same / Getting some fun out of life / Man I love / Travellin' all alone / Time on my hands / Laughing at life / Back in your own backyard / Georgia on my mind / Let's do it / Foolin' myself / Easy living / Say it with a kiss / You can't be mine (and someone else's too) / I can't believe that you're in love with me / She's funny that way / Romance in the dark / I must have that man
CD CD 53006
Giants Of Jazz / Mar '92 / Cadillac / Jazz Music / Target/BMG

LADY DAY'S 25 GREATEST HITS 1933-1944
Back in your own backyard / Did I remember / Easy living / Fine and mellow / Ghost of yesterday / He's funny that way / I can't give you anything but love / I love my man / I must have that man / I'll get by / I'll be the same / Long gone blues / You Mother's son in law / You go to my head / What a little moonlight can do / They can't take that away from me / Them there eyes / That ole devil called love / Swing, brother, swing / Strange fruit / Some other spring / No more / My last affair / Moanin' low / Miss Brown to you
CD CDAJA 5181
Living Era / Jan '96 / Select

LADY DAY'S IMMORTAL PERFORMANCES 1933-1942
CD Set CDB 1204
Giants Of Jazz / Apr '92 / Cadillac / Jazz Music / Target/BMG

LADY DAY'S IMMORTAL PERFORMANCES 1942-1957
CD Set CDB 1212
Giants Of Jazz / Jun '92 / Cadillac / Jazz Music / Target/BMG

LADY IN AUTUMN (2CD Set)
Body and soul / Strange fruit / Travellin' light / All of me / There is no greater love / I cover the waterfront / These foolish things / Tenderly / Autumn in New York / My man / Stormy weather / Yesterdays / He's funny that way / What a little moonlight can do / I cried for you / Too marvellous for words / I wished on the moon / I don't want to cry anymore / Prelude to a kiss / Nice work if you can get it / Come rain or come shine / What's new / God bless the child / Do nothin' 'til you hear from me / April in Paris / Lady sings the blues / Don't explain / Fine and mellow / I didn't know what time it was / Stars fell on Alabama / One for my baby (and one more for the road) / Gee baby ain't I good to you / Lover man / All the way / Don't worry 'bout me
CD 8494342
Verve / Mar '91 / PolyGram

LADY IN SATIN
I'm a fool to want you / For heaven's sake / You don't know what love is / I get along without you very well / For all we know / Violets for your furs / You've changed / Easy to remember / But beautiful / Glad to be unhappy / I'll be around / End of a love affair
CD 4508832
CBS / Jun '91 / Sony

LADY SINGS THE BLUES
Lady sings the blues / Travelling light / I must have that man / Some other Spring / Strange fruit / No-good man / God bless the child / Good morning heartache / Love me or leave me / Too marvellous for words / Willow weep for me / I thought about you / PS I love you / Softly / Stormy blues
CD 8337702
Verve / Nov '90 / PolyGram

LAST RECORDING
All of you / Sometimes I'm happy / You took advantage of me / When it's sleepy time down South / There'll be some changes / 'Deed I do / Don't worry 'bout me / All the way / Just one more chance / It's not for me to say / I'll never smile again / Baby, won't you please come home
CD 8353702
Verve / Dec '89 / PolyGram

LEGACY 1933-58, THE (3CD Set)
Your mother's son-in-law / I wished on the moon / What a little moonlight can do / Miss Brown to you / Saddest tale / If you were mine / These 'n' that 'n' those / You let me down / Life begins when you're in love / It's like reaching for the moon / These foolish things / Summertime / Billie's blues / Fine romance / I can't pretend / 1-2 button your shoe / Let's call a heart a heart / Easy to love / Pennies from Heaven / That's life, I guess / I can't give you anything but love / One never knows, does one / I've got my love to keep me warm / He ain't got rhythm / This year's kisses / Why was I born / I must have that man / Mood that I'm in / My last affair / Moaning low / Where is the sun / Let's call the whole thing off / Don't know if I'm coming or going / I'll get by / Foolin' myself / Easy living / I'll never be the same / Me, myself and I / Sailboat in the moonlight / Born to love / Without your love / They can't take that away from me / Swing brother swing / I can't get started (with you) / Who wants love / Travellin' all alone / He's funny that way / My man (mon homme) / Who want's love / I can't believe that you're in love with me / When a woman loves a man / You go to my head / Having myself a time / Says my heart / Very thought of you / I cried for you / Jeepers creepers / Long gone blues / Some other Spring / Them there eyes / Night and day / Man I love / Let's do it all / All of me / God bless the child / Gloomy Sunday / Until the real thing comes along / Fine and mellow / You've changed / For all we know
CD Set 4690492
Columbia / Nov '91 / Sony

LEGEND OF BILLIE HOLIDAY, THE
That ole devil called love / Lover man / Don't explain / Good morning heartache / There is no greater love / Easy living / Solitude / Porgy / My man (mon homme) / Them there eyes / Now or never / Ain't nobody's business if I do / Somebody's on my mind / Keeps on a rainin' / You're my thrill / God bless the child
CD MCLD 19216
MCA / Aug '93 / BMG

LEGEND, UNISSUED AND RARE MASTERS 1935-38
CD JZCD 305
Suisa / Feb '91 / Jazz Music / THE

LEGEND, UNISSUED AND RARE MASTERS 1939-52
CD JZCD 306
Suisa / Feb '91 / Jazz Music / THE

LEGEND, UNISSUED AND RARE MASTERS 1952-58
CD JZCD 307
Suisa / Feb '91 / Jazz Music / THE

LEGENDS IN MUSIC
CD LECD 071
Wisepack / Jul '94 / Conifer/BMG / THE

LIVE AND RARE 1937-56
CD 11049
Laserlight / '86 / Target/BMG

LOVE FOR SALE
CD CDSGP 0102
Prestige / May '94 / Else / Total/BMG

LOVE SONGS
All of me / You go to my head / Until the real thing comes along / My man / Very thought of you / Easy living / They can't take that away from me / I 've got my love to keep me warm / Them there eyes / Night and day / Man I love / Me, myself and I / Way you look tonight / If you were mine / I can't believe that you're in love with me / Let's do it
CD 4838782
Sony Jazz / Mar '96 / Sony

MAN I LOVE 1937-39, THE (Holiday, Billie & Lester Young)
This year's kisses / I must have that man / I'll get by / Mean to me / I'll never be the same / Easy living / Foolin' myself / Without your love / Me, myself and I / Sailboat in the moonlight / Travellin' all alone / She's funny that way / Getting some fun out of life / I can't believe that you're in love with me / Back in your own backyard / You can't be mine (and someone else's too) / Say it with a kiss / Man I love
CD CD 56008
Jazz Roots / Aug '94 / Target/BMG

MAN I LOVE, THE (Holiday, Billie & Lester Young)
CD CD 14529
Jazz Portraits / Jan '94 / Jazz Music

MASTERPIECES 1935-42
CD 158182
Masterpieces / Mar '94 / BMG

ME MYSELF I
CD 219912
Milan / Mar '95 / Conifer/BMG / Silva Screen

MISS BROWN TO YOU
What a little moonlight can do / Miss Brown to you / Twenty four hours a day / Yankee Doodle never went to town / If you were mine / These n'that n'those / Spreadin' rhythm around / Let's call a heart a heart / Please keep me in your dreams / I wish I had you / I'll never fail you / You're so desirable / You're gonna see a lot more of me / Hello my darling / Let's dream in the moonlight / More than you know / Under a blue jungle moon / Night and day / What is this going to get us / Loveless love / Georgia on my mind / Romance in the dark
CD GRF 075
Tring / '93 / Tring

MY FAVOURITE COLLECTION
God bless the child / My man / Please don't talk about me / Swing brother swing / Billie's blues / Lover come back to me / Don't be late / They can't take that away from me / Nice work if you can get it / Ain't nobody's business if I do / Don't explain / Miss Brown to you / I don't stand a ghost of a chance with you / He's funny that way / Lover man / Detour head
CD 100402
CMC / May '97 / BMG

MY MAN (Holiday, Billie & Teddy Wilson Orchestra)
CD CD 14536
Jazz Portraits / Jan '94 / Jazz Music

MY MAN (Holiday, Billie & Teddy Wilson Orchestra)
CD CD 56028
Jazz Roots / Jul '95 / Target/BMG

NIGHT AND DAY
I'm gonna lock my heart / Very thought of you / I can't get started (With you) / You can't be mine / Say it with a kiss / I'll never fail you / They say / That's all I ask of you / Yesterdays / Them there eyes / Night and day / You're just a no account / Body and soul / Falling in love again / I hear music / St. Louis blues / When you're smiling / I can't believe that you're in love with me / Now they call it the swing / On the sentimental side / Born to love / Without your love
CD RAJCD 857
Empress / Jul '97 / Koch

NIGHT AND DAY
What a little moonlight can do / Miss Brown to you / Twenty four hours a day / Yankee doodle never went to town / If you were mine / These 'n' that 'n' those / Spreadin' rhythm around / Let's call a heart a heart / Please keep me in your dreams / I wish I had you / I'll never fail you / You're gonna see a lot of me / Hello, my darling / Let's dream in the moonlight / More than you know / Night and day / What is this going to get us / Loveless love / Georgia on my mind / Romance in the dark
CD QED 027
Tring / Nov '96 / Tring

NO REGRETS
One two button my shoe / Let's call a heart a heart / Did I remember / No regrets / I can't give you anything but love / This years kisses / He aint' got rhythm / Let's call the whole thing off / They can't take that away from me / Sentimental and melancholy / Way I look tonight / I'll get by / Summertime / Who wants love / He's funny that way / Now they call it swing / Nice work if you can get it / Things are looking up / When you're smiling / If dreams come true / Fine romance / Billie's blues
CD PAR 2062
Parade / May '96 / Disc

ON THE SENTIMENTAL SIDE
CD PPCD 78117
Past Perfect / May '96 / Glass Gramophone Co.

PORTRAIT OF BILLIE HOLIDAY, A
CD GALE 409
Gallerie / May '97 / Disc / THE

PRICELESS JAZZ
Good morning heartache / My man / I loves you Porgy / Baby I don't cry over you / Lover man / Blues are brewin' / There is no greater love / You can't lose a broken heart / Big stuff / I'll look around / Now or never / Don't explain / Easy living / Crazy he calls me / My sweet hunk of trash / God bless the child
CD GRP 98712
GRP / Jul '97 / New Note/BMG

QUINTESSENCE, THE (1935-1944/2CD Set)
CD Set FA 209
Fremeaux / Oct '96 / ADA / Discovery

QUINTESSENTIAL VOL.1 1933-1935
Your mother's son-in-law / Riffin' the scotch / I wished on the moon / What a little moonlight can do / Miss Brown to you / Sun bonnet blue / What a night / What a moon / What a girl / I'm painting the town red / It's too hot for words / Twenty four hours a day / Yankee Doodle never went to town / Eeny meeny miney mo / If you were mine / These 'n' that 'n' those / You let me down / Spreadin' rhythm around
CD 4509872
Sony Jazz / Jan '95 / Sony

QUINTESSENTIAL VOL.2 1935-1936
Life begins when you're in love / It's like reaching for the moon / These foolish things / I cried for you / Guess who / Did I remember / No regrets / Summertime / Bille's blue / Fine romance / I can't pretend / 1-2 Button your shoe / Let's call a heart a heart / Easy to love / With thee I swing / Way you look tonight
CD 4600602
Sony Jazz / Jan '95 / Sony

QUINTESSENTIAL VOL.3 1936-1937
Who loves you / Pennies from Heaven / That's life I guess / I can't give you anything but love / One never knows, does one / I've got my love to keep me warm / If my heart could only talk / Please keep me in your dreams / He ain't got rhythm / This year's kisses / Why was I born / I must have that

man / Mood that I'm in / You showed me the way / Sentimental and melancholy / My last affair
CD ______ 4608202
Sony Jazz / Jan '95 / Sony

QUINTESSENTIAL VOL.4 1937
Carelessly / How could you / Moanin' low / Where is the sun / Let's call the whole thing off / They can't take away from me / I don't know if I'm coming or going / Sun showers / Yours and mine / I'll get by / Mean to me / Foolin' myself / Easy living / I'll never be the same / My, myself and I / Sailboat in the moonlight
CD ______ 4633332
Sony Jazz / Jan '95 / Sony

QUINTESSENTIAL VOL.5 1937-1938
Born to love / Without your love / Getting some fun out of life / Who wants love / Travellin' all alone / He's funny that way / Nice work if you can get it / Things are looking up / My man (mon homme) / Can't help lovin' dat man / My first impression of you / When you're smiling / I can't believe that you're in love with me / If dreams come true / Now they call it swing / On the sentimental side / Back in your own backyard / When a woman loves a man
CD ______ 4651902
Sony Jazz / Jan '95 / Sony

QUINTESSENTIAL VOL.6 1938
CD ______ 4663132
Sony Jazz / Jan '95 / Sony

QUINTESSENTIAL VOL.7 1938-1939
CD ______ 4669662
Sony Jazz / Jan '95 / Sony

QUINTESSENTIAL VOL.8 1939-1940
CD ______ 4679142
Sony Jazz / Jan '95 / Sony

QUINTESSENTIAL VOL.9 1940-1942
CD ______ 4679152
Sony Jazz / Jan '95 / Sony

SILVER COLLECTION, THE
I wished on the moon / Moonlight in Vermont / Say it isn't so / Our love is here to stay / Darn that dream / But not for me / Body and soul / Comes love / They can't take that away from me / Let's call the whole thing off / Gee baby ain't I good to you / Embraceable you / All or nothing at all / We'll be together again
CD ______ 8234492
Verve / Mar '92 / PolyGram

SOLITUDE
East of the Sun and West of the moon / Blue moon / You go to my head / You turned the tables on me / Easy to love / These foolish things / I only have eyes for you / Solitude / Everything I have is yours / Love for sale / Moonglow / Tenderly / If the moon turns green / Remember / Autumn in New York
CD ______ 5198102
Verve / Apr '93 / PolyGram

SONGS FOR DISTINGUE LOVERS
Day in, day out / Foggy day / Stars fell on Alabama / One for my baby (and one more for the road) / Just one of those things / I didn't know what time it was
CD ______ 8150552
Verve / Oct '84 / PolyGram

SPOTLIGHT ON BILLIE HOLIDAY
Lover man / Ain't nobody's business if I do / Billie's blues / Miss Brown to you / Good morning heartache / Why not take all of me / Do nothin' 'til you hear from me / My man / I cover the waterfront / Lover come back to me / Them there eyes / He's funny that way / You're driving me crazy / Fine and mellow
CD ______ HADCD 114
Javelin / Feb '94 / Henry Hadaway / THE

STAY WITH ME
I wished on the moon / Everything happens to me / Say it isn't so / I've got my love to keep me warm / Always / Do nothin' 'til you hear from me / How deep is the ocean / What a little moonlight can do / I cried for you
CD ______ 5115232
Verve / Feb '92 / PolyGram

STRANGE FRUIT
CD ______ CD 53085
Giants Of Jazz / May '93 / Cadillac / Jazz Music / Target/BMG

STRANGE FRUIT
CD ______ CWNCD 2014
Javelin / Jul '96 / Henry Hadaway / THE

SUMMER OF 1949
CD ______ BS 18004
Bandstand / Jul '96 / Swift

SUMMERTIME (Holiday, Billie & Her Orchestra)
CD ______ CD 14539
Jazz Portraits / Jan '94 / Jazz Music

SUMMERTIME 1936-1940
CD ______ CD 56035
Jazz Roots / Nov '94 / Target/BMG

THIS IS JAZZ
Miss Brown to you / Easy living / These foolish things / Some other spring / I wished on the moon / For heaven's sake / This years kisses / What a little moonlight can do / Sailboat in the moonlight / Fine romance / Mean to me / Fine and mellow / My man is easy to love / Pennies from heaven / You've changed / God bless the child
CD ______ CK 64622
Sony Jazz / Oct '96 / Sony

TWO ON ONE: BILLIE HOLIDAY & ELLA FITZGERALD (Holiday, Billie & Ella Fitzgerald)
CD ______ CDTT 9
Charly / Apr '94 / Koch

WISHING ON THE MOON (Life & Times Of Billie Holiday/Read By Annie Ross/ 2CD Set)
I wished on the moon / He ain't got rhythm / This year's kisses / Swing, brother swing / I'll get by / Easy living / Strange fruit / Some other spring / God bless the child / My sweet hunk o'trash / It ain't nobody's business if I do / My man / Lover come back to me / I thought about you / Fine and mellow / You've changed / For all we know
CD Set ______ 480947
Sony Jazz / Feb '97 / Sony

WITH TEDDY WILSON ORCHESTRA 1935-42 (Holiday, Billie & Teddy Wilson)
CD ______ CD 53055
Giants Of Jazz / Mar '90 / Cadillac / Jazz Music / Target/BMG

Hollaender, Friedrich

WENN ICH MIR WAS WUNSCHEN DURFTE (8CD Set) (Various Artists)
Jonny: *Weber, Marek* / Wenn der alte Motor wieder tackt: *Graetz, Paul* / Groschen: *Ebinger, Blandine* / Wenn ich mal tot bin: *Ebinger, Blandine* / Das ist der Hertzschlag, der zusammenhalt: *Graetz, Paul* / Liliput: *Weber, Marek* / Jonny: *Waldoff, Claire* / Dornroschen aus'm wedding: *Waldoff, Claire* / Ich tanz Charleston: *Charlie's Jazz Orchester* / Currendmadchen: *Ebinger, Blandine* / O Mond: *Ebinger, Blandine* / Die Hungerkunstlerin: *Ebinger, Blandine* / Das wunderkind: *Ebinger, Blandine* / Die hysterische Ziege: *Ebinger, Blandine* / Schiesshund: *Ebinger, Blandine* / Der Taler: *Ebinger, Blandine* / Die Trommlerin als Schiessbudenfigur: *Ebinger, Blandine* / Ich spiel so gern mit dir Klavier: *Ebinger, Blandine* / Raus mit den Mannern: *Waldoff, Claire* / O wie praktisch: *Waldoff, Claire* / Mit der hand uber'n Alexanderplatz: *Waldoff, Claire* / Das is bei mir so schon: *Graetz, Paul* / Die Herren Manner: *Hesterberg, Trude* / Lene Levi: *Hesterberg, Trude* / Bei uns um die Gedachtnischkirche rum: *Revue Ensemble* / Das sprichte band: *Revue Ensemble* / Der rote faden: *Revue Ensemble* / Zwei dunkle augen: *Hollaender, Friedrich* / Und immer noch spielen se blues: *Frohlich, Carl* / Nass oder trocken: *Godwin, Paul* / Ich tanz um die Welt mit dir: *Monosson, Leo* / Das nachtgespenst: *Gerron, Kurt* / Die Grosstadt Infanterie: *Gerron, Kurt* / Herr Doktor, Herr Doktor: *Gerron, Kurt* / Keiner weiss, wie ich bin nur du: *Keller, Greta* / Kitsch tango: *Bois, Curt* / Guck doch nicht immer nach dem Tangogeiger hin: *Bois, Curt* / Ich mache alles mit den beinen: *Bois, Curt* / Reizend: *Bois, Curt* / Solang wir jung sind Madame: *Bois, Curt* / Eine kleine sehnsucht: *Mosheim, Grete* / In St. Pauli bei Altona: *Mosheim, Grete* / Peter: *Dietrich, Marlene* / Jonny: *Dietrich, Marlene* / Der blaue Engel: *Dietrich, Marlene* / Ich bin die fesche Lola: *Dietrich, Marlene* / Nimm dich in acht vor blonden Frauen: *Dietrich, Marlene* / Kinder, heut' abend such ich mir was aus: *Dietrich, Marlene* / Ich bin von Kopf bis fuss auf liebe eingestelt: *Dietrich, Marlene* / Wenn ich mir was wunschen durfte: *Dietrich, Marlene* / Ich bin von Kopf bis fuss auf liebe eingestelt: *Weintraubs Syncopators* / Nimm dich in acht vor blonden Frauen: *Weintraubs Syncopators* / Wenn ich mir was wunschen durfte: *Keller, Greta* / Du hast ja eine trane im Knopfloch: *George, Heinrich* / Ich wunsch mir was: *Horn, Camilla* / Einbrecher: *Roberts, Ruhmann & Sargent* / Eine Liebelei, so nebenbei: *Harvey, Lilian* / Lass mich einmal deine Carmen sein: *Harvey, Lilian* / Ich lass mir mein Korper schwarz bepinseln: *Fritsch, Willy* / Kind, dein Mund ist musik: *Keller, Greta* / Also, das ist die liebe: *Keller, Greta* / Cocktail Lied: *Keller, Greta* / Baby (wo ist mein baby): *Comedy Harmonists* / Ich weiss nicht, zu wem ich gehore: *Sten, Anna* / Wie hab' ich nur leben konnen ohne dich: *Harvey, Lilian* / Jonny: *Dietrich, Marlene* / Awake in a dream: *Dietrich, Marlene* / You've got that look: *Dietrich, Marlene* / Boys in the backroom: *Dietrich, Marlene* / Little Joe the wrangler: *Dietrich, Marlene* / You've got that look: *Dietrich, Marlene* / St. Moritz waltz: *Robertson, Dick Studio Orchestra* / Eski-o-lay-li-mo: *Robertson, Dick Studio Orchestra* / Desire: *Lombardo, Carmen* / My heart & I: *Crosby, Bing* / House Jack built for Jill: *Crosby, Bing* / Moonlight & shadows: *Crosby, Bing* / Paradise in waltz time: *Swarthout, Gladys* / Moonlight & shadows: *Lamour, Dorothy* / Lovelight in the starlight: *Lamour, Dorothy* / Whispers in the dark: *Crosby, Bob & His Orchestra* / Whispers in the dark: *Boswell, Connee* / Thrill of a lifetime: *Leach, Billy* / True confession: *Armstrong, Louis* / True confession: *Wain, Bea* / It's raining sunbeams: *Durbin, Deanna* / Angel: *Paramount Studio Orchestra* / You leave me breathless: *Leonard, Jack* / You leave me breathless: *Keller, Greta* / Hello, my darling: *Holiday, Billie* / You & me: *Starr, Judy* / Stolen heaven: *Wain, Bea* / Mid night: *Carter, Benny & His Orchestra* / Strange enchantment: *Lamour, Dorothy* / Sentimental sandwich: *Lamour, Dorothy* / Palms of paradise: *Lamour, Dorothy* / Moon over Burma: *Lamour, Dorothy* / Man about town: *Ambrose & His Orchestra* / Man's in the navy: *Dietrich, Marlene* / I've been in love before: *Dietrich, Marlene* / Illusions: *Dietrich, Marlene* / Black market: *Dietrich, Marlene* / Ruins of Berlin: *Dietrich, Marlene* / Falling in love again: *Holiday, Billie* / Palms of paradise: *King, Henry* / Li'l boy love: *O'Neill, Dolores* / Arise my love: *O'Neill, Dolores* / This is the moment: *Stafford, Jo* / 5000 fingers of Dr.T: *Columbia Orchestra* / Dungeon ballet: *Columbia Orchestra* / Ten happy fingers: *Rettig, Tommy* / Dream stuff: *Rettig, Tommy* / Because we're kids: *Rettig, Tommy* / Get together weather: *Conrad, Healy & Hayes* / Dressing song: *Hayes, Peter* / Because we're kids: *Simpson, Carole* / Sabrina: *Gerhardt, Charles* / Falling in love again: *Britt, May* / Wenn ich mir was wunschen durfte: *Rampling, Charlotte* / Prolog: *Hollaender, Friedrich* / Das Spukschloss im Spessart: *Hollaender, Friedrich* / Der traum auf dem baum: *Hollaender, Friedrich* / Fur sie tun wir alles: *Hollaender, Friedrich* / Kleiner Rutsch in die Vergangenheit: *Hollaender, Friedrich* / Giftmischer rumba: *Hollaender, Friedrich* / Suleika: *Hollaender, Friedrich* / Kleider machen: *Hollaender, Friedrich* / Luete: *Hollaender, Friedrich* / Schiffs blues: *Hollaender, Friedrich* / Dazu gehoren zwei: *Hollaender, Friedrich* / Das wollen wir doch mal sein: *Hollaender, Friedrich* / Empfangsgesang: *Hollaender, Friedrich* / Giftmischer rumba (reprise): *Hollaender, Friedrich* / Hoppla auf's Sofa: *Ensemble Berlin* / Festival der goldenen zwanziger: *Ensemble Berlin* / Der song vom Stottern: *Wustenhagen, Harry & Rainer Bertram* / Ich ruf sie an: *Wustenhagen, Harry & Rainer Bertram* / Totale verfremdung: *Wustenhagen, Harry & Rainer Bertram* / Etikette a la Pappritz: *Maybach, Christianne* / Die neu neurose: *Maybach, Christianne* / Das wunderkind: *Eff, Barbara* / Der Rummelplatz blues: *Eff, Barbara* / Das Berg und Talbahngefhl: *Wustenhagen, Harry* / Stroganoff: *Wustenhagen, Harry* / Der Kopf unterm arm: *Bertram, Rainer* / Mainzer spezialitaten: *Vita, Helen & Edith Hancke* / Gesang der wasserman: *Vita, Helen & Edith Hancke* / Prinzesschen: *Vita, Helen & Edith Hancke* / Rote melodie: *Kuhl, Kate* / Die zersagte Dame: *Kuhl, Kate* / Dressur: *Hesterberg, Trude* / Ach lehne deine Wange: *Hesterberg, Trude* / Zieh dich aus Petronella: *Hesterberg, Trude* / Meine schwester liebt den Buster: *Dekowa, Victor* / Seit wann blast deine Grossmama Posaune: *Dekowa, Victor* / Duett im romanischen Cafe: *Sieg, Ursula & Lore Calvies* / Die kleptomanin: *Herking, Ursula* / Die kleine Internationale: *Stephan, Ruth* / An allem sind die Juden schuld: *Stephan, Ruth* / Sex appeal: *Lion, Margo* / Das Tauentzienmadel: *Bernhardt, Christa* / Wiener Schmarrn: *Vita, Helen* / Stroganoff: *Vita, Helen* / Chanson vom falschen Zug: *Schonbock, Karl* / Der Spuk personiich: *Pauli, Christiane* / Hochste Eisenbahn: *Strietzel, Achim* / Munchausen: *Thomas, Angelika* / Circe: *Wieder, Hanne* / Jonny wenn du geburtstag hast: *Ebinger, Blandine* / Die Schnapstrine: *Ebinger, Blandine* / Ick baumle mit de Beene: *Ebinger, Blandine* / Ilse: *Ebinger, Blandine* / Drei wunsche: *Ebinger, Blandine* / Dasm madchen mit den Schwefelholzern: *Ebinger, Blandine* / Chinesisches marchen: *Ebinger, Blandine* / Die roten schuhe: *Ebinger, Blandine* / Die trommlerin: *Ebinger, Blandine* / Ein volkslied: *Ebinger, Blandine* / In den abendwind geflustert: *Ebinger, Blandine* / Das wunderkind: *Ebinger, Blandine* / Currende: *Ebinger, Blandine* / Groschenlied: *Ebinger, Blandine* / Nachtgebet: *Ebinger, Blandine* / O Mond: *Ebinger, Blandine* / Wenn ich mal tot bin: *Ebinger, Blandine* / Giftmariechen: *Ebinger, Blandine* / Wiegenlied an eine Mutter: *Ebinger, Blandine* / Kinderlied oder der fliegende Jakob: *Ebinger, Blandine* / Kitsch: *Ebinger, Blandine* / Starker Tobak: *Ebinger, Blandine* / Das Berg und Tahlbahngefhl: *Hollaender, Friedrich* / Spotterdammerung: *Hollaender, Friedrich*
CD Set ______ BCD 16009
Bear Family / Nov '96 / Direct / Rollercoaster / Swift

Holland, Dave

DAVE HOLLAND & SAM RIVERS (Holland, Dave & Sam Rivers)
CD ______ 1238432
IAI / Mar '92 / Cadillac / Harmonia Mundi

DREAM OF THE ELDERS (Holland, Dave Quartet)
Winding way / Lazy snake / Claressence / Equality (vocal) / Ebb and flo / Dream of the edlers / Second thoughts / Equality (instrumental)
CD ______ 5290842
ECM / Feb '96 / New Note/Pinnacle

EMERALD TEARS
Spheres / Combination / Under Redwoods / Flurries / Emerald tears / B40, RS4W, M236k / Solar / Hooveling
CD ______ 5290872
ECM / Dec '95 / New Note/Pinnacle

EXTENSIONS (Holland, Dave Quartet)
Nemesis / Processional / Black hole / Oracle / 101 fahrenheit (slow meltdown) / Color of mind
CD ______ 8417782
ECM / Oct '90 / New Note/Pinnacle

JUMPIN' IN (Holland, Dave Quintet)
CD ______ 8174372
ECM / '88 / New Note/Pinnacle

LIFE CYCLE (Solo Cello)
CD ______ 8292002
ECM / Oct '86 / New Note/Pinnacle

ONES ALL
Homecoming / Three step dance / Pork pie hat / Jumpin' in / Reminiscence / Mr. PC / Little girl I'll miss you / Cashet / Blues for CM / Pass it on / God bless the child
CD ______ VBR 21482
Intuition / Jan '96 / New Note/Pinnacle

RAZOR'S EDGE, THE (Holland, Dave Quintet)
Brother Ty / Vedana / Razor's edge / Blues for CM / Vortex / Five four six / Wights waits for weights / Fight time
CD ______ 8330482
ECM / Oct '87 / New Note/Pinnacle

SEEDS OF TIME (Holland, Dave Quintet)
Uhren / Homecoming / Perspicuity / Celebration / World protection blues / Grid lock / Walk away / Good doctor / Double vision
CD ______ 8253222
ECM / Aug '85 / New Note/Pinnacle

TRIPLICATE (Holland, Dave Trio)
CD ______ 8371132
ECM / Sep '88 / New Note/Pinnacle

Holland, Jerry

FIDDLESTICKS COLLECTION, THE (1982-1992)
CD ______ GLCD 1156
Green Linnet / Dec '95 / ADA / CM / Direct / Highlander / Roots

Holland, Jools

A-Z OF PIANO
Brick Lane / Newgates Knocker / Temple Bar / Canary Wharf / Birdcage walk / Seven Dials / Rotten Row Boogie / Wapping Steps / St. Martin In The Fields / St. Andrews by the wardrobe / Between the dilly and the blue gate fields (city) / High street (ken) / Speaker's corner / Soho / Tranquil passage
CD ______ ALTGOCD 001
Alter Ego / Oct '92 / Vital

BOOGIE WOOGIE PIANO
CD ______ TMPCD 022
Temple / Oct '95 / BMG

FULL COMPLEMENT
Lost chord / One more time / Together again / No ones to blame / Baby, let me hold your hand / Lady don't fall backwards / Cackophony / Movin' on / Me - U = loneliness / Blue guitar / Shake, rattle and roll / Lady don't sing
CD ______ EIRSCD 1083
IRS/EMI / Jun '96 / EMI

JAZZ PIANO
CD ______ TMPCD 024
Temple / Oct '95 / BMG

LIVE PERFORMANCE
Bumble boogie / Bad luck blues / Skin the cat / Mean old man's world / Dr. Jazz / High street / I saw the light / Should've known better / Able Mable / Maiden's lament / Biggie wiggie / Maybe I need her / I gotta woman / Smoking shuffle / Hop, skip and jump
CD ______ BT 002CD
Beautiful / Nov '94 / Vital

RAG TIME PIANO
CD ______ TMPCD 023
Temple / Oct '95 / BMG

SEX'N'JAZZ'N'ROCK'N'ROLL
CD ______ HF 51CD
Coliseum / Oct '96 / Warner Music

WORLD OF HIS OWN
Architectural number / Maiden's lament / Honey dripper / Thursday in three movements / Harp solo / Biggy wiggy / Holy cow / In the heat of the night / We're through / Grand Hotel / Danger zone
CD ______ EIRSCD 1082
IRS/EMI / Jun '96 / EMI

Holland, Maggie

BY HEART
Oxford girl / Rosie / Only dreaming / Smokey's bar / Cathy come home / Catharine of Aragon's song / Rowan tree / May morning dew / Evergreen / Colorado song / Postcards from Scarborough / Tank park salute / Jack Haggerty / Company of strangers / Seven gypsies / Invitation to the blues / Taoist tale
CD ______ RHYD 5008
Rhiannon / Sep '95 / ADA / Direct / Vital

Holland, Nicky

SENSE AND SENSUALITY
Paperchase / Nobody's girl / Dear Ingrid / In a broken dream / Nothing / Falling water / New York inside my head / Cry to me / Hat full of stars / Lay down / John's first wedding
CD _______________ 4879922
Epic / Aug '97 / Sony

Hollander, Rick

ACCIDENTAL FORTUNE (Hollander, Rick Quartet)
Accidental fortune / My old flame / Point of the pen / I've grown accustomed to her face / Some lovely dreams / I should care / Big Stacey / Theme for Ernie / Beautiful friendship / Pull
CD _______________ CCD 4550
Concord Jazz / May '93 / New Note/ Pinnacle

ONCE UPON A TIME (The Music Of Hoagy Carmichael)
Skylark / Stardust / Baltimore Oriole / Georgia on my mind / Hong kong blues / Rockin' chair / Ivy / Nearness of you
CD _______________ CCD 4666
Concord Jazz / Sep '95 / New Note/ Pinnacle

Holley, Major

MULE
CD _______________ BB 8622
Black & Blue / Feb '96 / Discovery / Koch / Wellard

Holliday, Judy

HOLLIDAY WITH MULLIGAN (Holliday, Judy & Gerry Mulligan)
What's the rush / Loving you / Lazy / It must be Christmas / Party's over / It's bad for me / Suppertime / Pass that peace pipe / I gotta right to sing the blues / Summer's over / Blue prelude
CD _______________ CDSL 5191
DRG / Mar '87 / Discovery / New Note/ Pinnacle

Holliday, Michael

30TH ANNIVERSARY COLLECTION
Yellow rose of Texas / Gal with the yaller shoes / Love you darlin' / Keep your heart / Story of my life / Stairway of love / My heart is an open book / Palace of love / Life is a circus / For you, for you / I have waited / Steady game / Starry eyed / Dream talk / One finger symphony / Young in love / I wonder who's kissing her now / Miracle of Monday morning / Remember me / Dream boy dream / I don't want you to see me cry / Wishin' on a rainbow / Have I told you lately that I love you / Tears / I just can't win / Laugh and the world laughs with you / Just to be with you again / Drums / My last date with you
CD _______________ CDEMS 1509
EMI / Feb '94 / EMI

EMI PRESENTS THE MAGIC OF MICHAEL HOLLIDAY
Nothin' to do / Gal with the yaller shoes / Hot diggety / Ten thousand miles / Story of my life / In love / Stairway of love / I'll always be in love with you / Starry eyed / Skylark / Little boy lost / Have I told you lately that I love you / I wonder who's kissing her now / My house is your house / Folks who live on the hill / Yellow rose of Texas / Tears / Dear heart / Dream boy dream / Young in love / Palace of love / My last date (with you) / Old Cape Cod / Skye boat song / Rooney
CD _______________ CDMFP 6287
Music For Pleasure / May '97 / EMI

EP COLLECTION, THE
Runaway train / Yaller yaller gold / Darlin' Katie / Marrying for love / I'll be loving you too / Lonesome road / Just a wearyin' for you / Ramblin' man / Kentucky babe / In the good old summertime / Stairway of love / Four feather falls / Happy hearts and friendly faces / Way back home / Show me the way to go home / Side by side / Alexander's ragtime band / Just a prayer away / Careless hands / Dearest between hello and goodbye / Story of my life / I can't give you anything but love / Winter wonderland / Perfect day / Four walls / I Can't begin to tell you / Margie
CD _______________ SEECD 311
See For Miles/C5 / Feb '91 / Pinnacle

TOGETHER AGAIN (Holliday, Michael & Edna Savage)
Story of my life / Arrivederci darling / Rooney / Tear fell / Tip toe through the tulips / Once / Girl in the yaller shoes / Long ago and far away / We'll gather lilacs / 'S wonderful / In the wee small hours of the morning / My house is your house / Let me be loved / Hot diggity (dog ziggity boom) / Tea for two / Catch me a kiss / I promise you / Me head in de barrel / I saw Esau / Never leave me / I'll be seeing you / Why why why / Nothin' to do / Goodnight my love
CD _______________ CC 252
Music For Pleasure / May '90 / EMI

Holliday, Simon

RAGS, BOOGIE AND SWING
Should I reveal / As long as I live / Maple leaf rag / Airmail special / Climax rag / Boogie joys / All the things you are / Way down yonder in New Orleans / Winin' boy blues / Nagasaki
CD _______________ CMJCD 009
CMJ / Mar '90 / Jazz Music / Wellard

Hollies

AIR THAT I BREATHE, THE (The Best Of The Hollies)
Air that I breathe / Bus stop / Just one look / Yes I will / Look through my window / He ain't heavy, he's my brother / I can't let go / We're through / Searchin' / Stay, I'm alive / If I needed someone / Here I go again / Stop stop stop / On a carousel / Carrie Anne / King Midas in reverse / Jennifer Eccles / Listen to me / Sorry Suzanne / I can't tell the bottom from the top / Gasoline Alley bred / Hey Willy / Long cool woman in a black dress / Baby / Woman I love
CD _______________ CDEMTV 74
EMI / Mar '93 / EMI

AIR THAT I BREATHE, THE
CD _______________ BR 1302
BR Music / May '94 / Target/BMG

ALL THE WORLD IS LOVE
CD _______________ BR 1462
BR Music / Nov '94 / Target/BMG

ANOTHER NIGHT/RUSSIAN ROULETTE/ 5317704/BUDDY HOLLY (4 Hollies Originals/4CD Set)
Another night / 4th Of July, Asbury Park (Sandy) / Lonely hobo lullaby / Second hand hang-ups / Machine jive / I'm down / Look out Johnny (there's a monkey on your back) / Give me time / You gave me life (with that look on your eyes) / Lucy / Wiggle that wotsit / Forty eight hour parole / Thanks for the memories / My love / Lady of the night / Russian roulette / Draggin' my heels / Louise / Be with you / Daddy don't mind / Say it ain't so Jo / maybe it's dawn / Song of the sung / Harlequin / When I'm yours / Something to live for / Stormy waters / Boys in the band / Satelite three / It's in every one of us / Peggy Sue / Wishing / Love's made a fool of you / Take your time / Heartbeat / Tell me how / Think it over / Maybe baby / Midnight shifts / I'm gonna love you too / Peggy Sue got married / What to do / That'll be the day / It doesn't matter anymore / Everyday / Medley
CD Set _______________ CDHOLLIES 1
EMI / Feb '95 / EMI

BEST OF THE HOLLIES, THE (Centenary Collection)
On a carousel / Stop, stop, stop / Jennifer Eccles / He ain't heavy, he's my brother / Air that I breathe / Magic woman touch / Listen to me / Pay you back with interest / We're through / Yes I will / King Midas in reverse / Gasoline Alley bred / Sandy (4th July, Asbury Park) / Purple rain / Shine silently / Baby / Mighty Quinn / Peggy Sue / Look through any window / Just like me / Mickey's monkey / Stay / Holliedaze (medley)
CD _______________ CTMCD 311
EMI / Feb '97 / EMI

BUTTERFLY
Dear Eloise / Maker / Would you believe / Postcard / Try it / Step inside / Away away away / Pegasus / Wish you a wish / Charlie and Fred / Elevated observations / Butterfly
CD _______________ BGOCD 79
Beat Goes On / '89 / Pinnacle

CONFESSIONS OF THE MIND
Survival of the fittest / Man without a heart / Little girl / Isn't it nice / Confessions of a mind / Lady please / Frightened lady / Too young to be married / Seperated / I wanna shout
CD _______________ BGOCD 96
Beat Goes On / '89 / Pinnacle

DISTANT LIGHT
CD _______________ BGOCD 97
Beat Goes On / Jul '91 / Pinnacle

EP COLLECTION, THE
Woodstock / Here I go again / You know he did / What kind of boy / Baby that's all / Look through my window / What kind of love / When I'm not there / Rockin' Robin / Lucille / Memphis / Just one look / I'm alive / Come on back / We're through / I've got a way of my own / So lonely / To you my love / What'cha gonna do about it / Come on home / I can't let you go
CD _______________ SEECD 94
See For Miles/C5 / Mar '95 / Pinnacle

EVOLUTION
Then the heartaches begin / Water on the brain / Have you ever loved somebody / Heading for a fall / Ye olde toffee shoppe / When your lights turned on / Stop right there / Lullaby to Tim / You need love / Rain on the window / Leave me / Games we play
CD _______________ BGOCD 80
Beat Goes On / '89 / Pinnacle

FOR CERTAIN BECAUSE
CD _______________ BGOCD 9
Beat Goes On / Dec '89 / Pinnacle

HOLLIES LIVE
CD _______________ BRCD 123
BR Music / Jul '94 / Target/BMG

HOLLIES SING DYLAN
When the ship comes in / I'll be your baby tonight / I want you / This wheel's on fire / I shall be released / Blowin' in the wind / Quit your low down ways / Just like a woman / Times they are a changin' / All I really want to do / My back pages / Mighty Quinn
CD _______________ CZ 520
EMI / Jun '93 / EMI

HOLLIES, THE
CD _______________ BGOCD 25
Beat Goes On / May '91 / Pinnacle

HOUR OF THE HOLLIES, AN
Stop stop stop / Gasoline Alley bred / Searchin' / Listen to me / What kind of boy / Rockin' robin / Come on back / Memphis, Tennessee / Too young to be married / Dear Eloise / He ain't heavy, he's my brother / Sweet little sixteen / Nobody / Hey Willy / Just like me / Sorry Suzanne / Lucille / Keep off that friend of mine / On a carousel / Pay you back with interest / Clown / If I needed someone / Blowin' in the wind
CD _______________ CC 216
Music For Pleasure / '91 / EMI

IN THE HOLLIES STYLE
Nitty gritty / Something's got a hold on me / Don't you know / To you my love / It's in her kiss / Time for love / What kind of boy / Too much monkey business / I thought of you last night / Please don't feel too bad / Come on home / You'll be mine / Set me free
CD _______________ BGOCD 8
Beat Goes On / Oct '88 / Pinnacle

LOVE SONGS (22 Of Their Most Romantic Ballads)
I can't let go / Air that I breathe / Just one look / I can't tell the bottom from the top / Bus stop / Carrie Anne / Here I go again / Sorry Suzanne / Yes I will / To you my love / I'm alive / Come on back / Dear Eloise / Jennifer Eccles / What kind of boy / If I needed someone / You need love / King Midas in reverse / Too young to be married / Have you ever loved somebody / That's how strong my love is / Just like a woman
CD _______________ CDMFP 5883
Music For Pleasure / Aug '96 / EMI

NOT THE HITS AGAIN
Wings / It's in her kiss (Shoop shoop song) / You'll be mine / Take your time / I am a rock / Honey and wine / Very last day / It's only make believe / That's my desire / So lonely / Now's the time / Hard, hard year / Put yourself in my place / Please don't feel too bad / Nitty gritty-Something's got a hold on me / You better move on / I take what I want / Talkin 'bout you / Candy man / Set me free / Lawdy Miss Clawdy / Sweet little sixteen
CD _______________ SEECD 63
See For Miles/C5 / May '89 / Pinnacle

OTHER SIDE OF THE HOLLIES
'Cos you like to love me / Everything is sunshine / Signs that will never change / Not that way at all / You know he did / Do the best you can / So lonely / I've got a way of my own / Don't run and hide / Come on back / Open up your eyes / All the world is love / Whole world over / Row the boat together / Mad professor Blyth / Dandelion wine / Baby that's all / Nobody / Keep off that friend of mine / Running through the night / Hey what's wrong with me / Blowin' in the wind
CD _______________ SEECD 302
See For Miles/C5 / '90 / Pinnacle

ROMANY/WRITE ON/THE HOLLIES/A CRAZY STEAL (4 More Hollies Originals/4CD Set)
Won't you feel good that morning / Touch / Words don't come easy / Magic woman touch / Lizzy and the Rainman / Down river / Slow down / Delaware Taggett and the Outlaw Boys / Jesus was a crossmaker / Romany / Blue in the morning / Courage of your convictions / Star / Write on / Sweet country calling / Love is the thing / I won't move over / Narida / Stranger / Crocodile woman (she bites) / My island / There's always goodbye / Falling calling / It's a shame, it's a game / Don't let me down / Out on the road / Air that I breathe / Rubber Lucy / Transatlantic Westbound jet / Pick up the pieces again / Down on the run / Love makes the world go round / Day that Curly Billy shot down Crazy Sam McGee / Writing on the wall / What am I gonna do / Let it pour / Burn out / Hello to romance / Amnesty / Caraccas / Boulder to Birmingham / Clown service / Feet on the ground
CD Set _______________ CDHOLLIES 2
Premier/EMI / Feb '96 / EMI

SING HOLLIES
CD _______________ 175332
Magic / Jul '97 / Greyhound

SINGLES A'S AND B'S (1970-1989)
I can't tell the bottom from the top / Mad Professor Blyth / Gasoline alley bred / Dandelion wine / Hey Willy / Row the boat together / Long cool woman in a black dress / Cable car / Baby / Oh Granny / Day that Curly Billy shot crazy Sam McGhee / Born a man / Air that I breathe / No more riders / Star / Love is the thing / Hello to romance / Forty eight hour parole / Something to live for / Song of the sun
CD _______________ CDMFP 5980
EMI / Apr '93 / EMI

STAY WITH THE HOLLIES (Remastered)
Talkin' about you / You better move on / Lucille / Baby don't cry / Memphis / Stay / Rockin' Robin / What'cha gonna do about it / Do you love me / It's only make believe / What kind of girl are you / Little lover / Candy man / Mr. Moonlight / You better move on / Lucille / Baby don't cry / Memphis / Stay / Rockin' Robin / What'cha gonna do about it / Do you love me / It's only make believe / What kind of girl are you / Little lover / Talkin' about you / Mr. Moonlight / Candy man
CD _______________ DORIG 111
EMI / Jul '97 / EMI

Hollmer, Lars

12 SIBIRISKA CYKLAR/VILL DU HORA MER
CD _______________ RES 512CD
Resource / Dec '94 / ADA / Direct

LOOPING HOME
CD _______________ VICTOCD 024
Victo / Oct '94 / Harmonia Mundi / ReR Megacorp

SIBERIAN CIRCUS, THE
Boeves psalm / Inga pengar / Ante flottar ja te sjoss / Endlich ein zamba / Avlagsen strandvals / Starlep signs / 180 sekunder hemma / Vill du hora mer / Retsticka / Soldaten / Optimistbeat / Skar / Inte quantar / Onk kch onk kch / Skiss mellan brest och segosero / Simfageldans / Rindatrost / Spanksa trappan / Eyeliner / Karussellmusik/Utflykt med damcykel / Gitarette / Vendeltid
CD _______________ RESCD 502
Resource / Jul '97 / ADA / Direct

XII SIBIRISKA CYKLAR/VIII DU HORN MER
Avlagsen strandvals / Piano de jugugte / Hajar du idealfamiljen / Endlich ein zamba / Inga pengar / Kamelsvang / Ja ante flottar ja te sjoss / Boeves psalm / Jag vantar pa pelle / Bluesen / 44 sekunder kopt speldosa / Ung harald / Litet piano / Starlep signs / Sweet / Indojazz / Soldaten / En slags orfeo / Overgang / Baldis / Retsticka / Dragfragment / Glasmusik / Akarondo / Kuckeliku / Vill du hora mer / 180 sekunder hemma / Humanoid robottango / Finalvals
CD _______________ RESCD 512
Resource / Jul '97 / ADA / Direct

Hollow Rock String Band

TRADITIONAL DANCE TUNES
Kitchen girl / Clog / Waltz / Dinah / Richmond cotillion / Hog eyed man / Medley / Jawbones / Betty likens / Cabin creek / Folding down the sheets / Money musk / Devil on a stump / Over the waterfall / Fiddler's drunk and the fun's all over
CD _______________ COCD 2715
County / Jul '97 / ADA / Direct

Holloway, Laurie

ABOUT TIME
Tricrotism / Teach me tonight / For you / Quinta do lago / Nothing quite like love / Good to know / s'posin' / Gettin' there / Revelation / Love for sale / I Should n' ave ever / There is no greater love / Bye bye blues
CD _______________ C5CD 595
See For Miles/C5 / Jan '93 / Pinnacle

BLUE SKIES AND OTHER VISTAS
CD _______________ ELGIN 03
Elgin / Jan '97 / TKO Magnum

SHOWTIME (Holloway, Laurie Trio)
CD _______________ ELGIN 05
Elgin / Aug '97 / TKO Magnum

Holloway, Loleatta

HOTLANTA SOUL OF LOLEATTA HOLLOWAY
Cry to me / Go on that first plane / Part time lover, full time fool / I know where you're coming from / Mrs. So and So's daughter / I can't help myself / Just be true / Show must go on / Rainbow '71 / Casanova / We did it / Merrily / World don't owe you nothin' / Mother of shame / Bring it on up / Only a fool / So can I / (I love you) For sentimental reasons / What are you gonna do about tomorrow / Love woke me up / HELP ME MY LORD / Our love has just got to come together / This man's arms
CD _______________ CDKEND 135
Kent / Mar '96 / Pinnacle

LOLEATTA
Hit and run / Is it just a man's way / We're getting stronger / Dreamin' / Ripped off / Worn out broken heart / That's how heartaches are made / What now
CD _______________ CPCD 8063
Charly / Nov '94 / Koch

LOVE SENSATION
Love sensation / Dance what 'cha wanna / I'll be standing there / I've been loving you

too long / Short end of the stick / My way / Long hard climb to love / Two become a crowd
CD CPCD 8095
Charly / Apr '95 / Koch

RUNAWAY (The Best Of Loleatta Holloway)
CD CDGR 144
Charly / Apr '97 / Koch

Holloway, Miles

IN AT THE DEEP END (Holloway, Miles & Elliot Eastwick)
Glide by shooting: *Two Lone Swordsmen* / Danser: *New Phunk Theory* / Space groover: *Wulf n' Bear* / Chance: *Reel Houze* / Continuum: *Laj Gloves* / Fat Dan's rub a dub: *Paper Issue No.2* / Message: *Straight Life* / Journey into happiness: *Freaks* / Piano: *Housey Doingz* / Last chance to dance pt.1: *Urban Farmers* / I love what you're doing: *Dancer* / Summer daze: *Samba Magic* / Late nighter: *Loveys, Trevor* / Northern house: *Essa*
CD PAGANCD 1001
Pagan / Feb '97 / Vital

Holloway, Red

LOCKSMITH BLUES (Holloway, Red & Clark Terry Sextet)
CD CCD 4390
Concord Jazz / Nov '89 / New Note/ Pinnacle

RED HOLLOWAY AND COMPANY
But not for me / Caravan / Passion flower / Blues for QM / Well you needn't / What's new / Summertime / Tokyo express
CD CCD 4322
Concord Jazz / Jul '87 / New Note/Pinnacle

Holloway, Ron

SCORCHER
Hot house / Sidewinder / Everywhere calypso / Is that jazz / You and I / How high the moon / Red clay / Blue collar / Pulse
CD MCD 92572
Milestone / Oct '96 / Cadillac / Complete/ Pinnacle / Jazz Music / Wellard

Holloway, Stanley

PICK OOP THA MUSKET
Sam, pick oop tha musket / 'Alt, who goes theer / Marksman Sam / Sam's medal / Sam Small at Westminster / Up'ards / Three ha'pence a foot / 'Ole in the ark / With her head tucked underneath her arm / Lion and Albert / Song of the sea / Beefeater / Many happy returns / Gunner Joe / Beat the retreat / One each a piece all round / Sam Small's party
CD PASTCD 7021
Flapper / Aug '93 / Pinnacle

Holly, Buddy

20 GOLDEN GREATS: BUDDY HOLLY (Holly, Buddy & The Crickets)
That'll be the day / Peggy Sue / Words of love / Everyday / Not fade away / Oh boy / Maybe baby / Listen to me / Heartbeat / Think it over / It doesn't matter anymore / It's so easy / Well alright / Rave on / Raining in my heart / True love ways / Peggy Sue got married / Bo Diddley / Brown eyed handsome man / Wishing
CD DMCTV 1
MCA / Aug '93 / BMG

20 OF THE BEST (Holly, Buddy & The Crickets)
That'll be the day / Rave on / Peggy Sue / Words of love / Think it over / Bo Diddley / Maybe baby / Oh boy / Blue days, black nights / It's so easy / You've got the love / Deborah / Love's made a fool of you / Not fade away / Midnight shift / Lonesome tears / Baby my heart / Brown eyed handsome man / I fought the law / Early in the morning
CD NTMCD 537
Nectar / Mar '97 / Pinnacle

BUDDY HOLLY
Peggy Sue / Rock me my baby / Ready teddy / I'm looking for someone to love / Heartbeat / Well all right / That'll be the day / Every day / Baby I don't care / Rave on / Love me / Think it over / Maybe baby / It doesn't matter anymore / I'm changing all those changes / Early in the morning / Words of love / You've got love / Oh boy / It's so easy
CD 399541
Koch Presents / May '97 / Koch

BUDDY HOLLY/THAT'LL BE THE DAY (2CD Set)
I'm gonna love you too / Peggy Sue / Look at me / Listen to me / Valley of tears / Ready teddy / Everyday / Mailman bring me no more blues / Words of love / Baby I don't care / Rave on / Little baby / You are my one desire / Blue days black nights / Modern Don Juan / Rock around with Ollie Vee / Ting-a-ling / Girl on my mind / That'll be the day / Love me / I'm changing all those changes / Don't come back knockin' / Midnight shift / Rock around with Ollie Vee (alternative version)
CD Set MCD 33001
MCA / Jul '96 / BMG

BUDDY'S BUDDYS (The Buddy Holly Songbook) (Various Artists)
CD VSOPCD 175
Connoisseur Collection / Sep '92 / Pinnacle

DOUBLE EXPOSURE (Crickets)
My little girl / I fought the law / Oh boy / That'll be the day / When you ask about love / Tell me how / It doesn't matter anymore / Baby my heart / Rave on / Maybe baby / Brown eyed handsome man / Teardrops fall like rain / Everyday / Think it over / More than I can say / Don't ever change / Peggy Sue / Well alright / True love ways / (They call her) La bamba / It's so easy / Love's made a fool of you
CD RCCD 3006
Rollercoaster / Nov '93 / Rollercoaster / Swift

GOLDEN GREATS
Peggy Sue / That'll be the day / Listen to me / Everyday / Oh boy / Not fade away / Raining in my heart / Brown eyed handsome man / Maybe baby / Rave on / Think it over / It's so easy / It doesn't matter anymore / True love ways / Peggy Sue got married / Bo Diddley
CD MCLD 19046
MCA / Apr '92 / BMG

LEGEND LIVES, THE (15 Fantastic Guitar Instrumentals Of Classic Holly Hits) (Various Artists)
Everyday / Heartbeat / Learning the game / That'll be the day / Listen to me / True love ways / Oh boy / Not fade away / Wishing / Raining in my heart / Peggy Sue/Peggy Sue got married / Love's made a fool of you / Fool's paradise / It doesn't matter anymore / Girl in every song
CD 304552
Hallmark / Jul '97 / Carlton

LOVE SONGS
CD MCBD 19522
MCA / Jul '95 / BMG

NOT FADE AWAY (Remembering Buddy Holly) (Various Artists)
Peggy Sue got married: *Holly, Buddy & The Hollies* / True love ways: *Mavericks* / Well alright: *Griffith, Nanci & The Crickets* / Midnight shift: *Los Lobos* / Not fade away: *Band & The Crickets* / Think it over: *Tractors* / Wishing: *Carpenter, Mary Chapin & Kevin Montgomery* / Oh boy: *Ely, Joe & Todd Snider* / Crying, waiting, hoping: *Stuart, Marty & Steve Earle* / It doesn't matter anymore: *Bogguss, Suzy & Dave Edmunds* / Maybe baby: *Nitty Gritty Dirt Band* / Learning the game: *Jennings, Waylon & Mark Knopfler*
CD MCD 11260
MCA / Jan '96 / BMG

ORIGINAL VOICES OF THE CRICKETS, THE (Holly, Buddy & The Picks)
True loves ways / Every day / Love me / Don't come back knockin' / Baby I don't care / Reminiscing / Peggy Sue / Well alright / Midnight shift / Blue days black nights / That's what they say / Rock-a-bye rock / Heartbeat / Girl on my mind / Ting-a-ling / I'm gonna set my foot down / It's not my fault / Rock around with Ollie Vee / You are my one desire / Because I love you / Modern Don Juan / Words / You've lost that lovin' feelin'
CD CDMF 088
Magnum Force / Mar '96 / TKO Magnum

RAVIN' ON - FROM CALIFORNIA TO CLOVIS (Crickets)
CD RSRCD 002
Rockstar / Apr '94 / Direct / Nervous / Rollercoaster / TKO Magnum

SINGLES COLLECTION 1957-1961, THE (Holly, Buddy & The Crickets)
That'll be the day / I'm looking for someone to love / Oh boy / Not fade away / Maybe baby / Tell me how / Think it over / Fool's paradise / It's so easy / Lonesome tears / Love's made a fool of you / Someone someone / When you ask about love / Deborah / Baby my heart / More than I can say / Don't cha know / Peggy Sue got married / Sweet love / I fought the law
CD PWKS 4205
Carlton / May '94 / Carlton

THAT'LL BE THE DAY
You are my one desire / Blue days black nights / Modern Don Juan / Rock around with Ollie Vee / Ting a ling / Girl on my mind / Love me / I'm changing all those changes / Don't come back knockin' / Midnight shift
CD CLACD 309
Castle / Jan '96 / BMG

TRUE LOVE WAYS
Raining in my heart / Peggy Sue / That'll be the day / Oh boy / Everyday / True love ways / It doesn't matter anymore / Learning the game / I'm gonna love you too / Ready Teddy / Wishing / Well alright / Midnight shift / Love's made a fool of you / Reminiscing
CD TCD 2339
Telstar / Feb '89 / BMG

VERY BEST OF BUDDY HOLLY, THE
Heartbeat / It doesn't matter anymore / That'll be the day / Maybe baby / Peggy sue / Rave on / Oh boy / I'm gonna love you too / Well alright / Think it over / True love ways / Words of love / Raining in my heart / Wishing / It's so easy / Fool's paradise / Not fade away / Brown eyed handsome man / Early in the morning / Bo Diddley / Baby I don't care / Love's made a fool of you / Valley of tears / Peggy sue got married / Love is strange / Crying waiting hoping / Listen to me / Everyday
CD DINCD 133
Dino / Nov '96 / Pinnacle

VERY BEST OF BUDDY HOLLY, THE
CD MCBD 19535
MCA / Apr '97 / BMG

WORDS OF LOVE - 28 CLASSIC SONGS (Holly, Buddy & The Crickets)
Words of love / That'll be the day / Peggy Sue / Think it over / True love ways / What to do / Crying, waiting, hoping / Well alright / Love's made a fool of you / Peggy Sue got married / Valley of tears / Wishing / Raining in my heart / Oh boy / Rave on / Brown eyed handsome man / Bo Diddley / It's so easy / It doesn't matter anymore / Maybe baby / Early in the morning / Love is strange / Listen to me / I'm gonna love you too / Learning the game / Baby I don't care / Heartbeat / Everyday
CD 5144872
PolyGram TV / Feb '93 / PolyGram

Holly Golightly

GOOD THINGS, THE
CD DAMGOOD 65CD
Damaged Goods / Jun '95 / Shellshock/ Disc

LAUGH IT ALL UP
Sally go round the roses / If I could be loved by you / Mellow down easy / I can't stand it / Candy man / Look for me baby / Don't lie to me / Too much going for you / It's all over now / Troubles on my mind / Getting mighty crowded / You ain't no big thing / Sand / Hold me baby / This happens / Candle song / If I should ever leave / Mary Ann / Hold me baby / Good enough / High time / Until I find you
CD ASKCD 74
Vinyl Japan / Aug '97 / Plastic Head / Vinyl Japan

Hollyday, Christopher

CHRISTOPHER HOLLYDAY
Appointment in Ghana / Omega / Bloomdido / This is always / Koko / Little Melonae / Embraceable you / Blues inn / Be bop
CD PD 83055
Novus / Aug '89 / BMG

Hollyfaith

PURRR
Bliss / Who is you / Delicacies / Watching, waiting, turning / Zero / Voodoo doll / Whatsamatta / Whirlwind / Color of blood / Needs
CD CRECD 163
Creation / Aug '93 / 3mv/Vital

Hollywood Brats

HOLLYWOOD BRATS
Chez maximes / Another schoolday / Nightmare / Empty bottles / Courtesan / Then he kissed me / Tumble with me / Zurich 17 / Southern belles / Drowning sorrows / Sick on you
CD CDMRED 106
Cherry Red / Dec '93 / Pinnacle

Hollywood Fats Band

ROCK THIS HOUSE
CD BT 1097CD
Black Top / Jan '94 / ADA / CM / Direct

Hollywood Flames

HOLLYWOOD FLAMES, THE
Wheel of fortune / Later / Tabarin / Wine / My confession / Sound of your voice / Crazy / Buzz buzz buzz / Ooh baby ooh / This heart of mine / Little bird / Give me back my heart / Two little bees / It's love / Your love / Frankenstein's den / Strollin' on the beach / Chains of love / Let's talk it over / Star fell / I'll get by / Just for you / Hollywood Flames / I'll be seeing you / There is something on your mind / So good / Romance in the dark / Much too much
CD CDCHD 420
Ace / Sep '92 / Pinnacle

Hollywood Joe

JACK OF HEARTS
CD WHIT 001
Whitestone / Aug '96 / Nervous

Holm, Michael

MICHAEL HOLM
CD 16005
Laserlight / Aug '92 / Target/BMG

Holman, Bill

BILL HOLMAN BAND (Holman, Bill Band)
CD JD 3308
JVC / Sep '88 / Direct / New Note/ Pinnacle / Vital/SAM

BRILLIANT CORNERS (Holman, Bill Band)
Straight no chaser / Bemsha swing / Thelonious / 'Round midnight / Bye ya / Misterioso / Friday the 13th / Rhythm-a-ning / Ruby, my dear / Brilliant corners
CD JVC 90182
JVC / Jul '97 / Direct / New Note/Pinnacle / Vital/SAM

VIEW FROM THE SIDE, A (Holman, Bill Band)
No joy in mudville / Any dude'll do / But beautiful / Petaluma Lu / I didn't ask / Make my day / Peacock / Tennessee waltz / View from the side
CD JVC 20502
JVC / Aug '95 / Direct / New Note/Pinnacle / Vital/SAM

Holman, Eddie

EDDIE'S MY NAME
This can't be true / You can tell / I surrender / Return to me / Don't stop now / I'll cry 1000 tears / Where I'm not wanted / Hurt / Peace of mind / Never let me go / Been so long / Sexy Ed here wants a lonely girl / Eddie's my name / Sweet memories / Stay mine for heaven's sake / Free country / You know that I will / Am I a loser / I'm not gonna give up / I'll cry 1000 tears (unreleased version)
CD GSCD 031
Goldmine / Dec '93 / Vital

NIGHT TO REMEMBER, A
CD CPCD 8061
Charly / Nov '94 / Koch

Holmes Brothers

JUBILATION
CD CDRW 21
Realworld / Mar '92 / EMI

LOTTO LAND
CD TRIP 7714
Ruf / Apr '96 / Pinnacle

PROMISED LAND
Promised land / Start stoppin' / Train song / Easy access / You're good for me / You got to go / And I love her / There's a train / Got myself together / Thank God for you / New and improved me / I surrender all
CD ROUCD 2142
Rounder / Feb '97 / ADA / CM / Direct

SOUL STREET
CD ROUCD 2124
Rounder / Oct '93 / ADA / CM / Direct

WHERE IT'S AT
That's where it't at / Love is you / You can't hold on to a love that's gone / I've been a loser / Hi-heel sneakers / Worried life blues / Never let me go / Give it up / I've been to the well before / I saw the light / Drown in my own tears
CD ROUCD 2111
Rounder / Jun '95 / ADA / CM / Direct

Holmes, Chris

DAN LOVES PATTI
CD 7567927102
Atlantic / Feb '97 / Warner Music

Holmes, David

LET'S GET KILLED
CD 5391002
Go Beat / Sep '97 / PolyGram

THIS FILM'S CRAP LET'S SLASH THE SEATS
No man's land / Slash the seats / Shake ya brain / Got fucked up along the way / Gone / Atom and you / Minus 61 in Detroit / Inspired by Leyburn / Coming home to the sun
CD 8286312
Go Discs / Jul '95 / PolyGram

Holmes, Richard

AFTER HOURS (Holmes, Richard 'Groove')
Sweatin' / Jeannine / Minor surgery / This here / It might as well be Spring / Moose the Mooche / Groove's bag / Hallelujah, I love her so / After hours / Later / Do it my way / Secret love / Denise
CD CDP 8379862
Pacific Jazz / Jul '96 / EMI

BLUES ALL DAY LONG (Holmes, Richard 'Groove')
CD MCD 5358
Muse / Sep '92 / New Note/Pinnacle

GROOVE'S GROOVE
Grooves groove / California blues / What a wonderful world / Misty / Walking on a tightrope / Slow blues in G / Song for my father / My friend / Lonesome road blues / On say a joy / Danger zone is everywhere / Time has come
CD JHR 73585
Jazz Hour / Apr '95 / Cadillac / Jazz Music / Target/BMG

GROOVIN' WITH GROOVE (Holmes, Richard 'Groove')
Go away little girl / Young and foolish / It's impossible / You've got it bad / Choo choo / How insensitive / Red onion / No trouble on the mountain / Meditation / Good vibration / It's gonna take some time / Grooves groove
CD _______ CDC 9084
LRC / Apr '95 / Harmonia Mundi / New Note/Pinnacle

GROOVIN' WITH JUG (Holmes, Richard 'Groove' & Gene Ammons)
Happy blues (good vibrations) / Willow weep for me / Juggin' around / Hittin' the jug / Exactly like you / Groovin' with jug / Morris the monor / Hey you what's that
CD _______ CZ 257
Pacific Jazz / Jan '90 / EMI

NIGHT GLIDER (Holmes, Richard 'Groove')
CD _______ 500632
Musidisc / Jan '97 / Discovery

SOMETHIN' SPECIAL (Holmes, Richard 'Groove')
Somethin' special / Black groove / Me and groove / Comin' through the apple / I thought I knew you / Carma / Blow the man down / Satin doll
CD _______ CDP 8554522
Pacific Jazz / Mar '97 / EMI

SOUL MESSAGE (Holmes, Richard 'Groove')
CD _______ OJCCD 329
Original Jazz Classics / Dec '95 / Complete/Pinnacle / Jazz Music / Wellard

Holmstrom, Rick

LOOKOUT
CD _______ CDBT 1125
Black Top / Feb '96 / ADA / CM / Direct

Holocaust

HYPNOSIS OF BIRDS
Hypnosis of birds / Tower / Book of seasons / Mercier and camier / Small hours / Into Lebanon / Summer tides / Mortal Mother / Cairnpapple hill / In the dark places of the earth / Caledonia
CD _______ TRMCD 010
Taurus Moon / Apr '93 / Taurus Moon

SPIRITS FLY
CD _______ NM 006CD
Neat Metal / May '96 / Pinnacle

Holroyd, Bob

FLUIDITY & STRUCTURE
CD _______ BHCD 1001
Holroyd / Jul '94 / Direct

STAGES
CD _______ BHCD 2001
Soundscape / Jun '96 / Pinnacle

Holst, Ivan

PA FRI FUD
CD _______ MECCACD 1023
Music Mecca / Nov '94 / Cadillac / Jazz Music / Wellard

Holt, John

1000 VOLTS OF HOLT
Never never never / Morning of my life / Stoned out of my mind / Baby I want you / Help me make it through the night / Mr. Bojangles / I'd love you to want me / Killing me softly / You baby / Too much love / Girl from Ipanema / Which way you going, baby
CD _______ CDTRL 75
Trojan / Mar '94 / Direct / Jet Star

1000 VOLTS OF HOLT
CD _______ RN 7007
Rhino / Sep '96 / Grapevine/PolyGram / Jet Star

16 SONGS FOR SOULFUL LOVERS
I'd love you to want me / You'll never find / Too good to be forgotten / Help me make it through the night / Winter world of love / Killing me softly / If I were a carpenter / Rainy night in Georgia / I'll never fall in love again / Just the way you are / Wherever I lay my hat (that's my home) / Touch me in the morning / Love I can feel / Too much love / When I fall in love / I'll be there
CD _______ PLATCD 16
Platinum / Jul '89 / Prism

20 GOLDEN LOVE SONGS: JOHN HOLT
Never never never / I'd love you to want me / Killing me softly / You will never find another love like mine / When I fall in love / I'll take a melody / Just the way you are / Too good to be forgotten / Dr. Love / Help me make it through the night / Stoned out of my life / Touch me in the morning / I'll be lonely / Too much love / Love so right / Rainy night in Georgia / If I were a Carpenter / Everybody's talkin' / Baby don't get hooked on me / Last farewell
CD _______ CDTRL 192
Trojan / May '90 / Direct / Jet Star

20 GREAT HITS
Looking back / Stick by me / Lost love / Oh girl / Riding for a fall / Everybody needs love / I'll be lonely / Do you love me / Left with a broken heart / Release me / Stealing stealing / Wasted days and wasted nights / Here I come / I love my girl / Wolf and leopard / Born to lose / In the midnight hour / She want it / Homely girl / Party time
CD _______ CDSGP 067
Prestige / Oct '93 / Else / Total/BMG

2000 VOLTS OF HOLT/3000 VOLTS OF HOLT
Doctor love / Yester-me, yester-you, yesterday / Touch me in the morning / Keep on moving / I will / Alfie / I'll take a melody / My guiding star / On a clear day you can see forever / Peace and love / Take away my heart Teresa / For the love of you / Let's get it while it's hot / In the springtime / Till I'm gone / Let's kiss and say goodbye / Winter world of love / Oh what a day / Let's do it long / No place like home / Ungrateful lady / You will never find another love like mine
CD _______ CDTRL 380
Trojan / May '97 / Direct / Jet Star

COLLECTION, THE
CD _______ COL 069
Collection / Feb '95 / Target/BMG

GOLDEN HITS
CD _______ RNCD 2110
Rhino / Jun '95 / Grapevine/PolyGram / Jet Star

GREATEST HITS OF JOHN HOLT
CD _______ SOCD 1115
Studio One / Mar '95 / Jet Star

JOHN HOLT ARCHIVE
Baby I want you / Stealing stealing stealing / My desire / Never never never / Killing me softly with her song / Stoned out of my life / Help me make it through the night / I will / I'll be lonely / I'd love you to want me / My satisfaction / Wooden heart / Which way you going baby / Rainy night in Georgia / Tide is high / You baby / Everybody's talkin' / Doctor Love / Just the way you are / You'll never find another love like mine
CD _______ RMCD 212
Rialto / Sep '96 / Disc / Total/BMG

JOHN HOLT STORY, THE (2CD Set)
CD Set _______ JHCD 1/JHCD 2
Graylan / Jun '97 / Grapevine/PolyGram / Jet Star

LOVE I CAN FEEL
CD _______ SOCD 9017
Studio One / Mar '95 / Jet Star

LOVE SONGS VOL.2
CD _______ EPCD 1
Parish / Apr '92 / Jet Star

PARTY TIME (Holt, John & Dennis Brown)
CD _______ SONCD 0068
Sonic Sounds / Sep '94 / Jet Star

PEACEMAKER
Hey love / I hope we get to love in time / Hey world / Lucy and me pt.1 / Lucy and me pt.2 / I'm not gonna give you up / Peacemaker / You touch my life / Survival time pt.1 / Survival time pt.2
CD _______ CDSGP 049
Prestige / Jun '93 / Else / Total/BMG

PLEDGING MY LOVE
CD _______ RNCD 2019
Rhino / Sep '93 / Grapevine/PolyGram / Jet Star

REGGAE CHRISTMAS ALBUM, THE
CD _______ CDTRL 230
Trojan / Nov '95 / Direct / Jet Star

REGGAE MAX
CD _______ JSRNCD 5
Jet Star / Jun '96 / Jet Star

TIME IS THE MASTER
Time is the master / Everybody Knows / Riding For A Fall / Looking Back / Love is gone / Stick By Me / Lost Love / It May Sound Silly / Again / Oh Girl
CD _______ RNCD 2002
Rhino / Jun '92 / Grapevine/PolyGram / Jet Star

TONIGHT AT TREASURE ISLE
CD _______ RNCD 2081
Rhino / Dec '94 / Grapevine/PolyGram / Jet Star

TREASURE OF LOVE
CD _______ SONCD 0074
Sonic Sounds / Mar '95 / Jet Star

Holt, Nick

NICK HOLT
CD _______ WOLF 120883
Wolf / Jul '96 / Hot Shot / Jazz Music / Swift

Holt, Steve

CATWALK (Holt, Steve Jazz Quartet)
CD _______ SKCD 22032
Sackville / Feb '94 / Cadillac / Jazz Music / Swift

JUST DUET (Holt, Steve & Kieran Overs)
CD _______ SKCD 22025
Sackville / Jul '93 / Cadillac / Jazz Music / Swift

Holy Barbarians

CREAM
CD _______ BBQCD 182
Beggars Banquet / May '96 / RTM/Disc / Warner Music

Holy Gang

FREE TYSON FREE
Free Tyson free / Get chained / Power is my life / Murder as religion / Tyson Vs Washington (FTF) / Sanity fair / Sanity (Karaoke ambient) / Sanity B
CD _______ BIAS 270CD
Play It Again Sam / Sep '94 / Discovery / Plastic Head / Vital

Holy Ghost Inc.

MIND CONTROL OF CANDY JONES
CD _______ EFA 292562
Tresor / Oct '96 / 3mv/BMG / Prime / SRD

Holy Language

CHOOSE YOUR OWN
CD _______ EFA 004152
Space Teddy / Jul '96 / SRD

Holy Moses

NO MATTER WHAT'S THE CAUSE
CD _______ SPV 8476862
SPV / Oct '94 / Koch / Plastic Head

WORLD CHAOS
CD _______ 845700
SPV / Jul '90 / Koch / Plastic Head

Holy Terror

MIND WARS
CD _______ CDFLAG 25
Under One Flag / Oct '88 / Pinnacle

Holywell Ensemble

ENGLISH RHAPSODY, AN
CD _______ BML 010
British Music / Jan '96 / Forties Recording Company

HOWELLS & BRIDGE
CD _______ BML 003
British Music / Jan '96 / Forties Recording Company

Holzman, Adam

ADAM HOLZMAN
CD _______ LIP 890332
Lipstick / Oct '95 / Vital/SAM

BIG PICTURE, THE (Holzman, Adam & Brave New World)
Toxic waste introduction / Iron curtain / Mad cow disease / Longest day / Chaos theory / Second theory / Hot zone / Sky is falling / My game is strong / Comrad Russell / Fred Ex / Failed industrial belt
CD _______ ESC 036532
Escapade / Jun '97 / New Note/Pinnacle

Home

ALCHEMIST, THE
School days / Old man dying / Time passes by / Old man calling (save the people) / Disaster / Sun's revenge / Secret to keep / Brass band played / Rejoicing / Disaster return (Devastation) / Death of the alchemist / Alchemist
CD _______ 4809712
Columbia / Aug '95 / Sony

HOME
Dreamer / Knave / Shady Lady / Rise up / Dear Lord / Baby friend of mine / Western front / Lady of the birds
CD _______ 4844402
Columbia / Jul '96 / Sony

Home

HOME X
CD _______ EJ 10CD
Emperor Jones / Sep '96 / SRD

Home Bru

ROWIN FOULA DOON
CD _______ LDL 1230C
Lochshore / Jul '95 / ADA / Direct / Duncans

Home Grown

THAT'S BUSINESS
CD _______ BHR 045CD
Burning Heart / Jul '96 / Plastic Head

Home Service

EARLY TRANSMISSIONS
CD _______ RGF 28CD
Rgof / May '96 / ADA

WILD LIFE
CD _______ FLED 3001
Fledg'ling / Apr '95 / ADA / CM / Direct

Home T

HOLDING ON (Home T & Cocoa T/ Shabba Ranks)
CD _______ GRELCD 142
Greensleeves / Nov '89 / Jet Star / SRD

Homer & Jethro

WEIRD WORLD OF HOMER & JETHRO, THE (America's Song Butchers)
CD Set _______ RE 2130
Razor & Tie / Jul '97 / Koch

Homesick James

BLUES ON THE SOUTHSIDE
CD _______ OBCCD 529
Original Blues Classics / Nov '92 / Complete/Pinnacle / Wellard

JUANITA
CD _______ APCD 097
Appaloosa / Oct '95 / ADA / Direct / TKO Magnum

JUANITA
Juanita / My baby / Time is growin' near / Lonesome ol' train / Someday baby / Drivin' dog / Careless love / Right life / I can't hold out / Stop that thing
CD _______ ECD 26085
Evidence / Mar '97 / ADA / Cadillac / Harmonia Mundi

Homler, Anna

CORNE DE VACHE (Homler, Anna & Geert Waegeman/Pavel Fajt)
CD _______ VICTOCD 047
Victo / Jul '97 / Harmonia Mundi / ReR Megacorp

Hommage Aux Aines

C'EST LA FACON
CD _______ HAA 1994CD
Hommage / Apr '96 / ADA

Hone, Ged

SMOOTH SAILING
CD _______ LACD 52
Lake / Aug '95 / ADA / Cadillac / Direct / Jazz Music / Target/BMG

THROWING STONES AT THE SUN (Hone, Ged & New Orleans Boys)
Smile darn you smile / Montmartre / Africa blues / Throwing stones at the sun / Tuxedo rag / Maple leaf rag / Ella Speed / I can't sleep / Streamline train / Sobbin' blues / Japansy / Blue blood blues / West End blues / Smiling the blues away / I've got a feeling I'm falling in love / Ukelele lady / Climax rag
CD _______ LACD 28
Lake / Jun '93 / ADA / Cadillac / Direct / Jazz Music / Target/BMG

Honey Boy

LOVE YOU TONIGHT
CD _______ RNCD 2123
Rhino / Nov '95 / Grapevine/PolyGram / Jet Star

Honey Boy Hickling

STRAIGHT FROM THE HARP
CD _______ CMMR 943
Music Masters / Feb '95 / Midland CD Club

Honey Cone

ARE YOU MAN ENOUGH
CD _______ HDHCD 507
HDH / Nov '91 / Pinnacle

Honey Tongue

NUDE NUDES
CD _______ AMUSE 012CD
Playtime / Mar '95 / Pinnacle

Honeybus

AT THEIR BEST
Story / Fresher than the sweetness in water / Ceilings No. 1 / She said yes / I can't let Maggie go / Right to choose / Delighted to see you / Tender are the ashes / She sold Blackpool rock / Black mourning band / He was Columbus / Under the silent tree / I remember Caroline / Julie in my heart / Do I still figure in your life / Would you believe / How long / Scarlet lady / She's out there / Ceilings No.2 / Breaking up scene / Throw my love away / Girl of independent means / She sold Blackpool rock / How long
CD _______ SEECD 264
See For Miles/C5 / Jun '97 / Pinnacle

Honeycombs

HONEYCOMBS, THE
Have I the right / Can't get through to you / I want to be free / Leslie Anne / Colour slide / This year, Next year / That loving feeling / That's the way / It ain't necessarily

so / How the mighty have fallen / I'll cry tomorrow / I'll see you tomorrow / Is it because / She's too way out / Something better beginning / Eyes / Just a face in the crowd / Nice while it lasted / It's so hard / I can't stop / Don't love her no more / All systems go / Totem pole (Instrumental) / Emptiness / Oooee train / She ain't coming back / Something I got to tell you / Nobody but me / There's always me / Love in Tokyo
CD ______ CDEMS 1475
EMI / Feb '93 / EMI

Honeycrack

PROZAIC
King of misery / No please don't go / Go away / Powerless / Genius is loose / Good, good feeling / If I had a life / I hate myself and everybody else / Animals / Samantha Pope / Paperman / Sitting at home / Parasite
CD ______ 4842302
Epic / May '96 / Sony

Honeydippers

BIG E BOOGIE
CD ______ SHA 0112
Shattered / Feb '97 / Cargo / Nervous

Honeymoon Killers

SING SING (2CD Set)
CD Set ______ SFTRI 369
Sympathy For The Record Industry / Jan '97 / Cargo / Greyhound / Plastic Head

Hongjin, Liu

PIPES OF THE MINORITY PEOPLES
CD ______ VICG 50172
JVC World Library / Mar '96 / ADA / CM / Direct

Honing, Yuri

GAGARIN
Beauty of reason / Lodger / Gagarin / Nuku' alofa / On bare feet / Nelson's victory / Miradou
CD ______ AL 73025
Challenge / Mar '97 / ADA / Direct / Jazz Music / Wellard

STAR TRACKS (Honing, Yuri Trio)
Isobel / True colors / Some unexpected visitors / Walking on the moon / Waterloo / Body and soul / Basket case / True colors (reprise)
CD ______ 9920102
Via Jazz / Feb '97 / New Note/Pinnacle

Honkin' Hepcats

RANTIN' RAVIN' AND MISBEHAVIN'
CD ______ HHPC 40CD
Big 10 / Jun '96 / Vital/SAM

Honky

EGO HAS LANDED, THE
Who am I / Love thy neighbor / Hold it / Chains / Whistler / Supertight love / Honky doodle day / Stormy weather / Eazee street / KKK / Karaoke Joe / Eleven brides of Frankeneye / Wha ga do / Oranges and lemons / Goodnight from him
CD ______ 4509954552
WEA / Mar '94 / Warner Music

Honolulu Mountain Daffodils

ALOHA SAYONARA
Avenues and alleyways / Hurricane Marilyn / Electronic alcoholic / Drug dog girl / Rhine women and song / Farenheit 192 / Grungeda / Stigmata non starter / Psychic hitlists victim no.8 / Slaughterhouse blues / Chien d'enfer / Celestial siren / Song of the wind surgeons / Aloha seyonara / Kramer versus Williamson / Bathtime for beelzebub / Free men of mauna loa
CD ______ MISSCD 1991
Mission Discs / Aug '93 / Pinnacle

GUITARS OF THE OCEANIC UNDERGROWTH/TEQUILA DEMENTIA
Hanging on the crosses (by the side of the road) / Wolverine / Electrified sons of Randy Alvev / Guitars of the oceanic undergrowth / Sinner's club / Black car drives south / El muerto / Final solution / Disturbo charger / (I feel like a) Francis Bacon painting / Mule brain / Collector of souls / Also sprach Scott Thurston / Death bed bimbo / Menace in the front / Tequila dementia
CD ______ MISSCD 1992
Mission Discs / Aug '93 / Pinnacle

Honolulu Sunshine Band

BLUE HAWAII
Blue Hawaii / Hilo march / Honolulu march / Sanjornara / Warchant / Aloha oe / Dreams of the island / Hawaii tattoo / Danny boy / Hawaiian island / Wailana / Yellow bird
CD ______ 22516
Music / Feb '96 / Target/BMG

Honor Role

RECORDED HISTORY, THE
CD ______ MRG 041CD
Merge / Apr '97 / Cargo / Greyhound / SRD

Hood

SILENT '88
CD ______ SLR 059CD
Slumberland / Dec '96 / Cargo

STRUCTURED DISASTERS
CD ______ HAPPY 10CD
Happy Go Lucky / Jul '97 / Cargo

Hood, Robert

INTERNAL EMPIRE
CD ______ EFA 292772
Tresor / Aug '97 / 3mv/BMG / Prime / SRD
CD ______ 74321247722
Tresor / Jul '97 / 3mv/BMG / Prime / SRD

NIGHTMARE WORLD VOL.1
CD ______ CHEAPCD 2
Cheap / Oct '95 / Plastic Head / Vital

Hoodlum Priest

BENEATH THE PAVEMENT
Beneath the pavement
CD ______ CPRODCD 25
Concrete Productions / May '94 / Cargo / Plastic Head

Hoodoo Gurus

BLUE CAVE
CD ______ TVD 93455
Mushroom / Oct '96 / 3mv/Pinnacle

CRANK
Right time / Crossed wires / Quo vadis / Nobody / Form a circle / Fading slow / Gospel train / Less than a feeling / You open my eyes / Hypocrite blues / I see you / Judgement day / Mountain
CD ______ LD 9453CD
LD / Sep '94 / Vital

Hooka Hey

FURY IN THE SLAUGHTERHOUSE
CD ______ 0888402
SPV / May '91 / Koch / Plastic Head

Hooker, Earl

PLAY YOUR GUITAR, MR.HOOKER
CD ______ BT 1093CD
Black Top / Aug '93 / ADA / CM / Direct

SWEET BLACK ANGEL
CD ______ MCAD 22120
One Way / May '94 / ADA / Direct / Greyhound

TWO BUGS AND A ROACH
CD ______ ARHCD 324
Arhoolie / Apr '95 / ADA / Cadillac / Direct

Hooker, John Lee

1948-1949
Morning blues / Boogie awhile / Tuesday evening / Miss Pearl boogie / Good business / Mercy blues / Poor Slim / We gonna make / Low down boogie / Cotton pickin' boogie / Must I make / Roll me baby / I've been down so long / Christmas time blues
CD Set ______ KKCD 05
Krazy Kat / Oct '90 / Hot Shot / Jazz Music

ALONE
CD ______ 269 660 2
Tomato / Mar '90 / Vital

ALONE
I miss you so / Jesse James / Dark room / I'll never get out of these blues alive / Boogie chillun / When my first wife left me / Boom boom / One bourbon, one scotch, one beer
CD ______ TBA 13009
Blues Alliance / Aug '96 / New Note/ Pinnacle

ALTERNATIVE BOOGIE (Early Studio Recordings 1948-1952 - 3CD Set)
Come back baby / Forgive me / Streets is filled with women / Moon is rising / Whistle done blown / Turnin' gray blues / She was in Chicago / Lord taketh my baby away / Just like a woman / Throw this old dog a bone / Johnny Lee's mood / Miss Eloise, Miss Eloise / Crying all night / Welfare blues / Johnny Lee's original boogie / She left me by myself / Out the door I went / My baby she's long and tall / No mortgage on my soul / I come to you baby / I rule the den / Great disaster of 1936 / Winding highway / She quit me / How long can this go on / Can I say hello / I had a dream / Me and a woman / Throw my money around / Well I got to leave / I gotta be comin' back / I don't be welcome here / Two voice original mood / Three voice original mood / Johnny says come back / Story of a married woman / Snap them fingers boogie / Lord what more can I do / Baby, please don't go / I'm going away / Hummin' the blues / Johnny Lee and the thing / Slow down your chatter baby / I did everything / Someone to love / There's a day comin' baby / I was beggin' my baby / Nobody to talk to me / I'm gonna whip ya baby / It's a crime and a shame / I met the grindin' man / Louisiana blues for you / Long, long way from home / Sometime / TB's killin' me
CD Set ______ CDEM 1568
Premier/EMI / Feb '96 / EMI

AUDIO ARCHIVE
Dimples / Boom boom / Whiskey and wimmen / Frisco blues / Tupelo / Process / Good rockin' mama / No shoe / I'm in the mood / Dusty road / Boogie chillun / Hard hearted woman / Drug store woman / Hobo blues / Onions / Baby Lee / I'm leaving baby / Trouble blues / Little wheel / Old time shimmy
CD ______ CDAA 035
Tring / Jun '92 / Tring

BEST OF JOHN LEE HOOKER & CANNED HEAT, THE (Hooker, John Lee & Canned Heat)
You talk too much / Burning hell / Bottle up and go / World today / I got my eyes on you / Whiskey and wimmen / Just you and me / Let's make it / Peavine / Boogie chillen no.2
CD ______ DC 871802
Disky / Nov '96 / Disky / THE

BEST OF JOHN LEE HOOKER 1965-1974, THE
CD ______ MCAD 10539
MCA / May '93 / BMG

BEST OF JOHN LEE HOOKER, THE
I'm in the mood / Boogie chillun / Serves me right to suffer / This is hip / House rent boogie / I'm so excited / I love you honey / Hobo blues / Crawlin' kingsnake / Maudie / Dimples / Boom boom / Louise / Ground hog blues / Ramblin' by myself / Walkin' the boogie / One bourbon, one scotch, one beer / Sugar mama / Peace lovin' man / Leave my wife alone / Blues before sunrise / Time is marching
CD ______ MCCD 020
Music Club / Jun '91 / Disc / THE

BLUES BEFORE SUNRISE
CD ______ TKOCD 006
TKO / '92 / TKO

BLUES BROTHER
Boogie chillun / Rollin' blues / I need lovin' / Grinder man / Women in my life / My baby's got something / Momma poppa boogie / Sailing blues / Graveyard blues / Huckle up baby / Alberta / Three long years today / Do my baby think of me / Burnin' hell / Goin' on highway / Sail on little girl, sail on / Alberta No.2 / Find me a woman / Hastings street boogie / Canal street blues / War is over (Goodbye California) / Henry's swing club
CD ______ CDCHD 405
Ace / Nov '93 / Pinnacle

BLUES COLLECTION, THE
Don't look back / Boom boom / Process / Whiskey and wimmen / Mighty fire / Talk that talk / My first wife left me / Wednesday evening blues / Maudie / Birmingham blues / Crawlin' kingsnake / Time is marching / Love is a burning thing / Blues before sunrise / I want to shout / I'm leaving
CD ______ 100322
CMC / May '97 / BMG

BOOGIE CHILLUN
Dimples / Every night / Little wheel / You can lead me baby / I love you honey / Maudie / I'm in the mood / Boogie chillun / Hobo blues / Crawlin' kingsnake / Drive me away / Solid sender / No shoes / Want ad blues / Will the circle be unbroken / I'm goin' upstairs / Boom boom / Bottle up and go / This is hip / Big legs, tight skirt / Serves me right to suffer / Your baby ain't sweet like mine
CD ______ CPCD 8210
Charly / Feb '97 / Koch

BOOGIE CHILLUN
Tupelo / Boogie chillun / Dimples / Drug store woman / Boom boom / Frisco blues / No shoe / I'm in the mood / Hobo blues / Baby Lee / Trouble blues / Old time shimmy / Little wheel / Whiskey and wimmen / Process / Dusty road / Send me your pillow / I'm so excited / Onions / Good rockin' mama / Thelma / Keep your hands to yourself / What do you say / Lost a good girl / Let's make it / Hard hearted woman / I'm going upstairs / I'm leaving baby
CD ______ GRF 023
Tring / '93 / Tring

BOOGIE MAN, THE (4CD Set)
CD ______ CDDIG 5
Charly / Feb '95 / Koch

BOOM BOOM
Boom boom / I'm bad like Jesse James / Same old blues again / Sugar Mama / Trick bag / Boogie at Russian hill / Hittin' the bottle again / Bottle up and go / Thought I heard / I ain't gonna suffer no more / Hobo blues / I want to hug you / House rent boogie / Want ad blues / I'm so excited / Hard headed woman / I wanna walk / Onions / What do you say / She shot me down / Keep your hands to yourself / Dusty road / Send me your pillow / I want to shout / I'm leaving baby
CD ______ VPBCD 12
Pointblank / Oct '92 / EMI

BOOM BOOM
CD ______ CDSGP 066
Prestige / May '93 / Else / Total/BMG

BOOM BOOM
CD ______ 12333
Laserlight / May '94 / Target/BMG

BOOM BOOM
Tupelo / Boogie chillun / Dimples / Drug store woman / Boom boom / Frisco blues / No shoes / Hobo blues / Baby Lee / Trouble blues / Little wheel / Whisky and wimmen / Process / Send me your pillow / Good rockin' Mama / Thelma / She's mine (keep your hands to yourself) / What do you say / Lost a good girl / Let's make it / Hard headed woman / I'm going upstairs / I'm leaving
CD ______ QED 067
Tring / Nov '96 / Tring

BOSS, THE
CD ______ MATCD 320
Castle / Oct '94 / BMG

BOSS, THE
CD ______ PLSCD 124
Pulse / Apr '96 / BMG

BURNIN' HELL
Burning hell / Graveyard blues / Baby, please don't go / Jackson, Tennessee / You live your life and I'll live mine / Smokestack lightnin' / How can you do it / I don't want no woman if her hair ain't longer than mine / I rolled and turned and cried the whole night long / Blues for my baby / Key to the highway / Natchez fire
CD ______ OBCCD 555
Original Blues Classics / Feb '93 / Complete/Pinnacle / Wellard

CHILL OUT
Chill out (things gonna change) / Deep blue sea / Kiddio / Medley: Serves me right to suffer/Syndicator / One bourbon, one scotch, one beer / Tupelo / Woman on my mind / Annie Mae / Too young / Talkin' the blues / If you've never been in love / We'll meet again
CD ______ VPBCD 22
Virgin / Feb '95 / EMI

COLLECTION, THE (20 Blues Greats)
Dimples / I'm in the mood / Hobo blues / Boogie chillun / Boom boom / Blues before sunrise / Time is marching / Tupelo / Little wheel / Shake, holler and run / Want ad blues / Crawlin' kingsnake / Whisky and wimmen / Tease me baby / Wednesday evenin' blues / My first wife left me / Maudie / No shoes / I love you honey / Rock house boogie
CD ______ CCSCD 410
Castle / Feb '95 / BMG

COUNTRY BLUES OF JOHN LEE HOOKER
Black snake / How long blues / Wobblin' baby / She's long, she's tall, she weeps like a willow / Pea vine special / Tupelo blues / I'm prison bound / I rowed a little boat / Waterboy / Church bell tone / Bundle up and go / Good morning little school girl / Behind the plow
CD ______ OBCCD 542
Original Blues Classics / Nov '92 / Complete/Pinnacle / Wellard

CRAWLING KING SNAKE 1948-1952
CD ______ OCD 103
Opal / Nov '95 / ADA

CREAM, THE
Hey hey / Rock steady / Tupelo / You know it ain't right / She's gone / TB sheets / Sugar mama / One room country shack / Drug store woman / I want you to roll me / Bar room drinking / Little girl / Louise / When my first wife left me / Boogie on
CD ______ CPCD 8200
Charly / Feb '97 / Koch

DETROIT BLUES 1950-1952 (The Gotham Titles) (Hooker, John Lee & Eddie Burns)
House rent boogie / Wandering blues / Making a fool out of me / Questionnaire blues / Real gone gal / Squeeze me baby / Feed her all night / Gangsters blues / Where did you stay last night / My daddy was a jockey / Little boy blue / How long must I be your slave / Grieving blues / Ground hog blues / Mean old train / Catfish
CD ______ FLYCD 23
Flyright / Oct '90 / Hot Shot / Jazz Music / Wellard

DETROIT LION, THE
House rent boogie / I'm in the mood / Baby how can you do it / Let's talk it over / Yes, baby, baby, baby / I got the key / Four women in my life / Do my baby think of me / I'm gonna git me a woman / It hurts me so / Bluebird, bluebird, take a letter down South / Boogie chillun / Hello baby / This is 19 and 52, babe / Blues for Abraham Lincoln / Hey
CD ______ FIENDCD 154
Demon / Feb '90 / Pinnacle

DIMPLES (The Best Of John Lee Hooker/Original Hit Recordings)
Dimples / Boom boom / This is hip / I'm in the mood / I love you honey / Crawlin' kingsnake / Boogie chillun / I'm mad agin / Big legs, tight skirt / I'm going upstairs /

Onions / It serves me right to suffer / Send me your pillow / No shoes / I'm so excited / Hobo blues / Maudie / What do you say / She's mine / Don't look back
CD CDGR 151
Charly / Apr '97 / Koch

DON'T LOOK BACK
Dimples / Healing game / Ain't no big thing / Don't look back / Blues before sunrise / Spellbound / Travellin' blues / I love you honey / Frisco blues / Red house / Rainy day
CD VPBCD 39
Pointblank / Mar '97 / EMI

DON'T YOU REMEMBER ME
Stomp boogie / Who's been jivin' you / Black man blues / Poor Joe / Nightmare blues / Late last night / Wandering blues / Don't go baby / Devil's jump / I'm gonna kill that woman / Moaning blues / Numbers / Heart trouble blues / Slim's stomp / Thinking blues / Don't you remember me
CD CDCHARLY 245
Charly / Oct '90 / Koch

ELECTRIC
Onions / Dusty road / I'm in the mood / Blues before sunrise / Baby please don't go / Hobo blues / Boom boom / Whiskey and wimmen / Time is marching / Dimples / I'm so excited / Boogie chillun / Maudie / I'm gonna kill that woman / Slim's stomp / Crawlin' king snake
CD CDBM 117
Blue Moon / Sep '96 / Cadillac / Discovery / Greensleeves / Jazz Music / Jet Star / TKO Magnum

ENDLESS BOOGIE
(I got) a good 'un / Pots on, gas on high / Kick hit 4 hit kix u / I don't need no steam heat / We might as well call it through / Sittin' in my dark room / Endless boogie parts 27 and 28
CD BGOCD 70
Beat Goes On / Feb '90 / Pinnacle

ENDLESS BOOGIE/PLAYS AND SINGS THE BLUES (2CD Set)
(I got) a good 'un / Pots on, gas on high / Kick hit / I don't need no steam heat / We might as well call it through (I didn't get married) / Sittin' in my dark room / Endless boogie / Journey / I don't want your money / Hey baby, you look good to me / Mad man blues / Bluebird / Worried life blues / Apologise / Lonely boy boogie / Please don't go / Hey boogie / Just me and my telephone
CD Set MCD 33726
MCA / Jul '96 / BMG

EP COLLECTION, THE
Madman blues / You know, I know / Leave my wife alone / Down at the landing / Ground hog blues / High priced woman / Love blues / Union Station blues / Louise / One bourbon, one scotch, and one beer / Just me and my telephone / Apologise / Worried life blues / Journey / I don't want your money / Lonely boy boogie / Ramblin' by myself / Sugar Mama / It's my own fault / Women and money / Walking the boogie / Stella Mae / Let's go out tonight / Baby, please don't go
CD SEECD 402
See For Miles/C5 / Jul '94 / Pinnacle

EVERYBODY'S BLUES
Do my baby think of me / Three long years today / Strike blues / Grinder man / Walkin' this highway / Four women in my life / I need lovin' / Find me a woman / I'm mad / I been done so wrong / Boogie rambler / I keep the blues / No more doggin' (aka no more foolin') / Everybody's blues / Anybody's blues / Locked up in jail / Nothin' but trouble (don't take your wife's family in) / I need love so bad / I had a good girl / Odds against me (aka backbiters and syndicators)
CD CDCHD 474
Ace / Jun '93 / Pinnacle

FOLK BLUES OF JOHN LEE HOOKER, THE
Black snake / How long blues / Wobblin' baby / She's long, she's tall, she weeps like a willow / Pea vine special / Tupelo blues / I'm prison bound / I rowed a little boat / Waterboy / Church bell tone / Bundle up and go / Good morning little school girl / Behind the plow
CD CDCH 282
Ace / Nov '93 / Pinnacle

FREE BEER AND CHICKEN
Make it funky / Five long years / 713 blues / 714 blues / One bourbon, one scotch, one beer / Bluebird / Sittin' on top of the world / (You'll never amount to anything if you don't go to) College / I know how to rock / Nothin' but the best / Scratch
CD BGOCD 123
Beat Goes On / Sep '91 / Pinnacle

GET BACK HOME
CD ECD 260042
Evidence / Jan '92 / ADA / Cadillac / Harmonia Mundi

GOLD COLLECTION, THE
CD D2CD 07
Deja Vu / Dec '92 / THE

GRAVEYARD BLUES
War is over (Goodbye California) / Henry's swing club / Alberta / Street boogie / Build myself a cave / Momma poppa boogie / Graveyard blues / Burnin' hell / Sailing blues / Black cat blues / Miss Sadie Mae / Canal street blues / Huckle up baby / Goin' down highway / Sail on little girl, sail on / My baby's got something / Boogie chillun no. 2 / Twenty one boggie / Rollin' blues
CD CDCHD 421
Ace / Sep '92 / Pinnacle

HARD TIMES
Sally Mae / Rock with me / Hobo blues / Should've been gone / Hard times / Hooker's shuffle / I hate the day I was born
CD 3036000962
Carlton / Mar '97 / Carlton

HEALER, THE
Healer / I'm in the mood / Baby Lee / Cuttin' out / Think twice before you go / Sally Mae / That's alright / Rockin' chair / My dream / No substitute
CD ORECD 508
Silvertone / Mar '97 / Pinnacle

HOOKER 'N' THE HOGS (Hooker, John Lee & The Groundhogs)
Mai Lee / Losing you / Little girl / Lay down little dreamer / Don't be messin' with my bread / Lost everything / I cover the waterfront / I don't want nobody else / Storming on the deep blue sea / Crazy mixed up world / Seven days and seven nights / Wandering blues: *Hooker, John Lee* / Goin' mad blues: *Hooker, John Lee* / Black man blues: *Hooker, John Lee* / Helpless blues: *Hooker, John Lee*
CD IGOCD 2059
Indigo / Oct '96 / ADA / Direct

HOOKER SINGS THE BLUES
CD OBCCD 538
Original Blues Classics / Nov '92 / Complete/Pinnacle / Wellard

HOUSE RENT BOOGIE
Mambo chillun / Time is marching / Unfriendly woman / I'm so worried baby / Baby Lee / Road is so rough / Trouble blues / Everybody rockin' / I'm so excited / Crawlin' black spider / Little fine woman / Rosie Mae / You've taken my woman / Mama you've got a daughter / House rent boogie / I'm a stranger / I'm mad again / Hard hearted woman / I wanna walk / Run on / Blues before sunrise / Onions
CD CPCD 8212
Charly / Feb '97 / Koch

I WANNA DANCE ALL NIGHT
CD 500512
Musidisc / Oct '93 / Discovery

I'M IN THE MOOD
Baby Lee / Dimples / Blues before sunrise / I'm goin' upstairs / Thelma / I'm in the mood / Let's make it / Whiskey and wimmen / No shoes / Crawlin' kingsnake / Old time shimmy / Little wheel / Process / Good rockin' mama / When my first wife left me
CD CDSGP 027
Prestige / May '93 / Else / Total/BMG

IT SERVES YOU RIGHT TO SUFFER
Sugar mama / Decoration day / Money, that's what I want / Serves me right to suffer / Shake it baby / Country boy / Bottle up and go / You're wrong
CD BGOCD 335
Beat Goes On / Dec '96 / Pinnacle

JOHN LEE HOOKER (2CD Set)
CD Set R2CD 4007
Deja Vu / Jan '96 / THE

JOHN LEE HOOKER
CD GFS 074
Going For A Song / Jul '97 / Else / TKO Magnum

JOHN LEE HOOKER BOXSET (3CD Set)
Dusty road / My first wife left me / Maudie / Time is marching / Hug and squeeze / Blue before sunrise / Run on / That's my story / I wanna walk / Wenesday evening blues / You're leavin' me baby / I'm a stranger / Old time shimmy / No more doggin' / Solid sender / Syndicator / Tupelo / House rent boogie / Mama, you got a daughter / Tease me baby / Ground hog blues / Leave me alone / Dimples / Boom boom / Bottle up and go / Cry before I go / Back biter and syndicaters / Think twice before you go / I'm in the mood / Little wheel / Want ad blues / Whiskey and wimmen / Crawling king snake / Sugar Mama / Hobo blues / Baby Lee / I love you baby / Trouble blues / I'm so excited / She left me on bended knee / Process / Good rockin' Mama / No shoes / Send me the pillow you dream on / Onions / Frisco / Drug store woman / Let your Daddy ride / Don't you remember me / Boogie chillen
CD Set KBOX 345
Collection / Nov '95 / Target/BMG / TKO Magnum

JOHN LEE HOOKER COLLECTOR'S EDITION
CD DVBC 9012
Deja Vu / Apr '95 / THE

JOHN LEE HOOKER LIVE
CD 269 602 2
Tomato / May '88 / Vital

LEGENDARY JOHN LEE HOOKER
Boom boom / I'm going home / House rent boogie / Hobo blues / I love you honey / One way ticket / Whiskey and wimmen / I'm mad again / I'm in the mood / SDimples / I'm so excited / Dirty groundhog / Sally Mae / No shoes / Boogie chillen / Waterfront / Big legs tight skirt
CD NTMCD 561
Nectar / Aug '97 / Pinnacle

LEGENDARY MODERN RECORDINGS 1948-1954, THE
Boogie chillun / Sally Mae / Hoogie boogie / Hobo blues / Weeping willow boogie / Drifting from door to door / Crawlin' kingsnake / Women in my life / Howlin' Wolf / Playing the races / Let your Daddy ride / Queen bee / Wednesday evenin' blues / I'm in the mood / Tease me baby / Turn over a new leaf / Rock house boogie / Too much boogie / Need somebody / Gotta boogie / Jump me up one more time / Down child / Bad boy / Please take me back
CD CDCHD 315
Ace / Apr '93 / Pinnacle

LIVE AT CAFE AU GO GO
I'm bad like Jesse James / She's long, she's tall, she weeps like a willow / When my first wife left me / Heartaches and misery / One bourbon, one scotch, and one beer / I don't want no trouble / I'll never get out of these blues alive / Seven days
CD BGOCD 39
Beat Goes On / Oct '88 / Pinnacle

LIVE AT SUGARHILL VOL.1 & 2
I can't hold on much longer / Key to the highway / My babe / You been dealin' with the devil / Money / Run on / Matchbox / Night time is the right time / Boogie chillun / I'm gonna keep on walking / TB is killing me / This world (no man's land) / I like to see you walk / It's you I love, baby / Driftin' and driftin' / You're gonna miss me / You're nice and kind to me Lou Della / I want to get married
CD CDCHD 938
Ace / Nov '93 / Pinnacle

LONDON SESSIONS 1965
I don't want nobody else / Storming on the deep blue sea / I'm losing you / Go back to school, little girl / Don't be messing with my bread / Mary Lee / I cover the waterfront / Crazy mixed up world / Seven days / Little dreamer / Lost everything
CD NEBCD 657
Sequel / Jul '93 / BMG

MAMBO CHILLUN (Charly Blues - Masterworks Vol.19)
Mambo chillun / Wheel and deal / Unfriendly woman / Time is marching / I'm so married baby / Baby Lee / Road is so rough / Trouble blues / Stop talking / Everybody rockin' / I'm so excited / I see you when you're weak / Crawlin' black spider / Little fine woman / Rosie Mae / You can lead me baby
CD CDBM 19
Charly / Apr '92 / Koch

MORE REAL FOLK BLUES
This land is nobody's land / Deep blue sea / Nobody knows / Mustang Sally & GTO / Lead me / Catfish / I can't quit you baby / Want ad blues / House rent blues
CD MCD 09329
Chess/MCA / Apr '97 / BMG / New Note/ BMG

MR. LUCKY
I want to hug you / Mr. Lucky / Backstabbers / This is hip / I cover the waterfront / Highway 13 / Stripped me naked / Susie / Crawlin' kingsnake / Father was a jockey
CD ORECD 519
Silvertone / Mar '97 / Pinnacle

NOTHING BUT THE BLUES
I feel good / Baby baby / Dazie May / Stand by / Call it the night / Going home / We are cooking / Lookin' back over my day / Roll and tumble / Bottle of wine / Baby don't do me wrong
CD CDBM 070
Blue Moon / Apr '91 / Cadillac / Discovery / Greensleeves / Jazz Music / Jet Star / TKO Magnum

ORIGINAL FOLK BLUES...PLUS
Boogie chillun / Queen bee / Crawling king snake / Weeping willow boogie / Whistlin' and moanin' blues / Sally Mae / I need love so bad / Let's talk it over / Syndicator / Let your Daddy ride / Drifting from door to door / Baby, I'm gonna miss you / Cold chills / Cool little car / I wonder little darling / Jump me one more time / Lookin' for a woman / Ride till I die
CD CDCHM 530
Ace / Feb '94 / Pinnacle

REAL FOLK BLUES
Let's go out tonight / Peace lovin' man / Stella Mae / I put my trust in you / I'm in the mood / You know, I know / I'll never trust your love again / One bourbon, one scotch, one beer / Waterfront
CD CHLD 19097
Chess/MCA / Nov '91 / BMG / New Note/ BMG

RISING SUN COLLECTION
CD RSCD 001
Just A Memory / Apr '94 / New Note/ Pinnacle

SECOND CONCERT
Put your hand on your hip / Trying to survive / I won't be back no more / She left me on bended knee / You ain't too old to shift them gears / Hobo blues / I wish I could change your ways / Boogie chillen / Crawlin' king snake
CD TBA 130132
Blues Alliance / Jun '97 / New Note/ Pinnacle

SHAKE IT BABY (Charly Blues Masterworks Vol.45)
CD CDBM 45
Charly / Jun '93 / Koch

SIMPLY THE TRUTH
I don't wanna go to Vietnam / I wanna boogaloo / Tantalizing with the blues / I'm just a drifter / Mini skirts / Mean mean woman / One room country shack
CD MCAD 22136
One Way / Oct '94 / ADA / Direct / Greyhound

TANTALIZING WITH THE BLUES
Serves me right to suffer / Shake it up baby / Bottle up and go / Cry before I go / Backbiters and syndicators / Think twice before you go / I don't wanna go to Vietnam / Mini skirts / Mean mean woman / Tantalizing with the blues / I'm just a drifter / Kick hit / I'll never get out of these blues alive
CD MCLD 19033
MCA / Apr '92 / BMG

THAT'S MY STORY (NYC 1960)
CD CDCH 260
Ace / Nov '93 / Pinnacle

THAT'S MY STORY/ FOLK BLUES OF JOHN LEE HOOKER
I need some money / I'm wanderin' / Democrat man / I want to talk about you / Gonna use my rod / Wednesday evenin' blues / No more doggin' / One of these days / I believe I'll go back home / You're leavin' me, baby / That's my story / Black snake / How long blues / Wobblin' baby / She's long, she's tall, she weeps like a willow / Pea vine special / Tupelo blues / I rowed a little boat / Waterboy / Church bell tone / Bundle up and go
CD CDCH 927
Ace / '90 / Pinnacle

THAT'S WHERE IT'S AT
CD CDSXE 064
Stax / Jul '92 / Pinnacle

THIS IS HIP (Charly Blues - Masterworks Vol.7)
Dimples / Every night / Little wheel / Maudie / I'm in the mood / Boogie chillun / Hobo blues / Crawlin' kingsnake / Solid sender / Will the circle be unbroken / Boom boom / Thsi is hip / Big legs, tight skirt / Serves me right to suffer
CD CDBM 7
Charly / Apr '92 / Koch

TWO ON ONE: JOHN LEE HOOKER & MUDDY WATERS (Hooker, John Lee & Muddy Waters)
CD CDTT 3
Charly / Apr '94 / Koch

URBAN BLUES
Cry before I go / Boom boom / Backbiters and syndicators / Mr. Lucky / My own blues / I can't stand to leave you / Think twice before you go / I'm standing in line / Hot spring water / Motor city is burning / Want ad blues
CD BGOCD 122
Beat Goes On / Sep '91 / Pinnacle

VEE JAY YEARS 1955-1964 (6CD Set)
Unfriendly woman / Wheel and deal / Mambo chillun / Time is marching / I'm so worried baby / Baby Lee / Dimples / Every night / Road is so rough / Trouble blues / Stop talking / Everybody rockin' / I'm so excited / I can see you when you're weak / Crawlin' black spider / Little find woman / Rose Mae / You can lead me baby / I love you honey / You've taken my woman / Mama / You got a daughter / Nightmare / House rent boogie / Trying to find a woman / Drive me away / I'm goin' home / Love me all the time / Lou della / Bundle up and go / Wrong doin' woman / Maudie / Tennessee blues / I'm in the mood / Boogie chillun / Hobo blues / Crawlin' kingsnake / I wanna talk / Canal street blues / I'll know tonight / I can't believe / Goin' to California / Whiskey and wimmen / Run on / Solid sender / Sunnyland / Dusty road / I'm a stranger / No shoes / Five long years / I like to see you walk / Wednesday evenin' blues / Take me as I am / My first wife left me / You're looking good to me / You're gonna miss me when I'm gone / Dirty groundhog / She loves my best friend / Sally Mae / Moanin' blues / Hobo / Tupelo / Want ad blues / Will the circle be unbroken / I'm goin' upstairs / I left my baby / Hard headed woman / I'm mad again / Process / Thelma / What do you say / Boom boom / Blues before sunrise / I lost a good girl / She's mine / I got a letter this morning / New leaf / Let's make it / Drug store woman / Old time shimmy / Onions / You know I love you / Send me

your pillow / Big soul / Frisco blues / She shot me down / Take a look at yourself / Good rockin' mama / I love her / No one told me / Don't look back / One way ticket / Half a stranger / Bottle up and go / My grinding mill / I want to ramble / Sadie Mae / This is hip / Poor me / I want to shout / Love is a burning thing / I want to hug you / I'm leaving baby / Birmingham blues / I can't quit you now blues / Stop baby / Don't hold me / Bus station blues / Freight train to my friend / Talk that talk baby / Sometimes baby you make me feel so bad / You've got to walk yourself / Might fire / Big legs / Tight skirt / Flowers on the hour / Serves me right to suffer / It ain't no big thing / She left me one Wednesday / You can run / Your baby ain't sweet like mine / She's long / She's tall / You're mellow
CD Set CDREDBOX 6
Charly / Dec '92 / Koch

VERY BEST OF JOHN LEE HOOKER, THE
Boom boom / Shake it baby / Right time / Dimples / Boogie chillun / Mambo chillun / Wheel and deal / I'm so excited / Trouble blues / Everybody rockin' / Unfriendly woman / Time is marching / I see you when you're weak / I'm in the mood / Will the circle be unbroken / This is hip / Hobo blues / Solid sender
CD 500432
Musidisc UK / Jun '97 / Grapevine/ PolyGram

VERY BEST OF JOHN LEE HOOKER, THE (3CD Set)
High priced woman / Leave my wife alone / Ramblin' by myself / Walkin' the boogie / Love blues / Please don't go / Down at the landing / Mambo chillun / Time is marchin' / Dimples / Every night / Crawlin' black spider / I love you honey / House rent boogie / Trying to find a woman / Maudie / I'm in the mood / Boogie Chillun / Hobo blues crawlin' kingsnake / No shoes / Dirty ground hog / Hobo blues (AKA the hobo) / I'm goin' upstairs / I'm mad again / What do you say / Boom boom / She's mine / Drug store woman / You know I love you / Send me your pillow / Don't look back / One way ticket / Bottle up and go / This is hip / Big legs / Tight skirt / It serves me right to suffer / Stella Mae / One bourbon / One scotch / One beer / Waterfront / Stack O'Lee blues: *Hurt, 'Mississippi' John* / 44 Blues: *Sykes, Roosevelt* / Divin' duck blues: *Estes, 'Sleepy' John* / Gimme a pigfoot: *Smith, Bessie* / Revenue man blues / Sagefield woman blues: *Arnold, Kokomo* / Old times blues: *Martin, Carl* / Cross road blues: *Johnson, Robert* / Harmonica blues: *Terry, Sonny* / Easyrider: *Leadbelly* / Crawling king snake: *Hollins, Tony* / Can't you read: *Big Maceo* / Bad acting women: *Broonzy, 'Big' Bill* / Take a walk with me: *Waters, Muddy* / I got a break, baby: *Walker, T-Bone*
CD Set VBCD 301
Charly / Jul '95 / Koch

VERY BEST OF JOHN LEE HOOKER, THE (2CD Set)
Mambo chillun / Time is marchin' / Dimples / Every night / Baby Lee / Crawlin' black spider / I'm so excited / Mama, you got a daughter / I love you honey / House rent boogie / Trying to find a woman / Maudie / I'm in the mood / Boogie chillun / Hobo blues / Crawlin' kingsnake / Dusty road / No shoes / My first wife left me / Moanin' blues / Dirty groundhog / Hobo blues / Tupelo / I'm going upstairs / I'm mad again / Want ad blues / What do you say / Boom boom / She's mine / Drug store woman / You know I love you / Send me your pillow / Don't look back / One way ticket / Bottle up and go / This is hip / Half a stranger / Birmingham blues / It serves me right to suffer / Big legs, tight skirt
CD Set CPCD 82422
Charly / Oct '96 / Koch

WANDERIN' BLUES
CD MACCD 189
Autograph / Aug '96 / BMG

WATERFRONT GROUNDHOG
CD 3001072
Scratch / Jul '95 / Koch / Scratch/BMG

WHISKEY AND WOMEN
CD IMP 301
Iris Music / Jul '95 / Discovery

Hooker OK

HOOKER OK
CD SP 014
Sweet Pea / May '97 / Cargo

Hooker, William

ARMAGEDDON
CD HMS 2232
Homestead / Aug '95 / Cargo / SRD

ENVISIONING (Hooker, William & Lee Ranaldo)
CD KFWCD 159
Knitting Factory / Feb '95 / Cargo / Plastic Head

GIFT OF TONGUES, THE (Hooker, William & Lee Ranaldo/Andrea Parkins)
CD KFWCD 179
Knitting Factory / Oct '96 / Cargo / Plastic Head

RADIATION
CD HMS 2162
Homestead / Oct '94 / Cargo / SRD

SHAMBALLA (Hooker, William & Thurston Moore/Elliott Sharp)
CD KFWCD 151
Knitting Factory / Feb '95 / Cargo / Plastic Head

Hooligans

LAST CALL
CD SKIZ 002
Skizmatic / Dec '96 / Nervous

Hoopsnakes

HOOPSNAKES
CD MPD 6003
Mouthpiece / Aug '96 / Direct

JUMP IN AND HANG ON
CD MPD 6002
Flying Fish / Nov '94 / ADA / CM / Direct / Roots

Hoosegow

MIGHTY
CD T&M 008
Tradition & Moderne / Nov '96 / ADA / Direct

Hoosier Hot Shots

ARE YOU READY HEZZIE
CD CCD 905
Circle / Jan '94 / Jazz Music / Swift / Wellard

Hooters

HOOTERIZATION
And we danced / Nervous light / All you zombies / Satellite / Karla with a K / Where do the children go / 500 miles / Fightin' on the same side / Day by day / Lucy in the sky with diamonds / Heaven laughs / Brother don't you walk away / Johnny B / She comes in colours / Time after time / Beat up guitar
CD 4854922
Columbia / Oct '96 / Sony

NERVOUS NIGHT
We danced / Day by day / All you zombies / Don't take my car out tonight / Nervous night / Hanging on a heartbeat / Where do the children go / South ferry road / She comes in colours / Blood from a stone
CD 4624852
Columbia / May '94 / Sony

Hootie & The Blowfish

CRACKED REAR VIEW MIRROR
CD 7567826132
Atlantic / Feb '95 / Warner Music

FAIR WEATHER JOHNSON
Be the one / Sad caper / Tuckeris town / She crawls away / So strange / Old man and me / Earth stopped cold at dawn / Fair weather Johnson / Honeyscrew / Let it breath / Silly little pop song / Fool / Tootie / When I'm lonely
CD 7567828862
Atlantic / Apr '96 / Warner Music

Hooton 3 Car

CRAMP LIKE A FOX
CD CDWOOS 2
Out Of Step / Apr '96 / Pinnacle

Hoover

NEW STEREOPHONIC SOUND SPECTACULAR, A
Inhaler / 2 wicky / Wardrobe / Plus profond / Barabas / Cinderella / Nr 9 / Sarangi / Someone / Revolver / Innervoice
CD 4843892
Columbia / Jun '97 / Sony

Hoover, Louis

LOUIS HOOVER
ABC of love / I wanna be around / Lolita / This is all I ask / I got it bad and that ain't good / Keep it cool / Faccia di Luna / Spend a little time with her / On my own / Live, love and learn / It's funny how life can change / Should know better by now / Where in the world am I / Mack the knife
CD JHCD 054
Ronnie Scott's Jazz House / Aug '97 / Cadillac / Jazz Music / New Note/Pinnacle / TKO Magnum

Hope, Bob

BOB HOPE
CD DVGH 7102
Deja Vu / May '95 / THE

BOB HOPE AND HIS CHRISTMAS PARTY 1945
CD VJC 10312
Vintage Jazz Classics / '91 / ADA / Cadillac / CM / Direct

Hope, Elmo

ALL STAR SESSIONS, THE
CD MCD 47037
Milestone / Jun '95 / Cadillac / Complete/ Pinnacle / Jazz Music / Wellard

FINAL SESSIONS, THE (2CD Set)
I love you / Night in Tunisia / Stellations / Pam / Elmo's blues / Somebody loves me / Low tide / Bird's view / Roll on / Roll on / Vi-Ann / Vi-Ann / Toothsome threesome / Grammy / Kiss for my love / Something for Kenny / Punch that
CD Set ECD 221472
Evidence / Sep '96 / ADA / Cadillac / Harmonia Mundi

Hope, Lynn

JUICY (Hope, Lynn & Clifford Scott)
Juicy / Blue and sentimental / Hang out / Stardust / Oo wee / Tenderly / Shu-ee / Very thought of you / Shockin' / Rose room / Cutie / I don't stand a ghost of a chance with you / Little landslide / Full moon / Blue lady / Sands of the Sahara / Fros-tee nite / Body and soul
CD CDCHARLY 280
Charly / Oct '91 / Koch

Hopkin, Mary

EARTH SONG - OCEAN SONG
International / There's got to be more / Silver birch and weeping willow / How come the sun / Earth song / Martha / Streets of London / Wind / Water, paper and clay / Ocean song
CD CDP 7986952
Apple / Jun '92 / EMI

POSTCARD
Those were the days / Lord of the reedy river / Happiness runs (pebble and the man) / Love is the sweetest thing / Y blodyn gwyn / Honeymoon song / Puppy song / Inchworm / Voyage of the moon / Lullaby of the leaves / Young love / Someone to watch over me / Prince en avignon / Game / There's no business like show business / Turn turn turn (to everything there is a) / Those were the days (quelli erano giorni) / Those were the days (en aquellos dias)
CD CDP 7975782
Apple / Oct '91 / EMI

THOSE WERE THE DAYS
Those were the days / Goodbye / Temma harbour / think about your children / Knock knock who's there / Whatever will be will be (Que sera sera) / Lontano degli occhi / Sparrow / Heritage / Fields of St. Etienne / Jefferson / Let my name be sorrow / Kew Gardens / When I am old one day / Silver birch / Streets of London / Water, paper and clay
CD CDSAPCOR 23
Apple / Apr '95 / EMI

Y CANEUON CYNNAR (The Early Recordings)
Tro tro tro / Tami / Yn y bore / Gwrandewch ar y moroedd / Pleserau serch / Draw dros y moroedd / Aderyn llwyd / Y blodyn gwyn / Rhywbeth syml / Tyrd yn ol / Yfory
CD SCD 2151E
Sain / Feb '97 / ADA / Direct / Greyhound

Hopkins, Claude

CLAUDE HOPKINS 1932-34
CD CLASSICS 699
Classics / Jul '93 / Discovery / Jazz Music

CLAUDE HOPKINS 1934-35
CD CLASSICS 716
Classics / Jul '93 / Discovery / Jazz Music

CLAUDE HOPKINS 1937-40
CD CLASSICS 733
Classics / Jan '94 / Discovery / Jazz Music

MONKEY BUSINESS
Three little words / Margie / King Porter stomp / Monkey business / Mandy / Honey / Church Street / Sobbin' blues
CD HEPCD 1031
Hep / Jul '93 / Cadillac / Jazz Music / New Note/Pinnacle / Wellard

Hopkins, David

HEAR THE GRASS/ECHOES FROM THE WORLD OF BAMBOO
CD SM 10822
Wergo / Jun '91 / ADA / Cadillac / Harmonia Mundi

Hopkins, Lightnin'

1946-1960
CD SOB 35242CD
Story Of The Blues / Apr '95 / ADA / Koch

AUDIO ARCHIVE
Just sittin' down thinking / Don't keep my baby long / Tell me pretty mama / Bad luck and trouble / Needed time / Last affair / Santa Fe blues / Someday / Jake head boogie / Glory be / Sometimes she will / Shine on moon / Have you ever loved a woman / Shake that thing / I'm leaving you now / Walk a long time / Bring me my shotgun / Just pickin' / Last night / Mojo hand
CD CDAA 036
Tring / Jun '92 / Tring

AUTOBIOGRAPHY IN BLUES
CD TCD 1002
Tradition / Feb '96 / ADA / Vital

BLUES IN MY BOTTLE
Buddy Brown's blues / Wine drinkin' spo-dee-o-dee / Sail on little girl, sail on / DC-7 / Death bells / Goin' to Dallas to see my pony run / Jailhouse blues / Blues in the bottle / Beans beans beans / Catfish blues / My grandpa is old too
CD OBCCD 506
Original Blues Classics / Nov '92 / Complete/Pinnacle / Wellard

BLUES IN MY BOTTLE/WALKIN' THIS ROAD BY MYSELF
Buddy Brown's blues / Wine drinkin' spo-dee-o-dee / Sail on little girl, sail on / DC 7 / Goin' to Dallas to see my pony run / Jailhouse blues / Blues in the bottle / Beans beans beans / Catfish blues / My grandpa is old too / Walkin' this road by myself / Black gal / How many more years I got to let you dog me around / Baby don't you tear my clothes / Worried life blues / Happy blues for John Glenn / Good morning little school girl / Devil jumped the black man / Coffee blues / Black Cadillac
CD CDCHD 930
Ace / Mar '90 / Pinnacle

BLUES IS MY BUSINESS
CD EDCD 353
Edsel / Apr '95 / Pinnacle

BRAND NEW CAR
CD IMP 303
IMP / Apr '96 / ADA / Discovery

CALIFORNIA MUDSLIDE (AND EARTHQUAKE)
California muslide / Rosie Mae / Los Angeles Blues / Easy on your heels / New Santa Fe / Jesus will you come by here / No education / Antoinette's blues / Change my way of living / Los Angeles boogie / Call on my baby
CD CDCHM 546
Ace / Nov '94 / Pinnacle

CHICKEN MINNIE
CD TKCD 023
Magnum America / Nov '96 / TKO Magnum

COFFEE HOUSE BLUES (Charly Blues - Masterworks Vol.33)
Big car blues / Coffee house blues / Stool pigeon blues / Ball of twine / Mary Lou / Want to come home / Rolling and rolling / Devil is watching you / Please don't quit me / Coon is hard to catch / Heavy snow / Walking round in circles / War is starting again / Got me a Louisiana woman
CD CDBM 33
Charly / Jan '93 / Koch

COLLECTION, THE
CD COL 068
Collection / Feb '95 / Target/BMG

COMPLETE PRESTIGE AND BLUESVILLE RECORDINGS, THE (7CD Set)
CD Set 7PCD 4406
Prestige / Nov '91 / Cadillac / Complete/ Pinnacle

COUNTRY BLUES
CD TCD 1003
Tradition / Feb '96 / ADA / Vital

DOUBLE BLUES
Let's go sit on the lawn / I'm taking a devil of a chance / I got tired / I asked the bossman / Just a wristwatch on my arm / I woke up this morning / I was standing on 75 highway / I'm going to build me a heaven of my own / My babe / Too many drivers / I'm a crawling black snake / Rocky mountain blues / I mean goodbye / Howling wolf / Black ghost blues / Darling do you remember me / Lonesome graveyard
CD CDCH 354
Ace / Nov '93 / Pinnacle

FOREVER 1981
CD 157792
Blues Collection / Feb '93 / Discovery

FREE FORM PATTERNS
Mr. Charlie / To give me time to think / Fox chase / Mr. Ditta's grocery store / Open up your door / Baby child / Cooking's done / Got her letter this morning / Rain falling / Mini skirt
CD CPCD 8208
Charly / Feb '97 / Koch

GOIN' BACK HOME
Shaggy dog / Santa Fe blues / Shinin' moon / I'll be gone / Shake it baby / Goin' back home / Good times / I'm wit' it / Don't wake me / Talk of town / California landslide / Rosie Mae / Easy on your heels / Leave Jike Mary alone / You treat po' lightnin' wrong
CD CDSGP 090
Prestige / Nov '93 / Else / Total/BMG

GOLD STAR SESSIONS VOL.1
CD ARHCD 330
Arhoolie / Apr '95 / ADA / Cadillac / Direct

GOLD STAR SESSIONS VOL.2
CD ARHCD 337
Arhoolie / Apr '95 / ADA / Cadillac / Direct

GOOD ROCKIN' TONIGHT
Big black cadillac / Stool pigeon blues / Leave Jike Mary alone / Don't treat that man way you treat me / Gonna pull a party / Coffee house blues / You treat po' Lightnin' wrong / Short haired woman / Big car blues / I heard my children crying / 'Buked and scorned / I'm gonna meet my baby somewhere / Early morning blues / Get off my toe / Foot race is on / Good rockin' tonight
CD CDBM 118
Blue Moon / Sep '96 / Cadillac / Discovery / Greensleeves / Jazz Music / Jet Star / TKO Magnum

HOOTIN' THE BLUES
CD OBCCD 571
Original Blues Classics / Jul '95 / Complete/Pinnacle / Wellard

HOW MANY MORE YEARS I GOT
How many more years I got to let you dog me around / Walkin' this road by myself / Devil jumped the black man / My baby don't stand no cheatin' / Black cadillac / You is one black rat / Fox chase / Mojo hand / Mama blues / My black name / Prison farm blues / Ida Mae / I got a leak in this old building / Happy blues for John Glenn / Worried life blues / Sinner's prayer / Angel child / Pneumonia blues / Have you ever been mistreated
CD CDCH 409
Ace / Nov '92 / Pinnacle

IN NEW YORK
Take it easy / Mighty crazy / Your own fault, baby, to treat me the way you do / I've had my fun if I don't get well no more / Trouble blues / Lightnin's piano boogie / Wonder why / Mister Charlie
CD CCD 79010
Candid / Oct '93 / Cadillac / Direct / Jazz Music / Koch / Wellard

IT'S A SIN TO BE RICH
Roberta / Katie Mae / Howlin' wolf / It's a sin to be rich, it's a low-down shame to be poor / Y'all excuse me / Just out of Louisiana / Get out your pencil / I forgot to pull my shoes off / Turn on me / Candy kitchen
CD 5175142
EmArCy / Jun '93 / PolyGram

KING OF DOWLING STREET
Mean old twister / LA Blues / Little Mama boogie / Woman, woman (change your ways) / Mistreated blues / Liquor drinking woman / Shotgun blues / Rolling blues / Nightmare blues / Lightnin's boogie (Sis boogie) / Moon is rising / Have to let you go / Come back baby / Short haired woman / Big Mama jump / Thinkin' and worryin'
CD BGOCD 103
Beat Goes On / Sep '91 / Pinnacle

LAST NIGHT BLUES (Hopkins, Lightnin' & Sonny Terry)
CD OBCCD 548
Original Blues Classics / Nov '92 / Complete/Pinnacle / Wellard

LIGHTNIN'
CD ARHCD 390
Arhoolie / Apr '95 / ADA / Cadillac / Direct

LIGHTNIN'
CD OBCCD 532
Original Blues Classics / Nov '92 / Complete/Pinnacle / Wellard

LIGHTNIN' HOPKINS
CD CDSF 40019
Smithsonian Folkways / Aug '94 / ADA / Cadillac / CM / Direct / Koch

LIGHTNIN' HOPKINS (1946-1960)
CD SOB 35242
Story Of The Blues / Dec '92 / ADA / Koch

LIGHTNIN' IN NEW YORK
Take it easy / Mighty crazy / Your own fault, baby, to treat me the way you do / I've had my fun / Trouble blues / Lightnin's piano boogie / Wonder why / Mr. Charlie
CD CCD 9010
Candid / Feb '97 / Cadillac / Direct / Jazz Music / Koch / Wellard

LIVE AT THE RISING SUN
CD RS 0009CD
Rising Sun / Jul '95 / ADA

LONESOME DOG BLUES
Lonesome dog blues / Glory be / Sometimes she will / Shine on moon / Santa / Have you ever loved a woman / Shake that thing / I'm leaving you now / Walk a long time / Bring me my shotgun / Just pickin' / Last night / Mojo hand / Coffee for mama / Awful dreams / Black mare trot
CD GRF 060
Tring / '93 / Tring

LONESOME LIFE
Rainy days in Houston / You just gotta miss me / Pine gum boogie / Wake up the dead / How does it / Got a letter this morning / Stinking foot / Walking and walking / Good as old time religion / Born in the bottoms / Ballin' the Jack / World's in a tangle / Man like me is hard to find
CD CDBM 093
Blue Moon / Jul '92 / Cadillac / Discovery / Greensleeves / Jazz Music / Jet Star / TKO Magnum

MORNING BLUES (Charly Blues Masterworks Vol.8)
Found my baby crying / Letter to my back door friend) / Fishing clothes / Morning blues / Gambler's blues / Wig wearing woman / Lonesome dog blues / Last affair / Lovin' arms / Rock me mama / Mr. Charlie (Part 1) / Mr. Charlie (Part 2) / Play with your poodle / You're too fast / Love me this morning / I'm coming home / Ride in your new automobile / Breakfast time
CD CD BM 8
Charly / Apr '92 / Koch

NOTHIN' BUT THE BLUES
Blues in the bottle / Catfish blues / DC-7 / Death bells / Rock me baby / Shotgun
CD CD 52023
Blues Encore / Aug '92 / Target/BMG

PO' LIGHTNIN'
CD ARHCD 403
Arhoolie / Apr '95 / ADA / Cadillac / Direct

SHAKE IT BABY
Shining moon / I'll be gone / Shake it baby / Back home / Good times / What'd I say / Talk of the town / California landslide / Easy on your heels / Rosie mae / Leave jike mary alone / Don't you treat poor lightnin' wrong / Shaggy do fe blues
CD CWNCD 2013
Javelin / Jul '96 / Henry Hadaway / THE

SHAKE THAT THING
CD 422173
New Rose / May '94 / ADA / Direct / Discovery

SMOKES LIKE LIGHTNING
T model blues / Jackstropper blues / You cook alright / My black name / You never miss your water / Let's do the Susie-Q / Ida Mae / Smokes like lightning / Prison farm blues
CD OBCCD 551
Original Blues Classics / Jan '96 / Complete/Pinnacle / Wellard

SOUL BLUES
CD OBCCD 540
Original Blues Classics / Nov '92 / Complete/Pinnacle / Wellard

SWARTHMORE CONCERT
CD OBCCD 563
Original Blues Classics / Jul '94 / Complete/Pinnacle / Wellard

TEXAS BLUES MAN
Mojo hand / Cotton / Little wail / Hurricane Betsy / Take me back, baby / Really nothin' but the blues / Guitar lightnin' / Woke up this morning / Shake yourself / California showers / Goin' out / Tom Moore blues / I would if I could / At home blues / Watch my fingers / Bud Russell blues / Cut me out baby
CD ARHCD 302
Arhoolie / Apr '95 / ADA / Cadillac / Direct

TEXAS BLUES MAN
CD CD 52005
Blues Encore / '92 / Target/BMG

TEXAS COUNTRY BLUES (Hopkins, Lightnin' & Joel/John Henry)
CD ARHCD 340
Arhoolie / Apr '95 / ADA / Cadillac / Direct

Hopkins, Nicky

REVOLUTIONARY PIANO OF NICKY HOPKINS, THE
Mr. Big / Yesterday / Goldfinger / Don't get around much anymore / Jenni / Acapulco 1922 / You came a long way from St. Louis / Love letters / Unlonely bull / Satisfaction / Paris belles v the llejistry pig
CD 4785022
Columbia / Feb '95 / Sony

TIN MAN WAS A DREAMER, THE
Sundown in Mexico / Waiting for the band / Edward / Dolly / Speed on / Dreamer / Banana Anna / Lawyer's lament / Shout it out / Pigs boogie
CD 4809692
Columbia / Aug '95 / Sony

Hopkins, Rich

DIRT TOWN (Hopkins, Rich & Luminarios)
CD OUT 1182
Brake Out / Nov '94 / Direct

DUMPSTER OF LOVE (Hopkins, Rich & Luminarios)
CD OUT 1212
Brake Out / Aug '96 / Direct

Hopley, David

SEQUENCE SELECTION
CD SAV 238CD
Savoy / Dec '95 / Savoy / THE / TKO Magnum

Hopper

ENGLISH AND FRENCH
Bad kid / Placebo / Nice set up / Oh my heartless / 'Cause I rock / Someone phoned / Germolene / Ridiculous day / Four goodbyes / Interference / Homesick / English and french / Wasted / Joytown
CD FACD 210
Factory Too / Jul '96 / Pinnacle / PolyGram

Hopper & Sinclair

SOMEWHERE IN FRANCE
CD VP 133CD
Voiceprint / Dec '96 / Pinnacle

Hopper, Brian

BEGGARS FARM
Long time / Story / Tomorrow won't be long / Astral plane / Sea / You're not my girl at all / Living in a building / Looking back / Thinking of me / Your lovin' man / You forever
CD VP 145CD
Voiceprint / Apr '97 / Pinnacle

HUGE (Hopper, Brian & Kramer)
Huge: *Hopper & Kramer* / Ten mile mean streak: *Hopper & Kramer* / Tall as the Empire State Building: *Hopper & Kramer* / Terry Southern blues: *Hopper & Kramer* / Texas trombone: *Hopper & Kramer* / Only being: *Hopper & Kramer* / Celine's final breath: *Hopper & Kramer* / Einstein and Hawking: *Hopper & Kramer* / She's everything, Mr H: *Hopper & Kramer* / Waltz of the big brains: *Hopper & Kramer* / Manchester 96: *Hopper & Kramer*
CD BP 248CD
Blueprint / Apr '97 / Pinnacle

Hopper, Hugh

1984
CD MANTRA 061
Mantra / Nov '96 / Cargo / Direct / Discovery

ALIVE (Hopper, Hugh Band)
Glider / Forget the dots / Turfschip enterprise / Double booked / Nomali / Lullaby letter bomb / Hanging around for you / Just in time / Golden section
CD BP 150CD
Blueprint / Aug '96 / Pinnacle

BEST SOFT
CD 1059610
Mantra / Dec '96 / Cargo / Direct / Discovery

HOPPER TUNITY BOX
CD 3012842
Arcade / Feb '97 / Discovery

MERCY DASH
CD 3012802
Arcade / Feb '97 / Discovery

MONSTER BAND (Hopper, Hugh Monster Band)
Golden section / Sliding dogs / Churchy Lily Kong / 12-8 theme / Lily Kong / Nozzles / Tecalemit / Get together
CD 3012782
Arcade / Feb '97 / Discovery

Hopper, Kev

STOLEN JEWELS
CD GHETTCD 4
Ghetto / May '90 / Sony

Horde

HELLIG USVART
CD NB 1282
Nuclear Blast / Mar '95 / Plastic Head

Horiuchi, Glenn

HILLTOP VIEW (Horiuchi, Glenn Trio/ Unit)
CD CD 935
Music & Arts / Oct '96 / Cadillac / Harmonia Mundi

MERCY
CD CD 962
Music & Arts / Apr '97 / Cadillac / Harmonia Mundi

OXNARD BEET
CD 1212282
Soul Note / Sep '92 / Cadillac / Harmonia Mundi / Wellard

Horizon 222

3 OF SWANS
CD CHARRMCD 18
Charrm / Mar '94 / Plastic Head

THROUGH THE ROUND WINDOW
CD HY 39100252
Hyperium / Mar '94 / Cargo / Plastic Head

Horizontal Ladies Club

HORIZONTAL LADIES CLUB
I hate to think / Too blonde to see / Just another Doris Day / ODD equilibrium / God is a girl / Angel baby / Paleface / Be careful what u wish 4 / Fossil / Killing spiders / Nowhere to cry / Unprotected
CD DOMO 710022
Domo / Jun '96 / Pinnacle

Horlen, Johan

DANCE OF RESISTANCE
CD DRCD 260
Dragon / Oct '95 / ADA / Cadillac / CM / Roots / Wellard

Horler, John

GENTLE PIECE
This is my lovely day / Astra / Melancholia / Daisy / All the things you are / My funny valentine / Interlude / Gentle piece / Two bits / Solid silver / Whisper not
CD SPJCD 542
Spotlite / Feb '97 / Cadillac / Jazz Music / New Note/Pinnacle / Swift

LOST KEYS
I'm a fool to want you / Mood river / Abstract no.4 / Waltz / Blue in green / This is my lovely day / Lost keys / Re: Person I knew / Abstract no.2 / Mabel/Gentle peace
CD CHECD 00109
Master Mix / Jun '94 / Jazz Music / New Note/Pinnacle / Wellard

QUIET PIECE
CD SPJCD 542
Spotlite / May '93 / Cadillac / Jazz Music / New Note/Pinnacle / Swift

Horn, Jim

WORK IT OUT
CD 7599259112
WEA / Jan '96 / Warner Music

Horn, Paul

CHINA
CD CDKUCK 080
Kuckuck / Sep '87 / ADA / CM

INSIDE THE CATHEDRAL
Song for friendship / Song for peace / Moscow blues / Song for love / Syrinx / Song for understanding / Song for Eugene / Song for Edward / Song for Marina / Song for Riya / Oche cherrnouiye / Song for Rimsky / Song for Trane
CD CDKUCK 075
Kuckuck / Feb '87 / ADA / CM

INSIDE THE GREAT PYRAMID
Prologue / Inside / Mantra I / Meditation / Mutaz Mahal / Unity / Agra vibrations / Akasha / Jumma / Shah Jahan / Mantra II / Duality / Ustad Isa / Mantra III
CD Set CDKUCK 060/061
Kuckuck / Feb '87 / ADA / CM

INSIDE THE TAJ MAHAL
CD CDKUCK 11062
Kuckuck / Nov '89 / ADA / CM

PEACE ALBUM
CD CDKUCK 110832
Kuckuck / Dec '88 / ADA / CM

Horn, Shirley

CLOSE ENOUGH FOR LOVE
This can't be love / I got lost in his arms / Beautiful friendship / Baby baby all the time / Close enough for love / I wanna be loved / Come fly with me / Once I loved / But beautiful / Get out of town / Memories of you / It could happen to you / So I love you
CD 8379332
Verve / Aug '89 / PolyGram

HERE'S TO LIFE
Here's to life / Come a little closer / How am I to know / Time for love / Where do you start / You're nearer / Return to paradise / Isn't it a pity / Quietly there / If you love me (really love me) / Summer (Estate) / Wild is the wind
CD 5118792
Verve / Jan '92 / PolyGram

I LOVE YOU, PARIS
CD 5234862
Verve / Dec '94 / PolyGram

I THOUGHT ABOUT YOU
Something happens to me / Eagle and me / I got it bad and that ain't good / Our love is here to stay / Isn't it romantic / Summer / Nice 'n' easy / I thought about you / Great city / I wish I didn't love you so / Quiet nights
CD 8332352
Verve / Mar '93 / PolyGram

LIGHT OUT OF DARKNESS (A Tribute To Ray Charles)
Hit the road Jack / Just a little lovin' / You don't know me / Drown in my own tears / Hard hearted Hannah / Georgia on my mind / Makin' whoopee / Green / How long has this been going on / If you were mine / I got a man / Just for a thrill / Light out of darkness / Bye bye love / Sun died
CD 5197032
Verve / Feb '94 / PolyGram

LOADS OF LOVE/SHIRLEY HORN WITH HORNS
Wild is love / Loads of love / My future just passed / There's a boat that's leavin' soon

for New York / Ten cents a dance / Only the lonely / Second time around / Do it again / It's love / That's no joke / Love for sale / Who am I / On the street where you live / Great city / That old black magic / Mack the knife / Come dance with me / Let me love you / After you've gone / Wouldn't it be loverly / Go away little boy / I'm in the mood for love / Good life / In the wee small hours of the morning
CD 8434542
EmArCy / Apr '94 / PolyGram

LOVING YOU
CD 5370222
Verve / Mar '97 / PolyGram

MAIN INGREDIENT, THE
CD 5295552
Verve / Mar '96 / PolyGram

SOFTLY
CD Set APCD 224
Audiophile / Apr '89 / Jazz Music

YOU WON'T FORGET ME
Music that makes me dance / Come dance with me / Don't let the sun catch you crying / Beautiful love / Come back to me / Too late now / I just found out about love / It had to be you / Soothe me / Foolin' myself / If you go / You stepped out of a dream / You won't forget me / All my tomorrows
CD 8474822
Verve / May '91 / PolyGram

Horne, Lena

BEST OF LENA HORNE, THE
I wish I was back in my baby's arms / Love (can change the stars) / I got it bad and that ain't good / Love me or leave me / Honeysuckle rose / Poppa don't preach to me / Why was I born / Lady is a tramp / Lover man / My blue heaven / Can't help lovin' that man / From this moment on / Night and day / What'll I do / Cuckoo in the clock / At long last love / Old devil moon / Good for nothin' Joe / Take me / Nobody knows the trouble I've seen
CD PLSCD 119
Pulse / Dec '96 / BMG

ESSENTIAL LENA HORNE (Horne, Lena & Gabor Szabor)
CD ATJCD 5958
All That's Jazz / Jun '92 / Jazz Music / THE

EV'RY TIME WE SAY GOODBYE
When I fall in love / September song / I wish I'd met you / Fine romance / It could happen to you / Eagle and me / Look to the rainbow / Sing my heart / Roundabout / Joy / Ours / Close enough for love / I won't leave you again / Ev'ry time we say goodbye
CD QED 126
Tring / Nov '96 / Tring

FABULOUS LENA HORNE, THE (22 Hits 1936-1946)
I take to you: *Horne, Lena & Noble Sissle Orchestra* / That's what love did to me: *Horne, Lena & Noble Sissle Orchestra* / Good for nothin' Joe: *Horne, Lena & Charlie Barnet* / You're my thrill: *Horne, Lena & Charlie Barnet* / All I desire: *Horne, Lena & Charlie Barnet* / St. Louis blues: *Horne, Lena & Henry Levine/Dixieland Jazz Group* / Careless love: *Horne, Lena & Henry Levine/Dixieland Jazz Group* / Aunt Hagar's blues: *Horne, Lena & Henry Levine/Dixieland Jazz Group* / Beale Street blues: *Horne, Lena & Henry Levine/Dixieland Jazz Group* / Don't take your love from me: *Horne, Lena & Artie Shaw* / Out of nowhere: *Horne, Lena & Teddy Wilson Orchestra* / Prisoner of love: *Horne, Lena & Teddy Wilson Orchestra* / Stormy weather / What is this thing called love / Ill wind / Mad about the boy / Moanin' low / Where or when / One for my baby and one more for the road: *Horne, Lena & Horace Henderson Orchestra* / As long as I live: *Horne, Lena & Horace Henderson Orchestra* / How long has this been going on: *Horne, Lena & Phil Moore Four* / Frankie and Johnny
CD CDAJA 5238
Living Era / Jun '97 / Select

FEELIN' GOOD
On a wonderful day like today / Take the moment / I wanna be around / Feelin' good / Who can I turn to / Less than a second / Willow weep for me / Girl from Ipanema / Softly as I leave you / And I love him / Hello young lovers / Moon river / I love Paris / Never on Sunday / Somewhere / It's a mad mad mad mad world / What the world needs now is love / Let the little people talk / I get along without you very well / It had better be tonight
CD CDSL 8269
Music For Pleasure / Nov '95 / EMI

LA SELECTION 1936-41
CD 011
Art Vocal / Sep '93 / Discovery

LADY AND HER MUSIC, THE
As long as I live / Good for nothin' / Where or when / Ill wind / Careless love / Beale street blues / I gotta right to sing the blues / Man I love / Prisoner of love / Captain and his men / Haunted town / You're my thrill / St Louis blues / I didn't know about you / That's what love did to me / Don't take your love from me / Stormy weather / Out of nowhere / Hagar's blues / Mad about the boy / One for my baby (and one for the road)
CD PASTCD 7091
Flapper / Jul '96 / Pinnacle

LADY IS A TRAMP, THE
Why was I born / Love me of leave me / Love can change the stars / I wish I was back in my baby's arms / Good for nothing Joe / Old devil moon / I got it bad and that ain't good / Papa don't preach to me / Honeysuckle rose / Lady is a tramp / Lover man / Take me / My blue heaven / Can't help lovin' that man / From this moment on / Night and day / Cuckoo in the clock / What I'll do / At long last love / Nobody knows the trouble I've seen
CD CDSGP 059
Prestige / Aug '93 / Else / Total/BMG

LENA
CD CDPC 7900
Prestige / Aug '90 / Cadillac / Complete/ Pinnacle

LENA GOES LATIN
CD CDMRS 510
DRG / '88 / Discovery / New Note/ Pinnacle

LENA GOES LATIN AND SINGS YOUR REQUESTS
CD LDJ 274945
Radio Nights / Sep '92 / Cadillac / Harmonia Mundi

LENA SINGS THE STANDARDS
I got it bad and that ain't good / Lover man / Love can change the stars / Honeysuckle rose / Night and day / Old devil moon / Why was I born / Poppa don't preach to me / My blue heaven / From this moment on / Love me or leave me / Lady is a tramp / Once in a lifetime / Meditation / Good for nothin' Joe / I wish I was back in my baby's arms / Can't help lovin' that man / Cuckoo in the clock / Stormy weather / Take me
CD 300322
Hallmark / Jul '96 / Carlton

SONG FOR YOU, A
CD ATJCD 5962
All That's Jazz / Oct '92 / Jazz Music / THE

SPOTLIGHT ON LENA HORNE
Close enough for love / Ours / Every time we say goodbye / Fine romance / Round about / September song / Joy / Eagle and me / When I fall in love / Look for the rainbow / It could happen to you / Sing my heart / Don't squeeze me / Whispering / Hesitating blues / Beale Street blues
CD HADCD 129
Javelin / Feb '94 / Henry Hadaway / THE

STORMY WEATHER
Stormy weather / Good for nothin' Joe / Diga diga doo / I can't give you anything but love / Mad about the boy / As long as I live / 'Deed I do / Once in a lifetime / Meantime / Silent spring / Slowin' in the wind / Best things in life are free / Lost in the stars / Now / Wouldn't it be loverly / More than you know / At long last love / Nobody knows the trouble I've seen / Blue prelude / Little girl blue / It's a rainy day / Frankie and Johnny / Lady is a tramp
CD GRF 062
Tring / '93 / Tring

Horne, Marilyn

60TH BIRTHDAY
CD 09026625472
RCA Victor / Oct '94 / BMG

MEN IN MY LIFE, THE
Swinging on a star / Man I love / You're just in love / Blah blah blah/Just in time / Small world / Long before I knew you / Friendship / All the things you are / In the still of the night / Some enchanted evening / I get embarrassed / All through the night / Bewitched, bothered and bewildered / All I ask of you / Little things you do together / Love walked in/Our love is here to stay
CD 09026626472
RCA Victor / Nov '94 / BMG

Hornsby, Bruce

HARBOR LIGHTS
Harbour lights / Talk of the town / Long tall cool one / China doll / Fields of gray / Rainbow's cadillac / Passing through / Tide will rise / What a time / Pastures of plenty
CD 07863661142
RCA / Mar '93 / BMG

HOT HOUSE
Spider fingers / White wheeled limosine / Walk in the sun / Changes / Tango king / Big rumble / Country doctor / Longest night / Hot house ball / Swing street / Cruise control
CD 07863665842
RCA / Aug '95 / BMG

NIGHT ON THE TOWN, A (Hornsby, Bruce & The Range)
Night on the town / Fire on the cross / Across the river / Stander on the mountain / Another day / These arms of mine / Carry the water / Barren ground / Stranded on Easy Street / Lost soul / Special night
CD 74321160012
RCA / Sep '93 / BMG

SCENES FROM THE SOUTH SIDE (Hornsby, Bruce & The Range)
Look out any window / Valley Road / I will walk with you / Road not taken / Show goes on / Old playground / Defenders of the flag / Jacob's ladder / Till the dreaming's done
CD ND 90492
RCA / Nov '90 / BMG

WAY IT IS, THE (Hornsby, Bruce & The Range)
On the Western skyline / Every little kiss / Mandolin rain / Long race / Way it is / Down the road tonight / Wild frontier / River runs low / Red plains
CD 74321444212
RCA / Feb '97 / BMG

Horny Toad

THIRTEEN
Shiver / Youth / Long slow death / Fragile planet / Fire in the sky / Quicksand / Vampire ska / Eggfart / Signify / Ho / Brick / Give to me
CD DOMO 710132
Domo / Apr '97 / Pinnacle

Horo, Krachno

TRADITIONAL BULGARIAN
CD Y 225217CD
Silex / Oct '94 / ADA / Harmonia Mundi

Horo, Slobo

ESMA
CD ZENCD 2401
Rockadillo / Apr '95 / ADA / Direct

Horovitz, Wayne

WAYNE HOROVITZ & ZONY MASH (Horovitz, Wayne & Zony Mash)
CD KFWCD 201
Knitting Factory / Mar '97 / Cargo / Plastic Head

Horse

SAME SKY, THE
And she smiled / Speed of the beat of my heart / Never not going to / You are / Breathe me / You could be forgiven / Don't call me / Sweet thing / Stay / Careful
CD CDP 7489662
EMI / Apr '97 / EMI

Horse Latitudes

HORSE LATITUDES
Oh Caroline / What is more than life / Baby don't go / Harvest days / Thrown away / Building mansions / Northern country lie / I can't stop loving you / Younger generation / Someone / There I go again
CD CDBRED 90
Cherry Red / Sep '90 / Pinnacle

Horseflies

HUMAN FLY
Human fly / Hush little baby / Jenny on the railroad / Rub alcohol blues / Cornbread / Who throwed lye on my dog / I live where it's gray / Link of chain / Blueman's daughter
CD COOKCD 013
Cooking Vinyl / Jan '97 / Vital

Horslips

ALIENS
Before the storm / Wrath of the rain / Speed the plough / Sure the boy was green / Come Summer / Stowaway / New York wakes / Exiles / Second Avenue / Ghosts / Lifetime to pay
CD MOOCD 014
Outlet / Jan '95 / ADA / CM / Direct / Duncans / Koch / Ross

BEST OF HORSLIPS
My Lagan love (downtown) / Dearg doom / Green gravel / Oisin's tune / Bim Istigh ag ol / Johnny's wedding / Daybreak (opening the station) / More than you can chew / King of the fairies / Musical far East / High reel / Flower among them all
CD CMOD 021
Outlet / '89 / ADA / CM / Direct / Duncans / Koch / Ross

BOOK OF INVASIONS, THE
Daybreak / March into trouble / Trouble with a capital T / Power and the glory / Rocks remain / Dusk / Sword of light / Warm sweet breath of love / Fantasia (my lagan love) / King of morning, Queen of day / Sideways to the sun / Drive the cold winter away / Ride to hell / Dark
CD MOOCD 012
Outlet / Jan '95 / ADA / CM / Direct / Duncans / Koch / Ross

COLLECTION, THE
CD MOOCD 025
Outlet / Oct '95 / ADA / CM / Direct / Duncans / Koch / Ross

DANCEHALL SWEETHEARTS
Nightown boy / Blind can't lead the blind / Stars / We bring the Summer with us / Sunburst / Mad Pat / Blind man / King of the fairies / Lonely hearts / Best years of my life
CD MOOCD 007
Outlet / Jan '95 / ADA / CM / Direct / Duncans / Koch / Ross

DRIVE THE COLD WINTER AWAY
Rug muire mac do dhia / Sir Festus Burke/ Carolan's frolic / Snow that melts the soonest / Piper in the meadow straying / Drive the cold winter away / Thompson's cottage to the grove / Ny kirree fo naghtey / Crabs in the skillet / Dennis O'Connor / Do'n oiche i mbeithil / Lullaby / Snow and frosts are all over / Paddy Fahey's / When a man's in love
CD MOOCD 009
Outlet / Jan '95 / ADA / CM / Direct / Duncans / Koch / Ross

GUESTS OF THE NATION
King of the fairies / Flower among them all / Johnny's wedding / Daybreak / Furniture / King of the morning, Queen of the day / Dearg doom / Trouble with a capital T / Man who built America / I'll be waiting / Power and the glory / Speed the plough / Long weekend / Guests of the nation
CD MOOCD 024
Outlet / Jan '95 / ADA / CM / Direct / Duncans / Koch / Ross

HAPPY TO MEET, SORRY TO PART
Happy to meet / Hall of mirrors / Clergy's lanentation / An bratach ban / Shamrock shore / Flower among them all / Bim istigh ag ol / Furniture / Ace and deuce of pipering / Dance to your daddy / High reel / Scalloway rip off / Musical priest / Sorry to part
CD MOOCD 003
Outlet / Jan '95 / ADA / CM / Direct / Duncans / Koch / Ross

HORSLIPS LIVE
Mad Pat / Blindman / Silver spear / High reel / Stars / Hall of mirrors / If that's what you want (That's what you get) / Self defence / Everything will be alright / Rakish Paddy / King of the fairies / Furniture / You can't fool the beast / More than you can chew / Dearg doom / Comb your hair and curl it / Johnny's wedding
CD MOOC 010
Outlet / Jan '95 / ADA / CM / Direct / Duncans / Koch / Ross

HORSLIPS STORY - STRAIGHT FROM THE HORSE'S MOUTH
High reel / Night town boy / Flower among them all / Dearg doom / Faster than the hounds / Best years of my life / Man who built America / Guests of the nation / Daybreak / Everything will be alright / Power and the glory / Sword of light / Warm sweet breath of love / Speed the plough / Trouble with a capital T / Shamrock shore / King of the fairies / High volume love / An bratach ban / Silver spear
CD DHCD 802
Outlet / Feb '95 / ADA / CM / Direct / Duncans / Koch / Ross

HORSLIPS, THE
High reel / Dearg doom / Man who built America / Guests of the nation / Daybreak / Power and the glory / Sword of light / Speed the plough / Trouble (with a capital T) / King of the fairies / An Bratach Ban / Silver spear
CD KCD 450
Celtic Collections / Jan '97 / Target/BMG

LIVE IN BELFAST
Trouble with a capital T / Man who built America / Warm sweet breath of love / Power and the glory / Blindman / Shakin' all over / King of the fairies / Guests of the nation / Dearg doom
CD MOOCD 020
Outlet / Jan '95 / ADA / CM / Direct / Duncans / Koch / Ross

MAN WHO BUILT AMERICA
Man who built America / Tonight / I'll be waiting / If it takes all night / Green star liner / Loneliness / Homesick / Long weekend / Letters from home / Long time ago
CD MOOCD 017
Outlet / Jan '95 / ADA / CM / Direct / Duncans / Koch / Ross

SHORT STORIES TALL TALES
Guests of the nation / Law on the run / Unapproved road / Ricochet man / Back in my arms / Summer's most wanted girl / Amazing offer / Rescue me / Life you save / Soap opera
CD MOOCD 019
Outlet / Jan '95 / ADA / CM / Direct / Duncans / Koch / Ross

TAIN, THE
Setanta / Meave's court / Charolais / March / You can't fool the beast / Dearg doom / Ferdia's song / Gae bolga / Cu chulainn's lament / Faster than the hounds / Silver spear / More than you can chew / Morrigan's dream / Time to kill / March
CD MOOCD 005
Outlet / Jan '95 / ADA / CM / Direct / Duncans / Koch / Ross

TRACKS FROM THE VAULTS
Motorway madness / Johnny's wedding / Flower among them all / Green gravel / Fairy king / Dearg doom / High reel / King of the fairies / Phil the fluter's ball / Come back Beatles / Fab four-four / Daybreak / Oisin's tune
CD _______________ MOOCD 013
Outlet / Jan '95 / ADA / CM / Direct / Duncans / Koch / Ross

TRADITIONAL IRISH MUSIC
CD _______________ MOOCD 021
Outlet / Feb '95 / ADA / CM / Direct / Duncans / Koch / Ross

UNFORTUNATE CUP OF TEA
If that's what you want (That's what you get) / Ring-a-rosey / Flirting in the shadows / Self defence / High volume love / Unfortunate cup of tea / Turn your face to the wall / Snakes' farewell to the Emerald Isle / Everything will be alright
CD _______________ MOOCD 008
Outlet / Jan '95 / ADA / CM / Direct / Duncans / Koch / Ross

Horstall, Des

EASY ROAD
CD _______________ SBDCD 1
Southbound / Oct '96 / Grapevine/ PolyGram

Horta, Toninho

ONCE I LOVED
Pica pau / Lullaby of birdland / Stella by starlight / Waltz for Mariana / My funny valentine / Isn't it romantic / Once I loved / Footprints / Tarde / Minas train
CD _______________ 5135612
Verve / Apr '92 / PolyGram

Horton, Big Walter

ANN ARBOUR JAZZ & BLUES FESTIVAL VOL.4 (Horton, Big Walter & King Biscuit Boys)
Little car blues: *King Biscuit Boys* / Me & the devil blues: *King Biscuit Boys* / Down so long: *King Biscuit Boys* / Cool drink of water blues: *King Biscuit Boys* / Bricks in my pillow: *King Biscuit Boys* / Sweet black angel: *King Biscuit Boys* / It's too bad: *King Biscuit Boys* / Mr. Down Child: *King Biscuit Boys* / Walter's slow blues: *Horton, Big Walter* / Hard hearted woman: *Horton, Big Walter* / Swingin' blues: *Horton, Big Walter* / That ain't it: *Horton, Big Walter* / Trouble in mind: *Horton, Big Walter* / St. Louis blues: *Horton, Big Walter* / Honeydripper (Walter jumps one): *Horton, Big Walter* / It hurts me too: *Horton, Big Walter*
CD _______________ NEXCD 285
Sequel / Aug '96 / BMG

BIG WALTER HORTON WITH CAREY BELL (Horton, Big Walter & Carey Bell)
CD _______________ ALCD 4702
Alligator / May '93 / ADA / CM / Direct

LITTLE BOY BLUE
CD _______________ JSPCD 208
JSP / Jan '88 / ADA / Cadillac / Direct / Hot Shot / Target/BMG

MOUTH HARP MAESTRO
Jumpin' blues / Hard hearted woman / Cotton patch hot foot / I'm in love with you baby / What's the matter with you / Black gal / Go 'long woman / Little boy blues / Blues in the morning
CD _______________ CDCH 252
Ace / Nov '93 / Pinnacle

Horton, Johnny

1956-1960
I'm a one woman / Honky tonk man / I'm ready if you're willing / I got a hole in my pirogue / Take me like I am / Sugar coated baby / I don't like I did / Hooray for that little difference / I'm coming home / Over loving you / She know why / Honky tonk mind (the woman I need) / Tell me baby I love her / Goodbye lonesome, hello baby doll / I'll do it everytime / You're my baby / Let's take the long way home / Lover's rock / Honky tonk hardwood floor / Wild one / Everytime I'm kissing you / Lonesome and heartbroken / Seven come eleven / I can't forget you / Wise to the ways of a woman / Out in New Mexico / Tetched in the head / Just walk a little closer / Don't use my heart for a stepping stone / I love you baby / Counterfeit love / Mr. Moonlight / All grown up / Got the bull by the horns / When it's springtime in Alaska / Whispering pines / Battle of New Orleans / All for the love of a girl / Lost highway / Sam Magee / Cherokee Boogie / Golden Rocket / Joe's been a gittin' there / First train headin' South / Sal's got a sugar lip / Words / Johnny reb / Ole slew foot / They shined up rudolph's nose / Electrified donkey / Same old tale crow told me / Sink the Bismarck / Ole slew foot (CD 3) / Miss Marcy / Sleepy eyed John / Mansion you stole / They'll never take her love from me / Sinking of the Reuben James / Jim Bridger / Battle of Bull Run / Snow shoe thompson / John paul jones / Comanche / Young abe lincoln / O'leary's cow / Johnny freedom / Go north / North to alaska / Rock is / Land line / Hank and joe and me / Sleeping at the foot of the bed / Old blind barnabas / Evil hearted me / Hot in the sugarcane field / You don't move me anymore baby / Gosh darn wheel / Broken hearted gypsy / Church by the side of the road / Vanishing race / Broken hearted gypsy / That boy got the habit / Hot in the sugarcane field / You don't move anymore baby (CD 4) / Church by the side of the road (CD 4) / I just don't like this kind of livin' / Take it like a man / Hank and joe and me (CD 4) / Old blind baranbas (CD 4) / Empty bed blues / Rock Island line / Shake, rattle and roll / A / Sleeping at the foot of the bed / Old dan tucker / Gosh darn wheel (CD 4) / From memphis to mobile / Back up train / Schottische in texas / My heart stopped, trembled and died / Alley gir ways / How you gonna make it / Witch walking baby / Down that river road / Big wheels rollin' / I got a slow leak in my heart / What will i do without you / Janey / Streets of dodge / Give me back my picture and you can keep the frame
CD Set _______________ BCD 15470
Bear Family / May '91 / Direct / Rollercoaster / Swift

ROCKIN' ROLLIN' JOHNNY HORTON
Sal's got a sugar lip / Honky tonk hardwood floor / Honky tonk man / I'm coming home / Tell my baby I love her / Woman I need / First train headin' South / Lover's rock / All grown up / Electrified donkey / Sugar coated baby / Let's take the long way home / Ole slew foot / Sleepy eyed John / Wild one / I'm ready if you're willing
CD _______________ BCD 15543
Bear Family / Oct '90 / Direct / Rollercoaster / Swift

Horton, Pug

DON'T GO AWAY
By myself / Sweetheart o'mine / I'll string along with you / Don't go away / Tipperary / Miss my lovin' time / If / Breezin' along / I can dream / Melancholy / Send a little love my way / I found a new baby
CD _______________ ACD 212
Audiophile / Apr '94 / Jazz Music

Horzu

DIE RITTER DER SCHWARFELRUNDE
CD _______________ MOVE 7015CD
Move / Jul '95 / Plastic Head

Hosokawa, Masahiko

LIKE A SHIMMERING OF HOT AIR (2CD Set)
CD Set _______________ BELLE 96306
Belle Antique / Jun '97 / ReR Megacorp

Hostility

BRICK
CD _______________ CM 77103CD
Century Media / Jan '96 / Plastic Head

Hot Boogie Chillun

SWEETS
She's gone / Leave me alone / You better / I'm coming home / Dirty old man / Fucking sweet / Dirty robber / Shot of love / Talking 'bout you / Yes or no / Have love will travel / He's waiting / Dinosaur
CD _______________ FCD 3045
Fury / May '97 / Nervous / TKO Magnum

Hot Chocolate

COLLECTION, THE
Love is life / You could've been a lady / I believe (in love) / You'll always be a friend / Brother Louie / Rumours / Emma / Cheri babe / Disco queen / Child's prayer / You sexy thing / Don't stop it now / Man to man / Heaven is in the back seat of my cadillac
CD _______________ CDGOLD 1064
EMI Gold / Oct '96 / EMI

GIRL CRAZY
CD _______________ SE 865652
Disky / Mar '96 / Disky / THE

GREATEST HITS
You sexy thing / It started with a kiss / Brother Louie / Girl crazy / So you win again / Put your love in me / Love is life / I'll put you together again / No doubt about it / Every 1's a winner / Emma / I gave you my heart (Didn't I) / You could've been a lady / Don't stop it now / Child's prayer / What kinda boy you looking for (girl) / I believe (In love) / Are you getting enough happiness
CD _______________ CDEMTV 73
EMI / Mar '93 / EMI

GREATEST HITS
Love is life / You could've been a lady / I believe (in love) / You'll always be a friend / Brother Louie / Rumours / Emma / Cheri babe / Disco queen / Child's prayer / You sexy thing / Don't stop it now / Man to man / Heaven is in the back seat of my cadillac
CD _______________ CDMFP 6009
Music For Pleasure / Sep '87 / EMI

GREATEST HITS
So you win again / Put your love in me / Every 1's a winner / I'll put you together again / Mindless boogie / Going through the motions / No doubt about it / Are you getting enough of what makes you happy / Love me to sleep / You'll never be so wrong / Girl crazy / It started with a kiss / Chances / What kinda boy you looking for (girl) / Tears on the telephone / I gave you my heart (didn't I)
CD _______________ CDMFP 6130
Music For Pleasure / Nov '95 / EMI

REST OF THE BEST OF HOT CHOCOLATE, THE
Heaven is in the back seat of my cadillac / Man to man / You could've been a lady / Rumours / Mary Anne / You'll always be a friend / Mindless boogie / Heartache no.9 / Cheri babe / Going through the motions / Blue night / Every 1's a winner / You'll never be so wrong / I'm sorry / Chances / Tears on the telephone / Love me to sleep / You sexy thing (remix)
CD _______________ CDGO 2060
EMI / Sep '94 / EMI

Hot Club De Norvege

PORTRAIT OF DJANGO
CD _______________ HCRCD 83
Night & Day / Feb '97 / ADA / Direct / Discovery

SWINGIN' WITH JIMMY (Hot Club De Norvege & Jimmy Rosenberg)
CD _______________ HCRCD 82
Hot Club / Oct '94 / Cadillac

Hot Damn

HIGH HEELS SLUT
CD _______________ HELLYEAH 031CD
Hell Yeah / Sep '95 / Greyhound / Plastic Head

Hot Gammes

OUVERTURE
CD _______________ IMP 944
IMP / Nov '96 / ADA / Discovery

Hot Knives

WAY THINGS/BLACK (Hot Knives & Liquidators)
CD _______________ PHZCD 82
Unicorn / Sep '94 / Plastic Head

Hot Pastrami

WITH A LITTLE HORSERADISH ON THE SIDE
CD _______________ GV 158CD
Global Village / May '94 / ADA / Direct

Hot Rize

HOT RIZE (Red Knuckles & The Trailblazers)
Travellin' blues / Honky tonk man / Slade's theme / Dixie cannonball / I know my baby loves me / Trailblazers theme / Always late / Honky tonk song / Kansas city star / Waldo's discount donuts / Boot hill drag / Window up above / You're gonna change (or I'm gonna leave) / Long gone John from bowling green / Let me love you one more time / Goin' across the sea / My little darlin' / I've been all around this world / I'm gonna sleep with one eye open / Martha White theme / Sally Goodin / Your light leads me on / Sugarfoot rag / Intro of Red Knuckles and The Trailblazers / Texas hambone blues / Wendell's fly swatters / Oh Mona / Rank stranger / Shady grove
CD _______________ FF 70107
Flying Fish / '89 / ADA / CM / Direct / Roots

HOT RIZE
Blue night / Empty pocket blues / Nellie Kane / High on a mountain / Ain't I been good to you / Powwow the Indian boy / Prayer bells of heaven / This here bottle / Ninety nine years (and one dark day) / Old Dan Tucker / Country boy rock 'n' roll / Standing in the need of prayer / Durham's reel / Midnight on the highway
CD _______________ FF 70206
Flying Fish / Sep '96 / ADA / CM / Direct / Roots

SHADES OF THE PAST (Hot Rize Presents Red Knuckles & The Trailblazers) (Red Knuckles & The Trailblazers)
Travellin' blues / Honky tonk man / Slade's theme / Dixie cannonball / I know my baby loves me / Trailblazer theme / Always late / Honky tonk song / Kansas City song / Waldo's discount donuts / Boot hill drag / Window up above / You're gonna change (or I'm gonna leave) / Long gone John from Bowling Green
CD _______________ SHCD 3767
Sugar Hill / Jul '88 / ADA / CM / Direct / Koch / Roots

TAKE IT HOME
Colleen Malone / Rocky road blues / Voice in the wind / Bending blades / Gone fishing / Think of what you've done / Climb the ladder / Money to burn / Bravest cowboy / Lamplighting time in the valley / Where the wild river rolls / Old rounder / Tenderly calling (Home, come on home)
CD _______________ SHCD 3784
Sugar Hill / Oct '90 / ADA / CM / Direct / Koch / Roots

TRADITIONAL TIES
Hard pressed / If I should wander back tonight / Walk the way the wind blows / Hear Jerusalem moan / Frank's blues / Lost John / Montana cowboy / Footsteps so near / Leather britches / Working on a building / John Henry / Keep your lamp trimmed and burning
CD _______________ SHCD 3748
Sugar Hill / Mar '89 / ADA / CM / Direct / Koch / Roots

UNTOLD STORIES
Are you tired of me darling / Untold stories / Just like you / Country blues / Bluegrass / Won't you come and sing for me / Life's too short / You don't have to move the mountain / Shadows in my room / Don't make me believe / Wild ride / Late in the day
CD _______________ SHCD 3756
Sugar Hill / Mar '89 / ADA / CM / Direct / Koch / Roots

Hot Strings

I SAW STARS
CD _______________ JCD 267
Jazzology / Jun '96 / Jazz Music

Hot Stuff

CELEBRATING EARLY JAZZ
CD _______________ LACD 40
Lake / Feb '95 / ADA / Cadillac / Direct / Jazz Music / Target/BMG

Hot Toddy

THREE SHEETS TO THE WIND
Hogtie's reel / Dinkies / Jenny Dang the weaver / Wing commander Donald MacKenzie / MacArthur Road / Geese in the bog / Seagull / Curlew / New rigged ship / Three sheets to the wind / Jazz's broken bridge / Alessio's / Inverness gathering / Tam Bain's lum / Auld resting chair / Carnival reel / Old grey cat / La bastringue / Waiting for the federales / Walking on the moon / Think of a name for Friday / Neil Gow's lament / Euan's tune / Captain Campbell / Sailor's wife / Kiss for nothing / Troy's wedding / Paddy's leather breeches / Wind that shakes the barley / Carol wood / Glenburnie rant / Roscoff ferry / In and out of the harbour / Atholl highlanders / Long road home / Andy Renwick's ferret / Reconciliation / Dick Gossip's reel / Midshore / Wind on the heath / Cobbler's last waltz
CD _______________ CDLDL 1261
Lochshore / Jul '97 / ADA / Direct / Duncans

Hot Toddy Ceilidh Band

PURELY MEDICINAL
CD _______________ CDLOC 1092
Klub / Apr '96 / ADA / CM / Direct / Duncans / Ross

Hot Tuna

CLASSIC HOT TUNA - ACOUSTIC
CD _______________ REL 2075
Relix / Aug '96 / ADA / Greyhound

CLASSIC HOT TUNA - ELECTRIC
CD _______________ REL 2076
Relix / Aug '96 / ADA / Greyhound

DOUBLE DOSE
Winin' boy blues / Keep your lamp trimmed and burning / Embryonic journey / Killing time in the Crystal City / I wish you would / Genesis / Extrication love song / Talking about you / Funky No. 7 / Serpent of dreams / Bowlegged woman, knock kneed man / I see the light / Watch the north wind rise / Sunrise dance with the Devil / I can't be satisfied
CD _______________ EDCD 397
Edsel / Nov '94 / Pinnacle

HOT TUNA
CD _______________ EDCD 331
Edsel / Jul '91 / Pinnacle

TRIMMED & BURNING
CD _______________ EDCD 396
Edsel / Aug '94 / Pinnacle

Hotel Hunger

AS LONG AS
CD _______________ EIGEN 013CD
Pingo / Dec '94 / Plastic Head

Hotel X

ENGENDERED SPECIES
CD _______________ SST 304CD
SST / Jan '95 / Plastic Head

LADDERS
CD _______________ SST 317CD
SST / Nov '95 / Plastic Head

RESIDENTIAL SUITE
CD _______________ SST 301CD
SST / Jul '94 / Plastic Head

Houdinis

HYBRID
CD _______________ CHR 70004

Challenge / Aug '95 / ADA / Direct / Jazz Music / Wellard

PLAY THE BIG FIVE
CD _______ CHR 70027
Challenge / Nov '95 / ADA / Direct / Jazz Music / Wellard

Houghton Weavers

BEST OF HOUGHTON WEAVERS, THE
Ballad of Wigan Pier / Where do you go from here / We want to work / Martians have landed in Wigan / Blackpool belle / Maggie / All for me grog / Home boys home / When you were sweet sixteen / Rose of Tralee / Old miner / Mist over the Mersey / Room in the sky / Dutchman / On the banks of the roses / God must love the poor / That stranger is a friend / Will ye go lassie go / Success to the Weavers / Mingulay boat song
CD _______ CDSL 8272
Music For Pleasure / Sep '95 / EMI

Houl Yer Whist Folk Band

HISTORICAL FOLK SONGS OF ULSTER
On Boyne's red shore / William's march / My Grandfather died / Orange Maid of Silgo / Lurgan town / Biddy McDowell / Battle of Garagh / Derry's walls / Union crusade / Bleacher / Aghalee heroes / Drowning of Willie Robinson / Crimson Banner
CD _______ OASCD 3005
Outlet / Apr '97 / ADA / CM / Direct / Duncans / Koch / Ross

Houlind, Doc

LIVE AT THE FEMO JAZZ 1996 (Houlind, Doc Ragtime Band & John Boutte)
CD _______ MECCACD 2007
Music Mecca / May '97 / Cadillac / Jazz Music / Wellard

Houmark, Karsten

DAWN (Houmark, Karsten Quartet)
CD _______ STCD 4211
Storyville / May '97 / Cadillac / Jazz Music / Wellard

FOUR (Houmark, Karsten Quartet)
Four / Again and again / Rangoon / Little man / Simple song / Blue planet / B flat for Bob / Waltz for Kenny
CD _______ STCD 4197
Storyville / Mar '95 / Cadillac / Jazz Music / Wellard

Houn, Fred

TOMORROW IS NOW (Houn, Fred & The Afro-Asian Music Ensemble)
CD _______ 1211172
Soul Note / Nov '93 / Cadillac / Harmonia Mundi / Wellard

Hounslow, Keith

ELATION
CD _______ NEW 1033
Australian Jazz / Nov '96 / Jazz Music

House Band

ANOTHER SETTING
CD _______ GL 1143CD
Green Linnet / Jul '94 / ADA / CM / Direct / Highlander / Roots

GROUNDWORK
Trip to amnesia / Diamantina drover / Anti-social worker / For the sake of example / Tornado two-step/The Cooper/The woodpecker / Joy after sorrow / War party / Cobb/Slip jig/The metric fox / Pit stands idle / Here's the tender coming / Four courts/ Fox on the prowl / Major Harrison's fedora
CD _______ GLCD 1132
Green Linnet / Mar '94 / ADA / CM / Direct / Highlander / Roots

ROCKALL
CD _______ GLCD 1174
Green Linnet / Aug '96 / ADA / CM / Direct / Highlander / Roots

STONETOWN
Skepper schotish-schotish fra lyo / Lonesome drunkards walk stonetown / Eliz iza / Sunday's best / New tobacco / Rolling waves ryans / Final trawl / Killybegs highland / Charlie O'Neils / Rond De Loudeac / Here comes the weak / On the turn / Hernons / Phoenix / Geordie / Wals voor polle / Baldazka
CD _______ HARCD 019
Harbour Town / Nov '91 / ADA / CM / Direct / Roots

WORD OF MOUTH
CD _______ GLCD 3045
Green Linnet / Oct '93 / ADA / CM / Direct / Highlander / Roots

House Of Dreams

HOUSE OF DREAMS
CD _______ NAK 6124CD
Naked Language / Jun '94 / Koch

House Of Freaks

INVISIBLE JEWEL
CD _______ OUT 1172
Brake Out / Nov '94 / Direct

TANTILLA
When the hammer came down / Righteous will fall / White folk's blood / Birds of prey / King of kings / Family tree / Sun gone down / Kill the mockingbird / Broken bones / I want answers / Big houses / World of tomorrow
CD _______ 8122708462
WEA / Jul '93 / Warner Music

House Of Love

AUDIENCE WITH THE MIND
CD _______ 5148802
Fontana / Jun '93 / PolyGram

BABE RAINBOW
You don't understand / Crush me / Cruel / High in your face / Fade away / Feel / Girl with the loneliest eyes / Burn down the world / Philly Phile / Yer eyes
CD _______ 5125492
Fontana / Jul '92 / PolyGram

HOUSE OF LOVE
Hanah / Shine on / Beatles and the Stones / Shake and crawl / Hedonist / I don't know why I love you / Never / Somebody's got to love you / In a room / Blind / 32nd Floor / So dest
CD _______ 8422932
Fontana / Jan '96 / PolyGram

HOUSE OF LOVE/SPY IN THE HOUSE OF LOVE (2CD Set))
Hannah / Shine on / Beatles and the Stones / Snake and crawl / Hedonist / I don't know why I love you / Never / Somebody's got to love you / In a room / Blind / Thirty second floor / Se Dest / Safe / Marble / D song '89 / Scratched inside / Phone / Put the fool down / Ray / Love II / Baby teen / Love III / Soft as fire / Love IV / No fire / Love V
CD Set _______ 5286022
Fontana / Aug '95 / PolyGram

SPY IN THE HOUSE OF LOVE, A
Safe / Marble / D song 89 / Scratched inside / Phone / Cut the fool down / Ray / Love / Baby teen / Love 3 / Soft as fire / Love 4 / No fire / Love 5
CD _______ 8469782
Fontana / Oct '90 / PolyGram

House Of Pain

HOUSE OF PAIN
CD _______ XLCD 111
XL / Nov '92 / Warner Music

SAME AS IT EVER WAS
CD _______ XLCD 115
XL / Jun '94 / Warner Music

TRUTH CRUSHED TO EARTH
CD _______ TBCD 1161
Tommy Boy / Oct '96 / RTM/Disc

House, Simon

YASSASIM
Yassasim / Orion / Northlands / Omedlok rides again / Laithwaite stardrive / Neuroscape / Sherwood / Oldayze
CD _______ EBSSCD 115
Emergency Broadcast System / Nov '96 / BMG

House, Son

DEATH LETTER
Death letter / Pearline / Louise McGhee / John the revelator / Empire state express / Preachin' blues / Grinnin' in your face / Sundown / Levee camp moan
CD _______ EDCD 167
Edsel / Dec '90 / Pinnacle

DELTA BLUES (Congress Sessions From Field Recordings)
Levee camp blues / Government fleet blues / Walkin' blues / Shetland pony blues / Delta blues / Special rider blues / Low down dirty dog blues / Depot blues / American defense / Am I right or wrong / County farm blues / Pony blues / Jinx blues
CD _______ BCD 118
Biograph / Jul '91 / ADA / Cadillac / Direct / Hot Shot / Jazz Music / Wellard

FATHER OF THE DELTA BLUES (Complete 1965 Sessions/2CD Set)
Death letter / Pearline / Louise McGhee / John the revelator / Empire state express / Preachin' blues / Grinnin' in your face / Sundown / Levee camp moan / President Kennedy / Down the staff / Motherless children / Yonder comes my mother / Shake it and break it / Pony blues / Downhearted blues
CD Set _______ 4716622
Columbia / Jun '96 / Sony

LIBRARY OF CONGRESS SESSIONS, THE
Levee camp blues / Government fleet blues / Special rider blues / Low down dirty dog blues / Walkin' blues / Depot blues / Camp hollars
CD _______ TMCD 02
Travellin' Man / Apr '90 / Hot Shot / Jazz Music / Wellard

SON HOUSE AND THE GREAT DELTA BLUES SINGERS (1928-1930) (House, Son & The Great Delta Blues Singers)
CD _______ DOCD 5002
Document / Feb '92 / ADA / Hot Shot / Jazz Music

SON HOUSE IN CONCERT
It's so hard / Judgement day / New York central / True friend is hard to find / Preachin' the blues / Change your mind
CD _______ CDBM 020
Blue Moon / '91 / Cadillac / Discovery / Greensleeves / Jazz Music / Jet Star / TKO Magnum

Household Cavalry Band

BEATING RETREAT
CD _______ BNA 5088
Bandleader / Sep '93 / Conifer/BMG

Household Regiment Bands

GUARDS IN CONCERT, THE
Royale / Capital city / La Ronde / Academic festival overture / Arrival of the Queen of Sheba / Phantom of the opera / Intermezzo / Can can for band / Cavalry of the steppes / Entry of the boyards / Les miserables / Slave's chorus / Earl of Oxford's march / Sospan fach / Star of St. Patrick / Great gate of kiev
CD _______ BNA 5042
Bandleader / '91 / Conifer/BMG

Housemartins

LONDON 0 HULL 4
Happy hour / Get up off our knees / Flag day / Anxious / Reverend's revenge / Sitting on a fence / Sheep / Over there / Think for a minute / We're not deep / Lean on me / Freedom / I'll be your shelter (just like a shelter)
CD _______ 8283472
Go Discs / Jan '95 / PolyGram

NOW THAT'S WHAT I CALL QUITE GOOD (Greatest Hits)
I smell winter / Bow down / Think for a minute / There is always something there to remind me / Mighty ship / Sheep / I'll be your shelter (just like a shelter) / Five get over excited / Everybody's the same / Build / Step outside / Flag day / Happy hour / You've got a friend / He ain't heavy, he's my brother / Freedom / People who grinned themselves to death / Caravan of love / Light is always green / We're not deep / Me and the farmer / Lean on me
CD _______ 8283442
Go Discs / Jan '95 / PolyGram

PEOPLE WHO GRINNED THEMSELVES TO DEATH, THE
People who grinned themselves to death / I can't put my finger on it / Light is always green / World's on fire / Pirate aggro / We're not going back / Me and the farmer / Five get over excited / Johannesburg / Bow down / You better be doubtful / Build
CD _______ 8283312
Go Discs / Oct '92 / PolyGram

Housewreckers

FOR A FEW WRECKS MORE
CD _______ GRCD 6050
Goofin' / Nov '96 / Nervous / TKO Magnum

WATCH OUT
CD _______ GRCD 6021
Goofin' / Jan '97 / Nervous / TKO Magnum

Housey Doingz

DOING IT (LIVING IT, LOVING IT, LARGIN' IT)
Poet / Brothers / Piano I / Ride / Flying saucer / Lonely tribe / Ambidextrous left / Piano II / Curly wurly / No smoke: *Matthew B* / Space bunny: *Space Bunny* / Reggae's house: *Francis, Terry* / Lonely / As you cry: *Francis, Terry* / Naff off / Naff on
CD _______ PAGANCD 1002
Pagan / Jul '97 / Vital

Housley, Chris

TIME TO DANCE
CD _______ SAV 184CD
Savoy / May '93 / Savoy / THE / TKO Magnum

Housten, Day

MARIE'S HAEDWALTZ
CD _______ WB 1134CD
We Bite / Sep '95 / Plastic Head

Houston, Cisco

FOLKWAYS YEARS 1944-61
CD _______ SFCD 40059
Smithsonian Folkways / Jun '94 / ADA / Cadillac / CM / Direct / Koch

Houston, Cissy

FACE TO FACE
God don't ever change / Lord will make a way somehow / How sweet it is / I'm somebody / Amazing grace / Too close to Heaven / Without God / Something's bound to happen / Just tell him / Face to face / Go where I send thee / He is the music
CD _______ HBSCD 87007
House Of Blues / Apr '96 / ADA / BMG
CD _______ 70010870072
House Of Blues / Jun '96 / ADA / BMG

MIDNIGHT TRAIN TO GEORGIA (The Janus Years)
CD _______ SCL 2102
Ichiban Soul Classics / May '95 / Koch

Houston, Clint

WATERSHIP DOWN
CD _______ STCD 4150
Storyville / Feb '90 / Cadillac / Jazz Music / Wellard

Houston, Joe

CORNBREAD & CABBAGE GREENS
Cornbread and cabbage greens / Jay's boogie / Blues after hours / Sentimental journey / Celebrity club drag / Gordon's knot / All night long / Ruth's rock / Flying home / Walkin' home / Lester leaps in / I cover the waterfront / Troubles and worries / Huggy boy radio ad / Rockin' and boppin' / She's gone / Anything / Richie's roll / Thom's tune / Teen-age hop / Well, well my love / Mambo / Shake it up / Coastin' / Midnight
CD _______ CDCHD 395
Ace / Mar '92 / Pinnacle

Houston, Penelope

BIRD BOYS
Harry Dean / Talking with you / Voices / Living dolls / Out of my life / Waiting room / Bed of lies / Wild mountain thyme / Putting me in the ground / Full of wonder / Summers of war / Stoli / Rock 'n' roll show / All that crimson
CD _______ NORM 173CD
Normal / Nov '93 / ADA / Direct

KARMAL APPLE
CD _______ NORMAL 183CD
Normal / Dec '94 / ADA / Direct

SILK PURSE
CD _______ RTS 2CD
Normal / Mar '94 / ADA / Direct

WHOLE WORLD, THE
CD _______ NORMAL 153CD
Normal / Mar '94 / ADA / Direct

Houston, Whitney

I'M YOUR BABY TONIGHT
I'm your baby tonight / My name is not Susan / All the man that I need / Lover for life / Anymore / Miracle / I belong to you / Who do you love / We didn't know / After we make love / I'm knockin'
CD _______ 261039
Arista / Nov '90 / BMG

PREACHER'S WIFE, THE (Original Soundtrack)
I believe in you and me / Step by step / Joy / Hold on, help is on the way / Go to the rock / I love the Lord / Who'd imagine a king / Lord is my shepherd / Somebody bigger than you and I / My heart is calling / You were loved / I believe in you and me / Step by step / Joy to the world
CD _______ 74321441252
CD _______ 07822189512
Arista / Dec '96 / BMG

WHITNEY
I wanna dance with somebody (who loves me) / Just the lonely talking again / Love will save the day / Didn't we almost have it all / So emotional / Where you are / Love is a contact sport / You're still my man / For the love of you / Where do broken hearts go / I know him so well
CD _______ 258141
Arista / May '87 / BMG

WHITNEY HOUSTON
How will I know / Take good care of my heart / Greatest love of all / Hold me / You give good love / Thinking about you / Someone for me / Saving all my love for you / Nobody loves me like you do / All at once
CD _______ 610359
Arista / Aug '86 / BMG

Hoven Droven

GROV
Slentbjenn / Timas hans / Myhrpolska / Grovhaling / Tjangel / Okynnesvals / Klarinettpolska / Grottan / Kerstins brudpolska / LP Schottis / Skvadern / Stilla / Jaintlandssangvalsen
CD _______ XOUCD 114CD
Xource / May '97 / ADA / Direct

HIA HIA
Hia hia amour / Farmors brudpolska / Trallpolska / Lillht green / Arepolska / Kjellingen / Kottpolska / Skogspolska / Myhrhalling / Dajmen / Hamburger / Bruvals

CD XOUCD 110
Xource / May '97 / ADA / Direct

Hovercraft

AKATHISIA
Quiet room / Angular momentum / Haloparidol / Vagus nerve / De-orbit burn
CD BFFP 135CD
Blast First / Jan '97 / RTM/Disc

Hovhannessian, Karineh

MUSIC OF ARMENIA VOL.4, THE (The Kanon)
CD 131182
Celestial Harmonies / Nov '96 / ADA / Select

Howard, Adina

DO YOU WANNA RIDE
CD 7559617572
Atlantic / Feb '95 / Warner Music

WELCOME TO FANTASY ISLAND
Welcome to my Queendom / (Freak) And you know it / All about you / Personal freak / Crank me up / Sexual needs / Could've got away / Another level / T-shirt and panties / I'll be damned if I apologise / Don't come too fast / Take me home / Lay him down / Ain't no need / Satisfied
CD 7559620362
Mecca Don/Elektra / Jul '97 / Warner Music

Howard, Camille

ROCK ME DADDY
Boogie and the blues / You don't love me / You used to be mine / Unidentified boogie / Has your love grown cold / Mood I'm in / Gotta have a little lovin' / How long can I go on like this / Cry over you / O sole mio boogie / Within this heart of mine / Boogie in G / I'm blue / Rock me Daddy / Broken memories sad and blue / I ain't got the spirit / Shrinking up fast / Easy / Money blues / Schuberts serenade boogie / You lied to me baby / Real gone Daddy
CD CDCHD 511
Ace / Jan '94 / Pinnacle

Howard, Eddy

EDDY HOWARD
CD CCD 029
Circle / Oct '93 / Jazz Music / Swift / Wellard

Howard, George

ATTITUDE ADJUSTMENT
Watch your back / Best friend / One last time / Diana's blues / Attitude adjustment / Let's unwind / Been thinking / Whole lot of drum in you
CD GRP 98392
GRP / Jan '96 / New Note/BMG

HOME FAR AWAY, A
Miracle / If you were mine / Doria / Till tomorrow / You can make the story right / Grover's groove / No ordinary love / Home far away / For our fathers / Renewal
CD GRP 97802
GRP / Jul '94 / New Note/BMG

VERY BEST AND THEN SOME, THE
Love will follow / Baby come to me / Everything I miss at home / When summer comes / Diane's blues / Home far away / Midnight mood / Cross your mind / Find your way / Love will find a way / Miracle
CD GRP 98852
GRP / Jun '97 / New Note/BMG

Howard, Harlan

ALL TIME FAVOURITE COUNTRY SONGWRITER
Busted / I fall to pieces / Heartaches by the number / Pick me up on your way down / Too many rivers / Everglades / Blizzard / Mary Ann regrets / Call me Mister In-Between / I've got a tiger by the tail / Above and beyond / I don't believe I'll fall in love today
CD 379152
Koch International / Aug '96 / Koch

Howard, Joe

JAZZ HIGHWAY 20
CD PS 007CD
P&S / Sep '95 / Discovery

SWINGIN' CLOSE IN
CD PS 005CD
P&S / Sep '95 / Discovery

Howard, Johnny

BEST OF THE DANSAN YEARS VOL.6, THE (Howard, Johnny Orchestra & Ray McVay Orchestra)
CD DACD 006
Dansan / Jul '92 / Jazz Music / President / Target/BMG / Wellard

FOREVER DANCE (Howard, Johnny & His Orchestra)
CD CDTS 2001
Maestro / Nov '93 / Savoy

Howard, Kid

LAVIDA
CD AMCD 054
American Music / Oct '93 / Jazz Music

Howard, Miki

FEMME FATALE
Good morning heartache / This better earth / Hope that we can be together soon / Shining through / But I love you / Ain't nobody like you / I've been through it / Release me / Thank you for takin' me to Africa / Cigarette ashes on the floor
CD 07599244522
Giant / Oct '92 / BMG

Howard, Owen

SOJOURN
CD 378072
Koch Jazz / Sep '96 / Koch

Howard, Rosetta

ROSETTA HOWARD 1939-47
CD JPCD 1514
Jazz Perspectives / Dec '94 / Hot Shot / Jazz Music

Howe, Greg

GREG HOWE
CD RR 9531 2
Roadrunner / Aug '88 / PolyGram

Howe, Steve

EARLY YEARS, THE (Howe, Steve & Bodast)
Do you remember / Beyond winter / Once in a lifetime / Black leather gloves / I want you / Tired towers / Mr. Jones / 1000 years / Nether Street / Nothing to cry for
CD C5CD528
See For Miles/C5 / May '90 / Pinnacle

HOMEBREW (Unreleased Demos)
CD RPM 164
RPM / Jun '96 / Pinnacle

MOTHBALLED SESSIONS 1964-69
Maybellene / True to me / Howlin' for my baby / What to do / Leave me kitten alone / Don't know what to do / On the horizon / Stop, wait a minute / You're on your own / Why must I criticise / I don't mind / Finger poppin' / Mothballs / You never can stay in one place / Real life permanent dream / Claremount lake / Revolution / Hallucinations / Three jolly little dwarfs / My white bicycle / Kid was a killer / Come over stranger / Beyond winter / Nothing to cry for / Nether street
CD RPM 140
RPM / Oct '94 / Pinnacle

NOT NECESSARILY ACOUSTIC
CD CSA 104
RPM / Jun '95 / Pinnacle

SERAPHIM (Howe, Steve & Paul Sutin)
CD SPV 07689562
SPV / Mar '96 / Koch / Plastic Head

VOYAGERS (Howe, Steve & Paul Sutin)
CD SPV 07689572
SPV / Mar '96 / Koch / Plastic Head

Howell, Carol

MERRY DANCE
CD LCD 8008
Lizard / Aug '96 / Direct / RTM/Disc

Howell, Eddie

MAN FROM MANHATTAN, THE
Happy affair / First day in exile / Miss America / If I knew / Young Lady / Walls / Chicago kid / Man from Manhattan / Can't get over you / Waiting in the wings / Little crocodile / You'll never know / Enough for me / Don't say you love me
CD ZCDEH 014
Zok / Feb '97 / Grapevine/PolyGram / Total/BMG

Howell, Paul

OPUS ONE
CD CDGRS 1288
Grosvenor / May '96 / Grosvenor

Howell, Peg Leg

PEG LEG HOWELL - VOL.1 1926-27
Sadie Lee blues / Too tight blues / Moanin' and groanin' blues / Hobo blues / Peg Leg stomp / Doin' wrong / Skin game blues / Coal man blues / Tashomingo blues / New prison blues / Fo'day blues / New jelly roll blues / Beaver slide rag / Papa stobb blues
CD MBCD 2004
Matchbox / Jan '94 / Cadillac / CM / Jazz Music / Roots

PEG LEG HOWELL - VOL.2 1928-29
Please ma'am / Rock and gravel blues / Low down rounder blues / Fairy blues / Banjo blues / Turkey buzzard blues / Turtle dove blues / Walkin' blues / Broke and hungry / Rolling Mill blues / Ball and chain blues / Monkey man blues / Chittlin' supper / Away from home
CD MBCD 2005
Matchbox / Jan '94 / Cadillac / CM / Jazz Music / Roots

Howie B

MUSIC FOR BABIES
Music for babies / Cry / Shag / Allergy / Away again / How to suckie / Here comes the tooth / On the way
CD 5294642
Polydor / Mar '96 / PolyGram

TURN THE DARK OFF
Fizzy in my mouth/Your mouth / Hopscotch / Switch / Sore brown eyes / Take your partner by the hand: *Howie B & Robbie Robertson* / Limbo / Angels go bald too / Who's got the bacon / Baby sweetcorn (come here) / Butt meat
CD 5379342
Polydor / Jul '97 / PolyGram

Howie, Simon

SIMON HOWIE & HIS SCOTTISH DANCE BAND
CD SHCD 001
Howie / Jul '96 / Duncans

Howle, Danielle

ABOUT TO BURST
CD SMR 36CD
Simple Machines / Jun '96 / SRD

Howlin' Wolf

AIN'T GONNA BE YOUR DOG (2CD Set)
Look-a-here baby / California blues / Worried all the time / Everybody's in the mood / Color and kind / Dorothy Mae / Sweet woman / Decoration day / Oh red / I'm not joking / Highway my friend / Hold your money / California blues / Stay here 'til my baby comes back / Come to me baby / So glad / Bluebird / My life / You ought to know / Nature / Walk to camp hall / Poor boy / My baby told me / Midnight blues / You can't put me out / Getting late / Wolf in the mood / My people's gone / Mama's baby / Tail dragger / Long green stuff / Joy to my soul / Poor wind that never change / Pop it to me / I had a dream / Big house / Tired of crying / Rollin' and tumblin' / More Howlin' Wolf talks / I ain't gonna be your dog no more / Woke up this morning / Ain't going down that dirt road
CD Set MCD 09349
Chess/MCA / Apr '97 / BMG / New Note/ BMG

AUDIO ARCHIVE
Little red rooster / Moanin' at midnight / Down in the bottom / My life / Shake for me / Commit a crime / Back door man / You'll be mine / Highway 49 / Who's been talkin' / Goin' back home / Howlin' for my baby / Wang dang doodle / Tell me / Country sugar mama / Little baby / Hold onto your money / Spoonful / Built for comfort / Goin' down slow
CD CDAA 031
Tring / Jun '92 / Tring

COMPLETE RECORDINGS 1951-1967 (7CD Set)
Moaning at midnight / How many more years / Wolf is at your door (Howlin' for my baby) / Howlin' Wolf boogie / Getting old and gray / Mr. Highway man / Saddle my pony / Worried all the time / Oh red / My last affair / Baby ride with me (ridin' in the moonlight) / California boogie / Look a here baby / Everybody's in the mood / Color and kind / Bluebird / Sweet woman / Well that's alright / Decoration day / Dorothy Mae / Come back home / Smile at me / California blues / My baby walked off / My troubles and me / Chocolate drop / Drinkin' CV wine / Baby ride with me / I've got a woman / Just my kind / Work for your money / I'm not joking / Mama died and left me / Highway be my friend / Hold to your money / Streamline woman / Stay here 'till my baby comes / Crazy about you baby / All night boogie / I love my baby / No place to go / Neighbors / I'm the wolf / Rockin' daddy / Baby how long / Evil / I'll be around / Forty four / Who will be next / I have a little girl / Come to me baby / Don't mess with me baby / Smokestack lightnin' / You can't be beat / I asked for water (she gave me gasoline) / So glad / Break of day / Natchez burning / Going back home / My life / You ought to know / Who's been talkin' / Tell me / Somebody in my home / Nature / Walk to camp hall / Poor boy / My baby told me / Sittin' on top of the world / Howlin' blues / I better go now / I didn't know / Moaning for my baby / I'm leaving you / Can't put me out / Change my way / Getting late / I've been abused / Howlin' for my darling / My people's gone / Mr. Airplane man / Wang dang doodle / Back door man / Spoonful / Little baby / Down in the bottom / Shake for me / Little red rooster / You'll be mine / Just like I treat you / I ain't superstitious / Goin' down slow / Mama's baby / Do the do / Tail dragger / Long green stuff / Sugar mama / May I have a talk with you / Hidden charms / 300 pounds of joy / Joy to my soul / Built for comfort / Love me darlin' / Killing floor / My country sugar mama / Louise / I walked from Dallas / Tell me what I've done / Don't laugh at me / Ooh baby / Hold me / Poor wind that never change / New crawlin' king snake / My mind is ramblin' / Commit a crime / Pop it to me / I had a dream / Dust my broom / Mary Sue / Hard luck / Tired of crying / You gonna wreck my life / I'm leavin' you / You can't put me out / Wolf in the mood / Rollin' and tumblin' / Ain't goin' down that dirt road / Conversation
CD Set CDREDBOX 7
Charly / Jun '93 / Koch

GENUINE ARTICLE, THE (The Best Of Howlin' Wolf)
Moanin' at midnight / How many more years / I'm the wolf / Baby how long / Evil / Forty four / Smokestack lightnin' / I asked for water (she gave me gasoline) / Natchez burning / Who's been talkin' / Sittin' on top of the world / I've been abused / Howlin' for my baby (darling) / Wang dang doodle / Back door man / Spoonful / Down in the bottom / Little red rooster / I ain't superstitious / Goin' down slow / 300 pounds of joy / Killing floor / Dust my broom / Ain't goin' down that dirt road
CD MCD 11073
Chess/MCA / Apr '97 / BMG / New Note/ BMG

HIS BEST
CD MCD 09375
Chess/MCA / Jul '97 / BMG / New Note/ BMG

HOWLIN' AT THE SUN
Baby ride with me / How many more years / California boogie / Look a here baby / Smile at me / My baby walked off / My troubles and me / Mr. Highway man / Chocolate drop / Everybody's in the mood / Colour and kind / Bluebird / Dorothy Mae / Sweet woman (I got a woman) / Well that's alright / Decoration day / Oh red / Drinkin' CV wine / My last affair / Come back home / California blues
CD CPCD 8235
Charly / Jan '97 / Koch

HOWLIN' FOR MY BABY
My baby walked off / Smile at me / Bluebird blues / Everybody's in the mood / Chocolate drop / Come back home / Dorothy Mae / Highwayman / Oh Red / My last affair / Howlin' for my baby / Sweet woman / CV wine blues / Look-a-here baby / Decoration day / Well that's alright / California blues / My troubles and me / California boogie
CD CDCHARLY 66
Charly / Apr '87 / Koch

HOWLIN' WOLF COLLECTOR'S EDITION
CD DVBC 9022
Deja Vu / Apr '95 / THE

I AM THE WOLF
I've got a woman / Just my kind / Work for your money / All night boogie / I love you baby / No place to go / Neighbours / I am the wolf / Rockin' daddy / Baby how long / I'll be around / Who will be next / I have a little girl / You can't be beat / Goin' back home / My life / You ought to know / Tell me / Somebody in my home / Nature / Poor boy / My baby told me / Little baby / I ain't superstitious
CD CDRED 32
Charly / Jan '92 / Koch

KILLING FLOOR
Highway 49 / Dust my broom / Rockin' the blues / Forty-four / Do the do / Little red rooster / All my life / I didn't mean to hurt your feelings / Howlin' for my darlin' / Commit a crime / Wang dang doodle / Built for comfort / Killing floor / Poor boy / Worried 'bout you / Going down slow
CD CDBM 121
Blue Moon / Oct '96 / Cadillac / Discovery / Greensleeves / Jazz Music / Jet Star / TKO Magnum

LEGENDARY MASTERS SERIES, THE
CD COLLECT 3CD
Aim / Oct '95 / ADA / Direct / Jazz Music

LIVE IN CAMBRIDGE, MASS. 1966
CD 422329
Last Call / Feb '97 / Cargo / Direct / Discovery

MEMPHIS DAYS VOL.1 (Definitive Edition)
Oh red / My last affair / Come back home / California boogie / California blues / Look-a-here baby / Smile at me / My baby walked off / Drinkin' CV wine / My troubles and me / Chocolate drop / Mr. Highwayman / Bluebird blues / Color and kind / Everybody's in the mood / Dorothy Mae / I got a woman / Decoration day / Well that's alright / How many more years / Baby ride with me
CD BCD 15460
Bear Family / Apr '89 / Direct / Rollercoaster / Swift

MEMPHIS DAYS VOL.2 (Definitive Edition)
Baby ride with me / How many more years / Moanin' at midnight / Howlin' Wolf boogie / Wolf is at your door (howlin' for my baby) / Mr. Highwayman / Gettin' old and grey / Worried all the time / Saddle my pony / Oh red / My last affair / Come back home / Dorothy Mae / Oh red

CD BCD 15500
Bear Family / Sep '90 / Direct / Rollercoaster / Swift

MOANIN' AND HOWLIN'
Moanin' at midnight / How many more years / Evil / Forty four / Smokestack Lightnin' / I asked for water (she gave me gasoline) / Natchez burning / Bluebird / Who's been talkin' / Walk to camp hall / Sittin' on top of the world / Howlin' for my baby / Wang dang doodle / Back door man / Spoonful / Down in the bottom / Shake for me / Little red rooster / You'll be mine / Goin' down slow / Tail dragger / 300 pounds of joy / Built for comfort / Killing floor
CD CDRED 3
Charly / Oct '88 / Koch

POWER OF THE VOICE, THE
I ain't superstitious / Sittin' on top of the world / Built for comfort / Little red rooster / Highway 49 / Cause of it all / Killing floor / Brown skin woman / Sun is rising / I'm the wolf / House rockin' boogie / Dog me around / Keep what you got / My baby stole off / Crying at day break / Passing by blues / Poor boy / Commit a crime / Wang dang doodle / Do the do / Worried about my baby / Rockin' daddy
CD CD 52002
Blues Encore / '92 / Target/BMG

REAL FOLK BLUES
Killing floor / Louise / Poor boy / Sittin' on top of the world / Nature / My country sugar mama (aka Sugar Mama) / Tail dragger / 300 pounds of joy / Natchez burning / Built for comfort / Ooh baby, hold me / Tell me what I've done
CD CHLD 19098
Chess/MCA / Nov '92 / BMG / New Note/BMG

RED ROOSTER
CD IMP 302
Iris Music / Jul '95 / Discovery

RED ROOSTER, THE
Shake for me / Little red rooster / You'll be mine / Who's been talkin' / Wang dang doodle / Little baby / Spoonful / Goin' down slow / Down in the bottom / Back door man / Howlin' for my baby / Tell me / My baby walked off / Killing floor / Country sugar mama / My life / Goin' back home / Louise / Highway 49 / Hold onto your money / Built for comfort / I ain't superstitious / My last affair / Dorothy Mae / Commit a crime / Moanin' at midnight
CD GRF 026
Tring / '93 / Tring

RIDES AGAIN
House rockin' boogie / Crying at daybreak / Keep what you got / Dog me around / Moanin' at midnight / Chocolate drop / My baby stole off / I want your picture / Passing by blues / Worried about my baby / Driving this highway / Sun is rising / Riding in the moonlight / My friends / I'm the Wolf
CD CDCHD 333
Ace / Oct '91 / Pinnacle

SMOKESTACK LIGHTNIN'
CD MCSTD 1960
MCA / May '94 / BMG

SPOONFUL
Smokestack lightnin' / Back door man / Evil / Tell me / Watergate blues / Tail dragger
CD CDRB 2
Charly / Apr '94 / Koch

VERY BEST OF HOWLIN' WOLF, THE (& Roots Of The Blues vol.3 Compilation/ 3CD Set)
Moanin' at midnight / How many more years / Wolf is at your door / Dorothy Mae / Work for your money / All night boogie / Neighbours / I'm the wolf / Baby how long / Evil / Forty four / Who will be next / Smokestack lightnin' / I asked for water (she gave me gasoline) / Natchez burning / Tell me / Sittin' on top of the world / Moanin' for my baby / I'm leaving you / I've been abused / Wang dang doodle / Back door man / Spoonful / Little baby / Down in the bottom / Shake for me / Little red rooster / You'll be mine / I ain't superstitious / Goin' down slow / Do the do / Trail dragger / Long green stuff / 300 Pounds of joy / Built for comfort / Killing floor / What a woman / Who's been talkin' / Poor boy / Rockin' Daddy / Life savers blues: *Johnson, Lonnie* / Frankie: *Hurt, 'Mississippi' John* / Big fat Mama blues: *Johnson, Tommy* / Blind Arthur's breakdown: *Blind Blake* / Milk cow blues: *Estes, 'Sleepy' John* / Preachin' the blues: *Sun House* / Do your duty: *Smith, Bessie* / Brown skin girls: *Loften, Cripple Clarence* / Back door blues: *Weldon, Casey Bill* / Evil hearted woman blues: *Woods, Oscar 'Buddy'* / Love in vain: *Johnson, Robert* / Fox chase: *Terry, Sonny* / I done got wise: *Broonzy, 'Big' Bill* / Yancy stomp: *Yancey, Jimmy* / Leaving the blues: *Leadbelly* / You gonna miss me when I'm gone: *Waters, Muddy*
CD Set VBCD 303
Charly / Jul '95 / Koch

WOLF IS AT YOUR DOOR, THE (Charly Blues Masterworks Vol.5)
Moanin' at midnight / How many more years / Wolf is at your door (howlin' for my baby) / California blues / California boogie / Look-a-here baby / Howlin' wolf boogie / Smile at me / Getting old and gray / Mr. Highwayman / My baby walked off / Champagen velvet blues (CV Wine Blues) / My troubles and me / Chocolate drop / Highway man / Everybody in the mood / Bluebird / Saddle my pony
CD CD BM 5
Charly / Apr '92 / Koch

WOLF IS AT YOUR DOOR, THE (2CD Set)
Somebody's in my home / My mind is ramblin' / I walked from Dallas / Streamline woman / Cause of it all / Do the do / Worried about you / Poor boy / Shake for me / Little red rooster / You'll be mine / Who's been talkin' / Wang dang doodle / Little baby / Spoonful / Goin' down slow / Down in the bottom / Back door man / Howlin' for my baby / Tell me / My baby walked off / Killing floor / My country sugar mama / My life / Goin' back home / Louise / Highway 49 / Hold on to your money / Built for comfort / I ain't superstitious / My last affair / Dorothy Mae / Commit a crime / Moanin' at midnight / Riding in the moonlight / Everybody's in the mood / Wolf is at your door (howlin' for my baby) / I better go now
CD Set 422176
New Rose / May '94 / ADA / Direct / Discovery

Hoy, Johnny

TROLLING THE HOOTCHY (Hoy, Johnny & The Bluefish)
CD CDTC 1151
Tonecool / Apr '95 / ADA / Direct

YOU GONNA LOSE YOUR HEAD (Hoy, Johnny & The Bluefish)
You better listen / Glad she's gone / Made for one / Another / Stand tall / Gong gong / Believer's blues / I want to see her / Mellow chick swing / Red door / Beer bellied man / I ain't got no home / Nobody else / Can't stand to sleep alone / Just to be with you
CD CDTC 1157
Tonecool / Oct '96 / ADA / Direct

HP Lovecraft

HP LOVECRAFT LIVE
Wayfaring stranger / Drifter / It's about time / White ship / At the mountains of madness / Bag I'm in / I've never been wrong before / Country boy and Bleeker Street
CD EDCD 345
Edsel / Nov '91 / Pinnacle

THIS IS/HP II
CD 10
Britonic / Jun '97 / Greyhound

HP Zinker

AND THEN THERE WAS LIGHT
CD NECKCD 004
Roughneck / Jul '91 / RTM/Disc

HR

HUMAN RIGHTS
CD SST 117CD
SST / Mar '88 / Plastic Head

ROCK OF ENOCH
CD SST 274CD
SST / May '93 / Plastic Head

SINGIN' IN THE HEART
Fool's gold / Rasta time / Singin' in the heart / Treat street / Youthman sufferer / Fools gold (dub) / Don't trust no (shadows) / Youthman sufferer (dub)
CD SST 224CD
SST / Sep '89 / Plastic Head

Hradistan

MORAVIAN ECHOES
CD LT 0018
Lotos / Nov '95 / Czech Music Enterprises

Hsiao-Yueh, Tsai

NAN-KOUAN VOL.1
CD C 559004
Ocora / Sep '93 / ADA / Harmonia Mundi

NAN-KOUAN VOL.2
CD C 560037
Ocora / Sep '93 / ADA / Harmonia Mundi

NAN-KOUAN VOL.3
CD C 560038
Ocora / Sep '93 / ADA / Harmonia Mundi

NAN-KOUAN VOL.4-6
CD Set C 560039/41
Ocora / Sep '93 / ADA / Harmonia Mundi

Hua, Jiang Jian

EARTH, THE
Jiang jiao xing / Yang guan san die / Er wuan ying yue / Hana / Murika muchibushi / Tai hu chuan / Chang yuan zong sheng / Yang guang zhao yao ze ta shiku e can / Cao yuan shang / Shima uta
CD JVC 90092
JVC World Library / May '97 / ADA / CM / Direct

Hubbard, Freddie

ALL BLUES
All blues / God bless the child / Bolivia / Dear John
CD JWD 102217
JWD / Apr '95 / Target/BMG

ARTISTRY OF FREDDIE HUBBARD, THE
Caravan / Bob's place / Happy times / Summertime / Seventh day
CD IMP 11792
Impulse Jazz / Feb '96 / New Note/BMG

BACKLASH
Backlash / Return of the prodigal son / Little sunflower / On the que tee / Up jumped spring / Echoes of blue
CD 7567904662
Atlantic / Jul '93 / Warner Music

BALLADS
Body and soul / But beautiful / Mirrors / Weaver of dreams / I wished I knew / Lament for booker
CD CDP 8566912
Blue Note / Jul '97 / EMI

BODY AND THE SOUL, THE
Body and soul / Carnival / Chocolate snake / Dedicated to you / Clarence's place / Aries / Skylark / I got it bad / Thermo
CD IMP 11832
Impulse Jazz / Sep '96 / New Note/BMG

BOLIVIA
Homegrown / Bolivia / God bless the child / Dear John / Managua / Third world
CD 8208372
Limelight / Jul '91 / PolyGram

BORN TO BE BLUE
Gibraltar / True colors / Born to be blue / Joy spring / Up jumped spring
CD OJCCD 734
Original Jazz Classics / Jun '94 / Complete/ Pinnacle / Jazz Music / Wellard

HUB ART (Essence All-Stars)
CD HIBD 8005
Hip Bop / Feb '96 / Koch / Silva Screen

HUB OF HUBBARD, A
Without a song / Just one of those things / Blues for Duane / Things we did last summer / Muses for Richard Davis
CD 8259562
Polydor / '88 / PolyGram

HUB'S NUB
CD CD 53206
Giants Of Jazz / Jan '95 / Cadillac / Jazz Music / Target/BMG

KEYSTONE BOP VOL.2 (Friday/ Saturday)
One of another kind / 'Round midnight / Red clay / First light
CD PCD 241632
Prestige / Aug '96 / Cadillac / Complete/ Pinnacle

LIVE AT FAT TUESDAY'S (2CD Set)
Take it to the ozone / Egad / Phoebe's samba / But beautiful / One of a kind / CORE / Destiny's children / First light
CD 8442802
Limelight / Aug '90 / PolyGram

MINOR MISHAP
CD BLCD 760122
Black Lion / Aug '89 / Cadillac / Jazz Music / Koch / Wellard

NIGHT OF THE COOKERS VOL.1 & 2
Pensativa / Walkin' / Jodo / Breaking point
CD CDP 8288822
Blue Note / May '94 / EMI

OUTPOST
CD ENJACD 309523
Enja / Jan '95 / New Note/Pinnacle / Vital/ SAM

THIS IS JAZZ
Red clay / Spirits of trane / Sky dive / In a mist / First light / Here's that rainy day
CD CK 65041
Sony Jazz / May '97 / Sony

Hubbard, Joe

VANISHING POINT
CD CMMR 921
Music Maker / Jun '92 / ADA / Grapevine/ PolyGram

Hubbard, Ray Wylie

DANGEROUS SPIRITS
CD CSCCD 1004
Continental Song City / Mar '97 / Direct

Hucko, Peanuts

SWING THAT MUSIC
CD SLCD 9005
Starline / Feb '94 / Jazz Music

TRIBUTE TO BENNY GOODMAN (Hucko, Peanuts/Butterfield/Erstrand)
CD CDTTD 513
Timeless Traditional / Jul '94 / Jazz Music / New Note/Pinnacle

Huddersfield Choral Society

CAROLS ALBUM, THE
O come all ye faithful (Adeste Fidelis) / Unto us is born a son / I saw three ships / Joy to the world / Away in a manger / God rest ye merry gentlemen / It came upon a midnight clear / Shepherds farewell / Good Christian men rejoice / Good King Wenceslas / Once in Royal David's City / We three kings of Orient are / In the bleak midwinter / O come, o come Emmanuel / While shepherds watched their flocks by night / First Noel / Silent night / Angles from the realms of glory / As with gladness men of old / Hark the herald angels sing / See amid the winter's snow
CD CDMFP 6038
Music For Pleasure / Dec '94 / EMI

CHRISTMAS FANTASY
We wish you a Merry Christmas: *Huddersfield Choral Society/Black Dyke Mills Band* / O come all ye faithful (Adeste Fidelis): *Huddersfield Choral Society/Black Dyke Mills Band* / Sussex carol: *Huddersfield Choral Society/Black Dyke Mills Band* / Ding dong merrily on high: *Huddersfield Choral Society/Black Dyke Mills Band* / First Noel: *Huddersfield Choral Society/Black Dyke Mills Band* / In dulci jubilo: *Huddersfield Choral Society/Black Dyke Mills Band* / Silent night: *Huddersfield Choral Society/Black Dyke Mills Band*
CD CHAN 8679
Chandos / Nov '88 / Chandos

Hudson, Dean

DEAN HUDSON ORCHESTRA 1944-1950 (Hudson, Dean & His Orchestra)
CD CCD 13
Circle / Mar '97 / Jazz Music / Swift / Wellard

Hudson, Keith

BRAND
Image dub / National anthem dub / Feel the strain dub / Darkness dub / Highter hights dub / Leggo dub / Musicology dub / My eyes are red dub / Barrabas dub / Rub dub
CD CDPS 004
Pressure Sounds / Jul '95 / Jet Star / SRD

PICK A DUB
CD BAFCD 3
Blood & Fire / Oct '94 / Vital

STUDIO KINDA CLOUDY (Hudson, Keith & Friends)
CD CDTRL 258
Trojan / Sep '94 / Direct / Jet Star

TORCH OF FREEDOM
CD CONCD 003
Connexion / Nov '96 / Grapevine/ PolyGram

Hudson Swan Band

PROSPECT LANE
CD LDLCD 239
Lochshore / Jun '96 / ADA / Direct / Duncans

Hue & Cry

BEST OF HUE & CRY, THE
Labour of love / Looking for Linda / Under neon / Wide screen / Ordinary angel / Sweet invisibility / Peaceful face / I refuse / She makes a sound / Too shy to say / Mother Glasgow / Stars crash down
CD CDVIP 134
Virgin VIP / Apr '95 / EMI

JAZZ NOT JAZZ
CD AKD 057
Linn / Oct '96 / PolyGram

LABOURS OF LOVE - THE BEST OF HUE & CRY
Labour of love / I refuse / Sweet invisibility / Looking for Linda / My salt heart / Violently (Your words hit me) / Strength to strength / Ordinary angel / Long term lovers of pain / She makes a sound / Widescreen / Stars crash down / Peaceful face / Man with the child in his eyes / Truth / Labour of love (7" urban edit)
CD HACCD 1
Circa / Mar '93 / EMI

REMOTE
Ordinary angel / Looking for Linda / Guy on the wall / Violently / Dollar William / Under neon / Only thing (more powerful than the boss) / Where we wish to remain / Sweet invisibility / Three foot blasts of fire / Remote / Family of eyes
CD CDVIP 187
Virgin VIP / Apr '97 / EMI

REMOTE/BITTER SUITE (Limited Edition 2CD Set)
Mother Glasgow / Man with the child in his eyes / Shipbuilding / Rollin' home / Peaceful face / Widescreen (live) / O God head hid (live) / Looking for Linda (live) / Remote (live) / It was a very good year / 'Round midnight / Truth / Ordinary angel / Looking for Linda / Guy on the wall / Violently (your words hit me) / Dollar William / Only thing more powerful than the boss / Where we wish to remain / Sweet invisibility / Three foot blasts of fire / Remote

CD Set CDHUE 6
Circa / '89 / EMI

SEDUCED AND ABANDONED
Strength to strength / History city / Goodbye to me / Human touch / Labour of love / I refuse / Something warmer / Alligator man / Love is the master / Just one word / Truth
CD VI 874802
Disky / Nov '96 / Disky / THE

STARS CRASH DOWN
My salt heart / Life as text / She makes a sound / Making strange / Remembrance and gold / Long term lovers of pain / Stars crash down / Vera drives / Woman in time / Late in the day
CD CIRCD 15
Circa / Jun '91 / EMI

Hue B

GOOD IN A ME, THE
CD CRCD 31
Charm / Mar '94 / Jet Star

Huevos Rancheros

DIG IN
CD LOUDEST 7
One Louder / Apr '95 / Mo's Music Machine / Shellshock/Disc / SRD

Hufschmidt, Thomas

PEPILA (Hufschmidt, Thomas & Tyron Park)
CD BEST 1034CD
Acoustic Music / Nov '93 / ADA

Huge Baby

SUPER FRANKENSTEIN
CD PILLMCD 5
Placebo / Aug '94 / RTM/Disc

Huggy Bear

WEAPONRY LISTENS TO LOVE
Immature adolescence / Fuck your heart / Face down / Warming rails / On the wolves tip / Erotic bleeding / Sixteen and suicide / Obesity and speed / Insecure offenders / Why am I a lawbreaker / Local arrogance
CD WIJ 037CD
Wiiija / Oct '94 / RTM/Disc

Hughes, Brian

BETWEEN DUSK...AND DREAMING
CD JUST 362
Justin Time / Mar '92 / Cadillac / New Note/Pinnacle

UNDER ONE SKY
CD JUST 492
Justin Time / Jan '93 / Cadillac / New Note/Pinnacle

Hughes, Glenn

BEST OF GLENN HUGHES, THE (Various Artists)
Burn: *Hughes, Glenn* / I got your number: *Hughes, Glenn* / Still the night: *Phenomena* / Surrender: *Phenomena II* / So much love to give: *LA Blues Authority* / Face the truth: *Norum, John* / Only one: *Hughes, Glenn* / Cry for love: *Liesgang, Billy* / Into the void: *Hughes, Glenn* / You keep me moving: *Hughes, Glenn* / Live and learn: *Brazen Abbot* / Lay my body down: *Hughes, Glenn* / King of the western world: *Liesgang, Billy* / Pheonix rising: *Phenomena* / Make my day: *Amen* / In your eyes: *Norum, John* / Look in your eye: *Hughes, Glenn* / Kiss of fire: *Hughes, Glenn* / Reach for the sky: *Moore, Gary* / No stranger to love: *Black Sabbath*
CD 60234
Cargo / Nov '96 / Cargo

BLUES
Boy can sing the blues / I'm the man / Here comes the rebel / What can I do for ya / You don't have to save me anymore / So much love to give / Shake the ground / Hey buddy (you got me wrong) / Have you read the book / Life of misery / Can't take away my pride / Right to live
CD RR 90882
Roadrunner / Sep '96 / PolyGram

BURNING JAPAN LIVE
CD SPV 08518202
SPV / Jul '95 / Koch / Plastic Head

FEEL
CD CD 08589762
SPV / Nov '95 / Koch / Plastic Head

FROM NOW ON
CD RR 90072
Roadrunner / Sep '96 / PolyGram

PLAY ME OUT
I got it covered / Space high / It's about time / LA cut off / Well / Solution / Your love is like a fire / Destiny / I found a woman / Smile / Getting near to you / Fools condition / Take me with you / She knows
CD RPM 149
RPM / Jan '96 / Pinnacle

Hughes, Howard

CAR GOING OVER A BRIDGE
CD USRCD 3
Ultrasonic / Nov '93 / Pinnacle

Hughes, James

JAMES HUGHES PLAYS JAMES MOODY VOL.1
Rondo rococo / Duo baroque / Caprice / Ballet Imaginaire / Sonatina / Maid behind the bar / Moody's fancy / Down by the Tanyard side / Castle Dromore / Spanish lady / Gentle maiden / Love thee dearest / Next market day / Kathleen O'Moore / Down by the Sally Gardens / Trotting to the fair / My Lagan love / Meeting of the waters / Snowy breasted pearl / Cruiskeen lawn / Open the door softly / Echoes of Ireland
CD CDGRS 1291
Grosvenor / Aug '96 / Grosvenor

Hughes, Jerry

CELTIC WOMAN (Instrumentally Yours) (Hughes, Jerry & Alan Connaughton)
Orinoco flow / No frontiers / Woman's heart / Delaney's gone back on the wine / Nothing compares 2 U / After the ball / All the lies / Riverun / Teddy O'Neill / Summerfly
CD CHCD 030
Chart / Apr '96 / Direct / Koch

Hughes, Joe

DOWN AND DEPRESSED - DANGEROUS
CD NETCD 0044
Network / Jul '93 / Direct / Greensleeves / SRD

TEXAS GUITAR MASTER-CRAFTSMAN
CD DTCD 3019
Double Trouble / Aug '88 / CM / Hot Shot

TEXAS GUITAR SLINGER
CD MMBCD 1
Me & My / Oct '95 / Direct

Hughes, Spike

COMPLETE VOL.3 & 4
CD KCM 003/004
Kings Cross Music / Aug '95 / Cadillac / Harmonia Mundi / Wellard

HIS DECCA-DENTS, DANCE ORCHESTRA & HIS THREE BLIND MICE 1930
CD KCM 001/002
Kings Cross Music / Mar '95 / Cadillac / Harmonia Mundi / Wellard

SPIKE HUGHES & BENNY CARTER 1933 (Hughes, Spike & Benny Carter)
Nocturne / Someone stole Gabriel's horn / Pastorale / Bugle call rag / Arabesque / Fanfare / Sweet sorrow blues / Music at midnight / Sweet Sue just you / Air in D flat / Firebird / Music at sunrise / How come you do me like you do / Swing it / Synthetic love / Six bells stampede / Love you're not the one for me / Devil's holiday / Lonesome nights / Symphony in riffs / Blue Lou
CD RTR 79005
Retrieval / Nov '96 / Cadillac / Direct / Jazz Music / Swift / Wellard

Hugill, Stan

CHANTS PAS MARINS ANGLAIS
CD SCM 021
Diffusion Breizh / May '93 / ADA

Hula

BEST OF HULA, THE
Fever car / Get the habit / Freeze out / Ghost rattle / Black wall blue / Big heat / Mother courage / Walk on stalks of shattered glass / Tear up / Hard stripes / Poison (Club mix) / Give me money / Cut me loose / Seven sleepers / Junshi
CD CDGRAM 81
Anagram / Jun '94 / Cargo / Pinnacle

Hulbaekmo, Tone

KONKYLIE
CD GR 4095CD
Grappa / Apr '95 / ADA

Hulkkonen, Jori

SELKASAARI TRACKS
Flavataanssit / Sumthing / Blane Tudor's theme / Vinci / Mello dick track / 3rd line / Selkasaari / Cum off it / Heights
CD FO 52CD
F-Communications / Feb '97 / Prime / Vital

Hull, Alan

PIPEDREAM
Breakfast / Just another sad song / Money game / United states of mind / Country gentleman's wife / Numbers (travelling band) / For the bairns / Drug song / Song for a windmill / Blue murder / I hate to see you cry
CD CASCD 1069
Charisma / Feb '91 / EMI

STATUES AND LIBERTIES
CD TRACD 246
Transatlantic / Nov '96 / Pinnacle

Hullabaloo

LUBITORIUM
CD CZ 027CD
C/Z / Sep '91 / Plastic Head

REGURGITATED
CD EFA 11381CD
Musical Tragedies / Jun '93 / SRD

Hum Projimo

ALPENGLUH'N: SONGS FROM MURMI
CD EFA 112842
Glasnost / Oct '95 / SRD

Humair, Daniel

EDGES
CD LBLC 6545
Label Bleu / Jan '92 / New Note/Pinnacle

Human Beinz

NOBODY BUT ME
Nobody but me / Foxey lady / Shamen / Flower grave / Dance on through / Turn on your lights / It's fun to be clean / Black is the colour of my true love's hair / This lonely town / Sueno / Serenade to Sarah
CD SEECD 327
See For Miles/C5 / Jul '91 / Pinnacle

Human Chains

HUMAN CHAINS
Freely / My Girl / Antonia / Elderberries / La la la / Grinding to the miller men / Hollyhocks / Golden slumbers / Further away / Suguxhama / Jolobe / Ikebana / Bon / Nancy D / Death
CD AHUM 002
Ah-Um / Jun '89 / Cadillac / New Note/ Pinnacle

Human Clay

U41A
Lessons of love / King of the nation / Salvation / Pain and deception / Thin line / Speed demon / U4IA / Pretender / Stand 4 the fall / Survive
CD CDMFN 227
Music For Nations / Jul '97 / Pinnacle

Human League

CRASH
Money / Swang / Human / Jam / Are you ever coming back / I need your lovin' / Party / Love on the run / Real thing / Love is all that matters
CD CDV 2391
Virgin / May '86 / EMI

DARE
Things that dreams are made of / Open your heart / Sound of the crowd / Darkness / Do or die / Get Carter / I am the law / Seconds / Love action (I believe in love) / Don't you want me
CD CDV 2192
Virgin / Oct '81 / EMI

GREATEST HITS
Don't you want me / Love action / Mirror man / Tell me when / Stay with me tonight / Open your heart / (Keep feeling) Fascination / Sound of the crowd / Being boiled / Lebanon / Love is all that matters / Louise / Life on your own / Together in electric dreams / Human / Don't you want me (Snap remix)
CD CDV 2792
Virgin / Oct '95 / EMI

HYSTERIA
I'm coming back / I love you too much / Rock me again and again and again..... / Louise / Lebanon / Betrayed / Sign / So hurt / Life on your own / Don't you know I want you
CD CDV 2315
Virgin / Jul '87 / EMI

OCTOPUS
Tell me when / These are the days / One man in my heart / Words / Filling up with heaven / Housefull of nothing / John Cleese; is he funny / Never again / Cruel young lover
CD 4509987502
East West / Jan '95 / Warner Music

REPRODUCTION
Almost medieval / Circus of death / Path of least resistance / Blind youth / Word before last / Empire state human / Morale...You've lost that loving feeling / Austerity/Girl one (medley) / Zero as a limit
CD CDV 2133
Virgin / '87 / EMI

SOUNDTRACK TO A GENERATION
Human / Kiss the future / Together in electric dreams / Are you ever coming back / Betrayed / Hard times / Get it right this time / I need your loving / Do or die / Rebound / Soundtrack to a generation / Empire State human / Real thing / Don't you know I want you
CD VI 875302
Disky / Oct '96 / Disky / THE

TRANCE LEAGUE EXPRESS (A Tribute To The Human League) (Various Artists)
CD CLP 9934
Hypnotic / Mar '97 / Cargo / SRD

TRAVELOGUE
Black hit of space / Only after dark / Life kills / Dreams of leaving / Toyota city / Crow and a baby / Touchables / Gordon's gin / Being boiled / WXJL tonight
CD CDV 2160
Virgin / '87 / EMI

Human Remains

USING SICKNESS AS A HERO
CD RR 69272
Relapse / Feb '97 / Pinnacle / Plastic Head

Humara, Walter Salas

RADAR
CD NORMAL 193CD
Normal / Jan '96 / ADA / Direct

Humate

BEST OF HUMATE, THE (Various Artists)
Love stimulation: *Humate* / Bagdad: *Paragliders* / East: *Humate & Rabbit In The Moon* / East: *Humate & Rabbit In The Moon* / 3.1: *Humate* / 3.3: *Humate* / Sound: *Humate* / Feather: *Spicelab* / 1996 (part 1): *Spicelab* / 1996 (part 2): *Humate*
CD EFA 628192
Superstition / Mar '97 / Plastic Head / SRD / Vital

Humble Pie

COLLECTION, THE
Bang / Natural born bugie / I'll go alone / Buttermilk boy / Desperation / Nifty little number like you / Wrist job / Stick shift / Growing closer / As safe as yesterday / Heartbeat / Down home again / Take me back / Only you can see / Silver tongue / Every mother's son / Sad bag of Shaky Jake / Cold lady / Home and away / Light of love
CD CCSCD 104
Castle / Apr '94 / BMG

IMMEDIATE YEARS, THE (2CD Set)
Natural born bugie / Wrist job / Desperation / Stick shift / Buttermilk boy / Growing closer / As safe as yesterday is / Bang / Alabama 69 / I'll go alone / Nifty little number like you / What you will / Greg's song / Take me back / Sad bag of shaky Jake / Light of love / Cold lady / Down home again / Ollie Ollie / Every Mother's son / Heartbeat / Only you can see / Silver tongue / Home and away
CD Set CDIMMBOX 3
Charly / Aug '95 / Koch

PIECE OF THE PIE, A
CD 5401792
A&M / Apr '95 / PolyGram

TOWN AND COUNTRY
Take me back / Sad bag of Shaky Jake / Light of love / Cold lady / Down home again / Ollie Ollie / Every mother's son / Heartbeat / Only you can see / Silver tongue / Home and away
CD CDIMM 020
Charly / Feb '94 / Koch

Humblebums

BEST OF THE HUMBLEBUMS, THE
CD PDSCD 542
Pulse / Aug '96 / BMG

NEW HUMBLEBUMS, THE/OPEN UP THE DOOR
Look over the hill and far away / Saturday round about Sunday / Patrick / Everybody knows that / Rick rack / Her father didn't like me anyway / Please sing a song for us / Joe Dempsey / Blood and glory / Coconut tree / Silk pyjamas / Good-bye-ee / My apartment / I can't stop now / Open up the door / Mary of the Mountains / All the best people do it / Steamboat row / Mother / Shoeshine boy / Cruisin' / Keep it to yourself / Oh no / Song for Simon / Harry / My singing bird
CD ESMCD 498
Essential / Apr '97 / BMG

Humes, Helen

CLASSICS 1927-1945
CD CLASSICS 892
Classics / Sep '96 / Discovery / Jazz Music

LET THE GOOD TIMES ROLL
CD BB 8712
Black & Blue / Sep '96 / Discovery / Koch / Wellard

NEW YEARS EVE, THE
CD LDJ 274914
Radio Nights / Nov '91 / Cadillac / Harmonia Mundi

ON THE SUNNY SIDE OF THE STREET
Alright, OK you win / If I could be with you one hour tonight / Ain't nobody's business if I do / Kansas City / I'm satisfied / Blue because of you / On the sunny side of the street / I got it bad and that ain't good
CD **BLCD 760185**
Black Lion / Jul '93 / Cadillac / Jazz Music / Koch / Wellard

Hummel, Mark

FEEL LIKE ROCKIN'
Georgia slop / Rockin' all the time / So darn cute / Learned my lesson (changed my ways) / Everything / Nickels and dimes / Lost in the shuffle / Bad luck blues / I'm gonna quit / Where you at / City livin' / Coast to coast / Worried mind / Last time in Florida / Third time out / When I'm not with you
CD **FF 70634**
Flying Fish / Nov '94 / ADA / CM / Direct / Roots

HEART OF CHICAGO
My kind of baby / Rockin' at the riverside / Lost a good man / Rollin' from side to side / Tryin' to make a living / Love shock / I want your love / Peaches tree / Step back baby / But I forgive you / Out on a limb / Ready for Eddie / Drinkin' again / Living with the blues
CD **CDTC 1158**
Tonecool / Feb '97 / ADA / Direct

MARRIED TO THE BLUES
They don't want me to rock / I'm gone / Find some boogie / Rock and roll baby / Jungle scotch plaid / No buts, no maybes / Can't judge nobody / Can't live with 'em / High steppin' / Married to the blues / I got eyes / Trial by fire / Bluesman
CD **FF 70647**
Flying Fish / Oct '96 / ADA / CM / Direct / Roots

Hummon, Marcus

ALL IN GOOD TIME
Hittin' the road / God's country USA / One of these days / Honky tonk Mona Lisa / Next step / I do / Virginia reelin' / Somebody's leaving / Bless the broken road / As the crow flies / Bridges over blue / All in good time
CD **4810282**
Columbia / Jan '96 / Sony

Humperdinck, Engelbert

AFTER DARK
Love me like we'll never love again / If I could love you more / Once in a while / I could get used to this / Healing: *Humperdinck, Engelbert & Louise Sarah Dorsey* / Answered prayers / Stay with me / Great divide / Slide a little closer / I know you hear me / There's no song like a slow song
CD **ALPCD 100**
Alpha Entertainments / Mar '97 / Pinnacle

AND I LOVE YOU SO
CD **12567**
Laserlight / Oct '95 / Target/BMG

BEST OF ENGELBERT HUMPERDINCK, THE
CD **PLSCD 121**
Pulse / Apr '96 / BMG

BEST OF ENGELBERT HUMPERDINCK, THE
CD **TRTCD 219**
TrueTrax / Jul '96 / THE

CLOSE TO YOU
Close to you / My cherie amour / Everybody's talkin' / Killing me softly / Just the way you are / Love me tender / Raindrops keep falling on my head / And I love you so / Another time another place / You are the sunshine of my life / Something / Leaving on a jet plane / What I did for love / Help me make it through the night / Forever and ever (and ever) / Love me with all your heart / Without you / You light up my life
CD **CDMFP 5932**
Music For Pleasure / Oct '91 / EMI

COLLECTION, THE
Please release me / To all the girls I've loved before / Bella Italia / Les bicyclettes de Belsize / There goes my everything / One world / Last waltz / On the wings of a silverbird / Portofino / Spanish night is over / Under the man in the moon / I can't stop loving you / I can never let you go / Are you lonesome tonight
CD **262540**
Ariola / Feb '97 / BMG

ENGELBERT
Love can fly / Love was here before the stars / Don't say no (Again) / Let me into your life / Through the eyes of love / Les bicyclettes de belsize / Way it used to be / Marry me / To get to you / You're easy to love / True / Good thing going / Stay / Come over here / You love / If I were you / Two different worlds / Am I that easy to forget
CD **8205762**
London / Jan '93 / PolyGram

ENGELBERT HUMPERDINCK
I'm a better man (for having loved you) / Gentle on my mind / Love letters / Time for us / Didn't we / I wish you love / Aquarius / All you've got to do is ask / Signs of love / Cafe / Let's kiss tomorrow goodbye / Winter world of love / Those were the days / Can't take my eyes off you / Love was here before the stars / Stardust
CD **8205772**
London / Jan '93 / PolyGram

ENGELBERT HUMPERDINCK
CD **HM 011**
Harmony / Jun '97 / TKO Magnum

ENGELBERT HUMPERDINCK
Lovely way to spend an evening / Far away places / I'll walk alone / My foolish heart / Very thought of you / You belong to my heart / Red sails in the sunset / You'll never know / I wish I knew / Embraceable you / I don't want to walk without you / As time goes by / Long ago and far away / Night to remember
CD **GFS 068**
Going For A Song / Jul '97 / Else / TKO Magnum

ENGELBERT IN LOVE
Man without love / Killing me softly / Last waltz / Help me make it through the night / There goes my everything / My cherie amour / Winter world of love / Way it used to be / Something / Close to you / Am I that easy to forget / Love me tender / Release me / Quando, quando, quando (tell me when) / Most beautiful girl / Spanish eyes / Just the way you are / First time ever I saw your face / You are the sunshine of my life / And I love you so
CD **4625592**
Columbia / Feb '96 / Sony

FROM ENGELBERT WITH LOVE
I don't want to walk without you / Embraceable you / I wish I knew / You'll never know / Red sails in the sunset / You belong to my heart / Very thought of you / My foolish heart / I'll walk alone / Far away places / Lovely way to spend an evening / More I see you / In the still of the night / I'm getting sentimental over you / Moonlight becomes you / But beautiful / Harbour lights / They say it's wonderful / Long ago / As time goes by
CD **100532**
CMC / May '97 / BMG

GREATEST HITS
Release me / Man without love / Way it used to be / Quando, quando, quando / Everybody knows we're through / There's a kind of hush / There goes my everything / Les bicyclettes de Belsize / I'm a better man (for having loved you) / Winter world of love / My world / Ten guitars / Am I that easy to forget / Last waltz
CD **8203672**
London / Jul '89 / PolyGram

HIS ROMANTIC HITS
CD **CD 3503**
Cameo / Aug '94 / Target/BMG

IN THE STILL OF THE NIGHT
In the still of the night / I'm getting sentimental over you / I'll walk alone / Moonlight becomes you / You'll never know / I don't want to walk without you / Stardust / Embraceable you / You belong to my heart / Lovely way to spend an evening / Long ago and far away / Red sails in the sunset / Far away places / My foolishy heart / Very thought of you / They say it's wonderful / Harbour lights / More I see you / Yours / As time goes by
CD **MCCD 055**
Music Club / Mar '92 / Disc / THE

LAST WALTZ, THE
Last waltz / Dance with me / Two different worlds / If it comes to that / Walk hand in hand / Place in the sun / Long gone / All this world and the seven seas / Miss Elaine ES Jones / Everybody knows (we're through) / To the ends of the earth / That promise / Three little words / Those were the days / What now my love
CD **8205752**
London / Jul '91 / PolyGram

LIVE IN JAPAN
Intro / There's a kind of hush / All I ever need is you / Il mondo / Man without love / Stripper / Impressions / I'll be your baby tonight / Another time another place / Release me / Love is all / Without you / I can help / I never said goodbye / Last waltz / Quando quando / There goes my everything / Spanish eyes / Les bicyclettes de belsise
CD **12657**
Laserlight / May '96 / Target/BMG

LOVE IS ALL (3CD Set)
After the lovin' / Can't take my eyes off you / Another time another place / Love me with all your heart / And I love you so / You are the sunshine of my life / You'll never walk alone(live) / Help me make it through the night / Love is all / Close to you (they long to be) / Raindrops keep fallin' on my head / Can't smile without you / Leaving on a jet plane / Release me (live) / Killing me softly with his song / My cherie amour / Something / Without you / Forever and ever / Everybody's talkin' / Sweet Marjorene / First time in my life / In time / Most beautiful girl / I can't leave a dream / Baby I'm a want you / What now my love / Man without love / Just the way you are / Can't help falling in love / I'm stone in love with you / Much greater love / Let's kiss tomorrow goodbye / Just say I love her / Those were the days / Funny familiar forgotten feelings / You light up my life / What I did for love / Love me tender / And the day begins / Here you come again / Medley
CD Set **SA 872542**
Disky / Sep '96 / Disky / THE

LOVE SONGS
CD **CD 3028**
Scratch / Oct '94 / Koch / Scratch/BMG

LOVE UNCHAINED
Too young / Secret love / Unchained melody / Answer me / (Sittin' on the) dock of the bay / No other love / Stranger in paradise / I apologise / Smoke gets in your eyes / Such a night / Love me tender / Love is a many splendoured thing
CD **CDEMTV 94**
EMI / May '95 / EMI

MAN WITHOUT LOVE, A
Man without love / Can't take my eyes off you / From here to eternity / Spanish eyes / Man and a woman / Quando, quando, quando / Up, up and away / Wonderland by night / What a wonderful world / Call on me / By the time I get to Phoenix / Shadow of your smile / Stardust / Pretty ribbon / Dommage dommage / When I say goodnight / Funny familiar forgotten feelings / There goes my everything
CD **8207682**
London / Nov '88 / PolyGram

MASTERPIECES
CD **12329**
Laserlight / May '94 / Target/BMG

PACKET OF THREE VOL.10 (3CD Set) (Humperdinck, Engelbert/Donna Summer/Various Artists)
Lovely way to spend an evening: *Humperdinck, Engelbert* / Far away places: *Humperdinck, Engelbert* / I'll walk alone: *Humperdinck, Engelbert* / My foolish heart: *Humperdinck, Engelbert* / Very thought of you: *Humperdinck, Engelbert* / You belong to my heart: *Humperdinck, Engelbert* / Red sails in the sunset: *Humperdinck, Engelbert* / Embraceable you: *Humperdinck, Engelbert* / As time goes by: *Humperdinck, Engelbert* / Long ago and far away: *Humperdinck, Engelbert* / They say it's wonderful: *Humperdinck, Engelbert* / Harbour lights: *Humperdinck, Engelbert* / I'll be around: *Humperdinck, Engelbert* / Moonlight becomes you: *Humperdinck, Engelbert* / Getting sentimental over you: *Humperdinck, Engelbert* / In the still of the night: *Humperdinck, Engelbert* / More I see you: *Humperdinck, Engelbert* / I'll be seeing you: *Humperdinck, Engelbert* / Funstreet: *Summer, Donna* / Little Marie: *Summer, Donna* / Shout it out: *Summer, Donna* / They can't take away our music: *Summer, Donna* / Back off boogaloo: *Summer, Donna* / Jeannie: *Summer, Donna* / Nice to see you: *Summer, Donna* / Na na hey hey: *Summer, Donna* / Do what Mother do: *Summer, Donna* / When a man loves a woman: *Various Artists* / Love is all around: *Various Artists* / Love letters in the sand: *Various Artists* / Groovy kind of love: *Various Artists* / Moon river: *Various Artists* / My guy: *Various Artists* / Feel the need in me: *Various Artists* / Ain't no way to treat a lady: *Various Artists* / Breaking up is hard to do: *Various Artists* / Sorrow: *Various Artists* / My prayer: *Various Artists* / PPS I love you: *Various Artists* / By the time I get to Phoenix: *Various Artists* / Ruby, don't take your love to town: *Various Artists* / God bless the child: *Various Artists* / Love really hurts: *Various Artists* / I owe it all to you: *Various Artists* / Don't let the sun catch you crying: *Various Artists* / Stand by me: *Various Artists* / You'll never walk alone: *Various Artists*
CD Set **KLMCD 310**
BAM / Nov '96 / Koch / Scratch/BMG

RELEASE ME
CD **8204592**
London / Jan '93 / PolyGram

SIMPLY THE BEST - RELEASE ME
CD **WMCD 5694**
Disky / May '94 / Disky / THE

SINGS THE CLASSICS
CD **CCSCD 432**
Castle / Mar '95 / BMG

STARDUST
Stardust / I'll be seeing you / Yours / More I see you / In the still of the night / I'm getting sentimental over you / Moonlight becomes you / But beautiful / I'll be around / Harbour lights / They say it's wonderful / Long ago and far away
CD **MSCD 21**
Music De-Luxe / Jun '95 / TKO Magnum

STEP INTO MY LIFE
Red roses for my lady / You are so beautiful / I get lonely / Step into my life / Sentimental lady / You are my love / Sweet lady Jane / I wanna rock you / You're my heart my soul / Dancing with tears in my eyes
CD **CDWM 102**
Westmoor / '91 / Target/BMG

THROUGH THE EYES OF LOVE
There goes my everything / Walk through this world / Ten guitars / Dommage dommage / What now my love / Come over here / There's a kind of hush (all over the world) / This is my song / Stay / Misty blue / Take my heart / Funny familiar forgotten feelings / When I say goodnight / Release me
CD **5500222**
Spectrum / May '93 / PolyGram

VERY THOUGHT OF YOU, THE
Long ago and far away / Stardust / They say it's wonderful / I'll be around / But beautiful / Moonlight becomes you / I'm getting sentimental over you / In the still of the night / More I see you / I'll be seeing you / Lovely way to spend an evening / My foolish heart / Very thought of you / You belong to my heart / Red sails in the sunset / I wish I knew / Embraceable you / As time goes by
CD **EMPRCD 908**
Emporio / Jan '97 / Disc

Humpers

PLASTIQUE VALENTINE
CD **64832**
Epitaph / Feb '97 / Pinnacle / Plastic Head

Humpff Family

FATHER'S
That's what I see / Triangle / Magic journey / Can of beans / Future imperfect / Skye Bridge song / Love, death, divorce, prison, alcohol, rivers and trains / Be there / Joanie's letter / Mary's luck / Rain / Henryetta / Conduct of pigeons
CD **IGCD 208**
Iona Gold / Jul '94 / ADA / Total/BMG

MOTHERS
CD **IRCD 019**
Iona / Oct '91 / ADA / Direct / Duncans

Humphrey, Percy

PERCY HUMPHREY & MARYLAND JAZZBAND
CD **BCD 318**
GHB / Apr '94 / Jazz Music

Humphrey, Willie

NEW ORLEANS TRADITIONAL JAZZ LEGENDS
CD **MG 9002**
Mardi Gras / Feb '95 / Jazz Music

WILLIE HUMPHREY & NORBERT SUSEMIHL (Humphrey, Willie & Norbert Susemihl)
CD **BCD 248**
GHB / Nov '96 / Jazz Music

Humphries, Les

LES HUMPHRIES SINGERS, THE (Humphries, Les Singers)
CD **HM 015**
Harmony / Jun '97 / TKO Magnum

VERY BEST OF LES HUMPHRIES, THE
CD **10272**
CMC / Jun '97 / BMG

Humphries, Tony

KING STREET SOUNDS/MIX THE VIBE (Various Artists)
Tension: *Mateo & Matos* / Satisfaction: *Overtown & Shauna* / Got to have it: *Mood II Swing* / Privately: *Hall, Reggie* / It works for me: *Pope, Sabrynaah* / Back to Zanzibar: *Ly* / Only you: *Lovelace, Kimara* / Until we meet again: *Urban Soul* / Pick it up: *Harding, Carolyn* / Brighter days: *Big moses & Kenny Bobian* / Philadelphia: *Morales, David Brooklyn Friends* / Trust yourself: *Mentalinstrum & Giant Storm* / Hallelujah: *Chandler, Kerri* / Back together: *Urban Soul* / Souffles H: *Mondo Grosso*
CD **S3CD 1**
Sony S3 / Dec '96 / Sony

TAKE HOME THE CLUB
CD **BLRCD 30032**
Bassline / Jul '97 / Essential/BMG

Hundred Years

HUNDRED YEARS
CD **H 00392**
Hellhound / Jul '95 / Koch

SKYHOOK
Intuition time / Am I wrong / Mesmerized / When the day is here / Two wrong words / All man overboard / 30 Below / Dungeon hole / Liar / Fire from within / Relocation / Beds are burning / 13
CD **N 02812**
Noise / Mar '97 / Koch

Hunger

STRICTLY FROM HUNGER
CD **AFT 010**
Afterglow / Jun '97 / Greyhound

Hungry Chuck

SOUTH IN NEW ORLEANS
Hats off, America / Cruisin' / Old Thomas Jefferson / Play that country music / Find the enemy / People do / Watch the trucks go by / Dixie highway / You better watch it Ben / Someday you're gonna run out of gas / Hoona, spoona / All bowed down / Doin' the funky lunch box / Cruising / Play Old thomas jefferson
CD C5CD 590
See For Miles/C5 / Aug '92 / Pinnacle

Hunks, Beau

CELEBRATION ON THE PLANET MARS, A (A Tribute To Raymond Scott) (Hunks, Beau Sextette)
CD 379092
Koch International / Nov '95 / Koch

Hunningale, Peter

MR. GOVERNMENT
Mr. Songbird / Tweet dub / Jump / Babylon / War on babylon / Mr. Government / Downing St. dub / One people / One dub / Sensi sensi
CD ARICD 101
Ariwa Sounds / Apr '94 / Jet Star / SRD

MR. VIBES
CD ARKCD 102
Arawak / Jan '93 / Jet Star

NAH GIVE UP
Nah give up / Trust me / Lover's affair / Thinking about you / Praises / Good and ready / Roots and culture / Sorry / Waiting on your love / Declaration of rights / Perfect lady / Baby please
CD DTJCD 2
Down To Jam / Jan '97 / Grapevine/ PolyGram / Jet Star / Total/BMG

REGGAE MAX
CD JSRNCD 9
Jet Star / Apr '97 / Jet Star

SILLY HABITS
CD DTJCD 005
Down To Jam / Jul '97 / Grapevine/ PolyGram / Jet Star / Total/BMG

Hunt, Howard Slim

BEST OF HOWARD SLIM HUNT & THE SUPREME ANGELS, THE (Hunt, Howard Slim & The Supreme Angels)
CD NASH 4506
Nashboro / Feb '96 / Pinnacle

Hunt, Keith

SHAKIN' ALL OVER
CD MAGIM 901
Magnum Music / May '96 / TKO Magnum

Hunt, Marsha

WALK ON GILDED SPLINTERS
Walk on gilded splinters / Facing a dying nation / Hot rod Papa / Stacey Grove / No face, no name, no number / My world is empty without you / Moan, you moaners / Keep the customer satisfied / Long black veil / You ain't goin' nowhere / Woman child / Desdemona / Wild thing / Hippy Gumbo
CD CSAPCD 116
Connoisseur Collection / Jun '94 / Pinnacle

Hunt, Steve

HEAD, HEART AND HAND
CD IRR 015CD
Irregular / Dec '93 / ADA / Direct / Irregular

Hunt, Tommy

BIGGEST MAN, THE
Biggest man / I just don't know what to do with myself / Human / Lover / New neighbourhood / She'll hurt you too / You made a man out of me / I might like it / Didn't I tell you / Make the night a little longer / This and only this / Just a little taste (of your sweet lovin') / Coming on strong / How can I be anything (without you) / Everybody's got a home but me / Words can never tell it / False alarm / I am a witness / Your man / Don't make me over / It's all a bad dream / promised land / Paradise of broken hearts / Poor millionaire / So lonely / It's all in the game / Do you really love me / I'm wondering / Oh Lord what are you doing to me
CD CDKEND 145
Kent / Apr '97 / Pinnacle

Hunter, Alberta

20'S - 30'S
CD JCD 6
Jass / Jun '87 / ADA / Cadillac / CM / Direct / Jazz Music

ALBERTA HUNTER VOL.1 (1921-1923)
CD DOCD 5422
Document / Jul '96 / ADA / Hot Shot / Jazz Music

ALBERTA HUNTER VOL.2 (1923-1924)
CD DOCD 5423
Document / Jul '96 / ADA / Hot Shot / Jazz Music

ALBERTA HUNTER VOL.3 (1924-1927)
CD DOCD 5424
Document / Jul '96 / ADA / Hot Shot / Jazz Music

ALBERTA HUNTER VOL.4 (1927-1946)
CD DOCD 5425
Document / Jul '96 / ADA / Hot Shot / Jazz Music

ALTERNATE TAKES 1921-1924, THE
CD DOCD 1006
Document / May '97 / ADA / Hot Shot / Jazz Music

BEALE STREET BLUES
CD CBCD 006
Collector's Blues / Mar '96 / TKO Magnum

CHICAGO-THE LIVING LEGENDS (Hunter, Alberta & Lovie Austin)
St. Louis blues / Moanin' low / Downhearted blues / Now I'm satisfied / Sweet Georgia Brown / You better change / C jam blues / Streets paved with gold / Gallion stomp / I will always be in love with you
CD OBCCD 510
Original Blues Classics / Nov '92 / Complete/Pinnacle / Wellard

SONGS WE TAUGHT YOUR MOTHER (Hunter, Alberta/Victoria Spivey/Lucille Hegamin)
I got myself a workin' man / St. Louis blues / Black snake blues / I got a mind to ramble / You'll want my love / Going blues / You gotta reap what you sow / Arkansas blues / Got the blues so bad / Chirpin' the blues / Has anybody seen my Corine / Let him beat me
CD OBCCD 520
Original Blues Classics / Nov '92 / Complete/Pinnacle / Wellard

YOUNG AH, THE
CD JASSCD 6
Jass / '88 / ADA / Cadillac / CM / Direct / Jazz Music

Hunter, Alfonzo

BLACK A DA BERRY
Weekend thang / Blacka da berry / When you're ready / Keep it tight (interlude) / Slow motion / Crazy / Just the way (playas play) / Groove on / Would you be mine / Everything / Daddy's little baby / Rest in peace / Quiet time
CD CTCD 55
Cooltempo / Jan '97 / EMI

Hunter, Charlie

BING BING BING (Hunter, Charlie Trio)
Greasy granny / Wornell's Yorkies / Fistful of haggis / Come as you are / Scrabbling gor purchase / Bullethead / Bing, bing, bing, bing / Squiddlesticks / Lazy Susan (with a client now) / Elbo room
CD CDP 8318092
Blue Note / Jul '95 / EMI

CHARLIE HUNTER TRIO (Hunter, Charlie Trio)
Fred's life / Live oak / 20 30 40 50 60 dead / Funky niblets / Fables of Faubus / Dance of the jazz fascists / Telephone's a'ringin' / Rhythm comes in 12 tones / Mule / Faffer time
CD MR 0662
Mammoth / Mar '94 / Vital

READY...SET...SHANGO (Hunter, Charlie Quartet)
Ashby man / Teabaggin' / Let's get medieval / Shango / Dersu / 911 / Shango...the ballad / Thursday the 12th / Sutton
CD CDP 8371012
Blue Note / Jun '96 / EMI

Hunter, Ian

IAN HUNTER
Once bitten twice shy / Who do you love / Lounge lizard / Boy / 3000 miles from here / Truth / Whole truth nuthin' but the truth / It ain't easy when you fall / Shades off / I get so excited
CD 4773592
Columbia / Aug '94 / Sony

SHORT BACK 'N' SIDES PLUS LONG ODDS & OUTTAKES
Central park 'n' west / Lisa likes rock 'n' roll / I need your love / Old records never die / Noises / Rain / Gun control / Theatre of the absurd / Leave me alone / Keep on burning / Detroit (Rough mix instrumental) / Na na na / I need your love (Rough mix) / Rain (Alternative mix) / I believe in you / Listen to the eight track / You stepped into my dreams / Venus in a bathtub / Theatre of the absurd (Wessex mix) / Detroit (Out take 5 - Vocal) / Na na na (Extended mix) / China (Ronson vocal) / Old records never die (Version 1)
CD Set CDCHR 6074
Chrysalis / May '94 / EMI

WELCOME TO THE CLUB
FBI / Once bitten twice shy / Angeline / Laugh at me / All the way from Memphis / I wish I was your mother / Irene Wilde / Just another night / Cleveland rocks / Standin' in my light / Bastard / Walkin' with a mountain / All the young dudes / Slaughter on 10th Avenue / We gotta get out of here / Silver needles / Man 'o' war / Sons and daughters
CD Set CDCHR 6075
Chrysalis / May '94 / EMI

YOU'RE NEVER ALONE WITH A SCHIZOPHRENIC
Just another night / Wild east / Cleveland rocks / Ships / When the daylight comes / Life after death / Standin' in my light / Bastard / Outsider
CD CD25CR 03
Chrysalis / Mar '94 / EMI

Hunter, James

BELIEVE WHAT I SAY
Two can play / Way down inside / Very thought of you / It ain't funny / Turn on your love light / Let me know / I'll walk away / I wanna get old with you / Hallelujah I love her so / Believe what I say / Out of sight / Don't step on it / Hear me calling / Ain't nothing you can do
CD CDCHD 636
Ace / Oct '96 / Pinnacle

Hunter, Jim

CRACK O'NOON CLUB
CD CRACD 14
Watercolour / Mar '96 / ADA

FINGERNAIL MOON
CD COMD 2047
Temple / Feb '94 / ADA / CM / Direct / Duncans / Highlander

UPHILL SLIDE
CD COMD 2040
Temple / Feb '94 / ADA / CM / Direct / Duncans / Highlander

Hunter, Long John

BORDER TOWN LEGEND
CD ALCD 4839
Alligator / Feb '96 / ADA / CM / Direct

RIDE WITH ME
CD BMCD 9020
Black Magic / Apr '93 / ADA / Cadillac / Direct / Hot Shot

SWINGING FROM THE RAFTERS
Time and time again / I don't care / Stop what you're doing / Both ends of the world / Bugs on my window / Take it home with you / Trouble on the line / In the country / V-8 Ford / 30 days / I'm broke / Walking catfish / Locksmith man / Love prevails
CD ALCD 4853
Alligator / Jul '97 / ADA / CM / Direct

Hunter, Robert

BOX OF RAIN
Box of rain / Scarlet begonias / Franklin's tower / Jack Straw / Brown eyed women / Reuben and Cerise / Space / Deal / Promontory rider / Ripple / Boys in the bar room / Stella blue
CD RCD 10214
Rykodisc / Sep '91 / ADA / Vital

SENTINEL
Pride of bone / Gingerbread man / Idiot's delight (excerpt) / Red dog's decoration day / Trapping a muse / Jazz / Toad in love / Rimbaud at 20 / Rain in a courtyard / Way of the ride / Sentinel / Preserpie / Poets on poets / Like a basket / Yagritz / Cocktails with Hindemith / Blue moon alley / New jungle / Full moon cafe / Tango hit palace / Exploding diamond blues / Rainwater sea / Hologomena
CD RCD 20265
Rykodisc / Nov '93 / ADA / Vital

TALES OF THE GREAT RUM RUNNERS
Lady Simplicity / Dry dust road / Rum runners / Maybe she's a bluebird / It must have been the roses / Standing at your door / Keys to the rain / That train / I heard you singing / Children's lament / Boys in the bar room / Arizona lightning / Mad
CD GDCD 4013
Grateful Dead / May '89 / Pinnacle

TIGER ROSE
Tiger rose / Rose of Sharon / Dance a hole / Over the hills / Yellow moon / One thing to try / Wild Bill / Cruel white water / Last flash / Ariel
CD GDCD 4010
Grateful Dead / Jul '90 / Pinnacle

Hunter, Sonya

FAVOURITE SHORT STORIES
CD NORMAL 165
Normal / Nov '94 / ADA / Direct

FINDERS KEEPERS
CD RTS 19
Return To Sender / Aug '95 / ADA / Direct

GEOGRAPHY
Unlikely combinations / Can two worlds collide / Middle of somewhere / Atlases / Just a job / Heart cryin' in the wind / Mama sky / Baby girl / I can't reach you / Get back on that horse / London bridges
CD NORMAL 160CD
Normal / Mar '94 / ADA / Direct

PEASANT PIE
CD NORM 190CD
Normal / Apr '95 / ADA / Direct

Hunter, William

1982
CD CMCD 010
Celtic Music / Apr '94 / CM

LEAVING LERWICK HARBOUR (Hunter, William & Violet Tulloch)
Jackie Coleman/Sally Gardens / Leaving Lerwick Harbour / Chadwicks bog / Jamie's reel / Clarence Tough / Newcastle hornpipe/ Pat's reel / Caberfeidh / Randy wives of Fochabers / Carnival march / Sands of Murness / Kiwi reel / Laird o' Drumblair / De'il among the tailors / Ash plant / McGuire's welcome to Fermanagh / Alan Brown / Auld fiddler / Dumbarton Castle / Marquis of Huntley's farewell / Marquis of Tullybardine / Balkan Hills / Miller o' Hirn / Donald Stuart the piper / Weeping birches of Kilmorack / Grace Morrison of Borve / Cathie & Jim Lambie / Da grocer / Hjerdfeld / Laxo burn / Cape Breton Fiddler's welcome to Shetland / Peerie Willie / Lorna's reel
CD CDTRAX 106
Greentrax / Apr '96 / ADA / Direct / Duncans / Highlander

Hunters

COMPLETE COLLECTION, THE
CD BGOCD 325
Beat Goes On / Mar '97 / Pinnacle

Hunters & Collectors

CUT
CD TVD 93364
Mushroom / Feb '96 / 3mv/Pinnacle

DEMON FLOWER
CD TVD 93401
Mushroom / May '94 / 3mv/Pinnacle

Hunting Lodge

EIGHT BALL
CD Set NORMAL 61/62CD
Normal / '89 / ADA / Direct

NECROPOLIS
CD DV 17
Dark Vinyl / Jan '94 / Plastic Head / World Serpent

WILL
CD DV 10
Dark Vinyl / Mar '94 / Plastic Head / World Serpent

Huntley, George

BRAINJUNK
CD TVT 551CD
TVT / Apr '96 / Cargo / Greyhound

Huracan

VOICES OF THE WIND
CD PV 796011
Pierre Verany / Apr '96 / Discovery / Kingdom

Hurdy Gurdy

HURDY GURDY
CD HBG 122/11
Background / Apr '94 / Background / Greyhound

Hurleurs

BAZAR
Bazar / L'air du temps / Le ballade du corbeau / Sous le vent / Je suis tout petit / Dimanche / Pigeon / Lieder / Sans nom / Les roses de saadi / Marie / La petit mort / En votre absence / Kiki l'Indien
CD AC 6455
Chorus / Jan '97 / Harmonia Mundi

Hurley, Michael

WATERTOWER
CD HYMN 8
Fundamental / Aug '97 / Cargo / Plastic Head / Shellshock/Disc

WOLFWAYS
CD 379102
Koch Veracity / Jun '96 / Koch

Hurrah

SOUND OF PHILADELPHIA
CD CREV 014CD
Rev-Ola / Sep '93 / 3mv/Vital

Hurricane

AMERICA'S MOST HARDCORE (Hurricane & DFL)
Hurra: *Hurricane* / Can we get along: *Hurricane* / Elbow room: *Hurricane* / Pizza man: *DFL* / America's most hardcore: *DFL* / U don't understand: *DFL* / Knucklehead na-

tion: *DFL* / Think about the pit: *DFL* / Smoke bomb: *DFL* / My crazy life: *DFL*
CD _______________ WIJ 034CD
Wiiija / Apr '94 / RTM/Disc

Hurt, 'Mississippi' John

AIN'T NOBODY'S BUSINESS
Nobody's business but mine / Angels laid him away / Baby what's wrong with you / Casey Jones / Candy man / Lonesome blues / My creole belle / Make me a pallet on your floor / Trouble I had all my days / C-H-I-C-K-E-N blues / Coffee blues / Shake that thing / Monday morning blues / Frankie and Albert / Salty dog / Spike drivers blues / Here I am, Lord, send me / Talking Casey / Hot time in The Old Town tonight / I'm satisfied / Richland woman blues
CD _______________ CDSGP 037
Prestige / Jan '93 / Else / Total/BMG

AVALON BLUES 1963
CD _______________ ROUCD 1081
Rounder / Feb '92 / ADA / CM / Direct

COFFEE BLUES
CD _______________ IMP 309
IMP / Nov '96 / ADA / Discovery

IMMORTAL MISSISSIPPI JOHN HURT, THE
Since I've laid my burden down / Moaning the blues / Stocktime (Buck dance) / Lazy blues / Richland woman blues / Wise and foolish virgins / Hop joint / Monday morning blues / I've got the blues and I can't be satisfied / Keep on knocking / Chicken / Stagger Lee / Nearer my God to thee
CD _______________ VMD 79248
Vanguard / Oct '95 / ADA / Pinnacle

IN CONCERT
Nobody's business but mine / Angels laid him away / Baby what's wrong with you / Casey Jones / Candy man / Lonesome blues / My creole belle / Make me a pallet on the floor / Trouble I had all my days / C-H-I-C-K-E-N blues / Coffee blues / Shake that thing / Monday morning blues / Frankie and Albert / Salty dog / Spike driver's blues
CD _______________ CDBM 083
Blue Moon / Apr '91 / Cadillac / Discovery / Greensleeves / Jazz Music / Jet Star / TKO Magnum

LIBRARY OF CONGRESS RECORDINGS, THE
CD _______________ FLYCD 06
Flyright / Jun '89 / Hot Shot / Jazz Music / Wellard

MEMORIAL ANTHOLOGY
Slidin' delta / Salty dog / Louis Collins / stagger lee / Monday mornin' blues / Comin' home / Candy man blues / Hot time in the old town tonight / KC Jones blues / Make me a pallet on the floor / You can't come in / Joe Turner / Spanish flangdang / Lonesome am I / I shall not be moved / CC rider / Trouble blues
CD _______________ EDCD 381
Edsel / Feb '94 / Pinnacle

MEMORIAL ANTHOLOGY VOL.2
Lovin' spoonful / Richland woman blues / Frankie and Albert / Creole Bell / Chicken / Let the mermaids flirt with me / Nobody's dirty business / Stop time (buck dance) / Worried blues / Avalon blues
CD _______________ EDCD 446
Edsel / Apr '97 / Pinnacle

MISSISSIPPI JOHN HURT
CD _______________ DOCD 5003
Document / Feb '92 / ADA / Hot Shot / Jazz Music

SATISFIED LIVE
CD _______________ CWNCD 2024
Javelin / Jul '96 / Henry Hadaway / THE

TODAY
Pay day / I'm satisfied / Candy man / Make me a pallet on the floor / Talking Casey / Corinna Corinna / Coffee blues / Louis Collins / Hot time in the old time tonight / If you don't want me baby / Spike driver's blues / Beulah land
CD _______________ VMD 79220
Vanguard / Oct '95 / ADA / Pinnacle

WORRIED BLUES
CD _______________ ROUCD 1082
Rounder / Feb '92 / ADA / CM / Direct

Hurt, Peter

UMBRELLAS
Climbing / Between ourselves / So good / Les parapluies De Stoke Newington Part II / Triangle / Goat / Complications
CD _______________ ASCCD 10
ASC / Jun '96 / Cadillac / New Note/ Pinnacle

Hurvitz, Sandy

SANDY'S ALBUM IS HERE AT LAST
CD _______________ EDCD 399
Edsel / Nov '94 / Pinnacle

Hush

HUMAN
CD _______________ SHCD 5704
Shanachie / Oct '95 / ADA / Greensleeves / Koch

Husik, Lida

FLY STEREOPHONIC
Fly stereophonic / Fade sister cool / Sharon Hill shadows / Soundman / Cape fear / Cafe con leche / Death trip / Ein symphonie des grauens / Slide / Dead poets / Chocolate city / Dancing pants
CD _______________ A 121D
Alias / Jul '97 / Vital

GREEN BLUE FIRE
Bird / Bad head day / Haunt me / Wonderland / River Ouse / Just like candy / All hands on deck / Starburst 7 / Soul of God / Dead radio
CD _______________ ASW 6149
Astralwerks / Nov '96 / Cargo / Vital

Husker Du

CANDY APPLE GREY
Crystal / Don't want to know if you are lonely / I don't know for sure / Sorry somehow / Too far down / Hardly getting over it / Dead set on destruction / Eiffel Tower high / No promise have I made / All this I've done for you
CD _______________ 7599253852
WEA / Nov '92 / Warner Music

CASE CLOSED (A Tribute To Husker Du) (Various Artists)
CD _______________ SRC 19
SPV / May '94 / Koch / Plastic Head

EVERYTHING FALLS APART
From the gut / Blah blah blah / Punch drunk / Bricklayer / Afraid of being wrong / Sunshine superman / Signals from above / Everything falls apart / Wheels / Target / Obnoxious / Gravity / In a free land / What do I want / MIC / Statues / Let's go die / Amusement / Do you remember
CD _______________ 8122711632
WEA / Mar '93 / Warner Music

FLIP YOUR WIG
Flip your wig / Every everything / Makes no sense at all / Hate paper doll / Green eyes / Divide and conquer / Games / Find me / Baby song / Flexible flyer / Private plane / Keep hanging on / Wit and the wisdom / Don't know yet
CD _______________ SST 055CD
SST / May '93 / Plastic Head

LAND SPEED RECORD
CD _______________ SST 195CD
SST / Nov '88 / Plastic Head

LIVING END, THE
New day rising / Heaven hill / Standing in the rain / Back from somewhere / Ice cold ice / Everytime / Friend you're gonna fall / She floated away / From the gut / Target / It's not funny anymore / Hardly getting over it / Terms of psychic warfare / Powertime / Books about UFO's / Divide and conquer / Keep hanging on / Celebrated Summer / Now that you know me / Ain't no water in the well / What's going on / Data control / In a free land / Sheena is a punk rocker
CD _______________ 9362455822
WEA / May '94 / Warner Music

NEW DAY RISING
CD _______________ SST 031CD
SST / May '93 / Plastic Head

THERE'S A BOY WHO LIVES ON HEAVEN HILL (A Tribute To Husker Du) (Various Artists)
CD _______________ BHR 009CD
Burning Heart / Nov '94 / Plastic Head

WAREHOUSE SONGS AND STORIES
These important years / Charity, charity, prudence and hope / Standing in the rain / Back from somewhere / Ice cold ice / You're a soldier / Could you be the one / Too much spice / Friend, you've got to fall / She floated away / Bed of nails / Tell you why tomorrow / It's not peculiar / Actual condition / No reservations / Turn it around / She's a woman / Up in the air / You can live at home
CD _______________ 7599255442
WEA / Oct '92 / Warner Music

ZEN ARCADE
Something I learned today / Broken home broken heart / Never talking to you again / Chartered trips / Dreams reoccuring / Indecision time / Hare krishna / Beyond the threshold / Pride / I'll never forget you / Biggest lie / What's going on / Masochism world / Standing by the sea / Somewhere / One step at a time / Pink turns to blue / Newest industry / Monday will never be the same / Whatever / Tooth fairy and the princess / Turn on the news / Recurring dream
CD _______________ SST 027CD
SST / Jun '97 / Plastic Head

Husky & The Sandmen

ARABIAN NIGHTS
CD _______________ GASCD 1
Goofin' / Nov '96 / Nervous / TKO Magnum

Husky, Ferlin

CAPITOL COLLECTORS SERIES: FERLIN HUSKY
Feel better all over / I'll baby sit with you / Gone / Fallen star / My reason for living / Dragging the river / Wings of a dove / Waltz you saved for me / Somebody save me / I know it was you / Timber, I'm falling / I could sing all night / I hear Little Rock calling / Once / You pushed me too far / Just for you / That's why I love you so much / Every step of the way / Heavenly sunshine / Sweet misery
CD _______________ CZ 230
Capitol / Sep '89 / EMI

FERLIN HUSKY
Convoy / Truck drivin' sun of a gun / Don't fall asleep at the wheel / Giddy up go / Truck driving blues / Drunken driving / Hello I'm a truck / Wings of a dove / Little Joe / Phantom 309 / Me and old CB
CD _______________ PRACD 4005
Prairie / Jun '97 / Henry Hadaway

Hussain, Zakir

MAKING MUSIC (Hussain, Zakir & John McLaughlin)
Making music / Zakir / Water girl / Toni / Anisa / Sunjog / You and me / Sabah
CD _______________ 8315442
ECM / Jul '87 / New Note/Pinnacle

ZAKIR HUSSAIN & THE RHYTHM EXPERIENCE (Hussain, Zakir & The Rhythm Experience)
Balinese fantasy / Nines over easy / Lineage / Def and drum / Triveni / Rapanagutan / Ryupak / Rhythm sonata in E major
CD _______________ MRCD 1007
Moment / Jun '94 / ADA / Koch

Hustlers Of Culture

MANY STYLES
CD _______________ WALLLP 007
Wall Of Sound / Aug '95 / Prime / Soul Trader / Vital
CD _______________ WALLCD 008
Wall Of Sound / Mar '96 / Prime / Soul Trader / Vital

Hutcherson, Bobby

AMBOS MUNDOS (BOTH WORLDS)
Pomponio / Tin tin deo / Both worlds / Street song / Beep d' bop / Poema para ravel / Yelapa / Besame mucho
CD _______________ LCD 15222
Landmark / Nov '89 / New Note/Pinnacle

FAREWELL KEYSTONE
Crescent Moon / Short stuff / Prism / Starting over / Rubber man / Mapenzi
CD _______________ ECD 220182
Evidence / Jul '92 / ADA / Cadillac / Harmonia Mundi

FOUR SEASONS (Hutcherson, Bobby & George Cables)
I mean you / All of you / Spring is here / Star eyes / If I were a bell / Summertime / Autumn leaves
CD _______________ CDSJP 210
Timeless Jazz / Jan '87 / New Note/ Pinnacle

MIRAGE
Nascimento / Mirage / Beyond the bluebird / Pannonica / Del Valle / I am in love / Zingargo / Ground work / Love letters / Heroes
CD _______________ LCD 15292
Landmark / Aug '91 / New Note/Pinnacle

Hutchings, Ashley

ALBION JOURNEY, AN
CD _______________ HNCD 4802
Hannibal / May '89 / ADA / Vital

ASHLEY HUTCHINGS BIRTHDAY BASH CONCERT
CD _______________ HTD 39CD
HTD / Jul '95 / CM / Pinnacle

BATTER PUDDING FOR JOHN KEATS, A
CD _______________ HTDCD 62
HTD / Jun '96 / CM / Pinnacle

GUVNOR (4CD Set)
Washington at Valley Forge / Some sweet day / You're gonna need my help / Dear landlord / College grove/Silver spear / Lay down your weary tune / Four hand reel/St. Anne's reel / Horn fair / Lament / Sailor's life / Bluebell / Six days on the road / Albion band is here again / Lost in space / Elements lament / Angelina / 3 Brampton morris tunes / We lie / Didn't he ramble / You never wanted me / Sir Patrick Spens / Morris dance tunes / Rambling sailor / Cuckoos nest / Old Sir Simon the King / High level hornpipe / Don't be an outlaw / Spirit of the dance / Lay down your waery tune / Moon shine's bright / Rose and the rock / Sweet bird of paradise / Ninety miles an hour / I just got off the plane / Rainbow over the hill / Jerusalem ridge / Memories of you / Night in the city / Marcie / Harvest home / Fair maid of Islington / Three waltzes / Y'acre of land / Boycott's bouree / By the time it gets dark / Pain or paradise / Four tunes / Moon shine's bright / Princess Royal / Down the road / It doesn't matter anymore / Loose hornpipe / Spencer the rover / Cardhouse / Brief encounters / Oak / Both sides now / Fotheringay / Mistress's health / Quaker's wife / Here we come / Holms fancy / I'm looking through you / Simple melody / Electric guitar is king / Cecil sharp show / Personent Hodie / Love gets dangerous / Pa's piano stool / Turnpike reel / Willow / Not for the want of will / Swallow your gum / Wings
CD Set _______________ HTDBX 01
HTD / Aug '97 / CM / Pinnacle

GUVNOR VOL.1
CD _______________ HTDCD 23
HTD / Jul '94 / CM / Pinnacle

GUVNOR VOL.2
CD _______________ HTDCD 29
HTD / Mar '95 / CM / Pinnacle

GUVNOR VOL.3
CD _______________ HTDCD 38
HTD / Jul '95 / CM / Pinnacle

GUVNOR VOL.4
CD _______________ HTDCD 66
HTD / Aug '96 / CM / Pinnacle

KICKIN' UP THE SAWDUST
La russe (medley) / Buttered peas / Hullichan jig / Wave of joy / Heel and toe polka / Tavern in the town / Double quadrille / Jumping Joan / Dorset four hand reel / Hornpipes / Speed the plough / Cumberland square eight
CD _______________ BGOCD 244
Beat Goes On / Oct '94 / Pinnacle

RATTLEBONE AND PLOUGHJACK
CD _______________ BGOCD 353
Beat Goes On / Jun '97 / Pinnacle

SWAY WITH ME (Hutchings, Ashley & Judy Dunlop)
CD _______________ RGFCD 008
Road Goes On Forever / '92 / Direct

TWANGIN' AND A TRADDIN'
FBI / Sherwood handjive / Riff raff / Telstar / Walk don't run / Duane Eddy medley / Spyder walk
CD _______________ HTDCD 25
HTD / Sep '96 / CM / Pinnacle

Hutchinson, Frank

FRANK HUTCHINSON 1926-1929 VOL.1
CD _______________ DOCD 8003
Document / Mar '97 / ADA / Hot Shot / Jazz Music

Hutchinson, Leslie

CREAM OF HUTCH VOL.2, THE (Hutchinson, Leslie 'Hutch')
CD _______________ PASTCD 7036
Flapper / Aug '94 / Pinnacle

HUTCH (Hutchinson, Leslie 'Hutch')
I forgot the little things / Begin the beguine / Don't make me laugh / Broken hearted clown / Night and day / Dusty shoes / I need you / If I should lose you / Good night my beautiful / East of the sun and west of the moon / I couldn't believe my eyes / Turn on the old music box / You made me care / Kiss in the dark / My heart is haunted / Faithfull forever / That old feeling / Indian summer / Body and soul / I've got my eyes on you / I know now / You're just looking for romance
CD _______________ PASTCD 9755
Flapper / Aug '91 / Pinnacle

HUTCH SINGS COLE PORTER & NOEL COWARD (Hutchinson, Leslie 'Hutch')
Let's do it let's fall in love / I'm a gigolo / Looking at you / What is sthis thing called love / Two little babes in the wood / Night and day / Anything goes / Begin the beguine / Just one of those things / Easy to love / I've got you under my skin / It's delovely / Do I love you / I've got my eyes on you / You'd be so nice to come home to / Half caste woman / I'll follow my secret heart / I travel alone / Close your eyes / All I do is dream of you / I nearly let love go slipping through my fingers / Says my heart / You go to my head / Cole Porter medley (Parts one and two)
CD _______________ CDCHD 213
Happy Days / Mar '94 / Conifer/BMG

LESLIE 'HUTCH' HUTCHINSON (Hutchinson, Leslie 'Hutch')
Heartaches / Danger ahead / I promise you / Peg o' my heart / Seems liek old times / You stepped out of a dream / Flamingo / Till stars forget to shine / Way that the wind blows / Till then / There I've said it again / Sophisticated lady / Where in the world / Absent minded moon / Sand in my shoes / Manana / But beautiful / I never loved anyone / It only happens when I dance with you / Ask anyone who knows / You do / Tree in the meadow / You keep coming back like a song / I'm confessin' / Now is the hour
CD _______________ CDMFP 6357
Music For Pleasure / Jun '97 / EMI

TREASURED MEMORIES (Hutchinson, Leslie 'Hutch')
Begin the beguine / All the things you are / Mist on the rivers / I've got my eyes on you / Violins and violets / Man I love / Among my souvenirs / There's a small hotel / In-

termezzo / What is this thing called love / When love comes your way / Try a little tenderness / Don't make me laugh / It's a lovely day tomorrow / Shake down the stars / Should I tell you that I love you / Dusty shoes / It happens every day / Where or when / That's the beginning of the end / Let's fall in love / Cole Porter medley / Small cafe by Notre Dame / Careless / Rosita
CD _______ CDAJA 5084
Living Era / Mar '92 / Select

Hutson, Leroy

FEEL THE SPIRIT
CD _______ CPCD 8275
Charly / May '97 / Koch

HUTSON
CD _______ CPCD 8280
Charly / Jul '97 / Koch

HUTSON VOL.2
CD _______ CPCD 8283
Charly / Mar '97 / Koch

LOVE, OH LOVE
CD _______ CPCD 8156
Charly / Mar '96 / Koch

LUCKY FELLOW (The Best Of Leroy Hutson 1973-1979)
Lucky fellow / All because of you / Where did love go / Never know what you can do (give it a try) / So in love with you / Love to hold you close / Don't it make you feel good / Ghetto '74 / In the mood / Get to this (you'll get to me) / Lovers' holiday / So nice / When you smile
CD _______ CDNEW 101
Charly / Dec '96 / Koch

MAN, THE
Can't say enough about Mom / Gotta move gotta groove / Ella Weez / Give this love a try / Getto '74 / After the fight / Could this be love / Dudley Do-Right
CD _______ CPCD 8128
Charly / Oct '95 / Koch

VERY BEST OF LEROY HUTSON, THE (The Definitive Hits Collection)
Love the feeling / Classy lady / Ghetto '74 / So nice / All because of you / Lover's holiday / Lucky fellow / Get to this (you'll get to me) / Love to hold you close / Don't it make you feel good / Heaven right here (on earth) / More where that came from / Never know what you can do (give it a try) / Love oh love / Cool out / It's different
CD _______ DEEPM 007
Deep Beats / Feb '97 / BMG

Hutto, J.B.

HAWK SQUAT (Hutto, J.B. & His Hawks)
CD _______ DD 617
Delmark / Mar '95 / ADA / Cadillac / CM / Direct / Hot Shot

HIGH AND LONESOME
High and lonesome / JB's boogie / Feel so good / Too much alcohol / Hide and seek / Laundromat blues / Coo coo baby / Walking the dog / Come back baby / Kansas city
CD _______ 422330
WMD / Jan '97 / Discovery

LIVE AT THE SHABOO INN 1979
CD _______ 422327
Last Call / Feb '97 / Cargo / Direct / Discovery

MASTERS OF MODERN BLUES SERIES (Hutto, J.B. & His Hawks)
CD _______ TCD 5020
Testament / Apr '95 / ADA / Koch

SLIDESLINGER (Hutto, J.B. & The New Hawks)
CD _______ ECD 260092
Evidence / Jan '92 / ADA / Cadillac / Harmonia Mundi

Hutton, Joe

NORTHUMBRIAN PIPER
CD _______ EAR 15CD
East Allen / Oct '94 / ADA

Hutton, Tim

CONSCIOUS KIND, THE
CD _______ SBZCD 005
Some Bizarre / Dec '91 / Pinnacle

Huub De Lange

LIFE AND DEATH ON A STREET ORGAN
CD _______ PAN 145CD
Pan / Dec '94 / ADA / CM / Direct

Huun-Huur-Tu

IF I'D BEEN BORN AN EAGLE
CD _______ SH 64080
Shanachie / Feb '97 / ADA / Greensleeves / Koch

ORPHANS LAMENT
CD _______ SHAN 64058CD
Shanachie / Apr '95 / ADA / Greensleeves / Koch

SIXTY HORSES IN MY HERD (Old Songs & Tunes Of Tuva - Throat Singing)
CD _______ SHCD 64050
Shanachie / Mar '94 / ADA / Greensleeves / Koch

Huxley, George

SWING THAT MUSIC
CD _______ JCD 239
Jazzology / Mar '95 / Jazz Music

Huygen, Michel

BARCELONA 1992
Carvalho / Impossible love / Chase / Meeting at the hilton / Loneliness / Barcelona 1992 / Tonight
CD _______ CDTB 056
Thunderbolt / Feb '88 / TKO Magnum

INTIMO
Tenderness / Light being / When I stop the time / Remoteness / El mar de la Soledad / Tempestad cerebral / Vital breath / Infinite tenderness
CD _______ CDTB 092
Thunderbolt / Sep '90 / TKO Magnum

Hwan, Kang Tae

KANG TAE HWAN & SAINKHO NAMTCHYLAK LIVE (Hwan, Kang Tae & Sainkho Namtchylak)
CD _______ FINCD 9301
Free Improvision Network / Apr '94 / Harmonia Mundi

Hyatt, Walter

MUSIC TOWN
CD _______ SHCD 1039
Sugar Hill / Jan '94 / ADA / CM / Direct / Koch / Roots

Hybernoid

HYBERNOID
CD _______ D 00028CD
Displeased / Jan '95 / Plastic Head / RTM/Disc

LAST DAY
CD _______ FDN 2002CD
Foundation 2000 / Aug '95 / Plastic Head

Hybrid Kids

HONEYMOON IN BABYLON
CD _______ SPV 07745772
SPV / Mar '96 / Koch / Plastic Head

Hydra

SPOOKY WEIRDNESS
Comfort / Dream on / Let me be your worm / Clinging vine / Nowhere over the rainbow / Custer's last grand / Butterflies / Maid of grace / Nitro / W4 syndrome
CD _______ 5331262
Hi-Life / Mar '97 / PolyGram

Hydroplane

HYDROPLANE
CD _______ DRIVE 09
Drive-In / Jun '97 / Cargo

Hyenas In The Desert

DIE LAUGHING
Elephant graveyard / Can you feel it / Wild dogs / Longest night (journal #1) / Concubinez / Why me / Fresh meat / Hyenas in the desert / Other side of midnight
CD _______ 4843652
Columbia / Sep '96 / Sony

Hykes, David

CURRENT CIRCULATION (Hykes, David & The Harmonic Choir)
CD _______ CDCEL 13010
Celestial Harmonies / Nov '92 / ADA / Select

CURRENT MEETINGS (Hykes, David & The Harmonic Choir)
CD _______ CDCEL 14013
Celestial Harmonies / Nov '92 / ADA / Select

HARMONIC MEETINGS (Hykes, David & The Harmonic Choir)
CD Set _______ CDCEL 013/14
Celestial Harmonies / Jul '88 / ADA / Select

Hyla, Lee

IN DOUBLE LIGHT
CD _______ AVAN 015
Avant / Sep '93 / Cadillac / Harmonia Mundi

Hyland, Brian

VERY BEST OF BRIAN HYLAND
CD _______ MCCD 146
Music Club / Nov '93 / Disc / THE

Hylton, Jack

CREAM OF JACK HYLTON
Rhythm like this / Trouble in Paradise / Gold diggers song (We're in the money) / I can't remember / Hallelujah, I'm a tramp / Stormy weather / Shadow waltz / Dancing butterfly / With you here, and me here / Honeymoon hotel / You're an old smoothie / You are too beautiful / You've got me crying again / Close your eyes / (In) a shanty in old Shanty Town / Try a little tenderness / Ride tenderfoot ride / Good morning / Love makes the world go round / What goes on here
CD _______ PASTCD 9775
Flapper / Feb '92 / Pinnacle

JACK'S BACK (Hylton, Jack & His Orchestra)
Happy days are here again / Speaking of Kentucky days / My bundle of love / I'm looking over a four leaf clover / World's greatest sweetheart is you / Harmonica Harry / Gentlemen prefer blondes / Broadway melody / Happy feet / I wanna go places and do things / Guy that wrote 'The stein' song / Meadow lark / Choo choo / Life is just a bowl of cherries / Da da da / Under the ukelele tree / Hang on to me / When day is done
CD _______ CDAJA 5018
Living Era / '87 / Select

Hyman, Dick

CHEEK TO CHEEK (Hyman, Dick Trio)
CD _______ ARCD 19155
Arbors Jazz / May '97 / Cadillac

CONCORD DUO SERIES VOL.6 (Hyman, Dick & Ralph Sutton)
I've found a new baby / I'm gonna sit right down and write myself a letter / Always / I'm sorry I made you cry / Everything happens to me / All of me / Sunday / Ol' man river / Spider and the fly / World is waiting for the sunrise / Dinah / Emaline
CD _______ CCD 4603
Concord Jazz / Jul '94 / New Note/Pinnacle

DICK HYMAN PLAYS COLE PORTER: ALL THROUGH THE NIGHT
CD _______ MM 5060
Music Masters / Oct '94 / Nimbus

DICK HYMAN PLAYS FATS WALLER (Hyman, Dick & His Trio)
CD _______ RR 33CD
Reference Recordings / Sep '91 / Jazz Music / May Audio

FACE THE MUSIC (A Century Of Irving Berlin)
CD _______ MM 5002
Music Masters / Oct '94 / Nimbus

GERSHWIN SONGBOOK: JAZZ VARIATIONS
CD _______ MM 65094
Music Masters / Oct '94 / Nimbus

GREAT AMERICAN SONGBOOK, THE
CD _______ 01612651202
Music Masters / Sep '95 / Nimbus

KINGDOM OF SWING & THE REPUBLIC OF OOP BOP SH'BAM (Jazz In July Live)
Lester leaps in: *Jazz In July* / Joshua fit de battle of jericho: *Jazz In July*
CD _______ MM 5016
Music Masters / Oct '94 / Nimbus

LIVE AT THE 92ND STREET Y (Hyman, Dick Piano Players & Significant Others)
CD _______ MM 5042
Music Masters / Oct '94 / Nimbus

MANHATTAN JAZZ (Classics In Jazz) (Hyman, Dick & Ruby Braff)
Jubilee / You're lucky to me / Man I love / How long has this been going on / He loves and she loves / I'm crazy 'bout my baby / Some day you'll be sorry / Don't worry 'bout me / Jeepers creepers / I'm just wild about Harry / Man that got away / If only I had a brain / Somewhere over the rainbow / Blues for John W
CD _______ 8208122
Limelight / Oct '90 / PolyGram

MANHATTAN JAZZ (Hyman, Dick & Ruby Braff)
CD _______ MM 5031
Music Masters / Oct '94 / Nimbus

SWING IS HERE
CD _______ RR 72CD
Reference Recordings / Jul '96 / Jazz Music / May Audio

THEY GOT RHYTHM (Hyman, Dick & Derek Smith)
CD _______ JCD 635
Jass / Oct '93 / ADA / Cadillac / CM / Direct / Jazz Music

Hyman, Phyllis

BEST OF PHYLLIS HYMAN (The Buddah Years)
Loving you - losing you / No one can love you more / One thing on my mind / I don't want to lose you / Deliver the love / Night bird gets the love / Beautiful man of mine / Children of the world / Living inside your love / Sweet music / Answer is you / Love is free / Sing a song / Soon come again / Be careful (how you treat my love)
CD _______ NEXCD 138
Sequel / Oct '90 / BMG

Hype-A-Delics

MO' FUNK FOR YOUR ASS
CD _______ EFA 119352
Juiceful / Mar '94 / SRD

Hyper Go Go

NATIONAL ANTHEMS
CD _______ AVEXCD 32
Avex / Apr '96 / 3mv/Pinnacle

Hyperborea

SERPENTINE
CD _______ SC 469
Starc / Aug '96 / ADA / Direct

Hyperhead

METAPHASIA
CD _______ CDDVN 16
Devotion / Dec '92 / Pinnacle

Hypermodern Jazz 2000.5

HYPERMODERN JAZZ 2000.5
CD _______ EFA 006732
Mille Plateau / Apr '96 / SRD

Hypersax

STEPDANCE
Stepdance / Run for fun / Sailing around Greek islands / Princy palace / Long distance education / Update / Song for Contessa / Red Bank NJ / Solo in the night / Starlight / Rush hour / Rainy days / Pop song / VIBSAX
CD _______ 101 2 7054 2
New Note / Nov '92 / Cadillac / New Note/ Pinnacle

Hypnodance

HYPNODANCE
CD _______ CONTECD 129
Contempo / Nov '89 / Plastic Head

Hypnolovewheel

ALTERED STATES
You choose / Peace of mind / Watermelon song / Turn you off / I know / Model railroad / Right on / Dysfunctional friend / Electric brown / Nightly grind / Kerosene kiss / Dodge city
CD _______ A 034D
Alias / May '93 / Vital

ANGEL FOOD
CD _______ A 020D
Alias / Jun '92 / Vital

SPACE MOUNTAIN
CD _______ A 011D
Alias / Jul '92 / Vital

Hypnotone

AI
CD _______ CRECD 080
Creation / May '94 / 3mv/Vital

HYPNOTONE
CD _______ CRECD 067
Creation / May '94 / 3mv/Vital

Hypocrisy

ABDUCTED
CD _______ NB 133CD
Nuclear Blast / Jan '96 / Plastic Head

FOURTH DIMENSION, THE
CD _______ NB 112CD
Nuclear Blast / Oct '94 / Plastic Head

INFERIOR DEVOTIES
CD _______ NB 096CD
Nuclear Blast / Mar '94 / Plastic Head

MAXIMUM ABDUCTION
CD _______ NB 145CD
Nuclear Blast / May '96 / Plastic Head

OBSCULUM OBSCENUM
CD _______ NB 080CD
Nuclear Blast / Aug '93 / Plastic Head

OSCULUM OBSECNUM/INFERIOR DEVOTEES/PLEASURES OF MOLESTATION
CD _______ NB 215CD
Nuclear Blast / Nov '96 / Plastic Head

PENETRALLIA
CD _______ NB 164CD
Nuclear Blast / Jun '96 / Plastic Head

Hypocrite

EDGE OF EXISTENCE
CD _______ OW 003CD
Offworld / Jul '96 / Plastic Head

I

I

TINNED MUSIC
CD PODCD 033
Pod Communications / Feb '95 / Plastic Head

I Benjamin

RASTA 2000
CD OBCD 01
Obzaki / Jun '97 / Essential/BMG

I-Compani

LUNA TRISTE
CD BVHAASTCD 9012
Bvhaast / Oct '93 / Cadillac

SOGNI D'ORO
CD BVHAASTCD 9404
Bvhaast / Oct '94 / Cadillac

I-Cube

PICNIC ATTACK
CD VERCD 006
Versatile / May '97 / Amato Disco / Arabesque / Prime

I Found God

BEFORE HE TURNED THE GUN ON HIMSELF
CD OC 500022
Outcast / May '97 / Cargo

I-Roy

CRISUS TIME
Heart of a lion / Casmas Town / Tonight / Wrap 'n' bap 'n' / Union call / London / Roots man time / African tak / Crisus time / Equality and justice / Hypocrite back out / Musical injection / Don't touch I man locks / Satta a masagana / African herbsman / Love your neighbour / Send us little power oh jah / Moving on strong
CD CDFL 9015
Frontline / Jul '93 / EMI / Jet Star

DON'T CHECK ME WITH NO LIGHTWEIGHT STUFF (I-Roy 1972-1975)
CD BAFCD 16
Blood & Fire / Jan '97 / Vital

GREAT GODFATHER
CD RNCD 2079
Rhino / Dec '94 / Grapevine/PolyGram / Jet Star

KING TUBBY'S STUDIO (I-Roy & Dillinger)
CD LG 21116
Lagoon / Oct '95 / Grapevine/PolyGram

STRAIGHT TO I-ROY'S HEAD (Various Artists)
CD CC 2719
Crocodisc / Apr '95 / Grapevine/PolyGram

I-Salonisiti

CAFE VICTORIA
Los mareados / Poema valseado / Recuerdo / Coral / Romance de barrio / Uno / Payadora / Flores negras / Severina / Flor de lino / Contra bajilsmo
CD CDC 1695312
Harmonia Mundi / Jul '86 / Cadillac / Harmonia Mundi

I-Sharko

I SHARKO
CD BCD 4053
Bomp / Apr '96 / Cargo / Greyhound / RTM/Disc / Shellshock/Disc

I-Shen Sound

KING SIZE DUB
CD HYPOXIA 002CD
Hypoxia / Oct '95 / Plastic Head

I Start Counting

FUSED
CD CDSTUMM 50
Mute / Jun '89 / RTM/Disc

MY TRANSLUCENT HANDS
Introduction / My translucent hands / Catch that look / You and I / Lose him / Keep the sun away / Cranley Gardens / Which way is home / Letters to a friend / Still smiling / Small consolation / (There is always the) unexpected
CD CDSTUMM 30
Mute / Oct '86 / RTM/Disc

I Suanatori Delle Quatro ...

RACCONTI A COLORI (I Suanatori Delle Quatro Province)
CD NT 6720
Robi Droli / Jan '94 / ADA / Direct

i0

90 MINUTES IN THE EYES OF IO (i0 & Adsr)
CD CHEAP ONE
Cheap / Apr '95 / Plastic Head / Vital

Ian & Sylvia

END OF THE BEGINNING, THE
More often than not / Creators of rain / Summer wages / Midnight / Barney / Some kind of fool / Shark and the cockroach / Last lonely eagle / Lincoln feed me / Needle of death / Everybody has to say goodbye / Give it to the world / Jordan Station / Long Beach / Love is strange
CD BCD 15940
Bear Family / Dec '96 / Direct / Rollercoaster / Swift

SO MUCH FOR DREAMING
CD VMD 79241
Vanguard / Oct '96 / ADA / Pinnacle

Ian, Janis

AFTERTONES
Aftertones / I would like to dance / Love is blind / Roses / Belle of the blues / Goodbye to morning / Boy I really tried one on / This must be wrong / Don't cry / Old man / Hymn
CD GRACD 304
Grapevine / Jan '96 / Grapevine/PolyGram

BETWEEN THE LINES
When the party's over / At seventeen / From me to you / Bright lights and promises / In the Winter / Water colors / Between the lines / Come on / Light a tight / Tea and sympathy / Lover's lullaby
CD GRACD 303
Grapevine / Aug '95 / Grapevine/PolyGram

BREAKING SILENCE
All roads to the river / Ride me like a wave / Tattoo / Guess you had to be there / What about the love / His hands / Walking on sacred ground / This train still runs / Through the years / This house / Some people's lives / Breaking silence
CD 5196142
Polydor / Jul '93 / PolyGram

JANIS IAN
Grand illusion / Some people / Tonight will last forever / Hotels and one night stands / Do you wanna dance / Silly habits / Bridge / My mama's house / Street life serenaders / I need to live alone again / Hopper painting
CD GRACD 306
Grapevine / Jan '96 / Grapevine/PolyGram

MIRACLE ROW
Party lights / I want to make you love me / Sunset of your life / Take to the sky / Candlelight / Let me be lonely / Slow dance romance / Will you dance / I'll cry tonight / Miracle row / Maria
CD GRACD 305
Grapevine / Aug '95 / Grapevine/PolyGram

NIGHT RAINS
Other side of the sun / Fly too high / Memories / Photographs / Here comes the night / Day by day / Have mercy love / Lay low / Night rains / Jenny
CD GRACD 307
Grapevine / Jan '96 / Grapevine/PolyGram

OLD GREY WHISTLE TEST 1976
CD WHISCD 008
Whistle Test / Mar '96 / ADA

PRESENT COMPANY
Seaside / Present company / See my grammy ride / Here in Spain / On the train / He's a rainbow / Weary Lady / Nature's at peace / See the river / Let it run free / Alabama / Liberty / My land / Hello Jerry / Can you reach me / Sunlight
CD BGOCD 165
Beat Goes On / Nov '92 / Pinnacle

RESTLESS EYES
Under the covers / I remember yesterday / I believe I'm myself again / Restless eyes / Get ready to roll / Passion play / Down and away / Bigger than real / Dear Billy / Sugar mountain
CD GRACD 308
Grapevine / Jan '96 / Grapevine/PolyGram

REVENGE
CD GRACD 301
Grapevine / May '95 / Grapevine/ PolyGram

SOCIETY CHILD - THE VERVE YEARS
CD 5275912
Verve / Apr '96 / PolyGram

SOCIETY'S CHILD
Society's child / Too old to go 'way little girl / Hair of spun gold / Then the tangles of my mind / I'll give you a stone if you'll throw it / Pro-girl / Younger generation blues / New Christ cardiac hero / Everybody knows / Mistaken identity / Friends again / 42nd Street / Psycho blues / She's made of porcelain / Sweet misery / When I was a child / What do you think of the dead / Look to the rain
CD 5725912
Polydor / Jan '94 / PolyGram

STARS
Stars / Man you are in me / Sweet sympathy / Page nine / Thank yous / Dance with me / Without you / You've got me on a string / Applause
CD GRACD 302
Grapevine / Jan '96 / Grapevine/PolyGram

UNCLE WONDERFUL
CD GRACD 309
Grapevine / Jan '96 / Grapevine/PolyGram

Ibis

EARTH CITIZEN
CD 092032
Cobalt / Nov '92 / Grapevine/PolyGram

Ibrahim, Abdullah

AFRICAN PIANO (Brand, Dollar)
Bra Joe from Kilimanjaro / Selby that the eternal spirit / Is the only reality / Moon / Xaba / Sunset in the blue / Kippy / Jabulani / Tintinyana
CD 8350202
ECM / Sep '88 / New Note/Pinnacle

AFRICAN SKETCH BOOK (Brand, Dollar)
CD ENJACD 20262
Enja / Nov '94 / New Note/Pinnacle / Vital/ SAM

AFRICAN SPACE PROGRAMME (Brand, Dollar)
CD ENJACD 20322
Enja / Nov '94 / New Note/Pinnacle / Vital/ SAM

AFRICAN SUN (Brand, Dollar)
African sun / Bra Joe from Kilimanjaro / Rollin' / Memories of you / Sathima / African herbs / Nobody knows the trouble I've seen / Blues for B / Gwidza / Kamalie
CD KAZ CD 102
Kaz / Jul '88 / BMG

ANATOMY OF A SOUTH AFRICAN VILLAGE (Brand, Dollar & Gertze/ Ntshoko)
CD BLC 760172
Black Lion / Nov '92 / Cadillac / Jazz Music / Koch / Wellard

ANCIENT AFRICA
Bra Joe from Kilimanjaro / Mama / Tokai / Ilanga / Cherry / African sun / Tintinyana / Xaba / Peace - Salaam air
CD SKCD 23049
Sackville / Oct '94 / Cadillac / Jazz Music / Swift

BLUES FOR A HIP KING (Brand, Dollar)
Ornette's cornet: *Ibrahim, Abdullah* / All day and all night long: *Ibrahim, Abdullah* / Sweet Basil blues: *Ibrahim, Abdullah* / Blue monk: *Monk, Thelonious* / Tsakwe here comes the postman: *Ibrahim, Abdullah* / Blues for a hip king: *Ibrahim, Abdullah* / Blues for B: *Ibrahim, Abdullah* / Mysterioso: *Monk, Thelonious* / Just you, just me: *Green* / Eclipse at dawn: *Ibrahim, Abdullah* / King Kong: *Matshikiza* / Khumbula Jane: *Davashe* / Boulevarde East: *Ibrahim, Abdullah*
CD KAZ CD 104
Kaz / Oct '88 / BMG

CAPE TOWN FLOWERS
Excursions / Eleventh hour / Kofifi blue / Chisa / Song for Aggerey / Stride / Call / African marketplaace / Joan Cape Town Flower / Maraba blue / Monk in Harlem
CD 8888262
Tiptoe / May '97 / New Note/Pinnacle

DOLLAR BRAND (Brand, Dollar)
Little Niles / Resolution / Which way / On the banks of Allen Waters / Knights night / Pye R squared / Mood indigo/Don't get around much anymore/Take the A train / Stride / Tintiyana / Obluega
CD 8747112
DA Music / Jul '96 / Conifer/BMG

DUKES' MEMORIES (Brand, Dollar)
CD 233853
Black & Blue / '86 / Discovery / Koch / Wellard

ECHOES FROM AFRICA (Brand, Dollar)
CD ENJA 30472
Enja / Apr '90 / New Note/Pinnacle / Vital/ SAM

FATS, DUKE AND MONK
CD SKCD 3049
Sackville / Mar '97 / Cadillac / Jazz Music / Swift

GOOD NEWS FROM AFRICA (Brand, Dollar Duo)
CD ENJACD 20482
Enja / Nov '94 / New Note/Pinnacle / Vital/ SAM

KNYSNA BLUE
Knysna blue / You can't stop me now / Peace / Three no.1 / Kofifi / Three no.2 / Cape Town / Ask me now
CD 8888162
Enja / Jun '94 / New Note/Pinnacle / Vital/ SAM

LIVE AT MONTREUX: DOLLAR BRAND (Brand, Dollar)
CD ENJACD 30792
Enja / Nov '94 / New Note/Pinnacle / Vital/ SAM

MANTRA MODE
CD 8478102
New Note / Nov '91 / Cadillac / New Note/ Pinnacle

MEMORIES
CD WWCD 2029
West Wind / Apr '90 / Koch

MINDIF (Brand, Dollar)
CD ENJA 50732
Enja / Jul '88 / New Note/Pinnacle / Vital/ SAM

NO FEAR, NO DIE
Calypso minor / Angelica / Meditation / Nisa / Kata / Meditation / Calypso major
CD TIP 8888152
Tiptoe / Jul '93 / New Note/Pinnacle

ODE TO DUKE ELLINGTON (Brand, Dollar)
Impressions on a caravan / Ode to Duke / What really happened in the cornfield / Rose got it bad in Harlem / Solitude / In a sentimental mood / Two spirituals
CD WWCD 2020
West Wind / Dec '93 / Koch

REFLECTIONS (Brand, Dollar)
Honeysuckle rose / Resolution / Knight's night / Mood indigo / Don't get around much anymore / Take the 'A' train / Monk's mood / You are too beautiful / Little Niles / Pye R squared / On the banks of Allen Waters / Reflections / Which way
CD BLCD 760127
Black Lion / May '90 / Cadillac / Jazz Music / Koch / Wellard

ROUND MIDNIGHT AT MONTMARTRE (Brand, Dollar)
CD BLCD 76011
Black Lion / Feb '89 / Cadillac / Jazz Music / Koch / Wellard

WATER FROM AN ANCIENT WELL
Mandela / Song for Fathima / Manenberg revisited / Tuang Guru / Water from an ancient well / Wedding / Mountain / Sameeda
CD 8888122
Tiptoe / Feb '95 / New Note/Pinnacle

YARONA
Nisa / Duke / Cherry / Mannenberg / African river / Tuang guru / Stardance / African marketplace / Tintinyana / Barakaat
CD 8888202
Enja / Jul '95 / New Note/Pinnacle / Vital/ SAM

ZIMBABWE (Brand, Dollar)
CD ENJA 40562
Enja / '88 / New Note/Pinnacle / Vital/SAM

Ice

UNDER THE SKIN
CD PATH 11CD
NMC / Jul '93 / Total/Pinnacle

Ice

SAGA OF THE ICE KING
CD KSCD 9596
Kissing Spell / Jun '97 / Greyhound

Ice Age

LIFE'S A BITCH
CD HMIXD 154
FM / Aug '90 / Revolver / Sony

Ice Cold July

THERE WILL COME A DAY
CD SECT2 10002
Sector 2 / Jul '95 / Cargo / Direct

Ice Cube

AMERIKKKA'S MOST WANTED
Better off dead / Nigga ya love to hate / What they hittin foe / You can't fade me/ JD's gaffilin / Once upon a time in the projects / Turn off the radio / Endangered species (Tales from the darkside) / Gangsta's fairytale / I'm only out for one thang / Get off my dick and tell yo bitch to come here / Drive-by / Rollin' wit' tha lench mob / Who's the mack / Amerikkka's most wanted / It's a man's world / Bomb
CD ____ **IMCD 230**
Island / Sep '96 / PolyGram

BOOTLEGS & B-SIDES
Robbin' hood (cause it ain't all good) / What can I do / 24 with a L / You know how we do it / 2 n the morning / You don't wanna fuck with these / Lil ass gee / My skin is my sin / It was a good day / U ain't gonna take my life / When I get to heaven / D'Voidofpopniggafiedmegamix
CD ____ **IMCD 231**
Island / Sep '96 / PolyGram

DEATH CERTIFICATE
Funeral / Wrong nigga to fuck wit / My summer vacation / Steady mobbin / Robin Lench / Givin' up the nappy dug out / Look who's burnin / Bird in the hand / Man's best friend / Alive on arrival / Death / Birth / I wanna kill Sam / Horny Lil devil / True to the game / Color blind / Doing dumb shit / Us
CD ____ **IMCD 232**
Island / Sep '96 / PolyGram

KILL AT WILL
Endangered species (Tales from the darkside) / Jackin' for beats / Get off my dick and tell yo bitch to come here / Product / Dead homiez / JD gaffiliin / I gotta say what up
CD ____ **BRECD 572**
4th & Broadway / Mar '91 / PolyGram

LETHAL INJECTION
Shot / Really doe / Ghetto bird / You know how we do it / Cave bitch / Bop gun (one nation) / What can I do / Lil ass gee / Make it ruff, make it smooth / Down for whatever / Enemy / When I get to heaven
CD ____ **IMCD 229**
Island / Sep '96 / PolyGram

PREDATOR, THE
First day of school / When will they shoot / I'm scared / Wicked / Now I gotta wet 'cha / Predator / It was a good day / We had to tear this MF up / Dirty mack / Don't trust 'em / Gangsta's fairytale 2 / Check yo' self / Who got the camera / Integration / Say hi to the bad guy
CD ____ **IMCD 228**
Island / Sep '96 / PolyGram

WORLD IS MINE, THE
CD ____ **8941762**
Priority/Virgin / Mar '97 / EMI

Ice-T

CLASSIC COLLECTION, THE
Ice-a-mix / Coldest rap / Killers / Ya don't quit / Six in the mornin' / Body rock / Cold wind madness / Dog 'n the wax / Icapella / Ice-o-tek
CD ____ **8122711702**
Street Knowledge / May '93 / Warner Music

HOME INVASION
Warning / It's on / Ice M/F T / Home invasion / G style / Addicted to danger / Question and answer / Watch the ice break / Race war / That's how I'm livin' / I ain't new ta this / Pimp behind the wheels / Gotta lotta love / Shit hit the fan / Depths of hell / Ninety nine problems / Funky gripsta / Message to the soldier / Ain't a damn thing changed
CD ____ **RSYND 1**
Rhyme Syndicate / Mar '93 / EMI

ICEBERG/FREEDOM OF SPEECH
Shut up / Be happy / Iceberg / lethal weopon / You played yourself (aka the boss) / Peel their caps back / Girl tried to kill me / Black 'n' decker / Hit the deck / This one's for me / Hunted child / What ya wanna do (aka do you wanna go party) / Freedom of speach / my word is bond
CD ____ **9260282**
Street Knowledge / Oct '89 / Warner Music

OG ORIGINAL GANGSTER
First impression / Ziplock / New jack hustler / Bitches 2 / Straight up nigga / OG original gangster / House / Evil E - what about sex / Fly by / Fried chicken / Lifestyles of the rich and famous / Body Count / Prepared to die / Escape from the killing fields / Tower / Ya shoulda killed me last year / Home of the bodybag / Mic contract / Mind over matter / Ed / Midnight / MVPS / Street killer / Pulse of the rhyme
CD ____ **7599264922**
Street Knowledge / May '91 / Warner Music

POWER
Intro / Power / Drama / Heartbeat / I'm your pusher / LGBNAF / Syndicate / Radio suckers / Soul on ice / Outro / High rollers / Personal
CD ____ **9257652**
Street Knowledge / Sep '88 / Warner Music

RETURN OF THE REAL
Pimp anthem / Where the shit goes down / Bouncin' down the stezeet / Return of the real / I must stand / Alotta niggas / Rap games hijacked / How does it feel / Lane / Rap is fake / Make the loot loop / Syndicate 4 ever / 5th / It's goin' down / They want me back in / Inside of a gangsta / Forced to do dirt / Haters / Cramp your style / Real / Dear homie
CD ____ **RSYND 3**
Rhyme Syndicate / May '96 / EMI

RHYME PAYS
Intro / Six 'n the mornin' / Make it funky / Somebody gotta do it / 409 / I love ladies / Sex / Pain / Squeeze the trigger
CD ____ **7599256022**
Street Knowledge / Jan '93 / Warner Music

Iceburn

MEDITAVOULTIONS (Iceburn Collective)
CD ____ **REV 042CD**
Revelation / Apr '96 / Plastic Head

POETRY OF LIFE
CD ____ **REV 36CD**
Revelation / Jun '95 / Plastic Head

SPLIT EP (Iceburn & Engine Kid)
CD ____ **REVEL 034CD**
Revelation / Oct '94 / Plastic Head

Iced Earth

BURNT OFFERINGS
CD ____ **CM 770932**
Century Media / May '95 / Plastic Head

DARK SAGA, THE
CD ____ **CMCD 77131**
Century Media / Jun '96 / Plastic Head

DAYS OF PURGATORY (2CD Set)
CD Set ____ **CM 77165CD**
Century Media / May '97 / Plastic Head

ICED EARTH
CD ____ **8497142**
Century Media / Feb '91 / Plastic Head

Icho Candy

GLORY AND THE KING (Icho Candy & Jah Shaka)
CD ____ **SHAKACD 948**
Jah Shaka / Jul '93 / Jet Star / SRD

Ichor

NONPLUS
CD ____ **EFA 112372**
Danse Macabre / May '95 / SRD

Ichu

ICHU
CD ____ **BLR 84 023**
L&R / May '91 / New Note/Pinnacle

Icicle Works

BEST OF THE ICICLE WORKS
CD ____ **BEGA 124CD**
Beggars Banquet / Aug '92 / RTM/Disc / Warner Music

BLIND
Intro / Shit creek / Little Girl Lost / Starry blue eyed wonder / One true love / Blind / Two two three / What do you want me to do / Stood before Saint Peter / Here comes trouble / Kiss off / Walk a while with me
CD ____ **IWA 2CD**
Beggars Banquet / Apr '88 / RTM/Disc / Warner Music

ICICLE WORKS, THE
Chop the tree / Love is a wonderful colour / As the dragonfly flies / Lover's day / In the cauldron of love / Out of season / Factory in the desert / (Birds fly) Whisper to a scream / Nirvana / Reaping the rich harvest
CD ____ **BBL 50CD**
Lowdown/Beggars Banquet / Jul '88 / RTM/Disc / Warner Music

IF YOU WANT TO DEFEAT THE ENEMY SING HIS SONG
Hope springs eternal / Travelling chest / Sweet Thursday / Up here in the North of England / Who do you want for your love / When you were mine / Evangeline / Truck driver's lament / Understanding Jane / Walking with a mountain / Please don't let it rain on my parade / Everybody loves to play the fool / I never saw my hometown 'till I went around the world / Into the mystic
CD ____ **BBL 78CD**
Lowdown/Beggars Banquet / Feb '90 / RTM/Disc / Warner Music

SEVEN SINGLES DEEP
Hollow horse / Love is a wonderful colour / (Birds fly) Whisper to a scream / All the daughters / When it all comes down / Seven horses / Rapids
CD ____ **BBL 71 CD**
Lowdown/Beggars Banquet / Sep '88 / RTM/Disc / Warner Music

SMALL PRICE OF A BICYCLE, THE
Hollow horse / Perambulator / Seven horses / Rapids / Windfall / Assumed sundowns / Saint's sojourn / All the daughters / Book of reason / Conscience of Kings
CD ____ **BBL 61CD**
Lowdown/Beggars Banquet / Jan '89 / RTM/Disc / Warner Music

Ickes, Rob

HARD TIMES
No more my land / Down in the hole / Tom Dooley / Flat lonesome / Reuben / Song for Jennifer / Look ka py py / Hard times / Ashland breakdown / One bad case of the blues / How great thou art / Uptown blues
CD ____ **ROUCD 0402**
Rounder / May '97 / ADA / CM / Direct

Icky Joey

POOH
CD ____ **CZ 026CD**
C/Z / Sep '91 / Plastic Head

Icons Of Filth

MORPHATE PROJECTS, THE
CD ____ **MORTCD 005**
Mortarhate / Apr '96 / RTM/Disc

Idaho

THIS WAY OUT
Drop off / Drive it / Weird wood / Fuel / Still / Sweep / Glow / Taken / Crawling out / Zabo / Forever
CD ____ **QUIGD 7**
Quigley / Jan '95 / EMI

THREE SHEETS TO THE WIND
If you dare / Catapult / Pomegranate bleeding / Shame / Stare at the sky / No one's watching / Alive again / Sound awake / Glass bottom / Get you back
CD ____ **CAROL 001CD**
Caroline / Apr '96 / Cargo / Vital

YEAR AFTER YEAR
God's green earth / Skyscrape / Gone / Here to go / Sundown / Memorial day / One Sunday / Only road / Let's cheat death / Save / Year after year / Endgame
CD ____ **QUIGD 4**
Quigley / Sep '93 / EMI

Idee Des Nordens

ELATION, ELEGANCE, EXALTATION
CD ____ **EFA 155832**
Gymnastic / Apr '95 / SRD

Ides Of March

VEHICLE
CD ____ **175052**
Magic / Jul '97 / Greyhound

Ides Of May

FEED BACK
CD ____ **TRCD 9908**
Tramp / Nov '93 / ADA / CM / Direct

Idha

MELODYINN
CD ____ **CRECD 160**
Creation / Jan '94 / 3mv/Vital

TROUBLEMAKER
CD ____ **CRECD 184**
Creation / Aug '97 / 3mv/Vital

Idiots

IDIOTS MINI ALBUM
CD ____ **DIRTY 3CD**
Dirt / Mar '97 / Pinnacle

Idol, Billy

BILLY IDOL
Come come on / White wedding / Hot in the city / Dead on arrival / Ain't nobody's business if I do / Love calling / Hole in the wall / Shooting star / It's so cruel / Congo man
CD ____ **ACCD 1377**
Chrysalis / Jul '94 / EMI

CHARMED LIFE
Loveless / Pimping on steel / Prodigal blues / LA woman / Trouble with the sweet stuff / Cradle of love / Mark of Caine / Endless sleep / Love unchained / Right way / License to thrill
CD ____ **CCD 1735**
Chrysalis / Sep '97 / EMI

CYBERPUNK
Wasteland / Shock to the system / Tomorrow people / Adam in chains / Neuromancer / Power junkie / Love labours on / Heroin / Shangri la / Concrete kingdom / Venus / Then the night comes / Mother Dawn
CD ____ **CDCHR 6000**
Chrysalis / Jun '93 / EMI

IDOL SONGS (11 Of The Best)
Rebel yell / Hot in the city / White wedding / Eyes without a face / Catch my fall / Mony mony / To be a lover / Sweet sixteen / Flesh for fantasy / Don't need a gun / Dancing with myself
CD ____ **BIL CD 1**
Chrysalis / Jun '88 / EMI

VITAL IDOL
Dancing with myself / White wedding / Flesh for fantasy / Catch my fall / Mony mony / Love calling (dub) / Hot in the city
CD ____ **CCD 1502**
Chrysalis / '86 / EMI

Idols

IDOLS WITH SID VICIOUS (Idols & Sid Vicious)
CD ____ **422289**
Last Call / Feb '97 / Cargo / Direct / Discovery

If

FORGOTTEN ROADS
CD ____ **NEMCD 773**
Sequel / Oct '95 / BMG

IF
I'm reaching out on all sides / What did I say about the box Jack / What can a friend say / Woman can you see / Raise the level of your conscious mind / Dockland / Promised land
CD ____ **EDCD 505**
Edsel / Feb '97 / Pinnacle

IF 2
Sunday sad / Tarmac T Pirate and the lonesome nymphomaniac / I couldn't write and tell you / Shadows and echoes / Song for Elsa / Three days before her 25th birthday / Your city is falling
CD ____ **EDCD 506**
Edsel / Feb '97 / Pinnacle

Ifang Bondi

DARAJA
CD ____ **MWCD 3009**
Music & Words / Jul '94 / ADA / Direct

Ifield, Frank

REMEMBERING THE SIXTIES (3CD Set)
Did you see my Daddy over there / Suvla Bay / Come back Liza / Lucky Devil / Nobody else but you / Unchained melody / Gotta get a date / No love tonight / She's the girl who doesn't care / That's the way it goes / Hoebe Snow / I can't stop loving you / Your time will come / That's the way it is / Alone too long / Bigger than you or me / I remember you / Lovesick blues / She taught me how to yodel / Wayward wind / I'm smiling now / Lonely teardrops / San Antonio rose / (I heard) That lonesome whistle / Before this day ends / I just can't lose the blues / Nobody's darlin' but mine / You don't have to be a baby to cry / Mule train / One man's love / Confessin' that I love you / Waltzin' Matilda / My kind of girl / He'll have to go / I can't get enough of your kisses / Cold cold heart / Daybreak / Love song of the waterfall / Wolverton Mountain / Half as much / Funny how time slips away / Riders in the sky / I'd be a legend in my time / Scarlet ribbons for her hair / Don't blame me / Blue skies / Dark moon / Let me be the one / I'll be around / Tumblin' tumbleweeds / Sweet Lorraine / Angry at the big oak tree / Go tell it to the mountain / I should care / Another cup of coffee / Cat came back / Chivalrous man-eating shark / Me Japanese boy (I love you) / Don't make me laugh (don't make me cry) / Lonesome number one / I'm so lonesome I could cry / Hong Kong blues / Hold me thrill me kiss me / True love ways / Oh lonesome me / Love walked in / Stardust / Hey Joe / Fool such as I / Did I remember / I'll never fall this way again / I guess / Devoted to you / Lost love / Just one time / You came along from out of nowhere / Rainbows and roses / Cool water / Roses, moonlight and one little bottle of wine / All the time / Singing the blues / Days of wine and roses / Mood indigo / Fireball Mall / What's new / Adios Matador / Rovin' lover / Oh such a stranger / Goodbye now
CD Set ____ **IFIELD 3**
EMI / Mar '97 / EMI

REST OF THE EMI YEARS
Lucky devil / I remember you / She taught me how to yodel / Lovesick blues / Confessin' (that I love you) / Just one more chance / Nobody's darlin' but mine / Wayward wind / My blue heaven / Say it isn't so / Don't blame me / You came a long way from St. Louis / Summer is over / Once a jolly swagman / Botany Bay / Paradise / Wild rover / Call her your sweetheart / No one will ever know / Give me your word
CD ____ **CDEMS 1402**
EMI / May '91 / EMI

SOMEONE TO GIVE MY LOVE TO/AIN'T GONNA TAKE NO FOR AN ANSWER
Someone to give my love to / California cotton fields / Why can't people be people / I cry my heart out for you / Country comfort / Say goodbye to Angelina / Paint the world / Silver wings / Him big top, me the clown / Don't forget I still love you / My happiness / 'Til I waltz again with you / Where is tomorrow / Count up to ten / Make up of a clown / Nearness of you / Joanne / I remember you / Sad song without words / Ain't gonna take no for an answer / Cotton Jenny / Home isn't home anymore / Excuse me friend

CD SEECD 439
See For Miles/C5 / Mar '97 / Pinnacle

Iggy Pop

AMERICAN CAESAR
Character / Wild America / Mixin' the colors / Jealousy / Hate / It's our love / Plastic and concrete / Fuckin' alone / Highway song / Beside you / Sickness / Boogie boy / Perforation problems / Social life / Louie Louie / Caesar / Girls of NY
CD CDVUS 64
Virgin / Aug '93 / EMI

BEST OF IGGY POP LIVE, THE
Raw power / High on you / Nightclubbing / China girl / Blah blah blah / No fun / 1969 / Tv eye / Easy rider / I need somebody / 5 foot 1 / I wanna be your dog / Passenger / I got a right / Some weird sin / Real wild child / Lust for life / Search 'n' destroy
CD MCD 84021
MCA / Aug '96 / BMG

BLAH BLAH BLAH
Real wild child / Baby, it can't fall / Shades / Fire girl / Isolation / Cry for love / Blah blah blah / Hideaway / Winners and losers
CD CDMID 159
A&M / Oct '92 / PolyGram

BRICK BY BRICK
Home / I won't crap out / Butt town / Moonlight lady / Neon forest / Pussy power / Brick by brick / Main Street eyes / Candy / Undefeated / Something wild / Starry night / My baby wants to rock 'n' roll / Livin' on the edge of the night
CD CDVUS 19
Virgin / Apr '92 / EMI

COMPLETE RAW MIXES
I got a right / No fun / 1969 / I wanna be your dog / Not right / Little doll / Fun house / Down on the street / 1970 / TV eye / Dirt / Shake appeal / Search and destroy / Raw power / I need somebody / Rubber legs / Open up and bleed / Johanna
CD MIG 60
Revenge / Dec '96 / Cargo / Direct / Discovery

FUN HOUSE (Iggy & The Stooges)
Down on the street / Loose / TV eye / Dirt / 1970 / Fun house / LA Blues
CD 7559606692
Elektra / Oct '93 / Warner Music

I WANNA BE A STOOGE (Various Artists)
CD 642006
Wotre Music / Sep '96 / Discovery / New Note/Pinnacle

IDIOT, THE
Sister midnight / Nightclubbing / Fun time / Baby / China girl / Dum dum boys / Tiny girls / Mass production
CD CDOVD 277
Virgin / Apr '90 / EMI

IGGY POP (Interview)
CD 3D 013
Network / Dec '96 / Total/BMG

INSTINCT
Cold metal / High on you / Strong girl / Tom Tom / Easy rider / Power and freedom / Lowdown / Instinct / Tuff baby / Squarehead
CD 3951982
A&M / Dec '96 / PolyGram

KILL CITY (Iggy Pop & James Williamson)
Kill City / Sell your love / Beyond the law / I got nothing / Johanna / Night theme / Consolation prizes / No sense of crime / Lucky moments / Master charge
CD BCD 4042
Bomp / Jan '93 / Cargo / Greyhound / RTM/Disc / Shellshock/Disc

KILL CITY/I GOT A RIGHT (Iggy & The Stooges)
CD 890050
Revenge / Jul '96 / Cargo / Direct / Discovery

LIVE 1971 & EARLY LIVE RARITIES (Iggy & The Stooges)
CD 642011
New Rose / Sep '94 / ADA / Direct / Discovery

LIVE AT THE WHISKEY A GO GO (Iggy & The Stooges)
CD 895104
Wotre Music / Jan '97 / Discovery / New Note/Pinnacle

LIVE CHANNEL BOSTON MA 1988
CD 642005
New Rose / May '94 / ADA / Direct / Discovery

LIVE NEW YORK RITZ 1986
CD 642044
New Rose / May '94 / ADA / Direct / Discovery

LUST FOR LIFE
Lust for life / Sixteen / Some weird sin / Passenger / Tonight / Success / Turn blue / Neighbourhood threat / Fall in love with me
CD CDOVD 278
Virgin / Apr '90 / EMI

LUST FOR LIFE/THE IDIOT/BRICK BY BRICK (3CD Set)
CD Set TPAK 21
Virgin / Jan '93 / EMI

METALLIC KO (Iggy & The Stooges)
Raw power / Head on the curb / Gimme danger / Search and destiny / Heavy liquid / I wanna be your dog / Recital / Open up and bleed / I got nothing / Rich bitch / Cock in my pocket / Louie Louie
CD 622322
Skydog / Apr '88 / Discovery

MY GIRL HATES MY HEROIN (Iggy & The Stooges)
CD 7890028
Wotre Music / Jan '97 / Discovery / New Note/Pinnacle

NAUGHTY LITTLE DOGGIE
I wanna live / Pussy walk / Innocent world / Knucklehead / To belong / Keep on believing / Outta my head / Shoeshine girl / Heart is saved / Look away
CD CDVUS 102
Virgin / Feb '96 / EMI

NEW VALUES
Tell me a story / New values / Girls / I'm bored / Don't look down / Endless sea / Five foot one / How do you fix a broken heart / Angel / Curiosity / African man / Billy is a runaway
CD 260997
Arista / Nov '90 / BMG

NIGHT OF DESTRUCTION (Iggy & The Stooges)
CD 642100
New Rose / Jun '94 / ADA / Direct / Discovery

NUDE & RUDE (The Best Of Iggy Pop)
I wanna be your dog / No fun / Search & destroy / Gimme danger / I'm sick of you / Funtime / Nightclubbing / China girl / Lust for life / Passenger / Kill city / Real wild child / Cry for love / Cold metal / Candy / Home / Wild America
CD VUSCD 115
Virgin / Oct '96 / EMI

OPEN UP AND BLEED (Iggy & The Stooges)
CD 890016
Revenge / Jul '96 / Cargo / Direct / Discovery
CD BCD 4051
Bomp / Jan '97 / Cargo / Greyhound / RTM/Disc / Shellshock/Disc

PARIS HIPPODROME 1977
CD 893334
Revenge / Jul '96 / Cargo / Direct / Discovery

PARTY
Pleasure / Rock 'n' roll party / Eggs on plate / Sincerity / Houston is hot tonight / Pumpin' for Jill / Happy man / Bang bang / Sea of love / Time won't let me
CD 253806
RCA / Sep '89 / BMG

POP MUSIC
Loco mosquito / Bang bang / Tell me a story / Pumpin' for Jill / Take care of me / I need more / I'm bored / Knocking 'em down / I snub you / Sea of love / Play it safe / Dog food / Happy man / Time won't let me / Five foot one / Angel / Girls / New values / Pleasure / Houston is hot tonight
CD 74321415032
Camden / Oct '96 / BMG

POP SONGS
Loco mosquito / Bang bang / Pumpin' for Jill / Tell me a story / Take care of me / Mr. Dynamite / I'm bored / Sea of love / Play it safe / Endless sea / Pleasure / Five foot one / Houston is hot tonight / Dog food
CD 262178
Arista / Jan '92 / BMG

RAW MIXES VOL.1 (Iggy & The Stooges)
CD 895002
New Rose / Sep '94 / ADA / Direct / Discovery

RAW MIXES VOL.2 (Iggy & The Stooges)
CD 895003
New Rose / Sep '94 / ADA / Direct / Discovery

RAW MIXES VOL.3 - SEARCH & DESTROY (Iggy & The Stooges)
CD 895004
New Rose / Sep '94 / ADA / Direct / Discovery

RAW POWER (Iggy & The Stooges)
Search and destroy / Gimme danger / Your pretty face is going to hell / Penetration / Raw power / I need somebody / Shake appeal / Death trip
CD 4851762
Columbia / Apr '97 / Sony

ROUGH POWER (Iggy & The Stooges)
CD BCD 4049
Bomp / Jan '97 / Cargo / Greyhound / RTM/Disc / Shellshock/Disc

RUBBER LEGS (Iggy & The Stooges)
CD 422351
New Rose / May '94 / ADA / Direct / Discovery

SOLDIER
Loco mosquito / Ambition / Take care of me / Get up and get out / Play it safe / I'm a conservative / Dog food / I need more / Knocking 'em down (in the city) / Mr. Dynamite / I snub you
CD 251160
Arista / Apr '91 / BMG

STOOGES, THE (Iggy & The Stooges)
1969 / I wanna be your dog / We will fall / No fun / Real cool time / Ann / Not right / Little doll
CD 7559606672
Elektra / Oct '93 / Warner Music

STUDIO SESSIONS (Iggy & The Stooges)
Head on / Death trip / I got a right / Hard to beat / Cock in my pocket / Rubber legs / Johanna / Pin point eyes / Open up and bleed / Raw power
CD PILOT 008
Burning Airlines / Feb '97 / Total/Pinnacle

SUCK ON THIS
CD 642 050
NMC / May '93 / Total/Pinnacle

TILL THE END OF THE NIGHT (Iggy & The Stooges)
CD 642042
New Rose / Jun '94 / ADA / Direct / Discovery

TV EYE (1977 LIVE)
TV eye / Fun time / Sixteen / I got a right / Lust for life / Dirt / Nightclubbing / I wanna be your dog
CD CDOVD 448
Virgin / Jun '94 / EMI

WILD ANIMAL (Live USA 1977)
CD 642050
Revenge / Jul '96 / Cargo / Direct / Discovery

YEAR OF THE IGUANA (Iggy & The Stooges)
CD BCD 4063
Bomp / Mar '97 / Cargo / Greyhound / RTM/Disc / Shellshock/Disc

Iglesias, Julio

1,100 BEL AIR PLACE/STARRY NIGHT/ EMOCIONES (3CD Set)
All of you / Two lovers / Bambou medley / Air that I breathe / Last time / Moonlight lady / When I fall in love / Me va, me va / If / To all the girls I've loved before / Can't help falling in love / And I love her / Mona Lisa / Cryin' time / Yesterday when I was young / When I need you / 99 miles from LA / Vincent / If you go away / Love has been a friend to me / Me olvide de vivir / Voy a perder la cabeza por tu amor / Spanish girl / Pobre diablo / Quiereme / Preguntale / Quiereme mucho / Con una pinta asi / No vengo ni voy / Un dia tu, un dia yo
CD Set 4853182
Columbia / Oct '96 / Sony

1100 BEL AIR PLACE
All of you: *Iglesias, Julio & Diana Ross* / Two lovers / Bambou medley / Air that I breathe / Last time / Moonlight lady / When I fall in love / Me va, me va / If / To all the girls I've loved before: *Iglesias, Julio & Willie Nelson*
CD CD 86308
CBS / Sep '86 / Sony

BEGIN THE BEGUINE
Begin the beguine / Quiereme / Me olvide de vivir / Por un poco de tu amour / Grande, grande, grande / Como tu / Guantanamera / Quiereme mucho / Hey / Un dia ty, un dia yo / Soy un truhan, soy un senor / Candilejas / El amor / 33 anos / Isla en el sol
CD CD 85462
CBS / Aug '87 / Sony

CALOR/BEGIN THE BEGUINE
CD Set 4716012D
Columbia / Feb '93 / Sony

CRAZY
Crazy / Let it be me / Mammy blue / Fragile / Guajira/Oye como va / When you tell me that you love me / I keep telling myself / Pelo amor de uma mulher (Por el amor de una mujer) / Caruso / Song of joy
CD 4747382
Columbia / May '94 / Sony

DE NINA A MUJER
De nina a mujer / Volver a empezar / Despues de ti / Que nadie sepa mi sufrir / Isal en el sol / O me quieres o me dejas / Y pensar..si madam / Grande, grande, grande / Come tu
CD 4654502
Columbia / Oct '95 / Sony

HEY
For Elle / Amantes / Morrinas / Viejas tradiciones / Ron y coco cola / Hey / Sentimental / Paloma blanca / La Nave del Olvido / Pajaro chogui
CD 4510582
Columbia / Apr '94 / Sony

HEY/JULIO/LIBRA (3CD Set)
CD Set 4688082
Columbia / Jan '95 / Sony

JULIO
Begin the beguine / Forever and ever / Yours / La paloma / Pensami / D'abord..et puis / Never never never / Nathalie / Feelings / Hey, amor / Limelight / Rum and coca cola / Sono lo / Je nais pas change / So close to me
CD 4510772
CBS / Feb '88 / Sony

LA CARRETERA
La carretera / Cosae de la vida / Baila morena / Derroche el ultimo / Verano / Agua dulce, agua sala / Sin exasas ni rodeos / Mal de amores / Rumbas / Vuela alto
CD 4807042
Columbia / Jul '95 / Sony

NON STOP
Love is on our side again / I know it's over / Never never never / AE, AO / Words and music / My love (featuring Stevie Wonder) / Everytime we fall in love / Too many women / If I ever needed you (I need you now)
CD 4609902
Columbia / Oct '95 / Sony

STARRY NIGHT
Can't help falling in love / And I love her / Mona Lisa / Crying time / Yesterday when I was young / When I need you / Ninety nine miles from LA / Vincent (starry starry night) / If you go away / Love has been a friend to me
CD 4672842
Columbia / Mar '96 / Sony

TANGO
La cumparsita / El dia que me quieras / A media luz / Volver / Yira..yira / Mano a mano / El choclo / Adios / Pampa mia / Cambalanche / Uno... / Caminito / Mi buenos aires querido
CD 4866752
Columbia / Nov '96 / Sony

Ignatzek, Klaus

ANSWER, THE (Ignatzek, Klaus Quintet)
Answer / Altered moods / Number one / With pleasure / Claudio's delight / One milestone
CD CCD 79534
Candid / Feb '97 / Cadillac / Direct / Jazz Music / Koch / Wellard

RETURN VOYAGE (Ignatzek, Klaus Jazztet)
Calling Mr. Gillespie / Return voyage / Oscar for Gigi / Jay by Jay / Un abraco do Brasil (A salute to Brazil) / Flowers around midnight / Whisper yes / Blue energy
CD CCD 79716
Candid / Feb '97 / Cadillac / Direct / Jazz Music / Koch / Wellard

Ignite

FAMILY
CD LF 192CD
Lost & Found / Jul '95 / Plastic Head

IN MY TIME
CD LF 124CD
Lost & Found / Feb '95 / Plastic Head

SCARRED FOR LIFE
CD LF 104CD
Lost & Found / Aug '94 / Plastic Head

Ignition

COMPLETE SERVICES
CD DIS 88CD
Dischord / Mar '94 / SRD

Ignorance

CONFIDENT RAT, THE
CD CDZORRO 17
Metal Blade / Feb '91 / Pinnacle / Plastic Head

POSITIVELY SHOCKING
CD CDZORRO 48
Metal Blade / Sep '92 / Pinnacle / Plastic Head

IIIrd Tyme Out

LETTER TO HOME
CD ROUCD 0333
Rounder / Oct '95 / ADA / CM / Direct

LIVING ON THE OTHER SIDE
He'll take you in / I want to stroll over heaven / I'm working on the road to Gloryland / Everybody's gonna have a wonderful time up there / Giving my soul back to him / Across the miles / When we're living on the other side / Eternity has begun / Feed me Jesus / I feel closer to Heaven / Swing low, sweet chariot / Heading for that city
CD ROUCD 0393
Rounder / Sep '96 / ADA / CM / Direct

Ijahman Levi

AFRICA
CD CDJMI 400
Jahmani / Dec '95 / Grapevine/PolyGram / Jet Star / THE

ARE WE A WARRIOR
Are we a warrior / Moulding / Church / Miss Beverly / Two sides of love
CD _______________ RRCD 25
Reggae Refreshers / Nov '90 / PolyGram / Vital
CD _______________ CDJMI 200
Jahmani / Dec '95 / Grapevine/PolyGram / Jet Star / THE

BEAUTY AND THE LION
CD _______________ CDJMI 2300
Jahmani / Jan '97 / Grapevine/PolyGram / Jet Star / THE

BLACK ROYALITIES
CD _______________ CDJMI 1800
Jahmani / Dec '95 / Grapevine/PolyGram / Jet Star / THE

CULTURE COUNTRY
CD _______________ CDJMI 700
Jahmani / Dec '95 / Grapevine/PolyGram / Jet Star / THE

ENTITLEMENT
CD _______________ CDJMI 1600
Jahmani / Dec '95 / Grapevine/PolyGram / Jet Star / THE

FORWARD RASTAMAN
Waitin' on you / Gambler's blues / Tired of your jive / Night life / Buzz me / Sweet sixteen part 1 / Don't answer the door / Blind love / I know what you're puttin' down / Baby get lost / Gonna keep on loving you / Sweet sixteen part 2
CD _______________ CDJMI 800
Jahmani / Dec '95 / Grapevine/PolyGram / Jet Star / THE

GEMINI MAN
CD _______________ CDJMI 1500
Jahmani / Dec '95 / Grapevine/PolyGram / Jet Star / THE

HAILE I HYMN
Jah heavy load / Jah is no secret / Zion hut / I'm a levi / Praises in strange places / Marcus hero / Zion train
CD _______________ CDJMI 100
Jahmani / Dec '95 / Grapevine/PolyGram / Jet Star / THE

I DO (Ijahman Levi & Madge Sutherland)
CD _______________ CDJMI 600
Jahmani / Dec '95 / Grapevine/PolyGram / Jet Star / THE

IJAHMAN & FRIENDS
Master ideas / Mellow music / African train / Struggling dub / Extended dub / Master dub / Struggling times / Let him go / Jah is coming
CD _______________ CDJMI 900
Jahmani / Dec '95 / Grapevine/PolyGram / Jet Star / THE

IJAHMAN LEVI & BOB MARLEY IN DUB (Ijahman Levi & Bob Marley)
CD _______________ CDJMI 2200
Jahmani / Dec '95 / Grapevine/PolyGram / Jet Star / THE

INSIDE OUT
CD _______________ CDJMI 1100
Jahmani / Dec '95 / Grapevine/PolyGram / Jet Star / THE

KINGFARI
CD _______________ CDJMI 1400
Jahmani / Dec '95 / Grapevine/PolyGram / Jet Star / THE

LILY OF MY VALLEY
CD _______________ CDJMI 500
Jahmani / Dec '95 / Grapevine/PolyGram / Jet Star / THE

LIVE IN PARIS 1994
CD _______________ CDJMI 2000
Jahmani / Dec '95 / Grapevine/PolyGram / Jet Star / THE

LIVE OVER EUROPE
CD _______________ CDJMI 1000
Jahmani / Dec '95 / Grapevine/PolyGram / Jet Star / THE

LOVE SMILES
CD _______________ CDJMI 1200
Jahmani / Dec '95 / Grapevine/PolyGram / Jet Star / THE

ON TRACK
CD _______________ CDJMI 1300
Jahmani / Dec '95 / Grapevine/PolyGram / Jet Star / THE

SINGS BOB MARLEY
CD _______________ CDJMI 1900
Jahmani / Dec '95 / Grapevine/PolyGram / Jet Star / THE

TELL IT TO THE CHILDREN
CD _______________ CDJMI 300
Jahmani / Dec '95 / Grapevine/PolyGram / Jet Star / THE

TWO DOUBLE SIX 701
CD _______________ CDJMI 1700
Jahmani / Dec '95 / Grapevine/PolyGram / Jet Star / THE

Ikeda, Royoji

PLUS/MINUS
CD _______________ TO 30
Touch / Nov '96 / Kudos / Pinnacle

Ikettes

FINE, FINE, FINE
(He's gonna be) Fine fine fine / Can't sit down / Don't feel sorry for me / Camel walk / Blue on blue / I'm so thankful / You're trying to make me lose my mind / Sally go round the roses / Peaches and cream / Never more will I be lonely for you / Not that I recall / Your love is me / Biggest players / How come / Nobody loves me / It's been so long / Through with you / Cheater / I'm leaving you / You're still my baby / Give me a chance (try me) / Love of my man: *Ikettes & Venetta Fields* / Living for you: *Ikettes & Dee Dee Johnson* / I love the way you love: *Ikettes & Robbie Montgomery*
CD _______________ CDKEN 063
Kent / Sep '92 / Pinnacle

Ikhwani Safaa Musical Club

TAARAB MUSIC OF ZANZIBAR VOL.2
Usiji gambe / Nna zama / Pendo la wasikitisha / Nipe pee / Kanilemaza / Uki chungua / Waridi lisilo miba / Hidaya
CD _______________ CDORB 033
Globestyle / Oct '88 / Pinnacle

Ikon

FLOWERS OF THE GATHERING
CD _______________ NRE 01CD
Nightbreed / Apr '97 / Plastic Head

MOMENT IN TIME, A
CD _______________ EFA 121672
Apollyon / Nov '95 / SRD

Ildjarn

FOREST POETRY
CD _______________ NORSE 004
Napalm / Jun '96 / RTM/Disc

Ile Axe

BRAZILIAN PERCUSSION
CD _______________ PS 65059
PlayaSound / Nov '90 / ADA / Harmonia Mundi

Ilg, Dieter

SUMMERHILL
It's getting better / Spring fever / Shadows of the fall / Summerhill / All childrens love song / Somersault / Under the skin of the earth
CD _______________ LIP 890062
Lipstick / Feb '95 / Vital/SAM

Ill Wind

FLASHES
CD _______________ AFT 012
Afterglow / Jun '97 / Greyhound

Illapu

RAZA BRAVA
CD _______________ MCD 71811
Monitor / Jun '93 / CM

SERENO (Panpipe Instrumentals From The Andes)
Cariquima / Sol demaiz / Condorcanqui / Sereno / Chilhuanos / Paso de mulata / Bailando en Isluga / Sipassy / Cancisy / Labradores / Poblacires / O marqu waylas de cala cala / Baila caporal
CD _______________ HEMICD 26
Hemisphere / Jun '97 / EMI

Illdisposed

FOUR DEPRESSIVE SEASONS
CD _______________ NB 103
Nuclear Blast / Apr '94 / Plastic Head

HELVEDE
CD _______________ RRS 945CD
Lost & Found / Sep '95 / Plastic Head

RETURN FROM TOMORROW
CD _______________ NB 116
Nuclear Blast / Aug '94 / Plastic Head

SUBMIT
CD _______________ PCD 021
Progress / Nov '95 / Cargo / Plastic Head

Illusion

ENCHANTED CARESS
CD _______________ PL 92152
Promised Land / Aug '90 / Direct / Kingdom

OUT OF THE MIST / ILLUSION
Isadora / Roads to freedom / Beautiful country / Solo flight / Everywhere you go / Face of yesterday / Candles are burning / Madonna blues / Never be the same / Louis theme / Wings across the sea / Cruising nowhere / Man of miracles / Revolutionary
CD _______________ EDCD 369
Edsel / Mar '94 / Pinnacle

Illusion Of Safety

WATER SEEKS IT'S OWN LEVEL
CD _______________ SR 9351
Silent / Mar '94 / Cargo / Plastic Head

Illustrious

NO NO NO (Illustrious GY)
CD _______________ 74321157292
RCA / Nov '93 / BMG

Iluyenkori

CUBAN DRUMS
CD _______________ PS 65084
PlayaSound / Mar '92 / ADA / Harmonia Mundi

Imagination

NIGHT DUBBING
Flashback / Just an illusion / Music and lights / So good, so right / Body talk / Heart 'n' soul / Changes / Burning up
CD _______________ BX 4302
BR Music / Jun '96 / Target/BMG

VERY BEST OF IMAGINATION, THE
CD _______________ BX 4182
BR Music / Apr '95 / Target/BMG

Imago

SPIRIT DANCE, THE
CD _______________ DBCDA 202
Dancebeat / May '97 / Jet Star / Total/ BMG

Imai, Kazuo

HOW WILL WE CHANGE
CD _______________ PSFD 70
PSF / Feb '96 / Harmonia Mundi

Imlach, Hamish

MORE AND MERRIER
CD _______________ CDLDL 1238
Lochshore / Mar '96 / ADA / Direct / Duncans

SONNY'S DREAM
Cod liver oil and orange juice / Ballad of William Brown / Mary Anne / Reprobate's lament / Salonika / Kisses sweeter than wine / Smoker's song / Sonny's dream / If it wasn't for the union / Parcel o' rogues / I didn't raise my boy to be a soldier / Goodbye booze / D-day dodgers / Seven men of Knoydart
CD _______________ LCOM 7006
Lismor / May '95 / ADA / Direct / Duncans / Lismor

Immaculate Fools

KISS AND PUNCH
Little bird sing / Ready for me / Kiss and punch / No I don't think so / Love us / Government wall / Tinderbox / No gods no masters / Rain song / Hard peace / Killing field / Whole world down / El emanacer
CD _______________ COOKCD 096
Cooking Vinyl / Aug '97 / Vital

TOY SHOP
Stand down / Heaven down here / Political Wish / Cotillas / Leaving song / Wonder of things / Good times / Through these eyes / Bed of tears / How the west was won
CD _______________ 192092
Continuum / Oct '92 / Pinnacle

WOODHOUSE
Rain / Some of us / Ship song / Time to kill / Profit for prophets / Pass the jug / Rudy / Home / Bury my heart / Wish you were here / If you go
CD _______________ COOKCD 085
Cooking Vinyl / Jul '97 / Vital

Immature

PLAYTYME IS OVER
I don't mind / Never lie / Walk you home / Constantly / Broken heart / Summertime / Nothing but a party / Look into your eyes / Sweetest love / Just a little bit
CD _______________ MCLD 19337
MCA / Oct '96 / BMG

WE GOT IT
We got it / Lover's groove / Just a little bit / Please don't go / I don't know pager / Crazy / I can't stop the rain / Boy like me / Candy / When it's love / Pay you back / I feel the funk
CD _______________ MCD 11385
MCA / Mar '96 / BMG

Immersion

FULL IMMERSION
CD _______________ VWM 40
Swim / Jun '95 / Kudos / RTM/Disc / SRD

OSCILLATING
CD _______________ WM 4CD
Swim / Sep '94 / Kudos / RTM/Disc / SRD

Immolation

DAWN OF POSSESSION
CD _______________ RC 93102
RC / Jan '94 / Pinnacle

HERE IN AFTER
CD _______________ 3984102CD
Metal Blade / Jan '96 / Pinnacle / Plastic Head

STEPPING ON ANGELS...BEFORE DAWN
CD _______________ RPS 004CD
Repulse / Jan '95 / Plastic Head

Immortal

BATTLES IN THE NORTH
CD _______________ OPCD 027
Osmose / May '95 / Plastic Head

BLIZZARD BEASTS
CD _______________ OPCD 051
Osmose / Mar '97 / Plastic Head

PURE HOLOCAUST
CD _______________ OPCD 19
Osmose / Dec '93 / Plastic Head

Immortelle

DEW SCENTED
CD _______________ SPV 0851826
SPV / Mar '96 / Koch / Plastic Head

Impacts

DESERT ISLAND TREASURES
CD _______________ BA 1116CD
Bacchus Archives / Mar '97 / Cargo / Plastic Head

Impaled Nazarene

LATEX CULT
CD _______________ OPCD 038
Osmose / Apr '96 / Plastic Head

MOTORPENIS
CD _______________ OPCD 039
Osmose / Jun '96 / Plastic Head

SUOMI FINLAND
CD _______________ OPCD 026
Osmose / Apr '95 / Plastic Head

TOL CORMPT NORZ NORZ NORZ
CD _______________ OPCD 010LTD
Osmose / Nov '95 / Plastic Head

UGRA KARMA
CD _______________ OPCD 018
Osmose / Apr '94 / Plastic Head

Impatient Youth

ALL FOR FUN
CD _______________ LF 76CD
Lost & Found / Nov '94 / Plastic Head

Imperial Drag

IMPERIAL DRAG
Zodiac sign / Boy or a girl / Crosseyed / Man in the moon / Kiss it all goodbye / Playboy after dark / Illuminate / Spyder / Overnight sensation / Salvation Army band / Dandelion / Stare into the sun / Scaredy cats and egomaniacs / Down with the man
CD _______________ 4841782
Columbia / Oct '96 / Sony

Imperial Teen

SEASICK
Imperial teen / Water boy / Butch / Pig latin / Blaming the baby / You're one / Balloon / Tippy tap / Copafeelia / Luxury / Eternity
CD _______________ 8287282
Custom / Sep '96 / Pinnacle / PolyGram

Imperials

GOIN' OUT OF MY HEAD (Little Anthony & The Imperials)
CD _______________ BGOCD 309
Beat Goes On / Apr '96 / Pinnacle

Implant Code

BIODIGIT
CD _______________ MHCD 020
Minus Habens / Mar '94 / Plastic Head

Impreciation

THEURGIA GOETIA SUMMA
CD _______________ RSP 012CD
Repulse / May '96 / Plastic Head

Impressions

ALL THE BEST
Gypsy woman / It's alright / People get ready / Talking about my baby / I'm so proud / You must believe me / Woman's got soul / I've been trying / Amen / You've been cheating / I'm the one who loves you / We're a winner / Keep on pushing / Right on time / Move on up: *Mayfield, Curtis* / Freddie's dead: *Mayfield, Curtis* / First impressions
CD _______________ 3035900112
Carlton / Apr '96 / Carlton

CHANGING IMPRESSIONS (2CD Set)
For your precious love / Come back my love / Little young lover / At the country fair / Gypsy woman / Keep on pushin' / I'm so proud / I've been trying / Amen (1970) / Fool for you / Gone away / This is my country / Seven years / Wherever he leadeth me / Choice of colours / Mighty, mighty (Spade & Whitey) / (Baby) turn on to me / Check out your mind / We must be in love / Ain't got time / Times have changed / Inner city blues (make me wanna holler) / Potent love / Preacher man / Thin line / I'm a changed man (finally got myself together) / If it's in you to do wrong / I'll always be here / Make a resolution / Something's mighty, mighty wrong / Sooner or later / Same thing it took / First impressions / Sunshine / Loving power / All I want to do is make love to you / Fan the fire / I don't wanna lose your love / For your precious love
CD Set ______ **CPCD 82542**
Charly / Nov '96 / Koch

CHECK OUT YOUR MIND/TIMES HAVE CHANGED
Check out your mind / Can't you see / You're really something Sadie / Do you want to win / You'll be always mine / Only you / (Baby) turn onto me / Madam Mary / We must be in love / Say you love me / Stop the war / Times have changed / Inner city blues (make me wanna holler) / Our love goes on and on / Potent love / Need to belong to someone / This love's for real / Love me
CD ______ **NEMCD 843**
Sequel / Oct '96 / BMG

COME TO MY PARTY/FAN THE FIRE
CD ______ **CDGR 126**
Charly / Mar '97 / Koch

DEFINITIVE IMPRESSIONS, THE (28 Classic Soul Masters)
Gypsy woman / Grow closer together / Little young lover / Minstrel and queen / I'm the one who loves you / Sad, sad girl and boy / It's alright / Talking about my baby / I'm so proud / Keep on pushing / I've been trying / Girl you don't know me / I made a mistake / You must believe me / Amen / People get ready / Woman's got soul / Meeting over yonder / I need you / Just one kiss from you / You've been cheating / Since I lost the one I love / I can't satisfy / You always hurt me / I can't stay away from you / We're a winner / We're rolling on / I loved and I lost
CD ______ **CDKEND 923**
Kent / Oct '89 / Pinnacle

FIRST IMPRESSIONS/LOVING POWER
Sooner or later / Same thing it took / Old before my time / First impressions / Groove / I'm so glad / How high is high / Why must a love song be a sad song / Loving power / Sunshine / I can't wait to see you / If you have to ask / You can't be wrong / I wish I'd stayed in bed / Keep on trying
CD ______ **NEMCD 867**
Sequel / Aug '97 / BMG

IMPRESSIONS/THE NEVER ENDING IMPRESSIONS
It's alright / Gypsy woman / Grow closer together / Little young lover / You've come home / Never let me go / Minsterel and queen / I need your love / I'm the one who loves you / Sad, sad girl and boy / As long as you love me / Twist and limbo / Sister love / Little boy blue / Satin doll / Girl don't you know me / I gotta keep on moving / You always hurt the one you love / That's what love will do / I'm so proud / September song / Lemon tree / Ten to one / Woman who loves me
CD ______ **CDKEND 126**
Kent / Aug '95 / Pinnacle

KEEP ON PUSHING/PEOPLE GET READY
Keep on pushing / I've been trying / I ain't supposed to / Dedicate my song to you / Long, long winter / Somebody help me / Amen / I thank heaven / Talking about my baby / Don't let it hide / I love you / I made a mistake / Woman's got soul / Emotions / Sometimes I wonder / We're in love / Just another dance / Can't work no longer / People get ready / I've found that I've lost / Hard to believe / See the real me / Get up and move / You must believe me
CD ______ **CDKEND 130**
Kent / Feb '96 / Pinnacle

PREACHER MAN/FINALLY GOT MYSELF TOGETHER (2CD Set)
What it is / Preacher man / Simple message / Find the way / Thin line / Colour us all grey (I'm lost) / I'm loving you / If it's in you to do wrong / Finally got myself together / I'll always be here / Miracle woman / We go back a ways / Guess what I've got / Try me / Don't forget what I told you
CD Set ______ **NEMCD 866**
Sequel / Jul '97 / BMG

THIS IS MY COUNTRY/YOUNG MODS' FORGOTTEN STORY
CD ______ **NEMCD 782**
Sequel / Feb '96 / BMG
CD ______ **CDGR 108**
Charly / Mar '96 / Koch

Impromptu

SWEET KAFKA
Hiedeggar's lobster / Sweet Kafka / Avenue / Simply breathing / Fountain / Me and Louise / Med mig sjalv / Ginsberg / What can I say / Ten unicorns / Flay / La petite mort
CD ______ **RGM 194CD**
Red Gold Music / Dec '94 / Red Gold Music

Impulse

ONE-SIX-FOUR-ONE-SEVEN
CD ______ **K7R 010CD**
Studio K7 / Mar '97 / Prime / RTM/Disc

Impulse Manslaughter

LOGICAL END
CD ______ **NB 013CD**
Nuclear Blast / Jun '89 / Plastic Head

In Aura

ONE MILLION SMILES
100 degrees / This month's epic / 2-5 am / 90's itch / Virus / Desire / Sense / Soap opera / One million smiles / Las vegas leg
CD ______ **ORGAN 030CD**
Org / Aug '97 / Pinnacle

In Cahoots

PARALLEL
Simmer / Parallel / Ed or Ian / Half life / Sit down / Billow
CD ______ **CD 4CD**
Blueprint / Nov '96 / Pinnacle

RECENT DISCOVERIES
Riffy / Trick of the light / Opener / Recent discoveries / Chez gege / Tide / Breadhead
CD ______ **CD 003CD**
Voiceprint / Sep '94 / Pinnacle

In Crowd

NATURAL ROCK 'N' REGGAE
CD ______ **RNCD 2003**
Rhino / Nov '92 / Grapevine/PolyGram / Jet Star

WE PLAY REGGAE - A TRIBUTE
CD ______ **3021512**
Arcade / Jun '97 / Discovery
CD ______ **RN 7019**
Rhino / May '97 / Grapevine/PolyGram / Jet Star

In Flames

JESTER RACE, THE
CD ______ **NB 168CD**
Nuclear Blast / Sep '96 / Plastic Head

LUNAR STRIANS
CD ______ **WAR 003CD**
Wrong Again / Apr '96 / Plastic Head

In Folio

IN FOLIO
Amandine / Juggling in Central Park / Varan de komodo / Nain de jardin / Bascule / Da / Onze tetes de turc / Laurent d'arabie / Visitez la belgique en autocar / 5 AM / La soupe aux choux / All blues / Spopondrilloches
CD ______ **JMS 186812**
JMS / Apr '96 / New Note/BMG

In Gowan Ring

LOVE CHARMS
CD ______ **WSCD 006**
World Serpent / Oct '96 / World Serpent

TWIN TREES, THE
Rivertime tome / One silver ring / Twin trees / Stone song III / Lady beyond the river / By moss strand and waterspathe / Cupped hands spell / Our rainbowed paradox
CD ______ **LUNE 002CD**
Lune / Mar '97 / World Serpent

In My Rosary

STRANGE EP
CD ______ **SPV 06519042**
SPV / Aug '95 / Koch / Plastic Head

In Process

PARSEK
CD ______ **AS 20072**
Al Segno / Jun '96 / Vital/SAM

In The Nursery

AMBUSH OF GHOSTS, AN (Original Soundtrack)
CD ______ **TM 90382**
Roadrunner / Mar '96 / PolyGram

ANATOMY OF A POET
CD ______ **TM 89762**
Roadrunner / Mar '96 / PolyGram

DECO
CD ______ **CORP 014CD**
ITN Corporation / May '96 / Plastic Head

DUALITY
CD ______ **TM 91632**
Roadrunner / Mar '96 / PolyGram

IN THE CABINET OF DR. CALIGARI
CD ______ **CORP 015CD**
ITN Corporation / Nov '96 / Plastic Head

KODA
CD ______ **CORP 008CD**
ITN Corporation / Jun '95 / Plastic Head

L'ESPIRIT
CD ______ **TMCD 48**
Third Mind / Feb '90 / Pinnacle / Third Mind
CD ______ **CORP 010CD**
ITN Corporation / Jun '95 / Plastic Head

PRELUDE
CD ______ **CORP 007CD**
ITN Corporation / Jun '95 / Plastic Head

SCATTER
CD ______ **CORP 011CD**
ITN Corporation / Jun '95 / Plastic Head

SENSE
CD ______ **TM 92712**
Roadrunner / Mar '96 / PolyGram

TWINS
CD ______ **CORP 009CD**
ITN Corporation / Jun '95 / Plastic Head

In The Woods

HEART OF THE AGES
CD ______ **AMAZON 004CD**
Misanthropy / May '95 / Plastic Head

OMNIO
CD ______ **AMAZON 011CD**
Misanthropy / Jun '97 / Plastic Head

In Your Face

COLLECTIVE WORKS, THE
CD ______ **LF 106CD**
Lost & Found / Oct '94 / Plastic Head

Inanna

NOTHING
CD ______ **DVLR 08CD**
Dark Vinyl / Jun '95 / Plastic Head / World Serpent

Inbreds

KOMBINATOR
Kombinator / Round 12 / You will know / Any sense of time / Turn my head / Dale says / She's acting / Scratch / Link / Dangerous / Don't try so hard / Cruise control / Last flight / Amelia Earhart
CD ______ **926062**
Tag / Jan '96 / Vital

Incantation

BEST OF INCANTATION
On the wing of a condor / Cutimy / Saccaywaman / Dance of the flames / Sonccuiman / Noches de luna / Cacharpaya / Papel de plata / Virgins of the sun / Atahualpa / Dolencias / Festival of Yotala / Los senors de Potasi
CD ______ **NAGE 100CD**
Art Of Landscape / May '92 / Sony

INCANTATION
Ganado feroz / Wild / Herd / Brazfest / Reunion / Santa Cruz jit / Doina cestriana / Electric snake charmer / Llaulillay / Dawn at volcabamba / Serenading chango / Little flute player / Remembrance of Mary and Ellen / Cacharpaya shuffle
CD ______ **COOKCD 073**
Cooking Vinyl / Aug '97 / Vital

INCANTATION CHRISTMAS
What is this fragrance / I saw three ships come sailing by / Torches / Our lady / How hard it bloweth / Solis ortus / Cardine / Virgin Mother / Holly and the ivy / In dulci jubilo / Lullay thou tiny little child / Angel Gabriel / Child divine / Shepherd's story / Spiritual / Wexford Carol / Virgin most pure / Jesus redemption omniun
CD ______ **3036000102**
Carlton / Oct '95 / Carlton

MEETING, THE
De mis huellas / Antiguos duenos de las flechas / Old thatched cabin / Canto del agua / Scarborough Fair / On earth as it is in heaven (Theme from the mission) / Phuru runas/Waya yay / El amor es un camina / Cuando / Cancion de carnival Eddi's tune / Night shadows
CD ______ **COOKCD 068**
Cooking Vinyl / Jun '94 / Vital

PANPIPES OF THE ANDES
Amores hallaras / Cacharpaya / Papel de plata / Friends of the Andes / El pajaro madrugador / Condor dance / Sonccuiman / Dolencias / Winds on the mountain / On the wing of a condor / Sikuriadas / High flying bird
CD ______ **NAGE 101CD**
Art Of Landscape / Oct '92 / Sony

SERGEANT EARLY'S DREAM/ GHOST DANCES
May morning dew / Sergeant early's dream / Eighteen years old / Maid of mount / Sisco/Skylark/Richard Dwyers / Geordie / Love will you marry me/Plains of boyle / Black is the colour of my true love's hair / Peggy Gordon / Gospel ship / Barbara Allen / Junior Crehan's / Favourite/Corney is coming / Ojo azules / Huajra / Dolencias / Papel de plata / Mis Llamitas / Sikuriadas / Ojos azules
CD ______ **COOKCD 069**
Cooking Vinyl / Feb '95 / Vital

SONGS FOR THE SEASON
CD ______ **ACD 501CD**
Aeolian / Oct '94 / Carlton / Complete/ Pinnacle

Incantation

MORTAL THRONE OF NAZARENE
Golgotha / Devoured death / Blasphemous creations / Rotting spiritual embodiment / Unholy massacre / Entrantment of evil / Christening the afterbirth / Immortal cessation / Profanation / Deliverance of horrific prophecies
CD ______ **RR 69052**
Nuclear Blast / Jul '97 / Plastic Head

ONWARD TO GOLGOTHA
CD ______ **RR 60372**
Relapse / Jul '97 / Pinnacle / Plastic Head

Inch

DOT CLASS C
CD ______ **CRGD 82071**
Headhunter / Feb '97 / Cargo

STRESSER
Linger / No. 48 Vs SL/A / Kermit the hostage / Stresser / I'm the cat / Kane / Icepick / Surprise / Root canal/Manatoba / Oxidizer / Were riding
CD ______ **142522**
Seed / May '94 / Vital

Incognito

BENEATH THE SURFACE
Solar fire / Labour of love / Beneath the surface / Shade of blue / Without you / Misunderstood / Hold on to me / Living against the river / She wears black / Fountain of life / Out of the storm / Dark side of the cog
CD ______ **5340712**
Talkin' Loud / Oct '96 / PolyGram

BLUE MOODS
Colibri / Love is the colour / Magnetic ocean / Deep waters / L'arc en ciel de miles / Gypsy / Journey into sunlight / Sunchild / Millenium / Thinking bout tomorrow / Jcobs ladder / She wears black / Dark side of the cog
CD ______ **5347832**
Talkin' Loud / Apr '97 / PolyGram

INCOGNITO REMIXED
Always there / Good love / Jump to my love / I hear my name / Giving it up / Pieces of a dream / Jacobs ladder / Everyday / Barumba / Roots / Still a friend a mine / I hear your name / Still a friend of mine
CD ______ **5323092**
Talkin' Loud / Apr '96 / PolyGram

INSIDE LIFE
Metropolis / Smile / One step to a miracle / Can you feel me / Gypsy / Inside life / Love is the colour / Sketches in the dark / Soho / Always there
CD ______ **8485462**
Talkin' Loud / Jul '91 / PolyGram

ONE HUNDRED DEGREES AND RISING
Where did we go wrong / Good love / Hundred and rising / Roots / Everyday / Too far gone / After the fall / Spellbound and speechless / I hear your name / Barumba / Millenium / Time has come / Jacob's ladder
CD ______ **5280002**
Talkin' Loud / May '95 / PolyGram

POSITIVITY
Still a friend of mine / Smiling faces / Keep the fire burning / Do right / Positivity / Talkin' loud / Deep waters / Where do we go from here / Giving it up / Thinking about tomorrow
CD ______ **5182602**
Talkin' Loud / Nov '93 / PolyGram

TRIBES, VIBES AND SCRIBES
Colibri / Change / River in my dreams / Don't you worry about a thing / Magnet ocean / I love what you do for me / Closer to the feeling / L'Arc en ciel de miles / Need to know / Pyramids / Tribal vibes
CD ______ **5123632**
Talkin' Loud / Jun '92 / PolyGram

Incredible String Band

5000 SPIRITS OR THE LAYERS OF THE ONION
Chinese white / No sleep blues / Painting box / Mad hatter's song / Little cloud / Eyes of fate / Blues for the muse / Hedgehog's song / First girl I loved / You know that you could be / My name is death / Gently tender / Way back in the 1960's
CD ______ **HNCD 4438**
Hannibal / Jun '94 / ADA / Vital

BIG HUGE, THE
Maya / Greatest friend / Son of Noah's brother / Lordly nightshade / Mountain of God / Cousin caterpillar / Iron stone / Douglas Traherne Harding / Circle is unbroken

CD 7559615482
Elektra / Jul '93 / Warner Music

CHANGING HORSES
Big Ted / White bird / Dust be diamonds / Sleeper's awake / Mr. and Mrs. / Creation
CD HNCD 4439
Rykodisc / Nov '94 / ADA / Vital

CHELSEA SESSIONS 1967, THE
Lover man / Born in your town / First girl I loved / Gently tender / Little cloud / Blues for the muse / Eyes of fate / Mad hatters song / Alice is a long time gone / See your face and know you / Frutch / Iron stone / God dog
CD PWMD 5003
Pigs Whisker Music / Jun '97 / Pinnacle

HANGMAN'S BEAUTIFUL DAUGHTER
Koee / Addi there / Minotaur's song / Witches hat / Very cellular song / Mercy I cry city / Waltz of the new moon / Water song / Three is a green crown / Swift as the wind / Nightfall
CD HNCD 4421
Hannibal / Jun '94 / ADA / Vital

HARD ROPE AND SILKEN TWINE
Maker of islands / Cold February / Glancing love / Dreams of no return / Dumb Kate / Ithkos
CD EDCD 368
Edsel / Jan '93 / Pinnacle

I LOOKED UP
CD HNCD 4440
Rykodisc / Nov '94 / ADA / Vital

INCREDIBLE STRING BAND
Maybe someday / October song / When the music starts to play / Schaeffer's jig / Womankind / Tree / Whistle tune / Dandelion blues / How happy I am / Empty pocket blues / Smoke shovelling song / Can't keep me here / Good as gone / Footsteps of the heron / Niggertown / Everything's fine right now
CD HNCD 4437
Hannibal / Jun '94 / ADA / Vital

LIQUID ACROBAT AS REGARDS AIR
Talking of the end / Dear old battlefield / Cosmic boy / Worlds they rise and fall / Evolution rag / Painted chariot / Adam and Eve / Red hair / Here till here is there / Tree / Jigs / Darling belle
CD IMCD 130
Island / Jun '91 / PolyGram

NO RUINOUS FEUD
CD EDCD 367
Edsel / Nov '92 / Pinnacle

WEE TAM
Job's tears / Puppies / Beyond the sea / Yellow snake / Log cabin in the sky / You get brighter / Half remarkable question / Air / Ducks on a pond
CD HNCD 4802
Rykodisc / Nov '94 / ADA / Vital

Incredibles

HEART AND SOUL
Heart and soul / (I love you) for sentimental reasons / Lost without you / Standing here crying / I'll make it easy / Miss Treatment / Without a word / All of a sudden / Another dirty deal / There's nothing else to say baby / Fool, fool, fool (version 1) / Stop the raindrops / I found another love / Crying heart (version 1) / Without a word / Standing here crying / Miss Treatment (45 version) / I can't get over losing your love / Fool, fool, fool (version 2)
CD GSCD 018
Goldmine / Jul '93 / Vital

Incubus

BEYOND THE UNKNOWN
CD NB 039CD
Nuclear Blast / Jan '91 / Plastic Head

ENJOY INCUBUS
You will be a hot dancer / Shaft / Take me to your leader / Version / Azwethinkweiz hilikus / Hidden bonus
CD 4871022
Epic / Feb '97 / Sony

SERPENT TEMPTATION
CD RAD 124CD
Radiation / Apr '96 / Plastic Head

Incubus Succubus

WYTCHES
Wytches / Queen of the May / Pagan born / Gypsy lament / Leveller / Call out my name / Conquistadors / Burning times / Song to Pan / Enchantment / Catherine / Church of madness / Rape of Maude Bowen / Dark mother / Devils
CD PMRCD 7
Pagan Media / '96 / Pagan Media / Pinnacle

Index

BLACK LIGHT TWILIGHT
CD COPCD 023
Cop International / Nov '96 / Cargo

Indian Bingo

OVERWROUGHT
CD ROCK 60792
Rockville / Mar '93 / Plastic Head / SRD

PICTURE SHOP, THE
CD ROCK 61332
Rockville / Jan '94 / Plastic Head / SRD

Indicate

WHELM
CD TO 25
Touch / Jun '95 / Kudos / Pinnacle

Indigo

CARNETS DE VOL
CD 926642
BUDA / Feb '97 / Discovery

ONE
Indigo sunrise / As above, so below / Dream warriors / Beyond white mountains / Guarana / I morning-you bird / Fisherman's lament / Memories of Lhasa / Shell shocked / White horse dancing / Tomorrow is maybe / Aliens of Red Rock / Xingu river / Indigo sunset
CD PRMDCD 12
Premier/EMI / Sep '96 / EMI

Indigo Girls

4.5
Joking / Hammer and a nail / Kid fears / Galileo / Tried to be true / Power of two / Pushing the needle too far / Reunion / Closer to fine / Three hits / Least complicated / Touch me fall / Love's recovery / Land of Canaan / Ghost
CD 4804392
Epic / Jul '95 / Sony

RITES OF PASSAGE
Three hits / Galileo / Ghost / Joking / Jonas and Ezekial / Love will come to you / Romeo and Juliet / Virginia Woolf / Chicken man / Airplane / Nashville / Let it be me / Cedar tree
CD 4713632
Epic / '89 / Sony

SHAMING THE SUN
Shame on you / Get out the map / Shed your skin / It's alright / Caramia / Don't give that girl a gun / Leeds / Scooter boys / Everything in its own time / Cut it out / Burn all the letters / Hey kind friend
CD 4869822
Epic / May '97 / Sony

SWAMPOPHELIA
Fugitive / Least complicated / Language or the kiss / Reunion / Power of two / Touch me fall / Wood song / Mystery / Dead man's hill / Fare thee well / This train revised
CD 4759312
Epic / May '94 / Sony

Indigo Kennedy

ZET LONDON VOL.3
CD INGI 001CD
Zet / Jun '97 / Plastic Head

Indo Aminata

GREATEST DREAM
Love will be on your side / Dunigna colorila / Always / Leo Leo / I've waited for this love / Cruel love / When you have the greatest dream / Djeneba / Silan magninde / Follow me / Djiamma
CD 5328812
Manifesto / Nov '96 / PolyGram

Inducing The Pleasure Dreams

RADIO MOOG 1996
CD XTC 00000011CD
Apocalyptic Vision / Nov '96 / Cargo / Plastic Head / SRD

Industrial Terror Squad

TERROR DROME
CD 35286
Industrial Strength / Sep '96 / Mo's Music Machine / Vital

Inertia

INFILTRATOR
CD EFA 125292
Celtic Circle / Nov '95 / SRD

Infernal Majesty

NONE SHALL DEFY
CD D 00044
Displeased / Jun '96 / Plastic Head / RTM/Disc

Inferno

DEATH AND MADNESS
CD GTA 025
Grand Theft Auto / Mar '97 / Cargo / Plastic Head

PSYCHIC DISTANCE
CD MASSCD 043
Massacre / Jan '95 / Plastic Head

UTTER HELL
CD OPCD 044
Osmose / Oct '96 / Plastic Head

Infinite Wheel

BLOW
CD BRAINK 54
Brainiak / Jul '96 / 3mv/Sony / Arabesque / RTM/Disc

INFINITE WHEEL, THE
CD BRAINK 41CD
Brainiak / Oct '94 / 3mv/Sony / Arabesque / RTM/Disc

Infinity Project

MYSTICAL EXPERIENCES
CD BR 005CD
Blue Room Released / Jan '96 / Essential/ BMG / SRD

Infor/Mental

MIND DRONE
Mind drone / Wave / Pleasuredance / Dream mode mutation / Mental journey / Frenzy / Trance induction / Infection / Dream mode mutation (mix) / Insanity / Device trigger / Ambient one
CD LUDDITECD 066
Death Of Vinyl / Oct '93 / Vital

Ingham, Keith

KEITH INGHAM & MARTY GROSZ/ COSMOPOLITES (Ingham, Keith & Marty Grosz)
CD SOSCD 1285
Stomp Off / Mar '95 / Jazz Music / Wellard

OUT OF THE PAST
CD SKCD 23047
Sackville / '92 / Cadillac / Jazz Music / Swift

Ingleton Falls

ABSCONDED
CD CHARRMCD 20
Charrm / Mar '95 / Plastic Head

Ingman, Nick

HOME (Ingman, Nick & Friends)
Home: *Ingman, Nick* / Homeward bound: *Simon, Paul* / Now and then: *Davis, Gayle* / Just be close: *Ingman, Nick* / Making tracks: *Mindel, David* / Staying in: *Maliszewski, Aleksander* / Help me make it through the night: *Kristofferson, Kris* / Missing you again: *Aldrich, Ronnie* / Welcome home: *Maliszewski, Aleksander* / By your side: *Maliszewski, Aleksander* / Late night talking: *Ingman, Nick* / Woman: *Lennon, John* / Sunday morning: *Ingman, Nick* / Home is where the heart is: *Love, Geoff* / On the road: *Maliszewski, Aleksander* / Green green grass of home: *Putman, Curley* / When day is done: *Katscher, Robert & De Sylva* / Cosy: *Maliszewski, Aleksander* / Safe and sound: *Ingman, Nick* / Here where you are: *Goodwin, Ron*
CD BATCD 1001
Baton / Jul '89 / DI Music

Ingram, Adrian

DUETS (Ingram, Adrian & Andy MacKenzie)
Pick yourself up / Gravy waltz / Nivram / Django's bounce / Barney's bossa / Wes mode / Kenny's groove / Mr PM / Can't buy me love / Lover man / Lullaby of birdland / Rabbit waltz
CD IPCD 010
Crimson / Jun '97 / New Note/Pinnacle

SPREAD THE WORD (Ingram, Adrian & Ben Crossland Quartet)
Warm one / Seachange / Spread the word / Down at Pol's / Movin' on / Floating blue / Friday the 13th / We got it too / Peter the wolf / You don't know what love is / Ade's groove
CD JCCD 102
Jazz Cat / Nov '96 / New Note/Pinnacle

Ingram, Jack

LIVIN' OR DYIN'
Nothin' wrong with that / Big time / Ghost of a man / Flutter / Rita Ballou / She does her best / Dim lights, thick smoke (and loud, loud music) / Picture on my wall / That's not me / Don't you remember / Imitation of love / Dallas / I can't leave you / Airways motel
CD RTD 80370
Rising Tide / Apr '97 / BMG

Ingram, James

ALWAYS YOU
Someone like you / Let me love you this way / Always you / Treat her right / Baby's born / This is the night / You never know what you've got / Too much from this heart / Sing for the children / Any kind of love
CD 9362452752
Qwest / May '93 / Warner Music

POWER OF GREAT MUSIC, THE
Where did my heart go / How do you keep the music playing / Just once / Somewhere out there / I don't have the heart / There's no easy way / Get ready / Baby, come to me / Hundred ways / Yah mo be there / Remember the dream / Whatever we imagine
CD 7599267002
Qwest / Mar '94 / Warner Music

Inhaler

VOLUME
CD LLL 2030
Seriously Groovy / Dec '96 / Cargo

Iniquity

SERENADIUM
CD RRS 953CD
Progress / Jul '96 / Cargo / Plastic Head

Inishkea

PAN PIPES OF IRELAND
When you were sweet sixteen / Bunch of thyme / I'll take you home again Kathleen / Shepherd moon / Carrickfergus / Maggie / Pal of my cradle days / When Irish eyes are smiling / Molly Malone / Fields of Athenrey / Rose of Tralee / Have I told you lately / Mountains of Mourne / Leaving of Liverpool / Whiskey in the jar / Londonderry air
CD 307602
Hallmark / Jul '97 / Carlton

Ink, Mike

POLKA TRAX
CD WAPCD 82
Warp / Oct '96 / Prime / RTM/Disc

Ink Spots

18 HITS
CD KCD 5001
King / Apr '97 / Avid/BMG

BEST OF THE INK SPOTS
If I didn't care / Bless you for being an angel / When the swallows come back to Capistrano / Whispering grass / Maybe / Java jive / Do I worry / I don't want to set the world on fire / Every night about this time / Don't get around much anymore / To each his own / Ring, telephone, ring / I'd climb the highest mountain / Puttin' and takin' / Cow cow boogie: *Ink Spots & Ella Fitzgerald* / Into each life some rain must fall: *Ink Spots & Ella Fitzgerald* / Your feet's too big / I'll never smile again / It's a sin to tell a lie / Someone's rocking my dreamboat
CD CDMFP 6064
Music For Pleasure / May '89 / EMI

BEST OF THE INK SPOTS, THE
CD HMNCD 001
Half Moon / Jun '97 / BMG

BLESS YOU
Bless you / If I didn't care / Whispering grass / Stop pretending / When the swallows come back to Capistrano / So sorry / Do I worry / We'll meet again / I'd climb the highest mountain / Ring, telephone, ring / That cat is high / Memories of you / My prayer / Just for a thrill / We three / Someone's rocking my dreamboat / Maybe / I'll never smile again / I'm getting sentimental over you / Coquette / Oh red / When the sun goes down
CD PLCD 535
President / Mar '93 / Grapevine/PolyGram / President / Target/BMG

CLASSICS
Bless you / Don't get around much anymore / Ring telephone ring / So sorry / Someone's rocking my dreamboat / Do I worry / Whispering grass / Java jive / If I didn't care / I'd climb the highest mountain / When the swallows come back to Capistrano / Maybe / That cat is high / Stop pretending / With plenty of money and you / When the sun goes down / Who wouldn't love you / That's the way it is / To each his own / Everyone is saying hello again / Street of dreams / Someday I'll meet you again
CD RAJCD 886
Empress / Jul '97 / Koch

INK SPOTS GREATEST HITS VOL.1
CD BMCD 3037
Blue Moon / Jan '97 / Cadillac / Discovery / Greensleeves / Jazz Music / Jet Star / TKO Magnum

INK SPOTS GREATEST HITS VOL.2
CD BMCD 3038
Blue Moon / Jan '97 / Cadillac / Discovery / Greensleeves / Jazz Music / Jet Star / TKO Magnum

INK SPOTS, THE
CD CD 110
Timeless Treasures / Oct '94 / THE

JAVA JIVE
CD 15430
Laserlight / Jan '93 / Target/BMG

SENTIMENTAL OVER YOU
CD HADCD 194
Javelin / Nov '95 / Henry Hadaway / THE

SWING HIGH, SWING LOW (1936-1940)
Bless you / Java jive / When the swallows come back to Capistrano / My prayer / Christopher Columbus / I'll never smile again / Stompin' at the Savoy / Whispering grass / If I didn't care / I'm getting sentimental over you / Keep away from my doorstep / Let's call the whole thing off / Maybe / Oh Red / Slap that bass / Stop pretending / Swing high swing low / That cat is high / When the sun goes down / With plenty of money and you / Yes suh / Your feet's too big
CD ______ CDAJA 5082
Living Era / Apr '91 / Select

WHISPERING GRASS (The Very Best Of The Ink Spots)
If I didn't care / I'll never smile again / Java jive / Stop pretending / Maybe / Your feet's too big / I don't want to set the world on fire / When the swallows come back to Capistrano / Cat is high / Whispering grass (don't tell the trees) / Someone's rocking my dreamboat / Who wouldn't love you / Christopher Columbus / Do I worry / My prayer / Slap that bass / Don't get around much more / I'm getting sentimental over you / We three / Bless you
CD ______ 305522
Hallmark / Oct '96 / Carlton

WHISPERING GRASS
Bless you / Stop pretending / That cat is high / When the swallows come back to Capistrano / Mama don't allow it / My prayer / Whispering grass / We three (my echo, my shadow and me) / I'm getting sentimental over you / Java jive / With plenty of money and you / Keep away from my doorstep / Do I worry / I'll never smile again / Don't let old age creep up on you / Maybe / If I didn't care / Stompin' at the Savoy / Coquette / Swing high swing low / Your feet's too big / When the sun goes down
CD ______ PASTCD 9757
Pearl / Aug '91 / Harmonia Mundi

Inkubus Sukkubus

BELLADONNA & ACONITE
CD ______ ABCD 007
Resurrection / Mar '96 / Plastic Head

BELTHANE
CD ______ ABCD 11
Resurrection / Oct '96 / Plastic Head

HEATBEAT
CD ______ ABCD 005
Resurrection / Apr '96 / Plastic Head

Inkuyo

ANCIENT SUN - MUSIC OF THE ANDES
CD ______ 130932
Celestial Harmonies / Sep '96 / ADA / Select

Inmates

INMATES
CD ______ 892223
New Rose / May '94 / ADA / Direct / Discovery

INSIDE OUT
CD ______ 422178
New Rose / May '94 / ADA / Direct / Discovery

SILVERIO
CD ______ 3018322
Last Call / Feb '97 / Cargo / Direct / Discovery

WANTED
CD ______ 422460
New Rose / May '94 / ADA / Direct / Discovery

Inner Circle

BAD TO THE BONE
Sweat (a la la la la long) / Shock out Jamaican style / Bad to the bone / Rock with you / Long time / Hey love / Slow it down / Living it up / Stuck in the middle / Looking for a better way / Wrapped up in your love / Bad boys / Party party / Sunglasses at nite / Tear down these walls / Down by the river / Hold on to the ridim / Why them a gwan so
CD ______ 9031776772
Magnet / Dec '96 / Warner Music

BEST OF INNER CIRCLE
Rock the boat / Curfew / Duppy gunman / None shall escape the judgement / You make me feel brand new / Some guys have all the luck / Everything I own / TSOP (The sound of Philadelphia) / Westbound train / Book of rules / Natty dread / I shot the sheriff / Irie feelings / Forward Jah Jah children / Blame it on the sun / Curly locks / Your kiss is sweet / Burial / Roadblock / When will I see you again
CD ______ CDTRL 318
Trojan / Mar '94 / Direct / Jet Star

BEST OF INNER CIRCLE, THE
CD ______ CID 8007
Island / Jan '94 / PolyGram

DA BOMBE
CD ______ 0630151922
East West / Aug '96 / Warner Music

FORWARD JAH JAH PEOPLE
Rastaman / Forward Jah Jah children / Last crusade / Lively up yourself / Funky reggae / One love
CD ______ CPCD 8133
Charly / Oct '95 / Koch

ONE WAY
One way / Front and centre / Champion / Keep the faith / Love one another / Massive / Bad boys / Life / Stay with me
CD ______ RASCD 3030
Ras / Oct '87 / Direct / Greensleeves / Jet Star / SRD

REGGAE DANCER
CD ______ 4509961162
Magnet / Sep '94 / Warner Music

REGGAE THING
CD ______ NSPCD 510
Connoisseur Collection / Mar '95 / Pinnacle

Inner City

PARADISE
Inner city theme / Ain't nobody better / Big fun / Good life / And I do / Paradise / Power of passion / Do you love what you feel / Set your body free / Secrets of the mind
CD ______ VI 874812
Disky / Nov '96 / Disky / THE
CD ______ CDVIP 160
Virgin VIP / Oct '96 / EMI

PARADISE REMIXED
Big fun / Good life / Ain't nobody better / Do you love what you feel / What'cha gonna do with my lovin' / House fever / Paradise megamix
CD ______ XIDCD 81
10 / Feb '90 / EMI

PRAISE
One nation / Praise / Pennies from heaven / Hallelujah / Follow your heart / Slaves of dance / Let it reign / United / Faith / Save the children
CD ______ DIXCD 107
10 / Jun '92 / EMI

TESTAMENT '93
Good life / Pennies from heaven / Hallelujah / Praise / Follow your heart / Good life (Unity remix)
CD ______ CDOVD 438
Virgin / May '93 / EMI

Inner City Jazz Workshop

INSIDE DANCING ONLY
CD ______ MANU 1504
Manu / Feb '96 / ADA / Discovery

Inner City Unit

NEW ANATOMY
CD ______ 14845
Spalax / Feb '97 / ADA / Cargo / Direct / Discovery / Greyhound

Inner Sanctum

12 AM
CD ______ WDR 42101
Rock The Nation / Nov '94 / Plastic Head

Innersphere

OUTER WORKS
Out of body / Toys in the attic / Let's go to work / Mine drift / Infernal aftershock / Tuberculosis / Necronomicon / Biomechanoid / 3750 Miles / Out of body (Reprise)
CD ______ SBRCD 002
Sabrettes Of Paradise / Oct '94 / Vital

Innes, Heather

COAINEADH - SONGS FROM THE HEART
CD ______ FE 099CD
Fellside / Jun '94 / ADA / Direct / Target/ BMG

Innes, Neil

RE-CYCLED VINYL BLUES
Recycled vinyl blues / Angelina / Come out into the open / Prologue / Momma Bee / Lie down and be counted / Immortal invisible / Age of desperation / Topless a go-go / Feel no shame / How sweet to be an idiot / Dream on / L'amour perdu / Song for Yvonne / This love of ours / Fluff on the needle / Singing a song is easy / Bandwagon
CD ______ CZ 536
EMI / Aug '94 / EMI

Innisfree Ceoil

CELTIC AIRS VOL.1
CD ______ CHCD 2001
Chyme / Nov '96 / ADA / CM / Direct / Koch

CELTIC AIRS VOL.2
CD ______ CHCD 2002
Chyme / Nov '96 / ADA / CM / Direct / Koch

Innocence

BELIEF
Silent voice / Let's push it / Reflections / Natural thing / Matter of fact / Higher ground / Remember the day / Moving upwards / Come together / Reprise
CD ______ CCD 1797
Cooltempo / Oct '90 / EMI

BUILD
Family ties / I'll be there / Build / Looking for someone / Solitude / Family ties(Reprise) / One love in my lifetime / Promise of love / Hold on / Respect / No sacrifice / Build (reprise)
CD ______ CTCD 26
Cooltempo / Oct '92 / EMI

Innocents

COMPLETE INDIGO RECORDINGS
Gee whiz / Please Mr. Sun / Walking along / Once in a while / Pain in my heart / Chiquita / Girl in my dreams / Because I love you / Sleeping beauty / Donna / Kathy / My baby Hully Gullys / Honest I do / Beware / I'm a hog for you / When I become a man / Two young hearts / Dee dee di oh / I believe in you / It was a tear / You got me goin' / Little blue star / I know a valley / Time makes you change / In the beginning
CD ______ CDCHD 374
Ace / Jun '92 / Pinnacle

Inoue, Tetsu

OM/INSTANT ENLIGHTENMENT
CD ______ CS 8513
Mic Mac / Mar '96 / Vital/SAM

Inquisitor

WALPURGIS, SABBATH OF LUST
CD ______ SHR 018CD
Shiver / Jul '96 / Plastic Head

Insane Jane

EACH FINGER
CD ______ SKYCD 5041
Sky / Sep '94 / Greyhound / Koch / Vital/ SAM

GREEN LITTLE PILL
CD ______ SKYCD 5040
Sky / Sep '94 / Greyhound / Koch / Vital/ SAM

Insanity Sect

MANISOLA
CD ______ RBADCD 15
Beyond / Feb '96 / Kudos / Pinnacle

Insaurralde, Mirta

DE IGUAL A IGUAL (Insaurralde, Mirta & Ruben Ferrero)
Duerme negrito / Que he sacado con quererte / La vieja / El dia que me quieras / Patio de naranjos / Nunca se supo porque / Vidala para mi sombra / Tierra tiembla / Homenaje a Pablo Neruda / De igual a igual
CD ______ SLAMCD 502
Slam / Oct '94 / Cadillac

Insekt

DREAMSCAPE
CD ______ KK 074CD
KK / Mar '92 / Plastic Head

STRESS
CD ______ KK 054CD
KK / Mar '91 / Plastic Head

WE CAN'T TRUST THE INSEKT
CD ______ KK 036CD
KK / Jun '93 / Plastic Head

Inside Out

SHE LOST HER HEAD
CD ______ COX 032CD
Meantime / Apr '92 / Cadillac / Vital

Insides

CLEAR SKIN
CD ______ TU 7
4AD / Feb '94 / RTM/Disc

EUPHORIA
CD ______ GU 4CD
Guernica / Oct '93 / Pinnacle

Insomniacs

OUT OF IT
CD ______ ES 1233CD
Estrus / Apr '97 / Cargo / Greyhound / Plastic Head

Inspector Tuppence

PARADISO
CD ______ INSPEC 001
Inspec / Mar '97 / Nervous

Inspiral Carpets

BEAST INSIDE, THE
Caravan / Please be cruel / Born yesterday / Sleep well tonight / Grip / Beast inside / Niagara / Mermaid / Further away / Dreams are all we have
CD ______ DUNG 14CD
Cow / May '91 / Pinnacle

DEVIL HOPPING
CD ______ LDUNG 25CD
Cow / Feb '94 / Pinnacle

LIFE
CD ______ DUNG 008CD
Cow / Mar '90 / Pinnacle

REVENGE OF THE GOLDFISH
CD ______ DUNG 19CD
Cow / Oct '92 / Pinnacle

SINGLES, THE
CD ______ CDMOOTEL 3
Cow / Sep '95 / Pinnacle

TALKING WITH THE BEAST
CD ______ CBAK 4047
Baktabak / Jun '91 / Arabesque

Inspirational Choir

GOSPEL SONGS
Amazing grace / Rock of ages / He's got the whole world in his hands / Deep river / Every time I feel the spirit / Steal away / I've got a robe / Were you there / Old rugged cross / Old time religion / Abide with me / He's got the whole world in his hands
CD ______ 5501912
Spectrum / Sep '94 / PolyGram

SWEET INSPIRATION
Sweet inspiration / People get ready / Up where we belong / One love / Jesus dropped the charges / I've got a feeling / You light up my life / Morning has broken / Amazing grace / What a friend we have in Jesus / When He comes / God is / Abide with me
CD ______ CD 10048
CBS / Jan '86 / Sony

Inspirations

PAN PIPE IMAGES
CD ______ TCD 2819
Telstar / Mar '96 / BMG

PIANO REFLECTIONS
CD ______ PMCD 7024
Pure Music / Jan '96 / BMG

Instant Funk

FUNK IS ON, THE
It's cool / Funk is on / Funk 'n' roll / You want my love / What can I do for you / Everybody / Can you see where I'm coming from / You're not getting older
CD ______ CPCD 8097
Charly / Apr '95 / Koch

INSTANT FUNK
I got my mind made up (You can get it girl) / Crying / Never let it go away / Don't wanna party / Wide world of sports / Dark vader / You say you want me to stay / I'll be doggone
CD ______ CPCD 8075
Charly / Mar '95 / Koch

Insted

BONDS OF FRIENDSHIP
CD ______ LF 178CD
Lost & Found / Sep '96 / Plastic Head

Institute Of Dubology

S/T (Institute Of Dubology & Tuffhead)
CD ______ LIVESTOCK 2CD
Livestock / Jul '96 / Jet Star / SRD

Insult

MUTANT PUZZLE
CD ______ SPI 021CD
Spinefarm / Jun '95 / Plastic Head

Insult II Injury

POINT OF THIS
CD ______ CM 77086
Century Media / Jan '95 / Plastic Head

Insync & Mysteron

ANDROID ARCHITECTS
Gravity pull / Next world / Landing site / Human loop / Android architects / Science fact / Auto glide / Missing link / Dig deep / Train of thought / Naked I
CD ______ TPRCD 005
10th Planet / Mar '97 / Kudos / Pinnacle / Prime

Intastella

WHAT YOU GONNA DO
CD ______ SATURNCD 1
China / Oct '95 / Pinnacle

Integrated Circuits

PREDO
CD ______ DBMLABCD 6
Labworks / Oct '95 / RTM/Disc / SRD

Integrity

HOOKED LUNG STOLEN BREATH
CD _____ LF 112CD
Lost & Found / Nov '94 / Plastic Head

SEASONS IN THE SIZE OF DAYS
CD _____ VR 053CD
Victory / Jun '97 / Plastic Head

SYSTEMS OVERLOAD
CD _____ VE 023CD
Victory / Aug '95 / Plastic Head

TASTE EVERY SIN
CD _____ HT 004
Holy Terror / Jun '97 / Greyhound

THOSE WHO FEAR TOMORROW
CD _____ DEI 20212
Homestead / Mar '93 / Cargo / SRD

Intergrity

WHY I NEED A BEER
CD _____ WB 1135CD
We Bite / Apr '96 / Plastic Head

Interlect 3000

ELECTRIC ALLSORTS
Plastic mushroom / Ghost in the machine / Cyclogic / Evolutionary changes / Default / e-scape / Can't take it / Squirt transmission / Induction / White noise / Connect / Alien cargo / SOS
CD _____ ISLCD 1
Phantasm/Inspiral / Feb '97 / Vital/SAM

Interloper

AUGUR
CD _____ PLKCD 5
Plink Plonk / Jun '96 / Prime / SRD

Intermix

FUTURE PRIMITIVES
CD _____ SUN 49982
Mokum / Sep '96 / Pinnacle

International Children's Choir

O HOLY NIGHT
CD _____ 15302
Laserlight / Nov '95 / Target/BMG

International Language

WHERE THE BANDS ARE
CD _____ SFTRI 457
Sympathy For The Record Industry / Dec '96 / Cargo / Greyhound / Plastic Head

International People

INTERNATIONAL PEOPLE
CD _____ EMIT 3395
Time Recordings / Oct '95 / Pinnacle

International Strike Force

LOVE IS
CD _____ SLAMPT 41CD
Slampt Underground / Nov '96 / Shellshock/Disc

Inti-Illimani

ANDADAS
CD _____ GL 4009CD
Green Linnet / Oct '93 / ADA / CM / Direct / Highlander / Roots

CANTO DE PUEBLOS ANDINOS
CD _____ MCD 71787
Monitor / Jun '93 / CM

CANTO PARA MATAR UNA CULE
CD _____ MCD 71817
Monitor / Jun '93 / CM

DE CANTO Y BAILE
Mi chiquita / Dedica toria de un libro / Cantiga de la memoria rota / Bailando / Candidos / El colibri / El vals / La muerte no va conmigo / Danza di cala luna
CD _____ MES 159362
Messidor / Apr '93 / ADA / Koch

I WILL RISK MY SKIN
Medianoche / Maria Canela / El hacha / Entre nosotros / Quien eres tu / Arriesgare la piel / Kalimba / Cumpleanos 80 de nicanor / Caramba yo soy dueno del baron / El negro bembon / Kulliacas / Canto de las estrellas
CD _____ XENO 4049CD
Xenophile / Nov '96 / ADA / Direct

LA NUEVA CANCION CHILENA
CD _____ MCD 71794
Monitor / Jun '93 / CM

VIVA CHILE
CD _____ MCD 71769
Monitor / Jun '93 / CM

Inti-Raymi

INCA QUENA
CD _____ TUMICD 047
Tumi / '94 / Discovery / Stern's

INTI-RAYMI
CD _____ TUMICD 009
Tumi / Dec '90 / Discovery / Stern's

Intimate Orchestra

TENDER MOMENTS
With you I'm born again / Crying / Suddenly / One day I'll fly away / First time ever I saw your face / Sailing / Chi mai / Cavatina / For your eyes only / Woman / Memory / All out of love / Chariots of fire / Imagine / Bright eyes / Just when I needed you most / Don't cry for me Argentina / I'm not in love / If I fell / Concierto de aranjuez
CD _____ QED 175
Tring / Nov '96 / Tring

Intini, Cosmo

MY FAVOURITE ROOTS (Intini, Cosmo & The Jazz Set)
When Sunny gets blue / Powerful warrior / 'Round midnight / Fatherly love / My one and only love / Steps
CD _____ CDSJP 339
Timeless Jazz / Aug '90 / New Note/ Pinnacle

Into Another

IGNAURUS
CD _____ REVEL 35CD
Revelation / May '94 / Plastic Head

INTO ANOTHER
CD _____ WB 083CD
We Bite / Jan '92 / Plastic Head

SEEMLESS
CD _____ 1620082
Hollywood / Feb '96 / PolyGram

Into Paradise

UNDER THE WATER
Bring me closer / Here with you / Red light / Pleasure is you / Circus came to town / Bring me closer (version) / World won't stop / Hearts and flowers / Blue moon express / Say goodnight / Beautiful day / Going home
CD _____ SETCD 1
Setanta / Feb '90 / Vital

Into The Abyss

FEATHERED SNAKE, THE
CD _____ EFA 112832
Glasnost / Aug '95 / SRD

MARTYRIUM
CD _____ SPV 08425232
SPV / Feb '94 / Koch / Plastic Head

Intricate

(VA:1)
CD _____ CM 770612
Century Media / Jan '94 / Plastic Head

Intro

INTRO
Love thang / Let me be the one / Anyhting for you / Why don't you love me / It's all about you / Ribbon in the sky / Don't leave me / Come inside / One of a kind love / So many reasons / Ecstasy of love
CD _____ 7567824632
Atlantic / Apr '93 / Warner Music

NEW LIFE
Funny how time flies / Love me better / Strung out on your lovin' / New life / My love's on the way / Somebody loves you / My song / Spending my life with you / There is a way / Feels like the first time
CD _____ 7567826622
Atlantic / Nov '95 / Warner Music

Intruder

PSYCHO SAVANT
CD _____ CDZORRO 25
Metal Blade / Jul '91 / Pinnacle / Plastic Head

Intuition

INTUITION
CD _____ FAT 002CD
Fat Cat / Sep '93 / ADA / CM / Direct

Intveld, James

JAMES INTVELD
Perfect world / Blue blue day / Cryin' over you / I'm to blame / Barely hangin' on / Samantha / Standing on a rock / My heart is achin' for you / Important words / Your lovin' / You say goodnight, I'll say goodbye / I love you
CD _____ BCD 15900
Bear Family / Oct '95 / Direct / Rollercoaster / Swift

Invisible String Quartet

ENTOMIC
Insect flak / Traffic jam / Marsh ague / Reincarnation / 21cm band / Bee-line / Ephemera / Lagos holiday
CD _____ SLAMCD 210
Slam / Oct '96 / Cadillac

Invocator

DYING TO LIVE
CD _____ PCD 020
Progress / Sep '95 / Cargo / Plastic Head

EARLY YEARS, THE
CD _____ RRS 943CD
Pingo / Dec '94 / Plastic Head

EXCURSION DEMISE
CD _____ 8410582
Black Mark / Jan '92 / Plastic Head

WEAVE THE APOCALYPSE
CD _____ BMCD 34
Black Mark / Jul '93 / Plastic Head

INXS

ELEGANTLY WASTED
CD _____ 5346132
Mercury / Apr '97 / PolyGram

FULL MOON, DIRTY HEARTS
Days of rust / Gift / Make your peace / Time / I'm only looking / Please (You've got that) / Full moon, dirty hearts / Freedom deep / Kill the pain / Cut your roses down / Messenger / Viking juice
CD _____ 5186372
Mercury / Oct '93 / PolyGram

GREATEST HITS
Mystify / Suicide blonde / Taste it / Strangest party / Need you tonight / Original sin / Heaven sent / Disappear / Never tear us apart / Gift / Devil inside / Beautiful girl / Deliver me / New sensation / What you need / Listen like thieves / Bitter tears / Baby don't cry
CD _____ 5262302
Mercury / Oct '94 / PolyGram

INXS
On a bus / Doctor / Just keep walking / Learn to smile / Jumping / In vain / Roller skating / Body language / Newsreel babies / Wishy washy
CD _____ 8389252
Mercury / May '90 / PolyGram

INXS: INTERVIEW PICTURE DISC
CD _____ CBAK 4038
Baktabak / Apr '90 / Arabesque

KICK
Guns in the sky / New sensation / Devil inside / Need you tonight / Mediate / Loved one / Wild life / Never tear us apart / Mystify / Kick / Calling all nations / Tiny daggers
CD _____ 8327212
Mercury / Nov '87 / PolyGram

LISTEN LIKE THIEVES
What you need / Listen like thieves / Kiss the dirt / Shine like it does / Good and bad times / Biting bullets / This time / Three sisters / Same direction / One x one / Red red sun
CD _____ 8249572
Mercury / Jan '86 / PolyGram

LIVE BABY LIVE
New sensation / Mystify / Shining star / Mediate / Burn for you / This time / Suicide blonde / Never tear us apart / Guns in the sky / By my side / Need you tonight / One x one / One thing / Stairs / Hear that sound / What you need
CD _____ 5105802
Mercury / Nov '91 / PolyGram

SHABOOH SHOOBAH
CD _____ 8120842
Mercury / Jul '93 / PolyGram

SWING, THE
Original sin / Melting in the sun / Send a message / Dancing on the jetty / Swing / Johnson's aeroplane / Love is (what I say) / Face the change / Burn for you / All the voices
CD _____ 8185532
Mercury / Jul '84 / PolyGram

UNDERNEATH THE COLOURS
Stay young / Horizon / Big go go / Underneath the colours / Fair weather ahead / Night of rebellion / Follow / Barbarian / What would you do / Just to learn again
CD _____ 8387772
Mercury / Jul '89 / PolyGram

WELCOME TO WHEREVER YOU ARE
Questions / Heaven sent / Communication / Taste it / Not enough time / All around / Baby don't cry / Beautiful girl / Wishing well / Back on line / Strange desire / Men and women
CD _____ 5125072
Mercury / Aug '92 / PolyGram

X
Suicide blonde / Disappear / Stairs / Faith in each other / By my side / Lately / Who pays the price / Know the difference / Bitter tears / On my way / Hear that sound
CD _____ 8466682
Mercury / Sep '90 / PolyGram

Iona

BEYOND THESE SHORES
CD _____ WHAD 1300
What / Jul '96 / Nelson Word / Total/BMG

BOOK OF KELLS, THE
CD _____ WHAD 1287
What / Apr '95 / Nelson Word / Total/BMG

IONA
CD _____ WHAD 1266
What / May '95 / Nelson Word / Total/ BMG

JOURNEY INTO THE MORN
CD _____ ALCD 034
3 Chord / Oct '95 / Total/BMG

TREASURES (The Best Of Iona)
CD _____ WHAD 1303
3 Chord / Dec '96 / Total/BMG

Iona

HEAVEN'S BRIGHT SUN (2CD Set) (Iona, Andy & Islanders/Cliff Edwards)
CD Set _____ CORDCD 2
3 Chord / Jul '97 / Total/BMG

Iona Ac Andy

100 MILES
CD _____ SCD 2111
Sain / Feb '96 / ADA / Direct / Greyhound

SPIRIT OF THE NIGHT
CD _____ SCD 2071
Sain / Oct '94 / ADA / Direct / Greyhound

Ionatos, Angelique

DE LA SOURCE A LA MER
CD _____ A 6222
Tempo / Feb '96 / Discovery / Harmonia Mundi

PAROLE DE JUILLET DE ODYSSEUS ELYTIS
CD _____ 088532
Melodie / Jul '97 / ADA / Discovery / Grapevine/PolyGram / Greensleeves / Jet Star

Iowa Beef Experience

PERSONALIEN
Guilt and revenge / Hardcore fan / Cum soaked / Making the monster a snack / Pizenhead / Tools of the trade / Love muscle no.96 / Talented amature / Nonstop nacho / Dope smoking redneck...
CD _____ OINK 015 CD
Pigboy / Jan '93 / Vital

Ipsen, Kjeld

JAZZ CODE (Ipsen, Kjeld & Uffe Markussen)
CD _____ STCD 4208
Storyville / May '97 / Cadillac / Jazz Music / Wellard

IQ

ARE YOU SITTING COMFORTABLY
War heroes / Drive on / Nostalgia / Falling apart at the seams / Sold on you / Through my fingers / Wurensh / Nothing at all
CD _____ GEPCD 1013
Giant Electric Pea / Feb '95 / Pinnacle

EVER
CD _____ GEPCD 1006
Giant Electric Pea / Aug '94 / Pinnacle

J'AI POLLETE D'ARNU
CD _____ GEPCD 1001
Giant Electric Pea / Aug '93 / Pinnacle

LIVING PROOF
CD _____ GEPCD 1004
Giant Electric Pea / Aug '93 / Pinnacle

NOMZAMO
No love lost / Promises (as the years go by) / Nomzamo / Still life / Passing strangers / Human nature / Screaming / Common ground
CD _____ GEPCD 1012
Giant Electric Pea / Oct '94 / Pinnacle

TALES FROM THE LUSH ATTIC
Last human gateway / Awake and nervous / Enemy smacks / Just changing hands / Through the corridors / My baby treats me right, cause I'm a hard lovin' man all nig
CD _____ GEPCD 1010
Giant Electric Pea / Aug '94 / Pinnacle

WAKE, THE
Outer limits / Magic roundabout / Widow's peak / Headlong / Thousand days (demo) / Wake / Corners / Thousand days / Dans le Parc du chateau noir / Magic roundabout (demo)
CD _____ GEPCD 1011
Giant Electric Pea / Aug '94 / Pinnacle

Irakere

EN VIVO
Bacalao con pan / Moja el pan / Xiomara mayoral xiomara / Taka taka-ta / La similla / Dile a catalina / Baila mi ritmo / El coco / Aguanile bonko
CD _____ PSCCD 1005
Pure Sounds From Cuba / Feb '95 / Henry Hadaway / THE

EXUBERANCIA
Xiomara / El guayo de catalina / Chango / El recuentro / Samba para enrique / El guao

/ Brown music / Guan tan amera / Brown music (encore)
CD JHCD 009
Ronnie Scott's Jazz House / Feb '94 / Cadillac / Jazz Music / New Note/Pinnacle / TKO Magnum

FELICIDAD
Stella, Pete, Ronnie / La maquina del sabor / Contradanza / Anabis / Tributoa peruchin / La pastora
CD JHCD 014
Ronnie Scott's Jazz House / Jan '94 / Cadillac / Jazz Music / New Note/Pinnacle / TKO Magnum

GRANDES MOMENTOS
CD 74321327212
Milan / Nov '96 / Conifer/BMG / Silva Screen

HOMENAJE A BENY MORE
CD MES 259042
Messidor / Feb '93 / ADA / Koch

LEGENDARY - LIVE IN LONDON, THE
Bilando asi / Johana / Estela va a estallar (Stella by starlight) / Las margaritas / Lo que va a pasar / Duke
CD JHCD 005
Ronnie Scott's Jazz House / Jan '94 / Cadillac / Jazz Music / New Note/Pinnacle / TKO Magnum

MISA NEGRA (AFRICAN MASS)
CD MES 159722
Messidor / Dec '92 / ADA / Koch

Iration Steppas

ORIGINAL DUB DAT
CD ISCD 005
Iration Steppas / Jun '96 / SRD

Irazu

LA FIESTA DEL TIMBALERO
Timbalero / Laura / Me voy contigo / Salseando / A Puerto padre / El son de Irazu / Si vienes te quwdas / Anoranza / Danzon del corazon / Everything happens to me
CD CDLR 45039
L&R / Jan '92 / New Note/Pinnacle

Irigara, Carlos Alberto

NAVIDAD CRIOLLA
CD 262063
Milan / Oct '91 / Conifer/BMG / Silva Screen

Irini

DON'T MAKE ME WISH
CD HIICD 023
Here It Is / Jan '96 / Jet Star

Iris

CROSSING THE DESERT
CD IRISCD 001
Blueprint / Apr '97 / Pinnacle

Irish Guards Band

MUSIC FOR REMEMBRANCE
National anthem / March of the Royal British Legion / Heart of oak / Life on the ocean wave / Red, white and blue / Lass who loved a sailor / Great little army / WRAC march / Grey and scarlet / Old comrades / Ulster defence regiment march / Royal Air Force march past / Holyrood / Princess Royals red cross march / Boys of the old brigade / Sunset / Cwm Rhondda / Abide with me / Last post / Reveille / Eternal father strong to save / Rule Britannia / Minstrel boy / Men of Harlech / Isle of beauty / David of the white rock / Oft in the stilly night / Nimrod / Laid in earth / Solemn melody / Funeral march / O God our help in ages past / March melody / It's a long way to Tipperary / Pack up your troubles / There'll always be an England / Keep the home fires burning / Madamoiselle from Armentieres / Take me back to dear old blighty / Run rabbit run / Kiss me goodnight, Sergeant Major / Hang out the washing on the Siegfried line / Wish me good luck as you wave goodbye / Beer barrel polka / Lili Marlene / Walting Mathilda / Maple leaf forever / Maori battalion marching song
CD BNA 5014
Bandleader / Nov '87 / Conifer/BMG

Irish Rovers

RAMBLERS AND GAMBLERS (20 All Time Irish Favourites)
Wild rover / Wild mountain thyme / I'm a rambler, I'm a gambler / Last of the Irish rovers / Unicorn / Good luck to the barleymow / Lovely isle of Innisfree / Gypsy rover / My boy Willie / Orange and the green / Liverpool Lou / Caltan weaver / Mountain tay / Turra market / Sweet Strabane / Come by the hills / Black velvet band / Whiskey on a Sunday / Star of the County Down / Rolling home to Ireland
CD 3036001142
Carlton / Jul '97 / Carlton

Irish Soundscape

CELTIC INSPIRATIONS
CD CDC 012
Ceol / Feb '97 / CM

Irish Tradition

CORNER HOUSE, THE
CD GLCD 1016
Green Linnet / Sep '88 / ADA / CM / Direct / Highlander / Roots

TIMES WE'VE HAD, THE
Paddy Fahy's reel / Paddy O'Brien's reel / Shipyard apprentice / Quilty/Sault's hornpipe / Michael O'Connor / Paddy's lamentation / Festus Burke / Yellow tinker/Sally gardens / Lady fair / Happy days / Flight of wild geese / Wild rover / Lad O'Beirne's/ Small hills of Offaly
CD GLCD 1063
Green Linnet / Jun '93 / ADA / CM / Direct / Highlander / Roots

Irish Weavers

LIVE AT BLARNEY PARK
Irish Weavers song / All for me grog / Rambles of spring / Pinch of snuff / Miss Mcleod's reel / Coolin / Dunmore lasses / Ship in full sail / Trippin' up the stairs / Whisky in the jar / Quartermaster's stores / Copperplate reel / Peter Street / O'Donovan's reel / Cork loves a stranger / Jig o'slurs / Athol highlanders / Oldest swinger in town / Lonesome boatman / Ghost of '47 / Whistling gypsy / Red Rose Cafe / My Irish Molly-O / Nation once again / Wild rover / Cockles and mussels / Boys of Fair Hill / Coming round the mountain / Irish Weavers song (play off)
CD GRCD 76
Grasmere / Mar '96 / Highlander / Savoy / Target/BMG

Irmin's Way

OPUS DESTROY
CD KSCD 9569
Kissing Spell / Jun '97 / Greyhound

Iron Bong

BIG HITS
CD LOST 006
Lost / May '97 / Cargo

Iron Butterfly

IN-A-GADDA-DA-VIDA
Most anything you want / My mirage / Termination / Are you happy / In-a-gadda-da-vida / Flowers and beads
CD 8122721962
Atlantic / Jan '96 / Warner Music

LIGHT & HEAVY
Iron butterfly / Possession / Unconcious power / You can't win / So lo / In-a-gadda-da-vida / Most anything you want / Flowers and beads / My mirage / Termination / In the time of our lives / Soul experience / Real fright / In the crowds / It must be love / Belda beast / I can't help but deceive you little girl / New day / Stone believer / Soldier in our own town / Easy rider (let the wind pay the way)
CD 8122711662
Atlantic / Mar '93 / Warner Music

SUN AND STEEL
CD EDCD 408
Edsel / Feb '95 / Pinnacle

Iron Fist

MOTORSEXLE MANIA
CD FDN 2009CD
Foundation 2000 / Jul '94 / Plastic Head

Iron Horse

FIVE HANDS HIGH
CD LDL 1214CD
Lochshore / Aug '94 / ADA / Direct / Duncans

IRON HORSE
CD LDL 1202CD
Lochshore / Aug '94 / ADA / Direct / Duncans

THRO' WATER,EARTH & STONE
CD LDLCD 1206
Lochshore / May '93 / ADA / Direct / Duncans

VOICE OF THE LAND
CD CDLDL 1232
Lochshore / Sep '95 / ADA / Direct / Duncans

Iron Maiden

BEST OF THE BEAST, THE
Mumber of the beast / Can I play with madness / Fear of the dark / Run to the hills / Bring your daughter to the slaughter / Evil that men do / Aces high / Be quick or be dead / 2 Minutes to midnight / Man on the edge / Virus / Running free / Wasted years / Clairvoyant / Trooper / Hallowed be thy name
CD CDEMD 1097
EMI / Oct '96 / EMI

BEST OF THE BEAST, THE (2CD Set)
Virus / Sign of the cross / Man on the edge / Afraid to shoot strangers / Be quick or be dead / Fear of the dark / Bring your daughter to the slaughter / Holy smoke / Clairvoyant / Can I play with madness / Evil that men do / Heaven can wait / Wasted years / Rime of the Ancient Mariner / Running free / 2 minutes to midnight / Aces high / Where eagles dare / Number of the beast / Trooper / Run to the hills / Hallowed be thy name / Wrathchild / Phantom of the opera / Sanctuary / Strange world / Iron Maiden
CD Set CDEMDS 1097
EMI / Nov '96 / EMI

CAN I PLAY WITH MADNESS
Can I play with madness / Black Bart blues / Massacre / Evil that men do / Prowler '88 / Charlotte the harlot '88 / Listen with Nicko part ix
CD CDP 7940012
EMI / Apr '90 / EMI

FEAR OF THE DARK
Be quick or be dead / From here to eternity / Afraid to shoot strangers / Fear is the key / Childhood's end / Wasting love / Fugitive / Chains of misery / Apparition / Judas be my guide / Weekend warrior / Fear of the dark
CD CDP 7991612
EMI / May '92 / EMI

IN PROFILE (Interview Disc)
CD CDINPROF 001
EMI / Aug '97 / EMI

IRON MAIDEN
Prowler / Remember tomorrow / Running free / Phantom of the opera / Transylvania / Strange world / Charlotte the harlot / Iron Maiden
CD CDEMS 1538
EMI / Jul '94 / EMI

KILLERS
Ides of March / Wrathchild / Murders in the Rue Morgue / Another life / Genghis Khan / Innocent exile / Killers / Prodigal son / Purgatory / Drifter
CD CDEMS 1536
EMI / Jul '94 / EMI

LIVE AFTER DEATH
Aces high / Two minutes to midnight / Trooper / Revelations / Flight of Icarus / Rime of the ancient mariner / Powerslave / Number of the beast / Hallowed be thy name / Iron Maiden / Run to the hills / Running free
CD CDEMS 1535
EMI / Jul '94 / EMI

MAIDEN OVER
CD 3D 016
Network / Dec '96 / Total/BMG

NO PRAYER FOR THE DYING
Tailgunner / Holy smoke / No prayer for the dying / Public enema no.1 / Fates warning / Assassin / Run silent run deep / Hooks in you / Bring your daughter... to the slaughter / Mother Russia
CD CDEMS 1541
EMI / Jul '94 / EMI

NUMBER OF THE BEAST
Invaders / Children of the damned / Prisoner / 22 Acacia Avenue / Number of the beast / Run to the hills / Gangland / Hallowed be thy name
CD CDEMS 1533
EMI / Jul '94 / EMI

PIECE OF MIND
Where eagles dare / Revelations / Flight of Icarus / Die with your boots on / Trooper / Still life / Quest for fire / Sun and steel / To tame a land
CD CDEMS 1540
EMI / Jul '94 / EMI

PLAYING WITH MADNESS
CD CBAK 4035
Baktabak / Jan '92 / Arabesque

POWERSLAVE
Aces high / Two minutes to midnight / Losfer words (big 'Orra) / Flash of the blade / Duellists / Back in the village / Powerslave / Rime of the ancient mariner
CD CDEMS 1539
EMI / Jul '94 / EMI

REAL DEAD ONE, A
Number of the beast / Trooper / Prowler / Transylvania / Remember tomorrow / Where eagles dare / Sanctuary / Running free / Two minutes to midnight / Iron maiden / Hallowed be thy name
CD CDEMD 1048
EMI / Oct '93 / EMI

REAL LIVE ONE, A
Be quick or be dead / From here to eternity / Can I play with madness / Wasting love / Tailgunner / Evil that men do / Afraid to shoot strangers / Bring your daughter... to the slaughter / Heaven can wait / Clairvoyant / Fear of the dark
CD CDP 7814562
EMI / Sep '94 / EMI

SEVENTH SON OF A SEVENTH SON
Moonchild / Infinite dreams / Can I play with madness / Evil that men do / Seventh son of a seventh son / Prophecy / Clairvoyant / Only the good die young
CD CDEMS 1534
EMI / Jul '94 / EMI

SOMEWHERE IN TIME
Caught somewhere in time / Wasted years / Sea of madness / Heaven can wait / Loneliness of the long distance runner / Stranger in a strange land / Deja vu / Alexander the great
CD CDEMS 1537
EMI / Jul '94 / EMI

X FACTOR, THE
Sign of the cross / Lord of the flies / Man on the edge / Fortunes of war / Look for the truth / Aftermath / Judgement of heaven / Blood on the world's hands / Edge of darkness / 2 am / Unbeliever
CD CDEMD 1087
EMI / Sep '97 / EMI

Iron Man

BLACK NIGHT
CD HELL 022
Hellhound / Jul '93 / Koch

PASSAGE, THE
Fury / Unjust reform / Gargoyle / Harvest of earth / Passage / Iron warrior / Freedom fighters / Waiting for tomorrow / Time of indecision / Tony stark / End of the world
CD H 00222 CD
Hellhound / Oct '94 / Koch

Irresistable Force

FLYING HIGH
CD RSNCD 5
Rising High / Nov '92 / 3mv/Sony

GLOBAL CHILLAGE
CD RSNCD 24
Rising High / Nov '94 / 3mv/Sony

Irvine, Andy

ANDY IRVINE & PAUL BRADY (Irvine, Andy & Paul Brady)
Plains of Kildare / Lough Erne shore / Fred Finn's reel/Sailing into Walpole's marsh / Bonny woodhall / Arthur McBride / Jolly soldier / Blarney pilgrim / Autumn gold / Mary and the Soldier / Streets of Derry / Martinmas time / Little stack of wheat
CD GL 3201CD
Green Linnet / Jul '94 / ADA / CM / Direct / Highlander / Roots

EAST WIND (Irvine, Andy & Davy Spillane)
Chetvorno horo / Bear's rock / Dance of suleiman / Illyrian dawn / Two steps to the bar / Pride of Macedonia / Kadana / Hard on the heels
CD TARACD 3027
Tara / Apr '92 / ADA / CM / Conifer/BMG / Direct

RAINY SUNDAYS, WINDY DREAMS
Come to the land of sweet liberty / Farewell to old Ireland / Edward Connors / Longford weaver / Christmas Eve / farewell to Ballymoney / Romanian song / Paidushko horo / King Bore and sandman / Rainy Sundays
CD CDTUT 72141
Wundertute / '88 / ADA / CM / Duncans

RUDE AWAKENING
CD GLCD 1114
Green Linnet / Apr '92 / ADA / CM / Direct / Highlander / Roots

Irvine, Weldon

BEST OF WELDON IRVINE VOL.1, THE
Deja vu / Bananas / Turkish bath / Walk that walk, talk that talk / Mr Clean / We getting down / Jungle juice / Music is the key
CD CNMDCD 01
Timewarp / Jun '97 / Timewarp

LIBERATED BROTHER
CD HUBCD 12
Hubbub / Oct '96 / Beechwood/BMG / SRD / Timewarp

TIME CAPSULE
CD HUBCD 13
Hubbub / Oct '96 / Beechwood/BMG / SRD / Timewarp

Is

IS, THE
CD DMCD 1033
Demi-Monde / Feb '92 / RTM/Disc / TKO Magnum

Isaac, Ismael

TREICH FEELING
CD 3019522
Arcade / Feb '97 / Discovery

Isaacs, Barney

HAWAIIAN TOUCH
CD DCT 38026CD
Dancing Cat / Mar '96 / ADA

Isaacs, Barry

REVOLUTIONARY MAN
CD ROTCD 7
Reggae On Top / Sep '95 / Jet Star / SRD

Isaacs, Gregory

ABSENT
CD GRELCD 190
Greensleeves / Aug '93 / Jet Star / SRD

BAD BOY LOVER MAN (2CD Set)
CD Set CPCD 82782
Charly / Jul '97 / Koch

BLOOD BROTHERS (Isaacs, Gregory & Dennis Brown)
CD RASCD 3116
Ras / Feb '94 / Direct / Greensleeves / Jet Star / SRD

CALL ME COLLECT
CD RASCD 3067
Ras / Nov '90 / Direct / Greensleeves / Jet Star / SRD

CLASSIC HITS VOL.2
CD SONCD 0027
Sonic Sounds / Apr '92 / Jet Star

COME AGAIN DUB
CD RE 193CD
ROIR / Nov '94 / Plastic Head / Shellshock/Disc

COME CLOSER
CD 503382
Declic / Sep '94 / Jet Star

COOL DOWN
Cool down / Black kill a black / I am alright / Good luck and goodbye / Love is all I need / Come rain or come shine / Mr. Babylon / Don't want to be your man / Cross the line
CD CY 78935
Nyam Up / Mar '95 / Conifer/BMG

COOL RULER - SOON FORWARD - SELECTION
Native woman / John Public / Party in the slum / Uncle Joe / Word of the farmer / One more time / Let's dance / Created by the father / Raving tonight / Don't pity me
CD CDFL 9012
Frontline / Sep '90 / EMI / Jet Star

COOL RULER RIDES AGAIN, THE (22 Classics From 1978-1981)
Let's dance / Permanent lover / My only lover / Gi me / Poor natty / Mr. Brown / Raving tonight / Soon forward / Front door / Tribute to wa de / Poor and clean / Fugitive / If I don't have you / Few words / I am sorry / Protection / Confirm reservation / Once ago / One more time / Hush darling / My relationship / Slave market
CD NSCD 017
Nascente / Jul '97 / Disc / New Note/ Pinnacle

DANCE HALL DON
CD SHCD 45015
Shanachie / Jun '94 / ADA / Greensleeves / Koch

DANCING FLOOR
Dancing floor / Crown and anchor / Give it all up / Private lesson / Nobody knows / Dealing / Shower me with love / Opel ride / Chips is down / Rock me
CD MRCD 148
Munich / Jul '90 / ADA / CM / Direct / Greensleeves

DEM TALK TOO MUCH
CD CDTRL 355
Trojan / Jun '95 / Direct / Jet Star

DREAMING
CD CDHB 155
Heartbeat / Jul '95 / ADA / Direct / Greensleeves / Jet Star

EARLY YEARS, THE
Rock away / Sweeter the victory / Sinner man / Lonely lover / Loving pauper / Promised land / Love is overdue / Bad da / Way of life / Financial endorsement / Give a hand / All I have is love
CD CDTRL 196
Trojan / Mar '94 / Direct / Jet Star

ENCORE
Out Deh / Tune in / Top ten / Private secretary / My only lover / All I have is love / Love is overdue / Can't give my love / Cool down the pace / Oh what a feeling / Addicted to you / Night nurse
CD CDKVL 9030
Kingdom / Jan '88 / Kingdom

GREGORY ISAACS & FRIENDS
CD SHCD 150
Shanachie / Jun '94 / ADA / Greensleeves / Koch

GREGORY ISAACS COLLECTION, THE
CD RNCD 2102
Rhino / Apr '95 / Grapevine/PolyGram / Jet Star

HARDCORE
CD GSCD 70035
Greensleeves / Nov '92 / Jet Star / SRD

HEARTACHE AVENUE
CD WRCD 009
World / Jun '97 / Jet Star / TKO Magnum

HEARTBREAKER
CD RRTGCD 7788
Rohit / Jul '90 / Jet Star

HOLD TIGHT
Miss Cutie Cutie / Wah dee / Hold tight / Mi no want / Tan so back / Thank you Mr. Judge / Kill them with music / Lady on the frontline / Come make love to me / Get deport / Don't go / Motherless children / I miss you
CD CDHB 210
Heartbeat / May '97 / ADA / Direct / Greensleeves / Jet Star

I AM GREGORY
CD CRCD 22
Charm / Sep '93 / Jet Star

I AM THE INVESTIGATOR
CD CB 6006
Bluesilver / Jan '96 / Jet Star

I'LL NEVER TRUST YOU
CD LG 21098
Lagoon / May '94 / Grapevine/PolyGram

IOU
CD GRELCD 136
Greensleeves / Aug '89 / Jet Star / SRD

LADY OF YOUR CALIBRE
CD WRCD 013
World / Jun '97 / Jet Star / TKO Magnum

LEE PERRY PRESENTS GREGORY ISAACS
CD RNCD 2030
Rhino / Dec '93 / Grapevine/PolyGram / Jet Star

LIVE AT THE ACADEMY
My number one / All I ask is love / My only lover / Love overdue / Storm / Mr. Brown / Slave master / Oh what a feeling / Soon forward / Sunday morning / Addicted to you / Front door / Border / Can't give my love / Cool down the pace
CD CDKVL 9027
Kingdom / Jan '87 / Kingdom

LIVE IN FRANCE
CD SONCD 0060
Sonic Sounds / Mar '94 / Jet Star

LONELY DAYS
CD JMC 200205
Jamaican Gold / Sep '94 / Grapevine/ PolyGram / Jet Star

LONELY LOVER
Happy anniversary / Gi me / Tribute to Waddy / Poor and clean / Poor natty / I am sorry / Few words / Protection / Hard time / Tune in
CD RNCD 2047
Rhino / Mar '94 / Grapevine/PolyGram / Jet Star

LOOKING BACK
CD RASCD 3196
Ras / Aug '96 / Direct / Greensleeves / Jet Star / SRD

LOVE IS OVERDUE
CD CDHB 98
Heartbeat / Aug '96 / ADA / Direct / Greensleeves / Jet Star

MAXIMUM RESPECT
CD CDSGP 070
Prestige / Mar '94 / Else / Total/BMG

MEMORIES
Make love to me / Memories / Say a prayer / You keep me waiting / Spend sometime / Common sense / My apology / Love you more / Cry over me / Who will see / All in the game
CD 112082
Musidisc UK / Aug '95 / Grapevine/ PolyGram

MR. COOL
CD RFCD 001
Record Factory / Oct '95 / Jet Star

MR. ISAACS
CD OH 003
Ossie / Nov '95 / Jet Star

MR. LOVE
Mr. Brown / Word of the farmer / Black liberation struggle / Poor and clean / Slave market / Uncle Joe / Universal tribulation / Confirm reservation / Protection / Tribute to Waddy / Let's dance / One more time / John Public / Native woman / Lonely girl / If I don't have you / Poor millionaire / My only lover / Raving tonight / Hush darling / Soon forward
CD CDFL 9021
Frontline / Jun '95 / EMI / Jet Star

MY NUMBER ONE
CD CDHB 61
Heartbeat / Mar '90 / ADA / Direct / Greensleeves / Jet Star

MY POOR HEART
CD HBCD 167
Heartbeat / Aug '94 / ADA / Direct / Greensleeves / Jet Star

NIGHT NURSE
Material man / Not the way / Sad to know you're leaving / Hot stepper / Cool down the pace / Night nurse / Stranger in town / Objection overruled
CD RRCD 9
Reggae Refreshers / Sep '90 / PolyGram / Vital

NO INTENTIONS
CD VPCD 1133
RF / Jun '91 / Jet Star

NO LUCK
CD LG 21049
Lagoon / Nov '92 / Grapevine/PolyGram

NO SURRENDER
CD GVCD 2020
Greensleeves / Nov '92 / Jet Star / SRD

NOT A ONE MAN THING
CD RASCD 3145
Ras / Jul '95 / Direct / Greensleeves / Jet Star / SRD

NUMBER ONE
CD CPCD 8026
Charly / Feb '94 / Koch

ONCE AGO
Tribute to Waddy / Gimme / Poor and clean / Poor Natty / I am sorry / Few words / Protection / Hard time / Hush darling / Confirm reservation / Front door / Permanent lover / My only lover / If I don't have you / Substitute / Poor millionaire / Fugitive / Once ago
CD CDFL 9004
Frontline / Jul '90 / EMI / Jet Star

OUT DEH
Good morning / Private secretary / Yes I do / Sheila / Out deh / Star / Dieting / Love me with feeling
CD RRCD 46
Reggae Refreshers / Jul '94 / PolyGram / Vital

OVER THE YEARS VOL.2
CD AMCD 012
African Museum / Apr '96 / Jet Star

OVER THE YEARS VOL.3
CD KPAMCD 013
African Museum / Mar '97 / Jet Star

PARDON ME
CD RASCD 3100
Ras / Sep '93 / Direct / Greensleeves / Jet Star / SRD

PARDON ME (Dub Version)
CD 504992
Declic / May '96 / Jet Star

PRIVATE BEACH PARTY
Wish you were mine / Feeling irie / Bits and pieces / Let off supm / No rushings / Private beach party / Better plant some loving / Got to be in tune / Special to me / Promise is a comfort
CD GRELCD 85
Greensleeves / Jul '95 / Jet Star / SRD

PRIVATE LESSON
CD DUBID 2CD
Acid Jazz Roots / Sep '95 / Disc

RAS PORTRAITS
Private beach party / So much love / Rumours / Give in with caution / Special to me / Call me collect / Don't dis the dancehall / Nah lef the dance / Red rose for Gregory / Let off some supm / Break the ice / Intimate potential / Too good to be true / Enough is enough
CD RAS 3309
Ras / Jul '97 / Direct / Greensleeves / Jet Star / SRD

RED ROSE FOR GREGORY
CD GRELCD 118
Greensleeves / Sep '88 / Jet Star / SRD

REGGAE GREATS (Gregory Isaacs Live)
Number one / Tune in / Substitute / Soon forward / Mr. Brown / Sunday morning / Oh what a feeling / Love is overdue / Top 10 / Front door / Border
CD RRCD 42
Reggae Refreshers / Jan '94 / PolyGram / Vital

REGGAE MAX
CD JSRNCD 3
Jet Star / Mar '96 / Jet Star

RESERVED FOR GREGORY
CD EXCD 1
Exodus / Nov '95 / Jet Star

SET ME FREE
CD VYDCD 02
Vine Yard / Sep '95 / Grapevine/PolyGram

SINNER MAN
CD CSAPCD 121
Connoisseur Collection / Mar '96 / Pinnacle

SLUM IN DUB
CD CDTRL 344
Trojan / Jul '94 / Direct / Jet Star

SLY & ROBBIE PRESENT GREGORY ISAACS
CD RASCD 3206
Ras / Dec '95 / Direct / Greensleeves / Jet Star / SRD

SPECIAL GUEST
CD 3021442
Arcade / Jun '97 / Discovery
CD RN 7016
Rhino / May '97 / Grapevine/PolyGram / Jet Star

TWO BAD SUPERSTARS (Isaacs, Gregory & Dennis Brown)
CD CDTRL 335
Trojan / Mar '94 / Direct / Jet Star

TWO TIME LOSER
CD 792152
Melodie / Apr '96 / ADA / Discovery / Grapevine/PolyGram / Greensleeves / Jet Star

UNFORGETTABLE
CD RRTGCD 7736
Rohit / '88 / Jet Star

UNLOCKED
CD GRELCD 193
Greensleeves / Sep '93 / Jet Star / SRD

VICTIM
CD VPCD 1033
VP / Apr '89 / Greensleeves / Jet Star / Total/BMG

WATCHMAN OF THE CITY
CD RIFWLCD 9300
Rohit / Mar '88 / Jet Star

WILLOW TREE
CD JMC 200204
Jamaican Gold / Jun '94 / Grapevine/ PolyGram / Jet Star

WORK UP A SWEAT
CD AMCD 010
African Museum / Feb '95 / Jet Star

YESTERDAY
CD VPCD 14942
VP / Jul '97 / Greensleeves / Jet Star / Total/BMG

YOU'RE DIVINE
CD RB 3002
Reggae Best / May '94 / Grapevine/ PolyGram

Isaak, Chris

FOREVER BLUE
CD 9362458452
Reprise / May '95 / Warner Music

HEART SHAPED WORLD
Heart shaped world / I'm not waiting / Don't make me dream about you / Kings of the highway / Wicked game / Blue spanish sky / Wrong to love you / Forever young / Nothing's changed / In the heat of the jungle
CD 9258372
Reprise / Jun '89 / Warner Music

SAN FRANCISCO DAYS
San Francisco days / Beautiful homes / Round and round / Two hearts / Can't do a thing (to stop me) / Except the new girl / Waiting / Move along / I want your love / 5.15 / Lonely with a broken heart / Solitary man
CD 9362451162
Reprise / Apr '93 / Warner Music

SILVERTONE
Dancin' / Talk to me / Living for your lover / Back on your side / Voodoo / Funeral in the rain / Lonely one / Unhappiness / Tears / Gone ridin' / Pretty girls don't cry / Western stars
CD 9251562
Reprise / Dec '87 / Warner Music

WICKED GAME
Wicked game / You owe me some kind of love / Blue Spanish sky / Heart shaped world / Heart full of soul / Funeral in the rain / Blue Hotel / Dancin' / Nothings changed / Voodoo / Lie to me / Wicked game (instrumental)
CD 7599265132
Reprise / Jan '91 / Warner Music

Isalonisti

HUMORESQUE
Souvenir / Whispering flowers / Czardas / Come away to Madrid / My sweet little friend / On the sea shore / My heart only calls to you / Humoresque / Slavonic dance No.6 / Melody in F / Syncopation / Gypsy Capriccio / Poeme / Little Viennese march / Mill in the black forest / Maiden's prayer / We wander the world / Eight in the night / When a toreador falls in love
CD CDC 1695132
Harmonia Mundi / Oct '86 / Cadillac / Harmonia Mundi

Isan Slete

FLOWER OF ISAN, THE
Lai lam toei sam jangwa / Hua ngawk yawk sao / Sutsanaen-noeng mode / Lam phloen / Lai pu pa lan / Toei khong / Lam doeng dong / Lai-yai mode / Lam toei thammada / Lai ngua khuen phu / Lam kio / Lai phu thai / Sutsanaen mode / Kawn lawng la / Lai an nang-sue / Imae, imae
CD CDORB 051
Globestyle / Oct '89 / Pinnacle

Isbin, Gilbert

BLUE SOUNDS AND TOUCHES
Quite blue / Sueno / Tell me / In balance / Leon / Mosca Espagnola / Mar arbierto / Full moon and little bastion / Nenia / Blue 2 / Camino verde / Come into my door / A nice advance / Blue in blue / Ballad in a cave / HWYL
CD HWYLCD 4
Hwyl / Jun '91 / Hwyl

Isengard

HOSTMORKE
CD FOG 007CD
Moonfog / Jun '95 / Plastic Head

Isfort, Tim

TIM ISFORT ORCHESTRA (Isfort, Tim Orchestra)
CD EFA 121202
Moll / Jul '97 / SRD

Isham, Mark

BLUE SUN
Barcelona / Beautiful sadness / Trapeze / Lazy afternoon / Blue sun / In more than love / Miles to go before he sleeps / In a sentimental mood / Tour de chance
CD 4813042
Sony Jazz / Oct '95 / Sony

COOL WORLD
CD VSCD 5382
Varese Sarabande / Aug '92 / Pinnacle

SKETCH ARTIST
CD VSCD 53776
Varese Sarabande / Aug '92 / Pinnacle

TIBET
CD 01934110802
Windham Hill / Sep '95 / BMG

Ishii, Ken

INNERELEMENT
Encoding / AFIAC / Twist of space / QF / Flurry / Garden of the palm / Pneuma / Sponge / Radiation / Loop / Fragment of yesterday / Kala / Decoding
CD RS 94038CD
R&S / May '94 / Vital

JELLY TONES
Extra / Cocoa mousse / Stretch / Ethos 9 / Moved by air / Pause in herbs / Frame out / Endless season
CD RS 95065CD
R&S / Oct '95 / Vital

X-MIX (3LP Set)
Fool's paradise: *United Future Organisation* / Phantom: *Renegade Soundwave* / Bumbuphone: *Fretless AZM* / Theme from the innocent: *Innocent* / Fly life: *Basement Jaxx* / NP 21: *Flare* / Mood: *Symbols & Instruments* / Gyroscope: *Strange Attractor* / Drums in a grip: *De Wulf, Frank* / Pumpin' bass manoeuvres: *Ghetto Brothers* / Dance of the naughty knights: *Jedi Knights* / Atomic moog 2000: *Coldcut* / Buckfunk discoteque: *Buckfunk 3000* / DIRR: *Flare* / Circular motion / Echo exit / No-one in the world: *Locust* / Nautilus: *Slazenger, Jake* / Squarepusher theme: *Squarepusher* / Mass: *Silent Poets*
CD K7 057CD
Studio K7 / Apr '97 / Prime / RTM/Disc

Island, Johnny

REGGAE SOUNDS FROM JAMAICA (Island, Johnny Reggae Group)
CD 15287
Laserlight / '91 / Target/BMG

Islandica

SONGS AND DANCES FROM ICELAND
CD EUCD 1187
ARC / Apr '92 / ADA / ARC Music

Isley Brothers

3 + 3
That lady / Don't let me be lonely tonight / If you were there / You walk your way / Listen to the music / What it comes down to / Sunshine (go away today) / Summer breeze / Highways of my life
CD 4879372
Epic / Jul '97 / Sony

BEAUTIFUL BALLADS
Brown eyed girl / Hello it's me / Let's fall in love (parts 1 and 2) / You're the key to my heart / You're beside me / I once had your love (and I can't let go) / Caravan of love / All in my lovers eyes / Don't let me be lonely tonight / Make me say it again girl / Voyage to Atlantis / Choosey lover / Lay lady lay / Don't say goodnight
CD 4805042
Epic / May '95 / Sony

BEST OF THE ISLEY BROTHERS, THE
CD 12549
Laserlight / May '95 / Target/BMG

BROTHER BROTHER BROTHER
Brother brother brother / Put a little love in your heart / Sweet seasons/Keep on walkin' / Work to do / Pop that thang / Lay away / It's too late / Love put me on the corner
CD 4875122
Epic / Jul '97 / Sony

BROTHERS ISLEY, THE
I turned you on / Vacuum cleaner / I got to get myself together / Was it good to you / Blacker the berrie / My little girl / Get down off of the train / Holding on / Feels like the world
CD 4875152
Epic / Jul '97 / Sony

COMPLETE UA SESSIONS, THE (The Legends Of Rock & Roll Series)
Surf and shout / Please please please / She's the one / Tango / What'cha gonna do / Stagger Lee / You'll never leave him / Let's go, let's go, let's go / She's gone / Shake it with me baby / Long tall Sally / Do the twist / My little girl / Open up her eyes / Love is a wonderful thing / Footprints in the snow / Who's that lady / Basement / Conch / My little girl
CD CDGOLD 1024
EMI Gold / May '96 / EMI

GET INTO SOMETHING
Get into something / Freedom / Take inventory / Keep on doin' / Girls will be girls / I need you so / If he can you can / I got to find me one / Beautiful / Bless your heart
CD 4875142
Epic / Jul '97 / Sony

GIVIN' IT BACK
Ohio/Machine gun / Fire and rain / Lay lady lay / Spill the wine / Nothing to do but today / Cold Bologna / Love the one you're with
CD 4875132
Epic / Jul '97 / Sony

GREATEST HITS
Summer breeze / That lady / Harvest for the world / Hope you feel better love / Highways of my life / Caravan of love / Who loves you better / Work to do / Between the sheets / Don't let me be lonely / For the love of you / Pride / Love the one you're with / It's a disco night
CD 4879962
Epic / Jul '97 / Sony

LIVE
Here we go again / Between the sheets / Smooth sailin' tonight / Voyage to Atlantis / Take me to the next phase / Choosey lover / Footsteps in the dark / Groove with you / Hello it's me / Don't say goodnight (It's time for love) / Spend the night / Who's that lady / It's your thing / Shout / For the love / Fight the power / Make me say it again girl
CD 7559615382
Elektra / Sep '93 / Warner Music

MISSION TO PLEASE
CD 5242142
4th & Broadway / May '96 / PolyGram

MOTOWN EARLY CLASSICS
This old heart of mine (is weak for you) / There's no love left / Seek and you shall find / Leaving here / Baby don't you do it / Stop in the name of love / I guess I'll always love you / Tell me it's just a rumour baby / Why when love is gone / Catching up on time / One too many heartaches / Nevermore / It's out of the question / Whispers (gettin' louder) / Good things / Behind a painted smile / Save me from this misery / My love is your love (forever)
CD 5521222
Spectrum / Jul '96 / PolyGram

MOTOWN'S GREATEST HITS
This old heart of mine / Just ain't enough love / Put yourself in my place / I guess I'll always love you / There's no love left / It's out of the question / Take some time out for love / Whispers / Nowhere to run / Who could ever doubt my love / Behind a painted smile / That's the way love is / Tell me it's just a rumour baby / Take me in your arms / Got to have you back / Little Miss Sweetness / My love is your love (forever) / Why when the love has gone / All because I love you / I hear a symphony
CD 5300532
Motown / Jan '92 / PolyGram

PACKET OF THREE VOL.8 (3CD Set) (Isley Brothers/Walter Becker & Donald Fagen/Sam & Dave)
Twist and shout: *Isley Brothers* / Time after time: *Isley Brothers* / Hold on baby: *Isley Brothers* / Snake: *Isley Brothers* / Let's twist again: *Isley Brothers* / Don't you feel: *Isley Brothers* / Nobody but you: *Isley Brothers* / Twisting with Linda: *Isley Brothers* / Spanish twist: *Isley Brothers* / Drag: *Isley Brothers* / Don't be jealous: *Isley Brothers* / This is the end: *Isley Brothers* / Let's go, let's go, let's go: *Isley Brothers* / I'm laughing to keep from crying: *Isley Brothers* / Rubber leg twist: *Isley Brothers* / I say love: *Isley Brothers* / You better come home: *Isley Brothers* / Never leave me baby: *Isley Brothers* / Brooklyn: *Becker, Walter & Donald Fagen* / Mock turtle song: *Becker, Walter & Donald Fagen* / Soul ram: *Becker, Walter & Donald Fagen* / Any world: *Becker, Walter & Donald Fagen* / You go where I go: *Becker, Walter & Donald Fagen* / This seat's been taken: *Becker, Walter & Donald Fagen* / Berry Town: *Becker, Walter & Donald Fagen* / More to come: *Becker, Walter & Donald Fagen* / Android warehouse: *Becker, Walter & Donald Fagen* / Roaring of the lamb: *Becker, Walter & Donald Fagen* / Sun mountain: *Becker, Walter & Donald Fagen* / Stone patio: *Becker, Walter & Donald Fagen* / Parker's band: *Becker, Walter & Donald Fagen* / Caves of Altimura: *Becker, Walter & Donald Fagen* / Come back baby: *Becker, Walter & Donald Fagen* / Old regime: *Becker, Walter & Donald Fagen* / Let George do it: *Becker, Walter & Donald Fagen* / I can't function: *Becker, Walter & Donald Fagen* / Brain tap shuffle: *Becker, Walter & Donald Fagen* / Ida Lee: *Becker, Walter & Donald Fagen* / Wonderful world: *Sam & Dave* / Soul sister, brown sugar: *Sam & Dave* / Dock of the bay: *Sam & Dave* / You got me hummin': *Sam & Dave* / Gimme some lovin': *Sam & Dave* / Another Saturday night: *Sam & Dave* / Cupid: *Sam & Dave* / Hold on I'm coming: *Sam & Dave* / Summertime: *Sam & Dave* / Mustang Sally: *Sam & Dave* / Good lovin': *Sam & Dave* / Land of 1000 dances: *Sam & Dave* / Satisfaction guarenteed: *Sam & Dave* / You don't know what you mean to me: *Sam & Dave* / You send me: *Sam & Dave* / Soothe me: *Sam & Dave* / Bring it on home: *Sam & Dave* / I thank you: *Sam & Dave* / Said I wouldn't tell nobody: *Sam & Dave* / You don't know like I know: *Sam & Dave*
CD Set KLMCD 308
BAM / Nov '96 / Koch / Scratch/BMG

SHOUT
Shout (part 1) / Shout (part 2) / Tell me who / How deep is the ocean / Respectable / Say you love me too / Open up your heart / He's got the whole world in his hands / Without a song / Yes indeed / Ring-a-ling-a-ling / That lucky old sun / How deep is the ocean / Respectable / When the saints go marching in / Gypsy love song / St. Louis blues / (We're gonna) Rock around the clock / Turn to me / Not one minute more / I'm gonna knock on your door
CD BCD 15425
Bear Family / Dec '88 / Direct / Rollercoaster / Swift

SHOUT AND TWIST WITH RUDOLPH, RONALD AND O'KELLY
Twist and shout / Nobody but me / Crazy love / Snake / Make it easy on yourself / Right now / You better come home / Twistin' with Linda / Never leave me baby / Two stupid feet / Time after time / Let's twist again / Wah watusi / I say love / Rubberleg twist / Hold on baby / I'm laughing to keep from crying / Don't you feel / Spanish twist
CD CDCH 928
Ace / Apr '90 / Pinnacle

TRACKS OF LIFE
Get my licks in / No axe to grind / Searching for a miracle / Sensitive lover / Bedroom eyes / Lost in your love / Whatever turns you on / Morning love / Dedicate this song / Red hot / Koolin' out / Brazilian wedding song / I'll be there / Turn on the moon
CD 7599266202
WEA / Jun '92 / Warner Music

Isotope

ISOTOPE/ILLUSION
Then there were four / Do the business / Oh little fat man / Sunshine park / Bite on this / Upward curve / Retracing my steps / Windmills and waterfalls / Honkey donkey / Illusion / Rangoon creeper / Spanish sun / Edorian / Frog / Sliding dogs / Lion sandwich / Golden section / Marin county girl / Lily kong / Temper tantrums
CD SEECD 432
See For Miles/C5 / Aug '95 / Pinnacle

Israel Vibration

BEST OF ISRAEL VIBRATION, THE
CD NETCD 1001
Network / Jan '91 / Direct / Greensleeves / SRD

DUB THE ROCK
CD RASCD 3190
Ras / Aug '95 / Direct / Greensleeves / Jet Star / SRD

FOREVER
CD RASCD 3080
Ras / Sep '91 / Direct / Greensleeves / Jet Star / SRD

FREE TO MOVE
CD RASCD 3231
Ras / Sep '96 / Direct / Greensleeves / Jet Star / SRD

ISRAEL DUB
CD GRELCD 510
Greensleeves / Apr '91 / Jet Star / SRD

ISRAEL VIBRATION VOL.4
CD RASCD 3120
Ras / Aug '93 / Direct / Greensleeves / Jet Star / SRD

LIVE AGAIN (Israel Vibration & Roots Radics)
Rockford rock / Same song / Jailhouse rocking / Rudeboy shufflin' / Never gonna hurt me again / You never know / There is no end / On the rock / Greedy dog / Racial injustice / Red eyes / Strength of my life / Licks and kicks / War
CD RAS 3247
Ras / Jul '97 / Direct / Greensleeves / Jet Star / SRD

LIVE AT REGGAE SUNSPLASH (Israel Vibration & Gladiators)
CD NETCD 8925
Network / Nov '92 / Direct / Greensleeves / SRD

ON THE ROCK
CD RASCD 3175
Ras / Mar '95 / Direct / Greensleeves / Jet Star / SRD

PERFECT LOVE & UNDERSTANDING
CD NETCD 1006
Network / Jun '93 / Direct / Greensleeves / SRD

PRAISES
CD RASCD 3054
Ras / Jul '90 / Direct / Greensleeves / Jet Star / SRD

RAS PORTRAITS
Cool and calm / We a de rasta / Same song / Jailhouse rockin' / Livity in the dub / Rudeboy shufflin' / Highway robbery / Dub of conscience / Mr. Consular Man / Falling angels / Saviour in your dub / Dub in the Middle East / Feelin' irie / Strength of my dub / Red eyes
CD RAS 3317
Ras / Jul '97 / Direct / Greensleeves / Jet Star / SRD

RUDEBOY SHUFFLIN'
CD CRCDM 1
Ras / Aug '95 / Direct / Greensleeves / Jet Star / SRD

SAME SONG, THE
Same song / Weep and mourn / Walk the streets of glory / Ball of fire / I'll go through / Why worry / Lift up your conscience / Prophet has arisen / Jah time has come / Licks and kicks
CD CDPS 003
Pressure Sounds / Jun '95 / Jet Star / SRD
CD RASCD 3228
Ras / Sep '96 / Direct / Greensleeves / Jet Star / SRD

STRENGTH OF MY LIFE
CD RASCD 3037
Ras / Dec '88 / Direct / Greensleeves / Jet Star / SRD

SURVIVE
CD LG 21115
Lagoon / Oct '95 / Grapevine/PolyGram

UNCONQUERED PEOPLE
CD GRELCD 148
Greensleeves / Jul '90 / Jet Star / SRD

VIBES ALIVE
CD RASCD 3091
Ras / Nov '92 / Direct / Greensleeves / Jet Star / SRD

Israel, Yoron

GIFT FOR YOU, A (Israel, Yoron Connection)
CD FRLCD 024
Freelance / Jan '96 / Cadillac / Koch

Israelites

SENSI DUB VOL.8
CD OMCD 032
Original Music / Jun '96 / Jet Star / SRD

Israelvis

CHURCH OF ISRAELVIS
CD PRO 019
Progress / Feb '97 / Cargo / Plastic Head

EUROSIS
CD PRO 024
Progress / Apr '97 / Cargo / Plastic Head

It

ERA VULGARIS NCODED - DROP 6.3
CD MASOCD 90078
Materiali Sonori / Jul '97 / Cargo / Greyhound / New Note/Pinnacle

It

ON TOP OF THE WORLD
CD BCKCD 1
Black Market International / Jul '90 / Prime / Soul Trader / Vital

It Bites

BIG LAD IN THE WINDMILL
I got you eating out of my hand / All in red / Whole new world / Screaming on the beaches / Turn me loose / Cold, tired and hungry / Calling all the heroes / You'll never go to heaven / Big lad in the windmill / Wanna shout
CD CDV 2378
Virgin / Jul '86 / EMI

CALLING ALL THE HEROES (The Best Of It Bites)
Still too young to remember / Calling all the heroes / Strange but true / All in red / Kiss like Judas / Murder of the planet Earth / Midnight / Sister Sarah / Old man and the

angel / Underneath your pillow / Screaming on the beaches / Whole new world / Yellow christian / You'll never go to heaven
CD CDOVD 453
Virgin / Feb '95 / EMI

EAT ME IN ST. LOUIS
Positively animal / Underneath your pillow / Let us all go / Still too young to remember / Murder of the planet earth / People of America / Sister Sarah / Leaving without you / Till the end of time / Ice melts (into water) / Charlie / Having a good day / Reprise / Bullet in the barrel
CD CDV 2591
Virgin / Aug '91 / EMI

ONCE AROUND THE WORLD
Midnight / Kiss like Judas / Yellow christian / Rose Marie / Old man and the angel / Hunting the whale / Plastic dreamer / Once around the world / Black December
CD CDV 2456
Virgin / Aug '91 / EMI

THANK YOU AND GOODNIGHT (The Best Of It Bites)
Kiss like Judas / All in red / Underneath your pillow / Murder of the planet earth / Ice melts (into water) / Yellow christian / You'll never go to heaven / Calling all the heroes / Screaming on the beaches / Still too young to remember
CD VGDCD 3516
Virgin / Oct '91 / EMI

Italian Instabile Orchestra

SKIES OF EUROPE
Il maestro muratore / Squilli di morte / Corbu / Meru lo snob / L'arte mistica del vasaio / Il maestro muratore (reprise) / Du du duchamp / Quand duchamp joue du marteau / Il suono giallo / Mariene e gli ospiti misteriosi / Satie satin / Masse d'urto / Fellini song
CD 5271812
ECM / Mar '95 / New Note/Pinnacle

Itals

BRUTAL OUT DEH
CD NHCD 303
Nighthawk / '89 / ADA / Direct / Hot Shot

GIVE ME POWER
CD NHCD 307
Nighthawk / '89 / ADA / Direct / Hot Shot

Itch

AVENUE PARADE
Superficial girl / Happy and free / Uncertain / Boy in the corner / Plain in Summer / Get up, get down / Key to life / Not my friend / Don't blame me / Never listen / Eyes across the room / Beginner's luck
CD DRCD 012
Detour / Jun '97 / Detour / Greyhound

Ithaca

GAME FOR ALL WHO KNOW, A
CD HBG 122/3
Background / Jun '97 / Background / Greyhound

It's A Beautiful Day

LIVE AT THE CARNEGIE HALL
Give your woman what she wants / Hot summmer day / Angels and animals / Bombay calling / Going to another party / Good lovin' / Grand camel suite / White bird
CD 4809702
Columbia / Aug '95 / Sony

It's Alive

EARTHQUAKE VISIONS
CD CDMFN 177
Music For Nations / Dec '94 / Pinnacle

It's Immaterial

SONG
New Brighton / Endless holiday / Ordinary life / Heaven knows / In the neighbourhood / Missing / Homecoming / Summer winds / Life on the hill / Your voice
CD CDSRN 27
Siren / Apr '92 / EMI

Ivers, Eileen

EILEEN IVERS
CD GLCD 1139
Green Linnet / Apr '94 / ADA / CM / Direct / Highlander / Roots

KEEP IT REEL
CD PAG 001CD
PAG / Apr '96 / ADA

TRADITIONAL IRISH MUSIC
CD GL 1139CD
Green Linnet / Jun '94 / ADA / CM / Direct / Highlander / Roots

WILD BLUE
CD GLCD 1166
Green Linnet / Feb '96 / ADA / CM / Direct / Highlander / Roots

Iversen, Einor

WHO CAN I TURN TO
CD GMCD 73
Gemini / Jan '87 / Cadillac

Ives, Burl

BURL IVES
Fox / Waltzing Matilda / Blue tail fly / Goober peas / Down in the valley / John Henry / Old Dan Tucker / Cowboy's lament / That's my heart strings (That's my boy) / Eerie canal / Foggy, foggy dew / Git along little doggies / Molly Malone / Mrs. McGrath / Aunt Rhody / Haul away, Joe / Prisoner's song (Midnight special) / Vive la compagnie
CD CD 12533
Music Of The World / Jun '96 / ADA / Target/BMG

LITTLE BITTY TEAR, A (5CD Set)
Little bitty tear / Long black veil / Shanghai'd / Almighty dollar bill / Forty hour week / Delia / Oh my side / Lenora, let your hair hang down / Mocking bird hill / I walk the line / Drink to me only with thine eyes / Mama don't want no peas, no rice, no coconut oil / Empty saddles / Oregan trail / Home on the range / When the bloom is on the sage / My adobe hacienda / Cowboy's dream / Mexicali rose / Last round-up / Oh bury me not on the lone prairie / Jingle jangle jingle / Cool water / Tumbling tumbleweeds / Royal telephone / Holding hands for Joe / Sixteen fathoms down / What you gonna do Leroy / Brooklyn bridge / Poor little Jimmy / Thumbin' Johnny Brown / Funny way of laughing / That's all I can remember / Ninety nine / Call me Mr. In-between / I ain't comin' home tonight / How do you fall out of love / In foggy old London / Mother wouldn't do that / Bring them in / Let the lower lights be burning / Beulah land / Standing on the promises / Fairest Lord Jesus / We're marching to Zion / Sunshine in my soul / Blessed assurance / Leaning on the everlasting arms / Where he leads me / Will there be any stars / When they ring those golden bells / Same old hurt / Wishin' she was here (instead of me) / Busted / Poor boy in a rich man's town / Mary Ann regrets / Billy Bayou / Moon is high / Green turtle / Bury the bottle with me / Blizzard / It comes and goes / I'm the boss / Same old hurt (remake) / Curry road / Deepening snow / She didn't let the ink dry on the paper / Late movie / Home James / Man about town / She called me baby / My chicken run away to the bush / Baby come home to me / Roses and orchids / Lynching party / Hundred twenty miles from nowhere / Two car garage / I found my best friend in the dog pound / I'll hit it with a stick / Saskatoon, Saskatchewan / Some folks / I'll walk away smiling / There goes another pal of mine / This is your day / This is all I ask / Lower forty / Four initials on a tree / Someone hangin' round you all the time / Beautiful Annabelle Lee / Hobo jungle / Strong as a mountain / Can't you hear me / Cherry blossom song / What I want (I can never have) / Can angels fly over the Rockies / Legend of the T / Kentucky turkey buzzard / Funny little show / Hard luck and misery / Pearly shells / What little tears are made of / Short on love / Who done it / Two of the usual / Tell me / Among my souvenirs / Gater hollow / I ain't missing nobody / Catfish Bill / Time to bum again / Born for trouble / Unemployment check / Atlantic coastal line / Don't let love die / How deep is the ocean / Okeechobee ocean / My melancholy baby / Jealous / My gal Sal / By the light of the silvery moon / For me and my gal / Red sails in the sunset / Make believe / Oh how I miss you tonight / You know you belong to somebody else / Down in the Okefenokee / (I hear you) Call my name / Mr. Make-up man / River boy / Drifting and dreaming / Beyond the reef / My Isle of golden dreams / Now is the hour / Sweet Leilani / Moon of Manakoora / Song of the Islands / Keep your eyes on the hands / Hawaiian bells / Little brown girl / On the beach of Waikiki / Aloha oe / Thirty thousand feet over Denver / Betsy the cow
CD BCD 15667
Bear Family / Jul '93 / Direct / Rollercoaster / Swift

LITTLE BITTY TEAR, A
CD HMNCD 006
Half Moon / Jun '97 / BMG

POOR WAYFARING STRANGER
CD PASTCD 7090
Flapper / Mar '96 / Pinnacle

SINGS HIS FAVOURITES
Gypsy's wedding day / Jesse James / Three crows / Cowboy's lament / Wee cooper o'Fife / Edward / Tam Pierce / Young man who couldn't hoe corn / Little McGhee / I'm goin' down the road feelin' bad / Blue tail fly / Darlin' Cory / Old Bangum / Riddle song / On top of old smokey / Swapping song / Oh Sally, my dear / Golden vanity / I'm goin' away / As I went out one morning
CD CBCD 007
Collector's Edition / Sep '96 / TKO Magnum

SOME OF THE BEST
I'm thinking tonight of my blue eyes / Blue tailed fly / New York girls / Venezuela / Rodger Young / I know an old lady / Jack was every inch a sailor / Goober peas / Leave her, Johnny, leave her / Lydia, the tattooed lady / Kling, kling bird (on top of the divi-divi tree) / Hush little baby / Big rock candy mountain / There is a tavern in the town
CD 12649
Laserlight / May '97 / Target/BMG

VERY BEST OF BURL IVES
CD SOWCD 708
Sound Waves / May '93 / Target/BMG

WELL RESPECTED MAN
Galisteo / Snowbird / Time / Real roses / Roll up some inspiration / Another day another year / Raindrops keep falling on my head / One more time billy brown / Tied down here at home / Funny way of laughing / Coming after Jimmy
CD CWNCD 2021
Javelin / Jul '96 / Henry Hadaway / THE

Ivorys

BALA
CD WWCD 06
World / Dec '88 / Grapevine/PolyGram

Ivy

IN THE ABSENCE OF ANGELS
Could have been / Avenge / Bones / Israel / Wish you would / Unmindful of the night / At least it's warm in hell / Look who's laughing now / Trudi's right / How do you know it's for real
CD NBX 024
Noisebox / Sep '96 / RTM/Disc / Vital

Ivy NYC

REALISTIC
Get enough: *Ivy* / No guarantee: *Ivy* / Decay: *Ivy* / Fifteen seconds: *Ivy* / Everyday: *Ivy* / Point of view: *Ivy* / Don't believe word: *Ivy* / Beautiful: *Ivy* / Shallow: *Ivy* / In the shadows: *Ivy* / Dying star: *Ivy* / Over: *Ivy*
CD 142532
Seed / Feb '95 / Vital

Iwamoto, Yoshikazu

SHAKUHACHI FLUTE - THE SPIRIT OF THE WIND
CD 926402
BUDA / Mar '96 / Discovery

Iwan, Dafydd

CANEUON QWERIN
CD SCD 2062
Sain / Feb '95 / ADA / Direct / Greyhound

DALIGREDU
CD SCD 4053
Sain / Mar '95 / ADA / Direct / Greyhound

YMA O HYD (Iwan, Dafydd & Ar Log)
Y wen na phyla amser / Cwm ffynnon ddu / Adlais y gog lwydlas / Tra bo hedydd / Laura Llwelyn / Ffidl yn y to / Hoffedd Gwilym/Mynydd yr heliwr/Mans o'r felin / Hoffedd Jac Nurphy / Can Wiliam / Can y medd / Per oslef / Y chwe chant a naw / Yma o hyd
CD SCD 2063
Sain / Feb '95 / ADA / Direct / Greyhound

Izachaar, Hughie

PRAISE JAH
CD ROTCD 009
Reggae On Top / Apr '96 / Jet Star / SRD

Izadi, Kamyar

SANTOUR
Sur le mode Mahur / Sur le mode shur pich Daramad avaz-s reng / Sur le mode Esfahan
CD CP 10396
Cinq Planetes / May '97 / Harmonia Mundi

Izit

IMAGINARY MAN
Mother of mine / Just a matter of time / Architecture / Undiscovered land / I believe von daniken / Feel like makin' love / Change / Imaginary man / You're losing me / Oasis / This harmony / Elijah's blue
CD TNGCD 007
Tongue 'n' Groove / May '95 / Vital

J

J

WE ARE THE MAJORITY
Keep the promise / Beast no one ever tamed / Best thaing / School power / Randy / Born on the wrong side of town / First they came / Nightime / We are the majority / Badge of pride / In the trench / Take a chance / Come over here / Justice of burn / After
CD ______ **5177102**
A&M / Jan '93 / PolyGram

J-Bad

MAKE WAY FOR THE GRIMREAPER
CD ______ **RAP 60072**
Rapture / May '94 / Plastic Head

J-Church

ARBOR VITAE
Cigarettes kill / Racked / Drinking down / Church on fire / Your shirt / Without a single word / Contempt for modesty / Swallow / Switzerland / Waiting on the ground / Mr. Backrub / Stinking seas
CD ______ **HB 011**
Honey Bear / Dec '96 / Cargo

DRAMA OF ALIENATION, THE
CD ______ **DON 003CD**
Honest Don's / Nov '96 / Greyhound / Plastic Head

ECSTASY OF COMMUNICATION, THE
Bottom rung / Good judge of character / Yellow, blue and green / November / Kathi / My favourite phrase / Sound of Mariachi bands / Foreign films / No surprise / Why I liked bikini kill / Fascist radio / Lama people / My favourite place / Ivy league college / Sleep / Panama / Band your love to hate / Nostalgic for nothing / Analysis, yes, very nice / Kill your boss / Waiting on the ground / Cigarettes kill / Racked / Stinking sea
CD ______ **STAR 49142**
Startracks / Jul '97 / RTM/Disc

NOSTALGIA FOR NOTHING
CD ______ **SKIP 037CD**
Broken Rekids / Nov '95 / Cargo / Plastic Head

RECESSION OF SIMULACRA, THE
CD ______ **JT 1019CD**
Jade Tree / Jul '95 / Cargo / Greyhound / Plastic Head

WHOREHOUSE SONGS & STATEMENTS
CD ______ **DAMGOOD 103CD**
Damaged Goods / Sep '96 / Shellshock/ Disc

J-Quest

QUEST IS ON, THE
Given it all / Quest is on / It's gonna be alright / Brand new love / Up and down / Anything / Don't stop ya luv / From now on / Come and give it (you know what I want) / On my mind / Behind the scenes / Up and down (original mix)
CD ______ **5285342**
Mercury / Sep '95 / PolyGram

J To The D

LIVING ON THE EDGE
Detroit / Givin' you that funk / 2 make U dance / Sach chaser / Bay bay kids / Nympho / Caught up in the game / Murder game / Girls with game / Fuck that
CD ______ **CDWRA 8104**
Wrap / Feb '92 / Koch

J&W Crew

J&W CREW PRESENTS HIT ROCKERS OF THE 80'S (Various Artists)
CD ______ **JWCD 1**
Heavy Beat / Oct '96 / Jet Star

Jach'a Mallku

ESTO ES BOLIVIA
CD ______ **CD 064**
Tumi / Feb '97 / Discovery / Stern's

GRAN CONDOR
CD ______ **TUMICD 037**
Tumi / Jun '93 / Discovery / Stern's

Jacinta

AUTRES CHANSONS YIDDISH
CD ______ **C 560033**
Ocora / May '92 / ADA / Harmonia Mundi

TANGO, MI CORAZON
CD ______ **MES 159112**
Messidor / Jun '93 / ADA / Koch

Jack & The Beanstalk

...AND OTHER STORIES
CD ______ **PARCD 024**
Parasol / Feb '97 / Cargo

Jack

PIONEER SOUNDTRACKS
Of lights / Wintercomessummer / White jazz / Biography of a first son / Filthy names / I didn't mean it Marie / FU / Dress you in mourning / Hope is a liar
CD ______ **PURECD 055**
Too Pure / Jun '96 / Vital

Jack Frost

SNOW JOB
CD ______ **BEGL 183CD**
Beggars Banquet / Apr '96 / RTM/Disc / Warner Music

Jack O'Nuts

ON YOU
Hook / Citation / Q / Showcase / Chump change / Feelin' Freddy / Raw candle vote / Starbane
CD ______ **RDL 0062**
Radial / May '94 / Cargo / Vital

Jack Radics

I'LL BE SWEETER
CD ______ **PHCD 23**
Penthouse / Sep '93 / Jet Star

OPEN REBUKE
CD ______ **HBST 168CD**
Heartbeat / Aug '94 / ADA / Direct / Greensleeves / Jet Star

RADICAL
CD ______ **SHCD 45003**
Shanachie / Jun '93 / ADA / Greensleeves / Koch

SOMETHING
CD ______ **TOPCD 1**
Top Rank / Nov '92 / Jet Star

TEQUILA SUNSET
CD ______ **SFCD 002**
Sprint / Jul '95 / SRD

WHAT ABOUT ME
CD ______ **RN 0039**
Runn / Apr '97 / Grapevine/PolyGram / Jet Star / SRD

Jack Speed

SURGE
Emma / Blue bossa / Tangents / Storm / Construction / With the clouds / Tone control / Fission / CTC / Froing / Fast
CD ______ **RS 96067CD**
R&S / Jun '96 / Vital

Jack The Lad

IT'S JACK THE LAD
Boilermaker blues / Back on the road again / Plain dealing / Fast lane driver / Turning into winter / Why I can't be satified / Song without a band / Rosalie / Promised land / Corny pastiche / Black cock of Wickham/ Chief O'Neill's favourite / Golden rivet/ Staten Island/ The Cook in the kitchen / Lying in the water / One more dance / Make me happy
CD ______ **CASCD 1085**
Charisma / Nov '92 / EMI

ROUGH DIAMONDS
Rocking chair / Smokers coughin' / My friend, the drink / Letter from France / Gentlemen soldier / Gardener of eden / One for the boy / Beachcomber / Ballad of Winston O'Flaherty / Jackie Lusive / Draught genius / Baby let me take you home
CD ______ **CASCD 1110**
Charisma / Nov '92 / EMI

Jackass

REALITY BITES (IN SANTA BARBARA) EP
CD ______ **SMLX 009**
Smilex / Mar '97 / Cargo

Jackie & Roy

EAST OF SUEZ
CD ______ **CCD 4149**
Concord Jazz / Jul '96 / New Note/ Pinnacle

HIGH STANDARDS
I got rhythm / Stardust / Loving you / I watch you sleep / Too marvellous for words / Am I blue / Bidin' my time / Joy spring / Mine / Nobody's heart belongs to me
CD ______ **CCD 4186**
Concord Jazz / Nov '96 / New Note/ Pinnacle

SPRING CAN REALLY HANG YOU UP THE MOST
CD ______ **BLCD 760904**
Black Lion / Jun '88 / Cadillac / Jazz Music / Koch / Wellard

Jacklin, Tony

SWINGS INTO
CD ______ **CREV 46CD**
Rev-Ola / Sep '96 / 3mv/Vital

Jackman, Colin

ACTION TIME
CD ______ **CJ 0196CD**
Multimedia / Mar '97 / Jet Star

Jacks

WHY DON'T YOU WRITE ME VOL.2
Why don't you write me / Since my baby's been gone / Heaven help me / Do you wanna rock / Away / How soon / I cry / They turned the party out down at Bessie's house / Dream a little longer / Fine lookin' baby / So wrong / Wiggie waggie woo / I'm confessin' that I love you / Let's make up / If it is wrong / Annie meet Henry / My reckless heart / Why did I fall in love / I want you / You belong to me / Dancin' Dan / This empty heart / So will I / My Darling
CD ______ **CDCHD 535**
Ace / Apr '95 / Pinnacle

Jackson Five

ANTHOLOGY VOL.1 & 2 (2CD Set)
I hear a symphony / Dancing machine / Body language / Got to be there / Rockin' robin / Ben / Daddy's home / ABC / I want you back / I'll be there / Sugar daddy / Maybe tomorrow / Mama's pearl / I am love / Teenage symphony / Skywriter / Hallelujah day / Bogie man / Let's get serious / Let me tickle your fancy / You're supposed to keep your love for me / Love don't want to leave / That's how love goes / Just a little bit of you / We're almost there / I wanna be where you are / Forever came today / All I do is think of you / I was made to love her / Whatever you got, I want / Get it together
CD Set ______ **5301932**
Motown / Jan '92 / PolyGram

CHRISTMAS ALBUM, THE (Merry Christmas From Motown)
Have yourself a merry little Christmas / Santa Claus is coming to town / Christmas song / Up on the house top / Frosty the snowman / Little drummer boy / Rudolph the red nosed reindeer / Christmas won't be the same this year / Give love on Christmas Day / Some day at Christmas / I saw Mommy kissing Santa Claus
CD ______ **5501412**
Spectrum / Nov '96 / PolyGram

HISTORIC EARLY RECORDINGS
You've changed / We don't have to be over 21 (to fall in love) / Jam session / Big boy / Michael the lover / My girl / Soul jerk / Under the boardwalk / Saturday night at the movies / Tracks of my tears
CD ______ **CPCD 8122**
Charly / Oct '95 / Koch

JACKSON FIVE, THE
Big boy / You've changed / Michael the lover / My girl / Under the Boardwalk / Over 21 / Stormy Monday / Soul jerk / Saturday night at the movies / Jam session / Tracks of my tears / Monologue/Jam session
CD ______ **EXP 020**
Experience / May '97 / TKO Magnum

SOULSATION (4CD Set)
CD Set ______ **5304892**
Motown / Jul '95 / PolyGram

Jackson Singers

GOSPEL EMOTIONS
Storm is passing / This little light of mine / You've got to move / God has smiled on me / Over my head / Nobody knows the trouble I've seen / Put your trust in Jesus / I've decided to make Jesus my choice / Jesus said if you go / If it had not been for the Lord / Pass me not / Precious Lord
CD ______ **CDLR 44016**
L&R / May '92 / New Note/Pinnacle

Jackson, Alan

EVERYTHING I LOVE
Little bitty / Everything I love / Buicks to the moon / Between the devil and me / There goes / House with no curtains / Who's cheatin' who / Walk on the rocks / Must've had a ball / It's time you learned about goodbye
CD ______ **07822188132**
Arista / Nov '96 / BMG

GREATEST HITS COLLECTION
Chattahoochee / Gone country / She's got rhythm / Midnight in Montgomery / Tall, tall trees / Chasin' that neon rainbow / I'l try / Don't rock the jukebox / Livin' on love / Summertime blues / Love's got a hold on you / (Who says) You can't have it all / Home / Wanted / I don't even know your name / Dallas / Here in the real world / Someday / Mercury blues / I'd love you all over again
CD ______ **07822188012**
Arista / Oct '95 / BMG

HERE IN THE REAL WORLD
Ace of hearts / Blue blooded woman / Chasin' that neon rainbow / I'd love you all over again / Home / Here in the real world / Wanted / She don't get the blues / Dog river blues / Short sweet ride
CD ______ **260817**
Arista / Jul '90 / BMG

HONKY TONK CHRISTMAS
Honky tonk christmas / Angels cried / If we make it through December / If you don't wanna see Santa Claus cry / I only want you for christmas / Merry Christmas to me / Holly jolly christmas / There's a new kid in town / Santa's gonna come in a pickup truck / Please daddy (don't get drunk this Christmas)
CD ______ **7822187362**
Arista / Nov '95 / BMG

LOT ABOUT LIVIN', A (And A Little 'Bout Love)
Chattanoochee / She's got the rhythm (I got the blues) / Tonight I climbed the wall / I don't need the booze (To get a buzz on) / (Who says) You can't have it all / Up to my ears in tears / Tropical depression / She likes it too / If it ain't one thing (It's you) / Mercury blues
CD ______ **07822187112**
Arista / Jun '94 / BMG

WHO I AM
Summertime blues / Livin' on love / Hole in the wall / Gone country / Who I am / You can't give up on love / I don't even know your name / Song for the life / Thank God for the radio / All American country boy / Job description / If I had you / Let's get back to me and you / Chattahoochee
CD ______ **74321217682**
Arista / Aug '96 / BMG

Jackson, Billy

LONG STEEL RAIL
CD ______ **TCD 5014**
Testament / Dec '94 / ADA / Koch

MISTY MOUNTAIN (Jackson, Billy & Billy Ross)
Beinn a' cheataich / Landfall / Glen of copeswood / Lass o'glenshee / Boyne water / Guidnicht and joy be wi' ye a' / Country girl and the hungarian fiddler / Tar the house / Little cascade / Geil mill / First step / Trusdar bodaich, drochaid, luideach / Na'm faighinn gille 'ri cheannach / For our lang bidin' here / Meudail is m'aighear s'mo ghradh
CD ______ **IRCD 005**
Iona / '88 / ADA / Direct / Duncans

WELLPARK SUITE, THE (Jackson, Billy & Ossian)
Glasgow 1885 / Dear green place changed life in the city / March of the workers / Molendinar: The spring / Brewing / Fermentation / Glasgow celebration
CD ______ **IRCD 008**
Iona / Aug '91 / ADA / Direct / Duncans

Jackson, Bleu

GONE THIS TIME
CD ______ **TX 1005CD**
Taxim / Jan '94 / ADA

Jackson, Bull Moose

BAD MAN JACKSON, THAT'S ME
Big ten inch record / Bad man Jackson, that's me / Jammin' and jumpin / We ain't got nothin' but the blues / Bull Moose Jackson blues / Honey dripper / Hold him Joe / I want a bowlegged woman / Oh John / Fare thee well / Nosey Joe / Bearcat blues / Why don't you haul off and love me / Cherokee boogie / Meet me with your black dress on / Hodge podge / Big fat mamas are back in style again / All night long / Bootsie / If you ain't lovin' (you ain't livin') / I wanna hug ya, kiss ya, squeeze ya
CD ______ **CDCHARLY 274**
Charly / Jan '93 / Koch

Jackson, Carl

BANJO MAN (A Tribute To Earl Scruggs)
Earl's breakdown / John Henry / Grey eagle / You are my flower / Home sweet home / Careless love / Keep on the sunny side / Little darlin', pal of mine / Reuben / Ground speed / Banjo man
CD SHCD 3715
Sugar Hill / Jan '97 / ADA / CM / Direct / Koch / Roots

NASHVILLE COUNTRY
Gone gone gone: *Jackson, Carl & Ricky Scaggs* / To keep your memory green: *Jackson, Carl & Sharon White/Cheryl White* / Under your spell again: *Jackson, Carl & Emmylou Harris* / Walk through the world with me: *Jackson, Carl & Emmylou Harris* / All that's left for me / Something draws me to you: *Jackson, Carl & Emmylou Harris* / When my blue moon turns to gold again: *Jackson, Carl & Emmylou Harris* / You made a memory of me: *Jackson, Carl & Sharon White/Cheryl White* / I take the chance: *Jackson, Carl & Emmylou Harris* / Before I met you: *Jackson, Carl & Ricky Scaggs* / We must have been out of our minds: *Jackson, Carl & Emmylou Harris* / Dyin' on sorrow's wine / Best we could do / Nobody's darlin' but mine
CD CDSD 074
Sundown / Aug '97 / TKO Magnum

SPRING TRAINING (Jackson, Carl & John Starling/The Nash Ramblers)
CD SHCD 3789
Sugar Hill / Mar '89 / ADA / CM / Direct / Koch / Roots

Jackson, Chubby

HAPPY MONSTER, THE (Small Groups 1944-1947)
CD C&BCD 109
Cool & Blue / Oct '93 / Discovery / Jazz Music

Jackson, Chuck

ENCORE/MR. EVERYTHING
Tell him I'm not home / Blue holiday / Tomorrow / Two stupid feet / This broken heart (that you gave me) / Don't believe him, Donna / King of the Mountain / Invisible / Another day / Lonely am I / Go on Yak Yak / Getting ready for the heartbreak / Since I don't have you / I just don't know what to do with myself / I need you / I'm your man / Human / Love is a many splendoured thing / Work song / If I didn't love you / Something you've got / D-5 / Somebody new / Tears of joy
CD CDKEND 110
Kent / Aug '94 / Pinnacle

GOOD THINGS
Tell him I'm not home / Beg me / I keep forgettin' / Millionaire / Hand it over / Two stupid feet / Make the night a little longer / I wake up crying / I'm your man / Castanets / Who's gonna pick up the pieces / Good things come to those who wait / I don't want to cry / Breaking point / Any other way / Any day now / Since I don't have you / They don't give medals (to yesterday's heroes) / Where do I go from here / These chains of love (are breaking me down) / What's with this loneliness / Forget about me / I just don't know what to do with myself / I can't stand to see you cry
CD CDKEND 935
Kent / Aug '90 / Pinnacle

I DON'T WANT TO CRY/ANY DAY NOW
I don't want to cry / Tears on my pillow / My willow tree / In between tears / Tear of the year / I cried for you / Lonely teardrops / Don't let the sun catch you crying / Salty tears / I wake up crying / Tear / Man ain't supposed to cry / I keep forgettin' / Any day now / Just once / Same old story / What'cha gonna say tomorrow / Make the night a little longer / Who's gonna pick up the pieces / In real life / Angel of angels / Breaking point / Prophet / Everybody needs love
CD CDKEND 107
Kent / Aug '93 / Pinnacle

SOMETHING YOU GOT (Jackson, Chuck & Maxine Brown)
CD SCL 21172
Ichiban Soul Classics / Oct '96 / Koch

Jackson, Cliff

CAROLINA SHOUT
Honeysuckle rose / Ain't misbehavin' / 'S wonderful / Tin roof blues / You took advantage of me / Carolina shout / I'm coming Virginia / Crazy rhythm / Beale Street blues / Someday, sweetheart / Who's sorry now
CD BLC 760194
Black Lion / Mar '94 / Cadillac / Jazz Music / Koch / Wellard

Jackson, Cordell

LIVE IN CHICAGO
CD BH 0003
Bughouse / Jul '97 / Greyhound

Jackson, D.D.

PAIRED DOWN VOL.1
Rhythm and things / Ballad for miles / Reflections / Chick-isms / Fanfare and fiesta / Subliminal messages / African dreams / For Don / Bang's dream / Easy
CD JUST 992
Justin Time / Jul '97 / Cadillac / New Note/ Pinnacle

PEACE SONG
CD JUST 722
Justin Time / Apr '95 / Cadillac / New Note/Pinnacle

RHYTHM-DANCE
D D Blues / Nueve cancion / No boundaries / Some thoughts about you / Motion sickness / Rhythm-dance / Ayse / Dreams / Guitar song / For Mamma / Peace of mind
CD JUST 892
Justin Time / Aug '96 / Cadillac / New Note/ Pinnacle

Jackson, David

FRACTAL BRIDGE
Ecco soundbeam / Aloerotic / Three main dishes / Keystone / Wildman / Untouched by human hand / Songerie / Three kinds of rice / Hello / Ecco soundbeam reprise
CD FIE 9113
Fie / Oct '96 / Vital

Jackson, Duffy

SWING SWING SWING
CD MCD 9233
Milestone / Apr '96 / Cadillac / Complete/ Pinnacle / Jazz Music / Wellard

Jackson, Earl

BUSTIN' LOOSE (Jackson, Earl & The Jailbreakers)
CD POCD 016
Popcorn / Oct '96 / Nervous

Jackson, Franz

SNAG IT
CD DD 223
Delmark / Nov '93 / ADA / Cadillac / CM / Direct / Hot Shot

Jackson, Freddie

DO ME AGAIN
Don't it feel good / Love me down / Main course / It takes two / I'll be waiting for you / Don't say you love me / Do me again / Live for the moment / Second time for love / I can't take it / All over you
CD RE 21222
Razor & Tie / Dec '96 / Koch

DON'T LET LOVE SLIP AWAY
Nice 'n' slow / Hey lover / Don't let love slip away / Crazy (for me) / One heart too many / If you don't know me by now / You and I got a thang / Special lady / Yes, I need you / It's gonna take a long, long time
CD CZ 401
Capitol / Mar '91 / EMI

DON'T LET LOVE SLIP AWAY
CD RE 21212
Razor & Tie / Dec '96 / Koch

FREDDIE JACKSON STORY, THE (For Old Time's Sake)
I don't want to lose your love / I could use a little love (right now) / Look around / Second time for love / Me and Mrs Jones / Can we try / Love me down / Main course / Jam tonight / Rock me tonight (for old time's sake) / Have you ever loved somebody / You are my lady / Tasty love / Little bit more: *Jackson, Freddie & Melba Moore*
CD CTMCD 303
EMI / Feb '97 / EMI

GREATEST HITS OF FREDDIE JACKSON
Do me again / Rock me tonight / I don't want to lose your love / I could use a little love (right now) / Jam tonight / Nice and slow / You are my lady / Love me down / Have you ever loved somebody / Hey lover / Love is just a touch away / Tasty love / Christmas forever
CD CDEST 2226
Capitol / Feb '94 / EMI

HERE IT IS
Was it something / Comin' home II u / Here it is / How does it feel / Givin' my love / Paradise / Make love easy / Addictive 2 touch / I love / My family
CD 7863 663182
RCA / Jan '94 / BMG

JUST LIKE THE FIRST TIME
You are my love / Tasty love / Have you ever loved somebody / Look around / Jam tonight / Just like the first time / I can't let you go / I don't want to lose your love / Still waiting / Janay
CD CZ 118
Capitol / Jan '87 / EMI

ROCK ME TONIGHT
He'll never love you (like I do) / Love is just a touch away / I wanna say I love you / You are my lady / Rock me tonight / Sing a song of love / Calling / Good morning heartache
CD CZ 364
EMI / Oct '90 / EMI

Jackson, George

CAIRITIONA (Jackson, George & Maggie McInnes)
CD IRCD 006
Iona / '88 / ADA / Direct / Duncans

Jackson, J.J.

GREAT J.J. JACKSON, THE
But it's alright / Try me / That ain't right / You've got me dizzy / Change is gonna come / I dig girls / Come and see me (I'm your man) / Stones that I throw / Give me back the love / Ain't too proud to beg / Love is a hurtin' thing / Boogaloo baby / Let it out
CD SEECD 281
See For Miles/C5 / Feb '94 / Pinnacle

Jackson, Janet

CONTROL
Control / What have you done for me lately / You can be mine / Pleasure principle / When I think of you / He doesn't know I'm alive / Let's wait awhile / Funny how time flies / Nasty
CD CDMID 178
A&M / Mar '93 / PolyGram

CONTROL - THE REMIXES
Control / When I think of you / Pleasure principle / What have you done for me lately / Let's wait awhile / Nasty
CD CDMID 149
A&M / Aug '91 / PolyGram

DESIGN OF A DECADE 1986-1996
What have you done for me lately / Best things in life are free: *Jackson, Janet & Luther Vandross* / Nasty / Control / When I think of you / Pleasure principle / Escapade / Black cat / Miss you much / Rhythm nation / Whoops now / That's the way love goes / Love will never do (without you) / Come back to me / Alright / Let's wait awhile / Runaway / Twenty foreplay
CD 5404382
CD 5404002
CD Set 5404222
A&M / Sep '95 / PolyGram

JANET
Morning / That's the way love goes / You know... / You want this / Be a good boy / If / Back / This time / Go on Miss Janet / Throb / What'll I do / Lounge / Funky big band / Racism / New agenda / Love pt.2 / Because of love / Wind / Again / Another lover / Where are you now / Hold on baby / Body that loves you / Rain / Anytime anyplace / Are you still up / Sweet dreams / Whoops now
CD CDV 2720
Virgin / May '93 / EMI

JANET JACKSON
Say you do / You'll never find (a love like mine) / Young love / Love and my best friend / Don't mess up a good thing / Forever yours / Magic is working / Come give your love to me
CD CDMID 114
A&M / Oct '92 / PolyGram

JANET REMIXED
That's the way love goes / If / Because of love / And on and on / Throb / You want this / Anytime anyplace / Where are you now / 70's love groove / What'll I do / One more chance
CD CDVY 2720
Virgin / Mar '95 / EMI

RHYTHM NATION 1814
Rhythm nation / State of the world / Knowledge / Miss you much / Love will never do (without you) / Livin' in a world (they didn't make) / Alright / Escapade / Black cat / Lonely / Come back to me / Someday is tonight
CD CDA 3920
A&M / Sep '89 / PolyGram

Jackson, Javon

LOOK WITHIN, A
Assessment / Memoria e fado / Zoot allures / Country girl / Leap frog / Peggy's blue skylight / L'eau a la bouche / Hamlet's favorite son / Recado bossa nova
CD CDP 8364902
Blue Note / Sep '96 / EMI

ME AND MR. JONES (Jackson, Javon Quartet)
CD CRISS 1053CD
Criss Cross / May '92 / Cadillac / Direct / Vital/SAM

Jackson, Jerry

SHRIMP BOATS A-COMIN', THERE'S DANCIN' TONIGHT
Hey sugarfoot / Se habla espanol / Tell her Johnny said goodbye / La dee dah / You don't wanna hurt me / They really don't know you / If teardrops were diamonds / I don't play games / You might be there with him / Shrimp boats / It hurts me / Till the end of time / Blowin' in the wind / Blues in the night / Time / If I had only known / Are you glad when we're apart / Always / You're mine (and I love you) / Gone to pieces / Turn back / Wide awake in a dream / Gypsy feet / She lied
CD BCD 15481
Bear Family / May '90 / Direct / Rollercoaster / Swift

Jackson, Jim

COMPLETE RECORDED WORKS VOL.1
CD DOCD 5114
Document / Nov '92 / ADA / Hot Shot / Jazz Music

COMPLETE RECORDED WORKS VOL.2
CD DOCD 5115
Document / Nov '92 / ADA / Hot Shot / Jazz Music

Jackson, Joe

BODY AND SOUL
Verdict / Cha cha loco / Not here, not now / You can't get what you want / Go for it / Loisaida / Happy ending / Be my number two / Heart of ice
CD CDMID 118
A&M / Oct '92 / PolyGram

I'M THE MAN
On your radio / Geraldine and John / Kinda kute / It's different for girls / I'm the man / Band wore blue shirts / Don't wanna be like that / Amateur hour / Get that girl / Friday
CD CDMID 117
A&M / Oct '92 / PolyGram

JUMPIN' JIVE
Jumpin' with symphony Sid / Jack you're dead / Is you is or is you ain't my baby / We the cats (shall help ya) / San Francisco fan / Five guys named Moe / Jumpin' jive / You run your mouth, I'll run my business / What's the use of getting sober / You're my meat / Tuxedo junction / How long must I wait for you
CD 5500622
Spectrum / May '93 / PolyGram

LOOK SHARP
One more time / Sunday papers / Is she really going out with him / Happy loving couples / Throw it away / Baby stick around / Look sharp / Fools in love / Do the instant mash / Pretty girls / Got the time
CD CDMID 115
A&M / Oct '92 / PolyGram

NIGHT AND DAY
Another world / Chinatown / TV age / Target / Steppin' out / Breaking us in two / Cancer / Real men / Slow song
CD CDMID 158
A&M / Oct '92 / PolyGram

NIGHT AND DAY/LOOK SHARP (2CD Set)
CD Set CDA 24121
A&M / Jul '93 / PolyGram

NIGHT MUSIC
Nocturne no. 1 / Flying / Ever after / Nocturne no. 2 / Man who wrote Danny Boy / Nocturne no. 3 / Lullaby / Only the future / Nocturne no. 4 / Sea of secrets
CD CDVUS 78
Virgin / Oct '94 / EMI

STEPPIN' OUT (Very Best Of Joe Jackson)
Is she really going out with him / Fools in love / I'm the man / It's different for girls / Beat crazy / Jumpin' jive / Breaking us in two / Steppin' out / Slow song / You can't get what you want / Be my number two / Right and wrong / Home town / Down to London / Nineteen forever
CD 3970522
A&M / Sep '90 / PolyGram

THIS IS IT (Anthology/2CD Set)
Is she really going out with him / Fools in love / One more time / Sunday papers / Look sharp / Got the time / On your radio / It's different for girls / Don't wanna be like that / Amateur hour / I'm the man / Tilt / Someone up there / One to one / Beat crazy / Biology / Jumpin' jive / What's the use of getting sober / Is she really going out with him / Another world / Breaking us in two / Chinatown / Real men / Steppin' out / Slow song / You can't get what you want / Not here, not now / Be my number two / Happy ending / Wild West / Right and wrong / Home town / Precious time / Me and you (against the world) / Down to London / Nineteen forever / Human touch
CD Set 5404022
A&M / Feb '97 / PolyGram

Jackson, John

DON'T LET YOUR DEAL GO DOWN
CD ARHCD 378
Arhoolie / Apr '95 / ADA / Cadillac / Direct

Jackson, Latoya

BAD GIRL
Sexual feeling / You and me / He's my brother / Restless heart / Playboy / You can count on me / Somewhere / Bad girl / Be my lover / He's so good to me / Do the salsa / Piano man

CD CDTB 127
Magnum Music / Feb '92 / TKO Magnum

DANCE COLLECTION
CD 10212
CMC / Jun '97 / BMG

MY COUNTRY COLLECTION
Fanfare/Intro / Burnin' love / So in love with you / Georgia dreamin' / I've got to be bad / Crazy / Trash like you / Another heart / Dance away these blues tonight / What you don't say / Little misunderstood / One strike you're out / Break a leg / Boots
CD 100552
CMC / May '97 / BMG

SEXUAL FEELING
Sexual feeling / Be my lover / He's my brother / He's so good to me / Bad girl / You keep my restless heart / Playboy / You and me / You can count on me / Do the salsa / Piano man / Somewhere
CD 304472
Hallmark / Jul '97 / Carlton

SPOTLIGHT ON LATOYA JACKSON
Sexual feeling / You and me / He's my brother / Be my lover / Piano man / Restless heart / Do the salsa / Playboy / He's so good to me / Somewhere / Bad girl / You can count on me
CD HADCD 111
Javelin / Feb '94 / Henry Hadaway / THE

Jackson, Lil' Son

BLUES COME TO TEXAS
CD ARHCD 409
Arhoolie / Apr '95 / ADA / Cadillac / Direct

Jackson, Mahalia

BEST OF MAHALIA JACKSON
CD DLCD 4013
Dixie Live / Mar '95 / TKO Magnum

GOSPEL QUEEN
CD 304022
Carlton / May '97 / Carlton

GOSPELS, SPIRITUALS AND HYMNS (2CD Set)
CD Set 4686632
Columbia / May '94 / Sony

HE'S GOT THE WHOLE WORLD IN HIS HANDS
CD JW 77004
JWD / '90 / Target/BMG

I'M ON MY WAY
CD CD 12509
Music Of The World / Nov '92 / ADA / Target/BMG

MAHALIA JACKSON & OTHER GREAT GOSPEL PERFORMERS 1937-1950
CD DOCD 5463
Document / Jun '96 / ADA / Hot Shot / Jazz Music

QUEEN OF GOSPEL
CD MCCD 122
Music Club / Aug '93 / Disc / THE

QUEEN OF GOSPEL, THE
CD CD 53028
Giants Of Jazz / Mar '92 / Cadillac / Jazz Music / Target/BMG

SILENT NIGHT
Silent night / Go tell it on the mountain / Bless this house / Sweet little Jesus boy / Star stood still (Song of the nativity) / Hark the herald angels sing / Christmas comes to us all once a year / Joy to the world / O come all ye faithful (adeste fidelis) / O little town of Bethlehem / What can I give
CD CD 62130
Columbia / Nov '96 / Sony

WHEN THE SAINTS GO MARCHING IN
CD CD 3554
Cameo / Jul '95 / Target/BMG

Jackson, Michael

BAD
Bad / Way you make me feel / Speed demon / Liberian girl / Just good friends / Another part of me / Man in the mirror / I just can't stop loving you / Dirty Diana / Smooth criminal / Leave me alone
CD 4502902
Epic / Sep '87 / Sony

BEN
Ben / Greatest show on earth / People make the world go round / We've got a good thing going / Everybody's somebody's fool / My girl / What goes around comes around / In our small way / Sheebe-doo-be-doo-a-day / You can cry on my shoulder
CD 5301632
Motown / Sep '93 / PolyGram

BEST OF MICHAEL JACKSON AND THE JACKSON FIVE (Jackson, Michael/ Jackson Five)
I want you back: *Jackson Five* / ABC: *Jackson Five* / Love you save: *Jackson Five* / I'll be ther: *Jackson Five* / Mama's pearl: *Jackson Five* / Never can say goodbye: *Jackson Five* / Got to be there: *Jackson, Michael* / Rockin' robin: *Jackson, Michael* / Ain't no sunshine: *Jackson, Michael* / Lookin' through the windows: *Jackson Five* / Ben: *Jackson, Michael* / Doctor my eyes: *Jackson Five* / We're almost there: *Jackson, Michael* / Farewell my summer love: *Jackson, Michael* / Girl you're so together: *Jackson, Michael*
CD 5308042
PolyGram TV / Jun '97 / PolyGram

BIG BOY (Jackson, Michael/Jackson Five)
CD PLD 8122
Charly / Jul '95 / Koch

BLOOD ON THE DANCEFLOOR
Blood on the dance floor / Morphine / Superfly sister / Ghosts / Is it scary / Scream louder / Money / 2 Bad / Stranger in Moscow / This time around / Earth song / You are not alone / History
CD 4875002
MJJ Music / May '97 / Sony

DANGEROUS
Jam / Why you wanna trip on me / In the closet / She drives me wild / Remember the time / Can't let her get away / Heal the world / Black or white / Who is it / Give in to me / Will you be there / Keep the faith / Gone too soon / Dangerous
CD 4658022
Epic / Nov '91 / Sony

GOT TO BE THERE
Ain't no sunshine / I wanna be where you are / Girl don't take your love from me / In our small way / Got to be there / Rockin' robin / Wings of my love / Maria / Love is here and now you're gone / You've got a friend
CD 5301622
Motown / Aug '93 / PolyGram

HISTORY PAST PRESENT AND FUTURE VOL.1
Billie Jean / Way you make me feel / Black or white / Rock with you / She's out of my life / Bad / I just can't stop loving you / Man in the mirror / Thriller / Beat it / Girl is mine / Remember the time / Don't stop till you get enough / Wanna be startin' something / Heal the world / Scream / They don't care about us / Stranger in Moscow / This time around / Earth song / DS / Money / Come together / You are not alone / Childhood / Tabloid junkie / 2 Bad / History / Little Susie / Smile
CD Set 4747092
MJJ Music / Jun '95 / Sony

INTERVIEW DISC
CD SAM 7015
Sound & Media / Nov '96 / Sound & Media

MOTOWN EARLY CLASSICS (Jackson, Michael/Jackson Five)
I want you back / Can you remember / Who's lovin' you / True love can be beautiful / In our small way / Goin' back to Indiana / Can I see you in the morning / I'll bet you / Rockin' Robin / People make the world go round / Doggin' around / Never can say goodbye / Lookin' through the windows / We've got a good thing going / Young folks / My little baby / (We've got) Blue skies / With a child's heart
CD 5522242
Spectrum / Jul '96 / PolyGram

MOTOWN'S GREATEST HITS
I want you back / Doctor my eyes / One day in your life / Lookin' through the windows / Got to be there / I'll be there / Love you save / ABC / Rockin' Robin / Happy / Ben / Never can say goodbye / Farewell my summer love / I want you back (original) / Mama's pearl / Ain't no sunshine / Girl you're so together / Hallelujah day / Skywriter / We're almost there
CD 5300142
Motown / Feb '92 / PolyGram

OFF THE WALL
Don't stop till you get enough / Rock with you / Working day and night / Get on the floor / Off the wall / Girlfriend / She's out of my life / I can't help it / It's the falling in love / Burn this disco out
CD CD 83468
Epic / '83 / Sony

THRILLER
Wanna be startin' something / Baby be mine / Girl is mine / Thriller / Beat it / Billie Jean / Human nature / PYT (pretty young thing) / Lady in my life
CD CD 85930
Epic / '83 / Sony

Jackson, Michael Gregory

CLARITY
CD ESP 30282
ESP / Jan '93 / Jazz Music

KARMONIC SUITE
CD 1238572
IAI / Sep '93 / Cadillac / Harmonia Mundi

Jackson, Millie

21 OF THE BEST (1971-1983)
Child of God / Ask me what you want / My man, a sweet man / Breakaway / It hurts so good / How do you feel the morning after / (If loving you is wrong) I don't want to be right / Loving arms / Bad risk / You can't turn me off (in the middle of turning me on) / If you're not back in love by Monday / All the way lover / Go out and get some (get it out 'cha system) / Keep the home fire burnin' / Never change lovers in the middle of the night / Kiss you all over / This is it (part 2) / It's gonna take some time this time / Do you wanna make love / Blues don't get tired of me / I feel like walking in the rain
CD CDSEWD 100
Southbound / Sep '94 / Pinnacle

CAUGHT UP
(If loving you is wrong) I don't want to be right / Rap / All I want is a fighting chance / I'm tired of hiding / It's all over but the shouting / So easy going so hard coming back / I'm through trying to prove my love to you / Summer (first time)
CD CDSEWM 003
Southbound / Jun '89 / Pinnacle

ESP (Extra Sexual Persuasion)
Sexercise (Parts 1 and 2) / This girl could be dangerous / Slow tongue (Working your way down) / Why me / I feel like walking in the rain / Too easy being easy / Slow tongue / You're working me
CD CDSEWM 093
Southbound / Apr '94 / Pinnacle

FEELIN' BITCHY
All the way lover / Lovin' your good thing away / Angel in your arms / Little taste of outside love / You created a monster / Cheatin' is / If you're not back in love by Monday / Feeling like a woman
CD CDSEWM 042
Southbound / Oct '91 / Pinnacle

FOR MEN ONLY
This is where I came in / This is it / If that don't turn you on / I wish that I could hurt that way again / Fool's affair / You must have known I needed love / Despair / Not on your life / Ain't no coming back
CD CDSEWM 070
Southbound / Jun '93 / Pinnacle

FREE AND IN LOVE
House for sale / I'm free / Tonight I'll shoot the moon / There you are / Do what makes the world go round / Bad risk / I feel like making love / Solitary love affair / I'm in love again
CD CDSEW 032
Southbound / Aug '90 / Pinnacle

GET IT OUTCHA SYSTEM
Go out and get some (get it out 'cha system) / Keep the home fire burnin' / Logs and thangs / Put something down on it / Here you come again / Why say you're sorry / He wants to hear the words / I just wanna be with you / Sweet music man
CD CDSEWM 046
Southbound / Mar '92 / Pinnacle

HARD TIMES
Blufunkes / Special occasion / I don't want to cry / We're gonna make it / Hard times / Blues don't get tired of me / Mess on your hands / Finger rap / Mess on your hands (reprise) / Finger rap (reprise) / Feel love comin' on
CD CDSEWM 090
Southbound / Mar '94 / Pinnacle

HOT, WILD, UNRESTRICTED
Hot, wild, unrestricted, crazy love / Getting to know me / Imitation of love / Love stinks / Muffle that fart / I'm waiting baby / Will you love me tomorrow / Investigative reporting / Love is a dangerous game / Sho nuff danjus
CD 301122
Hallmark / Jun '97 / Carlton

I GOT TO TRY IT ONE TIME
How do you feel the morning after / Get your love right / My love is so fly / Letter full of tears / Watch the one who brings you the news / I got to try it one time / Gospel truth / One night stand / I gotta do something about myself / In the wash
CD CDSEW 023
Southbound / Feb '90 / Pinnacle

I HAD TO SAY IT
I had to say it / Loving arms / Rap / Stranger / I ain't no glory story / It's gonna take some time this time / Fancy this / Ladies first / Somebody's love died here last night / You owe me that much
CD CDSEWM 086
Southbound / Nov '93 / Pinnacle

IT HURTS SO GOOD
I cry / Hypocrisy / Two-faced world / It hurts so good / Don't send nobody else / Hypocrisy (reprise) / Good to the very last drop / Help yourself / Love doctor / Now that you got it / Close my eyes / Breakaway
CD CDSEW 019
Southbound / Nov '89 / Pinnacle

IT'S OVER
CD ICH 1502CD
Ichiban / Dec '95 / Direct / Koch

JUST A LIL' BIT COUNTRY
I can't stop loving you / Till I get it right / Pick me up on your way down / Loving you / I laughed a lot / Love on the rocks / Standing in your line / Rose coloured glasses / It meant nothing to me / Anybody that don't like Millie Jackson
CD CDSEWM 089
Southbound / Jan '94 / Pinnacle

LIVE AND UNCENSORED/LIVE AND OUTRAGEOUS (2CD Set)
Keep the home fire burnin' / Logs and thangs / Put something down on it / Da ya think I'm sexy / Just when I needed you most / Phuck u symphony / What am I waiting for / I still love you (you still love me) / All the way lover / Soaps / Hold the line / Be a sweetheart / Didn't I blow your mind this time / Give it up / Moment's pleasure / (If loving you is wrong) I don't want to be right / Rap / Never change lovers in the middle of the night / Sweet music man / It hurts so good / Passion / Horse or mule / Lovers and girlfriends / Don't you ever stop loving me / I had to say it / Still / Ugly men / This is it
CD Set CDSEW2 038
Southbound / Mar '91 / Pinnacle

LOVINGLY YOURS
You can't turn me off (in the middle of turning me on) / Something 'bout you / I'll continue to love you / I can't say goodbye / Love of your own / I'll live my love for you / Body movements / From her arms to mine / Help me finish my song / I'll be rolling
CD CDSEWM 037
Southbound / Feb '91 / Pinnacle

MILLIE JACKSON
If this is love / I ain't giving up / I miss you baby / Child of God / Ask me what you want / My man, a sweet man / You're the joy of my life / I gotta get away from my own self / I just can't stand it / Strange things
CD CDSEW 009
Southbound / Aug '89 / Pinnacle

MOMENT'S PLEASURE, A
Never change lovers in the middle of the night / Seeing you again / Kiss you all over / Moment's pleasure / What went wrong last night / Rising cost of love / We got to hit it off / Once you've had it
CD CDSEWM 053
Westbound / Sep '92 / Pinnacle

ROYAL RAPPIN'S (Jackson, Millie & Isaac Hayes)
Sweet music, soft lights and you / Feels like the first time / You never cross my mind / Love changes / I changed my mind / Do you wanna make love / If I had my way / If you had your way / You needed me
CD CDSEWM 059
Southbound / Jan '93 / Pinnacle

STILL CAUGHT UP
Loving arms / Making the best of a bad situation / Memory of a wife / Tell her it's over / Do what makes you satisfied / You can't stand the thought of another me / Leftovers / I still love you (you still love me)
CD CDSEW 027
Southbound / Jul '90 / Pinnacle

YOUNG MAN, OLDER WOMAN
CD ICH 1159CD
Ichiban / Feb '94 / Direct / Koch

Jackson, Milt

AIN'T BUT A FEW OF US LEFT (Jackson, Milt & Oscar Peterson/Grady Tate/Ray Brown)
Ain't but a few of us left / Time for love / If I should lose you / Stuffy / Body and soul / What am I here for
CD OJCCD 785
Original Jazz Classics / Jun '94 / Complete/ Pinnacle / Jazz Music / Wellard

BAGS MEETS WES (Jackson, Milt & Wes Montgomery)
CD OJCCD 234
Original Jazz Classics / Apr '86 / Complete/Pinnacle / Jazz Music / Wellard

BAGS' BAG
Blues for Roberta / Groovin' / How are you / Slow boat to China / I cover the waterfront / Rev / Tour angel / Blues for Tomi-Oka
CD PACD 23108422
Pablo / Oct '94 / Cadillac / Complete/ Pinnacle

BEBOP
Au privave / Good bait / Woody 'n' you / Now's the time / Ornithology / Groovin' high / Birk's works / Salt peanuts
CD 7567909912
Atlantic / Jul '93 / Warner Music

BEST OF MILT JACKSON
Once I loved / If you went away / Yes sir that's my baby / Three thousand miles ago / Ain't misbehavin' / My kind of trouble is you / Soul fusion / Blues for Edith
CD PACD 24054052
Pablo / Jul '94 / Cadillac / Complete/ Pinnacle

BIG BAGS
CD OJCCD 366
Original Jazz Classics / Nov '95 / Complete/Pinnacle / Jazz Music / Wellard

BIG THREE, THE (Jackson, Milt & Joe Pass/Ray Brown)
Pink panther / Nuages / Blue bossa / Come Sunday / Wave / Moonglow / You stepped out of a dream / Blues for Sammy
CD OJCCD 805

Original Jazz Classics / Jul '93 / Complete/ Pinnacle / Jazz Music / Wellard

BROTHER JIM (Jackson, Milt & His Gold Medal Winners)
Brother Jim: *Jackson, Milt* / Ill wind: *Jackson, Milt* / Rhythm-a-ning: *Jackson, Milt* / Sudden death: *Jackson, Milt* / How high the moon: *Jackson, Milt* / Back to Bologna: *Jackson, Milt* / Sleeves: *Jackson, Milt* / Lullaby of the leaves: *Jackson, Milt* / Weasel: *Jackson, Milt*
CD _______________ PACD 23109162
Pablo / Oct '94 / Cadillac / Complete/ Pinnacle

FEELINGS
Feelings / Come to me / Trouble is a man / Moody blue / Day it rained / My kind of trouble is you / If you went away / Tears / Blues for Edith / You don't know what love is
CD _______________ OJCCD 448
Original Jazz Classics / Jul '93 / Complete/ Pinnacle / Jazz Music / Wellard

FOR SOMEONE I LOVE
CD _______________ OJCCD 404
Original Jazz Classics / Jul '93 / Complete/Pinnacle / Jazz Music / Wellard

HAREM, THE
Blues for Gene / Holy land / Ellington's Strayhorn / Harem / NPS / Old folks / Olinga / All members / Every time we say goodbye
CD _______________ 8208362
Limelight / Jun '91 / PolyGram

HAREM, THE
CD _______________ MM 5061
Music Masters / Oct '94 / Nimbus

HIGH FLY (2CD Set)
Close your eyes / Here's that rainy day / Star eyes / Blues for Edith / Chicago / Time for love / Shiny stockings / Goodbye / Bye bye blackbird / Scrapple from the apple / I thought about you / High fly / If you never come to me / Li'l darlin' / Good bait
CD Set _______________ JLR 103602
Live At EJ's / May '96 / Target/BMG

IN THE BEGINNING (Jackson, Milt & Sonny Stitt)
CD _______________ OJCCD 1771
Original Jazz Classics / Oct '94 / Complete/Pinnacle / Jazz Music / Wellard

INVITATION (Jackson, Milt Sextet)
Invitation / Too close for comfort / Ruby my dear (Take 6) / Ruby my dear (Take 5) / Sealer / Poom-a-loom / Stella by starlight / Ruby / None shall wander (Take 8) / None shall wonder (Take 6)
CD _______________ OJCCD 260
Original Jazz Classics / Sep '93 / Complete/ Pinnacle / Jazz Music / Wellard

IT DON'T MEAN A THING IF YOU CAN'T TAP YOUR FOOT TO IT (Jackson, Milt Quartet)
Midnight waltz / Ain't that nuthin' / Stress and strain / Used to be Jackson / It don't mean a thing if it ain't got that swing / If I were a bell / Close enough for blood
CD _______________ OJCCD 601
Original Jazz Classics / Feb '92 / Complete/ Pinnacle / Jazz Music / Wellard

JACKSON
CD _______________ CD 20022
Pablo / May '86 / Cadillac / Complete/ Pinnacle

JACKSON, JOHNSON, BROWN AND COMPANY (Jackson, Milt & J.J. Johnson/Ray Brown)
Jaybone / Lament / Our delight / Bag's groove / Watch what happens / My one and only / Jumpin' blues
CD _______________ OJCCD 907
Original Jazz Classics / Jun '97 / Complete/ Pinnacle / Jazz Music / Wellard

LIVE AT THE VILLAGE GATE
Bags of blue / Little girl blue / Gemini / Gerri's blues / Time after time / Ignunt oil / Willow weep for me / All members
CD _______________ OJCCD 309
Original Jazz Classics / May '93 / Complete/ Pinnacle / Jazz Music / Wellard

LONDON BRIDGE, A
CD _______________ CD 2310932
Pablo / '93 / Cadillac / Complete/Pinnacle

MILT JACKSON
Wonder why / I should care / Stonewall / My funny Valentine / Nearness of you / Moonray
CD _______________ OJCCD 12
Original Jazz Classics / Mar '92 / Complete/ Pinnacle / Jazz Music / Wellard

MILT JACKSON & COUNT BASIE BIG BAND VOL.1 (Jackson, Milt & Count Basie Big Band)
9.20 special: *Jackson, Milt & Count Basie* / Moonlight becomes you: *Jackson, Milt & Count Basie* / Shiny stockings: *Jackson, Milt & Count Basie* / Blues for me: *Jackson, Milt & Count Basie* / Every tub: *Jackson, Milt & Count Basie* / Easy does it: *Jackson, Milt & Count Basie* / Lena and Lenny: *Jackson, Milt & Count Basie* / Sunny side of the street: *Jackson, Milt & Count Basie* / Back to the apple: *Jackson, Milt & Count Basie* / I'll always be in love with you: *Jackson, Milt & Count Basie* / Come back: *Jackson, Milt & Count Basie* / Basie: *Jackson, Milt & Count Basie* / Corner pocket: *Jackson, Milt & Count Basie* / Lady in lace: *Jackson, Milt & Count Basie* / Blues for Joe Turner: *Jackson, Milt & Count Basie* / Good time blues: *Jackson, Milt & Count Basie* / Li'l darlin': *Jackson, Milt & Count Basie* / Big stuff: *Jackson, Milt & Count Basie* / Blue and sentimental: *Jackson, Milt & Count Basie*
CD _______________ OJCCD 740
Original Jazz Classics / May '93 / Complete/ Pinnacle / Jazz Music / Wellard

MILT JACKSON & COUNT BASIE BIG BAND VOL.2 (Jackson, Milt & Count Basie)
9/20 special / Moonlight becomes you / Shiny stockings / Blues for me / Every tub / Easy does it / Lena and Lenny / Sunny side of the street / Back to the apple / I'll always be in love with you
CD _______________ OJCCD 741
Original Jazz Classics / May '93 / Complete/ Pinnacle / Jazz Music / Wellard

MILT JACKSON AT LONDON BRIDGE
CD _______________ PACD 23109322
Pablo / Jul '93 / Cadillac / Complete/ Pinnacle

MONTREUX 1977 (Jackson, Milt & Ray Brown)
Slippery / Beautiful friendship / Mean to me / You are my sunshine / CMJ / That's the way it is
CD _______________ OJCCD 375
Original Jazz Classics / Apr '93 / Complete/ Pinnacle / Jazz Music / Wellard

MOSTLY DUKE
CD _______________ PACD 23109442
Pablo / Jan '93 / Cadillac / Complete/ Pinnacle

NIGHT MIST
Blues in my heart / Double B / Blues for Clyde / Matter of adjustment / Night mist blues / Other bag blues / DB blues
CD _______________ OJCCD 827
Original Jazz Classics / Jul '93 / Complete/ Pinnacle / Jazz Music / Wellard

SOUL FUSION (Jackson, Milt & Monty Alexander)
Parking lot blues / Three thousand miles ago / Isn't she lovely / Soul fusion / Compassion / Once I loved / Yano / Bossa nova do marilla
CD _______________ OJCCD 731
Original Jazz Classics / '93 / Complete/Pinnacle / Jazz Music / Wellard

SOUL ROUTE (Jackson, Milt Quartet)
Sittin' in the sandtrap / Blues for Gene / How long has this been going on / Dejection blues / Soul route / Afterglow / In a mellow tone / My romance / Chloe
CD _______________ PACD 23109002
Pablo / Jul '93 / Cadillac / Complete/ Pinnacle

THAT'S THE WAY IT IS (Jackson, Milt & Ray Brown Quintet)
Frankie and Johnny / Here's that rainy day / Wheelin' and dealin' / Blues in the basement / Tenderly / That's the way it is
CD _______________ MCAD 33112
Impulse Jazz / Jan '90 / New Note/BMG

Jackson, Nicole

SENSUAL LOVING
Little dab / I like / Sensual loving / Nobody but you / Tell me how you like it / Don't make me wait / Love come down / Temporary love / Make you mine / Just in case / Good thang / Sooner or later / Family
CD _______________ XECD 4
Debut / Jun '95 / 3mv/Sony / Pinnacle

Jackson, P.J.

P.J. JACKSON
CD _______________ SP 1178CD
Stony Plain / Oct '93 / ADA / CM / Direct

Jackson, Papa Charlie

VOL.1 1924-1925
CD _______________ DOCD 5087
Document / '92 / ADA / Hot Shot / Jazz Music

VOL.2 1924-1925
CD _______________ DOCD 5088
Document / '92 / ADA / Hot Shot / Jazz Music

VOL.3 1924-1925
CD _______________ DOCD 5089
Document / '92 / ADA / Hot Shot / Jazz Music

Jackson, Paul

MR. DESTINY
CD _______________ SPCD 11
Spindle / Aug '95 / Else / Jet Star

Jackson, Rebbie

REBBIE JACKSON COLLECTION, THE (Expansion Collector Series)
This love is forever / Friendship song / Eternal love / Open up my love / Always wanting something / Ready for love / Hey boy / Fork in the road / Tonight I'm yours / Sweetest dreams / Centipede
CD _______________ EXCDG 2
Expansion / Jul '96 / 3mv/Sony

Jackson, Ron

SONG FOR LUIS
Time in a bottle / Reminiscing / Little Nick / Memories of you / I cant' explain / Make someone happy / You / Streike up the band / Sacred love / Little Willie leaps / Visitation / Song for Luis
CD _______________ CHECD 00115
Master Mix / Jul '96 / Jazz Music / New Note/Pinnacle / Wellard

Jackson, Ronald Shannon

RAVEN ROC (Jackson, Ronald Shannon Decoding Society)
CD _______________ DIW 862
DIW / Sep '92 / Cadillac / Harmonia Mundi

RED WARRIOR (Jackson, Ronald Shannon Decoding Society)
Red warrior / Ashes / Gate to heaven / In every face / Elders / What's not said
CD _______________ AXCD 3008
Axiom / Oct '91 / PolyGram / Vital

SHANNON'S HOUSE (Jackson, Ronald Shannon Decoding Society)
CD _______________ DIW 913
DIW / Dec '96 / Cadillac / Harmonia Mundi

Jackson, Steve

HOUSE THAT JACK BUILT, THE (Various Artists)
CD _______________ BDRCD 16
Breakdown / Sep '96 / Pinnacle

Jackson, Wanda

COUNTRY CLASSICS
Jambalalaya (On the bayou) / Let's have a party / Hot dog that made him mad / Fancy satin pillows / Because it's you / I may never get to heaven / Seven lonely days / Mean mean man / Long tall Sally / Fujiyama mama / Whole lotta shakin' goin' on / Yakety yak / Right or wrong / Stand by your man / In the middle of a heartache
CD _______________ CDMFP 6325
Music For Pleasure / Apr '97 / EMI

PARTY
Let's have a party / What in the world's come over you / Right or wrong / I fall to pieces / Rave on / Sweet dreams / Oh boy / Breathless / Sweet nothings / It's only make believe / Stupid cupid / Raining in my heart
CD _______________ 306062
Hallmark / Jan '97 / Carlton

RIGHT OR WRONG 1954-1962 (4CD Set)
If you knew what I know / Lovin' country style / Heart / You could have had / Right to love / You can't have my love / If you don't, somebody else will / You'd be the first one to know / It's the same world (Wherever you go) / Tears at the Grand Old Opre / Don't do the things he'd do / Nobody's darlin' but mine / Wasted / I cried again / I'd rather have a broken heart / You won't forget about me / Step by step / Half as good a girl / I gotta know / Cryin' thru the night / Baby loves him / Honey bop / Silver threads and golden needles / Hot dog that made him mad / Did you miss me / Cool love / Let me explain / Don'a Wan'a / No wedding bells for Joe / Fujiyama Mama / Just queen for a day / Making believe / Just call me lonesome / Happy, happy birthday / Let me go, lover / Let's have a party / Daydreaming / Heartbreak ahead / Here we are again / I wanna waltz / I can't make my dreams understand / Money Honey / Long tall Sally / Sinful heart / Mean mean man / Rock your baby / Date with Jerry / (Every time they play) our song / You've turned to a stranger / Reaching / I'd rather have you / Savin' my love / You're the one for me / In the middle of a heartache / Please call today / My destiny / Wrong kind of girl / Kansas City / Fallin' / Sparkling brown eyes / Hard headed woman / Baby, baby, bye bye / It doesn't matter anymore / Lonely weekends / Tweedle dee / Riot in cell block 9 / Little charm bracelet / Right or wrong / Funnel of love / Tongue tied / There's a party goin' on / Lost weekend / Man we had a party / Why I'm walkin / I may never get to heaven / Stupid cupid / Brown eyed handsome man / I cried again / Last letter / Who shot Sam / Slippin' and slidin' / My baby left me / So soon / Window up above / Sticks and stones / I don't wanta go / In the middle of a heartache / Little bitty tear / I'd be ashamed / Seven lonely days / Don't ask me why / I need you now / This should go on forever / Is it wrong / We could / You don't know baby / Before I lose my mind / Tip of my fingers / Let me talk to you / (Let's stop) Kickin' our hearts around / Between the window and the phone / If I cried every time you hurt me / I misunderstood / Let my love walk in / To tell you the truth / Greatest actor / You bug me bad / One teardrop at a time / Funny how time slips away / These empty arms / But I was lying / We haven't a moment to lose / How important can it be / Things I might've been / Little things mean a lot / Have you ever been lonely / Please love me forever / Since I met you baby / May you never be alone / Sympathy / Whirlpool / Pledging my love / What am I living for
CD Set _______________ BCD 15629
Bear Family / Mar '93 / Direct / Rollercoaster / Swift

ROCKIN' WITH WANDA JACKSON
CD _______________ MAR 045
Marginal / Jun '97 / Greyhound

SANTA DOMINGO (Her German Recordings)
CD _______________ BCD 15582
Bear Family / Apr '92 / Direct / Rollercoaster / Swift

WANDA JACKSON: CAPITOL COUNTRY MUSIC CLASSICS
I gotta know / Silver threads and golden needles / Cool love / Don'a wan'a / Fujiyama Mama / Making believe / Let's have a party / Long tall Sally / Mean mean man / Tweedle dee / Little charm bracelet / Right or wrong / There's a party goin' on / I may never get to heaven / Slippin' and slidin' / In the middle of a heartache / This should go on forever / (Let's stop) Kickin' our hearts around / Between the window and the phone / If I cried every time you hurt me / Slippin' / Violet and a rose / Box it came in / Blue yodel No. 6 / Because it's you / Tears will be a chaser for your wine / Both sides of the line / Girl don't have to drink to have fun / My big iron skillet / Woman lives for love / Fancy satin pillows
CD _______________ CDEMS 1485
Capitol / Apr '93 / EMI

Jackson, William

CELTIC SUITE FOR GLASGOW
Bird / Tree / Bell / Fish
CD _______________ CDTRAX 041
Greentrax / Dec '90 / ADA / Direct / Duncans / Highlander

CELTIC TRANQUILITY
Dove across the water / Light on a distant shore / Harvest of the fallen / Glasgow 1885 / Dear green place unchanged / Molendinar: The spring / Fermentation / Paradise valley, angels's ascent / Landfall / Fish
CD _______________ IR 016CD
Iona / Jun '92 / ADA / Direct / Duncans

HEART MUSIC
Lady Amelia Murray's strathspey / Breton march / Wauking o' the faulds / Port lennox / Strike the young harp / John Maclean of lewis / Paradise alley / Angel's ascent / Threefold flame / Air by fingal / Emigrant peak / St Kilda dance / Fair shoemaker / Rose without rue
CD _______________ IRCD 010
Iona / Sep '91 / ADA / Direct / Duncans

INCHCOLM
CD _______________ AKD 037
Linn / Mar '95 / PolyGram

Jackson, Willis

BAR WARS
CD _______________ MCD 6011
Muse / Sep '92 / New Note/Pinnacle

CALL OF THE GATORS
CD _______________ DD 460
Delmark / Jul '93 / ADA / Cadillac / CM / Direct / Hot Shot

PLEASE MR. JACKSON
CD _______________ OJCCD 321
Original Jazz Classics / Dec '95 / Complete/Pinnacle / Jazz Music / Wellard

Jackson, Yvonne

I'M TROUBLE
I'm trouble / Sweet memories / Woman in me / She set you free / No deposit, no return / What I'd do to get your love back / Common, ordinary housewife gone bad / What'cha gonna do about it / If tears are only water / I'm walking out
CD _______________ BLU 10162
Blues Beacon / Jun '94 / New Note/ Pinnacle

Jacksons

2300 JACKSON STREET
Art of madness / Nothin' (that compares 2 U) / Maria / Private affair / 2300 Jackson Street / Harley / She / Alright with me / Play it up / Midnight rendezvous / If you'd only believe
CD _______________ 4633522
Epic / Jul '97 / Sony

AMERICAN DREAM, AN
CD _______________ 5301192
Motown / Jan '94 / PolyGram

DESTINY
Blame it on the boogie / Push me away / Things I do for you / Shake your body / Destiny / Bless his soul / All night dancin' / That's what you get
CD _______________ 4688752
Epic / Jul '97 / Sony

DESTINY/TRIUMPH/VICTORY (3CD Set)
Blame it on the boogie / Push me away / Things I do for you / Shake your body (down to the ground) / Destiny / Bless his soul / All night dancin' / That's what you get (for being polite) / Can you feel it / Lovely one / Your ways / Everybody / This place hotel / Time waits for no one / Walk right now / Give it up / Wondering who / Torture / Wait / One more chance / Be not always / State of shock / We can change the world / Hurt / Body
CD Set 4853192
Epic / Jul '97 / Sony

GOIN' PLACES
Music's takin' over / Goin' places / Different kind of lady / Even though you're gone / Jump for joy / Heaven knows I love you, girl / Man of war / Do what you wanna / Find me a girl
CD 4688772
Epic / Jul '97 / Sony

JACKSONS, THE
Enjoy yourself / Think happy / Good times / Keep on dancing / Blues away / Show you the way to go / Living together / Strength of one man / Dreamer / Style of life
CD 4688772
Epic / Jul '97 / Sony

LIVE
Opening/Can you feel it / Things I do for you / Off the wall / BenBen / This place hotel / She's out of my life / Movie and rap / Excerpts / Medley / I'll be there / Rock with you / ovely one / Working day and night / Don't stop till you get enough / Shake your body down
CD 4668372
Epic / Jul '97 / Sony

TRIUMPH
Can you feel it / Lovely one / Your ways / Everybody / This place hotel / Time waits for no one / Walk right now / Give it up / Wondering who
CD CD 86112
Epic / Jul '97 / Sony

VICTORY
Torture / Wait / One more chance / Be not always / State of shock / We can change the world / Hurt / Body
CD 4504502
Epic / Jul '97 / Sony

Jackyl

NIGHT OF THE LIVING DEAD
CD CDMFN 199
Music For Nations / Feb '96 / Pinnacle

Jacob, Christian

MAYNARD FERGUSON PRESENTS CHRISTIAN JACOB
Remembrance / Tears of sadness / Top down / Playtime / Sergey suite / Our love is here to stay / Here's that rainy day / You don't know what love is / I've got rhythm / Still by me
CD CCD 47442
Concord Jazz / Feb '97 / New Note/ Pinnacle

Jacobites

HOWLING GOOD TIMES
CD JANIDA 004
Regency / May '94 / Total/Pinnacle

JACOBITES (Sudden, Nikki & Dave Kusworth)
CD JANIDA 001
Regency / May '93 / Total/Pinnacle

OLD SCARLETT
CD GRCD 382
Glitterhouse / Dec '95 / Avid/BMG

Jacob's Mouse

RUBBER ROOM
CD WIJ 040CD
Wiiija / Feb '95 / RTM/Disc

WRYLY SMILERS
Good / Dusty / Group of seven / Palace / Sag bag / Fandango widewheels / B12 Marmites / Three pound apathy / Keen apple / Lip and cheek
CD JCOB 001CD
Wiiija / Oct '94 / RTM/Disc

Jacob's Optical Stairway

JACOB'S OPTICAL STAIRWAY
Fragments of a lost language / Naphosisous wars / Chase the escape / Fusion formula (the meetamophosis) / Majestic 12 / Solar feelings / Jacob's optical illusion / Harsh realities / Engulfing whirlpool / Quatrain 72 (Red horizon) / 20 Degrees of Taurus
CD RS 95079CD
R&S / Jan '96 / Vital

Jacobs, Peter

PIANO MUSIC OF BILLY MAYERL
CD PRCD 399
Priory / Jul '92 / Priory

Jacobsen, Pete

EVER ONWARD
CD FMRCD 12
Future / Apr '95 / ADA / Harmonia Mundi

Jacquet, Illinois

BLACK VELVET BAND
Jet propulsion / King Jacquet / Try me one more time / Embryo / Riffin' at the 24th Street / Mutton leg / Symphony in Sid / Jacquet for Jack the Belboy / Big foot / Black velvet / B-yot / Adam's alley / Blue satin / My old gal / Slow down baby / Hot rod / You gotta change / Flying home
CD ND 86571
Bluebird / Nov '88 / BMG

COMEBACK, THE
CD BLCD 760160
Black Lion / Oct '92 / Cadillac / Jazz Music / Koch / Wellard

FLYING HOME - THE BEST OF THE VERVE YEARS
Speedliner / Pastel / Groovin' / Cotton tail / Boot 'em up / Bluesitis / Lean baby / Port of rico / Where are you / Heads / It's the talk of the town / Kid and the brute / Sophia / Honeysuckle rose / Stardust / Las Vegas blues / Achtung / Have you met Miss Jones / No sweat / Flying home
CD 5216442
Verve / Jun '94 / PolyGram

ILLINOIS JACQUET (Jacquet, Illinois & Wild Bill Davis)
CD 233044
Black & Blue / May '87 / Discovery / Koch / Wellard

ILLINOIS JACQUET
Frantic Fanny / Stella by starlight / Satin doll / Banned in Boston / Indiana (back home in Indiana) / Ydeen O / Imagination / How now / Reverie / Pucker up / Satin doll / Ydeen O / How now / Frantic Fanny / Stella by starlight
CD EK 64654
Sony Jazz / Feb '96 / Sony

ILLINOIS JACQUET AND ALL STAR NEW YORK BAND
CD JSPCD 212
JSP / Jan '88 / ADA / Cadillac / Direct / Hot Shot / Target/BMG

JACQUET'S STREET
CD BLE 591122
Black & Blue / Oct '94 / Discovery / Koch / Wellard

LOOT TO BOOT
CD CDC 9034
LRC / Jul '91 / Harmonia Mundi / New Note/Pinnacle

LOOT TO BOOT
Soft winds / Sweet Georgia Brown / How long / Racquet club / Loot to boot / No sweat / Blues for New Orleans / It don't mean a thing
CD 17131
Laserlight / May '97 / Target/BMG

MAN I LOVE, THE
CD BB 8652
Black & Blue / Apr '96 / Discovery / Koch / Wellard

Jad Fair

MONARCHS
CD DRJIM 20
Dr. Jim / Jul '97 / Cargo / Greyhound

Jade

JADE TO THE MAX
Don't walk away / I wanna love you / I want 'cha baby / That boy / Out with the girls / Hold me close / One woman / Give me what I'm missing / Looking for Mr. Do Right / Don't ask my neighbour / Blessed
CD 74321148002
Giant / Feb '96 / BMG

Jade Bridge

AMBUSH ON ALL SIDES
Bird in flight / Calm lake and Autumn moon / Ambushed from ten sides / Thunder ends the dry season / Journey to Gusu / Horse race / Street procession / Plow is coming / Purple bamboo / Moon reflected at Second Springs / Peking Opera fantasia
CD HSR 0004
Henry Street / Mar '97 / Direct

Jade Warrior

BREATHING THE STORM
CD CDR 105
Red Hot / Mar '94 / THE

DISTANT ECHOES
CD CDR 106
Red Hot / Jan '94 / THE

FLOATING WORLD
Clouds / Mountain of fruit and flowers / Waterfall / Red lotus / Rainflower / Easty / Monkey chant / Memories of a distant sea / Quba
CD IMCD 99
Island / Feb '90 / PolyGram

WAY OF THE SUN
Sun ra / Sun child / Moontears / Heaven stone / Way of the sun / River song / Carnival / Dance of the sun / Death of Ra
CD IMCD 100
Island / Feb '90 / PolyGram

Jadis

ACROSS THE WATER
CD GEPCD 1009
Giant Electric Pea / May '94 / Pinnacle

MORE THAN MEETS THE EYE
Sleepwalk / Hiding in the corner / G 13 / Wonderful world / More than meets the eye / Beginning and the end / Holding your breath
CD GEPCD 1002
Giant Electric Pea / Dec '93 / Pinnacle

SOMERSAULT
Live this lie / Batstein / Speechless / Losing my fear / Tomorrow always arrives / Falling away / Hear us
CD DMJAD 001
Dorian / Apr '97 / Pinnacle

Jaffa, Max

MUSIC FOR A GRAND HOTEL (Jaffa, Max Orchestra)
Roses from the South / Gypsy carnival / Great waltz / Canto amoroso / Fascination / Scarborough Fair / Some day I'll find you / Dobra dobra / Gentle maiden / I dream of Jeannie with the light brown hair / Memories of Richard Tauber / Adoration / Annen polka / Victor Herbert medley / Ave Maria
CD VALD 8057
Valentine / Feb '86 / Conifer/BMG

Jaffe, Andy

MANHATTAN PROJECTIONS (Jaffe, Andy Sextet)
CD STCD 549
Stash / '92 / ADA / Cadillac / CM / Direct / Jazz Music

Jag Panzer

DISSIDENT AGGRESSOR
CD 62292CD
SPV / Nov '94 / Koch / Plastic Head

Jagger, Chris

ATCHA
CD NEXCD 258
Sequel / Mar '94 / BMG

Jagger, Mick

PRIMITIVE COOL
Throwaway / Let's work / Radio control / Say you will / Primitive cool / Kowtow / Shoot off your mouth / Peace for the wicked / Party doll / War baby
CD 7567825542
East West / Sep '87 / Warner Music

SHE'S THE BOSS
Lonely at the top / Half a loaf / Running out of luck / Turn the girl loose / Hard woman / Just another night / Lucky in love / Secrets / She's the boss
CD 7567825532
East West / Apr '92 / Warner Music

WANDERING SPIRIT
Wired all night / Sweet thing / Out of focus / Don't tear me up / Put me in the trash / Use me / Evening gown / Mother of man / Think / Wandering spirit / Hang on to me tonight / I've been lonely for so long / Angel in my heart / Handsome Molly
CD 7567824362
East West / Feb '93 / Warner Music

Jagoda, Flory

GRANDMOTHER SINGS, THE (Jagoda, Flory & Family)
CD GV 155CD
Global Village / Nov '93 / ADA / Direct

Jagwarr, Don

FADED
Intro / Bad boy / What set U from / Whose is it / Steppin' / Who do you fear / My law / Skank wit' U / Cure / RESPECT / Roll 'em up / She loves me not / Rewind (live) (Outro)
CD CDPTY 112
Priority/Virgin / Dec '94 / EMI

Jah Lion

COLOMBIA COLLY
Wisdom / Dread ina Jamdong / Hay fever / Flashing whip / Colombia colly / Fat man / Bad luck Natty / Black lion / Little Sally Dater / Sata / Soldier and police war
CD RRCD 47
Reggae Refreshers / Jul '94 / PolyGram / Vital

Jah Messengers

REGGAE TIME
CD HBCD 115
Heartbeat / May '93 / ADA / Direct / Greensleeves / Jet Star

Jah Red

MR. BOGLE
CD JR 220561
Deleeuwauc / Mar '93 / Jet Star

Jah Screw

JAH SCREW PRESENTS DANCEHALL GLAMITY (Various Artists)
CD RASCD 3117
Ras / Sep '93 / Direct / Greensleeves / Jet Star / SRD

Jah Shaka

AT ARIWA SOUNDS (Jah Shaka & Mad Professor)
CD ARICD 20
Ariwa/Shaka / Sep '94 / SRD

COMMANDMENTS OF DUB VOL.1
CD SHAKACD 824
Jah Shaka / Sep '90 / Jet Star / SRD

COMMANDMENTS OF DUB VOL.9
CD SHAKACD 872
Jah Shaka / Sep '90 / Jet Star / SRD

DISCIPLES, THE
CD SHAKACD 871
Jah Shaka / Sep '90 / Jet Star / SRD

DUB SALUTE VOL.1
CD SHAKACD 940
Ariwa Sounds / Jul '94 / Jet Star / SRD

DUB SALUTE VOL.2
CD SHAKACD 941
Ariwa Sounds / Jul '94 / Jet Star / SRD

DUB SALUTE VOL.3
CD SHAKACD 942
Ariwa Sounds / Jul '94 / Jet Star / SRD

DUB SALUTE VOL.4
CD SHAKACD 953
Jah Shaka / Jul '95 / Jet Star / SRD

DUB SALUTE VOL.5
CD SHAKACD 954
Jah Shaka / Apr '96 / Jet Star / SRD

FARI SHIP DUB (Jah Shaka & Max Romeo)
CD SHAKACD 989
Jah Shaka / Nov '92 / Jet Star / SRD

JAH CHILDREN GATHER ROUND (Jah Shaka & Prince Allah)
CD SHAKACD 952
Jah Shaka / Dec '95 / Jet Star / SRD

JAH SHAKA & THE FASIMBAS IN THE GHETTO
CD SHAKACD 935
Jah Shaka / Dec '93 / Jet Star / SRD

JAH SHAKA MEETS HORACE ANDY
CD SHAKA CD947
Jah Shaka / Jul '93 / Jet Star / SRD

MESSAGE FROM AFRICA (Jah Shaka All Stars)
CD SHAKACD 848
Jah Shaka / Sep '90 / Jet Star / SRD

NEW DECADE OF DUB (Jah Shaka & Mad Professor)
CD ARICD 116
Ariwa Sounds / Apr '96 / Jet Star / SRD

NEW TESTAMENT OF DUB VOL.2
CD SHAKACD 936
Jah Shaka / Dec '93 / Jet Star / SRD

OUR RIGHTS (Jah Shaka & Max Romeo)
CD SHAKACD 951
Jah Shaka / Mar '95 / Jet Star / SRD

Jah Stitch

LOVE AND HARMONY
CD RNCD 2058
Rhino / May '94 / Grapevine/PolyGram / Jet Star

ORIGINAL RAGGAMUFFIN 1975-1977
Give Jah the glory / African people (3 in 1) / Raggamuffin style / Watch your step youthman / No dread can't dead / Sinners repent your soul / Judgement / Militant man / Real born African / Cool down youthman / African queen / King of the arena
CD BAFCD 10
Blood & Fire / Apr '96 / Vital

Jah Thomas

INA DANCEHALL STYLE (2CD Set) (Jah Thomas & Barrington Levy)
Praise God: *Jah Thomas* / Dance pon the corner / Dance with me: *Jah Thomas* / Shine eye gal / Happy birthday to you: *Jah Thomas* / Natty dread the traveller / New dress style: *Jah Thomas* / King of Kings / Advice from the doctor: *Jah Thomas* / Natty dread a de general / You no hear: *Jah Thomas* / Keep on dancing: *Jah Thomas* / Living in Jamaica: *Jah Thomas* / She nuh ready: *Jah Thomas* / Cricket lovely cricket: *Jah Thomas* / Best dress: *Jah Thomas & Errol Holt* / Mister Walker: *Jah Thomas* / Nuff boy a imitate: *Jah Thomas*
CD Set MRCD 4
Midnight Rock / Aug '97 / Grapevine/ PolyGram / Jet Star

JAH THOMAS MEETS KING TUBBY IN THE HOUSE OF DUB
CD _______ MRCD 1002
Majestic Reggae / Aug '96 / Direct

JAH THOMAS MEETS SCIENTIST IN DUB CONFERENCE
CD _______ MRCD 1001
Majestic Reggae / Aug '96 / Direct

LYRICS FOR SALE
CD _______ RNCD 2071
Rhino / Jul '94 / Grapevine/PolyGram / Jet Star

Jah Warrior

AFRICAN TRIBES DUB
CD _______ JWCD 005
Jah Warrior / Jun '97 / Jet Star / SRD

ONE OF THESE DAYS (Jah Warrior & Naph-Tali)
Humane beings / Humane dub / What about the story / What about the dub / One of these days / One of these dubs / Visionary dream / Visionary dub / Pollution / Pollution dub / Ini culture / Culture dub / 22nd book / 22nd dub / Visionary dub / Culture dub
CD _______ JWCD 008
Jah Warrior / May '97 / Jet Star / SRD

Jah Wobble

CELTIC POETS, THE (Jah Wobble's Invaders Of The Heart)
Dunes / Man I knew / Market rasen / Thames / Gone in the wind / Saturn / Bagpipe music / Third heaven / Star of the east / London rain
CD _______ 30HZCD 001
30 Hertz / Jun '97 / Vital

HEAVEN AND EARTH
Heaven and earth / Love song / Dying over Europe / Divine Mother / Gone to Croatan / Hit me / Om namah shiva / All life is sacred (part 1) / All life is sacred (part 2)
CD _______ CID 8044
Island / Nov '95 / PolyGram

INSPIRATION OF WILLIAM BLAKE
Songs of innocence / Lonely London / Bananas / Tyger tyger / Holy Thursday / Breathing out the world / Swallow in the world / Kings of Asia / Swallow in the world (reprise) / Bob and Harry / Angel / Gateway / Auguries of innocence
CD _______ ASCD 029
All Saints / Sep '96 / Discovery / Vital

PSALMS
CD _______ 185222
Southern / Jul '94 / SRD

REQUIEM
Requiem I / Requiem II / Requiem III / Father / Mother
CD _______ 30HZCD 002
30 Hertz / Jul '97 / Vital

RISING ABOVE BEDLAM (Jah Wobble's Invaders Of The Heart)
Visions of you / Relight the flame / Bomba / Ungodly kingdom / Rising above bedlam / Erzulie / Everyman's an island / Soledad / Sweet divinity / Wonderful world
CD _______ 9031754702
East West / Sep '91 / Warner Music

TAKE ME TO GOD (Jah Wobble's Invaders Of The Heart)
God in the beginning / Becoming more like God / Whisky priests / I'm an Algerian / Amor / Amor dub / Take me to God / Sun does rise / When the storm comes / I love everybody / Yoga of the nightclub / I am the music / Bonds of love / Angels / No chance is sexy / Raga / Forever
CD _______ CID 8017
Island / May '94 / PolyGram

WITHOUT JUDGEMENT (Jah Wobble's Invaders Of The Heart)
CD _______ KKUK 001CD
KK / '90 / Plastic Head

Jah Woosh

AT LEGGO SOUND
CD _______ OMCD 31
Original Music / Jan '96 / Jet Star / SRD

BEST OF JAH WOOSH, THE
CD _______ RNCD 2005
Rhino / May '93 / Grapevine/PolyGram / Jet Star

CHALICE BLAZE
CD _______ OMCD 033
Original Music / Jun '96 / Jet Star / SRD

DUB PLATE SPECIAL
CD _______ OMCD 024
Original Music / Jan '93 / Jet Star / SRD

MARIJUANA WORLD TOUR
CD _______ OMCD 17
Original Music / Dec '93 / Jet Star / SRD

WE CHAT YOU ROC (Jah Woosh & I Roy)
CD _______ CDTRL 296
Trojan / Jul '91 / Direct / Jet Star

Jahson, David

NATTY CHASE
CD _______ CC 2717
Crocodisc / Apr '95 / Grapevine/PolyGram

Jaildog

PUNKROCK, HIPHOP AND OTHER OBSCURE STUFF
CD _______ N 02512
Noise / Jul '95 / Koch

Jairo

ARGENTINA MIA...
CD _______ 3019502
Last Call / Feb '97 / Cargo / Direct / Discovery

Jakko

ARE MY EARS ON WRONG
Drowning not waving / Are my ears on wrong / Judy get down / I can't stand this pressure / Camera in your eyes / Cover up / Grown man immersed in tin tin / Shout / Sighing for the moon / Happy in the homelands / Tell her / When the taps run dry / Dangerous dreams
CD _______ RES 110CD
Resurgence / Apr '97 / Pinnacle

KINGDOM OF DUST
Hands of Che Guevara / Drowning in my sleep / It's only the moon / Judas kiss
CD _______ RES 101CD
Resurgence / Apr '97 / Pinnacle

MUSTARD GAS AND ROSES
Just another day / Little town / Devil's dictionary / Damn this town / Borders we traded / Perfect kiss / Saddleworth moor / Learning to cry / Handful of pearls / Then and now / Mustard gas and roses / We'll change the world
CD _______ RES 103CD
Resurgence / Apr '97 / Pinnacle

ROAD TO BALLINA
CD _______ RES 127CD
Resurgence / Jun '97 / Pinnacle

Jalal

FRUITS OF RAP
CD _______ EFA 187052
On The One / Feb '97 / New Note/ Pinnacle / SRD

MANKIND
CD _______ EFACD 0748
On-U Sound / Sep '93 / Jet Star / SRD

ON THE ONE
CD _______ EFA 187032
On The One / Mar '96 / New Note/ Pinnacle / SRD

Jale

SO WOUND
CD _______ SPCD 350
Sub Pop / Jun '96 / Cargo / Greyhound / Shellshock/Disc

Jam

ALL MOD CONS
All mod cons / To be someone / Mr. Clean / David Watts / English rose / In the crowd / Billy Hunt / It's too bad / Fly / Place I love / Bomb in Wardour Street / Down in the tube station at midnight
CD _______ 5374192
Polydor / Jul '97 / PolyGram

BEAT SURRENDER
Beat surrender / Town called Malice / Pretty green / That's entertainment / Gift / Carnaby Street / Batman / In the city / All mod cons / Modern world / When you're young / Funeral pyre / Private hell / In the midnight hour
CD _______ 5500062
Spectrum / May '93 / PolyGram

DIG THE NEW BREED
In the city / All mod cons / To be someone / It's too bad / Start / Big bird / Set the house ablaze / Ghosts / Standards / In the crowd / Going underground / Dreams of children / That's entertainment / Private hell
CD _______ 8100412
Polydor / Jun '90 / PolyGram

DIRECTION, REACTION, CREATION (5CD Set)
In the city / Takin' my love / Art school / I've changed my address / Slow down / I got by in time / Away from the numbers / Batman theme / Sounds from the street / Non stop dancing / Time for truth / Bricks and mortar / All around the world / Carnaby Street / Modern world / London traffic / Standards / Life from a window / Combine / Don't tell them you're sane / In the street today / London girl / I need you (for someone) / Here comes the weekend / Tonight at noon / In the midnight hour / News of the world / Aunties and Uncles (impulsive youths) / Innocent man / David Watts / A bomb in Wardour Street / Down in the tube station at midnight / So sad about us / Night / All mod cons / To be someone (didn't we have a nice time) / Mr. Clean / English rose / In the crowd / Billy Hunt / It's too bad / Fly / Place I love / Strange town / Butterfly collector / When you're young / Smithers Jones / Eton rifles / See saw / Girl on the phone / Thick as thieves / Private hell / Little boy soldiers / Wasteland / Burning sky / Smithers Jones / Saturday's kids / Heat wave / Going underground / Dreams of children / Start / Liza Radley / Pretty green / Monday / But I'm different now / Set the house ablaze / That's entertainment / Dream time / Man in the corner shop / Music for the last couple / Boy about town / Scrape away / Funeral pyre / Disguises / Absolute beginners / Tales from the riverbank / Town called Malice / Precious / Happy together / Ghosts / Just who is the 5 o'clock hero / Trans-global express / Running on the spot / Circus / Planner's dream goes wrong / Carnation / Gift / Great depression / Bitterest pill / Pity poor Alfie/Fever / Beat surrender / Shopping / Move on up / Stoned out of my mind / War / In the city / Time for truth / Sounds from the street / So sad about us / Worlds apart / Billy Hunt / It's too bad / To be someone / David Watts / Best of both worlds / That's entertainment / Rain / Dream time / Dead End Street / Stand by me / Every little bit hurts / Tales from the riverbank / Walking in Heaven's sunshine / Precious / Pity poor Alfie / Bitterest pill / Solid bond in your heart
CD Set _______ 5371432
Polydor / May '97 / PolyGram

EXTRAS
Dreams of the children / Tales from the riverbank / Liza radley / Move on up / Shopping / Smithers Jones / Pop art poem / Boy about town / Solid bond in your heart / No one in the world / And your bird can sing / Burning sky / Thick as thieves / Disguises
CD _______ 5131772
Polydor / Apr '92 / PolyGram

GIFT, THE
Happy together / Ghosts / Precious / Just who is the five o'clock hero / Trans-Global express / Running on the spot / Circus / Planner's dream goes wrong / Carnation / Town called Malice / Gift
CD _______ 5374222
Polydor / Jul '97 / PolyGram

GREATEST HITS
In the city / All around the world / News of the world / Modern world / David Watts / Down in the tube station at midnight / Strange town / When you're young / Eton rifles / Going underground / Start / That's entertainment / Funeral pyre / Absolute beginners / Town called malice / Precious / Just who is the five o'clock hero / Bitterest pill (I ever had to swallow) / Beat surrender
CD _______ 8495542
Polydor / Jul '91 / PolyGram

IN THE CITY
Art school / I've changed my address / Slow down / I got by in time / Away from the numbers / Batman / In the city / Sounds from the street / Non-stop dancing / Time for truth / Takin' my love / Bricks and mortar
CD _______ 5374172
Polydor / Jul '97 / PolyGram

IN THE CITY/THIS IS THE MODERN WORLD
Art school / I've changed my address / Slow down / I got by in time / Sway from the numbers / Batman / In the city / Sounds from the street / Non-stop dancing (Non stop) / Time for truth / Takin' my love / Bricks and mortar / Modern world / London traffic / Standards / Life from a window / Combine / Don't tell them you're sane / In the street today / London girl / I need you for someone / Here comes the weekend / Tonight at noon / In the midnight hour
CD _______ 8477302
Polydor / Jan '91 / PolyGram

JAM COLLECTION, THE (2CD Set)
Away from the numbers / I got by in time / I need you (for someone) / To be someone (didn't we have a nice time) / Mr. Clean / English rose / In the crowd / It's too bad / Butterfly collector / Thick as thieves / Private hell / Wasteland / Burning sky / Saturday's kids / Liza Radley / Pretty green / Monday / Man in the corner shop / Boy about town / Tales of the river bank / Ghost / Just who is the five o'clock hero / Carnation / Great depression / Shopping
CD Set _______ 5314932
Polydor / Jul '96 / PolyGram

LIVE JAM
Modern world / Billy Hunt / Thick as thieves / Burning sky / Mr. Clean / Smithers Jones / Little boy soldiers / Eton rifles / Away from the numbers / Down in the tube station at midnight / Strange town / When you're young / Bomb in Wardour Street / Pretty green / Boy about town / Man in the corner shop / David Watts / Funeral pyre / Move on up / Carnation / Butterfly collector / Precious / Town called malice / Heatwave
CD _______ 5196672
Polydor / Oct '93 / PolyGram

SETTING SONS
Burning sky / Eton rifles / Girl on the phone / Heatwave / Little boy soldiers / Private hell / Saturday's kids / Smithers Jones / Thick as thieves / Wasteland
CD _______ 5374202
Polydor / Jul '97 / PolyGram

SNAP
In the city / Away from the numbers / All around the world / Modern world / News of the world / Billy Hunt / English rose / Mr. Clean / David Watts / Bomb in Wardour Street / Down in the tube station at midnight / Strange town / Butterfly collector / When you're young / Smithers Jones / Thick as thieves / Eton rifles / Going underground / Dreams of children / That's entertainment / Start / Man in the corner shop / Funeral pyre / Absolute beginners / Tales from the riverbank / Town called Malice / Precious / Bitterest pill (I ever had to swallow) / Beat surrender
CD _______ 8217122
Polydor / Jul '97 / PolyGram

SOUND AFFECTS
Pretty green / Monday / But I'm different now / Set the house ablaze / Start / That's entertainment / Dreamtime / Man in the corner shop / Music for the last couple / Boy about town / Scrape away
CD _______ 5374212
Polydor / Jul '97 / PolyGram

THIS IS THE MODERN WORLD
Modern world / London traffic / Standards / Life from a window / Combine / Don't tell them you're sane / In the street today / London express / I need you for someone / Here comes the weekend / Tonight at noon / In the midnight hour
CD _______ 5374182
Polydor / Jul '97 / PolyGram

Jam & Spoon

KALEIDOSCOPE SKIES
Garden of eden / Kaleidoscope skies / Guiding light / Warm dead dog / Flame / You got to get in to get out / Kiss away / Usual suspect / El baile / So called techno track / Suspicious minds / Mark runs the voodoo down / Don't call it love / I pull my gun once / I pull my gun twice
CD _______ 4872622
Dance Pool / Jul '97 / Sony

TRIPOMATIC FAIRYTALES 2001
Heart of Africa / Odyssey to Anyoona / Two spys in the house of love / Stella / Neurotrance adventure / Operating spaceship Earth / Zen flash zen bones / Who opened the door to nowhere / Right in the night / Muffeled drums / Path of harmony / Paradise garage / Earth spirit / Stellas cry
CD _______ 4749282
Epic / Feb '94 / Sony

TRIPOMATIC FAIRYTALES 2002
Hermaphrodite / NASA Nocturnal Audio Sensory Awakening / LSD Nikon / Future is in small hands / Salinas afternoon / V Angel is calling / Words and Dana / Ancient dream / I saw the future / Castaneda future illuminations / Secret kind of love / World of X-T-C
CD _______ 4749182
Epic / Feb '94 / Sony

Jam Band

ROADRUNNER
CD _______ JBCD 0102
Boyson Inc. / May '97 / Jet Star

Jam Nation

WAY DOWN BELOW BUFFALO HELL
First time / Sleeping / Awakening / Sunstroke / She moved through the fair / Mekong / Meeting of the people / Harmonix / 454 / Pre-pubescent grand prix / La visite est terminee / Prehistoric (Bone us)
CD _______ CDRW 36
Realworld / Aug '93 / EMI

Jamaaladen, Tacuma

JUKEBOX
Metamorphosis / Rhythm of your mind / In the mood for mood / Naima / Time a place / Jam-all / Jukebox / Zam Zam was such a wonderful... / Solar system blues
CD _______ 1888032
Gramavision / Dec '88 / Vital/SAM

Jamaican Maroon Music

DRUMS OF DEFIANCE
CD _______ SFCD 40412
Sackville / Mar '93 / Cadillac / Jazz Music / Swift

Jamaicans

BABA BOOM TIME
CD _______ JMC 200231
Jamaican Gold / Oct '96 / Grapevine/ PolyGram / Jet Star

Jamal, Ahmad

AT THE PERISHING/BUT NOT FOR ME
But not for me / Surrey with the fringe on top / Moonlight in Vermont / (Put another nickel in) Music music music / No greater love / Poinciana / Woody 'n you / What's new
CD _______ MCD 0918

Chess/MCA / Apr '97 / BMG / New Note/ BMG

AWAKENING, THE
Awakening / I love music / Patterns / Dolphin dance / You're my everything / Stolen moments / Wave
CD _____ IMP 12262
Impulse Jazz / Apr '97 / New Note/BMG

BIG BYRD (The Essence Vol.2)
CD _____ 5334772
Verve / Oct '96 / PolyGram

CHICAGO REVISITED - LIVE AT JOE SEGAL'S JAZZ SHOWCASE
CD _____ CD 83327
Telarc / Feb '93 / Conifer/BMG

CRYSTAL
CD _____ 7567817932
Atlantic / Jul '93 / Warner Music

DIGITAL WORKS
Poinciana / But not for me / Midnight sun / Footprints / Once upon a time / One / La Costa / Misty / MASH (Suicide is painless) / Biencavo / Time for love / Wave
CD _____ 7567812582
Atlantic / Jun '93 / Warner Music

I REMEMBER DUKE, HOAGY & STRAYHORN
My flower / I got it bad and that ain't good / In a sentimental mood / Ruby / Don't you know I care (or don't you care to) / Prelude to a kiss / Do nothin' 'til you hear from me / Chelsea bridge / I remember Hoagy / Skylark / Never let me go / Goodbye
CD _____ CD 83339
Telarc / Mar '95 / Conifer/BMG

LIVE AT THE PERSHING & THE SPOTLIGHT CLUB
CD _____ JHR 73522
Jazz Hour / Sep '93 / Cadillac / Jazz Music / Target/BMG

LIVE IN PARIS 1992
Tube / Alone together / Laura / Wild is the wind / Caravan / Easy living / Acorn / Dreamy / Appreciation / Look for the silver lining / Aftermath
CD _____ 8494082
Birdology / Jan '93 / PolyGram

MONTREAL JAZZ FESTIVAL
CD _____ 7567816992
Atlantic / Jun '93 / Warner Music

MY FUNNY VALENTINE
CD _____ ATJCD 5955
All That's Jazz / '92 / Jazz Music / THE

NIGHT SONG
When you wish upon a star / Deja vu / Need to smile / Bad times / Touch me in the morning / Night song / MASH (Suicide is painless) / Something's missing in my life
CD _____ 5303032
Verve / Apr '94 / PolyGram

ROSSITER ROAD
CD _____ 7567816452
Atlantic / Jun '93 / Warner Music

Jamal, Khan

THINKING OF YOU
CD _____ STCD 4138
Storyville / Feb '89 / Cadillac / Jazz Music / Wellard

James

GOLD MOTHER
Come home / Government walls / God only knows / How much suffering / Crescento / How was it for you / Hang one / Walking the ghost / Gold mother / Top of the world / Lose control / Sit down
CD _____ 8487312
Fontana / Apr '91 / PolyGram

LAID
Out to get you / Sometimes / Dream thrum / One of the three / Say something / Five-O / PS / Everybody knows / Knuckle too far / Low low low / Laid / Lullaby / Skindiving
CD _____ 5149432
Fontana / Apr '94 / PolyGram

ONE MAN TALKING
CD _____ CBAK 4049
Baktabak / Jun '91 / Arabesque

SEVEN
Born of frustration / Ring the bells / Sound / Bring a gun / Mother / Don't wait that long / Live a love of life / Next lover / Heavens / Protect me / Seven
CD _____ 5109322
Fontana / Feb '92 / PolyGram

STRIP MINE
What for / Charlie dance / Fairground / Are you ready / Medieval / Not there / Ya ho / Riders / Vulture / Strip mining
CD _____ 9256572
Sire / Feb '95 / Warner Music

STUTTER
Skullduggery / Scarecrow / So many ways / Just hipper / John Yen / Summer songs / Really hard / Billy's shirts / Why so close / Withdrawn / Black hole
CD _____ 7599254372
Sire / Jul '91 / Warner Music

WHIPLASH
Tomorrow / Lost a friend / Waltzing along / She's a star / Greenpeace / Go to the bank / Play dead / Avalanche / Homeboy / Watering hole / Blue pastures
CD _____ 5343542
Fontana / Feb '97 / PolyGram

James Bong

C'EST TRES BONG
CD _____ TKCD 24
2 Kool / Sep '96 / Pinnacle / SRD

James, Bob

12
No pay no play / Courtship / Moonbop / I need more of you / Ruby Ruby Ruby / Midnight / Legacy
CD _____ ESMCD 466
Essential / Jan '97 / BMG

ALL AROUND THE TOWN LIVE
Touchdown / Stompin' / At the Savoy / Angela / We're all alone / Farandole / Westchester lady / Golden apple / Kari
CD _____ ESMCD 449
Essential / Nov '96 / BMG

BEST OF BOB JAMES, THE
CD _____ CCSCD 807
Renaissance Collector Series / Apr '96 / BMG

BJ4
Pure imagination / Where the wind blows free / Tappan zee / Nights are forever without you / Treasure Island / El verano
CD _____ ESMCD 429
Essential / Aug '96 / BMG

COOL (James, Bob & Earl Klugh)
Movin' on / As it happens / So much in common / Fugitive life / Night that love came back / Secret wishes / New York samba / Handara / Sponge / Terpsichore / San Diego stomp / Miniature
CD _____ 7599269392
WEA / Sep '92 / Warner Music

DOUBLE VISION (James, Bob & David Sanborn)
Maputo / More than friends / Moontune / Since I fell for you / It's you / Never enough / You don't know me
CD _____ 9253932
WEA / Jun '86 / Warner Music

FOXIE
Ludwig / Fireball / Zebra man / Miranda / Marco Polo / Calaban
CD _____ ESMCD 464
Essential / Jan '97 / BMG

GENIE...THEMES AND VARIATIONS FROM THE TV SERIES 'TAXI', THE
Brookly heights boogie / Genie / Last chance / Ballade / Groove for Julie / Hello Nardo / Marilu / New York mellow / Night moods / Angela
CD _____ ESMCD 465
Essential / Jan '97 / BMG

GRAND PIANO CANYON
Bare bones / Restoration / Wings for Sarah / Svengali / Worlds apart / Stop that / Xraxse / Just listen / Far from turtle
CD _____ 7599262562
WEA / Sep '90 / Warner Music

H
Snowbird fantasy / Shepherds song / Brighton by the sea / Walkman / Thoroughbred / Reunited
CD _____ ESMCD 447
Essential / Nov '96 / BMG

HANDS DOWN
Spunky / Macumba / Shamboozie / Janus / Roberta / It's only me
CD _____ ESMCD 463
Essential / Jan '97 / BMG

HEADS
Heads / We're alla lone / I'm in you / Night crawler / You are so beautiful / One loving night
CD _____ ESMCD 430
Essential / Aug '96 / BMG

LUCKY SEVEN
Rush hour / Blue lick / Look alike / Big stone city / Friends / Fly away
CD _____ ESMCD 446
Essential / Nov '96 / BMG

ONE
Valley of the shadows / In the garden / Soulero / Night on bald mountain / Feel like makin' love / Nautilus
CD _____ ESMCD 426
Essential / Aug '96 / BMG

ONE ON ONE (James, Bob & Earl Klugh)
Kari / After glow / Love lips / Mallorca / I'll never see you smile again / Winding river
CD _____ ESMCD 448
Essential / Nov '96 / BMG

RESTLESS
Lotus leaves / Under me / Restless / Kissing cross / Storm warning / Animal dreams / Back to Bali / Into the light / Serenissima / Awaken us to the blue
CD _____ 9362455362
Warner Bros. / Mar '94 / Warner Music

SIGN OF THE TIMES
Hypnotique / Steamin' feelin' / Enchanted forest / Unicorn / Sign of the times / Love power
CD _____ ESMCD 450
Essential / Nov '96 / BMG

SWAN, THE
Swan / La delaissado / Prospero / Water music / Ensenada madness / Quietly crazy for you
CD _____ ESMCD 467
Essential / Jan '97 / BMG

THREE
One mint julep / Women of Ireland / Westchester lady / Storm king / Jamaica farewell
CD _____ ESMCD 428
Essential / Aug '96 / BMG

TOUCHDOWN
Angela / Touchdown / I want to thank you (very much) / Sun runner / Caribbean nights
CD _____ ESMCD 431
Essential / Aug '96 / BMG

TWO
Take me to the Mardis Gras / I feel a song / Golden apple / Farandole / You're as right as rain / Dream journey
CD _____ ESMCD 427
Essential / Aug '96 / BMG

James, Boney

BACKBONE
CD _____ 9362456112
Warner Bros. / Feb '95 / Warner Music

James, Brian

BRIAN JAMES
CD _____ 422181
New Rose / May '94 / ADA / Direct / Discovery

James, Carla

SACRIFICE
Sacrifice / Round and round / Love will see us through / My very first lover / Virginia's secret / Something sacred / Oh mother / Things that we all do for love / No one else will do / So what's going on / Actions speak louder
CD _____ 5403782
A&M / Jul '95 / PolyGram

James, Colin

COLIN JAMES
Five long years / Voodoo thing / Down in the bottom / Chicks 'n' cars / Why'd you lie / Hidden charms / Bad girl / Dream of satin / Three sheets to the wind / Lone wolf
CD _____ CDV 2542
Virgin / Jul '93 / EMI

COLIN JAMES AND THE LITTLE BIG BAND
Cadillac baby / That's what you do to me / Sit right here / Three hours past midnight / Satellite / Surely (I love you) / Breakin' up the house / No more doggin' / Evening / Train kept a rollin' / Leading me on / Boogie twist (Part 2) / Cha shooky doo
CD _____ VPBCD 18
Pointblank / Jan '94 / EMI

SUDDEN STOP
CD _____ CDVUS 20
Virgin / Oct '90 / EMI

James, Danny

BOOGIE IN THE MUD - SOUTHERN SWAMP GUITAR
Boogie in the mud / Your gravy train came to a screeching halt / Please Mr. Sandman / Devil made me say that / That's right / No yo / Paper in my shoe / Soul & wine / Sick & tired / Lonely feeling / Intrusion / Switchit / Another day / Dark was the night / Tequila / Blue strain / Blue clouds / Crazy cat / Linda Lu / Baby you been to school / Lollypoluza / Appelousa / Peek-a-bou Lou / My river / Corpus Christi / Frosty / High camp
CD _____ CDCHD 626
Ace / Nov '96 / Pinnacle

Ellen James Society

RELUCTANTLY WE
CD _____ DR 01CD
Daemon / Sep '90 / Direct

James, Elmore

BEST OF THE EARLY YEARS, THE
Dust my broom / I held my baby last night / Baby, what's wrong / I believe / Sinful woman / Early in the morning / Hawaiian boogie / Can't stop lovin' / Make a little love / Strange kinda feeling / Please find my baby / Hand in hand / Make my dreams come true / Sho 'nuff I do / Dark and dreary / Rock my baby right / Sunnyland / Standing at the crossroads / Late hours at midnight / Way you treat me / Happy home / No love in my heart (For you) / Dust my blues / I was a fool / Blues before sunrise / Goodbye baby / Wild about you / Long tall woman
CD _____ CDCHD 583
Ace / Jun '95 / Pinnacle

CLASSIC EARLY RECORDINGS, THE (1951-1956/3CD Set)
Dust my broom / Please find my baby / Hawaiian boogie (take 1) / Hand in hand / Long tall woman / Rock my baby right / One more drink / My baby's gone / Lost woman blues / I believe / I held my baby last night / Baby what's wrong / Sinful woman / Round house boogie / Dumb woman blues / Saxony boogie / Kicking the blues around / I may be wrong, but I think you're wonderful / Sweet little woman / Early in the morning / Can't stop lovin' / Hawaiian boogie / Make a little love / My best friend / Make my dreams come true / Strange kinda feeling / Dark and dreary / Quarter past nine / Where can my baby be / Please come back to me (sho'nuff I do) / Session talk and sho'nuff I do / Sho'nuff I do (alternate take) / Sho'nuff I do / 1839 blues / I got a strange baby / Canton Mississippi breakdown / Standing at the crossroads / Late hours at midnight / Happy home / Sunnyland / Way you treat me / No love in my heart / Dust my blues / I was a fool / Blues before sunrise / Goodbye (baby) / So mean to me / Wild about you baby / Wild about you / Elmo's shuffle
CD Set _____ ABOXCD 4
Ace / Oct '93 / Pinnacle

COME GO WITH ME
Baby, please set a date / So unkind / Sunnyland train / Twelve year old boy / My kind of woman / Hand in hand / My baby's gone / Make my dreams come true / Anna Lee / Bobby's rock / Find my kinda woman / Stranger blues / Mean mistreatin' mama / I can't stop loving you / She moved / I'm worried / She done moved / My bleeding heart / Look on yonder wall / Early one morning / Strange angels / It hurts me too / Every day I have the blues / I have a right to love my baby / Standing at the crossroads
CD _____ CPCD 8205
Charly / Feb '97 / Koch

CROSSROADS
Dust my broom / Look on yonder wall / Mean mistreating mama / Fine little mama / Got to move / Rollin' and tumblin' / Coming home / It hurts me too / Standing at the crossroads / Everyday I have the blues / I done somebody wrong / Pickin' the blues / Anna Lee / Sunnyland train / One way out / Sky is crying
CD _____ 304012
Hallmark / Jun '97 / Carlton

ELMORE JAMES
Mean mistreatin' Mama / Dust my broom / Standing at the crossroads / Sky is crying / Coming home / Hand in hand / Held my baby last night / I believe / Pickin' the blues / Done somebody wrong / It hurts me too / Fine little Mama / Rollin' and tumblin' / Look on yonder wall
CD _____ BN 023
Blue Nite / Feb '97 / Target/BMG

IMMORTAL ELMORE JAMES, THE (King Of The Bottleneck Blues)
Dust my broom / Everyday I have the blues / Sky is crying / I'm worried / Coming home / Stranger blues / Fine little mama / Make my dreams come true / Early one morning / It hurts me too / Mean mistreatin' mama / Shake your moneymaker / Can't stop loving my baby / My bleeding heart / Look on yonder wall / Hand in hand / (I) done somebody wrong / Rollin' and tumblin' / Standing at the crosswords / I can't stop lovin' you
CD _____ MCCD 083
Music Club / Apr '92 / Disc / THE

KING OF THE SLIDE GUITAR, THE (The Complete Chief & Fire Sessions/3CD Set)
CD Set _____ CPBOX 301
Charly / Apr '97 / Koch

LET'S CUT IT (The Very Best Of Elmore James)
Dust my blues / Blues before sunrise / No love in my heart / Sho' nuff I do / Standing at the crossroads / I was a fool / Sunnyland / Canton Mississippi breakdown / Happy home / Wild about you baby / Long tall woman / So mean to me / Hawaiian boogie / Mean and evil / Dark and dreary / My best friend / I believe / Goodbye baby
CD _____ CDCH 192
Ace / Nov '93 / Pinnacle

MASTER OF BLUES, THE (A Tribute To Elmore James) (Various Artists)
CD _____ P 250569
Icehouse / Nov '96 / Hot Shot

RAW BLUES POWER
Dust my broom / Look on yonder wall / It hurts me too / Coming home / Sky is crying / Standing in the crossroads / Hand in my hand / Rollin' and tumblin' / Mean mistreatin' Mama / I done somebody wrong / Pickin' the blues / I believe / My bleeding heart
CD _____ CWNCD 2033
Crown / Jun '97 / Henry Hadaway

SKY IS CRYING, THE (Charly Blues - Masterworks Volume 12)
Sky is crying / Bobby's rock / Held my baby last night / Dust my broom / Baby please set a date / Rollin' and tumblin' / I'm worried / (I) done somebody wrong / Fine little mama / I can't stop lovin' you / Early one

morning / I need you / Strange angels / She done moved / Something inside of me / Stranger blues
CD ____ CDBM 12
Charly / Apr '92 / Koch

STANDING AT THE CROSSROADS (Charly BLues - Masterworks Vol. 28)
Anna Lee / Stranger blues / My bleeding heart / Standing at the crossroads / One way out / Person to person / My kind of woman / So unkind / Got to move / Shake your moneymaker / Mean mistreatin' mama / Sunnyland train / My baby's gone / Find my kinda woman
CD ____ CDBM 28
Charly / Apr '92 / Koch

STREET TALKIN' (James, Elmore & Jimmy Reed)
CD ____ MCD 5087
Muse / Sep '92 / New Note/Pinnacle

James, Ethan

ANCIENT MUSIC OF CHRISTMAS
Bring a torch Jeanette Isabella / From church to church/A virgin most pure/When Christ was bor / This is the truth sent from above / What lovely infant can this be/The Christmas child / Alleluya Christo lubelimus Alleluya / Balo Lammy/Three King's songs / Quem pastores Lauduere/On Christmas night / Now to conclude our Christmas mirth / Seven joys of Mary / Lullay lullay als I lay on yoolis night / Jerusalem gaude/Jesu redemptor omnium / O come O come Emmanuel / Sing we Noel/Goodnight/Christmas bells / Now we make joy / Lulajze Jezuniu/Come shepherds arise / Blessed be that maid Marie/The fleecy care / Canzone di Zampoignari
CD ____ HNCD 1398
Hannibal / Oct '96 / ADA / Vital

WHAT ROUGH BEAST
CD ____ EFA 121112
Moll / Apr '95 / SRD

James, Etta

BLUES IN THE NIGHT (James, Etta & Eddie 'Cleanhead' Vinson)
Kidney stew / Railroad porter blues / Something's got a hold on me / Medley: at last / Trust in me / Sunday kind of love / I just want to make love to you / Please send me someone to love / Love man / Misty
CD ____ FCD 9647
Fantasy / Apr '94 / Jazz Music / Pinnacle / Wellard

COME A LITTLE CLOSER
Out on the street again / Mama told me / You give me what I want / Come a little closer / Let's burn down the cornfield / Powerplay / Feeling uneasy / St. Louis blues / Gonna have some fun tonight / Sookie sookie
CD ____ MCD 91509
Chess/MCA / Apr '97 / BMG / New Note/ BMG

DEEP IN THE NIGHT
Laying beside you / Piece of my heart / Only women bleed / Take it to the limit / Lovesick blues / Strange man / Sugar on the floor / Sweet touch of love / I'd rather go blind
CD ____ CDBB 9579
Bullseye Blues / Jun '96 / Direct

GENUINE ARTICLE, THE (The Best Of Etta James)
I just want to make love to you / Sunday kind of love / I just want to be loved / I'd rather go blind / Tell mama / Stormy weather / Do right woman, do right man / Security / Miss Pitiful / You got it / It's alright / I found a love / At last / All I could do was cry / Spoonful: *James, Etta & Harvey Fuqua* / Don't blame me / 842-3089 (Call my name) / These foolish things / If I can't have you: *James, Etta & Harvey Fuqua* / Something's got a hold on me / Tell it like it is / WOMAN / I never meant to love him / Lovin' arms / My dearest darling
CD ____ CHD 9361
Chess/MCA / Feb '96 / BMG / New Note/ BMG

GOSPEL SOUL OF ETTA JAMES
CD ____ KWEST 5403
Kenwest / Sep '93 / THE

HER BEST
CD ____ MCD 09367
Chess/MCA / Jul '97 / BMG / New Note/ BMG

LATE SHOW, THE (James, Etta & Eddie 'Cleanhead' Vinson)
Cleanhead blues / Old maid boogie / Home boy / Cherry red / Baby, what you want me to do / Sweet little angel / I'd rather go blind / Teach me tonight / Only women bleed / He's got the whole world in his hands
CD ____ FCD 96552
Fantasy / Apr '94 / Jazz Music / Pinnacle / Wellard

LIVE FROM SAN FRANCISCO
CD ____ 01005821252
Private Music / Feb '95 / BMG

LOVE'S BEEN ROUGH ON ME
Rock / Cry like a rainy day / Love's been rough on me / Love it or leave it alone / Don't touch me / Hold me / If I had any pride left at all / I can give you everything / I've been loving you too long / Done in the dark
CD ____ 01005821402
Private Music / Apr '97 / BMG

MULTI-CULTURAL CHILDREN'S SONGS
CD ____ SFWCD 45045
Smithsonian Folkways / Nov '95 / ADA / Cadillac / CM / Direct / Koch

MYSTERY LADY
Don't explain / You've changed / Man I love / I don't stand a ghost of a chance with you / Embraceable you / How deep is the ocean / (I'm afraid) The masquerade is over / Body and soul / Very thought of you / Lover man / I'll be seeing you
CD ____ 01005821142
Private Music / Apr '94 / BMG

R & B DYNAMITE
WOMAN / Number one / I'm a fool / Strange things happening / Hey Henry / I hope you're satisfied / Good rockin' daddy / Sunshine of love / That's all / How big a fool / Market place / Tough lover / Do something crazy / Be my lovey dovey / Nobody loves you (like me) / Hickory dickory dock / You know what I mean / Wallflower / Baby, baby, every night / We're in love / Tears of joy / Pick-up
CD ____ CDCH 210
Ace / Nov '93 / Pinnacle

RESPECT YOURSELF
CD ____ IMP 304
IMP / Apr '96 / ADA / Discovery

RIGHT TIME, THE
I sing the blues / Love and happiness / Evening of love / Wet match / You're taking up another man's place / Give it up / Let it rock / Ninety nine and a half (won't do) / You've got me / (Night time) Is the right time / Down home blues
CD ____ 7559613472
WEA / Dec '96 / Warner Music

SOMETHING'S GOT A HOLD
CD ____ CDRB 3
Charly / Apr '94 / Koch

SOULFUL MISS PEACHES
Tell Mama / I'd rather go blind / Security / I'm loving you more everyday / Mellow fellow / In the basement / Love of my man / Same rope / I'm gonna take what he's got / Just a little bit / Steal away / I'm waiting for Charlie to come home / You got it / Almost persuaded / I got you babe / Losers weepers / All the way down / Let's burn down the cornfield / Feelin' uneasy / Out on the street again
CD ____ CPCD 8017
Charly / Feb '94 / Koch

STICKIN' TO MY GUNS
Whatever gets you through the night / Love to burn / Blues don't care / Your good thing is about to end / Get funky / Beware / Out of the rain / Stolen affection / Fool in love / I've got dreams to remember
CD ____ IMCD 191
Island / Jul '94 / PolyGram

TELL MAMA
If I can't have you / Spoonful / Nobody but you / Next door to the blues / Something's got a hold on me / (You better) do right / I'm loving you more everyday / Breaking point / Mellow fellow / Steal away / Just a little bit / Don't lose your good thing / Watchdog / I'm gonna take what he's got / I'd rather go blind / Love of my man / It hurts me so much / Same rope / I got you babe / I worship the ground you walk on / You got it / Fire / Miss Pitiful
CD ____ CDRED 7
Charly / Oct '88 / Koch

THESE FOOLISH THINGS
Only time will tell / I want to be loved (but only by you) / Prisoner of love / How do you speak to an angel / These foolish things / You can't talk to a fool / Again / Tommorrow night / Don't take your love from me / Lover man (oh, where can he be) / Don't blame me / I won't cry anymore / Tell it like it is / Hold back the tears
CD ____ MCD 09354
Chess/MCA / Apr '97 / BMG / New Note/ BMG

James Gang

JAMES GANG RIDES AGAIN
CD ____ BGOCD 121
Beat Goes On / Sep '91 / Pinnacle

LIVE IN CONCERT
CD ____ BGOCD 120
Beat Goes On / Sep '91 / Pinnacle

THIRDS
CD ____ BGOCD 119
Beat Goes On / Sep '91 / Pinnacle

TRUE STORY OF THE JAMES GANG...PLUS, THE
Take a look around / Bluebird / Collage / Wrap city in English / Yadig / Woman / Ashes the rain and I / It's all the same / Things I could be / Live my life again / I'll tell you why / Run run run / Midnight man / My door is open / Everybody needs a hero / Up to yourself / Funk 49
CD ____ SEECD 367
See For Miles/C5 / Aug '97 / Pinnacle

YER ALBUM
Take a look around / Bluebird / Stone rap / I don't have the time / Fred / Funk / Lost woman / Collage / Wrapcity in English / Stop
CD ____ BGOCD 60
Beat Goes On / Oct '90 / Pinnacle

James, Harry

1944-THE D-DAY REMOTES (James, Harry Orchestra)
CD ____ JH 1023
Ronnie Scott's Jazz House / Feb '93 / Cadillac / Jazz Music / New Note/Pinnacle / TKO Magnum

1946-55 (James, Harry Orchestra)
CD ____ CD 53185
Giants Of Jazz / Jan '95 / Cadillac / Jazz Music / Target/BMG

1948 - BROADCASTS (James, Harry Orchestra)
CD ____ JH 1007
Jazz Hour / Oct '91 / Cadillac / Jazz Music / Target/BMG

1954-1966 (James, Harry Orchestra)
CD ____ CD 53191
Giants Of Jazz / Sep '94 / Cadillac / Jazz Music / Target/BMG

1964 LIVE IN THE HOLIDAY BALLROOM (James, Harry Orchestra)
Ciribiribin / Cubana chant / In a mellow tone / Sultry serenade / I'm getting sentimental over you / Koo koo / Flyin' home / Two o'clock jump / Drum solo by Buddy Rich / Malaguena Saleroso / Blues inside out / Sunday morning / He's gone now / Tuxedo junction / King Porter stomp / Big time / Rainbow kiss
CD ____ JH 1001
Jazz Hour / Apr '90 / Cadillac / Jazz Music / Target/BMG

ALL OR NOTHING AT ALL (James, Harry & Frank Sinatra)
Ciribiribin / My buddy / Avalon / All or nothing at all / Mean to me / Melancholy mood / I found a new baby / From the bottom of my heart / Sweet Georgia Brown / To you / I poured my heart into a song / Japanese sandman / Here comes the night / Undecided / On a little street in Singapore / Let's disappear / I'm forever blowing bubbles
CD ____ HCD 263
Hindsight / Nov '95 / Jazz Music / Target/ BMG

ALL TIME STANDARDS 1938-1954 (James, Harry Orchestra)
CD ____ 11082
Laserlight / '88 / Target/BMG

BANDSTAND MEMORIES (James, Harry Orchestra)
CD Set ____ HBCD 503
Hindsight / Nov '94 / Jazz Music / Target/ BMG

BEST OF HARRY JAMES
CD ____ DLCD 4002
Dixie Live / Mar '95 / TKO Magnum

CLASSICS 1937-1939
CD ____ CLASSICS 903
Classics / Nov '96 / Discovery / Jazz Music

CLASSICS 1939
CD ____ CLASSICS 936
Classics / Jun '97 / Discovery / Jazz Music

COMPLETE RECORDINGS 1939, THE (James, Harry & Frank Sinatra)
From the bottom of my heart / Melancholy mood / My Buddy / It's funny to everyone but me / Here comes the night / All or nothing at all / On a little street in Singapore / Who told you I cared / Ciribiribin (they're so in love) / Every day of my life / Stardust / Wishing will make it so / If I didn't care / Lamp is low / My love for you / Moon love / This is no dream
CD ____ CK 66377
Columbia / Feb '96 / Sony

DREAM DUO, THE (James, Harry & Betty Grable)
CD ____ VJB 19482
Vintage Jazz Band / Nov '96 / Cadillac / Hot Shot / Jazz Music / Wellard

GREAT HARRY JAMES, THE
How high the moon / Blue skies / Come rain or come shine / My old flame / What is this thing called love / I may be wrong (but I think you're wonderful) / Between the devil and the deep blue sea / All of me / Don't get around much anymore / I cover the waterfront / Man I love / If I had you
CD ____ HCD 334
Hindsight / Apr '96 / Jazz Music / Target/ BMG

HARRY JAMES
CD ____ 22711
Music / Nov '95 / Target/BMG

HARRY JAMES & HIS GREAT VOCALISTS
I'll get by / I don't want to walk without you / It's the dreamer in me / One dozen roses / My silent love / I had the craziest dream / I've heard that song before / I'm beginning to see the light / It's been a long, long time / I can't begin to tell you / Who's sorry now / This is always / As long as I'm dreaming / You can do no wrong / What am I gonna do about you / You'll never know
CD ____ CK 66371
Columbia / Jul '95 / Sony

HARRY JAMES & HIS MUSIC MAKERS 1942-1944
CD ____ VJB 1945
Vintage Jazz Band / May '96 / Cadillac / Hot Shot / Jazz Music / Wellard

HARRY JAMES 1943-1946
If that's the way you want it, baby / Indiana / Body and soul / I'm satisfied / I couldn't sleep a wink last night / Rose room / All of me / Shorty George / On the sunny side of the street / Between the devil and the deep blue sea / Stardust / It't been so long / My baby just cares for me / Girl of my dreams / You go to my head / Shady lady bird
CD ____ HCD 102
Hindsight / Jul '96 / Jazz Music / Target/ BMG

HAVE TRUMPET, WILL TRAVEL
CD ____ CECD 10
Collector's Edition / Mar '96 / TKO Magnum

JAZZ MASTERS
CD ____ 5299022
Verve / Jun '96 / PolyGram

JUMP SAUCE (James, Harry & His Music Makers)
CD ____ VNG 201
Viper's Nest / Jul '94 / ADA / Cadillac / Direct / Jazz Music

LIVE FROM CLEARWATER VOL.1
CD ____ DAWE 76
Magic / Jul '96 / Cadillac / Harmonia Mundi / Jazz Music / Swift / Wellard

LIVE FROM CLEARWATER VOL.2
CD ____ DAWE 77
Magic / Jul '96 / Cadillac / Harmonia Mundi / Jazz Music / Swift / Wellard

LIVE IN CONCERT (James, Harry & His Music Makers)
Opener / King size blues / Shiny stockings / Harry's delight / Two o'clock jump / Jumpin' at the woodside / One on the house / Rockin' in rhythm / Don't get around much anymore / Tweet tweet
CD ____ DBCD 03
Dance Band Days / Jul '89 / Prism

LIVE IN HI-FI AT CULVER CITY 1945 (James, Harry Orchestra)
CD ____ JH 3006
Jazz Hour / Mar '97 / Cadillac / Jazz Music / Target/BMG

LIVE IN LONDON
Don't be that way / Moonglow / Opus / That's all / Charade / HJ blues / Apples / Two o'clock jump / Hits medley
CD ____ JASMCD 2533
Jasmine / Feb '95 / Conifer/BMG / Hot Shot / TKO Magnum

MISTER TRUMPET (James, Harry & His Band)
CD ____ HCD 702
Hindsight / Jul '94 / Jazz Music / Target/ BMG

RARE 1940 VARSITY TITLES (James, Harry & Dick Haymes)
CD ____ FLYCD 943
Flyright / Jun '95 / Hot Shot / Jazz Music / Wellard

RAZZLE DAZZLE
Carnival of Venice / (Back home again in) Indiana / I've heard that song before / Texas chatter / Eli-Eli / Trumpet blues and cantabile / Song of the wanderer / Back beat boogie / Duke's mixture / Record session / Concerto for trumpet / Flight of the bumble bee / Cherry / Trumpet rhapsody / Little bit of heaven / Let me up / I cried for you / Flat bush Flanagan / Sleepy time gal / memphis blues
CD ____ PASTCD 7044
Flapper / May '94 / Pinnacle

STOMPIN' AT THE SAVOY (James, Harry Orchestra)
CD ____ 15771
Laserlight / Jul '92 / Target/BMG

THERE THEY GO 1948-1949 (James, Harry Orchestra)
CD ____ FSCD 2014
Fresh Sound / Jan '97 / Discovery / Jazz Music

UNFORGETTABLE, THE
CD ____ ENTCD 227
Entertainers / Nov '87 / Target/BMG

YES INDEED
All or nothing at all: *James, Harry & Frank Sinatra* / Back beat boogie / Boo-woo / Ciribiribin / Everybody's laughing: *James, Harry & Billie Holiday* / Flash / I found a new

baby / I had the craziest dream: *James, Harry & Helen Forrest* / Jubilee: *James, Harry & Helen Humes* / Just a mood / Life goes to a party / Night special / Nobody knows the trouble I've seen / One o'clock jump / Out of nowhere / Shoe shiner's drag / Spreadin' knowledge around / Sugarfoot stomp / Two o'clock jump / Woo woo / Wrappin' it up / Yes indeed: *James, Harry & Dick Haymes* / You made me love you / Zoom, zoom, zoom
CD ______ CDAJA 5120
Living Era / Nov '93 / Select

James, Hilary

BURNING SUN
O'er the ocean / Busy old fool / La marche des Rois / Polly Vaughan / Two sisters / Bay of Biscay / Lascia ch'io Pianga / Seeds of love / Lonesome day / Les Berceaux / March borrowed from April / Sail away
CD ______ CDACS 016
Acoustics / Jun '97 / ADA / Koch

CHILDREN'S FAVOURITES - MUSICAL MYSTERY TOUR (James, Hilary & Simon Mayor)
Snowman's song / Magpie sitting on a broken chair / Parrot song / Chico the bandit / My bike / Big surprise / Slippery slimy trout / Road to Banbury / Old Dan Tucker's song / Give me a drum / Trumpet hornpipe / Fireman's song / Fat fat farmer / Farmyard tango / Gobble gobble gobble gobble gobble / King Wastelot and the Right Royal rubbish dump / Australian Santa Claus / Sally Ann Johnson / Up in a big balloon
CD ______ CDACS 002
Acoustics / Aug '93 / ADA / Koch

LOVE, LUST AND LOSS (James, Hilary & Beryl Marriott)
CD ______ CDACS 029
Acoustics / May '97 / ADA / Koch

James, Jan

COLOR OF THE ROSE
Missisipi man / To believe / Color of the rose / Come runnin' back / Down the river / Dance / Middle of fate / Shake / Treasure me / Please forgive me / Don't try to chain me down / Good woman / If I held on to you / Guilty man / Waste of my time
CD ______ PRD 70862
Provogue / Feb '96 / Pinnacle

LAST TRAIN
CD ______ PRD 70702
Provogue / Feb '95 / Pinnacle

SOUL DESIRE
CD ______ PRD 70992
Provogue / Mar '97 / Pinnacle

James, Jimmy

VAGABOND KING
Hi diddley dee dum dum (it's a good feeling) / I feel alright / I wanna be (your everything) / Come to me softly / This heart of mine / I don't wanna cry / I'm just a fool for you / Ain't no big thing / Do it right / Ain't love good, ain't love proud / Don't know what I'm gonna do / I can't get back home to my baby / Hungry for love / Never like this before / Little boy blue / It's growing / Wear it on our face / Courage ain't strength / No good to cry / Four walls / Good day sunshine / Cry like a baby / (I believe) love is a doggone good thing / Everybody loves a winner / If you're gonna love me, love me / Better by far / Who could be loving you / Red red wine
CD ______ NEMCD 942
Sequel / Jul '97 / BMG

James, John

SKY IN MY PIE/HEAD IN THE CLOUDS
And Sam came too / Sailor's farewell / Mammy o'mine / Easy street / Out on the rolling sea / Sky in my pie / Conquistador / Bach goes to town / Kicking up the dust / Nola / Quiet days / Weeping willow / Blap bam boom / Be mine or run / Turn your face / Georgemas Junction / Black and white rag / Head in the clouds / Slow drag / Wormwood tangle / Stranger in the world / Rags to riches / Blues for Felix / Heliotrope bouquet / Secrets in the sky / Stretching of a young girl's heart
CD ______ ESMCD 358
Essential / Jan '96 / BMG

James, Joni

LET THERE BE LOVE
Let there be love / You're my everything / You're fooling someone / Am I in love / My love, my love / Purple shades / Almost always / I'll be seeing you / When we come of age / These foolish things / It's talk of the town / Too late now / In love in vain / That old feeling / I'm through with love / Little girl blue
CD ______ JASCD 316
Jasmine / Jan '95 / Conifer/BMG / Hot Shot / TKO Magnum

James, Josie

CANDLES
Tell me / I don't wanna lose it / Candles / Looking for a man / Win your love / All over me / Take a little time / After the love / This time / Back in my arms / Cry
CD ______ XECD 7
Expansion / Feb '96 / 3mv/Sony

James, Laurence

THEATRE ORGAN, THE (Wurlitzer and Compton Theatre Organs) (James, Laurence & Ronald Curtis)
Whispering: *Curtis, Ronald* / Lullaby of the leaves: *Curtis, Ronald* / Alone: *Curtis, Ronald* / Five foot two, eyes of blue: *Curtis, Ronald* / Autumn concerto: *Curtis, Ronald* / Lover: *Curtis, Ronald* / Only make believe/ Why do I love you: *Curtis, Ronald* / Caribbean honeymoon: *Curtis, Ronald* / Nightingale sang in Berkeley Square: *Curtis, Ronald* / Only a rose: *Curtis, Ronald* / Top hat, white tie and tails: *Curtis, Ronald* / Funiculi, funicula: *Curtis, Ronald* / What a perfect combination: *Curtis, Ronald* / Over the rainbow: *Curtis, Ronald* / Falling in love with love: *Curtis, Ronald* / Bye bye blues: *Curtis, Ronald* / I know that you know: *James, Laurence* / It's the talk of the town: *James, Laurence* / Goody goody: *James, Laurence* / Kiss in the dark: *James, Laurence* / Lazy river: *James, Laurence* / I know why: *James, Laurence* / Tuxedo junction: *James, Laurence* / I won't dance: *James, Laurence* / All the things you are: *James, Laurence* / Alley cat: *James, Laurence* / Walkin' my baby back home: *James, Laurence* / After you've gone: *James, Laurence*
CD ______ CDSDL 392
Saydisc / Aug '91 / ADA / Direct / Harmonia Mundi

James, Paul

ACOUSTIC BLUES
CD ______ SP 1133CD
Stony Plain / Oct '93 / ADA / CM / Direct

ROCKIN' THE BLUES
CD ______ SP 1135CD
Stony Plain / Oct '93 / ADA / CM / Direct

James, Rick

GREATEST HITS
Super freak / You turn me on / You & I / Mary Jane / Ebony eyes / Give it to me baby / Dance wit' me / Cold blooded / 17
CD ______ 5516392
Spectrum / Sep '96 / PolyGram

STREET SONGS
Give it to me baby / Ghetto life / Make love to me / Mr. Policeman / Super freak / Fire and desire / Call me up / Below the funk
CD ______ 5302182
Motown / Sep '93 / PolyGram

James, Sian

CYSGODION KARMA
Dacw 'nghariad / Marchnad Llangollen / Mynwent eglwys / Ffarwel i ddociau lerpwl / Hiraeth am feirion / Going south / Camu nol (wrth gamu 'mlaen) / Merch ifanc o'n ben bore / Sgerbwd ar y bryn / Fy ngeneth fach / Mae'r rhod yn troi / Ev chistr 'ta laou
CD ______ SAIN 4037CD
Sain / Aug '94 / ADA / Direct / Greyhound

DISTAW
CD ______ SAIN 2025CD
Sain / Aug '94 / ADA / Direct / Greyhound

GWEINI TYMOR
Y gog lwydlas / Aderyn pur / Y gwydd / Merch ei mam / Peth mawr ydy cariad / Ei di'r deryn du / Si hei lwli / Cariad cyntaf / Deio bach / Mi fum yn gweini tymor / Mwynen merch / Ffarwel I langyelach lon / Broga bach
CD ______ SCD 2145
Sain / Feb '97 / ADA / Direct / Greyhound

James, Skip

COMPLETE 1931 RECORDINGS
CD ______ DOCD 5005
Document / Feb '92 / ADA / Hot Shot / Jazz Music

COMPLETE EARLY RECORDINGS, THE
CD ______ YAZCD 2009
Yazoo / Oct '94 / ADA / CM / Koch

GREATEST OF THE DELTA BLUES SINGERS
CD ______ BCD 122
Biograph / '92 / ADA / Cadillac / Direct / Hot Shot / Jazz Music / Wellard

SHE LYIN'
CD ______ EDCD 379
Edsel / Nov '93 / Pinnacle

SKIP'S PIANO BLUES
CD ______ EDCD 481
Edsel / Oct '96 / Pinnacle

TODAY
CD ______ VMD 79219
Vanguard / Jan '95 / ADA / Pinnacle

James, Steve

AMERICAN PRIMITIVE
CD ______ ANT 0030CD
Antones / Jul '94 / ADA / Hot Shot

TWO TRACK MIND
CD ______ ANTCD 0024
Antones / May '94 / ADA / Hot Shot

James, Tommy

1960'S FRENCH EPS COLLECTION, THE (James, Tommy & The Shondells)
CD ______ 175432
Magic / Jul '97 / Greyhound

CRIMSON & CLOVER/CELLOPHANE SYMPHONY (James, Tommy & The Shondells)
Crimson and clover / Kathleen McArthur / I am a tangerine / Do something for me / Crystal blue persuasion / Sugar on Sunday / Breakaway / Smoky roads / I'm alive / Crimson and clover (Reprise) / Cellophane symphony / Makin' good time / Evergreen / Sweet cherry wine / Papa rolled his own / Changes / Loved one / I know who I am / Love of a woman / On behalf of the entire staff and management
CD ______ NEMCD 647
Sequel / Nov '93 / BMG

HANKY PANKY/MONY MONY (James, Tommy & The Shondells)
Hanky panky / I'll go crazy / I'm so proud / Lover / Love makes the world go round / Good lovin' / Say I am / Cleo's mood / Don't throw our love away / Shake a tail feather / Soul searchin' baby / Lots of pretty girls / Mony mony / Do unto me / (I'm) Taken / Nightime (I'm a lover) / Run away with me / Somebody cares / Get out now / I can't go back to Denver / Some kind of love / Gingerbread man / 1-2-3 And I fell
CD ______ NEMCD 646
Sequel / Feb '94 / BMG

Jamieson, Ronnie

AALD NOOST
CD ______ AT 040CD
Attic / Jul '95 / ADA / CM

Jamiroquai

EMERGENCY ON PLANET EARTH
When you gonna learn / Too young to die / Hooked up / If I like it, I do it / Music of the mind / Emergency on planet Earth / Whatever it is I just can't stop / Blow your mind / Revolution 1993 / Didgin' out
CD ______ 4740692
Sony Soho2 / Jun '93 / Sony

RETURN OF THE SPACE COWBOY
Just another story / Stillness in time / Half the man / Light years / Manifest destiny / Kids / Mr. Moon / Scam / Journey to Arnhemland / Morning glory / Space cowboy
CD ______ 4778132
Sony Soho2 / Oct '94 / Sony

TRAVELLING WITHOUT MOVING
Virtual insanity / Cosmic girl / Use the force / Everyday / Alright / High times / Drifting along / Didjerama / Didjital vibrations / Travelling without moving / You are my love / Spend a lifetime / Funktion
CD ______ 4839992
CD ______ 4839999
Sony Soho2 / Sep '96 / Sony

Jamison, Mac

HOW CAN I EXPLAIN
CD ______ HBC 1218DAAD
Heartbeat City / Aug '94 / Jet Star

Jamma

JAMMA AND FRIENDS
CD ______ QRCD 003
Quartz / Dec '96 / Essential/BMG / Jet Star

Jammin' Unit

DEAF, DUB AND BLIND
CD ______ PLAN 4CD
Blue Planet / Mar '97 / 3mv/Sony / Prime

Jamming Arabs

NEVER BIN SURFIN'
CD ______ WIGCD 018
Alopecia / Jun '97 / Plastic Head

Jams

BASTARDMUSIK
CD ______ TUT 72156
Wundertute / Jan '94 / ADA / CM / Duncans

Jan & Dean

BEST OF JAN & DEAN, THE
CD ______ MATCD 329
Castle / Feb '95 / BMG

BEST OF JAN & DEAN, THE
CD ______ PLSCD 128
Pulse / Mar '96 / BMG

DEAD MAN'S CURVE/NEW GIRL IN SCHOOL, THE
Dead man's curve / Three window coupe / Bucket T / Rockin' little roadster / B gas rickshaw / Mighty GTO / New girl in school / Linda / Barons west LA / School days / It's as easy as 1,2,3 / Hey little freshman
CD ______ C5CD550
See For Miles/C5 / Jan '90 / Pinnacle

GREATEST HITS
Surfin' USA / Barbara Ann / Dead man's curve / I get around / Little old lady from Pasadena / Fun fun fun / California girls / Little Deuce coupe / Honolulu Lulu / Be true to your school / Surf city / New girl in school / Ride the wild surf / Drag city / Linda / Sidewalk surfin'
CD ______ 100702
CMC / May '97 / BMG

JAN & DEAN STORY, THE
CD ______ RNCD 1010
Rhino / Jun '93 / Grapevine/PolyGram / Jet Star

LITTLE OLD LADY FORM PASADENA, THE
Little old lady from Pasadena / Memphis / When it's over / Horace the swingin' school bus driver / Old ladies seldom power shift / Sidewalk surfin' / Anaheim, Azusa and Cucamonga sewing circle / Summer means fun / It's as easy as 1 2 3 / Move over little mustang / Skateboarding / One piece topless bathing suit
CD ______ C5CD 574
See For Miles/C5 / Oct '91 / Pinnacle

SURF CITY
Surf City / Detroit city / Tallahassee Lassie / Manhattan / I left my heart in San Francisco / Kansas City / Memphis / Soul City / Way down yonder in New Orleans / Philadelphia Pa / Honolulu Lulu / You came a long way from St. Louis
CD ______ C5CD 585
See For Miles/C5 / Apr '92 / Pinnacle

TAKE LINDA SURFIN'
Linda / Surfin' / Rhythm of the rain / Walk right in / Gypsy cried / When I learn to cry / Walk like a man / Let's turkey trot / Mr. Bass Man / Best friend I ever had / My foolish heart / Surfin' Safari
CD ______ C5CD 584
See For Miles/C5 / Apr '92 / Pinnacle

Jan & Kjeld

BANJO BOY
Banjo boy / Mach doch nicht immer soviel wind / Tingelingeling mein banjo singt / Penny melodie / Banjo swing / Itsy bitsy teenie weenie / Blacky and Johnny / Traumen kann man was man will / Viele bunte lichter / Hillbilly banjo / Hello Mary Lou / Sing cowboy sing / O du lieber Augustin / Hazel bleib' da / Ginny oh Ginny / Der kaffee kommt direkt uas Brasilien / Auf meinem alten banjo / Tausen schone madchen / Kommen sie mal nach Kopenhagen / Zwei kleine Italiener / Ich druck die daumen / Sugar boy and honey baby / Lederstrumpf / Piccolina / No no mady / Icht wolt' ein madchen kussen / Hallo Dolly / Hillbilly banjo / Stasera no / Candy girl
CD ______ BCD 15923
Bear Family / Dec '96 / Direct / Rollercoaster / Swift

TIGER RAG
Tiger rag / Buona sera / When the sints go marching in / Yes sir that's my baby / Grandfather's clock / When Irish eyes are smiling / Tutti frutti / Three bells / Darling Nellie Gray / Waterloo / Down by the riverside / Ballad of Tom Dooley / What you've done to me / I shall not be moved / Heartaches by the number / True true happiness / He's got the whole world in his hands / Born to late / Everybody loves Saturday night / Tell him no / When the red red robin comes bobbin' along / Can anyone explain / In the shade of the old apple tree
CD ______ BCD 15924
Bear Family / Dec '96 / Direct / Rollercoaster / Swift

TINGELINGELING MY BANGO SINGS
Tingelingeling my banjo sings / Penny melody / St. Louis blues / I can't give you anything but love / Mack the knife / Some of these days / Tisket-a-tasket / Oh Susanna / O mein Papa / Freight train / Carry me back to old Virginny / You are my sunshine / Sweet Sue / Dinah / Oh Susanna / Go down Moses / I love Susi / Polly wolly doodle / Taste of honey / Got no nickel to my name / Ein kuss zum abschied / Vergiss deine tranen / Schick die andern alle weg / Entscheide dich bald
CD ______ BCD 15941
Bear Family / Dec '96 / Direct / Rollercoaster / Swift

Jan, Anne-Marie

PARALLELES
CD ______ KMRSCD 214
Keltia Musique / Dec '94 / ADA / Discovery

Jane

AGE OF MADNESS
CD RR 7047
Repertoire / Jun '97 / Greyhound

Jane Pow

LOVE IT, BE IT
Sanitized / It's on its way / Walker / Get by / Sand barrier / Shutdown / 90's / Love it, be it / Track 9 / Playpower / Morningside / Out of it / On hold / Through / Latitude / Take / Jack Boot / Warm room / Bophia Green / Fruity
CD SLUM 025
Slumberland / Jul '93 / Vital

Jane's Addiction

JANE'S ADDICTION
Trip away / Rock 'n' roll / I would for you / Jane says / Pigs in zen / My time / Whores / Sympathy / Chip away / 1%
CD 7599265992
WEA / Dec '96 / Warner Music

NOTHING'S SHOCKING
Up the beach / Had a dad / Standing in the shower / Jane Says / Thank you boys / Mountain song / Summertime rolls / Ted, just admit it / Ocean size / Idiots rule / Pigs in Zen
CD K9257272
WEA / Mar '94 / Warner Music

RITUAL DE LO HABITUAL
Stop / No one's leaving / Ain't no right / Obvious / Been caught stealing / Three days / Then she did / Of course / Classic girl
CD 7599259932
WEA / Feb '95 / Warner Music

Jang, Jon

SELF DEFENSE (Jang, Jon & the Pan-Asian Arkestra)
CD 1212032
Soul Note / Nov '92 / Cadillac / Harmonia Mundi / Wellard

TIANANMEN (Jang, Jon & the Pan-Asian Arkestra)
CD 1212232
Soul Note / Nov '93 / Cadillac / Harmonia Mundi / Wellard

TWO FLOWERS ON A STEM (Jang, Jon Sextet)
CD 1212532
Soul Note / Oct '96 / Cadillac / Harmonia Mundi / Wellard

Janis, Conrad

CONRAD JANIS & HIS TAILGATE JAZZ BAND VOL.1 (Janis, Conrad Tailgate Jazz Band)
CD BCD 71
GHB / Jun '95 / Jazz Music

CONRAD JANIS & HIS TAILGATE JAZZ BAND VOL.2 (Janis, Conrad Tailgate Jazz Band)
CD BCD 81
GHB / Nov '96 / Jazz Music

Janitor Joe

LUCKY
CD ARRCD 52326
Amphetamine Reptile / May '94 / Plastic Head

Jankowski, Horst

BEST OF MR. BLACK FOREST, THE
CD ISCD 108
Intersound / Jun '95 / Jazz Music

PIANO INTERLUDE
CD ISCD 147
Intersound / Jun '95 / Jazz Music

Jannah, Denise

TAKE IT FROM THE TOP
Pennies from Heaven / Willow weep for me / Fragile / I've got the world on a string / I'm in a minor key today / I get along without you very well / Groovin' high / I'm a fool to want you / Sleepin' bee / My funny valentine
CD CDSJP 308
Timeless Jazz / Jan '92 / New Note/ Pinnacle

Janovitz, Bill

LONESOME BILLY
Girl's club / Think of all / Shoulder / Gaslight / Ghost in my piano / Strangers / My funny valentine / Peninsula / Talking to the Queen / Red balloon
CD BBQCD 186
Beggars Banquet / Dec '96 / RTM/Disc / Warner Music

Jansch, Bert

BERT AND JOHN (Jansch, Bert & John Renbourn)
East wind / Piano tune / Goodbye pork pie hat / Soho / Tic-tocative / Orlando / Red's favourite / No exit / Along the way / Time has come / Stepping stones / After the dance / Waggoner's lad / Lucky thirteen / In this game / Dissatisfied blues / Hole in the cole / Bells
CD HILLCD 8
Wooded Hill / Jan '97 / Direct / World Serpent

BERT JANSCH/IT DON'T BOTHER ME
CD ESMCD 407
Essential / Jul '96 / BMG

BIRTHDAY BLUES/ROSEMARY LANE
Come sing me a happy song / Bright new year / Tree song / Poison / Miss Heather Rosemary Sewell / I've got a woman / Woman like you / I am lonely / Promised land / Birthday blues / Wishing well / Blues / Tell me what is true love / Rosemary Lane / M'lady Nancy / Dream, a dream, a dream / Alman / Wayward child / Nobody's bar / Reynardine / Silly woman / Peregrinations / Sylvie / Sarabanda / Bird song
CD ESMCD 519
Essential / Jul '97 / BMG

BLACKWATER SIDE (2CD Set)
Rosemary lane / When I get home / First time ever... / Woe is love my dear / Blackwater side / I saw an angel / Little sweet sunshine / Life depends on love / Running from home / Market song / Wishing well / Tell me what is true love / I loved a lass / It don't bother me / No exit / Bruton town / Casbah / So long (been on the road) / Tinker's blues / Courting blues / Needle of death / Oh how your love is strong / Angie / Poison / Lucky 13 / Peregrinations / Soho / Woman like you / Rambling's gonna be... / Gardener / Tic-tocative / Nobody's bar / Train song / Reynardine / Sweet child / Come back baby / Rabbit run / Strolling down the highway / Go your way my love
CD Set SMDCD 153
Snapper / May '97 / Pinnacle

COLLECTION, THE
CD CCSCD 430
Castle / Mar '95 / BMG

GARDENER/ESSENTIAL BERT JANSCH 1965-71
CD TDEM 09
Trandem / Mar '94 / ADA / CM / Pinnacle

HEARTBREAK
Is it real / Up to the stars / Give me the time / If I were a carpenter / Wild mountain thyme / Heartbreak hotel / Sit down beside me / No rhyme, nor reason / Blackwater side / And not a word was said
CD HNCD 1312
Hannibal / Jul '93 / ADA / Vital

JACK ORION/NICOLA
Waggoner's lad / First time I ever saw your face / Jack Orion / Gardener / Nottamun town / Henry Martin / Blackwaterside / Pretty polly / Go your way my love / Woe is love my dear / Nicola / Come back baby / Little sweet sunshine / Love is teasing / Rabbit run / Life depends on love / Weeping willow / Box of love / Wish my baby was here / If the world isn't there
CD ESMCD 459
Essential / Jan '97 / BMG

LEATHER LAUNDERETTE (Jansch, Bert & Rod Clements)
Strolling down the highway / Sweet Rose / Brafferton / Ain't no more cane / Why me / Sundown station / Knight's move / Brownsville / Bogie's bonnie belle / Leather launderette / Been on the road so long
CD CROCD 218
Black Crow / Mar '88 / CM / Roots

LIVE AT THE 12 BAR
CD BJ 002CD
Jansch / Aug '96 / ADA / Direct

MOONSHINE
Yarrow / Brought with the rain / January man / Night time blues / Moonshine / First time ever I saw your face / Ramble away / Twa corbies / Oh my Father
CD BJ 001CD
Jansch / Jul '95 / ADA / Direct

ORNAMENT TREE, THE
CD D 271365
Jansch / Nov '96 / ADA / Direct

RARE CONUNDRUM, A
St Fiacre / If you see my love / Looking for a home / Poor mouth / Cat and mouse / Three chord trick / Lost love / Daybreak / One to a hundred / Pretty saro / Doctor, Doctor / 3 AM / Curragh of Kildare / Instrumentally Irish (per's hose pipe)
CD CASCD 1127
Charisma / Jun '97 / EMI

ROSEMARY LANE
Tell me what is true love / Rosemary Lane / M'lady Nancy / Dream, a dream, a dream / Alman / Wayward child / Nobody's bar / Reynardine / Silly woman / Peregrinations / Sylvie / Sarabande / Bird song
CD HILLCD 2
Wooded Hill / Sep '96 / Direct / World Serpent

SKETCHES
CD COMD 2035
Temple / Feb '94 / ADA / CM / Direct / Duncans / Highlander

THREE CHORD TRICK
Fresh as Sunday morning / Chambertin / One for Jo / Needle of death / Cluck old hen / Love anew / Lost and gone / Blues run the game / When the teardrops fell / Kingfisher / Daybreak / Doctor doctor / Curragh of Kildare / Looking for a home / Poor mouth / In the bleak midwinter
CD CDVM 9024
Virgin / Jul '93 / EMI

WHEN THE CIRCUS COMES TO TOWN
Walk quietly by / Open road / Back home / On one around / Step around / Step back / When the circus comes to town / Summer heat / Just a dream / Lady doctor from Ashington / Steal the night away / Honey don't you understand / Born with the blues / Morning brings peace of mind / Living in the shadows
CD COOKCD 092
Cooking Vinyl / Aug '95 / Vital

Jansen, Steve

BEGINNING TO MELT (Medium Series Vol.1) (Jansen, Steve & Richard Barbieri/Mick Karn)
Beginning to melt / Wilderness / March of the innocents / Human agie / Shipwrecks / Ego dance / Orange asylum
CD MPCD 001
Medium / Sep '96 / Pinnacle

OTHER WORLDS IN A SMALL ROOM (Jansen, Steve & Richard Barbieri)
Remains of a fragile illusion / Light years / Disturbed sense of distance / Breaking the silence / Blue lines / Way the light falls / Distant fire
CD MPCD 004
Medium / Mar '97 / Pinnacle

SEED (Jansen, Steve & Richard Barbieri/Mick Karn)
Beginning to melt / In the black of desire / Insect tribe / Prey
CD MPCD 002
Medium / Mar '97 / Pinnacle

STONE TO FLESH (Jansen, Steve & Richard Barbieri)
Mother London / Sleeper's awake / Ringing the bell backwards (pt 1 & 2) / Everything ends in darkness / Closer than I / Swim there
CD MPCD 003
Medium / Sep '96 / Pinnacle

STORIES ACROSS BORDERS (Jansen, Steve & Richard Barbieri)
Long tales, tall shadows / When things dream / Lumen / Insomniac's bed / Night gives birth / Celebration / Nocturnal night-seeing / One more zombie
CD CDVE 908
Virgin / Jul '94 / EMI

Janson, Claes

ALL OF ME
CD SITCD 9209
Sittel / Mar '94 / Cadillac / Jazz Music

Janssen, Gus

CLAVECIMBEL
CD GEESTCD 07
Geest Gronden / Aug '87 / Cadillac

PIANO/KLANKKAST
CD GEESTCD 09
Geest Gronden / Mar '89 / Cadillac

POK
CD GEESTCD 03
Geest Gronden / Oct '89 / Cadillac

Jansson, Lars

SADHANA
CD 1264
Caprice / Oct '92 / ADA / Cadillac / CM / Complete/Pinnacle

Jansson, Lena

EVERYTHING I LOVE
CD SITCD 9206
Sittel / Jun '94 / Cadillac / Jazz Music

LENA JANSSON & NILS LINDBERG BIG BAND 1983/1986 (Jansson, Lena & Nils Lindberg)
CD ABCD 3005
Bluebell / Feb '95 / Cadillac / Jazz Music

January's Little Joke

JANUARY'S LITTLE JOKE
CD BUTCD 3
But / Apr '97 / Pinnacle

Janvier, Phillipe

POUR LE COEUR D'UN MARINIER
CD KMCD 219
Keltia Musique / Mar '96 / ADA / Discovery

Jaojoby

SALEGY
CD XENO 404CD
Xenophile / May '96 / ADA / Direct

Japan

EXORCISING GHOSTS
Methods of dance / Swing / Gentlemen take polaroids / Quiet life / Foreign place / Night porter / My new career / Other side of life / Visions of China / Sons of pioneers / Talking drum / Art of parties / Taking islands in Africa / Voices raised in welcome, hands held in prayer / Life without buildings / Ghosts
CD VGDCD 3510
Virgin / Jan '85 / EMI

GENTLEMEN TAKE POLAROIDS
Gentlemen take polaroids / Swing / Burning bridges / My new career / Methods of dance / Ain't that peculiar / Nightporter / Taking islands in Africa
CD CDV 2180
Virgin / Jun '88 / EMI

GENTLEMEN TAKE POLAROIDS/TIN DRUM/OIL ON CANVAS (3CD Set)
CD Set TPAK 6
Virgin / Oct '90 / EMI

IN VOGUE
Unconventional / Lovers on main street / Transmission / I second that emotion / All tomorrows parties / Alien / Halloween / Surburban berlin / Quiet life / Love is infectious / Fall in love with me / Adolescent sex / European son / In vogue / Life in tokyo
CD 74321393382
RCA / Aug '96 / BMG

OIL ON CANVAS
Sons of pioneers / Cantonese boy / Visions of China / Ghosts / Voices raised in welcome, hands held in prayer / Nightporter / Still life in mobile homes / Methods of dance / Quiet life / Art of parties / Temple of dawn / Oil on canvas / Gentlemen take polaroids / Canton
CD CDVD 2513
Virgin / Apr '92 / EMI

SOUVENIR FROM JAPAN, A
I second that emotion / Life in Tokyo / Deviation / Surburban Berlin / Adolescent sex / European son / All tomorrow's parties / Communist China / State line / Rhodesia / Obscure alternatives / Quiet life
CD 260360
Arista / Dec '89 / BMG

TIN DRUM
Visions of China / Art of parties / Talking drum / Cantonese boy / Canton / Ghosts / Still life in mobile homes / Sons of pioneers
CD CDV 2209
Virgin / Jun '88 / EMI

Japhet, Paskaal

RAZANA
CD NDCD 002
Night & Day / Jun '97 / ADA / Direct / Discovery

Jara, Victor

15 YEARS OF TRADITIONAL PORTUGUESE MUSIC
CD PS 65111
PlayaSound / Nov '93 / ADA / Harmonia Mundi

CANTO LIBRE VOL.2
CD MCD 71799
Monitor / Jun '93 / CM

VIENTOS DEL PUEBLO
CD MCD 71778
Monitor / Jun '93 / CM

Jarboe

SACRIFICIAL CAKE
Lavender girl / Ode to V / Shimmer 1 / My buried child / Not logical / Spiral staircase / Yum yab / Surgical saviour / Cache toi / Tragic seed / Troll lullaby / Deflowered / Body lover / Shimmer 2 / Act 3 / Troll
CD YGCD 008
Young God / Jun '95 / Vital

Jarman, Joseph

AS IF IT WERE THE SEASONS (Jarman, Joseph Quartet)
CD DD 417
Delmark / Nov '96 / ADA / Cadillac / CM / Direct / Hot Shot

CONNECTING SPIRITS (Jarman, Joseph & Marilyn Crispell)
CD CD 964
Music & Arts / Jan '97 / Cadillac / Harmonia Mundi

EGWU ANWU (2CD Set)
CD Set IN 1033CD
India Navigation / Jun '97 / Discovery / Impetus

SONG FOR JOSEPH JARMAN
Little fox run / Non-cognitive aspects of the city / Adam's rib / Song for / Little fox run
CD DD 410
Delmark / Mar '97 / ADA / Cadillac / CM / Direct / Hot Shot

Jarocha, Alma

SONES JAROCHOS (Music Of Mexico Vol. 1) (Jarocha, Conjunto Alma)

CD ARHCD 354
Arhoolie / Apr '95 / ADA / Cadillac / Direct

Jarre, Jean Michel

CHRONOLOGIE
CD 4873792
Epic / Jun '97 / Sony

EQUINOXE
Equinoxe part 1 / Equinoxe part 2 / Equinoxe part 3 / Equinoxe part 4 / Equinoxe part 5 / Equinoxe part 6 / Equinoxe part 7 / Equinoxe part 8
CD 4873762
Epic / Jun '97 / Sony

HOUSTON-LYON CITIES IN CONCERT
Oxygene part 5 / Ethnicolour / Magnetic fields part 1 / Souvenir of China / Equinoxe part 5 / Rendezvous part 2-4 / Ron's piece
CD 4873772
Epic / Jun '97 / Sony

IMAGES (The Best Of Jean Michel Jarre)
Oxygene 4 / Equinoxe part 5 / Magnetic fields II / Oxygene 2 / Computer week-end / Equinoxe part 4 / Band in the rain / Rendezvous / London kid / Ethnicolor 1 / Orient express / Calypso 1 / Calypso 3 (fin de siecle) / Rendezvous / Moon machine / Eldorado / Globetrotter
CD 4873782
Epic / Jun '97 / Sony

MUSIC OF JEAN MICHEL JARRE, THE
Oxygene part iv / Equinox part 5 / Magnetic fields / Oxygene part 2 / Computer weekend / Equinox part 4 / Ethnicolor 1 / Moon machine / Eldorado / Globetrotter / Rendezvous / London / Band in the rain / Orient express / Calypso 1 / Calypso 3 / Rendezvous 4
CD 306232
Hallmark / Jan '97 / Carlton

OXYGENE
Oxygene part 1 / Oxygene part 2 / Oxygene part 3 / Oxygene part 4 / Oxygene part 5 / Oxygene part 6
CD 4873752
Epic / Jun '97 / Sony

OXYGENE 7-13
Oxygene 7:1a / Oxygene part 1:1b / Oxyegene part 2:1c / Oxygene part 3 / Oxygene 8 / Oxygene 9:3a / Oxygene part 1:3b / Oxygene part 2:3c / Oxygene 3 / Oxygene 10 / Oxygene 11 / Oxygene 12 / Oxygene 13
CD 4869842
Disques Dreyfus / Feb '97 / Sony

Jarreau, Al

AIN'T NO SUNSHINE (A Salute To Bill Withers)
Ain't no sunshine / Lean on me / Use me / Kissing my love / Grandma's hands / You / Lonely town / Lonely street / Same love that made me laugh
CD CDBM 011
Blue Moon / Jun '88 / Cadillac / Discovery / Greensleeves / Jazz Music / Jet Star / TKO Magnum

HEAVEN AND EARTH
What you do to me / It's not hard to love you / Blue angel / Heaven and earth / Superfine love / Whenever I hear your name / Love of my life / If I break / Blue in green (tapestry)
CD 9031774662
Warner Bros. / Jul '92 / Warner Music

IMPROVISATIONS
My favourite things / Stockholm sweetnin' / Sleepin' bee / Masquerade is over / Sophisticated lady / Joey / Come rain or shine / One note samba jobim, mendonca-de, hendricks / Ain't no sunshine / Lean on me / Use me / Kissing my love / Grandma's hands / You / Lonely town, lonely street / Same love that made me laugh / Livin' for you / Call me / Here I am / Let's get married / Let's stay together / You ought to be with me / Love and happiness / Tired of being alone / Look what you done for me / I'm still in love with you
CD CDBM 502
Blue Moon / Nov '96 / Cadillac / Discovery / Greensleeves / Jazz Music / Jet Star / TKO Magnum

KINGS OF SOUL (Jarreau, Al & Lou Rawls)
Ain't no sunshine: *Jarreau, Al* / Lean on me: *Jarreau, Al* / Sad song: *Rawls, Lou* / Kissing my love: *Jarreau, Al* / Season of the witch: *Rawls, Lou* / Use me: *Jarreau, Al* / I love you, yes I do: *Rawls, Lou* / I want to be loved: *Rawls, Lou* / Same love that made me laugh: *Jarreau, Al* / Your good thing is about to end: *Rawls, Lou* / Grandma's hands: *Jarreau, Al* / When a man loves a women: *Rawls, Lou* / You: *Jarreau, Al* / I wonder: *Rawls, Lou* / Lonely town, lonely street: *Jarreau, Al* / Trying as hard as I can: *Rawls, Lou*
CD 306192
Hallmark / Jan '97 / Carlton

LET'S STAY TOGETHER
Let's stay together / Call me / Tired of being alone / Living for you / You ought to be with me / Let's get married / Here I am / I'm still in love with you / Ain't no sunshine / Love and happiness / Look what you've done for me / Lean on me / Same love that made me laugh / Use me / You / Grandma's hands / Kissing my love / Lonely town, lonely street
CD 100492
CMC / May '97 / BMG

LIVING FOR YOU
Living for you / Call me / Here I am / Let's get married / Let's stay together / You ought to be with me / Love and happiness / Tired of being alone / Look what you done for me / Still in love with you
CD CDBM 107
Blue Moon / Oct '95 / Cadillac / Discovery / Greensleeves / Jazz Music / Jet Star / TKO Magnum

MASQUERADE IS OVER, THE
My favourite things / Stockholm sweetnin' / Sleepin' bee / (I'm afraid) the masquerade is over / Sophisticated lady / Joey / Come rain or come shine / One note samba
CD CDBM 079
Blue Moon / Nov '89 / Cadillac / Discovery / Greensleeves / Jazz Music / Jet Star / TKO Magnum

SPOTLIGHT ON AL JARREAU
Ain't no sunshine / Kissing my love / You / Same love that made me laugh / Rainbow in your eyes / Grandma's hands / Lonely town, lonely street / Lean on me / One good turn / We got by / Use me (till you use me up) / Loving you / Letter perfect
CD HADCD 115
Javelin / Feb '94 / Henry Hadaway / THE

Jarrett, Keith

ARBOUR ZENA
Dunes / Solara march / Mirrors
CD 8255922
ECM / Aug '85 / New Note/Pinnacle

AT THE DEER HEAD INN
Solar / Basin Street blues / Chandra / You don't know what love is / You and the night and the music / Bye bye blackbird / It's easy to remember
CD 5177202
ECM / May '94 / New Note/Pinnacle

BELONGING
Spiral dance / Blossom / Long as you know you're living yours / Belonging / Windup / Solstice
CD 8291152
ECM / Jun '86 / New Note/Pinnacle

BOOK OF WAYS (Solo Clavichord/2CD Set)
CD Set 8313962
ECM / Oct '87 / New Note/Pinnacle

BRIDGE OF LIGHT
Elegy / Adagio / Celebration / Song / Dance / Birth / Bridge of light
CD 4453502
ECM / May '94 / New Note/Pinnacle

BYE BYE BLACKBIRD (Jarrett, Keith & Jack DeJohnette/Gary Peacock)
Bye bye blackbird / You won't forget me / Butch and butch / Summer night / For miles / Straight no chaser / I thought about you / Blackbird bye bye
CD 5130742
ECM / May '93 / New Note/Pinnacle

CELESTIAL HAWK (For Orchestra, Percussion & Piano) (Jarrett, Keith & Syracuse Symphony)
CD 8293702
ECM / Aug '88 / New Note/Pinnacle

CHANGELESS (Jarrett, Keith & Jack DeJohnette/Gary Peacock)
Dancing / Endless / Lifeline / Ecstacy
CD 8396182
ECM / Oct '89 / New Note/Pinnacle

CHANGES (Jarrett, Keith & Jack DeJohnette/Gary Peacock)
Flying: *Jarrett, Keith* / Prism: *Jarrett, Keith*
CD 8174362
ECM / Oct '84 / New Note/Pinnacle

COMPLETE BLUE NOTE RECORDINGS, THE (6CD Set)
In your own sweet way / How long has this been going on / While we're young / Partners / No lonely nights / Now's the time / Lament / I'm old fashioned / Everything happens to me / If I were a bell / In the wee small hours of the morning / Oleo / Alone together / Skylark / Things 'ain't what they used to be / Autumn leaves / Days of wine and roses / Bop-be / You don't know what love is Muezzin / When I fall in love / How deep is the ocean / Close your eyes / Imagination / I'll close my eyes / I fall in love to easily / On Green Dolphin Street / My romance / Don't ever leave me / You'd be so nice to come home to / La valse bleue / Straight, no chaser / Time after time / For heaven's sake / Desert sun / How about you
CD Set 5276382
ECM / Oct '95 / New Note/Pinnacle

CONCERTS: BREGENZ
CD 8272862
ECM / Aug '88 / New Note/Pinnacle

CURE, THE (New York Town Hall/April 1990)
Old folks / Body and soul / Woody 'n' you / Things ain't what they used to be
CD 8496502
ECM / Oct '91 / New Note/Pinnacle

DARK INTERVALS
Opening / Hymn / Americana / Entrance / Parallels / Fire dance / Ritual prayer / Recitative
CD 8373422
ECM / Oct '88 / New Note/Pinnacle

EXPECTATIONS
Expectations / Take me back / Circular letter (for JK) / Sundance / Bring back the time when (if) / There is a road (God's River) / Common mama / Magician in you / Roussillon / Nomads
CD 4679022
Columbia / Jan '92 / Sony

EYES OF THE HEART
Eyes of the heart / Encore (A-B-C)
CD 8254762
ECM / Oct '85 / New Note/Pinnacle

FACING YOU
In front / Ritooria / Lalene / My lady: my child / Landscape for future earth / Starbright / Vapallia / Semblence
CD 8271322
ECM / Dec '85 / New Note/Pinnacle

FORT YAWUH
If the misfits wear it / Fort Yawuh / De drums / Still life, still life
CD MCAD 33122
Impulse Jazz / Oct '90 / New Note/BMG

IN THE LIGHT (2CD Set)
CD Set 8350112
ECM / Jul '88 / New Note/Pinnacle

INVOCATIONS: THE MOTH AND THE FLAME (2CD Set)
Invocations / Moth and the flame
CD Set 8254732
ECM / Oct '85 / New Note/Pinnacle

KOLN CONCERT, THE
CD 8100672
ECM / '83 / New Note/Pinnacle

LA SCALA
La scala part 1 / La scala part 2 / Over the rainbow
CD 5372682
ECM / Jun '97 / New Note/Pinnacle

LUMINESSENCE (Music For String Orchestra & Saxophone) (Jarrett, Keith & Jan Garbarek)
CD 8393072
ECM / Sep '89 / New Note/Pinnacle

MY SONG
Questar / My song / Tabarka / Mandela / Journey home
CD 8214062
ECM / '84 / New Note/Pinnacle

MYSTERIES
Rotation / Everything that lives laments / Flame / Mysteries
CD MCAD 33113
Impulse Jazz / Jan '90 / New Note/BMG

MYSTERIES (The Impulse Years 1975-1976/4CD Set)
Shades of jazz / Southern smiles / Rose petals / Diatribe / Shades of jazz / Southern smiles / Rose petals / Rose petals / Rotation / Everything that lives laments / Flame / Mysteries / Everything that lives laments / Playaround / Byablue / Konya / Rainbow / Trieste / Fantasm / Yahllah / Byablue / Trieste (intro) / Rainbow / Mushi mushi / Silence / Bop be / Pyramids moving / Gotta get some sleep / Blackberry winter / Pocketful of cherry / Gotta get some sleep / Blackberry winter
CD Set IMPD 4189
Impulse Jazz / Nov '96 / New Note/BMG

NUDE ANTS (Live At The Village Vanguard/2CD Set)
Chant of the soil / Innocence / Processional / Oasis / New dance / Sunshine song
CD Set 8291192
ECM / Jun '86 / New Note/Pinnacle

PARIS CONCERT (Solo Piano/October 17th 1988/Salle Pleyel)
October 17, 1988 / Wind / Blues
CD 8391732
ECM / Apr '90 / New Note/Pinnacle

RUTA AND DAITYA
CD 8293882
ECM / Oct '88 / New Note/Pinnacle

SACRED HYMNS OF G.I. GURDJIEFF
Reading of sacred books / Prayer and despair / Religious ceremony / Hymn / Orthodox hymn from Asia minor / Hymn for Good Friday / Hymn for Easter Thursday / Hymn to the endless creator / Hymn from a great temple / Story of the resurrection of Christ / Holy affirming, holy denying, holy reconciling / Easter night procession / Meditation
CD 8291222
ECM / Jun '86 / New Note/Pinnacle

SOLO CONCERTS - BREMEN/ LAUSANNE (2CD Set)
CD Set 8277472
ECM / Jul '86 / New Note/Pinnacle

SOMEWHERE BEFORE
My back pages / Pretty ballad / Moving son / Somewhere before / New rag / Moment for tears / Pout's over (and the day's not through) / Dedicated to you / Old rag
CD 7567814552
WEA / Mar '93 / Warner Music

SPHERES
Spheres
CD 8274632
ECM / Jul '86 / New Note/Pinnacle

SPIRITS (2CD Set)
CD Set 8294672
ECM / Oct '86 / New Note/Pinnacle

STAIRCASE (2CD Set)
Staircase / Hourglass / Sundial / Sand
CD Set 8273372
ECM / Dec '85 / New Note/Pinnacle

STANDARDS IN NORWAY
All of you / Little girl blue / Just in time / Old folks / Love is a many splendoured thing / Dedicated to you / I hear a rhapsody / How about you
CD 5217172
ECM / Apr '95 / New Note/Pinnacle

STANDARDS LIVE (Jarrett, Keith & Jack DeJohnette/Gary Peacock)
Stella by starlight: *Jarrett, Keith* / Wrong blues: *Jarrett, Keith* / Falling in love with love: *Jarrett, Keith* / Too young to go steady: *Jarrett, Keith* / Way you look tonight: *Jarrett, Keith* / Old country: *Jarrett, Keith*
CD 8278272
ECM / Feb '86 / New Note/Pinnacle

STANDARDS VOL.1 (Jarrett, Keith & Jack DeJohnette/Gary Peacock)
Meaning of the blues: *Jarrett, Keith* / All the things you are: *Jarrett, Keith* / It never entered my mind: *Jarrett, Keith* / (I'm afraid) the masquerade is over: *Jarrett, Keith* / God bless the child: *Jarrett, Keith*
CD 8119662
ECM / Aug '88 / New Note/Pinnacle

STANDARDS VOL.2 (Jarrett, Keith & Jack DeJohnette/Gary Peacock)
So tender: *Jarrett, Keith* / Moon and sand: *Jarrett, Keith* / In love in vain: *Jarrett, Keith* / Never let me go: *Jarrett, Keith* / If I should lose you: *Jarrett, Keith* / I fall in love too easily: *Jarrett, Keith*
CD 8250152
ECM / May '85 / New Note/Pinnacle

STILL LIVE (Jarrett, Keith & Jack DeJohnette/Gary Peacock)
My funny valentine / Autumn leaves / When I fall in love / Song is you / Come rain or come shine / Late lament / You and the night and the music / Someday my Prince will come / I remember Clifford
CD Set 8350082
ECM / May '88 / New Note/Pinnacle

SUN BEAR CONCERTS (Piano Solo/ Kyoto/Osaka/Tokyo/Sapporo November 1976/6CD Set)
Kyoto/November 5th 1976 / Osaka/November 8th 1976 / Tokyo/November 14th November / Sapporo/November 18th 1976
CD Set 8430282
ECM / Oct '90 / New Note/Pinnacle

SURVIVOR'S SUITE
CD 8271312
ECM / Dec '85 / New Note/Pinnacle

TRIBUTE (2CD Set) (Jarrett, Keith & Jack DeJohnette/Gary Peacock)
Lover man / I hear a rhapsody / Little girl blue / Solar / Sun prayer / Just in time / Smoke gets in you eyes / All of you / Ballad of the sad young man / All the things you are / It's easy to remember
CD Set 8471352
ECM / Nov '90 / New Note/Pinnacle

VIENNA CONCERT (Recorded At The Vienna State Opera)
Vienna / Vienna
CD 5134372
ECM / Sep '92 / New Note/Pinnacle

WELL TEMPERED CLAVIER BOOK, THE (2CD Set)
CD Set 8352462
ECM / Nov '88 / New Note/Pinnacle

WORKS: KEITH JARRETT
Country / Riootria / Journey / Staircase (Part II) / String quartet (2nd movement) / Invocations / Nagoya (Part 2B)(Encore)
CD 8254252
ECM / Jun '89 / New Note/Pinnacle

Jarrett, Winston

TOO MANY BOUNDARIES
CD RASCD 3167
Ras / Dec '95 / Direct / Greensleeves / Jet Star / SRD

TRIBUTE TO BOB MARLEY, A (Jarrett, Winston & The Righteous Flames)
CD OMCD 28
Original Music / Jul '94 / Jet Star / SRD

WISE MAN
CD TWCD 1001
Tamoki Wambesi / Apr '88 / Greensleeves / Jet Star / Roots Collective / SRD

Jars Of Clay

JARS OF CLAY
Liquid / Sinking / Love song for a saviour / Like a child / Art in me / He / Boy on a string / Flood / Worlds apart / Blind
CD ORECD 541
Silvertone / Oct '96 / Pinnacle

Jarvis, Jane

CUT GLASS
CD ACD 258
Audiophile / Apr '93 / Jazz Music

JANE JARVIS' LA QUARTET
CD ACD 248
Audiophile / '89 / Jazz Music

Jasani, Viram

RAGS, MALKAUNS AND MEGH (Jasani, Viram & Gurdev Singh/U.L.A. Khan)
Rag Malkauns / Rag Megh
CD CDSDL 377
Saydisc / Mar '94 / ADA / Direct / Harmonia Mundi

Jasmine Minks

JASMINE MINKS
CD CRECD 007
Creation / May '94 / 3mv/Vital

SCRATCH THE SURFACE
CD CRELP 044 CD
Creation / Feb '89 / 3mv/Vital

SOUL STATION
CD CRECD 112
Creation / Sep '91 / 3mv/Vital

Jason & The Scorchers

BLAZING GRACE, A
Cry by night operator / 200 Proof lovin' / Country roads / Where bridges never burn / Shadow of night / One more day of weekend / Hell's gate / Why baby why / Somewhere within / American legion party
CD MR 1012
Mammoth / Feb '95 / Vital

CLEAR IMPETUOUS MORNING
Self sabotage / Cappucino Rosie / Drug store truck drivin' man / 2+1 = Nothing / Victory Rd / Kick me down / Everything has a cost / To feel no love / Walking a vanishing line / Tomorrow comes today / Jeremy's legend / I'm sticking with you
CD MR 1472
Mammoth / Sep '96 / Vital

RECKLESS COUNTRY SOUL
Shot down again / Broken whiskey glass / I'm so lonesome (I could cry) / Jimmie Rodger's last blue yodel / Help there's a fire / I'd rather die young / Candy kisses / Pray for me Momma (I'm a gypsy now) / Hello walls / If you've got the love (I've got the time) / Gone gone gone
CD MR 1272
Mammoth / Feb '96 / Vital

Jaspar, Bobby

AT RONNIE SCOTT'S, 1962 (Jaspar, Bobby Quartet)
Be like Bud / Our delight / Darn that dream / Pent-up house / Oleo / Sonnymoon for two / Like someone in love / Stella by starlight
CD MOLECD 11
Mole Jazz / Nov '89 / Cadillac / Impetus / Jazz Music / Wellard

BOBBY JASPAR
CD OJCCD 1788
Original Jazz Classics / Feb '93 / Complete/Pinnacle / Jazz Music / Wellard

Jasper

LIBERATION
Liberation / Ain't no peace / Baby please don't go / Shelagh / Liberation interlude / Liberation interlude II / Confusion / St. Louis blues / Cutin' out / Beard / Liberation II / Finale
CD SEECD 438
See For Miles/C5 / Apr '96 / Pinnacle

Jasraj, Pandit

INVOCATION
CD WLAES 31CD
Waterlilly Acoustics / Nov '95 / ADA

TABLA (Jasraj, Pandit & Shri Swapan Chaudhuri)
CD WRCD 1009
Koch / Dec '94 / Koch

Jaume, Andre

ABBAYE DE L'EPAU (Jaume, Andre/ Charlie Haden/Olivier Clerc)
CD CELC C20
CELP / Mar '92 / Cadillac / Harmonia Mundi

GIACOBAZZI - "AUTOUR DE LA ROUTE" (Jaume, Andre/Barry Altschul)
CD CELPC 25
CELP / Nov '93 / Cadillac / Harmonia Mundi

PEACE/PACE/PAIX (Jaume, Andre/ Charlie Haden/Olivier Clerc)
CD CELP C19
CELP / Feb '92 / Cadillac / Harmonia Mundi

Javalins

JAVALINS BEAT
Caroline / Mr. Chang aus Chinatown / Al Capone / Javalin's beat / Sherry / Twisting away / Hey Hey Ha Ha / Joe der Gitarrenman / Hully gully hop / Lass sie reden / Scherben / Tanz doch mit mir Swim / Jenny Jenny / Monkey walk / Be my baby / Loveliest night of the year / Es gibt kein bier aus Hawaii / Ya Ya twist / Footpatter / Git it / Sweet Georgia Brown / Twist and shout
CD BCD 15798
Bear Family / May '94 / Direct / Rollercoaster / Swift

Javier

HARD WAY, THE (Javier & The Str8jackers)
Intro / Shoot out / F I U Jay / Other guy / Hammer break / Real deal / Talking shit / Plain ole gangster / Pass me da 40 ounce / Talkin' shit again / Jones / Never heard rappin' / Baddest M F out da ATL / Chillin' at da crib / Candy / Players dialogue / Player style / Str8jackin' / Wildest fantasy / Outtro
CD ICH 1109CD
Ichiban / Oct '93 / Direct / Koch

Jawara, Jali Musa

DIRECT FROM WEST AFRICA
Fote Mogoban / Haidari / Yeke yeke / Yasimika
CD GGXCD 1
Go Discs / Sep '88 / PolyGram

Jawbox

FOR YOUR OWN SPECIAL SWEETHEART
CD EFA 49322
City Slang / Mar '94 / RTM/Disc

GRIPPE
CD DIS 52CD
Dischord / May '94 / SRD

JAWBOX
CD EFA 049812
City Slang / Jun '96 / RTM/Disc

NOVELTY
CD DIS 69CD
Dischord / May '94 / SRD

Jaworzyn, Stefan

IN A SENTIMENTAL MOOD (Jaworzyn, Stefan & Alan Wilkinson)
CD INCUSCD 25
Incus / May '97 / Cadillac / Cargo

Jay-Z

REASONABLE DOUBT
Can't knock the hustle: *Jay-Z & Mary J. Blige* / Politics as usual / Brooklyn's finest: *Jay-Z & Notorious BIG* / Dead presidents II / Feelin' it: *Jay-Z & Mecca* / D'evils / 22 two's / Can I live / Ain't no nigga: *Jay-Z & Foxxy Brown* / Friend or foe / Coming of age: *Jay-Z & Memphis Bleek* / Cashmere thoughts / Bring it on: *Jay-Z & Big Jaz/ Sauce Money* / Regrets / Can't knock the hustle: *Jay-Z & Meli'sa Morgan*
CD 74321447202
Northwestside / Mar '97 / BMG

Jaye, Jerry

MY GIRL JOSEPHINE
My girl Josephine / Long black veil / In the middle of nowhere / Got my mojo working / Pipeliner blues / I'm in love again / Sugar bee / I washed my hands in muddy water / Honky tonk women love redneck men / Standing room only / Drinkin' my way back home / When morning comes to Memphis / Hot and still heating / Let your love flow / Forty days
CD HIUKCD 122
Hi / Feb '92 / Pinnacle

Jayhawks

HOLLYWOOD TOWN HALL
Waiting for the sun / Crowded in the wings / Clouds / Two Angels / Take me with you / Sister cry / Settle down like rain / Witghita / Nevada, California / Martin's song
CD 74321239942
American / Apr '95 / BMG

SOUND OF LIES
Man who loved life / Think about it / Trouble / It's up to you / Stick in the mud / Big star / Poor little fish / Sixteen down / Haywire / Dying on a vine / Bottomless cup / Sound of lies / I hear you cry
CD 74321464062
American / Apr '97 / BMG

TOMORROW THE GREEN GRASS
Blue / I'd run away / Miss Williams' guitar / Two hearts / Real light / Over my shoulder / Bad time / See him on the streets / Nothing left to borrow / Anne Jane / Pray for me / Red's song / Ten little kids
CD 74321236802
American / Feb '95 / BMG

Jays

UNFORGETTABLE TIMES
CD JJCD 027
Channel One / Apr '96 / Jet Star

Jaz Klash

THRU THE HAZE
Off the edge / Intrigue (Down for whatever) / BQE / Intoxicated / 97 / Traffic / Thru the haze / Finale / Gift / Party next door / One fine day
CD COTCD 008
Cup Of Tea / Jun '97 / Vital

Jazayer

JAZAYER (Jazayer & Ali Jihad Racy)
CD CDEB 2549
Earthbeat / May '93 / ADA / Direct

Jazz Artists Guild

JAZZ LIFE, THE
R and R / Black cat / Father and son / Lord, lord am I ever gonna know / Vassarlean / Oh yeah, oh yeah
CD CCD 9019
Candid / Feb '97 / Cadillac / Direct / Jazz Music / Koch / Wellard

NEWPORT REBELS
Mysterious blues / Cliff walk / Wrap your troubles in dreams (and dream your troubles away) / Ain't nobody's business if I do / Me and you
CD CCD 9022
Candid / Apr '87 / Cadillac / Direct / Jazz Music / Koch / Wellard

Jazz Butcher

BIG PLANET
CD CRECD 49
Creation / May '94 / 3mv/Vital

CONDITION BLUE
CD CRECD 110
Creation / Oct '91 / 3mv/Vital

CULT OF THE BASEMENT
Basement / Pineapple Tuesday / Daycare nation / Mr. Odd / Panic in room 109 / Turtle bait / She's on drugs / Onion field / My Zeppelin / After the euphrates / Girl go / Sister death
CD CRECD 62
Creation / May '94 / 3mv/Vital

DRAINING THE GLASS (The Jazz Butcher Conspiracy 1982-1986)
CD NTMCD 529
Nectar / Aug '96 / Pinnacle

EDWARD'S CLOSET
CD CRECD 078
Creation / Jun '89 / 3mv/Vital

ILLUMINATE (Jazz Butcher Conspiracy)
CD CRECD 182
Creation / Apr '95 / 3mv/Vital

WAITING FOR THE LOVE BUS
CD CRECD 156
Creation / May '93 / 3mv/Vital

WESTERN FAMILY
Southern Mark Smith / Shirley Maclaine / Sister death / Still and all / Pineapple Tuesday / Angles / Beautiful snow-white hair / She's on drugs / Girl-go / She's a yoyo / Racheland / Everybody's talkin' / Tugboat Captain / Over the rainbow
CD CRED 148
Creation / Jan '93 / 3mv/Vital

Jazz Classical Union

FREE FLIGHT
Blue rondo a la turk / Pavanne for a true musical prince (Don's song) / Chopin etude / Paganini caprice / Pachelbel canon / Peasant dance / Bach's groove / For Frederic and Bill / Con mucho gusto
CD HCD 609
Hindsight / Jul '97 / Jazz Music / Target/ BMG

Jazz Composer's Orchestra

COMMUNICATIONS
CD 8411242
ECM / Nov '89 / New Note/Pinnacle

Jazz Crusaders

LIVE AT THE LIGHTHOUSE 1996
Aleluia / Blues up tight / You don't know what love is / Miss it / 'Round midnight / Some other blues / Scratch / Doin' that thing / Milestones
CD CDP 8379882
Pacific Jazz / Jul '96 / EMI

Jazz Epistle

VERSE 1
CD 668922
Melodie / Mar '96 / ADA / Discovery / Grapevine/PolyGram / Greensleeves / Jet Star

Jazz Furniture

JAZZ FURNITURE
CD CAP 21449
Caprice / Oct '94 / ADA / Cadillac / CM / Complete/Pinnacle

Jazz Grass Ensemble

TICO BANJO
CD PV 758 091
Disques Pierre Verany / Feb '86 / Kingdom

Jazz Hot Ensemble

JAZZ HOT ENSEMBLE
CD JCD 242
Jazzology / Jun '95 / Jazz Music

Jazz Mentality

SHOW BUSINESS IS MY LIFE
CD 378352
Koch Jazz / Feb '97 / Koch

Jazz Passengers

CROSS THE STREET
Spirits of a flatbust / Basketballfish / Tintindeo / Somewhere in New Jersey / My Spanish cookies / Ghostly strange love / Little gold ring / Fathouse / You don't know what love is / Laura / Tikkun
CD TWI 1012
Les Disques Du Crepuscule / Apr '96 / Discovery

IMPLEMENT YOURSELF
CD NW 398
New World / Aug '92 / ADA / Cadillac / Harmonia Mundi

INDIVIDUALLY TWISTED
Babble a la Roy / Maybe I'm lost / Angel eyes / Pork chop / Aubergine / Ole / Imitation of a kiss / Jive samba / Doncha go 'way mad / Tide is high / It came from outer space
CD ESSCD 578
Essential / Jul '97 / BMG

JAZZ PASSENGERS IN LONDON
CD 72902103282
High Street / Mar '95 / BMG

LIVE AT THE KNITTING FACTORY
CD KFWCD 107
Knitting Factory / Nov '94 / Cargo / Plastic Head

PLAIN OLD JOE
CD KFWCD 139
Knitting Factory / Feb '95 / Cargo / Plastic Head

Jazz Police

LONG NIGHT COMING, A
CD CDPC 748
Prestige / Oct '90 / Else / Total/BMG

Jazz Posse

BLUE
Antistrophy / We know who we are / Woody / Gemini / Crescent / Integrate / Skag / Countdown / Juke joint / Horny / Un loco loco / Blue / Metafisico / Frog sauce / Anna
CD FSCD 004
Freak Street / Oct '95 / Pinnacle

Jazz Trio

'S WONDERFUL JAZZ
'S Wonderful / Cherokee / That old feeling / You are too beautiful / Bali Ha'i / Jitterbug waltz / You've changed
CD WCD 8418
Wilson Audiophile / Sep '91 / Quantum Audio

Jazz Vandals

CHANGE IN JAZZITUDE, A
CD JVCD 003
Burning / Aug '96 / Pinnacle

Jazz Warriors

OUT OF MANY ONE PEOPLE
Warriors / In reference to our forefathers' fathers' dreams / Minor groove / St. Maurice (of Aragon) / Many pauses
CD IMCD 111
Antilles/New Directions / May '91 / PolyGram

Jazz X

PEACE AND NICENESS
CD XEN 006CD
Funky Xen / Nov '96 / Timewarp

Jazzateers

I SHOT THE PRESIDENT
CD MA 30
Marina / May '97 / SRD

Jazzmeteors

UGLY BEAUTY
Evolution to the groove / Miles to go before I sleep / Chimichurri / Yet to come / De varkensslachterij / Why do they hate / Black satin / Falling / Boot des levens / Hallo
CD _______ 9920022
Via Jazz / Oct '96 / New Note/Pinnacle

Jazzsick

JAZZSICK
CD _______ EFA 120702
Hotwire / Apr '95 / SRD

Jazztet

MOMENT TO MOMENT
CD _______ SNCD 1066
Soul Note / '86 / Cadillac / Harmonia Mundi / Wellard

REAL TIME
Whisper not / Sad to say / Are you real / Autumn leaves / Along came Betty
CD _______ CCD 14034
Contemporary / Jan '94 / Cadillac / Complete/Pinnacle / Jazz Music / Wellard

JB Horns

FUNKY GOOD TIMES
CD _______ GCD 79485
Gramavision / Sep '95 / Vital/SAM

JB3

CLOSE GRIND
CD _______ NOMU 50CD
Nova Mute / Dec '96 / Prime / RTM/Disc

JC 001

RIDE THE BREAK (JC 001 & DJ D'Zire)
Never again / Favourite breaks / Sea of MC's / Cupid / Build the mutha up / Words within words / Flow / Ride the break / Virtual reality / All my children
CD _______ 4509914062
Anxious / Apr '93 / Warner Music

Jean, Wyclef

PRESENTS THE CARNIVAL FEATURING REFUGEE CAMP ALLSTARS
Intro/Court/Clef/Intro / Apocalypse / Guantanamera / Pablo diablo / Bubblegoose / Prelude/To all the girls / Down lo ho / Anything can happen / Gone till November / Words of wisdom / Year of the dragon / Sang Fezi / Fresh interlude / Mona Lisa / Street jeopardy / Killer MC / We trying to stay alive / Gunpowder / Closing arguments / Enter the Carnival / Jaspora / Yele / Carnival
CD _______ 4874422
Ruff House / Jun '97 / Sony

Jeane, Deborah

FLY
CD _______ 5679162
Music & Words / Aug '96 / ADA / Direct

Jeanneau, Francois

MALOYA TRANSIT
CD _______ LBLC 6546
Label Bleu / Jul '92 / New Note/Pinnacle

Jeck, Philip

LOOPHOLES
CD _______ TO 26
Touch / Jun '95 / Kudos / Pinnacle

Jedi Knights

NEW SCHOOL SCIENCE
CD _______ EVO 042CD
Universal Language / Feb '96 / Prime / RTM/Disc

Jeep Beat Collective

ATTACK OF THE WILD STYLE
CD _______ RUF 008
Ruf / Nov '96 / Plastic Head / SRD

Jefferson Airplane

BEST OF JEFFERSON AIRPLANE
Blues from an airplane / White rabbit / Somebody to love / Ballad of you and me and Pooneil / Crown of creation / Plastic fantastic lover / Volunteers / When the earth moves again / Aerie (gang of eagles) / Milk train / Mexico
CD _______ ND 89186
RCA / Jan '92 / BMG

JEFFERSON AIRPLANE LIVE
White rabbit / Somebody to love / She has funny cars / Ride / High flying bird / Would you love me / My best friend / Plastic fantastic lover / Don't slip away / 3/5 of a mile in ten seconds / It's no secret / Other side of life / Today / What you're asking / You're so loose / This is my life
CD _______ EXP 021
Experience / May '97 / TKO Magnum

JOURNEY (The Best Of Jefferson Airplane)
Embryonic journey / High flyin' bird / It's no secret / Come up the years / Somebody to love / Blues from a airplane / White rabbit / Plastic fantastic lover / Aerie (gang of eagles) / Ballad of you an me and pooneil / Crown of creation / Lather / Last wall of the castle / Greasy heart / Volunteers / When the earth moves again / Triad / We can be together / Wooden ships / Milk train / Have you seen the saucers
CD _______ 74321400572
Camden / Jan '97 / BMG

LIVE AT THE MONTEREY FESTIVAL
Somebody to love / Other side of this life / White rabbit / High flying bird / Today / She has funny cars / Young girl with Sunday blues / Ballad of you and me and Pooneil
CD _______ CDTB 074
Thunderbolt / May '90 / TKO Magnum

WE ALL ARE ONE (CD/Book Set)
CD _______ SB 03
Stampa Alternativa / Jan '97 / Cargo

WHITE RABBIT
CD _______ RMB 75065
Remember / Aug '93 / Total/BMG

Jefferson Starship

DEEP SPACE
Shadowlands / Ganja of love / Dark ages / I'm on fire / Papa John / Women who fly / Gold / Light / Crown of creation / Count on me / Miracles / Lawman / Wooden ships / Somebody to love / White rabbit
CD _______ ESMCD 493
Essential / Apr '97 / BMG

EARTH
Love too good / Count on me / Take your time / Crazy feelin' / Skateboard / Fire / Show yourself / Runaway / All nite long
CD _______ 07863668782
RCA / Jun '97 / BMG

GREATEST HITS (10 Years & Change 1979-1991) (Starship)
Jane / Find your way back / Stranger / No way out / Laying it on the line / Don't lose any sleep / We built this city / Sara / Nothing's gonna stop us now / It's not over ('til it's over) / It's not enough / Good enough
CD _______ 74321289902
RCA / Aug '95 / BMG

SPITFIRE
Cruisin' / Dance with the dragon / Hot water / St. Charles / Song to the sun / Don't let it rain / With your love / Switchblade / Big city / Love lovely love / Ozymandias
CD _______ 07863668762
RCA / Jun '97 / BMG

Jefferson, Blind Lemon

ALL TIME BLUES CLASSICS
CD _______ 8420282
Music Memoria / Oct '96 / ADA / Discovery

BEST OF BLIND LEMON JEFFERSON, THE
CD _______ WBJCD 016
Wolf / Jul '96 / Hot Shot / Jazz Music / Swift

BLIND LEMON JEFFERSON
CD _______ DVBC 9072
Deja Vu / May '95 / THE

BLIND LEMON JEFFERSON 1925-26
CD _______ DOCD 5017
Document / Aug '91 / ADA / Hot Shot / Jazz Music

CAT MAN BLUES
CD _______ ALB 1009CD
Aldabra / Mar '94 / CM / RTM/Disc

IN CHRONOLOGICAL ORDER
CD _______ DOCD 5018
Document / Nov '93 / ADA / Hot Shot / Jazz Music

MOANIN' ALL OVER
CD _______ TCD 1011
Tradition / May '96 / ADA / Vital

ONE DIME BLUES
CD _______ ALB 1006CD
Aldabra / Mar '94 / CM / RTM/Disc

Jefferson, Carter

RISE OF ATLANTIS, THE
Why / Rise of Atlantis / Wind chimes / Changing trains / Song for Gwen / Blues for wood
CD _______ CDSJP 126
Timeless Jazz / Mar '91 / New Note/Pinnacle

Jefferson, Eddie

BODY AND SOUL
See if you can get to that / Body and soul / Mercy mercy mercy / So what / There I go, There I go again / Psychedelic Sally
CD _______ OJCCD 396
Original Jazz Classics / Jan '94 / Complete/Pinnacle / Jazz Music / Wellard

HIPPER THAN THOU
So what / Moody's mood for love / Sister Sadie / It's only a paper moon / TD's boogie / Now's the time / Body and soul / Workshop / Sherry / Baby girl (These foolish things) / Memphis / Honeysuckle Rose / Preacher / Night train / NJR (I'm gone) / I got the blues / Silly little Cynthia / Red's new dream
CD _______ LDJ 274946
Radio Nights / Sep '92 / Cadillac / Harmonia Mundi

JAZZ SINGER, THE (Vocal Improvisations On Famous Jazz Solos)
So what / Moody's mood for love / Sister Sadie / Lester's trip to the moon (Paper moon) / TD's boogie woogie / Now's the time / Body and soul / Workshop / Sherry / Baby girl (These foolish things) / Memphis / Honeysuckle rose / Crazy romance / Night train / NJR (I'm gone) / I've got the blues / Silly little Cynthia / Red's new dream
CD _______ ECD 22062
Evidence / Oct '93 / ADA / Cadillac / Harmonia Mundi

LETTER FROM HOME
CD _______ OJCCD 307
Original Jazz Classics / Jan '94 / Complete/Pinnacle / Jazz Music / Wellard

THINGS ARE GETTING BETTER
Bitches brew / Things are getting better / Freedom jazz dance / Night in Tunisia / Trane's blues / I just got back in town / Billie's bounce / Thank you
CD _______ MCD 5043
Muse / Jul '96 / New Note/Pinnacle

Jefferson, Marshall

DAY OF THE ONION
CD _______ EFA 019532
KTM / Nov '96 / SRD

Jefferson, Paul

PAUL JEFFERSON
CD _______ ALMCD 13
Almo Sounds / Sep '96 / Pinnacle

Jefferson, Thomas

THOMAS JEFFERSON
CD _______ EDCD 416
Edsel / Mar '95 / Pinnacle

Jeffrey's Accordion Band

50 WARTIME MEMORIES VOL.3
CD _______ SOW 511
Sound Waves / May '94 / Target/BMG

Jeffreys, Garland

DON'T CALL ME BUCKWHEAT
Moonshine in the cornfield / Welcome to the world / Don't call me Buckwheat / Color line / Hail hail rock 'n' roll / I was afraid of Malcolm / Bottle of love / Answer / Racial repertoire / Spanish blood / Lonelyville / Murder jubilee / I'm not a know it all
CD _______ 74321330702
RCA / Feb '96 / BMG

Jeffries, Peter

AT SWIM TWO BIRDS (Jeffries, Peter & Jono Lonie)
CD _______ DFR 31
Drunken Fish / Apr '97 / Cargo

ELEVATOR MADNESS
CD _______ EJO 9CD
Emperor Jones / Oct '96 / SRD

Jegede, Tunde

LAMENTATION
Lamentation / Songs of the eternal / African path / Heat haze / Hill of solitude - valley of festivity / Caravans of gold / Buffalo's tail / Departure / Song of the waterfall / Island of cold
CD _______ TRICD 1001
Triciom / Oct '95 / New Note/Pinnacle

Jellyfish

BELLYBUTTON
Man I used to be / That is why / King is half undressed / I wanna stay home / She still loves him / All I want is everything / Now she knows she's wrong / Bed spring kiss / Baby coming back / Calling Sarah
CD _______ CDCUX 3
Charisma / Feb '92 / EMI

SPILT MILK
Joining a fan club / Sebrina, Paste and Plato / New mistake / Glutton of sympathy / Ghost at number one / Bye bye bye / All is forgiven / Russian hill / He's my best friend / Too much, too little, too late / Brighter day
CD _______ CDCUS 20
Charisma / May '93 / EMI

Jenkins, Billy

BLUE MOON IN A FUNCTION ROOM (Jenkins, Billy & The Voice Of God Collective)
Blue of the night / Vision on / Bye bye blue-bird / On the street where you live / Take five / Baby elephant walk / Ruby, don't take your love to town / Liebestraum / Pick a bale of cotton / Maria Elena / Georgia / Kalinka / Moon river
CD _______ BDV 9402
Babel / Mar '95 / ADA / Cadillac / Diverse / Harmonia Mundi

ENTERTAINMENT USA
CD _______ BDV 9401CD
Babel / Jul '94 / ADA / Cadillac / Diverse / Harmonia Mundi

FIRST AURAL ART EXHIBITION (Jenkins, Billy & The Voice Of God Collective)
Brilliant / Expensive equipment / Fat people / Blues / Sade's lips / Johnny Cash / Discoboats at two o'clock / Cooking oil / Donkey droppings / Elvis Presley
CD _______ VOCD 921
VOTP / Sep '92 / Diverse / VOTP

SAD (Jenkins, Billy & The Blues Collective)
CD _______ BDV 9615
Babel / Feb '97 / ADA / Cadillac / Diverse / Harmonia Mundi

SCRATCHES OF SPAIN
Monkey men / Cuttlefish / Barcelona / Benidorm motorway services / Bilbao/ St.Columbus day / Cooking oil / McDonalds
CD _______ BDV 9404
Babel / Oct '94 / ADA / Cadillac / Diverse / Harmonia Mundi

STILL SOUNDS LIKE BROMLEY
CD _______ BDV 9717
Babel / Aug '97 / ADA / Cadillac / Diverse / Harmonia Mundi

Jenkins, Ella

AND ONE AND TWO (& Other Songs For Pre School/Primary Children)
CD _______ SFWCD 45016
Smithsonian Folkways / Mar '96 / ADA / Cadillac / CM / Direct / Koch

EARLY EARLY CHILDHOOD SONGS (Jenkins, Ella & Lake Meadows Nursery School)
CD _______ SFWCD 45015
Smithsonian Folkways / Oct '96 / ADA / Cadillac / CM / Direct / Koch

HOLIDAY TIMES
CD _______ SFWCD 45041
Smithsonian Folkways / Nov '96 / ADA / Cadillac / CM / Direct / Koch

JAMBO (& Other Call And Response Songs/Chants)
CD _______ SFWCD 45017
Smithsonian Folkways / Oct '96 / ADA / Cadillac / CM / Direct / Koch

SONGS CHILDREN LOVE TO SING (Celebrating 40 Years Of Recordings)
CD _______ SFWCD 45042
Smithsonian Folkways / Oct '96 / ADA / Cadillac / CM / Direct / Koch

YOU'LL SING A SONG AND I'LL SING A SONG
CD _______ SF 45010CD
Smithsonian Folkways / Dec '94 / ADA / Cadillac / CM / Direct / Koch

Jenkins, Leroy

LEGEND OF AL GLATSON, THE
Al Glatson / Brax Stone / Albert Ayler / Tuesday child / What goes around comes around
CD _______ 1200222
Black Saint / Nov '90 / Cadillac / Harmonia Mundi

LIFELONG AMBITIONS (Jenkins, Leroy & Muhal Richard Abrams)
CD _______ 1200332
Black Saint / Jan '94 / Cadillac / Harmonia Mundi

LIVE
CD _______ 1201222
Black Saint / Sep '93 / Cadillac / Harmonia Mundi

Jenkins, Lillette

LILLETTE JENKINS PLAYS LIL HARLEM ARMSTRONG
CD _______ CRD 302
Chiaroscuro / Jan '93 / Jazz Music

Jenkins, Mark

SPACE DREAMS VOL.1
CD _______ AMPCD 015
AMP / Feb '95 / Cadillac / Discovery / TKO Magnum

SPACE DREAMS VOL.2
CD _______ AMPCD 030
AMP / Apr '97 / Cadillac / Discovery / TKO Magnum

Jenks, Glenn

DUETS OF RAGS (Jenks, Glenn & Dan Gunstead)

CD _____ SOSCD 1292
Stomp Off / Nov '95 / Jazz Music / Wellard

Jenney, Jack

STARDUST
Night is blue / High society / What is there to say / I'll get by / I've gone romantic on you / Stardust / Cuban boogie woogie / If you knew Susie
CD _____ HEPCD 1045
Hep / Mar '96 / Cadillac / Jazz Music / New Note/Pinnacle / Wellard

Jennings, John

BUDDY
Walking to China / It's only the rain / Do you want me now / Everybody wants me / Night will fall / Third of the world / Run run run / Another town / Willie Short / Monday night
CD _____ VCD 79496
Vanguard / Apr '97 / ADA / Pinnacle

Jennings, Waylon

ABILENE
CD _____ CDSGP 0129
Prestige / Jan '95 / Else / Total/BMG

BACK IN THE SADDLE
CD _____ HADCD 181
Javelin / Nov '95 / Henry Hadaway / THE

BEST OF WAYLON JENNINGS, THE
CD _____ MUCD 3010
Musketeer / Oct '94 / Disc

BEST OF WAYLON JENNINGS, THE
CD _____ 74321378392
RCA / Jul '96 / BMG

CLOVIS TO PHOENIX (The Early Years)
My baby walks all over me / Stage / Another blue day / My world / Never again / Jole Blon / When sin stops / Crying / Sally was a good ole girl / Burning memories / Big mambou / Money / Don't think twice, it's alright / Dream baby / It's so easy / Lorena / Love's gonna live here / Abilene / White lightning
CD _____ ZCD 2021
Zu Zazz / Aug '95 / Rollercoaster

ESSENTIAL WAYLON JENNINGS, THE
Only daddy that'll walk the line / Brown eyed handsome man / Taker / Good hearted woman / You asked me to / Amanda / Rainy day woman / Waymore's blues / Are you sure Hank done it this way / Wild side of life/It wasn't God who made honky tonk angels / Wurlitzer prize (I don't want to get over you) / Theme from Dukes of Hazard (Good ol' boys) / Storms never last: *Jennings, Waylon & Jessie Colter* / Just to satisfy you: *Jennings, Waylon & Willie Nelson* / Lucille (you won't do your daddy's will) / Never could toe the mark / America / Broken promised land / Drinkin' and dreamin' / Whatever happened to the blues
CD _____ 07863668572
RCA Nashville / Aug '96 / BMG

GREATEST HITS VOL.1
Lonesome, on'ry and mean / Ladies love outlaws / I've always been crazy / I'm a ramblin' man / Only daddy that'll walk the line / Amanda / Honky tonk heroes / Mamas don't let your babies grow up to be cowboys / Good hearted woman / Luckenbach, Texas (Back to the basics of love) / Texas / Are you sure Hank done it this way
CD _____ ND 90304
RCA / '90 / BMG

MAGIC OF WAYLON JENNINGS, THE
Sally was a good old girl / Big mamou / Don't think twice, it's alright / It's so easy / Love's gonna live here / White lightning / Crying / Burning memories / Dream baby / Abilene / Jolie blon / Money (that's what I want) / Lorena / When sin stops
CD _____ TKOCD 024
TKO / Apr '92 / TKO

OUTLAWS, THE (Jennings, Waylon & Willie Nelson)
CD _____ CTS 55407
Country Stars / Jan '92 / Target/BMG

WAYMORE'S BLUES (PART 2)
Endangered species / Waymore's blues (part 2) / This train (Russell's song) / Wild ones / No good for me / Old timer / Up in Arkansas / Nobody knows come back and see me / You don't mess around with me
CD _____ 7863664092
RCA / Oct '94 / BMG

WHITE LIGHTNING
CD _____ 15486
Laserlight / Dec '94 / Target/BMG

WHITE LIGHTNING
CD _____ MACCD 230
Autograph / Aug '96 / BMG

WILL THE WOLF SURVIVE
Will the wolf survive / They ain't got em' all / Working without a net / Where does love go / Dog won't hunt / What you'll do when I'm gone / Suddenly single / Shadow of your distant friend / I've got me a woman / Devil's right hand
CD _____ MCAD 5688
MCA / '88 / BMG

Jenny & Carolyn

FAREWELL ORKNEY
CD _____ AT 45
Attic / Aug '96 / ADA / CM

Jensen, Ingrid

HERE ON EARTH
Shiva's dance / Woodcarvings / Here on earth / Time remembered / You do something to me / Time of the barracudas / Ninety-one / Consolation / Fallin' / Avila and tequila
CD _____ ENJ 93132
Enja / Jun '97 / New Note/Pinnacle / Vital/SAM

VERNAL FIELDS
Marsh blues / Skookum spook / Vernal fields / Every time we say goodbye / I love you / Mingus that I knew / Stuck in the dark / Christiane / Be myself
CD _____ ENJ 90132
Enja / May '95 / New Note/Pinnacle / Vital/SAM

Jensen, Kurt

JAZZ CLASSICS AND EVERGREENS (Jensen, Kurt New Orleans Trio/Quartet)
CD _____ MECCACD 2003
Music Mecca / May '97 / Cadillac / Jazz Music / Wellard

Jensen, Nancy

BACH NATURALLY
CD _____ 2236
NorthSound / Aug '96 / Gallant

Jentekor, Sandefjord

PA FOLKEMUNNE
CD _____ BD 7023CD
Musikk Distribujson / Apr '95 / ADA

Jeremy Days

CIRCUSHEAD
Give it a name / Sylvia suddenly / My man / Mr. Judge / Virginia / Room to revolution / Red river / 1987 / History / Sleeping room / Circushead / What the wind's blowin roun / Clouds of maine / Sacrifice
CD _____ 8439982
Polydor / Mar '91 / PolyGram

Jerks

JERKS, THE
CD _____ OVER 65CD
Overground / May '97 / Shellshock/Disc / SRD

Jerling, Michael

NEW SUIT OF CLOTHES
CD _____ SHCD 8010
Shanachie / Dec '94 / ADA / Greensleeves / Koch

Jerolamon, Jeff

INTRODUCING (Jerolamon, Jeff & George Cables)
You stepped out of a dream: *Jerolamon, Jeff* / Dark side/light side: *Jerolamon, Jeff* / Straight no chaser: *Jerolamon, Jeff* / 'Round midnight: *Jerolamon, Jeff* / Quiet fire: *Jerolamon, Jeff* / Little B's poem: *Jerolamon, Jeff* / I thought about you: *Jerolamon, Jeff*
CD _____ CCD 79522
Candid / Feb '97 / Cadillac / Direct / Jazz Music / Koch / Wellard

SWING THING
Midget / You go to my head / Idaho / Avalon / Seven come-eleven / Nancy with the laughing face / Evidence/Just you just me / Overtime / My heart tell me / Dark eyes / Lover come back to me
CD _____ CCD 79538
Candid / Feb '97 / Cadillac / Direct / Jazz Music / Koch / Wellard

Jerry, Clark

FLUTIN' AND FLUGIN'
CD _____ ATJCD 5963
All That's Jazz / Jun '92 / Jazz Music / THE

Jerry's Kids

KILL, KILL, KILL
CD _____ T 027CD
Taang / Apr '89 / Cargo

Jeru The Damaja

WRATH OF THE MATH
Wrath of the math / Frustrated nigga / Black cowboy / Tha bullshit / Whatever / Physical stamina / One day / Revenge of the prophet / Scientifical madness / Not the average / Me or the papes / How I'm living / Too perverted / Ya playin' yaself / Invasion
CD _____ 8288462
FFRR / Oct '96 / PolyGram

Jerusalem

BOOK OF DAYS, THE
CD _____ EFA 121782
Apollyon / Jul '97 / SRD

Jerusalem Slim

JERUSALEM SLIM
CD _____ 5146802
Phonogram / Jan '93 / PolyGram

Jessamine

JESSAMINE
CD _____ KRANK 003CD
Kranky / Mar '97 / Cargo / Greyhound

LONG ARM OF COINCIDENCE
CD _____ KRANK 012CD
Kranky / Mar '97 / Cargo / Greyhound

Jesus & Mary Chain

AUTOMATIC
Here come Alice / Coast to coast / Blues from a gun / Between planets / UV ray / Her way of praying / Head on / Take it / Halfway to crazy / Gimme hell / Drop / Sunray
CD _____ K 2462212
Blanco Y Negro / Dec '96 / Warner Music

BARBED WIRE KISSES
Kill surf city / Head / Rider / Hit / Don't ever change / Just out of reach / Happy place / Psycho candy / Sidewalking / Who do you love / Surfin' USA / Everything's alright when you're down / Upside down / Taste of Cindy / Swing / On the wall-f hole / Bo Diddley is Jesus / Here it comes again / Cracked / Mushroom
CD _____ 2423312
Blanco Y Negro / Apr '88 / Warner Music

DARKLANDS
April skies / Happy when it rains / Down on me / Deep one perfect / Fall / About you / Cherry came too / On the wall / Nine million rainy days
CD _____ K 2421802
Blanco Y Negro / Nov '94 / Warner Music

HONEY'S DEAD
CD _____ 9031765542
Blanco Y Negro / Dec '96 / Warner Music

PSYCHO CANDY
Just like honey / Living end / Taste the floor / Hardest walk / Cut dead / In a hole / Taste of Cindy / Never understand / It's so hard / Inside me / Sowing seeds / My little underground / You trip me up / Something's wrong
CD _____ 2420002
Blanco Y Negro / Oct '86 / Warner Music

SOUND OF SPEED, THE
Snakedriver / Reverence / Heat / Teenage lust / Why'd you want me / Don't come down / Guitar man / Something I can't have / Sometimes / Write record release blues / Shimmer / Penetration / My girl / Tower of song / Little red rooster / Break me down / Lowlife / Deviant slice / Reverberation (doubt) / Sidewalking
CD _____ 4509931052
Blanco Y Negro / Jul '93 / Warner Music

STONED & DE-THRONED
CD _____ 4509967172
Blanco Y Negro / Dec '96 / Warner Music

Jesus Jones

ALREADY
Next big thing / Run on empty / Look out tomorrow / Top of the world / Rails / Wishing it away / Chemical no.1 / Motion / They're out there / For moment / Addiction / Obsession and me / February
CD _____ FOODCD 22
Food / Aug '97 / EMI

DOUBT
Trust me / Who, Where, Why / International bright young thing / I'm burning / Right here, right now / Nothing to hold me / Real real real / Welcome back Victoria / Two and two / Stripped / Blissed
CD _____ FOODCD 5
Food / Feb '94 / EMI

LIQUIDIZER
Move mountains / Never enough / Real world / All the answers / What's going on / Song 13 / Info freako / Bring it on down / Too much to learn / What would you know / One for the money / Someone to blame
CD _____ FOODCD 3
Food / Oct '89 / EMI

PERVERSE
Zeroes and ones / Devil you know / Get a good thing / From love to war / Yellow brown / Magazine / Right decision / Your crusade / Don't believe it / Tongue tied / Spiral / Idiot stare
CD _____ FOODCD 8
EMI / Nov '92 / EMI

Jesus Lizard

DOWN
CD _____ TG 131CD
Touch & Go / Aug '94 / SRD

GOAT
CD _____ TG 68CD
Touch & Go / Feb '91 / SRD

HEAD
CD _____ TGCD 54
Touch & Go / Jul '93 / SRD

LIAR
CD _____ TG 100CD
Touch & Go / Oct '92 / SRD

SHOT
Thumper / Blue shot / Thumbscrews / Good riddance / Mailman / Skull of a German / Trephination / More beautiful than Barbie / Too bad about the fire / Churl / Now then / Inamorata / Pervertedly slow
CD _____ CDEST 2284
Capitol / May '96 / EMI

Jesus Loves You

MARTYR MANTRAS, THE
Generations of love / One on one / Love's gonna let you get down / After the love / I specialize in loneliness / No clause / Love hurts / Siempre te amare / Too much love / Bow down mister
CD _____ CUMCD 1
More Protein / Mar '91 / Pinnacle / Total/BMG

Jesus Messerschmitt

JESUS MESSERSCHMITT
CD _____ 343752
No Bull / Sep '96 / Koch

Jet

CPH 2000
CD _____ APR 017CD
April / Apr '97 / Plastic Head / Shellshock/Disc

Jet Black Machine

JET BLACK MACHINE
CD _____ PPR 002
Phantom Power / Jun '96 / Nervous

Jet Red

JET RED
CD _____ CDMFN 94
Music For Nations / Aug '89 / Pinnacle

Jet Streams

SECRET GOLDFISH, THE
CD _____ MA 26
Marina / May '97 / SRD

Jeter, Rev. Claude

YESTERDAY AND TODAY
CD _____ SHCD 6010
Shanachie / Mar '95 / ADA / Greensleeves / Koch

Jethro Tull

20 YEARS OF JETHRO TULL
Stormy Monday blues / Love story / New day yesterday / Summer day sands / Coronach / March the mad scientist / Pibroch (pee break) / Black satin / Lick your fingers clean / Overhand / Crossword / Saturation / Jack-a-Lynn / Motoreyes / Part of the machine / Mayhem / Maybe / Kelpie / Under wraps 2 / Wond'ring aloud / Dun ringill / Life's a long song / Nursie grace / Witch's promise / Teacher / Living in the past / Aqualung / Locomotive breath
CD _____ CCD 1655
Chrysalis / Nov '89 / EMI

25TH ANNIVERSARY BOX SET (4CD Set)
My Sunday feeling (remix) / Song for Jeffrey (Remix) / Living in the past (Remix) / Teacher / Sweet dream / Cross-eyed Mary / Witch's promise / Life is a long song / Bungle in the jungle / Minstrel in the gallery / Cold wind to Valhalla / Too old to rock 'n' roll, too young to die / Songs from the wood / Heavy horses / Black Sunday / Broadsword / My God / With you there to help me / Song for Jeffrey / To cry you a song / Sossity, you're a woman / Reasons for waiting / We used to know / Guitar solo / For a thousand mothers / So much trouble / My Sunday feeling / Someday the sun won't shine for you / Living in the past / Bouree / With you there to help me / Thick as a brick / Cheerio / New day yesterday / Protect and survive / Jack-a-Lynn / Whistler / My God / Aqualung / To be sad is a mad way to be / Back to the family / Passion play extract / Wind-up/Locomotive breath/ Land of Hope and Glory/Wind-up / Seal driver / Nobody's car / Pussy willow / Budapest / Nothing is easy / Kissing Willie / Still loving you tonight / Beggar's farm/ Passion Jig / Song for Jeffrey (Live) / Living in the past (Live)
CD _____ CDCHR 6004
Chrysalis / Apr '93 / EMI

A
Crossfire / Flyingdale flyer / Working John, working Joe / Black Sunday / Protect and survive / Batteries not included / Uniform /

4 WD (low ratio) / Pine martin's jig / And further on / Bod
CD ____ CCD 1301
Chrysalis / Jan '89 / EMI

AQUALUNG
Aqualung / Cross-eyed Mary / Cheap day return / Mother goose / Wond'ring aloud / Up to me / My God / Hymn 43 / Slipstream / Locomotive / Breath / Wind up
CD ____ CD25CR 08
Chrysalis / Mar '94 / EMI

AQUALUNG (25th Anniversary Edition)
Aqualung / Cross eyed Mary / Cheap day return / Mother Goose / Wond'ring aloud / Up to me / My God / Hymn 43 / Slipstream / Locomotive breath / Wind up / Lick your fingers clean / Wind up / Excerpts from the Ian Anderson interview / Song for Jeffrey / Fat man / Bouree
CD ____ CD25AQUA 1
Chrysalis / Jun '96 / EMI

BENEFIT
With you there to help me / Nothing to say / Alive and well and living in / Son for Michael Collins / Jeffrey and me / To cry you a song / Time for everything / Inside / Play in time / Sossity / You're a woman
CD ____ CPCD 1043
Chrysalis / Jun '87 / EMI

BEST OF JETHRO TULL, THE (2CD Set)
Song for Jeffrey / Beggar's farm / Christmas song / New day yesterday / Bouree / Nothing is easy / Living in the past / To cry you a song / Teacher / Sweet dream / Cross-eyed Mary / Mother goose / Aqualung / Locomotive breath / Life is a long song / Thick as a brick / Passion play / Skating away (on the thin ice of the new day) / Bungle in the jungle / Minstrel in the gallery / Too old to rock and roll, too young to die / Songs from the wood / Jack in the green / Whistler / Heavy horses / Dun ringill / Flyingdale flyer / Jack-a-Lynn / Pussy willow / Broadsword / Under wraps 2 / Steel monkey / Farm on the freeway / Jump start / Kissing Willie / This is not love
CD Set ____ CDCHR 6001
Chrysalis / May '93 / EMI

BROADSWORD AND THE BEAST, THE
Beastie / Clasp / Fallen on hard times / Flying colours / Slow marching / Broadsword / Pussy willow / Watching me watching you / Seal driver / Cheerio
CD ____ CCD 1380
Chrysalis / Apr '82 / EMI

CATFISH RISING
This is not love / Occasional demons / Rocks on the road / Thinking round corners / Still loving you tonight / Doctor to my disease / Like a tall thin girl / Sparrow on the schoolyard wall / Roll yer own / Gold-tipped boots, black jacket and tie
CD ____ CCD 1886
Chrysalis / Sep '97 / EMI

CLASSIC CASE, A (The Music Of Jethro Tull Featuring Ian Anderson) (Palmer, David & The London Symphony Orchestra)
Locomotive breath / Thick as a brick / Elegy / Bouree / Fly by night / Aqualung / Too old to rock 'n' roll, too young to die / Teacher / Bungle in the jungle / Rainbow blues / Living in the past / War child
CD ____ 09026625102
RCA Victor / Apr '94 / BMG

CREST OF A KNAVE
Steel monkey / Farm on the freeway / Jump start / Said she was a dancer / Budapest / Mountain men / Raising steam / Waking edge / Dogs in the midwinter
CD ____ CCD 1590
Chrysalis / Sep '87 / EMI

HEAVY HORSES
And the mouse police never sleeps / Acres wild / No lullaby / Moths / Journeyman / Rover / One brown mouse / Heavy horses / Weathercock
CD ____ CCD 1175
Chrysalis / '86 / EMI

JETHRO TULL COLLECTION, THE
Acres wild / Locomotive breath / Dharma for one / Wind up / War child / Budapest / Whistler / We used to know / Beastie / Rare and precious chain / Quizz kid / Still loving you tonight / Living in the past
CD ____ DC 878612
Disky / Mar '97 / Disky / THE

LITTLE LIGHT MUSIC, A
Some day the sun won't shine for you / Living in the past / Life is a long song / Under wraps / Rocks on the road / Nursie / Too old to rock 'n' roll, too young to die / One white duck / New day yesterday / John Barleycorn / Look into the sun / Christmas song / From a dead beat to an old greaser / Bouree / Pussy willow
CD ____ CCD 1954
Chrysalis / Sep '97 / EMI

LIVING IN THE PAST
Witches promise / Song for Jeffrey / Love story / Christmas song / Living in the past / Driving song / Bouree / Sweet dream / Singing all day / Witch's promise / Inside / Just trying to be / By kind permission of you / Dharma for one / Wondering again / Locomotive breath / Life is a long song / Up the 'Pool / Dr. Bogenbroom / For later / Nursie
CD ____ CCD 1575
Chrysalis / Feb '94 / EMI

MINSTREL IN THE GALLERY
Minstrel in the gallery / Cold wind to Valhalla / Black satin dancer / Requiem / One white duck / O 10 equals nothing at all / Baker St. muse / Including pig me and the whore / Nice little tune / Crash barrier waltzer / Mother England reverie / Grace
CD ____ CCD 1082
Chrysalis / '86 / EMI

MU - THE BEST OF JETHRO TULL VOL.1
Teacher / Aqualung / Thick as a brick / Bungle in the jungle / Locomotive breath / Fat man / Living in the past / Passion play / Skating away (on the thin ice of the new day) / Rainbow blues / Nothing is easy
CD ____ ACCD 1078
Chrysalis / Dec '85 / EMI

NIGHT CAP - THE UNRELEASED MASTERS 1972-1991
First post / Animelee / Tiger toon / Look at the animals / Law of the bungle / Law of the bungle (part II) / Left right / Solitaire / Critique oblique / Post last / Scenario / Audition / No rehearsal / Paradise steakhouse / Sealion II / Piece of cake / Quartet / Silver river turning / Crew nights / Curse / Rosa on the factory floor / Small cigar / Man of principle / Commons brawl / No step / Drive on the young side of life / I don't want to be me / Broadford bazaar / Lights out / Truck stop runner / Hard liner
CD Set ____ CDCHR 6057
Chrysalis / Nov '93 / EMI

ORIGINAL MASTERS
Living in the past / Aqualung / Too old to rock 'n' roll, too young to die / Locomotive breath / Skating away (on the thin ice of the new day) / Bungle in the jungle / Sweet dream / Songs from the wood / Witches promise / Thick as a brick / Minstrel in the gallery / Life is a long song
CD ____ CCD 1515
Chrysalis / Apr '86 / EMI

PASSION PLAY, A
CD ____ CCD 1040
Chrysalis / Jan '89 / EMI

REPEAT (The Best Of Jethro Tull)
Minstrel in the gallery / Cross-eyed Mary / New day yesterday / Bouree / Thick as a brick / War child / Passion play / To cry you a song / Too old to rock 'n' roll, too young to die / Glory row
CD ____ CCD 1135
Chrysalis / Apr '86 / EMI

ROCK ISLAND
Kissing Willie / Rattlesnake trail / Ears of tin / Undressed to kill / Rock Island / Heavy water / Another Christmas song / Whaler's dues / Big riff and Mando / Strange avenues
CD ____ CCD 1708
Chrysalis / Sep '97 / EMI

ROOTS TO BRANCHES
Roots to branches / Rare and precious chain / Out of the noise / This free will / Valley / Dangerous veils / Beside myself / Wounded, old and treacherous / At last forever / Stuck in the August rain / Another Harry's bar
CD ____ CDCHR 6109
Chrysalis / Sep '97 / EMI

SONGS FROM THE WOOD
Songs from the wood / Jack in the green / Cup of wonder / Hunting girl / Ring out, Solstice bells / Velvet green / Whistler / Pibroch (cap in hand) / Fire at midnight
CD ____ ACCD 1132
Chrysalis / '86 / EMI

STAND UP
New day yesterday / Jeffrey goes to Leicester Square / Bouree / Back to the family / Look into the sun / Nothing is easy / Fat man / We used to know / Reasons for waiting / For a thousand mothers
CD ____ CCD 1042
Chrysalis / Jan '89 / EMI

STORM WATCH
North Sea oil / Orion / Home / Dark ages / Warm sporran / Something's on the move / Old ghosts / Dunringill / Flying Dutchman / Elegy
CD ____ CCD 1238
Chrysalis / Jan '89 / EMI

THICK AS A BRICK (25th Anniversary)
Thick as a brick / Thick as a brick / Thick as a brick
CD ____ CDCNTAV 5
EMI / Jun '97 / EMI

THIS WAS
My Sunday feeling / Someday the sun won't shine for you / For you / Beggar's farm / Move on alone / Serenadeto a cuckoo / Dharma for one / It's breaking me / Cat's squirrel / Song for Jeffrey / Round
CD ____ CCD 1041
Chrysalis / '86 / EMI

THIS WAS/STAND UP/BENEFIT (The Originals/3CD Set)
My Sunday feeling / Someday the sun won't shine for you / Beggar's farm / Move on alone / Serenadeto a cuckoo / Dharma for one / It's breaking me / Cat's squirrel / Song for Jeffrey / New day yesterday / Jeffery goes to Leicester Square / Bouree / Back to the family / Look into the sun / Nothing is easy / Fat man / We used to know / Reasons for waiting / For a thousand mothers / With you there to help me / Nothing to say / Alive and well and living in / Son for Michael Collins / Jeffrey and me / To cry you a song / Time for everything / Inside / Play in time / Sossity / You've a woman
CD Set ____ CDOMB 021
EMI / Mar '97 / EMI

THROUGH THE YEARS
Living in the past / Wind up / Warchild / Dharma for one / Acres wild / Budapest / Whistler / We used to know / Beastie / Locomotive breath / Rare and precious chain / Quizz kid / Still loving you tonight
CD ____ CDGOLD 1079
EMI Gold / Feb '97 / EMI

TO CRY YOU A SONG (A Tribute To Jethro Tull) (Various Artists)
CD ____ RR 88722
Roadrunner / Aug '96 / PolyGram

TOO OLD TO ROCK AND ROLL
Quizz kid / Crazed institution / Salamander / Taxi grab / From a dead beat to an old greaser / Bad eyed and loveless / Big dipper / Too old to rock 'n' roll, too young to die / Pied piper / Chequered flag (dead of alive)
CD ____ CCD 1111
Chrysalis / '86 / EMI

UNDER WRAPS
Lap of luxury / Under wraps / European legacy / Later the same evening / Saboteur / Radio free Moscow / Nobody's car / Heat / Under wraps 2 / Paparazzi / Apologee
CD ____ CCD 1461
Chrysalis / Sep '84 / EMI

Jets

ALL FIRED UP
CD ____ KRYPCD 202
Krypton / Aug '91 / TKO Magnum

ONE FOR THE ROAD
CD ____ KYPCD 204
Krypton / Apr '95 / TKO Magnum

STARE STARE STARE
CD ____ KRYPCD 205
Krypton / Feb '97 / TKO Magnum

Jetset

BEST OF THE JETSET TOO
CD ____ TANGCD 5
Tangerine / May '93 / RTM/Disc

BEST OF THE JETSET, THE
CD ____ TANGCD 1
Tangerine / Aug '92 / RTM/Disc

Jett, Joan

I LOVE ROCK 'N' ROLL (Jett, Joan & The Blackhearts)
I love rock 'n' roll / I'm gonna run away / Love is pain / Nag / Crimson and clover / Victim of circumstance / Bits and pieces / Be straight / You're too possessive / Oh woe is me / Louie louie intro / Louie louie / You don't know what you got
CD ____ 4865092
Columbia / Feb '97 / Sony

Jeune

BACK TO REALITY
CD ____ SR 40032
PLR / Oct '96 / Pinnacle

Jeunes Sonneurs

CENTRAL BRITTANY
CD ____ CD 437
Arfolk / Mar '96 / ADA / Discovery / Roots

Jewel

PIECES OF YOU
Who will save your soul / Morning song / Painters / Amen / Angel standing by / Daddy / Don't / You were meant for me / I'm sensitive / Adrian / Pieces of you / Little sister / Foolish games / Near you always
CD ____ 7567827002
Atlantic / Jun '96 / Warner Music

Jewish Theatre Orchestra

YIDDISH FOLKSONGS (Spiritual & Traditional Music)
CD ____ 15185
Laserlight / '91 / Target/BMG

Jezebelle

BAD ATTITUDE
Ain't no lady / Leave me alone / Travel on gypsy / Other side / Scandal / No mercy / Satisfaction guaranteed / Boulevard / Bum
CD ____ HMRXD 148
Heavy Metal / May '90 / Revolver / Sony

JFK

FOUR DAYS THAT SHOCK THE WORLD
CD ____ RPM 122
RPM / Oct '93 / Pinnacle

Jhana

SENTIENT BEING
CD ____ WIRED 229
Wired / May '97 / 3mv/Sony / Mo's Music Machine / Prime

Jhelisa

GALACTICA RUSH
Galactica rush / There's nothing wrong / Hold my peace / Whirl keeps turning / Death of a soul diva / Friendly pressure / Baby god / Sweet dreams (4UIC) / Secret place
CD ____ DOR 26CD
Dorado / Sep '94 / Pinnacle

LANGUAGE ELECTRIC
Language electric / Sending you a message / Freedom from pity / Sell me away (who will protect me from my own people) / Bete noir / That's bullshit Woody / My ego needs me tonight / Everybody jump off / Story of a musician's madness / Feeling that feeling / Live no lie
CD ____ DOR 56CD
Dorado / Mar '97 / Pinnacle

Jigsy King

ASHES TO ASHES
CD ____ VPCD 1427
VP / Sep '95 / Greensleeves / Jet Star / Total/BMG

HAVE TO GET YOU
CD ____ CRCD 19
Charm / Jul '93 / Jet Star

Jim & Jesse

BLUEGRASS AND MORE (5CD Set)
Stormy horizons / Gosh I miss you all the time / Flame of love / Beautiful moon of Kentucky / My empty arms / Diesel train / Voice of my darling / Uncle Will played the fiddle / Fireball / Heartaches and flowers / Sweet little miss blue eyes / Somebody loves you darlin' / She left me standing on the mountain / Don't say goodbye if you love me / Wish you knew / When it's time for the whippoorwill to sing / Grave in the valley / Blue bonnet lane / Are you missing me / Congratulations, anyway / Pickin' and a-grinnin / Stoney creek / Sixteen hundred miles from home / South bound train / Ballad of Thunder Road / Uncle Jimmy Lee / What about you / When my blue moon turns to gold again / Nine pound hammer / Little paper boy / I wonder where you are tonight / Just when I needed you / Las Cassas, Tennessee / Drifting and dreaming of you / Grass is greener / Violet and the rose / Take my ring from your finger / Why not confess / Better times a-coming / Wild Georgia boys / Cotton mill man / To the top of the world / Old time religion / Old camp meeting days / Old country church / Are you washed in the blood / It's a lonesome road / Swing low, sweet chariot / Kneel at the cross / Rock of ages / Where the roses never fade / Lord I'm coming home / This world is not my home / Where the soul never dies / Ole slew foot / Sleepy eyed John / Tell her lies and feed her candy / Y'all come / Company's coming / Stay a little longer / Rabbit in the log / Salty dog blues / Alabama / Good bunch of bisquits / Bluegrass banjo / Don't let nobody tie you down / Big hands / Dancing Molly / If you've seen one you've seen them all / Memphis / Maybellene / Johnny B Goode / Sweet little sixteen / Roll over Beethoven / Reelin' and rockin' / Brown eyed handsome man / Too much monkey business / Bye bye Johnny / Back in the USA / God moved in / I'll wear the banner / Weapon of prayer / Angel mother / Sing unto him a new song / In God's eyes / Who did, Jesus did / How much are you worth / He walks on the water / River of Jordan / Where the chilly winds don't blow / All for the love of a girl / Diesel on my tail / Truck driving man / Six days on the road / Sam's place / Ballad of Thunder Road / Lovin' machine / Hot rod race / Girl on the billboard / Give me forty acres / Tijuana taxi / Greenwich Village folksongs salesman / Pretty girls (in mini skirts) / Yonder comes a freight train / Rose City Chimes / Wildwood flower / Orange blossom special / Buckaroo / Remington ride / Sugarfoot rag / Maiden's prayer / Down yonder / Banderilla / We'll build a bridge / When the snow is on the roses / Then I'll stop goin' for you / Big job / Are you teasing me / I don't believe you've met my baby / My baby's gone / Cash on the barrelhead / Childish love / Must you throw dust in my face / When I stop dreaming / Knoxville girl / I take the chance / I'm hoping that you're hoping / Fire ball mail / Streamlined cannonball / Tennessee Central 9 / (I heard that) Lonesome whistle / Pan American / Golden rocket / Freight train in my mind / I like trains / Wabash cannonball
CD Set ____ BCD 15716
Bear Family / Sep '94 / Direct / Rollercoaster / Swift

CLASSIC RECORDINGS (1952-1955)
I'll wash your love from my heart / Just wondering why / Are you missing me / I will always be waiting for you / Virginia waltz / Are you lost in sin / Look for me (I'll be there) / Purple heart / Airmail special / My little honeysuckle rose / Waiting for a message / Too many tears / My darling's in heaven / Two arms to hold me / Is it true / Memory of you / I'll wear the banner / My garden of love / Tears of regret / I'll see you tonight (in my dreams)
CD BCD 15635
Bear Family / Apr '92 / Direct / Rollercoaster / Swift

Jimenez, Don Santiago

HIS FIRST AND LAST RECORDINGS
CD ARHCD 414
Arhoolie / Apr '95 / ADA / Cadillac / Direct

MONTELONGO
CD SCR 44
Strictly Country / Aug '96 / ADA / Direct

Jimenez, Fernando

LA FIESTA
CD TUMICD 012
Tumi / Apr '90 / Discovery / Stern's

Jimenez, Flaco

ARIBA EL NORTE
CD NETCD 1008
Network / Aug '94 / Direct / Greensleeves / SRD

AY TE DEJO EN SAN ANTONIO
CD ARHCD 318
Arhoolie / Apr '95 / ADA / Cadillac / Direct

ENTRE HUMO Y BOTELLAS
CD NETCD 1007
Network / Aug '94 / Direct / Greensleeves / SRD

FLACO'S AMIGOS
La tumba sera el final / Did I tell you / Jennette / Te quiero mas / Mi primer amor / Free Mexican air force / Lucerito / Espero tu regreso / Poquita fe / Feria polka / Para toda la vida / I'm gonna love you like there is no tomorrow / Yo quisiera saber / Atotonilco
CD ARHCD 3027
Arhoolie / Apr '95 / ADA / Cadillac / Direct

FLACO'S FIRST
CD ARHCD 370
Arhoolie / Apr '95 / ADA / Cadillac / Direct

PARTNERS
Change partners / Marina / Carmelita / El puente roto / Across the borderline / Me esta matando / Girl from Texas / West Texas waltz / Las golondrinas / Eres un encanto / Don't worry baby
CD 7599268222
WEA / Aug '92 / Warner Music

SAN ANTONIO SOUL
CD NETCD 1009
Network / Aug '94 / Direct / Greensleeves / SRD

TEX-MEX PARTY (Jimenez, Flaco/ Santiago Jimenez Jr.)
Mis movidas: *Jimenez, Flaco* / Victoria: *Jimenez, Flaco* / Eres un encanto: *Jimenez, Flaco* / El perdido: *Jimenez, Flaco* / Que lo sepa el mundo: *Jimenez, Flaco* / La esperanza: *Jimenez, Flaco* / La Hawaiana: *Jimenez, Santiago Jr.* / De San Antonio a Penjamo: *Jimenez, Santiago Jr.* / La mujer: *Jimenez, Santiago Jr.* / El corrido de Santiago Jimenez: *Jimenez, Santiago Jr.* / Ya llegaron a la luna: *Jimenez, Santiago Jr.* / Zulema waltz: *Jimenez, Santiago Jr.*
CD EDCD 7041
Easydisc / Jul '97 / Direct

UN MOJADA SIN LICENCIA (Original Hits 1955-1967)
CD ARHCD 396
Arhoolie / Apr '95 / ADA / Cadillac / Direct

VIVA SEGUIN
Viva sequin / La botellita / Hasta la vista / Los amores del flaco / Mi duice amor / Horalia / Arriba el norte / Polka town / La piedrera / Viajando en polka marianela / Adios muchachos
CD SCR 42
Strictly Country / Nov '95 / ADA / Direct

Jimenez, Rafael Jimenez

CANTE GITANO
CD 131122
Celestial Harmonies / Aug '96 / ADA / Select

Jimenez, Santiago Jr.

CAMA DE PIEDRA
CD 829462
BUDA / Jul '97 / Discovery

CANCIONES DE MI PADRE
CD WM 1019CD
Watermelon / May '94 / ADA / Direct

EL MERO, MERO DE SAN ANTONIO
CD ARHCD 317
Arhoolie / Apr '95 / ADA / Cadillac / Direct

LIVE IN HOLLAND
CD SCR 38
Strictly Country / Mar '95 / ADA / Direct

MUSICA DE TIEMPOS PASADOS DEL PRESENTE Y FUTURO
CD WM 1035
Watermelon / Jul '95 / ADA / Direct

Jimmies

COUNTDOWN
CD SCZZ 228
Schizophonic / Feb '97 / Cargo

Jimmy & Johnny

IF YOU DON'T SOMEBODY ELSE WILL
CD BCD 15771
Bear Family / Jun '97 / Direct / Rollercoaster / Swift

Jinda, George

BETWEEN DREAMS
CD SH 5020
Shanachie / Mar '96 / ADA / Greensleeves / Koch

RELIABLE SOURCES (Jinda, George & World News)
Reliable sources / Behind the scenes / Storyteller / High road / Overleafing a new turn / Code of silence / Serengeti sky / Force of habit / For the rain forest
CD JVC 20232
JVC / Nov '93 / Direct / New Note/Pinnacle / Vital/SAM

Jing, Pang

CLASSICAL CHINESE FOLK MUSIC (Jing, Pang & Ensemble)
CD EUCD 1186
ARC / Apr '92 / ADA / ARC Music

Jing Ying Soloists

EVENING SONG (Traditional Chinese Music)
Autumn moon / Ducks quacking / Love song of the grassland / Singing the night among fishing boats / Fishing song / Marriage of Chan Xian-Yuen / Moonlight over the spring river / Happy reunion / Bamboo song from the village / Variations on Yang City tune / Meditating on the past / Moon over Guan-Shan
CD CDSDL 368
Saydisc / Mar '94 / ADA / Direct / Harmonia Mundi

LIKE WAVES AGAINST THE SAND
Flowing streams / Suzhou scenery / Races / Love at the fair / High moon / Night / Chinese martial arts / Flower fair / Shenpadei folksong / Like waves against the sand / Bird song / Legend
CD CDSDL 325
Saydisc / Mar '94 / ADA / Direct / Harmonia Mundi

Jinmo

LIVE AT THE KNITTING FACTORY
CD KFWCD 129
Knitting Factory / Feb '95 / Cargo / Plastic Head

Jivaros Quartet

NEAR THE NOISE
CD L 8909301
Danceteria / Jan '90 / ADA / Plastic Head / Shellshock/Disc

Jive Bunny

NON STOP JUKE BOX
CD MCCD 239
Music Club / Mar '96 / Disc / THE

PARTY CRAZY
CD MCCD 286
Music Club / Mar '97 / Disc / THE

Jive Five

OUR TRUE STORY
My true story / Do you hear wedding bells / Beggin' you please / Rain / Johnny never knew / People from another world / What time is it / When I was single / These golden rings / Girl with the wind in her hair / I don't want to be without you baby / No not again / You know what I would do / Never never / Hully gully callin' time / Hurry back
CD CDCH 76
Ace / Aug '91 / Pinnacle

Jive Turkey

PERFUME EXPERIMENT
CD DANCD 042
Danceteria / Sep '90 / ADA / Plastic Head / Shellshock/Disc

Jives Aces

OUR KINDA JIVE
CD JACD 1000
Jive Aces / Jan '97 / Jazz Music

Joan Of Arc

PORTABLE MODEL OF...
CD JT 1033CD
Jade Tree / Jul '97 / Cargo / Greyhound / Plastic Head

Joao, Maria

FABULA
CD 5332162
Verve / Oct '96 / PolyGram

Jobim, Antonio Carlos

ANTONIO BRASILIERO
So danco samba / Piano na manguiera / How insensitive / Querida surfboard / Samba de maria luiza / Forever green / Maracangalha / Maricotinha pato preto / Meu amigo radames / Blue train (trem azul) / Radames y pele / Chora coracao / Trem de ferro
CD 4762812
Sony Jazz / May '95 / Sony

BLUE NOTE PLAYS JOBIM (Various Artists)
Desafinado: *Gilberto, Joao* / Waters of March: *Elias, Elaine* / Wave: *Turrentine, Stanley* / How insensitive: *Lagrene, Birelli* / O amore em paz: *Pearson, Duke* / Corcovado: *Green, Grant* / Useless landscape: *Jackson, Javon* / No more blues: *McRae, Carmen* / She's a carioca: *Turrentine, Stanley* / Se todas fossem iquais a voce: *Wilson, Jack* / Triste: *Klugh, Earl* / Girl from Ipanema: *Elias, Elaine* / Samba de uma nota so: *Gilberto, Joao*
CD CDP 8352832
Blue Note / Mar '96 / EMI

COMPOSER PLAYS, THE
Girl from Ipanema / O morro / Auga de beber / Dreamer / Favela / How insensitive / Corcovado / One note samba / Meditation / Jazz samba / Chega de saudade / Desafinado
CD 8230112
Verve / Mar '94 / PolyGram

DEDICATED TO ANTONIO CARLOS JOBIM VOL.1 (Various Artists)
Samba de uma nota so / Desafinado / Chega de saudade / Corcovado / Meditacao / O amor em paz / How insensitive / Outra vez (once again) / Disscissao / O Grand amor / Dreamer / Brigas, nunca maiss / So em tues bracos / So danco samba / Este seu olhar / A felicidade
CD CD 62083
Saludos Amigos / Jan '96 / Target/BMG

E CONVIDADOS
Waters of March / To say goodbye / For all my life / Seperation sonnet / Song of the jet / She's a carioca / Raining in the rose garden / Theme of love for Gabriella / Happiness / Longing for Bahia / Girl from Ipanema
CD 8266652
Verve / Sep '91 / PolyGram

ESTRADA BRANCA
CD KAR 27
Kardum / May '96 / Discovery

GIRL FROM IPANEMA, THE
CD CD 62084
Saludos Amigos / Jan '96 / Target/BMG

GIRL FROM IPANEMA, THE
Girl from Ipanema / Look to the sky / Antigua / Tema jazz / Caribe / Red blouse / Lamento / Carinhoso / Takatanga / Batidinha / Tide / Rockanalia / Mojave / Triste / Sue Ann / Captain bacardi / Dialogo / Wave / Remember
CD 5405822
A&M / Oct '96 / PolyGram

INEDITO (2CD Set)
CD Set 74321467062
Milan / May '97 / Conifer/BMG / Silva Screen

JAZZ MASTERS
Corcovado / Dreamer / So danco samba / Desafinado / Waters of March / O grande amor / Agua de beber / Double rainbow / O morro tem tem vez / How insensitive / Inutil paisasagem / Favela / Por todo minha vida / Triste / Borzeguim
CD 5164092
Verve / Apr '93 / PolyGram

JOBIM & FRIENDS (Live In Brazil 1993) (Various Artists)
CD 5315562
Verve / Jul '96 / PolyGram

LES PLUS BELLES CHANSONS DE (Jobim, Antonio Carlos & Vinicus De Moraes)
CD KAR 073
IMP / Apr '97 / ADA / Discovery

LIVE IN RIO DE JANEIRO (Jobim, Antonio Carlos & Vinicus De Moraes/ Toquinho/Miucha)
CD 1917462
EPM / Apr '97 / ADA / Discovery

SOME OF THE BEST
Double rainbow / Wave / Someone to light up my life / How insensitive / Anos durados / Janelas abertas / Love theme from The Adventures / Pardon my english / Estrada du sol / Triste / Waters of March / Caminhos cruzados / A felicidade
CD 12631
Laserlight / May '97 / Target/BMG

STONE FLOWER
Brazil / Stone flower / God and the devil in the land of the sun / Sabia / Choro / Andorinha / Amparo / Children's games / Tereza my love
CD 4722382
Sony Jazz / Jan '95 / Sony

TIDE
Girl from Ipanema / Carinhoso / Tema jazz / Sue Ann / Remember / Tide / Takatanga / Caribe / Rockanalia
CD 3930312
A&M / Jul '93 / PolyGram

WAVE
Wave / Red blouse / Look to the sky / Batidinha / Triste / Mojave / Dialogo / Lamento / Antigua / Captain Bacardi
CD 3930022
A&M / Jul '93 / PolyGram

Joboxers

ESSENTIAL BOXERBEAT
Boxerbeat / Crosstown walk up / Curious George / She's got sex / Hide nor hair / Crime of passion / Johnny friendly / Fully booked / Not my night / Just got lucky / Don't add up / Is this really the first time (you been in love) / Dead end streets / One in a milion / Some kind of heart / Strictly business / Don't keep the ladies waiting / Jealous love / Johnny friendly / She's got sex
CD 74321393412
RCA / Aug '96 / BMG

Jocasta

NO COINCIDENCE
Laughing / Go / Life in a day / Change me / Actress / Leave the light on / Something to say / Single as hell / Perfect / Face you / Crackbaby / Inside out
CD 4878612
Columbia / Jun '97 / Sony

Jock Scot

MY PERSONAL CULLODEN (Jock Scot & The Nectarine No.9)
Easy to wirte / Gay paean to Thierry / Above the volcanos / Someone's yearning / Tape your head on / Just another fucked up little druggy / Farewell to Ferodo / There's a hole in daddy's arm / Good God / Domestic bliss / Thunder over Kilburn / Certain beauty / Norman Vaughan's blues / Underdog / White car passing by / All over the world / Nuts going off someone
CD ST 1877
Sano / May '97 / Vital

Jocque, Beau

BEAU JOCQUE BOOGIE (Jocque, Beau & The Zydeco Hi-Rollers)
CD ROUCD 2120
Rounder / Jun '93 / ADA / CM / Direct

GIT IT BEAU JOCQUE (Jocque, Beau & The Zydeco Hi-Rollers)
CD ROUCD 2134
Rounder / Apr '95 / ADA / CM / Direct

GONNA TAKE YOU DOWNTOWN (Jocque, Beau & The Zydeco Hi-Rollers)
CD ROUCD 2150
Rounder / Sep '96 / ADA / CM / Direct

PICK UP ON THIS (Jocque, Beau & The Zydeco Hi-Rollers)
Give it to me / Gardez donci (look at that) / Zydeco boogie woogie / Mardi gras blues / Comin' / Don't tell your mama don't tell your papa / Yesterday / Do right sometime / Hucklebuck / Pick up on this / Cher mignonne / Hi-rollers theme-low rider
CD ROUCD 2129
Rounder / Apr '94 / ADA / CM / Direct

Jodeci

DIARY OF A MAD BAND
My heart belongs to you / Cry for you / Feenin' / What about us / Ride and slide / Alone / You got it / Won't waste you / In the meanwhile / Gimme all you got / Sweaty / Jodecidal hotline / Lately / Let's go through the motions / Success
CD MCLD 19316
MCA / Jul '96 / BMG

FOREVER MY LADY
CD MCLD 19307
MCA / Oct '95 / BMG

SHOW, THE AFTER-PARTY, THE HOTEL, THE
Show / Bring on da funk / Room 723 / Fun 2 nite / Room 577 / S-more / After party / Get on up / Room 499 / Can we flo / Zipper / Let's do it all / Pump it back / DJ Don Jeremy / Freek 'n you / Room 454 / Time and place / Fallin' / Love U 4 life / 4 U / Good luv
CD MCD 11258
MCA / Jul '95 / BMG

Jodimars

LETS ALL ROCK TOGETHER
CD ______ RSRCD 007
Rockstar / Jan '95 / Direct / Nervous / Rollercoaster / TKO Magnum

Joe

EVERYTHING
One for me / I'm in luv / All or nothing / It's alright / (If loving you is wrong) I don't want to be right / What's on your mind / Finally back / Get a little closer / I can do it right / Everything / Baby don't stop / Do me
CD ______ 5188072
Vertigo / Feb '94 / PolyGram

Joel, Billy

BRIDGE, THE
Running on ice / This is the time / Matter of trust / Baby grand / Big man on Mulberry street / Temptation / Code of silence / Getting closer / Modern woman
CD ______ 4655612
CBS / Feb '94 / Sony

FURTHER THAN HEAVEN
CD ______ JHD 004
Tring / Jun '92 / Tring

GLASS HOUSES
You may be right / Sometimes a fantasy / Don't ask me why / It's still rock and roll to me / All for Leyna / I don't want to be alone / Sleeping with the television on / C'etait toi / Close to the borderline / Through the long night
CD ______ 4500872
CBS / Apr '94 / Sony

GREATEST HITS VOL.1 & 2 (2CD Set)
Piano man / Say goodbye to Hollywood / New York state of mind / Stranger / Just the way you are / Movin' out (Anthony's song) / Only the good die young / She's always a woman / My life / Big shot / Honesty / You may be right / It's still rock and roll to me / Pressure / Allen town / Goodnight Saigon / Tell her about it / Uptown girl / Longest time / You're only human (Second wind) / Night is still young
CD ______ CD 88666
CBS / May '94 / Sony

INNOCENT MAN, AN
Easy money / Innocent man / Longest time / This night / Tell her about it / Uptown girl / Careless talk / Christie Lee / Leave a tender moment alone / Keeping the faith
CD ______ 4663292
CBS / Aug '90 / Sony

INNOCENT MAN, AN/STORM FRONT/ THE STRANGER (3CD Set)
Easy money / Innocent man / Longest time / This night / Tell her about it / Uptown girl / Careless talk / Chritie Lee / Leave a tender moment alone / Keeping the faith / That's not her style / We didn't start the fire / Downeaster 'Alexa' / I go to extremes / Shameless / Storm front / Leningrad / State of grace / When I Rome / And so it goes / Movin' out / Stranger / Just the way you are / Scenes from an Italian restaurant / Vienna / Only the good die young / She's always a woman / Get it right the first time / Everybody has a dream
CD Set ______ 4853202
Columbia / Oct '96 / Sony

INNOCENT MAN, AN/THE STRANGER (2CD Set)
CD Set ______ 4716042
Columbia / Jul '92 / Sony

KOHUEPT
Odoya / Angry young man / Honesty / Goodnight Saigon / Stiletto / Big man on Mulberry Street / Baby grand / Innocent man / Allentown / Matter of trust / Only the good die young / Sometimes a fantasy / Uptown girl / Big shot / Back in the USSR / Times they are a changin'
CD ______ 4674482
Columbia / May '92 / Sony

PIANO MAN
Travellin' prayer / Ain't no crime / You're my home / Ballad of Billy The Kid / Worst comes to worst / Stop in Nevada / If I only had the words (to tell you) / Somewhere along the line / Captain Jack
CD ______ CD 32002
CBS / Apr '89 / Sony
CD ______ 4879382
Columbia / Jul '97 / Sony

RIVER OF DREAMS
No man's land / Great wall of China / Blonde over blue / Minor variation / Shades of grey / All about soul / Lullaby (Goodnight, my angel) / River of dreams / Two thousand years / Famous last words
CD ______ 4738722
Columbia / Aug '93 / Sony

SONGS IN THE ATTIC
Miami 2017 / Summer, highland falls / Street life serenade / Los Angelenos / She's got a way / Everybody loves you now / Say goodbye to Hollywood / Captain Jack / You're my home / Ballad of Billy The Kid / I've loved these days
CD ______ CD 32364
CBS / Jun '89 / Sony

STORM FRONT
That's not her style / We didn't start the fire / Downeaster Alexa / I go to extremes / Shameless / Storm front / Leningrad / State of grace / When in Rome / And so it goes
CD ______ 4656582
CBS / Mar '96 / Sony

STRANGER, THE
Movin' out / Just the way you are / Scenes from an Italian restaurant / Vienna / Stranger / Only the good die young / She's always a woman / Get it right the first time / Everybody has a dream
CD ______ 4509142
CBS / Jun '89 / Sony

STREETLIFE SERENADE
Los Angelenos / Great suburban showdown / Root beer rag / Roberta / Entertainer / Last of the big time spenders / Street life serenade / Weekend song / Souvenir / Mexican connection
CD ______ 4844612
Columbia / Feb '97 / Sony

TURNSTILES
I've loved these days / Miami 2017 / Angry young man / Say goodbye to Hollywood / James / New York State of mind / Prelude / Angry young man / Summer / Highland falls / All you wanna do is dance
CD ______ 4746812
Columbia / Feb '97 / Sony

Joey Negro

DISCO HOUSE (Mixed By Joey Negro) (Various Artists)
CD ______ JAPECD 105
Escapade / Jul '95 / 3mv/Sony / Prime

GET DOWN TONIGHT (Joey Negro & Doc Livingstone)
CD ______ 336202
Koch Dance Force / Jun '97 / Koch

Jog, Pandit V.G.

VIOLIN
CD ______ MR 1003
Moment / Jul '93 / ADA / Koch

Jogi, Iqbal

PASSION OF PAKISTAN (Jogi, Iqbal & Party)
CD ______ TCD 1045
Tradition / Mar '97 / ADA / Vital

Johansen, Bjorn

DEAR HENRIK
CD ______ GMCD 152
Gemini / Oct '89 / Cadillac

Johansen, David

BUSTER'S HAPPY HOUR (Poindexter, Buster)
CD ______ RSFCD 818
Sequel / Oct '94 / BMG

Johansson, Jan

JAZZ PA UNGERSK/IN PLENO (Johansson, Jan & Svend Asmussen)
CD ______ HE 014CD
Heptagon / Aug '96 / ADA

Johansson, Ulf

BIG BAND WULF
I let a song go out of my heart / City express / In a mellow tone / I want to be happy / Ankbrand / Nuages / I won't dance / Bye bye blackbird
CD ______ NCD 8820
Phontastic / '93 / Cadillac / Jazz Music / Wellard

TRACKIN' THE WULF
Leopard shoe / Lover come back to me / China boy / Song of Sarek / Nice work if you can get it / Moose blues / Sweet Lorraine / 2.19 Blues
CD ______ NCD 8809
Phontastic / Dec '94 / Cadillac / Jazz Music / Wellard

John & Mary

VICTORY GARDENS
Red wooden beads / Azalea festival / Piles of dead leaves / We have nothing / Rags of flowers / I became alone / Open window / July 6th / Pram / Un Canadien errant
CD ______ RCD 10203
Rykodisc / Jul '91 / ADA / Vital

WEEDKILLERS DAUGHTER, THE
Two worlds parted / Angels of stone / Your return / Clare's scarf / Cemetary ridge / Nightfall / I wanted you / One step backward / Fly me to the north / Clouds of reason / Maid of the mist / Poor murdered woman
CD ______ RCD 10259
Rykodisc / Mar '93 / ADA / Vital

John Ac Alun

YR WYLAN WEN CHWARELWR
CD ______ SCD 2077
Sain / Dec '94 / ADA / Direct / Greyhound

John Came

RHYTHMICON
CD ______ CDSTUMM 140
Mute / Jun '95 / RTM/Disc

John, Elton

17.11.70
CD ______ 5281652
Rocket / Oct '95 / PolyGram

21 AT 33
Changing the crown / Dear God / Give me the love / Little Jeannie / Never gonna fall in love again / Sartorial eloquence / Take me back / Two rooms at the end of the world / White lady white powder
CD ______ 8000552
Rocket / '83 / PolyGram

BLUE MOVES (2CD Set)
Your starter tonight / One horse town / Chameleon / Boogie pilgrim / Cage the songbird / Crazy water / Shoulder holster / Sorry seems to be the hardest word / Out of the blue / Between 17 and 20 / Wide-eyed and laughter / Someone's final love song / Where's the shoorah / If there's a God in Heaven (what's he waiting for) / Idol / Non-existent TV series, A theme from / Bite your lip (get up and dance)
CD Set ______ 5325542
Rocket / Jun '96 / PolyGram

BREAKING HEARTS
Restless / Slow down Georgie / Who wears these shoes / Breaking hearts / Li'l refrigerator / Passengers / In neon / Burning bridges / Did he shoot her / Sad songs
CD ______ 8220882
Rocket / Jun '84 / PolyGram

CAPTAIN FANTASTIC & THE BROWN DIRT COWBOY
Captain Fantastic and the Brown Dirt Cowboy / Tower of Babel / Bitter fingers / Tell me when the whistle blows / Someone saved my life tonight / (Gotta get a) meal ticket / Better off dead / Writing / We all fall in love sometimes / Curtains / Lucy in the sky with diamonds / One day at a time / Philadelphia freedom
CD ______ 5281602
Rocket / Jul '95 / PolyGram

CARIBOU
Bitch is back / Pinky / Dixie Lily / Solar prestige a gammon / Don't let the sun go down on me / Ticking / Grimsby / You're so static / I've seen the saucers / Stinker / Pinball wizard / Sick city / Cold highway / Step into Christmas
CD ______ 5281582
Rocket / May '95 / PolyGram

CHARTBUSTERS GOES POP
Don't forget to remember / I can't tell the bottom from the top / Young, gifted and black / Signed, sealed, delivered (I'm yours) / Natural sinner / She sold me magic / Cotton fields / Spirit in the sky / Good morning freedom / Travelling band / In the summertime / Yellow river / United we stand / My baby loves lovin' / Love of the common people / Lady D'arbanville / Snake in the grass / Up around the bend
CD ______ RPM 142
RPM / Mar '95 / Pinnacle

DON'T SHOOT ME I'M ONLY THE PIANO PLAYER
Daniel / Teacher I need you / Elderberry wine / Blues for my baby and me / Midnight creeper / Have mercy on the criminal / I'm gonna be a teenage idol / Texan love song / Crocodile rock / High flying bird / Screw you / Jack Rabbit / Whenever you're ready (we'll go steady again) / Skyline pigeon
CD ______ 5281542
Rocket / May '95 / PolyGram

DUETS (John, Elton & Various Artists)
Teardrops: *John, Elton & k.d. Lang* / When I think about love (I think about you): *John, Elton & PM Dawn* / Power: *John, Elton & Little Richard* / Shaky ground: *John, Elton & Don Henley* / True love: *John, Elton & Kiki Dee* / If you were me: *John, Elton & Chris Rea* / Woman's needs: *John, Elton & Tammy Wynette* / Don't let the sun go down on me: *John, Elton & George Michael* / Old friend: *John, Elton & Nik Kershaw* / Go on and on: *John, Elton & Gladys Knight* / Don't go breaking my heart: *John, Elton & Rupaul* / Ain't nothing like the real thing: *John, Elton & Marcella Detroit* / I'm your puppet: *John, Elton & Paul Young* / Love letters: *John, Elton & Bonnie Raitt* / Born to lose: *John, Elton & Leonard Cohen* / Duet for one: *John, Elton*
CD ______ 5184782
Rocket / Dec '93 / PolyGram

ELTON JOHN
Your song / I need you to turn to / Take me to the pilot / No shoe strings on Louise / First episode at Heinton / Sixty years on / Border song / Greatest discovery / Cage / King must die / Bad side of the moon / Grey seal / Rock 'n' roll Madonna
CD ______ 5281562
Rocket / May '95 / PolyGram

ELTON JOHN SONGBOOK (Various Artists)
CD ______ VSOPCD 192
Connoisseur Collection / Oct '93 / Pinnacle

EMPTY SKY
Empty sky / Valhalla / Western Ford gateway / Hymn 2000 / Lady what's tomorrow / Sails / Scaffold / Skyline pigeon / Gulliver/ It's hay chewed/Reprise / Lady Samantha / All across the heavens / It's me that you need / Just like strange rain
CD ______ 5281572
Rocket / May '95 / PolyGram

FOX, THE
Breaking down barriers / Heart in the right place / Just like Belgium / Fox / Nobody wins / Fascist faces / Carla etude - fanfare / Chloe / Heels of the wind / Elton's song
CD ______ 8000632
Rocket / Jun '89 / PolyGram

GOODBYE YELLOW BRICK ROAD
Funeral for a friend (Love lies bleeding) / Candle in the wind / Benny and the jets / Goodbye yellow brick road / This song has no title / Grey seal / Jamaica jerk off / I've seen that movie too / Sweet painted lady / Ballad of Danny Bailey (1909-1934) / Dirty little girl / All the girls love Alice / Your sister can't twist (But she can rock 'n' roll) / Saturday night's alright for fighting / Roy Rogers / Social disease / Harmony
CD ______ 5281592
Rocket / May '95 / PolyGram

HERE AND THERE (Royal Festival Hall/ Madison Square Gardens 1974) (2CD Set)
Skyline pigeon / Border song / Take me to the pilot / Country comfort / Love song / Bad side of the moon / Burn down the mission / Honky cat / Crocodile rock / Candle in the wind / Your song / Saturday night's alright for fighting / Funeral for a friend (Love lies bleeding) / Rocket man / Take me to the pilot / Benny and the jets / Grey seal / Daniel / You're so static / Whatever gets you thru the night / Lucy in the sky with diamonds / I saw her standing there / Don't let the sun go down on me / Your song / Bitch is back
CD Set ______ 5281642
Rocket / Oct '95 / PolyGram

HONKY CHATEAU
Honky cat / Mellow / I think I'm going to kill myself / Susie (dramas) / Rocket man / Salvation / Slave / Amy / Mona Lisas and mad hatters / Hercules / Slave (alternative version)
CD ______ 5281622
Rocket / Jul '95 / PolyGram

ICE ON FIRE
This town / Cry to heaven / Soul glove / Nikita / Too young / Wrap her up / Satellite / Tell me what the papers say / Candy by the pound / Shoot down the moon
CD ______ 8262132
Rocket / Jan '95 / PolyGram

INTERVIEW DISC
CD ______ TELL 08
Network / Dec '96 / Total/BMG

JUMP UP
Dear John / Spiteful child / Ball and chain / Legal boys / I am your robot / Blue eyes / Empty garden / Princess / Where have all the good times gone / All quiet on the Western Front
CD ______ 8000372
Rocket / Jan '95 / PolyGram

LADY SAMANTHA
Rock 'n' roll Madonna / Whenever you're ready / Bad side of the moon / Jack rabbit / Into the old man's shoes / It's me that you need / Ho ho ho (Who'd be a turkey at Christmas) / Screw you / Skyline pigeon / Just like strange rain / Grey seal / Honey roll / Lady Samantha / Friends
CD ______ 8320192
Rocket / Jun '87 / PolyGram

LEATHER JACKETS
Leather jackets / Hoop of fire / Don't trust that woman / Go it alone / Gypsy heart / Slow rivers / Heartache all over the world / Angeline / Memory of love / Paris I fall apart
CD ______ 8304872
Rocket / Nov '86 / PolyGram

LIVE IN AUSTRALIA
Sixty years on / I need you to turn to / Greatest discovery / Tonight / Sorry seems to be the hardest word / King must die / Take me to the pilot / Tiny dancer / Have mercy on the criminal / Madman across the water / Candle in the wind / Burn down the mission / Your song / Don't let the sun go down on me
CD ______ 8324702
Rocket / Feb '87 / PolyGram

LOVE SONGS
Sacrifice / Candle in the wind / I guess that's why they call it the blues / Don't let the sun go down on me: *John, Elton & George Michael* / Sorry seems to be the hardest word / Blue eyes / Daniel / Nikita / Your song / One / Someone saved my life tonight / True love: *John, Elton & Kiki Dee* / Can you feel the love tonight / Circle of life / Blessed / Please / Song for Guy

CD 5287882
Rocket / Nov '95 / PolyGram

MADE IN ENGLAND
Believe / Made in England / House / Cold / Pain / Belfast / Latitude / Please / Man / Lies / Blessed
CD 5261852
Rocket / Mar '95 / PolyGram

MADMAN ACROSS THE WATER
Levon / Razor face / Madman across the water / Indian sunset / Holiday inn / Rotten peaches / All the nasties / Goodbye / Tiny dancer
CD 5281612
Rocket / Jul '95 / PolyGram

ONE, THE
Simple life / One / Sweat it out / Whitewash country / North / When a woman doesn't want you / Runaway train / Last song / Understanding women / On dark street / Emily
CD 5123602
Rocket / Jun '92 / PolyGram

RARE MASTERS
Madman across the water / Into the old man's shoes / Rock me when he's gone / Slave / Skyline pigeon / Jack rabbit / Whenever you're ready (we'll go steady again) / Let me be your car / Screw you / One day at a time / Cold highway / Sick city / Ho ho ho (Who'd be a turkey at Christmas) / Step into Christmas / I saw her standing there / House of cards / Planes / Sugar on the floor / Here's to the next time / Lady Samantha / All across the havens / It's me that you need / Just like strange rain / Bad side of the moon / Rock 'n' roll Madonna / Grey seal / Friends / Michelle's song / Seasons / Variation on Michelle's song / Can I put you on / Honey roll / Reprise seasons / Four moods / I meant to do my work today (a day in the country) / Variation on friends
CD Set 5143052
Rocket / Jan '93 / PolyGram

REG STRIKES BACK
Town of plenty / Word in Spanish / Mona Lisas and mad hatters part II / I don't wanna go on with you like that / Goodbye Marlon Brando / Heavy traffic / Poor cow / Camera never lies / Since God invented girls
CD 8347012
Rocket / Jan '95 / PolyGram

ROCK 'N' ROLL MADONNA
CD 5502132
Spectrum / Mar '94 / PolyGram

ROCK OF THE WESTIES
Yell help / Wednesday night / Ugly / Dan Dare (pilot of the future) / Island girl / Grow some funk of your own / I feel like a bullet (in the gun of Robert Ford) / Street kids / Hard luck story / Feed me / Billy Bones and the white bird / Don't go breaking my heart
CD 5281632
Rocket / Jul '95 / PolyGram

SINGLE MAN, A
Big dipper / Georgia / I don't care / It ain't gonna be easy / Madness / Part time love / Return to Paradise / Reverie / Shine on through / Shooting star / Song for Guy
CD 8268052
Rocket / Sep '89 / PolyGram

SLEEPING WITH THE PAST
Club at the end of the street / Durban deep / Sacrifice / Blue Avenue / Healing hands / Whispers
CD 8388392
Rocket / Sep '89 / PolyGram

SOLO PIANO PLAYS THE HITS OF ELTON JOHN (Various Artists)
CD GRF 233
Tring / Aug '93 / Tring

TO BE CONTINUED....THE VERY BEST OF ELTON JOHN (4CD Set)
Come back baby / Lady Samantha / It's me that you need / Your song / Rock 'n' roll Madonna / Bad side of the moon / Take me to the pilot / Border song / Sixty years on / Country comfort / Gray seal / Friends / Levon / Tiny dancer / Madman across the water / Honky cat / Mona Lisa's and mad hatters / Rocket man / Daniel / Crocodile rock / Benny and the jets / Goodbye yellow brick road / All the girls love Alice / Funeral for a friend (Love lies bleeding) / Love lies / Bleeding / Whenever you're ready (we'll go steady again) / Saturday night's alright for fighting / Jack Rabbit / Harmony / Young man's blues / Step into Christmas / Bitch is back / Pinball wizard / Someone saved my life tonight / Philadelphia freedom / One day at a time / Lucy in the sky with diamonds / I saw her standing there / Island girl / Sorry seems to be the hardest word / Don't go breaking my heart: *John, Elton & Kiki Dee* / I feel like a bullet (in the gun of Robert Ford) / Ego / Empty garden (hey hey Johnny) / I guess that's why they call it the blues / I'm still standing / Sad songs (say so much) / Act of war / Nikita / Candle in the wind / Carla etude / Don't let the sun go down on me / I don't want to go on with you like that / Give peace a chance / Sacrifice / Made for me / Easier to walk away / Understanding women / Suit of wolves
CD Set 8482362
Rocket / Nov '91 / PolyGram

TOO LOW FOR ZERO
Cold as Christmas / I'm still standing / Too low for zero / Religion / I guess that's why they call it the blues / Crystal / Kiss the bride / Whipping boy / My baby's a saint / One more arrow
CD 8110522
Rocket / '83 / PolyGram

TUMBLEWEED CONNECTION
Ballad of a well known gun / Come down in time / Country comfort / Son of your father / My father's gun / Where to now St. Peter / Love song / Amoreena / Talking old soldiers / Burn down the mission / Into the old man's shoes / Madman across the water
CD 5281552
Rocket / May '95 / PolyGram

TWO ROOMS (A Celebration Of The Songs Of Elton John & Bernie Taupin) (Various Artists)
Border song: *Clapton, Eric* / Rocket man: *Bush, Kate* / Come down in time: *Sting* / Saturday night's alright for fighting: *Who* / Crocodile rock: *Beach Boys* / Daniel: *Wilson Phillips* / Sorry seems to be the hardest word: *Cocker, Joe* / Levon: *Bon Jovi, Jon* / Bitch is back: *Turner, Tina* / Your song: *Stewart, Rod* / Philadelphia freedom: *Hall & Oates* / Don't let the sun go down on me: *Adams, Oleta* / Madman across the water: *Hornsby, Bruce* / Burn down the mission: *Collins, Phil* / Tonight: *Michael, George*
CD 8457492
Rocket / Oct '91 / PolyGram

VERY BEST OF ELTON JOHN, THE (2CD Set)
Your song / Rocket man / Honky cat / Crocodile rock / Daniel / Goodbye yellow brick road / Saturday night's alright for fighting / Candle in the wind / Don't let the sun go down on me / Lucy in the sky with diamonds / Philadelphia freedom / Someone saved my life tonight / Pinball wizard / Bitch is back / Don't go breaking my heart / Benny and the jets / Sorry seems to be the hardest word / Song for Guy / Part time love / Blue eyes / I guess that's why they call it the blues / I'm still standing / Kiss the bride / Sad songs / Passengers / Nikita / Sacrifice / You gotta love someone / I don't wanna go on with you like that / Easier to walk away
CD Set 8469472
Rocket / Oct '90 / PolyGram

VICTIM OF LOVE
Johnny B Goode / Warm love in a cold world / Born bad / Thunder in the night / Spotlight / Street boogie / Victim of love
CD 5128812
Rocket / Jan '95 / PolyGram

John F. Kennedy Memorial ...

PLAYING POPULAR IRISH MARCHES (John F. Kennedy Memorial Pipe Band)
CD IRB 1922CD
Outlet / May '95 / ADA / CM / Direct / Duncans / Koch / Ross

John, Little Willie

15 HITS
CD KCD 5004
King / Apr '97 / Avid/BMG

FEVER
Fever / I'm stickin' with you baby / Do something for me / Love, life and money / Suffering with the blues / Dinner date / All around the world / Need your love so bad / Young girl / Letter from my darling / I've got to go cry / My nerves
CD CDCHARLY 246
Charly / Oct '90 / Koch

SURE THINGS
CD KCD 739
King / Mar '90 / Avid/BMG

John, Mable

STAY OUT OF THE KITCHEN
Stay out of the kitchen / Leftover love / Able Mable / Shouldn't I love him / Catch that man / Ain't giving it up / Running out / Love tornado / Bigger and better / Sweet devil / It's catching / Drop on in / That woman will give it a try / That's what my love can do / I love you more than words can say / Have your cake / Be warm to me / I taught you how / If you give up what you got (see what you lost / Don't get caught / Man's too busy / I'm a big girl now / To love what I want, and want what I love / Sorry about that / I need your love so bad
CD CDSXD 048
Stax / Sep '92 / Pinnacle

John McGee Orchestra

SLINKY
CD CREV 047CD
Rev-Ola / Aug '97 / 3mv/Vital

John, Michael

SINGALONG PARTY (A Collection Of All-Time Favourite Songs/2CD Set) (John, Michael Singers)
I've got a loverly bunch of coconuts / Sweet Rosie O'Grady / On Ilkla moor baht 'at / There's a tavern in the town / John Peel / Early one morning / Little brown jug / White cliffs of Dover / Sweet Georgia Brown / Yes sir, that's my baby / Golden locket / Golden slippers / Blue tail fly / Old folks at home / Daisy, daisy / Baby face / Sunny side of the street / Comin' through the rye / Over the sea to Skye / Charlie is my darlin' / K K K Katy / I want a girl / Cockles and mussels / Last rose of summer / Minstrel boy / Goodnight Irene / Hello, hello, who's your lady friend / Finnegan's wake / Flash bang wallop / Sippin' cider / Back home / Lily of Laguna / In the shade of the old apple tree / Side by side / Come landlord / Fill the flowing bowl / Goodnight ladies / Red river valley / Ma, he's making eyes at me / Battle hymn of the republic / Poor old Joe / Marching through Georgia / If you were the only girl in the world / Something nice to say / Underneath the arches / Wi' a hundred pipers / My bonnie lies over the ocean / Loch Lomond / When I'm sixty four / Crazy / Danny boy / Harp that once / She'll be coming round the mountain / You are my sunshine / When Irish eyes are smiling / Sentimental journey / Don't dilly dally
CD Set 330332
Hallmark / Mar '97 / Carlton

John-Krol, Louisa

ARGO
Dunsany's hope / Hyperion / Argo / I'm not walking / Little wanderer / Inanna / Out of the eqipage / Inside the bubble / House of legend / Duncan the fiddler / Oak, ash and thorn / Healer's names
CD EV 0010
Evolving Discs / Jul '97 / Pinnacle

Johnboy

CLAIM DEDICATIONS
CD TR 27CD
Trance / Aug '94 / SRD

PISTOL SWING
CD TR 16CD
Trance / Jun '93 / SRD

Johnna

PRIDE
CD HF 50CD
PWL / Sep '96 / Warner Music

Johnnie & Jack

JOHNNIE AND JACK AND THE TENNESSEE MOUNTAIN BOYS (Johnnie & Jack & The Tennessee Mountain Boys)
Lord watch over my daddy / There's no housing shortage in heaven / Love in the first degree / Too many blues / This is the end / Paper boy / Sing Tom Kitty / Jolie blon / I'll be listening / This world can't stand long / Old country church / I heard my name on the radio / Turn your radio on / He will set your fields on fire / What about you / For old times sake / Just when I need you / She went with a smile / Trials and tribulations / Buried alive / I heard my saviour call / Pray together and we'll stay together / Shout / You better get down on your knees and pray / Too much sinning / Jesus hits like the atom bomb / Too far from God / Jesus remembered me / Poison love / Lonesome / I'm gonna love you one more time / Smile on my lips / Take my ring from your finger / I can't tell my heart that / Cryin' heat blues / Let your conscience be your guide / Hummingbird / How can I believe in you / You tried to ruin my name / Ashes of love / Three ways of knowing / When you want a little loving / You can't fool God / Precious memories / Shake my mothers hand for me / When the saviour reached down for me / Slow poison / But I love you just the same / Just for tonight / Don't show off / Heart trouble / Two timing blues / I've gone and done it again / Don't let the stars get in your eyes / Only one I ever loved I lost / Borrowed diamonds / Private property / SOS / Called from Potter's field / I'll live with God (to die no more) / Angel's rock me to sleep / Eastern gate / Hank Williams will live forever / South in New Orleans / You're my downfall / Winner of your heart / Don't say goodbye if you love me / Pig latin song / Love trap / Cheated out of love / From the manger to the cross / I'm ready to go / God put a rainbow in the clouds / Don't give away your bible / Crazy worried mind / Love's a pleasure not a habit in Mexico / You've got me in your power / Dynamite kisses / I loved you better than you knew / Pick-up date / I get so lonely / You're just what the doctor ordered / I ain't got time / All the time / Goodnight sweetheart, goodnight / Honey, I need you / Kiss crazy baby / Beware of it / Sincerely / Carry on / No one dear but you / We live in two different worlds / So lovely baby / Look out / Don't waste your tears / Weary moments / Dream when you're lonely / Tom cat's kittens / Feet of clay / I want to be loved / You can't divorce my heart / Baby, it's in the making / I wonder why you said goodbye / Love love love / What's the reason I'm not pleasin' you / Love fever / Live and let live / When my blue moon turns to gold again / Why not confess / Banana boat song (Day O) / Mr. Clock / Love me now / If tears would bring you back / That's why I'm leavin' / Oh boy, I love her / Baby I need you / Nothing but sweet lies / Move it on over / No one will ever know / I don't mean to cry / I wonder where you are tonight / Slowly / Wedding bells / I never can come back to you / You are my sunshine / Stop the world (and let me off) / Camel walk stroll / I've seen this movie before / Yeah / Leave our moon alone / Lonely island pearl / That's the way the cookie crumbles / Just when I needed you / With a smile on my lips / What do you know about heartaches / I wonder if you know / It's just the idea / Sailor man / Wild and wicked world / Sweetie pie / Happy, lucky love / Just like you / Dreams come true / She loves me no more / Country music has gone to town / Talkin' eyes / Lonesome night blues / Love problems / I'm always by myself when I'm alone / Smiles and tears / Uncle John's bongos / Let my heart be broken / Sweet baby / Moon is high and so am I / 36-22-36 / What do you think of her now / Bye bye love / Foolin' around / Waterloo / Little bitty tear / I overlooked an orchard / You'll never get a better chance than this
CD Set BCD 15553
Bear Family / Jun '92 / Direct / Rollercoaster / Swift

JOHNNY & JACK WITH KITTY WELLS AT KWKH
Raining on the mountain / Intro / Orange blossom special / White dove / Singing waterfall / Sweeping through the gate / Wake up Susan / I heard my mother weeping / My bucket's got a hole in it / This world can't stand / Cheatam country breakdown / Death of litty Kathy Fiscus / No letter in the mail today / I saw the light / Mississippi sawyer / Cotton eyed Joe / Little cabin home on the hill / Love or hate / He will set your fields on fire / It's raining on the mountain
CD BCD 15808
Bear Family / Nov '94 / Direct / Rollercoaster / Swift

Johnny & The Hurricanes

DEFINITIVE COLLECTION, THE (2CD Set)
Cross fire / Lazy / Red river rock / Buckeye / Reveille rock / Time bomb / Sand storm / Beatnik fly / Down yonder / Sheba / Rocking goose / Revival / Molly O / You are my sunshine / Ja-da / Mr. Lonely / High voltage / Old smokie / Traffic jam / Farewell farewell / Miserlou / Salvation / San Antonio rose / Come on train / Minnesota fats / Sheik of Araby / Whatever happened to Baby Jane / Greens and beans / Money honey / Shadows / Kaw-Liga / Rough road / Happy time / Cut out / Storm warning / Bam boo / Thunderbolt / Joy ride / Rock-cha / Kid / Bye bye blackbird / Teensville tonight / Mister Irving / Tom's tune / Corn pome / Milk shake / Cyclone / Travelin' / Beanbags / Rockin' T / Hot fudge / Corn bread / Catnip / 'Hep' canary / Oh du lieber augustin / James Bond theme / Hungry eye / It's a mad, mad world / That's all
CD Set CPCD 81932
Charly / Aug '96 / Koch

RED RIVER ROCK
CD RMB 75026
Remember / Nov '93 / Total/BMG

Johnny & The Roccos

GREAT SCOTS
Crazy baby / Cat talk / Rockabilly / My baby's crazy about Elvis / Don't wake up the kids / Sneaky Pete / Stompin with the wildcats / Blue blue day / Cherokee boogie / Rock 'n' roll record girl / Holocaust boogie / My baby left me / I'm a little mixed up / Honey rush / Flying saucers / Hey little girl / Beat / Feelings of love / Southern guitar boogie / Good rockin' tonight
CD CDMF 091
Magnum Force / Mar '95 / TKO Magnum

Johnny Hates Jazz

TURN BACK THE CLOCK
Shattered dreams / Heart of gold / Turn back the clock / Don't say it's love / What other reason / I don't want to be a hero / Listen / Different reasons / Don't let it end this way / Foolish heart / Turn back the clock (extended) / Heart of gold (extended) / Shattered dreams (extended)
CD CDV 2475
Virgin / '88 / EMI

VERY BEST OF JOHNNY HATES JAZZ
Shattered dreams / My secret garden / Me and my foolish heart / Living in the past / I don't want to be a hero / Cage / Turn the tide / Heart of gold / Don't say it's love / Let me change your mind tonight / Last to know / Fool's gold / Cracking up / Turn back the clock
CD CDVIP 119
Virgin VIP / Nov '93 / EMI

Johnny P

BAD IN A DANCEHALL
CD RRTGCD 7784
Rohit / Jul '90 / Jet Star

Johnny Violent

SHOCKER (2CD Set)
2 kicks for yes / E heads must die / North Korea goes bang / Gotterdammerung / Destructor lives / US intervention / Hardest gabba / Kamikaze / I'm gonna fuck you / Imploding head / Happy birthday / Johnny is a bastard / Pull the trigger / Burn out
CD _______ **MOSH 153CD**
CD Set _______ **MOSH 153CDL**
Earache / Oct '96 / Vital

Johnny Was

SUMMER LOVERS
CD _______ **CDREP 8013**
Candor / Mar '95 / Else

Johns, Bibi

BELLABIMBA
Night filled with echoes / Someone to kiss your tears away / Puppy love / Two faced clock / I could never be ashamed of you / I wish I was a puppet on a string / Auf Jamaika schenken abends die Maltrosen / Bella bimba / Ich habe solche Angst / Sehnsucht / Bye bye baby: *Johns, Bibi & Angele Durand* / Little rock: *Johns, Bibi & Angele Durand* / Bimbo / In Barrabana / An jedem finger zehn / Gilly gilly ossenfeffer Katzenellenbogen the sea / Carnavalito / Ro ro ro Robinson / Die gipsy band / Papa tanzt mambo / Nach uns die sintflut: *Johns, Bibi & Paul Kuhn* / Zwei herzen im mai / Ich mocht auf deiner hochzeit tanzen: *Johns, Bibi & Paul Kuhn*
CD _______ **BCD 15649**
Bear Family / Mar '92 / Direct / Rollercoaster / Swift

John's Black Dirt

PERPETUAL OPTIMISM IS A FORCE MULTIPLIER
CD _______ **GROW 202**
Grass / Oct '94 / Pinnacle / SRD

John's Children

LEGENDARY ORGASM ALBUM, THE
Smashed blocked / Just what you want, just what you'll get / Killer Ben / Jagged time lapse / Smashed blocked (Live) / You're a nothing / Not the sort of girl / Cold on me / Leave me alone / Let me know / Just what you want, just what you'll get / Why do you lie / Strange affair / But she's mine
CD _______ **CDMRED 31**
Cherry Red / Sep '96 / Pinnacle

PETALS AND FLOWERS
Desdemona / Remember Thomas A Beckett / It's been a long time / Arthur Green / Midsummer night's scene / Sarah crazy child / Jagged time lapse / Go go girl / Come and play with me in the garden / Perfumed garden of Gulliver Smith / Midsummer night's scene / Not the sort of girl you take to bed / Help / Casbah candy
CD _______ **PILOT 018**
Burning Airlines / Aug '97 / Total/Pinnacle

SMASHED BLOCKED
Smashed blocked / Just what you want, just what you'll get / Strange affair / But she's mine / Hippy gumbo / Jagged time lapse / Midsummer nights scene / Not the sort of girl you take to bed / Mustang Ford / Love I thought I'd found / Remember Thomas A' Beckett / Come and play with me in the garden / Daddy rolling stone / Hot rod Mama / Perfumed garden of Gulliver Smith / Sally was an angel
CD _______ **PILOT 012**
Burning Airlines / Aug '97 / Total/Pinnacle

Johns, Evan

BOMBS AWAY (Johns, Evan & The H-Bombs)
Love is gone / I'm a little mixed up / Done by me / Twister county / Dance, Frannie, Dance / Lessons that burn / Oh New Orleans / Boudin man / Pain of love / Tired of trash / Still feels good / Poor boy's dream
CD _______ **RCD 10117**
Rykodisc / Dec '92 / ADA / Vital

KINSFOLK
CD _______ **VIRUS 19CD**
Alternative Tentacles / Jun '93 / Cargo / Greyhound / Pinnacle

ROLLIN' THRU THE NIGHT (Johns, Evan & The H-Bombs)
CD _______ **VIRUS 47CD**
Alternative Tentacles / '92 / Cargo / Greyhound / Pinnacle

Johnson Mountain Boys

BLUE DIAMOND
Duncan and Brady / My better days / It don't bring you back to me / Christine Leroy / See God's ark movin' / Blue diamond mines / Teardrops like raindrops / Our last goodbye / Future remains / You done me wrong / Roll on blues / There goes my love / Only a hobo / Harbor of love
CD _______ **ROUCD 0293**
Rounder / Apr '93 / ADA / CM / Direct

FAVOURITES
CD _______ **ROUCD 11509**
Rounder / '88 / ADA / CM / Direct

LET THE WHOLE WORLD TALK
Let the whole world talk / Maury river blues / Memories cover everything I own / He said if I be lifted up / Goodbye to the blues / Virginia waltz / Maybe you will change your mind / Memories that we shared / Sweeter love than yours / I'll never know / Shouting in the air / Beneath the old Southern skies
CD _______ **ROUCD 0225**
Rounder / Aug '88 / ADA / CM / Direct

LIVE AT THE BIRCHMERE
CD _______ **ROUCD 0191**
Rounder / Oct '94 / ADA / CM / Direct

Johnson, 'Blind' Willie

COMPLETE RECORDINGS, THE (2CD Set)
I know his blood can make me whole / Jesus make up my dying bed / It's nobody's fault but mine / Mother's children have a hard time / Dark was the night / Cold was the ground / If I had my way I'd tear the building down / I'm gonna run to the city of refuge / Jesus is coming soon / Lord I can't just keep from crying / Keep your lamp trimmed and burning / Let your light shine on me / God don't never change / Bye and bye I'm going to see the King / Sweeter as the years roll by / You'll need somebody on your bond / When the war was on / Praise God I'm satisfied / Take your burden to the Lord and leave it / There / Take your stand / God moves on the water / Can't nobody hide from God / If it had not been for Jesus / Rain don't fall on me / Trouble will soon be over / Soul of a man / Everybody ought to treat a stranger right / Church, I'm fully saved today / John the revelator / You're gonna need somebody on your bond
CD Set _______ **4721902**
Columbia / Jun '96 / Sony

DARK WAS THE NIGHT
CD _______ **IGOCD 2024**
Indigo / Sep '95 / ADA / Direct

SWEETER AS THE YEARS GO BY
CD _______ **YAZCD 1078**
Yazoo / Apr '91 / ADA / CM / Koch

Johnson, Bob

KING OF ELFLANDS DAUGHTER, THE (Johnson, Bob & Peter Knight)
Request / Lirazel / Witch / Alveric's journey / Through Elfland / Rune of the elf king / Cooing of the troll / Just another day of searching / Too much magic / Beyond the fields / We know
CD _______ **EDCD 342**
Edsel / Feb '92 / Pinnacle

Johnson, Budd

BUDDY & ELLA JOHNSON 1953-1964 (Johnson, Budd & Ella)
CD Set _______ **BCD 15479**
Bear Family / Mar '92 / Direct / Rollercoaster / Swift

CLASSICS 1939-1942 (Johnson, Budd Band)
CD _______ **CLASSICS 884**
Classics / Jul '96 / Discovery / Jazz Music

JPJ QUARTET (Johnson, Budd & Dill Jones/Bill Pemberton/Oliver Jackson)
CD _______ **STCD 8235**
Storyville / May '96 / Cadillac / Jazz Music / Wellard

MR. BECHET
CD _______ **BB 882**
Black & Blue / Apr '97 / Discovery / Koch / Wellard

WALK 'EM (The Decca Sessions) (Johnson, Budd Orchestra)
Walk 'em / Since I fell for you / Baby you're always on my mind / Boogie woogie's mother-in-law / You gotta walk that chalk line / I don't know what's troublin' your mind / Be careful (if you can't be good) / Boot man blues / 'Til my baby comes back / I'm gonna jump in the river / Talking about another man's wife / No more love / Shake 'em up / Satisfy my soul / Stormy weather / Did you see Jackie Robinson hit that ball / That's the stuff you gotta watch / They all say I'm the biggest fool / Fine brown frame / You'll get them blues / Southern echoes / When my man comes home / Please Mr. Johnson / Shufflin' and rollin'
CD _______ **CDCHD 623**
Ace / Jun '96 / Pinnacle

Johnson, Bunk

BUNK & LU (Johnson, Bunk & Lu Watters)
CD _______ **GTCD 12024**
Good Time Jazz / Oct '93 / Complete/ Pinnacle

BUNK JOHNSON (Johnson, Bunk & His Superior Jazz Band)
Panama / Down by the riverside / Storyville blues / Ballin' the Jack / Make me a pallet on the floor / Weary blues / Moose march / Bunk's blues / Yes Lord I'm crippled / Bunk Johnson talking
CD _______ **GTCD 12048**
Good Time Jazz / Jul '94 / Complete/ Pinnacle

BUNK JOHNSON & HIS NEW ORLEANS BAND
CD _______ **DOCD 1001**
Document / Jun '96 / ADA / Hot Shot / Jazz Music

BUNK JOHNSON & LEADBELLY (Johnson, Bunk & Leadbelly)
CD _______ **AMCD 046**
American Music / Oct '93 / Jazz Music

BUNK JOHNSON 1944-45
CD _______ **AMCD 12**
American Music / Apr '94 / Jazz Music

BUNK JOHNSON AND HIS SUPERIOR JAZZ BAND
Panama / Down by the riverside / Storyville blues / Ballin' the Jack / Make me a pallet on the floor / Yes Lord I'm crippled / Weary blues / Moose march / Bunk's blues / Bunk Johnson talking
CD _______ **GTJCD 120482**
Good Time Jazz / Jul '94 / Complete/ Pinnacle

IN SAN FRANCISCO
CD _______ **AMCD 16**
American Music / Jan '93 / Jazz Music

KING OF THE BLUES
CD _______ **AMCD 1**
American Music / Oct '92 / Jazz Music

LAST TESTAMENT
CD _______ **DD 225**
Delmark / Mar '95 / ADA / Cadillac / CM / Direct / Hot Shot

Johnson, Candy

CANDY'S MOOD
CD _______ **BB 884**
Black & Blue / Apr '97 / Discovery / Koch / Wellard

Johnson, Dean

ARCHIVES OF OUR LIVES
CD _______ **FMRCD 281295**
Future / Apr '97 / Pinnacle

Johnson, Dean

TRAINING OF THE SHOE, THE
CD _______ **PULCD 0151**
Pulse / Sep '97 / Grapevine/PolyGram

Johnson, Dick

PLAYS ALTO SAX & FLUTE & SOPRANO SAX & CLARINET
All the things you are / I'm old fashioned / Donna Lee / Star crossed lovers / Kelly Green / When the world was young / Who cares / Kelly Blue / In a sentimental mood / Everything I love / Get out of time
CD _______ **CCD 4107**
Concord Jazz / Mar '92 / New Note/ Pinnacle

Johnson, Dink

PIANO PLAYERS, THE (Johnson, Dink & Charlie Thompson)
CD _______ **AMCD 11**
American Music / Jun '93 / Jazz Music

Johnson, Earl

COMPLETE RECORDED WORKS VOL.1 1927
CD _______ **DOCD 8005**
Document / Apr '97 / ADA / Hot Shot / Jazz Music

COMPLETE RECORDED WORKS VOL.2 1927-1931
CD _______ **DOCD 8006**
Document / Apr '97 / ADA / Hot Shot / Jazz Music

Johnson, Eric

VENUS ISLE
Venus Isle / Battle we have won / All about you / SRV / Lonely in the night / Manhattan / Camel's night out / Song for Lynette / When the sun meets the sky / Pavillion / Venus reprise
CD _______ **PRMDCD 11**
Premier/EMI / Sep '96 / EMI

Johnson, Freddy

CLASSICS 1933-1939
CD _______ **CLASSICS 829**
Classics / Sep '95 / Discovery / Jazz Music

Johnson, General

WHAT GOES AROUND COMES AROUND (Johnson, General & Chairmen Of The Board)
CD _______ **SUR 4168CD**
Ichiban / Feb '94 / Direct / Koch

Johnson, Henry

MISSING YOU
CD _______ **INAK 3029**
In Akustik / Oct '96 / Direct / TKO Magnum

NEW BEGINNINGS
CD _______ **101S 71382**
101 South / Jun '93 / New Note/Pinnacle

Johnson, Herman

LOUISIANA COUNTRY BLUES
CD _______ **ARHCD 440**
Arhoolie / May '96 / ADA / Cadillac / Direct

Johnson, Howard

ARRIVAL (Johnson, Howard's Nubia)
CD _______ **5239852**
Verve / May '95 / PolyGram

GRAVITY
CD _______ **5310212**
Verve / Apr '96 / PolyGram

Johnson, J.J.

BE BOP LEGENDS
CD _______ **MCD 0722**
Moon / Aug '95 / Cadillac / Harmonia Mundi

BRASS ORCHESTRA
CD _______ **5373212**
Verve / Jul '97 / PolyGram

GREAT KAI AND J.J. (Johnson, J.J. & Kai Winding)
This could be the start of something big / Georgia on my mind / Blue monk / Judy / Alone together / Side by side / I concentrate on you / Picnic / Trixie / Going going gone / Just for a thrill
CD _______ **IMP 12252**
Impulse Jazz / Apr '97 / New Note/BMG

LET'S HANG OUT
Friendship suite / Ode to GT / Let's hang out / Love you Nana / Reunion / Stir fry / It never entered my mind / Kenya / Beautiful love / It's you or no one / May I have this dance / Syntax / Hasten Jason / I got it bad and that ain't good
CD _______ **5144542**
EmArCy / Feb '93 / PolyGram

QUINTERGY (Live At The Village Vanguard)
When the saints go marching in / Blue bossa / Doc was here / Bud's blues / Quintergy / Lament / Why Indianapolis / Why not Indianaopolis / It's alright / Coppin' the bop / Nefertiti / You've changed / Communication
CD _______ **8483272**
EmArCy / Jan '93 / PolyGram

STANDARDS (Live At The Village Vanguard)
CC rider / Shortcake / Sweet Georgia Gillespie / My funny valentine / Just friends / Misterioso / You stepped out of a dream / Misty / Autumn leaves / What is this thing called love
CD _______ **8483282**
EmArCy / Jan '93 / PolyGram

TANGENCE
CD _______ **5265882**
Verve / May '95 / PolyGram

THINGS ARE GETTING BETTER (Johnson, J.J. & Al Grey)
Soft winds / Let me see / Softly as in a morning sunrise / It's only a paper moon / Boy meets horn / Things ain't what they used to be / Things are getting better all the time / Don't cha hear me callin' to ya
CD _______ **OJCCD 745**
Original Jazz Classics / May '93 / Complete/ Pinnacle / Jazz Music / Wellard

YOKOHAMA CONCERT, THE (2CD Set) (Johnson, J.J. & Nat Adderley)
Horace / Cyclops / Why not / It happens / Work song / Walkin' / Jiving / Lament / Hummin' / Melodee
CD Set _______ **2PACD 26201092**
Pablo / Aug '97 / Cadillac / Complete/ Pinnacle

Johnson, James

BLUES COME HOME TO ROOST (Johnson, James 'Super Chikan')
Down in the delta / Well gone dry / Crystal ball eyes / Super Chikan strut / Mama / Chillen (part 1) / What it is / Captain love juice / Camel toe / White rock rooster / Bleeding from the heart / Mr. Rich man / Rockin' that caine and rollin' Mary Jane / Real you / Mama and the chillen (part 2)
CD _______ **R 2634**
Rooster / Mar '97 / Direct

Johnson, James 'Stump'

JAMES 'STUMP' JOHNSON 1929-1933
CD _______ **DOCD 5250**
Document / May '94 / ADA / Hot Shot / Jazz Music

Johnson, James P.

CAROLINA SHOUT
Steeplechase rag / Twilight rag / Carolina shout / Baltimore buzz / Gypsy blues / Harlem strut / Eccentricity / Don't mess with me / Nervous blues / Ole Miss Blues / I ain't givin' nothin' away / Muscle shoal blues / Farewell blues / Charleston
CD _____ BCD 105
Biograph / Jul '91 / ADA / Cadillac / Direct / Hot Shot / Jazz Music / Wellard

CLASSICS 1921-1928
CD _____ CLASSICS 658
Classics / Nov '92 / Discovery / Jazz Music

CLASSICS 1928-1938
CD _____ CLASSICS 671
Classics / Nov '92 / Discovery / Jazz Music

CLASSICS 1943-1944
CD _____ CLASSICS 824
Classics / Jul '95 / Discovery / Jazz Music

CLASSICS 1944 VOL.1
CD _____ CLASSICS 835
Classics / Sep '95 / Discovery / Jazz Music

CLASSICS 1944 VOL.2
CD _____ CLASSICS 856
Classics / Feb '96 / Discovery / Jazz Music

FEELIN' BLUE
All that I had is gone / Snowy morning blues / Chicago blues / Mournful tho'ts / Riffs / Feelin' blue / Put your mind right on it / Fare thee honey blues / You don't understand / You've got to be modernistic / Crying for the Carolines / What is this thing called love / Jingles / Go Harlem / Just a crazy song
CD _____ DHDL 107
Halcyon / May '95 / Cadillac / Harmonia Mundi / Jazz Music / Swift / Wellard

HOT PIANO
CD _____ TPZ 1048
Topaz Jazz / Jun '96 / Cadillac / Pinnacle

INTRODUCTION TO JAMES P. JOHNSON 1921-1944, AN
CD _____ 4035
Best Of Jazz / Mar '95 / Discovery

JAMES P. JOHNSON 1938-1942
CD _____ CLASSICS 711
Classics / Jul '93 / Discovery / Jazz Music

ORIGINAL, THE
CD _____ SFWCD 40812
Smithsonian Folkways / Nov '96 / ADA / Cadillac / CM / Direct / Koch

RUNNIN' WILD
CD _____ TCD 1048
Tradition / May '97 / ADA / Vital

Johnson, Jimmy

BAR ROOM PREACHER
CD _____ ALCD 4744
Alligator / May '93 / ADA / CM / Direct

I'M A JOCKEY
That will never do / Jockey / Engine number 9 / My ring / Highway / As the years go passing by / Black and white wall / Highway is like a woman / In the midnight hour / End of a rainbow / Look over yonder's wall
CD _____ 5215862
Birdology / Apr '93 / PolyGram

JOHNSON'S WHACKS
CD _____ DD 644
Delmark / Dec '89 / ADA / Cadillac / CM / Direct / Hot Shot

Johnson, Johnnie

BLUE HANDED JOHNNIE
CD _____ ECD 26017
Evidence / Feb '93 / ADA / Cadillac / Harmonia Mundi

JOHNNY B. BAD
Tanqueray / Hush oh hush / Johnny B Badde / Creek mud / Fault line tremor / Stepped in what / Can you stand it / Key to the highway / Blues no. 572 / Baby what's wrong / Cow cow blues / Movin' out
CD _____ 7559611492
Nonesuch / Sep '91 / Warner Music

ROCKIN' EIGHTY-EIGHTS (Johnson, Johnnie, Clayton Love & Jimmy Vaughn)
CD _____ MBCD 1201
Modern Blues / Jun '93 / ADA / Direct

THAT'LL WORK (Johnson, Johnnie & Kentucky Headhunters)
That'll work / Sunday blues / Johnnie's breakdown / I'm not runnin' / Burned about love / Stumblin' / Back to Memphis / Feel / I know you can / She's got to have it / Derby day special / Tell me baby
CD _____ 7559614762
Elektra / Aug '93 / Warner Music

Johnson, L.V.

I GOT THE TOUCH
I got the touch / Take a little time to know her / Are you serious / I don't want to lose your love / What do you mean love ain't got nothing to do / I am missing you / I just can't get over you / Stroking kind (choking kind)
CD _____ ICH 1112CD
Ichiban / Oct '93 / Direct / Koch

IT'S SO COLD AND MEAN
Get him out of your system / It's so cold and mean (the drug scene) / One in a million you / Blues in the north / It's not my time / Make you mine / Steal away / How can I live without you
CD _____ ICH 1050CD
Ichiban / Oct '93 / Direct / Koch

UNCLASSIFIED
CD _____ ICH 1137CD
Ichiban / May '94 / Direct / Koch

Johnson, Larry

MIDNIGHT HOUR BLUES (Johnson, Larry & John Hammond)
Blood red river / One room country shack / Saturday evening blues / Peace breakin' people / Walking blues / Mama-less rag / Red river dam blues / Nobody's biz-ness / Midnight hour blues / When things go wrong / Tell me Mama
CD _____ BCD 138
Biograph / Jul '97 / ADA / Cadillac / Direct / Hot Shot / Jazz Music / Wellard

Johnson, Laurie

LONDON BIG BAND VOL.1 (Johnson, Laurie London Big Band)
Come rain or come shine / Isn't it romantic / Wasn't it romantic / Swanee / What makes the sunset / Mr. B / Lady is a tramp / By strauss / Someone to watch over me / From this moment on / Jeepers creepers / It could happen to you / It's easy for you to say / Embraceable you / Coasting / Avalon / Never stray / But beautiful / CTS Blues
CD _____ CDSIV 6144
Horatio Nelson / Jul '95 / Disc

LONDON BIG BAND VOL.2 (Johnson, Laurie London Big Band)
CD _____ CDSIV 6160
Horatio Nelson / Jul '96 / Disc

MUSIC OF LAURIE JOHNSON, THE
CD _____ UKCD 2057
Unicorn-Kanchana / Jul '92 / Harmonia Mundi

Johnson, Lem

COMPLETE LEM JOHNSON 1940-1953, THE
CD _____ BMCD 6004
Blue Moon / Jul '96 / Cadillac / Discovery / Greensleeves / Jazz Music / Jet Star / TKO Magnum

Johnson, Lil

COMPLETE RECORDED WORKS VOL.2 1936-1937
CD _____ DOCD 5308
Document / Dec '94 / ADA / Hot Shot / Jazz Music

HOTTEST GAL IN TOWN 1936-1937
CD _____ SOBCD 35132
Story Of The Blues / Mar '92 / ADA / Koch

LIL JOHNSON & BARRELHOUSE ANNIE 1937 (Johnson, Lil & Barrelhouse Annie)
CD _____ DOCD 5309
Document / Dec '94 / ADA / Hot Shot / Jazz Music

LIL JOHNSON VOL.1 1929-1936
CD _____ DOCD 5307
Document / Dec '94 / ADA / Hot Shot / Jazz Music

Johnson, Linton Kwesi

BASS CULTURE
Bass culture / Street 66 / Reggae fi peach / De black petty booshwah / Inglan is a bitch / Lorraine / Reggae sounds / Two sides of silence
CD _____ RRCD 26
Reggae Refreshers / Nov '90 / PolyGram / Vital

DREAD BEAT AND BLOOD
Dread beat and blood / Five nights of bleeding / Doun de road / Song of blood / It dread inna Inglun (for George Lindo) / Come wi goh dung deh / Man free (for Darcus Howe) / All wi doin' is defendin'
CD _____ CDFL 9009
Frontline / Sep '90 / EMI / Jet Star

FORCES OF VICTORY
Want fi goh rave / It noh funny / Sonny's lettah / Independent intavenshan / Fite dem back / Reality poem / Forces of vicktry / Time come
CD _____ RRCD 32
Reggae Refreshers / Sep '91 / PolyGram / Vital

IN CONCERT
CD _____ SHANCD 43034/5
Shanachie / '88 / ADA / Greensleeves / Koch

LKJ ACAPPELLA LIVE
CD _____ LKJCD 016
LKJ / Oct '96 / Grapevine/PolyGram / Jet Star

LKJ IN CONCERT
CD _____ LKJCD 03
LKJ / Mar '95 / Grapevine/PolyGram / Jet Star

LKJ IN DUB
Victorious dub / Reality dub / Peach dub / Shocking dub / Iron bar dub / Bitch dub / Cultural dub / Brain smashing dub
CD _____ RRCD 34
Reggae Refreshers / Sep '91 / PolyGram / Vital

LKJ IN DUB VOL.2
CD _____ LKJCD 02
LKJ / Mar '95 / Grapevine/PolyGram / Jet Star

REGGAE GREATS
Reggae sounds / Independent intavenshan / Street 66 / Bass culture / Di great insohreckshan / It noh funny / Sonny's lettah / Reggae fi radni / Fit dem back / Making history
CD _____ 5528812
Spectrum / Jul '97 / PolyGram

TINGS AND TIMES
CD _____ LKJCD 013
LKJ / Oct '95 / Grapevine/PolyGram / Jet Star

Johnson, Lonnie

ANOTHER NIGHT TO CRY
CD _____ OBCCD 550
Original Blues Classics / Nov '92 / Complete/Pinnacle / Wellard

BLUES & BALLADS (Johnson, Lonnie & Elmer Snowden)
CD _____ OBCCD 531
Original Blues Classics / Nov '92 / Complete/Pinnacle / Wellard

BLUES BY LONNIE JOHNSON
Don't ever love / No love for sale / There's no love / I don't hurt anymore / She devil / One-sided love affair / Big legged woman / There must be a way / She's drunk again / Blues 'round my door / You don't move me / You will need me
CD _____ OBCCD 502
Original Blues Classics / Nov '92 / Complete/Pinnacle / Wellard

BLUES IN MY FINGERS
CD _____ IGOCD 2009
Indigo / Nov '94 / ADA / Direct

BLUES, BALLADS AND JUMPIN' JAZZ VOL.2 (Johnson, Lonnie & Elmer Snowden)
CD _____ OBCCD 570
Original Blues Classics / Jul '95 / Complete/Pinnacle / Wellard

COMPLETE FOLKWAYS RECORDINGS
CD _____ SFWCD 40067
Smithsonian Folkways / Sep '94 / ADA / Cadillac / CM / Direct / Koch

COMPLETE RECORDINGS VOL.1
CD _____ BDCD 6024
Blues Document / Nov '92 / ADA / Hot Shot / Jazz Music

COMPLETE RECORDINGS VOL.2
CD _____ BDCD 6025
Blues Document / Nov '92 / ADA / Hot Shot / Jazz Music

COMPLETE RECORDINGS VOL.3
CD _____ BDCD 6026
Blues Document / Nov '92 / ADA / Hot Shot / Jazz Music

HE'S A JELLY ROLL BAKER
Why women go wrong / Nothing but a rat / Jersey belle blues / Loveless blues / I'm just dumb / Get yourself together / Crowing rooster blues / That's love / Somebody's got to go / Lazy woman blues / Chicago blues / I did all i could / In love again / Last call / Rambler's blues / Baby, remember me / He's a Jelly Roll Baker / When you feel low down / Victim of love / Watch shorty
CD _____ 07863660642
Bluebird / Oct '92 / BMG

IDLE HOURS (Johnson, Lonnie & Victoria Spivey)
CD _____ OBCCD 518
Original Blues Classics / Nov '92 / Complete/Pinnacle / Wellard

LOSING GAME
CD _____ OBCCD 543
Original Blues Classics / Nov '92 / Complete/Pinnacle / Wellard

ME AND MY CRAZY SELF
You can't buy love / It was all in vain / Nothing but trouble / Me and my crazy self / What do you want that I've got / Pretty boy / I'm guilty / What a woman / Falling rain blues / Playing around / It's too late to cry / Seven long days / Why should I cry / Friendless blues / Happy new year darling / You only want me when you're lonely / Old fashioned love / My my baby / Just another day / What a real woman / Can't sleep anymore
CD _____ CDCHARLY 266
Charly / Mar '91 / Koch

ORIGINATOR OF MODERN GUITAR BLUES
In love again / Rambler's blues / Keep what you got / Little rocking chair / Nothin' clickin' chicken / My mother's eyes / I can't sleep any more
CD _____ RBD 300
Mr. R&B / Dec '90 / CM / Swift / Wellard

PLAYING WITH THE STRINGS
CD _____ JSPCD 335
JSP / Dec '94 / ADA / Cadillac / Direct / Hot Shot / Target/BMG

STEPPIN' ON THE BLUES
Mr. Johnson's blues / Sweet potato blues / Steppin' on the blues / I done told you / Mean old bedbug blues / Toothache blues - (part 1) / Toothache blues - (part 2) / Have to change keys (to play these blues) / Guitar blues / She's making whoopee in hell tonight / Playing with the strings / No more women blues / Deep blue sea blues / No more troubles now / Got the blues for murder only / Untitled / 6-88 glide / Racketeer's blues / I'm nuts about that gal
CD _____ 4672522
Columbia / May '91 / Sony

STOMPIN' AT THE PENNY (Johnson, Lonnie & Jim McHarg's Metro Stompers)
China boy / Mr. Blues walks / Dippermouth blues / Trouble in mind / Bring it home to Mam / West End blues / Stompin' at the Penny / Old rugged cross / Go go swing / My mother's eyes / Canal street blues / 14th of July / Marines' hymn
CD _____ 4767202
Legacy / May '94 / Sony

TOMORROW NIGHT
You will need me / I don't hurt anymore / She's drunk again / Nothing but I trouble / She devil / Little rocking chair / Trouble ain't nothing but the blues / Leave me or love me / Tomorrow night / Blues 'round my door / Workin' man blues / Jelly roll baker / End it all / Blues stay away from me / Careless love / CC rider / Clementine blues / Backwater blues / Jelly jelly / Love is the answer / Keep what you got
CD _____ CD 52016
Blues Encore / '92 / Target/BMG

Johnson, Lou

SOUTHERN SOUL
CD _____ MAR 057
Marginal / Jun '97 / Greyhound

Johnson, Luther

GET DOWN TO THE NITTY GRITTY (Johnson, Luther 'Georgia Snake Boy')
CD _____ 422255
Last Call / Feb '97 / Cargo / Direct / Discovery

ON THE ROAD AGAIN (Johnson, Luther 'Georgia Snake Boy')
On the road again / Back door man / Things I used to do / Catfish blues / Aces blues / You move me / Rock me baby / She moves me / You've got me running / Hoochie coochie man / Impressions from France / Mellow down easy / Little red rooster
CD _____ ECD 260472
Evidence / Mar '94 / ADA / Cadillac / Harmonia Mundi

THEY CALL ME THE SNAKE (Johnson, Luther 'Georgia Snake Boy')
Woman don't lie / Take it off him and put it on me / Blues is something I'll never lose / Woman why treat me so mean / They call me the snake / Somebody loan me a dime / Slip it off your hips and move
CD _____ 422268
Last Call / Feb '97 / Cargo / Direct / Discovery

Johnson, Luther

COUNTRY SUGAR PAPA (Johnson, Luther 'Guitar Junior')
CD _____ BB 9546CD
Bullseye Blues / May '94 / Direct

DOIN' THE SUGAR TOO (Johnson, Luther 'Guitar Junior')
Doin' the sugar too / Flippin' and floppin' / I'm ready / I need some air / Woke up this mornin' / Hard times (have surely come) / Get on the floor / Time to make my getaway / Bad boy / You were wrong / Early in the mornin' blues / What you don't know won't hurt you / Doin' the sugar too
CD _____ CDBB 9563
Bullseye Blues / Feb '97 / Direct

IT'S GOOD TO BE ME (Johnson, Luther 'Guitar Junior')
Feel so bad / Come on back to me / Deep down in Florida / I'm leaving you / If you love me like you say / Ronettes / Stealin' chicken / It's good to me / Raise your window / Next door neighbour / That's all you need / In my younger days
CD _____ CDBB 9516
Bullseye Blues / Nov '92 / Direct

LUTHER'S BLUES (Johnson, Luther 'Guitar Junior')
CD ECD 260102
Evidence / Oct '94 / ADA / Cadillac / Harmonia Mundi

SLAMMIN' ON THE WEST SIDE (Johnson, Luther 'Guitar Junior' & The Magic Rockers)
Pretty girl (a Cadillac and some money) / She's lookin' good / Hey little girl / I ain't doin' too bad / It's good to me / Sittin' on the back seat of a Greyhound bus / Every woman needs to be loved / Stranded / Early in the morning blues / Another man / Hard times (have surely come) / Woman I love / Get up and go / Why am I treated so bad / Waiting at the station / Meet me with your black drawers on
CD CD 83389
Telarc / May '96 / Conifer/BMG

Johnson, Luther

HOUSEROCKIN' DADDY (Johnson, Luther 'Houserocker')
I'm Mr. Luck / Bad luck blues / You could have fooled me / Fool's advice / She wants to sell my monkey / Rockin' daddy / You know I love you baby / Something you got / Don't say that no more / Things I used to do
CD ICH 9010CD
Ichiban / Nov '91 / Direct / Koch

LONESOME IN MY BEDROOM (Johnson, Luther 'Houserocker')
CD ECD 260052
Evidence / Jan '92 / ADA / Cadillac / Harmonia Mundi

Johnson, Marc

2X4
Killer Joe / Spartacus / Dinner for one please James / One finger snap / Miss Teri / Monk's dream / Gary's theme / Beautiful love / Ain't misbehavin' / Time remembered / Goodbye porkpie hat
CD 8422332
EmArCy / Apr '91 / PolyGram

BASS DESIRES
Samurai hee-haw / Resolution / Black is the colour of my true love's hair / Bass desires / Wishing doll / Mojo highway / Thanks again
CD 8277432
ECM / Feb '86 / New Note/Pinnacle

RIGHT BRAIN PATROL
They love me fifteen feet away / Batuki Burundi / Netcong on my mind / Right brain patrol / Heru nazel / Inside four walls / You after you / Whispers / Log o'rhythm / Light in your eye / Call
CD 8491532
jMT / Apr '92 / PolyGram

SECOND SIGHT (Johnson, Marc Bass Desires)
Crossing the corpus callosum / Small hands / Sweet soul / Twister / Thrill seekers / Prayer beads / 1951 / Hymn for her
CD 8330382
ECM / Oct '87 / New Note/Pinnacle

Johnson, Margaret

MARGARET JOHNSON 1923-1927
CD DOCD 5436
Document / May '96 / ADA / Hot Shot / Jazz Music

Johnson, Mark

DAYDREAM
On the sky / Blue smoke / When you were mine / Way you do the things you do / Dim the lights / Gotta do it good / Daydream / Island lullaby / You're the one / Long goodbye
CD JVC 20432
JVC / Apr '95 / Direct / New Note/Pinnacle / Vital/SAM

DEEP FOCUS
I told you so / Ocean of love / Mediterranean / Deep focus / Smoke and mirrors / Don't turn away / Shades of Dre / Afrique / Tempted / And when the time comes
CD JVC 20582
JVC / Oct '96 / Direct / New Note/Pinnacle / Vital/SAM

MARK JOHNSON
Overture / Exit 33 / Gift for the ages / Street samba / Come on / Mud hut / She's so funktional / Bad influence / Funky James / Hipocket / Devotional
CD JVC 20322
JVC / Apr '94 / Direct / New Note/Pinnacle / Vital/SAM

Johnson, Marv

VERY BEST OF MARV JOHNSON, THE
Can't take another day / Paper kisses / Whole lotta shakin' in my heart / It's magic between us / Night / Something's burning my heart / Gonna fix yoy good (every time you're bad) / Look it's raining sunshine / Pull myself together / I'll pick a rose for my rose / Heart for sale / Better love next time / Another chance / Beware there's danger / Riding for a fall / Nothing can stop me / By hook or by crook / Come to me
CD 3035990032
Carlton / Oct '95 / Carlton

Johnson, Mary

COMPLETE RECORDED WORKS 1929-36
CD DOCD 5305
Document / Dec '94 / ADA / Hot Shot / Jazz Music

Johnson, Merline

YAS YAS GIRL 1937-1947, THE
CD WBJCD 006
Wolf / Jul '96 / Hot Shot / Jazz Music / Swift

YAS YAS GIRL VOL.1 1937-1938
CD DOCD 5292
Document / Dec '94 / ADA / Hot Shot / Jazz Music

YAS YAS GIRL VOL.2 1938-1939
CD DOCD 5293
Document / Dec '94 / ADA / Hot Shot / Jazz Music

YAS YAS GIRL VOL.3 1939-1940
CD DOCD 5294
Document / Dec '94 / ADA / Hot Shot / Jazz Music

YAS YAS GIRL VOL.4 1940-1941
CD DOCD 5295
Document / Dec '94 / ADA / Hot Shot / Jazz Music

Johnson, Paul

FEEL THE MUSIC
Relax with me / Little Suntin Suntin / You make me say do be do / Hear the music / About your love / Summer Heat / I wonder why / Groove
CD PF 056CD
Peacefrog / Nov '96 / Mo's Music Machine / Prime / RTM/Disc / Vital

SECOND COMING
CD ACVCD 017
ACV / Jun '96 / Plastic Head / SRD

Johnson, Pete

CENTRAL AVENUE BOOGIE
Pete Kay boogie / Central Avenue drag / Margie / 66 stop / Minuet boogie / Yancy street boogie / Swanee river / Hollywood boogie / Hollywood boogie / Hollywood boogie / Hollywood boogie / Plain food blues / Plain food blues / Wiley's boogie
CD DD 656
Delmark / Mar '97 / ADA / Cadillac / CM / Direct / Hot Shot

CLASSICS 1938-1939
CD CLASSICS 656
Classics / Nov '92 / Discovery / Jazz Music

CLASSICS 1939-1941
CD CLASSICS 665
Classics / Nov '92 / Discovery / Jazz Music

CLASSICS 1944-1946
CD CLASSICS 933
Classics / Apr '97 / Discovery / Jazz Music

KING OF THE BOOGIE
CD CDCH 546
Milan / Oct '91 / Conifer/BMG / Silva Screen

Johnson, Plas

BEST OF PLAS JOHNSON, THE
CD WBJCD 021
Wolf / Nov '96 / Hot Shot / Jazz Music / Swift

POSITIVELY
Positively / Lover man (Oh where can you be) / Let's get it all together / Easy for you to say / Never more / My foolish heart / Careless love / Cottage for sale / Dirty leg blues / Sea sea
CD CCD 4024
Concord Jazz / May '97 / New Note/ Pinnacle

Johnson, Puff

MIRACLE
Forever more / Outside my window / All over your face / Yearning / Love between you and me / Miracle / Because of you / God sent you / True meaning of love / Come closer / Please help me I'm falling (in love with you) / Hold on to this hand
CD 4837492
Work/Columbia / Feb '97 / Sony

Johnson, Robb

HEART'S DESIRE (Johnson, Robb & Pip Collins)
Weathering the storm / Merrie olde Englande / Tomorrow will be better / Happy song / After the rain / End of the day / Gliders for Tim / Eddie outside / Nobody but yours / Pity and mercy / Heart's desire / Sunlight on the harbour / Wall came down / Die Moorsoldaten / Bells of freedom / More than enough
CD IRR 014CD
Irregular / Aug '93 / ADA / Direct / Irregular

HELL'S KITCHEN (Johnson, Robb Roots Band)
Working on a river / U have 2 dance / Waiting for bluebirds / Cassandra's song / Room beside the sea / Motherland / Butcher's hand / Lottery land / Hell's kitchen / New moon / Permanent free zone / Armistice day / Red, white and moo
CD IRR 026
Irregular / Sep '96 / ADA / Direct / Irregular

LACK OF JOLLY PLOUGHBOY (Johnson, Robb & Pip Collins)
Welcome to the warehouse / Wendy and Michelle / Paper poppies / House with nobody home / Shame of the nation / Dancing on a Sunday / Uncle Cyril / Mother and the motorway / Turning year / James Dean and Sameena / We rise up / Lack of jolly ploughboy / Blame the snow for falling
CD IRR O17CD
Irregular / Oct '94 / ADA / Direct / Irregular

NIGHT CAFE
CD IRR 025CD
Irregular / May '96 / ADA / Direct / Irregular

OVERNIGHT
Fairy tales in Feltham / I remember Managua / Orange class news / Last time I saw Paris / Day before the war / Vic Williams / Overnight / 17 again tonight / Tourists and casualties / Winter turns to spring / Suicide tour / Rehoused in Hounslow / Acton Town / You don't have to say goodbye
CD IRR 027
Irregular / Feb '97 / ADA / Direct / Irregular

ROBB JOHNSON
CD IRR 018CD
Irregular / Aug '95 / ADA / Direct / Irregular

THIS IS THE UK TALKING
Amateur dramatics / Rosa's lovely daughters / I close my eyes / Jolly sailor / Animals song / Herald of free enterprise / Evergreen / Like a brother / Another cold Saturday in hell / Sunday morning St.Denis / Uprising / Justice in Knightsbridge / Wasted years / Not in my name / 6B go swimming / Hounslow boys / UK Talking / Undefeated
CD RHYD 5002
Rhiannon / Jul '96 / ADA / Direct / Vital

Johnson, Robert

ALL TIME BLUES CLASSICS
CD 8420272
Music Memoria / Oct '96 / ADA / Discovery

BLUES, THE (San Antonio-Dallas 1936-1937/2CD Set)
CD FA 251
Fremeaux / Feb '96 / ADA / Discovery

CROSSROAD BLUES
CD NTMCD 504
Nectar / Jun '95 / Pinnacle

DELTA BLUES VOL.1 (Myth & Reality)
Crossroads blues / Terraplane blues / Come on in my kitchen / Walking blues / Last fair deal gone down / 32-20 blues / Kindhearted women blues / If I had possession over judgement day / Preaching blues / When you got a good friend / Rambling on my mind / Stones in my passway / Travelling riverside blues / Milkcow's calf blues / Me and the devil blues / Hellhound on my trail
CD ALB 1001CD
Aldabra / Jul '96 / CM / RTM/Disc

DELTA BLUES VOL.2
CD ALB 1002CD
Aldabra / Jul '96 / CM / RTM/Disc

GOLD COLLECTION, THE
CD D2CD 14
Deja Vu / Dec '92 / THE

HELLHOUND ON MY TRAIL
CD IGOCD 2017
Indigo / Mar '95 / ADA / Direct

KING OF THE DELTA BLUES SINGERS
Crossroads blues / Terraplane blues / Come on in my kitchen / Walking blues / Last fair deal gone down / 32-20 blues / Kindhearted woman blues / If I had possession over judgement day / Preaching blues / When you got a good friend / Rambling on my mind / Stones in my passway / Traveling riverside blues / Milkcow's calf blues / Hellhound on my trail
CD 4844192
Mastersound / Sep '96 / Sony

LOVE IN VAIN
I'm a steady rollin' man / Sweet home Chicago / Cross road blues / Kind hearted woman blues / Love in vain / Stop breakin' down blues / Me and the devil blues / Phonograph blues / Drunken hearted man / Preaching blues (up jumped the devil) / Little queen of spades / Terraplane blues
CD 305672
Hallmark / Oct '96 / Carlton

ROBERT JOHNSON (2CD Set)
CD Set R2CD 4014
Deja Vu / Jan '96 / THE

ROBERT JOHNSON COLLECTOR'S EDITION
CD DVBC 9052
Deja Vu / Apr '95 / THE

ROBERT JOHNSON GOLD (2CD Set)
CD Set D2CD 4014
Deja Vu / Jun '95 / THE

ROOTS OF ROBERT JOHNSON (Various Artists)
CD YAZCD 1073
Yazoo / Apr '91 / ADA / CM / Koch

TRAVELING RIVERSIDE BLUES
Kind hearted woman blues / Sweet home Chicago / Ramblin' on my mind / I believe I'll dust my broom / When you got a good friend / Come on in my kitchen / Terraplane blues / Phonograph blues / 32-20 blues / They're red hot / Crossroads blues / Walkin' blues / Preachin' blues / If I had possession over Judgement Day / I'm a steady rollin' man / Little Queen of Spades / Me and the devil blues / Stop breakin' down blues / Travellin' riverside blues / Love in vain / Milkcow's calf blues
CD CD 52019
Blues Encore / Aug '92 / Target/BMG

Johnson, Robert

FEELS LIKE BUZZ ALDRIN (Johnson, Robert & Punchdrunks)
CD SE 001
Strange Edge / May '97 / Cargo

Johnson, Ronnie

GIVE THEM ENOUGH ROPE
CD BRGCD 01
Music Maker / Jul '94 / ADA / Grapevine/ PolyGram

HOW THE LAND LIES
CD BRGCD 06
Music Maker / Jul '94 / ADA / Grapevine/ PolyGram

Johnson, Ruby

I'LL RUN YOUR HURT AWAY
I'll run your heart away / What more can a woman do / Won't be long / Love of my man / Why not give me a chance / It's not that easy / Don't play that song (You lied) / Come to me my darling / It's better to give than to receive / keep on keepin' on / How strong is my love / Need your love so bad / Leftover love / I'd better check on myself / I'd rather fight than switch / No no no / If I ever needed love (I sure do need it now) / When my love comes down / Weak spot
CD CDSXD 049
Stax / Mar '93 / Pinnacle

Johnson, Shirley

LOOKING FOR LOVE
CD APCD 094
Appaloosa / Jul '94 / ADA / Direct / TKO Magnum

Johnson, Snuff

WILL THE CIRCLE BE UNBROKEN
CD BMCD 9026
Black Magic / Sep '94 / ADA / Cadillac / Direct / Hot Shot

Johnson, Syl

A SIDES, THE
Love you left behind / I wanna satisfy your every need / We did it / Back for a taste of your love / I'm yours / Let yourself go / I want to take you home (to see mama) / Take me to the river / I only have love / Star bright, star light / About to make me leave home / Fonk you / Stand by me / Mystery lady
CD HILOCD 06
Hi / Mar '94 / Pinnacle

BACK FOR A TASTE OF YOUR LOVE
CD HIUKCD 142
Hi / Jun '93 / Pinnacle

BACK IN THE GAME
Back in the game / I like your style / I can't stop / Please don't give up on me / Keep on loving me / Take me to the river / Ghetto woman / Watch what you do to me / Dipped in the water: *Johnson, Syl & Syleena Thompson* / Driving wheel / Anyway the wind blows / Clean up man / I will rise again / All of your love
CD DE 674
Delmark / Mar '97 / ADA / Cadillac / CM / Direct / Hot Shot

DRESSES TOO SHORT
CD CDKEND 148
Kent / Aug '97 / Pinnacle

IS IT BECAUSE I'M BLACK
Come on sock it to me / Dresses too short / I can take care of business / I'll take those skinny legs / I resign / Get ready / I feel an urge / I take care of homework / Is it because I'm black / Concrete reservation / Walk a mile in my shoes / I'm talkin' 'bout

freedom / Right on / Different strokes / Going to the shack / One way to nowhere / Thank you baby / One way ticket to nowhere / Kiss by kiss / Same kind of thing
CD ______ CPCD 8011
Charly / Feb '94 / Koch

MUSIC TO MY EARS
CD ______ HIUKCD 117
Hi / Jul '91 / Pinnacle

TOTAL EXPLOSION AND UPTOWN SHAKEDOWN
I only have love / Bustin' up or bustin' out / Star bright, star light / Watch what you do to me / Steppin' out / Take me to the river / It ain't easy / About to make me leave home / That's just my luck / Mystery lady / Let's dance for love / Gimme little sign / You're the star of the show / Blue water / Who's gonna love you / Otis Redding medley
CD ______ HIUKCD 143
Hi / Jun '93 / Pinnacle

Johnson, Tommy

COMPLETE RECORDINGS 1928-30
CD ______ WSECD 104
Wolf / Jan '94 / Hot Shot / Jazz Music / Swift

TOMMY JOHNSON 1928-1929
CD ______ DOCD 5001
Document / Aug '91 / ADA / Hot Shot / Jazz Music

Johnson, Wayne

KEEPING THE DREAM ALIVE (Johnson, Wayne Trio)
Bedrock / Kite music / Occasion for Jackson / Nu blooz / Wonder mountain / Keeping the dream alive / No excuse / Tangletown / Rock runner / Portrait of a yak / Blue solanum
CD ______ 5302562
MoJazz / Apr '94 / PolyGram

Johnson, Wilko

BARBED WIRE BLUES
CD ______ FREUDCD 26
Jungle / Nov '88 / RTM/Disc / SRD

ICE ON THE MOTORWAY
Bottle up and go / Cairo blues / Down by the waterside / Ice on the motorway / Can you please crawl out of your window / Leave my woman alone / When I'm gone / All right / Keep it out of sight / Long tall texan / Whammy
CD ______ BUTCD 001
Hound Dog / Jan '91 / Street link

Johnson, Willie Neal

BEST OF WILLIE NEAL JOHNSON & THE GOSPEL KEYNOTES, THE (Johnson, Willie Neal & The Gospel Keynotes)
CD ______ NASH 4501
Nashboro / Feb '96 / Pinnacle

Johnston, Bruce

SURFIN' ROUND THE WORLD
CD ______ SC 6100
Sundazed / Feb '97 / Cargo / Greyhound / Rollercoaster

Johnston, Daniel

YIP JUMP MUSIC
CD ______ HMS 1422
Homestead / Nov '94 / Cargo / SRD

Johnston, Freedy

CAN YOU FLY
Trying to tell you I don't know / In the new sunshine / Tearing down this place / Remember me / Wheels / Lucky one / Can you fly / Responsible / Mortician's daughter / Sincere / Down in love / California thing / We will shine
CD ______ 7559615872
Elektra / Sep '93 / Warner Music

NEVER HOME
On the way out / I'm not hypnotized / Western sky / One more thing to break / He wasn't murdered / You get me lost / Hotel seventeen / Gone to see the fire / Seventies girl / If it's true / Something's out there
CD ______ 7559619202
WEA / May '97 / Warner Music

THIS PERFECT WORLD
Bad reputation / Evie's tears / Can't sink this town / This perfect world / Cold again / Two lovers stop / Across the avenue / Gone like the water / Delores / Evie's garden / Disappointed man / I can hear the laughs
CD ______ 7559616552
Elektra / Jul '94 / Warner Music

TROUBLE TREE, THE
Innocent / Down on the moon no. 1 / No violins / That's what you get / Fun ride / Gina / Nauture boy / Bad girl / After my shocks / Tucumcari / Down on the moon no. 2 / Little red haired girl
CD ______ FIENDCD 208
Demon / '91 / Pinnacle

Johnston, Jan

NAKED BUT FOR LILIES
If heaven callz / Paris / I learned (you blew me out) / Wild child / Don't be lonely / Don't make promises / Calling you / Something's in the house / Alive / Strange day
CD ______ 5402422
A&M / Aug '94 / PolyGram

Johnston, Philip

BIG TROUBLE
CD ______ 1201522
Black Saint / Sep '93 / Cadillac / Harmonia Mundi

Johnstone, Arthur

NORTH BY NORTH
North by North / Oil beneath the sea / Tinkermans daughter / Christmas 1914 / Margaret and me / Benny Lynch / Doomsday in the afternoon / Take her in your arms / Raglan Road / Crooked Jack / It's my union / Ballad of Joe Hill / Bandiera Rosa
CD ______ LCOM 9039
Lismor / Apr '91 / ADA / Direct / Duncans / Lismor

Johnstone, Jim

TRIBUTE TO JIMMY SHAND
CD ______ COMD 2039
Temple / Feb '94 / ADA / CM / Direct / Duncans / Highlander

Johnstons

BARLEY CORN, THE/THE JOHNSTONS
CD ______ ESMCD 410
Essential / Jul '96 / BMG

COLOURS OF THE DAWN
Hello friend / Crazy Anne / Brightness she came / If I could / Angela Davis / Colours of the dawn / I'll be gone in the morning / Seems so long ago Nancy / Old man's tale
CD ______ HILLCD 9
Wooded Hill / Jan '97 / Direct / World Serpent

GIVE A DAMN/BITTER GREEN
Give a damn / You keep going your way / Urge for going / Port of Amsterdam / Funny in a sad, sad way / Hey that's no way to say goodbye / Both sides now / Julia / Sweet Thames flow softly / I loved / I don't mind the rain on Monday / Walking out on foggy mornings / Jesus was a carpenter / Gypsy / Lord Thomas and fair Ellender / Fiddler's green / Story of Isaac / Bitter green / Penny wager / Marcie / Spanish lady / Streets of London
CD ______ ESMCD 525
Essential / Jul '97 / BMG

TRANSATLANTIC YEARS
Fhir a bhata / O'Carolan's concerto / Lark in the morning / Apprentice song / You keep going your way / Urge for going / Hey, that's no way to say goodbye / Both sides now / Ye Jacobites by name / Coleraine regatta / Barleycorn / Flower of Northumberland / Fuigfidh mise'n baile sea / Story of Isaac / Bitter green / Marcie / Spanish lady / If I could / Colours of the dawn / If I sang my song / Continental trailways bus
CD ______ TDEM 13
Trandem / Mar '94 / ADA / CM / Pinnacle

Jolicard, Jean-Pierre

SUMMER SOLSTICE
CD ______ PV 796021
Pierre Verany / Mar '96 / Discovery / Kingdom

Jolley & Swain

BACKTRACKIN'
Autumn leaves / Walk on / Amazon / Backtrackin' / Journey / Patterns / Soul street / Lost in the night
CD ______ SAK 004
Scratch / Jul '97 / Koch / Scratch/BMG

Jolliffe, Steve

ALIEN
CD ______ HM 1000
Atlantis / Nov '96 / TKO Magnum

BEYOND THE DREAM
CD ______ WV 002
Waveform / Feb '92 / TKO Magnum

ESCAPE
CD ______ WV 004
Waveform / Feb '92 / TKO Magnum

JAPANESE WAY, THE
CD ______ WV 003
Waveform / Feb '92 / TKO Magnum

JOURNEYS OUT OF THE BODY
CD ______ WV 001
Waveform / Oct '92 / TKO Magnum

TEMMENU
CD ______ SIN 004
Sine / Jun '96 / Grapevine/PolyGram

WARRIOR
CD ______ WV 005
Waveform / Oct '92 / TKO Magnum

ZANZI
CD ______ HM 1001
Atlantis / Nov '96 / TKO Magnum

Jolly Boys

POP'N'MENTO
Mother and wife / Love in the cemetery / River come down / Ten dollars to two / Banana / Big bamboo / Ben Wood Dick / Touch me tomato / Shaving cream / Watermelon / Back to back / Nightfall
CD ______ COOKCD 040
Cooking Vinyl / Jun '90 / Vital

Jolson, Al

AL JOLSON COLLECTOR'S EDITION
CD ______ DVGH 7042
Deja Vu / Apr '95 / THE

AL JOLSON VOL.3
CD ______ PASTCD 7045
Flapper / Jan '96 / Pinnacle

AUDIO ARCHIVE
My mammy / There's a rainbow 'round my shoulder / Ma blushin' Rosie / I'm sitting on top of the world / Rock-a-bye your baby with a dixie melody / I only have eyes for you / California here I come / Let me sing and I'm happy / Swanee / When the red, red robin comes bob, bob, bobbin' along / Sonny Boy / For me and my gal / Oh you beautiful doll / You made me love you / Give my regards to Broadway / April showers / Anniversary song / After you've gone / Toot toot tootsie / Avalon
CD ______ CDAA 004
Tring / Jun '92 / Tring

BEST OF AL JOLSON, THE (25 Great Songs)
CD ______ CD 6038
Music / Sep '96 / Target/BMG

BEST OF AL JOLSON, THE (20 Timeless Classics)
Rock a bye your baby with a Dixie melody / When the red red robin comes bob bob bobbin' along / Sonny Boy / April showers / Swanee / For me and my gal / By the light of the silvery moon / Avalon / About a quarter to nine / Carolina in the morning / Toot, toot, tootsie / California here I come / There's a rainbow 'round my shoulder / Waiting for the Robert E Lee / Give my regards to Broadway / Little pal / I'm in seventh heaven / Anniversary song / Let me sing and I'm happy / My Mammy
CD ______ ECD 3260
K-Tel / Jan '97 / K-Tel

BEST OF AL JOLSON, THE
CD ______ HMNCD 004
Half Moon / Jun '97 / BMG

FIRST RECORDINGS, THE
CD ______ STCD 564
Stash / May '93 / ADA / Cadillac / CM / Direct / Jazz Music

GREATEST ENTERTAINER, THE
April showers / Rock-a-bye your baby / I'm sitting on top of the world / There's a rainbow 'round my shoulder / When the red, red robin comes bob, bob, bobbin' along / Tonight's my night with baby / My mammy / Swanee / When the little red roses / Liza / Hallelujah, I'm a bum / California here I come / One I love / Golden gate / Back in your own backyard / Sonny boy
CD ______ HADCD 157
Javelin / May '94 / Henry Hadaway / THE

I LOVE TO SING
CD ______ JASCD 100
Jasmine / Nov '95 / Conifer/BMG / Hot Shot / TKO Magnum

JAZZ SINGER, THE
California here I come / Pasadena / I'm sitting on top of the world / Blue river / Golden gate / Back in your own backyard / My Mammy / Dirty hands, dirty face / There's a rainbow 'round my shoulder / Sonny boy / I'm in seventh heaven / Little pal / Used to you / Why can't you / Liza / Let me sing and I'm happy / April showers / Rock-a-bye your baby with a Dixie melody
CD ______ JZCD 309
Suisa / Feb '91 / Jazz Music / THE

JOLSON SONGBOOK, THE
Rock-a-bye your baby / Swanee / My Mammy / April showers / California here I come / Toot toot Tootsie / Sonny Boy / Let me sing and I'm happy / You made me love you / Back in your own backyard / There's a rainbow 'round my shoulder / I'm sitting on top of the world / Waiting for the Robert E Lee / Me and my shadow / Carolina in the morning / Baby face / Give my regards to Broadway / Pretty baby / Bye Bye blackbird / For me and my gal
CD ______ 3036200292
Carlton / Feb '97 / Carlton

LET ME SING AND I'M HAPPY
Let me sing and I'm happy: *Jolson, Al & Bing Crosby* / Medley: *Jolson, Al & Bing Crosby* / Kate: *Jolson, Al & Bing Crosby* / Best things in life are free: *Jolson, Al & Bing Crosby* / Lazy / New Ashmolean marching society and students' conservatory ba: *Crosby, Bing* / Anniversary song: *Crosby, Bing & Jolson, Al* / When the red red robbin comes bob bob bobbin' along: *Jolson, Al & Bing Crosby* / I can dream, can't I: *Crosby, Bing* / Rock a bye your baby with a dixie melody: *Jolson, Al & Bing Crosby* / April showers: *Jolson, Al & Bing Crosby* / Ma blushin' Rosie: *Jolson, Al & Bing Crosby* / You're wonderful: *Crosby, Bing* / One I love belongs to somebody else: *Jolson, Al & Bing Crosby* / Avalon: *Jolson, Al & Bing Crosby* / That lucky old sun: *Crosby, Bing* / Toot, toot, tootsie / Medley: *Jolson, Al & Bing Crosby* / Bye bye baby: *Crosby, Bing* / My mammy / Rainy night in Rio: *Crosby, Bing* / Suebonnet Sue: *Jolson, Al & Bing Crosby* / Pretty girl is like a melody: *Jolson, Al & Bing Crosby* / Linda: *Crosby, Bing* / Swanee / My old Kentucky home: *Jolson, Al & Bing Crosby* / Ho time in the old time tonight: *Jolson, Al & Bing Crosby* / Nobody: *Crosby, Bing* / Comedy: *Jolson, Al & Bing Crosby* / Oh Susanna: *Jolson, Al & Bing Crosby* / Medley: *Jolson, Al & Bing Crosby* / Comedy: *Jolson, Al & Bing Crosby* / Alabamy bound: *Jolson, Al & Bing Crosby*
CD ______ RMB 75019
Remember / Nov '93 / Total/BMG
CD ______ PARCD 004
Parrot / Jan '96 / BMG / Jazz Music / THE / Wellard

LET ME SING AND I'M HAPPY (Al Jolson At Warner Bros. 1926-1936)
April showers / Rock-a-bye your baby with a Dixie melody / Dirty hands, dirty face / Toot, toot, tootsie / Blue skies / Mother of mine, I still have you / My mammy / It all depends on you / I'm sitting on top of the world / Spaniard that blighted my life / There's a rainbow round my shoulder / Golden gate / Sonny boy / Back in your own back yard / Used to you / I'm in seventh heaven / Let me sing and I'm happy / (Across the breakfast table) looking at you / Why do they all take the night boat to Albany / Liza Lee / Little sunshine / About a quarter to nine / I love to sing
CD ______ CDODEON 24
Soundtracks / Jan '97 / EMI

SALESMAN OF SONG 1911-1923
That haunting melody / Everybody snap your fingers with me / Revival day / Back to the Carolina you love / I sent my wife to the Thousand Isles / I'm saving up the means to get to New Orleans / Someone else may be there while I'm gone / Don't write me letters / Broken doll / Every little while / Wedding bells / I've got my captain working for me now / You ain't heard nothin' yet / I gave her that / Tell me / Chloe / In sweet September / O-hi-o / Yoo hoo / Angel child / Lost: a wonderful girl / Stella / You've simply got me cuckoo / That big blond mumma / Coal black Mammy of mine
CD ______ PASTCD 9796
Flapper / Jul '92 / Pinnacle

SINGING FOOL, THE (Jolson, Al & Bing Crosby)
CD ______ ENTCD 276
Entertainers / '88 / Target/BMG

STAGE HIGHLIGHTS, 1911-25
CD ______ PASTCD 9748
Flapper / Jul '91 / Pinnacle

VERY BEST OF AL JOLSON (20 greatest hits)
Swanee / Toot toot Tootsie / Mammy / California here I come / Sonny boy / April showers / You made me love you
CD ______ PLATCD 30
Platinum / Mar '92 / Prism

VERY BEST OF AL JOLSON
There's a rainbow 'round my shoulder / Let me sing and I'm happy / Carolina in the morning / Give my regards to Broadway / Is it true what thay say about Dixie / About a quarter to nine / April showers / I'm just wild about Harry / Rock-a-bye your baby / With a Dixie melody / For me and my gal / When the red, red robin comes bob, bob, bobbin' along / You made me love you / Baby face/I'm looking over a four leaf clover / My mammy / California here I come / De Campton races / Alabamy bound / Swanee / When you were sweet sixteen / I only have eyes for you / Pretty baby / I'm sitting on top of the world / Oh you beautiful doll / Toot toot tootsie goodbye / I want a girl - just like the girl that married dear old Dad / By the light of the silvery moon / Waiting for the Robert E Lee / Spaniard that blighted my life / Anniversary song
CD ______ MCCD 074
Music Club / Jun '92 / Disc / THE

WORLD'S GREATEST ENTERTAINER (Vintage Recordings 1913-1942)
My mammy / Let me sing and I'm happy / Little pal / There's a rainbow round my shoulder / I'm sitting on top of the world / When the red red robin comes a bob bob bobbin along / California here I come / April showers / Cheek to cheek / Liza (all the clouds I'll roll away) / Sonny boy / Dirty hands, dirty face / Ol' man river / Rock a bye your baby with a Dixie melody / I'll say she does / Avalon / Morning will come / Toot toot tootsie / You made me love you
CD ______ QED 108
Tring / Nov '96 / Tring

YOU AIN'T HEARD NOTHIN' YET
California here I come / Sonny boy / April showers / Pasadena / When the red, red

robin comes bob, bob, bobbin' along / You made me love you / I'm ka-razy for you / You ain't heard nothin' yet / Swanee / When the little red roses get the blues for you / Rock-a-bye your baby with a Dixie melody / Blue river / Used to you / Steppin' out / Spaniard that blighted my life / Golden gate / My Mammy / Miami
CD ___ CDAJA 5038
Living Era / Dec '85 / Select

YOU MADE ME LOVE YOU
CD ___ PLCD 542
President / Aug '95 / Grapevine/PolyGram / President / Target/BMG

Jomanda

NUBIA SOUL
Never / Don't deny / Just a little more time / I like it / I cried the tears / Does the music love you / Life / What you go through for love / Island / Don't fight the feelings / Kiss you / Back to you / Gotta be with you
CD ___ 7567805482
Atlantic / Dec '93 / Warner Music

SOMEONE TO LOVE ME
Make my body rock / Someone to love me / Share / Don't you want my love / You knew / Boy / Dance / Got a love for you / It ain't no big thing / When love hurts / True meaning of love / What's the deal / I will always be there for you / Without you
CD ___ 7599244142
Sire / Jul '91 / Warner Music

Jon

SMOKE
CD ___ TZ 7210
Tzadik / Oct '96 / Cargo

Jon & Vangelis

BEST OF JON AND VANGELIS
Italian song / I'll find my way home / State of independence / One more time / Play within a play / Friends of Mr. Cairo / Outside of this (inside of that) / He is sailing / I hear you now
CD ___ 8219292
Polydor / Aug '84 / PolyGram

CHRONICLES
I hear you now / He is sailing / Thunder / Beside / Bird song / Play within a play / When the night comes / Deborah / Curious electric / Friends of Mr. Cairo / Back to school / Italian song / Polonaise / Love is
CD ___ 5501962
Spectrum / Sep '94 / PolyGram

FRIENDS OF MR.CAIRO
Friends of Mr. Cairo / Back to school / Outside of this, inside of that / State of independence / Beside / Mayflower
CD ___ 8000212
Polydor / Jun '88 / PolyGram

PAGE OF LIFE
Wisdom chain / Page of life / Money / Jazzy box / Garden of senses / Is it love / Anyone can light a candle / Be a good friend of mine / Shine for me / Genevieve / Journey to Ixtlan / Little guitar
CD ___ 261373
Arista / Feb '94 / BMG

PRIVATE COLLECTION
And when the night comes / Deborah / He is sailing / Polonaise / Horizon / King is coming
CD ___ 8131742
Polydor / '83 / PolyGram

Jon B

BONA FIDE
Bona fide / Simple melody / Love is Candi / Mystery 4 two / Someone to love / Time after time / Overflow / Pretty girl / Pants off / Isn't it scary / Burning for you / Gone before light / Love didn't do
CD ___ 4805012
550 Music Yab Yub / Nov '95 / Sony

Jon The Dentist

PYRAMID
CD ___ TECLP 24CD
TEC / Sep '96 / SRD

Jonas Jinx

CASE OF..., A
CD ___ SPV 08445692
SPV / May '95 / Koch / Plastic Head

Jonathan Fire Eater

TREMBLE UNDER BOOM LIGHTS
Search for cherry red / Make it precious / Give me daughters / Beautican / Winston Plum: Undertaker / When Prince was a kid
CD ___ BLUFF 038CD
Deceptive / Jan '97 / Vital

Jones, Alan

SHADOW IN TIME, A
Shadow in time (part 1) / Don't be cruel / Will you still love me tomorrow / Good rockin' tonight / Let's have a party / All shook up / Blue moon of Kentucky / Do you wanna dance / C'mon everybody / Blue suede shoes / Shadow in time / Kansas city / Songbird / Ain't no sunshine / Sleepwalk/ Midnight medley / Apache wardance
CD ___ VIPCD 001
VIP / Nov '96 / Pinnacle

Jones, Aled

ALED JONES WITH THE BBC WELSH CHORUS
Away in a manger / Come unto Him / Sussex carol / O little town of Bethlehem / St. Joseph's carol / Christmas star / Ding dong merrily on high / Deck the halls with boughs of holly / Holy Boy / Jesus Christ the apple tree / Gabriel's message / Rocking / Ave Maria / My heart ever faithful / Good king Wenceslas / Hwiangerdd mair / Unto us is born a son
CD ___ CDVIP 104
Virgin VIP / Dec '94 / EMI

PIE JESU
Art thou troubled / If I can help somebody / Zion hears the watchmen's voices / Jesu joy of man's desiring / Lullaby / I'll walk beside you / Crown of roses / I know that my redeemer liveth / Lausanne / God so loved the world / At the end of the day / Pie Jesu / Laudate dominum
CD ___ CDVIP 107
Virgin VIP / Nov '93 / EMI

Jones, Andrew

I NEED TIME (Jones, Andrew 'Jr. Boy')
I got a stick / Hoochie Mama / I need time / These bills / Big leg, heavy brother / Blues joint / I'm with you / Jr Boy's jam / You're a dog / Gotta be foolin' you / Tribute to Freddie
CD ___ JSPCD 278
JSP / Feb '97 / ADA / Cadillac / Direct / Hot Shot / Target/BMG

Jones, Barbara

FOR YOUR EARS ONLY
CD ___ JMC 200216
Jamaican Gold / Jun '95 / Grapevine/ PolyGram / Jet Star

SAD MOVIES
CD ___ CDGR 118
Charly / Mar '97 / Koch

Jones, Brad

GILT FLAKE
CD ___ GR 1001
Ginger / Jun '97 / Cargo / Greyhound

Jones, Carlo

CARLO JONES & THE KASEKO SURINAM TROUBADOURS
CD ___ MWCD 3011
Music & Words / Jul '95 / ADA / Direct

Jones, Carol Elizabeth

LIGHT ENOUGH TO FIND MY WAY (Jones, Carol Elizabeth & James Leva)
Someday / Cold black heart / I tell you only / Back of your hand / Black as a crow / Light enough to find my way / Nothing but gold / North Country / Smoke and mirrors / I wait alone / Love beyond / Darlin' it's too good to be true
CD ___ ROUCD 0407
Rounder / Jun '97 / ADA / CM / Direct

Jones, Charles

LIFE BEHIND THE MICROPHONE
CD ___ ISS 003CD
Issues / Sep '94 / Plastic Head

Jones, Chris

BLINDED BY THE ROSE
CD ___ SCR 40
Strictly Country / Sep '95 / ADA / Direct

Jones, Curtis

CURTIS JONES VOL.1 1937-1938
CD ___ DOCD 5296
Document / Dec '94 / ADA / Hot Shot / Jazz Music

CURTIS JONES VOL.2 1938-1939
CD ___ DOCD 5297
Document / Dec '94 / ADA / Hot Shot / Jazz Music

CURTIS JONES VOL.3 1939-1940
CD ___ DOCD 5298
Document / Dec '94 / ADA / Hot Shot / Jazz Music

CURTIS JONES VOL.4 1941-1953
CD ___ DOCD 5299
Document / Dec '94 / ADA / Hot Shot / Jazz Music

IN LONDON
Shake it baby / Syl-vous play blues / Young generation boogie / Skid row / Honey dripper / Lonesome bedroom blues / Alley bound blues / Curtis Jones boogie / Dust my broom / Red river blues / Good woman blues / Please send me someone to love / You got good business / Roll me over
CD ___ 8206242
Limelight / Jul '91 / PolyGram

LONESOME BEDROOM BLUES
CD ___ 158312
Blues Collection / Apr '95 / Discovery

TROUBLE BLUES
Lonesome bedroom blues / Whole lot of talk for you / Suicide blues / Please say yes / Weekend blues / Good woman blues / Trouble blues / Love season / Low down worried blues / Good time special / Fool blues
CD ___ OBCCD 515
Original Blues Classics / Apr '94 / Complete/Pinnacle / Wellard

Jones, David

BRIDGES
Bridges / I found a honky tonk angel / Let's stop living together, alone / You don't miss what you got / I'm all that I got left / Blues after sundown / Nothing lasts forever / She's got that loved on look / You're no longer mine / Tears out weigh the whiskey
CD ___ ZNCD 1007
Zane / Oct '95 / Pinnacle

Jones, Donell

MY HEART
In the hood (Playas version) / Knocks me off my feet / No interruptions / Waiting on you / I want you to know / My heart / Yearnin' / Wish you were here / All about you / You should know / Natural thang / Believe in me / In the hood / Don't cry / Onlyone you need
CD ___ 73008260252
Arista / Jun '96 / BMG

Jones, Duke

THUNDER ISLAND
Little boy blues / No ordinary love / You and I (Thunder Island) / Let's have it all / You don't know what love is / Caribbean Windsor / Thunder (In the sky) / True lovers
CD ___ ESJCD 239
Essential Jazz / Oct '94 / BMG

Jones, Ed

PIPER'S TALE
So the story goes / Returning / Long days / Piper's tale / Out in the open / Past tense / Kindred spirit
CD ___ ASCCD 2
ASC / Jun '95 / Cadillac / New Note/ Pinnacle

Jones, Eddie

ONE STRING BLUES (Jones, Eddie 'One-String' & Edward Hazelton)
One string three-quarter banjo picker: *Jones, Eddie 'One-String'* / Rolling and tumbling blues: *Jones, Eddie 'One-String'* / Walk with me Lord: *Jones, Eddie 'One-String'* / Come back baby: *Jones, Eddie 'One-String'* / John Henry: *Jones, Eddie 'One-String'* / I'll be your chauffeur: *Jones, Eddie 'One-String'* / It's raining here: *Jones, Eddie 'One-String'* / Baby please don't go: *Jones, Eddie 'One-String'* / Dozens: *Jones, Eddie 'One-String'* / Mocking the train, mocking the dogs: *Hazelton, Edward* / Poor boy travelling from town to town: *Hazelton, Edward* / Hard rock is my pillow: *Hazelton, Edward* / Motherless children have a hard time: *Hazelton, Edward* / Throw a poor dog a bone: *Hazelton, Edward* / Red river blues: *Hazelton, Edward*
CD ___ CDTAK 1023
Takoma / Jun '96 / ADA / Pinnacle

Jones, Eddie Lee

YONDER GO THAT OLD BLACK DOG (Jones, Eddie Lee 'Mustright' & Family)
CD ___ TCD 5023
Testament / May '95 / ADA / Koch

Jones, Elvin

ELVIN
Lady Luck / Buzz-At / Shadowland / Pretty brown / Ray-El / Four on six / You are too beautiful
CD ___ OJCCD 259
Original Jazz Classics / Dec '96 / Complete/ Pinnacle / Jazz Music / Wellard

HEAVY SOUNDS (Jones, Elvin & Richard Davis)
Raunchy Rita / Shiny stockings / ME / Summertime / Elvin's guitar blues / Here's that rainy day
CD ___ MCAD 33114
Impulse Jazz / Jan '90 / New Note/BMG

IT DON'T MEAN A THING
Green chimneys / Lullaby of Itsugo village / It don't mean a thing if it ain't got that swing / Lush life / Zenzo spirit / Flower is a lovesome thing / Ask me now / Bopsy / Fatima's waltz / Change is gonna come
CD ___ ENJ 80662
Enja / Nov '94 / New Note/Pinnacle / Vital/ SAM

LIVE AT PITT INN (Jones, Elvin Quartet)
Love supreme / Dear Lord / Happy birthday for 'Yuka' / Blues to Veen
CD ___ 4878992
Sony Jazz / Jun '97 / Sony

LIVE AT THE VILLAGE VANGUARD VOL.1
It's easy to remember / Front line / Tohryanse, tohryanse / George and me / Love supreme
CD ___ LCDI 53423
Landmark / Nov '93 / New Note/Pinnacle

LIVE IN JAPAN 1978 (Jones, Elvin Jazz Machine)
Keiko's birthday march / Bessie's blues / Antigua / EJ blues / Love supreme
CD ___ KCD 5041
Konnex / Nov '92 / SRD

LOVE AND PEACE
Little rock blues / Hip Jones / Korina / For tomorrow / Sweet and lovely / Origin / House that love built
CD ___ ECD 220872
Evidence / Jun '94 / ADA / Cadillac / Harmonia Mundi

ON THE MOUNTAIN
CD ___ OW 30328
One Way / Sep '94 / ADA / Direct / Greyhound

VERY RARE
Sweet mama / Passion flower / Zange / Tin tin deo / Pitter pat / Witching hour / EJBlues / Love supreme
CD ___ ECD 22053
Evidence / Jul '93 / ADA / Cadillac / Harmonia Mundi

Jones, Etta

CHRISTMAS WITH ETTA JONES
CD ___ MCD 5411
Muse / Sep '92 / New Note/Pinnacle

DON'T GO TO STRANGERS
CD ___ OJCCD 298
Original Jazz Classics / Jul '93 / Complete/Pinnacle / Jazz Music / Wellard

FINE & MELLOW/SAVE YOUR LOVE FOR ME
CD ___ MCD 6002
Muse / Sep '92 / New Note/Pinnacle

I'LL BE SEEING YOU
CD ___ MCD 5351
Muse / Sep '93 / New Note/Pinnacle

LONELY AND BLUE
CD ___ OJCCD 702
Original Jazz Classics / Jan '94 / Complete/Pinnacle / Jazz Music / Wellard

MELODY LINGERS ON, THE
Somewhere in my lifetime / A-tisket a-tasket / For sentimental reasons / What a wonderful world / What a difference a day makes / I cover the waterfront / Mr Bojangles / I apologise / I'm having a good time / Misty
CD ___ HCD 7005
High Note / Apr '97 / New Note/Pinnacle

SOMETHING NICE
CD ___ OJCCD 221
Original Jazz Classics / Jun '95 / Complete/Pinnacle / Jazz Music / Wellard

SUGAR
CD ___ MCD 5379
Muse / Sep '92 / New Note/Pinnacle

Jones, Floyd

MASTERS OF MODERN BLUES SERIES (Jones, Floyd & Eddie Taylor)
CD ___ TCD 5001
Testament / Aug '94 / ADA / Koch

Jones, George

ALL AMERICAN COUNTRY (18 Original Country Classics)
CD ___ 5525622
Spectrum / Jan '97 / PolyGram

BARTENDER'S BLUES
Bartender's blues / I'll just take it out on love / If you loved a liar / Ain't your memory got no pride at all / I gave it all up for you / I don't want no stranger sleepin' in my bed / I ain't got no business doin' business today / Leaving love all over the place / When your phone don't ring (it'll be me) / Julianne
CD ___ RAZCD 2101
Razor & Tie / May '96 / Koch

COUNTRY CLASSICS
Race is on / You comb her hair / Not what I had in mind / Girl I used to know / She thinks I still care / Your heart turned left / We must have been out of our minds / Where does a little tear come from / Least of all / My tears are overdue / Running bear / You win again / I'm gonna change everything / Beggar to a king / Something I dreamed
CD ___ CDMFP 6326
Music For Pleasure / Apr '97 / EMI

DON'T STOP THE MUSIC
Into my arms again / Who shot Sam / You gotta be my baby / Mr. Fool / Time lock / Candy hearts / What'cha gonna do / Vita-

mins l-o-v-e / Don't stop the music / Accidentally on purpose / All I want to do / Giveaway girl / Cup of loneliness / Wanderin' soul / My sweet Imogene / Likes of you / What am I worth / Boogie woogie Mexican boy / I'm with the wrong one / With half a heart / Ship of love / Honky tonk downstairs
CD ______ CDCH 912
Ace / Nov '93 / Pinnacle

DOUBLE TROUBLE (Jones, George & Johnny Paycheck)
When you're ugly like us / Along came Jones / Proud Mary / You can have her / Smack dab in the middle / Maybellene / Roll over Beethoven / Kansas City / Tutti frutti / You better move on
CD ______ RAZCD 2100
Razor & Tie / May '96 / Koch

EMI COUNTRY MASTERS (2CD Set)
She thinks I still care / Sometimes you just can't win / Ragged but right / Color of the blues / We must have been out of our minds: *Jones, George & Melba Montgomery* / Open pit mine / Girl I used to know / Precious jewel / Lovin' lies / Running bear / Big fool of the year / Give my love to Rose / Beggar to a King / Wait a little longer, please Jesus: *Jones, George & Melba Montgomery* / Not what I had in mind / I saw me / Take me as I am (Or let me go) / You comb her hair / Ain't it funny what a fool will do / Wings of a dove / Seasons of my heart / Little bitty tear / My tears are overdue / What's in our heart: *Jones, George & Melba Montgomery* / Your heart turned left (And I was on the right) / Race is on: *Jones, George & Melba Montgomery* / Something I dreamed: *Jones, George & Melba Montgomery* / It scares me half to death: *Jones, George & Melba Montgomery* / Rose from a bride's bouquet / Where does a tear come from / Please be my love: *Jones, George & Melba Montgomery* / Gold and silver / Warm red wine / We could / Love's gonna live here / Multiply the heartaches / Don't let the stars get in your eyes / Least of all / Rollin' in my sweet baby's arms: *Jones, George & Melba Montgomery* / Book of memories / I'm gonna change everything / I've been known to cry / Wrong number / She's mine / What's money / I'm just blue enough (To do most anything) / Let's invite them over: *Jones, George & Melba Montgomery* / Where did the sunshine go / World's worst loser / Peace in the valley
CD Set ______ CDEM 1502
EMI / Aug '93 / EMI

FRIENDS IN HIGH PLACES
Few ole country boys: *Jones, George & Randy Travis* / All fall down: *Jones, George & Emmylou Harris* / Fiddle and guitar band: *Jones, George & Charlie Daniels* / All that we've got left: *Jones, George & Vern Gosdin* / Love's gonna live here: *Jones, George & Buck Owens* / If I could bottle this up: *Jones, George & Shelby Lynne* / I've been there: *Jones, George & Tim Mensy* / You can't do wrong and get by: *Jones, George & Ricky Skaggs* / It hurts as much in Texas (as it did in Tennessee): *Jones, George & Ricky Van Shelton* / Travellers prayer: *Jones, George & Sweethearts Of The Rodeo*
CD ______ 4680992
Epic / Apr '91 / Sony

GEORGE AND TAMMY (Jones, George & Tammy Wynette)
One / Old love thing / Whatever happend to us / Will you travel down this road with me / (She's just) an old love turned memory / If God met you / Just look what we've started again / All I have to offer you is me / They're playing our song / Solid as a rock
CD ______ MCD 11248
MCA / Aug '95 / BMG

GEORGE JONES & GENE PITNEY (Jones, George & Gene Pitney)
Why baby why / Someday you'll want me to want you / For me this is happy / That's all it took / I'm gonna listen to me / I'm a fool to care / She thinks I still care / Big job / I'm up to my neck in IOU's / Sweeter than the flowers / Wreck on the highway / More I saw of her / Thousand arms (five hundred arms) / I've got five dollars and it's Saturday night / Louisiana man / Drinking from the well of your love / Life to go / One has my name / Mockin' bird hill / I'd like to see me stop you / I can't stop loving you / Your old standby / Won't take long / I've got a new heartache / My shoes keep walking back to you / I really don't want to know / As long as I live / Born to lose / Don't rob another man's castle / Love bug / Y'all come
CD ______ BCD 15790
Bear Family / Feb '95 / Direct / Rollercoaster / Swift

GEORGE JONES COLLECTION, THE (She Thinks I Still Care)
CD Set ______ RE 2136
Razor & Tie / Jul '97 / Koch

GRAND TOUR, THE
Grand tour / Darlin' / Pass me by / She'll love the one she's with / Once you've had the best / Weatherman / Borrowed angel / She told me so / Mary don't go 'round / Who will I be loving now / Our private life
CD ______ RE 21152
Razor & Tie / Oct '96 / Koch

GREATEST COUNTRY HITS OF THE SIXTIES
CD ______ PWKS 4264
Carlton / Jul '95 / Carlton

HIGH TECH REDNECK
High tech redneck / I've still got some hurtin' left to do / Love in your eyes / Visit / Silent partners / Tear me out of the picture / Thousand times a day / Never bit a bullet like this / Forever's here to stay / Hello darlin'
CD ______ MCAD 10910
MCA / Mar '94 / BMG

I LIVED TO TELL
Honky tonk song / Back down to hung up on you / Billy b bad / Hundred proof memories / It ain't gonna worry my mind / Lone ranger / Tied to a stone / I'll give you something to drink about / I must have done something bad / Hello heart
CD ______ MCAD 11478
MCA / Aug '96 / BMG

IN A GOSPEL WAY
CD Set ______ RE 2138
Razor & Tie / Jul '97 / Koch

LEGEND LIVES ON, THE
Good year for the roses / Developing my pictures / Tender years / Say it's not you / From here to the door / If my heart had windows / My favourite lies / Accidentally on purpose / Where grass won't grow / Sweet dreams / Things have gone to pieces / White lightning / Four-o-thirty three / Take me / I'm a people / I'm wasting good paper / Old brush abors / Love bug / Walk through this world with me / Race is on
CD ______ MSCD 24
Music De-Luxe / Oct '95 / TKO Magnum

LIVE AT DANCETOWN USA
White lightning / Something I dreamed / Achin' breaking heart / Window up above / Bony Moronie / She thinks I still care / Ragged but right / Poor man's riches / Jolie blon / Where does a little tear come from / Big Harlan Taylor / She's lonesome again / Race is on
CD ______ CDCHM 156
Ace / May '92 / Pinnacle

TENDER YEARS
CD ______ 15488
Laserlight / Dec '94 / Target/BMG

TOGETHER AGAIN (Jones, George & Tammy Wynette)
CD ______ RAZCD 2094
Razor & Tie / Apr '96 / Koch

WALK THROUGH THE WORLD WITH ME
CD ______ CWNCD 2020
Javelin / Jul '96 / Henry Hadaway / THE

WAYS OF THE WORLD
Don't you ever get tired of hurting me / Open pity mind / On the banks of the old pontchartrain / House without love / Ways of the world / Please don't let that woman get me / Yes I know why / Jonesy / Old brush arbors / Liberty / Jambalaya / Cold cold heart / Ragged but right / Tarnished angel / Your tender years / Wedding bells / Things have gone to pieces / World of forgotten people / From now on all of my friends are gonna be strangers / I can't escape from you
CD ______ CDSB 008
Starburst / Apr '96 / TKO Magnum

WE LOVE TO SING ABOUT JESUS (Jones, George & Tammy Wynette)
We love to sing about Jesus / Old fashioned singing / He is me everything / Me and Jesus / Noah and the ark / Let's all go down to the river / Let's all sing ourselves to glory / Talkin' about Jesus / When Jesus takes his children home / Everything gonna be alright / Show him that you love him
CD ______ RE 21182
Razor & Tie / Dec '96 / Koch

Jones, Glenn

HERE I AM
Here I am / It's gonna be alright / Love song / Round and round / Make it up to you / Coming back to you / Give love a chance / Everything to me / Since you've been gone (a house is not a home) / Don't walk away / In you
CD ______ 7567825132
Warner Bros. / Apr '94 / Warner Music

HERE I GO AGAIN
Here I go again / I've been searchin' / Call me / Good thang / Open up your heart / Way you do / Baby, come to me / In you / Love is forever / Get it right / Say yeah
CD ______ 7567823522
Atlantic / Dec '96 / Warner Music

Jones, Gloria

VIXEN/WINDSTORM
I ain't going nowhere / High / Tell me now / Tainted love / Cry baby / Get it on (part 1) / Go now / Would you like to know / Get it on (part 2) / Drive me crazy (Disco lady) / Sailors of the highway / Stage coach
CD ______ C5HCD 637
See For Miles/C5 / Apr '96 / Pinnacle

Jones, Grace

ISLAND LIFE
Slave to the rhythm / Pull up to the bumper / Private life / La vie en rose / I need a man / My Jamaican guy / Walking in the rain / Libertango / Love is the drug / Do or die
CD ______ IMCD 16
Island / Apr '91 / PolyGram

LIVING MY LIFE
My Jamaican guy / Nipple to the bottle / Apple stretching / Everybody hold still / Cry now - laugh later / Inspiration / Unlimited capacity for love
CD ______ IMCD 18
Island / Jun '89 / PolyGram

NIGHTCLUBBIN'
Feel up / Walking in the rain / Pull up to the bumper / Use me / Art groupie / Libertango / I've done it again
CD ______ IMCD 17
Island / Jun '89 / PolyGram

PORTFOLIO
Send in the clowns / What I did for love / Tomorrow / La vie en rose / Sorry / That's the trouble / I need a man
CD ______ IMCD 19
Island / Jun '89 / PolyGram

SLAVE TO THE RHYTHM
Jones the rhythm / Fashion show / Frog and the princess / Operattack / Slave to the rhythm / Crossing (ooh the action) / Don't cry - it's only the rhythm / Ladies and gentlemen: Miss Grace Jones
CD ______ IMCD 65
Island / '89 / PolyGram

WARM LEATHERETTE
Warm leatherette / Private life / Rollin' stone / Love is the drug / Hunter gets captured by the game / Bullshit / Breakdown / Pars
CD ______ IMCD 15
Island / Jun '89 / PolyGram

Jones, Grandpa

EVERYBODY'S GRANDPA (5CD Set)
It's raining here this morning / Banjo Sam / My darling's not my darling anymore / Going 'cross the sea / Groundhog / Mighty long way to travel / Make the rafters ring / All night long / Count your blessings / East bound freight train / I guess you don't remember now / I've just been gone too long / Tritzem yodel / T for Texas / Any old time / Waitin' for a train / My Carolina sunshine girl / Dear old sunny south / My little lady / Brakeman's blues / Lullaby yodel / Peach picking time in Georgia / Hobo Bill / Away out on the mountain / Roll along Kentucky moon / Waiting for a train / You and my old guitar / T for Texas / Tritzem yodel / Ladies man / Thing / I don't love nobody / Hip cat's wedding / These hills / Billy Yank and Johnny Reb / Goodbye Reb / Willi Mayberry / Sweet fern / Night train to Memphis / Rosalee / (Somewhere) somebody's waiting (for you) / Kickin' mule / Liza's up the 'simmon tree / Chicken don't roost too high / Going from the cotton fields / Tragic romance / Methodist pie / Fatal wedding / What does the deep sea say / I'm tying the leaves (so they won't come down) / Oh captain captain / Devilish Mary / Ladies man / Hip cat's wedding / Night train to Memphis / Are you from Dixie / Root hog root / Falling leaves / Here comes the champion / Banjo am the instrument / Spring time comes but once a year / Eight more miles to Louisville / Little old lady / Springtime comes but once a year / Eight more miles to Louisville / Eight more miles to Louisville / On the Jericho Road / I'll meet you in the morning / Gone home / Keep on the firing line / Just over in Gloryland / Old camp meetin' time / Empty mansion / When I get to the end of the way / Glory Land war / Turn your radio on / No tears in heaven / Lonesome train (on a lonesome track): *Jones, Grandpa & Ramona Jones* / Sandy land: *Jones, Grandpa & Ramona Jones* / Send me a red rose: *Jones, Grandpa & Ramona Jones* / Christmas roses / Christmas guest / Heart full of love / Goin' down to the river / Moon of Arizona / Steady drips of water / Everything I had going for me is gone / Don't look back / Trouble in mind / Trouble in mind / That's all this old world needs / Bill's gonna soon be home / Mountain laurel / Smoke, smoke, smoke (but not around me) / I've learned to leave that to the Lord / Old troupe dog / Sweet lips (Battle of King's Mountain) / Plans / I'll just keep living along / King of the Cannon County hills / Mountain dew / Old rattler / Old blue / Grasshopper McClain / Old Bill / Goin' down to the river / Valley of the never do no good / Four stone walls / Dollar short / Coal camp / Here I am makin' plans / Green hills of home / Are you sleeping Daddy darlin' / Nashville on my mind / Mountain man / Deep dark corner of my mind / Baby-O / My old lady / Brown girl and fair Eleanor / Four winds a-blowin' / Intro / Fix me a pallet / Dooley / Air, the sunshine and the rain / Castles in the air / Old Rattler's pup / My bonnie lies over the ocean / Rocky top / I don't love nobody / John Henry / Last ol' shevel / Southern bound / 15 cents is all I got
CD Set ______ BCD 15788
Bear Family / Jan '97 / Direct / Rollercoaster / Swift

Jones, Hank

ARIGATO
CD ______ PCD 7004
Progressive / Oct '91 / Jazz Music

COMPASSION
CD ______ BB 879
Black & Blue / Apr '97 / Discovery / Koch / Wellard

HANDFUL OF KEYS (The Music Of Thomas 'Fats' Waller)
Handful of keys / I'm more than satisfied / How come you do me like you do / Ain't misbeahvin' / Honeysuckle rose / Please don't talk about me when I'm gone / What did I do to be so black and blue / Spreadin' rhythm around / I've got a feeling I'm falling in love / Your feet's too big / Squeeze me / Sunday / Jitterbug waltz / How ya baby / Keepin' out of mischief now / Believe it, beloved
CD ______ 5127372
EmArCy / May '92 / PolyGram

HANK
Just squeeze me / In a sentimental mood / Satin doll / Prelude to a kiss / What am I here for / Do nothin' 'til you hear from me / Sophisticated lady / Oh look at me now / Alone together / Don't blame me / Gone with the wind / My heart stood still / If I had you / Very thought of you
CD ______ AAJ 11003
Jazz Alliance / Jan '92 / New Note/Pinnacle

HANK JONES TRIO (Jones, Hank Trio)
CD ______ STCD 4180
Storyville / Jan '94 / Cadillac / Jazz Music / Wellard

I REMEMBER YOU
CD ______ BLE 233122
Black & Blue / Oct '94 / Discovery / Koch / Wellard

LAZY AFTERNOON
Speak low / Lazy afternoon / Intimidation / Comin' home baby / Sublime / Peedlum / Work song / Lament / Passing time / Arrival
CD ______ CCD 4391
Concord Jazz / '89 / New Note/Pinnacle

LIVE AT MAYBECK RECITAL HALL VOL.16
I guess I'll have to change my plan / It's the talk of the town / Very thought of you / Night we called it a day / Bluesette / Child is born / What is this thing called love / Oh what a beautiful mornin' / Six and four / I cover the waterfront / Memories of you / Blue monk / 'Round midnight / Oh, look at me now
CD ______ CCD 4502
Concord Jazz / Mar '92 / New Note/ Pinnacle

MEETS LOUIS BELLSON AND IRA SULLIVAN
CD ______ STCD 553
Stash / '92 / ADA / Cadillac / CM / Direct / Jazz Music

ORACLE, THE (Jones, Hank & Dave Holland/Billy Higgins)
Interface / Beautiful love / Oracle / Blues for CM / Yesterdays / Blood count / Maya's dance / Jacob's ladder / Trane connections
CD ______ 8463762
EmArCy / Apr '91 / PolyGram

SPIRIT OF 176, THE (Jones, Hank & George Shearing)
CD ______ CCD 4371
Concord Jazz / Apr '89 / New Note/ Pinnacle

Jones, Howard

12 INCH ALBUM, THE
Always asking questions / New song / What is love / Like to get to know you well / Pearl in the shell / Total conditioning
CD ______ 2405432
WEA / Jul '88 / Warner Music

BEST OF HOWARD JONES, THE
Look mama / Prisoner / Everlasting love / Lift me up / Tears to tell / Two souls / IGY / City song / What is love / New song / Pearl in the shell / Always asking questions / Things can only get better / Like to get to know you well / Life in one day / You know I love you don't you / Hide and seek / No one is to blame
CD ______ 4509927012
WEA / Dec '96 / Warner Music

CROSS THAT LINE
Prisoner / Powerhouse / Cross that line / Guardians of the breath / Wanders to you / Everlasting love / Last supper / Out of thin air / Fresh air waltz / Those who move clouds
CD ______ 2441762
WEA / Mar '89 / Warner Music

DREAM INTO ACTION
Things can only get better / Life in one day / Dream into action / No one is to blame / Look mama / Assault and battery / Automaton / Is there a difference / Elegy / Specialty / Why look for the key / Hunger for flesh
CD ______ 2406322
WEA / Apr '85 / Warner Music

HUMAN'S LIB
Conditioning / What is love / Pearl in the shell / Hide and seek / Hunt the self / New song / Don't always look at the rain / Equality / Natural / Human's lib
CD _____ K 240335 2
WEA / Jun '84 / Warner Music

IN THE RUNNING
Lift me up / Fallin' away / Show me / Voices are back / Exodus / Tears to tell / Two souls / Gun turned on the world / One last try / City song
CD _____ 9031763362
WEA / Dec '96 / Warner Music

LIVE ACOUSTIC AMERICA
CD _____ PLUCD 001
Plump / Mar '96 / Grapevine/PolyGram

ONE TO ONE
You know I love you don't you / Balance of love / All I want / Where are we going / Don't want to fight anymore / Step into these shoes / Will you still be there / Good luck bad luck / Give me strength / Little bit of snow
CD _____ 2420112
WEA / Oct '86 / Warner Music

Jones, Hughie

HUGHIE'S DITTY BAG
Champion of the seas / Marques / Coal, coal for Manchester / Christmas time odd-job man / Marco polo / Navvies' way / Fairlie duplex engine / Ellen Vannin tragedy / Stockholm tar / Shortness of sight / Greyblack stone of ffestinog / Wavertree / New York girls are pretty
CD _____ FECD 081
Fellside / Jan '97 / ADA / Direct / Target/BMG

Jones, Ivan

LEGENDS OF ACID JAZZ, THE (Jones, Ivan 'Boogaloo Joe')
Boogaloo Joe / Don't deceive me / Boardwalk blues / Dream on little dreamer / Atlantic city soul / 6.30 blues / Right on / Things ain't what they used to be / Poppin' / Someday we'll be together / Brown bag / Let it be me
CD _____ PRCD 24167
Prestige / Oct '96 / Cadillac / Complete/Pinnacle

MINDBENDER, THE/ MY FIRE (Jones, Ivan 'Boogaloo Joe')
Mindbender / There is a mountain / Games / Sticks and stones / Blues for Bruce / Beat goes on / Right now / Call me / Light my fire / For big Hal / St. James Infirmary / Take all / Time after time / Ivan the Terrible
CD _____ CDBGPD 067
Beat Goes Public / Jun '93 / Pinnacle

SNAKE RHYTHM ROCK/BLACK WHIP (Jones, Ivan 'Boogaloo Joe')
Hoochie coo chickie / Snake rhythm rock / First time ever I saw your face / He's so fine / Big bad midnight roller / Black whip / My love / Freak off / Daniel / Ballad of mad dogs and Englishmen / Crank me up
CD _____ CDBGPD 043
Beat Goes Public / Sep '92 / Pinnacle

SWEETBACK (Jones, Ivan 'Boogaloo Joe')
CD _____ LHCD 020
Luv n' Haight / Jul '96 / Timewarp

Jones, Jack

BEST OF JACK JONES
CD _____ DSHCD 7003
D-Sharp / Dec '92 / Pinnacle

BEST OF JACK JONES, THE
CD _____ HMNCD 010
Half Moon / Jul '97 / BMG

BEWITCHED
My kind of town (Chicago is) / Along the way / She loves me / Lollipops and roses / Gypsies, the jugglers and the clowns / From Russia with love / Carioca / Feeling good / My favourite things / I don't care much / You'd better love me / Bewitched / Beautiful friendship / I must know / Afterthoughts / Mood I'm in / Julie / I will wait for you / Far away / I'm all smiles / Brother, where are you / Wives and lovers / This is all I ask / Travellin' on
CD _____ 3035900042
Carlton / Oct '95 / Carlton

JACK JONES COLLECTOR'S EDITION
CD _____ DVAD 6042
Deja Vu / Apr '95 / THE

LIVE AT THE LONDON PALLADIUM
I had a dream / Gypsies, jugglers and clowns / Gershwin medley / Just one of those things / Child is born / Hopeless romantic / This all I ask / Falling in love / Right here waiting / Music of the night / Wives and lovers / Lady / Call me irresponsible / If / Soliloquy / Imagine / From a distance
CD _____ DSHCD 7009
D-Sharp / Sep '93 / Pinnacle
CD _____ EMPRCD 630
Emporio / Jun '96 / Disc

LIVE AT THE PALLADIUM
I had a dream / Gypsies juggers and clowns / Summertime medley / Just one of those things / Child is born / Hopeless romantic / This is all I ask / Falling in love with love / Right here waiting / Music of the night / Wives and lovers / Soliloquy / Imagine medley
CD _____ 3037300012
Carlton / Mar '96 / Carlton

LOOK OF LOVE, THE
Look of love / She / Make it with you / If you could read my mind / Without her / God only knows / All cried out / Once in a while / It's too late / Goin' out of my head / What are you doing the rest of your life / Mean to me / You and the night and the music / For all we know
CD _____ 74321339442
Camden / Jan '96 / BMG

Jones, Janie

I'M IN LOVE WITH THE WORLD OF JANIE JONES
Woman in white / Witches brew / Gunning for you / Go go away from me / Tickle me tootsie wootsies / High and dry / High and dry / Hammer toes / Time has come to choose / Time has come to choose / Psycho / Back on my feet again / Back on my feet again / Cross on the wall in Nashville / Charlie Smith / Nobody's perfect / Girl's song / I've never met a boy like you / Easy to remember / Take-a my tip / House of the ju ju queen: *Strummer, Joe* / House of the ju ju queen / Sex machine / Letter to Joe / Witches brew
CD _____ RPM 177
RPM / Jul '97 / Pinnacle

Jones, Jim

TRUST, CONTRAFUSION (Jones, Jim & The Kool Ade Kids)
CD _____ CC 004
Common Cause / Nov '93 / Plastic Head / SRD

Jones, Jimmy

ORIGINAL HANDY MAN, THE
Handy man / You got it / Part time sweetheart / Don't you just know it / Nights of Mexico / Itchin' (for love) / Snap my fingers / I told you so / Good timin' / Close your eyes / You're much too young / Ee-i-ee-i-oh / 39-21-40 shape / That's when I cried / Personal property
CD _____ 303172
Hallmark / Jun '97 / Carlton

Jones, Jo

JO JONES TRIO (Jones, Jo Trio)
CD _____ FSCD 40
Fresh Sound / Oct '90 / Discovery / Jazz Music

JO JONES TRIO (Jones, Jo Trio)
Sweet Georgia Brown / My blue Heaven / Jive at five / Greensleeves / When your lover has gone / Philadelphia bound / Close your eyes / I got rhythm / Embraceable you / Be bop Irishman / Little Susie
CD _____ 5125342
EmArCy / Apr '93 / PolyGram

Jones, Joe

YOU TALK TOO MUCH (The Best Of Joe Jones)
You talk too much / Take a little walk / McDonald's daughter / Tisket-a-tasket / One big mouth (two big ears) / Here's what you gotta do / Where is my baby / To prove my love to you / Big mule / I cried for you / Just write / You talk too much (original) / I'm glad for your sake / One big mouth (original) / I love you still / Every night about eight / Tell me what's happening / Please don't talk about me when I'm gone / I need someone / Always picking on me / California sun / Because I love you / I've got a uh-uh wife / Oh gee how I cried / Indian love call / Down by the river
CD _____ NEMCD 672
Sequel / Jun '94 / BMG

Jones, Johnny

AIN'T GONNA WORRY (Jones, Johnny 'Yard Dog')
CD _____ 4937 CD
Earwig / Dec '96 / ADA / CM

Jones, Jonah

JONAH JONES STORY 1936-1945, THE
CD _____ 158512
Jazz Archives / Jul '96 / Discovery

Jones, Keziah

AFRICAN SPACE CRAFT
African space craft / Million miles from home / Colorful world / Prodigal funk / Splash / Dear Mr. Cooper / Speech / Cubic space division / Funk 'n' circumstance / Man with the scar / Never gonna let you go / If you know
CD _____ CDDLB 14
Delabel / Oct '95 / EMI

BLUFUNK IS A FACT
CD _____ CDDLB 1
Delabel / Mar '92 / EMI

Jones, Leroy

PROPS FOR POPS
Props for pops / Struttin' with some barbecue / West End blues / Someday you'll be sorry / When it's sleepy time down south / Jeepers creepers / You must not be hearin' straight / Preacher / Ain't misbehavin' / Baby won't you please come home / What a wonderful world / Whoopin' blues / Louie's lamentation / Armstrong parade
CD _____ 4851412
Sony Jazz / Oct '96 / Sony

Jones, Linda

NEVER MIND THE QUALITY...FEEL THE SOUL (Live In Ohio 1970)
Introduction / If I had a hammer / That's when I'll stop loving you / For your precious love / You're so fine / I found a love
CD _____ NEBCD 990
Sequel / Jul '97 / BMG

YOUR PRECIOUS LOVE
Your precious love / I do / I love you (I need you) / I've given you the best years of my life / Don't go (I can't stand to be alone) / Not on the outside / Doggin' me around / Let it be me / Hypnotised / If only we had met sooner / Fugitive from love / I'm so glad I found you / Stay with me forever / Things I've been through / When hurt comes back / I can't make it alone / Behold / Dancing in the street
CD _____ NEXCD 167
Sequel / Jul '91 / BMG

Jones, Marti

LIVE AT SPIRIT SQUARE
Hiding the boy / Inside these arms / Cliche / Tourist town / Twisted vines / Living inside the wind
/ I've got second sight / Any kind of lie / Read my heart / Is this the game / Follow you all over / World / Wind in the trees / Real one / If you can love somebody / Just a memory / Old friend
CD _____ SHCD 5502
Sugar Hill / Jul '96 / ADA / CM / Direct / Koch / Roots

MY LONG-HAIRED LIFE
I love the sound of breaking glass / It's not what I want / Life's a game / Black coffee in bed / Champagne and wine / Sleep of the just / Put me on top / You got what it takes / Feather on a stone / Silent partner / Songs to aging children come
CD _____ SHCD 5503
Sugar Hill / Nov '96 / ADA / CM / Direct / Koch / Roots

Jones, Mazlyn

ANGELS OVER WATER
Eden / Flying / Water and stone / Kelda / Windsmith / First light / Angels over water / Great rock / Sea of glass (II) / Glistening waters (II)
CD _____ BWKD 211
Brainworks / Oct '95 / Pinnacle

LIVE (Jones, Mazlyn & Guy Evans/Nik Turner)
Someone at the door / Twentieth century / Spirit moves / Well beyond this point / Behind the stones / Windsmith / Unseen friends / Ship to shore / It's your world
CD _____ BP 250CD
Blueprint / Mar '97 / Pinnacle

Jones, Michael

AIR BORN
Air born / Summer in Chimo / Lark in the clear air / Voices in the wind
CD _____ ND 61042
Narada / Jul '94 / ADA / New Note/Pinnacle

TOUCH
Evening / Walking / Play / River / Rebirth / Longing / Storm / Grace / Delight / Touch
CD _____ ND 61057
Narada / Oct '96 / ADA / New Note/Pinnacle

Jones, Mike

OH LOOK AT ME NOW
CD _____ CRD 325
Chiaroscuro / Mar '96 / Jazz Music

RUNNIN' WILD
CD _____ CRD 336
Chiaroscuro / Mar '96 / Jazz Music

Jones, Nic

PENGUIN EGGS
Canadee-i-o / Drowned lovers / Humpback whale / Little pot stove / Courting is a pleasure / Barrack Street / Planxty Davis / Flandyke Shore / Farewell to the gold
CD _____ TSCD 411
Topic / Nov '90 / ADA / CM / Direct

Jones, Oliver

CLASS ACT, A
CD _____ JUST 412
Justin Time / Sep '91 / Cadillac / New Note/Pinnacle

COOKIN' AT SWEET BASIL
Hymn to a friend / You are too beautiful / Blue mountain / Young and foolish / Take the 'A' train / Pe gros bois blues / Fly me to the moon / Someone to watch over me
CD _____ BRMCD 020
Bold Reprive / Aug '88 / Harmonia Mundi

FROM LUSH TO LIVELY (Jones, Oliver Big Band)
Way you look tonight / Why think about tomorrow / Len's den / We will love again / Swinging on a star / Jazz gavotte / Very thought of you / Tetra tetra / (Our) Love is here to stay / Should I love again / Blues for Helene
CD _____ JUST 732
Justin Time / Apr '96 / Cadillac / New Note/Pinnacle

JAZZ & RIBS LIVE AT BIDDLE'S (Jones, Oliver Trio & Charles Biddle & Bernard Primeau)
CD _____ JUST 12
Justin Time / May '91 / Cadillac / New Note/Pinnacle

NORTHERN SUMMIT (Mones, Oliver)
CD _____ JUST 342
Justin Time / Apr '91 / Cadillac / New Note/Pinnacle

REQUESTFULLY YOURS
CD _____ JUST 112
Justin Time / May '91 / Cadillac / New Note/Pinnacle

SPEAK LOW SWING HARD
CD _____ BRMCD 019
Bold Reprive / Aug '88 / Harmonia Mundi

Jones, Paul

AMERICAN GUESTS VOL.1
CD _____ JSPCD 210
JSP / Oct '92 / ADA / Cadillac / Direct / Hot Shot / Target/BMG

I NEED A STORM (Jones, Paul Urbana)
CD _____ FF 606CD
Flying Fish / Feb '93 / ADA / CM / Direct / Roots

MY WAY
My way / Lady Godiva / It is coming closer / I can't hold on much longer / Baby tomorrow / You've got too much going for you / Very, very funny / High time / She needs company / When my little girl is smiling / Wait 'til morning comes / I can't break the news to myself
CD _____ DORIG 108
EMI / Aug '97 / EMI

SOLO YEARS VOL.1, THE (My Way)
CD _____ RPM 168
RPM / Nov '96 / Pinnacle

SOLO YEARS VOL.2, THE (Love Me, Love My Friends)
CD _____ RPM 169
RPM / Nov '96 / Pinnacle

Jones, Paul Ubana

PAUL UBANA JONES
CD _____ 8409422
Sky Ranch / Sep '96 / Discovery

Jones, Peter

WITH TUNNELS
CD _____ OZ 004
Ozone / Jan '94 / Mo's Music Machine / Pinnacle / SRD

Jones, Philly Joe

BIG BAND SOUNDS
Blue gwynn / Stablemates / Carioca (El tambores) / Tribal message / Cherokee / Land of the blue veils / Philly JJ
CD _____ OJCCD 1792
Original Jazz Classics / Apr '97 / Complete/Pinnacle / Jazz Music / Wellard

FILET DE SOLE
CD _____ 151972
Marge / Nov '92 / Discovery

MO' JOE
CD _____ BLC 760154
Black Lion / Apr '91 / Cadillac / Jazz Music / Koch / Wellard

Jones, Quincy

A&M GOLD SERIES
Ironside / Killer Joe / Midnight soul patrol / Tell me a bedtime story / My cherie amour / Velas / Body heat / Stuff like that / You have to do it yourself / Bluesette / Just once / Ai no corrida / Bridge over troubled water / Superstition / Brown ballad
CD _____ 3970742
A&M / Jul '93 / PolyGram

AI NO CORRIDA (1973-1981)
Stuff like that / Everything must change / Body heat / Betcha wouldn't hurt me / Killer

Joe / Ai no corrida / If I ever lose this Heaven / Just once / I'm gonna miss you in the morning / What's going on / Is it love that we're missin' / Sanford and son / Razzamatazz / Gula matari / One hundred ways / Things could be worse for me / You've got it bad girl / Boogie Joe, the grinder
CD _______ 3969582
A&M / Feb '91 / PolyGram

BACK ON THE BLOCK
Prologue (2 Q's rap) / Back on the block / I don't go for that / I'll be good to you / Verb: To be / Wee b dooinit / Places you find love / Jazz corner of the world / Birdland (Inst.) / Setembro / One man woman / Tomorrow (a better you, better me) / Prelude to the garden / Secret garden
CD _______ 9260202
Qwest / Dec '89 / Warner Music

BEST, THE
Ai no corrida / Betcha wouldn't hurt me / I'm gonna miss you in the morning / Body heat / Everything must change / Killer Joe / If I ever lose this Heaven / Just once / What's going on
CD _______ 3932002
A&M / Feb '94 / PolyGram

BODY HEAT
Body heat / Soul saga / Everything must change / Boogie Joe, the grinder / Everything must change / One track mind / Just a man / Along came Betty / If I ever lose this Heaven
CD _______ 3931912
A&M / Feb '93 / PolyGram

DUDE, THE
Ai no corrida / Dude / Just once / Betcha wouldn't hurt me / Something special / Razzamatazz / Hundred ways / Valas / Turn on the action
CD _______ CDMID 119
A&M / Oct '92 / PolyGram

FREE AND EASY (Live In Sweden 1960)
Moanin / Tickle toe / I remember Clifford / Whisper not / Phantom's blues / Birth of a band / Gypsy / Ghana / Walkin' / Big red
CD _______ ANC 9500
Ancha / Aug '94 / Cadillac / Jazz Music / Wellard

GENIUS OF QUINCY JONES, THE (Classic Jazz and Soul Arrangements)
Take five / Bossa Nova USA / Cast your fate to the wind / Exodus / Walk on the wild side / Gravy waltz / Back at the chicken shack / Watermelon man
CD _______ 306202
Hallmark / Jan '97 / Carlton

GULA MATARI (Jones, Quincy & His Orchestra)
Bridge over troubled water / Gula matari / Walkin' / Hummin'
CD _______ 3930302
A&M / Apr '93 / PolyGram

LISTEN UP - THE LIVES OF QUINCY JONES
Listen up (instrumental version) / Kansas city wrinkles / Killer Joe / Let the good times roll / Airmail special / Perry's theme / Kingfish / Birth of a band / Fly me to the moon / Midnight sun will never set / Rack 'em up / TV medley / Maybe God is tryin' to tell you somethin' / Walking in space / Pop medley / How do you keep the music playing / Back on the block album medley / Somewhere / Listen up (vocal version)
CD _______ 7599263222
Qwest / Sep '90 / Warner Music

LIVE LAUSANNE 1960 (Jones, Quincy & His Orchestra)
Cherokee / Chinese checkers / Birth of a band / I remember Clifford / Ghana / Big red / My reverie / Parisian thoroughfare / Moanin' / Soul / Midnight sun will never set / Phantom's blues / Airmail special / Airmail special (Encore)
CD _______ TCB 02012
TCB / Jul '94 / New Note/Pinnacle

PAWNBROKER, THE/THE DEADLY AFFAIR (Original Soundtracks) (Jones, Quincy & His Orchestra)
CD _______ 5312332
Verve / Jun '96 / PolyGram

Q'S JOOK JOINT
Intro / Let the good times roll / Cool Joe, mean Joe / You put a move on my heart / Rock with you / Moody's mood for love / Stomp / Reprise / Do nothin' 'til you hear from me / Is it love that we're missin' / Heaven's girl / Stuff like that / Slow jams / At the end of the day / Outro
CD _______ 9362458752
Qwest / Nov '95 / Warner Music

QUINTESSENCE
Quintessence / Robot portrait / Little Karen / Straight, no chaser / For Lena and Lennie / Hard sock dance / Invitation / Twitch
CD _______ IMP 12222
Impulse Jazz / Apr '97 / New Note/BMG

SMACKWATER JACK
Smackwater Jack / Cast your fate to the wind / Ironside / What's going on / Anderson tapes / Brown ballad / Hikky burr / Guitar blues odyssey: from roots to fruits
CD _______ 3930372
A&M / Apr '93 / PolyGram

SOUNDS...AND STUFF LIKE THAT
Stuff like that / Love I never had it so good / Superwoman / I'm gonna miss you in the morning / Love me by my name / Takin' it to the streets
CD _______ CDMID 120
A&M / Oct '92 / PolyGram

STRIKE UP THE BAND (1961-1963)
Baby elephant walk / Pink panther / Dreamsville / Soldier in the rain / Blues in the night / Take five / After hours / Desafinado / Cast your fate to the wind / Jive samba / Strike up the band / Dear old Stockholm / Gentle rain / Bossa nova USA
CD _______ 8307742
Mercury / Feb '88 / PolyGram

WALK ON THE WILD SIDE
CD _______ MSCD 18
Music De-Luxe / Apr '95 / TKO Magnum

WALKING IN SPACE (Jazz Heritage)
Dead end / Walking in space / Killer Joe / Love and peace / I never told you / Oh happy day
CD _______ 3969932
A&M / Mar '94 / PolyGram

WATERMELON MAN
CD _______ HADCD 182
Javelin / Nov '95 / Henry Hadaway / THE

Jones, Richard M.

CLASSICS 1923-1927
CD _______ CLASSICS 826
Classics / Sep '95 / Discovery / Jazz Music

CLASSICS 1927-1944
CD _______ CLASSICS 853
Classics / Feb '96 / Discovery / Jazz Music

RICHARD M. JONES VOL.1 (1923-1927)
CD _______ JPCD 1524
Jazz Perspectives / Jul '96 / Hot Shot / Jazz Music

RICHARD M. JONES VOL.2 (1927-1936)
CD _______ JPCD 1525
Jazz Perspectives / Jul '96 / Hot Shot / Jazz Music

Jones, Rickie Lee

FLYING COWBOYS
CD _______ GEFD 24246
Geffen / Nov '91 / BMG

GHOSTYHEAD
CD _______ 9362465572
WEA / Sep '97 / Warner Music

NAKED SONGS
CD _______ 9362459502
WEA / Sep '95 / Warner Music

PIRATES
We belong together / Living it up / Skeletons / Woody and Dutch on the slow train to Peking / Pirates / Lucky guy / Traces of western slopes / Returns
CD _______ 256816
WEA / Jan '86 / Warner Music

POP POP
CD _______ GFLD 19293
Geffen / Oct '95 / BMG

RICKIE LEE JONES
On Saturday afternoons in 1963 / Night train / Young blood / Easy money / Last chance Texaco / Danny's all star joint / Coolsville / Weasel and the white boy's cool / Company / After hours (12 bars past midnight) / Chuck E's in love
CD _______ K2 56628
WEA / '89 / Warner Music

TRAFFIC FROM PARADISE
Pink flamingoes / Alter boy / Stewart's coat / Beat angels / Tigers / Rebel rebel / Jolie jolie / Running from mercy a stranger's car / Albatross
CD _______ GED 24602
Geffen / Sep '93 / BMG

Jones, Robin

CHANGO (Jones, Robin & King Salsa)
Elugua / King Salsa theme / Vamonos Pa'l Monte / Sonando / Manteca / Controladora / Viva la vida contento / Mi songo / Mama guela / Mozambique pa'gozar / Bomba de salon / June / Tremendo / Songo for Jo / Dominican dream / Amor verdadero / Olufina / Chango
CD _______ PARCD 502
Parrot / Feb '96 / BMG / Jazz Music / THE / Wellard

Jones, Rodney

ARTICULATION
Articulation / 1978 / Hard New York swing / Interlude 1 / Childville / Blues for Wes / Nereda
CD _______ CDSJP 125
Timeless Jazz / Jun '91 / New Note/ Pinnacle

RIGHT NOW
CD _______ MM 801054
Minor Music / Jun '96 / Vital/SAM

Jones, Salena

SALENA SINGS JOBIM WITH THE JOBIMS (Jones, Salena & A. Carlos Jobim/Paulo Jobim/Daniel Jobim)
Antonio's song / Agua de beber / Useless landscape / Quiet night of quiet stars / Somewhere in the hills / Dindi / Desafinado / Girl (boy) from Ipanema / Once I loved / Meditation / One note samba / Bonita / Song of the jet / Abandoned garden
CD _______ VG 102
Vine Gate / Oct '96 / New Note/Pinnacle

Jones, Sam

CHANT, THE
Chant / Blues on down / Sonny boy / In walked Ray / Bluebird / Over the rainbow / Off-colour
CD _______ OJCCD 1839
Original Jazz Classics / Apr '97 / Complete/ Pinnacle / Jazz Music / Wellard

DOWN HOME
Unit 7 / Come rain come shine / 'Round midnight / OP / Thumbstring / Down home / Strollin' / Falling in love with love
CD _______ OJCCD 1864
Original Jazz Classics / Apr '97 / Complete/ Pinnacle / Jazz Music / Wellard

VISITATION
CD _______ SCCD 31097
Steeplechase / Jul '88 / Discovery / Impetus

Jones, Shirley

WITH YOU
Gonna get over you / What about me / I've been expecting you / Say / Come closer / Perfect love / Nights over Eygpt / With you / I just can't wait / Dreams do come true / I'm yours tonight / I ain't going nowhere
CD _______ DIVCD 3
Diverse / Jul '94 / Grapevine/PolyGram

Jones, Spike

AND HIS CITY SLICKERS
CD _______ ENTCD 247
Entertainers / Mar '92 / Target/BMG

BEST OF SPIKE JONES & HIS CITY SLICKERS, THE (Jones, Spike & His City Slickers)
Cocktails for two / William Tell overture / Chloe / My old flame / Glow worm / None but the lonely heart / Laura / Man on the flying trapeze / You always hurt the one you love / Der Fuhrer's face / Dance of the hours / Hawaiian war chant
CD _______ 74321135762
RCA / May '93 / BMG

DIRECT OFF THE AIR 1949
CD _______ HQCD 30
Harlequin / Jan '95 / Hot Shot / Jazz Music / Swift / Wellard

MUSICAL DEPRECIATION (Original Mono Recordings 1941-1945) (Jones, Spike & His City Slickers)
Cocktails for two / Chloe / Behind those two swingin' doors / Red wing / Covered wagon rolled right along / Clink, clink another drink / Little Bo Peep has lost her jeep / Pass the biscuits, Mirandy / Der Fuehre's face / I wanna go back to West Virginia / Hotcha cornia (black eyes) / Leave the dishes in the sink Ma / Serenade to a jerk / Holiday for strings / Blue Danube / You always hurt the one you love / Hawaiian war chant / Liebestraum / That old black magic / Nutcracker suite
CD _______ CDAJA 5189
Living Era / Jan '96 / Select

RADIO DAYS (Jones, Spike & His City Slickers)
CD _______ RMB 75017
Remember / Nov '93 / Total/BMG

RIOT SQUAD VOL.2 (Louder & Funnier/ 1942-1945) (Jones, Spike & His City Slickers)
Blacksmith song / Moo woo woo / Don't give the chair to Buster / Big bad Bill / Red grow the roses / Casey Jones / And the great big saw came nearer / No no Nora / That's what makes the world go round / Hey Mabel / Now laugh / Three little words / At last I'm first with you / Jamboree Jones / Chloe / Trailer Annie / Mary Lou / Barstool cowboy / From old Barstow / Row row row / Toot toot tootsie goodbye / Siam
CD _______ HQCD 02
Harlequin / Nov '86 / Hot Shot / Jazz Music / Swift / Wellard

Jones, Steve

FIRE AND GASOLINE
Freedom fighter / We're not saints / God in Louisisana / Fire and gasoline / Hold on / Trouble maker / I did U no wrong / Get ready / Gimme love / Wild wheels / Leave your shoes on / Suffragette city
CD _______ MAUCD 647
Mau Mau / Mar '97 / Pinnacle

MERCY
Give it up / That's enough / Raining in my heart / With or without you / Pleasure and pain / Pretty baby / Drugs suck / Through the night / Love letters / Mercy
CD _______ MAUCD 644
Mau Mau / Apr '96 / Pinnacle

Jones, Thad

GREAT CONCERT, THE (Jones, Thad & Mel Lewis)
CD _______ COD 017
Jazz View / Jun '92 / Harmonia Mundi

MAD THAD
CD _______ FSCD 117
Fresh Sound / Jan '91 / Discovery / Jazz Music

SWISS RADIO DAYS JAZZ SERIES VOL.4
Second race / Don't ever leave me / Waltz you swang for me / A - that's freedom / Come Sunday / Don't get sassy / Bible story / Groove merchant
CD _______ TCB 02042
TCB / Jan '95 / New Note/Pinnacle

THAD JONES AND THE DANISH RADIO BIG BAND (Jones, Thad & The Danish Radio Big Band)
CD _______ STCD 4172
Storyville / Feb '90 / Cadillac / Jazz Music / Wellard

Jones, Tom

13 SMASH HITS
Don't fight it / You keep me hangin' on / Hold on I'm comin' / I was made to love her / Keep on running / Get ready / I'll never fall in love again / I know / I wake up crying / Funny how time slips away / Danny boy / It's a man's man's man's world / Yesterday
CD _______ 8205242
London / Jan '93 / PolyGram

A-TOM-IC JONES
Dr. Love / Face of a loser / It's been a long, long time / Coming / In a woman's eyes / More / I'll never let you go / Loser / To make a big man cry / Key to my heart / True love comes only once in a lifetime / Little you / You're so good to me / Where do you belong / These things you don't forget / Stop breaking my heart / Hide and seek / Not responsible / This and that / Promise her anything / Thunderball
CD _______ 8205562
London / Jan '93 / PolyGram

ALONG CAME JONES
I've got a heart / It takes a worried man / Skye boat song / Once upon a time / Memphis, Tennessee / What'cha gonna do / I need your loving / It's not unusual / Autumn leaves / Rose / If you need me / Some other guy / Endlessly / It's just a matter of time / Spanish harlem / When the world was beautiful
CD _______ 8440252
London / Jan '93 / PolyGram

AT HIS BEST (2CD Set)
Delilah / Don't cry for me Argentina / On the road again / Love me tonight / Proud Mary / Let it be / Danny boy / Lady Madonna / Memphis / Long and winding road / My way / Twist and shout / I can't stop loving you / Back in the USSR / For once in my life / Can't buy me love / She's a lady / Lay down Sally / Satisfaction / Let your love flow / She believes in love / I who have nothing / Starting over / As time goes by / Cupid / Great balls of fire / I can see clearly now / Rockin' me / Oh, pretty woman / Yesterday / What's new pussycat / Georgia on my mind / Hound dog / Send in the clowns / We don't talk anymore / Honky tonk woman / Spanish eyes / Jailhouse rock / Green, green grass of home / On Broadway / Save the last dance for me
CD Set _______ PDSCD 549
Pulse / Jul '97 / BMG

COLLECTION, THE
CD _______ CCSCD 431
Castle / Mar '95 / BMG

COLLECTION, THE
It's not unusual / Spanish harlem / Detroit city / What's new pussycat / My prayer / Sixteen tons / Nearness of you / Not responsible / Loser / Lucille (live) / Cool water / This and that / I'll never let you go / Dr. Love / More / Ten guitars / If you need me / Green, green grass of home
CD _______ 5515202
Spectrum / Aug '95 / PolyGram

COMPLETE TOM JONES, THE
It's not unusual / Delilah / Kiss / I'll never fall in love again / She's a lady / Green green grass of home / Love me tonight (Alla fine della strada) / Without love (there is nothing) / Daughter of darkness / Boy from nowhere / What's new pussycat / I'm coming home / Help yourself / I who have nothing / Move closer / Detroit city / Couldn't say goodbye / Till / Something 'bout you baby I like / Young new Mexican puppeteer
CD _______ 8442862
London / Jun '92 / PolyGram

DELILAH
Delilah / Riders in the sky / To wait for love is to waste your life away / Funny familiar forgotten feelings / Get ready / Georgia on my mind / When I fall in love / Danny boy /

Begin the beguine / Help yourself / I was made to love her / Hey Jude / If you go away / Yesterday / My foolish heart / Let it be me / What's he got that I ain't got / One day soon / Weeping Annaleah / Make this heart of mine smile again / Lingering on / You can't stop love / My elusive dreams / Just out of reach / Only a fool breaks his own heart / Why can't I cry / Take me
CD 8204862
London / Jan '93 / PolyGram

DELILAH
CD 12575
Laserlight / Oct '95 / Target/BMG

FROM THE HEART
Begin the beguine / You came a long way from St. Louis / My foolish heart / It's magic / Someday (you'll want me to want you) / Georgia on my mind / Kansas city / Hello, young lovers / Taste of honey / Nearness of you / When I fall in love / If ever I would leave you / My prayer / That old black magic / Any day now / I'm coming home / Thing called love / Green green grass of home
CD 8205572
London / Apr '89 / PolyGram

GOLDEN HITS
Green green grass of home / I'm coming home / I'll never fall in love again / Not responsible / Help yourself / What's new pussycat / Love me tonight / It's not unusual... / Funny familiar forgotten feelings / Detroit city / With these hands / Minute of your time / Without love / Delilah
CD 8101922
London / Jan '93 / PolyGram

GREATEST HITS
It's not unusual / Delilah / Help yourself / Daughter of darkness / I'll never fall in love again / Without love / With these hands / I'm coming home / Funny familiar forgotten feelings / Green green grass of home / Detroit city / Something 'bout you baby I like / I who have nothing / Till
CD TCD 2296
Telstar / Nov '88 / BMG

GREEN GREEN GRASS OF HOME
Green green grass of home / She's a lady / Funny familiar forgotten feelings / Delilah / Not responsible / Detroit city / Help yourself / Till / Love me tonight / It's not unusual / I'll never fall in love again / Daughter of darkness / What's new pussycat / I'm coming home / Once upon a time / This and that / Riders in the sky / He'll have to go / Sixteen tons / Two brothers / My mother's eyes / Ring of fire / Field of yellow daisies / Wish I could say no to you / All I get from you is heartaches / Mohair Sam / Cool water
CD 8201822
London / Jan '93 / PolyGram

HELP YOURSELF
Help yourself / I can't break the news to myself / Bed / Isadora / Set me free / I get carried away / This house (the house song) / So afraid / If I promise / If you go away / My girl Maria / All I can say is goodbye / Ten guitars / What a party / Looking out my window / Can't stop loving you / Let there be love / Without love
CD 8205592
London / Jan '93 / PolyGram

IT'S NOT UNUSUAL (Greatest Hits)
It's not unusual / Green green grass of home / Help yourself / I'll never fall in love again / Not responsible / Love me tonight / Without love / Delilah / What's new pussycat / Detroit city / Once upon a time / Thunderball / Minute of your time / With these hands / Funny familiar forgotten feelings / I'm coming home / You keep me hangin' on / Land of 1000 dances
CD 8205442
London / Jul '87 / PolyGram

KISS
Kiss / What you have been missing / Move closer / After the tears / Who's gonna take you home tonight / Satisfaction / I'm counting on you / At this moment / Touch my heart / 'Til the end of time
CD EMPRCD 555
Emporio / Mar '95 / Disc
CD 100002
CMC / May '97 / BMG

KISS
Kiss / What you been missing / Move closer / After the tears / Who's gonna take you home tonight / Satisfaction / I'm counting on you / At this moment / Touch my heart / 'Til the end of time
CD QED 014
Tring / Nov '96 / Tring

LEAD AND HOW TO SWING IT, THE
If I only knew / A girl like you / I wanna get back with you / Situation / Something for your head / Fly away / Love is on our side / I don't think so / Lift me up / Show me / I'm ready / Changes
CD IND 92498
Interscope / Aug '96 / BMG

LEGENDARY TOM JONES, THE
CD 8445522
Deram / Jan '96 / PolyGram

LIVE AT CAESAR'S PALACE
Dance of love / Cabaret / Soul man / I who have nothing / Delilah / Bridge over troubled water / My way / God bless the children / Resurrection shuffle / She's a lady / Till / I'll never fall in love again / Daughter of darkness / Love me tonight / It's not unusual / Hi-heel sneakers / Johnny B Goode / Bony Moronie / Long tall Sally
CD CDMFP 5931
Music For Pleasure / Oct '91 / EMI

LIVE IN LAS VEGAS
Turn on your love light / Bright lights and you girl / I can't stop loving you / Hard to handle / Delilah / Danny boy / I'll never fall in love again / Help yourself / Yesterday / Hey Jude / Love me tonight / It's not unusual / Twist and shout
CD 8203182
London / Jan '93 / PolyGram

LOVE ALBUM, THE (Jones, Tom & Engelbert Humperdinck)
CD DCD 5385
Disky / Jul '94 / Disky / THE

SIMPLY THE BEST - SHE'S A LADY
CD WMCD 5693
Disky / May '94 / Disky / THE

SING FOR YOU (Jones, Tom/Englebert Humperdinck)
Witch queen of New Orleans: *Jones, Tom* / Tired of being alone: *Jones, Tom* / Woman you took my life: *Jones, Tom* / If: *Jones, Tom* / Young New Mexican Puppeteer: *Jones, Tom* / All I ever need is you: *Jones, Tom* / You've got a friend: *Jones, Tom* / Time to get it together: *Jones, Tom* / I won't be sorry to see Suzanne again: *Jones, Tom* / Kiss an angel good morning: *Jones, Tom* / Stardust: *Humperdinck, Engelbert* / I'll be seeing you: *Humperdinck, Engelbert* / More I see you: *Humperdinck, Engelbert* / In the still of the night: *Humperdinck, Engelbert* / Moonlight becomes you: *Humperdinck, Engelbert* / But beautiful: *Humperdinck, Engelbert* / I'll be around: *Humperdinck, Engelbert* / Harbor lights: *Humperdinck, Engelbert* / They say it's wonderful: *Humperdinck, Engelbert* / Long ago (and far away): *Humperdinck, Engelbert*
CD RMB 75087
Remember / Sep '96 / Total/BMG

STOP BREAKING MY HEART
Stop breaking my heart / Before / Once in a while / Triple cross / Shake / If I had you / It ain't gonna be that way / How do you say goodbye / Things I wanna do / For the first time in my life / Tupelo Mississippi Flash / Lonely one / Smile / Day by day / Out in the cold again / Unfinished song / Man who knows too much / Minute of your time / With one exception / It's not unusual
CD 8207732
London / Jan '93 / PolyGram

THIS IS TOM JONES
Fly me to the moon / Little green apples / Wichita lineman / (Sittin' on the) dock of the bay / Dance of love / Hey Jude / Without you / That's all a man can say / That wonderful sound / Only once / I'm a fool to want you / Let it be me
CD 8202342
London / Jan '93 / PolyGram

THIS IS TOM JONES
CD 6389623
Spectrum / Jun '96 / PolyGram

TOM JONES AT CAESARS PALACE
Dance of love / Cabaret / Soul man / I (Who have nothing) / Delilah / Bridge over troubled water / My way / God bless the children / Reserrective shuffle / She's a lady / Till / I'll never fall in love again / Daughter of darkness / Love me tonight / It's not unusual / High heel sneaker / Johnny B Good / Bony Maroni / Long Tall Sally
CD 12656
Laserlight / Jun '96 / Target/BMG

TOM JONES LIVE IN LONDON
Star theme / Ain't that good news / Hello, young lovers / I can't stop loving you / What's new pussycat / Not responsible / I believe / My yiddishe Momme / Shake / That lucky old sun / Thunderball / That old black magic / Green green grass of home / It's not unusual / Land of 1000 dances
CD 8205582
London / Jan '93 / PolyGram

TOUCH MY HEART (3CD Set)
She's a lady / Till / Daughter of darkness / Young New Mexican puppeteer / Try a little tenderness / After the tears / Women you took my life / At this moment / To all the girls I've loved before / If I sing you a love song / Tired of being alone / You're my world / Letter to Lucille / Whose gonna take you home / Impossible dream / Pledging my love / I (who have nothing) / You've got a friend / Nothing rhymed / Ain't no sunshine / If / Love is in the air / Venus / Proud Mary / I won't be sorry to see Suzanne again / Sugar sugar / Resurrection shuffle / All I ever need is you / Kiss an angel good morning / Anniversary sing / Memories don't leave like people do / You'll never walk alone / Take me tonight / You've lost that lovin' feelin' / Say you'll stay until tomorrow / Rescue me / Puppet man / Somethin' about you I like / Till I can't take it anymore / To love somebody / My way / Move closer / We had it all / Touch my heart / Without love / 'Till the end of time / Witch queen of New Orleans / Hit medley (live) / I'll never fall in love again/Daughter of darkness/Love me t / It's not unusual
CD Set SA 872502
Disky / Sep '96 / Disky / THE

VELVET & STEEL/GOLD (2CD Set)
CD Set 8440962
London / Jan '93 / PolyGram

VOICE, THE
It's not unusual / (Sittin' on the) dock of the bay / What's new pussycat / let it be me / Green green grass of home / It's magic / Memphis, Tennessee / I can't stop loving you / If you go away / Kansas City / Promise her anything / Detroit city / With these hands / I'll never fall in love again / My prayer / Love me tonight / I'm coming home
CD MCCD 057
Music Club / Mar '92 / Disc / THE

WHAT A PARTY
CD 8440262
London / Jan '93 / PolyGram

WHAT'S NEW PUSSYCAT
What's new pussycat / Some other guy / I've got a heart / Little by little / Won't you give him (one more chance) / Bama lama bama loo / With these hands / Untrue / To wait for love is to waste your life away / I tell the sea / Rose / Endlessly / Memphis, Tennessee / Kiss kiss / Once upon a time / What'cha gonna do
CD 8205232
London / Jan '93 / PolyGram

Jones, Tutu

BLUE TEXAS SOUL
CD CDBB 9571
Bullseye Blues / Aug '96 / Direct

I'M FOR REAL
Sweet woman / I'm for real / My own fault / Excited / (Do you love) steppin' on me / She's my woman / I still love you / Too blues to be true / Stubborn woman / I'm not your fool / Outstanding
CD JSPCD 252
JSP / Jun '94 / ADA / Cadillac / Direct / Hot Shot / Target/BMG

Jones, Vince

COMPLETE, THE
If you're going to the city / Lobster / Detour ahead / Nature boy / My ideal / Big city / Blue / Don't worry about a thing / Nature of power / Since I fell for you / I put a spell on you / Dream / Not much / Budgie / Sensual item / Never let me go
CD INT 30902
Intuition / Nov '93 / New Note/Pinnacle

FUTURE GIRL
CD INT 31092
Intuition / Oct '92 / New Note/Pinnacle

HERE'S TO THE MIRACLES
Luncheon with the president / Here's to the miracles / America / We're still friends / Love comes back / Lost in the stars / Bye bye love / Tribute two / Can't afford to live, can't afford to die / Take a love song
CD INT 31982
Intuition / Feb '97 / New Note/Pinnacle

ONE DAY SPENT
Detour ahead / Let's get lost / I wish you love / Since I fell for you / Afterthought / I thought about you / Time after time / Never let me go / Save your love for me / There'll never be another you
CD INT 30872
Intuition / Feb '92 / New Note/Pinnacle

TRUSTWORTHY LITTLE SWEETHEARTS
Big city / Don't worry about a thing / Stricken by a storm / Trustworthy little sweethearts / I'm a fool to want you / Like young / My only friend / That old feeling / In an attempt to be fascinating / I didn't know what time it was / Not much / Turn around / (I'm afraid) the masquerade is over
CD INT 3046 2
Intuition / Mar '91 / New Note/Pinnacle

WATCH WHAT HAPPENS
CD INT 30702
Intuition / Oct '91 / New Note/Pinnacle

Jones, Vivian

IJAHMAN
CD IHCD 007
Imperial House / Jul '95 / Jet Star / THE

LOVE IS FOR LOVERS
CD IHCD 006
Imperial House / Jun '95 / Jet Star / THE

REGGAE MAX
CD JSRNCD 12
Jet Star / Mar '97 / Jet Star

Jones, Wizz

LATE NIGHTS AND LONG DAYS (Jones, Wizz & Simeon)
CD FE 091CD
Fellside / Jul '93 / ADA / Direct / Target/BMG

VILLAGE TAPES
CD TUT 72157
Wundertute / Jan '94 / ADA / CM / Duncans

Jonsson, Cennet

TEN PIECES
CD PSCD 94
Phono Suecia / May '97 / Cadillac / Impetus

Jonsson, Lennart

I THOUGHT ABOUT YOU
CD SITCD 9220
Sittel / Aug '95 / Cadillac / Jazz Music

Jontef

KLEZMER & YIDDISH
CD EUCD 1303
ARC / Jul '95 / ADA / ARC Music

Joolz

HEX
Protection / Cat / Facade / Love is (sweet romance) / Stand / Storm / Mummy's boy / Ambition / House of dreams / Requiem / Musket fife and drum / Legend / Mad, bad and dangerous to know
CD CDGRAM 44
Anagram / Apr '90 / Cargo / Pinnacle

Joos, Herbert

DAYBREAK - THE DARK SIDE OF TWILIGHT
Why / When were you born / Leicester Court 1440 / Daybreak / Black trees / Fasten your seatbelt / Dark side of twilight
CD 8414792
ECM / Jan '90 / New Note/Pinnacle

HERBERT JOOS PLAYS BILLIE HOLIDAY SONGS
I'm a fool to want you / My man / No more / You don't know what love is / God bless the child / Don't explain / Crazy he tells me / When your lover has gone / Mood indigo
CD 5226342
EmArCy / Jan '95 / PolyGram

Joplin, Janis

18 ESSENTIAL SONGS
Trouble in mind / Down on me / Bye bye baby / Ball and chain / Piece of my heart / I need a man to love / Summertime / Try (just a little bit harder) / One good man / Kozmic blues / Raise your hand / Tell Mama / Move over / Mercedes Benz / Get it while you can / Me and Bobby McGee / Trust me / Half moon
CD 4785152
Columbia / Apr '95 / Sony

ANTHOLOGY (2CD Set)
Piece of my heart / Summertime / Maybe / Try (just a little bit harder) / To love somebody / Kozmic blues / Turtle blues / Oh sweet Mary / Little girl blue / Trust me / Move over / Half moon / Cry baby / Me and Bobby McGee / Mercedes Benz / Down on me / Bye bye baby / Get it while you can / Ball and chain
CD Set 4674052
Columbia / Jun '97 / Sony

CHEAP THRILLS/PEARL/KOZMIC BLUES (3CD Set)
Combination of the two / I need a man to love / Summertime / Piece of my heart / Turtle blues / Oh sweet Mary / Ball and chain / Move over / Cry baby / Woman left lonely / Half moon / Buried alive in the blues / My baby / Me and Bobby McGee / Mercedes Benz / Trust me / Get it while you can / Try / Maybe / One good man / As good as you've been to this / To love somebody / Kozmic blues / Little girl blue / Work me lord
CD Set 4853212
Columbia / Oct '96 / Sony

FAREWELL SONG
Tell mama / Magic of love / Misery 'n' / One night stand / Harry / Raise your hand / Farewell song / Amazing grace / Hi-heel sneakers / Catch me daddy
CD 4844582
Columbia / Feb '97 / Sony

GREATEST HITS
Piece of my heart / Summertime / Try (just a little bit harder) / Cry baby / Me and Bobby McGee / Down on me / Get it while you can / Bye bye baby / Move over / Ball and chain / Everybody loves you now / Why Judy why / Falling of the rain / Turn around / You look so good to me / Tomorrow is today / Nocturne / Got to begin again
CD CD 32190
CBS / May '90 / Sony

JANIS (3CD Set)
What can drinkin' do / Trouble in mind / Hesitation blues / Easy rider / Coo coo / Down on me / Last time / All is loneliness / Call on me / Women is losers / Intruder / Light is faster than sound / Bye bye baby / Farewell song / Flower in the sun / Misery'n / Roadblock / Ball and chain / Combination of the two / I need a man to love / Piece of my heart / Turtle blues / Oh sweet Mary /

Catch me daddy / Summertime / Kozmic blues / Try (just a little bit harder) / One good man / Dear landlord / To love somebody / As good as you've been to this world / Little girl blue / Work me Lord / Raise your hand / Maybe / Me and Bobby McGee / One night stand / Tell mama / Cry baby / Move over / Woman left lonely / Half moon / Happy birthday John (happy trails) / My baby / Mercedes Benz / Trust me / Get it while you can
CD Set ______ **CD 48845**
Columbia / Jan '94 / Sony

LIVE AT WOODSTOCK 1969
CD ______ **ITM 960007**
Koch / Sep '93 / Koch

MAGIC OF LOVE
CD ______ **ITM 96001**
ITM / Nov '92 / Koch / Tradelink

PEARL
Move over / Cry baby / Woman left lonely / Half moon / Buried alive in the blues / Me and Bobby McGee / Mercedes Benz / Get it while you can / Trust me / My baby
CD ______ **CD 64188**
CBS / Dec '85 / Sony
CD ______ **4804152**
Mastersound / Jul '95 / Sony

Joplin, Scott

ELITE SYNCOPATION
Elite syncopations / Country club / Paragon rag / Eugenia / Cleopha / Real slow rag / Scott Joplin's new rag / Leola / Lily Queen / Chrysanthemum / Heliotrope bouquet / Reflection rag / Maple leaf rag / Ole Miss Rag / Magnetic rag / Silver swan rag
CD ______ **BCD 102**
Biograph / Jul '91 / ADA / Cadillac / Direct / Hot Shot / Jazz Music / Wellard

ENTERTAINER, THE (Classic Ragtime From Rare Piano Rolls)
Maple leaf rag / Something doing / Weeping willow rag / Entertainer / Easy winners / Pineapple rag / Solace / Gladiolus rag / Ragtime dance / Sugarcane / Crush collision march / Bethena / Combination march / Breeze from Alabama
CD ______ **BCD 101**
Biograph / Jul '91 / ADA / Cadillac / Direct / Hot Shot / Jazz Music / Wellard

ENTERTAINER, THE
CD ______ **ENTCD 220**
Entertainers / Feb '88 / Target/BMG

ENTERTAINER, THE
CD ______ **SHAN 98016**
Shanachie / May '93 / ADA / Greensleeves / Koch

ENTERTAINER, THE (The Very Best Of Scott Joplin) (Rifkin, Joshua)
CD ______ **7559794492**
Nonesuch / Jan '97 / Warner Music

GOLD COLLECTION, THE
CD ______ **D2CD 13**
Deja Vu / Dec '92 / THE

JAZZ PORTRAITS
Chrisanthemum / Scott Joplin's new rag / Something doing / Original rags / Entertainer / Maple leaf rag / Sunflower slow drag / Elite syncopations / Eugenia / Paragon rag / Euphonic sounds / Pineapple rag / Stoptime rag / Reflection rag / Cleopha / Lily Queen / Heliotrope bouquet / Country club
CD ______ **CD 14518**
Jazz Portraits / May '94 / Jazz Music

KING OF RAGTIME
CD ______ **CD 53004**
Giants Of Jazz / Mar '92 / Cadillac / Jazz Music / Target/BMG

KING OF RAGTIME
Elite syncopations / Chrisanthemum / Scott Joplin new rag / Eugenia / Paragon rag / Euphonic sounds / Pineapple rag / Something doing / Original rags / Entertainer / Maple leaf rag / Sunflower slow drag / Stoptime rag / Reflection rag / Cleopha / Lily Queen / Heliotrope Bouquet / Country club / Areal slow drag / Leola
CD ______ **GRF 080**
Tring / Apr '93 / Tring

KING OF RAGTIME (3CD Set)
CD Set ______ **55542**
Laserlight / Oct '95 / Target/BMG

KING OF RAGTIME
CD ______ **CD 56056**
Jazz Roots / Mar '95 / Target/BMG

KING OF RAGTIME WRITERS
Cascades / Strenuous life / Felicity rag / swipsey cakewalk / Peacherine rag / Something doing / Search light / Rose leaf rag / Fig leaf rag / Rag medley no. 6 - pineapple rag / Euphonic sounds / Palm leaf rag / Kismet rag / Wall Street rag / Pleasant moments / Original rags / Sunflower slow drag / Maple leaf rag
CD ______ **BCD 110**
Biograph / Jul '91 / ADA / Cadillac / Direct / Hot Shot / Jazz Music / Wellard

MARCHES, WALTZES & RAGS
CD ______ **MM 67102**
Music Masters / Oct '94 / Nimbus

PIANO RAGS OF SCOTT JOPLIN
Entertainer / Peacherine rag / Original rags / Easy winners / Strenuous life / Elite syncopations / Breeze from Alabama / Sycamore / Maple leaf rag / Sunflower slow drag / Weeping willow / Something doing / Solace / Chrysanthemum / Palm leaf rag / Cascades
CD ______ **EMPRCD 539**
Empress / Sep '94 / Koch

PIANO RAGS PLAYED BY THE COMPOSER - 1896-07
CD ______ **JZCD 321**
Suisa / Feb '91 / Jazz Music / THE

PIANO RAGS PLAYED BY THE COMPOSER - 1907-17
CD ______ **JZCD 322**
Suisa / Feb '91 / Jazz Music / THE

PIANO RAGS, THE
CD ______ **CDSGP 0118**
Prestige / May '94 / Else / Total/BMG

SCOTT JOPLIN (2CD Set)
CD Set ______ **R2CD 4013**
Deja Vu / Jan '96 / THE

SCOTT JOPLIN GOLD (2CD Set)
CD Set ______ **D2CD 4013**
Deja Vu / Jun '95 / THE

SCOTT JOPLIN RAGS (Eaton, Roy)
CD ______ **SBK 62833**
Sony Classical / Jun '97 / Sony

SCOTT JOPLIN'S PIANO RAGS (Rifkin, Joshua)
CD ______ **7559791592**
Warner Bros. / Jan '95 / Warner Music

Jordan, Charley

CHARLEY JORDAN VOL.1 1930-1931
CD ______ **DOCD 5097**
Document / '92 / ADA / Hot Shot / Jazz Music

CHARLEY JORDAN VOL.2 1931-1934
CD ______ **DOCD 5098**
Document / '92 / ADA / Hot Shot / Jazz Music

CHARLEY JORDAN VOL.3 1935-1937
CD ______ **DOCD 5099**
Document / '92 / ADA / Hot Shot / Jazz Music

Jordan, Chris

TWILIGHT OF THE GODS
Pilgrims / Evening star / Grail / Dance for dead lovers / Prize / Rhinegold / Valkyrie's dream / Bride's lament
CD ______ **NAGE 14 CD**
Art Of Landscape / Jun '87 / Sony

Jordan, Clifford

CLIFF CRAFT
Laconia / Soul-lo blues / Cliff craft / Confirmation / Sophisticated lady / Anthropology
CD ______ **CDP 8565842**
Blue Note / Jun '97 / EMI

CLIFFORD JORDAN (Featuring Junior Cook) (Jordan, Clifford Quartet)
CD ______ **CRISS 1011CD**
Criss Cross / Nov '90 / Cadillac / Direct / Vital/SAM

ROYAL BALLADS (Jordan, Clifford Quartet)
CD ______ **CRISS 1025CD**
Criss Cross / Nov '91 / Cadillac / Direct / Vital/SAM

Jordan, Duke

DUKE'S ARTISTRY (Jordan, Duke Quartet)
CD ______ **SCCD 31033**
Steeplechase / Jul '88 / Discovery / Impetus

FLIGHT TO DENMARK (Jordan, Duke Trio)
CD ______ **SCCD 31011**
Steeplechase / Oct '90 / Discovery / Impetus

FLIGHT TO JORDAN
Flight to Jordan / Starbrite / Squawkin' / Deacon Joe / Split quick / Si Joya / Diamond stud / I should care
CD ______ **VGCD 650118**
Vogue / Oct '93 / BMG

JORDU
CD ______ **VGCD 655010**
Vogue / Oct '93 / BMG

KISS OF SPAIN
Kiss of Spain / When you wish upon a star / As time goes by / I can't get started / If you could see her / Misty Thursday / All the things you are / All of me / Someone to watch over me / I need your love
CD ______ **5123072**
EmArCy / Jan '92 / PolyGram

ONE FOR THE LIBRARY
CD ______ **STCD 4194**
Storyville / Aug '94 / Cadillac / Jazz Music / Wellard

OSAKA CONCERT VOL.1 (Jordan, Duke Trio)
CD ______ **SCCD 31271**
Steeplechase / Nov '90 / Discovery / Impetus

PARIS-NEW YORK (Original Vogue Masters) (Jordan, Duke & Bud Powell)
Just one of those things / Embraceable you / Minor escamp / Scotch blues / Confirmation / Darn that dream / They can't take that away from me / Wait and see / Just one of those things / Embraceable you / Buttercup / John's abbey / Sweet and lovely / Crossin' the channel
CD ______ **74321457272**
Vogue / May '97 / BMG

TIME ON MY HANDS (Jordan, Duke Trio)
CD ______ **SCCD 31232**
Steeplechase / Jul '88 / Discovery / Impetus

Jordan, Lorraine

CRAZY GUESSING GAMES
CD ______ **LDL 1212CD**
Lochshore / Mar '94 / ADA / Direct / Duncans

INSPIRATION
CD ______ **LDL 1205CD**
Lochshore / May '93 / ADA / Direct / Duncans

Jordan, Louis

AT THE SWING CATS' BALL, 1937-39
Gee but you're swell / Honey in the bee ball / Keep a knockin' / Doug the jitterbug / You're my meat
CD ______ **JSPCD 330**
JSP / Oct '91 / ADA / Cadillac / Direct / Hot Shot / Target/BMG

CLASSIC RECORDINGS
CD Set ______ **BCD 15557**
Bear Family / Apr '92 / Direct / Rollercoaster / Swift

CLASSICS 1934-1940
CD ______ **CLASSICS 636**
Classics / Nov '92 / Discovery / Jazz Music

CLASSICS 1940-1941
CD ______ **CLASSICS 663**
Classics / Nov '92 / Discovery / Jazz Music

CLASSICS 1943-1945
CD ______ **CLASSICS 866**
Classics / Mar '96 / Discovery / Jazz Music

CLASSICS 1945-1946
CD ______ **CLASSICS 921**
Classics / Apr '97 / Discovery / Jazz Music

COMPLETE ALADDIN SESSIONS (Jordan, Louis & His Tympany Five)
Yeah yeah baby / Louis blues / I've seen what you've done / Fat back and corn liquor / Put some money in the pot boy cause the juice is running low / Gotta go / Dipper / Time's a passin' / Whiskey do your stuff / Gal you need a whippin' / It's hard to be good / Dollar down / Dad gum ya hide, boy / Till we two are one / Ooo wee / Private property (no trespassing) / For you / Messy Bessy / I'll die happy / If I had any sense, I'd go back home / Hurry home
CD ______ **CZ 426**
EMI / May '91 / EMI

FIVE GUYS NAMED MOE
CD ______ **MCLD 19048**
MCA / Apr '92 / BMG

FIVE GUYS NAMED MOE - RADIO RARITIES
CD ______ **VJC 10372**
Vintage Jazz Classics / Oct '92 / ADA / Cadillac / CM / Direct

GOOD TIMES
Let the good times roll / Five guys named Moe / Daddy-O / Texas and the Pacific
CD ______ **BSTCD 9103**
Best Compact Discs / May '92 / Complete/ Pinnacle

HOW 'BOUT THAT
At the swing cats ball / Small town boy / I know you, I know what you wanna do / Pompton turnpike / Honeysuckle rose / I'm gonna leave you on the outskirts of town / That'll bout knock me out / GI jive / Green grass grows all round / Caldonia boogie / Two little squirrels (nuts to you) / Ain't going nowhere / Saxa-woogie / How 'bout that / Ration blues / Is you is or is you ain't my baby / Barnacle Bill the sailor / It's a low down dirty shame / Boogie woogie came to town / You run your mouth and I'll run my business / Oh boy I'm in the groove / Sam Jones done snagged his britches / Pan pan / Brotherly love / Mama, mama blues (rusty dusty blues)
CD ______ **302372**
Hallmark / Jul '97 / Carlton

I BELIEVE IN MUSIC
CD ______ **ECD 260062**
Evidence / Jan '92 / ADA / Cadillac / Harmonia Mundi
CD ______ **BB 8762**
Black & Blue / Feb '97 / Discovery / Koch / Wellard

JUMP JIVE JORDAN
Five guys named Moe / Choo choo ch' boogie / Mop mop / If you're so smart how come you ain't rich / Barnyard boogie / Fat Sam from Birmingham / Ain't nobody here but us chickens / Saturday night fish fry / Is you is or is you ain't my baby / Open the door Richard / What's the use of getting sober / Run Joe / Chartreuse / Tamburitza boogie / Hog wash / School days
CD ______ **MCCD 085**
Music Club / Dec '92 / Disc / THE

LIVE JIVE (Jordan, Louis & His Tympany Five)
Five guys named Moe / Buzz me / Knock me a kiss / Let the good times roll / I like 'em fat like that / Choo choo ch' boogie / On the sunny side of the street / All for the love of Lil / Safe, sane and single / Broke but happy / Texas and Pacific / Drippy drippers / Don't let the sun catch you crying / How long must I wait for you / Daddy-O / Jumping at the Jubilee / Baby that's alright for you
CD ______ **DATOM 4**
A Touch Of Magic / Jul '89 / Harmonia Mundi

LOUIS JORDAN & HIS TYMPANY FIVE
Sunday / Sweet Lorraine / Choo choo ch' boogie / Caldonia / Life is so peculiar / Ooo wee / (I'll be glad when you're dead) you rascal you / Messy Bessy / Saturday night fish fry / I never had a chance / I'm gonna move to the outskirts of town / Knock me a kiss / Let the good times roll / If I had any sense I'd go back home / For you / Private property (no trespassing) / I'll die happy / Petootie pie / Hurry home / Baby it's cold outside / Till we two are one / Dad gum ya hide, boy
CD ______ **CD 352**
Entertainers / Mar '96 / Target/BMG

LOUIS JORDAN & TYMPANY FIVE 1939-1944
CD ______ **158372**
Jazz Archives / Jul '95 / Discovery

LOUIS JORDAN 1941-1943
CD ______ **CLASSICS 741**
Classics / Feb '94 / Discovery / Jazz Music

LOUIS JORDAN AND CHRIS BARBER (Jordan, Louis & Chris Barber)
CD ______ **BLCD 760156**
Black Lion / '91 / Cadillac / Jazz Music / Koch / Wellard

NO MOE (Louis Jordan's Greatest Hits)
Saturday night fish fry / Is you is or is you ain't my baby / Don't let the sun catch you crying / Salt Pork West Virginia / Early in the morning / Sunday / Knock me a kiss / Ain't nobody here but us chickens / Slop / Let the good times roll / Sweet Lorraine / Run Joe / Choo choo ch' boogie / I'm gonna move to the outskirts of town / Beware brothers beware / Caldonia
CD ______ **5125232**
Verve / Apr '92 / PolyGram

ON FILM 1942-1948
CD ______ **KKCD 17**
Krazy Kat / Jun '96 / Hot Shot / Jazz Music

ROCK 'N' ROLL
Ain't nobody here but us chickens / Choo choo ch' boogie / Knock me a kiss / Caldonia / Let the good times roll / Is you is or is you ain't my baby / Beware brothers beware / Big Bess / Cat scratchin' / Don't let the sun catch you crying / I'm gonna move to the outskirts of town / Salt Pork West Virginia / Run Joe / Early in the morning / Morning light / Fire rock Doc / Ella Mae / Jamp / Saturday night fish fry / Got my mojo working
CD ______ **8382192**
Mercury / Apr '89 / PolyGram

ROCK 'N' ROLL CALL
It's been said / Whatever Lola wants (Lola gets) / Slo' smooth and easy / Bananas / Baby let's do it up / Chicken back / Baby you're just too much / Where can I go / Rock 'n' roll call / Man ain't a man / Texas stew / Hard head
CD ______ **07863661452**
Bluebird / Apr '93 / BMG

VERY BEST OF LOUIS JORDAN, THE
Five guys named Moe / Knock me a kiss / End of my worry / Bahama Joe / How high am I / I like 'em fat like that / Flat face / Do you call me that a buddy / Penthouse in the basement / Is you is or is you ain't my baby / You're my meat / Never let your left hand know what your right hand's doin' / Doug the jitterbug / T-bone blues / Nobody but me / GI jive
CD ______ **SUMCD 4035**
Summit / Nov '96 / Sound & Media

Jordan, Montell

MORE TO TELL
Non-believers (interlude) / Superlover man / All I need / Tricks on my mind / Falling / What's on tonight / I say yes (interlude) / I like: *Jordan, Montell & Slick Rick* / Let me be the one / Never alone (interlude) / Never alone / Everything is gonna be alright / Bounce 2 this
CD ____ 5331912
Def Jam / Sep '96 / PolyGram

THIS IS HOW WE DO IT
My Mommy intro / Somethin' 4 da honeyz / This is how we do it / Payback / I'll do anything / Don't keep me waiting / Comin' home / Introducing shaunta / It's over / Midnight interlude / I wanna / Down on my knees / Gotta get my roll on / Close the door / Daddy's home
CD ____ 5271272
Def Jam / May '95 / PolyGram

Jordan, Ronny

ANTIDOTE, THE
Get to grips / Blues grinder / After hours / See the new / So what / Nite spice / Summer smile
CD ____ CID 9988
Island / Feb '92 / PolyGram

BAD BROTHERS (Jordan, Ronny & DJ Krush)
Jackal / Shit goes down / Love I never had it so good / So what / Season for a change / Bad brother
CD ____ IMCD 8024
Island / Aug '94 / PolyGram

LIGHT TO DARK
Into the light / Homage / It's you / Law / Fooled / Closer than close / I see you / Downtime / Deep in your heart / Laidback / Light to dark / Last goodbye
CD ____ CID 8047
Island / Apr '96 / PolyGram

QUIET REVOLUTION, THE
Season for change / In full swing / Slam in a jam / Mr. Walker / Jackal / Come with me / Morning after / Under your spell / Tinseltown / Vanston place (00 am)
CD ____ CID 8009
Island / Sep '93 / PolyGram

Jordan, Sass

TELL SOMEBODY
CD ____ REV XD 193
FM / Nov '92 / Revolver / Sony

Jordan, Sheila

OLD TIME FEELING (Jordan, Sheila & Harvie Swartz)
CD ____ MCD 5366
Muse / Sep '92 / New Note/Pinnacle

PORTRAIT OF SHEILA JORDAN
Falling in love with love / If you could see me now / Am I blue / Dat dere / When the world was young / Let's face the music and dance / Laugh clown laugh / Who can I turn to now / Baltimore Oriole / I'm a fool to want you / Hum drum blues / Willow weep for me
CD ____ BNZ 230
Blue Note / Jan '90 / EMI

Jordan, Stanley

BEST OF STANLEY JORDAN, THE
Jumpin' Jack / Eleanor Rigby / Lady in my life / All the children / Impressions / My favourtie things / Georgia on my mind / Stairway to heaven / Flying home / Still got the blues / Over the rainbow
CD ____ CDP 8315022
Blue Note / Apr '95 / EMI

BOLERO
Bolero Parts 1-6 / Always and forever / Cheleon / Betcha by golly wow / Drifting / Plato's blues / Always and forever (solo)
CD ____ 07822187032
Arista / Feb '94 / BMG

STANDARDS VOL.1
Sound of silence / Sunny / Georgia on my mind / Send one your love / Moon River / Guitar man / One bell less to answer / Because / My favourite things / Silent night
CD ____ BNZ 56
Blue Note / Apr '87 / EMI

Jordan, Steve

HERE COMES MR. JORDAN
CD ____ ACD 114
Audiophile / Oct '93 / Jazz Music

MANY SOUNDS OF STEVE 'ESTEBAN' JORDAN, THE
CD ____ ARHCD 319
Arhoolie / Apr '95 / ADA / Cadillac / Direct

RETURN OF EL PARCHE, THE
CD ____ ROUCD 6019
Rounder / '88 / ADA / CM / Direct

Jordanaires

SING ELVIS'S FAVOURITE SPIRITUALS
Didn't it rain / Peace in the valley / Joshua fit de battle of Jericho / Search me lord / Dig a little deeper / You better run / Let us break bread together / Wonderful time up there / How great thou art / I'm a rollin' / Dip your fingers in some water / Roll Jordan roll / Onward christian soldiers
CD ____ PWKS 4216
Carlton / Oct '94 / Carlton

SONGS WE SANG WITH ELVIS
CD ____ WMCD 5691
Disky / Apr '94 / Disky / THE

TRIBUTE TO ELVIS
Return to sender / That's alright mama / Jailhouse rock / All shook up / Good luck charm / Got a lot of lovin' to do / Can't help falling in love / It's now or never / Love me tender / Are you lonesome tonight / Teddy bear / Don't be cruel / You're the devil in disguise / Wear my ring around your neck / Heartbreak hotel / Always on my mind
CD ____ 5501282
Spectrum / Oct '93 / PolyGram

Jorgensen, Knud

BOJANGLES (Jorgensen, Knud & Bengt Hanson)
CD ____ TMCD 002
Touche / May '97 / Cadillac

JAZZ TRIO
CD ____ OP 8401CD
Opus 3 / Sep '91 / Direct / Jazz Music

SKISS (Jorgensen, Knud Trio)
CD ____ TMCD 001
Touche / May '97 / Cadillac

Jormin, Anders

ONCE
CD ____ DRCD 308
Dragon / May '97 / ADA / Cadillac / CM / Roots / Wellard

Jory, Sarah

20 CLASSIC SONGS (The Early Years)
Walk the way the wind blows / Somewhere between / I'll leave this world loving you / Just out of reach / Why me Lord / Beyond the point of no return / Let me be there / Dear God / Always have, always will / How great thou art / Jones on the jukebox / Before I'm over you / Just because I'm a woman / Faded love / It is no secret / No time at all / Funny face / Yesterday just passed my way again / Beneath still waters / Old rugged cross
CD ____ RITZSCD 429
Ritz / Apr '93 / Pinnacle

20 STEEL GUITAR FAVOURITES
Sticky fingers / Deep in the heart of Texas / Orange blossom special / Jealous heart / Under the boardwalk / Careless hands / Steel line / Way to survive / San Antonio stroll / She believes in me / Oklahoma stomp / Highway 40 blues / Rose coloured glasses / Blue jade / Cold cold heart / Three of us / In the garden / City lights / Once upon a time in the West / Remington ride
CD ____ RITZSCD 428
Ritz / Apr '93 / Pinnacle

LOVE WITH ATTITUDE
CD ____ RITZCD 0076
Ritz / Oct '95 / Pinnacle

NEW HORIZONS
Never had it so good / Look at us / Take your memory with you / Strings that tie you down / Darlin' / Wind beneath my wings / Orange blossom special / Mississippi / How do / Till each tear becomes a rose / You'll never get to heaven (if you break my heart) / Take a love off my mind / Heartaches by the number / Sarah's dream
CD ____ RITZCD 0067
Ritz / May '92 / Pinnacle

WEB OF LOVE
Before I call it love / Even then / Candle burning / If I love you / Every time / Binding me like a chain / Web of love / When you walk in the room / Over you / Even a fool / Two sparrows in a hurricane / Who's crying now / On the way to a dream / Real slow / Stop playing with my heart
CD ____ CD 0073
Ritz / Jul '94 / Pinnacle

Jo's All Stars

BRIXTON CAT
CD ____ CDTBL 106
Trojan / Aug '96 / Direct / Jet Star

Joseph, Bradley

RAPTURE
Lover's return / Feel / Jewel / Healing the hollow man / Blue rock road / Robbin's Island / Stray / Stolen kiss / Gallery / Passage / Storyteller / Coastal highway / Be still
CD ____ ND 63038
Narada / Apr '97 / ADA / New Note/Pinnacle

Joseph, David

BRITISH HUSTLE (The Best Of David Joseph & Hi-Tension) (Joseph, David & Hi-Tension)
You can't hide (your love from me) / Hi-tension / Joys of life / Funktified / British hustle / There's a reason / Let's live it up (Nite people) / Latin inspiration / You're my girl / Discover / Expansions '86 expand your mind / Power and lighting / Peace on earth / You can't hide (your love from me)
CD ____ 5527372
Spectrum / Feb '97 / PolyGram

Joseph, Julian

LANGUAGE OF TRUTH, THE
Miss Simmons / Language of truth / Don't chisel the shisel / Art of the calm / Wash house / Other side of town / High priestess / Magical one / Brothers of the bottom row / Tyrannosaurus Rex / Ode to the time our memories forgot
CD ____ 9031751222
East West / Dec '96 / Warner Music

LIVE AT THE WIGMORE HALL
CD ____ 0630113702
East West / Dec '96 / Warner Music

REALITY
Bridge to the south / Body and soul / Easy for you to say / Look out for love / Dance in a perfect world / Swingstone / Empty dream / Reality / Jean-ee-t / Creation constellation / Whispering dome / My desire
CD ____ 4509930242
East West / Dec '96 / Warner Music

UNIVERSAL TRAVELLER
CD ____ 0630120422
East West / Jun '96 / Warner Music

Joseph, Margie

ATLANTIC SESSION, THE (The Best Of Margie Joseph)
CD ____ SCL 2503
Ichiban Soul Classics / Apr '95 / Koch

MAKES A NEW IMPRESSION/PHASE II
Women talk / Stop in the name of love / Punish me / Medicine bend / Come tomorrow / Sweeter tomorrow / Same thing / How beautiful the rain / I'm fed up / Make me believe you'll stay / Temptation's about to take your love / That other woman got my man and gone / My world is empty without you / I'll always love you / Strung out / Please don't stop loving me / I love you too much to say goodbye / Didn't have to tell me / Takin' all the love I can
CD ____ CDSXD 097
Stax / Jul '93 / Pinnacle

Joseph, Martyn

FULL COLOUR BLACK AND WHITE
CD ____ GRACD 222
Grapevine / May '97 / Grapevine/ PolyGram

MARTYN JOSEPH
Change your world / Gift to me / Between the raindrops / Talk about it in the morning / Everything in heaven comes apart / Home to you / If I should fall / If heaven's waiting / Condition of my heart / Cardiff bay / Carried in sunlight
CD ____ 4806572
Epic / Jul '95 / Sony

Josey Wales

COWBOY STYLE
CD ____ GRELCD 198
Greensleeves / Feb '94 / Jet Star / SRD

Joshi, Pandit Bhimsen

IN CELEBRATION
CD ____ NRCD 0075
Navras / Feb '97 / New Note/Pinnacle

VOCAL
CD ____ MR 1002
Moment / Apr '95 / ADA / Koch

Joshua

SURRENDER
Surrender love / Heart full of soul / Your love is gone / Hold on / Back to the rock / Rockin' the world / Stay alive / Loveshock / Reprise
CD ____ WKFMXD 64
FM / Mar '86 / Revolver / Sony

Josi, Christian

I WALKS WITH MY FEET OFF THE GROUND
Just in time / Whenever I take my sugar to tea / This time the dreams on me / Let's get lost / Sleepin' bee / Watch what happens / You've met your match / Azure te / Nightingale sang in Berkley square / Whenever that gal comes around / Gotta be this or that / Girl of my dreams / I concentrate on you / Forgetful / Birth of the blues / Party's over
CD ____ CHECD 00111
Master Mix / Aug '94 / Jazz Music / New Note/Pinnacle / Wellard

Jostyn, Mindy

FIVE MILES FROM HOPE
CD ____ FIENDCD 781
Demon / Jun '96 / Pinnacle

Jouissance

INFERNAL NEBULA
CD ____ MHCD 019
Minus Habens / Jul '94 / Plastic Head

Journey

CAPTURED
Majestic / Where were you / Just the same way / Line of fire / Lights / Stay awhile / Too late / Dixie highway / Feeling that way / Anytime / Do you recall / Walks like a lady / La do da / Lovin' touchin' squeezin' / Squeezin' / Wheel in the sky / Anyway you want it / Party's over
CD ____ 4866612
Columbia / Nov '96 / Sony

DEPARTURE
Anyway you want it / Walks like a lady / Someday soon / People and places / Precious time / Where were you / I'm cryin' / Line of fire / Departure / Good morning girl / Stay a while / Homemade love
CD ____ 4866672
Columbia / Nov '96 / Sony

ESCAPE
Don't stop believin' / Stone in love / Who's crying now / Keep on running / Still they ride / Escape / Lay it down / Dead or alive / Mother, Father / Open arms
CD ____ 4866622
Columbia / Nov '96 / Sony

EVOLUTION
Too late / Lovin' touchin' squeezin' / City of the angels / When you're alone it ain't easy / Sweet and simple / Lovin' you is easy / Just the same way / Do you recall / Daydream / Lady Luck / Majestic
CD ____ 4866662
Columbia / Nov '96 / Sony

FRONTIERS
Separate ways / Send her my love / Chain reaction / After the fall / Faithfully / Edge of the blade / Troubled child / Back talk / Frontier / Rubicon
CD ____ 4866632
Columbia / Nov '96 / Sony

GREATEST HITS
Only the young / Don't stop believin' / Wheel in the sky / Faithfully / I'll be alright without you / Anyway you want it / (Ask) the lonely / Who's crying now / Separate ways / Lights / Lovin' touchin' squeezin' / Open arms / Girl can't help it / Send her my love / Be good to yourself
CD ____ 4631492
Columbia / Apr '96 / Sony

INFINITY
Lights / Feeling that way / Anytime / La do da / Patiently / Wheel in the sky / Somethin' to hide / Winds of March / Can do / Open the door
CD ____ 4866652
Columbia / Nov '96 / Sony

JOURNEY
Of a lifetime / In the morning day / Kohoutek / To play some music / Topaz / In my lonely feeling/conversations
CD ____ 4778542
Columbia / Oct '94 / Sony

RAISED ON RADIO
Girl can't help it / Positive touch / Suzanne / Be good to yourself / Once you love somebody / Happy to give / Raised on radio / I'll be alright without you / It could have been you / Eyes of a woman / Why can't this night go on forever
CD ____ 4866642
Columbia / Nov '96 / Sony

TRIAL BY FIRE
Message of love / One more / When you love a woman / If he should break your heart / Forever in blue / Castles burning / Don't be down on me baby / Still she cries / Colours of the spirit / When I think of you / Easy to fall / Can't tame the lion / It's just the rain / Trial by fire / Baby I'm leaving you
CD ____ 4852642
Columbia / Oct '96 / Sony

Journeyman

JOURNEYMAN
CD ____ NTONELP 24
Ntone / Aug '97 / Kudos / Vital

NEW IDOL SON
New idol son
CD ____ RED 005
Redemption / Jun '93 / SRD

Journeymen

WANDERLUST
CD ____ CDLDL 1235
Lochshore / Nov '95 / ADA / Direct / Duncans

Joy Division

CEREMONIAL - TRIBUTE TO JOY DIVISION (Various Artists)
CD ____ EFA 064982
Tess / Mar '96 / SRD

MEANS TO AN END, A (The Music Of Joy Division) (Various Artists)
She's lost control: *Girls Against Boys* / Day of Lords: *Honeymoon Switch* / New dawn fades: *Moby* / Transmission: *Low* / Atmosphere: *Codeine* / Insight: *Further* / Love will tear us apart: *Stanton-Miranda* / Isolation: *Starchildren* / Heart and soul: *Smith, Kendra* / Twenty four hours: *Versus* / Warsaw: *Desert Storm* / They walked in line: *Godheadsilo* / Interzone: *Face To Face* / As you said: *Tortoise*
CD ______ **CDHUT 29**
Hut / Oct '95 / EMI

PERMANENT
Love will tear us apart / Transmission / She's lost control / Shadow play / Day of the lords / Isolation / Passover / Heart and soul / Twenty four hours / These days / Novelty / Dead souls / Only mistake / Something must break / Atmosphere
CD ______ **8286242**
London / Jun '95 / PolyGram

SUBSTANCE (1977-1980)
She's lost control / Dead souls / Atmosphere / Love will tear us apart / Warsaw / Leaders of men / Digital / Transmission / Autosuggestion
CD ______ **5200142**
London / Jul '93 / PolyGram

Joy Of Life

ENJOY
CD ______ **HY 39100292**
Hyperium / Nov '92 / Cargo / Plastic Head

Joyce

DELIRIOS DE ORFEU
CD ______ **BOM 03CD**
Backbeat / Jul '96 / Jet Star / Timewarp

TARDES CARIOCAS
Barracumbarra / Tardes cariocas / Duas ou tres coisas / Luz do chao / Curioso / Nuvem / Nacoional kid / Ela / Sour
CD ______ **FARO 0016CD**
Far Out / Jul '97 / Amato Disco / New Note/ Pinnacle

Joykiller

3
CD ______ **65022**
Epitaph / Aug '97 / Pinnacle / Plastic Head

JOYKILLER
CD ______ **864512**
Epitaph / Apr '95 / Pinnacle / Plastic Head

STATIC
CD ______ **864662**
Epitaph / Jul '96 / Pinnacle / Plastic Head

Joyland

SUN
CD ______ **NBX 014**
Noisebox / Jul '95 / RTM/Disc / Vital

Joyner, Bruce

HOT GEORGIA NIGHTS
CD ______ **ROSE 129CD**
New Rose / Dec '87 / ADA / Direct / Discovery

Joyrider

BE SPECIAL
Fabulae / Strike sparks everywhere / That tired / Said she to me / Bible blackbelt / I cursed you / Nobody home / Another skunk song / Vegetable animal mineral / I don't give in / Are you sure you're alright / Imagine dead language
CD ______ **PDOXCD 005**
Paradox / Aug '96 / PolyGram / Vital

SKID SOLO
Skid solo / Chop logic / What you think of me / Learn the ropes / Whole reason / Confession / Mongoose / Tonight is stolen / Day in the sun / Growing pains / Hub of the north / Wise is nice / Devil you know / Hit for fun
CD ______ **5407402**
A&M / May '97 / PolyGram

Joystick

HEAVY CHEVY
CD ______ **LOB 10005**
Lobster/Fat Wreck Chords / Apr '97 / Plastic Head

JP Nystroms

STOCKHOLM 1313KM
Spel nisses vals / Forsbergs polka / Matalan torpan balladi / Pojkarna pa landsvagen / Hambomazurka efter Blomqvistaru / Polska fran 1814 / Oceanangaren Titanics undergang / Sankte per / Tre broder / Kadrilj fran haparanda / Menuett fran oravais / Taitaa tulla / Lekande toner / Sa mork ar bimlen / Till havs i motorbat / Friarpolka fran Leipojarvi / Bjorn dansen
CD ______ **RESCD 514**
Resource / Jul '97 / ADA / Direct

THA
CD ______ **RES 514CD**
Resource / Aug '96 / ADA / Direct

JPP

KAUSTINEN RHAPSODY
CD ______ **OMCD 53**
Olarin Musiiki Oy / Dec '94 / ADA / Direct

JPS Experience

BLEEDING STAR
CD ______ **FNCD 246**
Flying Nun / Sep '93 / RTM/Disc

SIZE OF FOOD, THE
CD ______ **FNCD 122**
Flying Nun / Jul '96 / RTM/Disc

Jr. & His Soulettes

PSYCHODELIC SOUNDS
CD ______ **SH 954**
Shaft / Jun '97 / Greyhound

JSD Band

FOR THE RECORD
Sarah Jane / As I roved out / Cuckoo / Irish girl/Musical priest / Groundhog / Johnny O'Breadislea / Sunshine hornpipe/The mountain road / Darlin' Corey / Galway races / Goin' down the road / Don't think twice / Down the road / Morrison's jig/Cooley's reel / Over and over
CD ______ **CDLDL 1256**
Lochshore / May '97 / ADA / Direct / Duncans

Jubelklaenge

200 YEARS OF THE BAD BLEIBERG BRASS BAND
CD ______ **322766**
Koch / Oct '92 / Koch

Juber, Laurence

LAURENCE JUBER
CD ______ **BEST 1081CD**
Acoustic Music / Feb '96 / ADA

Jubilee Gospel Team

JUBILEE GOSPEL TEAM AND THE DEEP RIVER PLANTATION SINGERS (Jubilee Gospel Team & The Deep River Plantation Singers)
CD ______ **DOCD 5519**
Document / Mar '97 / ADA / Hot Shot / Jazz Music

Jubilee Hummingbirds

GUILTY OF SERVING GOD (Jubilee Hummingbirds & James Carr)
God is worthy to be praised / Guilty of serving God / My soul is satisfied / He'll be there / Jesus changed me / Doin' the best I can / In the name of Jesus / Where Jesus is / Jordan river
CD ______ **CDCHM 611**
Ace / Jul '95 / Pinnacle

Jubilees

REGGAE CARNIVAL
CD ______ **BRMCD 027**
Bold Reprive / Oct '88 / Harmonia Mundi

Judah, Levi

CREATION TRODDING (Nyabinghi)
CD ______ **ROTCD 013**
Reggae On Top / May '97 / Jet Star / SRD

Judas Priest

COLLECTION, THE
One for the road / Rocka rolla / Winter / Deep freeze / Winter retreat / Cheater / Never satisfied / Run of the mill / Dying to meet you / Victim of changes / Ripper / Dream deceiver / Prelude / Tyrant / Genocide / Epitaph / Island of domination
CD ______ **CCSCD 213**
Castle / Apr '89 / BMG

HERO HERO
Dreamer deceiver / Deceiver / Winter / Deep freeze / Winter retreat / Cheater / Diamonds and rust / Run of the mill / Genocide / Caviar and meths / Prelude / Tyrant / Rocka rolla / One for the road / Victim of changes / Dying to meet you / Never satisfied
CD ______ **CSAPCD 119**
Connoisseur Collection / Jul '95 / Pinnacle

LIVING AFTER MIDNIGHT
Better by you, better than me / Take on the world / Green Manalishi / Living after midnight / Breaking the law / United / Hot rockin' / You've got another thing comin' / Hellion/Electric eye / Freewheel burning / Some heads are gonna roll / Turbo lover / Locked in / Johnny B Goode / Ram it down / Painkiller / Touch of evil / Night crawler
CD ______ **4872422**
Columbia / Apr '97 / Sony

METAL WORKS 1973-1993 (2CD Set)
Hellion / Electric eye / Victim of changes / Painkiller / Eat me alive / Devil's child / Dissident aggressor / Delivering the goods / Exciter / Breaking the law / Hell bent for leather / Blood red skies / Metal gods / Before the dawn / Turbo lover / Ram it down / Metal meltdown / Screaming for vengeance / You've got another thing comin' / Beyond the realms of death / Solar angels / Bloodstone / Desert plains / Wild nights, Hot and Crazy Days / Heading out to the highway / Living after midnight / Touch of Evil / Rage / Night comes down / Sinner / Freewheel burning / Night crawler
CD Set ______ **4730502**
Columbia / Oct '95 / Sony

SIN AFTER SIN
Sinner / Diamonds and rust / Starbreaker / Last rose of summer / Let us prey / Call for the priest / Raw deal / Here come the tears / Dissident aggressor
CD ______ **4746842**
Epic / Feb '97 / Sony

TRIBUTE TO JUDAS PRIEST VOL.1 (Various Artists)
CD ______ **CM 77115CD**
Century Media / Jun '96 / Plastic Head

TRIBUTE TO JUDAS PRIEST VOL.2 (Various Artists)
CD ______ **CM 77125CD**
Century Media / Sep '96 / Plastic Head

TRIBUTE TO JUDAS PRIEST, A (Various Artists)
CD ______ **CM 77169CD**
Century Media / Mar '97 / Plastic Head

Judd, Wynonna

GREATEST HITS
No one else on earth / Making my way / Somebody to love / Change the world / Heaven help my heart / Healing / Rock bottom / To be loved by you / Father and son / Free bird / Let's make a baby king / Girls with guitars / Only love / I saw the light / She is his only need / My strongest weakness / Is it over yet / Tell me why
CD ______ **CURCD 041**
Curb / Apr '97 / Grapevine/PolyGram

WYNONNA
What it takes / She is his only need / I saw the light / My strongest weakness / When I reach the place I'm goin' / No one else on Earth / It's never easy to say goodbye / Little bit of love (goes a long long way) / All of that love from here / Live with Jesus
CD ______ **4716712**
Curb / May '92 / Grapevine/PolyGram

Judds

ESSENTIAL JUDDS, THE
Had a dream / John Deere tractor / Mama he's crazy / Why not me / Girls' night out / Lazy country evening / Rockin' with the rhythm of the rain / Grandpa (tell me 'bout the good old days) / Turn it loose / Sweetheart gift / Don't be cruel / Working in the coalmine / Old pictures / Guardian angels / Give a little love to me / More fun than the law allows / One little teardrop / Born to be blue / Love can build a bridge / Don't you hear Jerusalem moan
CD ______ **74321666802**
RCA / Feb '96 / BMG

JUDDS COLLECTION, THE
CD ______ **CURCD 024**
Curb / May '96 / Grapevine/PolyGram

Judge

NO APOLOGIES/CHUNG
CD ______ **LF 033CD**
Lost & Found / Apr '92 / Plastic Head

WHAT WE SAID
CD ______ **LF 217CD**
Lost & Found / Nov '95 / Plastic Head

Judge Dread

...NEVER MIND, UP WITH THE COCK
Big 7 / Je t'aime (moi non plus) / Y viva suspenders / Dread rock/Will I what / Big 10 / Up with the cock / Lover's rock / Big 9 / Big 1 / Winkle man
CD ______ **QED 223**
Tring / Nov '96 / Tring

40 BIG ONES VOL.1
Lover's rock / This little piece of dinkle / Banana throat song / Confessions of a bouncer / Y'viva suspenders / Six wives of Dread / Donkey dick / Fatty dread / Oh she is a big girl now / Big 7 / Dread rock / My ding a ling / Rasta chat / Big 6 / Come outside / One eyed lodger / Belle of Snodland Town / Workers lament / Big 5 / Up with the cock / Big punk / Look a pussy / Dr. Kitch / Winkle man / Jamaica jerk off / Grandad's flannelette nightshirt / Move over darling / Will I what / Big 1 / Rudeness train / Bring back the skins / Take off your clothes / Christmas in Dreadland / Rhyme in time / What kung fu dat / Big 10 / Je t'aime / Dread's law / Trenchtown Billy / Big everything
CD ______ **RNCD 2001**
Rhino / Jun '92 / Grapevine/PolyGram / Jet Star

40 BIG ONES VOL.2
CD ______ **RNCD 2121**
Rhino / Sep '95 / Grapevine/PolyGram / Jet Star

BEDTIME STORIES
CD ______ **RNCD 2013**
Rhino / Jun '93 / Grapevine/PolyGram / Jet Star

BIG HITS
Big one / Rudeness is all in the mind / Big five / Je t'aime (moi non plus) / Big six / Winkle man / Big seven / Y viva suspenders / Big eight / Molly / Big nine / Come outside / Big ten / Bring back the skins / Biggest bean you ever seen / Rhyme in time / Big punk / Dreadrock / My ding a ling / Big everything
CD ______ **SUMCD 4088**
Summit / Jan '97 / Sound & Media

BIG TWENTY FOUR, THE
CD ______ **CDTRL 333**
Trojan / Feb '94 / Direct / Jet Star

LAST OF THE SKINHEADS
CD ______ **RNCD 2023**
Rhino / Oct '93 / Grapevine/PolyGram / Jet Star

SKA'D FOR LIFE
CD ______ **CDBM 110**
Blue Moon / Jun '96 / Cadillac / Discovery / Greensleeves / Jazz Music / Jet Star / TKO Magnum

VERY BEST OF JUDGE DREAD, THE
Big 6 / Big 7 / Big 8 / Je t'aime / Big 9 / Big 10 / Come outside / Bring back the skins / Winkle man / Y viva suspenders / Will I what / Jamaica jerkoff / Up with the cock / Lover's rock / Dread rock / Big 1
CD ______ **MCCD 040**
Music Club / Sep '91 / Disc / THE

Judge Jules

JOURNEYS BY DJ VOL.10 (2CD Set) (Various Artists)
CD Set ______ **JDJCD 10**
JDJ / Mar '96 / 3mv/Pinnacle / SRD

SPERM BANK, THE (Various Artists)
Three minute warning: *Yum Yum* / Space grass: *Apply Within* / Livin' it up: *Yum Yum* / Headspace: *Yum Yum* / Bacchanal: *Scope* / Let me go: *Yum Yum* / Three minute warning: *Yum Yum* / Mind gap: *Yum Yum* / Inner space: *Boomerang* / So damn tuff: *Boomerang* / Free bass: *Yum Yum* / Funky cheeba: *Paradox* / Catch it: *Boomerang* / 5000 feet: *Apply Within* / Bacchanal: *Scope* / Loca motion: *Societe* / Pale drifter: *Societe* / Hypermania: *Yum Yum*
CD ______ **SPERM 2001**
Sperm / Mar '97 / Grapevine/PolyGram / Mo's Music Machine / Prime / SRD

Judge Smith, Chris

DEMOCRAZY
CD ______ **THEBES 001**
Oedipus / Jun '92 / Plastic Head

DOME OF DISCOVERY
CD ______ **THEBES 03CD**
Oedipus / Apr '94 / Plastic Head

Judybats

DOWN IN THE SHACKS WHERE THE SATELLITE DISHES GROW
Our story / She's sad she said / How it is / Down in the shacks where the satellite dishes grow / Margot known as missy / Witch's night / Is anything / Poor bruised world / Animal farm / Saturday / Lullaby/ Weren't we wild / When things get slow round here
CD ______ **7599268012**
Sire / Oct '92 / Warner Music

Juggernaut

BLACK PAGODA
Shedding / Bitter / Decide / Difference / Green lightening / IO / Reality easel / Whisper / Make it so hard / Machine / Cry me a river / Master of pricks / Searchin' for a better high
CD ______ **N 02152**
Noise / Sep '94 / Koch

Jughead's Revenge

13 KIDDIE FAVOURITES
CD ______ **EFA 127222**
Do It / May '95 / SRD

ELIMINATION
CD ______ **EFA 118722**
Do It / Mar '94 / SRD

IMAGE IS EVERYTHING
CD ______ **158082**
Nitro / Oct '96 / Pinnacle / Plastic Head

Juhnke, Harald

MIT BEIDEN HANDEN IN DEN TASCHEN
Ich glaube nicht / Von bar zu bar / Die fehler de ander'n / Mit ein paar blumen / Ich komm' mir vor / Ein whiskey zuviel / Zwischen nacht und morgen / Ich bin ich /

Die wand zwischen dir und mir / Das sprachtalent / Was hast du schon davon, wenn du ein playboy bist / Beide hande in den taschen / Mr. Brown Maaison / Was nutzt das schlechte leben / Eine schoner als die an dere / Die Dolly von den folies bergere / Was mir an Paris so gefalt / Ach lass' doch bloss den blonden pianisten / Ich versetze berge / Mich nennen alle frauen cassanova / Die dame mit dem gift grunen schleier / Der schwarze Joe aus Idaho
CD BCD 15968
Bear Family / Jul '96 / Direct / Rollercoaster / Swift

Juice With Soul

BODY ARMOR
Gang lingo / To the uumhm / It's on / Just because you're black / Kill or get killed / Money ain't shit when you're dead / Body armor / Like father, like son / Born suspect / Nickel plated funk / No bizness in show bizness / System / Juice with soul
CD 7567824682
Atlantic / Jul '93 / Warner Music

Juiceful Jazz

BETWEEN THE CHAPTERS
CD EFA 127572
Juiceful / Jul '95 / SRD

STREETZ OF DESIRE
CD EFA 126012
Juiceful / Aug '95 / SRD

Juicemen

META LUNA
CD MASSCD 029
Massacre / Apr '94 / Plastic Head

Juicy Eureka

THINKING UP THINGS AND THEN FORGETTING THEM
CD LISS 19
Lissy's / Jun '97 / SRD

Juicy Lucy

BEST OF JUICY LUCY
Who do you love / Midnight rider / Pretty woman / That woman's got something / Jessica / Willie the pimp/Lie back and enjoy it / Changed my mind, changed my sign / Just one time / I'm a thief / Built for comfort / Mr. Skin / Mr. A. Jones / Future days / Chicago north western / Hello LA, bye bye Birmingham / Thinking of my life
CD NEXCD 105
Sequel / Mar '90 / BMG

HERE SHE COMES AGAIN
Pretty woman / Try my love / Who do you love / Voodoo child / Saturday night / Up to the tracks / Talk to me / Drug squad
CD HTDCD 28
HTD / Sep '96 / CM / Pinnacle

JUICY LUCY/LIE BACK AND ENJOY IT
Mississippi woman / Who do you love / She's mine / She's yours / Just one time / Chicago North Western / Train / Nadine / Are you satisfied / Thinking of my life / Built for comfort / Pretty woman / Whiskey in my jar / Hello LA, bye bye Birmingham / Changed my mind / That woman's got something / Willie the pimp / Lie back and enjoy it
CD BGOCD 279
Beat Goes On / Jun '95 / Pinnacle

Julian, Don

HEAVEN AND PARADISE (Julian, Don & The Meadowlarks)
Heaven and paradise / Love only you / I got tore up / Untrue / Oop boopy oop / Devil or angel / Boogie woogie teenage / Blue moon / Please (say you love me) / Mine all mine / This must be paradise / Real pretty Mama / I am a believer / Big Mama wants to rock / Please love a fool / Thrill me night and day / LFMST Blues / Embarrasing moments / Always and always / Doin' the cha cha / Pass the gin
CD CDCHD 552
Ace / Aug '95 / Pinnacle

Julian, Richard

RICHARD JULIAN
CD 00897
Blackbird / May '97 / Grapevine/PolyGram

Julian's Treatment

TIME BEFORE THIS, A
First oracle / Coming of the mule / Phantom city / Black tower / Alda, dark lady of the outer worlds / Altarra, princess of the blue women / Second oracle / Twin suns of Centauri / Alkon, planet of Centauri / Terran / Fourth from the sun / Strange things / Time before this / Child of the night (1 and 2) / Stranger / Death of Alda / Cycles / Soldiers of time
CD SEECD 288
See For Miles/C5 / Jan '90 / Pinnacle

Julie Dolphin

LIT
CD TIMBCD 602
Timbuktu / Mar '94 / Pinnacle

Julinho

ACCORDEON DO BRASIL
CD BPE 107
Kardum / Nov '92 / Discovery

Juluka

SCATTERLINGS OF JULUKA
CD SHAKACD 2
Safari / Sep '91 / Pinnacle

Juma, Issa

SIGLAME VOL.2 (Juma, Issa & Les Wanyika)
Sigalame 2 / Money / Pole pole / Rafki uangu / Ateka / Sarah
CD AFRIZZ 008
Disc Afrique / May '90 / CM / Roots

Jumble Lane

JUMBLE LANE
CD HBG 123/3
Background / Apr '94 / Background / Greyhound

Jump

MYTH OF INDEPENDENCE, THE
Tower of babel / Princess of the people / On the wheel / Heaven and earth / Runaway / Keep the blues / Blind birds / Drivetime / Valediction / On my side / Shallow man
CD CYCL 027
Cyclops / Sep '95 / Pinnacle

Jump Cat Jump

HOT ROCKIN'
CD RKCD 9601
Rockhouse / Nov '96 / Nervous

Jumpin' The Gunn

SHADES OF BLUE
Cryin' blues / Green all over / Turtle blues / Crossed wires / More and more / Tired of tryin' / Shades of blue / Mind reader / Sweet Jesus / All I say to you
CD VPBCD 14
Pointblank / Apr '93 / EMI

Junaro, Emma

SI DE AMOR SE TRATA
CD TUMICD 015
Tumi / '92 / Discovery / Stern's

Juncosa, Sylvia

NATURE
CD SST 146CD
SST / Jun '93 / Plastic Head

Junction

SWINSSET
CD RED 014CD
Redemption / Jan '94 / SRD

June

I AM BEAUTIFUL
CD BBQCD 181
Beggars Banquet / Apr '96 / RTM/Disc / Warner Music

June Brides

1983 TO 1986
CD OVER 40CD
Overground / Jan '95 / Shellshock/Disc / SRD

June Of 44

ENGINE TAKES TO THE WATER
CD QS 32CD
Quarter Stick / Jun '95 / Cargo / SRD

TROPICS AND MERIDIANS
CD QS 44CD
Quarter Stick / Jun '96 / Cargo / SRD

Jung, Robert

DIE SCHONSTEN LIEDER VON
CD 15359
Laserlight / Nov '91 / Target/BMG

Jungle Band

JUNGLE GROOVE
Dancing in the street - part one / Jungle groove / You got to make it funky / Full speed ahead / Under the control of love / South fights back / Marvellous (red clay mix) / Dancing in the street - part two
CD CDCHARLY 134
Charly / Aug '88 / Koch

Jungle Brothers

DONE BY THE FORCES OF NATURE
Beyond this world / Feelin' alright / Sunshine / What U waitin' 4 / U make me sweat / Acknowledge your own history / Belly dancin' Dina / Good newz comin' / Done by the forces of nature / Beeds on a string / Tribe vibes / J Beez comin' through / Black woman / In dayz 2 come / Doin' our own dang / Kool accordin' 2 a Jungle Brother
CD 7599263642
Warner Bros. / Aug '90 / Warner Music

J BEEZ WIT THE REMEDY
Forty below trooper / Book of rhyme pages / My Jimmy weighs a ton / Good ole hype shit / Blahbludify / Spark a new flame / I'm in love with Indica / Simple as that / All I think about is you / Good lookin' out / J Beez comin' through / Spittin wicked randomness / For the headz at company Z / Man made material
CD 7599266792
Warner Bros. / Jun '93 / Warner Music

RAW DELUXE
CD GEE 1000282
Gee Street / May '97 / 3mv/Pinnacle

Jungr & Parker

CANADA
CD HARCD 023
Harbour Town / Oct '93 / ADA / CM / Direct / Roots

OFF THE PEG
CD UTIL 003 CD
Utility / Jun '90 / Grapevine/PolyGram

Junior Gone Wild

PULL THE GOALIE
CD TX 2011CD
Taxim / Jan '94 / ADA

TOO DUMB TO QUIT
CD SP 1160CD
Stony Plain / Oct '93 / ADA / CM / Direct

Junior MAFIA

CONSPIRACY
Intro / White chalk / Excuse me / Realms of Junior MAFIA / Players anthem / I need you tonight / Get money / I've been... / Crazaay / Backstabbers / Shot / Lyrical wizardry / Oh my Lord / Murder one / Outro
CD 7567926142
Atlantic / Sep '95 / Warner Music

Junk Head

ADDICTION
CD JUNKCD 001
Punk / Nov '95 / Plastic Head

Junk Monkeys

BLISS
CD CDZORRO 51
Metal Blade / Aug '92 / Pinnacle / Plastic Head

Junkera, Kepa

KALEJIRA AL-BUK
CD KDCD 386
Elkar / May '97 / ADA

LAU ESKUTARA (Junkera, Kepa & Julio Pereira)
CD KD 428CD
Elkar / Nov '96 / ADA

Junkyard Dogs

GOOD LIVIN' PLATTER
CD SFTRI 246CD
Sympathy For The Record Industry / Jun '97 / Cargo / Greyhound / Plastic Head

Juno Reactor

BEYOND THE INFINITE
CD BR 009CD
Blue Room Released / Mar '97 / Essential/ BMG / SRD

BIBLE OF DREAMS
CD BR 042CD
Blue Room Released / Jun '97 / Essential/ BMG / SRD

LUCIANA
CD INTA 002CD
Intermodo / Jul '94 / RTM/Disc

TRANSMISSIONS
CD NOMU 24CD
Mute / Sep '93 / RTM/Disc

Jura Ceilidh Band

JURA CEILIDH BAND
CD LDLCD 1240
Lochshore / Jun '96 / ADA / Direct / Duncans

Jurie, Renat

ENTRE LA RIVIERA ET LA MER
CD Y225025
Silex / Jun '93 / ADA / Harmonia Mundi

Juris, Vic

MOONSCAPE
CD SCCD 31402
Steeplechase / Apr '97 / Discovery / Impetus

MUSIC OF ALEX WILDER
Where is the one / Goodbye John / Winter of my discontent / Moon and sand / Blackberry winter / Long night / Lady sings the blues / That's my girl / While we're young / Homework / Such a lonely girl am I / Little circles
CD DTRCD 118
Double Time / Nov '96 / Express Jazz

NIGHT TRIPPER
CD SCCD 31353
Steeplechase / Sep '95 / Discovery / Impetus

Just, Andy

DON'T CRY
CD CCD 11044
Crosscut / Nov '94 / ADA / CM / Direct

Juster

REMEMBER THAT NIGHT
CD CDVEST 48
Bulletproof / Apr '95 / Pinnacle

WHAT I SEE WHAT I THINK
Boom boom boom / What I see / Buck your head / Blow the shack up / Common thief / I remember that night / For the mobiles / No room / Officer Murphy / Don't ask me why
CD CDVEST 54
Bulletproof / Aug '95 / Pinnacle

Justice League Of Zion

DISCOVERERS
CD CEND 1900
Century / Oct '94 / Shellshock/Disc

Justice, Jimmy

WHEN MY LITTLE GIRL IS SMILING/ BEST OF JIMMY JUSTICE
I understand / Bloodshot eyes / When love has left you / Teacher / Little bit of soap / Little lonely one / When my little girl is smiling / If I lost your love / Ain't that funny / One / My one sin / Spanish harlem / Write me a letter / Dawning / Too long will be too late / Early in the morning / Hallelujah, I love her so / World of lonely people / I wake up crying / Little cracked bell / Guitar player / Don't let the stars get in your eyes / Night has a thousand eyes / Save the last dance for me / Tell her / Folk singer / Can't get used to losing you / Up on the roof / You're gonna need my loving / Since you've been gone / Only heartbreaks for me / Everything in the garden
CD NEXCD 241
Sequel / Jun '93 / BMG

JVC Force

DOIN' DAMAGE
CD MIL 20102
Multimedia / Jun '97 / Jet Star

K

K-Hand

ON A JOURNEY
CD K7R 001CD
Studio K7 / Oct '96 / Prime / RTM/Disc

READY FOR THE DARKNESS
CD SUB 48362
Distance / Mar '97 / 3mv/Sony / Prime

SOUL
CD EFA 063382
Ausfahrt / May '97 / SRD

K-Ci & Jo Jo

LOVE ALWAYS
HBI / Last night's letter / Baby come back / Just for your love / Now and forever / Don't rush / You bring me up / Still waiting / Love ballad / How many times / All my life / How could you
CD MCD 11613
MCA / Jun '97 / BMG

K-Jacks

DOUBLE EXPOSURE
CD APR 019CD
April / Aug '97 / Plastic Head / Shellshock/ Disc

K-Klass

REMIX AND ADDITIONAL PRODUCTION BY... (Various Artists)
Question: *Seven Grand Housing Authority* / Mama said: *Anderson, Carleen* / Caught in the middle/I want you: *Roberts, Juliet* / Rapture: *Blondie* / Two can play that game: *Brown, Bobby* / Ruined in a day: *New Order* / U: *Clark, Loni* / Lover: *Roberts, Joe* / Freedom: *Shiva* / When: *Sunscreem* / What do you want from me: *Knuckles, Frankie* / Hideaway: *De'Lacy* / Love rendezvous: *M-People* / Come on come on: *Pearl*
CD 74321342082
De-Construction / Mar '96 / BMG

UNIVERSAL
1-2-3 / Rhythm is a mystery / Let me show you / Don't stop / Underground express / What you're missing / Taking me over / La cassa / Share your love / I can take some more
CD CDPCSD 149
EMI / Dec '93 / EMI

K-Passa

AFTER THE HEADRUSH
CD QP 6651CD
Que-P / Sep '94 / ADA / Direct

Ka-Spell, Edward

CHINA DOLL
CD STCD 090
Staalplaat / Sep '95 / Vital/SAM

DOWN IN THE CITY
CD SOL 29CD
Staalplaat / Feb '96 / Vital/SAM

KHATACLIMICI CHINA DOLL
CD 1009
Staalplaat / Feb '96 / Vital/SAM

TANITH AND THE LION TREE
CD TM 92671
Roadrunner / Oct '91 / PolyGram

Kaaos

TOTAL CHAOS
CD LF 130
Lost & Found / Mar '95 / Plastic Head

Kaapana, Ledward

LED LIVE SOLO
CD DCT 38008CD
Dancing Cat / Mar '96 / ADA

Kaasa, Anne Karin

SOLEFALLSTIME
CD FXCD 117
Kirkelig Kultuverksted / Jul '93 / ADA

SVALANDE VIND
CD FXCD 103
Kirkelig Kultuverksted / Jul '93 / ADA

Kaasinen, Sari

JOUKU JOULUN ALKKAA SAA (Kaasinen, Sari & Mari)
CD MIPU 205CD
Mipu / Dec '93 / ADA / Direct

TSIHI TSIHI (Kaasinen, Sari & Sirmakka)
CD 14753
F / Nov '96 / ADA

Kabalas

MARTINIS AND BAGELS
CD ID 123343CD
Dionysus / Oct '96 / Cargo / Greyhound / Plastic Head

Kada, Cheb

FROM ORAN TO PARIS
CD CHCD 64029
Shanachie / Jul '91 / ADA / Greensleeves / Koch

Kadekaru, Rinsho

FOLK SONGS OF OKINAWA
CD VICG 53602
JVC World Library / Feb '96 / ADA / CM / Direct

Kadison, Joshua

PAINTED DESERT SERENADE
Jessie / Painted desert serenade / Beau's all night radio love line / Invisible man / Mama's arms / Beautiful to my eyes / Picture postcards from LA / When a woman cries / Georgia rain
CD SBKCD 22
SBK / May '95 / EMI

Kadwaladyr

LAST HERO, THE
CD 4133CD
Musea / Aug '96 / ADA / Greyhound

Kaempfert, Bert

20 EASY LISTENING CLASSICS
CD 5294922
Polydor / Apr '96 / PolyGram

BLUE MIDNIGHT (Good Life Music Vol.1) (Kaempfert, Bert Orchestra)
CD 5339072
Polydor / Jun '97 / PolyGram

EVERGREENS (2CD Set) (Kaempfert, Bert Orchestra)
CD Set 5335552
Polydor / Jun '97 / PolyGram

MAGIC MUSIC OF BERT KAEMPFERT, THE
Strangers in the night / Afrikaan beat / Bass walks / Bye bye blues / Maltese melody / Red roses for a blue lady / Spanish eyes / Remember when / Swingin' safari / Love / Danke schon / Wonderland by night
CD 8439862
Polydor / May '91 / PolyGram

ORANGE COLOURED SKY (Good Life Music Vol.3) (Kaempfert, Bert Orchestra)
CD 5339092
Polydor / Jun '97 / PolyGram

RED ROSES
Red roses for a blue lady / Almost there / Blue midnight / Sentimental journey / Stardust / Dream / Wonderland by night / Moonglow / Three O'clock in the morning / Happy trumpeter / Swingin' safari / Wimoweh / Afrikaan beat / Zambesi
CD 5500962
Spectrum / Oct '93 / PolyGram

SPANISH EYES
CD PDSCD 522
Pulse / Sep '96 / BMG

STRANGERS IN THE NIGHT (The Bert Kaempfert Collection - 2CD Set)
Bye bye blues / Remember when / When you're smiling / Tahitian sunset / Once in a while / Steady does it / It makes no difference / You stepped out of a dream / Wiederseh n / I'm beginning to see the light / Melina / Out of nowhere / Take the 'A' train / Sunny side of life / My melancholy baby / Time to dream / What is this thing called love / Love's wonderland / Wheeling free / Good life / Bert's bossa No.2 / Skyliner / Manhattan merengue / Honeysuckle rose
CD Set 8437102
Polydor / May '91 / PolyGram

STRANGERS IN THE NIGHT (Good Life Music Vol.2) (Kaempfert, Bert Orchestra)
CD 5339062
Polydor / Jun '97 / PolyGram

SWING (Good Life Music Vol.4) (Kaempfert, Bert Orchestra)
CD 5339082
Polydor / Jun '97 / PolyGram

TROPICAL SUNRISE (Good Life Music Vol.5) (Kaempfert, Bert Orchestra)
CD 5339052
Polydor / Jun '97 / PolyGram

Kahn, Brenda

DESTINATION ANYWHERE
CD SHCD 5708
Shanachie / Jul '96 / ADA / Greensleeves / Koch

EPIPHANY IN BROOKLYN
I don't sleep, I drink coffee instead / Mojave winters / She's in love / Anesthesia / Mint juleps and needles / My lover / Sleepwalking / Lost / Great divide / Madagascar / Losing time / In Indiana
CD SHED 004CD
Creation / Aug '93 / 3mv/Vital

Kahn, Si

GOOD TIMES & BED TIMES
CD ROUCD 8027
Rounder / Dec '93 / ADA / CM / Direct

I HAVE SEEN FREEDOM
CD FF 70578
Flying Fish / Jul '92 / ADA / CM / Direct / Roots

I'LL BE THERE
CD FF 70509
Flying Fish / Oct '89 / ADA / CM / Direct / Roots

IN MY HEART
Gone gonna rise again / Aragon Mill / Mississippi river / Farewell to Ireland / Gentle with me darling / What you do with what you've got / Last good war / Senator / Brookside strike / Luray women / Children of Poland / What will I leave / Cold frosty morning / Wild rose of the mountain / Rock me, roll me / Curtains of old Joe's house / People like you / Crossing the border / Welcome to the world / Detroit December / If I live / Lady of the harbour / In my heart
CD PH 1169CD
Philo / May '94 / ADA / CM / Direct
CD SCR 33
Strictly Country / Mar '97 / ADA / Direct

NEW WOOD
CD PHCD 1168
Philo / Oct '94 / ADA / CM / Direct

Kahr, Jim

BACK TO CHICAGO
CD BEST 1027CD
Acoustic Music / Nov '93 / ADA

Kaia

KAIA
CD CHSW 14CD
Chainsaw / Dec '96 / Cargo

Kaiser & Kuriokhin

POPULAR SCIENCE
CD RCD 20118
Rykodisc / Nov '91 / ADA / Vital

Kaiser, Henry

ACOUSTICS
CD VICTOCD 025
Victo / Oct '94 / Harmonia Mundi / ReR Megacorp

ALTERNATIVE VERSIONS
CD SST 237CD
SST / Mar '89 / Plastic Head

DEVIL IN THE DRAIN
Sugagaki for conlon / King of the wild frontier / Dark memory / Smokestack lightnin' / Roadside picnic / Free to choose / Lost horizons / Devil in the drain / If this goes on...
CD SST 118CD
SST / May '93 / Plastic Head

ETERNITY BLUE
CD SHCD 6016
Shanachie / Dec '95 / ADA / Greensleeves / Koch

HEARTS DESIRE
Dark star / Rivers edge / Fishin' hole / Anyone who had a heart / Losing hand / Don't let a thief steal into your heart / Number 2 Klavierstuck III / Are you experienced / Lover / Flavor bud living / Ballad of Shane Muscatel / King Harvest (has surely come) / Black light / Buried treasure / Never again
CD CDRECK 19
Reckless / Jan '90 / RTM/Disc

IMPROVISED VANCOUVER (Kaiser, Henry & John Oswald)
CD INCUS 26CD
Incus / Mar '97 / Cadillac / Cargo

LEMON FRESH TWEEZER
CD RUNE 45
Cuneiform / Dec '89 / ReR Megacorp

OUTSIDE ALOHA PLEASURE
CD DEX 8
Dexter's Cigar / Dec '96 / Cargo

RE-MARRYING FOR MONEY
CD SST 222CD
SST / May '93 / Plastic Head

SWEET SUNNY NORTH (Kaiser, Henry & David Lindley)
CD SH 64057
Koch / Nov '94 / Koch

SWEET SUNNY NORTH VOL.2 (Kaiser, Henry & David Lindley)
CD SH 64061
Shanachie / Nov '96 / ADA / Greensleeves / Koch

TOMORROW KNOWS WHERE YOU LIVE (Kaiser, Henry & Jim O'Rourke)
CD VICTOCD 014
Victo / Nov '94 / Harmonia Mundi / ReR Megacorp

WIREWORKS (Kaiser, Henry & Derek Bailey)
CD SHAN 5011CD
Shanachie / Apr '95 / ADA / Greensleeves / Koch

WORLD OUT OF TIME VOL.1, A (Kaiser, Henry & David Lindley)
CD SHAN 64041CD
Shanachie / '92 / ADA / Greensleeves / Koch

WORLD OUT OF TIME VOL.2, A (Kaiser, Henry & David Lindley)
CD SHAN 64048CD
Shanachie / Aug '93 / ADA / Greensleeves / Koch

Kaisers

BEAT IT UP
Watcha say / Liquorice twist / She's gonna two time / Leave my kitten alone / I just don't understand / Watch your step / She's only doggin' around / Hippy hippy shake / Don't come back / Like I do / Loopy Lu / Theme from Vengeance / (Ain't that) just like me / Don't go with him / Let's stomp / You've got to keep her underhand
CD NOHITCD 017
No Hit / Apr '95 / Cargo / SRD

Kajagoogoo

TOO SHY - THE SINGLES...AND MORE
Too shy / Ooh to be ah / Hang on now / Big apple / Lion's mouth / Turn your back on me / Shouldn't do that / Only for love / Too much trouble / Never ending story / Love in your eyes / Inside to outside / Too shy (midnight mix) / Hang on now (extended version) / Turn your back on me (extended mix) / Never ending story (club mix)
CD CZ 524
EMI / Sep '93 / EMI

VERY BEST OF KAJAGOOGOO, THE
Big Apple / Charm of a gun / Too shy / Lion's mouth / Kajagoogoo / Ooh to be aah / Never ending story / Power to forgive / Turn your back on me / White feathers / Do I / Lies & promises / Only for love / Hang on now / Shouldn't do that / Big Apple (remix) / Too shy (12" mix)
CD CDGOLD 1038
EMI Gold / Jul '96 / EMI

Kala, Musa Dieng

SHAKAWTU - FAITH
CD SH 64072
Shanachie / Oct '96 / ADA / Greensleeves / Koch

Kalaf, Jerry

TRIO MUSIC (Kalaf, Jerry Group)
CD SBCD 3018
Sea Breeze / Jun '96 / Jazz Music

Kalahari Surfers

VOLUME 1 - THE 80'S
CD RERKS 1
ReR/Recommended / Oct '96 / ReR Megacorp / RTM/Disc

Kalaniemi, Maria

IHO
Lomasavel / Green score / Slingerdansin / Surin slimat / Iho / Triolopolska / Sofias flykt / Istunpa sankys laitalla / Sade / Linjarv / Napoleon
CD HNCD 1396
Hannibal / Jan '97 / ADA / Vital

Kalaschjan

RURAL & URBAN TRADITIONAL MUSIC FROM ARMENIA

CD SM 15052
Wergo / Jan '93 / ADA / Cadillac / Harmonia Mundi

Kaldor, Connie

SMALL CAFE
Someday / What do they know / If I was to tell you / Down to a river (Alan's song) / Coyote's call / Get lucky / Choppy water (rocky marriage breakdown) / I don't care / He's running in his sleep / Old friends (Mr. Settee's song) / Prairie moon / I love that dog
CD CDPH 1205
Philo / Jul '97 / ADA / CM / Direct

Kaleidoscope

BEACON FROM MARS, A
I found out / Greenwood sidee / Life will pass you by / Taxim / Baldheaded end of a broom / Louisiana man / You don't love me / Beacon from mars
CD EDCD 532
Edsel / Aug '97 / Pinnacle

BERNICE
Chocolate whale / Another love / Sneakin' thru the ghetto / To know is not to be / Lulu arfin nanny / Lie and hide / Ballad of Tommy Udo / Bernice / Soft and easy / New blue ooze
CD EDCD 534
Edsel / Aug '97 / Pinnacle

BLUES FROM BAGDAD
Egyptian gardens / If the night / Please / Keep your mind open / Pulsating dream / Oh death / Why try / Rampe rampe / I found out / Life will pass you by / Greenwood side / Beacon from Mars / Lie to me / Petite fleur / Banjo / Nobody / Elevator man / Hello trouble / Cuckoo / Sweet ate sweet
CD EDCD 375
Edsel / Aug '93 / Pinnacle

INCREDIBLE
Lie to me / Let the good love flow / Killing floor / Petite fleur / Banjo / Cuckoo / Seven ate sweet
CD EDCD 533
Edsel / Aug '97 / Pinnacle

SIDE TRIPS
Egyptian gardens / If the night / Please / Keep your mind open / Pulsating dream / Oh death / Come on in / Why try / Minnie the moocher
CD EDCD 531
Edsel / Aug '97 / Pinnacle

Kaleidoscope

DIVE INTO YESTERDAY
Dive into yesterday / Mr. Small the watch repair man / Flight from Ashiya / Murder of Lewis Tollani / (Further reflections) in the room of percussion / Dear Nellie Goodrich / Sky children / Dream for Julie / Faintly blowing / Poem / Snapdragon / Story from Tom Bitz / (Love song) for Annie / If you so wish / Opinion / Jenny Artichoke / Just how much you are / Bless the executioner / Black fjord / Feathered tiger / I'll kiss you once / Do it agin for Jeffrey / Music
CD 5340032
Fontana / Feb '97 / PolyGram

TANGERINE DREAM
Kaleidoscope / Please excuse my face / Dive into yesterday / Mr. Small, The watch repairer man / Flight from Ashiya / Murder of Lewis Tollani / Further reflections in the room / Dear nelle goodrich / Holidaymaker / Lesson perhaps / Sky children
CD CDTD 2165
Fingerprint / Jul '97 / Greyhound

Kaleidoscope

BEATZ 'N' PIECES
CD PNMCD 01
Pik 'n' Mix / Jun '97 / Kudos / Pinnacle / Prime / SRD

Kalenda Maya

ARMS OF THE GOD
CD PCOM 1126
President / Sep '92 / Grapevine/PolyGram / President / Target/BMG

Kalin Twins

WHEN
Sweet sweet sugar lips / Chicken chief / Oh my goodness / Jumpin' Jack / Clickety clack / Three o'clock thrill / Spider and the fly / No money can buy / When / Forget me not / Picture of you / Zing went the strings of my heart / Walkin' to school / Momma poppa / It's only the beginning / You mean the world to me
CD BCD 15597
Bear Family / Feb '92 / Direct / Rollercoaster / Swift

Kaliphz

SEVEN DEADLY SINS
Blood in blood out / Wass the deal / Bang bang boogie / Why im ez / Knockout position / Kloud 9 / Open up your mind / Rokk on shokk on / Sx horra vylence / Citi neva sleepz / Police n thievez / Eat the world / Kashflows / Props 2 tha thru skool
CD 8286752
Payday / Oct '95 / PolyGram / Vital

Kalis

ROCK AROUND
CD SYN CD 151
Topic / Apr '93 / ADA / CM / Direct

Kalle, Pepe

GIGANTAFRIQUE
Tiembe raid pa moli / Ce chale carnaval / Marche commun / Bilala lala / Pon moun paka bouge / Ndaka ya zeke
CD CDORB 062
Globestyle / Jul '90 / Pinnacle

L'ARGENT NE FAIT LE BONHEUR
CD KLCD 032
Gefraco / Nov '90 / Stern's / Triple Earth

Kallick, Kathy

CALL ME A TAXI
CD SHCD 3856
Sugar Hill / Nov '96 / ADA / CM / Direct / Koch / Roots

MATTERS OF THE HEART
CD SHCD 3820
Sugar Hill / Jan '94 / ADA / CM / Direct / Koch / Roots

USE A NAPKIN, NOT YOUR MOM
CD SHCD 3833
Sugar Hill / May '95 / ADA / CM / Direct / Koch / Roots

Kallmann, Gunter

SERENADE (Kallmann, Gunter Choir)
Elizabethan serenade / Bei walzermusick / Annabelle / Musik zum verlieben / Glocken serenade / Der reigen / Traum melodie / La montanara / Glocken klingen zu den sternen / Serenade / Oh mein Papa / Serenade / Edelweiss / Somewhere my love / La mer / My cherie amour / Romantica / Strangers in the night / Daydream / Day the rains came
CD CDMOIR 518
Memoir / Oct '96 / Jazz Music / Target/BMG

Kalmery, So

RASMI
CD 829222
BUDA / Oct '96 / Discovery

Kaloum Star

FELENKO
CD 829332
BUDA / Jan '97 / Discovery

Kalte Farben

TRUST
CD EFA 112352
Danse Macabre / Dec '94 / SRD

Kalyna Krasnaya

AT NARODA
CD SYN 189CD
Syncoop / Nov '95 / ADA / Direct

Kam

KAM
CD 7567617542
Street Knowledge / Mar '95 / Warner Music

MADE IN AMERICA
CD 7559617542
Street Knowledge / Dec '95 / Warner Music

NEVA AGAIN
Intro / Peace treaty / Stereotype / Still got love 4 'um / Hang 'um high / Drama / Neva again / Y'all don't hear me dough / Ain't that a bitch / Holiday madness / Watts riot / Outro
CD 7567922082
Street Knowledge / Mar '93 / Warner Music

Kamal

DANCE (Kamal & The Brothers)
CD NI 4022
Natasha / Nov '93 / ADA / Cadillac / CM / Direct / Jazz Music

Kamelot

DOMINION
Ascension / Heaven / Rise again / One day I'll win / We are not seperate / Birth of a hero / Creation / Sin / Song of Roland / Crossing two rivers / Troubled mind
CD N 02722
Noise / Nov '96 / Koch

Kamen, Michael

BRAZIL
CD 74321111242
RCA / Jun '96 / BMG

CONCERTO FOR SAXOPHONE (Kamen, Michael & David Sanborn)
Concerto for saxophone / Helen-Claire / Sasha / Zoe / Sandra / Waiting for daddy
CD 7599261572
WEA / Nov '90 / Warner Music

Kamikaze Ground Crew

MADAME MARIE'S TEMPLE OF KNOWLEDGE
CD 804382
New World / Sep '93 / ADA / Cadillac / Harmonia Mundi

SCENIC ROUTE, THE
CD NW 400
New World / Aug '92 / ADA / Cadillac / Harmonia Mundi

Kaminsky, Max

AT THE COPLEY TERRACE 1945 (Kaminsky, Max & Pee Wee Russell)
CD JCD 15
Jazzology / Jun '96 / Jazz Music

Kamkars

LIVING FIRE, THE (Live In Paris)
CD 122157
Long Distance / Feb '96 / ADA / Discovery

NIGHTINGALE WITH A BROKEN WING
Kosha hawraman / Awaz / Larzan / Bolboly bal shkaw / Amine to golakamy / Sheleren / Dekay ambar, dekay auber / Kajawa
CD WSCD 009
Womad Select / May '97 / ADA / Direct

Kamoze, Ini

HERE COMES THE HOTSTEPPER
Call the police / Rough / Here comes the hotstepper / Gunshot / World-a-music / Trouble you trouble me / General / Pull up the cork / Pirate / Babylon, Babylon, I want Ital / Burnin'
CD 4785362
Columbia / May '95 / Sony

ORIGINAL HOT STEPPER
CD RRCD 49
Reggae Refreshers / Jan '95 / PolyGram / Vital

SHOCKING OUT
Cool it off / Clown talking / Cone now / Boss / We run the country / Shocking out / Revolution / Girl E / Hole in the pumpkin / Spread out
CD GRELCD 115
Greensleeves / Jan '95 / Jet Star / SRD

Kamuca, Richie

JAZZ EROTICA
CD FSCD 500
Fresh Sound / Feb '88 / Discovery / Jazz Music

Kamusasadi, Vumvum

MUZ ANGOLA
CD 68971
Tropical / Apr '97 / Discovery

Kanabis The Edit Assassin

DIGITAL CONTACT (The First Generation)
Detroit winter / Walk under a full moon's light / Home grown (The Chatam Ontario flavour) / Blunt intermission / Circus of the confused / Peace in Detroit / Native noise interlude / Venus / Phat 107 bpm / Dee and Angel / EFW interlude / Some funk / Dedication to my Grandma
CD K7R 011CD
Studio K7 / May '97 / Prime / RTM/Disc

Kanchay

MACHU PICCHU
CD TUMICD 011
Tumi / Apr '90 / Discovery / Stern's

Kanda Bongo Man

AMOUR YOU
CD HNCD 1337
Hannibal / Jan '89 / ADA / Vital

KWASSA-KWASSA
CD HNCD 1343
Hannibal / May '89 / ADA / Vital

NON STOP NON STOP
Iyole / Ida / Djessy / Amina / Mazina
CD CDORB 005
Globestyle / Mar '90 / Pinnacle

SANGO
CD 795372
Melodie / Apr '96 / ADA / Discovery / Grapevine/PolyGram / Greensleeves / Jet Star

SOUKOUS IN CENTRAL PARK
Liza / Bedy / Yesu Christu / JT / Wallow / Luta / Sai / Lela lela
CD HNCD 1374
Hannibal / Mar '93 / ADA / Vital

WELCOME TO SOUTH AFRICA
CD 320052
Melodie / Apr '96 / ADA / Discovery / Grapevine/PolyGram / Greensleeves / Jet Star

ZING ZONG
Zing zong / Isambe / Mosali / Wallow / Monie / Yonde love me / Yesu Christu / Freres soki / Kadhi
CD HNCD 1366
Hannibal / Jul '91 / ADA / Vital

Kane, Candye

HOME COOKIN'
CD ANT 0033CD
Antones / Sep '94 / ADA / Hot Shot

Kane, Chet

TEARS FOR COLUMBIA
CD GRCD 315
Glitterhouse / Sep '94 / Avid/BMG

Kane, Eden

ALL THE HITS AND MORE
CD CDSGP 0241
Prestige / Feb '96 / Else / Total/BMG

HITS ALBUM, THE
CD MOGCD 005
Moggie / Dec '94 / Else

WELL I ASK YOU
CD 8209662
Deram / Jan '96 / PolyGram

Kane Gang

MOTORTOWN
Motortown / Amusement park / Smalltown creed / Brother brother / Mighty day / Crease in his hat / Giving up / Don't look any further / Finer place / Respect yourself / What time is it / Spend / It's a gift / King Street rain
CD 5501952
Spectrum / Mar '94 / PolyGram

Kane, Kieran

DEAD RECKONING
CD DR 0001
Dead Reckoning / Feb '96 / Avid/BMG

Kane, Ray

PUNAHELE
CD DCT 38001CD
Dancing Cat / Mar '96 / ADA

Kangaroo Moon

BAGPIPES ON THE BEACH
CD MS 117CD
Music Suite / Apr '94 / Direct / Music Suite

BELONGIL
CD KM 02CD
Kangaroo Moon / Jan '96 / ADA / Direct

KEEP THEM WARM
Keep them warm / Five fingers of the seventh wave / Bela Lughoti / Sally Sandwich / Whirlimix / Reggae reels / Open ones/ Don't forget to breath/Tunes
CD KM 03CD
Kangaroo Moon / Aug '96 / ADA / Direct

Kankawa

B III
St. Louis blues / Stone free / Hey Joe / Cat Street / Talkin' 'bout Mr. K / Impressions / Family / Tokyo intro / Tokyo / Green onions / Plant a tree, plant love
CD JVC 90122
JVC / Aug '97 / Direct / New Note/Pinnacle / Vital/SAM

Kanoute, Moussa

DANCE OF THE KORA
Windswept / Courage / Ledian dance / Caribe / From the source / Pensee la vie / Happiness / I shall be released / Mosque
CD R 272536
Earthbeat / Nov '96 / ADA / Direct

Kansas

AUDIO VISIONS
Relentless / Anything for you / Hold on / Loner / Curtain of iron / Got to rock on / Don't open your eyes / No one together / No room for a stranger / Back door
CD 4811612
Epic / Mar '96 / Sony

DRASTIC MEASURES
Fight fire with fire / Everybody's my friend / Mainstream / Andi / Going through the motions / Get rich / Don't take your love away / End of the age / Incident on a bridge
CD 4811632
Epic / Mar '96 / Sony

FREAKS OF NATURE
I can fly / Desperate times / Hope once again / Black fathom / Under the knife / Need / Freaks of nature / Cold grey morning / Peaceful and warm

CD ESMCD 492
Essential / Apr '97 / BMG

KANSAS
Can I tell you / Bringing it back / Lonely wind / Belexes / Journey from Mariabronn / Pilgrimage / Apercu / Death of Mother Nature suite
CD 4688832
Epic / Feb '97 / Sony

KANSAS BOXED SET, THE
Can I tell you / Death of mother nature suite / Journey from Mariabronn / Song for America / Devil game / Incomudro-hymm to the atman / Child of innocence / Icarus / Borne on wings of steel / Mysteries and mayhem / Pinnacle / Carry on wayward son / Wall / What's on my mind / Opus insert / Magnum opus / Father Padilla meets the perfect gnat / Howling at the moon / Industry on parade / Release the beavers / Gnat attack / Point of no return / Portrait (He Knew) / Dust in the wind / Closet chronicles / People of the south wind / On the other side / Glimpse of home / Relentless / Loner / Hold on / Wheels
CD Set CD 47364
Legacy / Jul '94 / Sony

VINYL CONFESSIONS
Play the game tonight / Right away / Fair exchange / Chaining shadows / Diamonds and pearls / Face it / Windows / Borderline / Play on / Crossfire
CD 4811622
Epic / Mar '96 / Sony

Kansas City Five

CLASSICS 1938-1944 (Kansas City 5, 6, 7)
CD CLASSICS 912
Classics / Jan '97 / Discovery / Jazz Music

Kansas City Stompers

40-ARS JUBILAEUM
CD MECCACD 1018
Music Mecca / Nov '94 / Cadillac / Jazz Music / Wellard

HAPPY JAZZ
CD MECCACD 1041
Music Mecca / Nov '94 / Cadillac / Jazz Music / Wellard

PA DANSK
CD MECCACD 1086
Music Mecca / May '97 / Cadillac / Jazz Music / Wellard

Kante, Mory

AKWABA BEACH
Yeke yeke / Deni / Inch Allah / Tama / Africa 2000 / Dia / Nanfoulen / Akwaba beach
CD 8331192
London / Apr '91 / PolyGram

Kanu Nan

CHIMBALOMA
CD TUMICD 027
Tumi / '91 / Discovery / Stern's

Kanyakumari, A

VADYA LAHARI (Kanyakumari, A & South Indian Music Ensemble)
CD CDT 125
Topic / Apr '93 / ADA / CM / Direct

KAOS

INTERNATIONAL DOPE DEALERS
CD EFA 610032
Blitzvinyl / May '94 / SRD

Kapel, Jons Jazz

LAZY 'SIPPI STEAMER
CD MECCACD 1019
Music Mecca / Nov '94 / Cadillac / Jazz Music / Wellard

Kapelye

KAPELYE: ON THE AIR (Old-Time Jewish American Radio)
CD SHCD 67005
Shanachie / Mar '95 / ADA / Greensleeves / Koch

Kapilow, Robert

GREEN EGGS AND HAM BY DR. SEUSS (Kapilow, Robert & Angelina Reaux/NJ Chamber Music Society)
CD 389002
Koch International / Aug '96 / Koch

Kaplansky, Lucy

FLESH AND BONE
CD RHRCD 92
Red House / Nov '96 / ADA / Koch

TIDE, THE
CD RHRCD 65
Red House / May '95 / ADA / Koch

Kapoor, Mahendra

FROM BIRMINGHAM TO SOUTHALL
CD DMUT 1069
Multitone / Apr '89 / BMG

Kapstad, Egil

CHEROKEE
CD GMCD 161
Gemini / Oct '90 / Cadillac

Karadjova, Nadka

BULGARIAN POLYPHONY VOL.3 (Karadjova, Nadka & The Bisserov Sisters)
CD VICG 52332
JVC World Library / Mar '96 / ADA / CM / Direct

Karaindrou, Eleni

MUSIC FOR FILMS
Farwell theme / Elegy for rosa / Fairytale / Parade / Return / Wandering in Alexandria / Voyage / Scream / Adagio / Rosa's song / Improvisation on farewell and waltz theme / Song / Waltz and farewell theme
CD 8476092
ECM / May '91 / New Note/Pinnacle

SUSPENDED STEP OF THE STORK, THE
Refugee's theme / Search - refugee's theme variation A / Suspended step / Train-car neighbourhood variation A / River / Refugee's theme symphonic variation No. 1 / Train-car neighbourhood variation B / Refugee's theme symphonic variation No. 2 / Hassaposerviko / Search - refugee's theme variation B / Waltz for the bride / Final
CD 5115142
ECM / Mar '92 / New Note/Pinnacle

Karate

IN PLACE
CD 185432
Southern / Apr '97 / SRD

KARATE
CD 185342
Southern / Mar '96 / SRD

Karayorgis, Pandelis

IN TIME (Karayorgis, Pandelis & Mat Maneri)
CD LABCD 002
Leo / Oct '94 / Cadillac / Impetus / Wellard

Karelia

DIVORCE AT HIGH NOON
Divorce at high noon / Love's a cliche / Say try / To his dietres / Life in a Barrat Garret / Crazy irritation / Remorse at high noon / Dancing along the nekrotaphion / Devil rides hyndland / Infinite duration / Nostalgia / Tension / Bleach yours / Exaggeration / Garavaughty butes
CD RR 88232
Roadrunner / Apr '97 / PolyGram

Karen

BETWEEN ME AND YOU
CD JJCD 1017
Beechwood / Jan '92 / Duncans / Ross

Kargaard, Morten

COLOUR OF A MOMENT
CD MECCACD 2004
Music Mecca / May '97 / Cadillac / Jazz Music / Wellard

Karklins, Ingrid

ANIMA MUNDI
CD GLCD 1141
Green Linnet / May '94 / ADA / CM / Direct / Highlander / Roots

DARKER PASSION, A
Leatherwing bat / Big one/Little one / Es apkalu ozolinu/Oceans apart / Hiro/Smitten / Time/Incredible march of the spiny lobsters / Kupla, kupla liepa auga / Crack the slab / Visas manas sikus dziesmas / Ar vilcinu riga braucu / Metenitis
CD GLCD 1118
Green Linnet / Mar '92 / ADA / CM / Direct / Highlander / Roots

Karlsson, Stefan

BELOW ZERO
CD JR 07032
Justice / Mar '94 / Koch

ROOM 292
CD JR 007012
Justice / Oct '92 / Koch

Karma To Burn

KARMA TO BURN
(Waltz of the) Playboy pallbearers / Bobbi, Bobbi, Bobbi - I'm not God / Patty Hearst's closet mantra / Mt Penetrator / Eight / Apalachian woman / Twenty four hours / Sixgun sucker punch / Thirteen six / Ma petite mort / Twin sisters and a half bottle of bourbon
CD RR 88622
Roadrunner / Feb '97 / PolyGram

Karminski Experience

ESPRESSO ESPRESSO (Various Artists)
CD 5355472
Deram / Aug '96 / PolyGram

Karn, Mick

BESTIAL CLUSTER
Bestial cluster / Back in the beginning / Beard in the letterbox / Drowning dream / Sad velvet breath of summer and winter / Saday, Maday / Liver and lungs / Bones of mud
CD CMP CD 1002
CMP / Jun '93 / Cargo / Grapevine/PolyGram / Vital/SAM

DREAMS OF REASON PRODUCE MONSTERS
First impression / Language of ritual / Buoy / Land / Three fates / When love walks in / Dream of reason / Answer
CD CDV 2389
Virgin / '87 / EMI

TITLES
Tribal dawn / Lost affections in a room / Passion in moisture / Weather the windmill / Saviour are you with me / Trust me / Sensitive / Piper blue
CD CDV 2249
Virgin / Oct '90 / EMI

TOOTH MOTHER, THE
Thundergirl mutation / Plaster the magic tongue / Lodge of skins / Gossip's cup / Feta funk / Tooth Mother / Little less hope / There was not anything but nothing
CD CMPCD 1008
CMP / May '95 / Cargo / Grapevine/PolyGram / Vital/SAM

Karoli, Michael

DELUGE (Karoli, Michael & Polly Eltes)
CD SPOONCD 16
The Grey Area / Mar '95 / RTM/Disc

Karolinka

SONGS AND DANCES FROM POLAND
CD EUCD 1124
ARC / '91 / ADA / ARC Music

Karp

KARP
CD KLP 67CD
K / Apr '97 / Cargo / Greyhound / SRD

SUPLEX
CD KLP 48CD
K / Oct '95 / Cargo / Greyhound / SRD

Karrer, Chris

DERVISH KISS
CD INDIGO 30542
Faruk / Dec '96 / Cargo

SUFUSTICATED
CD 1609002
Think Prog / Jun '97 / Greyhound

KAS Serenity

RETURN TO THE RAINBOW BRIDGE
CD PPP 4219
Ichiban / Mar '96 / Direct / Koch

Kashif

BEST OF KASHIF, THE
I just gotta have you (lover turn me on) / Baby don't break your baby's heart / Are you the woman: *Kashif & Whitney Houston* / Reservations for two: *Kashif & Dionne Warwick* / Love changes: *Kashif & Meli'sa Morgan* / Fifty ways (to fall in love): *Kashif & Whitney Houston* / Stay the night / Love me all over / Help yourself to my love / Dancing in the dark
CD 262817
Arista / Jun '92 / BMG

Kassav

KASSAV VOL.3
CD 3018842
Arcade / Jul '97 / Discovery

KASSAV VOL.4
CD 3018852
Arcade / Jul '97 / Discovery

LES INOUBLIABLES DE...
CD 472299
Flarenasch / Feb '97 / Discovery

PASSEPORT
CD 3021202
Arcade / Jul '97 / Discovery

Kastinen, Arja

IRO
Amut / Kotanen / Siera / Varpa / Tisvata / Siide / Hapenet / Heutuvoa / Usmakka / Varpa / Kotanen / Prisonkka / Sihku / Tuokko / Kanna / Helve / Voli
CD MIPUCD 401
Mipu / May '97 / ADA / Direct

Kastrierte Philosophen

LEIPZIG DC
CD NORMAL 124CD
Normal / Dec '90 / ADA / Direct

Kataklysm

MYSTICAL GATE OF REINCARNATION
CD NB 0932
Nuclear Blast / Feb '94 / Plastic Head

SORCERY
CD NB 1082
Nuclear Blast / May '96 / Plastic Head

TEMPLE OF KNOWLEDGE
CD NB 157CD
Nuclear Blast / Jul '96 / Plastic Head

Katatonia

BRAVE MURDER DAY
CD AV 022
Avant Garde / Nov '96 / Plastic Head / RTM/Disc

DANCE OF THE DECEMBER SOULS
CD NFR 005
No Fashion / Oct '94 / Plastic Head

Kater, Peter

COLLECTION 1983-1990, THE
CD SD 605
Silver Wave / Sep '92 / Jazzizit Organisation / New Note/Pinnacle

FOOL & THE HUMMINGBIRD, THE
CD SD 502
Silver Wave / Jan '93 / Jazzizit Organisation / New Note/Pinnacle

FOR CHRISTMAS
CD SD 503
Silver Wave / Jan '93 / Jazzizit Organisation / New Note/Pinnacle

GATEWAY
CD SD 161
Silver Wave / Jan '93 / Jazzizit Organisation / New Note/Pinnacle

HOMAGE
CD 1390172
Gaia / May '89 / New Note/Pinnacle

MOMENTS, DREAMS & VISIONS
CD SD 509
Silver Wave / Jan '93 / Jazzizit Organisation / New Note/Pinnacle

NATIVES
CD SD 601
Silver Wave / Jan '93 / Jazzizit Organisation / New Note/Pinnacle

ROOFTOPS
CD SD 608
Silver Wave / Sep '92 / Jazzizit Organisation / New Note/Pinnacle

SEASON, THE
CD SD 702
Silver Wave / Jan '93 / Jazzizit Organisation / New Note/Pinnacle

Katharconsoort

LA DIVINA COMEDIA
CD 21087
Sonifolk / Aug '96 / ADA / CM

Katharsis

EARTH...HEY
CD CLP 9883
Cleopatra / Apr '97 / Cargo / Greyhound / Plastic Head / RTM/Disc / SRD

Katie's Quartet

KATIE'S QUARTET
CD OHCD 003
Old Hat / Aug '96 / ADA / CM / Direct

Katmandu

CASE FOR THE BLUES, A
CD SARCD 007
Saraja / Apr '94 / THE

Kato, Ano

CHTES TA KANAME
CD CDPAN 144
Pan / Apr '93 / ADA / CM / Direct

Katon, Michael

BUSTIN' UP THE JOINT - LIVE
Rip it hard / Water won't boil / No more whiskey / Lucky, lucky, lucky / Love hoo doo / Rock around / Roadtested / Devil's daughter / Boogie whip / Two angels flyin' / Wake up call / Barbeque on my boogie / Get on the boogie train / Rock 'n' run
CD PRD 70962
Provogue / Nov '96 / Pinnacle

GET ON THE BOOGIE TRAIN
CD PRD 70492
Provogue / Apr '93 / Pinnacle

PROUD TO BE LOUD
CD PRD 70532
Provogue / Sep '93 / Pinnacle

RIP IT HARD
CD PRD 70642
Provogue / May '94 / Pinnacle

RUB
CD PRD 70792
Provogue / Mar '96 / Pinnacle

Katrina & The Waves

KATRINA & THE WAVES/WAVES
Red wine and whisky / Do you want crying / Qu te quiero / Machine gun Smith / Cry for me / Walking on sunshine / Going down to Liverpool / Mexico / Sun won't shine / Game of love / Is that it / Tears for me / Sun Street / Lovely Lindsey / Riding shotgun / Sleep on my pillow / Money chain / Mr. Star / Love that boy / Stop trying to prove (how much of a man you is) / Red wine and whiskey
CD BGOCD 330
Beat Goes On / Dec '96 / Pinnacle

VERY BEST OF KATRINA & THE WAVES, THE
Walking on sunshine / Red wine and whiskey / Do you want crying / Que te quiero / Going down to Liverpool / Machine gun Smith / Mexico / Game of love / Is that it / Tears for me / Sun street / Lovely Lindsay / I can dream about it / That's the way / Rock 'n' roll girl / (I've got a) Crush on you / Rock myself to sleep / We gotta get out of this place / Tears of a woman / I really taught me to watsui
CD CDEMC 3766
EMI / Apr '97 / EMI

WALK ON WATER
CD 0630198372
East West / Aug '97 / Warner Music

Katz, Bruce

TRANSFORMATION
Chicago transformation / Boppin' out of the abyss / Sweeper / What might have been / Larry the spinning poodle / Circular notion / Deep pockets / Crime novel / Window of soul / But now I see
CD AQCD 1026
Audioquest / Jul '95 / ADA / New Note/ Pinnacle

Katz, Dick

3 WAY PLAY
CD RSRCD 127
Reservoir Music / Nov '94 / Cadillac

Katze, Nav

NEVER MIND THE DISTORTION
CD SSR 154
SSR / Oct '95 / Amato Disco / Grapevine/ PolyGram / Prime / RTM/Disc

Kauffeld, Greetje

GREETJE KAUFFELD MIT PAUL KUHN
Leider nur eine schlechte kopie / Ruf an / Oh Charly boy / Nur wer liebt ist nie allein / Lebewohl Konny / Jeden tag da lieb' ich dich ein kleines bisschen mehr: *Kauffeld, Greetje & Paul Kuhn* / Jonny / Sunday melody / Benny's doodlin' band: *Kauffeld, Greetje & Paul Kuhn* / Der braune boy in baumwollfeld / Junge lieb im Mai / Wir konnen uns nur briefe schreiben / Musikant lass die geigen erklingen / Lieber guter alter mond: *Kauffeld, Greetje & Paul Kuhn* / Melodie poesie / I love you: *Kauffeld, Greetje & Paul Kuhn* / Tanz bitte noch einmal mit mir / Blue honeymoon: *Kauffeld, Greetje & Paul Kuhn* / Nur am abend / Das ist so schon, das wunsch ich mir / Nur bei dir fuhl ich mich zu haus: *Kauffeld, Greetje & Paul Kuhn* / Wenn es nacht wird / Groschen polka: *Kauffeld, Greetje & Paul Kuhn* / Hey hey big boy / Kopenhagen serenade: *Kauffeld, Greetje & Paul Kuhn* / Komm' dach zuruck zu mir / Blonder liebling / Ich lieb' immer dur nich: *Kauffeld, Greetje & Paul Kuhn* / Die stunde der liebe / Ich bin immer die andere / I love you because: *Kauffeld, Greetje & Paul Kuhn*
CD BCD 16146
Bear Family / Jan '97 / Direct / Rollercoaster / Swift

Kaufmann, Anna Maria

ANNA MARIA KAUFMANN
CD MSPCD 9502
Mabley St. / Sep '95 / Grapevine/ PolyGram

Kaulkin, Andy

SIX FOOT SEVEN AND RISING
CD BL 28
Bongload / Oct '96 / Cargo / Greyhound / Plastic Head

Kauriga Balalaika Ensemble

RUSSIAN DANCES
CD MCD 71789
Monitor / Jun '93 / CM

Kava Kava

YOU CAN LIVE HERE
Headset / Sync / Gil / Revenge of the pseuds / Tat tvam asi / Swivel / Beat their chests / Loudest lebenstraum / In transits destined / For Uranus / Hippy bollocks / Silliness
CD DELECCD 024
Delerium / Apr '95 / Cargo / Pinnacle / Vital

Kavana

KAVANA
Crazy chance / I can make you feel good / Where are you / MFEO / Holdin' back on U / Release it / Wait for the day / Time is right / For the very first time / Protected / Jealousy / Work
CD CDNMS 1
Nemesis / Apr '97 / EMI

Kavanagh, Niamh

FLYING BLIND
When there's time for love / Romeo's twin / White city of lights / Let's make trouble / Miles away / I can't make you love me / Whatever it takes / Don't stop now / Flying blind / Red roses for me
CD 74321255412
Arista / Oct '95 / BMG

Kavanagh, Richie

AON FOCAL EILE
CD LYNCD 001
Wag / Feb '97 / Total/BMG

Kay, Arthur

RARE 'N' TASTY
CD LOMACD 33
Loma / Aug '94 / BMG

Kay, Fiede

VOLKSSANGER AUS DEM NORDEN
CD EUCD 1118
ARC / '91 / ADA / ARC Music

Kay Gees

ESSENTIAL DANCEFLOOR ARTISTS VOL.5
You've got to / Keep on bumpin' / Get down / Masterplan / Hustle wit every muscle / Waiting at the bus stop / Cheek to cheek / I believe in music / Tango hustle / Killowatt / Killowatt/Invasion / Who's the man (with the master plan)
CD DGPCD 707
Deep Beats / Sep '94 / BMG

Kay, Janet

CAPRICORN WOMAN
CD ARKCD 3
Pressure / Sep '89 / Black Marketing / Jet Star

DUB DEM SILLY
CD ARKCD 105
Arawak / Dec '93 / Jet Star

I'LL ALWAYS LOVE YOU
CD JFRCD 001
Joe Frazier / Dec '93 / Jet Star

IMMACULATE COLLECTION
So amazing / Look what love can do / Almaz / Loving you / Moving away / Kiss away / Bad, bad girl / Chariots of fire / I'd rather go blind / Closer I get to you / For the good times / Music man / Dreams of emotion / Have you ever loved somebody / Since I fell for you / One day I'll fly away / He reminds me / Trade winds / Show me the way / So good, so right / Imagine / Computer love / I want to be the one / Love won't let me wait
CD JANETCD 2
New Name / Nov '93 / Jet Star

ORCHESTRAL DUB COLLECTION
CD JANETCD 3
Body Music / Jul '94 / Jet Star

SILLY GAMES
Silly games / Imagine that / Feel no way / Rock the rhythm / Closer to you / Do you love me / Can't give it up / That night / Capricorn woman
CD CECD 1001
Jet Star / Aug '90 / Jet Star

SO AMAZING (Part 1)
CD JANETCD 1
Body Music / Apr '94 / Jet Star

SWEET SURRENDER
CD JANETCD 5
Body Music / Jul '89 / Jet Star

ULTIMATE COLLECTION, THE
CD ARKCD 106
Arawak / Oct '95 / Jet Star

Kay Yn't Seil

T'MALLE SCHIP
CD SYNCD 164
Syncoop / Jun '94 / ADA / Direct

Kayak

ROYAL BED BOUNCER
CD CDP 1012DD
Pseudonym / Jun '97 / Greyhound

SEE SEE THE SUN
Reason for it all / Lyrics / Mouldy wood / Lovely Luna / Hope for a life / Ballet of the cripple / Forever is a lonely thought / Mammoth / See see the sun
CD CDP 1024DD
Pseudonym / Jun '97 / Greyhound

Kaye, Danny

VERY BEST OF DANNY KAYE (20 Golden Greats)
I'm Hans Christian Andersen / Inchworm / King's new clothes / Thumbelina / Ugly duckling / Wonderful Copenhagen / Tubby the tuba (parts 1 and 2) / Woody Woodpecker song / Popo the puppet / I taut I taw a puddy tat / Ballin' the Jack / Tchaikovsky / Civilization / Molly Malone / Oh by jingo, oh by gee / Candy kisses / St. Louis blues / Manic depressive parents lobby number part I and part II
CD MCLD 19049
MCA / Aug '94 / BMG

Kaye, Sammy

SAMMY KAYE 1944/LES ELGART 1946 (Kaye, Sammy & Les Elgart)
CD CCD 93
Circle / Aug '94 / Jazz Music / Swift / Wellard

Kayirebwa, Cecile

RWANDA
Rwanamiza / Tarihinda / Kana / Inkindi / Mundeke mbaririmbire / Urusamaza / Rubyiruko / Umulisa / Cyusa / Ndare / Umunezero
CD CDORBD 083
Globestyle / Aug '94 / Pinnacle

Kazazian, Georges

SABIL
CD ED 13034CD
L'Empreinte Digitale / Jul '95 / ADA / Harmonia Mundi

Kazda

NEW STRATEGIES OF RIDING
CD ITM 1492
ITM / Oct '95 / Koch / Tradelink

Kazjurol

DANCE TARANTELLA
CD CDATV 12
Active / Sep '90 / Pinnacle

KBZ 200

EXOTIC TRILOGY, THE
CD KBZ 200
Staalplaat / Dec '95 / Vital/SAM

KC & The Sunshine Band

BEST OF KC AND THE SUNSHINE BAND, THE
Sound your funky horn / Get down tonight / I'm your boogie man / (Shake shake shake) Your booty / Queen of clubs / That's the way (I like it) / Keep it comin' love / Please don't go / Boogie shoes / Let's go rock and roll / Give it up / Do you wanna go party / I like to do it / Shotgun shuffle / Wrap your arms around me / All I want
CD CDROU 5007
Roulette / Jul '90 / EMI

BEST OF KC AND THE SUNSHINE BAND, THE
CD 1120112
Vono Disc / Sep '96 / Koch

BEST OF KC AND THE SUNSHINE BAND, THE
That's the way I like it / Sound your funky horn / Queen of clubs / Let it go (part 1) / I'm so crazy / (Shake, shake, shake) Shake your body / Please don't go / I get lifted / Boogie shoes / Get down tonight / It's the same old song / Ain't nothin' wrong / Keep it coming love / I'm your boogie man / Baby I want your loving / Do it good
CD CDGOLD 1021
EMI Gold / May '96 / EMI

GET DOWN LIVE
Opening, KC, KC, KC / Give it up / Shake your booty / James Brown medley / Boogie man medley / Higher
CD CLACD 411
Castle / Nov '96 / BMG

KC & THE SUNSHINE BAND
Let it go / That's the way (I like it) / Get down tonight / Boogie shoes / Ain't nothin' wrong / I'm so crazy 'bout you / What makes you happy / I get lifted / Let it go
CD MUSCD 504
MCI Original Masters / Sep '94 / Disc / THE

SHAKE YOUR BOOTY
CD MSCD 027
Music De-Luxe / Mar '96 / TKO Magnum

KCL Project

MANY RIVERS TO CROSS
CD ORCCD 004
Octopus / Sep '97 / Kudos / Pinnacle

KCM Inc.

DOIN' IT FUNKY SMOOTH
Peachtowne party jam / Is it worth it / Love stepped / That love thang / Let me groove you / All 'n' all / It's all about lovin' you / Real love / Do you / Emotion
CD PEA 4110CD
Haven / Sep '91 / Pinnacle / Shellshock/ Disc

Ke

I AM
Strange world / Someday / I think it's time / I don't wanna go / Don't walk away / Endless blue (why) / All you ever wanted / Holding on / Will I ever dream / Lay down / I am
CD 74321352582
RCA / Apr '96 / BMG

Keane, Brian

BEYOND THE SKY (Keane, Brian & Omar Faruk Tekbilek)
Beyond the sky / Imaginary traveller / Kolaymi / Bridge / Chargah Sirto / Your Love Is My Cure / Selemet / Strange Little Corner / Sisler / Sweet Trouble / Al Fatiha
CD CDCEL 13047
Celestial Harmonies / Jul '92 / ADA / Select

SNOWFALLS
CD FFK 70452
Flying Fish / Oct '89 / ADA / CM / Direct / Roots

Keane, Conor

COOLEY'S HOUSE
CD CKCD 01CD
Conor Keane / Oct '94 / ADA / Direct

Keane, Dolores

DOLORES KEANE
Sister and brother / Drag lines / Heart like a wheel / Caledonia / Mouth music / Aragon mill / Died for love / May morning dew / Lili Marlene / Foolish you
CD RTMCD 1
Round Tower / Feb '96 / Avid/BMG

FAREWELL TO EIREANN (Keane, Dolores & John Faulkner/Eamonn Curran)
CD CDTUT 724004
Wundertute / Oct '89 / ADA / CM / Duncans

LION IN A CAGE
I feel it in my bones / Lion in a cage / Room / Moorlough shore / Across the bridge / Walking on seashells / One golden rule / Island / Hold me
CD RTMCD 7
Round Tower / Jan '94 / Avid/BMG

SAIL OG RUA (Keane, Dolores & John Faulkner)
CD CEFCD 101
Gael Linn / Jan '94 / ADA / CM / Direct / Grapevine/PolyGram / Roots

SOLID GROUND
CD SHCD 8007
Shanachie / Mar '93 / ADA / Greensleeves / Koch
CD DARACD 065
Dara / Mar '95 / ADA / CM / Direct / Else / Grapevine/PolyGram

THERE WAS A MAID
Generous lover / Bantry girl's lament / My match is made / Lord Gordon's reel / Laurel bush / Johnny and Molly / Shaskeen reel / Lament for Owen Roe O'Neill / Seven yellow gypsies / Tommy Coen's reel / There was a maid in her father's garden / Carraroe jig / Whelan's jig / Bonnie bunch of roses
CD CC 23CD
Claddagh / Nov '90 / ADA / CM / Direct

Keane, James

ROLL AWAY THE REEL WORLD
Crossing the Shannon / Blooming meadows / Maud Miller's reels/The sailor's return
CD GLCD 1026
Green Linnet / '92 / ADA / CM / Direct / Highlander / Roots

THAT'S THE SPIRIT
CD GLCD 1138
Green Linnet / Jan '95 / ADA / CM / Direct / Highlander / Roots

Keane, Peter

WALKIN' AROUND
CD FF 652
Flying Fish / Sep '96 / ADA / CM / Direct / Roots

Keane, Rita

AT THE SETTING OF THE SUN
CD FIENDCD 771
Demon / Apr '96 / Pinnacle

Keane, Sean

FIRE AFLAME, THE (Keane, Sean & Matt Molloy & Liam O'Flynn)
Wheels of the world / Pinch of snuff/Micho Russell's reel / Bellharbour hornpipe/Old ruined cottage in the Glen / Geese in the bog/ Little fair cannavans/Whelan's old sow / Maid of Ballingarry/Stack of barley / JB Reel/Lads of Laois/Rambling thatcher / Drunken sailor / Night fishing 30th January 1972/Rights of man / Johnny 'Watt' Henry's reel/Jerry McMahon's reel / Pat Ward's jig/ Dusty Miller / Ask my Father/Connaught heifer / Casadh na nGeanna / Ace and deuce of pipering / Eire / Sean Ryan's reel /Grand spey
CD ____ CCF 30CD
Claddagh / Feb '93 / ADA / CM / Direct

GUSTY'S FROLICS
CD ____ CC 17CD
Claddagh / Nov '95 / ADA / CM / Direct

JIG IT IN STYLE
Baker/Miss Mary Walkr/The hawk/Marquis of Huntley / O'Farrel's welcome to Limerick/ Kitty come down from Limerick / Kiss the Maid behind the barrel / Dark Lochnagar / McLean of Pennycross/Maggie Cameron/ Duntroon Castle / Maiden that jigs it in style/Girl in the big house/Alasdruim / Tennessee stud/Arkansas traveller/Miss Susan Cooper / Bereton's reel/Bucks of Oranmore / Heartbreak hotel/Cliffs of Moher / Golden eagle/Tommy Hill's favourite / Willie's single/Glen road to Carrick / Blue angel/Strike the gay harp / Willie's fling / Atlantic roar / Margaret Jackson/Reavy's reel
CD ____ CCF 25CD
Claddagh / '90 / ADA / CM / Direct

TURN A PHRASE
CD ____ IND 001
Ind / May '96 / ADA

Keane, Sean

21 IRISH ACCORDION FAVOURITES
CD ____ WMCD 2001
Westmoor / Sep '94 / Target/BMG

ALL HEART, NO ROSES
CD ____ CBM 007CD
Cross Border Media / Nov '93 / ADA / Direct / Grapevine/PolyGram

Keane, Tommy

PIPERS APRON, THE
CD ____ CLUNCD 052
Mulligan / Aug '86 / ADA / CM

WIND AMONG THE REEDS, THE
CD ____ MMCCD 51
Maree Music / Oct '95 / ADA / Direct

Keating, Matt

CANDY VALENTINE
Candy valentine / Lonely blue / Emily / That kind of girl / All the rest
CD ____ A 092
Alias / Feb '96 / Vital

KILLJOY
Killjoy / Don't go the road alone / Bowery heights / Fruit you can't trust / Emily / You and me and this TV / Just to feel something / By the way / Roundabout way to get wise / While we fiddle / L word / Happy again
CD ____ A 093D
Alias / Apr '97 / Vital

SCARYAREA
Boxed inn / McHappiness / (I thought I heard my) Head exploding / Way to go / Pull some strings / Wrong God / Opportunist / Never fit in / Later October / You other face / All the rest / Naggin' feelin'
CD ____ A 069D
Alias / Oct '94 / Vital

TELL IT TO YOURSELF
Sanity in the asylum / Don't suffer in silence / When you don't have to work / Little talk / Lonely blue / Arrangements / Show me how / Nostalgia / So near, so far / '92 / Lost again / Hard place to be
CD ____ A 035D
Alias / Jun '93 / Vital

Keatons

BEIGE ALBUM, THE
CD ____ FSHH 7
Dogfish / Oct '94 / Plastic Head / SRD

Keats

KEATS
Heaven knows / Tragedy / Fight to win / Walking on ice / How can you walk away / Avalanche / Turn your heart around / Hollywood heart / Ask no questions / Night full of voices
CD ____ SEECD 447
See For Miles/C5 / Jul '96 / Pinnacle

Keb Mo'

JUST LIKE YOU
That's not love / Perpetual blues machine / More than one way home / I'm on your side / Just like you / You can love yourself / Dangerous mood / Action / Hand it over / Standin at the station / Momma / Where's my Daddy / Last fair deal gone down / Lullaby baby blues
CD ____ 4841172
Epic / Jun '96 / Sony

KEB MO'
Am I wrong / Come on in my kitchen / Dirty low down and bad / Don't try to explain / Kind hearted woman blues / City boy / Every morning / Tell everybody I know / Love blues / Victims of comfort / Angelina / Anybody seen my girl / She just wants to dance
CD ____ 4781732
Epic / Jul '95 / Sony

Kebnekajse

ELECTRIC MOUNTAIN
Barkbrodslaten / Polska fran harjedalan / Horgalaten / Eklundapolskan / Skanklat till spelman / Polska fran bingsjo / Rattvikarnas ganglat / Halling fran eksharad / Ganglat fran dala jarna / Comanche spring
CD ____ RESCD 503
Resource / Jul '97 / ADA / Direct

Kee, John

COLOUR BLIND
CD ____ VTYCD 001
Verity / Jun '94 / Pinnacle

Keel

LARGER THAN LIFE
CD ____ SPV 08512102
SPV / Aug '95 / Koch / Plastic Head

Keel, Howard

ALL TIME FAVOURITES
Hello / I've never been to me / Sometimes when we touch / Yesterday/Something / Send in the clowns / And I love you so / MacArthur Park / If / Theme from 'love story' / You needed me / Yesterday when I was young / What 50 said / This is all I ask / Always on my mind / With you I'm born again / I just called to say I love you / Just the way you are / Lady / Feelings / To all the girls I loved before / Both sides now / Memory
CD ____ WB 872022
Disky / Mar '97 / Disky / THE

BEST OF HOWARD KEEL, THE
Yesterday when I was young / Love letters / With you I am born again / Memory / Ol' man river / Make believe / If / And I love you so / Oh what a beautiful morning / Surrey with the fringe on top / People will say we're in love / Oklahoma / Softly as I leave you / Love story / Mr. Bojangles / Impossible dream / September song
CD ____ JHD 014
Tring / Jun '92 / Tring
CD ____ EMPRCD 559
Emporio / Mar '95 / Disc

CLOSE TO MY HEART
There's no business like show business / O what a beautiful morning / Secret love / Surrey with the fringe on top / If I loved you / Bless your beautiful hide / Wind beneath my wings / So in love / Make believe / Love changes everything / Bring him home / Prelude into music of the night / Colours of my life / Rose Marie
CD ____ CDKEEL 1
Premier/MFP / Apr '91 / EMI

ENCHANTED EVENING WITH HOWARD KEEL, A
Oklahoma medley / Some enchanted evening / This nearly was mine / I won't send roses / If ever I would leave you / La Mancha medley / You needed me / Love story / Come in from the rain / Yesterday / Something / Once upon a time / What are you doing for the rest of your life / Wave / MacArthur Park / Send in the clowns / You were always on my mind / I've never been to me / Annie get your gun medley
CD ____ MCCD 006
Music Club / Feb '91 / Disc / THE

FILM AND MUSICAL FAVOURITES
CD ____ 15093
Laserlight / May '94 / Target/BMG

GREAT SONGS, THE
CD ____ MU 5024
Musketeer / Oct '92 / Disc

VERY BEST OF HOWARD KEEL, THE
Oklahoma medley / Some enchanted evening / You needed me / Come in from the rain / Yesterday / Something / MacArthur Park / Send in the clowns / You were always on my mind / I've never been to me / And I love you / Memory / If / Love Story / Bless your beautiful hide / Showboat medley / Born again
CD ____ SUMCD 4121
Sound & Media / May '97 / Sound & Media

Keelaghan, James

MY SKIES
CD ____ GLCD 2112
Green Linnet / Jun '93 / ADA / CM / Direct / Highlander / Roots

RECENT FUTURE, A
CD ____ GLCD 2120
Green Linnet / Aug '95 / ADA / CM / Direct / Highlander / Roots

Keen, Robert Earl

BIGGER PIECE OF THE SKY, THE
So I can take my rest / Whenever kindness fail / Amarillo highway / Night right for love / Jesse with the long hair...Blow you away / Here in Arkansas / Daddy had a buick / Corpus Christie / Crazy cowboy dream / Paint the town beige
CD ____ SHCD 1037
Sugar Hill / Jul '93 / ADA / CM / Direct / Koch / Roots
CD ____ SPDCD 1048
Special Delivery / May '93 / ADA / CM / Direct

GRINGO HONEYMOON
Think it over one time / Tom ames prayer / Gringo honeymoon / Raven and the coyote / Lonely feeling / Merry Christmas from the family / Barbeque / Lynville train / I'm comin' home / Dreadful selfish crime
CD ____ SPDCD 1051
Special Delivery / Oct '94 / ADA / CM / Direct
CD ____ SHCD 1044
Sugar Hill / Jan '97 / ADA / CM / Direct / Koch / Roots

LIVE ALBUM, THE
I wanna know / Torch song / Goin' down in style / If I were King / Copenhagen / I would change my life / Stewball / I'll go on downtown / Bluegrass widow / Who'll be lookin' out for me
CD ____ SHCD 1024
Sugar Hill / Mar '88 / ADA / CM / Direct / Koch / Roots

NO KINDA DANCER
No kinda dancer / Front porch song / Between hello and goodbye / Swervin' in my lane / Christabel / Willie / Young lovers waltz / Death of tail Fitzsimmons / Rolling by / Armadillo jackal / Lu Ann / Coldest day of Winter
CD ____ SHCD 1049
Sugar Hill / Apr '95 / ADA / CM / Direct / Koch / Roots

NO.2 LIVE DINNER
I'm going to town / Gringo honeymoon / Merry Christmas from the family / Five pound bass / Rollin' by / Sonora's death row / When the bluebonnets bloom / Think it over one time / Amarillo highway / Road goes on forever / Dreadful selfish crime / Mariano / I'm comin' home
CD ____ SHCD 1051
Sugar Hill / Dec '96 / ADA / CM / Direct / Koch / Roots

PICNIC
Undone / Over the waterfall / Levelland / I wonder where my baby is tonight / Oh Rosie / Runnin' with the night / Coming of the son and brother / Fourth of July / Then cam lo mein
CD ____ 07822188342
Arista Austin / Jul '97 / BMG

WEST TEXTURES
Leavin' Tennessee / Maria / Sing one for sister / Road goes on forever / Sonora's death row / Don't turn out the light / Five pound bass / It's the little things / Jennifer Johnson and me / Mariano / Love's a word I never throw around
CD ____ SPDCD 1032
Special Delivery / Feb '90 / ADA / CM / Direct
CD ____ SHCD 1028
Sugar Hill / Jan '97 / ADA / CM / Direct / Koch / Roots

Keen, Speedy

Y'KNOW WHAT I MEAN
CD ____ EDCD 462
Edsel / Apr '96 / Pinnacle

Keenan, Brian

SOLO PIANO
CD ____ SACD 096
Solo Art / Jun '96 / Jazz Music

Keenan, Paddy

NA KEEN AFFAIR
CD ____ HCR 01CD
Hot Conya / May '97 / ADA

POIRT AN PHIOBAIRE
CD ____ CEFCD 099
Gael Linn / Jan '94 / ADA / CM / Direct / Grapevine/PolyGram / Roots

Keene, Tommy

DRIVING INTO THE SUN
Places that are gone / Nothing happened yesterday / Baby face / Back to zero / When the truth is found / Hey little child / Something got a hold of me / Real underground / Misunderstood / That you do / Mr. Roland / Back again / Safe in the light / People with fast cars drive fast / Love is the only thing that matters / Dull afternoon / Tattoo / Don't sleep in the daytime / Hey man / Andrea / Something to rave about / Sleeping on a rollercoaster
CD ____ A 059D
Alias / Apr '94 / Vital

TEN YEARS AFTER
Going out again / Turning on blue / Today and tomorrow / If your heart beats alone / If you're getting married tonight / On the runway / We started over again / Good thing going / Compromise / You can't wait for time / Before the lights go down / It's now true
CD ____ OLE 1772
Matador / Feb '96 / Vital

Keene, Verill

AFTERNOON AFFAIR, AN
CD ____ DFCD 71259
Del-Fi / Nov '96 / Cargo / Koch

Keepers

EVERY DOG IS A STAR
CD ____ LCD 80010
Lizard / May '97 / Direct / RTM/Disc

LOOKING FOR A SIGN
CD ____ LIZARD 80003
Lizard / Mar '95 / Direct / RTM/Disc

Keezer, Geoff

GEOFF KEEZER TRIO 1993
CD ____ SKCD 2039
Sackville / Jul '96 / Cadillac / Jazz Music / Swift

OTHER SPHERES
CD ____ DIW 871
DIW / Jul '93 / Cadillac / Harmonia Mundi

Keiji, Haino

ALLEGORICAL MISUNDERSTANDING
CD ____ AVAN 008
Avant / Sep '93 / Cadillac / Harmonia Mundi

Keineg, Katell

JET
Battle of the trees / One hell of a life / Smile / Enzo '96 / Ole, conquistador / Leonor / Veni vidi vici / Venus / Mother's map / Marietta / Hoping and praying / There you go
CD ____ 7559620522
Elektra / Jul '97 / Warner Music

Keita, Salif

SORO
Wamba / Soro / Souareba / Sina / Cono / Sanni Kegniba
CD ____ STCD 1020
Stern's / Mar '89 / ADA / CM / Stern's
CD ____ IMCD 243
Island / Mar '97 / PolyGram

SOSIE
CD ____ DKMS 96001
Mellemfolkeligt / Jan '97 / Stern's

Keith, Ben

SEVEN GATES - A CHRISTMAS ALBUM
CD ____ 9362457732
Warner Bros. / Nov '94 / Warner Music

Keith, Bill

BEATING AROUND THE BUSH
Beating around the bush / Don't let your deal go down / Cherokee shuffle / Liebestraum / Bay state bounce / Step lively / Drop in the bucket / Little old log cabin / Old hickory / Ready for the times / Bending the strings / Hornswoggled / Crab waltz
CD ____ GLCD 2107
Green Linnet / Feb '93 / ADA / CM / Direct / Highlander / Roots

Keith, Toby

BLUE MOON
Lonely / Every night / Closin' time at home / Woman's touch / Does that blue moon ever shine on you / Lucky me / She's perfect / She's gonna get it / Me too / Hello
CD ____ 5311922
A&M / Aug '96 / PolyGram

Kellaway, Roger

ALONE TOGETHER (Kellaway, Roger & Red Mitchell)
Alone together / Just friends / I should care / I surrender dear / Blue blues / It's a wonderful world / Dear old Stockholm / Emily
CD ____ DRCD 168
Dragon / Apr '89 / ADA / Cadillac / CM / Roots / Wellard

FIFTY FIFTY (Kellaway, Roger & Red Mitchell)
CD ____ CDNI 4014
Natasha / Apr '93 / ADA / Cadillac / CM / Direct / Jazz Music

LIFE'S A TAKE (Kellaway, Roger & Red Mitchell)
If I were a bell / Mean to me / I have the feeling I've been here before / Life's a mistake / Lover man / It's a wonderful world /

Take the 'A' train / Have you met Miss Jones
CD CCD 4551
Concord Jazz / May '93 / New Note/ Pinnacle

LIVE AT MAYBECK RECITAL HALL VOL.11
How deep is the ocean / I'm still in love with you / Love of my life / Close your eyes / New Orleans / My one and only love / Creole love call / I'm getting sentimental over you
CD CCD 4470
Concord Jazz / Jul '91 / New Note/Pinnacle

PORTRAIT OF ROGER KELLAWAY
CD FSRCD 147
Fresh Sound / Dec '90 / Discovery / Jazz Music

ROGER KELLAWAY MEETS GENE BERTONCINI & MICHAEL MOORE (Kellaway, Roger & Gene Bertoncini/ Michael Moore)
CD CRD 315
Chiaroscuro / Mar '96 / Jazz Music

Keller, Greta

THESE FOOLISH THINGS (25 Romantic Songs 1931-1938)
These foolish things / I apologise / Blues in my heart / All of me / Just friends / Faded summer love / Speak to me of love / Paradise / I don't stand a ghost of a chance with you / Say it isn't so / Zwischen heute und morgen / Die musik spielt ganz leise / Kleine melodie / Sag beim abschied / Bird on the wing / Would you / Did you mean it / They can't take that from me / Thanks for the memory / Once in a while / My fine feathered friend / You leave me breathless / So little time / Lights out / Auf wiederseh'n, my dear
CD CDAJA 5193
Living Era / May '96 / Select

Kelley Deal 6000

GO TO THE SUGAR ALTAR
Canyon / How about hero / Dammit / Sugar / Hundred tires / Head of the cult / Nice / Trixie delicious / Marooned / Tick tock / Mr. Goodnight
CD BIT 007CD
Bittersweet / Aug '96 / Vital

Kellso, Jon Erik

CHAPTER 1
CD ARCD 9125
Arbors Jazz / Nov '94 / Cadillac

Kelly, Alan

OUT OF THE BLUE
Red haired lass / Fleur de Mandragore / Gusty's frolics / Beautiful lake Ainslie / Bearhaven lassies / Trip to Dingle / Lough Isle Castle / Dancing eyes / Commodore / Spootiskerry / Far road to Sligo / Reel de Pointe-au-pic
CD BMM 001CD
Black Box Music / May '97 / ADA / Direct

Kelly Brothers

SANCTIFIED SOUTHERN SOUL
Falling in love again / You're that great big feelin' / My love grows stronger / I've got my baby (and that's enough) / Make me glad / I'd rather have you / Counting on you / Time has made me / Got the feeling / You're the most / Love time / Can't stand it no longer / If that will hold you / How can true love be this way / Ouch oh baby / I'll be right there / Just walk on / You put your touch on me / Hanging in there / That's what you mean to me / Comin' on in / That's how I am / I got this feeling / Stop these tears / Haven't I been good to you / If it wasn't for your love / It takes you / My baby loves me
CD CDKEND 137
Kent / Aug '96 / Pinnacle

Kelly, Dave

BEST OF THE 80'S
CD RPM 118
RPM / Oct '93 / Pinnacle

DAVE KELLY BAND LIVE
CD APCD 033
Appaloosa / '92 / ADA / Direct / TKO Magnum

MAKING WHOOPEE 1979-1982 (Kelly, Dave Band)
makin' whoopee / Hey baby / Ungrateful / Return to sender / Put your money where your mouth is / I'm into something good / Best part of breaking up / It feels right / Dawn surprise / You're gonna make me lonesome when you go / Two more bottles of wine / Red red wine / House lights / Don't cha hang up the phone / Can't win 'em all / Time after time / When I'm dead and gone / That's why / My heart in your hands / Worried man / Lights out
CD RPM 118
RPM / Oct '93 / Pinnacle

STANDING AT THE CROSSROADS (Kelly, Dave Band)
One way out / When I itch / It hurts me to / Big river / Okie / Smokestack lightning / Worried man / Crossroads / Leaving / Weight / Grits and groceries / Back in the blues / To love somebody / Poor man
CD INAK 8807CD
In Akustik / Jul '97 / Direct / TKO Magnum

WAITING FOR BESSIE (Kelly, Dave Band)
Give me my money / Come back to me / Blind man / Back in the blues / Still believe in you / Waiting for Bessie / Mais oui / Just shouldn't be that way / Love is a compromise / It isn't love / Straight line (to my heart) / Come kiss me love / Crying in the rain / Tongue tied / Foreign station / Hard to find a heart / You rocked me / Gael's blue / Glad I'm living / Ee do do qua qua
CD GEMCD 009
Diamond / Feb '97 / Pinnacle

Kelly, Ed

ED KELLY & PHAROAH SANDERS (Kelly, Ed & Pharoah Sanders)
Rainbow song / Newborn / You send me / Pippin / Answer me my love / You've got to have freedom / Song for the street people / West Oakland strutt / Lift every voice / Just the two of us / Well you needn't
CD ECD 22056
Evidence / Jul '93 / ADA / Cadillac / Harmonia Mundi

Kelly Family

ALMOST HEAVEN
When the boys come into town / Every baby / I can't help myself / Nanana / You belong to me / Staying alive / Come back to me / Fell in love with an alien / Hey diddle diddle / Like a queen / Stars fall from heaven / Thunder / Calling heaven / Nothing like home
CD PRMDCD 21
Premier/EMI / Apr '97 / EMI

OVER THE HUMP
Why why why / Father's nose / First time / Baby smile / Cover the road / She's crazy / Ares qui / Key to my heart / Roses of red / Once in a while / Break free / Angel / Wolf / Santa Maria
CD CDEMC 3713
EMI / Jun '95 / EMI

Kelly, Gene

GENE KELLY
CD DVGH 7082
Deja Vu / May '95 / THE

Kelly, Jack

1933-1939 (Kelly, Jack & His South Memphis Jug Band)
CD BDCD 6005
Blues Document / '91 / ADA / Hot Shot / Jazz Music

Kelly, James

TRADITIONAL MUSIC OF IRELAND
CD SH 34014
Shanachie / Apr '95 / ADA / Greensleeves / Koch

Kelly, Jo Ann

JUST RESTLESS (Kelly, Jo Ann Band)
CD APCD 028
Appaloosa / Feb '96 / ADA / Direct / TKO Magnum

STANDING AT THE BURYING GROUND (Kelly, Jo Ann & 'Mississippi' Fred McDowell)
61 Highway / Red cross store / When I lay my burden down / Evil hearted woman / I asked for whiskey, she brought me gasoline / Standing at the burying ground / Glory hallelujah / Write me a few of your lines / My baby done me wrong / Shake 'em on down / Louise / My babe / Waves of the water / Kokomo
CD NEBCD 851
Sequel / Aug '96 / BMG

WOMEN IN (E)MOTION FESTIVAL
CD T&M 110
Tradition & Moderne / Dec '95 / ADA / Direct

Kelly, John

IN THE UNIQUE WEST CLARE STYLE (Kelly, John & James)
CD PTICD 1041
Outlet / Oct '95 / ADA / CM / Direct / Duncans / Koch / Ross

IRISH TRADITIONAL FIDDLE MUSIC (Kelly, John & James)
CD PTICD 1041
Pure Traditional Irish / Jul '95 / ADA / CM / Direct / Ross

Kelly, Kirk

GO MAN GO
CD SST 223CD
SST / Jan '89 / Plastic Head

Kelly, Luke

COLLECTION, THE
CD CHCD 1041
Chyme / Aug '94 / ADA / CM / Direct / Koch

IRISH FAVOURITES VOL.1 (Kelly, Luke & Dubliners)
Raglan Road / Whiskey in the jar / Donegal Danny / Old triangle / Spancil Hill / Black velvet band / Town I loved so well / Dirty old town / McAlpine's fusiliers / Song for Ireland / All for me grog / Molly Malone
CD CHCD 1033
Chyme / Apr '93 / ADA / CM / Direct / Koch

IRISH FAVOURITES VOL.2 (Kelly, Luke & Dubliners)
Rare ould times / Fiddlers green / Biddy Mulligan / Avondale / Wild rover / Seven drunken nights / Finnegan's wake / Weila weila weila / Foggy dew / Lord of the dance / Johnston's motorcar / Farewell to Ireland
CD Set CHCD 1034
Chyme / Apr '93 / ADA / CM / Direct / Koch

LUKE KELLY ALBUM, THE (Kelly, Luke & Dubliners)
Button pusher / Scorn not his simplicity / Sun is burning / Blantyre explosion / For what died the sons of Roisin / Town I loved so well / Rare ould times / Dirty old town / Foggy dew / Farewell to Carlingford / Parcel o' rogues / Bunclody / dainty Davie / Unquiet grave
CD CHCD 1016
Chyme / Jul '93 / ADA / CM / Direct / Koch

LUKE'S LEGACY (Kelly, Luke & Dubliners)
Song for Ireland / Wild rover / School days over / Monto / Joe Hill / Auld triangle / Whiskey in the jar / Raglan road / Hand me down me bible / Free the people / Peat bog soldiers / Lifeboat Mona / Springhill disaster / Gartan mothers lullaby
CD CHCD 1031
Chyme / May '89 / ADA / CM / Direct / Koch

Kelly, Nick

BETWEEN TRAPEZES
CD CDSP 001
Self Possessed / May '97 / Shellshock/ Disc

Kelly, Paul

COMEDY
CD TVD 93343
Mushroom / Jan '95 / 3mv/Pinnacle

DEEPER WATER
CD TVD 93340
Mushroom / Oct '95 / 3mv/Pinnacle

GONNA STICK & STAY
CD BB 9523CD
Bullseye Blues / May '93 / Direct

HIDDEN THINGS
CD D 30748
Mushroom / Mar '95 / 3mv/Pinnacle

LIVE
CD D 16061
Mushroom / Feb '95 / 3mv/Pinnacle

LOST
CD D 19467
Mushroom / Mar '95 / 3mv/Pinnacle

WANTED MAN
Summer rain / God's hotel / She's rare / Just like animals / Love never runs out on time / Song from thee 16th floor / Maybe this time for sure / Ball and chain / Still picking the same sore / Everybody wants to touch me / We've started a fire / Lately / Nuhkanya
CD FIENDCD 758
Demon / Aug '94 / Pinnacle

Kelly, Sandy

MUSICAL TRIBUTE TO PATSY CLINE, A
CD KCD 347
K-Tel / Mar '94 / K-Tel

Kelly, Sean

50 SCOTTISH CELILDH ACCORDION FAVOURTIES
CD CDSCOT 050
Outlet / Oct '95 / ADA / CM / Direct / Duncans / Koch / Ross

CELTIC JEWELS VOL.1 (A Classic Collection Of Irish Instrumental Airs & Melodies) (Kelly, Sean Ensemble)
CD CDIRISH 017
Outlet / Apr '97 / ADA / CM / Direct / Duncans / Koch / Ross

CELTIC TRANQUILITY (Kelly, Sean Ensemble)
CD CHCD 1043
Chyme / Jan '95 / ADA / CM / Direct / Koch

Kelly, Wynton

FULL VIEW (Kelly, Wynton Trio)
I want a little girl / I thought / What a difference a day made / Autumn leaves / Don'tcha hear me callin' to ya / On a clear day (you can see forever) / Scufflin' / Born to be blue / Walk on by
CD OJCCD 912
Original Jazz Classics / May '97 / Complete/ Pinnacle / Jazz Music / Wellard

LAST TRIO SESSION
CD DD 441
Delmark / Aug '94 / ADA / Cadillac / CM / Direct / Hot Shot

TAKIN' CHARGE
CD LEJAZZCD 16
Le Jazz / Jun '93 / Cadillac / Koch

Kelsall, Phil

ALL I ASK OF YOU
Clarinet polka / All I ask of you / Waltzing in the clouds / Two hearts in waltz time / I just called to say I love you / Circus Renz / Embraceable you / I got plenty o' nuttin' / Liza / Svanee / Swanee / Dizzy fingers / Music of the night / Rouge et noir / Come to Fiona's wedding / If I can help somebody / I only have eyes for you / My melancholy baby / Poor butterfly / Romeo / Don't say goodbye / Your eyes / Love is a many splendoured thing / I'm in the mood for love / I'll see you in my dreams
CD GRACC 23
Grasmere / May '94 / Highlander / Savoy / Target/BMG

BLACKPOOL MAGIC
Entry of the gladiators / Sanctuary of the heart / Chattanooga choo choo / You'll never know / September in the rain / Jeepers creepers / Shadows on the Seine / Russian flag / For you alone / Shuffle off to Buffalo / About a quarter to nine / Shadow waltz / Dames, young and healthy / Lullaby of Broadway / 42nd Street / Coronation scot / Dubarry waltz / Dardanella / Pied Piper / Chanson d'amour / Old fashioned way / Can't smile without you / Bless this house / Rag doll / Paradise for two / My gal's a yorkshire gal / In the twi-twi-twilight / In the shade of the old apple tree / Wonderful guy / My favourite things / Wonderful, wonderful day
CD GRCD 43
Grasmere / '91 / Highlander / Savoy / Target/BMG

BLUE VELVET
Delicado / I dreamed a dream / Doll dance / Drigo's seranade / Chihuahua / Wind beneath my wings / Easy winners / Bluebells polka / Voices of spring / Flea market / Music from across the way / In the shadows / Meditation from Thais / Tambourin / Blue velvet / Barcarolle / I'm getting sentimental over you / I don't want to walk without you / Goodnight sweetheart / Masquerade
CD GRCD 47
Grasmere / '92 / Highlander / Savoy / Target/BMG

CENTENARY SPECIAL
CD SOW 517
Sound Waves / Jul '94 / Target/BMG

COME DANCING AT THE TOWER BALLROOM
You're driving me crazy / I wonder where my baby is tonight / Lulu's back in town / Doin' the raccoon / Anniversary waltz / When I grow too old to dream / Tammy / Charmaine / Am I blue / September song / Blue moon / Sweet and lovely / Whatever Lola wants (Lola gets) / Adios muchachos / Tower ballroom tango / Should I / Sweet and gentle / Kiss me honey, honey kiss me / Greey eyes / Sway / More than ever / Magic is the moonlight / Pierrette / Mademoiselle from Armentieres / Man who broke the bank at Monte Carlo / Wot'cher (Knocked 'em in the Old Kent Road) / Constantinople / I'm Henery the Eighth (I am) / Down forget-me-not Lane / I leave my heart in an english garden / Try a little tenderness / Moonlight bay / Chalk farm to Camberwell Green / Are we to part like this, Bill / Let me call you sweetheart / Bird in a gilded cage / Kind regards / Tiddley on pom / Morning promenade / Cindy swing / Dear hearts and gentle people / Back in your own backyard / Nice people / What can I say after I say I'm sorry / Linger awhile
CD GRCD 50
Grasmere / '92 / Highlander / Savoy / Target/BMG

CONGRATULATIONS
CD GRCD 62
Grasmere / Mar '94 / Highlander / Savoy / Target/BMG

DANCING TIME
Dancing time / Dancing with my shadow / Good morning / All I do is dream of you / In Marble Halls / Zigeuner / I'll see you again / Over the rainbow / I know why (and so do you) / Love me or leave me / Lonesome and sorry / Annietamento / Midnight tango / Summertime in Venice / Non Dimenticar / Till the end of time / On Green Dolphin Street / Itsy bitsy teeny weeny yellow polka dot bikini / Talk to the animals / More I see you / No can do / It's a long way to Tipperary / Pack up your troubles / Who were you with last night / Just as long as the world goes 'round and around / 'Deed I do / Little Dolly Daydream / Little dutch mill / On the air / Moonlight brings memories /

Rock-a-bye your baby / Buddy can you spare a dime / Puff the magic dragon / I'd like to teach the world to sing / Oh oh Antonio / I'm shy Mary Ellen / Can't we sing love's old sweet song again / One day when we were young / Wonderful world of the young / Guaglione / Namur / I love the sunshine of your smile / Jolly good company / Heartaches / I found a new baby / Dinah / Bill Bailey, won't you please come home / She'll be comin' round the mountain / When the Saints
CD _ GRCD 74
Grasmere / Mar '96 / Highlander / Savoy / Target/BMG

I DO LIKE TO BE BESIDE THE SEASIDE
Oh I do like to be beside the seaside / Darling buds of May / Nights of gladness / Amazing grace / South Rampart street parade / At last / Goodbye blues / He loves and she loves / How long has this been going on / Our love is here to stay / Bye bye blues / Farewell blues / Soon / They all laughed / Liza / Blackpool belle / Friends for life (Amigos para siempre) / Crystal chandeliers / Crazy / Blanket on the ground / Colonel Bogey / Sprinkling tam / Parade of the tin soldiers / Holy city / Dance of comedians
CD _ GRCD 58
Grasmere / Jun '93 / Highlander / Savoy / Target/BMG

LOVE CHANGES EVERYTHING
Heyken's first serenade / Morgens um sieben / Happy talk / I enjoy being a girl / Hello, young lovers / Love changes everything / Roses from the South / True love / Let's do it / Wunderbar / Just one of those things / Choo choo samba / Trudie / Petite waltz / Plink plank plunk / Tango in D (Abeniz) / Exactly like you / Way down yonder in New Orleans / T'ain't what you do (it's the way that you do it) / Braes of Strathnaver / Two sleepy people / For all we know / World is waiting for the sunrise / Romeo / Don't say goodbye / Your eyes / Rouge et noir
CD _ GRCD 36
Grasmere / Sep '89 / Highlander / Savoy / Target/BMG

MEMORIES ARE MADE OF THIS
CD _ GRCD 67
Grasmere / Apr '95 / Highlander / Savoy / Target/BMG

MY WAY (Plays The Technics SX-FA 1)
Tritsch tratsch polka / Sailing by / Miss Chatelaine / Le cygne/The swan / Buffoon / Dear Lord and father of mankind / Salut d'amour / Mack and Mabel / Thunderbirds / Memories of Martha / Berceuse from the Dolly Suite / Bel viso polka / Folks who live on the hill/Can't help singing/I'm old fashio / Ball-scene / My way
CD _ GRCD 78
Grasmere / Oct '96 / Highlander / Savoy / Target/BMG

PHIL KELSALL AT THE YAMAHA FX20
hors d'oeuvres / I won't dance / Stepping out with my baby / Love's last word is spoken / Shadow waltz / Emmeline / Innamorata / If I didn't care / Body and soul / Unchained melody / Romance in A minor / Perhaps, perhaps, perhaps / Garden in Granada / More I see you / Amor / Cocktails for two / Tangerine / Carioca / South American way / It had better be tonight / Boogie woogie bugle boy from Company B / Dolores / Every little while / I don't want to set the world on fire / J'Attendrai / Chapel in the moonlight / Soldiers in the park / Soldiers of the Queen / Take me back to dear old blighty / Hold your hand out, naughty boy / Blame it on the Bossa Nova / Meditation / I was never kissed before / Someday my Prince will come / Say you will not forget / Love's dream after the ball / Tell me I'm forgiven / Cafe in Vienna / Whispering tango / Birth of the blues / Back home in Tennessee / Nevertheless / Music maestro please / We're gonna hang out the washing on the Siegfried Line / I've got sixpence / Five minutes more / Rolling around the world / Walking the floor / Please don't talk about me when I'm gone
CD _ GRCD 60
Grasmere / Oct '93 / Highlander / Savoy / Target/BMG

PHIL KELSALL SELECTION
Shuffle off to Buffalo / About a Quarter to Nine / Shadow waltz / Dames / Coronation Scot / Catari, catari / Come back to Sorrento / Santa Lucia / Oh Maria Mari, Funiculi, Funicula / Pretty little black eyed Susie / Singin' the blues / Chicka boom / Dance of the comedians / You're driving me crazy / I wonder where my baby is tonight / Pink Lady / Paradise / Wyoming lullaby / Put me amongst the girls / Jolly good company beside the sea / When the guards are on parade / Tower Ballroom tango / Dancing with tears in my eyes / Diane / I love the moon / Garden in the rain / Rose of Washington Square / I'll string along with you / Bless 'em all / Band played on / Ash Grove / Daisy Bell / Circus Renz / My song of love / Two hearts in waltz time / Waltzing in the clouds / Choo choo samba / Braes of Strathnaver / Flea market / I dreamed a dream / Phantom of the Opera
CD _ GROSCD 1
Grasmere / Oct '93 / Highlander / Savoy / Target/BMG

SEQUENCE OF DANCING FAVOURITES
I can't give you anything but love / Chicago / Hello Dolly / After you've gone / Dancing with tears in my eyes / Diane / I love the moon / Memories of you / Stars fell on Alabama / Make mine love / There's no other love / El choclo / Oh Rosalita / How wonderful to know / Always in my heart / Indian summer / A-you're adorable / One / Frenesi / Take the 'A' train / You're sixteen / Tower ballroom jive / That's my weekness now / Moonstruck / If I had a talking picture of you / Put me amongst the girls / Jolly good company beside the sea / When the guards are on parade / PS I love you / Louise / Polka dots and moonbeams / Meet me tonight in Dreamland / Three o'clock in the morning / Eton boating song / If I had my way / Glad rag doll / Broken doll / Goodbye-ee / In the good old summertime / Tulips from Amsterdam / By the side of the Zuyder Zee / Mother Machree / Keep young and beautiful / Varsity drag / Black bottom / Charleston
CD _ GRCD 39
Grasmere / May '90 / Highlander / Savoy / Target/BMG

SOME ENCHANTED EVENING
Phantom of the opera / Some enchanted evening / Thoroughly modern Millie / No no Nanette / Hey there / Can't help lovin' dat man / And this is my beloved / I've got the sun in the morning and the moon at night / I whistle a happy tune / Best of times / I don't know how to love him / March of the siamese children / Out of my dreams / Girl that I marry / Waltz at Maxim's / If I loved you / Wouldn't it be loverly / Spring, spring, spring / Mame / Any dream will do / Leap year waltz / Highwayman love / Fold your wings / One flower grows alone in your garden / One alone / Indian love call / Wonderful day like today / There is nothin' like a dame / Do re mi / I could have danced all night / Oklahoma
CD _ GRCD 54
Grasmere / Oct '92 / Highlander / Savoy / Target/BMG

SWINGING SLEIGH BELLS
CD _ GRCD 70
Grasmere / Oct '95 / Highlander / Savoy / Target/BMG

THANK YOU FOR THE MUSIC
Waterloo / Hasta Manana / Money, money, money / Cavatina / As time goes by / Thanks for the memory / Shine / God bless our love / Floral dance / Love story / Somewhere my love / Bridge too far / All creatures great and small / Pass me by / Stein song / Hey look me over / Around the world / Kiss me again / Dream lover / Whispering / Change partners / Five foot two, eyes of blue / Who pays the ferryman / Enemy at the door / Here, there and everywhere / When I'm sixty four / All my loving / Sailing / Casatschok / Rasputin / Midnight in Moscow / Devil's gallop / World of sport march / Out of the blue / Match of the day / Agadoo / Under the linden tree / Out of nowhere / Only you / When the day is done / Cha Cha Chas / In a little Spanish town / Want to be happy, I / Orange coloured sky / Home (when shadows fall) / She's funny that way / By a waterfall / Irish lullaby / How can you buy Killarney / Believe me, if all those endearing young charms / Everything stops for tea / Underneath the arches / Ragtime cowboy Joe / Crazy people / Sweet Sue, just you / If you knew Susie like I know Susie / Ma, he's making eyes at me / Scotch broth / Hundred pipers / Campbells are coming / Fernando / Dancing queen / Thank you for the music
CD Set _ CDDL 1206
Music For Pleasure / May '91 / EMI

TIME FOR DANCING
Mr. Sandman / Avalon / Crazy rhythm / Dancing with tears in my eyes / Diane / Love the moon / Memories of you / Stars fell on Alabama / Make mine love / Bewitched, bothered and bewildered / Love in bloom / Someone to watch over me / Here's that rainy day / La golondrina / Cherry pink and apple blossom white / Por favor / Skater's waltz / Spanish gypsy dance / Nagasaki / Little red monkey / One the prom prom promenade / Consider yourself / Garden in the rain / Rose of Washington Square / I'll string along with you / Girl from Ipanema / Destination love / There's no other love / El choclo / Oh Rosalita / La cumparsita / Pink Lady / Paradise / Wyoming lullaby / Little white lies / Happy feet / It's just the time for dancing / If I had my way / Glad rag doll / Broken doll / Goodbye-ee / Blees' em all / Band played on / Ash grove / Daisy bell / Tip toe through the tulips / Don't know why (I just do) / My Mammy / Scotch mist
CD _ PWKS 4210
Carlton / Aug '94 / Carlton

UP, UP AND AWAY
Czardas / Anything goes/You're the top/ Buddy beware / I get a kick out of you / I believe / South American Joe / Gold and silver waltz / Old rugged cross / Snowbird/ Happy anniversary/I love you because / Take me home country roads / Stardust / Gimme dat ding / Diamonds are a girls' best friend / Up, up and away / Under the double eagle / Among my souvenirs/An affair to remember / You're just in love / Mack the knife / Serenade in blue / Mattinata/Ciribiribin / Hawaiian samba / Be my love/Because / Come fly with me/You make me feel so young / Lady is a tramp
CD _ GRCD 80
Grasmere / Mar '97 / Highlander / Savoy / Target/BMG

Kelsey, Rev.

REV. KELSEY 1947-1951
CD _ DOCD 5478
Document / Sep '96 / ADA / Hot Shot / Jazz Music

Keltz

MYSTERY OF AMERGIN
Mystery of Amergin / Sineads reel / Vijays / Tune for Aidan / Leons jig / Little fiery one part 1 / Little fiery one part 2 / Garten mother's lullaby / Ginepo leer / Oak tree / Reel for Farzanch / Logan water / Blackbird
CD _ CDLDL 1247
Lochshore / Jan '97 / ADA / Direct / Duncans

PRINCE OF PEACE
Gate / Siyah Chal / Mountains of Sulaymaniyyih / Exile / Garden of Ridvan / Reel of revelation / Release jig / Ascension
CD _ IRCD 024
Iona / Jan '94 / ADA / Direct / Duncans

Kelvynator

REFUNKANATION
CD _ EMY 1302
Enemy / Mar '92 / Grapevine/PolyGram

Kemener, Yann-Fanch

ENEZ EUSA
CD _ L'OZ 02
L'Oz / May '96 / ADA

GWERZIOU AND SONIOU
CD _ YFK 01CD
YFK / Nov '96 / ADA

ILE EXIL (Kemener, Yann-Fanch & Didier Squiban)
CD _ L'OZ 011CD
L'Oz / Nov '96 / ADA

Kemp, Gary

LITTLE BRUISES
Standing in love (the still point) / Brother heart / Inexperienced man / Wasted / Little bruises / Ophelia drowning / She said / Shadowman / These are the days (born under twins) / My lady soul
CD _ 4795732
Columbia / Oct '95 / Sony

Kemp, Hal

HAL KEMP & ORCHESTRA 1934-36
CD _ CCD 25
Circle / Apr '94 / Jazz Music / Swift / Wellard

Kemp, Rick

ESCAPE
What you see is what you get / Brampton to Roadhead blues / Over my head / Deep in the darkest night / Nobody put you on the train / Waiting for a miracle / Queen of light / Phoenix / Genocide / Fighting on the same side / Escape / Somewhere along the road
CD _ FECD 114
Fellside / Jan '97 / ADA / Direct / Target/ BMG

Kemp, Tara

TARA KEMP
Prologue / Hold you tight / Be my lover / Too much / One love / Tara by the way / Piece of my heart / Together / Way you make me feel / Something to groove to / Monday love / Epilogue
CD _ 7599244082
WEA / May '91 / Warner Music

Kemperle, Bagad

KEJADENN
CD _ Y225023
Silex / Jun '93 / ADA / Harmonia Mundi

Kendall Turner Overdrive

DISPLACED LINKS
Turbine / Mechanism / Pedal stop / Sump / Cylinder / Shift / Beached driver / Dismantle
CD _ CDPSST 4
Mute / Feb '97 / RTM/Disc

Kendall, Steve

SCOTTISH COUNTRY DANCING (Kendall, Steve & The Glencastle Sound)
CD _ 300792
Hallmark / Jan '97 / Carlton

Kendrick, Graham

IS ANYONE THIRSTY
Is anyone thirsty / Psalm 126 / Wake up o sleeper / How good and how pleasant / I was made for this / Knowing you / For this I have Jesus / Let me fill the room / Day of his power / Declare his glory
CD _ ALD 035
Alliance Music / Sep '95 / EMI

LAMB OF GOD
Great is the Lord / Rejoice / Let praise arise / Sing for joy in the Lord / His love endures forever / Lord have mercy / Lamb of God / My heart overflows / Think about His love / Lord thy God / Steadfast love of the Lord / Thou art worthy / Song for the nations
CD _ HMD 505
Nelson Word / Jan '88 / Nelson Word

MEEKNESS AND MAJESTY
All heaven waits / Come and see Jesus / Stand among us / Led like a lamb / Like a candle flame / Lord, have mercy on us / Meekness and majesty / O Lord / Restore / O Lord, the clouds are gathering / Servant King / Shine, Jesus, shine / Price is paid / This is my beloved son / Who can sound the depths of sorrow
CD _ KMCD 931
Kingsway / Apr '97 / Complete/Pinnacle

Kendrick, Keith

HOME GROUND
CD _ FECD 118
Fellside / Mar '97 / ADA / Direct / Target/ BMG

Kendrick, Matt

COMPOSITE
CD _ ICH 1166CD
Ichiban / May '94 / Direct / Koch

Kendrick, Rodney

DANCE, WORLD, DANCE
Cogent / Santeria / Love is the answer / Totem / Son is / We need mercy / Little sweeter / Last day / Mr. Bruce is back
CD _ 5219372
Verve / Oct '94 / PolyGram

LAST CHANCE FOR COMMON SENSE
CD _ 5315362
Verve / Jul '96 / PolyGram

SECRETS OF RODNEY KENDRICK, THE
Slide the world into place / Ganawa in Paris / New world is ordered / Berkshire blues / Dig / Sharon / Slick exit / Takin' it with me / Down here below
CD _ 5175582
Verve / Jul '93 / PolyGram

Keneally, Mike

HALF ALIVE IN HOLLYWOOD (2CD Set) (Keneally, Mike & Beer For Dolphins)
CD Set _ TVDCD 204
Third Venture / Aug '97 / Grapevine/ PolyGram

Kenickie

AT THE CLUB
In your car / People we want / Spies / How I was made / Brother John / Millionaire sweeper / Robot song / Classy / Punka / Nightlife / PVC / Come out 2 nite / I never complain / Acetone / Montrose gimps it up for charity
CD _ ADISCCD 002
EMI / Sep '97 / EMI

Kenkulian, Hrant

UDI HRANT KENKILIAN
CD _ CD 4265
Traditional Crossroads / Dec '94 / CM / Direct

Kennedy, Brian

BETTER MAN, A
Better man / For one kiss / Won't you take me home / No other words / And so I will wait for you / Life, love and happiness / Oldest dream in the world / Put the message in the box / By the mountain road / Ghost music / Wish me well
CD _ 74321409132
RCA / Oct '96 / BMG

Kennedy, Fiona

MAIDEN IN HEAVEN
CD _ CD 001
Colin Campbell / Nov '95 / Duncans

Kennedy, Frankie

ALTAN (Kennedy, Frankie & Mairead)
Highlandman / An Seanchaileach Gallda / Ta mo Chleamhnas a Dheanamh / Cat that ate the candle / Ceol A'Phiobaire / Tommy Peoploe's loch Altan / Danny Meehan's / Rogha an Ghabha / Sunset / Thug me Ruide / Humours of whiskey / Jimmy Lyon's Les / Citi na cumann / Con Cassidy's highland reel
CD _ GLCD 1078

Green Linnet / Apr '93 / ADA / CM / Direct / Highlander / Roots

Kennedy, Joan

CANDLE IN THE WIND
CD 322543
Koch International / Dec '95 / Koch

HIGHER GROUND
CD 341072
Koch International / Dec '95 / Koch

Kennedy, Nigel

KAFKA
Autumn regrets / I believe in God / Transfigured night / Melody in the wind / From Adam to Eve / Fallen forest / Innig / Soleil levant sur la Seine / New road / Solitude / Breathing stone
CD CDEMD 1095
EMI / Jun '96 / EMI

Kennedy, Pete

LIFE IS LARGE (Kennedy, Pete & Maura)
CD GL 2123CD
Green Linnet / May '96 / ADA / CM / Direct / Highlander / Roots

RIVER OF FALLEN STARS (Kennedy, Pete & Maura)
River of fallen stars / Same old way / Month of hours / Wall of death / Day in and day out / Winterheart / Fortune Teller Road / Stephen's green / House on fire / Run the red horses / Life goes on without you / Chelsea Embankment / Spirit compass
CD GLCD 2116
Green Linnet / Feb '95 / ADA / CM / Direct / Highlander / Roots

Kennedy, Ronnie

THOSE WERE THE DAYS
Those were the days / Dingle regatta / Irish medley / Whistling Rufus / Alpine slopes/ Jacqueline waltz / Country favourites medley / Looking for a partner / Lara's theme / Scottish medley / Birdie song / Cuckoo waltz / Bluebell polka / Edelweiss
CD RITZCD 514
Ritz / '91 / Pinnacle

Kennedy, Ross

GATHERING STORMS (Kennedy, Ross & Archie McAllister)
CD CDLDL 1243
Lochshore / Aug '96 / ADA / Direct / Duncans

TWISTED SINGERS (Kennedy, Ross & Archie McAllister)
CD CDLDL 1218
Lochshore / Oct '94 / ADA / Direct / Duncans

Kennedy, Tom

BASSES LOADED
Songs for Sara / Caravan / Hey eyes / Alfred's book / Crystal / Made in New York / I'll see you / All of you / Oleo
CD TKM 50022
TKM / May '96 / New Note/Pinnacle

Kennel, Hans

MYTHA
CD ARTCD 6110
Hat Art / Aug '92 / Cadillac / Harmonia Mundi

MYTHAHORNS VOL.2
CD ARTCD 6151
Hat Art / Apr '95 / Cadillac / Harmonia Mundi

STELLA
Meltdown / Moosruef / No.17 / Stella by starlight / Snobben / Varvisa / Inca Princess / Du liebe bueb vom emmital
CD TCB 97102
TCB / Apr '97 / New Note/Pinnacle

Kenney, Beverly

COME SWING WITH ME
CD FSCD 560
Fresh Sound / Feb '88 / Discovery / Jazz Music

Kenny & The Kasuals

IMPACT
CD FLASH 26
Flash / Jul '97 / Greyhound

THINGS GETTING BETTER/NOTHING BETTER TO DO
CD EVA 642390B39
EVA / Nov '94 / ADA / Direct

Kenny G

BREATHLESS
Joy of life / Forever in love / In the rain / Sentimental / By the time this night is over / End on the night / Morning / Even if my heart would break / G bop / Sister Rose / Year ago / Homeland / Natural ride / Wedding song / Alone
CD 07822186462
Arista / Mar '93 / BMG

DUOTONES
You make me believe / Slip of the tongue / What does it take (to win your love) / Don't make me wait for love / Sade / Esther / Songbird / Champagne / Midnight / Three of a kind
CD 258497
Arista / Feb '96 / BMG

G FORCE
Hi, how ya doin' / I've been missing you / Tribeca / G force / Do me right / I wanna be yours / Sunset at noon / Help yourself to my love
CD 259059
Arista / May '88 / BMG

GRAVITY
Love on the rise / One man's poison (another man's sweetness) / Where do we take it (from here) / One night stand / Japan / Sax attack / Virgin island / Gravity / Last night of the year
CD 74321161642
Arista / Feb '94 / BMG

KENNY G
Mercy mercy mercy / Here we are / Stop and go / I can't tell you why / Shuffle / Tell me / Find a way / Crystal mountain / Come close
CD 259337
Arista / Sep '95 / BMG

MIRACLES - THE HOLIDAY ALBUM
Winter wonderland / White christmas / Have yourself a merry little christmas / Christmas song / Silent night / Brahms lullaby / Greensleeves / Miracles / Away in a manger / Chanukah song / Little drummer boy / Silver bells / Spring breeze
CD 07822187672
Arista / Oct '95 / BMG

MOMENT, THE
Moment / Passages / Havana / Always / That somebody was you / Champion's theme / Eastside jam / Moonlight / Gettin' on the step / Everytime I close my eyes / Northern lights / Innocence
CD 07822189682
Arista / Apr '97 / BMG

MONTAGE
Songbird / I can't tell you why / Tribeca / Virgin island / I've been missing you / Uncle Al / What does it take (to win your love): *Kenny G & Ellis Hall* / Silhouette / Midnight motion / Against doctor's orders / Hi, how ya doin' / Sade / Going home / We've saved the best for last: *Kenny G & Smokey Robinson*
CD 260621
Arista / Apr '90 / BMG

SILHOUETTE
Silhouette / We've saved the best for last / Trade winds / I'll be alright / Against doctor's orders / Pastel / All in one night / Let go / Home / Summer song
CD 259284
Arista / Jul '96 / BMG

Kenny, Gerard

EVENING WITH GERARD KENNY, AN
CD ACLCD 100
Westmoor / Jun '95 / Target/BMG

PLAY ME SOME PORTER PLEASE (Kenny, Gerard & Royal Philharmonic Orchestra)
Play me some Porter please / Anything goes / Night and day / Miss Otis regrets / True love / Begin the beguine / From this moment on / Every time we say goodbye / So in love / I've got you under my skin
CD CDWM 106
Westmoor / May '92 / Target/BMG

Kenny, John

VOICE OF THE CARNYX, THE
CD BML 016
British Music / Feb '96 / Forties Recording Company

Kenso

KENSO
CD ARC 1003
Arc / Jan '96 / Harmonia Mundi

YUME NO OKA
CD 14534
Spalax / Jul '97 / ADA / Cargo / Direct / Discovery / Greyhound

Kenstroll

MUSIQUES VIVANTES
CD KD 95CD
Kan Dazont / Mar '96 / ADA

Kent 3

STORIES OF THE NEW WEST
CD SUPER 08CD
Super Electro / May '97 / Cargo

Kent, Stacey

CLOSE YOUR EYES
More than you know / Dream dancing / Close your eyes / There's a lull in my life / It's de-lovely / There's no you / I'm old fashioned / You go to my head / Little white lies / Sleep warm / Day in, day out
CD CCD 79737
Candid / May '97 / Cadillac / Direct / Jazz Music / Koch / Wellard

Kent, Willie

AIN'T IT NICE
Memory of you / Check it out / Worry worry / One more mile / Ain't it nice / What you're doing to me / I'm good / Ma Bea's / Come home / Feel so good / Stranded
CD DD 653
Delmark / Mar '97 / ADA / Cadillac / CM / Direct / Hot Shot

LONG WAY TO OL' MISS
Long way to ol' miss / Blues in my bedroom / Dirty works / It ain't right / Ain't got long to stay / My friend / Don't know much about love / Extension 309 / All my life / Ain't no love in your heart / Don't drive me away / Black night / What you doin' to me
CD DE 696
Delmark / Jun '97 / ADA / Cadillac / CM / Direct / Hot Shot

TOO HURT TO CRY
Too hurt to cry / Going down the road / Man and the blues / Willie Mae / Blues train / Just sitting here thinking / Good man feeling bad / This thing called love / 911 / In case we both are wrong / Night time is the right time / Countdown / All nite long
CD DE 667
Delmark / Mar '97 / ADA / Cadillac / CM / Direct / Hot Shot

Kenton, Stan

18 ORIGINAL BIG BAND RECORDINGS
CD HCD 407
Hindsight / Sep '92 / Jazz Music / Target/ BMG

1952 - 1956 INTERMISSION RIFF (Kenton, Stan Orchestra)
CD CD 53109
Giants Of Jazz / Jun '92 / Cadillac / Jazz Music / Target/BMG

23 DEGREES NORTH, 82 DEGREES WEST (Live 1952-1953) (Kenton, Stan Orchestra)
Theme (Artistry in rhythm) and opening announcements: *Kenton, Stan* / Works: *Kenton, Stan* / Yesterdays: *Kenton, Stan* / Swinghouse: *Kenton, Stan* / Stan Kenton speaks: *Kenton, Stan* / Gone with the wind: *Kenton, Stan* / There will never be another you: *Kenton, Stan* / Theme (Artistry in rhythm) and opening announcements: *Kenton, Stan* / Love for sale: *Kenton, Stan* / Over the rainbow: *Kenton, Stan* / Hava Havana: *Kenton, Stan* / Frank speaking: *Kenton, Stan* / I'll remember April: *Kenton, Stan* / Young blood: *Kenton, Stan* / Street of dreams: *Kenton, Stan* / Blue moon: *Kenton, Stan* / Bill's blues: *Kenton, Stan* / Lover man: *Kenton, Stan* / Collaboration: *Kenton, Stan* / 23 degrees North, 82 degrees West: *Kenton, Stan* / My lady: *Kenton, Stan* / Bill's blues: *Kenton, Stan*
CD VN 1007
Viper's Nest / Nov '96 / ADA / Cadillac / Direct / Jazz Music

ARTISTRY IN RHYTHM
CD JHR 73540
Jazz Hour / May '93 / Cadillac / Jazz Music / Target/BMG

AT FOUNTAIN STREET CHURCH VOL.1
CD DSTS 1014
Status / Oct '95 / Harmonia Mundi / Jazz Music / Wellard

AT FOUNTAIN STREET CHURCH VOL.2
CD DSTS 1016
Status / Oct '95 / Harmonia Mundi / Jazz Music / Wellard

AT MARCH FIELD AIR FORCE BASE, CALIFORNIA DECEMBER 1959 (Previously Unissued Recordings) (Kenton, Stan Orchestra)
Street of dreams / I'm glad there is you / Young and foolish / Where or when / How deep is the ocean / My heart stood still / All of you / Early Autumn / Chocolate caliente / Night we called it a day / You better go now / They didn't believe me / Twilight riff / Take the 'A' train / September song/Stardust / Eager beaver/Dynaflow/Jump for Joe/Artistry in rhythm
CD DSTS 1011
Status / May '95 / Harmonia Mundi / Jazz Music / Wellard

AT THE HOLIDAY BALLROOM, CHICAGO 1962
CD DSTS 1018
Status / May '96 / Harmonia Mundi / Jazz Music / Wellard

AT THE PAVILION, HEMEL HEMPSTEAD 1973
CD DSTS 1017
Status / May '96 / Harmonia Mundi / Jazz Music / Wellard

AT THE RENDEZVOUS VOL.1
My old flame / Out of this world / Time on my hands / Tequila / I hear music / Cuban mumble / Artistry in rhythm / Jump for Joe / Kingfish / Eager beaver / Glad to be unhappy
CD STATUSCD 102
Status / Mar '90 / Cadillac

AT THE RENDEZVOUS VOL.2
Beyond the blue horizon / I concentrate on you / Begin the beguine / Everything happens to me / Get out of town / Nice work if you can get it / Old devil moon / Take the 'A' train / I get along without you very well / When Sunny gets blue / Nightingale / They didn't believe me / Street of dreams / Wind / I should care / I remember you
CD STATUSCD 108
Status / Nov '90 / Cadillac

BALLAD STYLE OF STAN KENTON
hen I'll be tired of you / More than you know / When stars looked down / End of a love affair / Sunday kind of love / Moon song / Early autumn / How am I to know / Things we did last summer / We'll be together again / How deep is the ocean / Night we called it a day / Ill wind
CD CDP 8566882
Capitol Jazz / Jul '97 / EMI

BEST OF STAN KENTON, THE
CD DLCD 4012
Dixie Live / Mar '95 / TKO Magnum

BEST OF STAN KENTON, THE
Artistry in rhythm / Eager beaver / Artistry jumps / Painted rhythm / Intermission riff / Collaboration / Lover / Unison riff / Peanut vendor / Interlude / Love for sale / Laura / Twelve degrees north / Invention for guitar and trumpet / Stompin' at the Savoy / La suerte de los tontos (fortune of fools) / Waltz of prophets / Malageuna
CD CDP 8315042
Capitol Jazz / Apr '95 / EMI

BROADCAST TRANSMISSIONS 1941-1945
CD CD 883
Music & Arts / Sep '95 / Cadillac / Harmonia Mundi

CLASSICS 1940-1944
CD CLASSICS 848
Classics / Nov '95 / Discovery / Jazz Music

CLASSICS 1945
CD CLASSICS 898
Classics / Oct '96 / Discovery / Jazz Music

CONCERT IN MINIATURE ENCORES 1952-53
CD N 14017
Natasha / Oct '93 / ADA / Cadillac / CM / Direct / Jazz Music

EARLY CONCEPTS
CD LEJAZZCD 54
Le Jazz / Jan '96 / Cadillac / Koch

FESTIVAL OF MODERN AMERICAN JAZZ
Opening / Theme of four valves / Saxonia / Sam meets the Mambo / Cuba jazz / Sweets / That old black magic / Pennies from heaven / Improvisation / Fearless Finlay
CD STATUSCD 101
Status / Mar '90 / Cadillac

LIVE AT BARSTOW 1960 (Kenton, Stan Orchestra)
CD DSTS 1001
Status / May '94 / Harmonia Mundi / Jazz Music / Wellard

LIVE AT CARTHAGE COLLEGE VOL.1 (Kenton, Stan Orchestra)
CD DAWE 69
Magic / May '94 / Cadillac / Harmonia Mundi / Jazz Music / Swift / Wellard

LIVE AT CARTHAGE COLLEGE VOL.2 (Kenton, Stan Orchestra)
Here's that rainy day / 2002 - Zarathustrevisited / Macarthur park / Peanut vendor / Street of dreams / Malaguena / Artistry in rhythm / Happy birthday to you / Take the 'A' train
CD DAWE 70
Magic / Jun '94 / Cadillac / Harmonia Mundi / Jazz Music / Swift / Wellard

LIVE AT PALO ALTO 1955
CD STATUSCD 112
Status / '92 / Cadillac

LIVE AT SALT LAKE CITY VOL.1
CD DAWE 56
Magic / Feb '94 / Cadillac / Harmonia Mundi / Jazz Music / Swift / Wellard

LIVE AT SALT LAKE CITY VOL.2
CD DAWE 57
Magic / Nov '92 / Cadillac / Harmonia Mundi / Jazz Music / Swift / Wellard

LIVE AT SALT LAKE CITY VOL.3
CD DAWE 58
Magic / Nov '92 / Cadillac / Harmonia Mundi / Jazz Music / Swift / Wellard

LIVE AT THE LAS VEGAS TROPICANA
Artistry in rhythm / Bernie's tune / Tuxedo junction / Street scene / Puck's blues / This is always / Don't get around much anymore / Design for blue / Home journey / String of pearls / It's alright with me / Intermission riff / I concentrate on you / End of a love affair / You and I and George / Sentimental riff / Random riff
CD CDP 8352452
Capitol Jazz / Apr '96 / EMI

LIVE AT THE LONDON HILTON 1973
CD DSTS 1003
Status / '94 / Harmonia Mundi / Jazz Music / Wellard

LIVE AT THE MACUMBA CLUB
El Congo Valiente / Fuego Cubano / Big chase / My funny valentine / Opener / I concentrate on you / I remember you / Harlem nocturne / Between the Devil and the deep blue sea / Swing house / Love for sale / Royal blue / Artistry in rhythm
CD DAWE 53
Magic / Nov '91 / Cadillac / Harmonia Mundi / Jazz Music / Swift / Wellard

LIVE AT THE MACUMBA CLUB - SAN FRANCISCO 1956
Walking shoes / Autumn nocturne / Artistry in rhythm / Winter in Madrid / My old flame / La suerte de los tontos (Fortune of fools) / I concentrate on you / Theme on variations / Young blood / Collaboration / Stella by starlight / Cherokee / Intermission riff / Laura / Stompin' at the Savoy / Out of nowhere
CD DAWE 50
Magic / '91 / Cadillac / Harmonia Mundi / Jazz Music / Swift / Wellard

LIVE AT THE SUNSET RIDGE CLUB 1976
CD DAWE 59
Magic / Cadillac / Harmonia Mundi / Jazz Music / Swift / Wellard

LIVE AT THE SUNSET RIDGE CLUB 1976 VOL.2
CD DAWE 61
Magic / Mar '93 / Cadillac / Harmonia Mundi / Jazz Music / Swift / Wellard

LIVE IN 1951
CD EBCD 21052
Flyright / Feb '94 / Hot Shot / Jazz Music / Wellard

LIVE IN BILOXI (Kenton, Stan Orchestra & The Four Freshmen)
Lasuerte de los tontos / I concentrate on you / Lullaby of Broadway / Nearness of you / Kingfish / Early Autumn / Love for sale / My old flame / Yesterdays / Out of nowhere / Night we called it a day / Everything happens to me / There will never be another you / So in love / With the wind and rain in your hair / Big chase
CD DAWE 32
Magic / Apr '89 / Cadillac / Harmonia Mundi / Jazz Music / Swift / Wellard

LIVE IN COLOGNE 1976 VOL.1
CD DAWE 64
Magic / Jul '93 / Cadillac / Harmonia Mundi / Jazz Music / Swift / Wellard

LIVE IN COLOGNE 1976 VOL.2
CD DAWE 65
Magic / Jul '93 / Cadillac / Harmonia Mundi / Jazz Music / Swift / Wellard

LIVE IN LONDON (1972)
CD 8204662
London / Aug '87 / PolyGram

LONDON HILTON VOL.2 1973
CD DSTS 1005
Status / Dec '94 / Harmonia Mundi / Jazz Music / Wellard

MELLOPHONIUM MAGIC 1962 (Kenton, Stan Orchestra & The Four Freshmen)
All the things you are / Suddenly it's Spring / Reuben's blues / Tuxedo blues / Tenderly / Foggy day / East of the sun and west of the moon / You stepped out of a dream / Take me in your arms / Saga of the blues
CD STATUSCD 103
Status / Mar '90 / Cadillac

MELLOPHONIUM MOODS 1962
Lullaby of Birdland / Reuben's blues / Like someone in love / Cha cha sombrero / Misty / Easy to love / Caress the sea / Exit stage left / Blues story / Angel eyes / Blue ointment / How long has this been going on / Dragonwyck / Night at the gold nugget / Fitz
CD STATUSCD 106
Status / Nov '90 / Cadillac

MORE MELLOPHONIUM MOODS
Fly me to the moon / Foggy day / Misty / You stepped out of a dream / Reuben's blues / Magic moment / Blues story / Easy to love / Warm blue stream / Lot of livin' to do / My one and only love / Maria / Time after time / Love walked in / Like someone in love / Eager beaver/Opus in chartreuse/ Dynaflow/Jump for Joe / Java junction/Tea for two / Artistry in rhythm
CD DSTS 1010
Status / Apr '95 / Harmonia Mundi / Jazz Music / Wellard

NEW CONCEPTS OF ARTISTRY IN RHYTHM (Kenton, Stan Orchestra)
Twenty three degrees north - eighty two degrees west / Portrait of a count / Invention for guitar and trumpet / My lady / Young blood / Frank speaking / Prologue (this is an orchestra) / Improvisation / Taboo / Lonesome train (on a lonesome track) / Swing house / You go to my head
CD CZ 299
Pacific Jazz / Apr '90 / EMI

ON AIR
CD DSTS 1019
Status / Jul '96 / Harmonia Mundi / Jazz Music / Wellard

ONE NIGHT STAND (Kenton, Stan Orchestra)
CD DAWE 66
Magic / Dec '93 / Cadillac / Harmonia Mundi / Jazz Music / Swift / Wellard

OPUS IN PASTELS
CD CD 56023
Jazz Roots / Aug '94 / Target/BMG

PLAYS BOB GRAETTINGER CITY OF GLASS
Thermopylae / Everything happens to me / Incident in jazz / House of strings / Horn / City of glass (first movements part 1 to 4) / Orchestra / Trumpet / You got to my head / Cello / Modern opus / Reflections / Dance before the mirror / Entrance into the city
CD CDP 8320842
Capitol Jazz / Aug '95 / EMI

RARE RECORDINGS
CD 15725
Laserlight / Sep '92 / Target/BMG

RED HILL INN PENNSAUKEN NEW JERSEY 1959
Home journey / Laura / Frenesi / Mexican jumping bean / Lazy afternoon / Street scene / Bernie's tune / Lush life / Night in Tunisia / Thrill is gone / Obu / Opas in pastels
CD STATUSCD 104
Status / Mar '90 / Cadillac

RENDEZVOUS OF STANDARDS AND CLASSICS (A Collection Of Five Albums 2CD Set)
Artistry in rhythm / Eager beaver / Collaboration / Peanut vendor / Intermission riff / Concerto to end all concertos / Artistry jumps / Sophisticated lady / Begin the beguine / Lover man / Pennies from heaven / Over the rainbow / Fascinating rhythm / There's a small hotel / Shadow waltz / Tampico / Artistry in boogie / Southern scandal / Machito / Her tears flowed like wine / Minor riff / Across the valley from the Alamo / Unison riff / April in Paris / How high the moon / Crazy rhythm / I got it bad and that ain't good / You and the night and the music / Under a blanket of blue / I've got you under my skin / Autumn in New York / With the wind and rain in your hair / Memories of you / These things you left me / Two shades of autumn / They didn't believe me / Walkin' by the river / High on a windy hill / Love letters / I get along without you very well / Desiderata / This is no laughing matters / I see your face before me
CD Set CDDL 1293
Music For Pleasure / Jun '95 / EMI

STAN KENTON
CD 22714
Music / Jul '95 / Target/BMG

STAN KENTON & HIS INNOVATIONS ORCHESTRA (Kenton, Stan Orchestra)
Spirals / Ennui / In Veradero / Shelly Manne / Conte Candoli / Art Pepper / Improvisation / Love for sale / Bob Cooper / Reflections
CD 15770
Laserlight / May '94 / Target/BMG

STAN KENTON & HIS INNOVATIONS ORCHESTRA/JUNE CHRISTY 1950 (2CD Set) (Kenton, Stan Innovations Orchestra & June Christy)
CD Set EBCD 2131/32
Jazzband / Apr '97 / Cadillac / Hot Shot / Jazz Music / Wellard

STAN KENTON & HIS ORCHESTRA
Artistry in rhythm / Intermission riff / Way you look tonight / When I fall in love / Lullaby of broadway / Party's over / I've never been in love before / You'd be so nice to come home to / Mission trail / How deep is the ocean / Tuxedo junction / Begin the beguine / Younger than springtime / Prelude to a kiss / Cha cha sombero / Stardust / Siesta / When your lover has gone / Medley
CD CD 53217
Giants Of Jazz / Jul '97 / Cadillac / Jazz Music / Target/BMG

STAN KENTON & JAZZ LADIES
And the bull walked around olay: *Kenton, Stan & Chris Connor* / All about Ronnie: *Kenton, Stan & Chris Connor* / Jeepers creepers: *Kenton, Stan & Chris Connor* / If I should lose you: *Kenton, Stan & Chris Connor* / I get a kick out of you: *Kenton, Stan & Chris Connor* / Lonesome train (on a lonesome track): *Kenton, Stan & Kay Brown* / Lot of livin' to do: *Kenton, Stan & Jean Turner* / It's a big, wide, wonderful world: *Kenton, Stan & Jean Turner* / Black coffee: *Kenton, Stan & Ann Richards* / Thrill is gone: *Kenton, Stan & Ann Richards* / Don't be that way: *Kenton, Stan & Ann Richards* / I got rhythm: *Kenton, Stan & Ann Richards* / Morning after: *Kenton, Stan & Ann Richards* / Daddy: *Kenton, Stan & June Christy* / Ain't no misery in me: *Kenton, Stan & June Christy* / Willow weep for me: *Kenton, Stan & June Christy* / Across the valley from the Alamo: *Kenton, Stan & June Christy* / It's been a long long time: *Kenton, Stan & June Christy* / Shoo fly pie and apple pan dowdy: *Kenton, Stan & June Christy* / Just a sittin' and a rockin': *Kenton, Stan & June Christy* / Tampico: *Kenton, Stan & June Christy* / And her tears flowed like wine: *Kenton, Stan & Anita O'Day* / Gotta be gettin': *Kenton, Stan & Anita O'Day* / Are you livin' old man: *Kenton, Stan & Anita O'Day* / I'm going mad for a pad: *Kenton, Stan & Anita O'Day*
CD CD 53240
Giants Of Jazz / Oct '96 / Cadillac / Jazz Music / Target/BMG

STAN KENTON IN HI FI
Artistry jumps / Interlude / Intermission riff / Minor riff / Collaboration / Painted rhythm / Southern scandal / Peanut vendor / Eager Beaver / Concerto to end all concertos / Artistry in boogie / Lover / Unison riff / Opus in pastels / Machito / Artistry in rhythm / Minor riff (alt. take)
CD CZ 511
Capitol / Jul '92 / EMI

STAN KENTON LIVE
CD NI 4017
Natasha / May '93 / ADA / Cadillac / CM / Direct / Jazz Music

STREET OF DREAMS (Kenton, Stan Orchestra & The Four Freshmen)
Send in the clowns: *Kenton, Stan* / Rhapsody in blue: *Kenton, Stan* / Street of dreams: *Kenton, Stan* / Body and soul: *Kenton, Stan* / Tiare: *Kenton, Stan* / Too shy to say: *Kenton, Stan* / My funny valentine: *Kenton, Stan*
CD STD 1079
GNP Crescendo / Jun '95 / ZYX

TRANSCRIPTION PERFORMANCES 1945-1946, THE
CD HEPCD 47
Hep / Jan '97 / Cadillac / Jazz Music / New Note/Pinnacle / Wellard

UKIAH, 1959
How deep is the ocean / Walking shoes / Nearness of you / Lullaby of Broadway / Where or when / End of a love affair / Artistry in rhythm / Jump for Joe / Tenderly
CD STATUSCD 109
Status / Jan '91 / Cadillac

UNCOLLECTED VOL.2 1941, THE
Congo clambake / Arkansas traveller / Shuffling the chords / Take sixteen / Opus in pastels / Reed rapture / Etude for saxophones / Tribute to flatted fifth / Quit your show / Underneath the stars / Let her go / Too soon / Hold back the dawn / Low bridge / Popocatepeil / Blue fafre
CD HCD 124
Hindsight / Apr '95 / Jazz Music / Target/ BMG

Kentucky Boys

FELT SO WILD
CD PT 612001
Part / Jun '96 / Nervous

I WANT IT HOT
CD PT 612003
Part / Dec '96 / Nervous

Kentucky Colonels

APPALACHIAN SWING
Clinch mountain backstep / Nine pound hammer / Listen to the mockingbird / Wild Bill Jones / Billy in the lowground / Lee Highway blues / I am a pilgrim / Prisoner's song / Sally Goodin / Faded love / John Henry / Flat fork
CD ROUSS 31CD
Rounder / Aug '93 / ADA / CM / Direct

KENTUCKY COLONELS
Clinch Mountain back-step / Nine pound hammer / Listen to the mocking bird / Wild Bill Jones / Billy in the low ground / Lee Highway / That's what you get for loving me / I am a pilgrim / Prisoner's song / Sally Goodin / Ballad of Farmer Brown / Faded love / John Henry / Flat fork
CD BGOCD 357
Beat Goes On / Jul '97 / Pinnacle

LONG JOURNEY HOME
Roll on buddy / Bill Cheetham / There ain't nobody gonna miss me when I'm gone / Shuckin' the corn / Beautiful life / Get down on your knees and pray / Over in the glory land / Sally Ann / Brakeman's blues / Soldier's joy / Listen to the mockingbird / Farewell blues / Lonesome road blues / Beaumont rag / Footprints in the snow / Long journey home / In the pines / Chicken reel / Old hickory / Auld lang syne / Nola / Flat fork / Shady grove
CD VCD 77004
Vanguard / Oct '95 / ADA / Pinnacle

Kentucky Minstrels

KENTUCKY MINSTRELS, THE
Banjo song medley / Holy city / White wings / Passing by / Song that reached my heart / Kentucky Minstrels plantation medley no.1 / Smilin' through / Last rose of summer / Rose of Tralee / Love's old sweet song / Carry me back to green pastures / I'll walk beside you / Bless this house / O dry those tears / Christopher Robin is saying his prayers / Homing
CD CDAJA 5229
Living Era / Jul '97 / Select

Kenyatta

KENYATTA
Touch me / Turn me on / Baby can I hold you / Good vibes / Love again / I wanna do something freaky to you / Keep me comin' / R U ready / Feels so nice / Thank you (for loving me like you do) / I wanna do something freaky to you (ragga mix) / Love again (Mix)
CD BRCDX 568
4th & Broadway / Apr '92 / PolyGram

Kenyatta, Robin

GHOST STORIES
CD ITM 970060
ITM / Apr '91 / Koch / Tradelink

ROBIN KENYATTA'S FREE STATE BAND
CD 500572
Musidisc / May '94 / Discovery

TAKE THE HEAT OFF ME
CD ITMP 970069
ITM / Mar '92 / Koch / Tradelink

Kepone

KEPONE
CD QS 46CD
Quarter Stick / Apr '97 / Cargo / SRD

SKIN
CD QS 33CD
Quarter Stick / Sep '95 / Cargo / SRD

UGLY DANCE
CD QS 27CD
Quarter Stick / Aug '94 / Cargo / SRD

Keppard, Freddie

COMPLETE FREDDIE KEPPARD 1923-27
CD KJ 111FS
King Jazz / Oct '93 / Cadillac / Discovery / Jazz Music

LEGEND, THE
CD TPZ 1052
Topaz Jazz / Aug '96 / Cadillac / Pinnacle

NEW ORLEANS GIANTS VOL.2 1922-28 (Keppard, Freddie & Ory/Dodds/carey)
CD 152222
Hot 'n' Sweet / Dec '93 / Discovery

Kerbdog

ON THE TURN
Sally / JJ's song / Didn't even try / Mexican wave / Severed / Pledge / On the turn / Secure / Lesser shelf / Pointless / Rewind / Sorry for the record
CD 5329992
Vertigo / Mar '97 / PolyGram

TOTALLY SWITCHED
End of green / Dry riser / Dead anyway / Cleaver / Earthworks / Dummy crusher / Inseminator / Clock / Schism / Scram
CD 5188662
Vertigo / Apr '94 / PolyGram

Kerleo, Gwenael

TERRE CELTE
CD KER 01CD
KER / Nov '96 / ADA

Kern, Jerome

ALL THE THINGS YOU ARE (Jerome Kern Songbook) (Various Artists)
CD 5299072
Verve / May '96 / PolyGram

FINE ROMANCE - THE JEROME KERN SONGBOOK (Various Artists)
CD 5238272
PolyGram Jazz / Jan '95 / PolyGram

GREAT MELODIES, THE (Kern, Jerome/ Irving Berlin)
Smoke gets in your eyes / Fine romance / I won't dance / All the things you are / Way you look tonight / Who / Dearly beloved / Song is you / Ol' man river / Alexander's ragtime band / Puttin' on the Ritz / White christmas / Cheek to cheek / I've got my love to keep me warm / Change partners / They say it's wonderful / Medley (tribute to Irving Berlin)
CD 300612
Hallmark / Jul '96 / Carlton

SITTING PRETTY
CD 803872
New World / Aug '92 / ADA / Cadillac / Harmonia Mundi

TRIBUTE TO JEROME KERN, A (Various Artists)
Folks who live on the hill: *Lee, Peggy* / Fine romance: *Tilton, Martha* / Last time I saw Paris: *Four Freshmen* / Way you look tonight: *Haymes, Dick* / I'm old fashioned: *Garland, Judy* / Look for the silver lining: *Brent, Tony* / Ol' man river: *Wiata, Iniate* / Yesterdays: *Stafford, Jo* / They don't believe me: *Alberghetti, Anna Maria* / Long ago and far away: *Cardinali, Roberto & the Rita Williams singers* / I still suits me: *Wiata, Iniate* / How do you like to spoon with me: *Hunt, Jan* / Why was I born: *Washington, Dinah* / Sure thing: *Simpson, Carole* / Bojangles of Harlem: *Gonella, Nat* / All through the day: *Geraldo* / Who: *Shore, Dinah* / Bill: *Laine, Cleo* / Lovely to look at: *MacRae, Gordon* / I won't dance: *Lee, Peggy* / Smoke gets in your eyes: *Hilton, Ronnie* / Song is you: *Smith, Keely* / Make believe: *Lee, Peggy* / Nobody else but me: *Laine, Cleo* / Who do I love you: *Dallas, Lorna* / Pick yourself up: *Cordell, Frank* / Can't help lovin' dat man: *Bassey, Shirley* / You were never lovelier: *Lewis, Archie* / Can I forget you: *Lewis, Archie* / You are love: *Dallas, Lorna* / Life upon the wicked stage: *Bryan, Dora* / I might fall back on you: *Bryan, Dora* / Moon love: *Silvester, Victor* / I've told every little star: *Vernon Girls* / You wouldn't be cuter: *Geraldo* / Waltz in swingtime: *Martin, Skip* / Dearly beloved: *Wilson, Nancy* / Daydreaming: *Osbourne, Tony* / All the things you are: *May, Billy* / In love in vain: *Horne, Lena*
CD Set ______ **CDDL 1290**
EMI / Jun '95 / EMI

YESTERDAYS (The Jerome Kern Songbook) (Various Artists)
CD ______ **5333312**
Verve / May '97 / PolyGram

Kern, Renate

DU BIST MEINE LIEBE
Kiss and shake / Die Welt ist so schon wie ein traum / Kommt nict in frage / Du bist meine liebe / Eine Welt fur uns zwei / Weine keine Abschiedstranen / Bis morgen / Ganz genau wie du / Lass den Dummen Kummer / Weinen tut so weh / An irgendeinem Tag / Du musst mir die Wahrheit sagen / Stop the beat / Damals in Napoli / Ein schlaflose nacht / Ein mann - ein wort / Lieber mal weinen im gluck / Traurigsein lohnt sich nicht / Du musst mit den Wimpern klimpern / Herbstwind / Lass doch den Sonnenschein / Meine welt ist schon / Now and then / You'll be the first one to know / I'll remember summer / Love me tonight / Happy heart
CD ______ **BCD 16201**
Bear Family / Jun '97 / Direct / Rollercoaster / Swift

ER NAHM EIN ANDERES MADCHEN
Lieber heute gekusst / Einsamkeit / 1990 / Come on let's dance / Der wasserman / Hor auf den herz / Supermann / Silber und gold / Alle blumen brauchen sonne / Das schonste land der welt / Warum willst du weinen / Er nahm ein anderes madchen / Lass mich heute nicht allein / Auf dir lacht einmal die liebe / Geh'mit Gott / Qua la Linta / Morgen fruh, da lachst du schon wieder / Rinaldo Rinaldini / Das macht diese Welt erst richtig schon / Meine welt ist von heute an deine welt / Andiamo, amigo / Mach es wie die Sonnenuhr / Adio / Non, jene regrette rien / You'll never walk alone
CD ______ **BCD 16202**
Bear Family / Jun '97 / Direct / Rollercoaster / Swift

Kerosene

ARRHYTHMIA
Spring / Everybody's icon / Worthless / Excess / Shame / Come alive / My friends / Everything / Mercy / So plain / Joanne / Feeling within
CD ______ **9362452792**
WEA / Oct '93 / Warner Music

Kerosene 454

CAME BY TO KILL ME
CD ______ **DIS 1115CD**
Dischord / Feb '^7 / SRD

Kerr, Alec

CELTIC SOFT WINDS
CD ______ **CHCD 020**
Chart / May '96 / Direct / Koch

ECHOES OF IRELAND (Kerr, Alec & Sandra Townsend/Brian Lynch)
Danny Boy / Carrickfergus / Moon behind the hill / Come back Paddy Reilly / Boolavogue / For Ireland I'd tell not her name / Rose of Tralee / Molly Malone / Banks of my own lovely Lee / Coulin / Sweet vale of Avoca / Mountains of Mourne / Spinning wheel / Caoineadh an spailpin / Green glens of Antrim / Noreen Bawn / Old bog road / Down by the Sally Gardens / Galway Bay / If we only had old Ireland over here / Forty shades of green / Flight of the Earls / Wind and the willows
CD ______ **CHCD 027**
Chart / May '96 / Direct / Koch

Kerr, Moira

ALL THE BEST
Maclain of Glencoe / Where eagles fly / Skye boat song / Loch Lomond / Dark island / Banquo's walk / Sands of time / Drifting away / Mingulay boat song / Everlasting visions / Paradise for two / Cuillin
CD ______ **MOICD 010**
Moidart / Nov '96 / Conifer/BMG

BE THOU MY VISION
Be thou my vision / Who would true valour see / I vow to thee my country / Holy holy holy / Teach me, my God and King / O thou camest from above / By cool Siloam's shady rill / Stand up, stand up for Jesus / Dear Lord and Father of mankind / Immortal, invisible, God only wise / Forty days and forty nights / Breathe on me, breath of God / Alleluia, sing to Jesus / Jerusalem
CD ______ **CFTMCD 01**
Tangmere / Mar '95 / Conifer/BMG

BRAVEST HEART
Bravest heart / Corryvreckan / She moved through the fair / Only a woman's heart / Island in the mist / Queens Four Marys / Fear a bhata / For justice and honour (Rob Roy) / Safely ashore / Long black veil / House carpenter / Highlanders
CD ______ **CDMAYK 09**
Mayker / Oct '95 / Conifer/BMG

CELTIC SOUL
MacLain of Glencoe / Will ye go lassie go / Where eagles fly / Sands of time / Corryvreckan / Skye boat song / Bravest heart / Loch Lomond / Island of Tiree / Flower of Scotland / Highlanders / Mingulay / Dark Island / Farewell to Tarwathie / Skye high / Drifting away
CD ______ **CDMAYK 10**
Mayker / May '97 / Conifer/BMG

GLENCOE THE GLEN OF WEEPING
Closer to heaven / This child / Oban bay / Loch Lomond hills / Three months of the year / Glen of weeping / Glean bhaile chaoil / When I dream / Curragh of Kildare / Isle of Innisfree / Arran, the island i love / You'll be there / Glen of weeping (instrumental)
CD ______ **CDMAYK 1**
Mayker / Nov '94 / Conifer/BMG

Kerr, Sandra

NEAT AND COMPLETE (Kerr, Sandra & Nancy)
Lads of Alnwick / Milkmaids / Wee weaver / David Malone's / James Fagan's / Shoemakker / Maid on the shore / Welcome home / Saucy Nancy / Seven yellow gypsies / Yellow haired laddie / Lovely Nancy / Great Silkie / Sheepcrook and black dog / Rusty gully / Go to Berwick Johnny / Jackie Munroe / George Collins
CD ______ **FECD 107**
Fellside / May '96 / ADA / Direct / Target/BMG

Kerrs Pink

ART OF COMPLEX SIMPLICITY
CD ______ **FGBG 4219AR**
Musea / Jul '97 / ADA / Greyhound

Kershaw, Doug

CAJUN GREATS
CD ______ **12474**
Laserlight / Jun '95 / Target/BMG

HOT DIGGITY DOUG
Cajun baby / Louisiana / Jambalaya / I wanna hold you / Callin' Baton rouge / My toot toot / Boogie queen / Just like you / Louisiana man / Mansion in Spain / Cajun stripper / Fiddlin' man
CD ______ **CDSD 066**
Sundown / Oct '89 / TKO Magnum

Kershaw, Martin

ACOUSTIC DREAMS
CD ______ **PDSCD 531**
Pulse / Aug '96 / BMG

Kershaw, Nik

COLLECTION, THE
CD ______ **MCLD 19309**
MCA / Oct '95 / BMG

WOULDN'T IT BE GOOD
Wouldn't it be good / Running scared / Radio Musicola / Wild horses / When a heart beats / LABATYD / Dancing girls / Nobody knows / Human racing / Violet to blue / Faces / Save the whale / Drum talk
CD ______ **PWKS 4177**
Carlton / Oct '93 / Carlton

Kershaw, Rusty

LOUISIANA MAN (Kershaw, Rusty & Doug)
Louisiana man / Diggy liggy lo / Cheated too / Cajun Joe / We'll do it anyway / Jolie blon / So lovely baby / Look around / Mr. Love / Going down the road / Never love again / Kaw-liga
CD ______ **CDSD 022**
Sundown / Mar '92 / TKO Magnum

NOW AND THEN
CD ______ **80022**
Domino / Feb '97 / TKO Magnum

Kershaw, Sammy

POLITICS, RELIGION AND HER
CD ______ **5288932**
Mercury / Aug '96 / PolyGram

Kessel, Barney

ARTISTRY OF BARNEY KESSEL, THE
CD ______ **FCD 60021**
Fantasy / Oct '93 / Jazz Music / Pinnacle / Wellard

AUTUMN LEAVES
CD ______ **BLCD 760112**
Black Lion / Jun '88 / Cadillac / Jazz Music / Koch / Wellard

GREAT GUITARS AT CHARLIE'S, GEORGETOWN (Kessel, Barney/ Charlie Byrd/ Herb Ellis)
Where or when / New Orleans / When the saints go marching in / Change partners / Opus one / Old folks / Get happy / Trouble in mind
CD ______ **CCD 4209**
Concord Jazz / May '94 / New Note/ Pinnacle

IT'S A BLUE WORLD
CD ______ **JHR 73526**
Jazz Hour / May '93 / Cadillac / Jazz Music / Target/BMG

JELLYBEANS (Kessel, Barney Trio)
CD ______ **CCD 4164**
Concord Jazz / Jul '96 / New Note/ Pinnacle

LIMEHOUSE BLUES (Kessel, Barney & Stephane Grappelli)
It don't mean a thing if it ain't got that swing / Out of nowhere / Tea for two / Limehouse blues / How high the moon / Willow weep for me / Little star / Undecided
CD ______ **BLCD 760158**
Black Lion / Oct '92 / Cadillac / Jazz Music / Koch / Wellard

LIVE AT SOMETIME
CD ______ **STCD 4157**
Storyville / Feb '90 / Cadillac / Jazz Music / Wellard

PLAYS "CARMEN"
CD ______ **OJCCD 269**
Original Jazz Classics / Feb '92 / Complete/Pinnacle / Jazz Music / Wellard

POLL WINNERS RIDE AGAIN, THE
CD ______ **OJCCD 607**
Original Jazz Classics / Feb '92 / Complete/Pinnacle / Jazz Music / Wellard

POLL WINNERS, THE (Kessel, Barney/ Ray Brown/Shelly Manne)
Jordu / Satin doll / It could happen to you / Mean to me / Don't worry 'bout me / On green dolphin street / You go to my head / Minor mood / Nagasaki
CD ______ **OJCCD 156**
Original Jazz Classics / Sep '93 / Complete/ Pinnacle / Jazz Music / Wellard

POOR BUTTERFLY (Kessel, Barney & Herb Ellis)
Dearly beloved / Monsieur Armand / Poor butterfly / Make someone happy / Early autumn / Hello / Blueberry Hill / I'm a lover / Brigitte
CD ______ **CCD 4034**
Concord Jazz / Aug '95 / New Note/ Pinnacle

RED, HOT AND BLUES
CD ______ **CCD 14044**
Contemporary / Mar '95 / Cadillac / Complete/Pinnacle / Jazz Music / Wellard

SOARING
You go to my head / Get out of town / Seagull / Like someone in love / You're the one for me / Beautiful love / Star eyes / I love you
CD ______ **CCD 6033**
Concord Jazz / Feb '92 / New Note/ Pinnacle

SOLO
Brazil / What are you doing the rest of your life / Happy little song / Everything happens to me / You are the sunshine of my life / Manha de carnaval / People / Jellybeans / Alfie
CD ______ **CCD 4221**
Concord Jazz / Nov '96 / New Note/ Pinnacle

TO SWING OR NOT TO SWING
Begin the blues / Louisiana / Happy feeling / Embraceable you / Wail Street / (Back home again in) Indiana / Moten swing / Midnight sun / Contemporary blues / Don't blame me / Twelfth St. rag
CD ______ **OJCCD 317**
Original Jazz Classics / '93 / Complete/Pinnacle / Jazz Music / Wellard

YESTERDAY (Recorded Live At The Montreux Festival 1973)
CD ______ **BLCD 760183**
Black Lion / Apr '93 / Cadillac / Jazz Music / Koch / Wellard

Kessinger Brothers

KESSINGER BROTHERS VOL.1 (1928-1929)
CD ______ **DOCD 8010**
Document / Jul '97 / ADA / Hot Shot / Jazz Music

KESSINGER BROTHERS VOL.2 (1929)
CD ______ **DOCD 8011**
Document / Jul '97 / ADA / Hot Shot / Jazz Music

KESSINGER BROTHERS VOL.3 (1929-1930)
CD ______ **DOCD 8012**
Document / Jul '97 / ADA / Hot Shot / Jazz Music

Kester Emeneya

VIVA LA MUSICA
CD ______ **CDS 7007**
Sonodisc / Jan '97 / Stern's

Ketama

KETAMA
Sueno Ipossible / Luna, Quedate commigo / Ketama / Me Ilama / Slo para dos / Domo arigato / No se si vivo o sueno / Vacio / Galuchi / Cuando salga la luna / Chupendi / Canasteros
CD ______ **HNCD 1336**
Hannibal / May '89 / ADA / Vital

Ketchum, Hal

HAL YES
CD ______ **CURCD 042**
Curb / Aug '97 / Grapevine/PolyGram

HITS, THE (2CD Set)
CD Set ______ **CURCD 026**
Curb / May '96 / Grapevine/PolyGram

PAST THE POINT OF RESCUE
Small town Saturday night / I know where love lies / Old soldiers / Somebody's love / Past the point of rescue / Five o'clock world / I miss my Mary / Don't strike a match (To the book of love) / Long day comin' / She found the place
CD ______ **CURCD 004**
Curb / Mar '94 / Grapevine/PolyGram

SURE LOVE
Sure love / Mama knows the highway / You lovin' me / Hearts are gonna roll / Softer than a whisper / Ghost town / Daddy's oldsmobile / Till the coast is clear / Trail of tears / Some place far away
CD ______ **CURCD 7**
Curb / Apr '94 / Grapevine/PolyGram

Ketting, Otto

LIGHT OF THE SUN
CD ______ **BVHAASTCD 9105**
Bvhaast / Oct '93 / Cadillac

Ketty, Rina

CHANSOPHONE 1936-1939
CD ______ **701292**
Chansophone / Jun '93 / Discovery

Keun

KEUN
CD ______ **GWP 008CD**
Diffusion Breizh / Aug '95 / ADA

Kevrenn Brest Sant Mark

OCEAN LIBERTY
CD ______ **KBSM 002CD**
KBSM / Nov '96 / ADA

Key Of Life

IMPRESSIONS FROM THE TOP OF THE WORLD
CD ______ **341122**
Koch / Apr '94 / Koch

VISIONS
CD ______ **341112**
Koch / Apr '94 / Koch

Key, Tara

BOURBON COUNTY
CD ______ **HMS 2102**
Homestead / Jan '94 / Cargo / SRD

Keyes, Colin

MAGIC OF THE PIANO, THE
Carpenters medley (we've only just begun,(they long to be) c / Windmills of your mind / Our world / I'll never fall in love again / Entertainer, The / Tribute to Nat 'King' Cole (when I fall in love, unforgettab / Birth of the blues / Passing strangers / Golden touch / TV themes medley (where everybody knows your name (theme fro / Nocturne in e flat / Wind beneath my wings / Manhattan / View from here / What are you doing the rest of your life / Memory
CD ______ **ECD 3084**
K-Tel / Jan '95 / K-Tel

Keynoters

ESSENTIAL KEYNOTE COLLECTION VOL.9 (Keynoters & Nat 'King' Cole)
You're driving me crazy / I'm in the market for you / Blue Lou / I found a new baby / I can't believe that you're in love with me / Way you look tonight / Airiness a la Nat / My old flame
CD 8309672
Mercury / Mar '93 / PolyGram

Keys, Will

BANJO ORIGINAL, A
Wearing of the green / Chinquapin hunting / Midnight on the water / Standing on the promises / Cat in the pear tree / Once more / Dead march / Silver bell / Eighth of January / My pretty quadroon / Snake chapman's tune / Down yonder / Cielito lindo / Texas gals / Waiting for the Robert E. Lee / Blow ye winds softly / Puncheon floor / There is a fountain / Black mountain rag / Are you from Dixie / Palms of victory / Goodbye girls I'm going to Boston
CD COCD 2720
County / Jul '97 / ADA / Direct

Keystone Trio

HEART BEATS
Speak low / I fall in love too easily / If I should lose you / It had to be you / How deep is the ocean / Dancin' in the dark / Bewitched, bothered & bewildered / Two hearts / Stay as sweet as you are
CD MCD 92562
Milestone / Dec '96 / Cadillac / Complete/ Pinnacle / Jazz Music / Wellard

Khabbra, Surinder

GOOD TIME
CD OZITCD 0026
Ozit / May '97 / Cargo / Direct

KHABBRA
You blow my mind / AMG / Fire / Wrong dream / Ocean green / Don't blame me / Your favourite things / Zebra / Light the blue touch paper / I can only be me
CD GT 1010
Good Time / May '97 / Direct

Khac Chi Ensemble

MOONLIGHT IN VIETNAM
On the mountain top / Forest love / Quan ho folk song / T'rung stream / Mountain cave / Highland dance / Spring is coming / Cai luong folk song / Farmer's song / Spring walk / Full moon dance / Native land / Northwest folk song
CD HSR 0005
Henry Street / May '97 / Direct

Khaled, Cheb

KUTCHE (Khaled, Cheb & Safy Boutella)
CD STCD 1024
Stern's / Mar '89 / ADA / CM / Stern's

SAHRA
CD 5334052
Mango / Mar '97 / PolyGram / Vital

Khan, Ali Akbar

DUET
CD RSMCD 103
Ravi Shankar Music Circle / Apr '94 / Conifer/BMG

LEGACY
Guru bandana / Hori - in Kukubh Bilawal / Tarana - in Adana / Tarana - in Bhimpalasri / Kheyal - in Gour Sarang / Dhrupad - in Sankara Bharan / Sadra / Tarana - in Milan Ki Malhar / Tara - in Bhupali / Hori - in Bhairavi / Prayer - in Bhairavi
CD 72162
Triloka / Mar '96 / New Note/Pinnacle

TRADITIONAL MUSIC OF INDIA
CD PRCD 24157
Prestige / Mar '96 / Cadillac / Complete/ Pinnacle

Khan, Amjad Ali

RAGA LALITADHVANI
Alap-jod-jhara / Gat
CD VICG 54512
JVC / Oct '96 / Direct / New Note/Pinnacle / Vital/SAM

Khan, Brenda

OUTSIDE THE BEAUTY SALON
CD SHCD 5721
Shanachie / Apr '97 / ADA / Greensleeves / Koch

Khan, Chaka

CHAKA
I'm every woman / Love has fallen on me / Roll me through the rushes / Sleep on it / Life is a dance / We got the love / Some love / Woman in a man's world / Message in the middle of the bottom / I was made to love him
CD 7599258662
WEA / Jan '96 / Warner Music

CK
Signed, sealed, delivered (I'm yours) / Soul talkin' / It's my party / Eternity / Sticky wicked / End of a love affair / Baby me / Make it last / Where are you tonight / I'll be around
CD WX 124CD
WEA / Nov '88 / Warner Music

EPIPHANY (The Best Of Chaka Khan)
CD 9362458652
Warner Bros. / Nov '96 / Warner Music

I FEEL FOR YOU
This is my night / Stronger than before / My love is alive / Eye to eye / La flamme / I feel for you / Hold her / Through the fire / Caught in the act / Chinatown
CD 9251622
WEA / Oct '84 / Warner Music

LIFE IS A DANCE (The Remix Project)
Life is a dance / This is my night / Slow dancing / I'm every woman / Ain't nobody / I feel for you / I know you, I live you / Eye to eye / Fate / Million kisses / Clouds / Clouds (classic trax version)
CD 9259462
WEA / May '89 / Warner Music

PERFECT FIT
CD 7599255422
Warner Bros. / Jan '97 / Warner Music

WHATCHA GONNA DO FOR ME
We can work it out / What'cha gonna do for me / I know you, I live you / Any old Sunday / We got each other / Night in Tunisia / Night moods / Heed the warning / Father he said / Fate / I know you, I live you (reprise)
CD 7599258672
WEA / Jan '96 / Warner Music

WOMAN I AM, THE
Everything changes / Give me all / Telephone / Keep givin' me lovin' / Facts of love / Love you all my lifetime / I want / You can make the story right / Be my eyes / This time / Woman I am / Don't look at me that way
CD 7599262962
WEA / Apr '92 / Warner Music

Khan, Nishat

MEETING OF ANGELS
CD ARNR 1096
Amiata / Dec '96 / Harmonia Mundi

RAG BHIMPALASI/RAG TILAK KAMOD (Khan, Nishat & Irshad)
CD NI 5233
Nimbus / Sep '94 / Nimbus

STRING CRAFT
CD VICG 54522
JVC / Oct '96 / Direct / New Note/ Pinnacle / Vital/SAM

Khan, Nusrat Fateh Ali

BACK TO QAWWALI
CD 122083CD
Long Distance / Apr '95 / ADA / Discovery

DEVOTIONAL SONGS
Allah hoo allah hoo / Yaad-e-nabi gulshan mehka / Haq ali ali haq / Ali maula ali maula ali dam dam / Mast nazroon se allah bachhae / Ni main jogi de naal
CD RWMCD 2
Realworld / Nov '92 / EMI

EN CONCERT A PARIS
CD C 570200CD
Ocora / Apr '96 / ADA / Harmonia Mundi

GREATEST HITS
CD SH 64091
Shanachie / Jun '97 / ADA / Greensleeves / Koch

IN CONCERT IN PARIS VOL.1
CD C558 658
Ocora / '88 / ADA / Harmonia Mundi

IN CONCERT IN PARIS VOL.2
CD C558 659
Ocora / '88 / ADA / Harmonia Mundi

INTOXICATED SPIRIT
CD SHCD 64066
Shanachie / Aug '96 / ADA / Greensleeves / Koch

LAST PROPHET, THE
Mani madni / Sahib teri bandi / Ganj-e-shakar / Sochan dongian
CD CDRW 44
Realworld / Apr '94 / EMI

LOVE SONGS
Woh hata rahe hain pardah / Yeh jo halka saroor hae / Biba sada dil morr de / Yaadan vichre sajan dian aiyan / Sanson ki mala / Un ke dar pen pohchne to payen
CD RWMCD 3
Realworld / Nov '92 / EMI

MISSIVES FROM ALLAH
Salkhi allah / Panjabi / Jinah jinah tave / Tua gal beh / Rah hassan / Muujah haave / Surnaaja heeyve urh
CD MPG 74045
Movieplay Gold / Jul '97 / Target/BMG

MUSTT MUSTT
CD CDRW 15
Realworld / Nov '90 / EMI

NIGHT SONG (Khan, Nusrat Fateh Ali & Michael Brook)
My heart, my life / Intoxicated / Lament / My comfort remains / Longing / Sweet pain / Night song / Crest
CD CDRW 50
Realworld / Mar '96 / EMI

ORIENTE/OCCIDENTE (Khan, Nusrat Fateh Ali & Novum Gaudium)
CD 1295700842
Materiali Sonori / Jan '97 / Cargo / Greyhound / New Note/Pinnacle

QAWWALI - THE ART OF THE SUFIS VOL.1
CD VICG 50292
JVC World Library / Mar '96 / ADA / CM / Direct

RAPTURE
CD NSCD 013
Nascente / Mar '97 / Disc / New Note/ Pinnacle

SHAHBAAZ
Beh haadh ramza dhasdha / Shahbaaz qalandar / Dhyahar eh isqmeh / Jewleh lal
CD CDRW 16
Realworld / '91 / EMI

VOL.3
CD CDSR 003
Star / Aug '90 / Pinnacle / Stern's

VOL.5
CD CDSR 017
Star / Aug '90 / Pinnacle / Stern's

Khan, Praga

SPOONFUL OF MIRACLE, A (Khan, Praga & Jade 4 U)
Injected with a poison / Phantasia forever / I feel good / Give me your lovin' / Rave alert / Moonday / Travel through time / God of Abraham / Flesh and blood / Love me baby / I will survive / Love peace freedom
CD FILECD 439
Profile / May '93 / Pinnacle

Khan, Salamat Ali

RAGAS GUNKALI
CD NI 5307
Nimbus / Sep '94 / Nimbus

Khan, Steve

CROSSINGS
Descargo Khanalonious / Think of one / What I'm said / Pee Wee / It's you or no-one / I love Paris / Capricorn / Melancholee / Inner urge / While my lady sleeps
CD 5232692
Verve / Apr '94 / PolyGram

HEADLINE
Tyrone / Blessing / Autumn in Rome / Turnaround / Ontem a noite / Water babies / All or nothing at all / Havensack / Caribbean fire dance
CD 5176902
Polydor / Mar '93 / PolyGram

LET'S CALL THIS
Let's call this / Masqualero / Backup / Out of this world / Played twice / Little sunflower / Buddy system / Street of dreams / Mr. Kenyatta
CD 8495632
Polydor / Jan '92 / PolyGram

Khan, Ustad Amir

RAGA MANDRAGA DARBAR
CD DSAV 1059
Multitone / Jul '96 / BMG

Khan, Ustad Amjad Ali

LIVE 50TH BIRTHDAY CONCERT
CD NRCD 0070
Navras / Feb '97 / New Note/Pinnacle

Khan, Ustad Imrat

AJMER
CD WLAES 17CD
Waterlilly Acoustics / Nov '95 / ADA

EK PRAKAR KI KAUNS
CD NRCD 0014
Navras / Mar '96 / New Note/Pinnacle

INDIAN MUSIC FOR SITAR AND SURBAHAR (Khan, Imrat & Sons)
CD LYRCD 7376
Lyrichord / '91 / ADA / CM / Roots

LALITA
CD WLAES 26CD
Waterlilly Acoustics / Nov '95 / ADA

RAG DARBARI/RAG CHANDRA KANHRA
CD NI 5118
Nimbus / Sep '94 / Nimbus

RAG JHINJOTI/RAG PILU
CD NI 5195
Nimbus / Sep '94 / Nimbus

RAG JOG KAUNS RAGA DURGA
CD ED 1013
Edelweiss / Mar '96 / Discovery / Planetarium

RAG MADHUR RANJANI
CD CDT 123
Topic / Apr '93 / ADA / CM / Direct

RAG MEGH BRIDABANI SARANG SUDH SARANG
CD ED 1018
Edelweiss / Mar '96 / Discovery / Planetarium

RAG MIYA KI TODI/RAG BILASKHANI TODI
CD NI 5153
Nimbus / Sep '94 / Nimbus

RAGA MARWA
CD NI 5356
Nimbus / Sep '94 / Nimbus

Khan, Ustad Rashid

RAGAS
CD NRCD 0071
Navras / Nov '96 / New Note/Pinnacle

Khan, Ustad Sabri

INDIAN SARANGI AND TABLA RECITAL (Khan, Ustad Sabri & Sawar Sabri)
CD EUCD 1172
ARC / '91 / ADA / ARC Music

Khan, Ustad Salamat Ali

BREATH OF THE ROSE
CD WLAES 18CD
Waterlilly Acoustics / Nov '95 / ADA

Khan, Ustad Sultan

SARANGI INDIA
CD RCD 10104
Rykodisc / Nov '91 / ADA / Vital

Khan, Ustad Vilayat

UPHAAR (Khan, Ustad Vilayat & Ustad Bismillah Khan)
Alap / Gat composition
CD NRCD 0079
Navras / Jul '97 / New Note/Pinnacle

Khanum, Farida

HITS OF FARIDA KHANUM, THE
CD PMUT 020
Multitone / Jul '96 / BMG

Khanyile, Noise

ART OF NOISE, THE
Igobondela / Izulu seliyaduma / Viva Scotch land / Mapantsula jive / Jika jika jive / Ugabuzela / Kwazamazama / USA special / Dlamini / Baba wami / Umamemeza / London Ave / Marimba jive / Groovin' jive (no. 1)
CD CDORB 045
Globestyle / Jun '89 / Pinnacle

Khassonka Dunun

TRADITIONAL MUSIC FROM MALI
CD PS 65187
PlayaSound / Jul '97 / ADA / Harmonia Mundi

Kiani, Madjid

TRADITION CLASSIQUE DE L'IRAN VOL.3 (Le Santour) (Kiani, Madjid & Djamchid Chemirani)
CD HMA 190395
Musique D'Abord / Nov '93 / Harmonia Mundi

Kiani, Mary

LONG HARD FUNKY DREAMS (2CD Set)
When I call your name / Till death do us disco / With or without you / Long hard funky dreams / If I see you again / Let the music play / We can be one / 100% / I imagine / Blame it on the night / I knew / Beautiful day / Memories / I give it all to you / When I call your name (Hardfloor vocal mix) / Let the music play (Perfecto vocal mix) / I imagine (Mr. Spring club mix) / 100% (Tall Paul remix) / Let the music play (Union Jack mix) / I give it all to you (Umboza mix) / When I call your name (Motiv 8 special club mix)
CD 5345122
CD Set 5345112
Mercury / Jun '97 / PolyGram

Kibwe, Talib

INTRODUCING
Is that so / Joy spring / Heaven scent / Hot house / Lady in white / Hi fly / Kim / Blues from Jali / Portrait of Lois Marie / Star eyes
CD ECD 221452
Evidence / Mar '96 / ADA / Cadillac / Harmonia Mundi

Kick La Luna

SECRET WAVES
CD _______ EFA 129162
Turbulent / May '96 / SRD

Kickback

CORNERED
CD _______ CM 77139CD
Century Media / Nov '96 / Plastic Head

Kicklighter, Richy

IN THE NIGHT
Night after night / Without you / Under another sky / Between the worlds / Lucky / Time will tell / Tamiami / Angel
CD _______ ICH 1051CD
Ichiban / Oct '93 / Direct / Koch

JUST FOR KICKS
Jungle Song / In the wind / Change love / Till then / Wind in the curtains / After You're Gone / Phantoms / Now and then
CD _______ ICH 1019CD
Ichiban / Oct '93 / Direct / Koch

Kid Creole

BEST OF KID CREOLE & THE COCONUTS (Kid Creole & The Coconuts)
Lifeboat party / Gina Gina / Me no pop I / Off the coast of me / Don't take my coconuts / Maladie d'amour / There's something wrong in paradise / Stool pigeon / Annie I'm not your daddy / Latin music / I'm a wonderful thing, baby / Imitation / Dear Addy / Back in the field again
CD _______ IMCD 216
Island / Mar '96 / PolyGram

FRESH FRUIT/ TROPICAL GANGSTERS (Kid Creole & The Coconuts)
CD Set _______ ITSCD 7
Island / Nov '92 / PolyGram

STOOL PIGEON (Kid Creole & The Coconuts)
CD _______ ST 5002
Star Collection / Nov '93 / BMG

TROPICAL GANGSTERS (Kid Creole & The Coconuts)
Annie (I'm not your daddy) / I'm a wonderful thing, baby / Imitation / I'm corrupt / Loving you made a fool out of me / Stool pigeon / Love we have / No fish today
CD _______ IMCD 6
Island / '89 / PolyGram

Kid Loops

TIMEQUAKE
CD _______ FILT 022CD
Filter / Jun '97 / Pinnacle / Prime / RTM/ Disc

Kid 'n' Play

FACE THE NATION
It's alright y'all / Back on wax / Got a good thing going on / Next question / Face the nation / Foreplay / Slippin' / Ain't gonna hurt nobody / Give it here / Bill's at the door / Toe to toe
CD _______ 3368612062
WEA / Oct '91 / Warner Music

Kid Rock

POLYFUZE METHOD
CD _______ CDCTUM 2
Continuum / Sep '93 / Pinnacle

Kid Rocker

I'M ON A ROLL (Kid Rocker & The Phantoms)
CD _______ JRCD 22
Jappin' & Rockin' / Oct '96 / Swift / TKO Magnum

Kid Sheik

CLEVELAND & BOSTON 1960-1961
CD _______ AMCD 69
American Music / Aug '94 / Jazz Music

KID SHEIK & PAUL BARBARIN (Kid Sheik & Paul Barbarin)
CD _______ BCD 227
GHB / Apr '97 / Jazz Music

KID SHEIK'S SWINGSTERS 1961
CD _______ AMCD 91
American Music / Mar '97 / Jazz Music

REAL NEW ORLEANS JAZZ 1960 (Kid Sheik & Charlie Love)
When you're smiling / Waltz of the bells / Don't go 'way nobody / Sheik's blues / Corine Corina / Georgia camp meeting / Then I'll be happy / What a friend we have in Jesus / Sheikh of araby / Near the cross / Over in the glory land / Cado blues / Down in honky tonk town / Bill Bailey, Won't you please come home / Indian Sagua
CD _______ 504CDS 21
504 / Jan '95 / Cadillac / Jazz Music / Target/BMG / Wellard

Kidd, Carol

ALL MY TOMORROWS
Don't worry 'bout me / I'm all smiles / Autumn in New York / My funny valentine / 'Round midnight / Dat dere / Angel eyes / When I dream / I thought about you / Folks who live on the hill / Haven't we met / All my tomorrows
CD _______ AKHCD 005
Linn / Aug '90 / PolyGram

CAROL KIDD
Then I'll be tired of you / We'll be together / You go to my head / It isn't so good it couldn't be better / More I see you / I've grown accustomed to your face / Yes, I know when I've had it / Waltz for Debby / Never let me go / Like someone in love / Trouble is a man / I'm shadowing you / Spring can really hang you up the most / I like to recognise the tune
CD _______ AKHCD 003
Linn / Aug '90 / PolyGram

CRAZY FOR GERSHWIN
CD _______ AKD 026
Linn / Apr '94 / PolyGram

I'M GLAD WE MET
Lean baby / Don't go to strangers / Bad, bad Leroy Brown / I guess I'll hang my tears out to dry / Georgia on my mind / You're cheating yourself / I wish I'd met you / You're awful / Don't take your love from me / I'm a fool to want you / Please don't talk about me when I'm gone / Sometimes (not often)
CD _______ AKD 017
Linn / Nov '91 / PolyGram

NICE WORK (If You Can Get It)
Nice work if you can get it / Havin' myself a time / Isn't it a pity / Bidin' my time / Sing for your supper / Daydream / I'll take romance / New York on Sunday / What is there to say / Mean to me / I guess I'll have to change my plan / Starting tomorrow / Confessions
CD _______ AKHCD 006
Linn / Aug '90 / PolyGram

NIGHT WE CALLED IT A DAY, THE
How little it matters, how little we know / Where or when / I fall in love too easily / I loved him / Night we called it a day / Where are you / Glory of you / I could have told you so / I think it's going to rain today / Gloomy Sunday
CD _______ AKHCD 007
Linn / Sep '90 / PolyGram

THAT'S ME
You don't bring me flowers / Send in the clowns / When the world was young / 'Round midnight / I can't get started (With you) / I'm always chasing rainbows / Let me sing and I'm happy / This bitter Earth / Somewhere over the rainbow / Trolley song / That's me
CD _______ AKD 044
Linn / Sep '95 / PolyGram

Kidd, Johnny

CLASSIC AND RARE (Kidd, Johnny & The Pirates)
I want that / So what / Feeling / Please don't touch / Restless / Let's talk about us / Birds and the bees / It's got to be you / Some other guy / Shakin' all over / I'll never get over you / Send me some lovin' / Fool / Hungry for love / Your cheatin' heart / My babe / Casting my spell / Big blon' baby
CD _______ SEECD 287
See For Miles/C5 / Jun '93 / Pinnacle

COMPLETE JOHNNY KIDD (Best Of The EMI Years/2CD Set) (Kidd, Johnny & The Pirates)
Please don't touch / Growl / Yes sir that's my baby / Steady date / Feelin' / If you were the only girl in the world / You got what it takes / Longin' lips / Shakin' all over / Restless / Magic of love / Linda Lou / Let's talk about us / Big blon' baby / Weep no more my baby / More of the same / I just want to make love to you / Please don't bring me down (version 2) / So what / Please don't bring me down / Hurry on back to love / I want that / I can tell / Shot of rhythm and blues / Some other guy / Then I got everything / Ecstacy / Hungry for love / Casting my spell: *Pirates* / My babe: *Pirates* / Dr. Feelgood / Always and ever / Whole lotta woman / Your cheatin' heart / Let's talk about us (alt. version) / Little bit of soap / Fool (version 2) / Oh boy / Send me some lovin' / Big blon' baby (#2) / Please don't touch (version 2) / Right string baby, but the wrong yo-yo / Shop around / I know / Jealous girl / Where are you / Don't make the same mistake as I did / Birds and the bees / Can't turn you loose / Gotta travel on / Bad case of love / You can have her / I hate getting up in the morning / This golden ring / It's got to be you / I hate getting up in the morning (version 2) / Send for that girl / Fool / Send for that girl
CD Set _______ CDKIDD 11
EMI / Aug '92 / EMI

RARITIES (Kidd, Johnny & The Pirates)
I Know / Where are you / Little bit of soap / Oh boy / Steady date / More of the same / I just want to make love to you / This golden ring / Right string baby, but the wrong yo-yo / Can't turn you loose / Shakin' all over / I hate getting up in the morning / Send for that girl / Hurry on back to love / You got what it takes / Fool / Ecstacy / Shop around / Weep no more, my baby / Whole lotta woman
CD _______ SEECD 120
See For Miles/C5 / Jan '97 / Pinnacle

VERY BEST OF JOHNNY KIDD & THE PIRATES, THE (Kidd, Johnny & The Pirates)
Please don't touch / If you were the only girl in the world / Feelin' / You got what it takes / Shakin' all over / Yes sir that's my baby / Restless / Hurry on back to love / Shot of rhythm and blues / I'll never get over you / Hungry for love / Always and ever / Dr. Feelgood / Whole lotta woman / Your cheatin' heart / Gotta travel on / Fool / Birds and the bees / Send me some lovin' / Some other guy
CD _______ CDSL 8256
EMI / Jul '95 / EMI

Kidjo, Angelique

AYE
Agolo / Adouma / Azan nan kpe / Tatchedogbe / Djan djan / Lon lon vadjro / Houngbati / Idje idje / Yemandja / Tombo
CD _______ IMCD 244
Island / Mar '97 / PolyGram

Kiem

YOU SHOULD TRY
CD _______ CD 029
Torso / Jul '87 / SRD

Kiermyer, Franklin

KAIROS
Kairos / Kukisha m'poko / John's mode / In the house of my fathers / Baka yelli / In your presence I behold / Basheret / Elephant feast / Around the world / Epi trapezios / I turn my face towards the sun / Dream of a grandfather / Fifty years (after the liberation of Auschwitz)
CD _______ ECD 221442
Evidence / Feb '96 / ADA / Cadillac / Harmonia Mundi

SOLOMON'S DAUGHTER
Three jewels / Akdemus / Peace on earth / Solomon's daughter / Birds of the Nile / If I die before I wake
CD _______ ECD 220832
Evidence / May '94 / ADA / Cadillac / Harmonia Mundi

Kiernan, Ken

ERINSAGA (Kiernan, Ken & Ger MacDonald)
I am Tuan / Vision / Belgatan (our will is strong) / Tailltu's lament / Crom cruach / Dream of nuada / Battle-frenzy / My love is yours / Last battle / Erinsaga
CD _______ ERCD 1
Round Tower / Nov '89 / Avid/BMG

Kiesewetter, Knut

HIS BEST SONGS
CD _______ EUCD 1182
ARC / Apr '92 / ADA / ARC Music

WENN WIEHNACHTEN KUMMT (Kiesewetter, Knut & Fiede Kay)
CD _______ EUCD 1130
ARC / '91 / ADA / ARC Music

WO GEIHST DU HEN
CD _______ EUCD 1117
ARC / '91 / ADA / ARC Music

Kihn, Greg

HORROR SHOW
Kay is the mouth of May / Noa noa / Horror show / Waterloo sunset / Come back baby / Talk of the town / JFK / Trials, troubles and tribulations / Alligator man / Beam the light / Wherever there's smoke / Vampira
CD _______ CCD 716
Clean Cuts / Nov '96 / Direct / Jazz Music / Wellard

KIHNSPIRACY (Kihn, Greg Band)
Jeopardy / Fascination / Tear that city down / Talkin' to myself / Can't love them all / I fall to pieces / Someday / Curious / How long / Love never fails / Breakup song (they don't write 'em) / Happy man / Sorry / For you / Reunited / Any other woman
CD _______ HILLCD 19
Wooded Hill / Jun '97 / Direct / World Serpent

MUTINY
Blood red roses / Mutiny / Sittin' on top of the world / Anniversary of my broken heart / Joshua gone Barbados / Anastasia / I wish it would rain / Not fade away Mona / Femme fatale / Shot in the dark / Subterranean homesick blues / Love of the land / Been on the job too long / Gwabi
CD _______ FIENDCD 755
Demon / Aug '94 / Pinnacle

Kikoski, Dave

PRESAGE
CD _______ FRLCD 011
Freelance / Oct '92 / Cadillac / Koch

Kikuchi, Masabumi

AFTER HOURS
CD _______ 5297472
Verve / Mar '96 / PolyGram

TETHERED MOON
You're my everything / Misterioso / So in love / Moniker / PS / Moor / Tethered moon
CD _______ ECD 220712
Evidence / Nov '93 / ADA / Cadillac / Harmonia Mundi

Kikuchi, Teiko

TRADITIONAL MUSIC OF JAPAN
CD _______ 824612
BUDA / Nov '90 / Discovery

Kila

MIND THE GAP
Tickelled / Feach / Finnegan / Odlum's wild oats / Tatiana / 5.30 / Juno humm / Delta / Baile bhoithin / Mind the gap / Sean deora / Ezekiel / Steps / Islandbridge
CD _______ KRCD 004
Kila / May '97 / ADA / Direct

TOG E GO BOG E
Gwerzy / On taubh tuathail amach / Rusty nails / Seige of Carrickfinn International Airport / Jasmine / Oh to kiss Katie / Tog e go bog e / Crann na bpingini / Dusty wine bottle / Tip toe / Double knuckle shuffle / Rila do / Bi ann / Leanfaidh me
CD _______ KRCD 005
Kila / May '97 / ADA / Direct

Kilbey, Steve

GILT TRIP (Kilbey, Steve & Russell)
CD _______ VSC 004
Vicious Sloth / Jun '97 / Greyhound

NARCOSIS PLUS
CD _______ VSC 005
Vicious Sloth / Jun '97 / Greyhound

UNEARTHED
CD _______ 3297 2
Enigma / Oct '87 / EMI

Kilbride, Pat

LOOSE CANNON
CD _______ GLCD 1148
Green Linnet / Feb '95 / ADA / CM / Direct / Highlander / Roots

ROCK AND MORE ROSES
CD _______ COMD 2011
Temple / Feb '94 / ADA / CM / Direct / Duncans / Highlander

UNDOCUMENTED DANCING
Live bait / Aires de Pontevedra / All the leaves / Hunter's house / Milestones and memories / Patrick / Unfinished revolution / Munster bacon and the jig of slurs / Wearing of the breeches / Blind Mary / Flower of Magherally / Piccadilly / Cittern jig
CD _______ GLCD 1120
Green Linnet / Feb '91 / ADA / CM / Direct / Highlander / Roots

Kilby, Cody

JUST ME
Backstep / Round up / Memories of you / St. Anne's reel / El cumbanchero / Washington County / Ocoee sunrise / Monroe's hornpipe / One legged gypsy / Tune for poppy / Shenandoah breakdown / Frosty morn / Tom and Jerry
CD _______ REBCD 1736
Rebel / Jul '97 / ADA / Direct

Kilduff, Vinnie

BOYS FROM BLUE HILL
CD _______ LUNCD 050
Mulligan / Jan '95 / ADA / CM

Kilgore, Merle

TEENAGER'S HOLIDAY
Ride Jesse ride / Hang doll / Everybody needs a little lovin' / Ernie / Start all over again / Tom Dooley Jr / More and more / It can't rain all the time / Seein' double, feelin' single / What makes me love you / Funny feeling / Now that you are leavin' / That's when my blues began / Teenager's holiday / Please please please / I feel guilty / Trying to find (someone like you) / Goodbye / Forty two in Chicago / Wicked city / I'll take Ginger and run away / Girl named Liz / Ain't nothin' but a man / Somethin' goin' on that I can't see / There's no food in this house / Lover's hell / Back street affair / Trouble at the tower / Love bug / I'll shake your hand
CD _______ BCD 15544
Bear Family / May '91 / Direct / Rollercoaster / Swift

Kilgore, Rebecca

NOT A CARE IN THE WORLD (Kilgore, Rebecca & Dave Frishberg)
CD ARCD 19169
Arbors Jazz / May '97 / Cadillac

Kilgour, David

SUGAR MOUTH
CD FNCD 282
Flying Nun / Oct '94 / RTM/Disc

Kill City Dragons

KILL CITY DRAGONS
CD WBRCD 002
Wideboy / Jan '91 / Vital

Kill Creek

PROVING WINTER CRUEL
Unsteady / All ears / Binky / With you around / Role model / Biggest rift / Lullaby / Chromosone / Falsified / Punishment
CD MR 1352
Mammoth / Jul '96 / Vital

ST. VALENTINE'S GARAGE
Cosmetic surgery / Busted / Stretch / Mother's friends / Gett on / Kelly's dead / 7-11 / Killing / Fruit pie / Million / Harass / Wuss cliff / Die young / Funeral
CD MR 0912
Mammoth / Oct '94 / Vital

Kill II This

ANOTHER CROSS II BARE
CD HR 02CD
Hardware / Mar '97 / Plastic Head / Vital

Kill Switch Klick

DEGENERATE
CD CLP 9928
Cleopatra / Mar '97 / Cargo / Greyhound / Plastic Head / RTM/Disc / SRD

Killa Instinct

ESCAPISM
CD MOVE 7013CD
Move / Mar '95 / Plastic Head

Killafornia

ORGANISATION
CD 50539
Raging Bull / Jun '97 / Prime / Total/BMG

Killarney Singers

50 FAVOURITE IRISH PUB SONGS
CD CDIRISH 001
Outlet / Jan '95 / ADA / CM / Direct / Duncans / Koch / Ross

Killdozer

GOD HEARS PLEAS OF THE INNOCENT
CD TG 139CD
Touch & Go / Feb '95 / SRD

WAR ON ART
CD TG 82CD
Touch & Go / '94 / SRD

Killer

FATAL ATTRACTION
CD 36700012
Mausoleum / Oct '91 / Grapevine/ PolyGram

MURDER ONE
Impaler / Beast arises / Children of the revolution / S and M / Takin' no prisoners / Marshall Lokjaw / Protector / Dream keeper / Awakening / Remember tomorrow
CD PD 90643
RCA / May '92 / BMG

Killer Bees

LIVE IN BERLIN
CD DANCD 053
ROIR / Nov '94 / Plastic Head / Shellshock/Disc

Killer Dwarfs

DIRTY WEAPONS
Dirty weapons / Nothin' gets nothin' / All that we dream / Doesn't matter / Last laugh / Comin' through / One way out / Appeal / Not foolin' / Want it bad
CD 4659082
Epic / Apr '90 / Sony

Killer Shrews

KILLER SHREWS
CD EMY 1412/1
Enemy / Nov '94 / Grapevine/PolyGram

Killermeters

METRIC NOISE (Killermeters & Soldiers Are Dreamers)
Why should it happen to me: *Killermeters* / Don't tell baby: *Killermeters* / Back in business: *Killermeters* / Cardiac arrest: *Killermeters* / Rhona: *Killermeters* / Love on the rebound: *Killermeters* / Wrong way: *Killermeters* / Can't help it: *Killermeters* / Look but don't touch: *Killermeters* / Only you (light my way): *Killermeters* / Midnight breakfast show: *Killermeters* / Open my eyes: *Killermeters* / Eight miles high: *Killermeters* / Twisted wheel: *Killermeters* / SX 225: *Killermeters* / Summertime: *Killermeters* / Cry: *Killermeters* / Which way kids: *Killermeters* / Go with the flow: *Soldiers Are Dreamers* / Tomorrow is a brighter day: *Soldiers Are Dreamers* / Midnight: *Soldiers Are Dreamers* / Dreaming my life away: *Soldiers Are Dreamers* / And I break: *Soldiers Are Dreamers* / GI Joe: *Soldiers Are Dreamers*
CD DRCD 013
Detour / Apr '97 / Detour / Greyhound

Killers

LIVE
CD HR 01CD
Hardware / Mar '97 / Plastic Head / Vital

MENACE TO SOCIETY
CD CDBLEED 11
Bleeding Hearts / Oct '94 / Pinnacle

Killing Floor

KILLING FLOOR
CD SYC 006CD
BGR / May '95 / Plastic Head

Killing Joke

BRIGHTER THAN A 1000 SUNS
Adorations / Sanity / Chessboards / Twilight of the moral / Love of the masses / Southern sky / Winter gardens / Rubicon / Goodbye to the village / Victory / Exile
CD EGCD 66
EG / Nov '86 / EMI

COURTAULD TALKS, THE
CD INV 004CD
Invisible / Jun '97 / Plastic Head

DEMOCRACY
CD BFLCD 17
Big Life / Apr '96 / Mo's Music Machine / Pinnacle / Prime

FIRE DANCES
Gathering / Fun and games / Rejuvenation / Frenzy / Harlequin / Feast of blaze / Song and dance / Dominator / Let's all go (to the fire dances) / Lust almighty
CD EGCD 60
EG / '87 / EMI

KILLING JOKE
Requiem / War dance / Tomorrow's World / Bloodsport / Wait / Complications / SO 36 / Primitive
CD EGCD 57
EG / '87 / EMI

LAUGH I NEARLY BOUGHT ONE
Turn to red / Pssyche / Requiem / Wardance / Follow the leaders / Unspeakable / Butcher / Exit / Hum / Empire song / Chop chop / Sun goes down / Eighties / Darkness before dawn / Love like blood / Wintergardens / Age of greed
CD CDV 2693
EG / Oct '92 / EMI

NIGHT TIME
Night Time / Darkness before dawn / Love like blood / Kings and Queens / Tabazan / Multitudes / Europe / Eighties
CD EGCD 61
EG / Jan '87 / EMI

OUTSIDE THE GATE
America / My love of this land / Stay one jump ahead / Unto the ends of the earth / Calling / Obsession / Tiahuanaco / Outside the gate / America (mix)
CD EGCD 73
EG / May '88 / EMI

PANDEMONIUM
Pandemonium / Exorcism / Millennium / Communion / Black moon / Labyrinth / Jana / Whiteout / Pleasures of the flesh / Mathematics of chaos
CD BFLCD 09
Big Life / Jul '94 / Mo's Music Machine / Pinnacle / Prime

WHAT'S THIS FOR
Fall of because / Tension / Unspeakable / Butcher / Who told you how / Follow the leader / Madness / Exit
CD EGCD 58
EG / '87 / EMI

WILFUL DAYS
Are you receiving / Follow the leaders / Sun goes down / Dominator / Me or you / Wilful days / Eighties / New day / Love like blood / Madding crowd / Ecstasy / America / Change
CD CDOVD 440
Virgin / May '95 / EMI

Killing Time

BRIGHTSIDE
CD LF 157CD
Lost & Found / Jul '95 / Plastic Head

METHOD, THE
Used to it / It must be nice / Cayce / Can't get around it / Quietly / Symptom / Personal hardcore / Pokerface / Outgroup / Sidelined / Method / Occupied / Junk drawer / Scared / Happy hour / Resume / And I... / Are you comfortable
CD BLK 035ECD
Blackout / Jun '97 / Plastic Head / Vital

Killjoys

MILLION SONGS, A
CD D 30930
Mushroom / Oct '93 / 3mv/Pinnacle

Killrays

ON COMMON GROUND
CD BYE 970132
Bite Your Ear / May '97 / Cargo

SPACE GIANT
CD LF 203CD
Lost & Found / Nov '95 / Plastic Head

Kilmarnock Edition

FROM FAR HORIZONS
CD MANU 1501CD
Manu / Nov '95 / ADA / Discovery

Kilo

BLUNTLY SPEAKING
CD WRA 8118CD
Wrap / May '94 / Koch

GET THIS PARTY STARTED
CD WRA 8147
Wrap / Aug '95 / Koch

GIT WIT DA PROGRAM
CD WRA 8123CD
Wrap / Feb '94 / Koch

Kilpatrick, Tom

FIFTY SHADES OF GREEN
CD CDITV 538
Scotdisc / Jul '91 / Conifer/BMG / Duncans / Ross

SHADES OF GREEN
CD PLATCD 3922
Platinum / May '94 / Prism

SHAMROCK STRAND, THE
CD CDITV 560
Scotdisc / Sep '92 / Conifer/BMG / Duncans / Ross

Kimball, Bobby

RISE UP
CD 9041012
Mausoleum / Jun '95 / Grapevine/ PolyGram

Kimbara Brothers

TIME TO LEAVE
CD MMKB 9015CD
Meadow Music / Mar '96 / ADA

Kimber, Paul

PECKHAM IN SPRING
Peckham in spring / Flying Joey / Must be a boon / Swing thing / Nine O'clock midnight / Slieve loughsbannagh / Ben's groove / Confidence / Happy
CD FMD 029
Fictional / Mar '97 / Jazz Music

Kimbrough, Junior

ALL NIGHT LONG
CD FIENDCD 742
Demon / Nov '93 / Pinnacle

Kimmel, Tom

5 TO 1
That's freedom / Shake / Tryin to dance / A to Z / True love / Heroes / On the defensive / Violet eyes / No tech / Five to one
CD 8322482
Vertigo / Nov '87 / PolyGram

Kina, Shoukichi

ASIA CLASSICS VOL.2 (The Best Of Shoukichi Peppermint Tea House)
CD 9362451592
Luaka Bop / Jul '94 / Warner Music

Kind Of Jazz

KIND OF JAZZ
CD MECCACD 2006
Music Mecca / May '97 / Cadillac / Jazz Music / Wellard

Kinder Der Erde

KINDER DER ERDE
CD EFA 119722
High Society / Apr '95 / SRD

Kindness Of Strangers

HOPE
Kindness of strangers / Across the border / Tomorrow / Memory takes my hand / Walk away / Oh my America / Live in the world / Sunday / Day that I found love / Shelter for love / Desira / Kindness of strangers (reprise)
CD 6544922412
East West / Feb '94 / Warner Music

Kindred

BOMB UP THE TOWN
CD GI 0052
GI Productions / Mar '97 / Cargo / Greyhound

Kindred, Bob

HIDDEN TREASURES
CD 74321357312
Milan / May '96 / Conifer/BMG / Silva Screen

Kinesthesia

EMPATHY BOX
CD CAT 022CDR
CD CAT 022CD
Rephlex / Apr '96 / Prime / RTM/Disc

Kinfolk

EACH AND EVERY DAY
Each and every day / Handle that shit / Trapped up in tha ghetto / Holdin' tank / Why ya wanna (lock me down) / Gotta make those endz / Deal wit tha real / Gangsta glide / Players / MsBehave / Summer again / Situation critical / Kinfolkatosis / Ya daughter gits it all / If I could / Faith / On B1/2 of nutty
CD 74321335182
American / Oct '96 / BMG

King, Albert

BLUES AT SUNRISE (Live At Montreux)
Don't burn the bridge (cause you might wanna come back... / For the love of a woman / I'll play the blues for you / Roadhouse blues / I believe to my soul / Blues at sunrise / Little brother (make a way)
CD CDSXE 017
Stax / Nov '88 / Pinnacle

BLUES AT SUNRISE
CD CD 52034
Blues Encore / May '94 / Target/BMG

BLUES AT SUNSET (Live At Wattstax 1972 & Montreux 1973)
Matchbox blues / Got to be some changes made / I'll play the blues for you / Killing floor / Angel of mercy / Matchbox blues / Watermelon man / Breaking up somebody's home / Stormy Monday
CD SCD 8581
Stax / Jun '96 / Pinnacle

BLUES DON'T CHANGE, THE
Blues don't change / I'm doing fine / Nice to be nice / Oh pretty woman / King of kings / Feel the need / Firing line / Pinch paid off (Part I) / Pinch paid off (Part II) / I can't stand the rain / Ain't it beautiful
CD CDSXE 085
Stax / Feb '93 / Pinnacle

BLUES FOR YOU (The Best Of Albert King)
Born under a bad sign / Killing floor / Breaking up somebody's home / Can't you see what you're doing to me / Going back to luka / Answer to the laundromat blues / That's what the blues is all about / Phone booth / I'll play the blues for you / Left hand woman (Get right with me) / Flat tire / Drowning on dry land / Pinch paid off / Sky is crying / Driving wheel / Everybody wants to go to heaven / Angel of mercy / Wrapped up in love again / Blues power / Crosscut saw
CD CDSXD 120
Stax / Sep '95 / Pinnacle

CHICAGO 1978
CD CDBL 754
Charly / Nov '94 / Koch

CROSSCUT SAW
Crosscut saw / Down don't bother me / Honey bee / Ask me no questions / I'm gonna move to the outskirts of town / They made the Queen welcome / Floodin' in California / I found love in the food stamp line / Matchbox blues / Why you so mean to me
CD CDSXE 076
Stax / Oct '92 / Pinnacle

FUNKY LONDON
Cold sweat / Can't you see what you're doing to me / Funky London / Lonesome / Bad luck / Sweet fingers / Finger on the trigger / Drivin' wheel / Lovingest woman in town
CD SCD 8586
Stax / Oct '96 / Pinnacle

GREAT KING ALBERT
CD 2696032
Tomato / May '88 / Vital

HARD BARGAIN
Overall junction / Funk shun / You sure drive a hard bargain / You're gonna need me / As the years go passing by / Drownin' on dry land / Heart fixing business / Sky is crying / I get evil / Shake 'em down / I believe to my soul / Got to be some changes made / Albert's groove
CD SCD 8594
Stax / Oct '96 / Pinnacle

I WANNA GET FUNKY
I wanna get funky / Playing on me / Walking the back streets and crying / Till my back ain't got no bone / Flat tire / I can't hear nothing but the blues / Travellin' man / Crosscut saw / That's what the blues is all about
CD ______ CDSXE 081
Stax / Jul '93 / Pinnacle

I'LL PLAY THE BLUES FOR YOU (The Best Of Albert King)
Born under a bad sign / Answer to The Laundromatt Blues / You threw your love on me too strong / Crosscut saw / I'll play the blues for you / Angel of mercy / Heart fixing business / Killing floor / Sky is crying / Going back to luka / Drowning on dry land / That's what the blues is all about / Left hand woman (get right with me) / Drivin' wheel / Firing line / Don't burn the bridge (cause you might wanna come back... / Can't you see what you're doing to me
CD ______ CDSX 007
Stax / Jan '90 / Pinnacle

I'LL PLAY THE BLUES FOR YOU (King, Albert & John Lee Hooker)
Born under a bad sign: *King, Albert* / Very thought of you: *King, Albert* / I worked hard: *King, Albert* / When you down: *King, Albert* / Feel good / Boom boom / Serves me right to suffer / One bourbon, one scotch, one beer / King snake
CD ______ CPCD 8166
Charly / Jun '96 / Koch

I'LL PLAY THE BLUES FOR YOU/ LOVEJOY
CD ______ CDSXD 969
Stax / Mar '91 / Pinnacle

I'M IN A PHONE BOOTH BABY
Phone booth / Dust my broom / Sky is crying / Brother go ahead and take her / Your bread ain't done / Firing line / Game goes on / Truck load of lovin / You gotta sacrifice
CD ______ CDSXE 083
Stax / Jul '93 / Pinnacle

I'M READY (Best Of The Tomato Years/ 2CD Set)
CD Set ______ CPCD 82652
Charly / Jan '97 / Koch

JUST PICKIN'
CD ______ MBCD 721
Modern Blues / Jun '93 / ADA / Direct

KING ALBERT
Love shock / You upset me baby / Chump chance / Let me rock you easy / Boot lace / Love mechanic / Call my job / Good time Charlie
CD ______ CPCD 8233
Charly / Oct '96 / Koch

KING DOES THE KING'S THINGS (Blues For Elvis)
Hound dog / That's alright Mama / All shook up / Jailhouse rock / Heartbreak hotel / Don't be cruel / One night / Blue suede shoes / Love me tender
CD ______ CDSXE 073
Stax / Sep '92 / Pinnacle

KING OF THE BLUES GUITAR
Cold feet / You're gonna need me / Born under a bad sign / I love Luzy / Crosscut saw / You sure drive a hard bargain / Oh pretty woman / Overall junction / Funk-shun / Laundromat blues / Personal manager
CD ______ 7567820172
Atlantic / Mar '93 / Warner Music

LET'S HAVE A NATURAL BALL
CD ______ MBCD 723
Modern Blues / Jun '93 / ADA / Direct

LIVE
Watermelon man / Don't burn down the bridge / Blues at sunrise / That's what the blues is all about / Stormy Monday / Kansas City / I'm gonna call you as soon as the sun goes down / Matchbox holds my clothes / Jam in a flat / As the years go passing by / Overall junction / I'll play the blues for you
CD ______ CDBM 18
Charly / Apr '92 / Koch

LIVE IN CANADA
King's groove / King's jump / Watermelon man / I'm gonna move to the outskirts of town / Kansas city / Someday baby / Truckers blues / As the years go by / Rainin' in California / I'll play the blues for you / Sky is crying
CD ______ CDCBL 755
Charly / Oct '95 / Koch

LIVE WIRE/BLUES POWER (Albert King Live At The Fillmore 1968)
Watermelon man / Blues power / Night stomp / Blues at sunrise / Please love me / Lookout
CD ______ CDSXE 022
Stax / Nov '89 / Pinnacle

LOST SESSION, THE
She won't gimme no lovin' / Cold in hand / Stop lying / All the way down / Tell me what true love is / Down the road I go / Money lovin' women / Sun gone down / Brand new razor / Sun gone down (take 2)
CD ______ CDSXE 066
Stax / Nov '92 / Pinnacle

NEW ORLEANS HEAT
Get out of my life woman / Born under a bad sign / Feeling / We all wanna boogie / Very thought of you / I got the blues / I get evil / Angel of Mercy / Flat tire
CD ______ CPCD 8211
Charly / Feb '97 / Koch

SO MANY ROADS (Charly Blues - Masterworks Volume 2) (King, Albert & Otis Rush)
Bad luck blues / Be on your merry way / Murder / Searching for a woman / California blues / Wild woman / Won't be hangin' around no more / Howlin' for my darling / So many roads, so many trains / I'm satisfied / So close / All your love / You know my love / I can't stop baby
CD ______ CD BM 2
Charly / Apr '92 / Koch

THURSDAY NIGHT IN SAN FRANCISCO (Albert King Live At The Fillmore 1968)
San-Ho-Zay / You upset me baby / Stormy Monday blues / Everyday I have the blues / Driftin' blues / I've made nights by myself / Crosscut saw / I'm gonna move to the outskirts of town / Ooh-ee baby
CD ______ CDSXE 032
Stax / Oct '90 / Pinnacle

TRUCKLOAD OF LOVIN'
Cold women with warm hearts / Gonna make it somehow / Sensation, communication, together / I'm your mate / Truckload of lovin' / Hold hands with one another / Cadillac assembly line / Nobody wants a loser
CD ______ CPCD 8201
Charly / Feb '97 / Koch

VINTAGE BLUES (King, Albert & Otis Rush)
Be on your merry way / Bad luck blues / Murder / Searchin' for a woman / California blues / Wild woman / Won't be hangin' around / Howlin' for my darling / So many roads, so many trains / I'm satisfied / So close / All your love / You know my love / I can't stop baby / It must have been the devil / Five spot / I'm leaving you / I'm in love with you baby / Ice cream man / Rattlesnake / Be careful / Tough times / You got me
CD ______ CDRED 9
Charly / May '89 / Koch

WEDNESDAY NIGHT IN SAN FRANCISCO (Albert King Live At The Fillmore 1968)
Watermelon man / Why you so mean to me / I get evil / Got to be some changes made / Personal manager / Born under a bad sign / Don't throw your love on me so strong
CD ______ CDSXE 031
Stax / Sep '90 / Pinnacle

YEARS GONE BY
Wrapped up in love again / Shimmy shimmy walk / Cockroach / Killing floor / Lonely man / If the washing don't get you, the rinsing will / Drownin' on dry land / Drownin' on dry land / Heart fixing business / You threw your love on to me too strong / Sky is crying / Can't you see what you're doing to me / Cold sweat / As the years go passing by / Drownin' on dry land / Don't you lie to me / Shake 'em down / I believe to my soul / Heart fixing business / Sky is crying / You're treating me mean
CD ______ CDSXD 045
Stax / Apr '92 / Pinnacle

King Alex

HOT AS A COFFEE POT (King Alex & The Untouchables)
Hot as a coffee pot / Never do you no wrong / Grandma's sweet potato pie / Just the one that I love / Overload of love / Red cabin / I want to come back / Sweetest thing / Right all the time / Cryin' eyes / Way you do that / Weekend blues / Time is right / Some peoples do some peoples don't
CD ______ BMCD 9035
Black Magic / Jul '97 / ADA / Cadillac / Direct / Hot Shot

King, B.B.

AUDIO ARCHIVE
Letter / Long nights / Catfish blues / BB boogie / Evil child / Walkin' and cryin' / Sweet sixteen / Please love me / Other night blues / Everyday I have the blues / New way of driving / How blue can you get / It's my own fault / Mr. Pawnbroker / You've done lost your good thing now / Paying the cost to be the boss / I'm working on the building / Save a seat for me
CD ______ CDAA 037
Tring / Jun '92 / Tring

BEST OF B.B. KING VOL.1, THE
You upset me baby / Everyday / Five long years / Sweet little angel / Beautician blues / Dust my broom / Three o'clock blues / Ain't that just like a woman / I'm King / Sweet sixteen / Whole lot of love / Mean ol' Frisco / Please accept my love / Going down slow / Blues for me / You don't know / Early every morning / Blues at sunrise / Please love me
CD ______ CDCH 908
Ace / '89 / Pinnacle

BEST OF B.B. KING, THE
Hummingbird / Cook County jail introduction / How blue can you get / Sweet sixteen / Ain't nobody home / Why I sing the blues / Thrill is gone / Nobody loves me but my mother / Caldonia
CD ______ MCLD 19099
Chess/MCA / Nov '90 / BMG / New Note/ BMG

BEST OF B.B. KING, THE
CD ______ DLCD 4026
Dixie Live / Mar '95 / TKO Magnum

BLUES COLLECTION, THE
BB boogie / New way of driving / Catfish blues / Walkin' and cryin' / How blue can you get / Mr. Pawnbroker / You've done lost your good thing now / It's my own fault baby / Paying the cost to be the boss / Sweet sixteen / Letter / Other night blues / Long nights / Evil child / Everyday I have the blues
CD ______ 100332
CMC / May '97 / BMG

BLUES IS KING
Waitin' on you / Gambler's blues / Tired of your jive / Night life / Buzz me / Sweet sixteen part 1 / Don't answer the door / Blind love / I know what you're puttin' down / Baby get lost / Gonna keep on loving you / Sweet sixteen part 2
CD ______ SEECD 216
See For Miles/C5 / Apr '92 / Pinnacle

BLUES ON TOP OF BLUES
Heartbreaker / Losing faith in you / Dance with me / That's wrong little mama / Having my say / I'm not wanted anymore / Worried dream / Paying the cost to be the boss / Until I found you / I'm gonna do what they do to me / Raining in my heart / Now that you've lost me
CD ______ BGOCD 69
Beat Goes On / '89 / Pinnacle

BLUES SUMMIT
Playin' with my friends: *King, B.B. & Robert Cray* / Since I met you baby: *King, B.B. & Katie Webster* / I pity the fool: *King, B.B. & Buddy Guy* / You shook me: *King, B.B. & John Lee Hooker* / Something you got: *King, B.B. & Koko Taylor* / There's something on your mind: *King, B.B. & Etta James* / Stormy Monday: *King, B.B. & Albert Collins* / You're the boss: *King, B.B. & Irma Thomas* / I gotta move out of this neighbourhood / Nobody loves me but my mother / Little by little: *King, B.B. & Lowell Fulson* / Everybody's had the blues: *King, B.B. & Joe Louis Walker*
CD ______ MCD 10710
MCA / Jun '93 / BMG

COLLECTION, THE (20 Blues Greats)
Help the poor / Everyday I have the blues / Woke up this morning / Worry worry / Sweet little angel / How blue can you get / You upset me baby / It's my own fault / Please love me / She don't love me no more / Three o'clock blues / Fine looking woman / Blind love / You know I love you / Ten long years / Mistreated woman / Shake it up and go / Sweet sixteen / You done lost your good thing now / Outside help
CD ______ CCSCD 412
Castle / Feb '95 / BMG

DO THE BOOGIE (B.B.King's Early 50's Classics)
Boogie woogie woman / Past day / I gotta find my baby / Woke up this morning (my baby's gone) / Please love me / Blind love / When my heart beats like a hammer / Whole lotta love / That ain't the way to do it / Everyday I have the blues / Let's do the boogie / Dark is the night (Part 1) / Dark is the night (Part 2) / Why I sing the blues / Everything I do is wrong / Woman I love / Jump with you baby / Troubles, troubles, troubles / Crying won't help you
CD ______ CDCHD 916
Ace / '89 / Pinnacle

EARLY BLUES BOY YEARS VOL.1
CD ______ OCD 101
Opal / Nov '95 / ADA

EARLY BLUES BOY YEARS VOL.2
CD ______ OCD 102
Opal / Nov '95 / ADA

FABULOUS B.B. KING, THE
Three o'clock blues / You know I love you / Please love me / You upset me baby / Bad luck / On my word of honor / Everyday I have the blues / Woke up this morning (my baby's gone) / When my heart beats like a hammer / Sweet little angel / Ten long years / Whole lotta love
CD ______ CDFAB 004
Ace / Aug '91 / Pinnacle

FRIENDS
Friends / I got them blues / Baby, I'm yours / Philadelphia / When everything else is gone / My song
CD ______ BGOCD 125
Beat Goes On / Sep '91 / Pinnacle

GREATEST HITS 1951-1960
Three o'clock blues / You know I love you / Boogie woogie woman / Woke up this morning / Please love me / You upset me baby / Whole lotta love / Sneaking around / Every day I have the blues / Crying won't help you / Sweet little angel / Bad luck / I want to get married / Troubles, troubles, troubles / Please accept my love / Sweet sixteen / (I've) got a right to love my baby / My fault / You done lost your good thing now
CD ______ CSAPCD 117
Connoisseur Collection / Aug '94 / Pinnacle

GUESS WHO
Summer in the city / Just can't please you / Any other you / You don't know nothin' about love / Found what I need / Neighborhood affair / It takes a young girl / Better lovin' man / Guess who / Shoudn't have left me / Five long years
CD ______ BGOCD 71
Beat Goes On / May '90 / Pinnacle

HEART AND SOUL (A Collection Of Blues Ballads)
Lonely and blue / Sneakin' around / You can't fool my heart / Story from my heart and soul / Don't get around much anymore / You know I love you / I'm king / Lonely lover's plea / My heart belongs to only you / Don't cry anymore / Please accept my love / Peace of mind / I was blind / On my word of honour / I'll survive / If I lost you / My reward / I am / I love you so / Key to my kingdom
CD ______ CDCH 376
Ace / Oct '92 / Pinnacle

HIS BEST - THE ELECTRIC KING
Tired of your jive / BB Jones / Paying the cost to be the boss / I done got wise / Sweet sixteen / I don't want you cuttin' your hair / Don't answer the door / All over again / Think it over / Meet my happiness / You put it on me
CD ______ BGOCD 37
Beat Goes On / Oct '88 / Pinnacle

HOW BLUE CAN YOU GET
Rock me baby / Blues at midnight / How blue can you get / You upset me baby / I done got wise / Lucille / Thrill is gone / Please accept my love / Ask me no questions / Five long years / To know you is to love you / Don't make me pay for his mistakes / Everyday I have the blues / Mother fuyer / Midnight believer / Better not look down / There must be a better world somewhere / Six silver strings / I'm movin' on
CD ______ NTRCD 013
Nectar / Feb '94 / Pinnacle

IN LONDON
Caldonia / Blue shadows / Alexis' boogie / We can't agree / Ghetto woman / Wet hayshark / Part time love / Power of the blues / Ain't nobody home
CD ______ BGOCD 42
Beat Goes On / Oct '88 / Pinnacle

INDIANOLA MISSISSIPPI SEEDS
Nobody loves me but my mother / You're still my woman / Ask me no questions / Until I'm dead and cold / King's special / Ain't gonna worry my life anymore / Chains and things / Go underground / Hummingbird
CD ______ BGOCD 237
Beat Goes On / Mar '95 / Pinnacle

INTRODUCING B.B. KING
Into the night / Better not look down / My Lucille / Caldonia / Sell my monkey / In the midnight hour / Thrill is gone / Broken heart / Victim / Sweet sixteen / Rock me baby
CD ______ MCLD 19036
MCA / Apr '92 / BMG

KANSAS CITY 1972
CD ______ CDCBL 752
Charly / Jan '94 / Koch

KING OF THE BLUES
(You've become a) Habit to me / Drowning in the sea of love / Can't get enough / Standing on the edge of love / Go on / Let's staighten it out / Change in your lovin' / Undercover man / Lay another log on the fire / Business with my baby tonight
CD ______ MCLD 19214
MCA / Aug '93 / BMG

KING OF THE BLUES
Early every morning / Sweet little angel / Three O'clock in the morning / Ain't that just like a woman / Dark is the night (part 1) / Dark is the night (part 2) / Rock me baby / I've got a right to love my baby / Bad luck soul / Did you ever love a woman / King of guitar / You upset me baby / Get out of here / Troubles, troubles, troubles / Sweet sixteen part 1 / Sweet sixteen Part 2 / That ain't the way to do it / Ten long years / Powerhouse / Going down slow
CD ______ PWKS 4211
Carlton / Mar '96 / Carlton

KING OF THE BLUES (4CD Set)
Miss Martha King / She's dynamite / Three O'clock blues / Please love me / You upset me baby / Everyday I have the blues / Rock me baby / Recession blues / Don't get around much anymore / I'm gonna sit in til you give in / Blues at midnight / Sneakin' around / My baby's coming home / Slowly losing my mind / How blue can you get / Rockin' awhile / Help the poor / Stop leadin' me on / Never trust a woman / Sweet little angel / All over again / Sloppy drunk / Don't answer the door / I done got wise / Think it over / Gambler's blues / Goin' down slow / Tired of your jive / Sweet sixteen / I'm gonna do what they do to me / Lucille / Watch yourself / You put it on me / Get my-

self somebody / I want you so bad / Why I sing the blues / Get off my back woman / Please accept my love / Fools get wise / No good / So exited / Thrill is gone / Confessin' the blues / Nobody loves me but my mother / Hummingbird / Ask me no questions / Chains and things / Eyesight to the blind / Niji baby / Blue shadows / Ghetto woman / Ain't nobody home / I got some help I don't need / Five long years / To know you is to love you / I like to live the love / Don't make me pay for his mistakes / Let the good times roll / Don't you lie to me / Mother fuyer / Never make a move too soon / When it all comes down (I'll still be around) / Better not look down / Caldonia / There must be a better world somewhere / Play with your poodle / Darlin' you know I love you / Inflation blues / Make love to me / Into the night / Six silver strings / When love comes to town / Right time, wrong place / Many miles travelled / I'm movin' on / Since I met you baby
CD Set ____ MCAD 410677
MCA / Oct '92 / BMG

LIVE AND WELL
Don't answer the door / Just a little love / My mood / Sweet little angel / Please accept my love / I want you so bad / Friends / Get off my back woman / Let's get down to business / Why I sing the blues
CD ____ BGOCD 233
Beat Goes On / Jun '94 / Pinnacle

LIVE AT COOK COUNTY JAIL (2CD Set)
CD Set ____ MCD 33007
MCA / Jul '96 / BMG

LIVE AT SAN QUENTIN
Intro / Let the good times roll / Everyday I have the blues / Whole lotta lovin' / Sweet little angel / Never make a move too soon / Into the night / Ain't nobody's business if I do / Thrill is gone / Peace to the world / Nobody loves me but my mother / Sweet sixteen / Rock me baby
CD ____ MCLD 19253
MCA / Nov '94 / BMG

LIVE AT THE APOLLO
When love comes to town / Sweet sixteen / Thrill is gone / Ain't nobody's business if I do / All over again / Nightlife / Since I met you baby / Guess who / Peace to the world
CD ____ MCD 9637
MCA / Jan '93 / BMG

LIVE AT THE REGAL
Everyday I have the blues / Sweet little angel / It's my own fault / How blue can you get / Please love me / You upset me baby / Worry worry / Woke up this morning / You done lost your good thing now / Help the poor
CD ____ BGOCD 235
Beat Goes On / Oct '94 / Pinnacle

LUCILLE
Lucille / You move me so / Country girl / No money no luck / I need your love / Rainin' all the time / I'm with you / Stop putting the hurt on me / Watch yourself
CD ____ BGOCD 36
Beat Goes On / Feb '89 / Pinnacle

LUCILLE AND FRIENDS
When love comes to town: *King, B.B. & U2* / Playin' with my friends: *King, B.B. & Robert Cray* / To know you is to love you: *King, B.B. & Stevie Wonder* / Caught a touch of your love: *King, B.B. & Grover Washington Jr.* / All you ever give me is the blues: *King, B.B. & Vernon Reid* / You shook me: *King, B.B. & John Lee Hooker* / Spirit in the dark: *King, B.B. & Diane Schuur* / Can't get enough: *King, B.B. & Mick Fleetwood/ Stevie Nicks* / Since I met you baby: *King, B.B. & Gary Moore* / BB's blues: *King, B.B. & Branford Marsalis* / Better not look down: *King, B.B. & The Crusaders* / Frosty: *King, B.B. & Albert Collins* / Hummingbird: *King, B.B. & Leon Russell/Joe Walsh* / Ghetto woman: *King, B.B. & Friends* / Let the good times roll: *King, B.B. & Bobby Bland*
CD ____ MCD 33008
MCA / Jul '95 / BMG

MY SWEET LITTLE ANGEL
My sweet little angel / Crying won't help you / Ten long years / Quit my baby / Don't look now but I've got the blues / You know I go for you / Why do everything happen to me / Worry worry / Shake yours / Please accept my love / Treat me right / Going down slow / Just like a woman / Time to say goodbye / Early every morning / You've been an angel
CD ____ CDCHD 300
Ace / Mar '92 / Pinnacle

SINGIN' THE BLUES AND THE BLUES
Please love me / You upset me baby / Everyday I have the blues / Bad luck / Three o'clock blues / Blind love / Woke up this morning (my baby's gone) / You know I love you / Sweet little angel / Ten long years / Did you ever love a woman / Crying won't help you / Why do everything happen to me / Ruby Lee / When my heart beats like a hammer / Past day / Boogie woogie woman / Early every morning / I want to get married / That ain't the way to do it / Troubles, troubles, troubles / Don't you want a man like me / You know I go for you / What can I do
CD ____ CDCHD 320
Ace / Apr '91 / Pinnacle

SPOTLIGHT ON LUCILLE
Six silver strings / Big boss man / In the midnight hour / Into the night / My Lucille / Memory blues / My guitar sings the blues / Double trouble / Memory lane
CD ____ CDCH 187
Ace / Sep '86 / Pinnacle

SWEET LITTLE ANGEL
You upset me baby / Everyday I have the blues / Sneakin' around / Woman I love / Please accept my love / 3 o'clock blues / Save a seat for me / Sweet sixteen / Sweet little angel / Let me love you / Rock me baby / Army of the lord / I've got a right to love my baby / Well baby look at me / Please love me / Woke up this morning
CD ____ 305972
Hallmark / Jan '97 / Carlton

THERE IS ALWAYS ONE MORE TIME
CD ____ MCAD 10295
MCA / Aug '91 / BMG

THERE MUST BE A BETTER WORLD SOMEWHERE
Victim / More, more, more / You're going with me / Life ain't nothing but a party / Born again human / There must be a better world somewhere
CD ____ BGOCD 124
Beat Goes On / Sep '91 / Pinnacle

TOGETHER FOR THE FIRST TIME (King, B.B. & Bobby Bland)
CD ____ BGOCD 161
Beat Goes On / Jun '94 / Pinnacle

King Bees

POLLENATIN' (King Bees & Jerry McCain/Chicago Bob Nelson)
CD ____ TRCD 9927
Tramp / Dec '96 / ADA / CM / Direct

King, Ben

CELTIC STRINGS & WINGS
CD ____ IAGO 203CD
Iago / Apr '96 / ADA

King, Ben E.

ANTHOLOGY (2CD Set)
There goes my baby / Dance with me / This magic moment / Lonely winds / Save the last dance for me / I count the tears / Brace yourself / Show me the way / Spanish harlem / First taste of love / Young boy blues / Stand by me / On the horizon / Here comes the night / Amor / Ectasy / Yes / Walking in the footstesps of a fool / Don't play that song (You lied) / How can I forget / Gypsy / I who have nothing / What now my love / Groovin' / That's when it hurts / Let the water run down / It's all over / River of tears / Seven letters / Record (Baby I love you) / She's gone again / Cry no more / Goodnight my love / Pleasant dreams / So much love / I swear by stars above / What is soul / Man without a dream / Tears, tears, tears / We got a thing going on / Don't take your love from me / It's amazing / Till I can't take it anymore / It ain't fair / Hey little one / Supernatural thing / Do it in the name of love / I had a love / Get it up for love / Star in the ghetto / Music trance
CD Set ____ 8122712152
Atlantic / Oct '93 / Warner Music

BROTHERS IN SOUL (The Best Of Ben E. King & The Drifters) (King, Ben E. & The Drifters)
Stand by me: *King, Ben E.* / Up on the roof: *Drifters* / Dance with me: *Drifters* / Don't play that song (You lied): *King, Ben E.* / On broadway: *Drifters* / This magic moment: *Drifters* / I who have nothing: *King, Ben E.* / Spanish Harlem: *King, Ben E.* / Saturday night at the movies: *Drifters* / Please stay: *Drifters* / There goes my baby: *Drifters* / Supernatural thing (Part 1): *King, Ben E.* / Under the boardwalk: *Drifters* / Save the last dance for me: *Drifters* / You send me: *Drifters* / Unchained melody: *Drifters*
CD ____ ECD 3044
K-Tel / Jan '95 / K-Tel

COLLECTION, THE
CD ____ COL 055
Collection / Jan '95 / Target/BMG

DEFINITIVE BEN E. KING ANTHOLOGY VOL.1, THE (Spanish Harlem/Classics From The Atco Masters)
Amor amor / Sway / Come closer to me / Perfida / Granada / Sweet and gentle / Perhaps, perhaps, perhaps / Frenesi / Souvenir of Mexico / Besame mucho / Love me, love me / Spanish Harlem / How often: *King, Ben E. & Lavern Baker* / Help each other romance: *King, Ben E. & Lavern Baker* / Tell Daddy / Too bad / Walking in the footsteps of a fool / Gloria Gloria / Auf wiedersehn, my dear / How can I forget
CD ____ RSACD 837
Sequel / Nov '96 / BMG

DEFINITIVE BEN E. KING ANTHOLOGY VOL.2, THE (Sings For Soulful Lovers/ Classics From The Atco Masters)
My heart cries for you / He will break your heart / Dream lover / Will you love me tomorrow / My foolish heart / Fever / Moon river / What a difference a day made / Because of you / At last / On the street where you live / It's all in the game / I could have danced all night / Gypsy / I (who have nothing) / Beginning of time / What now my love / Groovin' / Don't play that song (you lied) / Stand by me / What'd I say
CD ____ RSACD 838
Sequel / Sep '96 / BMG

DEFINITIVE BEN E. KING ANTHOLOGY VOL.3, THE (Don't Play That Song/ Classics From The Atco Masters)
Don't play that song (you lied) / Ecstasy / On the horizon / Show me the way / Here comes the night / First taste of love / Stand by me / Yes / Young boy blues / Hermit of misty mountain / I promise love / Brace yourself / That's when it hurts / Around the corner / What a man can do / Way you shake it / Not now, I'll tell you when
CD ____ RSACD 839
Sequel / Sep '96 / BMG

DEFINITIVE BEN E. KING ANTHOLOGY VOL.4, THE (Seven Letters/Classics From The Atco Masters)
Seven letters / River of tears / I'm standing by / Jamaica / Down home / Si senor / It's all over / Let the water run down / This is my dream / It's no good for me / In the middle of the night / Don't drive me away / Where's the girl / So much love / Man without a dream / Tears tears tears / She knows what to do for me / Don't take your sweet love away
CD ____ RSACD 853
Sequel / Nov '96 / BMG

DEFINITIVE BEN E. KING ANTHOLOGY VOL.5, THE (What Is Soul/Classics From The Atco Masters)
Record (baby I love you) / She's gone again / There's no place to hide / Cry no more / Goodnight my love (pleasant dreams) / Katherine / I can't break myself the news / I swear by stars above / Get in a hurry / They don't give medals to yesterday's heroes / Teeny weeny little bit / What is soul / Forgive this fool / Don't take your love from me / It's amazing / When you love someone / It ain't fair / Till I can't take it anymore / Hey little one / What'cha gonna do about it: *King, Ben E. & Dee Dee Sharp* / We got a thing going on: *King, Ben E. & Dee Dee Sharp* / Soul meeting: *Soul Clan* / That's how it feels: *Soul Clan*
CD ____ RSACD 854
Sequel / Nov '96 / BMG

DEFINITIVE BEN E. KING ANTHOLOGY VOL.6, THE (Supernatural Thing/ Originals From The Atco Masters)
Supernatural thing / Supernatural thing / Your lovin' ain't good enough / Drop my heart off / Extra extra / Do it in the name of love / Happiness is where you find it / Do you wanna do a thing / Imagination / What do you want me to do / Supernatural thing / Do it in the name of love
CD ____ RSACD 855
Sequel / Nov '96 / BMG

DEFINITIVE BEN E. KING ANTHOLOGY VOL.7, THE (Benny & Us/Classics From The Atco Masters) (King, Ben E. & Average White Band)
Get it up for love / Fool for you anyway / Star in the ghetto / Message / What is soul / Someday we'll all be free / Imagine / Keeping it to myself / Star in the ghetto / Star in the ghetto / Fool for you anyway / Message
CD ____ RSACD 856
Sequel / Nov '96 / BMG

GREATEST HITS
CD ____ CDSGP 045
Prestige / Apr '93 / Else / Total/BMG

LEGENDARY BEN E. KING, THE
CD ____ HADCD 180
Javelin / Nov '95 / Henry Hadaway / THE

STAND BY ME (The Ultimate Collection)
Stand by me / Save the last dance for me / I who have nothing / That's when it hurts / I could have danced all night / First taste of love / Dream lover / Moon river / Spanish harlem / Amor / I count the tears / Don't play that song (You lied) / This magic moment / Young boy blues / It's all in the game / Supernatural thing (part 1)
CD ____ 7802132
Atlantic / Feb '87 / Warner Music

WHAT'S IMPORTANT TO ME
CD ____ ICH 1133CD
Ichiban / Jan '94 / Direct / Koch

King, Bill

MAGNOLIA NIGHTS
CD ____ 1390232
Gaia / May '89 / New Note/Pinnacle

King Biscuit Boy

DOWN THE LINE
Georgia slop / Done everything I can / Mama Luchie / Neighbour, neighbour / Down the line / Hoodoo party / Route 90 / Terraplane blus / It's my soul / Necromonica / Get it right / Look out Mabel / Step back baby
CD ____ NEBCD 849
Sequel / Aug '96 / BMG

King, Bob

BOB KING AND THE COUNTRY KINGS
Laurel Lee / Give my love to Rose / Hey mommy / Waltz of two broken hearts / Going back to an old love affair / Why don't you leave me / My petite Marie / If the things they say are true / Be careful of stones are throw / She went without saying goodbye / Pray for me mother of mine / Let's take a fair trade / Nothing ventured nothing gained / Lonely city park / That's what's on my mind / All Canadian boy / My home by the fraser / My son calls another man daddy / Rose of ol' pawnee / I dreamed about mom last night / No parking here / Just call on me / Boy with a future / I've been dreaming / Between our hearts / It's goodbye and so long to you
CD ____ BCD 15719
Bear Family / Aug '93 / Direct / Rollercoaster / Swift

JUST ME AND MY GUITAR
You and my old guitar / Little shirt my mother made for me / Patanio, the pride of the plains / Mommy please stay home with me / I'm just here to get my baby out of jail / French song / On the banks of the old pontchartrain / When the work's all done this fall / Old log cabin for sale / Driftwood on the river / Strawberry roan / Rockin' alone in an old rocking chair / I've been down that road before / Ballad of the chapeau boys / Mary Ann regrets / Memories of you / Rescue from the moose river gold mine / When it's lamplighting time in the valley / Cat came back / Ballad of Jed Clampett / Bluest man in the town / Cowboy / Jimmie Brown / Newboy / Little Tom / Train of memories / French Canadian girl / Road paved with heartaches / It breaks a mother's heart / Once more / Coconut Joe
CD ____ BCD 15718
Bear Family / Aug '93 / Direct / Rollercoaster / Swift

King, Bobby

LIVE AND LET LIVE (King, Bobby & Terry Evans)
CD ____ SPCD 1016
Special Delivery / Apr '94 / ADA / CM / Direct

RHYTHM, BLUES, SOUL AND GROOVES (King, Bobby & Terry Evans)
CD ____ ROUCD 2101
Rounder / Dec '94 / ADA / CM / Direct

King, Carole

FANTASY
Fantasy (beginning) / You've been around too long / Being at war with each other / Directions / That's how things go down / Weekends / Haywood / Quiet place to live / Welfare symphony / You light up my life / Corazch / Believe in humanity / Fantasy end
CD ____ 4879392
Epic / Jul '97 / Sony

GREATEST HITS
Jazzman / So far away / Sweet seasons / I feel the earth move / Brother brother / Only love is real / It's too late / Nightingale / Smackwater Jack / Been to Caanan / Corazon / Believe in humility
CD ____ CD 32345
CBS / Mar '91 / Sony

HITS AND RARITIES
CD ____ MAR 010
Marginal / Jun '97 / Greyhound

IN CONCERT
Hard Rock Cafe / Up on the roof / Smackwater Jack / So far away / Beautiful / Natural woman / Hold out for love / Will you love me tomorrow / Jazzman / It's too late / Chains / I feel the Earth move / You've got a friend / Locomotion / You've got a friend: *King, Carole & David Crosby*
CD ____ NTMCD 531
Nectar / May '97 / Pinnacle

IN CONCERT - THE GREATEST HITS LIVE
CD ____ CKINGCD 01
Quality / Feb '94 / Pinnacle

JAZZMAN
CD ____ JHD 010
Tring / Jun '92 / Tring

LIVE AT CARNEGIE HALL
Feel the earth move / Home again / After all this time / Child of mine / Carry your load / No easy way down / Song of long ago / Snow Queen / Smackwater Jack / So far away / It's too late / Eventually / Way over yonder / Beautiful / You've got a friend: *King, Carole & James Taylor* / Will you still love me tomorrow: *King, Carole & James Taylor* / Some kind of wonderful: *King, Carole & James Taylor* / Up on the roof: *King, Carole & James Taylor* / (You make me feel like) A natural woman
CD ____ 4851042
Epic / Nov '96 / Sony

MUSIC
Brother brother / It's going to take some time / Sweet seasons / Some kind of wonderful / Surely / Carry your load / Music / Song of long ago / Brighter / Growing away from me / Too much rain / Back to California

CD 4844622
Epic / Feb '97 / Sony

NATURAL WOMAN: THE ODE COLLECTION 1968-1976 (2CD Set)
Now that everything's been said / Hi de ho / Up on the roof / Child of mine / I feel the earth move / So far away / It's too late / Home again / Beautiful / Way over yonder / Where you lead / Will you still love me tomorrow / Smackwater Jack / Tapestry / (You make me feel like) A natural woman / You've got a friend / Music / Brother brother / It's going to take some time / Sweet seasons / Bitter with the sweet / Goodbye don't mean I'm gone / Been to Canaan / Corazon / Believe in humanity (live at Carnegie Hall) / Jazzman / Wrap around joy / Nightingale / Really Rosie / Alligators all around / There's a space between us / Only love is real / Ties that bind / You've got a friend (live) / Pocket money / This time in my life
CD Set E2K 48833
Legacy / Oct '94 / Sony

PEARLS/TIME GONE BY
CD VSOPCD 199
Connoisseur Collection / Jun '94 / Pinnacle

SWEET SEASON
CD JHD 038
Tring / Jun '92 / Tring

TAPESTRY
I feel the earth move / So far away / Beautiful / You've got a friend / Where you lead / Will you still love me tomorrow / Smack water Jack / Tapestry / It's too late / Home again / Way over yonder / (You make me feel like) a natural woman
CD 4804222
Mastersound / Sep '95 / Sony

TAPESTRY REVISITED (A Tribute To Carole King) (Various Artists)
CD 7567926042
Atlantic / Nov '95 / Warner Music

WRAP AROUND JOY
Nightingale / Change in mind, change in heart / Jazzman / You go your way, I'll go mine / You're something new / We are all in this together / Wrap around joy / You gentle me / My lovin' eyes / Sweet Adonis / Night this side of dying / Best is yet to come
CD CDTB 137
Thunderbolt / Mar '92 / TKO Magnum

King, Charlie

FOOD, PHONE, GAS & LODGING
CD FF 536CD
Flying Fish / '92 / ADA / CM / Direct / Roots

King, Claude

MORE THAN CLIMBING THAT MOUNTAIN, WOLVERTON MOUNTAIN THAT IS (5CD Set)
Flying saucers / I want to be loved / Million mistakes / Why should I / Beers and pinballs / Fifty one beers / She knows why / She's my baby / Take it like a man / So close to me / Got the world by the tail / Slow thinking heart / I think of you and me / Now that I love you / My future life will be my past / Over again / Run baby run / Not sure of you / Big river, big man / Sweet loving / Comancheros / I can't get over the way you got over me / Give me your love and I'll give you mine / Pistol packin' papa / You're breaking my heart / I'm here to get my baby out of jail / Little bitty heart / Would you care / I backed out / Wolverton mountain / This land of yours and mine / Sheepskin valley / Burning of Atlanta / Don't that moon look lonesome / I've got the world by the tail / Culpepper community / Building a bridge / What will I do / Scarlet O'Hara / Hey Lucille / Where the red red roses grow / Sixteen tons: *Platters* / Lace mantilla and a rose of red / That's what makes the world go around / Sam Hill / Big ole shoulder / Whirlpool (of your love) / When you gotta go (you gotta go) / Tiger woman / Great big tears / I won't belong in your town / Hold that tiger (tiger rag) / That's the way the wind blows / Little buddy / Come on home / Ancient history / There ain't gonna be no more / It's good to have my baby back home / Catch a little raindrop / Anna / Right place at the right time / Little things that every girl should know / Juggler / Watchman / Laura / Goodbye my love / Green green grass of home / Ruby, don't take your love to town / Almost persuaded / Ninety nine years / Parchman farm blues / Birmingham bus station / Yellow haired woman / Power of your sweet love / Beertops and teardrops / Sweet love on your mind / Green mountain / Four roses / I remember Johnny / Honky tonk man / First train headin' South / Ole slewfoot / North to Alaska / Battle of New Orleans / Sink the bismarck / All for the love of a girl / Whispering pines / When it's springtime in Alaska / House of the rising sun / Friend, lover, woman, wife / When you're twenty-one / I'll be your baby tonight / Turn it around in your mind / Mary's vineyard / Heart / Johnny Valentine / Highway lonely / Chip 'n' Dale's place / Help me make it through the night / Lady of our town / Just as soon as I get over loving you / Sweet Mary Ann / (Darlin' raise the shade) let the sun shine in / I know it's not been easy lovin' me / I know it's not been easy lovin' me (with strings) / This time I'm through / He ain't country / If my heart could stop / Don't do me bad / It's such a perfect day for making love / Sometimes you lose, sometimes you win / Cotton Dan / I'll spend a lifetime loving you / Night I cried / Cry yourself a river / Sugar baby candy girl / How long would it take / Just a bum husband / Best mistake I ever made / Bucks worth of change / I wonder who she missed me with today / I sat down on a beartrap (just this morning) / It starts off good (and keeps gettin' better) / Times and things keep changing / Last days of love
CD Set BCD 15619
Bear Family / Feb '94 / Direct / Rollercoaster / Swift

King Crimson

B BOOM OFFICIAL LIVE IN ARGENTINA
Vroom / Frame by frame / Sex, sleep, eat, drink, dream / Red / One time / B'boom / Thrak / Two sticks / Elephant talk / Indiscipline / Vroom vroom / Matte kudasai / Talking drum / Lark's tongues in aspic (part 2) / Heartbeat / Sleepless / People / B'boom (Reprise)
CD DGM 9503
Discipline / Jul '95 / Pinnacle

BEAT
Neal and Jack and Me / Heartbeat / Sartori in Tangier / Waiting man / Neurotica / Two Hands / Howler / Requiem
CD EGCD 51
EG / Jan '87 / EMI

COMPACT KING CRIMSON, THE
Discipline / Thel hun ginjeet / Matte Kudasai / Three of a perfect pair / Frame by frame / Sleepless / Heartbeat / Elephant talk / 21st century schizoid man / I talk to the wind / Epitaph / March for no reason (part of Epitaph) / Tomorrow and tomorrow (part of Epitaph) / Red / Cat food / Court of the crimson king / Return of the fire witch / Dance of the puppets
CD EGCD 68
EG / Jan '86 / EMI

CONCISE KING CRIMSON, THE
21st Century schizoid man / Epitaph / In the court of the Crimson King / Cat food / Ladies in the road / Starless (abridged) / Red / Fallen angel / Elephant talk / Frame by frame / Matte kudesai / Heartbeat / Three of a perfect pair / Sleepless
CD CDV 2721
Virgin / Oct '93 / EMI

DISCIPLINE
Elephant talk / Frame by frame / Matte Kudasai / Indiscipline / Thel hun ginjeet / Sheltering sky / Discipline
CD EGCD 49
EG / Jun '88 / EMI

EPITAPH (King Crimson Live In 1969/ 2CD Set)
21st Century schizoid man / In the court of the crimson king / Get thy bearings / Epitaph / Man a city / Travel weary capricorn / Mars
CD Set DGM 9607
Discipline / Apr '97 / Pinnacle

FRAME BY FRAME (The Essential King Crimson - 4CD Set)
21st Century schizoid man / I talk to the wind / Epitaph / Moonchild / In the court of the crimson King / Peace - a theme / Cat food / Groon / Cadence and cascade / Ladies of the road / Sailor's tale / Bolero / Larks' tongues in aspic / Night watch / Great deceiver / Fracture / Starless / Red / Fallen angel / One more red nightmare / Elephant talk / Frame by frame / Matte Kudesai / Thela Hun Gingeet / Heartbeat / Waiting man / Neurotica / Requiem / Three of a perfect pair / Sleepless / Sheltering sky / Discipline / King Crimson barbershop / Get thy bearings and variations / Travel weary Capricorn / Mars / Talking drum / 21st Century schizoid man / Asbury Park / Larks' tongues in aspic part 3 / Sartori in Tangiers / Indiscipline
CD Set KCBOX 1
Virgin / Jul '95 / EMI

GREAT DECEIVER, THE (4CD Set)
CD Set KCDIS 1
Virgin / Nov '92 / EMI

IN THE COURT OF THE CRIMSON KING
21st century schizoid man / I talk to the wind / Epitaph / Tomorrow and tomorrow (part of Epitaph) / Moonchild / Illusion / Court of the Crimson King / Return Of The fire witch / Dance of the puppets / March for no reason (part of Epitaph) / Dream
CD EGCD 1
EG / Jan '87 / EMI

IN THE WAKE OF POSEIDON
Peace - a beginning / Pictures of a city / Cadence and cascade / In the wake of Poseidon / Peace - a theme / Cat food / Devil's triangle / Merday Morn (part 1 of the Devil's Triangle) / Hand of Sceiron / Garden of worm (part 3 of the Devil's triangle) / Peace - an end
CD EGCD 2
EG / Jul '92 / EMI

LARKS' TONGUES IN ASPIC
Lark's tongues in aspic (part 1) / Book of Saturday / Exiles / Easy Money / Talking drum / Lark's tongues in aspic (part 2)
CD EGCD 7
EG / Jul '92 / EMI

LIZARD
Cirkus / Indoor games / Happy family / Lady of the dancing water / Lizard / Prince Rupert awakes (part 1 of Lizard) / Bolero / Battle of glass tears / Dawn song (part a of battle of glass tears) / Last skirmish (part b of Battle of Glass Tears) / Prince Rupert's lament (Part C of Battle of Glass Tears) / Big top
CD EGCD 4
EG / '88 / EMI

LIZARD/IN THE WAKE OF POSEIDON/ IN THE COURT OF THE... (3CD Set)
CD Set TPAK 28
Virgin / Nov '93 / EMI

RED
Red / Fallen angel / One more red nightmare / Providence / Starless
CD EGCD 15
EG / Jan '87 / EMI

STARLESS AND BIBLE BLACK
Great deceiver / Lament / We'll let you know / Night watch / Trio / Mincer / Starless and bible black / Fracture
CD EGCD 12
EG / '87 / EMI
CD CDVKC 6
Virgin / Jul '97 / EMI

THRAK
Vroom / Coda: marine 475 / Dinosaur / Walking on air / B'boom / Thrak / Inner garden / People / Radio I / One time / Radio II / Inner garden II / Sex, sleep, eat, drink, dream / Vroom vroom / Vroom vroom coda
CD KCCDY 1
CD KCCDX 1
Virgin / Apr '95 / EMI

THREE OF A PERFECT PAIR
Model man / Sleepless / Man with an open heart / Nuages (that which passes, passes like clouds) / Dig me / No warning / Lark's tongues in aspic (part 3) / Three of a perfect pair / Industry
CD EGCD 55
EG / Jan '87 / EMI

VROOOM
Vroom / Sex, sleep, eat, drink, dream / Cage / Thrack / When I say stop, continue / One time
CD DGM 0004
Discipline / Oct '94 / Pinnacle

King Curry

BEYOND GOOD AND EVIL
CD 342562
No Bull / Jun '96 / Koch

King Curtis

BEST OF KING CURTIS, THE
Night train / One mint julep / Soul twist / Soul serenade / Honky tonk / Slow drag / Hide away / Strollin' home / Sister Sadie / Tanya / Summer dream / Hung over / Bill Bailey, won't you please come home / More soul / Shake / Change is gonna come
CD CDP 8365042
Capitol Jazz / Aug '96 / EMI

BLUES AT MONTREUX (King Curtis & Champion Jack Dupree)
Junker's blues / Sneaky Pete / Everything's gonna be alright / Get with it / Poor boy blues / I'm having fun
CD 7567813892
Atlantic / Jan '96 / Warner Music

CAPITOL YEARS, THE (1962-1965)
Turn 'em on / Beach party / Beautiful brown eyes / Your cheatin' heart / Tennessee waltz / Wagon wheels / High noon / Anytime / Home on the range / Night train to Memphis / I'm movin' on / Raunchy / Tumbling tumbleweeds / Walking the floor over you / Slow drag / New dance / Frisky / Alexander's ragtime band / Amorosa (Bossa Nova) / Strollin' home / Mess around / Sukiyaki / Summer dream / Do the monkey / Feel all right / Turn 'em on (Mono) / Theme from Lillies Of The Field (Amen) / More soul / Soul serenade / Honky tonk / Watermelon man / Memphis / Soul twist / Night train / Tequila / Wiggle wobble / One mint julep / Can't sit down / Swingin' shepherd blues / My last date / Hideaway / Harlem Nocturne / Java / Stranger on the shore / Melancholy serenade / Summer dream / Tanya / Hung over / Soul twine (Stereo) / Hungover / Soul twine (Mono) / Moon river / Girl from Ipanema / Sister Sadie / Something you've got / Take these chains from my heart / Let it be me / Hung over (Re-make) / Misty (Re-make) / Bill Bailey, Won't you please come home / Peter Gunn / Shake / Ain't that good news / Twistin' the night away / Good times / Send me some lovin' / Bring it on home to me / Change is gonna come / You send me / Cupid / Having a party / Chain gang / Prance / Something you've got (Overdub)
CD Set BCD 15670
Bear Family / Mar '93 / Direct / Rollercoaster / Swift

GROOVIN' WITH THE KING (The Best Of King Curtis)
Soul twist / Night train / Groovin' with the King / Midnight blue / Watermelon man / Peter Gunn / Soul serenade / Irresistible you / Big dipper / I know / Jack-o-wee / What'd I say / Wiggle wobble / Camp meetin' / Memphis
CD AIM 2010CD
Aim / May '97 / ADA / Direct / Jazz Music

IT'S PARTY TIME
Free for all / Easy like / Hot saxes / I'll wait for you / Party time twist / Low down / Keep movin' / (Let's do) the hully gully twist / Slow motion / Firefly / Something frantic
CD CDCH 262
Ace / Nov '93 / Pinnacle

OLD GOLD/DOING THE DIXIE TWIST
Fever / Honky tonk / So rare / Tippin' in / You came a long way from St. Louis / Tuxedo junction / Hucklebuck / Lean baby / Harlem nocturne / Night train / Soft / Sweet Georgia Brown / Alexander's ragtime band / (In) a shanty in old Shanty Town / St. Louis blues / Royal garden blues / When the saints go marching in / Basin Street blues / Muskrat ramble / Up a lazy river / St. James infirmary
CD CDCHD 614
Ace / Jul '95 / Pinnacle

SOUL TWIST (The Complete Enjoy Sessions) (King Curtis & The Knoble Knights)
CD CPCD 8195
Charly / Aug '96 / Koch

TROUBLE IN MIND
Trouble in mind / Jivin' time / Nobody wants you when you're down and out / Bad bad whiskey / I have to worry / Woke up this morning / But that's alright / Ain't nobody's business if I do / Don't deceive me / Deep fry
CD CDCHD 545
Ace / Jul '94 / Pinnacle

King Diamond

ABIGAIL
CD RR 349622
Roadrunner / Jun '87 / PolyGram

CONSPIRACY
At the graves / Lies / Wedding dream / Something weird / Let it be done / Sleepless nights / Visit from the dead / Amon belongs to them / Victimised / Cremation
CD RR 94612
Roadrunner / Aug '89 / PolyGram

DARK SIDES, THE
Halloween / Tem / No presents for Christmas / Shrine / Lake / Phone call
CD RR 24552
Roadrunner / Oct '88 / PolyGram

EYE, THE
CD RR 93462
Roadrunner / Nov '90 / PolyGram

FATAL PORTRAIT
CD RR 349721
Roadrunner / '87 / PolyGram

GRAVEYARD, THE
CD MASSDP 103
Massacre / Sep '96 / Plastic Head

IN CONCERT 1987
CD RR 92872
Roadrunner / Dec '91 / PolyGram

SPIDERS LULLABY, THE
CD MASSCD 062
Massacre / Jun '95 / Plastic Head

THEM
CD RR 95502
Roadrunner / Jul '88 / PolyGram

King, Diana

TOUGHER THAN LOVE
Love me thru the night / Shy guy / Love triangle / Ain't nobody / Tougher than love / Can't do without you / Slow rush / Treat her like a lady / Black roses / Tumble down
CD 47777562
Columbia / Jul '95 / Sony

King, Earl

GLAZED (King, Earl & Roomful Of Blues)
It all went down the drain / Your love was never there / Everybody's gotta cry sometime / Love rent / Iron cupid / Somebody's got a tail / I met a stranger / Mardi gras in the city / Those lonely lonely nights / One step beyond love
CD CD 1035
Black Top / '88 / ADA / CM / Direct

HARD RIVER TO CROSS
CD BT 1090CD
Black Top / Jun '93 / ADA / CM / Direct

MILL IS GONE, THE
CD ANDCD 4
Telstar / Nov '96 / BMG

NEW ORLEANS STREET TALKIN'
It all went down the drain / Everybody's gotta cry sometime / Clairvoyant lady / Sexual telepathy / Love is the way of life / Medieval days / Time for the sun to rise / Old Mr. Bad Luck / Always a first time / Hard river to cross / No city like New Orleans
CD ________ CDBTEL 7004
Black Top / May '97 / ADA / CM / Direct

SEXUAL TELEPATHY
Old Mr. Bad Luck / I'll take you back home / Weary silent night / Time for the sun to rise / No one more for the road / Going public / Love is the way of life / Sexual telepathy / Happy little nobody's waggy tail dog / Always a first time / Make a better world
CD ________ FIENDCD 168
Demon / Aug '90 / Pinnacle

King Ernest

KING OF HEARTS
I resign / I'm not the one / In the dark / Black bag blues / Better days / Long as I have you / Tell me what's the reason / Cryin' for my baby / Sadie / Forgive me
CD ________ ECD 260842
Evidence / Mar '97 / ADA / Cadillac / Harmonia Mundi

King, Evelyn

BEST OF EVELYN 'CHAMPAGNE' KING, THE (King, Evelyn 'Champagne')
Shame / I'm in love / If you want my lovin' / Just for the night / Betcha she don't love you / I'm so romantic / Back to love / I don't know if it's right / Love come down / Action / High horse / Get loose / Music box / Shake down / I can't stand it / Your personal touch
CD ________ ND 74538
RCA / Apr '90 / BMG

FLIRT (King, Evelyn 'Champagne')
Flirt / You can turn me on / Kisses don't lie / Stop it / Hold on to what you've got / When your heart says yes / Before the date / Whenever you touch me
CD ________ CDGOLD 1036
EMI Gold / May '96 / EMI

I'LL KEEP A LIGHT ON (King, Evelyn 'Champagne')
Fascinated / I think about you / I'll keep a light on / It doesn't really matter / When it comes down to it / Sweet funky thing / Lover I can love / Starchild / Love is love (All over the world) / It's not that kind of party / In it for me / Hold tight / Shame '95
CD ________ XECD 1
Expansion / Jul '95 / 3mv/Sony

King Felix

OWL PLANE CRASH
CD ________ SR 9450
Silent / May '94 / Cargo / Plastic Head

King Ferus

MACEDONIAN WEDDING SOUL COOKING
Revisko oro / Romaniada / Kumov cocek/ Olimpijski cocek / Basal ferus / Staro cunovo oro / Turska igra / Romska gajda / Stipski cocek / Romska riznica / Bugarsko K4 oro / Dada sali / Dikman / Stipski sa sa / Tikino sa sa / Kocovo oro
CD ________ CDORBD 089
Globestyle / May '95 / Pinnacle

King, Freddie

17 HITS
CD ________ KCD 5012
King / Apr '97 / Avid/BMG

BLUES GUITAR HERO: THE INFLUENTIAL EARLY SESSIONS
Hideaway / Lonesome whistle blues / San-Ho-Zay / I'm tore down / See see baby / Christmas tears / You've got to love her with a feeling / Have you ever loved a woman / You know that you love me / I love the woman / It's too bad things are going so tough / Sen-sa-shun / Takin' care of business / Stumble / Sittin' on the boat dock / Side tracked / What about love / Come on / Just pickin' / I'm on my way to Atlanta / In the open / (The welfare) turns its back on you / She put the whamee on me
CD ________ CDCHD 454
Ace / Aug '93 / Pinnacle

BOOGIE ON DOWN
Your move / Ain't gonna worry anymore / Hideaway / Guitar blues / Meet me in the morning / Sweet home Chicago / Boogie on down / Big legged woman / Hey baby / I'm tore down / Key to the highway / Have you ever loved a woman / Going down / Introduction / You're so good looking / Look on yonder wall / Ain't nobody's business / Big legged woman
CD ________ CDBM 503
Blue Moon / Sep '96 / Cadillac / Discovery / Greensleeves / Jazz Music / Jet Star / TKO Magnum

BURGLAR
Pack it up / My credit didn't go through / I got the same old blues / Only getting second best / Texas flyer / Pulp wood / She's a burglar / Sugar sweet / I had a dream / Come on (let the good times roll)
CD ________ BGOCD 137
Beat Goes On / Apr '92 / Pinnacle

FREDDIE KING
CD ________ DVBC 9062
Deja Vu / May '95 / THE

FREDDIE KING LIVE
Big legged woman / Woman across the river / Look on yonder wall / Ain't no sunshine / Red light / Green light / We're gonna boogie / Have you ever loved a woman / Let the good times roll / Going down (encore)
CD ________ CDCBL 759
Charly / May '95 / Koch

FREDDIE KING SINGS
CD ________ MBCD 722
Modern Blues / Jun '93 / ADA / Direct

HIDEAWAY
See see baby / You've got to love her with a feeling / Have you ever loved a woman / Hideaway / I love the woman / Country boy / That's what you think / Lonesome whistle blues / It's too bad things are going so tough / I'm tore down / Sen-sa-shun / Side tracked / Stumble / San-ho-zay / Christmas tears / In the open / Takin' care of business / Driving sideways / Someday after awhile (you'll be sorry) / (The welfare) turns it's back on you / Let me down easy
CD ________ CD 52041
Blues Encore / Oct '96 / Target/BMG

KING OF THE BLUES
Same old blues / Dust my broom / Worried life blues / Five long years / Key to the highway / Going down / Living on the highway / Walking by myself / Tore down / Palace of the king / Lowdown in Lodi / Reconsider baby / Big legged woman / Me and my guitar / I'd rather be blind / Can't trust your neighbour / You was wrong / How many more years / Ain't no sunshine / Sky is crying / That's alright Mama / Woman across the river / Hoochie coochie man / Danger zone / Boogie man / Leave my woman alone / Just a little bit / Yonder wall / Help me through the day / I'm ready / Trouble in my mind / You don't have to go / Please send me someone to love / Gimme some lovin' / Love her with a feeling / Boogie fuck / It hurts me too / Something you got / Ain't no big deal on you / I just want to make love to you / Hide away
CD ________ CDEM 1580
Premier/EMI / Nov '95 / EMI

LET'S HIDE AWAY AND DANCE AWAY
CD ________ KCD 773
King / Mar '90 / Avid/BMG

LIVE AT THE ELECTRIC BALLROOM 1974
CD ________ CDBT 1127
Black Top / Mar '96 / ADA / CM / Direct

LIVE AT THE LIBERTY HALL
Hey baby / Feeling alright / Ain't no sunshine / Going down / Have you ever loved a woman / My feeling for the blues / I love you so / Let the good times roll / Kansas City
CD ________ CDBM 097
Blue Moon / Jul '95 / Cadillac / Discovery / Greensleeves / Jazz Music / Jet Star / TKO Magnum

LIVE IN ANTIBES 1974
Going down the Highway / Woman across the river / Ain't nobody's business if I do / Let the good times roll / Big legged woman / Have you ever loved a woman / Hideaway
CD ________ FCD 111
France's Concert / Jun '88 / BMG / Jazz Music

LIVE IN NANCY 1975 VOL.1
CD ________ FCD 126
France's Concert / Jun '89 / BMG / Jazz Music

PALACE OF THE KING
Living in the palace of the king / Please accept my love / Shake your booty baby / Mojo boogie / Big legged man / Hey baby / Look on yonder wall / Woman across the river / Have you ever loved a woman / Rock me baby
CD ________ CDBM 089
Blue Moon / Feb '92 / Cadillac / Discovery / Greensleeves / Jazz Music / Jet Star / TKO Magnum

TEXAS CANNONBALL
Freddie Kings with the Buggs Henderson band / Spoken introduction / Your move / Ain't gonna worry anymore / Hideaway / Guitar blues / Meet me in the morning / Boogie on down / Sweet home Chicago
CD ________ CDBM 062
Blue Moon / Nov '90 / Cadillac / Discovery / Greensleeves / Jazz Music / Jet Star / TKO Magnum

TEXAS SENSATION
You've got to love her with a feeling / Hideaway / Have you ever loved a woman / Sen-sa-shun / Look ma, I'm cryin' / San-Ho-Zay / I'm tore down / Driving sideways / Takin' care of business / Someday after a while / Side tracked / You know that you love me / Teardrops on your letter / Stumble / She's put the whammy on me / Lonesome whistle blues / High rise / It's too bad (things are going so tough) / Welfare (turns its back on you) / Double eyed whammy
CD ________ CDCHARLY 247
Charly / Oct '90 / Koch

THIS IS THE BLUES
CD ________ IMP 701
Iris Music / Nov '95 / Discovery

King Galliard

ROCKY ROAD TO DUBLIN
CD ________ 15370
Laserlight / '91 / Target/BMG

King Hash

HUMDINGER
Hard as I try / I'm the one / Jessie May / Hey now / All I ever wanted was you / She's on the move / Deliver me from evil / What can I do / Leave a light on / Jack fell down / Jessie May (Reprise)
CD ________ IGCD 201
Iona / Jan '94 / ADA / Direct / Duncans

King Jammy

COMPUTER STYLE
CD ________ 792022
Ras / Nov '92 / Direct / Greensleeves / Jet Star / SRD

HITS STYLE
CD ________ 792032
Ras / Nov '92 / Direct / Greensleeves / Jet Star / SRD

ROOTS & HARMONY STYLE
CD ________ 792012
Ras / Nov '92 / Direct / Greensleeves / Jet Star / SRD

King, James

LONESOME AND THEN SOME
CD ________ ROUCD 0350
Rounder / Oct '95 / ADA / CM / Direct

THESE OLD PICTURES
CD ________ ROUCD 305
Rounder / Jan '94 / ADA / CM / Direct

King, Jimmy

SOLDIER FOR THE BLUES (King, Jimmy & The King James Version)
Living in the danger zone / Drawers / I'm doing fine / Life is hard / I don't need nobody that don't need me / We'll be together again / Soldier for the blues / You ain't bulletproof / It takes a whole lot of money / Don't wanna go home / It ain't the same no mo' / I got sick one day
CD ________ CDBB 9582
Bullseye Blues / Jul '97 / Direct

King, Johnny

MELTDOWN
Meltdoen / After six / Third rail / Quiet as it's kept / So sorry please / Jacqueline's chimes / Lady Macbeth / Wellspring / Cochabamba / For Tomorrow / Blues for Andrew Hill
CD ________ ENJ 93292
Enja / Sep '97 / New Note/Pinnacle / Vital/SAM

NOTES FROM THE UNDERGROUND
Gnosis / Notes from the underground / Soliloquy / Caffeine / Mean to me / Blow-up / Common law / Las ramblas
CD ________ ENJ 90672
Enja / Apr '96 / New Note/Pinnacle / Vital/SAM

King, Jonathan

ANTICLONING
CD ________ REVVC 1
Sounds Of Revolution / Dec '92 / Grapevine/PolyGram

CREATIONS AND RELATIONS (Various Artists)
Everyone's gone to the moon / Hooked on a feeling: *King, Jonathan* / Just like a woman: *King, Jonathan* / I'll slap your face: *King, Jonathan* / Una paloma blanca: *King, Jonathan* / It only takes a minute girl: *100 Ton & A Feather* / Loop di love: *Shag* / Chick-a-boom: *33 & A Third* / Piglets: *Johnny Reggae* / It's the same old song: *Weathermen* / Lick a smurf for Christmas: *Father Abraphart & The Smurps* / Sun has got it's hat on: *Nemo* / In the mood: *Sound 9418* / I can't get no satisfaction: *Bubblerock* / Sugar sugar: *Sakkarin* / Leap up and down (wave your knickers in the air): *St. Cecilia* / It's good news week: *Hedgehoppers Anonymous* / Rubber Bullets: *10cc* / Silent sun: *Genesis* / Time warp: *London Cast*
CD ________ SUMCD 4129
Sound & Media / Jun '97 / Sound & Media

MANY FACES OF JONATHAN KING
CD ________ MCCD 108
Music Club / May '93 / Disc / THE

King, Jonny

IN FROM THE COLD
CD ________ CRISS 1093CD
Criss Cross / Sep '95 / Cadillac / Direct / Vital/SAM

King Kong

FUNNY FARM
CD ________ DC 33
Drag City / Dec '96 / Cargo / Greyhound

ME HUNGRY
CD ________ DC 67CD
Drag City / Dec '96 / Cargo / Greyhound

King Krab

KICKING ROSE
CD ________ EAR 12
Earthling / Mar '93 / SRD

King Kurt

LIVE AND ROCKIN'
CD ________ LOMACD 18
Loma / Aug '94 / BMG

OOH WALLAH WALLAH
Zulu beat / Destination zululand / Bo Diddley goes east / King Kurt's hound dog / Wreck a party rock / Ghost riders in the sky / Gather your limbs / Rockin' Kurt / Lonesome train (on a lonesome track) / Mack the knife / Oedipus rex / Do the rat / She's as hairy / Mack the knife (Remix) / Wreck a party rock (Extended version) / Banana banana banana / Scraming abdabs / Ape hour
CD ________ DOJOCD 91
Dojo / Dec '92 / Disc

POOR MAN'S DREAM
CD ________ FIENDCD 761
Demon / Nov '94 / Pinnacle

King L

GREAT DAY FOR GRAVITY
Tragedy girl / Dumbest story / Tom Driver / Greedy / All hail the alien Queen / Back to loving arms / Life after you / That's how it works / Hoping they'll be open / First man on the sun / Two cars collide / Don't believe in Hollywood / Lost and found and lost again / My last cigarette
CD ________ CIRCD 32
Circa / Oct '95 / EMI

King, Lana

KING AND COUNTRY
Blue bayou / I will always love you / Stand by your man / Carolina moon / He'll have to go / Desperado / Don't it make my brown eyes blue / Take these chains / Will you still love me tomorrow / Make it through the night / Rose / Amazing grace
CD ________ SOV 001CD
Sovereign / '92 / Target/BMG

King, Little Jimmy

SOMETHING INSIDE OF ME
CD ________ BB 9537
Bullseye Blues / Apr '94 / Direct

King Loser

CAUL OF THE OUTLAW
Troubled land / 1692 / Band on the run / Cyclonic vibration / Situation / Alien presence / New age power / Solid sky line / Lazenby's folly / Shadow / Change the locks / Four from the dark side
CD ________ FNCD 382
Flying Nun / Apr '97 / RTM/Disc

YOU CANNOT KILL WHAT DOES NOT LIVE
CD ________ FNCD 309
Flying Nun / Oct '95 / RTM/Disc

King Memphis

ASTONISHING KING MEMPHIS, THE
Crazy alien chick / Little Joe from Chicago / C'mon pretty baby / Lone star / Mr. Clean / Let it go / She hit me with a whip / 1962 ragtop / Gonna have a ball / Baby baby / You gotta pay / Walkin' my baby back home / Big hair / Red hot and ready / Gas cap / I'm mad
CD ________ NERCD 086
Nervous / Jun '96 / Nervous / TKO Magnum

King Missile

HAPPY HOUR
Sink / Martin Scorsese / (Why are we) Trapped / It's Saturday / Vulvavoid / Metanoia / Detachable penis / Take me home / Ed / Anywhere / Evil children / Glass / And / King Murdock / I'm sorry / Heaven / Happy hour
CD ________ 7567824592
WEA / Feb '93 / Warner Music

KING MISSILE
Love is / What if / Let's have sex / Pigs will fly / These people / Open up / Wind up toys / Delores / Tongue / Dishwasher / Socks / Bloodletting / Lies / Commercial / King David's dirge / Psalm / Happy note
CD ________ 7567825892
WEA / Jun '94 / Warner Music

King, Morgana

ANOTHER TIME, ANOTHER SPACE
CD MCD 5339
Muse / Sep '92 / New Note/Pinnacle

EVERYTHING MUST CHANGE
CD MCD 5190
Muse / Feb '86 / New Note/Pinnacle

FOR YOU, FOR ME, FOR EVERMORE
For you, for me, for evermore / Here I'll stay / There's a lull in my life / It's de-lovely / Down in the depths / Song is you / In the wee small hours of the morning / Everything I love / If you could see me now / I'll string along with you / Everything I've got / You're not so easy to forget
CD 5140772
EmArCy / May '93 / PolyGram

SIMPLY ELOQUENT
CD MCD 5326
Muse / Sep '92 / New Note/Pinnacle

King, Nancy

CLIFF DANCE (King, Nancy & Glen Moore)
CD JR 08032
Justice / Jun '94 / Koch

POTATO RADIO (King, Nancy & Glen Moore)
CD JR 008022
Justice / Oct '92 / Koch

King Of Hearts

MIDNIGHT CROSSING
CD IRS 993167
Edge Of Fluke / Mar '97 / Cargo

King Of The Slums

BLOWZY WEIRDOS
Gone all weirdo / Smile so big / Casin' the joint / Hot pot shebeen / Keepin' it all sweet / Clubland gangs / Joy / Rimo / Mard arse / Mood on / Blowzy luv of life
CD CDBRED93
Cherry Red / Jul '91 / Pinnacle

King, Paul

HOUDINI'S MOON
CD ANDCD 5
Telstar / Nov '96 / BMG

King, Paul

BEEN IN THE PEN TOO LONG/ TROUBLE AT MILL (King, Paul/King Earl Boogie Band)
Grey eyed Athena / Jean Harlow / Sugarcane / Three dog night / Whoa Buck / Clockwork machine / Candy man / I've changed my face / One legged man in a goldfish bowl / Bad storm coming / Take me back / Live your own life / Bovver blues / Plastic Jesus / If the Lord don't got you / Goin' the German / Keep your hands off my woman / Go down you murderer
CD SEECD 429
See For Miles/C5 / Jul '95 / Pinnacle

King, Pee Wee

PEE WEE KING & THE GOLDEN WEST COWBOYS (7CD Set) (King, Pee Wee & The Golden West Cowboys)
That cheap look in your eye / You were the cause of it all / Texas Toni Lee / Tennessee central / Southland polka / Steel guitar rag / Hear you knockin' / Keep them cold icy fingers off of me / Don't feel sorry for me / Arkansas traveller / Out of my mind / Ten gallon boogie / Kentucky waltz / Don't forget / Jukebox blues / Chattanooga Bess / Say good mornin' Nellie / Forty nine women / Ghost and honest Joe / New York to New Orleans / I'm satisfied with you / Quit honkin' that horn / Oh Monah / Bull fiddle boogie / Tenesse waltz / Rootie tootie / Gotta climb those golden stairs / Every time I feel the spirit / Gospel boogie / Singin' as I go / Waltz of the Alamo / Whisper waltz / I lost my love (the color song) / Bonaparte's retreat / Bluegrass waltz / Alabama moon / Tennessee tears / Get together polka / Nashville waltz / Waltz of regret / Lonesome steel guitar / Cornbread, lasses and sassafras tea / Fire on the mountain / Shocking rye straw / Billy in the lowground / Devil's dream / Fisher's hornpipe / Sally Goodin / Whistling Rufus / Going back to LA / You call everybody darlin' / Battle hymn of the Republic / Black eyed Susie / When they played that old Missouri waltz / Blame it all on Nashville / Kissing dance / Rag mop / What, where and when / Birmingham bounce / We're gonna go fishin' (next Saturday night) / Cincinnati dancing pig / River road two step / Mop rag boogie / No one but you / Within my heart (la golondrina) / Helegged hilegged / You drifted / Strange little girl / Chew tabacco rag / Slow poke / You won't need my love anymore / Two roads / Railroad boogie / Makin' like a train / Crying steel guitar waltz / Ragtime Annie Lee / Slow bloke / Slow coach / Silver and gold / If and when / Busybody / I don't mind / Two-faced clock / Mighty pretty waltz / Tennessee tango / Crazy waltz / Varsoviana / San Antonio rose / My adobe hacienda / One rose (that's left in my heart) / Under the double eagle / Spanish two step / Over the waves / Screwball / Last night on the back porch / Till I waltz again with you / Gone / I'll go on alone / That's me without you / Your kisses aren't kisses anymore / Here lies my heart / Oh mis'rable love / Richochet / Dragnet / Deck of cards / Huggin' my pillow / Changin partners / Bimbo / Backward, turn backward / In a garden of roses / Red deck of cards / Keep your eye on my darling / Indian giver / Why don't you all go home / How long / Peek-a-boo waltz / Peaches and cream / I can't tell a waltz from a tango / Flying home / Woodchopper's ball / Seven come eleven / Farewell blues / Tippin' in / Melody of love / You can't hardly get them no more / Tweedle Dee / Plantation boogie / Jim, Johnny and Jonas / Nevermind / Beauty is as beauty does / Half a dozen boogie / Blue suede shoes / Tennessee dancin' doll / Ballroom baby / Catty town / Absolutely, positively / Hoot scoot / I'll be walking alone in a crowd / Sugar beet / (I tasted) tears on your lips / Catchy tune / My darlin' (we're not too young to know) / Do you remember / Congratulations Joe / Prelude to a broken heart / Unbreakable heart / Janie / Little bit about myself (a phonobiography)
CD Set BCD 15727
Bear Family / Feb '85 / Direct / Rollercoaster / Swift

King, Peter

SPEED TRAP
Mr. Silver / My man's gone now / TNK / Naima / Speed trap / Getting on
CD JHCD 041
Ronnie Scott's Jazz House / Feb '96 / Cadillac / Jazz Music / New Note/Pinnacle / TKO Magnum

TAMBURELLO
Dido's lament / You taught my heart how to sing / Boxer's demise / Leona / Bess, oh where's my Bess / My man's gone now / Yes or no / Imola / Ayrton / Tamburello / Theme from bartok's violin concert No.2 / Please don't ever leave me
CD MMCD 083
Miles Music / Jul '95 / Cadillac / New Note/ Pinnacle / Wellard

King Pin

GOD OF LOVE
CD ARICD 072
Ariwa Sounds / Apr '92 / Jet Star / SRD

LETTER FROM JAIL
CD ARICD 059
Ariwa Sounds / Sep '90 / Jet Star / SRD

King Pleasure

BETTER BEWARE (King Pleasure & The Biscuit Boys)
Better beware / That's what makes old KP fat / I'll wait for you / World of trouble / Hey babe rebop / Last laugh now / Hot beef / Don't you know / Love rollercoaster / Money can't buy love / Daddy of jive / Walk'em / Hop skip and jump / Feelin' happy / Let 'em roll again
CD ESJCD 544
Essential Jazz / Apr '97 / BMG

THIS IS IT (King Pleasure & The Biscuit Boys)
Mr Blues is coming to town / Squeeze me / Lovin' me / Bongo boogie / Fish man / House party / Jumpin' from six to six / This is it / Why don't you do right / Train kept a rollin' / Bad bad whiskey / Drinkin' wine spo-dee-o-dee / Ain't nobody here but us chickens / Chicken rhythm / All night long
CD ESJCD 540
Essential Jazz / Apr '97 / BMG

King Pleasure

KING PLEASURE & ANNIE ROSS SING (King Pleasure & Annie Ross)
Red top / Sometimes I'm happy / What can I say after I say I'm sorry / Parker's mood / Twisted / Time was right / Jumpin' with symphony sid / This is always / Don't get scared / I'm gone / Farmer's market / Annie's lament / I'm in the mood for love / Exclamation blues / You're crying / Funk junction
CD OJCCD 217
Original Jazz Classics / Apr '96 / Complete/ Pinnacle / Jazz Music / Wellard

King Prawn

FIRST OFFENCE
CD WOWCD 46
Words Of Warning / Dec '96 / SRD / Total/BMG

King Rosa

CHEATING ON ME (King Rosa & Upside Down)
CD BL 013
Bloomdido / Oct '93 / Cadillac

King, Sandra

CONCERT OF VERNON DUKE, A (King, Sandra & Pat Smythe)
CD ACD 197
Audiophile / Mar '95 / Jazz Music

SANDRA KING & FRIENDS
CD ACD 222
Audiophile / Aug '94 / Jazz Music

SONGS OF VERNON DUKE
CD ACD 187
Audiophile / Oct '93 / Jazz Music

King, Shirley

JUMP THROUGH MY KEYHOLE
CD GBW 007
GBW / Nov '92 / Harmonia Mundi

King, Sid

GONNA SHAKE THIS SHACK TONIGHT (King, Sid & The Five Strings)
Good rockin' baby / Put something in the pot boy / Drinkin' wine spoli-oli / When my baby left me / Gonna shake this shack tonight / It's true, I'm blue / Crazy little heart / Mama I want you / I like it / But I don't care / Warmed over kisses / What have ya got to lose / I've got the blues / Ooby dooby / Booger red / Twenty one / Sag, drag and fall / Blue suede shoes / Let 'er roll / Purr, kitty, purr
CD BCD 15535
Bear Family / Mar '92 / Direct / Rollercoaster / Swift

King Sisters

FOR YOU
For you / Just squeeze me / When the swallows come back to Capistrano / What's the use / Sophisticated lady / Everybody loves my baby / Stardust / Between the devil and the deep blue sea / At sundown / When my dreamboat comes home / Crazy rhythm / Miss Otis regrets / Red sails in the sunset / Man I love
CD HCD 168
Hindsight / Mar '96 / Jazz Music / Target/ BMG

King Sounds

I SHALL SING
CD VZA 002 CD
Viza / Jan '94 / Jet Star

King, Tempo

TEMPO KING 1936-1937
Bojangles of Harlem / I'll sing you a thousand love songs / Organ grinder swing / Papa tree top tall / William Tell / (I would do) anything for you / High hat, a piccolo and a cane / We can cuddle at home / You're giving me a song and a dance / Alabama barbecue / That's what you mean to me / Sweet Adeline / You've got something there / Through the courtesy of love / I was saying to the moon / One hour for lunch / To Mary, with love / Swingin' the jinx away / Keepin' out of mischief now / You turned the tables on me / Swing high swing low / Floating on a bubble / Gee but you're swell
CD CBC 1002
Timeless Historical / Jan '92 / New Note/ Pinnacle

King Tubby

CREATION DUB
CD LG 21111
Lagoon / Jul '95 / Grapevine/PolyGram

CROSSFIRE
CD LG 21050
Lagoon / Nov '92 / Grapevine/PolyGram

DANGEROUS DUB (King Tubby & Roots Radics)
Country gal dub / Loud mouth rock / Up town special / Hungry belly dub / Shepherd bush in dub / London Bridge special / Earthquake shake / Rice grain rock / Banana and yam skank / Knife and fork dubwise / King Stereo gav dub / King Tubby's hi-fi dub / Symbolic dub
CD GRELCD 229
Greensleeves / Nov '96 / Jet Star / SRD

DUB GONE 2 CRAZY (King Tubby & Prince Jammy)
CD BAFCD 13
Blood & Fire / Jul '96 / Vital

DUB GONE CRAZY (The Evolution Of Dub At King Tubby's 1975-79) (King Tubby & Friends)
Champion version / Satta dread dub / Real gone crazy dub / Exalted dub / Dreada version / No love version / Peace and love in the dub / Wreck up a version / Hold them in dub / Jah love rockers dub / Step it up in dub / Dub with a view / Dub to the rescue / Dub fi gwan
CD BAFCD 2
Blood & Fire / May '94 / Vital

FIRST PROPHET OR DUB
CD TWCD 1012
Tamoki Wambesi / Dec '95 / Greensleeves / Jet Star / Roots Collective / SRD

FREEDOM SOUNDS IN DUB (King Tubby & The Soul Syndicate)
CD BAFCD 11
Blood & Fire / May '96 / Vital

GREENWICH FARM RUB A DUB (King Tubby & Scientist)
CD BAFCD 1001
Blood & Fire / May '96 / Vital

HERBS OF DUB (King Tubby & Jah Lloyd)
CD TMCD 1
Teem / Aug '96 / SRD

HOUSE OF DUB (Channel One & King Tubby)
CD GR 006CD
Sprint / May '95 / SRD

I AM THE KING
CD SFCD 003
Sprint / Jul '95 / SRD

I AM THE KING VOL.2
CD SFCD 4
Sprint / May '95 / SRD

I AM THE KING VOL.3
CD SFCD 006
Sprint / Aug '96 / SRD

IN ROOTS VIBES (King Tubby & Augustus Pablo)
CD LG 221121
Lagoon / Mar '97 / Jet Star

KING TUBBY MEETS THE UPSETTER AT THE GRASS ROOTS OF DUB (King Tubby & The Upsetter)
Blood of Africa / African roots / Rain roots / Wood roots / Luke lane rock / People from the grass roots / Crime wave / No justice for the poor / 300 years at the grass roots / King and The Upsetter at Spanish town
CD STCD 001
Studio 16 / Jun '97 / Jet Star

KING TUBBY MEETS VIVIAN JACKSON (King Tubby & Vivian Jackson)
CD YVJ 002CD
Yabby You / May '95 / Jet Star / THE

KING TUBBY ON THE MIX VOL.2 (Various Artists)
CD OMCD 023
Original Music / Jul '93 / Jet Star / SRD

KING TUBBY'S SOUNDCLASH VOL.1 & 2
CD SONCD 0012
Sonic Sounds / Jan '91 / Jet Star

KING TUBBY'S SPECIAL 1973 - 1976
CD CDTRD 409
Trojan / Mar '94 / Direct / Jet Star

KING TUBBY'S STUDIO VS. CHANNEL 1
CD RNCD 2126
Rhino / Nov '95 / Grapevine/PolyGram / Jet Star

MEMORIAL DUB
CD RNCD 2060
Rhino / Sep '94 / Grapevine/PolyGram / Jet Star

ROOTS & SOCIETY
CD RB 3003
Reggae Best / May '94 / Grapevine/ PolyGram

SENSI DUB VOL.3 (King Tubby & Prince Jammy)
Black up (dub) / Sensi dub (part 3) / Free herb / Ministers (dub) / No bush (dub) / Meditation / Court house (dub) / Heavy metal
CD OMCD 16
Original Music / '92 / Jet Star / SRD

SHALOM DUB (King Tubby & The Aggrovators)
CD RNCD 2107
Rhino / Jun '95 / Grapevine/PolyGram / Jet Star

SURROUNDED BY THE DREADS AT THE NATIONAL ARENA
CD STCD 003
Studio 16 / May '93 / Jet Star

UPSET THE UPSETTERS
CD RNCD 2037
Rhino / Nov '93 / Grapevine/PolyGram / Jet Star

WATER DUB
CD LG 21055
Lagoon / Feb '93 / Grapevine/PolyGram

King Ubu Orchestra

BINAURALITY
CD FMPCD 49
FMP / Sep '87 / Cadillac

Kingdom Come

BAD IMAGE
Passion departed / You're the one / Fake believer / Friends / Mad queen / Pardon the difference (but I like it) / Little wild thing / Can't resist / Talked too much / Glove of stone / Outsider
CD 4509931482
WEA / Feb '94 / Warner Music

JAM
CD BP 163CD
Blueprint / Jun '97 / Pinnacle

Kingdom Folk Band

RESTLESS
De'il's awa / Trooper and the maid / Star of County Down / Starry night / Rovin' journeyman / McPherson's rant / Restless / Crazy love / Clare to here / Parcel o'rogues / Cunla / Ramblin' guy / Nothing to show / Scots wha hae
CD _______ **RECD 518**
REL / Jun '97 / CM / Duncans / Highlander

Kinglee, Fred

LACHEN SIE MIT FRED KINGLEE (Kinglee, Fred & Die King Kols/Gus P. Kinglee Trio)
Meine kleine melodie (o schnibedidabedidum) / Cement mixer / Manana / Quanto le gusta (cuanto le gusta) / Das warenhaus/ Der Russische salat / Schieb ab / Die samba / Sie, wenn sie mal'nen hund brauchen / Kleiner zinnsoldat / Piff-paff-boogie / Hey, ba-ba-re-bop / Wie komm ich bloss an diesem hund vorbei / La marchina / Tschagalag / Kennst du schon den rubezahl / Ei-weih / King-Kols jubilaums-mischung / Bi-bi-bitte schon/Cement mixer/ Das ding / Die radiobastler / Jimmy, Johnny, Josefin' / Der herr baron / Kinglee blues (c-jam blues) / Das gibt es nur in Texas / Joachimthalerstrasse / Heimwh nach dem Kurfurstendamm / Crawel in the left / Rosalie / Dunkel war's der mond schein helle / Das warenhaus / Der Russische salat
CD _______ **BCD 16007**
Bear Family / Apr '97 / Direct / Rollercoaster / Swift

Kingmaker

BLOODSHOT AND FANCY FREE (The Best Of & The Rest Of Kingmaker)
Ten years asleep / Armchair anarchist / Really scrape the sky / You and I will never see things eye to eye / Hard times / Two headed yellow bellied hole digger / Freewheeling / Everything's changed (since you've been to London) / Queen Jane / When Lucy's down / In the best possible taste / High as a kite / Frustrated gangster / In the best possible taste / Honesty kills / Don't come over
CD _______ **CDCHRM 104**
Chrysalis / Feb '97 / EMI

EAT YOURSELF WHOLE
Revelation / Really scrape the sky / Two headed, yellow bellied hole digger / When Lucy's down / Wave / Lady Shakespear's bomb / Everything in life / High as a kite
CD _______ **CCD 1878**
Chrysalis / Oct '91 / EMI

King's College Choir

ADVENT PROCESSION WITH CAROLS
CD _______ **CDM 5662432**
EMI Classics / Nov '96 / EMI

CAROLS FROM KING'S
Once in Royal David's city / Oh Christmas night / Jesus Christ the apple tree / Adam lay-y-bounden / O little town of Bethlehem / It came upon the Midnight clear / Lamb / Cherry tree carol / God rest ye merry gentlemen / Noel nouvelet / Infant Holy / King Jesus hath a garden / While shepherds watched their flocks by night / In the bleak midwinter / Tomorrow shall be my dancing day / Three Kings / O come all ye faithful (adeste fidelis) / In dulci jubilo
CD _______ **CFMCD 11**
Classic FM / Nov '96 / Conifer/BMG

CHRISTMAS MUSIC
CD _______ **CDM 5662442**
EMI Classics / Nov '96 / EMI

CHRISTMAS MUSIC FROM KINGS
CD _______ **CDM 7641302**
EMI Classics / Oct '91 / EMI

FAVOURITE CAROLS
CD _______ **CDM 5662412**
EMI Classics / Nov '96 / EMI

FESTIVAL OF LESSONS AND CAROLS
CD _______ **CDM 5662422**
EMI Classics / Nov '96 / EMI

KING'S CHRISTMAS COLLECTION (4CD Set)
CD Set _______ **CMS 5662452**
EMI Classics / Nov '96 / EMI

SOUND OF KING'S, THE
On Christmas night / Hodie Christus natus est / For unto us a child / Allegri / Miserere mei, Deus / Nunc dimittis / Funeral music for Queen Mary / Thou knowest, Lord / Dixit dominus (Psalm 109) / Nationibus / Pie Jesu / Ave verum corpus / Psalm 84 / O how amiable / No. 5 Antiphon / Gloria / Ceremony of carols / Agnus dei / In paradisum
CD _______ **CDKCC 1**
EMI / Oct '89 / EMI

King's Own Royal Border ...

BATTLE HONOURS (King's Own Royal Border Regiment)
CD _______ **BNA 5075**
Bandleader / Feb '93 / Conifer/BMG

King's Own Scottish Borderers

SPIRIT OF SCOTLAND
CD _______ **CDITV 623**
Scotdisc / Feb '97 / Conifer/BMG / Duncans / Ross

King's Singers

BEATLES CONNECTION
Penny Lane / Mother nature's son / Ob-la-di ob-la-da / Help / Yesterday / Hard day's night / Girl / Got to get you into my life / Back in the USSR / Eleanor Rigby / Blackbird / Lady Madonna / I'll follow the sun / Honey pie / Can't buy me love / Michelle / You've got to hide your love away / I want to hold your hand
CD _______ **CDC 7495562**
EMI / May '88 / EMI

CHANSONS D'AMOUR
CD _______ **9026614272**
WEA / Apr '93 / Warner Music

DECK THE HALL (Songs For Christmas)
CD _______ **CDM 7641332**
EMI Classics / Oct '91 / EMI

HERE'S A HOWDY DO
CD _______ **09026618852**
RCA / Dec '93 / BMG

MADRIGAL HISTORY TOUR
Amore vittorioso / Lirum bililirum / Il bianco e dolce cigno / La bella Franceschina / Ultimi mei sospiri / Alla cazza / Or si rallegri il cielo / Fine knacks for ladies / Who made thee, Hob, forsake the plough / Of all the birds that I do know / Too much I once lamented / Fair Phyllis I saw / Silver swan / Now is the month of maying / La Guerre / La la la je ne l'ose dire / Bon jour, et puis, quelles nouvelles / Mignonne, allons voir si la rose / Il est bel et bon / Margot labourez les vignes / Un gentil amoureux / Faulte d'argent / La tricota / Triste estaba el rey David / Cucu, cucu / Fatal la parte / Tres morillas m'enamoran / La bomba / Tanzen und Springen / Ach weh des Leiden / Vitrum nostrum gloriosum / Ach Elslein / Das g'laut zu Speyer / Herzliebstes bild
CD _______ **CDM 769 837 2**
EMI / Jul '89 / EMI

POPS ALBUM
CD _______ **9026609382**
WEA / Apr '93 / Warner Music

RENAISSANCE DESPREZ
CD _______ **09026618142**
RCA / Dec '93 / BMG

Kings X

DOGMAN
Dogman / Shoes / Pretend / Flies and blue skies / Black the sky / Fool you / Don't care / Sunshine rain / Complain / Human behaviour / Cigarettes / Go to hell / Pillow / Manic depression
CD _______ **7567825582**
Atlantic / Jan '94 / Warner Music

EAR CANDY
Train / Mississippi moon / Lies in the sand / Fathers / Picture / American cheese / Life going by / Run / 67 / Looking for love / (Thinking and wondering) what I'm gonna do / Box / Sometime
CD _______ **7567828802**
Atlantic / May '96 / Warner Music

GRETCHEN GOES TO NEBRASKA
Out of the silent planet / Over my head / Summer land / Everybody knows a little bit of something / Difference (in the garden of St. Anne's-on-the-hill) / I'll never be the same / Mission / Fall on me / Pleiades / Don't believe it (it's easier said than done) / Send a message / Burning down
CD _______ **7819972**
Atlantic / Jun '89 / Warner Music

Kingsmen

1960'S FRENCH EPS COLLECTION, THE
CD _______ **523272**
Magic / Jul '97 / Greyhound

JERK & TWINE TIME
You really got me / All day and all of the night / Money / Jolly green giant / Twine time / Land of 1000 dances / In crowd / Jerk / Jerktown / She's not there / Downtown / Limbo rock / In the misty moonlight / Beau and John interview
CD _______ **CDSC 6010**
Sundazed / Jan '94 / Cargo / Greyhound / Rollercoaster

KINGSMEN VOL.1 (Louie Louie)
Louie Louie / Waiting / Mojo workout / Fever / Money / Bent scepter / Long tall Texan / You can't sit down / Twist and shout / JAJ / Night train / Mashed potatoes / Haunted castle / Krunch / (You got) The gamma coochee
CD _______ **CDSC 6004**
Sundazed / Jan '94 / Cargo / Greyhound / Rollercoaster

KINGSMEN VOL.2
Kingsmen introduction / Little latin lupe lu / Long green / Do you love me / New Orleans / Walking the dog / David's mood / Something's got a hold on me / Let the good times roll / Ooh-poo-pah-doo / Great balls of fire / Linda Lou / Death of an angel / And you brought me / Give her lovin'
CD _______ **CDSC 6005**
Sundazed / Feb '94 / Cargo / Greyhound / Rollercoaster

KINGSMEN VOL.3
Over you / That's cool, that's trash / Jolly green giant / Don't you just know it / La do dada / Long green / Mother in law / Shout / Searchin' for love / Tall cool one / Comin' home baby / Since you been gone / It's only the dog / Wolf of Manhattan / I'll go crazy
CD _______ **CDSC 6006**
Sundazed / Jan '94 / Cargo / Greyhound / Rollercoaster

LIES
Lies / I can do it better / Can't you see I'm trying / Please don't fight it / Just one girl / I believe in her / Wishful thinking / You'll never walk alone / Your kind of lovin' / Harlem nocturne / It's not unusual / Turn to me / Just out of reach / Beau and John Charles interview
CD _______ **CDSC 6011**
Sundazed / Jan '94 / Cargo / Greyhound / Rollercoaster

LOUIE LOUIE
CD _______ **CPCD 8160**
Charly / Nov '95 / Koch

ON CAMPUS
Annie Fanny / Rosalie / Hard day's night / I like it like that / Stand by me / Little green thing / Climb / Sticks and stones / Peter Gunn / Sometimes / Shotgun / Genevieve / Get out of my life woman / Don't say no / My wife can't cook (mono)
CD _______ **CDSC 6014**
Sundazed / Jan '94 / Cargo / Greyhound / Rollercoaster

UP AND AWAY
Trouble / If I needed someone / Grass is green / Tossin' and turnin' / Under my thumb / Wild thing / (I have found) another girl / Daytime shadows / Shake a tail feather / Children's caretaker / Land of 1000 dances / Mustang Sally / Little Sally tease / Hush-a-bye / Killer Joe
CD _______ **CDSC 6015**
Sundazed / Jan '94 / Cargo / Greyhound / Rollercoaster

Kingston Trio

CAPITOL COLLECTORS SERIES; KINGSTON TRIO
Scarlet ribbons / Tom Dooley / Raspberries, strawberries / Tijuana trail / MTA / Worried man / Coo coo-u / El matador / Bad man's blunder / Everglades / Where have all the flowers gone / Scotch and soda / Jane Jane Jane / One more town / Greenback dollar / Reverend Mr. Black / Desert Pete / Ally ally oxen free / Patriot game / Seasons in the sun
CD _______ **CZ 384**
Capitol / Jan '91 / EMI

CHILDREN OF THE MORNING
CD _______ **FE 6017**
Folk Era / Aug '96 / ADA / CM

EP COLLECTION, THE
Across the wide Missouri / San Miguel / Greenback dollar / Take her out of pity / Ruby red / Worried man / All my sorrows / Sally / Molly Dee / Where have all the flowers gone / Tom Dooley / I'm going home / Farewell / Scarlett ribbons / Lemon tree / Sail away ladies / Unfortunate Miss Bailey / Scotch and soda / Hobo's lullaby / Turn around / Little play soldiers / Santy anno / Little boy / It was a very good year / Raspberries, strawberries
CD _______ **SEECD 454**
See For Miles/C5 / Oct '96 / Pinnacle

LIVE AT NEWPORT 1959
Introduction / Saro Jane / MTA / All my sorrows / Remember the Alamo / E inu takou e / Hard ain't it hard / Merry little minuet / When the saints go marching in / Three jolly coachmen / South coast / Scotch and soda / Zombie jamboree
CD _______ **VCD 77009**
Vanguard / Oct '95 / ADA / Pinnacle

NICK, BOB & JOHN
CD _______ **FE 5271**
Folk Era / Dec '94 / ADA / CM

ON STAGE
Tom Dooley / Greenback Dollar / Tijuana Jail / Where have all the flowers gone / Scotch and soda / Lion sleeps tonight / Early morning rain / Baby you've been on my mind / Shape of things to come / Hard ain't it hard / I'm goin' home / Colours / Hard travellin' / Tomorrow is a long time / Roving gambler / One too many mornings / Goodnight Irene / MTA / Get away John / When the saints go marching in
CD _______ **STOCD 103**
Start / Feb '97 / Disc

SPOTLIGHT ON KINGSTON TRIO
Tom Dooley / Lion sleeps tonight / Greenback dollar / Baby, you've been on my mind / Goodnight Irene / I'm goin' home / Roving gambler / Tijuana jail / Where have all the flowers gone / Colours / MTA / Early morning rain / Shape of things to come / Tomorrow is a long time / When the saints go marching in
CD _______ **HADCD 106**
Javelin / Feb '94 / Henry Hadaway / THE

STAY AWHILE
CD _______ **FE 5435**
Folk Era / Dec '94 / ADA / CM

Kingwell, Colin

ALWAYS FOR PLEASURE (Kingwell, Colin & His Jazz Bandits)
Fair & square in love / Beautiful Ohio / Vieux Carre blues / When we danced at the Mardi Gras / All I do is dream of you / In the sweet bye and bye / Did you mean it / Beg your pardon / Original Dixieland one-step / Your foolin' someone / Where could I go but to the Lord / I'll never say never again, again
CD _______ **LACD 59**
Lake / Mar '96 / ADA / Cadillac / Direct / Jazz Music / Target/BMG

Kinks

DEFINITIVE COLLECTION, THE
You really got me / All day and all of the night / Stop your sobbing / Tired of waiting for you / Everybody's gonna be happy / Set me free / See my friends / Till the end of the day / Where have all the good times gone / Well respected man / Dedicated follower of fashion / Sunny afternoon / Dead end street / Waterloo sunset / Death of a clown / Autumn almanac / Suzannah's still alive / David Watts / Wonder boy / Days / Plastic man / Victoria / Lola / Apeman / Come dancing / Don't forget to dance
CD _______ **5164652**
PolyGram TV / Mar '97 / PolyGram

EP COLLECTION VOL.2, THE
CD _______ **SEECD 329**
See For Miles/C5 / Sep '91 / Pinnacle

EP COLLECTION, THE
See my friends / I gotta move / I've got that feeling / Don't you fret / Things are getting better / Set me free / Wait till the summer comes along / Such a shame / David Watts / Lazy old sun / Death of a clown / Funny face / All day and all of the night / Louie Louie / Well respected man / It's alright / I gotta go now / You really got me / Till the end of the day / Dedicated follower of fashion / Two sisters / Situation vacant / Love me till the sun shines / Suzannah's still alive
CD _______ **SEECD 295**
See For Miles/C5 / Aug '90 / Pinnacle

FAB FORTY (The Kinks' Singles Collection 1964-1970/2CD Set)
I took my baby home / Long tall Sally / You still want me / You do something to me / You really got me / It's alright / All day and all of the night / I gotta move / Tired of waiting for you / Come on now / Everybody's gonna be happy / Who'll be next in line / I need you / Set me free / See my friends / Never met a girl like you before / Till the end of the day / Where have all the good times gone / Sunny afternoon / I'm not like everybody else / Dead end street / Big black smoke / Waterloo sunset / Act nice and gentle / Autumn almanac / Mr. Pleasant / Polly / Wonder boy / Days / She's got everything / King kong / Plastic man / This man he weeps tonight / Shangri la / Victoria / Mr. Churchill says / Lola / Berkeley mews / Rats / Apeman
CD Set _______ **CDLIK 74**
Decal / Jan '91 / Koch

GREATEST HITS
CD _______ **BRCD 15**
BR Music / May '94 / Target/BMG

HITS
CD _______ **DC 869822**
Disky / Aug '96 / Disky / THE

INTROSPECTIVE: KINKS
Waterloo sunset / Lola / Apeman / Interview part one / Where have all the good times gone / Dedicated follower of fashion / You really got me / Interview part two
CD _______ **CINT 5005**
Baktabak / Apr '91 / Arabesque

KINKS, THE
You really got me / Tired of waiting for you / Sunny afternoon / Autumn almanac / Lola / Days / Plastic man / Waterloo sunset / Dedicated follower of fashion / All day and all of the night / Victoria / See my friends / Death of a clown / Where have all the good times gone / Big black smoke / Powerman / I'm not like everybody else / Shangri la / Sittin' on my sofa / Top of the pops
CD _______ **CDMFP 5921**
Music For Pleasure / Oct '91 / EMI

LOLA
Lola / Tired of waiting for you / Victoria / So long / Got my feet on the ground / Dancing in the street / Nothing to say / Just friends / Got to be free / Dedicated follower of fashion / Village Green Preservation Society / Tin soldier man / Don't ever change / Dead End Street / Starstruck / Holiday in Waikiki / Milk cow blues / Dandy
CD _______ **5507232**
Spectrum / Jul '95 / PolyGram

REMASTERED
CD ESBCD 268
Essential / Mar '95 / BMG

TELLTALES (Interview Disc)
CD TELL 16
Network / Jun '97 / Total/BMG

TO THE BONE
CD KNKCD 1
Konk / Oct '94 / Grapevine/PolyGram

YOU REALLY GOT ME
You really got me / I need you / Till the end of the day / Come on now / Long tall Sally / Cadillac / Beautiful Delilah / Everybody's gonna be happy / Things are getting better / All day and all of the night / Stop your sobbing / Don't ever change / David Watts / You still want me / Wonder where my baby is tonight / Don't you fret / Just can't go to sleep / Well respected man / I'm not like everybody else / Tired of waiting for you
CD 5507222
Spectrum / Aug '94 / PolyGram

Kinlechene, Kee

SONGS OF THE NAVAJO (Kinlechene, Kee & Yatza)
CD VICG 5334
JVC World Library / Jun '96 / ADA / CM / Direct

Kinlochard Ceilidh Band

SLAINTE
CD CDITV 601
Scotdisc / Mar '95 / Conifer/BMG / Duncans / Ross

SPIRIT OF FREEDOM
CD CDITV 622
Scotdisc / Mar '97 / Conifer/BMG / Duncans / Ross

Kinnaird, Alison

HARP KEY, THE
CD COMD 1001
Temple / Apr '96 / ADA / CM / Direct / Duncans / Highlander

MUSIC IN TRUST (Kinnaird, Alison & The Battlefield Band)
CD COMD 2010
Temple / Feb '94 / ADA / CM / Direct / Duncans / Highlander

MUSIC IN TRUST VOL.2 (Kinnaird, Alison & The Battlefield Band)
CD COMD 2004
Temple / Feb '94 / ADA / CM / Direct / Duncans / Highlander

QUIET TRADITION, THE (Kinnaird, Alison & Christine Primrose)
CD COMD 2041
Temple / Feb '94 / ADA / CM / Direct / Duncans / Highlander

SCOTTISH HARP, THE
CD COMD 2005
Temple / Feb '94 / ADA / CM / Direct / Duncans / Highlander

Kinney, Fern

CHEMISTRY (The Best Of Fern Kinney)
Groove me / If tomorrow never comes / Together we are beautiful / Easy lovin' / Under fire / Nothing takes the place of you / Boogie box / Don't make me wait / Angel on the ground / I'm ready for your love / Sweet music man / Beautiful love song / Most girls / Sun, moon, rain / Baby let me kiss you / Pipin' hot / Pillow talk
CD MCCD 167
Music Club / Jul '94 / Disc / THE

Kinsey, Big Daddy

CAN'T LET GO (Kinsey, Big Daddy & Sons)
CD CDBP 73489
Blind Pig / May '94 / ADA / CM / Direct / Hot Shot

I AM THE BLUES
Ode to Muddy Waters / I am the blues / Baby don't say that no more / Somebody's gonna get hooked tonight / Nine below zero / Walking thru the park / Good mornin' Mississippi / Don't you lie to me / Queen without a King / Mannish boy / Little red rooster / Got my mojo working
CD 5191752
Verve / May '94 / PolyGram

Kinsey Report

CROSSING BRIDGES
Too early to tell / I take what I want / She's gone / Midnight drive / Strange things / Release yourself / Five women / Chicken heads / One too many / Key to your heart / Love is real / My kind of woman / Dancin' with the beast / I take what I want (version 2)
CD VPBCD 9
Pointblank / Mar '93 / EMI

EDGE OF THE CITY
Poor man's relief / I can't let you go / Got to play someday / Answering machine / Give me what I want / Full moon on Main Street / Lucky charm / Back door man / Game of love / Come to me
CD ALCD 4758
Alligator / May '93 / ADA / CM / Direct

MIDNIGHT DRIVE
CD ALCD 4775
Alligator / May '93 / ADA / CM / Direct

Kipper, Sid

LIKE A RHINESTONE PLOUGHBOY
CD LER 2115CD
Leader / Mar '94 / CM / Duncans / Roots / Ross

Kips Bay Ceili Band

DIGGING IN
You / Battle of New Orleans / Suite for Hillary / Affligem night / Talk to me / Place I am bound / Broken promises / Big dig / Boozoo goes to heaven / Crab song
CD GLCD 1130
Green Linnet / Jul '93 / ADA / CM / Direct / Highlander / Roots

INTO THE LIGHT
CD GLCD 1164
Green Linnet / May '96 / ADA / CM / Direct / Highlander / Roots

Kiraly, Erno

PHOENIX
CD REREK 1
ReR/Recommended / Jun '97 / ReR Megacorp / RTM/Disc

Kirby, John

BIGGEST LITTLE BAND IN THE LAND, THE (2CD Set) (Kirby, John Sextet)
It feels so good: *Kirby, John* / Effervescent blues: *Kirby, John* / Turf: *Kirby, John* / Dawn on the desert: *Kirby, John* / Anitra's dance: *Kirby, John* / Sweet georgia brown: *Kirby, John* / Drink to me only with thine eyes: *Kirby, John* / Minute waltz: *Kirby, John* / Front and center: *Kirby, John* / Royal garden blues: *Kirby, John* / Opus 5: *Kirby, John* / Fantasy impromptu: *Kirby, John* / Blue skies: *Kirby, John* / Rose room: *Kirby, John* / I may be wrong, but I think you're wonderful: *Kirby, John* / Little brown jug: *Kirby, John* / Nocturne: *Kirby, John* / One alone: *Kirby, John* / Humoresque: *Kirby, John* / Serenade: *Kirby, John* / Jumpin' in the pump room: *Kirby, John* / Milumbu: *Kirby, John* / You go your way: *Kirby, John* / Twentieth century closet: *Kirby, John* / St. Louis blues: *Kirby, John* / Hour of parting: *Kirby, John* / Temptation: *Kirby, John* / Blues petite: *Kirby, John* / On a little street in Singapore: *Kirby, John* / Chloe: *Kirby, John* / Andiology: *Kirby, John* / Can't we be friends: *Kirby, John* / Then I'll be happy: *Kirby, John* / I love you truly: *Kirby, John* / Frasquita serenade: *Kirby, John* / Sextet from 'Lucia': *Kirby, John* / Coquette: *Kirby, John* / Zooming at the zombie: *Kirby, John* / If I had a ribbon bow: *Kirby, John* / Who is Sylvia: *Kirby, John* / Molly Malone: *Kirby, John* / Barbara Allen: *Kirby, John* / Bounce of the sugar plum fairy: *Kirby, John* / Beethoven riffs on: *Kirby, John* / Double talk: *Kirby, John* / Cutting the campus: *Kirby, John*
CD 4776352
Sony Jazz / Jan '95 / Sony

CLASSICS 1938-1939
CD CLASSICS 750
Classics / Aug '94 / Discovery / Jazz Music

CLASSICS 1939-1941
CD CLASSICS 770
Classics / Aug '94 / Discovery / Jazz Music

CLASSICS 1941-1943
CD CLASSICS 792
Classics / Jan '95 / Discovery / Jazz Music

JOHN KIRBY
It feels good / Sweet Georgia Brown / Front and center / Andiology / Coquette / Zooming at the Zombie / Opus 5 / Blue skies / Jumpin' in the pump room / 20th Century closet / Blues petite / Royal garden blues / Can't we be friends / Beethoven riffs on / Rehearsin' for a nervous breakdown / Undecided / Echoes of Harlem / Blue fantasy / Revolutionary etude (Etude in C minor) / Peanut vendor / Prelude for trumpet
CD CD 53243
Giants Of Jazz / Jun '96 / Cadillac / Jazz Music / Target/BMG

JOHN KIRBY 1941-44
CD TAX 37142
Tax / Aug '94 / Cadillac / Jazz Music / Wellard

Kirby, Kathy

BEST OF THE EMI YEARS, THE
My way / My Yiddishe Momme / Time / Come back here with my heart / Wheel of fortune / So here I go / Turn around / In all the world / Yes I've got / Is that all there is / Little song for you / Oh pleasure man / Do you really have a heart / Please help me, I'm falling / Here, there and everywhere / Golden days / Little green apples / I'll catch the sun / Let the music start / My thanks to you
CD CDEMS 1452
EMI / Jun '92 / EMI

VERY BEST OF KATHY KIRBY, THE
Secret love / Sometimes I'm happy / Dance on / Way of love / Let me go lover / I wish you love / You're the one / Havah nagilah / I want to be happy / I belong / That wonderful feeling of love / Happiness is a thing called Joe / Love me baby / Body and soul / (All of a sudden) my heart sings / Ol' man Mose / Sweetest sounds / Make someone happy / Slowly / Where in the world
CD 5520972
Spectrum / Jan '97 / PolyGram

Kirchen, Bill

TOMBSTONE EVERY MILE
Bottle baby boogie / Tombstone every mile / Rockabilly funeral / Fool on a stool / One woman man / Lovin' cajun style / Think it over / Lover's rock / Cool lovin' baby / Secrets of love / Hole in my pirogue / Tell me the reason / Without love / No one to talk to but the blues / All tore up
CD BT 1109CD
Black Top / Oct '94 / ADA / CM / Direct

Kirk

MAKIN' MOVES
CD 7467826012
East West / May '94 / Warner Music

Kirk, Andy

12 CLOUDS OF JOY, THE (Kirk, Andy & Mary Lou Williams)
Bearcat shuffle / Big Jim Blues / Close to five / Corky stomp / Dunkin' a doughnut / Floyd's guitar blues / Froggy Bottom / Gettin' off a mess / In the groove / Jump Jack jump / Little Joe from Chicago / Loose ankles / Lotta sax appeal / Margie / Mary's idea / Mellow bit of rhythm / Mess-a-stomp / Moten swing / Puddin' head serenade / Steppin' pretty / Toadie toddle / Twinklin' / Walkin' and swingin' / Wednesday night hop / Wham
CD CDAJA 5108
Living Era / Apr '93 / Select

ANDY KIRK & HIS 12 CLOUDS OF JOY 1937-1938
CD CLASSICS 581
Classics / Oct '91 / Discovery / Jazz Music

ANDY KIRK & HIS 12 CLOUDS OF JOY 1940-1942 (Kirk, Andy & His Twelve Clouds of Joy)
CD CLASSICS 681
Classics / Mar '93 / Discovery / Jazz Music

CLASSICS 1929-1931
CD CLASSICS 655
Classics / Nov '92 / Discovery / Jazz Music

CLASSICS 1936-1937
CD CLASSICS 573
Classics / Oct '91 / Discovery / Jazz Music

CLASSICS 1938
CD CLASSICS 598
Classics / Sep '91 / Discovery / Jazz Music

CLASSICS 1939-1940
CD CLASSICS 640
Classics / Nov '92 / Discovery / Jazz Music

KANSAS CITY BOUNCE (Kirk, Andy & His Twelve Clouds of Joy)
CD BLE 592402
Black & Blue / Dec '92 / Discovery / Koch / Wellard

Kirk, Rahsaan Roland

CASE OF THE THREE SIDED DREAM IN AUDIO COLOR, THE
CD 7567813962
Atlantic / Apr '95 / Warner Music

DOES YOUR HOUSE HAVE LIONS (Rahsaan Roland Kirk Anthology)
Wham bam thank you ma'am / Bye bye blackbird / If I loved you / Old rugged cross / Ain't no sunshine / Volunteered slavery / Seasons / Going home / Black and crazy blues / I say a little prayer / This love of mine / Roots / Inflated tear / Blacknuss / I love you yes I do / Portrait of those beautiful ladies / Water for Robeson and Williams / Laugh for Rory / Entertainer (done in the style of blues) / Black root / Carney and Begard place / Anysha / Making love after hours / Freaks for the festival / Bye bye blackbird / Three for the festival / Bright moments
CD 8122714062
Atlantic / Feb '94 / Warner Music

GIFTS AND MESSAGES (Live At Ronnie Scott's 1964)
Ronnie's intro / Bags' groove / Roland's intro / It might as well be Spring / (On a) misty night / Come Sunday / Avalon / My ship / Stritch in time / Gifts and messages / Reeling and rhyming
CD JHAS 606
Ronnie Scott's Jazz House / Sep '96 / Cadillac / Jazz Music / New Note/Pinnacle / TKO Magnum

INFLATED TEAR, THE
Black and crazy blues / Laugh for Rory / Many blessings / Fingers in the wind / Inflated tear / Creole love call / Handful of fives / Fly by night / Lovelievelilloqui
CD 7567900452
Atlantic / Jul '93 / Warner Music

JAZZ MASTERS
Theme for the festival / Blue rol / Reeds and deeds / Hip chops / From Bechet, Fats and Byas / Berkshire blues / Nightingale sang in Berkeley Square / March on swan lake / Haunted melody / Meeting on Termini's corner / Rolando / Blues for Alice / Black diamond / You did it, you did it / Where Monk and Mingus live / Blues for C and T
CD 5220622
Verve / Feb '94 / PolyGram

KIRK'S WORK
Three for Dizzy / Makin' Whoopee / Funk underneath / Kirk's work / Doin' the sixty-eight / Too Late Now / Skater's waltz
CD OJCCD 459
Original Jazz Classics / '93 / Complete/Pinnacle / Jazz Music / Wellard

LIVE IN PARIS 1970 VOL.2
Sweet fire / Make me a pallet on the floor / Charlie Parker medley / Volunteer slavery / You did it, you did it / Satin doll
CD FCD 115
France's Concert / Jun '88 / BMG / Jazz Music

MUSIC OF RAHSHAAN ROLAND KIRK, THE (Various Artists)
CD NI 4024
Natasha / Nov '93 / ADA / Cadillac / CM / Direct / Jazz Music

RAHSAAN - THE COMPLETE MERCURY RECORDINGS 1961-1965 (11CD Set)
Blues for Alice / My delight / Haunted melody / Sackful of soul / We free Kings / Spring will be a little late this year / Moon song / Some kind of love / Three for the festival / You did it, you did it / Get out of town / Rolando / I believe in you / Where Monk and Mingus live - let's call this / Domino / Ed / I didn't know what time it was / Someone to watch over me / Meeting on Termini's corner / When the sun comes out / Ad lib / Stitt's tune / I see with my third I / If I had you/Alone together/For Heaven's sake / Afternoon in Paris / Lady E / Meeting on Termini's corner / Domino / 3 in 1 without the oil / Stritch in time / Lament / Breath in the wind / Land of peace / Lonesome August child / Limbo boat / Hay ro / Waltz of the friends / This is always / Reeds and deeds / Song of the countrymen / Ecclusiastics / By myself / Roland speaks / Nightingale sang in Berkeley Square / Variations on a theme of Hindemith / I've got your number / Between the fourth and fifth step / April morning / Get in the basement / Abstract improvisation / Narrow bolero / My heart stood still / No title no.1 / Mood indigo / Cabin in the sky / On the corner of King and Scott Streets / Untitled blues / Monkey thing / Will you still be mine / One for my baby (and one more for the road) / We'll be together again / Mingus-Griff song / Mood indigo / Rock-a-bye baby/Nearness of you/ No title no.3 / Half a triple / Japan / Berkshire blues / Dirty money blues / Ad lib (hip chops) / Things I love / Petite fleur / March on swan lake / Tears sent by you / My heart at thy sweet voice / Gifts and messages / Hit chops / Blues for C and T / Where does the blame lie / Vertigo ro / Jive elephant / I talk with the spirits / Serenade to a cuckoo / We'll be together again/People from 'Funny Girl' / Ruined castle / Trees / Fugue'n and alludin' / Django / My ship / Quote from Clifford Brown / Business ain't nothin' but the blues / No tonic press / From Bechet, Fats and Byas / Slippery, hippery, flippery / Black diamond / Rip, rig and panic / Once in a while / Mystical dreams / Walk on by / Juarez / Shakey money / Ebrauqs / Raouf / Nothing but the truth / Safari / It's all in the game / And I love her / Taste of honey / Dyna-soar / Soul bossa nova / Comin' home baby / Days of wine and roses / Moon river / Dreamsville / (I love you) and don't you forget it / Charade / Peter Gunn / I had a ball / Addie's at it again / Stritch in time
CD Set 8466302
Mercury / Feb '91 / PolyGram

RIP, RIG AND PANIC/NOW PLEASE DON'T YOU CRY, BEAUTIFUL EDITH (Kirk, Rahsaan Roland Quartet)
No tonic press / Once in a while / From Bechet, Fats and Byas / Mystical dreams / Rip, rig and panic / Black diamond / Slippery, hippery, flippery / Now please don't you cry, beautiful Edith / Blue rol / Alfie / Why don't they know / Silverlization / Fallout / Stompin' grounds / It's a grand night for swinging
CD 8321642
EmArCy / Jul '90 / PolyGram

SOUL STATION
Call / Soul station / Our waltz / Our love is here to stay / Spirit girl / Jack the ripper
CD _______ LEJAZZ 35
Le Jazz / Sep '94 / Cadillac / Koch

SOUVENIR DE MONTREUX
CD _______ 8122724532
Atlantic / Jul '96 / Warner Music

SWEET FIRE
CD _______ JHR 73579
Jazz Hour / Jun '94 / Cadillac / Jazz Music / Target/BMG

TALKIN' VERVE
CD _______ 5331012
Verve / Dec '96 / PolyGram

THIRD DIMENSION
CD _______ BET 6006
Bethlehem / Jan '95 / ADA / ZYX

THREE FOR THE FESTIVAL
CD _______ LEJAZZCD 6
Le Jazz / Mar '93 / Cadillac / Koch

WE FREE KINGS
Three for the festival / Moon song / Sackful of soul / Haunted melody / Blues for Alice / We free kings / You did it, you did it / Some kind of love / My delight
CD _______ 8264552
Mercury / Nov '86 / PolyGram

Kirk, Richard H.

AGENTS WITH FALSE MEMORIES
CD _______ ASH 31CD
Ash International / Nov '96 / Kudos / Pinnacle

BLACK JESUS VOICE
CD _______ KIRKCD 3
The Grey Area / Feb '95 / RTM/Disc

ELECTRONIC EYE
CD Set _______ RBADCD 8
Beyond / Aug '94 / Kudos / Pinnacle

HIGH TIME FICTION
CD _______ KIRK 2CD
The Grey Area / Oct '94 / RTM/Disc

NUMBER OF MAGIC, THE
CD _______ WARPCD 32
Warp / Jul '95 / Prime / RTM/Disc

UGLY SPIRIT
Emperor / Confession / Infantile / Frankie machine / Hollywood babylon / Thai / Voodoo / Frankie machine (II)
CD _______ KIRKCD 4
The Grey Area / Feb '95 / RTM/Disc

VIRTUAL STATE
CD _______ WARPCD 19
Warp / Feb '94 / Prime / RTM/Disc

Kirkintilloch Band

BRASS O' SCOTLAND
CD _______ BNA 5078
Bandleader / Mar '93 / Conifer/BMG

Kirkland, Eddie

ALL AROUND THE WORLD
Shake it up / All I've got to offer / Live with it / Forty days and forty nights / Pick up the pieces / All around the world / Love don't love nobody / Country boy / There's gonna be some blues / Big city behind the sun / Someone to stand by me
CD _______ DELCD 3001
Deluge / Jan '96 / ADA / Direct / Koch

HAVE MERCY
CD _______ ECD 26018
Evidence / Feb '93 / ADA / Cadillac / Harmonia Mundi

IT'S THE BLUES MAN
Down on my knees / Don't take my heart / Daddy please don't cry / Have mercy on me / Saturday night stomp / I'm gonna forget you / I tried / Man of stone / I'm goin' to keep loving you / Train done gone / Something's gone wrong in my life / Baby you know it's true
CD _______ OBCCD 513
Original Blues Classics / Apr '94 / Complete/Pinnacle / Wellard

SOME LIKE IT RAW
CD _______ DELCD 3007
Deluge / Dec '95 / ADA / Direct / Koch

WHERE YOU GET YOUR SUGAR
CD _______ DELD 3012
Deluge / Dec '95 / ADA / Direct / Koch

Kirkland, Mike James

HANG ON IN THERE
CD _______ LHCD 028
Luv n' Haight / Nov '96 / Timewarp

Kirkpatrick, Bob

GOING BACK TO TEXAS
Going back to Texas / Big feet / I don't know why / Every-ree day / Schefel / I've been down so long / I got love / Old friends of mine / House calls / Sad, sad blues / Little girl / I want to see her
CD _______ CD 269
JSP / May '96 / ADA / Cadillac / Direct / Hot Shot / Target/BMG

Kirkpatrick, John

EARTHLING
CD _______ MWCD 4006
Music & Words / Jul '94 / ADA / Direct

FORCE OF HABIT
CD _______ FLED 3007
Fledg'ling / Feb '96 / ADA / CM / Direct

PLAIN CAPERS
Glorishears / Hammersmith flyover / Old Molly Oxford / Black Jack/Old Black Joe / Blue eyed stranger/Willow tree / Brighton camp/March past / Bobby and Joan / Monk's march/Fieldtown professional / Sweet Jenny Jones/Sherbourne jig / Lumps of plum pudding / Highland Mary / Wheatley processional / Maid of the mill/Cuckoo's nest/William and Nancy / Buffoon/Fool's jig / Constant Billy
CD _______ TSCD 458
Topic / Aug '92 / ADA / CM / Direct

SHEEPSKINS
Last night with Archie / Three jolly black sheepskins / Mad moll - the lively jig / Over the moon / Ronnets so blue / There's no doubt about it / Beating the oak / Dick the Welshman / Todley Tome / Blue eyed stranger / Watterddy Lane / Tun dish / Maiden's prayer / Turn again Martha / Churning butter / Abram circle dance / Raddled tup / Hunting the squirrel / Zot for Joe / Four lane end / Cocking the chafer / Threepenny ha-'penny treacle / Martha's comet or the evening star / Three hand reel / Green and yellow handkerchief dance / Prince of Wales / Morning star / Half a farthing candle / Hindley circle dance
CD _______ MWCD 4002
Music & Words / Jun '93 / ADA / Direct

SHORT HISTORY OF JOHN KIRKPATRICK, A
CD _______ TSCD 473
Topic / Aug '94 / ADA / CM / Direct

STOLEN GROUND (Kirkpatrick, John & Sue Harris)
CD _______ TSCD 453
Topic / Aug '89 / ADA / CM / Direct

TRANS EUROPE DIATONIQUE (Kirkpatrick, J. & R. Tessi)
CD _______ Y225026
Silex / Jun '93 / ADA / Harmonia Mundi

WELCOME TO HELL
Step dance tunes / Golden grain/Golden hornpipe / Fields of gold / Lovely Nancy / Welcome to hell / Shropshire tunes / Accordion Joe / On the road to freedom / Fill 'em up Rosie / 49003/55005
CD _______ FLED 3011
Fledg'ling / May '97 / ADA / CM / Direct

Kirlian

CHICKEN WINGS AND BEEF FRIED RICE
CD _______ EFA 122802
Disko B / '95 / SRD

Kirtley, Peter

BUSH TELEGRAPH
Save a piece of your heart / Halfway to paradise / Bird chase bird / If the gentle rain that falls / Bush telegraph / Next year / Roman wall blues / Way of the world / Sweet talkin' blues / Let's go walkin' / Don't throw this love away / Nobody knows / Suppertime / Mrs. Bell
CD _______ PLANCD 13
Planet / Feb '97 / Direct

Kirwan, Dominic

BEST OF DOMINIC KIRWAN, THE
CD _______ RITZCD 0077
Ritz / Apr '96 / Pinnacle

EVERGREEN
Hold me just one more time / Only couple on the floor / My happiness / Picture of you / If you're ever in my arms again / I really don't want to know / Evergreen / Absent friends / Release me / One bouquet of roses / Way love's supposed to be / Hello Mary Lou / Bless this house
CD _______ CD 0065
Ritz / Nov '91 / Pinnacle

IRISH FAVOURITES
Through the eyes of an Irishman / Tipperary on my mind / Irish eyes / Star of the Country Down / If we only had old Ireland over here / Sprig of Irish heather / Medley / Village of Astee / Limerick you're a lady / My Galway queen / My mother's home / Rose of Tralee / My own Donegal / Song for Ireland / Medley / Cavan girl
CD _______ RITZRCD 539
Ritz / Aug '94 / Pinnacle

LOVE WITHOUT END
Like father, like son / Almost persuaded / Love letters in the sand / Straight and narrow / Just for old times sake / Stranger things have happened / Say you'll stay until tomorrow / When the girl in your arms (is the girl in your heart) / Love without end, amen / There's always me / Hand that rocks the cradle / Fool's pardon / Life is what you make it / Noreen Bawn
CD _______ RITZRCD 527
Ritz / Apr '93 / Pinnacle

ON THE WAY TO A DREAM
Where does love go when it dies / Tonight we just might fall in love again / Hands across the ocean / Northern lights are shining for me / On the way to a dream / Answer to everything / Our love / Someone in your eyes / We'll be together from now on / My love is like a red red rose / I won't forget you / In my sleepless nights / What am I gonna do with all this love / Thank you for being a friend
CD _______ CD 0074
Ritz / Mar '95 / Pinnacle

TODAY
CD _______ RITZCD 0071
Ritz / Oct '93 / Pinnacle

TRY A LITTLE KINDNESS
Oh lonesome me / I'll leave this world loving you / Achin' breaking heart / Before the next teardrop falls / Try a little kindness / More than yesterday / My beautiful wife / Sea of heartbreak / Heaven knows / Heartaches by the number / Careless hands / Golden dreams / Paper roses / St. Theresa of the roses
CD _______ RITZCD 504
Ritz / '91 / Pinnacle

Kishino, Yoshiko

PHOTOGRAPH
Night and day / Scarborough fair / Desert island / All blues / Longing for you / Alone together / Photograph / Alice in wonderland / On Green Dolphin Street / Love dance / J's waltz / Autumn
CD _______ GRP 98842
GRP / Jun '97 / New Note/BMG

Kiske, Michael

INSTANT CLARITY
Be true to yourself / Calling / Somebody somewhere / Burned out / New horizons / Hunted / Always / Time's passing by / So sick / Thanx a lot / Do I remember a life
CD _______ RAWCD 112
Raw Power / Sep '96 / Pinnacle

Kiss

ALIVE VOL.3
Creatures of the night / Deuce / I just wanna / Unholy / Heaven's on fire / Watchin' you / Domino / I was made for lovin' you / I still love you / Rock 'n' roll all nite / Lick it up / Forever / Take it off / I love it loud / Detroit rock city / God gave rock 'n' roll to you II / Star spangled banner
CD _______ 5148272
Mercury / May '93 / PolyGram

CRAZY NIGHTS
Crazy crazy nights / Hell to hold you / Bang bang you / No no no / Hell or high water / My way / When your walls come down / Reason to live / Good girl gone bad / Turn on the night / Thief in the night
CD _______ 8326262
Vertigo / Feb '91 / PolyGram

DOUBLE PLATINUM
Strutter / Do you love me / Hard luck woman / Calling Dr. Love / Let me go rock 'n' roll / Love gun / God of thunder / Firehouse / Hotter than hell / I want you / Deuce / 100,000 years / Detroit rock city / She / Rock 'n' roll all nite / Beth / Makin' love / C'mon and love me / Cold gin / Black diamond
CD _______ 8241552
Mercury / Apr '87 / PolyGram

FIFTEEN YEARS ON (The Interview)
CD _______ CBAK 4002
Baktabak / Apr '88 / Arabesque

GREATEST HITS
Crazy crazy nights / I was made for lovin' you / Detroit city rock / Lick it up / HArd luck woman / aCalling doctor love / Beth / Love gun / God of thunder / Sure know something / Deuce / Do you love me / Strutter / Rock and roll nite / Plaster caster / Hotter than hell / Shock me / Cold gin / Black diamond / God gave rock 'n' roll to you II
CD _______ 5361592
PolyGram TV / Jun '97 / PolyGram

GREATEST KISS
Detroit rock city / Black diamond / Hard luck woman / Sure know something / Love gun / Deuce / Goin' blind / Shock me / Do you love me / She / I was made for loving you / Shout it out loud / God of thunder / Calling Dr. Love / Beth / Strutter / Rock 'n' roll all nite / Cold gin / Plaster caster / God gave rock 'n' roll to you
CD _______ 5342992
Mercury / Nov '96 / PolyGram

HOT IN THE SHADE
Rise to it / Betrayed / Hide your heart / Prisoners of love / Read my body / Love's a slap in the face / Forever / Silver spoon / Cadillac dreams / King of hearts / Street giveth and the street taketh away / You love me to hate you / Somewhere between heaven and hell / Little Caesar / Boomerang
CD _______ 8389132
Mercury / Oct '93 / PolyGram

INTERVIEW DISC
CD _______ TELL 02
Network / Dec '96 / Total/BMG

INTERVIEW DISC
CD _______ KISSCD 2
CD _______ KISSCD 1
Wax / Jan '97 / RTM/Disc / Total/BMG

KISS (Interview)
CD _______ 3D 009
Network / Dec '96 / Total/BMG

LICK IT UP
Exciter / Not for the innocent / Lick it up / All hell's breakin' loose / Fits like a glove / And on the eighth day / Dance all over your face / Gimme more / Million to one / Young and wasted
CD _______ 8142972
Vertigo / PolyGram

SMASHES, THRASHES AND HITS
Let's put the X in sex / Crazy crazy nights / (You make me) rock hard / Love gun / Detroit rock city / I love it loud / Deuce / Lick it up / Heaven's on fire / Strutter / Beth / Tears are falling / I was made for lovin' you / Rock 'n' roll all nite / Shout it out loud
CD _______ 8364272
Vertigo / Nov '88 / PolyGram

TRIBUTE TO KISS (Various Artists)
CD _______ TR 006CD
Tribute / Jul '96 / Plastic Head

UNPLUGGED
Comin' home / Plaster caster / Goin' blind / Do you love me / Domino / Sure know something / World without heroes / Rock bottom / See you tonight / I still love you / Every time I look at you / 2000 man / Beth / Nothin' to lose / Rock 'n' roll all nite
CD _______ 5289502
Mercury / Mar '96 / PolyGram

YOU WANTED THE BEST, YOU GOT THE BEST (The Best Of Kiss Live)
Parasite / Firehouse / Rock bottom / Rock 'n' roll all nite / I stole your love / Calling Dr. Love / Shout it out loud / Beth / Room service / Two timer / Let me know / Take me
CD _______ 5327412
Mercury / Jul '96 / PolyGram

Kiss It Goodbye

SHE LOVES ME
CD _______ REV 058CD
Revelation / Apr '97 / Plastic Head

Kiss My Jazz

DOC'S PLACE FRIDAY EVENING
CD _______ KFWCD 196
Knitting Factory / Oct '96 / Cargo / Plastic Head

Kiss My Poodle's Donkey

NEW HOPE FOR THE DEAD
Sacred cow / Truck / Bad hair day / Psychoman / Mood B / Gett off / See my eye / Lizard
CD _______ HOT 1048CD
Hot / Feb '94 / Hot Records

Kiss Of Life

REACHING FOR THE SUN
Love has put a spell on me / Fiction in my mind / As long as we're together / Only a fool / Pushing in / Love connection / Heaven is waiting / Holding on to a dream / Reaching for the sun / Be strong
CD _______ CIRCD 26
Circa / Oct '93 / EMI

Kissoon, Mac & Katie

STAR COLLECTION
CD _______ STCD 1003
Disky / Jun '93 / Disky / THE

SWINGING SOUL OF MAC AND KATIE KISSOON
Hey you love / Pidgeon / Chirpy chirpy cheep cheep / It's a hang up world / Change it all / (I found my) freedom / True love forgives / It's all over now / Love will keep us together / Vow / Love grows (Where my Rosemary grows) / Bless me / Don't make me cry / Swinging on a star / Black skinned blue eyed boys / Sing along / Love me baby / Show me / Hey diddle diddle
CD _______ C5CD538
See For Miles/C5 / '89 / Pinnacle

Kitachi

STRONG UNIT, A (2CD Set)
Realms of dub / Heavyweight / Scratch / Spirit / Bad day / Remedy / Constructive / Stalking / Kitachi in dub / Kaos / Time out / Spirit / Scratch / Chronic / Spirit bass mix / Realms of Dub / Time out / Constructive / Spirit / Chronic / Heavyweight
CD Set _______ CDXDOP 004
React / Sep '97 / Arabesque / Prime / Vital

Kitaro

10 YEARS (2CD Set)
CD Set DOMO 710622
Domo / May '97 / Pinnacle

BEST OF KITARO VOL.1, THE
Morning prayer / Eternal spring / Oasis / Westbound / Silver moon / Four changes / Tunhuang / Scared journey II / Revelation / Silk road fantasy / Shimmering light / Everlasting road
CD DOMO 710582
Domo / Jan '97 / Pinnacle

BEST OF KITARO, THE
Morning prayer / Eternal springs / Oasis / Westbound / Silver moon / Four changes / Tunhuang / Sacred journey II / Revelation / Silk road fantasy / Shimmering light / Everlasting road
CD CDKUCK 073
Kuckuck / Feb '87 / ADA / CM

BEST OF TEN YEARS (2CD Set)
CD Set DOM 0710622
Domo / Jul '97 / Pinnacle

BEST SELECTION
CD P 3012
Kuckuck / Jan '86 / ADA / CM

DREAM
Symphony of the forest / Mysterious island / Lady of dreams / Drop of silence / Passage of life / Agreement / Dream of chant / Magical wave / Symphony of dreams / Island of life
CD GEFD 24477
Geffen / Jul '92 / BMG

ENCHANTED EVENING, AN
Mandala / Planet / Dance of Sarasvati / Silk road / Chants from the heart / Spirit of Tokyo / Kokoro / Heaven and earth
CD DOMO 710052
Domo / Nov '96 / Pinnacle

IN PERSON/DIGITAL
Prologue / Eternal spring / Westbound / Silver moon / Peace / Bell tower / Morning prayer / Tienshan / Four changes / Magical sand dancing
CD DOMO 710552
Domo / Apr '97 / Pinnacle

KI
Revelation / Stream of being / Kaleidoscope / Oasis / Sun / Endless water / Tree / Cloud in the sky
CD DOMO 710572
Domo / Apr '97 / Pinnacle

KITARO BOX SET (Original Album Collection/5CD Set)
Silk road / Bell tower / Heavenly father / Great river / Great wall of China / Flying celestial nymphs / Silk road fantasy / Shimmering light / Westbound / Time / Bodhisattva / Everlasting road / Peace / Takla Makan desert / Eternal spring / Silver moon / Magical sand dance / Year 40080 / Time travel / Reincarnation / Dawning / Tienshan / Mirage: *Kitaro & London Philharmonic Orchestra* / Flight: *Kitaro & London Philharmonic Orchestra* / Aurora: *Kitaro & London Philharmonic Orchestra* / Fire: *Kitaro & London Philharmonic Orchestra* / Spring of youth: *Kitaro & London Philharmonic Orchestra* / Simmering horizon: *Kitaro & London Philharmonic Orchestra* / Oasis: *Kitaro & London Philharmonic Orchestra* / Pilgrimage: *Kitaro & London Philharmonic Orchestra* / Jesu joy of man's desiring / Silent night / Angels we have heard on night / Joy to the world/First noel / Little drummer boy / Jingle bells / Rosa mystica / It came upon a midnight clear / God rest ye merry gentlemen / A la nanita nana / O holy night / Great spirit / Mandala / Planet / Dance of Sarasvati / Silk road / Chants from the heart / Spirit of Taiko / Kokoro / Heaven and earth
CD Set DOMO 91001
Domo / Nov '96 / Pinnacle

KITARO'S WORLD OF MUSIC (Kitaro & Nawang Khechog)
Ocean of wisdom / Karuna / Tibet / Rhythm of Dakini / Presence / Thanksgiving to mother earth / Journey with ancients / Peace through kindness
CD DOMO 710042
Domo / Jun '96 / Pinnacle

KITARO'S WORLD OF MUSIC (Kitaro & Yu-Xiao Guang)
40800 / Caravansary / Taklamakan desert / Mandala / Flying celestial nymphs / Silk road / Peace / Linden / Everlasting road
CD DOMO 710112
Domo / Nov '96 / Pinnacle

KOJIKI
CD DOMO 710632
Domo / Jul '97 / Pinnacle

LIGHT OF THE SPIRIT
Mysterious encounter / Sundance / Field / Light of the spirit / In the beginning / Journey of fantasy / Howling thunder / Moondance
CD DOMO 710612
Domo / Jun '97 / Pinnacle

MANDALA
Mandala / Planet / Dance of Sarasvati / Scope / Chant from the heart / Crystal tears / Winds of youth / Kokoro
CD DOMO 810012
Domo / Jan '97 / Pinnacle

OASIS
Morning player / Moro-rism / New wave / Cosmic energy / Eternal spring / Moonlight / Shimmering horizon / Fragrance of nature / Innocent people / Oasis
CD DOMO 710542
Domo / Nov '96 / Pinnacle

PEACE ON EARTH
Jesu joy of man's desiring / Silent night / Angels we have heard on night / Joy to the world/First noel / Little drummer boy / Jingle bells / Rosa mystica / It came upon a midnight clear / God rest ye merry gentlemen / A la nanita nana / O holy night / Great spirit
CD DOMO 710142
Domo / Nov '96 / Pinnacle

SILK ROAD SUITE
Tienshan / Peace / Journey / Silk road theme / Drifting sand / Fragrance of nature / Silk road fantasy / Time / Flying celestial nymphs / Silk road theme / Everlasting road / Bell tower / Sunset / Westbound / Magical sand dance
CD DOMO 710522
Domo / Nov '96 / Pinnacle

SILK ROAD VOL.1
Silk Road / Bell tower / Heavenly father / Great river / Great wall of China / Flying celestial nymphs / Silk Road fantasy / Shimmering light / Westbound / Time / Bodhisattva / Everlasting Road
CD DOMO 710502
Domo / Nov '96 / Pinnacle

SILK ROAD VOL.2
Peace / Takla Makan desert / Eternal spring / Silver moon / Magical sand dance / Year 40080 / Time travel / Reincarnation / Dawning / Tienshan
CD DOMO 710512
Domo / Nov '96 / Pinnacle

TENKU
Tenku / Romance / Wings / Aura / Message from the Cosmos / Time travel / Legend of the road / Milky Way
CD DOMO 710602
Domo / Jun '97 / Pinnacle

TUNHUANG
Lord of the wind / Fata Morgana / Sacred journey I / Lord of the sand / Tunhuang / Free flight / Mandala / Tao / Sacred journey II
CD DOMO 710562
Domo / Nov '96 / Pinnacle

WORLD OF KITARO, THE (Kitaro & London Philharmonic Orchestra)
Mirage / Flight / Aurora / Fire / Spring of youth / Simmering horizon / Oasis / Pilgrimage
CD DOMO 710532
Domo / Nov '96 / Pinnacle

Kitch

INCREDIBLE
CD JW 1018CD
JW / Jan '96 / Jet Star

Kitchen Radio

VIRGIN SMILE
CD GRCD 339
Glitterhouse / Dec '94 / Avid/BMG

Kitchens Of Distinction

COWBOYS & ALIENS
Sand on fire / Get over yourself / Thought he had everything / Cowboys and aliens / Come on now / Remember me / One of those sometimes is now / Here comes the swans / Now it's time to say goodbye / Pierced / Prince of Mars
CD TPLP 53CD
One Little Indian / Aug '94 / Pinnacle

DEATH OF COOL
CD TPCD 39
One Little Indian / Jul '92 / Pinnacle

LOVE IS HELL
CD TPCD 9
One Little Indian / May '89 / Pinnacle

STRANGE FREE WORLD
CD TPCD 19
One Little Indian / Apr '91 / Pinnacle

Kitt, Eartha

BACK IN BUSINESS
Back in business / Let's misbehave / Solitude / Why can't I / Ain't misbehavin' / Nearness of you / Close enough for love / Brother can you spare a dime / Angelitos negros / Moon river / Speak low / Here's to life
CD DRGCD 91431
DRG / Nov '94 / Discovery / New Note/ Pinnacle

BAD BUT BEAUTIFUL
CD MAR 038
Marginal / Jun '97 / Greyhound

BEST OF THE FABULOUS EARTHA KITT, THE
CD MCLD 19120
MCA / Oct '92 / BMG

EARTHA IN NEW YORK (Live At The Plaza/Ballroom New York 1975)
CD ITM 1493
ITM / Mar '96 / Koch / Tradelink

EARTHA KITT
CD DVAD 6092
Deja Vu / May '95 / THE

EARTHA-QUAKE
Annie doesn't live here any more / Lilac wine / I want to be evil / C'est si bon / Two lovers / Mountain high, valley low / Angelitos negros / Uska Dara / Avril au Portugal / African lullaby / Senor / Santa baby / Under the bridges of Paris / Oh John (please don't kiss me) / Let's do it / Salangadou / Sandy's tune / Smoke gets in your eyes / Blues / My heart belongs to Daddy / Lovin' spree / Somebody bad stole the wedding bell / Looking for a boy / Lonely girl / Easy does it / I wantcha round / Apres moi / Mink shmink / This year's Santa baby / Hey Jacques / Strangers in the starlight / Do you remember / Day that the circus left town / Heel / Mambo de Paree / I've got that lovin' bug itch / Dinner for one please James / My heart's delight / Freddy / Sweet and gentle / Sho-ji-jo / Nobody taught me / Nothin' for Christmas / Je cherche un homme / If I can't take it with me / Just an old fashioned girl / Mademoiselle Kitt / Oggere / No importa si menti / Lazy afternoon / There is no cure for l'amore / Lisbon Antigua / Lullaby of Birdland / Jonny / Fascinating man / Thursday's child / Le danseur de Charleston / Honolulu rock and roll / Vid kajen / Rosenkyssar / Put more wood on the fire / I'm a funny dame / Woman wouldn't be a woman / Toujour Gai / Waydown blues / Proceed with caution / Yomme, yomme / Take my love, take my love / Careless love / Beale Street blues / Hesitating blues / Memphis blues / Friendless blues / Yellow dog blues / Chantez les bas / St. Louis blues / Long gone / Steal away / Hist the window, Noah / Shango / Sholem / Torah dance / Tierra va temblar / Mack the knife / I'd rather be burned as a witch / Independent / Love is a gamble / Yellow bird / Jambo hippopotami / In the evening / Lamplight / Let's do it again / April in Portugal / Johnny with the gentle hands / Johnny with the gentle hands / Monotonus / Love is a simple thing / Bal petit bal / Overture / Dialogue : Mrs. Patterson / Mrs. Patterson / Devil scene / I was a boy / Fantasy / I wish I was a bumble-bee / Card game scene / Be good, be good, be good / Tea party scene / Tea in Chicago / My Daddy is a dandy / Finale / I can't give you anything but love / Solitude / Since I fell for you / What is this thing called love / Callete (caliente)
CD Set BCD 15639
Bear Family / Oct '93 / Direct / Rollercoaster / Swift

LIVE IN LONDON
CD JHD 083
Tring / Mar '93 / Tring

LIVE ON BROADWAY
CD LDJ 274930
Radio Nights / Nov '91 / Cadillac / Harmonia Mundi

MY WAY - A MUSICAL TRIBUTE TO MARTIN LUTHER KING (Live At The Caravan Of Dreams, Fort Worth, Texas 1987)
Introduction (Ms. Kitt) / God bless the child / Old ship of Zion / America the beautiful / Look where God has brought us / Commentary: Ms Kitt / Old rugged cross / Abraham, Martin and John / My way
CD BASIC 50015
ITM / Mar '96 / Koch / Tradelink

SENTIMENTAL EARTHA
It is love (por amor) / Wear your love like heaven / I remember the rhymes / Paint me black angels (angelitos negros) / Catch me the wind / My sentimental friend / Once we loved / Way you are (asi eres tu) / Geneis / Hurdy gurdy man
CD C5LCD 628
See For Miles/C5 / Sep '95 / Pinnacle

STANDARDS
CD ITM 1484
Hightone / Jul '94 / ADA / Koch

Kix

SHOW BUSINESS
CD CDMFN 159
Music For Nations / Mar '95 / Pinnacle

K'Jarkas

CANTO A LA MUJER DE MI PUEBLO
CD TUMICD 010
Tumi / Feb '90 / Discovery / Stern's

EL AMOR Y LA LIBERTAD
CD TUMICD 013
Tumi / Apr '90 / Discovery / Stern's

KK Null

NEW KIND OF WATER (KK Null & Jim O'Rourke)
CD CHCD 6
Charnel House / Jun '97 / Cargo / Greyhound

Klang

KLANG - WORKS FOR TAPE & TAPE INSTRUMENTS (Sonic Arts Network Collection Vol.1)
CD NMCD 035
NMC / Jun '96 / Complete/Pinnacle

Klange

TIME 2/TIME 3 (Time Cubed In Time Square)
CD MHCD 024
Minus Habens / Jan '95 / Plastic Head

Klasse Kriminal

CI INCONTREREMO
CD KOCD 024
Knock Out / Mar '97 / Cargo

HISTORY OF KLASSE KRIMINAL VOL.1, THE (1985-1993)
CD KONCD 008
Knock Out / Mar '97 / Cargo

Klaw, Irving

UTEK PAHTOO MOGOI (Klaw, Irving Trio)
CD ROCO 017CD
Road Cone / Jul '97 / Cargo

Klearview Harmonix

HAPPY MEMORIES VOL.1 & 2
CD DTCD 67
Discotex / Jul '92 / Jet Star

THOSE WERE THE DAYS VOL.1
CD DTCD 21
Discotex / May '94 / Jet Star

Klein, Guillermo

EL MINOTAURO
El minotauro / La manzana de las luces / Primer tango free / Lo perdido / La madre de mi hermana / Abismo / Technicolor
CD CCD 79706
Candid / May '97 / Cadillac / Direct / Jazz Music / Koch / Wellard

Klein Healy, Eloise

ARTENIS IN ECHO PARK
CD NAR 103CD
New Alliance / Jan '94 / Plastic Head

Klein, Oscar

MOONGLOW
CD CD 021
Nagel Heyer / May '96 / Jazz Music

TIMELESS BLUES (Klein, Oscar & Karsten Grettner/Charly Antolini)
There is no greater love / Remembering Cootie / Exactly like you / Lonely harp / Franco Nero / Timeless blues / Cute / With hot lips and sticks / Dein ist mein ganzes / New Orleans memories / Jessica / Italian blues / George's chords
CD CDSJP 436
Timeless / Oct '96 / New Note/Pinnacle

Kleinow, Pete

LEGEND AND THE LEGACY, THE
CD CDSD 076
Sundown / May '94 / TKO Magnum

Kleive, Iver

KYRIE
CD FXCD 142
Musikk Distribujson / Jan '95 / ADA

Klemmer, John

MOSAIC (The Best Of Of John Klemmer)
Touch / Talking hands / Free fall love / Waterfall / My love has butterfly wings / Barefoot ballet / Whisper to the wind / Body pulse / Walk wiht my love and dream / Tone row weaver / Quite afternoon
CD GRP 98382
GRP / Jan '96 / New Note/BMG

Kletka Red

HIJACKING
CD TZ 7111
Tzadik / Oct '96 / Cargo

Klezmer Conservatory Band

DANCING IN THE AISLES
Freylekh jamboree / Oy s'iz gut / Farges mikh nit / Doyne/Freylekhs / Kol rina / Gimpel the fool / Mayn freylekh lid / Miserlou / Meron nign / Slow hora/Freylekhs / Mayn Yiddishe Meydele / Freylekh fantastique / Hopkele/Dancing in the aisles / In memoriam: Yitzhak Rabin
CD ROUCD 3155
Rounder / Jun '97 / ADA / CM / Direct

JUMPIN' NIGHT IN THE GARDEN OF EDEN, A
CD ROUCD 3105
Rounder / '88 / ADA / CM / Direct

KLEZMER CONSERVATORY BAND LIVE
CD ROUCD 3125
Rounder / Jan '94 / ADA / CM / Direct

OY CHANUKAH
CD ROUCD 3102
Rounder / Oct '88 / ADA / CM / Direct

Klezmer Groove

TOO LOUD FOR DINNER
CD OOMCD 1
Oom-Cha / Jan '95 / ADA
CD MSPCD 9503
Mabley St. / Sep '95 / Grapevine/ PolyGram

Klezmer Orchestra

KLEZMER SUITE
CD SHCD 21005
Shanachie / May '95 / ADA / Greensleeves / Koch

Klezmorim

FIRST RECORDINGS 1976-78
CD ARHCD 309
Arhoolie / Apr '95 / ADA / Cadillac / Direct

IS GEWIJN A FOLK
CD EUCD 1059
ARC / '89 / ADA / ARC Music

SHALOM
CD EUCD 1060
ARC / '89 / ADA / ARC Music

KLF

CHILL OUT
Brownsville turnaround on the Tex-Mex border / Pulling out of Ricardo and the dusk is falling fast / Six hours to Louisiana, black coffee going cold / Dreamtime in Lake Jackson / Madrugada eterna / Justified and ancient seems a long time ago / Elvis on the radio, steel guitar in my soul / 3am somewhere out of Beaumont / Wichita Lineman was a song I once heard / Trancentral lost in my mind / Lights of Baton Rouge pass by / Melody from a past life keeps pulling me back / Rock radio into the nineties and beyond / Alone again with the dawn coming up
CD TVT 7155
TVT / Jun '97 / Cargo / Greyhound

Klinghagen, Goran

TIME AGIN
CD DRCD 247
Dragon / Oct '94 / ADA / Cadillac / CM / Roots / Wellard

Klingonz

BEST OF THE KLINGONZ, THE
CD DAGCD 005
Fury / Oct '96 / Nervous / TKO Magnum

BOLLOX
CD FCD 3030
Fury / Apr '95 / Nervous / TKO Magnum

FLANGE
CD FCD 3017
Fury / Apr '95 / Nervous / TKO Magnum

GHASTLY THINGS
CD RUMBCD 013
Rumble / Aug '92 / Nervous / Pinnacle

Klug, Roger

TOXIC AND 15 OTHER LOVE SONGS
CD MG 9002
Mental Giant / May '97 / Cargo

Klugh, Earl

BALLADS
This time / Waltz for Debby / If you're still in love with me / April fools / Rayna / Natural thing / Waiting for Cathy / Julie / Nature boy / Dream come true / Shadow of your smile / Christina
CD CDP 8273262
Capitol / Feb '94 / EMI

BEST OF EARL KLUGH
Tropical legs (Wishful thinking) / Amazon (Dream come true) / Magic in your eyes / Calypso getaway / Dr. Macumba / Long ago and far away / Angelina / Heart string / Livin' inside your love / Christina (Low ride) / Wishful thinking / I don't want to leave you alone anymore
CD BNZ 264
Blue Note / Mar '91 / EMI

BEST OF EARL KLUGH - VOL.2
Crazy for you / Night drive / Goodtime Charlie's got the blues / Cabo frio / Back in Central Park / Natural thing / Jolanta / Rainmaker / Captain Caribe / Cast your fate to the wind / I'll see you again / Right from the street
CD BNZ 307
Blue Note / Feb '93 / EMI

CRAZY FOR YOU
I'm ready for your love / Soft stuff (and other sweet delights) / Twinkle / Broadway ramble / Calypso getaway / Rainmaker / Ballad in A / Crazy for you

CD CDP 7483872
Blue Note / Feb '96 / EMI

FINGER PAINTING
Dr. Macumba / Long ago and far away / Cabo frio / Keep your eye on the sparrow / Catherine / Dance with me / Jolanta / Summer song / This time
CD CDP 7483862
Blue Note / '95 / EMI

LIVING INSIDE YOUR LOVE
Captain caribe / I heard it through the grapevine / Felicia / Living inside your love / Another time another place / April fools / Kiko
CD CDP 7483852
Blue Note / Feb '96 / EMI

LOVE SONGS
Heart string / Laughter in the rain / Summer song / Catherine / Balladina / Alicia / Sweet rum and starlight / Mirabella / Like a lover / I'm ready for your love / Julie / Night song
CD CDP 8533542
Blue Note / Nov '96 / EMI

MAGIC IN YOUR EYES
Magic in your eyes / Alicia / Julie / Lode star / Cast your fate to the wind / Rose hips / Good time Charlie's got the blues / Mayaguez / Cry a little while
CD CDP 7483892
Blue Note / Feb '96 / EMI

SUDDEN BURST OF ENERGY
CD 9362458842
WEA / Mar '96 / Warner Music

Kluner, Kerry

LIVE AT WEST END CULTURAL CENTRE (Kluner, Kerry Big Band)
CD JTR 84362
Justin Time / Jul '92 / Cadillac / New Note/Pinnacle

Kluster

LIVE IN VIENNA VOL.1 (Zwei Osterei)
CD CLP 97372
Hypnotic / Aug '97 / Cargo / SRD

LIVE IN VIENNA VOL.2 (Klopzeichen)
CD CLP 97242
Hypnotic / Aug '97 / Cargo / SRD

Klute, Martin

SWING (Klute, Martin & Mark Edwards/ Paul Cavacuiti)
CD TCF 1731
Top Cat / Apr '96 / Cadillac / Top Cat

KMD

MR. HOOD
Mr. Hood at Piocalles jewelry/crackpot, who me / Boogie man / Mr. Hood meets onyx / Subroc's mission / Humrush / Figure of speech / Bananapeel blues / Nitty gritty / Trial 'n error / Hard wit no hoe / Mr. Hood gets a haircut / 808 man / Boy who cried wolf / Peach fuzz / Preacher porkchop / Soulflexin'
CD 7559609772
WEA / Aug '91 / Warner Music

KMFDM

ANGST
CD RR 89872
Roadrunner / Jul '94 / PolyGram

NIHIL
CD IRS 993603CD
Intercord / Jan '96 / Plastic Head

WHAT DO YOU KNOW DEUTSCHLAND
CD CDSAW 004
Skysaw / Feb '88 / Pinnacle

WORLD VAIOE
CD SBR 032 CD
Strike Back / May '89 / Grapevine/ PolyGram / Vital

Knack

GET THE KNACK/BUT THE LITTLE GIRLS UNDERSTAND
Let me out / Your number or your name / Oh Tara / (She's so) selfish / Maybe tonight / Good girls don't / My Sharona / Heartbeat / Siamese twins / Lucinda / That's what the little girls do / Frustrated / Baby talks dirty / I want ya / Tell me you're mine / Mr. Handleman / Can't put a price on love / Hold on tight and don't let go / Hard way / It's you / End of the game / Feeling I get / (Havin' a) Rave up / How can love hurt so much
CD BGOCD 248
Beat Goes On / Dec '94 / Pinnacle

Knapsack

DAY THREE OF MY LIFE
Thursday side of the street / Courage was confused / Decorate the spine / Diamond mine / Simple favor / Boxing gloves / Henry hammers harder / Perfect / Heart carved tree / Steeper than we thought
CD A 095D
Alias / Mar '97 / Vital

SILVER SWEEPSTAKES
Cellophane / Trainwrecker / Effortless / Fortunate and holding / Silver sweepstakes / Addressee / True to form / Symmetry / Centennial / Makeshift / Casanova
CD A 075D
Alias / May '95 / Vital

Knauber, Carol

NOW YOU'RE TALKIN'
Away with words / Bubbles, giggles and chuckles / Swinging banana shuffle / Half time / PCL / Dangerous dreams / New day / Nr 1 funk / Casey's samba / Are you still thinking (Intro) / Now you're talkin'
CD 101S 70592
101 South / Nov '93 / New Note/Pinnacle

Knepper, Jimmy

CUNNINGBIRD
CD SCCD 31061
Steeplechase / Jul '88 / Discovery / Impetus

DREAM DANCING (Knepper, Jimmy Quintet)
CD CRISS 1024CD
Criss Cross / May '92 / Cadillac / Direct / Vital/SAM

I DREAM TOO MUCH (Knepper, Jimmy Sextet)
CD SNCD 1092
Soul Note / '86 / Cadillac / Harmonia Mundi / Wellard

SPECIAL RELATIONSHIP
John's bunch / Stella by starlight / Just friends / Yardbird suite / Aristocracy of Jean Lafitte / Sophisticated lady / Lester leaps / Primrose path / What is there to say / Gnome on the range / 'Round midnight / Latterday saint
CD HEPCD 2012
Hep / Mar '94 / Cadillac / Jazz Music / New Note/Pinnacle / Wellard

Knickerbockers

DRIVING RHYTHM GUITARS, WILD SOLOS...
Lies / One track mind / I can do it better / Just one girl / I must be doing something right / Chuck Berry medley / High on love / Stick with me / Love is a bird / I love / They ran for their lives / My feet are off the ground / She said goodbye / You're bad / What does that make you / Rumours, gossip, words untrue / Comin' generation / Can't you see I'm trying / Sweet green fields / Give a little bit / Guaranteed satisfaction / Little children
CD CDWIKD 122
Big Beat / Jan '94 / Pinnacle

KNICKERBOCKERISM (2CD Set)
CD Set SC 11040
Sundazed / Feb '97 / Cargo / Greyhound / Rollercoaster

Knight, Beverley

B FUNK, THE
B-funk / Moving on up / Mutual feeling / Flava of the old school / Remedy / Down for the one / Steppin' on my shoes / Promise you forever / It's your time / So happy / Cast all your cares / U've got it / In time / Goodbye innocence
CD DOMECD 6
Dome / Oct '95 / 3mv/Sony

Knight, Brian

BLUE EYED SLIDE (Featuring Laurence Scott)
CD LMCD 022
Lost Moment / Dec '94 / Else / Shellshock/Disc

FILE UNDER BLUES
CD CDEC 3
Blooze / Dec '94 / Else

Knight, Cheri

KNITTER, THE
Knitter / Megalith / Down by the water / Light in the road / Last barn dance / Wishing well / That I might see / Waiting for Sara / Spellbound / Paper wings / Very last time
CD ESD 81122
East Side Digital / Jul '96 / Vital

Knight, Curtis

LIVE IN EUROPE
CD 858817
SPV / '90 / Koch / Plastic Head

Knight, Frederick

I'VE BEEN LONELY FOR SO LONG
I've been lonely for so long / This is my song of love to you / Take me on home witcha / Friend / I let my chance go by / Your love's all over me / Pick 'um up, put 'um down / Now that I've found you / Lean on me / Trouble / Someday we'll be together
CD CDSXE 099
Stax / Nov '93 / Pinnacle

Knight, Gladys

17 GREATEST HITS: GLADYS KNIGHT
CD 5300432
Motown / Jan '92 / PolyGram

2ND ANNIVERSARY/PIPE DREAMS (Knight, Gladys & The Pips)
Money / Street brother / Part time love / At every end there's a beginning / Georgia on my mind / You and me against the world / Where do I put his memory / Summer sun / Feel like makin' love / So sad the song / Alaskan pipeline / Pot of Jazz / I'll miss you / Nobody but you / Pipe dreams / Everybody's got to find a way / I will follow my dream
CD NEXCD 236
Sequel / Mar '93 / BMG

ANTHOLOGY VOL.1 & 2 (Knight, Gladys & The Pips)
Every beat of my heart / Letter full of tears / Giving up / Just walk in my shoes / Do you love me just a little, honey / You don't love me no more / Take me in your arms and love me / Everybody needs love / I heard it through the grapevine / End of our road / I know better / Don't let her take your love from me / It should have been me / I wish it would rain / Valley of the dolls / Didn't you know (you'd have to cry sometime) / Got myself a good man / All I could do was cry / Friendship train / Tracks of my tears / You need love like I do / Every little bit hurts / If I were your woman / I don't want to do wrong / One less bell to answer / Is there a place (in his heart for me) / Master of my mind / No one could love you more / Can't give it up no more / For once in my life / Make me the woman that you come home to / Help me make it through the night / Neither one of us / Daddy could swear, I declare / All I need is time / Don't tell me I'm crazy / Oh what a love I have found / Only time you love me is when you're losing me / Between her goodbye and my hello
CD 5301872
Motown / Jan '92 / PolyGram

BEST OF GLADYS KNIGHT & THE PIPS, THE (1980-1985) (Knight, Gladys & The Pips)
Licence to kill / Taste of bitter love / Bourgie bourgie / Love overboard / I will fight / My time / Landlord / Baby don't change your mind / Come back and finish what you started / Nobody but you / Part time love / One and only / Midnight train to Georgia / Wind beneath my wings / Try to remember (the way we were) / Best thing that ever happened to me
CD 4720382
Sony Music / '93 / Sony

COLLECTION, THE (Knight, Gladys & The Pips)
CD COL 058
Collection / Feb '95 / Target/BMG

GLADYS KNIGHT
CD LECD 048
Dynamite / May '94 / THE

HIT SINGLE COLLECTABLES (Knight, Gladys & The Pips)
CD DISK 4506
Disky / Apr '94 / Disky / THE

KNIGHT, GLADYS & THE PIPS (Knight, Gladys & The Pips)
Every beat of my heart / Room in your heart / Guess who / Letter full of tears / You broke your promise / Operator / Goodnight my love / Love me again / Come see about me / One more lonely night / I really didn't mean it / Stay away / Get a hold of yourself / Jungle love / Running around / If ever I should fall in love / I want that kind of love / I can't stand by / What shall I do / Trust in you
CD QED 055
Tring / Nov '96 / Tring

MIDNIGHT TRAIN
Midnight train to Georgia / I've got to use my imagination / Best thing that ever happend to me / I feel a song in my heart / Storm of troubled times / Once in a lifetime thing / Where peaceful waters flow / Perfect love / I can see clearly now
CD MSCD 025
Music De-Luxe / Feb '96 / TKO Magnum

MIDNIGHT TRAIN
CD PDSCD 541
Pulse / Aug '96 / BMG

SINGLES ALBUM - GLADYS KNIGHT & THE PIPS (Knight, Gladys & The Pips)
Licence to kill / Help me make it through the night / Best thing that ever happened to me / Baby don't change your mind / Bourgie bourgie / Taste of bitter love / One and only / Just walk in my shoes / Midnight train to Georgia / Try to remember / Look of love / Part time love / Come back and finish what you started / So sad the song / Take me in your arms and love me / Love overboard / Lovin' on next to nothin' / Neither one of us
CD 8420032
PolyGram TV / Oct '89 / PolyGram

ULTIMATE COLLECTION, THE (Knight, Gladys & The Pips)
CD 472122
Flarenasch / May '96 / Discovery

VERY BEST OF GLADYS KNIGHT, THE
CD _______________ TRTCD 132
TrueTrax / Feb '96 / THE

WAY WE WERE, THE (Knight, Gladys & The Pips)
Midnight train to Georgia / So sad the song / Baby don't change your mind / Home is where the heart is / Nobody but you / I feel a song (in my heart) / Feel like makin' love / Hold on / Little bit of love / Try to remember (the way we were) / Come back and finish what you started / Part time love / It's a better than good time / Georgia on my mind / Make yours a happy home / Best thing that ever happened to me / We don't make each other laugh anymore / Sorry doesn't always make it right
CD _______________ MCCD 005
Music Club / Feb '91 / Disc / THE

Knight, Peter

NUMBER ONE (Knight, Peter & Danny Thompson)
CD _______________ RES 108CD
Resurgence / Apr '97 / Pinnacle

Knight Society

KNIGHT SOCIETY
CD _______________ INTER 0010
Jammin' / May '97 / Grapevine/PolyGram / Jet Star

Knights Of The Occasional ...

KNEES UP MOTHER EARTH (Knights Of The Occasional Table)
CD _______________ FUCD 1
Middle Earth / Mar '95 / RTM/Disc

LES ELEPHANTS DU PARADIS (Knights Of The Occasional Table)
CD _______________ MIDDL 5CD
Middle Earth / Sep '96 / RTM/Disc

PLANET SWEET, THE (Knights Of The Occasional Table)
CD _______________ MIDDL 2CD
Middle Earth / Jul '95 / RTM/Disc

Knochengirl

KNOCHEN = GIRL
CD _______________ EFA 127232
Fidel Bastro / Apr '95 / SRD

Knock Down Ginger

SNOWMANS LAND
CD _______________ ZULU 017CD
Zulu / Oct '95 / Plastic Head

Knopfler, Mark

GOLDEN HEART
Darling pretty / Imelda / Golden heart / No can do / Vic and Ray / Don't you get it / Night in summer long ago / Cannibals / I'm the fool / Je suis desole / Ridiger / Nobody's got the gun / Done with Bonaparte / Are we in trouble now
CD _______________ 5147322
Vertigo / Mar '96 / PolyGram

Know How

REALITY
CD _______________ 558442
P1 / '89 / Plastic Head

Knowles, Chris

FRAME OF HARMONY
CD _______________ FH 0010CD
Brenin / Apr '95 / ADA

Knox, Buddy

PARTY DOLL
CD _______________ RSRCD 004
Rockstar / Apr '94 / Direct / Nervous / Rollercoaster / TKO Magnum

Knox, Chris

SONGS OF YOU AND ME
CD _______________ FN 313
Flying Nun / Mar '95 / RTM/Disc

Knuckles, Frankie

WELCOME TO THE REAL WORLD (Knuckles, Frankie & Adeva)
Fanfare / Welcome to the real world / Too many fish / Love can change it / Keep it real / You're number one (in my book) / Passion and pain / What am I missin' / Whadda U want (from me) / Tell me why / Walkin' / Tribute / Reprise
CD _______________ CDVUS 82
Virgin / May '95 / EMI

Knudsen, Kenneth

COMPACKED
CD _______________ MECCACD 1008
Music Mecca / Nov '94 / Cadillac / Jazz Music / Wellard

I ME HIM
CD _______________ MECCACD 1007
Music Mecca / Nov '94 / Cadillac / Jazz Music / Wellard

Knutsson, Jonas

FLOWER IN THE SKY
Syskonoga / Polska efter per Johan Arnstrom, Vihelmina / Norrland / Polska efter Pekkos per, bingsjo / Take off / Hymn / Polsquette, grotesque, saquette / Vyer / Rod avgang / Flower in the sky / Arktis
CD _______________ 92482
Act / Mar '97 / New Note/Pinnacle

VIEWS
CD _______________ 1426
Caprice / Jan '89 / ADA / Cadillac / CM / Complete/Pinnacle

Koch, Hans

CHOCKSHUT
CD _______________ INTAKTCD 031
Intakt / Oct '94 / Cadillac

HEAVY CAIRO TRAFFIC (Koch, Hans & Martin Schutz/Fredy Studer)
Alaschaan aref albi ma 'ak / Makana / Tulli men el maschkabeia / 18, Maamal el sokar / Nightclubbing with Haschepsut / Qissa / Heavy Cairo traffic / El ghalla ghalletna / Malaib schiha / Belly button rave / Vice versa / Nubian bonus track
CD _______________ INT 31752
Intuition / Apr '97 / New Note/Pinnacle

Koda, Cub

JOINT WAS ROCKIN', THE (Koda, Cub & The Houserockers)
CD _______________ DELD 3015
Deluge / Oct '96 / ADA / Direct / Koch

Kode IV

BEST OF KODE IV
CD _______________ KK 149CD
KK / Mar '96 / Plastic Head

INSANE
CD _______________ KK 078CD
KK / Jun '92 / Plastic Head

POSSESSED
CD _______________ KK 052CD
KK / Sep '90 / Plastic Head

SILICON CIVILISATION
CD _______________ KK 109CD
KK / Feb '95 / Plastic Head

Koenig, Brian

WAKE UP (Koenig, Brian & The Standback Blues Band)
CD _______________ BLUELOONCD 027
Blue Loon / Jul '95 / Hot Shot

Koenig, Michael

ACOUSMATRIX 1/2
CD Set _______________ BHVAASTCD 9001/2
Bvhaast / Jan '92 / Cadillac

Koerner, John

BLUES, RAGS AND HOLLERS (Koerner, Ray & Glover)
CD _______________ RHRCD 76
Red House / Jul '95 / ADA / Koch

RAISED BY HUMANS
CD _______________ RHRCD 44
Red House / Oct '95 / ADA / Koch

STARGEEZER (Koerner, 'Spider' John)
CD _______________ RHRCD 84
Red House / Jun '96 / ADA / Koch

Kofi

FRIDAY'S CHILD
CD _______________ ARICD 064
Ariwa Sounds / Dec '94 / Jet Star / SRD

VERY REGGAE CHRISTMAS, A
Little drummer boy / Deck the halls / First noel/Christmas song / We three kings / Hark the herald angels sing / What child is this / God rest ye merry gentlemen / O little town of Bethlehem / Silent night
CD _______________ 7567827132
Atlantic / Nov '94 / Warner Music

WISHING WELL
CD _______________ ARICD 092
Ariwa Sounds / Jan '94 / Jet Star / SRD

Koga, Miyuki

DREAMIN'
My buddy / Do do do / I surrender dear / I don't know why / Blues serenade/Serenade in blue / Isn't it a lovely day / Put the blame on mame / When my sugar walks down the street / You made me love you / My melancholy baby / S'posin' / I know that you know / Let me sing and I'm happy
CD _______________ CCD 4588
Concord Jazz / Feb '94 / New Note/ Pinnacle

Koglmann, Franz

ABOUT YESTERDAY'S EZZTHETICS
CD _______________ ARTCD 6003
Hat Art / Jul '88 / Cadillac / Harmonia Mundi

CANTOS I-IV
CD _______________ ARTCD 6123
Hat Art / Jan '94 / Cadillac / Harmonia Mundi

L'HEURE BLEUE
CD _______________ ARTCD 6093
Hat Art / Jan '92 / Cadillac / Harmonia Mundi

SCHLAF SCHLEMMER, SCHLAF MAGRITTE
CD _______________ ARTCD 6108
Hat Art / Sep '92 / Cadillac / Harmonia Mundi

Koita, Oumar

BAMBE KA SO
CD _______________ BLVD 1529
Boulevard / Aug '96 / ADA

Koite, Habibe

MUSO KO (Koite, Habibe & Bamada)
I ka barra / Muso ku / Den ko / Nanale / Fatma / Sira bulu / Nimato / Cigarette a bana / Din din wo / Kunfe ta / Koulandian
CD _______________ 612501
Wotre Music / Jul '96 / Discovery / New Note/Pinnacle
CD _______________ MRCD 187
Munich / Jul '97 / ADA / CM / Direct / Greensleeves

Koken, Walt

BANJONIQUE
CD _______________ ROUCD 0337
Rounder / Oct '94 / ADA / CM / Direct

HEI-WA HOEDOWN
CD _______________ ROUCD 0367
Rounder / Nov '95 / ADA / CM / Direct

Koko

BALFONS & AFRICAN DRUMS VOL.2 (Music From Bakino Faso)
CD _______________ PS 65101
PlayaSound / Apr '93 / ADA / Harmonia Mundi

Kokubu, Hiroko

MORE THAN YOU KNOW
CD _______________ JD 3312
JVC / Oct '88 / Direct / New Note/ Pinnacle / Vital/SAM

PURE HEART
Barefoot steppin' / Luck in the rain / Smooth struttin' / Vitamina / Once and forever / Mrs. Robinson / Annabella / Weekend / It's cool / Happiest for you (for your wedding)
CD _______________ JVC 20422
JVC / Mar '95 / Direct / New Note/Pinnacle / Vital/SAM

Kol Aviv

CHANTS ET DANSES D'ISRAEL
Meh'ol halahat / Et dodim kala / Suite yemenite / Ai didididai / Bein n'har prat ounh'ar h'idekal / Hine ma tov / Chibolet basade / Suite h'assidique / Chnei h'alilim / Ke chochana / El ginat egoz / Debka rafiah / Leorh'i oukhekh / Rikoud harabbi / Debka druze / Debka kafrit / Chir Hanokdim / Im houpalnou-chevat ne'ourim
CD _______________ ARN 64033
Arion / '88 / ADA / Discovery

Kolinda

IL JU HARAMIA
CD _______________ 199722
Hexagone / Oct '93 / ADA / Discovery / Roots

OSZ
CD _______________ 669832
Melodie / Sep '96 / ADA / Discovery / Grapevine/PolyGram / Greensleeves / Jet Star

Koloc, Bonnie

WITH YOU ON MY SIDE
CD _______________ FF 70437
Flying Fish / Nov '94 / ADA / CM / Direct / Roots

Kolyma

SONGS OF NATURE AND ANIMALS
CD _______________ 925662
BUDA / Aug '93 / Discovery

Komariah, Euis

JAIPONGAN JAVA (Komariah, Euis & Jugala Orchestra)
Engalkeun / Bulan sapasi / Bardin / Toka toka / Seunggah / Teuteup abdi / Sinden beken / Daun pulus
CD _______________ CDORB 057
Globestyle / Apr '90 / Pinnacle

SOUND OF SUNDA, THE (Komariah, Euis & Yus Wiradiredja)
Sorban palid / Salam sono / Asa tos tepang / Bulan sapasi / Campaka kambar / Duh leung / Ramalan asih / Pengkolan / Dalingding asih
CD _______________ CDORB 060
Globestyle / Jul '90 / Pinnacle

Komeda

GENIUS OF KOMEDA, THE
CD _______________ NONS 262
Nons / Mar '97 / Pinnacle

Komeda, Krzysztof

CRAZY GIRL
CD _______________ PB 00145
Power Bros. / Apr '97 / Harmonia Mundi

Kommunity FK

VISION AND THE VOICE
CD _______________ CLEO 94152
Cleopatra / Nov '94 / Cargo / Greyhound / Plastic Head / RTM/Disc / SRD

Kondo, Toshinori

BRAIN WAR (Kondo, Toshinori & Ima)
Brain war / Blue stone / Dry throat / Fly, Jack / Invisible man / Fire makes darkness / Bone man / Marginal moon / Space radio / Ice city
CD _______________ JARO 41612
Jaro / Sep '92 / New Note/Pinnacle

THIS, THAT AND THE OTHER
CD _______________ BASIC 50007
ITM / Jul '96 / Koch / Tradelink

Kondole

PSYCHIC
CD _______________ TOPY 046CD
Temple / Dec '89 / Pinnacle / Plastic Head

Kone, Aicha

MANDINGO LIVE FROM COTE D'IVORIE
CD _______________ SM 15142
Wergo / Sep '93 / ADA / Cadillac / Harmonia Mundi

Koner, Thomas

PERMAFROST
CD _______________ BAR 9
Barooni / Jul '93 / Plastic Head / SRD

TEIMO/PERMAFROST (2CD Set)
CD Set _______________ EFA 006852
Mille Plateau / Feb '97 / SRD

Kong

EARMINED
CD _______________ RR 88122
Roadrunner / Jun '97 / PolyGram

MULTIPOETVOCALISER
CD _______________ CDKTB 1
Dreamtime / Aug '95 / Kudos / Pinnacle

PUSH COMES TO SHOVE
CD _______________ CDKTB 17
Dreamtime / Feb '95 / Kudos / Pinnacle

Kongos, John

TOKOLOSHE MAN...PLUS
Jubilee cloud / Gold / Lift me from the ground / Tomorrow I'll go / Can someone please direct me back to Earth / Try to touch just one / Weekend lady / I would have had a good time / Come on down Jesus / Sometimes it's not enough / He's gonna step on you again / Great white lady / Higher than God's hat / Ride the lightning / Tokoloshe man
CD _______________ SEECD 221
See For Miles/C5 / May '90 / Pinnacle

Konig, Klaus

REVIEWS
Sniffing attitudes / Harry laughs / Who's that guy / Mission to the stars / Multiple choice / Matter of taste / Tuba boons / Harry laughs still / Black polo-necks / Avantgarde noise pollution / Who would have thought that / Day after
CD _______________ ENJ 900612
Enja / Jul '96 / New Note/Pinnacle / Vital/ SAM

Konitz, Lee

12 GERSHWIN IN 12 KEYS (Konitz, Lee & D'Andrea, Franco)
CD _______________ W 3122
Philology / Aug '92 / Cadillac / Harmonia Mundi

ANTI-HEROES (Konitz, Lee & Gil Evans)
Orange was the colour of her dress, then silk blue / Moon struck one / Drizzling rain / Gee baby ain't I good to you / Buzzard song / How insensitive / Copenhagen sight
CD _______________ 5116222
Verve / Mar '92 / PolyGram

CHICAGO AND ALL THAT JAZZ
My own best friend / Razzle dazzle / Loopin' de loop / Funny honey / Class / Me and my baby / Roxie / Ten percent
CD _______________ CDC 7971

LRC / Nov '90 / Harmonia Mundi / New Note/Pinnacle
CD ______ 17089
Laserlight / Jan '97 / Target/BMG

DEARLY BELOVED (Konitz, Lee Quartet)
CD ______ SCCD 31406
Steeplechase / Apr '97 / Discovery / Impetus

FIGURE AND SPIRIT (Konitz, Lee Quintet)
CD ______ PCD 7003
Progressive / Oct '91 / Jazz Music

FREE WITH LEE
CD ______ W 622
Philology / Dec '95 / Cadillac / Harmonia Mundi

FRIENDS
CD ______ DRCD 240
Dragon / Feb '94 / ADA / Cadillac / CM / Roots / Wellard

FROM NEWPORT TO NICE
CD ______ CD 214 W652
Philology / May '92 / Cadillac / Harmonia Mundi

HEROES (Konitz, Lee & Gil Evans)
Prince of darkness / Reincarnation of a lovebird / Aprilling / What am I here for / All the things you are / Prelude #20 in C minor opus 28 / Zee zee / Lover man
CD ______ 5116212
Verve / Mar '92 / PolyGram

I CONCENTRATE ON YOU
CD ______ SCCD 31018
Steeplechase / Jul '88 / Discovery / Impetus

IDEAL SCENE
CD ______ 1211192
Soul Note / Cadillac / Harmonia Mundi / Wellard

IN HARVARD SQUARE
CD ______ BLCD 760928
Black Lion / May '97 / Cadillac / Jazz Music / Koch / Wellard

JAZZ AT STORYVILLE
CD ______ BLCD 760901
Black Lion / Jun '88 / Cadillac / Jazz Music / Koch / Wellard

JAZZ NOCTURNE
You'd be so nice to come home to / Everything happens to me / Alone together / Misty / Body and soul / My funny valentine / In a sentimental mood
CD ______ ECD 220852
Evidence / Jun '94 / ADA / Cadillac / Harmonia Mundi

KONITZ
Bop goes the leesel / Easy livin' / Mean to me / I'll remember April / Skylark / Nursery rhyme / Limehouse blues
CD ______ BL 760922
Black Lion / Oct '93 / Cadillac / Jazz Music / Koch / Wellard

KONITZ MEETS MULLIGAN (Konitz, Lee & Gerry Mulligan)
Too marvellous for words / Lover man / I'll remember April / These foolish things / All the things you are / Bernie's tune / Almost like being in love / Sextet / Broadway / I can't believe that you're in love with me / Oh lady be good / Oh lady be good
CD ______ CDP 7851082
Blue Note / Mar '95 / EMI

LEE KONITZ MEETS JIMMY GIUFFRE (2CD Set) (Konitz, Lee & Jimmy Giuffre)
CD Set ______ 5277802
Verve / Jan '97 / PolyGram

LIVE AT LAREN
April / Who you / Without a song / Moon dreams / Times lie / Matrix
CD ______ SNCD 1069
Soul Note / '86 / Cadillac / Harmonia Mundi / Wellard

LIVE AT THE HALF NOTE
CD ______ 5216592
Verve / Nov '94 / PolyGram

LIVE IN EUROPE
CD ______ COD 031
Jazz View / Jul '92 / Harmonia Mundi

LULLABY OF BIRDLAND (Konitz, Lee Quartet)
Lullaby of Birdland / This is always / Anthropology / Ask me know / East of the sun / Cherokee / 'Round midnight / Song is you
CD ______ CCD 79709
Candid / Feb '97 / Cadillac / Direct / Jazz Music / Koch / Wellard

LUNASEA (Konitz, Lee & Peggy Stern)
CD ______ 1212492
Soul Note / Sep '92 / Cadillac / Harmonia Mundi / Wellard

ONCE UPON A LINE (Konitz, Lee & Harold Danko)
CD ______ 500162
Musidisc / Nov '93 / Discovery

PALO ALTO 1949-1960
CD ______ CD 53182
Giants Of Jazz / Sep '94 / Cadillac / Jazz Music / Target/BMG

ROUND AND ROUND
Round and round / Someday my Prince will come / Luv / Nancy / Boo doo / Valse hot / Lover man / Bluesette / Giant steps
CD ______ 8208042
Limelight / Nov '89 / PolyGram

SPEAKIN' LOW (Konitz, Lee & R. Sellani)
CD ______ W 712CD
Philology / Jul '94 / Cadillac / Harmonia Mundi

STRINGS FOR HOLIDAY (Tribute To Billie Holiday)
Man I love / You've changed / God bless the child / But beautiful / I cried for you / Lover man / All of me / Good morning heartache / For heaven's sake / Easy living / These foolish things / For all we know
CD ______ ENJ 93042
Enja / Oct '96 / New Note/Pinnacle / Vital/SAM

SUBCONSCIOUS LEE
CD ______ OJCCD 186
Original Jazz Classics / Nov '95 / Complete/Pinnacle / Jazz Music / Wellard

TENORLEE
I remember you / Skylark / Thanks for the memory / You are too beautiful / Handful of stars / Autumn nocturne / Tangerine / Tenorlee / Lady be good / Gypsy / Tis autumn
CD ______ CHCD 71019
Candid / Mar '97 / Cadillac / Direct / Jazz Music / Koch / Wellard

THINGIN (Konitz, Lee & Don Friedman/ Attila Zoller)
CD ______ ARTCD 6174
Hat Art / Feb '96 / Cadillac / Harmonia Mundi

UNACCOMPANIED (Live In Yokohama)
CD ______ PSFD 83
PSF / May '97 / Harmonia Mundi

VENEZIA, A (Konitz, Lee & Il Suono Improvviso)
CD ______ W 532
Philology / Nov '93 / Cadillac / Harmonia Mundi

WILD AS SPRINGTIME
Ezz-thetic / Hairy canary / She's as wild as Springtime / Duende / It's you / Prelude no.20 / Spinning waltz / Silly samba / Hi Beck / KO / Hairy canary / Ezz-thetic
CD ______ CCD 79734
Candid / May '97 / Cadillac / Direct / Jazz Music / Koch / Wellard

ZOUNDS (Konitz, Lee Quartet)
CD ______ 1212192
Soul Note / Mar '92 / Cadillac / Harmonia Mundi / Wellard

Konkhra

LIVE ERASER
CD ______ PCD 031
Progress / Jul '96 / Cargo / Plastic Head

SEXUAL AFFECTIVE DISORDER
CD ______ NB 105CD
Nuclear Blast / Mar '94 / Plastic Head

SPIT OR SWALLOW
CD ______ PCD 019
Lost & Found / Sep '95 / Plastic Head

STRANDED
CD ______ CD 7913002
Progress Red / Jun '93 / Plastic Head

Konstruktivists

FORBIDDEN
CD ______ OGPU 002CD
Ogpu / Oct '96 / World Serpent

KONSTRUKTIVISTS LIVE
CD ______ OGPU 001CD
Ogpu / Oct '96 / World Serpent

Konte, Dembo

JALIOLOGY (Konte, Dembo & Kausu Kuyateh)
CD ______ XENO 4036CD
Xenophile / Jun '95 / ADA / Direct

Konte, Lamine

SONGS OF THE GRIOTS
CD ______ VICG 50082
JVC World Library / Mar '96 / ADA / CM / Direct

Kooky Scientist

UNPOPULAR SCIENCE
CD ______ PLUS 8064CD
Plus 8 / Jun '97 / Intergroove

Kool & The Gang

BEST OF KOOL & THE GANG 1969-1976, THE
Funky stuff / Who's gonna take the weight / Rhyme tyme people / Hollywood swinging / Love the life you live / Give it up / Chocolate buttermilk / Jungle boogie / Let the music take your mind / Open sesame / Kool it (here comes the fuzz) / Summer madness / NT / Pneumonia / Love and understanding / Spirit of the boogie
CD ______ 5148222
Mercury / Jun '93 / PolyGram

COLLECTION, THE
Celebration / Ladies night / Victory / Big fun / Take it to the top / If you feel like dancin' / Tonight's the night / Street kids / Place for us / Hi de hi, ho de ho / Take my heart (you can have it if you want it) / Funky stuff / I sweat / Surrender / Think it over / Just friends / Fresh / Cherish
CD ______ 5516352
Spectrum / Mar '96 / PolyGram

DANCE COLLECTION
Celebration / Get down on it / Let's go dancin' (ooh la la la) / Big fun / Ladies night / Take my heart (you can have it if you want it) / In the heart / Straight ahead / Hi de hi, hi de ho / Steppin' out / Good time tonight / Fresh / Peacemaker / Emergency / Victory
CD ______ 8425202
Mercury / Aug '90 / PolyGram

GREAT AND REMIXED '91
CD ______ 8486042
Mercury / Jul '91 / PolyGram

GREATEST HITS LIVE
CD ______ 74321400632
Milan / Oct '96 / Conifer/BMG / Silva Screen

KOOL & THE GANG
CD ______ GFS 067
Going For A Song / Jul '97 / Else / TKO Magnum

KOOL AND THE GANG
CD ______ 12607
Laserlight / Oct '95 / Target/BMG

LIVE ON STAGE
Victory / Ladies night / Fresh / Take my heart (you can have it if you want it) / Hollywood / Too hot / Joanna / Cherish / Ooh la la la (let's go dancin') / Get down / Celebration / Tonight / Emergency
CD ______ MSCD 7
Music De-Luxe / Nov '94 / TKO Magnum

NIGHT PEOPLE
Get down on it / Stand up and sing / Hangin' out / Morning star / Love and understanding / Be my lady / Caribbean festival / Emergency / Never give up / Good time tonight / Home is where the heart is / All she really wants to do is dance / September love / Night people
CD ______ 5501982
Spectrum / Aug '94 / PolyGram

NYC COOL
(Jump up on the) Rhythm and ride / I think I love you / Love come down / Pretty little sexy Miss / Better late than never / Heart / My search is over / Summer / Brown / Give right now to you / Weight / Show us the way to love / Unite / God will find you
CD ______ MDCD 4
Magnum Music / Jan '94 / TKO Magnum

STATE OF AFFAIRS
CD ______ CURCD 21
Curb / Jun '96 / Grapevine/PolyGram

TOO HOT - LIVE HITS EXPERIENCE
Victory / Ladies night / Fresh / Take my heart / Hollywood swinging / Too hot / Joanna / Cherish / Ohh la la la (let's go dancing) / Get down on it / Celebration / Tonight / Emergency
CD ______ EMPRCD 657
Emporio / Jun '96 / Disc

UNITE
(Jump up on the) Rhythm and ride / I think I love you / Love comes down / Sexy Miss / Better late than never / Heart / My search is over / Summer / Brown / Give right now / Weight / Show us the way / Unite / God will find you
CD ______ CDUNITE 1
Charly / Oct '93 / Koch
CD ______ 74321446152
Milan / Mar '97 / Conifer/BMG / Silva Screen

UNITE
CD ______ ST 5010
Star Collection / Apr '95 / BMG

Kool Ace

MACKATHERMASTATICZXONE
CD ______ MRR 4212CD
Ichiban / Aug '95 / Direct / Koch

Kool G Rap

456
Blowin' up in the wind / Fast life / Ghetto knows / It's a shame / Money on my brain / Intro / 4, 5, 6 / It's a shame / Take 'em to war / Executioner style / For da brothaz
CD ______ 4814722
Epic / Oct '95 / Sony

Kooper, Al

REKOOPERATION
Downtime / After the lights go down low / When the spell is broken / How am I ever gonna get over you / Sneakin' round the barnyard / Soul twist-ed / Looking for clues / Honky tonk / Clean up woman / Don't be cruel / Alvino Johnson's shuffle / Johnny B Goode / I wanna little girl
CD ______ 8444002
Limelight / May '94 / PolyGram

SOUL OF A MAN (2CD Set)
CD Set ______ MM 65113
Music Masters / Jan '97 / Nimbus

SUPERSESSION (Kooper, Al/Mike Bloomfield/Stephen Stills)
Alberts shuffle / Stop / Man's temptation / His holy modal majesty / Really / It takes a lot to laugh, it takes a train to cry / Season of the witch / You don't love me / Harvey's tune
CD ______ CK 64608
Columbia / Jul '95 / Sony

Koral, Rob

WAS IT SOMETHING YOU SAID (Koral, Rob & Sue Hawker)
Yesterday's / Polka dots and moonbeams / Dance with me / Little piece of heaven / 500 Miles high / Her ways / Remember this / Horizons / I could write a book / Stay away / Crazy Sunday / Waiting for Norman / Lies / He's funny that way / I need your love so bad / Just the way things are / Was it something you said / Perdido
CD ______ CHECD 00112
Master Mix / Jul '95 / Jazz Music / New Note/Pinnacle / Wellard

Korb, Kristin

INTRODUCING KRISTIN KORB WITH THE RAY BROWN TRIO (Korb, Kristin & Ray Brown Trio)
Night in Tunisia / Peel me a grape / Whirlybird fever / Straight no chaser / Black Orpheus / Yeh yeh / Ain't misbehavin' / These foolish things / Funky tune for Ray / Take the 'A' train
CD ______ CD 83386
Telarc / Oct '96 / Conifer/BMG

Korgis

BEST OF THE KORGIS
CD ______ 472136
Flarenasch / May '96 / Discovery

Korn

KORN
Blind / Ball tongue / Need to / Clown / Divine / Faget / Shoots and ladders / Predictable / Fake / Lies / Helmet in the bush / Daddy
CD ______ 4780802
Epic / Nov '95 / Sony

LIFE IS PEACHY
Twist / Chi / Lost / Swallow / Porno creep / Good God / Mr. Rogers / K@#0%# / No place to Hi / Wicked / Adidas / Lowrider / Ass itch / Kill you / Twist (acapella)
CD ______ 4853692
Epic / Oct '96 / Sony

Korn, Paddy

BACK BEAT INSPIRED (Korn, Paddy & White Bread)
CD ______ CDST 02
Stumble / Nov '95 / Direct

Korner, Alexis

ALEXIS KORNER MEMORIAL CONCERT VOL.1 (Various Artists)
CD ______ IGOCD 2050
Indigo / Dec '95 / ADA / Direct

ALEXIS KORNER MEMORIAL CONCERT VOL.2 (Various Artists)
CD ______ IGOCD 2051
Indigo / Dec '95 / ADA / Direct

ALEXIS KORNER'S BLUES INCORPORATED...PLUS (Korner, Alexis & Blues Incorporated)
Blue mink / Rainy Tuesday / Sappho / Preachin' the blues / Royal dooji / Captain's tiger / Anything for now / Little bit groovy / Chris Trundle's habit / Trundlin' / Taboo man / CC rider / Yogi / Navy blue
CD ______ SEECD 457
See For Miles/C5 / Oct '96 / Pinnacle

BLUES INCORPORATED
CD ______ PLSCD 102
Pulse / Apr '96 / BMG

BOOTLEG HIM
She fooled me / Hoochie coochie man / Yellow dog blues / I wonder who / Dee / Oh Lord don't let them drop that atomic bomb on me / Rockin' honesty / I got a woman / Might mighty spade and whitey / Corine Corina / Operator / Love you save / Jesus is just alright / That's all / Evil hearted woman / Clay House Inn / Love is gonna go / Sunrise / Hellhound on my trail
CD ______ CLACD 291
Castle / Feb '93 / BMG

COLLECTION 1961-1972, THE
She fooled me / Hoochie coochie man / Oh Lord don't let them drop that atomic bomb on me / I got a woman / Corine Corina / Everyday I have the blues / Operator / Rosie / Polly put the kettle on / I see it / You don't miss your water / Mighty mighty spade and

whitey / Lo and behold / Louisiana blues / Ooh wee baby / Rock me baby / Sweet sympathy / Country shoes
CD _____ CCSCD 150
Castle / Apr '94 / BMG

COLLECTION, THE
Gospel ship / Captain America / Thief / Robert Johnson / Get off my cloud / Honky tonk woman / Spoonful / Daytime song / Lend me some time / Hey pretty mama / Stump blues / I got my mojo working / Geneva / Wreck of ol' 97 / Casey Jones / Hi-heel sneakers / King BB / Juvenile delinquent
CD _____ CCSCD 192
Castle / Sep '88 / BMG

I WONDER WHO
Watermelon man / Streamline train / Rock me / Come back / Going down slow / 2.19 blues / River's invitation / I wonder who / Chicken shack back home / County jail blues / Roll 'em Pete / Betty and Dupree / CC rider
CD _____ BGOCD 136
Beat Goes On / Mar '92 / Pinnacle

LIVE IN PARIS (Korner, Alexis & Colin Hodgkinson)
Blue Monday / Key to the highway / Catcoke rag / Phonograph blues / Little bitty gal blues / Sweet home Chicago / Cherry red / I got my mojo working / Gospel ship / Geneva / Working in a coalmine / Flocking with you
CD _____ CDTB 109
Thunderbolt / '91 / TKO Magnum

LOST ALBUM, THE
CD _____ CDTB 162
Thunderbolt / Nov '94 / TKO Magnum

ME
Honky tonk woman / Louise / Hammer and nails / Santa Fe blues / How long blues / Roberta / Precious lord / Honour the young man / And again / East St. Louis blues
CD _____ CLACD 292
Castle / Feb '93 / BMG

ME/BOOTLEG HIM/THE PARTY ALBUM (3CD Set)
CD Set _____ CLA BX 914
Castle / Feb '92 / BMG

NEW GENERATION OF BLUES, A
Mary open the door / Little bitty girl / Baby don't you love me / Go down sunshine / Same for you / I'm tore down / In the evening / Somethin' you got / New worried blues / What's that sound I hear / Flower
CD _____ BGOCD 102
Beat Goes On / Jul '91 / Pinnacle

ON THE MOVE
Hey good lookin' / Rosie / Blood on the saddle / Fly united / Steal away / Bluebirds fresh daily / Thief / Working in a coalmine / Rock me / Honky tonk woman / I don't know / Little bitty gal blues / Engine 143 / Louisiana blues / You got the power / Vicksburg blues / Big boss man
CD _____ CCSCD 809
Renaissance Collector Series / Sep '96 / BMG

PARTY ALBUM
Things ain't what they used to be / Captain's tiger / Skipping / Spoonful / Finkless cafe / Dooji wooji / Whole mess of blues / Lining the track / Robert Johnson
CD _____ CLACD 290
Castle / Feb '93 / BMG

R & B FROM THE MARQUEE (Korner, Alexis & Blues Incorporated)
Gotta move / Rain is such a lonesome sound / I got my brand on you / Spooky but nice / Keep your hands off / I wanna put a tiger in your tank / I got my mojo working / Finkles cafe / Hoochie coochie man / Downtown / How long blues / I thought i heard that train whistle blow
CD _____ 8209862
Deram / Oct '91 / PolyGram

RED HOT FROM ALEX (Korner, Alexis & Blues Incorporated)
Woke up this morning / Skipping / Herbie's tune / Stormy Monday / It's happening / Roberta / Jones / Cabbage greens / Chicken shack / Haitian fight song
CD _____ HILLCD 17
Wooded Hill / May '97 / Direct / World Serpent

SKY HIGH (Korner, Alexis & Blues Incorporated)
CD _____ IGOCD 2012
Indigo / Dec '94 / ADA / Direct

TESTAMENT (Korner, Alexis & Colin Hodgkinson)
One scotch, one bourbon, one beer: *Korner, Alexis* / Stump blues: *Korner, Alexis* / Streamline train: *Korner, Alexis* / My babe: *Korner, Alexis* / 32-20 blues: *Korner, Alexis* / Hi-heel sneakers: *Korner, Alexis* / Will the circle be unbroken: *Korner, Alexis* / Mary open the door: *Korner, Alexis*
CD _____ CDTB 2026
Thunderbolt / '86 / TKO Magnum

Kornog

ON SEVEN WINDS
Gavotten ar menez / Sir Aldingar / Toniou Bale / Ronds de St. Vincent / Helen of Kirkconnel / Trip to Flagstaff / Shuttle rins / Dans plinn / Gavotten / Varbishka ratchenitza
CD _____ GLCD 1062
Green Linnet / Feb '92 / ADA / CM / Direct / Highlander / Roots

PREMIERE
CD _____ GLCD 1055
Green Linnet / Feb '90 / ADA / CM / Direct / Highlander / Roots

Korpse

PULL THE FLOOD
CD _____ CANDLE 005CD
Candlelight / May '94 / Plastic Head

REVIRGIN
CD _____ CANDLE 014CD
Candlelight / Jun '96 / Plastic Head

Korriganed

RU HA DU
CD _____ KEL 003CD
Diffusion Breizh / Aug '95 / ADA

Kortchmar, Danny

INNUENDO
CD _____ 7559611742
Elektra / Jan '97 / Warner Music

Kosek, Kenny

ANGELWOOD
Locks at Athy medley / Strictly from Dixie / Poppy's waltz / Visco City breakdown / Cemetry man / La Bataille/Booth shot Lincoln / John Morton rag / Sugar Hill / When you and I were young Maggie / Table Mountain road/Tilden / Evan's farewell / Stoney Creek
CD _____ ROUCD 0362
Rounder / Feb '97 / ADA / CM / Direct

Koskerien

EBREL
CD _____ KOS96 02
KOS / Nov '96 / ADA

Kosma

UNIVERSAL
CD _____ IC 018CD
Infracom / Oct '96 / Plastic Head / SRD

Kosmic Twins

PSYCHO CONNECTION
CD _____ DIS 009CD
Disturbance / Mar '94 / Plastic Head / Prime

Kosmik Kommando

FREQUENSEIZE
CD Set _____ CAT 010CD
Rephlex / May '94 / Prime / RTM/Disc

Kossoff, Paul

BACK STREET CRAWLER
I'm ready / Time away / Molton gold / Back-street crawler / Tuesday morning
CD _____ IMCD 84
Island / Feb '90 / PolyGram

BLUE SOUL
Over the green hills (Part 1): *Free* / Worry: *Free* / Moonshine: *Free* / Trouble on double time: *Free* / Crossroads: *Free* / Oh I wept: *Free* / We got time: *Uncle Dog* / Oh how we danced: *Capaldi, Jim* / Stealer: *Free* / Hold on: *Kossoff/Kirke/Tetsu/Rabbit* / Catch a train: *Free* / Come together in the morning: *Free* / Molten gold / I know why the sun don't shine: *Rumbledown Band* / Tricky Dicky rides again: *Capaldi, Jim* / I'm ready / Blue soul: *Back Street Crawler*
CD _____ IMCD 144
Island / Jul '92 / PolyGram

KOSSOFF, KIRKE, TETSU, RABBIT (Kossoff/Kirke/Tetsu/Rabbit)
Bluegrass / Sammy's alright / Anna / Just for the box / Hold on / Fool's life / Yellow house / Dying fire / I'm on the run / Colours
CD _____ IMCD 139
Island / Aug '91 / PolyGram

STONE FREE
Worm: *Free* / Songs of yesterday: *Free* / Mr. Big: *Free* / Time away / You and me / You've taken hold of me / Hole in the head: *Amazing Blondel* / Band plays on: *Back Street Crawler* / It's a long way down to the top: *Back Street Crawler* / Train song: *Back Street Crawler* / Stealing my way: *Back Street Crawler* / Blue soul: *Back Street Crawler* / Just for you: *Back Street Crawler* / Leaves in the wind: *Back Street Crawler* / Molten gold
CD _____ 3036000952
Carlton / Mar '97 / Carlton

Kostars

KLASSICS WITH A K
CD _____ GR 025CD
Grand Royal / Apr '97 / Cargo / Plastic Head

Kostia

10 PEBBLES
Invitation / For you / It's going to rain / American fields / Russian song / We / Interlude / Loneliness / Yarmarka / Snowy river / Home sweet home
CD _____ ND 61055
Narada / Jul '96 / ADA / New Note/Pinnacle

Koteron, Ibon

LEONEN ORROAK (Koteron, Ibon & Kepa Junkera)
CD _____ KDCD 449
Elkar / May '97 / ADA

Kotilainen, Esa

AAMU JOELLA
CD _____ 129412
Fazer / Apr '96 / ADA

Kottke, Leo

6 AND 12 STRING GUITAR
Driving of the year nail / Last of the Arkansas greyhound / Ojo / Crow river waltz / Sailor's grave on the prairie / Vaseline machine gun / Jack Fig / Watermelon / Jesu joy of man's desiring / Fisherman / Tennessee toad / Busted bicycle / Brain of the purple mountain / Coolidge rising
CD _____ CDTAK 1024
Takoma / Apr '96 / ADA / Pinnacle

BALANCE
Tell Mary / I don't know why / Embryonic journey / Disguise / Whine / Losing everything / Drowning / Dolores / Half acre of garlic / Learning the game
CD _____ BGOCD 263
Beat Goes On / Aug '95 / Pinnacle

BEST, THE
Machine no.11 / Cripple creek / Bourree / When shrimps learn to whistle / Bill Cheatham / Song of the swamp / Last steam engine train / Bean time / Spanish entomologist / Short stories / Hole in the day / Mona Roy / Venezuela, there you go / Monkey lust / Busted bicycle / June bug / Eggtooth / Stealing / Living in the country / Medley: Crow river waltz/Jesu joy of man's desiring/ Jack Fig / Standing in my shoes / Bumble bee / Eight miles high / Tilt blillings and the student prince / Pamela Brown / Standing on the outside / Power failure
CD _____ BGOCD 277
Beat Goes On / Jun '95 / Pinnacle

BURNT LIPS
Endless sleep / Cool water / Frank forgets / Sonora's death row / Quiet man / Everybody lies / I called back / Low thud / Orange room / Credits / Out takes from Terry's movie / Voluntary target / Burnt lips / Sand street / Train and the gate / From Terry's movie
CD _____ BGOCD 259
Beat Goes On / Dec '94 / Pinnacle

CHEWING PINE
Standing on the outside / Power failure / Venezuela, there you go / Don't you think / Regards from Chuck Pink / Monkey money / Scarlatti rip-off / Wheels / Grim to the brim / Rebecca / Trombone / Can't quite put it into words
CD _____ BGOCD 148
Beat Goes On / Mar '93 / Pinnacle

DREAMS & ALL THAT STUFF
CD _____ BGOCD 132
Beat Goes On / Nov '92 / Pinnacle

GREENHOUSE
CD _____ BGOCD 50
Beat Goes On / Oct '90 / Pinnacle

GUITAR MUSIC
Part 2 / Available space / Side one suite / Some birds / Slang / My double / Three walls and bars / Some birds (reprise) / Perforated sleep / Strange / Little shoes / Jib's hat / Tumbling tumbleweeds / Agile / Song for the night of the hunter / All I have to do is dream / Sleepwalk
CD _____ BGOCD 261
Beat Goes On / May '95 / Pinnacle

HEAR THE WIND HOWL
Eight miles high / Pamela Brown / Cripple creek / Hear the wind howl / You tell me why / Mona Ray / Don't you think / All through the night / June bug / Grim to the brim / Poor boy / Scarlatti rip-off / Standing in my shoes / Little bit of San Antonio Rose/ America the beautiful
CD _____ DC 868682
Disky / Nov '96 / Disky / THE

ICE WATER
CD _____ BGOCD 146
Beat Goes On / Jul '92 / Pinnacle

KOTTKE, LANG & FAHEY (Kottke, Leo & Peter Lang/John Fahey)
Cripple Creek: *Kottke, Leo* / Ice miner: *Kottke, Leo* / Red and white: *Kottke, Leo* / Anyway: *Kottke, Leo* / St. Charles shuffle: *Lang, Peter* / When Kings come home: *Lang, Peter* / As I lay sleeping: *Lang, Peter* / Thoth song: *Lang, Peter* / On the sunny side of the ocean: *Fahey, John* / Sunflower river blues: *Fahey, John* / Revolt of the Dyke Brigade: *Fahey, John* / In Christ there is no East & West: *Fahey, John*
CD _____ CDTAK 1040
Takoma / Jun '96 / ADA / Pinnacle

LEO KOTTKE
Buckaroo / White ape / Haysee suede / Rio Leo / Range / Airproofing / Maroon / Waltz / Death by reputation / Up tempo / Shadowland
CD _____ BGOCD 257
Beat Goes On / Oct '94 / Pinnacle

LEO KOTTKE LIVE
William Powell / Room at the top of the stairs / Airproofing / Jack gets up / Combat / Peg leg / Twilight time / Bean time / Roy Autry / Parade / I yell at traffic / Flattend brain / Little Martha / Oddball / Arms of Mary
CD _____ 01005821322
Private Music / Mar '96 / BMG

LIVE IN EUROPE
Train and the gate / Open country joy: Theme and adhesions / Airproofing / Tell Mary / Wheels / Up tempo / Palms blvd / Shadowland / Eggtooth / Pamela Brown / Range
CD _____ BGOCD 265
Beat Goes On / Aug '95 / Pinnacle

MUDLARK
CD _____ BGOCD 101
Beat Goes On / Apr '91 / Pinnacle

MY FEET ARE SMILING
CD _____ BGOCD 134
Beat Goes On / Feb '92 / Pinnacle

PECULIAROSO
Peg leg / Poor boy / Parade / Wonderland by night / World made to order / Room service / Turning into Randolph Scott (Humid child) / Porky and pale arms of Mary / Room at the stop of the stairs / Big situation / Twilight time
CD _____ 01005821112
Private Music / Apr '94 / BMG

STANDING IN MY SHOES
Standing in my shoes / World turning / Dead end / Vaseline machine gun / Corrina, Corrina / Realm / Cripple creek / Twice: *Kottke, Leo & Chet Atkins* / Across the street / Don't call me Ray / Itchy
CD _____ 1005821462
Private Music / May '97 / BMG

TIME STEP
Running all night long / Bungle party / Rings / Mr. Fonebone / Julie's house / Memories are made of this / Saginaw Michigan / I'll break out again / Wrong track / Starving / Here comes that rain again
CD _____ BGOCD 255
Beat Goes On / Apr '95 / Pinnacle

Kotto Bass

SOUKOUS FUSION
CD _____ SMCD 1157
Sonima / Jan '97 / Stern's

Koun

AN DRO
CD _____ KMCD 59
Keltia Musique / Feb '96 / ADA / Discovery

Koutev, Philip

BULGARIAN ACAPELLA (Koutev, Philip Folk Ensemble)
Kaji, kaji, Angjo / Vecherjal, Rado / Poleg-nala e Todora / Dumai Zlato / Dragana i slavej / Malka moma dvori mete / Dimjaninka / Dai si vasse rachizata / Stoyan ide ot grad zarigrad / Aide sanze zaide / Pilenze pee govori / Grozdanka / Protekla e voda / Pri-turi se planinata
CD _____ JVC 53892
JVC World Library / Sep '96 / ADA / CM / Direct

BULGARIAN POLYPHONY (Koutev, Philip Folk Ensemble)
CD _____ VICG 50012
JVC World Library / Mar '96 / ADA / CM / Direct

BULGARIAN POLYPHONY VOL.2 (Koutev, Philip Folk Ensemble)
CD _____ VICG 50022
JVC World Library / Mar '96 / ADA / CM / Direct

Kouyate, Bassi

SONGS OF BAMBARA GRIOT, MALI
CD _____ 926582
BUDA / Jan '97 / Discovery

Kouyate, Diaryatou

GUINEA : KORA & SONG N'GABU VOL.1 (Kouyate, Diaryatou & M'Bady)
CD _____ 926292
BUDA / Apr '97 / Discovery

GUINEA : KORA & SONG N'GABU VOL.2 (Kouyate, Diaryatou & M'Bady)
CD 926482
BUDA / Apr '97 / Discovery

Kouyate, Famoro

ASSUSU (Kouyate, Famoro & Kike)
CD OA 204
PAM / Feb '94 / ADA / Direct

Kouyate, Ousmane

DOMBA (Kouyate, Ousmane Band)
Djougouya / Domba / Kounady / Miriya / An' fananta lele / N'nafanta
CD STCD 1030
Stern's / May '90 / ADA / CM / Stern's

Kouyate, Tata Bambo

JATIGUI
Hommage a baba cissoko / Mama batchily / Goundo tandja / Ainana bah / Ahourou bocoum / Amadou traore
CD CDORB 042
Globestyle / Jun '89 / Pinnacle

Kovac, Boris

FROM RITUAL NOVA I & II
CD RERBKCD 1
ReR/Recommended / Feb '94 / ReR Megacorp / RTM/Disc

Koverhult, Tommy

JAZZ IN SWEDEN 1983
CD 1289
Caprice / Jan '83 / ADA / Cadillac / CM / Complete/Pinnacle

Kovriga Balalaika Orchestra

RUSSIAN FAVOURITES
CD MCD 71793
Monitor / Jun '93 / CM

Kowald, Peter

DUOS USA JAPAN
CD FMPCD 21
FMP / Sep '87 / Cadillac

Kox Box

FOREVER AFTER
CD HHCD 012
Harthouse / Jun '95 / Mo's Music Machine / Prime / Vital

LIVE FROM THE BURNING MAN
CD BR 031CD
Blue Room Released / Sep '97 / Essential/ BMG / SRD

Kpiaye, John

RED GOLD & BLUE
CD LJKCD 012
LKJ / Jun '94 / Grapevine/PolyGram / Jet Star

Kraftwerk

AUTOBAHN
Autobahn / Kometenmelodie 1 / Kometenmelodie 2 / Mitternacht / Morgenspaziergang
CD CDP 7461532
EMI / Aug '95 / EMI

CAPITOL YEARS BOX, THE
CD Set CLEO 94162
Cleopatra / May '97 / Cargo / Greyhound / Plastic Head / RTM/Disc / SRD

COMPUTER WORLD
Pocket calculator / Numbers / Computer world / Computer love / It's more fun to compute / Home computer
CD CDEMS 1547
Capitol / Apr '95 / EMI

ELECTRIC CAFE
Boing boom tschak / Techno pop / Musique non stop / Telephone call / Sex object / Electric cafe
CD CDEMS 1546
EMI / Aug '95 / EMI

MAN MACHINE
Robots / Spacelab / Metropolis / Model / Neon lights / Man machine
CD CDEMS 1520
Capitol / Apr '95 / EMI

MAN MACHINE
Robots / Spacelab / Metropolis / Model / Man machine / Die roboter / Das modell / Neon licht
CD CDCNTAV 4
EMI / Jun '97 / EMI

MIX, THE
Robots / Computer love / Pocket calculator / Dentaku / Autobahn / Radioactivity / Trans Europe express / Abzug / Metal on metal / Homecomputer / Musique non stop
CD CDEM 1408
EMI / May '95 / EMI

MODEL, THE (The Best Of Kraftwerk 1975-1978)
CD CLEO 57612
Cleopatra / May '97 / Cargo / Greyhound / Plastic Head / RTM/Disc / SRD

RADIO ACTIVITY
Geiger counter / Radioactivity / Radioland / Airwaves / Intermission / News / Voice of energy / Antenna / Radio stars / Uranium / Transistir / Ohm sweet ohm
CD CDEMS 1524
Capitol / Apr '95 / EMI

SHOWROOM DUMMIES
CD CLEO 6843CD
Cleopatra / May '97 / Cargo / Greyhound / Plastic Head / RTM/Disc / SRD

TRANCEWERK EXPRESS VOL.2 (A Tribute To Kraftwerk) (Various Artists)
Tour De France / Pocket Calculator / Numbers / Man Machine / Kometen Melodie / Robots / Computer love / Model / Trans-Europe Express
CD CLP 99042
Cleopatra / Jan '97 / Cargo / Greyhound / Plastic Head / RTM/Disc / SRD

TRANS - EUROPE EXPRESS
Europe endless / Hall of mirrors / Showroom dummies / Trans - Europe express / Metal on metal / Franz Schubert / Endless endless
CD CDP 7464732
EMI / Aug '95 / EMI

Krakatu

MATINALE
Matinale / Unseen sea scene / Jai ping / Rural / For Bernard Moore / Sarajevo / Shuka / Raging thirst
CD 5232932
ECM / Nov '94 / New Note/Pinnacle

VOLITION
Brujo / Volition / Nai / Changgo / Little big horn / Dalens ande
CD 5119832
ECM / May '92 / New Note/Pinnacle

Kral, Irene

WHERE IS LOVE
I like you, you're nice / When I look in your eyes / Time for love / Small world / Love came on stealthy fingers / Never let me go / Spring can really hang you up the most / Lucky to be me / Some other time / Don't look back / Where is love
CD CHCD 71012
Candid / Mar '97 / Cadillac / Direct / Jazz Music / Koch / Wellard

Kral, Ivan

NATIVE
CD ZS 124
Special Delivery / Jul '92 / ADA / CM / Direct

Krall, Diana

ALL FOR YOU (A Tribute To Nat 'King' Cole)
I'm an errand girl for rhythm / Gee baby ain't I good to you / You call it madness / Frim fram sauce / Boulevard of broken dreams / Baby baby all the time / Hit that jive Jack / You're looking at me / I'm thru with love / 'Deed I do / Blossom fell / If I had you
CD IMP 11642
Impulse Jazz / Mar '96 / New Note/BMG

LOVE SCENES
All or nothing at all / Peel me a grape / I don't know enough about you / I miss you so / They can't take that away from me / Lost mind / I don't stand a ghost of a chance with you / You're getting to be a habit with me / Gentle rain / How deep is the ocean (how high is the sky) / My love / Garden in the rain / That old feeling
CD IMP 12342
Impulse Jazz / Aug '97 / New Note/BMG

ONLY TRUST YOUR HEART
Is you is or is you ain't my baby / Only trust your heart / I love being here with you / Broadway / Folks who live on the hill / I've got the world on a string / Sqeeze me / All night long / CRS Craft
CD GRP 98102
GRP / Mar '95 / New Note/BMG

STEPPING OUT
This can't be love / Straighten up and fly right / Between the devil and the deep blue sea / I'm just a lucky so and so / Body and soul / 42nd Street / Do nothin' 'til you hear from me / Big foot / Frim fram sauce / Jimmie / As long as I live
CD JUST 502
Justin Time / Oct '96 / Cadillac / New Note/ Pinnacle

Kramer

RUBBER HAIR (Kramer & Daved Hild)
CD SHIMMY 087CD
Shimmy Disc / Mar '97 / Cargo

Kramer, Billy J.

EMI YEARS, THE (Kramer, Billy J. & The Dakotas)
Do you want to know a secret / Bad to me / I call your name / I'll keep you satisfied / I know / I'll be on my way / Cruel sea / Little children / Second to none / They remind me of you / From a window / Sneakin' around / I'll be doggone / Neon city / Take my hand / Trains and boats and planes / That's the way I feel / It's gotta last forever / We're doing fine / Forgive me / Going going gone / You can't live on memories
CD CDEMS 1392
EMI / May '91 / EMI

EP COLLECTION, THE (Kramer, Billy J. & The Dakotas)
I call your name / Bad to me / Do you want to know a secret / I'll be on my way / I'll keep you satisfied / Dance with me / It's up to you / I know / Little children / They remind me of you / Beautiful reminder / From a window / Second to none / Twelfth of never / Sugar babe / Tennessee waltz / Irresistible you / Twilight time / Cruel sea / Millionaire / Magic carpet / Humdinger / Trains and boats and planes
CD SEECD 422
See For Miles/C5 / May '95 / Pinnacle

Kramer, Wayne

CITIZEN WAYNE
Stranger in the house / Back when dogs could talk / Revolution in apt. 29 / Down on the ground / Shining Mr. Lincoln's shoes / Dope for democracy / No easy way out / You don't know my name / Count time / Snatched defeat / Doing the work / Farewell to whiskey
CD 64882
Epitaph / Apr '97 / Pinnacle / Plastic Head

DEATH TONGUE
CD ITEM CD2
Progress / Jul '92 / Vital

HARDSTUFF, THE
CD E 864472
Epitaph / Jan '95 / Pinnacle / Plastic Head

Krantz, Wayne

2 DRINK MINIMUM
Whippersnapper / Dove Gloria / Shirts off / Dream called love / AFKap / Isabelle / Alliance / Secrets / Lynxpaw
CD ENJ 90432
Enja / Jul '95 / New Note/Pinnacle / Vital/ SAM

LONG TO BE LOOSE
These instrumental pieces were / Not consciously written about / Specific people, places, things or ideas / Although one began / From a little croaking sound / Friend's DAT machine makes / What they were written about / Is something I don't understand yet / But I know it when I see it / And, hopefully, so will you
CD ENJ 70992
Enja / Jul '93 / New Note/Pinnacle / Vital/ SAM

SEPERATE CAGES (Krantz, Wayne & Leni Stern)
Saturday morning / Claudine / Something is wrong in Spanish / Point falling / Nicole / King's Cross / Veronique / Keep my heart / Leave softly / Silver line / November
CD ALCD 1007
Alchemy / Apr '97 / Pinnacle

SIGNALS
CD 60482
Enja / Nov '90 / New Note/Pinnacle / Vital/ SAM

Krasavik Ensemble

GRAMNITSY
CD B 6843
Auvidis/Ethnic / Mar '97 / ADA / Harmonia Mundi

Krashman

BLACK CIRCLE
Got you faded / Something for the player to roll on / It be's like that / Caught up / Gitten mine / Making of a madman / Booty mack / Sister Suzie / Down in the ghetto / Four 40's / Black circle / Watch yo bitch / Nuthin' but a party
CD BRCD 601
4th & Broadway / Sep '93 / PolyGram

Kraus, Peter

DIE SINGLES 1958-1960
Sugar baby / Ich denk'an dich / Honey baby (du passt so gut zu mir) / Come on and swing / Kitty kat / Havanna love / Wunderbar wie du / Hey du bist okay / Tiger / Ich bin ja so allein / Wenn / Oh Veronika / Die jungen Jahre / Wenn du heute ausgehst / Das ist prima / OK / Cowboy Billy / Sensationell / Auf wiederseh'n und lass dir's gut ergehen / Genau wie du / Ten o'clock rock / Keine nacht kann ich schlafen / Dream face / Nobody else/Du gehorst mir
CD BCD 15453
Bear Family / Apr '89 / Direct / Rollercoaster / Swift

DIE SINGLES 1960
Susi sagt es Gabi / Doll doll dolly / Alle Madchen wollen kussen / Wenn sie dich allein lasst / Va Bene / Sag mir was du denkst / Honeymoon / Mondschein und Liebe / Ein rendezvous mit dir / Rote rosen / Ein haus in Tennessee / Blue river / Cherie, cherie / Cowboy Jenny / Rose Marie / Alles ist anders / Ausgerechnet ich / Come on and swing (live) / Basin Street blues / When the saints go marching in / Get happy / Love me or leave me / Alright, OK you win / Nobody else
CD BCD 15457
Bear Family / Apr '89 / Direct / Rollercoaster / Swift

DIE SINGLES 1961-62
CD BCD 15527
Bear Family / Apr '92 / Direct / Rollercoaster / Swift

DIE SINGLES 1962-63
CD BCD 15528
Bear Family / Apr '92 / Direct / Rollercoaster / Swift

HERZLICHST IHR PETER KRAUS
CD BCD 15478
Bear Family / '88 / Direct / Rollercoaster / Swift

TEENAGERTRAUME, LIEBELEIEN UND SUGARBABIES (10CD Set)
Tutti frutti / Die strasse der vergessenen / O wie gut / Susi rock / Schau keinen anderen mann an / Ten o'clock rock / Lass mich bitte nie allein / Liebelei / Teddybar / Ich will nicht wissen / Es fing so wunderbar an / Wenn teenager traumen / Mach dich schon / Hafen rock / Diana / So wie damals baby / I love you baby / Du sollst mein schicksal dein / Rosmarie / Hula baby / Mit siebzehn / Du gehorst mir / Teenager melodie: *Kraus, Peter & Micky Mann* / Ich mocht' mit dir traumen: *Kraus, Peter & Micky Mann* / Sugar baby / Ich denk an dich / Du passt so gut zu mir: *Kraus, Peter & Danny Mann* / Come on and swing / Kitty kat / Havanna love / Wunderbar wie du / Hey du bist okay / Tiger / Ich bin ja so allein / Wenn: *James Brothers* / Oh Veronika: *James Brothers* / Die jungen jahre: *James Brothers* / Wenn du heut ausgehst: *James Brothers* / Das ist prima: *James Brothers* / OK: *James Brothers* / Cowboy Billy: *James Brothers* / Sensationell: *James Brothers* / Auf wiederseh'n und lass dir's gut ergeh'n: *James Brothers* / Genau wie du: *James Brothers* / Ten o'clock rock: *James Brothers* / Keine nacht kann ich schlafen / Dream face / Nobody else / Susi sagt es Gabi / Doll doll Dolly / Alle madchen wollen kussen / Wenn sie dich allein lasst / Va bene / Sag' mir was du denkst: *Kraus, Peter & Conny Froboess* / Honey moon: *Kraus, Peter & Alice/Ellen Kessler* / Mondschein und liebe: *Kraus, Peter & Alice/Ellen Kessler* / Ein rendezvous mit dir: *Kraus, Peter & Alice/Ellen Kessler* / Rote rosen: *James Brothers* / Eine haus in Tennesse: *James Brothers* / Blue river: *James Brothers* / Cherie cherie: *James Brothers* / Cowboy Jenny: *James Brothers* / Rosemarie: *James Brothers* / Alles ist anders / Ausgerechnet ich / Come on and swing / Basin Street blues / When the saints go marchin' in / Get happy / Love me or leave me / Alright, okay you win / Ich kann dir was erzahlen: *Kraus, Peter & Alice/Ellen Kessler* / Wundervoll: *Kraus, Peter & Alice/Ellen Kessler* / Sie hat so wunderschone augen: *James Brothers* / Tiger Lilly: *James Brothers* / Jedes madchen auf erden / Von Paris bis Hawaii / Hallo Blondie / Happy baby: *Kraus, Peter & Alice/Ellen Kessler* / Ich hab' dich noch genauso lieb / Mein neuer hut / Solo tu / Blue melodie / Morgen bist du alle sargen los: *James Brothers* / Wie eine kleine lady: *James Brothers* / Das fraulein Gerda / Unsere sprache ist musik: *Kraus, Peter & Sacha Distel* / Oh so wunderbar / Twenty four hours / Everybody else but me / Mission bell / Bella bella Marie / Long long ago / Ja pense a toi / C'est toi plus belle / Comme un tigre / Par le monde: *Kraus, Peter & Alice/Ellen Kessler* / Wenn das nicht so romantisch war: *Kraus, Peter & Alice/Ellen Kessler* / Teddy: *Kraus, Peter & Alice/Ellen Kessler* / Noch ein jahr: *Kraus, Peter & Alice/Ellen Kessler* / Heute und immer my love / Farah von Haifa / Ich habe alles was ich brauche: *Kraus, Peter & Alice/ Ellen Kessler* / Evelyn / Schwarze rose / Rosy oh Rosy: *James Brothers* / Beim candlelight: *James Brothers* / Ich hab' mich so an dich gewohnt: *James Brothers* / Hanna aus Havanna: *James Brothers* / Schou schou: *Twist Boys* / Twist twist: *Twist Boys* / Silver moon / Ein junges herz / Holiday lady: *James Brothers* / Komm wieder: *James Brothers* / Hallo Brigitte / Lang lang ist's her / Die ganze welt ist himmelblau / Das macht die liebe: *Kraus, Peter & Lil' Babs* / Darlin' meine liebe: *Kraus, Peter & Connie Francis* / Oh I like it: *Kraus, Peter & Connie Francis* / Heute und immer my love / Va bene / Blue melodie / Heute und immer my love / Strasse der sehnsucht / Sweety / Uns're reise fangt on / Western rose / Hande weg von den Frau'n: *Kraus, Peter & Gus Backus* / Das haben die madchen gern: *Kraus, Peter & Gus Backus* / Sonny boy sonny boy / Lorelei / Eine souvenir / Pico pico bello / Das blonde baby vom Broadway / Schenk mir einen talismann / Zucchero / Ricky ticky teeny weeny

twist express: *Kraus, Peter & Gina Dobra* / Weil es so schon ist bei dir: *Kraus, Peter & Lil' Babs* / Huh a hah alter schimmel: *James Brothers* / Weit ist die welt / Cry your eyes out / Bigger the fool / She used to be mine / Cry your eyes out / Here is a heart / Ton visage, ton image / Que demandent les jeunes / Danse avec moi / Moins de vingt ans / Madchen mit herz / Dein herr Papa / Der geist von Buffalo Bill / Wer dich sieht Evelyn / Wilde rose fern in Mexico / Sonne, pizza and amore: *Kraus, Peter & Lil' Babs* / Mein liebling ist mir treu: *Kraus, Peter & Lil' Babs* / Hey Isabell: *Kraus, Peter & Lil' Babs* / Ich traum vom honey moon: *Kraus, Peter & Lil' Babs* / Schon ist die liebe: *Kraus, Peter & Lil' Babs* / Kisses in the night / Lass kein madchen lange warten / Take it easy little girl / Heidi hodi / Vergiss sie / Wenn es nacht wird am blue river / Eine die so ist wie du / Remets nous la danse / Et la, elle a dit / Les snap / J'ai beaucoup d'amour / Piccolo piccolo / 20km al giorno / 100,000 kussen / Hou je van mij / Linda Lou / Leder uur / Diane / Raunchy: *Greger, Max* / Teenager's romance: *James Brothers* / Joker: *Greger, Max* / Kewpie doll: *Berg, Jorg Maria* / Was ein mann alles kann: *Greger, Max* / Piccolissima serenata: *James Brothers* / Mit siebzehen: *Greger, Max* / Catch a falling star / Sail along silvery moon: *Greger, Max* / I love you baby / Sugartime: *Greger, Max* / When: *James Brothers* / Tequila: *Greger, Max* / Volare / Singing hills: *Greger, Max* / White sport coat / Manakoora: *Greger, Max* / Patricia: *Berg, Jorg Maria* / Vielleicht in 3, 4, 5, 6 jahren: *Greger, Max* / Hula baby / La paloma: *Greger, Max* / Buona sera / Love and kisses: *Greger, Max* / Rock around the clock / Tutti frutti / Lonely blue boy / Charly Brown / Red river rock / Brauner bar und weisse taube / Wenn teenager traumen / My happiness / Souvenirs / See you later alligator / Shake, rattle and roll / Va bene / Apache / Heartbreak hotel / Jailhouse rock / Love me tender / Itsy bitsy teenie weenie / Buona sera / Volare / Marina / Ciao ciao bambina / Twist it up America: *Kraus, Peter & Lil' Babs* / Hatt ich einen hammer: *Kraus, Peter & Lil' Babs* / Derr mann im mond/ Schwarze Rose Marie: *Kraus, Peter & Gus Backus* / Capri fischer / Ein schiff fahrt nach Shanghai / Unter einem regenschirm am abend / Wenn die Elisabeth... / Unter der roten laterne von St. Pauli / So stell ich mir die liebe vor / Mexikanische serenade / Man musst klavier spielen konnen / Du sollst mein gluckstern sein / In einem kelinen cafe in Hernals / Ich nenne all frauen baby / Ich brauche keine millionen / Il nostro concerto / Cassetta in Canada / Drei munzen im brunnen / Die sussesten fruchte / Funiculi funicula / Come prima / O mia bella Napoli / O sole mio / Rumba Anna / Rosen aus Napoli / Florentinische nachte / Schau mich bitte nicht so an / Eso beso / Va bene / Am zuckerhut / Hab'n sie nicht 'ne frau fur mich / Desafinado / Amapola / Oh la la / Sweety / Bella bella Donna / Capri fischer / My golden baby / Sie sind mir so symphatisch / Zucchero / Va bene / Ich mocht' mit dir traumen: *Kraus, Peter & Conny Froboess* / Kitty kat: *Kraus, Peter & Conny Froboess* / Kuss mich: *Kraus, Peter & Vivi Bach* / Was ich will: *Kraus, Peter & Vivi Bach* / Alexander's ragtime band: *Kraus, Peter & Mina* / Las verita / Susi cacaracha / Darktown strutters ball: *Kraus, Peter & Gene Reed* / Die seidene leiter / You are my sunshine: *Kraus, Peter & Inge Bruck* / Hokus pokus: *Kraus, Peter & Inge Bruck* / Simsalabim: *Kraus, Peter & Inge Bruck* / Hokus pokus: *Kraus, Peter & Wencke Myrhe* / Verliebt verliebt: *Kraus, Peter & Wencke Myrhe* / Das alte haus von rocky doky / Und dann tanzen wir mambo / Ein kleines pferd aus holz / Teenager melodie: *Kraus, Peter & Conny Froboess*
CD Set ______ BCD 15871
Bear Family / Dec '96 / Direct / Rollercoaster / Swift

Krause, Bernie

GORILLAS IN THE MIX
CD ______ RCD 10119
Rykodisc / Dec '92 / ADA / Vital

Krause, Dagmar

SUPPLY AND DEMAND (Songs by Brecht, Weill & Eisler)
CD ______ HNCD 1317
Hannibal / Mar '86 / ADA / Vital

TANK BATTLES (The Songs Of Hanns Eisler)
Song of the whitewash / You have to pay / Ballad of the sack slingers / Perhaps song / Mankind / Song of a German mother / Bankenlied / Und endlich stirbt / Mother's hands / Genvieve: Ostern ist ball sur Seine / (I read about) tank battles / Chanson allemande / Mother Beimlein / Bettellied / Change the world - it needs it / Failure in loving / Ballad of (Bourgeois) welfare / Berlin 1919 / Rat men - the nightmare / Homecoming / To a little radio / Lied von der belebenden wirkung des geldes / Legende von der entstehung des buches Taoteking / And I shall never see again / Wise woman and the soldier
CD ______ BP 138CD
Blueprint / May '97 / Pinnacle

Krauss, Alison

EVERYTIME YOU SAY GOODBYE
Everytime you say goodbye / Another night / Last love letter / Cluck old hen / Who can blame you / It work this time / Heartstrings / I don't know why / Cloudy days / New fool / Shield of faith / Lose again / Another day another dollar / Jesus help me stand
CD ______ ROUCD 0285
Rounder / '92 / ADA / CM / Direct

I KNOW WHO HOLDS THE FUTURE (Krauss, Alison & The Cox Family)
CD ______ ROUCD 307
Rounder / Mar '94 / ADA / CM / Direct

I'VE GOT THAT OLD FEELING
I've got that old feeling / Dark skies / Wish I still had you / Endless highway / Winter of a broken heart / It's over / Will you be leaving / Steel rails / Tonight I'll be lonely too / One good reason / That makes two of us / Longest highway
CD ______ ROUCD 0275
Rounder / '90 / ADA / CM / Direct

NOW THAT I'VE FOUND YOU
Baby now that I've found you / Oh Atlanta / Broadway / Everytime you say goodbye / Tonight I'll be lonely too / Teardrops will kiss the morning dew / Sleep on / When God dips his pen of love in my heart / I will / I don't believe you've met my baby / Palm of your hand / When you say nothing at all
CD ______ ROUCD 0325
Rounder / Feb '95 / ADA / CM / Direct

SO LONG SO WRONG (Krauss, Alison & Union Station)
CD ______ ROUCD 0365
Rounder / Mar '97 / ADA / CM / Direct

TOO LATE TO CRY (Krauss, Alison & Various Artists)
Too late to cry / Foolish heart / Song for life / Dusty Miller / If I give my heart / In your eyes / Don't follow me / Gentle river / On the borderline / Forgotten pictures / Sleep on
CD ______ ROUCD 0235
Rounder / Aug '88 / ADA / CM / Direct

TWO HIGHWAYS (Krauss, Alison & Union Station)
Two highways / I'm alone again / Wild Bill Jones / Beaumont rag / Heaven's bright shore / Love you in vain / Here comes goodbye / As lovely as you / Windy City rag / Lord don't you forsake me / Teardrops will kiss the morning dew / Midnight rider
CD ______ ROUCD 0257
Rounder / '89 / ADA / CM / Direct

WHEN YOU SAY NOTHING AT ALL
CD ______ CRCDS 7
Rounder / Nov '95 / ADA / CM / Direct

Krauss, Briggan

GOOD KITTY
CD ______ KFW 178
Knitting Factory / Apr '97 / Cargo / Plastic Head

Kraut

LEWIS
CD ______ NOZACD 7
Ninebar / Aug '97 / Kudos / Prime / RTM/ Disc

Krauth, Phil

SILVER EYES
CD ______ TB 2052
Teenbeat / May '96 / Cargo / SRD / Vital

Kravitz, Lenny

ARE YOU GONNA GO MY WAY
Are you gonna go my way / Believe / Come on and love me / Heaven help / Just be a woman / Is there any love in your heart / Black girl / My love / Sugar / Sister / Eleutheria
CD ______ CDVUS 60
Virgin / Mar '93 / EMI

CIRCUS
Rock 'n' roll is dead / Circus / Beyond the 7th sky / Tunnel vision / Can't get you off my mind / Magdalene / God is love / Thin ice / Don't go and put a bullet in your head / In my life today / Resurrection
CD ______ CDVUS 86
Virgin / Sep '95 / EMI

LET LOVE RULE
Sittin' on top of the world / Let love rule / Freedom train / My precious love / I build this garden for us / Fear / Does anybody out there even care / Mr. Cabdriver / Rosemary / Be / Blues for sister someone / Empty hands / Flower child
CD ______ CDVUS 10
Virgin / May '90 / EMI

MAMA SAID
Fields of joy / Always on the run / Stand by my woman / It ain't over 'til it's over / More than anything in this world / What goes around comes around / Difference is why / Stop draggin' around / Flowers for Zoe / Fields of joy (reprise) / All I ever wanted / When the morning turns to night / What the fuck are we saying / Butterfly
CD ______ CDVUS 31
Virgin / Apr '91 / EMI

Kreator

OUT OF THE DARK
CD ______ N 02002
Noise / Sep '92 / Koch

OUTCAST
CD ______ GUN 140CD
Gun / Jun '97 / Plastic Head

RENEWAL
CD ______ N 01932
Noise / Oct '92 / Koch

SCENARIOS OF VIOLENCE
CD ______ N 02662
Noise / Feb '96 / Koch

Kreidler

RESPORT
CD ______ EFA 073232
Stewardess / Jun '97 / SRD

WEEKEND
CD ______ PIAS 556500420
Kiff SM / Nov '96 / Plastic Head / Vital

WEEKEND
Traffic way / Shaun / Spat / La capital / Sand colour classic / Lio / Polaroid / Desto / Reflections / Hillwood / Telefon / La fille en beige / If / Schodringers katze
CD ______ KIFF 004CD
Play It Again Sam / Jun '97 / Discovery / Plastic Head / Vital

Krekel, Tim

OUT OF THE CORNER
CD ______ APCD 083
Appaloosa / Jun '92 / ADA / Direct / TKO Magnum

Kremer, Gidon

HOMMAGE A PIAZZOLLA
Vardarito / Mi longa en re / Buenos Aires hora zero / Cafe 1930 / Oblivion / Esqualo / Soledad / Concierto para quintero / Celos / Le grand tango
CD ______ 7559794072
Nonesuch / May '97 / Warner Music

Kreusch, Cornelius C.

BLACK MUD SOUND
CD ______ ENJACD 90872
Enja / Sep '95 / New Note/Pinnacle / Vital/ SAM

Kreuz

KREUZ KONTROL
CD ______ DESCD 1
Diesel / Mar '95 / Jet Star

NEW GENERATION
Interlude / When you smile / Baby come back / Crush on you / Hush-hush / UK Swing / Do you right / That jazz feeling / Hangin' on / I never knew / Interlude (sunshine) / Deja vu / Don't take it off / New generation / 101% / Sunshine / You are the one
CD ______ 5302032
Motown / Apr '93 / PolyGram

Krewmen

ADVENTURES OF THE KREWMEN
CD ______ LMCD 008
Lost Moment / Jun '97 / Else / Shellshock/ Disc

FINAL ADVENTURES VOL.1
CD ______ LMCD 023
Lost Moment / Apr '92 / Else / Shellshock/ Disc

INTO THE TOMB
CD ______ LMCD 014
Lost Moment / Jun '97 / Else / Shellshock/ Disc

PLAGUE OF THE DEAD
CD ______ LMCD 020
Lost Moment / Oct '88 / Else / Shellshock/ Disc

POWER
CD ______ LMCD 021
Lost Moment / Sep '90 / Else / Shellshock/Disc

SINGLED OUT
CD ______ LMCD 024
Lost Moment / Oct '94 / Else / Shellshock/ Disc

SWEET DREAMS
CD ______ LMCD 010
Lost Moment / Jun '97 / Else / Shellshock/ Disc

Krimsky, Katrina

STELLA MALU (Krimsky, Katrina & Trevor Watts)
CD ______ 8335162
ECM / Jul '88 / New Note/Pinnacle

Krishan, Gopal

DHRUPAD AND KHYAL
CD ______ C 560078
Ocora / Feb '96 / ADA / Harmonia Mundi

NORTHERN INDIA - THE ART OF THE VICHITRA VEENA
CD Set ______ C 560048/49
Ocora / Jan '94 / ADA / Harmonia Mundi

Krishnan, Ramnad

SONGS OF THE CARNATIC TRADITION OF SOUTH INDIA
CD ______ 7559720232
Nonesuch / Jan '95 / Warner Music

Kriss Kross

YOUNG, RICH AND DANGEROUS
Some cut up / When the homies show up / Tonite's tha night / Interview / Young, rich and dangerous / Live and die for hip hop / Money, power and fame (three things that's necessities) / It's a group thang / Mackin' it ain't easy / Da streets ain't right / Hey sexy / Tonite's da night (remix)
CD ______ 4816052
Ruff House / Mar '96 / Sony

Kristina, Sonja

HARMONICS OF LOVE
CD ______ HTDCD 34
HTD / Apr '95 / CM / Pinnacle

Kristine W

LAND OF THE LIVING
CD ______ CHAMPCD 1029
Champion / Jul '97 / 3mv/BMG

Kristofferson, Kris

LEGENDARY YEARS, THE
Me and Bobby McGee / Josie / Lover please: *Kristofferson, Kris & Rita Coolidge* / Jesus was a Capricorn / Magdalene / Living legend / Help me make it through the night / Smokey put the sweat on me / Why me / Silver tongued devil / When she's wrong / I may smoke too much / Easter Island / It's never gonna be the same again / Golden Idol / I'd rather be sorry: *Kristofferson, Kris & Rita Coolidge* / Bigger the fool / Shake hands with the Devil / Nobody loves anybody anymore / Broken freedom song / Here comes that rainbow again / Epitaph (black and blue)
CD ______ KKVSOPCD 141
Connoisseur Collection / Apr '90 / Pinnacle

NATURAL ACT (Kristofferson, Kris & Rita Coolidge)
Blue as I do / Not everyone knows / I fought the law / Number one / You're gonna love yourself in the morning / Loving her was easier (than anything I'll ever do again) / Back in my baby's arms / Please don't tell me how the story ends / Hoola hoop / Love don't live here anymore / Silver mantis
CD ______ 5507702
Spectrum / Aug '94 / PolyGram

Krivda, Ernie

ART OF THE BALLAD, THE (Krivda, Ernie & Bill Dobbins)
CD ______ 378062
Koch Jazz / Oct '96 / Koch

Krog, Karin

GERSHWIN WITH KARRIN KROG
CD ______ CDMR 4
Meantime / Jun '96 / New Note/Pinnacle

HI FLY (Krog, Karin & Archie Shepp)
Sing me softly of the blues / Steam / Daydream / Solitude / Hi fly / Soul eyes
CD ______ CDMR 3
Meantime / Jun '96 / Cadillac / Vital

ONE ON ONE
Blues in heart / You'd be so nice to come home to / These foolish things / But not for me / God bless the child / Just in time / Song for you / Feeling too good today / Stardust / I won't dance / Medley / Scandia skies / I was doing all right / I got the right to sing the blues / Sometimes I feel like a Motherless child / Love supreme / As you are are / Going home
CD ______ MR 7
Meantime / May '97 / New Note/Pinnacle

SOMETHING BORROWED, SOMETHING NEW
Thrill is gone / Out of this world / If I should lose you / My foolish heart / Canto mai / I get a kick out of you / All blues / Meaning of the blues / This is new / Just one of those things / I'm beginning to see the light / Every time we say goodbye / Tivoli
CD ______ CDMR 2
Meantime / Jun '96 / Cadillac / Vital

YOU MUST BELIEVE IN SPRING (Krog, Karin & Palle Mikkelborg)
CD ______ CDMR 5
Meantime / Jun '96 / New Note/Pinnacle

Krokus

TO ROCK OR NOT TO BE
CD SPV 08543872
SPV / Aug '95 / Koch / Plastic Head

Kronos Quartet

BOXSET VOL.2
CD 7559793122
Nonesuch / Jul '94 / Warner Music

DREAMS AND PRAYERS OF ISAAC THE BLIND, THE (Kronos Quartet & David Krakauer)
Prelude, calmo, sospeso / Agitato, con fuoco, maestoso, senza misura, oscilante / Teneramenta, ruvido, presto / Calmo, sospeso, allegro pesante / Postlude, lento, liberamente
CD 7559794442
Nonesuch / Apr '97 / Warner Music

GHOST OPERA (Kronos Quartet & Wu Man)
Bach, monks and Shakespeare meet in water / Earth dance / Dialogue with 'little cabbage' / Metal and stone / Song of paper
CD 7559794452
Nonesuch / Apr '97 / Warner Music

HOWL USA
Howl / Sing sing / Barstow / Cold War suite
CD 7559793722
Nonesuch / Jul '96 / Warner Music

IN FORMATION
CD RR 9CD
Reference Recordings / Sep '91 / Jazz Music / May Audio

KRONOS QUARTET (Music Of Sculthorpe/Hendrix/Sallinen/Glass & Nancarrow)
CD 7559791112
Nonesuch / Jan '87 / Warner Music

PIECES OF AFRICA
CD 7559792752
Nonesuch / Jan '92 / Warner Music

RELEASED 1985-1995
Mai nozipo / Tango sensations / Amazing grace / Different trains / String quartet / Salome / Black angels / Fratres / String quartet / Cool wind is blowing / Adagio for strings / Dinner music / How it happens / Elvis everywhere / Purple haze
CD 7559793942
Nonesuch / Feb '96 / Warner Music

SHORT STORIES
CD 7559793102
Nonesuch / Jan '95 / Warner Music

WHITE MAN SLEEPS (Music Of Volans/Ives/Hassell/Coleman/Lee/Johnston & Bartok)
White man sleeps no 1 / White man sleeps no 3 / White man sleeps no 5 / Scherzo holding your own / Pano da costa (Cloth from the coast) / Lonely woman / Amazing grace
CD 7559791632
Nonesuch / Jul '88 / Warner Music

WINTER WAS HARD (Sallinen/Riley/Part/Zorn/Webern/Piazzolla/Schnittke/Barber)
Winter was hard / Fratres / Bella by barlight / Door is ajar / Half wolf dances mad in moonlight / Forbidden fruit / Quartet No 3
CD 7559791812
Nonesuch / '88 / Warner Music

Kropinski, Uwe

AFRICAN NOTEBOOK (Kropinski, Uwe & Michael Heupel)
Addababa / Addis Hotel / Vivo Antananarivo / Zanzibar / Harare
CD AHO 1024
ITM / Apr '96 / Koch / Tradelink

Kropotkins

KROPOTKINS, THE
CD 379242
Koch International / Sep '96 / Koch

Krosfyah

ULTIMATE PARTY-PUMP ME UP
CD CE 001
Steel Donkey / Apr '96 / Jet Star

KRS 1

KRS 1
Rappaz R N dainja / De automatic: *KRS 1 & Fat Joe* / MC's act like they don't know / Ah yeah / REALITY / Free mumia: *KRS 1 & Channel Live* / Hold / Wannabemceez: *KRS 1 & Mad Lion* / Represent the real hip hop: *KRS 1 & Das EFX* / Truth / Build ya skillz: *KRS 1 & Busta Rhymes* / Out for fame / Squash all beef / Health wealth self
CD CHIP 165
Jive / Mar '97 / Pinnacle

RETURN OF DA BOOM BAP
CD CHIP 142
Jive / Oct '93 / Pinnacle

Kruder & Dorfmeister

DJ KICKS
CD K7 046CD
Studio K7 / Aug '96 / Prime / RTM/Disc

Krunchjam

KRUNCHJAM
CD OME 4148CD
Ichiban / Feb '94 / Direct / Koch

Krupa, Gene

CLASSICS 1935-1938
CD CLASSICS 754
Classics / May '94 / Discovery / Jazz Music

CLASSICS 1938
CD CLASSICS 767
Classics / Aug '94 / Discovery / Jazz Music

CLASSICS 1939-1940
CD CLASSICS 834
Classics / Sep '95 / Discovery / Jazz Music

CLASSICS 1940 VOL.1
CD CLASSICS 859
Classics / Feb '96 / Discovery / Jazz Music

CLASSICS 1940 VOL.2 (Krupa, Gene & His Orchestra)
CD CLASSICS 883
Classics / Jul '96 / Discovery / Jazz Music

CLASSICS 1940 VOL.3
CD CLASSICS 917
Classics / Jan '97 / Discovery / Jazz Music

DRUM BOOGIE
CD 4736592
Columbia / Aug '93 / Sony

DRUMMER MAN
Starburst (Opening Theme) / Leave us leap / Whispering / Idaho / You go to my head / Star dust / Bolero at the Savoy / Sweet Lorriane / My ideal / Up and atom / Tea for two / How high the moon / Lyonaise potatoes and some pork chops / Gypsy mood / He's funny that way / Out you go
CD HCD 262
Hindsight / Jun '96 / Jazz Music / Target/BMG

DRUMMER'S BAND 1938-1945, THE
CD 158592
Jazz Archives / Jul '96 / Discovery

DRUMMER, THE
Drum boogie / Ta-ra-ra-boom-der-e (ta-ra-ra-boom-de-ay) / Rhythm jam / Moonlight serenade / Big do / Jam on toast / Meet the beat of my heart / My own / You're as pretty as a picture / I'm gonna clap my hands / I hope Gabriel likes my music / My old Kentucky home / You and your love / Jazz me blues / Tutti frutti / Wire brush stomp / Old black Joe / Daydreaming / Apurskody / Tropical magic / Last round-up / Blues of Israel
CD PASTCD 7008
Flapper / Mar '93 / Pinnacle

DRUMMIN' MAN
CD CD 56080
Jazz Roots / Mar '95 / Target/BMG

GENE KRUPA & HIS ORCHESTRA 1939
CD CLASSICS 799
Classics / Mar '95 / Discovery / Jazz Music

GENE KRUPA LIVE 1946 (Krupa, Gene & His Orchestra)
CD JH 1039
Jazz Hour / Feb '95 / Cadillac / Jazz Music / Target/BMG

HOP, SKIP AND JUMP VOL.3 (Krupa, Gene & His Orchestra)
All by myself / That old devil moon / Yes, yes honey / How deep is the ocean / Hop, skip and jump / Out of nowhere / What is this thing called love / Some day soon / USO / And then I looked at you / Bolero at the Savoy / King Porter stomp / Old folks at home / Idaho / Where or when / In the moon mist / Dark eyes / Sweet Lorraine / He's funny that way / (Otto make that) riff Staccato / Come to the Mardis Gras / As long as I'm dreaming / Leave us leap
CD HEPCD 51
Hep / Nov '96 / Cadillac / Jazz Music / New Note/Pinnacle / Wellard

IT'S UP TO YOU (1946 Vol. 2)
Blue Lou / Summertime / Hodge podge / Boogie blues / Bugle call rag / Ain't nowhere / Man I love / 10 Ritchie Drive / It's up to you / Yesterdays / Margie / Night and day / By the river Sainte Marie / These foolish things / Medley: Mood indigo/Prelude to a kiss/Solitude / Medley: In a sentimental mood/Sophisticated Lady / I hear you screaming / Baby, won't you please come home / How high the moon / Birdhouse / It's a good day / You be you / Dear Old Southland
CD HEPCD 46
Hep / May '95 / Cadillac / Jazz Music / New Note/Pinnacle / Wellard

KRUPA & RICH (Krupa, Gene & Buddy Rich)
Buddy's blues/Bernie's tune / Gene's blues / Sweethearts on parade / I never knew / Sunday / Monster
CD 5216432
Verve / Mar '93 / PolyGram

LEAVE US LEAP (Krupa, Gene & His Orchestra)
CD VJC 1047
Vintage Jazz Classics / Jul '93 / ADA / Cadillac / CM / Direct

LEAVE US LEAP (Krupa, Gene & His Orchestra)
Starbust (Theme song) / Blue moon / Cry and you cry alone / I should care / Leave us leap (No.1) / Coca-Cola theme / Starburst (Theme song) / Leave us leap (No.2) / Don't take your love from me / Someday soon / Invention / Maybe baby / Moontide / Big do / Linger awhile / Leave us leap (No.3) / These foolish things / It's only a paper moon / Dark eyes / Laura / Lover / Drum boogie / Disc jockey jump
CD JZCL 6006
Jazz Classics / Nov '96 / Cadillac / Direct / Jazz Music

MASTERPIECES VOL.13 1936-1942
CD 158302
Masterpieces / Mar '95 / BMG

RADIO YEARS, THE
CD JUCD 2021
Jazz Unlimited / Jul '96 / Cadillac / Jazz Music / Wellard

WHAT'S THIS (1946-1947) (Krupa, Gene & His Orchestra)
(Back home again in) Indiana / My old flame / Up and atom / Wings on my shoes / Calling Dr. Gillespie / They didn't believe me / Stompin' at the Savoy / What's this / Begin the beguine / My ideal / Love's in my heart / Tea for two / Bolero at the Savoy / Leave us leap / Stardust / King Porter stomp / I'll never be the same / Wire brush stomp / Otto make that riff staccato / You go to my head / Lyonaisse potatoes and some pork chops / Lover
CD HEPCD 26
Hep / Aug '93 / Cadillac / Jazz Music / New Note/Pinnacle / Wellard

WIRE BRUSH STOMP 1938-1941 (Krupa, Gene & His Orchestra)
CD RACD 7117
Aerospace / May '96 / Jazz Music / Montpellier

Kruse, Kathe

LE SEXE ROUGE
CD EFA 153852
Todliche Doris / Jul '97 / SRD

Kruth, John

BANSHEE MANDOLIN
CD FF 602CD
Flying Fish / May '93 / ADA / CM / Direct / Roots

Kryptasthesie

INNER WHIRL
Flying saucers / Watching the sky / Tree / Intruder / Evening following cuttlefish / Secret power / Red shift / Chocolate Queen / Pictor HH / Then my left eye began again / Enigma / His golden guitar
CD DELECCD 038
Delerium / May '96 / Cargo / Pinnacle / Vital

K's Choice

PARADISE IN ME
Wait / Paradise in me / My record company / Only dreaming / Dad / Old woman / Something's wrong / Not an addict / Sound that only you can hear / White kite fauna / Mr. Freeze / Song for Catherine / To this day / Iron flower
CD 4813052
Epic / Mar '96 / Sony

Kubek, Smokin' Joe

CHAIN SMOKIN' TEXAS STYLE (Kubek, Smokin' Joe Band)
CD BBCD 9524
Bullseye Blues / Jan '93 / Direct

CRYIN' FOR THE MOON
CD CDBB 9560
Bullseye Blues / May '95 / Direct

GOT MY MIND BACK (Kubek, Smokin' Joe Band)
Got my mind back / Got you by the tail / Can't see for lookin' / All the love there is / She's it / Let me take your picture / I'm here for you / Don't touch her / Cryin' by myself / Double or nothing
CD CDBB 9578
Bullseye Blues / Sep '96 / Direct

TEXAS CADILLAC (Kubek, Smokin' Joe Band)
CD BB 9543CD
Bullseye Blues / Feb '94 / Direct

Kubis, Tom

TOM KUBIS PLAYS STEVE ALLEN (Kubis, Tom Big Band)
CD SB 2079
Sea Breeze / Jan '97 / Jazz Music

Kuepper, Ed

BLACK TICKET
CD HOT 1040CD
Hot / Jul '95 / Hot Records

BUTTERFLY NET, THE
Not a soul around / At times, so emotional / Nothing changes in my house / Sometimes / Everything's fine / Also sprach / Ghost of an ideal wife / New bully in the town / Sea air / Electrical storm / What you don't know / Black ticket day / Way I made you feel / Real wild life / Always the woman pays / It's lunacy / Honey steel's gold / Everything I've got
CD HOT 1045CD
Hot / Mar '95 / Hot Records

CHARACTER ASSASSINATION
By the way / Little fiddle (And the ghost of Xmas past) / Cockfighter / My best interests at heart / Take it by the hand / La di doh / I'm with you / Ill wind / So close to certainty / Good soundtrack / Ring of fire / If I had a ticket
CD Set HOT 1049CD
Hot / Aug '94 / Hot Records

ELECTRICAL STORM
CD HOT 1020CD
Hot / Jul '95 / Hot Records

EVERYBODY'S GOT TO
Everybody's got to / Too many clues / When there's this party / Standing in the cold, in the rain / Lonely paradise / Burned my fingers / Not a soul around / Nothing changes in my house / Spartan spirituals / No skin off your nose
CD HOT 1044CD
Hot / Jul '95 / Hot Records

FRONTIERLAND
All of these things / Fireman Joe / Weepin' willow / How would you plead / MDDP Limited / Pushin' fear / Roughneck blues / Someone told me / Poor Howard
CD HOT 1058CD
Hot / Oct '96 / Hot Records

HONEY STEEL'S GOLD
King of vice / Everything I've got belongs to you / Friday's blue cheer/Libertines of Oxley / Honey Steel's gold / Way I made you feel / Not too soon / Closer (but disguised) / Summer field
CD HOT 1036CD
Hot / Mar '95 / Hot Records

KING IN THE KINDNESS ROOM, THE
Confessions of a window cleaner / Pissed off / Highway to hell / Messin' part II / They call me Mr Sexy / Sundown / Space pirate / Diving board
CD HOT 1052CD
Hot / Jul '95 / Hot Records

ROOMS OF THE MAGNIFICENT
Rooms of the magnificent / Also sprach the king of Euro-Disco / Sea air / Sixteen days / Without your mirror / No point in working / I am your prince / Spend five years / Show pony / Nothing you can do
CD HOT 1027CD
Hot / Jul '95 / Hot Records

SERENE MACHINE
When she's done / Sleepy head (serene machine) / Who's been talkin' / It's happening before / I wish you were here / Maria peripatetica / Sounds like mysterious wind / Reasons / This hideous place / (You) don't know what to steal / You can't please everybody / Married to my lazy life
CD HOT 1042CD
Hot / Mar '95 / Hot Records

SINGS HIS GREATEST HITS FOR YOU
Way I made you feel / Pissed off / Real wild life / If I had a ticket / Sleepy head / This hideous place / La di doh / It's lunacy / Highway to hell / I'm with you / Black ticket day / Everything I've got belongs to you / Confessions in paradise / I wish you were here / Sad dark eyes
CD HOT 1057CD
Hot / Mar '96 / Hot Records

STARSTRUCK
Lion to your lamb / Hardhats and handbags / No.3 runaway / Rape of Cornelius / Love and happiness / Eightball / Spook / Anne 1 / Spook strain / Spring is sprung / Rachel owns the creek / Favourite angel / Wenceslas' daughter / Too many things / Angel's lament / Messin' with the tall / Diving board / Love me splendour / Christmas cake / Tom's theme / Green hat / Paul and Laurie have a party / Supermarket/Heaven / Everybody's got to you / Pleading ignorance / International playboys vs. the third reich
CD HOT 1064CD
Hot / Jul '97 / Hot Records

TODAY WONDER
Horse under water / Always the woman pays / Everything I've got belongs to you / What you don't know / I'd rather be the devil / There's nothing natural / Medley /

Pretty Mary / Eternally yours / If I were a carpenter
CD ________ HOT 1032CD
Hot / Mar '95 / Hot Records

Kuhn, Joachim

NIGHTLINE NEW YORK
Yvonne takes a bath / April in New York / Yvonne / Nightline / Rubber boots
CD ________ INAK 869CD
In Akustik / Jul '97 / Direct / TKO Magnum

Kuhn, Josie

PARADISE
CD ________ RTMCD 41
Round Tower / Nov '92 / Avid/BMG

WALKS WITH LIONS
CD ________ RTMCD 68
Round Tower / Oct '95 / Avid/BMG

Kuhn, Judy

JUST IN TIME
CD ________ VSD 5472
Varese Sarabande / Feb '95 / Pinnacle

Kuhn, Rolf

BROTHERS (Kuhn, Rolf & Joachim)
Loverman / Express / Saturday blues / Walk / Opal / What is left / Love / Brothers / Evert time we say goodbye
CD ________ VBR 21842
Vera Bra / Jun '96 / New Note/Pinnacle / Pinnacle

Kuhn, Steve

LIVE AT MAYBECK RECITAL HALL VOL.13
Old folks / Solar / I remember you / Autumn in New York / Meaning of the blues
CD ________ CCD 4484
Concord Jazz / Oct '91 / New Note/ Pinnacle

LOOKING BACK (Kuhn, Steve Trio)
Looking back / Duke / How insensitive / Stella by starlight / Alone together / Gee baby ain't I good to you / Baubles, bangles and beads / Zingaro / Will you still be mine / Emmanuel
CD ________ CCD 4446
Concord Jazz / Feb '91 / New Note/ Pinnacle

MOSTLY BALLADS
Yesterdays gardenias / Tennessee waltz / Danny boy / Don't explain / Body and soul / Emily / Airegin / How high the moon
CD ________ NW 351
New World / May '87 / ADA / Cadillac / Harmonia Mundi

REMEMBERING TOMORROW
Rain forest / Oceans in the sky / Lullaby / Trance / Life's backward glance / All the rest is the same / Emmanuel / Remembering tomorrow / Feeling within / Bittersweet passages / Silver
CD ________ 5290352
ECM / May '96 / New Note/Pinnacle

YEARS LATER
Gloria's theme / Upper Manhattan medical group / Years later / In a sentimental mood / Ladies in Mercedes / Good bait / Sometime ago / Silver's serenade / Born to be blue / Soul eyes
CD ________ CCD 4554
Concord Jazz / Jun '93 / New Note/ Pinnacle

Kukl

EYE
CD ________ 19842CD
Crass / Mar '97 / SRD

Kukuruza

CROSSING BORDERS
CD ________ SHCD 3814
Sugar Hill / Mar '94 / ADA / CM / Direct / Koch / Roots

Kula Shaker

K
Hey dude / Knight on the town / Temple of everlasting light / Govinda / Smart dogs / Magic theatre / Into the deep / Sleeping Jiva / Tattva / Grateful when you're dead / 303 / Start all over / Hollow man
CD ________ SHAKER 1CD
Columbia / Sep '96 / Sony

Kullman, Charles

20 UNFORGETTABLE CLASSICS
Only my song / Her name is Mary / Love here is my heart / Ah sweet mystery of life / Goodnight / For the love of you / Castles in the air / I love thee / Still as the night / Beautiful garden of roses / Serenade / Thora / World is mine tonight / On the road to Mandalay / I'm falling in love with someone / Thine alone / When you're away / Gypsy love song / Smilin' through / Ahoi so tont es weithin uber's meer
CD ________ CWNCD 2038
Crown / Jun '97 / Henry Hadaway

SERENADE
CD ________ CDMOIR 429
Memoir / Aug '95 / Jazz Music / Target/ BMG

Kumar, Pramod

INDIA RAGA ROUTE
CD ________ ARN 64277
Arion / Oct '94 / ADA / Discovery

Kumara

CONFLUENCE
White spring / Red spring / Influence / Confluence
CD ________ KU 9471
CDS / Feb '95 / Pinnacle

Kumo

KAMINARI
Together / Butterfly / Kraken awakes / Am I (That I am) / Kick your ass / Tigerstyle / Remover of obstacles / 7 buckets / (I hear) Daruma / Hubble eyes / Armed response
CD ________ PSYCD 1
Psychomat / Mar '97 / SRD

Kunda, Jali

GRIOTS OF WEST AFRICA AND BEYOND
CD ________ ELLICD 3510
Ellipsis Arts / May '97 / ADA / Direct

Kundalini Flavours

REVOLUTION OF UNDOING
CD ________ HIGH 2
High Strangeness / Nov '96 / Cargo

Kunene, Madala

KING OF THE ZULU GUITAR LIVE VOL.1, THE
Indiza / Nqo nqo nqu / Amnandi amasi / Khono thwele / Cabazini / Apartheid / Gumbela
CD ________ BNETCD 001
Bootleg.Net / Feb '97 / Vital/SAM

Kuni Kids

CONGO SQUARE
CD ________ MWCD 3003
Music & Words / Jun '93 / ADA / Direct

Kunz, Charlie

CHARLIE KUNZ - THE MEDLEY KING
CD ________ PASTCD 9783
Flapper / Jun '92 / Pinnacle

CHARLIE KUNZ AND THE VOCALISTS
When my dreamboat comes home / Gypsy who has never been in love / Rhythm on the range medley / Everything is rhythm medley / I'm in a dancing mood / Heart of gold / Every night at eight / It's love again medley / Goodnight my love / Here's love in your eye / It's my Mother's birthday today / All alone in Vienna / Sailing home with the tide / Have you forgotten so soon / Misty islands of the highlands / Sweet dreams sweetheart / Let's sit this one out / On a steamer coming over / Looking for a liitle bit of blue / There was an old woman / On tour with Charlie Kunz
CD ________ PASTCD 7089
Flapper / Mar '97 / Pinnacle

CLAP HANDS, HERE COMES CHARLIE KUNZ
Clap hands, here comes Charlie / Feller that played the pianner / Solo medley / Juggler / Solo medley (r15) / He was a handsome young soldier / Solo medley of Astaire/Rogers hits / Solo medley (s15) / Life begins when you're in love / Solo medley (r22) / St. James's Park / Solo medley (r1) / Star fell out of heaven / Medley: Piccadilly pickle / I was in the mood for love / Solo medley (r18) / Intro (March winds and April showers)
CD ________ PASTCD 9730
Flapper / Jan '91 / Pinnacle

FAMOUS PIANO MEDLEYS
In the blue of evening / Heavenly music / Put your arms around me honey / Close to you / Be honest with me / If you please / Roll on tomorrow / Sunday Monday or always / With all my heart / Coming in on a wing and a prayer / In my arms / Take it from there / I never mention your name / If I had my way / Ten little men with feathers / You happen once in a lifetime / Someday we shall meet again / Pedro the fisherman / I couldn't sleep a wink last night / All of my life / Amor amor / I'll get by / Don't ask me why / Don't sweetheart me / Silver wings in the moonlight / I'd like to set you to music / Johnny zero / You rhyme with everything that's beautiful / What's the good word, Mr. Bluebird / Side by side / There are such things / Darling / I want somebody / I say / When you know you're not forgotten / Soldier boy from Caroline / Mairzy doats Dozy doats / A journey to a star / You're the rainbow / I'm sending my blessings / Pocket full o'pennies / Someday soon / I'll walk alone / Swinging on a star / Shine on victory moon / Spring will be a little late this year / Echo of a serenade / San Fernando Valley / Moonlight becomes you / I met her on Monday / Mary's a grand old name / Constantly / At last / When the lights go on again / Dearly beloved / As time goes by / A touch of Texas / Daybreak / For me and my gal / Yankee doddle boy / Love is a song / Question and answer / I've got a gal in Kalamazoo / You are my sunshine / My devotion / That's the moon my son
CD ________ RAJCD 855
Empress / Jul '97 / Koch

THERE GOES THAT SONG AGAIN
CD ________ PASTCD 7037
Flapper / Apr '94 / Pinnacle

Kunzel, Erich

AMEN
CD ________ CD 80315
Telarc / Aug '93 / Conifer/BMG

BOND AND BEYOND
CD ________ CD 80251
Telarc / Apr '91 / Conifer/BMG

MANCINI'S GREATEST HITS (Kunzel, Erich & The Cincinnati Pops Orchestra)
CD ________ CD 80183
Telarc / Aug '90 / Conifer/BMG

POMP AND PIZAZZ (Kunzel, Erich & The Cincinnati Pops Orchestra)
CD ________ CD 80122
Telarc / '88 / Conifer/BMG

ROUND UP
Sounds of the west / Gioacchino Rossini / Magnificent seven / Furles suite / Round up / How the west was won / Gunfight at the OK Corral / Pops Hoedown / Big country / High noon / Western medley / Silverado
CD ________ CD 80141
Telarc / Apr '87 / Conifer/BMG

SAILING (Kunzel, Erich & The Cincinnati Pops Orchestra)
Sailing / Great Whales (theme) / Dove / Love came for me / Wave / Under the sea / New Hampshire hornpipe / Ebb tide / Sea shanties / Beyond the sea / Lonely looking sky / Be / Dear Father / Banana boat song (Day O) / Sleepy lagoon / (Sittin' on the) dock of the bay / Sleepy shores / Margaritaville / Calypso
CD ________ CD 80292
Telarc / Jul '92 / Conifer/BMG

STAR TRACKS VOL.2 (Kunzel, Erich & The Cincinnati Pops Orchestra)
CD ________ CD 80146
Telarc / '88 / Conifer/BMG

VERY BEST OF ERICH KUNZEL
Round up / Star Trek / Sing sing sing / Tara's theme (Gone with the wind) / Unchained melody / Nessun dorma / Little fugue in G minor / Star Wars / Batman / Grand Canyon suite / From Russia with love / Olympic fanfare / Opening sequence from Chiller / Overture to the Phantom Of The Opera / Godfather / Pink Panther / O mio babbino caro / Non-stop fast polka / Op 112 / Honor, honor, do lord / Cybergenesis / Terminator / Jurassic lunch
CD ________ CD 80401
Telarc / Sep '94 / Conifer/BMG

YOUNG AT HEART (Kunzel, Erich & The Cincinnati Pops Orchestra)
CD ________ 80245
Telarc / Oct '92 / Conifer/BMG

Kuolema

NOISE NOT MUSIC
CD ________ AA 031
AA / Jul '97 / Cargo / Greyhound

Kupper, Leo

ELECTRO ACOUSTIC
CD ________ POGUS 210092
Pogus / Jun '97 / ReR Megacorp

Kurnia, Detty

COYOR PANON
CD ________ FLTRCD 519
Flame Tree / Sep '93 / Pinnacle

DARI SUNDA
Sorban palid / Dar der dor / Emansipasi / Bandondari / Si kabayan / Bengawan solo / Asih kuring / Duriran / Mamanis / Sunayama / Hana
CD ________ TUGCD 1011
Riverboat / Oct '95 / New Note/Pinnacle / Stern's

Kursaal Flyers

CHOCS AWAY/ THE GREAT ARTISTE
CD ________ FOAMCD 3
On The Beach / Jan '94 / Direct / Pinnacle

FORMER TOUR DE FORCE IS FORCED TO TOUR
CD ________ WF 044CD
Waterfront / Aug '88 / ADA / CM / Jazz Music

Kurva, Szeki

MUSIC FOR JOYRIDERS
CD ________ ILIGHT 002CD
Iris Light / May '97 / Kudos

Kuryahkin, Illyah

COUNT NO COUNT
CD ________ AR 006
Arena Rock / Mar '97 / Cargo

Kustbandet

IN SWEDEN
CD ________ CK 83401
Kenneth / Jun '94 / Cadillac / Jazz Music / Wellard

OSREGN (Kustbandet In Sweden)
F and B flat 7 / Heavenly music / Stackars VI / Snofall / Hon ar en skon juvel / En liten sang om dig / Honeymooning / Osregn / Rhythm in blue / Sla dig los och ta semester / Tillie / Archipelago / Drommen / Karlek ar karlek / Regntunga skyar
CD ________ CKS 3401
Kenneth / Jun '94 / Cadillac / Jazz Music / Wellard

Kustomized

AT THE VANISHING POINT
Handcuffs / Fingertips / Permission / Bored to death / One that got away / Hound / Amy Arrow / Camp climax / Yacky doo / You make me feel weird / Film
CD ________ OLE 1872
Matador / Mar '96 / Vital

BATTLE FOR SPACE, THE
Day I had some fun / Throw your voice / Puff piece / Fifth / Gorgeous / 33 1/3 / Place where people meet / Phantasmagoria, now / La guene / Air freshner
CD ________ OLE 1132
Matador / Feb '95 / Vital

Kusworth, Dave

ALL THE HEARTBREAK STORIES
CD ________ CRECD 108
Creation / Jun '94 / 3mv/Vital

Kut Klose

SURRENDER
Lay my body down / Don't change / Get up on it / Do me / Lovely thang / Surrender / I like / Keep on / Giving you my love again / Sexual baby / Like you've never been done
CD ________ 7559616682
Warner Bros. / Mar '95 / Warner Music

Kutbay, Aka Gunduz

PLAYS THE TURKISH NEY
CD ________ PS 65078
PlayaSound / Aug / ADA / Harmonia Mundi

Kuti, Fela

2000 BLACKS (Kuti, Fela & Roy Ayers)
CD ________ 760230
Justin / Nov '90 / Triple Earth

AFRO BEAT
CD ________ MPG 74024
Movieplay Gold / Jan '94 / Target/BMG

BUY AMERICA (Kuti, Fela Anikulapo)
Jayen Jayen / Egbe mio / Who are you / Buy America / Fight to the finish
CD ________ MPG 74036
Movieplay Gold / Jan '97 / Target/BMG

FELA'S LONDON SCENE
CD ________ STCD 3007
Stern's / Oct '94 / ADA / CM / Stern's

MR. FOLLOW FOLLOW (Kuti, Fela Anikulapo)
CD ________ TRCD 40022
Terrascape / Jan '97 / Stern's

MUSIC IS THE WEAPON 75-78
CD ________ 760443
Justin / Nov '90 / Triple Earth

MUSIC IS THE WEAPON 81-84
CD ________ 760444
Justin / Nov '90 / Triple Earth

MUSIC IS THE WEAPON 85-86
CD ________ 760445
Justin / Nov '90 / Triple Earth

MUSIC OF MANY COLOURS (Kuti, Fela & Roy Ayers)
2,000 blacks got to be free / Africa, centre of the world
CD ________ MPG 74042
Movieplay Gold / Jun '97 / Target/BMG

NO AGREEMENT (Kuti, Fela Anikulapo)
CD ________ TRCD 40032
Terrascape / Jan '97 / Stern's

UNDERGROUND SYSTEM
CD ________ STCD 1043
Stern's / Nov '92 / ADA / CM / Stern's

Kuti, Fela Ransome

LIVE (Kuti, Fela Ransome & Ginger Baker)
CD ________ TRCD 40012
Terrascape / Jan '97 / Stern's

Kuti, Femi

KUTI AND THE POSITIVE FORCE (Kuti, Femi Anikulapo)
CD ____ **340002**
Melodie / Mar '96 / ADA / Discovery / Grapevine/PolyGram / Greensleeves / Jet Star

Kwak

A DE VLOPE
CD ____ **082100**
Wotre Music / Sep '96 / Discovery / New Note/Pinnacle

A LA KWAKANS
CD ____ **082041**
Wotre Music / Sep '96 / Discovery / New Note/Pinnacle

LE GA' MECI
CD ____ **082079**
Wotre Music / Sep '96 / Discovery / New Note/Pinnacle

Kwan, Leonard

KE ALA'S MELE
CD ____ **DCT 38004CD**
Dancing Cat / Mar '96 / ADA

Kwest Tha Madd Ladd

THIS IS MY FIRST ALBUM
Everyone always said I should start my album off with a bang / 101 things to do while I'm with your girl / Disnexone / I met my baby at VIM / Base blah (off tha head) / Lubrication / What's the reaction / Daddiez home / Kwest's theme song / Skin care / Day in the life of my asspipe / Butta-few-co / Disk and dat / 125 pennies for your thoughts / Herman's head / Bludawnmeyesneekhuz / Damn / Say my name again
CD ____ **74321242292**
American / Apr '96 / BMG

KWS

ALBUM
CD ____ **KWSCD 1**
Network / Dec '92 / 3mv/Sony / Pinnacle

Kwyet Kings

CHERRY PIE
CD ____ **SCACD 109**
Screaming Apple / Jun '97 / Cargo / Greyhound

Kyao, Rao

FLAUTAS DA TERRA
CD ____ **68952**
Tropical / Apr '97 / Discovery

Kydd, Christine

HEADING HOME
CD ____ **FE 093CD**
Fellside / Oct '93 / ADA / Direct / Target/BMG

Kyle, Billy

BILLY KYLE 1937-1938
CD ____ **CLASSICS 919**
Classics / Mar '97 / Discovery / Jazz Music

CLASSICS 1939-1946
CD ____ **CLASSICS 941**
Classics / Jun '97 / Discovery / Jazz Music

Kyle, Jamie

BACK FROM HOLLYWOOD
CD ____ **NTHEN 028CD**
Now & Then / Nov '96 / Plastic Head

Kynard, Charles

REELIN' WITH THE FEELIN'/WA-TU-WA-ZUI
Reelin' with the feelin' / Soul reggae / Slow burn / Boogaloogin' / Be my love / Stomp / Wa-tu-wa-zui / Winter's child / Zebra walk / Something / Change up
CD ____ **CDBGPD 055**
Beat Goes Public / Aug '93 / Pinnacle

Kyoma

RIGHT HERE WAITING
CD ____ **CCD 7**
Music / Apr '95 / Jet Star

Kyoto Nohgaku Kai

JAPANESE NOH MUSIC
CD ____ **LYRCD 7137**
Lyrichord / Feb '94 / ADA / CM / Roots

Kyoto Temple Monks

BUDDHIST BELLS, DRUMS & CHANTS
CD ____ **LYRCD 7200**
Lyrichord / Dec '94 / ADA / CM / Roots

Kyser, Kay

KOLLEGE OF MUSICAL KNOWLEDGE
CD ____ **JH 1047**
Jazz Hour / Jul '96 / Cadillac / Jazz Music / Target/BMG

MUSIC MAESTRO PLEASE
Stairway to the stars / You don't know how much you can suffer / So you left me for the leader of a swing band / Havin' myself a time / On the Isle Of May / Indian summer / Lost and found / Two shadows / What have you got that gets me / You're lovely Madame / Music maestro please / I'm sorry for myself / Little red fox / Let this be a warning to you baby / Deep Purple / I get along without you very well / (I gotta get some) shuteye / Sixty seconds got together / Two sleepy people / Stand by for further announcements / Man and his dreams / Johnny Peddler
CD ____ **RAJCD 874**
Empress / Apr '97 / Koch

SONGS OF WORLD WAR II VOL.2 (Kyser, Kay Orchestra)
CD ____ **VJC 1042**
Vintage Jazz Classics / Feb '93 / ADA / Cadillac / CM / Direct

Kyuss

AND THE CIRCUS LEAVES TOWN
El rodeo / One inch man / Gloria Lewis / Jumbo blimp jumbo / Phototropic / Spaceship landing / Catamaran / Size queen / Tangy zizzle / Thee ol' boozeroony / Hurricane
CD ____ **7559618112**
Warner Bros. / Jun '95 / Warner Music

BLUES FOR THE RED SUN
Thumb / Green machine / Molten universe / Fifty Million year trip (Downside up) / Thong song / Apothecarie's weight / Caterpillar march / Freedom run / 800 / Writhe / Capsized
CD ____ **3705613402**
Warner Bros. / Feb '93 / Warner Music

WELCOME TO SKY VALLEY
Gardenia / Asteroid / Supa scoopa and mighty scoop / 100 Degrees / Space cadet / Demon cleaner / Odyssey / Conan troutman / NO / Whitewater
CD ____ **7559615712**
Warner Bros. / Jun '94 / Warner Music

L

L-Kage

BRAZILLIANT
CD _______________ TPLP 26 CD
One Little Indian / Jun '93 / Pinnacle

L-Big Band

ELLINGTON SACRED CONCERT
CD _______________ LBBCD 7
LBB / Jan '97 / Cadillac / Jazz Music

LIVE WITH BLUE BIRD
CD _______________ LBBCD 6
LBB / Oct '94 / Cadillac / Jazz Music

L7

BEAUTY PROCESS
Beauty process / Drama / Off the wagon / I need / Moonshine / Bitter wine / Masses are asses / Bad things / Must have more / Non existent Patricia / Me, myself and I / Lorenza, Giada, Alessandra / Guera
CD _______________ 8288682
Slash / Feb '97 / PolyGram

HUNGRY FOR STINK
Andres / Baggage / Can I run / Bomb / Questioning my sanity / Riding with a movie star / Stuck here again / Fuel my fire / Freak magnet / She has eyes / Shirley / Talk box
CD _______________ 8285312
Slash / Jul '94 / PolyGram

SMELL THE MAGIC
CD _______________ SPCD 79
Sub Pop / Oct '95 / Cargo / Greyhound / Shellshock/Disc

LA 1919

TO PLAY (Jour Speilen)
Drumming ralk / Red wire / Un mondo invisibile / Donne kamikaze / Qua qua qua singing ducks / Storie del dormiveglia / Fate fagotto / Sheffield Wednesday / Hanna seppellito l'uomo sbagliato
CD _______________ MASOCD 90063
Materiali Sonori / May '95 / Cargo / Greyhound / New Note/Pinnacle

La Argentinita

DUENDE Y FIGURA
CD _______________ 20062CD
Sonifolk / Nov '95 / ADA / CM

EL AMOR BRUJO
CD _______________ 20090CD
Sonifolk / Nov '96 / ADA / CM

La Bamboche

LA SAISON DES AMOURS
CD _______________ 14926
Spalax / Sep '96 / ADA / Cargo / Direct / Discovery / Greyhound

La Barriada

LA BARRIADA
CD _______________ 74321402452
Milan / Nov '96 / Conifer/BMG / Silva Screen

La Belle Epoque

MEXICAN LANDSCAPES VOL.6
CD _______________ PS 65906
PlayaSound / Feb '93 / ADA / Harmonia Mundi

LA Blues Authority

CREAM OF THE CROP
CD _______________ RR 89662
Roadrunner / Sep '96 / PolyGram

FIT FOR A KING
CD _______________ RR 90492
Roadrunner / Sep '96 / PolyGram

HATS OFF TO STEVIE RAY
CD _______________ RR 90502
Roadrunner / Sep '96 / PolyGram

LA BLUES AUTHORITY
CD _______________ RR 91862
Roadrunner / Sep '96 / PolyGram

La Bolduc

SONGS OF QUEBEC 1929-39
CD _______________ Y225108CD
Silex / Oct '94 / ADA / Harmonia Mundi

La Bottine Souriante

EN SPECTACLE
CD _______________ MPCD 3039
Mille Pattes / May '97 / ADA

JUSQU AUX P'TITES HEURES
CD _______________ MPCD 2037
Mille Pattes / Mar '96 / ADA

LA MISTRINE
CD _______________ MPCD 2038
Mille Pattes / Mar '96 / ADA

TOUT COMME AU JOUR DE L'AN
CD _______________ MMPCD 2035
Mille Pattes / Mar '96 / ADA

Y'A BEN DU CHANGEMENT
CD _______________ MMPCD 265
Mille Pattes / Mar '96 / ADA

La Bouche

SWEET DREAMS
Forget me nots / Sweet dreams / Be my lover / Fallin in love / I'll be there / Nice 'n' slow / Where do you go / I love to love / Do you still need me / Poetry in motion / Shoo be do bee do (I like that way) / Heat is on / Mama look (I love him)
CD _______________ 74321288882
Arista / Mar '96 / BMG

La Charanga Habanera

ME SUBE LA FIEBRE (Love Fever)
CD _______________ 74321362872
Milan / Jun '96 / Conifer/BMG / Silva Screen

La Ciapa Rusa

TEN DA CHEN L'ARCHET CHE LA SUNADA L'E LONGA
CD _______________ MWCD 4014
Music & Words / May '97 / ADA / Direct

La Costa Rasa

AUTOPILOT
CD _______________ 11316832
Merciful Release / Jul '94 / Warner Music

La Cucina

BLOOM
Through the eyes / Secrets / Devil / Who's in control / Desperado Dan / Half way to the moon / Malavita part 1 / Malavita part 2 / I nostri / Seven days / Fly away / Motivation / Picture
CD _______________ OSMOCD 012
Osmosys / Jul '97 / Direct

CHUCHERIA
Patagonia / Zio Pepe / Rain / Majnoon / Sucalo / Witless / Armageddon train / lato muerta / Carmen / Tour / Mare chiare / Windy windy dance night
CD _______________ LAC 123CD
La Cucina / Mar '94 / CM / Direct
CD _______________ OSMOCD 002
Osmosys / Oct '95 / Direct

NABUMLA
Embers / Buddhas (are we) / Light shine through / Heart again / Runner / Guy Debord is sleeping / L'Americana / Villa laterno / Struggle / Question / Naked in the sunshine
CD _______________ OSMOCD 007
Osmosys / Mar '96 / Direct

La Donnas

LADONNALAND
CD _______________ IFACD 015
IFA / Nov '95 / Plastic Head

SHADY LANE
No way to treat a lady / Junkman / O'Donna / Invasion / Dirty bird / Feel the pain / Death of Beewak / Long legs / Bring it on by / Counter unload / She pays the rent / Wake me / Scene's gonna get you tonight
CD _______________ PO 14CD
Scooch Pooch / Oct '96 / Cargo / Greyhound / Pinnacle
CD _______________ 206142
Scooch Pooch / Jul '97 / Cargo / Greyhound / Pinnacle

La Dusseldorf

FIRST ALBUM
CD _______________ CTCD 064
Captain Trip / Jul '97 / Greyhound

VIVA
Viva / White overalls / Rheinita / Vogel / Geld / Cha cha 2000
CD _______________ CTCD 065
Captain Trip / Jul '97 / Greyhound

La Famille Dembele

AIRA YO (La Danse Des Jeunes Griots)
CD _______________ ARNR 1596
Amiata / Aug '97 / Harmonia Mundi

La Faro, Scott

ALCHEMY OF SCOTT LA FARO, THE (Various Artists)
Too close for comfort / I've never been in love before / Time remembered / Jade visions / Variants on a theme of Thelonious Monk (criss cross) / C & D / First take / Alchemy of Scott La Faro
CD _______________ CD 53213
Giants Of Jazz / Jan '96 / Cadillac / Jazz Music / Target/BMG

La Flamme, David

WHITE BIRD/INSIDE OUT
White bird / Hot summer day / Swept away / Easy woman / This man / Baby be wise / Spirit of America / Who's gonna love me / My life / Night song / Forever and a day / Somewhere down the road / Where flamingos fly / Day you went away / Need somebody / Can't wait until tomorrow
CD _______________ EDCD 419
Edsel / Aug '95 / Pinnacle

La Floa Maldita

DEDICATION SEPERATION
CD _______________ EEFA 127522
Kodex / Nov '95 / SRD

L'OASIS
CD _______________ SPV 7625892
SPV / Oct '96 / Koch / Plastic Head

LA Four

EXECUTIVE SUITE
Blues wellington / Amazonia / You and I / Simple invention / Entr'Acte / My funny valentine / Chega de Saudade
CD _______________ CCD 4215
Concord Jazz / Nov '95 / New Note/Pinnacle

LA FOUR
Dindi / Rainbows / Rondo es pressivo / Manteca / St. Thomas / Concierto de Aranjuez
CD _______________ CCD 4018
Concord Jazz / Sep '86 / New Note/Pinnacle

LA FOUR SCORES
CD _______________ CCD 6008
Concord Jazz / Jul '88 / New Note/Pinnacle

LIVE AT MONTREUX
CD _______________ CCD 4100
Concord Jazz / Jul '96 / New Note/Pinnacle

MONTAGE
Madame butterball / Syrinx / Samba for Ray / Teach me tonight / Rado's got the blues / My romance / Bachianas brasilerias No.5 / Squatty roo
CD _______________ CCD 4156
Concord Jazz / Jan '95 / New Note/Pinnacle

ZACA
Zaca / You can't go home again / Child is born / O barquinho / Close ecounter for love / Pavanne op50 / Secret love
CD _______________ CCD 4130
Concord Jazz / Feb '94 / New Note/Pinnacle

La Gloria Matancera

EL LIMONCITO 1948-1952
CD _______________ TCD 071
Tumbao Cuban Classics / Jul '96 / Discovery

VENGO ARROLLANDO 1937-1949
CD _______________ TCD 066
Tumbao Cuban Classics / Jul '96 / Discovery

La Grand Rouge

TRAVERSER DU PAYS
CD _______________ 199732
Hexagone / Oct '93 / ADA / Discovery / Roots

La Grande Bande Des ...

FAUT QU' CA BRILLE (La Grande Bande Des Cornemuses)
CD _______________ B 6743CD
Auvidis/Ethnic / Jul '94 / ADA / Harmonia Mundi

LA Guns

AMERICAN HARDCORE
FNA / What I've become / Unnatural act / Give / Don't pray / Pissed / Mine / Kevorkian / Hey world / Next generation / Hugs and needles / I am alive
CD _______________ 06076862052
CMC / Apr '97 / BMG

La Lugh

BRIGHID'S KISS
CD _______________ LUGH 961CD
Lughnasa / Mar '96 / ADA / Direct

La Marienne

UN BAL EN VENDEE
CD _______________ MRV 797CD
MRV / Nov '95 / ADA

La Mirlitanouille

1975-1980
CD _______________ IG 7779CD
Diffusion Breizh / Aug '95 / ADA

La Misma Gente

EL LOCO
CD _______________ TUMICD 030
Tumi / '92 / Discovery / Stern's

LA Mix

ON THE SIDE
Get loose / You are the one / Breathe deep / Don't turn away / Love together / Just waiting / Mellow mellow / Don't stop / Check this out
CD _______________ CDA 9009
A&M / Sep '89 / PolyGram

La Moposina, Toto

CARMELINA
Chi chi mani / La ceiba / Ven pronto / Los sabores del porro / Indios farotos / La sombra negra / Carmelina / Las cuatro palomas / Mohana / Milo son / Agua / Hacha machete y garabato (La tres punta)
CD _______________ LBLC 2516
Indigo / Apr '97 / New Note/Pinnacle

LA CANDELA VIVA
Dos de febrero / Adios fulana / El pescador / La sombra negra / Dame la mano juancho / Malanga / Mapale / Curura / Chi chi mani / La candela viva / La acabacion
CD _______________ CDRW 31
Realworld / Jun '93 / EMI

La Moresca

SARACENIA
CD _______________ RD 5033CD
Robi Droli / Aug '96 / ADA / Direct

La Morte De La Maison

ARROND RED
CD _______________ SPV 08419592
SPV / May '95 / Koch / Plastic Head

La Muerte

RAW
Speed, steel and gasoline / Serial killer / Black God, white devil / Hate love / Power / Wild fucker / Cravacher / Burst my soul / I would die faster / Lucifer Sam / KKK / Couteau dans l'eau / Blood on the moon / Ecoute cette priere / Mannish boy / Shoot in your back / Kung fu fighting / Wild thing
CD _______________ BIAS 266CD
Play It Again Sam / May '94 / Discovery / Plastic Head / Vital

La Musgana

EL DIABLO COJUELO
CD _______________ H 028CD
Sonifolk / Jun '94 / ADA / CM

LAS SEIS TENTACIONES
CD _______________ XENO 4030
Xenophile / Apr '95 / ADA / Direct

LUBICAN
CD _______________ GL 4010CD
Green Linnet / Jan '94 / ADA / CM / Direct / Highlander / Roots

La Negra Graciana

SON JAROCHO
CD _______________ COCD 109
Corason / Oct '94 / ADA / CM / Direct

La Negra, Tona

ORACION CARIBE
CD _______________ ALCD 023
Alma Latina / Jul '96 / Discovery

La Nina De Los Peines

ART OF FLAMENCO VOL.7, THE
CD _______________ MAN 4856
Mandala / Oct '95 / ADA / Harmonia Mundi / Mandala

La Noche Celta

RAMON PRADA
CD _______________ **FA 8754CD**
Fono Astur / Nov '96 / ADA

La Orquesta Del Tango De ...

LA ORQUESTA DEL TANGO DE BUENOS AIRES (La Orquesta Del Tango De Buenos Aires)
CD _______________ **74321453312**
Milan Sur / Feb '97 / Conifer/BMG

La Palma

SUCCES ET RARETES 1930-1936
CD _______________ **701572**
Chansophone / Sep '96 / Discovery

La Piva Del Carner

LA PEGRA A LA MATEINE
CD _______________ **NT 6735CD**
Robi Droli / Apr '95 / ADA / Direct

La Secta

FUZZ GOD
CD _______________ **MRCD 119**
Munster / Jun '97 / Cargo / Greyhound / Plastic Head

La Sonora Majestad

LA NEGRA TOMASA
CD _______________ **TUMICD 026**
Tumi / '91 / Discovery / Stern's

La Sonora Matancera

EN GRANDE
CD _______________ **TUMICD 022**
Tumi / '91 / Discovery / Stern's

FROM CUBA TO NEW YORK
CD _______________ **CDHOT 603**
Charly / Jun '96 / Koch

LIVE ON THE RADIO 1952-1958
CD _______________ **HQCD 79**
Harlequin / Sep '96 / Hot Shot / Jazz Music / Swift / Wellard

La Sonora Poncena

OPENING DOORS
Bamboleo / La rumba es mia / Dejala que siga / Conga yumbambe / A la patria mia / Son matamoroscelia / La mora / Ese animal / Ese mar es mio / No me cambie camino / Cobarde / Quitate la mascara
CD _______________ **CDHOT 514**
Charly / Sep '94 / Koch

La Souris Deglinguee

LA SOURIS DEGLINGUEE
CD _______________ **ROSE 6CD**
New Rose / '88 / ADA / Direct / Discovery

LA Star

POETESS
Wonderous dream / NPT posse / Do you still love me / Swing to the beat / It's like that / Fade to black / My tale / It takes a real woman / Once upon a time / If you don't wanna party / NPT posse (UK remix)
CD _______________ **FILECD 290**
Profile / Jul '90 / Pinnacle

LA Synthesis

MATRIX SURFER
CD _______________ **PIAS 533010120**
Shield / Apr '97 / Plastic Head

La Touche

CAJUN DANCE PARTY
CD _______________ **PLATCD 3938**
Platinum / Mar '95 / Prism

La Veillee Est Jeune

JE SUIS MAL MARIE
CD _______________ **LVJ 002CD**
LVJ / Apr '96 / ADA

La Verne, Elisha

HER NAME IS
CD _______________ **ADPTCD 4**
Adept / Mar '97 / 3mv/Pinnacle

La Vienta

JAZZMENCO
CD _______________ **CD 83353**
Telarc / Aug '93 / Conifer/BMG

NIGHT DANCE
Journey / Love for Isabel / Ariana / Tranquilo / El gato negro / Ojo caliente carnival / Beto's turn / Goodbye tomorrow / En la cueva / Promise of St Matthew / Samba loco
CD _______________ **CD 83359**
Telarc / Jun '94 / Conifer/BMG

Lab Report

FIGURE X-71
CD _______________ **CDDVN 27**
Devotion / Dec '93 / Pinnacle

UNHEALTHY
CD _______________ **CDDVN 31**
Devotion / Jun '94 / Pinnacle

Labanda

NO TODO ES SEDA
CD _______________ **21065CD**
Sonifolk / Nov '95 / ADA / CM

LaBarbera, Joe

JMOG
Game's afoot / Elvin's share / Dark ocean / Sierra Nevada / Elk the moochie / Another rainy day / Night/Morning
CD _______________ **SKCD 22031**
Sackville / Jun '93 / Cadillac / Jazz Music / Swift

LaBeef, Sleepy

I'LL NEVER LAY MY GUITAR DOWN
CD _______________ **ROUCD 3142**
Rounder / Jun '96 / ADA / CM / Direct

LARGER THAN LIFE (6CD Set)
Baby let's play house / Don't make me go / All alone / I'm through / Lonely / All the time / All the time / Lonely / I ain't gonna take it / Little bit more / Ballad of a teenage Queen / You're so easy to love / I wish I was the moon / Ways of a woman / Home of the blues / You're the nearest thing to heaven / Guess things happen that way / Can't get you off my mind / I found out / Turn me loose / Ridin' fence / Ride on Josephine / Lonely / Just a closer walk with thee / I won't have to cross Jordan alone / Drink up and go home / Teardrop on a rose / Long time to forget / Goodnight Irene / Leave me alone with the blues / Oh so many years / Somebody's been beatin' my time / Bring around Rosie / Completely destroyed / Another mile to go / This new love / You can't catch me / Everybody's got to have somebody to love / Shame, shame, shame / Ain't got no home / I feel a lot more like I do now / I'm too broke to pay attention / Drinking again / Man in my position / Go ahead on / Schneider / Sure beats the heck outta' settlin' down / Too young to die / Two hundred pounds of hurt / If I go right, I'm wrong / Everyday / Man alone / Too much monkey business / Sixteen tons / Got you on my mind / Birds of all nations / Back of his hand / Asphalt cowboy / Blackland farmer / She's bringin' me down / Buying a book / Me & Bobby McGee / Boom, boom, boom / It ain't sanitary / Honey hush / Hundred pounds of lovin' / Ballad of Thunder Road / I'm ragged but I'm right / Tender years / Other side of you / Stormy Monday blues / Cool water / Mule train / Streets of Laredo / Ghost riders in the sky / Bury me not on the lone prairie / Tumbling tumbleweeds / Strawberry roan / High noon / Wagon wheels / Home on the range / There ain't much after taxes / Good rockin' boogie / Roll over Beethoven / Party doll / I'm gonna be a wheel someday / You can't have her / Mathilda / Faded love / From a Jack to a King / Send me some lovin' / You can't judge a book by it's cover / Young fashioned ways / Sittin' on top of the world / Matchbox / Corrine, Corrina / Let's turn back the years / What am I living for / Reconsider baby / Raining in my heart / Put your arms around me / Elvira / Polk salad Annie / I'm the man / Queen of the silver dollar / Long tall Texan / Stay all night, stay a little longer / Tall oak tree / Take me back to Tulsa / Blue moon of Kentucky / I'll keep on loving you / I won't have to cross Jordan alone / Just a closer walk with thee / Satisfied / Ezekiel's boneyard / I saw the light / I'll never let the Devil win / This train / I'll be somewhere listening / I feel like travelling on / Old country church / Standing in the shadows / Walk and talk with my Lord / Rock'n'roll Ruby / Big Boss man / I'm ready if you're willing / I'm coming home / I'm a one woman man / Shotgun boogie / Boogie woogie country girl / Mystery train / There is something on your mind / Jack & Jill boogie / Blues stay away from me / Honky tonk hardwood floor / Tore up / Flying saucers rock'n'roll / Red hot / Honky tonk man / My sweet love ain't around / If you don't love me someone else will / Milk cow blues / Ride, ride, ride / Are you teasing me / LaBoef's cajun boogie / Go ahead on baby / Sick & tired / Mind your own business / Lonesome for a letter / Detour / Cigarettes & coffee blues / Cut across Shorty / I'm feelin' sorry
CD Set _______________ **BCD 15662**
Bear Family / Nov '96 / Direct / Rollercoaster / Swift

NOTHIN' BUT THE TRUTH
Tore up over you / How do you talk to a baby / Milk cow blues / Just pickin' / Gunslinger / Ring of fire / Boogie at the Wayside Lounge / Worried man blues / Let's talk about us / My toot toot / Jambalaya / Whole lot of shakin'
CD _______________ **ROUCD 3072**
Rounder / Jul '91 / ADA / CM / Direct

ROCKIN' DECADE, A
CD _______________ **CPCD 8303**
Charly / May '97 / Koch

STRANGE THINGS HAPPENING
CD _______________ **ROUCD 3129**
Rounder / Apr '94 / ADA / CM / Direct

Labelle, Patti

EARLY YEARS, THE (Labelle, Patti & The Bluebells)
Sold my heart to the junkman / One phone call / Have I sinned / Academy award / Go on (This is goodbye) / Island of unbroken hearts / Impossible / Decatur street / Where are you / Down the aisle / Tear after tear / What kind of heart / Danny boy / Please hurry home / I believe / I walked right in / Itty bitty twist / When Johnny comes marching home / You'll never walk alone / Joke's on you / You will fill my eyes no more / Love me just a little / Cool water / My bridal gown / I sold my heart to the junkman
CD _______________ **CDCHD 441**
Ace / Feb '93 / Pinnacle

I SOLD MY HEART TO THE JUNKMAN
CD _______________ **HADCD 179**
Javelin / Nov '95 / Henry Hadaway / THE

LADY MARMALADE (The Best Of Patti Labelle)
Lady Marmalade / What can I do for you / Are you lonely / You turn me on / Messin with my mind / Take the night off / Get you someone new / Isn't it a shame / Joy to have your love / I think about you / You are my friend / Teach me tonight (me gusta tu baile) / Quiet time / It's all right with me / Don't make your angel cry / Come what may
CD _______________ **4805102**
Epic / May '95 / Sony

OVER THE RAINBOW (The Atlantic Sessions)
CD _______________ **SCL 2501**
Ichiban Soul Classics / Apr '95 / Koch

YOU ARE MY FRIEND (The Ballads)
Love and learn / Come what may / Find the love / Don't make your angel cry / Isn't it a shame / You are my friend / Little girls / Do I stand a chance / Last dance / I don't go shopping / Love has finally come
CD _______________ **4871192**
Epic / May '97 / Sony

Labeque, Katia

LITTLE GIRL BLUE
We will meet again / My funny valentine / On fire / Besame mucho / Prologo / Little girl blue / Quizas quizas quizas / Volcano for hire / Turn out the stars / Summertime / La comparsa
CD _______________ **FDM 361862**
Dreyfus / Oct '95 / ADA / Direct / New Note/ Pinnacle

Laberinto

PRIORITY
CD _______________ **M 7023CD**
Mascot / Oct '96 / Plastic Head

Labradford

LA BRADFORD
CD _______________ **BFFP 136CD**
Blast First / Nov '96 / RTM/Disc

PRAZISION
CD _______________ **FNCD 342**
Flying Nun / Feb '96 / RTM/Disc

Lacen, Anthony

ANTHONY 'TUBA FATS' LACEN/RUE CONTI JAZZBAND/D.KELLIN
CD _______________ **BCD 344**
GHB / Jun '95 / Jazz Music

Lachlan Young, Murray

VICE AND VERSE
Casual sex / MTV/Supermodel / One nation under a goatee / I'm being followed by the Rolling Stones / Closet heterosexual / Simply everyone's taking cocaine / WAH Wiggins - the boy who struck the record deal / Pro's and cons of superstardom / Just another night at the seaside / Life and death of art
CD _______________ **CDEMC 3767**
EMI / Aug '97 / EMI

Lacrimosa

INFERNO
CD _______________ **DW 088CD**
Deathwish / Jun '95 / Plastic Head

STILLE
CD _______________ **HOS 781CD**
Hall Of Sermon / Jun '97 / Plastic Head

Lacy, Steve

AXIEME
CD _______________ **1231202**
Red / Apr '93 / ADA / Cadillac / Harmonia Mundi

BLINKS (2CD Set)
CD Set _______________ **ARTCD 6189**
Hat Art / Jul '97 / Cadillac / Harmonia Mundi

CHIRPS (Lacy, Steve & Evan Parker)
CD _______________ **FMPCD 29**
FMP / Mar '87 / Cadillac

CLANGS (Lacy, Steve Double Sextet)
CD _______________ **ARTCD 6116**
Hat Art / Jan '94 / Cadillac / Harmonia Mundi

COMMUNIQUE (Lacy, Steve & Mal Waldron)
CD _______________ **1212982**
Soul Note / Aug '97 / Cadillac / Harmonia Mundi / Wellard

FIVE FACINGS
CD _______________ **FMPCD 85**
FMP / May '97 / Cadillac

FLAME, THE
CD _______________ **1210352**
Soul Note / Nov '90 / Cadillac / Harmonia Mundi / Wellard

FLIM-FLAM (Lacy, Steve & Steve Potts)
CD _______________ **ARTCD 6087**
Hat Art / Nov '91 / Cadillac / Harmonia Mundi

FOREST AND THE ZOO, THE
CD _______________ **ESP 10602**
ESP / Jan '93 / Jazz Music

IMAGE (DUO PERFORMANCES) (Lacy, Steve & Steve Arguelles)
CD _______________ **AHUM 001**
Ah-Um / Apr '89 / Cadillac / New Note/ Pinnacle

LET'S CALL THIS...ESTEEM (Lacy, Steve & Mal Waldron)
Let's call this / Monk's dream / In a sentimental mood / Snake out / Blues for Aida / Johnny come lately / What it is / Evidence / Epistrophy / Esteem
CD _______________ **SLAMCD 501**
Slam / Oct '96 / Cadillac

MORE MONK
CD _______________ **1212102**
Soul Note / Apr '91 / Cadillac / Harmonia Mundi / Wellard

PACKET (Lacy, Steve & Irene Aebi/ Frederic Rzewski)
CD _______________ **NA 080**
New Albion / Dec '95 / Cadillac / Harmonia Mundi

REFLECTIONS (Steve Lacy Plays Thelonious Monk)
Four in one / Reflections / Hornin' in / Bye-ya / Let's call this / Ask me now / Skippy
CD _______________ **OJCCD 63**
Original Jazz Classics / Sep '93 / Complete/ Pinnacle / Jazz Music / Wellard

REMAINS
CD _______________ **ARTCD 6102**
Hat Art / May '92 / Cadillac / Harmonia Mundi

SCHOOL DAYS (Lacy, Steve & Roswell Rudd Quartet)
CD _______________ **ARTCD 6140**
Hat Art / Apr '94 / Cadillac / Harmonia Mundi

SIDELINES (Lacy, Steve & Michael Smith)
CD _______________ **1238472**
IAI / Sep '92 / Cadillac / Harmonia Mundi

SOPRANO SAX
CD _______________ **OJCCD 130**
Original Jazz Classics / Nov '95 / Complete/Pinnacle / Jazz Music / Wellard

SPIRIT OF MINGUS (Lacy, Steve & Eric Watson)
CD _______________ **FRLCD 016**
Freelance / Oct '92 / Cadillac / Koch

STEVE LACY
Easy to love / Daydream / Let's cool one / Rockin in rhythm / Something to live for / Alone together / Work / Skippy / Monk's wood / Bye-ya
CD _______________ **CD 53260**
Giants Of Jazz / Jan '96 / Cadillac / Jazz Music / Target/BMG

STRAIGHT HORN OF STEVE LACY, THE
Louise / Introspection / Donna Lee / Played twice / Air / Criss cross
CD _______________ **CCD 79007**
Candid / Feb '97 / Cadillac / Direct / Jazz Music / Koch / Wellard

TRICKLES
CD _______________ **1200082**
Black Saint / Oct '90 / Cadillac / Harmonia Mundi

VESPERS (Lacy, Steve Octet)
CD _______________ **1212602**
Soul Note / Nov '93 / Cadillac / Harmonia Mundi / Wellard

WE SEE
CD _______________ **ARTCD 6127**
Hat Art / Sep '93 / Cadillac / Harmonia Mundi

WEAL AND WOE
CD _______ EM 4004
Emanem / Dec '95 / Cadillac / Harmonia Mundi

WINDOW, THE (Lacy, Steve Trio)
CD _______ 1211852
Soul Note / Oct '90 / Cadillac / Harmonia Mundi / Wellard

Ladae

LADAE
CD _______ 5305422
Polydor / Jul '96 / PolyGram

Ladnier, Tommy

TRUMPET STYLIST, A
CD _______ 414652
Music Memoria / Apr '96 / ADA / Discovery

Lady G

GOD DAUGHTER
CD _______ VPCD 1436
VP / Oct '95 / Greensleeves / Jet Star / Total/BMG

Lady June

LADY JUNE'S LINGUISTIC LEPROSY
Some day silly twenty three / Reflections / Am I / Everythingsnothing / Tunion / Tourist / Bars / Letter / Mangel/Wurzel / To whom it may not concern / Optimism / Touchdowner
CD _______ SEECD 350
See For Miles/C5 / Jun '97 / Pinnacle

Lady Saw

GIVE ME THE REASON
CD _______ RUSHCD 1
Diamond Rush / May '96 / Jet Star

PASSION
CD _______ VPCD 1493
VP / Jul '97 / Greensleeves / Jet Star / Total/BMG

Ladybug Transistor

BEVERLEY ATONALE
CD _______ MRG 121CD
Merge / Mar '97 / Cargo / Greyhound / SRD

Ladysmith Black Mambazo

BEST OF LADYSMITH BLACK MAMBAZO
CD _______ SHCD 43098
Shanachie / Jul '92 / ADA / Greensleeves / Koch

CLASSIC TRACKS
CD _______ SHANCD 43074
Shanachie / Oct '90 / ADA / Greensleeves / Koch

HEAVENLY
Inkanyesi nezazi / Yith umlilo ovuthayo / Knockin' on heaven's door / Oh happy day / People get ready / Take my hand precious Lord / Sohlabeleulu Hosana / I'll take you there / Rain rain beautiful rain / River of dreams / Jesus is my leader / Chain gang / He showed me his hands / Ilingelo Ngelakho
CD _______ 5407902
A&M / Aug '97 / PolyGram

INALA
Buya uz'ekhaya / That's why I choose you / Wahlala emnyango / Ngothandaza njalo / Kulomhlaba (thula) / Udla nge'nduku zabanye / Pauline / Isala kutshelwa / Kwashintsh's isthothobala / Uthando oluphelayo
CD _______ SHANCD 43040
Shanachie / Mar '89 / ADA / Greensleeves / Koch

INDUKU ZETHU
Mangosuthu / Induku selhu / Vukani / Kubi ukungalaeli / Ithemba lakho / Isono sami sentombi / Ingwe idla ngamabla / Umzalwane / Ifa lobukhosana / Wayabimba mfana / Watatazela / Bakhuphuka izwe lanke
CD _______ SHANCD 43021
Shanachie / '88 / ADA / Greensleeves / Koch

INKANYEZI NEZAZI
CD _______ FLTRCD 502
Flame Tree / Dec '92 / Pinnacle

JOURNEY OF DREAMS
Umusa kankulunkulu / Lindelani / Ukhalangami / Bhasobha / Hamba dompasi / Ungayoni into enhle / Amaphiko okundiza / Wayibambezeka / Ungakhowlwa rain / Amazing grace
CD _______ 9257532
WEA / Aug '88 / Warner Music

LIPH'IQINISO
CD _______ FLTRCD 522
Flame Tree / Feb '94 / Pinnacle

SHAKA ZULU
Unomathemba / Hello my baby / At Golgotha / King of kings / Earth is never satisfied / How long / Home of the heroes / These are the guys / Rain rain beautiful rain / Who were you talking to
CD _______ K 9255822
WEA / Mar '94 / Warner Music

STAR & THE WISE MAN, THE
CD _______ 669112
Melodie / Nov '92 / ADA / Discovery / Grapevine/PolyGram / Greensleeves / Jet Star

THUTHUKANI MGOXOLO - LET'S DEVELOP IN PEACE
CD _______ FLTRCD 528
Flame Tree / Apr '96 / Pinnacle

TWO WORLDS ONE HEART
Township jive / Ofana naye (nobody like him) / Bala ubhale (count and write) / Love your neighbor / Leaning on the everlasting arms / Rejoice / Hayi ngalesiskhathi (not right now) / Emhlabeni (in this world) / Isikhathi siyimal (time is money) / Ngomnyango (by the door)
CD _______ 7599261252
WEA / May '90 / Warner Music

UMTHOMBO WAMANZI
CD _______ SHANCD 43055
Shanachie / Aug '88 / ADA / Greensleeves / Koch

ZULU TRADITIONAL
CD _______ VICG 52302
JVC World Library / Mar '96 / ADA / CM / Direct

LaFarge, Peter

ON THE WARPATH/AS LONG AS THE GRASS SHALL GROW
Look again to the wind / Senecas / Damn redskins / Tecumseh / Take back your atom bomb / Vision of a past warrior / Coyote / My little brother / Alaska / Custer trail of tears / Hey Mr. President / Touriste / Last words / Ballad of Ira Hayes / Johnny half breed / Radioactive Eskimo / Crimson parson / Move over, grap a 'holt' / Gather round / If I could not be an Indian / Drums / White girl / I'm an Indian, I'm an alien / Stampede / Please come back, Abe-War Whoop Father
CD _______ BCD 15626
Bear Family / Jun '92 / Direct / Rollercoaster / Swift

SONGS OF THE COWBOYS/IRON MOUNTAIN SONGS
Whoopee ti yi yo / Chisholm trail / Sirey peaks / Lavendar cowboy / I've got no use for the women / I ride old paint / Cowboy's lament / Yavipii Pete / When the work's all done this fall / Cowboy's dream / Black walkin' / John Strawberry Roan / Rodeo hand / Cattle calls / Stumbling / Pop Reed / Pony called Nell / Marijuana blues / Snow bird blues / Hungry blues / Avril blues / Santa Fe / Alaska 49th State / Iron mountain / Falling stars / Abraham Lincoln / Cisco Houston
CD _______ BCD 15627
Bear Family / Jun '92 / Direct / Rollercoaster / Swift

LaFave, Jimmy

AUSTIN SKYLINE
CD _______ BBEAT 8004
Bohemia Beat / Jan '94 / ADA / CM / Direct

HIGHWAY TRANCE
CD _______ LDCD 80002
Lizard / Sep '94 / Direct / RTM/Disc

ROAD NOVEL
You'll never know / Hold on / Vast stretches of broken heart / Into your life / Ramblin' sky / Home sweet Oklahoma / Buckets of rain / Long ago with miles between / Long time since the last time / Never put the blame / Open space / You've got that right / Big wheels / Heart of a woman / Great night
CD _______ BBEA 7
Bohemia Beat / Jul '97 / ADA / CM / Direct

Laffy, Gerry

MUSIC AND THE MAGIC
CD _______ WKFMXD 152
FM / Jul '90 / Revolver / Sony

Lafitte, Guy

LOTUS BLOSSOM (Lafitte, Guy & Wild Bill Davis)
CD _______ BLE 591882
Black & Blue / Apr '91 / Discovery / Koch / Wellard

THINGS WE DID LAST SUMMER, THE
CD _______ BLE 591922
Black & Blue / Apr '91 / Discovery / Koch / Wellard

Lag Wagon

HOSS
CD _______ FAT 532CD
Fatwreck Chords / Nov '95 / Plastic Head

TRASHED
CD _______ FAT 5132
Fatwreck Chords / Feb '94 / Plastic Head

Lagaretta, Felix

PUPY Y SU CHARANGA
CD _______ TUMICD 033
Tumi / '93 / Discovery / Stern's

Lagonia

ETC, ETC
CD _______ HBG 122/12
Background / Apr '94 / Background / Greyhound

Lagowski

WIRE SCIENCE
CD _______ TEQM 93002
TEQ / Jun '97 / Cargo / Plastic Head

Lagrave, Jean-Francois

ZOUK MALOYA
CD _______ PS 65077
PlayaSound / Aug '91 / ADA / Harmonia Mundi

Lagrene, Birelli

ACOUSTIC MOMENTS
Made in France / Rhythm things / Claire Marie / All the things you are / Three views of a secret / Impressions / Stretch / Acoustic moments / Bass ballad / Metal earthquake
CD _______ CDP 795 263 2
Blue Note / Nov '90 / EMI

BIRELLI LAGRENE & LARRY CORYELL/ MIROSLAV VITOUS (Lagrene, Birelli & Larry Carlton/Miroslav Vitous)
PSP no.2 / Berga / All the things you are / Albi / Solo no.1 / Wawe / Gloria's step / All blues
CD _______ INAK 8610
In Akustik / Jul '97 / Direct / TKO Magnum

LIVE (Lagrene, Birelli Ensemble)
Birelli / Minor swing / Spain / Rue De Pierre / Ornithology / Sim / Nuits de St. Germain de pres / Night of a champion / I can't give you anything but love / Moll blues
CD _______ INAK 865CD
In Akustik / Jul '97 / Direct / TKO Magnum

LIVE AT CARNEGIE HALL - A TRIBUTE TO DJANGO REINHARDT
CD _______ CDJP 1040
Jazz Point / May '94 / Cadillac / Harmonia Mundi

LIVE IN MARCIAC
Softly as in a morning sunrise / Days of wine and roses / Donna Lee / Smile / Autumn leaves / Nuages / C'est si bon / Blues walk / Stella by starlight / I got rhythm
CD _______ FDM 365672
Dreyfus / Jul '94 / ADA / Direct / New Note/ Pinnacle

MY FAVOURITE DJANGO
Daphne / Moppin' the bride / Babik / Melodie au creuscule / Place de brouckere / Nuages / Blues for Ike / Nuits de St. Germain des pres / Clair de lune / Troublant bolero / Solo
CD _______ FDM 365742
Dreyfus / Oct '95 / ADA / Direct / New Note/ Pinnacle

Laguna Jazz & Blues Band

TIMELESS MOODS
CD _______ LA 9501
Laguna / Jul '96 / Jazz Music

Lahawns

LIVE AT WINKLES
CD _______ LM 001CD
LM / May '97 / ADA

Lahiri, Bappi

HEARTRAVE
CD _______ FLTRCD 515
Flame Tree / Sep '93 / Pinnacle

Lai, Francis

MAN AND A WOMAN, A
Man and a woman / Love in the rain / Intimate moments / Live for life / Bilitis / La ronde / Seduction / Solitude / Blue rose (la rose bleue) / Les unes et les autres / Whitechapel / Happy new year / African summer / Smic smac smoc / Emotion / Sur notre etoile / Par le sang des autres / Theme from 'love story'
CD _______ 305562
Hallmark / Oct '96 / Carlton

Laibach

ALSO SPRACH JOHANN PAUL II
CD _______ EFACD 204472
Robot / Jul '97 / SRD

BAPTISM, A
CD _______ SUB 3306779 CD
Sub Rosa / Dec '90 / Direct / RTM/Disc / SRD / Vital

JESUS CHRIST SUPERSTAR
CD _______ CDSTUMM 136
Mute / Oct '96 / RTM/Disc

KAPITAL
CD _______ CDSTUMM 82
Mute / Apr '92 / RTM/Disc

KRST POD TRIGLAVOM BAPTISM
CD _______ CD 0019
Sub Rosa / Aug '88 / Direct / RTM/Disc / SRD / Vital

LAIBACH
CD _______ EFA 131322
Nika / Aug '95 / SRD

LET IT BE
Get back / Dig a pony / Across the universe / Dig it / I've got a feeling / Long and winding road / One after 909 / Maggie Mae / For you blue
CD _______ CDSTUMM 58
Mute / Oct '88 / RTM/Disc

LJUBLIANA, ZAGREB, BEOGRAD
CD _______ NSK 1CD
The Grey Area / May '93 / RTM/Disc

MACBETH
Preludium / Agnus dei / Wutach schlucht / Die Zeit / Ohne geld / USA / 10th May 1941 / Expectans exprectavos / Coincidentia oppositorum / Wolf
CD _______ STUMM 70 CD
Mute / Jan '90 / RTM/Disc

MB DECEMBER 21ST 1984
Sodba veka / Ti, ki izzivas / Sila/Dokumenti / Sredi bojev / Nova akropola / Dokumenti II / Tito / Dokumenti III / Dokumenti IV
CD _______ NSK 3CD
The Grey Area / Jun '97 / RTM/Disc

NATO
CD _______ CDSTUMM 121
Mute / Oct '94 / RTM/Disc

NOVA AKROPOLA
Four personen / Nova akropola / Krvava fruda-plodna zemja / Vojna poena / Ti ki izzivas
CD _______ CDMRED 67
Cherry Red / Mar '95 / Pinnacle

OCCUPIED EUROPE NATO TOUR
CD _______ NSK 2CDX
The Grey Area / Aug '96 / RTM/Disc

OPUS DEI
Great seal / How the west was won / Transnational / Opus dei / Leben-tod / F I A T / Geburt einer nation / Leben heist leben
CD _______ CDSTUMM 44
Mute / Apr '87 / RTM/Disc

SLOVENSKA ARKOPOLA
CD _______ EFA 200252
Nika / Aug '95 / SRD

Laibman, David

RAGTIME GUITAR
Gladiolus rag / Ragtime nightingale / Contentment / Cottontail rag / Ethiopia rag / Alaskan rag / Silver swan rag / Solace - A Mexican serenade / Magnetic rag / Pleasant moments
CD _______ EDCD 7026
Easydisc / Feb '97 / Direct

Laika

AMAZING COLOSSAL BAND, THE (Laika & The Cosmonauts)
CD _______ UPSTART 10
Upstart / Mar '95 / ADA / Direct

INSTRUMENTS OF TERROR
CD _______ UPSTART 005
Upstart / Apr '94 / ADA / Direct

Laika

SILVER APPLES OF THE MOON
CD _______ PURECD 042
Too Pure / Oct '94 / Vital

SOUNDS OF THE SATELLITES
Prairie dog / Breather / Out of sight and snowblind / Almost sleeping / Starry night / Bedbugs / Martinis on the moon / Poor gal / Blood and bones / Shut off/Curl up / Spooky rhodes / Dirty feet and giggles
CD _______ PURECD 062
Too Pure / Feb '97 / Vital

Laine, Cleo

BEAUTIFUL THING, A
All in love is fair / Skip a long Sam / Send in the clowns / Least you can do is the best you can / They needed each other / I loves you Porgy / Until it's time for you to go / Life is a wheel / Summer knows / Beautiful thing
CD _______ 09026616642
RCA / Oct '94 / BMG

BLUE AND SENTIMENTAL
Lies of handsome men / I've got a crush on you / Blue and sentimental / Afterglow / Not you again / Primrose colour blue / What'll I do / Love me (if it takes you all night long) / Creole love call
CD _______ 09026614192
RCA / Sep '94 / BMG

CLEO AT CARNEGIE
Any place / I'm shadowing you / Crazy rhythm / Primrose colour blue / We are the music makers / You spotted snakes / Methuselah / When I was one and twenty / Sing me no song / Triboro' fair: *Dankworth, John & His Quintet* / You've got to do what

you've got to do / He was beautiful / Turkish delight / Never let me go / I want to be happy
CD CDXP 2101
DRG / Apr '87 / Discovery / New Note/ Pinnacle

CLEO'S CHOICE
CD RPM 160
RPM / Apr '96 / Pinnacle

I AM A SONG
I'm gonna sit right down and write myself a letter / Early Autumn / Friendly persuasion / There is a time / Day when the world comes alive / I am a song / It might as well be Spring / Music / But not for me / Two part invention / Talk to me baby / Thieving boy / Hi-heel sneakers
CD 09026616702
RCA / Oct '94 / BMG

SOLITUDE (Laine, Cleo & John Dankworth/Duke Ellington Orchestra)
Don't get around much anymore / Sophisticated lady / I'm beginning to see the light / All too soon / Take all my loves / I got it bad and that ain't good / Love call / Don't you know I care (Or don't you care to) / Solitude / Reflections / We're rockin' in rhythm / Come Sunday / September rain / Cleo's 'A' train
CD 09026681242
RCA Victor / Jul '95 / BMG

SOMETIMES WHEN WE TOUCH (Laine, Cleo & James Galway)
Drifting dreaming / Title track / Play it again sam / Skylark / How, where, when / Fluter's ball / Consuelo's love theme / Keep loving me / Anyone can whistle / Still was the night / Lo here the gentle lark / Like a sad song
CD RD 83628
RCA / Jan '87 / BMG

SPOTLIGHT ON CLEO LAINE
I want to be happy / I think of you / I can dream, can't I / I've got my love to keep me warm / I got it bad and that ain't good / I'm a dreamer (aren't we all) / Popular song / I'm just wild about Harry / On a slow boat to China / Perdido / They say it's wonderful / If we lived on top of a mountain / Peel me a grape / Song without words / Fascinating rhythm / Oh Lady be good / Little boat / I cover the waterfront / Bidin' my time / Come rain or come shine / Lines to Ralph Hodgeson, Esquire / Riding high / Woman talk / I could write a book / Second time around / On a clear day (You can see forever) / Complete works / Please don't talk about me when I'm gone
CD 8481292
Polydor / Jan '90 / PolyGram

VERY BEST OF CLEO LAINE, THE (2CD Set)
He was beautiful / I loves you Porgy / No one is alone / Birdsong / Solitude / Streets of London / I don't know why / Send in the clowns / Dreamsville / Gonna get through / Skylark / Creole love call / What'll I do / It don't mean a thing / You must believe in Spring / Wish you were here (I do miss you) / Bill / Lies of handsome men / Play it again Sam / I'm gonna sit right down and write myself a letter / If / Won't you tell me why / I remember / Just a-sittin' and a-rockin' / Woman talk / Sophisticated lady / Music / Bess, you is my woman now / My man's gone now / I'm beginning to see the light / Time for farewell / Turkish delight / Born on a Friday / Thieving boy
CD Set 74321432152
RCA Victor / May '97 / BMG

WORD SONGS
All the world's a stage / If music be the food of love / You spotted snakes / Winter, when icicles hang by the wall / Fear no more the heat o' the sun / It was a lover and his lass / Sigh no more ladies / Dunsinane blues / When that I was a little boy / Shall I compare thee to a summer's day / Blow, blow thou winter wind / O mistress mine, where you are roaming / Take all my loves / My love is as a fever / Who is Sylvia / Compleat works / Our revels now are ended / Lines to Ralph Hodgeson Esquire / Goe, and catche a falling starre / Bread and butter / Dr. David Mantle / Advice to a girl / O tell me the truth about love / In Tenebris 1 / Sun and fun / song / English teeth / Viva sweet love / Mungojerrie and rumpelteazer / Thieving boy / Sing me no song
CD 8304612
Philips / Feb '94 / PolyGram

Laine, Denny

BLUE NIGHTS
Wings on my feet / Japanese tears / Go now / Say you don't mind / Hometown girls / Weep for love / Send me the heart / Caribbean sun / If I tried / Money talks / Stay away / Roll the dice / Land of peace / Blue nights / Blushing bride
CD PCOM 1132
President / Feb '94 / Grapevine/PolyGram / President / Target/BMG

MASTER SUITE
Loving touch / Blue musician / Rory's theme / La Manzanera / Campfire / Read the cards / Thin air / Mountain pass / Highlands / Moors and Christmas / Old man loving / Diego

CD CDTB 058
Thunderbolt / '88 / TKO Magnum

REBORN
CD SCRCD 013
Scratch / Sep '96 / Koch / Scratch/BMG

ROCK SURVIVOR, THE
CD WCPCD 1008
West Coast / Sep '96 / Koch / Scratch/ BMG

Laine, Frankie

1947 (Laine, Frankie & the Carl Fischer Orchestra)
CD HCD 198
Hindsight / Jun '94 / Jazz Music / Target/ BMG

20 GREAT TRACKS (Laine, Frankie & Friends)
CD PRCDSP 301
Prestige / Aug '93 / Else / Total/BMG

ALL TIME HITS
High noon / I believe / Answer me / Granada / Jealousy / Rain rain rain / Cool water / Strange lady in town / Hummingbird / Sixteen tons / Woman in love / Moonlight gambler / Cry of the wild goose / Mule train / Jezebel / Wheel of fortune / Rose rose I love you / Rawhide / Don't fence me in / There must be a reason
CD CDMFP 5907
Music For Pleasure / Apr '91 / EMI

BALLADEER/WANDERLUST
Rocks and gravel / Old Virginny / Cherry red / On a Monday / Careless love / Sixteen tons / Jelly coal man / Lucy D / New orleans / Old blue / Stack of blues / And doesn't she roll / Love is where you find it / Serenade / Wagon wheels / I let her go / Misirlou / Riders in the sky / De glory road / What kind of fool am I / On the road to Mandalay / If I love again / Moment of truth / I'm gonna live till I die
CD 4871912
Columbia / Mar '97 / Sony

BEST OF FRANKIE LAINE, THE
I believe / Mule train / Jezebel / High noon / Answer me
CD MU 3011
Musketeer / Oct '92 / Disc

BEST OF FRANKIE LAINE, THE
CD PLSCD 118
Pulse / Apr '96 / BMG

COLLECTION, THE
CD COL 039
Collection / Apr '95 / Target/BMG

DEUCES WILD/CALL OF THE WILD
Hard way / Camptown races / Luck be a lady / Get rich quick / Horses and women / Moonlight gambler / Ace in the hole / Man who broke the bank at Monte Carlo / Dead man's hand / Roving gambler / Deuces wild / Gamblin' woman / Song of the open road / North to Alaska / Swamp girl / Beyond the blue horizon / Call of the wild / On the trail / Wayfaring stranger / Tumbling tumble weeds / High road / Rollin' stone / New frontier / Girl in the wood
CD 4810172
Columbia / Aug '95 / Sony

FRANKIE LAINE
CD CD 108
Timeless Treasures / Oct '94 / THE

GOIN' LIKE WILDFIRE (Laine, Frankie & Jo Stafford)
Pretty eyed baby / That's the one for me / That's good, that's bad / In the cool, cool, cool of the evening / Cambella / Hey good lookin' / Ham bone / Let's have a party / Settin' the woods on fire / Piece a puddin' / Christmas roses / Chow willy / Bushel and a peck / Floatin' down to cotton town / Way down yonder in New Orleans / Basin Street blues / High society / Back where I belong
CD BCD 15620
Bear Family / Nov '93 / Direct / Rollercoaster / Swift

GREATEST HITS
Rawhide / Moonlight gambler / I believe / Hummingbird / Don't fence me in / Strange lady in town / Red rose I love you / There must be a reason / Answer me / Jezebel / High noon / Mule train / Jealously / Sixteen tons / Cool water / Wheel of fortune / Rain rain rain / Woman in love / Granada / Cry of the wild goose
CD GRF 044
Tring / Feb '93 / Tring

HITMAKER
Jezebel / Don't fence me in / Wheel of fortune / Moonlight gambler / Granada / Rose, rose I love you / Hummingbird / High noon / Sixteen tons / I believe / Jealousy / Strange lady in town / Woman in love / Rain rain rain / Cool water / Cry of the wild goose / Mule train / There must be a reason / Answer me / Rawhide
CD 300272
Hallmark / Jul '96 / Carlton

I BELIEVE
Rawhide / Jealousy / Moonlight gambler / Cry of the wild goose / Hummingbird / Don't fence me in / Strange lady in town / Rose, Rose, I love you / There must be a reason / Answer me / Jezebel / High Noon (Do not forsake me) / Mule train / Sixteen tons / Cool water / Wheel of fortune / Rain rain rain / Woman in love / Granada / I believe
CD CD 6055
Music / Jan '97 / Target/BMG

INCOMPARABLE FRANKIE LAINE, THE (2CD Set)
I believe / Granada / Answer me / That's my desire / Jezebel / Rosetta / I may be wrong / All of me / Black and blue / Two loves have I / Jealousy / Shine / But beautiful / There must be a reason / That lucky old sun / Laughing at life / Your cheatin' heart / On the sunny side of the street / We'll be together again / Rain, rain, rain / Rawhide / (Ghost) Riders in the sky / Sixteen tons / Mule train / Cry of the wild goose / Cool water / Don't fence me in / Moonlight gambler / High noon / Hummingbird / It only happens once / Strange lady in town / Put yourself in my place, baby / Rose Rose I love you / Georgia on my mind / Baby, that ain't right / Don't blame me / Woman in love / Moonlight in Vermont / Wheel of fortune
CD Set MUCD 9503
Musketeer / May '96 / Disc

MEMORIES IN GOLD (20 Great Hits)
Memories in gold / Jealousy / High noon / On the sunny side of the street / Mule train / Cool water / Kid's last fight / Woman in love / Georgia on my mind / Moonlight gambler / You gave me a mountain / Jezebel / That's my desire / Cry of the wild goose / I believe / Your cheatin' heart / Rawhide / That lucky old sun / Shine / We'll be together again
CD CDPC 5004
Prestige / Mar '92 / Else / Total/BMG

ON THE TRAIL
High noon / Cool water / 3.10 to Yuma / Gunfight at the OK Corral / Wanted man / Bowie knife / Mule train / Hanging tree / Along the Navajo trail / City boy / Cry of the wild goose / Rawhide / Gunslinger / Green leaves of Summer / On the trail / North to Alaska / Call of the wild / Tumbling tumbleweeds / Ghost riders in the sky / Prairie bell / Lonely man
CD BCD 15480
Bear Family / Aug '90 / Direct / Rollercoaster / Swift

ON THE TRAIL AGAIN
Strange lady in town / Ramblin' man / Rawhide / Champion the wonderhorse / Black gold / Where the wind blows / I let her go / Drill ye tarriers drill / El diablo / Ride through the night / Ghost riders in the sky / Beyond the blue horizon / Swamp girl / Song of the open road / My journey's end / Wagon wheels / 3.10 to Yuma / Cool water / Gunfight at the OK Corral / High noon / New frontier / Deuces wild / Moonlight gambler / Wheel of fortune / Dead man's hand / Hard way / Wayfaring stranger / Roving gambler / El diablo
CD BCD 15632
Bear Family / Jun '92 / Direct / Rollercoaster / Swift

RETURN OF MR RHYTHM
CD HCD 256
Hindsight / May '95 / Jazz Music / Target/ BMG

SOMETHIN' OLD, SOMETHIN' NEW
CD PRCDSP 300
Prestige / Jun '92 / Else / Total/BMG

Laing, Robin

ANGEL'S SHARE, THE
More than just a dram / Our glens / Piper Macneil / Willie brewed a pack o' malt / Parish o' Dunkeld / Twelve and a tanner a bottle / Whiskey and women / Nancy's whiskey / De'il's awa' wi' tha exciseman / Bottle o' the best / John Barleycorn / Tell tale / Whiskey you're the devil / Tak a dram / Wee deoch an Doris
CD CDTRAX 137
Greentrax / Jul '97 / ADA / Direct / Duncans / Highlander

WALKING IN TIME
Soldier maid / Kilbowie hill / Summer of '45 / Punters / Unquiet grave / Lass O'Patie's mill / El punado de centeno / Jamie Foyers / Billy Taylor / Forth Bridge song / Loose noose / Deacon Brodie / When two hearts combine / Neil Gow lament / Calypso's Island
CD CDTRAX 072
Greentrax / Apr '94 / ADA / Direct / Duncans / Highlander

Laka, Don

DESTINY
Move on / mamelodi / Late again / Time and space / Destiny / Sway / Tlang sekolong / Still waters / Odyssey / You will know me / No clue at all / SO long Mr
CD 4874952
Sony Jazz / Aug '97 / Sony

Lakatos, Roby

IN GYPSY STYLE
CD MWCD 4010
Music & Words / Jul '95 / ADA / Direct

Lakatos, Sandor

GYPSY VIOLINS (Lakatos, Sandor & His Gypsy Band)
CD HMP 3903027
HM Plus/Quintana / Oct '94 / Harmonia Mundi

HUNGARY - MUSIC TZIGANE
CD HMP 393009
HM Plus/Quintana / Oct '94 / Harmonia Mundi

MUSIC FROM HUNGARY (Lakatos, Sandor & His Gypsy Band)
CD 15187
Laserlight / '91 / Target/BMG

Lake, Greg

FROM THE BEGINNING (The Greg Lake Retrospective/2CD Set)
Court of the Crimson King: *King Crimson* / Cat food: *King Crimson* / Knife edge: *Emerson, Lake & Palmer* / Lucky man: *Emerson, Lake & Palmer* / From the beginning: *Emerson, Lake & Palmer* / Take a pebble: *Emerson, Lake & Palmer* / Still: *Sinfield, Pete* / Still, you turn me on: *Emerson, Lake & Palmer* / Jerusalem: *Emerson, Lake & Palmer* / Karn evil 9: *Emerson, Lake & Palmer* / I believe in father christmas / C'est la vie / Closer to believing / Watching over you / 21st century schizoid man / Nuclear attack / Love too much / It hurts / Retribution drive / Lie / Let me love you once / Manoeuvres / I don't know why I still love you / Touch and go: *Emerson, Lake & Palmer* / Lay down your guns: *Emerson, Lake & Palmer* / Love under fire / Money talks / Black moon: *Emerson, Lake & Palmer* / Paper blood: *Emerson, Lake & Palmer* / Affairs of the heart: *Emerson, Lake & Palmer* / Daddy: *Emerson, Lake & Palmer* / Heart of ice: *Emerson, Lake & Palmer*
CD Set ESDCD 552
Essential / May '97 / BMG

Lake, Kirk

BLACK LIGHTS
CD IRE 1032
Che / Nov '96 / SRD

SO YOU GOT ANYTHING ELSE
CD CHE 27CD
Che / Apr '95 / SRD

Lake Of Dracula

LAKE OF DRACULA
CD GR 39CD
Skingraft / Jun '97 / SRD

Lake Of Tears

GREATER ART
CD BMCD 49
Black Mark / May '94 / Plastic Head

HEADSTONES
CD BMCD 072
Black Mark / Sep '95 / Plastic Head

Lake, Oliver

BOSTON DUETS (Lake, Oliver & Donal Leonellis Fox)
CD CD 732
Music & Arts / Sep '92 / Cadillac / Harmonia Mundi

COMPILATION
CD R 279458
Gramavision / Aug '94 / Vital/SAM

EDGE-ING
CD 1210142
Black Saint / Oct '94 / Cadillac / Harmonia Mundi

HEAVY SPIRITS
While pushing down turn / Owshet / Heavy spirits / Movement equals creation / Lonely blacks / Intensity
CD CDBLC 760209
Black Lion / Apr '96 / Cadillac / Jazz Music / Koch / Wellard

HOLDING TOGETHER
CD 1200092
Black Saint / Nov '90 / Cadillac / Harmonia Mundi

OTHERSIDE
CD 1889012
Gramavision / Feb '89 / Vital/SAM

ZAKI (Lake, Oliver Trio)
CD ARTCD 6113
Hat Art / Aug '92 / Cadillac / Harmonia Mundi

Lakeman Brothers

THREE PIECE SUITE
CD CRM 01CD
Crapstone / Jun '94 / ADA

Lakeside

BEST OF LAKESIDE
Shot of love / One minute after midnight / Given in to love / It's all the way live / Rough rider / If you like our music (Get on up and move) / Fantastic voyage / Your love is on

the one / We want you (On the floor) / Say yes / Ever ready man / I want to hold your hand / Raid / Outrageous / Bulls eye
CD NEMCD 681
Sequel / Aug '94 / BMG

FANTASTIC VOYAGE
Fantastic voyage / Your love is on the one / I need you / Strung out / Say yes / Ever-eady man / I love everything you do
CD NEBCD 792
Sequel / Apr '96 / BMG

Lalama, Ralph

CIRCLE LINE (Lalama, Ralph Quartet)
Circle line / My ideal / Giant steps / You are too beautiful / Fiesta espagnol / Dark chocolate / Homestretch / Without a song
CD CRISS 1132CD
Criss Cross / Jul '97 / Cadillac / Direct / Vital/SAM

FEELIN' AND DEALIN' (Lalama, Ralph & His Manhattan All Stars)
CD CRISS 1046CD
Criss Cross / May '91 / Cadillac / Direct / Vital/SAM

MOMENTUM (Lalama, Ralph Quartet)
CD CRISS 1063CD
Criss Cross / Oct '92 / Cadillac / Direct / Vital/SAM

YOU KNOW WHAT I MEAN
CD CRISS 1097
Criss Cross / Apr '95 / Cadillac / Direct / Vital/SAM

Lally, Michael

WHAT YOU FIND THERE
CD NAR 102CD
New Alliance / Jul '94 / Plastic Head

Lam, Bun-Ching

LIKE WATER
CD TZA 7021
Tzadik / Feb '97 / Cargo

Lam, Kine

PRAISE
CD SHCD 64062
Shanachie / Jan '96 / ADA / Greensleeves / Koch

Lama Karta

TCHEUD
CD 74321483912
Milan / Jun '97 / Conifer/BMG / Silva Screen

TIBETAN CHANTS (Buddhist Meditation)
CD 74321327202
Milan / Apr '96 / Conifer/BMG / Silva Screen

Lamarque, Libertad

INSPIRACION 1932-1948
CD EBCD 72
El Bandoneon / Jul '96 / Discovery

Lamb

LAMB
Lusty / God bless / Cotton wool / Trans fatty acid / Zero / Merge / Gold / Closer / Gorecki / Feela
CD 5329682
Fontana / Sep '96 / PolyGram

Lamb, Andrew

PORTRAIT IN THE MIST
Air and ear painters / Negretta Mia / Light of the whirling dervish / Bohemian love affair / Portrait in the mist / Eccentricity / Morning of the black swan
CD DE 479
Delmark / Mar '97 / ADA / Cadillac / CM / Direct / Hot Shot

Lamb, Barbara

FIDDLE FATALE
Sally Gooden / Panhandle rag / Good woman's love / Paddy on the turnpike/gone again / Montana glide / Herman's hornpipe / So what / Foster's reel / Old French reel / I'll never be free / Katy Hill / Princess Angeline / Ducks on the Millpond (ducks with bongas)
CD SHCD 3810
Sugar Hill / May '93 / ADA / CM / Direct / Koch / Roots

TONIGHT I FEEL LIKE TEXAS
CD SHCD 3860
Sugar Hill / Oct '96 / ADA / CM / Direct / Koch / Roots

Lamb, Natalie

I'M A WOMAN (Lamb, Natalie & The Perune Jazz Band)
CD BCD 329
GHB / Aug '94 / Jazz Music

Lamb, Paul

FINE CONDITION (Lamb, Paul & The King Snakes)
CD IGOCD 2019
Indigo / Mar '95 / ADA / Direct

SHE'S A KILLER (Lamb, Paul & The King Snakes)
She's a killer / Keep on dreaming / Girl for me / Texas hop / Blackjack game / Who can it be / Just a dream / My baby she don't look like that / Whoop and holler / Reconsider baby / Wild wild women / Jump for joy / Back at the chicken shack / You're the one / John's jump
CD IGOXCD 503
Indigo / Jun '96 / ADA / Direct

SHIFTING INTO GEAR (Lamb, Paul & The King Snakes)
Come on everybody / Hey woman / Evening sun / Didn't do me no good / Give up giving up / Feel so good / Shifting into gear / Must be more to life than this / One more time / Snakeskin jump / I need somebody to love / Once too often
CD IGOXCD 504
Indigo / Feb '97 / ADA / Direct

Lambayeque

TRADITIONAL MUSIC OF PERU VOL.4
CD SFWCD 40469
Smithsonian Folkways / Dec '96 / ADA / Cadillac / CM / Direct / Koch

Lambchop

HANK
CD EFA 049792
City Slang / Jul '96 / RTM/Disc

HOW I QUIT SMOKING
CD EFA 049692
City Slang / Jan '96 / RTM/Disc

I HOPE YOU'RE SITTING DOWN
CD EFA 049532
City Slang / Mar '95 / RTM/Disc

Lambert, Gary

GUITAR PICKIN' RARITIES (Lambert, Gary & Eddie Cochran)
CD SJCD 594
Sun Jay / Mar '92 / Rollercoaster / TKO Magnum

Lambert, Hendricks & Ross

HOTTEST NEW GROUP IN JAZZ, THE (2CD Set)
Charleston Alley / Moanin' / Twisted / Bijou / CLoudburst / Centerpiece / Gimme that wine / Sermonette / Summertime / Everybody's boppin' / Cotton tail / All too soon / Happy anatomy / Rocks in my bed / Main stem / I don't know what kind of blues I've got / Things ain't what they used to be / Midnight indigo / What am I here for / In a mellow tone / Caravan / Come on home / New ABC / Farmer's market / Cookin' at the continental / With malice toward none / Hi-fly / Home cookin' / Halloween spooks / Popity pop / Blue / Mr. PC / Preacher / Walkin' / This here (dis hyunh) / Swingin' til the girls come home / Twist city / Just a little bit of twist / Night in Tunisia
CD Set C2K 64933
Sony Jazz / Nov '96 / Sony

Lambeth Community Youth ...

BEST OF CARIBBEAN STEEL DRUMS (Lambeth Community Youth Steel Orchestra)
CD EUCD 1140
ARC / '91 / ADA / ARC Music

STEEL DRUMS PARTY (Lambeth Community Youth Steel Orchestra)
CD EUCD 1325
ARC / Nov '95 / ADA / ARC Music

Lambrettas

BEAT BOYS IN THE JET AGE
Da-a-ance / Cortina MkII / London calling / Poison ivy / Leap before you look / Beat boys in the jet age / Page three / Living for today / Watch out I'm back / Don't push me / Runaround / Face to face
CD DOJOCD 187
Dojo / Nov '94 / Disc

Lament

LEVITATE
CD TOODAMNHY 82
Too Damn Hype / Jan '95 / Cargo / SRD

Lammas

BROKEN ROAD, THE
CD EFZ 1015
EFZ / Jan '96 / Vital/SAM

SOURCEBOOK
Rapid steps / Oathlaw / Ay fond kiss / New weather / Is fada liom um I / Private enterprise for the public good / Agent Scully's wooden jodhpurs / Road to elsewhere / Dance / Rooks / Hulaho / Waltz for Rosa
CD EFZ 1022
EFZ / Jun '97 / Vital/SAM

Lamond, Don

DON LAMOND & HIS BIG SWING BAND/QUARTET
CD CCD 148
Circle / Jun '96 / Jazz Music / Swift / Wellard

Lamond, Mary Jane

BHO THIR NAN CRAOBH
O, tha mise fo ghruaimean / Air faillirinn iu / Cagaran gaolach / Domhnaill antaidh / A chuachag nam beann / He mo leannan / Bodach beag a loinean / Ho ro's toigh leam fhin thu / Cha bhi mi buan / Ba ba mo leanabh / Piuirt-a-beul / Dh'olainn deoch a laimh mo run / Oran gillean alasdair mhoir / Dan do shean ford
CD IRCD 045
Iona / Mar '97 / ADA / Direct / Duncans

FROM THE LAND OF THE TREES
CD BRCD 0001
Macmeanma / May '95 / ADA / CM / Duncans / Highlander

Lamont Cranston Blues Band

LAMONT CRANSTON BLUES BAND
I don't wanna know / Cold winds / Two way wishin' / Love grown cold / You don't even know / Stop on by / I got designs on you / Whole lotta lovin' / Too young to die / Fever
CD ATM 1119
Atomic Theory / Sep '96 / ADA / Direct

Lamothe, Rob

GRAVITY
CD DCD 9626
Dream Circle / Nov '96 / Cargo / Plastic Head

Lamour, Dorothy

MOON OF MANAKOORA, THE (25 Romantic Favourites)
Moonlight and shadows / Panamania / You took the words right out of my heart / Thanks for the memory / Lovelight in the starlight / Little lady make-believe / Tonight will live / On a tropic night / That sentimental sandwich / Man I love / You took me out of this world / I'm all a-tremble over you / Paradise / Sweet potato piper / Palms of paradise / Moon and the willow tree / Too romantic / I gotta right to sing the blues / It had to be you / Your kiss / This is the beginning of the end / Moon over Burma / Mexican magic / One rose that's left in my heart / Moon of Manakoora
CD CDAJA 5231
Living Era / Feb '97 / Select

Lan Doky, Niels

DAYBREAK
All or nothing at all / Why / Final decision / Jet lag / Natural / Daybreak
CD STCD 4160
Storyville / '88 / Cadillac / Jazz Music / Wellard

DREAMS
CD MCD 9178
Milestone / Oct '93 / Cadillac / Complete/Pinnacle / Jazz Music / Wellard

FRIENDSHIP
Real mccoy / Endless vision / Christmas song / Confidence / KS / Point of no return / Friendship / To the limit / Center of gravity
CD MCD 9183
Milestone / Oct '93 / Cadillac / Complete/Pinnacle / Jazz Music / Wellard

HERE OR THERE (Lan Doky, Niels Trio)
CD STCD 4117
Storyville / Feb '89 / Cadillac / Jazz Music / Wellard

TARGET, THE (Lan Doky, Niels Trio)
CD STCD 4140
Storyville / Feb '89 / Cadillac / Jazz Music / Wellard

TRUTH, THE (Live at Montmartre) (Lan Doky, Niels Trio)
CD STCD 4144
Storyville / Feb '89 / Cadillac / Jazz Music / Wellard

Lancaster, Alan

LIFE AFTER QUO
CD PJR 001CD
Blueprint / Aug '96 / Pinnacle

Lancaster, Jack

MARSCAPE (Lancaster, Jack & Robin Lumley)
CD ZCDMS 012
Zok / Nov '96 / Grapevine/PolyGram / Total/BMG

SKINNINGROVE BAY
CD CSC 7120CD
Viceroy / Jan '97 / TKO Magnum

Land

LAND
CD XCD 032
Extreme / May '95 / Vital/SAM

Land, Harold

MAPENZI (Land, Harold & Blue Mitchell Quintet)
CD CCD 4044
Concord Jazz / Dec '90 / New Note/Pinnacle

XOCIA'S DANCE
CD MCD 5272
Muse / Sep '92 / New Note/Pinnacle

Lande, Art

SKYLIGHT (Lande, Art & David Samuels/Paul McCandleless)
Skylight / Dance of the silver skeezix / Duck in a colourful blanket (for here) / Chillum / Moist window/Lawn party / Ente (to go) / Willow
CD 5310252
ECM / Feb '96 / New Note/Pinnacle

Lande, Vidar

FIDDLE & HARDINGER FROM ADGER, NORWAY
CD D 8063
Unesco / Apr '96 / ADA / Harmonia Mundi

SLATTER AAKHUSS
CD VL 001CD
VL / Aug '96 / ADA

SLATTER RYSSTAD
CD VL 002CD
VL / Aug '96 / ADA

Landgren, Nils

FOLLOW YOUR HEART
CD 21393
Caprice / Mar '89 / ADA / Cadillac / CM / Complete/Pinnacle

GOTLAND (Landgren, Nils & Tomasz Stanko)
Den blomstertid nu kommer / Gotland / Tjelvar / Alskar barnet modernfamnen / Olu / Guldrupe / Ainbusk / Vange / Rank / Emil Kahl
CD 92262
Act / Feb '96 / New Note/Pinnacle

LIVE IN STOCKHOLM
Traci / Soundcheck / Impressions / Cheyenne / Simple life / Chicken / Ain't nobody / So what / Mr. M / Red horn / Yo yo
CD 92232
Act / Jul '95 / New Note/Pinnacle

PAINT IT BLUE (Landgren, Nils Funk Unit)
Walk tall / You dig / Why am I treated so bad / Brother Nat / Inside straight / Cannonball / Mercy mercy mercy / Mother fonk / Primitivo / After the party / Love all, serve all / Julian
CD 92432
Act / Feb '97 / New Note/Pinnacle

Landreth, Sonny

OUTWARD BOUND
Soldier of fortune / Back to Bayou Teche / When you're away / Sacred ground / New landlord / Speak of the devil / Yokamoma / Planet cannonball / Common law love / Bad weather / Outward bound
CD 72445110322
Zoo Entertainment / Jul '92 / BMG

SOUTH OF 1-10
Shooting for the moon / Creole angel / Native stepson / Orphans of the motherland / Congo square / Turning wheel / South of 1-10 / Cajun waltz / Mojo boogie / C'est chaud / Great gulf wind
CD 72445110702
Zoo Entertainment / Mar '95 / BMG

Landry, Henri

VIOLONEUX DES CANTONS DE L'EST
CD 926432
BUDA / Jul '96 / Discovery

Landsborough, Charlie

SONGS FROM THE HEART
I dreamed I was in heaven / Sill blue / Things that my ears can do / Walking on my memories / Song of my heart / All over but crying / One more time / You and me / Constantly / I cried / You're not the only one / Fireside dreaming / Summer country skies / Close your eyes / lily of the valley / still blue
CD RITZRCD 521
Ritz / Jun '92 / Pinnacle

WHAT COLOUR IS THE WIND
Million ways to fall / Forever friend / Dream or two / When you're not a dream / What colour is the wind / Once bitten twice shy / Throw me away / When the counting's done / Funny way to say goodbye / Song of the ocean / Dance with me / White lies and windows

CD ______ RCD 542
Ritz / Sep '94 / Pinnacle

WITH YOU IN MIND
No time at all / How do you do those things / Part of me / Shine your light / Isle of Innisfree / Down to earth / I will love you all my life / Heaven knows / If only / I say you / Irish waltz / You stand all alone
CD ______ RITZCD 0078
Ritz / Sep '96 / Pinnacle

Landscape

FROM THE TEA ROOMS OF MARS... (To the Hell Holes of Uranus)
European man / Shake the West awake / Computer person / Alpine tragedy / Sisters / Face of the 80's / New religion / Einstein a go go / Norman Bates / Doll's house / From the tea rooms of Mars / Beguine / Mambo / Tango
CD ______ MAUCD 618
Mau Mau / Jul '92 / Pinnacle

Landstrumm, Neal

BEDROOMS AND CITIES
CD ______ EFA 292822
Tresor / Sep '97 / 3mv/BMG / Prime / SRD

BROWN BY AUGUST
Shuttlecock / DX Serve / Index revisited / Sibling rivalry / Shake the hog / Custard tracks / Finnish deception / Home delivery / Squeeze / She-ra extra speaker
CD ______ PF 040CD
Peacefrog / Nov '95 / Mo's Music Machine / Prime / RTM/Disc / Vital

UNDERSTANDING DISINFORMATION (2CD Set)
CD Set ______ EFA 018002
Tresor / Jul '96 / 3mv/BMG / Prime / SRD

Lane, Anita

PEARL & DIRTY
CD ______ CDSTUMM 81
Mute / Sep '93 / RTM/Disc

Lane, Frankie

DOBRO
CD ______ CEFCD 159
Gael Linn / Jan '94 / ADA / CM / Direct / Grapevine/PolyGram / Roots

Lane, Jimmy D.

LONG GONE
CD ______ APO 2003CD
Analogue / May '97 / ADA

Lane, Mickey Lee

ROCKIN' ON...AND BEYOND
(I wanna) rock the bop / Senior class / Shaggy dog / Oo oo / (I wanna) rock the bop / Tears uncried / She cried to me / Zoo / Little girl / She don't want to / (That's how you'll know) when you're in love / Of yesterday / Yesterday / Baby what you want me to do / I'm not sure...I still want you / Bo doofus / At the sound of the gong/WMIC radio theme / Where it's rocking / Zoo / Morley trucks commercial/Move it on / Put on your leather weather baby / Coffee and toast / (Baby) I wanna be loved / Toasted love / One and one is two: *Mickey & Shonnie* / In love with love: *2 Guys & A Gal* / Frank the frog: *2 Guys & A Gal* / Hey sahlo-ney: *2 Guys & A Gal* / Tutti frutti: *2 Guys & A Gal* / Kum ba yah: *2 Guys & A Gal* / Night cap: *2 Guys & A Gal* / Something to live on: *2 Guys & A Gal* / Recording silence with PPH: *2 Guys & A Gal*
CD ______ RCCD 3014
Rollercoaster / May '97 / Rollercoaster / Swift

Lane, Ronnie

ANYMORE FOR ANYMORE (2CD Set) (Lane, Ronnie & Slim Chance)
Roll on babe / Tell everyone / Amelia Earhardt / Anymore for anymore / Bird in a gilded cage / Chicken wired / Careless love / Don't you cry for me / Gonna see the King / Silk stockings / Poacher / Poacher / How come / Done this before / Gonna see the King / How come
CD Set ______ PILOT 015
Burning Airlines / Aug '97 / Total/Pinnacle

ANYMORE FOR ANYMORE...PLUS (Lane, Ronnie & Slim Chance)
How come / Careless love / Don't you cry for me / Bye and bye (Gonna see The King) / Silk stockings / Poacher / Roll on babe / Tell everyone / Amelia Earhart's last flight / Anymore for anymore / Only a bird in a gilded cage / Chicken wired / Done this one before
CD ______ SEECD 338
See For Miles/C5 / Jun '97 / Pinnacle

KUSCHTY RYE (The Singles)
How come / Tell everyone / Done this one before / Poacher / Bye and bye (gonna see the King) / Roll on babe / Anymore for anymore / What went down (that night with you) / Lovely / Brother can you spare a dime / Ain't no lady / Don't try and change my mind / Well well hello (the party) / Kuschty rye / You're so right / One step / Lad's got money / Stone / Sweet Virginia
CD ______ PILOT 019
Burning Airlines / Jul '97 / Total/Pinnacle

ONE FOR THE ROAD (Lane, Ronnie & Slim Chance)
CD ______ EDCD 464
Edsel / Feb '96 / Pinnacle

SEE ME
One step / Good ol' boys boogie / Lad's got money / She's leaving / Barcelona / Kuschty Rye / Don't tell me now / You're so right / Only you / Winning with women / Way up yonder
CD ______ EDCD 492
Edsel / Jul '96 / Pinnacle

SLIM CHANCE
CD ______ EDCD 463
Edsel / Apr '96 / Pinnacle

YOU NEVER CAN TELL (2CD Set) (Lane, Ronnie & Slim Chance)
Ooh la la / Careless love / Flags and banners / How come / Sweet Virginia / Lovely / Anniversary / Don't try and change my mind / One for the road / Steppin' and reelin' / All or nothing / Last orders / Roll on babe / Lost/How come / You're so rude / What went down / Chicken wired / Sweet Virginia / You never can tell / Anniversary / Don't try and change my mind / Walk on by / You never can tell / Steppin' and reelin' / Ooh la la
CD Set ______ PILOT 011
Burning Airlines / Jun '97 / Total/Pinnacle

Lane, Steve

EASY COME - EASY GO (Lane, Steve & Red Hot Peppers)
Sing baby sing / London blues / Weatherbird rag / Easy come, easy go / Roy 'n' Audrey's stomp / Hindu blues / I'd love to take orders from you / Just too bad / Shakin' the blues away / I guess it wasn't meant to be / I can't believe that you're in love with me / Gotcha / Lazybones / Them there eyes / Jazz me blues / Cabinet shuffle / You're getting to be a habit with me
CD ______ AZCD 14
Azure / Nov '92 / Azure / Cadillac / Jazz Music / Swift / Wellard

Lanegan, Mark

WHISKEY FOR THE HOLY GHOST
CD ______ SPCD 78249
Sub Pop / Jan '94 / Cargo / Greyhound / Shellshock/Disc

WINDING SHEET
CD ______ GR 095CD
Sub Pop / Mar '94 / Cargo / Greyhound / Shellshock/Disc

Lang, Eddie

BLUE GUITAR VOL.1 & 2 (Lang, Eddie & Lonnie Johnson)
CD ______ BGOCD 327
Beat Goes On / Dec '96 / Pinnacle

HANDFUL OF RIFFS, A
Eddie's twister / April kisses / Prelude / Melody man's dream / Perfect / Rainbow / Add a little wiggle / Jeannine / I'll never be the same / Church Street sobbin' blues / There'll be some changes made / Two tone stomp / Jet black blues / Blue blood blues / Bullfrog moan / Handful of riffs / Bugle call rag / Freeze and melt / Hot heels / Walking the dog / March of the hoodlums
CD ______ CDAJA 5061
Living Era / May '89 / Select

JAZZ GUITAR RARITIES
CD ______ JZCD 380
Suisa / Jun '93 / Jazz Music / THE

TROUBLES, TROUBLES (Lang, Eddie/ Edgar Blanchard & The Gondoliers)
CD ______ ROUCD 2080
Rounder / '88 / ADA / CM / Direct

Lang, Jonny

LIE TO ME
Lie to me / Darker side / Good morning little school girl / Still wonder / Matchbox / Back for a taste of your love / Quitter never wins / Hit the ground running / Rack 'em up / When I come to you / There's gotta be a change / Missing your love
CD ______ 5406402
A&M / Jun '97 / PolyGram

Lang, k.d.

ABSOLUTE TORCH AND TWANG (Lang, k.d. & The Reclines)
Luck in my eyes / Trail of broken hearts / Didn't I / Full moon full of love / Big big love / Walkin' in and out of your arms / Three days / Big boned gal / Wallflower waltz / Pullin' back the reins / It's me / Nowhere to stand
CD ______ K 9258772
Sire / Mar '94 / Warner Music

ALL YOU CAN EAT
If I were you / Maybe / You're OK / Sexuality / Get some / Acquiesce / This / World of love / Infinite and unforeseen / I want it all
CD ______ 9362460342
Warner Bros. / Oct '95 / Warner Music

ANGEL WITH A LARIAT (Lang, k.d. & The Reclines)
Turn me round / High time for a detour / Diet of strange places / Got the bull by the horns / Watch your step polka / Rose garden / Tune into my wave / Angel with a lariat / Pay dirt / Three cigarettes in an ashtray
CD ______ 7599254412
Sire / Aug '88 / Warner Music

DRAG
Don't smoke in bed / Air that I breathe / Smoke dreams / My last cigarette / Joker / Valley of the dolls / Your smoke screen / My old addiction / Till the heart caves in / Smoke rings / Hain't it funny / Love is like a cigarette
CD ______ 9362466232
Warner Bros. / Jun '97 / Warner Music

EVEN COWGIRLS GET THE BLUES
Just keep me moving / Much finer place / Or was I / Hush sweet lover / Myth / Apogee / Virtual vortex / Lifted by love / Overture / Kundalini yoga waltz / In perfect dreams / Curious soul astray / Ride of bonanza jellybean / Don't be a lemming polka / Sweet little Cherokee / Cowgirl pride
CD ______ 9362454332
WEA / Oct '93 / Warner Music

INGENUE
Save me / Mind of love / Miss Chatelaine / Wash me clean / So it shall be / Still thrives this love / Seasons of hollow soul / Outside myself / Tear of love's recall / Constant craving
CD ______ 7599268402
Sire / Dec '96 / Warner Music

SHADOWLAND (The Owen Bradley Sessions) (Lang, k.d. & The Reclines)
Western stars / Lock, stock and teardrops / Sugar moon / I wish I didn't love you so / Once again around the dance floor / Black coffee / Shadowland / Don't let the stars get in your eyes / Tears don't care who cry them / I'm down to my last cigarette / Too busy being blue / Honky tonk angel's medley
CD ______ 9257242
WEA / Apr '88 / Warner Music

Lang, Thierry

THIERRY LANG
Yellow story / Comrade Conrad / Angels fly / If I should lose you / My foolish heart / Blue peach / Oliver's song / Bop boy / 'Round midnight
CD ______ CDP 8562542
Blue Note / Aug '97 / EMI

Lang, Thomas

LOST LETTER Z, THE
CD ______ DRYC 10012
Dry Communications / Sep '91 / Total/ BMG

OUTSIDE OVER THERE
CD ______ DRYCCD 15
Dry Communications / Nov '92 / Total/ BMG

VERSIONS
CD ______ TLGCD 007
Telegraph / Oct '96 / Total/BMG

Lang, Tom

MEDIATOR
CD ______ 343432
Koch International / Mar '96 / Koch

Langa-Langa, Zaiko

GRAND SUCESS DE LANGA
CD ______ FLTRCD 521
Flame Tree / Dec '93 / Pinnacle

Langas & The Manganiars

SONGS OF THE DISTANT SANDS
CD ______ NRCD 0059
Navras / Sep '96 / New Note/Pinnacle

Lange, Katherina

DAS WUNDERKIND
Abzahlen / Mignon vom kietz / Ich bin von kopf bis fuss auf liebe eingestelt / Die praktische Berlinerin / Da muss ich fliegen / Das zersagte dame / Der mann mit dem kalten blut / Currende / Abzahlen / Song der guste / Ich baumle mit de beene / Drahtseil akt / Das wunderkind / Dornroschen aus'm wedding / Das jroschenlied / Die Hungerkunstlerin / Nachtgebet / Kindertragodie / Rattenfangerlied / Es hat jeschnappt / Mit einer scheusslichen puppe / Volkslied / Oh mond / Wenn ick mal tot bin / Ich weiss nicht, zu wem ich gehore / In den abendwind jeflustert / Drei wunsche / Finale
CD ______ BCD 16025
Bear Family / Dec '96 / Direct / Rollercoaster / Swift

Langeleik, Levande

LEVANDE LANGELEIK
CD ______ HCD 7106
Helio / Nov '95 / ADA

Langford, Frances

GETTIN' SENTIMENTAL
I'm in the mood for love / Once in a while / Sweet someone / Is it true what they say about Dixie / Silhouetted in the moonlight / I don't want to make history / Everything you said came true / Deep shadows / I've got you under my skin / Harbour lights / You are my lucky star / Let's call a heart a heart / So do I / Speaking confidentially / Melody from the sky / Can't teach my old heart new tricks / If it's the last thing I do / So many memories / Rap tap on wood / Sweet heartache / I'm gettin' sentimental over you
CD ______ CMSCD 002
Movie Stars / Feb '93 / Conifer/BMG

I'M IN THE MOOD FOR LOVE
I'm in the mood for love / I feel a song coming on / Is it true what they say about Dixie / Easy to love / Rap tap on wood / Swingin' the jinx away / Was it rain / So many memories / I'm getting sentimental over you / Please be kind / At long last love / I won't tell a soul / Gipsy love song / Get out of town / Falling in love with love / Moonglow / Blue moon / When you wish upon a star / In the cool of the evening / In Waikiki / Tropical magic / Serenade in blue / Why do I love you / At last
CD ______ CDAJA 5219
Living Era / Jul '97 / Select

SWEET HEARTACHE
Kiss in the dark / Nasty man / Why do I love you / Palms of paradise / With the wind and the rain in your hair / Falling in love with love / When you wish upon a star / This can't be love / Hurry home / Serenade in blue / Neath the southern moon / Easy to love / Two dreams met / At last / You hi-de-hi-ing me / You're nearer / Little love, a little kiss / Echoes of Hawaii / Smilin' thru / Our love affair / Sweet heartache / Then you've never been blue / I'm gettin' sentimental over you / Was it rain
CD ______ ROYCD 203
Flare / Jul '96 / Target/BMG

Lanham, Roy

SIZZLING STRINGS/THE FABULOUS GUITAR OF ROY LANHAM
Summit Ridge drive / Stomping at the Savoy / Sophisticated swing / Kerry dance / Lover / Tea for two / Air Mail special / If I had you / Slipped disc / Mellow mood / Eager beaver / Tuxedo Junction / Your heart darlin' / Holiday for strings / Roy's blues / Tuxedo Junction / We'll be together again / Brazil / In the mood / Under the Double Eagle / Brown's ferry blues / Carnival in Paris / One love / Can't we be friends
CD ______ BCD 16116
Bear Family / Nov '96 / Direct / Rollercoaster / Swift

Lanois, Daniel

ACADIE
Still water / Maker / O Marie / Jolie Louise / Fisherman's daughter / White mustang II / Under a stormy sky / Where the hawkwind kills / Silium's hill / Ice / St. Ann's gold / Amazing grace
CD ______ K 925969 2
WEA / Sep '89 / Warner Music

FOR THE BEAUTY OF WYNONA
Messenger / Brother LA / Still learning how to crawl / Beatrice / Waiting / Collection of Marie Claire / Death of a train / Unbreakable chain / Lotta love to give / Sleeping in the devil's bed / For the beauty of Wynona / Rocky world / Indian red
CD ______ 9362450302
Warner Bros. / Dec '96 / Warner Music

Lanphere, Don

DON LANPHERE AND LARRY CORYELL (Lanphere, Don & Larry Coryell)
Dragon gate / Very early / Ascending truth / Imagination / Green tutu / Spring can really hang you up the most / Sunset blues / My ideal / Beach at Nerja / Here they come, there they go / Peace
CD ______ HEPCD 2048
Hep / Dec '90 / Cadillac / Jazz Music / New Note/Pinnacle / Wellard

DON LOVES MIDGE (Lanphere, Don Quintet)
And the angels sing / Easy living / I remember Clifford / Try a little tenderness / Poor butterfly / I'll never be the same again / Once in a while / Old cape cod / God bless the child / Gone with the wind / Polka dots and moonbeams / Everything I have is yours / Put your dreams away / Soon / My foolish heart / There's a sweet spirit...
CD ______ HEPCD 2027
Hep / Sep '93 / Cadillac / Jazz Music / New Note/Pinnacle / Wellard

GO AGAIN (Lanphere, Don Sextet)
Which / Go again / Darn that dream / Shangri la / I love you / Midges late valentine / What are you doing for the rest of your life / Maddie's dance / Music that makes me dance / Darkness on the Delta / Maestro
CD ______ HEPCD 2040
Hep / Jul '90 / Cadillac / Jazz Music / New Note/Pinnacle / Wellard

LOPIN' (Lanphere, Don & Bud Shank & Denny Goodhew)
I really didn't think that / Love's question / Lighten up / Time for love / Lope of a dolt / Have you met Miss Jones / Fall / El balie de la munecas (Dance of the dolls) / MK and MK
CD ___ HEPCD 2058
Hep / Sep '94 / Cadillac / Jazz Music / New Note/Pinnacle / Wellard

Lanz, David

BELOVED
Beloved / Leaves on the seine / Madree de la tierra / Madrona / Return to the heart / First light / Courage of the wind / Summer's child / Before the last leaf falls / Reverie / Angel of hope / Cristofori's dream / Variations on a theme from pachebel's canon in D major
CD ___ ND 64009
Narada / Oct '95 / ADA / New Note/ Pinnacle

BRIDGE OF DREAMS (Lanz, David & Paul Speer)
Day in the life / Into the dream / And the world falls away / Whispered in signs / Bridge of dreams / She stands on the mountain, still / Veil of fears / Reverie / Walking with Alfredo / Out of the shadows / Ode to a dark star / Song of the east (in this dream)
CD ___ ND 63024
Narada / Oct '93 / ADA / New Note/ Pinnacle

CHRISTMAS EVE
CD ___ ND 61046
Narada / Oct '94 / ADA / New Note/ Pinnacle

DESERT VISION (Lanz, David & Paul Speer)
Eagle's path / Seguaro / Desert rain / Sculptures / Canyon lands / Carlsbad / White sands / Stormlight / Tawtoma
CD ___ CD 3003
Narada / Aug '92 / ADA / New Note/ Pinnacle

NATURAL STATES (Lanz, David & Paul Speer)
Miranova / Faces of the forest (part 1) / Faces of the forest (part 2) / Behind the waterfall / Mountain / Allegro 1985 / Lento 1984 / Rainforest / First light
CD ___ CD 3001
Narada / Aug '92 / ADA / New Note/ Pinnacle

RETURN TO THE HEART
Return to the heart / Near the still waters of Amsterdam / Madre de la Tierra / Sounds from Koepel / Heartsounds / Manana, mi amor / Cori, Rio, Corre / Behind the waterfall/Desert rain / White shade of pale / Heart of the night / Dream of the forgotten child / Out of the darkness / Cristofori's dream / Gli uccelli di carpi / Variations on a theme / Return to the heart (reprise)
CD ___ CD 4005
Narada / Jun '92 / ADA / New Note/ Pinnacle

SACRED ROAD
Dreamer's waltz / Path with a heart / Take the high road / Where the tall trees grow / Still life / Brother Quixote / Long goodbye / Prelude: The approaching night / Nocturne / Compassionata / On our way home / Circle of friends / Before the last leaf falls / Sacred road
CD ___ ND 64010
Narada / Jun '96 / ADA / New Note/ Pinnacle

SKYLINE FIREDANCE
CD Set ___ CD 4001
Narada / Aug '94 / ADA / New Note/ Pinnacle

Lanza, Mario

BE MY LOVE
Be my love / Temptation / Wanting you / I'll be seeing you / With a song in my heart / Without a song / Danny boy / My wild Irish rose / And this is my beloved / Because / Only a rose / Funiculi, funicula / Come back to Sorrento / Maria Maria / O sole mio / Neapolitan love song / Arrivederci Roma / Ah sweet mystery of life / Look for the silver lining / Memories / Song is you / Ave Maria / You'll never walk alone / Serenade
CD ___ GD 60720
RCA / Mar '91 / BMG

BE MY LOVE (Popular Songs & Ballads)
Donkey serenade / More than you know / Loveliest night of the year / I love thee / Kiss / Softly as in a morning sunrise / Song of songs / Granada / Without a song / My song my love / Diane / Thine alone / Rosary / Ave Maria / Lord's prayer / If / They didn't believe me / Cosi cosa / Funiculi-funicula / Because you're mine / Be my love
CD ___ PLATCD 148
Platinum / Mar '96 / Prism

CHRISTMAS WITH MARIO LANZA
Deck the halls with boughs of holly / Hark the herald angels sing / God rest ye merry gentlemen / Joy to the world / O Christmas tree / I saw three ships / It came upon the midnight clear / Ave Maria / O holy night / Virgin's slumber song / Pieta signore / First Noel / O come all ye faithful (adeste fidelis) / Away in a manger / We three kings / O little town of Bethlehem / Silent night / Guardian angels / I'll walk with God / Lord's prayer
CD ___ 74321411982
RCA Victor / Oct '96 / BMG

COLLECTION, THE
CD ___ COL 061
Collection / Jun '95 / Target/BMG

DON'T FORGET ME
CD ___ 09026614202
RCA / Jun '93 / BMG

ESSENTIAL COLLECTION, THE
Serenade / More than you know / Torna a surriento / Vogliatemi bene / Mamma mia che vo'sape / Because you're mine / Donkey serenade / Softly as in a morning sunrise / Song of songs / Loveleiest night of the year / I love thee / Ave Maria / Without a song / Catari, catari / Cosi, costa / Parig, O'Cara / Un di all azziro spazio / Une furtiva lagrima / O soave fanciulla / E lucevan le stelle / Parlami d'amore, mariu / Temptation / La donna e mobile / Kiss
CD ___ PWKS 4230
Carlton / Nov '94 / Carlton

FOR THE FIRST TIME/ THAT MIDNIGHT KISS
Come prima / Tarantella / O sole mio / Neapolitan dance / Hofbrauhaus song / O mon amour / Mazurka / Pineapple pickers / Pagliacci - vesta la giubba / Otello - finale / Aida - grand finale / Ich liebe dich / Ave Maria / La Boheme / Che gelida manina / Mamma mia che vo'sape / I know, I know, I know / They didn't believe me / Core 'ngrato / Aida - celeste Aida
CD ___ GD 60516
RCA / Mar '91 / BMG

GRANADA
CD ___ PLSCD 205
Pulse / Apr '97 / BMG

IN CONCERT
CD ___ CD 6017
Music / Apr '96 / Target/BMG

LEGENDARY VOICE OF MARIO LANZA, THE (2CD Set)
Serenade / Una furtiva lagrima / Catari, catari / Vogliatemi bene / Mama mia, che vo-'sape / Because you're mine / Donkey serenade / Softly as in a morning sunrise / Song of songs / Loveliest night of the year / My song my love / Granada / Diane / Funiculi funicula / Thine alone / Vesti la giubba / Vuchella / La spagnola / O paradiso / Marechiare / Rosary / Lolita / If / Mattinata / They didn't believe me / Lord's prayer / Be my love / I love thee / Ave Maria / Without a song / Torna a surriento / Cosi, casa / Parigi o cara / Un di all' azzurro spazio / Temptation / E lucevan la stelle / Parlami d'amore, mariu / More than you know / La donna e mobile / Kiss
CD Set ___ MUCD 9506
Musketeer / May '96 / Disc

LIVE IN LONDON
CD ___ 09026618842
RCA Victor / Nov '94 / BMG

LOVELIEST NIGHT OF THE YEAR, THE
CD ___ MU 5049
Musketeer / Oct '92 / Disc

MARIO LANZA
CD ___ ENTCD 245
Entertainers / Mar '92 / Target/BMG

MARIO LANZA
CD ___ MATCD 287
Castle / Mar '94 / BMG

MARIO LANZA
CD ___ HM 013
Harmony / Jun '97 / TKO Magnum

MARIO LANZA COLLECTION, THE
Be my love / I'll never love you / Because you're mine / Song angels sing / Drink, drink, drink / Serenade / Loveliest night of the year / Great / La donna e mobile / Because / For you alone / Golden days / Deep in my heart / If I loved you / Yours is my heart alone / One night of love / Beloved / Beautiful love / With a song in my heart / You are my love / Call me fool / All the things you are / My song, my love / Love is the sweetest thing / Will you remember / Granada / Lolita / Temptation / Lygia / Lady of Spain / This land / Lee ah loo / Tina-lina / Boom biddy boom boom / Bayou lullaby / Lord's prayer / And here you are / Song of songs / Somewhere a voice is calling / I never knew / Ciribiribin / Wonder why / Come dance with me / O sole mio / Younger than springtime / For the first time / Never till now / Arrivederci / If you were mine / Behold / Night to remember / Love in a home / Do you wonder / Softly as in a morning sunrise / One alone / Celeste aida / Flower song / Brindisi - libiamo, libiamo / Questa o quella / Vesti la giubba / Addio all madre
CD Set ___ GD 60889
RCA / Mar '92 / BMG

MARIO LANZA COLLECTION, THE (2CD Set)
CD Set ___ CDSR 123
Telstar / Mar '97 / BMG

MARIO LANZA LIVE
Funiculi, funicula / My song, my love / Granada / Diane / Thine alone / Vesti la giubba / Vuchella / Toselli's serenade / Because you're mine / Loveliest night of the year / O paradiso / Marechiare / Rosary / Lolita / If / Mattinata / They didn't believe me / Lord's prayer / Be my love
CD ___ DATOM 2
A Touch Of Magic / Apr '94 / Harmonia Mundi

MARIO LANZA ON RADIO (CBS Radio Show From The Fifties)
CD ___ CDMR 1121
Radiola / Oct '90 / Pinnacle

MARIO LANZA SHOWS, THE
Introduction / Granada / Oh lady be good: *Sinatra, Ray & His Orchestra* / Serenade / Hello young lovers: *MacKenzie, Giselle* / La Fiacre: *MacKenzie, Giselle* / Because / Dizzy fingers: *Sinatra, Ray & His Orchestra* / Be my love / Funiculi, Funicula / A vucchella / Continental: *Sinatra, Ray & His Orchestra* / Fairyland: *MacKenzie, Giselle* / I'm falling in love with someone / Fiddle faddle: *Sinatra, Ray & His Orchestra* / Cock-eyed optimist: *MacKenzie, Giselle* / Torne Sorrento / Closing
CD ___ OTA 101910
On The Air / Feb '97 / Target/BMG

MY SONG OF LOVE
Because / My song of love / Granada / Dianne / Vesti la Giubba / Funiculi funicula / Thine alone / A Vucchella / Toselli's serenade / O paradiso / Marechiare / Rosary / Lolita / If / Mattinata / They didn't believe me / Lord's prayer / Be my love / Loveliest night of the year
CD ___ QED 139
Tring / Nov '96 / Tring

SERENADE
Serenade / La donna e mobile / Because you're mine / Donkey serenade / Ave Maria / My song, my love / Diane / Loveliest night of the year / Funiculi funicula / Thine alone / Granada / Vesta la giubba / A vucella / Toselli's serenade / O paradiso / A marechiare / Rosary / If / Be my love / Lord's prayer
CD ___ SUMCD 4029
Summit / Nov '96 / Sound & Media

ULTIMATE COLLECTION, THE
Be my love / Drink, drink, drink / La donna e mobile / Danny Boy / Granada / Because you're mine / Ave Maria / Valencia / Loveliest night of the year / Song of India / Because / O sole mio / Donkey serenade / Vesti la giubba / Serenade / Funiculi, funicula / Golden days / Arrivederci Roma / You'll never walk alone / Beloved / Come prima / E lucevan le stelle / Santa Lucia / I'll walk with God
CD ___ 74321185742
RCA Victor / Jan '94 / BMG

UNFORGETTABLE CLASSICS
CD ___ MACCD 105
Autograph / Aug '96 / BMG

WITH A SONG IN MY HEART (The Love Collection)
With a song in my heart / Be my love / Because you're mine / Loveliest night of the year / Because / Temptation / Beloved / Song is you / Serenade (from the student prince) / Lover come back to me (from new moon) / My wild irish rose / More than you know / Younger than springtime / September song / On the street where you live / Only a rose / Falling in love with love / And this is my beloved / My romance / This nearly was mine / All the things you are / I'll be seeing you
CD ___ 74321400582
Camden / Jan '97 / BMG

WITHOUT A SONG
Cose cosa / Donkey serenade / Parliamo d'amore Maria / Kiss / Recondito armante / Softly as in a morning sunrise / Una furtiva lagrima / Song of songs / Mamma mia che vo'sape / Come back to sorrento / Without a song / O sole mio / Ave maria / Perigi o cara / Vogliddemi bene, un bene piccolino / O souve funchilla / More than you know / La spagnola
CD ___ MUCD 9019
Musketeer / Apr '95 / Disc

YOU'LL NEVER WALK ALONE
I'll walk with God / Trembling of a leaf / Lord's prayer / Love in a home / Somebody bigger than you and I / Through the years / Ave Maria / Without a song / Hills of home / I love thee / Rosary / Look for the silver lining / None but the lonely heart / My buddy / Guardian angels / Somewhere a voice is calling / Trees / Ave Maria / Because / Roses of Picardy / For you alone / You'll never walk alone
CD ___ 09026680732
RCA Victor / Jun '95 / BMG

Lao, Molam

MUSIC FROM SOUTHERN LAOS
CD ___ NI 5401CD
Nimbus / Jun '94 / Nimbus

LAPD

WHO'S LAUGHING
CD ___ TX 93152
Roadrunner / May '91 / PolyGram

LaPorta, John

MOST MINOR, THE (LaPorta, John Quartet)
CD ___ FSRCD 208
Fresh Sound / Oct '96 / Discovery / Jazz Music

Lara, Agustin

INTERPRETA SUS CANCIONES DE AMOR
CD ___ ALCD 018
Alma Latina / Jul '96 / Discovery

Lara, Catherine

LA ROCKEUSE DE DIAMANTS
CD ___ 71015AE880
Ariola / '88 / BMG

Laraaji

DAYS OF RADIANCE
Dance no. 1 / Dance no. 2 / Dance no. 3 / Meditation / Meditation no.2
CD ___ EEGCD 19
EG / '87 / EMI

FLOW GOES THE UNIVERSE
Being here / Space choir / Cave in England / Immersion / Zither dance / Mbira dance / Laughing in tongues / Deep celestial / In continuum / Silence I / Silence II / Silence III / Silence IV / Silence V
CD ___ ASCD 10
All Saints / Apr '96 / Discovery / Vital

Larade, Alexandra

VINI DAN TCHEW
CD ___ CD 84002
Sonodisc/Atis / Jan '97 / Stern's

Lard

PURE CHEWING SATISFACTION
CD ___ VIRUS 199CD
Alternative Tentacles / Jun '97 / Plastic Head

Lard Free

UNNAMED
CD ___ 14915
Spalax / Jun '97 / ADA / Cargo / Direct / Discovery / Greyhound

Larguinho, Mathilde

BEST OF FADO PORTUGUESE
CD ___ EUCD 1174
ARC / '91 / ADA / ARC Music

Lark

0002K
CD ___ 2100053
Indisc / Jun '93 / Pinnacle

Larkin

O'CEAN
Emergence / Communitizing
CD ___ ND 62812
Narada / Aug '97 / ADA / New Note/ Pinnacle

Larkin, Kenny

ART OF DANCE
CD ___ SUB 48062
Distance / Mar '96 / 3mv/Sony / Prime

METAPHOR
Intro / Metaphor / Nocturnal / Loop 1 / Java / Groove / Loop 15 / Catatonic part 2 / Catatonic (first state) / Loop 2 / Soul man / Sympthy / Butterflies / Amethyst
CD ___ RS 95954CD
R&S / Feb '95 / Vital

Larkin, Patty

ANGELS RUNNING
Who holds your hand / Do not disturb / Banish misfortune / Open hand / Might as well dance / Ain't that as good / Helen / I told him that my dog wouldn't run / Pundits and poets / Booth of glass / Winter wind
CD ___ 72902103182
High Street / Nov '93 / BMG

I'M FINE
Rescue me / Justine / Window / Dangerous / I'm fine / Pucker up / Lately / On the run / Don't want to give it up / Island of time / If I were made of metal / Caffeine / Valentine / Day to day
CD ___ CDPH 1115
Philo / Oct '88 / ADA / CM / Direct

STEP INTO THE LIGHT
CD ______ PH 1103CD
Philo / Apr '94 / ADA / CM / Direct

Larkins, Ellis

LIVE AT MAYBECK RECITAL HALL VOL.22
How'd ya like to love me / Perfume and rain / Oh lady be good / I don't want to cry anymore / Blue skies / No more/God bless' The Child / I let a song go out of my heart / Spring will be a little late this year / Leave me alone / Things ain't what they used to be / When a woman loves a man/I'm through with love
CD ______ CCD 4533
Concord Jazz / Nov '92 / New Note/ Pinnacle

SMOOTH ONE, A
CD ______ BLE 591232
Black & Blue / Oct '94 / Discovery / Koch / Wellard

Larrissey, Brendan

FLICK OF THE WRIST
CD ______ CBM 016CD
Cross Border Media / Jul '95 / ADA / Direct / Grapevine/PolyGram

Larsen, Grey

GATHERING, THE
CD ______ SHCD 1133
Sugar Hill / Jan '97 / ADA / CM / Direct / Koch / Roots

ORANGE TREE, THE (Larsen, Grey & Andre Marchand)
CD ______ SHCD 1136
Sugar Hill / Apr '94 / ADA / CM / Direct / Koch / Roots

Larsen, Morton Gunnar

JELLY ROLL (Larsen, Morton Gunnar & Vernel Bagneris)
CD ______ BCD 400
GHB / Mar '97 / Jazz Music

Larson, Nicolette

NICOLETTE
Lotta love / Rumba girl / You send me / Can't get away from you / Mexican divorce / Baby, don't you do it / Give a little / Angels / Rejoiced / French waltz / Come early mornin' last in love
CD ______ 7599273662
WEA / Jan '96 / Warner Music

La's

LA'S
Son of a gun / I can't sleep / Timeless melody / Liberty ship / There she goes / Doledrum / Feelin' / Way out / IOU / Freedom song / Failure / Looking glass
CD ______ 8282022
Go Discs / Nov '90 / PolyGram

Las Hermanas Mendoza

JUANITA Y MARIA
CD ______ ARHCD 430
Arhoolie / Jun '95 / ADA / Cadillac / Direct

LaSalle, Denise

HERE I AM AGAIN
Here I am again / Married, but not to each other / Share your man with me / I wanna do what's on your mind / Trying to forget / My brand on you / Stay with me awhile / Anytime is the right time / Don't nobody live here (by the name of fool) / Hit and run / We've got love / Get up off my mind / Who's the fool / Best thing I ever had
CD ______ CDSEW 066
Westbound / Sep '93 / Pinnacle

TRAPPED BY A THING CALLED LOVE/ ON THE LOOSE
Man size job / What it takes to get a good woman / Harper Valley PTA / What am I doing wrong / Breaking up somebody's home / There ain't enough hate around / Your man and your best friend / Lean on me / Making a good thing better / I'm over you / I'm satisfied / Trapped by a thing called love / Now run and tell that / Heartbreaker of the year / Goody goody getter / Catch me if you can / Hung up, strung out / Do me right / Deeper I go (better it gets) / You'll lose a good thing / Keeping it coming / It's too late
CD Set ______ CDSEWD 018
Westbound / Feb '92 / Pinnacle

Lascelles

ROCK OIL
CD ______ OERCD 003
Orange Egg / Jun '97 / Alphamagic / Pinnacle / Vital

Lascelles Jams

TURN OFF THE LIGHTS
CD ______ JASCD 3
Sarge / Apr '97 / Jet Star

Lashout

DARKEST HOUR, THE
CD ______ SSR 001
Stormstrike / Nov '94 / Plastic Head

WHAT ABSCENCE YIELDS
CD ______ SSR 008CD
Stormstrike / Jul '96 / Plastic Head

Lask, Ulrich

INDEAN POA
CD ______ CMPCD 62
CMP / Sep '95 / Cargo / Grapevine/ PolyGram / Vital/SAM

Lasley, Tony

LATIN MOON
CD ______ M 46CD
World Disc / Aug '96 / Gallant

LaSpina, Steve

WHEN I'M ALONE (LaSpina, Steve Quintet)
CD ______ SCCD 31376
Steeplechase / Feb '96 / Discovery / Impetus

Lassigue Bendthaus

MATTER
CD ______ KK 113
KK / Jan '94 / Plastic Head

RENDER
CD ______ KK 115CD
KK / May '94 / Plastic Head

Last

AWAKENING
CD ______ SST 230CD
SST / Jul '89 / Plastic Head

Last Dance

TRAGEDY
CD ______ EFA 121692
Apollyon / Jan '96 / SRD

Last, David

INTRODUCING DAVID LAST
Nocturne in eb / Skye boat song/Scottish soldier / Bewitched, bothered and bewildered / C'est si bon/I love Paris / Don't cry for me Argentina / Sometimes when we touch/Shenandoah / My boy lollipop / Swingin' safari / Lass of Richmond Hill / Farmer and the cowman/Alias Smith and Jones / Only you / Feelings/Music of the night / Tritsch tratsch polka / Eye level/Windmill in old Amsterdam / Unforgettable/When I fall in love / Minuet in G/Pathetique sonata
CD ______ CDTS 035
Maestro / Aug '93 / Savoy

MELODIES FOR YOU
CD ______ CDTS 038
Maestro / Sep '93 / Savoy

Last Delay

JAIL
CD ______ EFA 125332
Celtic Circle / Oct '95 / SRD

Last Exit

BEST OF LAST EXIT LIVE, THE
CD ______ EMCD 110
Enemy / Feb '90 / Grapevine/PolyGram

IRON PATH
Prayer / Iron path / Black bat / Marked for death / Fire drum / Detonator / Sand dancer / Cut and run / Eye for an eye / Devil's rain
CD ______ CDVE 38
Venture / Feb '89 / EMI

LAST EXIT
CD ______ EMY 1012
Enemy / Nov '94 / Grapevine/PolyGram

NOISE OF TROUBLE
CD ______ EMY 1032
Enemy / Oct '92 / Grapevine/PolyGram

Last Great Dreamers

RETROSEXUAL
CD ______ CDBLEED 10
Bleeding Hearts / Oct '94 / Pinnacle

Last Illusion

IN A ROOTSMAN STYLE
CD ______ JMF 001CD
Jah Mountain Fountain / Feb '95 / SRD

Last, James

AT ST. PATRICK'S CATHEDRAL, DUBLIN
In the cathedral / Ave Maria / Conversation / An caoineadh / Scherzo / Away in a manger / Intermezzo of Notre Dame / Darkest midnight / Cavalleria rusticana / Holly and the ivy / Coulin / Seinn ailliu / Abide with me
CD ______ 8236692
Polydor / Dec '84 / PolyGram

BEST FROM 150 GOLD, THE
Starparade / Hora staccato / Charmaine / Morgens um sieben (morning's at seven) / Don't cry for me Argentina / Happy music / La entrada del bilbao / Knock on wood / Ballade pour Adeline / Hppy heart / Der seinsamer hirte (the lonely shepherd) / Liechtensteiner polka / Romance for violin and orchestra / Anvil polka / Salome / Petersburger schlittenfahrt
CD ______ 8355622
Polydor / Oct '90 / PolyGram

BLUEBIRD
Morning at Cornwall / Proud as a peacock / Love bird / Sandpiper / Quiberon / Bird of paradise / Alassio / Night owl / Over valley and mountain / Bill MaGee / Kingfisher / Roter Milan
CD ______ 8115172
Polydor / '88 / PolyGram

BY REQUEST
Mornings at 7 / Elvira Madigan / Air that I breathe / Adagio from the New World Symphony / Lonely shepherd / Roses of the south / Sabre dance / Lonely bull / Tulips from Amsterdam / Seduction / Zip a dee doo dah / Spanish eyes / Valencia / That's life
CD ______ 8317862
Polydor / Apr '87 / PolyGram

CHRISTMAS ALBUM, THE
Ave verum corpus / Winter / Here I stand at your cradle / Largo / For unto us a child is born / Adagio / Largo / Christmas concerto / Thus loved God the world
CD ______ 5506412
Spectrum / Nov '96 / PolyGram

CLASSIC TOUCH
Overture marriage of Figaro / Traumerei / Eine kleine nachtmusik / Intermezzo from cavalleria rusticana / Chanson triste / Rodrigo's guitar concerto de Aranjuez / Barcarolle / In the hall of the mountain king / Adagio from the sonata pathetique no.8 / Libestraum / Elvira Madigan / Hungarian dance No. 5 / Ballet music / Bolero
CD ______ 5500982
Spectrum / Oct '93 / PolyGram

CLASSICS
Mascagni's cavalleria / Schumann's symphony no.2 / Bach's double violin concerto / Hayden's trumpet concerto / Symphonie fantastique / Mozart's symphony no.39 / Beethoven's romance no.1 / Gieg's incidental music to Peer Gynt / Brahms symphony no.3
CD ______ 8000172
Polydor / Sep '88 / PolyGram

CLASSICS BY MOONLIGHT
Bolero / Romeo and Juliet / Swan lake / New World symphony / Spring from 'The four seasons' / Rhapsody in blue / Morning / Blue danube / Rhapsody on a theme by Paganini / Nabucco
CD ______ 8432182
Polydor / Mar '90 / PolyGram

DANCE DANCE DANCE
You win again / Frankie / Reet petite / Love will save the day / Saving all my love for you / Power of love / You keep me hangin' on / Heaven is a place on earth / Respect yourself / Don't leave me this way / Everybody have fun tonight / Chain reaction / Gimme hope Jo'anna / Easy lover / Rhythm is gonna get you / Doctorin' the tardis / So macho / Always on my mind / Nothing's gonna stop us now / La Bamba / My toot toot
CD ______ 8374532
Polydor / Nov '88 / PolyGram

GAMES THAT LOVERS PLAY
Lara's theme / Man and a woman / Games that lovers play / This is my song / What now my love / Close your eyes / I left my heart in San Francisco / Fly me to the moon / Now I know / Elizabethan serenade / Never on Sunday / Sandy's theme
CD ______ 8216102
Polydor / PolyGram

HAPPY HEART
Happy heart / Amboss polka / Happy Luxemburg / Games that lovers play / Music from across the way / Mornings at seven / Fool / I left my heart in San Francisco / Happy music / Root beer rag / Lonely shepherd
CD ______ 8396132
Polydor / Aug '89 / PolyGram

IN IRELAND
CD ______ 8299272
Polydor / '88 / PolyGram

INSTRUMENTAL FOREVER
String of pearls / Tico tico / Granada / Brazil / St. Louis blues march / Havah nagilah / Petite fleur / Cherry pink and apple blossom white / You are my sunshine / La Bamba / Amor amor amor / Copacabana
CD ______ 8152502
Polydor / '89 / PolyGram

JAMES LAST IN SCOTLAND
Skye boat song / My love is like a red red rose / I love a lassie / Roamin' in the gloamin' / Scottish soldier / Will ye no' come back again / I belong to Glasgow / Flower of Scotland / Auld lang syne / Ye banks and braes o' bonnie Doon / Days of auld lang syne / Keel row / Barren rocks of Aden / Loch Lomond / My bonnie Mary of Argyle / Annie laurie
CD ______ 8237432
Polydor / Jun '85 / PolyGram

JAMES LAST PLAYS ANDREW LLOYD WEBBER
With one look / Jesus Christ Superstar / Memory / I don't know how to love him / Music of the night / Any dream will do / Love changes everything / Don't cry for me Argentina / Tell me on a Sunday / Take that look off your face / Phantom of the opera / Point of no return
CD ______ 5199102
Polydor / Nov '93 / PolyGram

LEAVE THE BEST TO LAST
Tell her about it / Karma chameleon / Wake me up before you go go / Heartbreaker / Take a chance on me / You can't hurry love / Uptown girl / Caribbean queen (no more love on the run) / That was yesterday / Ghostbusters / Hooray hooray it's a holiholiday / Agadoo / I just called to say I love you / Wanderer / Easy lover / Every breath you take / You're my heart you're my soul / Super trouper / Half a minute / Do the conga / Hello / One more night / Red red wine / Live is life / Imagine
CD ______ 8273932
Polydor / Sep '85 / PolyGram

LIVE IN LONDON
Intro '78 / Tiger feet / Radar love / Jesus loves you / Bridge over troubled water / I've got you under my skin / Was ich dir sagen will / Jog dig oas / Rum and coca cola / Quando, quando, quando / South America take it away / Lonely shepherd / Larry O'Gaff / Fire on the mountain / Center amigos / Schwarze estrella / Ay ay ay / Costa brava / Eso es el amor / Star Wars / West Side story / Silly love songs / With one more look at you / Watch closely now / Love me tender / Rip it up / Don't be cruel / Jailhouse rock / Hound dog / Chicken reel / Turkey in the straw / Orange blossom special / Cockles and mussels / Daisy Daisy / Abide with me / Yes sir, I can boogie / Sorry I'm a lady / Don't leave me this way / Don't cry for me Argentina / Games that lovers play
CD ______ 8438092
Polydor / Nov '90 / PolyGram

MAKE THE PARTY LAST
Cracklin' Rosie / Rose garden / Knock three times / Banks of the Ohio / Song sung blue / Tie a yellow ribbon round the ole oak tree / Summer knows / Close to you / Soley soley / Is this the way to Amarillo / You are the sunshine of my life / Never can say goodbye / La bamba / Hava nagila / Pushbike song / What have they done to my song Ma / Joy to the world / What now my love / I don't know how to love him / In the summertime / Goodbye Sam, hello Samantha / I hear you knocking / (We're gonna) Rock around the clock / See you later alligator / Hound dog
CD ______ 5500332
Spectrum / May '93 / PolyGram

MUSIC OF JAMES LAST, THE
CD ______ MACCD 240
Autograph / Aug '96 / BMG

MUSICAL STYLE OF JAMES LAST, THE (London Pops Orchestra)
Exodus theme / La bamba / You won't find another fool like me / Old fashioned way / Solitaire / Barbara Ann / Funny funny / Pushbike song / It never rains in Southern California / Help yourself / My name is Jack / La bamba / Cracklin' Rosie / Montego bay / Beautiful dreamer / Help yourself / Top of the world / Paper roses / Walk right back / Your Mama don't dance / Yellow river / Ob-la-di ob-la-da / Satisfaction / I've got you under my skin / My sweet Lord / Danny / MacArthur Park / Chitty chitty bang bang / When I'm dead and gone
CD ______ QED 177
Tring / Nov '96 / Tring

PEACE
CD ______ 5176392
Polydor / Jan '93 / PolyGram

PLAYS MOZART
CD ______ 8390432
Polydor / Mar '89 / PolyGram

POP SYMPHONIES (Last, James Orchestra)
Lady in red / Nights in white satin / Power of love / Another day in love / Hotel California / Living years / Sorry seems to be the hardest word / Broken wings / Africa / One more night / Hard to say i'm sorry / Angelia
CD ______ 8494292
Polydor / Jun '91 / PolyGram

ROSE OF TRALEE AND OTHER IRISH FAVOURITES
Maggie / Irish stew / Coulin / Come back to Erin / Ril mhor bhaile an chalaidh / An eriskay love lilt / On the banks of my own lovely Lee / Summer in Dublin / When Irish eyes are smiling / Rose of Tralee / Londonderry air / Sweepstake / Cockles and mussels / IRELAND
CD ______ 8159842
Polydor / '88 / PolyGram

ROSES FROM THE SOUTH (James Last Plays Johann Strauss)
Roses from the South / Leichtes blut / Tales from the Vienna Woods / Annen polka / Voices of spring / Waltz / Thunder and lightning / Emperor waltz / Eljen a magyar / Radetzky march
CD 8237382
Polydor / Aug '88 / PolyGram

TENDERLY
(I left my heart) In San Fransisco / Air that I breathe / Fly me to the moon / I don't know how to love him / This is my song / Man and a woman / Elizabethan serenade / Close your eyes / Hey Jude / What now my love / Games that lovers play / Whiter shade of pale / Speak softly love / Lara's theme / Now I know / Romeo and Juliet / Wedding song (there is love) / Tenderly
CD 5513192
Spectrum / Mar '96 / PolyGram

TWO SIDES OF JAMES LAST, THE (2CD Set)
CD Set 5338822
Polydor / Nov '96 / PolyGram

VERY BEST OF JAMES LAST, THE
Whiter shade of pale / Bolero / From a distance / Yesterday / Granada / Mornings at seven / Penny Lane / Loneley shepherd / House of the rising sun / In the mood / Sacrifice / Viva Espana / Maggie / Roses from the South / Everything I do (I do it for you) / Games that lovers play
CD 5295562
Polydor / Oct '95 / PolyGram

Last Poets

BEST OF THE LAST POETS, THE
CD CDNEW 105
Charly / Mar '97 / Koch

BEST OF THE PRIME TIME RHYME VOL.2
El pluribus unum / Tranquility / African slave / Beyonder / Oh my people / What will you do / Enough emotion / Unholy alliance
CD SP 21CD
On The One / Nov '95 / New Note/Pinnacle / SRD

CHASTISEMENT
Tribute to Obani / Jazzoetry / Black soldier / E pluribus unum / Hands off / Lone ranger / Before the white man came / Bird's word
CD CPCD 822
Charly / Apr '97 / Koch

DELIGHTS OF THE GARDEN (Last Poets & Bernard Purdie)
It's a trip / Ho Chi Minh / Blessed are those who struggle / Pill / Delights of the garden / Beyonder
CD CPCD 8191
Charly / Sep '96 / Koch

FREEDOM EXPRESS
Tough enough / Woodshed walk / Freedom express / Geronimo / Un-Holy alliance
CD MPG 74040
Movieplay Gold / Jan '97 / Target/BMG

HOLY TERROR
Invocation / Homesick / Black rage / Mentality / Last rite / Talk show / Illusion of self / If only we knew / Funk / Phelhourinho
CD RCD 10319
Black Arc / Mar '97 / Vital

LAST POETS
CD CPCD 8184
Charly / Jun '96 / Koch

OH MY PEOPLE
CD CPCD 8174
Charly / Mar '96 / Koch

THIS IS MADNESS
CD CPCD 8154
Celluloid / Nov '95 / Discovery / Koch

Last Real Texas Blues Band

LAST REAL TEXAS BLUES BAND
CD ANT 0036
Antones / May '95 / ADA / Hot Shot

Last Straw

ALONE ON A STONE
CD KSCD 9591
Kissing Spell / Jun '97 / Greyhound

Laswell, Bill

ASANA
Devabandha / Om namah shiva / Matra
CD ADC 7
Douglas Music / Jul '97 / Cadillac / New Note/Pinnacle

AXIOM AMBIENT - LOST IN THE TRANSLATION
Eternal drift / Peace / Aum / Cosmic Trigger / Dharmapala / Flash of panic / Holy mountain / Ruins / Eternal drift (Techno mix) / Aum (Drift mix)
CD Set 5240532
Axiom / Nov '94 / PolyGram / Vital

BASELINES
CD CPCD 8284
Charly / Apr '97 / Koch

CITY OF LIGHT
CD SR 114
Sub Rosa / Jun '97 / Direct / RTM/Disc / SRD / Vital

DIVINATION - LIGHT IN EXTENSION
Divination / Seven heavens / Erratta / Delta / Tian zhen / Agrippa / Godspeed / Ain soph aour / Najam-al-din / Dead slow / Baraka / Silent fields / Evil eye / Dream light / Journeys / Last words of hassan I sabbath
CD Set SHCDD 001
Stoned Heights / Jun '94 / PolyGram / Vital

DUB MELTDOWN (Laswell, Bill & Style Scott)
CD EFA 012212
Word Sound Recordings / Aug '97 / Cargo / SRD

EQUATIONS OF ETERNITY (Laswell, Bill & Mick Harris/Eraldo Bernochi)
CD WSCD 015
Word Sound Recordings / Jan '97 / Cargo / SRD

FUNKRONMICON
Order within the universe / Under the influence / If six was nine / Orbitron attack / Cosmic slop / Free bass / Tell the world / Pray my soul / Hideous mutant freekz / Sax machine / Animal behaviour / Trumpets and violins, violins / Telling time / Jungle free bass / Blackout / Sacred to the pain
CD Set 5240772
Axiom / Aug '95 / PolyGram / Vital

HEAR NO EVIL
Lost roads / Bullet hole memory / Illinois central / Assassin / Stations of the cross / Kingdom come
CD CDVE 12
Venture / Mar '88 / EMI

INTO THE OUTLANDS
Voice of thunder / Speed of light
CD MPG 74043
Movieplay Gold / Jun '97 / Target/BMG

OSCILLATIONS
CD QUANTUM 726
Sub Rosa / Sep '97 / Direct / RTM/Disc / SRD / Vital

PHAT DUB VOL.1
CD APC 003
APC Tracks / Jul '97 / Greyhound

PHAT DUB VOL.2
CD APC 004
APC Tracks / Jul '97 / Greyhound

SACRED SYSTEM
CD RUSCD 821
ROIR / Jul '96 / Plastic Head / Shellshock/ Disc

Lateef, Yusef

AFRICAN-AMERICAN EPIC SUITE
CD 892142
Act / Jun '94 / New Note/Pinnacle

BLUE YUSUF LATEEF, THE
CD 7567822702
WEA / Mar '93 / Warner Music

EASTERN SOUNDS
CD OJCCD 612
Original Jazz Classics / Feb '92 / Complete/Pinnacle / Jazz Music / Wellard

NOCTURNES
CD 7567819772
Atlantic / Jul '93 / Warner Music

Latimer

LATIMER
Neolida / Kiss / Stabs the reason / Carolida / Chicken the goon / Cold front killer / Dirgesque / Hold down / Auto-redeemer / Stringbender / Poseur / Rek O Kut
CD WDOM 016CD
World Domination / May '95 / Pinnacle / RTM/Disc

LIVE FROM SOUR CITY
Citizen jive / Bullseye / Used cars / Bloated in Detroit / Motel motel / Start with me / Competition no / Regressing / Beats sored / Ohio / Finger loss / Sour city
CD WD 00442
World Domination / Mar '97 / Pinnacle / RTM/Disc

Latimore

SWEET VIBRATIONS
Stormy Monday / Ain't nothin' you can do / Snap your fingers / Let's straighten it out / Keep the home fire burnin' / There's a redneck in the sould band / Qualified man / It ain't where you been / Something 'bout you / Sweet vibrations / I get lifted / Dig a little deeper / Long distance love
CD NEXCD 166
Sequel / May '91 / BMG

Latin Jazz Quintet

LATIN JAZZ QUINTET
CD FCD 24129
Fantasy / Oct '93 / Jazz Music / Pinnacle / Wellard

Latin Playboys

LATIN PLAYBOYS
Viva la raza / Ten believers / Chinese surprise / Mira / Manifold de amour / New zandu / Rudy's party / If / Same brown earth / Lagoon / Gone / Crayon sun / Pink steps / Forever nightshade Mary
CD 8282222
London / May '94 / PolyGram

Latin Quarter

BRINGING ROSA HOME
CD SPV 08544742
SPV / Mar '97 / Koch / Plastic Head

LONG PIG
Long pig / Better helter skelter / King for a day / Bitter to the south / Phil Ochs / More than a trace / Desert rose / Contention city / Hoopoe / Church on fire / Coming down to pray / Like a miracle / Faith and reason
CD CLD 91082
Cloud Nine / Jun '95 / Koch / Silva Screen

Latin Touch

FIESTA
La senorita / Loco / Misunderstood / Fiesta / Conchita / Adios amigo / Ti me cuando / My love / Viva / Soul mate / Without you / Please tell me (illusions)
CD 74321183242
Ariola Express / Feb '94 / BMG

Latryx

LATRYX
Latryx / Say that / Quickening (the wreckoning part II) / Balcony beach / Live at 903 '94 / Muzapper's mix (aim for the flickering flame/rankin no.1) / Funky granules / Bad news / Off (with) their heads (be prompt) / Interlude (a double deuce) / Burnt pride / Scratchapella (veinte tres segundos) / Wreckoning / Burning hot in Cali on a Saturday night
CD SLSCD 001
Solesides / Mar '97 / Cargo / Vital

Lattau, Kevin

KEVIN LETTAU
CD NOVA 9135
Nova / Jan '93 / New Note/Pinnacle

Lauder, Harry

I LOVE A LASSIE
I love a lassie / Roamin' in the gloamin' / Wedding of Sandy McNab / Waggle o' the kilt / O sing to me the auld Scotch songs / When I get back to bonnie Scotland / Keep right on to the end of the road / It's just like being at home / Bonnie Leezie Lindsay / I'm looking for a bonnie lass tae love me / Love makes the world a merry go round / She is my daisy / Wee Deoch an' Doris / I think I'll get wed in the summer / I like my old home town / I'm the boss of the hoose / I've loved her ever since she was a baby / Soosie MacLean
CD PASTCD 9719
Flapper / Oct '90 / Pinnacle

SIR HARRY LAUDER (Britain's First Knight Of The Music Hall)
Overture - The Harry Lauder medley / I love a lassie / Will you stop your tickling jock / Breakfast in bed / Roamin' in the gloamin' / Waggle o' the kilt / Soosie Maclean / There's a wee hoose' mang the heather / I've just got off the chain / Just a wee deoch an' Doris / We parted on the shore / Keep right on to the end of the road
CD LCOM 5232
Lismor / May '94 / ADA / Direct / Duncans / Lismor

Lauderdale, Jim

PERSIMMONS
Life by numbers / Do you like it / And that's a lot / Am I only dreaming this / Don't leave your light low / Seems like you're gonna take me back / I thought we had a deal / Tears so strong / Please pardon me / Some things are too good to last / Nobody's perfect / Had a little time / That's not right babe / Optimistic messenger / Jupiter's rising
CD UPSTART 035
Upstart / Oct '96 / ADA / Direct

PLANET OF LOVE
Heaven's flame / Maybe / Wake up screaming / I wasn't fooling around / Bless her heart / Where the sidewalk ends / Planet of love / King of broken hearts / What you don't know / My last request
CD 7599265562
Reprise / May '92 / Warner Music

Laudet, Francois

MY DRUMMER IS RICH... (Laudet, Francois Big Band)
CD BBRC 9312
Big Blue / Jan '94 / Harmonia Mundi

Laughing Clowns

GHOSTS OF AN IDEAL WIFE
Crystal clear / Diabolic creature / No words of honour / Winter's way / Ghosts of an ideal wife / Only one that knows / New bully in town / It gets so sentimental / Flypaper
CD HOT 1013CD
Hot / Nov '93 / Hot Records

GOLDEN DAYS WHEN GIANTS WALKED THE EARTH
Eternally yours / Theme from Mad flies, mad flies / Winter's way / Mr. Uddich-Smuddich / Holy Joe / I don't know what I want / Possessions / Eulogy / Flypaper / Every dog has it's day
CD HOT 1055CD
Hot / Aug '95 / Hot Records

Laughing Heads

LAUGHING HEADS
CD RR 800CD
Resounding / Nov '96 / ADA

Laughing Hyenas

CRAWL
CD TG 102CD
Touch & Go / Oct '92 / SRD

HARD TIMES
CD TG 136CD
Touch & Go / Feb '95 / SRD

MERRY GO ROUND
CD TG 25CD
Touch & Go / Sep '95 / SRD

Laughlin, Tim

NEW ORLEANS RHYTHM
CD JCD 235
Jazzology / Apr '94 / Jazz Music

NEW ORLEANS SWING
CD JCD 265
Jazzology / Dec '95 / Jazz Music

SWING THAT MUSIC (Laughlin, Tim & Jack Maheu)
CD JCD 245
Jazzology / Jun '95 / Jazz Music

Laughner, Peter

TAKE THE GUITAR PLAYER FOR A RIDE
Baudelaire / Rock it down / Sylvia Plath / Pledging my time / Lullaby / In the bar / Cinderlla backstreet / Only love can break your heart / Visions of Johanna / Amphetamine / Life stinks / What love is / Ain't it fun / Dear Richard / Calvary cross / Take your love away / Baby's on fire / Me and the devil blues
CD TK 92CD045
T/K / Aug '94 / Pinnacle

Laula, Carol

STILL
Bad case of you / Child of mine / It's true / Gonna bu / Home to sister / Stay with me angel / Restless / Old brick wall / By the minute / White dress / Stars with my coffee
CD IRCD 020
Iona / '93 / ADA / Direct / Duncans

Laundry

BLACK TONGUE
Windsheild / Blizzard face / Blacktongue / Monarch man / Canvas / Monkey's wrench / Misery alarm / Hole / Moss covered rocks / Skin / Stitch / Bloodclot / Laundry / Nineteen
CD MR 0982
Mammoth / Feb '95 / Vital

Lauper, Cyndi

HAT FULL OF STARS
That's what I think / Product of misery / Who let in the rain / Lies / Broken glass / Sally's pigeons / Feels like Christmas / Dear John / Like I used to / Someone like me / Part hate / Hat full of stars
CD 4730542
Epic / Sep '96 / Sony

NIGHT TO REMEMBER, A/SHE'S SO UNUSUAL/TRUE COLORS (3CD Set)
I drove all night / Primitive / My first night without you / Like a cat / Heading west / Night to remember / Unconditional love / Insecurious / Dancing with a stranger / I don't want to be your friend / Kindred spirit / Money changes everything / Girls just wanna have fun / When you were mine / Time after time / She bop / All through the night / Witness / I'll kiss you / She's so unusual / Yeah yeah / Change of heart / Maybe he'll know / Boy blue / True colors / Calm inside the storm / What's going on / Iko iko / Faraway nearby / 911 / One track mind
CD Set 4716222
Epic / Oct '94 / Sony

SHE'S SO UNUSUAL
Money changes everything / Girls just wanna have fun / When you were mine / Time after time / She bop / All through the night / Witness / I'll kiss you / He's so unusual / Yeah yeah
CD 4633622
Epic / Feb '89 / Sony

SHE'S SO UNUSUAL/A NIGHT TO REMEMBER
Money changes everything / Girls just wanna have fun / When you were mine / Time after time / She bop / All through the night / Witness / I'll kiss you / He's so unusual / Yeah yeah / Intro / I drove all night / My first night without you / Like a cat / Heading West / Night to remember / Unconditional love / Insecurious / Dancing with a stranger / I don't want to be your friend / Kindred spirit
CD Set 4784832
Epic / Mar '95 / Sony

SHE'S SO UNUSUAL/TRUE COLORS/A NIGHT TO REMEMBER (3CD Set)
Money changes everything / Girls just want to have fun / When you were mine / Time after time / She bop / All through the night / Witness / I'll kiss you / He's so unusual / Yeah yeah / Change of heart / Maybe he'll know / Boy blue / True colors / Calm inside the storm / What's going on / Iko iko / Faraway / Nearby / 911 / One track mind / Intro / I drove all night / Primitive / My first night without you / Like a cat / Heading West / Night to remember / Unconditional love / Insecurious / Dancing with a stranger / I don't want to be your friend / Kindred spirit
CD Set 4853222
Epic / Oct '96 / Sony

SISTERS OF AVALON
Sisters of Avalon / Ballad of Cleo and Joe / Fall into your dreams / You don't know / Love to hate / Hot gets a little cold / Unhook the stars / Searching / Say a prayer / Mother fearless / Brimstone and fire / Lollygagging
CD 4853702
Epic / Feb '97 / Sony

TRUE COLORS
Change of heart / Maybe he'll know / Boy blue / True colors / Calm inside the storm / What's going on / Iko iko / Faraway nearby / 911 / One track mind
CD 4624932
Portrait / Aug '90 / Sony

TWELVE DEADLY CYNS - AND THEN SOME
I'm gonna be strong / Girls just wanna have fun / Money changes everything / Time after time / She bop / All through the night / Change of heart / True colors / What's going on / I drove all night / World is stone / Who let in the rain / That's what I think / Sally's pigeons / Hey now (girls just wanna have fun) / Come on home
CD 4773632
Epic / Aug '94 / Sony

Laurel & Hardy

BEST OF LAUREL AND HARDY, THE (2CD Set)
CD Set LH 100CD
Another Fine Mess / Dec '96 / Total/BMG

SONGS AND DIALOGUE VOL.4
CD MESSCD 4
Wax / Jan '97 / RTM/Disc / Total/BMG

SONS OF THE DESERT
CD LHOST 2CD
Wax / Jan '97 / RTM/Disc / Total/BMG

Laurel Canyon Ramblers

BLUE RAMBLER
CD SHCD 3852
Sugar Hill / Jul '96 / ADA / CM / Direct / Koch / Roots

RAMBLER'S BLUES
Rambler's blues / Crossroads bar / To a heart always true / This heart of mine (can never say goodbye) / Yellowhead / He said if I be lifted up / She's no angel / Jordan / Love reunited / Flatland ramble / Jesus saviour, pilot me / Roll on
CD SHCD 3834
Sugar Hill / May '95 / ADA / CM / Direct / Koch / Roots

Lauren, Jessica

SIREN SONG
Leo rises / Fire monkey / Siren song / When you call my name / Serengeti / Just a dream / Dance for Lotte / Dangerous curves / Freefall
CD SJRCD 020
Soul Jazz / Sep '94 / New Note/Pinnacle / Timewarp / Vital

Laurence, Zack

SINGALONG PIANO, THE (Great Medleys Of All Time Favourites)
Beatles medley / USA medley / Italian medley / Irving Berlin medley / Jolson medley / European medley / Roaring twenties medley / Moonlight medley / Winter medley / Knees up medley / Waltz medley / Soft shoe medley / Oriental medley / Fats Waller medley / Spanish medley / Vaudeville medley / Ragtime medley / London medley / Girls medley / Big band medley
CD 304672
Hallmark / Jul '97 / Carlton

Laurent, Scott

CAPOSVILLE (Laurent, Scott Band)
Madison / Paul's song / Caposville / Afraid of the ground / It always happened in the fall / Blacktop and lines / Meant to be / Waiting for me to move / You know me well / It's not the way it used to be
CD MRCD 1296
Club De Musique / Feb '97 / Direct

Lauria, Nando

NOVO BRASIL
Doce morena / Thinking of recife / Just you / Tide / Shall we / Dreaming of you / Gabriel's song / Northeast wind / Don Juan / Revival
CD ND 63036
Narada / Jul '96 / ADA / New Note/Pinnacle

POINTS OF VIEW
Back home / After dawn / Take two / If I fell / Cry and the smile / Saudade (longing) / Que xote (what a rhythm) / Northeast tide / Episode: Prelude / Episode
CD ND 63026
Narada / Apr '94 / ADA / New Note/Pinnacle

Laurie Accordian Orchestra

SPIRIT OF SCOTLAND
CD CDLOC 1087
Lochshore / Jun '95 / ADA / Direct / Duncans

Laurie, Cy

CHATTANOOGA STOMP (The Delving Back Series Vol.1)
Chattanooga stomp / Goober dance / Tuxedo junction / Kansas city stomp / Clarinet rondo / Minuet wobble / We shall walk through the streets of the city / Bourbon St. Parade / Perdido St. Blues / Twelfth St. Rag / Dauphjin St. blues / Canal St. Blues / Beale St Blues / Blue blood blue / There'll come a day / Keyhole blues / Don't go away nobody / Melancholy blues / St. Phillips street breakdown
CD LACD 61
Lake / Jul '96 / ADA / Cadillac / Direct / Jazz Music / Target/BMG

Laurnea

BETTA LISTEN
Happy / Infatuation / Sun don't rain / Can't let go / Over and over / Superstar / Today / Have you ever / Days of youth / Been a long time / Betta listen / Gone
CD 4874092
Epic / Jun '97 / Sony

Laury, Booker T

BOOKER IN PARIS 1980
CD 157912
Blues Collection / Jun '93 / Discovery

NOTHIN' BUT THE BLUES
CD BB 9542CD
Bullseye Blues / Feb '94 / Direct

Lauth, Wolfgang

LAUTHER
Ice nenne alle frauen baby / Est ist nur die leibe / Durch dich wird diesse welt erst schon / Bei dir war es immer so schon / Mein herz hat heut premiere / Warum bist du fortegangen / Ich werede jede nacht von ihnen traumen / Kauf dir einen bunten luftballon / Lauther / Donald / Johnnie Walker / Cool cave / I only have eyes for you / Pastels / Lauthentic / Jeb / These foolish things / Indian summer / Goofy / French fries / Can't help lovin' dat man / Chicken feet / Date on wax
CD BCD 15717
Bear Family / May '93 / Direct / Rollercoaster / Swift

Lava Love

WHOLE LAVA LOVE
CD SKYCD 2003
Sky / Sep '94 / Greyhound / Koch / Vital/SAM

Lavelle, Brian

RADIOS VOL.2
CD FRR 023
Freek / Sep '96 / RTM/Disc / SRD

Lavelle, Caroline

SPIRIT
CD 4509981372
Warner Bros. / Mar '95 / Warner Music

Laverne, Andy

ANDY LAVERNE PLAYS TODD DAMERON
CD SCCD 31372
Steeplechase / Feb '96 / Discovery / Impetus

FIRST TANGO IN NEW YORK
CD 500472
Musidisc / Nov '93 / Discovery

LIVE AT MAYBECK RECITAL HALL VOL.28
Yesterdays / I loves you Porgy / Sweet and lovely / Star eyes / My melancholy baby / When you wish upon a star / Beautiful love / Turn out the stars / Moonlight in Vermont / Impression for piano / Stan Getz in Chappaqua
CD CCD 4577
Concord Jazz / Oct '93 / New Note/Pinnacle

NATURAL LIVING (Laverne, Andy & John Abercrombie)
CD 500092
Musidisc / Nov '93 / Discovery

TIME WELL SPENT
Common knowledge / There is no greater love / Cantaloupe island / On a misty night / Time well spent / I should care / Lover man / Singel petal of a rose / Fall / Blue interlude / Rhythm and blues
CD CCD 4680
Concord Jazz / Feb '96 / New Note/Pinnacle

Lavette, Bettye

NEARER TO YOU
CD CDCHARLY 276
Charly / Jan '91 / Koch

Lavin, Christine

ATTAINABLE LOVE
Attainable love / Castlemaine / Yonder blue / Sensitive new age guys / Victim/volunteer / Kind of love you never recover from / Fly on a plane / Venus kissed the moon / Moving target / Shopping cart of love:The play
CD CDPH 1132
Philo / Jul '90 / ADA / CM / Direct

BEAU WOES AND OTHER PROBLEMS
CD CDPH 1107
Philo / Oct '88 / ADA / CM / Direct

FUTURE FOSSILS
CD CDPH 1104
Philo / '86 / ADA / CM / Direct

GOOD THING HE CAN'T READ MY MIND
Good thing he can't read my mind / Bumble bees / Santa Monica Pier / Waltzing with him / Mysterious woman / Realities / Downtown / Never go back / Eighty five degrees / Somebody's baby / Ain't love grand
CD CDPH 1121
Philo / '88 / ADA / CM / Direct

LAUGH TRACKS VOL.1
CD SH 8022
Shanachie / Nov '96 / ADA / Greensleeves / Koch

LAUGH TRACKS VOL.2
CD SH 8023
Shanachie / Nov '96 / ADA / Greensleeves / Koch

LIVE AT THE CACTUS CAFE - WHAT WAS I THINKING
CD PH 1159CD
Philo / Jan '94 / ADA / CM / Direct

ON A WINTER'S NIGHT
CD PH 1167CD
Philo / Feb '94 / ADA / CM / Direct

PLEASE DON'T MAKE ME TOO HAPPY
CD SHAN 8016CD
Shanachie / Apr '95 / ADA / Greensleeves / Koch

SHINING MY FLASHLIGHT ON THE MOON
CD SH 8024
Shanachie / Mar '97 / ADA / Greensleeves / Koch

Lavitz, T

MOODSWING
CD NOVA 9134
Nova / Jan '93 / New Note/Pinnacle

Law

LAW, THE
For a little ride / Miss you in a heartbeat / Stone cold / Come save me (Julianne) / Laying down the law / Nature of the beast / Stone / Anything for you / Best of my love / Tough love / Missing you bad girl
CD 7567821952
East West / Apr '91 / Warner Music

Law, John

EXPLODED ON IMPACT (Law, John Quartet)
Couplets / Mother's lament / Pissed off tree / Kaleidoscope / Joyriding
CD SLAMCD 204
Slam / Oct '96 / Cadillac

EXTREMELY QUARTET
CD ARTCD 6199
Hat Art / Mar '97 / Cadillac / Harmonia Mundi

ONLIEST, THE (Pictures From A Monk Exhibition)
CD FMRCD 32
Future / Apr '97 / ADA / Harmonia Mundi

Law, Johnny

JOHNNY LAW
CD CDZORRO 18
Metal Blade / Apr '91 / Pinnacle / Plastic Head

Lawal, Gasper

KADARA
Kadara / Iregbogbo / Irin ajo / Oyeye / Ase / Omo araye / Ola / Awo
CD CDORB 071
Globestyle / Apr '91 / Pinnacle

Lawndale

SASQUATCH ROCK
CD SST 125CD
SST / May '93 / Plastic Head

Lawnmower Deth

BELLY
Somebody call me a taxi / Billy / I need to be my main / Squeeze / Do you wanna be a chuffed core / Buddy Holly never wrote a song called we're too punk / Up the junction / If it was grey you'd say it's black / Kids in America / March of the dweebs / Funny thing about it is / Purple haze
CD MOSH 098CD
Earache / Oct '93 / Vital

OOH CRIKEY IT'S...
CD MOSH 025CD
Earache / Sep '90 / Vital

Lawrence, Denise

CAN'T HELP LOVIN' THESE MEN OF MINE
My baby just cares for me / (I want to be) Seduced / Quiney St. Stomp / Jesus on the mainline / Fish seller / Can't help lovin' that man of mine / Honky-tonk train blues / Send me to the electric chair / Cottage for sale / Iko iko / Keepin' out of mischief now / Booze and blues / Everything happens to me
CD LACD 60
Lake / Apr '96 / ADA / Cadillac / Direct / Jazz Music / Target/BMG

LET IT SHINE
Papa de da da / Seven golden daffodils / Way you do the things you do / Saturday night function / Mardi Gras in New Orleans / Shady green pastures / Down in Honky Tonk Town / Wasted life blues / Let your light from the lighthouse shine on me / Around the clock / New Orleans wiggle / Nice feeling
CD LACD 37
Lake / Feb '95 / ADA / Cadillac / Direct / Jazz Music / Target/BMG

Lawrence, Steve

WE GOT US/EYDIE & STEVE SING THE GOLDEN HITS (Lawrence, Steve & Eydie Gorme)
We got us / Side by side / No two people / Darn it baby / That's love / Together / Flattery / This could be the start of something / I remember it well / Baby, it's cold outside / Two lost souls / Harmony / Cheek to cheek / I've heard that song before / I'll be with you in apple blossom time / Green eyes / I hear a rhapsody / And the angels sing / Who wouldn't love you / Bei mir bist du schon / Marie / I don't want to walk without you / I've got a gal in Kalamazoo / White Christmas / Sentimental journey
CD JASCD 600
Jasmine / Aug '96 / Conifer/BMG / Hot Shot / TKO Magnum

WE'LL TAKE ROMANCE (Lawrence, Steve & Eydie Gorme)
CD MCCD 168
Music Club / Jul '94 / Disc / THE

Lawrence, Syd

LIVE IN DUBLIN
Evening serenade / Strike up the band / Splanky / My kind of town (Chicago is) / You're driving me crazy / Bye bye blues / Holiday for tombones / On the sunny side of the street / Sing sing sing / Skyliner / Phil the fluter's ball / Molly Malone / Galway bay / Rose of Tralee / Rakes of mallow (piper's patrol) / When Irish eyes are smiling / Elmer's tune / Too little time / Trumpet blues a cantabile / Moonlight serenade / In the mood / Irish anthem
CD 3036100102
Pearls / Apr '96 / Carlton

PLAYS GLENN MILLER (Lawrence, Syd Orchestra)
In the mood / St. Louis blues / At last / Tuxedo junction / Chattanooga choo choo / String of pearls / Little brown jug / Anchors aweigh / American patrol / Stardust / I know why / Pennsylvania 6-5000 / Frenesi / Humpty Dumpty heart / Adios / Moonlight serenade
CD CDGM 1
Premier/MFP / Jul '92 / EMI

PLAYS THE MUSIC OF GLENN MILLER (Nice & Easy) (Lawrence, Syd Orchestra)
Moonlight serenade / Little brown jug / String of pearls / At last / I've got a gal in Kalamazoo / American patrol / Perfidia / Slumber song / Anchors aweigh / Elmer's tune / St. Louis blues / In the mood / Story of a starry night / I dream I dwelt in Harlem / Falling leaves / Pennsylvania 6-5000 / Caribbean clipper / Tuxedo junction / Stardust / Chattanooga choo choo / Frenesi / Adios
CD 8428272
Philips / Apr '94 / PolyGram

REMEMBERS GLENN MILLER
In the mood / Pennsylvania 6-5000 / American patrol / Tuxedo junction / Serenade in blue / Perfidia / Stardust / Moonlight serenade / I've got a gal in Kalamazoo / Little brown jug / St. Louis blues / Chattanooga choo choo / Falling leaves / Frenesi
CD 5501872
Spectrum / Mar '94 / PolyGram

Lawrence, Tracy

ALIBIS
I threw the rest away / Can't break it to my heart / We don't love here anymore / Crying ain't dying / Alibis / My second home / Don't talk to me that way / It only takes one bar (to make a prison) / Back to back / If the good die young
CD 7567824832
Atlantic / Jul '93 / Warner Music

Laws, Hubert

LAWS OF JAZZ/FLUTE BY-LAWS
Miss thing / All soul / Black eyes peas and rice / Bessie's blues / Don't you forget it / Bimbe blue / Bloodshot / Miedo / Mean lene / No you'd better not / Let me go / Strange girl / Baila cinderella
CD 8122716362
Atlantic / May '94 / Warner Music

MY TIME WILL COME
Malaguena / My time will come / It's so crazy / Shades of light / Valse / Make it last / Moonlight sonata
CD 5184432
Limelight / May '94 / PolyGram

ROMEO AND JULIET
CD CK 34330
Sony Jazz / Aug '97 / Sony

Laws, Ronnie

BEST OF RONNIE LAWS
Always there / Night breeze / Let's keep it together / Karmen / Friends and strangers / New day / Just love / Flame / Solid ground / Just as you are / Living love / Love is here / Saturday evening
CD BNZ 287
Blue Note / Feb '92 / EMI

DEEP SOUL
CD CPCD 8143
Charly / Nov '95 / Koch

PRESSURE SENSITIVE (Laws, Ronnie & Pressure)
Always there / Momma / Never be the same / Tell me something good / Nothing to lose / Tidal wave / Why do you laugh at me / Mis' Mary's place
CD CDP 7465542
EMI / Jun '95 / EMI

TRIBUTE TO THE LEGENDARY EDDIE HARRIS
Listen here / Freedom jazz dance / Boogie woogie bossa nova / Cold duck / Sham time / I don't want no-one but you / Hip hoppin' / Compared to what
CD CDP 8553302
Parlophone / Apr '97 / EMI

TRUE SPIRIT
Gotta say goodbye / Love this way again / Virgin winds / From a glance / Song for Hiram / Heart station / Favorite love / Imo
CD CPCD 8126
Charly / Oct '95 / Koch

Lawson, Doyle

GOSPEL COLLECTION VOL.1, THE (Lawson, Doyle & Quicksilver)
CD SHCD 9104
Sugar Hill / Jan '97 / ADA / CM / Direct / Koch / Roots

HEAVEN'S JOY AWAITS (Lawson, Doyle & Quicksilver)
CD SHCD 3760
Sugar Hill / Dec '87 / ADA / CM / Direct / Koch / Roots

HEAVENLY TREASURES (Lawson, Doyle & Quicksilver)
CD SHCD 3735
Sugar Hill / Oct '94 / ADA / CM / Direct / Koch / Roots

I HEARD THE ANGELS SINGING (Lawson, Doyle & Quicksilver)
Holy city / Stormy weather / Little mountain church house / In the shelter of his arms / I heard the angels singing / He's my guide / Little white church / City where's comes no strife / Rock of ages / I won't have to cross Jordan alone / That new Jerusalem / That home far away
CD SHCD 3774
Sugar Hill / Jul '89 / ADA / CM / Direct / Koch / Roots

I'LL WANDER BACK SOMEDAY (Lawson, Doyle & Quicksilver)
CD SHCD 3769
Sugar Hill / Mar '88 / ADA / CM / Direct / Koch / Roots

KEPT AND PROTECTED (Lawson, Doyle & Quicksilver)
CD SHCD 3867
Sugar Hill / Jun '97 / ADA / CM / Direct / Koch / Roots

MY HEART IS YOURS (Lawson, Doyle & Quicksilver)
All in my love for you / Still got a crush on you / Move to the top of the mountain / I don't care / My heart is yours / Dreaming of you / Look for me (I'll be there) / Date with an angel / Now there's you / Between us / I'm satisfied with you / We were made for each other
CD SHCD 3782
Sugar Hill / Oct '90 / ADA / CM / Direct / Koch / Roots

NEVER WALK AWAY (Lawson, Doyle & Quicksilver)
CD SHCD 3842
Sugar Hill / Oct '95 / ADA / CM / Direct / Koch / Roots

ROCK MY SOUL (Lawson, Doyle & Quicksilver)
CD SHCD 3717
Sugar Hill / Jan '97 / ADA / CM / Direct / Koch / Roots

THERE'S A LIGHT GUIDING ME (Lawson, Doyle & Quicksilver)
CD SHCD 3845
Sugar Hill / Jul '96 / ADA / CM / Direct / Koch / Roots

Lawson, Yank

SOMETHING OLD, SOMETHING NEW, SOMETHING BORROWED, SOMETHING (Lawson, Yank Jazzband)
CD APCD 240
Audiophile / Apr '89 / Jazz Music

WITH A SOUTHERN ACCENT (Lawson-Haggart 'azz Band)
CD JCD 203
Jazzology / Feb '93 / Jazz Music

YANK LAWSON & BOB HAGGART (Lawson, Yank & Bob Haggart)
CD JCD 183
Jazzology / Oct '92 / Jazz Music

Lay Quiet Awhile

DELICATE WIRE
CD 185172
Southern / Jun '94 / SRD

Lay, Sam

LIVE (Lay, Sam Band)
CD AP 115
Appaloosa / May '97 / ADA / Direct / TKO Magnum

STONE BLUES (Lay, Sam Blues Band)
29 miles / Walkin' thru the park / I got wise / Short haired woman / Birmingham / Hide and seek / Jelly jelly / Red, white and blues / Shuffle master / That's alright Mama / Stone blues
CD ECD 260812
Evidence / Sep '96 / ADA / Cadillac / Harmonia Mundi

Laye, Evelyn

GAIETY GIRL
New moon / Lover come back to me / One kiss / Wanting you / Madame pompadour / Love me now / Blue eyes / Do I do wrong / Princess charming / Near and yet so far / Brave hearts / Love is a song / Princess awakening / Night is young / When I grow too old to dream / Paganini / My Nicolo / Love never comes too late / Nobody could love you more / Love, live forever (and rule my heart) / Bitter sweet / I'll see you again / Zigeuner / Lights up / You've done something to my heart / Let the people sing / Only a glass of champagne / Three waltzes / Forever
CD CDAJA 55211
Living Era / Apr '96 / Select

Layhe, Edgerton

ROUGH AND TUMBLE
Buffalo blues / Eleanor / Why would she go / Billy can / Everybody needs something nobody knows / Teardrop whisky / Dancing down at the crossroads/The convenience reel / All the tears in Liverpool / Lonely as Los Angeles, restless as New York / I'm on your side / Six thousand shoes
CD FE 096CD
Fellside / Jan '94 / ADA / Direct / Target/ BMG

Layton & Johnstone

ALABAMY BOUND
Anytime anywhere / Up with the lark / Wedding of the painted doll / Alabamy bound / New kind of girl with a new kind of love form / Weary river / Paddlin' Madelin' home / Turner Layton piano medley / Birth of the blues / Coquette / Hillo, 'tucky / Don't put the blame on me / Hard hearted Hannah / It all depends on you / At dawning / Medley of Layton and Johnstone successes
CD PASTCD 9712
Flapper / '90 / Pinnacle

GETTING SENTIMENTAL OVER YOU
Auf wiedersehen my dear / Deep purple: *Layton, Turner* / Don't you ever cry: *Layton, Turner* / Home on the range / I wanna sing about you / I'm getting sentimental over you / It was so beautiful / I've got a feeling I'm falling in love / Love is the sweetest thing / Medley / Medley / Miracles sometimes happen: *Layton, Turner* / More than you know / Night and day / Nightfall / Nightingale sang in Berkeley Square: *Layton, Turner* / There's rain in my eyes: *Layton, Turner* / These foolish things: *Layton, Turner* / To be in love espesh'lly with you / We just couldn't say goodbye / We three: *Layton, Turner* / Where or when: *Layton, Turner* / Wind and the rain: *Layton, Turner* / Without a song
CD CDAJA 5111
Living Era / Jun '93 / Select

Layton, Eddie

YOU GOTTA HAVE HEART
Bring on the Yankees / Take me out to the ball game / Jersey bounce / When the saints go marching in / My kind of town / Stormy weather / When you're smiling / You've gotta have heart
CD SONGCD 912
Silva Screen / Apr '97 / Koch / Silva Screen

Lazarus, Ken

SINGS REGGAE OF THE 70'S
CD PKCD 61094
K&K / Sep '94 / Jet Star

Lazerboy

FALLEN WORLD
CD PROBEUP 44CD
Probe Plus/Up / Jul '97 / SRD

FORGET NOTHING
CD FRR 021
Freek / Jun '96 / RTM/Disc / SRD

Lazonby

YOUR HUMBLE SERVANT
CD BRAINK 44CD
Brainiak / Mar '95 / 3mv/Sony / Arabesque / RTM/Disc

Lazonby, Dave

WAR ALL THE TIME (Lazonby, Dave Group)
Mass / Journey to Sirius B to Earth / Bossa nova my arse / War all the time / Mass
CD SLAMCD 214
Slam / Oct '96 / Cadillac

Lazy Cowgirls

RAGGED SOUL
CD EFA 115912
Crypt / Jul '95 / Shellshock/Disc

Lazy Lester

HARP AND SOUL
I done got over it / I'm a man / Dark end of the street / Bye bye baby / Alligator shuffle / Take me in your arms / Patrol wagon / Raining in my heart / Bloodstains on the wall / Five long years
CD ALCD 4768
Alligator / May '93 / ADA / CM / Direct

I'M A LOVER NOT A FIGHTER
I'm a lover not a fighter / Sugar coated love / Lester's stomp / I told my little woman / Tell me pretty baby / Whoa now / I hear you knocking / Through the goodness of my heart / I love you, I need you / Late in the evening / Real combination for love / Bloodstains on the wall / You got me where you want me / I'm so tired / Patrol blues / I'm so glad / Sad city blues / If you think I've lost you / I made up my mind / Lonesome highway blues / You're gonna ruin me baby / Same thing could happen to you / Take me in your arms / You better listen to what I said
CD CDCHD 518
Ace / Apr '94 / Pinnacle

Lazy Sundays

TEXTURE AND THE FLAVOUR
CD 21107
Subterfuge / Jul '97 / SRD

LCD

MAD LOVE
CD CLP 9975
Cleopatra / Apr '97 / Cargo / Greyhound / Plastic Head / RTM/Disc / SRD

Le Gaulois, Maurice

MUSETTE ACCORDION 1895-1995
CD ARN 64366
Arion / Sep '96 / ADA / Discovery

Le Gop

LE GOP
CD Y 225030CD
Silex / Dec '93 / ADA / Harmonia Mundi

Le Grand Blues Band

LE GRAND BLUES
CD 422430
New Rose / May '94 / ADA / Direct / Discovery

Le Jazz Non

IT'S THE NEW THING
CD HERMES 014
Corpus Hermeticum / Apr '97 / Cargo

Le June, Iry

CAJUN'S GREATEST
Grande nuit especial / Grande bosco / Duraldo waltz / I went to the dance / La valse de bayou chene / I made a big mistake / Come and get me / Donnes moi mon chapeau / Waltz of the mulberry limb / Church point breakdown / La valse du grande chemin / Jolie catin / La fitte la vove / Bayou pon pon special / La valse de cajin / Don't get married / Convict waltz / It happened to me / Parting waltz / Evangeline special / Love bridge waltz / Teche special / Calcasieu waltz / Te mone / Lacassine special
CD CDCHD 428
Ace / Oct '92 / Pinnacle

Le Maistre, Malcolm

1968 SARAJEVO EP
CD 12032CD
Unique Gravity / Jul '95 / ADA / Pinnacle

Le Meut, Jean

PE YUVANKIZ KUHET
CD KM 44
Keltia Musique / Sep '94 / ADA / Discovery

Le Mystere Des Voix Bulgares

LE MYSTERE DES VOIX BULGARES
CD CAD 603 CD
4AD / May '87 / RTM/Disc

LE MYSTERE DES VOIX BULGARES VOL.2
CD CAD 801CD
4AD / Nov '88 / RTM/Disc

RITUAL (Bulgarian State Television Female Choir)
CD 7559793492
Nonesuch / Feb '96 / Warner Music

Le, Nguyen

3 TRIOS
Silk / Silver / Sand / Dance of the comet / Foow / Kinderhund / Woof / Idoma / La parfum / Blue monkey / Straight no chaser
CD 92452
Act / Mar '97 / New Note/Pinnacle

MILLION WAVES
Mille vagues / Trilogy / Be good / Mango blues / Butterflies and zebras / Little wing / El saola / Sledge / Moonshine / I feel good
CD 92212
Act / May '95 / New Note/Pinnacle

MIRACLES
CD 500102
Musidisc / Nov '93 / Discovery

TALES FROM VIETNAM
Wind blew it away / Black horse / Don't you go away, my friend / Trong com / Hen ho / Banyan tree song / Spring of life / Ting ning / Mangustao - part 1 / Mangustao - part 2
CD 92252
Act / Feb '96 / New Note/Pinnacle

ZANZIBAR
CD 500352
Musidisc / Feb '97 / Discovery

Le Pont, Jester

L'ESCAPADE
CD MINCD 594
Minuit / Mar '96 / ADA

Le Quintette De Cornemuses

MENAGERIE
CD B 6795CD
Auvidis/Ethnic / Jul '94 / ADA / Harmonia Mundi

Le Rue, Pierre

IN TWO WORLDS
CD GWCD 005
Weaving / Nov '95 / ADA / Direct / Koch

Le Thugs

LABF
CD ____ **VIRUS 93CD**
Alternative Tentacles / '92 / Cargo / Greyhound / Pinnacle

Lea, Barbara

ATLANTA JAZZ PARTY (Lea, Barbara & Ed Polcer)
CD ____ **JCD 218**
Jazzology / Jul '93 / Jazz Music

DEVIL IS AFRAID OF MUSIC (Lea, Barbara & Loonis McGlohon/Dick Cary Trio)
CD ____ **ACD 119**
Audiophile / Mar '97 / Jazz Music

DO IT AGAIN
CD ____ **ACD 175**
Audiophile / Jun '95 / Jazz Music

FINE AND DANDY (Lea, Barbara & Keith Ingham)
CD ____ **CHR 70029**
Challenge / Sep '96 / ADA / Direct / Jazz Music / Wellard

HOAGY'S CHILDREN (Lea, Barbara/Bob Dorough/Dick Sudhalter)
CD ____ **ACD 291**
Audiophile / Apr '94 / Jazz Music

HOAGY'S CHILDREN VOL.2
CD ____ **ACD 292**
Audiophile / Apr '94 / Jazz Music

REMEMBERING LEE WILEY
CD ____ **ACD 125**
Audiophile / Jun '96 / Jazz Music

SONGS FROM 'POUSSE CAFE' (Lea, Barbara & Ellis Larkin)
CD ____ **ACD 263**
Audiophile / Apr '93 / Jazz Music

Leach, Tom

TOM LEACH
Guitar / Confidence / Doris days / Yesterday's news / Hello friend / Ice below you / Guiatar / Guitar / Saviour / Rain, rain / Wine, cigarettes, tears / If I were you / She's coming of age / Send in the blues / Tomorrow comes / Guitar
CD ____ **SRRCD 027**
Slow River / Jul '97 / Cargo

Lead Into Gold

AGE OF REASON
CD ____ **CDDVN 7**
Devotion / Mar '92 / Pinnacle

Leadbelly

ALABAMA BOUND
Pick a bale of cotton / Whoa Buck / Midnight special / Alabamy bound / Good morning blues / Red Cross store blues / Alberta / You can't lose-a me cholly / Gray goose / Stewball / Can't you line 'em / Rock Island line / Easy rider / New York City / Roberta / On my last go round
CD ____ **ND 90321**
Bluebird / Oct '94 / BMG

ALL TIME BLUES CLASSICS
CD ____ **8420322**
Music Memoria / Oct '96 / ADA / Discovery

CONGRESS BLUES
CD ____ **ALB 1007CD**
Aldabra / Mar '94 / CM / RTM/Disc

CONVICT BLUES
CD ____ **ALB 1004CD**
Aldabra / Mar '94 / CM / RTM/Disc

GO DOWN OLD HANNAH (Library Of Congress Recordings)
CD ____ **ROUCD 1099**
Rounder / Apr '94 / ADA / CM / Direct

GOOD MORNING BLUES
CD ____ **IGOCD 2007**
Indigo / Nov '94 / ADA / Direct

GOOD MORNING BLUES
CD ____ **TPZ 1029**
Topaz Jazz / Oct '95 / Cadillac / Pinnacle

GOODNIGHT IRENE
CD ____ **TCD 1006**
Tradition / Feb '96 / ADA / Vital

GOODNIGHT IRENE
CD ____ **IMP 310**
IMP / Nov '96 / ADA / Discovery

GWINE DIG A HOLE TO PUT THE DEVIL IN
CD ____ **ROUCD 1045**
Rounder / Feb '92 / ADA / CM / Direct

IN THE SHADOWS OF THE GALLOWS POLE
CD ____ **TCD 1018**
Tradition / May '96 / ADA / Vital

IRENE GOODNIGHT
CD ____ **CD 52028**
Blues Encore / Nov '93 / Target/BMG

KING OF THE TWELVE STRING GUITAR
Packin' trunk / Becky Deem, she was gamblin' girl / Honey, I'm all out and down / Four day worry blues / Roberta part 1 / Roberta part 2 / Death letter / Death letter / Kansas city papa / Wort Worth and Dallas blues / You don't know my mind / Ox drivin' blues / Daddy I'm coming back to you / Shorty George / Yellow jacket / TB woman blues
CD ____ **4678932**
Columbia / Nov '91 / Sony

LAST SESSIONS
CD Set ____ **SFWCD 40068**
Smithsonian Folkways / Oct '94 / ADA / Cadillac / CM / Direct / Koch

LEADBELLY & JOSH WHITE/PEETIE WHEATSTRAW 1924-MID 1940'S (Leadbelly & Josh White/Peetie Wheatstraw)
CD ____ **DOCD 5461**
Document / Jun '96 / ADA / Hot Shot / Jazz Music

LEADBELLY 1939-40
CD ____ **DOCD 5226**
Document / Apr '94 / ADA / Hot Shot / Jazz Music

LEADBELLY 1940-43
CD ____ **DOCD 5227**
Document / Apr '94 / ADA / Hot Shot / Jazz Music

LEADBELLY 1943-44
CD ____ **DOCD 5228**
Document / Apr '94 / ADA / Hot Shot / Jazz Music

LEADBELLY 1944
CD ____ **DOCD 5310**
Document / Dec '94 / ADA / Hot Shot / Jazz Music

LEADBELLY 1944-46
CD ____ **DOCD 5311**
Document / Dec '94 / ADA / Hot Shot / Jazz Music

LEADBELLY LEGACY VOL.1 (Where Did You Sleep Last Night)
CD ____ **SFWCD 40044**
Smithsonian Folkways / Apr '96 / ADA / Cadillac / CM / Direct / Koch

LEADBELLY LEGACY VOL.2 (Bourgeois Blues)
CD ____ **SFWCD 40045**
Smithsonian Folkways / May '97 / ADA / Cadillac / CM / Direct / Koch

LEGENDARY MASTERS SERIES, THE
CD ____ **COLLECT 4CD**
Aim / Oct '95 / ADA / Direct / Jazz Music

LET IT SHINE ON ME
CD ____ **ROUCD 1046**
Rounder / Mar '92 / ADA / CM / Direct

MASTERS
Match box blues / Bourgeois blues / Medley / My friend Blind Lemon / Can't you line 'em / John Hardy / Gallis pole / Borrow love and go / Big fat woman / Baby don't you love me no more / Bull cow / Red river blues / Alberta / Poor Howard / Kansas city papa / CC rider
CD ____ **CDBM 119**
Blue Moon / Sep '96 / Cadillac / Discovery / Greensleeves / Jazz Music / Jet Star / TKO Magnum

MASTERS OF THE COUNTRY BLUES (Leadbelly & 'Blind' Willie McTell)
Death letter blues: *Leadbelly* / Death letter blues part 2: *Leadbelly* / Kansas city papa: *Leadbelly* / Daddy I'm coming back to you: *Leadbelly* / Shorty George: *Leadbelly* / Yellow jacket: *Leadbelly* / TB woman blues part 1: *Leadbelly* / TB woman blues part 2: *Leadbelly* / Chainey: *McTell, 'Blind' Willie* / Murderer's home blues: *McTell, 'Blind' Willie* / Kill-it -kid rag: *McTell, 'Blind' Willie* / I got to cross de river O'Jordan: *McTell, 'Blind' Willie* / Old time religion: *McTell, 'Blind' Willie* / Will Fox: *McTell, 'Blind' Willie* / Dying crapshooters blues: *McTell, 'Blind' Willie* / Amazing Grace: *McTell, 'Blind' Willie* / Just as well get ready: Climbing high mountains, tryin' to g: *McTell, 'Blind' Willie* / King Edwards blues: AKA: Baby it must be love: *McTell, 'Blind' Willie* / Delia: *McTell, 'Blind' Willie* / Boll weevil: *McTell, 'Blind' Willie* / I got to cross the River Jordan: *McTell, 'Blind' Willie*
CD ____ **BCD 144**
Biograph / Jun '97 / ADA / Cadillac / Direct / Hot Shot / Jazz Music / Wellard

MIDNIGHT SPECIAL
CD ____ **ROUCD 1044**
Rounder / Feb '92 / ADA / CM / Direct

NOBODY KNOWS THE TROUBLE I'VE SEEN (Library Of Congress Recordings)
CD ____ **ROUCD 1098**
Rounder / May '94 / ADA / CM / Direct

SINGS FOLK SONGS
CD ____ **SFWCD 40010**
Smithsonian Folkways / Aug '95 / ADA / Cadillac / CM / Direct / Koch

TITANIC, THE (Library Of Congress Recordings)
CD ____ **ROUCD 1097**
Rounder / Apr '94 / ADA / CM / Direct

TRIBUTE TO LEADBELLY, A (Various Artists)
Intro - Leadbelly / You must have that true religion / I know it was the blood / Intro - Leadbelly on the blues / Best of friends / Rock island line / Poor Howard / Baby please don't go / John Henry / Intro - Alan Lomax and Leadbelly on meter / Bourgeois blues / Redbird / In the pines (where did you sleep last night) / Kisses sweeter than wine pigmeat / Pigmeat / De grey goose / Ain't goin' down to de well no mo' / Intro - Pete Seeger / Bring me Lil' water silby / On a Monday / Midnight special / Meeting at the building / Good night Irene
CD ____ **TBA 130142**
Blues Alliance / Jun '97 / New Note/ Pinnacle

VERY BEST OF LEADBELLY, THE
CD ____ **MCCD 106**
Music Club / May '93 / Disc / THE

Leaf, Ann

MIGHTY WURLITZER, THE (Leaf, Ann & Gaylord Carter)
Great day: *Carter, Gaylord* / Strike up the band: *Leaf, Ann* / You do something to me: *Leaf, Ann* / Son of the Sheik: *Leaf, Ann* / You were meant for me / Orphans of the storm / Jeannine: *Carter, Gaylord* / For heaven's sake: *Carter, Gaylord* / My romance: *Carter, Gaylord* / Charmaine: *Carter, Gaylord* / Intolerance: *Carter, Gaylord* / Phantom of the opera: *Carter, Gaylord*
CD ____ **NW 227**
New World / Aug '92 / ADA / Cadillac / Harmonia Mundi

Leafhound

GROWERS OF MUSHROOM
Freelance fiend / Sad road to the sea / Drowned my life in fear / Work my body / Stray / With a minute to go / Growers of mushroom / Stagnant pool / Sawdust Caesar / It's going to get better
CD ____ **SEECD 403**
See For Miles/C5 / May '96 / Pinnacle

League Of Gentlemen

THRANG THRANG COZIMBULK
CD ____ **DGM 9602**
Discipline / May '96 / Pinnacle

Leander, Zarah

KANN DENN LIEBE SUNDE SEIN (8CD Set)
Gebundene hande / Eine frau von heut' / Merci, mon ami / Ich hab' vielleicht noch nie geliebt / Yes sir / Tiefe sehnsucht / Ich steh' im regen / Kinostar / Der wind hat mir ein lied erzahlt / Du kannst es nicht wissen / Eine frau wird erst schon durch die liebe / Drei sterne sah ich scheinen / Sag' mir nicht adieu, sag' nur auf wiedersehn / Cheri, du bist heut' so anders / Du bist genau wie die anderen / Ich bin eine stimme / Kann denn liebe sunde sein / Von der puszta will ich traumen / Lang ist's her / Ein kleiner akkord auf meinem klavier / Nur nicht aus liebe weinen / Schlafe, mein geliebter / Wo ist dein herz / Schlummerlied / Fatme, erzahl mir ein marchen / Sagt dir eine schone frau 'vielleicht' / Heut' abend lad' ich mir die liebe ein / Ein paar tranen werd' ich weinen um dich / Reite, kleiner reiter / Schiff ahoi / Du darfst mir nie mehr rote rosen schenken / Und dann tanz ich einen czardas / Er heisst Waldemar / Wen ich liebe / Ich will nicht vergessen / Ich sag' nicht ja, ich sag' nicht nein / Mein leben fur die liebe / Ich weiss, es wird einmal ein wunder geschehn / Davon geht die welt nicht unter / Blaue husaren / Einen wie dich konnt' ich lieben / So glucklich wie du und so selig wie ich / Die lustige witwe (potpourri teil 1) / Die lustige witwe (potpourri teil 2) / Frag mich nicht, ob ich dich liebe / Lass mich geh'n / Es gibt keine frau, die nicht lugt / Wenn der Hergott will / Wann wirst du mich fragen / Irgendwo, irgendwann fangt ein marchen an / Warum brauchen denn die manner soviel liebe / Du bist der, bei dem's moglich war / Servus, sagt die schone stadt der lieder / Wunderbar / Welterfolge mit Zarah Leander (teil 1) / Welterfolge mit Zarah Leander (teil 2) / Eine frau in meinem jahren / Du machst mich so nervos / Sag mir nie wieder je t'aime / Und wenn's auch sunde war / O wermeland, du schones / In meinem garten / Du glaubst doch nicht / Ich kann ganz ohne menschen sein / Var'e du / Orjanslaten mit polska / Tanzet, tanzet meine lieben madchen / Tanze aus Smaland / Du sagst, du warst der beste tanzer / Zwei tanze aus Skane / Mannertreu / Weisse weihnacht / Un desir pour toi / Le vent m'a dit une chanson / Il pleut sans treve / Ich steh' im regen / Yes sir / Ich hab eine tiefe sehnsucht in mir / Nur nicht aus liebe weinen / Kann denn liebe sunde sein / Der wind hat mir ein lied erzahlt / Davon geht die welt nicht unter / Wenn der Herrgott will / Mit roten rosen fangt die liebe meistens an / Er heisst Waldemar / Wen ich liebe / Ich kenn den Jimmy aus Havanna / Wenn die wilden rosen bluhn / Ave Maria / Drei sterne sah ich scheinen / Reite, kleiner reiter / Gebundene hande / Weil ich dich so liebe / So stell ich mir die liebe vor / Paradiesvogel / Frauen sind schwer zu durchschauen / Die alte liebe / Daran zerbricht man doch nicht / Mitternachtsblues (1 fassung) / Mitternachtsblues (2 fassung) / Warum soll eine frau kein verhaltnis haben / Schon war die zeit / Merci, mon ami, es war wunderschon / Nachts ging das telefon / Eine frau wird erst schon durch die liebe / Ein leben ohne liebe / Pardon meine damen, pardon meine herrn / Seit ich dich sah / Ein leben ohne liebe / Jose / Einsamkeit / Bleib' hier, dich furht kein weg zuruck / Nie wieder so einen wie Waldemar / Schatten der vergangenheit / Paradiesvogel / Frauen sind schwer zu durchschauen / Die rose von Nowgorod / Ein mann fur mich / Othello / Wenn du traumst / Einmal kommt die liebe / Antonius / Sag nicht adieu / Wunderbar / Mitternachtblues / Eine frau wird erst schon durch die liebe / Wunderland bei nacht / Mir kommen tranen / Good bye, Sonny boy / Deine welt ist die kleine welt / Mitternachtslied / Antonius / Das leben ist ein roman / Othello / Kleine geige, sag adieu / Das herz einer frau / Was wissen manner von liebe / Cabaret Paris / Ich bin eine frau mir vergangenheit / Die liebe geht seltsame wege / Heinrich der achte / Ich kann den fruhling kaum erwarten / Ich kann allem wiedersteh'n / Mich hat die welt kaltgestellt / Wodka fur die konigin / Wenn am schwarzen meer / Dante / Das ist die grosse zeit / Abenteuer sind am abend teuer / Wo deine wiege stand / Einer muss da sein / Das gibt ein wiedersehn / Each time a churchbell rings / Mein herz kann lachen, mein herz kann weinen / Fragen / Adieu / Munchner g'schichten / Fenster meines lebens / Sag mir nicht adieu / Ich kenn Jimmy aus Havanna / Soll man lachen oder weinen / Liasons / Fragen / Adieu / Die kleine dinge / Ganz leise kommt die nacht / Einmal wird frieden sein / Mir kommen die tranen / Ich bin ein star / Yes sir / Drei sterne sah ich scheinen / Der wind hat mir ein lied erzahlt / Ich bin eine frau mit vergangenheit / Ich kann ganz ohne menschen sein / Wenn die wilden rosen bluhen / Nur nicht aus liebe weinen / Frauen sind schwer zu durchshauen / Warum soll eine frau kein verhaltnis haben / Ich weiss, es wird einmal ein wunder geschehn / Wenn der Herrgott will / Wunderbar / Sag mir nicht adieu / Ich kenn den Jimmy aus Havanna / Sol man lachen oder weinen / Liaisons
CD Set ____ **BCD 16016**
Bear Family / Apr '97 / Direct / Rollercoaster / Swift

Leandre, Joelle

PALIMPSESTE (Leandre, Joelle & Eric Watson)
CD ____ **ARTCD 6103**
Hat Art / May '92 / Cadillac / Harmonia Mundi

Leary, Timothy

BEYOND LIFE WITH TIMOTHY LEARY
After life / Beyond life / While birds sing / Fifty million years / Star light: *Leary, Timothy & Dr. Fiorella Terenzi* / Eternal note: *Leary, Timothy & Liquid Mind* / Why not, why not, why not / Goodbye, goodbye / Legend of a mind: *Moody Blues* / Tale of the tribe: *Ginsberg, Allen* / Lion's mouth: *Leary, Timothy & Al Jourgensen*
CD ____ **5342162**
Mouth Almighty / May '97 / PolyGram

YOU CAN BE ANYONE THIS TIME AROUND
CD ____ **RCD 10249**
Rykodisc / May '96 / ADA / Vital

Leather Strip

RETROSPECTIVE
CD ____ **CLP 9978**
Cleopatra / Apr '97 / Cargo / Greyhound / Plastic Head / RTM/Disc / SRD

SELF INFLICTED
CD ____ **CDZOT 173**
Zoth Ommog / Jul '97 / Cargo / Plastic Head

SERENADE FOR THE DEAD
CD ____ **CDZOT 114**
Music Research / Oct '94 / Plastic Head

Leatherface

LAST, THE
CD ____ **WIGCD 10**
Domino / Mar '94 / Vital

MINX
CD ____ **NECKCD 011**
Roughneck / May '93 / RTM/Disc

MUSH
CD ____ **NECKCD 005**
Roughneck / Sep '91 / RTM/Disc

Leatherwolf

ENDANGERED SPECIES
CD ____ **HMAXD 39**
Heavy Metal / Jul '85 / Revolver / Sony

Leaves

1966
CD ____ **422194**

New Rose / May '94 / ADA / Direct / Discovery

Leaving Trains

BIG JINX
CD _______________ SST 293CD
SST / Jul '94 / Plastic Head

KILL TUNES
CD _______________ SST 071CD
SST / May '93 / Plastic Head

LOSER ILLUSION PART 0
CD _______________ SST 284CD
SST / May '93 / Plastic Head

LUMP IN MY FOREHEAD
CD _______________ SST 288CD
SST / May '93 / Plastic Head

ROCK'N'ROLL MURDER
CD _______________ SST 283CD
SST / May '93 / Plastic Head

SLEEPING UNDERWATER SURVIVORS
CD _______________ SST 271CD
SST / May '93 / Plastic Head

TRANSPORTATIONAL D VICES
CD _______________ SST 221CD
SST / Feb '89 / Plastic Head

Leblanc, Keith

KICKIN' LUNATIC BEATS
CD _______________ BLCCD 12
Blanc / Oct '96 / Pinnacle / Shellshock/ Disc

Lebombo

KHWELA JAZZ
CD _______________ BVHAASTCD 9220
Bvhaast / Jan '93 / Cadillac

Lebrijano, Juan Pena

ENCUENTROS
Vivir un cuento de hadas / Dame la libertad / Las mil y una noches / Desafinado / El anillo (chibuli) / Pensamientos / Amigo mio, no / Esos ojos asesinos
CD _______________ CDORB 024
Globestyle / Jan '89 / Pinnacle

L'Echo Desluthes

MUSIQUE DE HAUTE BRETAGNE
CD _______________ BUR 822CD
Escalibur / '88 / ADA / Discovery / Roots

Lectroluv

LECTROLUV REMIX PROJECT, THE
CD _______________ EBCD 4
Eightball / Jan '95 / Vital

RETURN OF LECTROLUV
CD _______________ PLUGCD 4
CD _______________ PLUGMD 4
Produce / Apr '96 / 3mv/Sony

Lecuona Cuban Boys

CONGAS AND RUMBAS
CD _______________ CD 62014
Saludos Amigos / Apr '94 / Target/BMG

HISTORIC RECORDINGS
Cafunga conga / Panama / Tabou / Hindou / Amapola / La conga / Canto indio / La cucaracha
CD _______________ CAL 50586
Calig / Apr '91 / Priory

IN VENEZUELA 1940
CD _______________ HQCD 54
Harlequin / Jun '95 / Hot Shot / Jazz Music / Swift / Wellard

LECUONA CUBAN BOYS IN SOUTH AMERICA 1940-1944
CD _______________ HQCD 85
Harlequin / Sep '96 / Hot Shot / Jazz Music / Swift / Wellard

LECUONA CUBAN BOYS VOL.1
CD _______________ HQCD 11
Harlequin / '91 / Hot Shot / Jazz Music / Swift / Wellard

LECUONA CUBAN BOYS VOL.2 1934-1944
Cuba / Carnaval el Uruguay / La chaparrita / Mambo de jaruco / El pinero / Petrol / Rumbas de jaruco / Coctel de congas / Jose Dolores / Colibri / Bimbasaro / Tendre bolero / Patica y mondonguito / Camina pa-'lante / Danza del fuego / Canto Caribe / Costa Rica / Conga de la Martinica / Tumbao / Mi ultima conga
CD _______________ HQCD 07
Harlequin / Oct '91 / Hot Shot / Jazz Music / Swift / Wellard

LECUONA CUBAN BOYS VOL.5 1932-1946
CD _______________ HQCD 35
Harlequin / Feb '94 / Hot Shot / Jazz Music / Swift / Wellard

Led Zeppelin

4 SYMBOLS
Black dog / Rock 'n' roll / Battle of Evermore / Stairway to heaven / Misty mountain hop / Four sticks / Going to California / When the levee breaks
CD _______________ 7567826382
Atlantic / Aug '97 / Warner Music

CODA
We're gonna groove / Poor Tom / I can't quit you baby / Walter's walk / Darlene / Ozone baby / Wearing and tearing / Bonzo's Montreux
CD _______________ 7567924442
Atlantic / Aug '96 / Warner Music

COMPLETE STUDIO RECORDINGS, THE
Good times, bad times / Babe I'm gonna leave you / You shook me / Dazed and confused / Your time is gonna come / Black mountain side / Communication breakdown / I can't quit you baby / How many more times / Whole lotta love / What is and what should never be / Lemon song / Thank you / Heartbreaker / Livin' lovin' maid (she's just a woman) / Ramble on / Moby Dick / Bring it on home / Immigrant song / Friends / Celebration day / Since I've been loving you / Out on the tiles / Gallows pole / Tangerine / That's the way / Bron-y-aur stomp / Hats off to (Roy) Harper / Black dog / Rock 'n' roll / Battle of Evermore / Stairway to heaven / Misty mountain hop / Four sticks / Going to California / When the levee breaks / Song remains the same / Rain song / Over the hills and far away / Crunge / Dancing days / D'yer mak'er / No quarter / Ocean / Achille's last stand / For your life / Royal Orleans / Nobody's fault but mine / Candy store rock / Hots on for nowhere / Tea for one / Custard pie / Rover / In my time of dying / Houses of the holy / Trampled underfoot / Kashmir / In the light / Bron-y-aur / Down by the seaside / Ten years gone / Night flight / Wanton song / Boogie with Stu / Black country woman / Sick again / In the evening / South bound saurez / Fool in the rain / Hot dog / Carouselambra / All my love / I'm gonna crawl / We're gonna groove / Poor Tom / Walter's walk / Ozone baby / Darlene / Bonzo's Montreux / Wearing and tearing / Baby, come on home / Travelling riverside blues / White summer/Black mountain side / Hey hey what can I do
CD Set _______________ 7567825262
Atlantic / Apr '94 / Warner Music

GRAF ZEPPELIN (Interview Discs/2CD Set)
CD Set _______________ CONV 007
Network / Mar '97 / Total/BMG

HOUSES OF THE HOLY
Song remains the same / Rain song / Over the hills and far away / Crunge / Dancing days / D'yer mak'er / No quarter / Ocean
CD _______________ 7567826392
Atlantic / Aug '97 / Warner Music

IN THROUGH THE OUT DOOR
In the evening / South bound saurez / Fool in the rain / Hot dog / Carouselambra / All my love / I'm gonna crawl
CD _______________ 7567924432
Atlantic / Aug '97 / Warner Music

INTERVIEW DISC
CD _______________ SAM 7010
Sound & Media / Nov '96 / Sound & Media

LED ZEPPELIN (BOX SET)
Whole lotta love / Heartbreaker / Communication breakdown / Babe I'm gonna leave you / Dazed and confused / Ramble on / Your time is gonna come / What is and what should never be / Thank you / I can't quit you baby / Friends / Celebration day / Travelling riverside blues / Hey hey what can I do / White summer/Black mountain side / Black dog / Over the hills and far away / Immigrant song / Battle of Evermore / Bron-y-aur stomp / Tangerine / Going to California / Since I've been loving you / D'yer mak'er / Gallows pole / Custard pie / Misty mountain hop / Rock 'n' roll / Rain song / Stairway to heaven / Kashmir / Trampled underfoot / For your life / No quarter / Dancing days / When the levee breaks / Song remains the same / Achille's last stand / Ten years gone / Candy store rock / Moby Dick / In my time of dying / In the evening / Ocean / Ozone baby / Houses of the holy / Wearing and tearing / Poor Tom / Nobody's fault but mine / Fool in the rain / In the light / Wanton song / I'm gonna crawl / All my love
CD Set _______________ 7567821442
Atlantic / Oct '90 / Warner Music

LED ZEPPELIN BOXED SET VOL.2
Good times, bad times / We're gonna groove / Night flight / That's the way / Baby, come on home / Lemon song / You shook me / Boogie with Stu / Bron-y-aur stomp / Down by the seaside / Out on the tiles / Black mountain side / Moby Dick / Sick again / Hot dog / Carouselambra / South bound saurez / Walter's walk / Darlene / Black Country woman / How many more times / Rover / Four sticks / Hats off to (Roy) Harper / I can't quit you baby / Hots on for nowhere / Livin' lovin' maid (She's just a woman) / Royal Orleans / Bonzo's Montreux / Crunge / Bring it on home / Tea for one
CD Set _______________ 7567824772
Atlantic / Sep '93 / Warner Music

LED ZEPPELIN I
Good times, bad times / Babe I'm gonna leave you / You shook me / Dazed and confused / Your time is gonna come / Black mountain side / Communication breakdown / I can't quit you baby / How many more times
CD _______________ 7567826322
Atlantic / Aug '97 / Warner Music

LED ZEPPELIN II
Whole lotta love / What is and what should never be / Lemon song / Thank you / Heartbreaker / Livin' lovin' maid (she's just a woman) / Ramble on / Moby Dick / Bring it on home
CD _______________ 7567826332
Atlantic / Aug '97 / Warner Music

LED ZEPPELIN III
Immigrant song / Friends / Celebration day / Since I've been loving you / Out on the tiles / Gallows pole / Tangerine / That's the way / Bron-y-aur stomp / Hats off to (Roy) Harper
CD _______________ 7567826782
Atlantic / Aug '97 / Warner Music

LED ZEPPELIN: INTERVIEW PICTURE DISC
CD _______________ CBAK 4042
Baktabak / Apr '90 / Arabesque

PHYSICAL GRAFFITI
Houses of the holy / Trampled underfoot / Kashmir / Custard pie / Rover / In my time of dying / In the light / Bron-y-aur stomp / Down by the seaside / Ten years gone / Night flight / Wanton song / Boogie with Stu / Black country woman / Sick again
CD _______________ 7567924422
Atlantic / Aug '97 / Warner Music

PRESENCE
Achille's last stand / For your life / Royal Orleans / Nobody's fault but mine / Candy store rock / Hots on for nowhere / Tea for one
CD _______________ 7567924392
Atlantic / Aug '97 / Warner Music

REMASTERS (2CD Set)
Communication breakdown / Babe I'm gonna leave you / Good times, bad times / Dazed and confused / Whole lotta love / Heartbreaker / Ramble on / Immigrant song / Celebration day / Since I've been loving you / Black dog / Rock 'n' roll / Battle of Evermore / Misty mountain hop / Stairway to heaven / Song remains the same / Rain song / D'yer mak'er / Ocean / Houses of the holy / Kashmir / Trampled underfoot / Nobody's fault but mine / Achille's last stand / All my love / In the evening
CD Set _______________ 7567804152
Atlantic / Aug '97 / Warner Music

SONG REMAINS THE SAME, THE (2CD Set)
Rock 'n' roll / Celebration day / Song remains the same / Rain song / Dazed and confused / No quarter / Stairway to heaven / Moby Dick / Whole lotta love
CD Set _______________ SK 289402
Swansong / Aug '97 / Warner Music

THROUGH THE YEARS (Interview Discs/2CD Set)
CD Set _______________ CONV 004
Network / Feb '97 / Total/BMG

WHOLE LOTTA LOVE (Bootleg Zep)
Whole lotta love / Communication breakdown / Black dog / Bring it on home / Good times bad times / Living loving maid / Heartbreaker / D'yer mak'er / Ocean / Rock 'n' roll / Lemon song / Immigrant song / Dazed and confused / Live loser / Rock 'n' roll part 2 / Stairway to heaven
CD _______________ QED 107
Tring / Nov '96 / Tring

Leda Trio

AIRS FOR THE SEASONS
CD _______________ SPRCD 1036
Springthyme / May '94 / ADA / CM / Direct / Duncans / Highlander / Roots

Ledernacken

BOOGALOO AND OTHER NATTY DANCERS
CD _______________ SBR 14CD
Strike Back / Oct '87 / Grapevine/ PolyGram / Vital

L
CD _______________ E 119302
Derriere / Dec '93 / SRD

SEX METAL
CD _______________ SBR 16 CD
Strike Back / Jan '89 / Grapevine/ PolyGram / Vital

Ledgerwood, Leeann

YOU WISH
Robbin's row / Taisho pond / Miss Perfect / Chance / Nardis / Afterglow / You wish / Smash and grab / Terribillis / I want to talk about you
CD _______________ 3201872
Triloka / May '92 / New Note/Pinnacle

LeDonne, Mike

COMMON GROUND (LeDonne, Mike Trio)
CD _______________ CRISS 1058CD
Criss Cross / May '92 / Cadillac / Direct / Vital/SAM

SOULMATES (LeDonne, Mike Sextet)
CD _______________ CRISS 1074CD
Criss Cross / Nov '93 / Cadillac / Direct / Vital/SAM

Lee, Alan

JAZZ AT HYDE PARK
CD _______________ RQCD 1511
Request / Nov '96 / Jazz Music / Wellard

Lee, Albert

ALBERT LEE & HOGAN'S HEROES - IN FULL FLIGHT
CD _______________ RTMCD 60
Round Tower / Jan '94 / Avid/BMG

HIDING
Country boy / Billy Tyler / Are you wasting my time / Now and then it's gonna rain / O a real good night / Setting me up / Ain't living long like this / Hiding / Hotel love / Come up and see me anytime
CD _______________ CDMID 121
A&M / Oct '92 / PolyGram

Lee, Alvin

LIVE IN VIENNA
CD _______________ CDTB 171
Thunderbolt / Oct '95 / TKO Magnum

NINETEEN NINETY FOUR
Keep on rockin' / Long legs / I hear you knocking / I want you (she's so heavy) / I don't give a damn / Give me your love / Play it like it used to be / Take it easy / My baby's come back to me / Boogie all day / Bluest blues / Ain't nobody's business if I do
CD _______________ CDTB 150
Thunderbolt / Mar '95 / TKO Magnum

PURE BLUES
Don't want you woman / Bluest blues / I woke up this morning / Real life blues / Stomp / Slow blues in C / Wake up Mama / Talk don't bother me / Every blues you've ever heard / I get all shook up / Lost in love / Help me baby / Outside my window
CD _______________ CDCHR 6102
Chrysalis / Jul '95 / EMI

RETROSPECTIVE
Johnny B Goode / Help me / Good morning little school girl / Slow blues in C / Love until I die / Love like a man / One more chance / You told me / I'm going home / Jenny Jenny / Little bit of love / Truckin' down the other way
CD _______________ MMGV 064
Magnum Music / Mar '95 / TKO Magnum

Lee, Arthur

ARTHUR LEE & LOVE (Lee, Arthur & Love)
CD _______________ 422214
New Rose / May '94 / ADA / Direct / Discovery

BLACK BEAUTY & RARITIES (Lee, Arthur & Love)
CD _______________ EVOL 1
Eva / Jul '97 / Greyhound

VINDICATOR
Sad song / You can save up to 50% / Love jumped through my window / Find somebody / He said she said / Every time I look up / Everybody's gotta live / You want change for your re-run / He knows a lot of good women / Hamburger breath stinkfinger / Ol' morgue mouth / Busted feet
CD _______________ 5406972
A&M / Feb '97 / PolyGram

Lee, Ben

GRANDPAW WOULD
CD _______________ GR 015CD
Grand Royal / Apr '97 / Cargo / Plastic Head

SOMETHING TO REMEMBER ME BY
CD _______________ GR 044CD
Grand Royal / May '97 / Cargo / Plastic Head

Lee, Bonnie

SWEETHEART OF THE BLUES
CD _______________ DE 676
Delmark / Aug '95 / ADA / Cadillac / CM / Direct / Hot Shot

Lee, Brenda

BEST OF BRENDA LEE
Sweet nothin's / I'm sorry / Emotions / Dum dum / Fool number one / You always hurt the one you love / Will you still love me tomorrow / When I fall in love / I'll be seeing you / Speak to me pretty / Here comes that feeling / It started all over again / My colouring book / Someday you'll want me to want you / End of the world / All alone am i /

Losing you / Ronettes / My whole world / Sweet impossible you / As usual / Is it true / Think / Love letters / Too many rivers / Make the world go away / Crying time / Sweet dreams / Yesterday / Always on my mind / For the good times / Feelings
CD ____ **MCBD 19518**
MCA / Apr '95 / BMG

BEST OF BRENDA LEE, THE
CD ____ **MCCD 213**
Music Club / Oct '95 / Disc / THE

BRENDA LEE
Wiedersehn ist wunderschon / Kansas City / Ohne dich / Drei rote rosen bluh'n / Ich will immer auf dich warten / No my boy / Geh am gluck nicht vorbei / Am strand von Hawaii / Darling bye bye / In meinen traumen / Wo und wann fangt die liebe an / Darling was ist los mit dir / La premiere fool / Pourqui jamais moi / Sono sciocca / Nulla di me
CD ____ **BCD 15644**
Bear Family / Jun '92 / Direct / Rollercoaster / Swift

BRENDA LEE
Sweet nothin's / Dum dum / Call me / If you love me / I'm sorry / I want to be wanted / All alone am I / As usual / Emotions / Losing you / My whole world is falling down / Is it true / Kansas City / Too many rivers / Fool No.1 / You can depend on me
CD ____ **12456**
Laserlight / Apr '96 / Target/BMG

BRENDA LEE
CD ____ **HM 014**
Harmony / Jun '97 / TKO Magnum

COMING ON STRONG
CD ____ **MU 5037**
Musketeer / Oct '92 / Disc

CONCERT COLLECTION
Coming on strong / Silver threads and golden needles / Johnny one time / You're the one that I want / You don't have to say you love me / Medley / How much love / All you gotta do / Your Mama don't dance / I'm sorry / Medley / Medley / Medley
CD ____ **PLATCD 166**
Platinum / Mar '96 / Prism

CRYING GAME, THE
Crying game / Can't help falling in love / September in the rain / When I fall in love / Will you still love me tomorrow / Close to you / Fools rush in / You always hurt the one you love / Words / If you go away / Let it be me / Our day will come / This girl's in love with you / You don't have to say you love me / If I didn't care / I'll be seeing you / Lover come back to me / Softly as I leave you / What kind of fool am I / End of the world
CD ____ **MCLD 19241**
MCA / May '94 / BMG

EP COLLECTION, THE
Rock the bop / Weep no more baby / (If I'm dreaming) Just let me dream / Crazy talk / Speak to me pretty / Here comes that feeling / Ring-a-my-phone / Love you till I die / Rock-a-bye baby blues / Thanks a lot / All alone am I / If you love me (really love me) / I'm sorry / Georgia on my mind / I left my heart in San Francisco / Your used to be / She'll never know / Coming on strong / That's all you gotta do / Let's jump the broomstick / Stroll / Kansas City / Bigelow 6200 / Sweet nothin's / Rockin' around the Christmas tree
CD ____ **SEECD 425**
See For Miles/C5 / May '95 / Pinnacle

FAVOURITES
Coming on strong / Silver threads and golden needles / Johnny one time / You're the one that I want / You don't have to say you love me / Jambalaya / Is it true / My whole world / Sweet nothin's / End of the world / All alone am I / Fool no.1 / Too many rivers / How much love / That's all you gotta do / I'm sorry / Mama don't dance / Good ole acapella (soul to soul) / Old landmarks / I'll flyaway some glad morning / Operator / Up above my head / Saved / When you're smiling / You ought to be in pictures / Put on a happy face / Smile / Baby face
CD ____ **MUCD 9001**
Musketeer / Apr '95 / Disc

GREATEST HITS
Coming on strong / Silver threads and golden needles / Johnny one time / You're the one that I want / You don't have to say you love me / Jambalaya / Is it true / My whole world is falling down / Sweet nothin's / End of the world / All alone am I / How much love / All you gotta do / You mama don't dance / I'm sorry / When you're smiling / You ought to be in pictures / Put on a happy face / Smile / Baby face / Soul to soul / Old landmarks / Some glad morning / Operator / Up above my head / Saved / Dum dum / Fool number one / Too mnay rivers
CD ____ **PLATCD 362**
Platinum / '91 / Prism

I'M SORRY
CD ____ **WMCD 5570**
Disky / Oct '94 / Disky / THE

LEGENDS IN MUSIC
CD ____ **LECD 058**
Wisepack / Jul '94 / Conifer/BMG / THE

LITTLE MISS DYNAMITE (4CD Set)
Jambalaya / Bigelow 6-200 / Bigelow 6-200 / Some people / Your cheatin' heart / Doodle bug rag / Christy Christmas / I'm gonna lasso Santa Claus / Fairyland / One step at a time / Dynamite / Ain't that love / Love you till I die / One teenager to another / Rock a baby blues / Rock the bop / Ring-a-my-phone / Golden key / Little Jonah (rock on your steel guitar) / My baby likes Western guys / Papa Noel / Rockin' around the Christmas tree / Bill Bailey, won't you please come home / Heading home / Let's jump the broomstick / Hummin' the blues over you / Stroll / Rock-a-bye your baby with a dixie melody / Pretty baby / St. Louis blues / Pennies from heaven / Baby face / Ballin' the jack / Just because / Side by side / Good man is hard to find / Some of these days / Back in your own backyard / Toot toot tootsie goodbye / Sweet nothin's / (If I'm dreaming) Just let me dream / Weep no more my baby / That's all you gotta do / I want to be wanted (per tutta la vita) / Just a little / Build a big fence / Be my love again / I'm sorry / Dynamite / Love and learn / Wee Wee Willie / Jambalaya / Do I worry (yes I do) / Emotions / I want to be wanted (per tutta la vita) / No one / Crazy talk / Big chance / It's never too late / I'm learning about love / Careless, that's all / We three (my echo, my shadow and me) / If I didn't care / When my dreamboat comes home / Walkin' to New Orleans / Hallelujah I love him so / I'm in the mood for love / Swanee river rock / Pretend / If I didn't care / If you love me (really love me) / Teach me tonight / Blueberry Hill / Around the world / Fools rush in / Someone to love (The prisoner's song) / Zing went the strings of my heart / Georgia on my mind / Just another lie / When I fall in love / Cry / Will you love me tomorrow / You can depend on me / Careless, that's all / Lover come back to me / Kansas City / On the sunny side of the street / All the way / How deep is the ocean (how high is the sky) / Tragedy / Talkin' 'bout you / Tables are turning / Funny feelin' / Eventually / Dum dum / Let me be the one / Speak to me pretty / Time is not enough / Here comes that feeling / Just forget / Break it to me gently / Fool no.1 / Anybody but me / So deep / Only you (and you alone) / You've got me crying again / It's the talk of the town / You always hurt the one you love / I miss you so / I'll be seeing you / Lazy river / Send me some lovin' / Hold me / I'll always be in love with you / Organ grinder's swing / Let the four winds blow / Everybody loves me but you / Heart in hand / She'll never know / Why me / It takes one to know one / Sweet lovin'
CD Set ____ **BCD 15772**
Bear Family / Oct '95 / Direct / Rollercoaster / Swift

LITTLE MISS DYNAMITE
CD ____ **CD 6012**
Music / Jun '96 / Target/BMG

LIVE DYNAMITE (2CD Set)
CD Set ____ **CPCD 82892**
Charly / Jul '97 / Koch

ROCKIN' AROUND WITH BRENDA LEE
(If I'm dreaming) Just let me dream / Ain't that love / Bigelow 6200 / Bill Bailey, won't you please come home / Dum dum / Dynamite / Jambalaya / Let's jump the broomstick / Little Jonah (Rock on your little guitar) / Love and learn / My baby likes western guys / One step at a time / Ring-a-my-phone / Rock the bop / Rock-a-bye baby blues / Rockin' around the Christmas tree / Sweet nothin's / That's all you gotta do / Wee wee Willie's / Weep no more my baby
CD ____ **PWKS 4232**
Carlton / Nov '94 / Carlton

SINGS HER MOST BEAUTIFUL SONGS
CD ____ **CD 3501**
Cameo / Aug '94 / Target/BMG

VERY BEST OF BRENDA LEE, THE
CD ____ **MCLD 19121**
MCA / Oct '92 / BMG

Lee, Bryan

BLUES IS..., THE (Lee, Bryan & Jump Street Five)
Circles / Think / Waiting on ice / Let me down easy / It's your move / Gelle / There it is / You done me wrong / So low down / Pretty Jeanine / I worry / Blues is...
CD ____ **BLU 10122**
Blues Beacon / Feb '92 / New Note/ Pinnacle

MEMPHIS BOUND
CD ____ **JUST 522**
Justin Time / Sep '93 / Cadillac / New Note/Pinnacle

Lee, Bunny

AGGROVATE LEE PERRY AND THE UPSETTERS (Lee, Bunny & The Aggrovators)
Badaration dub: *Aggrovators* / Dread locks rasta love dub: *Aggrovators* / Righteous people dub: *Aggrovators* / Warmonger dub: *Aggrovators* / Bad rude boy dub: *Aggrovators* / Straight to the Upsetterhead: *Aggrovators* / Straight to Lee Scratchperry head: *Aggrovators* / Aggrovator colt the game in dub: *Aggrovators* / Winning punch dub: *Aggrovators* / Golden cup dub: *Aggrovators* / Rubber dub prize dub: *Aggrovators* / Bless the cup dub: *Aggrovators* / Standing ovation dub: *Aggrovators* / Humble lion dub: *Upsetters* / Mouth murderer dub: *Upsetters* / Dub slaughterer dub: *Upsetters* / Mean dub killer dub: *Upsetters* / Straight to the Aggrovator head: *Upsetters* / Iron front war dub: *Upsetters* / Steel plate bullerproof vest dub: *Upsetters* / Iron teeth killer dub: *Upsetters* / Ghetto blast dub: *Upsetters* / Upsetter murderer dub: *Upsetters* / War and peace dub: *Upsetters* / Upsetters knife edge dub: *Upsetters* / Straight to Bunny Lee's head: *Upsetters*
CD ____ **RN 7015**
Rhino / Feb '97 / Grapevine/PolyGram / Jet Star

Lee, Byron

BEST OF SKA (Lee, Byron & The Dragonaires)
CD ____ **JMC 200104**
Jamaican Gold / Dec '92 / Grapevine/ PolyGram / Jet Star

BEST OF SKA VOL.2, THE
CD ____ **JMC 200105**
Jamaican Gold / Feb '93 / Grapevine/ PolyGram / Jet Star

BEST OF SKA VOL.3, THE
CD ____ **JMC 200106**
Jamaican Gold / Feb '93 / Grapevine/ PolyGram / Jet Star

CHRISTMAS IN JAMAICA (Lee, Byron & The Dragonaires)
CD ____ **NL 25252**
Jamaican Gold / Oct '96 / Grapevine/ PolyGram / Jet Star

JAMAICA'S GOLDEN HITS (Lee, Byron & The Dragonaires)
My boy lollipop / Easy snappin' / Tell me darling / Green island / Wings of a dove / Sammy dead / Oh Carolina / Oil in my lamp / Occupation / Behold / Jamaica ska
CD ____ **DYCD 3380**
Dynamic / Jun '96 / Jet Star

ORIGINAL BYRON LEE, THE (Lee, Byron & The Dragonaires)
CD ____ **KENTONE 106**
Kentone / Jul '93 / Jet Star

PLAY DYNAMITE SKA (Lee, Byron & The Dragonaires)
CD ____ **JMC 200276**
Jamaican Gold / Jun '93 / Grapevine/ PolyGram / Jet Star

REGGAE BLAST OFF (Lee, Byron & The Dragonaires)
Monkey man / Elizabethan reggae / Love at first sight / Birth control
CD ____ **JMC 200108**
Jamaican Gold / Jul '94 / Grapevine/ PolyGram / Jet Star

REGGAE EYES
CD ____ **JMC 200107**
Jamaican Gold / Jul '94 / Grapevine/ PolyGram / Jet Star

REGGAE HOT SHOTS
CD ____ **JMC 200118**
Jamaican Gold / Jul '96 / Grapevine/ PolyGram / Jet Star

SOCA ENGINE (Lee, Byron & The Dragonaires)
CD ____ **DYCD 3493**
Dynamic / Jun '96 / Jet Star

SOCAROBICS (Lee, Byron & The Dragonaires)
CD ____ **DYCD 3494**
Dynamic / Jun '97 / Jet Star

SOFT LEE (Lee, Byron & The Dragonaires)
CD ____ **DYCD 3423**
Dynamic / Oct '95 / Jet Star

SOFT LEE VOL.2 (Lee, Byron & The Dragonaires)
CD ____ **DYCD 3456**
Dynamic / Sep '95 / Jet Star

SOFT LEE VOL.3 (Lee, Byron & The Dragonaires)
CD ____ **DYCD 3460**
Dynamic / Sep '95 / Jet Star

SOFT LEE VOL.5 (Lee, Byron & The Dragonaires)
CD ____ **DYCD 3489**
Dynamic / Jan '94 / Jet Star

WINE DOWN (Lee, Byron & The Dragonaires)
CD ____ **DY 3479**
Dynamic / May '92 / Jet Star

Lee, Dee C.

THINGS WILL BE SWEETER
CD ____ **CTNCD 001**
Cleartone / Oct '95 / Pinnacle

Lee, Dino

NEW LAS VEGAN, THE
CD ____ **ROSE 127CD**
New Rose / Oct '87 / ADA / Direct / Discovery

Lee, Elizabeth

TEXAS BOUND
CD ____ **PT 617001**
Part / Jun '96 / Nervous

Lee, Frankie

GOING BACK HOME
CD ____ **BPCD 5013**
Blind Pig / Dec '94 / ADA / CM / Direct / Hot Shot

SOONER OR LATER (Lee, Frankie & the Bluzblasters)
CD ____ **FF 595CD**
Flying Fish / Feb '93 / ADA / CM / Direct / Roots

Lee Harvey Oswald Band

BLASTRONAUT
CD ____ **TG 154CD**
Touch & Go / Jul '96 / SRD

TASTE OF PRISON
CD ____ **TGCD 84**
Touch & Go / Feb '94 / SRD

Lee, Jack

PIPING CENTRE 1996 RECITAL SERIES VOL.1, THE (2CD Set) (Lee, Jack & Alasdair Gillies)
CD Set ____ **COMD 2064**
Temple / Jul '97 / ADA / CM / Direct / Duncans / Highlander

Lee, Jackie

DUCK, THE
CD ____ **GSCD 011**
Goldmine / Feb '93 / Vital

Lee, John

BAMBOO MADNESS (Lee, John & Gerry Brown)
Infinite Jones / Deliverance / Jua / Absitively posolutely / Rise on / Who can see the shadow of the moon / Bamboo madness
CD ____ **FCD 0001**
Limetree / Nov '95 / New Note/Pinnacle

Lee, Julia

GOTTA GIMME WHATCHA GOT
He's tall, dark and handsome / Won't you come over to my house / Come on over to my house / Trouble in mind / If it's good / Show me Missouri blues / Lotus blossom / Dream lucky blues / Julia's blues / Lies / Gotta gimme whatcha' got / When a woman loves a man / Oh Marie / I'll get along somehow / Porter's love song to a chambermaid / Have you ever been lonely / Since I've been with you / Out in the cold again / Young girl's blues / On my way out
CD ____ **PLCD 560**
President / Mar '97 / Grapevine/PolyGram / President / Target/BMG

KANSAS CITY STAR
Down home syncopated / Merritt stomp / If I could be with you one hour tonight / Paseo Street / Ruff scufflin' / St. James Infirmary / He's tall, dark and handsome / Won't you come over to my house / Come over to my house / Trouble in mind / It it's good / Missouri blues / Lotus blossom / Dream lucky blues / We baby blues / I've got a crush on the fuller brush man / Two loves have I / Some of these days / St. Louis blues / Shake that thing shake it and break it / Julia's blues / Lies gotta gimme what you got / When a woman loves a man / Oh Marie / I'll get along somehow / Porter's love song / Have you ever been lonely / Since I've been with you / Out in the cold again / Young girl's blues / On my way out there / Snatch and grab it / If you hadn't gone away / Nobody knows you (when you're down and out) / Curse of an aching heart bleeding hearted blues / Living backstreet for you / You're a wise guy / Mama don't allow it / Doubtful blues / Ain't it a crime knock me a kiss / Cold hearted Daddy / My sin / When you're smiling / I was wrong / Pagan love song / All I ever do is worry / Take it or leave it / That's what I like / King size papa blues for somebody / I'm forever blowing bubbles / Breeze (blow my baby back to me) / Spinach song / Crazy world / Tell me Daddy / Christmas spirits / Until the real thing comes along / Charmaine / Lotus blosson marijuana / Sit down and drink it over / Away from you / Glory of love / Tonight's the night / My man stands out / Do you want it / It comes in like a lion / Don't come to soon / Ugly Papa / Don't save it too long / After hours waltz / You ain't got it no more / When your lover has gone / Oh chuck it (in a bucket) / Woman blues / Draggin' my heart around / It won't be long / You're gonna miss it / Can't get enough of that stuff / When a man has two women / Scream in the night / I know it's wrong / Music maestro please / Pipe dreams /

When Jenny does that low down dance / If I didn't care / Lazy river / All this beef and big red tomatoes / Can't get you off my mind / I got news for you / Goin' to Chicago blues / Last call for alcohol kansas city boogie / Love in bloom / Keep 'em barefoot and busy baby / I'm through / Scat you cats / I can't see how / King size Papa / Bop and rock lullaby
CD Set _______________ BCD 15770
Bear Family / Mar '95 / Direct / Rollercoaster / Swift

UGLY PAPA (Lee, Julia & Boyfriends)
CD _______________ RBD 603
Mr. R&B / Oct '91 / CM / Swift / Wellard

Lee, Keiko

BEAUTIFUL LOVE
Beautiful love / Time for love / My romance / Summer knows / You've changed / Shadow of your smile / Don't let me be lonely tonight / I'll be around / Go away little boy / Love is all there is / If it's magic
CD _______________ 4881942
Sony Jazz / Aug '97 / Sony

KICKIN' IT
Come back bebop - lover come back to me / Night and day / Love dance / Come rain or come shine / We'll be together again / Mr. Wonderful / Man I love / I will wait for you / How long has this been going on / God bless the child
CD _______________ 4851352
Sony Jazz / Sep '96 / Sony

Lee, Laura

THAT'S HOW IT IS
Wanted: Lover no experience necessary / Up tight good man / Another man's woman / He will break your heart / Dirty man / Hang it up / Man with some backbone / T'ain't what you do (it's the way that you do it) / Meet love halfway
CD _______________ CDRED 27
Charly / Sep '91 / Koch

Lee, Michael

FIRKINS
Laughing stacks / Runaway train / Deja blues / Rain in the tunnel / Sargasso sea / 24 Grand Avenue / Cactus cruz / Space crickets / Hula hoops
CD _______________ RR 93992
Roadrunner / Aug '90 / PolyGram

Lee, Myron

AW C'MON (Lee, Myron & The Caddies)
CD _______________ CLCD 4439
Collector/White Label / May '97 / TKO Magnum

Lee, Peggy

AT HER BEST (2CD Set)
Love for sale / Misty / You gotta know how / Rodgers and Hart medley / Have a good time / Mr. Wonderful / Sing a rainbow / Make believe / Fever / Why don't you do right / I don't want to play in your yard / I'm not in love / Everything must change / Mack the knife / Folks who live on the hill / Lover / Here's to you / Come back to me / Moments like this / Big spender / Here and now / Misty / I go to Rio / Unforgettable / I can't stop loving you / Big bad Bill / Dreams of Summer / Train song / Fisherman's wharf / St. Louis blues / Kansas City / Goin' to Chicago / Boston beans / Basin Street blues / New York city blues / I'm not in love / Switchin' channels / Hungry years / Alright, OK, you win / What I did for love
CD Set _______________ PDSCD 543
Pulse / Jul '97 / BMG

BEST OF PEGGY LEE, THE
CD _______________ MCCD 157
Music Club / May '94 / Disc / THE

BEST OF PEGGY LEE, THE
CD _______________ MATCD 316
Castle / Dec '94 / BMG

CHRISTMAS ALBUM, THE
I like a sleighride (Jingle bells) / Christmas song / Don't forget to feed the reindeer / Star carol / Christmas list / Christmas carousel / Santa Claus is coming to town / Christmas waltz / Christmas riddle / Tree / Deck the halls with boughs of holly / White Christmas / Winter wonderland / Little drummer boy / Happy holiday / Christmas spell / Toys for tots
CD _______________ CDMFP 6149
Music For Pleasure / Oct '96 / EMI

CLOSE ENOUGH FOR LOVE
CD _______________ CDSL 5190
DRG / '88 / Discovery / New Note/ Pinnacle

EMI PRESENTS THE MAGIC OF PEGGY LEE
As time goes by / Basin Street blues / Stormy weather / Cheek to cheek / Come dance with me / Fever / Fly me to the moon / Folks who live on the hill / From now on (leave it to me) / Unforgettable / Hallelujah I love him so / Happy holiday / I am in love / I could have danced all night / I hear music / I'm a woman / Man I love / Lady is a tramp / Mack the knife / On the street where you live
CD _______________ CDMFP 6371
Music For Pleasure / May '97 / EMI

FEVER
CD _______________ PRS 23012
Personality / Aug '93 / Target/BMG

FEVER (The Best Of Peggy Lee)
CD _______________ PLSCD 144
Pulse / Apr '96 / BMG

FOR SENTIMENTAL REASONS (16 Tender & Romantic Hits)
Lady is a tramp / Too young / Just one more chance / Shanghai / Let there be love / He's just my kind / I'm confessin' / I gotta right to sing the blues / Oh what a beautiful morning / Love is just around the corner / September in the rain / I'm beginning to see the light / Nice work if you can get it / These foolish things / That old gang of mine / (I love you) for sentimental reasons
CD _______________ PLATCD 160
Platinum / Mar '96 / Prism

GREAT VOCALIST, THE
CD _______________ CDSR 051
Telstar / Nov '94 / BMG

IF I COULD BE WITH YOU
If I could be with you one hour tonight / Too young / Clarinade / Shangai / Guy is a guy / Lady is a tramp / Dorsey medley / These foolish things / Just one more chance / Make the man love me
CD _______________ JASMCD 2534
Jasmine / Jan '95 / Conifer/BMG / Hot Shot / TKO Magnum

IN CONCERT
Do I hear a waltz / By the time I get to Phoenix / Reason to believe / Didn't want to have to do it / Personal property / Hand on the plow / Until it's time for you to go / Something stupid / What is a woman / Alright, okay, you win / Here's to you / Come back to me / Day in, day out / Moments like this / Fever / Second time around / One kiss / My romance / Vagabond King waltz / I got a man / I love being with you / But beautiful / Them there eyes / Just for a thrill / Yes indeed
CD _______________ CD 346
Entertainers / Jun '96 / Target/BMG

IN THE BEGINNING (The Legend Of Peggy Lee)
On the sunny side of the street / Blues in the night / Where or when / Why don't you do right / How deep is the ocean / Everything I love / How long has this been going on / Let's do it / Full moon / That did it Marie / Not mine / My old flame / Winter weather / I see a million people (but all I can see is you) / Shady ladybird / All I need is you / Somebody else is taking my place / Somebody nobody loves / Way you look tonight / I got it bad and that ain't good / I threw a kiss in the ocean / We'll meet again
CD _______________ PASTCD 7801
Flapper / Nov '96 / Pinnacle

IT'S A GOOD DAY (Lee, Peggy & Bing Crosby)
It's a good day / Everything's movin' too fast / Baby you can count on me / Best man / I still suits me / You came a long way from... / Exactly like you / I got rhythm / Little bird told me / On a slow boat to China / Cuanta La Gusta / What is thing thing called love / He's just my kind: *Lee, Peggy* / Linger in my arms: *Lee, Peggy* / What more can a woman do/: *Lee, Peggy* / (I love you) for sentimental reasons: *Lee, Peggy* / It's all over now: *Lee, Peggy* / Nightingale can sing the blues: *Lee, Peggy* / I'll close my eyes: *Lee, Peggy* / It takes a long, long train with a red caboose: *Lee, Peggy* / Just an old love of mine: *Lee, Peggy* / Golden earrings: *Lee, Peggy* / Love, your magic spell is everywhere: *Lee, Peggy* / Top hat, white tie and tails: *Lee, Peggy & Bing Crosby/Fred Astaire* / Isn't this a lovely day (to be caught in the rain): *Lee, Peggy & Bing Crosby/Fred Astaire* / They can't take that away from me: *Lee, Peggy & Bing Crosby/ Fred Astaire* / Dearly beloved: *Lee, Peggy & Bing Crosby/Fred Astaire* / Catalogue: *Lee, Peggy & Bing Crosby/Fred Astaire* / Then I'll be happy: *Lee, Peggy & Bing Crosby/Fred Astaire* / Maybe you'll be there: *Lee, Peggy & Bing Crosby/Fred Astaire* / Cheek to cheek: *Lee, Peggy & Bing Crosby/Fred Astaire* / Fine romance: *Lee, Peggy & Bing Crosby/Fred Astaire* / Smoke gets in your eyes: *Lee, Peggy & Bing Crosby/Fred Astaire* / White Christmas: *Lee, Peggy & Bing Crosby/Fred Astaire* / Kahehameha day: *Lee, Peggy & Bing Crosby/Fred Astaire* / I got lucky in the rain: *Lee, Peggy & Bing Crosby/Fred Astaire*
CD _______________ PARCD 001
Parrot / Jan '96 / BMG / Jazz Music / THE / Wellard

LATIN A LA LEE/OLE A LA LEE
Heart / On the street where you live / I am in love / Hey there / I could have danced all night / Surrey with the fringe on top / Party's over / Dance only with me / Wish you were here / C'est magnifique / I enjoy being a girl / 'Til there was you / Come dance with me / By myself / You're so right for me / Just squeeze me / Fantastico / Love and marriage / Non dimenticar / From now on / You stepped out of a dream / Ole / I can't resist you / Together wherever we go
CD _______________ CTMCD 111
EMI / Mar '97 / EMI

LEGENDS IN MUSIC
CD _______________ LECD 092
Wisepack / Nov '94 / Conifer/BMG / THE

LET THERE BE LOVE
I gotta right to sing the blues / Let there be love / If I could be with you one hour tonight / These foolish things / Shanghai / Make the man love me / Lady is a tramp / It's all over now / It takes a long, long train with a red caboose / Golden earrings / I got lucky in the rain / He's just my kind / What is this thing called love / (I love you) for sentimental reasons / My last affair / Just one more chance / Love is just around the corner / Love, your magic spell is everywhere / OH what a beautiful morning / Linger in my arms a little longer
CD _______________ TRTCD 153
TrueTrax / Dec '94 / THE

LET THERE BE LOVE
CD _______________ PLSCD 214
Pulse / Apr '97 / BMG

LISTEN TO THE MAGIC
It's a good day / I don't know enough about you / As long as I'm dreaming / I'll close my eyes / (I love you) for sentimental reasons / You and I passing by / He's just my kind / Linger in my arms a little longer baby / It's all over now / What more can a woman do / Nightingale can sing the blues / Ain'tcha never coming back / It takes a long long train with a red caboose / Just an old love of mine / Golden earrings / Ridin' high / Let there be love / I gotta right to sing the blues / Oh what a beautiful morning / What is this thing called love / Love is just around the corner / 'Deed I do / Do I love you / Just one of those things / You / I've got the world on a string / Love, your magic spell is everywhere / I got lucky in the rain
CD _______________ PLCD 550
President / Nov '96 / Grapevine/PolyGram / President / Target/BMG

MACK THE KNIFE
CD _______________ TRTCD 209
TrueTrax / Jul '96 / THE

MAN I LOVE, THE/IF YOU GO
Man I love / Please be kind / Happiness is a thing called Joe / Just one way to say I love you / That's all / Something wonderful / He's my guy / Then I'll be tired of you / My heart stood still / If I should lose you / There is no greater love / Folks who live on the hill / As time goes by / If you go / Oh love hast thou forsaken me / Say it isn't so / I wish I didn't love you so / Maybe it's because (I love you too much) / I'm gonna laugh you out of my life / I get along without you very well (except sometimes) / (I love your) gypsy heart / When I was a child / Here's that rainy day / Smile
CD _______________ CTMCD 105
EMI / Jan '97 / EMI

PEGGY LEE
CD _______________ ENTCD 13012
Entertainers / Apr '94 / Target/BMG

PEGGY SINGS THE BLUES (Classics In Jazz)
CC rider / Basin Street blues / Squeeze me / You don't know / Fine and mellow / Baby please come home / Kansas City / Birmingham jail / Love me / Beale Street blues / Ain't nobody's business if I do / God bless the child
CD _______________ 8208092
Limelight / Nov '89 / PolyGram

SPOTLIGHT ON PEGGY LEE
I've got the world on a string / When a woman loves a man / I'm beginning to see the light / There is no greater love / Too close for comfort / Unforgettable / Close your eyes / If I should lose you / I'm just wild about Harry / Deep purple / It's been a long, long time / Man I love / Best is yet to come / Come rain or come shine / Fever / I wanna be around / I hear music / That's all
CD _______________ CDP 8285332
Capitol / Jul '95 / EMI

THERE'LL BE ANOTHER SPRING (The Peggy Lee Songbook)
Circle in the sky / He's a tramp / Johnny guitar / I'll give it all to you / Where can I go without you / Things are swingin' / Shining sea / I just want to dance all night / There'll be another Spring / Fever / Sans souci / Boomerang (I'll come back to you) / Over the wheel
CD _______________ 8208212
Limelight / Jul '90 / PolyGram

THINGS ARE SWINGIN'/JUMP FOR JOY
It's a wonderful world / Things are swingin' / Alright, okay, you win / Ridin' high / It's been a long, long time / Lullaby in rhythm / Alone together / I'm beginning to see the light / It's a good, good night / You're getting to be a habit with me / You're mine, you / Life is for livin' / Jump for joy / Back in your own backyard / When my sugar walks down the street / I hear music / Just in time / Old devil moon / What a little moonlight can do / Four or five times / Music music music / Cheek to cheek / Glory of love / Ain't we got fun
CD _______________ CTMCD 101
EMI / Nov '96 / EMI

TOUCH OF CLASS, A
Sneakin' up on you / Come dance with me / Fever / Light of love / Till there was you / My man / Hallelujah I love him so / I'm a woman / CC rider / Mack the knife / Lady is a tramp / Alright, okay, you win / Manana / Golden earrings / Is that all there is / Pass me by
CD _______________ TC 862652
Disky / May '97 / Disky / THE

UNCOLLECTED 1948, THE
CD _______________ HCD 220
Hindsight / Jul '94 / Jazz Music / Target/ BMG

WHY DON'T YOU DO RIGHT
Elmer's tune / I see a million people but all I can see is you / I got it bad and that ain't good / My old flame / How deep is the ocean / Somebody else is taking my place / How long has this been going on / Winter weather / Blues in the night / On the sunny side of the street / Way you look tonight / We'll meet again / Full moon / Why don't you do right / Ain't goin' no place / That old feeling / What more can a woman do / You was right, baby / Waitin' for the train to come in / I don't know enough about you / Everything's movin' too fast / Linger in my arms a little longer, baby / It's a good day / It's lovin' time / It's all over now
CD _______________ CDAJA 5237
Living Era / May '97 / Select

YOU GIVE ME FEVER
Misty / What I did for love / Every little movement / Mr. Wonderful (Live) / Is that all there is / Folks who live on the hill / Love for sale / Fever / Mack the knife (live) / Sing a rainbow / I'm not in love / Hungry years / Lover / Star sounds
CD _______________ 5500882
Spectrum / Oct '93 / PolyGram

Lee, Ranee

LIVE AT LE BIJOU
CD _______________ JUST 22
Justin Time / Sep '93 / Cadillac / New Note/Pinnacle

MUSICALS, THE (Jazz On Broadway)
CD _______________ JUST 422
Justin Time / Jun '92 / Cadillac / New Note/Pinnacle

YOU MUST BELIEVE IN SWING
Secret love / Nice and easy / Angel eyes / I've got the world on a string / Au privave / My baby just cares for me / Yesterday's / Stolen moments / My romance / Fine and mellow / You must believe in spring / What is this thing called love
CD _______________ JUST 882
Justin Time / Aug '96 / Cadillac / New Note/ Pinnacle

Lee, Riley

ORIENTAL SUNRISE
CD _______________ NARCD 3803
Narada / Jun '96 / ADA / New Note/ Pinnacle

SATORI (Music For Yoga And Meditation) (Lee, Riley & Gabriel)
Satori / Kazue / Nightingale / Spring rain / Temple steps / Wanderer / Searching / Dreams
CD _______________ ND 62807
Narada / May '97 / ADA / New Note/ Pinnacle

Lee, Shawn

DISCOMFORT
Buzz Jenkins present Shawn Lee / Cryin' blue ('til my eyes are red) / Hanging by a thread / Who do you think you are / Married / Getting closer / Real nice / December flowers / P's funky finger / Rose without a thorn / Circles / Transcendental medication / Don't let the past change the future / Porcelain china doll / I can't save you / Untitled
CD _______________ 5327982
Talkin' Loud / Oct '96 / PolyGram

Lee, Soren

SOREN LEE QUARTET
New York subway waltz / Dr. Jekyll / My funny valentine / Darn that dream / Blues in the closet / Secret love / Lee meets Ray / St. Thomas / Blues for Philly Joe
CD _______________ CDLR 45073
L&R / Sep '93 / New Note/Pinnacle

Lee, Tim

ALL THAT STUFF (2CD Set) (Lee, Tim 'Love')
CD Set _______________ HYMN 10
Fundamental / Jun '97 / Cargo / Plastic Head / Shellshock/Disc

CONFESSIONS OF A SELECTOR (Lee, Tim 'Love')
Incense: *Lee, Tim* / Ruffbutt: *Lee, Tim* / One word: *Lee, Tim* / Nu pholk sound: *Lee, Tim* / Everybody loves the jungle: *Lee, Tim* /

Badder bongo: *Lee, Tim* / Java jam: *Lee, Tim* / Love's gonna get you: *Lee, Tim* / Mo' bounce: *Lee, Tim* / This is a story: *Lee, Tim* / Sugar spankin' No.2: *Lee, Tim* / Wack wack: *Lee, Tim* / At the bedside: *Lee, Tim* / Again son...: *Lee, Tim*
CD **MBTT 007CD**
Tummy Touch / Jun '97 / RTM/Disc

Lee, Tracey

MANY FACEZ
CD **UD 53036**
Universal / Apr '97 / Jet Star

Lee, Will

OH
CD **GOJ 60172**
Go Jazz / Dec '95 / Vital/SAM

Leeb, Michel

CERTAINS LEEB JAZZ
Lady is a tramp / Autumn in New York / Come rain or come shine / Can't buy me love / What's new / Fly me to the moon / Angel eyes / Teach me tonight / Moonlight in Vermont / Best is yet to come / Where or when / LA afternoon / One for my baby
CD **FDM 365862**
Dreyfus / Aug '97 / ADA / Direct / New Note/ Pinnacle

Leech Woman

33 DEGREES
TK 421 / Illuminator / Sea shepherd / Spit / Tool / Fear and bullets / Legion / Ova / Silicon / Intolerance / Sea shepherd
CD **VIRUS 194CD**
Alternative Tentacles / Jun '97 / Cargo / Greyhound / Pinnacle

Leeman, Mark

MEMORIAL ALBUM (Leeman, Mark Five)
CD **SEECD 317**
See For Miles/C5 / Jun '91 / Pinnacle

Leer, Thomas

BRIDGE
CD **BRIDGE 1CD**
The Grey Area / Jun '92 / RTM/Disc

CONTRADICTIONS
Hear what I say / Mr. Nobody / Contradictions / Looks that kill / Soul gypsy / Choices / Gulf stream / Private plane / International / Kings of sham / Dry land / Don't / Letter from America / Tight as a drum / West End / All about you
CD **CDBRED 105**
Cherry Red / Dec '93 / Pinnacle

Leeway

ADULT CRASH
Simple life / You / Make a move / Three wishes / Withering heights / Ten years / Silver tongue / Grip / Roulaison / Clueless
CD **CDVEST 4**
Bulletproof / Mar '94 / Pinnacle

OPEN MOUTH KISS
Foot the bill / Compromise / I believe / Hornet's nest / Manufabricate / Comes back / Product / State / Novena / Jock hop show / Old man of of sorrow
CD **CDVEST 64**
Bulletproof / Oct '95 / Pinnacle

Lefebvre, Patrick

ACCORDEAN GAVOTTE
CD **CD 431**
Diffusion Breizh / Apr '95 / ADA

Lefevre, Raymond

DEMONSTRATION
CD **819 921 2**
Bar / '88 / Pinnacle

Left For Dead

BEATINGS FROM ORLANDO
CD **DR 0001**
Dead Records / Feb '97 / Cargo

Left Hand Frank

LIVE AT THE KNICKERBOCKER CAFE
CD **422428**
Last Call / Feb '97 / Cargo / Direct / Discovery

Left Hand Freddy

BLUE TONIGHT (Left Hand Freddy & The Aces)
CD **MWCD 2010**
Music & Words / Dec '95 / ADA / Direct

Left Hand Right Hand

LEGS AKIMBO
CD **TAK 10CD**
Tonus Kozmetica / Oct '96 / World Serpent

Left Hand Solution

FEVERED
CD **NB 239CD**
Nuclear Blast / Apr '97 / Plastic Head

Leftfield

BACKLOG
CD **OUTERCD 1**
Outer Rhythm / Dec '92 / Vital

LEFTISM
Release the pressure / Pressure / Afro left / Melt / Song of life / Original black flute / Space shanty / Inspection (check one) / Storm 3000 / Half fast dub / Open up / 21st Century poem
CD **HANDCD 2**
Columbia / Jan '95 / Sony

Leftover Salmon

ASK THE FISH
CD **ATFCD 1**
Bert / Apr '96 / ADA

Leftwich, Brad

SAY OLD MAN
CD **CUY 2714CD**
County / Aug '96 / ADA / Direct

Lefty Dizz

AIN'T IT NICE TO BE LOVED
Cloudy weather / That's alright in the dark / I feel like jumping / Bad avenue / Ain't it nice to be loved / look on yonder wall / Too late / Sadie / Where the hell were you when I got home
CD **JSPCD 259**
JSP / Mar '95 / ADA / Cadillac / Direct / Hot Shot / Target/BMG

Legacy, Doug

KING CAKE PARTY (Legacy, Doug & Zydeco Party Band)
King cake party / Zydeco shoes / Cakewalk into town / Crime don't pay / Evil / He hates his threads / Sweet cajun baby / Closin' time / Cakewalk / Smokey places / No self control / Ya ya
CD **FIENDCD 206**
Demon / Jan '91 / Pinnacle

Legal Weapon

SQUEEZE ME LIKE AN ANACONDA
CD **LRR 010**
Last Resort / Oct '96 / Cargo

TAKE OUT THE TRASH
CD **TX 92772**
Roadrunner / Sep '91 / PolyGram

Legend

LEGEND
Friendly fire / Don't believe it / Angela / After the fall / Carry me / Set this place on fire / Colours / They that wait / Lead me back / Always and forever
CD **70193002637**
Nelson Word / Apr '92 / Nelson Word

Legend

AD 1980
Legend / My heart is there / Forgotten self / Heaven sent / Advantages / Way love's meant to be / Fantasy / Behind locked doors / Inside out / Silent world / Wooden sword / AM static / Favour
CD **ETHEL 4**
Vinyl Tap / Dec '94 / Cargo / Greyhound / Vinyl Tap

Legend

LIGHT IN EXTENSION
Light in extension / Hold the flame / Nightshade / Windsong / Pipes of Pan / Chase / Lament / Evidence of autumn
CD **PMCD 001**
Pagan Media / '96 / Pagan Media / Pinnacle

SECOND SIGHT
Dance / New horizons / Healer / Wild hunt / Legend / I close my eyes / Mordred
CD **PMRCD 6**
Pagan Media / '96 / Pagan Media / Pinnacle

TRIPLE ASPECT
Cunning man / Holly King / Lyonesse / All Hallow's Eve / Triple aspect
CD **PMRCD 9**
Pagan Media / '96 / Pagan Media / Pinnacle

Legenda

AUTUMNAL
CD **HOLY 025CD**
Holy / Jun '97 / Plastic Head

Legendary Blues Band

KEEPING THE BLUES ALIVE
I don't wanna know / Stuck in the bottom / I love my woman / Cook me / Open your eyes / Nobody knows / Without her / What's wrong / Shake it for me / Reach way back / Steady worried man
CD **ICH 1052CD**
Ichiban / Oct '93 / Direct / Koch

LIFE OF EASE
CD **ROUCD 2029**
Rounder / Oct '94 / ADA / CM / Direct

MONEY TALKS
CD **DOG 9107CD**
Wild Dog / May '94 / Koch

RED HOT 'N' BLUE
CD **ROUCD 2035**
Rounder / Oct '94 / ADA / CM / Direct

WOKE UP WITH THE BLUES
Another mule / I woke up with the blues / Your daughter looks good to me / Honey bee / I need you so bad / Don't throw your love on me so strong / I'd like to have a girl like you / I've got to be with you tonight / You're looking good again tonight / Having a hard time
CD **ICH 1039CD**
Ichiban / Oct '93 / Direct / Koch

Legendary Pink Dots

9 LIVES TO WONDER
Madame Guillotine / On another shore / Softly, softly / Crumbs on the carpet / Hotel Z / Oasis malade / Crack in melancholy time / Siren / Angel trail / Nine shades to the circle / Terra firma welcome
CD **BIAS 280CD**
Play It Again Sam / Feb '94 / Discovery / Plastic Head / Vital

ASYLUM
CD **CDBIAS 012**
Play It Again Sam / Mar '88 / Discovery / Plastic Head / Vital

BRIGHTER NOW
CD **TK 001 CD**
Terminal Kaleidoscope / Aug '88 / Vital / World Serpent

CANTA MIENTRAS PUEDAS
Belladonna / I love you in your tragic beauty / Green gang / Princess coldheart / Disturbance / Grain kings / Prague spring / Triple moon salute / Joey the canary / Siren / Angel trail / Velvet resurrection / Friend
CD **BIAS 325CD**
Play It Again Sam / Jul '96 / Discovery / Plastic Head / Vital

CHEMICAL PLAYSCHOOL (2CD Set)
CD **TEKA 834**
Terminal Kaleidoscope / Oct '96 / Vital / World Serpent

CURSE
CD **TK 002 CD**
Terminal Kaleidoscope / Aug '88 / Vital / World Serpent

FACES IN THE FIRE
CD **CDBIAS 001**
Play It Again Sam / Aug '88 / Discovery / Plastic Head / Vital

ISLAND OF JEWELS
CD **CDBIAS 041**
Play It Again Sam / '88 / Discovery / Plastic Head / Vital

MARIA DIMENSION, THE
CD **BIAS 184 CD**
Play It Again Sam / Jan '91 / Discovery / Plastic Head / Vital

SHADOW WEAVER
Zero zero / Guilty man / Ghosts of unborn children / City of needles / Stitching time / Twilight hour / Key to heaven / Laughing guest / Prague spring / Leper colony
CD **BIAS 225CD**
Play It Again Sam / Aug '92 / Discovery / Plastic Head / Vital

SHADOW WEAVER VOL.2 - MALACHAI
Joey the canary / Kingdom of the flies / Encore une fois / Wildlife estate / Pavanne / Window on the world / On the boards / We bring the day / Paris 4am
CD **BIAS 236CD**
Play It Again Sam / Mar '93 / Discovery / Plastic Head / Vital

STORM CIRCLES
Love puppets / Black zone / Golden dawn / Curious day / Hanging gardens / Fifteen flies / Our lady in darkness / Apocalypse / Gladiators version
CD **BIAS CD 1001**
Play It Again Sam / Apr '89 / Discovery / Plastic Head / Vital

TOWER, THE
CD **TK 003 CD**
Terminal Kaleidoscope / Aug '88 / Vital / World Serpent

UNDER TRIPLE MOONS
CD **RUSCD 8231**
ROIR / Jun '97 / Plastic Head / Shellshock/Disc

Legendary Stardust Cowboy

RETRO-ROCKET BACK TO EARTH
CD **422458**
WMD / Jan '97 / Discovery

Legende

EN REVENANT DES GRANDES CHANTIERS
CD **CDLCD 1802**
Coerdelion / Apr '96 / ADA

RETOUR AUX SOURCES
CD **CDLCD 1818**
Coerdelion / Apr '96 / ADA

Legg, Adrian

MRS. CROWE'S BLUES WALTZ
Kinvarra's child / Frank the part-time clown / Mrs. Crowe's Blues waltz / Gebrauchmusik II / Brooklyn blossom / Sour grapes / Norah Handley's waltz / Kiss-curl / Lunch time at Rosie's / Paddy goes to Nashville / Green ballet II / Last track
CD **CDRR 9085 2**
Roadrunner / Mar '93 / PolyGram

WAITING FOR A DANCER
CD **RHRCD 99**
Red House / Mar '97 / ADA / Koch

Legion

DIE DATENSCHLEUDER
CD **HY 39100982**
Hyperium / Apr '94 / Cargo / Plastic Head

LEVIATHAN
CD **DFX 024CD**
Side Effects / Apr '97 / Plastic Head / World Serpent

Legrand, Michel

DOUCE FRANCE (Legrand, Michel & Stephane Grappelli)
CD **5298502**
Verve / May '96 / PolyGram

LEGRAND GRAPPELLI (Legrand, Michel & Stephane Grappelli)
Parlez moi d'amour / C'est si bon / Les feuilles mortes / Summer of '42 / Revoir Paris / Mon legionnaire / Good life / Clopin clopant / Mon homme / What are you doing for the rest of your life / Insensiblement / Les parapluies de Cherbourg / Milou en Mai / Irma la douce / Nuages
CD **5170282**
Verve / Mar '93 / PolyGram

LEGRAND JAZZ (Legrand, Michel Orchestra)
Jitterbug waltz / Nuages / Night in Tunisia / Blue and sentimental / Stompin' at the Savoy / Django / Wild man blues / Rosetta / 'Round midnight / Don't get around much anymore / In a mist
CD **8300742**
Philips / May '93 / PolyGram

LIVE AT FAT TUESDAY'S (Legrand, Michel Quintet)
Watch what happens / How do you keep the music playing / Windmills of your mind / Once upon a Summertime / Blues for Ray
CD **8434442**
Verve / Apr '92 / PolyGram

WINDMILLS OF YOUR MIND (The Very Best Of Michel Legrand)
Summer of '42 / Where love begins / They simply fade away / Street where they lived / Old lovers never die / On the road / Windmills of your mind / Concerto for cabs / Do you come here often / In love with Normandy / Paris was made for lovers / Pavanne for people / Where love ends / Sea and sky: *Legrand, Michel & Dusty Springfield* / Place in Paris: *Legrand, Michel & Matt Monro* / I still see you (theme from 'The go between')
CD **305572**
Hallmark / Oct '96 / Carlton

Legs Diamond

CAPTURED LIVE
CD **CDMFN 137**
Music For Nations / Jun '92 / Pinnacle

WISH
CD **CDMFN 154**
Music For Nations / Oct '93 / Pinnacle

Leicester City FC

FILBERT STREET BLUES (Leicester City FC/Supporters)
This is the season: *Leicester City FC 1974* / Yes we're back: *Back Five* / Oh Leicester City (calypso): *Back Five* / Follow the foxes: *Back Four* / Glory boys in blue: *Back Four* / Post horn gallop: *Back Five* / Blue army blues: *Wembley '94* / FNF rap: *Filbert Fox Songs* / Filbert Fox song: *Filbert Fox Songs* / This is the season for us: *Phil Bert & The Foxes* / Post horn gallop: *Royal Marines* / We're going up: *Blue Army* / Flowing tears: *Price, Kev & The City Strikers* / Leicester boys: *Price, Kev & The City Strikers* / At the top where we belong: *Tilbury, Steve & The Blue Team* / We're back where we belong: *Ray Nardfox* / Frank Worthington: *Joe Jordanaires* / Champions: *Leicester Lads* / Tank: *Leicester City FC 1974*
CD **CDGAFFER 16**
Cherry Red / Apr '97 / Pinnacle

Leich, Peter

EXHILARATION
CD ____ RSRCD 118
Reservoir Music / Nov '94 / Cadillac

Leigh, Carol

CAROL LEIGH & THE DUMDUSTIER STOMPERS
CD ____ BCD 341
GHB / Jun '95 / Jazz Music

CAROL LEIGH WITH ERNIE CARSON AND BOB HELM (Leigh, Carol & Ernie Carson/Bob Helm)
CD ____ BCD 167
GHB / Nov '96 / Jazz Music

YOU'VE GOT TO GIVE ME SOME
CD ____ BCD 136
GHB / Jun '96 / Jazz Music

Leighton, Violet

SPEAK LOW
CD ____ BJAZZ 01
Blu Jazz / Aug '97 / Grapevine/PolyGram

Leijonhufvud, Johan

HAPPY FARM (Leijonhufvud, Johan Quartet)
CD ____ SITCD 9231
Sittel / May '97 / Cadillac / Jazz Music

Leimgruber, Urs

BEHIND THE NIGHT
CD ____ BW 049
B&W / Feb '96 / New Note/Pinnacle / SRD / Vital/SAM

L'ENIGMATIQUE (Leimgruber, Urs & Fritz Hauser)
CD ____ ARTCD 6091
Hat Art / Jun '92 / Cadillac / Harmonia Mundi

Leiner, Robert

VISIONS OF THE PAST
Out of control / Visions of the past / Interval / To places you've never been / Aqua viva / Full moon ritual / Zenit / Dream or reality / From beyond and back / Northern dark
CD ____ AMB 3925CD
Apollo / Jan '94 / Vital

Leitch, Peter

ON A MISTY NIGHT
CD ____ CRISS 1026CD
Criss Cross / May '94 / Cadillac / Direct / Vital/SAM

RED ZONE
CD ____ RSRCD 103
Reservoir Music / Oct '89 / Cadillac

SPECIAL RAPPORT, A
CD ____ RSRCD 129
Reservoir Music / Nov '94 / Cadillac

UP FRONT
CD ____ RSRCD 146
Reservoir Music / May '97 / Cadillac

Leixapren

GAITROPOS
CD ____ J 1024CD
Sonifolk / Jun '94 / ADA / CM

LeJeune, Eddie

CAJUN SOUL
Le two-step a pop / Grand bosco / La valse de Samedi au soir / Don't cry my children / Le branche de murrier / Lascassine special / J'ai ete au bal / Mistake I made / Little broken heart / Love bridge waltz / Cher'ti monde / Saturday night special
CD ____ HNCD 1353
Hannibal / Feb '90 / ADA / Vital

IT'S IN THE BLOOD
Le l'ai rencontree / Duralde waltz / Boire mon whiskey / Happy hop / Valse criminelle / Madeleine / Les conseils j'ai ecoutes / Je seras la apres t'espere / J'ai quitte ma famille dans les miseres / Teche / Fille a 'n oncle Hilaire / Reve du saoulard / Donnez moi la / J'aimerais tu viens me chercher
CD ____ HNCD 1364
Hannibal / Jul '91 / ADA / Vital

Lellis, Tom

TAKEN TO HEART
Mountain flight / Taken to heart / I'm late/ Alice in wonderland/You can fly / Milton's moment / Nobody does it better / Love is / My one and only love / Dukedom / It never entered my mind / It's not where you think it is / Wistful thinking
CD ____ CCD 4574
Concord Jazz / Nov '93 / New Note/ Pinnacle

Lema, Ray

EURO AFRICAN SUITE (Lema, Ray & Joachim Kuhn)
CD ____ 925492
BUDA / Nov '92 / Discovery

GAIA
CD ____ CIDM 1055
Mango / Nov '90 / PolyGram / Vital

GREEN LIGHT
CD ____ 829182
BUDA / Mar '96 / Discovery

NANGADEF
Kamulang / HAI 99 / Moni mambo / Boyete / Afcoeur / Nangadef / Pongi / What we need / Orchestra of the forest
CD ____ CIDM 1000
Mango / Apr '89 / PolyGram / Vital

STOP TIME
CD ____ 829452
BUDA / Jun '97 / Discovery

Lemaitre, Christian

BALLADE A L'HOTESSE
CD ____ CD 858
Escalibur / Feb '96 / ADA / Discovery / Roots

Lemer, Peter

LOCAL COLOUR
CD ____ ESP 10572
ESP / Jan '93 / Jazz Music

Lemon, Brian

BEAUTIFUL FRIENDSHIP, A (Lemon, Brian & Roy Williams Quintet)
Them there eyes / Fine and dandy / Nobody else but me / What's new / This love of mine / Comes love / Makin whoopee / One morning in May / Just friends / As time goes by / Moten swing / Up with the lark / Skylark / Beautiful friendship
CD ____ ZECD 4
Zephyr / Jul '97 / Cadillac / Jazz Music / New Note/Pinnacle

BUT BEAUTIFUL
Ill wind / Old folks / Exactly like you / I thought about you / It's you or no one / But beautiful / In a sentimental mood / This can't be love / That old feeling / Gee baby ain't I good to you / I'm putting all my eggs in one basket / Blues for Suzanne / St. Thomas / My one and only love
CD ____ ZECD 1
Zephyr / Oct '95 / Cadillac / Jazz Music / New Note/Pinnacle

HOW LONG HAS THIS BEEN GOING ON
Sweet Georgia Brown / How long has this been going on / Georgia on my mind / Bye bye blues / I can't get started with you / Blues in the closet / In the wee small hours of the morning / I remember you / Tenderly / When I fall in love / I've found a new baby
CD ____ ZECD 5
Zephyr / Mar '96 / Cadillac / Jazz Music / New Note/Pinnacle

LEMON LOOKS BACK JUST FOR FUN (Lemon, Brian & Roy Williams)
At the jazz band ball / I hadn't anyone till you / Farewell blues / Am I blue / Jazz me blues / I never knew / On the Alamo / When day is done / When it's sleepy time down south / When your lover has gone / Cotton tail
CD ____ ZECD 14
Zephyr / May '97 / Cadillac / Jazz Music / New Note/Pinnacle

OLD HANDS/YOUNG MINDS (Lemon, Brian & Alan Barnes Octet)
Limehouse blues / Polkadots and moonbeams / Mood indigo / Just one of those things / Chelsea bridge / Secret love / I gotta right to sing the blues / Willow weep for me / Someday my prince will come / After supper
CD ____ ZECD 12
Zephyr / Sep '96 / Cadillac / Jazz Music / New Note/Pinnacle

OVER THE RAINBOW
Over the rainbow / What is this thing called love / I don't stand a ghost of a chance with you / Have you met Miss Jones / When lights are low / Dearly beloved / Secret love / Emily / Star eyes / Straight no chaser / Alone together / You don't know what love is
CD ____ ZECD 2
Zephyr / Oct '95 / Cadillac / Jazz Music / New Note/Pinnacle

Lemon Kittens

BIG DENTIST, THE
They are both dirty / Hospital hurts / Girl / Log and the pin / Nudies
CD ____ BOT131 05CD
Biter Of Thorpe / Oct '96 / World Serpent

Lemon Pipers

LEMON PIPERS, THE
CD ____ NEXCD 131
Sequel / Jul '90 / BMG

Lemon Sol

ENVIRONMENTAL ARCHITECTURE
Sun flash / Memorandum / Natural ratio / Polymorph / Red drift / Powers of invasion / Fuse / Universal / Environmental architecture
CD ____ GRCD 014
Guerilla / Jul '94 / Pinnacle

Lemongrowers

SEGMENTS
CD ____ NBX 011
Noisebox / Apr '95 / RTM/Disc / Vital

Lemonheads

CAR BUTTON CLOTH
It's all true / If I could talk I'd tell you / Break me / Hospital / Outdoor type / Losing your mind / Knoxville girl / 6ix / One more time / C'mon Daddy / Something's missing / Tenderfoot / Secular Rockulidge
CD ____ 7567927262
Atlantic / Sep '96 / Warner Music

COME ON FEEL THE LEMONHEADS
Great big no / Into your arms / It's about time / Down about it / Paid to smile / Big gay heart / Style / Rest assured / Dawn can't decide / I'll do it anyway / Rick James style / Being around / Favorite T / You can take it with you / Jello fund
CD ____ 7567825372
Atlantic / Oct '93 / Warner Music

CREATOR
Burying ground / Sunday / Clang bang clang / Out / Your home is where you're happy / Falling / Die right now / Two weeks in another town / Plaster caster / Come to the window / Take her down / Postcard / Live without
CD ____ ESMCD 470
Essential / Mar '97 / BMG

HATE YOUR FRIENDS
Eat it / 394 / Nothing true / Second chance / Sneakyville / Amazing grace / Belt / Hate your friends / Don't tell yourself / Uhh / Fed up / Rat velvet / Fucked up
CD ____ ESMCD 469
Essential / Mar '97 / BMG

IT'S A SHAME ABOUT RAY
Rockin' stroll / Confetti / It's a shame about Ray / Rudderless / Buddy / Turnpike down / Bit part / Alisons starting to happen / Hannah and Gabi / Kitchen / Ceiling fan in my spoon / Frank Mills / Mrs. Robinson
CD ____ 7567823972
Atlantic / Feb '95 / Warner Music

LICK
Mallow cup / Glad I don't know / Seven Powers / Circle of one / Cazzo di Ferro / Anyway / Luka / Come back DA / I am a rabbit / Sad girl / Ever / Strange / Mad
CD ____ ESMCD 471
Essential / Mar '97 / BMG

LOVEY
Ballarat / Half the time / Year of the cat / Ride with me / Li'l seed / Stove / Come downstairs / Left for dead / Brass buttons / Door
CD ____ 7567821372
Atlantic / Feb '93 / Warner Music

Lemos, Paul

MUSIC FOR STOLEN ICONS VOL.2
CD ____ EFA 119392
Artware / Jan '94 / Vital

Lemper, Ute

BERLIN CABARET SONGS (Lemper, Ute & Matrix Ensemble/Jeff Cohen)
Alles schwindel / Sex appeal / Peter Peter / Das gesellschaftslied / Meine beste Freundin / Ich bin ein vamp / L'heure bleue / Zieh dich aus Petronella / Raus mit den mannern / Der verflossene / Gesetzt den fall... / Ich weiss nicht / Das Lila lied / Maskulinum - femininum / Mir is heut so nach tamerlan / Eine kleine sehnsucht / Munchhausen
CD ____ 4526012
Entartete Musik / Nov '96 / PolyGram

BERLIN CABARET SONGS (English Version) (Lemper, Ute & Matrix Ensemble/Jeff Cohen)
It's all a muddle / Sex appeal / Peter Peter / Smart bet / My best friend / I am a vamp / L'heure bleue / Take it off Petronella / Away with the man / Washed up lover / Oh just suppose / I don't know / Lavender song / Maskulinim-femininum / Tamerlam / Little yearning / Oh how we wish we were kids again / Munchausen
CD ____ 4528492
Entartete Musik / Jan '97 / PolyGram

CITY OF STRANGERS
CD ____ 4444002
Decca / Feb '95 / PolyGram

Lennon Family

DANCE OF THE HONEY BEES
CD ____ CEFCD 167
Gael Linn / Dec '95 / ADA / CM / Direct / Grapevine/PolyGram / Roots

Lennon, John

DOUBLE FANTASY (Lennon, John & Yoko Ono)
(Just like) starting over / Kiss kiss kiss / Clean up time / Give me something / I'm losing you / I'm movin' on / Beautiful boy / Watching the wheels / I'm your angel / Woman / Dear Yoko / Every man has a woman who loves him / Hard times are over
CD ____ CDP 7914252
Capitol / Jan '89 / EMI

IMAGINE
Imagine / Crippled inside / Jealous guy / It's so hard / I don't want to be a soldier / Gimme some truth / Oh my love / How do you sleep / How / Oh Yoko
CD ____ CDP 7466412
EMI / May '87 / EMI

IMAGINE - THE MOVIE
Real love / Twist and shout: *Beatles* / Help: *Beatles* / In my life: *Beatles* / Strawberry fields forever: *Beatles* / Day in the life: *Beatles* / Revolution: *Beatles* / Ballad of John and Yoko: *Beatles* / Julia / Don't let me down: *Beatles* / Give me a chance: *Plastic Ono Band* / How / Imagine / God / Mother / Stand by me / Jealous guy / Woman / Beautiful boy / (Just like) starting over
CD ____ CDPCSP 722
Parlophone / Oct '88 / EMI

JOHN LENNON/PLASTIC ONO BAND
Mother / Hold on / I found out / Working class hero / Isolation / Remember / Love / Well well well / Look at me / God / My mummy's dead
CD ____ CDFA 3310
Fame / Nov '94 / EMI

LENNON (4CD Set)
Give peace a chance / Blue suede shoes / Money (that's what I want) / Dizzy Miss Lizzy / Yer blues / Cold turkey / Instant karma / Mother / Hold on / I found out / Working class hero / Isolation / Remember / Love / Well well well / Look at me / God / My mummy's dead / Power to the people / Well (baby please don't go) / Imagine / Crippled inside / Jealous guy / It's so hard / Give me some truth / Oh my love / How do you sleep / How / Oh Yoko / Happy Christmas (war is over) / Woman is the nigger of the world / New York City / John Sinclair / Come together / Hound dog / Mind games / Aisumasen (I'm sorry) / One day (at a time) / Intuition / Out the blue / Whatever gets you through the night / Going down on love / Old dirt road / Bless you / Scared / Number 9 dream / Surprise surprise (sweet bird of paradox) / Steel and glass / Nobody loves you (when you're down and out) / Stand by me / Ain't that a shame / Do you want to dance / Sweet little sixteen / Slippin' and slidin' / Angel baby / Just because / Whatever gets you through the night (live) / Lucy in the sky with diamonds / I saw her standing there / (Just like) starting over / Cleanup time / I'm losing you / Beautiful boy / Watching the wheels / Woman / Dear Yoko / I'm stepping out / I don't wanna face it / Nobody told me / Borrowed time / (Forgive me) my little flower princess / Every man has a woman who loves him / Boys and girls / Grow old with me
CD Set ____ CDS 7952202
Parlophone / Oct '90 / EMI

LENNON INTERVIEW DISC
CD ____ SNECD 001
Speak 'n' Easy / Jun '97 / Total/BMG

LIFE WITH THE LIONS (Unfinished Music No.2) (Ono, Yoko & John Lennon)
CD ____ RCD 10412
Rykodisc / Jun '97 / ADA / Vital

LIVE IN NEW YORK CITY
New York City / It's so hard / Woman is the nigger of the world / Well, well, well / Instant Karma / Mother / Come together / Imagine / Cold turkey / Hound dog / Give peace a chance
CD ____ CDP 7461962
Parlophone / May '86 / EMI

LIVE JAM (Plastic Ono Band)
Cold turkey / Don't worry Kyoko / Well (baby please don't go) / Jamrag / Scumbag / AU
CD ____ CDP 7467832
Parlophone / Aug '87 / EMI

LIVE PEACE IN TORONTO (Plastic Ono Band)
Blue suede shoes / Money (that's what I want) / Dizzy Miss Lizzy / Yer blues / Cold turkey / Give peace a chance / Don't worry Kyoko / John John let's hope for peace
CD ____ CDP 7904282
Apple / May '95 / EMI

MENLOVE AVE
Here we go again / Rock 'n' roll people / Angel baby / My baby left me / To know her is to love her / Steel and glass / Scared / Old dirt road / Nobody loves you (when you're down and out) / Bless you
CD ____ CDP 7465762
Parlophone / Apr '87 / EMI

MIND GAMES
Mind games / Tight as / Aisumasen (I'm sorry) / One day (at a time) / Bring on the Lucie / Nutopian international anthem / Intuition / Out of the blue / Only people / I know (I know) / You are here / Meat city
CD ____ CDP 7467692
Parlophone / Aug '87 / EMI

PLASTIC ONO BAND (Yoko Ono & The Plastic Ono Band)
CD RCD 10414
Rykodisc / Jun '97 / ADA / Vital

ROCK 'N' ROLL
Be bop a lula / Stand by me / Rip it up / You can't catch me / Ain't that a shame / Do you wanna dance / Sweet little sixteen / Slippin' and slidin' / Peggy Sue / Bring it on home to me / Bony Moronie / Ya ya / Just because / Ready teddy
CD CDP 7467072
Parlophone / May '87 / EMI

SHAVED FISH
Give peace a chance / Cold turkey / Instant karma / Power to the people / Mother / Woman is the nigger of the world / Imagine / Whatever gets you through the night / Mind games / No. 9 dream / Happy Christmas (war is over) / Give peace a chance (reprise)
CD CDP 7466422
EMI / May '87 / EMI

TESTIMONY
CD CDTB 095
Thunderbolt / Apr '91 / TKO Magnum

TWO VIRGINS (Unfinished Music No.1) (Ono, Yoko & John Lennon)
CD RCD 10411
Rykodisc / Jun '97 / ADA / Vital

WALLS AND BRIDGES
Going down on love / Whatever gets you through the night / Old dirt road / What you got / Bless you / Scared / No. 9 dream / Surprise surprise (sweet bird of paradox) / Steel and glass / Beef jerky / Nobody loves you (when you're down and out) / Ya ya
CD CDP 7467682
Parlophone / Jul '87 / EMI

WEDDING ALBUM (Ono, Yoko & John Lennon)
CD RCD 10413
Rykodisc / Jun '97 / ADA / Vital

WORKING CLASS HERO (A Tribute To John Lennon) (Various Artists)
I found out: *Red Hot Chili Peppers* / I don't want to be a soldier: *Mad Season* / Steel and glass: *Candlebox* / Imagine: *Blues Traveller* / Working class hero: *Screaming Trees* / Power to the people: *Minus 5* / How do you sleep: *Magnificent Bastards* / Nobody told you: *Flaming Lips* / Well well well: *Super Eight* / Cold turkey: *Cheap Trick* / Isolation: *Sponge* / Jealous guy: *Collective Soul* / Instant karma: *Toad The Wet Sprocket* / Grow old with me: *Carpenter, Mary-Chapin* / Mind games: *Clinton, George*
CD 6201152
Hollywood / Oct '95 / PolyGram

Lennon, Julian

SECRET VALUE OF DAYDREAMING, THE
Stick around / You get what you want / Let me tell you / I've seen your face / Coward till the end / This is my day / You didn't have to tell me / Everyday / Always think twice / I want your body
CD CASCD 1171
Charisma / Jul '87 / EMI

VALOTTE
Valotte / OK for you / On the phone / Space / Well I don't know / Too late for goodbyes / Lonely / Say your wrong / Jesse / Let me be
CD CDVIP 162
Virgin VIP / Oct '96 / EMI

Lennox, Annie

INTERVIEW DISC
CD SAM 7013
Sound & Media / Nov '96 / Sound & Media

MEDUSA
No more I love you's / Take me to the river / Whiter shade of pale / Don't let it bring you down / Train in vain / I can't get next to you / Downtown lights / Thin line between love and hate / Waiting in vain / Something so right
CD 74321257172
RCA / Mar '95 / BMG

Lennox CF

PICNICS & HOLIDAYS
CD BRAM 1989052
Brambus / Nov '93 / ADA

Lens Cleaner

WITH VOICE INSTRUMENTS
CD SAB 002CD
Sabotage / Nov '95 / Plastic Head

Leo, Phillip

DOWN 2 EARTH
CD ASPCD 002
Sharma / Jul '97 / Jet Star

JUST 4 U
CD ASPCD 001
Sharma / Jul '96 / Jet Star

SPACE DUB
CD ASPCD 003
Sharma / Jul '97 / Jet Star

Leonard, Deke

ICEBERG/KAMIKAZE
Razor blade and rattlesnake / I just can't win / Lisa / Nothing is happening / Looking for a man / Hard way to live / Broken ovation / Jesse / Ten thousand takers / Ghost of musket flat / Crosby (Second class citizen blues) / 7171 551 / Cool summer rain / Jayhawk special / Sharpended claws / Taking the easy way out / Black gates of death / Stacia / Broken glass and limejuice / April the third / Louisiana hoedown / In search of Sarah and twenty six horses / Devil's gloves
CD BGOCD 288
Beat Goes On / Aug '95 / Pinnacle

Leonard, Harlan

CLASSICS 1940 (Leonard, Harlan & His Rockets)
CD CLASSICS 670
Classics / Nov '92 / Discovery / Jazz Music

Leonhart, Jay

FOUR DUKE (Leonhart, Jay & Gary Burton)
In a mellow tone / Rockin' in rhythm / C jam blues / Love you madly / Azure / Cotton tail / Creole love song / Take the 'A' train / Squeeze me / Caravan / Ishfanhan / Satin doll
CD CDC 9089
LRC / Aug '95 / Harmonia Mundi / New Note/Pinnacle

LIFE OUT ON THE ROAD - JAZZ JOURNEY
CD CDSGP 0199
Prestige / Jun '96 / Else / Total/BMG

LIVE AT FAT TUESDAY'S (Leonhart, Jay & Friends)
Smile / Let the flower grow / Robert Frost / Lonely rider / Strangest thing / They're coming to get me / Unhappy / Momma don't you think we ought to be going / Impossible to sing and play the bass / Kentucky wild flower / Me and Lenny
CD 8439
DRG / Nov '93 / Discovery / New Note/ Pinnacle

Leo's Sunshipp

WE NEED EACH OTHER
Give me the sunshine / I'm back for more / Get down people / Madame Butterfly
CD EXCDM 2
Expansion / Sep '96 / 3mv/Sony

Leroi Brothers

CHECK THIS ACTION
Are you with me baby / I can't be satisfied / Ain't I'm a dog / Big time operator / Steady with Betty / Check this action / Chicken and honey / Rockin' Daddy / Cotton pickin' / Crazy crazy lovin' / Ballad of a juvenile delinquent / Till it's too late / Arms race / Damage / Little Miss Understanding / Straight jacket / Mad about the wrong boy / Motorworld / On the third stroke / Slow patience / La la la la la loved you / Single girl / Lonesome little town / Taste of poison / High rise housewife / Talk about me / Sad about girls / Camera camera / I feel like breaking up somebody's home / Why do I / Laughin' and clownin' / If I ever had a good thing / Scarred knees / From the heart / Your love is so doggone good / We don't see eye to eye / Roadblock / Teach me to forget
CD ROUCD 9034
Rounder / Nov '94 / ADA / CM / Direct

Les 4 Jeans

ENTENDS TU MA BLONDE LE TONNERRE QUI GRONDE
CD 49504CD
Acousteak / Nov '96 / ADA / Discovery

Les Aborigenes

SONGS AND DANCES FROM NORTH AUSTRALIA
CD ARN 64056
Arion / Apr '91 / ADA / Discovery

Les Angeles Prietos

AGUINALDOS
CD PS 65160
PlayaSound / Feb '96 / ADA / Harmonia Mundi

Les Ballets Africains

HERITAGE
CD 926342CD
Euda / Nov '95 / ADA

Les Calchakis

FLUTES DE PAN DES ANDES
Recuerdo azul / Lima morena / Presencia lejana / Coplas de marzo / El colibri / Linda cambita / Jesusana / Cuculi / Blanca palomita / Aires de mi tierra / Sol nocturno / Amankay / Tiempo de paz / Requiem para un afilador / Uskil / Kena y siku / Sikus del titicaca / Triste tondero / Urpillay / Acuarela de sikus
CD ARN 64005
Arion / '88 / ADA / Discovery

FLUTES DES TERRES INCAS
La pastora / El centinela et anata morena / Lejana purmamarca / La maye / Reservista purajhey / Soplo del oriente / El pastor / Sol de vilcabamba / La bocina / El sacha puma / Kacharpari / Crepusculo costeno / Tuntuneando / Kurikinga / Casi me quisiste / Himno al sol / Sanjuanero / Sonkoy / Selvas y valles / Kapullay
CD ARN 64002
Arion / '88 / ADA / Discovery

HARPE, MARIMBA ET GUITARS LATINO-AMERICAINES
Cambai / El toro rabon / Carta a Buenos Aires / Bailecito triple / Isla saca / Nieve viento y sol / La escala / Campanas a M Nunez / Angata / La rielera / Imagenes Argentinas / Cuerdita / Joropeando / Poncho verde / Bailecito Calchaki / Concierto en la llanura / La zandunga / Lunarcito / Madrecita / Bachue
CD ARN 64032
Arion / '88 / ADA / Discovery

PRESTIGE DE LA MUSIQUE LATINO-AMERICAINE
Quiero contarte / Hilanderita / Tema boliviano / Cotopaxi / Sube a nacer conmigo / Rasguido de la paz / Chimborazo / Papel de plata / El aguaceral / Kalahuayo yuyay / Si tu me olvidas / Cullaguada / Alejandra / Del otro lado del mar
CD ARN 64025
Arion / '88 / ADA / Discovery

Les Chiens Jaunes

TRIO DE VIELLES
CD MB 002CD
Le Micro Bleu / Aug '96 / ADA

Les Ecoliers De Saint Genest

DANCES FROM THE BERRY
CD B 6832CD
Auvidis/Ethnic / Aug '96 / ADA / Harmonia Mundi

Les Fleurs De Lys

REFLECTIONS
Circles / Mud in your eye / Gong with the luminous nose / Sugar love / Hold on / Prodigal son / One city girl / Daughter of the sun / Tick tock / I can see the light / Liar / I forgive you / So come on / Hammerhead / Stop crossing the bridge / I like what I'm trying to do / Hold on / Butchers and bakers / Wait for me / Reflections of Charlie Brown / Brick by brick / I've been trying / Moondreams / So many things
CD BP 256CD
Blueprint / May '97 / Pinnacle

Les Freres Guillemain

BERRY BOURBONNAIS
CD Y 225105CD
Silex / Oct '93 / ADA / Harmonia Mundi

HISTORICAL BAGPIPE/HURDY GURDY
CD Y 225105
Silex / Oct '93 / ADA / Harmonia Mundi

Les Halmas

PLUS ONE
CD IH 9601
ReR/Recommended / Jun '97 / ReR Megacorp / RTM/Disc

Les Hommes Qui Wear ...

KAIRO (Les Hommes Qui Wear Espadrillos)
CD EFA 127922
Blu Noise / Dec '95 / SRD

Les Joyaux De La Princesse ...

DIE WEISSE ROSE (Les Joyaux De La Princesse & Regard Extreme)
Tiefe sehnsucht (zu neuen ufern) / Die natur ist jetzt mit waffenkland erwacht / Jetzt aber tagts / Der reissen ninabschaumt / Rosen des lebens / Die jugend trauert (marche funebre) / Weisse blatter / Letze kampf des lebens / Die flammen entbunden / Weisse rose / Der abschied / Tiefe sensucht / Sag' mir adieu
CD SD 04CD
New European / Jul '97 / World Serpent

Les Jumeaux

FEATHERCUT
CD CORP 013CD
ITN Corporation / Jan '96 / Plastic Head

Les Maniacs

LIVE AT BUDOKAN
CD STOP 09CD
Danceteria / Feb '90 / ADA / Plastic Head / Shellshock/Disc

Les Mecenes

SAMEDI SOIR CHEZ NANA
CD 829172
Bleu Caraibes / Mar '96 / Discovery

Les Negresses Vertes

10 REMIXES 87-93
Face a la mer / Hou Mamma mia / Sous le soleil de bodega / 200 Ans d'hypocrisie / Orane / Voila l'ete / Dun de nuit / Famille heureuse / Les yeux de ton pere / Zobi la mouche / Sous le soleil de bogeda (Di moko) / Hou Mamma Mia (House mix)
CD CDDLB 9
Delabel / Jun '93 / EMI

FAMILLE HEUREUSE
CD CDDLB 2
Delabel / Feb '92 / EMI

GREEN BUS (2CD Set)
CD Set CDDLB 16
Delabel / Aug '96 / EMI

MLAH
La valse / Zobi la mouche / C'est pas la mer a boire / Voila l'ete / Orane / La faim des haricots / Les yeux de ton pere / Il / L'homme des marais / Les rablablas les roubliblis / Marcelle Ratafia / La danse des negresses vertes / Hey Maria / Le pere Magloire
CD CDDLB 5
Delabel / Apr '92 / EMI

ZIG-ZAGUE
Fanfaron / Tous des ouvriers / Apres la pluie / La main verte / Mambo show / Comme toujours / A quoi bon / Enfer et paradis / Bourre d'allegresse / Iza mellino/mellino / Le poete / Ivresse / Footballer du Dimanche / Tu m'as saoule
CD CDDLB 12
Virgin / Feb '95 / EMI

Les Nouvelles Polyphonies ...

IN PARADISO (Les Nouvelles Polyphonies Corses)
CD CD 5324532
Mercury / Feb '97 / PolyGram

IN PARADISU (Les Nouvelles Polyphonies Corses)
Perdonu mio diu / Introitu / Kyrie Eleison / Gloria / Sanctus / Credo / Agnus dei / Salutaris / Tantum ergo / Subvenite / Requiem / Kyrie Eleison defunti / Dies irae / Domine offertoriu / Sanctus defunti / Agnus dei defunti / Libera me / In paradisu / Stabat mater / Dio vi salci regina
CD 5324532
Mercury / Feb '97 / PolyGram

Les Pires

SAVA
CD 562023
Bondage / Apr '96 / Discovery

Les Quatre Guitaristes De ...

WORLD TOUR 1988 (Les Quatre Guitaristes De L'Apocalypso-Bar)
CD RERGQ 1
ReR/Recommended / Oct '96 / ReR Megacorp / RTM/Disc

Les Tambours Du Bronx

MONOSTRESS 225L
La Valse des Nuls / Tchi tchi ou la mort / Metropolis / Heya / Cadence 22 / Le crepuscle des Crapules / Locomotive / Monostress 225L
CD 592048
FNAC / Nov '93 / Discovery

Les Thugs

AS HAPPY AS POSSIBLE
CD SOL 39CD
Vinyl Solution / Oct '93 / RTM/Disc

Les Vice Barons

STEEL BLUE MOODS
CD NITR 009
Demolition Derby / Feb '97 / Greyhound / Nervous

Lesh, Lagen

SEASTONES
CD RCD 40193
Rykodisc / Dec '92 / ADA / Vital

Leslie, Chris

GIFT, THE
Tenpence coloured / Shaker music / Samuel's shoes/Imogen's reel / Sir John Fenwick's/John's fairy dance / No sleep for the wicked / Red haired man's wife / Eighteenth century English dances / Gow rediscovered / I wandered by a brookside / Linda's tune / Of all the ways the wind can blow / Cape Breton set / She once loved me / Buffoon/ Black joke / Highland medley
CD BEJOCD 5
Beautiful Jo / Jun '94 / ADA / Direct

L'Esprit

FAR JOURNEY
Complete / Turning of the tide / Trust / That special place / Far journey / Release / Bali sure / Highlands
CD _____ KCD 002
Ki-Productions / May '92 / Ki-Productions

LANGUAGE OF TOUCH
Kaira / Sea of change / Ripples / Shoji / Taiga / Language of touch / Verandah
CD _____ KCD 001
Ki-Productions / May '92 / Ki-Productions

Less Than Jake

PEZCORE
CD _____ AM 001
Asian Man / Feb '97 / Cargo / Greyhound / Plastic Head

Lester Bangs

JOOK SAVAGES ON THE BRAZOS (Lester Bangs & The Delinquents)
CD _____ EFA 121662
Moll / Mar '95 / SRD

Leston, Paul

CARNIVAL HITS 1997
CD _____ JW 124CD
JW / Jun '97 / Jet Star

WEAKNESS FOR SWEETNESS
CD _____ JW 098CD
JW / Apr '96 / Jet Star

Let Loose

LET LOOSE
Crazy for you / Seventeen / One night stand / Way I wanna be / I love your smile / Cardboard city / Shame / Super sexy real thing / Best in me / Devotion / I believe / Love like there's no tomorrow
CD _____ 5260182
A&M / Nov '94 / PolyGram

ROLLERCOASTER
Don't change a thing / Make it with you / Take it easy / Everybody say everybody do / I wanna be your lover / Darling be home soon / Who's gonna love me now / Beautiful is what you are / Colour of your love / Need / Sweetest thing / Rollercoaster
CD _____ 5329552
Mercury / Sep '96 / PolyGram

Let Me Dream

MY DEAR
CD _____ CDAR 027
Adipocre / Jun '95 / Plastic Head

Lethal

PROGRAMMED
Fire in your skin / Programmed / Plan of peace / Another day / Arrival / What they've done / Obscure the sky / Immune / Pray for me / Killing machine
CD _____ 398414210CD
Metal Blade / Nov '96 / Pinnacle / Plastic Head

YOUR FAVOURITE GOD
CD _____ CDMVEST 44
Bulletproof / Mar '95 / Pinnacle

Lettau, Kevyn

ANOTHER SEASON
Another season / Summer dreams / Morning kisses / Foundation of humanity / I've got a crush on you / Ella / You don't love me like you used to / Father, Mother / Colors of joy / Inside your love / Retrato em branco e petro / Shower the people
CD _____ JVC 20302
JVC / Mar '94 / Direct / New Note/Pinnacle / Vital/SAM

UNIVERSAL LANGUAGE
Tribute to you / Secretly begin / Universal language / Underneath / Seeing for the very first time / Our lasting love / Beatriz / Gentle flower / Three little words / Love is unconditional / Dein ist mein ganzes herz / Only trust your heart
CD _____ JVC 20482
JVC / May '95 / Direct / New Note/Pinnacle / Vital/SAM

Letters To Cleo

AURORA GORY ALICE
Big star / I see / Rim shak / Wasted / Get on with it / Here and now / From under the dust / Mellie's comin' over / Come around / Step back
CD _____ WOLCD 1057
China / Apr '95 / Pinnacle

Leukafe, Carl

WARRIOR (Leukaufe, Carl & Jodie Christian/Lin Halliday)
Airegin / Before you know it / Little warrior / Come rain or come shine / Vierd blues / Tricotism / Pannonica / Star eyes / Blues for John Gilmore / Man I love / Chant
CD _____ DE 491
Delmark / Jun '97 / ADA / Cadillac / CM / Direct / Hot Shot

Leukemia

SUCK MY HEAVEN
Into the morgue / I nearly forgot / Uncarved miseria / Wandering / Sick inside / You es of ey / Everything falls apart / Memorized / Different but same
CD _____ BMCD 029
Black Mark / Mar '93 / Plastic Head

Levallet, Didier

GENERATIONS (Levallet, Didier Tentet)
CD _____ EVCD 212
Evidence / Feb '94 / ADA / Cadillac / Harmonia Mundi

Levanders, Jan

MUSAIK (Levanders, Jan Octet)
CD _____ DRCD 232
Dragon / Oct '94 / ADA / Cadillac / CM / Roots / Wellard

Levant, Oscar

OSCAR LEVANT PLAYS GERSHWIN
Rhapsody in blue / Second rhapsody for piano and orchestra / I got rhythm / Preludes for piano / Piano concerto in F
CD _____ CD 47681
Sony Classical / Jan '92 / Sony

PLAYS LEVANT & GERSHWIN
Gershwin: A portrait by Levant / Liza / My cousin in Milwaukee / Foggy day / Half of it dearie blues / But not for me / Rhapsody in blue / Concerto in F (third movement) / Then farewell / King and country call / Ah romantic love dream / First movement: Con ritmo / Second movement: Andantion poco mosso / Third movement: Allegro deciso / Piano concerto / Young in heart
CD _____ DRGCD 13113
DRG / Oct '94 / Discovery / New Note/ Pinnacle

Level 42

FOREVER NOW
Forever now / Model friend / Tired of waiting / All over you / Love in a peaceful world / Romance / Billy's gone / One in a million / Sunbed song / Talking in your sleep / Don't bother me
CD _____ 74321189962
CD _____ LV 102CD
Resurgence / Sep '96 / Pinnacle

LEVEL 42
Turn it on / Forty three / Why are you leaving / Almost there / Heathrow / Love games / Dune tune / Starchild
CD _____ 8219352
Polydor / Jul '84 / PolyGram

LEVEL 42 REMIXES
CD _____ VSOPCD 227
Connoisseur Collection / Jun '96 / Pinnacle

LEVEL BEST
Running in the family / Sun goes down (Living it up) / Something about you / Tracie / Starchild / It's over / Hot water / Take care of yourself / Heaven in my hands / Children say / Love games / Chinese way / Leaving me now / Lessons in love / Micro kid / Take a look / To be with you again / Chant has begun
CD _____ 8413992
Polydor / Nov '89 / PolyGram

LIVE AT WEMBLEY
Heaven in my hands / To be with you again / Children say / Silence / It's over / Over there / Man / Love games / Take a look / Something about you / Running in the family / Lessons in love / Chinese way
CD _____ WFRCD 005
World Famous / Apr '96 / Grapevine/ PolyGram

PHYSICAL PRESENCE, A
Almost there / Turn it on / Mr. Pink / Eyes waterfalling / Kansas city milkman / Follow me / Foundation and empire / Chant has begun / Chinese way / Sun goes down (living it up) / Hot water / Love games / 88
CD _____ 8256772
Polydor / Jun '85 / PolyGram

PURSUIT OF ACCIDENTS, THE
Weave your spell / Pursuit of accidents / Last chance / Are you hearing (what I hear) / You can't blame Louis / Eyes waterfalling / Shapeshifter / Chinese way / Chinese way (extended) / You can't blame Louis (extended)
CD _____ 8100152
Polydor / Jun '90 / PolyGram

RUNNING IN THE FAMILY
Lessons in love / Children say / Running in the family / It's over / To be with you again / Two solitudes / Fashion fever / Sleepwalkers / Freedom someday
CD _____ 8315932
Polydor / Mar '87 / PolyGram

STANDING IN THE LIGHT
Micro-kid / Sun goes down (living it up) / Out of sight out of mind / Dance on heavy weather / Pharaoh's dream of endless time / Standing in the light / I want eyes / People / Machine stops
CD _____ 8138652
Polydor / Jun '90 / PolyGram

STARING AT THE SUN
Heaven in my hands / I don't know why / Take a look / Over there / Silence / Tracie / Staring at the sun / Two hearts collide / Man / Gresham blues
CD _____ 8372472
Polydor / Sep '88 / PolyGram

TRUE COLOURS
Chant has begun / Kansas City milkman / Seven days / Hot water / Floating life / True believers / Kouyate / Hours by the window
CD _____ 8235452
Polydor / '88 / PolyGram

TURN IT ON
Running in the family / Chinese way / Heaven in my hands / Are you hearing (what I hear) / Children say / (Flying on) The wings of love / Physical presence / Turn it on / Love meeting love / True believers / Two hearts collide / I sleep on my heart / Can't walk you home / Coup d'etat / Take care of yourself / Love games
CD _____ 5520182
Spectrum / Mar '96 / PolyGram

WORLD MACHINE
World machine / Physical presence / Something about you / Leaving me now / I sleep on my heart / It's not the same for us / Good man in a storm / Coup d'etat / Lying still / Dream crazy / Love games / Hot water / Sun goes down (living it up) (Mix) / Chinese way (US mix) / I sleep on my heart (remix) / Something about you
CD _____ 8274872
Polydor / Oct '85 / PolyGram

Levellers

BEST LIVE (Headlights, White Lines & Black Tar Rivers)
Sell out / Hope St. / Fifteen years / Exodus / Carry me / Boatman / Three friends / Men an tol / Road / One way / England my home / Battle of the beanfield / Liberty / Riverflow
CD _____ WOLCDX 1074
China / Aug '96 / Pinnacle

LEVELLERS
Warning / 100 years of solitude / Likes of you and I / Is this art / Dirty Davey / This garden / Broken circles / Julie / Player / Belaruse
CD _____ WOLCD 1034
China / Aug '93 / Pinnacle

LEVELLING THE LAND
One way / Game / Boatman / Liberty song / Far from home / Sell out / Another man's cause / Road / Riverflow / Battle of the beanfield / Fifteen years
CD _____ WOLCD 1022
China / Sep '91 / Pinnacle

MOUTH TO MOUTH
Dog train / What a beautiful day / Celebrate / Rain and snow / Far away / CCTV / Chemically free / Elation / Captain courageous / Survivors / Sail away / Too real
CD _____ WOLCD 1084
CD _____ WOLCDX 1084
China / Aug '97 / Pinnacle

WEAPON CALLED THE WORD, A
World freak show / Carry me / Outside/Inside / Together all the way / Barrel of the gun / Three friends / I have no answers / No change / Blind faith / Ballad of Robbie Jones / England my home / What you know / Social insecurity / Cardboard box city / Three friends (remix)
CD _____ 105572
Musidisc UK / May '90 / Grapevine/ PolyGram

ZEITGEIST
Hope St. / Fear / Maid of the river / Saturday to sunday / 4.am / Forgotten ground / Fantasy / PC Keen / Just the one / Haven't made it / Leave this town / Men an tol
CD _____ WOLCD 1064
China / Sep '95 / Pinnacle

Levellers 5

SPRINGTIME
CD _____ PROBE 26 CD
Probe Plus / Jul '90 / SRD

Leven, Jackie

FAIRYTALES FOR HARDMEN
Boy trapped in a man / Desolation blues / Extremely violent man / Old West African song / Saint Judas / Poortoun / Fear of woman / Walled covers of Ravenscraig / Sad polish song / Sexual danger / Jim o' Windygates / Mad as the mist and snow / Kirkconnell flow / Listening to crows pray / Sir Patrick Spens / Sunflower / Torture blues / Story which could be true / Scotland the brave
CD _____ COOKCD 115
Cooking Vinyl / Apr '97 / Vital

FORBIDDEN SONGS OF THE DYING WEST
Young male suicide blessed by invisible woman / Some ancient misty morning / Working alone/A blessing / Leven's lament / Marble city bar / Wanderer / Exultation / Men in prison / Birds leave shadows / Stornoway girl / Silver roof / Lammermuir hills / Come back early or never of come / By the sign of the shettered star / Scene that haunts my memory / My lord what a morning
CD _____ COOKCD 090
Cooking Vinyl / Sep '95 / Vital

MYSTERY OF LOVE IS GREATER THAN THE MYSTERY OF DEATH
Clay jug / Shadow in my eyes / Call Mother a lonely field / Crazy song / Farm boy / Garden / Snow in Central Park / Looking for love / Heartsick land / Gylen Gylen / I say a little prayer / Bars of Dundee / Donna Karan / Ballad of a simple heart / Stranger on the square / Horseshoe and jug / Mary Jones' dog / So my soul can sing
CD _____ COOKCD 064
Cooking Vinyl / Jul '97 / Vital

SONGS FROM THE ARGYLLE CYCLE VOL.1 (Vol.1)
Stranger on the square / Walking in Argyll / Honeymoon hill / Looking for love / Grievin' at the mish nish / Ballad of a simple heart / As we sailed into Skibbereen / Some ancient misty morning / History of rain / Gylen Gylen / Fly / Crazy song
CD _____ COOKCD 101
Cooking Vinyl / Apr '96 / Vital

Levene, Keith

VIOLENT OPPOSITION
CD _____ RCD 10049
Rykodisc / Mar '92 / ADA / Vital

Levert

FOR REAL THO'
Me 'n' you / Clap your hands / Tribute song / Good ol' days / She's all that (I've been looking for) / For real tho' / Quiet storm / Do the thangs / My place (your place) / Say you will / ABC 123
CD _____ 7567824622
East West / Mar '93 / Warner Music

Levert, Gerald

FATHER SON
CD _____ 7559618592
East West / Dec '95 / Warner Music

Leverton, Jim

FOLLOW YOUR HEART (Leverton, Jim & Geoffrey Richardson)
CD _____ MSECD 008
Mouse / May '95 / Grapevine/PolyGram

Levi, K.D.

WE GIVE THEE THANKS
CD _____ NGCD 548
Twinkle / Jul '96 / Jet Star / Kingdom / SRD

Leviathan

DEEPEST SECRETS BENEATH
CD _____ RTN 41201
Rock The Nation / Nov '94 / Plastic Head

RIDDLES, QUESTIONS, POETRY AND OUTRAGE
CD _____ CM 77143CD
Century Media / Nov '96 / Plastic Head

Leviev, Milcho

BLUES FOR THE FISHERMAN (Leviev, Milcho Quartet & Art Pepper)
CD _____ MOLECD 1
Mole Jazz / May '87 / Cadillac / Impetus / Jazz Music / Wellard

ORACLE, THE (Live at Suntory Hall) (Leviev, Milcho & Dave Holland)
Oracle / Everybody's song but my own / Thracian flamenco / New one / Andante tranquillo / You, I love / Samba Deborah / First snow / Shoobee doobee / Warm valley
CD _____ PMC 1112
Pan Music / May '94 / Harmonia Mundi

Levin, Pete

MASTERS IN THIS HALL
CD _____ GV 794262
Gramavision / Dec '90 / Vital/SAM

PARTY IN THE BASEMENT
Bells / For a place to sleep / Party in the basement / Gone / Ragtime: Saturday night at the Last Chance / Subway / Something I said / Hunter / Complaint department / One day in the schoolyard
CD _____ GV 794562
Gramavision / Apr '90 / Vital/SAM

SOLITARY MAN
Abraham / Solitary man / Gil sings with the angels / Either or up down / Sad truth / Street band / Best pasta in jamaica / Through rose glasses / Colossus
CD _____ GCD 79457
Gramavision / Sep '95 / Vital/SAM

Levin, Tony

WORLD DIARY
CD DGM 9601
Discipline / Jan '96 / Pinnacle

Levine, Duke

COUNTRY SOUL GUITAR
CD DARING 3011CD
Daring / Nov '94 / ADA / CM / Direct

LAVA
Quiz show / Lovers' Lane / Manhole / Lava / Force field / Buckaroo / Far away / Fever / North of the border / Stalkin' / In the dark
CD DARINGCD 3028
Daring / Jul '97 / ADA / CM / Direct

NOBODY'S HOME
CD DRCD 3005
Daring / Jan '93 / ADA / CM / Direct

Levine, Mike

SMILEY AND ME
Our delight / When your heart's on fire smoke gets in your eyes / Stablemates / Daydream / Stompin' at the Savoy / My little brown book / Social call / Now
CD CCD 4352
Concord Jazz / Feb '95 / New Note/ Pinnacle

Levitation

COTTERIE
CD TOPPCD 001
Ultimate / Jul '94 / Pinnacle

Levy, Barrington

20 VINTAGE HITS
CD SONCD 0025
Sonic Sounds / Apr '92 / Jet Star

COLLECTION, THE
CD CORCD 06
Time / Jul '91 / Jet Star / Pinnacle

DIVINE
CD RASCD 3124
Ras / '95 / Direct / Greensleeves / Jet Star / SRD

DJ COUNTERACTION
CD GRECD 216
Greensleeves / Jun '95 / Jet Star / SRD

HERE I COME
Here I come / Do the dance / Under me sensi / Vibes is right / Real thing / Cool and loving / Struggler / Live good / Moonlight lover / Ya we deh / Give me your love / Don't run away
CD GRELCD 501
Greensleeves / May '88 / Jet Star / SRD

LOVE THE LIFE YOU LIVE
Love the life you live / Girl, I like your style / Too experienced / Why you do it / Long time friction / I've caught you / My woman / Come on little girl, come on / Two sounds / She's mine
CD TORCD 100
Time / '89 / Jet Star / Pinnacle

MAKING TRACKS
CD RN 7022
Rhino / Jun '97 / Grapevine/PolyGram / Jet Star

RAS PORTRAITS
Do the dance / Prison oval rock / Robber man / Living dangerously / Under mi sensi / Looking my love / Little children cry / Hypocrites / Vibes is right / Here I come / Mary long tongue / Please jah jah
CD RAS 3323
Ras / Jul '97 / Direct / Greensleeves / Jet Star / SRD

REGGAE VIBES
CD RGCD 022
Rocky One / Nov '94 / Jet Star

TIME CAPSULE
CD RASCD 3222
Ras / Apr '96 / Direct / Greensleeves / Jet Star / SRD

Levy, Lou

LUNARCY
Lunarcy / Pathetique / Suddenly it's Spring / Dolphin/Carnival / Shadow of your smile / Zoot / I hadn't anyone till you / Beautiful friendship / Ah Moore
CD 5124362
EmArCy / May '92 / PolyGram

YA KNOW
CD 5197002
Verve / Jun '94 / PolyGram

Levy, Ron

B-3 BLUES & GROOVES (Levy, Ron Wild Kingdom)
CD BB 9532CD
Bullseye Blues / May '93 / Direct

RON LEVY'S WILD KINGDOM (Levy, Ron Wild Kingdom)
I know you know I know / Chicken fried snake / So many roads / Why you stay out so late / Party in Nogales / Big town playboy / My heart's in trouble / It's hot in here / Knee squeeze / Must have missed a turn somewhere
CD CD 1034
Black Top / '88 / ADA / CM / Direct

SAFARI TO NEW ORLEANS (Levy, Ron Wild Kingdom)
CD CD 1040
Black Top / '88 / ADA / CM / Direct

WILD KINGDOM/GLAZED (Levy, Ron & Earl King)
CD FIENDCD 712
Demon / Feb '92 / Pinnacle

Lew, Benjamin

LA PARFUM DU RAKI
Les versants d'un coteau / Ce qu'elle voulait que j'entende / Et tout est parti de la / Ces personnages / Les sentiment de la couleur / Le visage sale par l'ecume / la magnifique alcoolique / La parful du raki / Que de moment d'alerte / Le sol noir des faubourgs marchands / Les personnage principal est un peuple isole / Sebkha / Un mal sourd / Regardez encore
CD MTM 35
Made To Measure / May '96 / New Note/ Pinnacle

NEBKA (Lew, Benjamin & Steven Brown)
CD MTM 17
Made To Measure / Sep '88 / New Note/ Pinnacle

Lewie, Jona

HEART SKIPS BEAT
I think I'll get my hair cut / Cream Jacqueline strawberry / Stop the cavalry / Abracadabra / Louise / Seed that always dies / Heart skips beat / What have I done / You go / Guessing games / Rearranging the deckchairs on the Titanic
CD STIFFCD 09
Disky / Jan '94 / Disky / THE

Lewin, Hakan

HAKAN LEWIN & ALDO MERISTO (Lewin, Hakan & Aldo Meristo)
CD SITCD 9211
Sittel / Jun '94 / Cadillac / Jazz Music

Lewis, Barbara

HELLO STRANGER (The Best Of Barbara Lewis)
My heart went do dat da / My Mama told me / Puppy love / Hello stranger / Think a little sugar / Straighten up your heart / Snap your fingers / How can I say goodbye / Spend a little time / Someday we're gonna love again / Pushin' a good thing too far / Baby, I'm yours / Make me your baby / Don't forget about me / Make me belong to you / Baby, what you want me to do / I remember the feeling / I'll make him love me / Thankful for what I got / Sho' nuff (it's got to be your love)
CD 8122716192
Atlantic / Feb '92 / Warner Music

MANY GROOVES OF BARBARA LEWIS, THE
Baby that's a no no / Windmills of your mind / Slip away / How can I tell / I can't break away (from your love) / Oh be my love / Just the way you are today / Anyway / But you know I love you / You made me a woman / Stars / Do I deserve it baby / Ask the lonely / Why did it take you so long / That's the way I like it
CD CDSXE 077
Stax / Jul '93 / Pinnacle

Lewis, David

NO STRAIGHT LINE
CD DJD 3215
Dejadisc / Aug '95 / ADA / Direct

Lewis, Donna

NOW IN A MINUTE
CD 7567827622
Atlantic / Sep '96 / Warner Music

Lewis, George

AT HERBERT OTTO'S PARTY
CD AMCD 74
American Music / Apr '94 / Jazz Music

AT THE CLUB HANGOVER, SAN FRANCISCO 1953 VOL.1 (Lewis, George New Orleans Jazz Band)
CD STCD 6024
Storyville / May '97 / Cadillac / Jazz Music / Wellard

CLASSIC NEW ORLEANS JAZZ VOL.1
CD BCD 127
Biograph / Oct '93 / ADA / Cadillac / Direct / Hot Shot / Jazz Music / Wellard

GEORGE LEWIS & BARRY MARTYN BAND
CD BCD 37
GHB / Jan '94 / Jazz Music

GEORGE LEWIS & KID SHOTS (Lewis, George & Kid Shots)
CD AMCD 2
American Music / Oct '92 / Jazz Music

GEORGE LEWIS & PAPA BUES VIKING JAZZ BAND
CD STCD 6018
Storyville / Aug '94 / Cadillac / Jazz Music / Wellard

GEORGE LEWIS BANDS/TRIOS/ QUINTETS
CD AMCD 83
American Music / Aug '95 / Jazz Music

GEORGE LEWIS WITH KEN COLYER'S JAZZMEN 1957 VOL.1
CD 504CD 50
504 / Jun '95 / Cadillac / Jazz Music / Target/BMG / Wellard

GEORGE LEWIS WITH KEN COLYER'S JAZZMEN 1957 VOL.2
CD 504CD 51
504 / Jun '95 / Cadillac / Jazz Music / Target/BMG / Wellard

IN CONCERT MANCHESTER 1959 (Lewis, George Ragtime Band)
CD 504CD 58
504 / Nov '96 / Cadillac / Jazz Music / Target/BMG / Wellard

IN STOCKHOLM
CD DRAGONCD 221
Dragon / Sep '89 / ADA / Cadillac / CM / Roots / Wellard

JAZZ AT VESPERS
CD OJCCD 1721
Original Jazz Classics / Jun '94 / Complete/Pinnacle / Jazz Music / Wellard

JAZZ FUNERAL IN NEW ORLEANS
CD TCD 1049
Tradition / May '97 / ADA / Vital

JAZZ IN THE CLASSIC NEW ORLEANS TRADITION
St. Phillip's street breakdown / Salty dog / Old rugged cross / Red wing / Lou-easy-an-i-a / Careless love / Weary blues / Bill Bailey, won't you please come home / Tin roof blues / Dippermouth blues / It's a long way to Tipperary / Bugle call rag
CD OJCCD 1736
Original Jazz Classics / Mar '94 / Complete/ Pinnacle / Jazz Music / Wellard

OHIO UNION 1954 (2CD Set) (Lewis, George & His Jazzband)
CD STCD 6020/21
Storyville / Jul '96 / Cadillac / Jazz Music / Wellard

OXFORD SERIES VOL.1 (Lewis, George & His Ragtime Band)
CD AMCD 21
American Music / Oct '92 / Jazz Music

OXFORD SERIES VOL.10
CD AMCD 30
American Music / Jan '94 / Jazz Music

OXFORD SERIES VOL.11
CD AMCD 31
American Music / May '95 / Jazz Music

OXFORD SERIES VOL.12
CD AMCD 32
American Music / May '95 / Jazz Music

OXFORD SERIES VOL.13
CD AMCD 33
American Music / Apr '97 / Jazz Music

OXFORD SERIES VOL.14
CD AMCD 34
American Music / Apr '97 / Jazz Music

OXFORD SERIES VOL.2
CD AMCD 22
American Music / Oct '92 / Jazz Music

OXFORD SERIES VOL.5
CD AMCD 25
American Music / Apr '93 / Jazz Music

OXFORD SERIES VOL.6
CD AMCD 26
American Music / Apr '93 / Jazz Music

OXFORD SERIES VOL.7
CD AMCD 27
American Music / Jun '93 / Jazz Music

OXFORD SERIES VOL.8
CD AMCD 28
American Music / Jun '93 / Jazz Music

OXFORD SERIES VOL.9
CD AMCD 029
American Music / Oct '93 / Jazz Music

PORTRAIT OF GEORGE LEWIS, A
CD LACD 50
Lake / Aug '95 / ADA / Cadillac / Direct / Jazz Music / Target/BMG

SPIRIT OF NEW ORLEANS (Lewis, George & His Ragtime Band)
CD MECCACD 1014
Music Mecca / Jul '93 / Cadillac / Jazz Music / Wellard

TRIOS & BANDS
CD AMCD 4
American Music / Jan '93 / Jazz Music

WALKING WITH THE KING (1954-1955) (Lewis, George & His Ragtime Band/ New Orleans Stomper)
Walking with the king / Ol' man Rose / Gettysburg march / Mama don't allow it / Canal street blues / Just a close walk with thee / Bill Bailey / Over the waves / Burgundy Street blues / Mahogany hall stomp / Bucket's got a hole in it / High society / CC rider / Savoy blues / Heebie jeebies / I can't escape from you / When you wore a tulip / Ice cream
CD CD 53186
Giants Of Jazz / Oct '96 / Cadillac / Jazz Music / Target/BMG

Lewis, George

CHANGING WITH THE TIMES
CD 804242
New World / Nov '93 / ADA / Cadillac / Harmonia Mundi

HOMAGE TO CHARLES PARKER (Lewis, George & Anthony Davis)
CD 1200292
Black Saint / May '92 / Cadillac / Harmonia Mundi

MONADS/TRIPLE SLOW MIX
CD 120016
Black Saint / Apr '94 / Cadillac / Harmonia Mundi

REUNION (Lewis, George (2) & Don Ewell)
Ida / Of all the wrongs / Whispering / Waltz you saved for me / Toot Toot Tootsie / Yes yes in your eyes / Wabash blues / Someday sweetheart / Ole miss / Bucket's got a hole in it / Ida / Of all the wrongs / Whispering / Yes yes in your eyes
CD DE 220
Delmark / Jun '97 / ADA / Cadillac / CM / Direct / Hot Shot

VOYAGER
CD AVANT 014
Avant / Nov '93 / Cadillac / Harmonia Mundi

Lewis, Hopeton

GROOVING OUT OF LIFE
CD JMC 200109
Jamaican Gold / Sep '93 / Grapevine/ PolyGram / Jet Star

Lewis, Huey & The News

FORE
Jacob's ladder / Stuck with you / Whole lotta lovin' / Hip to be square / I know what I like / I never walk alone / Power of love / Naturally / Simple as that / Doin' it all for my baby
CD CCD 1534
Chrysalis / Jul '94 / EMI

FOUR CHORDS & SEVERAL YEARS AGO
Shake, rattle and roll / Blue Monday / Searching for my love / Some kind of wonderful / But it's alright / If you gotta make a fool of somebody / Mother in law / Little bitty pretty one / Good morning little school girl / Stagger lee / She shot a hole in my soul / Surely I love you / You left the water running / Your cash ain't nothin' but trash / Function at the junction / Better to have and not need / Going down slow
CD 7559615002
Warner Bros. / May '94 / Warner Music

HARD AT PLAY
Build me up / It hit me like a hammer / Attitude / He don't know / Couple days off / That's not me / We should be making love / Best of me / Do you love me, or what / Don't look back / Time ain't money
CD CCD 1847
Chrysalis / Feb '94 / EMI

HEART OF ROCK AND ROLL, THE (The Best Of Huey Lewis And The News)
Power of love / Hip to be square / Do you believe in love / If this is it / Some of my lies are true / Workin' for a livin' / Bad is bad / I want a new drug / Heart of rock and roll / Heart and soul / Jacob's ladder / Stuck with you / Trouble in paradise / Walking on a thin line / Perfect world / Small world / Back in time
CD CDCHR 1934
Chrysalis / Oct '92 / EMI

HUEY LEWIS & THE NEWS/PICTURE THIS/SPORTS (3CD Set)
Some of my lies are true (sooner or later) / Don't make me do it / Stop trying / Now here's you / I want you / Don't ever tell me that you love me / Hearts / Trouble in paradise / Who cares / If you really love me you'll let me / Change of heart / Tell me a little lie / Tattoo (giving it all up for love) / Hope you love me like you say you do / Workin' for a livin' / Do you believe in love / Is it me / Whatever happened to true love / Only one / Buzz buzz buzz / Heart of rock'n'roll / Heart and soul / Bad is bad / I want a new drug / Walking on a thin line / Finally found a home / If this is it / You crack me up / Honky tonk blues
CD Set CDOMB 010
Chrysalis / Oct '95 / EMI

Lewis, Jerry Lee

1960'S FRENCH EPS COLLECTION, THE
CD **528862**
Magic / Jul '97 / Greyhound

BEST OF JERRY LEE LEWIS
CD **MCCD 081**
Music Club / Sep '92 / Disc / THE

CHANTILLY LACE
Me and Bobby McGee / There must be more to love than this / What made Milwaukee famous (has made a loser out of me) / I'm so lonesome I could cry / Heartaches by the number / I'm left, you're right, she's gone / Cold cold heart / Chantilly lace / Would you take another chance on me / He'll have to go / I love you because / For the good times / Oh lonesome me / I can't stop loving you
CD **5501802**
Spectrum / Mar '94 / PolyGram

COLLECTION, THE
Be bop a lula / Dixie / Goodnight Irene / Great balls of fire / High school confidential / Lewis boogie / Matchbox / Money / Sixty minute man / Ubangi stomp / Whole lotta shakin' goin' on / Wine drinkin' spo-dee-o-dee / CC rider / Good golly Miss Molly / Good rockin' tonight / Hang up my rock 'n' roll shoes / Johnny B Goode / Long gone lonesome blues / Mean woman blues / Pumpin' piano rock / Sweet little sixteen / What'd I say / Will the circle be unbroken / Let the good times roll
CD **CCSCD 143**
Castle / Dec '90 / BMG

COMPLETE SUN RECORDINGS (8CD Box Set)
Crazy arms / End of the road / You're the only star in my blue heaven / Born to lose / Silver threads among the gold / I'm throwing rice (at the girl I love) / I love you so much it hurts / Deep Elem blues / Goodnight Irene / Goodnight Irene (undubbed master) / Honey hush / Crawdad song / Dixie / Marines' hymn / That lucky old sun / Hand me down my walking cane / You're the only star in my blue heaven (Lewis boogie) / I love you because / I can't help it / Cold cold heart / Shame on you / I'll keep on loving you / You are my sunshine / Tomorrow night / Sixty minute man / It all depends (who will buy the wine) / I don't love nobody / Whole lotta shakin' goin' on / It'll be me (alt.) / It'll be me (alt.2) / Whole lotta shakin' goin' on (master) / False start and It'll be me / Ole pal of yesterday / You win again / Love letters in the sand / Little green valley / Lewis boogie / Pumpin' piano rock / It'll be me / All night long / Old time religion / When the saints go marching in (undubbed master) / My Carolina sunshine girl / Long gone lonesome blues / Drinkin' wine spo-dee-o-dee / Singin' the blues / Keep your hands off it / Matchbox (undubbed master) / Matchbox / Ubangi stomp / Rock 'n' roll Ruby / So long I'm gone / Ooby dooby / I forgot to remember to forget (unissued) / You win again (undubbed master) / I'm feeling sorry / Mean woman blues / Turn around / Great balls of fire (movie cut) / Chatter/Great balls of fire / Why should I cry over you / Religious discussion / Great balls of fire (master) / You win again (overdubbed master) / Down the line (unissued) / Down the line (false start) / I'm sorry I'm not sorry / Down the line (master) / Sexy ways (false start) / Cool cool ways / Milkshake madamoiselle / Breathless (unissued) / Milkshake madamoiselle (false starts) / Breathless (master) / High school confidential (false start) / High school confidential (unissued) / High school confidential / Put me down (unissued) / Good rockin' tonight / Pink pedal pushers / Jailhouse rock / Hound dog / Don't be cruel / Someday / Jambalaya / Friday nights / Big legged woman / Hello hello baby / Frankie and Johnny / Your cheatin' heart / Lovesick blues / Goodnight Irene (overdubbed master) / When the saints go marching in (overdubbed master) / Matchbox (overdubbed master) / Put me down / Fools like me (undubbed master) / Carrying on (sexy ways) / Crazy heart (false start) / High school confidential (master) / Slippin' around / I'll see you in my dreams / Real wild child / Let the good times roll / Fools like me (overdubbed master) / Settin' the woods on fire (unissued) / Memory of you / Come what may / Break up / Crazy heart / Live and let live / I'll make it all up to you (false start) / Johnny B Goode / Settin' the woods on fire (false start) / Return of Jerry Lee / Break up (unissued) / I'll make it all up to you (unissued) / Break up (master) / I'll make it all up to you / I'll sail my ship alone / It hurt me so (chatter) / You're the only star in my blue heaven (unissued) / It hurt me so / Lovin' up a storm (unissued) / Big blon' baby / Lovin' up a storm / Sick and tired / Shanty town / Release me / I could never be ashamed of you (false start) / Near you (takes 1and2) / I could never be ashamed of you / Hillbilly fever / My blue heaven / Let's talk about us (false start) / Little Queenie / Home / Will the circle be unbroken / Ballad of Billie Joe / Sail away / Am I to be the one / Night train to Memphis / I'm the guilty one / Let's talk about us / Wild side of life (stereo) / Charming Billy (stereo) / Bonnie / Mexicali rose (slow) / Mexicali rose (fast) / Gettin' in the mood / In the mood / I get the blues when it rains / Don't drop it / Great speckled bird / Bonnie B / Baby, baby, bye bye / I can't help it (unissued and false starts) / Old black Joe / As long as I live (unissued) / As long as I live / What'd I say / Keep your hands off it (birthday cake) / Hang up my rock 'n' roll shoes / John Henry / What'd I say (stereo) / CC rider / When my blue moon turns to gold again (unissued) / Lewis workout / When my blue moon turns to gold again (stereo) / When I get paid / Love made a fool of me (stereo) / No more than I get (stereo) / Livin' lovin' wreck / Cold cold heart (stereo) / I forgot to remember to forget / It won't happen with me / I love you because (stereo) / Save the last dance for me / Hello Josephine / High powered woman / My blue heaven 1 (stereo) / My blue heaven 2 (stereo) / Sweet little sixteen / Ramblin' rose (master extended) / Money (stereo) / Rockin' the boat of love / Ramblin' rose / I've been twistin' / Whole lotta twistin' goin' on / I've been twistin' (stereo) / I know what it means / Sweet little sixteen / My girl Josephine (stereo) / Set my mind at ease / Waiting for a train 1 (stereo) / Waiting for a train 2 (stereo) / How's my ex treating you (stereo and unissued) / Good rockin' tonight (stereo) / Be bop a lula / My girl Josephine (stereo and unissued) / How's my ex treating you / Good golly Miss Molly (unissued) / I can't trust me (in your arms anymore) / My pretty quadroon (stereo) / Waiting for a train (unissued) / Teenage letter (stereo) / Seasons of my heart / Your lovin' ways / Just who is to blame / Just who is to blame (unissued) / Hong Kong blues / Love on Broadway (stereo) / One minute past eternity (stereo) / Invitation to your party / Invitation to your party (stereo) / I can't seem to say goodbye / Carry me back to old Virginny / Carry me back to old Virginny
CD Set **BCD 15420**
Bear Family / Aug '89 / Direct / Rollercoaster / Swift

COMPLETE SUN YEARS, THE (12CD Set)
CD Set **CDSUNBOX 4**
Charly / Feb '93 / Koch

COUNTRY CLASSICS
You win again / What made Milwaukee famous (has made a loser out of me) / I can't stop loving you / Your cheatin' heart / Middle aged crazy / Mexicali rose / Bootles and barstools / Cold cold heart / Another place another time / I'll find it where I can / Careless hands / There must be more to love than this / Touching home / You are my sunshine / Thirty nine and holding / Hey good lookin' / She even woke me up to say goodbye / Will the circle be unbroken
CD **MUCD 9018**
Musketeer / Apr '95 / Disc

EP COLLECTION PLUS, THE
Ballad of Billie Joe / Let's talk about us / Little Queenie / I could never be ashamed of you / It won't happen with me / Cold cold heart / Baby, baby, bye bye / Old black Joe / It hurt me so / I'll sail my ship alone / Ramblin' Rose / As long as I live / When I get paid / Mean woman blues / Down the line / Breathless / I'm feeling sorry / Matchbox / Ubangi stomp / Break up / I'll make it all up to you / Big blon' baby / High school confidential / Whole lotta shakin' goin' on / Hound dog / Good rockin' tonight / Drinkin' wine spo-dee-o-dee / Great balls of fire
CD **SEECD 397**
See For Miles/C5 / Mar '94 / Pinnacle

EP COLLECTION, THE
CD **SEECD 307**
See For Miles/C5 / Dec '90 / Pinnacle

ESSENTIAL COLLECTION, THE
CD Set **LECD 610**
Wisepack / Apr '95 / Conifer/BMG / THE

ESSENTIALS (Lewis, Jerry Lee & Roy Orbison)
CD **LECDD 631**
Wisepack / Aug '95 / Conifer/BMG / THE

FERRIDAY FIREBALL
Lewis boogie / It'll be me / High school confidential / Whole lotta shakin' goin' on / Good rockin' tonight / Big legged woman / Great balls of fire / Drinkin' wine spo-dee-o-dee / Matchbox / You win again / Will the circle be unbroken / That lucky old sun / Crazy arms / Break up / Memory of you / Johnny B Goode / Little Queenie / Milkshake mademoiselle / Big blon' baby / Breathless / Mean woman blues / Down the line / When the saints go marching in / End of the road / What'd I say
CD **CDCHARLY 1**
Charly / Mar '86 / Koch

GREAT BALLS OF FIRE
CD **CD 12332**
Laserlight / Apr '94 / Target/BMG

GREAT BALLS OF FIRE
Whole lotta shakin' goin' on / It'll be me / Lewis boogie / Drinkin' wine spo-dee-o-dee / Rock 'n' roll Ruby / Matchbox / Ubangi stomp / Great balls of fire / You win again / Mean woman blues / Milkshake madamoiselle / Breathless / Down the line / Good rockin' tonight / Jambalaya / High school confidential / Pink pedal pushers / Don't be cruel / Johnny B Goode / Break up / Big blon' baby / Lovin' up a storm / Little queenie / In the mood / What'd I say / Sweet little sixteen / Good golly Miss Molly / Be bop a lula / Teenage letter / Carry me back to old Virginny
CD **CPCD 8206**
Charly / Feb '97 / Koch

GREATEST LIVE SHOWS ON EARTH, THE
Jenny Jenny / Who will the next fool be / Memphis, Tennessee / Hound dog / Mean woman blues / Hi-heel sneakers / No particular place to go / Together again / Long tall Sally / Whole lotta shakin' goin' on / Little queenie / How's my ex treating you / Johnny B Goode / Green green grass of home / What'd I say (part 2) / You win again / I'll sail my ship alone / Crying time / Money / Roll over Beethoven
CD **BCD 15608**
Bear Family / Nov '91 / Direct / Rollercoaster / Swift

HEARTBREAK
What made Milwaukee famous (has made a loser out of me) / Careless hands / Who will the next fool be / Touching home / More to love than this / Cold cold heart / You win again / Your cheatin' heart / I can't stop lovin' you / Another place another time / Thirty nine and holding / She even woke me up / I wish I was eighteen again / Who is going to play this ole piano
CD **598 0067 29**
Tomato / Aug '93 / Vital

HEARTBREAKER
CD **CPCD 8175**
Charly / Jun '96 / Koch

HIGH SCHOOL CONFIDENTIAL
Whole lotta shakin' goin' on / Lovin' up a storm / When I get paid / Baby baby bye bye / Wild one / What'd I say / Sixty minute man / Sweet little sixteen / Hello Josephine / High school confidential / Just who is to blame / Be bop a lula / Breathless / Money / Good golly Miss Molly / Great balls of fire
CD **SUMCD 4004**
Summit / Nov '96 / Sound & Media

HONKY TONK ROCK'N'ROLL PIANO MAN
My fingers do the talkin' / Why you been gone so long / Daughters of Dixie / Teenage Queen / I'm looking over a four leaf clover / I am what I am / Better not look down / Only you / Honky tonk rock 'n' roll piano man / Circumstantial evidence / I'm lookin' under a skirt / Rock 'n' roll money / Forever forgiving (alternative take no.1) / Why you been gone so long (alt. take no.3) / Get out your big roll daddy
CD **CDCH 332**
Ace / Oct '91 / Pinnacle

IN CONCERT
CD **CDSGP 0163**
Prestige / Oct '95 / Else / Total/BMG

IN CONCERT
Great balls of fire / Whole lotta shakin' goin' on / Shake, rattle and roll/Flip flop and fly / Chantilly lace / What'd I say / Good Golly Miss Molly / Mona Lisa / Who's sorry now / Come on in / You win again / Honky tonk angels / Trouble in mind / Help me make it through the night / Middle age crazy / Sweet little sixteen / Think about it darlin' / High School confidential
CD **100412**
CMC / May '97 / BMG

JERRY LEE LEWIS
Meat man / Jailhouse rock / House of blue light / Rock 'n' roll funeral / Don't touch me / Changing mountains / Beautiful dreamer / I'm alone because I love you / Lucille / Seventeen / Mathilda / Wake up little Susie
CD **12658**
Laserlight / Sep '96 / Target/BMG

JERRY LEE LEWIS
Good golly Miss Molly / High school confidential / Great balls of fire / Night train to Memphis / When the saints go marching in / Frankie and Johnny / Good rockin' tonight / Whole lotta shakin' goin' on / You win again / Jambalaya / Matchbox / Breathless / Crazy arms / Break up / What'd I say / Whole lot of twistin' / I'll make it up to you / Be bop a lula
CD **399538**
Koch Presents / May '97 / Koch

KILLER CONCERT
Great balls of fire / What'd I say / Lucille / Brown eyed handsome man / Hey good lookin' / Roll over Beethoven / Chantilly lace / Little queenie / Johnny B Goode / No headstone on my grave / Mexicali rose / I'll find it where I can / High school confidential / Boogie woogie country man / You are my sunshine / Meat man / Big legged woman / Rockin' my life away / Who's gonna play this old piano / Whole lotta shakin' goin' on
CD **QED 038**
Tring / Nov '96 / Tring

KILLER HITS
High school confidential / Great balls of fire / Big blon'baby / You win again / Drinkin' wine spo-dee-o-dee / It'll be me / Milkshake Madamoiselle / Crazy arms / I've been twistin' / In the mood / What'd I say / Breathless / Mean woman blues / Little Queenie / Down the line / That lucky old sun / Lewis boogie / Wild one / Sweet little sixteen / Let's talk about us / Lovin' up a storm / Whole lotta shakin' goin' on
CD **PWKS 4255**
Carlton / Mar '96 / Carlton

KILLER, THE
CD **MSCD 029**
Music De-Luxe / Apr '96 / TKO Magnum

LEGENDS IN MUSIC
CD **LECD 079**
Wisepack / Jul '94 / Conifer/BMG / THE

LIVE AT THE STAR CLUB, HAMBURG
Mean woman blues / High school confidential / Money / Matchbox / What'd I say / Great balls of fire / Good golly Miss Molly / Lewis boogie / Your cheatin' heart / Hound dog / Long tall Sally / Whole lotta shakin' goin' on / Down the line
CD **BCD 15467**
Bear Family / Jul '89 / Direct / Rollercoaster / Swift

LIVE AT THE VAPORS CLUB
Don't put no headstone on my grave / Chantilly lace / I'll find it where I can / Drinkin' wine spo-dee-o-dee / Sweet little sixteen / Boogie woogie country man / Me and Bobby McGee / Rockin' my life away / Whole lotta shakin' goin' on / You can have her / Hey good lookin' / Will the circle be unbroken
CD **CDCH 326**
Ace / May '91 / Pinnacle

LIVE IN ITALY
Rollin' in my sweet baby's arms / High school confidential / Me and Bobby McGee / Jackson / There must be more to love than this / Great balls of fire / What'd I say / Jerry Lee's rock and roll revival show / I am what I am / Whole lotta shakin' goin' on / You win again / Mona Lisa / One of those things we all go through / Hang up my rock 'n' roll shoes
CD **CDMF 071**
Magnum Force / Jun '89 / TKO Magnum

LOCUST YEARS/RETURN TO THE PROMISED LAND (9CD Set)
Whole lotta shakin' goin' on / Crazy arms / Great balls of fire / High school confidential / I'll make it all up to you / Break up / Down the line / Hit the road Jack / End of the road / Your cheatin' heart / Wedding bells / Just because / Breathless / He took it like a man / Drinkin' wine spo-dee-o-dee / Johnny B Goode / Hallelujah, I love her so / You went back on your word / Pen and paper / Hole he said he'd dig for me / You win again / Fools like me / Hit the road Jack / I'm on fire / She was my baby (he was my friend) / Bread and butter man / I bet you're gonna like it / Got you on my mind / Mathilda / Corine Corina / Sexy ways / Wild side / Flip flop and fly / Don't let go / Maybellene / Roll over Beethoven / Just in time / I believe in you / Herman the hermit / Baby, hold me close / Skid row / This must be the place / Rockin' pneumonia and the boogie woogie flu / Seasons of my heart / Big boss man / Too young / Danny boy / City lights / Funny how time slips away / North to Alaska / Walk right in / Wolverton mountain / King of the road / Detroit city / Ring of fire / Baby, you got what it takes / Green green grass of home / Sticks and stones / What a heck of a mess / Lincoln limousine / Rockin' Jerry Lee / Memphis beat / Urge / Whenever you're ready / She thinks I still care / Twenty four hours a day / Swinging doors / If I had it all to do over / Just dropped in / It's a hang up / Holdin' on / Hey baby / Dream baby / Treat her right / Turn on your love light / Shotgun man / All the good is gone / Another place another time / Walking the floor over you / I'm a lonesome fugitive / Break my mind / Play me a song I can cry to / Before the next teardrop falls / All night long / We live in two different worlds / What made Milwaukee famous (has made a loser out of me) / On the back row / Slippin' around / Ahe still comes around / Today I started loving you again / Louisiana man / There stands the glass / I can't have a merry Christmas, Mary / Out of my mind / I can't get over you / Listen they're playing my song / Echoes / Release me / Let's talk about us / To make love sweeter for you / Don't let me cross over / Born to lose / You belong to me / Oh lonesome me / Sweet dreams / Cold cold heart / Fraulein / Why don't you love me like you used to do / Four walls / It makes no difference now / I love you because / I'm so lonesome I could cry / Jambalaya / More and more / One has my name (the other has my heart) / Burning memories / Mom and Dad's last waltz / Pick me up on your way down / Heartaches by the number / I can't stop loving you / My blue heaven / I wonder where you are tonight / Jackson / Sweet thang / He'll have to go / You've still got a place in my heart / I get the blues when it rains / Gotta travel on / Milwaukee here I come / Crying time / Secret places / Don't take it out on me / Earth up above / Waiting for a train / Love for all seasons / She even woke me up to say goodbye / When the grass grows over me / Wine me up / Since I met you baby / Workin' man blues / Once more with feeling / In loving memories / You went out of your

way (to walk on me) / My only claim to fame / Brown eyed handsome man
CD Set _______ BCD 15783
Bear Family / Nov '94 / Direct / Rollercoaster / Swift

PEARLS FROM THE PAST
CD _______ KLMCD 012
BAM / Apr '94 / Koch / Scratch/BMG

PRETTY MUCH COUNTRY
Honky tonk heaven / She never said goodbye / That was the way it was then / Candy kisses / I am what I am / Come as you were / She sang amazing grace / Have I got a song for you / Daughters of Dixie / Send me the pillow that you dream on / She sure makes leavin' look easy / My fingers do the talkin' / Honky tonk heart / Careless hands / Honky tonk rock 'n' roll piano man / Forever forgiving
CD _______ CDCH 348
Ace / Feb '92 / Pinnacle

RARE AND ROCKIN'
It won't happen with me / Teenage letter / Pink pedal pushers / Hillbilly music / Deep Elem blues / You win again / I'm feeling sorry / I'm the guilty one / It hurt me so / I love you because / Cold cold heart / Whole lotta shakin' goin' on / In the mood / Great balls of fire / I forgot to remember to forget / Turn around / It all depends (who will buy the wine) / It'll be me / Sixty minute man / Lovin' up a storm / Rockin' with red / Honey hush / Hound dog / Hang up my rock 'n' roll shoes
CD _______ CDCHARLY 70
Charly / Apr '87 / Koch

ROCKIN' MY LIFE AWAY
CD _______ 2696612
Tomato / Apr '90 / Vital

ROCKIN' UP A STORM (2CD Set)
Little Queenie / Lucille / I love you because / Break up / Crazy arms / Jailhouse rock / Matchbox / House of blue lights / Lovesick blues / Great balls of fire / That lucky old sun / Money (that's what I want) / How's my ex treatin' you / Be bop a lula / Bonnie B / Save the last dance for me / Good golly Miss Molly / Sweet little sixteen / Whole lotta shakin' goin' on / Let the good times roll / Don't be cruel / Lovin' up a storm / It'll be me / End of the road / Lewis boogie / Down the line / I've been twistin' / Good rockin' tonite / What'd I say / Livin' lovin' wreck / Wild one / Jambalaya / Sixty minute man / Hound dog / Ramblin' Rose
CD Set _______ 330142
Hallmark / Jul '96 / Carlton

SESSION, THE
Johnny B Goode / Trouble in mind / Early morning rain / No headstone on my grave / Pledging my love / Memphis / Drinkin' wine spo-dee-o-dee / Music to the man / Bad moon rising / Sea cruise / Sixty minute man / Movin' on down the line / What'd I say
CD _______ 8227512
Mercury / May '85 / PolyGram

SPOTLIGHT ON JERRY LEE LEWIS
Hey baby / Roll over Beethoven / Boogie woogie country man/Rockin' / Sweet Georgia Brown / Just because / You win again / Sweet little sixteen / I'll find it where I can / No headstone on my grave / Whole lotta shakin' goin' on / Hadacol boogie / Middle aged crazy / Who will the next fool be / Down the line
CD _______ HADCD 124
Javelin / Feb '94 / Henry Hadaway / THE

SUN CLASSICS (4CD Box Set)
Whole lotta shakin' goin' on / Great balls of fire / High school confidential / Be bop a lula / Good golly Miss Molly / Down the line / Lovin' up a storm / Wild one / Ooby dooby / End of the road / Pumping piano rock / Put me down / Don't be cruel / I'm feeling sorry / Home / Wild side of life / When my blue moon turns to gold again / I love you because / Born to lose / Jambalaya / You win again / Crazy heart / Long gone lonesome blues / Cold cold heart / I can't help it (If I'm still in love with you) / Your cheatin' heart / Big blon' baby / Rock 'n' roll Ruby / Breathless / I'm sorry I'm not sorry / Ubangi stomp / It'll be me / Milkshake Madamoiselle / Baby, baby, bye bye / Break up / It won't happen with me / Bonnie B / Livin' lovin' wreck / Your lovin' ways / Crazy arms / I'll make it all up to you / Let's talk about us / It hurt me so / As long as I live / How's my ex treating you / I can't seem to say goodbye / I'll sail my ship alone / Someday (you'll want me to want you) / Set my mind at ease / Seasons of my heart / It all depends (who will buy the wine) / Slippin' around / Night train to Memphis / Big legged woman / Rockin' with Red / Sixty minute man / I've been twistin' / Teenage letter / Mean woman blues / Drinkin' wine spo-dee-o-dee / Keep your hands off it (Birthday cake) / Money / Hound dog / Cool cool ways / Hello hello baby / I know what it means / It'll be me (alt.) / Hillbilly music / Turn around / Fools like me / I forgot to remember to forget / I can't trust me (In your arms anymore) / I'm the guilty one / Hand me down my walking cane / Crawdad song / Don't drop it / Memory of you / Crazy arms (Remake) / What I'd say / Honey hush / Tomorrow night / Carrying on (sexy ways) / Good rockin' tonight / Come what may / Hello Josephine / Little Queenie / Johnny B Goode / Hang up my rock 'n' roll shoes / Sweet little sixteen / Matchbox / CC rider / Lewis boogie / My pretty quadroon / That lucky old sun / Goodnight Irene / Will the circle be unbroken / Great speckled bird / John Henry / Frankie and Johnny / You're the only star in my blue heaven / Waiting for a train / Deep Elem blues / You are my sunshine / Carry me back to old Virginny
CD Set _______ CDDIG 8
Charly / Feb '95 / Koch

THAT BREATHLESS CAT
Ragtime doodle / Meat man / Lovin' up a storm / Ubangi stomp / Rock 'n' roll ruby / Piano doodle / House of blue lights / My life would make a damn good country song / Beautiful dreamer / Autumn leaves / Pilot baby / Room full of roses / Keep a knockin' / Silver threads among the gold / Alabama jubilee / Lazy river / Mama this song's for you / Breathless / Whole lotta shakin' goin' on
CD _______ STCD 2
Stomper Time / Feb '93 / TKO Magnum

TWO ON ONE: JERRY LEE LEWIS & CARL PERKINS (Lewis, Jerry Lee & Carl Perkins)
CD _______ CDTT 5
Charly / Apr '94 / Koch

UP THROUGH THE YEARS 1956-1963
End of the road / Crazy arms / It'll be me / Whole lotta shakin' goin' on / You win again / Mean woman blues / Great balls of fire / Down the line / Breathless / Don't be cruel / Put me down / Break up / I'll make it up to you / I'll sail my ship alone / Lovin' up a storm / Big blon' baby / Night train to Memphis / Little Queenie / John Henry / Livin' lovin' wreck / What'd I say / Cold cold heart / Sweet little sixteen / Carry me back to old Virginny
CD _______ BCD 15408
Bear Family / Dec '87 / Direct / Rollercoaster / Swift

VERY BEST OF JERRY LEE LEWIS, THE (2CD Set)
Whole lotta shakin' goin' on / Great balls of fire / You win again / Breathless / High school confidential / Fools like me / I'll make it all up to you / What'd I say / Cold cold heart / Invitation to your heart / One minute past eternity / I can't seem to say goodbye / Waiting for a train / Love on Broadway / Break up / I'll sail my ship alone / Lovin' up a storm / Lewis boogie / I won't happen with me / Livin' lovin' wreck / Big blon' baby / I know what it means / Milkshake mademoiselle / Hand me down my walking cane / End of the road / Wild one / Down the line / Mean woman blues / Crazy arms / Little Queenie / Hang up my rock 'n' roll shoes / be bop a lula / It hurt me so / Good golly Miss Molly / Don't be cruel / Hound dog / Hello Josephine / CC rider / Jailhouse rock / Johnny B Goode / Money / Matchbox / Let's talk about us / How's my ex treating you / Your cheatin' heart / Teenage letter / Good rockin' tonight / Honey hush / I've been twistin' / Big legged woman
CD Set _______ CPCD 82432
Charly / Oct '96 / Koch

WHOLE LOTTA HITS
CD _______ CPCD 8121
Charly / Aug '95 / Koch

WHOLE LOTTA SHAKIN'
Whole lotta shakin' / Don't be cruel / Down the line / Let the good times roll / Jambalaya / High school confidential / Jailhouse rock / Lewis boogie / Hound dog / What's I say / Lovin' up / Storm / Wild one / Great balls of fire / Singin' the blues / Little Queenie / Mean woman blues / Sixty minute man / Lovesick blues / Breathless / It'll be me
CD _______ QSCD 6010
Charly / Aug '93 / Koch

WORLD OF JERRY LEE LEWIS, THE
Whole lotta shakin' goin' on / Don't be cruel / Johnny B Goode / Shake, rattle and roll / Roll over Beethoven / Sea cruise / I'm on fire / Long tall Sally / Down the line / Working man blues / Dream baby / Sweet little sixteen / Treat her right / Haunted house / Sweet Georgia Brown / I'm left, you're right, she's gone / Big blon' baby / Hound dog / Drinkin' wine spo-dee-o-dee / Great balls of fire
CD _______ 5520642
Spectrum / May '96 / PolyGram

YOUNG BLOOD
CD _______ 7559617952
Warner Bros. / Jun '95 / Warner Music

Lewis, John

AMERICAN JAZZ ORCHESTRA PLAYS ELLINGTON
CD _______ 7567914232
Atlantic / Apr '95 / Warner Music

PRIVATE CONCERT
Saint Germain des pres / Opening bid / Down two spades / Morning in Paris / Milano / Afternoon in Paris / Don't blame me / Gemini / 'Round midnight / Midnight in Paris
CD _______ 8482672
EmArCy / May '91 / PolyGram

WONDERFUL WORLD OF JAZZ
CD _______ 7567909792
Atlantic / Apr '95 / Warner Music

Lewis, Laurie

EARTH AND SKY (The Songs Of Laurie Lewis)
Girlfriend guard your heart / Green fields / Don't get too close / Love chooses you / Texas bluebonnets / Fine line / Old friend / Maple's lament / Bear song / Light / Point of no return / Restless rambling heart / I'd be lost without you / Hills of my home / Haven of mercy / Magic light
CD _______ ROUCD 0400
Rounder / Jul '97 / ADA / CM / Direct

LOVE CHOOSES YOU
Old friend / Hills of home / Point of no return / I don't know why / I'd be lost without you / When the nightbird sings / Women of Ireland / Ryestraw / Light / Texas bluebonnets / Love chooses you
CD _______ FF 70487
Flying Fish / Nov '96 / ADA / CM / Direct / Roots

OAK AND THE LAUREL, THE (Lewis, Laurie & Tom Rozum)
CD _______ ROUCD 0340
Rounder / Jul '95 / ADA / CM / Direct

RESTLESS RAMBLING HEART
Bowling green / Cowgirl's song / Restless rambling heart / Cry cry darlin' / Stealin' chickens / Maple's lament / Here we go again / Green fields / Hold to a dream / I'm gonna be the wind / Haven of mercy
CD _______ FF 70406
Flying Fish / Nov '96 / ADA / CM / Direct / Roots

SINGIN' MY TROUBLES AWAY (Lewis, Laurie & Grant Street)
Diamond Joe / Don't get too close / Rope / Beautiful bouquet / Overdrive / Heartache / When the cactus is in bloom / I wish it had been a dream / New day / Singin' my troubles away / Hell among the yearlings / Raleigh and Spencer / I miss the Mississippi and you
CD _______ FF 70515
Flying Fish / Mar '97 / ADA / CM / Direct / Roots

TOGETHER (Lewis, Laurie & Kathy Kallick)
Going up the mountain / Just like the rain / Is the blue moon still shining / Don't you see the train / Hideaway / Touch of the master's hand / Lost John / Maverick / That dawn the day you left me / Count your blessings / Little Annie / Don't leave your little girl all alone / Gonna lay down my old guitar
CD _______ ROUCD 0318
Rounder / Feb '95 / ADA / CM / Direct

TRUE STORIES
CD _______ ROUCD 300
Rounder / Sep '93 / ADA / CM / Direct

Lewis, Linda

BEST OF LINDA LEWIS, THE
(Remember the days of) the old schoolyard / It's in his kiss / This time I'll be sweeter / Rock 'n' roller coaster / Not a little girl anymore / I do my best to impress / Baby I'm yours / May you never / Shining / You came / Come back and finish what you started / Light years away / My love is here to stay / My friend the sun / So many mysteries to find / All comes back to love / Flipped over your love / Never been done before / Can't we just sit down and talk it over / Winter wonderland
CD _______ 74321431562
Camden / Oct '96 / BMG

SECOND NATURE
CD _______ TPN 3CD
Turpin / Nov '95 / Pinnacle

Lewis, Margaret

LONESOME BLUEBIRD
Shake a leg / One day, another tomorrow / Goin' to St Louie / From the cradle to the blues / Roll over Beethoven / Love is a fortune / Birmingham valley blues / You can't break my heart no more / No no never / Cheater's can't win / That's why I cry / Raggedy Ann and the player piano / There was no you / Bow wow puppy love / Dust my blues / Those lonely lonely nights / Reconsider me / You ought to see my baby / It's alright (you can go) / John De Lee (I love you) / Full grown man / Emmitt Lee / Lover's land / Baby please forgive me / Every time you turn me down / My blue eyed boy / Look what you're doing to me
CD _______ CDCHD 572
Ace / Jan '95 / Pinnacle

Lewis, Meade 'Lux'

1939-54
CD _______ SOB 35062CD
Story Of The Blues / Apr '95 / ADA / Koch

BARRELHOUSE PIANO
Six wheel chaser / How long blues / Someday sweetheart / Bugle call rag / I ain't gonna give nobody none o' this jelly roll / Mike / Darktown strutters ball / Birth of the blues / Tidal boogie / Mardi Gras drag / Tishomingo blues / Jada / Basin Street blues / Fast 'A' blues / 12th Street blues / St. Louis blues
CD _______ JASMCD 2536
Jasmine / Mar '95 / Conifer/BMG / Hot Shot / TKO Magnum

CLASSICS 1927-1939
CD _______ CLASSICS 722
Classics / Dec '93 / Discovery / Jazz Music

CLASSICS 1941-1944
CD _______ CLASSICS 841
Classics / Nov '95 / Discovery / Jazz Music

LEWIS, AMMONS & JOHNSON 1929-1935 (Lewis, Meade 'Lux' & Albert Ammons/Pete Johnson)
CD _______ PYCD 21
Magpie / Jun '96 / Hot Shot / Jazz Music

LEWIS, AMMONS & JOHNSON 1936-1941 (Lewis, Meade 'Lux' & Albert Ammons/Pete Johnson)
CD _______ BDCD 6046
Blues Document / Jun '95 / ADA / Hot Shot / Jazz Music

MEADE LUX LEWIS 1939-41
CD _______ CLASSICS 743
Classics / Feb '94 / Discovery / Jazz Music

TIDAL BOOGIE
CD _______ TCD 1029
Tradition / Aug '96 / ADA / Vital

Lewis, Mel

DEDICATION (Lewis, Mel & Thad Jones)
Groove merchant / Big dipper / Central Park North / Tow away zone / Quietude / Jive samba / Dedication / It only happens every time / Tiptoe / Child is born
CD _______ 17093
Laserlight / Mar '97 / Target/BMG

DEFINITIVE THAD JONES VOL.1, THE (Live From The Village Vanguard) (Lewis, Mel Jazz Orchestra)
Low down / Quietude / Three in one / Walkin' about / Little pixie
CD _______ MM 5024
Music Masters / Oct '94 / Nimbus

DEFINITIVE THAD JONES VOL.2 (Live At The Village Vanguard) (Lewis, Mel Jazz Orchestra)
Second race / Tip toe / Don't get sassy / Rhoda map / Cherry juice
CD _______ 8208382
Limelight / May '90 / PolyGram
CD _______ MM 5046
Music Masters / Oct '94 / Nimbus

LOST ART, THE (Lewis, Mel Sextet)
Hello / Voyager / Bulgaria / Native American / Allanjuneally / Ballad medley / Till there was you / My ideal / Lost art / Trio for BB / One for Max / Cold ranger / Face value / Goodbye
CD _______ 8208152
Limelight / Oct '90 / PolyGram

NEW MEL LEWIS QUINTET LIVE, THE (Lewis, Mel New Quintet)
Once I loved / Tranquilo / Pell mel / Ending shuffle
CD _______ INAK 8611CD
In Akustik / Jul '97 / Direct / TKO Magnum

SOFT LIGHTS AND HOT MUSIC (Classics In Jazz) (Lewis, Mel & The Jazz Orchestra)
Soft lights and sweet music / Compensation / Lester left town / It could happen to you / Off the cuff / Our love is here to stay / Little man you've had a busy day / How long has this been going on / Touch of your lips
CD _______ 8208132
Limelight / Jul '90 / PolyGram
CD _______ MM 5012
Music Masters / Oct '94 / Nimbus

SOFT LIGHTS AND SWEET MUSIC (Lewis, Mel & The Jazz Orchestra)
CD _______ 50122C
Music Masters / Dec '94 / Nimbus

TO YOU (A Tribute To Mel Lewis) (Lewis, Mel Jazz Orchestra)
Paper spoons / Five and a half weeks / Nightingale sang in Berkeley Square / Nocturne / ABC blues / Bob Brookmeyer / To you
CD _______ 8208322
Limelight / Aug '90 / PolyGram

Lewis, Pete

SCRATCHIN' (Lewis, Pete/Jimmy Nolen/ Cal Green)
Strollin' with Nolen / Louisiana hop / How fine can you be / Scratchin' / You've been goofing / Crying with the rising sun / Way you do / Big push / Raggedy blues / I can't stand you no more / After hours / Harmonica boogie / Don't leave me no more / Chocolate pork chop man / Wipe your tears / Green's blues / It hurts me too / Blast / Strawberry jam / Ooh midnight / Movin' on down the line

CD CDCHARLY 268
Charly / Jun '91 / Koch

Lewis, Peter

PETER LEWIS
CD TX 2008CD
Taxim / Jul '95 / ADA

Lewis, Ramsey

16 GREATEST HITS
CD CD 8024
16 / May '94 / BMG

BETWEEN THE KEYS
Sun goddess 2000 / Cold and windy / I'll always be about you / Secret place / Between the keys / Les fleurs / Just a little loving / Hearts of fire / All around the world
CD GRP 98432
GRP / Jun '96 / New Note/BMG

COLLECTION, THE
Wade in the water / Something you got / Hard day's night / Hang on Sloopy / Ain't that peculiar / Blues for the night owl / Hi-heel sneakers / Function at the junction / Uptight (everything's alright) / Lonely avenue / Day tripper / 1-2-3 / Felicidade / Les fleurs / Caves / Since I fell for you / All my love belongs to you / He's a real gone guy / Soul man / In crowd
CD MOCD 3012
More Music / Feb '95 / Sound & Media

GREATEST HITS (Lewis, Ramsey Trio)
'In' crowd / My babe / Since I fell for you / Something you got / Hard day's night / Hang on sloopy / Caves / Dancing in the street / Felicidade (happiness) / Wade in the water / Ain't that peculiar / Blues for the night owl / Function at the junction / Lonely avenue / 1-2-3 / Look-a-here / High heel sneakers / Uptight (everything's alright)
CD MCD 06021
Chess/MCA / Apr '97 / BMG / New Note/BMG

IN CONCERT - 1965 (Lewis, Ramsey Trio)
Satin doll / And I love her / Come Sunday / Hard day's night / In crowd
CD CD 53108
Giants Of Jazz / May '92 / Cadillac / Jazz Music / Target/BMG

IVORY PYRAMID
Bazillica / People make the world go round / Ivory pyramid / Sarah Jane / Tequila mockingbird / Night in Bahia / Malachi / Pavanne / Love's gotta hold / Jackson park
CD GRP 96882
GRP / Nov '92 / New Note/BMG

LIVE (Lewis, Ramsey Trio)
CD JHR 73524
Jazz Hour / May '93 / Cadillac / Jazz Music / Target/BMG

SKY ISLANDS
Julia / Aprez vous / Who are you / Suavecito / Tonight / Sky islands / Song for you / Medley / Love will find a way / Come back to me / Tonight (instrumental version)
CD GRP 97452
GRP / Oct '93 / New Note/BMG

SUN GODDESS
CD CK 33194
Sony Jazz / Aug '97 / Sony

THIS IS JAZZ
Wade in the water / Love song / Tondelayo / Waltz for Debby / There's no easy way / Blues for the night / Owl / Time for love / Brazillica / Soul sister / Spiritual / Song without words (remembering)
CD CK 65043
Sony Jazz / May '97 / Sony

Lewis, Smiley

SHAME, SHAME, SHAME
Turn on your volume, baby / Here comes Smiley / Tee-nah-nah / Lowdown / Slide me down / Growing old / If you ever loved a woman / Dirty people / Where were you / My baby / Sad life / Bee's boogie / Don't jive me / My baby was right / Bells are ringing / Lillie Mae / You're gonna miss me / Gypsy blues / You're not the one / Gumbo blues / Ain't gonna do it / It's so peaceful / Calsonia's party / Lonesome highway / Standing on the corner / Oh baby / Big mamou / Play girl / (I love you) for sentimental reasons / Lying woman / Little Fernandez / It's music / Show me the way / Down the road / One night / Blue Monday / Rocks / Nothing but the blues / That certain door / Nobody knows / She's got me hook, line and sinker / Can't stop loving you / Baby please / Ooh la la / By the water / Too many drivers / Rootin' and tootin' / Lost weekend / Jailbird / Farewell / Please listen to me / No, no / Real gone lover / Bumpity bump / Someday you'll want me / I can't believe it / I hear you knocking / Hey girl / Down yonder we go ballin' / Come on / Queen of hearts / No letter today / Li'l Liza Jane / Mama don't like / I shall not be moved / Ain't goin there no more / Shame, shame, shame / Oh Red / Last night / I want to be with her / Shame, shame, shame / Tell me who / Stormy Monday blues / These bones / Goin' down the road / Sweeter words (have never been told) / Tore up / When did you leave Heaven / You are my sunshine / I'm coming down with the blues / I wake up screamin' / Tomorrow night / Go on fool / To the river / How long / Ronettes / Sometimes / Lookin' for my woman / Goin' to jump and shout / One night of sin / Sheikh of araby / Bad luck blues / Bells are ringing / School days are back again / Jump (Instrumental) / My love is gone / Walkin' the girl (Instrumental) / Oh Red / Ain't goin there no more
CD Set BCD 15745
Bear Family / Nov '93 / Direct / Rollercoaster / Swift

SMILEY LEWIS VOL.1
Lillie Mae / Gypsy blues / My baby was right / Blue Monday / Playgirl / Oh baby / Gumbo blues / No no / Oh Red, don't jive me / Big mamou
CD KCCD 01
KC / Apr '90 / Cadillac / CM / Wellard

SMILEY LEWIS VOL.2
Down the road / Rocks
CD KCCD 02
KC / Apr '90 / Cadillac / CM / Wellard

Lewis, Vic

CELEBRATION OF CONTEMPORARY WEST COAST JAZZ, A
CD CCD 79711
Candid / Feb '97 / Cadillac / Direct / Jazz Music / Koch / Wellard

PLAY BILL HOLMAN (Lewis, Vic West Coast All Stars)
Oleo / Yesterdays / Sizzler before lunch / When I fall in love / Easter parade / As we speak / Sizzler after lunch
CD CDMOLE 14
Mole Jazz / Jan '90 / Cadillac / Impetus / Jazz Music / Wellard
CD CCD 79535
Candid / Jan '97 / Cadillac / Direct / Jazz Music / Koch / Wellard

SHAKE DOWN THE STARS (The Music Of Jimmy Van Heusen) (Lewis, Vic West Coast All Stars)
Swinging on a star / But beautiful / Suddenly it's spring / I'll only miss her / Here's that rainy day / Polka dots and moonbeams / I thought about you / So would I / Shake down the stars / Collar 17
CD CCD 79526
Candid / Feb '97 / Cadillac / Direct / Jazz Music / Koch / Wellard

TRIBUTE TO STAN KENTON, A (Lewis, Vic & His Orchestra)
Hammersmith riff / Pepperpot / Man I love / Music for moderns / Design for brass / Theme for Alto / Theme for trombone / Over the rainbow / Serenade in blue / Hundred years from today / Love for sale / Where are you / Concerto to end all concertos / Heir to a chinese maiden / Cuban carnival / Porphyria's lover / Blues / For you a bone / Eindayz / Inspiration / Everywhere
CD VICD 567
Avid / Jul '96 / Avid/BMG / Koch / THE

Lewis, Victor

EEEYYESS
Eeeyyess / Vulnerability / Un-til / Buttercups / Alter ego / No more misunderstandings / Stamina / Here's to you baby / Shakehandre
CD ENJ 93112
Enja / Apr '97 / New Note/Pinnacle / Vital/SAM

Lewis, Walter 'Furry'

FOURTH AND BEALE
Going to Brownsville / John Henry / Casey Jones / St. Louis blues / Judge Boushe blues / Just a little fun / Going back to Gary / When the saints go marchin' in / Dog named blue
CD 5197262
Verve / Apr '93 / PolyGram

IN HIS PRIME (1927-29)
CD YAZCD 12050
Yazoo / Jun '91 / ADA / CM / Koch

SHAKE 'EM ON DOWN
John Henry / When my baby left me / Shake 'em on down / Big chief blues / Old blue / I'm going to Brownsville / Back on my feet again / White lightning / Roberta / St. Louis blues / Baby you don't want me / Done changed my mind / Goin' to Kansas city / Judge boushay blues / Casey Jones / This time tomorrow / I will turn your money green / Frankie and Johnny / Longing blues / Long tall gal blues
CD CDCH 486
Ace / Nov '93 / Pinnacle

Lewis, Webster

LIVE AT CLUB 7
CD CR 001CD
Counterpoint / Apr '97 / Timewarp

Lewis, Willie

CLASSICS 1932-1936
CD CLASSICS 822
Classics / Jul '95 / Discovery / Jazz Music

CLASSICS 1936-1938
CD CLASSICS 847
Classics / Nov '95 / Discovery / Jazz Music

CLASSICS 1941
CD CLASSICS 880
Classics / Jul '96 / Discovery / Jazz Music

Lex Talionis

INTO THE SHADE
CD EFA 084652
Dossier / Dec '94 / Cargo / SRD

Ley, Tabu

AFRICA WORLDWIDE
CD ROUCD 5039
Rounder / Feb '96 / ADA / CM / Direct

BABETI SOUKOUS
Presentation / Kinshasa / Soroza / Linga ngai / Moto akokufa / Nairobi / Seli ja / I need you / Amour nala / Tu as dit que / Sentimenta / Pitie / Mosola
CD RWCD 5
Virgin / Jun '89 / EMI

LES ANNEES 70 (Ley, Tabu Rochereau)
CD CD 36562
Sonodisc / Jan '97 / Stern's

MUZINA
CD ROUCD 5059
Rounder / Nov '94 / ADA / CM / Direct

Leyland DAF Band

ROMANCE IN BRASS
Love changes everything / Spring / Summer night / Song of the seashore / All I ask of you / Elvira Madigan / Drink to me only with thine eyes / Can't take my eyes off you / Romance from 'The Gadfly' / Anything but lonely / Romance from 'Fair Maid of Perth' / Someone to watch over me / Serenata / Flower duet / Forgotten dreams / Fanfare, romance and finale
CD QPRL 043D
Polyphonic / Jun '90 / Complete/Pinnacle

Leyland, Carl 'Sonny'

BOOGIE AND BLUES
CD SACD 117
Solo Art / Jul '96 / Jazz Music

Leyli

SPIRITUAL BELLY DANCE
CD EUCD 1251
ARC / Mar '94 / ADA / ARC Music

Leyton, John

JOHN LEYTON ARCHIVE
Johnny remember me / Wild wind / Six white horses / Son, this is she / Lone rider / Lonely city / I think I'm falling in love / Lonely Johnny / Oh lover / I don't care if the sun don't shine / I love you for sentimental reasons / That's how to make love / Voodoo woman / Land of love / Cupboard love / Fabulous / It would be easy / Beautiful dreamer / Another man / Make love to me
CD RMCD 207
Rialto / Sep '96 / Disc / Total/BMG

Leyton, Johnny

BEST OF JOHN LEYTON
Johnny remember me / Wild wind / Six white horses / Son this is she / Lone rider / Lonely city / I think I'm falling in love / Lonely Johnny / Oh lover / I don't care if the sun don't shine / (I love you) for sentimental reasons / That's how to make love / I'll cut your tail off / Land of love / Cupboard love / How will it end / It would be easy / Beautiful dreamer / Another man / Make love to me / You took my love for granted / I guess you are always on my mind / Funny man / Man is not supposed to cry / Girl on the floor above / Tell Laura I love her / On Lovers Hill / Too many late nights / Lover's lane / I'm gonna let my hair down / Don't let her go away / All I want is you / I want a love I can see
CD SEECD 201
See For Miles/C5 / Sep '87 / Pinnacle

EP COLLECTION, THE
Son this is she / That's a woman / Fabulous / Voodoo woman / Wild wind / Six white horses / Thunder and lightning / Goodbye to teenage love / You took my love for granted / I don't care if the sun don't shine / Down the River Nile / Terry Brown's in love with Mary Dee / Walk with me my angel / There must be / Cupboard love / I'll cut your tail off / Beautiful dreamer / Another man / Oh lover / Lone rider / Lonely city / Lonely Johnny / On Lovers Hill / (I love you) For sentimental reasons / That's how to make love / Johnny remember me / Make love to me
CD SEECD 401
See For Miles/C5 / Mar '94 / Pinnacle

LFO

ADVANCE
CD WARPCD 39
Warp / Jan '96 / Prime / RTM/Disc

FREQUENCIES
CD WARPCD 3
Warp / Apr '96 / Prime / RTM/Disc

Lhamo, Yungchen

TIBET, TIBET
CD CDRW 59
Realworld / Jul '96 / EMI

Li Calzi, Giorgio

GIORGIO LI CALZI
CD PHIL 672
Philology / Oct '94 / Cadillac / Harmonia Mundi

Li He

CHINESE CLASSICAL FOLK MUSIC
CD EUCD 1155
ARC / '91 / ADA / ARC Music

Liangxing, Tang

HIGH MOUNTAIN, FLOWING WATER
CD SHAN 65012CD
Shanachie / Oct '93 / ADA / Greensleeves / Koch

Liars In Wait

SPIRITUALLY UNKNOWN
CD BS 008CD
Burning Sun / Nov '96 / Plastic Head

Libana

BORDERLAND
CD SHCD 67003
Shanachie / Mar '94 / ADA / Greensleeves / Koch

Liberace

UNPLUGGED
CD IGCD 3001
Ignition / Feb '96 / ADA

Liberation Through Hearing

LIBERATION THROUGH HEARING
CD DELECCD 023
Delerium / Aug '94 / Cargo / Pinnacle / Vital

Liberator

FREEDOM FIGHTERS
CD BHR 038CD
Burning Heart / Apr '96 / Plastic Head

THIS IS LIBERATOR
CD BHR 047CD
Burning Heart / Jul '96 / Plastic Head

Liberman, Jeffrey

THEN AND NOW
CD SB 034
Second Battle / Jun '97 / Greyhound

Libertine, Eve

SKATING
CD RH 2CD
Red Herring / Nov '92 / SRD

Liberty

LIBERTY
CD BLIPCD 101
Urban London / Mar '94 / Jet Star / Pinnacle

Liberty Cage

SLEEP OF THE JUST
Everything's different now / Fires below / Throwing stones at the sea / On her majesty's service / Swimming against the tide / One for the road / Judgement day / You make my mind stand still / Mercy of the guards / Cat and mouse affair / Murder in cell no.9
CD LICD 901293
Line / Sep '94 / CM / Direct

Libido Boyz

OPGU
CD CDZORRO 42
Metal Blade / Jul '90 / Pinnacle / Plastic Head

Library Of Congress ...

MUSIC FOR THE GODS (Library Of Congress Endangered Music Project)
CD RCD 10315
Rykodisc / Feb '95 / ADA / Vital

Licht, Alan

EVAN DANDO OF NOISE, THE
CD HERMES 022
Corpus Hermeticum / May '97 / Cargo

Lick

BREECH
CD INV 046CD
Invisible / Jan '96 / Plastic Head

Lick 57's

...AND THE BAND PLAYED ON
CD SEMAPHORE 35954
Onefoot / Nov '96 / Cargo

Licursi, Silvana

FAR FROM THE LAND OF EAGLE
CD LYRCD 7413
Lyrichord / '91 / ADA / CM / Roots

Lid

IN THE MUSHROOM
Lid / Mary Agnes / Dream is over / In the mushroom / Window pain / R / You are here / Alive / Randy scouse git / For all my life
CD CDVILE 67
Peaceville / Jun '97 / Pinnacle

Liebmann, David

CLASSIC BALLADS
Out of nowhere / If I should lose you / Dancing in the dark / Skylark / Angel eyes / Stella by starlight / My funny Valentine / On green dolphin street
CD CCD 79512
Candid / Feb '97 / Cadillac / Direct / Jazz Music / Koch / Wellard

IF ONLY THEY KNEW (Liebmann, David Quintet)
If only they knew / Capistrano / Moontide / Reunion / Autumn in New York / Move on some
CD CDSJP 151
Timeless Jazz / Feb '91 / New Note/ Pinnacle

JOY (The Music Of John Coltrane)
After the rain / Untitled original / Alabama / India / Naima / Joy/Selflessness
CD CCD 79531
Candid / Feb '97 / Cadillac / Direct / Jazz Music / Koch / Wellard

OPAL HEART, THE (Liebmann, David Quartet)
Sunburst / Port Ligat / Opal hearted aborigine / Concentrate on you / Star crossed lovers / Down under
CD ENJACD 30652
Enja / Jun '97 / New Note/Pinnacle / Vital/ SAM

PLAY THE MUSIC OF COLE PORTER (Liebmann, David & Steve Gilmore/Bill Goodwin)
CD 1232362
Red / Apr '91 / ADA / Cadillac / Harmonia Mundi

QUEST VOL.2
CD STCD 4132
Storyville / Jul '96 / Cadillac / Jazz Music / Wellard

RETURN OF THE TENOR - STANDARDS
All the things you are / Bye bye blackbird / Loverman / Secret love / No greater love / There will never be another you / Yesterdays / Summertime / All of me
CD DTRCD 109
Double Time / Nov '96 / Express Jazz

SONGS FOR MY DAUGHTERS
CD 1212952
Soul Note / Sep '95 / Cadillac / Harmonia Mundi / Wellard

TREE, THE
CD 1211952
Soul Note / Nov '91 / Cadillac / Harmonia Mundi / Wellard

VOYAGE (Liebmann, David Group)
Open eyes / Dancing in the park / When to love / Drum thing / Cut / Gravel and the bird / Maiden voyage / Yildiz
CD ECD 221572
Evidence / Sep '96 / ADA / Cadillac / Harmonia Mundi

Liebzeit, Jaki

NOWHERE
CD SPOONCD 17
The Grey Area / Feb '95 / RTM/Disc

Liedes, Anna-Kaisa

KUUTTAREN KORET
CD OMCD 44
Olarin Musiikki Oy / Dec '93 / ADA / Direct

OI MIKSI
CD TUG 1099CD
Tugboat / Feb '95 / ADA

Liege Lord

MASTER CONTROL
CD 1995412
Metal Blade / Jan '89 / Pinnacle / Plastic Head

Lien, Annbjorg

ANNBJORG LIEN
CD FXCD 88
Kirkelig Kultuverksted / Jul '93 / ADA

FELEFEBER
CD GR 4081CD
Grappa / Dec '94 / ADA

PRISME
CD GR 4113CD
Grappa / Nov '96 / ADA
CD SHCD 64082
Shanachie / Apr '97 / ADA / Greensleeves / Koch

Liers In Wait

SPIRITUALY UNCONTROLLED ART
CD DOL 007CD
Dolores / Nov '92 / Plastic Head

Lieutenant Stitchie

BANGARANG
CD SHCD 45023
Shanachie / Aug '95 / ADA / Greensleeves / Koch

GHETTO SOLDIER
CD GRELCD 213
Greensleeves / Dec '94 / Jet Star / SRD

LIEUTENANT STITCHIE, BEENIE MAN, COBRA & FRIENDS (Lieutenant Stitchie & Beenie Man/Cobra)
CD RNCD 2070
Rhino / Jul '94 / Grapevine/PolyGram / Jet Star

RUDE BOY
Jamaican addiction / Cab / Can U read my mind / Prescription / Mr. Good stuff / Twenty one governor salute / Rude boy chat / Ton load a fat / Rough rider / Nurse me / (I need) sexual healing / Tug of war / Bad like yaws
CD 7567824792
Warner Bros. / May '93 / Warner Music

Life

COCOON
CD NTHEN 029CD
Now & Then / Apr '97 / Plastic Head

Life Force

LIFE FORCE
CD WB 1154CD
We Bite / Jun '97 / Plastic Head

Life Of Agony

RIVER RUNS RED
CD RR 90432
Roadrunner / Oct '93 / PolyGram

UGLY
CD RR 89242
CD RR 89249
Roadrunner / Oct '95 / PolyGram

Life Sex & Death

SILENT MAJORITY, THE
Blue velvet/we're here now / Jawohl asshole / School's for fools / Telephone call / Farm song / Fuckin' shit ass / Hey buddy / Train / Wet your lips / Tank / Raise a little hell / Guatemala / Big black bush / Rise above
CD 7599269582
WEA / Aug '92 / Warner Music

Life's Addiction

INNER SHADE
Cherry red / I do believe / Jesus coming in for the kill / Like me again / End of the road / Cool cool breeze / Inner shade / Couldn't sleep last night / Ocean / Lightning strikes
CD 8289102
FFRR / Aug '97 / PolyGram

Lifetime

JERSEY'S BEST DANCERS
CD JT 1034CD
Jade Tree / Jul '97 / Cargo / Greyhound / Plastic Head

Lifter Puller

LIFTER PULLER
CD RUNT 24
Runt / Mar '97 / Cargo / Greyhound / Plastic Head

Lig

BACTERIAL ACTIVITY
CD ABT 102CD
Abstract / Jun '97 / Cargo / Pinnacle / Total/BMG

Ligament

KIND DEEDS
CD FLOWCD 003
Flower Shop / Apr '96 / SRD

Liggins, Jimmy

JIMMY LIGGINS AND HIS DROPS OF JOY (Liggins, Jimmy & His Drops Of Joy)
I can't stop it / Troubles goodbye / Teardrop blues / Cadillac boogie / Move out baby / Careful love / Homecoming blues / Baby I can't forget you / Don't put me down / Nite life boogie / Mississippi boogie / Come back baby / Answer to Teardrop Blues / That song is gone / Saturday night boogie woogie man / Shuffle shock / Washboard special / That's what's knockin' me out / Hep cat boogie / I want my baby for Christmas / Train blues / Baby's boogie / Drunk / Going away / Come back home
CD CDCHD 306
Ace / Oct '90 / Pinnacle

ROUGH WEATHER BLUES VOL.2 (Liggins, Jimmy & His Drops Of Joy)
Bye bye baby goodbye / Lookin' for my baby / Rough weather blues / Misery blues / Give up little girl / Lonely nights blues / Saturday night boogie woogie man / Lover's prayer / Now's the time / Sincere lover's blues / Down and out blues / Unidentified instrumental / Blues for love / Brown skin baby / Stolen love / Jumpin' and stompin' / Low down blues / Cloudy day blues / Goin' down with the sun / Dark hour blues / Pleading my cause / I'll never let you go / Railroad blues / Drunk / I'll always love you
CD CDCHD 437
Ace / Jan '93 / Pinnacle

Liggins, Joe

JOE LIGGINS AND THE HONEYDRIPPERS (Liggins, Joe & His Honey Drippers)
Pink champagne / Ramblin' blues / Rag mop / Rhythm in the barnyard / Going back to New Orleans / I've got a right to cry / Honeydripper / I just can't help myself / Don't miss that train / Frankie Lee / Brand new deal in mobile / Little Joe's boogie / One sweet letter / Whiskey, gin and wine / Louisiana woman / Trying to lose the blues / Shuffle boogie blues / Rain rain rain / Flying Dutchman / Tanya / Blues for Tanya / Freight train blues / Whiskey, women and loaded dice / Big dipper / Do you love me pretty baby
CD CDCHD 307
Ace / Oct '90 / Pinnacle

Light, Allan

TWO NIGHTS (Light, Allan & Loren Mazzacane)
CD ROCO 012CD
Roadcone / Feb '97 / Cargo

Light Division

HORSE GUARDS PARADE (Massed Bands Of The Light Division)
Bugle calls / Light Division assembly / Advance / Sambre et meuse / Les clarions anglais / Mechanised infantry / Quick silver / Slave's chorus / Silver bugles / St. Mary / Run runaway / Light Cavalry / Keel row / Road to the Isles / Five to one / Three to one / Bugle boy / Secunderabad / Horse Guards echoes: *Massed Bands Of The Royal Air Force* / Great gate of Kiev / Fanfare Sir John Moore / Sunset / National Anthem / Light Infantry regimental march / Royal Green Jackets / No more parades today / High on a hill
CD BNA 5021
Bandleader / Jul '88 / Conifer/BMG

LIVE AT THE ALBERT HALL
Duke of Cambridge / Marvin Hamlisch showcase / March off / Bugle feature / March on / Bugle calls / Finale from trumpet concerto / Bohemian rhapsody / St. Marys / Royal green jackets / Nightfall in camp / Crown imperial / High on a hill / Light infantry
CD 3036100092
Pearls / Apr '96 / Carlton

LIVING TRADITION, A (Band & Bugles Of The Light Division)
Silver bugles / Zorba's dance / Rifle regiment / Sir John Moore / Let's face the music and dance / Here's that rainy day / Triomphale / Concerto for clarinet / Symphonic Beatles / Gavorkna fanfare / Drigo's serenade / Bill / Sabre dance / Auld lang syne/Last post / Light division marches
CD BNA 5123
Bandleader / Jun '96 / Conifer/BMG

Light Of Darkness

LIGHT OF DARKNESS
CD SB 019
Second Battle / Jun '97 / Greyhound

Light Of The World

BEST OF LIGHT OF THE WORLD, THE
CD MCCD 189
Music Club / Nov '94 / Disc / THE

VERY BEST OF LIGHT OF THE WORLD, THE
Somebody help me out: *Beggar & Co* / Swingin' / Keep the dream alive / I'm so happy / Midnight groovin' / Expansions / Parisienne girl: *Incognito* / London town / Pete's crusade / Time / I shot the sheriff / Got to get your own
CD MOCD 3007
More Music / Feb '95 / Sound & Media

Lightfoot, Gordon

DID SHE MENTION MY NAME/BACK HERE ON EARTH PLUS SPIN, SPIN
Did she mention my name / Wherefor and why / Last time I saw her / Black day in July / May I / Magnificent outpourings / Does your mother know / Mountains and Maryann / Pussy willows, cat tails / I want to hear from you / Something very special / Boss man / Long way back home / Unsettled ways / Long thin dawn / Bitter green / Circle is small / Marie Christine / Cold hands from New York / Affair on 8th Avenue / Don't beat me down / Gypsy / If I could / Spin, spin (New Yok remake version)
CD BGOCD 167
Beat Goes On / Mar '93 / Pinnacle

EARLY LIGHTFOOT/SUNDAY CONCERT
Rich man's spiritual / Long river / Way I feel / For lovin' me / First time / Changes / Early morning rain / Steel rail blues / Sixteen miles / I'm not saying / Pride of man / Ribbon of darkness / Oh Linda / Peaceful waters / In a windowpane / Lost children / Leaves of grass / Medley: I'm not sayin'; Ribbon of darkness / Apology / Bitter green / Ballad of Yarmouth Castle / Softly / Boss man / Pussy willows, cat tails / Canadian road trilogy
CD BGOCD 166
Beat Goes On / Apr '93 / Pinnacle

IF YOU COULD READ MY MIND
Minstrel of the dawn / Me and Bobby McGee / Approaching lavender / Saturday clothes / Cobwebs and dust / Poor little Allison / Sit down young stranger / If you could read my mind / Baby it's alright / Your love's return (song for Stephen Foster) / Pony man
CD 7599274512
WEA / Feb '92 / Warner Music

LIGHTFOOT
If you got it / Softly / Crossroads / Minor ballad / Go go round / Rosanna / Home from the forest / I'll be alright / Song for a winter's night / Canadian railroad trilogy / Way I feel / Rich man's spiritual / Long river / For lovin' me / First time / Changes / Early morning rain / Steel rail blues / Sixteen miles / I'm not saying / Pride of man / Ribbon of darkness / Oh Linda / Peaceful waters
CD BCD 15576
Bear Family / Apr '92 / Direct / Rollercoaster / Swift

SUNDAY CONCERT PLUS EXTRA STUDIO CUTS
In a windowpane / Lost children / Leaves of grass / I'm not sayin and ribbon of darkness / Apology / Bitter green / Ballad of Yarmouth Castle / Softly / Boss man / Pussy willows, cat tails / Canadian railroad trilogy / Just like Tom Thumb's blues / Movin' / I'll be alright / Spin, spin (Nashville version, Tk 8) / Movin'
CD BCD 15691
Bear Family / Mar '93 / Direct / Rollercoaster / Swift

SUNDOWN
Somewhere USA / High and dry / Seven Island suite / Circle of steel / Is there anyone home / Watchman's gone / Sundown / Carefree highway / List / Too late for pryin'
CD 7599272112
WEA / Feb '92 / Warner Music

WAY I FEEL, THE
Walls / If you got it / Softly / Crossroads / A-minor ballad / Go go round / Rosanna / Home from the forest / I'll be alright / Song for a winter's night / Canadian railroad trilogy / Way I feel
CD BGOCD 296
Beat Goes On / Nov '95 / Pinnacle

Lightfoot, Jerry

BURNING DESIRE (Lightfoot, Jerry & The Essentials)
CD CBHCD 2002
Connor Ray / Mar '96 / Direct

Lightfoot, Papa George

GOIN BACK TO THE NATCHEZ TRACE
My woman is tired of me lyin / New mean old train / Love my baby / Goin' down that muddy road / Ah come on honey / I heard somebody crying / Take it witcha / Nighttime / Early in the morning / Walkin' / Goin' back to Natchez / Baby, please don't go / Train tune / Papa George - Talkin' about it
CD CDCHD 548
Ace / Nov '94 / Pinnacle

Lightfoot, Terry

AT THE JAZZBAND BALL (Lightfoot, Terry & His Band)
CD BRMCD 028
Bold Reprive / Oct '88 / Harmonia Mundi

DOWN ON BOURBON STREET (Lightfoot, Terry & His Jazzmen)
Bourbon street parade / Do you know what it means to miss New Orleans / Eh la bas / When we danced at the Mardi Gras / Grandpa's spells / Closer walk with thee / Petite fleur / Chimes blues / Solace / Ole man mose / Hiawatha rag / Trouble in mind

/ Ice cream / Lonesome / Maryland / Ragtime music
CD ______ **CDTTD 581**
Timeless Jazz / Mar '94 / New Note/ Pinnacle

LIVE IN LEIPZIG
Rockin' in rhythm / West End blues / Sentimental journey / Summertime / Honeysuckle rose / Ol' man Mose / Honky tonk train blues / Tuxedo junction
CD ______ **BLCD 760513**
Black Lion / May '96 / Cadillac / Jazz Music / Koch / Wellard

SPECIAL MAGIC OF LOUIS ARMSTRONG, THE (Lightfoot, Terry & His Band)
Jeepers creepers / Muskrat ramble / Give me a kiss to build a dream on / You'll never walk alone / Mack the knife / Wonderful world / Hello Dolly / Tin roof blues / Dardanella / Now you has jazz / All the time in the world / Mame / Dippermouth blues / Lazy river / Faithful hussar / Cabaret / When it's sleepy time down South / Westherbird rag / Blueberry hill / Indiana
CD ______ **STOCD 104**
Start / Feb '97 / Disc

STARDUST (Lightfoot, Terry & His Band)
At the woodchoppers' ball / Just a gigolo / Fish seller / Stardust / Bad, Bad Leroy Brown / Undecided / Gone fishin' / Jumpin' at the woodside / Frim fram sauce / Ragtime music / Black and Tan fantasy / Big noise from Winnetka / Bye and bye / Drum boogie
CD ______ **URCD 104**
Upbeat / Dec '90 / Cadillac / Target/BMG

WHEN THE SAINTS GO MARCHING IN (Lightfoot, Terry & His Band)
When the Saints go marching in / Mame / At the jazzband ball / Every lonely river / Ballad of Jesse James / Wang wang blues / When you're smiling / Muskrat ramble / John Henry / Jazz me blues / Put down the glass / Drum boogie / Mack the knife / Who's gonna play that ragtime music / River stay 'way from my door / Nobody wants to know you when you're down and out
CD ______ **C5MCD 566**
See For Miles/C5 / Apr '96 / Pinnacle

Lighthouse

BEST OF LIGHTHOUSE - SUNNY DAYS AGAIN
One fine morning / Hats off to a stranger / Little kind words / 1849 / Sunny days / Sweet lullaby / Take it slow / Broken down guitar blues / I just wanna be your friend / You girl / Silver bird / Lonely places / Pretty lady / Can you feel it / Magic's in the dancing / Good day
CD ______ **CAN 9002**
Marquis / Oct '93 / Kingdom

BORN A NICE KID
CD ______ **ER 1033**
Elefant / Aug '97 / Greyhound / SRD

LIGHTHOUSE LIVE
Just wanna be your friend / Take it slow / Old man / Rockin' chair / You and me / Sweet lullaby / 1849 / Eight miles high / One fine morning / Insane
CD ______ **CAN 9010**
Marquis / Oct '93 / Kingdom

Lighthouse Family

OCEAN DRIVE
Lifted / Heavenly / Loving every minute / Ocean drive / Way you are / Keep remembering / Sweetest operator / What could be better / Beautiful night / Goodbye heartbreak
CD ______ **5237872**
Wild Card / Feb '96 / PolyGram

Lightnin' Rod

HUSTLER'S CONVENTION
Sport / Spoon / Cafe black rose / Brother hominy / Grit / Coppin' some fronts for the set / Hammock's hall was big (and there was a whole lot to dig) / Bones fly from spoon's hand / Break was so loud it hushed the crowd / Four bitches is what I got / Grit's den / Shit hits the fan again / Sentenced to the chair
CD ______ **CPCD 8177**
Charly / Jun '96 / Koch

Lightnin' Slim

BLUE LIGHTNING
Mama talk to your daughter / My baby left me this morning / It's mighty crazy / Caress me baby / I love you baby / Sky is crying / GI Slim / Help me spend my gold / My little angel child / Too close blues / I want you to love me / Bedbug blues / I'm tired waitin' baby / Ah'w baby
CD ______ **IGOCD 2002**
Indigo / Jul '95 / ADA / Direct

HIGH AND LOW DOWN/OVER EASY (Lightnin' Slim & Whispering Smith)
Rooster blues: *Lightnin' Slim* / Things I used to do: *Lightnin' Slim* / Bad luck blues: *Lightnin' Slim* / My babe: *Lightnin' Slim* / GI blues: *Lightnin' Slim* / Oh baby: *Lightnin' Slim* / That's alright Mama: *Lightnin' Slim* / Can't hold out much longer: *Lightnin' Slim* / Good morning heartaches: *Lightnin' Slim* / Hoodoo blues: *Lightnin' Slim* / What in the world's come over me: *Smith, Whispering* / Mojo hand: *Smith, Whispering* / Way you treat me: *Smith, Whispering* / I don't need no woman: *Smith, Whispering* / Everybody needs love: *Smith, Whispering* / I know I've got a sure thing: *Smith, Whispering* / Why am I treated so bad: *Smith, Whispering* / Rock me baby: *Smith, Whispering* / Married man: *Smith, Whispering* / I know you don't love me: *Smith, Whispering* / It's all over: *Smith, Whispering* / You want to do it again: *Smith, Whispering*
CD ______ **CDCHD 578**
Ace / Jul '95 / Pinnacle

IT'S MIGHTY CRAZY
Rock me Mama / Bad luck / West Texas / What evil have I done / Lightnin' blues / I can't be successful / I'm him / I can't understand / Just made twenty one / Sugar plum / Goin' home / Wonderin' and goin' / Bad luck and trouble / Have you way / I'm grown / Mean old lonesome train / Rocky mountain blues / Love me Mama / I'm a rollin' stone / Hoodoo blues / It's mighty crazy / Bedbug blues / Tom Cat blues / Farming blues
CD ______ **CDCHD 587**
Ace / Apr '95 / Pinnacle

NOTHIN' BUT THE DEVIL
Long leanie Mama / My starter won't work / It's mighty crazy / Blues at night / I'm leavin' you baby / Feelin' awful blue / Sweet little woman / Lightnin's problems / I gonna leave / Rooster blues / GI Slim / Driftin' blues / Too close blues / My little angel child / Greyhound blues / I just don't know / Somebody knockin' / Just a lonely stranger / Cool down baby / Nothin' but the devil / Goin' away blues / I'm tired waitin' baby / Death Valley blues / Hello Mary Lee
CD ______ **CDCHD 616**
Ace / Mar '96 / Pinnacle

ROOSTER BLUES
Rooster blues / Long leanie Mama / My starter won't work / GI Slim / Lightnin's troubles / Bedbug blues / Hoodoo blues / It's mighty crazy / Sweet little woman / Tom cat blues / Feelin' awful blues / I'm leavin' you baby / Lightnin' blues / I can't be successful / Sugar plum / Just made twenty one / Goin' home / Wonderin' and goin'
CD ______ **ELDIABLO 8038**
El Diablo / Mar '94 / Vital

ROOSTER BLUES/LIGHTNIN' SLIM' BELL RINGER
Rooster blues / Long Leanie Mama / My starter won't work / GI Slim / Lightnin' troubles / Bedbug blues / Hoodoo blues / It's mighty crazy / Sweet little woman / Tom cat blues / Feelin' awful blues / I'm leavin' you baby / Love me Mama / She's my crazy little baby / Have mercy on me baby / Winter time blues / If you ever need me / Mean old lonesome train / Baby please come back / Love is just a gamble / Somebody knockin' / You give me the blues / Don't start me talkin' / You move me baby
CD ______ **CDCHD 517**
Ace / Feb '94 / Pinnacle

Lightning

LIGHTNING
CD ______ **ANT 3811**
Anthology / Jul '97 / Cargo / Greyhound

Lightning Seeds

CLOUD CUCKOO LAND
All I want / Bound in a nutshell / Pure / Sweet dreams / Nearly man / Joy / Love explosion / Don't let go / Control the flame / Price / God help them
CD ______ **CDOVD 436**
Virgin / May '92 / EMI

DIZZY HEIGHTS
Imaginary friends / You bet your life / Waiting for today to happen / What if / Sugar coated iceberg / Touch and go / Like you do / Wishaway / Fingers and thumbs / You showed me / Ready or not / Fishes on the line
CD ______ **4866402**
Epic / Nov '96 / Sony

JOLLIFICATION
Perfect / Lucky you / Open goals / Change / Why why why / Marvellous / Feeling lazy / My best day / Punch and Judy / Telling tales
CD ______ **4772372**
Columbia / Sep '94 / Sony

PURE LIGHTNING SEEDS
Life of Riley / Sense / Blowing bubbles / Pure / Sweet dreams / All I want / Small slice of heaven / Love explosion / Don't let go / Joy / Price / Cool place / Happy / Tingle tangle / God help them / Bound in a nutshell / Nearly man / Thinking up, looking down
CD ______ **CDV 2805**
Virgin / Mar '96 / EMI

SENSE
Sense / Life of Riley / Blowing bubbles / Cool place / Where flowers fade / Small slice of heaven / Tingle tangle / Happy / Marooned / Thinking up, looking down
CD ______ **CDV 2690**
Virgin / Apr '92 / EMI

Lights In A Fat City

SOUND COLUMN
Taksu / Aluna / Surya / Memory ground
CD ______ **XCD 023**
Extreme / Nov '96 / Vital/SAM

Lights Of Euphoria

FAHRENHEIT
CD ______ **CDZOT 185**
Zoth Ommog / Jul '97 / Cargo / Plastic Head

Lightsey, Kirk

EVERYTHING HAPPENS TO ME (Lightsey, Kirk Trio)
CD ______ **CDSJP 176**
Timeless Jazz / Nov '90 / New Note/ Pinnacle

FROM KIRK TO NAT (Lightsey, Kirk Trio)
CD ______ **CRISS 1050CD**
Criss Cross / Nov '91 / Cadillac / Direct / Vital/SAM

GOODBYE MR. EVANS (Lightsey, Kirk Trio)
New blue / In your own sweet way / From Chopin to Chopin / Medley / Four in one / Habiba / Goodbye Mr. Evans
CD ______ **22165**
Evidence / Oct '96 / ADA / Cadillac / Harmonia Mundi

KIRK N' MARCUS (Lightsey, Kirk Quintet & Marcus Belgrave)
All my love / Loves I once knew / Windmill / Marcus' mates / Golden legacy / Lower bridge level / Lolita / Fixed wing
CD ______ **CRISS 1030CD**
Criss Cross / Feb '97 / Cadillac / Direct / Vital/SAM

TEMPTATION (Lightsey, Kirk Trio)
Society red / Brigette / Evidence / Temptation / Love is a many splendoured thing / Gibraltar
CD ______ **CDSJP 257**
Timeless Jazz / Aug '90 / New Note/ Pinnacle

Liimianarina

SUPERMARKET
CD ______ **DC 63CD**
Drag City / Dec '96 / Cargo / Greyhound

L'il Brian

FRESH (L'il Brian & The Zydeco Travellers)
CD ______ **ROUCD 2136**
Rounder / Apr '95 / ADA / CM / Direct

Lil' Devious

LIFTED
Lifted
CD ______ **STR 12007**
Stronghouse / Oct '96 / Amato Disco

Lil' Ed

CHICKEN, GRAVY AND BISCUITS (Lil' Ed & The Blues Imperials)
CD ______ **ALCD 4772**
Alligator / Oct '93 / ADA / CM / Direct

ROUGHHOUSIN' (Lil' Ed & The Blues Imperials)
CD ______ **ALCD 4749**
Alligator / May '93 / ADA / CM / Direct

WHAT YOU SEE IS WHAT YOU GET (Lil' Ed & The Blues Imperials)
Life is like gambling / Find my baby / Older women / Please help / Toothache / Living for today / Travellin' life / Out of the house / Upset man / Long long way from home / What you see is what you get / Bluesmobile / What am I gonna do / Packin' up
CD ______ **ALCD 4808**
Alligator / May '93 / ADA / CM / Direct

Lil' Kim

HARDCORE
No time / Intro in a minor / Big Momma thang: *Lil' Kim & JZ* / Spend a little doe / Take it / Scheamin' / We don't need it / Crush on you / Drugs / Player haters / Fuck you / Queen Bitch / R&B fantasies/Dreams / MAFIA land / Not tonight / Not tonight
CD ______ **7567927332**
Big Beat/Atlantic / Aug '97 / Warner Music

Lil' Mac

MAKIN' LOVE TO MONEY (Lil' Mac & DJ Trick)
CD ______ **WRA 8149**
Wrap / Jan '96 / Koch

Lilac Time

AND LOVE FOR ALL
Fields / All for love and love for all / Let our land be the one / I went to the dance / Wait and see / Honest to God / Laundry / Paper boat / Skabaskiblio / It'll end in tears (I won't cry) / Trinity / And on we go
CD ______ **8461902**
Fontana / Jan '96 / PolyGram

ASTRONAUTS
CD ______ **CRECD 098**
Creation / May '94 / 3mv/Vital

LILAC TIME, THE
Black velvet / Rockland / Return to yesterday / You've got to love / Love becomes a savage / Together / Road to happiness / Too sooner late than better / Trumpets from Montparnasse
CD ______ **8348352**
Fontana / Jan '96 / PolyGram

PARADISE CIRCUS
American eyes / Lost girl in the midnight sun / Beauty in your body / If the stars shine tonight / Days of the week / She still loves you / Paradise circus / Girl who waves at trains / Last to know / Father mother wife and child / Rollercoaster song / Work for the weekend / Twilight beer hall
CD ______ **8386412**
Fontana / Jan '96 / PolyGram

Lilier

BACK TO THE ROOTS (Lilier & Doc Houlind)
CD ______ **MECCACD 1020**
Music Mecca / Nov '94 / Cadillac / Jazz Music / Wellard

Lillian Axe

POETIC JUSTICE
CD ______ **CDMFN 131**
Music For Nations / Jul '92 / Pinnacle

PSYCHOSCHIZOPHRENIA
Crucified / Deep freeze / Moonlight in your blood / Stop the hate / Sign of the times / Needle and your pain / Those who prey / Voices in my walls / Now you know / Deep blue shadows / Day that I met you / Psychoschizophrenia
CD ______ **CDMFN 151**
Music For Nations / Sep '93 / Pinnacle

Lillie, Beatrice

UNIQUE, THE INCOMPARABLE BEA LILLIE, THE
There are fairies at the bottom of our garden / I'm a campfire girl / He was a gentleman / Nicodemus / Paree / Mad about the boy / Baby doesn't know / Marvellous party / I hate spring / Trains
CD ______ **PASTCD 7054**
Flapper / Nov '94 / Pinnacle

Lilly, John C.

ECCO
CD ______ **SR 9452**
Silent / Mar '94 / Cargo / Plastic Head

LILT

FOR THE CHILDREN
CD ______ **ETCD 191**
Alias / Nov '90 / Grapevine/PolyGram

Lilys

BETTER CAN'T MAKE YOUR LIFE BETTER
CD ______ **CHE 52CD**
Che / Sep '96 / SRD

Limerick, Alison

AND STILL I RISE
Make it on my own / Getting it right / Where love lives / Hear my call / Trouble / Come back (for real love) / Tell me what you mean / Let's make a memory / You and I / Difference is you
CD ______ **262365**
Arista / Aug '96 / BMG

CLUB CLASSICS
Where love lives / Make it on my own / Come back for real love / Love come down / Time of our lives / Getting it right
CD ______ **74321383102**
Arista / Jul '96 / BMG

Liminal

NOSFERATU
CD ______ **KFWCD 170**
Knitting Factory / Oct '96 / Cargo / Plastic Head

Liminal Lounge

EGO DUMP
CD ______ **KFWCD 202**
Knitting Factory / Jul '97 / Cargo / Plastic Head

Limp Bizkit

THREE DOLLAR BILL
CD ______ **IND 90124**
Interscope / Jul '97 / BMG

Lin, Caryn

TOLERANCE FOR AMBIGUITY
Call / In the abbey of Scartaglen / No lines drawn / Little king / At the risk of the sun / Tolerance for ambiguity / In cold blood
CD _______ ALCD 1010
Alchemy / Apr '97 / Pinnacle

Linares, Pepe

MISA FLAMENCA
CD _______ 172462
Musidisc / Mar '96 / Discovery

Lince, Louis

AT THE DOT (Lince, Louis Jelly Roll Kings)
CD _______ BCD 336
GHB / Aug '95 / Jazz Music

HOT AT THE DOT 1991 (Lince, Louis Jelly Roll Kings)
Panama / Memphis blues / Old spinning wheel / Mama's gone goodbye / One sweet letter from you / Royal telephone / Out of nowhere / Climax rag / Uptown bumps / Undecided
CD _______ JRKCD 510
JRK / Jun '96 / Jazz Music / Wellard

Lincoln Centre Jazz Orchestra

THEY CAME TO SWING
CD _______ 4772842
Sony Jazz / Jan '95 / Sony

Lincoln, Abbey

ABBEY IS BLUE
CD _______ OJCCD 69
Original Jazz Classics / Oct '92 / Complete/Pinnacle / Jazz Music / Wellard

DEVIL'S GOT YOUR TONGUE
Rainbow / Evalina Coffey / Story of my Father / Child is born / People in me / Circle of love / Jungle Queen / Merry dancer / Devil's got your tongue / Spring will be a little late this year / Music is my magic
CD _______ 5135742
Verve / Apr '92 / PolyGram

IT'S MAGIC
CD _______ OJCCD 205
Original Jazz Classics / Feb '92 / Complete/Pinnacle / Jazz Music / Wellard

PEOPLE IN ME
You and me love / Natas / Dorian / Africa / People in me / Living room / Kohjoh-notsuki / Naturally
CD _______ 5146262
Verve / Mar '94 / PolyGram

STRAIGHT AHEAD
Straight ahead / When Malindy sings / In the red / Blue monk / Left alone / African lady / Retribution
CD _______ CCD 79015
Candid / Feb '97 / Cadillac / Direct / Jazz Music / Koch / Wellard

THAT'S HIM
Strong man / Happiness is a thing called Joe / My man (mon homme) / Tender as a rose / That's him / Porgy / When a woman loves a man / Don't explain
CD _______ OJCCD 85
Original Jazz Classics / Oct '92 / Complete/Pinnacle / Jazz Music / Wellard

TURTLE'S DREAM, A
CD _______ 5273822
Verve / May '95 / PolyGram

WHEN THERE IS LOVE (Lincoln, Abbey & Hank Jones)
Part of me/There are such things / When there is love / Black butterfly / Angel face / Nearness of you/Can't help singing / Close your eyes / I should care / You came a long way from St. Louis / C'est si bon / Jitterbug waltz / Time after time / You won't forget me / First came a woman
CD _______ 5196972
Verve / Mar '94 / PolyGram

WHO USED TO DANCE
CD _______ 5335592
Verve / Mar '97 / PolyGram

WORLD IS FALLING DOWN, THE
World is falling down / First song / You must believe in Spring and love / I got thunder / How high the moon / When love was you and me / Hi-fly / Live for life
CD _______ 8434762
Verve / May '93 / PolyGram

YOU GOTTA PAY THE BAND
Bird alone / I'm in love / You gotta pay the band / Brother can you spare a dime / You made me funny / And how I hoped for your love / When I'm called home / Summer wishes, Winter dreams / Up jumped Spring / Time for love
CD _______ 5111102
Verve / Apr '91 / PolyGram

Lind, Ove

GERSHWIN - EVERGREEN
'S wonderful / Summertime / Swanee / Embraceable you / Bidin' my time / Our love is here to stay / But not for me / Changing my tune / Of thee I sing / Somebody loves me / Someone to watch over me / Oh lady be good / Aren't you kind of glad we did / I got plenty o' nuttin' / They can't take that away from me / Strike up the band / Man I love / Nice work if you can get it / Who cares / Love is sweeping the country / I've got a crush on you / Love walked in / Foggy day / My one and only / I was doing all right / They all laughed / How long has this been going on / Let's call the whole thing off
CD _______ PHONTCD 7410
Phontastic / Aug '94 / Cadillac / Jazz Music / Wellard

ONE MORNING IN MAY (Lind, Ove Quartet)
Just friends / Tangerine / Sky fell down / So would I / Cheek to cheek / I thought about you / Down by the old mill stream / Baby won't you please / I've got a feeling I'm falling in love / Stay as sweet as you are / I've got my eyes on you / True / One morning in May
CD _______ PHONTCD 7501
Phontastic / Aug '94 / Cadillac / Jazz Music / Wellard

ORCHESTRA SWEDISH EVERGREENS WITH CHARLIE PARKER
CD _______ PHONTCD 7408/9
Phontastic / Aug '94 / Cadillac / Jazz Music / Wellard

PHONTASTIC EVERGREENS VOL.1 (Lind, Ove Quartet/Sextet)
CD _______ PHONTCD 7401
Phontastic / Jul '96 / Cadillac / Jazz Music / Wellard

PHONTASTIC EVERGREENS VOL.2 (Lind, Ove Quintet/Sextet)
CD _______ PHONTCD 7403
Phontastic / Jul '96 / Cadillac / Jazz Music / Wellard

SUMMER NIGHT
Summer night / You leave me breathless / Say my heart / Changing my tune / Ill wind / You're a lucky guy / Oh lady be good / My cabin of dreams / You're the cream in my coffee / This heart of mine / Louise / Swinging on a star
CD _______ PHONTCD 7503
Phontastic / Aug '94 / Cadillac / Jazz Music / Wellard

Lindberg, John

DIMENSION 5 (Lindberg, John Quintet)
Eleven thrice / T'wixt C and D / T'wixt C and D (part 2) / Dimension 5
CD _______ 1200622
Black Saint / May '97 / Cadillac / Harmonia Mundi

DODGING BULLETS (Lindberg, John & Albert Mangelsdorff & Eric Watson)
CD _______ 12010502
Black Saint / Jan '93 / Cadillac / Harmonia Mundi

LUMINOSITY (Hommage To David Izenzon)
CD _______ CD 970
Music & Arts / Jul '97 / Cadillac / Harmonia Mundi

RESURRECTION OF A DORMANT SOUL
CD _______ 1201722
Black Saint / Dec '96 / Cadillac / Harmonia Mundi

Lindberg, Nils

O MISTRESS MINE
CD _______ ABCD 032
Bluebell / Oct '96 / Cadillac / Jazz Music

SAX APPEAL & TRISECTION
CD _______ DRAGONCD 220
Dragon / Jan '89 / ADA / Cadillac / CM / Roots / Wellard

SAXES & BRASS GALORE
CD _______ ABCD 3004
Bluebell / Jun '94 / Cadillac / Jazz Music

Lindbloom, Rolf

GERSHWIN
CD _______ PRCD 9001
Prestige / Aug '94 / Cadillac / Complete/Pinnacle

Lindemann, David

ANCIENT EVENINGS, DISTANT MUSIC
CD _______ CDSGP 9025
Prestige / Jun '95 / Else / Total/BMG

ETERNAL BOUNDARIES
CD _______ CDSGP 9002
Prestige / Apr '95 / Else / Total/BMG

Linden, Colin

THROUGH THE STORM
CD _______ FIENDCD 933
Demon / Aug '97 / Pinnacle

Lindgren, Erik

OIL ON LINEN
CD _______ AA 036
Arf Arf / Jul '97 / Greyhound

Lindgren, Kurt

LADY M
CD _______ DRCD 189
Dragon / Oct '88 / ADA / Cadillac / CM / Roots / Wellard

Lindgren, Lasse

TO MY FRIENDS
CD _______ DRCD 227
Dragon / Dec '88 / ADA / Cadillac / CM / Roots / Wellard

Lindgren, Ole 'Fessor'

BIG CITY SHUFFLE VOL.1 (Fessor's Big City Band)
CD _______ MECCACD 2014
Music Mecca / May '97 / Cadillac / Jazz Music / Wellard

BIG CITY SHUFFLE VOL.2 (Fessor's Big City Band)
CD _______ MECCACD 2015
Music Mecca / May '97 / Cadillac / Jazz Music / Wellard

JOYFUL NOISE, A (Fessor's Big City Band)
CD _______ MECCACD 1070
Music Mecca / May '97 / Cadillac / Jazz Music / Wellard

Lindisfarne

AMIGOS
One world / Everything changes / Working for the man / Roll on that day / You're the one / Wish you were here / Do it like this / Anyway the wind blows / Strange affair
CD _______ CLACD 384
Castle / May '93 / BMG

ANOTHER FINE MESS
Clear white light pt.2 / Squire / Lady Eleanor / Meet me on a corner / Evening / City song / One world / All fall down / Winter song / This heart of mine / We can make it / Road to kingdom come / Money / Run for home / Fog on the tyne
CD _______ GRACD 211
CD _______ GRAVD 211
Grapevine / Jul '96 / Grapevine/PolyGram

BACK AND FOURTH
Angels at eleven / Get wise / Jukebox gypsy / King X blues / Make me want to stay / Marshall Rileys army / Only alone / Run for home / Warm feeling / Woman / You and me
CD _______ CLACD 413
Castle / Oct '96 / BMG

BEST OF LINDISFARNE
Meet me on the corner / Lady Eleanor / All fall down / We can swing together / Fog on the Tyne / Road to Kingdom Come / Scarecrow song / Winter song / Clear white light / January song / Down / Walke up little sister / Together forever / Alright on the night / Go back / Don't ask me
CD _______ CDVIP 103
Virgin VIP / Dec '93 / EMI

BURIED TREASURES VOL.1
Buried treasures vol.1 / Red square dance / Finest hour / Together forever / Together crack - spoken word / Happy or sad / Way behind you / Behind crack - spoken word / Old peculiar feeling / True love / Love crack - spoken word / City song / Rock 'n' roll town / Swiss maid / Sporting life blues / Karen Marie / From my window / Window crack - spoken word / Run Jimmy run / Malvinas melody / Let's dance
CD _______ CDVM 9012
Virgin / Nov '92 / EMI

BURIED TREASURES VOL.2
Save our ales / Ale crack / Golden apples / Try giving everything / Nothing's gonna break us now / January song / Living on the baseline / On my own I built a bridge / Bridge crack / Roll on that day / Loving around the clock / Reunion / Reunion / Friday girl / Tomorrow if I'm hungry / Hungry crack / Fog on the Tyne / Winning the games / Peter Gunn theme / Run for home
CD _______ CDVM 9013
Virgin / Nov '92 / EMI

DANCE YOUR LIFE AWAY
Shine on / Love on the run / Heroes / All in the same boat / Dance your life away / Beautiful day / Broken doll / Hundred miles to Liverpool
CD _______ CLACD 383
Castle / Apr '93 / BMG

ELVIS LIVES ON THE MOON
Day of the Jackal / Soho Square / Old peculiar feeling / Mother Russua / Think / Spoken like a man / Heaven wails / Heeping the rage / Elvis lives on the moon / Don't leave me tonight / Demons
CD _______ ESMCD 391
Essential / Jul '96 / BMG

FOG ON THE TYNE
Meet me on the corner / Alright on the night / Uncle Sam / Together forever / January song / Peter Brophy don't care / City song / Passing ghosts / Train in G major / Fog on the Tyne / Scotch mist / No time to lose
CD _______ CASCD 1050
Charisma / '88 / EMI

LADY ELEANOR (2CD Set)
CD Set _______ SMDCD 159
Snapper / Jul '97 / Pinnacle

LINDISFARNE ON TAP (A Barrel Full Of Hits)
Run for home / Lady Eleanor / Meet me on the corner / We can make it / All fall down / Warm feeling / Winter song / Road to Kingdom come / Fog on the Tyne / Miracles / No time to lose / Running man / Elvis lives on the moon / Juke box gypsy / Dance your life away / Evening / Roll on that day / Clear white light
CD _______ ESMCD 399
Essential / Jul '96 / BMG

MAGIC IN THE AIR
Lady Eleanor / Road to kingdom come / Turn a deaf ear / January song / Court in the act / No time to lose / Winter song / Uncle Sam / Wake up little sister / All fall down / Meet me on the corner / Bye-bye birdie / Train in G major / Scarecrow song / Dingley dell / Scotch mist / We can swing together / Fog on the Tyne / Clear white light
CD _______ CCSCD 442
Castle / Oct '96 / BMG

NEWS, THE
Call of the wild / People say / 1983 / Log on your fire / Evening / Easy and free / Miracles / When Friday comes along / Dedicated hound / This has got to end / Good to be here
CD _______ CLACD 414
Castle / Oct '96 / BMG

NICELY OUT OF TUNE
Lady Eleanor / Road to Kingdom come / Winter song / Turn a deaf ear / Clear white light part 2 / We can swing together / Alan in the river with flowers / Down / Things I should have said / Jackhammer blues / Scarecrow song / Knackers yard blues / Nothing but the marvellous is beautiful
CD _______ CASCD 1025
Charisma / '88 / EMI

OTHER SIDE OF LINDISFARNE, THE
CD _______ CRESTCD 020
Mooncrest / Jun '96 / ADA / Direct

RUN FOR HOME (Lindisfarne Collected)
Run for home / Marshall Riley's army / Juke box gypsy / Winter song / Train in G major / When it gets the hardest / Brand new day / Good to be here / When Friday comes along / Sunderland boys / I must stop going to parties / Dance your life away / Love on the run / Clear white light / Meet me on the corner / Elvis on the moon / Day of the jackal / Fog on the Tyne
CD _______ MCCD 305
Music Club / Jun '97 / Disc / THE

SLEEPLESS NIGHTS
Nights / Start again / Cruising to disaster / Same way down / Winning the game / About you / Sunderland boys / Love is a pain / Do what I want / Never miss the water
CD _______ CLACD 382
Castle / Mar '93 / BMG

Lindley, David

OFFICIAL BOOTLEG VOL.1 (Playing Real Good) (Lindley, David & Hani Naser)
Bon ton roulie / Ain't no way / Her mind is gone / She took off my Romeos/Pretty girl rules the world / More than Eva Braun / Play it all night long / Cottonmill blues / Rag bag / Way out West in Kansas / Tiki torches at twilight / Mercury blues
CD _______ 753362
Pleemhead / Feb '97 / Direct

OFFICIAL BOOTLEG VOL.2 (Playing Even Better) (Lindley, David & Hani Naser)
Jimmy Hoffa memorial building blues / Meatman / How can a poor man face such times and live / Lick the tears / Afindrafindrao / Well well well / Tijuana / Poor old dirt farmer / About to make me leave home
CD _______ 756762
Pleemhead / Feb '97 / Direct

Lindner, Patrick

DIE KLEINEN DINGE DES LEBENS
Die kleinen dinge des lebens / Und wenn i tanz mit dir (des is a Wahnsinn) / A bisserl Abschied gibt's halt nicht / Und wenn's Nacht wird, Gibt's a Busserl / Dein kloaner Bua / Das Gefuhl Geborgenheit / Die stimme des Herzens / Manchmal braucht man was, an des ma glaub'n kann / Einmal noch mit dir / A wirtshaus und an Kramer-lad'n / Der liebe gott hat immer Zeit / Wenn i dich seh, muss i traumen
CD _______ DC 868232
Disky / Oct '96 / Disky / THE

DIE KLOANE TUR ZUM PARADIES
Die kloane tur zum paradies / Wenn d'sehnsucht a vogerl war / S'reserl vom mariental / Munchner kindl / Dann muB i hoam / Irgendwie hab i di gern / Kannst di net a bisserl freun / Arrivederci Maria Angela / Sowas liabs wie di / Zwei herzerln am birkenbaum / Immer wieder sind es lieder / Rosarot's brieaferl
CD _______ DCA 876932
Disky / Nov '96 / Disky / THE

EINE HANDVOLL HERZLICHKEIT
Die kloane aus der letzen Bank / Ich hatt / Heut nacht hab'n die sternl a pause / Du schaffst mi / Vergessen heiBt-halt immer an dich denken / Der anti-sorgen walzer / Der Mensch in dir / Wer einmal lugt / Eine Handvoll Herzlichkeit / Durfen darf ma alles / Ganseblumchen weinen nicht / LaB mei Herz a bisserl
CD ______ DC 868242
Disky / Oct '96 / Disky / THE

WEIHNACHTEN MIT
Kinder, kinder es ist winter / Weil's christkind bald Gerburtstag hat / Stille nacht / Der verlasse tannenbaum / Lasst uns mit den Hirten geh'n / Ein neues jahr / Lasst das licht in Eure Herzen / Still, still weil's kindlein schlafen will / Mandeln und zimt / Es wird scho glei dumpa / Frohliche weihnacht/kling glockchen / Weihnacht zu hause
CD ______ DC 868252
Disky / Oct '96 / Disky / THE

Lindo, Kashief

KASHIEF SINGS CHRISTMAS
CD ______ CRCD 37
Charm / Dec '94 / Jet Star

SOUL & INSPIRATION
CD ______ CRCD 45
Charm / Jan '96 / Jet Star

Lindsay, Arto

AGGREGATES
CD ______ KFWCD 164
Knitting Factory / Feb '95 / Cargo / Plastic Head

ENVY (Lindsay, Arto & The Ambitious Lovers)
Cross your legs / Troublemaker / Pagode Americano / Nothings monstered / Crowning roar / Too many mansions / Let's be adult / Venus lost her shirt / My competition / Babu / Dora / Beberibe / Locus coruleus
CD ______ CDOVD 469
Virgin / Jul '96 / EMI

HYPER CIVILIZADO (DJ Remixes)
Mundo civilizado / Complicity / Q samba / Q samba / Mundo civilizado / Complicity / Omulu / Complicity
CD ______ GCD 79519
Rykodisc / Jun '97 / ADA / Vital

MUNDO CIVILIZADO
Complicity / Q Samba / Simply beautiful / Mundo civilizado / Titles / Horizontal / Mar da gavea / Imbassai / Pleasure / Erotic city / Clown
CD ______ RCD 10410
Rykodisc / Jun '97 / ADA / Vital

O CORPO SUTIL (The Subtle Body)
4 skies / Child prodigy / Anima animale / Este seu olhar / My mind is going / Enxugar / No meu sotaque / Unbearable / Nobody in bed / Astronauts / Sovereign
CD ______ RCD 10369
Rykodisc / Aug '96 / ADA / Vital

Lindsay, Erica

DREAMER
Daydream / First movement / Walking together / Dreamer / At the last moment / Gratitude
CD ______ CCD 79040
Candid / Feb '97 / Cadillac / Direct / Jazz Music / Koch / Wellard

Lindsay, Reg

REASONS TO RISE
CD ______ LARRCD 300
Larrikin / Nov '94 / ADA / CM / Direct / Roots

Lindsey, Jimmy

FREE HAND (Lindsey, Jimmy & His Band)
CD ______ BYCD 1
Jim Lindsey / May '96 / Duncans

Lindup, Mike

CHANGES
Changes / Lovely day / Fallen angel / Spirit is free / Desire / West coast man / Judgement day / Life will never be the same / Paixao (Passion)
CD ______ LV 101CD
Voiceprint / Sep '94 / Pinnacle

Lingkungan Seni Degung ...

GAMELAN DEGUNG (Lingkungan Seni Degung Jugala)
CD ______ PAN 2053CD
Pan / Apr '96 / ADA / CM / Direct

Linhart, Peter

BLUE NIGHTS
CD ______ EFA 120652
Hotwire / Dec '94 / SRD

Link 80

17 REASONS
CD ______ AM 005CD
Asian Man / Feb '97 / Cargo / Greyhound / Plastic Head

Linka, Rudy

ALWAYS DOUBLE CZECH
Coming through / Room #428 / Air Jamaica / Our drives to K1 / Man from Waikiki / Bob's tune / Secret inside / Come rain or come shine / Way back / Now this / And how are you in the mornings
CD ______ ENJ 93012
Enja / Dec '96 / New Note/Pinnacle / Vital/ SAM

CZECH IT OUT
Old and new / Just on time / Uptown express / How deep is the ocean / Traveller / Welcome to the club / Folk song / At this point / Love letters
CD ______ ENJ 90012
Enja / Dec '94 / New Note/Pinnacle / Vital/ SAM

Linkchain, Hip

AIRBUSTERS
House cat blues / I had a dream / Blow wind blow / Bedbug blues / On my way / Keep on searching / Gambler's blues / I'll overcome / Strain on my heart / Take out your false teeth / Bad news / Airbusters / Fugitive / Diggin' my potatoes
CD ______ ECD 260382
Evidence / Sep '93 / ADA / Cadillac / Harmonia Mundi

Links II

NEW REASONS TO USE OLD WORDS
CD ______ EFA 127332
Musikerhof / Feb '96 / Cadillac / SRD

Linoleum

DISSENT
Restriction / Marquis / Dissent / Stay awhile / On a Tuesday / Dangerous shoes / Ray Liotta / She's sick / Twisted / Beds / Unresolved / Ways to escape / Ether
CD ______ LINO 005CD
CD ______ LINO 005CDS
Dedicated / Jul '97 / BMG / Vital

Linsky, Jeff

ANGEL'S SERENADE
Later / Black sand / Angel's serenade / Bop bop / In out heart / Leo / Over the rainbow / Can't dance / Beautiful love / Speak low
CD ______ CCD 4611
Concord Picante / Sep '94 / New Note/ Pinnacle

CALIFORNIA
Crossing / Murrietas' farwell / Samba cruz / For Elsa / Casa miguel / Second street / Pacifica / On the strand / Somoma / Highway one / Nightfall
CD ______ CCD 4708
Concord Vista / Jul '96 / New Note/Pinnacle

PASSPORT TO THE HEART
Passport to the heart / Mornin' / Love theme from Havana / Love club / Through the fire / Road to Akumal / Southern passage / Summer soft / While nature sleeps / Five reasons / Passport to the heart
CD ______ CCD 47642
Concord Vista / Jul '97 / New Note/Pinnacle

UP LATE
Armony / Besame mucho / Berimbau / Carlos / Hermosa / I didn't know what time it was / Lanikai / Monterrey / Up late / Wave
CD ______ CCD 4363
Concord Jazz / Nov '88 / New Note/ Pinnacle

Linton, Steffan

UNFINISHED AFFAIR
CD ______ DRCD 193
Dragon / Aug '88 / ADA / Cadillac / CM / Roots / Wellard

Linus

YOUGLI
CD ______ ELM 19CD
Elemental / Apr '94 / RTM/Disc

Linx, David

IF ONE MORE DAY
CD ______ TWI 972
Les Disques Du Crepuscule / May '96 / Discovery

Lionrock

INSTINCT FOR DETECTION, AN
Morning will come when I'm not ready / Straight at yer head / Peace repackaged / Death Valley clapperboard / Fire up the shoesaw / Don't die foolish / Depth / Snapshot on Pollard Street / Guide / Number nine / Bag of biros / Wilmslow Road
CD ______ 74321342812
De-Construction / Mar '96 / BMG

Lionsheart

LIONSHEART
CD ______ CDMFN 139
Music For Nations / Jul '92 / Pinnacle

PRIDE IN FACT
CD ______ CDMFN 167
Music For Nations / Nov '94 / Pinnacle

Lipovsky, Shura

MOMENTS OF JEWISH LIFE
CD ______ SYNCD 153
Syncoop / Jun '93 / ADA / Direct

Lipscomb, Mance

TEXAS BLUES GUITAR
CD ______ ARHCD 001
Arhoolie / Apr '95 / ADA / Cadillac / Direct

TEXAS SONGSTER
CD ______ ARHCD 306
Arhoolie / Apr '95 / ADA / Cadillac / Direct

YOU GOT TO REAP WHAT YOU SOW
CD ______ ARHCD 398
Arhoolie / Apr '95 / ADA / Cadillac / Direct

Liquid

LIQUID CULTURE
CD ______ XLCD 113
XL / Jul '95 / Warner Music

Liquid Hips

FOOL INJECTION
CD ______ EMY 1382
Enemy / Nov '94 / Grapevine/PolyGram

STATIC
CD ______ EMY 1422
Enemy / Nov '94 / Grapevine/PolyGram

Liquid Liquid

LIQUID LIQUID
Optimo / Cavern / Scraper / Out / Lock groove in / Lock groove out / Push / Zero leg / Eyes sharp / Groupmegroup / New walk / Lub dupe / Bell head / Rubbermiro / Lock groove / Groupmegroup / Bell head / Push
CD ______ MW 078CD
Mo Wax / Aug '97 / PolyGram / Vital

Liquid Lounge

URBAN SOULSCAPE
CD ______ SCAT 2CD
Scat / Jul '96 / Timewarp

Liquid Z

AMPHIBIC
CD ______ GAMMA 002CD
Gamma / Oct '95 / Plastic Head

Liquidators

LIQUIDATORS JOIN THE SKA TRAIN, THE (Various Artists)
Liquidator: *Harry J All Stars* / Phoenix city: *Alphonso, Roland* / Miss Jamaica: *Cliff, Jimmy* / Pressure drop: *Toots & The Maytals* / Skinhead moonstomp: *Symarip* / Guns of Navarone: *Skatalites* / 007: *Dekker, Desmond* / Shame and scandal: *Tosh, Peter & The Wailers* / Ethiopia: *Pyramids* / Johnny too bad: *Slickers* / Train to Skaville: *Ethiopians* / Monkey man: *Toots & The Maytals* / Rudie, a message to you: *Livingstone, Dandy* / It mek: *Dekker, Desmond* / Musical store room: *Drummond, Don* / Return of Django: *Upsetters* / Israelites: *Dekker, Desmond & The Aces* / Train to Rainbow City: *Pyramids* / Guns fever: *Brooks, Baba* / Double barrel: *Collins, Dave & Ansell* / Dollar in the teeth: *Upsetters* / Don't be a rude boy: *Rulers* / Twelve minutes to go: *McCook, Tommy* / Rudy's dead: *Pyramids*
CD ______ VSOPCD 136
Connoisseur Collection / Jul '89 / Pinnacle

Liquor Bike

NEON HOOP RIDE
CD ______ GROW 352
Grass / Feb '95 / Pinnacle / SRD

Liquor Giants

LIQUOR GIANTS
Chocolate clown / Fake love / Copycat / Cranium / 100 dollar car / Bastanchury Park / Awful good / Hideous pleasure / Hey you / Here / Jerked around / All I get / Thanksgiving in Zuma
CD ______ OLE 1812
Matador / Jun '96 / Vital

Liquorice

LISTENING CAP
Trump suite / Team player / Keeping the weekend free / Drive around / Cheap cuts / Trump suit edit / Jill of all trades / No excuses / Breaking the ice / Blew it
CD ______ CAD 5008CD
4AD / Jul '95 / RTM/Disc

Liquorice Roots

MELODEON
CD ______ MFR 0072
Mood Food / Jun '97 / Cargo

Lir

MAGICO MAGICO
CD ______ VELO 2003CD
Cross Border Media / Jan '94 / ADA / Direct / Grapevine/PolyGram

Lisa Gives Head

CLOSER LOOK AT THE GROUND, THE
CD ______ SPV 08436262
SPV / Mar '96 / Koch / Plastic Head

Listening Pool

STILL LIFE
Meant to be / Oil for the lamps of China / Follow where you go / Breathless / Somebody somewhere / Photograph of you / Promised the world / Blue Africa / Still life / Where do we go from here / Wild strawberries / Hand me that universe
CD ______ TLGCD 002
Telegraph / Feb '95 / Total/BMG

Lister, Anne

FLAME IN AVALON, A
CD ______ HFCD 003
Hearthfire / Apr '96 / ADA

SPREADING WINGS
CD ______ HFCD 02
Hearthfire / May '93 / ADA

Lister, Ayako

JAPANESE KOTO, THE
CD ______ EUCD 1105
ARC / '91 / ADA / ARC Music

Listing Attic

FLY LIKE AN EGO
CD ______ TEC 2
Three Id Cat / Jul '97 / Greyhound

Liston, Virginia

VIRGINIA LISTON VOL.1 1923-1924
CD ______ DOCD 5446
Document / May '96 / ADA / Hot Shot / Jazz Music

VIRGINIA LISTON VOL.2 1924-1926
CD ______ DOCD 5447
Document / May '96 / ADA / Hot Shot / Jazz Music

Litherland, James

4TH ESTATE
CD ______ CMMR 942
Music Maker / Nov '94 / ADA / Grapevine/ PolyGram

Lithium X-Mas

BAD KARMA
CD ______ LOST 007
Lost / May '97 / Cargo

Litter

$100 FINE
CD ______ TX 2004CD
Taxim / Jan '94 / ADA

DISTORTIONS
CD ______ TX 2003CD
Taxim / Jan '94 / ADA

DISTORTIONS + $100 FINE
CD ______ 842077
EVA / May '94 / ADA / Direct

Little Aida

CONFESSIONS
CD ______ DSL 002
Downsall Plastics / Jul '96 / Cargo / SRD

Little Angels

DON'T PREY FOR ME
Do you wanna riot / Kick hard / Big bad world / Kicking up dust / Don't prey for me / Broken wings of an angel / Bitter and twisted / Promises / When I get out of here / No solution / Pleasure pyre
CD ______ 8412542
Polydor / Jun '90 / PolyGram

JAM
Way that I live / Too much too young / Splendid isolation / Soap box / STW / Don't confuse sex with love / Womankind / Eyes wide open / Colour of love / I was not wrong / Sail away / Tired of waiting for you (So tired) / Reprise/STW / She's a little angel (live) / Product of the working class (Grooved and jammed) / I ain't gonna cry / Boneyard 1993 / Don't prey for me (Extended) / Won't get fooled again
CD ______ 5176762
Polydor / Jan '93 / PolyGram

TOO POSH TO MOSH
All roads lead to you / Forbidden fruit / I want love / Reach for me / Bad or just no good / Burning me / No more whiskey / Down in the night / Better than the rest / Too posh to mosh / Some kind of alien
CD ESMCD 398
Essential / Jan '97 / BMG

Little Annie

SHORT AND SWEET
CD ONUCD 16
On-U Sound / Jun '93 / Jet Star / SRD

Little Anthony & The ...

CAN'T TAKE IT (Little Anthony & The Locomotives)
CD DELCD 3005
Deluge / Mar '96 / ADA / Direct / Koch

DON'T WAIT ON ME (Little Anthony & The Locomotives)
CD DELCD 3013
Deluge / Jan '96 / ADA / Direct / Koch

Little Axe

WOLF THAT HOUSE BUILT, THE
CD WIRED 27
Wired / Jan '95 / 3mv/Sony / Mo's Music Machine / Prime

Little Bob

RENDEZVOUS IN ANGEL CITY
Isn't it enough / There'll never be another you / I can't wait / True love / Gimme you / Midnight crisis / As the lights go out / Keep on running / When the night falls / Never cry about the past
CD 104 182
Musidisc / Mar '90 / Discovery

Little Buster

LOOKIN' FOR A HOME (The Complete Little Buster Jubilee & Josie Sessions)
Lookin' for a home / I think I'm falling / It's loving time / All night worker / I got a good thing going / I proved I love you / But I do / I'm so lonely / Young boy blues / Cry me a river / You were meant for me / River's invitation / Whole lotta lovin' / He's gone / I knew it all the time / TCB / I love you, yes I do / I've got tears in my eyes / Just a letter / What a fool I've been / Why did it have to be me / All I could do was cry / I think I'm falling in love
CD NEMCD 768
Sequel / Jan '97 / BMG

RIGHT ON TIME (Little Buster & The Soul Brothers)
CD CDBB 9562
Bullseye Blues / Oct '95 / Direct

Little, Booker

FIRE WALTZ (Little, Booker & Eric Dolphy)
Number eight / Fire waltz / Bee vamp
CD ECD 220742
Evidence / Nov '93 / ADA / Cadillac / Harmonia Mundi

LIVE - THE COMPLETE CONCERT (Little, Booker & Teddy Charles Group)
CD COD 032
Jazz View / Jul '92 / Harmonia Mundi

OUT FRONT
We speak / Strength and sanity / Quiet, please / Moods in free time / Man of words / Hazy hues / New day
CD CCD 79027
Candid / Feb '97 / Cadillac / Direct / Jazz Music / Koch / Wellard

REMEMBERED LIVE AT SWEET BASIL (Little, Booker & Eric Dolphy)
Prophet / Aggression / Booker's waltz
CD ECD 220732
Evidence / Nov '93 / ADA / Cadillac / Harmonia Mundi

Little Caesar

LITTLE CAESAR
CD DGLD 19128
Geffen / May '92 / BMG

Little Charlie

ALL THE WAY CRAZY (Little Charlie & The Nightcats)
TV crazy / Right around the corner / Clothes line / Living hand to mouth / Suicide blues / Poor Tarzan / When girls do it / Eyes like a cat / I'll take you back / Short skirts
CD ALCD 4753
Alligator / May '93 / ADA / CM / Direct

BIG BREAK, THE (Little Charlie & The Nightcats)
CD ALCD 4776
Alligator / May '93 / ADA / CM / Direct

CAPTURED LIVE (Little Charlie & The Nightcats)
Tomorrow night / Run me down / Rain / Dump that chump / Ten years ago / Thinking with the wrong head / Wildcattin' / Crawlin' kingsnake / Smart like Einstein / Eyes like a cat
CD ALCD 4794
Alligator / Oct '93 / ADA / CM / Direct

DISTURBING THE PEACE (Little Charlie & The Nightcats)
That's my girl / Nervous / My money's green / If this is love / I ain't lyin' / She's talking / My last meal / Booty song / Don't boss me / V8 Ford blues / I feel so sorry / Run me down
CD ALCD 4761
Alligator / Apr '93 / ADA / CM / Direct

NIGHT VISION (Little Charlie & The Nightcats)
CD ALCD 4812
Alligator / May '93 / ADA / CM / Direct

STRAIGHT UP (Little Charlie & The Nightcats)
I could deal with it / I can't speak no spanish (No hablo espanol) / I'm just lucky that way / Turn my back on you / Me and my big mouth / You gonna lie / Hey gold digger / Homocide / Too close together / Gerontology / Playboy blues / Is that it / On the loose / My way or the highway
CD ALCD 4829
Alligator / Apr '95 / ADA / CM / Direct

Little Chief

SPIRIT
CD FGUTCD 001
Futgut / Jan '94 / CM

Little Feat

AIN'T HAD ENOUGH FUN
Drivin' blind / Blue jean blues / Cadillac hotel / Romance without finance / Big band theory / Cajun rage / Heaven's where you find it / Borderline blues / All that you can stand / Rock 'n' roll every night / Shaketown / Ain't had enough fun / That's a pretty good love
CD 72445110972
Zoo Entertainment / Jun '95 / BMG

AS TIME GOES BY (The Best Of Little Feat)
Dixie chicken / Willin' / Rock 'n' roll doctor / Two trains / Truck stop girl / Fat man in the bath tub / Trouble / Sailin' shoes / Spanish moon / Feats don't fail me now / Oh Atlanta / All that you dream / Long distance love / Mercenary territory / Rocket in my pocket / Texas twister / Let it roll / Hate to lose your lovin' / Old folks boogie / Twenty million things
CD 9548322472
WEA / Aug '93 / Warner Music

DIXIE CHICKEN
Dixie chicken / Two Trains / Roll um easy / On Your Way Down / Kiss it off / Fool yourself / Walkin' all night / Fat man in the bathtub / Juliet / Lafayette Railroad
CD K 246 200
WEA / Jul '88 / Warner Music

DOWN ON THE FARM
Down on the farm / Six feet of snow / Perfect imperfection / Kokomo / Be one now / Straight from the heart / Front page news / Wake up dreaming / Feel the groove
CD K2 56667
WEA / Jul '88 / Warner Music

FEATS DON'T FAIL ME NOW
Rock 'n' roll doctor / Cold cold cold / Tripe face boogie / Fan / Oh Atlanta / Skin it back / Down The Road / Spanish Moon / Feats Don't Fail Me Now
CD 256030
WEA / Jul '88 / Warner Music

LAST RECORD ALBUM, THE
Romance Dance / All that you dream / Long Distance Love / Day or Night / One Love / Down below the borderline / Somebody's leavin' / Mercenary Territory
CD K 256156
WEA / May '88 / Warner Music

LET IT ROLL
Hate to lose your lovin' / One clear moment / Cajun girl / Hangin' on to the good times / Listen to your heart / Let it roll / Long time till I get over you / Business as usual / Change in luck / Voices on the wind
CD 9257502
WEA / Aug '88 / Warner Music

LITTLE FEAT
Snakes on everything / Strawberry flats / Truck stop girl / Brides of Jesus / Willin' / Hamburger midnight / Forty four blues / How many more years / Crack in your door / I've been the one / Takin' my time / Crazy captain Gunboat Willie
CD 7599271892
WEA / Dec '96 / Warner Music

REPRESENTING THE MAMBO
Texas twister / Daily grind / Representing the mambo / Woman in love / Rad gumbo / Teenage warrior / That's her / She's mine / Feeling's all gone / Those feat'll steer ya wrong sometimes / Ingenue / Silver screen
CD 7599261632
WEA / Apr '90 / Warner Music

SAILIN' SHOES
Easy to slip / Cold cold cold / Trouble / Tripe face boogie / Willin' / Apolitical blues / Sailin' Shoes / Teenage nervous breakdown / Got no shadows / Cat fever / Texas Rose Cafe
CD 246156
WEA / '88 / Warner Music

TIME LOVES A HERO
Time loves a hero / Hi roller / New Delph freight train / Old folks boogie / Red streamliner / Keeping up with the Joneses / Rocket in my pocket / Missin' you / Day at the races
CD 256349
WEA / Jul '89 / Warner Music

WAITING FOR COLUMBUS
Join the band / Fat man in the bathtub / All that you dream / Oh Atlanta / Old folks' boogie / Time loves a hero / Day or night / Mercenary territory / Spanish moon / Dixie chicken / Tripe face boogie / Rocket in my pocket / Willin' / Don't Bogart that joint / Political blues / Sailin' shoes / Feats don't fail me now
CD 7599273442
WEA / Dec '96 / Warner Music

Little Hatch

WE'RE ALL RIGHT (Little Hatch & The Houserockers)
CD MB 1204
Modern Blues / Feb '94 / ADA / Direct

Little Isidore

INQUISITION OF LOVE (Little Isidore & The Golden Inquisitors)
CD HSAM 6061
Hy-Sam / Nov '96 / Nervous

Little Lenny

ALL THE GIRLS
CD GVCD 1700
Ras / Dec '95 / Direct / Greensleeves / Jet Star / SRD

GUN IN A BAGGY
Gun in a baggy / Fafunky man / Halla yea / Original / Healthy body / Wicked and wild / Champion bubbler / Glamity nuff / Teach reality / Diana
CD GRELCD 146
Greensleeves / Apr '90 / Jet Star / SRD

LITTLE LENNY IS MY NAME
CD VPCD 1172
Steely & Cleevie / Nov '92 / Jet Star

Little Mike & The Tornados

FLYNN'S PLACE
CD FF 641CD
Flying Fish / Jul '95 / ADA / CM / Direct / Roots

Little Milton

BLUES 'N' SOUL/WAITING FOR LITTLE MILTON
It's amazing / Who can handle me is you / Woman, you don't have to be so cold / Thrill is gone / Monologue 1 / That's how strong my love is / What it is / Little bluebird / Woman across the river / Behind closed doors / Sweet woman of mine / Worried dream / How could you do it to me / You're no good / Ain't nobody's business if I do / Hard luck blues
CD CDSXD 052
Stax / Jun '92 / Pinnacle

BLUES IS ALRIGHT, THE
Blues is alright / How could you do it to me / Bad luck is falling / Chains and things / Walking the back streets and crying / I'd rather drink muddy water / I'm digging you / Things have got to change
CD ECD 260262
Evidence / Feb '93 / ADA / Cadillac / Harmonia Mundi

COMPLETE STAX SINGLES, THE
If that ain't a reason (for your woman to leave you) / Mr. Mailman (I Don't want no letter) / I'm living off the love you give / That's what love will make you do / Before the honeymoon / Walking the back streets and crying / I'm gonna cry a river / What it is / Rainy day / Lovin' stick / Who can handle me is you / Tin pan alley / Sweet woman of mine / Behind closed doors / Bet you I win / Let me back in / Let your loss be your lesson / If you talk in your sleep / How could you do it to me / Packed up and took my mind
CD CDSXD 106
Stax / Jan '95 / Pinnacle

IF WALLS COULD TALK
If walls could talk / Baby I love you / Let's get together / Things I used to do / Kansas City / Poor man's song / Blues get off my shoulder / I play dirty / Good to me as I am to you / Your precious love / I don't know
CD MCD 09289
Chess/MCA / Apr '97 / BMG / New Note/ BMG

LIVE AT WESTVILLE PRISON
CD DE 681
Delmark / Dec '95 / ADA / Cadillac / CM / Direct / Hot Shot

TENDING HIS ROOTS (Charly R&B Masters Vol.17)
Feel so bad / If walls could talk / Life is like that / Sweet sixteen / I can't quit you baby / I'm mighty grateful / Don't talk back / Reconsider baby / Losing hand / We're gonna make it / Stormy Monday / Blind man / I'm gonna move to the outskirts of town / Blues in the night / Did you ever love a woman / Who's cheating who / Blues get off my shoulder / Things I used to do / Don't deceive me / Grits ain't groceries
CD CDRB 17
Charly / Mar '95 / Koch

Little Richard

20 CLASSIC CUTS
Long tall Sally / Ready Teddy / Girl can't help it / Rip it up / Miss Ann / She's got it / Lucille / Keep a knockin' / Good golly Miss Molly / Send me some lovin' / Tutti frutti / Hey hey hey / Slippin' and slidin' / Heebie jeebies / Baby face / Jenny Jenny / By the light of the silvery moon / Ooh my soul / True fine mama / Bama lama bama loo / I'll never let you go / Can't believe you wanna leave
CD CDCH 195
Ace / Jul '90 / Pinnacle

22 GREATEST HITS
CD 8308342
Polydor / '89 / PolyGram

BEST OF LITTLE RICHARD, THE
Long tall Sally / Lucille / Keep a knockin' / Jenny, Jenny / Tutti frutti / Rip it up / Girl can't help it / Good golly Miss Molly / Baby face / Cherry red / Groovy little Suzy / Money honey / Without love / Talking 'bout soul / Send me some lovin' / Hound dog
CD CDSGP 085
Prestige / Nov '93 / Else / Total/BMG

BOY CAN'T HELP IT, THE
CD QSCD 6008
Charly / Jan '94 / Koch

COLLECTION, THE
CD CCSCD 227
Castle / Jul '89 / BMG

EARLY STUDIO OUTTAKES
CD SJCD 565
Sun Jay / Sep '95 / Rollercoaster / TKO Magnum

EP COLLECTION, THE
Send me some lovin' / I'm just a lonely guy / Miss Ann / Oh why / Can't believe you wanna leave / She's got it / Girl can't help it / Jenny Jenny / Heebie jeebies / Slippin' and slidin' / Baby / Baby face / By the light of the silvery moon / She knows how to rock / Early one morning / keep a knockin' / Good golly Miss Molly / All around the world / True fine mama / Kansas city / Shake a hand / Chicken little baby / Whole lotta shakin' goin' on / Rip it up / Tutti frutti / Ready teddy / Long tall Sally
CD SEECD 366
See For Miles/C5 / Feb '93 / Pinnacle

ESSENTIAL COLLECTION, THE
CD Set LECD 609
Wisepack / Apr '95 / Conifer/BMG / THE

FABULOUS LITTLE RICHARD, THE
Tutti frutti / Long tall Sally / Slippin' and slidin' / Rip it up / Ready Teddy / She's got it / Jenny Jenny / Girl can't help it / Lucille / Baby face / Keep a knockin' / Good golly Miss Molly
CD CDFAB 001
Ace / Aug '91 / Pinnacle

FORMATIVE YEARS, THE (1951-1953)
Get rich quick / Why did you leave me / Taxi blues / Every hour / I brought it all on myself / Ain't nothing happening / Thinking 'bout my mother / Please have mercy on me / Little Richard's boogie / Directly from my heart / I love my baby / Maybe I'm right / Ain't that good news / Rice, red beans and turnip greens / Always
CD BCD 15448
Bear Family / Jul '89 / Direct / Rollercoaster / Swift

HERE'S LITTLE RICHARD/VOL.2/ FABULOUS LITTLE RICHARD (His 3 Original Specialty Albums/3CD Set)
Tutti frutti / True fine mama / Can't believe you wanna leave / Ready Teddy / Baby / Slippin' and slidin' / Long tall Sally / Miss Ann / Oh why / Rip it up / Jenny Jenny / She's got it / Keep a knockin' / By the light of the silvery moon / Send me some lovin' / I'll never let you go / Heebie jeebies / All around the world / Good golly Miss Molly / Baby face / Hey hey hey / Ooh my soul / Girl can't help it / Lucille / Shake a hand / Chicken little baby / All night long / Most I can offer / Lonesome and blue / Wonderin' / She knows how to rock / Kansas City / Directly from my heart / Maybe I'm right / Early one morning / I'm just a lonely guy / Whole lotta shakin' goin' on
CD Set ABOXCD 2
Ace / Oct '90 / Pinnacle

HIS GREATEST RECORDINGS
Ready Teddy / Rip it up / Girl can't help it / I'll never let you go / Miss Ann / Good golly Miss Molly / Lucille / Keep a knockin' / Can't believe you wanna leave / Tutti frutti / Heebie jeebies / Send me some lovin' /

Chicken little baby / Hey hey hey / She's got it / Long tall Sally
CD CDCH 109
Ace / Jul '90 / Pinnacle

HITS COLLECTION, THE
Lucille / Baby face / Tutti frutti / Good golly Miss Molly / Long tall Sally / Hound dog / Goodnight Irene / Rip it up / Whole lotta shakin' goin' on / Blueberry Hill / She's got it / Girl can't help it / Money honey / Jenny Jenny
CD 100442
CMC / May '97 / BMG

LITTLE RICHARD
Whole lotta shakin' goin' on / Rip it up / Baby face / Send me some lovin' / Girl can't help it / Lucille / Ooh my soul / Jenny Jenny / Good golly Miss Molly / Tutti frutti / Long tall Sally / Keep a knockin' / Money honey / Hound dog / Groovy little Suzie / Dancing all around the world / Slippin' and slidin' / Lawdy Miss Clawdy / Short fat Fanny / She's got it
CD LECD 036
Dynamite / May '94 / THE

LITTLE RICHARD
Keep a knockin' / Send me some lovin' / I'll never let you go / All around the world / By the light of the silvery moon / Good golly Miss Molly / Baby face / Hey hey hey / Ooh my soul / Lucille / Girl can't help it
CD CDCHM 131
Ace / Jul '89 / Pinnacle

LITTLE RICHARD
CD CD 106
Timeless Treasures / Oct '94 / THE

LITTLE RICHARD
Lucille / Long Tall Sally / Whole lotta shakin' goin' on / Good golly Miss Molly / Tutti frutti / Rip it up / Keep a knockin' / Ooh my soul / Jenny, Jenny / Girl can't help it / Slippin' and slidin' / She's got it / Money honey / Groovy little Suzy / Talking 'bout soul / Baby face / Blueberry Hill / Hound dog / Send me some lovin'
CD QED 086
Tring / Nov '96 / Tring

LITTLE RICHARD COLLECTION
CD COL 006
Collection / Jun '95 / Target/BMG

LUCILLE
Lucille / Long tall Sally / Baby face / Good golly Miss Molly / Tutti frutti / Whole lotta shakin' goin' on / Money, honey / Girl can't help it / Jenny Jenny / Hound dog
CD 15080
Laserlight / Aug '91 / Target/BMG

LUCILLE
Lucille / Good golly Miss Molly / Rip it up / Girl can't help it / Send me some lovin' / I don't know what you got / Ooh my soul / Long tall Sally / Tutti frutti / Whole lotta shakin' goin' on / Ready Teddy / Keep a knockin' / She's got it / Bama Lama Bama Loo / Blueberry Hill / Hound dog
CD 12660
Laserlight / Nov '96 / Target/BMG

NOW
CD RNCD 1007
Rhino / Jun '93 / Grapevine/PolyGram / Jet Star

PEARLS FROM THE PAST
CD KLMCD 004
BAM / Nov '93 / Koch / Scratch/BMG

RIP IT UP - THE LITTLE RICHARD MEGAMIX
Tutti frutti / Jenny Jenny / Keep a knockin' / Girl can't help it / Long tall Sally / Good golly Miss Molly / Lucille / Ooh my Sally / Ready Teddy / Can't believe you wanna leave / Baby face / She's got it / Rip it up / Slippin' and slidin' / By the light of the silvery moon / True fine Mama / All around the world / Bama lama bama loo / Miss Ann / Send me some lovin'
CD ECD 3070
K-Tel / Jan '95 / K-Tel

SECOND COMING, THE (2CD Set)
Whole lotta shakin' goin' on / Hound dog / Money honey / Lawdy Miss Clawdy / Good golly Miss Molly / Groovy little Susie / Short fat Fanny / Jenny Jenny / Lucille / Long tall Sally / She's got it / Girl can't help it / Rip it up / Tutti frutti / Slippin' and slidin' / Ooh my soul / Baby face / Keep a-knockin' / Send me some lovin' / Blueberry Hill / Dance what you wanna / Dancing all around the world / Going home tomorrow / Goodnight Irene / My wheels they are slippin' all the way / Something moves in my heart / It ain't what you do / Without love / Talkin' 'bout soul / I don't know what you've got but you've got me / Cherry red / Only you / Memories are made of this / I don't know what you've got but you've got me / Cross over / You better stop / Why don't you love me / Keep a-knockin' / Belle stars / Lucille / Long tall Sally / Funky dish rag
CD Set CPCD 82442
Charly / Nov '96 / Koch

SPECIALTY SESSIONS, THE (6CD Set)
CD Set ABOXCD 1
Ace / Jan '92 / Pinnacle

SPOTLIGHT ON LITTLE RICHARD
Babyface / Tutti frutti / Long tall Sally / Keep a knockin' / Groovy little Suzie / Cherry red / Good golly miss Molly / Girl can't help it / Without love / (Sittin' on the) dock of the bay / Rip it up / Money honey / Short fat Fanny / Slippin' and slidin' / Talkin' 'bout soul / She's got it
CD HADCD 117
Javelin / Feb '94 / Henry Hadaway / THE

TUTTI FRUTTI
Tutti frutti / Slippin' and slidin' / Lucille / Send me some lovin' / She's got it / Money honey / Baby face / Rip it up / Long tall Sally / Good golly Miss Molly / Ooh my soul / Girl can't help it / Short fat Fanny / Keep a knockin' / Jenny Jenny
CD 304292
Hallmark / Jun '97 / Carlton

VERY BEST OF LITTLE RICHARD, THE
Rip it up / Long tall Sally / Tutti frutti / She's got it / Girl can't help it / Lucille / Jenny Jenny / Keep a-knockin' / Good golly Miss Molly / Ooh my soul / Send me some lovin' / Whole lotta shakin' goin' on / Slippin' and slidin' / It ain't whatcha do / Dancin' all around the world / Baby face
CD SUMCD 4019
Summit / Nov '96 / Sound & Media

WILD AND WONDERFUL
CD QSCD 6002
Charly / Oct '91 / Koch

Little River Band

BEST OF LITTLE RIVER BAND, THE (Centenary Collection)
Lonesome loser / Help is on it's way / Other guy / Night owls / Lady / Man on your side / Take it easy on me / Happy anniversary / Cool change / Home on Monday / It's a long way there / Emma / Curiosity (killed the cat) / We two / St. Louis / Piece of the dream / Forever blue / Playing to win
CD CTMCD 308
EMI / Feb '97 / EMI

DIAMANTINA COCKTAIL
Help is on its way / Days on the road / Happy anniversary / Another runaway / Everyday of my life / Home on Monday / Inner light / Broke again / Take me home
CD DC 875522
Disky / May '97 / Disky / THE

IT'S A LONG WAY THERE
It's a long way there / Reminiscing / Night owls / Let's dance / One for the road / Man on the run / Down on the border / Emma / I'll always call your name / Take me home / Happy anniversary / Middle man / Hard life / It's not a wonder
CD DC 868702
Disky / Nov '96 / Disky / THE

Little Roy

COLUMBUS SHIP
CD COPCD 1
Copasetic / Oct '93 / BMG / Grapevine/ PolyGram / Jet Star / Pinnacle

LONGTIME
CD ONUCD 87
On-U Sound / Sep '96 / Jet Star / SRD

Little Sonny

ANN ARBOR BLUES VOL.2 (Various Artists)
Introduction/Creeper returns / They want money: *Willis, Aaron 'Little Sonny'* / Woman named trouble: *Crutcher, Betty* / Goin' down slow: *Oden, Jimmy* / Hot potatoes: *King Curtis* / Honest I do: *Reed, Jimmy* / Blues with a feeling: *Dixon, Willie* / Sad funk: *Willis, Aaron 'Little Sonny'* / No nights by myself: *Williamson, Sonny Boy* / Sweet little angel: *King, Riley B.* / Sweet sixteen: *King, Riley B.* / Interview: *Sinclair, John* / Creeper: *Willis, Aaron 'Little Sonny'* / Latin soul: *Willis, Aaron 'Little Sonny'* / Stretchin' out: *Willis, Aaron 'Little Sonny'* / Creeper returns: *Willis, Aaron 'Little Sonny'* / Interview: *Little Sonny*
CD NEXCD 279
Sequel / Apr '96 / BMG

BLACK AND BLUE
Hung up / Sonny's fever / You got a good thing / Woman named trouble / Honest I do / Wade in the water (instrumental) / Paying through the nose / Memphis B-K (instrumental) / Going home (where women got meat on their bones) / I found love / They want money
CD CDSXE 057
Stax / Jul '93 / Pinnacle

NEW KING OF THE BLUES HARMONICA/HARD GOIN' UP
Baby, what you want me to do / Eli's pork chop / Hey little girl / Hot potato / Don't ask me no questions / Tomorrow's blues today / Back down yonder / Sad funk / Creeper returns / It's hard going up (but twice as hard coming down) / My woman is good to me / You're spreading yourself a little too thin / Day you left me / You can be replaced / Do it right now / You made me strong / Sure is good / I want you
CD CDSXD 968
Stax / Jul '91 / Pinnacle

NEW ORLEANS RHYTHM & BLUES
CD BM 9023
Black Magic / Feb '94 / ADA / Cadillac / Direct / Hot Shot

SONNY SIDE UP
Sonny side up / Positive mind / I got to find my baby / Let me love you / Ready set go / Best of the best / I'm with you all the way / Tough times never last / Next dance with you
CD NEXCD 276
Sequel / Jun '95 / BMG

Little Steven

FREEDOM NO COMPROMISE
Freedom / Trail of broken treaties / Pretoria / Bitter fruit / No more party's / Can't you feel the fire / Native American / Sanctuary
CD NSPCD 511
Connoisseur Collection / Apr '95 / Pinnacle

MEN WITHOUT WOMEN (Little Steven & The Disciples Of Soul)
CD NSPCD 508
Connoisseur Collection / Mar '95 / Pinnacle

VOICE OF AMERICA
Voice of America / Justice / Checkpoint Charlie / Solidarity / Out of the darkness / Los desaparecidos (The disappeared ones) / Fear / I am not a patriot (and the river opens for the righteous) / Among the believers / Undefeated (everybody goes home)
CD NSPCD 512
Connoisseur Collection / Apr '95 / Pinnacle

Little Suzanne

BE HERE NOW
CD W 230093
Nettwerk / May '96 / Greyhound / Pinnacle / Vital

Little Texas

FIRST TIME FOR EVERYTHING
Some guys have all the luck / First time for everything / Down in the valley / You and forever and me / What you were thinkin' / Dance / Better way / I'd rather miss you / Just one more night / Cry on
CD 7599268202
Warner Bros. / May '92 / Warner Music

KICK A LITTLE
CD 9362457392
Warner Bros. / Nov '94 / Warner Music

Little Walter

BLUES WITH A FEELIN' (2CD Set)
Juke / Can't hold out much longer / Blue midnight / Fast boogie / Driftin' / Tonight with a fool / That's it / Blues with a feeling / My kind of baby / Last boogie / Come back baby / I love you so (oh baby) / Big leg mama / Mercy babe a/k/a My babe / Thunderbird / Crazy for my baby / Can't stop lovin' you / Who / Flying saucer / Teenage beat / Temperature / Shake dancer / Ah'w baby / Rock bottom / You gonna be sorry (someday baby) / Baby / My baby is sweeter / Crazy mixed up / Worried life blues / Everything's gonna be alright / Mean old Frisco / One of these mornings / Blue and lonesome / Me and Piney Brown / Break it up / Going down show / You're sweet / You don't know / I'm a business man / Chicken shack
CD MCD 09357
Chess/MCA / Apr '97 / BMG / New Note/ BMG

BLUES WORLD OF LITTLE WALTER
CD DD 648
Delmark / Nov '93 / ADA / Cadillac / CM / Direct / Hot Shot

BOSS BLUES HARMONICA
Juke / Can't hold out much longer / Mean ol' world / Sad hours / Tell me mama / Off the wall / Blues with a feeling / Too late / You're so fine / Last night / You better watch yourself / Blue light / My babe / Thunderbird / I got to go / Boom boom out go the lights / Flying saucer / It's too late brother / Teenage beat / Just a feeling / Shake dancer / Ah'w baby / Back track / Just your fool
CD CDRED 4
Charly / Aug '88 / Koch

CONFESSIN' THE BLUES
It ain't right / Rocker / I got to find my baby / Lights out / One more chance with you / Crazy legs / Temperature / I got to go / Crazy mixed up world / Quarter to twelve / Confessin' the blues / Toddle / Up the line / Rock bottom / Mean old Frisco
CD MCD 09366
Chess/MCA / Apr '97 / BMG / New Note/ BMG

ELECTRIC HARMONICA GENIUS, THE
Juke / Can't hold out much longer / Blue midnight / Mean ol' world / Sad hours / Quarter to twelve / Blues with a feeling / Last night / Mellow down easy / My babe / Hate to see you / Going down slow / It's too late brother / Everybody needs somebody / Confessin' the blues / Key to the highway / Walkin' on / Everything's gonna be alright / Blue and lonesome / I don't play / Peppers thing / Off the wall / You're so fine / Rocker
CD CD 52011
Blues Encore / '92 / Target/BMG

WINDY CITY BLUES (Little Walter & Otis Rush)
It's hard for me to believe baby / May be the last time / I feel good / Otis blues / Going down slow / Walter's blues / Lovin' you all the time / Blue mood
CD CDBM 028
Blue Moon / May '91 / Cadillac / Discovery / Greensleeves / Jazz Music / Jet Star / TKO Magnum

Little Whitt

MOODY SWAMP BLUES (Little Whitt & Big Bo)
CD ABP 1001
Alabama Blues Project / Apr '95 / ADA / Direct

Littlefield, Willie

GOING BACK TO KAY CEE (Littlefield, Little Willie)
Turn the lamp down low / Last laugh blues / Monday morning blues / Striking on you baby / Blood is redder than wine / KC lovin' / Pleading at midnight / Kansas City / Midnight hour was shining / Rock-a-bye baby / Miss KC's fine / Sitting on the curbstone / Jim Wilson's boogie / My best wishes and regards / Please dont go-o-o-oh / Falling tears / Goofy dust blues / Don't take my heart little girl
CD CDCHD 503
Ace / Jan '95 / Pinnacle

I'M IN THE MOOD (Littlefield, Little Willie)
CD OLCD 7002
Oldie Blues / Oct '93 / CM / Direct

YELLOW BOOGIE'N'BLUES (Littlefield, Little Willie)
CD OLCD 7006
Oldie Blues / Dec '94 / CM / Direct

Littlejohn, Johnny

CHICAGO BLUES STARS
CD ARHCD 1043
Arhoolie / Apr '95 / ADA / Cadillac / Direct

Litton, Martin

MARTIN LITTON
CD SACD 114
Solo Art / Aug '94 / Jazz Music

Live

MENTAL JEWELRY
Pain lies on the riverside / Operation spirit (the tyranny of tradition) / Beauty of gray / Brothers unaware / Tired of me / Mirror song / Waterboy / Take my anthem / You are the world / Good pain / Mother earth is a vicious crowd / 10,000 years (peace is now)
CD RARD 10346
Radioactive / Apr '92 / BMG / Vital

SECRET SAMADHI
Rattlesnake / Lakini's juice / Graze / Century / Ghost / Unsheathed / Insomnia and the hole in the universe / Turn my head / Gas hed goes west / Merica / Freaks / Heropsychodreamer
CD RAD 11590
Radioactive / Mar '97 / BMG / Vital

THROWING COPPER
CD RAD 10997
Radioactive / Oct '94 / BMG / Vital

Live Action Pussy Show

MONSTER LOVE
CD EFA 12292
Musical Tragedies / Aug '95 / SRD

Live Skull

POSITRACTION
CD GOES ON 29CD
What Goes On / Mar '89 / SRD

Live Wire

WIRED
CD ROUCD 281
Rounder / Dec '90 / ADA / CM / Direct

Lively Ones

SURF RIDER/SURF DRUMS
Surfbeat / Let's go trippin' / Misirlou / Guitar man / Caterpillar crawl / Walkin' the board / Paradise cove / Goofy foot / Surf rider / Happy gremmie / Hotdoggen / Surfer's lament / Tuff surf / Rik-a-tik / Wild weekend / Bustin' surfboards / Stoked / Surfer boogie / Surf drums / Shootin' the pier / Mr. Moto / Rumble / Forty miles of bad road / Hillbilly surf
CD CDCHD 957
Ace / Nov '90 / Pinnacle

Livengood, John

CYBORG SALLY
CD ____ **AMPCD 025**
AMP / Apr '95 / Cadillac / Discovery / TKO Magnum

Liverpool Cathedral Choir

CAROLS FROM LIVERPOOL
Maiden most gentle / Lulling her child / Gaudete, Christus natus est / On this day earth shall ring / Echo carol / Holly and the ivy / Away in a manger / Ding dong merrily on high / Little baby born at dark midnight / Christ is the flower / World's desire / Tomorrow shall be my dancing day / Spotless rose / Adam lay-y-bounden / In dulci jubilo / Noble stem of Jesse / Blessed song of God / Tyrley, tyrlow / Alleluia, a new work / Hark the herald angels sing / O come, all ye faithful / Once in Royal David's City
CD ____ **CDPS 386**
Alpha / Nov '91 / Abbey Recording

YOUR FAVOURITE HYMNS
CD ____ **VC 7912092**
Virgin Classics / Mar '92 / EMI

Liverpool FC

KOP CHOIR, THE (Liverpool's Own Football Sound) (Kop Choir)
CD ____ **CDGAFFER 14**
Cherry Red / Mar '97 / Pinnacle

YOU'LL NEVER WALK ALONE (Liverpool FC/Supporters)
CD ____ **CDGAFFER 4**
Cherry Red / Apr '96 / Pinnacle

Livin' Joy

DON'T STOP MOVING
Don't stop movin' / Follow the rules / Deep in you / Dreamer / Pick up the phone / Be original / Where can I find love / Don't cha wanna / Whenever you're lonely / Let me love you
CD ____ **MCD 60023**
MCA / Nov '96 / BMG

Living Color

GREATEST HITS
Pride / Sacred ground / Visions / Love rears its ugly head / These are happy times / Release the pressure / Memories can't wait / Cult of personality / Funny vibe / WTFF / Glamour boys / Open letter to a landlord / Solace of you / Nothingness / Type / Time's up / What's your favourite colour
CD ____ **4810212**
Epic / Feb '97 / Sony

Living End

STIFF MIDDLE FINGER
CD ____ **LRR 018**
Last Resort / Oct '96 / Cargo

Living In A Box

BEST OF LIVING IN A BOX, THE
CD ____ **DC 865922**
Disky / Mar '96 / Disky / THE

Livingston, Carlton

EMOTIONS
CD ____ **GVDCD 2025**
Grapevine / Jun '94 / Grapevine/PolyGram

Livingstone, Bill

WORLD'S GREATEST PIPERS VOL.9, THE (Livingstone, Pipe Major Bill)
CD ____ **LCOM 9045**
Lismor / Jul '91 / ADA / Direct / Duncans / Lismor

Lizard Music

DEAR CHAMP
Rebel without applause / (Theme from) We are the Egrets / My zebra / Things we did in slacks / Variations on a hallucination / Clam bake in C major / I would like to thank... / Care for any coffee / Sketchy angel / Hate you too / You're so young / Winter vacation / Imaginary toll / Plug it in/Clam bake
CD ____ **WD 00472**
World Domination / Jun '97 / Pinnacle / RTM/Disc

FASHIONABLY LAME
Esquire / Kill for a sprinkle / She's a very, very fat fat weirdo / Costume jewellry / Soft focus am / Goin' back to Orangeland / Routine / Jacko's book / Water / Deep in the heart of Texas / Howard's machinery / I see France / Frugal lame
CD ____ **WDOM 017CD**
World Domination / Jul '95 / Pinnacle / RTM/Disc

LOBSTER T
CD ____ **WDO 0392**
World Domination / Aug '96 / Pinnacle / RTM/Disc

Lizzy Borden

LOVE YOU TO DEATH
CD ____ **398414089CD**
Metal Blade / Sep '96 / Pinnacle / Plastic Head

MASTER OF DISGUISE
Master of disguise / One false move / Love is a crime / Sins of the flesh / Phantoms never too young / Be one of us / Psychodrama / Waiting in the wings / Roll over and play dead / Under the rose / We got the power
CD ____ **RR 94542**
Roadrunner / Aug '89 / PolyGram

MENACE TO SOCIETY
CD ____ **398414090CD**
Metal Blade / Sep '96 / Pinnacle / Plastic Head

MURDERESS METAL ROADSHOW, THE
CD ____ **398414092CD**
Metal Blade / Sep '96 / Pinnacle / Plastic Head

TERROR RISING/GIVE 'EM THE AXE
CD ____ **398414091CD**
Metal Blade / Sep '96 / Pinnacle / Plastic Head

VISUAL LIES
CD ____ **398414095CD**
Metal Blade / Sep '96 / Pinnacle / Plastic Head

LL Cool J

14 SHOTS TO THE DOME
How I'm comin' / Buckin' em down / Stand by your man / Little somethin' / Pink cookies in a plastic bag getting crushed by buildings / Straight from Queens / Funkadelic relic / All we got left is the beat / (NFA) No frontin' allowed / Back seat / Soul survivor / Ain't no stoppin' this / Diggy down / Crossroads
CD ____ **5234882**
Def Jam / Jan '96 / PolyGram

ALL WORLD
I can't live without my radio / Rock the bells / I'm bad / I need love / Going back to Cali / Jingling baby / Big ole butt / Boomin' system / Round the way girl / Mama said knock you out / Back seat / I need a beat / Doin' it / Loungin' (who do you love) / Hey lover: *LL Cool J & Boyz II Men*
CD ____ **5341252**
CD ____ **5343032**
Def Jam / Nov '96 / PolyGram

BIGGER AND DEFFER
I'm bad / Get down / Bristol Hotel / My rhyme ain't done / 357 - Break it on down / Go cut creator go / Breakthrough / I need love / Ahh, let's get ill / Doo wop / On the ill tip
CD ____ **5273532**
Def Jam / Jul '95 / PolyGram

MAMA SAID KNOCK YOU OUT
Boomin' system / Around the way girl / Eat 'em up L Chill / Mr. Good Bar / Murdergram (live at Rapmania) / Cheesy rat blues / Farmers boulevard (our anthem) / Mama said knock you out / Milky cereal / Jingling baby / To da break of dawn / Six minutes of pleasure / Illegal search / Power of God
CD ____ **5234772**
Def Jam / Jul '95 / PolyGram

MR. SMITH
Make it hot / Hip hop / Hey lover / Doin it / Life as / I shot ya / Mr. Smith / No aerplay / Loungin / Hollis to Hollywood / God bless / Get the drop on em
CD ____ **5297242**
Def Jam / Nov '95 / PolyGram

RADIO
I can't live without my radio / You can't dance / Dear Yvette / I can give you more / Dangerous / Rock the bells / I need a beat / You'll rock / I want you
CD ____ **5273522**
Def Jam / Jul '95 / PolyGram

WALKING WITH A PANTHER
Droppin' em / Smokin', dopin' / Fast peg / Clap your hands / Nitro / You're my heart / I'm that type of guy / Why do you think they call it dope / It gets no rougher / Big ole butt / One shot at love / 1-900 LL Cool J / Two different worlds / Jealous / Jingling baby / Def Jam in the motherland / Going back to Cali / Crime stories / Change your ways / Jack the ripper
CD ____ **5273552**
Def Jam / Jul '95 / PolyGram

Llan De Cubel

DEVA
CD ____ **FA 8701CD**
Fono Astur / Jul '95 / ADA

IV
Cabraliega / La Molinera / Pasucais de Xuan Martin/Munera de casu/Pasucais d'Amieva / Durme nenu / Alborada d'Amandi/Entemediu de Nemesio/Alborada'l tigre x / Lloxana / Fandangu puntiau/Alborada asturiana / Muneres de Tomaleo y d'os ozcos / Adios la mia vaca pinta / Pasucais d'Uvieu/Salon de casu/Marcha nupical de villaperi
CD ____ **IRCD 046**
Iona / Mar '97 / ADA / Direct / Duncans

L'OTRU DE LA MAR
CD ____ **FA 8734CD**
Fono Astur / Jul '95 / ADA

NA LLENDE
CD ____ **FA 8718CD**
Fono Astur / Apr '96 / ADA

Lloyd, A.L.

BALLADS ET SHANTIES (LLoyd, A.L. & Friends)
CD ____ **SCM 030CD**
Diffusion Breizh / Aug '94 / ADA

CLASSIC A.L. LLOYD
CD ____ **FE 098CD**
Fellside / Jul '94 / ADA / Direct / Target/ BMG

OLD BUSH SONGS
CD ____ **LRF 354**
Larrikin / Aug '96 / ADA / CM / Direct / Roots

Lloyd, Charles

ALL MY RELATIONS
Piercing the veil / Little peace / Thelonious theonlyus / Cape to Cairo suite / Evanstide, where lotus bloom / All my relations / Hymme to the Mother / Milarepa
CD ____ **5273442**
ECM / May '95 / New Note/Pinnacle

CALL, THE (Lloyd, Charles Quartet)
Nocturne / Song / Dwija / Glimpse / Imke / Amarma / Figure in blue, memories of Duke / Blessing / Brother on the rooftop
CD ____ **5177192**
ECM / Oct '93 / New Note/Pinnacle

CANTO
Tales of Rumi / How can I tell you / Desolation sound / Canto / Machiketa's lament / M / Durga durga
CD ____ **5373452**
ECM / Jun '97 / New Note/Pinnacle

FISH OUT OF WATER (Lloyd, Charles Quartet)
Fish out of water / Haghia Sophia / Dirge / Bharti / Eyes of love / Mirror
CD ____ **8410882**
ECM / Jan '90 / New Note/Pinnacle

NOTES FROM BIG SUR
Requim / Sister / Pilgrimage to the mountain / Sam song / Takur / Monk in Paris / When Miss Jessye sings / Pilgrimage to the mountain - part 2 surrender
CD ____ **5119992**
ECM / May '92 / New Note/Pinnacle

Lloyd, David

Y CANEUON CYNNAR (The Early Recordings 1940-1941)
Smilin' through / O loveliness beyond compare / Speak for me to my lady / All through the night / March of the men of Harlech / Jerusalem / England / Aberystwyth / Land of my fathers / Until / Serenade / Lovely maid in the moonlight / Bless this house / Sylvia / David of the white rock / Stars in heaven are bright / Over the stone / Cwm Rhondda
CD ____ **SCDC 2076**
Sain / Feb '97 / ADA / Direct / Greyhound

Lloyd, Floyd

MEET LAUREL AITKEN (Lloyd, Floyd & Potato Five)
CD ____ **GAZCD 001**
Gaz's Rockin' Records / '89 / Shellshock/ Disc

Lloyd, John

BY CONFUSION (Lloyd, John Quartet)
CD ____ **ARTCD 6198**
Hat Art / Apr '97 / Cadillac / Harmonia Mundi

SYZGY (Lloyd, John Quartet)
CD ____ **CDLR 173**
Leo / '90 / Cadillac / Impetus / Wellard

Lloyd-Langton, Huw

RIVER RUN (Lloyd-Langton, Huw Group)
CD ____ **LLG 6CD**
Allegro / Dec '94 / Plastic Head

Lloyd-Tucker, Colin

REMARKABLE
CD ____ **BAH 2**
Humbug / Apr '93 / Total/Pinnacle

SKYSCAPING
CD ____ **BAH 8**
Humbug / Jul '93 / Total/Pinnacle

SONGS OF LIFE, LOVE AND LIQUID
CD ____ **BAH 17**
Humbug / Apr '96 / Total/Pinnacle

Lloydie Crucial

JUNGLE IN THE SUBURBS
CD ____ **LCCD 002**
Lloydie Crucial / Feb '95 / Jet Star

JUNGLEMANIA VOL.1 (Lloydie Crucial & The Concrete Junglist Crew)
CD ____ **LCCDLP 001**
Lloydie Crucial / Oct '94 / Jet Star

Llwybr Llaethog

MAD
CD ____ **ANKSTCD 065**
Ankst / Jun '96 / Shellshock/Disc

MEWN DYB
CD ____ **RUSCD 8226**
ROIR / Jul '96 / Plastic Head / Shellshock/ Disc

Lo, Cheikh

NE LA THIASS
Ne la thiass / Set / Cheikh ibra fall / Bamba sunu goorgui / Guiss guiss / Boul di tagale / Ndogal / Boxandeme / Sant Maam
CD ____ **WCD 046**
World Circuit / Oct '96 / ADA / Cadillac / Direct / New Note/Pinnacle

Lo, Ismael

DIAWAR
CD ____ **STCD 1027**
Stern's / Nov '89 / ADA / CM / Stern's

Lo-Key

BACK 2 DA HOUSE
Welcome / Back 2 da howse / 26c / Don't trip on me / Getcha girlfriend / Li'l shumpin', shumpin' / Tasty / Play with me / Good ole fashion love / Turn around / Call my name / Interlude / My desire / We ain't right / Come on in
CD ____ **5490102**
Perspective / Dec '94 / PolyGram

Lobato, Chano

LA NUEZ MOSCA (Lobato, Chano & Pedro Bacan/Manuel Soler)
CD ____ **B 6840**
Auvidis/Ethnic / Oct '96 / ADA / Harmonia Mundi

Lobban, David

STEP BY STEP VOL.2
CD ____ **SEQCD 002**
Sound Waves / Jan '94 / Target/BMG

STEP BY STEP VOL.3
CD ____ **SEQCD 003**
Sound Waves / Jan '94 / Target/BMG

STEP BY STEP VOL.5
CD ____ **SEQCD 005**
Sound Waves / Jan '94 / Target/BMG

STEP BY STEP VOL.6
CD ____ **SEQCD 006**
Sound Waves / Jul '94 / Target/BMG

STEP BY STEP VOL.7
CD ____ **SEQCD 007**
Sound Waves / Jul '94 / Target/BMG

WURLITZER FAVOURITES
CD ____ **SOW 514**
Sound Waves / Jul '94 / Target/BMG

Lobe

LOBE
CD ____ **WM 7**
Swim / May '96 / Kudos / RTM/Disc / SRD

Lobi, Kakraba

WORLD OF KAKRABA LOBI, THE
CD ____ **VICG 50142**
JVC World Library / Mar '96 / ADA / CM / Direct

Lobotomy

LOBOTOMY
CD ____ **CHAOSCD 004**
Chaos / Jan '96 / Plastic Head

Local Area Network

LOCAL AREA NETWORK
CD ____ **A 5**
A-Musik / Jun '97 / SRD

Local H

AS GOOD AS DEAD
Manifest density (part 1) / High-fiving MF / Bound for the floor / Lovey dovey / I saw what you did and I know who you are / No problem / Nothing special / Eddie Vedder / Back in the day / Freeze dried (f)lies / Fritz's corner / OK / Manifest density (part 2)
CD ____ **5242022**
Island / Mar '97 / PolyGram

Locke, Jimmy

DANCETIME AT THE ORGAN VOL.3
CD SAV 236CD
Savoy / Dec '95 / Savoy / THE / TKO Magnum

IT'S DANCE TIME
CD SAV 188CD
Savoy / May '93 / Savoy / THE / TKO Magnum

JIMMY LOCKE PLAYS MUSIC MUSIC MUSIC
Heartaches / Amy / I'm a dreamer (aren't we all) / Little girl / I wonder who's kissing her now / True love / My mothers pearls / Memories / Foolishly yours / Yesterdays dreams / I apologise / How soon / Too young / Only you / Just loving you / Be careful it's my heart / Till / Petticoats of Portugal / From here to eternity / Return to me / In the spirit of the moment / I talk to the trees / Amapola / Strangers in the night / Oh Donna CLara / You were meant for me / Pretty baby / Heart of my heart / Breezin' along with the breeze / Someday (you'll want me to want you) / C'est magnifique / Rose of Washington Square / Whsipering / Broadway melody / Is it true what they say about Dixie / Baby face / I'll always be in love with you / Under the lidden tree the one rose / When your old wedding ring was new / Pal of my cradle days / Kiss me again / Cry / If I could only make you care / Sierra Sue / Nevertheless / You were only fooling / There must be a way
CD SAV 171CD
Savoy / Mar '92 / Savoy / THE / TKO Magnum

JIMMY'S MAGIC MELODIES
If your face wants to laugh/Follow the swallow / Three little words/Everything in rhythm with my heart / Silver wedding waltz/Last waltz of the evening / Kiss in your eyes/ Memories live longer than dreams / Look for the silver lining/When did you leave heaven / My gypsy dream girl/If I didn't care / Glory of love / Rock-a-bye your baby/Have you ever been lonely / It's magic/Don't take your love from me / Love is all / Fools rush in / Cherry pink and apple blossom white/Love me tender / Mr. Sandman/Five foot two, eyes of blue / Wait till the sun shines Nellie/ I'm nobody's baby / Please/Shine through my dreams / Once in a while/Prisoner of love / Your lips are red / Isle of Capri/Echo of a serenade / Maybe/Shepherd of the hills/Home / It had to be you/Love letters in the sand
CD SAV 175CD
Savoy / Jul '92 / Savoy / THE / TKO Magnum

Locke, Joe

RESTLESS DREAMS (Locke, Joe-Phil Markowitz Quartet)
Restless dreams / My foolish heart / Kahalid the warrior / May moon (Phil Markowitz) / You and I / Calypso nouveau
CD CHIEFCD 1
Chief / Mar '89 / Cadillac

Locke, Josef

HEAR MY SONG
Hear my song Violetta / Soldier's dream / March of the Grenadiers / Blaze away / Goodbye / If I were a blackbird / I'll walk beside you / At the end of the day / Mother Machree / Love's last word is spoken / Cara mia / O maiden, my maiden / If I could hear somebody / You are my heart's delight / Come back to Sorrento / I'll take you home again Kathleen / Holy City / Drinking song / Santa Lucia / When you were sweet sixteen / Count your blessings / My heart and I / Goodbye (from the The White Horse Inn) / Galway Bay / Macushla / Rose of Tralee / Bard of Armagh / When it's moonlight in Mayo / How can you buy Killarney / Dear old Donegal / Isle of Innisfree / Maire my girl / Shades of old Blarney / Shawl of Galway grey
CD Set CDDL 1033
EMI / Nov '92 / EMI

HEAR MY SONG - THE BEST OF JOSEF LOCKE
Hear my song Violetta / I'll take you home again Kathleen / Blaze away / Count your blessings / Oh maiden, my maiden / Drinking song / Love's last word is spoken / Charmaine / You are my heart's delight / If I can help somebody / Cara mia / Come back to Sorrento / It is no secret / When you were sweet sixteen / Rose of Slievenamon / You'll never forget about Ireland / Eileen O'Grady / I'll walk beside you / At the end of the day / My heart and I / How can you buy Killarney / When you talk about old Ireland / If I were a blackbird / Garden where the praties grow / Goodbye
CD CDGO 2034
EMI / Feb '92 / EMI

HEAR MY SONG VIOLETTA (The EMI Recordings 1947-1955 - 4CD Set)
Hear my song, Violetta / Santa Lucia / Goodbye / I'll take you home again Kathleen / Holy City / Come back to Sorrento / My heart & I / Star of Bethlehem / Dear old Donegal / When you were sweet sixteen / Rose of Tralee / Count your blessings / Galway Bay / Macushla / Rosary / Ave Maria / Husha bye Rose of Killarney / Song of songs / Old Bog Road / Strange music / Bless this house / When you're in love / Soldier's dream / Beneath thy window / While the angelus was ringing / Toselli's serenade / Will the angels play their harps for me / How can you buy Killarney / Shawl of Galway grey / Lay my head beneath a rose / Silent night / O come all ye faithful (adeste fidelis) / We all have a song in our hearts / Down in the Glen / In the chapel of San Remo / Ireland must be heaven / Within this heart of mine / Festival of roses / Christopher Robin is saying his prayers / Story of the sparrows / Teddy bears' picnic / Garden where the praties grow / Eileen O'Grady / If I were a blackbird / March of the Grenadiers / You are my heart's delight / When you talk about old Ireland / Take a pair of sparkling eyes / If I can help somebody / Keys to heaven / It is no secret / Nirvana / Dream / I'll walk beside you / Tonight beloved / At the end of the day / Charmaine / Love me little, love me long / Isle of Innesfree / Mother Machree / Wonderful Copenhagen / Love's last word is spoken / One little candle / Love me and the world is mine / It's a grand life in the army / You'll never forget about Ireland / Tear, a kiss, a smile / We'll pray for you / Shades of old Blarney / When you hear Big Ben / You're just a flower from an old bouquet / Tobermory Bay / Band of Armagh / Queen of everyone's heart / Daughter of Rose of Tralee / Rose of Slievenamon / Melba waltz / Maire my girl / When it's moonlight in Mayo / Drinking song / In the chapel in the moonlight / Cara Mia / Santo Natale / Brown bird singing / Bonnie Mary of Argyle / Blaze away / People like us / O maiden, my maiden / My mission
CD Set CDLOK 1
Premier/EMI / Apr '96 / EMI

HYMNS WE ALL LOVE
All people that on earth do dwell / When the roll is called up yonder / Old rugged cross / Lead kindly light / One love everlasting / There's a great new prospect in the sky / Onward Christian soldiers / It is no secret / Nearer my God to thee / Shall we gather at the river / Abide with me / God be with you till we meet again
CD DOCD 2027
Dolphin / Jul '96 / CM / Else / Grapevine/ PolyGram / Koch

IRISH FAVORITES
Blaze away / Old bog road / Slievenamon / I'll take you home again Kathleen / Danny Boy / Little grey home in the West / Sweet sixteen / Bold gendarmes / Town I loved so well / She moved through the fair / Old house / Lovely Derry on the banks of the Foyle / On the street where you live / My way / Mountains of Mourne / Goodbye
CD CDIRISH 009
Outlet / Mar '97 / ADA / CM / Direct / Duncans / Koch / Ross

LET THERE BE PEACE - COLLECTED SONGS
CD ARANCD 601
Aran / Nov '95 / CM

SINGALONG
In the shade of the old apple tree / My bonnie lies over the ocean / Daisy Daisy / East side, west side / Sweet Rosie O'Grady / She's only a bird in a gilded cage / In this good old summertime / If those lips could only speak / Clementine / Michael, row the boat ashore / He's got the whole world in his hands / John Brown's body / Red river valley / On top of old smokey / Beautiful brown eyes / Old faithful / Roll along covered wagon / South of the border (Down Mexico way) / Let him go, let him tarry / Ma goes Dixie / Rose of Tralee / Slaney Valley / Where the Blarney roses grow / Heaven street / Saints / Down by the Severnside / Loch Lomond / Annie Laurie / Will ye no' come back again / Oh Susanna / Beautiful dreamer / Camptown races / Quartermaster's stores / Old soldiers never die
CD DOCD 2026
Koch / Nov '93 / Koch

SONGS I LOVED SO WELL, THE
CD HMCD 5
Outlet / Jan '95 / ADA / CM / Direct / Duncans / Koch / Ross

TAKE A PAIR OF SPARKLING EYES
It's a grand life in the army / Take a pair of sparkling eyes / Macushla / Dear old Donegal / St. Lucia / Galway Bay / While the Angelus was ringing / Old bog road / Wonderful Copenhagen / Soldier's dream / Mother Machree / Maire my girl / Soldiers of the Queen / Shades of old Blarney / Rose of Tralee / When it's moonlight in Mayo / Toselli's serenade / Bless this house / Bard of Armagh / March of the grenadiers / Shawl of Galway grey / Tobermory bay / Isle of Innisfree / Ireland must be heaven / Ave Maria
CD CDP 7996402
EMI / Jun '92 / EMI

VERY BEST OF JOSEF LOCKE, THE
I'll take you home again Kathleen / Hear my song Violetta / Galway Bay / Macushla / Rose of Tralee / Bard of Armagh / When it's moonlight in Mayo / How can you buy Killarney / Marie my girl / Shawl of Galway grey / Come back to Sorrento / March of the Grenadiers / Soldier's dream / Holy city / Drinking song / Santa Lucia / When you were sweet sixteen / Count your blessings / My heart & I / Goodbye
CD CDMFP 6246
Music For Pleasure / Aug '96 / EMI

Locke, Kevin

FLASH OF THE MIRROR
CD 14937
Spalax / Jun '97 / ADA / Cargo / Direct / Discovery / Greyhound

Lockheart, Mark

MATHERAN (Lockheart, Mark & John Parricelli)
CD IS 02CD
Isis / Apr '94 / ADA / Direct

Locklin, Hank

MAGIC OF HANK LOCKLIN, THE
Please help me, I'm falling / Geisha girl / Happy birthday to me / Happy journey / Send me the pillow that you dream on / Let me be the one / It's a little more like heaven / Flying South / From here to there to you / I was coming home to you / We're gonna go fishin' / Queen of hearts / Mysteries of life / I'm lonely darling / Come share the sunshine with me / Year of time / To whom it may concern / Tell me you love me / Who you think you're foolin' / I could call you darling
CD TKOCD 025
TKO / May '92 / TKO

PLEASE HELP ME I'M FALLING (4CD Set)
CD BCD 15730
Bear Family / Jun '95 / Direct / Rollercoaster / Swift

SEND ME THE PILLOW YOU DREAM ON (3CD Set)
Rio Grande waltz / You've been talking in your sleep / Please come back and stay / I've got a feeling somebody's falling / I worship you / You've been talking in your sleep / Same sweet girl / Last look at Mother / One more mistake / Knocking at your door / Born to ramble / I'm lonely darling / Send me the pillow (you dream on) / Are you treating your neighbour as yourself / Fifty miles of elbow room / Crazy over you / Our love will show the way / Tho I've lost / Midnight tears / It's so hard to say I love you / Place and the time / You burned a hole in my heart / Pinball millionaire / Paper face / Come share the sunshine with me / No one is sweeter than you / Year of time / To whom it may concern / Song of the whispering leaves / Won't you change your mind / Holy train / Is there room for me / Who is knocking at my heart / Harvest is ripe (the labourers are few) / I could love you darling / Rio Grande waltz / Your house of love won't stand / Who do you think you're fooling / Sand me the pillow (you dream on) / I always lose / Stumpy Joe / I'm going to copyright your kisses / Down Texas way / Tomorrow's just another day to cry / Tell me you love me / Could you / Picking sweethearts / I like to play with your kisses / Golden wristwatch / (Sittin') alone at a table for two / I can't run away / Shadows / Red rose / Lessons in love / Let me be the one / I'm tired of bummin' around / I'll be blue til then / In the house of the Lord / Mysteries of life / Queen of hearts / Empty bottles, empty heart / Who will it be / Whispering scandal / Baby you can count me in / Let me confess / I'll always be standing by
CD Set BCD 15953
Bear Family / Jan '97 / Direct / Rollercoaster / Swift

VERY BEST OF HANK LOCKLIN, THE
Please help me I'm falling / Send me the pillow that you dream on / Baby I need you / There never was a time / Let me be the one / From here to there to you / Down on my knees / Happy birthday to me / Happy journey / These arms you push away / Night life queen / I was coming home to you / It's a little more like heaven / Geisha girl / Daytime love affair / Flying south / We're gonna go fishin'
CD 305712
Hallmark / Oct '96 / Carlton

Lockwood, Didier

NEW YORK RENDEZ-VOUS
Juggling in Central Park / Waltzy / Cousin William / Anbatole blues / Gordon / Reminiscence / Don't drive so fast / Eastern dance / Tom Thumb
CD JMS 186692
JMS / May '95 / New Note/BMG

STORYBOARD
Thought of a first Spring day / Back to Big Apple / En quittant kidonk / Mathilde / Tableau d'une exposition / Serie B / Storyboard / Irremediablement / Spirits of the forest
CD FDM 365822
Dreyfus / Dec '96 / ADA / Direct / New Note/ Pinnacle

Lockwood, Robert Jr.

PLAYS ROBERT JOHNSON
CD BLE 597402
Black & Blue / Sep '92 / Discovery / Koch / Wellard

STEADY ROLLIN' MAN
CD DD 630
Delmark / Jan '93 / ADA / Cadillac / CM / Direct / Hot Shot

Locomotive

WE ARE EVERYTHING YOU SEE
Overture / Mr. Armageddon / Now is the end, the end is when / Lay me down gently / Nobody asked me to come / You must be joking / Day in shining armour / Lovers of Augustus Abbey / Times of light and darkness / Broken heart / Rudie, a message to you / Rudi's in love / Never set me free / There's got to be a way / I'm never gonna let you go / Roll over Mary / Movin' down the line / Rudi the red nosed reindeer / White Christmas / Rudi catch the monster / My girl blue
CD BL 004
Shoestring / Jul '97 / Pinnacle

Locust

MORNING LIGHT
Your selfish ways / Morning light / Just like you / I am the murderer / Jukebox heart / Folie / One way or another / No-one in the world / Clouds at my feet / Summer rain / Ancient hometown / Girl with the fairytale dream / Let me take you back / Some love will remain unsaid / Shadow play / On the horizon
CD AMB 7942CD
Apollo / Jun '97 / Vital

TRUTH IS BORN OF ARGUMENTS
Truth is born of arguments / Penetration / I feel cold inside because of the things you say / Saturated love / When we coincide / I believe in a love I may never know / Optimist / I became overwhelmed / I am afraid of who I am / Inside I am crying / Love you cruelly gave me would not last
CD AMB 5940CD
R&S / Jun '95 / Vital

WEATHERED WELL
Prospero / Moist moss / Xenophobe / Weathered gate / Tamed / Still / Music about love / Lust / Fawn
CD AMB 3929CD
Apollo / Mar '94 / Vital

Locust Fudge

ROYAL FLUSH
CD GRCD 370
Glitterhouse / May '97 / Avid/BMG

Lodder, Steve

ABOVE THE CLOUDS (Lodder, Steve & Mark Ramsden)
Adrift in your dreams / Retrove / Andante / Juggler / Adagio / Confluence / Flos vernalis / Saint Chappelle / Adagio and Andante / While the pulse still beats / Tumbler / Above the clouds
CD BREATHE 001
Breathe / Apr '96 / New Note/Pinnacle

Lodestar

LODESTAR
Another day / Salter's ducks / Wait a minute / Representative / By halves / Better late than never / Aftertaste / Worthwhile / Soiled blood / Down in the mud / Lilac crest
CD TOPPCD 049
Ultimate / Oct '96 / Pinnacle

Lodge

SMELL OF A FRIEND
CD RES 122CD
Resurgence / Dec '96 / Pinnacle

Lodge, J.C.

I BELIEVE IN YOU
I believe in you / I found love / Let me down easy / Too good to be true / Night work / Cool mover / Given up / You don't want my love / Together we will stay / Happy now sorry later
CD RRTGCD 7712
Rohit / '88 / Jet Star

RAS PORTRAITS
Activate me / Make it up to you / Somewhere over the rainbow / Top of the line / Love for all seasons / Can't get over losing you / You carry the swing / Love you to the max / Work with me baby / Crysis
CD RAS 3310
Ras / Jun '97 / Direct / Greensleeves / Jet Star / SRD

SELFISH LOVER
Love's gonna break your heart / Conversations / Way up / I am in love / Sweet dreams / Cautious / Operator / Hardcore loving / Selfish love / Telephone love / Love me baby / Lonely nights / Since you came into my life

CD ________ GRELCD 143
Greensleeves / Apr '90 / Jet Star / SRD

SOMEONE LOVES YOU HONEY
CD ________ RGCD 6053
Rocky One / Mar '94 / Jet Star

SPECIAL REQUEST
CD ________ RASCD 3168
Ras / Jun '95 / Direct / Greensleeves / Jet Star / SRD

TO THE MAX
CD ________ RASCD 3128
Ras / Jan '94 / Direct / Greensleeves / Jet Star / SRD

Lodge, John

NATURAL AVENUE
Intro to children of rock 'n' roll / Natural Avenue / Summer breeze / Carry me / Who could change / Broken dreams, hard road / Piece of my heart / Rainbow / Say you love me / Children of rock 'n' roll / Street cafe
CD ________ JS 1
Halesouth / Mar '97 / Pinnacle

Loeb, Chuck

MUSIC INSIDE, THE
CD ________ SHCD 5022
Shanachie / Jul '96 / ADA / Greensleeves / Koch

Loeb, Lisa

TAILS (Loeb, Lisa & Nine Stories)
It's over / Snow day / Taffy / When all the stars are falling / Do you sleep / Hurricane / Rose-colored times / Sandalwood / Alone waiting for Wednesday / Lisa listen / Garden of delights / Stay
CD ________ GED 24734
Geffen / Sep '95 / BMG

Lofgren, Nils

ACOUSTIC LIVE
CD ________ FIENCD 934
Demon / Aug '97 / Pinnacle

ACROSS THE TRACKS (2CD Set)
CD Set ________ SMDCD 106
Snapper / Aug '97 / Pinnacle

BEST OF NILS LOFGREN, THE
CD ________ CDMID 160
A&M / Oct '92 / PolyGram

CODE OF THE ROAD
Secrets in the street / Across the tracks / Delivery night / Cry tough / Dreams die hard / Believe / Sun hasn't set on this boy yet / Code of the road / Moontears / Back it up / Like rain
CD ________ CLACD 311
Castle / '92 / BMG

CRY TOUGH
Cry tough / It's not a crime / Incidentally... it's over / It's over / For your love / Share a little / Mud in your eye / Can't get closer / You lit a fire / Jailbait
CD ________ CDMID 122
A&M / Oct '92 / PolyGram

DAMAGED GOODS
CD ________ ESSCD 337
Essential / Oct '95 / BMG

DON'T WALK, ROCK (The Best Of Nils Lofgren)
Moontears / Back it up / Keith don't go / Sun hasn't set on this boy yet / Goin' back / Cry tough / Jailbait / Can't get closer / Mud in your eye / I came to dance / To be a dreamer / No mercy / Steal away / Baltimore / Shine silently / Secrets in the street / Flip ya flip / Delivery night / Anytime at all
CD ________ VSOPCD 152
Connoisseur Collection / Jun '90 / Pinnacle

FLIP
Flip ya flip / Secrets in the street / From the heart / Delivery night / King of the rock / Sweet midnight / New holes in old shoes / Dreams die hard / Big tears fall / Beauty and the beast
CD ________ CLACD 312
Castle / Nov '92 / BMG

NILS
No mercy / I'll cry tomorrow / Baltimore / Shine silently / Steal away / Kool skool / Fool like me / I found her / You're so easy / This life holds something for me
CD ________ 5407072
A&M / Jan '97 / PolyGram

NILS LOFGREN
Be good tonight / Back it up / One more saturday night / If I say it, it's so / I don't want to know / Keith don't go / Can't buy a break / Duty the sun hasn't set on / Rock 'n' roll crook / Two by two / Goin' back / Girl don't come
CD ________ 5407022
A&M / Apr '97 / PolyGram

SHINE SILENTLY
Secrets in the street / Flip ya flip / King of the rock / Delivery night / New holes in old shoes / Keith don't go / Like rain / Shine silently / I came to dance / Anytime at all / Beauty and the beast / Dreams die hard / From the heart / Sweet midnight

CD ________ 5507502
Spectrum / Jan '95 / PolyGram

SILVER LINING
Silver lining / Valentine / Walkin' nerve / Live each day / Sticks and stones / Trouble's back / Little bit o' time / Bein' angry / Gun and run / Girl in motion
CD ________ ESMCD 145
Essential / Aug '96 / BMG

SOFT FUN TOUGH TEARS 1971-1979
CD ________ RVCD 44
Raven / Jun '95 / ADA / Direct

STEAL YOUR HEART AWAY (The Best Of Nils Lofgren/2CD Set)
Take you to the movies / Back it up / Incidentally... it's over / If I say it, it's so / Goin' back / You're the weight / Fool like me / Duty / Steal away / Shine silently / Cry tough / No mercy / Beggar's day / Like rain / I'll cry tomorrow / Keith don't go (Ode to the Glimmer Twin) / It's not a crime / For your love / Kool skool / Rock 'n' roll crook / I came to dance / Code of the road / I found her / Moon tears / You're so easy / Baltimore / One more Saturday night / Happy / Sun hasn't set on this boy yet
CD Set ________ 5404112
A&M / Apr '96 / PolyGram

Loft

ONCE AROUND THE FAIR
CD ________ CRECD 047
Creation / Jun '89 / 3mv/Vital

Loft Line

NINE STEPS
CD ________ BEST 1041CD
Acoustic Music / Nov '93 / ADA

VISITORS
CD ________ BEST 1085CD
Acoustic Music / Mar '96 / ADA

Loftus, Caroline

SUGAR
CD ________ LRF 268
Larrikin / Oct '93 / ADA / CM / Direct / Roots

Logan, Giuseppi

MORE GIUSEPPI LOGAN
CD ________ ESP 1013
ESP / Feb '93 / Jazz Music

Logan, Jack

BULK
Fuck everything / Shrunken head / Love not lunch / Female Jesus / Escape clause / Underneath your bed / Just go away / Lazy girl blues / New used car and a plate of Bar-B-Que / Opposite direction / Fifteen years in Indiana / Heart attack on the prairie / Optimist / Voodoo doll / Chloroform / Vegetable belt / Aloha-ha / Sweetest fruit / Lovely / Sometimes it's you / Monday night / Giant city, tiny town / Graves are fun to dig / Floating cowboy / Peace o' mind / Shipbuilding blues / Parishioners / Would I be happy then / Farsighted / On the beach / Yes I can / Grey steel train / Drunken arms / Good times, bad memories / Shit for brains / Heaven on earth / Idiot's waltz / Terminal gate / Weathermen / Tex / Cartoons / Town crier
CD Set ________ 892612
Medium Cool / Jul '94 / Vital

MOOD ELEVATOR
Teach me the rules / Unscathed / Chinese Lorraine / When it all comes down / My new town / Ladies and gentlemen / Just babies / Sky won't fall / No offense / Another life / Estranged / Neon tombstone / What's tickling you / What was burned / Vintage man / Suicide doors / Bleed
CD ________ 892902
Restless / Jan '96 / Vital

Logan, John 'Juke'

JUKE RHYTHM
CD ________ 8409432
Sky Ranch / Sep '96 / Discovery

Logan, Johnny

BEST OF JOHNNY LOGAN, THE
Hold me now / Stay / When your woman cries / I'm not in love / Helpless heart / Heartbroken man / Living a lie / Such a lady / Love letters / What's another year / Ginny come lately / Lovin' you / Love hurts / Saturday night at the movies / Take good care of my baby / Next time / When you walk in the room / Cryin' in the rain
CD ________ 4840472
Epic / May '96 / Sony

LIVING FOR LOVING
Living for loving / I don't want to fall in love / In London / Man with the accordion / Hey kid / Sad little woman / Carneval do Brazil / Honesty / Lonely tonight / Please please please
CD ________ PZA 002CD
Plaza / Feb '94 / Pinnacle

Logan, Willie

DEDICATIONS
2001 / Burning love / Don't believe a word / Wherever I lay my hat / I shot the sheriff / 20th Century boy / Crazy little thing called love / What a wonderful world / Watching the wheels / Summertime blues / Pretty woman / Dock of the bay / Goodbye love / Voodoo Chile / True love ways
CD ________ 3036400052
Hallmark / Apr '96 / Carlton

Logg

LOGG
You've got that something / Dancing into the stars / Something else / I know you will / Lay it on the line / Sweet to me
CD ________ CPCD 8076
Charly / Mar '95 / Koch

Logical Nonsense

EXPAND THE HIVE
CD ________ VIRUS 203CD
Alternative Tentacles / Jul '97 / Cargo / Greyhound / Pinnacle

Logsdon, Jimmy

I GOT A ROCKET IN MY POCKET
Hank Williams sings the blues no more / Death of Hank Williams / It's all over but the shouting / I can't make up my mind / No longer / I'm going back to Tennessee / Midnight boogie / My sweet French baby / Good deal Lucille / Pa-paya Mama / I got a rocket in my pocket / You're gone baby / Where the Rio de Rosa flows / You ain't nothing but the blues / Love you gave to me / One way ticket to nowhere / Let's have a happy time / As long as we're together / In the Mission of St. Augustine / Where the old red river flows / That's when I'll love you the best / Midnight blues / Cold, cold rain / I'll never know / These lonesome blues / I wanna be Mama'd / (We've reached the) Beginning of the end / Road of regret
CD ________ BCD 15650
Bear Family / Oct '93 / Direct / Rollercoaster / Swift

Logue & McCool

VERY BEST OF LOGUE & MCCOOL, THE
CD ________ DHCD 723
Homespun / Aug '96 / ADA / CM / Direct / Koch / Ross

Lohan, Sinead

WHO DO YOU THINK I AM
CD ________ DARA 186CD
Dara / Apr '95 / ADA / CM / Direct / Else / Grapevine/PolyGram
CD ________ GRACD 209
Grapevine / Oct '95 / Grapevine/PolyGram

Lois

BET THE SKY
CD ________ KLP 36CD
K / Nov '95 / Cargo / Greyhound / SRD

BUTTERFLY KISS
Davey / Narcissus / Press play and record / Staring at the sun / Valentine / Stroll always / Spray / Never last / Bonds in seconds / Sorara / Look who's sorry
CD ________ KLP 15CD
K / Nov '95 / Cargo / Greyhound / SRD

INFINITY PLUS
CD ________ KLP 58CD
K / Oct '96 / Cargo / Greyhound / SRD

STRUMPET
CD ________ KLP 21CD
K / Nov '95 / Cargo / Greyhound / SRD

Loitima

LOITIMA
CD ________ KICD 36
Kansanmusiikki Instituutti / Nov '95 / ADA / Direct

Loketo

EXTRA BALL
CD ________ SHCD 64028
Shanachie / Jul '91 / ADA / Greensleeves / Koch

Lol Interceps

MUSIC FOR MOVIES
CD ________ MHCD 023
Minus Habens / Nov '94 / Plastic Head

Loli & The Chones

PS WE HATE YOU
CD ________ RIPOFF 023CD
Rip Off / Mar '97 / Cargo / Greyhound

Lolitas

FUSEE D'AMOUR
CD ________ ROSE 170CD
New Rose / Apr '89 / ADA / Direct / Discovery

Lollipop

DOG PISS ON DOG
CD ________ ARRCD 74017
Amphetamine Reptile / Dec '96 / Plastic Head

Lombardi, Carlos

TANGO ARGENTINO
CD ________ SOW 90111
Sounds Of The World / Sep '93 / Target/ BMG

Lombardo, Guy

I'LL SEE YOU IN MY DREAMS (Lombardo, Guy & His Royal Canadians)
Deep purple / Boom / Faithful forever / Start the day right / Nearness of you / When the swallows come back to Capistrano / Scatterbrain / It's a hap-hap-happy day / I don't want to set the world on fire / Rainbow valley / Concerto in the park / Blues in the night / Along the Sante Fe trail / Tea for two / Hawaiian war chant / Who / Three little fishes / Cancel the flowers / Take it easy / I'll see you in my dreams / It's love love love / Goodnight sweetheart
CD ________ RAJCD 851
Empress / May '95 / Koch

LIVE AT THE WALDORF
When the saints go marchin' in / South Rampart street parade / Enjoy yourself / Too much mustard / Boo hoo / Cabaret / Give my regards to Broadway / Hello Dolly / Mack the knife / Silver dollar / Maple leaf rag / I want to be happy / Spanish eyes / Never on Sunday / Helena polka / Alley cat / Tarantella / Your cheatin' heart / High society / Dangerous Dan McGrew / Maria Elena / Johnson rag / Seems like old times / Show me the way to go home / Auld lang syne
CD ________ CDSIV 1141
Horatio Nelson / Jul '95 / Disc

UNCOLLECTED 1950, THE (Lombardo, Guy & His Royal Canadians)
CD ________ HCD 187
Hindsight / Jan '95 / Jazz Music / Target/ BMG

London Adventist Choral

DEEP RIVER
CD ________ PDSM 1
Paradisum / Aug '95 / Grapevine/ PolyGram

London Adventist Chorale

STEAL AWAY (London Adventist Chorale & Ruby Philogene)
CD ________ CDZ 5697072
EMI Classics / Apr '97 / EMI

London After Midnight

KISS
CD ________ EFA 015662
Apocalyptic Vision / Mar '96 / Cargo / Plastic Head / SRD

PSYCHO MAGNET
CD ________ EFA 015702
Apocalyptic Vision / Sep '96 / Cargo / Plastic Head / SRD

London All Stars Steel ...

LATIN AMERICAN HITS (London All Stars Steel Orchestra)
CD ________ EUCD 1161
ARC / '91 / ADA / ARC Music

London Beat

HARMONY
You bring the sun / Lover you send me colours / That's how I feel about you / Some lucky guy / Secret garden / Give a gift to yourself / Harmony / All born equal / Rainbow ride / Keeping the memories alive / Sea of tranquility
CD ________ 74321110602
RCA / Apr '94 / BMG

IN THE BLOOD
It's in the blood / Getcha ya ya / She broke my heart (in 36 places) / She said she loves me / No woman, no cry / This is your life / I've been thinking about you / Better love / In an I love you mood / You love and learn / Crying in the rain / Step inside my shoes
CD ________ 74321250352
RCA / Aug '95 / BMG

London Brompton Oratory ...

FESTIVAL OF NINE LESSONS & CAROLS (London Brompton Oratory Choir)
Once in Royal David's City / Adam lay y bounden / Of the Father's heart begotten / Great and mighty wonder / Gabriel's message / O little town / In dulci Jubilo / Personet Hodie / Adeste Fideles / Fantasia dulci Jubilo / This is the truth / I wonder as I wander / Alleluya a new work is come on hand / There is a flower / Rocking / Away in a manger / In the bleak midwinter / Hark the Herald Angels sing

CD CDCFP 5017
Classics For Pleasure / Oct '96 / EMI

London Community Gospel ...

GOSPEL GREATS (London Community Gospel Choir)
Swing low, sweet chariot / Precious Lord, amazing grace / Nobody knows the trouble I've seen / What a friend we have in Jesus / Kumbaya / Count your blessings / Love lifted me / When the saints go marching in / There is a green hill far away / Oh happy day / Old rugged cross
CD CDMFP 5731
Music For Pleasure / Apr '91 / EMI

London Drive

AWARE
CD 1333CD
Infinity / May '96 / Plastic Head

London Festival Orchestra

SILENT NIGHT
CD CNCD 5933
Disky / Nov '92 / Disky / THE

London Funk Allstars

FLESH EATING DISCO ZOMBIES VS THE BIONIC HOOKERS FROM MARS
Introduction / Old skool reunion / There's only one F in funk / Way out / Junkies bad trip / Allstars theme / Love is what we need / Knee deep in the beats Pt.1 / Never can get enough / Flesh eating disco zombies Vs the Bionic Hookers from Mars / UJ / Mad love / Chase / Give it to me raw / How to be a Ninja in one easy lesson
CD ZENCD 024
Ninja Tune / Aug '96 / Kudos / Pinnacle / Prime / Vital

LONDON FUNK VOL.1
Sure shot / Coolin' out / Booyakka / Six million dollar man / Listen to the beat / So good / Fetch / What's in the basket / Represent / Funky sweater / Chicago / Everybody get funky / Chun Li vs. Wah Wah Man / Wikki's revenge / Good life / Body rock / Can ya understand / Bang boogie boogie
CD ZENCD 016
Ninja Tune / May '95 / Kudos / Pinnacle / Prime / Vital

London Gabrieli Brass ...

UNDER THE INFLUENCE OF JAZZ (London Gabrieli Brass Ensemble)
CD CDTTD 569
Timeless Traditional / Mar '92 / Jazz Music / New Note/Pinnacle

London Jazz Composers ...

THREE PIECES FOR ORCHESTRA (London Jazz Composers Orchestra)
CD INTAKTCD 045
Intakt / May '97 / Cadillac

London Jazz Orchestra

DANCE FOR HUMAN FOLK (2CD Set)
CD Set HHCD 1016/17
Hot House / May '96 / Cadillac / Harmonia Mundi / Wellard

London, Jimmy

JIMMY LONDON COLLECTION, THE
CD BETA 1004CD
Beta / Jul '96 / Jet Star

London, Julie

ALL THROUGH THE NIGHT (Songs Of Cole Porter)
I've got you under my skin / You do something to me / Get out of town / All through the night / So in love / At long last love / Easy to love / My heart belongs to daddy / Every time we say goodbye / In the still of the night
CD JASCD 308
Jasmine / May '94 / Conifer/BMG / Hot Shot / TKO Magnum

AROUND MIDNIGHT/JULIE AT HOME
You'd be so nice to come home to / Lonesome road / They didn't believe me / By myself / Thrill is gone / You've gone / Goodbye / Sentimental journey / Give me the simple life / You stepped out of a dream / Let there be love / Everything happens to me / Around midnight / Lonely in Paris / Misty / Black coffee / Lush life / In the wee small hours of the morning / Don't smoke in bed / You and the night and the music / Something cool / How about me / But not for me / Party's over
CD CTMCD 100
EMI / Nov '96 / EMI

CRY ME A RIVER
Cry me a river / Boy on a dolphin / Saddle the wind / Must be catchin' / Come on-a my house / Broken hearted melody / Love letters / Besame mucho / Vaya con dios / I'm coming back to you / When snowflakes fall in the Summer / Say wonderful things / End of the world / Fascination / Second time around / More / Girl talk / I left my heart in San Francisco / Good life / Our day will come
CD CDSL 8267
Music For Pleasure / Nov '95 / EMI

EMI PRESENTS THE MAGIC OF JULIE LONDON
Cry me a river / Boy on a dolphin / Saddle the wind / Must be catchin' / Come on-a my house / Broken hearted melody / Love letters / Besame mucho / Vaya con dios / I'm coming back to you / When snowflakes fall in the summer / Say wonderful things / End of the world / Fascination / Second time around / More / Girl talk / I left my heart in San Francisco / Good life / Our day will come
CD CDMFP 6375
Music For Pleasure / May '97 / EMI

END OF THE WORLD/NICE GIRLS DON'T STAY FOR BREAKFAST
End of the world / I wanna be around / Call me irresponsible / Our day will come / I left my heart in San Francisco / Fly me to the moon / Days of wine and roses / I remember you / My coloring book / Chances are / Slightly out of tune (desafinado) / Good life / Nice girls don't stay for breakfast / When I grow too old to dream / I've got a crush on you / Everything I have is yours / You made me love you / Baby, won't you please come home / I didn't know what time it was / Give a little whistle / I surrender, dear / You go to my head / There will never be another you / Mickey Mouse march
CD CTMCD 114
EMI / Mar '97 / EMI

JULIE IS HER NAME VOL.1 & 2
CD CDP 7998042
Liberty / Oct '92 / EMI

SWING ME AN OLD SONG
CD MAR 040
Marginal / Jun '97 / Greyhound

London Philharmonic ...

ABIDE WITH ME (London Philharmonic Orchestra)
Pomp and circumstance / Zadok the priest / Bridal chorus / Londonderry air (Danny Boy) / Holy city / All people that on earth do dwell / Mine eyes have seen the glory / Rock of ages / Eternal father strong to save / Jerusalem / God that madest Earth and heaven / Hallelujah chorus / For unto us a child is born / For the wings of a dove / Abide with me / Brother James' air / Praise my soul the King of Heaven / God our help in ages past
CD 3036001022
Carlton / Apr '97 / Carlton

POP LEGENDS (Clark, Louis & The London Philharmonic Orchestra)
Oh pretty woman / You've lost that loving feeling / Dancing queen / Dancing in the dark / Will you still love me tomorrow / She's not there / When will I see you again / You can't hurry love / River deep, mountain high / MacArthur Park
CD WB 877072
Disky / Mar '97 / Disky / THE

TORVILL & DEAN'S FIRE AND ICE (London Philharmonic Orchestra)
Fire and Ice: Prelude/ Fire world / Ice world / Meeting / Ice court / Mask dance / Ice warriors / Skating lesson / Fire and ice(love duet) / Ambush / Lament/war dance / Melting/battle / After the war / Dance of hope
CD CASTCD 7
First Night / Nov '86 / Pinnacle

London Ragtime Orchestra

EASY WINNERS
Easy winners / Bright star blues / Mr. Jelly Lord / Pleasant moments / Do doodle oom / Ory's creole trombone / Magnetic rag / Louisiana swing / Solace / Black bottom stomp / Sunflower slow drag / Silver leaf rag / Wolverines / Kiss me sweet / Cornet chop suey / Heliotrope bouquet / Chant
CD LROCD 501
LRO / Jan '93 / Cadillac / Jazz Music

London Sound & Art Orchestra

48 HITS FROM THE AGE OF POP VOL.1 (3CD Set)
CD Set 290336
Column / Dec '96 / Total/BMG

48 HITS FROM THE AGE OF POP VOL.2 (3CD Set)
CD Set 290337
Column / Dec '96 / Total/BMG

London Studio Orchestra

MUSIC OF MORRICONE
CD ENTCD 269
Entertainers / Jul '88 / Target/BMG

London Symphony Orchestra

CLASSIC ROCK COUNTDOWN
Final countdown / Take my breath away / You can call me Al / Lady in red / Separate lives / We don't need another hero / It's a sin / She's not there / Don't give up / You're the voice / Abbey road medley / Golden slumbers / Carry that weight / End
CD 4604822
CBS / Mar '90 / Sony

CLASSIC ROCK VOL.2 (The Second Movement)
Eve of the war / Pinball wizard / Hey Joe / Day in the life / Question / Space oddity / God only knows / River deep, mountain high / American trilogy / Don't cry for me Argentina
CD TCD 6002
Telstar / Dec '88 / BMG

CLASSIC ROCK VOL.3 (Rhapsody In Black)
Fanfare intro-rhapsody in black / Reach out, I'll be there / You keep me hangin' on / First time ever I saw your face / Superstition / Standing in the shadows of love / Don't leave me this way / Tears of a clown / Rasputin / I heard it through the grapevine / Ain't no mountain high enough
CD TCD 6003
Telstar / Nov '86 / BMG

CLASSIC ROCK VOL.4 (Rock Classics)
Get back / Layla / Stairway to heaven / Baker Street / Another brick in the wall pt 2 / Jet / Ruby Tuesday / I don't like Mondays / Bright eyes / Hey Jude
CD TCD 6004
Telstar / Dec '88 / BMG

CLASSIC ROCK VOL.5 (Rock Symphonies)
Born to run / For your love / Chariots of fire / House of the rising sun / You really got me / MacArthur park / Eye of the tiger / Vienna / She's out of my life / Pictures of Lily / Since you've been gone / Gloria
CD TCD 6005
Telstar / Dec '88 / BMG

POWER OF CLASSIC ROCK (London Symphony Orchestra & London Choral Society)
Two tribes, relax: *London Symphony Orchestra* / I want to know what love is: *London Symphony Orchestra* / Drive: *London Symphony Orchestra* / Purple rain: *London Symphony Orchestra* / Time after time: *London Symphony Orchestra* / Born in the USA: *London Symphony Orchestra* / Power of love: *London Symphony Orchestra* / Thriller: *London Symphony Orchestra* / Total eclipse of the heart: *London Symphony Orchestra* / Hello: *London Symphony Orchestra* / Modern Girl: *London Symphony Orchestra* / Dancing in the dark: *London Symphony Orchestra*
CD 4634022
Epic / Feb '89 / Sony

POWER OF CLASSIC ROCK/LIVING YEARS/COUNTDOWN (3CD Set)
Two tribes/Relax / Drive / Purple rain / Time after time / I want to know what love is / Born in the USA/Dancing in the dark / Power of love / Thriller / Total eclipse of the heart / Hello / Modern girl / I want it all / Eternal flame / Against all odds / I still haven't found what I'm looking for / Sailing / Eloise / Smooth criminal / Clouds over aysgarth/In the air tonight / Prelude in motion/ The first time / Groovy kind of love / One moment in time / Living years / Final countdown / Take my breath away / You can call me Al / Lady in red / Separate lives / It's a sin / She's not there / Don't give up / You're the voice / Golden slumbers / Carry that weight / End
CD Set 4775172
Columbia / Oct '94 / Sony

ULTIMATE SYMPHONIC ROCK COLLECTION (3CD Set) (London Symphony Orchestra & London Pop Choir)
CD Set COLBX 002
Focus / Feb '97 / Koch

London Theatre Orchestra

NATIONAL ANTHEMS OF THE WORLD
God save the Queen (Great Britain) / Star spangled banner (USA) / La Marseillaise (France) / Deutcshland lied (Germany) / Inno di mameli (Italy) / Mazurek dabrowskiego (Poland) / Marcha real (Spain) / Segnorizo apo tin kopsi (Greece) / Hataikvah (Israel) / O Canada (Canada) / Kiminga yowa chiyoni (Japan) / Wilhemus van nassouwe (Holland) / Scotland the Brave (Scotland) / Amthran na bh fiann (Ireland) / Land of my fathers (Wales) / European anthem (Beethoven's 9th Symphony)
CD EMPRCD 581
Emporio / Oct '95 / Disc

London Trombone Quartet

SOME OF OUR BEST FRIENDS
Crack up / Talk time / Until / Not doon there / See you on the 8th / Eminance / Don't go changing / Off the rails / Welcome / Lost and found / Reverse gear
CD ASCCD 11
ASC / Nov '96 / Cadillac / New Note/ Pinnacle

London Welsh Male Voice ...

BEAUTIFUL SONG, THE (London Welsh Male Voice Choir)
Sailors chorus / Conspirators chorus / Sequidille / Yfory / Old woman / Ai am fod haul yn machlud / Suo gan / Love could I only tell thee / Aus der traube / Delilah / Bro aber / How green was my valley / Saint Saens organ symphony / You'll never walk alone / Soon ah will be done / Give me Jesus / Deep harmony / Mae d'eisiau di bob awr / American trilogy / Morte criste / Blaenwern
CD SCD 2131
Sain / Feb '97 / ADA / Direct / Greyhound

IN BRIGHT ARRAY ASSEMBLE (1000 Welsh Voices)
Roman war song / Soldier's farewell / Pilgrims / O Gymru / Myfanwy / Crimond / Tydi a roddast / Rhythm of life / Rose / Love changes everything / Casatschok / Dry bones / Y nefoedd / Timeless moment / Y dref wen / Where shall I be / An American triology / Finlandia / Bryn myrddin / Cwm rhondda
CD QPRZ 015D
Polyphonic / Jan '95 / Complete/Pinnacle

Lone Justice

LONE JUSTICE
East of Eden / After the flood / Ways to be wicked / Don't toss us away / Working late / Pass it on / Wait till we get home / Soap, soup and salvation / You are the light / Sweet sweet baby
CD GED 24060
Geffen / Nov '96 / BMG

SHELTER
I found love / Shelter / Reflected / Beacon / Wheels / Belfry / Dreams come true / Gift / Inspiration / Dixie storms
CD GED 24122
Geffen / Nov '96 / BMG

Lone Star

LONE STAR
She said / Lonely soldier / Flying in the reel / Spaceships / New day / Million stars / Illusions
CD 4844422
Columbia / '96 / Sony
CD 07863666422
RCA / Jun '96 / BMG

Lonely, Roy

ACTION SHOTS
CD USMCD 1024
Marilyn / Sep '93 / Pinnacle

Lonely Stranded Band

LONELY STRANDED BAND
CD CICD 116
CICD / Apr '96 / ADA

Lonesome Pine Fiddlers

WINDY MOUNTAIN
Pain in my heart / Lonesome sad and blue / Don't forget me / Will I meet Mother in Heaven / You broke your promise / I'm left alone / Nobody cares (not even you) / Twenty one years / My brown eyed darling / You left me to cry / That's why you left me so blue / I'll never make you blue / Honky tonk blues / You're so good / I'll never change my mind / Dirty dishes blues / Lonesome pine breakdown / Five string rag / Baby you're cheatin' / I'm feeling for you (but I can't reach you) / Some kinda sorry / Windy mountain / No curb service / New set of blues / There's just one you
CD ECD 501
Rollercoaster / Apr '92 / Rollercoaster / Swift

Lonesome River Band

OLD COUNTRY TOWN
CD SHCD 3818
Sugar Hill / Mar '94 / ADA / CM / Direct / Koch / Roots

ONE STEP FORWARD
CD SHCD 3848
Sugar Hill / Jul '96 / ADA / CM / Direct / Koch / Roots

Lonesome Standard Time

LONESOME AS IT GETS
CD SHCD 3839
Sugar Hill / Oct '95 / ADA / CM / Direct / Koch / Roots

LONESOME STANDARD TIME
Lonesome standard time / Delta queen / You can't do wrong and get by / Fields of home / Lower on the hog / Castellion springs / Down the road to gloryland / Kentucky king / Little Cecil / Old river rock / Highway 40 blues / Lonesome dove / You can't take it with you when you go
CD SHCD 3802
Sugar Hill / Sep '92 / ADA / CM / Direct / Koch / Roots

MIGHTY LONESOME
CD SHCD 3816
Sugar Hill / Mar '94 / ADA / CM / Direct / Koch / Roots

Lonesome Strangers

LONESOME STRANGERS
CD HCD 8016
Hightone / Sep '94 / ADA / Koch

Lonesome Sundown

BEEN GONE TOO LONG
They call me sundown / One more night / Louisiana lover man / Dealin' from the bottom / Midnight blues again / Just got to know / Black cat bone / I betcha / You don't miss your water / If you ain't been to Houston
CD HCD 8031
Hightone / Jun '94 / ADA / Koch

I'M A MOJO MAN
Gonna stick to you baby / I'm a mojo man / I stood by / Don't go / Lonely, lonely me / You know I love you / Learn to treat me better / Lonesome lonely blues / I'm glad she's mine / Sundown blues / My home ain't there / What you wanna do it for / I woke up crying (oh what a dream) / When I had, I didn't need (now I need, don't have a dime) / I'm a samplin' man / Hoodoo woman blues / I'm a young man / It's easy when you know how / I got a broken heart / Don't say a word / Lost without love / Leave my money alone / My home is a prison / Lonesome whistler
CD CDCHD 556
Ace / Feb '95 / Pinnacle

Loney, Roy

SCIENTIFIC BOMBS AWAY, THE (Loney, Roy & Phantom Movers)
CD AIM 1025CD
Aim / Oct '93 / ADA / Direct / Jazz Music

Long Decline

LONG DECLINE, THE
CD OVER 61CD
Overground / Apr '97 / Shellshock/Disc / SRD

Long Fin Killie

HOUDINI
Man Ray / How I blew it with Houdini / Homo Erectus / Heads of dead surfers / Montgomery / Love smothers allergy / Hollywood gem / Lamberton lamplighter / Corngold / Idiot hormone / Rockethead on mandatory surveillance / Flower carrier / Unconscious gangs of men
CD PURECD 047
Too Pure / Jun '95 / Vital

VALENTINO
Godiva / Pele / Kitten heels / 1,000 Wounded astronauts / Hands and lips / Valentino / Coward / Girlfriend / Matador / Cop / Cupid
CD PURECD 054
Too Pure / May '96 / Vital

Long Hind Legs

LONG HIND LEGS
CD KRS 274CD
Kill Rock Stars / Jan '97 / Cargo / Greyhound / Plastic Head

Long, Larry

HERE I STAND: ELDERS' WISDOM, CHILDREN'S SONG (Long, Larry & Youth/Elders Of Rural Alabama)
CD SFWCD 45050
Smithsonian Folkways / Aug '96 / ADA / Cadillac / CM / Direct / Koch

IT TAKES A LOT OF PEOPLE (A Tribute To Woody Guthrie)
CD FF 70508
Flying Fish / Oct '89 / ADA / CM / Direct / Roots

RUN FOR FREEDOM/SWEET THUNDER
Run for freedom / Grandma's penny sale / It feels OK / Blue highway / Sacred black hills / Anna Mae / Michael / American hymn / Grizzly bear / Mad about the way things are / Light a candle / Your love / Road to freedom / Water in the rain / Sweet thunder / Love will lay hatred down
CD CDFF 655
Flying Fish / Jun '97 / ADA / CM / Direct / Roots

Long, P.W.

WE DIDN'T SEE YOU ON SUNDAY (Long, P.W. & Reelfoot)
CD TG 178CD
Touch & Go / Jun '97 / SRD

Long River Train

ARGUMENTS FOR DRINKING
CD DEDCD 031
Dedicated / Apr '97 / BMG / Vital

Long Ryders

METALLIC BO
CD SID 001
Prima / Apr '95 / Direct

NATIVE SONS
I had a dream / Tell it to the judge on Sunday / Wreck of the 909 / Ivory tower / Too close to the lights / Still get by / Final wild son / (Sweet) mental revenge / Never got to meet the Mom / Fair game / Run Dusty run
CD DIAB 821
Diabolo / Jun '96 / Pinnacle

STATE OF OUR UNION
Looking for Lewis and Clarke / Lights of downtown / WDIA / Mason-Dixon line / Here comes that train again / Years long ago / Good times tomorrow, hard times today / Two kinds of love / You just can't ride the box cars anymore / Capturing the flag / State of my union
CD SID 003
Prima / Mar '95 / Direct

TWO FISTED TALES
Gunslinger man / I want you bad / Stitch in time / Light gets in the way / Prairie fire / Baby's in toyland / Long short story / Man of misery / Harriet Tubman's gonna carry me home / For the rest of my days / Spectacular fall
CD SID 005
Prima / Mar '96 / Direct

Long Tall Texans

ACES AND EIGHTS
Notice me / Nothing left but bone / Sister / I wish / Lip service / Everyday / Bloody / (Don't go back to) Rockville / Border radio / Tomorrow today / Innocent look / Piece of your love
CD CDMPSYCH 016
Anagram / Aug '97 / Cargo / Pinnacle

BEST OF THE TEXAS BEAT
One more time / Non stop lovin' / Nine hundred miles / Saints and sinners / Right first time / Poison / Get up and go / Off my mind / Should I stay or should I go / Indians / Texas beat / Gotta go / Get back wet back / Something's cookin' / Get your teeth out of my jugular / Don't I know it / Cairo / Shiver street / I get so excited / Heatwave / Breakaway / Alabama song / Smilin' eyes / Notice me / Bloody
CD CDMPSYCHO 10
Anagram / Jan '96 / Cargo / Pinnacle

IN WITHOUT KNOCKING
Poison / Rockin' Crazy / Mad About You / Saints and sinners / Gotta Go / Texas Beat / Right First Time / Rock 'n' Roll (Part 2)/ Endless Sleep / My Babe / Texas Boogie / Wreckin' me / Who's Sorry Now / Your Own Way / Get Back Wet Back / Long tall Texan / Get Up And Go / Paradise / My Idea Of Heaven / Indians / Off My Mind / Bloody / Dance Of The Headhunters / Should I stay or should I go
CD RAGECD 109
Rage / Aug '92 / Nervous / TKO Magnum

SINGING TO THE MOON
Singing to the moon / Rock Bottom Blues / Klub Foot Shuffle / Suicide At The Seaside / Winding me up / Reactor / Witch Hunting / Singing To The Moon / Axe To Grind / Smiling eyes / Alcohol / Indian Reservation / Nine Days Wonder / Senses six and seven / Alabama Song
CD RAGECD 108
Rage / Apr '91 / Nervous / TKO Magnum

Longjian, Tan

TAN LONGJIAN
CD OMCD 61
Olarin Musiikki Oy / Mar '96 / ADA / Direct

Longoria, Valerio

CABALLO VIEJO
CD ARHCD 336
Arhoolie / Apr '95 / ADA / Cadillac / Direct

TEXAS CONJUNTO PIONEER
CD ARHCD 358
Arhoolie / Apr '95 / ADA / Cadillac / Direct

Longpigs

SUN IS OFTEN OUT, THE
Lost myself / She said / Far / On and on / Happy again / All hype / Sally dances / Jesus Christ / Dozen wicked words / Elvis / Over our bodies
CD MUMCD 9602
Mother / Jun '96 / PolyGram

Longthorne, Joe

ESPECIALLY FOR YOU
CD CDSR 064
Telstar / May '95 / BMG

I WISH YOU LOVE
Young girl / Lady blue / So deep is the night / If I only had time / Mary in the morning / Say it with flowers / Where are you now / Runaway / Over and over / True love / My funny valentine / Never say never / Walk in the room / I wish you love
CD CEDMC 3662
EMI / Oct '93 / EMI

JOE LONGTHORNE SONGBOOK, THE
You're my world / My prayer / Always on my mind / My mother's eyes / Just loving you / It's only make believe / To all the girls I've loved before / End of the world / It was almost like a song / Hurt / Answer me / Danny boy / Don't laugh at me / When your old wedding ring was new
CD CDSR 059
Telstar / Aug '94 / BMG

LIVE AT THE ROYAL ALBERT HALL
Passing strangers / Mary in the morning / If I only had time / What's going on / Unchained melody / It's not unusual / To all the girls I've loved before / Daniel / I just called to say I love you / Stand by me / This is my life / I believe I'm going to love you / Whole lotta shakin' goin' on / Great balls of fire / Life on Mars / Lady is a tramp / Perfect love / You're the first, my last, my everything / Wind beneath my wings / Born free / Portrait of my life / If I never sing another song / Somewhere
CD CDDPR 134
Music For Pleasure / Dec '94 / EMI

Look People

BOOGASM
CD OUT 1122
Brake Out / Nov '94 / Direct

Looking East

LOOKING EAST
CD CDLDL 1258
Lochshore / Jun '97 / ADA / Direct / Duncans

Loomis, Hamilton

HAMILTON BLUES
CD HAMBONECD 301
Ham Bone / Jul '95 / Hot Shot

Loop

DUAL
Collision / Crawling / Thief of fire / Thief (Motherfucker) / Black sun / Circle grave / Mother sky / Got to get it over
CD REACTORCD 5
Reactor / Mar '94 / Vital

FADE OUT
Black sun / This is where you end / Fever knife / Torched / Fade out / Pulse / Vision stain / Got to get it over / Collision / Crawling heart / Thief of fire / Thief (motherfucker) / Mother sky
CD REACTORCD 4
Reactor / Mar '94 / Vital

GILDED ETERNITY, A
Vapour / Afterglow / Nail with burn / Blood / Breathe into me / From centre to wave / Be here now / Shot with a diamond / Nail with burn (burn out) / Arc-lite (sonar)
CD BBL 27CD
Beggars Banquet / Sep '95 / RTM/Disc / Warner Music

WOLF FLOW - JOHN PEEL SESSIONS 1987-90
Soundhead / Straight to you / Rocket USA / Pulse / This is where you end / Collision / From centre to wave / Afterglow / Sunburst
CD REACTORCD 3
Reactor / Mar '94 / Vital

WORLD IN YOUR EYES, THE
Sixteen dreams / Head on / Burning world / Rocket USA / Spinning / Deep hit / I'll take you there / Brittle head girl / Burning prisma / Spinning spun out
CD REACTORCD 2
Reactor / Mar '94 / Vital

Loop Guru

3RD CHAMBER
3rd Chamber parts 1-6
CD GURU 100CD
North South / Nov '96 / Pinnacle

AMRITA
CD GURU 200CD
North South / Mar '96 / Pinnacle

CATALOGUE OF DESIRES
CD GURU 300CD
North South / Apr '96 / Pinnacle

DUN-YA
CD NATCD 31
Nation / Apr '94 / RTM/Disc

PEEL SESSIONS, THE
CD SFRCD 139
Strange Fruit / Jul '96 / Pinnacle

Loopuyt, Marc

ORIENTS OF THE LUTE, THE (2CD Set)
CD Set 926742
BUDA / Jun '97 / Discovery

SUSPIRO DEL MORO
CD 926252
BUDA / Mar '96 / Discovery

Loos

FUNDAMENTAL
CD GEESTCD 10
Geest Gronden / Oct '87 / Cadillac

Loos, Charles

CHARLES LOOS AND ALI RYERSON (Loos, Charles & Ali Ryerson)
CD EMD 89012
Candid / May '89 / Cadillac / Direct / Jazz Music / Koch / Wellard

Loose

ESPECIALLY FOR YOU
CD LAZEYE 209CD
Lazy Eye / Oct '95 / Plastic Head

Loose Diamonds

BURNING DAYLIGHT
CD DOSCD 7001
Dos / May '93 / ADA / CM / Direct

NEW LOCATION
CD DOS 7010
Dos / Oct '95 / ADA / CM / Direct

Loose Ends

LOOK HOW LONG
Look how long / Don't you ever (try to change me) / Time is ticking / Love's got me / Don't be a fool / Cheap talk / Love controversy / Try my love / Hold tight / I don't need to love / Symptons of love
CD CDVIP 186
Virgin VIP / Apr '97 / EMI

REAL CHUCKEEBOO, THE
Watching you / (There's no) gratitude / Real chuckeeboo / You've just got to have it all / Life / What goes around / Easier said than done / Hungry / Is it ever too late / Remote control / Too much / Johnny broadhead
CD CDV 2528
10 / Jun '88 / EMI

SO WHERE ARE YOU
Magic touch / New horizon / If my lovin' makes you hot / So where are you / Golden years / Hangin' on a string / Give it all you got / Sweetest pain / You can't stop the rain / Silent talking
CD CDV 2340
10 / Feb '87 / EMI

TIGHTEN UP VOL.1
Magic touch / Gonna make you mine / Hangin' on a string / Choose me (rescue me) / Little spice / Slow down / Don't worry / Love's got me / Don't be a fool / Watching you / Tell me what you want / Ooh you make me feel / Hangin' on a string (original)
CD DIXCD 112
10 / Jul '92 / EMI

ZAGORA
Stay a little while child / Be thankful (Mama's song) / Slow down / Ooh you make me feel / Just a minute / Who are you / I can't wait / Nights of pleasure / Let's get back to love / Rainbow / Take the 'A' train
CD CDV 2384
10 / Jun '86 / EMI

Loosegoats

MEXICAN CAR IN A SOUTHERN FIELD, A
Slotmachines and busted dreams / War in my course / F as in dumped / Really Texan modesty / Country crook / It's so K / Ten speed / Stop drop-in inn / Broken babe / Mule habit / Destined to be a b-side / Independently correct / Surburban slut / Texan modesty / Telephone juncture / Slut / Molly coddle / Small planet / Freeloadin' / Towel
CD STAR 55202
Startracks / Aug '97 / RTM/Disc

Lopato, David

INSIDE OUTSIDE
CD EMY 1322
Enemy / Sep '92 / Grapevine/PolyGram

Lopes, Carlos

DREAMSVILLE
CD FMJXD 189
FM / Mar '93 / Revolver / Sony

Lopez, Belisario

PRUEBA MI SAZON 1942-1948 (Lopez, Belisario Orquesta)
CD TCD 069
Tumbao Cuban Classics / Jul '96 / Discovery

Lopez, Francisco

UNTITLED 74
CD TECHNETIUM 43
Table Of The Elements / Jul '97 / Cargo

Lopez, Isidro

EL INDIO
CD ARHCD 363
Arhoolie / Apr '95 / ADA / Cadillac / Direct

Lopez, Israel

DOS (Lopez, Israel 'Cachao')
CD CDGR 152
Charly / May '97 / Koch

MORE LEGENDARY DESCARGA SESSIONS (Lopez, Israel 'Cachao')
CD _____ CCD 510
Caney / Jul '96 / ADA / Discovery

Lopez, Juan

EL REY DE LA REDOVA
CD _____ ARHCD 407
Arhoolie / Apr '95 / ADA / Cadillac / Direct

Lopez, Oscar

HEAT
Forgive me / Thinking of you / Senitimento / Fire and fury / Fiesta latina / Distancia / Those times / Step by step / Way I am / Flight of the flamingo / Milonguita / Morenita / My heart in Rio / Tornado de amor / Desperate love
CD _____ ND 63040
Narada / Jul '97 / ADA / New Note/Pinnacle

Lopez, Trini

LA BAMBA (28 Greatest Hits)
CD _____ ENTCD 279
Entertainers / Oct '88 / Target/BMG

LEGENDS IN MUSIC
CD _____ LECD 098
Wisepack / Sep '94 / Conifer/BMG / THE

TRINI LOPEZ
CD _____ GRF 189
Tring / Jan '93 / Tring

TRINI LOPEZ
La bamba / If I had a hammer / Guantanamera / Blowin' in the wind / Adalita / America / Lemon tree / Shame and scandal / What'd I say / Bye bye blondie / Kansas city / El condor pasa / Amor, amor, amor / This land is your land / Quizas, quizas, quizas / Perfidia / Gotta travel on / Down by the riverside / Marianne / When the saints go marching in / Volare / Besame mucho
CD _____ 399531
Koch Presents / Jun '97 / Koch

TRINI LOPEZ LIVE
America / If I had a hammer / Bye bye blackbird / Cielito Lindo / This land is your land / What'd I say / La Bamba / Granada / Bye bye Blondie / Nie meir ohne (German) / Lebewohl daisy girl / Long ago / Folk medley / Unchain my heart
CD _____ BCD 15427
Bear Family / May '89 / Direct / Rollercoaster / Swift

VERY BEST OF TRINI LOPEZ, THE
CD _____ WMCD 5647
Woodford Music / Aug '92 / THE

Lopretti, Jose

CANDOMBE
CD _____ CHR 70013
Challenge / Apr '95 / ADA / Direct / Jazz Music / Wellard

Lorber, Alan

LOTUS PALACE, THE (Lorber, Alan Orchestra)
Up up and away / Where / Mas que nada / Echo of the night / Lucy in the sky with diamonds / Look of love / Flute thing / Hang on to a dream / Within you without you / Roopaka dha teri dhin dhin / Serpent and the hawk / Hollow in the wind / Where / Djellaba / I heard the rain
CD _____ CDWIKD 172
Big Beat / May '97 / Pinnacle

Lorber, Jeff

STATE OF GRACE
CD _____ 5315552
Verve/Forecast / Jul '96 / PolyGram

WORTH WAITING FOR
Rain song / Underground / Yellowstone / Punta del este / Lost with you / Worth waiting for / High wire / Wavelength / Columbus Ave / Do what it takes / Jazzery
CD _____ 5179982
Verve/Forecast / Jan '94 / PolyGram

Lorca, Federico Garcia

CANCIONES POPULARES ESPANOLAS
CD _____ J 105CD
Sonifolk / Jun '94 / ADA / CM

POETRY PUT TO SONG
CD _____ 7996502
Hispavox / Jan '95 / ADA

L'Orchestre Noir

CANTOS
Canto / Prologue / March of angels / Te arma lucis / Down these mean streets / Man must go / Assasins and other friends / Vetus et novum / In hell's mouth / Lake of bodies - Aqua morta / In Europe / Epilogue
CD _____ TURSA 013CD
Tursa / Mar '97 / World Serpent

Lord Belial

KISS THE GOAT
CD _____ NFR 010CD
No Fashion / May '95 / Plastic Head

Lord Blakie

RAW KAISO VOL.1 (Lord Blakie & Black Prince/Mighty Zandolie)
Introduction: *Lord Blakie* / Steelband clash: *Lord Blakie* / Maria: *Lord Blakie* / Hold de pussy: *Lord Blakie* / Calypso horrors: *Black Prince* / Friday evening: *Black Prince* / One lifetime ent nuff: *Black Prince* / Fry balls: *Black Prince* / De letter: *Black Prince* / Introduction to Mighty Zandolie: *Mighty Zandolie* / Iron man: *Mighty Zandolie* / Merchant of Venice: *Mighty Zandolie* / Whip: *Mighty Zandolie* / Man family: *Mighty Zandolie* / Stickman: *Mighty Zandolie*
CD _____ ROUCD 5074
Rounder / Feb '97 / ADA / CM / Direct

Lord Creator

DON'T STAY OUT LATE
CD _____ VPCD 2046
VP / Apr '96 / Greensleeves / Jet Star / Total/BMG

Lord High Fixers

WHEN
CD _____ ANDA 199
Au-Go-Go / Feb '97 / Cargo / Greyhound / Plastic Head

Lord, Jon

BEFORE I FORGET
Chance on a feeling / Tender babes / Hollywood rock and roll / Bach onto this / Before I forget / Say it's alright / Burntwood / Where are you / Lady / For a friend / Pavanne / Going home
CD _____ RPM 126
RPM / Mar '94 / Pinnacle

Lord Kitchener

STILL ESCALATING
CD _____ JW 055CD
Soca / Feb '94 / Jet Star

Lord, Mary Lou

MARY LOU LORD
Lights are changing / Helsinki / That kind of girl / He'd be a diamond / Bridge / I'm talking to you / His indie world / Speeding motorcycle
CD _____ KRS 238CD
Kill Rock Stars / Jan '95 / Cargo / Greyhound / Plastic Head

Lord Tanamo

IN THE MOOD FOR SKA
CD _____ CDTRL 313
Trojan / Mar '94 / Direct / Jet Star

Lordryk

LORDRYK
CD _____ VR 03CD
Vroe / Apr '96 / ADA

Lords Of The Underground

HERE COME THE LORDS
Here come the Lords / From da bricks / Funky child / Keep it underground / Check it / Grave digga / Lords prayer / Flow on (new symphony) / Madd skillz / Psycho / Chief rocka / Sleep for dinner / LOTUG (Lords Of The Underground) / Lord Jazz hit me one time (make it funky) / What's going on
CD _____ CTCD 41
Cooltempo / May '94 / EMI

KEEPERS OF THE FUNK
Intro / Ready or not / Tic toc / Keepers of the funk / Steam from da knot / What I'm after / Faith / Neva faded / No pain / Frustrated / Yes y'all / What U see / Outro
CD _____ CDCHR 6088
Cooltempo / Oct '94 / EMI

Lorelei

EVERYONE MUST TOUCH THE...
CD _____ SLR 044CD
Slumberland / Dec '96 / Cargo

HEADSTRONG
CD _____ LDL 1213CD
Lochshore / Jun '94 / ADA / Direct / Duncans

PROGRESSION
CD _____ CDLDL 1236
Lochshore / Nov '95 / ADA / Direct / Duncans

Lorellei

SPIRITUS BREATH OF LIFE
CD _____ SP 7156CD
Soundings Of The Planet / Jul '96 / Else

Lorenz, Trey

TREY LORENZ
Someone to hold / Photograph of Mary / Just to be to you / Run back to me / Always in love / Wipe all my tears away / Baby I'm in heaven / It only hurts when it's love / How can I say goodbye / Find a way / When troubles come
CD _____ 4721722
Epic / Dec '92 / Sony

Loretta's Doll

XXI DEGREES
CD _____ WSCD 004
World Serpent / Oct '96 / World Serpent

L'Orient Imaginaire

LABYRINTH (L'Orient Imaginaire/ Vladimir Ivanoff)
CD _____ 0630117562
Teldec Classics / Jul '96 / Warner Music

YEHUDI (Jewish Music From The Seraglio) (L'Orient Imaginaire/Vladimir Ivanoff)
CD _____ 0630116992
Teldec Classics / Aug '96 / Warner Music

Los Alfa 8

LA SALSA LLEGO
CD _____ TUMICD 029
Tumi / '92 / Discovery / Stern's

Los Alhama

FLAMENCO
CD _____ EUCD 1026
ARC / '89 / ADA / ARC Music

Los Amigos

SOUTH AMERICAN HOLIDAY
CD _____ CNCD 5962
Disky / Jul '93 / Disky / THE

Los Angeles

FALL AND RISE
CD _____ N 02572
Noise / Jul '95 / Koch

Los Assdraggers

ABBEY ROADKILL
CD _____ EFA 128802
Crypt / Nov '96 / Shellshock/Disc

Los Boleros

LOS BOLEROS
CD _____ 12462
Laserlight / Mar '95 / Target/BMG

Los Caimanes

MUSIC OF MEXICO VOL.3: LA HUASTECA (Los Caimanes & Los Caporales)
CD _____ ARHCD 431
Arhoolie / Jan '96 / ADA / Cadillac / Direct

Los Calchakis

LE CHANT DES POETES REVOLTES
CD _____ ARN 64374
Arion / Nov '96 / ADA / Discovery

Los Camperos De Valles

EL TRUNFO
CD _____ MT 007
Corason / Jan '94 / ADA / CM / Direct

MUSE
CD _____ CORA 124
Corason / Nov '95 / ADA / CM / Direct

Los Cenzontles

CO SU PERMISO, SENORES
CD _____ ARHCD 435
Arhoolie / Jan '96 / ADA / Cadillac / Direct

Los Chumps

PRETTY GIRLS EVERYWHERE
CD _____ TX 2103CD
Taxim / Jul '95 / ADA

Los Cincos

FIVE DEADLY SINS
CD _____ SFTRI 442CD
Sympathy For The Record Industry / Jan '97 / Cargo / Greyhound / Plastic Head

Los Del Rio

FIESTA MACARENA
La Nina / Tocala tocala / Macarena / San sereni / No te vay as todavia / Estas pillao / Pura carroceria / Tengo tengo / El sueno de la marisma / La polvareda / La Nina / Macarena / Macarena
CD _____ 74321346632
RCA / Jun '97 / BMG

Los Dos Gilbertos

ESTAMOS EN TEJAS
CD _____ EDCD 7042
Easydisc / Jul '97 / Direct

Los Gitanillos De Cadiz

FLAMENCO
CD _____ 401982
Musidisc / Aug '90 / Discovery

Los Gusanos

LOS GUSANOS
CD _____ 119312
Wowoka / Sep '97 / Grapevine/PolyGram

Los Hermanos Moreno

TOGETHER
Quimbombo / Hazme el amor / Sin ti no puedo vivir / Mas alla de todo / Quien como tu / Homenaje a mis colegas / Reunited / Por alguien como tu / Te quiero porqe te quiero / Maria Tomasa
CD _____ 66058007
RMM / Sep '93 / New Note/Pinnacle

Los Huertas

YO QUIERO MUSICA
CD _____ 322788
Koch / Oct '92 / Koch

Los Incas

ALGERIA
CD _____ 824132
BUDA / Nov '90 / Discovery

EL CONDOR PASA
CD _____ 824122
BUDA / Nov '90 / Discovery

Los Infernos

PLANET KAOS
CD _____ DD 0124
Dr. Dream / Apr '97 / Cargo

Los Latinos

BEST OF SALSA, THE
CD _____ EUCD 1125
ARC / '91 / ADA / ARC Music

Los Lobos

COLOSSAL HEAD
CD _____ 9362461722
Warner Bros. / Mar '96 / Warner Music

HOW WILL THE WOLF SURVIVE
Don't worry baby / Matter of time / Corrida No.1 / Our last night / Breakdown / I got loaded / Sere nata nortena / Evangeline / I got to let you know / Li'l king of everything / Will the wolf survive
CD _____ 8201842
Slash / Apr '89 / PolyGram

JUST ANOTHER BAND FROM EAST LA (2CD Set)
CD Set _____ 8284002
Slash / Jan '94 / PolyGram

KIKO
CD _____ 8282982
Slash / Jun '92 / PolyGram

NEIGHBORHOOD, THE
Down on the riverbed / Emily / I walk alone / Angel dance / Little John of God / Deep dark hole / Georgia slop / I can't understand / Giving tree / Take my hand / Jenny's got a pony / Be still / Neighborhood
CD _____ 8281902
Slash / Sep '90 / PolyGram

PAPA'S BREATH (Los Lobos & Lalo Guerrero)
CD _____ 942562
Music For Little People / Mar '95 / Direct

Los Machado

JIMENEZ - POETRY PUT TO SONG
CD _____ 7996542
Hispavox / Jan '95 / ADA

Los Machucambos

LA BAMBA
La Bamba / Mas que nada / Cuando calienta el sol / Pepito / Eso es el amor / Granada / Brazil / Con amor / Esperanza / Fio maravilha / Girl from Ipanema / Amor amor / Tres palabras / El condor pasa / Quiereme / Guantanamera / La cucaracha / Tristeza / Perfidia / Corcovado / La mama / Maria Elena / Tico-tico / Frenesie / El manisero
CD _____ 300052
Musidisc / Aug '90 / Discovery

Los Malaguenos

FLAMENCO
CD _____ HMA 190965CD
Musique D'Abord / Oct '94 / Harmonia Mundi

Los Masis

EL CORAZON DEL PUEBLO
CD _____ TUMICD 062
Tumi / Nov '96 / Discovery / Stern's

Los Munequitos De Matanzas

CANTAR MARAVILLOSO
Oyelos de nuevo / Lo que dice el abakua / Fundamento dilanga / El marino / Mi arer / Cantar maravilloso / Arague / A los embales
CD _______ **CDORB 053**
Globestyle / Feb '90 / Pinnacle

Los Paraguayos

MALAGUENA
CD _______ **CD 62005**
Saludos Amigos / Oct '93 / Target/BMG

MUSIC FROM THE ANDES
CD _______ **CD 12517**
Music Of The World / Jun '94 / ADA / Target/BMG

Los Pavos Reales

EARLY HITS
CD _______ **ARHCD 410**
Arhoolie / Apr '95 / ADA / Cadillac / Direct

Los Pinguinos Del Norte

CONJUNTOS NORTENOS (Los Pinguinos Del Norte & Conjunto Trio San Antonio)
CD _______ **ARHCD 311**
Arhoolie / Apr '95 / ADA / Cadillac / Direct

Los Pinkys

ESTA PASION
CD _______ **ROUCD 6064**
Rounder / Feb '96 / ADA / CM / Direct

SEGURO QUE SIL
CD _______ **ROUCD 6061**
Rounder / Dec '94 / ADA / CM / Direct

Los Pleneros De La 21

SOMOS BOROCUAS
CD _______ **HSR 0003**
Henry Street / Mar '96 / Direct

Los Quilla Huasi

SONGS OF THE ANDES VOL.2
CD _______ **VICG 53402**
JVC World Library / Mar '96 / ADA / CM / Direct

Los Reyes

GIPSY KINGS OF MUSIC, THE
CD _______ **EMPRCD 504**
Emporio / Apr '94 / Disc

GYPSY FAMILY VOL.2, THE
CD _______ **CD 15493**
Laserlight / Aug '93 / Target/BMG

Los Rupay

FOLKLORE DE BOLIVIA
CD _______ **EUCD 1001**
ARC / '91 / ADA / ARC Music

Los Sabandenos

ATLANTIDA
CD _______ **68975**
Tropical / Apr '97 / Discovery

Los Setenta

MARFIL
CD _______ **5041**
Divucsa / Oct '96 / Discovery

Los Straitjackets

LOS STRAITJACKETS
CD _______ **UPSTARTCD 015**
Upstart / Apr '95 / ADA / Direct

VIVA
Cavalcade / Casbah / Wrong planet / Lonely Apache / Outta gear / Pacifica / Espionage / Swampfire / Lawnmower / Lurking in the shadows / Brains and eggs / Venturing out / Tsunami / Nightmare in Monte Cristo
CD _______ **WENCD 014**
When / Aug '96 / Pinnacle

Los Timidos

DAME UN BESITO
CD _______ **TUMICD 018**
Tumi / '91 / Discovery / Stern's

Los Tres Paraguayos

CELITO LINDO
CD _______ **CD 3511**
Cameo / Nov '95 / Target/BMG

GUANTANAMERA & LATIN HITS
CD _______ **MCD 71490**
Monitor / Jun '93 / CM

Los Van Van

AZUCAR
CD _______ **GLCD 4025**
Green Linnet / Nov '94 / ADA / CM / Direct / Highlander / Roots

BEST OF LOS VAN VAN, THE
CD _______ **TUMICD 063**
Tumi / Nov '96 / Discovery / Stern's

BEST OF LOS VAN VAN, THE
CD _______ **74321424372**
Milan / Jun '97 / Conifer/BMG / Silva Screen

DE CUBA LOS VAN VAN WITH SALSA FORMELL
Nosotros los del Caribe / La Havana si / Si muere la tia / Por encima del nivel / Que pista / Que palo es ese / Canto la ceiba / Baila la palma real / Eso que anda
CD _______ **PSCCD 1003**
Pure Sounds From Cuba / Feb '95 / Henry Hadaway / THE

Los Yuras Of Bolivia

MUSIC FROM THE AYMARA AND QUECHUA ANDEAN CULTURES
Quimera / Ajayu / Hilanderita / Imilla / He venido a preguntarte / Jacha sicu / Ankatuma / Khunu / Caballito blanco / Chequela / Pa ja ra jita / Sicuridas / Mama India / Tema de la mina / Yo ya me estoy yendo / Tata calamani / Mi raza / Laimes pocoata
CD _______ **CDE 84352**
Meridian / May '97 / Nimbus

Loss, Joe

50 GREAT YEARS
I'll be faithful / Red sails in the sunset / Begin the beguine / Goodnight children everywhere / Thrill of a new romance / My prayer / Breeze and I / St. Mary's in the twilight / Stage coach / Tell me Marianne / Gal in calico / Oasis / No orchids for my lady / Put 'em in a box / Sabre dance / Ain't nobody here but us chickens / When it's evening / When you're in love / Enlloro / Flying saucer / With these hands / I wish I knew / Trumpet improptu parts 1 and 2 / Evermore / Crazy otto rag / Why don't you believe me / Be anything / This is heaven / My heart belongs to only you / I'll always love you / My darling, my darling / Luna rossa / Got you on my mind / Wake the town and tell the people / Take care of yourself / Wishing ring / Stardust / March of the mods / Wheels Caribbean clipper / In the mood / Love story / At the woodchoppers' ball / Sugar blues / So tired / Brazil
CD _______ **CDDL 1281**
EMI / Nov '94 / EMI

BRITISH DANCE BANDS (3CD Set) (Loss, Joe & Nat Gonella/Harry Roy)
Sioux Sue: *Loss, Joe* / Deep in the heart of Texas: *Loss, Joe* / You again: *Loss, Joe* / That lovely weekend: *Loss, Joe* / How green was my valley: *Loss, Joe* / Oasis: *Loss, Joe* / What more can I say: *Loss, Joe* / Hazy lazy lane: *Loss, Joe* / Concerto for two: *Loss, Joe* / Fur trappers ball: *Loss, Joe* / Baby mine: *Loss, Joe* / Soft shoe shuffle: *Loss, Joe* / When I see an elephant fly: *Loss, Joe* / Daddy: *Loss, Joe* / You say the sweetest things: *Loss, Joe* / I don't want to set the world on fire: *Loss, Joe* / There's a land of begin again: *Loss, Joe* / Johnny Pedler: *Loss, Joe* / Cornsilk: *Loss, Joe* / Bounce me brother with a solid four: *Loss, Joe* / Rancho pillow: *Loss, Joe* / Don't cry cherie: *Loss, Joe* / Georgia on my mind: *Gonella, Nat* / Tuxedo juntion: *Gonella, Nat* / Big noises from Winnekta: *Gonella, Nat* / I understand: *Gonella, Nat* / At the woodchoppers ball: *Gonella, Nat* / South of the border (Down Mexico way): *Gonella, Nat* / Hep hep the jumpin' jive: *Gonella, Nat* / Johnson rag: *Gonella, Nat* / If you were the only girl in the world: *Gonella, Nat* / Beat me Daddy eight to a bar: *Gonella, Nat* / In the mood: *Gonella, Nat* / Ay ay ay: *Gonella, Nat* / No Mama no: *Gonella, Nat* / I haven't time to be a millionaire: *Gonella, Nat* / Vox poppin': *Gonella, Nat* / Oh Buddy in my love: *Gonella, Nat* / It's a pair of wings for me: *Gonella, Nat* / Eep ipe wanna piece of pie: *Gonella, Nat* / Sunrise serenade: *Gonella, Nat* / Yes my darling daughter: *Gonella, Nat* / Plucking on the golden harp: *Gonella, Nat* / That's my home: *Gonella, Nat* / Tangerine: *Roy, Harry* / Hold your hats on: *Roy, Harry* / Oh the pity of it all: *Roy, Harry* / Humpt dumpty heart: *Gonella, Nat* / When I love I love: *Roy, Harry* / Was it love: *Roy, Harry* / Sentimental interlude: *Roy, Harry* / You bring the boogie woogie out in me: *Roy, Harry* / Greetings from you: *Roy, Harry* / Zoot suit: *Roy, Harry* / Do you care: *Roy, Harry* / When Daddy comes home: *Roy, Harry* / Darling Daisy: *Roy, Harry* / Elmer's tune: *Roy, Harry* / Madelaine: *Roy, Harry* / Chattanooga choo choo: *Roy, Harry* / Tica ti tica ta: *Roy, Harry* / It's funny to everyone but me: *Roy, Harry* / In the middle of a dance: *Roy, Harry* / Blues in the night: *Roy, Harry* / Green eyes: *Roy, Harry* / Shrine of St. Cecilia: *Roy, Harry*
CD Set _______ **EMPRESS 1001**
Empress / Jul '96 / Koch

EARLY YEARS, THE
My heart belongs to daddy / In the mood / Begin the beguine / Boo hoo / Toy trumpet / Little rendezvous in Honolulu / Red sails in the sunset / Happy ending / Over my shoulder / I double dare you / Ooooo-oh boom / Let's dance at the make believe ballroom / Scene changes / South of the border (Down Mexico way) / I've got my eyes on you / You must have been a beautifel baby
CD _______ **GRF 101**
Tring / '93 / Tring

GOLDEN SOUNDS OF JOE LOSS, THE
CD _______ **GS 863772**
Disky / Mar '96 / Disky / THE

HOUR OF SWING, AN (Loss, Joe & His Orchestra)
At the woodchoppers' ball / I'm getting sentimental over you / Stompin' at the Savoy / You made me love you / One o'clock jump / Take the 'A' train / Skyliner / Solitude / Don't be that way / Song of India / Begin the beguine / Trumpet blues and cantabile / Girl from Ipanema / Desafinado / Killing me softly / Sheikh of Araby / Five foot two, eyes of blue / It had to be you / Anvil chorus / Perfidia
CD _______ **CC 249**
Music For Pleasure / Sep '89 / EMI

IN THE MOOD
Begin the beguin / My heart belongs to daddy / In the mood / Don't sit under the apple tree / Put your arms around me honey / Wheels cha cha / Sucu sucu / Maigret theme / March of the mods / At last / American patrol / At Louis blues / Tuxedo junction / Toreando / Speak softly love / Moonlight serenade / Elmer's tune / Big ben to bow bells / Theme from the deerhunter / At the wood choppers ball
CD _______ **CDMFP 6393**
Music For Pleasure / Jul '97 / EMI

IT'S PARTY TIME WITH JOE LOSS (Loss, Joe & His Orchestra)
March of the mods / Zorba's dance / Finnjenka dance / Hey Jude / Entertainer / Charleston / This guy's in love with you / Twistin' in the mood / Celebration / Lily the pink / I came, I saw, I conga'd / (We're gonna) rock around the clock / Shake, rattle and roll / Tea for two / Hokey cokey / This is the life / Stripper / Simon says / Ob-la-di ob-la-da / Y viva Espana / Last waltz
CD _______ **CDMFP 5904**
Music For Pleasure / Oct '90 / EMI

JOE LOSS AND HIS BAND (Loss, Joe Band)
In the mood / Just a little cottage / I hear a rhapsody / Ridin' home in the buggy / Oasis / Down Forget-Me-Not Lane / Hey little hen / Honky tonk train blues / Home sweet home again / Shepherd's serenade / Blues upstairs and downstairs / Put that down in writing / Running wild / I'm nobody's baby / For all that I care / Down every street / Five o'clock whistle / Honeysuckle rose / Russian rose / You say the sweetest things / It's always you / First lullaby
CD _______ **PASTCD 9782**
Flapper / Jun '92 / Pinnacle

TIME TO DANCE (3CD Set)
In the mood / Some enchanted evening / Make believe / Why do I love you / Always / Tenderly / J'attendrai / Wedding samba / If I loved you / Brazil / Say it with music / At the Woodchopper's ball / We'll gather lilacs / Embraceable you / Fascination / Softly softly / Majorca / So deep is the night / You're the cream in my coffee / Button up your overcoat / Blue star / April in Paris / Room with a view / Foggy day / Song of the roses / Tango Capriccioso / Young and foolish / I'll get by / Hello young lovers / I'll see you again / World is waiting for a sunrise / I love my baby / Stardust / Mandolin serenade / I wish I knew / Mountain greenery / Mr. Wonderful / Tammy / April love / Love letters in the sand / I'm in a dancing mood / S'wonderland / Diane / Marie / Miss you / More than ever / Come dancing / After you've gone / Wait for me / If I didn't care / Twelfth Street rag / I'm in love for the very first time / Stairway of love / Exactly like you / Together / When I grow too old to dream / Venus / Blue moon / Cheek to cheek / Sugar time
CD Set _______ **CDTRBOX 220**
Trio / Jul '96 / EMI

WHAT MORE CAN I SAY (Loss, Joe Band)
Sioux Sue: *Loss, Joe Band & Harry Kay/The Lost Chords* / Deep in the heart of Texas: *Loss, Joe Band & Harry Kay/The Lost Chords* / You again: *Loss, Joe Band & Bette Roberts* / That lovely weekend: *Loss, Joe Band & Chick Henderson* / How green was my valley: *Loss, Joe Band & Pat McCormack* / Oasis: *Loss, Joe Band & Chick Henderson* / What more can I say: *Loss, Joe Band & Chick Henderson* / Hazy lazy lane: *Loss, Joe Band & Bette Roberts* / Concerto for two: *Loss, Joe Band & Chick Henderson* / Fur trappers ball: *Loss, Joe Band & Chick Henderson* / Baby mine: *Loss, Joe Band & Chick Henderson* / Soft shoe shuffle: *Loss, Joe Band & Chick Henderson* / When I see an elephant fly: *Loss, Joe Band & Chick Henderson* / Daddy: *Loss, Joe Band & Bette Roberts* / You say the sweetest things: *Loss, Joe Band & Yvette Darnal* / I don't want to set the world on fire: *Loss, Joe Band & Chick Henderson* / There's a land of begin again: *Loss, Joe Band & Chick Henderson* / Johnny Peddler: *Loss, Joe Band & Bette Roberts* / Cornsilk: *Loss, Joe Band & Chick Henderson* / Bounce me brother with a solid four: *Loss, Joe Band & Chick Henderson* / Rancho pillow: *Loss, Joe Band & Chick Henderson* / Don't cry Cherie: *Loss, Joe Concert Orchestra*
CD _______ **RAJCD 812**
Empress / Jan '97 / Koch

WORLD CHAMPIONSHIP BALLROOM DANCES (Loss, Joe & His Orchestra)
Dream / I only have eyes for you / Jealousy / Singin' in the rain / We make music / Toreando / Fascination / Can't help falling in love / Brazil / Something tells me / Mamma mia / Music to watch girls by / Cavatina / Forever and ever / Waltz is for dancing / Save your kisses for me / Don't it make my brown eyes blue / Till / Don't cry for me Argentina / Sunrise sunset / Mull of Kintyre / Spanish gypsy dance / Fernando / Tea for two / Copacabana / Rivers of Babylon / Guantanamera / Is this the way to Amarillo / What's happened to Broadway / I'd like to teach the world to sing / My resistance is low / How deep is your love
CD Set _______ **CDDL 1146**
Music For Pleasure / May '91 / EMI

Loss Of Centre

HUMANS LOSING HUMANITY
CD _______ **EFA 112862**
Glasnost / Jan '96 / SRD

Lost & Found

ACROSS THE BLUE RIDGE MOUNTAINS
CD _______ **REBCD 1121**
Rebel / Feb '96 / ADA / Direct

FOREVER LASTING PLASTIC WORDS
CD _______ **642420 B42**
EVA / Jan '95 / ADA / Direct

Lost

EARLY RECORDINGS 1965-1966
CD _______ **AA 059**
Arf Arf / Jul '97 / Greyhound

Lost Boyz

LEGAL DRUG MONEY
Intro / Yearn / Music makes me high / Jeeps, Lex Coups, Bimaz and Benz / Lifestyles of the rich and shameless / Renee / All right / Legal drug money / Get up / Is this da part / Straight from da ghetto / Keep it real / Channel zero / Da game / 1,2,3 / Lifestyles of the rich and shameless
CD _______ **UND 53010**
Universal / Jun '96 / BMG

LOVE, PEACE AND NAPPINESS
Intro / Summer time / Me and my crazy world / Beats from the East / LOve, peace and nappiness / Black hoodies / So love / My crew / What's wrong / Certain things we do / Games / Get your hustle on / Tight situations / Day / Why / From my family to yours
CD _______ **UND 53072**
MCA / Jun '97 / BMG

Lost Breed

EVIL IN YOU AND ME, THE
CD _______ **HELL 023CD**
Invisible / Jul '93 / Plastic Head

SAVE YOURSELF
Circles / BAC (What you fear) / Gears / Going strong / 472 C.I. of death / Lease on life / Chop / Dragon of chaos / You don't need to live / Tonga slut / Simulator / Up the hill
CD _______ **H 00332**
Hellhound / Aug '94 / Koch

Lost Generation

MIDNIGHT MEAT TRAIN
CD _______ **HMAXD 156**
Heavy Metal / Dec '90 / Revolver / Sony

Lost Gonzo Band

DEAD ARMADILLOS
CD _______ **EDCD 474**
Edsel / Apr '96 / Pinnacle

Lost Minds

EXPRESS JERKY MOTIONS
CD _______ **DRCD 010**
Detour / Mar '96 / Detour / Greyhound

Lost Soul Band

LAND OF DO AS YOU PLEASE
CD _______ **ORECD 524**
Silvertone / Oct '93 / Pinnacle

Lost Souls

CLOSE YOUR EYES AND IT WON'T HURT
CD _______ **RR 88832**
Roadrunner / Sep '96 / PolyGram

DEATHBEAT ROCK 'N' ROLL
CD _______ **BTCD 961**
Bone Tone / Mar '97 / Nervous

NEVER PROMISED YOU A ROSEGARDEN
CD _______ **SPV 08436192**
SPV / Oct '94 / Koch / Plastic Head

Lost Tribe

LOST TRIBE
Mythology / Dick Tracy / Procession / Letter to the editor / Eargasm / Rhinoceros / Mofungo / Space / Four directions / Fool for thought / TAthe W (Tender as the wind) / Cause and effect
CD 01934101432
Windham Hill / Nov '94 / BMG

SOULFISH
Walkabout / Whodunit / It's not what it is / Daze of ol' / Room of life / Steel orchards / La fontaine (the fountain) / Second story / Planet rock / Fuzzy logic
CD 72902103272
High Street / Nov '94 / BMG

Lost Trybe

LIFESTYLE
CD 36283
Raging Bull / May '97 / Prime / Total/BMG

Lost Weekend

LOST WEEKEND
CD LAST/VINTAP 1
Vinyl Tap / Jan '96 / Cargo / Greyhound / Vinyl Tap

Lothar

PRESENTING (Lothar & The Hand People)
CD OW S2117960
One Way / Sep '94 / ADA / Direct / Greyhound

THIS IS IT , MACHINES (Lothar & The Hand People)
Machines / Today is only yesterday's tomorrow / That's another story / Sister lonely / Sex and violence / You won't be lonely / It comes on anyhow / Wedding night for those who love / Yes, I love you / This is it / This may be goodbye / Midnight ranger / Ha (ho) / Sdrawkcab / Space hymn
CD SEECD 75
See For Miles/C5 / May '91 / Pinnacle

Lothian & Borders Police Band

CENTENNIAL (1890-1990)
Lothian and Borders Police centenary march / Slow air, hornpipe and jigs / March, strathspey and reel / 6/8 marches / Hornpipes / Strathspeys and reels / March medley / Drum fanfare / 2/4 marches / Slow air and jigs / Medley / March, strathspey and reel / Edinburgh City Police Pipe Band march
CD LCOM 5188
Lismor / Aug '96 / ADA / Direct / Duncans / Lismor

Lotion

NOBODY'S COOL
CD ABB 89CD
Big Cat / Jun '95 / 3mv/Pinnacle

Lotti, Paolo

HENDRIX (Lotti, Paolo & Harmonia)
CD 90090
Materiali Sonori / Jun '97 / Cargo / Greyhound / New Note/Pinnacle

Lotus Crown

CHOKIN' ON THE JOKES
Well (endless) / Well (of a Mother's symphony) / Circus circus / Swallow the bee / Strapped and tied / Blue arse fly / Shuttle weary / No title / Riddle me sober / Won't give up ('til I win your lovin') / Cynical clever / Beginnings
CD 9362461922
Reprise / Aug '97 / Warner Music

Louchie Lou

FREE 2 LIVE (Louchie Lou & Michie One)
CD WOLCD 1058
China / Aug '95 / Pinnacle

Loud

D GENERATION
CD WOLCD 1003
China / May '91 / Pinnacle

PSYCHE 21
CD WOLCD 1026
China / Jun '92 / Pinnacle

Loud Family

INTERBABE CONCERN
Sodium laureth sulfate / North San Bruno dishonor trip / Don't respond, she can tell / I'm not really a spring / Rise of the chokehold princess / Such little non-believers / Softest hip of her baby tongue / Screwed over by stylish introverts / Top dollar survivalist hardware / Not expecting both contempo and classique / I no longer fear the headless / Hot rox avec lying sweet talk / Uncle lucky / Just gone / Asleep and awake on the man's freeway / Where they go back to school but get depressed / Where they sell antique food / Where the flood waters soak their belongings / Where they walk over Saint Therese
CD A 098CD
Alcazar / Sep '96 / ADA

PLANTS AND BIRDS AND ROCKS AND THINGS
He do the police in different voices / Sword swallower / Aerodeliria / Self righteous boy reduced to tears / Jimmy still comes round / Take me down (Too halloo) / Don't thank me all at onece / Idiot son / Some grand vision of motives and irony / Spot the setup / Inverness / Rosy overdrive / Slit my wrists / Isaac's law / Second grade applauds / Last honest face / Even you / Ballad of how you can all shut up / Give in world
CD A033D
Alias / Feb '93 / Vital

SLOUCHING TOWARDS LIVERPOOL
Take me down / Come on / Back of a car / Slit my wrists / Aerodeliria / Erica's world
CD A 055D
Alias / Oct '93 / Vital

TAPE OF ONLY LINDA, THE
Soul drain / My superior / Marcia and Etrusca / Hyde street virgins / Baby hard-to-be-around / It just wouldn't be Christmas / Better nature / Still it's own reward / For beginners only / Ballet hetro
CD A 060D
Alias / Jan '95 / Vital

Loudblast

CROSS THE THRESHOLD
CD N 02232
Noise / Nov '93 / Koch

Loudermilk, John D.

BLUE TRAIN - 1961/1962
Blue train / Mr. Jones / Language of love / Jimmie's song / Angela Jones / Bully of the beach / Rhythm and blues / What would you take for me / Great snowman / Everybody knows / Google eye / Darling Jane / Song of the lonely teen / All of this for Sally / Roadhog / He's just a scientist (that's all) / Rocks of Reno / Big daddy / Callin' Dr Casey / You just reap what you sow / Little wind-up doll / Two strangers in love / Th'wife / Bad news / Run on home baby brother / Oh how sad
CD BCD 15421
Bear Family / Jun '89 / Direct / Rollercoaster / Swift

IT'S MY TIME
It's my time / No playing in the snow today / Little grave / I'm looking for a world / What is it / Bubble please break / Ma Baker's little acre / Mary's no longer mine / To hell with love / Talkin' silver cloud blues / Joey stays with me / Lament of the Cherokee reservation / Jones' / You're the guilty one / Where have they gone / Little bird / Brown girl / Givin' you all my love / I chose you / Honey / That ain't all / Interstate forty / Do you / Tobacco Road
CD BCD 15422
Bear Family / Jun '89 / Direct / Rollercoaster / Swift

SITTIN' IN THE BALCONY
Sittin' on the balcony / A-plus in love / It's gotta be you / Teenage queen / 1000c Concrete block / In my simple way / That's all I've got / Asiatic flu / Somebody sweet / They were right / Yearbook / Susie's house / Yo yo / Lover's lane / Goin' away to school / This cold war with you / Please don't play No.9 / Angel of flight 509 / Midnight bus / Red headed stranger / Tobacco road / Happy wonderer / March of the minute men
CD BCD 15875
Bear Family / Jun '95 / Direct / Rollercoaster / Swift

Loudon, Dorothy

BROADWAY BABY
Broadway baby / It all depends on you / After you / It all belongs to me / Bobo's / Pack up your sins and go to the devil / Any place I hang my hat is home / I got lost in his arms / They say it's wonderful / Do it again / He was too good to me / I had myself a true love / Ten cents a dance
CD CDSL 5203
DRG / Apr '87 / Discovery / New Note/Pinnacle

Louis, Big Joe

BIG 16
She was all the world to me / Back door slam / Christmas Eve 1993 / 3-6-9 / I've got to be more selective / Way I feel for you / Another married woman / Rock 'n' roll baby / Catfish / Ella Mae / Down Jamaica way / I can tell / Wine head / I took care of my homework (but Jody got my girl and gone) / Treat your daddy right / Leaving on my mind
CD CDCHD 622
Ace / Feb '96 / Pinnacle

Louis, Joe Hill

BE BOP BOY, THE
When I am gone / Dorothy Mae / She may be yours / Keep your arms around me / Got me a new woman / I'm a poor boy / In the mood / West winds are blowin' / Little Walter's boogie / Grandmother got Grandfather told / We all gotta go sometime / Walter's boogie / Come see me / Worry you off my mind / Reap what you sow / Walter's instrumental / Hydramatic / Woman tiger / Man keep your arms around me / She may be yours (take 3) / All gotta go sometime / Shine boy
CD BCD 15524
Bear Family / Jun '92 / Direct / Rollercoaster / Swift

Louis, Philippe

SUNSHINE
CD BAM 23
NMC / Jan '97 / Total/Pinnacle

Louisana Red

WALKED ALL NIGHT LONG (Louisiana Red & Lefty Dizz)
First degree / Bring me my machine gun / King Bee / Stole from me / Too poor to die / Walked allnight long / Cold white sheet / I'll pay the price / Going train blues / Going down Georgia / Ever heard a church bell sound / Mary / Got a gal with a dog won't bark / Whole world
CD TBA 130112
Blues Alliance / Jun '97 / New Note/ Pinnacle

Louise

NAKED
Naked / In walked love / Light of my life / Best that you bring / One kiss from heaven / Thinking about you baby / Discussions / Back to love / Never too late / Goodbye to love / That's the way I like it / I'll fly away / I gave you my love
CD CDEMC 3748
EMI / Jun '96 / EMI

Louise, Tina

IT'S TIME FOR TINA
Tonight is the night / Hand across the table / Snuggled on your shoulder / Embraceable you / I'm in the mood for love / Baby, won't you say you love me / It's been a long, long time / Hold me / I wanna be loved / Let's do it / How long has this been going on / Goodnight my love
CD Set DIW 322
DIW / Apr '90 / Cadillac / Harmonia Mundi

Louisiana Playboys

SATURDAY NIGHT SPECIAL
Lafayette / Why don't we do it in the road / Cajun blues / Saturday night special / Maggie Thatcher, won't you give me a hand / Louisiana playboy's theme / Memphis / Jolie blon / Mathilda / Te petite and te meon / Accordion waltz
CD JSPCD 225
JSP / Apr '89 / ADA / Cadillac / Direct / Hot Shot / Target/BMG

Louisiana Radio

BAYO
CD 343602
Koch International / May '96 / Koch

MAMA ROUX
CD MWCD 2011
Music & Words / Aug '94 / ADA / Direct

WULF
CD MWCD 2014
Music & Words / Dec '95 / ADA / Direct

Louisiana Red

ALWAYS PLAYED THE BLUES
CD JSPCD 240
JSP / Oct '91 / ADA / Cadillac / Direct / Hot Shot / Target/BMG

BLUES FOR IDA B.
CD JSPCD 209
JSP / Jan '88 / ADA / Cadillac / Direct / Hot Shot / Target/BMG

LOWDOWN BACK PORCH BLUES
Ride on Red, ride on / I wonder who (alternate) / Red's dream / Workin' man blues / I'm Louisiana Red / Sweet Alesse / Keep your hands off my woman / I'm a roaming stranger / Red on red, ride on / I wonder who / Seventh son / Sad news / Two fifty three / Don't cry / Sugar hips / I'm too poor to die / Don't cry (alternate)
CD NEX CD 213
Sequel / Jul '92 / BMG

MIDNIGHT RAMBLER
CD 269 607 2
Tomato / May '88 / Vital
CD CPCD 8168
Charly / Jun '96 / Koch

RISING SUN
CD RS 0006
Just A Memory / Oct '94 / New Note/ Pinnacle

Louisiana Repertory Jazz ...

HOT AND SWEET SOUNDS OF LOST NEW ORLEANS (Louisiana Repertory Jazz Ensemble)
CD SOSCD 1140
Stomp Off / Jan '88 / Jazz Music / Wellard

LOUISIANA REPERTORY JAZZ ENSEMBLE (Louisiana Repertory Jazz Ensemble)
CD SOSCD 1055
Stomp Off / May '93 / Jazz Music / Wellard

LOUISIANA REPERTORY JAZZ ENSEMBLE VOL.4 (Louisiana Repertory Jazz Ensemble)
CD SOSCD 1197
Stomp Off / Dec '94 / Jazz Music / Wellard

Louisiana Shakers

IN THE NEW ORLEANS REVIVAL STYLE
CD NEW 2015
Australian Jazz / Jul '96 / Jazz Music

Louisiana's LeRoux

BAYOU DEGRADABLE (The Best Of Louisiana's LeRoux)
CD RE 21142
Razor & Tie / Aug '96 / Koch

Louiss, Eddie

EDDIE LOUISS TRIO
Nardis / Blue tempo / Hot house / No smoking / You've changed / Don't want nothin'
CD FDM 365012
Dreyfus / May '94 / ADA / Direct / New Note/Pinnacle

FLOMELA
Saint Louis blues / Colchiques / Flomela / Pacha / Naissance / Comme un poisson dan le ciel / You can't see / Rene / Maxurka cacodou
CD FDM 365782
Dreyfus / May '96 / ADA / Direct / New Note/Pinnacle

MULTICOLOUR FEELING FANFARE
CD NTCD 105
Nocturne / Nov '96 / Discovery

MULTICOLOUR FEELING FANFARE LIVE
CD NTCD 108
Nocturne / Nov '96 / Discovery

PRESSE DE CONFERENCE (Louiss, Eddie & Michel Petrucciani)
Les grelots / Jean Philippe Herbien / All the things you are / I wrote you a song / So what / These foolish things / Amesha / Simply bop
CD FDM 365682
Dreyfus / Nov '94 / ADA / Direct / New Note/Pinnacle

SANG MELE
CD NTCD 101
Nocturne / Nov '96 / Discovery

WEBE
CD NTCD 109
Nocturne / Nov '96 / Discovery

Louiss, Pierre

CREOLE SWING
CD FA 042
Fremeaux / Nov '95 / ADA / Discovery

Lounge Lizards

LIVE 1979-1981
CD RE 136CD
ROIR / Nov '94 / Plastic Head / Shellshock/Disc

LIVE IN BERLIN
CD VBR 20442
Vera Bra / Sep '91 / New Note/Pinnacle / Pinnacle

LIVE IN BERLIN VOL.2
Remember / Evan's drive to Mombasa / King precious / Mr. Stinky's blues / Welcome herr Lazaro / What else is in there
CD VBR 20862
Vera Bra / Nov '92 / New Note/Pinnacle / Pinnacle

LOUNGE LIZARDS
Incident on South Street / Harlem nocturne / Do the wrong thing / Au contraire arto / Well you needn't / Ballad / Wangling / Conquest of Rah / Demented / I remember Coney Island / Fatty walks / Epistrophy / You haunt me
CD EEGCD 8
EG / Sep '90 / EMI

Loussier, Jacques

BACH: BRANDENBURG CONCERTOS (Nos. 5, 3 & 1)
CD 8440582
Limelight / Mar '91 / PolyGram

BEST OF BACH, THE
CD MCCD 113
Music Club / Jun '93 / Disc / THE

GREATEST BACH, THE (Loussier, Jacques Trio)
CD 8440592
Limelight / Mar '91 / PolyGram

JACQUES LOISSIER PLAYS BACH
CD 556604
Accord / Dec '89 / Cadillac / Discovery

JACQUES LOUSSIER PLAYS BACH
Fugue No.5 in D / Italian Concerto / Pastorale in C minor / Air on a G string / Toccata and fugue in D minor / Gavotte in D / Concerto in D minor
CD CD 83411
Telarc Jazz / Nov '96 / Conifer/BMG

PLAY BACH 2000
CD KAZCD 222
Kaz / Mar '95 / BMG

PULSION/SOUS LA MER
Pulsion / Caffeine / Mozart / Ludwig / Cubzac / Sous la mer / Minsk Greenwich / Madone / Birthday / Buda soupir
CD 8440602
Limelight / Mar '91 / PolyGram

VIVALDI - THE FOUR SEASONS (Loussier, Jacques Trio)
Spring / Summer / Autumn / Winter
CD CD 83417
Telarc Jazz / Jun '97 / Conifer/BMG

Louvin Brothers

CAPITOL COUNTRY MUSIC CLASSICS
Broadminded / Family who prays (Shall never part) / When I stop dreaming / Alabama / I don't believe you've met my baby / Hoping that you're hoping / Kentucky / Katy dear / Knoxville girl / Don't laugh / You're running wild / Cash on the barrelhead / Plenty of everything but you / Little light of mine / Tennessee waltz / Are you teasing me / My baby's gone / If I could only win your love / Satan is real / Christian life / Blues stay away from me / I love you best of all / How's the world treating you / Great atomic power / Must you throw dirt in my face / Stuck up blues / Thank God for my Christian home / What would you give me in exchange for my soul
CD CDEMS 1492
Capitol / Apr '93 / EMI

CLOSE HARMONY (8CD Set)
Alabama Alabama / Seven year blues / My love song for you / Get acquainted waltz / They've got the church outnumbered / Do you live what you preach / You'll be rewarded over there / I'll live with God (to die no more) / Rove of white / Great atomic power / Insured beyond the grave / Gospel way / Sons and daughters of God / Broadminded / Family who prays (shall never part) / I know what you're talking about / Let us travel on / I love God's way of living / Born again / Preach the gospel / From mother's arms to Korea / If we forget God / Satan and the Saint / Satan lied to me / God bless her ('cause she's my mother) / Last chance to pray / No one to sing for me / Swing low, sweet chariot / Nearer my God to thee / Make him a soldier / I can't say no / Just rehearsing / Love thy neighbour as thyself / Where will you build / Pray for me / When I stop dreaming / Pitfall / Alabama / Memories and tears / Don't laugh / I don't believe you've met my baby / Childish love / In the middle of nowhere / Hoping that you're hoping / First one to love you / I cried after you left / That's all he's asking of me / I'll be all smiles tonight / In the pines / What is home without love / Mary of the wild moor / Knoxville girl / Kentucky / Katy dear / My brother's will / Take the news to mother / Let her go God bless her / Tiny broken heart / Plenty of everything but you / Cash on the barrelhead / You're running wild / New partner waltz / I won't have to cross Jordan alone / Praying / Wait a little longer, please Jesus / This little light of mine / Steal away and pray / There's no excuse / Are you washed in the blood / Lord I'm coming home / Thankful / Take me back into your heart / Here today and gone tomorrow / We could / Tennessee waltz / Too late / Are you teasing me / Nobody's darling but mine / Don't let your sweet love die / I wonder where you are tonight / Why not confess / Making believe / Have I stayed away too long / Call me / I wish you knew / Dog sled / When I loved you / My baby's gone / She didn't even know I was gone / My baby came back / Are you wasting my time / My curly headed baby / Lorene / I wish it had been a dream / While you're cheatin' on me / If I could only win your love / You're learning / Blue from now on / Today / My heart was trampled on the street / Send me the pillow that you dream on / On my way to the show / Red hen hop / She'll get lonesome / I wonder if you know / Blue / Angels rejoiced last night / Dying from home and lost / Satan's jewelled crown / River of Jordan / I'm ready to go home / Kneeling drunkards plea / Satan is real / Christian life / Are you afraid to die / He can be found / There's is a higher power / Drunkard's doom / I see a bridge / Just suppose / Stagger / Nellie moved to town / What a change one day / Ruby's song / Last old shovel / Midnight special / Brown's ferry blues / Southern moon / Sand mountain blues / Nashville blues / Blues stay away from me / When it's time for the whippoorwill to sing / Put me on the train to Carolina / Freight train blues / Lonesome blues / Gonna lay down my old guitar / It's Christmas time / Santa's big parade / Love is a lonely street / If you love me stay away / I ain't gonna work tomorrow / I love you best of all / I can't keep you in love with me / Scared of the blues / I have found the way / He set me free / Kneel at the cross / Leaning on the everlasting arms / O why not tonight / You can't find the Lord too soon / Keep your eyes on Jesus / Almost persuaded / I feel better now / O who shall be able to stand / If today was the day / You'll meet him in the clowds / You'll meet him in the clouds (alt. take) / Away in a manger / Friendly beasts / Hark the herald angels sing / Good christian men rejoice / While shepherds watched their flocks by night / First Noel / It came upon a midnight clear / O come all ye faithful (Adeste Fidelis) / O little town of Bethlehem / Silent night / Deck the halls with boughs of holly / Joy to the world / It hurts me more the second time around / How's the world treating you / Every time you leave / Time goes slow / I died for the red, white and blue / Searching for a soldier's grave / At mail call today / Soldier's last letter / There's a star spangled banner waving somewhere / There's a grave in the wave of the ocean / Mother I thank you for the bible you gave / Seaman's girl / Robe of white / Weapon of prayer / Broken engagement / First time in life / There's no easy way / Love turned to hate / Must you throw dirt in my face / Great speckled bird / Wabash cannonball / Lonely mound of clay / Wreck on the highway / Wait for the light to shine / Low and lonely / We live in two different worlds / Precious jewel / Great judgement morning / Branded wherever I go / Not a word from home / Stuck up blues / Don't let them take the bible out of our school / I'm glad that I'm not him / Message to your heart / Thank God for my christian home / I'll never die / Price on the bottle / I've known a lady / He included me / Keep watching the sky / Now Lord, what can I do for you / Way up on a mountain / Gonna shake hands with mother over there / He was waiting at the altar / Oh Lord, my God / What would you take in exchange for my soul
CD Set BCD 15561
Bear Family / Jun '92 / Direct / Rollercoaster / Swift

RADIO FAVOURITES 1951-57
CD CMFCD 009
Country Music Foundation / Jul '93 / ADA / Direct

RUNNING WILD
When I stop dreaming / I don't believe you've met my baby / Hoping that you're hoping / You're running wild / Cash on the barrelhead / My baby's gone / Knoxville girl / I love you best of all / How's the world treating you / Must you throw dirt in my face / If I could only win your love
CD CDSD 044
Sundown / Jul '92 / TKO Magnum

SONGS OF THE LOUVIN BROTHERS (Various Artists)
Cash on the barrelhead: *Dreadful Snakes* / We live in two different worlds: *Skaggs, Ricky & Peter Rowan* / Are you afraid to die: *Nashville Bluegrass Band* / Make him soldier: *Whitstein Brothers* / Seven year blues: *Longview* / I'm gonna love you one more time: *Jim & Jesse & the Virginia Boys* / You're running wild: *Val, Joe & New England Bluegrass Boys* / Love and wealth: *Here Today* / Here today and gone tomorrow: *Dickens, Hazel & Johnson Mountain Boys* / My baby came back: *Lewis, Laurie & Tom Rozum* / When I stop dreaming: *McCoury, Del & The Dixie Pals* / I don't believe you've met my baby: *Moffatt, Hugh & Katy*
CD EDCD 7034
Easydisc / Jun '97 / Direct

Louvin, Charlie

LIVE IN HOLLAND
CD SCR 34
Strictly Country / Jul '95 / ADA / Direct

LONGEST TRAIN, THE
When I stop dreaming / In the pines / Cash on the barrelhead / I don't feel like dancing / Who knows where the times goes / Queen of the bayou / Are you wasting my time / Stone deaf, dumb and blind / My baby's gone / Christian life / I wanna die young (at a very old age) / Turn around
CD WMCD 1056
Watermelon / Nov '96 / ADA / Direct

Lovano, Joe

CELEBRATING SINATRA
I'll never smile again / Chicago / I'm a fool to want you / Imagination / I've got the world on a string / All the way / South of the border / In other words / I've got you under my skin / This love of mine / Someone to watch over me / One for my baby / Song is you
CD CDP 8377182
Blue Note / Jan '97 / EMI

LIVE AT THE VILLAGE VANGUARD (2CD Set) (Lovano, Joe Quartets)
Fort Worth / Birds of Springtime / I can't get started (With you) / Uprising / Sail away / Blue Note to lose / Song and dance / Lonnie's lament / Reflections / Little Willie leaps / This is all I ask / 26-2 / Duke Ellington's / Sounds of love / Sounds of joy
CD Set CDP 8291252
Blue Note / Feb '96 / EMI

RUSH HOUR
Prelude to a kiss / Peggy's blue skylight / Wildcat / Angel eyes / Rush hour on 23rd Street / Crepuscule with Nellie / Lament for M / Topsy turvy / Love I long for / Juniper's garden / Kathline Gray / Headin' out, movin' in / Chelsea bridge
CD CDP 8292692
Blue Note / Feb '95 / EMI

SOUNDS OF JOY
Sounds of joy / Strength and courage / I'll wait and prey / Cedar Avenue blues / Bass and space / Ettenro / Until the moment was now / This one's for Lacy / 23rd Street theme
CD ENJACD 70132
Enja / Mar '92 / New Note/Pinnacle / Vital/ SAM

Lovaz, Iren

ROSEBUDS IN A STONEYARD
CD 8557802
Origins / Jul '97 / Discovery

Love & Rockets

EARTH, SUN, MOON
Mirror people / Light / Welcome tomorrow / No new tale to tell / Here on earth / Lazy / Waiting for the flood / Rainbird / Telephone is empty / Everybody wants to go to heaven / Sun / Youth
CD BEGA 84CD
Beggars Banquet / Sep '87 / RTM/Disc / Warner Music

EXPRESS
It could be sunshine / Kundalini Express / All in my mind / Life in Laralay / Yin and Yang (the flower pot men) / Love me / All in my mind (acoustic version) / American dream
CD BBL 74CD
Beggars Banquet / Feb '90 / RTM/Disc / Warner Music

HOT TRIP TO HEAVEN
CD BBQCD 145
Beggars Banquet / Sep '94 / RTM/Disc / Warner Music

LOVE AND ROCKETS
No big deal / Purest blue / Motorcycle / I feel speed / Bound for hell / Teardrop collector / So alive / Rock 'n' roll Babylon / No words no more
CD BEGA 99CD
Beggars Banquet / Aug '89 / RTM/Disc / Warner Music

SEVENTH DREAM OF TEENAGE HEAVEN
If there's a heaven above / Private future / Dog end of a day gone by / Game / Seventh dream of teenage heaven / Haunted when the minutes drag / Saudade
CD BBL 66 CD
Lowdown/Beggars Banquet / Jan '89 / RTM/Disc / Warner Music

Love

COMES IN COLOURS
My little red book / Can't explain / Message to pretty / Softly to me / Hey Joe / Signed DC / And more / Seven and seven is / No 14 / Stephanie knows who / Orange skies / Que vida / Castle / She comes in colours / Alone again or / And more again / Old man / House is not a motel / Daily planet / Live and let live / Laughing stock / Your mind and we belong together / August / Arthur Lee interview
CD RVCD 29
Raven / Jan '93 / ADA / Direct

DA CAPO
Stepahnie knows who / Orange skies / Que vida / Seven and seven is / She comes in colours / Revelation / Castle
CD 9740052
Elektra / '89 / Warner Music

FALSE START
CD MCAD 22029
One Way / Apr '94 / ADA / Direct / Greyhound

FOREVER CHANGES
Alone again or / House is not a motel / And more again / Daily planet / Old man / Red telephone / Maybe the people would be the times / Live and let live / Good humour man he sees everything like this / Bummer in the summer / You set the scene
CD 9606562
Elektra / '89 / Warner Music

FOUR SAIL
August / Friends of mine / I'm with you / Good times / Singing cowboy / Dream / Robert Montgomery / Nothin' / Talking in my sleep / Always see your face
CD CDTB 047
Thunderbolt / Jun '88 / TKO Magnum

LOVE
My little red book / Can't explain / Message to pretty / My flash on you / Softly to me / No matter what you do / Emotions / You I'll be following / Gazing / Hey Joe / Signed DC / Coloured balls falling / Mushroom clouds / And more
CD 7559740012
Elektra / Dec '93 / Warner Music

OUT HERE
CD MCAD 22030
One Way / Apr '94 / ADA / Direct / Greyhound

OUT THERE
I'll pray for you / Love is coming / Signed DC / I still wonder / Listen to my song / Doggone / Nice to be / Stand out / Everlasting first / Gimmi a little break / Willow willow / You are something / Love is more than words / Gather round
CD CDWIKD 69
Big Beat / Jul '90 / Pinnacle

STUDIO/LIVE
CD MCAD 22036
One Way / Apr '94 / ADA / Direct / Greyhound

WE'RE ALL NORMAL AND WE WANT OUR FREEDOM (A Tribute To Arthur Lee & Love) (Various Artists)
Emotions: *Principle, Peter* / Robert Montgomery: *Urge Overkill* / Message to pretty: *Kilgour, David & Martin Phillips* / Which witch is which: *Hypnolovewheel* / Keep on shining: *Diesel Meat* / She comes in colours: *Mad Scene* / Car lights on in the daytime: *Jetty* / Signed DC: *Deer Team* / I'm down: *HP Zinker* / Between Clark and Hilldale: *Teenage Fanclub* / You are something: *TV Personalities* / Willow willow: *Eggs* / Dream: *Johnson* / Alone again or: *Gobblehoof* / Que Vidal: *Uncle Wiggly* / Softly to me: *Gamma Rays* / No matter what you do: *Love Battery* / My flash on you: *Fly Ashtray* / Bummer in the summer: *Smack Dab* / Stand out: *Das Damen* / Can't explain: *Tricycle*
CD A 058D
Alias / Jul '94 / Vital

Love 2 Be

ALBUM
CD FIRMCD 8
Firm / Oct '96 / Pinnacle

Love 666

AMERICAN REVOLUTION
CD AMREP 035CD
Amphetamine Reptile / Feb '95 / Plastic Head

PLEASE KILL YOURSELF SO I CAN ROCK
CD ARRCD 75018
Amphetamine Reptile / Dec '96 / Plastic Head

Love Affair

EVERLASTING LOVE AFFAIR, THE
Everlasting love / Hush / 60 minutes (of your love) / Could I be dreaming / First cut is the deepest / So sorry / Once upon a season / Rainbow valley / Day without love / Tobacco Road / Tree / Handbags and gladrags / Build on love / Please stay / Tale of two
CD 4836732
Columbia / Mar '96 / Sony

Love As Laughter

GREEKS BRING GIFTS, THE
CD KLP 51CD
K / Feb '96 / Cargo / Greyhound / SRD

Love, Charlie

CHARLIE LOVE WITH GEORGE LEWIS & LOUIS NELSON 1962 (Love, Charlie & George Lewis & Louis Nelson)
CD AMCD 60
American Music / Aug '94 / Jazz Music

Love City Groove

HARD TIMES
JUMP / Let's get funky / Love city groove / Soft spot / Spice (4am jam) / Trouble / Sentence of love / Inna city love / Gonna make it alright / Collioure / Blue / Love city groove (soul mix)
CD SATURN 2CD
Planet 3 / Feb '96 / Pinnacle

Love Coates, Dorothy

BEST OF DOROTHY LOVE COATES & THE GOSPEL HUMMINGBIRDS, THE (Love Coates, Dorothy & The Gospel Hummingbirds)
CD NASH 4508
Nashboro / Feb '96 / Pinnacle

GET ON BOARD
Peace, be still / Glory to his name / I'm sealed / Get away Jordan / Rest for the weary / Deliver me / Oh my Lord / Lead me

holy father / Old gospel train (the next stop is mine) / Get on board / Railroad / Plenty good room / Sometime / No hiding place / Waiting for me / Wade in the water / I wouldn't mind dying / I'll be with thee / He's calling me / Untitled instrumental / Thank you Lord for using me / These are they / 99 1/2 / That's enough
CD _______ CDCHD 412
Ace / Nov '93 / Pinnacle

VOL.1 & 2
He's calling me / One morning soon / You better run / No hiding place / When I reach my heavenly home on high / Get away Jordan / I'm sealed / That's enough / Ninety nine and a half (won't do) / Where shall I be / Jesus laid his hand on me / You can't hurry God / Jesus knows it all / You must be born again / These are they / Why not / I shall know him / Every day will be Sunday by and by / I wouldn't mind dying / Lord don't forget about me / There's a God somewhere / Just to behold his face / Am I a soldier / Heaven
CD _______ CDCHD 343
Ace / Nov '93 / Pinnacle

Love Corporation

DANCE STANCE
CD _______ CRECD 199
Creation / Jun '97 / 3mv/Vital

INTELLIGENTSIA
CD _______ CREDCD 116
Creation / May '94 / 3mv/Vital

LOVERS
CD _______ CRECD 068
Creation / May '94 / 3mv/Vital

TONES
CD _______ CRECD 056
Creation / May '94 / 3mv/Vital

Love Decade

DECADANCE
CD _______ GLOBECD 3
All Around The World / May '96 / Total/ BMG

Love Dogs

I'M YO DOG
CD _______ CDTC 1155
Tonecool / Jun '96 / ADA / Direct

Love, Geoff

BIG WAR MOVIE THEMES (Love, Geoff & His Orchestra)
Colonel Bogey / Lawrence of Arabia / Guns of Navarone / Battle of Britain / Longest Day / Where eagles dare / 633 Squadron / Dambusters march / Great escape / Green berets / Cavatina / Winds of war / Victory at sea extracts / We'll meet again / Is Paris burning / Reach for the Sky
CD _______ CC 211
Music For Pleasure / May '88 / EMI

GOING LATIN (Love, Geoff & His Orchestra)
La Bamba / Spanish harlem / Guantanamera / Sucu sucu / Girl from Ipanema / One note Samba / South of the border (Down Mexico way) / Maria Elena / Spanish eyes / Desafinado / Breeze and I / Mexican hat dance / Temptation / La Cumparsita / Blue tango / Spider of the night / Serenta / La Paloma / Jealousy / Adios muchachos / Ecstasy
CD _______ CC 270
Music For Pleasure / Aug '91 / EMI

IN THE MOOD - FOR LOVE (Love, Geoff & His Orchestra)
Cavatina / Annie's song / Chi Mai / Misty / Tara's theme / Begin the beguine / Time for us / We'll meet again / Summer knows / Godfather love theme / Summer place / Man and a woman / Secret love / When I fall in love / Love letters / Raindrops keep falling on my head / Falling in love with love / Where do I begin / Somewhere my love / Spartacus love theme / Love walked in / I wish you love / True love / I will wait for you
CD _______ CC 245
Music For Pleasure / Sep '89 / EMI

IN THE MOOD FOR WALTZING (Love, Geoff & His Orchestra)
Falling in love with love / Ramona / Anniversary song / Always / Beautiful dreamer / I'll see you again / Fascination / My wonderful one / Charmaine / Love's last word is spoken / Love's roundabout / Now is the hour / Desert song / Around the world / When I grow too old to dream / Vaya con dios / One night of love / Lover / Edelweiss / Song / Try to remember / Ask me why I love you / Waltz of my heart / Last waltz
CD _______ CC 261
Music For Pleasure / Oct '90 / EMI

MELODIES THAT LIVE FOREVER (In concert with) (Love, Geoff & His Orchestra)
Skater's waltz / Minute waltz / Destiny / Invitation to the dance / Morning: Peer Gynt / Elizabethan serenade / Largo / Moonlight sonata / Blue Danube / Sleeping beauty / Merry widow / Tales from the Vienna Woods / Dusk / Marriage of Figaro (overture) / Enigma variations: Nimrod / Air on a G string / Clair de Lune / Jesu joy of man's desiring / Ave Maria
CD Set _______ CDDL 1098
EMI / Nov '92 / EMI

SONGS THAT WON THE WAR (Love, Geoff Banjos)
Colonel Bogey / Sentimental journey / Lili Marlene / Good morning / You'll never know / Yours / Let the people sing / That lovely weekend / This is the army Mister Jones / Arm in arm / I'll be with you in apple blossom time / I don't want to set the world on fire
CD _______ CDMFP 5887
Music For Pleasure / Feb '95 / EMI

STAR WARS/CLOSE ENCOUNTER OF THE THIRD KIND (Love, Geoff & His Orchestra)
Star Wars / UFO / Star Trek / Barbarella / Space 1999 / Also sprach zarathustra / March from things to come / Thunderbirds / Star Wars / Dr. Who / Mars, Bringer of war from The Planets / Close Encounters Of The Third Kind / Logan's Run / Flight fantastic / Star Wars / Blake Seven / Omega Man
CD _______ CDMFP 6395
Music For Pleasure / Jun '97 / EMI

WHEN I FALL IN LOVE (Love, Geoff Singers)
Imagine / What are you doing the rest of your life / Moon river / If / I'm stone in love with you / When I fall in love / More I see you / I only have eyes for you / It's impossible / Annie's song / Without you / My eyes adored you / First time ever I saw your face / My cherie amour / Love story / Something / Don't cry for me Argentina / Vincent / Killing me softly / Snowbird / Send in the clowns / For once in my life / Michelle / You make me feel brand new / Just the way you are / Evergreen
CD Set _______ CDDL 1102
Music For Pleasure / May '92 / EMI

Love Groove

GLOBAL WARMING
CD _______ MILL 0112
Millenium / Mar '95 / Plastic Head / Prime / SRD

Love In Reverse

I WAS HERE
CD _______ 9362462212
Warner Bros. / Oct '96 / Warner Music

Love Inc.

LIFE'S A GAS
CD _______ FIM 1021
Force Inc. / Sep '96 / Amato Disco / Arabesque / SRD

Love Interest

BEDAZZLED
CD _______ INVCD 025
Invisible / Feb '94 / Plastic Head

Love Is Colder Than Death

OXEIA
CD _______ HY 39100952
Hyperium / Apr '94 / Cargo / Plastic Head

Love, Laura

LAURA LOVE COLLECTION, THE
CD _______ M 1182
Putumayo / Mar '97 / Grapevine/PolyGram

Love Like Blood

ECSTASY
CD _______ DW 20625CD
Deathwish / Jan '92 / Plastic Head

EXPOSURE
CD _______ 08545752
SPV / Jan '96 / Koch / Plastic Head

FLAGS OF REVOLUTION
CD _______ DW 21033CD
Deathwish / Jan '92 / Plastic Head

ODYSSEE
CD _______ SPV 08445552
SPV / Apr '94 / Koch / Plastic Head

Love, Mary

THEN AND NOW
I'm in your hands / Let me know / Because of you / I woke up / Hey stoney face / Lay this burden down / Satisfied feeling / I can't wait / Come out of the sandbox / Price / Baby I'll come / Move a little closer / More than enough love / Grace / I've gotta get you back / Talkin' about my man / Mr. Man / B Baby / Caught up / You turned my bitter into sweet / (I'm so glad) He uses me
CD _______ CDKEND 109
Kent / May '94 / Pinnacle

Love Nut

BASTARDS OF MELODY
She won't do me / Star / I'm a loser / Green tambourine / Images / Into battle / Jane / Touch / Please / Black cat
CD _______ OF 001CD
One Fifteen / Nov '95 / Vital

Love Parade

LOVE IS THE MESSAGE
CD _______ K7 037CD
Studio K7 / Jul '95 / Prime / RTM/Disc

Love Republic

IS NOTHING SACRED
CD _______ ARCHO 1666
TEQ / May '95 / Cargo / Plastic Head

Love Times Three

LOVE TIMES THREE
CD _______ TRI 4144CD
Ichiban / Feb '94 / Direct / Koch

Love Unlimited Orchestra

BEST OF LOVE UNLIMITED ORCHESTRA, THE
CD _______ 5269452
Mercury / Sep '95 / PolyGram

Love/Hate

I'M NOT HAPPY
CD _______ 08518222
SPV / Dec '95 / Koch / Plastic Head

Loved Ones

BETTER DO RIGHT
CD _______ HCD 8057
Hightone / Oct '94 / ADA / Koch

Loveland

WONDER OF LOVE, THE
CD _______ HF 45CD
PWL / Jun '95 / Warner Music

Loveless, Patty

TROUBLE WITH THE TRUTH, THE
Tear stained letter / Trouble with the truth / I miss who I was with you / Everybody's equal in the eyes of love / Lonely too long / You can feel bad / Thousand times a day / She drew a broken heart / To feel that way at all / Someday I will lead the parade
CD _______ 4814682
Epic / Feb '96 / Sony

WHEN ANGELS FLY
Handful of dust / Halfway down / When the fallen angels fly / You don't even know who I am / Feelin' good about feelin' bad / Here I am / I try to think about Elvis / Ships / Old weakness (coming on strong) / Over my shoulder
CD _______ 4771832
Columbia / Nov '94 / Sony

Lovelies

TUFF OF THE TRACK
CD _______ ER 1026
Elefant / Jul '97 / Greyhound / SRD

Lover Speaks

LOVER SPEAKS,THE
Every lover's sign / No more I love you's / Never to forget you / Face me and smile / Absent one / Love is: "I gave you everything" / This can't go on / Still faking this art of love / Tremble dancing / Of tears
CD _______ 3951272
A&M / Apr '95 / PolyGram

Love's Ugly Children

CAKEHOLE
CD _______ FNCD 324
Flying Nun / Nov '95 / RTM/Disc

Loveslug

CIRCLE OF VALUES
CD _______ GRCD KH
Glitterhouse / May '93 / Avid/BMG

Lovetrick

LOVETRICK
CD _______ 36700032
Mausoleum / Oct '91 / Grapevine/ PolyGram

Lovett, Eddie

BEST REGGAE HITS OF EDDIE LOVETT VOL.1, THE
CD _______ PKL 514912
K&K / Jul '93 / Jet Star

LET'S TRY AGAIN
CD _______ PKCD 33193
K&K / Jul '93 / Jet Star

Lovett, Lyle

I LOVE EVERYBODY
Skinny legs / Fat babies / I think you know what I mean / Hello Grandma / Creeps like me / Sonja / They don't like me / Record lady / Ain't it somethin' / Penguins / Fat girl / La to the left / Old friend / Just the morning / Moon on my shoulder / I've got the blues / Goodbye to Carolina / I love everybody
CD _______ MCD 10808
MCA / Sep '94 / BMG

JOSHUA JUDGES RUTH
CD _______ MCAD 10475
MCA / Mar '92 / BMG

LYLE LOVETT
CD _______ MCLD 19134
MCA / Oct '90 / BMG

LYLE LOVETT AND HIS LARGE BAND
Here I am / I know you know / I married her just because she looks / Once is enough / Stand by your man / Crying shame / What do you do / Nobody knows me / Which way does that old pony run / If you were to wake up
CD _______ DMCG 6037
MCA / Feb '89 / BMG

ROAD TO ENSENADA
Don't touch my hat / Her first mistake / Fiona / That's right (you're not from Texas) / Who loves you better / Private conversation / Promises / It ought to be easier / I can't love you anymore / Long tall Texan / Christmas morning / Road to Ensenada
CD _______ MCD 11409
MCA / Jun '96 / BMG

Lovette, Eddie

BEST REGGAE HITS OF...VOL.11
CD _______ PKCD 33094
K&K / Sep '94 / Jet Star

Lovich, Lena

FLEX
CD _______ STIFFCD 21
Disky / May '94 / Disky / THE

MARCH
Life / Wonderland / Nightshift / Hold on to love / Rage / Natural beauty / Make believe / Sharman / Vertigo / Shadow walk
CD _______ ECD 280012
Evidence / Oct '95 / ADA / Cadillac / Harmonia Mundi

NO MAN'S LAND
It's you only you (mein schmerz) / Blue hotel / Faces / Walking low / Special star / Sister video / Maria / Savages / Rocky road
CD _______ STIFFCD 22
Disky / May '94 / Disky / THE

STATELESS
CD _______ STIFFCD 20
Disky / May '94 / Disky / THE

STIFF YEARS, THE
CD _______ HRCD 8035
Disky / Jan '94 / Disky / THE

VERY BEST OF LENA LOVICH, THE
Lucky number / Tonight / Say when / Be stiff / What will I do without you / Angels / Too tender / New toy / Momentary breakdown / It's you, only you / One in a million / Home / Bird song / Writing on the wall / Telepathy / I think we're alone now / Special star / Big bird / Sleeping beauty
CD _______ DC 878582
Disky / May '97 / Disky / THE

Lovie, Robert

GENERATIONS OF CHANGE
Generations of change / Buchan vet / Yellow on the broom / Drumdelgie / North East shore / Wild geese / Auld folks on the wa' / Village where I went to school / Glorious North / It's lonely in the bothy / Road and the miles to Dundee / Chapelton / MacFarlane o' the sprots o' Burnieboozie / Old house / Come a' ye tramps and hawker lads / 'Tween Tyrie and the Dour / Bonnie Aiberdein
CD _______ CDGR 158
Ross / Dec '96 / CM / Duncans / Highlander / Ross

NORTH EAST SHORE, THE
North east shore / Guise o'tough / Banks o'red roses / Poem / Boggyclairts / Alex Green / Auld meal mill / Butter on the bow / I aince lo'ed a lass / Alford cattle show / Prince and Jean / Band selection / Silver darlings / McGinty's meal and ale / Parting song
CD _______ CDR 003
Donside / Jan '87 / Ross

Lovin' Spoonful

DAYDREAM
Daydream / There she is / It's not time now / Warm baby / Day blues / Let the boy rock 'n' roll / Jug band music / Didn't want to have to do it / You didn't have to be so nice / Bald headed Lena
CD _______ CLACD 194
Castle / Aug '90 / BMG

EP COLLECTION, THE
Did you ever... / Day blues / Blues in the bottle / There she is / Younger girl / Other side of this life / Sporting life / Fishin' blues / Jug band music / Loving you / Let the boy rock 'n' roll / Eyes / You baby / Butchie's tune / Wild about my lovin' / Voodoo in my basement / It's not time now / Didn't want

to have to do it / Coconut grove / Do you believe in music
CD SEECD 229
See For Miles/C5 / May '88 / Pinnacle

EVERYTHING PLAYING
She is still a mystery / Priscilla Millionaira / Boredom / Six o'clock / Forever / Younger generation / Money / Old folks / Only pretty, what a pity / Try a little bit / Close your eyes / Darling be home soon / Amazing air / Never going back / (Till I) run with you / Me about you
CD HILLCD 11
Wooded Hill / Jan '97 / Direct / World Serpent

HIT SINGLE COLLECTABLES
CD DISK 4503
Disky / Apr '94 / Disky / THE

SUMMER IN THE CITY
Daydream / Nashville cats / She is still a mystery / Didn't want to have to do it / Coconut grove / You didn't have to be so nice / Rain on the roof / Darling be home soon / Sittin' here lovin' you / On the road again / Do you believe in magic / Close your eyes / Jug band music / Summer in the city / Money / Warm baby / Night owl blues / Never going back (to Nashville)
CD 5507362
Spectrum / Jan '95 / PolyGram

Lovindeer

JAM LIKE A JAMAICAN
CD TSOJ 0311962
Sound Of Jamaica / Oct '96 / Jet Star

Low

CURTAIN HITS THE CAST, THE
Anon / Plan / Over the ocean / Mom says / Coat tails / Standby / Laugh / Lust / Stars gone out / Same / Do you know how to waltz / Prisoner / Tomorrow one
CD YARDCD 018
Vernon Yard / Aug '96 / Vital

LONG DIVISION
Violence / Below and above / Shame / Throw out the line / Swingin' / See-through / Turn / Caroline / Alone / Streetlight / Stay / Take
CD YARDCD 014
Vernon Yard / Feb '97 / Vital

Low 948

PACCARISCA
CD KICKCD 20
Kickin' / Jul '95 / Prime / SRD

Low Art Thrill

LOW ART THRILL
Sound of lust / Low rent lovers / Kilometre / Upside down / Baby's on fire / She'll kill you / European son / Cheap / Girlboy / Television / Jackdaw saw
CD FRUCD 1001
Fruition / Jun '97 / PolyGram / Vital

Low, Bruce

12 UHR MITTAGS
CD BCD 15511
Bear Family / Aug '90 / Direct / Rollercoaster / Swift

Low Flying Aircraft

LOW FLYING AIRCRAFT
Sybilization / Fourth dimension / Baptism by fire / Poolside / Abstract blue / Moronathon / Amnesia / Reflection / What did you do / Radically conservative
CD CDR 101
Red Hot / Mar '94 / THE

Low Pop Suicide

DEATH OF EXCELLENCE, THE
Bless my body / Almost said / Suicide ego / Zombie / Life and death / No genius / Humbled / More than this / Philo's snag / Sheep's clothing / Face to face / Tell them I was here
CD WDOM 012CD
World Domination / Jan '95 / Pinnacle / RTM/Disc

ON THE CROSS OF COMMERCE
Here we go / Kiss your lips / My way / Disengaged / It's easy / Your God can't feel my pain / Crush / Ride / Imagine my love / All in death is sweet
CD WDOM 007CD
World Domination / May '94 / Pinnacle / RTM/Disc

Low-Fi Generator

STEREO
CD NORMAL 207CD
Normal / Mar '97 / ADA / Direct

Lowe, Allen

DARK WAS THE NIGHT - COLD WAS THE GROUND (Lowe, Allen & The American Song Project)
CD CD 811
Music & Arts / May '94 / Cadillac / Harmonia Mundi

WOYZECK'S DEATH (Lowe, Allen & Roswell Rudd)
Cold as ice / Sun on her bones / Voices in the fiddles / Misery / Beautiful sins / Hard gray sky / On thing after another / Good and beautiful murder / Woyzeck's death / Bonehead / Concentration suite
CD ENJ 90052
Enja / May '95 / New Note/Pinnacle / Vital/ SAM

Lowe, Amanda

SPIRAL DANCE
CD GRIN 941CD
Grinnigogs / Jan '95 / ADA

Lowe, Frank

DECISION IN PARADISE
CD SNCD 1082
Soul Note / Jul '86 / Cadillac / Harmonia Mundi / Wellard

FRESH
Epistrophy / Play some blues / Fresh / Mysterioso / Chu's blues
CD CDBLC 760214
Black Lion / Apr '96 / Cadillac / Jazz Music / Koch / Wellard

LIVE FROM SOUNDSCAPE (Lowe, Frank Quintet)
CD DIW 399CD
DIW / Jul '94 / Cadillac / Harmonia Mundi

Lowe, Jez

BACK SHIFT
CD FE 089CD
Fellside / Nov '95 / ADA / Direct / Target/ BMG

BAD PENNY
Another man's wife / Small coal song / Midnight mail / Dandelion clocks / Land of the living / Nearer to Nettles / Father Mallory's dance / Yankee boots / New town incident
CD FE 070CD
Fellside / Feb '96 / ADA / Direct / Target/ BMG

BEDE WEEPS (Lowe, Jez & The Bad Pennies)
Call for the North country / These coal town days / Kid Canute / Scotty Moore's reel / Just like Moses / She'll always be freedom / Greek lightning / Dover / Delaware / Teardrop twostep / Too up and too down / Bulldog breed / Last of the widows / Mike Neville said it / Bede weeps
CD FE 094CD
Fellside / Nov '93 / ADA / Direct / Target/ BMG

BRIEFLY ON THE STREET (Lowe, Jez & The Bad Pennies)
You can't take it with you / Famous working man / One man bound / Old hammer-head / Boonas / Soda man / Davis and Golightly / Jordan/The begging bowl / Alice / Fun without fools / Swiss reel / New moon's arms
CD FECD 79
Fellside / Jun '96 / ADA / Direct / Target/ BMG

TENTERHOOKS (Lowe, Jez & The Bad Pennies)
CD GLCD 1161
Green Linnet / Jan '96 / ADA / CM / Direct / Highlander / Roots

Lowe, Mundell

MUNDELL LOWE QUARTET, THE
CD OJCCD 1773
Original Jazz Classics / Jul '94 / Complete/Pinnacle / Jazz Music / Wellard

Lowe, Nick

16 ALL-TIME LOWES
American squirm / Big kick, plain scrap / Born fighter / Cruel to be kind / Heart of the city / I love the sound of breaking glass / Little Hitler / Marie Provost / Nutted by reality / Skin deep so it goes / Switchboard Susan / They called it rock / When I write the book / Without love
CD DIAB 801
Diabolo / Oct '93 / Pinnacle

ABOMINABLE SHOWMAN
Wish you were here / Paid the price / Saint beneath the paint / Time wounds all heals / Tanque-Rae / Around with love / Cool reaction / Chicken and feathers / We want action / Ragin' eyes / How do you talk to an angel / Man or a fall
CD FIENDCD 184
Demon / Apr '90 / Pinnacle

BASHER: THE BEST OF NICK LOWE
So it goes / Heart of the city / I love the sound of breaking glass / Little Hitler / No reason / Thirty six inches high / Marie Provost / Nutted by reality / American squirm / Peace, love and understanding / Cracking up / Big kick, plain scrap / Born fighter / Switchboard Susan / Without love / Love so fine / Cruel to be kind / When I write the book / Heart / Stick it where the sun don't shine / Ragin' eyes / Time wounds all heels / Tanque-rae / Maureen / Half a boy and half a man / Breakaway / She don't love nobody / Seven nights to rock / Long walk back / Rose of England / I knew the bride / Lover's jamboree
CD FIENDCD 142
Demon / Aug '89 / Pinnacle

BOXED - 4CD SET (Jesus Of Cool/Rose Of England/Cowboy Outfit/Pinker &...)
CD Set NICK 1
Demon / Jan '94 / Pinnacle

IMPOSSIBLE BIRD
CD FIENDCD 757
Demon / Oct '94 / Pinnacle

JESUS OF COOL
Music for money / I love the sound of breaking glass / Little Hitler / Shake and pop / Tonight / So it goes / No reason / Thirty six inches high / Marie Provost / Nutted by reality / Heart of the city
CD FIENDCD 131
Demon / Oct '88 / Pinnacle

LABOUR OF LUST
Cruel to be kind / Cracking up / Big kick, plain scrap / Born fighter / You make me / Skin deep / Switchboard Susan / Endless grey ribbon / Without love / Dose of you / Love so fine
CD FIENDCD 182
Demon / Apr '90 / Pinnacle

NICK LOWE AND HIS COWBOY OUTFIT
Half a boy and half a man / You'll never get me up (in one of those) / Maureen / God's gift to women / Gee and the rick and the three card trick / Hey big mouth stand up and say that / Awesome / Breakaway / Love like a glove / Live fast love hard / LAFS
CD FIENDCD 185
Demon / May '90 / Pinnacle

NICK THE KNIFE
Burning / Heart / Stick it where the sun don't shine / Queen of Sheba / My heart hurts / Couldn't love you / Let me kiss ya / Too many teardrops / Ba doom / Raining / One's too many / Zulu kiss
CD FIENDCD 183
Demon / Apr '90 / Pinnacle

PARTY OF ONE PLUS
CD FIENDCD 767
Demon / Oct '95 / Pinnacle

PINKER & PROUDER THAN PREVIOUS
(You're my) wildest dream / Crying in my sleep / Big hair / Love gets strange / Black Lincoln Continental / Cry it out / Lover's jamboree / Geisha girl / Wishing well / Big big love
CD FIENDCD 99
Demon / Mar '88 / Pinnacle

ROSE OF ENGLAND
I knew the bride / Indoor fireworks / I'm right / I can be the one you love / Everyone / Bob Skaddidle daddle / Darlin' angel eyes / She don't love nobody / Seven nights to rock / Long walk back / Rose of England / Lucky dog
CD FIENDCD 73
Demon / Oct '88 / Pinnacle

WILDERNESS YEARS, THE
CD FIENDCD 203
Demon / Oct '90 / Pinnacle

Lowercase

ALL DESTRUCTIVE URGES
CD ARR 73016CD
Amphetamine Reptile / Jun '96 / Plastic Head

Lowery, Ian

KING BLANK TO... (Lowery, Ian Group)
Need / Sick little minds / Beach fire / One last blast / Kind of loathing / You're gonna pay / Party / Driver's arrived
CD SITL 24CD
Situation 2 / Nov '91 / Pinnacle

Lowground

SOUNDS FOR FREAKS
CD SIRE 003
Lowlands / Jan '97 / Cargo

Lowland Band & Pipers Of ...

EDINBURGH CASTLE (Lowland Band & Pipers Of The Scottish Division)
Scotland the brave / Bonnie black isle / Holyrood / Will ye no come back again / Pentland hills / Festoso / Edinburgh castle / Pipe set 3/4 marches / Hebrides suite / Ye banks and braes / Misty morn / Dunedin / Pipes set 6-8 marches / Garb of the old gaul / Dumbarton's drums / Regimental quick marches / Whistle o'er the lave / Blue bonnest o'er the border / Within a mile o'Edinboro' town
CD BNA 5115
Bandleader / Oct '95 / Conifer/BMG

Lowman, Annette

ANNETTE LOWMAN
CD MM 801050
Minor Music / Dec '95 / Vital/SAM

Loxam, Arnold

ARNOLD LOXAM CELEBRATES
Celebration march / Romance / Second waltz / Hawaiian holiday / This is my mother's day / Third Man theme / Jumpin' Charlie/In the pink / Audrey's melody / Spanish gypsy / Zuider Zee ballade / Mr. Snowman goes to town / Berliner Luft / Meditation / I got rhythm / Hors d'oeuvres / Cuckoo waltz / Old refrain / Amsterdam / Storm at sea / Come back to Sorrento
CD OS 223
OS Digital / Jul '96 / Conifer/BMG

BLACKPOOL MAGIC
Beside the seaside / Blackpool walk / Blackpool bounce / So blue / Carolina moon / Wyoming lullaby / Tammy / As time goes by / I'll string along with you / Angels never leave heaven / When my dreamboat comes home / Whispering / Shepherd of the hills / Let a smile be your umbrella / If you knew Susie like I know Susie / Bye bye blackbird / Ik hou van Holland / Sing something simple / Strollin' / Love letters in the sand / Bewitched, bothered and bewildered / Neighbours / One of those songs / Cabaret / Mr. Sandman / It's party time again / Stein song / GB junior club song / Delilah / Cruising down the river / Forever and ever / I just called to say I love you / Bunch of thyme / Love changes everything / Strangers in the night / I'm confessin' that I love you / In a little Spanish town / For me and my girl / Underneath the arches / Morningtown ride / Arm in arm / White cliffs of Dover / Blackpool lights / Last mile home / Who's taking you home / Goodnight (dear goodnight) / Now is the hour / It's a pity to say goodnight / It's a lovely day today / Here's to the next time / Wish me luck as you wave me goodbye
CD CDGRS 1215
Grosvenor / '91 / Grosvenor

STRANGER ON THE SHORE
CD CDGRS 1240
Grosvenor / Feb '93 / Grosvenor

WURLITZER SEASONS
Windermere march / Sunset over Morcambe bay / My darling Clementine / Grasshoppers dance / Perfect year / Dicky bird hop / Windmills of the Zuider Zee / Wear a smile / Londonderry air / End of the pier / To a wild rose / Wishing you were somehow here again / Four seasons in music / Roses of Picardy / Wurlitzer march / Narcissus / 12th Street rag / Kleine melody / Rock gospel melody
CD OS 212
OS Digital / Jun '95 / Conifer/BMG

Loy, Myrna

I PRESS MY LIPS
CD NORMAL 108CD
Normal / Aug '90 / ADA / Direct

Loyer, Jean-Paul

LE MESSAGER
CD OJNABCD 01
Ojnab / Apr '96 / ADA

Loza, Lori

THIS IS LOVE
CD CD 52202
Salt / Apr '96 / Else

LS Diezel

SUICIDAL DUB
Suicidal dub / Round the bend / Swamp dub / Skunk funk / Ragga / Get your spear out / Rockaholic / Ship hop / Dubcid / Eddidat / Secret Mexican trance / Fracid
CD LSDCD 001
LS Diezel / Nov '96 / Vital

LSG

LSG VOL.2
CD SUPER 2069CD
Superstition / Dec '96 / Plastic Head / SRD / Vital

RENDEZVOUS IN OUTER SPACE
Wrong time wrong place / Lonely casseopaya / My time is yours / Can you see the yellow turtles / Miss Understanding / Sweet gravity / Sweet g (#2) / Hidden sun of Venus / Lunar orbit / Everything is / Ebter - paradise / Fontana / Reprise
CD SUPER 2038CD
Superstition / Jun '95 / Plastic Head / SRD / Vital
CD EFA 698576
Superstition / Jul '97 / Plastic Head / SRD / Vital

LSO

SERENITY, TRANQUILITY & PEACE
CD TASTE 061CD
Taste / Aug '95 / Plastic Head / SRD

LTG Exchange

LTG EXCHANGE
CD DGPCD 725
Deep Beats / May '95 / BMG

LTJ Bukem

LOGICAL PROGRESSION VOL.1 (Various Artists)
Demons theme: *LTJ Bukem* / Links: *Links* / Music: *LTJ Bukem* / One & only: *PFM* / Bringing me down: *Aquarius & Tayla* / Sweet sunshine: *Ills & Solo* / Danny's song: *PFM* / Vocal: *Peshay* / Cool out: *LTJ Bukem* / Western: *PFM* / Horizons: *PFM* / Alright: *Funky Technicians* / Aura: *Ills & Solo* / Drum in a grip: *Wax Doctor* / Solution: *Ills & Solo* / Untitled: *Jam Master Jay* / So long: *Seb & Lo Tek* / Pharoah: *Photek* / After hours: *DJ Trance* / Universal: *Rob* / Mind games: *DJ Crystl*
CD 8287392
CD 8287472
FFRR / Apr '96 / PolyGram

LTJ BUKEM PRESENTS EARTH VOL.1 (Various Artists)
Rhyme goes on: *Poets Of Thought* / Travelling: *Appaloosa* / Faith: *Subject 13* / Above & beyond: *PHD & Technicians* / Samba with JC: *Poets Of Thought* / Revival: *Blame* / Do what you gotta do: *Pablo* / Jamming the session: *Poets Of Thought* / Moodswings: *LTJ Bukem* / Tokyo dawn: *Doc Scott*
CD EARTHCD 001
Good Looking / Oct '96 / Prime / Vital

REBIRTH, THE
CD YAMANCD 101
Yaman / May '96 / RTM/Disc

Lubert, Philip

RED LIGHTS AND LONELY FEELINGS
Maria / Lost soul / I just need to know / Lady / Blood / Fairytale / Eikosan / Les Jeux tu Joue / Highlander
CD XTRALUBE 001
Xtralube Productions / Jan '97 / Xtralube Productions

Lubke-Mayer, Coletta

CRIS DE BALAINES (Lubke-Mayer, Coletta Trio)
Invention / E flat blues / La Boheme / Misty cat / Corrida / Roberto / Onion field / Bravo / Three views / Circus / Cris de Balaines / Drum meets bum / Jamba
CD IOR 770302
In & Out / Oct '96 / Vital/SAM

Lubricated Goat

FORCES YOU DON'T UNDERSTAND
You remain anonymous / Next world / Crave the hedonists / Half life / Psychic detective / Lost time / Soul remains the pain / Twentieth century rake / Day in rock
CD PCP 0122
Matador / Aug '94 / Vital

PADDOCK OF LOVE
CD BLAKCD 6
Black Eye / Nov '94 / Direct

PSYCHEDELICATESSEN
CD BLACKCD 11
Normal / Mar '94 / ADA / Direct

SCHADENFREUDE
CD BLACKCD 3
Normal / Mar '94 / ADA / Direct

Lucas

LUCACENTRIC
CD 4509969252
Warner Bros. / Aug '94 / Warner Music

Lucas, Carrie

GREATEST HITS
Keep smilin' / Dance with you / It's not what you got but how you use it / Career girl / Show me where you're coming from / Hello stranger / Goin' in circles / Somebody said / Just a memory / Street corner symphony / Summer in the street / Rockin' for your love / I just can't do without your love
CD DEEPM 035
Deep Beats / Aug '97 / BMG

Lucas, Gary

BAD BOYS OF THE ARCTIC
CD EMY 1462
Enemy / Nov '94 / Grapevine/PolyGram

EVANGELINE
CD INDIGO 58522
Zensor / Dec '96 / Cargo

GODS AND MONSTERS
CD EMY 1332
Enemy / Sep '92 / Grapevine/PolyGram

SKELETON AT THE FEAST
CD EMY 1262
Enemy / Mar '92 / Grapevine/PolyGram

Lucas, Robert

BUILT FOR COMFORT
Built for comfort / Walkin' blues / Ringing that lonesome bell / Just a kid / Blues man from LA / Hawaiian boogie / My home is a burning / Change, change / Sleeping by myself / I miss you baby / Talk to me / Come on in my kitchen
CD AQCD 1011
Audioquest / Sep '95 / ADA / New Note/ Pinnacle

LUKE AND THE LOCOMOTIVE
Good morning little school girl / Big man mambo / Slide on outta here / Worried about it baby / Shed a tear / Feel like going home / Don't your peaches look mellow / Meet me in the bottom / Stranger / I'm so tired / Goodbye baby
CD AQCD 1004
Audioquest / Jul '95 / ADA / New Note/ Pinnacle

USIN' MAN BLUES
Usin' man / Ramblin' on my mind / What happend to my shoes / If I had possession over judgement day / If you see that woman / Moonshine 1 / I'm in jail again / Dancin' with Mr. Jones / Keep your business to yourself / Me and the devil / Jinx around my bed / Motherless children / It's Christmas time baby / New View / Moonshine 2
CD AQCD 1001
Audioquest / Jul '95 / ADA / New Note/ Pinnacle

Lucena, Luis

SELECCION DE ORO VOL.1
CD 9132
Divucsa / Oct '96 / Discovery

Luciano

BACK TO AFRICA
CD EXTCD 3
Exterminator / Sep '94 / Jet Star

DON'T GET CRAZY
CD CRCD 36
Charm / Dec '94 / Jet Star

DON'T GET CRAZY
CD SHRCD 6015
Sky High / Mar '96 / Direct / Jet Star

MESSENGER
Messenger / Life / Mama / Over the hills / Never give up my pride / Rainy days / Friend in need / How can you / Feel like moving / Carry Jah load / Guess what's happening
CD IJCD 3009
Island Jamaica / Oct '96 / Jet Star / PolyGram

MOVING UP
CD RASCD 3129
Ras / Jan '94 / Direct / Greensleeves / Jet Star / SRD

ONE WAY TICKET
CD VPCD 1386
VP / Jan '95 / Greensleeves / Jet Star / Total/BMG
CD CRCD 41
Charm / Jul '95 / Jet Star

REGGAE MAX
CD JSRNCD 13
Jet Star / Mar '97 / Jet Star

SHAKE IT UP TONIGHT
CD BSCD 3
Big Ship / Jul '97 / Jet Star

Lucid Dream

PURE PUNK
CD AA 003CD
A13 / Mar '97 / Kudos / Pinnacle / Vital

Lucid Dreams

LUCID DREAMS
CD EMIT 0096
Time Recordings / Mar '96 / Pinnacle

Lucie Cries

RES NON VERRA
CD AJE 09
Alea Jacta Est / Jun '94 / Plastic Head

Lucien, Jon

ENDLESS IS LOVE
CD SHCD 5031
Shanachie / May '97 / ADA / Greensleeves / Koch

MOTHER NATURE'S SON
How about you / But beautiful / You're sensational / Mother Nature's song / Mi vida / Mysteries / Once upon a time / Luna mi luna / Would you believe in me / Listen love
CD 5148942
Verve / Apr '94 / PolyGram

Luciferon

DEMONICATION (THE MANIFEST)
CD POSH 007CD
Osmose / Jun '95 / Plastic Head

Lucifer's Friend

SUMOGRIP
Get in / One way ticket to hell / You touched me / Step by step / Sheree / Intruder / Ride the sky / Get out / Heartbreaker / Don't look back / Cadillac / Rebound / Back in the track / Any day now / Free me / You touched me with your heart
CD ESMCD 489
Essential / Apr '97 / BMG

Lucky 15

COLOUR CODE WHITE
Medication through resonance / Terge / Stereo 1-5 / Monkey magic / Blue / Snowflakes in Hawaii
CD BU 009CD
Blow Up / Jun '97 / Arabesque / SRD

Lucky Bags

FOOD FOR THOUGHT
CD FECD 112
Fellside / Feb '97 / ADA / Direct / Target/ BMG

Lucky Dube

CAPTURED LIVE
CD SHCD 43090
Shanachie / Apr '93 / ADA / Greensleeves / Koch

SERIOUS REGGAE BUSINESS
CD CDLUCKY 10
Gallo / Nov '96 / Jet Star

TAXMAN
Guns and roses / Taxman / Is this the way / Take it to jah / Mirror, mirror / We love it / You've got a friend / Kiss no frog / Well fed slave/Hungry free man / Good hthings / Release me / I want to know what love is
CD TIMBCD 504
Timbuktu / Aug '97 / Pinnacle
CD CDLUCKY 11
Gallo / Jun '97 / Jet Star

TRINITY
CD 5504792
Tabu / Apr '95 / Jet Star

VICTIMS
CD FLTRCD 512
Flame Tree / Jul '93 / Pinnacle

Lucky Seven

ONE WAY TRACK
CD DEL 3008
Deluge / Dec '95 / ADA / Direct / Koch

Lucky Strikers

SLIP SLIDE AND HOPE
CD SPV 08498812
SPV / May '95 / Koch / Plastic Head

Ludichrist

IMMACULATE DECEPTION
CD WB 3034CD
We Bite / Sep '93 / Plastic Head

POWERTRIP
CD WB 035CD
We Bite / Oct '88 / Plastic Head

Luecking, Juliana

BIG BROAD
Oh / Fancy your hat / Gonna love a woman / 17-18-19 Grrrls / Pull the scam / Head and mouth / Come to Phoenix / Married in midair / Beefheart / Thanks for holding / Shiny blade / Rosita and Marita / 28 and 82 / Willy, Thelma and Kitty / Living legend / Stink / You the best / Margaret and Regina / Pretty girl / Esperanza dreams / Hide and seek / Growth spurt / Big broad / H-heart / Stick shift / Bed bath / Rescue squad / Leaf diving / To be touched / Catch
CD KRS 228CD
Kill Rock Stars / Sep '94 / Cargo / Greyhound / Plastic Head

Lujan, Tony

MAGIC CIRCLE
CD 74023
Capri / Nov '93 / Cadillac / Wellard

Lukather, Steve

LUKE
Real truth / Broken machine / Tears of my own shame / Love the things you hate / Hate everything about U / Reservations to live (the way it is) / Don't hang me on / Always be there for me / Open your heart / Bag o' tales / Bluebird
CD 4873602
Columbia / Jun '97 / Sony

Luke, Robin

SUSIE DARLIN'
Well oh well oh (don't you know) / Everlovin' / Five minutes more / You can't stop me from dreaming / Who's gonna hold your hand / Susie darlin' / Part of a fool / Poor little rich boy / So alone / All because of you / Make me a dreamer / Walkin' in the moonlight / My girl / Chicka chicka honey / School bus love affair / Strollin' blues
CD BCD 15547
Bear Family / Aug '93 / Direct / Rollercoaster / Swift

Lukie D

CENTRE OF ATTRACTION
CD VPCD 1451
VP / Jan '96 / Greensleeves / Jet Star / Total/BMG

Lull

COLD SUMMER
CD SNTX 490
Sentrax Corporation / Sep '94 / Plastic Head

CONTINUE
CD RR 69492
Relapse / Feb '97 / Pinnacle / Plastic Head

DREAMT ABOUT DREAMING
CD RWK 1111
Rawkus / Jun '97 / Cargo / Greyhound

JOURNEY THROUGH UNDERWORLDS
CD RKS 1112
Rawkus / Feb '97 / Cargo / Greyhound

Lullaby For The Working Class

BLANKET WARM
Good morning / Honey drop the knife / Turpentine / Spreading the evening sky with cows / Boar's nest / Eskimo song duel / Three peas in a pod / Rye / Queen of the long legged insects / Drama of your life / February North 24th Street / Wounded spider / Good night
CD RCD 10372
Rykodisc / Sep '96 / ADA / Vital

Lulu

ABSOLUTE
CD DOMECD 11
Dome / Jul '97 / 3mv/Sony

BEST OF LULU, THE
I'm a tiger / Boom bang-a-bang / Me the peaceful heart / Let's pretend / To Sir with love / Boy / Boat that I row / Day tripper / Love loves to love love / Take me in your arms and love me / You & I / March / To love somebody / Best of both worlds
CD 16153
Laserlight / Nov '96 / Target/BMG

EP COLLECTION, THE
Shout / Forget me baby / I am in love / Can't hear me no more / That's really some good / Here comes the night / Heatwave / What's easy for two is so hard for one / Satisfied / He don't want your love anymore / Surprise surprise / Leave a little love / Chocolate ace / Not in this whole world / So in love / He's sure the boy I love / What a wonderful feeling / Tossin' and turnin' / You touch me baby / You'll never leave her / Trouble with the boys / Nothing left to do but cry / Don't answer me / Boat that I row / Let's pretend
CD SEECD 452
See For Miles/C5 / Oct '96 / Pinnacle

GOLD COLLECTION, THE
Boom bang-a-bang / Boat that I row / I'm a tiger / Me the peaceful heart / Let's pretend / Boy / Love loves to love love / To sir with love / Take me in your arms and love me / Day tripper / Dreary days and nights / Best of both worlds / Morning dew / Rattler / You and I / Without him
CD CDGOLD 1005
EMI Gold / Mar '96 / EMI

SHOUT
CD DC 867412
Disky / Aug '96 / Disky / THE

VERY BEST OF LULU
CD BRCD 107
BR Music / Jan '95 / Target/BMG

WORLD OF LULU, THE
Shout / Try to understand / Heatwave / Just one look / Call me / Don't answer me / He don't want your love anymore / That's really some good / After you / What's easy for two is so hard for one / Can't hear you no more / Trouble with boys / Here comes the night / Take me as I am / Surprise surprise / Stubborn kind of fellow / I am in love / Nothing left to do but cry / Tossin' and turnin'
CD 5512702
Spectrum / May '96 / PolyGram

Luman, Bob

LORETTA
Loretta / It's a sin / If you don't love me / Love worked a miracle / Poor boy blues / Sentimental / You're welcome / Running scared / Freedom of living / Tears from out of nowhere / It's all over / Best years of my wife / Bigger man than I / Too hot to dance / I like your kind of love / Hardly anymore
CD CDSD 068
Sundown / Nov '89 / TKO Magnum

Lumiere, Jean

ETOILES DE LA CHANSON
CD 882502
Music Memoria / Aug '93 / ADA / Discovery

MONSIEUR CHARME
CD _______ 701632
Chansophone / Nov '96 / Discovery

Lumukanda

ARAGLIN
CD _______ NZCD 004
Nova Zembla / Feb '94 / Plastic Head

Luna

BEWITCHED
California (all the way) / Tiger Lily / Friendly advice / Bewitched / This time around / Great Jones Street / Going home / Into the fold / I know you tried / Sleeping pill
CD _______ 7559616172
WEA / Mar '94 / Warner Music

LUNAPARK
Slide / Anesthesia / Slash your tyres / Crazy people / Time / Smile / I can't wait / Hey sister / I want everything / Time to quit / Goodbye / We're both confused
CD _______ 7559613602
WEA / Aug '92 / Warner Music

PENTHOUSE
CD _______ BBQCD 178
Beggars Banquet / Jul '95 / RTM/Disc / Warner Music

PUP TENT
CD _______ BBQCD 194
Beggars Banquet / Aug '97 / RTM/Disc / Warner Music

Lunachicks

BABYSITTERS ON ACID
CD _______ BFFP 52CD
Blast First / Nov '89 / RTM/Disc

BINGE AND PURGE
CD _______ SPV 08445432
SPV / Mar '96 / Koch / Plastic Head

BINGE AND PURGE
CD _______ SH 21072
Safe House / Nov '96 / Cargo

JERK OF ALL TRADES
Drop dead / Fingerful / FDS / Light as a feather / Edgar / Dogyard / Butt plugg / Bitternes Barbie / Deal with it / Brickface and stucco / Jerk of all trades / Spoilt / Ring and run / Fallopian rhapsody / Insomnia / Why me
CD _______ GK 013CD
Go-Kart / May '97 / Greyhound / Pinnacle

PRETTY UGLY
CD _______ GK 024CD
Go-Kart / Mar '97 / Greyhound / Pinnacle

Lunar Drive

HERE AT BLACK MESA ARIZONA
CD _______ NR 1076CD
Nation / Oct '96 / RTM/Disc

Lunatic Calm

METROPOLE
CD _______ MCD 60043
MCA / Aug '97 / BMG

Lunatic Gods

INHUMAN AND INSENSIBLE
CD _______ POLYPH 002CD
Polyphemus / Jul '96 / Plastic Head

Lunceford, Jimmie

BABY WON'T YOU PLEASE COME HOME
Lonesome road / You set me on fire / Baby, won't you please come home / I've only myself to blame / You're just a dream / Easter parade / Blue blazes / Mixup / What is this thing called swing / Shoemaker's holiday / Ain't she sweet / Mandy / White heat / Well alright then / I love you / Oh why oh why / Who did you meet last night / You let me down / Sassin' the boss / I want the waiter (with the water) / You can fool some of the people (some of the time) / Think of me, little daddy / Liza / Belgium stomp / You let me down / I used to love you (but it's all over now)
CD _______ GRF 086
Tring / '93 / Tring

BLUES IN THE NIGHT (Lunceford, Jimmie & Orchestra)
T'ain't what you do (it's the way that you do it) / Blues in the night / Organ grinder swing / Margie / Le jazz hot / Uptown blues / Baby, won't you please come home / Twenty four robbers / I'm gonna move to the outskirts of town / For dancers only / Well alright then / Lonesome road / Cheatin' on me / Ain't she sweet / Mandy / Back door stuff / Harlem shout / Four or five times
CD _______ CD 56013
Jazz Roots / Sep '94 / Target/BMG

CLASSICS 1930-1934
CD _______ CLASSICS 501
Classics / Apr '90 / Discovery / Jazz Music

CLASSICS 1934-1935
CD _______ CLASSICS 505
Classics / Apr '90 / Discovery / Jazz Music

CLASSICS 1935-1937
CD _______ CLASSICS 510
Classics / Apr '90 / Discovery / Jazz Music

CLASSICS 1937-1939
CD _______ CLASSICS 520
Classics / Apr '90 / Discovery / Jazz Music

CLASSICS 1939
CD _______ CLASSICS 532
Classics / Dec '90 / Discovery / Jazz Music

CLASSICS 1939-1940
CD _______ CLASSICS 565
Classics / Oct '91 / Discovery / Jazz Music

CLASSICS 1940-41 (Lunceford, Jimmie & Orchestra)
CD _______ CLASSICS 622
Classics / Nov '92 / Discovery / Jazz Music

CLASSICS 1941-1945
CD _______ CLASSICS 862
Classics / Mar '96 / Discovery / Jazz Music

INTRODUCTION TO JIMMIE LUNCEFORD 1934-1942, AN
CD _______ 4002
Best Of Jazz / Dec '93 / Discovery

JIMMIE LUNCEFORD
CD _______ HEPCD 1017
Hep / Jan '91 / Cadillac / Jazz Music / New Note/Pinnacle / Wellard

JIMMIE LUNCEFORD & HIS ORCHESTRA (1934-1935) (Lunceford, Jimmie & Orchestra)
CD _______ 11088
Laserlight / '88 / Target/BMG

JIMMIE LUNCEFORD & ORCHESTRA (1934-1939) (Lunceford, Jimmie & Orchestra)
CD _______ BLE 592412
Black & Blue / Dec '92 / Discovery / Koch / Wellard

JIMMIE LUNCEFORD & ORCHESTRA 1934-42
CD _______ TPZ 1005
Topaz Jazz / Aug '94 / Cadillac / Pinnacle

LIVE AT JAFFERSON BARRACKS, MISSOURI (Lunceford, Jimmie & His Harlem Express)
CD _______ HCD 221
Hindsight / Sep '94 / Jazz Music / Target/BMG

LIVE BROADCASTS 1936-1943 (Lunceford, Jimmie Orchestra)
CD _______ JH 3004
Jazz Hour / Mar '97 / Cadillac / Jazz Music / Target/BMG

MUSIC OF JIMMIE LUNCEFORD, THE (American Jazz Orchestra)
Lunceford special / What's your story morning glory / Belgium stomp / I'm alone with you / Yard dog Mazurka / Hi spook / For dancers only / Uptown blues / Annie Laurie / Margie / I wanna hear swing songs / Organ grinder swing
CD _______ 8208462
Limelight / May '92 / PolyGram

POLISHED PERFECTION
CD _______ TOPAZ 1005
Topaz/ADA / Mar '95 / ADA

POWERHOUSE SWING
Well alright / You let me down / I want the waiter (with the water) / I used to love you (but it's all over now) / Belgian stomp / Think of me little Daddy / Liza / Rock it for me / I'm in an awful mood / Uptown blues / Lunceford special / Bugs parade / Blues in the groove / I got it / Chopins prelude No.7 / Swingin' in C / Let's try again / Monotony in four plats / Barefoot blues / Minnie the moocher is dead
CD _______ PAR 2012
Parade / Apr '94 / Disc

QUINTESSENCE, THE (1934-1941/2CD Set)
CD Set _______ FA 212
Fremeaux / Oct '96 / ADA / Discovery

RHYTHM IS OUR BUSINESS
Rhythm is our business / Stratosphere / Unsophisticated Sue / Four or five times / Bird of paradise / I'll take the South / Hittin' the bottle / Oh boy / Best things in life are free / Muddy water / Hell's bells / He ain't got rhythm / Slumming on Park Avenue / For dancers only / Posin' / Margie / Frisco fog / What is this thing called Swing / Ain't she sweet / Life is fine
CD _______ PPCD 78111
Past Perfect / Feb '95 / Glass Gramophone Co.

RHYTHM IS OUR BUSINESS
Baby, won't you please come home / Barefoot blues / Belgium stomp / Black and tan fantasy / Flaming reeds and screaming brass / For dancers only / Four or five times / Hittin' the bottle / I'm alone with you / Le jazz hot / Margie / My blue heaven / Organ grinder swing / Pigeon walk / Rhythm is our business / Shake your head / Since my best gal turned me down / Sleepy time gal / Sophisticated lady / T'ain't what you do (it's the way that you do it) / Time's a wastin' / Uptown blues / What's your story Morning Glory / While love lasts
CD _______ CDAJA 5091
Living Era / May '92 / Select

RHYTHM IS OUR BUSINESS (Lunceford, Jimmie & His Orchestra)
Organ grinder's swing / Strictly instrumental / I'm gonna move to the outskirts of town / Mood indigo / Yard dog mazurka / Posin' / Sophisticated lady / Margie / Runnin' a temperature / For dancers only / Rhythm is our business / Stratosphere / Annie Laurie / Black and tan fantasy / Twenty four robbers / Coquette / Blue prelude / Siesta at the fiesta / Knock me a kiss / Blues in the night
CD _______ 306312
Hallmark / Jan '97 / Carlton

Lunch, Lydia

RUDE HIEROGLYPHICS (Lunch, Lydia & Excene Cervenka)
CD _______ RCD 10326
Rykodisc / Oct '95 / ADA / Vital

SHOTGUN WEDDING
CD _______ WSP 002CD
UFO / Oct '91 / Pinnacle

TRANCE MUTATION/SHOTGUN WEDDING (2CD Set)
CD Set _______ TWIST 2
NMC / Jul '94 / Total/Pinnacle

TRANCEMUTATION (The Best Of Lydia Lunch)
CD _______ PILOT 009
Burning Airlines / Mar '97 / Total/Pinnacle

Lundeng, Susanne

AETTESYN
CD _______ FXCD 178
Kirkelig Kulturverksted / May '97 / ADA

DRAG
CD _______ FX 140CD
Kirkelig Kulturverksted / Dec '94 / ADA

Lundgren, Jan

CALIFORNIA COLLECTION (Lundgren, Jan & Peter Asplund Quartet)
CD _______ FLCCD 148
Four Leaf Clover / May '97 / Cadillac / Wellard

STOCKHOLM GET-TOGETHER (Lundgren, Jan Trio)
CD _______ FSR 5007CD
Fresh Sound / Jul '96 / Discovery / Jazz Music

Lundsten, Ralph

INSPIRATION - SWEDEN (Landscape Of Dreams)
CD _______ CDM 5658842
EMI Classics / Mar '96 / EMI

Lundy, Carmen

OLD DEVIL MOON
Star eyes / When your lover has gone / Just one more chance / You're not in love / I didn't know what time it was / Flying easy / I'm worried about you baby / At the end of my rope / In a sentimental mood / Love me forever
CD _______ JVC 90192
JVC / Jul '97 / Direct / New Note/Pinnacle / Vital/SAM

SELF PORTRAIT
Spring can really hang you up the most / Better days / My favourite things / Firefly / Forgive me / These things you are to me / Triste without you / I don't want to love without you / Old friend / My ship / 'Round midnight
CD _______ JVC 2047
JVC / Apr '95 / Direct / New Note/Pinnacle / Vital/SAM

Lundy, Curtis

JUST BE YOURSELF
Jabbo's revenge / Silver's serenade / Funny (not much) / Crossroads / Never gonna let you go / Just be yourself / Ballando / Shaw 'nuff
CD _______ ECD 221792
Evidence / Jul '97 / ADA / Cadillac / Harmonia Mundi

Lung

CACTII
CD _______ YELLOWBIKE 003
Plastic Head / Jul '92 / Plastic Head

Lung Leg

MAID TO MINX
CD _______ POMPCD 007
Vesuvius / Jul '97 / SRD

Lungfish

INDIVISIBLE
CD _______ DIS 106CD
Dischord / Apr '97 / SRD

PASS AND STOW
CD _______ DIS 92CD
Dischord / Sep '94 / SRD

RAINBOWS FROM ATOMS
CD _______ DIS 78 D
Dischord / Jun '93 / SRD

SOUND IN TIME
CD _______ DIS 97CD
Dischord / Feb '96 / SRD

Lungs

BETTER CLASS OF LOSER, A
CD _______ CDVEST 68
Bulletproof / Feb '96 / Pinnacle

Luniz

OPERATION STACKOLA
Intro / Put the lead on ya / I got 5 on it / Broke hos / Pimps, playas and hustlas / Playa hata / Broke niggaz / Operation stackola / 5150 / 900 Blame a nigga / Yellow brick road / So much drama / She's a freak / Plead guilty / I got 5 on it (Reprise) / Outro
CD _______ CDVUS 94
Virgin / Mar '96 / EMI

Lunny, Donal

DONAL LUNNY
CD _______ CEFCD 133
Gael Linn / Jan '94 / ADA / CM / Direct / Grapevine/PolyGram / Roots

Lunsford, Bascom Lamar

BALLADS, BANJO TUNES & SACRED SONGS OF NORTH CAROLINA
CD _______ SFWCD 40082
Smithsonian Folkways / May '96 / ADA / Cadillac / CM / Direct / Koch

Luomakunta

ROCK OK
CD _______ AA 030
AA / Jul '97 / Cargo / Greyhound

TAYSIN SYOTAVA
CD _______ AA 027
AA / Jul '97 / Cargo / Greyhound

Lupone, Patti

LUPONE LIVE
CD Set _______ 09026617972
RCA / Jul '93 / BMG

Lurie, Evan

HAPPY HERE NOW
CD _______ TWI 5742
Les Disques Du Crepuscule / Mar '96 / Discovery

PIECES OF BANDONEON
CD _______ TWI 8712
Les Disques Du Crepuscule / Mar '96 / Discovery

Lurie, John

MEN WITH STICKS (Lurie, John National Orchestra)
If I sleep the plane will crash / Men with sticks / Schnards live here
CD _______ MTM 34
Made To Measure / Apr '96 / New Note/Pinnacle

Lurkers

BEGGARS BANQUET PUNK SINGLES, THE
CD _______ CDPUNK 94
Anagram / May '97 / Cargo / Pinnacle

LAST WILL AND TESTAMENT
I'm on heat / Cyanide / Shadow / Wine drinker me / Out in the dark / Freak show / Jenny / Self destruct / Ain't got a clue / Take me back to Babylon / Total war / Love story / Then I kicked her / Just thirteen / New guitar in town / She knows
CD _______ BBL 2CD
Lowdown/Beggars Banquet / Jul '88 / RTM/Disc / Warner Music

NON STOP NITROPOP
CD _______ WLO 24602
Weser / Oct '94 / Plastic Head

POWERJIVE/KING OF THE MOUNTAIN
Powerjive / Lipstick and shampoo / Solitaire / Waiting for you / Things will never be the same / World of Jenny Brown / Walk like a superstar (talk like a zombie) / Go go girl / Strange desire (burn, burn, burn) / Raven's wing / I close my eyes / Lullaby / Barbara blue / Never had a beach head / Unfinished business / Going monkee again (hey hey hey) / King of the mountain (part 1) / Lucky John / King of the mountain (part 2)
CD _______ CDPUNK 69
Anagram / Nov '95 / Cargo / Pinnacle

WILD TIMES AGAIN
CD ____ WLO 24332
Weser / Oct '94 / Plastic Head

Luscious Jackson

FEVER IN, FEVER OUT
Naked eye / Don't look back / Door / Mood swing / Under your skin / Electric / Take a ride / Water your garden / Soothe yourself / Why do I lie / One thing / Parade / Faith / Stardust
CD ____ CDEST 2290
Grand Royal / Apr '97 / EMI

IN SEARCH OF MANNY
Let yourself get down / Life of leisure / Daughters of the kaos / Keep on rockin' it / She be wantin' it more / Bam-Bam / Satellite
CD ____ ABB 46XCD
Big Cat / Aug '95 / 3mv/Pinnacle
CD ____ GR 001CD
Grand Royal / Apr '97 / Cargo / Plastic Head

NATURAL INGREDIENTS
City song / Deep shag / Angel / Strongman / Energy sucker / Here / Find your mind / Pele Merengue / Rock freak / Rollin' / Surprise / LP Retreat
CD ____ CDEST 2234
Capitol / Aug '94 / EMI

Lush

LOVELIFE
Ladykillers / Heavenly nobodies / 50 / I've been here before / Papasan / Single girl / Ciao / Tralala / Last night / Runaway / Childcatcher / Olympia
CD ____ CAD 6004CD
4AD / Mar '96 / RTM/Disc

SCAR
CD ____ JADCD 911
4AD / Oct '89 / RTM/Disc

SPLIT
CD ____ GAD 4011CD
4AD / Feb '96 / RTM/Disc

SPOOKY
CD ____ GAD 2002CD
4AD / Feb '96 / RTM/Disc

Lusher, Don

JUST GOOD FRIENDS (Lusher, Don & Maurice Murphy/The Hammonds Sauce Works Band)
CD ____ DOYCD 020
Doyen / Feb '93 / Conifer/BMG

TRIBUTE TO THE GREAT BANDS VOL.1 (Lusher, Don Big Band)
Peanut vendor / Take the 'A' train / I'll never smile again / Don't be that way / I've got my love to keep me warm / Kid from Red Bank / Opus one / Adios / I get a kick out of you / Early Autumn / Caravan / Two o'clock jump
CD ____ CDSIV 110
Horatio Nelson / Jul '95 / Disc

TRIBUTE TO THE GREAT BANDS VOL.2 (Lusher, Don Big Band)
Trumpet blues and cantabile / Pennsylvania 6-5000 / That lovely weekend / That's right / Westlake / DL blues / Sing sing sing / April in Paris / I'm getting sentimental over you / Don't get around much anymore / Concerto to end all concertos
CD ____ CDSIV 1114
Horatio Nelson / Jul '95 / Disc

TRIBUTE TO THE GREAT BANDS VOL.3 (Lusher, Don Big Band)
Carnival / Benny rides again / Song of India / Cute / Wales '87 / Moonlight serenade / At the woodchoppers' ball / Boogie woogie / Love for sale / High and mighty / Cotton tail / Tea for two
CD ____ CDSIV 1125
Horatio Nelson / Jul '95 / Disc

TRIBUTE TO THE GREAT BANDS VOL.4 (Lusher, Don Big Band)
Mr. Anthony's boogie / Sunny side of the street / Continental / Isafahan / Mission to Moscow / Night in Tunisia / Apple honey / Wave / Shiny stockings / Liebestraum / String of pearls / One o'clock jump
CD ____ CDSIV 1133
Horatio Nelson / Jul '95 / Disc

Lussia

FLEUR DE MANDRAGORE
CD ____ 422471
New Rose / May '94 / ADA / Direct / Discovery

Lussier, Rene

CHANTS ET DANSES DU MONDE INANIME (Lussier, Rene & Robert Lepage)
CD ____ AM 001CD
Ambiances Magnetiques / Jun '97 / ReR Megacorp

FIN DE TRAVAIL
CD ____ AM 000CD
Ambiances Magnetiques / Jun '97 / ReR Megacorp

THREE SUITE PIECE (Lussier, Rene & Jean Derome/Chris Cutler)
CD ____ RERLDC 1
ReR/Recommended / Oct '96 / ReR Megacorp / RTM/Disc

Lustmord

LUSTMORD
CD ____ DV 04
Dark Vinyl / Jan '94 / Plastic Head / World Serpent

MONSTROUS SOUL
CD ____ DFX 14CD
Dark Vinyl / Oct '96 / Plastic Head / World Serpent

PARADISE DISOWNED
CD ____ SECD 07
Side Effects / Oct '96 / Plastic Head / World Serpent

PLACE WHERE THE BLACK STARS HANG, THE
CD ____ DFX 16CD
Dark Vinyl / Jan '95 / Plastic Head / World Serpent

Lutcher, Nellie

BEST OF NELLIE LUTCHER, THE
Hurry on down / One I love belongs to somebody else / You better watch yourself / Bub / My mother's eyes / He's a real gone guy / Let me love you tonight / Chi-Chi-Chi Chicago / Fine and mellow / I thought about you / Kinda blue and low / Song is ended (but the melody lingers on) / Lake Charles boogie / Fine brown frame / My man (mon homme) / Chicken ain't nothing but a bird / He sends me / My new Papa's got to have everything / Come and get it / Honey / That will just about knock me out, baby / What's your alibi / Pa's not home
CD ____ CDP 8350392
Capitol Jazz / Nov '95 / EMI

DITTO FROM ME TO YOU
Ditto from me to you / I took a trip on the train / One I love (belongs to somebody else) / Humoresque / Pig latin song / Imagine you having eyes for me / Princess Poo-Poo-Ly has plenty papya / Say a little prayer for me / Baby please stop and think about me / Only you / I really couldn't love you / He sends me / That's how it goes / Mean to me / If I didn't love you like I do / St. Louis blues
CD ____ RBD 1103
Mr. R&B / Oct '90 / CM / Swift / Wellard

NELLIE LUTCHER & HER RHYTHM (4CD Set)
One I love (belongs to someone else) / Hurry on down / Lady's in love with you / You better watch yourself Bub / Sleepy lagoon / My mother's eyes / He's a real gone guy / Let me love you tonight / Pig Latin song / Do you or don't you love me / Chi-Chi-Chi-Chicago / Loveable / Fine & mellow blues / There's another mule in your stall / I thought about you / Kinda blue & low / Reaching for the moon / Song is ended (but the melody lingers on) / So nice to see you baby / Lake Charles boogie / Fine brown frame / Humoresque / Imagine you having eyes for me / Alexander's Ragtime Band / Without a song / Wish I was in Walla Walla / Life is like that / Maid's prayer / Ditto from me to you / My man / I used to be dull / Dog fight song / Lutcher's leap / Say a little prayer for me / Cool water / Chicken ain't nothing but a bird / Princess Poo-Poo-Ly has plenty papaya / He sends me / My little boy / My new Papa's got to have everything / Come & get it honey / Little Sally Walker / To be forgotten / Darktown strutters ball / That will just about knock me out / Glad Rag doll / April in Paris / Only you / Kiss me sweet / Baby, please stop and think about me / That's aplenty / Baby, what's your alibi / I'll never get tired / For you my love / Can I come in for a second / Pa's not home / I really couldn't love you / Body & fender work / He couldn't care less / If you wanna get t'goin' / Mean to me / I want to be near you / Birth of the blues / Let the worry bird worry for you / What a difference a day made / That's how it goes / Heart of a clown / Keepin' out of mischief now / When they ask about you / How many more / Muchly verily / Whee baby / Takin' a chance on love / Takin' a chance on love / St. Louis blues / Bill Bailey, won't you please come home / Out of this world / It's been said / Blues in the night / Breezin' along with the breeze / Whose honey are you / Please come back / If I didn't love you like I do / Blue skies / Three little words / You made me love you / This can't be love / Nearness of you / It had to be you / On the sunny side of the street / Someone to watch over me / All of a sudden my heart sings / Rose coloured glasses / Ole buttermilk sky / Have you ever been lonely / Hurry on down / Let me tell you 'bout the city / If your face was as beautiful as your soul / He's a real gone guy / There's a reason / I'll never get tired / Heart of a clown / Reaching for the moon
CD Set ____ BCD 15910
Bear Family / Nov '96 / Direct / Rollercoaster / Swift

Lutefisk

BURN IN HELL FUCKERS
CD ____ BL 292
Bongload / Jan '97 / Cargo / Greyhound / Plastic Head

Luter, Claude

RED HOT REEDS
CD ____ BCD 219
GHB / Jul '93 / Jazz Music

Luxon, Benjamin

I LOVE MY LOVE (A Collection Of British Folk Songs) (Luxon, Benjamin & David Willison)
Jolly miller / Drink to me only with thine eyes / Foggy foggy dew / Isle of Cloy / Trees they grow so high / Died for love / Lovely Mollie / I love my love / Shooting of his dear / Down by the Sally Gardens / Old turf fire / Banks and braes / Barb'ra (H)ellen / Barbara Allen / She moved through the fair / Star of County Down / Sweet nightingale / Blow the wind southerly / British waterside / Press gang / Little Sir William / Sir Dukes went-a-fishin' / Sweet Polly Oliver / Bold William Taylor / Charlie is my darling / O Waly, Waly
CD ____ CHAN 8946
Chandos / Jun '92 / Chandos

TWO GENTLEMEN FOLK (Luxon, Benjamin & Friends)
CD ____ CD 84401
Telarc / '88 / Conifer/BMG

Luxuria

BEAST BOX
Beast box is dreaming / Stupid blood / Against the past / Our curious leader / We keep on getting there / Ticket / Animal in the mirror / Dirty beating heart / Smoking mirror / I've been expecting you / Karezza / Beast box / Jezebel
CD ____ BEGA 106CD
Beggars Banquet / May '90 / RTM/Disc / Warner Music

UNANSWERABLE LUST
Redneck / Flesh / Public highway / Pound / Lady 21 / Celebrity / Rubbish / Mile / Luxuria
CD ____ BEGA 90CD
Beggars Banquet / '88 / RTM/Disc / Warner Music

Luzzaschi, Luzzasco

SECRET MUSIC OF LUZZASCO LUZZASCHI
CD ____ CDSAR 58
Saydisc / Oct '92 / ADA / Direct / Harmonia Mundi

LV

I AM LV
CD ____ TBCD 1140
Tommy Boy / Mar '96 / RTM/Disc

Lwiro Children's Choir

AFRICAN MASS
CD ____ VICG 52292
JVC World Library / Mar '96 / ADA / CM / Direct

Ly, Mamadou

MANDINKA DRUM MASTER
CD ____ VPU 1001CD
Village Pulse / May '97 / ADA

Lyall, William

SOLO CASTING
Solo casting / Us / Playing in the sand / Supertrader / Reasons / Deeper you get / Maniac / Don't be silly / Take me up / Sleep
CD ____ SEECD 448
See For Miles/C5 / Jul '96 / Pinnacle

Lycia

DAY IN THE STARK CORNER, A
CD ____ HY 39100762CD
Hyperium / Oct '93 / Cargo / Plastic Head

IONIA
CD ____ PRO 32
Projekt / Jan '97 / Cargo

WAKE
CD ____ PRO 31
Projekt / Jan '97 / Cargo

Lydon, John

PSYCHO'S PATH
Grave ride / Dog / Psychopath / Sun / Another way / Dis-Ho / Take me / No and a yes / Stump / Armies / Open up / Grave ride / Sun / Psychopath / Stump
CD ____ CDVUS 130
Virgin / Jun '97 / EMI

Lyle, Bobby

JOURNEY, THE
CD ____ 7567821382
Atlantic / Jan '97 / Warner Music

PIANOMAGIC
CD ____ 7567823462
Atlantic / Jan '97 / Warner Music

SECRET ISLAND
CD ____ 7567824352
Atlantic / Dec '96 / Warner Music

Lyman, Arthur

BACHELOR'S DEN VOL.6
CD ____ DCC 96CD
DCC / Apr '96 / ADA

HAWAIIAN SUNSET
Hawaiian war chant / Sweet Leilani / Queen serenade / My Tani / Whispering reef / Song of the islands / Hi lawe / Island of golden dreams / Mapuano / Wapio / Kawohikukuplani / Ke kali ne au / Harbor lights / Blue Hawaii / Beyond the reef / Quiet village / Ahola-no Honolulu
CD ____ RCD 50365
Rykodisc / Sep '96 / ADA / Vital

SONIC SIXTIES
CD ____ TCD 1031
Tradition / Nov '96 / ADA / Vital

TABOO
Taboo / Katua / Ringo oiwake / Sea breeze / Miserlou / China clipper / Sim sim / Katsumi love theme / Caravan / Akaka falls / Dahil Sayo / Hilo march / Bwana A / Colonel Bogey's march / Waikiki serenade / Moon over a ruined castle
CD ____ RCD 50364
Rykodisc / Sep '96 / ADA / Vital

WITH A CHRISTMAS VIBE
Rudolph the red nosed reindeer / Winter wonderland / Mele Kalikimaka / Mary's boy child / O' holy night / Little drummer boy / We three Kings / White Christmas / Silver bells / Sleigh ride / Christmas song / Silent night / Joy to the world
CD ____ RCD 50363
Rykodisc / Oct '96 / ADA / Vital

Lymon, Frankie

BEST OF FRANKIE LYMON AND THE TEENAGERS
Why do fools fall in love / I want you to be my girl / I'm not a know it all / Who can exlain / I promise to remember / ABC's of love / Share / I'm not a juvenile delinquent / Baby baby / Paper castles / Teenage love / Out in the cold again / Goody goody / Creation of love / Please be mine / Love is a clown / Am I fooling myself again / Thumb thumb / Portable on my shoulder / Little bitty pretty one
CD ____ CZ 241
Roulette / Nov '89 / EMI

COMPLETE RECORDINGS (Lymon, Frankie & The Teenagers)
Why do fools fall in love / Please be mine / Love is a clown / Am I fooling myself again / I'm not a know it all / Who can explain / I promise to remember / ABC's of love (Version 2) / Share / I'm not a juvenile delinquent / Baby baby / Paper castles / Teenage love / Together / You / It would be so nice / Out in the cold again / Little white lies / Begin the beguine / Love is a clown (Alt) / I want you to be my girl / I'm not a know it all (Alt) / Who can explain (Alt) / ABC's of love (Version 1) / Promise to remember (Alt) / Share (Alt) / Fortunate fellow / Love put me out of my head / Lost without your love / I'll walk alone (Without love) / Everything to me / Flip flop / Good love / Flop hop / Mama wanna rock / My broken heart / Crying / Tonight's the night / Can you tell me why / Little wiser now / What's on your mind / Love me long / He's no lover / I hear the angels cry / Wild female / Jean of the ville / Draw / Goody goody / It's Christmas once again / Only way to love / Miracle in the rain / Yours / Glow worm / Good good (Version 1) / Love is the thing / You can't be true / Fools rush in / Too young / Over the rainbow / As time goes by / Don't take your love / I don't stand a ghost of a chance with you / Goody goody (Version 2) / Creation of love / Blue moon / These foolish things / You were only fooling / Guilty / So goes my love / My girl / My baby just cares for me / Somebody loves me / Silent night / Little girl / Let's fall in love / Thumb thumb / Portable on my shoulder / Footsteps / That's the way love goes / Wake up little Susie / Short fat Fannie / Waitin' in school / Next time you see me / Jailhouse rock / Send for me / Buzz buzz buzz / Searchin' / Silouettes / It hurts to be in love / Diana / Diana (Alt) / Little bitty pretty one / Mama don't allow it / Girls were made for boys / Campus queen / No matter what you've done / Melinda / Ain't she sweet / Almost out of my mind / Rockin' tambourine / Danny Boy / Up jumped the rabbit / Before I fall asleep / Prince or pauper / What a little moonlight can do / 'Deed I do / Since the beginning of time / Pardon me please / Magic song / Kiss from your lips / Joke (Version 1) / Rainbow / Joke (Version 2) / Goody good girl / Blessed are they / I'm not to young to dream / Almost out of my mind (Version 2) / Is you is or is you ain't my baby / Lover come back to me / Change partners / So young / I put the bomp / To each his own / Teacher, teacher / Roll off / Push and pull / Sweet and lovely / Somewhere /

Somewhere (Stereo) / I'm sorry / Sea breeze
CD Set BCD 15782
Bear Family / Jun '94 / Direct / Rollercoaster / Swift

ESSENTIAL RECORDINGS 1955-1961 (2CD Set)
Why do fools fall in love / Please be mine / I want you to be my girl / Im not a know it all / I promise to remember / Who can explain / ABC's of love / Share / I'm not a juvenile delinquent / Baby, baby / Teenage love / Paper castles / Love is a clown / Am I fooling myself again / Together / You / Out in the cold again / Miracle in the rain / Little white lies / It would be so nice / Fortunate fellow / Love put me out of my head / Begin the beguine / Goody goody / Creation of love / Flip flop / Everything to me / So goes my love / My girl / Footsteps / Thumb thumb / Little girl / Portable, on my shoulder / Mama don't allow it / My broken heart / Mama wanna rock / Waitin' in school / Wake up little Susie / Silhouettes / Next time you see me / Send for me / It hurts to be in love / Jailhouse rock / Diana / Buzz, buzz, buzz / Searchin' / Short fat Fannie / Little bitty pretty one / Melinda / Only way to love / No matter what you've done / Up jumped a rabbit / What a little moonlight can do / Before I fall asleep / Goody good girl / I'm not to young to dream / Tonight's the night / Crying / Little bit wiser now / Can you tell me / Change partners / So young / I put the bomp (in the bomp bomp bomp)
CD Set NEDCD 287
Sequel / Apr '97 / BMG

WHY DO FOOLS FALL IN LOVE
CD RMB 75034
Remember / Nov '93 / Total/BMG

Lynam, Ray

VERY BEST OF RAY LYNAM, THE
If we're not back in love by Monday / What a lie / He stopped loving her today / You put the blue in me / You win again / Gambler / Moon is still over her shoulder / Beautiful woman / To be lovers / Mona Lisa has lost her smile / Girls, women, and ladies / Hold her in your hand / Speak softly (you're talking to my heart) / I'll never get over you / Rainy days stormy nights / I don't want to see another town
CD RITZCD 513
Ritz / Dec '91 / Pinnacle

Lynch, Brian

IN PROCESS
Four flights up / Flamingo / On process / DTMYM (Do that make you mad) / After dark / New arrival / I should care / So in love / Brydflight
CD 66056011
Ken Music / Aug '92 / New Note/Pinnacle

PEER PRESSURE (Lynch, Brian Sextet)
Thomasville / Park Avenue petite / Peer pressure / Outlaw / Change of plan / Nother never
CD CRISS 1029CD
Criss Cross / Nov '91 / Cadillac / Direct / Vital/SAM

Lynch, Claire

MOONLIGHTER
CD ROUCD 0355
Rounder / Jun '95 / ADA / CM / Direct

Lynch, George

SACRED GROOVE
Memory Jack / Love power from the Mama head / Flesh and blood / We don't own this world / I will remember / Beast part 1 / Beast part 2 / Not necessary evil / Cry of the brave / Tierra del fuego
CD 7559614222
Elektra / Aug '93 / Warner Music

Lynch, Joe

LITTLE BIT OF IRELAND, A
CD MACCD 321
Autograph / Aug '96 / BMG

Lynch, Kenny

AFTER DARK
CD FRCD 100
Welfare / Jul '93 / Total/BMG

Lynch Mob

LYNCH MOB
Jungle of love / Tangled in the web / No good / Dream until tomorrow / Cold is the heart / Tie your mother down / Heaven is waiting / I want it / When darkness calls / Secret
CD 75596132212
Elektra / May '92 / Warner Music

WICKED SENSATION
Wicked sensation / River of love / Sweet sister mercy / All I want / Hell child / She's evil but she's mine / Dance of the dogs / Rain / No bed of roses / Through these eyes / For a million years / Street fighting man
CD 7559609542
Elektra / Oct '90 / Warner Music

Lynch, Ray

NO BLUE THING
No blue thing / Clouds below your knees / Here and never found / Drifted in a deeper land / Homeward at last / Evenings, yes / True spirit of mom and dad
CD 01934111192
Windham Hill / Jan '94 / BMG

NOTHING ABOVE MY SHOULDERS BUT THE EVENING
Over easy / Her knees deep in your mind / Passion song / Ivory / Mesquite / Only an enjoyment / Vanishing gardens of Cordoba
CD 01934111332
Windham Hill / Nov '93 / BMG

Lynch, Tomas

CRUX OF THE CATALOGUE, THE
CD LC 002CD
Linecheck / Apr '94 / ADA / Direct

Lynn, Barbara

ATLANTIC SESSION, THE (The Best Of Barbara Lynn)
CD SCL 2505
Ichiban Soul Classics / Apr '95 / Koch

SO GOOD
CD BB 9540CD
Bullseye Blues / Feb '94 / Direct

Lynn, Cheryl

GOOD TIME
CD AVEXCD 31
Avex / Mar '96 / 3mv/Pinnacle

GOT TO BE
CD AVEXCD 50
Avex / Jul '96 / 3mv/Pinnacle

GOT TO BE REAL
Got to be real / Give my love to you / All my lovin' / Star love / Shake it up / Tonight / I've got just what you need / I've got faith in you / Keep it hot / Day after day / Sleep walkin' / Believe in me / If this world were mine / Encore / It's gonna be right / Georgy Porgy
CD 4842752
Columbia / May '97 / Sony

Lynn, Loretta

CLASSIC COUNTRY
CD CDSR 069
Telstar / May '95 / BMG

COAL MINER'S DAUGHTER
CD WMCD 5667
Disky / Oct '94 / Disky / THE

COAL MINER'S DAUGHTER (Live)
Hey Loretta / Coal miner's daughter / Let your love flow / You're looking at country / Me and Bobby McGee / Your squaw is on the warpath / We've come a long way baby / Fist City / Spring fever / Medley / Somebody somewhere / Out of my head and back in my bed / They don't make them like Daddy anymore / Pill / You'll come / You ain't woman enough
CD 100222
CMC / May '97 / BMG

COAL MINER'S DAUGHTER LIVE
Hey Loretta / Coal miner's daughter / Let your love flow / You're lookin' at country / Me and Bobby McGee / One's on the way/ The pill / Out of my head and back in my bed / Somebody somewhere (don't know what he's missin' tonight) / Medley no.1 / Back in my baby's arms/She's got you / They don't make 'em like my Daddy / Your squaw is on the warpath / Spring fever / Fist city / Y'all come
CD CTS 55443
Country Stars / Feb '97 / Target/BMG

EVENING WITH LORETTA LYNN, AN
CD MU 5069
Musketeer / Oct '92 / Disc

GOLDEN GREATS
Before I'm over you / Wine, women and song / Happy birthday / Blue Kentucky girl / You ain't woman enough to take my man / Don't come home a drinkin' / Fist city / Woman of the world / Coalminer's daughter / One's on the way / Love is the foundation / Hey Loretta / Trouble in paradise / Somebody, somewhere / She's got you / Out of my head and back in my bed
CD MCLD 19040
MCA / Apr '92 / BMG

GREATEST HITS
Hey Loretta / You're looking at country / Let your love flow / We've come a long way baby / Spring fever / Your squaw is on the warpath / Fist city / I fall to pieces / Walkin' after midnight / Crazy / Back in baby's arms / She's got you / Me and Bobby McGee / Somebody, somewhere / Out of my head and back in my bed / Coal miner's daughter / They don't make 'em like my daddy / One's on the way / Pill / Y'all come / You ain't woman enough to take my man
CD PLATCD 363
Platinum / '91 / Prism

HER COUNTRY HITS SHOW
CD CD 3502
Cameo / Aug '94 / Target/BMG

LEGENDS IN MUSIC
CD LECD 059
Wisepack / Jul '94 / Conifer/BMG / THE

VERY BEST OF LORETTA LYNN
Coal miner's daughter / You're looking at country / Blue Kentucky girl / Wine, women and song / She's got you / One's on the way / Happy birthday / Before I'm over you / Out of my head and back in my bed / Woman of the world / Trouble in paradise / Hey Loretta / You ain't woman enough to take my man / Fist city / Somebody, somewhere / Don't come a drinkin'
CD PLATCD 308
Platinum / Dec '88 / Prism

WOMAN OF THE WORLD (The Best Of Loretta Lynn)
CD MCCD 142
Music Club / Nov '93 / Disc / THE

Lynn, Trudy

24 HOUR WOMAN
CD ICH 1172CD
Ichiban / Jun '94 / Direct / Koch

COME TO MAMA
Right back in the water / When something is wrong with my baby / Come to Mama / When you took your love from me / One woman man / Woman's gotta have it / Do I need you (too) / Fish girl blues / Making love to me
CD ICH 1063CD
Ichiban / Oct '93 / Direct / Koch

TRUDY SINGS THE BLUES
Sittin' and drinkin' / Just a little bit / I can tell / Trudy sings the blues / Dr. Feelgood / Do I need you / Bring the beef home to me / Ball and chain
CD ICH 1043CD
Ichiban / Oct '93 / Direct / Koch

WOMAN IN ME, THE
Woman in me / My baby can / Speak now or forever hold your peace / You owe it to yourself / Can't nothin' keep me from you / Still on my mind / I've been thinkin' / Feel you, feel me / Spare the rod (love the child)
CD ICH 1125CD
Ichiban / Oct '93 / Direct / Koch

Lynn, Vera

48 GOLDEN GREATS
CD DBG 53039
Double Gold / Jan '95 / Target/BMG

BEST OF VERA LYNN, THE (25 Great Songs)
(There'll be blue birds over) The white cliffs of Dover / Mexicali rose / It's a sin to tell a lie / Garden in Grenada / I won't tell a soul (I love you) / Maybe / Over the rainbow / I hear a dream (come again) / Goodnight wherever you are / Be like the kettle and sing / London I love / Only forever / There'll come another day / You'll never know / That lovely weekend / Over the hill / Cinderella (stay in my arms) / Up the wooden hill to Bedfordshire / Really and truly / I had the craziest dream / White Christmas / When they sound the last all clear / So many memories / Two sleepy people / We'll meet again
CD CD 6035
Music / Sep '96 / Target/BMG

CLOSE TO YOU
I'm yours sincerely / I had the craziest dream / Close to you / Really and truly / Little King without a crown / First lullaby / Little rain must fall / Concerto for two / That autumn in old London town / White cliffs of Dover / I'll be with you in apple blossom time / We three / Who am I / Woodpecker song / You'll never know / Who's taking you home tonight / Goodnight and God bless you / With all my heart / All the world sings a lullaby / You're breaking my heart all over again
CD RAJCD 820
Empress / May '97 / Koch

COLLECTION, THE
CD COL 053
Collection / Jun '95 / Target/BMG

GOLDEN HITS
Yours / Wishing (will make it so) / General's fast asleep / Harbour lights / Who's taking you home tonight / Be like the kettle and sing / It's a lovely day tomorrow / There's a new world over the skyline / Jealousy / Nightingale sang in Berkeley Square / We three (my echo, my shadow and me) / More and more / Only forever / London I love / Star fell out of Heaven / Little boy that Santa Claus forgot / Goodnight children everywhere / When the lights go on again / White cliffs of Dover / We'll meet again / Goodnight wherever you are
CD PASTCD 7805
Flapper / Jan '97 / Pinnacle

HARBOUR LIGHTS
CD WMCD 5690
Disky / May '94 / Disky / THE

IT'S A LOVELY DAY TOMORROW - A TRIBUTE VOL.2
White cliffs of Dover / Be like the kettle and sing / Goodnight children everywhere / It's a lovely day tomorrow / Only forever / There'll come another day / Anniversary waltz / London I love / Something to remember you by / Over the hill / Harbour lights / That lovely weekend / Cinderella / Mexicali rose / Jealousy / When the lights go on again / Nightingale sang in Berkeley Square / Bells of St. Mary's / It's a sin to tell a lie / I'm in the mood for love / Love bug will bite you / Heart and soul
CD PASTCD 7030
Flapper / Jan '94 / Pinnacle

IT'S LIKE OLD TIMES
After a while / I hope to die / Do you ever dream of tomorrow / For sweetheart's everywhere / I could never tell / Symphony / How green was my valley / I couldn't sleep a wink last night / Long ago and far away / You're breaking my heart all over again / Where in the world / I had the craziest dream / Someone's rocking my dreamboat / I've heard that song before / Please think of me / It always rains before the rainbow / Who am I / It's like old times / There's a new world over the skyline
CD RAJCD 854
Empress / Nov '96 / Koch

LET'S MEET AGAIN
We'll meet again / Wishing (will make it so) / Mexicali rose / I paid for the lie that I told you / I shall be waiting / Who's taking you home tonight / My own / Goodnight children everywhere / Little boy that Santa Claus forgot / Little Sir Echo / Bell's of St Mary's / Harbour lights / It's a sin to tell a lie / Lonely sweetheart / Memory of a rose / It's a lovely day tomorrow / I'll pray for you / Nightingale sang in Berkeley Square / Medley: I hear a dream / Medley: So rare/ You're here you're there, you're everywhere
CD PAR 2010
Parade / Feb '95 / Disc

SINCERELY YOURS - A TRIBUTE VOL.1
Wish me luck as you wave me goodbye / Who's taking you home tonight / I'll pray for you / Garden in Granada / Now it can be told / First quarrel / When Mother Nature sings her lullaby / We'll meet again / Love makes the world go round / I won't tell a soul (that I love you) / Over the rainbow / I hear a dream (come again) / It always rains before a rainbow / I'll walk beside you / Wishing (will make it so) / We both told a lie / I'll think of you / I'll remember / Yours / Goodnight wherever you are / I shall be waiting / Maybe
CD PASTCD 9778
Flapper / Mar '94 / Pinnacle

SOMETHING TO REMEMBER - WARTIME MEMORIES
Something to remember you by / Yours / Wish me luck as you wave me goodbye / I'll pray for you / White cliffs of Dover / I shall be waiting / Over the hill / That lovely weekend / You'll never know / Who's taking you home tonight / Nightingale sang in Berkeley Square / It's a lovely day tomorrow / London I love / When they sound the last All Clear / Wishing (Will make it so) / It's a sin to tell a lie / Be like the kettle and sing / There'll come another day / Only forever / Anniversary waltz / When the lights go on again / We'll meet again
CD JASMCD 2541
Jasmine / May '95 / Conifer/BMG / Hot Shot / TKO Magnum

THANK YOU FOR THE MUSIC
CD MATCD 223
Castle / Dec '92 / BMG

THANK YOU FOR THE MUSIC
CD PLSCD 171
Pulse / Apr '97 / BMG

THERE'S A LAND OF BEGIN AGAIN
CD PASTCD 7064
Flapper / May '95 / Pinnacle

VERA LYNN REMEMBERS
White cliffs of Dover / Red sails in the sunset / It's a sin to tell a lie / Roll out the barrel / You'll never know / Nightingale sang in Berkeley Square / Sailing / Harbour lights / Auf wiedersehen / Yours / From the time you say goodbye / My mother's eyes / That lovely weekend / Land of hope and glory / Coming in on a wing and a prayer / We'll meet again / Be like the kettle and sing
CD CDSIV 1120
Horatio Nelson / May '95 / Disc

VERA LYNN REMEMBERS (The Songs That Won World War 2)
Yours / Medley / Somewhere in France with you / Medley / Medley / London pride / Nightingale sang in Berkeley Square / White cliffs of Dover / Medley / I'll be seeing you / You'd be so nice to come home to / Room five-hundred-and-four / That lovely weekend / Besame mucho / There'll always be an England / You'll never know / It had to be you / Lili Marlene / Medley / Medley / Land of hope and glory
CD CDEMS 1515
EMI / May '94 / EMI

VERA LYNN REMEMBERS VOL.2
CD _______________ CDSIV 1140
Horatio Nelson / Apr '93 / Disc

WE'LL MEET AGAIN (The Early Years)
Be careful it's my heart / Careless / Cinderella / Goodnight and God bless you / I had the craziest dream / I paid for the lie that I told you / I'll be with you in apple blossom time / I'll never smile again / It's a sin to tell a lie / Rosalie / Roses in December / Smilin' through / Someone's rocking my dreamboat / Something to remember you by / There'll come another day / We'll meet again / When they sound the last All Clear / When you wish upon a star / Where in the world / White cliffs of Dover / Wishing / You made me care / You'll never know / Yours
CD _______________ CDAJA 5145
Living Era / Oct '94 / Select

WE'LL MEET AGAIN
We'll meet again / Bells of St. Mary's / Wish me luck as you wave me goodbye / Love makes the world go round / Over the rainbow / I'll walk beside you / London I love / Up the wooden hill to Bedfrodshire / Cinderella / Really and truly / I had the craziest dream / Two sleepy people / You'll never know / That lovely weekend / Over the hill / After a while / Coming home / When they sound the last All Clear
CD _______________ MUCD 9020
Musketeer / Apr '95 / Disc

WE'LL MEET AGAIN (Her Classic Performances)
It's a lovely day tomorrow / Goodnight children / Lonely sweetheart / Little sir echo / I'll pray for you / It's a sin to tell a lie / Mexicali rose / Nightingale sang in Berkeley square / Bells of St. Mary's / Who's taking you home tonight / Harbour lights / My own / Memory of a rose / I shall be waiting / Wishing (will make it so) / Wish me luck (as you wave me goodbye) / We'll meet again / I paid for the lie / I hear a dream / You're hear you're there you are everywhere / So rare / White cliffs of dover
CD _______________ 305532
Hallmark / Oct '96 / Carlton

YOURS
Yours / Be like the kettle and sing / Jealousy / I'll pray for you / It's a sin to tell a lie / Up the wooden hill to Befordshire / Who's taking you home tonight / Cinderella (stay in my arms) / It's a lovely day tomorrow / When the lights go on again / White Cliffs Of Dover / Harbour lights / Over the hill / With all my heart / Goodnight children everywhere
CD _______________ PWKS 4250
Carlton / Feb '96 / Carlton

Lynne

VOID
Into the void / All life is one part 3 / Electroglow / Dar shan / On the edge / Truth or sanity (Part 3) / Relentless / Signals / Who knows / Nothing
CD _______________ CYCL 051
Cyclops / Mar '97 / Pinnacle

Lynne, Bjorn

DREAMSTATE
Universe of the mind / Material matters / Now what / All life is one / Time and growth / Emptiness / Cycle / Mania / Digital phoenix / Mesmerized / Dark star / Sequences / Progress
CD _______________ CENCD 009
Centaur / Mar '95 / Pinnacle

Lynne, Gloria

GLORIA, MARTY AND STRINGS
CD _______________ FSRCD 221
Fresh Sound / Jul '97 / Discovery / Jazz Music

HE NEEDS ME
CD _______________ FSRCD 222
Fresh Sound / Jul '97 / Discovery / Jazz Music

I'M GLAD THERE IS YOU
CD _______________ FSRCD 223
Fresh Sound / Jul '97 / Discovery / Jazz Music

JUST IN TIME
CD _______________ FSRCD 227
Fresh Sound / Jul '97 / Discovery / Jazz Music

LONELY AND SENTIMENTAL
CD _______________ FSRCD 224
Fresh Sound / Jul '97 / Discovery / Jazz Music

MELLOW AND THE SWINGING, THE
CD _______________ FSRCD 226
Fresh Sound / Jul '97 / Discovery / Jazz Music

MISS GLORIA LYNNE
CD _______________ ECD 220092
Evidence / Jul '92 / ADA / Cadillac / Harmonia Mundi

TIME FOR LOVE, A
CD _______________ MCD 5381
Muse / Sep '92 / New Note/Pinnacle

TRY A LITTLE TENDERNESS
CD _______________ FSRCD 225
Fresh Sound / Jul '97 / Discovery / Jazz Music

Lynott, Phil

LIZZY SONGS, THE (A Tribute To Phil Lynott) (Various Artists)
CD _______________ TR 008CD
Tribute / Jun '97 / Plastic Head

SOLO IN SOHO
Solo in Soho / King's call / Child lullaby / Tattoo / Dear Miss Lonely Hearts / Yellow pearl / Girls / Ode to a black man / Jamaican rum / Talk in 79 / So what / Turn the hands of time
CD _______________ 8425632
Vertigo / Jul '90 / PolyGram

Lynton, Jackie

ALL OF ME
Over the rainbow / High in the sky / Wishful thinking / Don't take away your love / All of me / I'd steal / I believe / Girl in the wood / Teddy bear's picnic / Jeannie with the light brown hair / I'm talkin' 'bout you / Lawdy Miss Clawdy / Little child / Never a mention / Laura / Ebb tide / What'd I say / Three blind mice / Corrina corrina / He'll have to go / Only you / Decision / Sporting life / Answer me / I never loved a girl like you / Audrey / Ballad of Hank McCain / Did you ever hear
CD _______________ GEMCD 010
Diamond / Feb '97 / Pinnacle

QUICK AS A ROOF
CD _______________ ANDCD 6
Telstar / Nov '96 / BMG

Lynwood Slim

LOST IN AMERICA
CD _______________ BMCD 9017
Black Magic / Nov '93 / ADA / Cadillac / Direct / Hot Shot

SOUL FEET
I'm to blame / Hoy hoy hoy / I refuse / Do nothin' 'til you hear from me / Messin' with my bread / Reach for your telephone / Things gon' change / Doo's groove / Soul feet / Nothing takes the place of you / I've been around / Bad case of love / Too poor / Wipe your tears / Look the whole world over
CD _______________ ATM 1121
Atomic Theory / Oct '96 / ADA / Direct

Lynyrd Skynyrd

DEFINITIVE LYNYRD SKYNYRD, THE (3CD Set)
CD _______________ MCAD 310390
MCA / Feb '92 / BMG

FREEBIRD
Saturday night special / Whiskey rock'n'roller / Working for MCA / I ain't the one / Sweet home Alabama / Ballad of Curtis Loew / Call me the breeze / Needle and spoon / Swamp music / Gimme 3 steps / Tuesday's gone / Freebird / Gimme back my bullets / What's your name / That smell / You got that right
CD _______________ NTRCD 015
Nectar / Feb '94 / Pinnacle

FREEBIRD - THE MOVIE (Live At Knebworth 1976)
Workin' for MCA / I ain't the one / Saturday night special / Whisky rock-a-roller / Travellin' man / Searching / What's your name / That smell / Gimme three steps / Call me the breeze / T for Texas (blue yodel no.1) / Sweet home Alabama / Free bird / Dixie
CD _______________ MCD 11472
MCA / Sep '96 / BMG

GIMME BACK MY BULLETS (2CD Set)
CD Set _______________ MCD 33002
MCA / Jul '96 / BMG

LAST REBEL, THE
Good lovin's hard to find / One thing / Can't take that away / Best things in life / Last rebel / Outta hell in my dodge / Kiss your freedom goodbye / South of heaven / Love don't always come easy / Born to run
CD _______________ 7567824472
WEA / Feb '93 / Warner Music

LYNYRD SKYNYRD 1991
Smokestack lightnin' / Keeping the faith / Southern women / Pure and simple / I've seen enough / Backstreet crawler / Good thing / Money man / It's a killer / Mama (afraid to say goodbye) / End of the road
CD _______________ 7567822582
East West / Jun '91 / Warner Music

NUTHIN' FANCY
Made in the shade / Saturday night special / Cheatin' woman / Railroad song / I'm a country boy / On the hunt / Am I losin' / Whiskey rock'n'roller
CD _______________ MCLD 19074
MCA / Nov '92 / BMG

OLD TIME GREATS (2CD Set)
CD Set _______________ RR 4637
Repertoire / Jun '97 / Greyhound

ONE MORE FOR THE ROAD
Workin' for MCA / I ain't the one / Searching / Tuesdays gone / Saturday night special / Travellin' man / Whiskey rock'n'roller / Sweet home Alabama / Gimme three steps / Call me the breeze / T for Texas / Needle and spoon / Crossroads / Freebird
CD Set _______________ MCLDD 19139
MCA / Dec '92 / BMG

PRONOUNCED LEH-NERD SKIN-NERD
I ain't the one / Tuesday's gone / Gimme three steps / Simple man / Things goin' on / Mississippi kid / Poison whiskey / Freebird
CD _______________ MCLD 19072
MCA / Nov '91 / BMG

SECOND HELPING
Sweet home Alabama / I need you / Don't ask me no questions / Workin' for MCA / Ballad of Curtis Loew / Swamp music / Needle and spoon / Call me the breeze
CD _______________ MCLD 19073
MCA / Oct '92 / BMG

SKYNYRDS INNYRDS
CD _______________ DMCG 6046
MCA / Apr '89 / BMG

SOUTHERN BY THE GRACE OF GOD
Swamp music / Call me the breeze / Dixie / Freebird / Workin' for MCA / That smell / I know a little / Comin' home / You got that right / What's your name / Gimme back my bullets / Sweet home Alabama
CD _______________ MCLD 19010
MCA / Apr '92 / BMG

SOUTHERN KNIGHTS (2CD Set)
Working for MCA / Ain't the one / Saturday night special / Down south jukin / Double trouble / T For Texas / Devil in the bottle / That smell / Simple man / Whiskey rock and roller / What's your name / Gimme 3 steps / Sweet home / Freebird
CD Set _______________ SPV 08744192
SPV / Jul '96 / Koch / Plastic Head

STREET SURVIVORS
What's your name / That smell / One more time / I know a little / You got that right / I never dreamt / Honky tonk night time man / Ain't no good life
CD _______________ MCLD 19248
MCA / Oct '94 / BMG

TWENTY
We ain't much different / Bring it on / Voodoo lake / Home is where the heart is / Travellin' man / Talked myself right into it / Never too late / QRR / Blame it on a sad song / Berneice / None of us are free / How soon we forget
CD _______________ SPV 08544392
SPV / May '97 / Koch / Plastic Head

VERY BEST OF LYNYRD SKYNYRD, THE
CD _______________ MCLD 19140
MCA / Jul '92 / BMG

Lyons, Jimmy

BURNT OFFERING (Lyons, Jimmy & Andrew Cyrille)
CD _______________ 1201302
Black Saint / Jun '91 / Cadillac / Harmonia Mundi

GIVE IT UP (Lyons, Jimmy Quintet)
CD _______________ BSR 0087
Black Saint / '86 / Cadillac / Harmonia Mundi

JUMP UP
CD _______________ ART 6139CD
Hat Art / Apr '94 / Cadillac / Harmonia Mundi

Lyres

EARLY YEARS
CD _______________ EFA 11578
Crypt / Apr '97 / Shellshock/Disc

LYRES, LYERS
CD _______________ ROSE 103CD
New Rose / Nov '86 / ADA / Direct / Discovery

NOBODY BUT ME
CD _______________ TAANG 058CD
Taang / Jan '93 / Cargo

ON FYRE
CD _______________ ROSE 35CD
New Rose / Jul '84 / ADA / Direct / Discovery

PROMISE IS A PROMISE, A
Promise is a promise / Here's a heart on fyre / Every man for himself / Feel good / I'll try you anyway / Worried about nothing / Touch / Running through the night / She's got eyes that tell lie / Jagged time lapse / Knock my socks off / Sick and tired / Trying just to please / Witch
CD _______________ ROSE 153CD
New Rose / Aug '88 / ADA / Direct / Discovery

SOME LYRES
CD _______________ TAANG 82
Taang / Aug '94 / Cargo

Lytle, Cecil

READING OF A SACRED BOOK
CD Set _______________ CDCEL 028/29
Celestial Harmonies / Feb '89 / ADA / Select

SEEKERS OF THE TRUTH
CD Set _______________ CDCEL 020/21
Celestial Harmonies / Oct '88 / ADA / Select

Lytle, Johnny

LOOP/NEW & GROOVY
Loop / More I see you / Man / Time after time / Big Bill / Possum grease / Cristo redentor / Shyster / My romance / Hot sauce / Snapper / Summertime / Selim / Shadow of your smile / Come and get it / Pulpit / Too close for comfort / Chanukah / Screamin' loud / El marcel
CD _______________ CDBGPD 961
Beat Goes Public / Oct '90 / Pinnacle

Lyttelton, Humphrey

BEANO BOOGIE (Lyttelton, Humphrey & His Band)
Say forward I'll march / Ficklefanny strikes again / Apple honey / Do you call that a buddy / Sixth form / Beano boogie / Little king / Echoes of the jungle / Gnasher and me / Strange Mr. Peter Charles/Cop out / In swinger / Yorkville
CD _______________ CLGCD 021
Calligraph / Jun '92 / Cadillac / Jazz Music / New Note/Pinnacle / Wellard

DELVING BACK WITH HUMPH
Thin red line / Melancholy blues / Cakewalkin' babies / If you see me comin' / Panama / Working man blues / Fidgety feet / Weary blues / Ole Miss Rag / Vox humana / Elizabeth / Blue for Waterloo / First of many / Blues for two / High society / Royal Garden blues / Who's sorry now / Humph meets Trog / Bugle call rag / That da da strain / Sugar
CD _______________ LACD 72
Lake / Feb '97 / ADA / Cadillac / Direct / Jazz Music / Target/BMG

ECHOES OF THE DUKE (Lyttelton, Humphrey & His Band & Helen Shapiro)
Take the 'A' train / I got it bad and that ain't good / Caravan / Just squeeze me / Drop me off in Harlem / Solitude/Mood indigo / Echoes of The Duke / I ain't got nothin' but the blues / 'Cross a busy street / I let a song go out of my heart / Don't get around much anymore / It don't mean a thing if it ain't got that swing / Do nothin' 'til you hear from me / Pritti Nitti / Just a sittin' and a rockin'
CD _______________ CLGCD 002
Calligraph / Jun '92 / Cadillac / Jazz Music / New Note/Pinnacle / Wellard

GIGS (Lyttelton, Humphrey & His Band)
Stanley steams in / Black butterfly / Ah mersey / Golden gumboot / Grey turning blue / Barnes bridge
CD _______________ CDGCD 015
Calligraph / Nov '87 / Cadillac / Jazz Music / New Note/Pinnacle / Wellard

HEAR ME TALKIN' TO YA (Lyttelton, Humphrey & His Band)
Hear me talkin' to ya / Someone to watch over me / Madly / Blues for Zoe / Serenade to Sweden / Lord is listenin' to ya, hallelujah / Good buzz (take it from the top) / One for Al / Swinging scorpio / Beale Street blues / Moten swing / St. James infirmary / Mezzrow / I got rhythm
CD _______________ CLGCD 029
Calligraph / Aug '93 / Cadillac / Jazz Music / New Note/Pinnacle / Wellard

HUMPH 'N' HELEN (I Can't Get Started) (Lyttelton, Humphrey & Helen Shapiro)
Perdido / It might as well rain until September / I can't get started (with you) / Eventide / Music goes 'round and around / Make the man love me / Elmer's tune / Bye bye blackbird / Indian summer / Brazil / I'll never smile again / After you've gone / Crazy he calls me / Why don't you do right / Choo choo ch' boogie / Flying home
CD _______________ CLGCD 025
Calligraph / Jun '92 / Cadillac / Jazz Music / New Note/Pinnacle / Wellard

JAZZ AT THE ROYAL FESTIVAL HALL
Onions / Old grey mare / New Orleans stomp / Canal Street blues / Big cat little cat / Randolph Turpin
CD _______________ DM 22 CD
Dormouse / Aug '91 / Jazz Music / Target/BMG

LAY 'EM STRAIGHT (Lyttelton, Humphrey & His Band)
Lay 'em straight / Porgy / Love for sale / Some other Spring / Things ain't what they used to be / Last laugh / Song for Ruby / Zoltan's dream / Echoes of the duke / Satin doll / Ostendatious / Late night final / Bondo's blues / Only for men
CD _______________ CLGCD 033
Calligraph / Feb '97 / Cadillac / Jazz Music / New Note/Pinnacle / Wellard

MORE HUMPH & ACKER (Lyttelton, Humphrey & Acker Bilk)
Senora / Sugar / Maybe / I'd climb the highest mountain / Ludo / I told you once, I told you twice / Tiz-dum, tiz-dum / Mound bayou / Bessie couldn't help it / How long has this been going on / Russian lullaby / Blues and sentimental / Maritiniquen song / Three in the morning / Last smile blues / Easter parade
CD ____________________ CLGCD 030
Calligraph / Feb '95 / Cadillac / Jazz Music / New Note/Pinnacle / Wellard

MOVIN' AND GROOVIN'
CD ____________________ BLCD 760504
Black Lion / Oct '90 / Cadillac / Jazz Music / Koch / Wellard

PARLOPHONE YEARS, THE
Memphis blues / Snake rag / Bad penny blues / Lady in red / Lightly and politely / Blues excursion / London blues / Onions / Dallas blues / Dormouse
CD ____________________ DM 21 CD
Dormouse / Feb '89 / Jazz Music / Target/ BMG

ROCK ME GENTLY
Rock me gently / Top 'n' tail / Jack the bear / My funny valentine / Frankie and Johnny / Sea-lion's siesta / Lester and Herschel / Heads or tails / Royal flush / Sidney my man / Tribal dance / If we never meet again / Lady of the lavender mist / St. Louis blues
CD ____________________ CLGCD 026
Calligraph / Sep '91 / Cadillac / Jazz Music / New Note/Pinnacle / Wellard

TAKE IT FROM THE TOP (A Dedication To Duke Ellington)
CD ____________________ CDBLC 760516
Black Lion / Apr '96 / Cadillac / Jazz Music / Koch / Wellard

TROGLADYTES (Lyttelton, Humphrey & Wally Fawkes)
CD ____________________ SOSCD 1238
Stomp Off / May '93 / Jazz Music / Wellard

M

M-Age

UNDER A CUBIC SKY
CD _______________ RSNCD 29
Rising High / Jan '95 / 3mv/Sony

M-Man

LISTEN, SING AND DANCE MY LOVE
CD _______________ JBF 100196
M-Man Productions / May '96 / Jet Star

M-People

BIZARRE FRUIT
Sight for sore eyes / Search for the hero / Open up your heart / Love rendez-vous / Precious pearl / Sugar town / Walk away / Drive time / Padlock / And finally
CD _______________ 74321240812
De-Construction / Nov '94 / BMG

ELEGANT SLUMMING
One night in heaven / Moving on up / Renaissance / You just have to be there / Love is in my soul / Don't look any further / Natural thing / Little packet / La vida loca / Melody of life
CD _______________ 74321166782
De-Construction / Jul '96 / BMG

NORTHERN SOUL
Colour my life / How can I love you more / Inner city cruise / It's your world / Someday / Sexual freedom / Kiss it better / Tumbling down / Landscape of love / Life / Inner city dub / Colour my life (part 2) / Kiss it better / Platini / Excited / Man Smart / Colour my life (part 3) / Excited
CD _______________ 74321117772
De-Construction / Jul '96 / BMG

M3

M-3
CD _______________ NAR 057CD
New Alliance / Dec '93 / Plastic Head

Maar, Doe

4 US
CD _______________ CDM 183
RCA/Camden / '88 / BMG

Maas

LATITUDE
Festina / Upstate / Michigan breaks / Look at me now, falling / Esplanade / Suture / Shrift / Eurostar / Another Saturday night / Lost soul
CD _______________ SOMACD 7
Soma / Apr '97 / RTM/Disc

Mabern, Harold

FOR PHINEAS (Mabern, Harold & Geoff Keezer)
CD _______________ SKCD 2041
Sackville / Jul '96 / Cadillac / Jazz Music / Swift

LOOKIN' ON THE BRIGHT SIDE (Mabern, Harold Trio)
CD _______________ DIW 614
DIW / Nov '93 / Cadillac / Harmonia Mundi

PHILADELPHIA BOUND
CD _______________ SKCD 23051
Sackville / Oct '94 / Cadillac / Jazz Music / Swift

STRAIGHT STREET (Mabern, Harold Trio)
CD _______________ DIW 608
DIW / Sep '91 / Cadillac / Harmonia Mundi

Maboul, Aksak

UN PEU DE L'AME DES BANDITS
Modern lesson / Palmiers en pots / Geistige nacht / I viaggi formano la gioventu / Inoculating rabies / Ce qu'on peut voir avec un bon microscope / Alluvions / Azinou crapules / Age route brra / Bosses de crosses
CD _______________ CRAM 002
Crammed Discs / Apr '96 / Grapevine/PolyGram / New Note/Pinnacle / Prime / RTM/Disc

Mabsant

HUMOUR & SONG WITH MABSANT & EIRY PALFREY
CD _______________ SAIN 2029CD
Sain / Aug '94 / ADA / Direct / Greyhound

MABSANT (GYDA EIRY PALFREY)
Carol y blwch / Diary / Suai'r gwynt / Child's Christmas / Ar gyfer hiddiw'r bore / Red cock / Curlews / Dear John / Y wasael / Maggie fach / Holiday memory / Ar kan y mor / Local boy/Sell out / Gwenynen / Mrs. Evans/Meanwhile Dai / Y deryn du / Blodeuwedd / Moliannwn
CD _______________ SCD 2029
Sain / Oct '87 / ADA / Direct / Greyhound

Mabuses

MELBOURNE METHOD, THE
My brilliant way / Glass of bourbon / Tongues / Keeler joins the joyce gang / Whose party is this / Rooms / Paper plane / Lynched / Picnic at the red house / Fetch the hammer / Oscar / Narc fears / She went wild
CD _______________ R 3132
Rough Trade / Apr '94 / Pinnacle

Mac-Talla

MAIRIDH GAOL IS CEOL
Boys be happy / Old hunting song / Beloved Gregor / Mouth music / Tailor's dowry / Barcelona / Brown haired Alan / Mrs. Jamieson's favourite / Mouth music / Beautiful girl / Setting a course for Lewis / Uig Brae
CD _______________ COMD 2054
Temple / Feb '94 / ADA / CM / Direct / Duncans / Highlander

Macabre

SINISTER SLAUGHTER
CD _______________ NB 070CD
Nuclear Blast / Jun '93 / Plastic Head

Macaire, Mack

SOUCI Y A LA VIE
CD _______________ JIP 064
JIP / Jan '96 / Jet Star

McAlmont

MCALMONT
Either / Not wiser / Unworthy (edit) / Misunderstood / Is it raining / Conversation / He loves you / Worn away / It's always this way / My grey boy / They hide / Through the door / Placed aside / Unworthy / As if I'd known
CD _______________ CDHUT 12
Hut / Jan '95 / EMI

McAlmont & Butler

SOUND OF MCALMONT AND BUTLER, THE
Yes / What's the excuse this time / Right thing / Although / Don't call it soul / Disappointment / Debitor / How about you / Tonight / You'll lose a good thing / You do
CD _______________ CDHUT 32
Hut / Nov '95 / EMI

MacAlpine, Tony

EDGE OF INSANITY
CD _______________ RR 349706
Roadrunner / '89 / PolyGram

EVOLUTION
Sage / Overseas evolution / Eccentrist / Time table / Seville / Futurism / Etude no 5 opus 10 F / Powerfield / Plastic people / Sinfonia / Asturias kv 467
CD _______________ CDRR 89012
Roadrunner / Oct '95 / PolyGram

FREEDOM TO FLY
CD _______________ RR 91572
Roadrunner / Sep '96 / PolyGram

PREMONITION
CD _______________ RR 89652
Roadrunner / Sep '94 / PolyGram

McAnuff, Winston

ONE LOVE
CD _______________ CC 2716
Crocodisc / Apr '95 / Grapevine/PolyGram

MacAskill, Paula

CRYSTAL
CD _______________ CDRPM 0016
RP Media / May '97 / Essential/BMG

McAuley, Jack-E

FRETWORK
All jokers are wild / Gone crazy on you / SOS Crumlin Road / Danger money / Lay your load on me / Kerry red / Zoom zoom / This must be love, Theresa / Johnny forty coats / When Mama got the blues/Goodnight waltz / No mans land / Gael force West
CD _______________ RGFCD 032
Road Goes On Forever / Oct '96 / Direct

JACKIE MCAULEY...PLUS
CD _______________ SEECD 315
See For Miles/C5 / Apr '91 / Pinnacle

McBee, Cecil

ALTERNATE SPACES
CD _______________ IN 1043CD
India Navigation / Jan '97 / Discovery / Impetus

McBride, Christian

GETTIN' TO IT
CD _______________ 5239892
Verve / Mar '95 / PolyGram

NUMBER TWO EXPRESS
CD _______________ 5295852
Verve / Apr '96 / PolyGram

McBride, Joe

KEYS TO YOUR HEART
CD _______________ INAK 30352
In Akustik / Aug '96 / Direct / TKO Magnum

McBride, Martina

WAY THAT I AM, THE
Heart trouble / My baby loves me / That wasn't me / Independence day / Where I used to have a heart / Goin' to work / She ain't seen nothing yet / Life / Strangers / Ashes
CD _______________ 74321192292
RCA / Mar '94 / BMG

WILD ANGELS
Wild angels / Phones are ringin' all over town / Great disguise / Swingin' doors / All the things we've never done / Two more bottles of wine / Cry on the shoulder of the road / You've been driving all the time / Born to give my love to you / Beyond the blue / Safe in the arms of love
CD _______________ 07863665092
RCA / Oct '95 / BMG

McBride, Owen

LAWEESH ROCK AND OTHER SONGS
CD _______________ CIC 072CD
Clo Iar-Chonnachta / Nov '93 / CM

McBroom, Amanda

LIVE FROM RAINBOW & STARS, NEW YORK
September song / No fear / I love this place / Everybody wants to be Sondheim / Days of wine and roses / Time after time / I love men / Ship in a bottle / Here and now / Portrait / Rose / Carousel / Errol Flynn / Dieter's prayer / Baltimore Oriole / Breathing / My foolish heart / I can't make you love me
CD _______________ DRGCD 91432
DRG / Feb '95 / Discovery / New Note/ Pinnacle

Macc Lads

ALE HOUSE ROCK
CD _______________ DOJOCD 250
Dojo / Mar '96 / Disc

BEER NECESSITIES, THE
Alcohol / Germans / Fallatio Nell, son / Desperate Dan / Grease stop / Apprentice dentist / Man in the boat / Newcy Brown / Macavity / Chester Zoo / Naughty boy / Mr. Methane / More tea vicar / Two stroke Eddie / Animal testing / Don't fear the sweeper / Poodles
CD _______________ DOJOCD 158
Dojo / May '94 / Disc

BEER, SEX, CHIPS AND GRAVY
Lads from Macc / Beer, sex and chips 'n' gravy / Boddies / Sweaty Betty / England's glory / Blackpool / Miss Macclesfield / God's gift to women / Get weavin' / Now he's a poof / Nagasaki sauce / Saturday night / Buenos aires / Charlotte / Failure with girls / Do you love me / Dan's underpants / Twenty pints / Macc Lads party
CD _______________ WKFMXD 110
FM / Aug '89 / Revolver / Sony

BITTER, FIT CRACK
Barrel's round / Guess me weight / Uncle Knobby / Maid of ale / Dan's big log / Got to be Gordon's / Bitter fit crack / Julie the schooly / Doctor doctor / Torremolinos / Al o'peesha
CD _______________ WKFMXD 100
FM / Feb '91 / Revolver / Sony
CD _______________ DOJOCD 155
Dojo / Nov '93 / Disc

FROM BEER TO ETERNITY
Alton Towers / Geordie girl / No sheep 'til Buxton / All day drinking / Tab after tab / Lucy Lastic / My pub / Dead cat / Lady Muck / Gordon's revenge / Pie taster / Dans round yer 'andbag / Ben Nevis / Fluffy pup / Stoppyback / Ugly women
CD _______________ DOJOCD 157
Dojo / May '94 / Disc

LIVE AT LEEDS (The Who?)
Sweaty Betty / Ben Nevis / Bloink / Do you love me / God's gift to women / Charlotte / Blackpool / Lads from Macc / Now he's a poof / Doctor doctor / Julie the schooly / Guess me weight / Miss Macclesfield / Fat bastard / Get weavin / Barrels' round / Dan's underpants
CD _______________ WKFMXD 115
FM / Aug '88 / Revolver / Sony
CD _______________ DOJOCD 161
Dojo / Mar '94 / Disc

ORIFICE AND A GENITAL, AN (Outtakes 1986-1991)
Eh up lets sup / Fat bastard / Baggy Anne / Head kicked in / Knutsford / No sheep 'til Buxton / Pie taster / I love Macc / Made of ale / Knock knock / Brevil brevil / Manfred Macc / Buenos Aires '90 / Fellatio Nell, son / Two stroke Eddie / Even uglier women
CD _______________ DOJOCD 141
Dojo / Feb '94 / Disc

McCafferty, Dan

DAN MCCAFFERTY
Honky Tonk downstairs / Cinnamon girl / Great pretender / Boots of Spanish leather / What'cha gonna do about it / Out of time / You can't lie to a liar / Trouble / You got me hummin' / Stay with me baby / Nightingale
CD _______________ NEMCD 640
Sequel / Jun '94 / BMG

McCaffrey, Frank

PLACE IN MY HEART, A
Clock in the tower / Place in my heart / Day the world stood still / Drive safely darlin' / I'd rather be sorry / Annie's story / Blackboard of my heart / All alone in New York City / It's our anniversary / Give a lonely heart a home / Rose / Always Mayo
CD _______________ RITZCD 512
Ritz / '91 / Pinnacle

TODAY
Today / Things I wish I'd said / Silver medals and sweet memories / I wish it was me / You make me feel like a man / Forever lovers / In dreams / Wedding song / Broken wings / Lady from Glenfarn / Memories of Mayo / Sarah's smile
CD _______________ RITZCD 0063
Ritz / Apr '91 / Pinnacle

VERY BEST OF FRANK MCCAFFREY
It's our anniversary / Blackboard of my heart / I'll take you home again Kathleen / Ring your mother wore / Silver medals and sweet memories / Little grey home in the West / I wish it was me / Daisy a day / Place in my heart / Memories of Mayo / More than yesterday / If we only had old Ireland over here / Clock in the tower / Give a lonely heart a home / Moonlight in Mayo / My lady from Glenfarne / Things I wish I'd said / Broken wings / Day the world stood still / Wedding song
CD _______________ RITZCD 532
Ritz / Apr '93 / Pinnacle

YOUR SPECIAL DAY
Here's my native country / Midnight to midnight / I'm a fool / Always on my mind (forever in my heart) / Nobody's Darlin' but mine / Emigrant eyes / When your old wedding ring was new / You special day / Forty shades of green / Cr oce di oro / You're a friend of mine / Less of me / Our Lady of knock / Heart that beats in Ireland
CD _______________ RCD 548
Ritz / May '95 / Pinnacle

McCain, Jerry

STRANGE KIND OF FEELIN' (McCain, Jerry 'Boogie' & Tiny Kennedy, Clayton Love)
CD _______________ ALCD 2701
Alligator / Oct '93 / ADA / CM / Direct

McCall, Darrell

REAL MCCALL, THE (5CD Set)
This old heart / Excuse me (I think I've got a heartache) / Lonely River Rhine / Heart to heart talk: *McCall, Darrell & Harold Weakely* / Polka on the banjo / Fallen angel / Five brothers / North to Alaska / My kind of lovin' / My girl / Beyond imagination / What'll I do (call the zoo) / Loneliness / I gotta have you / Dear one / Up to my ears in tears / I've been known / For your sweet love / Stranger was here / I'm a little bit lonely / I can take his baby away / Man can change / Hud / No place to hide / Keeping my feet on the ground / Got my baby on my mind / Step by step / Hello world / Marionette / I love you baby / I'd love to live with you again / I'd die to see you smile / Wrong kind of man / Blame me / Hurry up / Wall of pictures / Tiny ribbons / Big oak tree / Bury the bottle

with me / Stranger was here / Wedding band / Hide & go cheat / New rich friend / First year / Likes of Polly / Yours & his / Don't tell my wife / Right to do wrong / Sally Bryson / Arms of my weakness / Heart of Dixie / Loser / Fiddlin' of Jacque Pierre Bordeaux / I'll break out again tonight / Mixing memories / It's the water / Rainbow at midnight / Eleven roses / Goodbye of the year / I still want you / Warm red wine (you're my sunshine) / Man you're most likely to forget / This time I won't cheat on her again / Loser never had a better friend / Here we go again / There's still a lot of love in San Antone / Texas honky tonk / Yours and his / I am love / Where is all that love you talked about / If you don't know your roses / Genuine healer of time / Never some night / Eleven roses / Champagne ladies & blue ribbon babies / Letting her be free / Face to the wall / Cold beer signs & country songs / If you don't believe I love you / She'll keep bringing all her love to me / Helpless / Pins & needles (in my heart) / Every girl I see / Waltz of the angels / I just destroyed the world / Tennessee / I come home to face the music / Are you teasing me / Sad songs & waltzes / Days when you were still in love with me / Dreams of a dreamer / It's my lazy day / It's been so long darlin' / Lily Dale: *McCall, Darrell & Willie Nelson* / Please don't leave me: *McCall, Darrell & Willie Nelson* / Half beered up & drinkin' / Weeds outlived the the roses / Old memory's arms / Down the roads of Daddy's dreams / Love didn't drive my good woman wild / Willie B / It took us all night to say goodbye / Long line of empties / I wonder which one of us is to blame / Married women / Afternoon rendezvous: *McCall, Darrell & Mona* / Just ridin' through / Sourwood Mountain / Don't wait till tomorrow / Strange little melody / Picture on the wall / Cindy / Rosewood casket / I'll cry again tomorrow / If you've got the money, I've got the time / Oh lonesome me / Heartbreak Avenue / Peace in the valley / Release me / Answer to anymore / Ages & ages ago / Under your spell again / Sweet dreams / Accidentally on purpose / Dear one / I can take his baby away / Another day, another dollar / Stranger was here / There's still a lot of love in San Antone / Helpless / It's the water / Eleven roses / Lone Star beer commercial / Coors beer commercial / Bad mouthin' / This I gotta see
CD Set ______ BCD 15846
Bear Family / Nov '96 / Direct / Rollercoaster / Swift

McCalla

HOT FROM THE SMOKE
Cause and effect / Family affair / Count all your blessings / Simmer down / Fly like an eagle / Lay you low / Ain't no sunshine / Your happiness / Let's go deeper / International love
CD ______ SEA 41622
Uplands / Oct '95 / Total/BMG

McCallister, Don Jr.

DON MCCALLISTER JR. & HIS COWBOY JAZZ REVUE
CD ______ DJD 3206
Dejadisc / May '94 / ADA / Direct

MacCallum, Hugh A.

WORLD'S GREATEST PIPERS VOL.2, THE
MacNeils of Ugadale / Sweet maid of Mull / Arniston castle / Caberfeidh / Grey bob / Willie Murray / Iain Rhuadh's lament / Donald, Hugh and his dog / Rosshire volunteers / John MacFadyen of Melfort / Joe McGann's fiddle / P/M George Allan / Clan MacColl / Tulloch castle / Major D Manson / Mhairi van og (Fair young Mary) / Battle of the Somme / Archie McKinlay / Miss Ada Crawford / Captain Home / Duke of Gordon's birthday / Sleepy Maggie / Dancing feet / Tail toddle / Allan MacPherson of Mosspark / Herring wife / Lament for Mary MacLeod
CD ______ LCOM 5147
Lismor / May '96 / ADA / Direct / Duncans / Lismor

McCallum

BIG BIGG MARKET
CD ______ BIGCD 1
Mawson & Wareham / Dec '94 / BMG

McCallum, Craig

IN A DIFFERENT LIGHT (McCallum, Craig Scottish Dance Band)
Gay Gordons / Dumbarton's drums / Pride of Erin Waltz / Canadian Barn dance / Pipe medley / Eva three step / Wild geese / Military two step / Irish reels / Highland Schottische / Circle waltz / Strip the willow / Party polka / Dashing white sergeant
CD ______ CDTRAX 037
Greentrax / Oct '90 / ADA / Direct / Duncans / Highlander

McCallum, David

OPEN CHANNEL D
CD ______ CREV 43CD
Rev-Ola / Sep '96 / 3mv/Vital

McCallum, William

HAILEY'S SONG
CD ______ COMD 2060
Temple / Oct '95 / ADA / CM / Direct / Duncans / Highlander

PIPERS OF DISTINCTION
CD ______ CDMON 801
Monarch / Dec '89 / ADA / CM / Direct / Duncans

McCalmans

FESTIVAL LIGHTS
Don't call me early in the morning / Pills / Far down the line / Highland road / Some hae meat / Tearing our industry down / Golden arches / Shanties / Bonnie barque the bergen / Barnyards of Delgaty / Goodnight sweetheart / Festival lights
CD ______ CDTRAX 097
Greentrax / Oct '95 / ADA / Direct / Duncans / Highlander

FLAMES ON THE WATER
Ah'm e man at muffed it / Isle of Eigg / Devolution anthem / Farewell tae the haven / Sounding / Hawks and eagles / Siege / Who pays the piper / Festival lights / Shian Road / Men o' worth / Curtain call
CD ______ CDTRAX 036
Greentrax / Jul '90 / ADA / Direct / Duncans / Highlander

HIGH GROUND
Cancel Marie's wedding / Lochs of the Tay / Don't sit on my Jimmy Shands / They sent a woman / Five o'clock in the morning / No one left but me / Upstairs, doonstairs / Take her in your arms / Don't waste my time / High ground / Wrecked again / White horses / Cholesterol / Libertas Ragusta
CD ______ CDTRAX 138
Greentrax / Aug '97 / ADA / Direct / Duncans / Highlander

HONEST POVERTY
Man's a man for a' that / Single handed sailor / Your daughters and your sons / Neil Gow's apprentice / Children are running away / Kelvingrove/Paddy's leather britches/Behind the haystack / War outside/ The white collar holler / I feel like Buddy Holly / Parade / Portnahaven / 8-2-0 / Wha'll be King but Charlie / Father Mallory's dance / New Year's Eve song / Harmless
CD ______ CDTRAX 067
Greentrax / Sep '93 / ADA / Direct / Duncans / Highlander

IN HARMONY - 30TH ANNIVERSARY COMPILATION ALBUM
Pace egging song / Sun rises bright in France / Broom / Windmills / My Johnny is a shoemaker / Smuggler / Ye Jacobites by name / Farewell to Sicily / Burn the witch / Ladies evening song / Kelty clippie / Bonnie maid of fire / Scotland / Bonnie lass o'Gala water / Mothers, daughters, wives / Rambling rover / Farewell tae the haven / Last session / Man's a man for a' that / Bound to go
CD ______ CDTRAX 086
Greentrax / Jan '95 / ADA / Direct / Duncans / Highlander

LISTEN TO THE HEAT - LIVE
I have seen the Highlands / Town of Kiandra / Mount and go / Sister Josephine / 23rd June / Prisoner's song / Song song / Rambling Rover / Rory Murphy / First Christmas / Lakewood / Thriepmuir hornpipe / Royal Belfast / President's men / Air fa la la la lo / Sickening thank you song
CD ______ CDTRAX 019
Greentrax / Aug '88 / ADA / Direct / Duncans / Highlander

PEACE AND PLENTY
Tullochgorum / Bells of the town / Song of the plough / Colliery gate / No you won't get me down in your mines / Black bear / Drover's lad / Top house / South Australia / Esikibo river / Blood red roses / Little Sally Rackett / Up and rin awa' Geordie / Mothers, daughters, wives / Highland road / Barratt's privateers / Men of the sea / Song for Europe / Tae the weavers gin ye gang / Leave her Johnny
CD ______ CDTRAX 002
Greentrax / Feb '89 / ADA / Direct / Duncans / Highlander

SMUGGLER/BURN THE WITCH
Smuggler / If mother should die / Gardens / Hornpipe/Reels / Mount and go / Boatie rows/Carls O'Dysart / Flowers o'the forest / Barnyards o'Delgaty / Bar-room / No churchman am I / Silkie of Sule Skerry / Man's a man for a'that / Johnnie Cope / Skye boat song / Tammy Traddlefeet/The rising / Fare ye well ye Mormond braes / Lion / Jennie Lusswade / Farewell to Novia Scotia / Aye walkin o / Gin I were where the gaudie rins / Burn the witch / Bonnie lass o'Gala Water / Jock Stuart / March of the Cameron men / Phantom whistler/Random jig / Doon in the wee room
CD ______ ESMCD 521
Essential / Apr '97 / BMG

SONGS FROM SCOTLAND
Boys that broke the ground / Tiree love song / Highland laddie / Roll the woodpile down / Hundred years ago / Westering home / Last session / All the tunes in the world / Most amazing thing of all / I will go / Widow MacKay / April waltz / Up and awa' wi' the Laverock / Scarce o'tatties / Lark in the morning / Ainster Harbour / Twa recruitin' / Sergeants / Rollin' home
CD ______ CDTRAX 045
Greentrax / Jul '91 / ADA / Direct / Duncans / Highlander

McCann, Eamon

EVERYTHING THAT I AM
Love is blind / Small town saturday night / Hey good lookin' / Past the point of rescue / It's all over now / Don't call me, I'll call you / Everything that I am / I promised you the world / When you come to land / Can't break it to my heart / Life after you / Gift of love / Bunch of bright red roses / Mother nature's son / I'm no stranger to the rain / Only when I laugh
CD ______ RCD 544
Ritz / Oct '94 / Pinnacle

GOLD IN THE MOUNTAIN
CD ______ RITZRCD 554
Ritz / Mar '96 / Pinnacle

McCann, Jim

GREATEST HITS
Galway races / Spancil hill / Easy and slow / Follow me up to Carlow / Next market day / Times have changed / Town of Ballybay / Carrickfergus / Lord of the dance / Go lassie go
CD ______ CDIRISH 019
Outlet / Mar '97 / ADA / CM / Direct / Duncans / Koch / Ross

McCann, Les

BEST OF LES MCCANN, THE
Fish this week, but next week chitlins / Truth / For Carl Perkins / Vakushna / Little 3/4 time for God and co / Shout / Doreen don't cry / Big Jim / Gone on and get that church / Pretty lady / Someone stole my chitlins / Shampoo
CD ______ CDP 8522162
Blue Note / Aug '96 / EMI

ON THE SOUL SIDE
Shambalala / Early riser / Black rub / Vu jade / New blues / Lift every voice and sing God Bless America / Ignominy / Children / Dippermouth / Look to your heart
CD ______ 5224312
Verve / Feb '92 / PolyGram

SOUVENIR DE MONTREUX (McCann, Les & Eddie Harris)
Step right up: *Kirk, Rahsaan Roland* / Music from the seeker: *Kirk, Rahsaan Roland* / Satin doll: *Kirk, Rahsaan Roland* / Balm to Gedeon: *Kirk, Rahsaan Roland* / Blue rot no.2: *Kirk, Rahsaan Roland* / You did it, you did it: *Kirk, Rahsaan Roland* / Misty: *Kirk, Rahsaan Roland* / Ragman and the junkman: *Kirk, Rahsaan Roland* / Volunteered: *Kirk, Rahsaan Roland* / Black boot: *Kirk, Rahsaan Roland* / Cuckoo: *Kirk, Rahsaan Roland* / You never can say goodbye: *Kirk, Rahsaan Roland*
CD ______ 8122724522
Atlantic / Jul '96 / Warner Music

McCann, Phillip

ALL OF THE WORLD'S MOST BEAUTIFUL MELODIES (5CD Set)
CD Set ______ CHAN 4536
Chandos / Sep '95 / Chandos

WORLD'S MOST BEAUTIFUL MELODIES VOL.5, THE (McCann, Phillip & Sellers Engineering Band)
Meditation from Thais / Salut d'amour / Suo gan / Beau soir / La calinda / Pavanne / I'll walk beside you / Clair de Lune / Exotica / On wings of song / Largo / Eriskay love lilt / Vissi d'arte / To a wild rose / Sheep may safely graze / Adagio from Symphony No. 2 / Czardas
CD ______ CHAN 4532
Chandos / Aug '94 / Chandos

McCann, Susan

20 COUNTRY CLASSICS
CD ______ CDC 004
Ceol / Feb '97 / CM

COUNTRY LOVE AFFAIR
Never ending love affair / Johnny lovely Johnny / Blue velvet / Forever and ever Amen / Little ole wine drinker me / Travellin' light / Let the rest of the world go by / Two broken hearts / Someone is looking for someone like you / Irish eyes / Boy in your arms / Wind in the willows / Mother's love's a blessing / Patches in heaven / How great thou art / When the sun says goodbye to the mountain
CD ______ IHCD 482
Irish Heritage / Nov '90 / Prism

DIAMONDS AND DREAMS
Love me one more time / When I hear the music / Have you ever been lonely / String of diamonds / Always / You're never too old to love / He never will be mine / Loving you / I vow to thee my country / Yellow roses / Sonny's dream / Broken speed of the sound of the loneliness / Rose of my heart / Hillbilly girl with the blues / Everything is beautiful / Give me more time
CD ______ IHCD 591
Irish Heritage / Oct '91 / Prism

MEMORIES
Softly, softly / String of diamonds / Whatever happened to old fashioned love / Irish memories / Dreaming of a little island / Help me make it through the night / Bus To LA / Penny arcade / If the whole world stopped loving / Once A Day / Love Has Joined Us Together / Since Johnny went away / Darlin' / Angels, Roses And Rain
CD ______ IHCD 592
Irish Heritage / Nov '92 / Prism

SUSAN MCCANN'S IRELAND
CD ______ TSCD 220
Outlet / Jan '95 / ADA / CM / Direct / Duncans / Koch / Ross

McCarthy

I'M A WALLET/BANKING, VIOLENCE & INTERNATIONAL NARCOTICS
CD ______ CDMRED 138
Cherry Red / Feb '97 / Pinnacle

THAT'S ALL VERY WELL BUT...
CD ______ CDMRED 125
Cherry Red / Apr '96 / Pinnacle

McCarthy, Cormac

PICTURE GALLERY BLUES
CD ______ GLCD 2122
Green Linnet / Aug '95 / ADA / CM / Direct / Highlander / Roots

McCarthy, Jimmy

SONG OF THE SINGING HORSEMAN, THE
On my enchanted sight / Hard man to follow / Mystic lipstick / Missing you / Ride on / No frontiers / Mad lady and me / Grip of parallel / Bright blue rose / Ancient rain / Song of the singing horseman
CD ______ LUNCD 053
Mulligan / Jan '91 / ADA / CM

McCartney, Paul

ALL THE BEST
Coming up / Ebony and ivory / Listen to what the man said / No more lonely nights / Silly love songs / Let 'em in / C moon / Pipes of peace / Live and let die / Another day / Maybe I'm amazed / Goodnight tonight / Once upon a long ago / Say say say / With a little luck / My love / We all stand together / Mull of Kintyre / Jet / Band on the run
CD ______ CDPMTV 1
Parlophone / Nov '87 / EMI

CHOBA B CCCP
Kansas City / Twenty flight rock / I'm in love again / Lawdy Miss Clawdy / Bring it on home to me / Lucille / Don't get around much anymore / I'm gonna be a wheel someday / That's alright Mama / Summertime / Ain't that a shame / Crackin' up / Just because / Midnight special
CD ______ CDPCSD 117
Parlophone / Aug '91 / EMI

FAMILY WAY, THE (Aubut, Carl & Claudel String Quartet)
CD ______ 4542302
Philips / Jun '96 / PolyGram

FLAMING PIE
Song we were singing / World tonight / If you wanna / Somedays / Young boy / Calico skies / Flaming pie / Heaven on a Sunday / Used to be bad / Souvenir / Little willow / Really love you / Beautiful night / Great day
CD ______ CDPCSD 171
Parlophone / Jun '97 / EMI

FLOWERS IN THE DIRT
My brave face / Rough ride / You want her too / Distractions / We got married / We got there / Figure of eight / This one / Don't be careless love / That day is done / How many people / Motor of love / Ou est le soleil
CD ______ CDPMCOL 16
Parlophone / Jun '93 / EMI

LIVERPOOL ORATORIO (Various Artists)
CD ______ CDPAUL 1
EMI Classics / Oct '91 / EMI

LIVERPOOL ORATORIO (HIGHLIGHTS) (Various Artists)
CD ______ CDC 7546422
EMI Classics / Oct '92 / EMI

MCCARTNEY
Lovely Linda / That would be something / Valentine's day / Every night / Hot as sun glasses / Junk / Man we was lonely / Oo you / Momma Miss America / Teddy boy / Singalong junk / Maybe I'm amazed / Kree nakoorie

CD CDPMCOL 1
Parlophone / Apr '93 / EMI

MCCARTNEY VOL.2
Coming up / Temporary secretary / On the way / Waterfalls / Nobody knows / Front parlour / Summer's day song / Frozen jap / Bogey music / Dark room / One of these days / Check my machine / Secret friend
CD CDPMCOL 11
Parlophone / Jun '93 / EMI

OFF THE GROUND
Off the ground / Looking for changes / Hope of deliverance / Mistress and maid / I owe it all to you / Biker like an icon / Peace in the neighbourhood / Golden earth girl / Lovers that never were / Get out of my way / Winedark open sea / C'mon people
CD CDPCSD 125
Parlophone / Nov '92 / EMI

PAUL IS LIVE
Drive my car / Let me roll it / Looking for changes / Peace in the neighbourhood / All my loving / Robbie's bit / Good rockin' tonight / We can work it out / Hope of deliverance / Michelle / Biker like an icon / Here, there and everywhere / My love / Magical mystery tour / C'mon people / Lady Madonna / Paperback writer / Penny Lane / Live and let die / Kansas City / Welcome to soundcheck / Hotel in Benidorm / I wanna be your man / Fine day
CD CDPCSD 147
Parlophone / Nov '93 / EMI

PIPES OF PEACE
Pipes of peace / Say say say / Other me / Keep under cover / So bad / Man / Sweetest little show / Average person / Hey hey / Tug of peace / Through our love
CD CDPMCOL 13
Parlophone / Jun '93 / EMI

PRESS TO PLAY
Stranglehold / Good times coming / Talk more talk / Footprints / Only love remains / Press / Pretty little head / Move over busker / Angry / However absurd / Write away / It's not true / Tough on a tightrope / Feel the sun / Once upon a long ago (long version) / Spies like us
CD CDPMCOL 15
Parlophone / Jun '93 / EMI

RAM (McCartney, Paul & Linda)
Too many people / Three legs / Ram on / Dear boy / Uncle Albert / Smile away: *McCartney, Paul* / Heart of the country: *McCartney, Paul* / Monkberry moon delight / Eat at home / Long haired lady / Backseat of my car: *McCartney, Paul*
CD CDPMCOL 2
Parlophone / Apr '93 / EMI

RED ROSE SPEEDWAY (McCartney, Paul & Wings)
Big barn bed / My love / Get on the right thing / One more kiss / Little lamb dragonfly / Single pigeon / When the night / Loup (1st indian on the moon) / Hold me tight / Lazy dynamite / Hands of love / Power cut / Mony mony (instrumental version)
CD CDPMCOL 4
Parlophone / Apr '93 / EMI

TRIPPING THE LIVE FANTASTIC
Showtime / Figure of eight / Jet / Rough ride / Got to get you into my life / Band on the run / Birthday / Ebony and ivory / We got married / Inner city madness / Maybe I'm amazed / Long and winding road / Crackin' up / Fool on the hill / Sergeant Pepper's lonely hearts club band / Can't buy me love / Matchbox / Put it there / Together / Things we said today / Eleanor Rigby / This one / My brave face / Back in the USSR / I saw her standing there / Twenty flight rock / Coming up / Sally / Let it be / Ain't that a shame / Live and let die / If I were not upon the stage / Hey Jude / Yesterday / Get back / Golden slumbers / Don't let the sun catch you crying
CD Set CDPCST 73461
Parlophone / Nov '90 / EMI

TRIPPING THE LIVE FANTASTIC - HIGHLIGHTS
Got to get you into my life / Birthday / We got married / Long and winding road / Sergeant Pepper's lonely hearts club band / Can't buy me love / All my trials / Things we said today / Eleanor Rigby / My brave face / Back in the USSR / I saw her standing there / Coming up / Let it be / Hey Jude / Get back / Golden slumbers / Carry that weight
CD CDPCSD 114
Parlophone / Nov '90 / EMI

TUG OF WAR
Tug of war / Take it away / Always somebody who cares / What's that you're doing / Here today / Ballroom dancing / Pound is sinking / Wanderlust / Get it / Be what you see / Dress me up as a robber / Ebony and ivory
CD CDPMCOL 12
Parlophone / Jun '93 / EMI

UNPLUGGED (The Official Bootleg)
Be bop a lula / I lost my little girl / Here, there and everywhere / Blue moon of Kentucky / We can work it out / San Francisco Bay blues / I've just seen a face / Every night / She's a woman / Hi-heel sneakers / And I love her / That would be something / Blackbird / Ain't no sunshine / Good rockin' tonight / Singin' the blues / Junk
CD CDPCSD 116
Parlophone / May '91 / EMI

McCarty, K.

DEAD DOG'S EYEBALL - SONGS OF DANIEL JOHNSTON
Intro / Walking the cow / Rocket ship / Living life / I had a dream / I am a baby (in my universe) / Hey Joe / Like a monkey in a zoo / Sorry entertainer / Desperate man blues / Oh no / Hate song / Golly gee / Going down / Museum of love / Wild West Virginia / Running water / Grievances / Creature
CD JUSCD 002
Justine / Jul '95 / Vital

MacCaskill, Ishbel

SIODA
CD SKYECD 006
Macmeanma / Jan '95 / ADA / CM / Duncans / Highlander

McCaslin, Mary

BEST OF MARY MCCASLIN
Things we said today / Northfield / Wayward wind / Prairie in the sky / San Bernardino waltz / Dealers / Ghost riders in the sky / Cole Younger / Living without you / Circle of friends / Blackbird / Bramble and the rose / Last cannonball / Way out west / My world is empty without you / Young Westertly / Back to Salinas / Old friends
CD PHCD 1149
Philo / '92 / ADA / CM / Direct

BROKEN PROMISES
CD PH 1160CD
Philo / May '94 / ADA / CM / Direct

OLD FRIENDS
Things we said today / Oklahoma hills / Wendigo / Way out there / Pinball wizard / My world is empty without you babe / Wayward wind / Blackbird / Don't fence me in / Old friends
CD CDPH 1046
Philo / Nov '96 / ADA / CM / Direct

PRAIRIE IN THE SKY
Pass me by / Priscilla Drive / Ballad of Weaverville / Back to Silas / Ghost riders in the sky / Last cannonball / It's my time / Cornerstone cowboy / Prairie in the sky / Cole Younger / Dealers / My love
CD CDPH 1024
Philo / Nov '95 / ADA / CM / Direct

McCavity's Cat

GENEVER CONVENTION, THE
CD MWCD 1003
Music & Words / Apr '93 / ADA / Direct

SCRATCH
CD MWCD 1006
Music & Words / Dec '95 / ADA / Direct

McClain, Sam

KEEP ON MOVIN'
CD AQ 1031
Audioquest / May '95 / ADA / New Note/ Pinnacle

McClatchy, Debby

LIGHT YEARS AWAY
Wild rose of the mountain / Charlie Poole's ramble / Girl I left in sunny Tennessee / Abe's retreat/Big siota / Run sister run / Mississippi moon / Sweet sunny South / When I got home I'm gonna be satisfied / Light years away / Hale's rag / Ballad of soulful Sam / Milwaukee blues / Brothers from York / Liza Jane / Glendy Burke
CD PLCD 084
Plant Life / Jan '93 / ADA / Soundalive / Symposium

McClennan, Grant

IN YOUR BRIGHT RAY
In your bright ray: *McLennan, Grant* / Cave in: *McLennan, Grant* / One plus one: *McLennan, Grant* / Sea breeze: *McLennan, Grant* / Malibu 69: *McLennan, Grant* / Who said love was dead: *McLennan, Grant* / Room for skin: *McLennan, Grant* / All them pretty angels: *McLennan, Grant* / Comet scar: *McLennan, Grant* / Down here: *McLennan, Grant* / Lamp by lamp: *McLennan, Grant* / Do you see the lights: *McLennan, Grant* / Parade of shadows: *McLennan, Grant*
CD BBQCD 192
Beggars Banquet / Jul '97 / RTM/Disc / Warner Music

McClennan, Tommy

GUITAR KING 1939-1942, A
CD 158702
Blues Collection / Jan '97 / Discovery

TRAVELLIN' HIGHWAY MAN - 1939-1942
You can mistreat me here / New shake 'em on down / Bottle it up and go / Boogie woogie woman / Mr. So and so blues / I love my baby / It's hard to be lonesome / Blue as I can be / Roll me baby / New highway 51
CD TMCD 06
Travellin' Man / Oct '90 / Hot Shot / Jazz Music / Wellard

McClinton, Delbert

DELBERT MCCLINTON
Sun medley / Tell me about it / Weatherman / Mary Lou / Have a little faith in me / Wanderer / Just you and me / One more last chance / Lay around and love on you / He will break your heart / Outskirts of town
CD CURBCD 008
Curb / Mar '94 / Grapevine/PolyGram

LIVE FROM AUSTIN
CD ALCD 4773
Alligator / May '93 / ADA / CM / Direct

NEVER BEEN ROCKED ENOUGH
Every time I roll the dice / I used to worry / Miss you fever / Why me / Have a little faith in me / Never been rocked enough / Blues as blues can get / Can I change my mind / Cease and desist / Stir it up / Good man, good woman
CD CURBCD 005
Curb / Mar '94 / Grapevine/PolyGram

VICTIM OF LIFE'S CIRCUMSTANCES/ GENUINE COWHIDE
Victim of life's circumstances / Honky tonkin' (I guess I done me some) / Two more bottles of wine / Lesson in the pain of love / Do it / Object of my affection / Ruby Louise / Real good itch / Solid gold plated fool / Morgan City fool / Troubled woman / It's love baby (24 hours a day) / Please please please / Lovey dovey / Before you accuse me / Blue Monday / I'm dyin' fast as I can / Lipstick, powder and paint / Pledging my love / One kiss led to another / (When she wants good lovin') my baby comes to me / Special love song / Let the good times roll / Love rustler / Let love come between us / Under suspicion / Some people
CD RVCD 65
Raven / Feb '97 / ADA / Direct

McClure, Bobby

BOBBY MCCLURE & WILLIE CLAYTON (McClure, Bobby & Willie Clayton)
CD HIUKCD 134
Hi / Aug '92 / Pinnacle

McClure, Ron

CLOSER TO YOUR TEARS
CD SCCD 31413
Steeplechase / Jul '97 / Discovery / Impetus

PINK CLOUD (McClure, Ron Quartet)
CD 860022
Naxos Jazz / Jun '97 / Select

YESTERDAY'S TOMORROW (McClure, Ron/John Abercrombie/Aldo Romano)
CD EPC 884
European Music Production / Feb '92 / Harmonia Mundi

McCluskey Brothers

AWARE OF ALL
CD ASKCD 13
Vinyl Japan / Jul '92 / Plastic Head / Vinyl Japan

FAVOURITE COLOURS
Perfect afternoon / Lonely satelite / Favourite colours / She said to the driver / 1000 Years / Better days / Cinder street / When the loving comes / Slip away / Passport
CD KF 001 CD
Kingfisher / Jan '93 / Vital

WONDERFUL AFFAIR
CD KF 002
Kingfisher / Jun '96 / Grapevine/PolyGram

MacColl, Angus

CLAN MACCOLL, THE
2/4 marches / Seagull jigs / Reels / March/ strathspey/reel / Archie beag jigs / 6/8 marches / Strathspey/reels / Tommy Tully's air / Gaelic airs/reel / Swallows tail reels / Gaelic air jigs
CD LCOM 5255
Lismor / Nov '96 / ADA / Direct / Duncans / Lismor

MacColl, Ewan

BLACK AND WHITE (The Definitive Ewan MacColl Collection)
Ballad of accounting / Driver's song / My old man / Dirty old town / Black and white / Brother did you weep / Press gang / Shoals of herring / Sheath and knife / Highland muster roll / Cam ye o'er frae France / Maid gaed tae the mill / Nobody knew she was there / Looking for a job / Kilroy was here / First time ever I saw your face / Foggy dew / Joy of living
CD COOKCD 038
Cooking Vinyl / Feb '95 / Vital

BLOW, BOYS, BLOW (MacColl, Ewan & A.L. Lloyd)
CD TCD 1024
Tradition / Aug '96 / ADA / Vital

BOTHY BALLADS
CD OSS 101CD
Ossian / Apr '94 / ADA / CM / Direct / Highlander

CLASSIC SCOTS BALLADS (MacColl, Ewan & Peggy Seeger)
CD TCD 1051
Tradition / Jul '97 / ADA / Vital

EFDSS & 70TH BIRTHDAY CONCERTS
Thirty foot trailer / Shoals of herring / Fish gutter's song / First time ever / White wind / Berry fields of Blair / Going to West / Invader / My old man / Spinning wheel / Joy of living / Ewan MacColl in conversation with Jim Lloyd
CD MASHCD 002
Cooking Vinyl / Jun '96 / Vital

JACOBITE REBELLIONS, THE
Ye Jacobites by name / Such a parcel of rogues in a nation / Will ye go to Sherriffmuir / Wae's me for Prince Charlie / Charlie is my darling / Haughs o' Cromdale / Bonnie moorhen / Johnny Cope / Cam ye o'er frae France / There's three brave loyal fellows / This is no my ain house / Piper o'Dundee / Donald MacGillavry / MacLean's welcome / Will ye no' come back again
CD OSS 103CD
Ossian / Apr '94 / ADA / CM / Direct / Highlander

LEGEND OF EWAN MACCOLL
CD NTMCD 502
Nectar / Jun '95 / Pinnacle

NAMING OF NAMES (MacColl, Ewan & Peggy Seeger)
Economic miracle / Just the tax for me / Grocer / Not going to give it back / Sellafield child / Bring the Summer home / Maggie went green / Nuclear means jobs / Hose hunting blues / Dracumag / Rogue's gallery / Island / We remember (naming of names)
CD COOKCD 036
Cooking Vinyl / May '90 / Vital

REAL MACCOLL, THE
Ye Jacobites by name / Johnny Cope / Cam ye o'er frae France / Haughs o' Cromdale / Such a parcel of rogues in a nation / Farewell to Sicily / Derek Bentley / Johnny O'Breadislee / Go down ye murderers / Van Diemen's land / Minorie / Sheep crook and black dog / Bramble briar / One night as I lay on my bed / Grey cock / Blantyre explosion / Gresford disaster / Four loom weaver / Song of the iron road / Dirty old town
CD TSCD 463
Topic / May '93 / ADA / CM / Direct

SCOTTISH POPULAR SONGS
CD OSS 105CD
Ossian / Apr '94 / ADA / CM / Direct / Highlander

SONGS OF ROBERT BURNS
CD OSS 102CD
Ossian / Apr '94 / ADA / CM / Direct / Highlander

TRADITIONAL SONGS & BALLADS
CD OSS 104CD
Ossian / Apr '94 / ADA / CM / Direct / Highlander

MacColl, Kirsty

ELECTRIC LANDLADY
Walking down Madison / All I ever need / Children of the revolution / Halloween / My affair / Lying down / He never mentioned love / We'll never pass this way again / Hardest word / Maybe it's imaginary / My way home / One and only
CD CDV 2663
Virgin / Jul '91 / EMI

ESSENTIAL COLLECTION, THE
CD STIFFCD 17
Disky / Aug '96 / Disky / THE

GALORE (The Best Of Kirsty MacColl)
They don't know / There's a guy works down the chip shop swears he's Elvis / New England / He's on the beach / Fairytale of New York / Miss Otis regrets / Free world / Innocence / You just haven't earned it yet baby / Days / Don't come the cowboy with me Sonny Jim / Walking down Madison / My affair / Angel / Titanic days / Can't stop killing you / Caroline / Perfect day
CD CDV 2763
Virgin / Mar '95 / EMI

KITE
Innocence / Mother's ruin / No victims / Don't come the cowboy with me Sonny Jim / What do pretty girls do / End of a perfect day / Free world / Days / Fifteen minutes / Tread lightly / Dancing in limbo / You and me baby / You just haven't earned it yet baby / La foret de mimosas / Complainte pour ste Catherine
CD CDKM 1
Virgin / Apr '89 / EMI

TITANIC DAYS
You know it's you / Soho sqaure / Angel / Last day of summer / Bad / Can't stop killing you / Titanic days / Don't go home / Big

boy on a Saturday night / Just woke up / Tomorrow never comes
CD 4509947112
WEA / Dec '96 / Warner Music

McColley, Laurie

PSEUDONYMOUS
CD MUDCD 022
Mud / Oct '96 / Cargo

McComb, Dave

LOVE OF WILL
CD D 31071
Mushroom / Mar '94 / 3mv/Pinnacle

McComiskey, Billy

MAKIN' THE ROUNDS
CD GLCD 1034
Green Linnet / '92 / ADA / CM / Direct / Highlander / Roots

McConnell, Cathal

FOR THE SAKE OF OLD DECENCY (McConnell, Cathal & Len Graham)
CD SA 22012CD
Sage Arts / Jan '94 / ADA

McConnell, Rob

BRASS IS BACK, THE (McConnell, Rob & The Boss Brass)
Strollin' / All the things you are / Love of my life / Who asked / Slow grind / Winter in Winnipeg / Days gone by / Them there eyes
CD CCD 4458
Concord Jazz / May '91 / New Note/ Pinnacle

BRASSY AND SASSY (McConnell, Rob & The Boss Band)
Strike up the band / Hey / Very early / Things ain't what they used to be / Scrapple from the apple / Embraceable you/Why did I choose you / Blue serge suit / Club Sirocco / Samnamblues / Blues unblue
CD CCD 4508
Concord Jazz / Jun '92 / New Note/ Pinnacle

DON'T GET AROUND MUCH ANYMORE (McConnell, Rob & The Boss Brass)
Don't get around much anymore / Waltz you knew was blue / Once I loved / If you never came to me / Crazy rhythm / Gee baby ain't I good to you / (Back home again in) Indiana / Donna Lee / Bad and the beautiful / Robin / Back beat / Rockin' in rhythm
CD CCD 4661
Concord Jazz / Aug '95 / New Note/ Pinnacle

EVEN CANADIANS GET THE BLUES (McConnell, Rob & The Boss Brass)
Blue tag / Even Canadians get the blues / Clarinet is black and blue / Do you mean it / Blue hodge / Sixth sense / Countless blues / Shuffle boogie swamp groove blues / O Canada
CD CCD 4722
Concord Jazz / Sep '96 / New Note/ Pinnacle

JAZZ ALBUM, THE (McConnell, Rob & The Boss Brass)
CD SB 2080
Sea Breeze / Jan '97 / Jazz Music

OUR 25TH YEAR (McConnell, Rob & The Boss Brass)
4 BC / Imagination / What am I here for / Just tell me yes or no / Riffs I have known / TQ2 / Nightfall / Broadway / My bells / Flying home
CD CCD 4559
Bellaphon / Jun '93 / New Note/Pinnacle

OVERTIME (McConnell, Rob & The Boss Brass)
Overtime / Touch of your lips / Stella by starlight / Hawg jawz / After you / Alone together / This may be your lucky day / Wait and see
CD CCD 4618
Concord Jazz / Nov '94 / New Note/ Pinnacle

THREE FOR THE ROAD (McConnell, Rob & Ed Bickert/Don Thompson)
Sleepin' bee / Dream a little dream of me / Two for the road / Royal blue / Dreamsville / I'm thru with love / Seems like old times / Dream dancing / Our waltz / I don't know enough about you / Last night when we were young / Young and foolish / In the blue of evening
CD CCD 47652
Concord Jazz / Apr '97 / New Note/ Pinnacle

TRIO SKETCHES (McConnell, Rob & Ed Bickert/Neil Swanson)
Snow White / My ideal / I have dreamed / Can't we be friends / Baubles, bangles and beads / This is love of mine, this is always / Long ago and far away / I'm gonna sit right down and write myself a letter / Ornithardy / 'Deed I do
CD CCD 4591
Concord Jazz / Mar '94 / New Note/ Pinnacle

McConville, Tom

CROSS THE RIVER
Hurleys / Homes of Donegal / Tone Rowe's/ Smithy's baccy tin / Caliope house / How can my poor heart / Frenchie's reel / President Garfield's reel / Johnny miner / Gold ring / Cross the river / Lark in the morning / Goodnight waltz / Overgate / Calum Donaldson/Mick Johnson's parrot/Da grocer / Wish the wars were all over / Ben's foot/ Birmingham fling
CD OBMCD 01
Old Bridge / Feb '96 / ADA / Direct / Highlander

FIDDLER'S FANCY
Quayside / Champion hornpipe / Cliff / Hill's no. 8 / Gateshead hornpipe / Pear tree / Cage / High level hornpipe / Flight of fancy / Hawk polka / Barber's pole / Beeswing / Lads like beer/Marquis of Waterford / Hawk / Proudlock's fancy / Fiddler's fancy / Bottle bank / Blaydon flats / Earl Grey
CD OBMCD 04
Old Bridge / Feb '96 / ADA / Direct / Highlander

McCoo, Marilyn

I HOPE WE GET TO LOVE IN TIME (McCoo, Marilyn & Billy Davis Junior)
CD RAZCD 2098
Razor & Tie / May '96 / Koch

McCook, Tommy

COOKIN'
CD CDHR 706
Trojan / Jun '96 / Direct / Jet Star

DOWN ON BOND STREET
Inez / Yellow basket, The (a tisket a tasket) / Down on Bond Street / Wall Street shuffle / Moody ska / Real cool / Tommy's rocksteady / Soul serenade / Persian cat (in a Persian market) / Saboo / Shadow of your smile / Music is my occupation / Our man Flint / Mad mad mad / Ode to billy joe / Heatwave / World needs love / Flying home / Mary Poppins / Second fiddle
CD CDTRL 326
Trojan / Mar '94 / Direct / Jet Star

McCorkle, Susannah

FROM BESSIE TO BRAZIL
Love / People that you never get to love / Thief in the night / Waters of March / Accentuate the positive / How deep is the ocean / Lady is a tramp / Quality time / My sweetie went away / Still crazy after all these years / Adeus America / That ole devil called love / Hit the road to dreamland / You go to my head
CD CCD 4547
Concord Jazz / May '93 / New Note/ Pinnacle

FROM BROADWAY TO BEBOP
Guys and dolls / Once you've been in love / Chica chica boom chic / My buddy / It's easy to remember / Don't fence me in / One of the good guys / I don't think I'll end it all today / Moody's mood / He loves me / Friend like me / I remember Bill
CD CCD 4615
Concord Jazz / Oct '94 / New Note/ Pinnacle

I'LL TAKE ROMANCE
Beautiful friendship / My foolish heart / I'll take romance / Get out of town / It never entered my mind / Let's get lost / Spring is here / Taking a chance on love / I concentrate on you / Lover man / That old feeling / Zing went the strings of my heart / Where do you start / I thought about you
CD CCD 4491
Concord Jazz / Jan '92 / New Note/ Pinnacle

LET'S FACE THE MUSIC (The Songs Of Irving Berlin)
I'd rather lead a band / Let's face the music and dance / Isn't this a lovely day (to be caught in the rain) / Heat wave / How deep is the ocean / Medley / There's no business like showbusiness / Cheek to cheek / Love and the weather / Supper time / Medley / Better luck next time / Let yourself go / Waiting at the end of the road
CD CCD 47592
Concord Jazz / Jun '97 / New Note/ Pinnacle

NO MORE BLUES
CD CCD 4370
Concord Jazz / Apr '89 / New Note/ Pinnacle

OVER THE RAINBOW (The Songs Of E.Y. 'Yip' Harburg)
Old devil moon / Begat / If I only had a heart / Ding dong, the witch is dead / Over the rainbow / Poor you / Napoleon / What is there to say / Thrill me / Happiness is a thing called Joe / Eagle and me / Moanin' in the mornin' / Down with love / Here's to your illusions/In times like these
CD TJA 10033
Jazz Alliance / Dec '96 / New Note/Pinnacle

PEOPLE THAT YOU NEVER GET TO LOVE, THE
No more blues / Bye bye country boy / Rain sometimes / Lady's in love with you / I have the feeling I've been here before / I won't dance / Hungry years / People that you never get to love / Call of the city / Alone too long / Foodophobia / I've grown accustomed to his face / Feeling of Jazz / I'm pulling through
CD TJA 100342
Jazz Alliance / Sep '97 / New Note/Pinnacle

SABIA
Tristeza / Estate / Dilemma / Dreamer / Sabia / So many stars / So danco samba / Manha de carnaval / P'ra machucar meu coracao / Travessia / A felicidade
CD CCD 4418
Concord Jazz / Oct '90 / New Note/ Pinnacle

SONGS OF COLE PORTER, THE
Night and day / Anything goes / Just one of those things / It's alright with me / Weren't / From this moment on / Who wants to be a millionaire / Why don't we try staying home / You do something to me / Easy to love / Goodbye little dream, goodbye / You'd be so nice to come home to / Let's do it / Ev'rytime we say goodbye
CD CCD 4696
Concord Jazz / May '96 / New Note/ Pinnacle

SONGS OF JOHNNY MERCER, THE
At the jazz band ball / Fools rush in / I'm old fashioned / Blues in the night / My new celebrity is you / Skylark / Any place I hang my hat is my home / Talk to me baby / This time the dream's on me / Dream / How little we know / Harlem butterfly / Arthur Murray taught me dancing in a hurry / Love's got me in a lazy mood / One for my baby (and one more for the road)
CD TJA 10031
Jazz Alliance / Apr '96 / New Note/Pinnacle

McCormack, John

CHRISTIAN CELEBRATION, A (Favourite Hymns, Carols & Sacred Music)
CD GEMMCD 9990
Pearl / Nov '92 / Harmonia Mundi

COUNT JOHN MCCORMACK VOL.7
Snowy breasted pearl / Meeting of the waters / When shall the day break in Erin / Molly Bawn / Irish emigrant / Avourneen / Killarney / Green Isle of Erin / Love thee dearest, love thee / Believe me, if all those endearing young charms / Norah the pride of Kildare / Come back to Erin / Eleen Alannah, Augus Asthore / Minstrel boy / Foggy dew / Kathleen Mavoureen / Dear little shamrock / Lily of Killarney / Once again / Wearing of the green / God save Ireland / Boys of Wexford / Nation once again / Croppy boy / Home to Athlone
CD Set OPAL CDS9847
Opal / Aug '91 / Harmonia Mundi

GREEN ISLE OF ERIN
CD CDC 006
Ceol / Feb '97 / CM

JOHN MCCORMACK
I'll walk beside you / Green bushes / Jeannie with the light brown hair / Star of County Down / Village that nobody knows / She is far from the land / Passing by / Drink to me only with thine eyes / Sweetly she sleeps, my Alice fair / Old house / Maureen / Lass with the delicate air / Child's prayer / Harp that once thro' Tara's hall / Bard of Armagh / Terence's farewell to Kathleen / O Mary dear / Believe me / If all those endearing young charms / Ye banks and braes o' bonnie Doon / Silent moon / Meeting of the waters / Gentle maiden / Love thee, dearest, love thee / Off to Philadelphia / Oft in the stilly night
CD CDMFP 6358
Music For Pleasure / Jun '97 / EMI

JOHN MCCORMACK IN AMERICAN SONG
CD GEMMCD 9971
Pearl / Oct '92 / Harmonia Mundi

KERRY DANCE (And Other Fine Irish Ballads)
Come back to Erin / She is far from the land / Irish emigrant / Low backed car / My lagan loce / Kathleen Mavoureen / Killarney / Macushla / Molly Brannigan / Eileen Alannah / Mother Machree
CD CDCH 207
Happy Days / Jun '93 / Conifer/BMG

MINSTREL BOY, THE
Minstrel boy / Nirvana / My dreams / Little love, a little kiss / Angel's serenade / Ave Maria / Serenata / Barcarolle / Before my window / Swans / Come, my beloved / Moonlight and roses / I look into your garden / Bird songs at eventide / By the short cut to the roses / Fairy tree / Harp that once thro' tara's halls / Once in a blue moon / Charm me asleep / Vespers / Sweetly she sleeps, my Alice fair / Song remembered / Dawning of the day / House, love, made for you and me / Old houses
CD CDAJA 5224
Living Era / Apr '97 / Select

POPULAR SONGS & IRISH BALLADS
Garden where the praties grow / Believe me, if all those endearing young charms / Star of County Down / Bless this house / Terence's farewell to Kathleen / I'll walk beside you / Believe me, if all those endearing young charms / Drink to me only with thine eyes / Green isle of Erin / Jeanie with the light brown hair / Kerry dance / O Mary dear / Linden lea / Little silver ring / Old house / She is far from the land / Oft in the stilly night / Meeting of the waters / Bard of Armagh / Down by the Sally gardens / She moved through the fair / Green bushes / Off to Philadelphia / Bantry Bay / I hear you calling me / I know of two bright eyes / Sweetly she sleeps / Kashmiri song / Passing by
CD CDH 7697882
HMV / May '93 / EMI

SCOTTISH & IRISH SONGS
Trottin' to the fair / Bonnie wee thing / My lagan love / Bonnie Mary of Argyle / Snowy breasted pearl / Turn ye to me / Wearing of the green / When the dew is falling / Low backed car / Annie Laurie / When you and I were young Maggie / Auld Scotch sangs / Irish emigrant / Maiden of morven / She moved through the fair / Ye banks and braes o' bonnie Doon / Green bushes / Song to the seals / Maureen / Star O' the country down
CD MIDCD 005
Moidart / Apr '95 / Conifer/BMG

SONGS OF JOHN MCCORMACK
CD CDIRISH 014
Outlet / Oct '95 / ADA / CM / Direct / Duncans / Koch / Ross

WHEN IRISH EYES ARE SMILING
Angels guard thee / Bard of Armagh / Believe me, if all those endearing young charms / Brown bird singing / Come into the garden Maud / Dear old pal of mine / Dream once again / Flirtation / Garden where the praties grow / I hear you calling me / I'll sing thee songs of Araby / Irish emigrant / Jeanie with the light brown hair / Kerry dance / Macushla / She moved through the fair / Since you went away / South winds / Star of County Down / Sunshine of your smile / Turn ye to me / Venetian song / Waiting for you / When Irish eyes are smiling / When you and I were young Maggie
CD CDAJA 5119
Living Era / Mar '94 / Select

WHERE THE RIVER SHANNON FLOWS
Londonderry air / When Irish eyes are smiling / Garden where the praties grow / Eileen Alannah / Mother in Ireland / Ballynore ballad / Harp that once through Tara's halls / Kathleen Mavoureen / Padraic the fiddiler / Mother Machree / Bard of Armagh / My Irish song of songs / Norah O'Neale / By the short cut of the Rosses / Irish Emigrant / Snowy breasted pearl / My dark Rosaleen / Love's old sweet song / Macushla / Low back'd car / Where the River Shannon flows / Foggy dew / Rose of Tralee / Kitty my love / Star of the County Down
CD PASTCD 7022
Flapper / Mar '94 / Pinnacle

McCormick, John

MERCURY'S WELL
CD PH 009CD
Phantom / Jul '95 / ADA

McCoury Brothers

MCCOURY BROTHERS
CD ROUCD 0230
Rounder / Apr '95 / ADA / CM / Direct

RONNIE & ROB MCCOURY
CD ROUCD 0353
Rounder / Oct '95 / ADA / CM / Direct

McCoury, Del

BLUE SIDE OF TOWN, THE
Beauty of my dreams / Queen Anne's Lace / If you need a fool / Old memories mean nothing to me / Try me one more time / Before the fire comes down / Blue side of town / Seasons in my heart / That's alright mama / Make room for the blues / High on the mountain / I believe
CD ROUCD 0292
Rounder / '92 / ADA / CM / Direct

COLD HARD FACTS, THE (McCoury, Del Band)
Cold hard facts / Blue darlin' / Smoking gun / Love is a long road / Henry Walker / Baltimore Jonny / Blackjack county chains / Hard on my heart / Snake in the house / First time she left / Loggin' man / Member of the blues
CD ROUCD 0363
Rounder / Oct '96 / ADA / CM / Direct

DEEPER SHADE OF BLUE, A
CD ROUCD 303
Rounder / Jan '94 / ADA / CM / Direct

HIGH ON A MOUNTAIN (McCoury, Del & The Dixie Pals)
CD ROUCD 0019
Rounder / Sep '95 / ADA / CM / Direct

I WONDER WHERE YOU ARE TONIGHT
CD ARHCD 5006
Arhoolie / Apr '95 / ADA / Cadillac / Direct

McCowan, Andrew

FLING TIME
CD CDMON 823
Monarch / May '95 / ADA / CM / Direct / Duncans

FLING TIME VOL.2
CD CDMON 824
Monarch / May '95 / ADA / CM / Direct / Duncans

McCoy, Charlie

GREATEST HITS
CD 4658622
Monument / Aug '90 / Sony

McCoy, Clyde

CLYDE MCCOY & HIS ORCHESTRA 1951 (McCoy, Clyde Orchestra)
CD CCD 082
Circle / Jul '96 / Jazz Music / Swift / Wellard

McCoy, Hank

MOHAWK STREET (McCoy, Hank & The Dead Ringers)
CD OK 33026CD
Okra / Feb '95 / ADA / Direct

McCoy, John

THINK HARD AGAIN
Freemind / Demon rose / Loving lies / Hell to play / Heads will roll / Ride the night / Fear of the morning / Jerusalem / Oh well / Night lights / Sound of thunder / Temporary threshold shift / Because you lied / Night lights / Oh well
CD SJPCD 001
Angel Air / Jan '97 / Pinnacle

McCoy, Neal

NEAL MCCOY
CD 7567829072
Atlantic / Jul '96 / Warner Music

McCoys

HANG ON SLOOPY (The Best Of The McCoys)
Meet the McCoys / Hang on sloopy / I can't explain / Fever / Sorrow / Up and down / If you tell a lie / Come on let's go / Little people / Smoky Joe's cafe / Mr. Summer / Everyday I have to cry / (You make me feel) So good / Runaway / Gaitor tails and monkey ribs / Koko / Bald headed Lena / Say those magic words / Don't worry Mother (Your son's heart is pure) / I got to go back (And watch that little girl dance) / Dynamite / Beat the clock
CD ZK 47074
Columbia / Jul '95 / Sony

McCrackin, Bill

I AM THE EGGMAN
CD SH 41CD
Shredder / Jun '97 / Cargo / Greyhound / Plastic Head

McCracklin, Jimmy

HIGH ON THE BLUES
CD CDSXE 072
Stax / Jul '93 / Pinnacle

MERCURY RECORDINGS, THE
Wobble / Georgia slop / Hitched / No one to love me / (I'll be glad when you're dead) you rascal you / By myself / Doomed lover / With your love / Let's do it / Bridge / What's that (part 1) / What's that (part 2) / Folsom prison blues
CD BCD 15558
Bear Family / Mar '92 / Direct / Rollercoaster / Swift

TASTE OF THE BLUES, A
CD BB 9535CD
Bullseye Blues / Aug '94 / Direct

WALK, THE (Jimmy McCracklin At His Best)
CD RE 2124
Razor & Tie / Mar '97 / Koch

McCrae, George

DO SOMETHING
CD 343312
Koch International / Mar '96 / Koch

ROCK YOUR BABY
Rock your baby / I can't leave you alone / You got my heart / You can have it all / Look at you / Make it right / I need somebody like you / I get lifted
CD MUSCD 503
MCI Original Masters / Sep '94 / Disc / THE

McCrae, Gwen

BEST OF GWEN MCCRAE
Rockin' chair / For your love / It's worth the hurt / 90% of me is you / It keeps on raining / He don't ever lose his groove / Winners together or losers apart: *McCrae, Gwen & George* / Let your love do the talkin': *McCrae, Gwen & George* / You and I were made for each other: *McCrae, Gwen & George* / Damn right it's good / Love without sex / Starting all over again / Tonight's the night / Let's straighten it out / Love insurance / Cradle of love / Maybe I'll find somebody new / Melody of life / All this love I'm giving
CD NEXCD 189
Sequel / May '92 / BMG

GIRLFRIEND'S BOYFRIEND
CD HGCD 5
Homegrown / Mar '96 / Jet Star / Mo's Music Machine

PSYCHIC HOT LINE
CD GWX 42212
Ichiban / Aug '96 / Direct / Koch

McCray, Larry

DELTA HURRICANE
Delta hurricane / Adding up / Last four nickels / Soul shine / Not that much / Last hand of the night / Witchin' moon / Blue river / Hole in my heart / Three straight days of rain / Blues in the city
CD VPBCD 10
Pointblank / May '93 / EMI

MEET ME AT THE LAKE (McCray, Larry & The Bluegills)
Too much rooster / More walk, less talk / In a funk, in a phone booth / Hell to pay / Look around / No letter / Havoc / Never let it happen again / Moon is full / Spend it
CD ATM 1124
Atomic Theory / Nov '96 / ADA / Direct

McCready, Mindy

TEN THOUSAND ANGELS
Ten thousand angels / Guys do it all the time / All that I am / Maybe he'll notice her now / Girl's gotta do (What a girl's gotta do) / Have a nice day / It ain't a party / Without love / Tell me something I don't know / Breakin' it
CD 7863668062
BNA / Mar '97 / BMG

McCready, Rich

THAT ABOUT COVERS IT
CD MGO 115
MGO / Jul '97 / Greyhound

McCue, Bill

A' THE BEST FROM BILL MCCUE
Bonnie Scotland / Star o'Rabbie Burns / Annie Laurie / Poem (of a' the airts) / Address to the haggis / Whispering hope / If I were a rich man / Nameless lass / Auld lang syne
CD CDITV 587
Scotdisc / Oct '96 / Conifer/BMG / Duncans / Ross

COUNT YOUR BLESSINGS
Count your blessings / Softly and tenderly Jesus is calling / Where we'll never grow old / What a friend we have in Jesus / Lord's prayer / If I can help somebody / Going home / Beautiful Isle of somewhere / Shall we gather at the river / Bless this house / Whispering hope / Little drummer boy / Blessed assurance / Amazing grace
CD CDITV 467
Scotdisc / Dec '88 / Conifer/BMG / Duncans / Ross

HEART OF SCOTLAND, THE (McCue, Bill & Kinlochard Ceilidh Band)
Broadsword of Scotland / Irish reels / Ye banks and braes o' bonnie Doon / Waltz for Elizabeth / Ca' the Yowes / Military two step / Slow air / Hiking song / Jimmy Shand hornpipes / Bonnie Strathyre / Margaret's waltz / Rob Roy MacGregor / Loch Ard / Strip the willow / Christine McRichie / Whispering Hope / Amazing grace
CD CDITV 552
Scotdisc / Apr '94 / Conifer/BMG / Duncans / Ross

LUCKY WHITE HEATHER
CD CDITV 484
Scotdisc / Jul '89 / Conifer/BMG / Duncans / Ross

SCOTLAND'S ROYAL HIGHLAND SHOW
CD CDITV 594
Scotdisc / Jun '95 / Conifer/BMG / Duncans / Ross

MacCuish, Alasdair

BLACK ROSE
CD CDLOC 1086
Lochshore / May '95 / ADA / Direct / Duncans

WEST COAST AND BEYOND
CD CDLOC 1093
Lochshore / Jun '96 / ADA / Direct / Duncans

McCulloch, Danny

BEOWULF (McCulloch, Danny & Friends)
Hallowed ground / Cat house / Mary Jane / Waitin' for a dream / Mama sure could swing a deal / Headin' out East / Love me / Praise the Lord and pass the soup / You're the one to blame / Mind your business
CD EDCD 423
Edsel / Jul '95 / Pinnacle

McCulloch, Gordeanna

IN FREENSHIP'S NAME
Shuttle rins / Bawbee birlin' / Johnny my lad / Laird o'the dainty dounby / My bonnie laddie's lang a growin' / Shepherd's wife / Skippin' barfit thro' the heather / Tam bowie / Laird o' warriston / Tail toddle / Ploonan laddies / Willie's droon'd in yarrow / Laird o'drum / In freenship's name
CD CDTRAX 123
Greentrax / Mar '97 / ADA / Direct / Duncans / Highlander

SHEATH AND KNIFE
Kirk o' Birnie Bouzle / Dowie Dens o' Yarrow / Lichtbob's lassie / Will ye gang love / Bleacher lassie o' Kelvinhaugh / Yowie wi' the crookit horn / There's a herrin' in the pan / Sheath and knife / Jock since ever I saw yer face / Chevy Chase / Captain Wedderburn / Gallant weaver / Fence upon a time / Caw the yowes / Bawbie Allan / Hielan' laddie / Be kind tae yer nainsel
CD FECD 117
Fellside / Mar '97 / ADA / Direct / Target/BMG

McCulloch, Ian

CANDLELAND
Flickering wall / White hotel / Proud to fall / Cape / Candleland / Horse's head / Faith and healing / I know you well / In boom / Start again
CD K 2462252
WEA / Sep '89 / Warner Music

McCulloch, Jimmy

COMPLETE (McCulloch, Jimmy & White Line)
CD MSCD 004
Mouse / Feb '95 / Grapevine/PolyGram

McCurdy, Ed

COWBOY SONGS
CD TCD 1025
Tradition / Aug '96 / ADA / Vital

McCusker, John

JOHN MCCUSKER
CD COMD 2059
Temple / Apr '95 / ADA / CM / Direct / Duncans / Highlander

McCutcheon, John

BETWEEN THE ECLIPSE
CD ROUCD 0336
Rounder / Oct '94 / ADA / CM / Direct

BIGGER THAN YOURSELF
CD ROUCD 8044
Rounder / Aug '97 / ADA / CM / Direct

FAMILY GARDEN
CD ROUCD 8026
Rounder / May '93 / ADA / CM / Direct

FINE TIMES AT OUR HOUSE
CD GR 70710
Greenhays / Dec '94 / ADA / CM / Direct / Duncans / Jazz Music / Roots

GONNA RISE AGAIN
CD ROUCD 0222
Rounder / Aug '88 / ADA / CM / Direct

HOWJADOO
CD ROUCD 8009
Rounder / '88 / ADA / CM / Direct

NOTHING TO LOSE
CD ROUCD 0358
Rounder / Oct '95 / ADA / CM / Direct

SIGNS OF THE TIMES (McCutcheon, John & Si Kahn)
CD ROUCD 4017
Rounder / Aug '94 / ADA / CM / Direct

SPROUT WINGS AND FLY
CD ROUCD 0406
Rounder / Mar '97 / ADA / CM / Direct

STEP BY STEP
CD ROUCD 0216
Rounder / Aug '88 / ADA / CM / Direct

SUMMERSONGS
CD ROUCD 8036
Rounder / Apr '95 / ADA / CM / Direct

WINTER SOLSTICE
CD ROUCD 0192
Rounder / Dec '86 / ADA / CM / Direct

McDaniel, Floyd

LET YOUR HAIR DOWN (McDaniel, Floyd & Blues Swingers)
Raggedy ride / Blue mood / Mary Jo / Strange things happening / It don't mean a thing / I want a little girl / St. Louis blues / God bless the child / Sent for you yesterday / RM blues / Christopher Columbus / West side baby / Beale Street baby / Let your hair down / Nobody knows you when you're down and out / Why's life got to be this way / Caldonia
CD DE 671
Delmark / Mar '97 / ADA / Cadillac / CM / Direct / Hot Shot

McDermott's Two Hours

ENEMY WITHIN, THE
CD HAGCD 2
Hag / Aug '94 / Pinnacle / Shellshock/Disc

McDermott, Josie

DARBY'S FAREWELL (Traditional Songs Played On Flute & Whistle)
CD OSS 20CD
Ossian / Mar '94 / ADA / CM / Direct / Highlander

McDermott, Kevin

LAST SUPPER, THE (McDermott, Kevin Orchestra)
CD IGCDM 207
Iona Gold / Jun '94 / ADA / Total/BMG

MOTHER NATURE'S KITCHEN (McDermott, Kevin Orchestra)
Wheels of wonder / Slow boat to something better / King of nothing / Diamond / Mother nature's kitchen / Into the blue / Where we were meant to be / Statue to a stone / What comes to pass / Suffocation blues / Angel / Healing at the harbour
CD CID 9920
Island / Jul '91 / PolyGram

McDevitt, Chas

FREIGHT TRAIN (McDevitt, Chas & Nancy Whisky)
Freight train / Badman Stackolee / County jail / I'm satisfied / She moved through the fair / My old man / Poor Howard / Greenback dollar / Sing sing sing / BB Blues / Deep down / Born to be with you / I want a little girl / Across the bridge / Come all ye fair and tender maidens / Sportin' life / Trottin' to the fair / Everyday of the week / Face in the rain / Goin' home / Tom Hark / It makes no difference now / Good mornin' blues / Real love / Pop pourri / Everyday I have the blues / I dig you baby / Ace in the hole / Tom Hark
CD Set RCCD 3007
Rollercoaster / Nov '93 / Rollercoaster / Swift

MacDhonnagain, Tadhg

RAIFTEIRI SAN UNDERGROUND
CD CICD 094
Clo Iar-Chonnachta / Jan '94 / CM

MacDonald, Catriona

OPUS BLUE
CD ARADCD 103
Acoustic Radio / May '94 / CM

MacDonald, Jeanette

VERY BEST OF JEANETTE MACDONALD, THE
CD SWNCD 005
Sound Waves / Oct '95 / Target/BMG

WHEN I'M CALLING YOU (MacDonald, Jeanette & Nelson Eddy)
Ah sweet mystery of life / At the Balalaika / Beyond the blue horizon / Dear when I met you / Farewell to dreams / I'm falling in love with someone / Indian love call / Isn't it romantic / Lover come back to me / March of the grenadiers / Mounties / One kiss / One hour with you / Rose Marie / Smilin' through / Softly as in a morning sunrise / Sun up to sundown / Toreador's song / Tramp, tramp, tramp along the highway / Vilia / Waltz aria / Will you remember
CD CDAJA 5124
Living Era / Mar '94 / Select

MacDonald, John

SCOTTISH ACCORDION BY THE FIRESIDE
Scottish sing-a-long / Bonny Dundee/ Muckin' o'Geordie's byre/With a hundred pipers / Scottish soldier / My home / Northern light of old Aberdeen/I belong to Glasgow / Amazing grace / Scotland the brave medley / Roamin' in the gloamin/I love a lassie/Road to the Isles / It's a long way to Tipperary / Mull of Kintyre / Road and the miles to Dundee / Hail Caledonia medley / Click go the shears/On the road to Gunagai / Annie Laurie
CD HADCD 214
Spotlight On / Jun '97 / Henry Hadaway

MacDonald, Kenneth

SOUND OF KINTAIL FEATURING KENNETH MACDONALD
John MacColl's march to Kilbowie cottage / Col David Murray's welcome to Kintail / Tullock Castle / Piobaireacho, Donald Gruanach's / Gregory Blend and Roddy MacDonald / Boys of Glendale / I'm going home to Kintail

CD _______ CDITV 460
Scotdisc / Oct '88 / Conifer/BMG / Duncans / Ross

MacDonald, Pat

SLEEPS WITH HIS GUITAR
CD _______ ARKK 10060
ARKK / May '97 / Greyhound

MacDonald, Rod

BRING ON THE LIONS
CD _______ BRAM 1989082
Brambus / Nov '93 / ADA

MAN ON THE LEDGE, THE
CD _______ SHCD 8011
Shanachie / Dec '94 / ADA / Greensleeves / Koch

WHITE BUFFALO
CD _______ BRAM 1991292
Brambus / Nov '93 / ADA

McDonald, Alastair

HEROES AND LEGENDS OF SCOTLAND
CD _______ CBNCD 019
Corban / Sep '96 / CM / Duncans

HONEST POVERTY
De'il's awa' wi' tha exciseman / Green grow the rashes / Rattlin' roarin' Willie / O wert thou in the cauld blast / Man's a man (for a' that, an' a' that) / Mary Morrison / I am a son of Mars / Ca' the ewes / Duncan Gray / We're a'noddin' / Up wi' the Carls o' Dysart / There'll never be peace till Jamie comes hame / Willie Wastle (sic a wife as Willie had) / Ay waukin o / Scots wha hae / Rantin' rovin' Robin / Such a parcel of rogues in a nation
CD _______ LCOM 5250
Lismor / Feb '96 / ADA / Direct / Duncans / Lismor

SINGS ROBERT BURNS
CD _______ LBP 2020CD
Lochshore / Mar '96 / ADA / Direct / Duncans

SONGS GRETNA TO GLENCOE
CD _______ CDITV 547
Scotdisc / Sep '91 / Conifer/BMG / Duncans / Ross

VELVET & STEEL
Jamie Foyers / Bruce / Bonnie Earl O'Moray / Harlaw / Seer / Lock the door / Haughs o' Cromdale / Killiecrankie / My bonnie Mary / Blue bonnets / Flodden/Flooers o' the forest / Culloden's harvest / Fyvie / Sheep and stag remain
CD _______ CDTRAX 078
Greentrax / Mar '95 / ADA / Direct / Duncans / Highlander

McDonald, Angus

A' SIREADH SPORS
CD _______ COMD 2043
Temple / Feb '94 / ADA / CM / Direct / Duncans / Highlander

WORLD'S GREATEST PIPERS VOL.1, THE (MacDonald, Pipe Major Angus)
Lord MacPherson of Drumochter / Major John MacLennan / Susan MacLeod / Mrs. MacPherson of Inveran / Bobs of Balmoral / I laid a herring in saut / Fair maid of Barra / Pinney's of Scotland / Caledonian Society of London / Cameron highlanders / Banks of Allan Water / Highland brigade at Magersfontein / Road to Sham Shui Poh / Jim Tweedie's sea legs / High level / Flowers of the forest / 93rd, of Modder river / Braes of Castle Grant / Wiseman's exercise / Fiddler's joy / Smith's a gallant fireman / Laird of Drumblair / Brolum / Kalabakan / Tam bain's lum / Willie's brogues / Liverpool hornpipe / Kesh jig / Rocking the baby / Give me a drink of water / Conundrum / P/M Willie Gray's farewell to the Glasgow Police / Lament for the children
CD _______ LCOM 5143
Lismor / Jun '93 / ADA / Direct / Duncans / Lismor

McDonald, Country Joe

CARRY ON
Picks and lasers / Lady with the lamp / Joe's blues / Hold on to each other / Stolen heart blues / Trilogy / Going home / Carry on / My last song
CD _______ SHCD 8019
Shanachie / Jul '96 / ADA / Greensleeves / Koch

CLASSICS
CD _______ CDWIK 108
Big Beat / Jul '92 / Pinnacle

COLLECTORS ITEMS (The First Three EPs) (Country Joe & The Fish)
I feel like I'm fixin' to die rag / Super bird / (Thing called) love / Bass strings / Section 43 / Fire in the city: *Krug, Peter* / Johnny's gone in the war: *Krug, Peter* / Kiss my ass: *Country Joe & Grootna* / Tricky dicky: *Country Joe & Grootna* / Free some day: *Country Joe & Grootna*
CD _______ NEXCD 228
Sequel / Nov '92 / BMG

ELECTRIC MUSIC FOR THE MIND AND BODY (Country Joe & The Fish)
Flying high / Not so sweet Martha Lorraine / Death sound blues / Porpoise mouth / Section 43 / Super bird / Sad and lonely times / Love / Bass strings / Masked marauder / Grace
CD _______ VMCD 79244
Vanguard / Oct '95 / ADA / Pinnacle

I FEEL LIKE I'M FIXIN' TO DIE (Country Joe & The Fish)
Fish cheer and I feel like I'm fixing to die rag / Who am I / Pat's song / Rock coast blues / Magoo / Though dream / Thursday / Eastern jam / Colors for Susan
CD _______ VMD 79266
Vanguard / Oct '95 / ADA / Pinnacle

LIVE AT THE FILLMORE WEST 1969 (Country Joe & The Fish)
Rock and soul music/Love / Here I go again / It's nice to have your love / Flying high / Doctor of electricity / Donovan's reef jam
CD _______ VCD 139
Vanguard / Aug '96 / ADA / Pinnacle

THINKING OF WOODY GUTHRIE
Pastures of plenty / Talkin' dust bowl blues / Blowing down that dusty road / So long (it's been good to know yuh) / Tom Joad / Sinking of the Reuben James / Roll on Columbia / Pretty boy Floyd / When the curfew blows / This land is your land
CD _______ VMD 6546
Vanguard / Jan '97 / ADA / Pinnacle

TOGETHER (Country Joe & The Fish)
Rock and soul music / Susan / Mojo navigator / Bright suburban Mr. and Mrs. clean machine / Good guys/Bad guys cheer and the streets of your town / Fish moan / Harlem song / Waltzing in the moonlight / Away bounce my bubbles / Catacean / Untitled protest
CD _______ VMD 79277
Vanguard / Oct '95 / ADA / Pinnacle

McDonald, Fergie

AGUS NA MUIDEARTAICH
Ceili music / Hebridean reels / Bothan ballads (Fergie's Gaelic waltz) / Hooligan's jig / Moidart reels / Benbecula barn dance / Real Fergie jigs / Tribute to Bobby Macleod / Jig Runrig / Button box schottische / Ian MacFarlane "On the fiddle" / Jigs / Talla a'bhaile reels / Ceilidh on the croft / Isle of Skye reels / Ceol eirainn
CD _______ LCOM 5222
Lismor / Oct '93 / ADA / Direct / Duncans / Lismor

McDonald, Michael

SWEET FREEDOM (The Best Of Michael McDonald)
Sweet freedom / I'll be your angel / Yah mo be there / I gotta try / I keep forgettin' / Our love / On my own / No lookin back / Any foolish thing / That's why / What a fool believes / I can let go now
CD _______ 2410492
WEA / Nov '86 / Warner Music

TAKE IT TO HEART
All we got / Get the word started / Love can break your heart / Take it to heart / Tear it up / Lonely talk / Searchin' for understanding / Homeboy / No amount of reason / One step away / You show me
CD _______ 7599259792
WEA / May '90 / Warner Music

McDonald, Steve

SONS OF SOMERLED
Introduction / Sons of somerled / Live on my warrior son / All you can know / Loch Lomond / Soldier's lament / Come to the Isle of Skye / Scotland the brave / Celtic segue / Celtic warrior / I will return / Wild mountain thyme / Per mare, per terras / Lordship of the isles / Journey of the warrior soul
CD _______ 9734776012
Strathan / Jul '97 / Duncans / Strathan

MacDonnchadha, Johnny ...

CONTAE MHUIGHEO (MacDonnchadha, Johnny Mhairtin Learai)
CD _______ CICD 013
Clo Iar-Chonnachta / Dec '93 / CM

McDonough, Megon

MY ONE AND ONLY LOVE
CD _______ SH 5027
Shanachie / Nov '96 / ADA / Greensleeves / Koch

McDougall, Ian

WARMTH OF THE HORN, THE
Warm / You go to my head / Like someone in love / Blue Daniel / Sixth sense / Lament / I remember you / How long has this been going on / Centerpiece / Blue skies / Mc not Mac and two L's
CD _______ CCD 4652
Concord Jazz / Jul '95 / New Note/Pinnacle

McDougall, John

WORLD'S GREATEST PIPERS VOL.8, THE
2/4 marches / Strathspeys and reels / Slow air and jigs / 6/8 marches / Strathspeys and reels / Lady Margaret MacDonald's salute / 2/4 marches / Hornpipe / Slow air and march / Strathspeys and reels / 6/8 marches / Battle of the Pass of Crieff
CD _______ LCOM 5189
Lismor / Feb '97 / ADA / Direct / Duncans / Lismor

MacDowell, Al

MESSIAH (MacDowell, Al & Timepiece)
Messiah / Powerful one / Playing in the sand / Close to the edge / Jamming in the pyramids / Offset / Second calling / Let the music sing / Latin lady / Here we come again
CD _______ GV 794512
Gramavision / May '91 / Vital/SAM

TIME PEACE
Fantastic voyage / St. Alban's tango / Nina's line of no return / Somewhere / Fantasia / Maybe / Peng shui / Ode bra / View from a window / Come see tomorrow / Blue age
CD _______ GCD 79450
Gramavision / Sep '95 / Vital/SAM

MacDowell, Lenny

MAGIC FLUTE
CD _______ BLR 84 027
L&R / May '91 / New Note/Pinnacle

McDowell, Fred

AMAZING GRACE (McDowell, 'Mississippi' Fred)
CD _______ TCD 5004
Testament / Aug '94 / ADA / Koch

GOOD MORNING LITTLE SCHOOLGIRL (McDowell, 'Mississippi' Fred)
CD _______ ARHCD 424
Arhoolie / Apr '95 / ADA / Cadillac / Direct

I DO NOT PLAY ROCK 'N' ROLL (2CD Set - The Complete Sessions) (McDowell, 'Mississippi' Fred)
Baby, please don't go / Good morning little school girl / Kokomo me baby / That's all right baby / Red Cross store / Everybody's down on me / 61 Highway / Glory hallelujah / Jesus is on the mainline / Someday / Write me a few of your lines / Mortgage on my soul / Baby let me lay down (in your cool iron bed) / Drop down Mama / Rap/Louise / Somebody keeps callin' me / Eyes like an eagle / My baby she gonna jump and shout / Long line Skinner / Baby, please don't go (alternate)
CD Set _______ CDEM 1582
Premier/EMI / Feb '96 / EMI

LONG WAY FROM HOME (McDowell, 'Mississippi' Fred)
CD _______ OBCCD 535
Original Blues Classics / Nov '92 / Complete/Pinnacle / Wellard

MISSISSIPPI BLUES (McDowell, 'Mississippi' Fred)
CD _______ BLCD 760179
Black Lion / Mar '93 / Cadillac / Jazz Music / Koch / Wellard

MISSISSIPPI FRED MCDOWELL (McDowell, 'Mississippi' Fred)
CD _______ ROUCD 2138
Rounder / Sep '95 / ADA / CM / Direct

MY HOME IS IN THE DELTA BLUES & SPIRITUALS (McDowell, 'Mississippi' Fred & Annie Mae)
CD _______ TCD 5019
Testament / Apr '95 / ADA / Koch

REAL BLUES (McDowell, 'Mississippi' Fred)
CD _______ IMP 307
IMP / Sep '96 / ADA / Discovery

SHAKE 'EM ON DOWN (McDowell, 'Mississippi' Fred)
Shake 'em on down / I'm crazy about you baby / John Henry / You got to move / Someday / Mercy / Lovin' blues / White lightnin' / Baby please don't go
CD _______ CPCD 8165
Charly / Apr '97 / Koch

STEAKBONE SLIDE GUITAR (McDowell, 'Mississippi' Fred)
CD _______ TCD 1012
Tradition / May '96 / ADA / Vital

THIS AIN'T NO ROCK 'N' ROLL (McDowell, 'Mississippi' Fred)
CD _______ ARHCD 441
Arhoolie / Sep '95 / ADA / Cadillac / Direct

WHEN I LAY MY BURDEN DOWN (McDowell, 'Mississippi' Fred & Furry Lewis)
If you see my baby / John Henry / Louise / 61 highway blues / Big fat mama / When I lay my burden down / Dankin farm / Casey Jones / Harry furry blues / Everyday in the week / Grieve my mind / Beale Street blues
CD _______ BCD 130
Biograph / Jun '94 / ADA / Cadillac / Direct / Hot Shot / Jazz Music / Wellard

YOU GOT TO MOVE (McDowell, 'Mississippi' Fred)
Some day baby / Milk cow blues / Train I ride / Over the hill / Goin' down to the river / I wished I were in heaven sittin' down / Louise
CD _______ ARHCD 304
Arhoolie / Apr '95 / ADA / Cadillac / Direct

McDuff, Jack

ANOTHER REAL GOOD 'UN
Another real good 'un / Summertime / Off the beaten path / Long day blues / Rock candy / I can't get started (with you) / I cover the waterfront
CD _______ MCD 5374
Muse / Sep '92 / New Note/Pinnacle

COLOUR ME BLUE (McDuff, Jack & Friends)
CD _______ CCD 4516
Concord Jazz / Aug '92 / New Note/ Pinnacle

DOWN HOME STYLE (McDuff, 'Brother' Jack)
Vibrator / Down home style / Memphis in June / Theme from electric surfboard / It's all a joke / Butter (for yo popcorn) / Groovin' / As she walked away
CD _______ CDP 8543292
Blue Note / Feb '97 / EMI

HEATIN' SYSTEM, THE
601 1/2 No. Poplar / Put on a happy face / Sundown / Mr. T / Jimmy Smith / In a sentimental mood / Fly away / Pink Panther / Playoff
CD _______ CCD 4644
Concord Jazz / Jun '95 / New Note/ Pinnacle

HONEYDRIPPER, THE
CD _______ OJCCD 222
Original Jazz Classics / Dec '95 / Complete/Pinnacle / Jazz Music / Wellard

HOT BARBEQUE/LIVE (AT THE FRONT ROOM) (McDuff, 'Brother' Jack)
Hot barbeque / Party's over / Briar patch / Hippy dip / 601 1/2 No. poplar / Cry me a river / Three day thang / Rock candy / It ain't necessarily so / Sanctified samba / Whistle while you work / Real good'n / Undecided
CD _______ CDBGPD 053
Beat Goes Public / Apr '93 / Pinnacle

SCREAMIN' (McDuff, 'Brother' Jack)
He's a real gone guy / Soulful drums / After hours / Screamin' / I cover the waterfront / One o'clock jump
CD _______ OJCCD 875
Original Jazz Classics / Jun '96 / Complete/ Pinnacle / Jazz Music / Wellard

THAT'S THE WAY I FEEL ABOUT IT (McDuff, 'Brother' Jack)
Age of Aquarius / Blooze in G / Theme from Mission Impossible / hat's the way I feel about it / Six am / Saturday night fish fry / Old folks / Flamingo / Moody's mood for love
CD _______ CCD 47602
Concord Jazz / Jul '97 / New Note/Pinnacle

WRITE ON CAP'N
Spec-tator / From the pulpit / Killer Joe / Room / Night in Tunisia / Captain's quarters / Billyjack / Out of my head / Goin' to the wall / Havin' a good time
CD _______ CCD 4568
Concord Jazz / Sep '93 / New Note/ Pinnacle

McDuff, Larry

RE-ENTRY, THE
CD _______ MCD 5361
Muse / Sep '92 / New Note/Pinnacle

McEachern, Malcolm

MALCOLM MC EACHERN
Oh ruddier than the cherry / Lord is a man of war / Honour and arms / Arm, arm ye brave / Lord God of Abraham / Revenge, Timotheus cries / I am a roamer / O tu palermo / Le veau d'or / Sperate, O Figli...d'egitto la sui lidi / Mighty deep / On the road to Mandalay / Australian bush songs / Excelsior: *McEachern, Malcolm & Frank Titterton* / Blow, blow thou winter wind / Danny Deever / Song of the Volga boatmen / Hundred pipers / Drinking / Gendarmes duet
CD _______ GEMMCD 9455
Pearl / '90 / Harmonia Mundi

McElroy, Bill

SLIMLINE DADDY (McElroy, Bill & The Prairie Boys)
CD _______ NERCD 089
Nervous / Sep '96 / Nervous / TKO Magnum

McEntire, Reba

FOR MY BROKEN HEART
For my broken heart / Is there life out there / Bobby / He's in Dallas / All dressed up

(with nowhere to go) / Night the lights went out in Georgia / Buying her roses / Greatest man I never knew / I wouldn't go that far / If I had only know
CD _______________ MCLD 19346
MCA / Oct '96 / BMG

GREATEST HITS
Just a little love / He broke your memory last night / How blue / Somebody should leave / Have I got a deal for you / Only in my mind / Whoever's in New England / Little rock / What am I gonna do about you / One promise too late
CD _______________ MCLD 19177
MCA / Mar '94 / BMG

GREATEST HITS VOL.2
Does he love you / You lie / Fancy / For my broken heart / Love will find it's way to you / They asked about you / Is there life out there / Rumour has it / Walk on / Greatest man I never knew
CD _______________ MCD 10906
MCA / Oct '93 / BMG

IT'S YOUR CALL
It's your call / Straight from you / Take it back / Baby's gone blues / Heart won't lie / One last good hand / He wants to get married / For herself / Will he ever go away / Lighter shade of blue
CD _______________ MCD 10673
MCA / Jan '93 / BMG

READ MY MIND
Everything that you want / Read my mind / I won't stand in line / I wish that I could tell you / She think's his name was John / Why haven't I heard from you / Still / Heart is a lonely hunter / I wouldn't want to be you / Till you love me
CD _______________ MCD 10994
MCA / Jun '94 / BMG

STARTING OVER
Talking in your sleep / Please come to Boston / On my own / I won't mention it again / You're no good / Ring on her finger, time on her hands / 500 miles away from home / Starting over again / You keep me hangin' on / By the time I get to Phoenix
CD _______________ MCD 11264
MCA / Oct '95 / BMG

WHAT IF IT'S YOU
How was I to know / Fear of being alone / What if it's you / I'd rather ride around with you / It don't matter / State of grace / Close to crazy / She's callin' it love / Just looking for him / Never had a reason to
CD _______________ MCD 11500
MCA / Nov '96 / BMG

Maceration

SERENADE OF AGONY, A
CD _______________ CD 7913004
Progress Red / Jun '93 / Plastic Head

McEvoy, Catherine

TRADITIONAL IRISH MUSIC (McEvoy, Catherine & Felix Dolan)
CD _______________ CICD 117
CICD / May '97 / ADA

McEvoy, Eleanor

ELEANOR MCEVOY
Finding myslef lost again / Only a woman's heart / Apologise / Boundaries of your mind / For you / Go now / It's mine / Not quite love / Promises we keep / Music of it all / Leave her now / Breathing hope / Stray thoughts
CD _______________ GED 24606
Geffen / Jun '97 / BMG

McEvoy, Johnny

20 GREATEST HITS (Ireland's Favourite Folk Singer)
CD _______________ TVCD 1
Dolphin / Sep '96 / CM / Else / Grapevine/ PolyGram / Koch

CELEBRATION (2CD Set)
CD Set _______________ JMCD 30
Dolphin / Mar '96 / CM / Else / Grapevine/ PolyGram / Koch

FAVOURITES
CD _______________ CDC 011
Ceol / Feb '97 / CM

JOHNNY MCEVOY SINGS COUNTRY AND IRISH
CD _______________ PLSCD 237
Pulse / Jul '97 / BMG

SONGS OF IRELAND
Home boys home / Red is the rose / Black velvet band / Maggie / Good ship Kangaroo / Wild mountain thyme / I wish I had someone to love me / Town of ballybay / Molly,my Irish Molly / Rare ould times / Streets of New York / Travelling people / shores of amerikkay / Bunch of thyme / Irish soldier laddie / Song for Ireland
CD _______________ MCBD 19520
MCA / Apr '95 / BMG

McEvoy, Michael J.

NIGHT SEA JOURNEY
My old school daze / Goodbye to yesterday / Shifting stones / Broken words / Heaven's cage / Calypso smile / No place like home / Tears from the sun / Ocean of you / Mission man
CD _______________ ATMM 002
All That / Aug '96 / New Note/Pinnacle

MacEwan, Sydney

FOLK SONGS AND BALLADS
Bonnie Earl O'Moray / Lark in the clear air / She moved thro the fair / O men from the fields / Dawning of the day / Mowing the barley / Silent O'Moyle / Duna / Since first I saw your face / In summertime in Bredon / Foggy dew / Pleading / Coronach / Green bushes / Banks of Allan Water / Jeanie with the light brown hair / Macishia / As I sit here / Maiden of Morven
CD _______________ MIDCD 007
Moidart / May '95 / Conifer/BMG

GREAT SCOTTISH TENOR, THE (MacEwan, Father Sydney)
Turn ye to me / Duna / Mowing the barley / Annie Laurie / Mother of mercy / Foggy dew / Maiden of Morven
CD _______________ GEMMCD 9107
Pearl / May '94 / Harmonia Mundi

SONGS OF SCOTLAND
Road to the isles / Peat fire flame / Maighdeanan na h-airidh / Island moon / Morag bheag / Bonnie banks of Loch Lomond / Ye banks and braes o' bonnie Doon / Togorm mo phiob / When the kye come home / Rowan tree / An eriskay love lilt / Herding song / Mnhathan a ghlinne
CD _______________ MIDCD 002
Moidart / Jan '95 / Conifer/BMG

MacEwan, William

WILLIAM MCEWAN (The Original Glasgow Street Singer-Evangelist)
Sunrise / Pull for the shore / Throw out the lifeline / I would be like Jesus / Merrily sing / Sweetest song I know / Pardoning grace / Not now but in the coming years / When the roll is called up yonder / We will talk it o'er together by and by / Old rugged cross / God be with you till we meet again / Will the circle be unbroken / My mothers hand is on my brow / Sinking sands (In loving kindness Jesus came) / He died of a broken heart / God will take care of you / I know my heavenly father knows / Someday / My ain countrie
CD _______________ LCOM 5235
Lismor / May '94 / ADA / Direct / Duncans / Lismor

McFadden & Whitehead

AIN'T NO STOPPIN' US NOW
CD _______________ KWEST 5406
Kenwest / May '93 / THE

McFadden, Charlie

CHARLIE 'SPECKS" MCFADDEN 1929-1940 (McFadden, Charlie 'Specks')
CD _______________ BDCD 6041
Blues Document / May '93 / ADA / Hot Shot / Jazz Music

McFadden, Gerry

IRISH TRADITIONAL UILLEANN PIPES
CD _______________ PTICD 1031
Outlet / Oct '95 / ADA / CM / Direct / Duncans / Koch / Ross

UILLEANN PIPES
CD _______________ PTI 1031CD
Pure Traditional Irish / Jul '95 / ADA / CM / Direct / Ross

MacFayden, Iain

CEOL MOR-CEOL BEAG
CD _______________ COMD 2018
Temple / Apr '96 / ADA / CM / Direct / Duncans / Highlander

WORLD'S GREATEST PIPERS VOL.7, THE
March, strathspey and reel / 6/8 marches / Gaelic air and hornpipes / Jigs / 9/8 marches / Piobaireachd / 6/8 march and jig / 2/4 marches / 6/8 marches / Strathspeys and reels / Piobaireachd
CD _______________ LCOM 5180
Lismor / Mar '95 / ADA / Direct / Duncans / Lismor

McFerrin, Bobby

BANG ZOOM
Bang zoom / Rememberance / Friends / Selim / Freedom is a voice / Heaven's design / My better half / Kid's toys / Mere words
CD _______________ CDP 8316772
Blue Note / Jan '96 / EMI

BEST OF BOBBY MCFERRIN, THE
Don't worry be happy / Friends / Thinkin' about your body / Spain / Freedom is a voice / Drive my car / Another night in Tunisia / Blue Bossa / Turtle shoes / Good lovin' / From me to you / Bang zoom
CD _______________ CDP 8533292
Blue Note / Nov '96 / EMI

CIRCLESONGS
CD _______________ SK 62734
Sony Classical / Jun '97 / Sony

JAZZ MASTERS
CD _______________ CDMFP 6303
Music For Pleasure / Mar '97 / EMI

PAPERMUSIC
CD _______________ SK 64600
Sony Classical / Jan '97 / Sony

MacGabhann, Antoin

AR AON BHUILE
CD _______________ CICD 105
CICD / Jan '95 / ADA

McGann, Andy

ANDY MCGANN & PADDY REYNOLDS FIDDLE (McGann, Andy & Paddy Reynolds)
CD _______________ SHANCD 34008
Shanachie / Jan '95 / ADA / Greensleeves / Koch

IT'S A HARD ROAD TO TRAVEL
CD _______________ SHCD 34011
Shanachie / Jul '95 / ADA / Greensleeves / Koch

TRADITIONAL MUSIC OF IRELAND (McGann, Andy & Paul Brady)
CD _______________ SHAN 34011CD
Shanachie / Apr '95 / ADA / Greensleeves / Koch

McGann, John

UPSIDE
CD _______________ GLCD 2118
Green Linnet / Mar '95 / ADA / CM / Direct / Highlander / Roots

McGarrigle, Kate & Anna

DANCER WITH BRUISED KNEES
Dancer with bruised knees / Southern boys / Biscuit song / First born / Blanche comme la neige / Perrine etait servante / Be my baby / Walking song / Naufragee du tendre / Hommage a grungie / Kitty come home / Come a long way / No biscuit blues
CD _______________ 7599259582
Warner Bros. / Jun '94 / Warner Music

FRENCH RECORD
Enter la jeunesse et la sagesse / Complainte pour Ste Catherine / Mais quand tu danses / Cheminant a la ville / Excursion a venise / En filant ma quenouille / La belle est etourdie / Maufragee du tendre / Avant la querre / Boire / Prends ton manteau
CD _______________ HNCD 1302
Hannibal / Mar '97 / ADA / Vital

HEARTBEATS ACCELERATING
Heartbeats accelerating / I eat dinner / Rainbow ride / Mother, mother / Love is / DJ serenade / I'm losing you / Hit and run love / Leave me be / St. James Hospital
CD _______________ 261142
Private Music / Nov '90 / BMG

KATE & ANNA MCGARRIGLE
Kiss and say goodbye / My town / Blues in D / Heart like a wheel / Foolish you / Talk to me of Mendocino / Complainte pour Ste Catherine / Tell my sister / Swimming song / Jigsaw puzzle of Life / Go leave / Travelling on for Jesus
CD _______________ 9362456772
Warner Bros. / Jun '94 / Warner Music

LOVE OVER AND OVER
Move over moon / Sun son (shining on the water) / I cried for us / Love over and over / Star cab company / Tu vas m'accompagner / On my way to town / Jesus lifeline / Work song / St. Valentine's day 1978 / Midnight flight
CD _______________ 8411012
Polydor / Jul '94 / PolyGram

MATAPEDIA
Matapedia / Goin' back to Harlan / I don't know / Hang out your heart / Arbre / Jacques et Gilles / Why must we die / Song for Gaby / Talk about it / Bike song
CD _______________ HNCD 1394
Hannibal / Sep '96 / ADA / Vital

McGear, Mike

MCGEAR (McCartney, Mike)
Sea breezes / Norton / Have you got problems / Casket / Rainbow lady / Givin' grease a ride / What do we really want to know / Leave it / Dance the do / Sweet baby / Simply love you / Man who found God in the moon
CD _______________ SEECD 339
See For Miles/C5 / Jun '94 / Pinnacle

WOMAN
Woman / Please Mr. Witness / Jolly good show / Roamin' Road / Sit down sister / Wishin' and washin' / I'm just a young man / Edward Heath / Butterscotch / Uptown downtown / Tiger
CD _______________ EDCD 507
Edsel / Feb '97 / Pinnacle

McGee, Dennis

COMPLETE EARLY RECORDINGS, THE (Early American Cajun Classics)
CD _______________ YAZCD 2012
Yazoo / Dec '94 / ADA / CM / Koch

McGee, Kieran

LEFT FOR DEAD
CD _______________ CCD 717
Clean Cuts / Aug '97 / Direct / Jazz Music / Wellard

McGhee, Brownie

AT THE 2ND FRET (McGhee, Brownie & Sonny Terry)
CD _______________ OBCCD 561
Original Blues Classics / Jan '94 / Complete/Pinnacle / Wellard

BROWNIE MCGHEE - 1944-1955
Watch out / Dissatisfied woman / Rum cola papa / My baby likes to shuffle / Daybreak / Doggin' blues / I'm gonna rock / Evil but kindhearted / Drinkin' wine spo-dee-o-dee
CD _______________ TMCD 04
Travellin' Man / Oct '90 / Hot Shot / Jazz Music / Wellard

BROWNIE'S BLUES
CD _______________ OBCCD 505
Original Blues Classics / Nov '92 / Complete/Pinnacle / Wellard

COMPLETE BROWNIE MCGHEE, THE (2CD Set)
Picking my tomatoes / Me and my dog blues / Born for bad luck / I'm callin Daisy / Step it up and go / My barkin' bulldog blues / Let me tell you 'bout my baby / Prison woman blues / Back door stranger / Be good to me / Not guilty blues / Coal miner's blues / Step it up and go 2 / Money spending woman / Death of Blind Boy Fuller / Got to find my little woman / I'm a black woman's man / Dealing with the devil / Double trouble / Woman I'm done / Key to my door / Million lonesome woman / Ain't no tellin' / Try me one more time / I want to see Jesus / Done what my Lord said / I want King Jesus / What will I do (Without the Lord) / Key to the highway / I don't believe in love / So much trouble / Goodbye now / Jealous of my woman / Unfair blues / Barbecue any old time / Workin' man blues / Sinful disposition woman / Back home blues / Deep sea diver / It must be love / Studio chatter / Swing soldier swing
CD Set _______________ 4757002
Columbia / Jun '96 / Sony

NOT GUILTY BLUES
CD _______________ CBCD 004
Collector's Blues / May '96 / TKO Magnum

RAINY DAY
CD _______________ CPCD 8167
Charly / Jun '96 / Koch

McGhee, Howard

DIAL MASTERS, THE
Intersection / Lifestream / Mop mop / Stardust / You / Stop time blues / Sleepwalker boogie / Surrender / Turnip blood / Night music / Coolie-rini / Night mist / Dorothy / High wind in Hollywood / Up in Dodo's room / Midnight at Mintons / Dialated pupils / Therodynamics / Trumpet at Tempo
CD _______________ SPJCD 131
Spotlite / Jul '95 / Cadillac / Jazz Music / New Note/Pinnacle / Swift

MCGHEE SPECIAL
McGhee special / Sportsman's hop / Bean stalking / Ready for love / April in Paris / Rifftide / Ventura jump / Hollywood stampede / Too much of a good thing / Bean soup / Intersection / Life stream / Mop mop / Stardust / I found a new baby / Windjammer / Skylark / Be bop / Trumpet at tempo / Thermodynamics / Dial-ated pupils / Midnight at Minton's / Up in Dodo's room / High wind in Hollywood
CD _______________ TPZ 1062
Topaz Jazz / Feb '97 / Cadillac / Pinnacle

SHARP EDGE
CD _______________ BLCD 760110
Black Lion / Dec '88 / Cadillac / Jazz Music / Koch / Wellard

SUNSET SWING (McGhee, Howard & Previn/Edison/Thompson)
CD _______________ BLCD 760171
Black Lion / Mar '93 / Cadillac / Jazz Music / Koch / Wellard

McGhee, Stick

NEW YORK BLUES (McGhee, Stick & His Spo-Dee-O-Dee Buddies)
Real good feeling: *Collins, Tom* / Heartache blues: *Collins, Tom* / Heartbreakin' woman: *Collins, Tom* / Watchin' my stuff: *Collins, Tom* / Gonna hop on down the line: *Willis, Ralph* / Do right: *Willis, Ralph* / Why'd you do it: *Willis, Ralph* / Door bell blues: *Willis, Ralph* / I'm doin' all this time (and you put me down): *McGhee, Stick* / Wiggle waggie

woo: *McGhee, Stick* / Dealin' from the bottom: *McGhee, Stick* / Whiskey, women and loaded dice: *McGhee, Stick* / Little things we used to do: *McGhee, Stick* / Blues in my heart and tears in my eyes: *McGhee, Stick* / Head happy with wine: *McGhee, Stick* / Jungle juice: *McGhee, Stick* / Sad, bad, glad: *McGhee, Stick* / Six to eight: *McGhee, Stick* / Get your mind out of the gutter: *McGhee, Stick* / Double crossin' liquor: *McGhee, Stick*
CD ____ **CDCHD 502**
Ace / Jan '95 / Pinnacle

McGhee, Wes

BACKBEAT
Voices from exile / Long nights and banjo music / Voices from exile / Light at the end of the line / Mailman (bring me no more blues) / Contrabandistas / Ain't that lovin' you baby / (It's no use bein' a fast draw) if you can't shoot straight / Mezcal Road / This time / I feel strange / Wee freakings / Justine / (I don't wanna hang up my) rock 'n' roll shoes / Extranjero / She almost reminds me of you / Every night about this time / Here on a Saturday night / Voices from exile / Heat of the highway
CD ____ **RGFCD 022**
Road Goes On Forever / May '97 / Direct

BORDER GUITARS
CD ____ **RGFCD 018**
Road Goes On Forever / Jul '94 / Direct

HEARTACHE AVENUE (Classic & Unreleased Recordings 1978-1992)
CD ____ **RGFCD 017**
Road Goes On Forever / Aug '96 / Direct

McGillivray, James

WORLD'S GREATEST PIPERS VOL.10, THE
CD ____ **LCOM 5216**
Lismor / Oct '90 / ADA / Direct / Duncans / Lismor

McGlohon, Loonis

LOONIS IN LONDON 1981
Foggy day / Send in the clowns / Time for love / Where's the child I used to hold / Lazybones / Blackberry winter / Songbird / Get me to the church on time / I've grown accustomed to her face
CD ____ **ACD 166**
Audiophile / Mar '97 / Jazz Music

McGlynn, Arty

MCGLYNN'S FANCY
Carolan's draught / Floating crowbar / I wish my love was a red, red rose / Peter Byrne's fancy / Blackbird / Creeping Docken / Charles O'Connor / Arthur Darley / Hills above Drumquin / Sally gardens / Sonny brogan's fancy / Brian Kiely's Delight
CD ____ **BERCD 011**
Emerald / Nov '94 / CM / Direct / Ross
CD ____ **MCLD 19351**
MCA / Oct '96 / BMG

McGoldrick, Michael

MORNING RORY
Jenny picking cockles/Earl's chair / Glens of Aherlow/Trip to Herve's / Copperplate/Green mountain/Controversial / History man / Knocknamoe jig/Custy's/Trip to Brittany / Peter Brown's/Mamma's pet/Sailor on the rock / My mind will never be easy/Baby Rory's slip jig / Larkin's beehive/McGann's/Amazing adventures of Dr.Moriarty / Gan ainm/Lavery's 1/Lavery's 2/September reel / Maid of Monisco/Galway rambler / Dub reel
CD ____ **AUGH 01**
Aughrim / Nov '96 / Direct

McGough, Roger

SUMMER WITH MONIKA
Prelude / Prologue / Epic film / I have lately learned to swim / Ten milk bottles / Big bad dark / You are so very beautiful / Sunday morning / Sky has nothing to say / Ring / Tightrope / Nobody's fool / Soup / Trench warfare / Last waltz / Porrige / Teethings / Epilogue
CD ____ **EDCD 508**
Edsel / Feb '97 / Pinnacle

MacGowan, Shane

SNAKE, THE (MacGowan, Shane & The Popes)
Church of the Holy spook / That woman's got me drinking / Song with no name / Aisling / I'll be your handbag / Her Father didn't like me anyway / Mexican funeral in Paris / Snake with the eyes of garnet / Donegal express / Victoria / Rising of the moon / Bring down the lamp
CD ____ **0630104022**
ZTT / Dec '96 / Warner Music

McGowan, Geraldine

RECONCILIATION
CD ____ **CMBCD 014**
Cross Border Media / Jan '95 / ADA / Direct / Grapevine/PolyGram

McGrattan, Paul

FROST IS ALL OVER, THE
Speed the plough / Abbey reel/Primrose lass / Hare in the corn/Grainne's welcome / Sailor's return/Chattering magpie/House on the hill / Slan le Maigh/Tailor's twist/Mayo reels / Stone in the field/John Egan's reel/Dublin porter / Up and away/Mountain pathway/Egan's polkas / Skylark/Jenny Dang the weaver / Frost is all over/Coleman's jig/Rambling pitchfork / Johnny O'Leary's/Padraig O'Keeffe's slide / Byrne's hornpipes / Gehan's reel/Crosses of Annagh/An untitled reel / Tracey's jig/Rose in the heather/Blackthorn stick / Hardiman the fiddler/Taim in arrears / Christmas eve/Old bush/The scholar reel / Tommy People's reel
CD ____ **CC 58CD**
Claddagh / Jan '93 / ADA / CM / Direct

PAUL MCGRATTAN & PAUL O'SHAUGHNESSY (McGrattan, Paul & Paul O'Shaughnessy)
CD ____ **SPINCD 1000**
Spin / Oct '96 / Direct

WITHIN A MILE OF DUBLIN (McGrattan, Paul & Paul O'Shaughnessy)
CD ____ **SPIN 1000CD**
Foetain / Aug '96 / ADA

McGraw, Tim

ALL I WANT
CD ____ **CURCD 16**
Curb / Sep '95 / Grapevine/PolyGram

EVERYWHERE
CD ____ **CURCD 039**
Curb / Jun '97 / Grapevine/PolyGram

MacGregor, Hamish

TRIP TO SCOTLAND (MacGregor, Hamish & The Blue Bonnets)
Flowers of Edinburgh/St. Kilda's wedding / Loch Lomond/Loch Ruan/Loch Maree / Pennan den / Stones of Stenness/Killiecrankie / Arniston Castle/Inver lassies / Dark Lochnagar / Roslin Castle/Stirling Castle/Roxburgh Castle / Kelso races/Miss Ann Cameron of Balvenie/Hoddom Castle / Banks of Loch Ness/Ben Nevis / Ye banks and braes of bonnie Doune/Farewell to Fuinary / Road and the miles to Dundee/Morag of Dunvegan / Glasgow hornpipe/Inverness gathering/Perth assembly / Skye boat song / Spootiskerry/Da Scallowa lasses/Bonnie Isle of Whalsay
CD ____ **CDTT 1001**
Tartan Tapes / Jul '97 / Duncans

McGregor, Chris

COUNTRY COOKING
Country cookin' / Bakwetha / Sweet as honey / You and me / Big G / Maxine / Dakar / Thunder in the mountains
CD ____ **CDVE 17**
Venture / May '88 / EMI

GRANDMOTHER'S TEACHING
CD ____ **ITM 1428**
ITM / Jan '91 / Koch / Tradelink

IN MEMORIUM (McGregor, Chris & Brotherhood Of Breath)
CD ____ **ITMP 970086**
ITM / Oct '95 / Koch / Tradelink

THUNDERBOLT (McGregor, Chris & The South African Exiles)
CD ____ **PAMCD 405**
Popular African Music / May '97 / Cadillac

McGregor, Freddie

ALL IN THE SAME BOAT
All in the same boat / Hungry belly pickney / Push comes to shove / Jah a the don / I'm coming home / Glad you're here with me / I don't want to see you cry / Somewhere / Mama Mama / Peace in the valley
CD ____ **RASCD 3014**
Ras / May '87 / Direct / Greensleeves / Jet Star / SRD

BIG SHIP
Big ship / Sweet lady / Peaceful man / Stop loving you / Get serious / Don't play the fool / Get united / Let me be the one / Roots man skanking / Holy Mount Zion
CD ____ **GRELCD 39**
Greensleeves / May '89 / Jet Star / SRD

CARRY GO BRING COME
CD ____ **GRELCD 197**
Greensleeves / Dec '93 / Jet Star / SRD

COME ON OVER
Shirley come on over / Apple of my eye / Go away pretty woman / Stand up and fight / Shortman / Are you crazy / Reggae feeling / Rhythm so nice / Natty dread / Brother man
CD ____ **RASCD 3002**
Ras / Apr '92 / Direct / Greensleeves / Jet Star / SRD

COMPILATION
CD ____ **RNCD 2131**
Rhino / Nov '95 / Grapevine/PolyGram / Jet Star

EARLY YEARS (McGregor, Freddie & The Clarendonians)
CD ____ **RN 7004**
Rhino / Sep '96 / Grapevine/PolyGram / Jet Star

FOREVER MY LOVE
CD ____ **RASCD 3160**
Ras / Aug '95 / Direct / Greensleeves / Jet Star / SRD

HARD TO GET
CD ____ **GRELCD 175**
Greensleeves / Nov '92 / Jet Star / SRD

JAMAICAN CLASSICS VOL.1
CD ____ **BSCD 1**
Jet Star / Oct '91 / Jet Star

JAMAICAN CLASSICS VOL.2
CD ____ **BSCD 2**
Big Ship / Jul '97 / Jet Star

JAMAICAN CLASSICS VOL.3
CD ____ **BSCD 7**
Big Ship / Jun '96 / Jet Star

LEGIT (McGregor, Freddie & Cocoa T/ Dennis Brown)
CD ____ **GRELCD 189**
Greensleeves / Aug '93 / Jet Star / SRD

LIVE IN LONDON 1991
CD ____ **CPCD 8027**
Charly / Feb '94 / Koch

MAGIC IN THE AIR
CD ____ **BSCD 5**
Big Ship / Aug '95 / Jet Star

NOW
CD ____ **VPCD 1163**
Steely & Cleevie / Jun '91 / Jet Star

PRESENTING FREDDIE MCGREGOR
CD ____ **RNCD 2136**
Rhino / Apr '96 / Grapevine/PolyGram / Jet Star

PUSH ON
CD ____ **BSCD 4**
Big Ship / Apr '94 / Jet Star

RAS PORTRAITS
Push come to shove / Go away pretty woman / Freddie / Apple of my eye / Across the border / Rastaman camp / Mama mama / Sweet child / Somewhere / Forever my love
CD ____ **RAS 3305**
Ras / Jun '97 / Direct / Greensleeves / Jet Star / SRD

REGGAE MAX
CD ____ **JSRNCD 7**
Jet Star / Mar '97 / Jet Star

REGGAE ROCKERS
CD ____ **RRTGCD 7714**
Rohit / '89 / Jet Star

RUMOURS
Tin soldier / She's gone / Rumours / Graveyard in Africa / Want more loving / Stay with me tonight / Woke up smiling / If you're the one / If I should fall in love / Come on over / Who is he / Stolen legacy / Mix up and blenda / Beautiful woman / Saying goodbye
CD ____ **GRELCD 236**
Greensleeves / Mar '97 / Jet Star / SRD

ZION CHANT
CD ____ **HB 138CD**
Heartbeat / Sep '94 / ADA / Direct / Greensleeves / Jet Star

McGriff, Jimmy

BLUES GROOVE (McGriff, Jimmy & Hank Crawford Quartet)
Movin' upside the blues / Splanky / Frame for the blues / Lew's piece / All blues / Sermon / When I fall in love / Could be / Don't cry baby / Mercy mercy mercy
CD ____ **CD 83381**
Telarc / Mar '96 / Conifer/BMG

ELECTRIC FUNK
Back on the track / Chris cross / Miss Poopie / Bird wave / Spear for moon dog - Part 2 / Tight times / Spinning the wheel / Funky junk
CD ____ **CDP 7843502**
Blue Note / Jan '97 / EMI

GEORGIA ON MY MIND
Let's stay together / Shaft / What's going on / Georgia on my mind / April in Paris / Everyday I have the blues / Yardbird suite / It's you I adore / Lonesome road / Mack the knife / There will never be another you / Canadian sunset / Mr. Lucky / Moonglow / Red sails in the sunset / Secret love
CD ____ **CDC8513**
LRC / Nov '90 / Harmonia Mundi / New Note/Pinnacle

JIMMY MCGRIFF FEATURING HANK CRAWFORD (McGriff, Jimmy & Hank Crawford)
CD ____ **CDC 9001**
LRC / Oct '90 / Harmonia Mundi / New Note/Pinnacle

PULLIN' OUT THE STOPS - BEST OF JIMMY MCGRIFF
All about my girl / I've got a woman / Discotheque / Kiko / CC rider / Cash box / Gospel time / Where it's at / Last minute / Blue juice / Step one / Chris cross / South Wes / Black pearl / Worm / Ain't it funky now / Fat cakes
CD ____ **CDP 8307242**
Blue Note / Sep '94 / EMI

RED BEANS
Red beans and rice / Big booty bounce / Space cadet / Alive and well / Sweet love / Love is my life / It feels so nice / Green machine / Please don't take me out / Overweight shark bait
CD ____ **CDC 9083**
LRC / Apr '95 / Harmonia Mundi / New Note/Pinnacle

SONNY LESTER COLLECTION
CD ____ **CDC 9070**
LRC / Nov '93 / Harmonia Mundi / New Note/Pinnacle

TRIBUTE TO BASIE (McGriff, Jimmy Big Band)
CD ____ **CDC 9027**
LRC / Mar '91 / Harmonia Mundi / New Note/Pinnacle

TRIBUTE TO COUNT BASIE
Hob nail boogie / Cherry point / Swingin' the blues / Lil' darlin' / Splanky / Slow but sure / Blues go away / Avenue C / Cute / Everyday
CD ____ **17094**
Laserlight / Jan '97 / Target/BMG

McGuinn, Roger

LIVE FROM MARS
CD ____ **1620902**
Polydor / Jan '97 / PolyGram

RETURN FLYTE (McGuinn & Clark)
CD ____ **EDCD 358**
Edsel / Dec '92 / Pinnacle

RETURN FLYTE VOL.2 (McGuinn, Roger & Gene Clark/Chris Hillman)
Little mama / Stopping traffic / Feelin' higher / Release me girl / Bye bye baby / One more chance / Won't let you down / Street talk / Deeper in / Painted fire / Mean streets / Entertainment / Soul shoes / Love me tonight / Secret side of you / Ain't no money / Making movies
CD ____ **EDCD 373**
Edsel / Jun '93 / Pinnacle

McGuinness Flint

CAPITOL YEARS, THE
When I'm dead and gone / Lazy afternoon / Bondang buck / Mister mister / Heritage / I'm letting you know / Let it ride / Dream darlin' dream / Who you got to love / International / Malt and barley blues / Rock on / Happy birthday Ruthy baby / Conversation / When I'm alone with you / Fixer / Faith and gravy / Klondike / Reader to writer / Changes / Friends of mine / Piper of dreams / Jimmy's song / Sparrow / Wham bam / Back on the road again
CD ____ **CDGO 2070**
EMI Gold / Oct '96 / EMI

LO AND BEHOLD
Eternal circle / Lo and behold / Let me die in my footsteps / Open the door Homer / Lay down your weary tune / Don't you tell Henry / Get your rocks off / Death of Emmett Till / Odds and ends / Tiny Montgomery / I wanna be your lover / Sign on the cross / Eternal circle
CD ____ **RVCD 62**
Raven / Oct '96 / ADA / Direct

McGuinness, Lyle

ELISE ELISE (McGuinness, Lyle Band)
CD ____ **GEMCD 015**
Diamond / Mar '97 / Pinnacle

McGuire Sisters

DO YOU REMEMBER WHEN/WHILE LIGHTS ARE LOW
Do you remember when / Sometimes I'm happy / June night / All by myself / Tip toe through the tulips with me / Them there eyes / Mississippi mud / Cuddle up a little closer / Lovely mine / Does your heart beat for me / Somebody loves me / 'S wonderful / Blue skies / I'm in the mood for love / Don't take your love from me / My darling, my darling / Moonglow / Tenderly / I hadn't anyone till you / If you were only mine / Wonderful one / I'm confessin' that I love you / Moon song / Love is here to stay / Think of me kindly
CD ____ **JASCD 601**
Jasmine / Aug '96 / Conifer/BMG / Hot Shot / TKO Magnum

McGuire, Barry

EVE OF DESTRUCTION MAN, THE
CD ____ **14528**
Spalax / Jan '97 / ADA / Cargo / Direct / Discovery / Greyhound

McGuire, Seamus

CAROUSEL (McGuire, Seamus & Manus McGuire/Daithi Sproule)
CD ____ **CEFCD 105**
Gael Linn / Jan '94 / ADA / CM / Direct / Grapevine/PolyGram / Roots

MISSING REEL, THE (McGuire, Seamus & John Lee)
CD _______ CEFCD 146
Gael Linn / Jan '94 / ADA / CM / Direct / Grapevine/PolyGram / Roots

WISHING TREE, THE
CD _______ GL 1151CD
Green Linnet / Jul '95 / ADA / CM / Direct / Highlander / Roots

McGuire, Sean

BROTHERS TOGETHER (McGuire, Sean & Jim)
CD _______ PTICD 1055
Pure Traditional Irish / Apr '94 / ADA / CM / Direct / Ross

CHAMPION OF CHAMPIONS
Cronin's reels / Key west / Poppy leaf / McCormack's / Coulin / Carolan's concerto / Maids of Tulla / Harvest home / High level / Strike the gay harp / Rose wood / Ned of the hill / O'Neills / Triumphal / Centenary / Planxty McGuire / Dear Irish boy / O'Rourke's boy / O'Rourke's reel / Wild Irishman / Jenny's welcome to Charlie
CD _______ PTICD 1005
Pure Traditional Irish / Mar '97 / ADA / CM / Direct / Ross

HAWKS AND DOVES
Planxty McGuire / Farl O'Gara / Liffey banks / High reels / Brian Boru / Glantan glas gweedore / Going to the well for water / Low level / Smedley's hornpipe / Dancer - Reavey's No.10 / Kerry Reel / Erin's my home / Larry O'Gaff / Jig No.3 / Maid behind the bar / Auld fiddler / Bert Murray's set reel & Lord Pottinger set / Cuckoo's nest hornpipe / End house of Connaught reel / Gypsy hornipipe / Yiddish flavoured reel / Gypsy hornpipe / An coulin / McCleod's reel / Bonny Kate / Danny boy / Humours of Westport / Andy McGann's reel
CD _______ PTICD 1089
Pure Traditional Irish / Mar '97 / ADA / CM / Direct / Ross

IRISH TRADITIONAL FIDDLING
Cronin's fancy / Tom Ward's downfall / Two reevy's / Cas an tugan / Slievenamon / Duke of Leinster and his wife / Pullet wants cock / Dairymaid / Holy land / Jackie Coleman's / Roger's fancy / Golden ring / Se fayh mo bhuartha / Two Andy McGann's / Mama's pet / Banks / Hinchie's delight / Tone rowe's
CD _______ PTICD 1002
Pure Traditional Irish / Mar '97 / ADA / CM / Direct / Ross

TWO CHAMPIONS (McGuire, Sean & Joe Burke)
Farl O'Gara / Trim the velvet / Copper plate No.1 / Copper plate No.2 / Old grey goose / Crooked road to Dublin / Concert / Flowing tide / Galway / Dr. Gilbert / Queen of the May / Old Blackthorn / Green groves / Paddy Ryan's dream / Ballinasloe fair / Burying poteen / Cup of tea / Kesh jig / Morrison's / Cronin's / George White's fancy / Tomorrow Morning / Friendly visit / Tom Clark's fancy / Longford collector / Ships are sailing / Bird in the bush
CD _______ PTICD 1014
Pure Traditional Irish / Mar '97 / ADA / CM / Direct / Ross

MacGuish, Alasdair

ALASDAIR MACGUISH & THE BLACK ROSE CEILIDH BAND
CD _______ LOC 1086CD
Lochshore / Jul '95 / ADA / Direct / Duncans

McHael, Allan

NEW RIVER TRAIN
CD _______ FE 1408
Folk Era / Nov '94 / ADA / CM

OLD COUNTRY RADIO SONGS (McHael, Allan & Old Time Radio Gang)
CD _______ FE 2062CD
Folk Era / Dec '94 / ADA / CM

McHaile, Tom

PURE TRADITIONAL TIN WHISTLE
CD _______ PTICD 1001
Pure Traditional Irish / Apr '94 / ADA / CM / Direct / Ross

McHargue, Rosy

OH HOW HE CAN SING
CD _______ SOSCD 1253
Stomp Off / Jul '93 / Jazz Music / Wellard

Machete Ensemble

MACHETE ENSEMBLE, THE
CD _______ CDEB 2501
Earthbeat / May '93 / ADA / Direct

Machin, Antonio

ANTONIO MACHIN VOL.1 1930-1932
Adela / Suavecito / A baracoa me voy / Pobre corazon / Damelo / Se va el dulcerito / Quisiera morirme / La rosa Oriental / Oprobio / El heurfanito / Illusion China / Ojeras / Las flores de mi jardin / Buey viejo / Sigue tu senda / Triguenita / Lamento Cubano / Esperanzas muertas / Junto a un canaveral / Munequita
CD _______ HQCD 24
Harlequin / Oct '96 / Hot Shot / Jazz Music / Swift / Wellard

ANTONIO MACHIN VOL.2 1932-1933
Entre tinieblas / Don lengua / Mujer / El caramelero / Las perlas de tu boca / Cuartito Sagrado / De que te vale / Recordando a un vendedor / Lucero de mis noches / La sitiera / Asi como suena mi son / El castigador / Para que no pago o dale que ya monte / Echale salsita / El guanajo relleno / Ese hombre es un diablo / Rumba tambah: *Orquesta Antiliana* / Menealo que se empelota: *Orquesta Antiliana* / Clara / Repellito
CD _______ HQCD 32
Harlequin / Oct '96 / Hot Shot / Jazz Music / Swift / Wellard

ANTONIO MACHIN VOL.3 1933-1934
CD _______ HQCD 58
Harlequin / Jan '97 / Hot Shot / Jazz Music / Swift / Wellard

CANTA A CUBA Y SUS COMPOSITORES
CD _______ CCD 803
Caney / Jan '97 / ADA / Discovery

CANTA A MEXICO Y SUS COMPOSITORES
CD _______ CCD 804
Caney / Jan '97 / ADA / Discovery

ESE SOY YO
CD _______ ALCD 025
Alma Latina / Apr '97 / Discovery

Machin, James

GUITAR AND ELECTRONICS MUSIC (Machin, James & Steve Pittis)
CD _______ DPROMCD 44
Dirter Promotions / Feb '97 / Cargo / Pinnacle / World Serpent

Machine Head

BURN MY EYES (2CD Set)
Davidian / Old / Thousand eyes / None but my own / Rage to overcome / Death church / I'm your God now / Blood for blood / Nation on fire / Real eyes, realize, real lies / Block
CD _______ RR 90165
CD _______ RR 90162
Roadrunner / May '95 / PolyGram
CD Set _______ RR 90160
Roadrunner / Feb '97 / PolyGram

MORE THINGS CHANGE, THE
10 ton hammer / Take my scars / Struck a nerve / Down to none / Frontlines / Spine / Bay of pigs / Violate / Blistering / Blood of the zodiac / Possibility of life's destruction / My misery / Colors
CD _______ RR 88605
CD _______ RR 88602
Roadrunner / Mar '97 / PolyGram

Machine In The Garden

VEILS AND SHADOWS EP
CD _______ ISOL 80022
Isol / Feb '95 / Plastic Head

Machines Of Loving Grace

CONCENTRATION
CD _______ 4509968522
WEA / Nov '94 / Warner Music

GILT
CD _______ 0086522CTR
Edel / Apr '96 / Pinnacle

MACHINES OF LOVING GRACE
CD _______ MR 00292
Mammoth / Feb '92 / Vital

Machito

AFRO CUBAN JAZZ (Machito & Charlie Parker/Stan Kenton)
CD _______ CD 53170
Giants Of Jazz / Aug '95 / Cadillac / Jazz Music / Target/BMG

BONGO FIESTA
Adios / Holiday mambo / Bongo fiesta / Mambo mucho mambo / Negro nanamboro / Ay que mate / Mambo inn / Zambia / Blem blem blem / Beerebee cum bee / Tremendo cumban / Hay que recordar / Freezelandia / Oboe mambo / Donde estabas tu / Mambo a la savoy
CD _______ CD 62070
Saludos Amigos / Apr '95 / Target/BMG

MACHITO & HIS AFRO-CUBANS 1948-1950
CD _______ HQCD 87
Harlequin / Jul '96 / Hot Shot / Jazz Music / Swift / Wellard

MACHITO & HIS ORCHESTRA (Machito & His Orchestra)
CD _______ CD 62045
Saludos Amigos / Nov '93 / Target/BMG

MAMBO IN JAZZ
CD _______ CD 62015
Saludos Amigos / Jan '93 / Target/BMG

RITMO PA' GOZAR (Machito & His Orchestra)
CD _______ CCD 511
Caney / Jul '96 / ADA / Discovery

SALSA BIG BAND 1982 (Machito & His Salsa Big Band)
Elas de la rumba / Quimbobo / Piniero tenia razon / Caso perdido / Manicero / Sambia / Yerbero
CD _______ CDSJP 161
Timeless Jazz / '89 / New Note/Pinnacle

Machlis, Paul

BRIGHT FIELD, THE (Machlis, Paul & Alasdair Fraser)
CD _______ CULD 107
Culburnie / Jun '95 / ADA / CM / Direct / Duncans / Highlander / Ross

McIlwaine, Ellen

LOOKING FOR TROUBLE
CD _______ SPCD 1110
Stony Plain / Apr '94 / ADA / CM / Direct

MacInnes, Mairi

CAUSEWAY
Clachan uaine (The green village) / Mendocino / Puirt a beul (mouth music) / Eala bhan (The white swan) / Eilidh / Cuachag nana craobh (The tree cuckoo) / Morag's na horo gheallaidh (walking song) / Mairead og / Soraidh le eilean a'cheo / (Back home again in) Indiana / Tuireadh mhic criomain (MacCrimmon's lament) / Mo chridhe trom's duilich leam / Everlasting gun
CD _______ LCOM 9018
Lismor / Oct '92 / ADA / Direct / Duncans / Lismor

THIS FEELING INSIDE
Puert a beul / Follow the light / Cum ar'naire / Come back to me / Neamhnaid gheal dochais / Sit at my table / Fraoch a ronaidh / Far from home / Fear a'bhata / Precious days / Mile marphaisg air a ghaol / Eilean m'araich / Puirt a beul / This feeling inside
CD _______ CDTRAX 092
Greentrax / Jul '95 / ADA / Direct / Duncans / Highlander

MacInnis, Jamie

FOSGAIL AN DORUS (MacInnis, Jamie & Paul MacNeil)
Thig a staigh / DNA / Newmarket House / Paul's solo / Rothesay / Milling set / Cape Breton set / Eireann's / Gun oran binn, no canain grinn / Jamie's solo / Ian Ruadh / Electric set
CD _______ IRCD 044
Iona / Jan '97 / ADA / Direct / Duncans

McIntyre, Kalaparusha Maurice

FORCES AND FEELINGS
Behold God's sunshine / Fifteen or sixteen / Sun spots / Ananda / Twenty-one lines / Behold God's sunshine / Ananda
CD _______ DE 425
Delmark / Nov '96 / ADA / Cadillac / CM / Direct / Hot Shot

PEACE AND BLESSINGS (McIntyre, Kalaparusha Maurice Quartet)
CD _______ 1200372
Black Saint / Oct '96 / Cadillac / Harmonia Mundi

McIntyre, Ken

COMPLETE UA SESSIONS, THE (2CD Set)
Miss Ann / Lois Marie / Chittlin's and cavyah / Permanentity / Tip top / Kaijee / Reflections / Say what / 96.5 / Arisin' / Laura / Speak low / Cosmos / Sendai / Undulation / Turbospacey / Bootsie / New time / Naomi / Someday / Mercedes
CD Set _______ CDP 8572002
Blue Note / Aug '97 / EMI

INTRODUCING THE VIBRATIONS (McIntyre, Ken Sextet)
CD _______ SCCD 31065
Steeplechase / Dec '95 / Discovery / Impetus

LOOKING AHEAD (McIntyre, Ken & Eric Dolphy)
Lautir / Curtsy / Geo's tune / They all laughed / Head shakin'
CD _______ OJCCD 252
Original Jazz Classics / Jun '96 / Complete/Pinnacle / Jazz Music / Wellard

MacIsaac, Ashley

HI HOW ARE YOU TODAY
Beaton's delight / Sleepy Maggie / Rusty D-con-Struck-tion / Devil in the kitchen / MacDougall's pride / Spoonboy / What an idiot he is / Sophia's pipes / Sad wedding day / Wing-stock / Hills of Glenorchy / Brenda Stubbert
CD _______ 5405222
A&M / Jun '96 / PolyGram

Mack, Bobby

RED HOT & HUMID
Black Jack / In the open / Maudie / Look watcha done / She's so fine / Phillip West / Ain't nobody's business if I do / Change my mind / All night long / Take it home
CD _______ PRD 70692
Provogue / Aug '94 / Pinnacle

SAY WHAT
CD _______ PRD 70502
Provogue / Apr '93 / Pinnacle

SUGAR ALL NIGHT
CD _______ PRD 70812
Provogue / Feb '96 / Pinnacle

Mack, Craig

PROJECT: FUNK DA WORLD
Project: Funk da world / Get down / Making moves with puff / That y'all / Flava in ya ear / Funk wit da style / Judgement day / Real raw / Mainline / When God comes / Welcome to 1994
CD _______ 78612730012
Arista / Oct '94 / BMG

Mack, Jimmy

JOY SOMETHING FOR EVERYONE
CD _______ LDRCD 021
Londisc / Nov '96 / Jet Star

MANKIND
CD _______ ORCD 008
Original Music / Jul '96 / Jet Star / SRD

Mack, Leroy

LEROY MACK & FRIENDS
CD _______ REB 1729CD
Rebel / Aug '96 / ADA / Direct

Mack, Lonnie

ATTACK OF THE KILLER V (Lonnie Mack Live)
CD _______ ALCD 4786
Alligator / May '93 / ADA / CM / Direct

HOME AT LAST
CD _______ OW S2117963
One Way / Sep '94 / ADA / Direct / Greyhound

LONNIE MACK & PISMO
CD _______ OW S2117964
One Way / Sep '94 / ADA / Direct / Greyhound

LONNIE ON THE MOVE
I found a love / Soul express / I've had it / Wildwood flower / Snow on the mountain / I washed my hands in muddy water / Shotgun / Sticks and stones / Jam and butter / One mint julep / Florence of Arabia / Lonnie on the move / Sa-ba-hoola / Money (that's what I want) / Dorothy on my mind / Men at play / Oh boy / Stand by me / Don't make my baby blue
CD _______ CDCH 352
Ace / Feb '92 / Pinnacle

SECOND SIGHT
Me and my car / Rock 'n' roll bones / Tough on me tough on you / Camp Washington Chili / Cincinnati / Rock people / Buffalo woman / Ain't nobody / Back on the road again / Song I haven't sung
CD _______ ALCD 4750
Alligator / Oct '93 / ADA / CM / Direct

STRIKE LIKE LIGHTNING
Hound dog man / Satisfy Susie / Stop / Long way from Memphis / Double whammy / Strike like lightning / Falling back in love with you / If you have to know / You ain't got me / Oreo cookie blues
CD _______ ALCD 4739
Alligator / May '93 / ADA / CM / Direct

Macka B

BUPPIE CULTURE
CD _______ ARICD 48
Ariwa Sounds / Jan '91 / Jet Star / SRD

DISCRIMINATION
CD _______ ARICD 098
Ariwa Sounds / Jun '94 / Jet Star / SRD

HERE COMES TROUBLE
Promises / Here comes trouble / Do the butterfly / Getting blacker / Don't worry / Thank you Father / Squeeze me / Reggae on the rampage / Crackpot / Rottweiler
CD _______ ARICD 088
Ariwa Sounds / Oct '93 / Jet Star / SRD

HOLD ON TO YOUR CULTURE
Bob / Legalize the herb / Beautiful eyes / Greetings / Hold on to your culture / Give the workers / Woman / Put down the gun / Tribute to Garnett Silk
CD _______ ARICD 108
Ariwa Sounds / Oct '95 / Jet Star / SRD

JAMAICA, NO PROBLEM
CD _______ ARICD 078
Ariwa Sounds / May '92 / Jet Star / SRD

PEACE CUP
CD _______ ARICD 068
Ariwa Sounds / Jul '91 / Jet Star / SRD

ROOTS RAGGA
Roots Ragga / (Get up I feel like being a) sex machine / Drink too much / Revelation time / Big mack / Devil dance / Rodney King medley / One man, one vote / Unemployment blues / Proud to be black / Back off / Buppie / Respect to the mother / Apartheid
CD ARICD 082
Ariwa Sounds / Nov '92 / Jet Star / SRD

SIGN OF THE TIMES
CD ARICD 028
Ariwa Sounds / Feb '89 / Jet Star / SRD

SUSPICIOUS
CD ARICD 138
Ariwa/Shaka / May '97 / SRD

McKagan, Duff

BELIEVE IN ME
Believe in me / Man in the meadow / (Fucked up) Beyond belief / Could it be U / Just not there / Punk rock song / Majority / Ten years / Swamp song / Trouble / Fuck you / Lonely tonite
CD GED 24605
Geffen / Sep '93 / BMG

MacKay, Andy

RESOLVING CONTRADICTIONS
Iron blossom / Trumpets on the mountains/ Off to work / Loyang tractor factory / Rivers / Battersea rise / Skill and sweet / Ortolan bunting (A sparrow falls) / Inexorable sequence / Song of friendship / Alloy blossom trumpet in the suburbs / Green and gold
CD EXVP 6CD
Expression / Jan '97 / Pinnacle

McKay, Alex Francis

LIFELONG HOME, A
Rosin the bow / Duke of Athole / Earl Grey / Lady Mary Ramsey / Highland society / McGlashan jig / Coilsfield house / Christy's quickstep / Craigaillichie bridge / Welcome to your feet / Mrs Garden of Troup / Double kisses / Dunkeld hermitage / Jenny Carouthers
CD ROUCD 7020
Rounder / May '97 / ADA / CM / Direct

MacKay, Iain

SEOLADH
CD SKYECD 07
Macmeanma / Sep '95 / ADA / CM / Duncans / Highlander

McKay, Kris

THINGS THAT SHOW
CD SHCD 8020
Shanachie / Jul '96 / ADA / Greensleeves / Koch

MacKay, Rhona

CEOL NA CLARSAICH
CD LCOM 5130
Lismor / Oct '96 / ADA / Direct / Duncans / Lismor

McKee, Maria

LIFE IS SWEET
Searlover / This perfect dress / Absolutely barking stars / I'm not listening / Everybody / Smarter / What else you wanna know / I'm awake / Human carried / Life is sweet / Afterlife
CD GED 24819
Geffen / Feb '96 / BMG

MARIA MCKEE
I've forgotten what it was in you / To miss someone / Am I the only one (who ever felt this way) / Nobody's child / Panic beach / Can't pull the wool down (over the little lamb's eyes) / More than a heart can hold / This property is condemned / Breathe / Has he got a friend for me / Drinkin' in my Sunday dress
CD GED 24229
Geffen / Nov '96 / BMG

YOU GOTTA SIN TO GET SAVED
I'm gonna soothe you / My lonely sad eyes / My girlhood among the outlaws / Only once / I forgive you / I can't make it alone / Precious time / Way young lovers do / Why wasn't I more grateful (when life was so sweet) / You gotta sin to get saved
CD GFLD 19290
Geffen / Oct '95 / BMG

McKellar, Kenneth

LAND OF HEART'S DESIRE
Think on me / Old turf fire / Fairy lullaby / Ho ro my nut brown maiden / David of the White Rock / MacPherson's farewell / Land of heart's desire / Star of County Down / Ellan Vannin / Bonnie Earl O'Moray / Wee Cooper o' Fife / Old house / O' are ye sleepin' Maggie / She moved through the fair / Durisdeer / Next market day / Watching the wheat / Twa corbies / My Irish jaunting car / O' a the airts / Wee Hughie / Gortnamona
CD LCOM 9044
Lismor / Aug '91 / ADA / Direct / Duncans / Lismor

LAUGHTER AND THE TEARS, THE (Songs Of The Jacobite Risings - Vol. 2)
Wah widna' fecht for Charlie / Charlie is my darling / Hey Johnny Cope / Our ain countrie / Your welcome Charlie Stuart / Kenmore's up and awa' / Come o'er the stream Charlie / Highland laddie / There'll never be peace till Jamie comes hame / Wi' a hundred pipers / Twa bonnie maidens / Women are a' gane wud / Highland widows lament / Campbells are coming / Sound the pibroch / We will take the good old way / Loch Lomond
CD LCOM 6036
Lismor / Dec '93 / ADA / Direct / Duncans / Lismor

MIST COVERED MOUNTAINS OF HOME, THE
Mist covered mountains of home / Bonnie Strathyre / Nicky Tams / Oor ain fireside / O gin I were whar' gadie rins / To people who have gardens / Amazing grace / Kelvin Grove / Corn rigs / Bonnie lass o' Fyvie / O gin I were a baron's heir / Wee cock sparra / Iona boat song / Pan drap song / Flowers of the forest / Scotland the brave
CD LCOM 6043
Lismor / Nov '95 / ADA / Direct / Duncans / Lismor

SCOTTISH JOURNEY VOL.2, A
This is Scotland / Mingulay boat song / Island of Tiree / Hieland laddie / Corn rigs / Scots wha hae / Come o'er the stream Charlie / Royal Mile / Sing to me the old Scots songs medley / Wee cooper of Fife / Bonnie Dundee / Saturday dance / Northern lights of old Aberdeen / Nicky tams / Amazing grace / Pan drap song / Oor ain fireside / Scotland the brave
CD LCOM 6044
Lismor / Feb '97 / ADA / Direct / Duncans / Lismor

SCOTTISH JOURNEY, A
CD LISMOR 6037
Lismor / Jan '95 / ADA / Direct / Duncans / Lismor

SONGS OF THE JACOBITE RISINGS
Bluebells of Scotland / Piper O'Dundee / Lewie Gordon / Cam ye by Atholl / Farewell to Glenshalloch / Ye Jacobites by name / Blackbird / Braes o'Killecrankie / Flora MacDonald's lament / Highland muster roll / Skye boat song / Ower the water to Charlie / Wae's me for Prince Charlie / Bonnets o' bonnie Dundee / Will ye no' come back again
CD LCOM 6028
Lismor / Aug '96 / ADA / Direct / Duncans / Lismor

TODAY
Island of Tiree / Flower of Scotland / Braes o'Balquhidder / Old ballad (the farmer's daughter) / Northern lights of old Aberdeen / Rowan tree / Glencoe (the massacre of) / Wee place in the Highlands / Jean / Scotland again / Thou Bonnie Wood O Craigelea / Mingulay boat song / Clyde medley / Star O' rabbie burns / Mull of the cool bens / Eriskay love lilt / Ye banks and braes o' bonnie Doon
CD LCOM 9011
Lismor / Aug '91 / ADA / Direct / Duncans / Lismor

VERY BEST OF KENNETH MCKELLAR, THE
My love is like a red red rose / Skye boat song / Cockles and mussels / Wi' a hundred pipers / Stranger in paradise / Villikins and Dinah / Ye banks and braes / Serenade from the fair maid of Perth / Danny boy / Island moon / Sweet lass of Richmond Hill / There was a lad was born in Kyle / Dance to your Daddy / Twa corbies / Greensleeves / Ball of Kirriemuir / O waly waly / Last rose of summer / Bonnie labouring boy / Rising of the lark
CD 5520952
Spectrum / Jan '97 / PolyGram

McKendree Spring

GOD BLESS THE CONSPIRACY
No regrets / Spock / Morning glory / Fire and rain / Susie Susie / Got no place to fall / Down by the river / Fading lady / Heart like a wheel / Hobo lady / Oh in the morning / God bless the conspiracy / Light up the skies / Man in me / What was gained
CD EDCD 497
Edsel / Oct '96 / Pinnacle

McKenna, Dave

CELEBRATION OF HOAGY CARMICHAEL
Stardust / Riverboat shuffle / One morning in May / Moon country / Two sleepy people / Come easy, go easy love / Nearness of you / Lazybones / Sky lark / Georgia / Lazy river
CD CCD 4227
Concord Jazz / May '94 / New Note/ Pinnacle

CONCORD DUO SERIES VOL.2 (McKenna, Dave & Gray Sargent)
Sheikh of Araby / Girl of my dreams / Red woods in the sunset / I'm gonna sit right down and write myself a letter / Blue and sentimental / 'Deed I do / Time after time/ time on my hands / Exactly like you
CD CCD 4552
Concord Jazz / May '93 / New Note/ Pinnacle

DAVE MCKENNA QUARTET FEATURING ZOOT SIMS (McKenna, Dave & Zoot Sims)
CD CRD 136
Chiaroscuro / Mar '96 / Jazz Music

EASY STREET
Broadway / Basin Street blues / Street of dreams / Don't forget 127th street / Easy street / On Green Dolphin Street / On the street where you live / Cat's cradle / My honey's lovin' arms / When your lover is gone / Now that you're gone / After you've gone / Gone with the wind / Theodore the thumper
CD CCD 4657
Concord Jazz / Jul '95 / New Note/Pinnacle

GIANT STRIDES
If dreams come true / Yardbird suite / Windsong / Dave's blues / I've got the world on a string / Love letter / Cherry / Lulu's back in town / Walkin' my baby back home / Underdog / I've found a new baby
CD CCD 4099
Concord Jazz / Feb '95 / New Note/ Pinnacle

HANDFUL OF STARS, A
Estrela, estrela / Stella by starlight / Star eyes / Star kissed / Handful of stars / Stardreams / Stairway to the stars / Estrellita / Stardust / Song from the stars / Swinging on a star / I've told every little star / Lost in the stars / When you wish upon a star / Stars fell on Alabama / Estrela, estrela (reprise)
CD CCD 4580
Concord Jazz / Nov '93 / New Note/ Pinnacle

HANGIN' OUT
Have you met Miss Jones / Just as though you were here / (Back home again in) Indiana / Splendid splinter / I'll be seeing you / Wrap your troubles in dreams (and dream your troubles away) / Easy living / Mixed emotions / When day is done / Thanks for the memories
CD CCD 4123
Concord Jazz / Feb '92 / New Note/ Pinnacle

MY FRIEND THE PIANO
Margie / Only trust your heart / Mean to me / Slowly / You're driving me crazy / Summer medley: guess I'll go back home this su / Indian summer / Baby, baby, all the time / Always medley: It's always you / Always / This is always
CD CCD 4313
Concord Jazz / Jul '87 / New Note/Pinnacle

NO BASS HIT
But not for me / If dreams come true / Long ago and far away / Drum boogie / I love you, samaritan / I'm gonna sit right down and write myself a letter / Easy to love / Get happy
CD CCD 4097
Concord Jazz / Oct '91 / New Note/ Pinnacle

NO MORE OUZO FOR PUZO (McKenna, Dave Quartet)
Look for the silver lining / Smile / For you, for me, for evermore / You and I / You brought a new kind of love to me / Talk of the town / Shake down the stars / Lonesome me / No more ouzo for Puzo / I keep going back to Joe's / Talk to me / Please don't talk about me when I'm gone
CD CCD 365
Concord Jazz / Jan '89 / New Note/ Pinnacle

PIANO SCENE OF DAVE MCKENNA, THE
CD 378092
Koch Jazz / May '96 / Koch

SOLO PIANO
CD CRD 119
Chiaroscuro / Feb '95 / Jazz Music

SUNBEAM AND THUNDERCLOUD (McKenna, Dave & Joe Temperley)
Once in a while / Sunbeam and Thundercloud / Sunset and the mockingbird / Gone with the wind / Black and tan fantasy / I let a song go out of my heart / Lotus blossom / Tricrotism / Nightingale / I can't believe that you're in love with me / I wish I knew / I got rhythm
CD CCD 4703
Concord Crossover / Jul '96 / New Note/ Pinnacle

YOU MUST BELIEVE IN SWING (McKenna, Dave & Buddy DeFranco)
You must believe in swing / Invitation / Song is you / If you could see me now / Darn that dream / Autumn nocturne / Poor butterfly / Detour ahead / Anthropology / You must believe in spring
CD CCD 47562
Concord Jazz / May '97 / New Note/ Pinnacle

McKenna, Joe

AT HOME (McKenna, Joe & Antoinette)
CD GRACC 27
Grasmere / May '94 / Highlander / Savoy / Target/BMG

HIS ORIGINAL RECORDINGS
CD JMCK 1
John McKenna Society / Nov '94 / Direct

MAGENTA MUSIC (McKenna, Joe & Antoinette)
CD SHCD 79076
Shanachie / Jun '91 / ADA / Greensleeves / Koch

McKenna, Mae

MIRAGE & REALITY
CD HY 200121CD
Hypertension / Sep '93 / ADA / CM / Direct / Total/BMG

McKenna, Terence

DREAM MATRIX TELEMETRY (McKenna, Terence & Zuvuya)
CD DELECCD 2012
Delerium / Nov '93 / Cargo / Pinnacle / Vital

McKennitt, Loreena

ELEMENTAL
CD QRCD 101
Quinlan Road / Oct '94 / ADA / Direct

MASK & THE MIRROR, THE
Mystic's dream / Bonny swans / Dark night of the soul / Marrakesh night market / Full circle / Santiago / Ce he mise le ulaingt / Two trees / Prospero's speech
CD 4509952962
WEA / May '95 / Warner Music

PARALLEL DREAMS
CD QRCD 103
Quinlan Road / Oct '94 / ADA / Direct

TO DRIVE THE COLD WINTER AWAY
CD QRCD 102
Quinlan Road / Dec '94 / ADA / Direct

VISIT, THE
All souls night / Bonny Portmore / Between the shadows / Lady of Shalott / Greensleeves / Tango to evora / Courtyard lullaby / Old ways / Cymbeline
CD 9031751512
WEA / May '95 / Warner Music

WINTER GARDEN, A
CD 0630122902
Quinlan Road / Dec '95 / ADA / Direct

MacKenzie, Eilidh

RAIMENT OF THE TALE, THE
CD COMD 2048
Temple / Feb '94 / ADA / CM / Direct / Duncans / Highlander

MacKenzie, Kate

AGE OF INNOCENCE
CD RHRCD 91
Red House / Nov '96 / ADA / Koch

LET THEM TALK
CD RHRCD 66
Red House / May '95 / ADA / Koch

MacKenzie, Malcolm M.

MACKENZIES PIPES AND BANJO (MacKenzie, Pipe Major Malcolm M.)
CD CDLOC 1059
Lochshore / Dec '90 / ADA / Direct / Duncans

MACKENZIES PIPES AND STRINGS (MacKenzie, Pipe Major Malcolm M.)
Maggie / Bunch of thyme / Silver threads among the gold / Canon in D / Annie Laurie / Rose of Tralee / Penhalonga piper / Way old friends do / MacKenzies tune / Danny boy / Scotland the brave / Isle of Arran / Mull of Kintyre / Will ye no' come back again / Amazing grace / Flower of Scotland / Bright eyes
CD CDLOC 1033
Lochshore / Jun '87 / ADA / Direct / Duncans

MacKenzie, Talitha

SOLAS
CD TUGCD 1007
Riverboat / Mar '94 / New Note/Pinnacle / Stern's

SPIORAD
CD SH 78003
Shanachie / Oct '96 / ADA / Greensleeves / Koch

McKenzie, Red

1935-37
Murder in the moonlight (it's love in the first degree) / Let's swing it / Double trouble / That's what you think / Georgia rockin' chair / Monday in Manhattan / Every now and then / Wouldn't it be a wonder / Sing me an old fashioned song / I'm building up to

an awful let-down / Don't count your kisses (before you're kissed) / When love has gone / I don't know your name (but you're beautiful) / Moon rose / I can't get started (with you) / I can pull a rabbit out of my hat / Sweet Lorraine / Wanted / I cried for you / Trouble with me is you / Farewell my love / You're out of this world / Sail along silv'ry moon / Georgianna
CD CBC 1019
Timeless Historical / Aug '94 / New Note/ Pinnacle

McKeown, Susan

BONES (McKeown, Susan & Chanting House)
CD SNG 701CD
Sheila-Na-Gig / Nov '95 / ADA

Mackey, Steve

LOST AND FOUND
CD BRI 9065
Bridge / Jul '96 / Complete/Pinnacle / Koch

Mackie Ranks

LICK OUT
CD HCD 7001
Hightone / Aug '94 / ADA / Koch

McKillop, Jim

TRADITIONAL IRISH FIDDLE AND PIANO (McKillop, Jim & Josephine Keegan)
CD PTICD 1045CD
Pure Traditional Irish / Jul '95 / ADA / CM / Direct / Ross

McKinley

MCKINLEY
CD BCD 00222
Burnside / May '96 / Koch

McKinley, Ray

BACK TO THE MILLER SOUND (McKinley, Ray & New Glenn Miller Orchestra)
Jeep Jockey jump / On the street where you live / Am I blue / Howdy friends / Laura / Here we go again / I'm thrilled
CD DAWE 46
Magic / Nov '93 / Cadillac / Harmonia Mundi / Jazz Music / Swift / Wellard

CLASS OF '49, THE
It's only a paper moon / Blue moon / Stompin' at the savoy / Stardust / Laura / How high the moon / Lullabye in rhythm / Harlem nocturne / I gotta right to sing the blues / Don't be that way
CD HEPCD 4
Hep / Dec '95 / Cadillac / Jazz Music / New Note/Pinnacle / Wellard

JAZZ PORTRAIT
CD CD 14586
Complete / Nov '95 / THE

JIMINY CRICKETS
CD AERO 1033
Aerospace / Jul '96 / Jazz Music / Montpellier

MCKINLEY TIME (McKinley, Ray & His Orchestra)
Rowdy friends / Carioca / Soon / Hard hearted Hannah / Jiminy crickets / I kiss your hand Madame / How high the moon / Along with me / Celery stalks at midnight / Pancho Maximillian Hernandez (The Best President we ever had / Blue moon / Star dest / I'm tired of waiting for you / It's only a paper moon / Laura / Stompin' at the Savoy / Tacos, enchiladas and beans / Borderline / (Where are you now) Now that I need you / Harlem nocturne / Lullaby in rhythm / Waitin' for the evenin' mail / Pete's cafe / Howdy friends
CD VN 1001
Viper's Nest / Nov '96 / ADA / Cadillac / Direct / Jazz Music

McKinney's Cotton Pickers

1928-29
CD CLASSICS 609
Classics / Oct '92 / Discovery / Jazz Music

CLASSICS 1930-1931
CD CLASSICS 649
Classics / Nov '92 / Discovery / Jazz Music

MCKINNEY'S COTTON PICKERS - 1929-30
CD CLASSICS 625
Classics / Nov '92 / Discovery / Jazz Music

McKinney, Carlos

UP FRONT
You and the night and the music / Prince of jade / If I should lose you / All because of you / Mademoiselle Gregoire / Black beauty / Obelisk / Seer / Door of no return
CD SJL 1002
Sirocco / Sep '97 / New Note/Pinnacle

MacKinon, Maeve

FO SMUAIN
CD SKYECD 08
Macmeanma / Mar '96 / ADA / CM / Duncans / Highlander

MacKintosh, Iain

GENTLE PERSUASION (MacKintosh, Iain & Brian McNeill/Alan Reid)
Tomorrow you're gone / Uncle Walter / Run the film backwards / My old man / It's so easy to dream / When I'm gone / January man / Farm auction / Wheelchair talking blues / Song of the pineapple rag / First you lose the rhyming / Waltzing around in the nude / Five ways to kill a man
CD CDTRAX 014
Greentrax / Feb '97 / ADA / Direct / Duncans / Highlander

RISKS AND ROSES
If I had a boat / Remember when the music / I wish I was in Glasgow / Cheeky young lad / Rats are winning / King of Rome / Flowers are red / My home town / Roses from the wrong man / Acceptable risks / Dill pickle rag / Annie McKelvie / Kilkelly / Hug song
CD CDTRAX 043
Greentrax / Feb '91 / ADA / Direct / Duncans / Highlander

STAGE BY STAGE (MacKintosh, Iain & Brian McNeil)
Plainstanes / Glasgow magistrate / Wind and rain / Sea maiden / Balkan hills / Bonny wee lassie who never said no / Holyrood house / Generations of change / Dallas domestic / Smoky mokes / Beautiful dreamer / Traveller's moon / Summer of love / Recruited collier / Tank / Cronin's / Fisherman's lilt / What you do with what you've got / Black swan / Roslin Castle / You can't take it with you when you go
CD CDTRAX 101
Greentrax / Nov '95 / ADA / Direct / Duncans / Highlander

MacKintosh, Ken

BLUES SKIES
CD DLD 1014
Dance & Listen / '92 / Savoy / Target/ BMG

McKnight, Brian

I REMEMBER YOU
CD 5284302
Talkin' Loud / Aug '95 / PolyGram

McKoy

FULL CIRCLE
CD TUMCD 1
Right Track / Apr '94 / Jet Star

McKuen, Rod

FRENCH CONNECTION, THE
CD 12444
Laserlight / Mar '95 / Target/BMG

GREATEST HITS
CD BX 4082
BR Music / Mar '94 / Target/BMG

ROD MCKUEN SINGS JACQUES BREL
CD BX 4072
BR Music / Mar '94 / Target/BMG

McKusick, Hal

EAST COAST JAZZ (McKusick, Hal Quartet)
CD FSCD 41
Fresh Sound / Oct '90 / Discovery / Jazz Music

McLachlan, Craig

CULPRITS (McLachlan, Craig & The Culprits)
CD RR 88442
Roadrunner / Oct '96 / PolyGram

McLachlan, Ian

ISLAND HERITAGE, AN
Donald McLean's farewell / Cameron's got his wife again / March/Reels/Strathspeys / Dark Island / Ale is dear / Calum Crubach / Reels / Conundrum / Highland Harry / Jig of slurs / Devil in the kitchen / Hornpipes / Cuttie's wedding / Puirt a beul / Pipe reels
CD SPRCD 1022
Springthyme / Jul '97 / ADA / CM / Direct / Duncans / Highlander / Roots

KINGS OF THE BUTTON KEYED BOX (McLachlan, Ian & Fergie MacDonald)
From Lewis to Glencoe: *McLachlan, Ian* / Goes Irish trad: *McDonald, Fergie* / Dark island: *McLachlan, Ian* / Mouth music on button box: *McDonald, Fergie* / Jiggin' across the Minch: *McLachlan, Ian* / Iain Rhuadh's lament: *McDonald, Fergie* / Gay gordons on button box: *McLachlan, Ian* / Three jigs for three friends: *McDonald, Fergie* / Two pipe marches: *McLachlan, Ian* / Two tunes for two bonnie lasses: *McDonald, Fergie* / Gaelic waltz hebridean style: *McLachlan, Ian* / Clanranald Hotel barn dance: *McDonald, Fergie* / Old flame: *McLachlan, Ian* / Fergie's own jigs: *McDonald, Fergie* / 2/4 marches: *McLachlan, Ian/Fergie MacDonald*
CD LCOM 5160
Lismor / Feb '97 / ADA / Direct / Duncans / Lismor

McLachlan, Sarah

FUMBLING TOWARDS ECSTASY
Possession / Wait / Plenty / Good enough / Mary / Elsewhere / Circle / Ice / Hold on / Ice cream / Fear / Fumbling towards ecstasy
CD 74321190322
Arista / Oct '94 / BMG

McLain, 'Mighty' Sam

SLEDGEHAMMER SOUL AND DOWN HOME BLUES
Slegehammer soul and down home blues / Where you been so long / Trying to find myself / Things ain't what they used to be / When the hurt is over / Pray / They call me mighty / Dancin' to the music of love / Hey Miss Bea / If you could see / Bridge of faith / Don't write me off
CD AQCD 1042
Audioquest / Dec '96 / ADA / New Note/ Pinnacle

McLain, Raymond W.

PLACE OF MY OWN, A
CD FF 597CD
Flying Fish / Feb '93 / ADA / CM / Direct / Roots

McLain, Tommy

SWEET DREAMS
Sweet dreams / Before I grow too old / Think it over / Barefootin' / I can't take it no more / Try to find another man / When a man loves a woman / After loving you / Tribute to Fats Domino / Going home / Poor me / Going to the river / Just because / Legend in my time / Together again / I thought I'd never fall in love again / So sad (to watch good love go bad) / Sticks and stones / Mu heart remembers
CD CDCH 285
Ace / Jan '90 / Pinnacle

McLaren, Malcolm

DUCK ROCK
Obatala / Buffalo gals / Merengue / Punk it up / Legba / Jive my baby / Song for Chango / Soweto / World's famous / Duck for the oyster / Double Dutch
CD MMCD 1
Charisma / Apr '88 / EMI

LARGEST MOVIE HOUSE IN PARIS, THE
CD NOCD 12
No / Apr '96 / 3mv/Sony

PARIS
CD NOMC 100
No / Aug '94 / 3mv/Sony

ROUND THE OUTSIDE (McLaren, Malcolm & World Famous Supreme Team)
CD CDV 2646
Virgin / Apr '92 / EMI

WALTZ DARLING
House of the blue Danube / Waltz darling / Deep in vogue / Algernon's simply awfully good at ... / Something's jumping in your shirt / Shall we dance / Call a wave / I like you in velvet
CD 4607362
Epic / Jul '89 / Sony

McLaughlin, Billy

FINGERDANCE
Fingerdance / Blaise's ballad / Helms place / Happy archer / Breaking of the shells / While she sleeps / Hurricane Bob / Lila's healing / So long / Good wife / Stormseeker / Dreaming on a runway / Coffee break
CD ND 61058
Narada / Dec '96 / ADA / New Note/ Pinnacle

McLaughlin, John

ADVENTURES IN RADIOLAND (McLaughlin, John & Mahavishnu Orchestra)
Wait / Just ideas / Jozy / Half man half cookie / Florianopolis / Gotta dance / Wall will fall / Reincarnation / Mitch match / 20th Century Ltd
CD 5193972
Verve / Feb '93 / PolyGram

AFTER THE RAIN
CD 5274672
Verve / Jun '95 / PolyGram

APOCALYPSE (Mahavishnu Orchestra)
CD 4670922
Sony Jazz / Jan '95 / Sony

BEST OF SHAKTI, THE (McLaughlin, John & Shankar/Zakir Hussain)
CD MRCD 1010
Koch / Jan '95 / Koch

BEST OF THE MAHAVISHNU ORCHESTRA (Mahavishnu Orchestra)
Birds of fire / Open country joy / Wings of Karma / Sister Andrea / Dance of Maya / Meeting of the spirits / Lila's dance / Be happy
CD 4682262
Sony Jazz / Jan '95 / Sony

BETWEEN NOTHING AND ETERNITY LIVE (Mahavishnu Orchestra)
CD BGOCD 31
Beat Goes On / Dec '88 / Pinnacle

BIRDS OF FIRE (McLaughlin, John & Mahavishnu Orchestra)
Birds of fire / Miles beyond / Celestial terrestrial commuters / Sapphire bullets of pure love / Thousand Island park / Hope / One word / Sanctuary / Open country / Resolution
CD 4682242
Columbia / Jan '92 / Sony

COLLECTION, THE
CD CCSCD 305
Castle / Oct '91 / BMG

DEVOTION
Marbles / Don't let the dragon eat your Mother / Purpose of when / Dragon song / Devotion
CD CPCD 8232
Charly / Dec '96 / Koch

ELECTRIC DREAMS (McLaughlin, John & The One Truth Band)
Guardian angels / Miles Davis / Electric dreams / Electric sighs / Love and understanding / Desire and the comforter / Singing earth / Dark prince / Unknown dissident
CD 4722102
Sony Jazz / Jan '95 / Sony

ELECTRIC GUITARIST
New York on my mind / Friendship / Every tear from every eye / Do you hear the voices you left behing / Are you the one / Pehnomenon / Compulsion / My foolish heart
CD 4670932
Columbia / Jan '95 / Sony

EXTRAPOLATION
Extrapolation / It's funny / Arjen's bag / Pete the poet / This is for us to share / Spectrum / Blinky's beam / Really you know / Two for two / Peace piece
CD 8415982
Polydor / Oct '90 / PolyGram

INNER WORLDS
CD 4769052
Sony Jazz / Jan '95 / Sony

LIVE AT THE ROYAL FESTIVAL HALL (27th November 1989) (McLaughlin, John Trio)
Blue in green / Just ideas/Jozy Florianapolis / Pasha's love / Mother tongues / Blues for LW
CD 8344362
jMT / Apr '90 / PolyGram

MY GOAL'S BEYOND (McLaughlin, John & Mahavishnu Orchestra)
CD RCD 10051
Rykodisc / May '92 / ADA / Vital

PASSION, GRACE AND FIRE (McLaughlin, John & Al Di Meola/Paco De Lucia)
Aspen / Orient blue / Chiquito / Sichia / David / Passion, grace and fire
CD 8113342
Philips / Jun '83 / PolyGram

PROMISE, THE
CD 5288282
Verve / Mar '96 / PolyGram

QUE ALEGRIA (McLaughlin, John Trio)
Belo Horizonte / Baba / Reincarnation / One nite stand / Marie / Hijacked / Milas repa / Que alegria / 2 willows
CD 8372802
Verve / Jan '92 / PolyGram

SHAKTI & JOHN MCLAUGHLIN (McLaughlin, John & Shakti)
CD 4679052
Sony Jazz / Jan '95 / Sony

THIS IS JAZZ
Birds of fire / Lotus feet / Love supreme / Do you hear the voices that you left behind / Guardian angel / Dark prince / Aspan / Are you the one / Dance of Maya / Until such time
CD CK 64971
Sony Jazz / Oct '96 / Sony

TIME REMEMBERED (John McLaughlin Plays Bill Evans)
Prologue / Very early / Only child / Waltz for Debby / Homage / My/Bells / Time remembered / Song for Helen / Turn out the stars / We will meet again / Epilogue
CD 5198612
Verve / Feb '94 / PolyGram

TOKYO LIVE (The Free Spirits Featuring John McLaughlin)
One nite stand / Hijched / When love is far away / Little Miss Valley / Juju at the crossroads / Vuhovar / No blues / Mattinale
CD 5218702
Philips / May '94 / PolyGram

VISIONS OF THE EMERALD BEYOND (Mahavishnu Orchestra)
CD _______ 4679042
Sony Jazz / Jan '95 / Sony

WHERE FORTUNE SMILES
Glancing backwards (For junior) / Earth bound hearts / Where fortune smiles / New place, old place / Hope
CD _______ BGOCD 191
Beat Goes On / Jun '93 / Pinnacle

McLaughlin, Pat

GET OUT AND STAY OUT
CD _______ DOS 7012
Dos / Oct '95 / ADA / CM / Direct

UNGLUED
CD _______ DOSCD 7005
Dos / Apr '94 / ADA / CM / Direct

MacLean, Dougie

CRAIGIE DHU
Gin I were a baron's heir / Read for the storm / It was a' for our rightful king / High flying seagull / Edmonton airbus / Craigie Dhu / Bonnie Bessie Logan / Seanair's song / It fascinates me / Tullochgorum / Caledonia
CD _______ DUNCD 001
Dunkeld / Feb '90 / ADA / CM / Direct

DOUGIE MACLEAN COLLECTION
CD _______ M 1172
Putumayo / Jan '97 / Grapevine/PolyGram

DOUGIE MACLEAN'S CALEDONIA (The Plant Life Years)
Plooboy laddies / Johnny teasie weasle / Over my mountain / Mistress MacKinley's breakfast surreals / Northern cowboy / I lo'e nae a lassie but ane / Rattlin' roarin' Willie / Mormond braes / Caledonia / Jock Stewart / Leis a lurighan / Rolling home / Mill brae / Lassies trust in providence / Bonnie Isle O'Whalsay / Ye banks and braes o' bonnie doon
CD _______ OSMOCD 004
Osmosys / Oct '95 / Direct

FIDDLE
Osprey / Bob MacIntosh Atholl Arms kuring-gai chase / Farewell to Craigie Dhu / Tattie ball / When are you coming over / Mr. and Mrs. MacLean of Snaigow / Roy Ashby's buckny burn / One summer's morning / Ferry / Spoutwells riechip leduckie / Centre / Gin I were a baron's heir
CD _______ DUNCD 002
Dunkeld / Oct '93 / ADA / CM / Direct

INDIGENOUS
CD _______ DUNCD 015
Dunkeld / Feb '89 / ADA / CM / Direct

MARCHING MYSTERY
CD _______ DUN 019CD
Dunkeld / Jul '94 / ADA / CM / Direct

REAL ESTATE
CD _______ DUNCD 008
Dunkeld / Nov '92 / ADA / CM / Direct

RIOS
CD _______ DUNCD 021
Dunkeld / Aug '97 / ADA / CM / Direct

SEARCH, THE
CD _______ DUNCD 011
Dunkeld / Nov '89 / ADA / CM / Direct

SINGING LAND
Singing land / Desperate man / This love will carry / Kelphope glen / Another story / Bonnie woods o'Hatton / Other side / Tumbling down / Guillotine release / Goodnight and joy
CD _______ DUNCD 004
Dunkeld / Oct '93 / ADA / CM / Direct

SUNSET SONG
CD _______ DUNCD 17
Dunkeld / Oct '93 / ADA / CM / Direct

TRIBUTE
CD _______ DUNCD 020
Dunkeld / Nov '95 / ADA / CM / Direct

WHITEWASH
CD _______ DUNCD 010
Dunkeld / Jul '90 / ADA / CM / Direct

McLean, Andy

ANDY'S THEME
Two hearts / Funny / Saliya / Take 5 and 6 / Please stay / Andy's theme / Is this for real / Make it last / Summer song / Early bird
CD _______ CALLCD 001
Callisto / Sep '94 / Timewarp

McLean, Don

AMERICAN PIE
American pie / Till tomorrow / Vincent / Crossroads / Winterwood / Empty chairs / Everybody loves me / Fatima / Grave / Babylon
CD _______ CDFA 3023
Fame / May '88 / EMI

BEST OF DON MCLEAN
American pie / Castles in the air / Dreidel / Winterwood / Everyday / Sister Fatima / Empty chairs / Birthday song / Wonderful baby / La la I love you / Vincent / Crossroads / And I love you so / Fools paradise / If we try / Mountains of Mourne / Grave / Respectable / Going for the gold / Crying
CD _______ CDMTL 1065
EMI Manhattan / Dec '91 / EMI

DON MCLEAN
If we try / Narcissima / Dreidel / Bronco Bill's lament / Birthday song / Pride parade / More you pay (The more it's worth) / Falling through time / On the Amazon / Oh my what a shame
CD _______ BGOCD 246
Beat Goes On / Mar '95 / Pinnacle

HOMELESS BROTHER
Winter has me in its grip / La la means I love you / Homeless brother / Sunshine life for me / Legend of Andrew McCrew / Wonderful baby / You have lived / Great big man / Tangled / Crying in the chapel / Did you know
CD _______ BGOCD 247
Beat Goes On / Oct '94 / Pinnacle

PLAYIN' FAVORITES
Mule skinner blues / Bill Cheatham = Old Joe Clark / Love O love / Fool's paradise / Mountain's O'Mourne / Lovesick blues / Sitting on top the world / Ancient history / Everyday / Over the mountains / Living with the blues / Happy trails
CD _______ BGOCD 21
Beat Goes On / Apr '95 / Pinnacle

RIVER OF LOVE, THE
CD _______ CURCD 19
Curb / Nov '95 / Grapevine/PolyGram

SOLO
Magdalene lane / Masters of war / Wonderful baby / Where were you baby / Empty chairs / Geordie's lost his penker / Babylon / I love you so / Mactavish is dead / Cripple creek/Muleskinner blues / Great big man / Bronco Bill's lament / Happy trails / Circus song / Birthday song / On the Amazon / American pie / Over the waterfall/Arkansas traveller / Homeless brother / Castles in the air / Three flights up / Lovesick blues / Winter has me in it's grip / Legend of Andrew McCrew / Dreidel / Vincent / Till tomorrow
CD _______ BGOCD 300
Beat Goes On / Sep '95 / Pinnacle

TAPESTRY
Castles in the air / General store / Magdalene Lane / Tapestry / Respectable / Orphans of wealth / Three flights up / I love you so / Bad girl / Circus song / No reason for your dreams
CD _______ BGOCD 232
Beat Goes On / Jun '94 / Pinnacle

McLean, Jackie

DEMON'S DANCE
Toyland / Boo Ann's grand / Sweet love of mine / Floogeh / Message from Trane / Demon's dance
CD _______ CDP 7843452
Blue Note / Feb '97 / EMI

DR. JACKIE (McLean, Jackie Quartet)
CD _______ SCCD 36005
Steeplechase / Oct '90 / Discovery / Impetus

HAT TRICK
Little Malonae / Cottage for sale / Solar / Bag's groove / Will you still be mine / Left alone / Jackie's hat / Sentimental journey / Bluesnik
CD _______ CDP 8383632
Blue Note / Oct '96 / EMI

JACKIE MAC ATTACK (Jackie McLean Live)
Cyclical / Song for my Queen / Dance little mandissa / Minor march / 'Round midnight / Five
CD _______ 5192702
Birdology / May '92 / PolyGram

JACKIE'S BLUES BAG (A Tribute To Jackie McLean) (Various Artists)
CD _______ HIBD 8015
Hip Bop / Mar '97 / Koch / Silva Screen

LET FREEDOM RING
Melody for Melonae / I'll keep loving you / Rene / Omega
CD _______ BNZ 58
Blue Note / May '87 / EMI

LIGHTS OUT (McLean, Jackie Quintet)
Lights out / Up 4:44 / Lorraine / Foggy day / Kerplunk / Inding
CD _______ OJCCD 426
Original Jazz Classics / Jun '96 / Complete/ Pinnacle / Jazz Music / Wellard

NEW AND OLD GOSPEL
Lifeline / Offering / Midway / Vernzone / Inevitable end / Old gospel / Strange as it seems
CD _______ CDP 8533562
Blue Note / Nov '96 / EMI

NEW YORK CALLING
CD _______ SCCD 31023
Steeplechase / Jul '88 / Discovery / Impetus

RHYTHM OF THE EARTH
Rhythm of the Earth / For hofsa / Sirius system / Explorers / Oh children rise / Osyris returns / Collective expression / Dark castle
CD _______ 5139162
Birdology / Apr '92 / PolyGram

SWING SWANG SWINGIN'
What's new / Let's face the music and dance / Stablemates / I remember you / I love you / I'll take romance / 116th and Lennox
CD _______ CDP 8565822
Blue Note / Jun '97 / EMI

McLean, John

MEN ARE LOVERS TOO
Life after you / Can't hold on / Time for love / Playboy / Love at first sight / Spreading rumours / Proud to be your lover / Never risk / We both belong to someone else / Dedication of love
CD _______ ARICD 104
Ariwa Sounds / Oct '94 / Jet Star / SRD

MacLellan, Colin

WORLD'S GREATEST PIPERS VOL.11, THE
2/4 Marches / Strathspeys and reels / Retreat marches / 6/8 Marches / Slow air and jigs / March, strathspey and reel / Hornpipes / Slow air / Strathspeys and reels / Piobaireachd
CD _______ LCOM 5219
Lismor / Jan '93 / ADA / Direct / Duncans / Lismor

MacLellan, John A.

SCOTTISH BAGPIPES (MacLellan, Pipe Major John A.)
CD _______ OSS 113CD
Ossian / Apr '94 / ADA / CM / Direct / Highlander

MacLennan, Ken

HIGHLAND TEMPEST (MacLennan, Ken & Storm)
Tempest reel no.1 / Golden dream / Bealach na spainnteach (spaniard's pass) / Skye boat song / Laid to rest/thunder reel / She moved thro' the fair / Hornpipe suite / Scandinavian mist / Tempest reel no.2 / Highland storm
CD _______ MOICD 011
Moidart / Dec '96 / Conifer/BMG

McLennan, Grant

FIREBOY
CD _______ BBQCD 127
Beggars Banquet / Mar '93 / RTM/Disc / Warner Music

HORSEBREAKER STAR
CD _______ BEGA 162CD
Beggars Banquet / Sep '95 / RTM/Disc / Warner Music

SIMONE & PERRY
CD _______ BBQ 57CD
Beggars Banquet / Jun '95 / RTM/Disc / Warner Music

WATERSHED
When word gets around / Haven't I been a fool / Haunted house / Stones for you / Easy come, easy go / Black mule / Putting the wheel back on / You can't have everything / Sally's revolution / Broadway bride / Just get that straight / Dream about tomorrow
CD _______ BEGACD 118
Beggars Banquet / Jun '91 / RTM/Disc / Warner Music

MacLeod, Donald

NEW YORK RECORDINGS 1967, THE
Cock of the North/The Campbell's are coming/Pibroch of Donal / Devil in the kitchen/ Craig-a-Bodich/Louden's bonnie Woods an / Reel of Tulloch/High road to Linton/Mrs. MacLeod of Raasay / Cronan (na Callaich)/ An Island lullaby/The man from Skye / 79th's farewell to Gibraltar/The Atholl and Breadalbane Gath / Donald Dugal MacKay / Colonel Robertson/Leaving Port Askaig / Lochaber no more/Banks of the lossie / Wee Highland laddie/Meeting of the waters/ Hen's march / Irish washerwife/Pipe Major George Allan / Donald MacLellan of Rothesay/Delvinside/Miss Proud / Invercharrow Highland gathering / All the blue bonnets over the border / Cronan na Caillach / Susan MacLeod/Thompson's dirk / Malcolm Ferguson/MacKenzie of Torridon / Mist covered mountains/My home/Mairi's wedding / Dolan's ass/Lord Panmure's march / Highland Brigade at Waterloo / Dr. Ross's 50th welcome to the Argyllshire Gathering / Pretty Dirk
CD _______ LCOM 8004
Lismor / Oct '96 / ADA / Direct / Duncans / Lismor

MacLeod, Doug

AIN'T THE BLUES EVIL
CD _______ VCD 3409
Volt / Apr '92 / Pinnacle

COME TO FIND
CD _______ AQ 1027
Audioquest / May '95 / ADA / New Note/ Pinnacle

NO ROAD BACK HOME
CD _______ HCD 8002
Hightone / Jun '94 / ADA / Koch

MacLeod, Jim

CEILIDH
CD _______ CDITV 604
Scotdisc / Oct '95 / Conifer/BMG / Duncans / Ross

JIM MACLEOD'S ALLSTAR SCOTTISH DANCE BAND (MacLeod, Jim Allstar Band)
Amazing grace / Scotland the brave / Bonnie Dundee / Loch Lomond / Ballad of Glencoe / Bluebell polka / Dark island / Black bear / Dashing white Sergeant
CD _______ CDITV 615
Scotdisc / Oct '96 / Conifer/BMG / Duncans / Ross

JIM MACLEOD'S DANCE PARTY FAVOURITES
Bluebell polka / Will you save the last dance just for me / Just for old times sake / Come by the hills / Dashing white sergeant / Dashing white sergeant (encore) / Do you think you could love me again / Amazing grace / Pittenweem Jo / Shetland reels / Cruising down the river / Loch Lomond / After all these years / Gay Gordons / Gay Gordons (encore) / Leaving Dundee / Shufflin' Sammy
CD _______ CD ITV 422
Scotdisc / Dec '86 / Conifer/BMG / Duncans / Ross

JIM MACLEOD'S HOGMANAY PARTY
Auld lang syne / Gay Gordons / Waltz / Strip the willow / Whistle and I'll dance / Bonnie lass o'Bon Accord / St. Bernard's waltz / Dashing white sergeant / My love is like a red red rose / Pipe selection / Barn dance / Crooked bawbee / Military two step
CD _______ CD ITV 444
Scotdisc / Dec '87 / Conifer/BMG / Duncans / Ross

LAND OF MACLEOD, THE (MacLeod, Jim & His Band)
CD _______ CDITV 548
Scotdisc / Aug '91 / Conifer/BMG / Duncans / Ross

PLAY SELECTED SCOTTISH COUNTRY DANCES (MacLeod, Jim & His Band)
CD _______ CDITV 491
Scotdisc / Oct '89 / Conifer/BMG / Duncans / Ross

ROAD AND MILES, THE (MacLeod, Jim & His Band)
CD _______ CDITV 583
Scotdisc / Nov '94 / Conifer/BMG / Duncans / Ross

SCOTTISH TOUR, A (MacLeod, Jim & His Band)
CD _______ CDITV 565
Scotdisc / Aug '93 / Conifer/BMG / Duncans / Ross

WELCOME TO MY WORLD
CD _______ CDITV 461
Scotdisc / Nov '89 / Conifer/BMG / Duncans / Ross

MacLeod, John

MACLEOD OF DUNVEGAN
Scots wha hae / Ae fond kiss / Birlinn ghoraidh chro'bhain / Barbara Allen / Bonnie Strathyre / Mo nighean chiuin donn / Ca' the yowes / Bonnie Earl O'Moray / Ho ro mo nighean donn bhoid heach / Mary Macneil / Maiden of Morven / Cha tillmaccrimmon / Foot of Benachie / O my love is like a red red rose / Mo run geal dileas / O'er the moor / Loch Lomond / Soiriidh / Skye boat song / Tog orm mo phiob
CD _______ LCOM 5206
Lismor / Mar '92 / ADA / Direct / Duncans / Lismor

MacLeod, Roderick J.

WORLD'S GREATEST PIPERS VOL.6, THE
Donald MacLean of Lewis / Portree Bay / Balmoral castle / John Mackenzie of Garrynahine / Stirling Castle / Farmer's daughter / Piper & the dairymaid / Be sid an gille truagh / Se siabost as boidliche leau / Donella Beaton / Turf lodge / Willie Gray's farewell to the Glasgow police / Donald MacLean's farewell to Oban / Train journey north / Crossing the Minch / Brigadier General Ronald Cheape of Tiroran / Piper's bonnet / Charlie's welcome / James MacLellan's favourite / Tenpenny bit / I ha'e a wife of my ain / Brose & butter / Grinder / Arniston Castle / Lady Mackenzie of Gareloch / Sheepwife / Broadford Bay / Mull of the mountains / Mo chuachag Laghach Thu / Irish traditional reel / Reel of Tulloch / Piobaireachd
CD _______ LCOM 5177
Lismor / Aug '96 / ADA / Direct / Duncans / Lismor

McLeod, Bobby

GENUINE ARTICLE, THE
Highland two step / Strathspeys / Waltz / Irish two step / Pride of Erin / Party pieces / Traditional selection / Traditional polka / Waltz valeta / Dunoon barn dance / Kerrera polka / Eva three step
CD _______________ LCOM 5127
Lismor / Nov '96 / ADA / Direct / Duncans / Lismor

McLeod, Enos 'Genius'

ENOS IN DUB
CD _______________ CEND 2004
Century / Oct '96 / Shellshock/Disc

GENIUS OF ENOS, THE
CD _______________ PSCD 008
Pressure Sounds / Mar '96 / Jet Star / SRD

GOODIES BEST
CD _______________ CEND 2003
Century / Oct '96 / Shellshock/Disc

RAM JAM PARTY
Ram jam party / Lipstick on my collar / I'm just a man / Beat of my heart / Tear drop / Satta a masagana / Tell you goodbye / Sweet sexy / Always / Dancehall style / Making love / Wish he didn't trust me so much / Puppet on a string / Woman at the house / Cash and carry / Headmistress
CD _______________ PRCD 606
President / Sep '96 / Grapevine/PolyGram / President / Target/BMG

McLeod, Rory

ANGRY LOVE
Farewell welfare / Shirley's her name / Stop the apartheid fascists / Pauline's song / Wind is getting stronger / Angry love / Walking towards each other / Passing the pain down / Criminals of hunger
CD _______________ COOKCD 051
Cooking Vinyl / Feb '95 / Vital

FOOTSTEPS AND HEARTBEATS
Love like a rock (in a stormy sea) / Till I don't know who I am / Collectorman / Moments shared / Wandering fool / Take me home / Singing copper / Kind of loneliness / Mariachis love song
CD _______________ COOKCD 018
Cooking Vinyl / Feb '95 / Vital

KICKING THE SAWDUST
Baksheesh dance / Huge sky / Rip Van Winkle / Kicking the sawdust / Dad's dance song / Sssh baby / Interrogations and confessions / Dance of measureless love / Hug you like a mountain / In the ghetto of our love / When children starve in peacetime / Strangers / Everything is provocative / Immaculate deception / Ambitious to love you / Harmonkikas dreams / Last tree / Divorcee blues / Old brigades song / Commentator cried / Hymn for her
CD _______________ COOKCD 067
Cooking Vinyl / Mar '94 / Vital

LULLABY'S FOR BIG BABIES
Be my rambling woman / Big eyes / Ballad of Spitalfields market / Night watchman / Forigner forever / Grandma's grave / Tea martoonies / Come with me when I go / Looking for you / Laredo / Punchinello's confession / Body search / Long lost friend / My two feet carry me home / Horse radish / Let him go
CD _______________ COOKCD 125
Cooking Vinyl / Jun '97 / Vital

TRAVELLING HOME
CD _______________ COOKCD 048
Cooking Vinyl / Feb '95 / Vital

McLeod, Zan

RING SESSIONS, THE (McLeod, Zan & James Kelly)
CD _______________ SPIN 99CD
Spin / Jan '96 / ADA / Direct

McLoughlin, Noel

20 BEST OF IRELAND
CD _______________ EUCD 1079
ARC / '89 / ADA / ARC Music

20 BEST OF SCOTLAND
CD _______________ EUCD 1080
ARC / '89 / ADA / ARC Music

BEST OF IRELAND
CD _______________ EUCD 1111
ARC / '91 / ADA / ARC Music

CHRISTMAS AND WINTER SONGS FROM IRELAND
CD _______________ EUCD 1086
ARC / '91 / ADA / ARC Music

MacLure, Pinkie

FAVOURITE
CD _______________ PILLCD 7
Placebo / May '95 / RTM/Disc

THIS DIRTY LIFE
CD _______________ BND 5 CD
One Little Indian / Feb '90 / Pinnacle

McMahan, Ken

KEN MCMAHAN & SLUMPY BOY
CD _______________ DFGCD 8434
Dixie Frog / Jun '96 / Direct / TKO Magnum

MacMahon, Tony

I GCNOC NA GRAI (MacMahon, Tony & Noel Hill)
CD _______________ CEFCD 114
Gael Linn / Jan '94 / ADA / CM / Direct / Grapevine/PolyGram / Roots

TONY MACMAHON
CD _______________ SHCD 34006
Claddagh / May '93 / ADA / CM / Direct

TRADITIONAL IRISH ACCORDION
CD _______________ CEFCD 033
Gael Linn / Jan '94 / ADA / CM / Direct / Grapevine/PolyGram / Roots

McManus, Ross

ELVIS' DAD SINGS ELVIS
Blue suede shoes / Suspicious minds / All shook up / Don't cry daddy / It's now or never / Hound dog / (Let me be your) teddy bear / In the ghetto / Heartbreak hotel / Love me tender / If I can dream / Jailhouse rock
CD _______________ 306602
Hallmark / Jun '97 / Carlton

McManus, Tony

TONY MCMANUS
Doherty's / Return to Milltown / Tommy Peoples / Sweetness of Mary / Piper's bonnet / Emigrant's farewell / Flanagan Brothers jig / Dermot Byrnes / Miss Sarah Mcfadyen / Jackie Coleman's / Millner's daughter / Rakish Paddy / Connor Dunn's / Breizh / Duck / Seagull / Humours of Barrack Street / Letterkenny blacksmith / Ar bhruach na laoi / Snowy path / Harper's chair / Gavotte de marcel / Dans fisel / Hector the hero / Girls at Martinfield / Johnstown reel / What a wonderful world / Charlie Hunter's / Humours of Tulla
CD _______________ CDTRAX 096
Greentrax / Dec '95 / ADA / Direct / Duncans / Highlander

MacMaster, Natalie

COMPILATION, A
CD _______________ CDTRAX 140
Greentrax / Jul '97 / ADA / Direct / Duncans / Highlander

FIT AS A FIDDLE
John Campbell's/Miss Ann Moir's birthday / Lady Georgina Campbell/Angus on the turnpike/Sheehan's reel / My Dungannon sweetheart/Scaffies Cairet/Juniper jig / Carnival march / Miller of Drone/MacKinnon's brook / Lucy Campbell/Annie is my darling/ Gordon Cote/Bird's nest / Man behind the bar/Nancy's waltz / Compliments to Sean Maguire / President Garfield/Miss Watt/ Casa Loma Castle / O'r the moor among the heather / Traditional/Lady Mary Ramsay / Jenny Dang the weaver/Lassies of Stewarton/Garfield Vale / Jean's reel / I'll always remember you / Girls at Martinfield/ Bennets favorite/Greenfields of Glentow / Counselor's/Rakes of Kildare/The lark in the morning / Lass of Carrie Mills/Lennox's love to Blantyre / Archie Menzies/Reichwall Forest / If ever you were mine / MacNeil's of Ugadale / MacLaine of Loch Buie/Colville's rant/Pibroch O'Donal Dhu
CD _______________ NMAS 1972CD
CBC Maritimes / Jul '95 / ADA
CD _______________ CDTRAX 141
Greentrax / Jul '97 / ADA / Direct / Duncans / Highlander
CD _______________ ROUCD 7022
Rounder / Mar '97 / ADA / CM / Direct

NO BOUNDARIES
Honeysuckle set / My friend Buddy / Fiddle and bow / Reel Beatrice / Paddy LeBlanc's set / Silver wells / Drunken piper / Catharsis / Where's Howie / Bill Crawford's set / Beaumont rag / Autograph / Rev Archie Beaton
CD _______________ ROUCD 7023
CD _______________ CDTRAX 142
Greentrax / Aug '97 / ADA / Direct / Duncans / Highlander

MacMathuna, Padraic

HIVES OF HONEYED SOUND
CD _______________ CEFCD 157
Gael Linn / Jan '94 / ADA / CM / Direct / Grapevine/PolyGram / Roots

McMeen, El

IRISH GUITAR ENCORES
CD _______________ SHCD 97017
Shanachie / Apr '92 / ADA / Greensleeves / Koch

OF SOUL AND SPIRIT
CD _______________ SHCD 97012
Shanachie / Jun '91 / ADA / Greensleeves / Koch

McMurdo, Dave

LIVE AT MONTREAL BISTRO (McMurdo, Dave Jazz Orchestra)
CD _______________ SKCD 22029
Sackville / Jun '93 / Cadillac / Jazz Music / Swift

McMurty, James

IT HAD TO HAPPEN
CD _______________ SCHD1058
Sugar Hill / Jul '97 / ADA / CM / Direct / Koch / Roots

McNabb, Ian

HEAD LIKE A ROCK
Fire inside my soul / You must be prepared to dream / Child inside a father / Still got the fever / Potency / Go into the light / As a life goes by / Sad strange solitary catholic mystic / This time is forever / May you always
CD _______________ IMCD 233
Island / Sep '96 / PolyGram

MERSEYBEAST
Merseybeast / Affirmation / Beautiful old mystery / Love's young dream / Camaraderie / Don't put your spell on me / Heydays / Little bit of magic / You stone my soul / Too close to the sun / They settled for less than they wanted / I'm a genius / Available light / Merseybeast (reprise)
CD _______________ 5242152
This Way Up / Apr '96 / PolyGram / SRD

MERSEYBEAST/NORTH WEST COAST (2CD Set)
CD Set _______________ 5242402
This Way Up / May '96 / PolyGram / SRD

TRUTH AND BEAUTY
(I go) My own way / These are the days / Great dreams of heaven / Truth and beauty / I'm game / If love was like guitars / Story of my life / That's why I believe / Trip with me / Make love to you / Presence of the one
CD _______________ 5143782
Phonogram / Jan '93 / PolyGram

McNally, James

EVERYBREATH
Black is the colour / Woman's heart / I still haven't found what I'm looking for / Bandia/ Homes of Donegal/Island / Everybreath you take / Mo gra / Song for Ireland/Coming home / Irish boy / Fairytale of New York / Lonesome boatman 2000 / Foggy dew / Raglan road / Isle of Innisfree / Sheas mo chroa / Belfast child / Saviour
CD _______________ 74321443722
RCA / Jul '97 / BMG

McNally, John

EVERGREENS
Galway bay / When Irish eyes are smiling / If I only had time / Danny boy / Bless this house / He ain't heavy he's my brother / I'll walk with God / Morning has broken / Mary in the morning / Song of joy / I believe / May each day / He'll have to go / Impossible dream / Croppy boy / I'll take you home again Kathleen / You light up my life / And I love her / You don't bring me flowers / Evergreen
CD _______________ EMPRCD 561
Emporio / Mar '95 / Disc

McNally, Larry John

VIBROLUX
CD _______________ DIGIT 5679152
Dig It / Jun '96 / ADA / Direct

MacNamara, Mary

TRADITIONAL MUSIC FROM EAST CLARE
Cailleach an airgid / Kerfunten jig / Rolling in the barrel / Tap room / Earl's chair / Humours of Tullycrine / Mikey Callaghan's / Pigeon on the gate / Lad O'Beirne's / John Naughton's / Reel with the birl / Paddy Lynn's delight / Connie Hogan's / Kitty goes milking / Killavil jig / Have a drink with me / Toss the feathers / Boys of Ballisodare / Fisherman's lilt / My love is in America / Rooms of Doogh / Walls of Liscarroll / Caoilte mountains / Green gowned lass / John Naughton's jigs / McGreevy's favourite / Miss McGuinness / Sweetheart reel / Maghera mountain / Huomours of Castlefin / Glen of Ahelow / Killarney boys of pleasure
CD _______________ CC 60CD
Claddagh / Oct '94 / ADA / CM / Direct

MacNamara, Paddy

IRISH PARTY
CD _______________ SOW 90124
Sounds Of The World / Apr '94 / Target/ BMG

MacNamara, Pat

TWO SIDES OF PAT MAC, THE
CD _______________ GTDCD 006
GTD / Jan '95 / ADA / Else

McNaughtan, Adam

LAST STAND AT MOUNT FLORIDA
Dear green place / Cholesterol / You've got to get your folios done / Scottish song / Soor mulk cairt / Shy lover / Old man Noah / Green belongs to Glasgow's folk / Weaver's lament / Coming hame/My grandfather's socks / Thomas Muir of Huntershill / Erchie Cathcairt / Twin-towered stand
CD _______________ CDTRAX 120
Greentrax / Sep '96 / ADA / Direct / Duncans / Highlander

McNaughton's Vale Of Atoll ...

LIVE 'N' WELL (McNaughton's Vale Of Atoll Pipe Band)
Il paco grande / Showaco set / Inveran set / MacCrimmon will never return set / Gargoyles set / Dugald NcColl's set / France set / Nameless piobaireachd set / Molendinar - The Wellpark Suite Set / Maclain of Glencoe / Smeceno horo set / Bu deonach leam tilleadh set / Steam train to Mallaig / Eileen Mary Connolly set / Il Paco grande (Encore)
CD _______________ CDTRAX 111
Greentrax / Jul '96 / ADA / Direct / Duncans / Highlander

McNeely, 'Big' Jay

BLUES AT DAYBREAK (McNeel, Big Jay & C. Rannenberg)
CD _______________ BEST 1018CD
Acoustic Music / Nov '93 / ADA

McNeely, James

LIVE AT MAYBECK RECITAL HALL VOL.20
There will never be another you / Zingaro / Bye ya / 'Round midnight / Touch / All the things you are / Body and soul / Breaking up breaking out
CD _______________ CCD 4522
Concord Jazz / Sep '92 / New Note/ Pinnacle

PLOT THICKENS, THE
CD _______________ MCD 5378
Muse / Sep '92 / New Note/Pinnacle

RAIN'S DANCE
CD _______________ SCCD 31412
Steeplechase / Jul '97 / Discovery / Impetus

MacNeil, Flora

CRAOBH NAN UBHAL
CD _______________ COMD 1002
Temple / Jan '94 / ADA / CM / Direct / Duncans / Highlander

MacNeil, Rita

FLYING ON YOUR OWN
Flying on your own / Neon city / She's called Nova Scotia / Baby baby / Leave her memory / Fast train to Tokyo / Everybody / Used to you / Loser (when it comes to love) / Realised your dreams
CD _______________ 8434232
Polydor / Jul '92 / PolyGram

HOME I'LL BE
CD _______________ 5112772
Polydor / Jul '92 / PolyGram

REASON TO BELIEVE
Walk on through / Two steps from broken / City child / Doors of the cemetary / Reason to believe / When the loving is through / Causing the fall / Music's going round again / Sound your own horn / Working man / Good friends
CD Set _______________ D 5177793
LPO / Oct '94 / Total/BMG

WORKING MAN (The Best Of Rita MacNeil)
CD _______________ 5178612
Polydor / Sep '90 / PolyGram

McNeil, John

EMBARKATION (McNeil, John Quintet)
CD _______________ SCCD 31099
Steeplechase / Oct '95 / Discovery / Impetus

THINGS WE DID LAST SUMMER
CD _______________ SCCD 31231
Steeplechase / Jul '88 / Discovery / Impetus

McNeill, Brian

BACK O' THE NORTH WIND, THE (Tales Of The Scots In America)
Back o' the North wind / Entail / Strong women rule us with their tears / Rock and the tide / Destitution road / Muir and the master builder / Atlantic reels / Best o' the barley / Ewen and the gold / Drive the golden spike / Lang Johnnie More / Steel man / Bridal boat
CD _______________ CDTRAX 047
Greentrax / Sep '91 / ADA / Direct / Duncans / Highlander

BUSKER AND THE DEVIL'S ONLY DAUGHTER, THE
CD COMD 2042
Temple / Feb '94 / ADA / CM / Direct / Duncans / Highlander

HORSES FOR COURSES
CD CDTRAX 071
Greentrax / Mar '94 / ADA / Direct / Duncans / Highlander

MONKSGATE
CD CDTRAX 062
Greentrax / May '93 / ADA / Direct / Duncans / Highlander

NO GODS
No gods and precious few heroes / Miss Michison regrets / Any Mick'll do / Drover's road / Breton wedding march / Trains and my grandfather / Tommy Sheridan's / Annie Lawson / Jocky's treble tops / Assynt crofters / Montrose / Inside the whale / Princess Augusta / Fighter / Alison Hargreaves / Veillon's / Young master Haigh / Steady as she goes / Bring back the wolf
CD CDTRAX 098
Greentrax / Dec '95 / ADA / Direct / Duncans / Highlander

NO GOODS
CD TRAX 098CD
Greentrax / Mar '96 / ADA / Direct / Duncans / Highlander

McNeir, Ronnie

LOVE SUSPECT
Love suspect / Lately / Summertime medley / Sexy Mama / Everybody's in a hurry / I'll be loving you / Follow your heart / Tying to keep my heart / Please come and be with me
CD EXCDP 1
Debut / Jun '93 / 3mv/Sony / Pinnacle

RARE MCNEIR
Baby I know / Different kind of love / Lonely superstar / Southern pearl / Ain't no woman like my baby / This is my prayer / I want to thank you / Strong for each other / Good side of your love / Your best friend and me / I'll come running back / Remember baby / I got someone
CD ATCD 024
ATR / Aug '95 / Beechwood/BMG

McNerney, Steve

SHE'S A FUNNY BLOKE (McNerney, Steve & Changing Man)
CD DOMCD 008
Public Domain / Mar '97 / RTM/Disc

McPartland, Marian

AMBIANCE
What is this thing called love / Aspen / Sounds like seven / Ambiance / Rime / Three little words / Hide and seek with the bombay bicycle club / Afterglow / Lost one / Wisdom of the heart / Glimpse
CD TJA 10029
Jazz Alliance / Feb '96 / New Note/Pinnacle

AT THE FESTIVAL
I love you / Willow weep for me / Windows / In the days of our love / Cotton tail / Here's that rainy day / On green dolphin street / Oleo
CD CCD 4118
Concord Jazz / Oct '94 / New Note/ Pinnacle

AT THE HICKORY HOUSE
I hear music / Tickle toe / Street of dreams / How long has this been going on / Let's call the whole thing off / Lush life / Mad about the boy / Love you madly / Skylark / Ja da / I've told every little star / Moon song
CD JASCD 312
Jasmine / Aug '95 / Conifer/BMG / Hot Shot / TKO Magnum

FROM THIS MOMENT ON
From this moment on / Emily / Sweet and lovely / Ambiance / You and the night and the music / If you could see me now / Lullaby of the leaves / There is no greater love / Polka dots and moonbeams
CD CCD 4086
Concord Jazz / Aug '91 / New Note/ Pinnacle

IN MY LIFE
CD CCD 4561
Concord Jazz / May '94 / New Note/ Pinnacle

LIVE AT YOSHI'S NITESPOT
Like someone in love / In a sentimental mood / Pretty woman / Come rain or shine / Shine / Straight, no chaser / Silent pool / Steeplechase / Pensativa / Bemsha swing / Warm valley / If I should lose you / Turn around
CD CCD 4712
Concord Crossover / Jul '96 / New Note/ Pinnacle

MARIAN MCPARTLAND PLAYS THE MUSIC OF ALEC WILDER
Jazz waltz for a friend / Why / While we're young / Lullaby for a lady / Inner circle / I'll be around / Trouble is a man / Homework / Where are the good companions / It's so peaceful in the country
CD TJA 10016
Jazz Alliance / Oct '92 / New Note/Pinnacle

PERSONAL CHOICE
I hear a rhapsody / Meditation / In your own sweet way / Sleepin' bee / I'm old fashioned / When the sun comes out / Tricrotism / Melancholy mood
CD CCD 4202
Concord Jazz / Mar '87 / New Note/ Pinnacle

PIANO JAZZ (McPartland, Marian & Dave Brubeck)
St. Louis blues: *McPartland, Marian* / Thank you: *McPartland, Marian* / Duke: *McPartland, Marian* / In your own sweet way: *McPartland, Marian* / One moment worth years: *McPartland, Marian* / Summer song: *McPartland, Marian* / Free piece: *McPartland, Marian* / Polytonal blues: *McPartland, Marian* / Take five: *McPartland, Marian*
CD TJA 12001
Bellaphon / Jun '93 / New Note/Pinnacle

PIANO JAZZ (McPartland, Marian & Teddy Wilson)
CD TJA 12002
Jazz Alliance / Jul '93 / New Note/ Pinnacle

PIANO JAZZ (McPartland, Marian & Dizzy Gillespie)
Con alma: *McPartland, Marian* / In a mellow tone: *McPartland, Marian* / On the alamo: *McPartland, Marian* / Manteca: *McPartland, Marian* / For Dizzy: *McPartland, Marian* / Lullaby of the leaves: *McPartland, Marian* / 'Round midnight: *McPartland, Marian* / Portrait of Diz: *McPartland, Marian* / Night in Tunisia: *McPartland, Marian*
CD TJA 12005
Jazz Alliance / Feb '94 / New Note/Pinnacle

PIANO JAZZ (McPartland, Marian & Eubie Blake)
Betty Washboard rag: *McPartland, Marian* / Valse Marion: *McPartland, Marian* / Song for Marian (Margaret): *McPartland, Marian* / You're lucky to me: *McPartland, Marian* / Charlston rag: *McPartland, Marian* / Dream rag: *McPartland, Marian* / For the last time call me sweetheart: *McPartland, Marian* / Stars and stripes forever: *McPartland, Marian* / Falling in love with someone: *McPartland, Marian* / Kiss me again: *McPartland, Marian* / St. Louis blues: *McPartland, Marian* / I'm just wild about Harry: *McPartland, Marian* / Little gypsy sweetheart: *McPartland, Marian*
CD TJA 12006
Jazz Alliance / Mar '94 / New Note/Pinnacle

PIANO JAZZ (McPartland, Marian & Dick Wellstood)
Ain't misbehavin': *McPartland, Marian* / Medley: *McPartland, Marian* / Lulu's back in town: *McPartland, Marian* / 'Deed I do: *McPartland, Marian* / Gee baby ain't I good to you: *McPartland, Marian* / Detour ahead: *McPartland, Marian* / Fine and dandy: *McPartland, Marian*
CD TJA 12007
Jazz Alliance / May '94 / New Note/Pinnacle

PIANO JAZZ (McPartland, Marian & Barbara Carroll)
Too soon: *McPartland, Marian* / My man's gone now: *McPartland, Marian* / This time the dream's on me: *McPartland, Marian* / Imagination: *McPartland, Marian* / Old friends: *McPartland, Marian* / Marbara: *McPartland, Marian* / There will never be another you: *McPartland, Marian*
CD TJA 12008
Jazz Alliance / Jun '94 / New Note/Pinnacle

PIANO JAZZ
Snapper / Come Sunday / There'll be other times / Mumbles / Simple waltz / Michelle / Memories of you / Wham
CD TJA 12009
Jazz Alliance / Aug '94 / New Note/Pinnacle

PIANO JAZZ (McPartland, Marian & Bobby Short)
Mood indigo: *McPartland, Marian* / Nobody's heart: *McPartland, Marian* / Experiment: *McPartland, Marian* / 'Round midnight: *McPartland, Marian* / I guess I'll have to change my plan: *McPartland, Marian* / Just one of those things: *McPartland, Marian* / Reflections in D: *McPartland, Marian* / My shining hour: *McPartland, Marian* / It don't mean a thing if it ain't got that swing: *McPartland, Marian*
CD TJA 12010
Jazz Alliance / Sep '94 / New Note/Pinnacle

PIANO JAZZ (McPartland, Marian & Dick Hyman)
Carousel memories: *McPartland, Marian* / Relax: *McPartland, Marian* / Handful of keys: *McPartland, Marian* / Gone with the wind: *McPartland, Marian* / Body and soul: *McPartland, Marian* / Flower is a lovesome thing: *McPartland, Marian* / This time the dream's on me: *McPartland, Marian* / Delicate balance: *McPartland, Marian* / Skylark: *McPartland, Marian* / Lover come back to me: *McPartland, Marian*
CD TJA 12012
Jazz Alliance / Nov '94 / New Note/Pinnacle

PIANO JAZZ (McPartland, Marian & Red Richards)
Have you met Miss Jones: *McPartland, Marian* / What a wonderful world: *McPartland, Marian* / Tangerine: *McPartland, Marian* / Hundred years from today: *McPartland, Marian* / Keepin' out of mischief now: *McPartland, Marian* / Echoes of spring: *McPartland, Marian* / Someday you'll be sorry: *McPartland, Marian* / Talk of the town: *McPartland, Marian* / Running wild: *McPartland, Marian*
CD TJA 12011
Jazz Alliance / Oct '94 / New Note/Pinnacle

PIANO JAZZ (McPartland, Marian & Stanley Cowell)
Top of your head blues / Stella by starlight / 'Round midnight / Juan Valdez / Watergate blues / Equipoise / You took advantage of me / God bless the child / Cherokee
CD TJA 12013
Jazz Alliance / Feb '95 / New Note/Pinnacle

PIANO JAZZ (McPartland, Marian & Mercer Ellington)
C Jam blues / Kinda dukish / Caravan / Prelude to a kiss / Chelsea bridge / Moon mist / Thing's aint' waht they used to be / Portrait of Mercer Ellington / Solitude
CD TJA 12014
Jazz Alliance / Feb '95 / New Note/Pinnacle

PIANO JAZZ (McPartland, Marian & Benny Carter)
Easy money / Faraway / Blues in my heart / Lonely woman / Only trust your heart / Evening star / Kiss from you / Key largo / Summer serenade / When lights are low
CD TJA 12015
Jazz Alliance / Feb '95 / New Note/Pinnacle

PIANO JAZZ (McPartland, Marian & Milt Hinton)
Milt's rap (MH solo): *McPartland, Marian* / All the things you are: *McPartland, Marian* / My one and only love (Duet): *McPartland, Marian* / Joshua: *McPartland, Marian* / Willow weep for me: *McPartland, Marian* / Old man time (duet): *McPartland, Marian* / These foolish things: *McPartland, Marian* / Stranger in a dream: *McPartland, Marian* / How high the moon: *McPartland, Marian*
CD TJA 12016
Jazz Alliance / Apr '95 / New Note/Pinnacle

PIANO JAZZ (McPartland, Marian & Jack DeJohnette)
Freddie freeloader / I loves you Porgy / It could happen to you / Alice in wonderland / Ambiance / Blue in green / Silver hollow / Mr. PC
CD TJA 12018
Jazz Alliance / May '95 / New Note/Pinnacle

PIANO JAZZ (McPartland, Marian & Jess Stacy)
Dancing fool / Lover man / Oh baby / Keepin' out of mischief now / Improv in A minor / Autumn of New York / I would do most anything for you / Moon mist / Heavy hearted blues / St. Louis blues
CD TJA 12017
Jazz Alliance / May '95 / New Note/Pinnacle

PIANO JAZZ (McPartland, Marian & Mary Lou Williams)
Space playing blues / Baby man / What's your story Morning Glory / Scratchin' in the gravel / Medi no 2 / Rosa Mae / Caravan / I can't get started (with you) / Jeep is jumpin' / Exit playing
CD TJA 12019
Jazz Alliance / Jul '95 / New Note/Pinnacle

PIANO JAZZ (McPartland, Marian & Kenny Burrell)
Listen to the dawn / 'Round midnight / I'm old fashioned / All too soon / Don't worry 'bout me / Spring can really hang you up the most / I'm just a lucky so and so / Raincheck
CD TJA 12021
Jazz Alliance / Aug '95 / New Note/Pinnacle

PIANO JAZZ (McPartland, Marian & Amina Claudine)
B I / Mood indigo / Windows / So what / Call him / Do you wanna be saved / Free impro / Have mercy upon us / Portrait of Amina / Sonnymoon for two
CD TJA 12022
Jazz Alliance / Oct '95 / New Note/Pinnacle

PIANO JAZZ (McPartland, Marian & Dave McKenna)
Cat's cradle / Theodore the thumper / Just the way you are / I'm a fool to want you / Let's get away from it all / My cherie amour / All in love is fair / Isn't she lovely / I'll never be the same / Struttin' with some barbeque
CD TJA 12023
Jazz Alliance / Nov '95 / New Note/Pinnacle

PIANO JAZZ (McPartland, Marian & Henry Mancini)
Two for the road / Meggie's theme / Pink Panther / Mr. Lucky / Dreamsville / Charade / Baby elephant walk / Moon river / Days of wine and roses
CD TJA 12024
Jazz Alliance / Dec '95 / New Note/Pinnacle

PIANO JAZZ (McPartland, Marian & Roy Eldridge)
Fast booie / Ball of fire / Une petite laitue / Rockin' chair / I want a little girl / Indian summer / M & R Blues
CD TJA 12025
Jazz Alliance / Feb '96 / New Note/Pinnacle

PIANO JAZZ (McPartland, Marian & Lee Konitz)
I'm gettin' sentimental over you / All the things you are / Stella by starlight / In your own sweet way / Body and soul / Tactile talk / Little girl blue / Naima / Like someone in love
CD TJA 12026
Jazz Alliance / Feb '96 / New Note/Pinnacle

PIANO JAZZ (McPartland, Marian & Joe Williams)
Who she do / Embraceable you / Twilight world / I'm confessin' that I love you / Prelude to a kiss / Nobody's heart / Just friends / I'm beginning to see the light
CD TJA 12027
Jazz Alliance / Mar '96 / New Note/Pinnacle

PIANO JAZZ (McPartland, Marian & Oscar Peterson)
Old folks / Place St Henri / Like someone in love / Body and soul / Emily / Take the 'A' train / Falling in love with love / Willow creek / Cotton tail
CD TJA 12028
Jazz Alliance / Apr '96 / New Note/Pinnacle

PIANO JAZZ (McPartland, Marian & Lionel Hampton)
Teach me tonight / Sweet Georgia Brown / Midnight sun / How high the moon / What's new / Mack the knife / Flyin' home
CD TJA 12029
Jazz Alliance / May '96 / New Note/Pinnacle

PIANO JAZZ (McPartland, Marian & Jay McShann)
Vine Street boogie / Georgia on my mind / 'Deed I do / Living back street for you / My chile / Tain't nobody's bizness if I do / What's your story morning glory / Confessin' the blues / Oh lady be good
CD TJA 12030
Jazz Alliance / Jun '96 / New Note/Pinnacle

PIANO JAZZ (McPartland, Marian & Charles Brown)
These blues / All my life / Is you is or is you ain't my baby / Drifting blues / There is no greater love / 'Round midnight / Sweet slumber / Joyce's boogie / Seven long days
CD TJA 12032
Jazz Alliance / Sep '96 / New Note/Pinnacle

PIANO JAZZ (McPartland, Marian & Les McCann)
Every time I see a butterfly / Prince of peace / Marian and Les together / Just squeeze me / My funny valentine / With these hands / Bill Evans / Why / Compared to what
CD TJA 12031
Jazz Alliance / Oct '96 / New Note/Pinnacle

PLAYS THE BENNY CARTER SONG BOOK
When lights are low / I'm in the mood for swing / Kiss from you / Key largo / Another time another place / Summer serenade / Doozy / Lonely woman / Only trust your heart / Evening star / Easy money
CD CCD 4412
Concord Jazz / Jun '90 / New Note/ Pinnacle

PLAYS THE MUSIC OF BILLY STRAYHORN
Intimacy of the blues / Isfahan / Lotus blossom / Raincheck / Lush life / UMMG / Flower is a lovesome thing / Take the 'A' train / Daydream / After all
CD CCD 4326
Concord Jazz / Oct '87 / New Note/ Pinnacle

PLAYS THE MUSIC OF MARY LOU WILLIAMS
Scratchin' the gravel / Lonely moments / What's your story Morning Glory / Easy blues / Threnody (a lament) / It's a grand night for swingin' / In the land of Oo-Bla-Dee / Dirge blues / Koolbonga / Walkin' and swingin' / Cloudy / My blue heaven / Mary's waltz / St. Martin de Porres
CD CCD 4605
Concord Jazz / Jul '94 / New Note/Pinnacle

PORTRAIT OF MARIAN MCPARTLAND
CD CCD 4101
Concord Jazz / Oct '91 / New Note/ Pinnacle

SENTIMENTAL JOURNEY, A (McPartland, Marian & Jimmy)
Royal garden blues / Sentimental journey / Blue prelude / Dinah / Basin Street blues / When you wish upon a star / Avalon / Perdido / Willow weep for me / I'm gonna sit right down and write myself a letter / Polka dots and moonbeams / Wolverine blues
CD TJA 10025
Jazz Alliance / Oct '94 / New Note/Pinnacle

SILENT POOL (McPartland, Marian & Strings)
For Dizzy / Twilight world / Stranger in a dream / Delicate balance / Ambiance / Silent pool / Castles in the sand / Melancholy mood / Threnody / Time and time again / There'll be other times / With you in mind
CD CCD 47452
Concord Jazz / Feb '97 / New Note/ Pinnacle

McPhatter, Clyde

BEST OF CLYDE MCPHATTER, THE
CD RSACD 812
Sequel / Oct '94 / BMG

LOVE BALLADS
Heartaches / Come what may / Rock and cry: *McPhatter, Clyde & Ruth Brown* / That's enough for me / I gotta have you / Just to hold my hand / Long lonely nights / When you're sincere / No matter what / No love like her / You'll be there / Love has joined us together: *McPhatter, Clyde & Ruth Brown* / Go yes go / Let me know / Just give me a ring / I can believe
CD RSACD 802
Sequel / Nov '96 / BMG

MacPhee, Catherine-Anne

CANAN NAN GAIDHEAL
Hi ri rio ra ill o / Nighean nan geug taladh / Puirt a buel / Soiridh leis a' bhreacan ur / Iomair thusa, choinnich chridhe / Ca' nan gaidheal / 'S fliuch an oidhche / Onan an Iolaire / Cearcall a' chuain / Ataireach ard
CD CDTRAX 009
Greentrax / May '93 / ADA / Direct / Duncans / Highlander

CHI MI'N GEAMHRADH (I SEE WINTER)
Chi mi'n geamhradh / Chaidh mo dhunnchadh dha'n bheinn / Oh hi ri lean / Bidh clann ulaidh / Mile marbhphaisg air a' ghaol / Seathan bu deonach leam tilleadh / 'S muladach mi 's mi air m'aineol / Bothan airigh am braigh rainneach / Tha na h-uain air an tulaich / Na libh o ho I
CD CDTRAX 038
Greentrax / Apr '91 / ADA / Direct / Duncans / Highlander

SINGS MAIRI MHOR
Nuair bha mi og / Coinneamh nan croiteran / Eilean a cheo / Soraidh leis an nollaig uir / Soraidh le eilean a'cheo / Oran beinn / Camanachd glaschu / Oran sarachaidh / Clach agus mairi / Luchd na beurla / Mar a tha / Faistneachd agus / Beannachd di na caidheil
CD CDTRAX 070
Greentrax / Jun '94 / ADA / Direct / Duncans / Highlander

McPhee, Joe

AT WBAI'S 1971 (McPhee, Joe & Survival Unit 11)
CD ARTCD 6197
Hat Art / Feb '97 / Cadillac / Harmonia Mundi

IMPRESSIONS OF JIMMY GIUFFRE (McPhee, Joe Trio)
CD CELPC 21
CELP / Jan '93 / Cadillac / Harmonia Mundi

LINEAR B (McPhee, Joe PO Music)
CD ARTCD 6057
Hat Art / Dec '91 / Cadillac / Harmonia Mundi

OLD EYES AND MYSTERIES (McPhee, Joe PO Music)
CD ARTCD 6047
Hat Art / Apr '92 / Cadillac / Harmonia Mundi

SWEET FREEDOM - NOW WHAT
CD ARTCD 6162
Hat Art / Sep '95 / Cadillac / Harmonia Mundi

McPhee, Tony

BLEACHING THE BLUES
When you're down / All your women / There's a light / Went in like a lamb / When your man has gone / Many times / All last night / When you're walking down the street / Meeting of the minds / Bleaching the blues / If I had possession / Love in vain / Floatin' bridge / Terraplane blues / Little red rooster
CD HTDCD 72
HTD / Apr '97 / CM / Pinnacle

FOOLISH PRIDE
Foolish pride / Every minute / Devil you know / Masqueradin' / Time after time / On the run / Took me by suprise / Whatever it takes / Been there, done that / I'm gonna win
CD HTDCD 10
HTD / Sep '96 / CM / Pinnacle

ME AND THE DEVIL/I ASKED FOR WATER, SHE GAVE ME GASOLINE
Rollin' and tumblin' / Duckin' and dodgin' / Death letter / Elevator woman / Make me a pallat / Heartstruck sorrow / When you got a good friend / Me and the devil / You better mind / Hard time killing floor / Same thing on my mind / Broke down engine / Arkansas woman / No more doggin' / Buy you a diamond ring / Oh death / She's gone / Factory blues / Boogie woman / Nervous / Crazy with the blues / Lord I feel tired / Gasoline / Rock me / London's got the blues / Love's in vain / Dust my blues / Built my hopes too high / Don't pass the hat around / When my woman is with me / I'm so tired
CD BGOCD 332
Beat Goes On / Dec '96 / Pinnacle

SLIDE T.S. SLIDE
Reformed man / Mean disposition / Slide to slide / From a pawn to a King / Tell me baby / Hooker 'n' The Hogs / Someday baby / Driving duck / No place to go / Me and the devil
CD HTDCD 26
HTD / Sep '96 / CM / Pinnacle

WHO SAID CHERRY RED (McPhee, Tony & The Groundhogs)
Rocking chair / Man trouble / Married men / BDD / Times / Natchez burning / Status people / Rich man, poor man / Darkness is no friend / Junkman / Year in the life / Sad is the hunter / Earth shanty / Mr. Hooker Sir John
CD IGOCD 2058
Indigo / Oct '96 / ADA / Direct

MacPherson, Donald

MASTER PIPER, THE
CD LCDM 9013
Lismor / '90 / ADA / Direct / Duncans / Lismor

MacPherson, Fraser

ELLINGTON 1987
CD SKCD 22043
Sackville / Jan '97 / Cadillac / Jazz Music / Swift

ENCORE (MacPherson, Fraser Quartet)
CD JTR 84202
Justin Time / Jan '94 / Cadillac / New Note/Pinnacle

IN THE TRADITION (MacPherson, Fraser Quintet)
Louisiana / Why am I blue / Struttin' with some barbecue / Hundred years from today / Constantly / When it's sleepy time down South / Desolation blues / You're lucky to me / If you could see me now / Dream of you / Ol' Bill's blues
CD CCD 4506
Concord Jazz / May '92 / New Note/ Pinnacle

MacPherson, Sandy

I'LL PLAY FOR YOU
I'll play to you / Vilia / Dancing on the ceiling / Room with a view / My heart stood still / June night on Marlow Reach / Was it a dream / Wonderful one / Till we meet again / It's a lovely day tomorrow / Who's taking you home tonight / Over the rainbow / Humoresque / Nobody knows the trouble I've seen / O Peter go ring-a-dem bells / Swing low, sweet chariot / Desert song / One flower / One alone / Can't help lovin' dat man / Why do I love you / Ol' man river / There's a boy coming home on leave / In an old Dutch garden / Woodpecker's song / Totem Tom / Indian love call / Rose Marie / Merry widow waltz / Dancing my way to heaven / Over my shoulder / When you've got a little springtime in your heart / March of the Bowmen / Oh Mama Mia / You made me care / My Capri serenade / Riff song / Waltz duet / Foreign legion / 'Tis me O Lord / Deep night / I got a robe / I've got no strings / Little wooden head / Give a little whistle / Carissima / Starlight / I do like to be beside the seaside / I've got to sing a torch song / Keep smiling / Oh Mr. Porter / Rhapsody in blue
CD RAJCD 861
Empress / Apr '96 / Koch

McPherson, Charles

CHARLES MCPHERSON
CD PCD 24135
Prestige / Nov '95 / Cadillac / Complete/ Pinnacle

COME PLAY WITH ME
Get happy / Lonely little chimes / Marionette / Pretty girl blues / Darn that dream / Bloomdido / Jumping Jacks / Fun house / Blues for Camille
CD AJ 0117
Arabesque / Oct '95 / New Note/Pinnacle

FIRST FLIGHT OUT
Lynn grins / Lizabeth / Blues for Chuck / Nostalgia in Times Square / Well you needn't / Seventh Dimension / Goodbye Pork Pie Hat / Deep night / Portrait / Karen / My funny valentine / First flight out
CD AJ 0113
Arabesque / Jan '95 / New Note/Pinnacle

McRackins

BACK TO THE CRACK
CD LOUDEST 20
One Louder / Oct '96 / Mo's Music Machine / Shellshock/Disc / SRD

BEST FRIEND
CD SH 40
Shredder / Jan '97 / Cargo / Greyhound / Plastic Head

McRae, Carmen

BEST OF CARMEN MCRAE, THE
Like a lover / I have the feeling I've been here before / Man I love / Would you believe / Child is born / Star eyes / Miss Otis regrets / Too close for comfort / Old folks / Dindi / Ain't nobody's business if I do
CD CDP 8335782
Capitol Jazz / Nov '95 / EMI

BLACK MAGIC 'LIVE'
CD JHR 73558
Jazz Hour / Oct '92 / Cadillac / Jazz Music / Target/BMG

CARMEN MCRAE
CD 15745
Laserlight / Apr '94 / Target/BMG

CARMEN MCRAE (Bethlehem Jazz Classics)
CD CDGR 129
Charly / Apr '97 / Koch

CARMEN MCRAE LIVE
CD CDGATE 7001
Kingdom Jazz / Sep '88 / Kingdom

CARMEN MCRAE SINGS LOVER MAN (& Other Billie Holiday Classics)
Them there eyes / Yesterdays / I'm gonna lock my heart (and throw away the key) / Strange fruit / Miss Brown to you / My man / I cried for you (now it's your turn to cry over me) / Lover man / Trav'lin' light / Some other Spring / What a little moonlight can do / God bless the child / If the moon turns green / Christmas song
CD CK 65115
Sony Jazz / Jun '97 / Sony

EVERYTHING HAPPENS TO ME
CD JHR 73582
Jazz Hour / Dec '94 / Cadillac / Jazz Music / Target/BMG

GREAT AMERICAN SONGBOOK, THE
Satin doll / At long last love / If the moon turns green / Day by day / What are you doing the rest of your life / I only have eyes for you / Easy living / Days of wine and roses / It's impossible / Sunday / Song for you / I cried for you / Behind the face / Ballad of Thelonious Monk / There's no such thing as love / Close to you / Three little words / Mr. Ugly / It's like reaching for the moon / I thought about you
CD 7567813232
Atlantic / Jun '93 / Warner Music

I'LL BE SEEING YOU (2CD Set)
Something to live for / Speak low / But beautiful / Midnight sun / Good morning heartache / I don't stand a ghost of a chance with you / We'll be together again / Star eyes / Whatever Lola wants (Lola gets) / Lush life / Until the real thing comes along / You don't know me / Skyliner / Party's over / East of the sun and west of the moon / Dream of life / Perdido / Exactly like you / I'm through with love / I'll see you again / Invitation / Bye bye blackbird / Flamingo / Oh yes, I remember Clifford / If I were a bell / Any old time / What's new / Night we called it a day / Please be kind / Thrill is gone / My myself / Do you know why / More I see you / When your lover has gone / If I could be with you one hour tonight / I only have eyes for you / I'm glad there is you / Ain't misbehavin' / I'll be seeing you
CD GRP 2647
GRP / Aug '95 / New Note/BMG

IN CONCERT
CD DM 15020
DMA Jazz / Jul '96 / Jazz Music

IT TAKES A WHOLE LOT OF HUMAN FEELING
CD CDGR 170
Charly / Jul '97 / Koch

MASQUERADE IS OVER, THE
CD CDSGP 0183
Prestige / May '96 / Else / Total/BMG

SONG TIME
CD HCD 602
Hindsight / Sep '96 / Jazz Music / Target/ BMG

VELVET SOUL
Nice work if you can get it / It takes a whole lot of human feeling / I fall in love too easily / Hey John / Where are the words / Straighten up and fly right / Inside a silent tear / Imagination / Right to love / All the things you are / You're mine you / You and I / How could I settle for less / Good life / Sunshine of my life / Exactly like you / There will come a time / (I'm afraid) the masquerade is over
CD CDC 7970
LRC / Nov '90 / Harmonia Mundi / New Note/Pinnacle

YOU'D BE SO EASY TO LOVE (The Finest Of Carmen McRae - The Bethlehem Years)
CD BET 6018
Bethlehem / Jan '95 / ADA / ZYX

YOU'RE LOOKING AT ME
I'm an errand girl for rhythm / Beautiful moons ago / Frim fram sauce / Come in and out of the rain / How does it feel / If I had you / I can't see for lookin' / Sweet Lorraine / You're lookin' at me / Just you, just me
CD CCD 4235
Concord Jazz / Sep '86 / New Note/ Pinnacle

MacRae, Gordon

BEST OF GORDON MACRAE, THE
Dear hearts and gentle people / Mule train / Sunshine of your smile / Younger than Springtime / Lover's waltz / On Rosary Hill / My Buick, my love and I / If someone had told me / How do you speak to an angel / Face to face / Be my little baby bumble bee / By the light of the silvery moon / Beela notte / Who are we / People will say we're in love / Surrey with the fringe on top / Woman in love / I've grown accustomed to her face / Sound of music / If ever I would leave you
CD CDSL 8275
Music For Pleasure / Nov '95 / EMI

CAPITOL YEARS, THE
Stranger in paradise / June in January / My funny valentine / It might as well be Spring / So in love / Spring is here / I'll remember April / Where or when / That's for me / All the things you are / Begin the beguine / Indian summer / September song / Autumn leaves / And this is my beloved / Without a song
CD CDEMS 1352
Capitol / Feb '90 / EMI

McShane, Ian

FROM BOTH SIDES NOW
Avalon / Fool (if you think it's over) / This guy's in love with you / I'd really love to see you tonight / From both sides now / I don't mind / I'm not in love / I could have been a sailor / Drive / Every breath you take / Reason to believe / Little in love / Shadow of your smile
CD 5176192
PolyGram TV / Nov '92 / PolyGram

McShann, Jay

1941-43
CD CLASSICS 740
Classics / Feb '94 / Discovery / Jazz Music

AIRMAIL SPECIAL
CD SKCD 23040
Sackville / '88 / Cadillac / Jazz Music / Swift

AT CAFE DES COPAINS
CD SKCD 22024
Sackville / Jun '93 / Cadillac / Jazz Music / Swift

BEST OF FRIENDS (McShann, Jay & Al Casey)
'Deed I do / One o'clock jump / Going to Kansas City / One sweet blues / How deep is the ocean / Anything / Hello little girl / Honky tonk train blues / Oh lady be good / Casey's shuffle / Stroll / Mess of trouble / Noodlin' / Al's theme
CD JSPCD 291
JSP / Jul '97 / ADA / Cadillac / Direct / Hot Shot / Target/BMG

CONFESSIN' THE BLUES
CD BB 8672
Black & Blue / Apr '96 / Discovery / Koch / Wellard

GOING TO KANSAS CITY (McShann, Jay & The All Stars)
CD NW 358
New World / '88 / ADA / Cadillac / Harmonia Mundi

JUST A LUCKY SO 'N' SO
CD SKCD 3035
Sackville / Jul '96 / Cadillac / Jazz Music / Swift

LAST OF THE WHOREHOUSE PIANO PLAYERS
CD CRD 306
Chiaroscuro / Mar '96 / Jazz Music

MAN FROM MUSKOGEE, THE
Vine Street boogie / Staggers / Yardbird waltz / My Chile / Confessin' the blues / Moten swing / Man from Muskogee / Blues for on old cat / I ain't mad at you / Do wah doo / Dexter blues
CD SKCD 3005
Sackville / Jul '96 / Cadillac / Jazz Music / Swift

MISSOURI CONNECTION, THE (McShann, Jay & John Hicks)
CD RSRCD 124
Reservoir Music / Nov '94 / Cadillac

PARIS ALL STAR BLUES (A Tribute To Charlie Parker) (McShann, Jay Kansas City Band)
Jumpin' blues / Moten swing / I'm just a lucky so and so / Lonely boy blues / Parker's mood / Say forward, I'll march / Tender touch / Swingin' the blues / Have you ever had the blues / Sebastian / Vine street boogie / Hootie blues
CD 8208332
Limelight / May '91 / PolyGram
CD MM 5052
Music Masters / Oct '94 / Nimbus

PIANO SOLOS
CD SWAGGIECD 401
Swaggie / Jul '93 / Jazz Music

SOME BLUES
CD ______ CRD 320
Chiaroscuro / Mar '96 / Jazz Music

SWINGMATISM (McShann, Jay & Don Thompson/Archie Alleyne)
CD ______ SKCD 23046
Sackville / Jun '93 / Cadillac / Jazz Music / Swift

VINE STREET BOOGIE
My chile / Hootie blues / Satin doll / I'm beginning to see the light / Vine Street boogie / Confessin' the blues / Yardbird waltz / Hootie's ignorant oil
CD ______ BLCD 760187
Black Lion / Jul '93 / Cadillac / Jazz Music / Koch / Wellard

McShee, Jacqui

ABOUT THYME
Jabalpur / Lovely Joan / Thyme / Factory girl / Would you / Little voices (Leah's song) / Sandalwood down to Kyle / Indiscretion / Don't turn on the light / Wife of Usher's well
CD ______ GJSCD 012
GJS / Jul '95 / Pinnacle

McTell, 'Blind' Willie

1927 - 1935
CD ______ YAZCD 1037
Yazoo / Apr '91 / ADA / CM / Koch

BLIND WILLIE MCTELL VOL.1 1927-1931
CD ______ DOCD 5006
Document / Feb '92 / ADA / Hot Shot / Jazz Music

BLIND WILLIE MCTELL VOL.2 1931-1933
CD ______ DOCD 5007
Document / Feb '92 / ADA / Hot Shot / Jazz Music

COMPLETE BLIND WILLIE MCTELL, THE (2CD Set)
Alanta strut / Travellin' blues / Come on round to my house Mama / Kind Mama / Talking to myself / Razor ball / Southern can is mine / Broke down engine blues / Stomp down rider / Scary day blues / Rough alley blues / Experience blues / Painful blues / Low riders blues / Georgia rag / Low down blues / Warm it up to me / It's your time to worry / It's a good little thing / You was born to die / Dirty mistreater / Lord have mercy if you please / Don't you see how this world made a change / Savannah Mama / Broke down engine No.2 / My baby's gone / Love makin' Mama / Death room blues / Death room blues / Death cells blues / Lord send me an angel / Lord send me an angel / B and O Blues No.2 / B and O BLues No.2 / Weary hearted blues / Bell St. lightening / Southern can Mama / Runnin' me crazy / East Saint Louis blues (Fare you well)
CD Set ______ 4757012
Columbia / Jun '96 / Sony

LAST SESSION
CD ______ OBCCD 517
Original Blues Classics / Nov '92 / Complete/Pinnacle / Wellard

LIBRARY OF CONGRESS RECORDINGS - 1940
CD ______ BDCD 6001
Blues Document / '91 / ADA / Hot Shot / Jazz Music

PIG 'N' WHISTLE RED
CD ______ BCD 126
Biograph / May '93 / ADA / Cadillac / Direct / Hot Shot / Jazz Music / Wellard

STATESBORO BLUES
CD ______ IGOCD 2015
Indigo / Feb '95 / ADA / Direct

McTell, Ralph

BEST OF RALPH MCTELL, THE
CD ______ TRTCD 206
TrueTrax / Feb '96 / THE

BLUE SKIES, BLACK HEROES
CD ______ TPGCD 10
Leola / Dec '94 / ADA / Direct

BOY WITH A NOTE, THE
CD ______ TPGCD 11
Leola / Dec '94 / ADA / Direct

COMPLETE ALPHABET ZOO, THE
CD ______ RGFCD 016
Road Goes On Forever / Jan '94 / Direct

GREATEST HITS
CD ______ CD 845008
Bluebird / Jan '94 / BMG

SAND IN MY SHOES
CD ______ TRACD 119
Transatlantic / Apr '96 / Pinnacle

SILVER CELEBRATION
CD ______ 08431822
CTE / Dec '95 / Koch

SLIDE AWAY THE SCREEN
Love grows (Where my Rosemary grows) / One heart / Gold in California / Van nuys, cruise night / London apprentice / Traces / Heroes and villains / Harry / Autumn / Promises / White dress / Save the last dance for me
CD ______ RGFCD 021
Road Goes On Forever / Sep '94 / Direct

SONGS FOR SIX STRINGS VOL.2
Gypsy / Mrs. Adlam's angels / Mermaid and the seagull / Lovin' I crave / Factory girl / From Clare to here / Red and gold / Summer girls / Fingerbuster / Near enough / Proposal / Slip shod tap room dance / Old brown dog / Girl from the hiring fair / Setting / First and last man / Affairs of the heart / Response / When did you leave heaven / Great dreams of heaven
CD ______ OLA 15B2CD
Leola / Feb '97 / ADA / Direct

SPIRAL STAIRCASE
Streets of London / Mrs. Aalam's angels / Wino and the mouse / England 1914 / Last train and ride / Fairground / Spiral staircase / Kind hearted woman blues / Bright and beautiful things / Daddy's here / Rizraklaru / (My) baby keeps staying out all night long / Terminus
CD ______ HILLCD 5
Wooded Hill / Sep '96 / Direct / World Serpent

SPIRAL STAIRCASE (2CD Set)
Summer come along / Terminus / Michael in the garden / Nanna's song / Last train and ride / Wino and the mouse / Clown / Willoughby's farm / Mermaid and the seagull / Eight frames a second / Wait until the snow / Hesitation blues / England 1914 / Girl on a bicycle / Mrs Adlam's angel / Granny takes a trip / Blind Blake's rag / Spiral staircase / Father forgive them / All things change / Streets of London / Factory girl / Bright and beautiful things / Father forgive them / Michael in the garden / I've thought about it / Blues in more than 12 bars / Rizraklaru / Factory girl / Siver birch and weeping willow / Louise / Too tight drag / Kew gardens / Fairground / Sleepy time blues / Daddy's here / Morning dew / I'm sorry I must leave
CD Set ______ SMDCD 151
Snapper / May '97 / Pinnacle

STREETS
Streets of London / You make me feel good / Grande affaire / Seeds of Heaven / El progresso / Red apple juice (trad) / Heron song / Pity the boy / Interest on the loan / Jenny Taylor - Je n'tais la / Lunar lullaby
CD ______ TPGCD 12
Leola / Apr '95 / ADA / Direct

STREETS OF LONDON (The Best Of Ralph McTell)
CD ______ PLSCD 164
Pulse / Apr '97 / BMG

McTells

WHAT HAPPENS NEXT
Expecting Joe / Trash can man / Everytime / Uncle Joe / All the time / Villiers Street / Buffalo / Jesse Rae / That / Sweetly breathing / Never look down / Francis said / Fridge freezer / This afternoon / Shadders / Secret wish / Everything heaven sent you / Theme / Back of my hand / Of only if / It happens / Side by side / Snowy white / Right way round / Rotten / Take the car / Virginia MC / Sometimes
CD ______ ASKCD 040
Vinyl Japan / Jun '94 / Plastic Head / Vinyl Japan

McWilliams, Brigette

TAKE ADVANTAGE OF ME
Set up / Cherish this love / Baby don't play me / Take advantage of me / No groove sweatin' (A funky space reincarnation) / Gotta be down / It's on / I get the job done / That's on me / Blankets of playboys / You got someth'n I want / (Don't let me catch you) slippin' / I'm ready
CD ______ CDVUS 77
Virgin / Jul '94 / EMI

Mad Cow Disease

TANTRIC SEX DISCO
My death squad / Craw / As good a place as any / Goatsucker / Exit / White dove / Annie Leiboritz version / Keep smiling / Elevator (going down) / Unicycle / Plague song / Epic departure
CD ______ 118052
CD Set ______ 118042
Musidisc / Sep '95 / Discovery

Mad Doctor X

HIP HOP EXPERIMENT ESCAPES FROM THE LAB
Mad(e) in London / I like my beats hard / Bounce / Dirty old man / Realism / Believe in your stealth / Mean machine
CD ______ FUNKRCD 005
Ninja Tune / Aug '96 / Kudos / Pinnacle / Prime / Vital

Mad Jocks

TAKE JOCK AND PARTY (Mad Jocks & Jockmaster BA)
Auld lang syne / Christmas cracker / No lager / Vicar / Jock party mix / Brigadier / Zorba's dance / Religious experience / Here we go again / Kennel talk / Jock jack mix / Pensioners / Guaglione / Daddy's tales / Auld lang syne
CD ______ CDSKM 1
SMP / Nov '96 / 3mv/Sony

Mad Lads

BEST OF THE MAD LADS, THE
So nice / Make room / Seeing is believing / Make this young lady mine / Love is here today / Cry baby / By the time I get to Phoenix / Gone the promise of yesterday / Did my baby call / No strings attached / These old memories / I forgot to be your lover / I'm so glad I fell in love with you / Let me repair your heart
CD ______ CDSXE 114
Volt / Jul '97 / Pinnacle

THEIR COMPLETE EARLY VOLT RECORDINGS
Don't have to shop around / I want someone / Come closer to me / I'm learning / (You're) My inspiration / Michael (The lover) / You mean so much to me / Land of 1000 dances / Nothing can break through / She's the one / Get out of my life / Sugar sugar / Tear-maker / What will love tend to make you do / I want a girl / Patch my heart / For these simple reasons / I don't want to lose your love / Mr. Fix it / Whatever hurts you / No time is better than right now / Please wait until I'm gone / Candy / Cloudburst
CD ______ CDSXD 111
Stax / Jun '97 / Pinnacle

Mad Lion

REAL LOVER
CD ______ VPCD 1402
VP / Mar '95 / Greensleeves / Jet Star / Total/BMG

Mad Monster Party

WANDERING
CD ______ BNVCD 09
Black & Noir / Jan '92 / Plastic Head

Mad Parade

CAT BITTEN TONGUE
CD ______ LF 256CD
Lost & Found / Dec '96 / Plastic Head

CLOWN TIME IS OVER
CD ______ LRR 025
Last Resort / Mar '97 / Cargo

CRAWL
CD ______ LF 208CD
Lost & Found / Apr '96 / Plastic Head

THIS IS LIFE
CD ______ LF 166CD
Lost & Found / Aug '95 / Plastic Head

Mad Professor

ADVENTURES OF A DUB SAMPLER, THE
CD ______ ARICD 033
Ariwa Sounds / Oct '92 / Jet Star / SRD

AT CHECKPOINT CHARLIE
CD ______ DANCD 089
Danceteria / Jul '97 / ADA / Plastic Head / Shellshock/Disc

BEYOND THE REALMS OF DUB
CD ______ AFRICD 003
Ariwa Sounds / Jan '91 / Jet Star / SRD

BLACK LIBERATION DUB VOL.1
Psychological warfare / Black liberation dub / Riot in Capetown / Slavery 21st century / Freedom must be taken / Chip on the slave master shoulder / When revolution comes / Black skin white minds / Tribal dub / Dub in D minor / Medicine doctor / Colonial mentality
CD ______ ARICD 095
Ariwa Sounds / Mar '94 / Jet Star / SRD

BLACK LIBERATION DUB VOL.2 (Anti-Racist Dub Broadcast)
Anti-racist dub broadcast / Dangerous escapades of dub / King Jimmy's dub / Basking in colonialism / Petty bourgeois dub / Pandora's box / Battle of Ciskei / Buthelezi trump card / Lion's domain / Rough rough dub / Legacy of Mussolini / Ethnic cleansing dub
CD ______ ARICD 100
Ariwa Sounds / Sep '94 / Jet Star / SRD

BLACK LIBERATION DUB VOL.3 (Evolution Of Dub)
Harder than babylon / No man's land / Kunte 96 / Solar system / Kathmandu dub / Cultural explosion / Gringo dread / Cosmic ray / Village gossip / Atonement dub / Kiwi culture
CD ______ ARICD 110
Ariwa Sounds / Apr '96 / Jet Star / SRD

DUB ME CRAZY VOL.1
CD ______ ARICD 001
Ariwa Sounds / Mar '97 / Jet Star / SRD

DUB ME CRAZY VOL.12 (Dub Maniacs On The Rampage)
CD ______ ARICD 075
Ariwa Sounds / Oct '92 / Jet Star / SRD

DUB ME CRAZY VOL.3 (The African Connection)
CD ______ ARICD 005
Ariwa Sounds / Aug '94 / Jet Star / SRD

DUB ME CRAZY VOL.9 (Science & The Witchdoctor)
Anansi skank / Blue ball fire / Cry of thee old higue / Coming of the obeahe man / Witch's brew / Mistaken identity / Natural fact / Jumbie umbrella / Bacoo in the bottle / Bohra seed / Holokoko dub
CD ______ ARICD 045
Ariwa Sounds / May '89 / Jet Star / SRD

DUB YOU CRAZY WITH LOVE
CD ______ ARICD 124
Ariwa Sounds / Feb '97 / Jet Star / SRD

FEAST OF YELLOW DUB, A
CD ______ RAS 3069CD
Ras / Feb '91 / Direct / Greensleeves / Jet Star / SRD

IN A RUB A DUB STYLE
Dubbing Jah / Bad man dubbing / Lighting dub / Cruel dub / Classic dub / True skank / Wicked skank / Skanking girl / Wolf skank / Skanking princess
CD ______ CDBM 105
Blue Moon / Jun '95 / Cadillac / Discovery / Greensleeves / Jazz Music / Jet Star / TKO Magnum

IT'S A MAD MAD MAD MAD PROFESSOR
CD ______ CRMCD 1
CRS / Jun '95 / ADA / Direct / Jet Star
CD ______ ARICD 105
Ariwa Sounds / Jun '96 / Jet Star / SRD

JAH SHAKA MEETS MAD PROFESSOR AT ARIWA SOUNDS (Mad Professor & Jah Shaka)
CD ______ ARICD 020
Ariwa Sounds / Sep '94 / Jet Star / SRD

LOST SCROLLS OF MOSES, THE
African Hebrew chant / African Hebrew dub / Land of Canaan / Moses in the bullrushes / Jordan crossing / Fire on Mount Sinai / Dub on Mount Sinai / Amorites dub / Dead Sea scrolls / Subversive literature / Bogle soca / Los Lomas
CD ______ ARICD 087
Ariwa Sounds / Jul '93 / Jet Star / SRD

MAD PROFESSOR CAPTURES PATO BANTON (Mad Professor & Pato Banton)
CD ______ ARICD 023
Ariwa Sounds / Oct '94 / Jet Star / SRD

PSYCHEDELIC DUB
CD ______ ARICD 057
Ariwa Sounds / Sep '90 / Jet Star / SRD

RAS PORTRAITS
Dub science / Beyond the realms dub / Zion / Holokoko dub / Sistren Version / Buccaneer's cove / Rasta chase / Hi-jacked to Jamaica / Cool runnings Mandela / Fire on Mt.Sinai / Black skin white minds / Anti racist broadcast / Harder than Babylon
CD ______ RAS 3329
Ras / Jul '97 / Direct / Greensleeves / Jet Star / SRD

TRUE BORN AFRICAN DUB
CD ______ ARICD 073
Ariwa Sounds / May '92 / Jet Star / SRD

WHO KNOWS THE SECRET OF THE MASTER TAPE
CD ______ ARICD 021
Ariwa Sounds / Aug '94 / Jet Star / SRD

Mad Pudding

DIRT AND STONE
Indian reels / Dirt & stone / Toast part 1 / Toast part 2 / Dewy dells of Yarrow / Crazy Creek set / Patchwork / Air / Dance of the hungry panda / Hey to the pipes / Ploughman's son / Heather Bonn / Service / Spanish lady / Brandon Town / Big John McNeil
CD ______ IRCD 040
Iona / Aug '96 / ADA / Direct / Duncans

Mad River

MAD RIVER
Merciful monks / High all the time / Amphetamine gazelle / Eastern light / Wind chimes / War goes on / Julian Hush
CD ______ EDCD 140
Edsel / Mar '85 / Pinnacle

PARADISE BAR AND GRILL
Harfy magnum / Paradise bar and grill / Love's not the way to treat a friend / Leave me stay / Copper plates / Equinoxe / They bought sadness / Revolution's in my pockets / Academy cemetry / Cherokee queen
CD ______ ED CD 188
Edsel / May '86 / Pinnacle

Mad Sin

AMPHIGORY
CD ______ FCD 3019
Fury / Oct '96 / Nervous / TKO Magnum

Madame Christine

REAL EXPERIENCE
CD ______ SUNCD 006
Sunvibe / May '93 / Jet Star

Madball

BALL OF DESTRUCTION
CD ______ CMCD 77130
Century Media / May '96 / Plastic Head

DEMONSTRATING MY STYLE
CD ______ RR 88752
Roadrunner / Jun '96 / PolyGram

SET IT OFF
Set it off / Lockdown / New York City / Never had it / It's time / CTYC / Across your face / Down by law / Spit on your grave / Face to face / Smell the bacon / Get out / World is mine / Friend or foe
CD ______ RR 89912
Roadrunner / Aug '94 / PolyGram

Madden, Glyn

CHRISTMAS WISHES
Winter wonderland / Silver bells / Fist Noel / I'm walking in the air / In the bleak midwinter / God rest ye merry gentlemen / Rudolph the red nosed reindeer / I saw Mommy kissing Santa Claus / Ave Maria / O little town of Bethlehem / Silent night / Frosty the snowman / Once in Royal David's City / Christmas tree with its candles gleaming / Dance of the snowmen / Sleigh ride / Have yourself a merry little Christmas / Christmas song / Ding dong merrily on high / White Christmas / O come all ye faithful (Adeste fidelis) / Jingle bells / Here we come a-wassailing / I heard the bells on Christmas day / O little one sweet / We wish you a Merry Christmas
CD ______ CDGRS 1221
Grosvenor / '91 / Grosvenor

TICO TICO
CD ______ CDGRS 1234
Grosvenor / Feb '93 / Grosvenor

ZWEI NACHTS IN EINER GROSSEN STADT
CD ______ CDGRS 1250
Grosvenor / Feb '93 / Grosvenor

Madden, Joanie

SONG OF THE IRISH WHISTLE
CD ______ HS 11060
Hearts Of Space / Mar '96 / ADA

WHISTLE ON THE WIND
CD ______ GL 1142CD
Green Linnet / Aug '94 / ADA / CM / Direct / Highlander / Roots

Madder Rose

BRING IT DOWN
Beautiful John / While away / Bring it down / Twenty foot red / Swim / Lay down low / Altar boy / Lights go down / (Living a) daydream / Sugarsweet / Razor pilot / Waiting for engines / Pocket fulla medicine
CD ______ 142292
Seed / Jun '93 / Vital

TRAGIC MAGIC
CD ______ 7567830092
Atlantic / Jun '97 / Warner Music

Madding Crowd

I HATE FLIES
CD ______ FETMC 1
Fuller's Earth / Mar '95 / Else

Maddox Brothers

AMERICA'S MOST COLOURFUL HILLBILLY BAND (Maddox Brothers & Rose Maddox)
CD ______ ARHCD 391
Arhoolie / Apr '95 / ADA / Cadillac / Direct

AMERICA'S MOST COLOURFUL HILLBILLY BAND VOL.2 (Maddox Brothers & Rose Maddox)
CD ______ ARHCD 437
Arhoolie / Sep '95 / ADA / Cadillac / Direct

ON THE AIR: THE 1940'S (Maddox Brothers & Rose Maddox)
Cowboy has to yell / Let me ride my pony down the sunset trail / Once I had a darling Mother / Hold that critter down / I'm talking about you / I'm going to the hoedown / Small town Mama / Mama please stay home with me / If you ain't got the do-re-mi / I might have known / I'll reap my harvest in Heaven / Don't hang around me anymore / Sinner's prayer is never answered / Girl I love don't pay me no mind / Write me sweetheart / I'm a handy man to have around / I've rambled around / Gathering flowers for the master's bouquet / I couldn't believe it was true / KTRB theme/Regal Pale Beer ad / Goldrush is over / Almost / Too old to cut the mustard / Breathless love / Walkin' in my sleep / Introduction by Fred and Rose / Fried potatoes / Nobody's love is like mine / Meanest man in town / Freight train boogie / KTRB theme out
CD ______ ARHCD 447
Arhoolie / Nov '96 / ADA / Cadillac / Direct

Maddox, Rose

$35 & A DREAM
CD ______ ARHCD 428
Arhoolie / Apr '95 / ADA / Cadillac / Direct

ONE ROSE, THE (4CD Set)
What makes me hang around / Bill Cline / Gambler's love / Lies and alibis / Custer's last stand / I lost today / Live and let live / My little baby / Philadelphia lawyer / Tramp on the street / Gathering flowers for the master's bouquet / I'm happy every day I live / Sally let your bangs hang down / Whoa sailor / On the banks of the old Ponchartrain / Honky tonkin' / At the first fall of snow / Why don't you haul off and love me / Chocolate ice cream cone / Move it on over / Shining silver, gleaming gold / Down down down / Please help me, I'm falling / Johnny's last kiss / Philadelphia lawyer / Johnny's last kiss / Wait a little longer, please Jesus / Empty mansions / Great speckled bird / This world is not my home / That glory bound train / Drifting too far from the shore / When I take my vacation in heaven / How beautiful heaven must be / I'll reap my harvest in heaven / Smoke, fire and brimstone / Will the circle be unbroken / Kneel at the cross / There's better times a comin' / I want to live again / Kissing my pillow / Dime a dozen / Loose talk / Mental cruelty / Conscience I'm guilty / Read my letter once again / Tall men / Early in the morning / There ain't no love / What am I living for / Stop the world (and let me off) / Jim Dandy / North to Alaska / Lonely Street / Gotta travel on / Just one more time / Don't tell me your troubles / There ain't no love / Your kind of lovin' won't do / Take me back again / Fool me again / Long journey home / From a beggar to a Queen / Let's pretend we're strangers / If you see my baby / Let those brown eyes smile at me / When the sun goes down / Alone with you / My life has been a pleasure / Curly Joe / Here we go again / Long black limousine / White lightning / Uncle Pen / Footprints in the snow / Blue moon of Kentucky / My rose of old Kentucky / Molly and Tenbrooks / Rollin' in my sweet baby's arms / Cotton fields / Each season changes you / Old crossroad is waitin' / I'll meet you in church Sunday morning / Down down down / Lonely teardrops / Sing a little song of heartache / Tie a ribbon in the apple tree / George Carter / Let me kiss you for old times / I don't hear you / Down to the river / Somebody told somebody / Sweethearts in heaven / We're the talk of the town / Back street affair / No fool like an old fool / I won't come in while he's there / Silver threads and golden needles / Bluebird let me tag along / That's a mighty long way to fall / Stand up fool / Silver threads and golden needles / Great pretender / Tia Lisa Lynn / Lonely one / Big Ball in Cowtown / Wabash cannonball / I'll always be loving you / Mad at the world / Big big day tomorrow / Cotton wood road / Down to the river (live)
CD Set ______ BCD 15743
Bear Family / Oct '93 / Direct / Rollercoaster / Swift

ROSE OF THE WEST COUNTRY
CD ______ ARHCD 314
Arhoolie / Apr '95 / ADA / Cadillac / Direct

Maderna, Bruno

OBOE CONCERTOS
CD ______ BVHAASTCD 9302
Bvhaast / Oct '94 / Cadillac

Madison, Art

LET IT FLOW
CD ______ 7567820042
Atlantic / Apr '90 / Warner Music

Madness

7
Cardiac arrest / Shut up / Sign of the times / Missing you / Mrs. Hutchinson / Tomorrows dream / Grey day / Pac-a-mac / Promises, promises / Benny bullfrog / When dawn arrives / Opium eaters / Day on the town
CD ______ CDOVD 135
Virgin / Nov '89 / EMI

ABSOLUTELY
Baggy trousers / Embarrassment / ERNIE / Close escape / Not home today / On the beat Pete / Solid gone / Take it or leave it / Shadow of fear / Disappear / Overdone / In the rain / You said / Return of the Los Palmas 7
CD ______ CDOVD 134
Virgin / Nov '89 / EMI

BUSINESS, THE (The Definitive Singles Collection/3CD Set)
Prince / Madness / One step beyond / Mistakes / Nutty theme / My girl / Stepping into line / In the rain / Night boat to Cairo / Deceives the eye / Young and the old / Don't quote me on that / Baggy trousers / Business / Embarrassment / Crying shame / Return of the Los Palmas 7 / That's the way you do it (aka odd jobman) / My girl (demo version) / Swan lake / Grey day / Memories / Shut up / Town with no name / Never ask twice (aka airplane) / It must be love / Shadow on the house / Cardiac arrest / In the city / House of fun / Don't look back / Driving in my car / Terry Wogan jingle / Animal farm / Riding on my bike / Walking with Mr. Wheeze / Our house (stretch mix) / Tomorrow's just another day / Madness / Wings of a dove / Behind the eight ball / One's second thoughtlessness / Sun and the rain / Fireball XL5 / Visit to Dracstein castle / Michael Caine / If you think there's something / One better day / Guns / Victoria gardens / Sarah / Yesterday's men / All I knew / It must be love (live) / Uncle Sam / David Hamilton jingle / Inanity over Christmas / Please don't go / Sweetest girl / Jennie / Tears you can't hide / Call me / Waiting for the ghost train / One step beyond (Italian version) / Maybe in another life / Seven year scratch / Release me / Carols on 45 / National anthem
CD Set ______ MADBOX 1
Virgin / Dec '93 / EMI

COMPLETE MADNESS
Embarrassment / Shut up / My girl / Baggy trousers / It must be love / Prince / Bed and breakfast man / Night boat to Cairo / House of fun / One step beyond / Cardiac arrest / Grey day / Take it or leave it / In the city / Madness / Return of the Los Palmas 7
CD ______ HITCD 1
Virgin / Jul '86 / EMI

DIVINE MADNESS
Prince / One step beyond / My girl / Night boat to Cairo / Baggy trousers / Embarrassment / Return of the Los Palmas 7 / Grey day / Shut up / It must be love / Cardiac arrest / House of fun / Driving in my car / Our house / Tomorrow's just another day / Wings of a dove / Sun and the rain / Michael Caine / One better day / Yesterday's men / Uncle Sam / Waiting for the ghost train
CD ______ CDV 2692
Virgin / Feb '92 / EMI

IT'S MADNESS
House of fun / Don't look back / Wings of a dove / Young and the old / My girl / Stepping into line / Baggy trousers / Business / Embarrassment / One's second thoughtlessness / Grey day / Memories / It must be love / Deceives the eye / Driving in my car / Animal farm
CD ______ CDVIP 105
Virgin VIP / Mar '94 / EMI

IT'S MADNESS TOO
Prince / Madness / One step beyond / Mistakes / Return of the Los Palmas 7 / Night boat to Cairo / Shut up / Town with no name / Cardiac arrest / In the city / Our house / Walking with Mr. Wheeze / Tomorrow's just another day / Victoria Gardens / Sun and the rain / Michael Caine
CD ______ CDVIP 117
Virgin / Jun '94 / EMI

KEEP MOVING
Keep moving / Michael Caine / Turning blue / One better day / March of the gherkins / Waltz into mischief / Brand new beat / Victoria gardens / Samantha / Time for tea / Prospects / Give me a reason
CD ______ CDOVD 191
Virgin / Nov '89 / EMI

MAD NOT MAD
I'll compete / Yesterday's men / Uncle Sam / White heat / Mad not mad / Sweetest girl / Burning the boats / Tears you can't hide / Time / Coldest day
CD ______ JZCD 1
Zarjazz / Jul '87 / EMI

MADNESS, THE
Nail down the days / What's that / I pronounce you / Oh / In wonder / Song in red / Nightmare nightmare / Thunder and lightning / Beat the bride / Gabriel's horn / Eleventh hour / Be good boy / Flashings / 4BF
CD ______ CDV 2507
Virgin / Aug '91 / EMI

MADSTOCK
One step beyond / Prince / Embarrassment / My girl / Sun and the rain / Grey day / It must be love / Shut up / Driving in my car / Bed and breakfast man / Close escape / Wings of a dove / Our house / Night boat to Cairo / Madness / House of fun / Baggy trousers / Harder they come
CD ______ 8283672
Go Discs / Nov '92 / PolyGram

ONE STEP BEYOND
One step beyond / My girl / Night boat to Cairo / Believe me / Land of hope and glory / Prince / Tarzan's nuts / In the middle of the night / Bed and breakfast man / Razor blade alley / Swan lake / Rockin' in AB / Mummy's boy / Chipmunks are go
CD ______ CDOVD 133
Virgin / Apr '90 / EMI

ONE STEP BEYOND/ABSOLUTELY/RISE AND FALL (3CD Set)
CD Set ______ TPAK 8
Virgin / Oct '90 / EMI

RISE AND FALL
Rise and fall / Tomorrow's just another day / Blue skinned beast / Primrose hill / Mr. Speaker gets the word / Sunday morning / Our house / Tiptoes / New Delhi / That face / Calling cards / Are you coming (with me) / Madness
CD ______ CDOVD 190
Virgin / Nov '89 / EMI

UTTER MADNESS
Our house / Driving in my car / Michael Caine / Wings of a dove / Yesterday's men / Tomorrow's just another day / I'll compete / Waiting for the ghost train / Uncle Sam / Sun and the rain / Sweetest girl / One better day / Victoria gardens
CD ______ JZCD 2
Zarjazz / Nov '86 / EMI

Madonna

BEDTIME STORIES
Survival / Secret / I'd rather be your lover / Don't stop / Inside of me / Human nature / Forbidden love / Love tried to welcome me / Sanctuary / Bedtime story / Take a bow
CD ______ 9362457672
Maverick / Oct '94 / Warner Music

EROTICA
Erotica / Fever / Bye bye baby / Deeper and deeper / Where life begins / Bad girl / Waiting / Thief of hearts / Words / Rain / Why's it so hard / In this life / Did you do it / Secret garden
CD ______ 9362450312
Sire / Oct '92 / Warner Music

FIRST ALBUM, THE
Lucky star / Borderline / Burning up / I know it / Holiday / Think of me / Physical attraction / Everybody
CD ______ 9238672
Sire / Oct '84 / Warner Music

GIVE IT TO ME
Give it to me / Shake / Get down / Time to dance / Wild dancing / Let's go dancing / Cosmic / On the street
CD ______ RM 1549
BR Music / Jun '97 / Target/BMG

I'M BREATHLESS
He's a man / Sooner or later / Hanky panky / I'm going bananas / Cry baby / Something to remember / Back in business / More / What can you lose / Now I'm following you / Vogue
CD ______ 7599262092
Sire / May '90 / Warner Music

IMMACULATE COLLECTION (Best Of Madonna)
Holiday / Lucky star / Borderline / Like a virgin / Material girl / Crazy for you / Into the groove / Live to tell / Papa don't preach / Open your heart / La Isla Bonita / Like a prayer / Express yourself / Cherish / Vogue / Justify my love / Rescue me
CD ______ 7599264402
Sire / Nov '90 / Warner Music

INTERVIEW COMPACT DISC: MADONNA
CD ______ CBAK 4019
Baktabak / Nov '89 / Arabesque

INTERVIEW DISC
CD ______ TELL 01
Network / Dec '96 / Total/BMG

INTERVIEW DISC - LIVE TO TELL
CD ______ DIST 006
Disturbed / Jun '96 / Total/BMG

LIFE AND TIMES OF MADONNA, THE (2CD Set)
CD Set ______ OTR 1100035
Metro Independent / Jun '97 / Essential/BMG

LIKE A PRAYER
Like a prayer / Love song / Promise to try / Dear Jessie / Keep it together / Act of contrition / Express yourself / Till death do us part / Cherish / Oh Father / Spanish eyes
CD ______ K 925844 2
Sire / Mar '94 / Warner Music

SALUTE TO MADONNA (Various Artists)
Like a virgin / Into the groove / Angel / Justify my love / Express yourself / Holiday / Human nature / Borderline / Papa don't preach / Dress you up / Deeper and deeper / Like a prayer / Vogue / La isla bonita / Bedtime story / True blue
CD ______ 306782
Hallmark / May '97 / Carlton

SOMETHING TO REMEMBER
I want you: *Madonna & Massive Attack* / I'll remember / Take a bow / You'll see / Crazy for you / This used to be my playground / Live to tell / Love don't live here anymore / Something to remember / Forbidden love / One more chance / Rain / Oh father / I want you (orchestral): *Madonna & Massive Attack*
CD ______ 9362461002
Maverick / Nov '95 / Warner Music

TRUE BLUE
Papa don't preach / Open your heart / Love makes the world go round / Jimmy Jimmy / La Isla Bonita / True blue / Where's the party / Live to tell / White heat
CD ______ K 9254422
Sire / Mar '94 / Warner Music

WILD DANCING (Madonna & Otto Van Wernherr)
CD ______ DS 2301
BR Music / May '96 / Target/BMG

WOW (Madonna & Otto Van Wernherr)
CD ____ **DS 2302**
BR Music / May '96 / Target/BMG

YOU CAN DANCE
Spotlight / Holiday / Everybody / Physical attraction / Over and over / Into the groove / Where's the party / Holiday (dub) / Into the groove (dub) / Over and over (dub)
CD ____ **9255352**
Sire / Feb '95 / Warner Music

Madou, Cora

SUCCES ET RARETES 1926-1935
CD ____ **701612**
Chansophone / Nov '96 / Discovery

Madredeus

O ESPIRITO DA PAZ
Concertino / Minueto / Allegro / Destino / Selenco / Os Senhores da Guerra / Pregao / O Mar / Os Moinhos / Tres Illusoes / Sentimento / Culpa / Amargura / As Cores do Sol / Ao Longe o Mar / Vem / Ajuda / O Pastor
CD ____ **PRMDCD 6**
Premier/EMI / Jul '96 / EMI

Madsen, Katrine

I'M OLD FASHIONED (Madsen, Katrine Swing Quintet)
CD ____ **MECCACD 1095**
Music Mecca / May '97 / Cadillac / Jazz Music / Wellard

Madsen, Peter

DRIP SOME GREASE (Madsen, Peter & Dwayne Dolphin/Bruce Cox)
CD ____ **MM 801056**
Minor Music / Jun '96 / Vital/SAM

Madura

MUSIQUE SAVANTE (Music From Indonesia)
CD ____ **C 560083**
Ocora / Dec '95 / ADA / Harmonia Mundi

Mady, Kasse

FODE
CD ____ **STCD 1025**
Stern's / Mar '89 / ADA / CM / Stern's

Maerz, Marion

ER IST WIEDER DA
Er ist wieder da / Terry / Liebe auf den ersten Blick / Andy / Er und ich / Mister boyfriend / Blau, blau, blau / Wie soll es weitergehn / Versprich mir nicht zuviel / Wenn das kein zufall ist / Da gehoren zwei dazu / Ich hab einen guten freund gehabt / Wer die liebe sucht / So fing es an / Auf, auf und davon / Weit, weit, weit / Klopf auf holz / Bis ans ende aller tage / Wenn du da bist / Sugar, sugar / Nur du / Falt ein stern zur welt / Mach nicht tur zu / Nichts als sorgen macht er mir / Hinter flas / Wir halten zusammen / Du bist genau wie die andern / Nur beim abschied nicht weinen / Du wirst schon seh'n was du davon hast / Round and round
CD ____ **BCD 15964**
Bear Family / Jul '96 / Direct / Rollercoaster / Swift

Maes, Christian

TILTED HOUSE (Maes, Christian & Sandi Miller)
CD ____ **KM 43CD**
Keltia Musique / Feb '94 / ADA / Discovery

Mafia & Fluxy

REVIVAL HITS VOL.3
CD ____ **MFCD 009**
Mafia/Fluxy / Mar '97 / Jet Star / SRD

Magadini, Pete

BONES BLUES (Magadini, Pete Quartet)
Old devil moon / Freddie freeloader / Poor butterfly / Solar / I remember Clifford / What a time we had / Bones blues / Freddie freeloader no. 2
CD ____ **SKCD 24004**
Sackville / Jun '93 / Cadillac / Jazz Music / Swift

NIGHT DREAMS (Magadini, Pete Quintet)
Friendly imposition / Exchanging love / Sunny side / Giant steps / Carolyn / Shutterbug / In a sentimental mood / Stablemates
CD ____ **CDSJP 317**
Timeless Jazz / Aug '91 / New Note/ Pinnacle

Magazine

CORRECT USE OF SOAP, THE
Because you're frightened / Model worker / I'm a party / You never knew me / Philadelphia / I want to burn again / Thank you (falettinme be mice elf agin) / Sweetheart contract / Stuck / Song from under the floorboards
CD ____ **CDV 2156**
Virgin / '88 / EMI

MAGIC, MURDER AND THE WEATHER
About the weather / So lucky / Honeymoon killers / Vigilance / Come alive / Great man's secrets / This poison / Naked eye / Suburban Rhonda / Garden
CD ____ **CDV 2200**
Virgin / '88 / EMI

PLAY
Give me everything / Song from under the floorboards / Permafrost / Light pours out of me / Model worker / Parade / Thank you (falettinme be mice elf agin) / Because you're frightened / Twenty years ago / Definitive gaze
CD ____ **CDV 2184**
Virgin / '88 / EMI

RAYS AND HAIL 1978-1981 (The Best Of Magazine)
Shot by both sides / Definitive gaze / Motorcade / Light pours out of me / Feed the enemy / Rhythm of cruelty / Back to nature / Permafrost / Because you're frightened / You never knew me / Song from under the floorboards / I want to burn again / About the weather / Parade
CD ____ **CDVM 9020**
Virgin / Jul '94 / EMI

REAL LIFE
Definitive gaze / My tulpa / Shot by both sides / Recoil / Burst / Motorcade / Great beautician in the sky / Light pours out of me / Parade
CD ____ **CDV 2100**
Virgin / '88 / EMI

SCREE (Rarities 1976-1981)
My mind ain't so open / Touch and go / Goldfinger / Give me everything / I love you big dummy / Rhythm of cruelty / TV baby / Book / Light pours out of me / Feed the enemy / Twenty years ago / Shot by both sides / In the dark / Operative
CD ____ **CDOVD 312**
Virgin / Jul '90 / EMI

SECONDHAND DAYLIGHT
Feed the enemy / Rhythm of cruelty / Cut out shapes / Talk to the body / I wanted your heart / Thin air / Back to nature / Believe that I understand / Permafrost
CD ____ **CDV 2121**
Virgin / '88 / EMI

Magdallan

BIG BANG
CD ____ **FLD 9098**
Frontline / Apr '92 / EMI / Jet Star

Magellan

IMPENDING ASCENSION
Estadium Nacional / Waterfront weirdos / Songsmith / Virtual reality / No time for words / Storms and mutiny / Under the wire
CD ____ **RR 90572**
Roadrunner / Jun '93 / PolyGram

TEST OF WILLS
CD ____ **RR 88172**
Roadrunner / Jun '97 / PolyGram

Magic

ENCLOSED
CD ____ **FLASH 44**
Flash / Jul '97 / Greyhound

Magic Affair

OMEN - THE STORY CONTINUES
Communication / Omen III / In the middle of the night / Homicidal / Fire / Water of sin / Under the sea / Carry on / Make your mind up / Give me all your love / Wonderland / Thin line
CD ____ **CDEMC 3686**
EMI / Sep '97 / EMI

Magic Carpet

MAGIC CARPET
CD ____ **MC 1001CD**
Magic Carpet / Oct '96 / Greyhound

ONCE MOOR
CD ____ **MC 1004CD**
Magic Carpet / Dec '96 / Greyhound

Magic Dick

BLUESTIME (Magic Dick & Jay Geils)
CD ____ **NETCD 51**
Network / '95 / Direct / Greensleeves / SRD

LITTLE CAR BLUES (Magic Dick & Jay Geils)
CD ____ **ROUCD 3141**
Rounder / Aug '96 / ADA / CM / Direct

Magic Fingers

WIRING IT UP
CD ____ **BAS 004**
Baseline / Jun '97 / Timewarp

Magic Hour

NO EXCESS IS ABSURB
CD ____ **CHE 20CD**
Che / Oct '94 / SRD

WILL THEY TURN YOU ON OR WILL THEY TURN ON YOU
CD ____ **CHE 30CD**
Che / Jun '95 / SRD

Magic Mushroom Band

FRESHLY PICKED
CD ____ **EYECD 7**
Magick Eye / Feb '93 / Cargo / SRD

SPACED COLLECTION, THE
CD ____ **CLP 9949**
Cleopatra / Apr '97 / Cargo / Greyhound / Plastic Head / RTM/Disc / SRD

SPACED OUT
CD ____ **EYECDLP 6**
Magick Eye / Aug '94 / Cargo / SRD

Magic Sam

BLACK MAGIC (Magic Sam Blues Band)
CD ____ **DD 620**
Delmark / Mar '95 / ADA / Cadillac / CM / Direct / Hot Shot

GIVE ME TIME
CD ____ **DD 654**
Delmark / Sep '91 / ADA / Cadillac / CM / Direct / Hot Shot

MAGIC BLUES GENIUS
CD ____ **CWNCD 2016**
Javelin / Jul '96 / Henry Hadaway / THE

MAGIC SAM LEGACY, THE
I feel so good / Lookin' good / Walkin' by myself / Hoochie coochie man / That ain't it / That's all I need / What have I done wrong / I just want a little bit / Everything's gonna be alright / Keep on doin' what you're doin' / Blues for Odie Payne / Easy baby / Keep on lovin' me baby
CD ____ **DE 651**
Delmark / Jul '97 / ADA / Cadillac / CM / Direct / Hot Shot

MAGIC TOUCH
CD ____ **BT 1085CD**
Black Top / May '93 / ADA / CM / Direct

WEST SIDE SOUL (Charly Blues - Masterworks Vol. 29)
All your love / Love me with a feeling / Everything gonna be alright / Look watcha done / All night long / All my whole life / Easy baby / Twenty one days in jail / Love me this way / Magic rocker / Roll your moneymaker / Call me if you need me / Every night about this time / Blue light boogie / Out of bad luck / She belongs to me
CD ____ **CDBM 29**
Charly / Apr '92 / Koch

Magic Slim

CHICAGO BLUES SESSION (Magic Slim & The Teardrops)
CD ____ **WOLF 120870**
Wolf / Jul '96 / Hot Shot / Jazz Music / Swift

GRAVEL ROAD (Magic Slim & The Teardrops)
CD ____ **BPCD 73690**
Blind Pig / Nov '96 / ADA / CM / Direct / Hot Shot

HIGHWAY IS MY HOME
CD ____ **ECD 260122**
Evidence / Jan '92 / ADA / Cadillac / Harmonia Mundi

RAW MAGIC (Magic Slim & The Teardrops)
CD ____ **ALCD 4728**
Alligator / May '93 / ADA / CM / Direct

SCUFFLIN' (Magic Slim & The Teardrops)
Think / Hole in the wall / Scufflin' / Down in Virginia / I'm not the same person / Just before you go / I'm gonna send you back to Georgia / Room 109 / I need lovin' / I'm gonna get you babe / Lookin' for a lover / Can't get no grindin'
CD ____ **BPCD 5036**
Blind Pig / Nov '96 / ADA / CM / Direct / Hot Shot

Magical Strings

BELL OFF THE LEDGE
CD ____ **FF 70631CD**
Flying Fish / Apr '94 / ADA / CM / Direct / Roots

CROSSING TO SKELLIG
CD ____ **FF 531CD**
Flying Fish / '92 / ADA / CM / Direct / Roots

ISLANDS CALLING
Ferry to Islesboro / Malagasy greeting / Warm island / Holy Island / Jamaican port o' call / Twilight over cove / Winter into Spring / Bahamian Time / Moussa's Kora / Dance of the Valiha / Father Dollard's hornpipe / Farewell
CD ____ **935282**
Earthbeat / Nov '96 / ADA / Direct

Magick Brothers

LIVE AT THE WITCHWOOD
CD ____ **BP 107CD**
Blueprint / Feb '97 / Pinnacle

Magick Heads

BEFORE WE GO UNDER
CD ____ **FNCD 290**
Flying Nun / Apr '95 / RTM/Disc

Magick Lantern Cycle

CHIMAERA
CD ____ **DURTRO 015CD**
Durtro / Oct '96 / World Serpent

Magid, Yakov

LEKHAYM YIDN
CD ____ **MU 3101762**
Multisonic / Dec '93 / Koch / Priory

Maglio, Juan 'Pacho'

EL LEGENDARIO 1927-1930
CD ____ **EBCD 86**
El Bandoneon / Apr '97 / Discovery

Magma

1001 CENTIGRADES
CD ____ **REX 6**
Rex / Apr '91 / Pinnacle

ATTAHK
Last seven minutes / Spiritual / Rinde / Lirik necronomicus kant / Maahnt / Dondai / Nono
CD ____ **CPCD 8170**
Charly / Apr '96 / Koch

INEDITS
CD ____ **REX 19**
Seventh / Jun '97 / Cadillac / Harmonia Mundi / ReR Megacorp

LES VOIX - CONCERT 1992
CD ____ **AKT 1**
AKT / Nov '92 / Cadillac / Harmonia Mundi

MAGMA
CD Set ____ **REX 4/5**
Seventh / Mar '93 / Cadillac / Harmonia Mundi / ReR Megacorp

MAGMA LIVE
Kohntark / Kobah / Lihns / Khat / Mekanik zain
CD ____ **CPCD 8171**
Charly / Jun '96 / Koch

MYTHS & LEGENDS (1969-1972)
CD ____ **REX 14**
Seventh / Mar '93 / Cadillac / Harmonia Mundi / ReR Megacorp

OPERA DE RHEIMS 1976 (3CD Set)
CD Set ____ **AKT 1X**
AKT / Jan '97 / Cadillac / Harmonia Mundi

RETROSPEKTIW VOL.3
CD ____ **REX 15**
Seventh / Mar '93 / Cadillac / Harmonia Mundi / ReR Megacorp

UDU WUDU
Udu wudu / Weidorje / Troller tanz / Soleil d'ork / Zombies / De futura
CD ____ **CPCD 8169**
Charly / Apr '96 / Koch

Magna Carta

IN CONCERT
CD ____ **HTDCD 69**
HTD / Dec '96 / CM / Pinnacle

LORD OF THE AGES
Wish it was / Two old friends / Lord of the ages / Isn't it funny (and not a little bit strange) / Song of evening / Father John / That was yesterday / Falkland grene
CD ____ **8464482**
Vertigo / Jul '90 / PolyGram

MAGNA CARTA
Times of change / Daughter daughter / Old John Parker / I am no more / Ballad of Francis Alabadeleio / Spinning wheels of time / Romeo Jack / Mid Winter / Shades of grey / Emily thru the window pane / Sea and sand / 7 o'clock hymn
CD ____ **HTDCD 68**
HTD / Dec '96 / CM / Pinnacle

SEASONS
Airport song / Autumn song / Elizabethan / Epilogue / Give me no goodbye / Goin' my way / Road song / Prologue / Ring of stones / Scarecrow / Spring poem / Spring song / Winter song
CD ____ **8464472**
Vertigo / Jul '90 / PolyGram

Magnapop

HOT BOXING
Slowly slowly / Texas / Lay it down / Here it comes / Piece of cake / Free mud / Leo / Crush / Ride / In the way / Idiot song / Get it right / Emergency / Skinburns

CD ______ BIAS 251CD
Play It Again Sam / Feb '94 / Discovery / Plastic Head / Vital

MAGNAPOP
Garden / Guess / Ear / Thirteen / Spill it / Chemical / Favourite writer / Complicated / Merry
CD ______ BIAS 220CD
Play It Again Sam / Jul '92 / Discovery / Plastic Head / Vital

RUBBING DOESN'T HELP
This family / I don't care / Open the door / Come on inside / Down on me / An apology / My best friend / Juicy fruit / Firebrand / Cherry bomb / Radio waves / Snake / Dead letter
CD ______ BIAS 321CD
Play It Again Sam / May '96 / Discovery / Plastic Head / Vital

Magnarelli, Joe

WHY NOT
CD ______ CRISS 1104
Criss Cross / Oct '95 / Cadillac / Direct / Vital/SAM

Magnetic Fields

CHARM OF THE HIGHWAY STRIP, THE
Lonely highway / Long vermont roads / Born on a train / I have the moon / Two characters in search of a country song / Crowd of drifters / Fear of trains / When the open road in closing in / Sunset city / Dustbowl
CD ______ SETCD 021
Setanta / Aug '95 / Vital

GET LOST
With whom to dance / Smoke and mirrors / All the umbrellas in London / Why I cry / Save a secret for the moon / Don't look away / Love is lighter than air / Desperate things you made me do / You and me and the moon / Village in the morning / Famous / When you're old and lonely / Dreaming moon
CD ______ SETCD 023
CD ______ SETCD 023L
Setanta / Mar '96 / Vital

Magnificat

VOICES OF ANGELS
CD ______ NTMCD 539
Nectar / Apr '97 / Pinnacle

Magnificent

HIT AND RUN
CD ______ AHOY 30
Captain Oi / Dec '94 / Plastic Head

Magnificent VII

LIVE AT THE HILTON
CD ______ ARCD 19123
Arbors Jazz / Nov '94 / Cadillac

Magnog

MAGNOG
CD ______ KRANK 010CD
Kranky / Mar '97 / Cargo / Greyhound

Magnolia Jazz Band

CHRISTMAS WITH THE MAGNOLIA JAZZ BAND
CD ______ BCD 420
GHB / Jan '97 / Jazz Music

MAGNOLIA ANYTIME
CD ______ BCD 220
GHB / Aug '95 / Jazz Music

Magnolias

OFF THE HOOK
CD ______ A 024D
Alias / Jun '92 / Vital

Magnolias Milan

2K
CD ______ BBPTC 68
Black Bean & Placenta Tape Club / Jul '97 / Cargo

Magnum

ARCHIVE
CD ______ JETCD 1005
Jet / Apr '93 / Total/Pinnacle

CHASE THE DRAGON
Lights burned out / We all play the game / Teacher / Spirit / Soldier of the line / On the edge of the world / Walking the straight line / Sacred hour
CD ______ WKFMXD 112
FM / Jun '88 / Revolver / Sony
CD ______ CLACD 222
Castle / '91 / BMG

COLLECTION, THE
CD ______ CCSCD 272
Castle / Oct '90 / BMG

ELEVENTH HOUR, THE
Prize / Great disaster / Vicious companions / One night of passion / Word / Road to paradise / Breakdown / So far away / Hit and run / Young and precious souls
CD ______ WKFMXD 111
FM / Jun '88 / Revolver / Sony
CD ______ CLACD 223
Castle / '91 / BMG

FIREBIRD
Back to earth / Prize / So far away / Hit and run / Lights burned out / Soldier of the line / Changes / Foolish heart / All of my life / Great adventure / Invasion / Kingdom of madness / Universe / Firebird
CD ______ 5507372
Spectrum / Jun '95 / PolyGram

FOUNDATION
CD ______ WKFMBXD 145
FM / Apr '90 / Revolver / Sony

GOODNIGHT LA
Rockin' chair / Only a memory / Matter of survival / Heartbroke and busted / No way out / Born to be king / Mama / Reckless man / What kind of love is this / Shoot / Cry for you
CD ______ 8435682
Polydor / Jul '90 / PolyGram

KEEPING THE NITE LITE BURNING
CD ______ JETCD 1006
Jet / Nov '93 / Total/Pinnacle

KINGDOM OF MADNESS
In the beginning / Baby rock me / Universe / Kingdom of madness / All that is real / Bringer / Invasion / Lords of chaos / All come together
CD ______ CLACD 126
Castle / '86 / BMG
CD ______ WKFMXD 118
FM / Jan '89 / Revolver / Sony

MAGNUM VOL.2
Great adventure / Changes / Battle / If I could live forever / Reborn / So cold the night / Foolish heart / Stayin' alive / Firebird / All of my life
CD ______ CLACD 125
Castle / Mar '87 / BMG
CD ______ WKFMXD 119
FM / Jan '89 / Revolver / Sony

MIRADOR
Just like an arrow / Soldier of the line / Changes / Sacred hour / Great adventure / Lights burned out / In the beginning / How far Jerusalem / Spirit / Word / Prize / Kingdom of madness / If I could live forever / Lords of chaos / Storyteller's night
CD ______ WKFMXD 106
FM / Nov '87 / Revolver / Sony

ON A STORYTELLER'S NIGHT
How far Jerusalem / Just like an arrow / Before first light / On a storytellers night / Les morts dansant / Endless love / Two hearts / Steal your heart / All England / Last dance
CD ______ WKFMXD 34
FM / May '85 / Revolver / Sony
CD ______ JETCD 1007
Jet / Jul '93 / Total/Pinnacle

ROCK ART
We all need to be loved / Hard hearted woman / Back in your arms again / Rock heavy / Tall ships / Tell tale eyes / Love's a stranger / Hush-a-bye baby / Just this side of heaven / I will decide myself / On Christmas Day
CD ______ CDEMD 1066
EMI / Jun '94 / EMI

SLEEP WALKING
CD ______ CDMFN 143
Music For Nations / Oct '92 / Pinnacle

STRONGHOLD (2CD Set)
CD Set ______ RRDCD 007
Receiver / Jun '97 / Grapevine/PolyGram

UNCORKED - THE BEST OF MAGNUM
CD ______ JETCD 1008
Jet / Jun '94 / Total/Pinnacle

VINTAGE MAGNUM
How far Jerusalem / Two hearts / On a storyteller's night / All England's eyes / Just like an arrow / Les morts dansant / Last dance / Kingdom of madness / Foolish heart / Endless love / Prize / Soldier of the line / One night of passion / Lonely nights / Start talking love / Lights burned out
CD ______ EMPRCD 596
Emporio / Oct '95 / Disc

Magoo

SOATERAMIC SOUNDS OF MAGOO, THE
CD ______ CHEM 012CD
Chemikal Underground / Apr '97 / SRD

Magpie Lane

OXFORD RAMBLE, THE
Magpie Lane / As I walked through the meadows / First of May / Oxford city / Oxfordshire Damosel / John Barleycorn / Johnny so long/Eynsham poaching song / Old Molly Oxford / Boar's head carol / Oxford scholar / Great Tom is cast / Old Tom of Oxford/Bonny Christ church bells / Astley's ride / Oxford ramble / Trunkles / Near Woodstock town / Double lead through / Princess Royal / Husbandman and servingman / Banbury Bill/As I was going to Banbury / Adderbury medley / May Day carol
CD ______ BEJOCD 3
Beautiful Jo / Jun '94 / ADA / Direct

SPEED THE PLOUGH
Carter's health / Regent's fete/Sir Roger de Coverley / Green bushes / Highwayman outwitted / Jockey to the fair / Bonny at Morn / Davy, Davy, knick-knack / Poor old horse / Kempshott hunt/Death of the fox / Swaggering Boney / Painful plough / Fool's jig / Mistress's health / Girl with the blue dress on/Swiss boy / Bushes and briars / Reading summer dance / Beverly maid and the tinker / Turtle dove/Bobbing Joe / Shepherd's song / Shooter's hornpipe / Bill Brown / Streets of Oxford / We're all jolly fellows that follow the plough / Speed the plough
CD ______ BEJOCD 4
Beautiful Jo / Jun '94 / ADA / Direct

Maguire, Sean

SEAN MAGUIRE
Someone to love / Love by candlelight / Take this time / My heart won't let you go / No choice in the matter / Suddenly / As soon as you know / Sun shines from you / Devotion / It's always Christmas time
CD ______ CDPCSD 164
Parlophone / Nov '94 / EMI

SPIRIT
Good day / Treat me / You to me are everything / If you really care / I'll be good for you / If I surrender / Now I've found you / Your love / Don't pull you love / Sweet town / Where do broken hearts go / Make it right
CD ______ CDPCSD 169
Parlophone / Jun '96 / EMI

Mahaleo

MAHALEO (Music From Madagascar)
CD ______ PS 65157
PlayaSound / Oct '95 / ADA / Harmonia Mundi

Maharaj, Pandit Kishan

LIVE TABLA SOLO RECITAL, A
CD ______ NRCD 0051
Navras / Jul '96 / New Note/Pinnacle

Maharishi Mahesh Yogi

MAHARISHI MAHESH YOGI
Love / Untapped source of power that lies within
CD ______ BGOCD 331
Beat Goes On / Dec '96 / Pinnacle

Mahavishnu Orchestra

BETWEEN NOTHINGNESS AND ETERNITY
CD ______ CK 32766
Sony Jazz / Aug '97 / Sony

Maher, Tony

IRISH TRANQUILITY
CD ______ HCD 009
GTD / Apr '95 / ADA / Else

Mahieddine

MAHIEDDINE
CD ______ AAA 138
Club Du Disque Arabe / Dec '96 / ADA / Harmonia Mundi

Mahlathini

KING OF THE GROANERS
Umkhovu / Intombi emnyama / Nomacala / Wavutha umlilo / Woza zoxolisa / Isitha ihliziyo / Mtaka mama / Umona / Isikhonyane / We-somhlolo / Ithemba alibulali / Ngizothi mamakubani / Mbaka aka / Umama ithembalmi / Guluva / Izandile jive / Selimathunzi / Normalanga / Inkosi yomkulo / Umkhenyana
CD ______ CDEWV 29
Earthworks / Mar '93 / EMI

LION OF SOWETO
Baba-ye / Bayasazi / Kudala besifuna / Kwa mfazi onge mama / Bhula mngoma / Kumnyama endlini / Kumnandi Emgababa / Amagoduka / Mahlalela / Abake ba bonana / Bayasimenmeza / Ngibuzindela
CD ______ CDEWV 4
Earthworks / '87 / EMI

LION ROARS, THE (Mahlathini & The Mahotella Queens)
Lion roars
CD ______ SHCD 43081
Shanachie / Jun '91 / ADA / Greensleeves / Koch

MBAQANGA (Mahlathini & The Mahotella Queens)
Mbaqanga / Yuya / Bayeza / Umashihlalisane / Jive motella / Thonthodi / Hayi kabi / Stop crying / Bon jour / Josefa / Noluthando / Kwa makhutha
CD ______ KAZ CD 901
Kaz / Oct '91 / BMG

STOKI STOKI (Mahlathini & The Mahotella Queens)
CD ______ SH 64068
Shanachie / Aug '96 / ADA / Greensleeves / Koch

THOKOZILE (Mahlathini & The Mahotella Queens)
Thokozile / Lilileza mililileza / Sibuyile / Nina Majuba / I wanna dance / Uyavutha umlilo / Sengikala Ngiyabaleka / Izulu liyaduduma
CD ______ CDEWV 6
Earthworks / Feb '88 / EMI

Mahogany Hall Stompers

MAHOGANY HALL STOMPERS
CD ______ SOSCD 1221
Stomp Off / Oct '92 / Jazz Music / Wellard

Mahogany Rush

DRAGONFLY (The Best Of Frank Marino & Mahogany Rush) (Marino, Frank & Mahogany Rush)
CD ______ RE 21052
Razor & Tie / Jul '96 / Koch

LEGENDARY MAHOGANY RUSH, THE (Child Of The Novelty/Maxoom/Strange Universe)
Look outside / Thru the milky way / Talking 'bout a feelin' / Child of the novelty / Makin' my wave / New rock and roll / Changing / Plastic man / Guit war / Chains of (s)pace / Maxoom / Buddy / Magic man / Funky woman / Madness / All in your mind / Blues / Boardwalk lady / Back on home / New beginning / Tales of the Spanish warrior / King who stole (The universe) / Satisfy your soul / Land of 1000 nights / Moonlight lady / Dancing lady / Once again / Tryin' anyway / Dear music / Strange universe
CD ______ CDWKM2 149
Big Beat / Jul '95 / Pinnacle

Mahogany, Kevin

DOUBLE RAINBOW
All blues / Confirmation / Save that time / Double rainbow / Our love remains / Dat dere / Little butterfly (Pannonica) / My dungeon shook / Since I fell for you / Three little words / Duke Ellington's sound of love / No one knows what love holds in store (two degrees east, thr / Bring it on home
CD ______ ENJ 70972
Enja / Jul '93 / New Note/Pinnacle / Vital/SAM

SONGS AND MOMENTS
Coaster / West coast blues / City lights / Night flight / Next time you see me / Songs and moments / Caravan / My foolish heart / Red top / Jim's ballad / Take the 'A' train / When I fall in love
CD ______ ENJ 80722
Enja / Oct '94 / New Note/Pinnacle / Vital/SAM

YOU GOT WHAT IT TAKES
Baby you got what it takes / Stockholm sweetnin' / Just in time / Sophisticated lady / Route 66 / Here's the rainy day / Yardbird suite / My funny valentine / Old times sake / BG's groove / God bless the children / Little Sherri / Please send me someone to love
CD ______ ENJ 90392
Enja / Oct '95 / New Note/Pinnacle / Vital/SAM

Mahotella Queens

PUTTING ON THE LIGHT (Mahotella Queens, Mahlathini & Others)
Umthakathi: *Mahotella Queens & Mbazo* / Uyagiyaumahlathini: *Mahlathini & The Mahotella Queens* / Umoya: *Mahotella Queens* / Imbodlomane: *Indodaumahlathini* / Izulungelami: *Mahotella Queens* / Duduzile: *Mahlathini* / Sithunyiwe: *Mahotella Queens* / Ukohhliwe: *Mahlathini* / Dolly swidilami: *Mthunzini Girls* / Thina siyakhanyisa: *Mahotella Queens* / Gabi gabi: *Indodamahlathini* / Bantwanyana: *Mahotella Queens*
CD ______ HNCD 4415
Hannibal / Jul '93 / ADA / Vital

WOMEN OF THE WORLD
CD ______ FLTRCD 510
Flame Tree / Jun '93 / Pinnacle

Maids Of Gravity

FIRST SECOND, THE
Half awake / Don't you disagree / Light you gave / No room / Another one / Golden harm / Can't lose / Looks the same / Islands / Live and die / In the days / It don't have to be
CD ______ VYD 019
Vernon Yard / Mar '97 / Vital

STRANGE CHANNEL
Your ground / Slave and rule / Moonspiders / Taste / In other words
CD ______ CDVUSM 85
Virgin / Apr '95 / EMI

Mailhes, Rene

GOPALINE (Mailhes, Rene Trio)
CD ______ IMP 922
Iris Music / Nov '95 / Discovery

Main

CORONA
CD ___ **HERTZ 1**
Beggars Banquet / Jun '95 / RTM/Disc / Warner Music

FIRMAMENT VOL.2
CD ___ **BBQCD 168**
Beggars Banquet / Nov '94 / RTM/Disc / Warner Music

FIRMAMENT VOL.3
CD ___ **BBQMCD 179**
Beggars Banquet / Nov '96 / RTM/Disc / Warner Music

HERTS SERIES, THE
CD ___ **HERT 16CD**
Beggars Banquet / Jan '96 / RTM/Disc / Warner Music

HYDRA/CALM
CD ___ **SITL 39CD**
Situation 2 / Jun '92 / Pinnacle

MAIN
CD ___ **HSRTZ 3**
Beggars Banquet / Aug '95 / RTM/Disc / Warner Music

MOTION POOL
CD ___ **BBQCD 148**
Beggars Banquet / Apr '94 / RTM/Disc / Warner Music

NEPER
CD ___ **HERT 26**
Beggars Banquet / Nov '95 / RTM/Disc / Warner Music

Main Ingredient

I JUST WANNA LOVE YOU
CD ___ **8412492**
Polydor / Mar '90 / PolyGram

Main Source

FUCK WHAT YOU THINK
Diary of a hit man / Only the real survive / What you need / Merrick Boulevard / Down low / Intermission / Where we're coming from / Hellavision / Fuck what you think / Set it off / Scrach and kut 94
CD ___ **CDPITCH 002**
Wild Pitch / Mar '94 / EMI

Main Stream Power Band

MEMORIES IN SWING
Music makers / Flight of the foo birds / In a persian market / Empty roads / Sailor's boogie / Way down yonder in New Orleans / Fantail / Down South camp meetin' / Soho beat / Main stream boogie / Lovely rose / When the saints go marching in / Bakerloo non-stop / Splanky / Memories in swing / Wrappin' it up / Jumping duck / Hampstead Saturday night / Merry go round / Hot pink / Saxes on fire / What's the trouble / If dreams come true / Play bounce
CD ___ **MONTCD 001**
Montpellier / May '96 / Jazz Music / Montpellier

Mainer, J.E.

RUN MOUNTAIN
CD ___ **ARHCD 456**
Arhoolie / Feb '97 / ADA / Cadillac / Direct

Mainesthal

OUT TO LUNCH
CD ___ **CDZOT 117**
Zoth Ommog / Aug '94 / Cargo / Plastic Head

Mainieri, Mike

AMERICAN DIARY, AN
Somewhere / King Kong / Piano sonata (vivace) / Piano sonato No 1 / Town meeting / Overture to the school for scandal / Hudson river valley / Sometimes I feel like a Motherless child / Song of my people / In the gloaming / Out of the cage / In the universe of Ives
CD ___ **NYC 60152**
NYC / Jul '95 / New Note/Pinnacle

AMERICAN DIARY, AN (The Dreamings)
'R' is for riddle / Los dos lorettas / Dreamings / Schecharchoret / Bashi-bazouk / Dear, my friend (the gift) / Planting rice is never fun / Straphangin' / An American tale / Peyote prayer / One night in paradise / Why gypsies are scattered all over the earth
CD ___ **NYC 60262**
NYC / Mar '97 / New Note/Pinnacle

COME TOGETHER
Come together / She's leaving home / Here, there and everywhere / And I love her / Michelle / Something / Eleanor Rigby / Norwegian wood / Blackbird / Within you without you / Yesterday
CD ___ **NYC 60042**
NYC / Jun '93 / New Note/Pinnacle

LIVE AT SEVENTH AVENUE SOUTH
Tee bag / Flying colours / Song for Seth / Bullet train / Sara's touch / Bamboo / Crossed wires
CD ___ **NYC 60222**
NYC / Jun '96 / New Note/Pinnacle

MAN BEHIND BARS
ESP / Trinary motion / Push-pull / Equinox / Satyr dance / Momento No 1 / Nearness of you / Momento No 2 / All the things you are / Binary motion
CD ___ **NYC 60192**
NYC / Dec '95 / New Note/Pinnacle

WANDERLUST
Bullet train / Sara's touch / Crossed wires / Flying colours / L'image / Bamboo / Wanderlust
CD ___ **NYC 60022**
NYC / Oct '92 / New Note/Pinnacle

WHITE ELEPHANT
Peace of mind / Jones / Battle royal / Look in his eyes / White elephant / Easy on / Animal fat / Monkey
CD ___ **NYC 60082**
NYC / Oct '94 / New Note/Pinnacle

WHITE ELEPHANT VOL.2
More to love / Broadway Joe / Dreamsong / Gunfighter / Right back / Sunshine clean / Save the water / Auld lang syne / Field song / Battle royal
CD ___ **NYC 60112**
NYC / Feb '96 / New Note/Pinnacle

Mainliner

MAINLINER SONIC
CD ___ **100252**
Charnel House / May '97 / Cargo / Greyhound

Mainstream Power Band

DATE WITH SWING, A (Mainstream Power Band & Heinz Schonberger)
CD ___ **MONTCD 002**
Montpellier / Jan '97 / Jazz Music / Montpellier

HOLIDAY FOR SWING
CD ___ **MONTCD 003**
Montpellier / Nov '96 / Jazz Music / Montpellier

Maipu

MUSIC FROM THE ANDES
CD ___ **15496**
Laserlight / Jan '94 / Target/BMG

Maisonneuve, Arnaud

OUILET MEN DEULAGAD
CD ___ **RSCD 222**
Keltia Musique / Jul '96 / ADA / Discovery

Maitre, Pandit Kamalesh

TABLA TARANG - RAGAS ON DRUMS (The World's Musical Traditions #10)
CD ___ **SFWCD 40436**
Smithsonian Folkways / Mar '96 / ADA / Cadillac / CM / Direct / Koch

Majella

SPINNING WHEEL, THE (24 Traditional Irish Favourites) (Majella & The Don Lowes Orchestra)
I know where I'm going / Leaving of Liverpool / Merskeen durkin / Song of Derry / Will ye go lassie go / She moves through the fair / Whiskey in the jar / Green glens of Antrim / Old maid in the garret / Connemara cradle song / Courtin' in the kitchen / Forty shades of green / Wild colonial boy / Irish soldier laddie / Galway boy / If we only had old Ireland over here / Rose of Tralee / It's Heaven around Galway Bay / Mountains of Mourne / Mary from Dungloe / Danny boy / Hanningan's hooley
CD ___ **306862**
Hallmark / Jul '97 / Carlton

Majestic

NO WORDS, NO MISUNDERSTANDINGS
CD ___ **EFA 125172**
Celtic Circle / Sep '95 / SRD

Major Worries

BABYLON BOOPS
CD ___ **792082**
Jammy's / Apr '93 / Jet Star

Majumdar, Ronu

REVERIE
CD ___ **NRCD 0073**
Navras / Feb '97 / New Note/Pinnacle

Make Up

AFTER DARK
CD ___ **DIS 105CD**
Dischord / Feb '97 / SRD

LOVE LIVE
CD ___ **DIS 99CD**
Dischord / Apr '96 / SRD

SOUND VERITE
CD ___ **KLP 64CD**
K / Mar '97 / Cargo / Greyhound / SRD

Makeba, Miriam

AFRICA
Mbube / Nomeva / Olilili / Suliram / Retreat song / Click song / Saduva / Iya guduza / Lakutshon ilanga / Umhome / Amanpondo / Dubula / Kwendini / Umhome / Pole mze / Le fleuve / Qhude / Mayibuye / Maduna / Kilimanjaro / Kwazulu (in the land of the Zulus) / Nongqongqq (To those we love) / Khawuleza / Ndodemnyama (Beware, Verwoerd)
CD ___ **ND 83155**
Novus / Jan '92 / BMG

FOLK SONGS FROM AFRICA
CD ___ **CD 12514**
Music Of The World / Jun '94 / ADA / Target/BMG

LIVE FROM PARIS AND CONAKRY
Kilmandjaro / I shall sing / Kulala / Malaika / Jolinkomo / Measure the valley / Ring bell / Pata pata / I'mm you'mm we'mm / U shaka / Tonados del media noche / Malcolm X / Tutu Maramba / Amampondo / West wind / Mas que nada / Forbidden games / Ngoma kurila / Congas / I phin dlela / Tutu marmamba
CD ___ **DRGCD 5234**
DRG / Jul '96 / Discovery / New Note/ Pinnacle

WELELA
Amampondo / African sunset / Diju de galinha / A luta continua / Soweto blues / Welela / Hapo zamani / Pata pata / Saduva / Africa
CD ___ **8382082**
Philips / May '89 / PolyGram

Makem, Tommy

CLASSIC GOLD (Makem, Tommy & Liam Clancy)
CD ___ **TF 1010**
Third Floor / Oct '94 / ADA / Direct / Total/ BMG

COLLECTION, THE (Makem, Tommy & Liam Clancy)
CD ___ **TFCB 1009CD**
Third Floor / Oct '94 / ADA / Direct / Total/ BMG

DUTCHMAN, THE (Makem, Tommy & Liam Clancy)
CD ___ **SHCD 52005**
Shanachie / May '93 / ADA / Greensleeves / Koch

FROM THE ARCHIVES
CD ___ **SHCD 52040**
Shanachie / Mar '95 / ADA / Greensleeves / Koch

IN CONCERT (Makem, Tommy & Liam Clancy)
CD ___ **TF 1002**
Third Floor / Oct '94 / ADA / Direct / Total/ BMG

LARK IN THE MORNING, THE (Makem, Tommy & Liam Clancy)
CD ___ **TCD 1001**
Tradition / Feb '96 / ADA / Vital

REUNION (Makem, Tommy & The Clancy Brothers)
CD ___ **TF 5009**
Third Floor / Oct '94 / ADA / Direct / Total/ BMG

SONGS OF TOMMY MAKEM, THE
CD ___ **TCD 1054**
Tradition / Jul '97 / ADA / Vital

TOMMY MAKEM'S CHRISTMAS
CD ___ **SHCD 52041**
Shanachie / Nov '96 / ADA / Greensleeves / Koch

Makers

HIP-NOTIC/SHOUT ON
CD ___ **SFTR 1470CD**
Sympathy For The Record Industry / May '97 / Cargo / Greyhound / Plastic Head

HUNGER
CD ___ **ES 1232CD**
Estrus / Mar '97 / Cargo / Greyhound / Plastic Head

SHOUT ON
CD ___ **SFTRI 470**
Sympathy For The Record Industry / Jun '97 / Cargo / Greyhound / Plastic Head

Makowicz, Adam

CLASSIC JAZZ DUETS (Makowicz, Adam & George Mraz)
CD ___ **NI 4021**
Natasha / Feb '94 / ADA / Cadillac / CM / Direct / Jazz Music

CONCORD DUO SERIES VOL.5 (Makowicz, Adam & George Mraz)
Don't ever leave me / 400 West d-flat / Where is love / Anything goes / Mito / Say it isn't so / Culebra / Concordance / I loves you Porgy / Cherokee
CD ___ **CCD 4597**
Concord Jazz / Jun '94 / New Note/ Pinnacle

MUSIC OF JEROME KERN, THE (Makowicz, Adam Trio)
All the things you are / Way you look tonight / Who / Song is you / I won't dance / Ol' man river / Long ago and far away / Smoke gets in your eyes / Yesterdays / Dearly beloved / I'm old fashioned
CD ___ **CCD 4575**
Concord Jazz / Nov '93 / New Note/ Pinnacle

MY FAVOURITE THINGS (The Music Of Richard Rodgers)
Where or when / I didn't know what time it was / Surrey with the fringe on top / My favourite things / Lady is a tramp / This can't be love / My funny valentine / My romance / Lover / It might as well be spring / Have you met Miss Jones
CD ___ **CCD 4631**
Concord Jazz / Feb '95 / New Note/ Pinnacle

SOLO ALBUM - ADAM IN STOCKHOLM
Blues for Stockholm / Scandinavia / 'Round midnight / Castle Hotel / I surrender dear / Yesterdays / Snowflower / Body and soul / Song for Tung / Summertime
CD ___ **5178882**
Verve / Jan '94 / PolyGram

Makulis, Jimmy

GITARREN KLINGEN LEISE DURCH DIE NACHT
Gitarren klingen leise durch die Nacht / Addio mein blondes Madel / Tahiti / Das wunder einer Sternenacht / Ein boot, eine Mondnacht und du / Nachts in Rom / Am Lido wartet eine Gondel / Weites Land / Sweetheart guitar / Das Tal der weissen rose / Ich habe im leben nur dich / Keiner weiss wohin / Maro, Maro / Weil ich weiss, dass wir uns wiedersehn / Horst du das lied aus alter zeit / Der bunte Hochzeitswagen / Traumen van der Sudsee / Eine Insel aus Traumen geboren / Lebe wohl, du blume von Tahiti / Der wind hat sich gedreht / Bald kommt der tag / Gold im sonnenschein / Vaya con dios / Aloha oe / Fontana di Trevi (Es war wie ein Marchen) / So kommt ein Stern in der nacht
CD ___ **BCD 15922**
Bear Family / May '96 / Direct / Rollercoaster / Swift

Malach, Bob

SEARCHER, THE
CD ___ **GOJ 60152**
Go Jazz / Sep '95 / Vital/SAM

Malaise

FIFTY TWO WAYS
CD ___ **MEMO 015CD**
Nightbreed / Jan '97 / Plastic Head

Malaria

REVISITED
CD ___ **DANCD 083**
Danceteria / Jul '97 / ADA / Plastic Head / Shellshock/Disc

Malavoi

DIAMOND COLLECTION, THE
CD ___ **3004402**
Arcade / Feb '97 / Discovery

Malayev, Ilyas

AT THE BAZAAR OF LOVE (Timeless Central Asian Maqam Music) (Malayev, Ilyas Ensemble)
CD ___ **SH 64081**
Shanachie / Feb '97 / ADA / Greensleeves / Koch

Malcahy, Mick

MICK MULCAHY AND FRIENDS
CD ___ **CEFCD 143**
Gael Linn / Jan '94 / ADA / CM / Direct / Grapevine/PolyGram / Roots

Malcolm X

ROOTS OF DUB VOL.3, THE
CD ___ **DTCD 25**
Discotex / Apr '96 / Jet Star

Malcolm, James

SCONEWARD
Scotch blues / Neptune / Losin' auld reeki / Wild geese / Scotlandshire / Achiltibuie / Lochs of the Tay / Wisest fool / Noran water / Barrenlands / Grandfathers / Party / Flowers of Edinburgh
CD ___ **CDTRAX 083**
Greentrax / Mar '95 / ADA / Direct / Duncans / Highlander

Malevolent Creation

ETERNAL
CD ___ **CDVEST 52**
Bulletproof / Mar '96 / Pinnacle

IN COLD BLOOD
CD ___ **PM 32258CD**
Pavement / Jun '97 / Plastic Head

Mali Rain

FORECAST FOR STORMS
Forecast for storms / Koan / Sentinel / Via Dolorosa / Khat / Statikat / Cove / Pende / Optimist castle / Basking / Octane / Pulse
CD STONE 024CD
3rd Stone / Apr '96 / Plastic Head / Vital

WE SHALL RETURN TO THE SEA
Basking / Arp-aht / Statikat / Simms / Tranquility bass / Canopy / Callow Hill 508 AM / Peyostasia / Octane / Koan
CD STONE 017CD
3rd Stone / Aug '95 / Plastic Head / Vital

Malicious Onslaught

BRUTAL CORE
CD USR 007CD
Unisound / Jan '96 / Plastic Head

REBELLIOUS MAYHEM
CD BROO 1CD
Brain Crusher / Nov '92 / Plastic Head

Malicorne

BALANCOIRE ENFEU
CD BPCD 9331
Boucherie Productions / Feb '96 / ADA

EN PUBLIC
CD BPCD 9311
Boucherie Productions / Feb '96 / ADA

L'EXTRAORDINAIRE
CD BPCD 9301
Boucherie Productions / Feb '96 / ADA

LE BESTIAIRE
CD BPCD 9321
Boucherie Productions / Feb '96 / ADA

LEGENDE: DEUXIEME EPOQUE
Le Prince D'Orange / Le ballet des coqs / Compagnons qui roulez en provence / La mule la conduite / Pierre De Grenoble / Vive la lune / La dance des dames / La Chasse Gallery / La nuit des sorcieres / Dormeur / L'ecolier assassin / Beau charpentier / Quand le cypes
CD HNCD 1360
Hannibal / Jul '91 / ADA / Vital

VOX
CD BPCD 9291
Boucherie Productions / Feb '96 / ADA

Malie

DANCE MUSIC FROM TONGA
CD PANCD 2011
Pan / May '93 / ADA / CM / Direct

Malik, Raphe

21ST CENTURY TEXTS
CD FMPCD 43
FMP / Sep '89 / Cadillac

Malika

TARABU (Music From The Swahili Of Kenya)
CD SH 64089
Shanachie / Jun '97 / ADA / Greensleeves / Koch

Malinga, Joe

ITHI GQI (Malinga, Joe Group)
CD BRAM 1990112
Brambus / Nov '93 / ADA

Malinverni, Pete

THIS TIME
CD RSRCD 147
Reservoir Music / May '97 / Cadillac

Malka Spiget

ROSH BALLATA
CD WM 1
Swim / Mar '94 / Kudos / RTM/Disc / SRD

Malkowsky, Liselotte

SONNTAGNACHT AUF DER REEPERBAHN
Sonntagnacht auf der Reeperbahn / Der alte Seemann kann nachts nicht sclafen / Auf dem Meeresgrunde / Meine stille liebe ist Elbe / Marju, gruss mir mein St. Pauli / Geht ein Schiff in see / Eine einsame harmonika / Fang' keine liebe mit Matrosen an / Das rote Licht an backbord / Das Herz von St. Pauli / Er war in Hamburg / Eine kleiner Akkordeonspieler / Jim spiele harmonika / Was macht der seeman, wenn er sehnsucht hat / Warum zahlen die Matrosen nachts die Sterne / Ein Herz und eine Rose / Schone insel Hawaii / Ja wenn das Meer nicht war / Mein schiff hab' gute Reise / In der bar 'Zum gold'nen anker' / Auf St. Pauli spielt der Jonny Mundharmonika / Ein seemann bleibt nicht zu hause / Wenn die schiffe den hafen verlassen / Fahr mich in die Ferne, mein blonder Matrose / Seemann, komm' doch nach haus' / Der alte Matrose
CD BCD 15955
Bear Family / May '96 / Direct / Rollercoaster / Swift

Malkuri

TRADITIONAL MUSIC OF THE ANDES
CD SP 7143CD
Soundings / Aug '96 / ADA / Else

Mallan, Peter

SCOTLAND IN SONG
CD CDLOC 1088
Lochshore / Jul '95 / ADA / Direct / Duncans

Mallett, David

FOR A LIFETIME
For a lifetime / Sweet Tennessee / My old man / Some peace will come / Night on the town / Hometown girls / This city life / Lost in a memory of you / Light at the end of the tunnel / Summer of my dreams
CD FF 70497
Flying Fish / Jul '89 / ADA / CM / Direct / Roots

OPEN DOORS AND WINDOWS
CD FF 70291
Flying Fish / Feb '95 / ADA / CM / Direct / Roots

Mallku De Los Andes

ON THE WINGS OF THE CONDOR
CD TUMICD 004
Tumi / '86 / Discovery / Stern's

Malmkvist, Siw

HARLEKIN
CD BCD 15661
Bear Family / Oct '93 / Direct / Rollercoaster / Swift

LIEBESKUMMER 1961-1968
CD BCD 15660
Bear Family / Oct '93 / Direct / Rollercoaster / Swift

Malmquist, Dan Gisen

NATTLJUS
Nattljus / Spegling / Speldosan / Motvals / Glasskapet / Sorg / Pavag / Gycklaren / Fallande angel / Gryningen / Kluring / Svanen / Kneppolskan / Festen ar over
CD XOUCD 116
Xource / May '97 / ADA / Direct

VATTENRINGER
CD RES 516CD
Resource / Jul '97 / ADA / Direct

Malmsteen, Yngwie

FIRE AND ICE
CD 7559611372
Elektra / Feb '92 / Warner Music

INSPIRATION (2CD Set)
CD CDMFN 200
Music For Nations / Oct '96 / Pinnacle

MAGNUM OPUS
Vengeance / No love lost / Tomorrows gone / Only one / Die without you / Overture 1622 / Voodoo / Cross the line / Time will tell / Fire in the sky / Amber dawn / Cantabile
CD CDMFN 188
Music For Nations / Jul '95 / Pinnacle

MARCHING OUT (Malmsteen, Yngwie & Rising Force)
Prelude / I'll see the light tonight / Don't let it end / Disciples of hell / I'm a viking / Overture 1383 / Anguish and fear / On the run again / Soldier without faith / Caught in the middle / Marching out
CD 8257332
Polydor / Aug '85 / PolyGram

ODYSSEY (Malmsteen, Yngwie & Rising Force)
Rising force / Hold on / Heaven tonight / Dreaming (tell me) / Bite the bullet / Riot in the dungeons / Deja vu / Crystal ball / Now is the time / Faster than the speed of light / Krakatau / Memories
CD 8354512
Polydor / Mar '96 / PolyGram

RISING FORCE
Black star: *Malmsteen, Yngwie & Rising Force* / Far beyond the sun / Now your ships are burned / Evil eye / Icarus' dream suite / As above so below: *Malmsteen, Yngwie & Rising Force* / Little savage / Farewell
CD 8253242
Polydor / May '88 / PolyGram

SEVENTH SIGN
Never die / I don't know / Meant to be / Forever one / Hairtrigger / Brothers / Seventh sign / Bad blood / Prisoner of your love / Pyramid of cheops / Crash and burn / Sorrow
CD CDMFN 158
Music For Nations / Mar '94 / Pinnacle

YNGWIE MALMSTEEN COLLECTION, THE
Black star / Far beyond the sun / I'll see the light tonight / You don't remember, I'll never forget / Liar / Queen in love / Hold on / Heaven tonight / Deja vu / Guitar solo / Spanish castle magic / Judas / Making love / Eclipse
CD 8492712
Polydor / Mar '96 / PolyGram

Malone, Debbie

GOOD LIFE
CD PULSECD 6
Pulse / Nov '92 / BMG

Malone, Michelle

NEW EXPERIENCE
CD SKYCD 5025
Sky / Sep '94 / Greyhound / Koch / Vital/SAM

Maloney, Bunny

SINGS OLDIES IN A REGGAE
CD HM 501172
Mudies / Sep '95 / Jet Star

Malope, Rebecca

FREE AT LAST (South African Gospel)
Mmele Wajeso (Kebophelo) / Uhlal'ekhona / Kojabula / Take my hand / Buyani / Emadleweni / In his hands / Umoya wam ngegazi lemvana / I'll bide my time / Vuselela / I'll be free / Shwele baba
CD HEMICD 27
Hemisphere / Jun '97 / EMI

Malta

CINEMATRIX
Aphrodite / EOS / Danae / Cassandra / Donky King / Donky queen / Shaista / Blackjack / P S I luv you / Whiter shade of pale
CD JVC 90222
JVC / Aug '97 / Direct / New Note/Pinnacle / Vital/SAM

HIGH PRESSURE
CD JD 3303
JVC / Jul '88 / Direct / New Note/Pinnacle / Vital/SAM

MY BALLADS
CD JD 3315
JVC / May '89 / Direct / New Note/ Pinnacle / Vital/SAM

OBSESSION
CD JD 3310
JVC / Oct '88 / Direct / New Note/ Pinnacle / Vital/SAM

UK UNDERGROUND
Songs for my father / Nica's dream / So what / Moanin' / Crisis / Sidewinder / Along came Betty / Les liaisons dangereuses / 'Ascenseur pour L'echafaud' Generique / Donna Lee / Brother Mason / London funktion / Half Moon street
CD JVC 90042
JVC / Aug '96 / Direct / New Note/Pinnacle / Vital/SAM

Maltese

COUNT YOUR BLESSINGS
CD CDATV 21
Active / Jul '92 / Pinnacle

Mama Sana

MUSIC FROM MADAGASCAR
CD SHCD 65010
Shanachie / May '95 / ADA / Greensleeves / Koch

Mamamax

AUDIOTRONIC
CD RR 69632
Relapse / Aug '97 / Pinnacle / Plastic Head

Mamas & The Papas

20 GREATEST HITS
California dreamin' / I saw her again / I call your name / Twist and shout / Sing for your supper / Look through my window / Do you wanna dance / Dancing in the street / You baby / Dedicated to the one I love / Monday, Monday / Words of love / Glad to be unhappy / Go where you wanna go / Safe in my garden / Spanish Harlem / Trip, stumble and fall / My girl / Creeque Alley / Dream a little dream of me: *Mama Cass*
CD CDMFP 50493
Music For Pleasure / Dec '92 / EMI

BEST OF THE MAMAS & PAPAS
CD MCBD 19519
MCA / Apr '95 / BMG

CALIFORNIA DREAMIN' (The Best Of The Mamas & The Papas)
California dreamin' / Dedicated to the one I love / Monday Monday / Dream a little dream of me / Creeque Alley / I saw her again / It's getting better / Words of love / In crowd / Dancing in the street / Spanish Harlem / Twist and shout / Do you wanna dance / Go where you wanna go / Look through my window / You baby / For the love of Ivy / Make your own kind of music / Twelve thirty (Young girls are coming to the canyon) / I call your name / My girl / California earthquake / Straight shooter / Glad to be unhappy
CD 5239732
Polydor / Jul '96 / PolyGram

CREEQUE ALLEY
CD MCLD 19124
MCA / Sep '94 / BMG

ELLIOTT, PHILLIPS, GILLIAM, DOCHERTY
California dreamin' / Dedicated to the one I love / Even if I could / Once there was a time I thought / You baby / In crowd / I saw her again / Did you ever want to cry / John's music box / Too late / Go where you wanna go / Midnight voyage / Creeque alley / Strange young girls / Dancing bear / No salt on her tail / My cart stood still / Dream a little dream of me: *Mama Cass* / California earthquake / Somebody groovy / Sing for your supper / Free advice / String man / I can't wait
CD VSOPCD 119
Connoisseur Collection / Jul '88 / Pinnacle

EP COLLECTION, THE
California dreamin' / Somebody groovy / Monday, Monday / In crowd / I saw her again / Go where you wanna go / Look through my window / Trip, stumble and fall / Dedicated to the one I love / Free advice / Straight shooter / Get a feeling / Hey girl / You baby / Even if I could / I call your name / Words of love / Dancing in the street / I can't wait / That kind of girl
CD SEECD 333
See For Miles/C5 / Aug '97 / Pinnacle

GOLDEN GREATS
Dedicated to the one I love / Monday, Monday / Look through my window / California dreamin' / I call your name / My girl / Dream a little dream of me: *Mama Cass* / Go where you wanna go / Got a feelin' / I saw her again / Words of love / Twelve thirty / Dancing in the street / Glad to be unhappy / Creeque alley / Midnight voyage / Spanish Harlem / You baby / Do you wanna dance / Twist and shout / Safe in my garden / California earthquake
CD MCLD 19125
MCA / Jul '92 / BMG

HITS OF GOLD
California dreamin' / Dedicated to the one I love / Monday, Monday / I saw her again / Creeque alley
CD MCLD 19050
MCA / Apr '92 / BMG

MAMAS & THE PAPAS
CD GFS 070
Going For A Song / Jul '97 / Else / TKO Magnum

VERY BEST OF MAMAS & PAPAS, THE
Monday, Monday / California dreamin' / Dedicated to the one I love / Creeque alley / It's getting better / Straight shooter / Spanish Harlem / Twelve thirty / Go where you wanna go / I saw her again / People like us / My girl / California earthquake / For the love of Ivy / Got a feelin'
CD PLATCD 302
Platinum / Dec '88 / Prism

Mambo

MAMBOS QUE HICIERON HISTORIA
CD 995202
EPM / Aug '93 / ADA / Discovery

Mambo Macoco

MAMBO MACOCO WITH TITO PUENTE AND HIS ORCHESTRA (Mambo Macoco & Tito Puente Orchestra)
CD TCD 018
Fresh Sound / Dec '92 / Discovery / Jazz Music

Mambossa

MAMBOSSA
CD BOM 06CD
Bomba / Jul '96 / Amato Disco / Mo's Music Machine / Prime / Timewarp

Mamduko

MUNDIALISTAS
CD TUMICD 020
Tumi / '92 / Discovery / Stern's

Mammoth

MAMMOTH
All the days / Can't take the hurt / Dark star / Long time coming / Home from the storm / Fat man / Thirty pieces of silver / Bet you wish / Bad times
CD SJPCD 006
Blueprint / Apr '97 / Pinnacle

Mamu

TOWNSHIP BOY
What a lie / Soweto so where to / Mpoho / We don't buy from town / Love / Township boy / Today someone died / Prologue/ monologue / Don't bother me / War is declared
CD KAZ CD 9
Kaz / Nov '89 / BMG

Man

2OZ OF PLASTIC WITH A HOLE IN THE MIDDLE
Prelude / Storm / It is as it must be / Spunk box / My name is Jesus Smith / Parchment and candles / Brother Arnold's red and white striped tent
CD _______ SEECD 273
See For Miles/C5 / Nov '89 / Pinnacle

ALL'S WELL THAT ENDS WELL
Let the good times roll / Welsh connection / Ride and the view / Hard way to live / Born with a future / Spunkrock / Romain
CD _______ PNTVP 103CD
Point / Jul '97 / Pinnacle

BACK INTO THE FUTURE
CD _______ BGOCD 211
Beat Goes On / Nov '93 / Pinnacle

BE GOOD TO YOURSELF AT LEAST ONCE A DAY
C'mon / Keep on crinting / Bananas / Life on the road
CD _______ BGOCD 14
Beat Goes On / Jul '89 / Pinnacle

CHRISTMAS AT THE PATTI
Welcome to the party / Boogaloo babe / My way / Jambalaya / Jingle bells/Run run Rudolph / Mona / Eddie Waring / Life on the road / Shuffle
CD _______ PNTVP 110CD
Point / Sep '97 / Pinnacle

DAWN OF MAN (2CD Set)
CD Set _______ SMDCD 124
Snapper / Jul '97 / Pinnacle

GREASY TRUCKERS PARTY
Spunkrock / Angel easy / Andy Dunkley
CD _______ PNTVP 104CD
Point / Jul '97 / Pinnacle

LIVE IN LONDON
7171-551 / Hard way to die / Breaking up once again / Life on the road / Day and night / Someone is calling / Many are called but few get up / Brazilian cucumber meets Deke's new nose
CD _______ PNTVP 101CD
Point / Jul '97 / Pinnacle

LIVE OFFICIAL BOOTLEG
CD _______ EFA 035052
Think Progressive / Apr '97 / Greyhound / SRD

MAXIMUM DARKNESS
7171-551 / Codine / Babe I'm gonna leave you / Many are called but few get up / Bananas
CD _______ BGOCD 43
Beat Goes On / Nov '91 / Pinnacle

OFFICIAL BOOTLEG, THE
C'mon / Mad on her / Even visionaires go blind / Chinese cut / Wings of mercury / Slide guitar intro to... / Ride and view / Feather on the scales of justice / Bananas
CD _______ PNTVP 109CD
Point / Sep '97 / Pinnacle

RHINOS, WINOS AND LUNATICS
CD _______ BGOCD 208
Beat Goes On / Oct '93 / Pinnacle

SLOW MOTION
CD _______ BGOCD 209
Beat Goes On / Oct '93 / Pinnacle

TO LIVE FOR TO DIE
Spunk box / Conscience / Storm / Would the christians wait five minutes / Alchemist of the mind / Daughter of the fireplace / Scholar of consciousness
CD _______ PNTVP 108CD
Point / Sep '97 / Pinnacle

WELSH CONNECTION
Ride and the view / Out of your head / Love can find a way / Welsh connection / Something is happening / Car toon / Born with a future
CD _______ PNTVP 102CD
Point / Jul '97 / Pinnacle

Man Mouse

HEROIC COUPLET
Fuck the lottery / I don't care what you say, think or do / Hex / Spin / Towards tomorrow / Testify / Rejecting the authority of Vedas / England's glory, my shame / Blowhole / No extra track / You're going down with the Mackems
CD _______ HOVE 1CD
Stereophonic Hovesound / Dec '94 / Hovesound

Man Called Adam

APPLE
CD _______ BLRCD 7
Big Life / Oct '91 / Mo's Music Machine / Pinnacle / Prime

Man Is The Bastard

SUM OF MEN
CD _______ VFMCD 9
Vermiform / Apr '96 / Cargo / Greyhound / Plastic Head

Man Or Astro Man

DESTROY ALL ASTRO MEN
CD _______ ESD 1215
Estrus / Jul '95 / Cargo / Greyhound / Plastic Head

EXPERIMENT ZERO
CD _______ LOUDEST 12
One Louder / Apr '96 / Mo's Music Machine / Shellshock/Disc / SRD

INTRAVENOUS TELEVISION CONTINUUM
CD _______ LOUDEST 8
One Louder / Jul '95 / Mo's Music Machine / Shellshock/Disc / SRD

IS IT
CD _______ ESD 129
Estrus / Jul '95 / Cargo / Greyhound / Plastic Head

LIVE TRANSMISSIONS FROM URANUS
CD _______ LOUDEST 6
One Louder / Mar '95 / Mo's Music Machine / Shellshock/Disc / SRD

PROJECT INFINITY
CD _______ ES 1221CD
Estrus / Jul '95 / Cargo / Greyhound / Plastic Head

WHAT REMAINS INSIDE A BLACK HOLE
CD _______ ANDA 191
Au-Go-Go / Jan '97 / Cargo / Greyhound / Plastic Head

YOUR WEIGHT ON THE MOON
CD _______ LOUDEST 4
One Louder / Aug '94 / Mo's Music Machine / Shellshock/Disc / SRD

Man Will Surrender

MAN WILL SURRENDER
CD _______ CR 019CD
Conversion / Jul '96 / Plastic Head

Man With No Name

MOMENT OF TRUTH
CD _______ DICCD 125
Beggars Banquet / Feb '96 / RTM/Disc / Warner Music

Man, Wu

CHINESE TRADITIONAL AND CONTEMPORARY MUSIC (Man, Wu & Ensemble)
Xiyang xiaogu / Niao tou lin / Han'gong qiuyue / Xiao ou'an zhou / Shimian maifu / Yang'guan san die / Run / CAGE IV / Gu yun san die
CD _______ NI 5477
Nimbus / Mar '96 / Nimbus

SOLO PIPA (Man, Wu & Ensemble)
CD _______ NI 5368
Nimbus / Mar '95 / Nimbus

Manahedji, Behnam

MASTER OF THE PERSIAN SANTOOR
CD _______ SM 15082
Wergo / Feb '94 / ADA / Cadillac / Harmonia Mundi

Manasseh

SHINING (Manasseh & The Equaliser)
CD _______ DUBIDCD 6
Acid Jazz / Aug '96 / Disc

Mance, Junior

AT THE VILLAGE VANGUARD (Mance, Junior Trio)
Looptown / Letter from home / Girl of my dreams / 63rd street theme / Smokey blues / 9.20 special / Bingo domino / You are too beautiful
CD _______ OJCCD 204
Original Jazz Classics / Jan '97 / Complete/ Pinnacle / Jazz Music / Wellard

JUBILATION
CD _______ SKCD 22046
Sackville / Jan '97 / Cadillac / Jazz Music / Swift

JUNIOR MANCE AT THE TOWN HALL VOL.1
CD _______ ENJACD 90852
Enja / Dec '95 / New Note/Pinnacle / Vital/ SAM

JUNIOR MANCE AT THE TOWN HALL VOL.2
Blues in the closet / Some other blues / My romance / Do nothin' 'til you hear from me / Mercy mercy mercy
CD _______ ENJACD 90952
Enja / Feb '97 / New Note/Pinnacle / Vital/ SAM

JUNIOR MANCE QUARTET PLAY THE MUSIC OF DIZZY GILLESPIE (Mance, Junior Quintet)
CD _______ SKCD 23050
Sackville / Feb '93 / Cadillac / Jazz Music / Swift

JUNIOR MANCE SPECIAL
CD _______ SKCD 23043
Sackville / Oct '92 / Cadillac / Jazz Music / Swift

SMOKEY BLUES (Mance, Junior Trio)
CD _______ JSPCD 219
JSP / Jul '88 / ADA / Cadillac / Direct / Hot Shot / Target/BMG

SOFTLY AS IN A MORNING (Mance, Junior Trio)
CD _______ ENJACD 80802
Enja / Jan '95 / New Note/Pinnacle / Vital/ SAM

TRIO BLUE MANCE (Mance, Junior Trio)
CD _______ CRD 331
Chiaroscuro / Mar '96 / Jazz Music

Manchester Utd FC

FOOTBALL CLASSICS - MANCHESTER UNITED (Various Artists)
Manchester United calypso / Red Devils / Ryan Giggs we love you / George Best - Belfast boy / I love George Best / Echoes of the cheers / Manchester United football double / United, Manchester United / Look around / Yellow submarine / Oh what a lovely morning / Storm in a teacup / Precious memories / Congratulations / Never be alone / Chirpy chirpy cheep cheep / Love again, live again / Saturday afternoon at the football / Raindrops keep falling on my head / Munich air disaster - Flowers of Manchester
CD _______ MONDE 16CD
Cherry Red / Apr '95 / Pinnacle

GLORY GLORY MAN UNITED
United united: *Stretford End Boys* / We will stand together / Red devils: *Georgie Boys* / Ryan Giggs we love you: *Rainbow Choir* / Le diable rouge: *Stretford End Boys* / United / Look around / Yellow submarine / Oh what a lovely morning / Storm in a teacup / Precious memories / Congratulations / Never be alone / Chirpy chirpy cheep cheep / Love again live again / Saturday afternoon (at the football) / Raindrops keep falling on my head / Glory glory Man Utd / We're the most united team in the land / Belfast boy: *Fardon, Don*
CD _______ EMPRCD 629
Emporio / Jun '96 / Disc

MANCHESTER UNITED: THE RED ALBUM (Various Artists)
Glory glory Man United / We are the champions / Denis the menace / Manchester United calypso / Willie Morgan on the wing / Ryan Giggs we love you / Rah rah rah for Man Utd / Manchester United football double / Georgie El Beatle / Cantona superstar / Song for Matt Busby / I love George Best / Euro Cup's all yours / Flowers of Manchester / Very great Bryan Robson / George Best's dream home / Georgie you've broken my heart / Belfast boy / George Best's ideal woman / Always look on the bright side of life
CD _______ PELE 006CD
Exotica / May '97 / SRD / Vital

Manchild

POWER AND LOVE/FEEL THE PHUFF
CD _______ CDGR 128
Charly / Mar '97 / Koch

Mancini, Henry

BEST OF HENRY MANCINI, THE
Breakfast at Tiffany's / Pink Panther / Days of wine and roses / Moon river / Shot in the dark / Love story / Raindrops keep fallin' on my head / Mr. Lucky / Peter Gunn / Experiments in terror / Windmills of your mind / Dream a little dream of me / Love is a many splendoured thing / By the time I get to Phoenix / Charade / Shadow of your smile / Evergreen / Midnight cowboy / Till there was you / Summer knows / Baby elephant walk / Hatari / Blue satin / Moment to moment
CD _______ 74321476762
Camden / Apr '97 / BMG

BLUES AND THE BEAT, THE
Blues / Smoke rings / Misty / Blue flame / After hours / Mood indigo / Beat / Big noise from Winnetka / Alright, OK you win / Tippin' in / How could you do a thing like that to me / Sing sing sing / House of the rising sun / C jam blues / Green onions / Night train
CD _______ 74321260472
RCA / Jun '95 / BMG

IN THE PINK
Pink Panther theme / Moon river / Days of wine and roses / Baby elephant walk / Theme from Hatari / Charade / Thorn birds theme / Blue satin / Two for the road / My lucky / Theme from the Molly Maguires / Moment to moment / As time goes by / Shot in the dark / Misty / Love Story / Pennywistle jig / Everything I do (I do it for you) / Moonlight sonata / Tender is the night / Theme from Mommie Dearest / Raindrops keep falling on my head / Crazy world / Mona Lisa / Peter Gunn / Unchained melody / Summer knows / Experiment in terror / Windmills of your mind / Til there was you / Speedy gonzales / Sweetheart tree / Love theme from Romeo and Juliet / Dream a little dream of me / Lonesome / Pie in the face polka / Love is a many splendoured thing / By the time I get tp Phoenix / Dear heart / Charade (opening tides) / Shadow of your smile / One for my baby (and one more for the road) / Breakfast at Tiffany's / That old black magic / Evergreen / Midnight cowboy
CD _______ 74321242832
RCA / Nov '95 / BMG

MANCINI TOUCH, THE
Bijou / Mostly for lovers / Like young / My one and only love / Politely / Trav'lin light / Let's walk / Snowfall / Cool shade of blue / Robbin's nest / Free and easy / That's all
CD _______ 74321357442
RCA / Jun '96 / BMG

MERRY MANCINI CHRISTMAS, A
Little drummer boy / Jingle bells / Sleigh ride / Christmas song / Winter wonderland / Silver bells / Frosty the snowman / Rudolph the red nosed reindeer / White Christmas / Carol for another Christmas / Silent night / O holy night / O little town of Bethlehem / God rest ye merry gentlemen / Deck the halls with boughs of holly / Hark the herald angels sing / We three kings of Orient are / O come all ye faithful (Adeste Fidelis) / Joy to the world / It came upon a midnight clear / Away in a manger / First Noel
CD _______ ND 81928
Arista / Nov '96 / BMG

ROMANTIC MOMENTS
CD _______ VSD 5530
Varese Sarabande / Nov '94 / Pinnacle

Mandala

LIVE FROM VENUS
CD _______ MANCD 111
Mandala / May '96 / Total/Pinnacle

Mandala Jati Ensemble

GAMELAN SEMARPEGULINGAN
CD _______ VICG 50252
JVC World Library / Feb '96 / ADA / CM / Direct

Mandalaband

EYE OF WENDOR, THE
Eye of Wendor / Florians song / Ride to the city / Almar's tower / Like the wind / Tempest / Dawn of a new day / Departure from Carthillias Elsethea / Witch of Waldow wood / Silesandre / Aenord's lament / Funeral of the king / Coronation of Damien
CD _______ RPM 105
RPM / Jul '93 / Pinnacle

MANDALABAND
Om mani padme hum (in four movements) / Determination / Song for a king / Roof of the world / Looking in
CD _______ EDCD 343
Edsel / Feb '92 / Pinnacle

Mandators

POWER OF THE PEOPLE
CD _______ CDBH 156
Heartbeat / Apr '94 / ADA / Direct / Greensleeves / Jet Star

Mandel, Harvey

BABY BATTER
Baby batter / One way street / Freedom ball / Hank the ripper / Midnight sun / Morton grove Mama / El stinger
CD _______ BGOCD 252
Beat Goes On / Feb '95 / Pinnacle

Mandingo

LO MEJER DE LA SALSA VENEZOLANA
CD _______ EUCD 1258
ARC / Mar '94 / ADA / ARC Music

NEW WORLD POWER
CD _______ AXCD 3004
Axiom / Sep '90 / PolyGram / Vital

WATTO SITTA
CD _______ CPCD 8153
Celluloid / Nov '95 / Discovery / Koch

Mandinka

INDEPENDENCE
CD _______ VICP 5646
JVC World Library / Jun '96 / ADA / CM / Direct

Mandolin Allstars

MANDOLIN ALLSTARS
CD _______ ACS 27CD
Acoustics / Aug '95 / ADA / Koch

Mandukhai Ensemble

MANDUKHAI ENSEMBLE OF MONGOLIA
CD _______ PS 65115
PlayaSound / Nov '93 / ADA / Harmonia Mundi

Mandville-Greeson, Liz

LOOK AT ME
CD 4938 CD
Earwig / Dec '96 / ADA / CM

Mane, Malang

BALANTA BALO (Talking Wood Of Casamance)
CD VPU 1006CD
Village Pulse / May '97 / ADA

Maneri, Joe

DAHABENZAPPLE
CD ARTCD 6188
Hat Art / Dec '96 / Cadillac / Harmonia Mundi

IN FULL CRY (Maneri, Joe Quartet)
Coarser and finer / Tenderly / Outside the dance hall / Kind of birth / Seed and all / Pulling the boat in / Nobody knows the trouble I've seen / In full cry / Shaw was a good man / Lift / I feel like a motherless child / Prelude to a kiss
CD 5370482
ECM / Aug '97 / New Note/Pinnacle

THREE MEN WALKING (Maneri, Joe & Joe Morris/Mat Maneri)
Calling / What's new / Bird's in the Belfry / If not now / Let me tell you / Through the glass / Three men walking / Deep paths / Diuturnal / Fevered / Gestalt / To Anne's eye's / Arc and point / For Josef Schmid
CD 5310232
ECM / Apr '96 / New Note/Pinnacle

Manet, Raghunath

MUSIC AND DANCE (2CD Set)
CD Set FA 414
Fremeaux / Oct '96 / ADA / Discovery

PONDICHERY
CD FA 419
Fremeaux / Jun '97 / ADA / Discovery

Manfila, Kante

KANKAN BLUES (Manfila, Kante & Balia Kalia)
CD OA 201
PAM / Feb '94 / ADA / Direct

N'NA NIWALE: KANKAN BLUES VOL.2
CD PAM 402CD
PAM / Mar '94 / ADA / Direct

NI KANU
Ni kanu / Fenko / Akadi / Koufenko / Akassa / Djanfa / L'unite / Foya / Denko / N'tesse / Dinyiya
CD CDEMC 3705
EMI / Sep '97 / EMI

Manfred Mann

20 YEARS OF MANFRED MANN'S EARTHBAND (Manfred Mann's Earthband)
Blinded by the light / Joybringer / Somewhere in Africa / You angel you / Questions / For you / California / Tribal statistics / Davy's on the road again / Runner / Mighty quinn / Angels at the gate
CD BOMME 1CD
Cohesion / Nov '90 / Grapevine/PolyGram

AGES OF MANN
5-4-3-2-1 / Pretty flamingo / Do wah diddy diddy / Sha la la / If you gotta go, go now / Oh no not my baby / Come tomorrow / My name is Jack / One in the middle / I put a spell on you / Just like a woman / Poison Ivy / Mighty quinn / Semi-detached suburban Mr. James / Ha ha said the clown / Raggamuffin man / Hubble bubble (toil and trouble) / There's no living without your loving / You gave me somebody to love / Got my mojo working / With God on our side / Fox on the run
CD 5143262
PolyGram TV / Sep '95 / PolyGram

ANGEL STATION (Manfred Mann's Earthband)
Don't kill it Carol / You angel you / Hollywood town / Belle of the earth / Platform end / Angels at the gate / You are / I am / Waiting for the rain / Resurrection
CD COMMECD 4
Cohesion / Nov '90 / Grapevine/PolyGram

ASCENT OF MANN, THE (2CD Set)
Just like a woman / I wanna be rich / Trouble and tea / Each and every day / Smemi detached surburban Mr. James / Morning after the party / Box office draw / Let it be me / All I wanna do / Vicar's daughter / I love you / Autumn leaves / Feeling so good / Mohair Sam / Love bird / Brown and Prter's meat exporters lorry / Its dso easy falling / Now and then thing / Another kind of music / Ha ha said the clown / Eastern street / Funniest gig / Miss JD / By request Edwin Garvey / Sunny / Wild thing / A 'B' side / Last train to Clarksvile / Budgie / So long Dad / Please Mrs. Henry / Mighty quinn / Sunshine superman / Big Betty / As long as I have loving / Each other's company / Sweet pea / My name is Jack / Sleeply hollow / Harry the one man band / Sitting alone in the sunshine / Dealer dealer / Everyday another hair turns grey / Fox on the run / Country dancing / Up the junction / I think it's gonna rain today / There is a man / Cubist town / One way / Too many people / Ragamuffin man
CD Set 5348062
Mercury / Jun '97 / PolyGram

BEST OF MANFRED MANN 1964-1966, THE
Do wah diddy diddy / 5-4-3-2-1 / Sha la la / Hubble bubble (toil and trouble) / If you gotta go, go now / Oh no not my baby / Bare hugg / Got my mojo working / Hoochie coochie man / Smokestack lightnin' / Pretty flamingo / You gave me somebody to love / Don't ask me what I say / I'm your kingpin / It's gonna work out fine / Hi lili hi lo / Stormy Monday blues / Abominable snowman / Since I don't have you / Come tomorrow
CD CDMFP 5994
Music For Pleasure / Dec '93 / EMI

BEST OF THE EMI YEARS 1963-1965, THE
Do wah diddy diddy / Cock-a-hoop / Got my mojo working / Sticks and stones / 5-4-3-2-1 / Why should we not / I'm your kingpin / Without you / I put a spell on you / Hubble bubble (toil and trouble) / Dashing away with a smoothing iron / Sha la la / Hi lili hi lo / I can't believe what you say / One in the middle / Watermelon man / With God on our side / Come tomorrow / I think it's gonna work out fine / She / Oh not my baby / My little red book / Come home baby / Pretty flamingo / If you gotta go, go now / Tired of trying, bored with lying, scared of dying / There's no living without your loving / You gave me somebody to love / Do wah diddy diddy (Unedited)
CD CDEMS 1500
EMI / May '93 / EMI

CHANCE (Manfred Mann's Earthband)
Lies (through the 80's) / One the run / For you / Adolescent dream / Fritz the blank / Stranded / This is your heart / No guarantee / Heart on the street
CD COMMECD 9
Cohesion / Nov '90 / Grapevine/PolyGram

CRIMINAL TANGO (Manfred Mann's Earthband)
Going underground / Who are the mystery kids / Banquet / Killer on the loose / Do anything you wanna do / Rescue / You got me right through the heart / Hey bulldog / Crossfire
CD DIXCD 35
10 / Jul '86 / EMI

EP COLLECTION, THE
5-4-3-2-1 / Cock-a-hoop / Without you / Groovin' / Do wah diddy diddy / Can't believe it / One in the middle / Watermelon man / What am I to do / With God on our side / There's no living without your loving / Tired trying, bored of lying, scared of dying / I can't believe what you say / That's all I ever want from you baby / It's getting late / Machines / She needs company / Tenessee waltz / When will I be loved / I got you babe
CD SEECD 252
See For Miles/C5 / Oct '94 / Pinnacle

FIVE FACES OF MANFRED MANN
Smokestack lightning / Don't ask me what I say / Sack o' woe / What you gonna do / Hoochie coochie man / I'm your kingpin / Down the road apiece / I've got my mojo working / It's gonna work out fine / Mr. Anello / Untie me / Bring it to Jerome / Without you / You've got to take it
CD DORIG 121
EMI / Jul '97 / EMI

FOUR MANFRED MANN ORIGINALS (4CD Set)
Do-wah-diddy diddy / Don't ask me what I say / Sack o' woe / What you gonna do / Hoochie coochie man / Smokestack lightning / Got my mojo working / It's gonna work out fine / Down the road apiece / Untie me / Bring it to Jerome / Without you / Sha la la / Come tomorrow / She / Can't believe it / John Hardy / Did you have to do that / Watermelon man / I'm your kingpin / Hubble bubble (toil and trouble) / You've got to take it / Groovin' / Dashing away with the smoothing iron / My little red book / Oh no, not my baby / What am I to do / One in the middle / You gave me somebody to love / You're for me / Poison ivy / Without you / Brother Jack / Love like yours (don't come knocking every day) / I can't believe what you say / With God on our side / Pretty flamingo / Let's go get stoned / Tired of trying, bored with lying, scared of dying / I put a spell on you / It's getting late / You're standing by / Machines / Stay around / Tennessee waltz / Driva man / Did you have to do that
CD Set CDMANFRED 1
Premier/EMI / Feb '96 / EMI

GLORIFIED MAGNIFIED (Manfred Mann's Earthband)
Meat / Look around / One way glass / I'm gonna have you all / Down home / Our friend George / Ashes to the wind / Wind / It's all over now / Baby blue / Glorified magnified
CD MFMCD 11
Cohesion / Nov '93 / Grapevine/PolyGram

GOOD EARTH, THE (Manfred Mann's Earthband)
Give me the good earth / Launching place / I'll be gone / Earth hymn (parts 1 and 2) / Sky high / Be not too hard
CD MFMCD 12
Cohesion / Nov '93 / Grapevine/PolyGram

GROOVIN' WITH THE MANFRED'S (The Manfred Mann R&B Album)
Groovin' / Can't believe it / What you gonna do / Don't ask me what I say / Hoochie coochie man / Smokestack lightning / I'm your kingpin / Bring it to Jerome / Without you / Let's go get stoned / Watermelon man / I put a spell on you / Driva man / Call it stormy Monday / What did I do wrong / Got my mojo working / Down the road apiece / Watch your step / LSD / One in the middle / Did you have to do that / Sticks and stones / Cock-a-hoop / Way you do the things you do / You've got to take it / Hubble bubble (toil and trouble)
CD CDEMS 1601
EMI / Oct '96 / EMI

LIVE IN BUDAPEST (Manfred Mann's Earthband)
Spirits in the night / For you / Lies (through the 80's) / Redemption song / Demolition man / Davy's on the road again / Blinded by the light / Mighty Quinn
CD COMMECD 10
Cohesion / Nov '90 / Grapevine/PolyGram

MANFRED MANN CHAPTER THREE VOL.1 (Manfred Mann Chapter 3)
CD MFMCD 14
Cohesion / Feb '94 / Grapevine/PolyGram

MANFRED MANN CHAPTER THREE VOL.2 (Manfred Mann Chapter 3)
CD MFMCD 15
Cohesion / Feb '94 / Grapevine/PolyGram

MANFRED MANN'S EARTHBAND (Manfred Mann's Earthband)
California coastline / Captain Bobby Stout / Sloth / Living without you / Tribute / Please Mrs. Henry / Jump sturdy / Prayer / Part time man / Up and leaving
CD COMMECD 6
Cohesion / Nov '90 / Grapevine/PolyGram

MASQUE (Manfred Mann's Earthband)
Joybringer / Billie's orno bounce / What you give is what you get / Rivers run dry / Planets schmanets / Geronimo's cadillac / Sister Billie's bounce / Telegram to Monica / Couple of mates, A (from Mars and Jupiter) / Neptune (icebringer) / Hymn (from Jupiter) / We're going wrong
CD DIXCD 69
10 / Apr '92 / EMI

MESSIN' (Manfred Mann's Earthband)
Messin' / Buddah / Cloudy eyes / Get your rocks off / Sad joy / Black and blue / Mardi Gras day
CD COMMECD 7
Cohesion / Nov '90 / Grapevine/PolyGram

NIGHTINGALES AND BOMBERS (Manfred Mann's Earthband)
Spirits in the night / Countdown / Time is right / Cross fade / Visionary mountains / Nightingales and bombers / Fat Nelly / As above so below
CD COMMECD 8
Cohesion / Nov '90 / Grapevine/PolyGram

PRETTY FLAMINGO
Do wah diddy diddy / 5-4-3-2-1 / Hubble bubble (toil and trouble) / Sha la la / Got my mojo working / Stormy Monday blues / If you gotta go, go now / Pretty flamingo / Oh no not my baby / Come tomorrow / You gave me somebody to love / Since I don't have you / One in the middle / Hi lili hi lo
CD 16140
Laserlight / Sep '96 / Target/BMG

ROARING SILENCE, THE (Manfred Mann's Earthband)
Blinded by the light / Singing the dolphin through / Waiter, there's a yawn in my ear / Road to Babylon / This side of paradise / Starbird / Questions
CD COMMECD 2
Cohesion / Nov '90 / Grapevine/PolyGram

SOFT VENGEANCE (Manfred Mann's Earthband)
CD GRACD 213
Grapevine / Jun '96 / Grapevine/PolyGram

SOLAR FIRE (Manfred Mann's Earthband)
CD COMMECD 1
Cohesion / Nov '90 / Grapevine/PolyGram

SOMEWHERE IN AFRICA (Manfred Mann's Earthband)
Tribal statistics / Eyes of Nostradamus / Third world service / Demolition man / Brothers and sisters / To Bantustan (Africa suite) / Koze kobenini / Lalela, redemption song (no kwazulu) / Somewhere in Africa
CD COMMECD 5
Cohesion / '90 / Grapevine/PolyGram

SPOTLIGHT (Manfred Mann's Earthband)
CD MFMCD 013
PolyGram TV / Sep '92 / PolyGram

WATCH (Manfred Mann's Earthband)
CD COMMECD 3
Cohesion / Nov '90 / Grapevine/PolyGram

WORLD OF MANFRED MANN, THE
Mighty Quinn / Ha ha said the clown / Vicar's daughter / Semi-detached suburban Mr. Jones / I wanna be rich / My name is Jack / A 'B' side / Fox on the run / It's so easy falling / Ragamuffin man / Trouble and tea / Box office draw / Sweet pea / Up the junction / Feeling so good / So long Dad / Each other's company / Just like a woman
CD 5523572
Spectrum / Apr '96 / PolyGram

Mangalam

FUNKY CLASSICAL INDIAN MUSIC
Twisted sara / Alex / Five it up / Anjneyar / Rainy sara / Dee I / Deetune Kedar / Jhaan
CD 8888272
Tiptoe / Jun '97 / New Note/Pinnacle

Mangas, Yiorgos

YIORGOS MANGAS
Tsifteteli rok / Roumaniko / Autoschediasmos / Ibon / Chorepste / Ta chrysa dactyla / Yia tous anthropous pou agapao / Skaros / To diko mou
CD CDORB 021
Globestyle / Jul '90 / Pinnacle

Mangelsdorff, Albert

WIDE POINT, THE/TRILOGUE/LIVE IN MONTREUX (Three Originals/2CD Set)
Up and down man / Mayday Hymn / Oh horn / I mo take you to the hospital and cut your liver out / Mood indigo / Wide point / For Peter / Trilogue / Zores Mores / Foreign fun / Accidental meeting / Ant steps on an elephant's toe / Dear Mr. Palmer / Mood azur / Stay on the carpet / Rip off
CD Set 5192132
MPS Jazz / Apr '94 / PolyGram

Mangione, Chuck

A&M GOLD SERIES
Feels so good / Hill where the Lord hides / You're the best there is / Fun and games / Cannonball run / Land of make believe / Give it all you got / Hide and seek / Children of Sanchez / Chase the clouds away / Bellavia / Doin' everything with you / Maui waui
CD 3970752
A&M / Mar '94 / PolyGram

Mango Jam

FLUX
CD SHCD 5710
Shanachie / Sep '96 / ADA / Greensleeves / Koch

Mangual, Jose Jr.

TRIBUTE TO CHANO POZO VOL.2, A
CD MIC 921
Fresh Sound / Nov '96 / Discovery / Jazz Music

Manhattan Jazz Quintet

FUNKY STRUT
Swing street / Hot grits / Mercy mercy mercy / Sister Sadie / Song for my father / Funky strut / Foxy little thang
CD 66055006
Sweet Basil / Oct '91 / New Note/Pinnacle

MY FAVOURITE THINGS
CD K32Y 6210
Electric Bird / Sep '88 / New Note/ Pinnacle

Manhattan New Music Project

MOOD SWING
CD 1212072
Soul Note / Apr '93 / Cadillac / Harmonia Mundi / Wellard

Manhattan Project

DREAMBOAT
Dreamboat / Cape Town ambush / Misty / Depth / I remember / Sacrifice / Someday my Prince will come / I didn't know what time it was / Alluding to
CD CDSJP 327
Timeless Jazz / Aug '90 / New Note/ Pinnacle

Manhattan Transfer

BEST OF MANHATTAN TRANSFER
Tuxedo Junction / Boy from New York City / Twilight zone / Body and soul / Candy / Four brothers / Birdland / Gloria / Trickle trickle / Operator / Java jive / Nightingale sang in Berkeley Square
CD 2508412
WEA / Aug '84 / Warner Music

BOP DOO WOP
Unchained melody / Route 66 / My cat fell in the well / Duke of Dubuque / How high the moon / Baby come back to me / Safronia B / Heart's desire / That's the way it goes
CD 7567812332
WEA / Mar '93 / Warner Music

BRASIL
Soul food to go / Zoo blues / So you say / Capim / Metropolis / Hear the voices / Agua / Jungle pioneer / Notes from the underground
CD ____ 7567818032
WEA / Mar '93 / Warner Music

COMING OUT
Don't let go / Zindy Lou / Chanson d'amour / Helpless / Scotch and soda / Speak up mambo / Cuentame / Poinciana / SOS / Popsicle toes / It wouldn't have made any difference / Thought of loving you
CD ____ 7567815022
WEA / Mar '93 / Warner Music

DOWN IN BIRDLAND
Trickle trickle / Gloria / Operator / Helpless / Ray's rockhouse / Heart's desire / Zindy Lou / Mystery / Baby come back to me (morse code of love) / Route 66 / Java jive / Chanson d'amour / Foreign affairs / Smile again / Spice of life / Speak up Mambo / Soul food to go (Sina) / So you say (Esquinas) / Boy from New York City / Twilight zone / Twilight tone / Four brothers / Bee blop blues / Candy / Gal in Calico / Love for sale / On a little street in Singapore / Tuxedo junction / That cat is high / Body and soul / Meet Benny Bailey / Sing joy spring / To you / Down south camp meeting / Until I met you / Why not / Another night in Tunisia / Capim / Nightingale sang in Berkley Square / Birdland (Vocal)
CD ____ 8122710532
WEA / Jan '94 / Warner Music

EXTENSIONS
Birdland / Wacky dust / Nothin' you can do about it / Coo coo-u / Body and soul (Eddie and the bean) / Twilight zone (part 1) / Twilight zone (part 2) / Trickle trickle / Shaker song / Foreign affair
CD ____ 7567815652
WEA / Mar '93 / Warner Music

LIVE
Four brothers / Rambo / Meet Benny Bailey / Airegin / To you / Sing joy Spring / Move / That's killer Joe / Duke of Dubuque / Gloria / On the boulevard / Shaker song / Ray's rockhouse
CD ____ 7567817232
WEA / Oct '87 / Warner Music

MANHATTAN TRANSFER
Tuxedo Junction / Sweet talking guy / Operator / Candy / Gloria / Clap your hands / That cat is high / You can depend on me / Blue champagne / Occapella / Heart's desire
CD ____ 7567814932
WEA / '87 / Warner Music

MECCA FOR MODERNS
On the Boulevard / Boy from New York City / Smile again / Wanted dead or alive / Spies in the night / Corner pocket / Confirmation / Kafka / Nightingale sang in Berkeley Square
CD ____ 7567814822
WEA / Mar '93 / Warner Music

PASTICHE
Four brothers / Gal in Calico / Love for sale / Je voulais (te dire que je t'attends) / On a little street in Singapore / In a mellow tone / Walk in love / Who, what, when, where and why / It's not the spotlight / Pieces of dreams / Where did our love go
CD ____ 8122718092
WEA / Jan '95 / Warner Music

TOUCH OF CLASS, A
Chicken bone bone / I need a man / You're a viper / Fair and tender ladies / Rosianna / Sunny disposish / Java jive / One more time around / Rosie / Guided missiles / Roll Daddy roll
CD ____ TC 877002
Disky / May '97 / Disky / THE

Manhattans

DEDICATED TO YOU/ FOR YOU AND YOURS
Follow your heart / That new girl / Can I / Boston monkey / I've got everything but you / Manhattan stomp / Searchin' for my baby / Our love will never die / I'm the one love forgot / What's it gonna be / Teach me (the Philly dog) / Baby I need you / I call it love / I betcha / Sweet little girl / There goes a fool / Alone on New Year's Eve / All I need is your love / I wanna be / When we're made as one / Call somebody please / For the very first time / It's that time of year / Baby I'm sorry
CD ____ CDKEND 103
Kent / Jun '93 / Pinnacle

KISS AND SAY GOODBYE
Kiss and say goodbye / Don't take your love / There's no me without you / Wish that you were mine / Day the robin sang to me / That's how much I love you / Hurt / La la la wish upon a star / I kinda miss you / It feels good to be loved so bad / Am I losing you / Everybody has a dream / Shining star / I'll never find another (find another like you) / Just one moment away / I was made for you / Just the lonely talking again / You send me / Goodbye is the saddest word
CD ____ 4808992
Columbia / Jan '96 / Sony

Manhole

ALL IS NOT WELL
Hypocrite / Sickness / Kiss or kill / Break / Empty / Put your head out / Victim / Clean / Roughness / Six feet deep / Cycle of violence / Down / Down (reprise)
CD ____ N 02682
Noise / May '96 / Koch

Manic Eden

MANIC EDEN
CD ____ NTHEN 15
Now & Then / Sep '95 / Plastic Head

Manic P

GOD'S TEARS
CD ____ HY 39100742CD
Hyperium / Oct '93 / Cargo / Plastic Head

Manic Street Preachers

EVERYTHING MUST GO
Elvis impersonator: Blackpool Pier / Design for life / Kevin Carter / Enola alone / Everything must go / Small black flowers that grow in the sky / Girl who wanted to be God / Removables / Australia / Interiors (song for Willem De Kooning) / Further away / No surface all feeling
CD ____ 4839302
Epic / May '96 / Sony

GENERATION TERRORISTS
Slash 'n' burn / Nat West-Barclays-Midland-Lloyds / Born to end / Motorcycle emptiness / You love us / Love's sweet exile / Little baby nothing / Repeat (stars and stripes) / Tennessee / Another invented disease / Stay beautiful / So dead / Repeat (UK) / Spectators of suicide / Damn dog / Crucifix kiss / Methadone pretty / Condemned to rock 'n' roll
CD ____ 4710602
Columbia / Jun '92 / Sony

GOLD AGAINST THE SOUL
Sleepflower / From despair to where / La tristesse durera (scream to a sigh) / Yourself / Life becoming a landslide / Drug drug druggy / Roses in the hospital / Nostalgic pushead / Symphony of tourette / Gold against the soul
CD ____ 4740642
Columbia / Sep '96 / Sony

HOLY BIBLE
Yes / Ifwhiteamericatoldthetruthforonedayitsworldwouldfallapart / Of walking abortion / She is suffering / Archives of pain / Revol / 4st 7lb / Faster / This is yesterday / Die in the summertime / Intense humming of evil / PCP / Mausoleum
CD ____ 4774212
Columbia / Feb '97 / Sony

MANIC STREET PREACHERS INTERVIEW 1991
CD ____ MSPCD 1
Total / May '96 / Total/BMG

Manilla Road

CIRCUS MAXIMUS
CD ____ BDCD 53
Black Dragon / Oct '92 / Else

Manilow, Barry

BARRY - LIVE IN BRITAIN
It's a miracle / Old songs medley / Stay / Beautiful music / I made it through the rain / Bermuda Triangle / Break down the door / Who's been sleeping in my bed / Copacabana / Could it be magic / Mandy / London - we'll meet again / One voice
CD ____ 261320
Arista / Apr '91 / BMG

EVEN NOW
Copacabana / Somewhere in the night / Linda song / Can't smile without you / Leavin' in the morning / Where do I go from here / Even now / I was a fool (to let you go) / Losing touch / I just want to be the one in your life / Starting again / Sunrise
CD ____ 251125
Arista / Oct '88 / BMG

GREATEST HITS
Ships / Some kind of friend / I made it through the rain / Put a quarter in the jukebox / One voice / Old songs / Let's hang on / Memory / You're looking hot tonight
CD ____ 258552
Arista / May '88 / BMG

GREATEST HITS
Mandy / Can't smile without you / Looks like we made it / Tryin' to get the feeling again / I made it through the rain / Read 'em and weep / Somewhere in the night / Lonely together / Stay / If I should love again / I write the songs / One voice (live) / Bermunda triangle / Hey mambo / I wanna do it with you / Let's hang on / Some kind of friend / Copacabana (1993 remix) / I'm your man / Could it be magic
CD ____ 74321175452
Arista / Apr '96 / BMG

IF I SHOULD LOVE AGAIN/ONE VOICE/ BARRY (3CD Set)
CD Set ____ 354296
Arista / Feb '93 / BMG

LIVE ON BROADWAY
Sweet life / It's a long way up / Brooklyn blues / Memory / Upfront / God bless the other 99 / Mandy / It's a miracle / Some good things never last / If you remember me / Do like I do / Best seat in the house / Gonzo hits medley / If I can dream
CD ____ 353785
Arista / Feb '90 / BMG

MANILOW
At the dance / If you were here with me tonight / Sweet heaven / Ain't nothing like the real thing / It's a long way up / I'm your man / It's all behind us now / In search of love / He doesn't care (but I do) / Some sweet day
CD ____ PD 87044
Arista / Feb '86 / BMG

MANILOW MOODS (20 Instrumental Versions Of Barry Manilow's Classic Hits) (Evolution)
Mandy / Trying to get the feeling again / It's a miracle / I don't want to walk without you / Ships / I made it through the rain / I wanna do it with you / Even now / Ready to take a chance again / Looks like we made it / Bermuda triangle / Can't smile without you / Old songs / Could it be magic / One voice / New York city rhythm / Somewhere in the night / Weekend in New England / Copacabana / I write the songs
CD ____ 3036000752
Carlton / Mar '97 / Carlton

SINGING WITH THE BIG BANDS
Sentimental journey / And the angels sing / Green eyes / I should care / On the sunny side of the street / All or nothing at all / I'm getting sentimental over you / I'll never smile again / Don't get around much anymore / I can't get started (with you) / Chattanooga choo choo / Moonlight serenade / Don't sit under the apple tree / I'll be with you in apple blossom time / Where does the time go
CD ____ 07822187712
Arista / Oct '94 / BMG

SONGS 1975-1990, THE
I write the songs / One voice / Old songs / Don't want to walk without you / Some good things never last / Somewhere down the road / When I wanted you / Stay / Even now / Read 'em and weep / Somewhere in the night / I made it through the rain / Daybreak (live) / Please don't be scared / Looks like we made it / Mandy / If I should love again / All the time / Copacabana / Keep each other warm / Weekend in New England / Lonely together / Can't smile without you / Trying to get the feeling again / Could it be magic / Brooklyn blues / Who needs to dream / Ready to take a chance again / If I can dream
CD ____ 353868
Arista / Jun '90 / BMG

SONGS TO MAKE THE WHOLE WORLD SING
Please don't be scared / One that got away / Keep each other warm / Once and for all / When the good times come again / In another world / My moonlight memories of you / Little travelling music please / Some good things never last / You begin again / Anyone can do the heartbreak
CD ____ 259927
Arista / May '89 / BMG

SUMMER OF '78 (Love Songs Of The 70's)
Summer of '78 / Interlude - Love's theme / Reminiscing / I go crazy / When I need you / Air that I breathe / Bluer than blue / We've got tonite / I'd really love to see you tonight / Sometimes when we touch / Never my love / Just remember I love you
CD ____ 7822188092
Arista / Nov '96 / BMG

Manly, Gill

DETOUR HEAD
CD ____ PARCD 505
Parrot / Dec '94 / BMG / Jazz Music / THE / Wellard

Mann, Aimee

I'M WITH STUPID
Long shot / Choice in the matter / Sugarcoated / You could make a killing / Superball / Amateur / All over now / Par for the course / You're with stupid now / That's just what you are / Frankenstein / Ray / It's not safe
CD ____ GED 24951
Geffen / Oct '95 / BMG

WHATEVER
I should've known / Fifty years after the fair / 4th of July / Could've been anyone / Put me on top / Stupid thing / Say anything / Jacob Marley's chain / Mr. Harris / I could hurt you now / I know there's a word / I've had it / Way back when
CD ____ GFLD 19319
Geffen / Jul '96 / BMG

Mann, Carl

MONA LISA (4CD Set)
Gonna rock and roll tonight / Rockin' love / Mona Lisa (master) / Foolish one / Rockin' love (master) / Pretend / I can't forget you / Some enchanted evening / I'm coming home / South of the border (Down Mexico way) / Ain't got no home / If I ever needed you / Island of love / Walkin' and thinkin' / Baby I don't care / I'm bluer than anyone can be / Wayward wind / Born to be bad / If I could change you / When I grow too old to dream / Mountain dew / Mona Lisa (alt.) / Look at that moon / Rockin' love (alt.) / Too young / Take these chains from my heart / I can't forget you (undubbed) / South of the border (Down Mexico way) / Kansas city / Today is Christmas / Crazy fool / Blueberry Hill / I'll always love you darlin' / Ain't you got no lovin' for me / Then I turned and walked slowly away / Serenade of the bells / It really doesn't matter now / Sentimental journey / Born to be bad (undubbed) / I love you, I adore you / Are you teasing me / Stop the world (and let me off) / I don't care / I'm walking the dog / Ubangi stomp / Don't let the stars get in your eyes / Long black veil / Canadian sunset / Even tho' / Chinatown, my Chinatown / Because of you / Till the end of forever / Mexicali rose / Hey doll baby / Vanished / Down to my last forgive you / Blue river / Yesterday is gone / Burnin' holes in the eyes of Abraham Lincoln / German town / She was young / Paying for the crimes / Met her in Alaska / Funny way of gettin' over someone else / When the leaves turn brown / Everyday grows sweet with the wine / More to life / Going to church with mama / It really matters / Toast to a fool / I'm married friend / My favorite bunch of roses / Ballad of Johnny Clyde / Cheatin' time / Keep feeding her the wine / Let's turn back the pages / If I ever love again / Make a man want to / Neon lights / I'm just about out of my mind / It's not the coffee that's keeping me awake / No easy way to say goodbye / Back lovin' / Annie over time / I've got feelings too / Twilight time / Eighteen yellow roses / Belly rubbin' country soul / Tennemonk, Georgia / She loves to love for the feeling / Love died a long time ago / Darling of Atlanta / Country was the song / Second guessing / One last goodbye / On the back streets of Dallas / Tripping on teardrops / I love you too much
CD Set ____ BCD 15713
Bear Family / Aug '93 / Direct / Rollercoaster / Swift

ROCKIN' MANN
Mona Lisa / Foolish one / Rockin' love / Pretend / Some enchanted evening / I can't forget you / Look at that moon / Take these chains from my heart / Too young / South of the border / Kansas City / Wayward wind / Ain't got no home / Blueberry Hill / I'll always love you darling / Baby I don't care / I don't care / Ubangi stomp / I'm comin' home / Born to be bad / Ain't you got no lovin' for me / Don't let the stars get in your eyes / When I grow too old to dream / Mountain dew / If I could change you / Even tho' / Because of you / Long black veil
CD ____ CPCD 8234
Charly / Nov '96 / Koch

Mann, Dany

SEXIE HEXY
CD ____ BCD 15483
Bear Family / '88 / Direct / Rollercoaster / Swift

Mann, Geoff

IN ONE ERA
Piccadilly square / I wouldn't lie to you / Kingdom come / Afterwards / For God's sake / Green paper snow / My soul / Slow one / Creation / Dance / Gethsemane / Waves / Flowers
CD ____ CYCL 004
Cyclops / Jun '97 / Pinnacle

LOUD SYMBOLS
CD ____ CDGRUB 15
Food For Thought / Jul '91 / Pinnacle

MINISTRY OF THE INTERIOR (Mann, Geoff Band)
CD ____ CDGRUB 21
Food For Thought / Sep '91 / Pinnacle

PEACE OFFERING
CD ____ CYCL 042
Cyclops / Nov '96 / Pinnacle

Mann, Herbie

AT THE VILLAGE GATE
Comin' home baby / Summertime / It ain't necessarily so
CD ____ 7567813502
Atlantic / Mar '93 / Warner Music

BEST OF HERBIE MANN, THE
Comin' home baby / Memphis underground / Philly dog / Man and a woman / This little girl of mine
CD ____ 7567813692
Atlantic / Mar '93 / Warner Music

COPACABANA
CD ____ CD 62059
Saludos Amigos / May '94 / Target/BMG

DEEP POCKET
Down in the corner / Knock on wood / Moanin' / When something is wrong with my baby / Papa was a rollin' stone / Sunny

/ Mercy mercy mercy / Go home / Amazing grace
CD _______________ KOKO 1296
Kokopelli / Sep '94 / New Note/Pinnacle

EPITOME OF JAZZ
CD _______________ BET 6011
Bethlehem / Jan '95 / ADA / ZYX

EVOLUTION OF MANN, THE (2CD Set/ The Herbie Mann Anthology)
Baghdad/Asia minor / Sawa sawa de / This little girl of mine / Comin' home baby / One note samba / Blues walk / Gymnopedie / I love you / Soul guajira / Mushi mushi / Feeling good / Philly dog / Memphis underground / Claudia pie / Muscle shoals nitty gritty / Yesterday's kisses / Push push / Hold on I'm comin' / In memory of Elizabeth Reed / Mellow yellow / Hijack / Lugar comun (Common place) / Draw your breaks / Cricket dance / Birdwalk / Aria / Dona primeira / Amazing grace
CD Set _______________ 8122716342
Atlantic / May '94 / Warner Music

FLAMINGO VOL.2 (Mann, Herbie Quartet)
CD _______________ BET 6007
Bethlehem / Jan '95 / ADA / ZYX

FLUTE SOUFFLE (Mann, Herbie & Bobby Jaspar)
Tel aviv / Somewhere else / Let's march / Chasin' the Bird
CD _______________ OJCCD 760
Original Jazz Classics / Apr '93 / Complete/ Pinnacle / Jazz Music / Wellard

HERBIE MANN PLAYS (Bethlehem Jazz Classics)
CD _______________ CDGR 133
Charly / Apr '97 / Koch

HERBIE MANN-SAM MOST QUINTET, THE (Mann, Herbie & Sam Most)
CD _______________ BET 6008
Bethlehem / Jan '95 / ADA / ZYX

JAZZ MASTERS
CD _______________ 5299012
Verve / Jun '96 / PolyGram

JUST WAILIN'
Minor groove / Blue echo / Blue dip / Gospel truth / Jumpin' with Symphony Sid / Trinidad
CD _______________ OJCCD 900
Original Jazz Classics / Sep '96 / Complete/ Pinnacle / Jazz Music / Wellard

LOVE AND THE WEATHER (Mann, Herbie Orchestra)
CD _______________ BET 6009
Bethlehem / Jan '96 / ADA / ZYX

MEMPHIS UNDERGROUND
Memphis underground / New Orleans / Hold on I'm comin' / Chain of fools / Battle hymn of the Republic
CD _______________ 7567813642
Atlantic / Sep '95 / Warner Music

NIRVANA (Mann, Herbie & Bill Evans)
Nirvana / Gymnopedie / I love you / Willow weep for me / Lover man / Cashmere
CD _______________ 7567901412
Atlantic / Jun '95 / Warner Music

OPALESCENCE
Dona Palermeira / Comin' home baby / Song for Lea / Bahia de tadas as contas / Dry land / Two rivers (Do oiapoque ao chui) / Sir Charles Duke / Number fifty-five / Calling you
CD _______________ KOKO 1298
Kokopelli / Sep '94 / New Note/Pinnacle

PEACE PIECES
Peri's scope / Funkallero / Interplay / Turn out the stars / We will meet again / Blue in green / Waltz for Debby / Very early / Peace piece
CD _______________ KOKO 1306
Kokopelli / Feb '96 / New Note/Pinnacle

PUSH, PUSH
CD _______________ 7567903062
Atlantic / Jul '93 / Warner Music

Mann, John

ASPECTS OF MUSIC
All the world's a stage / My heart and I / Annen polka / Kiss me / Romantica / Lost chord / Me and my girl / Love makes the world go round / Leaning on a lamp-post / Lambeth walk / Sun has got his hat on / Music in May / Czardas / Non, je ne regrette rien / L'accordeoniste / Hymne a l'amour / Funiculi, funicula / Melody of love / My blue heaven / Happy days and lonely nights / Bells are ringing / Ave Maria / Mistakes / Where is your heart (Moulin Rouge) / Gigi / Waltz at Maxim's / Night they invented champagne / Thank heavens for little girls / I remember it well / Parisians, I'll be seeing you
CD _______________ CDGRS 1232
Grosvenor / '91 / Grosvenor

EVERGREENS
Medley: Our Gracie Fields / Medley: De Sylva Brown and Henderson / Medley: Rodgers and Hammerstein / Intermezzo from Cavalleria Rusticana / Thunder and lightning polka / Dolores / Song of paradise / Blue tango / Brown bird singing / Post horn gallop / Medley: Off to the sea / Medley: Minstrel magic
CD _______________ CDGRS 1263
Grosvenor / Mar '95 / Grosvenor

MOONLIGHT AND ROSES
Theme from the last rhapsody / Varsity drag / Doin' the raccoon / Don't bring Lulu / Charleston / Barney Google / Nagaski / Minuet from Berenice / Maiden's prayer / Cavatina / Delicado / Irving Berlin's popular waltzes / Sheep may safely graze / Love is the sweetest thing / Makin' whoopee / You made me love you / Meditation / Moonlight and roses / Serenade / Camelot / If ever I would leave you / Thank heavens for little girls / Rain in Spain / Wouldn't it be loverly / Wandering star / I talk to the trees / Parisians / Lovely way to spend an evening / Nola / Send in the clowns
CD _______________ CDGRS 1266
Grosvenor / Feb '95 / Grosvenor

THAT'S ENTERTAINMENT
And all that jazz / Dreaming ballerina / La cumparsita / Marigold / My curly headed baby / Nicola / Summer in Venice / My foolish heart / Amor amor / Narcissus / It had to be you / Hello Dolly / Walking my baby back home / Any dream will do / Vienna / Neapolitan serenade / Flirtation waltz / Temptation rag / Grasshoppers dance / Catari, catari / Roses of Picardy / Windows of Paris / Bye bye blues
CD _______________ PLATCD 3918
Platinum / Apr '93 / Prism

VIENNA CITY OF MY DREAMS
CD _______________ CDGRS 1254
Grosvenor / Feb '93 / Grosvenor

Mann, Woody

HEADING UPTOWN
CD _______________ SHCD 8025
Shanachie / Apr '97 / ADA / Greensleeves / Koch

STAIRWELL SERENADE
CD _______________ BEST 1072CD
Acoustic Music / Aug '95 / ADA

STORIES
CD _______________ GR 70724
Greenhays / Nov '94 / ADA / CM / Direct / Duncans / Jazz Music / Roots

Manna

MANNA
From heaven / Secret life of bass / Mr. Echo (go to hell) / Eat it, weave it and wear it / Kelham's island / Transport of delight / Lonely tones
CD _______________ AMB 5937CD
Apollo / Jan '95 / Vital

Manne, Shelly

ALIVE IN LONDON
Three on a match / Once again / Big oak basin / Illusion / Don't know
CD _______________ OJCCD 773
Original Jazz Classics / Jan '94 / Complete/ Pinnacle / Jazz Music / Wellard

AT THE BLACK HAWK VOL.1 (Manne, Shelly & His Men)
Summertime / Our delight / Poinciana / Blue Daniel / Blue Daniel (alternate version) / Theme: A gem from Tiffany
CD _______________ OJCCD 656
Original Jazz Classics / Apr '93 / Complete/ Pinnacle / Jazz Music / Wellard

AT THE BLACK HAWK VOL.2 (Manne, Shelly & His Men)
CD _______________ OJCCD 657
Original Jazz Classics / Mar '93 / Complete/Pinnacle / Jazz Music / Wellard

AT THE BLACK HAWK VOL.3 (Manne, Shelly & His Men)
CD _______________ OJCCD 658
Original Jazz Classics / Mar '93 / Complete/Pinnacle / Jazz Music / Wellard

AT THE BLACK HAWK VOL.4 (Manne, Shelly & His Men)
CD _______________ OJCCD 659
Original Jazz Classics / Mar '93 / Complete/Pinnacle / Jazz Music / Wellard

AT THE BLACK HAWK VOL.5 (Manne, Shelly & His Men)
CD _______________ OJCCD 660
Original Jazz Classics / Mar '93 / Complete/Pinnacle / Jazz Music / Wellard

MY FAIR LADY (Manne, Shelly/Andre Previn/Leroy Vinnegar)
Get me to the church on time / I've grown accustomed to her face / Ascot gavotte / With a little bit of luck / On the street where you live / Wouldn't it be loverly / Show me / I could have danced all night
CD _______________ OJCCD 336
Original Jazz Classics / Jan '92 / Complete/ Pinnacle / Jazz Music / Wellard

PERK UP
Perk up / I married an angel / Seer / Come back / Yesterdays / Drinking and driving / Bleep / Bird of paradise
CD _______________ CCD 4021
Concord Jazz / Aug '95 / New Note/ Pinnacle

SHELLY MANNE & HIS FRIENDS (Manne, Shelly & His Friends)
Tea for two / How high the moon / When we're alone / On the sunny side of the street / Time on my hands / Moonglow / Them there eyes / Sarcastic lady / Night and day / Flamingo / Steps steps up / Steps steps down
CD _______________ OJCCD 240
Original Jazz Classics / Oct '92 / Complete/ Pinnacle / Jazz Music / Wellard

SWINGING SOUNDS (Manne, Shelly & His Men)
Dart game / Bea's flat / Parthenia / Un poco loco / Bernie's tune / Doxy / Slan / Gem from Tiffany
CD _______________ OJCCD 267
Original Jazz Classics / Jan '97 / Complete/ Pinnacle / Jazz Music / Wellard

WEST COAST SOUND VOL.1, THE (Manne, Shelly & His Men)
CD _______________ OJCCD 152
Original Jazz Classics / Feb '93 / Complete/Pinnacle / Jazz Music / Wellard

Mannheim Steamroller

CHRISTMAS
Deck the halls with boughs of holly / We three kings / Bring a torch, Jeannette, Isabella / Coventry carol / Good king Wenceslas / Wassail, wassail / Carol of the birds / I saw three ships / God rest ye merry Gentlemen / Stille nacht
CD _______________ AGCD 1984
American Gramophone / Nov '94 / New Note/Pinnacle

FRESH AIRE CHRISTMAS, A
Hark the herald trumpets sing / Hark the herald angels sing / Veni veni Emmanuel / Holly and the ivy / Little drummer boy / Still, still, still / Lo how a rose e'er blooming / In dulci jubilo / Greensleeves / Carol of the bells / Traditions of Christmas / Cantique de noel (o holy night)
CD _______________ AGCD 1988
American Gramophone / Nov '94 / New Note/Pinnacle

FRESH AIRE VOL.1
CD _______________ AGCD 355
American Gramophone / Dec '88 / New Note/Pinnacle

FRESH AIRE VOL.2
CD _______________ AGCD 359
American Gramophone / Dec '88 / New Note/Pinnacle

FRESH AIRE VOL.3
CD _______________ AGCD 365
American Gramophone / Dec '88 / New Note/Pinnacle

FRESH AIRE VOL.4
CD _______________ AGCD 370
American Gramophone / Dec '88 / New Note/Pinnacle

FRESH AIRE VOL.5
CD _______________ AGCD 385
American Gramophone / Dec '88 / New Note/Pinnacle

FRESH AIRE VOL.6
CD _______________ AGCD 386
American Gramophone / Dec '88 / New Note/Pinnacle

Manning, Anthony

CHROMIUM NEBULAE
CD _______________ 56IRDAEV3CD
Irdial / Nov '95 / RTM/Disc

Manning, Barbara

1212
Fireman / Evil plays piano / Evil craves attention/Our son/10X10 / Trapped and drowning / End of the rainbow / Blood of feeling / Rickity tikity tin / Syain on the sun / Isn't lonely lovely / That kid / First line (seven the row) / Marcus Leid / Stammtisch
CD _______________ OLE 2212
Matador / Jun '97 / Vital

ONE PERFECT GREEN BLANKET
CD _______________ NORMAL 138CD
Normal / Mar '94 / ADA / Direct

Manning, Lynn

CLARITY OF VISION
CD _______________ NAR 093CD
New Alliance / Sep '94 / Plastic Head

Manning, Matt

WALTZIN' AN ANGEL
CD _______________ RTMCD 80
Round Tower / Oct '96 / Avid/BMG

Manning, Roger

ROGER MANNING
Busy body blues (E5th Street blues) / Take back the night / No. 19 blues (pearly blues no.3) / Hitchhiker's blues no.2 (pearly blues no.3) / Traitors / Radical blues / Speaker phone / Persia blues / Unrequited / Waterloo blues / Subway blues / Waterloo calling/ Parade account / Pacifica blues / Dallas blues / Serious blues (no.18 blues) / Tompkins Square blues no.99 / Gallows pole / Sub folk
CD _______________ SH 5718
Shanachie / Feb '97 / ADA / Greensleeves / Koch

Mannsfield, Rodney

LET'S GET IT ON
Dance for me / I adore you / I can't live / Let me know / How can this be / Are you ever coming back / I wanna get it on / Nobody else / No way / Call me
CD _______________ XECD 2
Expansion / Sep '96 / 3mv/Sony

Mano Negra

KING OF BONGO
Bring the fire / King of bongo / Don't want you no more / Le bruit du frigo / Letter to the censors / El jako / It's my heart / Madman's dead / Out of time man / Madame Oscar / Welcome in occident / Furious fiesta / Fool / Paris la nuit
CD _______________ CDVIR 5
Virgin / Jul '91 / EMI

PUTA'S FEVER
Man negra / Rock 'n' roll band / King kong five / Soledad / Sidi hbibi / Rebel spell / Peligro / Pas assez de toi / Magic dice / Mad house / Guayaquil City / Voodoo / Patchanka / La rancon du succes / Devil's call / Roger Cageot / El sur / Patchuko hop
CD _______________ CDV 2608
Virgin / Jan '90 / EMI

Manolin

PARA MI GENTE
CD _______________ 74321401372
Milan / Sep '96 / Conifer/BMG / Silva Screen

Manone, Wingy

CLASSICS 1927-1934
CD _______________ CLASSICS 774
Classics / Aug '94 / Discovery / Jazz Music

CLASSICS 1935-1936
CD _______________ CLASSICS 828
Classics / Sep '95 / Discovery / Jazz Music

CLASSICS 1936
CD _______________ CLASSICS 849
Classics / Nov '95 / Discovery / Jazz Music

CLASSICS 1936-1937
CD _______________ CLASSICS 887
Classics / Jul '96 / Discovery / Jazz Music

COLLECTION VOL.1, THE
CD _______________ COCD 03
Collector's Classics / Jan '89 / Cadillac / Complete/Pinnacle / Jazz Music

SWINGIN' AT THE HICKORY HOUSE (His 24 Greatest)
San Sue strut: *Arcadian Serenaders* / Fidgety feet: *Arcadian Serenaders* / Cat's head: *Manone, Joe 'Wingy' Harmony Kings* / Wailin' blues: *Cellar Boys* / Shake that thing: *Barbecue Joe & His Hot Dogs* / Tar paper stomp: *Barbecue Joe & His Hot Dogs* / In the slot: *Manone, Wingy Orchestra* / Never had no lovin': *Manone, Wingy Orchestra* / Panama blues: *New Orleans Rhythm Kings* / Tin roof blues: *New Orleans Rhythm Kings* / Royal Garden blues: *Manone, Wingy Orchestra* / Blues have got me: *Manone, Wingy Orchestra* / Swing brother swing: *Manone, Wingy Orchestra* / Isle of Capri: *Manone, Wingy Orchestra* / Swingin' at the Hickory House: *Manone, Wingy Orchestra* / Dallas blues: *Manone, Wingy Orchestra* / Sweet Lorraine: *Manone, Wingy Orchestra* / Oh say can you swing: *Manone, Wingy Orchestra* / Loch Lomond: *Manone, Wingy Orchestra* / Limehouse blues: *Manone, Wingy Orchestra* / Dinner for the Duchess: *Manone, Wingy Orchestra* / Mama's gone goodbye: *Manone, Wingy Orchestra* / Shake the blues away: *New Orleans Buzzards* / Where can I find a cherry: *Manone, Wingy & His Cats*
CD _______________ CDAJA 5241
Living Era / Jul '97 / Select

WINGY MANONE & HIS ORCHESTRA 1934-35
CD _______________ CLASSICS 798
Classics / Mar '95 / Discovery / Jazz Music

WINGY MANONE AND HIS CATS
CD _______________ FLYCD 945
Flyright / Jul '96 / Hot Shot / Jazz Music / Wellard

WINGY MANONE COLLECTION VOL.4 1935-1936
Every little moment / Black coffee / Sweet and slow / Lulu's back in town / Let's swing it / Little door, little lock, little key / Love and kisses / Rhythm is our business / From the top of your head / Takes two to make a bargain / Smile will go a long, long way / I'm gonna sit right down and write myself a letter / Every now and then / I've got a feelin' you're foolin' / You're my lucky star / I've

got a note / I've got a note / I'm shooting high / Music goes 'round and around / You let me down / I've got my fingers crossed / Rhythm in my nursery rhymes / Old man mose / Broken record / Please believe me
CD COCD 20
Collector's Classics / Nov '94 / Cadillac / Complete/Pinnacle / Jazz Music

Manouri, Olivier

CUMPARSITA - TANGOS (Manouri, Olivier & E. Pascualla)
CD Y225212
Silex / Jun '93 / ADA / Harmonia Mundi

Manowar

ANTHOLOGY
CD VSOPCD 235
Connoisseur Collection / Apr '97 / Pinnacle

HAIL TO ENGLAND
Blood of my enemies / Each dawn I die / Kill with power / Hail to England / Army of the immortals / Black arrows / Bridge of death
CD GED 24539
Geffen / Nov '93 / BMG

HELL OF STEEL, THE (The Best Of Manowar)
Fighting the world / Kings of metal / Demon's whip / Warriors prayer / Defender / Crown and the ring / Blow your speakers / Metal warriors / Black wind, fire and steel / Hail and kill / Power of thy sword / Herz aus stahl / Kingdom come / Master of the wind
CD 7567805792
Atlantic / Feb '92 / Warner Music

INTO GLORY RIDE
Warlord / Secret of steel / Gloves of metal / Gates of Valhalla / Hatred / Revelation (death's angel) / March for revenge / By the soldiers of death
CD GED 24538
Geffen / Nov '93 / BMG

LOUDER THAN HELL
Return of the warlord / Brothers of metal pt.1 / Gods made heavy metal / Courage / Number 1 / Outlaw / King / Today is a good day to die / My spirit lives on / Power
CD GED 24925
Geffen / Nov '96 / BMG

TRIUMPH OF STEEL
Achilles, agony and ecstacy in eight parts / Metal warriors / Ride the dragon / Spirit of the cherokee / Burning / Power of sword / Demon's whip / Master of the wind
CD 7567824232
Atlantic / Oct '92 / Warner Music

Manring, Michael

THONK
Big fungus / Snakes got legs / Monkey businessman / Disturbed / On a day of many angels / My three moons / Cruel and unusual / Bad hair day / Adhan / You offered only parabolas / Enormous room
CD 72902103222
High Street / Feb '94 / BMG

Manson, Charles

COMPLETE STUDIO RECORDINGS, THE
CD GM 05CD
Grey Matter / Jan '97 / Cargo

FAMILY JAMS (2CD Set) (Manson Family)
CD Set ARO 002CD
Aoroa / May '97 / Cargo

LIVE AT SAN QUENTIN
CD GM 01CD
Grey Matter / Jan '97 / Cargo

Manson, Jean

COUNTRY GIRL (2CD Set) (Manson, Jeane)
CD 3008272
Arcade / Feb '97 / Discovery

Mansun

ATTACK OF THE GREY LANTERN
Chad who loved me / Mansun's only love song / Taxloss / You, who do you hate / Wide open space / Stripper vicar / Disgusting / She makes my nose bleed / Naked twister / Egg shaped Fred / Dark Mavis
CD CDPCS 7387
Parlophone / Jun '97 / EMI

Mantaray

REDS AND THE BLUES, THE
Know where to find you / I don't make promises / Always tomorrow / Look after myself / Just a ride / Something special / Everybody looks the same / Rise above it all / Blackburn / Behind the clouds / Patient man / Don't believe in me
CD 5342052
Fontana / May '97 / PolyGram

Mantas

WINDS OF CHANGE
Hurricane / Desperado / Sionara / Nowhere to hide / Deceiver / Let it rock / King of the rings / Western days / Winds of change
CD NEATCD 1042
Neat / Jan '96 / Pinnacle

Mantilla, Ray

HANDS OF FIRE (Mantilla, Ray Space Station)
CD 1231742
Red / Apr '93 / ADA / Cadillac / Harmonia Mundi

SYNERGY (Mantilla, Ray Space Station)
CD 1231982
Red / Apr '94 / ADA / Cadillac / Harmonia Mundi

Mantler, Karen

FAREWELL
Farewell / Mister E / Brain dead / Arnold's dead / I'm his boss / My life is hell / Help me / Bill / Con Edison / I hate money / Beware
CD 5315572
Watt / Jul '96 / New Note/Pinnacle

GET THE FLU (Mantler, Karen & Her Cat Arnold)
Flu / I love Christmas / Let's have a baby / My organ / Au lait / Waiting / Call a doctor / Good luck / I'm not such a bad guy / Mean to me
CD 8471362
ECM / Nov '90 / New Note/Pinnacle

MY CAT ARNOLD
CD 839 093 2
ECM / Jun '89 / New Note/Pinnacle

Mantler, Michael

ALIEN
Alien
CD 8276392
ECM / Dec '85 / New Note/Pinnacle

HAPLESS CHILD, THE
CD 8318282
ECM / Jul '87 / New Note/Pinnacle

I SEARCH FOR AN INNOCENT LAND
CD 5270922
ECM / Jul '95 / New Note/Pinnacle

LIVE
Preview - no answer / Slow orchestra piece no.3 (Prisonniers) / For instance / Slow orchestra piece no.8 (A l'abattoir) / When I run / Remembered visit / Slow orchestra piece no.6 / Hapless child / Doubtful guest
CD 8333842
ECM / Oct '87 / New Note/Pinnacle

MANY HAVE NO SPEECH
CD 8355802
ECM / Jul '88 / New Note/Pinnacle

SOMETHING THERE
CD 8318292
ECM / Jul '87 / New Note/Pinnacle

Mantovani

ALL TIME FAVOURITES (Mantovani & His Orchestra)
CD MU 5010
Musketeer / Oct '92 / Disc

ALL TIME FAVOURITES (2CD Set) (Mantovani Orchestra)
Tango / Zigeunerweisen / Hungarian dances No.5 / Solveig's song / Schon rosemarin / Ave Maria / Spanish dance / Tristesse op 10-3 etude in E major / Largo / Barcarolle / Meditation / Air on the G string / Clair De Lune / Song of India / None but the lonely heart / Slavonic dances no.2 in E minor / Chanson du matin / On wings of song / Come Prima / Stardust / Anima e core / Sunrise sunset / Over the rainbow / Lovely way to spend an evening / Andalucia / Limelight / Amapola / Three coins in a fountain / Smoke gets in your eyes / I left my heart in San Francisco / Autumn leaves / Tonight / Malaguena / Swedish rhapsody / La vie en rose / Jalousie
CD Set 330402
Hallmark / Mar '97 / Carlton

AND I LOVE YOU SO
CD 8441852
Decca / '88 / PolyGram

CHANSON D'AMOUR (Mantovani Orchestra)
CD PLSCD 208
Pulse / Apr '97 / BMG

CHRISTMAS
First Noel / Good King Wenceslas / O Holy night / God rest ye merry gentlemen / Nazareth / Holly and the ivy / Midnight waltz / O little town of Bethlehem / White Christmas / O tannenbaum / Toy waltz / O come all ye faithful (Adeste fidelis) / Mary's boy child / O thou that tellest good tidings / Skater's waltz / Silent night
CD 5501432
Spectrum / Nov '96 / PolyGram

CLASSIC MELODIES
Spanish dance no.5 / Solveig's song / Ave Maria / Etude no.3 / Barcarolle / Schon Rosemarin / On wings of song / Slavonic dance no.2 / Hungarian dance no.5 / Tango in D / Air on a G string / Claire de lune / Song of India / Meditation from Thais / None but the lonely heart / Largo from Xerxes / Chanson du matin
CD 12574
Laserlight / Dec '96 / Target/BMG

CLASSICAL LOVE THEMES
CD Set MBSCD 430
Castle / Nov '93 / BMG

ESSENTIAL MANTOVANI
CD Set TFP 023
Tring / Nov '92 / Tring

GOLDEN AGE OF MANTOVANI, THE
Siboney / Woman in love / Amazing grace / Candy man / Nessun Dorma / Italian Medley / I'll get By / Good life / Zorba the Greek / Ben Hur / Tara's Theme / Ay ay ay / Tie A Yellow Ribbon / People / Cara mia / Elizabethan serenade / For All We Know / Green Cockatoo / Big Country / Legend Of The Glass Mountain / Yellow rose of Texas / Sweetest sounds / Dream of Olwen / Trolley Song
CD CDSIV 6128
Horatio Nelson / Jul '95 / Disc

GOLDEN HITS
Charmaine / Moon river / Moulin Rouge / Summertime in Venice / Diane / Exodus / Greensleeves / True love / La vie en rose / Around the world / Some enchanted evening / Swedish Rhapsody
CD 8000852
Decca / '88 / PolyGram

GOLDEN HITS VOL.2
Tonight / Andalucia / Jealousy / La vie en rose / Smoke gets in your eyes / I left my heart in San Francisco / Limelight / Over the rainbow / Amapola / Malaguena / Sunrise, sunset / Anema e core / Lovely way to spend an evening / Come prima / Stardust
CD 12573
Laserlight / Sep '96 / Target/BMG

GREATEST HITS (Mantovani Orchestra)
CD MACCD 157
Autograph / Aug '96 / BMG

INTERNATIONAL HITS (Mantovani Orchestra)
CD PWK 079
Carlton / Jan '89 / Carlton

LATINO CONNECTION
CD 12307
Music Of The World / Apr '94 / ADA / Target/BMG

LOVE ALBUM - 20 ROMANTIC FAVOURITES, THE
Some enchanted evening / Very thought of you / I can't stop loving you / April love / It's impossible / My cherie amour / Shadow of your smile / Lovely way to spend an evening / Love is all / Charmaine / Hello, young lovers / Man and a woman / Dear heart / For all we know / She / I will wait for you / And I love you so / What are you doing the rest of your life / Spanish eyes / More
CD PLATCD 14
Platinum / Dec '88 / Prism

LOVE THEMES, THE
Charmaine / Love story / For once in my life / Shadow of your smile / If I loved you / Love letters / Stardust / Long ago and far away / Some enchanted evening / Embraceable you / Moon river / Tenderly / When I fall in love / Most beautiful girl / And I love you so / Till there was you / Way you look tonight / Love me with all your heart / Nearness of you / You are beautiful / Tea for two / Lover / Till / I have dreamed / September song / I wish you love / My prayer / Very thought of you
CD CDSIV 6101
Horatio Nelson / Jul '95 / Disc

MAGIC OF MANTOVANI
CD DCD 5301
Disky / Dec '93 / Disky / THE

MANHATTAN
Give my regards to Broadway / Autumn in New York / Bowery / Harlem nocturne / Slaughter on 10th Avenue / Manhattan serenade / Take the 'A' train / Manhattan lullaby / Maria / Somewhere / Belle of New York / Tenement symphony
CD 8204752
London / Jun '87 / PolyGram

MANTOVANI ORCHESTRA (Mantovani Orchestra)
Superman / Memory / I just called to say I love you / Medley / Medley / Canon / Nessun dorma / Medley / Chariots of fire / Flamingo / Midnight cowboy / Colours of my life / La mer / Begin the beguine / Tenderly / Live and let die
CD QED 059
Tring / Nov '96 / Tring

NOBODY DOES IT BETTER (Mantovani Orchestra)
CD MACCD 153
Autograph / Aug '96 / BMG

ROMANTIC MELODIES (Mantovani Orchestra)
CD DCD 5392 LM/VM
Disky / Apr '94 / Disky / THE

SERENADE
Around the world / Elizabethan serenade / Stardust / Old fashioned way / As time goes by / Anniversary waltz / And I love you so / Blue Danube / Very thought of you / Walk in the Black Forest / Stranger in paradise / Londonderry air / Spanish eyes / Swedish rhapsody
CD 5500172
Spectrum / May '93 / PolyGram

SOUND OF MANTOVANI, THE (Mantovani Orchestra)
CD KLMCD 056
BAM / Jun '97 / Koch / Scratch/BMG

TENDERLY (Mantovani Orchestra)
Flamingo: *Mantovani & His Orchestra* / Midnight cowboy: *Mantovani & His Orchestra* / La mer: *Mantovani & His Orchestra* / Begin the beguine: *Mantovani & His Orchestra* / Send in the clowns: *Mantovani & His Orchestra* / Song of Skye: *Mantovani & His Orchestra* / Autumn leaves: *Mantovani & His Orchestra* / Some enchanted evening: *Mantovani & His Orchestra* / Love is a many splendoured thing: *Mantovani & His Orchestra* / Deep purple: *Mantovani & His Orchestra* / Swedish rhapsody: *Mantovani & His Orchestra* / What are you doing for the rest of your life: *Mantovani & His Orchestra* / Tenderly: *Mantovani & His Orchestra* / Colours of my life: *Mantovani & His Orchestra* / Three coins in the fountain: *Mantovani & His Orchestra* / Charmaine: *Mantovani & His Orchestra*
CD PWK 031
Carlton / '88 / Carlton

VINTAGE MANTOVANI (Mantovani & His Tipica Orchestra)
Raggamuffin / Fete in Santa Lucia / Have you forgotten so soon / Madame, you're lovely / You're laughing at me / Spider of the night / No more you / In a German beergarden / September in the rain / Aromas mendocinas / Marcay / Eto nutche / Traumerei / Romany / Speak to me of love / Smoke gets in your eyes / Her name is Mary / Rose dreams / Nothing lives longer than love / Serenade / Ten pretty girls
CD PASTCD 9724
Flapper / Nov '90 / Pinnacle

WAY WE WERE, THE
CD DCDCD 210
Castle / Aug '96 / BMG

Mantra, Michael

SONIC ALTAR
CD SR 9449
Silent / Mar '94 / Cargo / Plastic Head

Manu Lann Huel

CADOU
CD RS 209CD
Keltia Musique / May '94 / ADA / Discovery

Manual Scan

PLAN OF ACTION
CD FUN 003
Snap / Jul '97 / Greyhound

Manuel

GOLDEN SOUNDS OF MANUEL & THE MUSIC OF THE MOUNTAINS, THE (Manuel & The Music Of The Mountains)
CD GS 863552
Disky / Mar '96 / Disky / THE

INSTRUMENTAL LOVE SONGS (3CD Set) (Manuel & Geoff Love)
Moon river: *Manuel* / Begin the beguine: *Manuel* / Very thought of you: *Manuel* / Smoke gets in your eyes: *Manuel* / All the things you are: *Manuel* / Moonlight serenade: *Manuel* / Clair de Lune: *Manuel* / What are you doing the rest of your life: *Manuel* / Chanson d'amour: *Manuel* / And I love you so: *Manuel* / How deep is your love: *Manuel* / Romeo and Juliet: *Manuel* / Amor amor: *Manuel* / Somewhere my love: *Manuel* / You'll never find another love like mine: *Manuel* / Twelfth of never: *Manuel* / You make me feel brand new: *Manuel* / You are the sunshine of my life: *Manuel* / Feelings: *Manuel* / Fernando: *Manuel* / Way we were: *Manuel* / As time goes by: *Manuel* / Forever and ever: *Manuel* / Misty: *Love, Geoff* / Dream lover: *Love, Geoff* / When I fall in love: *Love, Geoff* / I wish you love: *Love, Geoff* / Girl from Ipanema: *Love, Geoff* / Tara's theme (Gone with the wind): *Love, Geoff* / Stranger on the shore: *Love, Geoff* / Chi Mai: *Love, Geoff* / Annie's song: *Love, Geoff* / Cavatina: *Love, Geoff* / In the mood: *Love, Geoff* / Summer place: *Love, Geoff* / Love is blue: *Love, Geoff* / Falling in love with love: *Love, Geoff* / Love Story: *Love, Geoff* / Secret love: *Love, Geoff* / Love letters: *Love, Geoff* / Portrait of my love: *Love, Geoff* / Our love is here to stay: *Love, Geoff* / Plaisir d'amour: *Love, Geoff* / You made me love you: *Love, Geoff* / True love: *Love, Geoff* / Love walked in: *Love, Geoff*

CD Set CDTRBOX 116
Trio / Oct '94 / EMI

MAGIC OF MANUEL AND THE MUSIC OF THE MOUNTAINS
Somewhere my love / Sunrise sunset / Love story / Shadow of your smile / Spanish Harlem / Strangers in the night / If / Bali Ha'i / El condor pasa / Cuando calienta el sol / Spartacus love theme / Moonlight serenade / Sun, sea and the sky / Do you know the way to San Jose / Cavatina / Autumn leaves / Ebb tide / Moon river / Begin the beguine / Stranger on the shore / Misty / What are you doing the rest of your life / And I love you so / Killing me softly
CD Set CDDL 1086
Music For Pleasure / Nov '91 / EMI

MANUEL WITH LOVE
Windmills of your mind / As time goes by / Very thought of you / La vie en rose / Strangers in the night / I wish you love / Evergreen / When I need you / If / How near am I to love / How deep is your love / Way we were / You light up my life / And this is my beloved / Yesterday / Moonlight serenade / All the things you are / On days like these / One and only / Somewhere my love
CD CC 289
Music For Pleasure / Dec '92 / EMI

MOUNTAIN FIESTA (Manuel & The Music Of The Mountains)
Moonlight fiesta / Windmills of your mind / Stranger in Paradise / On days like these / Girl from Ipanema / Bossa de Cid / Carlos' theme / Little sparrow of Paris / La golondrina / Wandering star / You and the night and the music / Time for love is anytime / Umbrellas of Cherbourg / Stella by starlight / Malaguena / Singer not the song / Carnival / Gardens in Ibiza / Al di la / Boa noite
CD CC 253
Music For Pleasure / May '90 / EMI

Manuel, Manny

REY DE CORAZONES
Mi problema / Estrellita / Distanciado / Los hombres no debenllorar / Pero que necesidad / Se acabo lo que de daba / Si una vez / Rey de corsazones / Maniqui / Illusionado
CD 66058055
RMM / Feb '95 / New Note/Pinnacle

Manusardi, Guido

COLORED PASSAGES (Manusardi, Guido & Garzone/Lockwood/Gullotti)
CD RMCD 4504
Ram / Nov '93 / Cadillac / Harmonia Mundi

TOGETHER AGAIN (Manusardi, Guido & Red Mitchell)
CD 1211812
Soul Note / Nov '91 / Cadillac / Harmonia Mundi / Wellard

Manuskript

DIVERSITY OF LIFE, THE
CD ABCD 12
Resurrection / Oct '96 / Plastic Head

I CAN'T BELIEVE
CD ABCD 008
Resurrection / Jul '96 / Plastic Head

Manzanera, Phil

801 LIVE
Lagrima / TNK (Tomorrow never knows) / East of Asteroid / Rongwrong / Sombre reptiles / Baby's on fire / Diamond head / Miss Shapiro / You really got me / Third uncle
CD EGCD 26
EG / '87 / EMI

GUITARISSIMO
La Escena / Criollo / Diamond head / You are here / Rude awakening / Listen now / Big dome (part 2) / Caracas / Lagrima / Europe 70-1 / Island / That falling feeling / Big dome (part 1) / City of light / Initial speed
CD EGCD 69
EG / '87 / EMI

LIVE AT THE KARL MARX THEATRE (Manzanera, Phil & Moncada)
Yo te queria Maria / Mama Hue / Yolanda/ Pablo Milanes / Caiman no come caiman / Mi canto sube / Cantar el son de Cuba / Southern cross / Astrud / Musica / Corazon corazon
CD EXVP 4CD
Expression / Mar '97 / Pinnacle

MAINSTREAM (Quiet Sun)
Bargain classics / Mummy was an asteroid, Daddy was a non-stick kitchen utensil / RFD / Rongwrong / Sol caliente / Trot / Trumpets with motherhood
CD BP 246CD
Blueprint / Mar '97 / Pinnacle

MANZANERA AND MACKAY (Manzanera, Phil & Andy Mackay)
Black gang chine / Free yourself / Built for speed / Many are the ways / I can be tender / Dreams of the East / Sacrosanct / Every king of stone / Men with extraordinary / Safe in the arms of love / Forgotten man
CD EXVP 5CD
Expression / Feb '97 / Pinnacle

MANZANERA COLLECTION, THE (2CD Set)
Tomorrow never knows / Over you / Out of the blue / Fat lady of Limbourg / Impossible guitar / Charlie / Take a chance with me / Frontera / Diamond head / Needle in a camel's eye / Miss Shapiro / End / Gun / Europe 70-1 / Leyenda / Frontera 91 / Southern cross / Sphinx / Amazona / Million reasons why / Fifth wheel / It's just love / Talk to me / Suzanne / Blackgang Chine / Lorelei / Criollo / Mama hue / Corazon Corazon / Flor de azalea / Espiritu
CD CDVDM 9033
Virgin / May '95 / EMI

MILLION REASONS WHY, A
Million reasons why / Tambor / Great leveller / Astrud / Southern cross / Blood brother / Guantanamera / Rich and poor / Dance (break this trance) / Verde / De Fidel / Vencermos
CD EXVP 1CD
Expression / Apr '97 / Pinnacle

ONE WORLD (Manzanera, Phil & John Wetton)
It's just love / Keep on loving yourself / You don't have to leave my life / Suzanne / Round in circles / Do it again / Every trick in the book / One world / Can't let you go / Have you seen her tonight / Talk to me
CD BP 241CD
Blueprint / Mar '97 / Pinnacle

SOUTHERN CROSS
CD EXPCD 1
Expression / Oct '90 / Pinnacle

Manzarek, Ray

LOVE LION (Manzarek, Ray & M. McClure)
CD SHAN 5006CD
Shanachie / Oct '93 / ADA / Greensleeves / Koch

Manzi, Homero

HOMENAJE A LOS POETAS DEL TANGO
CD EBCD 78
El Bandoneon / Jul '96 / Discovery

Mao Tse Tung Experience

ARMOURER
CD RTD 19519092
Our Choice / Nov '94 / Pinnacle

Mapfumo, Thomas

CHIMURENGA FOREVER (The Best Of Thomas Mapfumo)
Serevende / Mhondoro / Vanhu vetama / Nyoka musango / Hanzvadzi / Nyarara mukadzi wangu / Zvenyika / Hondo / Ndave kuende / Shumba / Zvandivringa / Hwa hwa
CD CDEMC 3722
Hemisphere / Oct '95 / EMI

Maphis, Joe

FLYING FINGERS
Flying fingers / Lorrie Ann / Guitar rock 'n' roll / Randy Lynn rag / Sweet fern / Twin banjo special / Fire on the strings / Bully of the town / Town Hall shuffle / Floggin' the banjo / Tennessee two step / Katy Warren breakdown / Bye, bye: *Maphis, Joe & Larry Collins* / Early American: *Maphis, Joe & Larry Collins* / Rockin' gypsy: *Maphis, Joe & Larry Collins* / Hurricane: *Maphis, Joe & Larry Collins* / Short recess / Moonshot / Del Rio / Mavajo (war party) / Jubilo / Marching through Georgia / Water baby boogie / Black sombrero
CD BCD 16103
Bear Family / Jan '97 / Direct / Rollercoaster / Swift

LIVE AT THE TOWN HALL 1958-1961
CD RFDCD 16
Country Routes / Jan '97 / Hot Shot / Jazz Music

Mar-Keys

BACK TO BACK (Mar-Keys/Booker T. & MG's)
Introduction / Green onions / Red beans and rice / Tic-tac toe / Hip hug-her / Philly dog / Grab this thing / Last night / Gimme some lovin' / Booker-loo / Outrage
CD 7567903072
Atlantic / Feb '93 / Warner Music

GREAT MEMPHIS SOUND, THE
Honey pot / Plantation Inn / I've been loving you too long / Cleo's back / Grab this thing / Philly dog / Walking with the Duke / Girl from Ipanema / In the mood / Dear James
CD 7567823392
Atlantic / Jul '93 / Warner Music

Mara

DON'T EVEN THINK
CD SSMCD 042
Sandstock / May '94 / ADA / CM / Direct

IMMIGRI (Mara & Jalal)
CD BARBARITY 016
Barbarity / Jun '97 / Stern's

POETRY & MOTION
CD CDVEST 11
Bulletproof / May '94 / Pinnacle

Marachi Sol

MEXICO LINDO
CD EUCD 1249
ARC / Mar '94 / ADA / ARC Music

Maraire, Dumisani

CHAMINUKA
CD CDC 208
Music Of The World / Jun '93 / ADA / Target/BMG

SHONA SPIRIT (Maraire, Dumisani & Ephat Mujuru)
CD T 136
Music Of The World / Aug '96 / ADA / Target/BMG

Maralung, Alan

BUNGGRIDJ-BUNGGRIDJ: WANGGA SONGS FROM NORTHERN AUSTRALIA
CD SFCD 40430
Smithsonian Folkways / Jan '94 / ADA / Cadillac / CM / Direct / Koch

Marascia

ATOMICI
CD UCD 003
Undercontrol / Mar '96 / SRD

REWORKED
CD ICDIG 001
Illegal Gathering / Sep '96 / SRD

Maraya

NO HOPE FOR HUMANITY
CD 35786
Rising Sun / Nov '96 / Cargo / Plastic Head

Marbele, Aurulus

SEBENE DANCE
CD JIP 51
JIP / Jan '96 / Jet Star

Marbles

PYRAMID LANDING
CD SPART 53CD
Spin Art / Feb '97 / Cargo

Marc, Julian

BEACH SAMBA
CD 5331412
PolyGram TV / Aug '96 / PolyGram

Marcano, Pedro

PEDRO MARCANO 1935-1940
CD HQCD 86
Harlequin / Jun '97 / Hot Shot / Jazz Music / Swift / Wellard

Marce Et Tumpak

ZOUK CHOUV
Gren-n lanmou / Chien cho / Zouk chouv / Lans difou / Lese woule
CD CDORB 035
Globestyle / May '89 / Pinnacle

Marcello, Melis

FREE TO DANCE
CD 1200232
Black Saint / Oct '94 / Cadillac / Harmonia Mundi

Marcels

MARCELS COMPLETE COLPIX SESSIONS, THE
Blue moon / Goodbye to love / Loved her the whole week through / Peace of mind / I'll be forever loving you / Most of all / Sunday kind of people / Two people in the world / Sweet was the wine / Fallen tear / Over the rainbow / Crazy bells / Tetter totter love / Hold on / Footprints in the sand / You are my sunshine / Find another fool / Summertime / Flower pot / Heartaches / Allright, okay, you win / My love for you / Don't cry for me this xmas / Merry twistmas / Twistin' fever / My melancholy baby / Really need your love / Don't turn your back on me / That old black magic / Give me back your love / Tell them about it / Baby where y'been / I wanna be the leader / Friendly loans / Blue heartaches / Lollipop baby / One last kiss / Honestly sincere
CD NEDCD 264
Sequel / Nov '93 / BMG

March

TURN
CD NS 009CD
Network Sound / Jul '96 / Plastic Head

March, 'Little' Peggy

ICH DENK ZURUCK AN DIE ZEIT
Ich denk zuruck an die Zeit / Gib mir deine hand / Mein baum / Carmen aus Sevilla / Ich schau in deine augen / Sing, wenn du glucklich bist / Lieben ist schoner als traumen / Sonne und Wein / Hey Jude / Die Stadt im Meer / Ich geh mit dir / Eleanor Rigby / Die schonsten Zeiten der Erinnerung / Nie war diese Welt so schon / Kinder ohne Sonne / Zeig mir den Weg ins Gluck / Frag mich nie danach / Auf wiedersehen und gute nacht / Amerika nein sagt sich so leicht / Chim chim cheree / Ganz Paris traumt von der liebe / Der Weg in die Seligkeit / Superstar
CD BCD 15969
Bear Family / Nov '96 / Direct / Rollercoaster / Swift

IN DER CARNABY STREET
CD BCD 15967
Bear Family / Jun '96 / Direct / Rollercoaster / Swift

MEMORIES OF HEIDELBERG
Memories in Heidelberg / Antwort weiss ganz allein der wind / Tausend steine: *March, 'Little' Peggy & Benny Thomas* / Lass mich nie allein / Romeo und Julia / Fallt der regen in das meer / Spar dir deine dollar / Mississippi shuffle boat / Ender der zwanziger jahre / Es war hochste eisenbahn / Bahama lullaby / Telegramm aus Tennessee / Das ist musik fur mich / Ein zigeuner ohne geige / Wedding in my dreams / Du, du, du gehst mir im kopf herum / Die sonne kommt ja wieder / Hey (das ist musik fur dich) / Ich frage die zigeunerin / Weil die liebe zaubern kann / Der mond scheint schon / Mr. Giacomo Puccini / 1969 (weil es so schon war) / Male nicht den teufel an die wand / Yesterday waltz / Canale grande / Wiedersehn
CD BCD 15602
Bear Family / Nov '91 / Direct / Rollercoaster / Swift

MIT SIBZEHN HAT MAN NOCH TRAUME
CD BCD 15536
Bear Family / Mar '91 / Direct / Rollercoaster / Swift

ULTIMATE
CD MAR 046
Marginal / Jun '97 / Greyhound

March Violets

BOTANIC VERSES
CD FREUDCD 42
Jungle / Sep '93 / RTM/Disc / SRD

Marchand, Erik

ERIK MARCHAND
CD Y 225043CD
Silex / Oct '94 / ADA / Harmonia Mundi

Marclay, Christian

RECORDS 1981-1989
CD ALP 62CD
Atavistic / Aug '97 / Cargo / SRD

Marconi, Nestor

UN BANDONEON DE BUENOS AIRES
CD 74321453292
Milan Sur / Feb '97 / Conifer/BMG

Marcotulli, Rita

NIGHT CALLER
CD LBLC 6551
Label Bleu / Jan '93 / New Note/Pinnacle

Marcus, Hannah

RIVER OF DARKNESS
CD NORMAL 178CD
Normal / Mar '96 / ADA / Direct

Marcus, Michael

REACHIN'
Picnic in blue / Constant / Reachin' / Forgotten paradise / Psalm walk / Along the line / Into Nowhersville / Stritch 'n' / With you in mind / Feels like home
CD JUST 872
Justin Time / Aug '96 / Cadillac / New Note/ Pinnacle

UNDER THE WIRE
CD 60642
Enja / Apr '91 / New Note/Pinnacle / Vital/ SAM

Marcus, Steve

201
CD 4722082
Sony Jazz / Nov '92 / Sony

Mardones, Benny

STAND BY YOUR MAN
CD CURCD 030
Hit / Nov '96 / Grapevine/PolyGram

Marduk

DARK ENDLESS
CD NFR 003
No Fashion / Oct '94 / Plastic Head

GLORIFICATION
CD ______ OPCD 043
Osmose / Oct '96 / Plastic Head

HEAVEN SHALL BURN WHEN WE ARE GATHERED
CD ______ OPCD 40
Osmose / Jul '96 / Plastic Head

LIVE IN GERMANY
CD ______ OPCD 054
Osmose / Jun '97 / Plastic Head

OPUS NOCTURNE
CD ______ OPCD 028
Osmose / Jan '95 / Plastic Head

Margitza, Rick

GAME OF CHANCE
Good question / August in Paris / 13 bar blues / Careless / Blades run / Bird shit (for Charlie Parker) / Jazz prelude no.9 / No minor affair / Cidade vazia / Game of chance
CD ______ CHR 70044
Challenge / Jul '97 / ADA / Direct / Jazz Music / Wellard

HANDS OF TIME
CD ______ CHR 70021
Challenge / Sep '95 / ADA / Direct / Jazz Music / Wellard

Margo

IRELAND ON MY MIND
I would like to see you again / Poverty / Tribute to Packie Bonner / Tipperary far away / Born in Ireland / Consider the children / Little town on the Shannon / Man from the glen / Rented room / Little white house / Ireland on my mind / How far is heaven
CD ______ RITZRCD 516
Ritz / Apr '92 / Pinnacle

NEW BEGINNINGS
You'll remember me / Eyes of a child / Back in baby's arms / Irish harvest day / Home is where the heart is / Infamous angel / Memories of Mayo / I'll forgive and I'll try to forget / Pick me up on your way down / Paper mansions / If I kiss you / To my children I'm Irish / Sitting alone / Friends
CD ______ RITZCD 540
Ritz / Aug '94 / Pinnacle

Margolin, Bob

DOWN IN THE ALLEY
CD ______ ALCD 4816
Alligator / Nov '93 / ADA / CM / Direct

MY BLUES AND MY GUITAR
CD ______ ALCD 4835
Alligator / Nov '95 / ADA / CM / Direct

UP AND IN
Window / Alien's blues / Imagination / She and the devil / Blues for bartenders / Why are people like that / Goin' back out on the road / Up and in / Coffee break / 'Bout out / Not what you said last night / Long ago and far away / Just because / Later for you
CD ______ ALCD 4851
Alligator / May '97 / ADA / CM / Direct

Margy, Lina

ETOILES DE LA CHANSON
CD ______ 882402
Music Memoria / Aug '93 / ADA / Discovery

Maria, Tania

BEST OF TANIA MARIE
I don't go / Made in New York / I do I love you / Valeu / Bronx / Tanoca Vignette / Chuleta / Please don't stay / O bom e / Ca c'est bon / Marguerita / 210 West
CD ______ CDP 7986342
World Pacific / Jun '93 / EMI

BLUESILIAN
Yes, is the way to go / Eric's blues / Zaza / Bluesilian / Feeling the air / Rebordosa / All alone together / Please me / If I could change / From my window / Oxala
CD ______ TKM 50032
TKM / May '96 / New Note/Pinnacle

COME WITH ME
Sangria / Embraceable you / Lost in Amazonia / Come with me / Sementes, graines and seeds / Nega / Euzinha / It's all over now
CD ______ CCD 4200
Concord Picante / Jul '95 / New Note/ Pinnacle

EUROPE
Funky tamborine / Chuleta / I can do it / Senso unico / O bom e / She's outrageous / Bom bom bom (Chi chi chi)
CD ______ NNCD 1003
New Note / May '97 / Cadillac / New Note/ Pinnacle

LOVE EXPLOSION
Funky tambourine / It's all in my hands / You've got me feeling your love / Love explosion / Bela la bela / Rainbow of your love / Deep cove view / Pour toi
CD ______ CCD 4230
Concord Jazz / Dec '86 / New Note/ Pinnacle

NO COMMENT
Pelham melody / Liqued groove / Keep in mind / Desire / Marvin my love / Who knows / Jack Hammer / Gotcha / Fanatic / Bali / Something for now
CD ______ TKM 50012
TKM / May '95 / New Note/Pinnacle

OUTRAGEOUS
Dear Dee Vee / Confusion / She's outrageous / Bom bom bom / Happiness / Amei demais / Ta tudo cetto / I can do it / Minha Moe / Happiness / Granada
CD ______ CCD 4563
Concord Picante / Aug '93 / New Note/ Pinnacle

PIQUANT
CD ______ CCD 4151
Concord Jazz / Jul '88 / New Note/ Pinnacle

REAL TANIA MARIA-WILD, THE
Yatra - ta / A cama na varanda / Vem pra roda / Come with me / Funy tamborine / 2 a.m. / Sangria
CD ______ CCD 4264
Concord Jazz / Nov '86 / New Note/ Pinnacle

TAURUS
CD ______ CCD 4175
Concord Picante / Oct '87 / New Note/ Pinnacle

Maria-Jose

ETOILES DE LA CHANSON
CD ______ 882412
Music Memoria / Aug '93 / ADA / Discovery

Mariachi Azteca

BEST OF MARIACHI AZTECA, THE
CD ______ EUCD 1119
ARC / '91 / ADA / ARC Music

Mariachi Cobre

MARIACHI COBRE
CD ______ CDKUCK 11095
Kuckuck / Jun '92 / ADA / CM

XXV ANIVERSARIO 1971-1996
CD ______ 150222
Celestial Harmonies / Aug '96 / ADA / Select

Mariachi Jalisco

SINGS TO THE HOMELAND
CD ______ ARN 64342
Arion / Feb '96 / ADA / Discovery

Mariachi Reyes Del Aserradero

SONES FROM JALISCO
CD ______ CO 108
Corason / Feb '94 / ADA / CM / Direct

Mariachi Sol

CU CU RRU CU CU PALOMA
CD ______ EUCD 1246
ARC / Nov '93 / ADA / ARC Music

Mariano, Cesar Camargo

NATURAL
Maracatu / Manha da carnaval / Choro por Clare / Trocando em / Mudos / O nosso amor / Zazueira / Endlessley / Pamela / Tristeza de nos dois / Curitiba
CD ______ 5148512
Verve World / Mar '94 / PolyGram

Mariano, Charlie

70 (Mariano, Charlie & Friends)
Il Piacere / Everybody's song / Deep river / Rabou abou kabou / Crystal bells / Seva la murga
CD ______ VBR 21492
Vera Bra / Feb '94 / New Note/Pinnacle / Pinnacle

ALTO SAX...FOR YOUNG MODERNS (Mariano, Charlie, Quartet)
Johnny one note / Very thought of you / Smoke gets in your eyes / King for a day / Darn that dream / Floormat / Blues / I heard you cry last night
CD ______ BET 6013
Bethlehem / Jan '95 / ADA / ZYX

BOSTON DAYS 1954 (Mariano, Charlie Quintet)
CD ______ FSRCD 207
Fresh Sound / Nov '94 / Discovery / Jazz Music

CHARLIE MARIANO PLAYS
CD ______ BET 6012
Bethlehem / Jan '95 / ADA / ZYX

FRIENDS (Mariano, Charlie & Stephen Diez)
CD ______ ISCD 121
Intersound / '91 / Jazz Music

FROM ME TO YOU
CD ______ ISCD 148
Intersound / Jun '95 / Jazz Music

JYOTHI
Voice solo / Vandanam / Varshini / Saptarshi / Kartik / Bhajan
CD ______ 8115482
ECM / Aug '86 / New Note/Pinnacle

Mariano, Torcuato

LAST LOOK
Africa / Everything I couldn't say with words / Last look / In the rhythm of my heart / Very special place / Secrets / Ocean way / Walking on clouds / Rio stomp / Dindi
CD ______ 01934111672
Windham Hill / Oct '95 / BMG

PARADISE STATION
Train to Uberaba / Upon the sea / Just for you / I can't help it / Other side / On a summer night / Xufle / Sincere lies / Eastern winds / Paradise station / Mariana and Paula good night
CD ______ 01934111372
Windham Hill / Feb '94 / BMG

Marias, Gerard

EST
CD ______ HOP 200001
Label Hopi / May '94 / Harmonia Mundi

Marie, Donna

REGGAE LOVE MUSIC VOL.1
CD ______ PICD 202
Pioneer / Jun '97 / Jet Star

Marie, Teena

GREATEST HITS
I'm a sucker for your love / Don't look back / Behind the groove / I need your lovin' / Square biz / It must be magic / Ballad of Cradle Rob & me / Portugese love / Aladdin's lamp / Irons in the fire / I'm gonna have my cake (and eat it too) / Yes indeed / Deja vu (I've been there before) / Opus III (does anybody care)
CD ______ 5525462
Spectrum / Sep '96 / PolyGram

LOVERGIRL (The Teena Marie Story)
Just us two / Ooo la la la / Sugar shack / If I were a bell / Stop the world / My dear Mr. Gray / Shadow boxing / Light / Out on a limb / Lovergirl / Dear lover / Fix it / Casanove Brown
CD ______ 4871202
Epic / May '97 / Sony

STAR CHILD
Lovergirl / Help youngblood get to the freaky party / Out on a limb / Alibi / Jammin' / Star child / We've got to stop (meeting like this) / My Dear Mr.Gaye / Light
CD ______ 7464395282
Epic / Feb '85 / Sony

Marienthal, Eric

EASY STREET
CD ______ 5373382
ie music / May '97 / PolyGram

ERIC MARIENTHAL COLLECTION
Oasis / Hustlin' / Sun was in my eyes / Written in the wind / Brazilian dream / That's the way / Walk through the fire / Where are you / Hold on my heart / Where you belong / Street dance / Legenda
CD ______ GRP 98532
GRP / Feb '97 / New Note/BMG

ONE TOUCH
No doubt about it / That's the way / One for James / Walk through the fire / Ouch / Westland / Village / Tanto amor / Backtalk / Where are you
CD ______ GRP 96912
GRP / May '93 / New Note/BMG

STREET DANCE
Street dance / Kids stuff / Moment of silence / Shake it loose / Fafaru / Legenda / Nothin' but everything / Where you belong / Yosemite / Hold on to my heart / Forces of nature / Have I told you lately that I love you
CD ______ GRP 97992
GRP / Nov '94 / New Note/BMG

Marilla

SWEET SOUNDS OF CHRISTMAS, THE
Ding dong merrily on high / Once in royal David's city / O come all ye faithful (adeste fidelis) / When a child is born / Away in a manger / Drummer boy / Do you hear what I hear / In the bleak mid Winter / Angels we have heard on high / O little town of Bethlehem / It came upon the midwinter clear / Silent night / Mary's boy child / O holy night
CD ______ MLM 114
One Stop / Dec '96 / Koch

Marillion

AFRAID OF SUNLIGHT
Gazpacho / Cannibal surf babe / Beautiful / Afraid of sunrise / Out of this world / Afraid of sunlight / Beyond you / King
CD ______ CDEMD 1079
EMI / Jun '95 / EMI

B'SIDES THEMSELVES
Grendel / Charting the single / Market square heroes / Three boats down from the Candy / Cinderella search / Lady Nina / Freaks / Tux on / Margaret
CD ______ CZ 39
EMI / Jul '88 / EMI

BEST OF BOTH WORLDS, THE (2CD Set)
Script for a jesters tear / Market square heroes / He knows you know / Forgotten sons / Garden party / Assassing / Punch and Judy / Kayleigh / Lavender / Heart of Lothian / Incommunicado / Warm wet circles / That time of the night (the short straw) / Sugar mice / Uninvited guest / Easter / Hooks in you / Space / Cover my eyes (pain and heaven) / No one can / Dry land / Waiting to happen / Great escape / Alone again in the lap of luxury / Made again / King / Afraid of sunlight / Beautiful / Cannibal surf babe
CD Set ______ CDEMC 3761
EMI / Feb '97 / EMI

BRAVE
Bridge / Living with the big lie / Runaway / Goodbye to all that / Wave / Mad / Opium den / Slide / Standing in the swing / Hard as love / Hollow man / Alone again in the lap of luxury / Now wash your hand / Paper lies / Brave / Great escape / Last of you / Falling from the moon / Made again
CD ______ CDEMD 1054
EMI / Feb '94 / EMI

CLUTCHING AT STRAWS
Hotel hobbies / Warm wet circles / That time of the night / Going under / Just for the record / White Russian / Incommunicado / Torch song / Slainte Mhath / Sugar mice / Last straw
CD ______ CZ 214
EMI / '89 / EMI

COLLECTION, THE
Grendel / He knows you know / Jigsaw / Punch and Judy / Cinderella search / Kayleigh / Lavender / Lady Nina / Torch song
CD ______ CDGOLD 1058
EMI Gold / Oct '96 / EMI

FUGAZI
Assassing / Punch and Judy / Jigsaw / Emerald lies / She chameleon / Incubus / Fugazi
CD ______ CDEMC 3682
EMI / May '94 / EMI

HOLIDAYS IN EDEN
Splintering heart / Cover my eyes (pain and heaven) / Party / No one can / Holidays in Eden / Dry land / Waiting to happen / This town / Rakes progress / 100 nights
CD ______ CDEMD 1022
EMI / Jun '91 / EMI

MADE AGAIN (Live)
Splintering heart / East / No one can / Waiting to happen / Cover my eyes / Space / Hooks in you / Beautiful / Kayleigh / Lavender / Afraid of sunlight / King / Bridge / Living with the big lie / Runaway / Goodbye to all that / Wave / Mad / Opium den / Slide / Standing in the swing / Hard as love / Hollow man / Alone again in the lap of luxury / Now wash your hands / Paper lies / Brave / Great escape / Last of you / Falling from the moon / Made again
CD ______ CDEMD 1094
EMI / Mar '96 / EMI

MISPLACED CHILDHOOD
Pseudo-silk kimono / Kayleigh / Lavender / Bitter suite / Heart of Lothian / Waterhole / Lords of the backstage / Blind curve / Childhood's end / White feather
CD ______ CDEMC 3684
EMI / May '94 / EMI

REAL TO REEL/BRIEF ENCOUNTER (2CD Set)
Assasing / Incubus / Cinderella search / Emerald lies / Forgotten sons / Garden party / Market square heroes / Lady Nina / Freaks / Kayleigh / Fugazi / Script for a jester's tear
CD Set ______ CDEM 1603
EMI / Jun '97 / EMI

SCRIPT FOR A JESTER'S TEAR
He knows you know / Web / Garden party / Chelsea Monday / Forgotten sons / Script for a jester's tear
CD ______ CDGOLD 1012
EMI Gold / Mar '96 / EMI

SCRIPT FOR A JESTER'S TEAR/ FUGAZI/MISPLACED CHILDHOOD (The Originals/3CD Set)
Script for a jester's tear / He knows you know / Web / Garden party / Chelsea Monday / Forgotten sons / Punch and Judy / Jigsaw / Emerald lies / She chameleon / Incubus / Fugazi / Pseudo silk kimono / Kayleigh / Lavender / Bitter suite / Heart of Lothian / Waterhole (Expresso Bongo) / Lords of the backstage / Blind curve / Childhood's end / White feather
CD Set ______ CDOMB 015
EMI / Mar '97 / EMI

SEASONS END
King of Sunset town / Easter / Uninvited guest / Season's end / Holloway girl / Berlin / After me / Hooks in you / Space

CD ________ CDEMD 1011
EMI / Aug '89 / EMI

SINGLES COLLECTION 1982-1992, A
Cover my eyes (pain and heaven) / Kayleigh / Easter / Warm wet circles / Uninvited guest / Assassing / Hooks in you / Garden party / No one can / Incommunicado / Dry land / Lavender / I will walk on water / Sympathy
CD ________ CDEMD 1033
EMI / May '92 / EMI

THIEVING MAGPIE, THE (La Gazza Ladra)
La gazza ladra / Slainte Mhath / He knows you know / Chelsea Monday / Freaks / Jigsaw / Punch and Judy / Sugar mice / Fugazi / Script for a jester's tear / Incommunicado / White Russian / Pseudo-silk kimono / Kayleigh / Lavender / Bitter suite / Heart of Lothian / Waterhole / Lords of the backstage / Blind curve / Childhood's end / White feather
CD Set ________ CDMARIL 1
EMI / Nov '88 / EMI

THIS STRANGE ENGINE
Man of a thousand faces / One fine day / 80 Days / Estonia / Memory of water / An accidental man / Hope for the future / This strange engine
CD ________ RAWDP 121
CD ________ RAWCD 121
Raw Power / Apr '97 / Pinnacle

Marilyn Decade

MARILYN DECADE CD, THE
CD ________ FRR 015
Freek / Dec '95 / RTM/Disc / SRD

Marilyn Manson

ANTICHRIST SUPERSTAR
Irresponsible hate anthem / Beautiful people / Dried up tied up and dead to the world / Tourniquet / Little Horn / Cryptorchid / Deformography / Wormboy / Mister superstar / Angel with the scabbed wings / Kinderfeld / Antichrist superstar / 1996 / Minute of decay / Reflecting God / Man that you fear
CD ________ IND 90086
Interscope / Oct '96 / BMG

GET YOUR GUN
CD ________ INTDM 95902
Interscope / Dec '96 / BMG

LUNCHBOX
CD ________ INTDM 95806
Interscope / Dec '96 / BMG

PORTRAIT OF AN AMERICAN FAMILY
CD ________ IND 92344
Interscope / Jul '96 / BMG

SMELLS LIKE CHILDREN
Hands of small children / Diary of a dope fiend / Shitty chicken gang bang / Kiddie grinder / Sympathy for the parents / Sweet dreams (are made of this) / Everlasting cuntsucker / Fuck frankie / I put a spell on you / May cause discolouration of the urine or feces / Scab, guns and peanut butter / Dance of the dope hats / White trash / Dancing with the one-legged... / Rock 'n' roll nigger
CD ________ IND 92641
Interscope / Aug '96 / BMG

Marine Girls

LAZY WAYS/BEACH PARTY
CD ________ CDMRED 44
Cherry Red / Aug '88 / Pinnacle

Marini, Giovanna

DEPARTURES (Twenty Years After The Death Of Pier Paolo Pasolini) (Marini, Giovanna Vocal Quartet)
Il galeone / Il mio prino incontro con Pier Paolo Pasolini / Mi pesa andar lontano / E adesso / Miserere di Santu Lussurgiu / Amour mi amour/Dansa di narcis / Pauli/ Madonuta / Stornelli e Discanti all cepranese / Montefiori dall'aso / Stabermater / Eccoci bella mia buongiorno / Calpastevano mosaico / Si lui la vole / Sono arrivati i barbari / El di de la me muart / Lied / Lamento per la morte di Pasolini / Biva biva
CD ________ Y 225065
Silex / Jan '97 / ADA / Harmonia Mundi

PASOLINI PARTENZE (Marini, Giovanna Vocal Quartet)
CD ________ Y 225065CD
Silex / May '97 / ADA / Harmonia Mundi

Marino

AFTER FOREVERS GONE
Northern sky (part 1) / Jasmine / El Salvador / Look into the sun / After forever's gone / Fishermen (part II) / Borderline / Ian's garden / Did I say that / Northern sky (part II) / Present light / Northern sky (part III)
CD ________ WKFMCD 139
FM / Mar '90 / Revolver / Sony

BLUES FOR LOVERS
CD ________ WKFMXD 167
FM / Mar '91 / Revolver / Sony

Marion

THIS WORLD AND BODY
Fallen through / Sleep / Let's all go together / Wait / Only way / I stopped dancing / All for love / Toys for boys / Time / Vanessa / Your body lies / My children
CD ________ 8286952
London / Feb '96 / PolyGram

Marionettes

MEPHISTO'S MOB
CD ________ Z 910062
Jungle / May '93 / RTM/Disc / SRD

RISE
CD ________ BACCYCD 005
Diversity / Oct '95 / 3mv/Vital

Mariteragi, Marie

TUAMOTU AND BORA BORA ISLANDS
CD ________ S 65817CD
Manuiti / Apr '95 / Harmonia Mundi

Maritime Crew

HURRAH FOR OUR CAPTAIN
CD ________ CDMANU 1533
ODE / Jul '97 / CM / Discovery

Marjane, Leo

CHANSOPHONE 1937-1942
CD ________ 701282
Chansophone / Jun '93 / Discovery

HER FAVOURITE MOVIE SONGS
CD ________ 995702
EPM / Jul '96 / ADA / Discovery

Mark B

UNDERWORLD CONNECTION
CD ________ JFRCD 008
Jazz Fudge / Jul '97 / Pinnacle

Mark F.

RESULT OF RANDOM
CD ________ ZETD 04
Zeitgest / Jun '94 / Plastic Head

Mark, Jon

ALHAMBRA
CD ________ CDKUCK 11100
Kuckuck / Nov '92 / ADA / CM

CELTIC STORY, A
CD ________ WCL 11002
White Cloud / May '94 / Select

LAND OF MERLIN
Land of Merlin / Tintagel / Birth of Arthur / Child grows / Merlin and the unicorn / Dream of Arthur / Perilous and mystical journey / King, Queen and castle
CD ________ CDKUCK 11094
Kuckuck / Apr '92 / ADA / CM

STANDING STONES OF CALLANDISH
CD ________ CDKUCK 110822
Kuckuck / Dec '88 / ADA / CM

SUNDAY IN AUTUMN, A
CD ________ WCL 110032
White Cloud / May '95 / Select

Mark Of Cain

BATTLESICK
CD ________ 213CD 010
2.13.61 / Feb '97 / Pinnacle

Mark T

GARDEN OF LOVE, THE
CD ________ FSCD 20
Folksound / '92 / CM / Roots

Mark-Almond Band

NIGHTMUSIC
CD ________ WCL 110262
White Cloud / Sep '96 / Select

Marketts

BATMAN THEME
CD ________ EVA 642360B36
EVA / Nov '94 / ADA / Direct

Marks, Kenny

MAKE IT RIGHT
CD ________ DAYCD 4151
Dayspring / Nov '87 / Nelson Word

Marks, Louisa

BREAKOUT
CD ________ BFMCD 101
Bushranger / Jan '97 / Jet Star

Marley Booker, Cedella

AWAKE ZION
CD ________ DANCD 067
Danceteria / Jun '97 / ADA / Plastic Head / Shellshock/Disc

Marley, Bob

24 GREATEST HITS
CD ________ ENTCD 282
Entertainers / Mar '92 / Target/BMG

36 REGGAE SONGS (2CD Set)
Duppy conqueror / Trench Town rock / Lively up yourself / Rainbow country / Sun is shining / Soul almighty / All in one / Can't you see / Chances are / Hammer / Mellow mood / Mr. Brown / Reaction / Soon come / There she goes / Touch me / It's alright / Stop the train / Rebel's hop / Natural mystic / Treat you right / 400 years / Corner stone / Soul captive / African herbsman / Do it twice / Back out / No sympathy / No water / Small axe / Soul shakedown party / Try me / Brain washing / Caution / Don't rock my boat / I gotta keep on moving
CD Set ________ TNC 96202
Natural Collection / Aug '96 / Target/BMG

AFRICAN HERBSMAN
Lively up yourself / Small axe / Keep on moving / Duppy conqueror / Trenchtown rock / African herbsman / Fussing and fighting / All in one / Stand alone / Don't rock the boat / Put it on / Sun is shining / Kaya / 400 years / Riding high / Brain washing
CD ________ CDTRL 62
Trojan / Mar '94 / Direct / Jet Star

ALL THE HITS
CD ________ RRTGCD 7757
Rohit / Apr '91 / Jet Star

AUDIO ARCHIVE
CD ________ CDAA 047
Tring / Jun '92 / Tring

BABYLON BY BUS (Marley, Bob & The Wailers)
Positive vibration / Funky reggae party / Exodus / Rat race / Lively up yourself / Rebel music / War / No more trouble / Stir it up / Concrete jungle / Kinky reggae / Is this love / Heathen / Jamming
CD ________ TGDCD 1
Tuff Gong / Jan '94 / Jet Star / PolyGram

BEST OF BOB MARLEY, THE (1968-1972)
Trenchtown rock / Don't rock the boat / Kaya / Soul shakedown party / Cheer up / Keep on moving / Try me / Lively up yourself / All in one / Soul rebel / Duppy conqueror / Keep on skanking / Caution / Mr. Brown
CD ________ CSAPCD 107
Connoisseur Collection / Jun '90 / Pinnacle

BEST OF THE WAILERS (Marley, Bob & The Wailers)
CD ________ 444032
Rhino / Jan '97 / Grapevine/PolyGram / Jet Star

BEST, THE
CD ________ 15499
Laserlight / Nov '92 / Target/BMG

BOB MARLEY (The Great Legend Of Reggae)
Soul rebel / Caution / Treat me right / How many times / There she goes / Mellow mood / Tell me / Hammer / Touch me / Chances are / More axe / You can't do that to me / Corner stone / Reaction / No sympathy / Keep on skanking / Soul shakedown party / Try me / Wisdom / African herbsman / No water / Brainwashing / All in one / It's alright / Thank you lord / Adam and Eve / Brand new second hand / Jah is mighty / This train / Turn me loose / Mr. Brown / My cup
CD ________ 24336
Laserlight / Nov '96 / Target/BMG

BOB MARLEY (4CD Set)
Trench town rock / Medley (Bend down low, Nice time, One love, Simmer down, It / Soul rebel / Try me / It's alright / No sympathy / No water / Reaction / Rainbow country / Natural mystic / There she goes / Mellow mood / Treat you right / Chances are / Hammer / Touch me / Soul shakedown party / Stop that train / Caution / Soul captives / Go tell it to the mountain / Can't you see / Soon come / Cheer up / Back out / Do it twice / Keep on moving / Don't rock my boat / Put it on / Fussing and fighting / Duppy conqueror / Small axe / Riding high / Kaya / African herbsman / Stand alone / Sun is shining / Mr. Brown / 400 years / Lively up yourself / Soul almighty / My cup / Corner stone / Brain washing / Rebel's hop / You can't do that to me / How many times
CD Set ________ QUAD 004
Tring / Nov '96 / Tring

BOB MARLEY (CD/CD Rom Set)
CD Set ________ WWCDR 004
Magnum Music / Apr '97 / TKO Magnum

BOB MARLEY 50TH ANNIVERSARY (Various Artists)
CD Set ________ CDTAL 800
Trojan / Jan '96 / Direct / Jet Star

BOB MARLEY AND THE WAILERS (Upsetter Record Shop Pt.1) (Marley, Bob & The Wailers)
CD ________ LG 21040
Lagoon / Aug '92 / Grapevine/PolyGram

BOB MARLEY AND THE WAILERS (Upsetter Record Shop Pt.2) (Marley, Bob & The Wailers)
CD ________ LG 21044
Lagoon / Aug '92 / Grapevine/PolyGram

BOB MARLEY ARCHIVE
Mr. Brown / Soul rebel / Duppy conqueror / Four hundred years / Try me / African herbsman / Keep on moving / Fussing and fighting / Stand alone / My cup / Put it on / Sun is shining / Rebel's hop / Brand new secondhand / Cornerstone / No water / Jah is mighty / Riding high / Brainwashing / Dreamland
CD ________ RMCD 206
Rialto / Sep '96 / Disc / Total/BMG

BOB MARLEY COLLECTION, THE
Don't rock my boat / Soul shakedown party / There she goes / Stop the train / Mellow mood / Caution / Treat you right / Soul almighty / Sun is shining / Chances are / Kaya / Back out / Hammer / Lively up yourself / Cheer up / Mr. Brown / Reaction / Riding high / Rainbow country / Small axe / Soul captives / Kinky reggae / Can't you see / Natural mystic / Soon come / Trenchtown rock / No sympathy / Do it twice / Keep on moving / My cup / Put it on / Fussing and fighting / Corner stone / African herbsman / No water / Stand alone / Brain washing / Rebel's hop / Go tell it to the mountains / All in one / 400 years / Duppy conqueror / Soul rebel / You can't do that to me / Touch me / Try me / How many times / Memphis / It's alright
CD Set ________ TFP 010
Tring / Nov '92 / Tring

BOB MARLEY VOL.1
CD ________ EXP 022
Experience / May '97 / TKO Magnum

BOB MARLEY VOL.2
CD ________ KLMCD 038
BAM / Nov '94 / Koch / Scratch/BMG

BOB MARLEY VOL.2
CD ________ EXP 023
Experience / May '97 / TKO Magnum

BURNIN' (Marley, Bob & The Wailers)
Get up stand up / Hallelujah time / I shot the sheriff / Burnin' and lootin' / Put it on / Small axe / Pass it on / Duppy conqueror / One foundation / Rastaman chant
CD ________ TGLCD 2
Tuff Gong / Jan '94 / Jet Star / PolyGram

BUSTIN' OUT OF TRENCH TOWN (2CD Set)
CD Set ________ SMDCD 108
Snapper / Jul '97 / Pinnacle

CATCH A FIRE
Concrete jungle / 400 years / Stop the train / Baby we got a date / Rock it baby / Kinky reggae / No more trouble / Midnight ravers
CD ________ TGLCD 1
Tuff Gong / Jan '94 / Jet Star / PolyGram

COLLECTION, THE
CD ________ COL 024
Collection / Apr '95 / Target/BMG

CONFRONTATION (Marley, Bob & The Wailers)
Chant down Babylon / Buffalo soldier / Jump Nyabinghi / Mix up, mix up / Give thanks and praises / Blackman redemption / Trench town / I know / Stiff necked fools / Rastaman live up
CD ________ TGLCD 10
Tuff Gong / Jan '94 / Jet Star / PolyGram

DREAMS OF FREEDOM
CD ________ 5244192
Axiom / Sep '97 / PolyGram / Vital

EARLY COLLECTION (Marley, Bob & The Wailers)
Wings of a dove / Do you remember / Love and affection / Donna / It hurts to be alone / Do you feel the same way / Dancing shoes / I'm still waiting / I made a mistake / One love / Maga dog / Nobody knows / Lonesome feeling / Let him go / Lonesome track / I'm going home
CD ________ 4679542
Columbia / Oct '95 / Sony

EXODUS (Marley, Bob & The Wailers)
Natural mystic / So much things to say / Guiltiness / Heathen / Exodus / Jamming / Waiting in vain / Turn your lights down low / Three little birds / One love - people get ready
CD ________ TGLCD 6
Tuff Gong / Jan '94 / Jet Star / PolyGram

GREAT VOL.2, THE
CD ________ GLD 63185
Gold / Apr '95 / TKO Magnum

IN MEMORIAM (3CD Set)
CD Set ________ CDTAL 400
Trojan / Mar '94 / Direct / Jet Star

IN THE BEGINNING
Soul shakedown party / Adam and Eve / Brand new secondhand / Cheer up / This train / Jah is mighty / Caution / Thank you Lord / Keep on skanking / Wisdom / Stop the train / Mr. Chatterbox / Turn me loose
CD ________ CDTRL 221
Trojan / Mar '94 / Direct / Jet Star

INTERVIEW DISC
CD ______ SAM 7022
Sound & Media / Nov '96 / Sound & Media

JAMAICAN SINGLES VOL.1
CD ______ 60012
Declic / Nov '95 / Jet Star

JAMAICAN SINGLES VOL.2 (Dub Versions)
CD ______ 60022
Declic / Nov '95 / Jet Star

KAYA (Marley, Bob & The Wailers)
Easy skanking / Is this love / Sun is shining / Satisfy my soul / She's gone / Misty morning / Crisis / Kaya / Running away / Time will tell
CD ______ TGLCD 7
Tuff Gong / Jan '94 / Jet Star / PolyGram

LEE PERRY SESSIONS, THE
Lively up yourself / Small axe / Trenchtown rock / Sun is shining / Kaya / African herbsman / Brainwashing / Mr. Brown / Try me / No sympathy / Duppy conqueror / Stand alone / Fussing and fighting / Rebel's hop / Soul almighty / It's alright / Don't rock the boat / Put it on / All in one / Keep on moving
CD ______ CPCD 8009
Charly / Oct '93 / Koch

LEGEND (Marley, Bob & The Wailers)
Is this love / Jamming / No woman, no cry / Stir it up / Get up and stand up / Satisfy my soul / I shot the sheriff / One love / Buffalo soldier / Exodus / Redemption song / Could you be loved / Want more
CD ______ BMWCDX 1
Tuff Gong / May '91 / Jet Star / PolyGram

LEGEND IN SAX
CD ______ AACD 88
A&A Productions / Jun '95 / Jet Star

LEGENDARY BOB MARLEY, THE (3CD Set)
Trench Town rock / Rebels hop / Soul shake down party / Mr. Brown / My cup / Fussin' and fightin' / Treat you right / Reaction / Soul almighty / You can't do that to me / Riding high / Duppy conquerer / Sun is shining / Rainbow country / Chances are / Stop that train / Kaya / Mellow moods / Soul captives / Put it on / Can't you see / All in one / How many times / Hammer / Caution / Try me / Small axe / Brain washing / African Herbsman / Touch me / 400 years / Lively up yourself / Go tell it to the mountain / Don't rock my boat / Soul shake down party / Soul rebel / Cheer up / Corner stone / Stand alone / It's alright / Do it twice / Keep on moving / Back out / Soon come / Natural mystic / No sympathy / No water
CD Set ______ 101162
CMC / May '97 / BMG

LIVE (Wailers)
CD ______ SUB 48482
Melting Pop / Jun '97 / 3mv/Sony

LIVE AT THE LYCEUM (Marley, Bob & The Wailers)
Trenchtown rock / Burnin' and lootin' / Them belly full (But we hungry) / Lively up yourself / No woman, no cry / I shot the sheriff / Get up stand up
CD ______ TGLCD 4
Tuff Gong / Jan '94 / Jet Star / PolyGram

LIVELY UP YOURSELF
Soul shakedown party / Lively up yourself / Riding high / It's alright / Reaction / My cup / Can't you see / No water / Trenchtown rock / No sympathy / Stop the train
CD ______ CDSGP 056
Prestige / May '93 / Else / Total/BMG

LIVELY UP YOURSELF
Soul shakedown party / Stop that train / Caution / Soul captives / Go tell it on the mountain / Can't you see / Soon come / Cheer up / Back out / Do it twice / Keep on moving / Don't rock my boat / Put it on / Fussing and fighting / Duppy conqueror / Small axe / Riding high / Kaya / African herbsman / Stand alone / Sun is shining / Mr. Brown / 400 years / Lively up yourself
CD ______ QED 005
Tring / Apr '96 / Tring

LIVELY UP YOURSELF
Soul shakedown / Put it on / Fussin' and fightin' / Kaya / Lively up yourself / Trench Town Rock / Soul rebel / Soul captives / Natural mystic / There she goes / Mellow mood / Treat you right / Hammer / You can't do
CD ______ PLATCD 132
Platinum / Feb '97 / Prism

LIVELY UP YOURSELF
Lively up yourself / Go tell it to the mountain / Don't rock my boat / Soul shake down party / Soul rebel / Cheer up / Corner stone / Stand alone / It's alright / Do it twice / Keep on moving / Back out / Soon come / Natural mystic / No sympathy / No water
CD ______ 100062
CMC / May '97 / BMG

MAJESTIC WARRIORS (Wailers)
CD ______ 3640022
A&M / Oct '91 / PolyGram

MARLEY FAMILY ALBUM (Various Artists)
CD ______ HBCD 160
Heartbeat / Feb '95 / ADA / Direct / Greensleeves / Jet Star

MARLEY MAGIC (Live In Central Park At Summerstage/2CD Set) (Various Artists)
Lion in the morning: *Marley, Julian* / Me name Jr Gong/Crazy bald heads: *Marley, Damian 'Jr. Gong'* / Same old story: *Marley, Julian* / Searching: *Marley, Damian 'Jr. Gong'* / Babylon cookie jar: *Marley, Julian* / Love and inity: *Marley, Damian 'Jr. Gong'* / Exodus: *Marley, Julian* / We need love: *Yvad* / Music is the food of love: *Yvad* / No peace: *Yvad* / Freedom: *Yvad* / So much things to say: *Marley, Rita* / Good girls culture: *Marley, Rita* / That's the way: *Marley, Rita* / Harambe: *Marley, Rita* / To love somebody: *Marley, Rita* / Guava jelly/No woman no cry: *Marley, Rita* / Jammin'/Lively up yourself: *Marley, Rita* / Natty dread: *Marley, Ziggy & The Melody Makers* / Positive vibration: *Marley, Ziggy & The Melody Makers* / Stir it up: *Marley, Ziggy & The Melody Makers* / Get up stand up: *Marley, Ziggy & The Melody Makers* / Water and oil: *Marley, Ziggy & The Melody Makers* / Sun is shining: *Marley, Ziggy & The Melody Makers* / Free like we want to be: *Marley, Ziggy & The Melody Makers* / Could you be loved: *Marley, Ziggy & The Melody Makers*
CD Set ______ HBECD 20603
Heartbeat / May '97 / ADA / Direct / Greensleeves / Jet Star

NATTY DREAD (Marley, Bob & The Wailers)
Lively up yourself / No woman, no cry / Them belly full (But we hungry) / Rebel music / So yah say / Natty dread / Bend down low / Talkin' blues / Revolution
CD ______ TGLCD 3
Tuff Gong / Jan '94 / Jet Star / PolyGram

NATURAL MYSTIC
CD ______ AVC 506
Avid / Dec '92 / Avid/BMG / Koch / THE

NATURAL MYSTIC
Trench town rock / All in one / Soul rebel / Try me / It's alright / No sympathy / No water / Reaction / Rainbow country / Natural mystic / There she goes / Mellow mood / Treat you right / Chances are / Hammer / Touch me
CD ______ QED 030
Tring / Nov '96 / Tring

NATURAL MYSTIC - THE LEGEND LIVES ON
Natural mystic / Easy skanking / Iron Lion Zion / Crazy baldheads / So much trouble in the world / War / Africa unite / Trenchtown rock / Keep on moving / Sun is shining / Who the cap fits / One drop / Roots, rock, reggae / Pimpers paradise / Time will tell
CD ______ BMWCD 2
Tuff Gong / May '95 / Jet Star / PolyGram

NEVER ENDING WAILERS, THE (Wailers)
CD ______ RASCD 3501
Ras / Feb '94 / Direct / Greensleeves / Jet Star / SRD

ONE LOVE (Various Artists)
CD ______ 5320622
Antilles/New Directions / Jul '96 / PolyGram

ONE LOVE/ROOTS VOL.2
CD ______ CDBM 052
Blue Moon / Mar '95 / Cadillac / Discovery / Greensleeves / Jazz Music / Jet Star / TKO Magnum

PEARLS FROM THE PAST
CD ______ KLMCD 003
BAM / Nov '93 / Koch / Scratch/BMG

PLATINUM COLLECTION, THE (2CD Set)
African herbsman / Don't rock my boat / Stand alone / Cheer up / Mellow mood / Duppy conqueror / Reaction / Brain washing / Rebel's hop / 400 years / Back out / Small axe / Lively up yourself / Fussing and fighting / Do it twice / Hammer / Mr. Brown / Kaya / Put it on / Trenchtown rock / My cup / Caution / All in one / Natural mystic / Chances are / Corner stone / Can't you see / Treat you right / Riding high / Soon come / Soul rebel / Go tell it on the mountain / Soul captive / It's alright / No sympathy / Rainbow country / How many times / Keep on moving / No water / Try me
CD Set ______ PC 614
Start / Jul '97 / Disc

POWER
Redder than red / My cup (I've got to cry) / Power and more power / Hypocrites / Thank you Lord / Mr. Chatterbox / Soul almighty / Nice time / Try me (I've got the action) / Mellow mood / Redder than red / My cup (I've got to cry) / Power and more power / Hypocrites / Thank you Lord / Mr. Chatterbox / Hey happy people / Nice time / Try me (I've got the action) / Mellow mood
CD ______ MOCD 3014
More Music / Nov '96 / Sound & Media

RARITIES VOL.1, THE (Marley, Bob & The Wailers)
Shocks of mighty / All in one / Copasetic / More axe / Axe man / Duppy conquer / Zig zag / Run for cover / Picture on the wall version 3 / Picture on the wall version 4 / Man to man / Nicoteen / Rock my boat / Like it like this
CD ______ JMC 200229
Jamaican Gold / May '96 / Grapevine/ PolyGram / Jet Star

RARITIES VOL.2, THE (Marley, Bob & The Wailers)
Dreamland / Dreamland version 2 / Jah is mighty / Turn me loose / Second hand / Second hand, part 2 / Brand new second hand / Love life / Keep on moving / Keep on skanking / Mr. Brown / Mr. Brown Version / Send me that love
CD ______ JMC 200230
Jamaican Gold / May '96 / Grapevine/ PolyGram / Jet Star

RASTAMAN (2CD Set)
Soul shakedown party / Caution / Do it twice / Back out / Try me / Corner stone / No water / Soul almighty / I made a mistake / Let him go / I'm going home / Nobody knows / Wings of a dove / Soul captive / Don't rock my boat / Stand alone / Love and affection / One love / Mega dog / Donna / Lonesome feeling / It hurts to be alone / Who feels it / Dancing shoes / Lonesome talk / Ten commandments of love / Chances are
CD Set ______ CDBM 501
Blue Moon / Sep '95 / Cadillac / Discovery / Greensleeves / Jazz Music / Jet Star / TKO Magnum

RASTAMAN VIBRATION (Marley, Bob & The Wailers)
Positive vibration / Roots, rock, reggae / Johnny was / Cry to me / Want more / Crazy baldheads / Who the cap fits / Night shift / War / Rat race
CD ______ TGLCD 5
Tuff Gong / Jan '94 / Jet Star / PolyGram

REACTION
Reaction / I gotta keep on moving / Put it on / Go tell it on the mountain / Can't you see / Cheer up - good times are comin' / Don't rock the boat / Fussing and fighting / Memphis / African herbsman / Stand alone / Sun is shining / Brain washing / Mr. Brown / All in one / Soul rebel / Try me / Caution / No sympathy / It's alright
CD ______ PWK 072
Carlton / Sep '88 / Carlton

REAL SOUND OF JAMAICA (Marley, Bob & The Wailers)
Concrete jungle / Satisfy my soul / Rainbow country / Put it on / Don't rock my boat / Keep on movin' / Redder than red / Power and more power / Hypocrites / Thank you Lord / Mellow mood / Soul rebels / Reaction / Try me / Soul almighty
CD ______ 74321440032
Milan / Apr '97 / Conifer/BMG / Silva Screen

REBEL MUSIC (Marley, Bob & The Wailers)
Rebel music / So much trouble in the world / Them belly full (But we hungry) / Rat race / War / Roots / Slave driver / Ride natty ride / Crazy baldheads / Get up stand up / No more trouble
CD ______ TGLCD 11
Tuff Gong / Jan '94 / Jet Star / PolyGram

REBEL REVOLUTION (2CD Set) (Marley, Bob & The Wailers)
Small axe / My cup / Keep on moving / Try me / Don't rock the boat / 400 Years / Put it on / Cornerstone / Fussing and fighting / No water / Duppy conqueror / Reaction / Memphis / Soul almighty / It's alright / Riding high / Soul rebel / Kaya / African herbsman / Satisfy my soul / Stand alone / Rebels hop / Sun is shining / Love life / Brain washing / Mr. Brown / Long long winter
CD Set ______ JMC 200277
Jamaican Gold / May '96 / Grapevine/ PolyGram / Jet Star

REGGAE ROOTS
CD ______ 901622
FM / '91 / Revolver / Sony

RIDING HIGH (Marley, Bob & The Wailers)
CD ______ CPCD 8029
Charly / Feb '94 / Koch

ROOTS
I made a mistake / Let him go / I'm going home / Nobody knows / Wings of a dove / Soul captives / Don't rock my boat / Stand alone / Soul shakedown party / Caution / Do it twice / Back out / Try me / Corner stone / No water / Soul almighty
CD ______ CDBM 032
Blue Moon / Mar '95 / Cadillac / Discovery / Greensleeves / Jazz Music / Jet Star / TKO Magnum

ROOTS OF A LEGEND (2CD Set) (Marley, Bob & The Wailers)
Duppy conqueror / Try me / Keep on skanking / Small axe / Kaya / Brain washing / Put it on / Fussing and fighting / Mr. Brown / No sympathy / Lively up yourself / Fussing and fighting / More axe / Corner stone / Riding high / Trench Town rock / Turn me loose / It's alright / Sun is shining / Caution / Stand alone / Stand alone / 400 years / All in one / Duppy conqueror / Soul shakedown party / Adam and Eve / Brand new second hand / Soul rebel / My cup / No water / Reaction / African herbman / Stop the train / There she goes / How many times / Rebel hop / Chances are / Hammer / Treat me right / Cheer up / Touch me / Rainbow country / Soon come / Long, long winter / Mellow mood / Soul almighty / Don't rock the boat / Keep on movin' / Memphis
CD Set ______ CPCD 82462
Charly / Nov '96 / Koch

ROOTS VOL.2 (One Love)
One love / Love and affection / Mega dog / Donna / Lonesome feeling / It hurts to be alone / Who feels it / Dancing shoes / Lonesome talk / Ten commandments of men / Soul rebel / Chances are
CD ______ CDBM 1052
Blue Moon / '89 / Cadillac / Discovery / Greensleeves / Jazz Music / Jet Star / TKO Magnum

SATISFY MY SOUL
Satisfy my soul / Soul rebels / Concrete jungle / Soul almighty / Redder than red / My cup (I've got to cry) / Don't rock my boat / Try me (I've got the action) / Thank you Lord / Nice time / Try me / (I've got the action) / One love / Love life / Rainbow country / Long long winter / Corner stone / Reaction / It's all right / No water can quench my thirst / Keep on moving / Put it on
CD ______ CD 6074
Music / Apr '97 / Target/BMG

SIMMER DOWN AT STUDIO ONE (Marley, Bob & The Wailers)
CD ______ CDHB 171
Heartbeat / May '95 / ADA / Direct / Greensleeves / Jet Star

SONGS OF FREEDOM (3CD Set)
Judge not / One cup of coffee / Simmer down / I'm still waiting / One love / Put it on / Bus dem shut (pyaka) / Mellow mood / Bend down low / Hypocrites / Stir it up / Nice time / Thank you Lord / Hammer / Caution / Back out / Soul shakedown party / Do it twice / Soul rebel / Sun is shining / Don't rock the boat / Small axe / Duppy conqueror / Mr. Brown / Screwface / Lick samba / Trenchtown rock / Craven choke puppy / Guava jelly / Acoustic medley / High tide or low tide / Slave driver / No more trouble / Concrete jungle / Get up stand up / Rastaman chant / Burnin' and lootin' / Iron lion zion / Lively up yourself / Natty dread / I shot the sheriff / No woman, no cry / Who the cap fits / Jah live / Crazy baldheads / War / Johnny was / Rat race / Jammin' / Waiting in vain / Exodus / Natural mystic / Three little birds / Running away / Keep on moving / Easy skanking / Is this love / Smile Jamaica / Time will tell / Africa unite / Survival / One drop / One dub / Zimbabwe / So much trouble in the world / Ride natty ride / Babylon system / Coming in from the cold / Real situation / Bad card / Could you be loved / Forever loving Jah / Rastaman live up / Give thanks and praise / One love/ People get ready (12" mix) / Why should I / Redemption song
CD Set ______ TGCBX 1
Tuff Gong / Sep '92 / Jet Star / PolyGram

SOUL ALMIGHTY (Natural Mystic II)
Try me / Touch me / Soul almighty / Do it twice / Back out / Cheer up / Put it on / Kaya / Fussin' and fightin' / Corner stone / African herbman / No water / Stand alone / Rebels hop / All in one / Duppy conqueror / 400 years / You can't do that to me / How many times
CD ______ AVC 563
Avid / Dec '95 / Avid/BMG / Koch / THE

SOUL ALMIGHTY (The Formative Years)
CD ______ ANANCD 001
Anansi / Jun '96 / Pinnacle

SOUL CAPTIVE (Marley, Bob & The Wailers)
CD ______ RB 3010
Reggae Best / Nov '94 / Grapevine/ PolyGram

SOUL OF THE GONG (Bob Marley's Greatest Hits) (Various Artists)
CD ______ RNCD 2134
Rhino / Feb '96 / Grapevine/PolyGram / Jet Star

SOUL OF THE GONG IN DUB (Bob Marley's Greatest Hits In Dub) (Various Artists)
CD ______ RNCD 2135
Rhino / Feb '96 / Grapevine/PolyGram / Jet Star

SOUL REBEL
CD ______ EMPRCD 698
Emporio / Apr '97 / Disc

SOUL REBEL (Marley, Bob & The Wailers)
Soul rebel / There she goes / Treat me right / Put it on / Tell me / How many times / Mellow mood / Chances are / Hammer / Touch me
CD ______ 306542
Hallmark / Jun '97 / Carlton

SOUL REVOLUTION VOL.1 & 2 (2CD Set) (Marley, Bob & The Wailers)
Keep on moving / Don't rock my boat / Fussing and fighting / Put it on / Memphis / Soul rebel / Riding high / Kaya / Stand alone / African herbsman / Brain washing / Mr. Brown
CD Set ______ **CDTRD 406**
Trojan / Mar '94 / Direct / Jet Star

STOP THAT TRAIN
Stop that train / Kaya / Mellow moods / Soul captives / Put it on / Can't you see / All in one / How many times / Hammer / Caution / Try me / Small axe / Brain washing / African herbsman / Touch me / 400 years
CD ______ **100072**
CMC / May '97 / BMG

SURVIVAL (Marley, Bob & The Wailers)
So much trouble / Africa unite / Babylon system / Ride Natty ride / One prop / Fighting against ism and skism / Top ranking / Wake up and live / Survival / Zimbabwe
CD ______ **TGLCD 8**
Tuff Gong / Jan '94 / Jet Star / PolyGram

TALKIN' BLUES (Marley, Bob & The Wailers)
Talkin' blues / Burnin' and lootin' / Kinky reggae / Get up, stand up / Slave driver / Walk the proud land / You can't blame the youth / Rastaman chant / Am-a-do / Bend down low / I shot the sheriff
CD ______ **TGLCD 12**
Tuff Gong / Feb '91 / Jet Star / PolyGram

TRENCH TOWN ROCK
Trench Town rock / Rebels hop / Soul shake down / Mr. Brown / My cup / Fussin' and fightin' / Treat you right / Reaction / Soul almighty / You can't do that to me / Riding high / Duppy conqueror / Sun is shining / Rainbow country / Chances are
CD ______ **101202**
CMC / May '97 / BMG

TRIBUTE TO BOB MARLEY VOL.1, A (Various Artists)
CD ______ **CDTRL 332**
Trojan / Mar '94 / Direct / Jet Star

TRIBUTE TO BOB MARLEY VOL.1, A (Various Artists)
CD ______ **RNCD 2089**
Rhino / Feb '95 / Grapevine/PolyGram / Jet Star

TRIBUTE TO BOB MARLEY VOL.2, A (Various Artists)
CD ______ **CDTRL 341**
Trojan / May '94 / Direct / Jet Star

TRIBUTE TO BOB MARLEY VOL.2, A (Various Artists)
CD ______ **RNCD 2117**
Rhino / Sep '95 / Grapevine/PolyGram / Jet Star

TRIBUTE TO BOB MARLEY VOL.3, A (Various Artists)
(Marley's gone) his songs live on: *Hibbert, Toots* / Bend down low: *Groovers* / I'm still waiting: *Edwards, Jackie* / Mellow mood: *Gaytones* / Simmer down: *Clarke, Johnny* / Hypocrites: *Campbell, Al* / You poured sugar on me: *Smith, Ernie* / Duppy conqueror: *Lazarus, Ken* / My sympathy (400 years): *Upsetters* / Natty dread: *Shervington, Pluto* / No woman no cry: *Clarke, Johnny* / War: *Jarrett, Killerman* / I shot the sheriff: *Shervington, Pluto* / Time will tell: *Clarke, Johnny* / Talking blues: *Maroons* / Guava jelly: *Fab Five Inc.* / Easy skanking: *Clarke, Johnny* / I'm still waiting: *Brown, Dennis* / (Marley's gone) his songs live on: *Hibbert, Toots*
CD ______ **CDTRL 372**
Trojan / Sep '96 / Direct / Jet Star

TRIBUTE TO BOB MARLEY, A (Various Artists)
CD ______ **CC 2709**
Crocodisc / Apr '94 / Grapevine/PolyGram

TRIBUTE TO BOB MARLEY, A (An All Star Tribute To The Reggae Legend) (Various Artists)
Buffalo soldier: *Thomas, Ruddy* / I shot the sheriff: *Blues Busters* / Nice time: *Dunkley, Errol* / Soul rebel: *Romeo, Max* / Bend down low: *Clarke, Johnny* / Get up stand up: *Mafia & Fluxy* / Could you be loved: *Thomas, Ruddy* / Put it on: *Aggrovators & The Wailers* / Jammin': *Spence, Michael* / Thank you lord: *Romeo, Max* / No woman no cry: *Clarke, Johnny* / Small axe: *Hammond, Beres & Zappow* / Is this love: *Thomas, Ruddy* / Hypocrites: *Campbell, Al* / Simmer down: *Aggrovators & The Wailers* / Exodus: *Mafia & Fluxy* / Stir it up: *Edwards, Jackie* / Redemption song: *Frazer, Dean*
CD ______ **ECD 3296**
K-Tel / Feb '97 / K-Tel

UPRISING (Marley, Bob & The Wailers)
Coming in from the cold / Real situation / Bad card / We and them / Work / Zion train / Pimpers paradise / Could you be loved / Forever loving Jah / Redemption song
CD ______ **TGLCD 9**
Tuff Gong / Jan '94 / Jet Star / PolyGram

VERY BEST OF THE EARLY YEARS (Marley, Bob & The Wailers)
Trenchtown rock / Lively up yourself / Soul almighty / Wisdom / Caution / Cheer up / Thank you lord / Stop the train / This train / Small axe / More axe / Don't rock my boat / Keep on moving / Brand new secondhand / Kaya / Turn me loose / Sun is shining / Keep on skanking
CD ______ **MCCD 033**
Music Club / Sep '91 / Disc / THE

WAILING WAILERS AT STUDIO ONE (Marley, Bob & The Wailers)
CD ______ **CDHB 172**
Heartbeat / May '95 / ADA / Direct / Greensleeves / Jet Star

WAILING WAILERS, THE (Wailers)
CD ______ **SOCD 1001**
Studio One / Aug '94 / Jet Star

Marley, Damian

MR. MARLEY (Marley, Damian 'Jr. Gong')
Trouble / Love and inity / 10,000 chariots / Old war chant / Party time / Kingston 12 / Keep on grooving / Searching (so much bubble) / One more cup of coffee / Julie / Me name Jr Gong / Mr. Marley
CD ______ **HBECD 20602**
Heartbeat / May '97 / ADA / Direct / Greensleeves / Jet Star

Marley, Julian

LION IN THE MORNING
Loving clear / Blossoming and blooming / Lion in the morning / Now you know / Babylon cookie jar / Same old story / Attack back / Arm your soul / Ease these pains / When the sun comes up / Got to be
CD ______ **HBECD 20601**
Heartbeat / May '97 / ADA / Direct / Greensleeves / Jet Star

Marley, Kymani

LIKE FATHER LIKE SON
CD ______ **RN 7001**
Rhino / Aug '96 / Grapevine/PolyGram / Jet Star

Marley, Rita

HARAMBE
CD ______ **SHANCD 43010**
Shanachie / Nov '87 / ADA / Greensleeves / Koch

WE MUST CARRY ON
CD ______ **SHCD 43082**
Shanachie / Jun '91 / ADA / Greensleeves / Koch
CD ______ **322573**
Koch International / Apr '97 / Koch

WHO FEELS IT KNOWS IT
CD ______ **SHANCD 43003**
Shanachie / '87 / ADA / Greensleeves / Koch

Marley, Ziggy

CONSCIOUS PARTY
Conscious party / Tumblin' down / Who a say / Have you ever been to hell / Lee and Molly / Tomorrow people / We propose / What's true / Dreams of home / We a guh some weh / New love
CD ______ **CDV 2506**
Virgin / Mar '88 / EMI

CONSCIOUS PARTY/JAHMEKYA/ONE BRIGHT DAY (3CD Set) (Marley, Ziggy & The Melody Makers)
CD Set ______ **TPAK 31**
Virgin / Nov '93 / EMI

FALLEN IS BABYLON (Marley, Ziggy & The Melody Makers)
Fallen is Babylon / Everyone wants to be / People get ready / Postman / Brotherly sisterly love / Born to be lively / Long winter / I remember / Day by day / Five days a year / Notice / Diamond City / Jah bless / People get ready (remix)
CD ______ **7559620322**
Elektra / Jul '97 / Warner Music

JAHMEKYA (Marley, Ziggy & The Melody Makers)
Raw riddin' / Kozmik / Rainbow country / Drastic / Good time / What conquers defeat / First night / Wrong right wrong / Herbs an' spices / Problem with my woman / Jah is true and perfect / Small people / So good, so right / Namibia / New time and age / Generation
CD ______ **CDVUS 35**
Virgin / Apr '92 / EMI

JOY AND BLUES (Marley, Ziggy & The Melody Makers)
CD ______ **CDVUS 65**
Virgin / Jul '93 / EMI

ONE BRIGHT DAY
Black my story (not history) / One bright day / Who will be there / When the lights gone out / Problems / All love / Look who's dancing / Justice / Love is the only law / Pains of life / Ur-ban music / Give it all you got / When the light's gone out (Jamaican style)
CD ______ **CDVUS 5**
Virgin / Aug '91 / EMI

TIME HAS COME - THE BEST OF ZIGGY MARLEY & MELODY MAKERS (Marley, Ziggy & The Melody Makers)
Give a little love / Get up jah jah children / Freedom road / Children playing in the streets / Lyin' in bed / Aiding and abetting / Say people / Natty dread rampage / Naah leggo / Met her on a rainy day / Reggae revolution / Reggae is now
CD ______ **CDFA 3221**
Fame / Mar '90 / EMI

Marlo, Clair

BEHAVIOUR SELF
CD ______ **WLD 9208**
Varese Sarabande / Apr '95 / Pinnacle

Marmalade

COLLECTION, THE
CD ______ **CCSCD 436**
Castle / Apr '96 / BMG

FALLING APART AT THE SEAMS... PLUS
CD ______ **C5CD 578**
See For Miles/C5 / Mar '92 / Pinnacle

MARMALADE
CD ______ **HM 016**
Harmony / Jun '97 / TKO Magnum

REFLECTIONS OF THE MARMALADE
Super clean Jean / Carolina in my mind / I'll be home (in a day or so) / And yours is a piece of mine / Some other guy / Kaleidoscope / Dear John / Fight say the mighty / Reflections of my life / Life is / Rainbow / Ballad of Cherry Flavar / My little one / Sarah / Just one woman / Cousin Norman / Back on the road / Radancer
CD ______ **8205624**
London / Jan '93 / PolyGram

Marmarosa, Dodo

DIAL MASTERS
Deep purple / Bird lore / Midnight at Mintons / High wind in Hollywood / Tone paintings II / Dodo's dance / Dary departs / Tea for two / Dilated pupils / Up in Dodo's room / Tone paintings I / Bopmatism / Trade winds / Cosmo Street
CD ______ **SPJCD 128**
Spotlite / Feb '96 / Cadillac / Jazz Music / New Note/Pinnacle / Swift

DODO LIVES
Moose / Summertime / Don't blame me / Mellow mood / Deep purple / Boyd meets Stravinsky / Yardbird suite / Dodo's bounce / Smooth sailing / Dodo's lament
CD ______ **TPZ 1058**
Topaz Jazz / Sep '97 / Cadillac / Pinnacle

Maroa

ASTIMETRIX : NEW DIRECTIONS IN JAZZ
CD ______ **DIS 80018**
Dorian Discovery / Jan '94 / Conifer/BMG / Select

Marocana

TESTAMENT
Testament / Arab zenith / First light / Blue town / Evocation / Marooned / Desert uprising / Memories / Betrayal / 1000 years / New dawn / Slaves of time / Crucifixion
CD ______ **MDMCD 004**
Moidart / Nov '95 / Conifer/BMG

Marohnic, Chuck

COPENHAGEN SUITE (Marohnic, Chuck Quartet)
CD ______ **SCCD 31408**
Steeplechase / Apr '97 / Discovery / Impetus

PAGES OF STONE (Marohnic, Chuck, David Friesen & Joe Labarbera)
CD ______ **ITMP 970064**
ITM / Apr '92 / Koch / Tradelink

Marqua Y Su Combo

SABOR TROPICAL
CD ______ **TUMICD 016**
Tumi / '91 / Discovery / Stern's

Marques, Fernando

VERSAS Y TROVAS
CD ______ **7432144812**
Milan / Jun '97 / Conifer/BMG / Silva Screen

Marquet, Alain

CLARINET JOY (Marquet, Alain & Reimer von Essen)
CD ______ **SOSCD 1259**
Stomp Off / Jul '93 / Jazz Music / Wellard

HOP SCOT BLUES
CD ______ **SOSCD 1229**
Stomp Off / Nov '92 / Jazz Music / Wellard

Marr, Hank

GREASY SPOON
Ram-bunk-shush / Greasy spoon / Push / Mellow thing / Let's cut one / Tonk game / Number two / Wild shindig / Foggy night / Hank's idea / Molasses / Late freight / Silver spoon / Sabotage / Headache (donkey walk) / Travellin' heavy / Squash / Jim Dawg / Mexican vodca (bossa nova sandman) / Black slop
CD ______ **CDCHARLY 271**
Charly / Jun '91 / Koch

GROOVIN' IT
Soft winds / Killer Joe / Jim Dawg / Misty (ballad) / Battle hymn of the republic / Easy talk / Just friends / And what if I don't / Tenderly / Teach me tonight / Misty (swing)
CD ______ **DTRCD 112**
Double Time / Nov '96 / Express Jazz

IT'S 'BOUT TIME
One for Daddy-O / Chicken pickin' / Emily / It's 'bout time / Sweet Nancy / Amazing Grace / Home at last / Soul eyes / I thought about you / Never let me go / What, not another greasy spoon
CD ______ **DTRCD 102**
Double Time / Nov '96 / Express Jazz

Marra, Michael

CANDY PHILOSOPHY
Land of golden slippers / Don't look at me / Johnny Hallyday (Je vous salue) / True love (something no one should ever be without) / Violin lesson / To beat the drum / Painters painting paint / King Kong's visit to Glasgow / Guernsey kitchen porter / Australia instead of stars / O fellow man / This evergreen bough
CD ______ **ECLCD 9309**
Eclectic / Jan '96 / ADA / New Note/ Pinnacle

GAELS BLUE
Mincing wi' Chairlhi / Racing from Newburgh / Angus man's welcome to Mary Stuart / King George III's return to sanity / General Grant's visit to Dundee / Black babies / Monkey hair / Altar boys / Gael's blue / Happed in mist
CD ______ **ECLCD 9206**
Eclectic / Jan '96 / ADA / New Note/ Pinnacle

ON STOLEN STATIONERY
Margaret Reilly's arrival at Craiglockhart / Wise old men of Mount Florida / Under the ullapool moon / Rats / Hamish / Harmless / Neil Gow's apprentice / Humphrey Kate's song / Like another rolling stone / Here come the weak / Bawbee birlin' / O penitence
CD ______ **ECLCD 9104**
Eclectic / Jan '96 / ADA / New Note/ Pinnacle

PAX VOBISCUM (In Concert)
CD ______ **ECLCD 9616**
Eclectic / Jul '96 / ADA / New Note/ Pinnacle

Marriott, Beryl

WEAVE THE MIRROR
Big strong lad herding the goats/High road to Linton / Phantasy in fives/Searching for lambs/Bold fisherman / Cam ye by athol/ Laird O'Drumblair/Glengarry's march / Whelan's jig/Morrison's jig/McFadden's favourite/Smokey hous / Jenny Nettles/Give me your hand/March of the King of Laoise / Dance of the kings of man/Gillie Callum / Y deryn pur / Bridget cruise/Carolan's cup / Kid on the mountain / Lochaber no more / Carolan's welcome / Black nag/Nonsuch
CD ______ **WRCD 016**
Woodworm / Jan '92 / Pinnacle

Marriott, Steve

30 SECONDS TO MIDNIGHT
Knocking on your door / All or nothing / One more heartache / Um um um um um song / Superlungs my supergirl / Get up stand up / Rascal you / Life during wartime / Phone call away / Clapping song / Shakin' all over / Gypsy woman
CD ______ **CLACD 386**
Castle / Mar '93 / BMG

ALL STARS
Over you / Midnight rollin' / Times they are a-changin' / Wonderful world / Where're you going tonight / Factory girl / Soldier / Where're you going tonight / Things you do / Ruthy / Gimme some lovin' / Soldier / Vagabond lady / Midnight rollin' / Wham bam thank you Mam / Nobody but you
CD ______ **PILOT 022**
Burning Airlines / Aug '97 / Total/Pinnacle

DINGWALLS 6.7.84
CD ______ **MAUCD 609**
Mau Mau / Sep '91 / Pinnacle

INTERPRETATIONS (Documentary/Live)
CD ______ **OTR 1100023**
Metro Independent / Jun '97 / Essential/ BMG

LIVE AT THE PALACE (Marriot, Steve & A Packet Of Three)
CD _______________ OTR 1100020
Metro Independent / Jun '97 / Essential/ BMG

MARRIOTT ANTHOLOGY, THE (Interview/2CD Set)
CD Set _______________ OTR 1100021
Metro Independent / Jun '97 / Essential/ BMG

Mars

MARS LIVE
CD _______________ CDSA 54025
Semantic / Feb '94 / Plastic Head

Mars

'78 RE-ISSUE
CD _______________ ALP 48CD
Atavistic / Apr '97 / Cargo / SRD

Mars Accelerator

I AM THE SOUTH POLE
CD _______________ RXR 007CD
RX Remedy / Nov '96 / Cargo

Mars, Johnny

KING OF THE BLUES HARP
Horses and places / Rocket 88 / Johnny's groove / Desert island / I'll go crazy / Imagination / Mighty Mars / Cash ain't nothing / If I had a woman
CD _______________ JSPCD 217
JSP / Jul '88 / ADA / Cadillac / Direct / Hot Shot / Target/BMG

LIFE ON MARS
Born under a bad sign / Don't start me talkin' / Back door man / Steal away / Standing in line / Hot lips boogie / I can't take a jealous woman / Get on up / Desert island / Keep on swinging
CD _______________ BGOCD 159
Beat Goes On / Oct '93 / Pinnacle

Marsala, Joe

CLASSICS 1936-1942
CD _______________ CLASSICS 763
Classics / Jun '94 / Discovery / Jazz Music

CLASSICS 1944-1945
CD _______________ CLASSICS 902
Classics / Nov '96 / Discovery / Jazz Music

Marsalis, Branford

BEAUTYFUL ONES ARE NOT YET BORN, THE
Roused about / Beautyful ones are not yet born / Xavier's lair / Gilligan's Isle / Cain and Abel / Citizen Tain / Dewey baby / Beat's remark
CD _______________ 4688962
Columbia / Jan '95 / Sony

DARK KEYS, THE (Marsalis, Branford Trio)
Dark keys / Hesitation / Thousand autumns / Sentinels / Lykeif / Judas Iscariot / Blutain / Schott happens
CD _______________ 4866682
Sony Jazz / Nov '96 / Sony

I HEARD YOU TWICE THE FIRST TIME
Brother trying to catch a cab / (On the East side) blues / BB's blues / Rib tip Johnson / Mabel / Sidney in da haus / Berta Berta / Stretto from the ghetto / Dance of the Hei Gui / Road you choose / Simi valley blues
CD _______________ 4721692
Columbia / Jul '93 / Sony

RANDOM ABSTRACT
Yes and no / Crescent city / Broadway fools / Lonjellis / I thought about you / Lonely woman / Steep's theme
CD _______________ 4687072
Sony Jazz / Jan '95 / Sony

ROYAL GARDEN BLUES
Swingin' at the haven / Dienda / Strike up the band / Emanon / Royal Garden blues / Shadows / Wrath of Tain
CD _______________ 4687042
Sony Jazz / Jan '95 / Sony

SCENES IN THE CITY
No backstage pass / Scenes in the city / Solstice / Waiting for Tain / No sidestepping / Parable
CD _______________ 4684582
Sony Jazz / Jan '95 / Sony

Marsalis, Delfeayo

PONTIUS PILATE'S DECISION
Pontius Pilate's decision / Adam's ecstasy / Eve's delight / Barabbas / Weary ways of Mary Magdalene / Nicodemus / Son of the Virgin Mary / Reverend Judas Escariot / Simon's journey / Last supper / Crucifixion
CD _______________ PD 90669
Novus / Jun '92 / BMG

Marsalis, Ellis

CLASSIC MARSALIS, THE
Monkey puzzle / Whistle stop / After / Dee Wee / Twelve's it / Yesterdays / Magnolia triangle / Little joy / Swinging at the Haven / 'Round midnight / Night in Tunisia
CD _______________ CDBOP 016
Boplicity / Apr '93 / Pinnacle

LOVED ONES (Marsalis, Ellis & Branford)
Delilah / Maria / Lulu's back in town / Miss Otis regrets / Angelica / Stella by starlight / Louise / Bess, you is my woman now / Liza / Nancy / Laura / Alice in wonderland / Sweet Lorraine / Dear Dolores
CD _______________ 4836242
Sony Jazz / Mar '96 / Sony

NIGHT AT SNUG HARBOR, NEW ORLEANS, A
Introduction / Nothin' but the blues / Call / After / Some monk funk / I can't get started (With you) / Jitterbug / Very thought of you / Night in Tunisia
CD _______________ ECD 221292
Evidence / Sep '95 / ADA / Cadillac / Harmonia Mundi

PIANO IN E - SOLO PIANO
Hallucinations / Django / Jitterbug waltz / Nica's dream / So in love / Fourth autumn / Zee blues
CD _______________ CD 2100
Rounder / May '91 / ADA / CM / Direct

WHISTLE STOP
Whistle stop / Dee wee / Moment alone / Magnolia triangle / Mozartin' / Cry again / Cochise / Li'l boy man / Monkey puzzle / After / Beautiful old ladies / Little joy / When we first met
CD _______________ 4745552
Columbia / Apr '94 / Sony

Marsalis, Wynton

AMERICAN HERO, AN
One by one / My funny valentine / 'Round midnight / ETA / Time will tell / Blakey's theme
CD _______________ CDGATE 7018
Kingdom Jazz / Nov '86 / Kingdom

BLACK CODES (From The Underground)
Black codes / For wee folks / Delfeayo's dilemma / Phryzzian march / Aural oasis / Chambers of Tain / Blues
CD _______________ 4687112
Columbia / Feb '94 / Sony

BLOOD ON THE FIELDS (3CD Set)
Calling the Indians out / Move over / You don't hear no drums / Market place / Soul for sale / Plantation coffle / March / Work song (blood on the fields) / Lady's lament / Flying high / Oh we have a friend in Jesus / God don't like ugly / Juba and a O'Brown squaw / Follow the drinking gourd / My soul fell down / Forty lashes / What a fool I've been / Back to basics / I hold out my hand / Look and see / Sun is gonna shine / Will the sun come out / Sun is gonna shine / Chant to call the Indians out / Calling the Indians out / Follow the drinking gourd / Freedom is in the trying / Due North
CD Set _______________ CXK 57694
Sony Jazz / Jun '97 / Sony

BLUE INTERLUDE
CD _______________ 4716352
Sony Jazz / Jan '95 / Sony

CARNAVAL (Marsalis, Wynton & Eastman Wind Ensemble)
Variations on Le Carnaval de Venise: *Marsalis, Wynton* / Grand Russian fantasia: *Marsalis, Wynton* / Debutante: *Marsalis, Wynton* / Believe me, if all those endearing young charms: *Marsalis, Wynton* / Moto perpetuo: *Marsalis, Wynton* / 'Tis the last rose of Summer: *Marsalis, Wynton* / Flight of the bumble bee: *Marsalis, Wynton* / Napoli: *Marsalis, Wynton* / Variations on a Neapolitan song: *Marsalis, Wynton* / Fantasie brillante: *Marsalis, Wynton* / Sometimes I feel like a Motherless child: *Marsalis, Wynton* / Valse brillante: *Marsalis, Wynton*
CD _______________ MK 42137
CBS / Apr '87 / Sony

CITI MOVEMENT (Griot New York) (Marsalis, Wynton Septet)
CD _______________ 4730552
Sony Jazz / Jan '95 / Sony

CRESCENT CITY CHRISTMAS CARD
Carol of the bells / Silent night / Hark the herald angels sing / Little drummer boy / We three kings of Orient are / Oh tannenbaum / Sleigh ride / Let it snow, let it snow, let it snow / God rest ye merry gentlemen / Winter wonderland / Jingle bells / O come all ye faithful (Adeste Fidelis) / 'Twas the night before Christmas
CD _______________ 4658792
CBS / Dec '89 / Sony

FIRST RECORDINGS WITH ART BLAKEY
Angel eyes / Bitter dose / Wheel within a wheel / Gypsy / Jody
CD _______________ CDGATE 7013
Kingdom Jazz / Oct '87 / Kingdom

HOT HOUSE FLOWERS
Stardust / Lazy afternoon / For all we know / When you wish upon a star / Django / Melancholia / Hot house flowers / Confession
CD _______________ 4687102
Columbia / Feb '94 / Sony

IN GABRIEL'S GARDEN (Marsalis, Wynton & English Chamber Orchestra/ Anthony Newman)
CD _______________ SK 66244
Sony Classical / Jul '96 / Sony

IN THIS HOUSE, ON THIS MORNING (2CD Set) (Marsalis, Wynton Septet)
CD Set _______________ 4745522
Columbia / Apr '94 / Sony

J MOOD
J mood / Presence that lament brings / Insane asylum / Skain's domain / Melodique / After / Much later
CD _______________ 4687122
Sony Jazz / Jan '95 / Sony

JOE COOL'S BLUES (Marsalis, Wynton & Ellis)
Linus and Lucy / Buggy ride / Peppermint Patty / On Peanuts playground / Oh good grief / Wright Brothers rag / Charlie Brown / Little Red Haired Girl / Pebble Beach / Snoopy and Woodstock / Little birdie / Why Charlie Brown / Joe Cool's blues
CD _______________ 4782502
Sony Jazz / May '95 / Sony

LIVE AT BUBBA'S 1980 (Marsalis, Wynton & Art Blakey's Jazz Messengers)
CD Set _______________ JWD 102311
JWD / Oct '94 / Target/BMG

LIVE AT BUBBA'S JAZZ RESTAURANT VOL.1
CD _______________ DM 15012
DMA Jazz / Jul '96 / Jazz Music

LIVE AT BUBBA'S JAZZ RESTAURANT VOL.2
CD _______________ DM 15013
DMA Jazz / Jul '96 / Jazz Music

LONDON CONCERT, THE
CD _______________ SK 57497
Sony Classical / Jan '96 / Sony

MAJESTY OF THE BLUES, THE
Majesty of the blues (Puheeman strut) / Hickory dickory dock / New Orleans function / Death of jazz / Premature autopsies (sermon) / Oh, but on the third day (happy feet blues)
CD _______________ 4651292
Sony Jazz / Jan '95 / Sony

MARSALIS STANDARD TIME
Caravan / April in Paris / Cherokee / Goodbye / New Orleans / Soon all will know / Foggy day / Song is you / Memories of you / In the afterglow / Autumn leaves
CD _______________ 4510392
CBS / Oct '87 / Sony

MASTER OF TRUMPET
One by one / My funny valentine / 'Round midnight / ETA / Time will tell / Blakey's theme / Jody
CD _______________ 722008
Scorpio / Sep '92 / Complete/Pinnacle

MY IDEAL
CD _______________ JHR 73562
Jazz Hour / Oct '92 / Cadillac / Jazz Music / Target/BMG

PORTRAIT
CD _______________ SK 44726
Sony Classical / Jan '96 / Sony

SOUL GESTURES IN SOUTHERN BLUE VOL.1 (Thick In The South)
CD _______________ 4686592
Sony Jazz / Jan '95 / Sony

SOUL GESTURES IN SOUTHERN BLUE VOL.2 (Uptown Ruler)
CD _______________ 4686602
Columbia / Jul '94 / Sony

SOUL GESTURES IN SOUTHERN BLUE VOL.3 (Levee Low Moan)
CD _______________ 4686582
Sony Jazz / Jan '95 / Sony

THINK OF ONE
Think of one / Knozz-Moe-King / Fuschia / My ideal / What is happening here (now) / Bell ringer / Later / Melancholia
CD _______________ 4687092
Columbia / Feb '94 / Sony

TIME WILL TELL
CD _______________ JHR 73561
Jazz Hour / Oct '92 / Cadillac / Jazz Music / Target/BMG

WYNTON MARSALIS
Father time / I'll be there when the time is right / RJ / Hesitation / Sister Cheryl / Who can I turn to / Twilight / Knozz-Moe-King / Just friends / Knozz-moe-king (Interlude) / Juan / Cherokee / Delfeayo's dream / Chambers of Tain / Au privave / Do you know what it means to miss New Orleans / Juan (Skip Mustaad) / Autumn leaves / Skain's domain / Much later
CD _______________ 4687082
Columbia / Nov '93 / Sony

WYNTON MARSALIS STANDARD TIME VOL.1
CD _______________ 4687132
Sony Jazz / Jan '95 / Sony

WYNTON MARSALIS STANDARD TIME VOL.2 (Intimacy Calling)
CD _______________ 4682732
Sony Jazz / Jan '95 / Sony

WYNTON MARSALIS STANDARD TIME VOL.3 (The Resolution Of Romance)
CD _______________ 4668712
Sony Jazz / Jan '95 / Sony

Marscape

MARSCAPE
CD _______________ OZ 0052
Ozone / Jun '96 / Mo's Music Machine / Pinnacle / SRD

Marsden, Bernie

AND ABOUT TIME TOO
You're the one / Song for Fran / Love made a fool of me / Here we go again / Still the same / Sad clown / Brief encounter / Are you ready / Head the ball
CD _______________ RPM 152
RPM / Oct '95 / Pinnacle

GREEN AND BLUES
CD _______________ ESSCD 324
Essential / Nov '95 / BMG

LOOK AT ME NOW
Look at me now / So far away / Who's foolin' who / Always love you so / Behind your dark eyes / Byblos shack / Thunder and lightnng / Can you do it / After all the madness
CD _______________ RPM 153
RPM / Oct '95 / Pinnacle

Marsden, Gerry

TRIBUTE TO LENNON AND MCCARTNEY, A
Pipes of peace / Yellow submarine / Fool on the hill / Silly love songs / Yesterday / Woman / Ebony and ivory / Let it be / Long and winding road / My love / With a little luck / Imagine / It's for you / Love / You've got to hide your love away / Just like starting over / Mull of Kintyre / Give peace a chance
CD _______________ ECD 3138
K-Tel / Jan '95 / K-Tel

Marsh, Hugh

BEAR WALKS, THE
CD _______________ VBR 20112
Vera Bra / Dec '90 / New Note/Pinnacle / Pinnacle

Marsh, Josephine

JOSEPHINE MARSH
CD _______________ JMCD 001
Josephine Marsh / Feb '96 / Direct

Marsh, Warne

DUO - LIVE AT THE SWEET BASIL 1980 (Marsh, Warne & Red Mitchell)
CD _______________ FSCD 1038
Fresh Sound / Nov '94 / Discovery / Jazz Music

NEWLY WARNE
CD _______________ STCD 4162
Storyville / Feb '90 / Cadillac / Jazz Music / Wellard

TWO DAYS IN THE LIFE OF...
CD _______________ STCD 4165
Storyville / Feb '90 / Cadillac / Jazz Music / Wellard

UNISSUED COPENHAGEN STUDIO RECORDINGS, THE (Marsh, Warne Trio)
CD _______________ STCD 8278
Storyville / May '97 / Cadillac / Jazz Music / Wellard

Marshal, King Wasiu Ayinde

TALAZO FUJI MUSIC PARTY
Fuji collections / Talazo / Ultimate / Consolidation / Eyo / Series
CD _______________ WSCD 101
Womad Select / Jul '97 / ADA / Direct

Marshall Law

MARSHALL LAW
Armageddon / Under the hammer / Rock the nation / Marshall law / Hearts and thunder / Screaming / We're hot / Feel it / System X / Future shock / When will it end
CD _______________ HMRXD 138
FM / Dec '89 / Revolver / Sony

Marshall, Amanda

AMANDA MARSHALL
Let it rain / Birmingham / Fall from grace / Dark horse / Beautiful goodbye / Sitting on top of the world / Last exit to Eden / Trust me this is love / Let's get lost / Promises
CD _______________ 4837912
Epic / Jul '96 / Sony

Marshall, Evan

IS THE LONE ARRANGER
CD ROUCD 0338
Rounder / May '95 / ADA / CM / Direct

Marshall, John

KEEP ON KEEPING ON (Marshall, John Quintet)
You / Waltz for Birks / Nobody else but me / All through the night / Thrill is gone / Keep on keepin' on / That ole devil called love / Houston St. beat / Off minor / Theme of Kareem
CD MR 874774
Mons / Jun '97 / Montpellier

Marshall, Julian

CELEBRATION
CD C5CD561
See For Miles/C5 / Jul '91 / Pinnacle

Marshall, Larry

I ADMIRE YOU
CD HBCD 57
Greensleeves / Dec '92 / Jet Star / SRD

THROW MI CORN
CD OMCD 29
Original Music / Sep '94 / Jet Star / SRD

Marshall, Mike

GATOR STRUT
CD ROUCD 0208
Rounder / Aug '88 / ADA / CM / Direct

Marshall, Peter

CHANNEL ONE REVISITED
CD TBXCD 002
Top Beat / Oct '95 / Jet Star / SRD

Marshall, Wayne

90 DEGREES AND RISING
90 degrees / Hump tonight / King of sex and soul / Sexual thing / Your G-spot / Kinky sex / Shake it / Touch and kiss you / Goodie goodie / Slow down / Love life satisfaction / So bad / For those who've got the juice / Juice me
CD SOULCD 31
Soultown / Jun '94 / Jet Star / Pinnacle

BLESSED IS THE CHILD
CD EWCD 003
Teams / May '95 / Jet Star

CENSORED
CD SOULCD 34
Soultown / Dec '94 / Jet Star / Pinnacle

DOUBLE X-POSURE
CD SOUL 0042CD
Soultown / Feb '96 / Jet Star / Pinnacle

Marshes

FLEDGLING
CD BC 1706
Blitzcore / Feb '97 / Cargo

Marshmallow Overcoat

MARSHMALLOW OVERCOAT
CD 36T 0002CD
360 Twist / Jul '97 / Greyhound

Martains

LOW BUDGET STUNT KING
CD ALLIED 057CD
Allied / Nov '95 / Cargo / Greyhound / Plastic Head

Martell, Lena

BEST OF LENA MARTELL
CD MATCD 220
Castle / Dec '92 / BMG

FEELINGS - BEST OF LENA MARTELL
One day at a time / Don't cry for me Argentina / Nevertheless (I'm in love with you) / Let me try again / Old fashioned way / Running bear / Call collect / Old rugged cross / Danny come home / Six weeks every summer / Movin' on / Until it's time for you to go / Pledging my love / Love letters / Why did I choose you / Make the world go away / Everybody get together / Feelings / Call / Four and twenty hours / Forever in blue jeans
CD TRTCD 131
TrueTrax / Oct '94 / THE

ONE DAY AT A TIME (The Best Of Lena Martell)
One day at a time / Movin' on / Until it's time for you to go / Pledging my love / Love letters / First time ever I saw your face / Make the world go away / Running bear / Call collect / Old rugged cross / Danny come home / Six weeks every summer / Stay away from the apple tree / Everybody get together / Hillbilly hoedown / Feelings / Call / Four and twenty hours / Forever in blue jeans / I'm gonna be a country girl again / Help me make it through the night / (It looks like) I'll never fall in love again
CD PLSCD 169
Pulse / Feb '97 / BMG

Martha & The Muffins

FARAWAY IN TIME
Echo beach / Paint by number heart / Saigon / Indecision / Terminal twilight / Hide and seek / Monotone / Sinking land / Revenge (against the world) / Cheesies and gum / Insect love / About insomnia / Motor bikin' / Suburban dream / Was ezo / Women around the world at work / This is the ice age
CD COMCD 12
Virgin / May '88 / EMI

Marthely, J.P.

MARTHELOI (Marthely, J.P. & P. St. Eloi)
CD CD 84707
Sonodisc / Jan '97 / Stern's

Martignon, Hector

PORTRAIT IN WHITE AND BLACK
Teorema / Gabriela / She said she was from Sarajevo / Portrait in white and black / Coqueteos / Laura / Colombaiao / Noviembre / Susurro y cumbia / La puerta / Hell's kitchen / Sarabande / La candelaria / Tomorrow's past / You and the night and the music
CD CCD 79727
Candid / Jul '97 / Cadillac / Direct / Jazz Music / Koch / Wellard

Martika

12" TAPE: MARTIKA
More than you know (House mix part 1) / Toy soldiers (Special version) / Martika's kitchen (mix) / Coloured kisses / I feel the earth move
CD 4730402
Columbia / Mar '93 / Sony

MARTIKA
If you're Tarzan, I'm Jane / Cross my heart / More than you know / Toy soldiers / You got me into this / I feel the earth move / Water / It's not what you're doing / See if I care / Alibis
CD 4633552
Columbia / Oct '91 / Sony

MARTIKA'S KITCHEN
Martika's kitchen / Spirit / Love... thy will be done / Magical place / Coloured kisses / Safe in the arms of love / Pride and prejudice / Take me to forever / Temptation / Don't say U love me / Broken heart / Mi tierra
CD 4671892
Columbia / Apr '94 / Sony

Martin, Billie Ray

DEADLINE FOR MY MEMORIES
Hands up and amen / Running around town / Still waters / Deadline for my memories / Imitation of life / I try / True moments of my world / We shall be true / I don't believe / Space oasis / You and I (keep holding on) / Your loving arms / Big tears and make-up
CD 0630121802
Magnet / Jan '96 / Warner Music

Martin, Carl

MARTIN, BOGAN & ARMSTRONG/ OLD GANG OF MINE (Martin, Carl & Ted Bogan/Howard Armstrong)
CD FF 003CD
Flying Fish / Feb '93 / ADA / CM / Direct / Roots

Martin, Carl

CARL MARTIN 1930-6/WILLIE BLACKWELL 1941 (Martin, Carl & Willie Blackwell)
CD DOCD 5229
Document / Apr '94 / ADA / Hot Shot / Jazz Music

Martin, Claire

DEVIL MAY CARE
Devil may care / Victim of circumstance / If love were all / Devil's gonna git you / By myself / Close enough for love / Cant's give enough / Sun was falling from the sky / October thoughts / On thin ice / Save your love for me
CD AKD 021
Linn / Apr '93 / PolyGram

MAKE THIS CITY OURS
CD AKD 066
Linn / Mar '97 / PolyGram

OFFBEAT
Offbeat / Buy and sell / Come back to me / I'll close my eyes / Monk's new tune / I do it for your love / Worth the wait / Wishful thinking / Comes love / Would you believe / Lost in his arms / Something real / Make sure you're sure / Some other time
CD AKD 046
Linn / Nov '95 / PolyGram

OLD BOYFRIENDS
When the sun comes out / Close as pages in a book / Partners in crime / Chased out / Moon ray / Old boyfriends / Out of my continental mind / I've got news for you / Wheelers and dealers / I was telling him about you / Gentleman friend / Killing time
CD AKD 028
Linn / Sep '94 / PolyGram

WAITING GAME, THE
You hit the spot / Be cool / This funny world / Better than anything / If you could see me now / Some cats / Four AM / People that you never get to love / Tight / Everything happens to me / Key to your Ferrari
CD AKD 018
Linn / Mar '92 / PolyGram

Martin, Daisy

DAISY MARTIN & OZIE MCPHERSON 1921-1926 (Martin, Daisy & Ozie McPherson)
CD DOCD 5522
Document / Mar '97 / ADA / Hot Shot / Jazz Music

Martin, Dean

ALL THE HITS 1948-63
CD PRS 23015
Personality / Jan '94 / Target/BMG

ALL THE HITS 1964-69
CD PRS 23016
Personality / Jan '94 / Target/BMG

BEST OF DEAN MARTIN (The Capitol Years)
That's amore / Kiss / Memories are made of this / Sway / Money burns a hole in my pocket / Hey brother pour the wine / Naughty lady of Shady Lane / Man who plays the mandolino / Mambo Italiano / Innamorata / Volare / Relax-ay-voo: *Martin, Dean & Line Renaud* / All in a nights work / Return to me / Cha cha cha d'amour / Just in time
CD CDEMS 1297
Capitol / Jan '89 / EMI

BEST OF DEAN MARTIN
CD CPCD 8150
Charly / Nov '95 / Koch

BEST OF DEAN MARTIN, THE (1962-1968 Reprise Recordings)
CD CDGR 106
Charly / Jan '96 / Koch

CAPITOL YEARS 1950-1962, THE (2CD Set)
Memories are made of this / Powder your face with sunshine (smile smile smile) / You was: *Martin, Dean & Peggy Lee* / Dreamy old New England moon / I'm gonna paper all my walls with your love letters / I'll always love you (day after day) / Solitaire / Night train to Memphis / Pretty as a picture / Oh Marie / You belong to me / Susan / Peanut vendor / I'm yours / That's amore / I'd cry like a baby / Hey brother, pour the wine / Every street's a boulevard (in old New York): *Martin, Dean & Jerry Lewis* / I'll gladly make the same mistake again / Open up the doghouse (two cats are coming in): *Martin, Dean & Nat 'King' Cole* / Carolina in the morning / In Napoli / Inamorata / I'm gonna steal you away: *Martin, Dean & The Nuggets* / Only trust your heart / Beau James / Good mornin' life / Return to me / Volare / On an evening in Rome / All I do is dream of you / Medley / My guiding star / Until the real thing comes along / Ain't that a kick in the head / Just in time / Be an angel / Non dimenticar / Somebody loves you / It's 1200 miles from Palm Springs to Texas
CD Set PRDFCD 2
Capitol / Aug '96 / EMI

COLLECTION, THE
Everybody loves somebody / My heart cries for you / I'll hold you in my heart / In the chapel in the moonlight / Release me / Born to lose / Somewhere there's a someone / Green green grass of home / You've still got a place in my heart / You'll always be the one I love / Door is still open / Welcome to my world / In the misty moonlight / Room full of roses / I wonder who's kissing her now / Crying time / One I love (belongs to somebody else) / I'm so lonesome I could cry / Take these chains from my heart / I can't help it (if I'm still in love with you)
CD CCSCD 207
Castle / Nov '88 / BMG

DEAN MARTIN
CD DVGH 7092
Deja Vu / May '95 / THE

DEAN MARTIN SINGS COUNTRY
Send me the pillow that you dream on / Green green grass of home / Crying time / (Remember me) I'm the one who loves you / Little ole wine drinker, me / Lay some happiness on me / Born to lose / Detroit city / My heart cries for you / In the misty moonlight / You've still got a place in my heart / First thing every morning (and the last thing every night) / Detour / I take a lot of pride in what I am / Where the blue and lonely go / Little green apples
CD CTS 55438
Country Stars / May '96 / Target/BMG

DINO - THE GOLDEN YEARS 1962-1973 (4CD Set)
Face in a crowd / Everybody loves somebody / Door is still open to my heart / Send me the pillow you dream on / (Remember me) I'm the one who loves you / Houston / I will / Somewhere there's a someone / Come running back / Million and one / Shades / Nobody's baby again / (Open up the door) let the good times in / Lay some happiness on me / In the chapel in the moonlight / Little ol' wine drinker me / You've still got a place in my heart / April again / That old time feelin' / Five card stud / Not enough Indians / Gentle on my mind / I take a lot of pride in what I am / She's a little bit country / Get on with your livin' / My shoes keep walking back to you / I'm gonna change everything / Crying time / Once a day / Ain't gonna try anymore / Any time / I'll hold you in my heart (till I can hold you in my arms ag / Candy kisses / Middle of the night is my cryin' time / Detour / Bouquet of roses / Nobody but a fool / Make it rain / If you ever get around to loving me / Pride / Just a little lovin' / You're the reason I'm in love / Sneaky little side of me / If I ever get back to Georgia / One cup of happiness (and one peace of mind) / Hammer and nails / Down home / Everybody but me / Bumming around / Blue, blue day / Ramblin' rose / You're nobody till somebody loves you / I don't know why (I just do) / Blue moon / Smile / Corrine Corrina / Born to lose / Release me / My heart cries for you / It keeps right on-a hurtin' / Wallpaper roses / Hey good lookin' / What a difference a day made / Guess who / South of the border / Poor people of Paris / Things we did last summer / In a little Spanish town / I love Paris / La paloma / C'est si bon / Wedding bells / In the misty moonlight / Everybody loves somebody / I'll be seeing you / Singin' the blues / I can't help it (if I'm still in love with you) / Tips of my fingers / He's got you / Things / I'm so lonesome I could cry / You better move on / Take these chains from my heart / Where the blue and lonely go / Clinging vine / My heart is an open book / I walk the line / Room full of roses / My woman, my woman, my wife / Together again / Detroit city / Walk on by / Shutters and boards / Georgia sunshine / Kiss the world goodbye / Honey / Here we go again / For the good times / By the time I get to Phoenix / For once in my life
CD Set CDDIG 19
Charly / Oct '96 / Koch

DINO: ITALIAN LOVE SONGS/CHA CHA DE AMOR
Just say I love her / Arriverderci Roma / My heart reminds me / You're breaking my heart / Non dimenticar / Return to me / Vieni su / On an evening in Roma / Pardon / Take me in your arms / I have but one heart / There's no tomorrow / Somebody loves you / My one and only love / Love (your spell is everywhere) / I wish you love / Cha cha d'amour / Hundred years from today / I love you much too much / (I love you) for sentimental reasons / Let me love you tonight / Amor / Two loves have I / If love is good to me
CD CTMCD 108
EMI / Jan '97 / EMI

GREAT GENTLEMEN OF SONG, THE
All I do is dream of you / Please don't talk about me when I'm gone / Things we did last summer / Mean to me / Wrap your troubles in dreams (and dream your troubles away) / Imagination / Sleepy time gal / You're nobody til' somebody loves you / Dream / Someday (you'll want me to want you) / June in January / I can't believe that you're in love with me / Dream a little dream of me / Just in time / Cuddle up a little closer / Lovely mine / Until the real thing comes along / Hit the road to dreamland / Goodnight sweetheart
CD CDP 8320982
Capitol / Aug '95 / EMI

MEMORIES ARE MADE OF THIS (3CD Set)
Memories are made of this / That's amore / Come back to Sorrento / Cha cha cha d'amour / Angel baby / I've got my love to keep my warm / Kiss / Please don't talk about me when I'm gone / Dream a little dream of me / All I do is dream of you / Things we did last summer / How do you speak to an angel / Young and foolish / Standing on the corner / In Napoli / That lucky old son / Volare (nel blu dipinto di blu) / Dream / Hey, brother pour the wine / Buona sera / June in January / Hit the road to dreamland / Imagination / Let me go lover / Every street's a boulevard / There's my lover / Long long ago: *Martin, Dean & Nat 'King' Cole* / In the cool cool of the evening / Just one more chance / Two sleepy people: *Martin, Dean & Line Renaud* / Me 'n' you 'n' the moon / Return to me (rittorna a me) / Baby it's cold outside / Rio bravo / Goodnight sweetheart / I have but one heart (O Marenarillo) / You're nobody till somebody loves you / When you're smiling / Under the bridges of Paris / Somebody loves you / You can't love them all / Pretty as a picture / You was with Peggy Lee / Love me, my love / Night train to Memphis / On a evening in Roma / Watching the world go by
CD Set SA 872662
Disky / Sep '96 / Disky / THE

SINGLES, THE
You was: *Lee, Peggy & Dean Martin* / That lucky old sun / Night train to Memphis / In

the cool, cool, cool of the evening / Kiss / There's my lover / When you're smiling / Pretty as a picture / How do you speak to an angel / Every street's a boulevard: *Martin, Dean & Jerry Lewis* / Long long ago / Let me go, lover / Under the bridges of Paris / Two sleepy people: *Martin, Dean & Line Renaud* / Young and foolish / Just one more chance / Standing on the corner / Me 'n' you 'n' the moon / You can't love 'em all / I wish you love
CD _______ CDMFP 6129
Music For Pleasure / Sep '94 / EMI

SINGS THE ALL TIME GREATEST HITS (2CD Set)
Little ole wine drinker me / Raindrops keep fallin' on my head / Turn the world around / For once in my life / Everybody loves somebody / Sweetheart / Tie a yellow ribbon round the old oak tree / Red roses for a blue lady / Welcome to my world / Release me / We'll sing in the sunshine / Singing the blues / King of the road / Birds and the bees / Make the world go away / Together again / It keeps right on a-hurtin' / I'm gonna change everything / Things / Send me the pillow you dream on / My heart cries for you / Take these chains from my heart / Green, green grass of home / Detroit city / Houston / Gentle on my mind / Little green apples / For the good times / La paloma / La vie en rose / Glory of love / What a diff'rence a day made / Snap your fingers / I'm confessin' / Fools rush in / I will / By the time I get to Phoenix / Raining in my heart / Send me some lovin' / Take good care of her / Invisible tears / Ramblin' Rose / Cryin' time / Let the good times in / In the chapel in the moonlight / Clinging vine / My heart is an open book / My woman, my woman / My wife / You're the best thing that's ever happened to me / I'll be seeing you
CD Set _______ CPCD 81992
Charly / Aug '96 / Koch

SLEEP WARM
Sleep warm / Hit the road to dreamland / Dream / Cuddle up a little closer / Sleepy time gal / Goodnight sweetheart / All I do is dream of you / Let's put out the lights / Dream a little dream of me / Wrap your troubles in dreams (and dream your troubles away) / Goodnight my love / Brahms lullaby
CD _______ PRMCD 3
Premier/EMI / Apr '96 / EMI

VERY BEST OF DEAN MARTIN, THE
Return to me / Angel baby / Rio bravo / I've got my love to keep me warm / Baby, it's cold outside / Buona sera / That's amore / Goodnight sweetheart / Volare / Write to me from Naples / Memories are made of this / June in January / Come back to Sorrento / Hey brother pour the wine / Cha cha cha d'amour / I have but one heart
CD _______ CDMFP 6032
Music For Pleasure / Sep '88 / EMI

Martin, Doc

UNLOCK YOUR MIND
CD _______ MM 800552
Moonshine / Sep '96 / Mo's Music Machine / Prime / RTM/Disc

Martin, Emile

EMILE MARTIN
CD _______ BCD 317
GHB / Oct '93 / Jazz Music

Martin, Helene

CHANTE LES POETES
CD _______ 983862
EPM / Sep '96 / ADA / Discovery

LUCIENNE DESNOUES PAR H MARTIN
CD _______ 983922
EPM / Feb '97 / ADA / Discovery

Martin, Janis

FEMALE ELVIS, THE
Drug store rock 'n' roll / Will you Willyum / Love and kisses / My boy Elvis / Crackerjack / Bang bang / Ooby dooby / Barefoot baby / Good love / Little bit / Two long years / All right baby / Billy boy my Billy boy / Let's elope baby / Love me love / Love me to pieces / William / Here today and gone tomorrow / Teen street / Hard times ahead / Cry guitar / Just squeeze me / One more year to go / Blues keep calling / Please be my love / I don't hurt anymore / Half loved / My confession / I'll never be free
CD _______ BCD 15406
Bear Family / Jul '87 / Direct / Rollercoaster / Swift

Martin, Jimmy

JIMMY MARTIN & THE SUNNY MOUNTAIN BOYS (Martin, Jimmy & The Sunny Mountain Boys)
Save it save it / Chalk up another one / I pulled a boo boo / They didn't know the difference (but I did) / 20/20 Vision / That's how I count on you / Before the sun goes down / Skip, hop and wobble / You'll be a lost ball / Hitparade of love / Grand ole opry song / I'm the boss (of this here house) / Dog bite your hide / I'll drink no more wine / Ocean of diamonds / Sophronie / I'll never take no for an answer / Rock hearts / I like to hear 'em preach it / Voice of my saviour / Night / It's not like home / She's left me again / Hold what cha got / Bear tracks / Cripple creek / In foggy old London / Joke's on you / Wooden shoes / Home run man / Who'll sing for me / God is always the same / All the good times are past and gone / You don't know my mind / Homesick / Old fashioned christmas / He-de diddle / Don't cry to me / My walking shoes / Hold to God's unchanging hand / Undo what's been done / Deep river / What was I supposed to do / I can, I will, I do believe / There was a love / Poor little bull frogs / Steppin' stones / There ain't nobody gonna miss me / Little angels in heaven / Pretending I don't care / Leavin' town / Don't give your heart to a rambler / God guide our leader's hand / Train 45 / Mr. Engineer / This world is not my home / Drink up and go home / Lord I'm coming home / Goodbye / Pray the clouds away / Give me the roses now / Prayer bell of heaven / Moonshine hollow / Give me your hand / Stormy waters / What would you give in exchange / Shut in's prayer / Beautiful life / Little white church / Old man's drunk again / Hey lonesome / Tennessee / Widow maker / I'm thinking tonight of my blue eyes / Red river valley / John Henry / Truck driving man / There's more pretty girls than one / Six days on the road / Truck driver's queen / I'd rather have America / Little Robin / There's better times a coming / Guitar picking president / It takes one to know one / Sunny side of the mountain / Snow white grave / Poor Ellen Smith / Shenandoah waltz / Coming back but I don't know when / In the pines / Last song / Sweet Dixie / Wild indian / Run boy run / Theme time / Orange blossom special / I can't quit cigarettes / Lost highway / Good things out weigh the bad / Summer's come and gone / Fraulein / You're gonna change (or I'm gonna leave) / Tennessee waltz / Little Maggie, she's so sweet / Big country / Little red rooster / Crow on the banjo / You are my sunshine / Going up dry branch / Living like a fool / Union county / Uptown blues / Goin' ape (over you) / Steal away somewhere and die / Freeborn man / Losing you / Just and old standby / Slowly / Lonesome prison blues / Shackles and chains / Doin' my time / Milwaukee here I come / Arab bounce / (I've got my) Future on ice / Midnight rambler / Between fire and water / Singing all day / Lift your eyes to Jesus / Shake hands with Mother again / When the saviour reached down for me / Help thy brother / My Lord keeps a record / I'd like to be sixteen again / I cried again / Chattanooga dug / Mary Ann / I buried my future / Just plain yellow / Fly me to Frisco / Grave upon the green hillside / Lost to a stranger / Beautiful brown eyes
CD Set _______ BCD 15705
Bear Family / Sep '94 / Direct / Rollercoaster / Swift

YOU DON'T KNOW MY MIND
CD _______ ROUCD 5521
Rounder / Dec '90 / ADA / CM / Direct

Martin, Juan

ANDALUCIAN SUITES, THE
CD _______ CDFV 01
Flamencovision / Jun '91 / Pinnacle

GUITARRA FLAMENCA
CD _______ 31837
Divucsa / Oct '96 / Discovery

LUNA NEGRA
CD _______ CDFV 02
Flamencovision / May '93 / Pinnacle

MUSICA ALHAMBRA
CD _______ FVRPM 0042
Flamencovision / Nov '96 / Pinnacle

PICASSO PORTRAITS
Harlequin / Desire caught by the tail / Three musicians / Sleeping girl / Self portrait / Aficionado / Girls of Algiers / Weeping woman / Piccador
CD _______ CDFV 03
Flamencovision / Apr '94 / Pinnacle

Martin Luther Lennon

MUSIC FOR A WORLD WITHOUT LIMITATIONS
CD _______ NL 0039
Not Lame / Feb '97 / Cargo / Greyhound

Martin, Marilyn

MARILYN MARTIN
Body and the beat / Night moves / Too much too soon / Turn it on / Thank you / One step closer to you / Beauty or the beast / Move closer / Dream is always the same / Here is the news
CD _______ 7567802112
Atlantic / Jan '96 / Warner Music

Martin, Mary

DECCA YEARS 1938-1946, THE
CD _______ 379062
Koch International / Nov '95 / Koch

Martin, Mel

PLAYS BENNY CARTER
Kiss from you / Hello / Zanzibar / When lights are low / Summer serenade / Souvenir / Another time, another place / Wonderland / Only trust your heart
CD _______ ENJ 90412
Enja / Jul '95 / New Note/Pinnacle / Vital/ SAM

Martin, Mick

LONG DISTANCE CALL (Martin, Mick Bluesrockers)
CD _______ DTCD 3038
Double Trouble / Apr '97 / CM / Hot Shot

Martin, Moon

SHOTS FROM A COLD NIGHTMARE/ ESCAPE FROM DOMINATION
Hot nite in Dallas / Victim of romance / Nite thoughts / Paid killer / Cadillac walk / Bad case of lovin' you / Hands down / All I've got to do / You don't care about me / She's a pretender / I've got a reason / She made a fool of you / Dreamer / Gun shy / Hot house baby / Feeling's right / Rolene / No chance / Dangerous / Bootleg woman
CD _______ EDCD 432
Edsel / Jul '95 / Pinnacle

STREET FEVER/MYSTERY TICKET
CD _______ EDCD 433
Edsel / Oct '95 / Pinnacle

Martin, Nicholas

HAPPY DAYS ARE HERE AGAIN (At The Wurlitzer Organ)
CD _______ GRCD 49
Grasmere / '92 / Highlander / Savoy / Target/BMG

Martin, Sallie

PRECIOUS LORD (Martin, Sallie Singers)
Precious Lord / That's what he done for me / Old ship of Zion / Own me as a child / Search my heart / God is moving / Let me cross over / There's not a friend / No one ever cared / God is here / I need him / Nothing but the grace of God / He's in my heart / Seeking for me / Let Jesus come into my heart / When he comes / Keep me Jesus / Closer to Jesus / I was glad when they said to me / Jesus I love you
CD _______ CPCD 8116
Charly / Jul '95 / Koch

THROW OUT THE LIFELINE (Martin, Sallie Singers & Cora Martin)
God is a battle axe / Didn't it rain / I'll make it somehow / Oh yes, he set me free / He's able to carry me through / Oh what a time / Throw out the lifeline / Eyes hath not seen / Good old way / Jesus is waiting / Great day / I know it's well with my soul / Jesus said / I called the Lord and got an answer / There is a fountain filled with blood / It's a long, long way / I'm bound for the promised land / Hold to God's unchanging hand / Ain't that good news / (There is no sorrow) that heaven cannot heal / I'm getting nearer to my Lord / Every once in a while / One of these mornings / Thy servant's prayer / On the other side / He put his trust in me / I know that he cares for me / Lord I need you every day of my life
CD _______ CDCHD 481
Ace / Jul '93 / Pinnacle

Martin, Tony

SOMETHING IN THE AIR
Rainbow on the river / Star fell out of heaven / It's love I'm after / Where the lazy river goes by / Afraid to dream / By a wishing well / My sweetheart / That week in Paris / When did you leave Heaven / Loveliness of you / Sweetheart let's grow old together / There's something in the air / Mist is over the moon / You're slightly terrific / Song of old Hawaii / This may be the night / So do I / World is mine tonight
CD _______ CMSCD 004
Movie Stars / '88 / Conifer/BMG

THIS MAY BE THE NIGHT
By a wishing well / Cancel the flowers / Donkey serenade / Dream valley / Flamingo / I hadn't anyone till you / Island of Maui Hula / Just let me look at you / Last time I saw Paris / Marching along with time / My sweetheart / Now it can be told / One love affair / Rhythm of the waves / Song of old Hawaii / That week in Paris / This may be the night / 'Tis Autumn / Too beautiful to last / Where in the world / You couldn't be cuter / You stepped out of a dream
CD _______ CDAJA 5099
Living Era / Dec '92 / Select

Martinez, Narciso

FATHER OF TEX MEX CONJUNTO (1948-1960)
CD _______ ARHCD 361
Arhoolie / Apr '95 / ADA / Cadillac / Direct

Martinez, Pepe

ART OF FLAMENCO VOL.8, THE (1923-1984)
CD _______ MAN 4865
Mandala / Feb '96 / ADA / Harmonia Mundi / Mandala

Martino, Al

AL MARTINO
Spanish eyes / Red roses for a blue lady / My way / Hey Mama / Sweet Caroline / Everybody's talkin'
CD _______ 16114
Laserlight / May '94 / Target/BMG

AL MARTINO IN CONCERT
CD _______ CDPT 841
Prestige / Feb '91 / Else / Total/BMG

CONCERT COLLECTION
Song is you / I have but one heart / Cuando cuando cuando / Feelings / More I see you / Somewhere my love / Mary in the morning / Spanish eyes / Strangers in the night / To the door of the sun / Man without love / Because you're you / I love you more and more everyday / Painted tainted rose / Speak softly love / End of the line / I've got to be me / Can't help falling in love with you / Volare
CD _______ PLATCD 152
Platinum / Mar '96 / Prism

GREATEST HITS
Song is you / I have but one love / Cuando cuando cuando / Feelings / More I see you / Somewhere my love / Mary in the morning / Spanish eyes / Strangers in the night / As long as you're with me / Lonely is a man without love / I love you because / I love you more and more every day / Wild and lovely rose / Speak softly love / End of the line / Come into my life / I've got to be me / Can't help falling in love / Volare
CD _______ PLATCD 364
Platinum / '91 / Prism

HITS OF AL MARTINO, THE
Here in my heart / Spanish eyes / Granada / Wanted / Story of Tina / Now (before another day goes by) / Mary in the morning / White rose of Athens / Man from Laramie / Volare / Painted tainted rose / To the door of the sun / Rachel / I won't last a day without you / Take my heart / I love you because
CD _______ CDMFP 6030
Music For Pleasure / Jul '88 / EMI

LIVE IN CONCERT
Quando quando quando / You will be my music / Song is you / You will be my music / I have but one heart / Feelings / More I see you / Some where my love / Mary in the morning / Spanish eyes / Strangers in the night / To the door of the sun / Man without love / I love you because / I love you more and more everybody / Painted tainted rose / Speak softly love / End of the line / Come into my life / I've gotta be me / Can't help falling in love / Volare
CD _______ EMPRCD 634
Emporio / Jun '96 / Disc

QUANDO QUANDO QUANDO
CD _______ WMCD 5695
Disky / Oct '94 / Disky / THE

SPANISH EYES
CD _______ MU 5063
Musketeer / Oct '92 / Disc

SPANISH EYES
Now / Say you'll wait for me / Way paesano / There'll be no teardrops tonight / Wanted / Give me something to go with the wine / No one can change destiny / I still believe / No one but you / Not as a stranger / Don't go to strangers / Snowy, snowy mountains / To please my lady / Small talk / Somebody else is taking my place / What now my love / Melody of love / Spanish eyes / My love forgive me / You belong to me
CD _______ CDMFP 6176
Music For Pleasure / Nov '95 / EMI

SPANISH EYES
Spanish eyes / Quando quando quando / Feelings / More I see you / Somewhere my love (Lara's theme) / Mary in the morning / This song is you / Strangers in the night / Can't help falling in love / I love you because I love you more and more each day / Volare / Lonely is a man without love / I've got to be me / Come into my life / End of the line / Speak softly love / Painted tainted love
CD _______ CD 6067
Music / Apr '97 / Target/BMG

SPANISH EYES
Spanish eyes / Strangers in the night / You will be my music/The song is you / Quando, quando, quando / Speak softly love / Can't help falling in love / Mary in the morning / Feelings / Volare (nel blu dipinte di blu) / More I see you / Somewhere my love / I've gotta be me / Lonely is a man without love / Come into my life / I love you because you're you / I love you more and more every day
CD _______ 100712
CMC / May '97 / BMG

THIS IS MY SONG (3CD Set)
Volare (nel blu dipinto di blu) / Here in my heart / Can't take my eyes off you / Wanted / Now / Granada / White rose of Athens / Walking in the sand (and the seasons come and go) / Unchained melody / Story of Tina / Don't go to strangers / Melody of love / Mary in the morning / Man from Laramie / Always together / Can't help falling in love / Spanish eyes / I won't last a day without you / Speak softly love / My cherie / Never my love / No other arms, no other lips / Rachel / No one but you / Love is blue / I love you because / Give me something to go with the wine / Painted tainted rose / Have I told you lately that I love you / Way Paesano / Tears and roses / I can't help it if I'm still in love with you / To the door of the sun / Take my heart / Vaya con dios / What now my love / Shadow of my smile / True love / I still believe / This guy's in love with you / Somebody else is taking my place / There'll be no teardrops tonight / I started loving you again / To please my lady / Small talk / If I were a carpenter / You belong to me / Let it be me
CD Set ____ SA 872822
Disky / Sep '96 / Disky / THE

TOUCH OF CLASS, A
Here in my heart / Take my heart / Now / Rachel wanted / Story of Tina / Spanish eyes / Summertime / Man from Laramie / Painted, tainted rose / Tears and roses / Mary in the morning / Volare / Always together / Love is blue / Vaya con dios
CD ____ TC 862642
Disky / May '97 / Disky / THE

Martino, Pat

ALL SIDES NOW
Too high / Two of a kind / Progression / I'm confessin' (that I love you) / Ellipsis / Ayako / Two days old / Outrider / Never and after
CD ____ CDP 8376272
Blue Note / Aug '97 / EMI

DESPERADO
Blackjack / Dearborn walk / Oleo / Deperado / Portrait of Diana / Express
CD ____ OJCCD 397
Original Jazz Classics / Apr '93 / Complete/ Pinnacle / Jazz Music / Wellard

EAST
East / Close your eyes / Park Avenue petite / Lazy bird
CD ____ OJCCD 248
Original Jazz Classics / May '97 / Complete/ Pinnacle / Jazz Music / Wellard

Martins, Carlos

PASSAGEM
Sofia / Mali m'blue baaba / Duo / A Espera / Working blues / Round trip / Passado presente / I trust on you / Sophisticated lady / Naif
CD ____ ENJ 90732
Enja / May '97 / New Note/Pinnacle / Vital/ SAM

Martins, Vasco

ISLAND OF THE SECRET SOUNDS
CD ____ 669752
Melodie / Mar '96 / ADA / Discovery / Grapevine/PolyGram / Greensleeves / Jet Star

Martland, Steve

MARTLAND - FACTORY MASTERS
Babi Yar / Drill / Crossing the border / Principia / American invention / Re-mix / Shoulder to shoulder
CD ____ 09026683982
Catalyst / Nov '95 / BMG

PATROL
CD ____ 09026626702
Catalyst / Sep '94 / BMG

Marton, Tolo

MY PLACE IS CLOSE TO YOU
Certitude of laundromats / Alpine valley / See what you've done to me / Music lady / Plains of joy / Rainy day / Back to my youth / I don't wanna be alone / My place is close to you / Wake up / Pinto creek
CD ____ PRD 70922
Provogue / May '96 / Pinnacle

Martve Boys Choir

GEORGIAN POLYPHONY VOL.2
CD ____ VICG 50042
JVC World Library / Mar '96 / ADA / CM / Direct

Martyn, Barry

BARRY MARTYN
CD ____ SKCD 23056
Sackville / Jun '94 / Cadillac / Jazz Music / Swift

ON TOUR
CD ____ BCD 255
GHB / Aug '94 / Jazz Music

VINTAGE BARRY MARTYN
CD ____ BCD 75
GHB / Apr '97 / Jazz Music

Martyn, Jean

BLACKPOOL TOWER, THE WURLITZER AND ME
Oklahoma selection / Red River valley/Nut rocker / Rule Brittania/A life on the ocean wave/Anchors aweigh / Sailor's hornpipe/ Skye boat song/Lead us heavenly father / We are sailing / Wurli bird / Somewhere over the rainbow / California, here I come/ Mammy / Toot toot Tootsie/Goodbye / Blackpool Belle / Under the Double Eagle / What a friend we have in Jesus/And it can be / Will your anchor hold/Old rugged cross / Blessed assurance/How great thou art / You're a lady / Way you look tonight/Dream / Radetsky march / Breeze and I/September in the rain / Tenderly/Sentimental over you / When day is done
CD ____ CDGRS 1294
Grosvenor / Feb '97 / Grosvenor

REFLECTIONS
CD ____ CDGRS 1276
Grosvenor / Mar '95 / Grosvenor

Martyn, John

AND
Sunshine's better / Suzanne / Downward pull of human nature / All in your favour / Little strange / Who are they / Step it up / Carmine / She's a lover / Sunshine's better
CD ____ 8287982
Go Discs / Jul '96 / PolyGram

APPRENTICE, THE
Live on love / Look at that gun / Send me one line / Hold me / Apprentice / River / Income town / Deny this love / UPO / Patterns in the rain
CD ____ HY 2001101CD
Hypertension / Sep '93 / ADA / CM / Direct / Total/BMG

BLESS THE WEATHER
Go easy / Bless the weather / Sugar lump / Walk to the water / Just now / Head and heart / Let the good things come / Back down the river / Glistening Glyndebourne / Singin' in the rain
CD ____ IMCD 135
Island / Jul '91 / PolyGram

COOLTIDE
Hole in the rain / Annie says / Jack the lad / Number nine / Cure / Same difference / Father Time / Call me / Cooltide
CD ____ HY 200116CD
Hypertension / Jul '97 / ADA / CM / Direct / Total/BMG

ELECTRIC JOHN MARTYN, THE
Johnny too bad / Certain surprise / Sweet little mystery / Dancing
CD ____ IMCD 66
Island / '89 / PolyGram

FOUNDATIONS
Mad dog days / Angeline / Apprentice / May you never / Deny this love / Send me one line / John Wayne / Johnny too bad / Over the rainbow
CD ____ IMCD 180
Island / Mar '94 / PolyGram

GRACE AND DANGER
Some people are crazy / Grace and danger / Lookin' on / Johnny too bad / Sweet little mystery / Hurt in your heart / Baby please come home / Save some for me / Our love
CD ____ IMCD 67
Island / '90 / PolyGram

HIDDEN YEARS, THE
CD ____ ARTFULCD 2
Artful / Jan '97 / Pinnacle / Total/BMG

INSIDE OUT
Fine lines / Eibi gheal chiuin ni chearbhaill / Ain't no saint / Outside in / Glory of love / Look in / Beverley / Make no mistake / Ways to cry / So much in love with you
CD ____ IMCD 172
Island / Mar '94 / PolyGram

LONDON CONVERSATION
Fairytale lullaby / Sandy Grey / London conversation / Ballad of an elder woman / Cocaine / Run honey run / Back to stay / Rollin' home / Who's grown up now / Golden girl / This time / Don't think twice, it's alright
CD ____ IMCD 134
Island / Jun '91 / PolyGram

ONE WORLD
Dealer / One world / Smiling stranger / Big muff / Couldn't love you anymore / Certain surprise / Dancing / Small hours
CD ____ IMCD 86
Island / Feb '90 / PolyGram

PIECE BY PIECE
Nightline / Lonely lover / Angeline / One step too far / Piece by piece / Serendipity / Who believes in angels / Love of mine / John Wayne
CD ____ IMCD 68
Island / Nov '89 / PolyGram

ROAD TO RUIN, THE (Martyn, John & Beverley)
Primrose Hill / Parcels / Auntie Aviator / New day / Give us a ring / Sorry to be so long / Tree green / Say what you can / Road to ruin
CD ____ IMCD 165
Island / Mar '93 / PolyGram

SAPPHIRE
Over the rainbow / You know / Watching her eyes / Acid rain / Sapphire / Fisherman's dream / Mad dog days / Climb the walls / Coming in on time / Rope souled
CD ____ IMCD 164
Island / Mar '93 / PolyGram

SOLID AIR
Over the hill / Don't want to know / I'd rather be the devil / Go down easy / Dreams by the sea / May you never / Man in the station / Easy blues / Solid air
CD ____ IMCD 85
Island / Feb '90 / PolyGram

STORMBRINGER (Martyn, John & Beverley)
Go out and get it / Can't get the one I want / Stormbringer / Sweet honesty / Woodstock / John the baptist / Ocean / Traffic light lady / Tomorrow time / Would you believe me
CD ____ IMCD 131
Island / Jun '91 / PolyGram

SUNDAY'S CHILD
One day without you / Lay it all down / Root love / My baby girl / Sunday's child / Spencer the rover / Clutches / Message / Satisfied mind / You can discover / Call me crazy
CD ____ IMCD 163
Island / Mar '93 / PolyGram

SWEET LITTLE MYSTERIES - ISLAND ANTHOLOGY (2CD Set)
Bless the weather / Head and heart / Glistening Glyndebourne / Solid air / Over the hill / Don't want to know / I'd rather be the devil / May you never / Fine lines / Make no mistake / One day without you / Lay it all down / Root love / Sunday's child / Spencer the rover / You can discover / Call me crazy / Couldn't you love me more / Certain surprise / Dancing / Small hours / Dealer / One world / Some people are crazy / Lookin' on / Johnny too bad / Sweet little mystery / Hurt in your heart / Baby please come home / Sapphire / Fisherman's dream / Angeline / Send me one line / eibhli ghail chuin ni chearbaill
CD Set ____ CRNCD 4
Island / Jun '94 / PolyGram

TUMBLER, THE
Sing a song of summer / River / Goin' down to Memphis / Gardener / Day at the sea / Fishin' blues / Dusty / Holto train / Winding boy / Fly on home / Kuckledy crunch and slipledge slee song / Seven black roses
CD ____ IMCD 173
Island / Mar '94 / PolyGram

VERY BEST OF JOHN MARTYN, THE
CD ____ ARTFULCD 4
Artful / Apr '97 / Pinnacle / Total/BMG

Martyr Whore

ROSEYDOLVET BALLET
CD ____ EFA 121612
Apollyon / Aug '95 / SRD

Martyrium

MARTYRIUM
CD ____ MRCD 002
Modern Invasion / Jul '95 / Plastic Head

Marusia, Sergei

RUSSIAN GYPSY SONGS
CD ____ MCD 71565
Monitor / Jun '93 / CM

Marvelettes

HITS AND RARITIES
CD ____ MAR 033
Marginal / Jun '97 / Greyhound

VERY BEST OF THE MARVELETTES, THE
Make it right / Blame it on yourself / Ride the storm / Secret love affair / Right away / For the rest of my life / Just in the nick of time / Bad case of nerves / My wheel of fortune / When you're young and in love / Pushing too hard / Time has a new meaning / Holding on with both hands / We're gonna stay in love / You're my remedy / All things abide / Special feeling / Universal love
CD ____ 3035990022
Carlton / Oct '95 / Carlton

Marvellous Caine

GUN TALK
CD ____ SUBBASE CD3
Suburban Base / Nov '95 / Pinnacle / Prime

Marvin & Johnny

CHERRY PIE
Cherry pie / Tick tock / Forever / Kiss me / Sugar / Dear one / Honey girl / Little honey / Vip vop / Kokomo / Sometimes I wonder / Baby, won't you marry me / I love you, yes I do / Butter ball / Sugar Mama / Oh me oh my / Sweet dreams / Will you love me / I wanna / Let me know / Ain't that right / Sweet potato / Wonderful, wonderful one / Yes I do / Tell me darling / Have mercy Miss Percy / Have mercy Miss Percy (Take 1)
CD ____ CDCHD 509
Ace / Feb '94 / Pinnacle

FLIPPED OUT
Wine woogie / Old man's blues / Dream girl / As long as you're satisfied / My baby won't let me in / Sun was shining / Baby doll / I'm not a fool / Jo Jo / Honey / How long she been gone / If I should lose you / Boy loves girl / School of love / I want lovin' / Day in, day out / What's the matter / Flip / Hunter Hancock radio ad / Mamo mamo / Ding dong baby / Tell me darling / Yak yak woman / Pretty one / Bye bye my baby
CD ____ CDCHD 385
Ace / May '92 / Pinnacle

Marvin, Greg

I'LL GET BY
Ding dong the witch is dead / Our angel / Devil's dream / I'll get by / Over the rainbow / How deep is the ocean / Old faithful / 317 East 32nd / Tuesday / Yesterdays / I'm with you
CD ____ CDSJP 347
Timeless Traditional / Oct '91 / Jazz Music / New Note/Pinnacle

Marvin, Hank

HANK MARVIN AND JOHN FARRAR (Marvin, Hank & John Farrar)
CD ____ SEECD 322
See For Miles/C5 / Jul '91 / Pinnacle

HANK MARVIN GUITAR SYNDICATE
New Earth / Have you never been mellow / St. Louis blues / I've got you under my skin / Syndicated / Ebb tide / Bird of beauty / Thunder thumbs and lightnin' licks / Flamingo / Silvery rain / You are everything
CD ____ SEECD 289
See For Miles/C5 / Apr '93 / Pinnacle

HANK MARVIN LIVE
Live and let die / Devil woman / Summer holiday / Foot tapper / Living doll / Pipeline / Medley / Sleepwalk / Atlantis / Savage / Young ones / Travellin' light / Eleanor Rigby / Guitar tango / Hound dog / Mystery train / Wonderful land / Theme from the Deer Hunter (Cavatina) / Rise and fall of Flingel Bunt / Apache / Move it
CD ____ 5374282
PolyGram TV / Mar '97 / PolyGram

HANK PLAYS CLIFF
CD ____ 5294262
Polydor / Oct '95 / PolyGram

HANK PLAYS HOLLY
Peggy Sue / It's so easy / Raining in my heart / Oh boy / Peggy Sue got married / Listen to me / Wishing / Well...all right / It doesn't matter anymore / That'll be the day / Brown eyed handsome man / Everyday / Rave on / True love ways / Maybe baby / Not fade away / Heartbeat
CD ____ 5337132
PolyGram TV / Nov '96 / PolyGram

HEARTBEAT
CD ____ 5213222
PolyGram TV / Nov '93 / PolyGram

INTO THE LIGHT
We are the champions / Pipeline / Sylvia / Jessica / Another day in paradise / Everybody wants to rule the world / Don't know much / Road train / Sumiko / Into the light / Everything I do (I do it for you) / Rikki don't lose that number / Scirocco / Moontalk / Tailspin / Steel wheel
CD ____ 5171482
Polydor / Oct '92 / PolyGram

MARVIN, WELCH & FARRAR (Marvin, Welch & Farrar)
CD ____ SEECD 324
See For Miles/C5 / Jul '91 / Pinnacle

SECOND OPINION (Marvin, Welch & Farrar)
CD ____ SEECD 325
See For Miles/C5 / Jul '91 / Pinnacle

TWANG (A Tribute To Hank Marvin) (Various Artists)
Apache: *Blackmore, Ritchie* / FBI: *May, Brian* / Wonderful land: *Iommi, Tony* / Savage: *Stevens, Steve* / Rise and fall of Fingel Bunt: *Marvin, Hank* / Midnight: *Green, Peter Splinter Group* / Spring is nearly here: *Young, Neil & Randy Bachman* / Atlantis: *Knopfler, Mark* / Frightened city: *Frampton, Peter* / Dance on: *Urban, Keith* / Stingray: *Summers, Andy* / Stranger: *Fleck, Bela*
CD ____ PRMDCD 25
Premier/EMI / Mar '97 / EMI

WOULD YOU BELIEVE IT... PLUS
Aquarius / Born free / This guy's in love with you / Tokyo guitar / Chameleon / Lara's theme / Big Country / Love and occasional rain / Georgia on my mind / Windmills of your mind / Sacha / High sierra / Evening comes / Wahine / Morning star / Sunday for seven days / Boogatoo / Would you believe it / Midnight cowboy / Goodnight Dick
CD ____ SEECD 210
See For Miles/C5 / May '89 / Pinnacle

Marx, Richard

FLESH AND BONE
Fool's game / You never take me dancing / Touch of heaven / What's the story / Can't lie to my heart / Until I find you again / My confession / Surrender to me / Eternity / What's wrong with that / Image / Too shy to say / Talk to ya later / Breathless / Miracle
CD _____ CDEST 2294
Capitol / Jun '97 / EMI

PAID VACATION
Way she loves me / One more try / Silent scream / Nothing to hide / Whole world to save / Soul motion / Now and forever / Goodbye / Hollywood / Heaven's waiting / Nothing left behind us / What you want / One man / Miami 2017 / Baby blues
CD _____ CDESTU 2208
EMI / Feb '94 / EMI

REPEAT OFFENDER
Nothin' you can do about it / Satisfied / Angelia / Too late to say goodbye / Right here waiting / Heart on the line / Living in the real world / That was Lulu / Wait for the sunrise / Children of the night
CD _____ CDEST 2153
Capitol / Oct '91 / EMI

RICHARD MARX
Should've known better / Don't mean nothing / Endless Summer nights / Lonely heart / Hold on to the nights / Have mercy / Remember Manhattan / Flame of love / Rhythm of life / Heaven only knows
CD _____ CDEST 2152
Capitol / Oct '91 / EMI

RUSH STREET
Playing with fire / Love unemotional / Keep coming back / Take this heart / Hazard / Hands in your pocket / Calling you / Superstar / Street of pain / I get no sleep / Big boy now / Chains around my heart / Your world
CD _____ CDESTU 2158
Capitol / Nov '91 / EMI

Marxer, Marcy

JUMP CHILDREN
CD _____ ROUCD 8012
Rounder / '88 / ADA / CM / Direct

VOICE ON THE WIND (Marxer, Marcy & Fink & Cathy)
CD _____ ROUCD 0408
Rounder / Mar '97 / ADA / CM / Direct

Marxman

TIME CAPSULE
CD _____ ZCDKR 5
More Rockers / Nov '96 / 3mv/Sony

Mary Beats Jane

LOCUST
Homecoming / Blackeye / Pure / Day in day out / Dogrelish / Fall / Flowered / Corrosion / Cradlewake / Cut / Nail me
CD _____ UMD 80371
Universal / May '97 / BMG

MARY BEATS JANE
CD _____ MCD 11135
MCA / Oct '94 / BMG

Mary My Hope

MUSEUM
Wildman childman / Suicide king / Communion / Heads and tales / Death of me / It's about time / Untitled / I'm not singing / I'm not alone
CD _____ ORECD 504
Silvertone / Mar '94 / Pinnacle

Maryland Jazzband

MARYLAND JAZZ BAND
CD _____ BCD 358
GHB / Nov '96 / Jazz Music

Mary's Danish

CIRCA
CD _____ 5117862
Morgan Creek / Jun '92 / PolyGram

Mas Optica

CHOOSE TO SEE MORE
CD _____ IRS 972234
Rising Sun / Jun '94 / Cargo / Plastic Head

Masaray

COSMIC TRANCER
CD _____ PSY 017CD
PSY Harmonics / Oct '95 / Plastic Head

Maschinenzimmer 412

NACHT DURCH STIMME
CD _____ DVLR 7CD
Dark Vinyl / Mar '95 / Plastic Head / World Serpent

Masekela, Hugh

AFRICAN BREEZE
Don't go lose it baby / African breeze / Rainmaker (Motla le pula) / It's raining / Grazing in the grass / Wimoweh / Lady / Politician / Joke of life / Ritual dancer / Zulu wedding / Run no more
CD _____ MOCD 3013
More Music / Feb '95 / Sound & Media

AFRICAN BREEZE
Don't go lose it baby / Motla le pula / African breeze / Seven riffs of Africa / Lion never sleeps, Isikhokhyana / Grazing in the grass / Joke of life / Lady / U-Dwi / Coal train / Zulu wedding / Run no more / Tonight
CD _____ EMPRCD 656
Emporio / Jun '96 / Disc

BEATIN' AROUN' DE BUSH
Steppin' out / Ngena-ngena (instrumental) / Ngena (acapella) / Batsumi (mayibuye i Afrika) / Rock with you / Polina / Languta / Sekunjalo / U-mama / Beatin' aroun' de bush
CD _____ PD 90686
Novus / Jul '92 / BMG

HOPE
Abangoma / Uptownship / Mandela (Bring him back home) / Grazin in the grass / Lady / Until when / Languta / Nomali / Market place / Ntyilo ntyilo (The love bird) / Ha le se (The dowry song) / Stimela (coaltrain)
CD _____ 3202032
Triloka / Feb '94 / New Note/Pinnacle

LASTING IMPRESSIONS OF OOGA BOOGA, THE
Bajabula bonke / Dzinorabiro / Unhlanhia / Cantelope island / U-owi / Masuenada / Abangoma / Mixolydia / Con mucho carino / Where are you going / Mocolo / Bo Masekela / Unohila
CD _____ 5316302
Verve / Aug '96 / PolyGram

NOTES OF LIFE
Mama / Heart breaker / Moments of love / Father of our nation / Whooh Africa / No more cryin' / Talking thoughts / Bone thru the nose / Baby ngiya ku thanda / Somebody is stealin' my car / Thank you Madiba
CD _____ 4844502
Sony Jazz / Jul '96 / Sony

STIMELA
Languta / Child of the earth / Ha lese le di khanna / Coincidence / Bajabula bonke (the healing song) / Grazing in the grass / If there's anybody out there / Mace and grenades / Felicidade / African secret society / Been such a long time / Stimela (coaltrain)
CD _____ VSOPCD 200
Connoisseur Collection / Jun '94 / Pinnacle

Mashu

ELEPHANTS IN YOUR HEAD
Used to / Chariot / Sea beyond / Jus de peche / Elephant / Bell and clay / Passage thru NW / Afaiu / Chariot repriese
CD _____ VP 188CD
Voiceprint / May '97 / Pinnacle

Maslak, Keshavan

EXCUSE ME MR. SATIE (Maslak, Keshavan & Katsuyuki Itakura)
CD _____ CDLR 199
Leo / Oct '94 / Cadillac / Impetus / Wellard

MOTHER RUSSIA
CD _____ CDLR 177
Leo / '90 / Cadillac / Impetus / Wellard

NOT TO BE A STAR (Maslak, Keshavan & Paul Bley)
CD _____ 1201492
Black Saint / Sep '93 / Cadillac / Harmonia Mundi

Masochistic Religion

AND FROM THIS BROKEN CROSS
CD _____ EL 111
Electrip / Sep '94 / Plastic Head

SONIC REVOLUTION
CD _____ EL 102
Electrip / Nov '92 / Plastic Head

Mason, Allison

ISIM SKISM
CD _____ NGCD 549
Twinkle / Jul '96 / Jet Star / Kingdom / SRD

Mason, Barbara

PHILADELPHIA'S LADY LOVE (Best Of Barbara Mason)
Give me your love / Bed and board / Shackin' up / Caught in the middle / 1-2-3 / There's one man between us / You can be with the one you don't love / So he's yours now / Yes I'm ready / From his woman to you / Me and Mrs. Jones / Your old flame / What am I gonna do / Let me in your life / (He wants) the two of us / I miss you Gordon
CD _____ NEXCD 115
Sequel / May '90 / BMG

VERY BEST OF BARBARA MASON, THE
CD _____ NEMCD 680
Sequel / May '96 / BMG

Mason, Ian

AT FARNHAM MALTINGS (Mason, Ian & Rod Mason)
CD _____ BCD 335
GHB / Aug '95 / Jazz Music

Mason, Phil

HERE'S TO YOU (Mason, Phil New Orleans All-Stars)
CD _____ LACD 41
Lake / Mar '95 / ADA / Cadillac / Direct / Jazz Music / Target/BMG

PHIL MASON & NEW ORLEANS ALL STARS
CD _____ BCD 315
GHB / Apr '94 / Jazz Music

SPIRITUALS AND GOSPELS (Mason, Phil New Orleans All-Stars)
Sing on / Let God abide / Precious Lord / Nobody knows the trouble I've seen / Storm is passing over / Lilly of the valley / It is no secret / In the garden / Sweet fields / We shall not be moved / Just a closer walk with thee / When I move to the sky / We shall walk through the streets of the city / Higher ground / Over in the gloryland / When the saints go marching in
CD _____ LACD 64
Lake / Jun '96 / ADA / Cadillac / Direct / Jazz Music / Target/BMG

YOU DO SOMETHING TO ME (Mason, Phil New Orleans All-Stars & Christine Tyrrell)
I wish I were in Dixie / Jersey lightning / My curly headed baby / You do something to me / Bugle call rag / Gulf coast blues / Dreaming the hours away / Mahogany Hall stomp / That teasin' rag / When I grow too old to dream / Sheikh of Araby / My silent love / In the mood / Fair and square / Squeeze me / High society
CD _____ LACD 33
Lake / Jan '95 / ADA / Cadillac / Direct / Jazz Music / Target/BMG

Mason, Rod

STRUTTIN' WITH SOME BARBECUE
CD _____ BLCD 760511
Black Lion / Jun '94 / Cadillac / Jazz Music / Koch / Wellard

Mason, Steve

CONCEPTION VESSEL ONE
CD _____ EXGCD 001
Experience Grooves / Jun '97 / Prime

Mason-Dixon Hobos

MESSERS
CD _____ PT 604001
Part / Jun '96 / Nervous

Masonna

HYPER CHAOTIC
CD _____ V 001
V / Feb '97 / Cargo

Masqualero

RE-ENTER
Re-enter / Li'l Lisa / Heimo gardsjenta / Gaia / Little song / This is no jungle in Baltimore / Find another animal / Stykkevis og delt
CD _____ 8479392
ECM / May '91 / New Note/Pinnacle

Mass Psychosis

FACE
CD _____ 341912
No Bull / Nov '95 / Koch

Massacre

ENJOY THE VIOLENCE
CD _____ SHARK 018 CD
Shark / Mar '91 / Plastic Head

FINAL HOLOCAUST
CD _____ SHARK 014 CD
Shark / Apr '90 / Plastic Head

FROM BEYOND
CD _____ MOSH 027CD
Earache / Jul '91 / Vital

KILLING TIME
CD _____ RECDEC 906
ReR/Recommended / Nov '93 / ReR Megacorp / RTM/Disc

PROMISE
Nothing / Forever torn / Black soil nest / Promise / Bitter end / Bloodletting / Unnameable / Where dwells sadness / Suffering / Inner demon
CD _____ MOSH 096CD
Earache / Jul '96 / Vital

Massed Bands Of HM Forces

MILITARY PAGEANT, A
CD _____ TRTCD 201
TrueTrax / Jun '95 / THE

Massed Pipes & Drums

MARIE CURIE FIELDS OF HOPE
CD _____ LCOM 5247
Lismor / May '95 / ADA / Direct / Duncans / Lismor

Massengill, David

COMING UP FOR AIR
CD _____ FF 590CD
Flying Fish / Apr '94 / ADA / CM / Direct / Roots

RETURN, THE
CD _____ PLUCD 5
Plump / Jun '96 / Grapevine/PolyGram

Massey, Cal

BLUES TO COLTRANE
Blues to Coltrane / What's wrong / Bakai / These are soulful days / Father and son
CD _____ CCD 79029
Candid / Feb '97 / Cadillac / Direct / Jazz Music / Koch / Wellard

Massey, Zane

BRASS KNUCKLES
CD _____ DD 464
Delmark / Aug '94 / ADA / Cadillac / CM / Direct / Hot Shot

SAFE TO IMAGINE
Blues for Awliya / Lady Charlotte / Telekinetics / Sun of son / Saminiego / Quiet dawn / Myra's maya / Things have got to change
CD _____ DE 487
Delmark / Jun '97 / ADA / Cadillac / CM / Direct / Hot Shot

Massive Attack

BLUE LINES
Safe from harm / One love / Blue lines / Be thankful for what you've got / Five man army / Unfinished sympathy / Daydreaming / Lately / Hymn of the big wheel
CD _____ WBRCD 1
Wild Bunch / Jun '91 / EMI

NO PROTECTION (Massive Attack & The Mad Professor)
Radiation ruling the nation / Bumper ball dub / Trinity dub / Cool monsoon / Eternal feedback / Moving dub / I spy / Backward sucking
CD _____ WBRCD 3
Wild Bunch / Feb '95 / EMI

PROTECTION
Protection / Karmacoma / Three / Weather storm / Spying glass / Better things / Euro child / Sly / Heat miser / Light my fire
CD _____ WBRCD 2
Wild Bunch / Sep '94 / EMI

Masso, George

JAZZ IN AMERIKA HAUS VOL.4 (Masso, George Quintet)
CD _____ CD 014
Nagel Heyer / May '96 / Jazz Music

JUST FOR A THRILL
Summer night / Child is born / You brought a new kind of love to me / Soft lights and sweet music / Just for a thrill / Love walked in / Touch of your lips / I remember you / That old feeling / Half of it dearie blues / Sleepin' bee / Fred
CD _____ SKCD 22022
Sackville / Jun '93 / Cadillac / Jazz Music / Swift

LET'S BE BUDDIES (Masso, George & Dan Barrett)
CD _____ ARCD 19127
Arbors Jazz / Nov '94 / Cadillac

MASSO/POLCER/NEW YORK ALLSTARS 1992-1993 (Masso, George Allstars & Ed Polcer/New York Allstars)
CD _____ CD 008
Nagel Heyer / May '96 / Jazz Music

SHAKIN' THE BLUES AWAY (Masso, George & Brian Lemon/Roy Williams)
Lester leaps in / Love is just around the corner / My funny valentine / Shakin' the blues away / Keepin' out of mischief / I've got it bad and that ain't good / Stompin' at the Savoy / There is no greater love / Up a lazy river / Watch what happens / By George / This is all I ask / Sometimes I'm happy
CD _____ ZECD 6
Zephyr / May '97 / Cadillac / Jazz Music / New Note/Pinnacle

WONDERFUL WORLD OF GEORGE GERSHWIN, THE (Masso, George Allstars)
CD _____ CD 001
Nagel Heyer / May '96 / Jazz Music

Master

MASTER
CD NB 040
Nuclear Blast / Jan '91 / Plastic Head

ON THE 7TH DAY GOD CREATED MASTER
CD NB 054CD
Nuclear Blast / Feb '92 / Plastic Head

Master Ace

SLAUGHTAHOUSE
Walk through the valley / Slaughtahouse / Late model sedan / Jeep ass niguh / Big east / Jack B Nimble / Boom bashin' / Mad wunz / Style wars / Who you jackin' / Rollin' wit' um dada / Ain't u da masta / Crazy drunken style / Don't fuck around outro / Saturday nite live
CD BRCD 602
4th & Broadway / Aug '93 / PolyGram

Master Musicians Of Jajouka

JOUJOUKA BLACK EYES
CD SR 87
Le Coeur Du Monde / Jan '96 / Direct

Mastermind

MASTERMIND VOL.2 (Brainstorm)
1st Futility / Code of honor / Wake up America / William Tell overture / Resurrection / Tormented heart / Hammer of fate / Aspirations / Prelude / Ride of the Valkyrie / Nowhere in sight / Firefly / Resolution / Dance of the demons / From the ashes / Breakdown
CD CYCL 052
Cyclops / Apr '97 / Pinnacle

TRAGIC SYMPHONY
Tiger tiger / Power and the passion / All the king's horses / Tragic symphony / Sea of tears / Nothing left to say / Into the void
CD CYCL 026
Cyclops / Jul '95 / Pinnacle

UNTIL ETERNITY
CD CYCL 043
Cyclops / Oct '96 / Pinnacle

Masters At Work

MASTERWORKS (Masters At Work - The Essential Kenlou House Mixes) (Various Artists)
I can't get no sleep: *Masters At Work* / Only love can break your heart: *St. Etienne* / Beautiful people: *Tucker, Barbara* / Buddy: *Cherry, Neneh* / Voices in my mind: *Voices* / Photograph of Mary: *Lorenz, Trey* / My love: *Masters At Work* / We can make it: *Sole Fusion* / Moonshine: *Kenlou* / Can't play around: *Brown, Kathy* / Souffles H: *Mondo Grosso* / I like: *Shanice* / Bounce: *Kenlou*
CD HARMCD 001
Harmless / Sep '95 / RTM/Disc

Masters Hammer

RITUAL
CD OPCD 031
Osmose / Feb '95 / Plastic Head

SLAGRY
CD KRONH 03CD
Osmose / Feb '96 / Plastic Head

Masters Of Reality

SUNRISE ON SUFFERBUS
She got me (when she got her dress on) / JB Witchdance / Jody sings / Rolling green / Ants in the kitchen / VHV / Bicycle / 100 years (of tears on the wind) / TUSA / Tilt-a-whirl / Rabbit one / Madonna / Gimme water / Moon in your pocket
CD 5149472
American / Jun '93 / BMG

Masters, Frank

FRANKIE MASTERS
CD CCD 048
Circle / Oct '93 / Jazz Music / Swift / Wellard

FRANKIE MASTERS & HIS ORCHESTRA 1947 (Masters, Frank Orchestra)
CD CCD 063
Circle / Jul '96 / Jazz Music / Swift / Wellard

Masters, Mark

PRIESTESS (Masters, Mark Jazz Composers Orchestra)
CD 74031
Capri / Nov '93 / Cadillac / Wellard

Masterson, Declan

END OF THE HARVEST
CD CEFCD 148
Gael Linn / Jan '94 / ADA / CM / Direct / Grapevine/PolyGram / Roots

TROPICAL TRAD
Tropical trad / Down the back lane/Kit O'Mahony's / Ravelled Hank of Yarn/Picking the spuds/London jig / Kildare fancy/ Jimmy Reilly's / Young Tom Ennis/King of the pipers / Aisling gheal / Mistress/John Kelly's / When you go home/Caterpillar / Jack Rowe's/The gooseberry bush / Lady Gethin / Munster bank/The mile bush / Hazel woods / Boys of the town/James Kelly's/Bernie Cunnion's jig / Conor Tully's/ Chattering magpie / Hibernian/Contentment is wealth/Katie's fancy / Cambar lassies/ Crowley's/James Kelly / Full moon/Trail of tears/Keep her going
CD SCD 1093
Starc / Jan '94 / ADA / Direct

Masuda, Mikio

SMOKIN' NIGHT
CD JD 3313
JVC / Oct '88 / Direct / New Note/ Pinnacle / Vital/SAM

Masuka, Dorothy

PATA PATA
CD CIDM 1074
Mango / Jul '91 / PolyGram / Vital

Matalex

JAZZ GRUNGE
CD LIP 890382
Lipstick / Feb '96 / Vital/SAM

Matata

FEELIN' FUNKY
Wanna do my thing / Return to you / Good good understanding / Gettin' together / I believed her / Good samaritan / I feel funky / I don't have to worry / Something in mind / I want you / Love is the only way / Gimme some lovin / Talkin' talkin
CD PCOM 1134
President / Mar '94 / Grapevine/PolyGram / President / Target/BMG

WILD RIVER
Wild river / Beautiful burra / Mayo mayo / Jungle warrior / Wowo wowo / I need somebody / Vuana Africa / Pigha yako / Mosala tokosalaka / You've gotta find me / Maendeleo yakenya / Ulimwengu
CD PCOM 1133
President / Mar '94 / Grapevine/PolyGram / President / Target/BMG

Matchbox

MATCHBOX LIVE
CD PEPCD 102
Pollytone / Jan '95 / Nervous / Pollytone

SHADES OF GENE
Dance in the street / In my dreams / Got my eyes on you / Summertime / Everybody's talkin' 'bout Gene / Wedding bells / Ain't misbehavin' / Right here on Earth / Woman love / Be bop a lula / Lonesome fugitive / Git it / Sure fire way / Rocky road blues
CD PEPCD 108
Pollytone / Mar '95 / Nervous / Pollytone

Matching Mole

BBC RADIO 1 IN CONCERT
Instant pussy / Litheing and graceing / Marchides / Part of the dance / Brandy as benge
CD WINCD 063
Windsong / Jun '94 / Pinnacle

LITTLE RED BOOK
Starting in the middle of the day / Marchides / Nan's true hole / Righteous rumba / Brandy as in Benj / Gloria gloom / Flora fidgit / Smoke signal
CD 4714892
Columbia / Mar '97 / Sony

LITTLE RED RECORD
Glora Gloom / God song / Flora Fidgit / Smoke signal / Starting in the middle of the day / Marchides / Nan True's hole / Righteous rhumba / Brandy as in Benj
CD BGOCD 174
Beat Goes On / Jun '93 / Pinnacle

MATCHING MOLE
O Caroline / Instant pussy / Signed curtain / Part of the dance / Instant karma / Dedicated to you but you weren't listening / Beer as in braindeer / Immediate curtain
CD BGOCD 175
Beat Goes On / Mar '93 / Pinnacle

Matera

SAME HERE
CD CDWHIP 024
Sub/Mission / Mar '97 / Cargo

Material

LIVE FROM SOUNDSCAPE
CD DIW 389
DIW / Feb '94 / Cadillac / Harmonia Mundi

MEMORY SERVES
Memory serves / Disappearing / Upriver / Metal test / Conform to the rhythm / Unauthorised / Square dance / Silent land
CD CPCD 8285
Charly / Apr '97 / Koch

ONE DOWN
Take a chance / I'm the one / Time out / Let me have it all / Come down / Holding on / Memories / Don't lose control / Busting out
CD CPCD 8282
Charly / Jan '97 / Koch
CD MPG 74047
Movieplay Gold / Jul '97 / Target/BMG

SECRET LIFE (1979-1981)
CD FREUDCD 011
Jungle / Aug '91 / RTM/Disc / SRD

TEMPORARY MUSIC
OAO / White man / On sadism / Process/ Motion / Discourse / Slow murder / Secret life / Reduction / Heritage / Dark things / Detached / Ciquiri
CD MPG 74044
Movieplay Gold / Jul '97 / Target/BMG
CD CPCD 8286
Charly / May '97 / Koch

Mateu, Jaque

DE VILLAVICENCIO
CD 21044CD
Sonifolk / Jun '94 / ADA / CM

Matheson, Karen

DREAMING SEA
CD SURCD 020
Survival / Oct '96 / ADA / Pinnacle

Matheson, William

SCOTTISH TRADITION VOL.16 (Gaelic Bards & Minstrels)
CD CDTRAX 9016
Greentrax / Feb '94 / ADA / Direct / Duncans / Highlander

Mathews, Ronnie

SHADES OF MONK
CD SSCD 8064
Sound Hills / Jan '96 / Cadillac / Harmonia Mundi

SONG FOR LESLIE
CD RED 1231622
Red / Aug '95 / ADA / Cadillac / Harmonia Mundi

Mathey

CLEPO
CD 087882
Lusafrika / Jan '97 / Stern's

Mathieson, Robert

EBB-TIDE (Mathieson, Pipe Major Robert)
CD LCOM 9038
Lismor / Oct '90 / ADA / Direct / Duncans / Lismor

GRACE NOTES (Mathieson, Pipe Major Robert)
Hornpipes / Air and jigs / March, strathspey and reel / Galician dance / Irish reels and hornpipe / Mazurka / Air and jigs / Dance and jig / Hornpipes / Slip jig and Viennese waltz / Jigs / Airs and reels
CD LCOM 5171
Lismor / Oct '92 / ADA / Direct / Duncans / Lismor

Mathieu, Mireille

CHANTE PIAF
CD 4509940242
Carrere / Apr '97 / Warner Music

Mathis, Johnny

16 MOST REQUESTED SONGS
Chances are / It's not for me to say / Misty / Wild is the wind / Wonderful, wonderful / Maria / Twelfth day of never / Small world / Evergreen / Time for us (Theme from Romeo and Juliet) / What will my Mary say / When Sunny gets blue / Certain smile / Love story / Didn't we / Gina
CD CD 57059
CBS / '91 / Sony

ALL ABOUT LOVE
Let your heart remember / I will walk away / Every beat of my heart / Why goodbye / Like no one in the world / One more night / Let me be the one / Welcome home / Sometime's love's not enough / Could it be love this time
CD 4839312
Columbia / Jun '96 / Sony

CELEBRATION - THE ANNIVERSARY ALBUM
You saved my life / Wonderful, wonderful / It's not for me to say / Chances are / When a child is born / Too much, too little, too late / Last time I felt like this / Stop, look, listen (to your heart) / With you I'm born again / Three times a lady / She believes in me / I will survive / Evergreen / When I need you / Sweet surrender / How deep is your love / We're all alone / Misty / I'd rather be here with you / If it's magic
CD 4674522
CBS / Oct '90 / Sony

COLLECTION, THE
CD CCSCD 343
Castle / Jun '92 / BMG

GLOBAL MASTERS
Bye bye Barbara / Call me irresponsible / April love / Laura / Shangri La / Dream dream dream / When you wish upon a star / Beyond the blue horizon / Limehouse blues / Touch of your lips / More / Granada / After the storm / Hello Dolly / Manhattan / On a wonderful day / Sweetheart tree / Danny boy / Lovers in New York / Something's coming / On a clear day / So nice / Music that makes me dance / Somewhere my love
CD 4871182
Columbia / May '97 / Sony

HITS OF JOHNNY MATHIS, THE
Misty / Love story / Time for us / Twelfth of never / Look of love / This guy's in love with you / When will I see you again / I'm stone in love with you / Killing me softly / Me and Mrs. Jones / First time ever I saw your face / Do you know where you're going to / Moon river / Feelings / How deep is your love / When a child is born
CD 4679532
Columbia / Oct '95 / Sony

LOVE SONGS
Man and a woman / Feelings / Help me make it through the night / How deep is your love / I'll never fall in love again / I'm stone in love with you / I only have eyes for you / Killing me softly with her song / Mandy / Misty / Twelfth of never / First time (ever I saw your face) / Most beautiful girl / Way we were / Too much, too little, too late: *Mathis, Johnny & Deniece Williams* / When I need you / When will I see you again / Where do I begin (love story) / With you I'm born again / Without you / You are the sunshine
CD 4781712
Columbia / Sep '96 / Sony

MERRY CHRISTMAS
Winter wonderland / Christmas song / Sleigh ride / Blue Christmas / I'll be home for christmas / White Christmas / O holy night / What child is this / First Noel / Silver bells / It came upon a midnight clear / Silent night
CD 4814382
Columbia / Nov '96 / Sony

RAINDROPS KEEP FALLING ON MY HEAD/LOVE STORY (2CD Set)
Man and a woman / Odds and ends / Jean / Everybody's talkin' / Bridge over troubled water / Raindrops keep falling on my head / Honey come back / Watch what happens / Something / Alfie / Midnight cowboy / Love story / Rose garden / Ten times forever more / It's impossible / I was there / What are you doing the rest of your life / We've only just begun / Traces / For the good times / My sweet lord / Loss of love
CD Set 4775942
Columbia / Oct '94 / Sony

THAT'S WHAT FRIENDS ARE FOR (Mathis, Johnny & Deniece Williams)
You're all I need to get by / Until you come back to me / You're a special part of my life / Ready or not / Me for you, you for me / Your precious love / Just the way you are / That's what friends are for / I just can't get over you / Touching me with love
CD 4879512
Columbia / Jul '97 / Sony

Matipo Pyramid

AOTEAROA
CD MPP 001
Matipo Pyramid / Jan '97 / Shellshock/ Disc

Matire

MATIRE
CD DOMCD 015
Dominator / Apr '95 / Plastic Head

Matlock, Glen

WHO'S HE WHEN HE'S AT HOME
CD CRECD 191
Creation / May '96 / 3mv/Vital

Matlubeh

TURQUOISE OF SAMARKAND, THE
CD LD 122039
Long Distance / Sep '96 / ADA / Discovery

Matos, Bobby

CHANGO'S DANCE
CD CBCD 001
Cubop / Jul '96 / Timewarp

FOOTSTEPS
CD CBCD 005
Cubop / Nov '96 / Timewarp

Matt Bianco

BEST OF MATT BIANCO, THE
Don't blame it on that girl / Yeh yeh / Sneaking out the back door / Half a minute / Dancing in the street / Fire in the blood / Wap bam boogie / Good times / More than I can bear / Get out of your lazy bed / Matt's mood / Just can't stand it / Whose side are

you on / Say it's not too late / Nervous / We've got the mood
CD 9031725902
WEA / Dec '96 / Warner Music

WHOSE SIDE ARE YOU ON
More than I can bear / No no never / Half a minute / Matt's mood / Get out of your lazy bed / It's getting late / Sneaking out the back door / Riding with the wind / Matt's mood II / Whose side are you on / Big Rosie / Other side
CD 2404722
WEA / Aug '84 / Warner Music

Mattea, Kathy

LOVE TRAVELS
Love travels / Sending me angels / Patiently waiting / If that's what you call love / Further and further away / 455 rocket / I'm on your side / Bridge / All roads to the river / End of the line / Beautiful fool
CD 5328992
Mercury / Jan '97 / PolyGram

READY FOR THE STORM (Favourite Cuts)
Rock me on the water / Last night I dreamed of loving you / Nobody's gonna rain on our parade / Ready for the storm / I will / Standing knee deep in a river (Dying of thirst) / Untasted honey / Mary did you know / Asking us to dance / Few good things remain / Summer of my dreams / Late in the day
CD 5280062
Mercury / Apr '95 / PolyGram

WALKING AWAY A WINNER
CD 5188522
Mercury / May '94 / PolyGram

Matthew's Southern Comfort

MATTHEW'S SOUTHERN COMFORT/ SECOND SPRING
CD BGOCD 313
Beat Goes On / Jun '96 / Pinnacle

Matthews, David

AMERICAN PIE (Matthews, David Trio & Gary Burton)
American pie / Mr. Tambourine man / My back pages / Sound of silence / Sunny / Como en Vietnam / Taste of honey / Moonlight melody
CD 66055005
Sweet Basil / Jul '91 / New Note/Pinnacle

Matthews, David

CRASH
So much to say / Two steps / Crash into me / Too much / # 41 / Say goodbye / Drive in drive out / Let you down / Lie in our graves / Cry freedom / Tripping billies / Proudest monkey
CD 7863669042
RCA / Jul '96 / BMG

UNDER THE TABLE AND DREAMING
Best of what's around / What would you say / Satellite / Rhyme and reason / Typical situation / Dancing nannies / Ants marching / Lover lay down / Jimi thing / Warehouse / Pay for what you get / No 34
CD 07863664492
RCA / Mar '95 / BMG

Matthews, Eric

IT'S HEAVY IN HERE
CD SPCD 312
Sub Pop / Mar '96 / Cargo / Greyhound / Shellshock/Disc

Matthews, Iain

DARK SIDE, THE
CD WM 1025
Watermelon / Oct '94 / ADA / Direct

GOD LOOKED DOWN
CD WMCD 1055
Watermelon / Sep '96 / ADA / Direct

JOURNEYS FROM GOSPEL OAK
Things you gave me / Tribute to Hank Williams / Met her on a plane / Do right woman, do right man / Knowing the game / Polly / Mobile blue / Bride 1945 / Franklin Avenue / Sing me back home
CD CRESTCD 004
Mooncrest / Mar '91 / ADA / Direct

NIGHT IN MANHATTAN
CD TX 2001CD
Taxim / Dec '93 / ADA

ORPHANS & OUTCASTS
CD CDL 102
Dirty Linen / Jun '94 / ADA / Direct

PURE AND CROOKED
Like dominoes / Mercy Street / Hardly innocent mind / Rains of '62 / New shirt / Bridge of Cherokee / Busby's babes / Say no more / Perfect timing / Out of my range / This town's no lady
CD WMCD 1029
Watermelon / Dec '94 / ADA / Direct

SOME DAYS YOU EAT
CD 7559611682
Elektra / Mar '97 / Warner Music

VALLEY HI
CD 7559611692
Elektra / Mar '97 / Warner Music

Matthews, Jessie

DANCING ON THE CEILING
Dancing on the ceiling / When you've got a little springtime in your heart / It's love again / Gangway / Everything's in rhythm with my heart / Your heart skips a beat / One little kiss from you / When you gotta sing you gotta sing / Tony's in town / By the fireside / Head over heels in love / Lord and Lady Whoozis / One more kiss and then goodnight / Let me give my happiness to you / Tinkle tinkle tinkle / Just by your example / I'll stay with you / Three wishes / May I have the next romance with you / Looking around corners for you / Souvenir of love / My river
CD CDAJA 5063
Living Era / Jul '89 / Select

MY HEART STOOD STILL
CD PASTCD 9746
Flapper / Aug '91 / Pinnacle

Matthews, Julie

SUCH IS LIFE
CD RGFCD 030
Road Goes On Forever / Mar '96 / Direct

Matthews, Ronnie

AT CAFE DES COPAINS
CD SKCD 22026
Sackville / Jun '93 / Cadillac / Jazz Music / Swift

DARK BEFORE THE DAWN
CD DIW 604
DIW / Jun '91 / Cadillac / Harmonia Mundi

LAMENT FOR LOVE
CD DIW 612
DIW / Jan '93 / Cadillac / Harmonia Mundi

SELENA'S DANCES
In a sentimental mood / My funny valentine / Stella by starlight / Selena's dance / Body and soul / There is no greater love / Blue bossa / Fee fi fo fum
CD CDSJP 304
Timeless Jazz / Aug '90 / New Note/ Pinnacle

Matthews, Wall

COLOUR OF DUSK, THE (Songs Set To Poems By Dolores Kendrick) (Matthews, Wall & Aleta Greene)
Jenny in love / Ndzeli in passage/Jenny in love / Jenny in tears/Jenny in love / Leah in freedom / Prunella's picnic/Jenny in love / Tildy's prayer / Julia carrying water / Lucy sleeps with Master Muford / Slightly coloured lady / Harriet in mid air / Prayin' ground / Canticle of a black lady
CD CCD 715
Clean Cuts / Nov '96 / Direct / Jazz Music / Wellard

GATHERING THE WORLD
Where the rainbow ends / Go down old Hannah / Night waterman / Pastures of plenty / Clementine / Gathering of the world / She comes from the sea / Ada / Whale
CD CCD 712
Clean Cuts / Nov '96 / Direct / Jazz Music / Wellard

HEART OF THE WINTER, THE
Oh Holy night / Joy to the world/Here we come a-wassailing / We three Kings of Orient are / Greensleeves / Carol of the bells / Little drummer boy / O come o come Emmanuel / Sing we Noel / Hark the herald angels sing/Decks the halls/Angels we have h / Good King Wenceslas/I saw three ships / God rest ye merry gentlemen/Masters in the hall / O little town of Bethlehem / First Noel/Silent night / Jingle bells
CD CCD 710
Clean Cuts / Nov '96 / Direct / Jazz Music / Wellard

RIDING HORSES
Traveller / Rain tin / Maybe next year / Riding horses / Clowns / Old woman / Evening watch / By the fire light / Lion's tooth / Cloak of sorrow / Across the universe / I don't know what to say to you but I love you / Fol de rol / Lover of night / Stolen child
CD CCD 709
Clean Cuts / Nov '96 / Direct / Jazz Music / Wellard

Matthews, Wendy

LILY
Friday's child / Walk away / TKO / Mother can't do / Quiet art / Day you went away / If only I could / Homecoming song / Face of Appalachia / Naming names / Inexorably yours
CD 4509905472
East West / Mar '93 / Warner Music

Mattlar, Marja

LUMI
CD 829322
BUDA / Feb '97 / Discovery

Matto Congrio

MATTO CONGRIO
CD F 1031CD
Sonifolk / Jun '94 / ADA / CM

Matveinen, Liisa

OTTILIA
CD OMCD 55
Olarin Musiiki Oy / Mar '96 / ADA / Direct

Maubuissons

TREONVEL TRANSIT
CD MB 194CD
MB / Nov '96 / ADA

Mauger, Jacques

SHOWCASE FOR TROMBONE
CD DOYCD 027
Doyen / Nov '93 / Conifer/BMG

Maulidi & Musical Party

MOMBASA WEDDING SPECIAL
Mkufu / Hukomi mpelelezi / Shuga dedi / Mume ni moshi wa koko / Fadhila kama kukopa / Vishindo vya mashua / Ukiondoka mpenzi / Hasidi
CD CDORBD 058
Globestyle / May '90 / Pinnacle

Mauriat, Paul

ESCAPADES
CD 3019362
Arcade / Apr '97 / Discovery

LOVE IS BLUE (Best Collection)
CD 3019352
Arcade / Apr '97 / Discovery

SOUNDTRACKS
CD 3019372
Arcade / Apr '97 / Discovery

Maurinier, Charles

ZOUK POWER
CD MCD 51349
Sonodisc / '91 / Stern's

Maurizio

MAURIZIO
CD EFA 222222
M / Jun '97 / SRD

Mauro, Jose

OBNOXIUS
CD CDRSQ 1
Quartin / Feb '96 / New Note/Pinnacle

Mauro, Renata

BALLADS
CD RTCL 805CD
Right Tempo / Jul '96 / New Note/ Pinnacle / Timewarp

Mauro, Turk

JAZZ PARTY
CD BL 011
Bloomdido / Oct '93 / Cadillac

LIVE IN PARIS
CD BL 006
Bloomdido / Oct '93 / Cadillac

PLAYS LOVE SONGS
CD BL 009
Bloomdido / Oct '93 / Cadillac

Mausardi, Guido

ALLA STUDIO 7 (Mausardi, Guido Trio)
CD RTCL 808CD
Right Tempo / Jul '96 / New Note/ Pinnacle / Timewarp

Mause

TEEN RIOT GUNTHER - STRACKTURE
CD EFA 692922
Morbid / Aug '97 / SRD / Vital

Mavericks

MAVERICKS, THE
CD MCAD 10544
MCA / Mar '94 / BMG

SONGS FOR ALL OCCASIONS
Foolish heart / One step away / Here comes the rain / Missing you / All you ever do is bring me down / My secret flame / Writing on the wall / Loving you / If you only knew / I'm not gonna cry for you / Something stupid / Blue moon
CD MCD 11344
MCA / Oct '95 / BMG

WHAT A CRYING SHAME
There goes my heart / What a crying shame / Pretend / I should have been true / Things you said to me / Just a memory / All that heaven will allow / Neon blue / O what a thrill / Ain't found nobody / Losing side of me
CD MCLD 19353
MCA / Apr '97 / BMG

Max Polo

ELEVATION ZERO
CD ACCD 018
ACV / Nov '96 / Plastic Head / SRD

Max Romeo

CROSS OR THE GUN
CD TZ 018
Tappa / Apr '94 / Jet Star

MCCABEE VERSION
CD SONCD 0078
Sonic Sounds / May '95 / Jet Star

ON THE BEACH
CD LG 21042
Lagoon / Feb '93 / Grapevine/PolyGram

WET DREAM
CD CC 2705
Crocodisc / Aug '93 / Grapevine/PolyGram

Maxeen

DIARY, THE
CD SOULCD 35
Soultown / Jan '96 / Jet Star / Pinnacle

Maxi Jazz

ORIGINAL GROOVE JUICE VOL.1 (Maxi Jazz & The Soul Food Cafe)
CD REVCC 012
Revco / Jul '96 / Grapevine/PolyGram / Timewarp

Maximalist

WHAT THE BODY DOESN'T REMEMBER
CD SUBCD 00826
Sub Rosa / '89 / Direct / RTM/Disc / SRD / Vital

Maximum Penalty

INDEPENDENT
CD IJT 003
IJT / Mar '97 / Cargo / Greyhound

Maximum Style

STYLIN'
CD 74321476752
RCA / May '97 / BMG

Maxwell

MAXWELL UNPLUGGED
Suite urban theme / Mello sumthin / Lady suite / This womans work / Whenever wherever whatever / Ascension / Gotta get closer / Til the cops come knockin'
CD 4882922
Columbia / Jul '97 / Sony

MAXWELL'S URBAN HANG SUITE
Urban theme / Welcome / Sumthin' sumthin' / Ascension (don't ever wonder) / Dancewitme / Til the cops come knockin / Whenever wherever whatever / Lonely's the only company / Reunion / Suitelady / Suite theme
CD 4836992
Columbia / Feb '97 / Sony

Maxwell House

MAXWELL HOUSE
Sparticus / River Karnack / Brogal frets / Hilton box / Blossom cod / Cats phat / Window in the mix
CD PF 052CD
Peacefrog / Sep '96 / Mo's Music Machine / Prime / RTM/Disc / Vital

MAXWELL HOUSE VOL.2
Arena of the odd / Stuck up pylons / Almulantarah / In time with nine / Mild flowers / Dream / Finger movement one / Mid heaven express / Tony's phones / Odd
CD PF 067CD
Peacefrog / Apr '97 / Mo's Music Machine / Prime / RTM/Disc / Vital

Maxwell Street Klezmer Band

YOU SHOULD BE SO LUCKY
CD SH 67006
Shanachie / May '96 / ADA / Greensleeves / Koch

Maxwell, David

MAXIMUM BLUES PIANO
Blues don't bother me / Breakdown on the bayou / After hours / Sister Laura Lee / Down at PJ's place / Honky tonk train / Heart attack / Deep into it / Walk the walk / Manhattan wax (boppin' wit da chippies) / Take me on home
CD CDTC 1160
Tonecool / Jun '97 / ADA / Direct

Maxx

TO THE MAXIMUM
CD PULSE 15CD
Pulse 8 / Jul '94 / BMG

May, Billy

BEST OF BILLY MAY VOL.1, THE
CD _______ AERO 1013
Aerospace / Jul '96 / Jazz Music / Montpellier

BEST OF BILLY MAY VOL.2, THE (May, Billy & His Orchestra)
CD _______ AERO 1014
Aerospace / Jul '96 / Jazz Music / Montpellier

CAPITOL YEARS, THE
Mad about the boy / When your lover has gone / Perfidia / Top hat, white tie and tails / You're driving me crazy / If I had you / Lulu's back in town / Rose Marie / Show me the way to go home / Say it isn't so / Star eyes / March of the toys / If I were a bell / Till there was you / Brassmens holiday / Pawn ticket / Rhythm is our business / Blues in the night / In the mood cha cha / Autumn leaves / No strings / Loads of love / Late late show
CD _______ CDEMS 1472
Capitol / Mar '93 / EMI

GIRLS AND BOYS ON BROADWAY/ SWEETEST SWINGIN' SOUNDS OF...
Girls against the boys / My darling, my darling / If I were a bell / Where did we go / Out / Guys and dolls / Rich butterfly / Heart / Old fashioned girl / Till there was you / Girls and boys / I've never been in love / I gotta have you / No strings / Sweetest sounds / Love makes the world go / Nobody told me / Loads of love / Maine / Eager beaver / Look no further / Orthadox fool / La la la / Man whose has everything / Be my host
CD _______ CTMCD 118
EMI / Jun '97 / EMI

SORTA MAY/ SORTA DIXIE (May, Billy & His Orchestra)
Thou swell / Blues in the night / Chicago / All you want to do is dance / You go to my head / Soon / In a Persian market / Just one of those things / You're the top / Donkey serenade / Deep purple / They didn't believe me / Oh, by jingo / South Rampart street parade / Down home rag / Sugar foot strut / Sheik of Araby / Sorta blues / Panama / Riverboat shuffle / Five foot two / Eyes of blue (has anybody seen my gal)
CD _______ STD 1051
Creative World / '87 / Swift / Wellard

May, Brian

BACK TO THE LIGHT
Dark / Back to the light / Love token / Resurrection / Too much love will kill you / Driven by you / Nothin' but blue / I'm scared / Last horizon / Let your heart rule your head / Just one life / Rollin' over
CD _______ CDPCSD 123
Parlophone / Oct '92 / EMI

LIVE AT THE BRIXTON ACADEMY
Back to the light / Driven by you / Tie your mother down / Love token / Headlong / Love of my life / Let your heart rule your head / Too much love will kill you / Since you've been gone / Now I'm here / Guitar extravaganza / Resurrection / Last horizon / We will rock you / Hammer to fall
CD _______ CDPCSD 150
Parlophone / Jan '94 / EMI

May, Brian

THEMES AND DREAMS AND LOVE SONGS
CD _______ HADCD 190
Javelin / Nov '95 / Henry Hadaway / THE

May, Brother Joe

BEST OF BROTHER JOE MAY, THE
CD _______ NASH 4507
Nashboro / Feb '96 / Pinnacle

LIVE 1952-1955
God leads his children along / I'm a child of the king / Move on up a little higher / He's waiting for me / Old ship of Zion / Vacation in heaven / Jesus is real to me / All of my burdens (ain't that good news) / He's the one / I want Jesus on the road I travel / How I got over / Hold to God's unchanging hand / By and by when I get home / Speak, Lord Jesus / He'll understand and say well done
CD _______ CDCHD 565
Ace / Mar '94 / Pinnacle

THUNDERBOLT OF THE MIDDLE WEST
Old ship of zion (live) / WDIA plug / Search me lord / How much more of life's burden can we bear / In that day / I'm gonna live the life I sing about in my songs / Day is past and gone / Do you know him / I just can't keep from cryin' sometime / I want Jesus on the road I travel / Precious Lord / What do you know about Jesus / Our father / I'll make it somehow / Your sins will find you out / Remember me / I claim Jesus first / It's a long, long way / Don't forget the name of the lord / He'll understand and say Well Done / I'm happy working for the Lord / Grow closer / Jesus knows / Vacation in heaven / Going home
CD _______ CDCHD 466
Ace / Mar '93 / Pinnacle

May, Derrick

MAYDAY MIX
Mayday's intro / Message is love: *Fruit Loop* / Dance: *Earth People* / Make up your mind: *Groove Essentials* / French kiss: *Lil' Louis* / Lonely disco dancer: *House Proud People* / You are my heaven/Scuba: *King Britt* / Soundz in my head: *DJ Sneak* / Prelude: *New Soul Fusion* / Little suntin suntin: *Johnson, Paul* / Time for love: *House Of Jazz* / Preacher man: *Green Velvet* / Cosmic coast: *Farris, Gene* / Tribal life: *Andre, Hayden Project* / What has joined by GOD: *Dashwood, Kramer* / Alarm: *Mills, Jeff* / Spank spank: *Phuture* / 1999: *DJ Milton* / Good girls: *Designer Music* / Club MCM: *Club MCM* / Masterplan: *Mills, Jeff* / Serial operations: *Foundation Sounds* / Dancer: *Purpose Maker* / Mindless funk: *Freaks* / Fructose: *Styles Of The Abstract* / Convextion: *Convextion* / Relish: *Substance* / Get horny: *Basement Jaxx* / Shimmer: *Aubrey* / Nite drive: *Jibaros* / Eu nao: *Basement Jaxx* / Meditative fusion: *Silent Phase*
CD _______ OPENCD 005
CD Set _______ OPENLP 005
Open / Jul '97 / Amato Disco / Pinnacle / Prime / Vital

May Linn

MAY LINN
Soldier / Joey don't care / In the shelter of the night / Breakout / Dangerous games / Backstreet life / Fit for fight / Long way from home
CD _______ SHARK 007CD
Shark / Jun '88 / Plastic Head

May, Simon

NEW VINTAGE
CD _______ CDART 102
ARC / Oct '94 / ADA / ARC Music

May, Tina

FUN (May, Tina Quartet)
CD _______ 33JAZZ 013CD
33 Jazz / Jun '93 / Cadillac / New Note/ Pinnacle

IT AIN'T NECESSARILY SO
It ain't necessarily so / Maestro / Rosy glow / Chelsea bridge / They can't take that away from me / Wanting to be home / Les feuilles mortes / Solitude / Writers block
CD _______ 33JAZZ 017
33 Jazz / May '95 / Cadillac / New Note/ Pinnacle

NEVER LET ME GO (May, Tina Quartet)
CD _______ 33JAZZ 005CD
33 Jazz / Jun '93 / Cadillac / New Note/ Pinnacle

TIME WILL TELL
Stolen moments / Only time will tell / 'Round midnight / Do nothin' 'til you hear from me / I'd rather be in Hippodelphia / Where is love / Look of love / Hawk-man / After the love has gone / What's new
CD _______ 33JAZZ 029
33 Jazz / May '96 / Cadillac / New Note/ Pinnacle

May, Tom

RIVER AND THE ROAD
CD _______ FE 1420
Folk Era / Dec '94 / ADA / CM

Maya

CROSS OF SILENCE
CD _______ MAYACD 1
Maya / May '95 / Direct

Mayafra Combo

MAYAFRA
CD _______ RTCL 802CD
Right Tempo / Jul '96 / New Note/ Pinnacle / Timewarp

Mayall, John

1982 REUNION CONCERT, THE
CD _______ OW 30008
One Way / Apr '94 / ADA / Direct / Greyhound

BANQUET IN BLUES, A
CD _______ MCAD 22075
One Way / Apr '94 / ADA / Direct / Greyhound

BARE WIRES (Mayall, John & The Bluesbreakers)
Bare wires suite / Where did I belong / Start walking / Open a new door / Fire / I know now / Look in the mirror / I'm a stranger / No reply / Hartley quits / Killing time / She's too young / Sandy
CD _______ 8205382
London / Jun '88 / PolyGram

BLUES ALONE, THE
Brand new start / Please don't tell / Down the line / Sonny boy blow / Marsha's mood / No more tears / Catch that train / Cancelling out / Harp man / Brown sugar / Broken wings / Don't kick me
CD _______ 8205352
London / Jun '88 / PolyGram

BLUES BREAKERS (Mayall, John & Eric Clapton)
All your love / Hideaway / Little girl / Another man / Double crossin' time / What'd I say / Key to love / Parchman farm / Have you heard / Ramblin' on my mind / Steppin' out / It ain't right
CD _______ 8000862
Deram / Aug '90 / PolyGram

BLUES FOR THE LOST DAYS
Dead city / Stone cold deal / All those heroes / Blues for the lost days / Trenches / One in a million / How can you live like that / Some other day / I don't mind / It ain't safe / Sen-say-shun / You are for real
CD _______ ORECD 547
Silvertone / Apr '97 / Pinnacle

BLUES FROM LAUREL CANYON
Vacation / Walking on sunset / Laurel Canyon home / 2401 / Ready to ride / Medicine man / Somebody's acting like a child / Bear / Miss James / First time alone / Long gone midnight / Fly tomorrow
CD _______ 8205392
Deram / Jan '88 / PolyGram

CROSS COUNTRY BLUES
CD _______ OW 30009
One Way / Apr '94 / ADA / Direct / Greyhound

CRUSADE (Mayall, John & The Bluesbreakers)
Oh pretty woman / Stand back baby / My time after awhile / Snowy wood / Man of stone / Tears in my eyes / Driving sideways / Death of JB Lenoir / I can't quit you baby / Streamline / Me and my woman / Checkin' up on my baby
CD _______ 8205372
Deram / Jun '88 / PolyGram

DIARY OF A BAND VOL.2, THE (Mayall, John & The Bluesbreakers)
CD _______ 8440302
Deram / '92 / PolyGram

HARD CORE PACKAGE, A
CD _______ MCAD 22071
One Way / Apr '94 / ADA / Direct / Greyhound

HARD ROAD, A (Mayall, John & The Bluesbreakers)
Hard road / It's over / You don't love me / Stumble / Another kinda love / Hit the highway / Leaping Christine / Dust my blues / There's always work / Same way / Supernatural / Top of the hill / Some day after a while (you'll be sorry) / Living alone
CD _______ 8204742
London / Jul '89 / PolyGram

JOHN MAYALL
CD _______ EXP 024
Experience / May '97 / TKO Magnum

LAST OF THE BRITISH BLUES, THE
Tucson lady / Parchman farm / There's only now / Teaser / Hideaway / Bear / Lonely birthday / Lowdown blues / It must be there
CD _______ MCAD 22074
One Way / Apr '94 / ADA / Direct / Greyhound

LIFE IN THE JUNGLE (Charly Blues - Masterworks Vol. 4)
Ridin' on the L and M / Help me / All your love / I ain't got you / One life to live / Last time / Fascinating lover / Life in the jungle
CD _______ CDBM 4
Charly / Apr '92 / Koch

LOOKING BACK (Mayall, John & The Bluesbreakers)
Mr. James / Blues city shake down / They call it stormy Monday / So many roads / Looking back / Sitting in the rain / It hurts me too / Double trouble / Suspicions (part 2) / Jenny / Picture on the wall
CD _______ 8203312
Deram / Jan '89 / PolyGram

LOTS OF PEOPLE (Live In L.A. 1976)
CD _______ MCAD 22073
One Way / Apr '94 / ADA / Direct / Greyhound

NEW YEAR, NEW BAND, NEW COUNTRY (Live In L.A. 1976)
CD _______ MCAD 22072
One Way / Apr '94 / ADA / Direct / Greyhound

NOTICE TO APPEAR
CD _______ MCAD 22070
One Way / Apr '94 / ADA / Direct / Greyhound

PRIMAL SOLOS
Intro (Maudie) / It hurts to be in love / Have you ever loved a woman / Bye bye bird / Hoochie coochie man / Intro (Look at the girl) / Wish you were mine / Start walking
CD _______ 8203202
Deram / Nov '88 / PolyGram

RETURN OF THE BLUESBREAKERS
CD _______ AIM 1004CD
Aim / Oct '93 / ADA / Direct / Jazz Music

ROADSHOW BLUES
Why worry / Road show / Mama talk to your daughter / Big man / Lost and gone / Mexico City / John Lee Boogie / Reaching for a mountain / Baby, what you want me to do
CD _______ CDTB 060
Thunderbolt / Oct '88 / TKO Magnum

ROOM TO MOVE (2CD Set)
Laws must change / California / Room to move / Don't waste my time / Counting the days / When I go / To a Princess / Nature's disappearing / Took the car / My pretty girl / Prisons on the road / Accidental suicide / Boogie Albert / Television eye / Memories / Nobody cares / Bad luck time / Country road / Dry throat / Worried man / Red sky / Ten years are gone / Driving til the break of day / Better pass you by / I still care / Brand new band / Gasoline blues / Going to make my time / Deep down feelings
CD Set _______ 5172912
Polydor / Apr '96 / PolyGram

SENSE OF PLACE, A (Mayall, John & The Bluesbreakers)
I want to go / Send me down to Vicksburg / Sensitive kid / Let's work together / Black cat moan / All my life / Congo square / Without her / Jacksborn highway / I can't complain / Sugarcane
CD _______ IMCD 167
Island / Mar '93 / PolyGram

SPINNING COIN
CD _______ ORECD 537
Silvertone / Mar '97 / Pinnacle

STORMY MONDAY
Oh pretty woman / Sitting in the rain / Long gone midnight / No reply / Hartley quits / Jenny / Room to move / They call it Stormy Monday / Don't pick a flower / Thinking of my woman / Don't waste my time / Plan your revolution / Took the car / Time's moving on
CD _______ 5507172
Spectrum / Sep '94 / PolyGram

THRU THE YEARS
Crocodile walk / My baby is sweeter / Crawling up a hill / Mama talk to your daughter / Alabama blues / Out of reach / Greeny / Curly / Missing you / Please don't tell / Your funeral and my trial / Suspicions (part 1) / Knockers step forward / Hide and seek
CD _______ 8440282
Deram / Jan '91 / PolyGram

TURNING POINT
Laws must change / Saw Mill Gulch Road / I'm gonna fight for you JB / So hard to share / California / Thoughts about Roxanne / Room to move
CD _______ BGOCD 145
Beat Goes On / Jun '92 / Pinnacle

WAKE UP CALL
CD _______ ORECD 527
Silvertone / Apr '93 / Pinnacle

Mayaula Mayoni

TO DO ONE'S BEST (Mayaula Mayoni & Tpok Jazz)
CD _______ NG 025
Ngoyarto / Jan '97 / Stern's

Mayer, John

ASIAN AIRS (Mayer, John Indo-Jazz Fusions)
Chakkar / Megha / Yaman / Song before sunrise / Pilu / Bear / Jhaptal / Mela / Asian airs
CD _______ NI 5499
Nimbus / Nov '96 / Nimbus

Mayerl, Billy

BILLY MAYERL
CD _______ PASTCD 7053
Flapper / Oct '94 / Pinnacle

BILLY MAYERL FAVOURITES
In my garden / Hop-o-my thumb / Four aces suite / Ten cents a dance / Jasmine / Mignonette / Limehouse blues / Eskimo shivers / All-of-a-twist / Sing you sinners / Millionaire kid medley / Chopsticks / Puppets suite no 3 / Nimble fingered gentleman / Ace of spades / Balloons / Aquarium suite / Desert song medley / Anytime's the time to fall in love / Match parade
CD _______ CDGRS 1265
Grosvenor / Jun '93 / Grosvenor

VERSATILITY OF BILLY MAYERL
Golliwog / Judy / Punch / Honky tonk - A rhythmical absurdity / Sweet nothin's / Wistaria / Personal course in modern syncopation / Rag doll / Sennen Cove / Wedding of the painted doll / Old fashioned girls / He loves and she loves / It don't do nothing but rain / Drink to me only with thine eyes / Rainbow / Chopsticks / Masculine women, feminine men / Lay me down to sleep in Carolina / I ain't got nobody / Toodle-oo-sal / Hire purchase system / When lights are low in Cairo / More we are together
CD _______ PASTCD 9708
Flapper / '90 / Pinnacle

Mayes, Sally

OUR PRIVATE WORLD
CD _______ VSD 5529
Varese Sarabande / Mar '95 / Pinnacle

Mayfield, Curtis

BACK TO THE WORLD
Back to the world / Future shock / Right on for the darkness / Future song (love a good woman, love a good man) / If I were a child again / Can't say nothin' / Keep on trippin'
CD _______ **MPG 74029**
Movieplay Gold / Jan '94 / Target/BMG
CD _______ **CPCD 8040**
Charly / Jun '94 / Koch

BBC RADIO 1 IN CONCERT
Superfly / It's alright / I'm so proud / Billy Jack / Freddie's dead / People get ready / We've gotta have peace / Homeless / Move on up / Invisible / (Don't worry) If there's a hell below, we're all gonna go
CD _______ **WINDCD 052**
Windsong / Jan '94 / Pinnacle

BEST OF CURTIS MAYFIELD, THE
Move on up / Get on down / Pusherman / Superfly / (Don't worry) if there's a hell below, we're all gonna go / Freddie's dead / Give me your love / We got to have peace / Tripping out / So in love / People get ready / Right on for the darkness / Wild and free / Do wap is strong in here / Keep on keeping on
CD _______ **NTMCD 538**
Nectar / Feb '97 / Pinnacle

BEST OF CURTIS MAYFIELD, THE
Move on up / Give me your love / Never stop loving me / Tripping out / Soul music / Right combination / Hard times / So in love / Freddie's dead / (Don't worry) If there's a hell below, we're all gonna go / Future shock
CD _______ **SUMCD 4119**
Sound & Media / May '97 / Sound & Media

CURTIS
(Don't worry) If there's a hell below, we're all gonna go / Other side of town / Wild and free / Makings of you / Miss Black America / Move on up / We the people who are darker than blue / Give it up
CD _______ **MPG 74026**
Movieplay Gold / Jan '94 / Target/BMG
CD _______ **CPCD 8036**
Charly / Jun '94 / Koch

CURTIS IN CHICAGO
Superfly / For your precious love / I'm so proud / Preacher man / If I were a child again / Duke of Earl / Love oh love / Amen
CD _______ **CPCD 8046**
Charly / Sep '94 / Koch

CURTIS LIVE (2CD Set)
Mighty mighty / I plan to stay a believer / We've only just begun / People get ready / Star and stare / Check out your mind / Gypsy woman / Makings of you / We the people who are darker than blue / (Don't worry) If there's a hell below, we're all gonna go / Stone junkie / We're a winner
CD _______ **CPCD 8038**
Charly / Jun '94 / Koch
CD Set _______ **MPG 74176**
Movieplay Gold / Mar '94 / Target/BMG

CURTIS MAYFIELD
Move on up / Soul music / In your arms again (shake it) / Do do wap is strong in here / Hard times / So in love / You are, you are / Pusherman / Never stop loving me / Tripping out / Ain't no love lost / Superfly / Freddie's dead / This year / Give me your love / (Don't worry) If there's a hell below, we're all gonna go
CD _______ **12364**
Laserlight / May '94 / Target/BMG

CURTIS MAYFIELD'S CHICAGO SOUL (Various Artists)
You can't hurt me no more: *Opals* / What would you do: *Jackson, Walter* / I'm the one who loves you: *Major Lance* / I can't work no longer: *Butler, Billy & The Enchanters* / Good times: *Chandler, Gene* / Monkey time: *Major Lance* / Patty cake: *Artistics* / (I've got a feeling) You're gonna be sorry: *Butler, Billy & The Enchanters* / Think nothing about it: *Major Lance* / Nevertheless (I love you): *Butler, Billy & The Enchanters* / It's all over: *Jackson, Walter* / Found true love: *Butler, Billy & The Enchanters* / You'll want me back: *Major Lance* / That's what mama say: *Jackson, Walter* / Gotta get away: *Butler, Billy & The Enchanters* / Funny (not much): *Jackson, Walter* / You're gonna be sorry: *Opals* / Gonna get married: *Major Lance*
CD _______ **4810292**
Columbia / Jan '96 / Sony

DEFINITIVE COLLECTION, THE (2CD Set)
(Don't worry) if there's a hell below, we're all gonna go / Get down / Give it up / We got to have peace / Beautiful brother of mine / Move on up / Superfly / Freddie's dead / Future shock / If I were only a child again / Kung fu / To be invisible / Sweet exorcist / Billy Jack / So in love / Mothers' son / Only you babe / Soul music / Party night / I'm gonna win your love / Need someone to love / Do wap is strong in here / Short eyes/Freak free free free / Do it all night / This year / You're so good to me / Between you baby and me / Tripping out / Something to believe in / Love's sweet sensation / Baby it's you / Homeless / Do be down
CD Set _______ **CPCD 81892**
Charly / Oct '96 / Koch

DO IT ALL NIGHT
Do it all night / No goodbyes / Party party / Keeps me loving you / In love, in love, in love / You are, you are
CD _______ **CPCD 8050**
Charly / Sep '94 / Koch

GET DOWN TO THE FUNKY GROOVE
Get down / Superfly / Freddie's dead / Move on up / Wild and free / (Don't worry) If there's a hell below, we're all gonna go / Little child runnin' wild / Pusherman / If I were only a child again / Beautiful brother of mine / Now you're gone / Keep on trippin' / Right on for the darkness
CD Set _______ **CPCD 8034**
Charly / Feb '95 / Koch

GIVE GET TAKE AND HAVE
CD _______ **CPCD 8070**
Charly / Jun '94 / Koch

GOT TO FIND A WAY
Love me (right in the pocket) / So you don't love me / Prayer / Mother's son / Cannot find a way / Ain't no love lost
CD _______ **CPCD 8048**
Charly / Sep '94 / Koch

GROOVE ON UP
CD _______ **CPCD 8043**
Charly / Jun '94 / Koch

HEARTBEAT
Tell me, tell me / What is my woman for / Between you baby and me / Victory / Over the hump / You better stop / You're so good to me / Heartbeat
CD _______ **CPCD 8071**
Charly / Jun '94 / Koch

I'M SO PROUD (A Jamaican Tribute To Curtis Mayfield) (Various Artists)
It's all right: *Morgan, Derrick* / Keep on pushing: *Lloyd & Glen* / Queen majesty: *Techniques* / My voice is insured for half a million dollars: *Alcapone, Dennis* / Dedicate my song to you: *Jamaicans* / Gypsy woman: *Uniques* / Rocksteady time: *Progressions* / I'm so proud: *White, Joe* / Little boy blue: *Pat Kelly* / Man's temptation: *Brown, Noel 'Bunny'* / He will break your heart: *Silvertones* / My woman's love: *Uniques* / That's what love will do: *Gaylads* / Long long winter: *Marley, Bob & The Wailers* / Soulful love: *Pat Kelly* / Closer together: *Smith, Slim* / I've been trying: *Heptones* / I gotta keep on moving: *Marley, Bob & The Wailers* / Queen Majesty: *Chosen Few* / Gypsy man: *Griffiths, Marcia*
CD _______ **CDTRL 376**
Trojan / May '97 / Direct / Jet Star

LIVE IN EUROPE
Intro / Freddie's dead / We gotta have peace / People get ready / Move on up / Back to the world / Gypsy woman / Pusherman / We've only just begun / When seasons change / (Don't worry) If there's a hell below, we're all gonna go
CD _______ **CPCD 8178**
Charly / Mar '96 / Koch

LOVE IS THE PLACE/HONESTY
CD _______ **NEMCD 783**
Sequel / Mar '96 / BMG

MAN LIKE CURTIS, A
Move on up / Superfly / (Don't worry) If there's a hell below, we're all gonna go / You are, you are / Give me your love / Never stop loving me / Tripping out / Soul music / This year / Ain't no love lost / Pusherman / Freddie's dead / Do do wap is strong in here / Hard times / In your arms again (Shake it) / So in love
CD _______ **MUSCD 007**
MCI Music / Nov '92 / Disc / THE

MOVE ON UP
Move on up / Pusherman / Get down / Future shock / Superfly / We got to have peace / Beautiful brother of mine / Can't say nothin' / Freddie's dead / Kung Fu / So in love / (Don't worry) If there's a hell below, we're all gonna go / If I were only a child again
CD _______ **APH 102802**
Audiophile Legends / Apr '96 / Total/BMG

MOVE ON UP
Move on up / Love to keep you in mind / In your arms again (Shake it) / Power for the people / Eddie you should know better / Soul music / Superfly / Makings of you / Hard times / Ain't no love lost / Keeps me loving you / Miss Black America
CD _______ **306532**
Hallmark / May '97 / Carlton

NEVER SAY YOU CAN'T SURVIVE
Show me / Just want to be with you / When we're alone / Never say you can't survive / I'm gonna win your love / All night long / When you used to be mine / Sparkle
CD _______ **CPCD 8049**
Charly / Sep '94 / Koch

NEW WORLD ORDER
CD _______ **9362463482**
Warner Bros. / Feb '97 / Warner Music

PEACE, LOVE AND UNDERSTANDING (3CD Set)
CD Set _______ **NXTCD 286**
Sequel / Mar '97 / BMG

PEOPLE GET READY (Live At Ronnie Scott's)
Little child runnin' wild / It's alright / People get ready / Freddie's dead / Pusherman / I'm so proud / We've gotta have peace / Billy Jack / Move on up / To be invisible
CD _______ **CLACD 329**
Castle / '93 / BMG

ROOTS
Get down / Keep on keeping on / Underground / We got to have peace / Beautiful brother of mine / Now you're gone / Love to keep you in my mind
CD _______ **MPG 74027**
Movieplay Gold / Jan '94 / Target/BMG
CD _______ **CPCD 8037**
Charly / Jun '94 / Koch

SHORT EYES (Original Soundtrack)
Do wap is strong in here / Back against the wall / Need someone to love / Heavy dude / Short eyes / Break it down / Another fool in love / Father confessor
CD _______ **CPCD 8183**
Charly / Jun '96 / Koch

SOMETHING TO BELIEVE IN
Love me love me now / Never let me go / Tripping out / People never give up / It's alright / Something to believe in / Never stop loving me
CD _______ **CPCD 8073**
Charly / Jun '94 / Koch

SUPERFLY (Original Soundtracks)
CD _______ **CPCD 8039**
Charly / Jun '94 / Koch

SWEET EXORCIST
Ain't got time / Sweet exorcist / To be invisible / Power to the people / Kung fu / Suffer / Make me believe in you
CD _______ **CPCD 8047**
Charly / Sep '94 / Koch

TAKE IT TO THE STREETS
Homeless / Got to be real / Do be down / Who was that lady / On and on / He's a fly guy / Don't push / I mo git U sucka
CD _______ **CPCD 8179**
Charly / Apr '96 / Koch

THERE'S NO PLACE LIKE AMERICA TODAY
Billy Jack / When seasons change / So in love / Jesus / Blue monday people / Hard times / Love to the people
CD _______ **CPCD 8069**
Charly / Jun '94 / Koch

TRIBUTE TO CURTIS MAYFIELD, A (Various Artists)
Choice of colors: *Knight, Gladys* / It's alright: *Winwood, Steve* / Let's do it again: *Repercussions & Cutis Mayfield* / Billy Jack: *Kravitz, Lenny* / Look into your heart: *Houston, Whitney* / Gypsy woman: *Springsteen, Bruce* / You must believe me: *Clapton, Eric* / I'm so proud: *Isley Brothers* / Fool for you: *Marsalis, Branford & The Impressions* / Keep on pushing: *Campbell, Tevin* / Making of you: *Franklin, Aretha* / Woman's got soul: *King, B.B.* / People get ready: *Stewart, Rod* / (Don't worry) If there's a hell below, we're all gonna go: *Walden, Narada Michael* / I've been trying: *Collins, Phil* / I'm the one who loves you: *Wonder, Stevie* / Amen: *John, Elton & The Sounds of Blackness*
CD _______ **9362455002**
WEA / Feb '94 / Warner Music

TRIPPING OUT
CD _______ **CPCD 8065**
Charly / Nov '94 / Koch

VERY BEST OF CURTIS MAYFIELD, THE
CD _______ **CCSCD 806**
Castle / Apr '96 / BMG

Mayfield, Percy

MEMORY PAIN
Please send me someone to love / Strange things happen / Two hearts are greater than one / Big question / My blues / Nightless lover / How deep is the well / Ruthie Mae / My heart / Lonesome highway / Lonely one / I ain't gonna cry no more / Memory pain / You are my future / Kiss tomorrow goodbye / Advice (For men only) / I need love so bad / Does anyone care for me / It's good to see you baby / Sugar mama - Peachy papa / You were lyin' to me / Voice within / Please believe me / Diggin' the moonglow / Hit the road Jack
CD _______ **CDCHD 438**
Ace / Jan '93 / Pinnacle

POET OF THE BLUES
Please send me someone to love / Prayin' for your return / Strange things happening / Life is suicide / What a fool I was / Lost love / Nightless lover / Advice (for men only) / Cry baby / Lost mind / I dare you baby / Hopeless / Hunt is on / River's invitation / Big question / Wasted dream / Louisiana / Bachelor blues / Get way back / Memory pain / Loose ups / You don't exist anymore / Nightmare / Baby, you're rich / My heart is cryin'
CD _______ **CDCHD 283**
Ace / Oct '90 / Pinnacle

Mayhams, Norridge

NORRIDGE MAYHAMS & THE BLUE CHIPS 1936 (Mayhams, Norridge & The Blue Chips)
CD _______ **DOCD 5488**
Document / Nov '96 / ADA / Hot Shot / Jazz Music

Mayhem

DE MYSTERIIS DOM SATHANAS
CD _______ **ANTIMOSH 006CD**
Deathlike Silence / Mar '94 / Plastic Head

DEATHCRUSH
CD _______ **ANTIMOSH 003CD**
Deathlike Silence / Oct '96 / Plastic Head

LIVE IN LEIPZIG
CD _______ **AV 004**
Avant Garde / Aug '96 / Plastic Head / RTM/Disc

TRIBUTE TO EURONYMOUS (Various Artists)
CD _______ **NR 009CD**
Necropolis / Sep '96 / Plastic Head

Mayko

RASA BHAVA
CD _______ **SR 9606**
Silent / Feb '97 / Cargo / Plastic Head

Mayock, Emer

MERRY BITS OF TIMBER
CD _______ **KEY 121CD**
Key / Nov '96 / ADA / CM

Mayoiga

HIMEKAMI
CD _______ **21089**
Sonifolk / Aug '96 / ADA / CM

Mayor, Simon

ENGLISH MANDOLIN, THE
St. Paul's suite 1 / Molly on the shore / Nell Gwyn / Three English folk tune settings / Musick's hand-maid / Capriol suite
CD _______ **ACS 025CD**
Acoustics / Jul '95 / ADA / Koch

MANDOLIN ALBUM, THE
Jump the gun/Reelin' over the rooftops / Two seagulls call from my Birch Tree / Maple flames / Arrival of the Queen Of Sheba / Exchange / When summer comes again / Concerto for Mandolin / Villanelle / Tune for a mop fair / Jericho waltz / Wheelin' and dealin' / Sarabande / Double / Mosstrooper medley
CD _______ **CDACS 012**
Acoustics / May '97 / ADA / Koch

SECOND MANDOLIN ALBUM, THE
Hungarian dance no. 1 / Buttermere waltz / Huppings / Finale spirituoso / Three part invention / Pipped at the post / Two days in Tuscany / Great bear / Concerto for two mandolins / Old man of the mountain / Sonata / Hornpipe / Dead sea dances
CD _______ **CDACS 014**
Acoustics / Jul '97 / ADA / Koch

WINTER WITH MANDOLINS
CD _______ **CDACS 015**
Acoustics / Aug '95 / ADA / Koch

Mayor, Violaine

DANSE AVEC LES FEES
CD _______ **VM 01CD**
Hent Telenn / Nov '96 / ADA

Mays, Bill

CONCORD DUO SERIES VOL.7 (Mays, Bill & Ed Bickert)
Sometime ago / Taking a chance on love / Gee baby ain't I good to you / On the trail / Quietly / Do nothin' 'til you hear from me / Crazy she calls me / Bick's bag
CD _______ **CCD 4626**
Concord Jazz / Nov '94 / New Note/ Pinnacle

ELLINGTON AFFAIR, AN
I'm just a lucky so and so / Satin doll / Something to live for / My azure / Don't you know / Dancers in love / Single petal of a rose / Passion flower / Little African flower / Wig wise / Daydream / I let a song go out of my heart
CD _______ **CCD 4651**
Concord Jazz / Jul '95 / New Note/Pinnacle

GONE WITH THE WIND (Mays, Bill & Keith Copeland/Martin Wind)
Gone with the wind / I remember you / Lagrimo agradecida (A thankful tear) / Black Jack / Najul / Someone to watch over me / Born to be blue / High street / Sevillo / I should care / Sad story / Midnight song for Thalia / Gone with the wind (Bass solo)
CD _______ **CD 5116**
September / Feb '94 / Cadillac / Kingdom

LIVE AT MAYBECK RECITAL HALL VOL.26
Nightingale sang in Berkeley Square / I wish I knew / Stompin' at the Savoy / Boardwalk blues / Lush life / I'm confessin' that I love you / Guess I'll hang my tears out to dry /

Jitterbug waltz / Thanksgiving prayer / Why did I choose you / Never let me go / Grandpa's spells
CD _____ CCD 4567
Concord Jazz / Aug '93 / New Note/ Pinnacle

MAYS IN MANHATTAN
Manhattan / Summer in Central Park / UMMG (Upper Manhattan Medical Group) / New York state of mind / All across the city / Sunday in New York / 317 E. 32nd St. / Autumn in New York / '39 World's fair
CD _____ CCD 4738
Concord Jazz / Dec '96 / New Note/ Pinnacle

Mays, Lyle

LYLE MAYS
Highland aire / Teiko / Slink / Mirror of the heart / Alaskan suite: Northern Lights invocation ascent / Close to home
CD _____ GFLD 19193
Geffen / Mar '93 / BMG

SWEET DREAMS
Feet first / August / Chorinho / Possible straight / Hangtime / Before you go / Newborn / Sweet dreams
CD _____ GFLD 19194
Geffen / Mar '93 / BMG

Mayte

CHILD OF THE SUN
Child of the sun / In your gracious name / If I love U 2nite / Rhythm of your heart / Ain't no place like u / House of brick / Love's no fun / Baby don't cry / However much u want / Mo' better / If I love u 2nite / Most beautiful boy in the world
CD _____ 0061622NPG
Edel / Jul '97 / Pinnacle

Maytones

BROWN GIRL IN THE RING
CD _____ CDTRL 363
Trojan / Oct '95 / Direct / Jet Star

FUNNY MAN
CD _____ JMC 200206
Jamaican Gold / Nov '93 / Grapevine/ PolyGram / Jet Star

LOVER MAN
Lover man / Ready baby / People are changing / Jah is the master / How long / Show us the way / No ease up / Never gonna run away / One awy / Judgement day / Serious world / Who feel it / Don't show off / Take your time
CD _____ RN 7027
Rhino / Aug '97 / Grapevine/PolyGram / Jet Star

LOVING REGGAE
Let it be me / Loving reggae / Funny man / Serious love / Billy Goat / Ital Queen / Cool you up / As long as you love me / One way / Contiquros / Take your time / Come along / Baby give me the right loving / Ready baby / Zion land / Do good / Africa we want to go / De dey wid di money / Lover man / Holy ground / Be careful / Don't show off / Boat to Zion
CD _____ CDGR 127
Charly / Apr '97 / Koch

Mayweather, George

WHUP IT, WHUP IT (Mayweather, George 'Earring')
CD _____ CDTC 1147
Tonecool / May '94 / ADA / Direct

Maze

ANTHOLOGY
While I'm alone / Lady of magic / Working together / Golden time of day / Feel that you're feelin' / Lovely inspiration / Southern girl / Joy and pain / Happy feelings / Reason / Running away / Before I let go / Love is the key / Never let you down / I wanna thank you / Your own kind / Back in stride / Too many games / I wanna be with you / When you love someone
CD Set _____ CTMCD 332
EMI / Aug '97 / EMI

BACK TO BASICS
Nobody knows what you feel inside / Love is / Morning after / Laid back girl / What goes up / In time / All night long / Don't wanna lose your love / Twilight
CD _____ 9362452972
Warner Bros. / Sep '93 / Warner Music

CAN'T STOP THE LOVE (Maze & Frankie Beverly)
Back in stride / Can't stop the love / Reaching down inside / Too many games / I want to feel I'm wanted / Magic / Place in my heart
CD _____ MUSCD 502
MCI Original Masters / Sep '94 / Disc / THE

JOY AND PAIN (Maze & Frankie Beverly)
Changing times / Look in your eyes / Family / Roots / Joy and pain / Southern girl / Happiness
CD _____ RE 2092
Razor & Tie / Jun '96 / Koch

LIFELINES VOL.1 (Maze & Frankie Beverly)
Joy and pain / golden time of day / Happy feelin's / Back in stride / Before I let go / Running away / while I'm alone / Southern girl / Joy and pain (original LP version) / Before I let go
CD _____ CDEST 2111
Capitol / Nov '89 / EMI

MAZE LIVE IN NEW ORLEANS
You / Changing times / Joy and pain / Happy feelin's / Southern girl / Look at California / Feel that you're feelin / Look in your eyes / Running away / Before I let you go / We need love to live / Reason
CD _____ CUTLEGCD 1
Beechwood / Jul '95 / Beechwood/BMG / Pinnacle

SILKY SOUL
Silky soul / Can't get over you / Just us / Somebody else's arms / Love's on the run / Change our ways / Songs of love / Mandela / Midnight / Africa
CD _____ K 9258022
WEA / Mar '94 / Warner Music

Maze Of Torment

FORCE, THE
CD _____ CR 6503CD
Corrosion / Jun '97 / Plastic Head

Mazelle, Kym

GOLD COLLECTION, THE
Woman of the world / No one can love you more than me / Useless (I don't need you now) / Don't scandalize my name / Love strain / Never in a million years / Was that all it was / If it's love you want / Skin I'm in / Crazy 'bout the man / This love will never die / Wait / Just what it takes / Got to get you back
CD _____ CDGOLD 1018
EMI Gold / Mar '96 / EMI

Mazeltones

LATKES & LATTES
CD _____ GV 159CD
Global Village / May '94 / ADA / Direct

Mazetier, Louis

ECHOES OF CAROLINA (Mazetier, Louis & Francois Rilhac)
CD _____ SOSCD 1218
Stomp Off / Oct '92 / Jazz Music / Wellard

IF DREAMS COME TRUE (Mazetier, Louis & Neville Dickie)
CD _____ SOSCD 1289
Stomp Off / Nov '95 / Jazz Music / Wellard

Mazey Fade

SECRET WATCHERS BUILT THE WORLD
CD _____ WIGCD 9
Domino / Apr '94 / Vital

Mazinga Phaser

CRUISING IN THE NEON
CD _____ MAZPHA 007
Womb Tunes / May '97 / Greyhound

Mazur, Marilyn

CIRCULAR CHANT (Mazur, Marilyn & Pulse Unit)
Circular chant / Celldance / Louise / Pulsens sang / Gong piece 1 / Reeds duo / Amulu / Chordal piece / Gong piece 2 / Green bones / Balophone tune / Circular chant
CD _____ STCD 4200
Storyville / Mar '95 / Cadillac / Jazz Music / Wellard

FUTURE SONG
First dream / Saturn song / When I go to the mountain / Urstro / Rainbow birds / Aina's travels / Rainbow birds / Well of clouds / Rainbow birds / Seventh dream
CD _____ VBR 21052
Vera Bra / Aug '92 / New Note/Pinnacle / Pinnacle

SMALL LABYRINTHS
World of gates / Drum tunnel / Electric cave / Dreamcatcher / Visions in the wood / Back to the dreamfrog mountain / Creature talk / See there / Valley of fragments / Enchanted place / Castle of air / Holey
CD _____ 5336792
ECM / Mar '97 / New Note/Pinnacle

Mazurek, Robert

BADLANDS (Mazurek, Robert/Eric Anderson)
Arthur's seat / Angel eyes / Badlands / Deep purple / Kay's birthday / Evert time we say goodbye / Edinburgh nights / Stranger in paradise / I fall in love to easily / Nomad
CD _____ HEPCD 2065
Hep / Jun '95 / Cadillac / Jazz Music / New Note/Pinnacle / Wellard

GREEN AND BLUE (Mazurek, Robert & Eric Alexander)
Streets of Raith/Uptown / 5000 miles away / White river / In walked boom / Green and blue / Black river / Skylark / Other place
CD _____ HEPCD 2067
Hep / Jan '97 / Cadillac / Jazz Music / New Note/Pinnacle / Wellard

MAN FACING EAST
Manaus / Pretty blue butterfly / Flora's house / Tenderly / Man facing east / Roselis / Freddies blues / I wish I knew / Dragoon blue
CD _____ HEPCD 2059
Hep / Sep '94 / Cadillac / Jazz Music / New Note/Pinnacle / Wellard

Mazzy, Jimmy

HALFWAY TO HEAVEN (Mazzy, Jimmy & Eli Newberger/Joe Muranyi)
CD _____ SOSCD 1319
Stomp Off / Mar '97 / Jazz Music / Wellard

SHAKE IT DOWN (Mazzy, Jimmy & Eli Newberger)
CD _____ SOSCD 1109
Stomp Off / Jan '97 / Jazz Music / Wellard

Mazzy Star

AMONG MY SWAN
Disappear / Flowers in December / Rhymes of an hour / Cry, cry / Take everything / Still cold / All your sisters / I've been let down / Roseblood / Happy / Umbilical / Look on down from the bridge
CD _____ CDEST 2288
Parlophone / Nov '96 / EMI

SHE HANGS BRIGHTLY
Halah / Blue flower / She hangs brightly / I'm sailing / Give you my lovin / Be my angel / Taste of blood / Ghost highway / Free / Before I sleep
CD _____ CDEST 2196
Capitol / May '93 / EMI

SO TONIGHT THAT I MIGHT SEE
Fade into you / Bells ring / Mary of silence / Five string serenade / Blue light / She's my baby / Unreflected / Wasted / Into dust / So tonight that I might see
CD _____ CDEST 2206
Capitol / Sep '97 / EMI

Mbango, Charlotte

CHARLOTTE MBANGO VOL.3
CD _____ CD 54681
Sonodisc / '91 / Stern's

Mbarga, Prince Nico

AKI SPECIAL
CD _____ ROUCD 11545
Rounder / May '88 / ADA / CM / Direct

M'boom

COLLAGE
Circles / It's time / Jamaican sun / Street dance / Mr. Seven / Quiet place
CD _____ SNCD 1059
Soul Note / '86 / Cadillac / Harmonia Mundi / Wellard

Mbuli, Mzwakhe

CHANGE IS PAIN
Many years ago / Behind the bars / Drumbeats / Now is the time / Change is pain / Day shall dawn / Ignorant / Triple M / What a shame / I have travelled / Spear has fallen / Last struggle / Ngizwa ubgina bguzwa usajako / Sisi bayasinyanyisa
CD _____ PIR 3 CD
World Circuit / Sep '88 / ADA / Cadillac / Direct / New Note/Pinnacle

MC 900ft Jesus

HELL WITH THE LID OFF
Greater God / UFO's are real / I'm going straight to heaven / Talking to the spirits / Place of lonliness / Real black angel / Shut up / Spaceman / Too bad
CD _____ NETCD 015
Nettwerk / Feb '90 / Greyhound / Pinnacle / Vital

ONE STEP AHEAD OF THE SPIDER
New moon / But if you go / If I only had a brain / Stare and stare / Buried at sea / Tiptoe through the inferno / Garacias pepe / New Year's eve / Bill's dream / Rhubarb
CD _____ 74321242312
American / Mar '95 / BMG

WELCOME TO MY DREAM
CD _____ NET 035CD
Nettwerk / Oct '91 / Greyhound / Pinnacle / Vital

MC Brainz

BRAINWASHED
CD _____ WRA 81532
Wrap / Jun '96 / Koch

MC Breed

BEST OF MC BREED, THE
CD _____ WRA 8150
Wrap / Nov '95 / Koch

FUNKAFIED
CD _____ RAP 60132
Rapture / Sep '94 / Plastic Head

NEW BREED, THE
CD _____ WRA 81202CD
Wrap / Jan '94 / Koch

TO DA BEAT CH'ALL
CD _____ WRA 81542
Wrap / Jul '96 / Koch

MC Det

OUT OF DET
Stick up / So simple / Can't sample det / Freeform reality / We nuh ease up / Abducted / Junglist massive / Elevate / Can U feel / Dub plate special / Amber / Nuclear det / Hands clappin' / Let me recommend / Tonic's reality
CD _____ SOURCD 005
SOUR / Jul '96 / SRD

MC Duke

ORGANISED RHYME
Organised rhyme / We go to work / Free / Throw your hands in the air / I'm riffin' / Miracles / For the girls / Gotta get your own / Running man / Alternative argument
CD _____ DUKE 1CD
Music Of Life / Nov '89 / Grapevine/ PolyGram

MC Hammer

FUNKY HEADHUNTER, THE
Oaktown / It's all good / Somethin' for the OG's / Don't stop / Pumps and a bump / One mo time / Clap yo' hands / Break 'em off somethin' propa / Don't fight the feeling / Goldie in me / Sleepin' on a master plan / It's all that / Funky headhunter / Pumps and a bump reprise (bump Teddy bump) / Help Lord (won't you come) / Do it like this / Heartbreaka (is what they call me)
CD _____ 74321188622
RCA / Mar '94 / BMG

GREATEST HITS
U can't touch this / Too legit to quit / Turn this mutha out / Pray / Addams groove / Do not pass me by / Here comes the Hammer / Have you seen her / Gaining momentum / Pump it up (here's the news) / They put me in the mix
CD _____ CTMCD 300
Capitol / Feb '97 / EMI

LET'S GET IT STARTED
Intro (Turn this mutha out) / Let's get it started / Ring 'em / Cold go MC Hammer / You're being served / Turn this mutha out / It's gone / They put me in the mix / Son of the king / That's what I said / Feel my power / Pump it up (here's the news)
CD _____ CDEST 2140
Capitol / Apr '91 / EMI

MC Lyte

AIN'T NO OTHER
Intro / Brooklyn / Ruffneck / What's my name yo / Li'l Paul / Ain't no other / Hard copy / Fuck that motherfucking bullshit / Intro / I go on / One nine nine three / Never heard nothin' like this / Can I get some dap / Let me adem / Steady fucking / Who's house / I cram to understand U
CD _____ 7567922302
Elektra / Jul '93 / Warner Music

BAD AS I WANNA B
CD _____ 7559617812
Atlantic / Aug '96 / Warner Music

MC Potts

STRAIGHT TO YOU
CD _____ AVEXCD 45
Avex / Jun '96 / 3mv/Pinnacle

MC Shy D

COMEBACK, THE
CD _____ WRA 81242
Wrap / Apr '94 / Koch

MC Solaar

PARADISIAQUE
Intro / Gangster moderne / Zoom / Dakota / Les temps changent / Les boys bandent / Wonderbra / Protege tibia / Paradisiaque / Tournicotic / Le sens de la vie / Illico presto / Daydreamin' / Les pensees sont des flowers / Le 11eme choc / Quand le soleil devient froid
CD _____ 5337692
Talkin' Loud / Jun '97 / PolyGram

PROSE COMBAT
Aurade / Obsolette / Nouveau Western / A la claire fontaine / Superstarr / La concubine de l'hemoglobine / Devotion / Temps mort / L'nmiaccd htck72kpdp / Sequelles / Dieu ait son ame / A dix de mes disciples / La paim justifie les moyene / Relations humaines / Prose combat

CD 5212892
Talkin' Loud / Apr '94 / PolyGram

MC5

AMERICAN RUSE, THE
CD NERCD 2001
Alive / Feb '95 / RTM/Disc / Shellshock/ Disc

BABES IN ARMS
Shakin' street / American ruse / Skunk (sonically speaking) / Tutti frutti / Poison / Gotta keep movin' / Tonite / Kick out the jams / Sister / Future now / Gold / I can only give you everything / One of the guys / I just don't know / Looking at you
CD RE 122CD
ROIR / Nov '94 / Plastic Head / Shellshock/ Disc

BACK IN THE USA
Tutti frutti / Tonight / Teenage lust / Let me try / Looking at you / High school / Call me animal / American ruse / Shakin' street / Human being lawnmower / Back in the USA
CD 8122710332
Atlantic / Mar '93 / Warner Music

HIGH TIME
Sister Anne / Baby won't ya / Miss X / Gotta keep movin' / Future/now / Poison / Over and over / Skunk (sonically speaking)
CD 8122710342
WEA / Mar '93 / Warner Music

ICE PICK SLIM
CD ALIVECD 8
Alive / Feb '97 / RTM/Disc / Shellshock/ Disc

KICK OUT THE JAMS
Ramblin' rose / Kick out the jams / Come together / Rocket reducer No.62 / Borderline / Motor city is burning / I want you right now / Starship
CD 7559740422
Elektra / Jan '93 / Warner Music

LIVE DETROIT 68/69
Intro / Come together / I want you right now / I believe / Come on down (High rise) / It's a man's man's man's world / Looking at you / Fire of love
CD 895050
New Rose / Nov '94 / ADA / Direct / Discovery

POWER TRIP
CD ALIVE 005CD
Alive / Oct '94 / RTM/Disc / Shellshock/ Disc

M'Carver, Kimberly

BREATHE THE MOONLIGHT
Silver wheeled pony / Whistle down the wind / Cryin' wolf / Borrowed time / Only in my dreams / Jose's lullaby / Springtime friends / My way back home to you / Carnival man / Serious doubt / Texas home
CD CDPH 1129
Philo / '90 / ADA / CM / Direct

INHERITED ROAD
CD CDPH 1179
Philo / Dec '94 / ADA / CM / Direct

MD 45

CRAVING, THE
Hell's motel / Day the music died / Fight hate / Designer behaviour / Creed / My town / Voices / Nothing is something / Hearts will bleed / No pain / Roadman
CD CDEST 2286
Capitol / Jun '96 / EMI

MDC

HEY COP, IF I HAD A FACE LIKE YOURS
CD MDC 812
R Radical / Mar '92 / SRD

METAL DEVIL COKES
CD WB 3110CD
We Bite / Apr '94 / Plastic Head

MILLIONS OF DAMN CHRISTIANS
CD WB 3022CD
We Bite / Sep '93 / Plastic Head

MILLIONS OF DEAD COPS
Business on parade / Dead cops / America's so straight / Born to die / Corporate deathburger / I remember / Violent rednecks / John Wayne was a nazi / Dick for brains / I hate work / My family is a little weird / Greedy and pathetic / Church and state / Kill the light / American achievements
CD WB 3109CD
We Bite / Apr '94 / Plastic Head

MORE DEAD COPS
CD WB 3033CD
We Bite / Sep '93 / Plastic Head

SHADES OF BROWN
CD WB 3112CD
We Bite / Apr '94 / Plastic Head

SMOKE SIGNALS
CD WB 3155CD
We Bite / Oct '96 / Plastic Head

Me

HARMONISE OR DIE
Together alone / We must be / Funny thing / Here comes everybody / Dreambleeding / To the stars / Yousong / Water / Where do you think / Guilty feet fall foul / Quester / Paul / Happy place / Threticular grussock / Can't stop / Sweepin dust / Upsmile down / Don't paint me in your colours / Pygmy songs
CD PGCD 026
Pop God / Jun '93 / Vital

Me First & The Gimme ...

HAVE A BALL (Me First & The Gimme Gimmes)
CD FAT 554CD
Fatwreck Chords / May '97 / Plastic Head

Mead, Steven

EUPHONY (Mead, Steven & Royal Northern College Of Music Brass Band)
Euphonium concerto / Carrickfergus / Euphony / Aubade / Return to Sorrento / Euphonium music / Nappoli / Midnight euphonium / Better world
CD QPRL 082D
Polyphonic / Dec '96 / Complete/Pinnacle

WORLD OF THE EUPHONIUM VOL.2, THE
Concert gallop / Solo de Concurse / Fantasia / Swan / Fantasie contertante / Song for Ina / Ransomed / Libesfreud / Largo elegaico / Panache / Two Faure duets / Ball of fire / Horo staccato
CD QPRZ 017D
Polyphonic / Nov '95 / Complete/Pinnacle

WORLD OF THE EUPHONIUM, THE
Sonata in F / Partita Op 89 / Vocalise / Soliloquy IX / Fantasy for euphonium / Variations for ophicleide / Sonata euphonica / Apres un reve / Weber's last waltz / Heart to heart / Barcarolle / New carnival of Venice
CD QPRZ 014D
Polyphonic / Jul '92 / Complete/Pinnacle

Meade, Tyson

MOTORCYCLE CHILDHOOD
CD ECHO 100
Echo Static / Apr '97 / Cargo

Meadows, Marion

BODY RHYTHM
My cherie amour / Be with you / South beach / Later on / Get involved / One more chance / Kool / Marion's theme / Wanna be loved by you / Body rhythm / Deep waters / Summer's over / Lift
CD 07863666232
Novus / Aug '95 / BMG

FORBIDDEN FRUIT, THE
Red lights / Always on my mind / Asha / Forbidden fruit / Whenever your heart wants to song / You will never know what you're missing / Back2back / Save the best for last / Somewhere island / Comin' home to you / Nocturnal serenade
CD 01241631672
Novus / Mar '94 / BMG

Mean Cat Daddies

GHOST OF YOUR LOVE
Sally-Ann / Just a memory / Sign of the times / Why do I cry / Drivin' all night / I can tell / Decision time / Tell me / Am I the one / Ghost of your love / Midnight cruise / Losing game / Waiting for you / This is the end
CD NERCD 079
Nervous / Oct '94 / Nervous / TKO Magnum

Mean Red Spiders

DARK HOURS
Love in a bottle / Live and let live / Arms open wide / Just can't stop / Feel so bad / Drunken fool / Dangerous game / Heaven above / Teacher / Happy on my own / Murder my baby / Love won't save you now / Sure can't hide / Lie and cheat you blind / No more work song / Coming back for more / Call me long distance
CD GBCD 1
Gray Brothers / Sep '95 / Pinnacle

Mean Season

GRACE
CD NA 024CD
New Age / Jul '96 / Plastic Head

Meanies

GANGRENOUS
CD EFA 123012
Vince Lombard / Mar '94 / SRD

Meanstreak

ROADKILL
Roadkill / Nostradamus / Lost stranger / Congregation / Searching forever / It seems to me / Warning
CD CDMFN 89
Music For Nations / Oct '88 / Pinnacle

Meantime

WELCOME: MOTHER EARTH
Crusin' the hood / Lugnut / Down by the farm intro / Down by the farm / Tortoise shell sky / Detour / Two in one / Welcome Mother Earth
CD JUST 802
Justin Time / Aug '96 / Cadillac / New Note/ Pinnacle

Meantime

UNSOPHISTICATED
CD SPV 08056822
Wolverine / Sep '94 / Cargo / Plastic Head

Meanwhile

REMAINING RIGHT
CD RAD 001CD
Nuclear Blast / Jun '95 / Plastic Head

Meat Beat Manifesto

99%
CD BIAS 180 CD
Play It Again Sam / May '90 / Discovery / Plastic Head / Vital

ORIGINAL FIRE
CD INTD 90127
Nothing / Jun '97 / Arabesque

SATYRICON
Postsounds / Mindstream / Drop / Original control (version 1) / Your mind belongs to the state / Circles / Sphere / Brainwashed this way/Zombie/That shirt / Original control (version 2) / Euthanasia / Edge of no control (part 1) / Edge of no control (part 2) / Untold stories / Son of Sam / Track 15 / Placebo
CD BIAS 202CD
Play It Again Sam / Aug '92 / Discovery / Plastic Head / Vital

SUBLIMINAL SANDWICH
Sound innovation / Nuclear bomb / Long periods of time / 1979 / Future worlds / What's your name / She's unreal / Phone calls from the dead / Asbestos lead asbestos / Mass producing hate / Radio mellotron / Assasinator / Cancer / We done / Transmission / No purpose no design / Addiction / Lucid dream
CD BIAS 302CD
CD BIAS 302CDX
Play It Again Sam / May '96 / Discovery / Plastic Head / Vital

VERSION GALORE
CD BIAS 192CD
Play It Again Sam / Feb '91 / Discovery / Plastic Head / Vital

Meat Loaf

12" MIXES
Bat out of hell / Dead ringer for love / Read 'em and weep / If you really want to / Razor's edge
CD 4501312
Epic / Mar '93 / Sony

ALIVE IN HELL
CD PMCD 7002
Pure Music / Oct '94 / BMG

BAD ATTITUDE
Bad attitude / Modern girl / Nowhere fast / Surf's up / Piece of the action / Jumping the gun / Cheatin' in your dreams / Don't leave your mark on me / Sailor to a siren
CD 259049
Arista / Dec '93 / BMG

BAT OUT OF HELL
You took the words right out of my mouth / Heaven can wait / All revved up and no place to go / Two out of three ain't bad / Bat out of hell / For cryin' out loud / Paradise by the dashboard light / Praying for the end of time / Man and woman / Dead ringer for love
CD 4804112
Epic / Jul '95 / Sony

BAT OUT OF HELL VOL.2 (Back Into Hell)
I'd do anything for love (But I won't do that) / Life is a lemon and I want my money back / Rock 'n' roll dreams come through / It just won't quit / Out of the frying pan (and into the fire) / Objects in the rear view mirror may appear closer... / Wasted youth / Everything louder than everything else / Good girls go to heaven (bad girls go everywhere) / Back into hell / Lost boys and golden girls
CD CDV 2710
Virgin / Aug '93 / EMI

BLIND BEFORE I STOP
Execution day / Rock 'n' roll mercenaries / Getting away with murder / One more kiss (night of the soft parade) / Blind before I stop / Burning down / Standing on the outside / Masculine / Man and a woman / Special girl / Rock 'n' roll here
CD 257741
Arista / Dec '93 / BMG

COLLECTION, THE
Bat out of hell / Bad attitude / One more kiss (Night of the soft parade) / Execution day / Jumpin' the gun / Sailor to a siren / Modern girl / Special girl / Standing on the outside / Cheatin' in your dreams / Masculine / Rock 'n' roll mercenaries
CD 74321152182
Ariola Express / Sep '93 / BMG

DEAD RINGER
Peel out / I'm gonna love her for both of us / More than you deserve / I'll kill you if you don't come back / Read 'em and weep / Nocturnal pleasure / Dead ringer for love / Everything is permitted
CD CD 83645
Epic / Nov '87 / Sony

DEAD RINGER/MIDNIGHT AT THE LOST AND FOUND (2CD Set)
Peel out / I'm gonna love her for both of us / More than you deserve / I'll kill you if you don't come back / Read 'em and weep / Nocturnal pleasure / Dead ringer for love / Everything is permitted / Razor's edge / Midnight at the lost and found / Wolf at your door / Keep driving / Promised land / You never can be too sure about the girl / Priscilla / Don't you look at me like that / If you really want to / Fallen angel
CD Set 4784862
Epic / Mar '95 / Sony

HITS OUT OF HELL
Bat out of hell / Read 'em and weep / Midnight at the lost and found / To out of three ain't bad / Dead ringer for love / Modern girl / I'm gonna love her for both of us / You took the words right out of my mouth / Razor's edge / Paradise by the dashboard light
CD 4504472
Epic / Mar '91 / Sony

LIVE AND KICKING
Bat out of hell / Two out of three ain't bad / Modern live / Blind before I stop / Piece of the action / Rock 'n' roll mercenaries / Paradise by the dashboard light / Masculine / Took the words / Midnight at the lost and found / Bad attitude / Medley: Johnny B Goode/Slow down/Jailhouse rock/Blue suede
CD 74321339422
Camden / Jan '96 / BMG

MEAT LOAF & FRIENDS
Paradise by the dashboard light / Holding out for a hero: *Tyler, Bonnie* / You took the words right out of my mouth / We belong to the night: *Foley, Ellen* / Bad for good: *Steinman, Jim* / What's the matter baby: *Foley, Ellen* / Two out of three ain't bad / Faster than the speed of night: *Tyler, Bonnie* / Dead ringer for love / Night out: *Foley, Ellen* / Total eclipse of the heart: *Tyler, Bonnie* / Left in the dark: *Steinman, Jim*
CD 4724192
Epic / Oct '94 / Sony

MIDNIGHT AT THE LOST AND FOUND
Razor's edge / Midnight at the Lost and found / Wolf at your door / Keep driving / Promised land / You never can be too sure about the girl / Priscilla / Don't you look at me like that / If you really want to / Fallen angel
CD 4503602
Epic / Jan '94 / Sony

PRIMECUTS
Modern girl / Getting away with murder / Bat out of hell / Surf's up / Blind before I stop / Bad attitude / Jumpin' the gun / Two out of three ain't bad / Paradise by the dashboard light (live) / Rock 'n' roll mercenaries
CD 260363
Arista / Dec '89 / BMG

ROCK 'N' ROLL HERO
Bad attitude / Sailor to a siren / One more kiss / Jumpin' the gun / Special girl / Modern girl / Masculine / Don't leave your mark on me / Rock 'n' roll mercenaries / Cheatin' in your dreams / Blind before I stop / Piece of the action / Rock 'n' roll hero / Paradise by the dashboard light / Bat out of hell
CD 74321393362
Camden / Jun '96 / BMG

WELCOME TO THE NEIGHBOURHOOD
When the rubber meets the road / I'd lie for you (and that's the truth) / Original sin / 45 seconds of ecstasy / Runnin' for the red light (I gotta life) / Fiesta de Las Almas Perdidas / Left in the dark / Not a dry eye in the house / Amnesty is granted / If this is the last kiss (let's make it last all night) / Martha / Where angels sing
CD CDV 2799
Virgin / Oct '95 / EMI

Meat Puppets

1
CD SST 009CD
SST / May '93 / Plastic Head

HUEVOS
CD SST 150CD
SST / May '93 / Plastic Head

II
CD SST 019CD
SST / May '93 / Plastic Head

MIRAGE
CD SST 100CD
SST / Jul '87 / Plastic Head

MONSTERS
CD ______ SST 253CD
SST / Oct '89 / Plastic Head

NO JOKE
Scum / Nothing / Head / Taste of the sun / Vampires / Predator / Poison arrow / Eyeball / For free / Cobbler / Inflatable / Swet ammonia / Chemical garden
CD ______ 8286652
London / Oct '95 / PolyGram

NO STRINGS ATTACHED
CD ______ SST 265CD
SST / May '93 / Plastic Head

OUT MY WAY
CD ______ SST 049CD
SST / Sep '87 / Plastic Head

TOO HIGH TO DIE
Violet eyes / Never to be found / We don't exist / Severed Goddess head / Flaming heart / Shine / Backwater / Roof with a hole / Station / Things / Why / Evil love / Comin' down / Lake of fire
CD ______ 8284842
London / Feb '94 / PolyGram

UP ON THE SUN
CD ______ SST 039CD
SST / Aug '87 / Plastic Head

Meatfly

FATNESS
CD ______ DISC 1CD
Vinyl Japan / '92 / Plastic Head / Vinyl Japan

Meathead

MEATHEAD AGAINST THE WORLD (Various Artists)
Introoutofthisworld / Large Amerikan jaw: *Meathead* / Schweinhund: *Cop Shoot Cop* / Filler: *Meathead* / Black room: *Zeni Geva* / Disgraceland: *Meathead* / Cancer beat: *Babyland* / Godbastardgod: *Meathead* / Digraceland: *Meathead* / Possible end, 47: *Meathead* / Tigress of Babylon: *Pain Teens* / Godbastardgod: *Meathead* / Schweinhund: *Cop Shoot Cop* / Large Amerikan Jaw: *Meathead*
CD ______ WHIP 023
Submission / Dec '96 / SRD

PROTECT ME FROM WHAT I WANT
Would u / Feel like / Pool / Let it out-hit me / Wipeout / Rotula / Pianola / Broken spine / My money / Timoti / Gravida code / Wipe out all their pain / Canterbury
CD ______ DY 00232
Dynamica / May '97 / Koch

Meathook Seed

EMBEDDED
Famine sector / Furned grave / My infinity / Day of conceiving / Cling to an image / Wilted remnant / Forgive / Focal point blur / Embedded / Visible shallow self / Sea of tranquility
CD ______ MOSH 088CD
Earache / Mar '93 / Vital

Meatlocker

TRIANGLE OF PAIN
CD ______ PRLCD 7913011
Progress Red / Apr '95 / Plastic Head

Meatmen

CRIPPLED CHILDREN SUCK
CD ______ TG 59 CD
Touch & Go / Feb '91 / SRD

WAR OF THE SUPERBIKE
CD ______ GK 022CD
Go-Kart / Oct '96 / Greyhound / Pinnacle

Mecano

AIDALAI
El fallo positivo / El uno, el dos, el tres / Bilando salsa / El 7 Septiembre / Naturaleza muerta / 1917 / Una rosa es una rosa / El lago artificial / Tu / Dalai Lama / El peon del rey de negras / JC Sentia
CD ______ 261786
Ariola / Nov '91 / BMG

Mecca Normal

EAGLE AND THE POODLE, THE
Breathing in the dark / Her ambition / Revival of cruelty / Rigid man in an ice age / When you build a house without doors / Prize arm / Mrs. McGillvary / Now that you're here / Kingdom without weather / Cave in / Drive at / Peach-a-vanilla / When you know
CD ______ OLE 1862
Matador / Apr '96 / Vital

SITTING ON SNAPS
Vacant night sky / Something to be said / Crimson dragnet / Frozen rain / Only heat trapped / Inside your heart / Alibi / Pamela makes waves / Bepo's room / Cyclone / Gravity believes
CD ______ OLE 1122
Matador / Feb '95 / Vital

Meco

BEST OF MECO, THE
Star Wars theme/Cantina / Empire strikes back medley / Close Encounters / Wizard Of Oz / Star Trek medley / Topsy / Meco's theme/3W57 / Moondancer / Spooky / Can you read my mind / Werewolf (loose in London) / Star Wars / Other galactic funk / Asteroid field/Finale
CD ______ 5532552
Mercury / Mar '97 / PolyGram

Mecolodians

JOE BAIZA/RALPH GORODETZSKY/ TONY CICERO
CD ______ EMY 1472
Enemy / Nov '94 / Grapevine/PolyGram

Medalark 11

MEDALARK 11
Cute / Smoke / Coffee / Throw down a rope / Metalark / Snake / Socket / Call your name / Diving / Querelcia / Big sharp
CD ______ CRECD 145
Creation / Dec '93 / 3mv/Vital

Medallions

SPEEDIN'
Speedin' / Magic mountain / I wonder wonder wonder / Letter / Dance and swing / Dear and darling / Push button automobile / Lover's prayer / Edna / '59 Volvo / Unseen / Ticket to love / I'm in love with you / Buick '59 / Behind the door / Don't shoot baby / I want a love / My Mary Lou / For better or for worse / Give me the right / Telegram / Rocket ship / Did you have fun / Coupe de ville baby / Shedding tears for you
CD ______ CDCHD 536
Ace / Mar '96 / Pinnacle

Medardo Y Su Orquesta

LA BODA
CD ______ TUMICD 032
Tumi / '92 / Discovery / Stern's

Medeski, John

FRIDAY AFTERNOON IN THE UNIVERSE (Medeski, John & Billy Martin/Chris Wood)
Lover / Paper bass / House mop / Last chance to dance trance (perhaps) / Baby clams / We're so happy / Shack / Tea / Chinoiserie / Between two limbs / Sequel / Friday afternoon in the universe / Billy's tool box / Chubb sub / Khob khun krub
CD ______ GCD 79503
Gramavision / Mar '95 / Vital/SAM

IT'S A JUNGLE IN HERE (Medeski, John & Billy Martin)
Beeah / Where's sly / Shuck it up / Sand / Worms / bemsha swing / Moti mo / It's a jungle in here / Syeeda's song flute / Wiggles way
CD ______ GCD 79495
Gramavision / Sep '95 / Vital/SAM

SHACK MAN (Medeski, John & Billy Martin/Chris Wood)
Is there anybody here that loves my Jesus / Think / Dracula / Bubble house / Henduck / Strance of the spirit red gator / Spy kiss / Lifeblood / Jelly belly / Night marchers / Kenny
CD ______ GCD 79514
Gramavision / Oct '96 / Vital/SAM

Media Form

BEAUTY REPORTS
CD ______ SOHO 18CD
Suburbs Of Hell / Nov '94 / Kudos / Pinnacle / Plastic Head

Medicine

BURIED LIFE
CD ______ ARBCD 5
Beggars Banquet / Oct '93 / RTM/Disc / Warner Music

HER HIGHNESS
All good things / Wash me out / Candy Candy / Feel nothing at all / Fractured smile / Farther down / Aarhus / Seen the light alone / Heads
CD ______ 74321287572
American / Nov '95 / BMG

SHOT FORTH SELF LIVING
One More / Aruca / Defective / Short happy life / 5ive / Sweet Explosion / Queen of tersion / Miss Drugstore / Christmas Song
CD ______ CRECD 142
Creation / Oct '92 / 3mv/Vital

Medicine Head

MEDICINE HEAD LIVE
CD ______ RMCCD 0201
Red Steel / Aug '96 / Pinnacle

TIMEPEACE (BOOM, HOWL AND MOAN)
CD ______ RMOCD 0201
Red Steel / Sep '95 / Pinnacle

Medicine Man

DARK AND DANGEROUS RHYTHM
Sell me the dream / Frozen heart / Take me home / Fatal cure / Morning runs quickly / New rules / Look around / This is your news today
CD ______ MMRCD 002
Cyclops / Jul '97 / Pinnacle

Medicine Rain

NATIVE
CD ______ MACDL 945
Resurrection / Nov '96 / Plastic Head

Meditation Dub

MEDITATION DUB
CD ______ WRCD 15
Techniques / Oct '92 / Jet Star

Meditation Singers

GOOD NEWS
My soul looks back and wonders / Ain't that good news / You don't know how blessed you are / He's alright with me / Remember me / One river to cross / Know the day is over / Make a step in the right direction / Day is past and gone / I'm saying yes / I'm determined to run this race / Do you know Jesus / Promise to meet me there / Until I reach my heavenly home / He made it all right / Jesus is always there / Too close to heaven / God is good to me / WDIA plug / My soul looks back in wonders
CD ______ CDCHD 465
Ace / Mar '93 / Pinnacle

Meditations

DEEPER ROOTS
CD ______ HBCD 158
Heartbeat / Jun '94 / ADA / Direct / Greensleeves / Jet Star

FOR THE GOOD OF MAN
Mr. Vulture man / Roots man party / Tin sardin / Wallah up / For the good of man / Bourgeois game / Dem a fight / Man no better than woman / Woman woman / Rocking in America
CD ______ GRELCD 114
Greensleeves / Aug '88 / Jet Star / SRD

NO MORE FRIEND
No more friend / Forcing me / Jack on top / Mother love / Book of history / Carpenter rebuild / Fuss and fight / Slick chick / Talk of the town / Big city
CD ______ GRELCD 52
Greensleeves / Aug '95 / Jet Star / SRD

RETURN OF THE MEDITATIONS
CD ______ HBCD 130
Heartbeat / Nov '92 / ADA / Direct / Greensleeves / Jet Star

Medium Cool

IMAGINATION
How long has this been going on / That old feeling / I fall in love too easily / Look for the silver lining / My foolish heart / Like someone in love / Let's get lost / My buddy / Imagination / Little girl blue
CD ______ COOKCD 055
Cooking Vinyl / Apr '93 / Vital

Medlow, Junior

THRILL FOR THRILL
CD ______ LIZARD 80006
Lizard / Aug '95 / Direct / RTM/Disc

Mednick, Lisa

ARTIFACTS OF LOVE
CD ______ DJD 3209
Dejadisc / May '94 / ADA / Direct

Medusa Cyclone

MEDUSA CYCLONE
CD ______ 3G 11
Third Gear / Jun '97 / Cargo / Greyhound

Meek, Gary

LIVE AT RONNIE SCOTT'S
On the road / Time one / Eva Marie / Sierra highway / Song for Donna / Sun is out
CD ______ BNETCD 005
Bootleg.Net / Feb '97 / Vital/SAM

TIME ONE
Time one / Misturada / Eva Marie / Bosporous blues / Sierra highway / For a long time / On the road / New day / Sun is out / Free
CD ______ BW 057
B&W / Nov '96 / New Note/Pinnacle / SRD / Vital/SAM

Meek, Joe

I HEAR A NEW WORLD (Meek, Joe & The Blue Men)
Love dance of the Saroos / Glob waterfall / Magnetic field / Valley of the Saroos
CD ______ RPM 103
RPM / Jan '92 / Pinnacle

INTERGALACTIC INSTROS (Various Artists)
Night of the vampire: *Moontrekkers* / Just for chicks: *Ramblers* / Oo la la: *Jay, Peter & The Jaywalkers* / Red rocket: *Laverne, Roger & The Microns* / Hatahiai: *Moontrekkers* / Green jeans: *Fabulous Flee Rekkers* / West point: *Checkmates* / Keep moving: *Sounds Incorporated* / Spook walks: *Spooks* / Lawrence of Arabia: *Tornados* / Pinto: *Stonehenge Men* / Bogey man: *Tornados* / Totem pole: *Jay, Peter & The Jaywalkers* / Saxon way cry: *Saxons* / Union pacific: *Original Checkmates* / Cerveza: *Fabulous Flee Rekkers* / Melodie d'amore: *Moontrekkers* / Take it away: *Ramblers* / Big feet: *Stonehenge Men* / There's something at the bottom of the well: *Moontrekkers* / Dodge city: *Ramblers* / Order of the keys: *Sounds Incorporated* / Spy: *Original Checkmates* / Sunday sunset: *Moontrekkers* / Jaywalker: *Jay, Peter & The Jaywalkers* / You are my sunshine: *Fabulous Flee Rekkers* / John Brown's body: *Moontrekkers* / Poet and peasant: *Jay, Peter & The Jaywalkers* / Telstar: *Tornados* / Exodus: *Tornados* / Czardas: *Tornados* / Telstar demo: *Meek, Joe*
CD ______ GEMCD 002
Diamond / Oct '96 / Pinnacle

JOE MEEK - THE PYE YEARS VOL.2 (304 Holloway Road) (Various Artists)
Pocket full of dreams and eyes full of tears: *Gregory, Iain* / Night you told a lie: *Gregory, Iain* / Who's the girl: *Jay, Peter* / Bittersweet love: *Riot Squad* / Try to realise: *Riot Squad* / When love was young: *Rio, Bobby & the Revelles* / Happy talk: *Saints* / Midgets: *Saints* / Parade of the tin soldiers: *Saints* / Baby I go for you: *Blue Rondos* / What can I do: *Blue Rondos* / May your hearts stay young forever: *Reader, Pat* / Goodness knows: *Wayne, Ricky & the Off-Beats* / Baby I like the look of you: *London, Peter* / Fickle heart: *Garfield, Johnny* / Stranger in paradise: *Garfield, Johnny* / As time goes by: *Dean, Alan & His Problems* / Cool water: *Cameron, Chick Ted Group & The D.J.'s* / Rescue me: *Wayne, Ricky* / It can happen to you: *Conrad, Jess* / There and Bach again: *Cook, Peter* / Sing C'est la vie: *Collins, Glenda* / I'm not made of clay: *Rio, Bobby* / My saddest day: *Austin, Reg* / Two timing baby: *Carter-Lewis & The Southerners* / Tell me: *Carter-Lewis & The Southerners*
CD ______ NEXCD 216
Sequel / Feb '93 / BMG

JOE MEEK STORY VOL.5, THE (The Early Years) (Various Artists)
Georgia's got a moon: *Miller, Betty* / Robin Hood: *Miller, Gary* / Cry me a river: *Ryan, Marion* / Rhythm and blues: *Winston, Eric* / 16 Tons: *Hockridge, Edmund* / Sugarfree: *Lotis, Dennis* / Garden of eden: *Miller, Gary* / Love is strange: *Donegan, Lonnie* / Bye bye love: *Fraser, Johnny* / Freight train: *Seeger, Peggy* / Wild eyes and tender lips: *Hicks, Colin & The Cabin Boys* / Land of make believe: *Davis, Jackie* / Story of my life: *Miller, Gary* / Mule skinner blues: *Donegan, Lonnie* / Cerveza: *Wainer, Cherry* / Weekend: *Price, Red Band* / Charlie Brown: *Ellington, Ray* / Venus: *Valentine, Dickie* / Yashmak: *Arnaz, Chico* / Allentown jail: *Roza, Lita* / Hold back tomorrow: *Miki & Griff* / What do you want to make those eyes at me for: *Ford, Emile & The Checkmates* / Dear Daddy: *Clark, Petula* / Mr Blue: *MacBeth, David* / This love I have for you: *Fortune, Lance*
CD ______ NEMCD 882
Sequel / Mar '97 / BMG

LET'S GO WITH JOE MEEK'S GIRLS (Various Artists)
CD ______ RPM 166
RPM / Jun '96 / Pinnacle

RGM RARITIES VOL.1 (The Joe Meek Collection) (Various Artists)
CD ______ GEMCD 012
Diamond / Jun '97 / Pinnacle

RGM RARITIES VOL.2 (The Beat Group Era/The Joe Meek Collection) (Various Artists)
That's my plan: *Beat Boys* / Third time lucky: *Beat Boys* / You're holding me down: *Beat Boys* / I gotta buzz: *Buzz* / Sticks and stones: *Checkmates* / Right girl for me: *Chris, Peter & The Outcasts* / I've got you out of my mind: *Cristo, Bobby & The Rebels* / Singin' the blues: *Eddie, Jason & The Centremen* / True to you: *Eddie, Jason & The Centremen* / Whatcha gonna do: *Eddie, Jason & The Centremen* / Come on baby: *Eddie, Jason & The Centremen* / Man's gotta stand tall: *Four Matadors* / I don't love her no more: *Hotrods* / Ain't coming back no more: *Hotrods* / Too far out: *Impac* / Kansas city: *Jay, Peter & The Jaywalkers* / I love to see you strut: *John, David & The Mood* / Bring it to jerome: *John, David & The Mood* / Diggin' for gold: *John, David & The Mood* / She's fine: *John, David & The Mood* / Summer without the sun: *Kingsley, Charles Creation* / sStill in love with you: *Kingsley, Charles Creation* / Wishing well: *Kingsley, Charles Creation* / Boys and girls: *Parker, Benny & The Dynamics* / Bluebirds over the mountain: *Joey, Shade & The Night Owls* / Every once in a while: *Shakeouts* / Who told you: *Starr, Freddie & the Midnigh-*

ters / It's shakin' time: *Starr, Freddie & the Midnighters*
CD GEMCD 016
Diamond / Jul '97 / Pinnacle

WORK IN PROGRESS
CD RPM 121
RPM / Oct '93 / Pinnacle

Meeks, Carl

JACKMANDORA
CD GRELCD 132
Greensleeves / Jul '89 / Jet Star / SRD

Mega Banton

FIRST POSITION
CD VPCD 1343
VP / Jan '94 / Greensleeves / Jet Star / Total/BMG

NEW YEAR, NEW STYLE (Mega Banton & Friends)
CD SHCD 45020
Shanachie / Dec '94 / ADA / Greensleeves / Koch

SHOWCASE (Mega Banton & Ricky General)
CD BSCCD 17
Black Scorpio / Dec '93 / Jet Star

Mega City Four

INSPIRINGLY TITLED - THE LIVE ALBUM
Thanx / Shivering sand / Props / Messenger / Stop / Revolution / Words that say / Callous / Lipscar / Peripheral / Clown / Open / What you've got / Don't want to know if you are lonely / Who cares / Finish
CD MEGCD 2
Big Life / Nov '92 / Mo's Music Machine / Pinnacle / Prime

MAGIC BULLETS
Perfect circle / Drown / Rain man / Toys / Iron sky / So / Enemy skies / Wallflower / President / Shadow / Underdog / Greener / Speck
CD MEGCD 003
Big Life / May '93 / Mo's Music Machine / Pinnacle / Prime

SEBASTOPOL RD
Ticket collector / Scared of cats / Callous / Peripheral / Anne Bancroft / Prague / Clown / Props / What's up / Vague / Stop / Wasting my breath
CD MEGCD 1
Big Life / Feb '92 / Mo's Music Machine / Pinnacle / Prime

SOULSCRAPER
CD FIRECD 54
Fire / Mar '96 / Pinnacle / RTM/Disc

Mega Drums

LAYERS OF TIME
Ancient feelings / Layers of time / Olua / Mahakal / Bardo / Tschung mori / Parabao / Ga ma la / Gecko's in bahia
CD INT 31732
Intuition / Sep '96 / New Note/Pinnacle

Mega, Tom

FOR YOU ONLY
CD ITM 001485
ITM / Dec '93 / Koch / Tradelink

Megabyte

POWERPLAY
Glow energy / My father was a teacher / Skyline sculptures / Powerplay / Hello, Ralph here / Secret destination
CD CDTB 2049
Thunderbolt / Jan '88 / TKO Magnum

Megadeth

COUNTDOWN TO EXTINCTION
Skin o' my teeth / Symphony of destruction / Architecture of aggression / Foreclosure of a dream / Sweating bullets / This was my life / Countdown to extinction / High speed dirt / Psychotron / Captive honour / Ashes in your mouth
CD CDESTU 2175
Capitol / Jun '92 / EMI

CRYPTIC WRITINGS
Trust / Almost honest / Use the man / Mastermind / Disintegrators / I'll get even / Sin / Secret place / Have cool, will travel / She-wooolf / Vortex / FFF
CD CDEST 2297
Capitol / Jun '97 / EMI

PEACE SELLS...BUT WHO'S BUYING/ SO FAR, SO GOOD, SO WHAT/RUST (The Originals/3CD Set)
Wake up dead / Conjuring / Peace sells / Devil's Island / Good morning / Bad omen / I ain't superstitious / My last words / Black Friday / Into the lungs of hell / Set the world afire / Anarchy in the UK / Mary Jane / 502 / In my darkest hour / Liar / Hook in mouth / Holy wars...the punishment due / Hangar 18 / Take no prisoners / Five magics / Poison was the cure / Lucretia / Tornado of souls / Dawn patrol / Rust in peace...Polaris
CD Set CDOMB 019
EMI / Mar '97 / EMI

RUST IN PEACE
Holy wars... the punishment due / Hangar 18 / Take no prisoners / Five magics / Poison was the cure / Lucretia / Tornado of souls / Dawn patrol / Rust in peace...Polaris
CD CDEST 2132
Capitol / Sep '90 / EMI

SO FAR SO GOOD SO WHAT
Into the lungs of hell / Set the world afire / Anarchy in the UK / Mary Jane / 502 / In my darkest hour / Liar / Hook in mouth
CD CDEST 2053
Capitol / Mar '88 / EMI

YOUTHANASIA
Reckoning day / Train of consequences / Addicted to chaos / Tout le monde / Elysian fields / Killing road / Blood of heroes / Family tree / Youthanasia / I thought I knew it all / Black curtains / Victory / No more Mr. Nice Guy / Breakpoint / Go to hell / Angry again / Ninety nine ways to die / Paranoid / Diadems / Problems
CD CDEST 2244
Capitol / Oct '94 / EMI

Megakronkel

MEGAKRONKEL
CD K 148D
Konkurrel / Mar '93 / SRD

Megalon

PANDORA'S BOX
CD PLKCD 002
Plink Plonk / Oct '94 / Prime / SRD

Megashira

ZERO HOUR
CD IC 0262
Infracom / Jun '97 / Plastic Head / SRD

Megora

WAITING
CD SPV 08496742
SPV / Dec '94 / Koch / Plastic Head

Meices

DIRTY BIRD
CD 8286812
London / Jan '96 / PolyGram

GREATEST BIBLE STORIES EVER TOLD
CD EFA 113822
Empty / Sep '94 / Cargo / Greyhound / Plastic Head / SRD

TASTES LIKE CHICKEN
That good one / Good one / Daddy's gone to California / All time high / Light 'em up / Slide / Until the weekend / Lettuce is far out / Big shitburger / Untruly / Hopin' for a ride / Now / That other good one / Don't let the soap run out / Alex put something in his pocket / Pissin' in the sink / Number one
CD BLUFF 013CD
Deceptive / Feb '95 / Vital

Mejia, Miguel Aceves

SUS GRANDES EXITOS VOL.2
CD ALCD 022
Alma Latina / Jul '96 / Discovery

SUS GRANDES EXITOS VOL.3
CD ALCD 024
Alma Latina / Jul '96 / Discovery

Mekon

WELCOME TO TACKLETOWN
Phatty's lunchbox / Freestyle / Rock 'n' roll / Revenge of the Mekon / Hook link / Mr Sophistication / Welcome to tackletown / Mekon Vs Artery / Broken synth lead / Skool's out / Agent mekon
CD WALLCD 006
Wall Of Sound / May '97 / Prime / Soul Trader / Vital

Mekong Delta

PICTURES AT AN EXHIBITION
Promenade / Gnomus / Interludium / Il veccio castello / Interludium / Tuileries / Bydtlo / Interludium / Ballet / Samuel / Limoges / Catacombae / Lingua mortis / Hut on chicken's legs / Heroic gate (in the old capital of Kiev)
CD CDVEST 78
Bulletproof / Feb '97 / Pinnacle

Mekons

DEVIL'S RATS AND PIGGIES (A Special Message From Godzilla)
CD QS 66CD
Quarter Stick / Aug '97 / Cargo / SRD

MEKONS
Snow / St. Patrick's day / DP Miller / Institution / I'm so happy / Chopper squad / Business / Trimden grange explosion / Karen / Corporal chalkie / John Barry / Another one
CD CDMGRAM 76
Cherry Red / Feb '94 / Pinnacle

PUSSY, KING OF THE PIRATES (Featuring Kathy Acker)
CD QS 36CD
Quarter Stick / Feb '96 / Cargo / SRD

RETREAT FROM MEMPHIS
CD QS 26CD
Quarter Stick / Jun '94 / Cargo / SRD

ROCK 'N' ROLL
Memphis, Egypt / Club Mekon / Only darkness has the power / Ring o'roses / Learning to live on your own / Cocaine Lil / Empire of the senseless / Someone / Amnesia / I am crazy / Heaven and back / Blow your tuneless trumpet / Echo / When darkness falls
CD BFFP 40CD
Blast First / '89 / RTM/Disc

Mel & Kim

FLM
FLM / Showing out / Respectable / Feel a whole lot better / I'm the one who really loves you / More than words can say / System / From a whisper to a scream / Who's gonna catch you / Showing out (remix) / Respectable (remix)
CD CDGOLD 1006
EMI Gold / Mar '96 / EMI

Mel & Tim

GOOD GUYS ONLY WIN IN THE MOVIES
CD SC 6078
Sundazed / Nov '96 / Cargo / Greyhound / Rollercoaster

STARTING ALL OVER AGAIN
Don't you mess with my money, my honey or my woman / Starting all over again / I may not be what you want / Carry me / Free for all / Heaven knows / Wrap it up / What's your name / I'm your puppet / Too much wheelin' and dealin' / Forever and a day / It's those little things that count / Same folks / Yes we can-can
CD CDSXE 078
Stax / Jan '93 / Pinnacle

Melanie

BEST OF MELANIE, THE
Ruby Tuesday / Brand new key / Animal crackers / Mr. Tambourine man / Baby day / Beautiful people / Save the night / Lay down (candles in the rain) / Close it all / What have they done to my song Ma / Lay lady lay / Some day I'll be a farmer / Good book / Peace will come / Gardens in the city / Nickel song / Pebbles in the sand / Tell me why
CD MCCD 011
Music Club / Feb '91 / Disc / THE

BORN TO BE
In the hour / Bo Bo's party / Momma momma / Animal crackers / Close to it all / I'm back in town / Mr. Tambourine man / Really loved Harold / Christopher Robin / Merry Christmas
CD C5CD 582
See For Miles/C5 / Apr '92 / Pinnacle

COLLECTION, THE
Somebody loves me / Beautiful people / In the hour / I really loved Harold / Johnny boy / Any guy / I'm back in town / What have they done to my song Ma / Lay down (candles in the rain) / Peace will come / Good book / Nickle song / Babe rainbow (reprise) / Carolina on my mind / Ruby Tuesday / Sign in the window / Lay lady lay / Christopher Robin / Animal crackers / I don't eat animals / Psychotherapy / Leftover wine
CD CCSCD 195
Castle / Jun '88 / BMG

FOUR SIDES OF MELANIE, THE
Somebody loves me / Beautiful people / In the hour / I really loved Harold / Johnny boy / Any guy / I'm back in town / What have they done to my song Ma / Lay down (candles in the rain) / Peace will come / Good book / Nickle song / Babe rainbow / Mr. Tambourine man / Carolina in my mind / Ruby Tuesday / Lay lady lady / Christopher Robin / Animal crackers / I don't eat animals / Leftover wine
CD HILLCD 10
Wooded Hill / Jan '97 / Direct / World Serpent

FROM WOODSTOCK TO THE WORLD (2CD Set)
Brand new key / Long long time / Beautiful people / Lay down / Peace will come / Look what they've done to my song / Ruby Tuesday / Babe rainbow / Close to it all / Ring around the moon / Ring the living bell / Nickel song / Summer of love / Good book / Estate sale / Alexander Beetle / I don't eat animals / Purple haze / Silence is King / Christopher Robin / Arrow / These nights / Something warm / Look what they've done to my song
CD Set 24337
Laserlight / Nov '96 / Target/BMG

GOOD BOOK, THE
Good book / Babe rainbow / Sign on the window / Saddest thing / Nickel song / Isn't it a pity / My father / Chords of fame / You can go fishin / Birthday of the sun / Prize
CD C5CD 597
See For Miles/C5 / Feb '93 / Pinnacle

HIT SINGLE COLLECTABLES
CD DISK 4505
Disky / Apr '94 / Disky / THE

OLD BITCH WARRIOR
CD 74321293572
RCA / Feb '96 / BMG

RUBY TUESDAY
Mr. Tambourine man / Beautiful people / Carolina in my mind / Lay lady lay / Kansas / My bonny lies over the ocean / Someday I'll be a farmer / Nickel song / Happy birthday / Ruby Tuesday / What have they done to my song Ma / Somebody loves me / Tell me why / Candles in the rain / Leftover wine / Brand new key / Stop, I don't wanna hear it anymore / Peace will come
CD 5507512
Spectrum / Jan '95 / PolyGram

UNPLUGGED
Ruby Tuesday / Look what they've done to my song / Brand new key / Beautiful people / Freedom knows my name / Lay down (candles in the rain) / Ballerina / Peace will come / Sun and moon / Life will not go away / Babe rainbow / Ring around the moon / Arrow / Close to it all / Long long time / Purple haze
CD DC 879982
Disky / May '97 / Disky / THE

Meldonian, Dick

DICK MELDONIAN & SONNY IGOE BIG BAND 1980-1982 (Meldonian, Dick & Sonny Igoe)
CD CCD 73
Circle / Nov '96 / Jazz Music / Swift / Wellard

DICK MELODIAN TRIO (Meldonian, Dick Trio)
CD JCD 164
Jazzology / Aug '94 / Jazz Music

SWING ALTERNATE (Meldonian, Dick & Orchestra)
CD CLCD 150
Circle / Mar '90 / Jazz Music / Swift / Wellard

SWING OF ARR. OF GENEROLA (Meldonian, Dick & Orchestra)
CD CCD 150
Circle / Oct '91 / Jazz Music / Swift / Wellard

YOU'VE CHANGED (Meldonian, Dick Quartet)
CD PCD 7052
Progressive / Jun '93 / Jazz Music

Melek-Tha

ASTRUM ARGENTINIUM
CD CDAR 032
Adipocre / Apr '96 / Plastic Head

Melford, Myra

ALIVE IN THE HOUSE OF SAINTS (Melford, Myra Trio)
CD ARTCD 6136
Hat Art / Nov '93 / Cadillac / Harmonia Mundi

JUMP
CD EMY 1152
Enemy / Nov '94 / Grapevine/PolyGram

NOW & NOW (Melford, Myra Trio)
CD EMY 1312
Enemy / Oct '92 / Grapevine/PolyGram

SAME RIVER TWICE, THE
Bound unbound / Crush / Changes / Drawing in the dark / Large ends the way
CD GCD 79513
Gramavision / Oct '96 / Vital/SAM

Melis, Efisio

LAUNEDDAS
CD RD 5025CD
Robi Droli / Mar '96 / ADA / Direct

Mellencamp, John

AMERICAN FOOL (Mellencamp, John Cougar)
Can you take it / Hurts so good / Jack and Diane / Hand to hold on to / Danger list / Can you fake it / Thundering hearts / China girl / Close enough / Weakest moments
CD 8149932
Mercury / '88 / PolyGram

BIG DADDY (Mellencamp, John Cougar)
Big daddy of them all / To live / Martha say / Theo and weird Henry / Jackie Brown / Pop singer / Void in my heart / Mansions in heaven / Sometimes a great notion / Country gentleman / JM's question
CD 8382202
Mercury / May '89 / PolyGram

JOHN COUGAR
Little night dancin' / Miami / Do you think that's fair / Welcome to Chinatown / Pray for me / Small paradise / Great midwest / I need a lover / Sugar Marie / Taxi dancer

CD 8149952
Mercury / Jan '86 / PolyGram

LONESOME JUBILEE, THE
Paper in fire / Down and out in paradise / Check it out / Real life / Cherry bomb / We are the people / Empty hands / Hard times for an honest man / Hot dogs and hamburgers / Rooty toot toot
CD 8324652
Mercury / Jul '92 / PolyGram

MR. HAPPY GO LUCKY
Overture / Jerry / Key West intermezzo / Just another day / This may not be the end of the world / Emotional love / Mr. Bellows / Full catastrophe / Circling around the moon / Large world turning / Jackamo Road / Life is hard
CD 5328962
Mercury / Oct '96 / PolyGram

SCARECROW
Rain on the scarecrow / Grandmas's theme / Small town / Minutes to memories / Lonely ol' night / Face of the nation / Justice and independence '85 / Between a laugh and a tear / Rumbleseat / You've got to stand for something / ROCK in the USA / Kind of fella I am
CD 8248652
Mercury / Nov '85 / PolyGram

UH-HUH
Crumblin' down / Pink houses / Authority song / Hurts so good / Thundering hearts / Warmer place to sleep
CD 8144502
Mercury / Oct '91 / PolyGram

WHENEVER WE WANTED
Love and happiness / Now more than ever / I ain't never satisfied / Get a leg up / Crazy ones / Last chance / They're so tough / Melting pot / Whenever we wanted / Again tonight
CD 5101512
Mercury / Oct '91 / PolyGram

Meller, Raquel

SUCCES ET RARETES 1926-1932
CD 701562
Chansophone / Sep '96 / Discovery

Melling, Steve

UN LOCO POCO
What is this thing called love / Prelude to a kiss / Night and day / In a monochrome / Leona / Janas delight / Eronet / Un poco loco / Wise one / Some other time
CD JHCD 045
Ronnie Scott's Jazz House / Feb '96 / Cadillac / Jazz Music / New Note/Pinnacle / TKO Magnum

Mellow Candle

SWADDLING SONGS
Heaven Heath / Sheep season / Silversong / Poet and the witch / Messenger birds / Dan the wing / Reverend Sisters / Break your token / Buy or beware / Vile excesses / Lonely man / Boulders on my grave
CD SEECD 404
See For Miles/C5 / May '96 / Pinnacle

VIRGIN PROPHET
CD KSCD 9520
Kissing Spell / Jun '97 / Greyhound

Mellow Fellows

STREET PARTY
I've got to find a way / Street party / I've got a feeling / Feels like rain / Drivin' wheel / We'll be friends / Don't turn your heater down / Since I fell for you / Last night / Me and my woman / Broad daylight
CD ALCD 4793
Alligator / May '93 / ADA / CM / Direct

Mellowtrons

EVACUATE
CD CHILLCD 009
Chillout / Jul '96 / Kudos / Pinnacle / RTM/Disc

Mellstock Band

CAROLS & DANCES OF HARDY'S WESSEX
CD CDSDL 360
Saydisc / Oct '92 / ADA / Direct / Harmonia Mundi

SONGS OF THOMAS HARDY'S WESSEX (With Sally Dexter/Julie Murphy/Ian Giles/Andy Turner)
Foggy dew / Jockey to the fair/Dame Durden / Mistletoe bough / Cupid's garden / Queen Eleanor's confession / Spotted cow / Seeds of love / Barley mow / Prentice boy / I have parks, I have hounds / Break o'the day / Sheepshearing song / Tailor's breeches / Downhills of life / I wish I wish / Joan's ale / Outlandish knight / Such a beauty I did grow / Banks of Allan Water / King Arthur had three sons / Light of the moon
CD CDSDL 410
Saydisc / Mar '95 / ADA / Direct / Harmonia Mundi

TENANTS OF THE EARTH
CD WGS 281CD
Wild Goose / Nov '96 / ADA

Melly, George

ANYTHING GOES
CD PLSCD 112
Pulse / Mar '96 / BMG

BEST OF GEORGE MELLY LIVE, THE
CD LCD 7019
D-Sharp / Jul '95 / Pinnacle

BEST OF GEORGE MELLY, THE
CD KAZCD 22
Kaz / Jul '92 / BMG

BEST OF GEORGE MELLY, THE
Anything goes / Oh Chubby, stay the way you are / House of the rising sun / Porter's love song / Nobody knows you (When you're down and out) / Hard hearted Hannah / Puttin' on the ritz / I ain't got nobody / Someday sweetheart / Route 66 / September song / Maybe not at all / It had to be you / Wrap your troubles in dreams (and dream your troubles away) / Chicago (That toddling town) / I hate a man like you / Sundown mamma / I don't want to set the world on fire
CD TRTCD 160
TrueTrax / Dec '94 / THE

HOT DOG MAN, THE
Glory of love / Nuts / Crazy rhythm / My honey's lovin' arms / Living on my own / Frankie and Johnny / Take me for a buggy ride / Waiter and the porter / Sweet substitute / Salty dog / I wish I were twins / You call it joggin' / Riverboat shuffle / (I wanna) hot dog
CD 303192
Hallmark / Jun '97 / Carlton

Melochita

MI SON SABROSON
CD 1004CD
Fresh Sound / Nov '96 / Discovery / Jazz Music

Melodian Pops Orchestra

TIJUANA TRUMPET
Pan pot dixie / O sole mio / Mextet / Bossa nova scotia / Taste of honey / Pedro Smith / Ghost of influence / Little zab / Bell and the bugle / Soft waving with a tik / Guantanamera / Furlough for two / Arena Santa Monica / Tijuana sleigh ride / Trouble spot / Studying for elephant / Last train to Tampico / Down the road a piece / EL tora bravo / Rambling swallow
CD 302562
Hallmark / Jul '97 / Carlton

Melodians

SWING & DINE
CD HBCD 129
Heartbeat / Nov '92 / ADA / Direct / Greensleeves / Jet Star

Melodie E Canzoni

ERIK SATIE
CD NT 6717
Robi Droli / Jan '94 / ADA / Direct

Melonz Bustin'

WATCH YOUR SEEDS POP OUT
CD CDCTUM 9
Continuum / Sep '94 / Pinnacle

Melt Banana

SCRATCH OR STITCH
CD GR 34CD
Skingraft / May '96 / SRD

Melusine

FRANCE FOLK
CD B 6833CD
Auvidis/Ethnic / Aug '96 / ADA / Harmonia Mundi

VOIX CONTREVOIX
CD 140192
Musidisc / Mar '96 / Discovery

Melvin, Brian

NIGHT FOOD
Ain't nothin' but a party / Don't forget the bass / Night food / Zen turtles / For Max / Polly wanna rhythm / Primalass / Warrior / Continuum
CD CDSJP 214
Timeless Jazz / '88 / New Note/Pinnacle

NIGHT FOOD (FEATURING JACO PASTORIUS) (Melvin, Brian's Nightfood)
Sexual healing / Fever / CIA / Dania / Did you hear that Monie / Mercy mercy mercy / Bahama Mama / JP's shuffle / Milers mode
CD 66052003
Global Pacific / Feb '91 / Pinnacle

STANDARDS ZONE (Melvin, Brian Trio & Jaco Pastorius)
Morning star / Days of wine and roses / Wedding waltz / Moon and sand / So what / Fire water / If you could see me now / Out of the night / Tokyo blues / Village blues
CD 66052008
Global Pacific / May '91 / Pinnacle

Melvin, Harold

IF YOU DON'T KNOW ME BY NOW (The Best Of Cabaret) (Melvin, Harold & The Bluenotes)
Cabaret / Love I lost / If you don't know me by now / Don't leave me this way / I'm weak for you / Everybody's talkin' / Hope that we can be together soon / Keep on lovin' you / Tell the world how I feel about cha baby / I miss you / Satisfaction guaranteed / Yesterday I had the blues / Yesterday / Wake up everybody / Where are all my friends / Bad luck
CD 4805092
Epic / May '95 / Sony

SATISFACTION GUARANTEED (The Best Of Harold Melvin & The Blue Notes) (Melvin, Harold & The Bluenotes)
Don't leave me this way / Satisfaction guaranteed / Love I lost / Wake up everybody / Hope that we can be together soon / You know how to make me feel so good / Be for real / Nobody could take your place / Bad luck / Where are all my friends / Keep on loving you / Tell the world how I feel about cha baby / To be true / I'm searching for a love / To be free to be who we are / If you don't know me by now
CD 4720392
Epic / Jul '92 / Sony

SOUND OF PHILADELPHIA LIVE IN LONDON (Melvin, Harold & The Bluenotes/Three Degrees/Billy Paul)
Introduction/Love I lost: *Melvin, Harold & The Bluenotes* / If you don't know me by now: *Melvin, Harold & The Bluenotes* / Hope that we can be together soon: *Melvin, Harold & The Bluenotes* / Don't leave me this way: *Melvin, Harold & The Bluenotes/Billy Paul* / Wake up evrybody: *Melvin, Harold & The Bluenotes/Billy Paul* / Me and Mrs Jones: *Melvin, Harold & The Bluenotes/Billy Paul* / TSOP (The Sound Of Philadelphia): *Three Degrees* / My simple heart: *Three Degrees* / Medley: *Three Degrees* / Woman in love: *Three Degrees* / Dirty ol' man: *Three Degrees* / When will I see you again: *Three Degrees* / Love train
CD QED 016
Tring / Nov '96 / Tring

WAKE UP EVERYBODY (Melvin, Harold & The Bluenotes)
If you don't know me by now / Love I lost / Satisfaction guaranteed / Where are all my friends / Bad luck / Hope that we can be together soon / Wake up everybody / You know how to make me feel so good / Be for real / Nobody could take your place / Keep on lovin' you / To be true / I'm searching for love / To be free to be who we are / Do it any way you wanna
CD RMB 75086
Remember / Mar '96 / Total/BMG

Melvins

HONKY
CD ARRCD 81024
Amphetamine Reptile / Apr '97 / Plastic Head

HOUDINI
Hooch / Night goat / Lizzy / Goin' blind / Honey bucket / Hag me / Set me straight / Sky pup / Joan of arc / Teet / Copache / Pearl bomb / Spread eagle beagle
CD 7567825322
Atlantic / Sep '93 / Warner Music

LYSOL
CD TUP 422
Tupelo / Nov '92 / RTM/Disc

MELVINS: LIVE
CD YCR 012CD
Your Choice / '92 / Plastic Head

PRICK
CD ARRCD53 333
Amphetamine Reptile / Sep '94 / Plastic Head

STAG
CD 7567828782
Atlantic / Jul '96 / Warner Music

STONER WITCH
CD 7567827042
WEA / Nov '94 / Warner Music

Members

SOUND OF THE SUBURBS (A Collection Of The Members' Finest)
Handling the big jets / Sally / GLC / Offshore banking business/Pennies in the pound / Soho a go-go / Muzak machine / Rat up a drainpipe / Sound of the suburbs / Phone-in show / Brian was / Killing time / Clean men / Romance / Flying again / Solitary confinement / Chelsea nightclub / Gang war / Police car
CD CDOVD 455
Virgin / Feb '95 / EMI

Members Only

MEMBERS ONLY WITH NELSON RANGELL (Members Only & Nelson Rangell)
CD MCD 5332
Muse / Sep '92 / New Note/Pinnacle

TOO
CD MCD 5348
Muse / Sep '92 / New Note/Pinnacle

Membranes

BEST OF THE MEMBRANES, THE
Ice age / Fashionable junkies / Muscles / High St. yanks / Man from moscow / Kafka's dad / Spike Milligan's tape recorder / Myths and legends / Shine on pumkin moon / I am fish eye / Mr. Charisma brain / Everything's brilliant / Kennedy '63 / Spaceships / Everyone's going triple bad acid yeah / Time warp 1991 / Love your puppy / Electric storm / Tatty seaside town / Voodoo chile
CD CDMGRAM 112
Anagram / Jun '97 / Cargo / Pinnacle

TO SLAY THE ROCK PIG
CD SUK 9CD
Vinyl Drip / Nov '89 / RTM/Disc

WRONG PLACE AT THE WRONG TIME
CD CCON 001CD
Constrictor Classics / Jul '93 / SRD

Memento Mori

LIFE, DEATH AND OTHER MORBID TALES
CD BM 051CD
Black Mark / Aug '94 / Plastic Head

Memorandum

ARS MORIENDI
CD EFA 01556CD
Apocalyptic Vision / Sep '96 / Cargo / Plastic Head / SRD

Memphis Horns

MEMPHIS HORNS
Take me to the river / Fa fa fa fa fa (Sad song) / I've been loving you too long / Somebody have mercy / Break the chain / Holding on to love / I'm just another soldier / Rumours / Rollercoaster / You don't miss your water / Desire in your eyes
CD CD 83344
Telarc / Jul '95 / Conifer/BMG

Memphis Jug Band

1932-34
CD BDCD 6002
Blues Document / '91 / ADA / Hot Shot / Jazz Music

MEMPHIS JUG BAND
CD YAZCD 1067
Yazoo / Apr '91 / ADA / CM / Koch

MEMPHIS JUG BAND VOL.1
CD JSPCD 606
JSP / Oct '93 / ADA / Cadillac / Direct / Hot Shot / Target/BMG

MEMPHIS JUG BAND VOL.2
CD DOCD 5022
Document / Nov '93 / ADA / Hot Shot / Jazz Music

Memphis Minnie

ANTHOLOGY 1929-1944
CD EN 520
Encyclopaedia / Sep '95 / Discovery

CITY BLUES
CD ALB 1008CD
Aldabra / Mar '94 / CM / RTM/Disc

HOT STUFF
Hot stuff / I hate to see the sun go down / Memphis minnie-jitis / Frankie / She put me outdoors / I don't want that junk outta you / Biting bug blues / Moonshine / Chicksaw train blues / Down by the riverside / I called you this morning / Man you won't give me no money / Keep on sailing / It's hard to be mistreated / New bumble bee / Me and my chauffeur blues / Good morning / Ice man
CD CBCD 2
Collector's Blues / Feb '96 / TKO Magnum

IN MY GIRLISH DAYS
CD CD 52036
Blues Encore / May '94 / Target/BMG

ME AND MY CHAUFFER 1935-1946
CD 158822
Blues Collection / Feb '97 / Discovery

MEMPHIS MINNIE & KANSAS JOE (Memphis Minnie & Kansas Joe)
CD DOCD 5031
Document / Nov '93 / ADA / Hot Shot / Jazz Music

TRAVELLING BLUES
CD ALB 1005CD
Aldabra / Mar '94 / CM / RTM/Disc

Memphis Pilgrims

MECCA
CD REL 2077
Relix / Aug '96 / ADA / Greyhound

Memphis Roots

GOOD NOISE (The Best Of Western Line Dancing)
CD 3036000442
Carlton / May '97 / Carlton

Memphis Slim

4.00 BLUES
4.00 Blues / Trouble in mind / Worried life blues / Cow cow blues / Lonesome in my bedroom / Diggin' my potatoes / In the evening / Blue and disgusted / Miss Ida Bea / I'll take her to Chicago / Lonesome / Cold blooded woman / One man's mad / Let the good times roll creole / What is the mare rack / Pigalle love / Four walls / It's been too long / Big Bertha / I'm lost without you / I'll just keep on singing the blues / True love
CD GRF 059
Tring / '93 / Tring

ALL KINDS OF BLUES
Blues is trouble / Grinder man blues / Three in one boogie / Letter home / Churnin' man blues / Two of a kind / Blacks / If you see Kay / Frankie and Johnny Boogie / Mother earth
CD OBCCD 507
Original Blues Classics / Nov '92 / Complete/Pinnacle / Wellard

ALONE WITH MY FRIENDS
Highway 51 blues / I feel so good / Rock me Momma / Goin' down slow / Sittin' on top of the world / Sunnyland train / Goin' down to the river / I just want to make love to you / I can hear my name a-ringin' / Going back to my plow
CD OBCCD 581
Original Blues Classics / Oct '96 / Complete/Pinnacle / Wellard

AUX TROIS MAILLETZ (Memphis Slim & Willie Dixon)
Rock 'n' rolling the house / Baby please come home / How make you do me like you do / Way she loves a man / New way to love / African hunch with a boogie beat / Shame / Pretty girls / Baby baby baby / Do de do / Cold blooded / Just you and I / Pigalle love / All by myself
CD 5197292
Verve / Mar '94 / PolyGram

BABY PLEASE COME HOME (Memphis Slim & Willie Dixon In Paris) (Memphis Slim & Willie Dixon)
Rock 'n' rolling the house / Baby please come home / How come you do me like you do / Way she loves a man / New way to love / African hunch with a boogie beat / Shame pretty girls / Baby baby baby / Do de do / Cool blooded / Just you and I / Pigalle love / All by myself
CD OBCCD 582
Original Blues Classics / Oct '96 / Complete/Pinnacle / Wellard

BLUE THIS EVENING
CD BLCD 760155
Black Lion / '91 / Cadillac / Jazz Music / Koch / Wellard

BLUEBIRD RECORDINGS 1940-1941, THE
Beer drinkin' woman / You didn't mean me no good / Grinder man blues / Empty room blues / Shelby County blues / I see my great mistake / Old Taylor / I believe I'll settle down / Jasper's gal / You got to help me some / Two of a kind / Whiskey store blues / Maybe I'll loan you a dime / Me, myself and I / Whiskey and gin blues / You gonna worry too / This life I'm livin' / Caught the old coon at last / Don't think that you're smart / Lend me your love
CD 07863667202
Bluebird / Feb '97 / BMG

BLUES BEFORE SUNRISE
CD TKOCD 017
TKO / '92 / TKO

COMPLETE RECORDINGS 1940-41
CD 158032
Blues Collection / Jun '93 / Discovery

DIALOGUE IN BOOGIE (Memphis Slim & Philippe Lejeune)
Rockin' / EEC boogie / C'est normal, c'est normand / Jefferson county blues / Fourth and beale / This is the way I feel / Three, two, one boogie / Midnite tempo / Cooky boogie / C and L boogie
CD 157112
Blues Collection / Feb '93 / Discovery

I AM THE BLUES
CD CDSGP 080
Prestige / Jan '95 / Else / Total/BMG

LIFE IS LIKE THAT
Life is like that / Nobody loves me / Sometimes I feel like a Motherless child / Pacemaker boogie / Harlem bound / Darling / I miss you so / Lend me your love / Cheatin' around / Letter home / Now I got the blues / Grinder man blues / Don't ration my love / Slim's boogie / Little Mary / Mistake in life / Messin' around with the blues / Midnight jump
CD CDCHARLY 249
Charly / Oct '90 / Koch

LONDON SESSIONS, THE
Help me some / Fattenin' frogs for snakes / I feel so good / Every day / One more time / I feel so good (Take 2) / Every day (Take 1) / Blues in London / Ain't nobody's business if I do / Messin' around / Worried life / Messin' around (Take 4) / Ain't nobody's business if I do / Fattenin' frogs for snakes (Take 1)
CD NEXCD 252
Sequel / Sep '93 / BMG

MEMPHIS HEAT (Memphis Slim & Canned Heat)
Back to Mother Earth / Trouble everywhere I go / Black cat cross my trail / Mr. Longfingers / Five long years / When I was young / You don't know my mind / Boogie duo / Down the big road / Whizzle wham / Paris
CD 5197252
Verve / Feb '94 / PolyGram

MEMPHIS SLIM
CD DVBC 9082
Deja Vu / May '95 / THE

MEMPHIS SLIM USA
Born with the blues / Just let it be me / Red haired boogie / Blue and disgusted / New key to the highway / I'd take her to Chicago / Harlem bound / El capitan / I just landed in your town / John Henry / I believe I'll settle down / Bad luck and trouble / Late afternoon blues / Memphis Slim USA
CD CCD 79024
Candid / Feb '97 / Cadillac / Direct / Jazz Music / Koch / Wellard

MOTHER EARTH
CD OW 30007
One Way / Jul '94 / ADA / Direct / Greyhound

RAINING THE BLUES
Beer drinking woman / Teasing the blues / IC Blues / Baby doll / Just blues / Blue and disgusted / Blue brew / Rack 'em back Jack / Motherless child / Brenda / When your dough roller is gone / Hey slim / Darling I miss you so / Lonesome traveller / No strain / Don't think you're smart / Raining the blues / You're gonna need my help one day / Angel child / Fast and free / My baby left me / Lucille / Nice stuff
CD CDCH 485
Ace / Nov '93 / Pinnacle

REAL FOLK BLUES
My baby / Trouble trouble / Slim's blues / Tiajuana / I guess I'm a fool / Really got the blues / Feeling low / For a day / Mother Earth / Blues for my baby / What is the mare rack / Having fun
CD MCD 09270
Chess/MCA / Apr '97 / BMG / New Note/ BMG

ROCKIN' THE BLUES
Gotta find my baby / Come back / Messin' around / Sassy Mae / Lend me your love / Guitar cha cha / Stroll on little girl / Rockin' the house / Wish me well / Blue and lonesome / My gal keeps me crying / Slim's blues / Steppin' out / Mother Earth / What's the matter / This time I'm through
CD CDBM 21
Charly / Apr '92 / Koch

STEADY ROLLIN' BLUES
CD OBCCD 523
Original Blues Classics / Nov '92 / Complete/Pinnacle / Wellard

STEPPIN' OUT (Live At Ronnie Scott's)
Health shaking / Mother earth / Rock this house tonight / If you see Kay / Feel so good / Tribute to Gaillard / Four hundred years / Steppin' out / Baby please come home / Where do I go from here / Didn't we / Christina / Animal / Beer drinking woman / What is this world coming to / Bye bye blues
CD CLACD 334
Castle / '93 / BMG

TRAVELLING WITH THE BLUES
Memphis boogie / St. Louis blues / Santa Fe blues / Chicago new home of the blues / Chicago house / Rent party blues / Arkansas road house blues / Midnight jump / Goodbye blues / Reminiscin' with the blues / Good rockin' blues / Blues confession / Boogie woogie / Blues made up / Worries all the time
CD STCD 8021
Storyville / Mar '95 / Cadillac / Jazz Music / Wellard

TRIBUTE TO BIG BILL BROONZY
I feel so good / Rockin' chair blues / Baby gone / Cow cow blues / Miss Ida B / Forty-four blues / Trouble in my mind / Worried life blues / Don't want my rooster crowin' after the sun goes down / Lonesome in my bedroom / Diggin' my potatoes / In the evening
CD CCD 79023
Candid / Feb '97 / Cadillac / Direct / Jazz Music / Koch / Wellard

Memphis Willie B

HARD WORKING MAN BLUES
CD OBCCD 578
Original Blues Classics / Jan '96 / Complete/Pinnacle / Wellard

MEN

I FEEL
CD CDRPM 0011
RP Media / Mar '97 / Essential/BMG

Men At Work

BUSINESS AS USUAL
Who can it be now / I can see it in your eyes / Down under / Underground / Helpless automaton / People just love to play with words / Be good Johnny / Touching the untouchables / Catch a star / Down by the sea
CD 4508872
Epic / Apr '94 / Sony

CARGO
Dr. Heckyll and Mr. Jive / Overkill / Settle down my boy / Upstairs in my house / No sign of yesterday / It's a mistake / Highwire / Blue for you / I like to / No restrictions
CD 4746832
Columbia / Feb '97 / Sony

CARGO/BUSINESS AS USUAL
Dr. Heckyll and Mr. Jive / Overkill / Settle down my boy / Upstairs in my house / No sign of yesterday / It's a mistake / Highwire / Blue for you / I like to / No restrictions / Who can it be now / I can see it in your eyes / Down under / Underground / Helpless automaton / People just love to play with words / Be good Johnny / Touching the untouchables / Catch a star / Down by the sea
CD Set 4610232
Columbia / Jul '92 / Sony

CONTRABAND (The Best Of Men At Work)
Who can it be now / It's a mistake / Hard luck story / Still life / Underground / Upstairs in my house / I live to / High wire / Maria / Be good Johnny / Dr. Jheckyll and Mr. Jive / Overkill / Man with two hearts / Snakes and ladders / Down by the sea
CD 4840112
Columbia / Jul '96 / Sony

Men Of Vizion

MEN OF VIZION
Personal / That's alright / Instant love / House keeper / When you need someone / Forgive me / Personal joyride / You told me you loved me / Do thangz / Show you the way to go / It's only just a dream / Night and day
CD 4841122
MJJ Music / Jun '96 / Sony

Men They Couldn't Hang

BIG SIX PACK, THE
CD VEXCD 15
Demon / Jun '97 / Pinnacle

FIVE GLORIOUS YEARS
CD ORECD 509
Silvertone / Nov '89 / Pinnacle

HOW GREEN IS THE VALLEY
Gold strike / Ghosts of Cable Street / Bells / Shirt of blue / Tiny soldiers / Parted from you / Gold rush / Dancing on the pier / Going back to Coventry / Rabid underdog / Parade
CD MCLD 19075
MCA / Nov '92 / BMG

NEVER BORN TO FOLLOW
CD FIENDCD 788
Demon / Oct '96 / Pinnacle

NIGHT OF A THOUSAND CANDLES
Day after / Jack Dandy / Night to remember / Johnny come home / Green fields of France / Iron masters / Hush little baby / Walkin' talkin' / Kingdom come / Scarlet ribbons
CD FIENDCD 50
Demon / '88 / Pinnacle

WELL HUNG
CD CDAFTER 10
Fun After All / Mar '91 / Pinnacle

Menace

GLC - RIP
CD AHOY 17
Captain Oi / Nov '94 / Plastic Head

Menace To Society

PURE AND UNCUT
CD TX 51234CD
Triple X / Oct '96 / Plastic Head

Menano, Antonio

ARQUIVOS DO FADO
CD HTCD 31
Heritage / Jun '95 / ADA / Direct / Hot Shot / Jazz Music / Swift / Wellard

Menard, D.L.

NO MATTER WHERE YOU AT, THERE YOU ARE
Wildwood flower / I passed in front of your door / Let's gallop to Mamou / Convict waltz / Big Texas / Heart of the city / I went to the dance last night / Little black eyes / Water pump / Every night / Lafayette two-step / No christmas for the poor
CD HNCD 1352
Hannibal / Feb '90 / ADA / Vital

SWALLOW RECORDINGS, THE (Menard, D.L. & Austin Pitre)
Louisiana aces special: *Badeaux & The Louisiana Aces* / Back door: *Badeaux & The Louisiana Aces* / I can't forget you: *Badeaux & The Louisiana Aces* / She didn't know I was married: *Badeaux & The Louisiana Aces* / Bachelor's life: *Badeaux & The Louisiana Aces* / Valse de Jolly Rodgers: *Badeaux & The Louisiana Aces* / Miller's cave: *Menard, D.L.* / Water pump: *Menard, D.L.* / It's too late you're divorced: *Menard, D.L.* / Riches of a musician: *Menard, D.L.* / Vail and the crown: *Menard, D.L.* / I can live a better life: *Badeaux & The Louisiana Aces* / Rebecca Ann: *Badeaux & The Louisiana Aces* / Two step de bayou teche: *Pitre, Austin* / Opelousas waltz: *Pitre, Austin* / Two step a tante adele: *Pitre, Austin* / Rainbow waltz: *Pitre, Austin* / Rene's special: *Pitre, Austin* / Grand mamou blues: *Pitre, Austin* / Flumes d'enfer: *Pitre, Austin* / Chinaball blues: *Pitre, Austin* / Le pauvre hobo: *Pitre, Austin* / Pretty rosie cheeks: *Pitre, Austin* / Don't shake my tree: *Pitre, Austin* / La valse d'amour: *Pitre, Austin* / Jungle club waltz: *Pitre, Austin* / J'ai coiner a ta porte: *Pitre, Austin* / Chataigner waltz: *Pitre, Austin*
CD CDCHD 327
Ace / Jul '91 / Pinnacle

Mendelssohn, Felix

FELIX MENDELSSOHN & HIS HAWAIIAN SERENADERS 1940-1945 (Mendelssohn, Felix & His Hawaiian Serenaders)
CD HQCD 93
Harlequin / Apr '97 / Hot Shot / Jazz Music / Swift / Wellard

Mendes, Sergio

BRASILEIRO
Fanfarra / Magalenha / Indiado / What is this / Lua soberana / Sambadouro / Senhoras do amazonas / Kalimba / Barabare / Esconjuros / Pipoca / Magano / Chorado
CD 7559613152
Elektra / May '92 / Warner Music

DANCE MODERNO
CD P 630991CD
Rare Brazil / Apr '97 / Cargo

GREATEST HITS
Mas que nada / Scarborough Fair / With a little help from my friends / Like a lover / Look of love / Night and day / Masquerade / Fool on the hill / Goin' out of my head / Look around / So many stars / Day tripper / Pretty world / What the world needs now is love
CD CDMID 123
A&M / Oct '92 / PolyGram

OCEANO
Rio De Janeiro / Trilhos urbanos / Holografico olodu / Anos dourados / Madalena / Puzzle of hearts / Capivara / Anjo de mim / Vale da ribeira / Maracatudo / Los aveux / Un oceano silenzi
CD 5328022
Verve / Oct '96 / PolyGram

VERY BEST OF SERGIO MENDES & BRASIL '66, THE (Mendes, Sergio & Brasil '66)
Mas que nada / So many stars / Viola / With a little help from my friends / Wichita lineman / Batacuda / Dois dias / Easy to be hard / Roda / Some time ago / Masquerade / Fool on the hill / You stepped out of a dream / Moanin' / Salt sea / For me / Stillness / Cinnamon and clove / Going out of my head / Look who's mine / Like a lover / Ye-me-le / Day tripper / Viramundo / Wave / What the world needs now / For what it's worth / Where are you coming from / Chelsea morning / Lost in paradise / Joker / Night and day / Scarborough Fair/Canticle / Tim-Dom-Dom / Pretty world / Righteous life / Look of love / One note samba / Agua de beber / Cancao do nosso amor / Empty faces / Triste / Norwegian wood / Bim-Bom / So danco samba / Sometimes in winter / Constant rain / Pradizer Adeus
CD Set 5407522
A&M / Aug '97 / PolyGram

Mendoza, Celeste

LA REINA DEL GUAGUANCO
Papa ogun / Estas acabando / Recordare / Mi rumba echando candela / Yo le llamo vivir / A ti na ma / Que me castigue dios / Muere la luz / carinto ven / Lo que vale mi querer / Si yo fuera / En la cumbre
CD PSCCD 1009
Pure Sounds From Cuba / Feb '95 / Henry Hadaway / THE

Mendoza, Lydia

FIRST QUEEN OF TEJANO MUSIC
CD _______ ARHCD 392
Arhoolie / Apr '96 / ADA / Cadillac / Direct

LA GLORIA DE TEXAS
CD _______ ARHCD 3012
Arhoolie / Apr '95 / ADA / Cadillac / Direct

Mendoza, Victor

IF ONLY YOU KNEW
Para gozar un poquinto / If only you knew / Siempre caliente / Terri by the sea / Snow samba / At the tortilla factory / Cancao da noite / Santa Fe
CD _______ CDLR 45019
L&R / Nov '90 / New Note/Pinnacle

Mendoza, Vince

JAZZ PANA (Mendoza, Vince & Arif Mardin)
El vito cante / Tangos / Entre tinieblas / Tanguillo / Soy gitano / Buleria / Suite fraternidad / El vito en gran tamano
CD _______ 92122
Act / Apr '94 / New Note/Pinnacle

SKETCHES
CD _______ 892152
Act / Jul '94 / New Note/Pinnacle

Menezes, Margareth

LUZ DOURADA
Vou mandar / Black show / Luz dourada / Vai mexer / Novos rumos / Mar de amor / Raca negra / Desabalada / Club de brown benjor / Ate rir o mar / Olho do farol / Chegar a Bahia
CD _______ 5195372
Verve / Jan '94 / PolyGram

Mengelberg, Misha

DUTCH MASTERS (Mengelberg, Misha/ Steve Lacy/George Lewis)
CD _______ 1211542
Soul Note / Mar '92 / Cadillac / Harmonia Mundi / Wellard

IMPROMPTUS
CD _______ FMPCD 07
FMP / May '86 / Cadillac

WHO'S BRIDGE
CD _______ DIW 036
DIW / May '95 / Cadillac / Harmonia Mundi

Menhaden Countrymen

WON'T YOU HELP ME TO RAISE 'EM
CD _______ GV 220CD
Global Village / Nov '93 / ADA / Direct

Menswear

NUISANCE
125 West 3rd Street / I'll manage somehow / Sleeping in / Little Miss Pin Point Eyes / Daydreamer / Hollywood girl / Being brave / Around you again / One / Stardust / Piece of me / Stardust (Reprise)
CD _______ 8286762
Laurel / Mar '96 / Pinnacle / PolyGram

Mental Hippie Blood

MENTAL HIPPIE BLOOD
CD _______ SPV 08476752
SPV / Oct '94 / Koch / Plastic Head

Mental Overdrive

PLUGGED
CD _______ LDO 001CD
Love OD Communications / Sep '96 / Plastic Head

Mentallo & The Fixer

NO REST FOR THE WICKED
CD _______ BIOCD 02
Messerschmitt / Mar '94 / Plastic Head

WHERE ANGELS FEAR TO TREAD
CD _______ CDZOT 108
Zoth Ommog / Mar '94 / Cargo / Plastic Head

Mentally Damaged

PUNK GRUNK
CD _______ SPV 08456802
Wolverine / Oct '94 / Cargo / Plastic Head

Mentaur

DARKNESS BEFORE DAWN
CD _______ CYCL 033
Cyclops / Jan '97 / Pinnacle

Menuhin, Yehudi

MENUHIN & GRAPPELLI PLAY BERLIN/ KERN/PORTER (Menuhin, Yehudi & Stephane Grappelli)
Cheek to cheek / Isn't this a lovely day (to be caught in the rain) / Piccolino / Change partners / Top hat, white tie and tails / I've got my love to keep me warm / Heatwave / Way you look tonight / Pick yourself up / Fine romance / All the things you are / Why do I love you / I get a kick out of you / Night and day / Looking at you / Just one of those things / My funny valentine / Thou swell / Lady is a tramp / Blue room
CD _______ CDM 769 219 2
EMI / Feb '88 / EMI

MENUHIN AND GRAPPELLI PLAY 'JEALOUSY' (And Other Great Standards) (Menuhin, Yehudi & Stephane Grappelli)
Jealousy / Tea for two / Limehouse blues / These foolish things / Continental / Nightingale sang in Berkeley Square / Sweet Sue, just you / Skylark / Laura / Sweet Georgia Brown / I'll remember April / April in Paris / Things we did last summer / September in the rain / Autumn leaves / Autumn in New York / Button up your overcoat
CD _______ CDM 769 220 2
EMI / Mar '88 / EMI

MENUHIN AND GRAPPELLI PLAY GERSHWIN (Menuhin, Yehudi & Stephane Grappelli)
Fascinating rhythm / Summertime / Nice work if you can get it / Foggy day / 'S wonderful / Man I love / I got rhythm / They all laughed / Funny face / Oh lady be good
CD _______ CDM 769 218 2
Angel / Mar '88 / EMI

Menxperience

LA MANCHA NEGRA
CD _______ TKCD 21
2 Kool / Apr '97 / Pinnacle / SRD

Menzies, Ian

GREAT BRITISH TRADITIONAL JAZZBANDS VOL.9 (Menzies, Ian & His Clyde Valley Stompers)
Roses of picardy / Beale St. Blues / Gettysburg march / Swinging seamus / Ace in the hole / Sailing down chesapeake bay / In a Persian market / There'll be a hot time in the old town tonight / Mack the knife / World is waiting for the sunrise / Scotland the brave / Salty dog / Fish man / Royal garden blues / Irish black bottom / Yellow dog blues / Just a closer walk with thee / Tres moutarde
CD _______ LACD 79
Lake / Apr '97 / ADA / Cadillac / Direct / Jazz Music / Target/BMG

Meow

GOALIE FOR THE OTHER TEAM
CD _______ OUT 1202
Brake Out / Aug '96 / Direct

Mephisto

SUBTERRANEAN SOUND, THE
CD _______ SSR 162CD
SSR / Feb '96 / Amato Disco / Grapevine/ PolyGram / Prime / RTM/Disc

Mephisto Waltz

CROCOSMIA
CD _______ EFA 15564
Gymnastic / Apr '93 / SRD

ETERNAL DEEP, THE
CD _______ CLEO 63082
Cleopatra / Apr '94 / Cargo / Greyhound / Plastic Head / RTM/Disc / SRD

TERROR REGINA
CD _______ CLEO 92592
Cleopatra / Mar '94 / Cargo / Greyhound / Plastic Head / RTM/Disc / SRD

THALIA
CD _______ CLEO 95112
Cleopatra / Aug '95 / Cargo / Greyhound / Plastic Head / RTM/Disc / SRD

Mera

HUNGARIAN FOLK MUSIC FROM TRANSYLVANIA
CD _______ SYN 188
Syncoop / Nov '95 / ADA / Direct

Merauder

MASTER KILLER
CD _______ CM 77104CD
Century Media / Nov '95 / Plastic Head

Mercer, Johnny

MY HUCKLEBERRY FRIEND
CD _______ DRGCD 5244
DRG / May '96 / Discovery / New Note/ Pinnacle

PARDON MY SOUTHERN ACCENT
CD _______ CDHD 203
Happy Days / Aug '93 / Conifer/BMG

SONGWRITER SERIES VOL.3 (Old Music Master)
CD _______ PASTCD 7094
Flapper / Jun '96 / Pinnacle

STARS SALUTE JOHNNY MERCER, THE (Tribute To A Songwriting Legend) (Various Artists)
That old black magic: *Eckstine, Billy* / Goody, goody: *Goodman, Benny Orchestra* / Day in, day out: *McRae, Carmen* / GI jive: *Jordan, Louis & His Tympany Five* / Trav'lin light: *Holiday, Billie* / Jeepers creepers: *Bennett, Tony & Count Basie* / Arthur Murray taught me dancing in a hurry: *Dorsey, Jimmy Orchestra* / Laura: *Sinatra, Frank* / Dearly beloved: *Richards, Ann* / Lazy bones: *Carmichael, Hoagy* / Accentuate the positive: *Mercer, Johnny* / Cuckoo in the clock: *Horne, Lena* / Blues in the night: *Herman, Woody Orchestra* / Bernadine: *Boone, Pat* / Out of this world: *Connor, Chris* / Fools rush in: *Miller, Glenn Orchestra* / Skylark: *O'Day, Anita* / I'm an old cowhand: *Crosby, Bing* / Dream: *Washington, Dinah* / Moon river: *Butler, Jerry*
CD _______ 305842
Hallmark / Oct '96 / Carlton

SWEET GEORGIA BROWN
CD _______ HCD 152
Hindsight / Nov '95 / Jazz Music / Target/ BMG

TOO MARVELLOUS FOR WORDS (The Songs Of Johnny Mercer) (Various Artists)
Too marvelous for words: *Crosby, Bing & Jimmy Dorsey Orchestra* / Out of breath and scared to death of you: *Arden, Victor & Phil Ohman Orchestra* / Lazybones: *Mills Brothers* / I'm an old cowhand: *Crosby, Bing & Jimmy Dorsey Orchestra* / Jeepers creepers: *Mills Brothers* / You must have been a beautiful baby: *Crosby, Bing & Bob Crosby Orchestra* / And the angels sing: *Goodman, Benny Orchestra & Martha Tilton* / Fools rush in: *Sinatra, Frank & Tommy Dorsey Orchestra* / Mister Meadowlark: *Crosby, Bing & Johnny Mercer/Victor Young Orchestra* / Waiter and the porter and the upstairs maid: *Martin, Mary & Bing Crosby/Jack Teagarden Orchestra* / This time the dream's on me: *Miller, Glenn Orchestra* / Tangerine: *Dorsey, Jimmy Orchestra* / Blues in the night: *Shore, Dinah & Leonad Joy/RCA Victor Orchestra* / That old black magic: *Miller, Glenn Orchestra & Skip Nelson/The Modernaires* / Skylark: *Shore, Dinah & Rosario Bourdon/ RCA Victor Orchestra* / I'm old fashioned: *Astaire, Fred & John Scott Trotter Orchestra* / Old music master: *Mercer, Johnny & Jack Teagarden/Paul Whiteman Orchestra* / Dearly beloved: *Astaire, Fred & John Scott Trotter Orchestra* / One for my baby and one more for the road: *Horne, Lena & Horace Henderson Orchestra* / Accentuate the positive: *Crosby, Bing & Andrews Sisters/ Vic Schoen Orchestra* / Laura: *Haymes, Dick & Victor Young Orchestra* / On the Atchison Topeka and the Santa Fe: *Garland, Judy & Lennie Hayton Orchestra* / Come rain or come shine: *Haymes, Dick & Helen Forrest/Victor Young Orchestra* / Hit the road to dreamland: *Whiting, Margaret & Freddie Slack Orchestra*
CD _______ CDAJA 5230
Living Era / Sep '97 / Select

Merceron, Mariano

YO TENGO UN TUMBAO 1940-1946
CD _______ TCD 064
Tumbao Cuban Classics / Jul '96 / Discovery

Mercey, Larry

FULL SPEED AHEAD
CD _______ 322544
Koch / Jul '91 / Koch

Merchant

EARLY YEARS
CD _______ JW 1016CD
JW / Oct '96 / Jet Star

Merchant, Natalie

TIGERLILY
CD _______ 7559617452
Elektra / Jun '95 / Warner Music

Merciless

TREASURES WITHIN, THE
CD _______ CDATV 26
Active / Jun '92 / Pinnacle

UNBOUND
CD _______ NFR 007
No Fashion / Oct '94 / Plastic Head

Merciless

LEN OUT MI MERCY
CD _______ ANXCD 1
Annex / Jun '95 / Jet Star

Mercury Rev

BOCES
CD _______ BBQCD 140
Beggars Banquet / May '93 / RTM/Disc / Warner Music

YERSELF IS STEAM/LEGO IS MY EGO
CD _______ BBQCD 125
Beggars Banquet / Nov '92 / RTM/Disc / Warner Music

Mercury Rising

UPON DEAF EARS
Upon deaf ears / Light to grow / Halfway to forever / Minute man / Zeros and ones / It's war / Prayer / Where fear ends
CD _______ N 02782
Noise / Feb '97 / Koch

Mercury, Freddie

BARCELONA (Mercury, Freddie & Montserrat Caballe)
Barcelona / Fallen priest / Golden boy / Guide me home / Overture piccante / La japonaise / Ensueno / Guid me home / How can I go on
CD _______ 8372772
Polydor / Oct '88 / PolyGram

FREDDIE MERCURY ALBUM, THE
Great pretender / Foolin' around / Time / Your kind of lover / Exercises in free love / In my defence / Mr. Bad Guy / Let's turn it on / Living on my own / Love kills / Barcelona
CD _______ CDPCSD 124
Parlophone / Nov '92 / EMI

MAN FROM MANHATTAN, THE (Mercury, Freddie & Brian May & Eddie Howell)
CD _______ BUD 002CD
Voiceprint / Feb '95 / Pinnacle

Mercy

WITCHBURNER
CD _______ ERCD 921
Now & Then / Jul '92 / Plastic Head

Mercyful Fate

BEGINNING, THE
CD _______ RR 349603
Roadrunner / Nov '87 / PolyGram

BELLWITCH
CD _______ 398417027CD
Metal Blade / Feb '97 / Pinnacle / Plastic Head

DON'T BREAK THE OATH
CD _______ RR 349835
Roadrunner / '89 / PolyGram

MELISSA
CD _______ RR 349898
Roadrunner / '89 / PolyGram

RETURN OF THE VAMPIRE
CD _______ RR 91842
Roadrunner / May '92 / PolyGram

TIME
CD _______ 398417028CD
Metal Blade / Feb '97 / Pinnacle / Plastic Head

Mercyland

SPILLAGE
Minutes and parts / Who hangs behind your eyes / Mr. Right / Service economy / Uncle / Eula Geary is dead / Like a whore / Waiting for the garbage can / John D White / Freight truck / Touch ass knives / Do you know what I mean / Tears towards heaven / Guessing time is gone / Fall of the city / Imperial vision / Black on black on black / Ciderhead / Amerigod / Burning bath
CD _______ RCD 10314
Rykodisc / Oct '94 / ADA / Vital

Mercyless

ABJECT OFFERINGS
CD _______ FT 05035
Flametrader / Apr '94 / Plastic Head

COLOURED FUNERAL
CD _______ CM 770542
Century Media / Nov '93 / Plastic Head

Merdy Girl

TWIST HER
CD _______ NL 13CD
No Life / Oct '96 / Cargo / Greyhound

Meridian

SUNDOWN EMPIRE
Descent into solitude / Dreams unveiled / Call / This masquerade / Hiding / Surreal embrace / Athanasia / Revelations in black / Wail in weep / Messiah / Children / Gatekeeper
CD _______ CDMFN 210
Music For Nations / Dec '96 / Pinnacle

Meridian Arts Ensemble

TAXIN/BARBER/RADZYNSKI/ SAMPSON/ROBLES
CD _______ CCS 9496
Channel Classics / Jul '96 / Select / Vital/ SAM

Meridian Dream

HOW ABOUT NOW
Aurora / Dwellers in the sky world / 333 / Automatic transmission / Omega / Nazarene / Syncretize / Insect soul dream / Chicone

CD NW 50042
Extreme Noteworks / Jun '97 / Vital/SAM

Merino Brothers

VALLENTINO DYNAMOS
De mi vida una ilusion / Acompaname a sufrir / Mal procedimiento / La democracia / Riquezas de la vida / Minutos felices / Ese soy yo / Maria Elena / Noches de desvelos / Mi padre el campesino
CD CDORB 049
Globestyle / Nov '89 / Pinnacle

Merlons Of Nehemiah

CANTONEY
CD EFA 113952
Musical Tragedies / Jan '94 / SRD

ROMANOIR
CD EFA 122222
Musical Tragedies / Apr '95 / SRD

Merman, Ethel

AMERICAN LEGENDS
I get a kick out of you / Heatwave / Make it another old fashioned, please / Blow, Gabriel, blow / But not for me / You're the top / Hot and happy / Down in the depths on the ninetieth floor / It's delovely / I'll pay the check / Marching along with time / Friendship / You're the top
CD 12741
Laserlight / May '97 / Target/BMG

I GET A KICK OUT OF YOU
CD PASTCD 7056
Flapper / Jan '95 / Pinnacle

MERMAN SINGS MERMAN
You're the top / I got rhythm / You're just in love / Alexander's ragtime band / I got lost in his arms / Eadie was a lady / There's no business like show business / They say it's wonderful / It's de-lovely / I get a kick out of you / Everything's coming up roses / Blow Gabriel blow
CD 8440862
Deram / Aug '92 / PolyGram

Mermen

GLORIOUS LETHAL EUPHORIA, A
CD 7567926342
Warner Bros. / Mar '96 / Warner Music

Merricks

IN SCHWIERIGKEITEN
CD EFA 155462
Sub Up / Apr '95 / SRD

SOUND OF MUNICH, THE
CD EFA 155502
Sub Up / Jun '97 / SRD

Merrill, Helen

BLOSSOM OF STARS
My romance / Willow weep for me / What is this thing called love / Autumn leaves / You'd be so nice to come home to / All of you / Misty Summertime / In a mellow tone / Quand tu dors pres de moi / 'S wonderful / We are not alone
CD 5146522
EmArCy / Feb '94 / PolyGram

BROWNIE
CD 5223632
Verve / Dec '94 / PolyGram

CLEAR OUT OF THIS WORLD
Out of this world / Not like this / I'm all smiles / When I grow too old to dream / Some of these days / Maybe / Tender thing is love / Soon it's gonna rain / Willow weep for me
CD 5106912
EmArCy / Jun '92 / PolyGram

COLLABORATION (Merrill, Helen & Gil Evans)
Summertime / Where flamingoes fly / Dream of you / I'm a fool to want you / Troubled waters / I'm just a lucky so and so / People will say we're in love / By myself / Any place I hang my hat is home / I've never seen / He was too good to me / New town is a blue town
CD 8342052
EmArCy / Apr '93 / PolyGram

DREAM OF YOU
People will say we're in love / By myself / Any place I hang my hat is home / I've never seen / He was too good to me / New town is a blue town / You're lucky to me / Where flamingos fly / Dream of you / I'm a fool to want you / I'm just a lucky so and so / Troubled waters / Alone together / Glad to be unhappy / This is my night to cry / How's the world treating you
CD 5140742
EmArCy / Feb '93 / PolyGram

DREAM OF YOU
Dream of you / People will say we're in love / You'd be so nice to come home to / Any place I hang my hat is home / 'S wonderful / I'm a fool to want you / What's new / Don't explain / By myself / You're lucky to me / Where flamingos fly / Falling in love with love / Yesterdays / I'm just a lucky so and so / Born to be blue / I've never seen / He was too good to me / Troubled waters
CD CD 53234
Giants Of Jazz / Jun '96 / Cadillac / Jazz Music / Target/BMG

HELEN MERRILL WITH CLIFFORD BROWN/GIL EVANS (Merrill, Helen & Clifford Brown/Gil Evans)
Don't expain / You'd be so nice to come home to / What's new / Falling in love with love / Yesterdays / Born to be blue / 'S wonderful / He was too good to me / I've never seen / I'm a fool to want you / Troubled waters / By myself / People will say we're in love / You're lucky to me / Dream of you
CD 8382922
EmArCy / Jan '93 / PolyGram

IN ITALY
CD IRS 0063/5
Liuto / Aug '91 / Cadillac / Harmonia Mundi

JUST FRIENDS (Merrill, Helen & Stan Getz)
Cavatina / It never entered my mind / Just friends / It don't mean a thing if it ain't got that swing / Baby ain't I good to you / It's not easy being green / If you go away / Yesterdays / Music maker
CD 8420072
EmArCy / Apr '93 / PolyGram

OUT OF THIS WORLD
CD 5106912
Philips / Feb '92 / PolyGram

Merry Pranksters

RUMPUS ROOMS, THE (2CD Set)
CD Set NOZACD 01
Ninebar / Apr '96 / Kudos / Prime / RTM/Disc

Merry Thoughts

PSYCHOCULT
CD SPV 08561392
SPV / May '97 / Koch / Plastic Head

Merseybeats

MERSEY SOUNDS
CD HADCD 202
Javelin / Jul '96 / Henry Hadaway / THE

VERY BEST OF THE MERSEYBEATS, THE
I think of you / Don't let it happen to us / Wishin' and hopin' / I love you, yes I do / I stand accused / Last night (I made a little girl cry) / Long tall Sally / It would take a long long time / Milkman / It's love that really counts / Fortune teller / Mr. Moonlight / Hello young lovers / He will break your heart / Really mystified / Good good lovin' / Don't turn around / See me back / Jumping Jonah / All my life
CD 5521022
Spectrum / Jan '97 / PolyGram

Mertens, Wim

AFTER VIRTUE
CD TWICD 825
Les Disques Du Crepuscule / Sep '88 / Discovery

ALLE DINGHE (3CD Set)
CD Set TWI 9432
Les Disques Du Crepuscule / Mar '96 / Discovery

DIVIDED LOYALTIES (2CD Set)
It serves you right / What's mine is yours / Letter of intent / Quotable lines / How about it / How about what / Now you see it, now you don't
CD Set TWI 1004
Les Disques Du Crepuscule / Feb '95 / Discovery

EDUCES ME
CD TWICD 808
Les Disques Du Crepuscule / Sep '88 / Discovery

EPIC THAT NEVER WAS
Circular breathing / Multiple 12 / Land beyond the sunset / Voo outro / Humility / La femme de nulle part / Iris / Kanaries/Night creature / Belly of an architect / Close cover
CD TWI 9832
Les Disques Du Crepuscule / Apr '94 / Discovery

FOR AMUSEMENT ONLY
Insert coin / Deluxe / 8 ball / Mystik / Fireball / Invader / Dog in / Gorf
CD TWI 048CD
Les Disques Du Crepuscule / Jul '88 / Discovery

GAVE VAN NIETS (3CD Set)
De blik omhoog / Ofwel daar, Ofwel Hier / Van wie je alles verwacht / Do komst van een ander / Buiten het oog / Zie niet / Hoor niet / Wees niet / Altijd haast / Waar ik heers / Schillen / Schorsen / Alles gisteren / Het lied / Restorica
CD Set TWI 1005
Les Disques Du Crepuscule / Feb '95 / Discovery

INSTRUMENTAL SONGS
CD TWICD 666
Les Disques Du Crepuscule / Dec '86 / Discovery

JARDIN CLOS
CD TWI 1020
Les Disques Du Crepuscule / Oct '96 / Discovery

JEREMIADES
Kaf / Kof / Mem / Alef / Gimel / Jod
CD TWI 1019
Les Disques Du Crepuscule / Jun '95 / Discovery

MAN WITH NO FORTUNE/WITH A NAME TO COME
CD TWICD 748
Les Disques Du Crepuscule / Nov '86 / Discovery

MAXIMIZING THE AUDIENCE
CD TWI 4802
Les Disques Du Crepuscule / '89 / Discovery

MOTIVES FOR WRITING
CD TWI 8262
Les Disques Du Crepuscule / '89 / Discovery

RECULER POUR MIEUX SAUTER (3CD Set)
Plus grandes les parts du mort / Plus grandes les parts de vie / Trouver les repos / Les saisons qui apportent / Tout / Ce qui arrive / Ce qui se produit / Ce qui a lieu / Le vrai / Le heros / Le cas / Le propos / La mesure
CD Set TWI 1006
Les Disques Du Crepuscule / Feb '95 / Discovery

SHOT AND ECHO
Their duet / His own thing / Watch over me / One who matters / Silver lining / Shot one / We'll find out / Let him go / Wandering eyes
CD TWI 9502
Les Disques Du Crepuscule / May '93 / Discovery

SOURCES OF SLEEPLESSNESS (2CD Set)
CD Set TWI 9412
Les Disques Du Crepuscule / Mar '96 / Discovery

STRATEGIE DE LA RUPTURE
CD TWI 9562
Les Disques Du Crepuscule / Mar '96 / Discovery

WHISPER ME
CD 01934111412
Windham Hill / Sep '95 / BMG

YOU'LL NEVER BE ME (2CD Set)
No - men / Chasms / Leaps / Laid back / Wo - men
CD Set TWI 1003
Les Disques Du Crepuscule / Feb '95 / Discovery

Merton, Johnny

PARTY HITS NON-STOP (Merton, Johnny Party Sound)
Let's twist again / Roll over Beethoven / Rock 'n' roll music / Hound dog / Twist and shout / Baby come back / Black is black / Hippy hippy shake / Bend me shape me / Back in the USSR / Massachussetts / San Francisco / Air that I breathe / All I have to do is dream / California dreamin' / Keep on running / Hey tonight / Girls, girls, girls / Fox on the run / Whiskey in the jar / Relax / Like a virgin / Super trouper / Final countdown / Mr. Vain / Sing hallelujah / Don't talk just kiss / Rhythm is dancer / It's my life
CD 333304
Music / Dec '95 / Target/BMG

Merton Parkas

COMPLETE MOD COLLECTION, THE
CD CDMGRAM 111
Anagram / May '97 / Cargo / Pinnacle

Merzbow

AGE OF 369/CHANT 2
Age of 369 / Chant 2 / Ho makai / Bonus track
CD XLTD 002
Extreme / Mar '97 / Vital/SAM

AKASHA GULVA
CD ALIENCD1
Alien8 / Nov '96 / Cargo / Harmonia Mundi

HYBRID NOISEBLOOM
CD VC 113
Vinyl Communication / Jun '97 / Cargo / Greyhound / Plastic Head

LOVES EMIL BEAULIEAU
CD PURE 45
Pure / Jun '97 / Greyhound

MERZBOW/BASTARD NOISE (Merzbow/ Bastard Noise)
CD RR 9646
Release / Nov '96 / Cargo

MUSIC FOR BONDAGE PERFORMANCE VOL.2
CD XCD 034
Extreme / Oct '96 / Vital/SAM

OERSTED
CD VC 104CD
Vinyl Communication / Oct '96 / Cargo / Greyhound / Plastic Head

RAINBOW ELECTRONICS VOL.2
CD DEX 6
Dexter's Cigar / Dec '96 / Cargo

RECTAL ANARCHY (Merzbow/Gore Beyond)
Punks not Dead Kennedys rectal anarchy / Chaos disorder rectal anarchy / Pretty vacant panty rectal anarchy / Love me Suicidal Tendencies rectal anarchy / Sunlight path rectal anarchy / Between nothingness and eternity rectal anarchy / Split crotch disorder rectal anarchy / Snatch punk rectal anarchy / Pussy poking disorder chaos anarchy rectal anarchy / In tight disorder rectal anarchy / Tits 4 chaos rectal anarchy / Finger friggin' in grind rectal anarchy / Melon and mounds rectal mosh anarchy / There way all the mosh rectal anarchy / Say ah punks rectal anarchy / That takes balls rectal anarchy / Ski meat funky rectal anarchy / Jeff Stryker super star rectal anarchy / Horse named rectal anarchy / Heritage banner dictate passion hate rectal anarchy / Force dead face apathy under the rectal anarchy / London calling chaos damnation action violent anarchy / Parricide blaze of socialized rectal anarchy / Agent orange country war feast rectal anarchy / Release from agony state of processsion rectal anarchy / Morbid shit confusion anarchy / Violent rectal anarchy / Manta size shit body pollution hate rectal anarchy / Up her shit emotion disregarded qrectal anarchy / He can fly them against cruel no harm shit rectal anarchy
CD RR 69622
Relapse / May '97 / Pinnacle / Plastic Head

SCUMTRON
House of kaya: *O'Rourke, Jim* / Eat beat eat: *O'Rourke, Jim* / Elephants memory: *Panasonic* / Anmon: *Rehberg & Bauer* / Micromedley: *Haswell, Russell* / Ecobondage: *Autechre* / Eat beat eat 1 / Untitled: *Gunter, Bernhard*
CD BFFP 138CD
Blast First / Jun '97 / RTM/Disc

SPIRAL HONEY
CD WIP 004
Work In Progress / Oct '96 / Cargo

TINT
CD VC 110CD
Vinyl Communication / Jun '97 / Cargo / Greyhound / Plastic Head

VENEREOLOGY
Ananga-ranga / Kloken phantasie / I lead you / Towards glorious times / Slave new desert
CD RR 69102
Relapse / Jul '97 / Pinnacle / Plastic Head

Merzy

MERZY
CD MMT 3303CD
Shark / May '90 / Plastic Head

Mesa Music Consort

SPIRITS OF THE WILD
CD TTCD 131
Talking Taco / Mar '96 / ADA

Meshuggah

CONTRADICTIONS COLLAPSE
CD NB 049CD
Nuclear Blast / Jun '96 / Plastic Head

DESTROY ERASE IMPROVE
CD NB 121DCD
Nuclear Blast / May '95 / Plastic Head

NONE
CD NB 102CD
Nuclear Blast / Jun '95 / Plastic Head

Mess Of Booze

STAATSFEIND NR.1
CD PT 615001
Part / Jun '96 / Nervous

Messaoud, Bellemou

LE PERE DU RAI
CD WCD 011
World Circuit / May '89 / ADA / Cadillac / Direct / New Note/Pinnacle

Messer, Michael

MOONBEAT
CD APCD 123
Appaloosa / Nov '95 / ADA / Direct / TKO Magnum

NATIONAL AVENUE
CD SCRD 018
Scratch / Apr '97 / Koch / Scratch/BMG

Messiah

21ST CENTURY JESUS
Age of the machine / Beyond good and evil / Defiance / There is no law / Temple of dreams / Creator / Peace and tranquility / Thunderdome / Destroyer / I feel love / 20,000 hardcore members / Desire
CD 4509943932
WEA / Dec '93 / Warner Music

Messiah

PSYCHOMORPHIA
CD N 01803
Noise / '91 / Koch

ROTTEN PERISH
CD N 01952
Noise / Jul '92 / Koch

UNDERGROUND
CD N 02442
Noise / Jun '94 / Koch

Messiah Force

LAST DAY, THE
Sequel / Watch out / White night / Hero's saga / Third one / Call from the night / Spirit killer / Silent tyrant / Last day
CD BRMCD 022
Bold Reprive / Oct '88 / Harmonia Mundi

Messina, Jim

WATCHING THE RIVER RUN
CD FIENDCD 935
Demon / Aug '97 / Pinnacle

Mestisay

LA ROSA DE LOS VIENTOS
Sulema / Fado de mar / Donde te Lleva/El Corazon / Son del tronquillo / La flor de Guinea / La Rosa de Los Vientos / Canta Machin / Olvidarme de querer / Canciones del sur / Asi / Estrella y ana / Sangueo
CD INT 32072
Intuition / Aug '97 / New Note/Pinnacle

Meta

SONGS AND DANCES FROM HUNGARY
CD EUCD 1068
ARC / '89 / ADA / ARC Music

WINTER AND CHRISTMAS SONGS FROM HUNGARY
CD EUCD 1085
ARC / '91 / ADA / ARC Music

Metal Church

HANGING IN THE BALANCE
CD SPV 08562170
SPV / May '94 / Koch / Plastic Head

Metal Molly

SURGERY FOR ZEBRA
CD ORECD 544
Silvertone / Nov '96 / Pinnacle

Metal Sound

METAL SOUND
CD 503412
Declic / Apr '95 / Jet Star

Metallica

AND JUSTICE FOR ALL
Blackened / Eye of the beholder / Shortest straw / Frayed ends of sanity / Dyes eve / And justice for all / One / Harvester of sorrow / To live is to die
CD 8360622
Vertigo / Oct '88 / PolyGram

BAY AREA THRASHERS, THE (Interview/2CD Set)
CD Set OTR 1100060
Metro Independent / Aug '97 / Essential/ BMG

INTERVIEW DISC
CD SAM 7012
Sound & Media / Nov '96 / Sound & Media

KILL 'EM ALL
Hit the lights / Four horsemen / Motorbreath / Jump in the fire / Pulling teeth (Anasthesia) / Whiplash / Phantom lord / No remorse / Seek and destroy / Metal militia
CD 8381422
Vertigo / May '89 / PolyGram

LOAD
Ain't my bitch / 2X4 / House that Jack built / Until it sleeps / King nothing / Hero of the day / Bleeding me / Cure / Poor twisted me / Wasting my hate / Mama said / Thorn within / Ronnie / Outlaw thorn
CD 5326182
Vertigo / Jun '96 / PolyGram

MASTER OF PUPPETS
Battery / Master of puppets / Thing that should not be / Welcome home (Sanitarium) / Disposable heroes / Leper messiah / Orion / Damage Inc
CD 8381412
Vertigo / May '89 / PolyGram

METAL MILITIA (A Tribute To Metallica) (Various Artists)
Disposable heroes / Leper messiah / For whom the bell tolls / Fight fire with fire / Battery / Escape / Motorbreath / Thing that should not be / Damage Inc / Eye of the beholder / Fade to black
CD BS 01CD
Dolores / Feb '95 / Plastic Head

METALLIC-ERA (Various Artists)
CD NM 011CD
Neat Metal / Oct '96 / Pinnacle

METALLICA
Enter sandman / Sad but true / Holier than thou / Unforgiven / Wherever I may roam / Don't tread on me / Through the never / Nothing else matters / Of wolf and man / God that failed / My friend of misery / Struggle within
CD 5100222
Vertigo / Aug '91 / PolyGram

METALLICA: INTERVIEW COMPACT DISC
CD CBAK 4016
Baktabak / Nov '89 / Arabesque

METALLICA: INTERVIEW COMPACT DISC VOL.2
CD CBAK 4053
Baktabak / Apr '92 / Arabesque

PLAYS METALLICA BY FOUR CELLOS (Apocalyptica)
CD 5327072
Vertigo / Sep '96 / PolyGram

RE-LOAD (Interview Disc)
CD DIST 007
Disturbed / Aug '96 / Total/BMG

RIDE THE LIGHTNING
Fight fire with fire / Ride the lightning / For whom the bell tolls / Fade to black / Trapped under ice / Escape / Creeping death / Call of Ktulu
CD 8381402
Vertigo / May '89 / PolyGram

TRIBUTE TO METALLICA VOL.2, A (Various Artists)
CD TR 001CD
Tribute / Apr '96 / Plastic Head

Metamatics

METAMATICS PRODUCTION, A
CD CLR 429CD
Clear / Apr '97 / Prime / RTM/Disc

Metamora

GREAT ROAD, THE
CD SHCD 1134
Sugar Hill / Jan '97 / ADA / CM / Direct / Koch / Roots

METAMORA
CD SHCD 1131
Sugar Hill / May '95 / ADA / CM / Direct / Koch / Roots

Meteors

BASTARD SONS OF A ROCK 'N' ROLL DEVIL
CD HELLRAISER 001CD
Hellraiser / Jan '97 / Cargo

BEST OF THE METEORS, THE
Voodoo rhythm / Graveyard stomp / Wreckin' crew / Mutant rock / Hills have eyes / Johnny remember me / When a stranger calls / I don't worry about it / I'm just a dog / Stampede / Fire, fire / Hogs and cuties / Bad moon rising / Rhythm of the bell / Surf city / Go Buddy go / Don't touch the bang bang fruit / Swamp thing / Rawhide / Surfin' on the planet zorch / Somebody put something in my drink / Please don't touch / Chainsaw boogie / Madman roll / Who do you love
CD CDMGRAM 66
Anagram / Sep '93 / Cargo / Pinnacle

GRAVEYARD STOMP (Best Of The Meteors 1981-1988)
Voodoo rhythm / Graveyard stomp / Wreckin' crew / Sick things / Blue sunshine / Mutant rock / Hills have ears / Michael Myers / Bad moon rising / Fire fire / Power of steel / Eat the baby / Rhythm of the bell / Surf city / Go Buddy go / Somebody put something in my drink / Don't touch the bang bang fruit / Corpse grinder
CD NTMCD 508
Nectar / Sep '95 / Pinnacle

IN HEAVEN
In Heaven / Shout so loud / Earwigs in my brain / In the cards / Attack of the zorch men / Crazed / Get off my cloud / Love you to death / Teenagers from outer space / Maniac / Into the darkness / Death dance / Psycho for your love / Room / Rockabilly psychosis
CD EDCD 509
Edsel / Feb '97 / Pinnacle

INTERNATIONAL WRECKERS VOL.2 (The Lost Tapes Of Zorch)
Shout so loud / Death dance / Michael Myers / Sweet love on my mind / I'm just a dog / Stampede / Kit boy / Hills have eyes / Long blond hair / Graveyard stomp / Ain't gonna bring me down / Hoover rock / Love you to death / In the cards / Rockhouse / When a stranger calls / I ain't ready / Maybe tomorrow
CD RRCD 230
Receiver / Oct '96 / Grapevine/PolyGram

LIVE STYLES OF THE SICK AND SHAMELESS
Ex-men boogie / Wipeout / Rattlesnakin' daddy / Mutant rock / Maniac / Blue sunshine / Mind over matter / These boots / Lil' red riding hood / Hill have eyes / Wild thing / I go to bed (with the undead) / Voodoo rhythm / I ain't ready / Wreckin' crew / Lonesome train (on a lonesome track) / Rock bop / Ain't gonna bring me down / Graveyard stomp
CD SUMCD 4109
Sound & Media / Mar '97 / Sound & Media

MUTANT MONKEY AND THE SURFERS FROM ZORCH
Swamp thing / Electro II (the revenge) / Side walk psycho / I'm invisible man / She's my baby again / Surfin' on the planet Zorch / Spine bender / Dance crazy baby / Rawhide / Oxygen dog / Yellow zone / Meet me in the morgue
CD CDMPSYCHO 12
Anagram / Feb '97 / Cargo / Pinnacle

ONLY THE METEORS ARE PURE PSYCHOBILLY
Voodoo rhythm / Graveyard stomp / Wreckin' crew / Sick things / Blue sunshine / Mutant rock / Hills have eyes / Fire, fire / Power of steel / Eat the baby / Rhythm of the bell / Sure city / Go buddy go / Somebody put something in my drink
CD SUMCD 4089
Summit / Jan '97 / Sound & Media

SEWERTIME BLUES
Ain't taking a chance / So sad / Here's Johnny / Mind over matter / Acid and psyam / Sewertime blues / Return of Ethel Merman / Deep dark jungle / Never get away / I bury the living / Vibrate / Surf city / Go Buddy go / Midnight people / Low livin' daddy / Your worst nightmare / Wildkat ways / Repo man / Don't touch the bang bang fruit / Crack me up / Shaky shaky / Psycho kat / Let's go / Revenge of the el trio los bastados
CD CDMPSYCHO 3
Anagram / Apr '95 / Cargo / Pinnacle

STAMPEDE/MONKEY BREATH
Ex man boogie / Power of steel / Hoover rock / Kit boy / Maybe tomorrow / Electro / Stampede / Just a dog / In too deep / Cecil drives a combine harvester / Michael Myers / Only a fury in my heart / Hogs and cuties / Alligator man / Rhythm of the bell / You're out of time / Ain't gonna bring me down / Night of the werewolf / Take a ride / Just the three of us / Meat is meat / Jobba's revenge
CD CDMSPSYCHO 9
Anagram / Oct '95 / Cargo / Pinnacle

TEENAGERS FROM OUTER SPACE
Voodoo rhythm / Maniac rockers from hell / My daddy is a vampire / You can't keep a good man down / Graveyard stomp / Radioactive kid / Leave me alone / Dog eat robot / Walter Mitty blues / Just the three of us / Blue sunshine / Insight / Attack of the zorch men / Jupiter stroll / Another half hour till sunrise / Island of lost souls / Napoleon solo / Get me to the world on time
CD CDWIK 47
Big Beat / May '86 / Pinnacle

UNDEAD, UNFRIENDLY AND UNSTOPPABLE
Razor back / Disneyland / My kind of rockin' / Lonesome train (on a lonesome track) / Johnny God / I go to bed with the undead / Out of the attic / Brains as well / Charlie Johnny Rawhead and me / Lies in wait / Surf mad pig / Please don't touch
CD CDMPSYCHO 2
Cherry Red / Apr '95 / Pinnacle

WELCOME TO THE WRECKIN' PITT
CD RRCD 217
Receiver / Apr '96 / Grapevine/PolyGram

Meters

CRESCENT CITY GROOVE MERCHANTS
CD CPCD 8066
Charly / Nov '94 / Koch

FUNDAMENTALLY FUNKY
CD CPCD 8044
Charly / Jun '94 / Koch

FUNKY MIRACLE
CD CDNEV 2
Charly / Mar '91 / Koch

GOOD OLD FUNKY MUSIC
Look-ka-py-py / Seahorn's farm / Art / Ease back / Cissy strut / Message from the Meters / Thinking / Good old funky music / Live wire / Stretch your rubber band / Doodle-opp / Tippi toes / Rigor mortis / Nine to five / Sophisticated Cissy / Chicken strut / Here come the metermen / Darling darling / Dry spell / Ride your pony
CD ROUCD 2104
Rounder / Dec '94 / ADA / CM / Direct

ORIGINAL FUNKMASTERS, THE
Sophisticated Sissy / Funky miracles / Look-ka py py / Ease back / Ride your pony / Stormy / Dry spell / Cissy strut / Tippi toes / Chicken strut / I need more time / Live wire / Handclapping song / Message from The Meters / Here comes The Metermen
CD CPCD 8229
Charly / Sep '96 / Koch

SECOND HELPING (Meters & The JB Horns)
CD LAKE 2026
Lakeside / Aug '95 / TKO Magnum

UPTOWN RULERS (Live On The Queen Mary 1975)
Fire on the bayou / Africa / It ain't no use / Make it with you / Cissy strut / Cardova / It's your thing / Love the one you're with / Rockin' pneumonia and the boogie woogie flu / I know / Everybody loves a lover / Liar / Mardi gras mambo / Hey pocky away
CD NEXCD 220
Sequel / Sep '92 / BMG

Meth OD

TEXAS GOD STARVATION
Long distance voyeurism / Produktiv konduktor / First zen temple of New York / Dbug now / High school high / August / Goldinger / Big dipper / Kaptain clearview / Bastard Tarantino
CD HCCD 002
Human Condition / Mar '97 / RTM/Disc

Metheny, Pat

80-81 (2CD Set)
Goin' ahead / Two folk songs / Bat / Turn around / Open / Pretty scattered / Everyday I thank you
CD Set 843 169 2
ECM / Oct '90 / New Note/Pinnacle

AMERICAN GARAGE
(Cross the) Heartland / Airstream / Search / American garage / Epic
CD 8271342
ECM / Dec '85 / New Note/Pinnacle

AS FALLS WICHITA, SO FALLS WICHITA FALLS (Metheny, Pat & Lyle Mays)
As falls Wichita, so falls Wichita Falls / September 15th / It's for you / Estupenda graca
CD 8214162
ECM / Jul '85 / New Note/Pinnacle

BRIGHT SIZE LIFE
Bright size life / Sirabhorn / Unity village / Missouri incompromised / Midwestern nights dream / Unquity road / Omaha celebration / Round trip-Broadway blues
CD 8271332
ECM / Dec '86 / New Note/Pinnacle

FIRST CIRCLE (Metheny, Pat Group)
Forward march / Yolanda / You learn / First circle / If I could / Tell it all / End of the game / Mas alla (beyond) / Praise
CD 8233422
ECM / Nov '84 / New Note/Pinnacle

NEW CHAUTAUQUA
New chautauqua / Country poem / Long ago child / Fallen star / Hermitage / Sueno con Mexico / Daybreak
CD 8254712
ECM / Aug '85 / New Note/Pinnacle

OFFRAMP
Barcarolle / Are you going with me / Au lait / Eighteen / Offramp / James / Bat (part 2)
CD 8171382
ECM / Sep '84 / New Note/Pinnacle

PAT METHENY GROUP (Metheny, Pat Group)
San Lorenzo / Phase dance / Jaco / Aprilwind / April joy / Lone jack
CD 8255932
ECM / Aug '88 / New Note/Pinnacle

PAT METHENY/PAUL WERTICO/GREGG BENDIAN/DEREK BAILEY (3CD Set) (Metheny, Pat & Paul Wertico/Gregg Bendian/Derek Bailey)
CD KFWCD 197
Knitting Factory / May '97 / Cargo / Plastic Head

QUARTET
Introduction / When we were free / Montevideo / Take me there / Seven days / Oceania / Dismantling Utopia / Double blind / Second thought / Mojave / Badland / Glacier / Language of time / Sometimes I see / As I am
CD GED 24978
Geffen / Jan '97 / BMG

QUESTION AND ANSWER (Metheny, Pat/Dave Holland/Roy Haynes)
Solar / Question and answer / H and H / Never too far away / Law years / Change of heart / All the things you are / Old folks / Three flights up
CD GFLD 19197
Geffen / Mar '93 / BMG

REJOICING
Lonely woman / Tears inside / Humpty dumpty / Blues for Pat / Rejoicing / Story from a stranger / Calling / Waiting for an answer

CD 8177952
ECM / Jun '84 / New Note/Pinnacle

ROAD TO YOU, THE
Have you heard / First circle / Road to you / Half life of absolution / Last train home / Better days ahead / Naked moon / Beat 70 / Letter from home / Third wind / Solo from More travels
CD GED 24601
Geffen / Jul '93 / BMG

SECRET STORY
Above the treetops / Facing west / Cathedral in a suitcase / Finding and believing / Longest summer / Sunlight / Rain river / Always and forever / See the world / As a flower blossoms (I am running to you) / Antonia / Truth will always be / Tell her you saw me / Not to be forgotten (our final our)
CD GEFD 24468
Geffen / Jul '92 / BMG

STILL LIFE TALKING (Metheny, Pat Group)
Minuano / So may it secretly begin / Last train home / It's just talk / Third wind / Distance / In her family
CD GFLD 19196
Geffen / Mar '93 / BMG

TRAVELS (2CD Set) (Metheny, Pat Group)
Are you going with me / Fields, the sky / Goodbye / Phase dance / Straight on red / Farmer's trust / Extradition / Goin' ahead / As falls Wichita, so falls Wichita Falls / Travels / Song for Bilbao / San Lorenzo
CD Set 8106222
ECM / Aug '86 / New Note/Pinnacle

WATERCOLORS
Watercolors / Icefire / Lakes / River Quay / Florida Greeting song / Legend of the fountain / Sea song
CD 8274092
ECM / Feb '86 / New Note/Pinnacle

WE LIVE HERE
Here to stay / And then I knew / Girls next door / To the end of the world / We live here / Episode d'azur / Something to remind you / Red sky / Stranger in town
CD GED 24729
Geffen / Jan '95 / BMG

WORKS: PAT METHENY
Sueno con Mexico / (Cross the) Heartland / Travels / James / It's for you / Everyday I thank you / Goin' ahead
CD 8232702
ECM / Jun '89 / New Note/Pinnacle

ZERO TOLERANCE FOR SILENCE
CD GED 24626
Geffen / Apr '94 / BMG

Method Man

TICAL
Tical / Biscuits / Bring the pain / All I need / What the blood clot / Meth vs. Chef / Subcrazy / Release yo'self / PLO style / I get my thang in action / Mr. Sandman / Stimulation / Method man / I'll be there for you/ You're all I need to get by: *Method Man & Mary J. Blige*
CD 5238392
Def Jam / Dec '94 / PolyGram

Methodist Central Hall Choir

20 FAVOURITE HYMNS OF CHARLES WESLEY
O for a thousand tongues to sing / Lo he comes with clouds descending / Father of everlasting grace / Forth in thy name, O lord, I go / Charge to keep I have / Captain of Istael's host / Happy the man that finds the grace / All praise to our redeeming lord / Jesu lover of my soul / Ye servants of God / Come sinners to the gospel feast / Christ, whose glory fills the skies / Jesus the first and last / Thou God of truth and love / Earth rejoice, our lord is king / What shall I do my lord to love / O thou who camest from above / Let earth and heaven agree / Come thou long expected Jesus / And can it be that I should gain
CD CDMVP 828
SCS Music / Apr '94 / Conifer/BMG

Metri

METRI
CD SAHK 0006
Sahko / Apr '94 / Plastic Head / SRD

Metro

TREE PEOPLE
CD LIP 890312
Lipstick / Sep '95 / Vital/SAM

Metroshifter

METROSHIFTER, THE
CD CR 021CD
Conversion / Jul '96 / Plastic Head

Metura, Philip

SENTIMENTAL LOVE
CD LM 60732
Melodie / '91 / ADA / Discovery / Grapevine/PolyGram / Greensleeves / Jet Star

Metz, Henrik

HENRIK METZ, FREDRIK LUNDIN & NIELS PEDERSON (Metz, Henrik & Fredrik Lundin/Niels Pederson)
CD MECCACD 1024
Music Mecca / Oct '93 / Cadillac / Jazz Music / Wellard

Meurkens, Hendrik

CLEAR OF CLOUDS
Samba for Claudio / Clear of clouds / Seu acalento / Mambo inn / Estate / Chega de saudade/To Brenda with love / Hesitation / Beauty and the priest / You go to my head / Joe's donut / Allan's theme
CD CCD 4531
Concord Picante / Nov '92 / New Note/ Pinnacle

OCTOBER COLORS
October colors / Who did it / In motion / Night in the afternoon / Brigas, nunca mais / Footprints / Chorinho no 1 / Summer in San Francisco / Tranchan / High tide
CD CCD 4670
Concord Jazz / Nov '95 / New Note/ Pinnacle

POEMA BRASILEIRO
Her smile / Boa Noticia / Desperar jamais / Chelsea nocturne / Angel eyes / Saindo de mim / Felicidade / Peach (Chorinho No.4) / One note samba / Passarin / Manhattan samba
CD CCD 4728
Concord Picante / Sep '96 / New Note/ Pinnacle

SLIDIN'
Come rain or come shine / Have you met Miss Jones / Slidin' / Cottage / Bolero para paquito / All of you / Stolen moments / Fortuna / Tribute / Voyage / Once was / Talking trout
CD CCD 4628
Concord Jazz / Jan '95 / New Note/ Pinnacle

VIEW FROM MANHATTAN, A
Meet you after dark / Whisper not / Park Avenue South / Speak low / Naima / Prague in March / Monster and the flower / Body and soul / Madison Square / Moment's notice / Child is born
CD CCD 4585
Concord Jazz / Dec '93 / New Note/ Pinnacle

Meuross, Reg

GOODBYE HAT, THE
CD RTMCD 75
Round Tower / Feb '96 / Avid/BMG

Meves, Carol

NATURAL FLUTE, THE
CD 2685
NorthSound / Aug '96 / Gallant

Mevlevi Ensemble

WHEREVER YOU TURN IS THE FACE OF GOD
CD WLAES 50CD
Waterlilly Acoustics / Feb '96 / ADA

Mexican Mariachi Band

MARIACHI FROM MEXICO
CD 15284
Laserlight / '91 / Target/BMG

Mexican Pets

HUMBUCKER
Hill of beans / Machu picchu / No distance / Supermarket / Versus Jesus / Sunny day / Western union / If only never / Roses / Nancy / Used gettin' used
CD BLUNT 016
Blunt / Apr '97 / Vital

NOBODY'S WORKING TITLE
Stigmata errata / Subside / Magnet force / How to have more fun / Bruise / Merry hell
CD BLUNT 013
Blunt / Mar '96 / Vital

VOICE OF TRUCKER YOUTH, THE
Diana the moon / Magnet force / Mackerel sky high / Subside / Daktari / Stigmata errata / How to have more fun / Where's my pony / Bruise / Scarper / Secret saviour / Merry hell
CD BLUNT 014
Blunt / Jul '96 / Vital

Mexico 70

DUST HAS COME TO STAY, THE
Wonderful lie / Just like we never came down / What's in your mind / Sacred heart / I feel fine / Drug is the love / All day long / Find someone else to play Misty / For you / Always by your side / Queen of swords / You make it worse / Make it right / Kenton's lane
CD CDBRED 101
Cherry Red / Jun '92 / Pinnacle

Mey, Reinhard

DIE GROSSEN ERFOLGE
CD INT 860 191
Interchord / '88 / CM

DIE ZWOLFTE
CD INT 865 001
Interchord / '88 / CM

Meyer, Liz

WOMANLY ARTS
CD SCR 37
Strictly Country / Dec '94 / ADA / Direct

Meyer, Peter 'Banjo'

JAZZ PARTY
CD CD 009
Nagel Heyer / May '96 / Jazz Music

Meyer, Richard

LETTER FROM THE OPEN SKY, A
CD SHCD 8012
Shanachie / Dec '94 / ADA / Greensleeves / Koch

Meyers, Augie

WHITE BOY
CD MWCD 2019
Music & Words / Dec '95 / ADA / Direct

Meza, Lisandro

AMOR LINDO
CD TUMICD 017
Tumi / '91 / Discovery / Stern's

CUMBIAS COLOMBIANAS
CD TUMICD 046
Tumi / '94 / Discovery / Stern's

Mezcla

FRONTERAS DE SUENOS
La Guagua / Fronteras de Suenos / La mulata de Caramelo / Ikiri adda / Rio quibu / Vivir para ver / Como una campana de cristal / Muros transparentes / Ando buscando uno amor
CD INT 30472
Intuition / Feb '91 / New Note/Pinnacle

Mezquida, Allen

GOOD THING, A
CD 378222
Koch Jazz / Aug '96 / Koch

Mezzoforte

RISING
Check it in / Take off / Happy hour / Waves / Blizzard / Solid / Northern comfort / Fiona rising / Check it out
CD ZYX 100232
ZYX / Nov '96 / ZYX

Mezzrow, Mezz

KING JAZZ VOL.1 (Mezzrow-Bechet Quintet & Septet)
CD KJ 101FS
King Jazz / Oct '93 / Cadillac / Discovery / Jazz Music

KING JAZZ VOL.2 (Mezzrow-Bechet Quintet & Septet)
CD KJ 102FS
King Jazz / Oct '93 / Cadillac / Discovery / Jazz Music

KING JAZZ VOL.3 (Mezzrow-Bechet Quintet & Septet)
CD KJ 103FS
King Jazz / Oct '93 / Cadillac / Discovery / Jazz Music

KING JAZZ VOL.4 (Mezzrow-Bechet Quintet & Septet)
CD KJ 104FS
King Jazz / Oct '93 / Cadillac / Discovery / Jazz Music

MEZZ MEZZROW 1928-36 (Mezzrow, Milton 'Mezz')
CD CLASSICS 713
Classics / Jul '93 / Discovery / Jazz Music

MEZZ MEZZROW 1936-1939 (Mezzrow, Milton 'Mezz')
CD CLASSICS 694
Classics / May '93 / Discovery / Jazz Music

MEZZROW/BECHET QUINTET/SEPTET (Mezzrow-Bechet Quintet & Septet)
CD STCD 8212
Storyville / May '93 / Cadillac / Jazz Music / Wellard

MEZZROW/BECHET QUINTET/SEPTET VOL.2 (Mezzrow-Bechet Quintet & Septet)
CD STCD 8213
Storyville / May '93 / Cadillac / Jazz Music / Wellard

MEZZROW/BECHET QUINTET/SEPTET VOL.3 (Mezzrow, Milton 'Mezz')
CD STCD 8214
Storyville / May '93 / Cadillac / Jazz Music / Wellard

MEZZROW/BECHET QUINTET/SEPTET VOL.4 (Mezzrow, Milton 'Mezz')
CD STCD 8215
Storyville / May '93 / Cadillac / Jazz Music / Wellard

MF Pitbulls

FIRST SIN
First sin / Magnetize / Goodbye man / I kill for me / Lube / Senile / All gone / Contemplate / King of decay / She is coming / Religion / Green eyed lady / Right here in hell
CD RAWCD 119
Raw Power / Oct '96 / Pinnacle

MFSB

LOVE IS THE MESSAGE
Interlude / Love is the message / Poinciana / Freddie's dead / My one and only love / Sexy / Something for nothing / Zack's fanfare (I hear music) / Back Stabbers / Bitter sweet / TSOP (The sound of Philadelphia) / Cheaper to keep her / My mood / TLC (Tender lovin' care) / Philadelphia freedom / Smile happy
CD 4809042
Columbia / Jan '96 / Sony

Mhlongo, Busi

BABHEMU
Izinziswa / Ting-tingu (Cash dispenser) / Unomkhubulwane (African angel) / Umenthisi (Matches) / Shosholoza (Keep going) / Mfazonga phesheva (Woman from abroad) / Ujantshi (Rails) / Ntandane (Orphan)
CD STCD 1053
Stern's / Mar '94 / ADA / CM / Stern's

Mhoireach, Anna

INTO INDIGO
Finbarr Saunders: *Campbell, Rory* / Gaol na h-oige, na goisidich: *Campbell, Rory* / Tar the house / Medley / Zeto the bubbleman / Medley / Tarruing teann an crios / Medley / Ballivanich / Medley / Miss Campbell of Sheerness / Medley / Medley / Medley
CD CDLDL 1249
Lochshore / Mar '97 / ADA / Direct / Duncans

OUT OF THE BLUE
CD CDLDL 1219
Lochshore / Nov '94 / ADA / Direct / Duncans

Miaabal, Robert

SONG CARRIER
CD MTI 1295
MTI / Aug '96 / ADA

Miah, Shahjahan

MYSTICAL BAUL SONGS OF BANGLADESH
CD AUW 260039
Auvidis/Ethnic / Feb '93 / ADA / Harmonia Mundi

Miasma 1195

EMIT 1195
CD EMIT 1195
Time Recordings / Mar '95 / Pinnacle

Mic Force

IT AIN'T OVER
CD MOVE 7009CD
Move / Apr '94 / Plastic Head

Micaelli, Jacky

CORSICA SACRA
Agnus dei / Lamentu di Ghjesu / Kyrie / Perdono mio dio / Stabat mater / Tota pulchra / L'amica / Sanctus / Adoriamo / Lodi al sepolcro / Dio vi salvi regina / Misere mini mei
CD B 6842
Auvidis/Ethnic / Jan '97 / ADA / Harmonia Mundi

Michael Learns To Rock

MICHAEL LEARNS TO ROCK
My blue angel / Looking at love / Kiss in the rain / Actor / Messages / I still carry on / Crazy dream / African Queen / Come on and dance / Let's build a room
CD CDEMC 3625
Impact / Aug '92 / EMI

Michael, George

FAITH
Faith / Father figure / I want your sex / One more try / Hard day / Hand to mouth / Look at your hands / Monkey / Kissing a fool / Last request (I want your sex, pt 3)
CD 4600002
Epic / Nov '87 / Sony

INTERVIEW DISC
CD _______ **SAM 7024**
Sound & Media / Jan '97 / Sound & Media

LISTEN WITHOUT PREJUDICE VOL.1
Praying for time / Freedom 90 / They won't go when I go / Something to save / Cowboys and angels / Waiting for that day / Mothers pride / Heal the pain / Soul free / Waiting (Reprise)
CD _______ **4672952**
Epic / Sep '90 / Sony

OLDER
Jesus to a child / Fastlove / Older / Spinning the wheel / It doesn't really matter / Strangest thing / To be forgiven / Move on / Star people / You have been loved / Free
CD _______ **CDV 2802**
Virgin / Apr '96 / EMI

Michael, Walt

MUSIC FOR HAMMERED DULCIMER
CD _______ **EP 101**
Eastwick Productions / Mar '94 / Inform

STEP STONE
CD _______ **FF 70480**
Flying Fish / Apr '94 / ADA / CM / Direct / Roots

Michaels, Lee

COLLECTION, THE
CD _______ **8122703742**
WEA / Jul '93 / Warner Music

Michel, Matthieu

ESTATE
Leaving / Never let me go / Moon princess / It could be worse / Estate / Round trip / Sail away / Caruso / On the spot / Moment to moment
CD _______ **TCB 95802**
TCB / Dec '95 / New Note/Pinnacle

Michigan & Smiley

DOWNPRESSION (Michigan, Papa & General Smiley)
Downpression / Natty heng on in deh / Come when Jah call you / Ghetto man / Jah army / Diseases / Living in a babylon / Jah know / Arise / Come on black people
CD _______ **GRELCD 42**
Greensleeves / Aug '95 / Jet Star / SRD

RUB-A-DUB STYLE
CD _______ **HBCD 3512**
Heartbeat / May '92 / ADA / Direct / Greensleeves / Jet Star

SUGAR DADDY
CD _______ **RASCD 3004**
Ras / Nov '92 / Direct / Greensleeves / Jet Star / SRD

Michigan State University

TRIBUTE (Featuring Steven Mead)
Original fantasie / Night in June / From the shores of the mighty Pacific / Rhapsody / Beautiful Colorado / Concertino / Fanrasia di concerto / Estrellita / Atlantic Zephyrs / Believe me, if all those endearing young charms / Flower Song / Auld lang syne
CD _______ **QPRM 118D**
Polyphonic / Aug '92 / Complete/Pinnacle

Michiru, Monday

DELICIOUS POISON (Michiru, Monday & The Paradox Band)
CD _______ **5376412**
Verve / Jul '97 / PolyGram

Mickey & Ludella

BEDLAM A GO-GO
That look that you gave to me / I believed your lies / Stop and listen / Ain't nobody's friend / I'm afraid they're all talkin about me / Tell me / Surfin' snow matador / Bedlam a go-go / Bring it back / Do I expect to much / Standing next to the railway track / We're gonna get married / I'm on the way down / She's drunk / Well now
CD _______ **ASKCD 052**
Vinyl Japan / Jan '96 / Plastic Head / Vinyl Japan

Mickey & Sylvia

LOVE IS STRANGE (2CD Set)
Forever and a day / Se de boom run dun / I'm so glad / Rise Sally rise / Seems like just yesterday / Peace of mind / No good lover / Love is strange / Walkin' in the rain / Two shadows on your window / Who knows why / In my heart / I'm going home / Two shadows on your window (with chorus) / There oughta be a law / Dearest / Where is my honey / Too much weight / Let's have a picnic / New idea on love / Say the word / Love will make you fail in school / I gotta be home by ten / Love is a treasure / Loving you darling / I'm working at the five and dime / Shake it up / There'll be no backin' out / Summertime / Rock and stroll room (take 1) / Rock and stroll room (take 12) / It's you love / True, true, love / Bewildered / Oh yeah Uh huh / To the valley / Mommy out de light / Gonna work out fine / What would I do / Sweeter as the days goes by / I'm glad for your sake / I hear you knocking / Love lesson / This is my story / Baby you're so fine / Love is the only thing / Dearest / From the beginning of time / Fallin' in love / Gypsy / Yours / Let's shake some more
CD Set _______ **BCD 15438**
Bear Family / May '90 / Direct / Rollercoaster / Swift

WILLOW SESSIONS
Love is strange / He gave me everything / Love drops / Hucklebuck / Baby you're so fine / Mickey's blues / Anytime / Darling (I miss you so) / Walking in the rain / I'm guilty / Loving you darling / Sylvia's blues / Since I fell for you / Love is the only thing / I can't help it / Our name (alternative take) / Because you do it to me / Soulin' with Mickey and Sylvia
CD _______ **NEM 763**
Sequel / Jan '96 / BMG

Microdisney

BIG SLEEPING HOUSE (A Collection Of Choice Cuts)
Horse overboard / Loftholdingswood / Singer's Hampstead home / She only gave in to her anger / Gale force wind / I can't say no / Angels / Mrs. Simpson / Armadillo man / And he descended into hell / Rack / Big sleeping house / Back to the old town / Send Herman home / Town to town / Begging bowl
CD _______ **CDOVD 452**
Virgin / Feb '95 / EMI

CLOCK COMES DOWN THE STAIRS, THE
CD _______ **CREV 41CD**
Rev-Ola / May '96 / 3mv/Vital

EVERYBODY IS FANTASTIC
CD _______ **CREV 40CD**
Rev-Ola / May '96 / 3mv/Vital

LOVE YOUR ENEMIES
CD _______ **CREV 42CD**
Rev-Ola / May '96 / 3mv/Vital

Microstoria

INIT DING
CD _______ **EFA 006672**
Mille Plateau / Oct '95 / SRD

MICROSTORIA
CD _______ **THRILL 035CD**
Thrill Jockey / Oct '96 / Cargo / Greyhound

REPROVISERS
CD _______ **EFA 006872**
Mille Plateau / Mar '97 / SRD

REPROVISERS
CD _______ **THRILL 042**
Thrill Jockey / Jun '97 / Cargo / Greyhound

SND
CD _______ **EFA 006752**
Mille Plateau / Jun '96 / SRD

Microwave Dave

NOTHIN' BUT THE BLUES (Microwave Dave & The Nukes)
CD _______ **DFGCD 8448**
Dixie Frog / Jul '96 / Direct / TKO Magnum

Micus, Stephan

ATHOS
CD _______ **5232922**
ECM / Sep '94 / New Note/Pinnacle

DARKNESS AND LIGHT
CD _______ **8472722**
ECM / Dec '90 / New Note/Pinnacle

EAST OF THE NIGHT
East of the night / For Nobuko
CD _______ **8256552**
ECM / Mar '88 / New Note/Pinnacle

LISTEN TO THE RAIN
For Abai and Togshan / Dancing with the morning / Listen to the rain / White paint on silver wood
CD _______ **8156142**
ECM / '88 / New Note/Pinnacle

OCEAN
Part 1 / Part II / Part III / Part IV
CD _______ **8292792**
ECM / Jun '86 / New Note/Pinnacle

TILL THE END OF TIME
CD _______ **5137862**
ECM / '88 / New Note/Pinnacle

TO THE EVENING CHILD
Nomad song / Yuko's eyes / Young moon / To the evening child / Morgenstern / Equinox / Desert poem
CD _______ **5137802**
ECM / Sep '92 / New Note/Pinnacle

TWILIGHT FIELDS
CD _______ **8350852**
ECM / Feb '88 / New Note/Pinnacle

WINGS OVER WATER
CD _______ **8310582**
ECM / Aug '88 / New Note/Pinnacle

Micus, Stephen

GARDEN OF MIRRORS
Earth / Passing cloud / Violeta / Flowers in chaos / In the high valleys / Gates of fire / Mad bird / Night circles / Words of truth
CD _______ **5371622**
ECM / Aug '97 / New Note/Pinnacle

Middle Of The Road

MIDDLE OF THE ROAD
CD _______ **295594**
Ariola / Dec '92 / BMG

TODAY
Midnight blue / Samson and Delilah / Love takes prisoners / Sacramento / Dance with me / South America / Soley Soley / Turn on your radio / Chirpy chirpy cheep cheep / Tweedle dee - Tweedle dum / Kailakee Kailakee / Fall / One kiss
CD _______ **399368**
Koch Presents / Jun '97 / Koch

Middleton, Arthur

HARMONICA FAVOURITES
CD _______ **CDR 012**
Donside / Oct '89 / Ross

Middleton-Pollock, Marilyn

DOLL'S HOUSE, A
CD _______ **FE 086CD**
Fellside / Feb '87 / ADA / Direct / Target/ BMG

RED HOT AND BLUE
CD _______ **LACD 42**
Lake / Jan '95 / ADA / Cadillac / Direct / Jazz Music / Target/BMG

THOSE WOMEN OF THE VAUDEVILLE BLUES
Miss Jenny's blues / Aggravatin' papa / Handyman / Barrelhouse blues / It's tight like that / Moanin' the blues / Mighty tight woman / Trouble in mind / Hot time in the old town / Last journey blues / Wild women don't get the blues / Dark man / I got a mind to ramble / St. Louis blues / Women don't need no mens / Nobody knows you (when you're down and out) / Some of these days
CD _______ **LACD 18**
Lake / Feb '91 / ADA / Cadillac / Direct / Jazz Music / Target/BMG

Midget

TOGGLE SWITCH, THE
CD _______ **ANDA 203**
Au-Go-Go / Mar '97 / Cargo / Greyhound / Plastic Head

Midi Rain

ONE
CD _______ **STEAM 56CD**
Vinyl Solution / Jul '94 / RTM/Disc

Midler, Bette

BETTE MIDLER
Skylark / Drinking again / Breaking up somebody's home / Surabaya Johnny / I shall be released / Optimistic voices / Lullaby of broadway / In the mood / Uptown / Da doo ron ron / Twisted / Higher and higher
CD _______ **7567827792**
Atlantic / Jan '94 / Warner Music

BETTE OF ROSES
CD _______ **7567828232**
Atlantic / Nov '95 / Warner Music

BROKEN BLOSSOM
Empty bed blues / Dream is a wish your heart makes / Paradise / Yellow umbrella / La vie en rose / Make yourself comfortable / You don't know me / Say goodbye to Hollywood / I never talk to strangers / Storybook children / Red
CD _______ **7567827802**
Atlantic / Dec '93 / Warner Music

DIVINE MADNESS
CD _______ **7567827812**
Atlantic / Jun '94 / Warner Music

DIVINE MISS M, THE
Do you want to dance / Chapel of love / Superstar / Daytime hustler / Am I blue / Friends / Hello in there / Leader of the pack / Delta dawn / Boogie woogie bugle boy
CD _______ **7567827852**
Atlantic / Mar '92 / Warner Music

EXPERIENCE THE DIVINE BETTE MIDLER (The Greatest Hits Of Bette Midler)
Hello in there / Do you want to dance / From a distance / Chapel of love / Only in Miami / When a man loves a woman / Rose / Miss Otis regrets / Shiver me timbers / Wind beneath my wings / Boogie woogie bugle boy / One for my baby (and one more for the road) / Friends / In my life
CD _______ **7567824972**
Atlantic / Oct '93 / Warner Music

NO FRILLS
Is it love / (You're my) favourite waste of time / All I need to know / Only in Miami / Heart over head / Let me drive / My eye on you / Beast of burden / Soda and a souvenir / Come back Jimmy Dean
CD _______ **7567827832**
Atlantic / Mar '92 / Warner Music

SOME PEOPLE'S LIVES
One more round / Some people's lives / Miss Otis regrets / Spring can really hang you up the most / Night and day / Girl is on to you / From a distance / Moonlight dancing / He was too good to me/Since you stayed here / All of a sudden / Gift of love
CD _______ **7567821292**
Atlantic / Sep '90 / Warner Music

SONGS FOR THE NEW DEPRESSION
Strangers in the night / I don't want the night to end / Mr. Rockefeller / Old Cape Cod / Buckets of rain / Shiver me timbers / Samedi et vendredi / No jestering / Tragedy / Marahuana / Let me just follow behind
CD _______ **7567827842**
Atlantic / Mar '92 / Warner Music

THIGHS AND WHISPERS
Big noise from Winnetka / Millworker / Cradle days / My knight in black leather / Hang on in there baby / Hurricane / Rain / Married men
CD _______ **7567827862**
Atlantic / May '93 / Warner Music

Midnight Choir

MIDNIGHT CHOIR
Talk to me / Don't turn out the light / Gypsy rider / What am I worth to you / Turning of the tide / Hearts gone wild / Mercy on the street / Rock bottom / Lonesome drifter / Lift me up
CD _______ **119742**
Musidisc UK / Sep '96 / Grapevine/ PolyGram

Midnight Configuration

GOTHTEC
CD _______ **NIGHTMCD 001**
Nightbreed / Mar '94 / Plastic Head

SPECTARAL DANCE
CD _______ **NIGHTMAXICD 003**
Nightbreed / Nov '94 / Plastic Head

Midnight Oil

BLUE SKY MINING
Blue sky mining / Stars of Warburton / Bedlam bridge / Forgotten years / Mountains of Burma / King of the mountain / River runs red / Shakers and movers / One country / Antarctica
CD _______ **465653 2**
Columbia / Sep '93 / Sony

BREATHE
Underwater / Surf's up tonight / Common ground / Time to heal / Sins of omission / One too many / Times / Star of hope / In the rain / Bring on the change / Home / E-beat / Barest degree / Gravelrash
CD _______ **4854029**
Columbia / Oct '96 / Sony

DIESEL AND DUST
Beds are burning / Put down that weapon / Dreamworld / Arctic world / Warakuma / Dead heart / Woah / Bullroarer / Sell my soul / Sometimes
CD _______ **4600052**
CBS / May '88 / Sony

MIDNIGHT OIL
Powderworks / Head over heels / Dust used and abused / Surfing with a spoon / Run by night / Nothing lost, nothing gained
CD _______ **4509022**
CBS / Feb '94 / Sony

SCREAM IN BLUE
Scream in blue / Read about it / Dreamworld / Brave faces / Only the strong / Stars of Warburton / Progress / Beds are burning / Sell my soul / Sometimes / Hercules / Powderworks / Burnie
CD _______ **41714532**
Columbia / May '92 / Sony

Midnight Star

BEST OF MIDNIGHT STAR, THE
I've been watching you / Hot spot / Feels so good / Playmates / Scientific love / Headlines / Don't rock the boat / I won't let you be lonely / Wet my whistle / Curious / Let's celebrate / Operator / Midas touch
CD _______ **NEMCD 682**
Sequel / Nov '94 / BMG

HEADLINES
Searching for love / Headlines / Get dressed / Stay here by my side / Midas touch / Close encounter / Engine no.9 / Dead end / Headlines / Engine no.9
CD _______ **NEBCD 786**
Sequel / Jul '96 / BMG

NO PARKING ON THE DANCE FLOOR
Electricity / Night rider / Feels so good / Wet my whistle / No parking (on the dance floor) / Freak-a-zoid / Slow jam / Play mates
CD _______ **NEBCD 787**
Sequel / Jul '96 / BMG

VERY BEST OF MIDNIGHT STAR, THE
Headlines / Midas touch / Freakazoid / Operator / Engine No. 9 / Electricity / No

parking on the dancefloor / Make it last / Slow jam / Luv u up / Wet my whistle / Victory / Money can't buy you love / Work it out / Snake in the grass / Heartbeat
CD ____ CCSCD 805
Renaissance Collector Series / Sep '95 / BMG

VICTORY/PLANETARY INVASION
Victory / Move me / Make time (to fall in love) / Hot spot / You can't stop me / Be with you / Operator / Body snatchers / Scientific love / Let's celebrate / Curious / Planetary invasion / Can you stay with me
CD ____ DEEPM 030
Deep Beats / Aug '97 / BMG

Midnight Well

MIDNIGHT WELL
CD ____ LUNCD 011
Mulligan / Mar '96 / ADA / CM

Midway Still

DIAL SQUARE
CD ____ NECKCD 008
Roughneck / Apr '92 / RTM/Disc

LIFE'S TOO LONG
CD ____ NECKCD 12
Roughneck / Jun '93 / RTM/Disc

Miel, Melinda

KISS ON A TEAR, A
CD ____ NORM 161CD
Normal / Mar '94 / ADA / Direct

LAW OF THE DREAM, THE
CD ____ NORMAL 113CD
Normal / Mar '94 / ADA / Direct

Migenes Johnson, Julia

JULIA MIGENES JOHNSON (Greatest Hits)
I could have danced all night / Oh mein papa / Tonight / Chim chim cheree / Johnny Guitar / So in love / La Paloma / Someone's waiting for you / Man I love / Embraceable you / Someone to watch over me / Summertime
CD ____ 610 232
Eurodisc / Oct '91 / BMG

LIVE AT OLYMPIA
CD ____ CDCH 503
Milan / Mar '90 / Conifer/BMG / Silva Screen

MY FAVOURITE SONGS
CD ____ 8478842
Polydor / Jul '93 / PolyGram

Mighty Baby

MIGHTY BABY
Egyptian tomb / Friend you know but never see / I've been down so long / Same way from the sun / House without windows / Trials of a city / I'm from the country / At a point between fate and destiny / Only dreaming / Dustbin full of rubish / Understanding love / My favourite day / Saying for today
CD ____ CDWIKD 120
Big Beat / Feb '94 / Pinnacle

Mighty Bop

AUTRES VOIX AUTRES BLUES
CD ____ YP 013ACD
Yellow / Nov '96 / Timewarp

LA VAGUE SENSORIELLE
CD ____ YP 008ACD
Yellow / Jul '96 / Timewarp

Mighty Clouds Of Joy

POWER
In God's will / Have you told him lately / We will stand / He saw me / I'm ready / I've been in the storm to long / What a wonderful God / Hold on / Nearer my God to thee / Hour of the holy ghost
CD ____ CDK 9147
Alliance Music / Aug '95 / EMI

Mighty Diamonds

BEST OF MIGHTY DIAMONDS, THE
CD ____ MDRP 001CD
Hitbound / Jul '97 / Jet Star

BUST OUT
Screechie 'cross the border / Cool it / Africans / I need a roof / Bogle / Love me girl / Hotter the battle / In de dance again / Tell the heathen / Declaration of rights / Came, saw and conquered / Fight fire with fire
CD ____ GRELCD 188
Greensleeves / Aug '93 / Jet Star / SRD

GET READY
Schoolmate / Another day another raid / Tonight I'm gonna take it easy / Idlers' corner / Cannot say you didn't know / Sensimillia / My baby / Get ready / Up front / Modeller
CD ____ GRELCD 112
Greensleeves / Jun '88 / Jet Star / SRD

GO SEEK YOUR RIGHTS
Right time / Why me black brother why / Have mercy / Shame and pride / Gnashing of teeth / Them never love poor Marcus / One brother short / Masterplan / I need a roof / Go seek your rights / Bodyguard / Natural Natty / Africa / Sweet lady / Got to get away / Let the answer be yes
CD ____ CDFL 9002
Frontline / Jul '90 / EMI / Jet Star

HEADS OF GOVERNMENT
CD ____ PHCD 2046
Penthouse / Oct '96 / Jet Star

LIVE IN EUROPE
Party time / Country living / Mr. Botha / Have mercy / I need a roof / My baby / Puttin' on the Ritz / Real enemy / I don't mind / Right time / Africa / Keep on moving / Heavy load
CD ____ GRELCD 124
Greensleeves / Feb '89 / Jet Star / SRD

MIGHTY DIAMONDS MEETS DON CARLOS & GOLD AT CHANNEL 1 STUDIO (Mighty Diamonds & Don Carlos)
CD ____ JJ 084085
Jet Star / Jun '94 / Jet Star

PAINT IT RED
CD ____ RASCD 3114
Ras / Jun '93 / Direct / Greensleeves / Jet Star / SRD

RAS PORTRAITS
Gone bad / Bodygaurd / Posse are you ready / Knock knock / Corrupt cop / Anti-crack / This time / Putting up the ritz / Kick up rumpus / Gold digger
CD ____ RAS 3326
Ras / Jul '97 / Direct / Greensleeves / Jet Star / SRD

REAL ENEMY
Real enemy / Gang war / Play girl / Babylon is dangerous / Dem a worry / Free Africa / Right feelin' / I say no / Mr. Botha / Chant down war
CD ____ GRELCD 102
Greensleeves / Sep '88 / Jet Star / SRD

REGGAE STREET
CD ____ SHANCD 43004
Shanachie / May '90 / ADA / Greensleeves / Koch

RIGHT TIME
Right time / Why me black brother why / Shame and pride / Gnashing of teeth / Them never love poor Marcus / I need a roof / Go seek your rights / Have mercy / Natural natty / Africa
CD ____ SHANCD 43014
Shanachie / Jan '84 / ADA / Greensleeves / Koch

STAND UP TO YOUR JUDGE
CD ____ JJCD 020
Channel One / Apr '96 / Jet Star

Mighty House

LOVE THE SEA IS BLUE
CD ____ CDGOLD 1
Mighty House / May '96 / Else

Mighty Lemon Drops

ROLLERCOASTER (The Best Of The Mighty Lemon Drops 1986-1989)
Happy head / Into the heart of love / My biggest thrill / Inside out / Other side of you / Out of hand / Like an angel / Fall down (like the rain) / Splash #1 (now I'm home) / Beautiful shame / Rollercoaster / In everything you do / Uptight / Shine / Where do we go from (heaven) / Count me out / Something happens / Sympathise with us / Now she's gone
CD ____ CDCHRM 103
Chrysalis / Feb '97 / EMI

Mighty Loverboy

CASSAVA MAN
CD ____ TRCD 6103
Taso / May '97 / Jet Star

Mighty Ryeders

HELP US SPREAD THE MESSAGE
CD ____ LHCD 017
Luv n' Haight / Jul '96 / Timewarp

Mighty Sparrow

EXPLODES INTO CALYPSO TIME
Obeah wedding / Bongo / Lion and donkey (rematch) / Wood in the fire / Congo man / Dan is the man (in the van) / Sparrow dead / Sell the pussy / Same time, same place / Carnival woman / Du du yemi / Miss universe / Idi Amin / Soca man / Rose / Madam dracula
CD ____ SEECD 446
See For Miles/C5 / Jul '96 / Pinnacle

SALVATION WITH SOCA BALLADS
CD ____ BLSCD 1017
Soca / Feb '94 / Jet Star

Mighty Truth

FROM THE CITY TO THE SEA
Rebirth / Is it a wizard or a blizzard / Don't you ever learn / Connexion / Blowing for the 6th sign / Hear the voice / End of an era / Heavy knowledge / Miro / City to the sea / Wandering world / Pure as the driven
CD ____ TNGCD 006
Tongue 'n' Groove / May '95 / Vital

Mikami, Kan

TOGE NO SHONIN (Merchant On The Pass)
CD ____ PSFD 84
PSF / May '97 / Harmonia Mundi

Mike & Rich

EXPERT KNOB TWIDDLERS
CD ____ CAT 027CD
Rephlex / Jun '96 / Prime / RTM/Disc

Mike & The Mechanics

BEGGAR ON A BEACH OF GOLD
Beggar on a beach of gold / Another cup of coffee / You've really got a hold on me / Mea Culpa / Over my shoulder / Someone always hates someone / Ghost of sex and you / Web of lies / Plain and simple / Something to believe in / House of many rooms / I believe (when I fall in love it will be forever) / Going, going... home
CD ____ CDV 2772
Virgin / Mar '95 / EMI

LIVING YEARS, THE
Nobody's perfect / Seeing is believing / Nobody knows / Poor boy down / Blame / Don't / Black and blue / Beautiful day / Why me / Living years
CD ____ CDV 2825
Virgin / Feb '97 / EMI

MIKE & THE MECHANICS HITS
All I need is a miracle / Over my shoulder / Word of mouth / Living years / Another cup of coffee / Nobody's perfect / Silent running / Nobody knows / Get up / Time and place / Taken in / Everybody gets a second chance / Beggar on a beach of gold
CD ____ CDV 2797
Virgin / Feb '96 / EMI

MIKE AND THE MECHANICS
Silent running / All I need is a miracle / Par avion / Hanging by a thread / I get the feeling / Take the reins / You are the one / Call to arms / Taken in
CD ____ CDV 2824
Virgin / Feb '97 / EMI

WORD OF MOUTH
Get up / Word of mouth / Time and place / Yesterday, today, tomorrow / Way you look at me / Everybody gets a second chance / Stop baby / My crime of passion / Let's pretend it didn't happen / Before (the next heartache falls)
CD ____ CDV 2662
Virgin / May '91 / EMI

Mike & The Mellotones

LIVE MAGIC
Not fade away / Love gone sour / Louise / Careless rooster blues / Louisiana nights / Travelin' blues / So glad to have you / Song for a friend / I'd hate you if I didn't love you / Love don't love nobody
CD ____ LCD 80007
Lizard / Nov '96 / Direct / RTM/Disc

Mike Ink

GOLDEN
CD ____ STUDIO 001
Studio One / Apr '97 / Jet Star

Mike Stuart Span

TIMESPAN
CD ____ WHCD 003
Wooden Hill / Mar '97 / Wooden Hill

Mikey Dread

AFRICAN ANTHEMS
Saturday night style / Industrial spy / Headline news / Mikey Dread in action / Resignation dub / Technician selection / Comic strip / Pre-dawn dub / Operator's choice
CD ____ ABB 108CD
Big Cat / Apr '96 / 3mv/Pinnacle

BEST SELLERS
CD ____ RCD 20178
Rykodisc / Aug '91 / ADA / Vital

BEYOND WORLD WAR III
Break down the walls / Jah jah love (in the morning) / Jumping master / Israel (12 tribe) stylee / Warrior stylee / Money dread / Rockers delight / Mental slavery / World war III
CD ____ ABB 109CD
Big Cat / Apr '96 / 3mv/Pinnacle

DUB PARTY
CD ____ RUSCD 8208
ROIR / Jul '95 / Plastic Head / Shellshock/ Disc

PAVE THE WAY
CD ____ HBCD 31
Heartbeat / Oct '95 / ADA / Direct / Greensleeves / Jet Star

Mikey General

XTERMINATOR
Sinners / I'm going home / Women of Israel / Tired of it / I'm wondering / I know I love you / New name / I'll never be / Rastaman have to be strong / Black and comey / Deh pon derm / Many have fallen
CD ____ CRCD 43
Charm / Sep '95 / Jet Star

Mikey Roots

PRAISE AND HONOUR
Uncle Tom / Plastic City / Give thanks and praise / Praise and honour / Fi wi time / Life at the top / We a watch dem / Jesus Jesus Jesus / Paradise / Girl you turn me on / Sweet feeling / I'll never get you (out of my mind) / Great is Jah / Life is for real
CD ____ SPV 0855212
SPV / Aug '96 / Koch / Plastic Head

Mikey Spice

ALL ABOUT YOU
So much things to say / Goodbye to you / Lady / Where do love go / All about you / I will stand tall / Rock you / I can't get over you / Give thanks and praise / Baby / Lucky girl lucky boy / You make me / Let's work it out: *Mikey Spice & Luciano*
CD ____ RASCD 3192
Ras / Nov '96 / Direct / Greensleeves / Jet Star / SRD

BORN AGAIN
CD ____ VPCD 1465
VP / Feb '96 / Greensleeves / Jet Star / Total/BMG

CLOSE THE DOOR
Way you are / What the world need now / Close the door / Deeper and deeper / Am I losing you / Can't get enough / Loving you / Baby come back / Real good men / Sunday morning / Winter of a loving heart / Be my friend
CD ____ CRCD 52
Charm / Jan '96 / Jet Star

HAPPINESS
CD ____ RN 0042
Runn / Apr '95 / Grapevine/PolyGram / Jet Star / SRD

IT'S ALL ABOUT TIME
CD ____ FHCD 1
Firehouse / Mar '97 / Jet Star / SRD

JAH LIFTED ME
CD ____ VPCD 1488
VP / Apr '97 / Greensleeves / Jet Star / Total/BMG

SO MUCH THINGS TO SAY
CD ____ BSCD 6
Big Ship / Oct '96 / Jet Star

TOE 2 TOE (Mikey Spice & Garnet Silk)
CD ____ CRCD 66
Charm / Jun '97 / Jet Star

Miki & Griff

BEST OF MIKI & GRIFF, THE
CD ____ PLSCD 227
Pulse / Jul '97 / BMG

LITTLE BITTY TEAR
CD ____ SSLCD 203
Savanna / Jun '95 / THE

MIKI & GRIFF
CD ____ MATCD 259
Castle / Apr '93 / BMG

VERY BEST OF MIKI & GRIFF, THE
CD ____ SOW 702
Sound Waves / May '94 / Target/BMG

Mila Et Loma

TAHITI: BELLE EPOQUE VOL.2
CD ____ S 65809
Manuiti / Jul '92 / Harmonia Mundi

Milanes, Pablo

ADEMAS LA SALSA
CD ____ 74321401842
Milan / Feb '97 / Conifer/BMG / Silva Screen

ANIVERSARIO
CD ____ 74321401852
Milan / Feb '97 / Conifer/BMG / Silva Screen

CANTOS DE AMOR Y DESAMOR
CD ____ 74321434702
Milan / Feb '97 / Conifer/BMG / Silva Screen

DE TODO PARA BAILAR (Milanes, Pablo & Adalberto Alvarez/Isaac Delgado)
CD ____ 74321401822
Milan / Feb '97 / Conifer/BMG / Silva Screen

IDENTIDAD
CD ____ 74321402852
Milan / Feb '97 / Conifer/BMG / Silva Screen

PROPOSICIONES
CD 74321401832
Milan / Feb '97 / Conifer/BMG / Silva Screen

Milder, Joakim

STILL IN MOTION
CD DRCD 188
Dragon / Jan '88 / ADA / Cadillac / CM / Roots / Wellard

WAYS
CD DRCD 231
Dragon / Jan '89 / ADA / Cadillac / CM / Roots / Wellard

Miles, Buddy

HELL AND BACK (Miles, Buddy Express)
Born under a bad sign / Change / All along the watchtower / Let it be me / Come back home / Be kind to your girlfriend / Decision / Nothing left to lose
CD RCD 10305
Black Arc / Jun '94 / Vital

MIGHTY RHYTHM TRIBE
CD LAKE 2020
Lakeside / Aug '95 / TKO Magnum

TRIBUTE TO JIMI HENDRIX, A
Bad bad misses / Knock on wood / Red house / Come together / Peter Gunn / Take higher / Superstition / Life is what you make it
CD IRSCD 993013
Intercord / Nov '96 / Plastic Head
CD SPV 03442072
Hengest / Feb '97 / Grapevine/PolyGram

Miles, Butch

COOKIN'
CD CD 020
Nagel Heyer / May '96 / Jazz Music

LIVE (Miles, Butch & Kansas City Big Band)
CD MECCACD 1013
Music Mecca / Nov '94 / Cadillac / Jazz Music / Wellard

Miles, Floyd

GOIN' BACK TO DAYTONA
Same thing / Goin' back to Daytona / Mean heartbreaker / No life at all / Oh, Mary / Two against them all / All the love I can / Samson and Delilah / That's why I'm here tonight / Love on the rocks
CD FCD 752
Demon / Jun '94 / Pinnacle

Miles, Gerry

GERRY MILES (Miles, Gerry & Alan Licht/Keijo Haino)
CD ALP 71CD
Atavistic / Mar '97 / Cargo / SRD

Miles, John

REBEL
Music / Everybody wants some more / High fly / You have it all / Rebel / When you lose someone so young / Lady of my life / Pull the damn thing down / Music (reprise)
CD 8200802
London / Mar '87 / PolyGram

Miles, Josie

JOSIE MILES VOL.1 (1922-1924)
CD DOCD 5466
Document / Jul '96 / ADA / Hot Shot / Jazz Music

JOSIE MILES VOL.2 (1924-1925)
CD DOCD 5467
Document / Jul '96 / ADA / Hot Shot / Jazz Music

Miles, Lizzie

LIZZIE MILES
CD AMCD 73
American Music / Feb '95 / Jazz Music

LIZZIE MILES VOL.1 1922-1923
CD DOCD 5458
Document / Jun '96 / ADA / Hot Shot / Jazz Music

LIZZIE MILES VOL.2 1923-1928
CD DOCD 5459
Document / Jun '96 / ADA / Hot Shot / Jazz Music

LIZZIE MILES VOL.3 1928-1929
CD DOCD 5460
Document / Jun '96 / ADA / Hot Shot / Jazz Music

Miles, Lynn

SLIGHTLY HAUNTED
CD CDPH 1190
Philo / Mar '96 / ADA / CM / Direct

Miles, Robert

DREAMLAND (Remixes/2CD Set)
CD Set 74321429742
De-Construction / Nov '96 / BMG

Miles, Ron

MY CRUEL HEART
CD GCD 79510
Gramavision / Jun '96 / Vital/SAM

WITNESS
CD 740142
Capri / '90 / Cadillac / Wellard

WOMAN'S DAY
Dew / Belly / Born liar / You taste / Jesus / Woman's day / Bath / Longing / Cobain / Linen / Mommy on top / Goodnight
CD GCD 79516
Gramavision / Mar '97 / Vital/SAM

Milk & Honey Band

ROUND THE SUN
Tin cans / Not heaven / Another perfect day / Out of nowhere / Tea / Round the sun / Pier view / Puerto / Off my hands / Light / Raining / Bird song
CD R 3572
Rough Trade / Oct '94 / Pinnacle

Milk

TANTRUM
CD CDEVER 007
Eve / Oct '91 / Grapevine/PolyGram

Milkshakes

107 TAPES (Early Demos & Live Recordings)
Pretty baby / Ruhrge beat / Well well / I want you / Flat foot / I say you lie / Shed country 81 / Don't love another / Mumble the peg / You did her wrong / Red monkey / Let's stomp / Eaten more honey / Tell me where's that girl / Girl called mine / Little Queenie / Jaguar / Cadillac / Black sails (In the moonlight) / Sit right down and cry / She tells me she loves me / Soldiers of love / Monkey business / Let me love you / El Salvador / Boys
CD ASK 8CD
Vinyl Japan / '91 / Plastic Head / Vinyl Japan

19TH NERVOUS SHAKEDOWN
It's you / Please don't tell my baby / Shed country / Pretty baby / Don't love another / Another midnight / Seven days / Black sails (In the moonlight) / Cadalina / You did her wrong / Shimmy shake / Hide and scatter / El Salvador / Jaguar / General Belgrano / Klansmen kometh / Brand new Cadillac / Love can lose / Little Bettina / I'm the one for you / Let me love you / Quiet lives / Wounded knee / I'm needing you / Red monkey / Ambassador of love / Can't seem to love that girl / Cassandra / Green hornet / Out of control
CD CDWIKD 939
Big Beat / Jul '90 / Pinnacle

20 ROCK'N'ROLL HITS OF THE 50'S & 60'S
Hippy hippy shake / Rip it up / I'm gonna sit right down and cry over you / Say mama / Peggy Sue / Jaguar and the thunderbirds / Comanche / I'm talking about you / Sweet little sixteen / Money (that's what I want) / Carol / Boys / Something else / Some other guy / Who do you love / Jezebel / Hidden charms / Little Queenie / Ya ya twist / I wanna be your man
CD CDWIKM 20
Big Beat / Mar '91 / Pinnacle

AFTER SCHOOL
CD SCRAG 10CD
Hangman's Daughter / Apr '97 / Shellshock/Disc / SRD

MILKSHAKES REVENGE, THE
Let me love you / I want you / If I saw you / Graveyard words / Boys / Little girl be good / Pipeline / She tells me loves me / Little girl (mumble the peg) / Every girl I meet / One I get / Baby what's wrong
CD HOG1
Hangman's Daughter / Sep '94 / Shellshock/Disc / SRD

STILL TALKIN' BOUT
CD ASK 10CD
Vinyl Japan / Nov '92 / Plastic Head / Vinyl Japan

TALKING 'BOUT - MILKSHAKES
She'll be mine / Pretty baby / For she / I want'cha for my little girl / Ruhrge beat / After midnight / Bull's nose / Shed country / Don't love another / Tell me where's that girl / Can'tcha see / Love you the whole night through / Nothing you can say or do / I say you lie
CD SCRAG 4CD
Hangman's Daughter / Jul '95 / Shellshock/Disc / SRD

Milky Way

MILKY WAY
CD CDLR 45012
L&R / Jun '89 / New Note/Pinnacle

Milky Wimpshake

BUS ROUTE TO YOUR HEART
CD SLAMPT 48CD
Slampt Underground / May '97 / Shellshock/Disc

Milladoiro

AS FADAS DE ESTRANO NOME
Polca dos campaneiros / O nosso tempo / Vals de libunca / Foliada de berducido / Alala das marinas / Foliada de santirso / Xota para aida / Brincadeiro / As fadas de estrano nome / Danza e contradanza de darbo / Aires de pontevedra / Invernia / O voo da pomba / Danza de alberllos / Clumsy lover
CD GLCD 3118
Green Linnet / Mar '97 / ADA / CM / Direct / Highlander / Roots

GALICIA NO TEMPO
CD GLCD 3073
Green Linnet / Feb '93 / ADA / CM / Direct / Highlander / Roots

GALLAECIA FVLGET
CD DM 1003CD
Discmedia / Aug '96 / ADA

Millar Brass Ensemble

WORLD ANTHEMS VOL.1
USA / UK / Canada / Italy / Argentina / South AFrica / Ukraine / India / Hungary / France / China / Slovakia / Czech Republic / Venezuela / Egypt / Russia / Spain / Trinidad & Tobago / Jordan / Belgium / Ireland / Greece / Chile / Finland / Kenya / South Korea / Israel / Denmark / Bulgaria / Brazil / Japan / Monaco / Latvia / Mexico / New Zealand / Ethiopia / Sweden / Poland / Lithuania / Taiwan / Indonesia / Germany / Estonia / Netherlands / Norway / Austria / Turkey / Australia
CD DE 3199
Delos / Jul '96 / Nimbus

Millencolin

FOR MONKEYS
CD BHR 056CD
Burning Heart / Apr '97 / Plastic Head

LIFE ON A PLATE
CD BHR 033CD
Burning Heart / Apr '97 / Plastic Head

SAME OLD TUNES
CD BHR 019CD
Burning Heart / Apr '97 / Plastic Head

SKAUCH
CD BHR 016CD
Burning Heart / Oct '94 / Plastic Head

STORY OF MY LIFE
CD BHR 032CDS
Burning Heart / Apr '97 / Plastic Head

TINY TUNES
CD BHR 019CD
Burning Heart / Feb '95 / Plastic Head

Millennium

21ST CENTURY BEBOP
CD REVCC 014
Revco / Nov '96 / Grapevine/PolyGram / Timewarp

Miller, Al

COMPLETE RECORDED WORKS 1927-36
CD DOCD 5306
Document / Dec '94 / ADA / Hot Shot / Jazz Music

WILD CARDS
I don't play / Stuck in Chicago / Seventy-four / Long grey mare / Can't stay here no more / Special way / Deal the cards / Red top boogie / Fallin' rain / I had a dream / Jockey blues / Big 'C' blues / Blues for John Littlejohn / Sittin' here thinkin'
CD DE 675
Delmark / Mar '97 / ADA / Cadillac / CM / Direct / Hot Shot

Miller Bros.

MILLER BROTHERS BAND, THE
CD CLCD 2853
Collector/White Label / Jul '97 / TKO Magnum

Miller, Buddy

YOUR LOVE AND OTHER LIES
CD HCD 8063
Hightone / Aug '95 / ADA / Koch

Miller, Byron

GIT WIT ME
CD NOVA 9029
Nova / Jan '93 / New Note/Pinnacle

Miller, Cercie

DEDICATION
CD ST 580
Stash / Jun '94 / ADA / Cadillac / CM / Direct / Jazz Music

Miller, Dave

FINGER PICKING RAGS AND OTHER DELIGHTS
Sweet Georgia Brown / Stagger Lee / God bless the child / Cheap wine / Chattanooga choo-choo / Inflation blues / Bicycle built for two/Sidewalks of New York / Air on a G string / Too tite rag / Pitschel Players theme / Amtrak shuffle / Blue prelude / Take it on the run / Nice work if you can get it / Son of Diddie / Birth of the blues / Shelley's swing / Fleabites / Little fugue / Hey Jude / Boys from Blue Hill
CD KMCD 3904
Kicking Mule / Jul '97 / Pinnacle

Miller, Ed

AT HOME WITH THE EXILES
Pittenween Jo / Darling Allie / John McLean march / Blood upon the grass / Bottle o'the best / Mistress / Yellow on the broom / Jute Mill song / Crooked Jack / Broom o'the cowdenknowes / Generations of change / Man's man / At home with the exiles / Tak a dram
CD CDTRAX 089
Greentrax / Jul '95 / ADA / Direct / Duncans / Highlander

Miller, Frankie

BBC LIVE IN CONCERT
Free and safe on the road / Play something sweet (Brickyard blues) / It takes a lot to laugh, it takes a train to cry / With you in mind / Rock / Be good to yourself / Fool in love / Jealous guy / I can't break away / Double heart trouble / Stubborn kind of fellow / Falling in love / Goodnight sweetheart / Woman to love / When I'm away from you / When something is wrong with my baby / Darlin' / Ain't got no money
CD WINDCD 054
Windsong / Feb '94 / Pinnacle

BEST OF FRANKIE MILLER, THE
Darlin' / When I'm away from you / Be good to yourself / I can't change it / Highlife/ Brickyard blues / Fool in love / Have you seen me lately Joan / Love letters / Caledonia / Stubborn kind of fellow / Devil gun / Hard on the levee / Tears / I'm ready / Shoo-rah shoo-rah / Double heart trouble / So young, so young
CD CDCHR 1981
Chrysalis / Feb '94 / EMI

LOVE LETTERS
CD DC 864322
Disky / Mar '96 / Disky / THE

Miller, Frankie

SUGAR COATED BABY
Sugar coated baby / Love me now / Living doll / This lonely heart / Power of love / I don't know / I won't forget / I'm still in love with you / I'm gettin' rid of you / You just had / Bare foot blues / I'm only wishin' / I'm so blue I don't know what to do / I dreamed you were here last night / Baby we're really in love / I can't run away / I'd still want you / I don't know what to tell my heart / Hey where ya goin' / You'll never be true / It's no big thing to me / What have I ever done / Paid in full / My wedding song to you / You're going to cry on my shoulder again / You don't show me much / What you do from now on / Paint, powder & perfume / Day by day / I don't know why I love you
CD BCD 15909
Bear Family / May '96 / Direct / Rollercoaster / Swift

Miller, Glenn

1938-42 BROADCAST VERSIONS (Miller, Glenn Orchestra)
CD JH 1004
Jazz Hour / Feb '91 / Cadillac / Jazz Music / Target/BMG

1941 SUNSET SERENADE-CAFE ROUGE
CD JH 1021
Jazz Hour / Feb '93 / Cadillac / Jazz Music / Target/BMG

1942 CHESTERFIELD SHOWS (Miller, Glenn Orchestra)
CD JH 1028
Jazz Hour / Feb '93 / Cadillac / Jazz Music / Target/BMG

20 GREATEST HITS
CD ENTCD 201
Entertainers / '88 / Target/BMG

ABBEY ROAD RECORDING
CD AMSC 575
Avid / Aug '96 / Avid/BMG / Koch / THE

AMERICAN PATROL VOL.2 (Miller, Glenn Orchestra)
CD DAWE 55
Magic / Nov '93 / Cadillac / Harmonia Mundi / Jazz Music / Swift / Wellard

ARMY AIR FORCE BAND 1943-44, THE
St. Louis blues march / Peggy, the pin-up girl / Speak low / Tail-end Charlie / Anvil

chorus / Oh what a beautiful morning / There are Yanks / Everybody loves my baby / Enlisted mens mess / I'll be around / There'll be a hot time in the town of Berlin / People will say we're in love / Pearls on velvet / Poinciana / It must be jelly, 'cause jam don't shake like that / Jeep jockey jump / Victory polka
CD ND 86360
Bluebird / Jun '88 / BMG

ARMY AIRFORCE ORCHESTRA VOL.2
CD DAWE 78
Magic / Jul '96 / Cadillac / Harmonia Mundi / Jazz Music / Swift / Wellard

AT MEADOWBROOK 1939 (Miller, Glenn Orchestra)
Moonlight serenade (theme) / Little brown jug / Blue rain / Oh johnny oh johnny oh / In an old Dutch garden / Tiger rag / Love with a capital you / Bugle call rag / Blue moonlight / Indian summer / Why couldn't it last last night / This changing world / I just got a letter / On a little street in Singapore / Faithful to you / Farewell blues / Moonlight serenade (theme and fadeout)
CD DAWE 34
Magic / Sep '89 / Cadillac / Harmonia Mundi / Jazz Music / Swift / Wellard

AUDIO ARCHIVE
Moonlight serenade / Pennsylvania 6-5000 / Don't sit under the apple tree / In the mood / St. Louis blues march / Little brown jug / Anvill chorus / My blue heaven / Sun valley jump / Sunrise serenade / Chattanooga choo choo / Indian summer / Tuxedo junction / Pin ball Paul / Song of the Volga boatmen / Woodpecker song / Begin the beguine / Over there / String of pearls / Slumber song
CD CDAA 011
Tring / Jun '92 / Tring

BBC BIG BAND PLAYS GLENN MILLER (BBC Big Band)
In the mood / American patrol / I've got a gal in Kalamazoo / Little brown jug / Chattanooga choo choo / Pennsylvania 6-5000 / String of pearls / Anvil chorus / Moonlight serenade / Tuxedo junction / Don't sit under the apple tree / Song of the Volga boatmen / Begin the beguine / St. Louis blues
CD QED 138
Tring / Nov '96 / Tring

BEST OF GLENN MILLER, THE
CD DCD 5333
Disky / Dec '93 / Disky / THE

BEST OF GLENN MILLER, THE
CD DLCD 4006
Dixie Live / Mar '95 / TKO Magnum

BEST OF GLENN MILLER, THE (2CD Set)
CD Set MOVCDD 1
Wax / Sep '96 / RTM/Disc / Total/BMG

BEST OF GLENN MILLER, THE
CD MACCD 178
Autograph / Aug '96 / BMG

BEST OF GLENN MILLER, THE
In the mood / American patrol / String of pearls / Tuxedo junction / Take the 'A' train / King Pavior stomp / Sun valley jump / Old black magic / Rhapsody in blue / I got rhythm / Little brown jug / Don't sit under the apple tree / I've got a girl in Katamazoo / Pennsylvania 65000 / Chattanooga choo choo / Beat me Daddy, eight to the bar / St. Louis blues / Georgia on my mind / In a sentimental mood / Moonlight serenade
CD CD 601
Music / Apr '97 / Target/BMG

BEST OF GLENN MILLER, THE (The Lost Recordings/The Secret Broadcasts)
In the mood / Army air corps song: *Desmond, Johnny* / Music stopped: *Desmond, Johnny* / Snafu jump / Summertime / Victory polka: *Glee Club* / Moonlight serenade / Mission to Moscow / Oh, what a beautiful mornin': *Desmond, Johnny & The Crew Chiefs* / Caribbean clipper / Jeanie with the light brown hair / Beat me Daddy, eight to the bar / String of pearls / Anvil chorus / Speak low: *Desmond, Johnny* / Tuxedo junction / Stealin' apples / Jeep jockey jump / Poinciana: *Desmond, Johnny & The Crew Chiefs* / Song of the Volga boatmen / American patrol / Little brown jug
CD 75605522902
Happy Days / Sep '97 / Conifer/BMG

BEST OF GLENN MILLER, THE
Moonlight serenade / Hallelujah / In a sentimental mood / Back to back / Jumpin' jive / In the mood / Chattanooga choo choo / Happy in love / Serenade in blue / Don't sit under the apple tree / Moonlight cocktail / Pensylvania 6-5000
CD 399233
Koch Presents / Jun '97 / Koch

BEST OF THE BIG BANDS, THE
Blues serenade / Moonlight on the Ganges / I got rhythm / Sleepy time gal / Community swing / Time on my hands / My fine feathered friend / Humoresque / Doin' the jive / Silhouetted in the moonlight / Every day's a holiday / Sweet stranger / Don't wake up my heart / Why'd ya make me fall in love / Sold American / Dippermouth blues
CD 4716562
Columbia / Jun '92 / Sony

BIG BAND BASH
Moonlight serenade / Pennsylvania 6-5000 / American patrol / Tuxedo junction / I've got a gal in Kalamazoo / String of pearls / Song of the Volga boatmen / Perfidia / In the mood / Chattanooga choo choo / St. Louis blues march / Anvil chorus / Johnson rag / My melancholy baby / Sun valley jump / Sunrise serenade / Jumpin' jive / Farewell blues / Little brown jug / Hallelujah / Under a blanket of blue
CD CD 53024
Giants Of Jazz / Mar '90 / Cadillac / Jazz Music / Target/BMG

CHATTANOOGA CHOO CHOO (The No.1 Hits)
Wishing (will make it so) / Stairway to the stars / Moon love / Over the rainbow / Man with the mandolin / Blue orchids / In the mood / Careless / Tuxedo junction / When you wish upon a star / Woodpecker / Imagination / Fools rush in / Blueberry Hill / Song of the Volga boatmen / You and I / Chattanooga choo choo / Elmer's tune / String of pearls / Moonlight cocktail / Don't sit under the apple tree / I've got a gal in Kalamazoo / That old black magic
CD ND 90584
Bluebird / Oct '91 / BMG

CLASSIC GLENN MILLER, THE (2CD Set) (Miller, Glenn Orchestra)
Moonlight serenade / Sunlight serenade / Wishing (will make it so) / Lady in love with you / Stairway to the stars / Little brown jug / Moon love / Over the rainbow / Man with the mandolin / Blue orchids / My prayer / Careless / When you wish upon a star / Indian summer / Tuxedo Junction / Woodpecker song / Imagination / Shake down the stars / Say it / Slow freight / Fools rush in / Nearness of you / Pennsylvania 6-5000 / When the swallows come back to Capistrano / Adios / In the mood / Blueberry Hill / Five o'clock whistle / Nightingale sang in Berkeley Square / Along the Santa Fe trail / Song of the Volga boatmen / I dreamt I dwelt in Harlem / Perfidia / You and I / Chatanooga choo choo / I know why (and so do you) / Elmer's tune / String of pearls / White cliffs of Dover / Moonlight cocktail / Skylark / Don't sit under the apple tree / American patrol / I've got a gal in Kalamazoo / At last / Serenade in blue / Dearly beloved / Moonlight becomes you / That old black magic / Juke box Saturday night
CD Set CPCD 82492
Charly / Oct '96 / Koch

CLASSIC YEARS, THE (Miller, Glenn Orchestra)
CD CDSGP 092
Prestige / Oct '93 / Else / Total/BMG

COLLECTION, THE
CD COL 025
Collection / Apr '95 / Target/BMG

COMMEMORATION 1944-1994
CD OVCCD 002
Satellite Music / May '94 / THE

COMPLETE GLENN MILLER, THE (1938-1942) (13CD Set) (Miller, Glenn Orchestra)
My reverie / By the waters of Minnetonka / King Porter stomp / Shut eye / How I'd like to be with you in Bermuda / Cuckoo in the clock / Romance runs in the family / Chestnut tree / And the angels sing / Moonlight serenade / Lady's in love with you / Wishing (will make it so) / Three little fishes (Itty bitty poo) / Sunrise serenade / Little brown jug / My last goodbye / But it don't mean a thing / Pavanne / Running wild / To you / Stairway to the stars / Blue evening / Lamp is low / Rendezvous time in Paris / We can live on love / Cinderella / Moon love / Guess I'll go back home / I'm sorry for myself / Back to back / Sliphorn jive / Oh you crazy moon / Ain't cha comin' out / Day we meet again / Wanna hat with cherries / Solid American / Pagan love song / Ding dong the witch is dead / Over the rainbow / Little man who wasn't there / Man with the mandolin / Starlit hour / Blue orchids / Glen Island special / Love with a capital you / Baby me / In the mood / Wah (re-bop-boom-bam) / Angel in a furnished room / Twilight interlude / I want to be happy / Farewell blues / Who's sorry now / My isle of golden dreams / My prayer / Blue moonlight / Basket weaver man / Melancholy baby / (Why couldn't it last) last night / Out of space / So many times / Blue rain / Can I help it / I just got a letter / Bless you / Bluebirds in the moonlight / Faithful forever / Speaking of Heaven / Indian summer / It was written in the stars / Johnson rag / Ciribiribin / Careless / Oh Johnny oh Johnny oh Johnny oh / In an old Dutch garden / This changing world / On a little street in Singapore / Vagabond dreams / I beg your pardon / Faithful to you / Gaucho serenade / Sky fell down / When you wish upon a star / Give a little whistle / Missouri waltz / Beautiful Ohio / What's the matter with me / Say si si / Fhumba jumps / Stardust / My melancholy baby / Let's all sing together / Rug cutter's swing / Woodpecker song / Sweet potato piper / Too romantic / Tuxedo junction / Danny boy / Imagination / Shake down the stars / I'll never smile again / Starlight and music / Polka dots and moonbeams / My my / Say it / Moments in the moonlight / Hear my song Violetta / Sierra Sue / Boog it / Yours is my heart alone / I'm stepping out with a memory tonight / Alice blue gown / Wonderful one / Devil may care / April played the fiddle / Fools rush in / I haven't time to be a millionaire / Slow freight / Pennsylvania 6-5000 / Bugle call rag / Nearness of you / Mr. Meadowlark / My blue heaven / When the swallows come back to Capistrano / Million dreams ago / Blueberry Hill / Cabana in Havana / Be happy Angel child / Call of the Canyon / Our love affair / Crosstown / What's your story Morning Glory / Fifth Avenue / I wouldn't take a million / Handful of stars / Old black Joe / Yesterthoughts / Falling leaves / Shadows on the sand / Goodbye little darlin' goodbye / Five o'clock whistle / Beat me Daddy, eight to the bar / Ring, telephone, ring / Make believe ballroom time / You've got me this way / Nightingale sang in Berkeley Square / I'd know you anywhere / Fresh as a daisy / Isn't that just like love / Along the Santa Fe trail / Do you know why / Somewhere / Yes my darling daughter / Stone's throw from heaven / Helpless / Long time no see baby / You are the one / Anvil chorus (parts 1 and 2) / Frenesi / Mem'ry of a rose / I do, do you / Chapel in the valley / Prairieland lullaby / Ida, sweet as apple cider / Song of the Volga boatmen / One I love (belongs to somebody else) / You stepped out of a dream / I dreamt I dwelt in Harlem / Sun Valley jump / What that man is dead and gone / Spirit is willing / Little old church in England / Perfidia / It's always you / Spring will be so sad (when she comes this year) / Airminded executive / Below the equator / Boulder buff / Bogglie wogglie piggy / Chattanooga choo choo / I know why / Don't cry cherie / Cradle song / Sweeter than the sweetest / I guess I'll have to dream the rest / Take the 'A' train / Peek-a-boo to you / Angels came thru / Under blue Canadian skies / Cowboy serenade / You and I / Adios / It happened in Sun Valley / I'm thrilled / Kiss polka / Delilah / From one love to another / Elmer's tune / Says who, says you, says I / Orange blossom lane / Dear Arabella / Man in the moon / Ma-ma-Maria / This time the dream is on me / Dreamsville / Ohio / Papa Niccolini / Jingle bells / This is no laughing matter / Humpty dumpty heart / Everything I love / String of pearls / Baby mine / Long tall mama / Daydreaming / Moonlight sonata / Slumber song / White cliffs of Dover / We're the couple in the castle / It happened in Hawaii / Moonlight cocktail / Happy in love / Fooled / Keep 'em flying / Chip off the old block / Story of a starry night / At the President's birthday ball / Angels of mercy / On the old assembly line / Let's have another cup of coffee / Skylark / Dear Mom / When the roses bloom again / Always in my heart / Shhh, it's a military secret / Don't sit under the apple tree / She'll always remember / Lamplighter's serenade / When Johnny comes marching home / American patrol / Soldier, let me read your letter / Sleep song / Sweet Eloise / I've got a gal in Kalamazoo / Serenade in blue / At last / Lullaby of the rain / Knit one, purl two / That's sabotage / Conchita, Marquita, Lolita, Pepita, Rosita, Juanita Lopez / Hummingbird / Yesterday's gardenias / Dearly beloved / Moonlight mood / Caribbean clipper / Here we go again / That old black magic / Moonlight becomes you / Jukebox Saturday night / It must be jelly, 'cause jam don't shake like that / I'm old fashioned / Pink cocktail for a blue lady / Rainbow rhapsody / Sleepy town train / Rhapsody in blue / Mr. Meadlowlark / Beat me daddy, eight to the bar / Anvil chorus (part 2)
CD Set ND 90600
Bluebird / Nov '91 / BMG

DANCE TIME USA 1939-1940 (Miller, Glenn Orchestra)
Slumber song / Song of the Volga boatmen / You walk by / There I go / Oh so good / Stone's throw from Heaven / I dreamt I dwelt in Harlem / Moonlight serenade / Beer barrel polka / Cinderella / Back to back / Pagan love song / Dippermouth blues / Moon love / Guess I'll go back home / Moon is a silver dollar / Heaven can wait / Bugle call rag / Sometime
CD DAWE 51
Magic / Nov '93 / Cadillac / Harmonia Mundi / Jazz Music / Swift / Wellard

DECEMBER 25TH 1943 (Miller, Glenn & The Army Airforce Orchestra)
CD JH 1041
Jazz Hour / Feb '95 / Cadillac / Jazz Music / Target/BMG

DEFINITIVE COLLECTION
Moonlight serenade / Hallelujah / In a sentimental mood / Back to back / Jumpin jive / In the mood / Chattanooga choo choo / Happy in love / Serenade in blue / Don't sit under the apple tree (with anyone else but me) / Moonlight cocktail / Pensylvania 6-5000 / Johnson rag / St Louis blues / My prayer / Anchors aweigh / I've got a girl in Kalamazoo / Woodpecker song / I know why / Medley (my melancholy baby, moon love, stomping at the Savoy
CD ECD 3112
K-Tel / Jan '95 / K-Tel

EARLY YEARS, THE
CD DHDL 129
Magic / Oct '96 / Cadillac / Harmonia Mundi / Jazz Music / Swift / Wellard

ESSENTIAL GLENN MILLER ORCHESTRA, THE
CD 4715582
Sony Jazz / Jan '95 / Sony

ESSENTIAL GLENN MILLER, THE
Moonlight serenade / Wishing / Sunrise serenade / Little brown jug / Running wild / Stairway to the stars / Moon love / Over the rainbow / My isle of golden dreams / In the mood / Indian summer / It's a blue world / Gaucho serenade / When you wish upon a star / Say si si / Stardust / Tuxedo junction / Danny Boy / Imagination / Fools rush in / Pennsylvania 6-5000 / Nearness of you / When the swallows come back to Capistrano / Million dreams ago / Nightingale sang in Berkeley Square / Along the Santa Fe trail / Yes my darling daughter / Anvil chorus / Song of the Volga boatmen / Perfidia / Chattanooga choo choo / I know why / You and I / Adios / Elmer's tune / String of pearls / White cliffs of Dover / Moonlight cocktail / Skylark / Always in my heart / Don't sit under the apple tree / American patrol / I've got a gal in Kalamazoo / Serenade in blue / At last / Old black magic / Jukebox Saturday night
CD 07863766520
Bluebird / Apr '95 / BMG

ESSENTIAL V-DISCS, THE
CD JZCD 302
Suisa / Feb '91 / Jazz Music / THE

ESSENTIAL WARTIME RECORDINGS
CD MCCD 249
Music Club / Jun '96 / Disc / THE

FRESH AS A DAISY (Miller, Glenn Orchestra)
Cabana in Havana / Fresh as a daisy / Stardust / Sweeter than the sweetest / Don't cry cherie / Blue moonlight / Farewell blues / Who's sorry now / I dreamt I dwelt in Harlem / Let's have another cup of coffee / It was written in the stars / My melancholy lullaby / All I do is dream of you / Blue orchids / Blue rain / Wonderful one / Twilight interlude / Pagan love song / Running wild / Ciribiribin / My Isle of golden dreams / In the mood
CD RAJCD 841
Empress / Feb '95 / Koch

GLENN MILLER (2CD Set)
CD Set R 2CD4001
Deja Vu / Jan '96 / THE

GLENN MILLER (4CD Set)
American patrol / Serenade in blue / That old black magic / You and I / Moonlight cocktail / Under a blanket of blue / Perfidia / Stardust / At last / Adios / Elmer's tune / Little man who wasn't there / This time the dream's on me / Everything I love / Skylark / There'll be bluebirds over the white cliffs of Dover / I dreamt I dwelt in Harlem / Starlit hour / Danny boy / I've got a gal in Kalamazoo / Moonlight serenade / Sunrise serenade / Don't sit under the apple tree with anyone else but me / Lady's in love with you / Anvil chorus / Indian summer / I got rhythm / Blue skies / Johnson rag / St. Louis blues / Pennsylvania 6-5000 / String of pearls / I know why / One o'clock jump / Farewell blues / Caribbean clipper / On a little street in Singapore / Hop / In the mood / My melancholy baby / Little brown jug / Tuxedo junction / I wan't to be happy / My blue heaven / I wanna hat with cherries / Begin the beguine / Say it / Dearly beloved / Song of the Volga boatmen / Moonlight becomes you / It must be jelly / Fools rush in / Chattanooga choo choo / You are always in my heart / And the angels sing / When Johnny comes marching home / Running wild / Slip horn jive / Seven-o-five / Falling leaves
CD Set QUAD 007
Tring / Dec '96 / Tring

GLENN MILLER (CD/CD Rom Set)
In the mood / Chatanooga choo choo / Tuxedo Junction / Kalamazoo / Song of the Volga boatman / Pennsylvania 6-5000 / Moonlight serenade / Little brown jug / String of pearls / American patrol / Anvil chorus / I dreamt I dwelt in Harlem / Serenade in blue / April in Paris / Sunrise serenade / Starlit hour / Sun valley jump
CD Set WWCDR 003
Magnum Music / Apr '97 / TKO Magnum

GLENN MILLER
In the mood / Sunrise serenade / American patrol / My melancholy baby / Anvil chorus / Stardust / Juke box Saturday night / String of pearls / Johnson rag / I've got a gal in Kalamazoo / Moonlight serenade / Song of the Volga boatmen / Sun Valley jump / I know why / St. Louis blues march / Chattanooga choo choo / Pennsylvania 6-5000 / Perfidia
CD 399529
Koch Presents / May '97 / Koch

GLENN MILLER & HIS AMERICAN BAND 1945
CD DAWE 72
Magic / Dec '94 / Cadillac / Harmonia Mundi / Jazz Music / Swift / Wellard

GLENN MILLER & HIS ARMY AIR FORCE ORCHESTRA 1944
CD _______________ **DAWE 62**
Magic / Jul '93 / Cadillac / Harmonia Mundi / Jazz Music / Swift / Wellard

GLENN MILLER 1943-1944
CD _______________ **PHONTCD 9307**
Phontastic / Aug '94 / Cadillac / Jazz Music / Wellard

GLENN MILLER AND HIS ORCHESTRA 1938-1940 (Miller, Glenn Orchestra)
CD _______________ **VJC 10142**
Vintage Jazz Classics / Oct '92 / ADA / Cadillac / CM / Direct

GLENN MILLER ARMY AIR FORCE BAND 1943-1944, THE
Anvil chorus / Stormy weather / Jukebox Saturday night / Jeep jockey jump / All the things you are / Song of the Volga boatmen / With my head in the clouds / I hear you screaming / Long ago and far away / Cherokee / Peggy and the pin-up girl / In the mood / Holiday for strings / String of pearls / Don't be that way
CD _______________ **ND 89767**
Jazz Tribune / Jun '94 / BMG

GLENN MILLER COLLECTOR'S EDITION
CD _______________ **DVX 8022**
Deja Vu / Apr '95 / THE

GLENN MILLER GOLD (2CD Set)
CD Set _______________ **D2CD 4001**
Deja Vu / Jun '95 / THE

GLENN MILLER LIVE 1940
CD _______________ **TAX 37042**
Tax / Aug '94 / Cadillac / Jazz Music / Wellard

GLENN MILLER ORCHESTRA
Moonlight serenade / Sunrise serenade / Don't sit under the apple tree / Bugle call rag / Anvil chorus / Moonlight cocktail / Indian summer / Sun Valley jump / Farewell blues / Under a blanket of blue / Penfida / Stardust / At last / St. Louis blues march / Adios / Little brown jug / American patrol / Tuxedo junction / Slumber song / My blue heaven / Blues in my heart / Begin the beguine / Everybody loves my baby / Over there / Song of the Volga boatmen / Enlisted mens blues / It must be jelly, 'cause jam don't shake like that / Rainbow rhapsody / Londonderry air / I've got a gal in Kalamazoo / Pennsylvania 6-5000 / String of pearls / April in Paris / Little man who wasn't there / Georgia on my mind / Baby me / Chestnut tree / Kings march / I dreamt I dwelt in Harlem / Starlit hour / Glenn Island line / That old black magic / In the mood / Serenade in blue / Pin ball Paul / Chatanooga choo choo / String of pearls / Blue champagne / When Johnny comes marching home / Jeanie with the light brown hair / Serenade in blue / In a sentimental mood / Elmer's tune / Seven-o-five / Falling leaves / Caribbean clipper / My love for you / Lover / Woodpecker song / Hallelujah
CD Set _______________ **TFP 017**
Tring / Nov '92 / Tring

GLENN MILLER ORCHESTRA
CD _______________ **KLMCD 047**
BAM / Jan '95 / Koch / Scratch/BMG

GLENN MILLER VOL.1
CD _______________ **15701**
Laserlight / Apr '97 / Target/BMG

GLENN MILLER VOL.2
CD _______________ **15712**
Laserlight / Apr '94 / Target/BMG

GLENN MILLER'S MEN IN PARIS (Various Artists)
CD _______________ **STD 1**
Starlite / Nov '95 / Jazz Music / Wellard

GLENN MILLER/DUKE ELLINGTON/ BENNY GOODMAN (Miller, Glenn & Duke Ellington/Benny Goodman)
CD Set _______________ **MAK 104**
Avid / Nov '94 / Avid/BMG / Koch / THE

GO TO WAR (Radio Broadcasts From The 1940's) (Miller, Glenn Orchestra)
CD _______________ **CDMR 1160**
Radiola / Nov '90 / Pinnacle

GOLD COLLECTION, THE
CD _______________ **D2CD 01**
Deja Vu / Dec '92 / THE

GOLDEN GREATS (Miller, Glenn & Dorsey Brothers)
CD _______________ **ATJCD 5956**
All That's Jazz / '92 / Jazz Music / THE

GREAT BRITISH DANCE BANDS SALUTE GLENN MILLER (2CD Set) (Various Artists)
I've got a gal in Kalamazoo / You'll never know / Don't sit under the apple tree / Take the 'A' train / Always in my heart / Shoo shoo baby / Deep in the heart of Texas / Lamplighter's serenade / I'm old fashioned / Sweet Eloise / Blues in the night / This is no laughing matter / Dearly beloved / Elmer's tune / My devotion / Yes my darling / I'd know you anywhere / American patrol / Chattanooga choo choo / I'll never smile again / Is my baby blue tonight / I know why / In the mood / String of pearls / Moonlight cocktail / Little brown jug / Five o' clock whistle / St. Louis blues / Serenade in blue / Pennsylvania 6-5000 / Beat me Daddy, eight to the bar / I guess I'll have to dream the rest / I don't want to set the world on fire / Miss you / Humpty dumpty heart / Sierra Sue / Bugle call rag / Falling leaves / April played the fiddle / Farewell blues / Sleep song / Sunrise serenade / Johnson rag / I haven't time to be a millionaire / Tuxedo junction / Stardust / Moonlight serenade
CD Set _______________ **CDDL 1251**
Music For Pleasure / Dec '93 / EMI

GREAT INSTRUMENTALS 1938-1942 (Miller, Glenn Orchestra)
CD _______________ **RTR 79001**
Retrieval / May '96 / Cadillac / Direct / Jazz Music / Swift / Wellard

GREATEST HITS
In the mood / String of pearls / Pennsylvania 6-500 / Chattanooga choo choo / Tuxedo junction / Little brown jug / I've got a gal in Kalamazoo / American patrol / Moonlight serenade / Don't sit under the apple tree (with anyone else but me) / Serenade in blue / Song of the Volga boatmen
CD _______________ **74321339352**
Camden / Jan '96 / BMG

GREATEST HITS LIVE 1940-42 (Miller, Glenn Orchestra)
CD _______________ **DLWE 1**
Magic / Nov '93 / Cadillac / Harmonia Mundi / Jazz Music / Swift / Wellard

HANDFUL OF STARS 1940, A
CD _______________ **DAWE 71**
Magic / '94 / Cadillac / Harmonia Mundi / Jazz Music / Swift / Wellard

HIS GREATEST BAND (Miller, Glenn & The Army Airforce Orchestra)
CD _______________ **3037300042**
Carlton / May '97 / Carlton

I SUSTAIN THE WINGS VOL.2 (USA 1943) (Miller, Glenn & The Army Airforce Orchestra)
CD _______________ **DAWE 67**
Magic / Jan '94 / Cadillac / Harmonia Mundi / Jazz Music / Swift / Wellard

IN REAL HI-FI STEREO 1941 (Miller, Glenn Orchestra)
CD _______________ **JH 1042**
Jazz Hour / Feb '95 / Cadillac / Jazz Music / Target/BMG

IN THE MOOD (1939-1940)
Blueberry Hill / Bugle call rag / Careless / Danny Boy / Imagination / In the mood / Indian summer / It's a blue world / Moonlight serenade / My My / Nearness of you / Out of space / Pennsylvania 6-5000 / Rug cutters' swing / Say it / Slow freight / Stairway to the stars / Stardust / Sunrise serenade / Tuxedo junction / Wishing / Woodpecker song
CD _______________ **CDAJA 5078**
Living Era / Apr '91 / Select

IN THE MOOD
CD _______________ **QSCD 6003**
Charly / Oct '91 / Koch

IN THE MOOD
In the mood / Pennsylvania 6-5000 / Moonlight becomes you / Sunrise serenade / Moonlight serenade / Elmer's tune / Jukebox Saturday night / Tuxedo junction / Chattanooga choo choo / Caribbean clipper / Moonlight cocktail / American patrol / I got a gal in Kalamazoo / Danny Boy / Serenade in blue / String of pearls / At last / Going home / I know why / Don't sit under the apple tree
CD _______________ **MUCD 9010**
Musketeer / Apr '95 / Disc

IN THE MOOD
String of pearls / Pennsylvania 6-5000 / Moonglow / Slaughter on 10th Avenue / Moonlight serenade / American patrol / Sentimental journey / Little brown jug / Anvil chorus / Elmer's tune / Begin the beguine / Flag waver / In the mood / Chattanooga choo choo / Don't sit under the apple tree / Get happy / Swing low, sweet chariot
CD _______________ **100612**
CMC / May '97 / BMG

IN THE MOOD - GLENN MILLER AND HIS ORCHESTRA 1939-1944
In the mood / Pennsylvania 6-5000 / Moonlight serenade / American patrol / Sunrise serenade / Jumpin' jive / Tuxedo junction / Anvil chorus / Chattanooga choo choo / Johnson rag / String of pearls / St. Louis blues march / I've got a gal in Kalamazoo / Song of the Volga boatmen / Perfidia / Little brown jug / My melancholy baby / Serenade in blue
CD _______________ **CD 56006**
Jazz Roots / Aug '94 / Target/BMG

IN THE MOOD - THE BEST OF GLENN MILLER
CD _______________ **TRTCD 192**
TrueTrax / Jun '95 / THE

INTRODUCTION TO GLENN MILLER 1935-1942, AN
CD _______________ **4033**
Best Of Jazz / Jul '96 / Discovery

JAZZ PORTRAITS (Miller, Glenn Orchestra)
In the mood / Pennsylvania 6-5000 / Moonlight serenade / American patrol / Sunrise serenade / Jumpin' jive / Tuxedo junction / Anvil chorus / Chattanooga choo choo / Johnson rag / String of pearls / St. Louis blues march / I've got a gal in Kalamazoo / Song of the Volga boatmen / Perfidia / Little brown jug / My melancholy baby / Serenade in blue
CD _______________ **CD 14502**
Jazz Portraits / May '94 / Jazz Music

L'INCONTOURNABLE
CD _______________ **3014642**
Arcade / Apr '97 / Discovery

LEGEND LIVES ON, THE (The Civilian Orchestra 1938-1941/4CD Set)
Theme / Moonlight serenade / Butcher boy / Don't wake up my heart / Cowboy from Brooklyn / My best wishes / I know that you know / On the sentimental side / On the Alamo / Dipsy doodle / Theme / Moonlight serenade / Sold American / Please come out of your dream / Poinciana / Lady's in love with you / Wishing / Pavanne / And the angels sing / King Porter stomp / Moon is a silver dollar / Sometime / Hold tight / Moonlight serenade / Glen island special / Lamp is low / Jumpin' jive / My blue heaven / Runnin' wild / Moonlight serenade / I've got no string / Theme, Moonlight Serenade / Woodpecker song / Sweet and lovely / Sierra Sue / Very thought of you / Blue evening/Tiger rag / Boog It / Anchors aweigh / Moonlight serenade / Let's all sing together / Say it / On the Alamo / Fools rush in / Slow freight / Woodpecker song / By the waters of Minnetonka / Runnin' wild / Solitude / On the Alamo / King Porter stomp / Wham / Solid as a Stonewall Jackson / Jeannie with the light brown hair / I never took a lesson in my life / I want to be happy / Farewell blues / Fifth avenue / Sophisticated lady / Isn't it romantic / Shadows on the sand / Blue prelude / Moonlight serenade / Midnight on the Nile / Shadows on the sand / Limehouse blues / Handful of stars / Crosstown / Tiger rag / In a sentimental mood / Beat me daddy / Eight to the bar / Bugle woogie / High on a windy hill / Goin' home / You walk by / Georgia on my mind / Morning after / In the mood / Moonlight serenade / Sun valley jump / Chattanooga choo-choo / It happened in sun valley / Spirit is willing / I know why / Measure for measure / Whatcha' know, Joe / Are you Rusty Gate / Love song hasn't been sung / Just a little bit north of south Carolina / Here we go again / Song of the Volga boatmen / Hereafter / Moonlight serenade/Jingle bells / Nobody ever wants me / Sun valley jump/Moonlight serenade
CD Set _______________ **FBB 902**
Ember / Nov '96 / TKO Magnum

LEGEND, THE
Jeep jockey jump / Symphony / Rhapsody in blue / Seven-o-five / Killarney / I've got a heart filled with love / Wabash blues / Everybody loves my baby / In the mood / There'll be a hot time in the town of Berlin / Speak low / Keep 'em flying / Moonlight serenade / Why dream / Here we go again / Fellow on a furlough / Passage interdit / Little brown jug / Deep purple / Jukebox Saturday night / Now I know / Bubble bath / Closing time
CD _______________ **DBCD 01**
Dance Band Days / Oct '87 / Prism

LEGENDARY PERFORMER, A
Moonlight serenade / Sunrise serenade / Little brown jug / Danny boy / Tuxedo junction / My melancholy baby / Pennsylvania / So you're the one / Sentimental me / Song of the Volga boatmen / Jack and Jill / String of pearls / Stardust / Everything I love / Jingle bells / In the mood / Chattanooga choo choo / At last / Moonlight cocktail / I've got a gal in Kalamazoo / Jukebox Saturday night
CD _______________ **ND 90586**
Bluebird / Oct '91 / BMG

LITTLE BROWN JUG
CD _______________ **VJC 10382**
Vintage Jazz Classics / Oct '92 / ADA / Cadillac / CM / Direct

LIVE 1938/39 PARADISE RESTAURANT NEW YORK (Miller, Glenn Orchestra)
Lovelight in the starlight / How'd ya like to love me / You leave me breathless / Please come out of your dream / What have you got that get's me / Room with a view / Wait until
CD _______________ **DAWE 42**
Magic / '89 / Cadillac / Harmonia Mundi / Jazz Music / Swift / Wellard

LIVE AT CAFE ROUGE 1940 (Miller, Glenn Orchestra)
CD _______________ **JH 1037**
Jazz Hour / Feb '95 / Cadillac / Jazz Music / Target/BMG

LIVE AT THE HOLLYWOOD PALLADIUM 1946
CD _______________ **CD 53200**
Giants Of Jazz / Aug '95 / Cadillac / Jazz Music / Target/BMG

LIVE FROM MEADOWBROOK BALLROOM 1939 VOL.2
CD _______________ **DAWE 81**
Magic / Jul '97 / Cadillac / Harmonia Mundi / Jazz Music / Swift / Wellard

LIVE IN HI-FI, GLEN ISLAND 1939 (Miller, Glenn Orchestra)
CD _______________ **JH 1012**
Jazz Hour / '91 / Cadillac / Jazz Music / Target/BMG

LOST RECORDINGS VOL.1, THE (Conducted By Glenn Miller - 1944) (American Band Of The Allied Expeditionary Force)
In the mood / Stardust / Song of the Volga boatmen / Long ago and far away / Is you is or is you ain't my baby / American patrol / Summertime / Tuxedo junction / Begin the Beguine / Anvil chorus / Here we go again / My heart tells me / String of pearls / Stormy weather / Poinciana / All I do is dream of you / Where or when / Cow cow boogie
CD _______________ **CD 53288**
Giants Of Jazz / Jul '97 / Cadillac / Jazz Music / Target/BMG

LOST RECORDINGS VOL.2, THE (Conducted By Glenn Miller - 1944) (American Band Of The Allied Expeditionary Force)
Stardust / Farewell blues / I've got a heart filled with love (for you dear) / Caribbean clipper / Smoke gets in your eyes / Little brown jug / Holiday for strings / Tail end Charlie / Begin the Beguine / Everybody loves my baby / Jeep jockey jump / Great day / All the things you are / Swing low, sweet chariot / Body and soul / Beat me daddy, eight to the bar / Get happy / Moonlight serenade
CD _______________ **CD 53289**
Giants Of Jazz / Jul '97 / Cadillac / Jazz Music / Target/BMG

LOST RECORDINGS, THE
In the mood / Stardust / Song of the Volga boatmen / Long ago and far away / Is you is or is you ain't my baby / Great day / Summertime / Tuxedo junction / Begin the beguine / Anvil chorus / Poinciana / American patrol / Here we go again / My heart tells me / String of pearls / Stormy weather / Little brown jug / Where or when / Cow cow boogie / Holiday for strings / All I do is dream of you / Farewell blues / I've got a heart filled with love / Dear / Caribbean clipper / Smoke gets in your eyes / Tail end Charlie / Everybody loves my baby / Jeep jockey jump / All the things you are / Swing low, sweet chariot / Body and soul / Beat me Daddy, eight to the bar / Eight to the bar / Get happy / Moonlight serenade
CD Set _______________ **CDHD 4012**
Happy Days / Feb '95 / Conifer/BMG

MAGIC OF GLENN MILLER (4CD Set)
CD _______________ **CDDIG 14**
Charly / Apr '95 / Koch

MAJOR GLENN MILLER ARMY AIRFORCE OVERSEAS ORCHESTRA (Miller, Glenn Orchestra)
Flying home / Long ago and far away / Moonlight serenade / I can't give you anything but love / Symphony / Cherokee / Laura
CD _______________ **DAWE 47**
Magic / Nov '93 / Cadillac / Harmonia Mundi / Jazz Music / Swift / Wellard

MARVELLOUS MILLER MAGIC (2CD Set)
String of pearls / I've got a gal in Kalamazoo / In the mood / Tuxedo junction / Wishing / Moon love / I dreamt I dwelt in Harlem / Juke box Saturday night / Stairway to the stars / My blue heaven / Elmers tune / Skylark / I know why / Sunrise serenade / Pennsylvania 6-5000 / Little brown jug / Rainbow rhapsody / Blueberry Hill / Serenade in blue / Adios / Don't sit under the apple tree / American patrol / Fools rush in / At last / Moonlight cocktail / Nightingale sang in Berkeley Square / Song of the Volga Boatmen / Over the rainbow / Take the 'A' train / When you wish upon a star / It's a blue world / Long tall mama / You and I / Stardust / Chatanooga choo choo / Slow freight / Danny Boy / Old black magic / Rhapsody in blue / Moonlight serenade
CD Set _______________ **330022**
Hallmark / Jul '96 / Carlton

MEMORIAL FOR GLENN MILLER VOL.2
King's march / Tuxedo Junction / All the things you are / April in Paris / American patrol / Song of the Volga boatmen / Night and day / Baby me / Georgia on my mind / Dream / Over the rainbow / Running wild / Stormy weather / Man I love / Lady is a tramp / Adios / Tisket-a-tasket
CD _______________ **139 005**
Accord / Dec '86 / Cadillac / Discovery

MEMORIAL FOR GLENN MILLER VOL.3
CD _______________ **139 218**
Accord / Dec '86 / Cadillac / Discovery

MISSING CHAPTERS VOL.1 (American Patrol)
Sun valley jump / Pearls on velvet / With my head in the clouds / Speak low / Here we go again / Rhapsody in blue / Dipsy doodle / String of pearls / Cherokee / Music

stopped / It must be jelly / Songs my Mother taught me / Stompin' at the Savoy / Poinciana / Tail-end Charlie / Summertime / Song of the Volga boatmen / Oh what a beautiful morning / Suddenly it's Spring / Honeysuckle rose / Stardust / Anvil chorus
CD AMSC 556
Avid / Dec '95 / Avid/BMG / Koch / THE

MISSING CHAPTERS VOL.2 (Keep 'Em Flying)
Bubble bath / Blue Danube / Everybody loves my baby / Blues in the night / In the mood / In the gloaming / Over there / Stormy weather / Victory polka / Tuxedo junction / I love you / Holiday for strings / Jeanie with the light brown hair / Enlisted men's mess / Now I know / Guns in the sky / Don't be that way / All through the night / Put your arms around me / Moondreams / Keep 'em flying / All the things you are / Music makers / Squadron song
CD AMSC 557
Avid / Dec '95 / Avid/BMG / Koch / THE

MISSING CHAPTERS VOL.3 (All's Well Mademoiselle)
Moonlight serenade / 705 / Sweet Lorraine / Tuxedo junction / Jeannie with the light brown hair / Begin the beguine / Blue rain / Down the road apiece / Great day / Jerry's Aachen back / Anchors aweigh / Song of the Volga boatmen / Little brown jug / Parachute jump / Wham / Mission to Moscow / Git along song / What is this thing called love / Time alone will tell / All's well Madamoiselle / Hog snortin' romp / I sustain the wings / I'll see you again / Londonderry air / Way you look tonight / I'll be seeing you / I sustain the wings
CD AMSC 558
Avid / Dec '95 / Avid/BMG / Koch / THE

MISSING CHAPTERS VOL.4 (The Red Cavalry March)
Moonlight serenade / Song of the Volga boatmen / Laura / Get happy / Drink to me with thine eyes / There goes that song again / Music makers / Farewell blues / Red cavalry march / I've got sixpence / String of pearls / Trolley song / Shoo shoo baby / Time alone will tell / My guy's come back / Everybody loves my baby / Moonlight serenade / Here we go again / I'll be seeing you / Swing low, sweet chariot / Poinciana / Moonlight serenade
CD AMSC 559
Avid / Dec '95 / Avid/BMG / Koch / THE

MISSING CHAPTERS VOL.5 (The Complete Abbey Road Recordings)
Moonlight serenade / In the mood / Stardust / Song of the Volga boatmen / Long ago and far away / Is you is or is you ain't my baby / Great day / Moonlight serenade / American patrol / Summertime / Tuxedo junction / Now I know / Begin the beguine / Anvil chorus / Moonlight serenade / Hre we go again / My heart tells me / String of pearls / Stormy weather / Poinciana / Moonlight serenade
CD AMSC 560
Avid / Dec '95 / Avid/BMG / Koch / THE

MISSING CHAPTERS VOL.6 (Blue Champagne)
Army Air Corps/I sustain the wings / Sun valley jump / Suddenly it's Spring / All through the night / I love you / Take it easy / Blue Hawaii / Juke box Saturday night / Pearls on velvet / There are Yanks / I sustain the wings / My ideal / Holiday for strings / Goin' home / Dipsy doodle / Speak low / It must be jelly / Annie Laurie / In the mood / In an 18th century drawing room / Guns in the sky / Deep purple / Oh what a beautiful morning / Now I know / Put your arms around me honey / Blue champagne / Snafu jump / Army Air Corps song
CD AMSC 561
Avid / Dec '95 / Avid/BMG / Koch / THE

MISSING CHAPTERS VOL.7 (S'wonderful)
I sustain the wings / In the mood / My heart tells me / Holidays for strings / Victory polka / Wigan pier wiggle / Going my way / Everybody loves my baby / Song and dance / Long long ago / Music stopped / Dipsy doodle / Blues in my heart / Eyes and ears of the world / Waiting for the evening mail / She's funny that way / 9.20 Special / S'wonderful / You, fascinating you / Sleepy town train / I heard you screamin'
CD AMSC 588
Avid / Mar '97 / Avid/BMG / Koch / THE

MISSING CHAPTERS VOL.8 (Get Happy)
Song and dance / Somebody's wrong / Whatcha know Joe / I dream of you / Plain and fancy blues / Moonlight serenade / In the mood / More and more / Get happy / Old black Joe / Someone to love / Here we go again / My prayer / Her tears flowed like wine / Schubert's serenade / Some other time / Little brown jug / Under a blanket of blue / No compris / With my head in the clouds / I sustain the wings / Spring will be a little late this year / I dream of Jeannie with the light brown hair / Lover come back to me
CD AMSC 589
Avid / Mar '97 / Avid/BMG / Koch / THE

MOOD SWINGS
Moonlight serenade / Serenade in blue / Chattanooga choo choo / It happened in Sun Valley / American patrol / Bugle call rag / I've got a gal in Kalamazoo / Spirit is willing / Tuxedo junction / I know why / At last / String of pearls / Measure for measure / Pennsylvania 6500 / Sun Valley jump / In the mood
CD SUMCD 4017
Summit / Nov '96 / Sound & Media

MOONLIGHT COCKTAIL (Miller, Glenn & Ray Eberle)
Too romantic / Imagination / Danny boy / Say it / Hear my song violetta / Pennsylvania 6-5000 / Sierra Sue / Devil may care / Bugle call rag / Nearness of you / Moonlight cocktail / Story of a starry night / Sleep song / Serenade in blue / At last / Beethoven's moonlight sonata / Who's sorry now / Out of space / One I love / Brahms cradle song / Slow freight / Blue orchids
CD CDMOIR 309
Memoir / Apr '95 / Jazz Music / Target/BMG

MOONLIGHT COCKTAIL
American patrol / Serenade in blue / That old black magic / Bugle call rag / Moonlight cocktail / Under a blanket of blue / Penfida / Stardust / At last / Adios / April in Paris / Little man wasn't there / Georgia on my mind / Baby me / Chestnut tree / Kings march / I dreamt I dwell in Harlem / Starlit hour / Glen island line / Rainbow rhapsody / Londonderry air / Kalamazoo
CD GRF 271
Tring / Apr '93 / Tring

MOONLIGHT COCKTAIL
American patrol / Serenade in blue / That old black magic / You and I / Moonlight cocktail / Under a blanket of blue / Perfidia / Stardust / At last / Adios / Elmer's tune / Little man who wasn't there / This time the dream's on me / Everything I love / Skylark / White cliffs of Dover / I dreamt I dwelt in Harlem / Starlit hour / Londonderry air / I've got a gal in kalamazoo
CD QED 218
Tring / Nov '96 / Tring

MOONLIGHT SERENADE
Moonlight serenade / King Porter stomp / Little brown jug / In the mood / Tuxedo junction / Pennsylvania 6-5000 / String of pearls / Elmer's tune / Chattanooga choo choo / Don't sit under the apple tree / American patrol
CD ND 90626
Bluebird / Apr '92 / BMG

MOONLIGHT SERENADE
Moonlight serenade / Wham / Sunrise serenade / Ciribiribin / Bluebirds in the moonlight / My prayer / Little brown jug / Nearness of you / Fresh as a daisy / Blueberry Hill / Booglie wooglie piggy / When the swallows come back to Capistrano / Boulder buff / Handful of stars / Kiss polka / I know why / Chattanooga choo choo / It happened in Sun Valley / Let's have another cup of coffee / Story of a starry night / Don't sit under the apple tree / Jukebox Saturday night / Adios
CD CDHD 210
Happy Days / Feb '97 / Conifer/BMG

MOONLIGHT SERENADE
Moonlight serenade / Little brown jug / Sunrise serenade / Pin ball Paul / Indian summer / Woodpecker song / Pennsylvania 6-5000 / Slumber song / Chatanooga choo choo / String of pearls / Don't sit under the apple tree / My blue heaven / In the mood / Sun Valley jump / Farewell blues / Tuxedo junction / Blues in my heart / Begin the beguine / Anvill chorus / St. Louis blues march / Everybody loves my baby / Over there / Song of the Volga boatmen / Enlisted mens' Miss / It must be jelly, 'cause jam don't shake like that
CD GRF 076
Tring / Apr '93 / Tring

MOONLIGHT SERENADE
Moonlight serenade / Pennsylvania 6-5000 / Johnson rag / Blue orchids / American patrol / Moonlight cocktail / Little brown jug / Frenesi / Elmer's tune / Slip horn jive / Don't sit under the apple tree / String of pearls / Chattanooga choo choo / Take the 'A' train / Perfidia / Tuxedo Junction / Nightingale sang in Berkeley Square / Boulder buff / Story of a starry night / At last / Serenade in blue / I've got a gal in Kalamazoo / In the mood
CD PPCD 78116
Past Perfect / Feb '95 / Glass Gramophone Co.

ON THE AIR
Pennsylvania 6-5000 / My isle of golden dreams / Booglie wooglie piggy / Tuxedo junction / People like you and me / Bless you / Fresh as a daisy / Limehouse blues / Woodpecker song / Sweet and lovely/Sierra Sue/Very thought of you/Blue evening / Keep 'em flying / Jingle bells / Introduction to a waltz / Five o'clock whistle / Here we go again / St. Louis blues / I've got no strings / Handful of stars / Baby me / Blueberry hill / Chattanooga choo choo / Song of the Volga boatmen / Everybody loves my baby / Rumba jumps
CD AVC 550
Avid / Jun '95 / Avid/BMG / Koch / THE

ON THE RADIO (1939-41) (Miller, Glenn Orchestra)
CD DAWE 63
Magic / Sep '93 / Cadillac / Harmonia Mundi / Jazz Music / Swift / Wellard

ORIGINAL GLENN MILLER & HIS ORCHESTRA, THE (Miller, Glenn Orchestra)
When Johnny comes marching home / man with the mandolin / American patrol / Sweet Eloise / Chip off the old block / My blue heaven / Sweet potato piper / Wishing / My, my / Let's have another cup of coffee / Over the rainbow / Boog it / Chattanooga choo choo / Alice blue gown / Wonderful one / Day we meet again / Boulder buff / Frenesi / Booglie wooglie piggy / I know why / Anvil chorus
CD PASTCD 7011
Flapper / Apr '93 / Pinnacle

PACKET OF THREE VOL.9 (3CD Set) (Miller, Glenn Orchestra/Mantovani/ Various Artists)
Little brown jug: *Miller, Glenn Orchestra* / Pennsylvania 6-5000: *Miller, Glenn Orchestra* / Chattanooga choo choo: *Miller, Glenn Orchestra* / String of pearls: *Miller, Glenn Orchestra* / Sunrise serenade: *Miller, Glenn Orchestra* / Johnson rag: *Miller, Glenn Orchestra* / American patrol: *Miller, Glenn Orchestra* / Kalamazoo: *Miller, Glenn Orchestra* / Bugle call rag: *Miller, Glenn Orchestra* / Anvil chorus: *Miller, Glenn Orchestra* / Moonlight cocktail: *Miller, Glenn Orchestra* / Sun Valley jump: *Miller, Glenn Orchestra* / Stardust: *Miller, Glenn Orchestra* / Hallelujah: *Miller, Glenn Orchestra* / Don't sit under the apple tree: *Miller, Glenn Orchestra* / Little man wasn't there: *Miller, Glenn Orchestra* / Georgia on my mind: *Miller, Glenn Orchestra* / In the mood: *Miller, Glenn Orchestra* / Baby me: *Miller, Glenn Orchestra* / Chesnut tree: *Miller, Glenn Orchestra* / Charmaine: *Mantovani* / Some enchanted evening: *Mantovani* / Love is a many splendoured thing: *Mantovani* / Hello Dolly: *Mantovani* / Whispering: *Mantovani* / Smile: *Mantovani* / Count of Luxembourg waltz: *Mantovani* / Dance of the comedians: *Mantovani* / Chitty chitty bang bang: *Mantovani* / Chim chim cheree: *Mantovani* / When you wish upon a star: *Mantovani* / La la la lu: *Mantovani* / Beauty and the beast: *Mantovani* / Zip a dee doo dah: *Mantovani* / Song for Nana: *Mantovani* / Song of Tchaikovsky: *Mantovani* / When a man loves a woman: *Various Artists* / Love is all around: *Various Artists* / Love letters in the sand: *Various Artists* / Groovy kind of love: *Various Artists* / Moon river: *Various Artists* / My guy: *Various Artists* / Feel the need in me: *Various Artists* / Ain't no way to treat a lady: *Various Artists* / Breaking up is hard to do: *Various Artists* / Sorrow: *Various Artists* / My prayer: *Various Artists* / PS I love you: *Various Artists* / By the time I get to Phoenix: *Various Artists* / Ruby, don't take your love to town: *Various Artists* / God bless the child: *Various Artists* / Love really hurts: *Various Artists* / I owe it all to you: *Various Artists* / Don't let the sun catch you crying: *Various Artists* / Stand by me: *Various Artists* / You'll never walk alone: *Various Artists*
CD Set KLMCD 309
BAM / Nov '96 / Koch / Scratch/BMG

PORTRAIT OF GLENN MILLER, A
CD GALE 410
Gallerie / May '97 / Disc / THE

RARITIES 1938-40
CD JZCD 337
Suisa / Jan '93 / Jazz Music / THE

RETURN TO THE CAFE ROUGE
CD DAWE 38
Magic / '89 / Cadillac / Harmonia Mundi / Jazz Music / Swift / Wellard

SECRET BROADCASTS (3CD Set)
I sustain the wings / Mission to Moscow / Army Air Corps song/Music stopped: *Desmond, Johnny* / Long tall mama / Blue Danube / I've got a heart filled with love (for you dear): *Desmond, Johnny & The Crew Chiefs* / Summertime / Caribbean clipper / Army Air Corps song/Irresistible you: *Desmond, Johnny & The Crew Chiefs* / Our waltz / Everybody loves my baby / Along the Santa Fe trail / Keep 'em flying / Songs my mother taught me / Over there: *Crew Chiefs* / Pearls on velvet / My blue heaven / Here we go again / Moon dreams: *Desmond, Johnny & The Crew Chiefs* / Oh lady be good / Begin the beguine / Caprice Viennois / Tuxedo junction / Squadron song: *Desmond, Johnny & The Crew Chiefs/The Glee Club* / Stompin' at the Savoy / Swing low, sweet Chariot / I sustain the wings / I sustain the wings / Bubble bath / Way you look tonight / Going my way: *Desmond, Johnny* / Snafu jump / Rhapsody in blue / Oh, what a beautiful mornin': *Desmond, Johnny & The Crew Chiefs* / In the gloamin' / In the mood / Suddenly it's Spring: *Desmond, Johnny* / Dipsy doodle / Stardust / There'll be a hot time in the town of Berlin: *McKinley, Ray & The Crew Chiefs/Glee Club* / Blue is the night / Tail-end Charlie / I love you: *Desmond, Johnny* / American patrol / All the things you are / Put your arms arouond me honey: *Desmond, Johnny & The Crew Chiefs* / Lovely way to spend an evening: *Desmond, Johnny & The Crew Chiefs* / 7-0-5 (Seven-o-five) Goin' home / Don't be that way / With my head in the clouds: *Desmond, Johnny & The Crew Chiefs* / Farewell blues / Anvil chorus / I sustain the wings / I sustain the wings / Stealin' apples / Army Air Corps song/Fellow in a furlough: *Desmond, Johnny* / Cherokee / Stormy weather / Guns in the sky: *Desmond, Johnny & Ensemble* / Jeanie with the light brown hair / Music makers / Summertime / It must be jelly ('cause jam don't shake like that) / Holiday for strings / Victory Polka: *Glee Club* / String of pearls / Moonlight serenade / Speak low: *Desmond, Johnny* / Sun valley jump / Annie Laurie / Enlisted men's mess / Poinciana: *Desmond, Johnny & The Crew Chiefs* / Song of the Volga boatmen / All through the night / 9.20 Special / Now I know: *Desmond, Johnny* / Jeep jockey jump / Goodnight wherever you are: *Desmond, Johnny & The Crew Chiefs* / I sustain the wings
CD Set 75605525002
Happy Days / Nov '96 / Conifer/BMG

SINGALONG PARTY
String of pearls / Song of the Volga boatmen / Chatanooga choo choo / Pennsylvania 6-5000 / Don't sit under the apple tree / American patrol / Sun valley jump / Little brown jug / In the mood / Tuxedo junction / St. Louis blues / My blue heaven / Anvil chorus / Over there / Indian summer / Moonlight serenade / Miller's megamix / Swingalong megamix
CD GRF 152
Tring / '93 / Tring

SPIRIT IS WILLING 1939-1942, THE
King Porter stomp / Slip horn jive / Pagan love song / Glen island special / I want to be happy / Farewell blues / Johnson rag / Rug cutter's swing / Slow freight / Bugle call rag / My blue heaven / I dreamt I dwelt in Harlem / Sun valley jump / Spirit is willing / Boulder buff / Take the 'A' train / Long tall Mama / Keep 'em flying / Caribbean clipper / Here we go again / Rainbow rhapsody / Rhapsody in blue
CD 07863665292
Bluebird / Apr '95 / BMG

SPOTLIGHT ON GLENN MILLER (Biography/Classic Tracks)
Moonlight serenade / King Porter stomp / Little brown jug / In the mood / Tuxedo junction / American patrol / Don't sit under the apple tree / Chattanooga choo choo / Elmer's tune / String of pearls / Pennsylvania
CD VLF 5
Talking Volumes / Apr '95 / BMG

SPOTLIGHT ON GLENN MILLER & THE DORSEY BROTHERS (Miller, Glenn & Dorsey Brothers)
Boogie woogie: *Dorsey, Tommy* / Moonlight serenade: *Miller, Glenn* / String of pearls: *Miller, Glenn* / Amapola: *Dorsey, Jimmy* / Little brown jug: *Miller, Glenn* / Chattanooga choo choo: *Miller, Glenn* / Green eyes: *Dorsey, Jimmy* / In the mood: *Miller, Glenn* / Serenade in blue: *Miller, Glenn* / I'm getting sentimental over you: *Dorsey, Tommy* / Over the rainbow: *Miller, Glenn* / Song of India: *Dorsey, Tommy* / So rare: *Dorsey, Jimmy* / I've got a gal in Kalamazoo: *Miller, Glenn* / Sunrise serenade: *Miller, Glenn*
CD HADCD 128
Javelin / Feb '94 / Henry Hadaway / THE

STORY OF A MAN AND HIS MUSIC, THE
CD 11017
Laserlight / '86 / Target/BMG

STRING OF PEARLS, A
Little brown jug / Sunrise serenade / In the mood / I'm sitting on top of the world / Jumpin' jive / Moonlight Bay / String of pearls
CD BSTCD 9107
Best Compact Discs / May '92 / Complete/ Pinnacle

STRING OF PEARLS, A
Always in my heart / American patrol / At last / Chip off the old block / Don't sit under the apple tree / Elmer's tune / Humpty Dumpty heart / I guess I'll have to dream the rest / It must be jelly, 'cause jam don't shake like that / I've got a gal in Kalamazoo / Jukebox Saturday night / Lamplighter's serenade / Let's have another cup of coffee / Moonlight cocktail / Moonlight becomes you / Serenade in blue / Skylark / Story of a starry night / String of pearls / Sweet Eloise / Take the 'A' train / That old black magic / This is no laughing matter / When Johnny comes marching home
CD CDAJA 5109
Living Era / Jun '93 / Select

STRING OF PEARLS, A
CD PLSCD 113
Pulse / Apr '96 / BMG

STRING OF PEARLS, A
CD MACCD 222
Autograph / Aug '96 / BMG

SUN VALLEY SERENADE/ORCHESTRA WIVES
CD BMCD 7001
Blue Moon / Jan '95 / Cadillac / Discovery / Greensleeves / Jazz Music / Jet Star / TKO Magnum

SUNSET SERENADE BROADCAST 22 NOV 1941 (Miller, Glenn Orchestra)
Intro / Tuxedo junction / Dreamsville Ohio / Chattanooga choo choo / I know why / It happened in Sun Valley / Everything I love / V Hop / In a sentimental mood / I guess I'll have to dream the rest / Do you care / Tschaikovsky's piano concerto / Till reveille / I don't want to set the world on fire / Papa Niccolini / In the mood / Close
CD Set _____ JH 1002
Jazz Hour / Apr '90 / Cadillac / Jazz Music / Target/BMG

SUSTAINING REMOTE BROADCASTS VOL.1 & 2, THE (2CD Set) (Miller, Glenn Orchestra)
Moonlight serenade: *Miller, Glenn & His Orchestra* / I never knew (I could love anybody like I'm loving you): *Miller, Glenn & His Orchestra* / This can't be love: *Miller, Glenn & His Orchestra* / What have you got that gets me: *Miller, Glenn & His Orchestra* / Change partners: *Miller, Glenn & His Orchestra* / When paw was courtin' maw: *Miller, Glenn & His Orchestra* / Why doesn't somebody tell me these things: *Miller, Glenn & His Orchestra* / Without you on my mind: *Miller, Glenn & His Orchestra* / Down South camp greetin': *Miller, Glenn & His Orchestra* / Moonlight serenade: *Miller, Glenn & His Orchestra* / Lady's in love with you: *Miller, Glenn & His Orchestra* / Twilight interlude: *Miller, Glenn & His Orchestra* / Dong dong the witch is dead: *Miller, Glenn & His Orchestra* / Bugle call rag: *Miller, Glenn & His Orchestra* / Moonlight serenade: *Miller, Glenn & His Orchestra* / Moonlight serenade: *Miller, Glenn & His Orchestra* / Pennsylvania 6-5000: *Miller, Glenn & His Orchestra* / Call of the canyon: *Miller, Glenn & His Orchestra* / Gentleman needs a shave: *Miller, Glenn & His Orchestra* / Handful of stars: *Miller, Glenn & His Orchestra* / Moonlight serenade: *Miller, Glenn & His Orchestra* / On, brave old army team: *Miller, Glenn & His Orchestra* / When the swallows come back to Capistrano: *Miller, Glenn & His Orchestra* / Down for the count: *Miller, Glenn & His Orchestra* / Glenn Miller speaks: *Miller, Glenn & His Orchestra* / Slumber song: *Miller, Glenn & His Orchestra* / Lady's in love with you: *Miller, Glenn & His Orchestra* / Rendezvous time in Paree: *Miller, Glenn & His Orchestra* / (Hep hep) the jumpin' jive: *Miller, Glenn & His Orchestra* / Farewell blues: *Miller, Glenn & His Orchestra* / Moonlight serenade: *Miller, Glenn & His Orchestra* / Moonlight serenade: *Miller, Glenn & His Orchestra* / Glen island special: *Miller, Glenn & His Orchestra* / Why couldn't it last last night: *Miller, Glenn & His Orchestra* / Wham (re bop boom bam): *Miller, Glenn & His Orchestra* / Indian summer: *Miller, Glenn & His Orchestra* / King porter stomp: *Miller, Glenn & His Orchestra* / It's a blue world: *Miller, Glenn & His Orchestra* / I wanna hat with cherries: *Miller, Glenn & His Orchestra* / My blue heaven: *Miller, Glenn & His Orchestra* / Moonlight serenade: *Miller, Glenn & His Orchestra* / Moonlight serenade: *Miller, Glenn & His Orchestra* / Johnson rag: *Miller, Glenn & His Orchestra* / Gaucho serenade: *Miller, Glenn & His Orchestra* / Boog it: *Miller, Glenn & His Orchestra* / Sky fell down: *Miller, Glenn & His Orchestra* / I want to be happy: *Miller, Glenn & His Orchestra* / Starlit hour: *Miller, Glenn & His Orchestra* / Glenn Miller speaks: *Miller, Glenn & His Orchestra* / Tuxedo junction: *Miller, Glenn & His Orchestra* / Too romantic: *Miller, Glenn & His Orchestra* / Glenn Miller speaks again: *Miller, Glenn & His Orchestra* / My my: *Miller, Glenn & His Orchestra*
CD Set _____ JZCL 5011
Jazz Classics / Nov '96 / Cadillac / Direct / Jazz Music

SUSTAINING REMOTE BROADCASTS VOL.2, THE (Miller, Glenn Orchestra)
CD _____ VJC 10222
Vintage Jazz Classics / '91 / ADA / Cadillac / CM / Direct

SWING ALONG PARTY
String of pearls / Song of the Volga boatmen / Chattanooga choo choo / Pennsylvania 6-5000 / Don't sit under the apple tree / American patrol / Sun valley jump / Little brown jug / In the mood / Tuxedo junction / St. Louis blues / My blue heaven / Anvil chorus / Over there / Indian summer / Moonlight serenade / Medley 1 / Medley 2
CD _____ QED 100
Tring / Nov '96 / Tring

SWINGING MR. MILLER
It happened in Sun Valley / When Johnny comes marching home / American patrol / I got a gal in Kalamazoo / Ida, sweet as apple cider / Song of the Volga boatmen / Sun valley jump / Frenesi / Five o'clock whistle / Beat me Daddy, eight to the bar / Yes my darling daughter / Pennsylvania 6-5000 / My blue heaven / Caribbean clipper / Old black magic / Jukebox Saturday night / It must be jelly, 'cause jam don't shake like that / Pagan love song / Glen island special / Take the 'A' train / Tuxedo junction / Wonderful one
CD _____ RAJCD 807
Empress / Apr '97 / Koch

TWO ON ONE: GLENN MILLER & BENNY GOODMAN (Miller, Glenn & Benny Goodman)
CD _____ CDTT 10
Charly / Apr '94 / Koch

ULTIMATE GLENN MILLER, THE
In the mood / Little brown jug / Sliphorn jive / My prayer / Tuxedo junction / Fools rush in / Pennsylvania 6-5000 / Blueberry Hill / Song of the Volga boatmen / Perfidia / Chattanooga choo choo / I know why / Adios / String of pearls / Skylark / Don't sit under the apple tree / American patrol / Serenade in blue / I've got a gal in Kalamazoo / St. Louis blues march / At last / Moonlight serenade
CD _____ 74321131372
RCA / Feb '93 / BMG

UNFORGETTABLE GLENN MILLER, THE
CD _____ PD 89260
RCA / Apr '84 / BMG

Miller, Herb

REMEMBER GLENN MILLER (Miller, Herb Orchestra)
Sun Valley jump / I'm thrilled / Johnson rag / Angel divine / Bugle call rag / Quiet nights of quiet stars / Long tall mama / Slumber song / Caribbean clipper / Remember Glenn Miller / Anchors aweigh / Days of wine and roses / Here we go again / Skylark / I dreamt I dwelt in Harlem
CD _____ CDPT 504
Prestige / Jan '94 / Else / Total/BMG

Miller, Jacob

I'M JUST A DREAD
CD _____ RGCD 6016
Rocky One / Mar '94 / Jet Star

JACOB MILLER MEETS FATMAN RIDDIM SECTION
CD _____ CC 2715
Crocodisc / Apr '95 / Grapevine/PolyGram

MIXED UP ROOTS
CD _____ CC 2707
Crocodisc / Jan '94 / Grapevine/PolyGram

NATTY CHRISTMAS
CD _____ RASCD 3103
Ras / Nov '92 / Direct / Greensleeves / Jet Star / SRD

REGGAE GREATS (Miller, Jacob & Inner Circle)
Shaky girl / Tenement yard / Suzy Wong / Sinners / Healing of the nation / 80,000 careless Ethiopians / I've got the handle / Tired fe lickweed in a bush / Roman soldiers of Babylon / Standing firm / All night 'til daylight / Forward Jah Jah children
CD _____ 5527382
Spectrum / Jul '97 / PolyGram

WHO SAY JAH NO DREAD
CD _____ GRELCD 166
Greensleeves / Jul '97 / Jet Star / SRD

WITH THE INNER CIRCLE BAND & AUGUSTUS PABLO
CD _____ LG 21053
Lagoon / Nov '92 / Grapevine/PolyGram

Miller, Jerry

LIFE IS LIKE THAT (Miller, Jerry Band)
CD _____ MRSCD 004
Messaround / Jun '97 / Greyhound

Miller, Julie

BLUE PONY
CD _____ HCD 8079
Hightone / Jun '97 / ADA / Koch

INVISIBLE GIRL
CD _____ SPARK 7037CD
Spark / Feb '95 / ADA

MEET JULIE MILLER
CD _____ MYRRH 5610CD
Myrrh / Feb '95 / Nelson Word

ORPHANS AND ANGELS
CD _____ MYRRH 7616CD
Myrrh / Jan '95 / Nelson Word

Miller, June

WHEN LIFE HURTS
CD _____ GMICD 066
Spark / May '96 / ADA

Miller, Lisa

QUIET GIRL WITH A CREDIT CARD
Big American car / You're a big girl now / Guitar boat / Nobody's an angel / I'm gonna live my life (I'm gonna take my time) / Hang my head / Woman left lonely / False waltz / Too dark to see / Long wide load / Big small town
CD _____ FIENDCD 794
Demon / May '97 / Pinnacle

Miller, Luella

LUELLA MILLER & LONNIE JOHNSON
CD _____ DOCD 5183
Document / Oct '93 / ADA / Hot Shot / Jazz Music

Miller, Marcus

LIVE AND MORE
Intro / Panther / Tutu / Funny (all she needs is love) / Strange fruit / Summertime / Maputo / People make the world go round / Sophie / Jazz in the house
CD _____ FDM 365852
Dreyfus / Mar '97 / ADA / Direct / New Note/ Pinnacle

SUN DON'T LIE, THE
Panther / Steveland / Rampage / Sun don't lie / Scoop / Mr. Pastorius / Funny (all she needs is love) / Moons / Teen town / Ju Ju / King is gone (for miles)
CD _____ FDM 365602
Dreyfus / Aug '93 / ADA / Direct / New Note/ Pinnacle

TALES
Blues / Tales / Eric / True geminis / Rush over / Running through my dreams / Ethiopia / Strange fruit / Visions / Brazilian rhyme / Forevermore / Infatuation / Tales (reprise) / Come together
CD _____ FDM 365712
Dreyfus / Apr '95 / ADA / Direct / New Note/ Pinnacle

Miller, Max

CHEEKY CHAPPIE (Holborn Empire & Finsbury Park 1936-39)
Max with the band / Max on stage - Holborn Empire / Max on stage - Holborn Empire / Max on stage - Finsbury Park Empire
CD _____ PASTCD 9714
Flapper / '90 / Pinnacle

CHEEKY CHAPPIE ENTERTAINS, THE (3CD Set)
Lulu / She said she wouldn't / Doing all the nice things / With a bit of luck / Influence / Mother Brown Story / There's always someone worse / Mary from the dairy (introduction) / Passing the time away / Hearts and flowers / Be sincere / Girls I like / Fan dancer (oh, Dear what can the matter be) / Mary Anne (the five year plan) / Josephine / Twin sisters / On the banks of the Nile / Hiking / Tit bits / Market song / When we go on our holiday / Cheeky chappie tells a few / I thought we came here to pick some flowers / All becuase I rolled my eyes / Girls who work where I work / Every Sunday afternoon / New kind of old fashioned girl / Cheeky chappie picks from the white book and blue book / Is there no end to his cleverness / What ju-ju wants ju-ju must have / Stringing along with you / Sitting in the old armchair / Jean Carr asks some questions but Max knows all the answers / Max gives Jean some chocolates / Hiking song / Do re mi / No, no, no / Cheeky chappie tells some / Cheeky Chappie chats about etiquette and manners / Down where the rambling roses grow / I don't like the girls / All good stuff lady / Mary Anne
CD Set _____ MAGPIE 4
See For Miles/C5 / Sep '95 / Pinnacle

CHEEKY CHAPPIE...PLUS
Lulu / Lulu (Reprise) / She said she wouldn't / Doing all the nice things / With a little bit of luck / Influence / Mother Brown story / There's always someone worse off than you
CD _____ C5LCD 613
See For Miles/C5 / Sep '94 / Pinnacle

MAX AT THE MET/THAT'S NICE MAXIE
Mary from the dairy / Hearts and flowers / Be sincere (Introduction) / Fan dancer (Oh dear what can the matter be) / Mary Ann (The five year plan) / Twin sister / Tit bits / Passing the time away / Be sincere / Girls I like / Hikin / Josephine / On the banks of The Nile / Market song
CD _____ C5LCD 598
See For Miles/C5 / Sep '94 / Pinnacle

MAX MILLER VOL.2 (The Pure Gold Of Music Hall)
Julietta / Love bug will bite you / Max with the forces: *Miller, Max & Jean Carr* / Confessions of a cheeky chappy / Woman improver / Weeping willow / You can't blame me for that / Backscratcher / Impshe / Max the auctioneer / Girl next door / How the so-and-so can I be happy / Do re mi / Everything happens to me / At the bathing parade / No, no, no
CD _____ PASTCD 9736
Flapper / Feb '91 / Pinnacle

THERE'LL NEVER BE ANOTHER/THE ONE AND ONLY
Mary from the dairy / When we go on our honeymoon / Cheeky chappie tells a few / I thought we came here to pick some flowers / All because I rolled my eyes / Girls who work where I work / Every Sunday afternoon / New kind of old fashioned girl / From the white book / And the blue book / Is there no end to his cleverness / What Ju Ju wants Ju Ju must have / Stringing along with you / Sitting in the old armchair / Hiking song / Doh-re-me / No, no, no / Cheeky chappie tells some / Passing the time away / About etiquette and manners / Cheeky chappie tells some more / Down where the rambling roses grow / I don't like the girls / All good stuff lady / Mary Ann
CD _____ C5LCD 631
See For Miles/C5 / Feb '96 / Pinnacle

Miller, Mulgrew

COUNTDOWN, THE
CD _____ LCD 15192
Landmark / Apr '89 / New Note/Pinnacle

GETTING TO KNOW YOU
Eastern joy dance / Second thoughts / Sweet Sioux / Getting to know you / Whisper / Didn't we / Fool on the hill / I don't know how to love him / If I should lose you / Nandhi
CD _____ 01241631882
Novus / Feb '96 / BMG

HAND IN HAND
CD _____ 01241631532
Novus / Jul '93 / BMG

WINGSPAN
CD _____ LCD 15152
Landmark / Jul '88 / New Note/Pinnacle

Miller, Ned

FROM A JACK TO A KING
From a jack to a king / Parade of broken hearts / Turn around / Lights in the street / Old mother nature and old father time / Roll o' rollin' stone / One among the many / Man behind the gun / Another fool like me / Magic moon / Sunday morning tears / Big love / Old restless ocean / Invisible tears / Do what you do do well / Dusty guitar / Just before dawn / Go on back you fool / Dark moon / Cold grey bars / My heart waits at the door / Big lie / Heart without a heartache / Billy Carino / Cry of the wild goose / Long shadow / Mona Lisa / Stage coach / You belong to my heart / King of fools / Girl across the table
CD _____ BCD 15496
Bear Family / Feb '91 / Direct / Rollercoaster / Swift

Miller, Pat

RADIO DAYS (Miller, Pat & Mike Edwards)
CD _____ NEW 1006
Australian Jazz / Nov '96 / Jazz Music

Miller, Paul D.

VIRAL SONATA
Prologue / Indra's net / Morphic interlude / Invisual ocean / Striated interlude no.1 / Necrologue / Striated interlude no.2 / City on the edge of forever / Zona rosa / Colophon / Striated interlude no.3 / Primary inversion / Striated interlude no.4 / Epilogue
CD _____ EFA 709762
Asphodel / Aug '97 / Cargo / SRD

Miller, Phil

CUTTING BOTH WAYS
Green and purple extract / Hic haec hoc / Simple man / Eastern region / Hard shoulder / Figures of speech / Green and purple
CD _____ RUNE 11
Cuneiform / Dec '89 / ReR Megacorp

DIGGING IN
CD _____ RUNE 34
Cuneiform / Oct '90 / ReR Megacorp

IN CAHOOTS - LIVE IN JAPAN
No holds barred / Bass motives / Speaking to Lydia / Truly yours / Second sight / Green and purple extract / Digging in extract
CD _____ CD 2CD
Crescent Discs / Jun '93 / Vital

SPLIT SECONDS
CD _____ CDRECK 8
Reckless / Mar '89 / RTM/Disc

Miller, Punch

ICON
CD _____ AMCD 52
American Music / May '95 / Jazz Music

LARRY BORENSTEIN VOL.5
CD _____ 504CD 34
504 / Oct '94 / Cadillac / Jazz Music / Target/BMG / Wellard

PUNCH MILLER
CD _____ 504CD 40
504 / Dec '95 / Cadillac / Jazz Music / Target/BMG / Wellard

PUNCH MILLER 1925-30
CD _____ JPCD 1517
Jazz Perspectives / May '95 / Hot Shot / Jazz Music

Miller, Rodney

AIRPLANG
Sail away ladies/Waynesboro / Erin/Soulmate / Hangman's reel / In Christ there is no east or west/Salimony waltz / Contrazz/ Old Joe / Dancing bear / Elvira/Asher / Nancy's waltz/Dark island / Fair Jenny / Cotton Eyed Joe
CD _____ CMCD 075
Celtic Music / Jul '97 / CM
CD _____ ROUCD 0193
Rounder / May '97 / ADA / CM / Direct

GREASY COAT
CD _____ SA 1301CD
Sage Arts / Apr '94 / ADA

Miller, Roger

BEST OF ROGER MILLER, THE
CD _______________ **MATCD 327**
Castle / Feb '95 / BMG

BEST OF ROGER MILLER, THE
CD _______________ **PLSCD 126**
Pulse / Apr '96 / BMG

DANG ME (Greatest Hits)
CD _______________ **15479**
Laserlight / Aug '94 / Target/BMG

KING OF THE ROAD
You're part of me / Fair Swiss maiden / Every which a way / It happened just that way / I get up early in the morning / I catch myself crying / I'll be somewhere / Little green apples / I know who it is (and I'm gonna tell on him) / But I love you more / If you want me too / Burma shave / You don't want my love / Sorry Willie / You can't do me that way / When two worlds collide / Lock, stock and teardrops / Trouble on the turnpike / Hey little star / Footprints in the snow / Hitch hiker / Dang me / King of the road / Chug-a-lug / Engine no.9 / Kansas City star / England swings / Do wacka do / One dyin' and a buryin'
CD _______________ **BCD 15477**
Bear Family / Feb '90 / Direct / Rollercoaster / Swift

KING OF THE ROAD
CD _______________ **WMCD 5658**
Woodford Music / Jul '92 / THE

KING OF THE ROAD
Engine engine no.9 / England swings / Kansas city star / King of the road / Dang me / Chug-a-lug / Husbands and wives / Walking in the sunshine / My uncle used to love me but she died / When two worlds collide / You can't rollerskate in a buffalo herd / Me and Bobby McGee / Please release me / In the summertime / Last word is lonesome / My elusive dreams / Everything's coming up roses / Do-wacka-do / Billy Bayou / Burning bridges
CD _______________ **PLATCD 216**
Platinum / Feb '97 / Prism

LEGENDS IN MUSIC
CD _______________ **LECD 083**
Wisepack / Jul '94 / Conifer/BMG / THE

WORLD OF ROGER MILLER, THE
King of the road / Engine / Kansas City star / England swings / Little green apples / Dang me / Husbands and wives / Boeing Boeing 707 / Chug-a-lug / (You had a) do-wacka-do / You can't roller skate in a buffalo herd / My Uncle used to love me but she died / Walkin' in the sunshine / Me and Bobby McGee / By the time I get to Phoenix / Gentle on my mind / Ruby, don't take your love to town / Everybody's talking
CD _______________ **5511112**
Spectrum / May '96 / PolyGram

Miller, Roger

ELEMENTAL GUITAR
CD _______________ **SST 318CD**
SST / Aug '95 / Plastic Head

OH
We grind open (in) / Meltdown man / Chinatown samba / Firetruck / Cosmic battle / You son of a bitch / War bolts / Fun world reductions / Space is the place / Forest / Kalgastak
CD _______________ **NAR 097**
New Alliance / Mar '94 / Plastic Head

UNFOLD (Miller, Roger Exquisite Corpse)
CD _______________ **SST 307CD**
SST / Sep '94 / Plastic Head

Miller, Sing

BLUES, BALLADS & SPIRITUALS
CD _______________ **MG 9006**
Mardi Gras / Feb '95 / Jazz Music

Miller, Steve

BEST OF THE STEVE MILLER BAND 1968-1973, THE (Miller, Steve Band)
Joker / Livin' in the USA / My dark hour / Going to the country / Shu ba da du ma ma ma / Going to Mexico / Come on into the kitchen / Evil / Song for our ancestors / Your saving grace / Quicksilver girl / Seasons / Space cowboy / Gangster of love / Kow kow calqulator / Little girl / Don't let nobody turn you around / Jackson-Kent blues / Sugar babe
CD _______________ **CDEST 2133**
Capitol / Oct '90 / EMI

GREATEST HITS (Decade Of American Music 1976-1986) (Miller, Steve Band)
Space intro / Fly like an eagle / Bongo bongo / Rock 'n' me / Jet airliner / Take the money and run / Mercury blues / Swing town / Shangri la / Abracadabra / Italian x rays / Out of the night / Who do you love / Harmony of the spheres
CD _______________ **8309782**
Mercury / May '87 / PolyGram

JOKER, THE (Miller, Steve Band)
Sugar babe / Mary Lou / Shu ba da du ma ma ma / Your cash ain't nothin' but trash / Joker / Lovin' cup / Come on in my kitchen / Evil / Something to believe in
CD _______________ **CDP 7944452**
EMI / Sep '96 / EMI

SAILOR (Miller, Steve Band)
Song for our ancestors / Dear Mary / My friend / Living in the USA / Quicksilver girl / Lucky man / Gangster of love / You're so fine / Overdrive / Dime-a-dance romance
CD _______________ **CDFA 3254**
Fame / Apr '91 / EMI

WIDE RIVER (Miller, Steve Band)
Wide river / Midnight train / Blue eyes / Lost in your eyes / Perfect world / Horse and rider / Circle of fire / Conversation / Cry cry cry / Stranger blues / Walks like a lady / All your love (I miss loving)
CD _______________ **5194412**
Polydor / Jul '93 / PolyGram

Millinder, Lucky

BACK BEATS
Swingin' in E flat / African lullaby / Dancing dogs / back beats / Spitfire / Harlem heat / Trouble in mind / Slide Mr. Trombone / Ride Red Ride / Rock Daniel / Big fat Mama / Shout sister shout / Apollo jump / Rock me / Let me off uptown / That's all / I want a tall skinny Papa / Savoy / Mason flyer / Little John special / Shipyard social function / Hurry hurry / Who threw the whiskey in the well / All the time
CD _______________ **TPZ 1056**
Topaz Jazz / Oct '96 / Cadillac / Pinnacle

LUCKY MILLINDER 1941-42
CD _______________ **CLASSICS 712**
Classics / Jul '93 / Discovery / Jazz Music

RAM-BUNK-SHUSH
Ram-bunk-shush / Oh babe / Please open your heart / Silent George / I'm waiting just for you / No one else could be / It's been a long, long time / Please be careful / Loaded with love / When I gave you my love / Heavy sugar / Old spice / I'm here love / It's a sad, sad feeling / Owl / Goody good love
CD _______________ **CDCHARLY 288**
Charly / Sep '91 / Koch

Million Dollar Quartet

COMPLETE MILLION DOLLAR QUARTET
You belong to my heart / When God dips his love in my heart / Just a little talk with Jesus / Walk that lonesome valley / I shall not be moved / Peace in the valley / Down by the riverside / I'm in the crowd but oh so alone / Farther along / Blessed Jesus hold my hand / As we travel along the Jericho road / I just can't make it by myself / Little cabin home on the hill / Summertime is passed and gone / I hear a sweet voice calling / Sweetheart you done me wrong / Keeper of the key / Crazy arms / Don't forbid me / Brown eyed handsome man / Out of sight out of mind / Brown eyed handsome man (take 2) / Don't be cruel / Don't be cruel (take 2) / Paralysed / Don't be cruel (take 3) / There's no place like home / When the saints go marching in / Softly and tenderly / Is it so strange / That's when the heartaches begin / Brown eyed handsome man (take 3) / Rip it up / I'm gonna bid my blues goodbye / Crazy arms (take 2) / That's my desire / End of the road / Jerry's boogie / You're the only star in my blue heaven / Elvis, farewell
CD _______________ **CDCHARLY 102**
Charly / Jan '88 / Koch

Millman, Jack

FOUR MORE (Millman, Jack Quartet/Quintet)
CD _______________ **FSRCD 217**
Fresh Sound / Jan '97 / Discovery / Jazz Music

Mills Blue Rhythm Band

BLUE RHYTHM
CD _______________ **HEPCD 1008**
New Note / Aug '92 / Cadillac / New Note/Pinnacle

CLASSICS 1931
CD _______________ **CLASSICS 660**
Classics / Nov '92 / Discovery / Jazz Music

CLASSICS 1931-1932
CD _______________ **CLASSICS 676**
Classics / Mar '93 / Discovery / Jazz Music

INTRODUCTION TO MILLS BLUE RHYTHM BAND 1931-1937, AN
CD _______________ **4009**
Best Of Jazz / Mar '95 / Discovery

MILLS BLUE RHYTHM BAND 1934-36
CD _______________ **CLASSICS 710**
Classics / Jul '93 / Discovery / Jazz Music

MILLS BLUE RHYTHM BAND 1936-37
CD _______________ **CLASSICS 731**
Classics / Jan '94 / Discovery / Jazz Music

RHYTHMS SPASM
Cabin in the cotton / Minnie the moocher's wedding day / Growl / Might sweet / Rhythm spasm / Swanee lullaby / White lightning / Wild waves / Sentimental gentlemen from Georgia / You gave me everything but love / Ol' yazoo / Reefer man / Jazz cocktail / Smoke rings / Ridin' in rhythm / Weary traveller / Buddy's Wednesday outing / Harlem after midnight / Jazz martini / Feelin' gay / Break it down / Kokey Joe / Love's serenade
CD _______________ **HEPCD 1015**
Hep / Jun '93 / Cadillac / Jazz Music / New Note/Pinnacle / Wellard

Mills Brothers

CHRONOLOGICAL VOL.2
CD _______________ **JSPCD 302**
JSP / Apr '89 / ADA / Cadillac / Direct / Hot Shot / Target/BMG

CHRONOLOGICAL VOL.3
CD _______________ **JSPCD 303**
JSP / Apr '89 / ADA / Cadillac / Direct / Hot Shot / Target/BMG

CHRONOLOGICAL VOL.4
CD _______________ **JSPCD 304**
JSP / Oct '88 / ADA / Cadillac / Direct / Hot Shot / Target/BMG

CLASSICS
Put another chair at the table / Meet me tonight in Dreamland / Don't be a baby, baby / There's no-one but you / I'll be around / I wish / I'm afraid to love you / Till then / Flat foot floogie / Organ grinder's swing / Jeepers creepers / Swanee river / Georgia on my mind / Shine / In the shade of the old apple tree / Caravan / It don't mean a thing / Paper doll / Smoke rings / I guess I'll get the papers / Boog it / Too many irons in the fire
CD _______________ **RAJCD 883**
Empress / Jul '97 / Koch

DARLING NELLY GRAY 1936-1940
CD _______________ **CD 56072**
Jazz Roots / Jul '95 / Target/BMG

I'VE FOUND A NEW BABY 1932-34
CD _______________ **CD 56057**
Jazz Roots / Jul '95 / Target/BMG

JAZZ PORTRAIT VOL.1
CD _______________ **CD 14584**
Complete / Nov '95 / THE

JAZZ PORTRAIT VOL.2
CD _______________ **CD 14587**
Complete / Nov '95 / THE

JAZZ PORTRAIT VOL.3
CD _______________ **CD 14577**
Complete / Nov '95 / THE

LA SELECTION 1931-38
CD _______________ **012**
Art Vocal / Sep '93 / Discovery

MILLS BROTHERS MEET ARMSTRONG (Mills Brothers & Louis Armstrong)
CD _______________ **BMCD 3056**
Blue Moon / Apr '97 / Cadillac / Discovery / Greensleeves / Jazz Music / Jet Star / TKO Magnum

MILLS BROTHERS VOL.2 1931-1934
CD _______________ **CD 53086**
Giants Of Jazz / May '92 / Cadillac / Jazz Music / Target/BMG

MILLS BROTHERS VOL.2, THE
Sweet Sue, just you / Goodbye blues / How 'm I doin', hey-hey / Baby, won't you please come home / (I'll be glad when you're dead) you rascal you / Tiger rag / My romance / Old man of the mountains / Anytime, anyday, anywhere / That's Georgia / Jungle fever / Swing it, sister / Smoke rings / I heard / Put on your old grey bonnet / Sleepy head / Lazybones / Old-fashioned love / Miss Otis regrets / Sweeter than sugar / Ida, sweet as apple cider / Limehouse blues / Shuffle your feet / Bandana babies / My little grass shack in Kealakekua Hawaii
CD _______________ **CD 53273**
Giants Of Jazz / Jun '96 / Cadillac / Jazz Music / Target/BMG

MILLS BROTHERS VOL.3, THE
Rockin' chair swing / Love bug will bite you / Big boy blue: *Mills Brothers & Ella Fitzgerald* / Dedicated to you: *Mills Brothers & Ella Fitzgerald* / Rhythm saved the world / Solitude / Lulu's back in town / Sweet and slow / Shoe shine boy / London rhythm / Swing is the thing / 'Long about midnight / Pennies from heaven / Swing for sale / Sweet Lucy Brown / Song is ended / Don't be afraid to tell your Mother / Since we fell out of love / Moanin' for you / What's the reason (I'm not pleasin' you) / Caravan / Little old lady / When lights are low / I found the thrill again
CD _______________ **CD 53276**
Giants Of Jazz / Feb '97 / Cadillac / Jazz Music / Target/BMG

MILLS BROTHERS VOL.4 1937-1940
Flat foot floogie / My walking stick / Song is ended / Organ grinder's swing / Let me dream / Caravan / Carry me back to old Virginny / Darling Nellie Gray / In the shade of the old apple tree / Old folks at home / Funiculi' funicula' / Asleep in the deep / Side kick Joe / Julius Ceasar / Cherry / Marie / Boog it / WPA / Lambeth walk / Yam / Just a kid named Joe / Sixty seconds got together / Elder Eatmore's sermon on throwing stones / Elder eatmore's sermon on generosity
CD _______________ **CD 53279**
Giants Of Jazz / Jul '97 / Cadillac / Jazz Music / Target/BMG

MILLS BROTHERS, THE
Swing is the thing / Stardust / Shoe-shine boy / Nagasaki / Flat foot floogie / Window washing man / How did she look / Boog it / When you were sweet sixteen / (I'll be glad when you're dead) you rascal you / It don't mean a thing if it ain't got that swing / Caravan / Georgia / Jeepers creepers / Organ grinder swing / Lazybones / FDR Jones / My Gal Sal / Sleepy time gal / Shine / Smoke rings / London rhythm
CD _______________ **PASTCD 7049**
Flapper / May '94 / Pinnacle

PAPER DOLL
Paper doll / Lazy river / Old fashioned love / Limehouse blues / You tell me your dreams / You broke the only heart that loved you / Lazy bones / Two blocks down / Standing on the corner / Gloria / Ida, sweet as apple cider / On the banks of the Wabash / Across the alley from the Alamo / Goodbye blues
CD _______________ **100422**
CMC / May '97 / BMG

SWEETER THAN SUGAR
Tiger rag / Old-fashioned love / Fiddlin' Joe / Smoke rings / I've found a new baby / Chinatown, my Chinatown / Lazybones / Diga diga doo / Nagasaki / Sweeter than sugar / Miss Otis regrets / Ida, sweet as apple cider / Rockin' chair / Some of these days / Sweet Georgia Brown / Nobody's sweetheart
CD _______________ **CDAJA 5032**
Living Era / Feb '87 / Select

TIGER RAG (1931-1932)
CD _______________ **CD 56050**
Jazz Roots / Nov '94 / Target/BMG

Mills, Jeff

JEFF MILLS LIVE AT THE LIQUID ROOM, TOKYO (Various Artists)
Utopia: *Mills, Jeff* / Extremist: *Mills, Jeff* / Life cycle: *Mills, Jeff* / Untitled A: *Mills, Jeff* / 19: *Mills, Jeff* / Changes of life: *Mills, Jeff* / Ax-009: *Mills, Jeff* / Detached: *Mills, Jeff* / Loop 3: *Mills, Jeff* / Untitled B: *Mills, Jeff* / Growth: *Mills, Jeff* / Casa: *Mills, Jeff* / Magneze: *Surgeon* / Move: *Surgeon* / Start it up: *Beltram, Joey* / Gameform: *Beltram, Joey* / Step to enchantment: *Milsart* / Work that body: *DJ Funk* / Run (UK): *DJ Funk* / Play with the voice in USA: *Vannelli, Joe T.* / Clementina: *Wicked Wipe* / Overkill: *Circuit Breaker* / Wet floor: *Traxmen* / Nocturnal: *Young, Claude* / Bad boy: *Advent* / 187 Skillz: *DJ Skull* / Strings of life: *Rhythm Is Rhythm* / Extra: *Ishii, Ken* / Avion: *Wild, Damon* / Intro: *X-120* / Suspense: *H&M* / Other side: *Shadow* / Flowerchild: *Morgan, Dan* / Bazetoya: *Hell & Jonzon*
CD _______________ **REACTCD 077**
React / May '96 / Arabesque / Prime / Vital

OTHER DAY, THE
Solarized / Gamma player / Sleeping giants / I9 / Time out of mind / Growth / Gateway of zen / Medusa / Man from tomorrow / Spider formation / Childhood / Humana / Inner life
CD _______________ **REACTCD 105**
React / May '97 / Arabesque / Prime / Vital

WAVE FORM TRANSMISSION VOL.3
CD _______________ **EFA 292762**
Tresor / Aug '97 / 3mv/BMG / Prime / SRD

WAVEFORM TRANSMISSION VOL.1
CD _______________ **EFA 01742CD**
Tresor / Feb '93 / 3mv/BMG / Prime / SRD
CD _______________ **74321212372**
RCA / Aug '96 / BMG

Mills, Stephanie

PERSONAL INSPIRATIONS
I had a talk with God / Sweepin' through the city / He cares / In the morning time / Everything you touch / Everybody ought to know / Power of God / People get ready / He cares (reprise) / I'm gonna make you proud
CD _______________ **GCD 2123**
Alliance Music / Jul '95 / EMI

Milltown Brothers

VALVE
When it comes / Turn off / Killing all the good men, Jimmy / Pictures (Round my room) / Turn me over / Trees / Sleepwalking / Falling straight down / Crawl with me / Someday / It's all over now baby blue / Cool breeze
CD _______________ **5401322**
A&M / Apr '95 / PolyGram

Milsap, Ronnie

ESSENTIAL RONNIE MILSAP, THE
Stranger things have happened / She keeps the home fires burning / Nobody likes sad songs / Any day now / Woman in love /

Cowboys and clowns / Snap your fingers / He got you / Where do the nights go / Stranger in my house / All is fair in love and war / Happy, happy birthday baby / (There's) no getting over me / Make no mistake, she's mine / How do I turn you on / I wouldn't have missed it for the world / Why don't you spend the night / Lost in the Fifties tonight / Don't you ever get tired / Turn that radio on
CD _____ 74321665342
RCA / Feb '96 / BMG

Milteau, J.J.

J.J. MILTEAU LIVE
CD _____ 192007
Saphir / Sep '95 / New Note/Pinnacle

Milton, Richie

STRAIGHT AHEAD, NO STOPPIN' (Milton, Richie & The Lowdown)
CD _____ RTCD 017
Right Track / Jul '95 / Hot Shot

Milton, Roy

ROY MILTON VOL.1 (Milton, Roy & His Solid Senders)
Milton's boogie / RM blues / True blues / Camille's boogie / Thrill me / Big fat mama / Keep a dollar in your pocket / Everything I do is wrong / Hop, skip and jump / Porter's love song to a chamber maid / Hucklebuck / Information blues / Where there is no love / Junior jives / Bartender's boogie / Oh babe / Christmas time blues / It's later than you think / Numbers blues / I have news for you / T town twist / Best wishes / So tired / Night and day I miss you / Blue turning grey over you
CD _____ CDCHD 308
Ace / Oct '90 / Pinnacle

ROY MILTON VOL.2 (Groovy Blues) (Milton, Roy & His Solid Senders)
Groovy blues / Rhythm cocktail / On the sunny side of the street / Little boy blue / Pack your sack Jack / Roy rides / Cryin' and singin' the blues / Unidentified shuffle blues / I want a little girl / My blue heaven / T'ain't me / Junior jumps / Sympathetic blues / Oh Marie / Waking up baby / Playboy blues / Bye bye baby blues / Don't you remember baby / One O'clock jump / Marie / Unidentified novelty song No.1 / That's the one for me / Cold blooded woman / Short, sweet and snappy / I stood by
CD _____ CDCHD 435
Ace / Jan '93 / Pinnacle

ROY MILTON VOL.3 (Blowin' With Roy) (Milton, Roy & His Solid Senders)
Coquette / Song is ended (but the melody lingers on) / Them there eyes / When I grow too old to dream / What's the use / Train blues / LA Hop / Blue skies / If you don't know / Along the navajo trail / You mean so much to me / New year's resolution / I've had my moments / Ol' man river / Everything I do is wrong / There is something missing / My sweetheart / Believe me baby / Blowin' with Roy / Thelma Lou / Sad feeling / Practice what you preach / If you love me baby / Blues ain't news / Cool down
CD _____ CDCHD 575
Ace / Jul '94 / Pinnacle

Milwaukee Slim

LEMON AVENUE
CD _____ BLUELOONCD 016
Blue Loon / Jul '95 / Hot Shot

Mimani Park Orchestra

SUNGI
CD _____ PAM 403
PAM / Dec '94 / ADA / Direct

Mimms, Garnet

CRY BABY/WARM AND SOULFUL
For your precious love / Cry to me / Nobody but you / Until you were gone / Baby don't you weep / Anytime you need me / Runaway lover / Cry baby / Don't change your heart / Quiet place / So close / Wanting you / I'll take good care of you / Looking for you / It won't hurt (half as much) / It was easier to hurt her / Thinkin' / Prove it to me / More than a miracle / As long as I have you / One girl / There goes my baby / It's just a matter of time / Little bit of soap / Look away / I'll make it up to you
CD _____ BGOCD 268
Beat Goes On / Apr '95 / Pinnacle

Min, Jung Jung

SIMCHONGGA
CD _____ VICG 50192
JVC World Library / Mar '96 / ADA / CM / Direct

Min, Xiao Fen

SPRING, RIVER, FLOWER, MOON, NIGHT
CD _____ EFA 709742
Asphodel / Jul '97 / Cargo / SRD

Minafra, Pina

NOCI ... STRANI FRUTTI (Minafra, Pina & Reijseger/Bennik)
CD _____ CDLR 176
Leo / '90 / Cadillac / Impetus / Wellard

Minales, Pablo

ANTOLOGIA
CD _____ 68968
Tropical / Jul '97 / Discovery

Mind Doctors

ON THRESHOLD OF REALITY
CD _____ KSCD 9597
Kissing Spell / Jun '97 / Greyhound

Mind Funk

PEOPLE WHO FELL FROM THE SKY
CD _____ CDMFN 182
Music For Nations / Mar '95 / Pinnacle

Mind Over 4

HALF WAY DOWN
Introduction (Charged) / Honor / Barriers and passages / Cycle of experience / Unknown peers / Faith / My name is nothing / Struggle / Conscience of nation / Then and now / Funny pocket / Coffee
CD _____ CDRR 9072 2
Roadrunner / Apr '93 / PolyGram

Mind Over Matter

SECURITY
CD _____ WAR 0152CD
Wreckage / Aug '94 / Plastic Head

Mind Over Rhythm

WINTER SUN
Time's up / Skyclad / Mongoose / Sniper / Refugee / Kitchen sync / Mojo fly / Winter sun / Ebe's campfire stories
CD _____ RUMBLE 152
Rumble / Jul '97 / Nervous / Pinnacle

Mind Riot

PEAK
CD _____ GOD 012CD
Godhead / May '95 / Plastic Head

Mindbomb

TRIPPIN' THRU THE MINEFIELD VOL.1
CD _____ RUF 009CD
Ruf / Nov '96 / Plastic Head / SRD

TRIPPIN' THRU THE MINEFIELD VOL.2
CD _____ RUFCD 010
Ruf / Nov '96 / Plastic Head / SRD

Mindheavy Mustard

CHEMICALS, CIGARETTES AND LA WOMEN
Bitterness / Complication / Cocaine / Say it / Auto pilot / Chemicals / Interwine / Adopted / Co-pilot / Off ramp / Razor blade / Bungalow / Sing-a-long pizza / Nicole Eggert
CD _____ N 02482
Noise / Sep '96 / Koch

Mindjive

CHEMICALS
CD _____ BHR 040CD
Burning Heart / Apr '96 / Plastic Head

MINDJIVE
CD _____ BHR 020CD
Burning Heart / Feb '95 / Plastic Head

Mindrot

DAWNING
CD _____ NB 138CD
Nuclear Blast / Nov '95 / Plastic Head

Mindset

MINDSET
Shed the skin / 2am / Cosmic Charles / Shoe shine boy / Ihateyoudon'tleaveme / Nosebleed / Sleeping pills / If the devil wore Adidas / Great unwashed / Delilah / Home grown God / Monster in the closet / Psycho sound wave / Faced
CD _____ N 02732
Noise / Mar '97 / Koch

Mindstorm

LOVE GOES BLIND
CD _____ PRS 10292
Provogue / Sep '91 / Pinnacle

Ming-Yeuh Ling, David

DIALOGUE WITH THE OCEAN
CD _____ 68920
Tropical / Jul '97 / Discovery

DREAM OF THE BUTTERFLY
CD _____ 68928
Tropical / Jul '97 / Discovery

Minger, Pete

LOOK TO THE SKY
(I'm afraid) the masquerade is over / Night has a thousand eyes / Make someone happy / Falling in love with love / Soon / Moose the mooche / Like someone in love / Blue 'n' boogie / I hear a rhapsody / Look to the sky
CD _____ CCD 4555
Concord Jazz / Jun '93 / New Note/ Pinnacle

Mingus Big Band

LIVE IN TIME
Number 29 / Dianne/Alice's wonderland / Boogie stop shuffle / Sue's changes / This subdues my passion / Children's hour of dream / Baby take a chance with me / So long Eric / Moanin' Mambo / Chair in the sky / E's flat, ah's flat too / Shoes of the fisherman's wife are some jive-ass slippers / Us is two / Man who never sleeps/East coasting / Wednesday night prayer meeting
CD _____ FDM 365832
Dreyfus / Feb '97 / ADA / Direct / New Note/ Pinnacle

Mingus, Charles

AT BOTTOM LINE (Mingus Dynasty Band)
CD _____ WWCD 2060
West Wind / Jan '91 / Koch

BLACK SAINT AND THE SINNER LADY, THE
Solo dancer / Group and solo dancers / Single solos and group dance / Trio and group dancers / Group dancers freewoman / Duet solo dancers / Stop, look and listen / Sinner Jim Whitney / Heart's beat and shades in physical embraces / Stop, look and sing songs of revolutions / Saint and sinner join in merriment on battle front / Group and solo dance of love / Pain and passioned revolt then / Farewell my beloved
CD _____ IMP 11742
Impulse Jazz / Nov '95 / New Note/BMG

BLUES AND ROOTS
Wednesday night prayer meeting / Cryin' blues / Moanin' / Tension / My Jelly Roll soul / E's flat ah's flat too
CD _____ 7567813362
Atlantic / Mar '93 / Warner Music

CHANGES ONE
Remember rockefeller at Attica / Sue's changes / Devil blues / Duke Ellington's sound of love
CD _____ 8122714042
CD _____ 8122714032
Atlantic / Jul '96 / Warner Music

CHANGES TWO
Free cell block F tis Nazi USA / Orange was the colour of her dress, then silk blue / Black bats and poles / Duke Ellington's sound of love / For Harry Carney
CD _____ 8122710422
Atlantic / Jul '96 / Warner Music

CHARLES MINGUS
Caroline Keikki Mingus / It might as well be Spring / Peggy's blue skylight / Duke Ellington's sound of love / What is this thing called love / Fables of Faubus / Slop / So long Eric / Farewell blues / Just for laughs part 1
CD _____ BN 029
Blue Nite / Feb '97 / Target/BMG

CHARLES MINGUS AND FRIENDS (2CD Set)
Jump monk / ESP / Ecclusiastics / Eclipse / Us is two / Taurus in the arena of life / Mingus blues / Little royal suite / Strollin' / I of hurricane Sue / E's flat, ah's flat too / Ool-ya-koo / Portrait / Don't be afraid, the clown's afraid too
CD Set _____ C2K 64975
Sony Jazz / Nov '96 / Sony

CHARLES MINGUS AT CARNEGIE HALL
CD _____ 7567813952
Atlantic / Jun '95 / Warner Music

CLOWN, THE
CD _____ 7567901422
Rhino / Dec '96 / Warner Music

COLLECTION, THE
CD _____ CCSCD 382
Castle / Nov '93 / BMG

COMPLETE DEBUT RECORDINGS 1951-1958, THE (12CD Set)
What is this thing called love / Darn that dream / Yesterdays / Body and soul / Blue moon / Blue tide / Darn that dream / Jeepers creepers / Jeepers creepers / Portrait / Portrait / I've lost my love / I've lost my love / Extra sensory perception / Extra sensory perception / Precognition / Make believe / Paris in blue / Montage / Day dream / Day dream / Rhapsody in blue / Rhapsody in blue / Jet / Jet / You go to my head / Can you blame me / You and me / Be bopper / Cupid / Drum conversation / I've got you under my skin / Embraceable you / Sure thing / Cherokee / Hallelujah / Lullaby of Birdland / Wee Allen's alley / Hot house / Night in Tunisia / Perdido / Salt peanuts / All the things you are / 52nd Street theme / Perdido / Salt peanuts / All the things you are / 52nd Street theme / Wee Allen's alley / Hot house / Night in Tunisia / Bass-ically speaking / Bass-ically speaking / Bass-ically speaking / Bass-ically speaking / Wee dot (blues for some bones) / Stardust / Move / I'll remember April / Now's the time / Trombosphere / Ow / Chazzanova / Yesterdays / Kai's day / Pink topsy / Miss Bliss / Blue tide / Pink topsy / Eclipse / Eclipse / Opus 1 / Opus 1 / (Teapot) walkin' / Like someone in love / I can't get started / Spontaneous combustion / Theme / Split kick / This time the dream's on me / Zootcase / Santa Claus is coming to town / Pendulum at falcon's lair / Jack the fieldstalker / Stockholm sweetnin' / Low and behold / Elusive / Chazzanova / I'll remember April / Bitty ditty / Sombre intrusion / You don't know what love is / Like someone in love / Peace of mind / Lament / Jeep is jumpin' / Git up from there / Lament / One more / I can't get started / More of the same / Get out of town / One more / Get out of town / Ensenada / Machajo / Cherokee / Seven moons / Seven moons / All the things you are / All the things you are / Cherokee / Nature boy / Alone together / There's no you / Easy living / Edge of love / Makin' whoopee / Fanny / Portrait / Jump Monk / Serenade in blue / Percussion discussion / Work song / Septemberly / All the things you C# / I remember April / Love chant / Foggy day / Drums / Haitain fight song / Lady Bird / Jump Monk / All the things you C(#2) / Drums / Drums / I'll remember April / Foggy day / Portrait of Bud Powell / Haitian fight song / Love chant / Lady Bird / What is this thing called love / Latter day Saint / Cunningbird / Jumpin' blues / Masher / Latter day Saint / Latter day Saint / Masher / Latter day Saint / Untitled original blues / Stella by starlight / Stella by starlight / Untitled original composition / Untitled original composition / Autumn in New York / Autumn in New York / Long ago and far away / Long ago and far away / Long ago and far away / Untitled original blues / Joldi / Joldi / Untitled percussion composition
CD Set _____ 12DCD 4402
Debut / Nov '96 / Cadillac / Complete/ Pinnacle

COMPLETE TOWN HALL CONCERT, THE
Freedom / Osmotin / Epitaph (pt 1) / Peggy's blue skylight / Epitaph (pt 2) / My search / Portrait / Duke's choice (Don't come back) / Please don't come back from the moon / In a mellow tone / Epitaph
CD _____ CDP 8283532
Blue Note / Jul '94 / EMI

CONCERTGEBOUW AMSTERDAM APRIL 1964 VOL.1
CD _____ 087112
Ulysse / Sep '95 / Discovery

CONCERTGEBOUW AMSTERDAM APRIL 1964 VOL.2
CD _____ 087122
Ulysse / Sep '95 / Discovery

CUMBIA & JAZZ FUSION
CD _____ 8122717852
Atlantic / Sep '94 / Warner Music

DEBUT RARITIES VOL.1 (Mingus, Charles Octet/Jimmy Knepper Quintet)
CD _____ OJCCD 1807
Original Jazz Classics / Apr '93 / Complete/Pinnacle / Jazz Music / Wellard

DEBUT RARITIES VOL.2
What is this thing called love / Blue moon / Blue tide / Jeepers creepers / Daydream / Rhapsody in blue
CD _____ OJCCD 1808
Original Jazz Classics / Apr '93 / Complete/ Pinnacle / Jazz Music / Wellard

DEBUT RARITIES VOL.3
CD _____ OJCCD 1821
Original Jazz Classics / Apr '93 / Complete/Pinnacle / Jazz Music / Wellard

DEBUT RARITIES VOL.4
CD _____ OJCCD 1829
Original Jazz Classics / Apr '93 / Complete/Pinnacle / Jazz Music / Wellard

EAST COASTING (Mingus, Charles Sextet)
Memories of you / East coasting / West Coast ghost / Celia / Conversation / Fifty First Street blues
CD _____ CDGR 120
Charly / Mar '97 / Koch

FINAL WORK, THE
CD _____ DM 15007
DMA Jazz / Jul '96 / Jazz Music

GOODBYE PORK PIE HAT
CD _____ JHR 73516
Jazz Hour / '91 / Cadillac / Jazz Music / Target/BMG

GREAT CONCERT - PARIS 1964
CD _____ 500072
Musidisc / Nov '93 / Discovery

GUNSLINGING BIRDS (Mingus Big Band)
Gunslinging birds / Reincarnation of a lovebird / O P / Please don't come back from the moon / Fables of Faubus / Jump monk / Noon night / Hog callin' blues / Started melody

CD FDM 365752
Dreyfus / Jul '95 / ADA / Direct / New Note/ Pinnacle

HIS FINAL WORK
Just for laughs / Peggy's blue skylight / Caroline Keikki Mingus / Fables of Faubus / Duke Ellington's sound of love / Farewell farewell / So long Eric / Slop / It might as well be spring
CD CDGATE 7016
Kingdom Jazz / Oct '87 / Kingdom

IMMORTAL CONCERTS (Antibes Jazz Festival 13th July 1960) (Mingus, Charles & Eric Dolphy)
Better git it in your soul / Wednesday night prayer meeting / Prayer for passive resistance / I'll remember April / What love / Folk forms 1
CD CD 53013
Giants Of Jazz / Mar '90 / Cadillac / Jazz Music / Target/BMG

IN A SOULFUL MOOD
CD MCCD 201
Music Club / May '95 / Disc / THE

IN EUROPE
CD ENJACD 30492
Enja / Nov '94 / New Note/Pinnacle / Vital/ SAM

JAZZ EXPERIMENTS OF CHARLES MINGUS
CD BET 6016
Bethlehem / Jan '95 / ADA / ZYX

JAZZ WORKSHOP
CD VGCD 650132
Vogue / Oct '93 / BMG

JAZZICAL MOODS (Mingus, Charles & John LaPorta)
CD OJCCD 1857
Original Jazz Classics / Apr '93 / Complete/Pinnacle / Jazz Music / Wellard

LIVE AT BIRDLAND 1962
CD COD 028
Jazz View / Mar '92 / Harmonia Mundi

LIVE AT THE T.T.B. PARIS VOL.1 (Big Band Charlie Mingus)
CD 1211922
Soul Note / Nov '93 / Cadillac / Harmonia Mundi / Wellard

LIVE AT THE T.T.B. PARIS VOL.2 (Big Band Charlie Mingus)
CD 1211932
Soul Note / Nov '93 / Cadillac / Harmonia Mundi / Wellard

LIVE AT THE VILLAGE VANGUARD (Mingus Dynasty Band)
CD STCD 4124
Storyville / Feb '90 / Cadillac / Jazz Music / Wellard

LIVE IN CHATEAUVALLON 1972
CD FCD 135
France's Concert / '89 / BMG / Jazz Music

LIVE IN COPENHAGEN
CD LS 2905
Landscape / Nov '92 / THE

LIVE IN OSLO 1964
Fables of Faubus / Ow / Orange was the colour of her dress, then silk blue / Take the 'A' train
CD LS 2913
Landscape / Feb '93 / THE

LIVE IN PARIS 1964 VOL.2
CD FCD 110
France's Concert / Jun '88 / BMG / Jazz Music

MEDITATION
Peggy's blue skylight / Orange was the colour of her dress, then silk blue / Meditation for integration / Fables of Faubus
CD FCD 102
Esoldun / Jan '88 / Target/BMG

MINGUS
MDM / Stormy weather / Lock 'em up
CD CCD 79021
Candid / Feb '97 / Cadillac / Direct / Jazz Music / Koch / Wellard

MINGUS AH UM
Better git it in your soul / Goodbye Pork Pie Hat / Boogie stop shuffle / Self portrait in three colours / Open letter to Duke / Bird calls / Fables of Faubus / Pussy cat dues / Jelly roll
CD 4504362
Columbia / Oct '93 / Sony

MINGUS AT ANTIBES
Wednesday night prayer meeting / Prayer for passive resistance / What love / I'll remember April / Folk forms 1 / Better git it in your soul
CD 7567905322
Atlantic / Mar '93 / Warner Music

MINGUS AT CARNEGIE HALL
C jam blues / Perdido
CD 8122722852
Atlantic / Mar '96 / Warner Music

MINGUS AT THE BOHEMIA
CD OJCCD 45
Original Jazz Classics / Oct '92 / Complete/Pinnacle / Jazz Music / Wellard

MINGUS DYNASTY
Slop / Diane / Song with orange / Gunslinging birds / Things ain't the way they used to be / Far wells / Mill valley / New now, know how / Mood indigo / Put me in that dungeon
CD 4729952
Columbia / Feb '94 / Sony

MINGUS MOVES
Canon / Opus 4 / Moves / Flowers for a lady / Newcomer / Opus 3 / Big Alice / Call
CD 8122714542
Atlantic / Jul '96 / Warner Music

MINGUS PLAYS PIANO
Myself when I am real / I can't get started (with you) / Body and soul / Roland Kirk's message / Memories of you / She's just Miss Popular hybrid / Orange was the colour of her dress, then silk blue / Meditations for Moses / Old portrait / I'm getting sentimental over you / Compositional theme story
CD IMP 12172
Impulse Jazz / Apr '97 / New Note/BMG

MINGUS REVISITED
Take the 'A' train / Prayer for passive resistance / Eclipse / Mingus fingus no.2 / Weird nightmare / Do nothin' 'til you hear from me / Bemoanable lady / Half mast inhibition
CD 8264962
Verve / Feb '97 / PolyGram

MINGUS THREE
Yesterdays / Back home blues / I can't get started / Hamp's new blues / Summertime / Dizzy moods / Laura
CD CDP 8571552
Roulette / Jul '97 / EMI

MINGUS, MINGUS, MINGUS, MINGUS, MINGUS
II BS / I x love / Celia / Mood indigo / Better git it in your soul / Theme for Lester Young / Hora decubitus
CD MCAD 39119
Impulse Jazz / Jun '89 / New Note/BMG

MODERN JAZZ SYMPOSIUM OF MUSIC AND POETRY (Bethlehem Jazz Classics)
CD CDGR 131
Charly / Apr '97 / Koch

MYSTERIOUS BLUES
Mysterious blues / Wrap your troubles in dreams (and dream your troubles away) / Body and soul / Vassarlean / Reincarnation of a love bird / Me and you blues / Melody for the drums
CD CCD 79042
Candid / Feb '97 / Cadillac / Direct / Jazz Music / Koch / Wellard

NEW TIJUANA MOODS
Dizzy moods / Ysabel's table dance / Los mariachis (the street musicians) / Flamingo / Tijuana gift shop
CD 09026685912
RCA Victor / Oct '96 / BMG

NOSTALGIA IN TIMES SQUARE (Mingus Big Band '93)
Nostalgia in Times Square / Moanin' / Self portrait in three colours / Don't be afraid... / Duke Ellington's Sound of love / Mingus fingers / Weird nightmare / Open letter to Duke / Invisible lady / Ecclusiastics
CD FDM 365592
Dreyfus / Aug '93 / ADA / Direct / New Note/ Pinnacle

OH YEAH
Hog callin' blues / Devil woman / Wham bam thank you ma'am / Ecclusiastics / Oh Lord don't let them drop that atomic bomb on me / Eat that chicken / Passion of a man
CD 7567906672
Atlantic / Mar '93 / Warner Music

ORANGE
CD MCD 078
Moon / Dec '95 / Cadillac / Harmonia Mundi

ORIGINAL FAUBUS FABLES
CD ATJCD 5965
All That's Jazz / Jul '92 / Jazz Music / THE

PARIS 1964
CD LEJAZZCD 19
Le Jazz / Jun '93 / Cadillac / Koch

PARIS 1967 VOL.2 (Mingus, Charles & Sonny Stitt)
So long Eric / Parkeriana
CD LEJAZZCD 38
Le Jazz / May '95 / Cadillac / Koch

PARIS TNP OCTOBER 1970
CD 087312
Ulysse / Sep '95 / Discovery

PARIS, 1947
CD CD 56047
Jazz Roots / Nov '94 / Target/BMG

PITHYCANTHROPUS ERECTUS
CD 7567814562
Atlantic / Jul '96 / Warner Music

PLUS MAX ROACH (Mingus, Charles & Max Roach)
Drums / Haitian fight song / Ladybird / I'll remember April / Love chant
CD OJCCD 440
Original Jazz Classics / Sep '93 / Complete/ Pinnacle / Jazz Music / Wellard

PRESENTS CHARLES MINGUS
Folk forms No.1 / Original Faubus fables / What love / All the things you could be by now if Sigmund Freud's wife..
CD CCD 79005
Candid / Feb '97 / Cadillac / Direct / Jazz Music / Koch / Wellard

REINCARNATION (Mingus Dynasty Band)
CD SNCD 1042
Soul Note / '86 / Cadillac / Harmonia Mundi / Wellard

REINCARNATION OF A LOVE BIRD
Reincarnation of a love bird / Wrap your troubles in dreams / Body and soul / Bugs / R and R
CD CCD 79026
Candid / Feb '97 / Cadillac / Direct / Jazz Music / Koch / Wellard

REVENGE
CD 32002CD
32 / May '96 / ADA

RIGHT NOW: LIVE AT THE JAZZ WORKSHOP
New fables / Meditation
CD OJCCD 237
Original Jazz Classics / Sep '93 / Complete/ Pinnacle / Jazz Music / Wellard

THIS IS JAZZ
Better git it in your soul / Goodbye Pork Pie Hat / Fables of faubus / Self portrait in three colours / Slop / Song with orange / Gunslinging bird / Far Wells, Mill Valley / New now, know how / Shoes of the fisherman's wife are some jive ass slippers / Please don't come back from the moon
CD CK 64624
Sony Jazz / May '96 / Sony

THREE OR FOUR SHADES OF BLUE
Better git it in your soul / Goodbye Pork Pie Hat / Noddin ya head blues / Three or four shade of blues / Nobody knows
CD 7567814032
Atlantic / Mar '93 / Warner Music

TOWN HALL CONCERT
So long Eric / Praying with Eric
CD OJCCD 42
Original Jazz Classics / Sep '93 / Complete/ Pinnacle / Jazz Music / Wellard

WEDNESDAY NIGHT PRAYER MEETING
Better git it in your soul / Wednesday night prayer meeting / Wednesday night prayer meeting / Folk forms no.2
CD 306662
Hallmark / Jun '97 / Carlton

WONDERLAND
Nostalgia in Times Square / I can't get started (with you) / No private income blues / Alice's wonderland
CD CDP 8273252
Blue Note / Feb '94 / EMI

Minh Doky, Christian

APPRECIATION
CD STCD 4169
Storyville / Feb '90 / Cadillac / Jazz Music / Wellard

SEQUEL, THE
Fall / Certified / Message / Alone / Sequel / Falling in love with love / Brother / Let's pretend
CD STCD 4175
Storyville / Feb '90 / Cadillac / Jazz Music / Wellard

Minhinnet, Ray

DON'T GET MAD GET EVEN
CD SPRAYCD 107
Making Waves / Oct '93 / CM

Miniature

I CAN'T PUT MY FINGER ON IT
Zilla / Jersey devil / PG suggested / Combat / Aspetta / Lowball / Luna / Bullfrog breath / Who's vacant / Weasels in the bush / Dink
CD 8491472
jMT / Oct '91 / PolyGram

MINIATURE
Ethiopian boxer / Circular prairie song / Hong Kong sad song / Lonely mood / Narlin' / Peanut / Abeetah / Sanctuary
CD 8344232
jMT / Feb '89 / PolyGram

Minimal Compact

DEADLY WEAPONS/NEXT ONE IS REAL
CD CRAM 3032
Crammed Discs / Nov '88 / Grapevine/ PolyGram / New Note/Pinnacle / Prime / RTM/Disc

FIGURE ONE CUTS
CD CRAM 055
Crammed Discs / Oct '87 / Grapevine/ PolyGram / New Note/Pinnacle / Prime / RTM/Disc

LOWLANDS FLIGHT
CD MTM 10CD
Made To Measure / '88 / New Note/ Pinnacle

MINIMAL COMPACT LIVE
CD CRAM 061
Crammed Discs / Nov '88 / Grapevine/ PolyGram / New Note/Pinnacle / Prime / RTM/Disc

ONE PLUS ONE BY ONE
CD CRAM 1521
Crammed Discs / Nov '88 / Grapevine/ PolyGram / New Note/Pinnacle / Prime / RTM/Disc

RAGING SOULS
CD CRAM 042
Crammed Discs / '88 / Grapevine/ PolyGram / New Note/Pinnacle / Prime / RTM/Disc

Minimal Man

HUNGER IS ALL SHE'S EVER KNOWN/ MOCK HONEYMOON
CD BIAS 071CD
Play It Again Sam / '90 / Discovery / Plastic Head / Vital

Ministry

FILTH PIG
Reload / Filth pig / Crumbs / Useless / Lava / Dead guy / Face / Brick windows / Game show / Lay lady lay / Reload (edit)
CD 9362458382
WEA / Jan '96 / Warner Music

LAND OF RAPE AND HONEY
Stigmata / Missing / Deity / Golden dawn / Destruction / Land of rape and honey / You know what you are / Flashback / Abortive / Hizbollah / I prefer
CD 7599257992
WEA / Nov '92 / Warner Music

LIVE - IN CASE YOU DIDN'T FEEL LIKE SHOWING UP
Missing / Deity / So what / Burning inside / Thieves / Stigmata
CD 7599262662
WEA / Nov '92 / Warner Music

MIND IS A TERRIBLE THING TO TASTE, THE
Thieves / Never believe / Breathe / Burning inside / Cannibal song / So what / Test / Dream song / Faith collapsing
CD 7599260042
WEA / Mar '94 / Warner Music

PSALM 69
NWO / Just one fix / TV II / Hero / Jesus built my hotrod / Scarecrow / Psalm 69 / Corrosion / Grace
CD 7599267272
WEA / Dec '96 / Warner Music

Ministry Of Ska

RARIN' TO GO
Skankin' with the torreadores / Rarin' to go / Saint / Ras / Dangerman / Skaty / Rawhide / Tell William / Condoms / Head 'em up, move 'em out / Norman / Skanking with the torreadores
CD FLEGCD 6
Future Legend / Jun '96 / Future Legend / Pinnacle

Ministry Of Terror

FALL OF LIFE
CD FDN 2011CD
Foundation 2000 / Jun '95 / Plastic Head

Mink Deville

CABRETTA/RETURN TO MAGENTA
Venus of Avenue D / Little girl / One way street / Mixed up, shook up girl / Gunslinger / Can't do without it / Cadillac walk / Spanish stroll / She's so tough / Party girls / Guardian angel / Soul twist / A train lady / Rolene / Desperate days / Just your friends / Steady drivin' man / Easy slider / I broke that promise / Confidence to kill
CD RVCD 59
Raven / Oct '96 / ADA / Direct

CABRETTA/RETURN TO MAGENTA/LE CHAT BLEU (3CD Set)
Venus of Avenue D / Little girl / One way street / Mixed up / Shook up girl / Gunslinger / Can't do without it / Cadillac Walk / Spanish stroll / She's so tough / Party girl / Guardian angel / Soul twist / A-train lady / Rolene / Desperate days / Just your friends / Steady drivin' man / Easy slider / I broke that promise / Confidence to kill / This must be the night / Savoire faire / That world outside / Slow drain / You just keep holding on / Lipstick traces / Just to walk that little girl home / Turn you every way but loose / Bad boy / Heaven stood still
CD Set CDOMB 013
EMI / Oct '95 / EMI

LE CHAT BLEU
This must be the night / Savoir faire / That world outside / Slow drain / You just keep holding on / Lipstick traces / Bad boy / Mazurka / Just to walk that little girl home / Heaven stood still
CD ______ WM 339002
Wotre Music / Jun '93 / Discovery / New Note/Pinnacle

RETURN TO MAGENTA
Just your friends / Soul twist / A train lady / Rolene / Desperate days / Guardian angel / Steady drivin' man / Easy slider / I broke that promise / Confidence to kill
CD ______ WM 339003
Wotre Music / Jun '93 / Discovery / New Note/Pinnacle

SPANISH STROLL
CD ______ RVCD 32
Raven / Jun '93 / ADA / Direct

Mink Stole

EATS HEAD
CD ______ SPV 07745582
SPV / Jul '94 / Koch / Plastic Head

Minnelli, Liza

COLLECTION, THE
Cabaret / Look of love / On a slow boat to China / Man I love / Stormy weather / Leavin' on a jet plane / Liza (with a Z) / Everybody's talkin'/Good morning starshine / Come rain or come shine / Love story / Love for sale / Can't help lovin' dat man / I will wait for you / Nevertheless (I'm in love with you) / For no-one / Macarthur Park / Lazybones / God bless the child / Maybe this time / How long has this been going on
CD ______ 5518152
Spectrum / Nov '95 / PolyGram

GENTLY
Chances are: *Minnelli, Liza & Johnny Mathis* / You stepped out of a dream / Embraceable you / Close your eyes / Some cats know / Lost in you / I got lost in his arms / It had to be you / Never let me go / Does he love you: *Minnelli, Liza & Donna Summer* / In the wee small hours of the morning
CD ______ CDQ 8354702
Angel / Jun '96 / EMI

LIVE AT CARNEGIE HALL
CD ______ CD 85502
Telarc / '88 / Conifer/BMG

RESULTS
I want you now / Losing my mind / If there was love / So sorry, I said / Don't drop bombs / Twist in my sobriety / Rent / Love pains / Tonight is forever / I can't say goodnight
CD ______ 4655112
Epic / Oct '89 / Sony

Minogue, Kylie

CELEBRATION (Greatest Hits)
CD ______ HFCD 25
PWL / Aug '92 / Warner Music

ENJOY YOURSELF
Hand on your heart / Wouldn't change a thing / Enjoy yourself / Tell tale signs / Tears on my pillow / Never too late / Nothing to lose / Heaven and earth / I'm over dreaming (over you) / My secret heart
CD ______ HFCD 9
PWL / Oct '89 / Warner Music

INTERVIEW COMPACT DISC: KYLIE & JASON (Minogue, Kylie & Jason Donovan)
CD ______ CBAK 4026
Baktabak / Nov '89 / Arabesque

KYLIE - THE ALBUM
I should be so lucky / Locomotion / Je ne sais pas pourquoi / It's no secret / Got to be certain / Turn it into love / I miss you / I'll still be loving you / Look my way / Love at first sight
CD ______ HFCD 3
PWL / Jul '88 / Warner Music

KYLIE MINOGUE
Confide in me / If I was your lover / Where is the feeling / Put yourself in my place / Dangerous game / Automatic love / Where has the love gone / Falling / Time will pass you by
CD ______ 74321227492
De-Construction / Jun '96 / BMG

LET'S GET TO IT
CD ______ HFCD 21
PWL / Oct '91 / Warner Music

RHYTHM OF LOVE
CD ______ HFCD 18
PWL / Nov '90 / Warner Music

Minor Forest

FLEMISH ALTRUISM
CD ______ THRILL 34CD
Thrill Jockey / Jul '97 / Cargo / Greyhound
CD ______ RUNT 27
Runt / Mar '97 / Cargo / Greyhound / Plastic Head

Minor Threat

COMPLETE DISCOGRAPHY
CD ______ DISCHORD 40
Dischord / Mar '90 / SRD

Minott, Sugar

20 SUPER HITS
CD ______ SONCD 0009
Sonic Sounds / Oct '90 / Jet Star

AFRICAN SOLDIER
CD ______ HBCD 49
Heartbeat / '88 / ADA / Direct / Greensleeves / Jet Star

BLACK ROOTS
Mankind / Hard time pressure / River Jordan / Jailhouse / I'm gonna hold on / Oppressors oppression / Two time loser / Black roots / Clean runnings / Mr. Babylon man
CD ______ RRCD 39
Reggae Refreshers / Jul '92 / PolyGram / Vital

BREAKING FREE
CD ______ RAS 3176
Ras / Aug '96 / Direct / Greensleeves / Jet Star / SRD

CHANNEL ONE COLLECTION
CD ______ SMCD 1
Channel One / Feb '96 / Jet Star

COLLECTION, THE
All kind a style / Musical murder / Lovers rock medley / Power of love / I am a man / Let love come in / Keep the crowd coming / Forever in love / We rule rythem / Hot fe the riddim / Play this rub a dub / Gone away / Freedom for the people / Mind what you say / No turning back / Love we know / Teach the youth the truth / Got to live in love / Lets make things right / Rocking from dust to dawn
CD ______ RN 7011
Rhino / Feb '97 / Grapevine/PolyGram / Jet Star

COLLECTORS COLLECTION VOL.1
CD ______ CDHB 206
Heartbeat / Aug '96 / ADA / Direct / Greensleeves / Jet Star

EASY SQUEEZE
CD ______ WRCD 007
World / Jun '97 / Jet Star / TKO Magnum

GOOD THING GOING
Good thing going / High up above / Never my love / House on a hill / My sister / Jasmine / Life without money / Lonely days / Walk on by / Family affair
CD ______ HBCD 13
Heartbeat / Aug '88 / ADA / Direct / Greensleeves / Jet Star

GOOD THING GOING
CD ______ CDSGP 0146
Prestige / Jul '95 / Else / Total/BMG

INNA REGGAE DANCE HALL
CD ______ HBCD 29
Heartbeat / Jul '88 / ADA / Direct / Greensleeves / Jet Star

INTERNATIONAL
CD ______ RASCD 3197
Ras / Jan '96 / Direct / Greensleeves / Jet Star / SRD

JAH MAKE ME FEEL SO GOOD
CD ______ EXTCD 4
Exterminator / Mar '97 / Jet Star

RAS PORTRAITS
Ain't nobody move me / Sprinter stayer / Run things / Herbsman hustling / Dancehall fever / Devil's pickney / Gun gang / Ramdance master / International herbalist / A just rasta / Break free / Rub-a-dub sound / Heads of conference
CD ______ RAS 3319
Ras / Jul '97 / Direct / Greensleeves / Jet Star / SRD

REGGAE LOVE SONGS
Good thing going / Lovers rock / Lonely days / Now we know / Just don't wanna be lonely / Make it with you / Missing you / Show me that you love me / Girl is in love / Sandy / You've lost that loving feeling / Never too young / Can you remember / House is not a home
CD ______ CD 6064
Music / Apr '97 / Target/BMG

REGGAE MAX
CD ______ JSRNCD 16
Jet Star / Jun '97 / Jet Star

SHOWDOWN VOL.1 (Minott, Sugar & Frankie Paul)
CD ______ 78249700160
Channel One / Apr '95 / Jet Star

SLICE OF THE CAKE
CD ______ HBCD 24
Heartbeat / '88 / ADA / Direct / Greensleeves / Jet Star

SUGAR MINOTT STORY, THE
CD ______ UPTCD 25
Uptempo / Jul '97 / Jet Star

TOUCH OF CLASS, A
CD ______ JMCD 001
Jammy's / Mar '91 / Jet Star

WITH LOTS OF EXTRA
CD ______ 78249700120
Channel One / Apr '95 / Jet Star

Minstrels Of Annie Street

ORIGINAL TUXEDO RAG
CD ______ SOSCD 1272
Stomp Off / Apr '94 / Jazz Music / Wellard

Mint 400

INTERCOMFORT
CD ______ HIPCD 16
Backs / Jun '96 / RTM/Disc

Mint Condition

DEFINITION OF A BAND
Intro / Change your mind / You don't have to hurt no more / Gettin' it on / What kind of man would I be / Let me be the one / Definition of a band / Ain't hookin' me up enough / Funky weekend / I want it again / On and on / Never that you'll never know / Asher in Rio interlude / Raise up / On and on / Sometimes / Missing / If it wasn't for your love - dedication
CD ______ 5490282
Polydor / Jun '97 / PolyGram

Mint Juleps

ONE TIME
CD ______ STIFFCD 15
Disky / Jan '94 / Disky / THE

WOMEN IN (E)MOTION FESTIVAL
CD ______ T&M 104
Tradition & Moderne / Nov '94 / ADA / Direct

Minty

OPEN WIDE
Procession / Minty / That's nice / Plastic bag / Useless man / Homage / Manners mean / King size / Hold on / Nothing / Homme aphrodite / Dream / Art / Jeremy
CD ______ CAN 2CD
Candy / Jul '97 / RTM/Disc

Mintzer, Bob

LIVE AT THE BERLIN JAZZ FESTIVAL
CD ______ BASIC 50003
ITM / Jun '96 / Koch / Tradelink

Minucci, Chieli

JEWELS
Courageous cats / Phat city / Only you / Sitting in limbo / Hideaway / Dig the dirt / Mountains / Realm of the senses / Moment of love / Jewels
CD ______ JVC 20442
JVC / May '95 / Direct / New Note/Pinnacle / Vital/SAM

RENAISSANCE
Big sky country / Renaissance / Cause we-'ve ended as lovers / Come as you are / Anything and everything / Shine / In your arms / Spirit / Sun will always shine / Cacoutra / Leilani / Mixomelodia / Reunion / Faith
CD ______ JVC 20562
JVC / Jun '96 / Direct / New Note/Pinnacle / Vital/SAM

Minus 5

OLD LIQUIDATOR
CD ______ GRCD 350
Glitterhouse / Dec '94 / Avid/BMG

Minus, Rich

BORDERLINE BLUES
CD ______ 422432
New Rose / Feb '97 / ADA / Direct / Discovery

COLLECTION, THE
CD ______ 422231
New Rose / Feb '97 / ADA / Direct / Discovery

RICH MINUS 3
CD ______ 422497
New Rose / Feb '97 / ADA / Direct / Discovery

Minute By Minute

DON'T MESS WITH FIRE
Don't mess with fire / Long hot night / A million miles away / Short Avenue / Go back to sleep / Black and blue / I'll be back / It'll be all right on the night / Tijuana holiday / Three times your age / Homesick / Katie's love
CD ______ SRH 803
Start / Feb '97 / Disc

Minutemen

3 WAY TIE (FOR LAST)
CD ______ SST 058CD
SST / Feb '86 / Plastic Head

BALLOT RESULT
CD ______ SST 068CD
SST / May '93 / Plastic Head

BUZZ OR HOWL UNDER THE INFLUENCE OF HEAT
CD ______ SST 016CD
SST / May '93 / Plastic Head

DOUBLE NICKELS ON THE DIME
CD ______ SST 028CD
SST / Oct '87 / Plastic Head

FAT
CD ______ SST 214CD
SST / Nov '88 / Plastic Head

POLITICS OF TIME
CD ______ SST 277CD
SST / May '93 / Plastic Head

POST-MERSH VOL.1
CD ______ SST 138CD
SST / May '93 / Plastic Head

POST-MERSH VOL.2
CD ______ SST 139CD
SST / May '93 / Plastic Head

POST-MERSH VOL.3
CD ______ SST 165CD
SST / May '93 / Plastic Head

PROJECT MERSH
CD ______ SST 034CD
SST / May '93 / Plastic Head

PUNCH LINE, THE
CD ______ SST 004CD
SST / May '93 / Plastic Head

WHAT MAKES A MAN START FIRES
CD ______ SST 014CD
SST / May '93 / Plastic Head

Minxus

PABULUM
Minxus / Silk purse / I know you want to stop / Pabulum / Falcon contract / Vultura / Wonderful pair / Get / I live on sand / Monkey theme / Liberty bodice / Fecund girls / Sunshine / X Y Zoom / Ever since forever
CD ______ PURECD 043
Too Pure / Jan '95 / Vital

Mion, Philippe

LEONE
CD ______ IMED 9632
Diffunzioni Musicali / Jun '97 / ReR Megacorp

Mioritza

SONGS AND DANCES FROM ROMANIA
CD ______ EUCD 1070
ARC / '89 / ADA / ARC Music

Mira

NEW HOPE FOR THE DEAD
CD ______ JVC 90062
JVC / Feb '97 / Direct / New Note/ Pinnacle / Vital/SAM

Miracle Workers

ANATOMY OF A CREEP
CD ______ TX 51156CD
Triple X / Feb '96 / Plastic Head

INSIDE OUT
CD ______ VOXXCD 2031
Voxx / '94 / Else / RTM/Disc

ROLL OUT THE RED CARPET
CD ______ TX 93162
Roadrunner / Apr '91 / PolyGram

Miranda

PHENOMENA
CD ______ SUB 48372
Distance / Feb '97 / 3mv/Sony / Prime

Miranda Sex Garden

FAIRYTALES OF SLAVERY
CD ______ CDSTUMM 120
Mute / May '94 / RTM/Disc

IRIS
Lovely Joan / Falling / Fear / Blue light / Iris
CD ______ CDSTUMM 97
Mute / May '92 / RTM/Disc

Miranda, Carmen

BRAZILIAN BOMBSHELL, THE
CD ______ LEGEND CD 6005
Fresh Sound / Dec '92 / Discovery / Jazz Music

CARMEN MIRANDA
CD ______ HQCD 33
Harlequin / Oct '93 / Hot Shot / Jazz Music / Swift / Wellard

CARMEN MIRANDA
CD ______ 883723
Milan / May '97 / Conifer/BMG / Silva Screen

SOUTH AMERICAN WAY
South American way / Mama eu tuero (I want my mama) / I yi yi yi yi (I like you very much) / Chica chica boom chic / Weekend

in Havana / When I love I love / Chattanooga choo choo / Manuelo / O passo du kanguru / Bambu bambu / Cae cae / Turadas em madrid / Tic tac do meu coracao / Co co co co ro / Cuanto Lagusta / Wedding samba
CD _______ JASCD 317
Jasmine / Nov '93 / Conifer/BMG / Hot Shot / TKO Magnum

Miranda, Marçia

UNBOUNDED
CD _______ JMC 1143CD
JMC / Mar '97 / Jet Star

Miranda, Marlui

TODOS OS SONS
Tchori Tchori / Pame Daworo / Tche nane / Naumu / Awina/Ijain Je E' / Araruna / Mena Barsaa / Bep / Festa da flauta / Yny maj Hyrynh / Hirigo / Wine merewa / Meko merewa / Ju parana / Kworo kango / Mito - Metumji laren / 15 variacoes de Hai Nai Hai
CD _______ ACT 50052
Act / Aug '97 / New Note/Pinnacle

Mireille

MIREILLE & JEAN SABLON/PILLS & TABET (2CD Set) (Mireille & Jean Sablon)
CD _______ FA 043
Fremeaux / Feb '96 / ADA / Discovery

Mirrors Over Kiev

NORTHERN SONGS
Jane's farewell / Midnight sky / Rolling in the hay / By your side / Arrows in your eyes / All his women / My cheatin' heart / Scars are healing / Northern song / Dance you through / Hang down your head
CD _______ RRACD 014
Run River / Sep '91 / ADA / CM

Mirwais

MIRWAIS
CD _______ ROSE 235 CD
New Rose / Feb '91 / ADA / Direct / Discovery

Mirza

ANADROMOUS
CD _______ DRL 043CD
Darla / Jul '97 / Cargo

Misanthrope

666 THEATRE BIZARRE
CD _______ HOLY 016CD
Holy / Nov '95 / Plastic Head

MIRACLES TOTEM TABOO
CD _______ HOLY 06CD
Holy / Jul '94 / Plastic Head

VARIATION ON INDUCTIVE THEORIES
CD _______ HOLY 2CD
Holy / May '94 / Plastic Head

Mischo, R.J.

COOL DISPOSITION (Mischo, R.J. Red Hot Blues Band)
(Everybody's) in the mood / I should be dead / Cold hearted woman / Get your money / Second wind / Love my baby / Taste of my own medicine / Main Street strut / Little village / A-OK / Don't bring a friend / Skinny woman / High maintainance woman / Dangerous boy / Travellin' all day
CD _______ CCD 11055
Crosscut / Jun '97 / ADA / CM / Direct

READY TO GO (Mischo, R.J. & Teddy Morgan Band)
She's murder / Rockin' the mule / You're sweet / Kidstuff / Had my fun / Forty days / Baby I don't care / RJ's jump / Change your way / I got to find my baby / McCabe's 88's / Can't get nothing / Evil / Lightnin' blues
CD _______ ATM 1126
Atomic Theory / Feb '97 / ADA / Direct

Miscreant

DREAMING ICE
CD _______ WAR 004CD
Wrong Again / Apr '96 / Plastic Head

Misery

WHO'S THE FOOL
CD _______ SKULD 020CD
Skuld / Jan '97 / Cargo

Misery Index

MISERY INDEX
CD _______ MIS 001
Misery Index / Jan '97 / Nervous

Misery Loves Co

HAPPY
Happy / Strain of frustration / This is no dream / Private hell / Kiss your boots / Sonic attack
CD _______ MOSH 151CD
Earache / Mar '96 / Vital

MISERY LOVES CO
My mind still speaks / Kiss your boots / Need another one / Sonic attack / This is no dream / Happy / Scared / I swallow / Private hell / Only way / Two seconds
CD Set _______ MOSH 133CDB
Earache / Aug '95 / Vital
CD _______ MOSH 133CD
Earache / Sep '97 / Vital

Misfits

AMERICAN PSYCHO
Abominable Dr. Phibes / American psycho / Speak of the devil / Walk among us / Hunger / From hell they came / Dig up her bones / Blacklight / Resurrection / This island Earth / Crimson ghost / Day of the dead / Haunting / Mars attacks / Hate the living, love the dead / Shining / Don't open til Doomsday
CD _______ GED 24939
Geffen / May '97 / BMG

EARTH AD (Earth AD/Die Die My Darling)
CD _______ PL9CD 02/3
Plan 9/Caroline / Jan '97 / Cargo / Vital

EVILIVE
20 eyes / Night of the living dead / Astro zombies / Horror business / London dungeon / Nike a go go / Hate breeders / Devil's whorehouse / All hell breaks loose / Horror hotel / Ghouls night out / We are 138
CD _______ PL9CD 08
Plan 9/Caroline / Mar '97 / Cargo / Vital

HELL ON EARTH (A Tribute To The Misfits) (Various Artists)
CD _______ TR 004CD
Tribute / Dec '96 / Plastic Head

LEGACY OF BRUTALITY
CD _______ PL9CD 06
Plan 9/Caroline / Jan '97 / Cargo / Vital

MISFITS BOX SET (4CD Set)
CD Set _______ CDCAR 7529
Caroline / Jan '97 / Cargo / Vital

MISFITS COLLECTION VOL.1
Bullet / Horror business / Teenager's from Mars / Night of the living / Where eagles dare / Vampira / Skulls / I turned into a martian / Eyes / Violent world / London dungeon / Ghoul's night out / Halloween / Die die my darling / Mommy, can I go out and kill tonight
CD _______ PL9CD 1
Plan 9/Caroline / Jan '97 / Cargo / Vital

MISFITS COLLECTION VOL.2
CD _______ CAROL 75152
Caroline / Jan '97 / Cargo / Vital

STATIC AGE
Static age / TV casualty / Some kinda hate / Last caress / Return of the fly / Hybrid moments / We are 138 / Teenagers from mars / Come back / Angelfuck / Hollywood Babylon / Attitude / Bullet / Theme for a Jackal / She / Spinal remains / In the doorway
CD _______ CAROL 75202
Caroline / Jul '97 / Cargo / Vital

VIOLENT WORLD (A Tribute To The Misfits) (Various Artists)
She: *Snapcase* / Astro zombies: *Pennywise* / 20 eyes: *Shades Apart* / TV casualty: *Tanner* / Where eagles dare: *Therapy* / London dungeon: *Prong* / Death comes ripping: *108* / Mommy, can I go out and kill tonight: *Bouncing Souls* / Ghouls night out: *Goldfinger* / Horror business: *Deadguy* / All hell breaks loose: *Sick Of It All* / Last caress: *NOFX* / Earth AD: *Earth Crisis* / Return of the fly: *Farside*
CD _______ CAROL 006CD
Caroline / Feb '97 / Cargo / Vital

Misha

CONNECTED TO THE UNEXPECTED
Si kuku ni ta kuja / Thoughts the rain / 1 and the 9 / Black ballet / Poet in the trash can / Who are you / Electrified / Donde estan mis zapatos / Moon over my ami / Smooth / Moonlight serenade
CD _______ JVC 20552
JVC / Jun '96 / Direct / New Note/Pinnacle / Vital/SAM

Mishra, Rajan Sajan

RAGAS, DESI AND SHUDDH BHAIRAVI
CD _______ NRCD 0057
Navras / May '96 / New Note/Pinnacle

Mishra, Sanjay

BLUE INCANTATION (Mishra, Sanjay & Jerry Garcia)
My meditation / Monsoon / For Julia / Allegro / Clouds / Passage of time / Self portrait / Bach in time / Nocturne / Before summer rain
CD _______ RCD 10409
Rykodisc / Apr '97 / ADA / Vital

Misiani, Daniel Owino

PINY OSE MER/THE WORLD UPSIDE DOWN (Misiani, Daniel Owino & Shirati Band)
Isabella Muga / Rose Akoth / Margret Odero / Piny Ose Mer / Makuru bor / Otieno anyango / Wuoth iye tek / Dora Mamy
CD _______ CDORB 046
Globestyle / Jul '89 / Pinnacle

Misra, Pandit Lalmani

MUSIC OF PANDIT LALMANI MISRA, THE
CD _______ D 8627
Unesco / Feb '96 / ADA / Harmonia Mundi

Miss Alans

LEDGER
CD _______ WD 352
World Domination / Aug '96 / Pinnacle / RTM/Disc

Miss Bliss

MISS BLISS
CD _______ MDR 10CD
Meltdown / Jul '97 / Cargo

Miss Lou

YES M'DEAR
CD _______ SONCD 0079
Sonic Sounds / Nov '95 / Jet Star

Miss Murgatroid

METHYL ETHYL KEY TONES
CD _______ WOE 24
Worrybird / Nov '93 / SRD

Miss World

MISS WORLD
First female serial killer / Nine steps to nowhere / Watch that man weep / Blow / What a wonderful world / British pharmaceuticals / Highway of dead roads / Mother Mary / Speak / Troubled blood / Love is the whole of the law / Thief inside / Dead flowers
CD _______ 4509903522
Anxious / Nov '92 / Warner Music

Missing Brazilians

WARZONE
CD _______ ONUCD 18634
On-U Sound / Aug '97 / Jet Star / SRD

Mission

BLUE
CD _______ SMEECD 002
Equator / Jun '96 / Pinnacle

CARVED IN SAND
Amelia / Into the blue / Butterfly on a wheel / Sea of love / Deliverance / Grapes of wrath / Belief / Paradise (will shine like the moon) / Hungry as the hunter / Lovely
CD _______ 8422512
Mercury / Jan '90 / PolyGram

CHILDREN
Beyond the pale / Wing and a prayer / Heaven on earth / Tower of strength / Kingdom come / Breathe / Shamera Kye / Black mountain mist / Heat / Hymn (for America)
CD _______ 8342632
Mercury / Feb '88 / PolyGram

CHILDREN/CARVED IN SAND (2CD Set)
Amelia / Into the blue / Butterfly on a wheel / Sea of love / Deliverance / Grapes of wrath / Breathe / Child's play / Shamera Kye / Black mountain mist / Dream on / Heat / Hymn for America / Beyond the pale / Wing and a prayer / Fabienne / Heaven on earth / Tower of strength / Kingdom come / Belief / Paradise (will shine like the moon) / Hungry as the hunter / Lovely
CD Set _______ 5286052
Mercury / Aug '95 / PolyGram

FIRST CHAPTER, THE
Over the hills and far away / Serpent's kiss / Crystal ocean / Dancing barefoot / Like a hurricane / Naked and savage / Garden of delight / Wake / Tomorrow never knows / Wishing well
CD _______ 8325272
Mercury / May '88 / PolyGram

GRAINS OF SAND
Hands across the ocean / Grip of disease / Divided we fall / Mercenary / Mr. Pleasant / Kingdom come / Heaven sends you / Sweet smile of mystery / Love / Bird of passage
CD _______ 8469372
Mercury / Oct '90 / PolyGram

MASQUE
Never again / Shades of green (pat II) / Even you may shine / Trail of scarlet / Spider and the fly / She conjures me wings / Sticks and stones / Like a child again / Who will love me tomorrow / You make me breathe / From one Jesus to another / Until there's another sunrise
CD _______ 5121212
Mercury / Jun '92 / PolyGram

NEVERLAND
Raising cain / Sway / Lose myself in you / Swoon / Afterglow (reprise) / Stars don't shine without you / Celebration / Cry like a baby / Heaven knows / Swim with the dolphins / Neverland (vocal) / Daddy's going to heaven now
CD _______ SMEECD 001
Equator / Feb '95 / Pinnacle

SUM AND SUBSTANCE (The Best Of The Mission)
CD _______ 5184472
Mercury / Jan '94 / PolyGram

Mission Of Burma

FORGET
CD _______ TAANG 24CD
Taang / Nov '92 / Cargo

MISSION OF BURMA
CD _______ RCD 40072
Rykodisc / Jun '92 / ADA / Vital

Mississippi Sheiks

MISSISSIPPI SHEIKS VOL.1 1930
CD _______ DOCD 5083
Document / '92 / ADA / Hot Shot / Jazz Music

MISSISSIPPI SHEIKS VOL.2 1930-1931
CD _______ DOCD 5084
Document / '92 / ADA / Hot Shot / Jazz Music

MISSISSIPPI SHEIKS VOL.3 1931-1934
CD _______ DOCD 5085
Document / '92 / ADA / Hot Shot / Jazz Music

MISSISSIPPI SHEIKS/CHAPMAN BROTHERS VOL.4 1934-1936
CD _______ DOCD 5086
Document / '92 / ADA / Hot Shot / Jazz Music

Mista

MISTA
Everything must change / What about us / I'll sweat you / Crossroads / Tears scars lies / Things you do / If my baby / I think that I should be / Heart is / Lady / Fresh groove / Blackberry molasses
CD _______ 7559619122
Elektra / Sep '96 / Warner Music

Mistakes

MISTAKES, THE
CD _______ TVCD 203
Third Venture / Apr '96 / Grapevine/ PolyGram

Mistinguett

1926-31
CD _______ 124
Chansophone / Nov '92 / Discovery

EMPRESS OF THE MUSIC HALL, THE
CD _______ 995732
EPM / Jul '97 / ADA / Discovery

Misty In Roots

CHRONICLES: THE BEST OF MISTY IN ROOTS
CD _______ KAZCD 903
Kaz / Jun '94 / BMG

EARTH
CD _______ KAZCD 601
Kaz / Aug '95 / BMG

FORWARD
Fiesta / Midas touch / Hawks on the street / Save a thought / Forward / Jah see Jah know / Envy us / Look before you leap / Feelings / Sinner
CD _______ KAZCD 900
Kaz / Aug '91 / BMG

JAH SEES...JAH KNOWS (2CD Set)
Food, clothes and shelter / Live up / Follow fashion / Earth / Wondering wanderer / Wise and foolish / Musi o tunya / Poor and needy / Dreadful dread / Peace and love / West livity / Bail out / Ireation / Economical slavery / Salvation / Rich man / Jah bless Africa / Introduction / Man kind / Ghetto of the city / How long Jah / Oh wicked man / Judas Iscariote / See them ah come / Sodom and Gomarrah
CD Set _______ SMDCD 107
Snapper / May '97 / Pinnacle

LIVE AT THE COUNTER EUROVISION
Introduction / Mankind / Ghetto of the city / How long Jah / Oh wicked man / Judas Iscariot / See them a-come / Sodom and Gomorrah
CD _______ KAZCD 12
Kaz / Jun '90 / BMG

MUSI O TUNYA
CD _______ KAZCD 602
Kaz / Aug '95 / BMG

WISE AND FOOLISH
CD _______ KAZCD 603
Kaz / Aug '95 / BMG

Misunderstood

BEFORE THE DREAM FADED
Children of the sun / My mind / Who do you love / Unseen / Find a hidden door / I can take you to the sun / I'm not talking / Who's been talkin' / I need your love / You don't have to go / I cried my eyes out / Like I do / Crying over love
CD ______ CDBRED 32
Cherry Red / Sep '96 / Pinnacle

LEGENDARY GOLD STAR, THE/ GOLDEN GLASS
Blues with a feeling / Who's been talking / You got me dizzy / You don't have to go / Goin' to New York / Shake your money maker / I just want to make love to you / I'm not talking / Never had a nice girl / Golden glass / I don't want to discuss it / Little red rooster / Tuff enough / Freedom / Keep on running / I'm cruising
CD ______ CDBRED 142
Cherry Red / Mar '97 / Pinnacle

Mitchell's Christian Singers

MITCHELL'S CHRISTIAN SINGERS VOL.1 1934-1936
CD ______ DOCD 5493
Document / Nov '96 / ADA / Hot Shot / Jazz Music

MITCHELL'S CHRISTIAN SINGERS VOL.2 1936-1938
CD ______ DOCD 5494
Document / Nov '96 / ADA / Hot Shot / Jazz Music

MITCHELL'S CHRISTIAN SINGERS VOL.3 1938-1940
CD ______ DOCD 5495
Document / Nov '96 / ADA / Hot Shot / Jazz Music

MITCHELL'S CHRISTIAN SINGERS VOL.4/WRIGHT BROTHERS GOSPEL SI (Mitchell's Christian Singers/Wright Brothers Gospel Singers)
CD ______ DOCD 5496
Document / Nov '96 / ADA / Hot Shot / Jazz Music

Mitchell, Blue

BIG SIX
CD ______ OJCCD 615
Original Jazz Classics / Nov '95 / Complete/Pinnacle / Jazz Music / Wellard

BLUE SOUL
Minor vamp / Head / Way you look tonight / Park avenue petite / Top shelf / Waverley street / Blue soul / Polka dots and moonbeams / Nica's dream
CD ______ OJCCD 765
Original Jazz Classics / Jun '94 / Complete/ Pinnacle / Jazz Music / Wellard

DOWN WITH IT
Hi-heel sneakers / Perception / Alone, alone, alone / March on Selma / One shirt / Samba de Stacy
CD ______ CDP 8543272
Blue Note / Feb '97 / EMI

OUT OF THE BLUE
CD ______ OJCCD 667
Original Jazz Classics / Nov '95 / Complete/Pinnacle / Jazz Music / Wellard

SMOOTH AS THE WIND
Smooth as the wind / But beautiful / Best things in life are free / Peace / For Heaven's sake / Nearness of you / Blue time / Strollin' / For all we know / I'm a fool to want you
CD ______ OJCCD 871
Original Jazz Classics / Aug '96 / Complete/ Pinnacle / Jazz Music / Wellard

Mitchell, Bobby

YOU ALWAYS HURT THE ONE YOU LOVE (2CD Set)
I'm crying / Rack 'em back / I'm a young man / Angel child / Wedding bells are ringing / Meant for me / One Friday morning / 4 x 11 = 44 / Baby's gone / Sister Lucy / I cried / I wish I knew / I'm in love / Try rock 'n' roll / I fell for you / You are my angel / No no no / I try so hard / Goin' round in circles / I've got my fingers crossed / How long (must I wait) / Sixty four hours / You always hurt the one you love / I love to hold you (more and more) / I would like to know / I'm gonna be a wheel someday / You better go home / You're going to be sorry / Hearts of fire / Well I done got over it / Just say you love me / Send me your picture / You're doing me wrong / There's only one of you / Mama don't allow / When we first met / I'll fiddle while you cry / Oh yeah / My Southern belle / Got to call that number / I never knew what hit me / I don't want to be a wheel no more / Walking in circles / You got the nerve
CD Set ______ BCD 15961
Bear Family / Jan '97 / Direct / Rollercoaster / Swift

Mitchell, Chad

VIRGO MOON
CD ______ SCD 91590
Folk Era / Dec '94 / ADA / CM

Mitchell, George

DOWN MEMORY LANE (3CD Set) (Mitchell, George Minstrels)
Ring up the curtain / Ring ring the banjo / When the saints go marching in / Chicago / You made me love you / Mr. Gallagher and Mr. Shean / Put your arms around me honey / Down where the Swanee river flows / While strolling through the park one day / In the good old summertime / Sweet Rosie O'Grady / I'll be your sweetheart / Little Annie Rooney / And the band played on / Alabamy bound / Swanee / Is it true what they say about Dixie / Carolina / Toot Toot Tootsie goodbye / Old ark's a' movering / Along the Navajo trail / In ol' Oklahoma / Old Dan Tucker / Country Style / Skip to my Lou / Buffalo gal / Singin' in the rain / Together / No two people / My blue Heaven / Falling in love with love / Maria from Bahia / I yi yi yi yi (I like you very much) / When I love I love / Bandit / Cielito lindo / Cuonto le Gusta / I'll si si ya in Bahia / Hard times come again no more / Gentle Annie / Way down upon the Swanee river / Tell me pretty maiden / Put on your tata, little girlie / Hello hello, who's your lady friend / I was a good girl until I met you / In the twi-twi-twilight / Two little girls in blue / North and south / You're in Kentucky sure as you're born / Yellow rose of Texas / Georgia on my mind / Stars fell on Alabama / I'm going back to old Nebraska / Dixieland / Carry me back to old Virginny / Lady is a tramp / (In) a shanty in old Shanty Town / Ain't we got fun / I'm sittin' high on a hill top / Big rock candy mountain / Side by side / Widdicombe fair / Home on the range / Back in those old Kentucky days / I went down to Virginia / Sonny boy / Goin' to the county fair / Dicky bird hop / Cuckoo waltz / She was one of the early birds / When the red, red robin comes bob, bob, bobbin' along / Too-Whit Too-Whoo / Chee Chee oo Chee / Let's all sing like the birdies sing / Load of hay / 1-2 Button your shoe / You are my sunshine / Bei mir bist du schon / Memories are made of this / Sing a song of sunbeams / South of the border (Down Mexico way) / Where or when / Frog and the mouse / Long long ago / Roamin' in the gloamin' / Let me call you sweetheart / Meet me tonight in dreamland / Pack up your troubles in your old kit bag / Till we meet again / Roses of Picardy
CD Set ______ CDDL 1096
Music For Pleasure / Nov '91 / EMI

Mitchell, Guy

16 MOST REQUESTED SONGS
My heart cries for you / Pittsburgh, Pennsylvania / Roving kind / Knee deep in the blues / Belle belle, my liberty belle / Pretty little black eyed Susie / There's always room at our house / Chicka boom / Sparrow in the tree top / Christopher Columbus / My truly truly fair / She wears red feathers / Feet up pat him on the po po / Day of jubilo / Crazy with love / Singin' the blues
CD ______ 4720482
Columbia / Jul '92 / Sony

20 GREATEST HITS
My truly fair / Chick a boom / Pretty little black eyed susie / Sparrow in the tree top / My heart cries for you / Call Rosie on the phone / Singin' the blues / Knee deep in the blues / Roving kind / There's a pawn shop on the corner in Pittsburg, Pennsylvania / Feet up pat him on the po po / Music music music / She wears red feathers / My shoes keep walking back / Cuff of my shirt / Sippin' soda / Cloud lucky seven / Rock-a-billy
CD ______ 300372
Hallmark / Jul '96 / Carlton

20 GREATEST HITS
CD ______ CDSGP 0279
Prestige / Jun '97 / Else / Total/BMG

ALL TIME HITS
She wears red feathers / Pretty little black eyed Susie / Feet up / Chicka boom / Cloud lucky seven / Cuff of my shirt / Sippin' soda / Side by side / My heart cries for you / Singin' the blues / Knee deep in the blues / Rockabilly / Call Rosie on the 'phone / Heartaches by the number / Pittsburgh, Pennsylvania / Music music music / Sparrow in the tree top / My truly, truly fair / My shoes keep walking back to you / Roving kind
CD ______ CDMFP 5908
Music For Pleasure / Apr '91 / EMI

BEST OF ALL, THE (18 Greatest Hits)
My truly truly fair / Chick-a-boom / Pretty little black eyed Sue / Sparrow in the tree top / Side by side / My heart cries for you / Call Rosie on the phone / Singin' the blues / Heartaches by the number / Pittsburg Pennsylvania / Feet up (pat him on the po po) / Music music music / She wears red feathers / My shoes keep walking back / Cuff of my heart / Sippin' soda / Cloud lucky seven / Rock-a-billy
CD ______ PLATCD 161
Platinum / Mar '96 / Prism

BEST OF GUY MITCHELL, THE
Singin' the blues / Roving kind / Cut of my shirt / She wears red feathers / Chicka boom / Belle, belle my liberty belle / Rock-a-billy / My truly, truly fair / Feet up (pat him on the po-po) / Look at that girl / Sparrow on the treetops / My heart cries for you / Pittsburgh, Pennsylvania / There's always room at my house / Crazy with love / Cloud lucky seven / Dime and a dollar / Heartaches by the number / Knee deep in the blues / Christopher Columbus / Pretty little black eyed Susie / Sippin' soda / Day of jubilo / Call Rosie on the phone
CD ______ 4840392
Columbia / May '96 / Sony

CLASSIC ALBUM, THE (2CD Set)
CD Set ______ KCD 7000
King / Apr '97 / Avid/BMG

GREATEST HITS
CD ______ WMCD 5671
Woodford Music / Feb '93 / THE

GUY MITCHELL
CD ______ GRF 237
Tring / Aug '93 / Tring

HEARTACHES BY THE NUMBER
Heartaches by the number / Miracle of love / Rockabilly / Singin' the blues / Notify the FBI / Same old me / Sunshine guitar / My shoes keep walking back to you / Sweet stuff / Hoot owl / Knee deep in the blues / Take me back baby / Because I love you / Pittsburgh, Pennsylvania / Roving kind / My heart cries for you / Dime and a dollar / My truly, truly fair / House of the swinging bamboo / Sparrow on the tree-top / Christopher Columbus / Belle belle, my liberty belle / Ninety nine years / Pretty little black eyed Susie / Unless
CD ______ BCD 15454
Bear Family / May '90 / Direct / Rollercoaster / Swift

SINGING THE BLUES
My truly, truly fair / Knee deep in the blues / Cloud lucky seven / Music music music / She wears red feathers / Roving kind / Pretty little black-eyed Susie / Pittsburgh Pennsylvannia / Chicka boom / Heartaches by the number / Singin' the blues / Side by side / Sparrow in the treetop / My shoes keep walking back to you / Sippin' soda / Rock-a-billy / Cuff of my shirt / Rosie on the 'phone / My heart cries for you / Feet up
CD ______ QED 058
Tring / Nov '96 / Tring

Mitchell, Joni

BLUE
All I want / My old man / Little green / Carey / Blue / California / This flight tonight / River / Case of you / Last time I saw Richard
CD ______ K 244 128
Reprise / Jan '87 / Warner Music

CHALK MARK IN A RAINSTORM
My secret place / Number one / Lakota / Tea leaf prophecy / Dancing clown / Cool water / Beat of black wings / Snakes and ladders / Recurring dream / Bird that whistle
CD ______ GFLD 19199
Geffen / Aug '93 / BMG

CLOUDS
Tin angel / Chelsea morning / I don't know where I stand / That song about the Midway / Roses blue / Gallery / I think I understand / Songs to ageing children come / Fiddle and the drum / Both sides now
CD ______ K2 44070
Reprise / Jan '88 / Warner Music

COURT AND SPARK
Court and spark / Help me / Free man in Paris / People's parties / Same situation / Car on a hill / Down to you / Just like this train / Raised on robbery / Trouble child / Twisted
CD ______ 2530022
Asylum / May '83 / Warner Music

DOG EAT DOG
Good friends / Fiction / Three great stimulants / Tax free / Smokin' / Dog eat dog / Shiny toys / Ethiopia / Impossible dreamer / Lucky girl
CD ______ GED 24074
Geffen / Nov '96 / BMG

FOR THE ROSES
Banquet / Cold blue steel and sweet fire / Barangrill / Lesson in survival / Let the wind carry me / For the roses / You see sometime / Electricity / You turn me on, I'm a radio / Blonde in the bleachers / Woman of heart and mind / Judgement of the moon and stars
CD ______ 253007
Asylum / Dec '87 / Warner Music

GHOSTS
CD ______ OTR 1100027
Metro Independent / Jun '97 / Essential/ BMG

HEJIRA
Coyote / Amelia / Furry sings the blues / Strange boy / Hejira / Song for Sharon / Black crow / Blue motel room / Refuge of the roads
CD ______ 2530532
Asylum / Oct '87 / Warner Music

HISSING OF SUMMER LAWNS, THE
In France they kiss on Main Street / Jungle line / Edith and the kingpin / Don't interrupt the sorrow / Shades of scarlet conquering / Hissing of summer lawns / Boho dance / Harry's house / Sweet bird / Shadows and light
CD ______ 253018
Asylum / Dec '87 / Warner Music

HITS
Urge for going / Chelsea morning / Big yellow taxi / Woodstock / Circle game / Carey / California / You turn me on, I'm a radio / Raised on robbery / Help me / Free man in Paris / River / Chinese cafe / Come in from the cold / Both sides now
CD ______ 9362463262
Reprise / Oct '96 / Warner Music

JONI MITCHELL
I had a King / Michael from the mountains / Night in the city / Marcie / Nathan La Franeer / Sisotowbell Lane / Dawntreader / Pirate of penance / Song to a seagull / Cactus tree
CD ______ 244051
Reprise / '87 / Warner Music

JONI MITCHELL
CD ______ EXP 025
Experience / May '97 / TKO Magnum

LADIES OF THE CANYON
Morning Morgantown / For free / Conversation / Ladies of the canyon / Willy / Arrangement / Rainy night house / Priest / Blue boy / Big yellow taxi / Woodstock / Circle game
CD ______ K 244085
Reprise / Jul '88 / Warner Music

MINGUS
Happy birthday / God must be a boogie man / Funeral / Chair in the sky / Wolf that lives in Lindsey / Is a muggin' / Dry cleaner from Des Moines / Lucky / Goodbye Pork Pie Hat / Sweet sucker dance / Coin in the pocket
CD ______ 253091
Asylum / '88 / Warner Music

MISSES
Passion play / Nothing can be done / Case of you / Beat of black wings / Dog eat dog / Wolf that lives in Lindsay / Magdalene laundries / Impossible dreamer / Sex kills / Reoccuring dream / Harry's house / Arrangement / For the roses / Hejira (travelling)
CD ______ 9362463582
Reprise / Oct '96 / Warner Music

NIGHT RIDE HOME
Night ride home / Passion play (When all the slaves are free) / Cherokee Louise / Windfall (Everything for nothing) / Slouching towards Bethlehem / Come in from the cold / Nothing can be done / Only joy in town / Ray's dad's Cadillac / Two grey rooms
CD ______ GEFD 24302
Geffen / Feb '91 / BMG

TURBULENT INDIGO
Sunny Sunday / Sex kills / How do you stop / Turbulent indigo / Last chance lost / Magdalene laundries / Not to blame / Borderline / Yvette in English / Sire of sorrow (Job's sad song)
CD ______ 9362457862
Asylum / Oct '94 / Warner Music

WILD THINGS RUN FAST
Chinese cafe / Unchained melody / Wild things run fast / Ladies man / Moon at the window / Solid love / Be cool / Baby I don't care / You dream flat tires / Man to man / Underneath the streetlight / Love
CD ______ GFLD 19129
Geffen / Jul '92 / BMG

Mitchell, Kevin

I SANG THE SWEET REFRAIN
CD ______ CDTRAX 108
Greentrax / Apr '96 / ADA / Direct / Duncans / Highlander

Mitchell, Prince Phillip

LONER
While the cat's away / Starting from scratch / Come to bed / Can't nobody love you better than me / Never let her down / Nothing hurts like love / You did what you had to do / Loner / She's a party animal
CD ______ ICH 1110CD
Ichiban / Oct '93 / Direct / Koch

Mitchell, Red

ALONE TOGETHER
CD ______ DRAGONCD 168
Dragon / Jan '88 / ADA / Cadillac / CM / Roots / Wellard

EVOLUTION
CD ______ DRCD 191
Dragon / Jan '89 / ADA / Cadillac / CM / Roots / Wellard

MITCHELL/KELLAWAY/MILDER (Mitchell, Red & Roger Kellaway/Joakim Milder)
CD ______ DRCD 219
Dragon / Oct '94 / ADA / Cadillac / CM / Roots / Wellard

TALKING
CD ______ 74016
Capri / Nov '93 / Cadillac / Wellard

VERY THOUGHT OF YOU, THE
CD DRAGONCD 161
Dragon / Jan '89 / ADA / Cadillac / CM / Roots / Wellard

Mitchell, Roscoe

3 X 4 EYE
CD 120050
Black Saint / Apr '94 / Cadillac / Harmonia Mundi

HEY DONALD
CD DE 475
Delmark / Oct '95 / ADA / Cadillac / CM / Direct / Hot Shot

LIVE AT THE KNITTING FACTORY (Mitchell, Roscoe & The Sound Ensemble)
CD 1201202
Black Saint / May '92 / Cadillac / Harmonia Mundi

LRG/THE MAZE/S II EXAMPLES
CD CHIEFCD 4
Chief / Jun '89 / Cadillac

SONGS IN THE WIND
CD VICTOCD 011
Victo / Nov '94 / Harmonia Mundi / ReR Megacorp

SOUND
Ornette / Sound 1 / Little suite / Ornette / Sound 2
CD DE 408
Delmark / Nov '96 / ADA / Cadillac / CM / Direct / Hot Shot

SOUND SONGS (2CD Set)
Let's get ready to rumble / They all had new clothes / Messenger in traffic / Fallen heroes / Full frontal saxophone / Down at the pond / 4.50 express / Meeting / For Lester B / Near and far / Song for percussion and bamboo sax / Play / Garden / Night / On the country road / Side one / Other side / Side two / First sketches of Leola / Appear and disappear / Dream machine / For Madeline / Closer
CD Set 2DE 493
Delmark / Jul '97 / ADA / Cadillac / CM / Direct / Hot Shot

THIS DANCE IS FOR STEVE MCCALL (Mitchell, Roscoe & The Note Factory)
CD 1201502
Black Saint / Nov '93 / Cadillac / Harmonia Mundi

Mitchell, Ross

ALL NIGHT LONG (Mitchell, Ross & His Band & Singers)
CD DLD 1037
Dance & Listen / May '93 / Savoy / Target/BMG

BAM-BOOM
CD DLD 1023
Dance & Listen / '92 / Savoy / Target/BMG

BEST OF THE DANSAN YEARS VOL.2, THE (Mitchell, Ross Band & Singers)
CD DACD 002
Dansan / Jul '92 / Jazz Music / President / Target/BMG / Wellard

BEST OF THE DANSAN YEARS VOL.3, THE (Mitchell, Ross Band & Singers)
CD DACD 003
Dansan / Jul '92 / Jazz Music / President / Target/BMG / Wellard

CFD VOL.6
CD DLD 1062
Dance & Listen / Dec '95 / Savoy / Target/BMG

DON'T STOP
CD DLD 1016
Dance & Listen / '92 / Savoy / Target/BMG

GO DANCING
CD DLD 1028
Dance & Listen / Jul '92 / Savoy / Target/BMG

MERRY CHRISTMAS (Mitchell, Ross & His Band & Singers)
CD DLD 1006
Dance & Listen / Jul '92 / Savoy / Target/BMG

OPENING NIGHT (Mitchell, Ross & His Band & Singers)
CD DLD 1031
Dance & Listen / May '93 / Savoy / Target/BMG

RAINBOW COLLECTION, THE
CD DLD 1004
Dance & Listen / Jul '92 / Savoy / Target/BMG

ROSS MITCHELL PRESENTS CFD
CD DLD 1027
Dance & Listen / May '92 / Savoy / Target/BMG

STANDARD AND LATIN DANCES
CD DLD 1042
Dance & Listen / Nov '93 / Savoy / Target/BMG

STAR REQUESTS (Mitchell, Ross & His Band & Singers)
I won't dance / Tap your troubles away / Desert song / Kisses in the dark / Fascination / Wish upon a star / Jealousy / Star / Tea for two / Brazil / Shall we dance / All I ask of you / I won't send roses / Wake up little Susie
CD DLD 1003
Dance & Listen / Oct '88 / Savoy / Target/BMG

ZING '90
CD DLD 1010
Dance & Listen / '92 / Savoy / Target/BMG

ZING VOL.2 (Mitchell, Ross & His Band & Singers)
Baubles, bangles and beads / Dancing in the dark / London by night / Where is your heart / Swingin' down the lane / One / Rain in Spain / Wrap your troubles in dreams (and dream your troubles away) / Sway / Zambesi / Quand tu chantes / If I loved you / With a song in my heart / Trickle trickle
CD DLD 1002
Dance & Listen / Apr '88 / Savoy / Target/BMG

Mitchell, Warren

ALF GARNETT'S MUSIC HALL
At Trinity church / Old rustic bridge by the mill / I live in Trafalgar Square / Gilbert the filbert / Down the road / Bill Bailey / In the twi-twi-twilight / If it wasn't for the 'ouses in between / It's a great big shame / Every little while / When father papered the parlour / Hold your hand out naughty boy / Let's all go down the strand / Honeysuckle and the bee / My grandfather's clock
CD 306592
Hallmark / May '97 / Carlton

Mitchell, Willie

OOH BABY YOU TURN ME ON/LIVE AT THE ROYAL
CD HIUKCD 132
Hi / Jun '93 / Pinnacle

SOLID SOUL
Prayer meetin' / Grazing in the grass / Windy / Sunrise serenade / Horse / Groovin' / San-Ho-Zay / Uphard / Monkey jump / Strawberry soul / Hideaway / Willie-wam
CD HIUKCD 120
Hi / Jul '91 / Pinnacle

SPARKLE
Sparkle / Reaching out / Honey bear / Midnight rhapsody / Give the world more love / Sugar candy / Expressions / Happy hour
CD C5CD517
See For Miles/C5 / Jun '88 / Pinnacle

WALKIN' WITH WILLIE
CD RCCD 3009
Rollercoaster / Jun '94 / Rollercoaster / Swift

Mitchum, Robert

CALYPSO
Jean and Dinah / From a logical point of view / Not me / What is this generation coming to / Tic tic tic / Beauty is only skin deep / I learn a merengue, mama / Take me down to lover's row / Mama look a boo boo / Coconut water / Matilda Matilda / They dance all night
CD CREV 037CD
Rev-Ola / Jul '95 / 3mv/Vital

THAT MAN
You deserve each other / Walker's woods / Wheels (it's rollin' time again) / In my place / Ballad of Thunder Road / That man right there / Litle ole wine drinker me / Ricardo's mountain / Sunny / They dance all night / Matilda Matilda / Coconut water / Boo Boo (shut your mouth go away) / Mama look / Take me down to lovers row / Meremgue, Mama / I learn A / Beauty is only skin deep / Tic, tic, tic (lost watch) / What is this generation coming to / Not me / From a logical point of view / Jean and dinah / Gotta travel on / Whip-poor-will / Little white lies
CD BCD 15890
Bear Family / Jun '95 / Direct / Rollercoaster / Swift

Mittoo, Jackie

EVENING TIME
CD SOCD 8014
Studio One / Mar '95 / Jet Star

KEEP ON DANCING
CD CSCD 8020
Studio One / Mar '96 / Jet Star

KEYBOARD LEGEND
CD SONCD 0073
Sonic Sounds / Apr '95 / Jet Star

SHOWCASE VOL.3
CD JIMCD 4957
A&A Productions / Jun '95 / Jet Star

TRIBUTE TO JACKIE MITTOO
CD CDHB 189190
Heartbeat / Aug '95 / ADA / Direct / Greensleeves / Jet Star

Mixed Emotions

BEST OF MIXED EMOTIONS, THE
You want love (Maria, Maria) / It's over now / One way love / Bring back (sha na na) / Changin' light of love / Love is so easy now / Just for you / Sweetheart-darlin'-my dear / Children of a lesser paradise / Chiquitita Renita / I never give up / Sentimental song / Over the limit / Close to heaven now
CD DC 871102
Disky / Nov '96 / Disky / THE

Mixman

EARLY DUB TAPES, THE
CD BLKMCD 011
Blakamix / Oct '94 / Jet Star / SRD

NEW DIMENSIONS DUB
CD BLKCD 002
Blakamix / Sep '92 / Jet Star / SRD

SEEK AND YOU WILL FIND - THE DUB PIECES
CD BLKCD 16
Blakamix / Nov '95 / Jet Star / SRD

Mixmaster Morris

DREAMFISH VOL.2 (Mixmaster Morris & Pete Namlock)
CD PW 016
Fax / Nov '95 / Plastic Head

Mixon, Donovan

LOOK MA, NO HANDS
CD W 1122
Philology / Sep '93 / Cadillac / Harmonia Mundi

Miyati, Kohachiro

SHAKUHACHI, THE JAPANESE FLUTE
CD 7559720762
Nonesuch / Jan '95 / Warner Music

Mizarolli, John

MESSAGE FROM THE 5TH STONE
No magic love / Granny did it / Ain't nobody gonna bring me down / Message from the 5th stone / Lost your love my love / Wake up and live / Is mamma the president / Menopause / Mama never told you
CD INAK 867 CD
In Akustik / '88 / Direct / TKO Magnum

MK

REMIXED, REMADE, REMODELLED
CD ACTIVCD 10
Activ / Aug '97 / Total/BMG

SURRENDER (MK & Alana)
Crazy, crazy / Always / Only you / Almost gave up / Burning / Love changes / Surrender / MK Apella / Reality / Precious jewels / Games / Hot stuff
CD ACTIVCD 2
Activ / Jun '95 / Total/BMG

MK Ultra

THIS IS THIS
CD 13318162
Merciful Release / Jul '94 / Warner Music

MKB

FRENCHIE'S BAD INDIANS
CD ODE 003
Odessa / Mar '94 / Plastic Head

MLO

IO
CD RSNCD 16
Rising High / Apr '94 / 3mv/Sony

PLASTIC APPLE (3CD Set)
DJ Food's sonic soup / New generation / Samarkand / Garden / Samarkand / Two voyages / Out of the blue / Gun crazy / New generation / Sleeper / Dreamlab / Blowpipe / Samarkand / Two voyages / One beat too many / Out of the blue / Garden / Long and winding / New generation / Aqua / Birds 'n' flutes 'n' shit
CD Set SUCD 5
Aura Surround Sounds / Oct '96 / Arabesque / Grapevine/PolyGram / Mo's Music Machine / Pinnacle

MN8

FREAKY
Tuff act to follow / Dreaming / Freaky / I'll give you my everything / Baby I surrender / Beautiful body / It's all on you / Shake it / This heart / I promise / Keep it in the family / Talk to you
CD 4852992
Columbia / Nov '96 / Sony

TO THE NEXT LEVEL
I've got a little something for you / If you only let me in / Happy / Pathway to the moon / Lonely / Baby it's you / Black pearl / I'll be gone / Holding hands / I will be there / Touch the sky
CD 4802802
Columbia / May '95 / Sony

Mnemonic

WEAPONS
CD APR 008CD
April / Aug '96 / Plastic Head / Shellshock/Disc

Mo, Billy

MISTER RHYTHM KING
Swing Methusalem / Buona Sera / Oh Marie / Gonggonza / Ding dong / Darling du weisst ja / Regenbogen blues / La Paloma / Habe mitleid / Mary my girl / Oh Jennilie / Billy boy / Tatalee / Mister Rhythm King / Nevada swing / Das fraulein Gerda / Salambuli / You are my sunshine / Smoke like it hot / Baby / Golden River / Dickie Doo / Dolly Doo / Lass mich rein Barberina / Susie / Pinguin jive / Ay, ay, ay / Mitternachts blues / Ich kauf mir lieber einen Tirolerhut
CD BCD 15966
Bear Family / May '96 / Direct / Rollercoaster / Swift

Mo Boma

MYTHS OF THE NEAR FUTURE
CD XCD 025
Extreme / Feb '95 / Vital/SAM

MYTHS OF THE NEAR FUTURE VOL.3
CD XCD 035
Extreme / Jun '96 / Vital/SAM

Mo Rag's Marauders

NOO VOL.2
CD LCOM 5256
Lismor / Nov '96 / ADA / Direct / Duncans / Lismor

Mo Thugs

FAMILY SCRIPTURES
Intro / Searchin' 4 peace / Ghetto Bluez / Killing fields / Mo' murder / Ain't no reason / Take your time / Welcome to my world / Thug devotion / Here with me / Player in me no pretender / Rumors and wars / 2 Tru / Low Down / Family scriptures
CD 4867412
Relativity / Nov '96 / Sony

Moal, Gildas

AN DISPUT (Moal, Gildas & Rene Chaplain)
CD CD 438
Arfolk / Sep '96 / ADA / Discovery / Roots

Moaning Wind

VISIONS OF FIRE
CD CR 6502CD
Corrosion / Jun '97 / Plastic Head

Mob

MOB, THE
Maybe I'll find a way / Once a man, twice a child / (I'd like to see) more of you / Lost / Give it to me / For a little while / Goodtime baby / I dig everything about you / Love's got a hold on me / Back on the road again / Savin' my love for you / Everyday people/ Love power / Make me yours / All I need / I feel the earth move / Money (that's what I want) / Where you lead / Two and two together / Uh-uh-uh-uh-uh-uh
CD NEMCD 724
Sequel / May '95 / BMG

Mob

LET THE TRIBE INCREASE
Youth / Crying again / Witch hunt / Shuffling souls / No doves fly here / I hear you laughing / Mirror breaks / Stay / Another day, another death / Cry of the morning / Dance on (you fool) / Raised in a prison / Slayed / Our life, our world / Gates of hell / I wish / Never understood / Roger
CD SEEP 012CD
Rugger Bugger / Oct '95 / Shellshock/Disc

Mob 47

GARANTEART MANGEL
CD DISTCD 022
Distortion / Nov '95 / Plastic Head

Mobb Deep

HELL ON EARTH
Animal instinct: *Mobb Deep & Ty Nitty/ Gambino* / Drop a gem on 'em / Bloodsport / Extortion: *Mobb Deep & Method Man* / More trife life / Man down: *Mobb Deep & Big Noyd* / Can't get enough of it: *Mobb Deep & General C* / Nightime vultures: *Mobb Deep & Chef Raekwon* / GOD part 3 / Get dealt with / Shook ones part 1 / Front lines (hell on earth) / Give it up fast: *Mobb Deep & Nas/Big Noyd* / Still shinin' / Apostles warning
CD 74321425582
Loud / Nov '96 / BMG

INFAMOUS MOBB DEEP, THE
Infamous
CD 07863664802
RCA / Apr '95 / BMG

Mobido, Askia

WASS REGGAE
CD STCD 1060
Stern's / May '96 / ADA / CM / Stern's

Mobley, Bill

TRIPLE BILL (Mobley, Bill Sextet)
Prelude / 49th Street / I concentrate on you / Mulgrew's motif / I love it when you dance that way / Three gifts / They say it's wonderful / Panon impressions / I didn't know what time it was
CD ECD 221632
Evidence / Sep '96 / ADA / Cadillac / Harmonia Mundi

Mobley, Hank

BEST OF HANK MOBLEY, THE
Avila & Tequila / Funk in deep freeze / Fin de l'affaire / Take your pick / This I dig of you / Smokin' / Recado bossa nova / No room for squares / Turnaround / 3rd time around
CD CDP 8370522
Blue Note / Apr '96 / EMI

HANK MOBLEY & HIS ALL STARS
Reunion / Lower stratosphere / Don't walk / Ultramarine / Mobley's musings
CD CDP 8376882
Blue Note / Jun '96 / EMI

ROLL CALL
Roll call / My groove your move / Take your pick / Baptist beat / Baptist beat, A (alternate take) / More I see you / Breakdown
CD CDP 7468232
Blue Note / Feb '97 / EMI

Moby

AMBIENT
CD ATLASCD 002
Arctic / Oct '93 / Pinnacle

ANIMAL RIGHTS (2CD Set)
CD CDSTUMM 150
CD Set LCDSTUMM 150
Mute / Sep '96 / RTM/Disc

END OF EVERYTHING, THE (Voodoo Child)
CD CDIDIOT 1
Mute / Jul '96 / RTM/Disc

EVERYTHING IS WRONG (2CD Set)
Hymn / Feeling so real / All that I need is to be loved / Let's go free / Everytime you touch me / Bring back my happiness / What love / First cool hive / Into the blue / Anthem / Everything is wrong / God moving over the face of the waters / When it'sl'd like to die
CD CDSTUMM 130
CD LCDSTUMM 130
Mute / Mar '95 / RTM/Disc
CD Set XLCDSTUMM 130
Mute / Jan '96 / RTM/Disc

HYMN
CD CDMUTE 161
Mute / May '94 / RTM/Disc

STORY SO FAR
CD ATLASCD 001
Equator / Jul '93 / Pinnacle

Moby Grape

VINTAGE - THE VERY BEST OF MOBY GRAPE (2CD Set)
Hey grandma / Mr. Blues / Fall on you / 8.05 / Come in the morning / Omaha / Naked, if I want to / Rounder / Someday / Ain't no use / Sitting by the window / Changes / Lazy me / Indifference / Looper / Sweet ride / Bitter wind / Place and the time / Miller's blues / Big / Skip's song / You can do anything / Murder in my heart / For the judge / Can't be so bad / Just like Gene Autry / Foxtrot / He / Motorcycle Irene / Funky tunk / Rose coloured eyes / If you can't learn from your mistakes / Ooh mama ooh / Ain't that a shame / Trucking man / Captain Nemo / What's to choose / Going nowhere / I am not willing / It's a beautiful day today / Right before my eyes / Truly fine citizen / Hoochie / Soul stew / Seeing
CD Set 4839582
Columbia / Jun '96 / Sony

Moco, Maio

PORTUGAL NOVO
CD PS 65071
PlayaSound / May '91 / ADA / Harmonia Mundi

MOD

DEVOLUTION
CD CDMFN 163
Music For Nations / Jun '94 / Pinnacle

DICTATED AGRESSION
CD CDMFN 201
Music For Nations / May '96 / Pinnacle

LOVED BY THOUSANDS HATED BY MILLIONS
Noize / Aren't you hungry / Spandex enormity / Aids / Hate tank / Goldfish / Surfin USA / Surfs up / Mr. Oofus / No glove no love / True colours / Livin in the city / Get up and dance / Rhymestein / Irresponsible / Rally (NYC) / Ballad of Dio / Bubble butt / Short but sweet / Ode to Harry / Vents / Theme song / Bonanza / Buckshot blues / Clubbin seals / US Dreams / He's dead Jim / Get the boot
CD CDVEST 66
Bulletproof / Oct '95 / Pinnacle

Model 500

CLASSICS
No UFO's / Chase / Off to battle / Night drive / Electric entourage / Electronic / Ocean to ocean / Techno music / Sound of stereo
CD RS 931CD
R&S / Jul '93 / Vital

DEEP SPACE
Milky Way / Orbit / Flow / Warning / Astralwerks / Starlight / Last transport (to Alpha Centauri) / I wanna be there / Lightspeed
CD RS 95066CD
R&S / May '95 / Vital

Modern English

AFTER THE SNOW
I melt with you / Tables turning / Carry me down
CD CAD 206CD
4AD / Nov '92 / RTM/Disc

MESH AND LACE
Sixteen days / Just a thought / Move in light / Grief / Token man / Viable commercial / Black houses / Dance of devotion (love song)
CD CAD 105CD
4AD / Nov '92 / RTM/Disc

RICOCHET DAYS
CD CAD 402CD
4AD / Nov '92 / RTM/Disc

Modern Folk Quartet

AT CHRISTMAS
CD FE 1404
Folk Era / Nov '94 / ADA / CM

Modern Jazz

IN A CROWD
Pyramid / In a crowd / Mean to me / Winter tale / Bag's groove / I should care / Sheriff
CD ADC 2
Douglas Music / May '97 / Cadillac / New Note/Pinnacle

Modern Jazz Quartet

2 DEGREES EAST 3 DEGREES WEST
CD VN 161
Viper's Nest / May '95 / ADA / Cadillac / Direct / Jazz Music

40TH ANNIVERSARY CELEBRATION
Bag's groove / All the things you are / Cherokee / (Back home again in) Indiana / Come rain or come shine / Willow weep for me / Memories of you / Blues for Juanita / There will never be another you / Easy living / Django / Darn that dream / Billie's bounce
CD 7567825382
Atlantic / Feb '93 / Warner Music

ARTISTRY OF THE MODERN JAZZ QUARTET
CD FCD 60016
Fantasy / Oct '93 / Jazz Music / Pinnacle / Wellard

BEST OF MODERN JAZZ QUARTET, THE
Valeria / Le cannet / Nature boy / Watergate blues / Connie's blues / Reunion blues / Echoes
CD PACD 24054232
Pablo / Apr '94 / Cadillac / Complete/Pinnacle

BLUES ON BACH
Regret / Blues in B flat / Rise up in the morning / Blues in A minor / Precious joy / Blues in C minor / Don't stop this train blues in H / Tears from the children
CD 7567813932
Atlantic / Mar '93 / Warner Music

DJANGO
CD OJCCD 572
Original Jazz Classics / Feb '92 / Complete/Pinnacle / Jazz Music / Wellard

ECHOES/TOGETHER AGAIN
CD CD 2312142
Pablo / Oct '92 / Cadillac / Complete/Pinnacle

FIRST RECORDINGS
CD JW 77014
JWD / May '93 / Target/BMG

FONTESSA
CD CD 53219
Giants Of Jazz / Nov '95 / Cadillac / Jazz Music / Target/BMG

IMMORTAL CONCERTS (Scandinavia, April 1960)
Django / Bluesology / La ronde / I remember Clifford / Vendome / Odds against tomorrow / Pyramid / It don't mean a thing if it ain't got that swing / 'Round midnight / Bag's Groove / I'll remember April / Skating in Central Park / I should care / Festival sketch
CD CD 53012
Giants Of Jazz / Mar '90 / Cadillac / Jazz Music / Target/BMG

LAST CONCERT, THE
Softly as in a morning sunrise / Cylinder / Summertime / Travellin' blues / One never knows, does one / Bag's groove / Confirmation / 'Round midnight / Night in Tunisia / Golden striker / Skating in Central Park / Django / What's new
CD 7567819762
Atlantic / Apr '95 / Warner Music

LEGENDARY PERFORMANCES, THE
CD JZCD 340
Suisa / Jan '93 / Jazz Music / THE

LONGING FOR THE CONTINENT
Animal dance / Django / England's carol / Bluesology / Bag's groove / Sketch 3 / Ambiquite / Midsummer
CD CDC 7678
LRC / Nov '90 / Harmonia Mundi / New Note/Pinnacle

LOOKING FOR THE CONTINENT
Animal dance / Django / England's carol / Bluesology / Bags' groove / Sketch / Ambiquite / Midsummer
CD 17077
Laserlight / Jan '97 / Target/BMG

MJQ BOX, THE (Concorde/Django/3CD Set)
Ralph's new blues / All of you / I'll remember April / Gershwin medley / Softly as in a morning sunrise / Concorde / Django / One bass hit / La ronde suite / Queen's fancy / Delaunay's dilemma / Autumn in New York / But not for me / Milano / All the things you are / La ronde / Vendome / Rose of the Rio Grande / Opus de funk / I've lost your love / Buhaina / Soma
CD Set 3PRCD 7711
Prestige / Nov '96 / Cadillac / Complete/Pinnacle

MJQ FOR ELLINGTON
It don't mean a thing (if it ain't got that swing) / Come Sunday / For Ellington / Prelude to a kiss / Rockin' in rhythm / Jack the bear / Maestro EKE / Ko-ko / Sepia panorama
CD 7567909262
Atlantic / Mar '93 / Warner Music

MODERN JAZZ QUARTET (Modern Jazz Quartet & Milt Jackson Quintet)
CD OJCCD 125
Original Jazz Classics / May '93 / Complete/Pinnacle / Jazz Music / Wellard

MODERN JAZZ QUARTET LIVE 1956
CD 550062
Jazz Anthology / Oct '89 / Cadillac / Discovery / Harmonia Mundi

SPACE
Visitor from Venus / Visitor from Mars / Here's that rainy day / Dilemma / Adagio from Concierto de Aranjuez
CD CDSAPCOR 10
Apple / Oct '96 / EMI

TOGETHER AGAIN (Live At The Montreux Jazz Festival 1982)
Django / Cylinder / Martyr / Really true blues / Odds against tomorrow / Jasmine tree / Monterey mist / Bag's new groove / Woody 'n' you
CD CD 2308244
Pablo / Jun '93 / Cadillac / Complete/Pinnacle

TOPSY THIS ONE'S FOR BASIE
Reunion blues: *Basie, Count* / Nature boy: *Basie, Count* / Topsy: *Basie, Count* / D and E blues: *Basie, Count* / Valeria: *Basie, Count* / Milano: *Basie, Count* / Le cannet: *Basie, Count*
CD CD 2310917
Pablo / Apr '94 / Cadillac / Complete/Pinnacle

UNDER THE JASMINE TREE
Blue necklace / Three little feelings (parts 1, 2 and 3) / Exposure / Jasmine tree
CD CDP 7975802
Apple / Oct '91 / EMI

Modern Klezmer Quartet

HORA AND BLUE
CD GV 156CD
Global Village / May '94 / ADA / Direct

Modernaires Orchestra

TRIBUTE TO GLENN MILLER VOL.1, A
CD ROSSCD 66212
Ross / Feb '89 / CM / Duncans / Highlander / Ross

TRIBUTE TO GLENN MILLER VOL.2, A
CD ROSSCD 66222
Ross / Feb '89 / CM / Duncans / Highlander / Ross

TRIBUTE TO GLENN MILLER VOL.3, A
CD ROSSCD 66152
Ross / Feb '89 / CM / Duncans / Highlander / Ross

Modernettes

GET IT STRAIGHT
CD ZULU 013CD
Zulu / Oct '95 / Plastic Head

Modest Proposal

CONTRAST
CD BAR 999D
Barooni / Mar '93 / Plastic Head / SRD

Mods

TWENTY TWO MONTHS
CD OPM 2106CD
Other People's Music / Oct '96 / Greyhound / Plastic Head

Modugno, Paolo

LE BALA ET LA MOUCHE
CD NT 6732
New Tone / Aug '96 / ADA / Impetus

Moebius

DOUBLE CUT (Moebius & Beerbohm)
CD SKYCD 3091
Sky / May '95 / Greyhound / Koch / Vital/SAM

RASTAKRAUT PASTA/MATERIAL (Moebius & Plank)
CD SKYCD 32/105-106
Sky / Jun '97 / Greyhound / Koch / Vital/SAM

STRANGE MUSIC (Moebius & Beerbohm)
CD SKYCD 870305
Sky / Jun '96 / Greyhound / Koch / Vital/SAM

TONSPUREN
CD SKYCD 3083
Sky / Feb '95 / Greyhound / Koch / Vital/SAM

ZERO SET (Moebius & Plank/Neumer)
CD SKYCD 3085
Sky / Feb '95 / Greyhound / Koch / Vital/SAM

Moer, Paul

PLAYS THE MUSIC OF ELMO HOPE (Moer, Paul Trio)
CD FSR 5008CD
Fresh Sound / Jul '96 / Discovery / Jazz Music

Moffatt, Hugh

DANCE ME OUTSIDE (Moffatt, Hugh & Katy)
It's been decided / We'll sweep out the ashes in the morning / On the borderline / I don't believe you've met my baby / Dance me outside / Right over me / La Luna / Making new / Walking on the moon / Dark end of the street
CD PH 1144CD
Philo / '92 / ADA / CM / Direct

HEART OF A MINOR POET
CD WM 1047CD
Watermelon / Aug '96 / ADA / Direct

LIVE AND ALONE
CD BRAM 1991182
Brambus / Nov '93 / ADA

LOVING YOU
When you held me in your arms / Mama Rita / Old flames (can't hold a candle to you) / Words at twenty paces / Slow movin' freight train / No stranger to the blues / Loving you / Tomorrow is a long time / Carolina star / Jack and Lucy / Roll with weather
CD PH 1111CD
Philo / '88 / ADA / CM / Direct

TROUBADOUR
Way love is / Rose of my heart / I'll leave the rest to you / Somewhere in Kansas / How could I love her so much / Roses, love and promises / Hard times come again no more / Praise the Lord and send the money / Devil took the rest / Old songs / For Mary
CD BD 500CD
Breakdown / Feb '90 / Pinnacle

WOGNUM SESSIONS, THE (Moffatt, Hugh Trio)
CD SCR 32
Strictly Country / Dec '94 / ADA / Direct

Moffatt, Katy

CHILD BRIDE
Child bride / In a moment / Lonely avenue / Look out it must be love / Playin' fool / We ran / You better move on / Anna / Settin' the woods on fire
CD PH 1133CD
Philo / '90 / ADA / CM / Direct

MIDNIGHT RADIO
CD RTMCD 81
Round Tower / Jun '96 / Avid/BMG

WALKIN' ON THE MOON
Walkin' on the moon / I'm sorry darlin' / If anything comes to mind / Papacita (Mama Rita) / Mr. Banker / Borderline / Fire in your

eyes / I'll take the blame / Hard time on Easy street / I know the difference now
CD RTM 59CD
Round Tower / Jun '97 / Avid/BMG

Moffett, Cody

EVIDENCE
CD CD 83343
Telarc / Oct '93 / Conifer/BMG

Mofungo

BUGGED
CD SST 191CD
SST / May '93 / Plastic Head

Mogel

SCREAM
CD KAMEL 016
Kamel / Oct '96 / Cargo

Moggsway

EDGE OF THE WORLD
Change brings a change / All out of luck / Gravy train / Fortune town / Highwire / Saving me from myself / Mother Mary / House of pain / It's a game / History of flames / Spell on you / Totaled
CD RR 88042
Roadrunner / Jul '97 / PolyGram

Mogwai

TEN RAPID
CD TWA 05CD
Jetset / Jun '97 / Cargo / Greyhound

Mohamed, Pops

HOW FAR HAVE WE COME
CD BW 088
B&W / Feb '97 / New Note/Pinnacle / SRD / Vital/SAM

Mohead, John

LULA CITY LIMITS
CD OKRATONE 4961
Okratone / Aug '95 / ADA / Direct

Moher

OUT ON THE OCEAN
CD CBMCD 013
Cross Border Media / Jan '95 / ADA / Direct / Grapevine/PolyGram

Mohiuddin, Dagar Zia

RAGA YAMAN
CD NI 5276
Nimbus / Sep '94 / Nimbus

Moholo, Louis

BUSH FIRE (Moholo, Louis & Evan Parker Quintet)
CD OGCD 009
Ogun / May '97 / Cadillac / Jazz Music / Wellard

VIVA LA BLACK
CD OGCD 006
Ogun / Sep '94 / Cadillac / Jazz Music / Wellard

Moiseyev Dance Co.

RUSSIAN FOLK DANCES
CD MCD 71310
Monitor / Jun '93 / CM

Moist

SILVER
Push / Believe me / Kill for you / Silver / Freaky be beautiful / Break her down / Into everything / Picture Elvis / Machine punch through / This shrieking love / Low low low
CD CDCHR 6080
Chrysalis / Sep '94 / EMI

Moist Fist

MOIST FIST
CD RR 1212
Rise / Jul '93 / Pinnacle

Moistboyz

MOISTBOYZ
CD GR 004CD
Grand Royal / Apr '97 / Cargo / Plastic Head

MOISTBOYZ VOL.2
It ain't rude / Secondhand smoker / Lazy and cool / Rock, stock and barrel / Man of the year / American made and duty free / Crank / Powervice / Keep the fire alive / Good morning America
CD GR 037CD
Grand Royal / Nov '96 / Cargo / Plastic Head

Moity, Francoise

OPENING NIGHT
CD 829372
BUDA / Feb '97 / Discovery

Mojave 3

ASK ME TOMORROW
Love songs on the radio / Sarah / Tomorrow's taken / Candle song 3 / You're beautiful / Where is the love / After all / Pictures / Mercy
CD BAD 5013CD
4AD / Oct '95 / RTM/Disc

Mojo

TRA MOR
Dial y dail / Rhy hwyr / Byd yn bwysicach na dyn / Chwilio am yr hen fflam / Tro ar ol tro / Chwilio am dy galon / Dawnsio o flaen dy delyn / Gwyr y craig / Sefyll yn f'unfan / Daw'r cyflawn yn rhydd / Eiliad mewn einioes / Pan fo'r cylch yn cau / Byd mewn crud / I sycharth yn ol
CD SCD 2137
Sain / Nov '96 / ADA / Direct / Greyhound

Mojos

EVERYTHING'S ALRIGHT
CD 8209622
London / Jan '90 / PolyGram

Mokave

AFRIQUE
Sun bone / Africa 3/2 / Fragements/Whispers / Parable / Gloria's step / Bugle Ann / Afrique / Mr. Moore's neighbourhood / Country
CD AQCD 1024
Audioquest / Sep '95 / ADA / New Note/Pinnacle

Mokenstef

AZZ IZZ
Sex in the rain / Just be gentle / Azz izz / He's mine / Don't go there / Stop callin' me / It happens / Laid back / Let him know / It goes on / I got him all the time
CD 5273642
Def Jam / Sep '95 / PolyGram

Mola, Tony

BRAGADA
Pega pega / Tribal / Abracadabra / Vem benzinho / Arma som / Tem dende / Baby volta pra mim / De gray / Abebe / Pisa na barata
CD BJAC 50062
Blue Jackel / Sep '97 / New Note/Pinnacle

Moland, Joey

PILGRIM, THE
CD RCD 10212
Rykodisc / Jun '92 / ADA / Vital

Molard, Patrick

ER BOLOM KOH (Molard, Patrick & Y. Le Bihan)
CD GWP 007CD
Diffusion Breizh / Jul '95 / ADA

PIOBAIREACHD
CD GWP 003CD
Gwerz / Aug '93 / ADA / Discovery

Moleque De Rua

STREET KIDS OF BRAZIL
Pregoes do Rio / Rap do moleque / Louco e triste / Zumbi / Nao vou pagar pra ser boiada / Dor de dente / Herodes / O sosia / Filosofia do bom malandro / Assaltar papai noel / Ze do Brazil / Ensaio geral
CD MOL 91002
Cramworld / Aug '96 / New Note/Pinnacle

Molest

MILKFISH
CD PCD 023
Progress / Nov '95 / Cargo / Plastic Head

Moller, Ale

HASTEN OCH TRANAN
CD AM 732
Amigo / May '96 / ADA / Cadillac / CM / Wellard

VIND
Klavaheilagt / Skalhallingar / Gauketrail/ Vigstadmoin / Lugum leik / Jakup lom / Mikaelidagen/Kladdlaten / Finn hanses ganglat / Tre stromningar / Fodelsedagsvisan/ Gratlaten / Fars lilla / Liabekken/Gammelhusin/Sylfest mork / Mans nerhole / Munnharpevals / Gjermundhalling / Drang jerkpolska / Jubelskagget / Kopmanpolska / Guns brudvals / Havamal
CD XOU 106CD
Xource / May '97 / ADA / Direct

Molloy, Matt

CONTENTMENT IS WEALTH (Molloy, Matt & Sean Keane)
CD GLCD 1058
Green Linnet / Jun '93 / ADA / CM / Direct / Highlander / Roots

HEATHERY BREEZE
CD SHAN 79064CD
Shanachie / Aug '93 / ADA / Greensleeves / Koch

MATT MOLLOY
CD LUNCD 004
Mulligan / Aug '94 / ADA / CM

SHADOWS ON STONE
Morning thrush / Crib of perches/Carmel Mahoney Mulhaire's / Wind in the woods / Garret Barry's jig/Paddy Rafferty's favourite / Mulvihill's/Wallop the spot / Mason's apron / Fig for a kiss/Poll Ha'penny/Merry sisters / Chinese lake reflections / Music of the seals / Banshee / Sirius reel / Humours of Max / Babbling brook / Galway piper/ Sligo polka / Skylark/Finbar Dwyer's
CD CDVE 930
Venture / May '97 / EMI

STONY STEPS
McFadden's favourite / Boys of the town / City of Savannah / Primrose lass mullinger races / Parting of friends / Stony steps/Michael Dwyers's favourite / Mrs. Kenny's barndance / Paddy Murphy's wife / Jig of slurs / O Rathaille's grave / Miss Mcguiness/Reel of mullinavat / Frank Roche's favourite / Johnny 'Watt' Henry's favourite / Gravel walk / Slip jig
CD CCF 18 CD
Claddagh / May '88 / ADA / CM / Direct

Molly Hatchet

DEVIL'S CANYON
Down from the mountain / Rolling thunder / Devil's canyon / Heartless land / Never say never / Tatanka / Come hell or high water / Look in your eyes / Eat your heart out / Journey / Dreams I'll never see
CD SPV 08544352
SPV / Aug '96 / Koch / Plastic Head

LIGHTNING STRIKES TWICE
CD SPV 08544342
SPV / Dec '96 / Koch / Plastic Head

NO GUTS NO GLORY
What does it matter / Ain't even close / Sweet dixie / Fall of the peacemakers / What's it gonna take / Kinda like love / Under the gun / On the prowl / Both sides
CD 4736932
Epic / Feb '97 / Sony

Moloney, Mick

3 WAY STREET (Moloney, Mick & Eugene O'Donnell & Seamus Egan)
CD GLCD 1129
Green Linnet / Jul '93 / ADA / CM / Direct / Highlander / Roots

MICK MOLONEY WITH EUGENE O'DONNELL (Moloney, Mick & Eugene O'Donnell)
Joseph Baker / John Dwyer's reel/Lasses of Castlebar / Killin's fairy hill / Limerick rake / Clar hornpipe/Pride of Moyvane/Humours of Newcastle West / Blackthorn stick/Poet Carney / Bantry girl's lament / Fairie's hornpipe / Winnie Greene's reel/Boston boys / John of dreams / Kilkenny races / Sean Reid's reel/Toss the feathers / Paddy O'Brien's jig/King of the pipers / Irish maid
CD GLCD 1010
Green Linnet / Oct '88 / ADA / CM / Direct / Highlander / Roots

STRINGS ATTACHED
My love is in America/Lisdoonvarna reel / Arthur Darley's reel/Over the hills to Runbush / Munster grass/Peacock's feathers / Gooseberry bush/Charlie Mulvihill's reels / Loftus Jones / Dunmore lassies/McFadden's handsome daughter / Off to Puck Fair / Ricky's white fence/Top of the stairs / Bush on the hill / Bellharbour reel / Miss Lyon's fancy / Tom of the hill / Jackson's morning brush/Paddy Reynold's dream / Coyle's piano reels
CD CDGL 1027
Green Linnet / Oct '88 / ADA / CM / Direct / Highlander / Roots

THERE WERE ROSES
Ballad of Jack Dolan / Allastromm's/Julia Clifford's / Drimin Donn Dilis (Dear brown cow) / Redican's mother/Gan ainm/Blast of wind / Almost every circumstance / I will leave this town / There were roses / Fair haired cassidy/Paddy Gavin/Priest's boots / Commodore/Charleston reel / Mickey dam / Harvey Street hornpipe/Birds/O'Connor's frolics / Here I am from Donegal
CD GLCD 1057
Green Linnet / Oct '88 / ADA / CM / Direct / Highlander / Roots

UNCOMMON BONDS (Moloney, Mick & Eugene O'Donnell)
St. Brendan's fair Isle / Road to Dunmore / Bow legged tailor/Galway jig/April fool/ O'Lochlainn's / Miss Fogarty's christmas cake / Sean McGlynn's mazurka / Bonny blue-eyed Nancy / O'Hara, Hughes, McCreesh and Sands / Blackbird and hen/ Keane's farewell to Nova Scotia / Mary in the morning / Farewell my gentle harp / Muldoon the solid man / Curlew's reel/Derry reel/Hanly's / Bay of Biscay
CD GLCD 1053
Green Linnet / Oct '88 / ADA / CM / Direct / Highlander / Roots

Molsky, Bruce

BIG HOEDOWN (Molsky, Bruce & Big Hoedown)
Sugar babe / Five miles out of town / Pretty saro / Half past four / Wagoner's lad / Shove the pig's foot a little bit further into the fire / John Henry / Rocky mountain / Paddy won't you drink some good old cider / Robert's serenade / Old paint / We'll all go to Heaven when the devil goes blind / Shady grove / Train on the island/Golden chain tree / Blue tail fly / Clyde's hiccups
CD ROUCD 0421
Rounder / Jul '97 / ADA / CM / Direct

LOST BOY
CD ROUCD 361
Rounder / Feb '96 / ADA / CM / Direct

Molton, Flora

UNITED STATES - GOSPEL (Molton, Flora & Eleanor Ellis)
CD C 580053
Ocora / May '94 / ADA / Harmonia Mundi

Moment

MOD GODS
CD TANGCD 10
Tangerine / Mar '96 / RTM/Disc

Moments

GREATEST HITS
Lovely way she loves / My thing / If I didn't care / Nine times / To you with love / Girls / Jack in the box / Gotta find a way / All I have / Sexy Mama / Love on a two way street / With you / Life and breath / I do / Not on the outside / Lucky me / What's your name / Dolly my love / Look at me (I'm in love) / Girls (french lyrics)
CD NEMCD 614
Sequel / May '91 / BMG

MOMENTS TO REMEMBER (Every Hit & More/2CD Set)
Not on the outside / Sunday / I do / I'm so lost / Lovely way she loves / Love on a two-way street / If I didn't care / All I have / I can't help it / That's how it feels / Lucky me / To you with love / Thanks a lot / Just because he wants to make love (don't mean he loves you) / My thing / Gotta find a way / Sexy mama / Sho 'nuff boogie / What's your name / Girls pt.1 / Sweet sweet lady / Dolly my love / Jack in the box / Look at me (I'm in love) / Nine times / With you / (We) don't cry out loud / I don't wanna go / Oh I could have loved you / It don't rain in my backyard / Just to spend some time / Gonna keep you busy / Sleep won't come / More than that / So in love / We finally found us / If you could be my sweet baby / Lady in blue / I may be right, I may be wrong / I've got to keep my head
CD Set DEEPD 021
Deep Beats / Apr '97 / BMG

Momus

20 VODKA JELLIES
CD CDMRED 133
Cherry Red / Sep '96 / Pinnacle

CIRCUS MAXIMUS
Lucky like St. Sebastian / Lesson of Sodom / John The Baptist Jones / King Solomon's song and mine / Little Lord Obedience / Day the circus came to town / Rape of Lucretia / Paper wraps rock / Rules of the game of quoits
CD ACME 2CD
El / Jun '97 / Pinnacle

HIPPOPOTAMOMUS
CD CRECD 097
Creation / May '94 / 3mv/Vital

HOLD BACK THE NIGHT
CD CRECD 52
Creation / Nov '89 / 3mv/Vital

MONSTERS OF LOVE
CD CRECD 059
Creation / May '94 / 3mv/Vital

PHILOSOPHY OF MOMUS
Toothbrushead / Madness of Lee Scratch Perry / It's important to be trendy / Quark and Charm, the robot twins / Girlish boy / Yokohama Chinatown / Withinity / K's diary / Virtual Valerie / Red pyjamas / Cabinet of Kuniyoshi Kaneko / Slide projector lie detector / Microworlds / Complicated / I had a girl / Philiosophy of Momus / Loneliness of lift music / Paranoid acoustic seduction machine / Sadness of things
CD CDBRED 119
Cherry Red / May '95 / Pinnacle

POISON BOYFRIEND
CD CRECD 021
Creation / Apr '88 / 3mv/Vital

SLENDER SHERBERT (Readings Of My Early Years)
Complete history of sexual jealousy / Guitar lesson / Closer to you / Homosexual / Charm of innocence / Lucky like St Sebastian / I was a maoist intellectual / Lifestyles of the rich and famous / Angels are voyeurs

/ Hotel Marquis De Sade / Gatecrasher / Hairstyle of the devil / Bi shonen / Angels reprise
CD _______ CDBRED 123
Cherry Red / Oct '95 / Pinnacle

TENDER PERVERT
CD _______ CRECD 036
Creation / Nov '88 / 3mv/Vital

TIMELORDS
CD _______ CRECD 151
Creation / Oct '93 / 3mv/Vital

ULTRACONFORMIST (Live Whilst Out Of Fashion)
Sinister themes / Last of the window cleaners / Ladies understand / Cape and stick gang / Ultraconformist / Mother In Law / La catrina / Cheques in the post / Spy on the moon / Forests
CD _______ MONDE 3CD
Cherry Red / Jun '97 / Pinnacle

VOYAGER
CD _______ CRECD 113
Creation / Jun '92 / 3mv/Vital

Mona Lisa

11-20-79
CD _______ 5242442
4th & Broadway / Jul '96 / PolyGram

Monaco

MUSIC FOR PLEASURE
What do you want from me / Shine / Sweet lips / Buzz gum / Blue / Junk / Billy bones / Happy Jack / Tender / Sedona
CD _______ 5372422
Polydor / Jun '97 / PolyGram

Monastery

MONASTRY/ANARCHUS (Monastery/ Anarchus)
CD _______ SLAP 152
Slap A Ham / Mar '93 / Cargo / Greyhound / Plastic Head

Monastyr

NEVER DREAMING
CD _______ MN 03CD
Nuclear Blast / Jan '95 / Plastic Head

Mondo Grosso

INVISIBLE MAN
CD _______ 99 2135
Ninetynine / Jul '96 / Timewarp

LIVE AND REMIXED
CD _______ 99124CD
Ninetynine / Nov '96 / Timewarp

MARBLE
CD _______ 99 2125
Ninetynine / Jul '96 / Timewarp

MONDO GROSSO
CD _______ 99 2122
Ninetynine / Jul '96 / Timewarp

Mondo Topless

50,000 DOLLAR HAND JOB
CD _______ 36T 0001CD
360 Twist / Jul '97 / Greyhound

Mondonga, Lomani

LA PLEINE LUNE DES ELEPHANTS
CD _______ AT 8009
Night & Day / Apr '97 / ADA / Direct / Discovery

Mondschein Trio

AUF GEHT'S BEIM
CD _______ 15251
Laserlight / Nov '91 / Target/BMG

Money Mark

MARK'S KEYBOARD REPAIR
Pretty pain / No fighting / Ba ba ba boom / Have clav will travel / Don't miss the boat / Sunday garden Blvd / Insects are all around us / Scenes from / Poet's walk / Spooky / Cry / Flute / Hand in your head / That's for sure / Stevie / Time lapse / Sly / Sometimes / Latin
CD _______ MW 034CD
Mo Wax / Aug '95 / PolyGram / Vital

THIRD VERSION
Sometimes you gotta make it alone / Revolt of the octopi / Slow flames / Hard ass / From the beginning to the end / Function / World lesson pt. 2 / Inner laugh / Grade / Mark's keyboard repair
CD _______ MW 043CD
Mo Wax / Mar '96 / PolyGram / Vital

Monger, Eileen

LILTING BANSHEE, THE (Airs & Dances For Celtic Harp)
King of the fairies / Lilting banshee / O South wind / Great high wind / Wild geese / Bonnie Portmore / Morning dew / Ivy leaf / Limerick's lamentation / Give me your hand / Neil Gow's lament / Farewell to Craigie Dhu / Fingal's cave
CD _______ CDSDL 348
Saydisc / Mar '94 / ADA / Direct / Harmonia Mundi

Moniars

EVEN GRANNY WAS DANCING
CD _______ CRAICD 62
Crai / Feb '96 / ADA / Direct

Y GORAU O DDAU FYD
CD _______ CRAICD 045
Crai / Dec '94 / ADA / Direct

Monica

MISS THANG
Miss Thang / Don't take it personal (just one of dem days) / Like this and like that / Get down / With you / Skate / Angel / Woman in me / Tell me if you still care / Let's straighten it out / Before you walk out of my life / Now I'm gone / Why I love you so much / Never can say goodbye / Forever always
CD _______ 75444370062
Rowdy / Sep '95 / BMG

Monifah

MOODS...MOMENTS
Intro / You / It's alright / You don't have to love me / Nobody's body / Don't waste my time / Lay with you / Interlude / I miss you (come back home) / All I want / You've got my heart / Everything you do / You should have told me / Jesus is love / I miss you (come back home)
CD _______ UPTD 53004
Universal / May '96 / BMG

Monk & Canatella

CARE IN THE COMMUNITY
Darkus twisted / Out of here / Flying high / Apology / Roughead / Forthcoming / Chelsea smile / This time it's different / Top yourself / Lucy Gray / I can water my plants / Trout
CD _______ COTCD 005
Cup Of Tea / Apr '97 / Vital

Monk, Meredith

BOOK OF DAYS
Early morning melody / Dawn / Traveller 4 / Churchyard entertainment / Afternoon melodies / Field/Clouds / Dusk / Eva's song / Evening / Travellers / Jewish storyteller/ Dance/Dream / Plague / Madwoman's vision / Cave song
CD _______ 8396241
ECM / Apr '90 / New Note/Pinnacle

DO YOU BE
Scared song / I don't know / Window in 7's / Double fiesta / Do you be / Panda chant 1 / Memory song / Panda chant 11 / Quarry lullaby / Shadow song / Astronaut anthem / Wheel
CD _______ 8317822
ECM / Jul '87 / New Note/Pinnacle

DOLMEN MUSIC
Gotham lullaby / Travelling / Biography / Tale / Dolmen music
CD _______ 8254592
ECM / Oct '85 / New Note/Pinnacle

Monk, Thelonious

5 BY MONK BY 5
CD _______ OJCCD 362
Original Jazz Classics / Feb '92 / Complete/Pinnacle / Jazz Music / Wellard

ALONE IN SAN FRANCISCO
CD _______ OJCCD 231
Original Jazz Classics / Feb '92 / Complete/Pinnacle / Jazz Music / Wellard

AND THE JAZZ GIANTS
Bemsha swing / Crepuscule with Nellie / Nutty / I mean you / Pea eye / In walked Bud / Little Rootie Tootie / Played twice / San Francisco holiday
CD _______ FCD 60018
Fantasy / Apr '94 / Jazz Music / Pinnacle / Wellard

AT THE BLACKHAWK
CD _______ OJCCD 305
Original Jazz Classics / Feb '92 / Complete/Pinnacle / Jazz Music / Wellard

AT TOWN HALL
CD _______ OJCCD 135
Original Jazz Classics / Feb '92 / Complete/Pinnacle / Jazz Music / Wellard

BEMSHA SWING
CD _______ ATJCD 5966
All That's Jazz / Jul '92 / Jazz Music / THE

BEST OF THELONIOUS MONK, THE
Thelonious / Ruby my dear / Well you needn't / April in Paris / Monk's mood / In walked Bud / 'Round midnight / Evidence / Misterioso / Epistrophy / I mean you / Four in one / Criss cross / Straight no chaser / Ask me now / Skippy
CD _______ BNZ 261
Blue Note / Mar '91 / EMI

BIG BAND AND QUARTET IN CONCERT (2CD Set)
Bye-ya / I mean you / Evidence / Epistrophy / When it's darkness on the delta / Played twice / Misterioso / Light blue / Oskat / Four in one
CD Set _______ 4768982
Columbia / Aug '94 / Sony

BLUE MONK
CD _______ JHR 73501
Jazz Hour / Sep '93 / Cadillac / Jazz Music / Target/BMG

BLUE MONK (Blue Note Plays Monk's Music) (Various Artists)
Bemsha swing: *Peterson, Ralph Trio* / Rocky mount: *Tracey, Stan Octet* / Monk's dream: *Young, Larry* / Monk in wonderland: *Moncur, Grachan III* / Blue Monk: *Tyner, McCoy & Bobby Hutcherson* / 'Round midnight: *Evans, Gil* / Round midnight: *Gonzales, Babs & Jimmy Smith* / Epistrophy: *Taylor, Art* / Straight no chaser: *Three Sounds* / Well you needn't: *Rubalcaba, Gonzala* / Hat & beard: *Dolphy, Eric*
CD _______ CDP 8354712
Blue Note / Oct '95 / EMI

BRILLIANT CORNERS (Monk, Thelonious & Sonny Rollins)
CD _______ OJCCD 262
Original Jazz Classics / Feb '92 / Complete/Pinnacle / Jazz Music / Wellard

COMPLETE BLUE NOTE RECORDINGS, THE (4CD Set)
Humph / Evonce (alt. take) / Evonce / Suburban eyes / Suburban eyes (alt. take) / Thelonious / Nice work if you can get it (alt. take) / Nice work if you can get it / Ruby my dear (alt. take) / Ruby my dear / Well you needn't / Well you needn't (alt. take) / April in Paris (alt. take) / April in Paris / Off minor / Introspection / In walked Bud / Monk's mood / Who knows / 'Round midnight / Who knows (alt. take) / All the things you are / I should care (alt. take) / I should care / Evidence / Misterioso / Misterioso (alt. take) / Epistrophy / I mean you / Four in one / Criss cross (alt. take) / Eronel / Straight no chaser / Ask me now / Ask me now (alt. take) / Willow weep for me / Skippy / Skippy (alt. take) / Hornin' in (alt. take) / Hornin' in / Sixteen (first take) / Sixteen (second take) / Carolina moon / Let's cool one / I'll follow you / Reflections / Crepuscule with Nellie / Trinkle tinkle
CD Set _______ CDP 8303632
Blue Note / Oct '94 / EMI

COMPLETE RIVERSIDE RECORDINGS 1955-1961, THE (15CD Set)
It don't mean a thing if it ain't got that swing / Sophisticated lady / I got it bad and that ain't good / Black and tan fantasy / Mood indigo / I let a song go out of my heart / Solitude / Caravan / Liza / All the clouds'll roll away / Memories of you / Honeysuckle rose / Darn that dream / Tea for two / You are too beautiful / Just you, just me / Ba-lue Bolivar ba-lues are / Pannonica / Pannonica / Brilliant corners / Bemsha swing / I surrender dear / I don't stand a ghost of a chance with you / I don't stand a ghost of a chance with you / I should care / I should care / I should care / 'Round midnight / Round midnight / April in Paris / I'm getting sentimental over you / Monk's mood / Monk's mood / Functional / Functional / All alone / Crepuscule with Nellie / Crepuscule with Nellie / Blues for tomorrow / Off minor / Off minor / Abide with me / Crepuscule with Nellie / Crepuscule with Nellie / Epistrophy / Epistrophy / Well you needn't / Well you needn't / Ruby my dear: *Monk, Thelonious & Coleman Hawkins* / Ruby my dear: *Monk, Thelonious & John Coltrane* / Nutty / Trinkle tinkle / Straight no chaser / Straight no chaser / Rhythm-a-ning / I mean you / I mean you / I mean you / Round midnight / Decidedly / Decidedly / Sweet and lovely / Coming on the Hudson / In orbit / One foot in the gutter / Trust in me / Let's cool one / Pea eye / Argentia / Moonlight fiesta / Buck's business / Flugelin' the blues / Very near blues / Evidence / Blues five spot / In walked Bud/Epistrophy / Nutty / Blue five spot / Let's cool one / In walked Bud / Misterioso / Epistrophy / I walked Bud / Blue Monk / Unidentified solo piano / Bye-ya/Epistrophy / Round midnight / Bye-ya/Epistrophy / Light blue / Coming on the Hudson / Rhythm-a-ning / Just a gigolo / Blue Monk / Evidence / Epistrophy / Rhythm-a-ning / Monk's mood / Friday the 13th / Little rootie tootie / Off minor / Thelonious / Crepuscule with Nellie / Little rootie tootie / Played twice / Played twice / Played twice / Straight no chaser / Ask me now / I mean you / Jackie-ing / Round lights / Pannonica / Blue Monk / Ruby my dear / There's danger in your eyes Cherie / Cherie / There's danger in you eyes cherie / Everything happens to me / Reflections / Remember / Bluehawk / You took the words right out of my heart / San Francisco holiday / Just you, just me / Round midnight / San Francisco holiday / I'm getting sentimental over you / Evidence / Epistrophy / Epistrophy / Four in one / Let's call this / Round midnight / San Francisco holiday / Four in one / Epistrophy / Well you needn't / Crepuscule with Nellie / Jackie-ing / Body and soul / Off minor / April in Paris / I mean you / Rhythm-a-ning / Just a gigolo / Hackensack / Epistrophy / I'm getting sentimental over you / Jackie-ing / Body and soul / Straight no chaser / Crepuscule with Nellie / Bemsha swing / San Fransisco holiday / Rhythm-a-ning / Epistrophy
CD Set _______ RCD 0222
Riverside / Nov '96 / Cadillac / Complete/ Pinnacle / Jazz Music

COMPOSER, THE
'Round midnight / Bemsha swing / Rhythm-a-ning / Reflections / Straight no chaser / Brilliant corners / Ruby my dear / Well you needn't / Blue monk / Criss cross / Crepuscule with Nellie
CD _______ 4633382
Sony Jazz / Jan '95 / Sony

ESSENTIAL THELONIOUS MONK, THE
CD _______ 4685712
Sony Jazz / Jan '95 / Sony

EVIDENCE
Rhythm-a-ning / Ruby my dear / Bright Mississippi / 'Round midnight / Evidence / Jackie-ing / Stuffy / Blue monk
CD _______ FCD 105
Esoldun / Jan '88 / Target/BMG

FIRST EUROPEAN CONCERT '61, THE
CD _______ MRCD 120
Magnetic / Sep '91 / TKO Magnum

GENIUS OF MODERN MUSIC VOL.1
'Round midnight / Off minor / Ruby my dear / I mean you / April in Paris / In walked Bud / Thelonious / Epistrophy / Misterioso / Well you needn't / Introspection / Humph / Evonce / Evonce (alt. take) / Suburban eyes (alt. take) / Nice work if you can get it / Nice work if you can get it (alt. take) / Ruby my dear (alt. take) / Well you needn't (alt. take) / April in Paris (alt. take) / Monk's mood / Who knows / Who knows (alt. take)
CD _______ BNZ 244
Blue Note / Sep '92 / EMI

GENIUS OF MODERN MUSIC VOL.2
Carolina moon / Hornin' in / Skippy / Let's cool one / Suburban eyes / Evonce / Straight no chaser / Nice work if you can get it / Monk's mood / Who knows / Ask me now / Four in one / Criss cross (alt. take) / Eronel / Ask me now (alt. take) / Willow weep for me / Skippy (alt. take) / Hornin' in (alt. take) / Sixteen (first take) / Sixteen (second take) / I'll follow you
CD _______ CDP 7815112
Blue Note / Mar '95 / EMI

IN ACTION (Monk, Thelonious Quartet)
CD _______ OJCCD 103
Original Jazz Classics / '92 / Complete/ Pinnacle / Jazz Music / Wellard

IN ITALY
Jackie-ing / Epistrophy / Body and soul / Straight no chaser / Beshma swing / San Francisco holiday / Crepuscule with Nellie / Rhythm-a-ning
CD _______ OJCCD 488
Original Jazz Classics / Apr '93 / Complete/ Pinnacle / Jazz Music / Wellard

IN JAPAN 1963 (Monk, Thelonious Quartet)
Evidence / Blue monk / Just a gigolo / Bolivar blues / Epistrophy
CD _______ PRCDSP 202
Prestige / Aug '93 / Else / Total/BMG

IT'S MONK'S TIME
Lulu's back in town / Memories of you / Stuffy turkey / Brake's sake / Nice work if you can get it / Shuffle boil
CD _______ 4684052
Sony Jazz / Jan '95 / Sony

JAZZ MASTERS
CD _______ CDMFP 6300
Music For Pleasure / Mar '97 / EMI

JAZZ PORTRAITS
'Round midnight / Thelonious / Off minor / Well you needn't / Ruby my dear / Epistrophy / Evidence / Mysterioso / Ask me now / Criss cross / Straight no chaser / Hornin' in / Let's cool one / Little rootie tootie / Monk's dream / Bemesha swing / Reflections / Let's call this
CD _______ CD 14510
Jazz Portraits / May '94 / Jazz Music

LIVE AND RARE IN EUROPE - 1967
CD _______ JZCD 356
Suisa / Feb '92 / Jazz Music / THE

LIVE AT THE JAZZ WORKSHOP (2CD Set)
CD _______ 4691832
Sony Jazz / Jan '95 / Sony

LIVE IN PARIS 1967
Presentation A Francis / Ruby my dear / We see / Epistrophy / Oska T / Evidence / Blue monk / Epistrophy
CD _______ FCD 113
France's Concert / Jun '88 / BMG / Jazz Music

LIVE IN PARIS, 1964 VOL.1
CD _______ FCD 132
France's Concert / '89 / BMG / Jazz Music

LONDON COLLECTION VOL.1
Trinkle tinkle / Crepuscule with Nellie / Darn that dream / Little rootie tootie / Meet me tonight in dreamland / Nice work if you can

get it / My melancholy baby / Jackie-ing / Lover man / Blue sphere
CD BLCD 760101
Black Lion / Jun '88 / Cadillac / Jazz Music / Koch / Wellard

LONDON COLLECTION VOL.2
CD BLCD 760116
Black Lion / Oct '94 / Cadillac / Jazz Music / Koch / Wellard

LONDON COLLECTION VOL.3
CD BLCD 760142
Black Lion / Oct '90 / Cadillac / Jazz Music / Koch / Wellard

MEMORIAL ALBUM
CD MCD 47064
Milestone / Oct '93 / Cadillac / Complete/ Pinnacle / Jazz Music / Wellard

MISTERIOSO
CD 4684062
Sony Jazz / Jan '95 / Sony

MONK
CD 4684072
Sony Jazz / Jan '95 / Sony

MONK AND ROLLINS (Monk, Thelonious & Sonny Rollins)
CD OJCCD 592
Original Jazz Classics / Feb '92 / Complete/Pinnacle / Jazz Music / Wellard

MONK IN COPENHAGEN (Monk, Thelonious Quartet)
CD STCD 8283
Storyville / May '97 / Cadillac / Jazz Music / Wellard

MONK IN FRANCE
CD OJCCD 670
Original Jazz Classics / '93 / Complete/ Pinnacle / Jazz Music / Wellard

MONK ON TOUR IN EUROPE
Oska T / Epistrophy / Evidence / Blue monk / Monk's mood / We see / Hackensack / Lulu's back in town / I mean you / 'Round midnight
CD CDCHARLY 122
Charly / Jun '88 / Koch

MONK QUINTET
CD OJCCD 162
Original Jazz Classics / Feb '92 / Complete/Pinnacle / Jazz Music / Wellard

MONK'S BLUES
Let's cool one / Reflections / Rootie tootie / Just a glance at love / Brilliant corners / Consecutive seconds / Monk's point / Trinkle tinkle / Straight no chaser / Blue Monk / 'Round midnight
CD 4756982
Columbia / Feb '94 / Sony

MONK'S DREAM (1952-1956) (Monk, Thelonious Quartet)
Monk's dream / Body and soul / Bright Mississippi / Five spot blues / Bolivar blues / Just a gigolo / Bye ya / Sweet and lonely
CD 4600652
Sony Jazz / Jan '95 / Sony

MONK'S MUSIC
Abide with me / Well you needn't / Ruby my dear / Epistrophy / Crepuscule with Nellie
CD OJCCD 842
Original Jazz Classics / Feb '92 / Complete/ Pinnacle / Jazz Music / Wellard

MULLIGAN MEETS MONK (Monk, Thelonious & Gerry Mulligan)
'Round midnight / Rhythm-a-ning / Sweet and lonely / Decidedly / Straight no chaser / I mean you
CD OJCCD 301
Original Jazz Classics / Oct '92 / Complete/ Pinnacle / Jazz Music / Wellard

NEW YORK 1958 (Monk, Thelonious & Johnny Griffin)
CD CD 53112
Giants Of Jazz / Nov '92 / Cadillac / Jazz Music / Target/BMG

NONET LIVE, THE
CD LEJAZZCD 7
Le Jazz / Mar '93 / Cadillac / Koch

PIANO SOLO 1954 (Original Vogue Masters)
'Round midnight / Evidence / Smoke gets in your eyes / Well you needn't / Reflections / Wee see / Eronel / Off minor / Hackensack
CD 74321429242
Vogue / Apr '97 / BMG

ROUND MIDNIGHT
'Round midnight / Off minor / Mysterioso / Criss cross / Hornin' in well / You needn't / Ruby my dear / Let's cool one / Straight no chaser / Ask me now / Thelonious / Evidence / Epistrophy / Monk's dream / Little rootie tootie / Reflections / Blue monk / Let's call this / Bemesha swing / Rhythm-a-ning
CD CD 53008
Giants Of Jazz / Mar '92 / Cadillac / Jazz Music / Target/BMG
CD CD 56022
Jazz Roots / Aug '94 / Target/BMG

SAN FRANCISCO HOLIDAY
CD MCD 9199
Milestone / Oct '93 / Cadillac / Complete/ Pinnacle / Jazz Music / Wellard

SOLO MONK
CD 4712482
Sony Jazz / Jan '95 / Sony

STANDARDS
CD 4656812
Sony Jazz / Jan '95 / Sony

STRAIGHT NO CHASER
Locomotive / I didn't know about you / Straight, no chaser / Japanese folk song / Between the devil and the deep blue sea / We see / This is my story, this is my song / I didn't know about you / Green chimneys
CD CK 64886
Sony Jazz / Sep '96 / Sony

SWEET AND LOVELY
CD MCD 079
Moon / Dec '95 / Cadillac / Harmonia Mundi

THELONIOUS HIMSELF
April in paris / I don't stand a ghost of a chance with you / Functional / I'm getting sentimental over you / I should care / All alone / Monk's mood / 'Round midnight
CD OJCCD 254
Original Jazz Classics / Feb '92 / Complete/ Pinnacle / Jazz Music / Wellard

THELONIOUS MONK TRIO (Monk, Thelonious Trio)
CD OJCCD 102
Original Jazz Classics / Feb '92 / Complete/Pinnacle / Jazz Music / Wellard

THELONIUS MONK & JOHN COLTRANE (Monk, Thelonious & John Coltrane)
CD OJCCD 392
Original Jazz Classics / Feb '92 / Complete/Pinnacle / Jazz Music / Wellard

THIS IS JAZZ
'Round midnight / Well you needn't / Bemsha swing / Ruby my dear / Straight no chaser / Blue Monk / Rhythm-a-ning / Monk's dream / Misterioso / Epistrophy
CD CK 64625
Sony Jazz / May '96 / Sony

TRIO AND BLUE MONK VOL.2
CD CDJZD 009
Prestige / Nov '91 / Cadillac / Complete/ Pinnacle

UNDERGROUND
CD 4600662
Sony Jazz / Jan '95 / Sony

UNIQUE, THE
CD OJCCD 642
Original Jazz Classics / Feb '92 / Complete/Pinnacle / Jazz Music / Wellard

Monkees

BIRDS, BEES & THE MONKEES
CD 4509976562
Warner Bros. / Dec '94 / Warner Music

CHANGES
CD 4509976572
Warner Bros. / Dec '94 / Warner Music

HEADQUARTERS
CD 4509976622
Warner Bros. / Jan '95 / Warner Music

INSTANT REPLAY
CD 4509976612
Warner Bros. / Jan '95 / Warner Music

JUST US
CD ARTFULCD 6
Artful / Jan '97 / Pinnacle / Total/BMG

MONKEES PRESENT..., THE
CD 4509976602
Warner Bros. / Dec '94 / Warner Music

MONKEES' GREATEST HITS, THE
CD PLATCD 05
Platinum / '88 / Prism

MONKEES, THE
CD 4509976552
Warner Bros. / Dec '94 / Warner Music

MORE OF THE MONKEES
She / When love comes knockin' / Mary Mary / Hold on girl / Your Auntie Grizelda / Look out (here comes tomorrow) / Kind of girl I could love / Day we fell in love / Sometime in the morning / Laugh / I'm a believer
CD 4509976582
Warner Bros. / Dec '94 / Warner Music

PISCES, AQUARIUS, CAPRICORN & JONES LTD.
CD 4509976632
Warner Bros. / Jan '95 / Warner Music

POOL IT
Heart and soul / I'd go the whole wide world / Long way home / Secret heart / Gettin' in / I'll love you forever / Every step of the way / Don't bring me down / Midnight / She's movin' in with Rico / Since you went away / Counting on you
CD 8122721542
Rhino / Nov '95 / Warner Music

Monkey Beat

SHAKE
CD LUCKY 79207
Lucky Seven / Mar '95 / ADA / CM / Direct

Monkey Business

IN A TIME LIKE THIS
Much too much / Bad Daddy B / Money / Conga bop / Let your body go / No time / Love your neighbour / Tea for two / In a time like this
CD ME 000292
Soulciety/Bassism / Oct '95 / EWM

Monkey Island

MERE PRAWNS TO ME
CD ULR 001
Ultra Recordings / Feb '97 / SRD

Monkey Mafia

LIVE AT THE SOCIAL VOL.2 (Mixed By John Carter) (Various Artists)
Supa: *Dope, Kenny & The Mad Racket* / He ya hey: *Budha Baboons* / Gucci dance live: *Sam The Beast* / I'm the magnificent: *Special Ed* / Real McCoy (ah ah ah): *Rankin' Don* / Play wit fire: *Yard Boy Ten* / Bells of NY: *Slo Moshun* / That other hop hop track: *Bitch* / Here comes the hotstepper: *Kamoze, Ini* / A buen a ting: *DJ Doubles* / Ain't nothin' to it: *K-9 Posse* / Program: *Morales, David & The Bad Yard Club/Papa San* / Yeah: *Audioweb* / Come togther: *Transplant* / Request the style: *Top Cat* / Peckings: *Ballistic Brothers* / Opus Vol.2: *Bass Bin Twins* / Revenge of the Mekon: *Mekon & Mad Frankie Fraser* / Everybody thinks I'm high: *DJ Voodoo & The Liquid Method* / Sine eye: *Ragga Twins* / Assault 1: *Melting Pot* / Carry go bring home: *McGregor, Freddie* / Say Party: *Shut Up & Dance* / Mr. Loverman: *Shabba Ranks*
CD HVNLP 15CD
Heavenly / Aug '96 / 3mv/Pinnacle / BMG / Vital

Monkhouse

CAKEY PIG
CD DAMGOOD 55CD
Damaged Goods / Apr '95 / Shellshock/ Disc

DEAD ROOM/GLUE BAG (Monkhouse & Striknien DC)
CD REJ 1000003
Rejected / Aug '96 / Shellshock/Disc

FINAL INDIGNITY
CD REJ 1000006
Rejected / Dec '96 / Shellshock/Disc

Monks

SUSPENDED ANIMATION
Don't want no reds / Suspended animation / Don't bother me I'm a Christian / James Bondage / Grown ups / Oxford street / Cool way to live / Go / I can do anything you like / Plastic Max / King dong / Space fruit / Gold and silver / Lost in romance / Slimy gash / Beast in cages / Ann Orexia / Cybernetic sister
CD CYBVP 001CD
Cyberdisk / Jul '97 / Pinnacle

Monks Of Bodnath Monastery

TIBETAN RITUAL
Rituel du soir
CD PS 65183
PlayaSound / May '97 / ADA / Harmonia Mundi

Monks Of Zhihuasi Temple

BUDDHIST MUSIC OF THE MING DYNASTY
CD VICG 52592
JVC World Library / Mar '96 / ADA / CM / Direct

Monne, Joan

SON SONG
CD FSNT 010
Fresh Sound / Feb '96 / Discovery / Jazz Music

Mono

FORMICA BLUES
Life in mono / Silicone / Slimcea girl / Outsider / Disney town / Blind man / High life / Playboys / Penguin freud / Hello Cleveland
CD ECHCD 017
Echo / Aug '97 / EMI / Vital

Mono Junk

MIND WONDER
CD DUM 017CD
Dum / Jul '95 / Plastic Head

Mono Men

BENT PAGES
CD ANDA 215CD
Au-Go-Go / May '97 / Cargo / Greyhound / Plastic Head

LIVE AT TOM'S
CD ES 108CD
Estrus / Jun '95 / Cargo / Greyhound / Plastic Head

STOP DRAGGIN' ME DOWN
CD ESCD 1R
Estrus / Sep '94 / Cargo / Greyhound / Plastic Head

WRECKAGE
CD ESD 123
Estrus / Sep '94 / Cargo / Greyhound / Plastic Head

Mono Puff

UNSUPERVISED
Guitar was the case / Unsupervised, I hit my head / Don't break the heart / Nixon's the one / To serve mankind / Don't I have the right / Careless Santa / So long, mockingbird / Dr. Kildare / Hello hello / What bothers the spaceman / Devil went down to Newport / Distant antenna
CD RCD 10360
Rykodisc / Jun '96 / ADA / Vital

Monochrome Set

BLACK & WHITE MINSTRELS 1975-1979
CD CDMRED 118
Cherry Red / Jan '95 / Pinnacle

CHARADE
Overture / Forever young / Clover / Snow girl / My white garden / Her pain / Little noises / Crystal chamber / Girl / Angie / Talking about you / (I've got) No time (for girls) / Christine / Tilt
CD CDBRED 102
Cherry Red / Jan '93 / Pinnacle

DANTE'S CASINO
CD ASK 4CD
Vinyl Japan / '92 / Plastic Head / Vinyl Japan

ELIGIBLE BACHELORS
Jet set junta / I'll cry instead / On the 13th day / Cloud 10 / Mating game / March of the eligible bachelors / Devil rides out / Fun for all the family / Midas touch / Ruling class / Great barrier riff
CD SUMCD 4096
Summit / Feb '97 / Sound & Media

GOOD LIFE, THE
He's Frank / Martians go home / Straits of Malacca / Sugar plum / B-I-D spells bid / Alphaville / Heaven can wait / Goodbye Joe / Strange boutique / Strange boutique (reprise) / Jacob's ladder / Wallflower / Apocalypso / Mr. Bizarro / I'll cry instead / Espresso / 405 lines / Eine symphonie des grauns / Monochrome Set
CD MONDE 8CD
Richmond / Oct '92 / Pinnacle

HISTORY: 1978-1996
CD CDBRED 128
Cherry Red / May '96 / Pinnacle

MISERE
Milk and honey / Pauper / Dr. Robinson / Achilles / Leather jacket / Someone has been sleeping / Handsome boy / Ethereal one / UFO 10 / Integrate me / Twang 'em high
CD CDBRED 114
Cherry Red / May '94 / Pinnacle

TOMORROW WILL BE TOO LONG
Monochrome Set (I presume) / Lighter side of dating / Expresso / Puerto Rican fence climber / Tomorrow will be too long / Martians go home / Love goes down the drain / Ici les enfants / Etcetera stroll / Goodbye Joe / Strange boutique / Love zombies / O come all ye faithful (Adeste fidelis) / 405 lines / B-I-D spells bid / RSVP / Apocalypso / Karma suture / Man with the black moustache / Weird, wild, wonderful world of Tony Potts / In love, Cancer
CD CDOVD 458
Virgin / Feb '95 / EMI

TRINITY ROAD
Flame dials / All over / April dance affair / Bliss / Bar Madiera / Hob's end / Golden apples of the sun / Worst is yet to come / Two fits / Albert bridge / Hula honey / Snake-fingers / Mousetrap / Kissy kissy / I love Lambeth
CD CDBRED 122
Cherry Red / Sep '95 / Pinnacle

VOLUME, CONTRAST, BRILLIANCE...
Eine symphonie des grauns / Jet set junta / Love zombies / Silicon carne / Ruling class / Viva death row / Man with the black moustache / He's Frank / Fun for all the family / Lester leaps in / Ici les enfants / Fat fun / Alphaville / Avanti
CD CDBRED 47
Cherry Red / May '93 / Pinnacle

WESTMINSTER AFFAIR
Jet set junta / Cast a long shadow / Ruling class / Lester leaps in / Mating game / On the 13th day / March of the eligible bachelors / Devil rides out / Fun for all the family / Andiamo / Cowboy country / JDHANEY / Noise / Eine symphonie des grauns / Viva

death row / Jacob's ladder / Ici les enfants / Avanti
CD ACME 17 CD
El / Aug '88 / Pinnacle

Monolith

TALES OF THE MACABRE
Morbid curiosity / Sleep with the dead / Misery / Undead burial / Devoured from within / Locked in horror / Catalogue of carnage / Maceration
CD SOL 036CD
Vinyl Solution / Mar '93 / RTM/Disc

Monomorph

ALTERNATIVE FLUID
CD DIS 016CD
Disturbance / Sep '94 / Plastic Head / Prime

Monotonic

ELECTRALUX
CD HUK 002CD
Headhunter / Jun '97 / Cargo

Monro, Matt

CAPITOL YEARS, THE
Put on a happy face / I'm glad there's you / Laura / Real live girl / Born free / Wednesday's child / I'll take romance / If she walked into my life / Strangers in the night / In the arms of love / Here's to my lady / When Joanna loved me / You've got possibilities / People / Sunrise sunset / Man and a woman / And we were lovers / Georgy girl / On days like these / Come back to me
CD CZ 354
Capitol / Nov '90 / EMI

EMI YEARS, CAPITOL YEARS & THROUGH THE YEARS, THE (2CD Set)
My kind of girl / Portrait of my love / From Russia with love / Who can I turn to / Let's face the music and dance / Jeannie / April fool / Cheek to cheek / Softly as I leave you / Here and now / Love is a many splendoured thing / How little it matters, how little we know / Stardust / Small fry / Skylark / One morning in May / I get along without you very well / Memphis in June / Blue orchids / I have dreamed / Put on a happy face / I'm glad there is you / Laura / Real live girl / Born free / Wednesday's child / I'll take romance / If she walked into my life / Strangers in the night / In the arms of love / Here's to my lady / When Joanna loved me / You've got possibilities / People / Sunrise sunset / Man and a woman / We were lovers / Georgy girl / On days like these / Come back to me / As long as I am singing / Fools rush in / Ethel baby / Ebb tide / Hava nagila / Fly me to the moon / Good life / Autumn leaves / Did it happen / Maria / Let me sing a happy song / Spring is here / Spanish eyes / If you go away (no me dejes) / Come sta / Roses and roses / You made me so very happy / My way / This is all I ask / Party's over
CD Set MONRO 1
EMI / Feb '95 / EMI

GREAT GENTLEMEN OF SONG, THE
My kind of girl / I'm glad there is you / I get along without you very well / I'll take roamnce / When I fall in love / Laura / Time after time / Real live girl / Autumn leaves / Ebb tide / When Sunny gets blue / From Russia with love / Sweet Lorraine / Stardust / When Joanna loved me / This is all I ask / Good life / September song
CD CDP 8293942
Capitol / Aug '95 / EMI

HOLLYWOOD AND BROADWAY
Look for small pleasures / Stranger in paradise / Impossible dream / Apple tree / I'll only miss her when I think of her / Come back to me / Hello Dolly / Sunrise sunset / Walking happy / If she walked into my life / Put on a happy face / Till the end of time / Charade / Green leaves of summer / Second time around / Everybody's talkin' / Shadow of your smile / I've grown accustomed to her face / Chattanooga choo choo / Pretty Polly
CD CDMFP 6137
Music For Pleasure / Oct '94 / EMI

LOVE SONGS (2CD Set)
Softly as I leave you / Portrait of my love / Somewhere / From Russia with love / On days like these / Michelle / Speak softly love / My love and devotion / This time / Can this be love / When love comes along / I will wait for you / Time after time / Love walked in / And we were lovers / Time for love / Till then my love / With these hands / Let's face the music and dance / When I fall in love / Autumn leaves / Sweet Lorraine / Stardust / Didn't we / My kind of girl / And you smiled / Eye level theme / Cheek to cheek / Love is a many splendored thing / How little we know / Skylark / I have dreamed / Girl I love / I'm glad there is you / I'll take romance / Strangers in the night / Walk away / One day / Unchained melody / In the arms of love / Man and a woman / Hello young lovers / You light up my life / Maria / I've grown accustomed to her face / Precious moments / Let there be love / Real live girl / September song / You're sensational / All my loving / I get along without you very well / Fools rush in / In other words (fly me to the moon) / If you go away
CD Set CDTRBOX 256
Music For Pleasure / Jan '97 / EMI

MATT MONRO SINGS
I have dreamed / Who can I turn to / My friend, my friend / Love is a many splendoured thing / It's a breeze / Without the one you love / Once in every long and lonely while / All my loving / If this should be a dream / How soon / Exodus / Here and now / Friendly persuasion / Start living / Stardust / Small fry / How little it matters, how little we know / Nearness of you / Georgia on my mind / Skylark / One morning in May / I get along without you very well / Memphis in June / I guess it was you all the time / Blue orchids / Rockin' chair / You're sensational / Love walked in / Yesterday / Alfie / Hello, young lovers / Michelle / Softly as I leave you / Here, there and everywhere / Somewhere / From Russia with love
CD Set CDDL 1072
Music For Pleasure / May '91 / EMI

MATT SINGS MONRO (Monro, Matt Jr. & Matt Monro Sr.)
We're gonna change the world / Did it happen / More / You and me against the world / You've made me so very happy / For all we know / He ain't heavy, he's my brother / If i never sing another song / Long and winding road / On days like these / I'll never fall in love again / I close my eyes and count to ten / Jean / Didn't we
CD CDMFP 6279
Music For Pleasure / Nov '96 / EMI

MOMENT TO MOMENT (3CD Set)
Portrait of my love / My kind of girl / Yesterday / For mama / Why not now / Alfie / Cheek to cheek / Let's face the music and dance / Spring is here / Laura / Nearness of you / Green leaves of summer / Softly as I leave you / Sweet Lorraine / Everybody's talkin' / How little we know / Born free / Gonna build a mountain / Walk away / And you smiled / When love comes along / Didn't we / Hello dolly / Autumn leaves / Ebb tide / Shadow of your smile / For all we know / Love is a many splendoured thing / April fool / Moment to moment / Come sta / Here and now / Unchained melody / From Russia with love / My love and devotion / Without you / Georgia on my mind / Strangers in the night / With these hands / Sunrise sunset / Fools rush in / Fly me to the moon / Maria / Spanish eyes / If you go away (no me dejes) / You've made me so very happy / Answer me / My way
CD Set SA 871692
Disky / Sep '96 / Disky / THE

SOFTLY AS I LEAVE YOU
Born free / On days like these / Walk away / Softly as I leave you / Michelle / Who can I turn to / Love is a many splendoured thing / From Russia with love / One morning in May / For all we know / I have dreamed / All my loving / Stardust / Portrait of my love / Nearness of you / Unchained melody / Hello, young lovers / Alfie / September song
CD CDMFP 6003
Music For Pleasure / Oct '87 / EMI

THIS IS
Portrait of my love / Walk away / Time after time / Cheek to cheek / On a wonderful day like today / For once in my life / Laura / Girl I love / Choose / On days like these / Born free / Why not now / Moment to moment / Singin' in the rain / When Sunny gets blue / This is the life / You're gonna hear from me / Party's over / Who can I turn to / Softly as I leave you / From Russia with love / My kind of girl / Days of wine and roses / Precious moments / Ten out of ten / As long as she needs me / One day / Happy / Sweet Lorraine / Can this be love / Yesterday / Michelle / If she should come to you / You and me against the world / I'm glad I'm not young anymore / This way Mary / Happening / What to do / My love and devotion / Speak softly love
CD CDDL 1257
Music For Pleasure / Jan '94 / EMI

THIS IS THE LIFE/HERE'S TO MY LADY
I'm glad there's you / This is the life / You're gonna hear from me / I'll take romance / Strangers in the night / On a clear day (you can see forever) / Sweet Lorraine / My best girl / On a wonderful day like today / Merci cherie / Honey on the vine / When Joanna loved me / Real live girl / When sunny gets blues / Laura / People / Here's to my lady / Good life / You've got possibilities / Rain sometimes / Sweet talkin' Hannah / Nina never knew
CD CTMCD 107
EMI / Jan '97 / EMI

THROUGH THE YEARS
As long as I am singing / Fools rush in / Ethel baby / Ebb tide / Hava nagila / Fly me to the moon / Good life / Autumn leaves / Did it happen / Maria / Let me sing a happy song / Spring is here / Spanish eyes / If you go away (no me dejes) / Come sta / Roses and roses / You've made me so very happy / My way / This is all I ask / Party's over
CD CDEMS 1544
EMI / Feb '95 / EMI

TIME FOR LOVE, A
Portrait of my love / Softly as I leave you / Why not now / Can this be love / My kind of girl / When love comes along / Without you / Speak softly love / Wednesday's child / I will wait for you / Time after time / Love walked in / And we were lovers / Time for love / With these hands / Answer me / Till then my love / Man and a woman / On days like these / Didn't we / Alguien Canto (The music played) / Be my love / In the arms of love / You light up my life
CD CDMFP 6070
Music For Pleasure / Aug '89 / EMI

VERY BEST OF MATT MONRO, THE
Born free / Softly as I leave you / From Russia with love / On days like these / Walk away / Around the world / My love and devotion / Michelle / On a clear day (You can see forever) / Somewhere / Impossible dream / Gonna build a mountain / Who can I turn to / Portrait of my love / Speak softly love / My kind of girl / For mama / Yesterday / This time / We're gonna change the world
CD CDMFP 5568
Music For Pleasure / Aug '96 / EMI

Monroe, Bill

BLUEGRASS 1950-1958 (4CD Set)
Bluegrass ramble / New muleskinner blues / My little Georgia rose / Memories of you / I'm on my way to the old home / Alabama waltz / I'm blue, I'm lonesome / I'll meet you in church Sunday morning / Boat of love / Old fiddler / Uncle Pen / When the golden leaves begin to fall / Lord protect my soul / River of death / Letter from my darling / On the old Kentucky shore / Rawhide / Poison love / Kentucky waltz / Prisoner's song / Swing low, sweet chariot / Angels rock me to sleep / Brakeman's blues / When the cactus is in bloom / Sailors plea / My Carolina sunshine girl / Ben Dewberry's final run / Peach pickin' time in Georgia / Those gamblers blues / Highway of sorrow / Rotation blues / Lonesome truck driver's blues / Sugar coated love / You're drifting away / Cabin of love / Get down on your knees and pray / Christmas time's a coming / First whippoorwill / In the pines / Footprints in the snow / Walking in Jerusalem / Memories of Mother and Dad / Little girl and the dreadful snake / Country waltz / Don't put it off till tomorrow / My dying bed / Mighty pretty waltz / Pike County breakdown / Wishing waltz / I hope you have learned / Get up John / Sittin' alone in the moonlight / Plant some flowers by my grave / Changing partners / Y'all come / On and on / I believed in you darling / New John Henry blues / White House blues / Happy on my way / I'm working on a building / Voice from on high / He will set your fields on fire / Close by / Blue moon of Kentucky / Wheel hoss / Cheyenne / You'll find her name written there / Roanoke / Wait a little longer, please Jesus / Let the light shine down on me / Used to be / Tall timbers / Brown County breakdown / Fallen star / Four walls / Good woman's love / Cry cry darlin' / I'm sitting on top of the world / Out in the cold world / Roane Country prison / Goodbye old pal / In despair / Molly and tenbrooks / Come back to me in my dreams / Sally Jo / Brand new shoes / Lonesome road / I saw the light / Lord build me a cabin / Lord lead me on / Precious jewel / I'll meet you in the morning / Life's railway to heaven / I've found a hiding place / Jesus hold my hand / I am a pilgrim / Wayfaring stranger / Beautiful life / House of gold / Panhandle country / Scotland / Gotta travel on / No one but my darlin' / Big mon / Monroe's hornpipe
CD Set BCD 15423
Bear Family / Jul '89 / Direct / Rollercoaster / Swift

BLUEGRASS 1959-1969 (4CD Set)
When the phone rang / Tomorrow I'll be gone / Dark as the night, blue as the day / Stoney lonesome / Lonesome wind blues / Thinking about you / Come go with me / Sold down the river / Linda Lou / You live in a world all your own / Little Joe / Put my rubber doll away / Seven year blues / Time changes everything / Lonesome road blues / Big river / Flowers of love / It's mighty dark to travel / Bluegrass / Little Maggie / I'm going back to old Kentucky / Toy heart / Shady grove / Nine pound hammer / Live and let live / Danny boy / Cotton fields / Journey's end / John Hardy / Bugle call rag / Old Joe Clark / There was nothing we could do / I was left on the street / Cheap love affair / When the bees are in the hive / Big ball in Brooklyn / Columbus / Stockade blues / Blue Ridge mountain blues / How will I explain about you / Foggy river / Old country Baptising / I found the way / This world is not my home / Way down deep in my soul / Drifting too far from the shore / Going home / On the Jericho road / We'll understand it better / Somebody touched me / Careless love / I'm so lonesome I could cry / Jimmie brown the newsboy / Pass me not / Gloryland, way / Farther along / Big Sandy river / Baker's breakdown / Darling Corey / Cindy / Master builder / Let me rest at the end of the day / Salt Creek / Devil's dream / Sailor's hornpipe / Were you there / Pike county breakdown / Shenandoah breakdown / Santa Claus / I'll meet you in church Sunday morning / Mary at the home place / Highway of sorrow / One of God's sheep / Roll on Buddy roll on / Legend of the Blue Ridge mountains / Last old dollar / Bill's dream / Louisville breakdown / Never again / Just over in the Gloryland / Fire on the mountain / Long black veil / I live in the past / There's an old old house / When my blue moon turns to gold again / I wonder where you are tonight / Turkey in the straw / Pretty fair maiden in the garden / Log cabin in the lane / Paddy in the turnpike / That's alright Mama / It makes no difference now / Dusty Miller / Midnight on the stormy deep / All the good times are past and gone / Soldier's joy / Blue night / Grey eagle / Gold rush / Sally Goodin / Virginia darlin' / Is the blue moon still shining / Train 45 / Kentucky mandolin / I want to go with you / Crossing the Cumberlands / Walls of time / I haven't seen Mary in years / Fireball male / Dead march / Cripple creek / What about you / With body and soul / Methodist preacher / Walk softly on my heart / Tall pines / Candy gal / Going up Caney / Lee wedding tune / Bonnie / Sweet Mary and the miles between
CD Set BCD 15529
Bear Family / Feb '91 / Direct / Rollercoaster / Swift

BLUEGRASS 1970-1979 (4CD Set)
McKinley's march / Texas gallop / Road of life / It's me again Lord / Beyond the gate / I will sing for the glory of God / Kentucky waltz / Girl in the blue velvet band / Lonesome moonlight waltz / Tallahassee / Summertime is past and gone / Rocky road blues / Mule skinner blues / Katy hill / Poor white folks / Old grey mare come tearing out / Kiss me waltz / Jenny Lynn / Heel and toe polka / Milenburg joys / Sweetheart you done me wrong / Banks of the Ohio / Tall pines / Mother's only sleeping / Foggy mountain top / Love please come home / What would you give in exchange / When the golden leaves begin to fall / Walls of time / My old Kentucky and you / Mule skinner blues / You won't be satified that way / Uncle pen / Blue moon of Kentucky / Ole slewfoot / Sweet little miss blue eyes / Please be my love / I wish you knew / Train 45 / Bonny / When my blue moon turns ot gold again / Hit parade of love / Mary Ann / Sunny side of the mountain / Freeborn man / Tennessee / Rollin' in my sweet baby's arms / Feudin' banjos / Ballad of Jed Clampett / I wonder where you are tonight / Orange blossom special (instrumental) / Fiddler roll call / Down yonder / Soldier's joy / Grey eagle / Swing low, sweet chariot / Clinging to a saving hand / Show me the way / Jerusalem ridge / Ashland breakdown / Mary Jane, won't you be mine / Old old house / Watson's blues / Thank God for Kentucky / Reasons why / Weary traveller / My cabin in Caroline / No place to pillow my head / My sweet blue eyed darling / Monroe's blues / First whippoorwill / Lucky lady / My Louisiana love / Christmas time's a coming / Texas blue-bonnet / Sunset trail / My sweet memory / She's young and I'm growing old / Blue goose / My Florida sunshine / Wabash cannonball / Hard times have been here (but they've gone) / Six feet under the ground / Who's gonna shoe your pretty little feet / Jake Satterfield / Muddy waters / Corine Corina / Have a feast here tonight / Golden river / I'm going back to Old Kentucky / Those memories of you / Intro (Watermelon hangin) / John Henry / Dog house blues / Old mountaineer / Little cabin home on the hill / Orange blossom special / Molly and the Tenbrooks medley: Little Magggie, Train 45 / Little girl and the dreadful snake / In despair / Y'all come
CD Set BCD 15606
Bear Family / Apr '94 / Direct / Rollercoaster / Swift

BLUEGRASS BREAKDOWN (Monroe, Bill & His Bluegrass Boys)
Bluegrass breakdown / No letter in the mail / Uncle Pen / Orange blossom special / Footprints in the snow / I saw the light / Shady grove / Muleskinner blues / Shenandoah breakdown / Prison song / Blue moon of Kentucky / Can't you hear me calling / Nine pound hammer
CD PRACD 4003
Prairie / Jun '97 / Henry Hadaway

OFF THE RECORD VOL.1 (Live Recordings 1956-1969) (Monroe, Bill & His Bluegrass Boys)
CD SF 40063CD
Smithsonian Folkways / Nov '94 / ADA / Cadillac / CM / Direct / Koch

OFF THE RECORD VOL.2 (Live Duets From 1963-1980) (Monroe, Bill & Doc Watson)
CD SFWCD 40064
Smithsonian Folkways / Aug '95 / ADA / Cadillac / CM / Direct / Koch

TRUE LIFE BLUES (The Songs Of Bill Monroe - An All Star Tribute) (Various Artists)
CD SHCD 2209
Sugar Hill / Nov '96 / ADA / CM / Direct / Koch / Roots

Monroe, Marilyn

COLLECTION, THE
CD COL 042
Collection / Mar '95 / Target/BMG

DIAMOND COLLECTION, THE
CD WWRCD 6002
Wienerworld / Jun '95 / THE

DIAMONDS ARE A GIRL'S BEST FRIEND
CD WMCD 5675
Woodford Music / Feb '93 / THE

DIAMONDS ARE A GIRL'S BEST FRIEND
CD CDGFR 135
Tring / Jun '92 / Tring

ESSENTIAL COLLECTION, THE
CD Set LECD 621
Wisepack / Apr '95 / Conifer/BMG / THE

ESSENTIAL RECORDINGS, THE
I wanna be loved by you / Diamonds are a girl's best friend / Some like it hot / I'm gonna file my claim / You'd be surprised / She acts like a woman should / Fine romance / Bye bye baby / Do it again / Running wild / When love goes wrong / Lazy / I'm through with love / River of no return / Heatwave / Kiss / My heart belongs to daddy / Little girl from Little Rock / Happy birthday Mr. President
CD MCCD 062
Music Club / '92 / Disc / THE

KISS
CD CD 3555
Cameo / Mar '96 / Target/BMG

LEGENDS IN MUSIC
CD LECD 067
Wisepack / Jul '94 / Conifer/BMG / THE

MARILYN MONROE
CD 15443
Laserlight / Jan '93 / Target/BMG

MARILYN MONROE
CD DVGH 7072
Deja Vu / May '95 / THE

MARILYN MONROE
I wanna be loved by you / Two little girls from Little Rock: *Monroe, Marilyn & Jane Russell* / I'm gonna file my claim / My heart belongs to Daddy / Runnin' wild / Fine romance / You'd be surprised / Diamonds are a girl's best friend / Bye bye baby / I'm through with love / Specialisation: *Monroe, Marilyn & Frankie Vaughan* / Heatwave / Do it again / When love goes wrong, nothing goes right: *Monroe, Marilyn & Jane Russell* / After you get whet you want, you don't want it / River of no return / Lazy / Kiss / When I fall in love / Happy Birthday Mr. President
CD 399534
Koch Presents / May '97 / Koch

MARILYN MONROE ESSENTIALS
CD LECDD 621A
Wisepack / Aug '95 / Conifer/BMG / THE

PORTRAIT: MARILYN MONROE
I wanna be loved by you / Diamonds are a girl's best friend / Little girl from Little Rock / When love goes wrong / Bye bye baby / My heart belongs to Daddy / I'm gonna file my claim / River of no return / Do it again / Kiss / You'd be surprised / This is a fine romance / I'm through with love / Heatwave / Running wild / Lazy / Happy birthday Mr. President
CD PLATCD 3905
Platinum / Dec '88 / Prism

SOME LIKE IT HOT
Diamonds are a girl's best friend / Man chases a girl / Every baby needs a da da daddy / Happy birthday Mr. President / Incurably romantic / Down in the meadow / Some like it hot / I found a dream / Anyone can see I love you / Specialization / Heatwave / Ladies of the chorus / When I fall in love / Let's make love / Bye bye baby / Fine romance / One silver dollar / That old black magic / There's no business like show business / I wanna be loved by you
CD HADCD 153
Javelin / May '94 / Henry Hadaway / THE

Monroe, Vaughan

VAUGHAN MONROE 1943 (Monroe, Vaughan Orchestra)
CD CCD 045
Circle / Jun '96 / Jazz Music / Swift / Wellard

VAUGHAN MONROE 1943-1944 (Monroe, Vaughan Orchestra)
CD CCD 116
Circle / Jun '96 / Jazz Music / Swift / Wellard

Monsoon

THIRD EYE
Wings of the dawn / Tomorrow never knows / Third eye and Tikka TV / Eyes / Shauti / Ever so lonely / You can't take me with you / And I you / Kashmir / Watchers of the night
CD PIPCD 001
Great Expectations / Jun '89 / BMG

Monster Magnet

DOPES TO INFINITY
Dopes to Infinity / Negasonic teenage warhead / Look to your orb for warning / All friends and kingdom come / Ego, the living planet / Blow 'em off / Third alternative / I control, I fly / King of Mars / Dead Christmas / Theme from Masterburner / Vertigo / Forbidden planet
CD 5403152
A&M / Feb '95 / PolyGram

SPINE OF GOD
CD GR 0172
Glitterhouse / Jun '92 / Avid/BMG

Monster Zero

WRECK
CD EVRCD 13
Eve / Nov '92 / Grapevine/PolyGram

Monsterland

AT ONE WITH TIME
At one with time / Jane Wiedlin used to be a Go-Go / Your touch is uncomfortable to me / Chewbacca / Blank / Girlfriend on drugs
CD 959282
Seed / Mar '94 / Vital

DESTROY WHAT YOU LOVE
Insulation / Rid of you / Lobsterhead / Nobody loves you / Car on fire / Twice at the end / At one with time / Fish eye / Crashing teenage crush / Angel scraper / Bursitis
CD 142362
Seed / Nov '93 / Vital

Monstertruckfive

COLUMBUS OHIO
CD SFTRI 367CD
Sympathy For The Record Industry / Aug '95 / Cargo / Greyhound / Plastic Head

Monstrosity

IMPERIAL DOOM
CD NB 055CD
Nuclear Blast / Feb '92 / Plastic Head

MILLENNIUM
CD NB 208CD
Nuclear Blast / Nov '96 / Plastic Head

Montana, Dick

DEVIL LIED TO ME, THE (Montana, 'Country' Dick)
CD 7422511
Last Call / Nov '96 / Cargo / Direct / Discovery

Montanablue

CHAINED TO AN ELEPHANT
CD 57291144
Pinpoint / '90 / SRD

Montand, Yves

SINGER (Original Recordings 1948-1955)
Le gamin de Paris / C'est si bon / Clopin clopant / Quand un soldat / La goualante du pauvre Jean / Le tete a l'ombre / Grands boulevards / La galerien / Les feuilles mortes / Le musicien / Actualites / Rue lepic / Le roi renaud de guerre revient / La complainte de madrin / J'avions recu commandement / Aux marches du palais / Le roi a fait battre tambour / Chanson du capitaine (Je me suis t'engage) / Le soldat mecontent / Les canuts / Le temps de cerises / La butte rouge / Girofle, girofla / Le chant de la liberation (Le chant des partisans)
CD CDEMS 1486
EMI / May '93 / EMI

SONGS OF PARIS
CD MCD 61535
Monitor / Jun '93 / CM

Montaro, Francisco

STRICTLY BALLROOM - CHA CHA (Montaro, Francisco Ensemble)
Mr. Lucky / 'Til there was you / Por favor / Patricia / Teach me tonight / Guantanamera / Sway / Dansaro yellow days (la mentira) / I just called to say I love you
CD QED 145
Tring / Nov '96 / Tring

STRICTLY BALLROOM - FAVOURITES (Montaro, Francisco Ensemble)
Mr. Lucky / Frenesi / Copy cabana / All my lovin' / Blue Tango / I only have eyes for you / Miami Beach Rhumba / Blue Danube waltz / Begin the beguine / Matilda
CD QED 154
Tring / Nov '96 / Tring

STRICTLY BALLROOM - FOX TROT (Montaro, Francisco Ensemble)
I only have eyes for you / April in Paris / Our love is here to stay / All the things you are / It had to be you / Entertainer / Sweet Caroline / After the lovin' / Morning train / Michelle
CD QED 148
Tring / Nov '96 / Tring

STRICTLY BALLROOM - LATIN (Montaro, Francisco Ensemble)
Marina / Begin the beguine / Preciosa / Matilda / Manha de carnival / How insensitive / Mary Ann medley / Wedding samba / Tico tico / Espana cani
CD QED 151
Tring / Nov '96 / Tring

STRICTLY BALLROOM - MAMBO (Montaro, Francisco Ensemble)
Asi mambo / Mambo inn / Tequila / Mas que nada / Come a little bit closer / St. Thomas / Say si si / Frenesi / Mambo jambo / Karma chameleon
CD QED 150
Tring / Nov '96 / Tring

STRICTLY BALLROOM - RHUMBA (Montaro, Francisco Ensemble)
Miami Beach Rhumba / Siboney / Flamingo / Besame mucho / Que reste-t-il / And I love her / If / Serenata / Speak low / Cherish
CD QED 152
Tring / Nov '96 / Tring

STRICTLY BALLROOM - SAMBA (Montaro, Francisco Ensemble)
Anna / Delicado / Quando quando / Samba de orpheu / Copy cabana / Brazil / El cambanchero / One note samba / Amor / It had better be tonight
CD QED 146
Tring / Nov '96 / Tring

STRICTLY BALLROOM - TANGO (Montaro, Francisco Ensemble)
Blue Tango / Orchids in the moonlight / Softly as in a morning sunrise / La paloma / Jalousie / No other love / Tango of roses / Adios muchachos / Hernandos hideaway / La cumparsita
CD QED 149
Tring / Nov '96 / Tring

STRICTLY BALLROOM - TRIPLE SWING (Montaro, Francisco Ensemble)
Honky tonk / Kansas City / Leroy Brown / Work song / I'm getting sentimental over you / All my lovin' / On the sunny side of the street / Walk between the raindrops / Wake me up before you go go / I ain't got nobody/just a Gigolo
CD QED 153
Tring / Nov '96 / Tring

STRICTLY BALLROOM - WALTZ (Montaro, Francisco Ensemble)
Petite waltz / Blue Danube waltz / Somewhere my love / French waltz medley / Baubles bangles and beads / Hello young lovers / Do I hear a waltz / Girl next door / Moon river / Could I have the dance
CD QED 147
Tring / Nov '96 / Tring

Montbel, Eric

CHABRETAS, LES CORNEMUSES A MIROIRS DU LIMOUSIN
CD ALCD 156
Al Sur / Nov '96 / ADA / Discovery

L'ART DE CORNEMUSE VOL.1
CD ARN 60347
Arion / Feb '97 / ADA / Discovery

Monte Cazazza

POWER VERSUS WISDOM
CD DFX 015CD
Side Effects / Apr '97 / Plastic Head / World Serpent

Monte, Marisa

GREAT NOISE, A
Arrepio: *McLean, Jackie* / Magla Malabaris / Chuva no Brejo / Cerebro eletronico / Tempos modernos / Maraca / Panis et circencis / De noi te na Cama / Beija eu / Give me love / Aindo me lembro / A Menina Danca / Danca de Soliao / Ao meu redor / Bem de leve / Segue o seco / Xote das meni nas
CD CDP 8533532
Metro Blue / Nov '96 / EMI

ROSE AND CHARCOAL
Maria de Verdade / Na Estrada / Ao meu redor / Seque o seco / Pale blue eyes / Danca da Solidao / De Mais / Ninguem / Alta noite / O Ceu / Bem leve / Balanca pema / Enquanto isso / Esta melodia
CD CDP 8300802
Blue Note / Oct '94 / EMI

Montego Joe

MONTEGO JOE
CD PRCD 24139
Prestige / Jul '93 / Cadillac / Complete/ Pinnacle

Monteiro, Alcimar

VAQUEJADAS BRASILEIRAS
CD 829162
BUDA / Feb '96 / Discovery

Montero, Germaine

GERMAINE MONTERO: SINGS
CD Set LDX 274959/60
La Chant Du Monde / Mar '93 / ADA / Harmonia Mundi

Monterose, J.R.

LITTLE PLEASURE, A (Monterose, J.R. & Tommy Flanagan)
CD RSRCD 109
Reservoir Music / Dec '94 / Cadillac

Montez, Chris

LET'S DANCE
Let's dance / You're the one / It takes two / Tell me (it's not over) / No no no / Monkey fever / I feel like dancing / Rock 'n' blues / Chiquita mia / He's been leading you on / In an English town / Say you'll marry me / Shoot that curl / Let's do the limbo / All you had to do (was tell me) / It's not puppy love / My baby loves to dance / Love me / I ran / Some kinda fun
CD MOCD 3008
More Music / Feb '95 / Sound & Media

LET'S DANCE (The Monogram Sides)
Let's dance / No no no / Some kinda fun / It takes two / I ran / It's not puppy love / Shoot that curl / My baby loves to dance / All you had to do (was tell me) / Rockin' blues / Chiquita Mia / You're the one / Let's do the limbo / Tell me (it's not over) / I feel like dancing / He's been leading you on / In an English town (in a Turkish town) / Monkey fever / Say you'll marry me / Love me
CD CDCH 369
Ace / Mar '92 / Pinnacle

Montez, Manuelo

STRICTLY DANCING: PASODOBLES (Montez, Manuelo Orchestra)
CD 15334
Laserlight / May '94 / Target/BMG

Montgomery Brothers

GROOVE YARD
Back to back / Groove yard / If I should lose you / Delirium / Just for now / Doujie / Remember
CD OJCCD 139
Original Jazz Classics / Jun '96 / Complete/ Pinnacle / Jazz Music / Wellard

Montgomery, Buddy

LIVE AT MAYBECK RECITAL HALL VOL.15
Since I fell for you / Man I love / Cottage for sale / Who cares / Night has a thousand eyes / How to handle a woman / What'll I do / You've changed / Money blues / By myself / This time I'll by sweeter / Soft winds / My lord and master/Something wonderful
CD CCD 4494
Concord Jazz / Jan '92 / New Note/ Pinnacle

SO WHY NOT
CD LCD 15182
Landmark / Apr '89 / New Note/Pinnacle

TIES OF LOVE
CD LCD 1512
PolyGram TV / Aug '88 / PolyGram

Montgomery, James

OVEN IS ON, THE (Montgomery, James Band)
CD CDTC 1145
Tonecool / May '94 / ADA / Direct

Montgomery, John Michael

JOHN MICHAEL MONTGOMERY
CD 7567827282
Warner Bros. / Apr '95 / Warner Music

KICKIN' IT UP
Be my baby tonight / Full time love / I swear / She don't need a band to dance / All in my heart / Friday at five / Rope the moon / If you've got skin / Oh how she shines / Kick it up
CD 7567825592
Warner Bros. / Feb '92 / Warner Music

Montgomery, Little Brother

1930-36
CD DOCD 5109
Document / Nov '92 / ADA / Hot Shot / Jazz Music

BAJEZ COPPER STATION
CD BLU 10022
Blues Beacon / Jun '93 / New Note/ Pinnacle

CHICAGO - THE LIVING LEGENDS
Home again blues / Up the country blues / Saturday night function / Michigan water blues / Sweet daddy (your mam's done gone mad) / Prescription for the blues / 44 Vicksburg / Trouble in mind / Riverside boogie / Oh daddy blues / Somethin' keep worryin' me
CD OBCCD 525
Original Blues Classics / Apr '94 / Complete/Pinnacle / Wellard

GOODBYE MISTER BLUES
CD DD 663
Delmark / May '94 / ADA / Cadillac / CM / Direct / Hot Shot

LITTLE BROTHER MONTGOMERY 1930-54
CD _______________ BDCD 6034
Blues Document / Apr '93 / ADA / Hot Shot / Jazz Music

TASTY BLUES
CD _______________ OBCCD 554
Original Blues Classics / Jan '94 / Complete/Pinnacle / Wellard

Montgomery, Marian

FOR THE LOVE OF MERCER VOL.1
CD _______________ ELGIN 01
Elgin / Jan '97 / TKO Magnum

FOR THE LOVE OF MERCER VOL.2
CD _______________ ELGIN 02
Elgin / Jan '97 / TKO Magnum

I GOTTA RIGHT TO SING
In the dark / 'Deed I do / Love dance / People will say we're in love / That old black magic / You came a long way from St. Louis / Mean to me / Ol' man river / Georgia on my mind / Yesterday's wine / I gotta right to sing the blues / He's my guy / Lady is a tramp
CD _______________ JHCD 003
Ronnie Scott's Jazz House / Jan '94 / Cadillac / Jazz Music / New Note/Pinnacle / TKO Magnum

MAKIN' WHOOPEE (Montgomery, Marian & Mart Rodgers Manchester Jazz)
Way down yonder in New Orleans / You took advantage of me / Mean to me / Shake it and break it / Kansas City Man blues / If I ever cease to love / I get the blues when it rains / Sobbin' blues / Dinah / After you've gone / Then it changed / Canal Street blues / My melancholy baby / You're a sweetheart / I'm crazy 'bout my baby / Makin' whoopee / Froggie Moore / Love me or leave me / Riverboat shuffle
CD _______________ OWSCD 2602
Bowstone / May '93 / Cadillac / Wellard

MELLOW
Where or when / Dancing in the dark / I've got you under my skin / Long ago and far away / I thought of you last night / Never let me go / When the world was young / Speak low / It's not over / Skylark / Ill wind / Secret love / Why can't you behave / I guess I'll hang my tears out to dry / Remind me / I got lost in his arms / Why did I choose you
CD _______________ C5HCD 594
See For Miles/C5 / Aug '96 / Pinnacle

NICE AND EASY (Montgomery, Marian & Richard Rodney Bennett)
Ain't no sunshine / It amazes me / Man I love / Loads of love / I wonder what became of me / Partners in crime / In the wee small hours of the morning / Summertime / Nice work if you can get it/Easy to love / But not for me / Blues in the night / If you can't keep the one you love / Bye bye blackbird
CD _______________ JHCD 011
Ronnie Scott's Jazz House / Jan '94 / Cadillac / Jazz Music / New Note/Pinnacle / TKO Magnum

SOMETIMES IN THE NIGHT
Man I love / Somebody loves me / Just in time / People that you never get to love / My foolish heart / Maybe (if he knew me) / Tell me softly / You're the best love / I don't want to walk without you / But love (that's another game) / Very thought of you / You've come a long way from St Louis / Not funny / Tender trap / You are my lucky star / Sometimes in the night
CD _______________ C5CD 532
See For Miles/C5 / May '89 / Pinnacle

Montgomery, Monty

MASSIVE, ARE YOU READY
CD _______________ NAK 61112
Naked Language / Feb '94 / Koch

Montgomery, Roy

TEMPLE IV
CD _______________ KRANK 009
Kranky / Mar '97 / Cargo / Greyhound

Montgomery, Wes

ALTERNATIVE, THE
Born to be blue / Come rain or come shine / Fried pies / Besame mucho / Way you look tonight / Stairway to the stars / Jingles / Back to back / Movin' along / Body and soul / Tune up
CD _______________ MCD 47065
Milestone / Jul '94 / Cadillac / Complete/ Pinnacle / Jazz Music / Wellard

ARTISTRY OF WES MONTGOMERY, THE
'Round midnight / Four on six / Klactoveesedstein / Says you / Remember / Cotton tail / Jingles / Cariba / Tune up / Dearly beloved / Freddie the freeloader
CD _______________ FCD 60019
Fantasy / Oct '93 / Jazz Music / Pinnacle / Wellard

BODY AND SOUL
Sonny boy / Wes easy blues / Solo ballad in A major / Gone with the wind / Broadway / Body and soul / I'll remember April / Here's that rainy day / Words from Wes
CD _______________ JHAS 604
Ronnie Scott's Jazz House / May '96 / Cadillac / Jazz Music / New Note/Pinnacle / TKO Magnum

BOSS GUITAR
Besame mucho / Dearly beloved / Days of wine and roses / Trick bag / Canadian sunset / Fried pies / Breeze and I / For Heaven's sake
CD _______________ OJCCD 261
Original Jazz Classics / Feb '92 / Complete/ Pinnacle / Jazz Music / Wellard

CALIFORNIA DREAMIN'
CD _______________ 8278422
Verve / Mar '97 / PolyGram

COMPLETE RIVERSIDE RECORDINGS, THE (12CD Set)
'Round midnight / Satin doll / Satin doll / Missile blues / Missile blues / Jingles / Whisper not / End of a love affair / Too late now / Ecaroh / Yesterdays / Airegin / West Coast blues / Four on six / D natural blues / In your own sweet way / Mister Walker / Polka dots and moonbeams / Gone with the wind / Sack o' woe / Work song / Scrambled eggs / Pretty memory / Fall out / My heart stood still / Mean to me / Violets for your furs / I've got a crush on you / Compulsion / Terrain / Klactoveesedstein / Ursula / West Coast blues / Don't explain / Lolita / Chant / Azule serape / Never will I marry / Yours is my heart alone / Au privare / Au privare / Tune up / Tune up / Body and soul / Body and soul / Body and soul / Sandu / Sandu / So do it / So do it / Movin' along / Moin' along / Movin' along / I don't stand a ghost of a chance with you / Says you / Doujie / Doujie / Just for now / Groove yard / Heart strings / Remember / Delirium / Bock to bock / Bock to bock / If I should lose you / If I should lose you / Doujie / Somethin' like Bags / I'm just a lucky so and so / Cotton tail / Twisted blues / I wish I knew / Repetition / While we're young / One for my baby (and one more for the road) / Darn that dream / Darn that dream / And then I wrote / Double deal / No hard feelings / Love walked in / Love walked in / Lois Ann / Enchanted / Love for sale / Stranger in paradise / Mambo in chimes / Mambo in chimes / Lamp is low / Blue Roz / Jingles / Jingles / Stairway to the stars / Stairway to the stars / Stablemates / Stablemates / Sam Sack / Sam Sack / SKJ / SKJ / Delilah / Delilah / Come rain or come shine / Born to be blue / Blue 'n' boogie / Cariba / SOS / Come rain or come shine / Born to be blue / Full house / Cariba / Blue 'n' boogie / SOS / I've grown accustomed to her face / In the wee small hours of the morning / Pretty blue / Girl next door / Girl next door / God bless the child / God bless the child / My romance / Prelude to a kiss / Prelude to a kiss / All the way / Somewhere / Tune up / Tune up / Tune up / Baubles, bangles and beads / Baubles, bangles and beads / Trick bag / Trick bag / Days of wine and roses / Canadian sunset / Dearly beloved / For Heaven's sake / Besame mucho / Fried pies / Fried pies / Breeze and I / Moanin' / Dreamsville / Freddie Freeloader / Movin' along / Mi cosa / For all we know / Way you look tonight / Way you look tonight / Yesterday's child / Geno / Dangerous / Lolita / Blues riff / Blues riff / Moanin'
CD Set _______________ 12RCD 44082
Riverside / Nov '96 / Cadillac / Complete/ Pinnacle / Jazz Music

ENCORES VOL.1 (Body & Soul)
Body and soul / So do it / Movin' along / Doujie / Blue Roz / Stablemates / Sam Sack / SKJ
CD _______________ MCD 9252
Milestone / Aug '96 / Cadillac / Complete/ Pinnacle / Jazz Music / Wellard

ENCORES VOL.2 (Blues 'N' Boogie)
Born to be blue / Blue 'n' boogie / Cariba / Girl next door / God bless the child / Prelude to a kiss / Tune-up / Baubles, bangles and beads / Trick bag / Movin' along
CD _______________ MCD 92612
Milestone / Mar '97 / Cadillac / Complete/ Pinnacle / Jazz Music / Wellard

FINGERPICKIN'
Sound carrier / Bud's beaux arts / Back to back / Lois Ann / All the things you are / Fingerpickin' / Stranger in Paradise / Baubles, bangles & beads / Not since Ninevah
CD _______________ CDP 8379872
Pacific Jazz / Jul '96 / EMI

FULL HOUSE (Montgomery, Wes & Johnny Griffin)
CD _______________ OJCCD 106
Original Jazz Classics / Feb '92 / Complete/Pinnacle / Jazz Music / Wellard

FULL HOUSE
CD _______________ LEJAZZCD 13
Le Jazz / Jun '93 / Cadillac / Koch

FUSION
CD _______________ OJCCD 368
Original Jazz Classics / Feb '92 / Complete/Pinnacle / Jazz Music / Wellard

GUITAR ON THE GO (Montgomery, Wes Trio)
Way you look tonight (alternate take) / Way you look tonight / Dreamsville / Geno / Missile blues / For all we know / Fried pies / (Unidentified solo guitar)
CD _______________ OJCCD 489
Original Jazz Classics / Apr '93 / Complete/ Pinnacle / Jazz Music / Wellard

JAZZ MASTERS
Goin' out of my head / Impressions / My one and only love / Tequila / Bumpin' / What the world needs now is love / No blues / Shadow of your smile / Caravan / Bumpin' on sunset / Twisted blues / Oh you crazy moon / Con alma / Thumb
CD _______________ 5198262
Verve / Apr '93 / PolyGram

JAZZ MASTERS
CD _______________ CDMFP 6302
Music For Pleasure / Mar '97 / EMI

LIVE 1961
CD _______________ MRCD 124
Magnetic / Sep '91 / TKO Magnum

LIVE IN EUROPE: WES MONTGOMERY
CD _______________ CD 214 W972
Philology / Feb '92 / Cadillac / Harmonia Mundi

MOVIN' ALONG
Movin' along / Tune up / I don't stand a ghost of a chance with you / Sandu / Body and soul / So do it / Says you
CD _______________ OJCCD 892
Original Jazz Classics / Feb '92 / Complete/ Pinnacle / Jazz Music / Wellard

MOVIN' WES
West coast blues / Caravan / Movin' Wes / Moca flor / Matchmake / Theodora / In and out / Born to be blue / People / Phoenix love theme
CD _______________ 8100452
Verve / Mar '89 / PolyGram

PORTRAIT OF WES
CD _______________ OJCCD 144
Original Jazz Classics / Feb '92 / Complete/Pinnacle / Jazz Music / Wellard

PRIVATE RECORDINGS
CD _______________ JZCD 378
Suisa / Jun '93 / Jazz Music / THE

ROUND MIDNIGHT
Four on six / Girl next door / Mr. Walker / Here's that rainy day / 'Round midnight / Impressions
CD _______________ LEJAZZCD 34
Le Jazz / Sep '94 / Cadillac / Koch

SILVER COLLECTION, THE
If you could see me now / Impressions / Four on six / Unit 7 / Mellow mood / James and Wes / What's new / Misty / Portrait of Jennie / Here's that rainy day
CD _______________ 8234482
Verve / Nov '84 / PolyGram

STRAIGHT NO CHASER
CD _______________ BS 18002
Bandstand / Jul '96 / Swift

TEQUILA
Tequila / Little child / What the world needs now is love / Big hurt / Bumpin' on sunset / How insensitive / Thumb / Midnight mood / Wives and lovers / Bumpin' on sunset / Big hurt / Tequila
CD _______________ 8316712
Verve / Aug '87 / PolyGram

TWISTED BLUES (Montgomery, Wes Quartet)
CD _______________ JHR 73569
Jazz Hour / Nov '93 / Cadillac / Jazz Music / Target/BMG

WES MONTGOMERY TRIO, THE (Montgomery, Wes Trio)
'Round midnight / Yesterdays / End of a love affair / Whisper not / Ecaroh / Satin doll / Missile blues / Too late now / Jingles
CD _______________ OJCCD 342
Original Jazz Classics / Feb '92 / Complete/ Pinnacle / Jazz Music / Wellard

Montoliu, Tete

BODY AND SOUL
CD _______________ CDBLC 760212
Black Lion / Apr '96 / Cadillac / Jazz Music / Koch / Wellard

BODY AND SOUL (Montoliu, Tete Trio)
CD _______________ CDG 813
Helix / Nov '96 / Discovery

EN EL SAN JUAN
CD _______________ NM 15690CD
Fresh Sound / Apr '97 / Discovery / Jazz Music

MAN FROM BARCELONA, THE (Montoliu, Tete Trio)
Concierto de Aranjuez / Stella by starlight / Easy living / Autumn leaves / For you my love / Tune up / I fall in love too easily / Django / When lights are low / Please, I like to be gentle / Night in Tunisia
CD _______________ CDSJP 368
Timeless Jazz / Feb '92 / New Note/ Pinnacle

MUSIC I LIKE TO PLAY VOL.3
CD _______________ 1212302
Soul Note / Jan '92 / Cadillac / Harmonia Mundi / Wellard

MUSIC I LIKE TO PLAY VOL.4 (Soul Eyes)
CD _______________ 1212502
Soul Note / Jan '93 / Cadillac / Harmonia Mundi / Wellard

TETE
CD _______________ SCCD 31029
Steeplechase / Jul '88 / Discovery / Impetus

TOOTIE'S TEMPO
CD _______________ SCCD 31108
Steeplechase / Jul '88 / Discovery / Impetus

TRIO LIURE JAZZ (Montoliu, Tete Trio)
CD _______________ CDG 812
Helix / Nov '96 / Discovery

Montoya, Carlos

AIRES FLAMENCOS
CD _______________ CD 12510
Music Of The World / Nov '92 / ADA / Target/BMG

FLAMENCO
CD _______________ TCD 1008
Tradition / Feb '96 / ADA / Vital

Montoya, Coco

YA THINK I'D KNOW BETTER
CD _______________ BLPCD 5033
Blind Pig / Sep '96 / ADA / CM / Direct / Hot Shot

Montoya, Ramon

ART OF FLAMENCO VOL.4, THE
CD _______________ MAN 4840CD
Mandala / Apr '95 / ADA / Harmonia Mundi / Mandala

Montreal Jubilation Gospel ...

CAPPELLA, A (Montreal Jubilation Gospel Choir)
Lord I know I've been changed / There is a balm in Gilead / Ezekiel saw de wheel / Deep river / In that great gettin' up morning / Swing low, sweet chariot / Soon ah will be done
CD _______________ BLU 10142
Blues Beacon / Nov '92 / New Note/ Pinnacle

GLORY TRAIN (Montreal Jubilation Gospel Choir)
CD _______________ 10082
Blues Beacon / Mar '91 / New Note/ Pinnacle

JUBILATION - JOY TO THE WORLD (Montreal Jubilation Gospel Choir)
CD _______________ JUST 542
Justin Time / Feb '94 / Cadillac / New Note/Pinnacle

JUBILATION VOL.2 (Montreal Jubilation Gospel Choir)
CD _______________ 10062
Blues Beacon / Mar '91 / New Note/ Pinnacle

Montrose, J.R.

MESSAGE, THE
CD _______________ FSRCD 7001
Fresh Sound / Jul '97 / Discovery / Jazz Music

Monty

NAPOLEON COMPLEX, THE
Napoleon complex / Don't make me love you / Angel delight / 89 St. James' Square / Time machine / Love me to death / Haunted / Lion in Windsor / Kensington girl / All my birthdays / So non e vero (e bon trovato)
CD _______________ BAH 29
Humbug / Oct '96 / Total/Pinnacle

TYPICAL SCORPIO, A
Mr. Inconsistent / I'm Spartacus / Will I ever learn / Understanding Alfie / Ah Voodoo / Baby octopus / Moving the goalposts / Signorina / Come into my parlour / Can you do the mashed potato / Marianne / Say the word / Apple for the teacher / Bitten by the lovebug
CD _______________ BAH 6
Humbug / Oct '93 / Total/Pinnacle

Monty's Sunshine Jazz Band

YOU ARE MY SUNSHINE
You are my sunshine / Peoria / Yellow dog blues / Just a little while to stay here / Wildcat blues / Mama / Magnolia's wedding day / Hindustan / In the sweet bye and bye / Lover / Black cat on the fence / Far away blues / Sweet Georgia brown / Glory of love / Curse of an arching heart / Till we meet again
CD _______________ CDTTD 609
Timeless / Jun '97 / New Note/Pinnacle

Monumentum

IN ABSENTIA CHRISTI
CD AMAZON 007CD
Misanthropy / Oct '95 / Plastic Head

Mooch

3001
CD TASTE 44CD
Taste / Nov '94 / Plastic Head / SRD

POST VORTA
CD TASTE 48
Taste / Jan '95 / Plastic Head / SRD

STARHENGE
CD TASTE 057CD
Taste / Aug '95 / Plastic Head / SRD

Mood Six

BEST OF MOOD SIX, THE
Hanging around / She's too far / Rain falls on Mary / It's your life / Plastic flowers / Party time / Victim / I wanna destroy you / What have you ever done / Intruder / Contemporary scene / When the time comes / Voice of reason / Game show / I saw the light / You could be my soul / I'll keep holding on / Mad about the boy / Flowers and boxes / Look at me now / Shake some action / Somebody
CD CDMRED 141
Cherry Red / Mar '97 / Pinnacle

Moodie

EARLY YEARS, THE
CD MMCD 1052
Moodie / Jul '94 / Jet Star / SRD

Moods Orchestra

HOLDING BACK THE YEARS
CD MACCD 329
Autograph / Aug '96 / BMG

NIGHTS IN WHITE SATIN
CD MACCD 331
Autograph / Aug '96 / BMG

POWER OF LOVE, THE
CD MACCD 330
Autograph / Aug '96 / BMG

WOMAN IN LOVE, A
CD MACCD 328
Autograph / Aug '96 / BMG

Moodswings

LIVE AT LEEDS
CD 74321186312
Arista / Feb '94 / BMG

PSYCHEDELICATESSEN
Lifeforce in a pizza / Crysmile / Undistracted / Dancing is important / Together as one (luminous) / Great sound of letting go / Sugarush / Destruction and destroy / Indian drug carpet / Spore / Redemption song (oh happy day) / Horrozontal / Vibratonik / Okinawa / Hinkenlooper's eclipse / God knows what I want / Happy piano
CD 74321442172
Arista / May '97 / BMG

Moody Blues

CAUGHT LIVE AND FIVE
CD 8201612
London / Jan '97 / PolyGram

DAYS OF FUTURE PASSED (Moody Blues/London Festival Orchestra/Peter Knight)
Day begins / Dawn - dawn is a feeling / Morning / Another morning / Lunch break / Peak hour / Afternoon / Forever afternoon (Tuesday?) / Time to get away / Evening / Sunset / Twilight time / Night / Nights in white satin
CD 8200062
London / May '86 / PolyGram

EVERY GOOD BOY DESERVES FAVOURS
Procession / Story in your eyes / Our guessing game / Emily's song / After you came / One more to live / Nice to be here / You can never go home / My song
CD 8201602
London / '86 / PolyGram

GO NOW
CD CD 12209
Laserlight / Aug '93 / Target/BMG

GREATEST HITS
Your wildest dreams / Voice / Gemini dream / Story in your eyes / Tuesday afternoon (Forever Afternoon) / Isn't life strange / Nights in white satin / I know you're out there somewhere / Ride my see-saw / I'm just a singer (in a rock 'n' roll band) / Question
CD 8406592
Polydor / Jan '90 / PolyGram

IN SEARCH OF THE LOST CHORD
Departure / Ride my see-saw / Dr. Livingstone, I presume / House of four doors / Legend of a mind / House of four doors (part 2) / Voices in the sky / Best way to travel / Visions of paradise / Actor / Word / Om
CD 8201682
London / '86 / PolyGram

IN WORDS AND MUSIC
CD OTR 1100025
Metro Independent / Jun '97 / Essential/BMG

KEYS OF THE KINGDOM
Say it with love / Bless the wings (That bring you back) / Is this heaven / Say what you mean / Lean on me (Tonight) / Hope and pray / Shadows on the wall / Celtic sonant / Magic / Never blame the rainbows for the rain
CD 8494332
Polydor / Jul '91 / PolyGram

LIVE AT RED ROCKS
Overture with excerpts / Late lament / Tuesday afternoon (Forever afternoon) / For my lady / Lean on me (Tonight) / Lovely to see you / I know you're out there somewhere / Voice / Your wildest dreams / Isn't life strange / Other side of life / I'm just a singer (in a rock 'n' roll band) / Nights in white satin / Question / Ride me see-saw
CD 5179772
Polydor / Mar '96 / PolyGram

LONG DISTANCE VOYAGER
Voice / Talking out of turn / Gemini dream / In my world / Meanwhile / 22,000 days / Nervous / Painted smile / Reflective smile / Veteran cosmic rocker
CD 8201052
London / '86 / PolyGram

ON THE THRESHOLD OF A DREAM
In the beginning / lovely to see you / Dear diary / Send me no wine / To share our love / So deep within you / Never comes the day / Lazy day / Are you sitting comfortably / Dream / Have you heard (part 1) / Voyage / Have you heard (part 2)
CD 8201702
London / '86 / PolyGram

OTHER SIDE OF LIFE
Your wildest dreams / Talkin talkin / Rock 'n' roll over you / I just don't care / Running out of love / Other side of life / Spirit / Slings and arrows / It may be a fire
CD 8291792
Polydor / Jan '90 / PolyGram

PRESENT, THE
Blue world / Meet me halfway / Sitting at the wheel / Going nowhere / Hole in the world / Under my feet / It's cold outside of your heart / Running water / I am / Sorry
CD 8101192
London / Apr '91 / PolyGram

QUESTION OF BALANCE, A
Question / How is it (we are here) / And the tide rushes in / Don't you feel small / Tortoise and the hare / It's up to you / Minstrel's song / Dawning is the day / Melancholy man / Balance
CD 8202112
London / Jul '92 / PolyGram

SEVENTH SOJOURN
Lost in a lost world / New horizons / For my lady / Isn't life strange / You and me / Land of make believe / When you're a free man / I'm just a singer (in a rock 'n' roll band)
CD 8201592
London / Sep '86 / PolyGram

SUR LA MER
I know you're out there somewhere / Want to be with you / River of endless love / No more lies / Here comes the weekend / Vintage wine / Breaking point / Miracle / Love is on the run / Deep
CD 8357562
Polydor / Mar '96 / PolyGram

TIME TRAVELLER
CD Set 5164362
Polydor / Sep '94 / PolyGram

TO OUR CHILDREN'S, CHILDREN'S, CHILDREN
Higher and higher / Eyes of a child / Floating / Eyes of a child II / I never thought I'd live to be a hundred / Beyond / Out and in / Gypsy / Eternity road / Candle of life / Sun is still shining / I never thought I'd live to be a million / Watching and waiting
CD 8203642
London / Aug '86 / PolyGram

VERY BEST OF THE MOODY BLUES, THE
Go now / Tuesday afternoon / Nights in white satin / Ride my see-saw / Voices in the sky / Question / Story in your eyes / Isn't life strange / I'm just a singer / Blue guitar / Steppin' on a slide zone / Forever Autumn / Voice / Gemini dream / Blue world / Your wildest dreams / I know you're out there somewhere
CD 5358002
PolyGram TV / Sep '96 / PolyGram

VOICES IN THE SKY
Ride my see-saw / Talking out of question / Driftwood / Never comes the day / I'm just a singer (in a rock 'n' roll band) / Gemini dream / Voice / After you came / Question / Veteran cosmic rocker / Isn't life strange / Nights in white satin
CD 8201552
London / Apr '91 / PolyGram

Moody Boyz

PRODUCT OF THE ENVIRONMENT
Shango / Pigmy song / Fight back / Head in the sky / Elite presents this / Just out of Africa / July / Glich / Shango (Black dog) / Ogdon / Elite dubs the snooze the sequel / Funny thing happened to me on Wednesday
CD GRCD 013
Guerilla / Jul '94 / Pinnacle

RECYCLED EP
CD GREP 006CD
Guerilla / Jul '94 / Pinnacle

Moody Brothers

CARLTON MOODY & THE MOODY BROTHERS
Shame on me / I tried at first not to / You turned the light on / Aunt Bea's breakdown / I'll know you're gonna cheat on me / You / You left the water running / Dreaming / Showboat gambler / Little country county fair / Start with the talking / Drive over the mountain
CD LR 10157
Sundown / Dec '87 / TKO Magnum

COTTON EYED JOE
Midnight flyer / My mind's already home / Let me dance with you / Redneck girl / It's my turn to sing with ol' Willie / Southern railroad / Brown eyed girl / When she tells you goodbye / Line dancing / Our love / Cotton eyed Joe
CD LRCD 101162
Sundown / '89 / TKO Magnum

Moody, James

FEELIN' IT TOGETHER
Anthropology / Dreams / Autumn leaves / Wave / Morning glory / Kriss kross
CD MCD 5020
Muse / May '95 / New Note/Pinnacle

MOODY'S PARTY
Birthday tribute / Groovin' high / It might as well be spring / Parker's moon / Eternal triangle / Polka dots and moonbeams / Benny's from heaven / Be bop
CD CD 83382
Telarc / Oct '95 / Conifer/BMG

RETURN FROM OVERBROOK
Flute 'n the blues / Birdland story / It could happen to you / I cover the waterfront / Body and soul / Breaking the blues / Parker's mood / Easy living / Boo's tune / Richard's blues
CD GRP 18102
GRP / Apr '96 / New Note/BMG

Moody, Lloyd

BLACKSLATE MEETS SOUL SYNDICATE
CD MMCD 95
Moody Music / Sep '94 / Else / Jazz Music

Moody Marsden Band

TIME IS RIGHT, THE
CD ESDCD 225
Essential / Sep '94 / BMG

Moog Cookbook

MOOG COOKBOOK, THE
Black hole sun / Buddy Holly / Basket case / Come out and play / Free fallin' / Are you gonna go my way / Smells like teen spirit / Evenflow / One I love / Rockin' in the free world
CD 729142
Restless / Jun '96 / Vital

Moom

TOOT
Prelude / Sally / Astronaught / Void is clear / Babbashagga / Higher the sun / Crocodillian suite / Waiting for the sphere eye / I can't remember the sixties
CD DELECD 035
Delerium / Jul '95 / Cargo / Pinnacle / Vital

Moon & The Banana Tree

NEW GUITAR MUSIC FROM MADAGASCAR
CD SH 64074
Shanachie / Dec '96 / ADA / Greensleeves / Koch

Moon Lay Hidden Beneath A ...

AMARA TANTA TYRI (Moon Lay Hidden Beneath A Cloud)
CD ART 2CD
Arthur's Round Table / Oct '96 / World Serpent

MOON LAY HIDDEN (Moon Lay Hidden Beneath A Cloud)
CD ART 1CD
Arthur's Round Table / Oct '96 / World Serpent

NEW SOLDIER, A (Moon Lay Hidden Beneath A Cloud)
CD ART 3CD
Arthur's Round Table / Oct '96 / World Serpent

SMELL OF BLOOD BUT VICTORY, THE (2CD Set)
CD Set ART 11CD
Arthur's Round Table / Apr '97 / World Serpent

Moon Of Sorrow

CRYSTAL EMOTION
CD IGN 1M
Ignition / Nov '93 / Plastic Head

NEW DAWN, A
CD IGN 4M
Ignition / Jun '95 / Plastic Head

Moon Seven Times

SUNBURNT
Further / Through the roses / Nashville / Thirteen days / What you said / Bug collection / Neither luminary / Some of them burn / Montgomery L / You look past me / Fat dog / Full moon
CD RR 89112
Roadrunner / Jul '97 / PolyGram

Moonboot Oz

MUSIC FROM THE PSYCHEDELIC CAFE
CD ARDCD 1
Chameleon / May '97 / SRD

Moon'doc

GET MOONED
CD 341342
No Bull / Oct '96 / Koch

MOON'DOC
CD 342052
No Bull / Oct '95 / Koch

Moondogg

FAT LOT OF GOOD
CD BETCD 002
CD BETCD 002L
Better / Jun '96 / 3mv/Vital

MOONDOG
Caribea / Lullaby / Tree trail / Death when you come to me / Big cat / Frog bog / To a sea horse / Dance rehearsal / Surf session / Tree against the sky / Tap dance / Ooo debut / Drum suite / Street scene
CD OJCCD 1741
Original Jazz Classics / May '93 / Complete/Pinnacle / Jazz Music / Wellard

MORE
CD OJCCD 1781
Original Jazz Classics / Jun '93 / Complete/Pinnacle / Jazz Music / Wellard

Mooney, Claire

DRAWING BREATH SKETCHING DREAMS
CD RED 002CD
Red / Apr '95 / ADA / Cadillac / Harmonia Mundi

Mooney, Gordon

OVER THE BORDER
CD COMD 2031
Temple / Feb '94 / ADA / CM / Direct / Duncans / Highlander

Mooney, John

AGAINST THE WALL
Sacred ground / Doggone thing / Sweat 'n' bone / Broken mould / Late on in the evening / Three sides / Bitter pill / You told me / One step forward / Somebody been missing somebody (too long)
CD 70010870062
House Of Blues / Jun '96 / ADA / BMG

DEALING WITH THE DEVIL
Mighty / Dead or alive / Trouble / Junky Heaven / You never can tell / Later / Is it any wonder / Over my shoulder / Are you waiting for me / Intuition / William's lamentation / Myopia / I'm ready
CD T&M 007
Tradition & Moderne / Nov '96 / ADA / Direct

TRAVELLIN' ON (Mooney, John & Bluesiana)
CD CCD 10032
Crosscut / May '93 / ADA / CM / Direct

Moonglows

GREATEST HITS
CD MCD 09379
Chess/MCA / Jul '97 / BMG / New Note/BMG

Moonlight Serenaders

STARDUST MEMORIES (Hits Of The 1930's/1940's)

Change partners / Night and day / Cheek to cheek / Let's face the music and dance / Way you look tonight / You're the top / Zing went the strings of my heart / Nice work if you can get it / We're in the money / I've got a gal in Kalamazoo / In the mood / Chattanooga choo choo / Moonlight serenade / Boogie woogie bugle boy / Don't sit under the apple tree / White cliffs of Dover / Easter parade / Trolley song
CD PWKM 4038
Carlton / Feb '96 / Carlton

Moonlighters

RUSH HOUR
This livin' ain't lovin / Wait in line / I'm gonna put a bar in the back of my car / Coming up on happiness / All tore up / Soul cruisin' / World to lose / Big noise in the neighbourhood / Here she comes / I feel like a motor / Seven nights to rock / Workman on the nightshift
CD DIAB 806
Diabolo / Feb '94 / Pinnacle

Moonshake

BIG GOOD ANGEL
Two trains / Capital letters / Girly loop / Seance / Flow / Helping hands
CD PURECD 022
Too Pure / May '93 / Vital

DIRTY AND DIVINE
CD WDOM 028CD
World Domination / Oct '96 / Pinnacle / RTM/Disc

EVA LUNA
Wanderlust / Tar Baby / Seen and not heard / Bleach and salt water / Little Thing / City Poison / Sweetheart / Spaceship Earth / Beautiful Pigeon / Mugshot Heroine
CD PURECD 016
Too Pure / Sep '92 / Vital

SOUND YOUR EYES SHOULD FOLLOW
CD PURECD 033
Too Pure / Apr '94 / Vital

Moonspell

IRRELIGIOUS
CD CMCD 77123
Century Media / Jul '96 / Plastic Head

UNDER THE MOONSPELL
CD CDAR 021
Adipocre / Jan '97 / Plastic Head

WOLFHEART
CD CM 77112CD
Century Media / Jan '96 / Plastic Head

Moorcock, Michael

NEW WORLD FAIR, THE
CD DOJOCD 88
Dojo / May '95 / Disc

Moore, Aaron

HELLO WORLD
Hello world / What did you do to me / I just called / You got good business / Keep lovin' me / I feel alright again / Why you so mean to me / So long / Security / Searching for love / I once was lost / Castle Rock boogie / Lonely blues / True love is like that / It's all over
CD DE 695
Delmark / Jun '97 / ADA / Cadillac / CM / Direct / Hot Shot

Moore, Abra

SING
CD BBEA 4
Bohemia Beat / Aug '95 / ADA / CM / Direct

Moore, Alex

FROM NORTH DALLAS TO THE EAST SIDE (Moore, 'Whistlin' Alex)
CD ARHCD 408
Arhoolie / Apr '95 / ADA / Cadillac / Direct

WHISTLIN' ALEX MOORE - 1929-1951 (Moore, 'Whistlin' Alex)
CD DOCD 5178
Document / Oct '93 / ADA / Hot Shot / Jazz Music

WIGGLE TAIL
CD ROUCD 11559
Rounder / '88 / ADA / CM / Direct

Moore, Anthony

FLYING DOESN'T HELP
Judy get down / Ready ready / Useless moments / Lucia / Caught being in love / Timeless strange / Girl it's your time / War / Just us / Twilight, Uxbridge Rd
CD VP 177CD
Voiceprint / Oct '94 / Pinnacle

OUT
Stitch in time / Thousand ships / River / Please go / You tickle / Lover of mine / Johnny's dead / Dreams of his laughter / Driving blind / Pilgrim / Catch a falling star / Wrong again
CD VP 165CD
Voiceprint / Jul '97 / Pinnacle

Moore, Brew

SVINGET 14
CD BLCD 760164
Black Lion / Oct '93 / Cadillac / Jazz Music / Koch / Wellard

Moore, Chante

LOVE SUPREME, A
Intro / Searchin' / This time / My special perfect one / I'm what you need / Your love's supreme / Old school lovin' / Free/Sail on without your love / I want to thank you / Mood / Thank you for loving me / Soul dance / Am I losing you / Thou shalt not
CD MCD 11197
MCA / Nov '94 / BMG

Moore, Christy

AT THE POINT - LIVE
CD GRACD 203
Grapevine / Jan '95 / Grapevine/PolyGram

COLLECTION 1981-91, THE
Ordinary man / Mystic lipstick / Lakes of Ponchartrain / City of Chicago / Faithful departed / Don't forget your shovel / Delirium tremens / Knock song / Messenger boy / lisdoonvarna / Voyage / Missing you / Night visit / Biko drum / Time has come / Easter snow / Bright blue rose / Reel in the flickering light / Nancy Spain / Ride on
CD 903173512
WEA / Sep '91 / Warner Music

GRAFFITI TONGUE
CD GRACD 215
Grapevine / Sep '96 / Grapevine/PolyGram

IRON BEHIND THE VELVET (Moore, Christy & Friends)
Patrick was a gentleman / Sun is burning / Morrissey and the Russian sailor / Foxy devil / Three reels / Trip to Jerusalem / Three reels / Patrick's arrival / Gabriel McKeon's / Dunlavin Green / Joe McCann
CD TARACD 2002
Tara / Apr '95 / ADA / CM / Conifer/BMG / Direct

KING PUCK
Before the deluge / Two Conneeleys / Lawless / Yellow furze woman / Guiseppe / Sodom and Begorra / Johnny Connors / King Puck / Away ye broken heart / Me and the rose
CD ATLASCD 003
Equator / Oct '93 / Pinnacle

LIVE IN DUBLIN (Moore, Christy/Donal Lunny/Jimmy Faulkner)
Hey Sandy / Boys of Barr Na Sraide / Little mother / Clyde's bonnie banks / Pretty boy Floyd / Bogey's bonnie banks / Crack was ninety in the Isle of Man / Black is the colour of my true love's hair / One last cold kiss
CD TARACD 2005
Tara / Feb '95 / ADA / CM / Conifer/BMG / Direct

PROSPEROUS
Raggle taggle Gipsies / Tabhair dom do lamh / Dark eyed sailor / I wish I was in England / Lock hospital / James Connolly / Hackler from Grouse Hall / Tribute to Woody / Ludlow massacre / Letter to Syracuse / Spancillhill / Cliffs of Dooneen / Rambling Robin
CD TARACD 2008
Tara / Feb '95 / ADA / CM / Conifer/BMG / Direct

RIDE ON
City of Chicago / Vive la quinte brigada / Song of wandering aengus / Mcilhatton / Lisdoonvarna / Wicklow hills / Sonny's dream / Dying soldier / El Salvador / Back home in Derry / Least we can do
CD 2292404072
WEA / Jul '95 / Warner Music

SMOKE AND STRONG WHISKEY
CD CM 00022
Newberry / May '91 / Pinnacle

UNFINISHED REVOLUTION
Biko drum / Natives / Metropolitan Avenue / Unfinished revolution / Other side / Messenger boy / On the bridge / Suffocate / Derby day / Dr. Vibes / Pair of brown eyes
CD 2292421342
WEA / Jul '95 / Warner Music

VOYAGE
Mystic lipstick / Voyage / Mad lady and me / Deportees club / Night visit / All for the roses / Missing you / Bright blue rose / Farewell to pripchat / Muscha God help her / First time ever I saw your face / Middle of the island
CD 2292461562
WEA / Jul '95 / Warner Music

Moore, Gary

AFTER HOURS
Cold day in hell / Don't you lie to me / Story of the blues / Since I met you baby / Separate ways / Only fool in town / Key to love / Jumpin' at shadows / Blues is alright / Hurt inside / Nothing's the same
CD CDV 2684
Virgin / Mar '92 / EMI

AFTER THE WAR
After the war / Speak for yourself / Livin' on dreams / Led clones / Running from the storm / This thing called love / Ready for love / Blood of emeralds / Messiah will come again / Dunluce (pts 1 and 2) / Dunluce
CD CDV 2575
Virgin / Dec '88 / EMI

AFTER THE WAR/RUN FOR COVER/ WILD FRONTIER (3CD Set)
CD Set TPAK 18
Virgin / Nov '91 / EMI

BALLADS AND BLUES (1982-1994)
Always gonna love you / Still got the blues / Empty rooms / Parisienne walkways / One day / Separate ways / Story of the blues / Crying in the shadows / With love (remember) / Midnight blues / Falling in love with you / Jumpin' at shadows / Blues for Narada / Johnny boy
CD CDV 2738
Virgin / Nov '94 / EMI

BLUES ALIVE
Cold day in hell / Walking by myself / Story of the blues / Oh pretty woman / Separate ways / Too tired / Still got the blues / Since I met you baby / Sky is crying / Further on up the road / King of the blues / Parisienne walkways / Jumpin' at shadows
CD CDVX 2716
Virgin / May '93 / EMI

BLUES FOR GREENY
If you be my baby / Long grey mare / Merry go round / I loved another woman / I need your love so bad / Same way / Supernatural / Driftin' / Showbiz blues / Love that burns / Looking for somebody
CD CDV 2784
Virgin / May '95 / EMI

CORRIDORS OF POWER
Don't take me for a loser / Always gonna love you / Wishing well / Gonna break my heart again / Falling in love with you / End of the world / Rockin' every night / Cold hearted / I can't wait until tomorrow
CD CDV 2245
Virgin / Jul '85 / EMI

DARK DAYS IN PARADISE
One good reason / Cold wind blows / I have found my love in you / One fine day / Like angels / What are we here for / Always there for tomorrow / Where did we go wrong / Business as usual / Dark days in paradise
CD CDV 2826
Virgin / May '97 / EMI

DIRTY FINGERS
Hiroshima / Dirty fingers / Bad news / Don't let me be misunderstood / Run to your Mama / Nuclear attack / Kidnapped / Really gonna rock / Lonely nights / Rest in peace
CD CLACD 131
Castle / Apr '87 / BMG

G-FORCE (G-Force)
You / White knuckles / Rockin' and rollin' / She's got you / I look at you / Because of your love / You kissed me sweetly / Hot gossip / Woman's in love / Dancin'
CD CLACD 212
Castle / Feb '91 / BMG

LIVE AT THE MARQUEE
Back on the streets / Run to your mama / Dancin' / She's got you / Parisienne walkways / You / Nuclear attack / Dallas warhead
CD CLACD 211
Castle / Feb '91 / BMG

LOOKING AT YOU (2CD Set)
Nuclear attack / Dirty fingers / Dancin' / Really gonna rock / She's got you / Hiroshima / I look at you / Kidnapped / Because of your love / Lonely nights / Woman's in love / You kissed me sweetly / Rest in peace / White knuckles / Rockin' and rollin' / Don't let me be misunderstood / Bad news / Run to your Mama / Hot gossip / Back on the streets / Run to your Mama / Dancin' / She's got you / Parisienne walkways / Nuclear attack / Dallas warhead / You / You
CD Set SMDCD 123
Snapper / May '97 / Pinnacle

PARISIENNE WALKWAYS
Back on the streets / Fanatical fascists / Don't believe a word / Spanish guitar / Parisienne walkways / Put it this way / Desperado / Castles / Fighting talk / Scorch
CD MCLD 19076
MCA / Jun '92 / BMG

ROCKIN' EVERY NIGHT (Live In Japan)
Rockin' every night / Wishing well / I can't wait until tomorrow / Nuclear attack / White knuckles / Rockin' and rollin' / Back on the streets / Sunset
CD XIDCD 1
10 / Jun '88 / EMI

RUN FOR COVER
Out in the fields / Reach for the sky / Run for cover / Military man / Empty rooms / Nothing to lose / Once in a lifetime / All messed up / Listen to your heartbeat / Out of my system
CD DIXCD 16
10 / Feb '86 / EMI

STILL GOT THE BLUES
Moving on / Oh pretty woman / Walking by myself / Still got the blues / Texas strut / All your love / Too tired / King of the blues / As the years go passing by / Midnight blues / That kind of woman / Stop messin' around
CD CDV 2612
Virgin / Mar '90 / EMI

VICTIMS OF THE FUTURE
Murder in the skies / All I want / Hold on to love / Law of the jungle / Victims of the future / Teenage idol / Shape of things to come / Empty rooms
CD DIXCD 2
10 / Jun '88 / EMI

WALKWAYS
Don't let me be misunderstood / Hot gossip / Really gonna rock tonight / Back on the streets / Dallas warhead / Parisienne walkways / Nuclear attack / Run to your Mama / Woman's in love / Kidnapped / Dirty fingers / Dancin' / White knuckles/Rockin' and rollin' / Hiroshima
CD 5507382
Spectrum / Sep '94 / PolyGram

WE WANT MOORE
Murder in the skies / Shape of things to come / Victims of the future / Cold hearted / End of the world / Back on the streets / So far away / Empty rooms / Don't take me for a loser / Rockin' and rollin'
CD Set GMDLD 1
10 / Apr '92 / EMI

WILD FRONTIER
Over the hills and far away / Wild frontier / Take a little time / Loner / Friday on my mind / Strangers in the darkness / Thunder rising / Johnny boy / Wild frontier / Over the hills and far away (12" version) / Crying in the shadows
CD DIXCD 56
10 / Feb '87 / EMI

Moore, Glen

DRAGONETTI'S DREAM
Oxeye / Beautiful swan lady / If you can't beat em, beat em / Red and black / Dragonetti's dream / Jade visions / Walcott's pendulum / Enter the king / Vertebra / Travels with my foot / Put in a quarter / Burning fingers / Fat horse / Four queasy pieces / Appalachian dance
CD VBR 21542
Vera Bra / Feb '96 / New Note/Pinnacle / Pinnacle

Moore, Grace

ONE NIGHT OF LOVE
CD CDMOIR 424
Memoir / Sep '94 / Jazz Music / Target/ BMG

Moore, Hamish

BEES KNEES, THE (Moore, Hamish & Dick Lee)
Thunderhead / Easy club reel / Rumblin' brig / Boatman Bill / Iain McGhee's Romanian boots / Birnam triangle / Nigheann dubh alainn / Teapot jig / Rock and Wee Pickle tow / Bannocks of Beremeal / Song for Julie / Thoir a nall ailean thugam / Jenny's chickens / Jenny dang the weaver / Maggie's reel / Slippit bar / Paddy in the sauna / Slow hare / Mongoose in the Byre / bee's knees / Staten island / Trip to Pakistan / Anne's tune / Buccleuch Street / Famous ballymoate
CD HARCD 014
Harbour Town / '90 / ADA / CM / Direct / Roots

FAREWELL TO DECORUM (Moore, Hamish & Dick Lee)
Third movement of a concerto for bagpipes and jazz orchestra / Autumn returns / Galician jigs / Cat's pyjamas, The/The Mental blockade / Farewell to Nigg / Resolution No. 9 / Ye banks and braes/Malts on the optics/ Farewell to decorum / Round dawn / Forest lodge/Primrose lass/Miss Girdle / Monster / 12.12.92 (A march for democracy) / Freedom come all ye
CD CDTRAX 063
Greentrax / Sep '93 / ADA / Direct / Duncans / Highlander

STEPPING ON THE BRIDGE
King George IV strathspey / King's reel / Blue bonnets / Margaret MacLachlan / Back of the change house / Lucy Campbell / Go immediatley / High road to Linton / Father John MacMillian of Barra / Sprig of ivy / St Josephs / Mrs. Gregor's search / Cameron's strathspley / Crippled boy / Helen Black of Inveran / Dal nahas ag / Sparks rant / Drose and butter / Stumpie
CD CDTRAX 073
Greentrax / Jul '94 / ADA / Direct / Duncans / Highlander

Moore, Johnny B.

911 BLUES
CD WOLF 120873
Wolf / Jul '96 / Hot Shot / Jazz Music / Swift

LIVE AT BLUE CHICAGO
Rollin' and tumblin' / Turn on your love light / Same thing / Sweet little angel / All my whole life / Back door friend / All of your love / Mean mistreater / You can't lose what you never had / If you don't put nothin' in it / Straight from the shoulder / Boogie chillen'
CD DE 688
Delmark / Jun '97 / ADA / Cadillac / CM / Direct / Hot Shot

TROUBLED WORLD
Troubled world / Keep it to yourself / Sittin' here thinkin' / I'm going upside your head / Things that I used to do / Why you wanna do me like that / Stoop down baby / Broke your promise / Walkin' through the park / Think twice / It's too late brother
CD DE 701
Delmark / Jun '97 / ADA / Cadillac / CM / Direct / Hot Shot

Moore, Junia

LOVE ME LIKE YESTERDAY
Love me today like yesterday / Stay / If I knew / Woman / Love is a disease / To hell I love you / On your patio / Put your head on my shoulder / Bring it back to me / Hello good looking
CD CY 78938
Nyam Up / Apr '95 / Conifer/BMG

Moore, Kid Prince

KID PRINCE MOORE
CD DOCD 5180
Document / Oct '93 / ADA / Hot Shot / Jazz Music

Moore, Melba

LITTLE BIT MORE, A
I'm not gonna let you go / Falling / Mind up tonight / How's love been treating you / Little bit more: *Moore, Melba & Freddie Jackson* / Stay / Love's comin' at ya / Livin' for your love / Lean on me / I'm in love: *Moore, Melba & Kashif* / Underlove / I can't complain: *Moore, Melba & Freddie Jackson* / (Can't take half) all of you: *Moore, Melba & Lillo Thomas* / Let's stand together: *Moore, Melba & Lillo Thomas*
CD CTMCD 316
EMI / Apr '97 / EMI

Moore, Merrill E.

BOOGIE MY BLUES AWAY (2CD Set)
Rock rock ola / House of blue lights / Big bug boogie / Saddle boogie / Corine Corina / Red light / Bartender's blues / Hard top race / Nola boogie / Bell bottom boogie / Doggie house boogie / Sweet Jenny Lee / Fly right boogie / It's a one-way door / Snatchin' and grabbin' / I think I love you too / Ten ten am / Yes indeed / Five foot two, eyes of blue / Cow cow boogie / Boogie my blues away / Rock Island line / King Porter stomp / Cooing to the wrong pigeon / She's gone / Down the road apiece / Gotta gimme whatcha got / Nursery rhyme blues / Buttermilk baby / Barrel house Bessie / Tuck me to sleep in my old Kentucky home / Music music music / Sun Valley walk / Lazy river / (Back home again in) Indiana / South / (In) a shanty in old Shanty Town / Sweet Georgia Brown / Nobody's sweetheart / Jumpin' at the woodside / Somebody stole my gal / Moore blues / Sentimental journey
CD Set BCD 15505
Bear Family / Sep '90 / Direct / Rollercoaster / Swift

Moore, Michael

CHICOUTIMI
CD RAMBOY 06
Bvhaast / Oct '94 / Cadillac

CONCORD DUO SERIES VOL.9
I remember you / Just me, just me / If I loved you / Limehouse blues / Come Sunday / Ain't she sweet / I should care / Zoot's suite / All the things you are / Old new waltz / Seven, come eleven / Liebst du um schonheit / Cotton tail / Deep summer music
CD CCD 4678
Concord Jazz / Dec '95 / New Note/ Pinnacle

DOUBLE BASS DELIGHTS (Moore, Michael & Rufus Reid)
Tea for two / All blues / Satin doll / It's the nights I like / You're my everything / Cotton tail / Stompin' at the Savoy / Recordame / Sophisticated lady / Lover / Sonnymoon for two / Seven minds / They can't take that away from me
CD DTRCD 117
Double Time / Dec '96 / Express Jazz

PLAYS GERSHWIN
Summertime / Love walked in / Shall we dance / Embraceable you / He loves, she loves / But not for me / 'S Wonderful / Foggy day / They all laughed / I've got a crush on you / Someone to watch over me / Who cares
CD CHECD 00110
Master Mix / Mar '95 / Jazz Music / New Note/Pinnacle / Wellard

Moore, Monette

1923-1924 VOL.1
CD DOCD 5338
Document / May '95 / ADA / Hot Shot / Jazz Music

1924-1932 VOL.2
CD DOCD 5339
Document / May '95 / ADA / Hot Shot / Jazz Music

Moore, Ralph

ROUND TRIP
CD RSRCD 104
Reservoir Music / Oct '89 / Cadillac

Moore, Rebecca

ADMIRAL CHARCOAL'S SONG
CD KFWCD 162
Knitting Factory / Feb '95 / Cargo / Plastic Head

Moore, Rudy Ray

GOOD OLE BIG ONES
Fast black / Silent George / Good ole big ones / He can give it / Hell of a blow job / Period / Black topping / White beans / Sack of nookie and others / Dirty dozens, Hercules / Catch me some nuts / Grow by the minute / St. Peter & Bro. rap
CD CDPS 002
Pulsar / Nov '95 / TKO Magnum

Moore, Scotty

GUITAR THAT CHANGED THE WORLD, THE
Hound dog / Loving you / Money honey / My baby left me / Heartbreak hotel / That's alright Mama / Milk cow blues / Don't / Mystery train / Don't be cruel / Love me tender / Mean woman blues
CD 4809662
Epic / Aug '95 / Sony

Moore, Seamus

WINNING DREAM, THE
CD HRCD 1030
Hazel / Apr '94 / BMG

Moore, Thomas

DREAMER IN RUSSIA
Molenie o lybuvi (Prayer for love) / Michael Michael / Lake of Ponchartrain / Schlar / Fog in Monterey / No clouds / Sonya and Amy in Grey / Crooked road / Believe me Sligo
CD SUNCD 2
Sound / '90 / ADA

GORGEOUS AND BRIGHT
CD SCD 1294
Starc / Feb '95 / ADA / Direct

Moore, Thurston

BAREFOOT IN THE HEAD (Moore, Thurston & Jim Sauter/Don Dietrich)
CD FE 015
Forced Exposure / Dec '96 / Cargo

KLANGFARBENMELODIE
CD HERMES 011
Corpus Hermeticum / Apr '97 / Cargo

PIECE FOR JETSUN DOLMA
CD VICTOCD 045
Victo / Mar '97 / Harmonia Mundi / ReR Megacorp

PILLOW WAND (Moore, Thurston & Nels Cline)
CD LB 011CD
Little Brother / Jul '97 / Cargo

PSYCHIC HEARTS
Queen bee and her pals / Ono soul / Psychic hearts / Pretty bad / Patti Smith math scratch / Blues from beyond the grave / See through playmate / Hang out / Feathers / Tranquilizer / Staring statues / Cindy (Rotten Tanx) / Cherry's blues / Female cop / Elegy for all the dead rock stars
CD GED 24810
Geffen / Sep '96 / BMG

Moore, Vinnie

MIND'S EYE
In control / Saved by a miracle / Lifeforce / Mind's eye / Journey / Daydream / Hero without honour / NNY / Shadows of yesterday
CD RR 349635
Roadrunner / Feb '87 / PolyGram

OUT OF NOWHERE
CD CDMFN 194
Music For Nations / Feb '96 / Pinnacle

Moorish, Lisa

I'VE GOT TO HAVE IT ALL
CD 8287502
Go Beat / Aug '96 / PolyGram

Moose

HONEY BEE
Uptown invisible / Meringue / Mondo cane / You don't listen / Joe courtesy / Asleep at the wheel / I wanted to see you to see if I wanted you / Around the warm bend / Stop laughing / Dress you the same / Hold on
CD BIAS 260CD
Play It Again Sam / Oct '93 / Discovery / Plastic Head / Vital

LIVE A LITTLE, LOVE A LOT
Play God / Man who hanged himself / First balloon to Nice / Rubdown / Poor man / Eve in a dream / Old man time / Love on the dole / So much love so little time / Last of the good old days / Regulo 7
CD BIAS 320CD
Play It Again Sam / Feb '96 / Discovery / Plastic Head / Vital

SONNY AND SAM
CD HUT 011CD
Hut / Feb '92 / EMI

XYZ
Soon is never soon enough / I'll See You In My Dreams / High Flying Bird / Screaming / Friends / XYZ / Slip and slide / Little Bird / Don't Bring Me Down / Polly / Whistling Song / Everybody's talkin' / River is nearly dry / Live At The Happy Moustache / Early Morning Rain / Moon Is Blue
CD CDHUT 005
Hut / Aug '92 / EMI

MOP

FIRING SQUAD
Intro / Firing squad / New jack city / Stick to ya gunz / Anticipation / Born 2 Kill / Brownsville / Salute / World famous / Downtown swinga / Lifestyle of a ghetto child / Revolution / Illside of town / Nothin to lose / Dedication / Dead and gone
CD 4867372
Relativity / Nov '96 / Sony

Moped, Johnny

BASICALLY (Studio Recordings/Live At The Roundhouse 19th Feb 1978)
No one / VD boiler / Panic button / Little Queenie / Maniac / Darling, let's have another baby / Groovy Ruby / 3D time / Wee wee / Make trouble / Wild breed / Hell razor / Incendiary device / Somethin' else / Groovy Ruby (Live) / VD boiler (Live) / Little Queenie (Live) / Wee wee (Live) / Panic button (Live) / Make trouble (Live) / Somethin' else (Live) / Incendiary device (Live) / Hard lovin' man (Live) / Wild breed (Live) / Hell razor (Live) / Starting a moped / Groovy Ruby / It really digs / Mystery track
CD CDWIKD 144
Chiswick / Sep '95 / Pinnacle

Moped Lads

KICKED OUT '77
CD NV 44CD
Nasty Vinyl / Oct '96 / Cargo

Moradi, Shahmirza

MUSIC OF LORESTAN
CD NI 5397
Nimbus / Sep '94 / Nimbus

Moraes, Angel

HOT 'N' SPYCY - THE ALBUM
CD SUB 17D
Subversive / Jun '96 / 3mv/Sony / Amato Disco / Mo's Music Machine / Prime / Vital

NEW YORK IN THE MIX VOL.1
CD SUB 5D
Subversive / Nov '95 / 3mv/Sony / Amato Disco / Mo's Music Machine / Prime / Vital

Moraito

FLAMENCO VIVO COLLECTION (Morao Y Oro)
CD AUB 6772
Auvidis/Ethnic / Feb '93 / ADA / Harmonia Mundi

Moral Crusade

ACT OF VIOLENCE, AN
CD CMFTCD 5
CMFT / Jul '90 / Plastic Head

Morales, Noro

BROADCASTS & TRANSCRIPTIONS 1942-1948
CD HQCD 78
Harlequin / Nov '96 / Hot Shot / Jazz Music / Swift / Wellard

Morath, Max

LIVING A RAGTIME LIFE
CD SACD 110
Solo Art / Jul '93 / Jazz Music

REAL AMERICAN FOLK SONGS
CD SACD 120
Solo Art / Mar '95 / Jazz Music

Moravenka Band

MUSIC FOR PLEASURE
CD VA 0039
Musicvars / Nov '95 / Czech Music Enterprises

Moraz, Patrick

OUT IN THE SUN
Out in the sun / Rana batucada / Nervous breakdown / Silver screen / Tentacles / Kabala / Love hate sun rain you / Time for a change
CD CDOVD 445
Virgin / May '94 / EMI

STORY OF I, THE
Impact / Warmer hands / Storm / Cachaca / Intermezzo / Indoors / Best years of our lives / Descent / Incantation (procession) / Dancing now / Impressions (the dream) / Like a child in disguise / Rise and fall / Symphony in the space
CD CDOVD 446
Virgin / May '94 / EMI

Morbid Angel

ABOMINATIONS
CD MOSH 048CD
Earache / Jan '93 / Vital

ALTARS OF MADNESS
Visions from the darkside / Chapel of ghouls / Maze of torment / Damnation / Bleed for the devil
CD MOSH 011CD
Earache / Sep '89 / Vital

BLESSED ARE THE SICK
CD MOSH 031CD
Earache / May '91 / Vital

COVENANT
Rapture / Pain divine / World of shit / Vengeance is mine / Lion's den / Blood on my hands / Angel of disease / Sworn to black / Nar mattaru / God of emptiness
CD MOSH 081CD
Earache / Sep '97 / Vital

DOMINATION
Dominate / Where the slime live / Eyes to see, ears to hear / Melting / Nothing to fear / Dawn of the angry / This means war / Caesar's Palace / Dreaming / Inquisition (burn with me) / Hatework
CD MOSH 123CDSL
Earache / Sep '95 / Vital
CD MOSH 134CD
Earache / Sep '97 / Vital

ENTANGLED IN CHAOS
Immortal rites / Blasphemy of the holy ghost / Sworn to the black / Lord of all fevers and plague / Blessed are the sick / Days of suffering / Chapels of ghouls / Maze of torment / Rapture / Blood on my hands / Dominate
CD MOSH 167CD
Earache / Nov '96 / Vital

Morbid Saint

SPECTRUM OF DEATH
CD GCI 89803
Plastic Head / Jun '92 / Plastic Head

Morbius

ALIENCHRIST
CD CYBERCD 16
Cyber / May '95 / Amato Disco / Arabesque / Plastic Head

Morcheeba

WHO CAN YOU TRUST
Moog island / Trigger hippie / Post houmous / Tape loop / Never an easy way / Howling / Small town / Enjoy the wait / Col / Who can you trust / Almost done / End theme
CD ZEN 009CD
Indochina / Apr '96 / Pinnacle

Mordred

FOOLS GAME
CD CDNUK 135
Noise / May '89 / Koch

NEXT ROOM, THE
CD N 02112
Noise / Aug '94 / Koch

More, Benny

BAILA MI SON
CD CCD 506
Caney / Jul '96 / ADA / Discovery

BOLEROS DE ORO
Mi amor fugaz / No te atrevas / Preferi perderte / Mi corazon lloro / Corazon rebelde / Dolor y perdon / Por que pensar asi / No puedo callar / Fiebre de ti / Y te encontre / Que me hace dano / Como fue / Esta noche corazon / Mucho corazon
CD CD 62103
Saludos Amigos / Oct '96 / Target/BMG

CARICIAS CUBANA
CD SON 035
Iris Music / Jul '95 / Discovery

EL BARBARO DEL RITMO
Te quedaras / Encatidando de la vida / En el tiempo de la colonia / Oh vida / Locas por el mambo / Mi chiquita / Barbaro del ritmo / A media noche / Cinturita / Corazon rebelde / El bobo de la yuca / Me voy pa'el / Pueblo
CD ______ **PSCCD 1004**
Pure Sounds From Cuba / Feb '95 / Henry Hadaway / THE

VOZ Y OBRA
CD ______ **74321283412**
Milan / Jun '96 / Conifer/BMG / Silva Screen

More Fiends

TOAD LICKIN'
CD ______ **SR 330290CD**
Semaphore / Dec '90 / Plastic Head

More, Keith

GUITAR STORIES
Unopened book / Festival / Self inflicted part 1 / Self inflicted part 2 / Angeline / Farewell bop / Retribution / Silver bullet / Rascal / Farewell
CD ______ **SKMCD 001**
Selective / Sep '96 / Pinnacle

More Rockers

DUB PLATE SELECTION VOL.1
CD ______ **ZCDKR 1**
More Rockers / Feb '95 / 3mv/Sony

Moreau, Jean

JEAN MOREAU
I'm losing my mind / Life is fleeting / Skin, Leon / Nothing happens anymore / Ask for me, I prefer / Lazy blues / Life of leisure / Man to love / Clockmaker / Neither too soon, nor too late / Lies / Love out of focus / I'll never tell you that I'll love you forever / All blue / I once had a friend / Words about nothing / Anonymous / Farewell to life / You bother me / Sometimes red sometimes blue / Le Tourbillon
CD ______ **DRGCD 5567**
DRG / Aug '96 / Discovery / New Note/ Pinnacle

Moreira, Airto

COLOURS OF LIFE, THE (Moreira, Airto & Flora Purim)
CD ______ **IORCD 001**
In & Out / Sep '88 / Vital/SAM

FORTH WORLD (Moreira, Airto & Forth World)
CD ______ **JHRCD 026**
Ronnie Scott's Jazz House / Sep '92 / Cadillac / Jazz Music / New Note/Pinnacle / TKO Magnum

KILLER BEES (Moreira, Airto & The Gods Of Jazz)
Banana jam / Be there / Killer bees / City sushi / See ya later / Never mind / Communion / Nasty moves / Chicken in the mind
CD ______ **BW 041**
B&W / Dec '93 / New Note/Pinnacle / SRD / Vital/SAM

OTHER SIDE OF THIS, THE
CD ______ **RCD 10207**
Rykodisc / Jun '92 / ADA / Vital

Morel Inc

NYC JAM SESSION
CD ______ **SR 320CD**
Strictly Rhythm / Jun '95 / Prime / RTM/ Disc / SRD / Vital

Moreland, Ace

I'M A DAMN GOOD TIME
CD ______ **ICH 9014CD**
Ichiban / Jun '94 / Direct / Koch

Morello, Joe

CAN'T BE DENIED
CD ______ **JSPCD 287**
JSP / Feb '97 / ADA / Cadillac / Direct / Hot Shot / Target/BMG

Morellos

CRAZY RHYTHM
Manoir des mes reves / Jeepers Creepers / Crazy rhythm / Embraceable you / Bolero / Buona sera / Bonjour mon amour / Pennies from heaven / Paper moon / Zing went the strings
CD ______ **33JAZZ 028**
33 Jazz / Aug '96 / Cadillac / New Note/ Pinnacle

Moreno, Antonita

CARRETERA DE ASTURIAS
CD ______ **9175**
Divucsa / Oct '96 / Discovery

Moreno, Buddy

BUDDY MORENO ORCHESTRA 1947-1949 (Moreno, Buddy Orchestra)
CD ______ **CCD 49**
Circle / Nov '96 / Jazz Music / Swift / Wellard

Moreno, Tutti

TENDIDO (Moreno, Tutti & Friends & Joyce)
CD ______ **F 006CD**
Far Out / Jul '96 / Timewarp

TOCANDO, SENTINDO, SUANDO (Playing, Feeling, Sweating) (Moreno, Tutty & Joyce)
Magica / Algo sobre nos / Pricesinha / Costelacao / Pega leve / Pianco / GB / Camaleao
CD ______ **FARO 006**
Far Out / Aug '96 / Amato Disco / New Note/Pinnacle

Moreton, Ivor

NIMBLE FINGERS (Moreton, Ivor & Dave Kay)
Aurora / It always rains before a rainbow / Ridin' home on the buggy / That lovely weekend / Sand in my shoes / Do you care / Wrap yourself in cotton wool / Shepherd serenade / Elmer's tune / Sailor with the navy blue eyes / Baby mine / When I love I love / Deep in the heart of Texas / Tica ti tica ta / Tomorrow's sunrise / I don't want to walk without you / Flamingo / Someone's rocking my dreamboat / Arm in arm / Time was / In an old dutch garden / Lamplighter's serenade/Sometimes/Somebody else is taking my / Where in the world/Always in my heart/Soft shoe shuffle / Jersey bounce / Three little sisters / Tell me teacher / Only you / Idaho / It costs so little / Mean to me / Time on my hands / If I had you / Be careful it's my heart / Love is a song/Here you are / Love is a song / Here you are / This is worth fighting for / You walked by / Lovenest / Whispering grass / Three dreams/ There's a harbour of dreamboats / Where's my love/Lady who don't believe in love/ Keep an eye o / Why don't you fall in love with me/All our tomorrows/There a / Hit the road to dreamland/I spy/Let's get lost / I can't hear you anymore / I haven't time to be a millionaire / We'll go smiling along / All over the place/Maybe/Where was I / All the things you are/Bluberry Hill/Sierra Sue / In the blue hills of Maine / Zoot suit / When your old wedding ring was new
CD ______ **RAJCD 822**
Empress / May '97 / Koch

Moretti, Dan

SAXUAL
Waiting for the call / Hot summer night / Just a matter of time / Midnight layer cake / First love / Cru-cre corroro / Keepin' up the magic / Serenade / Tune for Tina / Be my guest
CD ______ **PAR 2019CD**
PAR / Apr '94 / Koch

Morgan, Derrick

21 HITS SALUTE
CD ______ **SONCD 0077**
Sonic Sounds / May '95 / Jet Star

BLAZING FIRE
CD ______ **PHZCD 80**
Unicorn / Nov '93 / Plastic Head

CLASSICS OF YESTERDAY
CD ______ **HRCD 200**
Hop / Sep '96 / Jet Star

I AM THE RULER
Teach my baby / Hop / Forward march / Housewives' choice / Gypsy woman / Blazing fire / No raise no praise / Look before you leap / I found a Queen / Don't you worry / It's alright / Got you on my mind / You never miss your water / I am the ruler / I want to go home / Conquering ruler / Gimme back / Tears on my pillow
CD ______ **CDTRL 300**
Trojan / Mar '94 / Direct / Jet Star

ROCKSTEADY
CD ______ **RNCD 2103**
Rhino / Apr '95 / Grapevine/PolyGram / Jet Star

SKA MAN CLASSICS
CD ______ **CDBH 170**
Heartbeat / Nov '95 / ADA / Direct / Greensleeves / Jet Star

TIME MARCHES ON
Time marches on / Fatman / You're a pest / I wish I were an apple / Love not to brag / Lover boy / Do the beng beng / Father Killam / Bad luck on me / Ain't that crazy / Tears on my pillow / Lagga head / Stumbling block / Conquering ruler / Top the pop / What a bam bam / Searching so long / Reggae train / Rudies don't fear / I shot the deputy / Moon hop
CD ______ **CDHB 153**
Heartbeat / Jul '97 / ADA / Direct / Greensleeves / Jet Star

Morgan, Frank

BEBOP LIVES (Morgan, Frank Quintet)
What is this thing called love / Parker's mood / Well you needn't / Little Melonae / Come Sunday / All the things you are / Night in Tunisia
CD ______ **CCD 14026**
Contemporary / Apr '94 / Cadillac / Complete/Pinnacle / Jazz Music / Wellard

BOP (Morgan, Frank & The Rodney Kendrick Trio)
Milano / Well, you needn't / KC blues / Night in Tunisia / Blue monk / Half Nelson / Lover man / 52nd Street theme
CD ______ **CD 83413**
Telarc Jazz / Mar '97 / Conifer/BMG

DOUBLE IMAGE (Morgan, Frank & George Cables)
All the things you are / Virgo / Blues for Rosalinda / After you've gone / Helen's song / Love dance / Love story / I told you so / Blue in green
CD ______ **CCD 14035**
Contemporary / Apr '94 / Cadillac / Complete/Pinnacle / Jazz Music / Wellard

LISTEN TO THE DAWN
CD ______ **5189792**
Antilles/New Directions / Aug '94 / PolyGram

LOVE, LOST AND FOUND
Nearness of you / Last night when you were young / What is this thing called love / Skylark / Once I loved / I can't get started with you / It's only a paper moon / My one and only love / Someday my prince will come / All
CD ______ **CD 83374**
Telarc / Oct '95 / Conifer/BMG

YARDBIRD SUITE (Morgan, Frank Quartet)
Yardbird suite / Night in Tunisia / Billie's bounce / Star eyes / Scrapple from the apple / Skylark / Cheryl
CD ______ **CCD 14045**
Contemporary / Apr '94 / Cadillac / Complete/Pinnacle / Jazz Music / Wellard

Morgan, George

CANDY KISSES (9CD Set)
All I need is some more lovin' / Candy kisses / Rainbow in my heart / Please don't let me love you / Silver river / Don't make me sorry / Put all your lovin' on a cookie jar / Room full of roses / I love everything about you / Ring on your finger / Cry baby heart / Why in heaven's name / Shoe is on the other / Wedding dolls / Greedy fingers / Angel mother / Lucky seven / You wind the bride / So far / Warm hands, cold heart / Don't be afraid to love me / I know you'll never change / Pardon me for being a fool / D-A-R-L-I-N-G / Somebody robbed my beehive / I love no one but you / Broken candy heart / I wish I may, I wish I might / Tennessee hillibilly ghost / Waltzing by the Ohio / My heart keeps telling me / Fresh red apple cheeks / My baby lied to me / Strangers in the night / Mansion over the hilltop / Cry of the lamb / You're a little doll / Almost / Every little thing rolled into one / Be sure you know / Whistle my love / One woman man / Please believe / Harbor of broken hearts / Will the angel let me play / Can you trust me again / You're the only one / Withered roses / You love me just enough to hurt me / Grapevine swing / Ain't love grand / Lovers' quartet / Honky tonk street / Most of all / Every prayer is a flower / How many times / I passed by your window / Lonesome waltz / I'll furnish the shoulder you cry on / Half hearted / Look what followed me home tonight / No one knows it better than me / Love, love, love / First time I told you a lie / It's been nice / Walking shoes / I think I'm going to cry / Sweetheart / Cheap affair / So lonesome / I'd like to know / Shott / Shot in the dark / Best mistake / Wither thou goest / Oceans of tears / Oh, gentle shepherd / You don't have to walk alone / Lonesome record / Ever so often / Little pioneer / She's back in town / Jesus savior pilot me / Stay away from my baby / Take a look at yourself / Send for my baby / Now you know / There goes my love / Way of a hopeless love / Perfect romance / Can I be dreaming / Don't cry, for you I love / Sweet, sweet lips / Tears behind the smile / Don't knock it / Our summer vacation / It always ends too soon / Late date / My house is divided / It's a sin / One rose / White azaleas / You're th only star in my blue heaven / I'm not afraid / Loveable you / Rockabilly bungalow / Come away from his arms / I'm in love again / Touch of your sweet lips / It was all in your mind / Little dutch girl / Last thing I want to know / You're the only good thing / One empty chair / Where there's a will there's a way / Who knows you best / It's best you know / Little green men / Only one minute more / Day will come / Trees / Mother Machree / Smilin' thru / Mighty like a rose / Beautiful dreamer / Galway Bay / Memories / Danny Boy / Rosary / Old refrain / Across the wide Missouri / Dear little boy of mine / Every day of my life / Don't you know me / Our love / Lonely room / Let me live and love today / I can hear my heart break / Have you ever been untrue / Blue snowfall / Beyond my heart / Macht michts / Where is my love / Tender lovin' care / Would you believe / Whose memory are you / All right / One dozen roses / You're not home yet / Back again / Just like a fool / We could / Almost all the time / In your eyes / Your lonely nights are over / Just out of reach / Sin and silver / Slipping around / I love you so much it hurts / Country boy - city girl / Just your conscience / Too busy saying goodbye / Tears and roses / Dear John / Happy endings / Please help me I'm falling / Slowly / How can we plan the future / Beginning of the end / Eyes of the world / I'm thinking tonight of my blue eyes / I'll call you Charlie / Yesterday's roses / Bouquet of roses / Teardrops on the roses / Petal from a faded rose / Convict and the rose / Roses / Violet and a rose / Roses are red / By the river of the roses / Picture that's new / Bring your roses to her now / Red roses for a blue lady / It's all coming home to you but me / Not from my world / Saving all my love / Home is where the heart is / No man should hurt as bad as I do / There goes my world / Married / Wheel of hurt / Speak well of me
CD Set ______ **BCD 15851**
Bear Family / Jul '96 / Direct / Rollercoaster / Swift

ROOM FULL OF ROSES
CD ______ **RE 21092**
Razor & Tie / Oct '96 / Koch

Morgan, Greg

SPIRIT OF LIGHT VOL.1
Spirit of light
CD ______ **SLAMCD 221**
Slam / Oct '96 / Cadillac

Morgan, Jane

BEST OF JANE MORGAN, THE
CD ______ **MAR 061**
Marginal / Jun '97 / Greyhound

Morgan, Lee

AT THE LIGHTHOUSE 70 (Morgan, Lee Quintet)
CD ______ **FSRCD 140**
Fresh Sound / Dec '90 / Discovery / Jazz Music

BEST OF LEE MORGAN (Blue Note Years)
Ceora / Speedball / Night in Tunisia / Since I fell for you / Rumproller / I remember Clifford / Mr. Kenyatta / Cornbread / Sidewinder
CD ______ **BNZ 144**
Blue Note / Dec '88 / EMI

CARAMBA
Caramba / Suicide city / Cunning Lee / Soulita / Helen's ritual / Baby's smile
CD ______ **CDP 8533582**
Blue Note / Nov '96 / EMI

EXPOOBIDENT
Expoobident / Easy living / Triple threat / Fire / Just in time / Hearing / Lost and found / Terrible 'T' / Mogie / I'm a fool to want you / Running brook / Off spring / Bess
CD ______ **LEJAZZCD 39**
Le Jazz / May '95 / Cadillac / Koch

JAZZ PROFILE
CTA / Trapped / Twilight mist / Our man Higgins / Procrastinator / Sidewinder
CD ______ **CDP 8549012**
Blue Note / May '97 / EMI

LIVE AT THE LIGHTHOUSE (3CD Set)
Introduction / Beehive / Absolutions / Peyote / Speedball / Nommo / Neophilia / Something like this / I remember Britt / Aon / Yunjanna / 416 East 10th Street / Sidewinder
CD Set ______ **CDP 8352282**
Blue Note / May '96 / EMI

MINOR STRAIN (Morgan, Lee & Thad Jones)
Suspended sentence / Minor strain / Bid for Sid / Subtle rebuttal / Tip toe / H and T blues / Friday the 13th
CD ______ **CDROU 1015**
Roulette / Jun '90 / EMI

RUMPROLLER, THE
Rumproller / Desert moonlight / Eclypso / Edda / Lady / Venus de mildew
CD ______ **CDP 7464282**
Blue Note / Feb '97 / EMI

SIDEWINDER
Sidewinder / Totem pole / Gary's notebook / Boy what a night / Hocus pocus
CD ______ **CDP 7841572**
Blue Note / Mar '95 / EMI

TAKE TWELVE (Morgan, Lee Quintet)
Raggedy Ann / Waltz for Fran / Lee sure time / Little spain / Take twelve / Second's best
CD ______ **OJCCD 310**
Original Jazz Classics / Apr '93 / Complete/ Pinnacle / Jazz Music / Wellard

TRIBUTE TO LEE MORGAN (Various Artists)
Lion and the wolf / Sidewinder / Ceora / Speedball / You don't know what love is / Kozo's waltz / Yama / Ca-lee-so / Search for the new land

CD NYC 601062
NYC / Jul '95 / New Note/Pinnacle

WE REMEMBER YOU
CD FSCD 1024
Fresh Sound / Oct '93 / Discovery / Jazz Music

Morgan, Lorrie

GREATER NEED
Soldier of love / I just might be / Greater need / Steppin' stones / I can buy my own roses / Don't stop in my world / By my side / Reading my heart / Good as I was to you / She walked beside the wagon / Back among the living
CD 7863668472
BNA / Jul '96 / BMG

GREATEST HITS
CD 7863665082
RCA / Jul '95 / BMG

Morgan, Meli'sa

DO YOU STILL LOVE ME (The Best Of Meli'sa Morgan)
CD RE 21132
Razor & Tie / Jul '96 / Koch

STILL IN LOVE WITH YOU
Still in love with you / Bring you joy / Never had a love like this / Can't wait / Through the tears / I'm gonna be your lover (tonight) / Let's be real / Release me / Now I have someone / What change have you made lately
CD 3360612732
Cooltempo / May '92 / EMI

Morgan, Mike

AIN'T WORRIED NO MORE (Morgan, Mike & The Crawl)
CD BT 1102CD
Black Top / Apr '94 / ADA / CM / Direct

LET THE DOGS RUN (Morgan, Mike & Jim Suhler)
CD BT 1106CD
Black Top / Oct '94 / ADA / CM / Direct

LOWDOWN AND EVIL (Morgan, Mike & The Crawl/Jim Suhler)
I don't want you hangin' around / She's taking me to Heaven / Lowdown and evil / Frankie's blues / Where'd you get your sugar from / Looky here / I just want to get to know you / I'm worried / You ain't like you used to be / Blue cat blues / I gotta leave / I ain't worried no more / Kiss me baby / Should've done better
CD MMBCD 703
Me & My Blues / Jun '97 / CM / Direct

Morgan, Russ

22 ORIGINAL BIG BAND RECORDINGS (Morgan, Russ & His Orchestra)
CD HCD 404
Hindsight / Oct '92 / Jazz Music / Target/BMG

Morgan, Sonny

COCO DE MER (Morgan, Sonny & Seychellois)
Reggae creole / L'echo des isles / A la creole / Island way of life / Koz mwan / Femme napa marie / Coco de mer / La digue / Gros Claire / Aroa / Libre pou choisir / Tropical girls / Mahe island
CD MISSCD 1990
See For Miles/C5 / Aug '93 / Pinnacle

Morgan, Tudur

BRANWEN
O Eire/Llongau ddaeth/Efnisien/Wedi'r wledd / Ffarwel i'r marian / Hiraeth am Feirion / Cefnfor Erin / Bryniau Iwerddon / Damhsa tara / Ar lannau Llinnon / Gwern / Drudwy Branwen/Hiraeth / Cenad Aber Menai / Bendigeidfran a brwydrau Erin / Ffarwel Erin / Alaw'r Alaw / Llongau aeth / Hedd i ti Branwen / Cyn delwyf i Gymru'n ol / Yr eneth glaf / Titrwm tatrwm / Suo gan / Bryniau Wicklow / Mil harddach wyt / Mae 'nghariad i'n fenws
CD SCD 4074
Sain / Feb '95 / ADA / Direct / Greyhound

Morgana Lefay

PAST, PRESENT, FUTURE
CD BMCD 084
Black Mark / Nov '95 / Plastic Head

SANCTIFIED
CD BMCD 063
Black Mark / Mar '95 / Plastic Head

SECRET DOCTRINE, THE
CD BMCD 42
Black Mark / May '94 / Plastic Head

Morgane

BLUES AND CHANSONS OF DANIELLE MESSIA
CD KM 47CD
Keltia Musique / Jan '95 / ADA / Discovery

Morganelli, Mark

SPEAK LOW (Morganelli, Mark & The Jazz Forum All Stars)
Speak low / Dreams / Blues for Ian / When I fall in love / Summertime / Opus 15 / Lamb kurma / Child is born / Jolly jumper
CD CCD 79054
Candid / Feb '97 / Cadillac / Direct / Jazz Music / Koch / Wellard

Morganistic

FLUIDS AMNIOTIC
CD INMCD 1
GPR / Nov '94 / 3mv/Vital

Morgen

MORGEN
CD EVA 842144B19
EVA / Nov '94 / ADA / Direct

Morgion

AMONG MAJESTIC RUIN
Relic of a darkened past / In ashen tears (thus I cry) / Travesty / Basking under a blacksun dawning / Invalid prodigy
CD RR 69242
Relapse / Mar '97 / Pinnacle / Plastic Head

Morgoth

CURSED
CD CM 97192
Century Media / Sep '94 / Plastic Head

ETERNAL FALL
Burnt identity / White gallery / Eternal sanctify / Female infanticide / Pits of utumno
CD 8497082
Century Media / Aug '90 / Plastic Head

ETERNAL FALL & RESURRECTION ABSURD
CD CM 97082
Century Media / Sep '94 / Plastic Head

FEEL SORRY FOR THE FANATIC
CD CM 77119CD
Century Media / Oct '96 / Plastic Head

ODIUM
CD 8497492
Century Media / Jun '93 / Plastic Head

Moria Falls

LONG GOODBYE
Waking up screaming / Traveller / Out of darkness / Still raining / Mists / Frost / Perfect world / Long goodbye
CD VRCDMF 003
Cyclops / Nov '95 / Pinnacle

Morin, Christian

ESQUISSE
CD 3052
Deesse / Nov '92 / Discovery

Morissette, Alanis

INTERVIEW CD
CD UFOMWW 3CD
UFO / Nov '96 / Pinnacle

INTERVIEW DISC
CD SAM 7027
Sound & Media / Jan '97 / Sound & Media

JAGGED LITTLE PILL
All I really want / You oughta know / Perfect / Hand in my pocket / Right through you / Forgiven / You learn / Head over feet / Mary Jane / Ironic / Not the doctor / Wake up / You oughta know (version) / Your house
CD 9362459012
Maverick / Jun '95 / Warner Music

PILL (Interview Disc)
CD CONV 002
Network / Feb '97 / Total/BMG

Moritz, Christoph

YELLOW SIX
Green country / Yellow six / Spin / Welcome / Listen from behind / Blue world / Skyline / Brainland / Il conte / Song for Alex / Stop thinking / Half moon
CD 101 S 7053 2
New Note / Nov '92 / Cadillac / New Note/Pinnacle

Moriyama, Takeo

LIVE AT LOVELY
CD DIW 820
DIW / Mar '97 / Cadillac / Harmonia Mundi

Mork Gryning

TUSEN AR HAR GATT
CD NFR 012CD
No Fashion / Jan '96 / Plastic Head

Morley, Michael

PAVILLION OF FOOLS
CD BHC 004CD
Black Halo / Jul '97 / Cargo

Mormos

GREAT WALL OF CHINA
CD 14540
Spalax / Jul '97 / ADA / Cargo / Direct / Discovery / Greyhound

MAGIC SPELL OF MOTHER'S WRATH
CD 14541
Spalax / Jul '97 / ADA / Cargo / Direct / Discovery / Greyhound

Morning Glories

FULLY LOADED
CD SCANCD 06
Radarscope / Oct '95 / Pinnacle

LET THE BODY HANG
CD HED 069
Headhunter / Jun '97 / Cargo

Morohas, Hiroshi

TIME NOTE
CD PIAS 533010320
Shield / Jun '97 / Plastic Head

Morphew, Jason

TRANSPARENT
CD BING 009
Ba Da Bing / Apr '97 / Cargo

Morphine

BUENA
CD RCD 51035
Rykodisc / Mar '94 / ADA / Vital

CURE FOR PAIN
Dawna / Buena / I'm free now / All wrong / Candy / Head with wings / In spite of me / Thursday / Cure for pain / Mary won't you call my name / Let's take a trip together / Sheila / Miles Davis' funeral
CD RCD 10262
Rykodisc / Mar '97 / ADA / Vital

GOOD
Good / Saddest song / Claire / Have a lucky day / You speak my language / You look like rain / Do not go quietly unto your grave / Lisa / Only one / Test tube baby/Shoot'm down / Other side / I know you
CD RCD 10263
Rykodisc / Mar '97 / ADA / Vital

LIKE SWIMMING
Lilah / Potion / I know you pt.3 / Early to bed / Wishing well / Like swimming / Murder for the money / French fries with pepper / Empty box / Eleven o'clock / Hanging on a curtain / Swing it low
CD RCD 10362
Rykodisc / Mar '97 / ADA / Vital

THURSDAY
CD RCD 1036
Rykodisc / May '94 / ADA / Vital

YES
Honey white / Scratch / Radar / Whisper / Yes / All your way / Super sex / I had my chance / Jury / Sharks / Free love / Gone for good
CD RCD 10320
Rykodisc / Mar '97 / ADA / Vital

Morphogenesis

CHARIVARI MUSIC
CD PD 902
Paradigm / Jun '97 / ReR Megacorp

Morris, Butch

DUST TO DUST
CD 804082
New World / Jun '91 / ADA / Cadillac / Harmonia Mundi

TESTAMENT: A CONDUCTION COLLECTION (10CD Set)
CD Set 804782
New World / Dec '95 / ADA / Cadillac / Harmonia Mundi

Morris, Joe

SYMBOLIC GESTURE
CD SN 1212042
Soul Note / Oct '94 / Cadillac / Harmonia Mundi / Wellard

YOU AND ME (Morris, Joe Quartet)
CD 1213042
Soul Note / Jul '97 / Cadillac / Harmonia Mundi / Wellard

Morris, Lynn

BRAMBLE AND THE ROSE (Morris, Lynn Band)
Blue skies and teardrops / Coat of many colours / Engineers don't wave from trains anymore / Why tell me why / Love grows cold / Bramble and the rose / I'll pretend it's raining / Hey porter / New patches / My younger days / Red line too Shady Grove / Heartstrings
CD ROUCD 0288
Rounder / Feb '92 / ADA / CM / Direct

LYNN MORRIS BAND (Morris, Lynn Band)
My heart skips a beat / You'll get no more me / Adams county breakdown / Black pony / Come early morning / Help me climb that mountain / Kisses don't die / Handyman / What was I supposed to do / If lonely was the wind / Don't tell me stories / Valley of peace
CD ROUCD 0276
Rounder / '90 / ADA / CM / Direct

MAMA'S HAND
CD ROUCD 0328
Rounder / Oct '95 / ADA / CM / Direct

Morris On

MORRIS ON
Bean setting / Shooting / I'll go and enlist for a sailor / Princess Royal / Cuckoo's nest / Morris off / Morris call / Greensleeves / Nutting girl / Old woman tossed up in a blanket / Shepherd's hey / Trunkles / Staines morris / Lads a bunchum / Young Collins / Vandals of Hammerwich / Willow tree
CD HNCD 4406
Hannibal / Jan '87 / ADA / Vital

Morris, R.B.

TAKE THAT RIDE
World owes me / Ridin' with O'Hanlon / They say there's a time / Hell on a poor boy / Take time to love / Ballad of Thunder Road / Take that ride / Roy / Dog days / Pot hole street / Bottom of the big black hull / Glory dreams
CD OBR 016CD
Oh Boy / May '97 / ADA / CM / Direct

Morris, Sarah Jane

BLUE VALENTINE
CD JHCD 038
Ronnie Scott's Jazz House / Apr '95 / Cadillac / Jazz Music / New Note/Pinnacle / TKO Magnum
CD IRMA 4838002
Ronnie Scott's Jazz House / Aug '96 / Cadillac / Jazz Music / New Note/Pinnacle / TKO Magnum

Morris, Sonny

BLUES FOR THE GOOD OLD BOYS (Morris, Sonny & The Delta Jazz Band)
Do what Ory say / Black cat on a fence / Yellow dog blues / Dr. Jazz / Sensation rag / Dallas rag / Hiawatha rag / Blue for the good old boys / Girls go crazy / Silver birches / Joe Avery's piece / In the gloaming / Trombonium
CD LACD 63
Lake / Jul '96 / ADA / Cadillac / Direct / Jazz Music / Target/BMG

GLORYLAND (Morris, Sonny & The Delta Jazz Band)
CD PKCD 024
PEK / Jul '96 / Cadillac / Jazz Music / Wellard

SONNY MEETS PAT (Morris, Sonny & The Delta Jazz Band/Pat Halcox)
Bogalusa strut / Bugle boy march / One sweet letter from you / Poor little green bean / Climax rag / There's yes, yes in your eyes / Tin roof blues / Panama rag / You took advantage of me / Flee as a bird/Didn't he ramble / Home
CD LACD 81
Lake / Jun '97 / ADA / Cadillac / Direct / Jazz Music / Target/BMG

SONNY SIDE UP (Morris, Sonny & The Delta Jazz Band)
CD PARJ 501
Parrot / May '93 / BMG / Jazz Music / THE / Wellard

SPIRIT LIVES ON, THE (Morris, Sonny & The Delta Jazz Band)
Yaaka hula hickey dula / Hesitation blues / While we danced at the Mardi Gras / Canal street blues / Dusty rag / If I had my life to live over / When you and I were young Maggie / I can't escape from you / Barefoot boy / Sometimes my burden is so hard to bear / Mandy, make up your mind / Give me a june night / Wabash blues / Looks like a big time tonight
CD LACD 46
Lake / Apr '95 / ADA / Cadillac / Direct / Jazz Music / Target/BMG

Morris, Thomas

CLASSICS 1923-1927
CD CLASSICS 823
Classics / Jul '95 / Discovery / Jazz Music

WHEN A 'GATOR HOLLERS (Thomas Morris 1926)
Lazy drag / Jackass blues / Charleston stampede / Georgia grind / Ham gravy / Who's dis heah stranger / When a 'gator hollers, folks say it's a sign of rain / My baby doesn't squawk / King of the Zulus / South Rampart Street blues / Blues for the Everglades / PDQ blues / Mess / Chinch
CD DGF 1
Frog / May '95 / Cadillac / Jazz Music / Wellard

Morrisey, Louise

WHEN I WAS YOURS
I couldn't leave you if I tried / He thinks I still care / Old flames / Blue eyes cryin' in the rain / Oh what a love / I still love you / Night Daniel O'Donnell came to town / When I was yours / Tipperary on my mind / Rose of Allendale / Hills of Killinaule / Green willow / Slievenamon / Roses and violets / Amazing grace
CD RITZCD 508
Ritz / '91 / Pinnacle

YOU'LL REMEMBER ME
Just in case / Out of sight out of mind / Waltzing with you tonight / That's the way to my heart / Come back Paddy Reilly to Ballyjamesduff / Precious memories / Don't say goodbye / You'll remember me / I'd live my life over you / You make me feel like a woman / I'll bet my heart on you / Getting over getting over you / Heaven I call home / Hills I used to roam
CD RITZRCD 546
Ritz / Nov '94 / Pinnacle

Morrison, Alexander

SCOTTISH MEMORIES
CD CDLOC 1089
Lochshore / Jun '95 / ADA / Direct / Duncans

Morrison, Fred

BROKEN CHANTER, THE
Reels / Strathspeys and reels / Jigs / Hornpipes / Malcolm Ferguson / Irish reels / Polkas / 2/4 Marches / Jigs / Hector the hero / Strathspeys and reels / Piobaireachd
CD LCOM 5223
Lismor / Sep '93 / ADA / Direct / Duncans / Lismor

Morrison, Frieda

FLYING BY THE SUN
CD BLR 101
Smiddymare / May '97 / Duncans / Highlander

Morrison, Junie

WESTBOUND YEARS
Junie / Tightrope / Walt's first trip / Place / When we do / Johnny Carson samba / Loving arms / Junie II / Not as good as you should / Cookies will get you / Freeze / Super J / Granny's funky rolls royce / Junie III / Surrender / Suzie / Super groupie / Suzy Thundertussy / Spirit / Junie's ultimate departure
CD CDSEWD 064
Westbound / Apr '94 / Pinnacle

Morrison, Mark

ONLY GOD CAN JUDGE ME (Verse I Chapter II)
Headlines / Who's the mack / Lord's prayer / Only God can judge me / NEC '96 / Mac life / Lisa at lunchtime / Blackstabbers / Lord's prayer
CD 0630195392
Warner Bros. / Sep '97 / Warner Music

RETURN OF THE MACK
Home / Crazy / Let's get down / Get high with me / Moan and groan / Return of the mack / I like / Trippin' / Tears for you / Horny / I really love you / Crazy / Home
CD 0630145862
WEA / Apr '96 / Warner Music

Morrison, Peter

LAND OF THE EAGLE
Land of the eagle / Ae fond kiss / Crinan canal / Hundred pipers / Culloden's harvest / Roses of Prince Charlie / Caledonia / Muckin' 'o' Geordie's byre / Mary Morrison / Bonnie Well's O'Wearie / Niel Gow's farewell to whiskey / Marching medley
CD CDGR 155
Ross / Jul '96 / CM / Duncans / Highlander / Ross

TOAST TO THE MUSIC OF SCOTLAND, A
Toast is music / There was a lad / Roamin' in the gloamin' / Wee Deoch an' Doris / I love a lassie / My love is like a red red rose / Calling me home / Man's a man for a' that / Lass I lo'v ye dearly / Bonnie lass O'Ballochmyle / Dancing in Kyle / Of a the airts / Think on me / Hail Caledonia
CD LCOM 6015
Lismor / Aug '96 / ADA / Direct / Duncans / Lismor

Morrison, Van

ASTRAL WEEKS
Astral weeks / Beside you / Sweet thing / Cyprus Avenue / Young lovers do / Madame George / Ballerina / Slim slow rider
CD 7599271762
Warner Bros. / Jan '95 / Warner Music

AVALON SUNSET
Whenever God shines his light / Contacting my angel / I'd love to write another song / Have I told you lately that I love you / Coney island / I'm tired Joey Boy / When will I ever learn to live in God / Orangefield / Daring night / These are the days
CD 8392622
Polydor / May '89 / PolyGram

BANG MASTERS
Brown eyed girl / Spanish rose / Goodbye baby (baby goodbye) / Ro ro Rosy / Chicka boom / It's alright / Send your mind / Smile you smile / Back room / Midnight special / TB sheets / He ain't give you none / Who drove the red sports car / Beside you / Joe Harper saturday morning / Madame George / Brown eyed girl (alternate take) / I love you (the smile you smile)
CD 4683092
Legacy / Mar '92 / Sony

BEAUTIFUL VISION
Celtic ray / Northern music / Dweller on the threshold / She gives me religion / Beautiful vision / Aryan mist / Across the bridge where angels dwell / Vanlose stairway / Scandinavia / Cleaning windows
CD 8396012
Polydor / Aug '89 / PolyGram

BEST OF VAN MORRISON VOL.1, THE
Whenever God shines his light: *Morrison, Van & Cliff Richard* / Jackie Wilson said (I'm in heaven when you smile) / Brown eyed girl / Brown side of the road / Have I told you lately that I love you / Moondance / Here comes the night / Domino / Gloria / Baby, please don't go / And it stoned me / Sweet thing / Warm love / Wild night / Cleaning windows / Did ye get healed / Dweller on the threshold / Queen of the slipstream / Wonderful remark / Full force gale
CD 8419702
Polydor / Feb '90 / PolyGram

BEST OF VAN MORRISON VOL.2, THE
Real real gone / When will I ever learn to live in God / Sometimes I feel like a Motherless child / In the garden / Sense of wonder / Carrickfergus / Coney island / Enlightenment / Rave on, John Donne / Don't look back / It's all over now baby blue / One Irish rover / Mystery / Hymns to the silence / Evening meditation
CD 5177602
Polydor / Jan '93 / PolyGram

BLOWIN' YOUR MIND
Brown eyed girl / He ain't give you none / TB Sheets / Spanish rose / Goodbye baby (baby goodbye) / Ro ro Rosy / Who drove the red sports car / Midnight special
CD 4804212
Mastersound / Jun '95 / Sony

BROWN EYED GIRL
Brown eyed girl / Goodbye baby (baby goodbye) / Ro Ro Rosey / Back room / Midnight special / He ain't give you none / Who drove the red sports car / Joe Harper Saturday morning / Madame George / Spanish rose / Chick-a-boom / Smile you smile / It's alright / TB Sheets / Beside you / I love you (the smile you smile) / Send your mind
CD APH 102805
Audiophile Legends / Apr '96 / Total/BMG

COMMON ONE
Haunts of ancient peace / Summertime in England / Satisfied / When heart is open / Wild honey / Spirit
CD 8396002
Polydor / Aug '89 / PolyGram

DAYS LIKE THIS
Perfect fit / Russian roulette / Raincheck / You don't know me / No religion / Underlying depression / Songwriter / Days like this / I'll never be free / Melancholia / Ancient highway / In the afternoon
CD 5273072
Polydor / Jun '95 / PolyGram

ENLIGHTENMENT
Real real gone / Enlightenment / So quiet in here / Avalon of the heart / See me through / Youth of 1,000 summers / In the days before rock 'n' roll / Start all over again / She's a baby / Memories
CD 8471002
Polydor / Oct '90 / PolyGram

HARD NOSE THE HIGHWAY
Snow in San Anselmo / Warm love / Hard nose the highway / Wild children / Great deception / Bein' green / Autumn song / Purple heather
CD 5374522
Polydor / Jun '97 / PolyGram

HEALING GAME, THE
Rough God goes riding / Fire in the belly / This weight / Waiting game / Piper at the gates of dawn / Burning ground / It once was my life / Sometimes we cry / If you love me / Healing game
CD 5371012
Polydor / Mar '97 / PolyGram

HIS BAND & STREET CHOIR
Domino / Crazy face / Give me a kiss / I've been working / Call me up in Dreamland / I'll be your lover too / Blue money / Virgo clowns / Gypsy queen / Sweet Jannie / If I ever needed someone / Street choir
CD 7599271882
Warner Bros. / Oct '93 / Warner Music

HOW LONG HAS THIS BEEN GOING ON
CD 5291362
Verve / Dec '95 / PolyGram

HYMNS TO THE SILENCE (2CD Set)
Professional jealousy / I'm not feeling it anymore / Ordinary life / Some peace of mind / So complicated / I can't stop loving you / Why must I always explain / Village idiot / See me through / Take me back / By his grace / All Saints Day / Hymns to the silence / On Hyndford Street / Be thou my vision / Carrying a torch / Green mansions / Pagan streams / Quality Street / I must be you / I need your kind of love
CD Set 8490262
Polydor / Sep '91 / PolyGram

INARTICULATE SPEECH OF THE HEART
Higher than the world / Connswater / River of time / Celtic swing / Rave on, John Donne / Inarticulate speech of the heart / Irish heartbeat / Street only knew your name / Cry for home / Inarticulate speech of the heart no.2 / September night
CD 8396042
Polydor / Feb '94 / PolyGram

INTO THE MUSIC
Bright side of the road / Full force gale / And the healing has begun / Steppin' out queen / Troubadors / Rolling hills / You make me feel so free / Angelou / It's all in the game / You know what they're writing about
CD 8396032
Polydor / Feb '94 / PolyGram

IRISH HEARTBEAT (Morrison, Van & The Chieftains)
Star of County Down / Irish heartbeat / Ta mo chleamhnas deanta / Raglan Road / She moved through the fair / I'll tell me ma / Carrickfergus / Celtic ray / My lagan love / Marie's wedding
CD 8344962
Mercury / Jun '88 / PolyGram

IT'S TOO LATE TO STOP NOW (2CD Set)
Ain't nothin' you can do / Warm love / Into the mystic / These dreams of you / I believe in my soul / I've been working / Help me / Wild children / Domino / I just want to make love to you / Bring it on home to me / St. Dominic's preview / Take your hand out of my pocket / Listen to the lion / Here comes the night / Gloria / Caravan / Cyprus Avenue
CD Set 5374532
Polydor / Jun '97 / PolyGram

LIVE AT THE GRAND OPERA HOUSE, BELFAST
Into the mystic / Inarticulate speech of the heart / Dweller on the threshold / It's all in the game / You know what they're writing about / She gives me religion / Haunts of ancient peace / Full force gale / Beautiful vision / Vanlose stairway / Rave on, John Donne / Rave on, John Donne / Northern muse / Cleaning windows
CD 8396022
Polydor / Aug '89 / PolyGram

MOONDANCE
Stoned me / Moondance / Crazy love / Caravan / Into the mystic / Come running / These dreams of you / Brand new day / Everyone / Glad tidings
CD 246040
Warner Bros. / Jan '86 / Warner Music

NEW YORK SESSIONS 1967, THE (2CD Set)
Brown eyed girl / He ain't give you none / TB sheets / Spanish rose / Goodbye baby (baby goodbye) / Ro ro Rosey / Who drove the red sportscar / Midnight special / Beside you / It's alright / Madame George / Send your mind / Smile you smile / Back room / Joe Harper Saturday morning / Chick-a-boom / I love you (the smile you smile) / Brown eyed girl / Jam session
CD Set PILOT 006
Burning Airlines / Feb '97 / Total/Pinnacle

NIGHT IN SAN FRANCISCO, A (2CD Set)
Did ye get healed / It's all in the game/Make it real one more time / I've been working / I forgot that love existed / Vanlose stairway/ Trans-Euro train/Fool for you / You make me feel so free / Beautiful vision / See me through/Soldier of fortune/Thankyou falettinmebemicel / Ain't that lovin' you baby / Stormy Monday/Have you ever loved a woman/No rollin' blues / Help me / Good morning little school girl / Tupelo honey / Moondance/My funny valentine / Jumpin' with symphony Sid / It fills you up / I'll take care of you/It's a man's man's man's world / Lonely avenue/4 o' clock in the morning / So quiet in here/That's where it's at / In the garden/You send me/Allegheny / Have I told you lately that I love you / Shakin' all over/Gloria
CD Set 5212902
Polydor / Apr '94 / PolyGram

NO GURU, NO METHOD, NO TEACHER
Got to go back / Oh the warm feeling / Foreign window / Town called Paradise / In the garden / Tir na nog / Here comes the knight / Thanks for the information / One Irish rover / Ivory tower
CD 8496192
Polydor / Feb '94 / PolyGram

NO PRIMA DONNA (A Tribute To Van Morrison) (Various Artists)
You make me feel so free: *O'Connor, Sinead* / Queen of the slipstream: *Kennedy, Brian* / Coney Island: *Neeson, Liam* / Crazy love: *Wilson, Cassandra* / Bright side of the road: *Hothouse Flowers* / Irish heartbeat: *Kennedy, Brian & Shana Morrison* / Full force gale: *Costello, Elvis* / Tupelo honey: *Coulter, Phil Orchestra* / Madame George: *Faithfull, Marianne* / Friday's child: *Stansfield, Lisa*
CD 5233682
Polydor / Jul '94 / PolyGram

PAYIN' DUES (The Best Of The 1965 Studio Recordings/2CD Set)
Brown eyed girl / He ain't give you none / TB Sheets / Spanish rose / Goodbye baby (Baby goodbye) / Ro ro Rosy / Who drove the red sports car / Midnight special / Beside you / It's alright / Madame George / Send your mind / Smile you smile / Back room / Joe Harper Saturday morning / Chicka boom / I love you (The smile you smile) / Brown eyed girl / Twist and shake / Shake and roll / Stomp and scream / Scream and holler / Jump and thump / Drivin' wheel / Just ball / Shake it Mable / Hold on George / Big royalty check / Ring worm / Savoy Hollywood / Freaky if you got this far / Up your mind / Thirty two / All the bits / You say France and I whistle / Blow in your nose / Nose in your blow / La mambo / Go for yourself / Want a Danish / Here comes dumb George / Chickee coo / Do it / Hang on groovy / Goodbye George / Dum dum George / Walk and talk / Wobble / Wobble and ball
CD Set CPCD 80352
Charly / Aug '96 / Koch

PERIOD OF TRANSITION, A
You gotta make it through the world / It fills you up / Eternal Kansas City / Joyous sound / Flamingoes fly (heavy connection) / Cold wind in August
CD 5374572
Polydor / Jun '97 / PolyGram

PHILOSOPHER'S STONE, THE (2CD Set)
Really don't know / Ordinary people / Wonderful remark / Not supposed to break down / Laughing in the wind / Madame Joy / Bright side of the road / I'm ready / Street theory / Real real gone / Showbusiness / For Mr. Thomas / Crazy Jane on God / Song of a being a child / High spirits / Contemplation Rose / Don't worry about tomorrow / Try for sleep / Lover's prayer / Drumshanbo hustle / Twilight zone / Foggy mountain top / Naked in the jungle / There there child / When I deliver / John Henry / John Brown's body / I have finally come to realise / Flamingoes fly / Stepping out Queen part 2
CD Set 5317892
Polydor / Jul '96 / PolyGram

POETIC CHAMPIONS COMPOSE
Spanish Steps / Mystery / Queen of the slipstream / I forgot that love existed / Sometimes I feel like a Motherless child / Celtic excavation / Someone like you / Alan Watts Blues / Give me my rapture / Did ye get healed / Allow me
CD 5172172
Polydor / Mar '94 / PolyGram

SENSE OF WONDER, A
Tore down a'la rimbaud / Ancient of days / Evening meditation / Master's eyes / What would I do / Sense of wonder / Boffyflow and Spike / If you only knew / Let the slave
CD 8431162
Polydor / May '90 / PolyGram

ST. DOMINIC'S PREVIEW
Jackie Wilson said (I'm in heaven when you smile) / Gypsy / I will be there / Listen to the lion / St. Dominic's preview / Redwood tree / Almost Independence Day
CD 5374512
Polydor / Jun '97 / PolyGram

TB SHEETS
He ain't give you none / Beside you / It's all right/For sentimental reasons / Madame George / TB Sheets / Who drove the red sports car / Ro Ro Rosy / Brown eyed girl
CD 4678272
Columbia / May '91 / Sony

TOO LONG IN EXILE
Too long in exile / Big time operators / Lonely avenue / Ball and chain / In the forest / Till we get the healing done / Gloria / Good morning little school girl / Wasted years / Lonesome road / Moody's mood for love / Close enough for jazz / Before the world was made / Medley: I'll take care of you
CD 5192192
Polydor / Jun '93 / PolyGram

TUPELO HONEY
Wild night / Straight to your heart like a cannonball / Old old Woodstock / Starting a new life / You're my woman / Tupelo honey / I wanna roo you / When that evening sun goes down / Moonshine whisky
CD 5374502
Polydor / Jun '97 / PolyGram

VAN MORRISON SONGBOOK, THE (Various Artists)
Cleaning windows: *Whitfield, Barrence & Tom Russell* / Jackie Wilson said (I'm in heaven when you smile): *Dexy's Midnight Runners* / I shall sing: *Garfunkel, Art* / Madame George: *Energy Orchard* / Angeliou: *Deacon Blue* / I wanna roo you: *Hawn, Gol-*

die / Have I told you lately: *Emilio* / Brown eyed girl: *Steel Pulse* / Tupelo honey: *Springfield, Dusty* / Irish heartbeat: *Connolly, Billy* / Moondance: *McFerrin, Bobby* / My lonely sad eyes: *McKee, Maria* / Sweet thing: *Waterboys* / Mercy, mercy, mercy/ Vanlose stairway: *Fame, Georgie & The Blue Flames* / Gloria: *Eddie & The Hot Rods*
CD VSOPCD 233
Connoisseur Collection / Mar '97 / Pinnacle

VEEDON FLEECE
Fair play / Linden Arden stole the highlights / Who was that masked man / Streets of Arklow / You don't pull no punches but you don't push the river / Bulbs / Cul de sac / Comfort you / Come here my love / Country fair
CD 5374562
Polydor / Jun '97 / PolyGram

WAVELENGTH
Kingdom Hall / Checking it out / Natalia / Venice USA / Lifetimes / Wavelength / Santa Fe: Beautiful obsession / Hungry for your love / Take it where you find it
CD 5374582
Polydor / Jun '97 / PolyGram

Morrison, William

PIPERS OF DISTINCTION
CD MON 821CD
Monarch / Oct '94 / ADA / CM / Direct / Duncans

Morrissey

BEETHOVEN WAS DEAF
You're the one for me fatty / Certain people I know / National front disco / November spawned a monster / Seasick, yet still docked / Loop / Sister I'm a poet / Jack the ripper / Such a little thing makes such a big difference / I know it's gonna happen someday / We'll let you know / Suedehead / He knows I'd love to see him / You're gonna need someone on your side / Glamorous glue / We hate it when our friends become successful
CD CDCSD 3791
HMV / May '93 / EMI

BONA DRAG
Piccadilly palare / Interesting drug / November spawned a monster / Will never marry / Such a little thing makes such a big difference / Last of the famous international playboys / Ouija board, ouija board / Hairdresser on fire / Everyday is like Sunday / He knows I'd love to see him / Yes, I am blind / Luckylisp / Suedehead / Disappointed
CD CDCLP 3788
HMV / Mar '94 / EMI

KILL UNCLE
Our Frank / Asian rut / Sing your life / Mute witness / King Lear / Found found found / Driving your girlfriend home / Harsh truth of the camera eye / (I'm) the end of the family line / There's a place in hell for me and my friends
CD CDCSD 3789
HMV / Feb '91 / EMI

MALADJUSTED
Maladjusted / Alma matters / Ambitious outsiders / Trouble loves me / Papa Jack / Ammunition / Wide to receive / Roy's keen / He cried / Satan rejected my soul
CD CID 8059
Island / Aug '97 / PolyGram

SOUTHPAW GRAMMAR
Teachers are afraid of the pupils / Reader meet author / Boy racer / Operation / Dagenham Dave / Do your best and don't worry / Best friend on the payroll / Southpaw
CD 74321299532
RCA / Aug '95 / BMG

VAUXHALL AND I
Now my heart is full / Spring heeled Jim / Billy Budd / Hold on to your friends / More you ignore me, the closer I get / Why don't you find out for yourself / I am hated for loving / Lifeguard sleeping, girl drowning / Used to be a sweet boy / Lazy sunbathers / Speedway
CD CDPCSD 148
HMV / Mar '94 / EMI

VIVA HATE
Alsatian cousin / Little man, what now / Everyday is like Sunday / Bengali in platforms / Angel, angel, down we go together / Late night, Maudlin Street / Suedehead / Break up the family / Ordinary boys / I don't mind if you forget me / Dial a cliche / Margaret on the guillotine
CD CDCNTAV 2
Parlophone / Mar '97 / EMI

WORLD OF MORRISSEY, THE
Whatever happens I love you / Billy Budd / Jack the ripper / Have-a-go merchant / Loop / Sister I'm a poet / You're the one for me fatty / Boxers / Moonriver / My love life / Certain people I know / Last of the famous international playboys / We'll let you know / Spring heeled Jim
CD CDPCSD 163
HMV / Feb '95 / EMI

YOUR ARSENAL
You're gonna need someone on your side / Glamorous glue / We'll let you know / National front disco / Certain people I know / We hate it when our friends become successful / You're the one for me fatty / Seasick, yet still docked / I know it's gonna happen someday / Tomorrow
CD CDCSD 3790
HMV / Jul '92 / EMI

Morrissey, Bill

FRIEND OF MINE (Morrissey, Bill & Greg Brown)
CD PH 1151CD
Philo / May '93 / ADA / CM / Direct

NIGHT TRAIN
CD PH 1154CD
Philo / Jan '94 / ADA / CM / Direct

Morrissey, Dick

THERE AND BACK (Morrissey, Dick Quartet)
CD JHAS 607
Ronnie Scott's Jazz House / Feb '97 / Cadillac / Jazz Music / New Note/Pinnacle / TKO Magnum

Morriston Orpheus Choir

60 YEARS OF SONG
Rhyfelgrch gwyr Harlech (march of the men of Harlech) / Way you look tonight / Morte Criste (When I survey the wondrous cross) / Memory / How great thou art / Bugeilio'r gwenith gwyn / Did those feet in ancient time (Jerusalem) / Speed your journey (va pensiero from Nabucco) / Old rugged cross / In my Father's house / Drinking song (from the Student Prince) / You'll never walk alone / Gwahoddiad / Amazing grace / Llanfair / Myfanwy
CD CDPR 133
Premier/MFP / Feb '95 / EMI

ALWAYS ON MY MIND
Morte christie (When I survey the wonderous cross) / Always on my mind / Just a closer walk with thee / Non nobis, domine / Y nefoedd / Nidaros / Rhythm of life / Give me Jesus / When I fall in love / Where could I go but to the Lord / Sound an alarm / There is a balm in gilead / My wish for you / Cwm rhondda
CD GRCD 59
Grasmere / Jun '93 / Highlander / Savoy / Target/BMG

CHRISTMAS FROM THE LAND OF SONG
Have yourself a merry little Christmas / Joy to the world / When a child is born / Ding dong merrily on high / Silent night / God rest ye merry gentlemen / Do they know it's Christmas / Saviour's day / Mistletoe and wine / Happy Christmas (war is over) / Hark the herald angels sing / Winter wonderland / Holly and the ivy / Deck the halls with boughs of holly / See amid the winter's snow / Child this day is born / O little town of Bethlehem / Good King Wenceslas / Away in a manger / We three Kings / I saw three ships / O come all ye faithful (Adeste Fidelis) / White Christmas
CD CDXMAS 1
Premier/MFP / Dec '94 / EMI

LAND OF MY FATHERS
Land of my fathers (Hen wlad fy nhadau) / It's now or never / Moonlight and memory / Funiculi, funicula / gloria / Be still my soul / Where shall I be / By babylon's wave / Aberystwyth / Calon lan / Onward, ye peoples / Sanctus / Arwelfa / Do you hear the people sing / I dramed a dream / Master of the house / On my own / Drink with me / Empty chairs at empty tables
CD GRCD 40
Grasmere / Sep '90 / Highlander / Savoy / Target/BMG

LET'S FACE THE MUSIC
Tribute to the USA / Non ti scordar di me / True love / Let's face the music and dance / Very best time of year / Nos a bore / In the spirit / Memories of Martha / La vergine degli angeli / I bob un sy'n Ffyddion / Smilin' through / Flower that shattered the stone / They led my Lord away / Jesus Christ Superstar medley
CD GRCD 81
Grasmere / Mar '97 / Highlander / Savoy / Target/BMG

MORRISTON ORPHEUS CHOIR & FRIENDS
Cwm Rhondda (Guide me O thou great redeemer) / Wynwbwn 'fory pan ddan (Let's face the music and dance) / Cymru fach / Nessun dorma / Bugeilio'r Gwenith Gwyn / Llanfair / Ceidward y goleudy / Law yn llaw / Un ydym ni / Finlandia / Y nefoedd / Ni cherdd'n unig fyth (You'll never walk alone)
CD CDMFP 6213
Music For Pleasure / Feb '96 / EMI

MYFANWY
Myfanwy / With a voice of singing / Kula serenade / High on a hill / Ave verum corpus / Come back to Sorrento / Old rugged cross / Love could I only tell thee / Roll Jordan roll / Scarborough Fair / My little Welsh home / We'll gather lilacs / How soon / Gloria in excelsis / Amazing grace / Eli Jenkin's prayer / Speed your journey / Battle hymn of the Republic / Little drummer boy
CD CDMFP 6027
Music For Pleasure / Jul '88 / EMI

YOU'LL NEVER WALK ALONE
Dies irae / Let it be me / Anvil chorus / Miserere / Rise up shepherd and follow / You'll never walk alone / Cymru fach / Creation's hymn / Old folks at home (Swanee river) / Li'l Liza Jane / My hero / Martyrs of the arena
CD GRACC 7
Grasmere / May '94 / Highlander / Savoy / Target/BMG

Morro, Henry J.

SOMOZAS TEETH
CD NAR 112CD
New Alliance / Nov '94 / Plastic Head

Morrow, Buddy

NIGHT TRAIN
CD AERO 1034
Aerospace / Jul '96 / Jazz Music / Montpellier

Mors Syphilitica

MORS SYPHILITICA
CD EFA 01568CD
Apocalyptic Vision / Sep '96 / Cargo / Plastic Head / SRD

Morse, Steve

STRESSFEST
Stressfest / Rising power / Eyes of a child / Nightwalk / Brave new world / Four minutes to live / Easy way / Glad to be / Delicate business / Live to ride
CD 72902103482
High Street / Jun '96 / BMG

STRUCTURAL DAMAGE (Morse, Steve Band)
Sacred ground / Good to go / Dreamland / Barbary Coast / Smokey Mountain Drive / Slice of time / Native dance / Just out of reach / Rally cry / Foreign exchange / Structural damage
CD 72902103322
High Street / Feb '96 / BMG

Morta Skuld

DYING REMAINS/AS HUMANITY FADES
CD CDVILE 60
Peaceville / May '95 / Pinnacle

FOR ALL ETERNITY
Bitter / For all eternity / Vicious circle / Justify / Tears / Germ farm / Second thought / Bleeding heart / Crawl inside / Burning daylight
CD CDVILE 57
Peaceville / Oct '95 / Pinnacle

Mortal Constraint

LEGEND OF DEFORMATION, THE
CD GLA 112692
Glasnost / Apr '94 / SRD

Mortal Memories

STONE AND THE GRAIL, THE
CD FREQCD 005
Hyperium / Jul '93 / Cargo / Plastic Head

Mortal Sin

EVERY DOG HAS ITS DAY
CD CDFLAG 61
Under One Flag / Sep '91 / Pinnacle

Mortals

LAST TIME AROUND
CD ES 1228CD
Estrus / Sep '96 / Cargo / Greyhound / Plastic Head

Mortician

HACKED UP FOR BARBECUE
CD RR 69522
Relapse / Feb '97 / Pinnacle / Plastic Head

HOUSE BY THE CEMETERY
Intro/Defiler of the dead / Barbaric cruelties / World domination / Driller killer / House by the cemetery / Procredtion (of the wicked) / Scum / Gateway to beyond / Flesheaters / Noturam demondo
CD RR 69332
Relapse / Jul '97 / Pinnacle / Plastic Head

Mortification

BLOOD WORLD
CD NB 1182
Nuclear Blast / May '95 / Plastic Head

ENVISION EVANGELENE
CD NB 159CD
Nuclear Blast / Jul '96 / Plastic Head

MORTIFACTION
CD NB 101CD
Nuclear Blast / Mar '94 / Plastic Head

POST MOMENTARY AFFLICTION
CD NB 082
Nuclear Blast / Nov '93 / Plastic Head

POST MOMENTARY AFFLICTION/ SCROLLS OF THE MONOLITH
CD NB 214CD
Nuclear Blast / Nov '96 / Plastic Head

PRIMITIVE RHYTHM MACHINE
CD NB 134CD
Nuclear Blast / Aug '95 / Plastic Head

Mortiis

FOOD TIL A HERSKE
CD MA 003CD
Malicious / Oct '95 / Plastic Head

Mortimer, Harry

KING OF BRASS (Various Artists)
Mikado / Lost chord / Hallelujah chorus / Solemn melody / Colonel Bogey on parade / William Tell overture - finale / Onward christian soldiers / Grand march from Aida / Nimrod / Finlandia / Hunting medley / Semper sousa / When the saints go marching in / Gallop / Londonderry air / Hailstorm / Waltzing trumpets / Parade of the tin soldiers / March: Kenilworth suite
CD CC 283
Music For Pleasure / Jul '92 / EMI

TRIBUTE IN MUSIC, A
Cossack / Yeoman of the guard / Three jolly sailormen / Shipbuilders / Trumpet voluntary / Relaxation / Force of destiny / Medallion / Grandfather's clock / Jesu joy of man's desiring / Alla hornpipe / All in the April evening / Life divine / Praise my soul
CD QPRL 050D
Polyphonic / Jun '92 / Complete/Pinnacle

Morton, Benny

CLASSICS 1934-1945
CD CLASSICS 906
Classics / Nov '96 / Discovery / Jazz Music

Morton, Eddy

TATTERDEMALION
CD MM 014CD
New Mountain / Nov '96 / ADA

Morton, Jelly Roll

ANTHOLOGY 1926-1939
CD EN 515
Encyclopaedia / Sep '95 / Discovery

BLUES AND STOMPS FROM RARE PIANO ROLLS
Jelly Roll blues / Mr. Jelly Lord / London blues / Sweet man / Grandpa's spells / Stratford hunch / Shreveport stomp / Tom cat blues / King Porter stomp / Midnight mama / Tin roof blues / Dead man blues / Pep / Naked dance
CD BCD 111
Biograph / Jul '91 / ADA / Cadillac / Direct / Hot Shot / Jazz Music / Wellard

CLASSIC YEARS, THE
CD CDSGP 0174
Prestige / Feb '96 / Else / Total/BMG

CLASSICS 1923-1924
CD CLASSICS 584
Classics / Oct '91 / Discovery / Jazz Music

CLASSICS 1924-1926
CD CLASSICS 599
Classics / Sep '91 / Discovery / Jazz Music

CLASSICS 1926-1928
CD CLASSICS 612
Classics / Feb '92 / Discovery / Jazz Music

CLASSICS 1928-1929
CD CLASSICS 627
Classics / Nov '92 / Discovery / Jazz Music

CLASSICS 1929-1930
CD CLASSICS 642
Classics / Nov '92 / Discovery / Jazz Music

CLASSICS 1930-1939
CD CLASSICS 654
Classics / Nov '92 / Discovery / Jazz Music

CLASSICS 1939-1940
CD CLASSICS 668
Classics / Nov '92 / Discovery / Jazz Music

COMPLETE JELLY ROLL MORTON'S RED HOT PEPPERS
CD MM 30380
Music Memoria / Apr '91 / ADA / Discovery

COMPOSITIONS OF JELLY ROLL MORTON, THE (Various Artists)
Froggie Moore / London (Cafe) Blues / Kansas city stomps / Milenberg joys / Granpa's spells / Chicago breakdown / King Porter stomp / Dead man blues / Black bottom stomp / Sidewalk blues / Schreeveport

stomp / Midnight Mama / Windy city blues (Stomp) / Wild man blues / Jelly roll blues / Jungle blues / New King Porter stomp / Sweetheart O'mine / Wolverine blues / Shoe shiner's drag / Pearls / Original Jelly Roll blues
CD _______________ CBC 1027
Timeless Jazz / Aug '96 / New Note/ Pinnacle

DOCTOR JAZZ
CD _______________ JHR 73521
Jazz Hour / '91 / Cadillac / Jazz Music / Target/BMG

DOCTOR JAZZ (His Greatest Recordings)
Ballin' the Jack / Black bottom stomp / Burnin' the iceberg / Chant / Deep Creek / Dirty, dirty, dirty / Dr. Jazz / Don't you leave me here / Freakish / Grandpa's spells / King Porter stomp / Low gravy / Mama Nita / Mamie's blues / Michigan water blues / Mint Julep / Mournful serenade / Pearls / Ponchatrain blues / Seattle hunch / Shreveport stomp / Tia Juana / Turtle twist / Winin' boy blues / Wolverine blues
CD _______________ CDAJA 5125
Living Era / Mar '94 / Select

DOCTOR JAZZ
Doctor Jazz / Pearls / High society / Climax rag / Beale St. blues / Ballin' the jack / Red hot peppers / Black bottom stomp / Mint julep / Jersey Joe / Mushmouth shuffle / Gambling Jack / Oh didn't he ramble / Wolverine blues / Original Jelly Roll blues / Wild man blues / Kansas City stomps / Grandpa's spells / Strokin' away / Low gravy / Smilin' the blues away / Try me out / Shreveport
CD _______________ 74321500212
Camden / Jun '97 / BMG

INTRODUCTION TO JELLY ROLL MORTON 1926-1939, AN
CD _______________ 4008
Best Of Jazz / May '94 / Discovery

JELLY ROLL MORTON
CD _______________ RTR 79002
Retrieval / Nov '95 / Cadillac / Direct / Jazz Music / Swift / Wellard

JELLY ROLL MORTON 1923/24
King Porter stomp / New Orleans joys / Grandpa's spells / Kansas city stomp / Wolverine blues / Pearls / Tia Juana / Shreveport stomp / Froggie Moore rag / Mamanita / Jelly roll blues / Big foot ham blues / My gal / Muddy water blues / Steady roll / Fish tail blues / High society / Weary blues / Tiger rag
CD _______________ MCD 47018
Milestone / Jun '93 / Cadillac / Complete/ Pinnacle / Jazz Music / Wellard

JELLY ROLL MORTON 1924-26
CD _______________ CD 599
Classic Jazz Masters / Sep '91 / Wellard

JELLY ROLL MORTON VOL.1
CD _______________ KJ 105FS
King Jazz / Oct '93 / Cadillac / Discovery / Jazz Music

JELLY ROLL MORTON VOL.2
CD _______________ KJ 106FS
King Jazz / Oct '93 / Cadillac / Discovery / Jazz Music

JELLY ROLL MORTON VOL.4 (Alternative Takes)
Chant / Sidewalk blues / Dead man blues / Someday sweetheart / Grandpa's spells / Original Jelly Roll blues / Mournful serenade / Pearls / Georgia swing
CD _______________ JSPCD 324
JSP / Apr '91 / ADA / Cadillac / Direct / Hot Shot / Target/BMG

JELLY ROLL MORTON VOL.4 1928-29
CD _______________ 152132
Hot 'n' Sweet / Oct '93 / Discovery

JELLY ROLL MORTON'S JAMS (Various Artists)
CD _______________ 5177772
Verve / Jan '93 / PolyGram

LAST SESSIONS
Sporting house rag (perfect rag) / Original rags / Crave / Naked dance / Mister Joe / King porter stomp / Winin' boy blues (wineing boy) / Animule dance / Buddy Bolden's blues / Naked dance / Don't you leave me here / Mamie's blues / Michigan water blues / Sweet substitute / Panama / Good old New York / Big lip blues / Why / Get the bucket / If you knew / Shake it / Dirty, dirty, dirty / Swinging the elkes / Ma-ma's got a baby / My home is a Southern town
CD _______________ CMD 14032
Commodore Jazz / Feb '97 / New Note/ BMG

LIBRARY OF CONGRESS RECORDINGS (3CD Set)
CD _______________ CDAFS 10103
Affinity / Oct '92 / Cadillac / Jazz Music / Koch

LIBRARY OF CONGRESS RECORDINGS 1938 VOL.1 (Kansas City Stomp)
CD _______________ ROUCD 1091
Rounder / Jan '94 / ADA / CM / Direct

LIBRARY OF CONGRESS RECORDINGS 1938 VOL.2 (Anamule Dance)
CD _______________ ROUCD 1092
Rounder / Jan '94 / ADA / CM / Direct

LIBRARY OF CONGRESS RECORDINGS 1938 VOL.3 (The Pearls)
CD _______________ ROUCD 1093
Rounder / Jan '94 / ADA / CM / Direct

LIBRARY OF CONGRESS RECORDINGS 1938 VOL.4 (Winin' Boy Blues)
CD _______________ ROUCD 1094
Rounder / Jan '94 / ADA / CM / Direct

LIBRARY OF CONGRESS RECORDINGS VOL.1
CD _______________ SACD 11
Solo Art / Jul '93 / Jazz Music

MR. JELLY LORD
Dr. Jazz / Original Jelly Roll blues / Mr. Jelly Lord / Beale Street blues / Oh, didn't he ramble / High society / I thought I heard Buddy Holden say / Kansas city stomp / Shoe shiner's drag / Shreveport stomp / Turtle twist / Georgia swing / Wild man blues / Black bottom stomp / Cannonball blues / Wolverine blues / Boogaboo / Grandpa's spell
CD _______________ CD 56017
Jazz Roots / Aug '94 / Target/BMG

OH DIDN'T HE RAMBLE
CD _______________ CDSGP 065
Prestige / Aug '93 / Else / Total/BMG

PIANO BLUES AND RAG 1924/25
CD _______________ 550122
Jazz Anthology / Jan '94 / Cadillac / Discovery / Harmonia Mundi

PIANO ROLLS, THE
CD _______________ 7559793632
Nonesuch / Jul '97 / Warner Music

QUINTESSENCE, THE (1923-1940/2CD Set)
CD Set _______________ FA 203
Fremeaux / Oct '96 / ADA / Discovery

RARITIES AND ALTERNATIVE 1923-1940
CD _______________ JZCD 358
Suisa / Feb '91 / Jazz Music / THE

RED HOT PEPPERS, NEW ORLEANS JAZZMEN & TRIOS
Oh, didn't he ramble / West End blues / High society / I thought I heard Buddy Bolden say / Kansas city stomp / Shoe shiner's drag / Deep creek / Chant / Original Jelly Roll blues / Mr. Jelly Lord / Shreveport stomp / Turtle twist / Beale Street blues / Georgia swing / Wild man blues / Black bottom stomp / Grandpa's spells / Dr. Jazz / Cannonball blues / Wolverine blues / Boogaboo / Winin' boy blues / Ballin' the Jack
CD _______________ CD 53018
Giants Of Jazz / Jun '88 / Cadillac / Jazz Music / Target/BMG

SWEET & HOT
CD _______________ TPZ 1003
Topaz Jazz / Jul '94 / Cadillac / Pinnacle

Morton, Mandy

MAGIC LADY (Morton, Mandy & Spriguns)
CD _______________ ENG 1011
English Garden / Apr '94 / Background

Morton, Pete

COURAGE LOVE & GRACE
CD _______________ HARDCD 029
Harbour Town / May '95 / ADA / CM / Direct / Roots

MAD WORLD BLUES
CD _______________ HARCD 018
Harbour Town / Oct '93 / ADA / CM / Direct / Roots

ONE BIG JOKE
Prisoner / Simple love / Water from the houses of our fathers / First day / Little boy's room / Another train / Lucy / Old grey moon / One big joke / Girls like you / River of love / Somewhere in love / Live your life
CD _______________ HARCD 004
Harbour Town / Oct '93 / ADA / CM / Direct / Roots

URBAN FOLK VOL.1 & 2 (Morton, Pete & Roger Wilson/Simon Edwards)
Love's trainee / Fox / Hey Joe / Lord Randall / Absent love / Old Joe Clark/The Louisiana two step / Della / Bleak mist / Rambleaway / False bride / Shadow of an absent friend / It takes a lot to laugh, it takes a train to cry / Running outta lovin' / When you see those flying saucers / Little musgrave / Goodbye my love / Belly boys / Cuckoo's nest / O' Reilly / Swimming song / None so fair / Love hurts / Derwentwater's farewell
CD _______________ HARCD 032
Harbour Town / Mar '97 / ADA / CM / Direct / Roots

Mortuary

BLACKENED IMAGES
CD _______________ BR 003CD
Brain Crusher / Nov '92 / Plastic Head

Morwells

DUB ME (Morwell Unlimited & King Tubby)
Sky ride / Bald head / Morwell's star / Jah star / John Bull / Lightning and thunder / Pegasus rock / Morwell's theme / Concord / Jungle shuffle / Swing and dub / Morpheus special / Ethiopians special / Stepping in HQ
CD _______________ BAFCD 018
Blood & Fire / May '97 / Vital

Mosalini, Juan Jose

BORDONEO Y 900
Bordoneo Y 900 / Lo que vendra / Alma de bohemio / Don goyo / Al maestro con nostagias / Retrato a julio ahumada / De contrapunto / Ojos negros / Danzarin / Adios nonino / Fuego lento / Bien al mango / Dominguera / La bordona / Tres Y dos / Cabulero
CD _______________ LBLC 2507
Indigo / Nov '95 / New Note/Pinnacle

LA BORDONA (Mosalini, Juan Jose/ Gustavo Beytelmann/Patrice Caratini)
La bordona / El choclo / Cardo y malvon / Nocturna / La cumparsita / Inspiracion / Palomita blanca / Contrajeando la cumparsita / Inspiracion / Palomita blanca
CD _______________ LBLC 6548
Label Bleu / Jan '92 / New Note/Pinnacle

Mosby, Curtis

ON THE WEST COAST AND IN LONDON (Mosby, Curtis & Henry Starr)
CD _______________ BDW 8003
Jazz Oracle / Nov '96 / Jazz Music

Moscheles, Gary

SHAPED TO MAKE YOUR LIFE EASIER
CD _______________ SSR 171CD
SSR / Nov '96 / Amato Disco / Grapevine/ PolyGram / Prime / RTM/Disc

Moses, Bob

DEVOTION
CD _______________ 1211732
Soul Note / Dec '96 / Cadillac / Harmonia Mundi / Wellard

EAST SIDE (Moses, Bob & Billy Martin)
CD _______________ ITM 1415
ITM / '89 / Koch / Tradelink

STORY OF MOSES
CD _______________ 1887032
Gaia / May '89 / New Note/Pinnacle

TIME STOOD STILL
Prelude: Simul-Circular loopology in A minor / Felonious thunk / Time stood still - Africa and back in a day / Jaco / Gregarious chants / Elegant blue ghosts - Dance like clouds over mean street US / Lost in your eyes / Word from the RA / Mbira Tanzania / Black east blues / Deusa do amour / Once in a blue moon / Prayer
CD _______________ GCD 79493
Gramavision / Sep '95 / Vital/SAM

VISIT WITH THE GREAT SPIRIT
Fan man / Deepest blues / Machupicchu / Visit with the great spirit / Monktional / Carinhoso / Suite Bahia
CD _______________ GCD 79507
Gramavision / Jun '96 / Vital/SAM

WHEN ELEPHANTS DREAM OF MUSIC
Trevor / Picolo and Lulu / Everybody knows when you're up and in / Lava flow / Happy to be here today / For miles / Black orchid / Disappearing blues / Blame it on the egg / River / Embraceable Jew / Bugs Bunny / Ripped Van Twinkle
CD _______________ GCD 79491
Gramavision / Sep '95 / Vital/SAM

Moses, Pablo

MISSION, THE
Will power / Brain wash / He was bad / Tick tock / One shot / Too much / Never seen / You got a spell / Stand off back off / These are the days / Live up woman / Mission
CD _______________ RASCD 3158
Ras / Jul '95 / Direct / Greensleeves / Jet Star / SRD
CD _______________ 111962
Musidisc UK / Jun '97 / Grapevine/ PolyGram

REVOLUTIONARY DREAM
I love I bring / Be not a dread / Give I fe I name / Come mek we run / Revolutionary dream / Where am I / I man a grasshopper / Corrupted man / Blood money / Lonely singer
CD _______________ 198832
Musidisc UK / Feb '94 / Grapevine/ PolyGram

Moskowitz, Joseph

ART OF THE CYMBALOM, THE
CD _______________ ROUCD 1126
Rounder / Mar '96 / ADA / CM / Direct

Mosley, Rev. W.M.

REV. W.M. MOSLEY 1926-1931
CD _______________ DOCD 5480
Document / Sep '96 / ADA / Hot Shot / Jazz Music

Moss, Anne Marie

TWO FOR THE ROAD (Moss, Anne Marie & Vivian Lord)
CD _______________ STCD 554
Stash / '92 / ADA / Cadillac / CM / Direct / Jazz Music

Moss, Buddy

ATLANTA BLUES LEGEND
Hurry home / Red river / Pushin' it / Comin' home / How I feel today / That'll never happen no more / Oh lawdy mama / I'm sitting on top of the world / Kansas city / It was in the weary hour night / Chesterfield / I've got to keep to the highway / Come on round to my house / Step it up and go / Everyday seems like Sunday / I got a woman don't mean me no good / Betty and Dupree / Every day every day
CD _______________ BCD 139
Biograph / Jun '97 / ADA / Cadillac / Direct / Hot Shot / Jazz Music / Wellard

BUDDY MOSS 1930-41
I'm on my way down home / Diddle da diddle / She looks so good / She's coming back some cold rainy day / Bye bye mama / Unfinished business / I'm sittin' here tonight / Joy rag / You need a woman / Who stole de lock / Tampa strut / Jealous hearted man / Mistreated boy
CD _______________ TMCD 05
Travellin' Man / Oct '90 / Hot Shot / Jazz Music / Wellard

BUDDY MOSS VOL.1 1933
CD _______________ DOCD 5123
Document / Oct '92 / ADA / Hot Shot / Jazz Music

BUDDY MOSS VOL.3 1935-1941
CD _______________ DOCD 5125
Document / Oct '92 / ADA / Hot Shot / Jazz Music

Moss, Danny

BIRDLAND, HAMBURG (Moss, Danny Quartet & Jeanie Lambe)
CD _______________ CD 019
Nagel Heyer / May '96 / Jazz Music

THA GOOD (Moss, Danny & Jack Jacobs)
CD _______________ PCD 7018
Progressive / Aug '94 / Jazz Music

WEAVER OF DREAMS (Moss, Danny Quartet)
CD _______________ CD 017
Nagel Heyer / May '96 / Jazz Music

Moss, David

MY FAVOURITE THINGS
CD _______________ INTAKTCD 022
Intakt / Mar '92 / Cadillac

TEXTURE TIME
CD _______________ INTAKTCD 034
Intakt / Oct '94 / Cadillac

Moss Icon

LYBURNUM
CD _______________ VMFM 013CD
Vermiform / May '97 / Cargo / Greyhound / Plastic Head

Mosser, Jonell

AROUND TOWNES
CD _______________ WH 3308CD
Winter Harvest / Aug '96 / ADA / Direct

Mossman, Mike

GRANULAT (Mossman, Mike & Daniel Schnyder)
CD _______________ 1232402
Red / Nov '91 / ADA / Cadillac / Harmonia Mundi

Moten, Bennie

1930-1932 (Moten, Bennie Kansas City Orchestra)
CD _______________ CD 591
Classic Jazz Masters / Sep '91 / Wellard

CLASSICS 1923-1927 (Moten, Bennie Kansas City Orchestra)
CD _______________ CLASSICS 549
Classics / Dec '90 / Discovery / Jazz Music

CLASSICS 1927-1929
CD _______________ CLASSICS 558
Classics / Oct '91 / Discovery / Jazz Music

CLASSICS 1929-1930
CD _______________ CLASSICS 578
Classics / Oct '91 / Discovery / Jazz Music

CLASSICS 1930-1932
CD ______ **CLASSICS 591**
Classics / Sep '91 / Discovery / Jazz Music

INTRODUCTION TO BENNIE MOTEN 1923-1932, AN
CD ______ **4027**
Best Of Jazz / Nov '95 / Discovery

Moth Macabre

MOTH MACABRE
All great architects are dead / Amazing / Elizabeth / Pale / Blow / Two days / Malibu / Glass eye / Screwdriver girl / Lemuria / AEIOU
CD ______ **7567922372**
WEA / Jun '93 / Warner Music

Mother

WATAMANU
CD ______ **SIXXCD 5**
Six6 / Nov '96 / 3mv/Sony / Pinnacle

Mother Carey's Chickens

I'LL TELL ME MA
CD ______ **MCC 010694CD**
MCC Music / Aug '94 / Direct

Mother Earth

DESIRED EFFECT
CD ______ **FOCUSCD 18**
Focus / May '96 / Pinnacle

PEOPLE TREE
Institution man / Jesse / Stardust bubblegum / Mr. Freedom / Warlocks of the mind / Dragster / Find it / People tree / Apple green / Time of the future / Saturation 70 / Illusions / Trip down brain lane
CD ______ **JAZIDCD 083**
Acid Jazz / Feb '94 / Disc

STONED WOMAN
CD ______ **JAZIDCD 048**
Acid Jazz / May '92 / Disc

YOU HAVE BEEN WATCHING
CD ______ **FOCUSCD 11**
Focus / Oct '95 / Pinnacle

Mother Hen

MOTHER HEN
Sing evermore / My granny's face / Goodbye old razzle dazzle / Lookout Charlie / Man from Aberdeen / America the landlord's dream / Naked king / He's alive and remembers / Old before your time / Passage back
CD ______ **EDCD 349**
Edsel / Jun '92 / Pinnacle

Mother Hips

BACK TO THE GROTTO
Hey Emille / Portrero Road / Run around me / Chum / Back to the grotto / This is a man / Precious opal / Two young queens / Stephanie's for LA / Figure 11 / Hot lunch / Turtle bones
CD ______ **74321254512**
American / Jul '95 / BMG

PART TIMER GOES FULL
Shut the door / Stoned up the road / Mona Lisa / Poison / Afternoon after afternoon / Magazine / Are you breathing / Petfoot / Sunshine feel / Tehachapi / Beat carousel / Bad Marie / Been lost once / Trunk box
CD ______ **74321289772**
American / Nov '95 / BMG

SHOOTOUT (ON 22ND AVENUE)
I can't sleep at all / Mother Hips / Honey dew / Collected some nerve / Single spoon / So much more to learn / Transit / Wind / Shootout on 22nd Avenue / Two river blues / Engagement ring / Whiskey on a southbound / Picture of him / Emergency exit / Super winners
CD ______ **74321403052**
American / Feb '97 / BMG

Mother Love Bone

STARDOG CHAMPION
This is Shanrila / Stardog champion / Holy roller / Bone china / Come bite the apple / Stargazer / Heartshine / Captain Hi-top / Man of golden words / Capricorn sister / Gentle groove / Mr. Danny Boy / Crown of thorns / Thru fade away / Mindshaker meltdown / Half ass monkey boy / Chloe dancer/Crown of thorns / Lady Godiva blues
CD ______ **5141772**
Polydor / Jul '92 / PolyGram

Mother May I

SPLITSVILLE
Poison dart / Teenage Jesus / Painted on / Something better / Birthday wish / Disk and Jane / Meet you there / In a box / Never ending riddle / In between / Bastard / All the way in
CD ______ **4782032**
Columbia / Nov '95 / Sony

Mother Station

BRAND NEW BAG
CD ______ **7567923662**
Warner Bros. / Oct '94 / Warner Music

Mother Superior

MOTHERSHIP HAS LANDED, THE
CD ______ **SPV 08545892**
SPV / May '97 / Koch / Plastic Head

Motherlight

BOBAK, JONS & MALONE
CD ______ **MER IV**
Merlin / Jun '97 / Greyhound

Mother's Finest

BEST OF MOTHER'S FINEST, THE (Not Yer Mothers Funk)
CD ______ **RE 2137**
Razor & Tie / Jul '97 / Koch

Mothers

FIRST BORN
Miracle man / Sponge / Even if we lose / Kingfisher rock / Lady leave the pain / Oasis / Drag racer / Make no mistakes / Pond / Night is my day / Truly
CD ______ **7559610222**
Elektra / Apr '91 / Warner Music

Moths

HERON'S DAUGHTER
CD ______ **KSCD 9470**
Kissing Spell / Jun '97 / Greyhound

Motian, Paul

BILL EVANS
Show type tune / Turn out the stars / Walkin' up / Very early / Five / Time remembered / 34 skidoo / Re: person I knew / Children's play song
CD ______ **8344452**
jMT / May '91 / PolyGram

CONCEPTION VESSEL
Georgian bay / Ch'I energie / Rebica / Conception vessel / American Indian:Song of sitting bull / Inspiration from a Vietnamese lullaby
CD ______ **5192792**
ECM / Jun '93 / New Note/Pinnacle

DANCE
CD ______ **5192822**
ECM / Jul '94 / New Note/Pinnacle

IT SHOULD'VE HAPPENED A LONG TIME AGO (Motian, Paul Trio)
CD ______ **8236412**
ECM / Apr '85 / New Note/Pinnacle

JACK OF CLUBS (Motian, Paul Quintet)
CD ______ **SN 1124**
Soul Note / '86 / Cadillac / Harmonia Mundi / Wellard

LE VOYAGE
Folk song for Rosie / Abacus / Cabla/Drum music / Sunflower / Le voyage
CD ______ **5192832**
ECM / Mar '94 / New Note/Pinnacle

LIVE IN TOKYO
From time to time / Shakalaka / Kathelin Gray / Hoax / Mumbo jumbo / Bird song / Move V1 / Two women from Padua / It is / Bird song
CD ______ **8491542**
jMT / Oct '91 / PolyGram

MONK IN MOTIAN
Crepuscle with Nellie / Justice / Ruby my dear / Straight no chaser / Bye-ya / Ugly beauty / Trinkle tinkle / Epistrophy / Off minor / Reflections
CD ______ **8244212**
jMT / Feb '89 / PolyGram

PAUL MOTIAN & THE ELECTRIC BEBOP BAND
Shaw nuff / I waited for you / Dance of the infidels / Darn that dream / Hot house / Dizzy atmosphere / Scrapple from the apple / Monk's dreams
CD ______ **5140042**
jMT / Jan '93 / PolyGram

PAUL MOTIAN ON BROADWAY VOL.1
Liza / Somewhere over the rainbow / They didn't believe me / What is this thing called love / My heart belongs to Daddy / Last night when we were young / I concentrate on you / Someone to watch over me / So in love
CD ______ **8344302**
jMT / Jan '90 / PolyGram

PAUL MOTIAN ON BROADWAY VOL.2
Good morning heartache / You and the night and the music / Moonlight becomes you / But not for me / Bess, oh where's my Bess / I got rhythm / All the things you are / Nice work if you can get it / It might as well be spring / Look to the rainbow / Body and soul
CD ______ **8344402**
jMT / May '90 / PolyGram

PAUL MOTIAN ON BROADWAY VOL.3
How deep is the ocean / I wish I knew / Just one of those things / Crazy she calls me / Tico tico / Weaver of dreams / Way you look tonight / Handful of stars / Pennies from Heaven / Skylark
CD ______ **8491572**
jMT / May '93 / PolyGram

PSALM (Motian, Paul Band)
Psalm / White magic / Boomerang / Fantasm / Mandeville / Second hand / Etude / Yahllah
CD ______ **8473302**
ECM / Mar '92 / New Note/Pinnacle

REINCARNATION OF A LOVEBIRD
CD ______ **5140162**
jMT / Mar '95 / PolyGram

TRIBUTE
Victoria / Tuesdays ends Saturdays / War orphans / Sod house / Song for Che
CD ______ **51928122**
ECM / Nov '93 / New Note/Pinnacle

TRIOISM (Motian, Paul Trio)
It should've happened a long time ago / Cosmology / Blue midnight / Congestion / Monica's garde / Jack of clubs / Play / In rememberance of things past / Zabel / Endgame
CD ______ **5140122**
jMT / Jun '94 / PolyGram

YOU TOOK THE WORDS OUT OF MY HEART (Live At The Village Vanguard)
CD ______ **5140282**
jMT / Apr '96 / PolyGram

Motions

IMPRESSIONS OF WONDERFUL
CD ______ **CDP 1004DD**
Pseudonym / Jun '97 / Greyhound

Motley Crue

DECADE OF DECADENCE '81-'91
Live wire / Piece of your action / Shout at the devil / Looks that kill / Home sweet home / Smokin' in the boys room / Girls, girls, girls / Wild side / Dr. Feelgood / Kickstart my heart / Teaser / Rock 'n' roll junkie / Primal scream / Angela / Anarchy in the UK
CD ______ **7559612042**
Elektra / Oct '91 / Warner Music

DECADENT DISCUSSION
CD ______ **CBAK 4031**
Baktabak / Mar '92 / Arabesque

DOCTOR FEELGOOD
Same old situation / Slice of your pie / Rattlesnake shake / Kickstart my heart / Without you / Don't go away mad / She goes down / Sticky sweet / Time for a change / T'n'T (Terror 'n Tinseltown) / Dr. Feelgood
CD ______ **9608292**
Elektra / Sep '89 / Warner Music

GENERATION SWINE
Find myself / Afraid / Flush / Generation swine / Confessions / Beauty / Glitter / Anybody out there / Let us prey / Rocketship / Rat like me / Shout at the devil '97 / Brandon
CD ______ **7559619012**
Elektra / Jun '97 / Warner Music

MOTLEY CRUE
Power to the music / Uncle Jack / Hooligan's holiday / Misunderstood / Loveshine / Poison apples / Hammered / Till death do us part / Welcome to the numb / Smoke the sky / Droppin' like flies / Drift away
CD ______ **7559615342**
Elektra / Mar '94 / Warner Music

THEATRE OF PAIN
City boy blues / Fight for your rights / Use it or lose it / Smokin' in the boys room / Louder than hell / Keep your eye on the money / Home sweet home / Tonight (we need a lover) / Save our souls / Raise your hands to rock
CD ______ **9604182**
Elektra / Jul '86 / Warner Music

Motley, Frank

BEST OF WASHINGTON DC R'N'B, THE (Motley, Frank & TNT Tribble)
Duel trumpet blues / Bow wow wow / That's alright with me / Herbert's jump / Hurricane lover / Movin' man / Fat man / Groove / Good mama / Half a pint of whiskey / Oh babe / Red hot boogie / Long gone / Annie's boogie
CD ______ **FLYCD 32**
Flyright / Apr '91 / Hot Shot / Jazz Music / Wellard

Motocaster

STAY LOADED
CD ______ **BBQCD 165**
Beggars Banquet / Oct '94 / RTM/Disc / Warner Music

Motor Totemist Guild

ARCHIVE ONE
CD ______ **NML/MTG 1**
ReR/Recommended / Jun '97 / ReR Megacorp / RTM/Disc

Motorbass

PANSOUL
Fabulous / Ezio / Flying fingers / Les ondes / Neptune / Wan dence / Genius / Pariscyde / Bad vibes / Off
CD ______ **DIF 001CD**
Different / Oct '96 / PolyGram

Motorcycle Boy

SCARLET
CD ______ **CCD 1689**
Chrysalis / Sep '89 / EMI

Motorhead

ACE OF SPADES
Ace of spades / Bite the bullet / Chase is better than the catch / Dance / Fast and loose / Fire, fire / Hammer / Jailbait / Live to win / Love me like a reptile / We are the road crew / Shoot you in the back
CD ______ **ESMCD 312**
Essential / Aug '96 / BMG

ALL THE ACES
CD ______ **CCSCD 427**
Castle / May '95 / BMG

ANOTHER PERFECT DAY
Back at the funny farm / Shine / Dancing on your grave / Rock it / One track mind / Another perfect day / Marching off to war / I got mine / Tales of glory / Die you bastard / Turn you around again / Hoochie coochie man / (Don't need) religion
CD ______ **ESMCD 438**
Essential / Sep '96 / BMG

BOMBER
Dead men tell no tales / Lawman / Sweet revenge / Sharp shooter / Poison / Stone dead forever / All the aces / Step down / Talking head / Bomber
CD ______ **ESMCD 311**
Essential / Aug '96 / BMG

BORN TO LOSE - LIVE TO WIN (The Best Of Lemmy) (Various Artists)
It's alright: *Rockin' Vickers* / Watcher: *Hawkwind* / Lost Johnny: *Hawkwind* / Iron horse: *Motorhead* / Leavin' here: *Motorhead* / Motorhead: *Motorhead* / Louie Louie: *Motorhead* / Dead men tell no tales: *Motorhead* / Stay clean: *Motorhead* / Ace of spades: *Motorhead* / Please don't touch: *Headgirl* / Motorhead (live): *Motorhead* / Stand by your man: *Williams, Wendy O. & Lemmy* / Night of the hawks: *Hawkwind* / Count down: *Jarvinen, Albert Band* / Blue suede shoes: *Lemmy & The Upsetters* / Paradise: *Lemmy & The Upsetters*
CD ______ **VSOPCD 206**
Connoisseur Collection / Oct '94 / Pinnacle

COLLECTION, THE (Bear Trap)
Motorhead / Overkill / Talking head / Rock it / Iron fist / I got mine / Steal your face / We are the road crew / Swaggletooth / Stay clean / Iron horse / One track mind / Speedfreak / Loser / (Don't need) religion / Stone dead forever / Sweet revenge / Capricorn / Love me like a reptile / Ace of spades
CD ______ **CCSCD 237**
Castle / Mar '90 / BMG

FROM THE VAULTS
CD ______ **NEXCD 136**
Sequel / Nov '90 / BMG

IRON FIST
Iron fist / Heart of stone / I'm the doctor / Go to hell / Loser / Sex and outrage / America / Shut it down / Speed freak / Don't let them grind ya down / (Don't need) religion / Bang to rights
CD ______ **ESMCD 372**
Essential / Aug '96 / BMG

IRON FIST/HORDES FROM HELL
CD ______ **CLEO 94132**
Cleopatra / Dec '94 / Cargo / Greyhound / Plastic Head / RTM/Disc / SRD

KEEP US ON THE ROAD
Motorhead / Vibrator / Keep us on the road / Watcher / Iron horse / Leaving here / On parole / I'm your witchdoctor / Train kept a rollin' / City kids / White line fever
CD ______ **CDRIA 1001**
Rialto / Sep '96 / Disc / Total/BMG

LIFELINES (The Complete Collection) (Rockin' Vickers)
I go ape / Someone like me / Zing went the strings of my heart / Stella / It's alright / Stay by me / Dandy / I don't need your kind / Baby never say goodbye / I just stand there / Say Mama / Shake, rattle and roll / What's the matter Jane / Little Rosey
CD ______ **RETRO 803**
RPM / Jul '95 / Pinnacle

LIVE
CD ______ **JHD 081**
Tring / Mar '93 / Tring

LIVE 1983
Back to the funny farm / Tales of glory / Shoot you in the back / Marching off to war / Iron horse / Another perfect day / (Don't need) Religion / One track mind / Go to hell / America / Shine / Dancing on your grave

/ Rock it / I've got mine / Bite the bullet / Chase is better than the catch
CD DOJOCD 108
Dojo / Feb '94 / Disc

MOTORHEAD
Motorhead / Vibrator / Lost Johnny / Iron horse / Born to lose / White line fever / Keep us on the road / Watcher / Train kept a rollin' / City kids / Beer drinkers and hell raisers / On parole / Instro / I'm your witch doctor
CD CDWIK 2
Chiswick / Jun '88 / Pinnacle

MOTORHEAD
CD GFS 073
Going For A Song / Jul '97 / Else / TKO Magnum

MOTORHEAD LIVE AND LOUD
Motorhead / I'll be your sister / Keep us on the road / Louie louie / Love me like a reptile / Vibrator / Iron horse / Watcher / Ace of spades / Fast and loose / Leavin' here / Tear you down / Train kept a rollin' / On parole / City kids / Road crew
CD EMPRCD 575
Emporio / Jul '95 / Disc

MOTORHEAD VOL.1 - ACES HIGH
Stone dead forever / All the aces / Poison / Ace of spades / Live to win / America / Jailbait / Please don't touch / Iron fist / Go to hell / Don't let 'em grind ya down / Dance / Heart of stone / I got mine / Tales of glory / Overkill
CD 5507242
Spectrum / Aug '94 / PolyGram

NO REMORSE
Ace of spades / Motorhead / Jailbait / Stay clean / Too late too late / Killed by death / Bomber / Iron fist / Shine / Dancing on your grave / Metropolis / Snaggletooth / Overkill / Please don't touch / Stone dead forever / Like a nightmare / Emergency / Steal your face / Louie Louie / No class / Iron horse / We are the road crew / Leaving here / Locomotive / Under the knife / Under the knife / Masterplan / No class / Stand by your man
CD ESDCD 371
Essential / Sep '96 / BMG

NO SLEEP 'TIL HAMMERSMITH
Ace of spades / Stay clean / Metropolis / Hammer / Iron horse / No class / Overkill / We are the road crew / Capricorn / Bomber / Motorhead
CD ESMCD 313
Essential / Aug '96 / BMG

NO SLEEP AT ALL
Dr. Rock / Dogs / Built for speed / Deaf forever / Killed by death / Traitor / Ace of spades / Eat the rich / Just coz you got the power / Overkill / Stay clean / Metropolis
CD ESMCD 558
Essential / Jul '97 / BMG

ON PAROLE
Motorhead / On parole / Vibrator / Iron horse / Born to lose / City kids / Fools / Watcher / Leaving here / Lost Johnny
CD CDFA 3251
Fame / Oct '90 / EMI

ON PAROLE (Remastered)
Motorhead / On parole / Vibrator / Iron horse/Born to lose / City kids / Watcher / Leaving here / Lost Johnny / Fools / On parole / City kids / Motorhead / Leaving here
CD CDGO 2072
EMI Gold / Feb '97 / EMI

ORGASMATRON
Deaf forever / Nothing up my sleeve / Ain't my crime / Claw / Mean machine / Built for speed / Ridin' with the driver / Dr. Rock / Orgasmatron / On the road / Steal your face / Claw
CD ESMCD 557
Essential / Jul '97 / BMG

OVERKILL
Overkill / Stay clean / (I won't) Pay your price / I'll be your sister / Capricorn / No class / Damage case / Tear ya down / Metropolis / Limb from limb
CD ESMCD 310
Essential / Aug '96 / BMG

OVERNIGHT SENSATION
CD CD 08518302
SPV / Nov '96 / Koch / Plastic Head

PROTECT THE INNOCENT 1975-1992 (4CD Set)
On parole / Leaving here / White line fever / Motorhead / Beer drinkers and hell raisers / City kids / Louie Louie / Tear ya down / Overkill / Too late, too late / No class / Like a nightmare / Stay clean / Metropolis / Bomber / Over the top / Dead men tell no tales / Stone dead forever / All the aces / Ace of spades / Dirty love / Please don't touch: *Motorhead & Girlschool* / Jailbait / We are the roadcrew / Chase is better than the catch / Train kept a rollin' / Motorhead / Hammer / Capricorn / Iron horse / Iron fist / Remember me, I'm gone / Heart of stone / America / Don't let 'em grind ya down / Stand by your man / I got mine / Turn you round again / Tales of glory / Shine / Hoochie coochie man / Dance on your grave / Another perfect day / Snaggletooth / Under the knife / Under the knife / Deaf forever / On the road / Steal your face / Orgasmatron / Dr. Rock / Rock 'n' roll / Dogs / Eat the rich / Wolf / Cradle to the grave / Just 'cos you got the power / Killed by death / Built for speed / Traitor / One to sing the blues / Deadman's hand / Eagle rock / Shut you down / I ain't no nice guy / You better run
CD Set ESBCD 562
Essential / Aug '97 / BMG

ROCK 'N' ROLL
Rock 'n' roll / Eat the rich / Black heart / Stone deaf in the USA / Wolf / Traitor / Dogs / All for you / Boogeyman / Cradle the the grave / Just 'cos you got the power
CD ESMCD 556
Essential / Jul '97 / BMG

SACRIFICE
CD SPV 08576942
SPV / Dec '96 / Koch / Plastic Head

STONE DEAD FOREVER
CD RRCD 238
Receiver / Feb '97 / Grapevine/PolyGram

TAKE NO PRISONERS (2CD Set)
Overkill / Stay clean / No class / Bomber / All the aces / Dead men tell no tales / Please don't touch / Ace of spades / Iron fist / Don't need religion / Another perfect day / I got mine / Shine / Killed by death / Deaf forever / Orgasmatron / Rock 'n' roll / Eat the rich / Dirty love / We are the road crew / Fast and loose / Shoot you in the back / Bastard / Stone dead forever / Love me like a reptile / Louie Louie / Jailbait / Tear ya down / Sharpshooter / Motorhead / Leaving here / Train kept a rollin' / On parole / City kids / White line fever
CD Set SMDCD 127
Snapper / May '97 / Pinnacle

WE'RE MOTORHEAD AND WE'RE GONNA KICK YOUR ASS
CD CD 08576942
Steamhammer / Nov '96 / Pinnacle / Plastic Head

Motorpsycho

8 SOOTHING SONGS FOR RUT
CD VOW 027C
Voices Of Wonder / Jan '94 / Plastic Head

ANGELS AND DAEMONS AT PLAY (3CD Set)
CD Set PBMEGA 007
Stickman / Jun '97 / Cargo / Pinnacle
CD PSYCHOBABBLE 007CD
Stickman / Mar '97 / Cargo / Pinnacle

BLISSARD
CD INDIGO 39022
Indigo / Nov '96 / Cargo
CD PSYCHOBABBLE 003
Stickman / Apr '97 / Cargo / Pinnacle

DEMON BOX
CD VOW 030CD
Voices Of Wonder / Jun '93 / Plastic Head

LOBOTOMIZER
CD VOW 026C
Voices Of Wonder / Jan '94 / Plastic Head

TIMOTHY'S MONSTER
CD PSYCHOBABBLE 002
Stickman / Nov '96 / Cargo / Pinnacle

Motors

AIRPORT (The Motors' Greatest Hits)
Dancing the night away / Sensation / Airport / Metropolis / Love and loneliness / Forget about you / Emergency / Tenement steps / Today / Freeze / That's what John said / You beat the hell outta me / Soul redeemer / Cold love / Time for make up / Love round the corner / Here comes the hustler
CD CDVM 9032
Virgin / Jan '95 / EMI

APPROVED BY
Airport / Mama rock 'n' roller / Forget about you / Do you mind / You beat the hell outta me / Breathless / Soul redeemer / Dreaming your life away / Sensation / Today
CD CDV 2101
Virgin / Oct '90 / EMI

Mott The Hoople

ALL THE YOUNG DUDES
All the young dudes / Honaloochie boogie / All the way from Memphis / Roll away the stone / Golden age of rock 'n' roll / Foxy foxy / Saturday gig / She's a star / Yesterday / Forgotten dreams / Steamer / Yes
CD RM 1547
BR Music / Apr '97 / Target/BMG

BALLAD OF MOTT, THE (A Retrospective/2CD Set)
Rock 'n' roll Queen / Walkin' with a mountain / Waterlow / Sweet Angeline / All the young dudes / Momma's little jewel / One of the boys / Sucker / Sweet Jane / Sea diver / Reach for love/After lights / Ballad of Mott The Hoople / Drivin' sister / Violence / Rose / I wish I was your mother / Honaloochie boogie / All the way from Memphis / Whizz kid / Hymn for the dudes / Golden age of rock 'n' roll / Rest in peace / Marionette / Crash street kidds / Born late '58 / Roll away the stone / Where do you all come from / Henry and the H-bomb / Foxy foxy / Saturday gigs / Lounge lizard / Through the looking glass / American pie
CD Set 4744202
Columbia / Jun '96 / Sony

DRIVE ON
By tonight / Monte Carlo / She does it / I'll tell you something / Stiff upper lip / Love now / Apologies / Great white wail / Here we are / It takes one to know one / I can show you how it is
CD 4872372
Columbia / Mar '97 / Sony

GREATEST HITS
All the way from Memphis / Honaloochie boogie / Hymn for the dudes / Born late '58 / All the young dudes / Roll away the stone / Ballad of Mott the Hoople / Golden age of rock 'n' roll / Foxy foxy / Saturday gigs
CD CD 32007
CBS / Apr '89 / Sony

MOTT
All the way from Memphis / Whizz kid / Hymn for the dudes / Honaloochie boogie / Violence / Drivin' sister / Ballad of Mott the Hoople / I'm a Cadillac / El camino dolo roso / I wish I was your mother
CD 4674022
Columbia / Mar '95 / Sony

MOTT THE HOOPLE
Dear Louise / Hot footin' / World cruise / Brother soul / 1-2-3-4 Kickalong blues / Wild in the streets
CD SEACD 7
See For Miles/C5 / May '93 / Pinnacle

MOTT THE HOOPLE
CD GFS 065
Going For A Song / Jul '97 / Else / TKO Magnum

MOTT THE HOOPLE/MAD SHADOWS
You really got me / At the crossroads / Laugh at me / Backsliding fearlessly / Rock 'n' roll Queen / Rabbit food and Toby time / Half moon bay / Wrath and roll / Thunderbuck ram / No wheels to ride / You are one of us / Walkin' with a mountain / I can feel / Threads of iron / When my minds gone
CD EDCD 361
Edsel / Jan '93 / Pinnacle

ORIGINAL MIXED UP KIDS (The BBC Sessions 1970-1971)
CD WINCD 084
Windsong / Jul '96 / Pinnacle

PHILADELPHIA 1972
CD PILOT 005
Burning Airlines / Apr '97 / Total/Pinnacle

WALKING WITH A MOUNTAIN (The Best Of Mott The Hoople 1969-1972)
Rock 'n' roll queen / At the crossroads / Thunderbuck ram / Whiskey woman / Waterlow / Moon upstairs / Second love / Road to Birmingham / Black scorpio (momma's little jewel) / You really got me / Walkin' with a mountain / No wheels to ride / Keep a knockin' / Midnight lady / Death may be your Santa Claus / Darkness darkness / Growing man blues / Black hills
CD IMCD 87
Island / Jun '90 / PolyGram

Mould, Bob

BLACK SHEETS OF RAIN
Black sheets of rain / One good reason / Hanging tree / Hear me calling / Disappointed / It's too late / Stop your crying / Last night / Out of your life / Sacrifice / Let there be peace
CD CDVUS 21
Virgin / Apr '92 / EMI

BOB MOULD
CD CRECD 188
Creation / Apr '96 / 3mv/Vital

POISON YEARS
Black sheets of rain / It's too late / Stop your crying / Out of your life / Hanging tree / Sacrifice / Wishing well / See a little light / All those people know / Compositions for the young and old / If you're true / Poison years / Brasilia crossed with Trenton / Shoot out the lights
CD CDVM 9030
Virgin / May '94 / EMI

WORKBOOK
Sunspots / Wishing well / Heartbreak a stranger / See a little light / Poison years / Sinners and their repentances / Brasilia crossed with Trenton / Compositions for the young and old / Lonely afternoon / Dreaming, I am whichever way the wind blows
CD CDVUS 2
Virgin / Jul '89 / EMI

Moulin, Marc

SAM SUFFY
CD CR 003CD
Counterpoint / Apr '97 / Timewarp

Mound City Blues Blowers

1935-36
What's the reason I'm not pleasin' you / She's a Latin from Manhattan / You've been taking lessons in love (from somebody new) / (Back home again in) Indiana / Red sails in the sunset / I'm sittin' high on a hilltop / On Treasure Island / Thanks a million / Eeny meeny miney Mo / Little bit independent / I'm shootin' high / I've got my fingers crossed / High Society / Muskrat ramble / Broken record / Music goes 'round and around / I'm gonna sit right down and write myself a letter / Mama don't allow it / Rhythm in my nursery rhymes / I hope Gabriel likes my music / You hit the spot / Spreadin' rhythm around / Saddle your blues to a wild mustang / Wah-hoo / I'm gonna clap my hands
CD CBC 1018
Timeless Historical / Aug '94 / New Note/ Pinnacle

CLASSICS 1935-1936
CD CLASSICS 895
Classics / Oct '96 / Discovery / Jazz Music

Mounsey, Paul

NAHOO
Passing away / Alba / Journeyman / Dalmore / Stranger in a strange land / As terras baixas da / Hollanda / From ebb to flood / I will go / My faithful fond one / Illusion
CD IRCD 029
Iona / Jan '95 / ADA / Direct / Duncans

Mount Shasta

PUT THE CREEP ON
CD GR 013CD
Skingraft / Apr '94 / SRD

WHO'S THE HOTTIE
CD GR 31CD
Skingraft / May '95 / SRD

Mountain

BEST OF MOUNTAIN
Never in my life / Taunta (Sammy's tune) / Nantucket sleighride / Roll over Beethoven / For Yasgur's farm / Animal trainer and the toad / Mississippi Queen / Kings Chorale / Boys in the band / Don't look around / Crossroader
CD 4663352
CBS / Aug '90 / Sony

CLIMBING
Mississippi queen / Theme for an imaginary western / Never in my life / Silver paper / For Yasgur's farm / To my friend / Laird / Sittin' on a rainbow / Boys in the band
CD 4721802
Columbia / Feb '95 / Sony

FLOWERS OF EVIL
CD BGOCD 113
Beat Goes On / Jun '97 / Pinnacle

NANTUCKET SLEIGHRIDE (The Best Of Mountain)
Don't look around / You can't get away / Tired angels / My lady / Great train robbery / Taunta (Sammy's tune) / Nantucket sleighride / Animal trainer and the toad / Travellin' in the dark
CD BGOCD 32
Beat Goes On / Mar '89 / Pinnacle

OVER THE TOP (2CD Set)
Blood of the sun / Long red / Blind man / Dreams of milk and honey / Southbound train / Never in my life / Silver paper / For yasgur's farm / To my friend / Sittin' on a rainbow / Stormy Monday / Waiting to take you away / Don't look around / Taunta (Sammy's tune) / Nuntucket sleighride (To Owen Coffin) / You can't get you away / Animal trainer and the toad / My lady / Travellin' in the dark (To EMP) / Great train robbery / Flowers of evil / One last cold kiss / Crossroader / Roll over Beethoven / Back where I belong / Bardot damage / Shimmy on the footlights / Talking to the angels
CD Set 4848982
Columbia / Jun '96 / Sony

ROAD GOES ON FOREVER, THE (Mountain Live)
CD BGOCD 111
Beat Goes On / Jun '97 / Pinnacle

Mountain Ash Band

HERMIT, THE
CD DORIS 2
Vinyl Tap / Jan '96 / Cargo / Greyhound / Vinyl Tap

Mountain Bus

SUNDANCE
CD EVA 852121B32
EVA / Nov '94 / ADA / Direct

Mountain Goats

BEAUTIFUL RAT SUNSET
CD SHR 99
Shrimper / Dec '96 / Cargo

FULL FORCE GALESBURG
CD EJ 11CD
Emperor Jones / Jun '97 / SRD

NINE BLACK POPPIES
CD EJ 02CD
Emperor Jones / Nov '95 / SRD

SWEDEN
CD SHR 68CD
Shrimper / Dec '96 / Cargo

Moura, Paulo

RIO NOCTURNES
Guadeloupe / Capricornio / Rio nocturne / Baleias / Jumento elegante / Barbara's vatapa / Sereia do leblon / Mulatas / Tumbalele / Concierto brasitalian / Tarde de chuva / Casamento em xaxei
CD 158162
Messidor / Aug '92 / ADA / Koch

Mourn

MOURN
CD RISE 10CD
Rise Above / Jun '95 / Plastic Head / Vital

Mourning

GREETINGS FROM HELL
CD FDN 2005CD
Foundation 2000 / Jul '93 / Plastic Head

Mourning Phase

MOURNING PHASE
CD KSCD 9440
Kissing Spell / Jun '97 / Greyhound

Mourning Sign

ALIENOR
CD GOD 015CD
Godhead / Jun '95 / Plastic Head

MOURNING SIGN
CD GOD 016CD
Godhead / Oct '95 / Plastic Head

MULTIVERSE
CD GOD 022CD
Godhead / Jan '97 / Plastic Head

Mouse & The Traps

FRATERNITY YEARS, THE
Public execution / Maid of sugar, maid of spice / Nobody cares / Cryin' inside / I'm a man: *St. John, Chris* / Lie, beg, borrow and steal / I've got her love: *St. John, Chris* / I am the one / Like I know you do / Sometimes you just can't win / All for you / Do the best you can / Look at the sun / You don't love me (you don't care): *St. John, Chris* / Promises promises / I satisfy / Requiem for Sarah / LOVE love / Ya ya / Good times / Hand in hand / You are my sunshine / I wonder where the birds fly / Mohair Sam / As far as the sea: *St. John, Chris*
CD CDWIKD 171
Big Beat / May '97 / Pinnacle

PUBLIC EXECUTION
CD 842088
EVA / May '94 / ADA / Direct

Mouse On Mars

AUTODITACKER
Sui shop / Juju / Twirt shoeblade / Das tamagnochi / Dark FX / Scat / Tux and damask / Sehnsud / X-files / Scnick schnack melt made / Rodio / Maggots hell wings
CD PURECD 070
Too Pure / Aug '97 / Vital

IAORA TAHITI
Stereomission / Kompod / Staurday night world / Cup fieber / Schunkel / Gocard / Kanu / Bib / Schlecktron / Preprise / Pap Antoine / Omnibuzz / Hallo / Die innere orange
CD PURECD 048
Too Pure / Aug '95 / Vital

VULVA LAND
CD PURECD 036
Too Pure / Jun '94 / Vital

Mousetrap

CEREBRAL REVOLVER
Cerebral revolver
CD GROW 0032
Grass / Jul '93 / Pinnacle / SRD

LOVER
CD GROW 0232
Grass / Jun '94 / Pinnacle / SRD

Mouskouri, Nana

MAGIC OF NANA MOUSKOURI
Only love / White rose of Athens / Never on a Sunday / Yesterday / Amazing grace / Try to remember / Power of love / Bridge over troubled water / Only time will tell / Morning has broken / And I love you so / Ave Maria / Love me tender / Nights in white satin / Song for liberty / Lonely shepherd
CD 8307642
Polystar / Jul '93 / PolyGram

NANA
Johnny / Half a crown / Just a ribbon / If you love me / Love we never knew / I love my man / Ballinderry / I gave my love a cherry / He didn't know me / Tiny sparrow / My kind of man
CD 8100552
Mercury / Sep '84 / PolyGram

PASSPORT
Amazing grace / And I love you so / Bridge over troubled water / Cu-cu-rru-cu-cu-paloma / Day is done / Enas mithos / Four and twenty hours / I have a dream / If you love me / Last rose of Summer / Loving song / Milisse Mou / My friend the sea / Never on Sunday / Odos oniron / Over and over / Plaisir d'amour / Seasons in the sun / Try to remember / Turn on the Sun / White rose of Athens
CD 8307642
Philips / '88 / PolyGram

RETURN TO LOVE
CD 5345732
Mercury / May '97 / PolyGram

Mouth Music

MODI
CD TRECD 111
Triple Earth / Feb '95 / Grapevine/ PolyGram / Stern's

MOUTH MUSIC
Bratach bana / Mor a' cheannaich / Chi mi na morbheana / Mile marbh'aisg a'ghaol / Froach a ronaigh / Co ni mire rium / Martin Martin / I bhi a da / Air fair a lail o
CD TERRACD 109
Triple Earth / Aug '90 / Grapevine/PolyGram / Stern's

SHORELIFE
CD TRECD 113
Triple Earth / Oct '94 / Grapevine/ PolyGram / Stern's

Mouthpiece

WHAT WAS SAID
CD NA 020CD
New Age / Jul '96 / Plastic Head

Mouzon, Alphonse

MIND TRANSPLANT
Mind transplant / Snowbound / Carbon dioxide / Ascorbic acid / Happiness is loving you / Some of the things people do / Golden rainbows / Nitroglycerin / Real thing
CD RPM 116
RPM / Sep '93 / Pinnacle

MORNING SUN
I'm glad that you're here / When Linda smiles / Lullaby for little alphonse / To Mom with love / Tell me / Morning sun / If tomorrow comes / Just because of you / Do I have to / Space invaders
CD TENAC 92102
Tenacious / Aug '97 / New Note/Pinnacle

NIGHT IS STILL YOUNG
Protocol / Daddy's blues / Daddy's little girl / Promise kept / Waltz for Emma / To drum or not to drum / What are you doing later on / Seduction / Night is still young / Slammin' / Just another Samba / Undulation / Africa
CD TENAC 92112
Tenacious / Mar '97 / New Note/Pinnacle

SKY IS THE LIMIT, THE
Why don't you break it / Jean-Pierre / Do you wanna dance / Making love with you / Come and see what I've got / Sky is the limit, The / Starting all over again / Rock 'n' roll waltz / Don't break my funk / Old friends / Night for love / One more time / I'm glad that you're here
CD TENAC 92082
Tenacious / Aug '97 / New Note/Pinnacle

Move

BEST OF THE MOVE
Blackberry Way / Curly / Yellow rainbow / I can hear the grass grow / Fire brigade / Hey Grandma / Kilroy was here / Night of fear / Feel too good / Brontosaurus / Flowers in the rain / Walk upon the water / Stephanie knows who / Turkish tram conductor blues / Useless information / Weekend / Cherry blossom clinic revisited / So you want to be a rock 'n' roll star
CD MCCD 009
Music Club / Feb '91 / Disc / THE

COLLECTION, THE
Night of fear / I can hear the grass grow / Wave your flag and stop the train / Flowers in the rain / Fire brigade / Wild tiger woman / Blackberry way / Curly / Brontosaurus / So you want to be a rock 'n' roll star / Something else / It'll be me / Sunshine help me / When Alice comes back to the farm / Zing went the strings of my heart / Cherry blossom clinic revisited / Hello Susie / Kilroy was here / Last thing on my mind / Here we go round the lemon tree / Field's of people / Don't make my baby blue / Yellow rainbow / Walk upon the water
CD CCSCD 135
Castle / '86 / BMG

MESSAGE FROM THE COUNTRY
Message from the country / Ella James / No time / Don't mess up / Until your Mama's gone / It wasn't my idea to dance / Minister / Ben Crawley steel company / Words of Aaron / My Marge
CD BGOCD 238
Beat Goes On / Jun '94 / Pinnacle

MOVE, THE
CD CUCD 15
Disky / Oct '94 / Disky / THE

Move D

EXPLORING THE PSYCHEDELIC LANDSCAPE (Move D & Peter Namlook)
CD PK 08121
Fax / Dec '96 / Plastic Head

Mover

ORIGINAL RECIPE
CD MR 068CD
Man's Ruin / May '97 / Cargo / Greyhound / Plastic Head

Movietone

MOVIETONE
CD PUNK 10CD
Planet / Nov '95 / SRD

Moving Cloud

MOVING CLOUD
CD GLCD 1150
Green Linnet / Feb '95 / ADA / CM / Direct / Highlander / Roots

Moving Hearts

DARK END OF THE STREET
CD 229250144
WEA / May '95 / Warner Music

LIVE HEARTS
CD 2292402302
WEA / May '95 / Warner Music

STORM, THE
Lark / Storm / Tribute to Peardar O Donnell / Titanic / Finore / May morning dew
CD BUACD 892
Son / Feb '89 / Total/BMG

Moving Targets

BRAVE NOISE
CD TAANG 030CD
Taang / Jan '93 / Cargo

FALL
CD TG 93042
Roadrunner / May '91 / PolyGram

TAKE THIS RIDE
CD TAANG 73CD
Taang / Jun '93 / Cargo

Moviola

GLEN ECHO AUTOHARP
CD SO 7
Spirit Of Orr / Feb '97 / Cargo

YEAR YOU WERE BORN
CD AW 040
Anyway / Dec '96 / Cargo

Mowatt, Judy

BLACK WOMAN
Strength to go through / Concrete jungle / Slave queen / Put it on / Zion chant / Black woman / Down in the valley / Joseph / Many are called / Sisters chant
CD GRELCD 111
Greensleeves / Jul '88 / Jet Star / SRD

LOVE IS OVERDUE
Sing our own song / Love is overdue / Try a little tenderness / Long long time / Rock me / Get up and chant / Screwface / Hold dem jah / One more time / Who is he
CD GRELCD 103
Greensleeves / Jul '87 / Jet Star / SRD

ONLY A WOMAN
CD SHANCD 43007
Shanachie / '88 / ADA / Greensleeves / Koch

WORKING WONDERS
CD SHANCD 43028
Shanachie / Aug '85 / ADA / Greensleeves / Koch

Mowrey, Dude

DUDE MOWREY
CD 07822186782
Arista / Jul '94 / BMG

Moxham, Stuart

CARS IN THE GRASS (Moxham, Stuart & The Original Artists)
My criteria / Hello world / Return to work / Tug of love / Night by night / Soft eject / Against creating war / God knows / Appropriate response / Cars in the grass / Drifting west
CD ASKCD 035
Vinyl Japan / Mar '95 / Plastic Head / Vinyl Japan

SIGNAL PATH (Moxham, Stuart & The Original Artists)
Over the sea / Between edits / Her shoes (are right) / Knives (always fall) / Broken heart blues / It says here / No one road / That's my love / I wonder why / Remember / It took you / Mutual gaze / Yeah x 3 / Unit of desire
CD FGAO 015
Feel Good All Over / Mar '93 / Cargo

Moxy Fruvous

BARGAINVILLE
CD 4509931342
WEA / Apr '94 / Warner Music

Moyet, Alison

ALF
Love resurrection / Honey for the bees / For you only / Invisible / Steal me blind / All cried out / Money mile / Twisting the knife / Where hides sleep
CD 4838362
Columbia / Sep '96 / Sony

ESSEX
Falling / Whispering your name / Getting into something / Dorothy / So am I / And I know / Ode to boy / Satellite / Another living day / Boys own / Take of me / Ode to boy II / Whispering your name (mix)
CD 4759552
Columbia / Mar '94 / Sony

HOODOO
Footsteps / It won't be long / This house / Rise / Wishing you were here / (Meeting my man) main man / Hoodoo / Back where I belong / My right ARM / Never too late / Find me
CD 4682722
Columbia / Apr '91 / Sony

RAINDANCING
Weak in the presence of beauty / Ordinary girl / You got me wrong / Without you / Sleep like breathing / Is this love / Blow wind blow / Glorious love / When I say (no giveaway) / Stay
CD 4501522
Columbia / Mar '90 / Sony

SINGLES
First time I ever saw your face / Only you / Nobody's diary / Situation / Love resurrection / All cried out / Invisible / That ole devil called love / Is this love / Weak in the presence of beauty / Ordinary girl / Love letters / It won't be long / Wishing you were here / This house / Falling / Whispering your name / Getting into something / Ode to boy II / Solid wood
CD 4806632
Columbia / May '95 / Sony

SINGLES/LIVE (2CD Set)
Fist time ever I saw your face / Only you / Nobody's diary / Situation / Love resurrection / All cried out / Invisible / That ole devil called love / Is this love / Weak in the presence of beauty / Ordinary girl / Love letters / It won't be long / Wishing you were here / This house / Falling / Whispering your name / Getting into something / Ode to boy II / Solid wood / Getting into something / Chain of fools / Love letters / All cried out / Dorothy / Falling / Ode to boy / Is this love / Nobody's diary / Whispering your name / There are worse things I could do
CD Set 4806339
Columbia / Apr '96 / Sony

Mr. B

SHINING THE PEARLS
CD BP 71886
Blind Pig / Dec '95 / ADA / CM / Direct / Hot Shot

Mr. Barth

MY OLD BLUES SUITS
CD PLUMPCD 101
Plumphouse / Mar '97 / Prime

Mr. Big

BIG, BIGGER, BEST
Addicted to that rush / Rock 'n' roll over / Green-tinted sixties mind / To be with you / Just take my heart / Daddy, brother, lover, little boy / Wild world / Colorado bulldog / Nothing but love / Promise her the moon / Take cover / Goin' where the wind blows / Seven impossible days / Not one night / Unnatural / Stay together
CD 7567806852
East West / Apr '97 / Warner Music

BUMP AHEAD
Colorado bulldog / Price you gotta pay / Promise her the moon / What's it gonna be / Wild world / Mr. Gone / Whole world's gonna know / Nothing but love / Temperamental / Ain't seen love like that / Mr. Big
CD 7567824952
Atlantic / Sep '93 / Warner Music

HEY MAN
CD 7567806482
Atlantic / Feb '96 / Warner Music

LEAN INTO IT
Daddy / Brother / Lover / Little boy / Alive and kickin' / Green tinted sixties mind / CDFF-Lucky this time / Voodoo kiss / Never say never / Just take my heart / My kinda woman / Little loo loose / Road to ruin / To be with you
CD 7567822092
Atlantic / Apr '91 / Warner Music

LIVE - MR BIG
Daddy, brother, lover, little boy (the electric drill song) / Alive and kickin' / Green tinted sixties mind / Just take my heart / Road to

ruin / Lucky this time / Addicted to that rush / To be with you / Thirty days in the hole / Shy baby / Baba O'Riley
CD 7567805232
Atlantic / Nov '92 / Warner Music

MR. BIG
Addicted to that rush / Wind me up / Merciless / Had enough / Blame it on my youth / Take a walk / Big love / How can you do what you do / Anything for you / Rock 'n' roll over
CD 7819902
Atlantic / Jul '89 / Warner Music

Mr. Bloe

GROOVIN' WITH MR. BLOE
Groovin' with Mr. Bloe / Straight down the line / Smokey Joe / Mighty mouse / Land of 1000 dances / Dancing machine / Chicken feed / If you've gotta make a fool of somebody / Sugar sugar / Doo-di-dog-dad / Ja da / Curried soul
CD 5526362
Spectrum / Feb '97 / PolyGram

Mr. Bungle

DISCO VOLANTE
Everyone I went to High School with is dead / Chemical marriage / Carry stress in the jaw / Desert search for techno Allah / Violenza domestica / After school special / Phlegmatics / Ma meeshka mow skwoz / Bends / Backstrokin' / Platypus / Merry go bye bye
CD 8286942
Slash / Jan '96 / PolyGram

MR. BUNGLE
Quote, unquote / Slowy growing deaf / Squeeze me macaroni / Carousel / Egg / Stubb (a dub) / My ass is on fire / Girls of porn / Love is a fist / Dead goon
CD 8282762
Slash / Sep '91 / PolyGram

Mr. C

DJ COLLECTION VOL.3 (Various Artists)
CD FANTA 10CD
Fantazia / Mar '97 / 3mv/Sony / Prime

X-MIX VOL.6 (Electronic Storm) (Various Artists)
CD K7 044CD
Studio K7 / Apr '96 / Prime / RTM/Disc

Mr. Doo

PRESENTS THE DOO EXPERIENCE
CD FILERCD 418
Profile / Nov '91 / Pinnacle

Mr. Electric Triangle

KOSMOSIS IN DUB
CD TKCD 38
2 Kool / Sep '96 / Pinnacle / SRD

KOSMOSIS OF THE HEART
CD TKCD 20
2 Kool / Oct '95 / Pinnacle / SRD

Mr. Epp

RIDICULING THE APOCALYPSE
CD SUPER 06
Super Electro / Nov '96 / Cargo

Mr. Fox

MR. FOX/THE GIPSY
Join us in our game / Hanged man / Gay goshawk / Rip Van Winkle / Mr. Trill's song / Little woman / Salisbury plain / Ballad of Neddy Dick / Leaving the dales / Mr. Fox / Gipsy / Aunt Lucy Broadwood / House carpenter / Elvira Madigan / Dancing song / All the good times
CD ESMCD 433
Essential / Oct '96 / BMG

Mr. Gloria's Head

DARLING'S OUT OF COCKTAIL
CD ALIVE 0026
Bomp / Nov '96 / Cargo / Greyhound / RTM/Disc / Shellshock/Disc

Mr. Gone

LOOKING AT THE FUTURE IN THE REARVIEW MIRROR
Equation: boogie / Mosquito coast '94-'96 / Les cinq notes magiques / Is it modern interlude 2 / I love Paris interlude 3 / Looking at the future in the rearview mirror / La pomme d'Adam / Souvenirs sapphique / No disrespect interlude 1 / I love jazz / That's an earthquake / Les cinq notes magiques
CD IBCD 8
Internal Bass / Apr '97 / Prime / Timewarp / Total/BMG

Mr. Hageman

TWIN SMOOTH SNOUTS
CD STAR 5CD
Starlight / Dec '96 / Cargo

Mr. President

UP 'N' AWAY
CD 4509997002
East West / Jun '95 / Warner Music

WE SEE THE SAME SUN
Intro / Coco jamboo / Side to side / Goodbye, lonely heart / I give you my heart / Love zone / Show me the way / Olympic dreams / You can get it / Don't you ever stop / Turn it up / I love the way you love me / I love to love / Where the sun goes down / Outro
CD 0630149462
Warner Bros. / Jul '97 / Warner Music

Mr. Review

MR. REVIEW/SPY EYE (Mr. Review/Spy Eye)
CD PHZCD 81
Unicorn / Nov '94 / Plastic Head

Mr. Scruff

MR. SCRUFF
Sea mammal / Tubby mechanical friend / Bass baby / Chicken in a box / Night time / Limbic funk / Bobby's jazz pony / Jazz potato / Crisps / Wail
CD JOYCD 13
Pleasure / May '97 / Pinnacle / RTM/Disc

Mr. So & So

COMPENDIUM
Closet skeletons / Missionary / Bolton-eeny-noo / Tick a box / Primrose days / Sixes and sevens / Hobson the traveller
CD CYCL 014
Cyclops / Jul '97 / Pinnacle

PARAPHERNALIA
So near so far / Hypnotic / Again / Stand tall / Sea / It's irrelevant / Mr. So & So / Circus
CD PMCD 004
Pagan Media / '96 / Pagan Media / Pinnacle

Mr. Spats

DREAM PATROL
CD NOVA 8913
Nova / Jan '93 / New Note/Pinnacle

Mr. T Experience

ALTERNATIVE IS HERE TO STAY
CD LOOKOUT 126CD
Lookout / Sep '95 / Cargo / Greyhound / Shellshock/Disc

BIG BLACK BUGS BLEED BLUE BLOOD
CD LOOKOUT 145CD
Lookout / May '97 / Cargo / Greyhound / Shellshock/Disc

EVERYONE'S ENTITLED TO THEIR OWN OPINION
CD LOOKOUT 39CD
Lookout / Jul '95 / Cargo / Greyhound / Shellshock/Disc

LOVE IS DEAD
CD LOOKOUT 134CD
Lookout / Jan '96 / Cargo / Greyhound / Shellshock/Disc

OUR BODIES
CD LOOKOUT 80CD
Lookout / Jul '95 / Cargo / Greyhound / Shellshock/Disc

Mr. Z

DOT'S POLKATAINMENT
CD TCD 1034
Tradition / Nov '96 / ADA / Vital

Mraz, George

JAZZ
Moonlight in Vermont / Cinema paradiso (love theme) / Infant eyes / Happy saint / Foolish door / Your story / Spring is here / Pepper / Time remembered / Peacocks / Cinema paradiso (reprise)
CD MCD 92482
Milestone / Jan '97 / Cadillac / Complete/Pinnacle / Jazz Music / Wellard

Mrs. Mills

EP COLLECTION, THE
CD SEECD 332
See For Miles/C5 / Sep '91 / Pinnacle

PIANO FAVOURITES
Put your arms around me honey / I'm in the mood for love / Yes sir that's my baby / Moonlight and roses / Oh Johnny oh Johnny oh / Give me the moonlight, give me the girl / Winchester Cathedral / Green green grass of home / I'm nobody's baby / In the good old Summertime / Tiptoe through the tulips / You are my sunshine / April showers / Down at the Old Bull and Bush / Cruising down the river / Shine on harvest moon / I do like to be beside the seaside / Out of town / Let's all sing like the birdies sing / Good morning / Me and my shadow / My melancholy baby / Second hand rose / There's a blue ridge 'round my heart, Virginia / Virginia / Let him go, let him tarry / I belong to Glasgow / Over the rainbow / Get out and get under the moon

CD CC 269
Music For Pleasure / Aug '91 / EMI

MSB & Dosezero

CONTROL REMOTO 2.0
CD EFAO 15652
Apocalyptic Vision / Mar '96 / Cargo / Plastic Head / SRD

Mseleku, Bheki

BEAUTY OF SUNRISE
CD 5318682
Verve / Jul '97 / PolyGram

CELEBRATION
CD WCD 028
World Circuit / Apr '92 / ADA / Cadillac / Direct / New Note/Pinnacle

MEDITATIONS
CD 5213372
Verve / Jan '95 / PolyGram

TIMELESSNESS
CD 5213062
Verve / Feb '94 / PolyGram

MSI/Asylum

TAKEZ TIME
Intro / Msylum thing / Bwoy wha yuh tek dis fah / Cell wardenz / Whutz da reason / Fuck da dat / Takez time / Naughty but nice / Snide / Takez time / No known kure / Rapperz / Natural (headtop) / Whutz da reason / None ov diss
CD CZCD 002X
Central Zone / Nov '96 / Plastic Head

MT

LORD HAVE MERCY ON MY SOUL
CD FILECD 465
Profile / Mar '96 / Pinnacle

MTA

BY THE BULLET OR THE BALLOT
CD MIA 002CD
MIA / Sep '94 / Plastic Head

Mu

BAND FROM A LOST CONTINENT, THE
CD XMCD 1
Xotic Mind / Jun '97 / Greyhound

BEST OF MU, THE
CD CDRECK 4
Reckless / Oct '89 / RTM/Disc

MU (2CD Set)
CD Set SC 11037
Sundazed / Jun '97 / Cargo / Greyhound / Rollercoaster

MU330

CHUMPS ON PARADE
CD AM 008CD
Asian Man / Jun '97 / Cargo / Greyhound / Plastic Head

PRESS
CD AM 007CD
Asian Man / May '97 / Cargo / Greyhound / Plastic Head

Mua, Boua Zou

MUSIC OF THE HMONG PEOPLE OF LAOS
CD ARHCD 446
Arhoolie / Apr '96 / ADA / Cadillac / Direct

Mucky Pup

ACT OF FAITH
CD CM 9731 CD
Century Media / Jul '92 / Plastic Head

ALIVE AND WELL
CD SPV 08489222
SPV / Dec '96 / Koch / Plastic Head

CAN'T YOU TAKE A JOKE
CD RR 95532
Roadrunner / Feb '93 / PolyGram

FIVE GUYS IN A REALLY HOT GARAGE
CD SPV 08544022
SPV / Jan '96 / Koch / Plastic Head

LEMONADE
CD CM 77058
Century Media / Jan '94 / Plastic Head

NOW
Hippies hate water / Three dead gophers / Jimmy's / Baby / She Quieffed / Feeling sick / Headbangers balls and 120 minutes / My hands, your neck / Face / Hotel Penitentiary / Mucky pumpin' beat / I know nobody / Walkin' with the devil / Yesterdays / To be lonely
CD RO 93402
Roadrunner / Feb '93 / PolyGram

Mud

DYNAMITE
CD BX 4212
BR Music / Jul '94 / Target/BMG

DYNAMITE
CD SE 865642
Disky / Mar '96 / Disky / THE

GOLD COLLECTION, THE
Dynamite / Tiger feet / Cat crept in / Secrets that you keep / Oh boy / Blue moon / Hippy hippy shake / Tallahassee lassie / Living doll / Diana / End of the world / One night / Crazy / Hypnosis / Moonshine Sally / Rocket
CD CDGOLD 1003
EMI Gold / Mar '96 / EMI

Mud

TRAIN TO FOREVER
CD DIS 1095CD
Radiopaque / Mar '97 / Cargo

Mudane

SEED
CD BMCD 075
Raw Energy / Jun '95 / Plastic Head

Mudboy

NEGRO STREETS AT DAWN (Mudboy & The Neutrons)
CD 422469
New Rose / May '94 / ADA / Direct / Discovery

THEY WALK AMONG US (Mudboy & The Neutrons)
CD 379132
Koch International / Nov '95 / Koch

Muddle

MUDDLE
CD SST 310CD
SST / Jul '95 / Plastic Head

Mudhoney

EVERY GOOD BOY DESERVES FUDGE
Generation genocide / Let it slide / Good enough / Something so clear / Thorn / Into the drink / Broken hands / Who you drivin' now / Move out / Shoot the moon / Fuzzgun '91 / Pokin' around / Don't fade IV / Check out time
CD SPCD 105
Sub Pop / Jan '94 / Cargo / Greyhound / Shellshock/Disc

MY BROTHER, THE COW
CD 9362458402
WEA / Mar '95 / Warner Music

PIECE OF CAKE
No end in sight / Make it now / When in Rome / Suck you dry / Blinding sun / Thirteenth floor opening / Youth body expression explosion / I'm spun / Take me there / Living wreck / Let me let you down / Ritzville / Acetone
CD 4509900732
WEA / Oct '92 / Warner Music

Mudshark

MUDSHARK
Wall of fame / Showtime / Cut on the grain / Cold moon rain / Natural / Gangway / Broadway bound / Put out the word / Out of my hands / It won't shine
CD PONYLPCD 001
Pony / Sep '95 / Vital

Muffin Men

MULM
CD EFA 034082
Muffin / Jul '94 / SRD

PLAY UNCLE FRANK LIVE
CD EFA 034172
Muffin / Jan '97 / SRD

SAY CHEESE AND THANKYOU
CD EFA 034022
Muffin / Jan '94 / SRD

Muffins

185
CD CUNEIFORM 55013
Cuneiform / Jun '97 / ReR Megacorp

Muffs

BLONDER AND BLONDER
CD 9362458522
Warner Bros. / Apr '95 / Warner Music

MUFFS, THE
Lucky guy / Saying goodbye / Everywhere I go / Better than me / From your girl / Not like me / Baby go round / North pole / Big mouth / Every single thing / Don't waste another day / Stupid jerk / Another day / Eye to eye / I need you / All for nothing
CD 9362452512
Warner Bros. / Aug '93 / Warner Music

Mugam Ensemble

AZERBAIJAN - LAND OF FLAMES (Mugam Ensemble Jabbar Karyagdy)
CD PANCD 2012
Pan / Oct '93 / ADA / CM / Direct

Muhammad, Abu Al-Ila

ABU AL-ILA MUHAMMAD
CD AAA 114
Club Du Disque Arabe / Oct '95 / ADA / Harmonia Mundi

Muhammad, Idris

BLACK RHYTHM REVOLUTION/PEACE AND RHYTHM
Express yourself / Soulful drums / Super bad / Wander / By the red sea / Peace / Rhythm / Brother you know you're doing wrong / Don't knock my love / I'm a believer
CD CDBPGD 046
Beat Goes Public / Oct '92 / Pinnacle

KABSHA
Kabsha / I want to talk to you / Little feet / GCCCG Blues / Soulful drums / St. M / Kabsha (Alternate take) / GCCG Blues
CD ECD 220962
Evidence / Jul '94 / ADA / Cadillac / Harmonia Mundi

MY TURN
Piece o' cake / Free / There is a girl / Dark road / Dracula / This love / Happenstance / Stranger / Where did we go wrong
CD LIP 890022
Lipstick / Feb '95 / Vital/SAM

Mujician

JOURNEY, THE
CD RUNE 42
Cuneiform / Dec '87 / ReR Megacorp

Mujuru, Ephat

RHYTHMS OF LIFE
CD LYRCD 7407
Lyrichord / '91 / ADA / CM / Roots

Mukherjee, Budhaditya

RAG BAGESRI/RAG DES
CD NI 5268
Nimbus / Sep '94 / Nimbus

RAG RAMKALI/RAG JHINJOTI
CD NI 5221
Nimbus / Sep '94 / Nimbus

Muld, Sorten

SORTEN MULD
CD INT 33
Inter Music / May '96 / ADA

Muldaur, Maria

FANNING THE FLAMES
Home of the blues / Somebody was watching over me / Trust in my love / Stand by me / Well, well, well / Fanning the flames / Heaven on earth / Brotherly love / Talk real slow / Stop running from your own shadow / Can't pin yo' spin on me / Strange and foreign land
CD CD 83394
Telarc Jazz / Nov '96 / Conifer/BMG

MARIA MULDAUR
Any old time / Midnight at the oasis / My Tennessee mountain home / I never did sing you a love song / Work song / Don't you feel my leg / Walking one and only / Long hard climb / Three dollar bill / Vaudeville man / Mad mad mad
CD 7599272082
Reprise / Sep '93 / Warner Music

MEET ME AT MIDNIGHT
CD BT 1107CD
Black Top / Oct '94 / ADA / CM / Direct

SWEET & SLOW
CD SP 1183CD
Stony Plain / Oct '93 / ADA / CM / Direct

Muldrow, Ronald

DIASPORA
CD ENJACD 80862
Enja / May '95 / New Note/Pinnacle / Vital/SAM

FACING WES
On the fritz / Facing wes / Andrea / Granite green / Oliver's moments / Our day will come / Minus mingus / Cryin' blues / Little white lies / Three quarter miles
CD KOKO 1311
Kokopelli / Aug '96 / New Note/Pinnacle

GNOWING YOU (Muldrow, Ronald Trio)
Quasimodal / Deaceleration / Soleshia / Georgia Ann / Gnowing you / Polka dots and moonbeams / Little Wes
CD CDLR 45047
L&R / Feb '92 / New Note/Pinnacle

Mule

IF I DON'T SIX
CD QS 29CD
Quarter Stick / Sep '94 / Cargo / SRD

MULE
CD QS 15 CD
Quarter Stick / Feb '93 / Cargo / SRD

Mullican, Moon

MOON'S ROCK
Moon's rock / Jenny Lee / Pipeliner blues / Sweet rockin' music / That's me / Cush cush ky yay / Writing on the wall / Wedding of the bugs / Nobody knows but my pillow / My love / I'm waiting for the ships that never come in / You don't have to be a baby to cry / I'll sail my ship alone / I was sorta wonderin' / Every which a way / I don't know why (I just do) / Sweeter than the flowers / Leaves mustn't fall / Anything that's part of you / Early morning blues / My baby's gone / Colinda / Make friends / Cajun coffee song / Quarter mile rows / Just to be with you / I'll pour the wine / Fools like me / Big big city / Mr. Tears / She once lived here / This glass I hold
CD BCD 15607
Bear Family / Apr '92 / Direct / Rollercoaster / Swift

MOONSHINE JAMBOREE
Hey Mr. Cotton Picker / Leaving you with a worried mind / What's the matter with the mill / Pipeliner blues / Triflin' woman blues / Nine tenths of the Tennessee River / Cherokee boogie / All I need is you / I'll sail my ship alone / Good deal Lucille / Moonshine blues / Rocket to the moon / Downstream / I done it / Goodnight Irene / Rheumatism boogie / Well oh well / Don't ever take my picture down / Lonesome hearted blues / It's a sin to love you like I do / I'm gonna move home and bye and bye / I left my heart in Texas / I'll take your hat right off my rack
CD CDCHD 458
Ace / Sep '93 / Pinnacle

Mulligan, Gerry

AT BIRDLAND NEW YORK 1960
CD 550072
Jazz Anthology / Jan '94 / Cadillac / Discovery / Harmonia Mundi

BEST OF GERRY MULLIGAN
CD DLCD 4018
Dixie Live / Mar '95 / TKO Magnum

BEST OF GERRY MULLIGAN WITH CHET BAKER
Bernie's tune / Nights at the turntable / Freeway / Soft shoe / Walkin' shoes / Makin' whoopee / Carson city stage / My old flame / Love me or leave me / Swing house / Jeru / Darn that dream / I'm beginning to see the light / My funny valentine / Festive minor
CD CZ 416
Pacific Jazz / Sep '92 / EMI

CONCERT IN THE RAIN
CD EBCD 2129
Jazzband / Jun '96 / Cadillac / Hot Shot / Jazz Music / Wellard

DRAGONFLY (Mulligan, Gerry Quartet)
Dragonfly / Brother blues / I'm not rappaport / Backstage / Little glory / Art of trumpet / Listening to Astor / Ninth life / Underneath a pale blue moonlight / Start all over again
CD CD 83377
Telarc / Feb '96 / Conifer/BMG

DREAM A LITTLE DREAM
Nobody else but me / Home (when shadows fall) / Dream a little dream / I'll be around / They say it's wonderful / Real thing / Here's that rainy day / Georgia on my mind / My funny valentine / As close as pages in a book / My shining hour / Walking shoes / Song for Strayhorn
CD CD 83364
Telarc / Nov '94 / Conifer/BMG

GERRY MEETS HAMP (Mulligan, Gerry & Lionel Hampton)
CD JHR 73555
Jazz Hour / Jan '93 / Cadillac / Jazz Music / Target/BMG

GERRY MULLIGAN & CONCERT JAZZ BAND
CD 5233422
Verve / Apr '94 / PolyGram

GERRY MULLIGAN MEETS BEN WEBSTER (Mulligan, Gerry & Ben Webster)
Chelsea Bridge / Cat walk / Sunday / Who's got rhythm / Tell me when / Go home / In a mellotone / What is this thing called love / For Bessie / Fajista / BLues in B flat
CD 8416612
Verve / Aug '90 / PolyGram

GERRY MULLIGAN QUARTET WITH CHET BAKER (Mulligan, Gerry & Chet Baker)
CD CD 53027
Giants Of Jazz / Aug '88 / Cadillac / Jazz Music / Target/BMG

GERRY MULLIGAN SEXTET: 1955-56
CD CD 53141
Giants Of Jazz / Nov '92 / Cadillac / Jazz Music / Target/BMG

GERRY MULLIGAN/ASTOR PIAZZOLLA 1974 (Mulligan, Gerry & Astor Piazzolla)
CD 556642CD
Accord / Aug '94 / Cadillac / Discovery

GERRY MULLIGAN/PAUL DESMOND QUARTET (Mulligan, Gerry & Paul Desmond)
Blues in time / Body and soul / Stand still / Line for Lyons / Wintersong / Battle hymn of the republican / Fall out / Tea for two / Wintersong / Lover
CD 5198502
Verve / Mar '94 / PolyGram

IDOL GOSSIP (Mulligan, Gerry & His New Sextet)
CD CRD 155
Chiaroscuro / Mar '96 / Jazz Music

IMMORTAL CONCERTS
I may be wrong, but I think you're wonderful / Gold rush / Makin' whoopee / Laura / Soft shoe / Nearness of you / Love me or leave me / Bernie's tune / Walking shoes / Five brothers / Lullaby of the leaves / Limelight / Come out wherever you are / Moonlight in Vermont / Lady is a tramp / Bark for Barksdale
CD CD 53020
Giants Of Jazz / Jun '88 / Cadillac / Jazz Music / Target/BMG

IN CONCERT (Mulligan, Gerry Quartet)
CD RTE 760463
RTE / May '95 / ADA / Koch

JAZZ PROFILE
Disc jockey jump / Venus de Milo / Revelation / Walkin' shoes / Five brothers / My funny Valentine / Open country / Western reunion / Red door
CD CDP 8549052
Blue Note / May '97 / EMI

JERU
Get out of town / Here I'll stay / Inside impromptu / Blue boy / You've come home / Lonely town / Capricious
CD 4736852
Columbia / Nov '93 / Sony

LIMELIGHT
CD DM 15016
DMA Jazz / Jul '96 / Jazz Music

LIVE IN STOCKHOLM 1957
Come out wherever you are / Birth of the blues / Moonlight in Velmont / Lullaby of the leaves / Open country / I can't get started (with you) / Frenesi / Baubles, bangles and beads / Yardbird suite / Walkin' shoes / My funny valentine / Blues at the roots / Introduction / Bernie's tune
CD MCD 0462
Moon / Nov '93 / Cadillac / Harmonia Mundi

LONESOME BOULEVARD
Rico Apollo / I heard the shadows dancing / Lonesome boulevard / Curtains / Ring around a bright star / Splendor in the grass / Good neighbour / Thelonious / Wallflower / Flying Scotsman / Etude for Franca
CD 3970612
A&M / Mar '94 / PolyGram

MULLIGAN
Jeru / Festive minor / Rose room / North Atlantic run / Taurus moon / Out back of the barn
CD 17081
Laserlight / Jan '97 / Target/BMG

MULLIGAN IN THE MAIN (Newport Jazz Festival July 3rd/6th 1958)
CD NCD 8814
Phontastic / '93 / Cadillac / Jazz Music / Wellard

MULLIGAN SONGBOOK, THE
Four and one more / Crazy day / Turnstile / Sextet / Disc jockey jump / Venus de Milo / Revelation / May-reh / Preacher / Good bait / Bags' groove
CD CDP 8335752
Pacific Jazz / Jan '96 / EMI

NEWS FROM BLUEPORT (Mulligan, Gerry & Art Farmer)
CD JHR 73577
Jazz Hour / May '94 / Cadillac / Jazz Music / Target/BMG

NIGHT LIGHTS
Morning of the carnival / Prelude in E minor / Night lights / Festive minor / Tell me when / In the wee small hours of the morning
CD 8182712
Mercury / Aug '84 / PolyGram

PARAISO (Mulligan, Gerry & Jane Duboc)
CD CD 83361
Telarc / Oct '93 / Conifer/BMG

PARIS 1954/LA 1953 (Mulligan, Gerry Quartet)
Soft shoes / Five brothers / Lullaby of the leaves / Limelight / Come out wherever you are / Motel / My funny valentine / Turnstile / Speak low / Ladybird / Love me or leave me / Swing house / Varsity drag / Half Nelson
CD VG 655616
Vogue / Nov '92 / BMG

PLEYEL CONCERT 1954 VOL.1 (Original Vogue Masters) (Mulligan, Gerry Quartet)
Bernie's tune / Presentation of the musicians / Walkin' shoes / Nearness of you / Motel/Utter chaos / Love me or leave me / Soft shoe / Bark for Barksdale / My funny valentine / Turnstile/Utter chaos / I may be wrong / Five brothers / Gold rush / Makin' whoopee
CD 74321429232
Vogue / Apr '97 / BMG

PLEYEL CONCERT 1954 VOL.2 (Original Vogue Masters) (Mulligan, Gerry Quartet)
Lady is a tramp / Laura / Motel / Five brothers / Lullaby of the leaves / Nearness of you / Limelight / Come out come out wherever you are / Makin' whoopee / Love me or leave me / Laura / Line for Lyons / Moonlight in Vermont / Bark for Barksdale/Utter chaos
CD 74321429222
Vogue / Apr '97 / BMG

SHADOW OF YOUR SMILE (Mulligan, Gerry Quartet)
CD MCD 003
Moon / Sep '89 / Cadillac / Harmonia Mundi

SILVER COLLECTION, THE (Gerry Mulligan Meets The Saxophonists)
Chelsea Bridge / Tell me when / Bunny / 18 carrots for rabbit / Come rain or come shine / Red door / Scrapple from the apple / This can't be love / Line for Lyons / Body and soul
CD 8274362
Verve / Feb '93 / PolyGram

SOFT LIGHTS AND SWEET MUSIC (Mulligan, Gerry & Scott Hamilton)
Soft lights and sweet music / Gone / Do you know what I see / I've just seen her / Noblesse / Ghosts / Port of Baltimore blues
CD CCD 4300
Concord Jazz / Jan '87 / New Note/ Pinnacle

STOCKHOLM 1959 (Mulligan, Gerry Quartet)
CD TAXCD 3711
Tax / Jan '93 / Cadillac / Jazz Music / Wellard

SYMPHONIC DREAMS (Mulligan, Gerry Quartet)
Entente / Sax chronicles / Song for Strayhorn / Sax chronicles / K4 Pacific
CD SION 18130
Sion / Jul '97 / Direct

THIS IS JAZZ
Line for Lyons / Festive minor / As catch can / What is there to say / You've come home / Bernie's tune / Utter chaos / My funny valentine / Lullabye de Mexico
CD CK 64972
Sony Jazz / Oct '96 / Sony

WALKING SHOES
CD BS 18008
Bandstand / Jul '96 / Swift

WALKING SHOES 1959/NEW YORK 1977
CD Set JWD 102310
JWD / Oct '94 / Target/BMG

WHAT IS THERE TO SAY (Mulligan, Gerry Quartet)
What is there to say / Just in time / News from blueport / Festive minor / My funny valentine / As catch can / Blueport / Utter chaos
CD 4756992
Columbia / Feb '94 / Sony

Mulligan, Mick

MEET MICK MULLIGAN & GEORGE MELLY (Mulligan, Mick & George Melly)
Young & healthy / Button up your overcoat / All I do is dream / I'm crazy 'bout my baby / All of me / Rocking chair / Bei mir bist du schon / There'll be some changes made / Girl of my dreams / Ace in the hole / Alexander's ragtime band / Oh you beautiful doll / Muscrat ramble / Sweet Lorraine / When you're smiling / After you've gone / I'll see you in my dreams / Mama don't allow
CD LACD 66
Lake / Aug '96 / ADA / Cadillac / Direct / Jazz Music / Target/BMG

Mullins, Rob

5TH GEAR
CD NOVA 8810
Nova / Jan '93 / New Note/Pinnacle

JAZZ JAZZ
CD NOVA 8918
Nova / Jan '93 / New Note/Pinnacle

ONE NIGHT IN HOUSTON
Polka dot dress / Very blue / Quick call the note police / Jazz man / One night in Houston / Plus three / Quiet fire / Holiday / Too cold
CD AQCD 1020
Audioquest / Sep '95 / ADA / New Note/ Pinnacle

TOKIO NIGHTS
CD NOVA 9026
Nova / Jan '93 / New Note/Pinnacle

Mulo, Alman

AFRODIZIAC DREAMTIME (Mulo, Alman Band)

CD TASTE 41CD
Southern / Nov '93 / SRD

DIAMONDS AND TOADS (Mulo, Alman Band)
CD TASTE 46
Taste / Jan '95 / Plastic Head / SRD

ORISHA (Mulo, Alman Band)
CD TASTE 37
Taste / Jan '95 / Plastic Head / SRD

Mulqueen, Ann

MO GHRASA THALL NA DEISE (Memorable Songs In The Munster Tradition)
CD CIC 080CD
Clo Iar-Chonnachta / Jan '93 / CM

Mulu

SMILES LIKE A SHARK
She smiles / Filmstar / Deowarfe / Pussycat / Eyesight / Bitesize / Sink / Pink pony cafe / Desire / Trixter / Isit me / Peaceful and quiet / Rainy days
CD DEDCD 033
Dedicated / Aug '97 / BMG / Vital

Mulvihill, Brendan

FLAX IN BLOOM, THE
Flax in bloom/Honeymoon / Crabs in the skillet / Concertina/The circus / Lament for O'Donnell / John Grady's downfall/The flogging reel / Pigeon on the gate/Miss Monahan's reel / Dr. O'Neill's reel / Home ruler / Brigade / Fermoy lassies/Bunker hill / Hardlman's fancy/Billy Rush's own / First house in Connaught/Dairy maid
CD GLCD 1020
Green Linnet / Feb '93 / ADA / CM / Direct / Highlander / Roots

MORNING DEW, THE (Mulvihill, Brendan & Donna Long)
Morning dew/Grants / Brian Maguire/Thomas Judge/The broken pledge/McGlinchey's/Th / Rathlin Island / Shandon bells/Boys of the town/Rakes of Clonmel/ Girls of the / Festus Burke/John Drury / An ceileabrad caoine / Morgan Magan/Greig's pipes / Mrs. Judge / Down the broom/Joseph Bank / Kean and Colonel O'Hara/Flaggon reel/Dublin lasses
CD GLCD 1128
Green Linnet / Jul '93 / ADA / CM / Direct / Highlander / Roots

Mumbleskinny

HEAD ABOVE WATER
CD SECT2 10011
Sector 2 / Jul '95 / Cargo / Direct

Munarriz, Valeria

TANGO
CD MES 159172
Messidor / Feb '93 / ADA / Koch

Munde, Alan

BLUE RIDGE EXPRESS
CD ROUCD 0301
Rounder / Apr '94 / ADA / CM / Direct

FESTIVAL FAVOURITES REVISITED
CD ROUCD 0311
Rounder / Apr '93 / ADA / CM / Direct

Mundell, Hugh

AFRICA MUST BE FREE BY 1983
Let's all unite / My mind / Africa must be free by 1983 / Why do blackmen fuss and fight / Book of life / Run revolution come / Day of judgement / Jah will provide / Ital sip
CD GRELCD 94
Greensleeves / May '90 / Jet Star / SRD

ARISE
CD NETCD 1003
Network / '92 / Direct / Greensleeves / SRD
CD CONCD 002
Conqueror / Oct '96 / Grapevine/PolyGram / Jet Star

BLACK MAN FOUNDATION
CD SHANCD 43012
Shanachie / Jun '85 / ADA / Greensleeves / Koch

MUNDELL
Jacqueline / Rasta have the handle / Going places / Red, gold and green / Tell I a lie / Twenty four hours a day / Jah music / Your face is familiar
CD GRELCD 36
Greensleeves / Jul '97 / Jet Star / SRD

Mundy

JELLY LEGS
Reunion / Pardon me / Life's a cinch / Song for my darlin' / Gin and tonic sky / Blown away / To you I bestow / Stone / Springtown / Sisters / Arrow of gold / Private paradise / Mundy in wonderland
CD MUNDY 3CD
CD MUNDY 3CDS
Epic / Oct '96 / Sony

Mungo Jerry

ALL THE HITS PLUS MORE
CD CDPT 002
Prestige / Jun '92 / Else / Total/BMG

BEST OF MUNGO JERRY, THE
Lana / It's a secret / Hello Nadine / Let's get started / Forgotten land / Drum song / In the summertime / Lady Rose / Somebody stole my wife / Alright, alright / Long legged woman / Sugar Mama / That's my baby / Angel Mama / I'm gonna bop till I drop / Rockin' on the road / Baby jump / You don't have to be in the army to fight the war / Open up / Wild love
CD 4776449
Columbia / Aug '95 / Sony

BEST OF MUNGO JERRY, THE (Alright, Alright, Alright)
In the summertime / Baby jump / Open up / John B. Badde / Lady Rose / Little Miss Hipshake / Long legged woman dressed in black / Mighty man / Don't stop / Alright alright alright / Somebody stole my wife / You don't have to be in the army to fight in the war / Maggie / Wild love / Hey Rosalyn / Northcote arms / Gonna bop till I drop / Have a whiff on me / Summer's gone
CD MCCD 292
Music Club / May '97 / Disc / THE

GREATEST HITS
In the summertime / Wild love / Baby jump / Mighty man / Another bad day / Callin' / Long legged woman dressed in black / Lady Rose / Alright, alright, alright / Open up / Feels like I'm in love / Keep me up all night / Hello Nadine / You don't have to be in the army to fight in the war
CD 399360
Koch Presents / Jun '97 / Koch

MUNGO JERRY/ELECTRONICALLY TESTED
Baby let's play house / Johnny B Badde / San Francisco Bay blues / Sad eyed Joe / Maggie / Peace in the country / See me / Movin' on / My friend / Mother fucker boogie / Tramp / Daddie's brew / She rowed / I just want to make love to you / In the summertime / Somebody stole my wife / Baby jump / Follow me down / Memoirs of a stockbroker / You better leave that whiskey alone / Coming back to you when the time comes
CD BGOCD 286
Beat Goes On / Oct '96 / Pinnacle

SUMMERTIME
In the summertime / Baby jump / Lady Rose / Alright alright alright / Wild love / My girl and me / Maggie / Johnny B Badde / Don't stop / Long legged woman dressed in black / All dressed up and no place to go / I don't wanna go back to school / Baby let's play house / Gonna bop till I drop / Brand new car / Somebody stole my wife / Sweet Mary Jane / Too fast to live, too young to die
CD 5507492
Spectrum / Jan '95 / PolyGram

VERY BEST OF MUNGO JERRY, THE
In the summertime / Hello Nadine / Alright, alright, alright / Baby jump / Snakebite / All I wanna do / Heartbreak avenue / Girl like you / Red leather and chrome / Sugar in the bowl / Jesse James / Remember me / Rock 'n' roll-rock 'n' roll / Right on / Lady Rose / Long legged dressed in black / Open up / It's a secret / Let's get started / Forgotten land
CD SUMCD 4090
Summit / Jan '97 / Sound & Media

VERY BEST OF MUNGO JERRY, THE
In the summertime / Alright, alright, alright / Dancing in the street / Rocking on the road / Mighty man / It's a secret / Dance rave / Red leather and chrome / Forgotten land / Open up / Girl like you / Maggie / Bottle of beer / Baby jump
CD 100622
CMC / May '97 / BMG

YOU DON'T HAVE TO BE IN THE ARMY/BOOT POWER (2CD Set)
You don't have to be in the army to fight the war / Ella speed / Pigeon stew / Take me back / Give me love / Hey Rosalyn / Northcote arms / There's a man going round taking names / Simple things / Keep your hands off her / On a sunday / That old dust storm / Open up / She's gone / Lookin' for my girl / See you again / Demon / My girl and me / Sweet Mary Jane / Lady Rose / Dusty road / Brand new car / 46 an' on
CD Set BGOCD 292
Beat Goes On / Oct '96 / Pinnacle

Munyon, David

ACRYLIC TEEPEES
CD GRCD 393
Glitterhouse / Nov '96 / Avid/BMG

CODE NAME: JUMPER
CD GRCD 307
Glitterhouse / May '97 / Avid/BMG

Munzer, Fritz

STRAIGHT OFF (Munzer, Fritz Sound Express)
CD ISCD 112
Intersound / Oct '91 / Jazz Music

Muppets

CHRISTMAS TOGETHER, A (Denver, John & Muppets)
CD MCCDX 007
Music Club / Nov '94 / Disc / THE

KERMIT UNPIGGED (Various Artists)
CD 74321233382
BMG Kidz / Oct '94 / BMG

Mur, Mona

WARSZAW
CD SPLCD 1
Solid Pleasure / Jul '92 / Pinnacle

Muranyi, Joe

JOE MURANYI WITH THE ORIENT DIXIELAND JAZZ BAND
CD JCD 266
Jazzology / Jun '96 / Jazz Music

Murata, Yoichi

DOUBLE EDGE
Return of prodigal son / Some skunk funk / Wrecker / Good-bye pork pie hat / Squib cakes / Shuffling jazzmen / Reflections / Freedom jazz dance / Manteca / Sweet Henry
CD JVC 90052
JVC / Aug '96 / Direct / New Note/Pinnacle / Vital/SAM

WHAT'S BOP (Murata, Yoichi & Solid Brass)
Be bop - what's the matter / Teen town / Snapping turtle / Ponta march / Acute angles / Three views of a secret / Bring back / High old time / Come Sunday / Port to port
CD JVC 90162
JVC / Aug '97 / Direct / New Note/Pinnacle / Vital/SAM

Murder Inc.

MURDER INC
CD INVCD 013
Invisible / Feb '94 / Plastic Head

MURDER INC.
Supergrass / Murder Inc / Mania / Hole in the wall / Uninvited guest / Gambit / Red black / Last of the urgents / Mrs. Whiskey name
CD CDDVN 9
Devotion / May '92 / Pinnacle

Murderer's Row

MURDERER'S ROW
CD A2Z 85012CD
A-Z / Jul '96 / Plastic Head

Murmur

SEXPOWDER 2000 VOLTS
CD RAIN 013CD
Cloudland / Apr '95 / Plastic Head / SRD

Murphy, Column

IRISH DRUM, THE
CD CEFCD 175
Gael Linn / Mar '96 / ADA / CM / Direct / Grapevine/PolyGram / Roots

Murphy, David Lee

GETTING OUT THE GOOD STUFF
Every time I get around you / Road you leave behind / She's really something to see / Genuine rednecks / 100 years too late / Born that way / Breakfast in Birmingham / Getting out the good stuff / I've been a rebel (and it don't pay) / Pirates cove
CD MCAD 11423
MCA / Jun '96 / BMG

Murphy, Dennis

MUSIC FROM SLIABHRA LUCHRA
CD RTE 183CD
RTE / Jan '95 / ADA / Koch

Murphy, Donal

SLIABH NOTES (Murphy, Donal & Matt Cranitch/Tommy O'Sullivan)
CD CBMCD 018
Cross Border Media / Jul '96 / ADA / Direct / Grapevine/PolyGram

Murphy, Elliott James

12
CD 422244
New Rose / May '94 / ADA / Direct / Discovery

AFFAIRS ETC.
CD 422237
New Rose / May '94 / ADA / Direct / Discovery

CHANGE WILL COME
CD 422239
New Rose / May '94 / ADA / Direct / Discovery

IF POETS WERE KING
CD 422240
New Rose / May '94 / ADA / Direct / Discovery

LIVE HOT POINT
CD 422241
New Rose / May '94 / ADA / Direct / Discovery

MILWAUKEE
CD ROSE 99CD
New Rose / Nov '86 / ADA / Direct / Discovery

PARIS-NEW YORK
CD 422401
New Rose / May '94 / ADA / Direct / Discovery

PARTY GIRLS/BROKEN POETS
CD DJD 3201
Dejadisc / May '94 / ADA / Direct

Murphy, Jimmy

SIXTEEN TONS ROCK'N'ROLL
Sixteen tons rock'n'roll / My gal Dottie / Grandpaw's cat / Baboon boogie / I'm looking for a mustard patch / Put some meat on them bones / Here Kitty Kitty / Sweet sweet lips (unissued) / Electricity / Big mama blues / That first guitar of mine / Love that satisfies / Educated fool / Rambling heart / We live a long, long time / Mother where is your daughter
CD BCD 15451
Bear Family / Sep '90 / Direct / Rollercoaster / Swift

Murphy, Maggy

LINKIN' O'ER THE LEA
CD VT 134CD
Veteran Tapes / Aug '96 / ADA / Direct

Murphy, Mark

BEAUTY AND THE BEAST
CD VGCD 600606
Vogue / Jan '93 / BMG

NIGHT MOODS (The Music Of Ivan Lins)
CD MCD 9145
Milestone / Jan '92 / Cadillac / Complete/ Pinnacle / Jazz Music / Wellard

RAH
CD OJCCD 141
Original Jazz Classics / Jun '95 / Complete/Pinnacle / Jazz Music / Wellard

Murphy, Matt

WAY DOWN SOUTH
Way down South / Big 6 / Gonna be some changes made / Big city takedown / Buck's boogie / Thump tyme / Matt's guitar boogie / Low down and dirty / Gimme somma dat / Blue walls
CD ANTCD 0013
Antones / Mar '91 / ADA / Hot Shot

Murphy, Maurice

LIGHTER SIDE OF MAURICE MURPHY
CD DOYCD 007
Doyen / Oct '91 / Conifer/BMG

STARS IN BRASS (Murphy, Maurice/Guy Barker/Derek Watkins)
Trumpet blues and cantabile / Charivari / Anyone can whistle / Carnival of Venice / Softly as I leave you / Stardust / Our love is here to stay / Maiaguena / Li'l darlin' / Street scene / Here comes that rainy day / Norwiegian wood / Memories of you / Bess you is my woman now / We've only just begun / Three kings swing
CD DOYCD 035
Doyen / Oct '94 / Conifer/BMG

Murphy, Pat J.

BYGONE DAYS
CD CDC 009
Ceol / Feb '97 / CM

Murphy, Peter

CASCADE
CD BBQCD 175
Beggars Banquet / Apr '95 / RTM/Disc / Warner Music

DEEP
Deep ocean vast sea / Crystal wrists / Seven veils / Cuts you up / Roll call / Shy / Marlene Dietrich's favourite poem / Line between the devil's teeth / Strange kind of love / Roll call (reprise)
CD BEGA 107CD
Beggars Banquet / '88 / RTM/Disc / Warner Music

LOVE HYSTERIA
All night long / His circle and hers meet / Dragnet drag / Socrates the python / Indigo eyes / Time has nothing to do with it / Blind sublime / My last two years / Fun time
CD BEGA 92CD
Beggars Banquet / Mar '88 / RTM/Disc / Warner Music

SHOULD THE WORLD FAIL TO FALL APART
Light pours out of me / Confessions / Should the world fail to fall apart / Never man / God sends / Blue heart / Answer is clear / Final solution / Jemal
CD ______ BBL 69CD
Lowdown/Beggars Banquet / Jul '88 / RTM/ Disc / Warner Music

Murphy, Phil

TRIP TO CULLENSTOWN, THE (Murphy, Phil, John & Pip)
Flogging reel/Kathy jones/The honeymoon / Shores of Lough Gowna/Humours of Kesh / Wexford and Bannow Bay hornpipes / Pete's polka/The happy polka / Micky the moulder/Tatter Jack Welsh / Shepherd's love dream / Kitty come over/The mug of brown ale / Ballygow reel / Trip to Cullenstown / Congress/The heather breeze/Earl's chair / Lakes of Kincora/Cronin's hornpipe / Mummer's jigs / Pete Bate's hornpipe/Joe Kearne's favourite / Ballygow polka / Wistful lover / Kerry hills / King of Clans/Castlekelly / Listowel polka
CD ______ CC 55CD
Claddagh / Nov '92 / ADA / CM / Direct

Murphy, Rose

LIVE IN CONCERT 1982
CD ______ EQCD 7002
Equinox / Jan '95 / Discovery

ROSE MURPHY
CD ______ ACD 70
Audiophile / Jul '96 / Jazz Music

Murphy, Turk

BEST OF TURK MURPHY, THE
CD ______ MMRCCD 2
Merry Makers / Jul '93 / Jazz Music

CONCERT IN THE PARK (Murphy, Turk Jazz Band)
CD ______ MMRCD 12
Merry Makers / Jul '96 / Jazz Music

ITALIAN VILLAGE 1952-53 (Murphy, Turk Jazz Band)
CD ______ MMRCD 11
Merry Makers / Aug '95 / Jazz Music

SAN FRANCISCO JAZZ (Murphy, Turk Jazz Band)
CD ______ MMRCCD 3
Merry Makers / Jun '88 / Jazz Music

SAN FRANCISCO JAZZ VOL.2 (Murphy, Turk Jazz Band)
CD ______ CMMRC 115
Merry Makers / Jun '88 / Jazz Music

TURK MURPHY AND HIS SAN FRANCISCO JAZZ BAND (Murphy, Turk San Francisco Jazz Band)
CD ______ BCD 91
GHB / Oct '93 / Jazz Music

TURK MURPHY AND HIS SAN FRANCISCO JAZZ BAND VOL.2
CD ______ BCD 92
GHB / Jan '93 / Jazz Music

Murphy, Willie

HUSTLIN' MAN BLUES (Murphy, Willie & The Angel-Headed Hipsters)
CD ______ MU 1
Muff Ugga / Apr '97 / Hot Shot

MONKEY IN THE ZOO
Keep on rocking the boat / World is a neighbourhood / Keep on running / Kamikaze / I just wanna be / Open letter / Time (is running out) / Midnight hour / Great balls of fire / Monkey in the zoo
CD ______ ATM 1125
Atomic Theory / May '97 / ADA / Direct

Murrain

FAMINE, THE
CD ______ MAB 003CD
MAB / Jul '93 / Plastic Head

Murray, Anne

BEST OF ANNE MURRAY SO FAR, THE
Snowbird / Now and forever (you and me) / Danny's song / Nobody loves me like you do / Love song / Time don't run out on me / You won't see me / Just another woman in love / You needed me / Little good news / I just fall in love again / Somebody's always saying goodbye / Broken hearted me / Could I have this dance / Daydream believer / Another sleepless night / Shadows in the moonlight / Blessed are the believers / Make love to me / Over you
CD ______ CDP 8311582
EMI / Jul '95 / EMI

CROONIN'
Old cape cod / Wayward wind / Secret love / Fever / When I fall in love / Allegheny moon / You belong to me / Born to be with you / True love / Teach me tonight / Cry me a river / Make love to me / Hey there / It only hurts for a little while / I'm confessin' I'm a fool to care / Wanted / I really don't want to know / Moments to remember
CD ______ CDEMC 3672
EMI / Mar '94 / EMI

THERE GOES MY EVERYTHING
CD ______ HADCD 183
Javelin / Nov '95 / Henry Hadaway / THE

Murray, David

ACOUSTIC OCTFUNK
CD ______ SSCD 8051
Sound Hills / Apr '94 / Cadillac / Harmonia Mundi

BALLADS FOR BASS CLARINET (Murray, David Quartet)
CD ______ DIW 880
DIW / Jan '94 / Cadillac / Harmonia Mundi

BLACK & BLACK
CD ______ 4715772
Sony Jazz / Nov '92 / Sony

BODY AND SOUL (Murray, David Quartet)
CD ______ 1201552
Black Saint / Nov '93 / Cadillac / Harmonia Mundi

CHILDREN
CD ______ BSR 0089
Black Saint / '86 / Cadillac / Harmonia Mundi

DARK STAR (The Music Of The Grateful Dead)
Shakedown Street / Sampson and Delilah / Estimated prophet / China doll / One more Saturday night / Should have been me
CD ______ TCD 4002
Astor Place / Jul '96 / New Note/Pinnacle

DAVID MURRAY BIG BAND
CD ______ DIW 851
DIW / Nov '91 / Cadillac / Harmonia Mundi

DEATH OF A SIDEMAN (Murray, David Quintet)
CD ______ DIW 866
DIW / Feb '93 / Cadillac / Harmonia Mundi

FLOWERS FOR ALBERT (2CD Set) (Murray, David & Low Class Conspiracy)
CD Set ______ IN 1026CD
India Navigation / Jun '97 / Discovery / Impetus

FO DEUK REVUE
Blue muse / Evidence / One world family / Too many hungry people / Chant africain / Abdoul aziz sy / Village urbana / Thilo
CD ______ JUST 942
Justin Time / Jun '97 / Cadillac / New Note/ Pinnacle

FOR AUNT LOUISE
CD ______ DIW 901
DIW / Dec '95 / Cadillac / Harmonia Mundi

HEALERS, THE (Murray, David & Randy Weston)
CD ______ 1201182
Black Saint / Cadillac / Harmonia Mundi

HOME (Murray, David Octet)
Home / Santa Barbara and Crenshaw / Follies / Choctaw blues / Last of the hipmen / 3-D family
CD ______ BSRCD 055
Black Saint / Sep '85 / Cadillac / Harmonia Mundi

HOPE SCOPE (Murray, David Octet)
CD ______ 1201392
Black Saint / Apr '91 / Cadillac / Harmonia Mundi

I WANT TO TALK ABOUT YOU (Murray, David Quartet)
CD ______ 1201052
Black Saint / Sep '89 / Cadillac / Harmonia Mundi

INTERBOOGIEOLOGY
CD ______ 1200182
Black Saint / Nov '90 / Cadillac / Harmonia Mundi

LIVE AT SWEET BASIL VOL.1 (Murray, David Big Band)
Lovers / Bechet's bounce / Silence / Duet for big band
CD ______ BSRCD 085
Black Saint / '86 / Cadillac / Harmonia Mundi

LIVE AT SWEET BASIL VOL.2 (Murray, David Big Band)
CD ______ BSRCD 0095
Black Saint / '86 / Cadillac / Harmonia Mundi

LIVE AT THE LOWER MANHATTAN OCEAN CLUB
CD ______ IN 1032CD
India Navigation / Jan '97 / Discovery / Impetus

LOVE AND SORROW
CD ______ DIW 921
DIW / Feb '97 / Cadillac / Harmonia Mundi

MING (Murray, David Octet)
Fast life / Hill / Ming / Jasvan / Dewey's circle
CD ______ BSRCD 045
Black Saint / Sep '85 / Cadillac / Harmonia Mundi

MODERN PORTRAIT OF LOUIS ARMSTRONG, A (Murray, David, Doc Cheatham, Loren Schoenburg, Allen Lowe)
CD ______ STCD 563
Stash / May '93 / ADA / Cadillac / CM / Direct / Jazz Music

MORNING SONG (Murray, David Octet)
Morning song / Body and soul / Light blue / Jitterbug waltz / Off season / Duet
CD ______ BSRCD 075
Black Saint / Sep '85 / Cadillac / Harmonia Mundi

MURRAY'S STEPS (Murray, David Octet)
CD ______ BSR 0065
Black Saint / '86 / Cadillac / Harmonia Mundi

PICASSO (Murray, David Octet)
CD ______ DIW 879
DIW / Jan '94 / Cadillac / Harmonia Mundi

REAL DEAL (Murray, David & Milford Graves)
CD ______ DIW 867
DIW / Jan '93 / Cadillac / Harmonia Mundi

REMEMBRANCES (Murray, David Quintet)
CD ______ DIW 849
DIW / Nov '91 / Cadillac / Harmonia Mundi

SANCTUARY WITHIN, A
CD ______ 1201452
Black Saint / Nov '92 / Cadillac / Harmonia Mundi

SHAKILL'S VOL.2
CD ______ DIW 884
DIW / Oct '94 / Cadillac / Harmonia Mundi

SHAKILL'S WARRIOR (Murray, David Quartet)
CD ______ DIW 850
DIW / Nov '91 / Cadillac / Harmonia Mundi

TENORS (Murray, David Quartet)
CD ______ DIW 881
DIW / Jan '94 / Cadillac / Harmonia Mundi

TIP, THE
CD ______ DIW 891
DIW / Mar '95 / Cadillac / Harmonia Mundi

Murray, Diedre

FIRESTORM (Murray, Diedre & Fred Hopkins)
CD ______ VICTOCD 020
Victo / Nov '94 / Harmonia Mundi / ReR Megacorp

STRINGOLOGY (Murray, Diedre & Fred Hopkins)
CD ______ 1201432
Black Saint / May '94 / Cadillac / Harmonia Mundi

Murray, Keith

ENIGMA
CD ______ CHIP 172
Jive / Nov '96 / Pinnacle

MOST BEAUTIFULLEST THING IN THE WORLD, THE
Live from New York / Sychosymatic / Dip dip di / Most beautifullest thing in the world / Herb is pumpin' / Sychoward / Straight Loonie / Danger / Get lifted / How's that / Chase / Take it to the streetz / Born born zee / Countdown / Escapism / Most beautifullest thing in this world
CD ______ CHIP 159
Jive / Mar '97 / Pinnacle

Murray, Martin

DARK HORSE, A
CD ______ CBM 021CD
Cross Border Media / Nov '96 / ADA / Direct / Grapevine/PolyGram

Murray, Pauline

PAULINE MURRAY & THE INVISIBLE GIRLS (Murray, Pauline & The Invisible Girls)
CD ______ PILOT 002
Burning Airlines / Mar '97 / Total/Pinnacle

Murray, Ruby

EMI PRESENTS THE MAGIC OF RUBY MURRAY
Heartbeat / Mr. Wonderful / Little white lies / Have you ever been lonely / When Irish eyes are smiling / Let him go, let him tarry / Goodbye Jimmy goodbye / Knock on any door / Passing stranger / Dear ol' Donegal / I'll come when you call / Nevertheless (I'm in love with you) / Softly softly / Danny boy / Let him go lover / Honestly I do / Evermore / Make him jealous / Two kinds of tears / Galway Bay / How can you buy Killarney / O'Malley's tango / Smile / Happy days / Lonely nights / Mountains of Mourne
CD ______ CDMFP 6293
Music For Pleasure / May '97 / EMI

HOUR OF RUBY MURRAY, AN
Softly, softly / Happy days and lonely nights / I'll come when you call / When Irish eyes are smiling / If anyone finds this, I love you / Heartbeat / Mr. Wonderful / Danny boy / You are my sunshine / Smile / When I grow too old to dream / Trottin' to the fair / Let me go, lover / Let him go, let him tarry / Evermore / Real love / Get well soon / Nevertheless (I'm in love with you) / You are my first love / Goodbye Jimmy goodbye / Cockles and mussels / Button up your overcoat / Pennies from Heaven / Now is the hour
CD ______ CC 219
Music For Pleasure / May '88 / EMI

WHEN IRISH EYES ARE SMILING/IRISH AND PROUD OF IT
CD ______ CTMCD 110
EMI / Mar '97 / EMI

Murray, Sunny

13 STEPS ON GLASS
CD ______ ENJACD 80942
Enja / Sep '95 / New Note/Pinnacle / Vital/ SAM

Murrell, Christopher

GOSPELS & SPIRITUALS (Murrell, Christopher & Robert Irving)
CD ______ NHRSP 3
Nagel Heyer / Jul '96 / Jazz Music

Musavi, Mohammad

NEY OF MOHAMMAD MUSAVI, THE
CD ______ 926452
BUDA / Sep '96 / Discovery

Muschalle, Frank

BATTIN' THE BOOGIE
CD ______ DOCD 7002
Document / Mar '97 / ADA / Hot Shot / Jazz Music

Musci, Roberto

LOSING THE ORTHODOX PATH (Musci, Roberto & Giovanni Venosta/Massimo Mariani)
CD ______ VICTOCD 049
Victo / Jul '97 / Harmonia Mundi / ReR Megacorp

MESSAGES AND PORTRAITS (Musci, Roberto & Giovanni Venosta)
CD ______ RERMVCD
ReR/Recommended / Jan '93 / ReR Megacorp / RTM/Disc

NOISE, A SOUND, A (Musci, Roberto & Giovanni Venosta)
CD ______ RERMVCD 2
ReR/Recommended / Oct '96 / ReR Megacorp / RTM/Disc

Muse

INNOCENT VOICES
CD ______ 3031282
Arcade / Jul '97 / Discovery

Mushroams

ICH ZAHLE TAGLICH MEINE SORGEN
Ich zahle taglich meine Sorgen / Motorbiene / Rote lippen soll man kussen
CD ______ BCD 15999
Bear Family / Nov '96 / Direct / Rollercoaster / Swift

Music De Madrid

LA FOILE DE LA SPAGNA
CD ______ HM 90 1050
Harmonia Mundi / Oct '88 / Cadillac / Harmonia Mundi

Music Revelation Ensemble

IN THE NAME OF
CD ______ DIW 885
DIW / Oct '94 / Cadillac / Harmonia Mundi

Musica De La Tierra

INSTRUMENTAL & VOCAL MUSIC VOL.2
CD ______ CDC 207
Music Of The World / Jun '93 / ADA / Target/BMG

Musica Electronica Viva

LEAVE THE CITY
CD ______ 14968
Spalax / Jun '97 / ADA / Cargo / Direct / Discovery / Greyhound

Musica Transonic

WORLD OF MUSICA TRANSONIC, THE
CD ______ PSFD 91
PSF / Jul '97 / Harmonia Mundi

Musicians Of The Nile

CHARCOAL GYPSIES
Bitnadini tani lih / Eb'at Djawaben / Sq Al-Manadl / Mawwal-doha / Rais al-bahr / Al-

ward Al-foll / Ramla / Salamat / Walla zaman
CD CDRW 63
Realworld / Nov '96 / EMI

Musicians Union Band

MUSICIANS UNION BAND, THE
Poor misguided woman / In my room / City ride / Caroline belie / Bad boy / Your man / Put your trust in the Lord / Sugar lipped Sal / My babe / Let the circle be unbroken / Elvis lives / Heartbreak hotel / Love me tender / One night / Jailhouse rock / Beggar man / Funky / Shake your moneymaker / Put your trust in the Lord / Part 2 / Yes it must be Spring / Side step
CD SJPCD 010
Angel Air / Jul '97 / Pinnacle

Musikklag, Eikanger-Bjorsvik

KING'S MESSENGER
Songs for BL / King messenger / Frogs of aristophanes / River dance / Arctic funk / Intrada / Concertine for trombone / Alle fugler / American dream
CD DOYCD 047
Doyen / Oct '95 / Conifer/BMG

Musillami, Michael

GLASS ART
Glass art / Shoeshine / Mars bars / Out of balance / Cousin Jim / Haberdasher blues / I wait for the summertime / Grey Cypress
CD ECD 220602
Evidence / Nov '93 / ADA / Cadillac / Harmonia Mundi

YOUNG CHILD, THE
CD STCD 556
Stash / Jan '93 / ADA / Cadillac / CM / Direct / Jazz Music

Muslimgauze

AZZAZIN
CD MUSLIMLIM 003
Staalplaat / Jun '96 / Vital/SAM

CITADEL
CD XCD 026
Extreme / Feb '95 / Vital/SAM

INFIDEL
CD XEP 026
Extreme / Feb '95 / Vital/SAM

INTIFAXA
CD XCD 002
Extreme / May '95 / Vital/SAM

ISLAMAPHOBIA
CD MUSLIMLIM 101
Staalplaat / Feb '96 / Vital/SAM

MAROON
CD STCD 084
Staalplaat / Sep '95 / Vital/SAM

MUSLIMGAUZE REMIXES
Re-mix / Loop / Re-edit / Themselves
CD SOL 37CD
Staalplaat / Mar '97 / Vital/SAM

ZUL'M
Fakir / Curfew gaza / Afghan black / Indian summer of Benazir Bhutto / Tehran via train / Shiva hooka / Tehran via train
CD XCD 012
Extreme / Jun '97 / Vital/SAM

Musselwhite, Charley

ACE OF HARPS
Blues overtook me / She may be your woman / River hip mama / Leaving your town / Hello pretty baby / Mean ol' Frisco / Kiddio / Yesterdays / Hangin' on / My road lies in darkness
CD ALCD 4781
Alligator / May '93 / ADA / CM / Direct

HARMONICA ACCORDING TO CHARLEY MUSSELWHITE, THE
CD BPCD 5016
Blind Pig / Dec '94 / ADA / CM / Direct / Hot Shot

IN MY TIME
CD ALCD 4818
Alligator / Mar '94 / ADA / CM / Direct

MELLOW DEE
Hey Miss Bessie / Need my baby / I'll get a break / Peach orchard mama / Ask me nice / Come back baby / Comin' home baby / Baby, please don't go / Lotsa poppa / Steady on your trail / Can't you see what you're doing to me / Christo redemptor
CD CCD 11013
Crosscut / Nov '88 / ADA / CM / Direct

MEMPHIS CHARLEY
CD ARHCD 303
Arhoolie / Apr '95 / ADA / Cadillac / Direct

ROUGH NEWS
Both sides of the fence / I sat and cried / Sleepwalk / Natural born lover / Darkest hour / Harlem nocturne / Drifting boy / Rough dried woman / Feel it in your heart / Rainy highway / Clarksdale boogie / Rough news
CD VPBCD 42
Pointblank / Apr '97 / EMI

SIGNATURE
Make my getaway / Blues got me again / Mama long legs / 38 special / It's gettin' warm in here / What's new again / Hey Miss Bessie / Me and my baby and the blues / Catwalk / Cheatin' on me
CD ALCD 4801
Alligator / May '93 / ADA / CM / Direct

STAND BACK (Here Comes Charley Musselwhite's South Side Band)
Baby will you please help me / No more lonely nights / Cha cha the blues / Christo redemptor / Help me / Chicken shack / Strange land / 39th and Indiana / My baby / Early in the morning / 4 pm / Sa day
CD VMD 79232
Vanguard / Oct '95 / ADA / Pinnacle

STONE BLUES (Musselwhite, Charley Blues Band)
My buddy buddy friends / Everything's gonna be alright / My baby's sweeter / Clay's tune / Gone and left me / Cry for me baby / Hey baby / Juke / She belongs to me / Bag gloom brews
CD VMD 79287
Vanguard / Oct '95 / ADA / Pinnacle

TAKING CARE OF BUSINESS
Louisiana fog / Takin' care of business / Big legged woman / Riffin' / Leavin' / Just a little bit / Fell on my knees / Directly from my heart / Fat city
CD CDTB 172
Thunderbolt / Nov '95 / TKO Magnum

Musso, Robert

TRASONIC
CD AW 013CD
Ambient World / Dec '96 / Plastic Head

Mussolini Headkick

BLOOD ON THE FLAG
CD WD 6663CD
World Domination / Oct '90 / Pinnacle / RTM/Disc

Mussolini, Romano

SOFT AND SWING
CD RTCL 809CD
Right Tempo / Jul '96 / New Note/ Pinnacle / Timewarp

Mustafa, Melton

BOILING POINT (Mustafa, Melton Orchestra)
Boiling point (3 in 1 blues) / Blind love blues / Bridging the gap / Some kind of blues / I can sing / Easy as it goes (A night at El Morocco) / Upsy Daisy / Let it be known / Where there's smoke / Swinging my lady / Gift of knowledge (El don del conocimiento)
CD CCD 14075
Contemporary / Jul '96 / Cadillac / Complete/Pinnacle / Jazz Music / Wellard

Mustang Ford

CHATTERBOX
CD SISSY 004
Sticksister / May '97 / Cargo

Mustang Lightning

MUSTANG LIGHTNING
CD 422499
New Rose / May '94 / ADA / Direct / Discovery

Mustard Plug

EVIL DOERS BEWARE
CD HR 6202
Hopeless / Jun '97 / Cargo / Greyhound

Mustard Seeds

MUSTARD SEEDS
CD 87902IDE
Edel / May '96 / Pinnacle

Mutabaruka

BLAKK WI BLAK..K..K
CD 322574
Koch / Oct '91 / Koch

CHECK IT
CD ALCD 8306
Alligator / Aug '92 / ADA / CM / Direct

MELANIN MAN
CD SHCD 45013
Shanachie / Apr '94 / ADA / Greensleeves / Koch

MYSTERY UNFOLDS,THE
Leaders speak / Dub poem / Revolutionary words / My great shun / Old cut bruk / Bun dung Babylon / Mustery unfolds / Dis poem / Famine injection / Eyes of liberty / Walkin' on gravel / Voice
CD SHANCD 43037
Shanachie / Aug '87 / ADA / Greensleeves / Koch

OUT CRY
CD SHANCD 43023
Shanachie / Nov '87 / ADA / Greensleeves / Koch

ULTIMATE COLLECTION, THE
CD GRELCD 224
Greensleeves / May '96 / Jet Star / SRD

Mute Beat

MUTE BEAT IN DUB
CD RUSCD 8227
ROIR / Sep '96 / Plastic Head / Shellshock/Disc

Mute Drivers

EVERYONE
CD BND 4CD
One Little Indian / Feb '90 / Pinnacle

Muthspiel, Christian

MUTHSPIEL - PEACOCK - MUTHSPIEL - MOTIAN (Muthspiel, Christian & Wolfgang/Gary Peacock/Paul Motian)
Jodler / Chill out honey pie / Eight slash eight / Hanne / Mupemo / One for Igor / After all / Gnome's run / (Grand) canon
CD 5196762
Amadeo / Mar '94 / PolyGram

OCTET OST
Introitus / VII / Interlude / II / Interlude / II continues / Interlude / VII / Interlude / I / Interlude / IV / X / Interlude / III / Interlude / XIV / Extroitus
CD 5133292
Amadeo / May '94 / PolyGram

OCTET OST VOL.2 (Indirect View Of Beauty)
Part one / Song nine / Part two
CD 5218232
Amadeo / May '94 / PolyGram

Muthspiel, Wolfgang

BLACK AND BLUE (Muthspiel, Wolfgang Sextet)
Dance / North shore / Swords crossing / Duet / Miles / Square 1 / Rules of the game / Visions / Bliss and other short stories
CD 5176532
Amadeo / May '94 / PolyGram

PERSPECTIVE
CD 5334662
Amadeo / Nov '96 / PolyGram

PROMISE, THE
TG / Sonic presence of David Lee / My funny valentine / Promise / No luck in Paris / New York was another story / La Nevada / End of the day / Trackings
CD 8470232
Amadeo / May '94 / PolyGram

TIMEZONES (Muthspiel, Wolfgang Trio)
My hill / Chip / Asleep (for Christine) / Introduction / Everything happens to that dog / On the edge / Singing beach / Timezones / Blue morning rays (for Menga)
CD 8390132
Amadeo / May '94 / PolyGram

Mutilation

AGGRESSION IN EFFECT
CD Set BR 002CD
Brain Crusher / Nov '92 / Plastic Head

Mutiny

AFTERSHOCK 2005
Growl / It's all good / No choice / Passion / Tickin' like a time bomb / Rock the boat / Desires / Moments
CD RCD 10334
Black Arc / Feb '96 / Vital

Mutter

HAUPTSACHE MUSIK
CD EFA 047032
DEG / Jul '94 / SRD

ICH SCHANE MICH GEDANKEN ZU HAB
CD EFA 047012
DEG / Jul '94 / SRD

Mutton Birds

ENVY OF ANGELS
Straight to your head / She's been talking / Trouble with you / April / Like this train / Another morning / Ten feet tall / Come around / Crooked mile / While you sleep / Inside my skin / Envy of angels
CD CDVIR 55
Virgin / Jun '97 / EMI

NATURE
Nature / Dominion Road / Anchor me / Heater / Giant friend / Your window / White valient / In my room / Thing well made / Queen's English / There's a limit / Too close to the sun
CD CDVIR 39
Dindisc / Sep '95 / EMI

Mutton Gun

AMPLEXUS
Aimless / Thanks, but no thanks / Don't talk to your mother like that / Cutfleisch / Sound track / Kansas / Ruby / Das lied fur dong / Aldgate / Poor unfortunate lovers
CD MINTCD 1
Mint Sauce / Jul '90 / Jet Star

INTO THE HOGGER
CD MINTCD 3
Mint Sauce / Dec '90 / Jet Star

MUTTONGUN 111
Rain rain / Turkey / Better / Demon honey / End of it all / Bullet for a guide / Good dog bad dog / Turquoise blue / Chucky bear / Young / Thought for the day / Enter the hogger / Summer in the city
CD KOKOPOP 005CD
Kokopop / Feb '94 / Vital

Muzsikas

BLUES FOR TRANSYLVANIA
CD HNCD 1350
Hannibal / Feb '90 / ADA / Vital

KETTO
CD MRCD 175
Munich / Sep '95 / ADA / CM / Direct / Greensleeves

MARAMAROS (The Lost Jewish Music Of Transylvania)
Hasid wedding dances / Rooster is crowning / Dance from maramures / Lamenting song / Anne Maamini / I have just come from gyula / Farewell to Saturday evening / Jewish dance from Szaszregan / Hat ein jid ein wejbele / Jewish csardas series from szek / Hassid dance / Greeting of the bride / Haneros halelu / Farewell to the guests
CD HNCD 1373
Hannibal / Mar '93 / ADA / Vital

MORNING STAR (Muzsikas & Marta Sebestyen)
Wedding in Fuzes village / Song from Madocsa / Roun dance of Gyimes / My mother's rosebush / Oh, the road is long / If I were a rose / Trouble trouble / Cry only on Sundays / Oh evening star farewell to soldiers
CD HNCD 1401
Hannibal / Sep '97 / ADA / Vital

PRISONER'S SONG, THE (Muzsikas/ Marta Sebestyen)
CD HNCD 1341
Hannibal / Jan '89 / ADA / Vital

Muzur, Virgil

MASTER OF THE ROMANIAN FIDDLE, THE
CD B 6821CD
Auvidis/Ethnic / Aug '96 / ADA / Harmonia Mundi

MX 80

DAS LOVE BOAT
CD ALP 56CD
Atavistic / Apr '97 / Cargo / SRD

HARD ATTACK/BIG HITS EP
Man on the move / Kid stuff / Fascination / Summer '77 / PCB's / Crushed ice / Theme from checkmate / Facts/facts / You're not alone / Civilised/Dem' eyes / Afterbirth/Aftermath / Boy trouble/Girl trouble / Myonga von bontee / SCP / You turn me on / Train to loveland / Till death do us part / Tidal wave
CD ALP 30CD
Atavistic / Apr '97 / Cargo / SRD

I'VE SEEN ENOUGH
CD ALP 67CD
Atavistic / Apr '97 / Cargo / SRD

OUT OF CONTROL
CD ALP 32CD
Atavistic / Apr '97 / Cargo / SRD

My Bloody Valentine

ISN'T ANYTHING
Soft as snow / Lose my breath / Cupid come / You're still in a dream / No more sorry / All I need / Feed me with your kiss / Sueisfine / Several girls galore / You never should / Nothing much to lose / I can see it
CD CRECD 040
Creation / Nov '88 / 3mv/Vital

LOVELESS
Only shallow / Loomer / Touched / To here knows when / When you sleep / I only said / Come in alone / Sometimes / Blown a wish / What you want / Soon
CD CRECD 060
Creation / Nov '91 / 3mv/Vital

My Dad Is Dead

FOR RICHER, FOR POORER
CD EJ 01CD
Emperor Jones / Nov '95 / SRD

LET'S SKIP THE DETAILS
CD HMS 109CD
Homestead / Jul '88 / Cargo / SRD

SHINE(R)
CD EJ 05
Emperor Jones / Jun '96 / SRD

My Drug Hell

THIS IS MY DRUG HELL
CD VTONECD 001X
Voltone / May '97 / Shellshock/Disc

My Dying Bride

ANGEL AND THE DARK RIVER (2CD Set)
CD Set CDVILE 50
Peaceville / Apr '96 / Pinnacle

AS THE FLOWER WITHERS
CD CDVILE 32
Peaceville / Apr '95 / Pinnacle

LIKE GODS OF THE SUN
Like Gods of the sun / Dark caress / Grace unhearing / Kiss to remember / All swept away / For you / It will come / Here in the throat / For my fallen angel
CD CDXVILE 65
CD CDVILE 65
Peaceville / Oct '96 / Pinnacle

STORIES, THE
Symphonaire infernus et spera empyrium / God is alone / De sade soliloquay / Thrash of naked limbs / Le cerf malade / Gather me up forever / I am the bloody earth / Transcending (Into the exquisite) / Crown of sympathy
CD Set VILE 045CD
Peaceville / Oct '94 / Pinnacle

TRINITY
Symphonaire infernus / Thrash of naked limbs / I am the bloody earth / God is alone / Le cerf malade / Sexuality of bereavement / De sade soliloquy / Gather me up forever / Crown of sympathy
CD CDVILE 46
Peaceville / Sep '95 / Pinnacle

TURN LOOSE THE SWANS
Sear me MCMXC111 / Songless bird / Snow in my hand / Crown of sympathy / Turn loose the swans / Black God
CD CDVILE 39
Peaceville / Mar '95 / Pinnacle

My Friend The Chocolate Cake

BROOD
CD D 31136
Mushroom / Mar '95 / 3mv/Pinnacle

GOOD LUCK
CD TVD 93462
Mushroom / Aug '96 / 3mv/Pinnacle

REVIEW
CD MUSH 4CD
Mushroom / Jul '97 / 3mv/Pinnacle

My Life In Rain

SLOWBURN
CD ALLIED 81
Allied / Jan '97 / Cargo / Greyhound / Plastic Head

My Life Story

MORNINGTON CRESENT
CD MOTHERCD 1
Mother Tongue / Jan '95 / RTM/Disc

My Name

MEGACRUSH
CD CZ 046CD
C/Z / Aug '92 / Plastic Head

My Own Victim

BURNING INSIDE
CD CM 77105CD
Century Media / Jan '96 / Plastic Head

MY OWN VICTIM
CD CM 770822
Century Media / Mar '95 / Plastic Head

My Sister's Machine

DIVA
Hands and feet / Pain / I hate you / Wasting time / Love at high speed / I'm sorry / Walk all over you / Sunday / Monster box / Diva
CD CARCD 18
Caroline / Apr '92 / EMI

WALL FLOWERS
Inside of me / Broken land / This is fear / Steamy swamp thang / Feed / Empty room / Sixteen ways to go / Enemy / I slip away / Burn / Mockingbird / Cracking new ground
CD 3705615122
WEA / Jul '93 / Warner Music

My Solid Ground

MY SOLID GROUND
CD SB 035
Second Battle / Jun '97 / Greyhound

Myaz, Benjy

INTIMATE RELATIONSHIP
CD VPCD 1495
VP / May '97 / Greensleeves / Jet Star / Total/BMG

Myers, Amina Claudine

COUNTRY GIRL
CD MMCD 801012
Minor Music / Apr '90 / Vital/SAM

SALUTES BESSIE SMITH
CD CDLR 103
Leo / Feb '89 / Cadillac / Impetus / Wellard

WOMEN IN (E)MOTION FESTIVAL
CD T&M 102
Tradition & Moderne / Nov '94 / ADA / Direct

Myers, Fraser

FRASER MYERS BIG BAND
CD VCTMD 1
Vocal Cords / Nov '93 / Grapevine/ PolyGram

Myers, Hazel

HAZEL MEYERS VOL.1
CD DOCD 5430
Document / Jul '96 / ADA / Hot Shot / Jazz Music

Myers, Louis

I'M A SOUTHERN MAN
CD TCD 5026
Testament / Aug '95 / ADA / Koch

Myles, Alannah

ALANNAH
CD 7567828422
Atlantic / May '93 / Warner Music

ALANNAH MYLES
Still got this thing / Black velvet / Lover of mine / If you want to / Who loves you / Love is / Rock this joint / Kickstart my heart / Just one kiss / Make love
CD 7819562
Atlantic / Nov '89 / Warner Music

ROCKING HORSE
Our world our times / Make me happy / Sonny say you will / Tumbleweed / Livin' on a memory / Song instead of a kiss / Love in the big town / Last time I saw William / Lies and rumours / Rocking horse
CD 7567824022
WEA / Nov '92 / Warner Music

Myles, Heather

JUST LIKE OLD TIMES
Love lyin' down / Why I'm walkin' / Changes / Rum and rodeo / Make a fool out of me / Other side of town / Just like old times / Stay out of my arms / I love you, goodbye / Lovin' the bottle / One good reason why / Playin' in the dirt
CD FIENDCD 717
Demon / Apr '92 / Pinnacle

SWEET LITTLE DANGEROUS
CD FIENDCD 772
Demon / Feb '96 / Pinnacle

UNTAMED
And it hurts / Just leave me alone / When you walked out on me / Cadillac cowboy / Until I couldn't have you / Indigo moon / It ain't over / Begging to you / How could she / Coming back to me / Gone too long / Untamed
CD FIENDCD 763
Demon / Jan '95 / Pinnacle

Mylett, Peter

SOMETHING OLD, SOMETHING NEW
CD FRCD 030
Foam / Oct '94 / CM

Mynediad Am Ddim

MYNEDIAD AM DDIM 1974-92
Wa MacSpredar / P-Pendyffryn / Arica / Beti Wyn / Fi / Llwch y glo / Padi / Mi ganaf gan / Ceidwad y goleudy / Ynys Llanddwyn / Mynd yn bell i ffwrdd / y gwrthodedig / Yn y dre / Hi yw fy ffrind / Mae'r byd yn wag / Cofio dy wyneb / Pappagio's / Gwaed i'r llwch / Can y cap / Wini / Casa eroti / Y storu wir
CD SCD 2003
Sain / Feb '95 / ADA / Direct / Greyhound

Mynox Layh

TERMINUS CLARITATAS
CD HY 39100962
Hy-Ritual / Jun '94 / Plastic Head

Mynta

FIRST SUMMER
CD XOUCD 117
Xource / May '97 / ADA / Direct

NANDUS DANCE
Nandu's dance / Tarana / Tove / What's the bag dad / Kamala / Sounds / Hey-ho / She survived / Emma / Indian summer / Faroe Islands
CD XOUCD 107
Xource / May '97 / ADA / Direct

Myrick, Gary

TEXAS GLITTER AND TOMBSTONE TALES (Myrick, Gary & Havana 3am)
CD BCD 00242
Burnside / Sep '96 / Koch

Myrna Loy

IMMERSCHON
CD NORM 158CD
Normal / Nov '93 / ADA / Direct

Myro

LET'S GO DISTORTION KIDS
CD LIQ 005CD
Liquid / Jun '97 / Intergroove / SRD

Myster-Me

LET ME EXPLAIN (Myster-Me & DJ 20/20)
What's the word / Can't fuck with the record / If ever / Playtime's over / Unsolved mysterme / Myster Master / Call me Myster / Happy like death / Whatever whatever / Peepin' the wreck / Hoodie down / Under the influence
CD GEECD 15
Gee Street / Jul '94 / PolyGram

Mysteries Of Life

FOCUS ON THE BACKGROUND
CD FLT 108
Flat Earth / Mar '97 / Cargo

Mysteries Of Science

EROTIC NATURE OF AUTOMATED UNIVERSE, THE
CD IAE 005CD
Instinct Ambient Europe / Jul '95 / Plastic Head

Mystery Machine

10 SPEED
CD W 230098
Nettwerk / Oct '95 / Greyhound / Pinnacle / Vital

GLAZED
Shaky ground / Everyone's alright / Valley song / Ride / Stay high / Hooked / Floored / Hi-test / Invitation / Salty / Underground / Broken / Slack / Stain master
CD NET 043CD
Nettwerk / Mar '93 / Greyhound / Pinnacle / Vital

Mystic Astrologic

FLOWERS NEVER CRY
CD DOCD 1993
Drop Out / Jul '91 / Pinnacle

Mystic Charm

SHADOWS OF THE UNKNOWN
CD SHR 008CD
Shiver / Aug '95 / Plastic Head

Mystic Forces

ETERNAL QUEST
CD IRS 972030
Rising Sun / Dec '93 / Cargo / Plastic Head

TAKE COMMAND
CD CMFTCD 7
CMFT / Nov '90 / Plastic Head

Mystic Revealers

JAH WORKS
CD RASCD 3123
Ras / Sep '93 / Direct / Greensleeves / Jet Star / SRD

RAS PORTRAITS
Space and time / Remember Romeo / Saw you smiling / Righteous / Religion / Religion dub / We and dem / Got to be a better way / Space and dub / Dem problem / Mash down aparthied / World War Three
CD RAS 3328
Ras / Jul '97 / Direct / Greensleeves / Jet Star / SRD

SPACE AND DUB
CD RASCD 3173
Ras / Apr '96 / Direct / Greensleeves / Jet Star / SRD

SPACE AND TIME
CD RASCD 3170
Ras / Aug '95 / Direct / Greensleeves / Jet Star / SRD

YOUNG REVOLUTIONARIES
CD RAS 3226
Ras / Mar '96 / Direct / Greensleeves / Jet Star / SRD

Mystic Siva

MYSTIC SIVA
CD MR 1
Mystic / Jul '97 / Cargo / Greyhound / Plastic Head

Mystic Tide

SOLID SOUND/SOLID GROUND
CD DR 1006
Distortions / Jun '97 / Greyhound

Mystifier

GOETIA
CD OPCD 16
Osmose / Nov '93 / Plastic Head

IF THE WORLD IS SO GOOD (THAT WHO MADE IT DOESN'T LIVE HERE ANYMORE)
CD OPCD 042CD
Osmose / Sep '96 / Plastic Head

Mystik

PERPETUAL BEING
CD MASSCD 028
Massacre / Apr '94 / Plastic Head

Myth Science

LOVE IN OUTER SPACE
CD KFWCD 183
Knitting Factory / Oct '96 / Cargo / Plastic Head

Mythos

DREAMLAB
CD SPALAX 14206
Spalax / Nov '96 / ADA / Cargo / Direct / Discovery / Greyhound

PAIN AMPLIFIER
CD EOR 0002
Evil Omen / Feb '95 / Plastic Head

N

N2 Deep

BACK TO THE HOTEL
CD FILERCD 427
Profile / May '92 / Pinnacle

N-Joi

INSIDE OUT
Set smart / Trauma / Never let you go / Ease yourself / Papillon 2 / Chaser / Zeus / Bad things / Games / Papillon / On the move / Anthem
CD 74321256872
De-Construction / Jun '97 / BMG

N-Trance

ELECTRONIC PLEASURE
What is your pleasure / Electronic pleasure / Stayin' alive / I will take you there / (Just) Let it go / Set you free / Softly (Dragging me down) / Do you wanna rock / Gimme 1 2 3 4 5 / Turn up the power / I don't wanna lose your love again / That's all we need
CD GLOBECD 2
All Around The World / Jun '95 / Total/BMG

Na Casaidigh

1691
CD CEFCD 154
Gael Linn / Jan '94 / ADA / CM / Direct / Grapevine/PolyGram / Roots

Na Fili

PURE TRADITIONAL MUSIC OF IRELAND
CD PTICD 1010
Pure Traditional Irish / Apr '94 / ADA / CM / Direct / Ross

Na Firein

NA FIREIN
CD CEFCD 162
Gael Linn / Jan '94 / ADA / CM / Direct / Grapevine/PolyGram / Roots

Na Lua

CONTRADANZAS
CD GCDF 1002CD
Sons Galiza / Apr '95 / ADA

PELIQUEIRO
CD SGF 1021CD
Sons Galiza / Apr '95 / ADA

Naa, D.K.

GIFTY
CD CD 4398
Gifty / May '96 / Jet Star

Naam, Fong

JAKAJAN (Music From New Siam)
CD NI 5486
Nimbus / Aug '96 / Nimbus

NANG HONG SUITE
CD NI 5332
Nimbus / Sep '94 / Nimbus

SLEEPING ANGEL, THE
CD NI 5319
Nimbus / Sep '94 / Nimbus

Nabat

NATI PER NIENTE
CD BB 023CD
Banda Bannot / Oct '96 / Cargo

Nada

CELMETRA
CD CC 006CD
Common Cause / Oct '94 / Plastic Head / SRD

Nada Surf

HIGH/LOW
Popular / Plan / Sleep / Psychic caramel / Stalemate / Hollywood / Zen brain / Icebox / Treehouse / Deeper well
CD 7559619132
Elektra / Oct '96 / Warner Music

Nagflar

VITTRA
CD WAR 008CD
Wrong Again / Apr '96 / Plastic Head

Nagle, Paul

EARTHSHAPER
CD AMPCD 034
AMP / Apr '97 / Cadillac / Discovery / TKO Magnum

Nagourney, Jan

THREE AND ONE
Tadd's delight / Byrd in hand / Gregory is here / Dancing on the ceiling / In the wee small hours of the morning / Split kick / Three and one / Thanks for Hanks / Juicy Lucy / We're all together / Koolin' on the street
CD LICD 3168
Liphone / Jan '97 / Cadillac / Jazz Music

Naif

WAITING IS OVER
CD ZYX 204262
ZYX / Jan '97 / ZYX

Nail, Jimmy

BIG RIVER
Big river / I think of you / Can't hold on / Right to know / Love / What kind of man am I / Something that we had / What's the use / Hands of time / I wonder
CD 0630128232
East West / Nov '95 / Warner Music

CROCODILE SHOES VOL.1
CD 4509985562
East West / Nov '94 / Warner Music

CROCODILE SHOES VOL.2
CD 0630169352
East West / Nov '96 / Warner Music

GROWING UP IN PUBLIC
Ain't no doubt / Reach out / Laura / Waiting for the sunshine / Real love / Only love (can bring us home) / Wicked world / Beautiful / I believed / Absent friends
CD 4509901442
East West / Dec '94 / Warner Music

TAKE IT OR LEAVE IT
That's the way love is / Airwaves / Walk away / Your decision today / Ladies and gentlemen of South Africa / Rain burns / Same again / Further on / One more day / Love don't live here anymore
CD CDVIP 111
Virgin VIP / Nov '93 / EMI

Nailbomb

POINT BLANK
CD RR 90552
Roadrunner / Jul '95 / PolyGram

Naive, Steve

IT'S RAINING SOMEWHERE
CD KFWCD 198
Knitting Factory / Oct '96 / Cargo / Plastic Head

Najma

ATISH
CD TRECD 108
Triple Earth / Nov '93 / Grapevine/ PolyGram / Stern's

FORBIDDEN KISS
CD SH 64063
Shanachie / Aug '96 / ADA / Greensleeves / Koch

QAREEB
Neend koyi / Har sitani aap ka / Zikar hai apna mehfil mehfil / Karcon na yad magar / Jane kis tarjha / Dil laga ya tha
CD TRECD 103
Triple Earth / Nov '93 / Grapevine/PolyGram / Stern's

Nakagawa, Masami

PRELUDE FOR AUTUMN
CD JD 3304
JVC / Jul '88 / Direct / New Note/Pinnacle / Vital/SAM

TOUCH OF SPRING
CD JD 3311
JVC / Oct '88 / Direct / New Note/ Pinnacle / Vital/SAM

Nakai, R. Carlos

DESERT DANCE (The Spirit Of The Native American)
CD 130332
Celestial Harmonies / Dec '95 / ADA / Select

ISLAND OF BOWS
CD CRCD 7018
Canyon / Mar '96 / ADA

KOKOPELLI'S CAFE
CD CR 7013CD
Canyon / Nov '96 / ADA

SPIRIT HORSES
CD CRCD 7014
Canyon / Mar '96 / ADA

SUNDANCE SEASON
CD CDCEL 024
Celestial Harmonies / Feb '89 / ADA / Select

Nakamoto, Mari

WHAT IS LOVE
I could write a book / If I were a bell / Whisper not / All of me / All too soon / In a mellow tone / Speak low / Easy to love / What is this thing called love / You don't know what love is
CD JVC 90082
JVC / Feb '97 / Direct / New Note/Pinnacle / Vital/SAM

Naked

NAKED
CD RAACD 003
Red Ant / Jun '97 / Pinnacle

Naked City

ABSINTHE
CD AVAN 004
Avant / Jan '94 / Cadillac / Harmonia Mundi

BLACK BOX (2CD Set)
CD Set TZA 73122
Tzadik / Feb '97 / Cargo

GRAND GUIGNOL
CD AVANT 002
Avant / Jan '93 / Cadillac / Harmonia Mundi

HERETIC - JEUX DES DAMES CRUELLES
CD AVANT 001
Avant / Aug '92 / Cadillac / Harmonia Mundi

RADIO
CD AVAN 003
Avant / Jan '94 / Cadillac / Harmonia Mundi

Naked Ear

ACOUSTIC GUITAR DUOLOG
CD BEST 1022CD
Acoustic Music / Nov '93 / ADA

Naked Funk

VALIUM
CD PUSSYCD 003
Pussy Foot / Jul '96 / RTM/Disc

Naked Ray Gun

ALL RISE
CD HMS 045CD
Homestead / Jul '88 / Cargo / SRD

THROB THROB
CD HMS 008CD
Homestead / Jul '88 / Cargo / SRD

Naked Rhythm

FATBOX
CD MASSCD 038
Massacre / Nov '94 / Plastic Head

Namlook, Pete

2350 BROADWAY 3 (Namlook, Pete & Tetsuo Inuoe)
CD PW 025CD
Fax / Feb '96 / Plastic Head

4 SEASONS
CD SEA 00
Fax / Oct '96 / Plastic Head

DARK SIDE OF THE MOOG VOL.4 (Namlook, Pete & Bill Laswell)
CD PH 08112
Fax / Apr '96 / Plastic Head

DARK SIDE OF THE MOOG VOL.5 (Namlook, Pete & Bill Laswell)
CD PK 08123CD
Fax / Dec '96 / Plastic Head

DREAMFISH (Namlook, Pete & Mixmaster Morris)
CD AW 012CD
Ambient World / Oct '96 / Plastic Head

ELECTRONIC MUSIC CENTRE
CD PK 08119
Fax / Oct '96 / Plastic Head

JET CHAMBER
CD PK 08115CD
Fax / May '96 / Plastic Head

KOOLFANG VOL.2 (Namlook, Pete & David Monfang)
CD PK 08106CD
Fax / Jan '96 / Plastic Head

NAMLOOK ATOM
CD PK 08107CD
Fax / Jan '96 / Plastic Head

NAMLOOK XI
CD PK 08113CD
Fax / May '96 / Plastic Head

OUTLAND VOL.2 (Namlook, Pete & Bill Laswell)
CD PW 028CD
Fax / Apr '96 / Plastic Head

OZOONA (Namlook, Pete & Gordon)
CD PW 030
Fax / Sep '96 / Plastic Head

PSYCHONAVIGATION VOL.2 (Namlook, Pete & Bill Laswell)
CD PW 024CD
Fax / Nov '95 / Plastic Head

SHADES OF ORION
CD PW 029CD
Fax / May '96 / Plastic Head

SULTAN
CD PW 027CD
Fax / Apr '96 / Plastic Head

TIME VOL.2 (Namlook, Pete & Tetsuo Inuoe)
CD PW 032CD
Fax / Dec '96 / Plastic Head

Namtchylak, Sainkho

LOST RIVERS
CD FMPCD 42
FMP / Mar '87 / Cadillac

Namyslowski, Zbigniew

KUJAVIACK GOES FUNKY
CD PBR 33859
Power Bros. / Aug '95 / Harmonia Mundi

ZBIGNIEW NAMYSLOWSKI QUARTET
CD PBR 33861
Power Bros. / Oct '95 / Harmonia Mundi

Nanaco

LOVE IS A DRUG
CD HYD 10012
CDS / Jun '96 / Pinnacle

Nancy Boy

PROMOSEXUAL
CD BENDCD 001
Equator / Oct '95 / Pinnacle

Nannini, Gianna

LATIN LOVER
CD 811 669 2
Ricordi / '88 / Discovery

PUZZLE
CD 813 387 2
Ricordi / '88 / Discovery

Naos

MELANCHOLIA
CD NIHIL 15CD
Cacophonous / Aug '96 / Plastic Head / RTM/Disc

Napalm

CRUEL TRANQUILITY
Mind melt / AOA / Shake it off / Gag of steel / Devastation / Combat zone / Immoral society / Attack on America / Reanimate / Act of betrayal / Nightmare administrator / Practice what you preach / Kranked up and out
CD 857565
Steamhammer / Jun '89 / Pinnacle / Plastic Head

ZERO TO BLACK
CD 847622
Steamhammer / Nov '90 / Pinnacle / Plastic Head

Napalm Death

DEATH BY MANIPULATION
CD MOSH 051CD
Earache / Sep '94 / Vital

DIATRIBES
Greed killing / Glimpse into genocide / Ripe for the breaking / Cursed to crawl / Cold forgiveness / My own worst enemy / Just rewards / Dogma / Take the strain / Corrosive elements / Placate, sedate, eradicate / Diatribes / Take the stain
CD MOSH 141CDD
CD MOSH 141CD
Earache / Jan '96 / Vital

FEAR, EMPTINESS, DESPAIR
Twist the knife (slowly) / Hung / Remain nameless / Plague rages / More than meets the eye / Primed time / State of mind / Ar-

mageddon X 7 / Retching on the dirt / Fasting on deception / Throwaway
CD MOSH 109CD
Earache / Sep '97 / Vital

FROM ENSLAVEMENT TO OBLITERATION
Evolved as one / It's a MAN's world / Lucid fairytale / Private death / Unchallenged hate / Uncertainty blurs / Vision / Retreat to nowhere / Display to me / From enslavement / Blind to the truth / Emotional suffocation / Practice what you preach / Mentally murdered / Worlds apart
CD MOSH 008CD
Earache / Sep '94 / Vital

HARMONY OF CORRUPTION
CD MOSH 019CD
Earache / Sep '94 / Vital

INSIDE THE TORN APART
Breed to breathe / Birth in regress / Section / Reflect on conflict / Down in the zero / Inside the torn apart / If systems persist / Prelude / Indispose / Purist realist / Low point / Lifeless alarm / Time will come / Bled dry / Ripe for the breaking
CD MOSH 171CD
CD MOSH 171CDL
Earache / Jun '97 / Vital

PEEL SESSIONS, THE (13.9.87/8.3.88)
Kill / Prison without walls / Dead part 1 / Deceiver / Lucid fairytale / In extremis / Extremis / Blind to the truth / Negative approach / Common enem6y / Obstinate direction / Life / You suffer pt. 2 / Multinational cooporations / Instinct of survival / Stigatised / Parasites / Moral crusade / Worlds apart / MAD / Divine death / C 9 / Control / Walls / Raging in hell / Conform or die / SOB
CD SFPMCD 201
Strange Fruit / '89 / Pinnacle

UTOPIA BANISHED
CD MOSH 053CD
Earache / Sep '97 / Vital

Napoleon, Phil

LIVE AT NICK'S
CD JCD 39
Jazzology / Nov '96 / Jazz Music

Narayan, Aruna

SARANGI
CD NI 5447
Nimbus / Nov '95 / Nimbus

Narayan, Brij

RAGA LALIT/RAGA BAIRAGI BHAIRAV (Narayan, Brij & Zakir Hussain)
CD NI 5263
Nimbus / Sep '94 / Nimbus

Narayan, Pandit Ram

RAG BHUPAL TORI/RAG BATDIP
CD NI 5119
Nimbus / Sep '94 / Nimbus

RAG LALIT
CD NI 5183
Nimbus / Sep '94 / Nimbus

RAG SHANKARA/RAG MALA IN JOGIA
CD NI 5245
Nimbus / Sep '94 / Nimbus

Narcotica

DRUG FREE AMERICA
Narcotica / Sewers of paradise / Fear and adrenalin / Baby doll / Ransacking the earthnet / Soap opera and Brown / Drop zone / Baby doll (Reprise)
CD CDKTB 21
Dreamtime / Jul '95 / Kudos / Pinnacle

Nardini, Peter

SCREAMS & KISSES
Don't know / Light up the sky / Wid became an astronaut / And I will fly / She said, O, is that right / Kiss from Wishaw cross / Another star / Zak Anderson / Double take / You're like a rock / Don't shut the door ma / River without you
CD ECLCD 9307
Eclectic / Jan '96 / ADA / New Note/ Pinnacle

Nardo Ranks

COOL AND HUMBLE
CD CDHB 183
Heartbeat / Aug '95 / ADA / Direct / Greensleeves / Jet Star

Narell, Andy

DOWN THE ROAD
CD 01934101392
Windham Hill / Sep '95 / BMG

LONG TIME BAND, THE
Bacchanal / Jenny's rooms / De long time band / You the man / Play one for Keith / Groove town / Dance class / Canboulay / De long time band (conclusion)
CD 01934111722
Windham Hill / Oct '95 / BMG

Narita

NARITA
CD SHARK 022
Shark / Oct '92 / Plastic Head

Nas

ILLMATIC
Genesis / NY State of mind / Life's a bitch / World is yours / Half time / Memory lane (sittin' in da park) / One love / One time 4 your mind / Represent / It ain't hard to tell
CD 4759592
Columbia / Feb '97 / Sony

IT WAS WRITTEN
Intro / Message / Street dreams / I gave you power / Watch dem niggas / Take it in blood / Nas is coming / Affirmative action / Set up / Black girl lost / Suspect / Shootouts / Live nigga rap / If I ruled the world (imagine that)
CD 4841962
Columbia / Jul '96 / Sony

Nascimento, Milton

ANGELUS
Seis horas da tarde / Estrelada / De um modo geral / Angelus / Coisas de minas / Hello goodbye / Sofro calado / Clube da Esquina No.2 / Meu veneno / Only a dream in Rio / Qualquer coisa a haver com o paraiso / Vera cruz / Novena / Amor amigo
CD 9362454992
Warner Bros. / Jul '94 / Warner Music

CLUBE DA ESQUINA VOL.1
Tudo que voce podia ser / Cais / O trem azul - part esp: Lo borges / Saidas e bandeiras no.1 - part esp: Beto guedes / Nuvem cigana / Cravo e canela / Dos cruces / Um girassol da cor de seu cabelo - part esp: Lo borges / San Vincente / Estralas - part esp: Lo Borges / Clube da Esquina no. 2 / Paisagem da Janela - part esp: Lo Borges / Me deixz em pas - part esp:: Alaide Costa / Os povos / Saidas e bandeiras no.2 - part esp: Beto guedes / Um gosto de sol / Pelo amor de deus / Lilia / Trem de doido - part esp: Lo Borges / Nada sera como antes - part esp: Beto Guedes / Ao que vai nascer
CD CDEMC 3702
EMI / Mar '95 / EMI

CLUBE DA ESQUINA VOL.2 (2CD Set)
Credo / Nascente / Ruas da cidade / Paiuxao e fe / Casmiento de Negros / Olho d'agua / Canoa, canoa / O que foi feito devera (De Vera) / Misterios / Pao e agua / E dai (A Queda) / Cancao Amiga / Cancion por la unidad Latinoamericana / Tanto / Dona Olimpia / Testamento / A sede do peixe (Para o que nao tem solucao) / Leo / Maria Maria / Meu Menino / Toshiro / Reis e rainhas do Maracatu / Que bom, amigo
CD Set CDEM 1550
Hemisphere / Mar '95 / EMI

COURAGE
Bridges / Vera cruz / Tres pontas / Outubro / Courage / Rio vermelho / Gira girou / Morro velho / Catavento / Cancao do sol
CD 3930192
A&M / Feb '93 / PolyGram

MILAGRE DOS PEIXES
Os escravos de jo / Carlos, Lucia, Chico e Tiago / Milagre dos peixes / A chamada / Cade-canto:Nico e Telo / Pablo no 2 / Tema dos deuses / Hoje e dia de el-ray / Ultima sessao de musica / Sacramento / Pablo-canto:Nico
CD INT 30082
Intuition / Sep '96 / New Note/Pinnacle

MILTON NASCIMENTO
CD 9362462482
Warner Bros. / Jun '96 / Warner Music

SENTINELA
O velho / Peixinhos do mar / Tudo / Cancao da America / Sueno con serpientes / Roupa nova / Povo da raca Brasil / Sentinela / Catinga caico / Bicho homem / Itamarandiba / Um gafune, na cabeca malandro, eu quero ate de macao / Peixinhos do mar
CD 8133572
Verve / Jan '90 / PolyGram

Nascimento, Toninho

ADORADA ESTRELA GUIA
A beleza du amor / Tropicana / Zoraide / Men curacao e quem diz / Ladeira / Segredos de mulher / Daqui algum tempo / Adorada estrela guia / Passarinho cantador / Samba de avias / Morro velho
CD TCB 03022
TCB / '96 / New Note/Pinnacle

Nash, Johnny

BEST OF JOHNNY NASH, THE
I can see clearly now / Dream lover / Hold me tight / There are no more questions than answers / Let's be friends / Cupid / Reggae on Broadway / Let's move and groove together / Guava jelly / What a wonderful world / Stir it up / Ooh what a feeling / Loving you / Tears on my pillow (I can't take it) / All I have to do is dream / Halfway to paradise
CD 4688592
Columbia / Feb '96 / Sony

I CAN SEE CLEARLY NOW
I can see clearly now / Let's be friends / Cream puff / Reggae on Broadway / Wonderful world / Ooh what a feeling / Birds of a feather / Cupid / Tears on my pillow / Guava jelly / That woman / Dream lover / There are more questions than answers / All I have to do is dream / Nice time / You got soul / My merry go round / Halfway to paradise / Stir it up
CD 4653062
Epic / May '89 / Sony

Nash, Lewis

RHYTHM IS MY BUSINESS
Let me try / 106 Nix / Sing me a song everlasting / My shining hour / Sabuku / Omlette / When you return / Monk's dream / Danuelle's waltz / Pranayama
CD ECD 22041
Evidence / Mar '93 / ADA / Cadillac / Harmonia Mundi

Nashville All-Stars Country ...

AFTER THE RIOT IN NEWPORT (Nashville All-Stars Country Band)
Relaxin' / Nashville to Newport / Opus de funk / Wonderful / 'Round midnight / Frankie and Johnny / Riot-chorus
CD BCD 15447
Bear Family / Jun '89 / Direct / Rollercoaster / Swift

COUNTRY ALL THE WAY (Nashville All-Stars Country Band)
Most beautiful girl / Oh lonesome me / Rocky mountain high / There's a heartache following me / Snowbird / Rhinestone cowboy / Take these chains from my heart / Jolene / Have I told you lately that I love you / Last train to San Fernando / From a Jack to a king / Release me / Welcome to my world / Adios amigos / It's four in the mornin' / Your cheatin' heart / Heartaches by the number / Make the world go away
CD 306612
Hallmark / May '97 / Carlton

Nashville Bluegrass Band

BOYS ARE BACK IN TOWN, THE
Get a transfer to home / Long time gone / Big river / Hard times / Connie and Buster / Don't let our love die / I'm rollin' through this unfriendly world / Rock bottom blues / Diamonds and pearls / Ghost of Eli Renfro / Weary blues from waiting / Big cow in Carlisle / Dark as the night, blue as the day / Boys are back in town
CD SHCD 3778
Sugar Hill / Jul '90 / ADA / CM / Direct / Koch / Roots

HOME OF THE BLUES
CD SHCD 3793
Sugar Hill / Jan '97 / ADA / CM / Direct / Koch / Roots

IDLE TIME
Idle time / Old devil's dream / Two wings / I closed my heart's door / All I want is you / Angeline the baker / Little Maggie / Last night I dreamed of loving you / No one but my darling / My Lord heard Jerusalem when she moaned / Old timey risin' damp / Train carryin' Jimmie Rodgers home
CD ROUCD 0232
Rounder / Aug '88 / ADA / CM / Direct

MY NATIVE HOME
CD ROUCD 0212
Rounder / Jul '93 / ADA / CM / Direct

TO BE HIS CHILD
Goodnight the Lord's coming / Every humble knee must bow / No hiding place / You're drifting away / Hold fast to the right / Child enters life / To be his child / Gospel plow / Are you afraid to die / I'll be rested / Old Satan / New born soul
CD ROUCD 0242
Rounder / Aug '88 / ADA / CM / Direct

UNLEASHED
CD SHCD 3843
Sugar Hill / Oct '95 / ADA / CM / Direct / Koch / Roots

WAITIN' FOR THE HARD TIMES TO GO
Back trackin' / Waitin' for the hard times to go / Kansas City railroad line / Open pit mine / Train of yesterday / Father I stretch my arms to thee / When I get where I'm goin' / Waltzing's for dreamers / I ain't goin' down / We decided to make Jesus our choice / On again off again / Soppin' the gravy
CD SHCD 3809
Sugar Hill / May '93 / ADA / CM / Direct / Koch / Roots

Nashville Voices

NEW COUNTRY HITS
CD 12504
Laserlight / Jun '95 / Target/BMG

Nastasee

TRIM THE FAT
CD SPV 08544122
SPV / May '96 / Koch / Plastic Head

Nasty, Billy

RACE DATA ETA (2CD Set)
CD Set AVEXCD 55
Avex / Jun '97 / 3mv/Pinnacle

Nasty Idols

CRUEL INTENTION
Way ya walk / Cool way of living / American nights / Don't tear it down / Alive 'n' kickin' / House of rock and roll / BITCH / Can't get ya off my mind / Devil in disguise / Westcoast city rockers / Trashed and dirty / Can't get ya off my mind
CD BMCD 022
Black Mark / Apr '92 / Plastic Head

Nasty Savage

INDULGENCE/ABSTRACT REALITY
CD 398414064CD
Metal Blade / Nov '96 / Pinnacle / Plastic Head

NASTY SAVAGE
CD 398414063CD
Metal Blade / Nov '96 / Pinnacle / Plastic Head

I'M A ZYDECO HOG
CD ROUCD 2143
Rounder / Aug '97 / ADA / CM / Direct

Nathan & Zydeco Cha Cha's

CREOLE CROSSROADS
CD ROUCD 2137
Rounder / Oct '95 / ADA / CM / Direct

FOLLOW ME CHICKEN
CD ROUCD 2122
Rounder / Aug '93 / ADA / CM / Direct

I'M A ZYDECO HOG
CD ROUCD 2143
Rounder / Aug '97 / ADA / CM / Direct

Nathanson, Roy

COMING GREAT MILLENNIUM, THE (Nathanson, Roy & Anthony Coleman)
CD KFWCD 119
Knitting Factory / Oct '92 / Cargo / Plastic Head

I COULD'VE BEEN A DRUM (Nathanson, Roy & Anthony Coleman)
CD TZA 7113
Tzadik / Feb '97 / Cargo

LOBSTER & FRIEND (Nathanson, Roy & Anthony Coleman)
CD KFWCD 147
Knitting Factory / Feb '95 / Cargo / Plastic Head

Nation Of Ulysses

13 POINT PROGRAM...
CD DIS 57CD
Dischord / Feb '97 / SRD

PLAYS PRETTY FOR BABY
CD DIS 71VCD
Dischord / Oct '92 / SRD

National Gallery

KEEP IT CLEAN
Lost lover blues / Trouble in mind / Keep it clean / Weeping willow blues / When I lay my burden down / Wini' boy blues / From four till late / Sundown / Worried life / Come back baby / Drunken hearted man / Big road blues / Special rider blues / Sittin' on top of the world / Electric chair blues / Police dog blues / Ballad of Fulton Allen / Travellin' light
CD RHYD 5007
Rhiannon / Jul '97 / ADA / Direct / Vital

National Health

DS AL CODA
Flanagan's people / Toad of toad hall / Portrait of a shrinking man / Tales of a damson knight / Black hat / TNTFX / Feel a night coming on / Arriving twice / Shining water
CD BP 129CD
Blueprint / Sep '96 / Pinnacle

MISSING PIECES
CD VP 113CD
Voiceprint / Nov '96 / Pinnacle

NATIONAL HEALTH
Tenemos roads / Brujo / Borogroves / Elephants
CD CDCRH 113
Charly / Feb '97 / Koch
CD 14827
Spalax / Jun '97 / ADA / Cargo / Direct / Discovery / Greyhound

OF QUEUES AND CURES
Bryden 2 step (for amphibians) / Collapso / Squarer for Maud / Dreams wide awake / Binoculars / Phlakaton / Bryden 2 step (for amphibians)
CD CDCRH 117
Charly / Feb '97 / Koch

National Heroes

ONCE AROUND THE SUN
CD FFR 016
Freek / Apr '96 / RTM/Disc / SRD

Native Colours

ONE WORLD
Pumpkin's delight / Freedom / Girlie's world / Highest mountain / Reflections in D / One world / Nature boy / I'm glad there is you / Orion's belt / Time was
CD CCD 4646
Concord Jazz / Jun '95 / New Note/ Pinnacle

Native Son

CROSSFIRE
CD RMCCD 0192
Red Steel / Aug '96 / Pinnacle

NO MAN'S LAND
CD RMCCD 0194
Red Steel / Aug '96 / Pinnacle

SOLID GROUND
CD RMCCD 0191
Red Steel / Jul '96 / Pinnacle

Natural Born Groovers

GROOVEBIRD SYSTEM, THE
CD ZYX 204372
ZYX / Jul '97 / ZYX

Natural Four

HEAVEN RIGHT HERE ON EARTH
CD CPCD 8155
Charly / Mar '96 / Koch

NATURAL FOUR
Can this be real / You bring out the best inme / Try love again / You can't keep running away / This is what's happening now / Love that really counts / Try to smile / Love's society / Things will be better tomorrow
CD CPCD 8127
Charly / Oct '95 / Koch

Nature & Organisation

BEAUTY REAPS THE BLOOD OF SOLITUDE
CD DURTRO 021CD
Durtro / Oct '96 / World Serpent

Naturel, Gilles

NATUREL
Feeling of jazz / Trusting / Nice reed / Little world / Ray's blues / Trois bornes / I had a dream
CD JMS 186762
JMS / Mar '96 / New Note/BMG

Naturists

FRIENDLY ISLANDS
Shaving cream / Boogie 2 shoes / Green green grass of home / Mavis Riley / Mission impossible / Lost in Tonga
CD ACTIVE 001CD
Interactive / Jan '94 / 3mv/Sony

Naundorf, Frank

FRANK NAUNDORF & BAND
CD BCD 316
GHB / Apr '94 / Jazz Music

Nauseef, Mark

SNAKE MUSIC, THE (Nauseef, Mark & Miroslav Tadic)
Lizard on a hot rock / Wind cries Mary / Peacock on a hot rock / Rope ladder to the moon / Armacord / Who are the brain police / Hamburg 2 / All souls day / Trio / Walls of the vortex / Fourths
CD CMPCD 60
CMP / Jul '94 / Cargo / Grapevine/PolyGram / Vital/SAM

Navarro, Fats

AT THE ROYAL ROOST VOL.1 (Navarro, Fats & Tadd Dameron)
CD COD 010
Jazz View / Mar '92 / Harmonia Mundi

AT THE ROYAL ROOST VOL.2 (Navarro, Fats & Tadd Dameron)
CD COD 025
Jazz View / Jun '92 / Harmonia Mundi

COMPLETE BLUE NOTE & CAPITOL RECORDINGS, THE (2CD Set) (Navarro, Fats & Tadd Dameron)
Chase / Chase / Squirrel / Squirrel / Our delight / Our delight / Dameronia / Dameronia / Jahbero / Jahbero / Lady Bird / Lady Bird / Symphonette / Symphonette / I think I'll go away / Sid's delight / Casbah / John's delight / What's new / Heaven's doors are wide open / Focus / Skunk / Boperation / Boperation / Skunk / Double talk / Double talk / Bouncing with Bud: *Navarro, Fats & Bud Powell* / Dancing with Bud: *Navarro, Fats & Bud Powell* / Bouncing with Bud: *Navarro, Fats & Bud Powell* / Wall: *Navarro, Fats & Bud Powell* / Dance of the infidels: *Navarro, Fats & Bud Powell* / Dance of the Infidels: *Navarro, Fats & Bud Powell* / 52nd Street: *Navarro, Fats & Bud Powell* / Steekin' apples: *Navarro, Fats & Bud Powell*
CD Set CDP 8333732
Blue Note / Oct '95 / EMI

FATS NAVARRO 1946-1949
CD CD 53076
Giants Of Jazz / Mar '92 / Cadillac / Jazz Music / Target/BMG

Navarro, Jose Angel

MIEL
CD ASHECD 2002
Ashe / Nov '96 / Direct

Nawazish, Shabnu

TAMANNA
CD DMUT 1188
Multitone / Mar '96 / BMG

Naylor, Oliver

OLIVER NAYLOR 1924-1925
High society / Oh Johnny, please don't, Mom Ma / Ringelberg blues / Hugo (I go where you go) / She wouldn't do what I asked her to / I've got a cross eyed Papa (but he looks straight at me) / You / 31st Street blues / Ain't that hateful / Twilight rose / So I took the $50,000 / Driftwood / Say say Sadie / Susquehanna home / You and I / Take me / Bye bye baby / Headin' for Louisville / Carolina stomp / Sweet Georgia Brown / Slowin' down blues
CD RTR 79008
Retrieval / Feb '97 / Cadillac / Direct / Jazz Music / Swift / Wellard

Nazareth

2XS
Love leads to madness / Boys in the band / You love another / Gatecrash / Games / Back to the trenches / Dream on / Lonely in the night / Preservation / Take the rap / Mexico
CD CLACD 217
Castle / Feb '91 / BMG

CHAMPIONS OF ROCK
CD CR 867112
Disky / Mar '96 / Disky / THE

CLOSE ENOUGH FOR ROCK 'N' ROLL
Telegram / Vicki / Homesick again / Vancouver shakedown
CD CLACD 182
Castle / Aug '90 / BMG

EXERCISES
I will not be led / Cat's eye, apple pie / In my time / Woke up this morning / Called her name / Fool about you / Love now you're gone / Madelaine / Sad song / 1692 (Glencoe massacre)
CD CLACD 220
Castle / Feb '91 / BMG

EXPECT NO MERCY
All the king's horses / Expect no mercy / Gimme what's mine / Gone dead train / Kentucky fried blues / New York broken toy / Place in your heart / Revenge is sweet / Shot me down / Busted
CD CLACD 187
Castle / Aug '90 / BMG

FOOL CIRCLE, THE
Dressed to kill / Another year / Moonlight eyes / Pop the silo / Let me be your leader / We are the people / Every young man's dream / Little part of you / Cocaine / Victoria
CD CLACD 214
Castle / Dec '90 / BMG

FROM THE VAULTS
Friends / If you see my baby / Hard living / Spinning top / Love hurts / Down / My white bicycle / Holy roller / Railroad boy / You're the violin / Good love / Greens / Desolation road / Heart's grown cold / Razamanaz / Hair of the dog / Talkin' to one of the boys / Morning dew / Juicy Lucy / On the run
CD NEMCD 639
Sequel / Mar '93 / BMG

GREATEST HITS
CD BRCD 1392
BR Music / Jun '94 / Target/BMG

GREATEST HITS
Razamanaz / Holy roller / Shanghai'd in Shanghai / Love hurts / Turn on your receiver / Bad bad boy / This flight tonight / Broken down angel / Hair of the dog / Sunshine / My white bicycle / Woke up this morning / Morning dew / Love now your gone / Carry out feelings / I want to do everything for you / Expect no mercy
CD ESMCD 369
Essential / Oct '96 / BMG

HAIR OF THE DOG
Hair of the dog / Miss Misery / Guilty / Changing times / Beggar's day / Rose in the heather / Whisky drinkin' woman / Please don't Judas me / Love hurts / Railroad boy
CD ESMCD 550
Essential / May '97 / BMG

LOUD 'N' PROUD
Go down fighting / Not faking it / Turn on your receiver / Teenage nervous breakdown / Free wheeler / This flight tonight / Child in the sun / Ballad of Hollis Brown / This flight tonight / Go down fighting / Ballad of Hollis Brown
CD ESMCD 379
Essential / Sep '96 / BMG

MALICE IN WONDERLAND
Holiday / Showdown at the border / Talkin' to one of the boys / Heart's grown cold / Fast cars / Big boy / Talkin' 'bout love / Fallen angel / Ship of dreams / Turning a new leaf
CD CLACD 181
Castle / Aug '90 / BMG

MOVE ME
Let me be your dog / Can't shake these shakes / Crack me up / Move me / Steamroller / Stand by your beds / Rip it up / Demon alcohol / You had it comin' / Bring it on home to mama / Burning down
CD ESMCD 503
Essential / May '97 / BMG

NAZARETH
Witchdoctor woman / Dear John / Empty arms, empty heart / I had a dream / Red light lady / Fat man / Country girl / Morning dew / King is dead
CD CLACD 286
Castle / Jun '92 / BMG

NO MEAN CITY
Claim to fame / Just to get into it / May the sunshine / No mean city / Simple solution / Star / Whatever you want babe / What's in it for me
CD CLACD 213
Castle / Dec '90 / BMG

PLAY 'N' THE GAME
Somebody to roll / Down home girl / Flying / Waiting for the man / Born to love / I want to do everything for you / I don't want to go on without you / Wild honey / LA girls
CD CLACD 219
Castle / Feb '91 / BMG

RAMPANT
Silver dollar forger / Glad when you're gone / Loved and lost / Shanghai'd in Shanghai / Jet lag / Light my way / Sunshine / Shapes of things / Space safari / Down
CD ESMCD 551
Essential / May '97 / BMG

RAZAMANAZ
Razamanaz / Alcatraz / Vigilante man / Woke up this morning / Night woman / Bad bad boy / Sold my soul / Too bad, too sad / Broken down angel / Hard living / Spinning top / Woke up this morning / Witchdoctor woman
CD ESMCD 370
Essential / Sep '96 / BMG

SINGLES COLLECTION, THE
Broken down angel / Bad bad boy / This flight tonight / My white bicycle / Out of time / Shanghai'd in Shanghai / Love hurts / Hair of the dog / Holy roller / Carry out feelings / You're the violin / Somebody to roll / I don't want to go on without you / Gone dead train / Place in your heart / May the sunshine / Star / Dressed to kill / Morning dew / Games / Love leads to madness
CD CCSCD 280
Castle / Dec '90 / BMG

SNAKES AND LADDERS
We are animals / Lady luck / Hang on to a dream / Piece of my heart / Trouble / Key / Back to school / Girls / Donna, get off that crack / See you, see me / Helpless / Winner on the night
CD ESMCD 501
Essential / May '97 / BMG

SNAZ
Telegram / Razamanaz / I want to do everything for you / This flight tonight / Beggar's day / Every young man's dream / Heart's grown cold / Java blues / Cocaine / Big boy / So you want to be a rock 'n' roll star / Holiday / Let me be your leader / Dressed to kill / Hair of the dog / Expect no mercy / Shapes of things / Love hurts / Morning dew / Juicy Lucy / On your way
CD ESMCD 531
Essential / May '97 / BMG

SOUND ELIXIR
All nite radio / Milk and honey / Whipping boy / Rain on the window / Back room boy / Why don't you read the book / I ran / Rags to riches / Local still / Where are you now
CD CLACD 218
Castle / Feb '91 / BMG

Nazeri, Sharam

NOWRUZ
CD 58395CD
World Network / Apr '96 / ADA

Nazgul

TOTEM
CD VAMP 7495CD
Vampire / Jan '96 / Plastic Head

Nazia & Zoher

CAMERA
CD TIMBCD 500
Timbuktu / Sep '92 / Pinnacle

NCE Engine

GRAVITY WELL
CD SH 1872203
Interfere Chrome / Nov '95 / Plastic Head

Ndai Ndai

EN CONCERT
CD MW 3013CD
Music & Words / Nov '96 / ADA / Direct

Ndegeocello, Me'shell

PEACE BEYOND PASSION
CD 9362460332
Maverick / Jun '96 / Warner Music

PLANTATION LULLABIES
Plantation lullabies / I'm diggin' you (like an old soul record) / If that's your boyfriend (he wasn't last night) / Shoot'n up and gett'n high / Dred loc / Untitled / Step into the projects / Soul on ice / Call me / Outside your door / Picture show / Sweet love / Two lonely hearts (on the subway)
CD 9362457542
Maverick / Jul '94 / Warner Music

Ndere Troupe

KIKWABANGA
CD PAN 2016CD
Pan / Oct '93 / ADA / CM / Direct

N'Dour, Youssou

BEST OF YOUSSOU N'DOUR
Set / Shakin' the tree: *N'Dour, Youssou & Peter Gabriel* / Sinebar / Medina / Lion - Gaiende / Toxiques / Fenene / Miyoko / Bamako / Fakastalu / Bes / Hey you / Macoy / Immigres bitim rew / Xale rewmi / Kocc barma
CD CDV 2773
Virgin / Oct '94 / EMI

EYES OPEN
New Africa / Live television / No more / Country boy / Hope / Africa remembers / Coupl's choice / Yo le le (Fulani groove) / Survie / Am am / Marie-Madeleine La Sainte-Louisienne / Useless weapons / Same / Things unspoken
CD 4711862
Columbia / Jun '92 / Sony

GAINDE (N'Dour, Youssou & Yande Codou Sene)
CD 53891
World Network / Mar '96 / ADA

GUIDE (WOMMAT)
Leaving / Old man / Without a smile / Mame bamba / Seven seconds / How are you / Generations / Tourista / Undecided / Love one another / Life / My people / Oh boy / Silence / Chimes of freedom
CD 4765082
Columbia / Feb '97 / Sony

HEY YOU (The Essential Collection 1988-1990)
Lion / Hey you / Fenene / Sinebar / Fakastalu / Set / Bes / Miyoko / Shakin' the tree / Immigres/Bitim rew / Medina / Sabar / Bamako / Toxiques / Macoy
CD NSCD 018
Nascente / Jul '97 / Disc / New Note/ Pinnacle

LION, THE
Lion / Gaiende / Shakin' the tree / Kocc barma / Bamako / Truth / Old tucson / Macdy / My daughter (sama doom) / Bes
CD CDV 2584
Virgin / Jun '89 / EMI

SET
Set / Alboury / Sabar / Toxiques / Sinebar / Medina / Miyoko / Xale rewmi / Fenene / Fakastalu / Hey you / Oneday / Ay chono la
CD CDV 2634
Virgin / Sep '90 / EMI

NDR Big Band

MAGIC NIGHT
CD ISCD 164
Intersound / Jul '96 / Jazz Music

Neal & Leandra

ACCIDENTAL DREAMS
CD RHRCD 85
Red House / May '96 / ADA / Koch

HEARTS AND HAMMERS
CD RHRCD 62
Red House / Jul '95 / ADA / Koch

Neal, Kenny

BAYOU BLOOD
CD ALCD 4809
Alligator / May '93 / ADA / CM / Direct

BIG NEWS FROM BATON ROUGE
CD ALCD 4764
Alligator / Apr '93 / ADA / CM / Direct

DEVIL CHILD
CD ALCD 4774
Alligator / May '93 / ADA / CM / Direct

HOODOO MOON
CD ALCD 4825
Alligator / Nov '94 / ADA / CM / Direct

WALKING ON FIRE
Look but don't touch / Truth hurts / I put my trust in you / Blues stew / Morning after / IOU / My only good thing / I been missing you too / Caught in the jaws of a vice / Things to get better / Walking on fire / Bad luck card
CD ALCD 4795
Alligator / May '93 / ADA / CM / Direct

Neal, Raful

LOUISIANA LEGEND
CD ALCD 4783
Alligator / May '93 / ADA / CM / Direct

Neanders Jazzband

OH DIDN'T HE RAMBLE
CD MECCACD 1027
Music Mecca / Nov '94 / Cadillac / Jazz Music / Wellard

Near Castlegar

IN JANUARY
CD SHR 72
Shrimper / Dec '96 / Cargo

Neary, Paddy

MUSICAL GEMS
CD CDITV 512
Scotdisc / Oct '90 / Conifer/BMG / Duncans / Ross

Necessary Evils

SPIDER FINGERS
CD ITR 045CD
In The Red / Jun '97 / Cargo / Greyhound

Neckbones

SOULS ON FIRE
Dead end kids / Souls on fire / It ain't enough / Don't ya leave me / Hit me / Keep driving / Crack Whore blues / Dolly / Superstar Chevrolet / You can't touch her / Skronky tonk / Art school drop out / Love ya rock 'n' roll / Can't drive you / Shouldn't call your man a fool / Gambling
CD 03042
Fat Possum / Aug '97 / Cargo / Pinnacle

Necromantia

ANCIENT PRIDE
CD OPMCD 048
Osmose / Mar '97 / Plastic Head

CROSSING THE FIERY PATH
CD OPCD 021
Osmose / Feb '94 / Plastic Head

SCARLET EVIL WITCHING BLACK
CD OPCD 036
Osmose / Nov '95 / Plastic Head

Necronomicon

DEVIL'S TONGUE, THE
CD 15197
Laserlight / Aug '91 / Target/BMG

Necrony

NECRONYCISM
CD SPV 06557722
Poserslaughter / Jun '94 / Plastic Head

Necrophobic

NOCTURNAL SILENCE
CD BMCD 40
Black Mark / Aug '93 / Plastic Head

Necrosanct

INCARNATE
Ritual acts / Inevitable demise / Undeath dead dying / Abhorrence / Incarnate / Necronomicon / Exiternity / Restless dead / Solace / Ominous despair / Oblivion seed
CD BMCD 021
Black Mark / Apr '92 / Plastic Head

Necrosis

ACTA SANCTORUM
CD BMCD 045
Black Mark / Jun '95 / Plastic Head

Nectarine

STERLING BEAT
CD GROW 0342
Grass / May '95 / Pinnacle / SRD

Nectarine No.9

SAINT JACK
Saint Jack / Curdled fragments / Fading memory babe / Can't scratch out / This arsehole's been burned too many time before / It's not my baby putting me down / My trapped lightening / Just another fucked up little druggy on the scene / Couldn't phone potatoes / Dead horse arum / Firecrackers / Un-loaded for you / Clipped wings and power stings / Tape your gead on
CD DUBH 951CD
Postcard / Jun '95 / Vital

SEA WITH THREE STARS, A
Pop's love thing / She's a nicer word to sing / Holes of corpus christi / Beautiful car / Twenty two blue / Peanut brain / Smith's new automatic / Sea with three stars / No, you mean / Don't worry babe, you're not the only one awake / Trace nine / Chocolate swastika
CD DUBH 931CD
Postcard / Feb '93 / Vital

Ned's Atomic Dustbin

05.22
Saturday night / Scrawl / Aim / Bite / Faceless / I've never been to me / Grey cell green / Cut up (Tartan Shoulders mix) / Kill your remix / Wirey / Flexible head / Sentence / Prostrate / Terminally groovie / NAD V NDX equals Intact / Twenty three hour toothache / Titch / Plug me in / That's nice / NAD V NDX equals NSA / Perfectly rounded / Forty five second blunder
CD 4779842
Furtive / Nov '94 / Sony

ARE YOU NORMAL
Suave and suffocated / Walking through syrup / Legoland / Swallowing air / Who goes first / Tantrum / Not sleeping around / You don't want to do that / Leg end in his own boots / Two and two make five / Fracture / Spring / Intact
CD 4726332
Sony Soho2 / Sep '96 / Sony

BITE
CD CHAPCD 058
Chapter 22 / Sep '91 / Vital

GOD FODDER
Kill your television / Less than useful / Selfish / Grey cell green / Cut up throwing things / Capital letters / Happy / Your complex / Nothing like until you find out / You / What gives my son
CD 4681122
Furtive / Apr '95 / Sony

Neel, Johnny

COMIN' ATCHA LIVE
CD BIGMO 10272
Big Mo / Aug '95 / ADA / Direct

Neely, Don

DON NEELY AND HIS ROYAL SOCIETY JAZZ ORCHESTRA (Neely, Don & His Royal Society Jazz Orchestra)
CD MMRCCD 6
Merry Makers / Feb '94 / Jazz Music

DON'T BRING... (Neely, Don & His Royal Society Jazz Orchestra)
CD SOSCD 1250
Stomp Off / May '93 / Jazz Music / Wellard

ROLL UP (Neely, Don & His Royal Society Jazz Orchestra)
CD CCD 147
Circle / Aug '95 / Jazz Music / Swift / Wellard

Nefertiti

FROM 18TH DYNASTY
CD FILERCD 421
Profile / Nov '91 / Pinnacle

Negativland

ESCAPE FROM NOISE
CD SST 133CD
SST / May '93 / Plastic Head

FREE
CD SEELAND 009
Seeland / Jun '93 / Cargo / SRD

GUNS
CD SST 291CD
SST / May '93 / Plastic Head

HELTER STUPID
CD RECDEC 29
Rec Rec / Jul '93 / Cadillac / Plastic Head / ReR Megacorp / SRD
CD SST 252CD
SST / May '93 / Plastic Head

LETTER U & THE NUMBER 2, THE
CD RECDEC 51
Rec Rec / Jul '93 / Cadillac / Plastic Head / ReR Megacorp / SRD

NEGATIVE CONCERT LAND
CD Set 180G
ReR/Recommended / Jan '94 / ReR Megacorp / RTM/Disc

Negazione

BEHIND THE DOOR
CD WB 05051CD
We Bite / '90 / Plastic Head

LITTLE DREAMER
CD WB 030CD
We Bite / '89 / Plastic Head

LO SPIRITO CONTINUA
CD TVOR 04CD
Plastic Head / Jan '92 / Plastic Head

WILD BUNCH
CD 846113
SPV / Aug '90 / Koch / Plastic Head

Neglect

END IT
CD WB 21132
We Bite / Oct '94 / Plastic Head

FOUR YEARS OF HATE (2CD Set)
CD Set GG 006CD
Gain Ground / Dec '96 / Cargo

Negra, Pata

BLUES DE FRONTORA
CD HNCD 1309
Hannibal / May '89 / ADA / Vital

Negrete, Jorge

SUS GRANDES EXITOS VOL.3
CD ALCD 021
Alma Latina / Jul '96 / Discovery

Negro, Gato

BLACK CAT DUB
CD RE 203CD
ROIR / Nov '94 / Plastic Head / Shellshock/Disc

VITAL FORCE DUB
CD RUSCD 8210
ROIR / May '97 / Plastic Head / Shellshock/Disc

Negrocan

MEDIA MUNDO
CD DEPE 01CD
Deep South / Jul '96 / Timewarp

Neighb'rhood Childr'n

LONG YEARS IN SPACE
CD SC 11041
Sundazed / Jun '97 / Cargo / Greyhound / Rollercoaster

Neil

NEIL'S HEAVY CONCEPT ALBUM
Hello vegetables / Hole in my shoe / Heavy potato encounter / My white bicycle / Neil the barbarian / Lentil nightmare / Computer alarm / Wayne / Gnome / Cosmic jam / Golf girl / Bad karma in UK / Our tune / Ken / End of the world cabaret / God save the Queen / Floating / Hurdy gurdy man / Paranoid mix / Amoeba song
CD 4509948522
WEA / Jan '94 / Warner Music

Neil, Alan

STEPPING OUT VOL.1
CD DLD 1025
Dance & Listen / '92 / Savoy / Target/ BMG

STEPPING OUT VOL.2
CD DLD 1032
Dance & Listen / Mar '93 / Savoy / Target/ BMG

Neil, Fred

EVERYBODY'S TALKIN'
CD CREV 021CD
Rev-Ola / Jan '94 / 3mv/Vital

Neil, Vince

CARVED IN STONE
CD 9362458772
Warner Bros. / Jul '95 / Warner Music

EXPOSED
Look in her eyes / Sister of pain / Can't have your cake / Edge / Can't change me / Fine, fine wine / Living is a luxury / You're invited but your friend can't come / Gettin' hard / Forever
CD 9362452602
Warner Bros. / Apr '93 / Warner Music

Neill, Ben

TRIPTYCAL
CD 5331842
Antilles/Verve / Mar '97 / PolyGram

Neither Neither World

ALIVE WITH THE TASTE OF HELL
CD WSCD 011
World Serpent / Oct '96 / World Serpent

MADDENING
CD DVLR 010CD
Dark Vinyl / Nov '95 / Plastic Head / World Serpent

Nekromantix

BROUGHT BACK TO LIFE
CD INTCD 009
Nervous / May '95 / Nervous / TKO Magnum

CURSE OF THE COFFIN
CD NERCD 063
Nervous / '91 / Nervous / TKO Magnum

DEMONS ARE A GIRL'S BEST FRIEND
CD RMD 96042
Record Music / Dec '96 / Nervous

HELLBOUND
CD TBCD 2001
Nervous / Mar '93 / Nervous / TKO Magnum

Nell, Bob

WHY I LIKE COFFEE
CD 804192
New World / Sep '92 / ADA / Cadillac / Harmonia Mundi

Nelson

IMAGINATOR
CD VICP 5817
Victor / May '97 / Greyhound

Nelson, Bill

AFTER THE SATELLITE SINGS
Deeply dazed / Tomorrow yesterday / Flipside / Streamliner / Memory babe / Skull baby cluster / Zoom sequence / Rocket to Damascus / Beautiful nudes / Old goat / Squirm / Wow it's Scootercar Sexkitten / Phantom sedan / Ordinary idiots / V-ghost / Blink agog
CD RES 114CD
Resurgence / Apr '97 / Pinnacle

BLUE MOONS AND LAUGHING GUITARS
Ancient guitars / Girl from another planet / Spinnin' around / Shaker / God man slain / Dead we wake with the upstairs drum / New moon rising / Glory days / Wishes / Angel in my system / Wings and everything / Boat to forever / Invisible man and the unforgettable girl / So it goes / Fires in the sky / Dream ships set sail
CD CDVE 912
Venture / Aug '92 / EMI

BUDDHA HEAD
My philosophy / Killing my desires / Buddha head / Way / Big river / Karma kisses / We will rise / Signs and signals / Lotus in the stream / Enlightenment / Eternally / Duality / Perfect world / Heart has its reasons / Sun will rise / Big illumination / Life as we know it
CD POPU 004CD
Populuxe / Mar '97 / Pinnacle

CONFESSIONS OF A HYPERDREAMER (2CD Set)
Sun at six windows / Bird ornaments / My favourite atom / Girl I never forgot / Circle the world in a paper canoe / Queer weather / Astro-coaster / Brutal Tinkerbell / Waltz at the end of the world / Secret agent at Science Park / Twentieth century / Aura hole / Radiant nature knows not the workers sorrow / Essoldo stripshow / Rain and neon / Candyland / Birds and blue stuff / Radiated robot men / Coney Island / Weird critters / Golden satellites / Brotherhood of sleeping car porters / Quarter moons and stars / Wonder story / Cool blue heaven / Far too flip / Realm rider / Angels in Arcadia
CD Set POPBOXCD 1
Populuxe / Jan '97 / Pinnacle

CRIMSWORTH
CD RES 104CD
Resurgence / Apr '97 / Pinnacle

DEEP DREAM DECODER
Things to come / God bless me / Rise (above these things) / Snowing outside / It's all true / Head full of lights and a hat full of haloes / Girls I've loved / Amazing things / Deep dream decoder / Dissolve / Year 44 (the birthday song) / Wing and a prayer / Dreamnoise and angel / Tired eyes / Golden girl / Spark
CD POPU 005CD
Populuxe / Jun '97 / Pinnacle

ELECTRICITY MADE US ANGELS
Begin to burn / Heaven's happy hemisphere / God in her eyes / Float away / Big blue day / Sweet is the mystery / If wishes were horses / Fair winds and flying boats / Ocean over blue / River of love / This is destiny / Wonders never cease / Nothing yet / God thundered boy / She sends me
CD POPU 003CD
Populuxe / Feb '97 / Pinnacle

NORTHERN DREAM
CD SM 777CD
Blueprint / Mar '96 / Pinnacle

PRACTICALLY WIRED
Roses and rocketships / Spinning planet / Thousand fountain island / Piano 45 / Pink buddha blues / Kid with cowboy tie / Royal ghosts and great fires / Her presence in flowers / Big noise in Twanagton / Tiny little thing / Wild blues sky / Every moment infinite / Friends from heaven / Eternal for a-ton / Soapland
CD ASCD 022
All Saints / Mar '95 / Discovery / Vital

Nelson, David

LIMITED EDITION (Nelson, David Band)
CD DNB 95001
Icenine / Jun '97 / Greyhound

Nelson, Louis

LOUIS NELSON BIG FOUR VOL.1
CD BCD 25
GHB / Jun '96 / Jazz Music

LOUIS NELSON BIG FOUR VOL.2
CD BCD 26
GHB / Jun '96 / Jazz Music

Nelson, Oliver

AFRO AMERICAN SKETCHES (Nelson, Oliver Orchestra)
Message / Jungleaire / Emancipation blues / There's a yearnin' / Going up North / Disillusioned / Freedom dance
CD OJCCD 1819
Original Jazz Classics / Jun '96 / Complete/ Pinnacle / Jazz Music / Wellard

BLUES AND THE ABSTRACT TRUTH
Stolen moments / Hoedown / Cascades / Yearnin' / Butch and butch / Teenie's blues
CD MCAD 5659
Impulse Jazz / Nov '91 / New Note/BMG

JAZZ MASTERS
CD 5276542
Verve / Mar '96 / PolyGram

MEET OLIVER NELSON
CD OJCCD 227
Original Jazz Classics / Nov '95 / Complete/Pinnacle / Jazz Music / Wellard

MORE BLUES AND THE ABSTRACT TRUTH
Blues and the abstract truth / Blue o'mighty / Mr. Broadway / Midnight blue / Critic's choice / One for Bob / Blues for Mr. Broadway / Goin' to Chicago blues
CD IMP 12122
Impulse Jazz / Apr '97 / New Note/BMG

SCREAMIN' THE BLUES
Screamin' the blues / March on, march on / Drive / Meetin' / Three seconds / Alto-itis
CD OJCCD 80
Original Jazz Classics / Nov '95 / Complete/ Pinnacle / Jazz Music / Wellard

STRAIGHT AHEAD (Nelson, Oliver & Eric Dolphy)
CD OJCCD 99
Original Jazz Classics / Nov '95 / Complete/Pinnacle / Jazz Music / Wellard

Nelson, Ozzie

HEAD OVER HEELS IN LOVE
CD HCD 259
Hindsight / Oct '95 / Jazz Music / Target/ BMG

NELSON TOUCH, THE (25 Band Hits 1931-1941) (Nelson, Ozzie & Harriet)
It's gonna be you / Dream a little dream of me / Yes suh / Got you where I want you (Right in my arms) / By a waterfall / Oh Susanna, dust off that old pianna / Rigamarole / About a quarter to nine / Swamp fire / And them some / Tiger rag / But where are you / Wave-a-stick blues / Our penthouse on third avenue / Subway / Roses in December / Says my heart / Ramblin wreck from Georgia tech / That sly old gentlemen from Featherbed Lane / Yours for a song / I want the waiter with the water / I'm looking for a guy who plays alto and baritone and double / Jersey jive / Swingin' on the golden gate / Central Avenue shuffle
CD CDAJA 5197
Living Era / Jun '96 / Select

OZZIE NELSON
CD CCD 027
Circle / Oct '93 / Jazz Music / Swift / Wellard

Nelson, Portia

LET ME LOVE YOU (The Songs Of Bart Howard)
Beautiful woman / On the first warm day / Thank you for the lovely summer / One love affair / Fly me to the moon / Be my all / Let me love you / Never kiss / If you leave Paris / It was worth it / Year after year / Music for lovers
CD DRGCD 91442
DRG / Dec '95 / Discovery / New Note/ Pinnacle

THIS LIFE
Confession of a New Yorker / It's the little things / Gentle love / I don't smoke / I never planned to love you / Let me be the music / Pieces / Decisions / Gettin' over the blues / Pony, pony / Love on the rocks / Such a man / As I remember him / Autobiography in five short chapter / This life / Make a rainbow
CD DRGCD 91445
DRG / May '96 / Discovery / New Note/ Pinnacle

Nelson, Red

RED NELSON 1935-1947
CD OTCD 6
Old Tramp / Jul '95 / Hot Shot / Swift

Nelson, Rick

ALL MY BEST
Travellin' man / Hello Mary lou / Poor little fool / Stood up / You are the only one / It's late / You know what I mean / Young world / Lonesome town / I got a feeling / Just a little too much / Believe what you say / It's up to you / Waitin' in school / Never be anyone elese but you / Don't leave me this way / Fools rush in / Teenage idol / I'm walkin' / Mighty good / Sweeter than you / Garden party
CD CDMF 081
Magnum Force / Mar '92 / TKO Magnum

ANTHOLOGY (2CD Set)
CD Set CPCD 82902
Charly / Jul '97 / Koch

BEST OF RICKY NELSON, THE
CD MATCD 328
Castle / Feb '95 / BMG

BEST OF RICKY NELSON, THE
CD PLSCD 127
Pulse / Mar '96 / BMG

COUNTRY MUSIC
CD CD 336
Entertainers / Aug '94 / Target/BMG

EP COLLECTION, THE
I'm in love again / Baby I'm sorry / Boppin' the blues / There goes my baby / Your true love / Stood up / Down the line / Don't leave me this way / If you can't rock me / Stop sneakin' around / Hello Mary Lou, goodbye heart / Lucky star / Young world / Mad mad world / It's up to you / Have I told you lately that I love you / Never be anyone else but you / I can't help it / Someday / Poor little fool / It's late / There's good rockin' tonight / I'm feelin' sorry / You tear me up / Believe what you say
CD SEECD 483
See For Miles/C5 / Aug '97 / Pinnacle

GARDEN PARTY
Let it bring you along / Garden party / So long Mama / I wanna be with you / Are you really real / I'm talking about you / Nightime lady / Flower opens gently by / Don't let your goodbye stand / Palace guard
CD WMCD 5696
Disky / Oct '94 / Disky / THE

GARDEN PARTY (Nelson, Rick & Stone Canyon Band)
CD NTMCD 540
Nectar / Mar '97 / Pinnacle

GARDEN PARTY/WINDFALL (Nelson, Rick & Stone Canyon Band)
Let it bring you along / Garden party / So long Mama / I wanna be with you / Are you really real / I'm talking about you / Nighttime lady / Flower opens gently by / Don't let your goodbye stand / Palace guard / Legacy / Someone to love / How many times / Evil woman child / Don't leave me here / Wild nights in Tulsa / Lifestream / One night stand / I don't want to be lonely tonight / Windfall
CD BGOCD 333
Beat Goes On / Nov '96 / Pinnacle

GREATEST HITS
CD MU 5019
Musketeer / Oct '92 / Disc

GREATEST HITS
Hello Mary Lou / Garden party / Fools rush in / Travellin' man / Poor little fool / Lonesome town / It's late / Never be anyone else but you / Teenage idol / I'm walkin' / Young world / I got a feeling / Mighty good / Don't leave me this way / You know what I mean / Believe what you say / Waitin' in school / Stood up / Just a little too much / It's up to you / Sweeter than you / You are the only one
CD 100202
CMC / May '97 / BMG

HELLO MARY LOU (GOODBYE HEART) (The Best Of Rick Nelson)
Hello Mary Lou (goodbye heart) / Never be anyone else but you / Be bop baby / Stood up / I got a feeling / Someday (you'll want me to want you) / Poor little fool / Waitin' in school / It's late / Lonesome town / Sweeter than you / Have I told you lately that I love you / You are the only one / Mighty good / Yes sir that's my baby / Just a little too much / Everlovin' / (It's a) young world / It's up to you / Travellin' man / If you can't rock me / Young emotions / Today's teardrops / Wonder like you
CD CZ 560
Premier/EMI / Feb '96 / EMI

IN CONCERT (From Chicago To LA)
Stood up / Waitin' in school / I got a feeling / Travellin' man / Hello Mary Lou / Garden party / You know what I mean / That's alright mama / Believe what you say / Milk cow blues boogie / Never be anyone else but you / Fools rush in / It's up to you / Poor little fool / It's late / Honky tonk woman / My bucket's got a hole in it / Boppin' the blues / Lonesome town

CD CDMF 083
Magnum Force / Jan '92 / TKO Magnum

LIVE
CD 15178
Laserlight / Aug '91 / Target/BMG

LIVE AT THE ALADDIN
Garden party / Poor little fool / My bucket's got a hole in it / Last time around / Milkcow blues / She belongs to me / Lonesome town / Travelling man / Hello Mary Lou / It's late / Merry Christmas baby / Mystery train
CD CDMF 078
Magnum Force / Feb '91 / TKO Magnum

RICK NELSON & THE STONE CANYON BAND VOL.1
CD EDCD 417
Edsel / Mar '95 / Pinnacle

RICK NELSON & THE STONE CANYON BAND VOL.2 (Nelson, Rick & Stone Canyon Band)
Hello Mary Lou / I'm walkin' / Believe what you say / Violets of dawn / Red balloon / Louisiana man / Easy to be free / We've got a long way to go / Sweet Mary / Look at Mary / Mr Dolphin / How long / Reason why / Just like a woman / Honky tonk women / Feels so good / Night time lady / Palace guard / I'm talking about you / Windfall / Don't leave me here
CD EDCD 521
Edsel / Apr '97 / Pinnacle

ROCKIN' WITH RICK
Travellin' man / Hello Mary Lou / Poor little fool / Garden party / Young world / Don't leave me this way / I'm walkin' / Lonesome town / Just a little too much / You are the only one / Stood up / Waitin' in school / I got a feeling / You know what I mean / That's alright mama / Believe what you say / Milk cow blues / It's late / Boopin' the blues / Fools rush in
CD CPCD 8004
Charly / Oct '93 / Koch

ROCKIN' WITH RICKY
Mighty good / Milk cow blues / If you can't rock me / Be bop baby / Good rockin' tonight / It's late / Waitin' in school / Shirley Lee / There goes my baby / Boppin' the blues / I got a feeling / My babe / Stood up / Down the line / One of these mornings / Your true love / Ain't nothin' but love / Believe what you say / My bucket's got a hole in it / Whole lotta shakin' goin' on / I'm in love again / You tear me up / You'll never know what you're missin' / Just a little too much / You're so fine / Break my chain / Oh yeah I'm in love / Stop sneakin' around / I'll make believe / Today's teardrops / Poor loser / I've been thinkin'
CD CDCHD 85
Ace / Apr '96 / Pinnacle

WINDFALL (Nelson, Rick & Stone Canyon Band)
CD LICD 9012730
Line / Nov '96 / CM / Direct

Nelson, Sandy

BEAT THAT DRUM/BE TRUE TO YOUR SCHOOL
You name it / Shuckin' / Turf rider / Here we go / Puttin' it on / Diddley walk / Lonesome drums / Rockin' party / Drummin' good time / Viva Nelson / Alexes / Wiggle walk / Be true to your school / School days / High school USA / Hey little girl (in the High School sweater) / Waitin' in school / Teen march / Cheer leader / School's out / Rock around the clock / Charley Brown / Moments to remember / Graduation day
CD C5HCD 650
See For Miles/C5 / Aug '96 / Pinnacle

COUNTRY STYLE/TEENAGE HOUSE PARTY
North wind / Wolverton mountain / Battle of New Orleans / Geisha girl / On a honky tonk hardwood floor / Bimbo / Waterloo / Wild side of life / Tijuana jail / Fraulein / Four walls / Chew tobacco rag / House party rock / Hearts of stone / Let the four winds blow / Tweedle dee / Let the good times roll / Feel so good / Day train / Night train / Limbo rock / Dumplins / Teenage party
CD C5HCD 649
See For Miles/C5 / Aug '96 / Pinnacle

DRUMMIN' UP A STORM/COMPELLING PERCUSSION
Castle rock / Sandy / I'm in love again / All night long / C jam blues / Here we go again / All around the world with drums / Tub thumpin' / Drummin' up a storm / Civilization / And then there were drums / Alexes / Chicka boom / Jump time / Drums - For drummers only / Drums - For strippers only
CD C5HCD 641
See For Miles/C5 / Jun '96 / Pinnacle

GOLDEN HITS/BEST OF THE BEATS
Live it up / Splish splash / Kansas city / Early in the morning / Rock house / Walking to New Orleans / What'd I say / Honky tonk / Bony Moronie / I'm gonna be a wheel someday / I want to walk you home / Be bop baby / Let's go / Yakety yak / Yakety yakety / My wife can't cook / Stagger Lee / All shook up / Don't be cruel / La bomba bossa nova / Wiggle wobble / Ooh pooh pah doo / Willy and the hand jive / Stood up / Mother In Law

CD C5HCD 648
See For Miles/C5 / Aug '96 / Pinnacle

KING OF DRUMS (His Greatest Hits)
Teen beat / There were drums / In beat / Cool operator / Ooh-poo-pah-doo / Freak beat / Big noise from the jungle / You name it / Blues theme / Let there be drums / Mr. John Lee (parts 1 and 2) / Swamp beat / Quite a beat / Drum stuff / Let there be drums and brass / Drums are my beat / Teen beat '65 / Gimme some skin / Drum stomp / Drums a go go / Drummin' up a storm / Soul drums / Live it up / Kitty's theme
CD SEECD 423
See For Miles/C5 / Jul '95 / Pinnacle

LET THERE BE DRUMS/DRUMS ARE MY BEAT
Slippin' and slidin' / Tequila / My girl Josephine / Big noise from Winnetka / Let there be drums / Bouncy / Birth of the beat / Quite a beat / Get with it drum roll / My blue heaven / Hawaiian war chant / Caravan / Drums are my beat / Day drumming / Drum stomp / Hum drum / Topsy / City
CD C5HCD 640
See For Miles/C5 / Jun '96 / Pinnacle

ROCK 'N' ROLL DRUM BEAT
Day train / Slippin' and slidin' / Willie and the hand jive / All night long / My girl Josephine / All shook up / Sandy / Alexis / Let's go / City / Linda Lu / Bullfrog / Bony Moronie / Tough beat / Yakety yak / La bamba bossa nova / Jivin' around / Don't be cruel (to a heart that's true) / Flip / Be bop baby / Live it up / Dumplin's / Wiggle wobble / Limbo rock / School day / In the mood / Charlie Brown / My wife can't cook / I'm gonna be a wheel someday / Let there be drums
CD CDCHD 586
Ace / Oct '95 / Pinnacle

TEEN BEAT/HE'S A DRUMMER BOY
Teen beat / Jivin' around / Funny face / Wiggle / Rainy day / Drum party / In the mood / Alexes / Lost dreams / I'm walkin' / Boom chicka boom / Party time / Cool operator / Feel beat / Linda Lou / Bullfrog / Tough beat / Raunchy / Jive talk / Jumpin' jungles / Flip / Big noise from the jungle / Walkin' to Hartford / Tim tam
CD C5HCD 639
See For Miles/C5 / Jun '96 / Pinnacle

Nelson, Shara

FRIENDLY FIRE
Rough with the smooth / Movin' on / Poetry / I fell (so you could catch me) / Footprint / Between the lines / After you / Exit 1 / Friendly fire / Keeping out the cold / Segabeats
CD CTCD 48
Cooltempo / Sep '95 / EMI

WHAT SILENCE KNOWS
Nobody / Pain revisited / One goodbye in ten / Inside out / Chance / Uptight / Down that road / Thoughts of you / How close / What silence knows
CD CTCD 35
Cooltempo / Sep '93 / EMI

Nelson, Steve

COMMUNICATIONS (Nelson, Steve Quartet)
CD CRISS 1034CD
Criss Cross / Nov '90 / Cadillac / Direct / Vital/SAM

Nelson, Tracy

HOMEMADE SONGS/COME SEE ABOUT ME
God's song / I've been there before / Ice man / Summer of the silver comet / Tightrope / You don't need to move a mountain / She's taking my part / Friends of a kind / Sounds of the city / Suddenly / Come see about me / Done got over / Holiday / It's growing / Walk away / Tears / Hold on I'm coming / See saw / River's invitation / You're my world
CD FF 70052
Flying Fish / Sep '96 / ADA / CM / Direct / Roots

I FEEL SO GOOD
CD ROUCD 3133
Rounder / Feb '95 / ADA / CM / Direct

IN THE HERE AND NOW
CD ROUCD 3123
Rounder / Jun '93 / ADA / CM / Direct

MOVE ON
CD ROUCD 3143
Rounder / Aug '96 / ADA / CM / Direct

Nelson, Willie

20 OF THE BEST
Funny how time slips away / Night life / My own peculiar way / Hello walls / Mr. Record man / To make a long story short (she's gone) / Good times / She's still gone / Little things / Pretty paper / Bloody Mary morning / What can you do to me now / December days / Yesterday's wine / Me and Paul / Goodhearted woman / She's not for you / It should be easier now / Phases and stages / Circles, cycles and scenes

CD ND 89137
RCA / Mar '91 / BMG

ALWAYS ON MY MIND
Will you remember mine / Some other time / I hope so / Is there something on your mind / Broken promises / Blame in on the times / Face of a fighter / Shelter of your arms / End of understanding / Home is where you're happy / And so will you my love / Waiting time / No tomorrow in sight / Everything but you / Happiness lives next door / Right from wrong / Go away / I'll stay around / Always on my mind
CD SUMCD 4007
Summit / Nov '96 / Sound & Media

AUGUSTA (Nelson, Willie & Don Cherry)
CD CDSD 080
Sundown / Oct '95 / TKO Magnum

BEST OF WILLIE NELSON, THE
Georgia on my mind / Help me make it through the night / Highwayman / Don't get around much anymore / Someone to watch over me / For the good times / Mamas don't let your babies grow up to be cowboys / Good hearted woman / Blue eyes crying in the rain / Mona Lisa / Stardust / City of New Orleans / As time goes by / Moonlight in Vermont / Amazing grace / Lovin' her was easier (than anything I'll ever do) / Always on my mind
CD 4840412
Columbia / May '96 / Sony

BEST OF WILLIE NELSON, THE
CD 74321378402
RCA / Jul '96 / BMG

BEST OF WILLIE NELSON, THE (Funny How Time Slips Away)
Fire and rain / Me and Paul / Crazy arms / Night life / Funny how time slips away / Hello walls / If you can touch her at all / Yesterday's wine / Help me make it through the night / Good times / Mountain dew / You ought to hear me cry / One in a row / She's not for you / San Antonio rose / Once more with feeling / I'm a memory / Pretty paper / Sweet memories / Little things / Laying my burdens down / Party's over
CD 74321487272
Camden / May '97 / BMG

CLASSIC AND UNRELEASED COLLECTION, A
CD 8122714622
WEA / Jan '96 / Warner Music

COLLECTION, THE
On the road again / To all the girls I've loved before: *Nelson, Willie & Julio Iglesias* / Whiter shade of pale / They all went to Mexico: *Nelson, Willie & Carlos Santana* / Golden earrings / Always on my mind / City of New Orleans / Seven Spanish angels: *Nelson, Willie & Ray Charles* / Georgia on my mind / Highwayman / Over the rainbow / Let it be me
CD 4609302
CBS / Mar '88 / Sony

COLLECTION, THE
CD COL 026
Collection / Oct '95 / Target/BMG

COUNTRY LOVE SONGS
Home is where you're happy / I let my mind wonder / I can't find the time / You'll always have someone / December days / Suffering in silence / I feel sorry for him / Blame it on the time / I just don't understand / Shelter of my arms / Any old arms won't do / Slow down old world / I didn't sleep a wink / And so will you my love / Things to remember / One step beyond / Undo the wrong / Healing hands of time / Why are you picking on me / You wouldn't cross the street to say goodbye
CD 100342
CMC / May '97 / BMG

ESSENTIAL COLLECTION, THE
CD Set LECD 617
Wisepack / Apr '95 / Conifer/BMG / THE

ESSENTIAL WILLIE NELSON, THE
Me and Paul / Yesterday's wine / December day / Bloody Mary morning / Healing hands of time / Darkness on the face of the earth / Funny how time slips away / Family bible / My own peculiar way / Mr. Record Man / I gotta get drunk / Hello walls / Sweet memories / Night life / Waltz across Texas / Party's over / Some other world / Goin' home / Once more with feeling / Phrases, stages, circles, cycles and scenes
CD 74321665902
RCA / Feb '96 / BMG

FACE OF A FIGHTER
CD MU 5067
Musketeer / Oct '92 / Disc

FACE OF A FIGHTER
And so will you my love / Will you remember mine / Home is where you're happy / I hope so / Some other time / Is there something on your mind / Broken promises / Waiting time / Face of a fighter / No tomorrow in sight / Everything but you / Shelter of your arms / Happiness lives next door / End of understanding / Go away / Blame it on the times / Right from wrong / I'll stay around
CD 300042
Hallmark / Jul '96 / Carlton

GOLD
CD GOLD 032
Gold / Aug '96 / Else

GREATEST HITS
Railroad lady / Heartaches of a fool / Blue eyes cryin' in the rain / Whiskey river / Goodhearted woman / Georgia on my mind / If you've got the money, I've got the time / Look what thoughts will do / Uncloudy day / Mamas don't let your babies grow up to be cowboys / My heroes have always been cowboys / Help me make it through the night / Angel flying too close to the ground / I'd have to be crazy / Faded love / On the road again / Heartbreak hotel / If you could touch her at all / Till I gain control again / Stay a little longer
CD 4714122
Columbia / '92 / Sony

HEALING HANDS OF TIME
Funny how time slips away / Crazy / Night life / Healing hands of time / (How will I know) I'm falling in love again / All the things you are / Oh what is seemed to be / If I had my way / I'll be seeing you / There are worse things that being alone
CD CDEMC 3695
EMI / Oct '94 / EMI

HEARTACHES
CD CDSGP 052
Prestige / Apr '93 / Else / Total/BMG

HOW GREAT THOU ART
CD FA 9605CD
Fine Arts / Aug '96 / ADA

IS THERE SOMETHING ON YOUR MIND
Ghost / Let's pretend / I'm gonna lose a lot of teardrops / Wastin' time / Go away / No tomorrow in sight / New way to cry / Broken promises / I let my mind wander / December days / I can't find the time / I didn't sleep a wink / You wouldn't cross the street to say goodbye / Suffering in silence / I feel sorry for him / You'll always have someone / I just don't understand / Building heartaches / Pages / Is there something on your mind / Face of a fighter / I hope so / Everything but you / Moment isn't very long / Some other time / Shelter of my arms / Blame it on the times / End of an understanding / One step beyond
CD GRF 032
Tring / Feb '93 / Tring

LEGEND BEGINS, THE
Some other time / I hope so / Will you remember mine / Is there something on your mind / Everything but you / Moment isn't very long / Blame it on the times / Face of a fighter / Shelter of my arms / End of understanding
CD CDMF 086
Magnum Force / Nov '92 / TKO Magnum

NIGHTLIFE
CD 15485
Laserlight / May '94 / Target/BMG

OLD TIME RELIGION (Nelson, Willie & Bobby Nelson)
CD 12114
Laserlight / May '93 / Target/BMG

ONE STEP BEYOND
I let my mind wander / December days / I can't find the time / I didn't sleep a wink / You wouldn't cross the street to say goodbye / Suffering in silence / I feel sorry for him / You'll always have someone / I just don't understand / Pages / Any old arms won't do / Slow down old world / Healing hands of time / And so will you my love / Things to remember / One step beyond / Undo the wrong / Home is where you're happy / Why are you picking on me / I hope so
CD CDSGP 096
Prestige / Jun '94 / Else / Total/BMG

ORIGINAL OUTLAWS (Nelson, Willie & Waylon Jennings)
Crying / Ghost / Sally was a good old girl / Let's pretend / Abilene / I'm gonna lose a lot of teardrops / It's so easy / Waiting time / Love's gonna live here / Go away / Don't think twice / No tomorrow in sight / Dream baby / New way to cry / Lorena / Broken promises / Burning memories / Let my mind wander / White lightning / Moment isn't very long / Big mamou / I can't find the time / Money / I feel sorry for him
CD QED 116
Tring / Nov '96 / Tring

OUTLAW REUNION (Nelson, Willie & Waylon Jennings)
Some other time: *Nelson, Willie* / Is there something on your mind: *Nelson, Willie* / Broken promises: *Nelson, Willie* / End of our understanding: *Nelson, Willie* / Home is where you're happy: *Nelson, Willie* / Waiting time: *Nelson, Willie* / I'll stay around: *Nelson, Willie* / Happiness lives next door: *Nelson, Willie* / Sally was a good old girl: *Jennings, Waylon* / White lightning: *Jennings, Waylon* / Love's gonna live here: *Jennings, Waylon* / Burning memories: *Jennings, Waylon* / Don't think twice: *Jennings, Waylon* / Lorena: *Jennings, Waylon* / Dream baby: *Jennings, Waylon* / It's so easy: *Jennings, Waylon*
CD ECD 3344
K-Tel / May '97 / K-Tel

PEACE IN THE VALLEY (Nelson, Willie & Willie Nelson Jr.)
CD PLMCD 052158
Promised Land / Nov '94 / Direct / Kingdom

REVOLUTIONS OF TIME - THE JOURNEY 1975-1993 (3CD Set)
Time of the preacher / Blue eys crying in the rain / If you've got the money I've got the time / Uncloudy day / Always late with your kisses / Georgia on my mind / Blue skies / Whiskey river / Stay a little longer / Mr. Record Man / Loving her was easier / Mammas don't let you babies grow up to be cowboys / It's not supposed to be that way / On the road again / Angel flying too close to the ground / Mona Lisa always on my mind / Last thing I needed the first thing this morning / Party's over / Summertime: *Nelson, Willie & Leon Russell* / Faded love: *Nelson, Willie & Ray Price* / Pancho and lefty: *Nelson, Willie & Merle Haggard* / Old friends: *Nelson, Willie & Roger Miller/Ray Price* / In the jailhouse again: *Nelson, Willie & Webb Pierce* / Everything's beautiful (in it's own way): *Nelson, Willie & Dolly Parton* / Take it to the limit: *Nelson, Willie & Waylon Jennings* / To all the girls I loved before: *Nelson, Willie & Julio Iglesias* / How do you feel about foolin' around: *Nelson, Willie & Kris Kristofferson* / Seven Spanish angels: *Nelson, Willie & Ray Charles* / Hello walls: *Nelson, Willie & Faron Young* / I'm movin' on: *Nelson, Willie & Hank Snow* / Highwayman: *Nelson, Willie & J. Cash/W. Jennings/K. Kristofferson* / Slow movin' outlaw: *Nelson, Willie & Lacy J Dalton* / Are there any more real cowboys: *Nelson, Willie & Neil Young* / They all went to Mexico: *Nelson, Willie & Carlos Santana* / Half a man: *Nelson, Willie & George Jones* / Texas on a Saturday night: *Nelson, Willie & Mel Tillis* / Heartland: *Nelson, Willie & Bob Dylan* / Nobody slides my friend / Little old fashioned karma / Harbour lights / Without a song / Good time Charlie's got the blues / City of New Orleans / Who'll buy my memories / Write your own songs / Forgiving you was easy / Me and Paul / When I dream / My own peculiar way / Living in the promiseland / There is no easy way (but there is a way) / Buttermilk sky / Horse called music / Nothing I can do about it now / Is the better part over / Ain't necessarily so / Still is still moving to me
CD Set C3K 64796
Columbia / Nov '95 / Sony

SHOTGUN WILLIE
Shotgun Willie / Whiskey river / Sad songs and waltzes / Local memory / Slow down old world / Stay all night (stay a little longer) / Devil in a sleepin' bag / She's not for you / Bubbles in my beer / You look like the devil / So much to do / Song for you
CD 7567814262
WEA / Mar '93 / Warner Music

SIX HOURS AT PEDERNALES
Nothings changed / Chase the moon / Are you sure / Party's over / We're not talking anymore / Turn me loose / Once your past the blues / It won't be easy / Stray cats, cowboys and girls of the night / Best worst thing / It should be easier now / My own peculiar way
CD SORCD 0084
D-Sharp / Oct '94 / Pinnacle

SPIRIT
CD 5342422
This Way Up / May '96 / PolyGram / SRD

SPOTLIGHT ON WILLIE NELSON
I just don't understand / I didn't sleep a wink / Blame it on the times / I let my mind wander / Shelter of my arms / And so will you my love / Home is where you're happy / I feel sorry for him / Slow down old world / Why are you picking on me / Any old arms won't do / Broken promises / I can't find the time / Things to remember / You always have someone / One step beyond
CD HADCD 132
Javelin / Feb '94 / Henry Hadaway / THE

STARDUST
Stardust / Georgia on my mind / Blue skies / All of me / Unchained melody / September song / On the sunny side of the street / Moonlight in Vermont / Don't get around much anymore / Someone to watch over me
CD CK 57206
Mastersound / Nov '95 / Sony

THINGS TO REMEMBER
CD CTS 55401
Country Stars / Jan '92 / Target/BMG

VERY BEST OF WILLIE NELSON, THE
Country Willie / Night life / There'll be no teardrops tonight / Funny how time slips away / Hello walls / Crazy / Touch me / Wake me when it's over / Seasons of my heart / Columbus Stockade blues / San Antonio blues / Heartaches by the number / Wabash cannonball / Family bible / Goodhearted woman / Home in San Antone / Have I told you lately that I love you / Help me make it through the night / I love you because / Mr. Record man
CD CDMFP 6110
Music For Pleasure / Dec '93 / EMI

WILLIE NELSON
CD 295047
Ariola / Oct '94 / BMG

WILLIE NELSON
Let's pretend / I'm gonna lose a lot of teardrops / Go away / No tomorrow in sight / New way to cry / Broken promises / I let my mind wander / I can't find the time / I didn't sleep a wink / Building heartaches / Pages / Is there something on your mind / Face of a fighter / I hope so / Everything but you / Moment isn't very long / Some other time / Blame it on the times / End of understanding / One step beyond
CD QED 068
Tring / Nov '96 / Tring

WILLIE NELSON COLLECTION, THE
Shelter of my arms / Face of a fighter / Things to remember / Moment isn't very long / Blame it on the times / Building heartaches / Undo the right / Will you remember mine / Any old arms won't do / Slow down old world / And so will you my love / Why are you picking on me / I hope so / Everything but you / Healing hands of time / No tomorrow in sight / One step beyond / Go away
CD ECD 3073
K-Tel / Jan '95 / K-Tel

WILLIE NELSON VOL.1
CD DS 008
Desperado / Jun '97 / TKO Magnum

WILLIE NELSON VOL.2
CD DS 009
Desperado / Jun '97 / TKO Magnum

Nembrionic Hammerdeath

NEMBRIONIC HAMMERDEATH/ CONSOLATION SPLIT ALBUM (Nembrionic Hammerdeath & Consolation)
CD D 00027
Displeased / Mar '94 / Plastic Head / RTM/Disc

Nemesis

PEOPLE WANT BASS
CD FILECD 461
Profile / May '95 / Pinnacle

TEMPLE OF BOOM
Temple of boom / Nemesis on the premises / Deep up on it / Cantfiguritout / Big, the bad, the bass / Get ya flow on / Str8jackin' / Hard from birth / Parkin' lot on Dixon / Go Ron C / Brand new team / Cloud 7
CD FILECD 441
Profile / Jun '93 / Pinnacle

Nemeth, Yoska

GYPSY KINGS (Nemeth, Yoska & Paul Toscano)
Les deus guitares / Je vous al aimee / Cocher vite chez yar / Czardas / Le chant de l'alouette / Fascination / Le temps de cerises / Suite hongroise / Cocher, ralentis tes chevaux / Romance et czardas hongroises / Airs populaires roumains / Confidences de roses rouges / Joue jusqu'au matin / Beltz scha stil / Reviens / Souika hora / Petites clochettes monotones / L'ame des violons / Romance et danse caucasiennes
CD 300062
Musidisc / Aug '90 / Discovery

Nemirovski, Bielka

DE LA MER BLANCE A LA MER NOIRE
CD 8558392
Origins / Jul '97 / Discovery

Neolithic

PERSONAL FRAGMENT
CD CDAR 028
Adipocre / Jun '95 / Plastic Head

Neon Hearts

BALL AND CHAIN
CD OVER 64CD
Overground / Jul '97 / Shellshock/Disc / SRD

Neon Judgement

ALASKA HIGHWAY
CD BIAS 167 CD
Play It Again Sam / Jun '90 / Discovery / Plastic Head / Vital

FIRST JUDGEMENTS
CD CDBIAS 070
Play It Again Sam / Sep '87 / Discovery / Plastic Head / Vital

Neotropic

15 LEVELS OF MAGNIFICATION
NW37th / Laundry pt.3 / La centinela / Laundry pt.1 / 15 levels of magnification / Weeds / Nana / Nincompoop / Electric bud / CCTV / Neotropic / Beautiful pool / Regents park / Your turn to wash up / Aloo gobi / Frozen hands
CD NTONECD 017
Ntone / Sep '96 / Kudos / Vital

Neptune Towers

CARAVANS TO EMPIRE ALGOL
CD _____ FOG 002
Moonfog / Dec '94 / Plastic Head

TRANSMISSIONS FROM EMPIRE ALGOL
CD _____ FOG 008CD
Moonfog / Nov '96 / Plastic Head

Neptune, John Kaizan

TOKYOSPHERE
CD _____ JD 3316
JVC / May '89 / Direct / New Note/ Pinnacle / Vital/SAM

Nerell, Loren

LILEN DEWA
CD _____ DFX 026CD
Side Effects / May '97 / Plastic Head / World Serpent

Nerem, Bjarne

BJARNE NAREM & AL GREY
CD _____ GMCD 162
Gemini / Oct '88 / Cadillac

EVERYTHING HAPPENS TO ME
CD _____ GMCD 71
Gemini / Jan '89 / Cadillac

HOW LONG HAS THIS BEEN GOING ON
CD _____ GMCD 72
Gemini / Jan '90 / Cadillac

MOOD INDIGO
CD _____ GMCD 159
Gemini / Jan '90 / Cadillac

MORE THAN YOU KNOW
When your lover has gone / Everything I have is yours / Easy to love / Autumn nocturne / Miss Mopay / More than you know / Gone with the wind / Cabin in the sky / Emaline
CD _____ GMCD 156
Gemini / Jan '88 / Cadillac

THIS IS ALWAYS
CD _____ GMCD 147
Gemini / Mar '89 / Cadillac

Nerf Herder

NERF HERDER
CD _____ MY 8052CD
My Records / Sep '96 / Plastic Head
CD _____ 07822189542
Rhythm King / Jul '97 / 3mv/Pinnacle / BMG

Nergal

WIZARD OF NERATH, THE
CD _____ USR 016CD
Unisound / Jan '96 / Plastic Head

Nerious Joseph

GUIDANCE
CD _____ FADCD 023
Fashion / Nov '92 / Jet Star / SRD

REJOICE
CD _____ CRCD 64
Charm / Mar '97 / Jet Star

Nerney, Declan

PART OF THE JOURNEY
Part of the journey / With this ring / In your arms / I really don't want to know / Anna from Fernangh / You in the morning / Lovely Derry on the banks of the Foyle / Honky tonk girl / Blue side of lonesome / Born to hang / Half as much / Cottage on the borderline / Tonight we just might fall in love again / Love me
CD _____ RCD 549
Ritz / Jul '95 / Pinnacle

WALKIN' ON NEW GRASS
Walkin' on new grass / Among the Wicklow hills / I found my girl in the USA / Give an Irish girl to me / North to Alaska / Just call me lonesome from now on / Stand at your window / Crazy dreams / Tipperary on my mind / Never again will I knock on your door / I still miss someone / I'd rather love and lose you / World of our own / Molly Bawn
CD _____ RITZRCD 526
Ritz / Apr '93 / Pinnacle

Nero Circus

HUMAN PIGS
CD _____ GOD 018CD
Godhead / Jul '95 / Plastic Head

Nero's Acolytes

ALBATROCITY
Blonde in black / Low point x / If if if / Cloning by numbers / Venus in furs / Nightmare trip III / Sex kills II / Fetch a gaoler / High flyer no safety net / Monster mash / Inner space / Join the system / Insatiable / Blinded by delight / Triggerman / My roots are wheels / Kiss of death / Remember me this way
CD _____ EXIT 001CD
Exoteric / May '97 / Else

Nerve

CANCER OF CHOICE
Coins / Fragments / Oil / Rage / Closedown / Water / Seed / Dedalus / Trust / Waters / Thirties
CD _____ BIAS 261CD
Play It Again Sam / Oct '93 / Discovery / Plastic Head / Vital

Nervous

SON OF THE GREAT OUTDOORS
CD _____ GRACD 214
Grapevine / Aug '96 / Grapevine/PolyGram

Nervous Fellas

BORN TO BE WILD
CD _____ NERCD 055
Nervous / '90 / Nervous / TKO Magnum

Nervous Project

BACK TO BASICS
CD _____ DBMLABCD 8
Labworks / Mar '96 / RTM/Disc / SRD

Nesby, Ann

I'M HERE FOR YOU
Let the rain fall / I'm still wearing your name / If you love me / Invitation / (What a) Lovely evening / I'll do anything for you / String interlude / Thrill me / Hold on / In the spirit / This weekend / Can I get a witness / I'm here for you / I'll be your everything / Let old memories be / Lord how I need you
CD _____ 5490222
Perspective / May '96 / PolyGram

Nesmith, Michael

AND THE HITS JUST KEEP ON COMING (Nesmith, Michael & Countryside Band)
CD _____ AWCD 1027
Awareness / Nov '91 / ADA

INFINITE RIDER
CD _____ AWCD 1031
Awareness / Mar '92 / ADA

LOOSE SALUTE (Nesmith, Michael & The First National Band)
Silver moon / I fall to pieces / Thanx for the ride / Dedicated friend / Conversations / Tengo amore / Listen to the band / Bye bye bye / Lady of the valley / Hello lady
CD _____ AWCD 1024
Awareness / Mar '91 / ADA

MAGNETIC SOUTH (Nesmith, Michael & The First National Band)
Calico girlfriend / Nine times blue / Little red rider / Crippled lion / Joanne / First national rag / Mama Nantucket / Keys to the car / Hollywood / One rose / Beyond the blue horizon
CD _____ AWCD 1023
Awareness / Mar '91 / ADA

NEVADA FIGHTER (Nesmith, Michael & The First National Band)
Grand ennui / Propinquity (I've begun to care) / Here I am / Only bound / Nevada fighter / Texas morning / Tumbling tumbleweeds / I looked away / Rainmaker / Rene
CD _____ AWCD 1025
Awareness / Mar '91 / ADA

NEWER STUFF, THE
CD _____ AWCD 1014
Awareness / Apr '89 / ADA

OLDER STUFF, THE
CD _____ AWCD 1032
Awareness / Mar '92 / ADA

TANTAMOUNT TO TREASON
Mama Rocker / Lazy lady / You are my one / In the afternoon / Highway 99 with Melange / Wax minute / Bonaparte's retreat / Talking to the wall / She thinks I still care
CD _____ AWCD 1026
Awareness / Sep '91 / ADA

Ness, Marilla

ABBA MY FATHER
CD _____ MLM 116
One Stop / Apr '96 / Koch

Netherworld

NETHERWORLD
CD _____ HNF 025CD
Head Not Found / Mar '97 / Plastic Head

Neto, Jose

IN MEMORY OF THUNDER
For the gypsies / Leave a fax or send a message / Silvia / Moonlight with strings / Savannah / Airbourne / Deer park / Redemption song / In memory of thunder
CD _____ BW 056
B&W / Nov '96 / New Note/Pinnacle / SRD / Vital/SAM

Networks 3

INTELLIGENT COMPILATION, AN
CD _____ K7 047CD
Studio K7 / Sep '96 / Prime / RTM/Disc

Netzer, Effi

HAVA NAGILA
CD _____ EUCD 1052
ARC / '89 / ADA / ARC Music

Neu

LA NEU DUSSELDORF
CD _____ CTCD 051
Captain Trip / Jun '97 / Greyhound

NEUK

STATE OF MIND
CD _____ BRC 101CD
Black Mail / Jul '95 / Plastic Head

Neumann, Alberto

PERPETUAL TANGO VOL.1
CD _____ 926302
BUDA / Feb '96 / Discovery

PERPETUAL TANGO VOL.2
CD _____ 926512
BUDA / Jul '96 / Discovery

Neural Network

KINESTHETICS
CD _____ BIOCD 06
Messerschmitt / Jun '94 / Plastic Head

Neuro

ELECTRIC MOTHERS OF INVENTION
CD _____ 3BTTCD 2
3 Beat / Nov '93 / PolyGram

Neuronium

ABSENCE OF REALITY
CD _____ TUXCD 5016
Tuxedo / May '95 / TKO Magnum

CHROMIUM ECHOES
Prelude / Chromium echoes / Neutron age
CD _____ CDTB 057
Thunderbolt / Jul '89 / TKO Magnum

FROM MADRID TO HEAVEN
Intro / Part 1 / Part 2 / Part 3 / Part 4
CD _____ CDTB 2064
Thunderbolt / '89 / TKO Magnum

HERITAGE
CD _____ TUXCD 5009
Tuxedo / May '95 / TKO Magnum

INVISIBLE VIEWS
CD _____ TUXCD 5017
Tuxedo / May '95 / TKO Magnum

NEW DIGITAL DREAM
CD _____ TUXCD 5013
Tuxedo / May '95 / TKO Magnum

NUMERICA
500 years / Deep illness of love / Promenade / Power of your smile / Numerica / Maze extreme limits / Au revoir
CD _____ CDTB 082
Thunderbolt / Apr '90 / TKO Magnum

OLIM
CD _____ TUXCD 5018
Tuxedo / May '95 / TKO Magnum

SUPRANATURAL
When the goblins invade Madrid / Digitron / Priorite absolue / Europe is Europe / Sundown at Tanah Lot
CD _____ CDTB 055
Thunderbolt / Mar '88 / TKO Magnum

Neuropolitique

BEYOND THE PINCH
CD _____ ELEC 33CD
New Electronica / Jun '97 / Beechwood/ BMG / Plastic Head

MENAGE A TROIS
CD _____ IRDMAT 004CD
Irdia / May '94 / Vital

NOMENCLATURE (2CD Set)
Factory junction / Can't get off the slide / Mind you don't slip / Gene pools / No feet on stage / Remote phrases / Artemis / In the mix / Menage a trois / 1494 backslash 48207 / Large spoon / Mind mirror / Idiotic lantern / Neu arena / Express triangle / Fusion neu / Report / Ad nauseum / 1492 backslash 48207 / Box / Faze / Wide / 365 Fellatio / Animated data
CD Set _____ ELEC 29CD
New Electronica / Jun '96 / Beechwood/ BMG / Plastic Head

Neurosis

THROUGH SILVER IN BLOOD
CD _____ ICR 002CD
Iron City / Jun '96 / Plastic Head

Neurotic Outsiders

NEUROTIC OUTSIDERS
CD _____ 0630155362
Maverick / Aug '96 / Warner Music

Neutral Milk Hotel

ON AVERY ISLAND
CD _____ FIRECD 53
Fire / Sep '96 / Pinnacle / RTM/Disc

Neutron 9000

LADY BURNING SKY
CD _____ RSNCD 233
Rising High / Sep '94 / 3mv/Sony

WALRUS
CD _____ FILERCD 407
Profile / May '91 / Pinnacle

Neuwirth, Bob

LOOK UP
CD _____ WM 1050CD
Watermelon / Aug '96 / ADA / Direct

Nevada Beach

ZERO DAY
CD _____ CDZORRO 13
Metal Blade / Sep '90 / Pinnacle / Plastic Head

Neven

TWIN CYCLES
CD _____ LOW 007
Lowlands / Jul '96 / Greyhound / ReR Megacorp / SRD

Neverland

SURREAL WORLD
CD _____ ESM 007
Escape / Nov '96 / Cargo

Nevermore

IN MEMORY
CD _____ CM 77121CD
Century Media / Jul '96 / Plastic Head

NEVERMORE
CD _____ CM 77091CD
Century Media / Apr '95 / Plastic Head

POLITICS OF ECSTACY, THE
CD _____ CM 77132CD
Century Media / Nov '96 / Plastic Head

Nevil, Robbie

C'EST LA VIE
Just a little closer / Dominoes / Limousines / Back to you / C'est la vie / Wot's it to ya / Walk your talk / Simple life / Neighbours / Look who's alone tonight
CD _____ NSPCD 513
Connoisseur Collection / Apr '95 / Pinnacle

Neville Brothers

BROTHERS KEEPER
Brother blood / Steer me right / Sons and daughters / Jah love / Witness / Sons and daughters (reprise) / Bird on the wire / Brother Jake / Fearless / Fallin' rain / River of life / My brother's keeper / Mystery train
CD _____ 3953122
A&M / Aug '90 / PolyGram

FAMILY AFFAIR, A (A History Of The Neville Brothers/2CD Set)
Over you: *Neville, Aaron* / Funky miracle: *Meters* / Little girl from the candy store: *Neville, Art* / Show me the way: *Neville, Aaron* / Sophisticated cissy: *Meters* / I'm waiting at the station: *Neville, Aaron* / My baby don't love me anymore: *Neville, Art* / 6V6 love: *Meters* / Ride your pony: *Meters* / Wrong number: *Neville, Aaron* / Cardova: *Meters* / I need some Art: *Neville, Art* / How could I help but love you: *Neville, Aaron* / Cissy strut: *Meters* / Humdinger: *Neville, Aaron* / That rock 'n' roll beat: *Neville, Art* / Chicken strut: *Meters* / Don't cry: *Neville, Aaron* / All these things: *Neville, Art* / Britches: *Meters* / Even though (reality): *Neville, Aaron* / Get out of my life: *Neville, Aaron* / Darling don't leave me this way: *Neville, Art* / Live wire: *Meters* / House on the hill (rock 'n' roll hootenanny): *Neville, Art* / Dry spell: *Meters* / Humdinger: *Neville, Art* / Tippi-toes: *Meters* / Hook, line and sinker: *Neville, Art* / For everybody there's a girl: *Neville, Aaron* / Art: *Meters* / Same old thing: *Meters* / You won't do right: *Neville, Art* / Everyday: *Neville, Aaron* / Sweet little mama: *Neville, Aaron* / Pains in my heart: *Neville, Art* / Joog: *Meters* / Tell it like it is: *Neville, Aaron* / Hercules: *Neville, Aaron* / I'm gonna put some hurt on you: *Neville, Art* / Make me strong: *Neville, Aaron* / Kook-ka py py: *Meters* / All those things: *Neville, Aaron* / Ease back: *Meters* / Bo Diddley: *Neville, Art* / Heartaches: *Neville, Aaron* / Been so wrong: *Neville, Aaron* / Message from the Meters: *Meters* / Going home: *Neville, Aaron* / Dance your blues away: *Neville, Charles*
CD Set _____ CPCD 82482
Charly / Nov '96 / Koch

FAMILY GROOVE
Fly like an eagle / One more day / I can see it in your eyes / Day to day thing / Line of fire / Take me to heart / It takes more / Family groove / True love / On the other side of paradise / Let my people go / Saxafunk / Maori chant / Good song

CD 3971802
A&M / Apr '92 / PolyGram

FIYO ON THE BAYOU
Hey pocky away / Sweet honey dripper / Fire on the Bayou / Ten commandments / Sitting in limbo / Brother John / Iko iko / Mona lisa / Run Joe
CD CDMID 187
A&M / Jan '94 / PolyGram

LEGACY (A History Of The Nevilles/2CD Set)
Mardi Gras mambo: *Hawketts* / Over you: *Neville, Aaron* / Funky miracle: *Meters* / Little girl from the candy store: *Neville, Art* / Show me the way: *Neville, Aaron* / Sophisticated Cissy: *Meters* / I'm waiting at the station: *Neville, Aaron* / My baby don't love me anymore: *Neville, Art* / 6v6 LA: *Meters* / Ride your pony: *Meters* / Wrong number: *Neville, Aaron* / Cardova: *Meters* / I need someone: *Neville, Art* / How could I help but love you: *Neville, Aaron* / Cissy strut: *Meters* / Humdinger: *Neville, Aaron* / That rock'n'roll beat: *Neville, Art* / Chicken strut: *Meters* / Don't cry: *Neville, Aaron* / All these things: *Neville, Art* / Britches: *Meters* / Even though (reality): *Neville, Aaron* / Get out of my life: *Neville, Aaron* / Darling don't leave me this way: *Neville, Art* / Live wire: *Meters* / House on the hill (rock 'n' roll hootenanny): *Neville, Art* / Tippi toes: *Meters* / Hook, line and sinker: *Neville, Art* / For every boy there's a girl: *Neville, Aaron* / Art: *Meters* / Same old thing: *Meters* / You won't do right: *Neville, Art* / Everyday: *Neville, Aaron* / Sweet little mama: *Neville, Aaron* / Pains in my heart: *Neville, Art* / Joog: *Meters* / Tell it like it is: *Neville, Aaron* / Hercules: *Neville, Aaron* / I'm gonna put some hurt on you: *Neville, Art* / Make me strong: *Neville, Aaron* / Look ka py py: *Meters* / Ease back: *Meters* / Bo Diddley: *Neville, Art* / Speak to me: *Neville, Aaron* / Cry me a river: *Neville, Aaron* / Heartaches: *Neville, Art* / Been so wrong: *Neville, Aaron* / Message from the Meters: *Meters* / Going home: *Neville, Aaron*
CD Set CDNEV 1
Charly / Apr '90 / Koch

LIVE AT TIPITINA'S VOL.2
Wishin' / Rock 'n' roll medley / All over again / Everybody's got to wake up / Dance your blues away / Little Liza Jane / Wildflower / My girl / Riverside / Saib's groove / Pocky way / Doo wop medley / Rockin' pneumonia and the boogie woogie flu / Something you got / I know / Everybody loves a lover
CD CLACD 347
Castle / Jun '94 / BMG

LIVE ON PLANET EARTH
Shake your tambourine / Voodoo / Dealer / Junk man / Brother Jake / Sister Rosa / Yellow moon / Her African eyes / Sands of time / Congo Square / Love the one you're with/ You can't always get what you want / Let my people go/Get up stand up / Amazing Grace / One love/People get ready/Sermon
CD 5402252
A&M / Apr '95 / PolyGram

MITAKUYE OYASIN OYASIN
Love spoken here / Sound / Holy spirit / Soul to soul / Whatever you do / Saved by the grace of your love / You're gonna make your Momma cry / Fire on the mountain / Ain't no sunshine / Orisha dance / Sacred ground
CD 5405212
A&M / May '96 / PolyGram

NEVILLE-IZATION
Fever / Woman's gotta have it / Mojo Hannah / Tell it like it is / Why you wanna hurt my heart / Fear, hate, envy, jealousy / Caravan / Big chief / Africa
CD FIENDCD 31
Demon / Nov '86 / Pinnacle

TELL IT LIKE IT IS
Tell it like it is: *Neville, Aaron* / Over you: *Neville, Aaron* / That rock 'n' roll beat: *Neville, Art* / For every boy there's a girl: *Neville, Aaron* / I'm waiting at the station: *Neville, Aaron* / House on the hill (rock 'n' roll hootenanny): *Neville, Art* / How many times: *Neville, Aaron* / How could I help but love you: *Neville, Aaron* / All these things: *Neville, Art* / Cry me a river: *Neville, Aaron* / Speak to me: *Neville, Aaron* / Hook, line and sinker: *Neville, Art* / Mardi Gras mambo: *Hawketts* / Cardova: *Meters* / Funky miracle: *Meters* / Ride your pony: *Meters* / Struttin' on Sunday: *Neville, Aaron* / Make me strong: *Neville, Aaron* / Heartaches: *Neville, Art* / Show me the way: *Neville, Aaron* / Wrong number: *Neville, Aaron* / You won't do right: *Neville, Art* / Get out of my life: *Neville, Aaron* / Hercules: *Neville, Aaron*
CD MCCD 022
Music Club / May '91 / Disc / THE

UPTOWN
Whatever it takes / Forever...for tonight / You're the one / Money back guarantee (my love is guaranteed) / Drift away / Shek-a-na-na / Old habits die hard / I never need no one / Midnight key / Spirits of the world
CD CDGOLD 1028
EMI Gold / May '96 / EMI

WITH GOD ON OUR SIDE (2CD Set)
Ten commandments of love / I owe you one / Change is gonna come / Bells / Will the circle be unbroken / Sitting in limbo / Yellow moon / Fearless / Brother Jake / Love the one you're with/You can't always get what you want / Bird on a wire / Fallin' rain / Louisiana 1927 / Mona Lisa / Ave Maria / That's the way she loves / Song of Bernadette / Close your eyes / Ain't no way / Feels like rain / Don't go, please stay / Don't fall apart on me tonight / Betcha by golly, wow / My brother, my brother / La vie dansante / True love / On the other side of paradise / Let my people go/Get up stand up / Take me to heart / With you in mind / One more day / Amazing grace / O holy night / Lord's prayer / With god on our side
CD Set 5406912
A&M / Jun '97 / PolyGram

YELLOW MOON
My blood / Yellow moon / Fire and brimstone / Change is gonna come / Sister Rosa / With God on our side / Wake up / Voodoo / Ballad of Hollis Brown / Will the circle be unbroken / Healing chant / Wild injuns
CD 3952402
A&M / Apr '95 / PolyGram

Neville, Aaron

AARON NEVILLE'S SOULFUL CHRISTMAS
CD 5401272
A&M / Nov '93 / PolyGram

GRAND TOUR
CD 5401002
A&M / Jan '94 / PolyGram

HERCULES
Over you / Show me the way / How could I help but love you / Get out of my life / Wrong number / I'm waiting at the station / I found another love / How many times / Hey little Alice / Let's live / Tell it like it is / Struttin' on Sunday / Make me strong / Hercules / Been so wrong / Cry me a river / Greatest love / One fine day / All these things / Performance
CD CPCD 8016
Charly / Feb '94 / Koch

MAKE ME STRONG
Struttin' on Sunday / Hercules / Make me strong / All these things / Baby I'm a want you / Performance / Mojo Hannah / Greatest love / One fine day / Tell it like it is / Cry me a river / Been so wrong / Speak to me / Wild flower / Feelings / Nadie / For the good times / She's on my mind
CD CPCD 8213
Charly / Jun '96 / Koch

ORCHIDS IN THE STORM
CD 8122709562
Rhino / May '95 / Warner Music

SHOW ME THE WAY
How could I help but love you / Over you / Even though (reality) / Humdinger / Show me the way / I found another love / How many times / Everyday / Hey little Alice / Sweet little mama / Don't cry / Ticks of the clock / For every boy there's a girl / I'm waiting at the station / Wrong number / I've done it again / Let's live / Get out of my life
CD CDCHARLY 162
Charly / Aug '89 / Koch

TATTOOED HEART
Can't stop my heart from loving you (The rain song) / Show some emotion / Everyday of my life / Down into muddy water / Some days are made for rain / Try (a little harder) / Beautiful night / My precious star / Why should I fall in love / Use me / For the good times / In your eyes / Little thing called life / Crying in the chapel
CD 5403492
A&M / May '95 / PolyGram

WARM YOUR HEART
Louisiana 1927 / Everybody plays the fool / It feels like rain / Somewhere, somebody / Don't go please stay / With you in mind / That's the ways she loves / Angola bound / Close your eyes / La vie dansante / Warm your heart / I bid you goodnight / Ave Maria / House on a hill
CD 3971482
A&M / Jul '91 / PolyGram

Neville, Art

HIS SPECIALTY RECORDINGS 1956-58
Please believe me / Standing on the highway / Please don't go / When my baby went away / Please listen to my song / Lover's song / Oooh-baby / Whiffenpoof song / Oooh-wee baby / Let's rock / Back home to me / Zing zing / Cha dooky-doo / That old time Rock 'N' Roll / Arabian love call / Rockin' pneumonia and the boogie woogie flu / What's going on / Belle amie / Dummy / I'm a fool to care
CD CDCHD 434
Ace / Jan '93 / Pinnacle

KEYS TO THE CRESCENT (Neville, Art & Eddie Bo/Charles Brown/Willie Tee)
CD ROUCD 2087
Rounder / Sep '91 / ADA / CM / Direct

MARDI GRAS ROCK 'N' ROLL
Zing zing / Oooh-wee baby / Bella Mae / I'm a fool to care / Cha dooky-doo / Back home to me / What's going on / Old time rock 'n' roll / Rockin' pneumonia and the boogie woogie flu / Bring it on home to me / Dummy / Let's rock / Arabian love call / Please listen to my song / Whiffenpoof song
CD CDCHD 188
Ace / Oct '90 / Pinnacle

Neville, Charles

CHARLES NEVILLE & DIVERSITY (Neville, Charles & Diversity)
Diverse / Summertime / Woman's place / Baluba / Ladies / Samba de orpheus / God bless the child / Jamaica John / Nyomba / Moose the mooche / Jitterbug waltz / Jiminy Syndicate
CD 17045
Laserlight / Jul '96 / Target/BMG

Neville, Charmaine

IT'S ABOUT TIME
Playing on the front porch / Rocket V / Barbecue Bess / Two to mars / Dance / Softly as in a morning sunrise / Staurday night fish fry / Don't stop the carvival / Right key but the wrong keyhole
CD ME 000392
Soulciety/Bassism / Oct '95 / EWM

Neville, Cyril

FIRE THIS TIME, THE (Neville, Cyril & The Uptown Allstars)
CD CD 08544112
SPV / Jul '96 / Koch / Plastic Head

Neville, Ivan

IF MY ANCESTORS COULD SEE ME NOW
CD CD 08544102
SPV / Jul '96 / Koch / Plastic Head

THANKS
CD CD 08544092
SPV / Jul '96 / Koch / Plastic Head

New & Used

2ND
CD KFWCD 163
Knitting Factory / Feb '95 / Cargo / Plastic Head

NEW AND USED
CD KFWCD 125
Knitting Factory / Nov '92 / Cargo / Plastic Head

New Age Radio

SURVIVAL SHOW
CD MANCD 1999
Mandala / Nov '95 / Total/Pinnacle

New Age Steppers

MASSIVE HITS VOL.1
CD ONUCD 10
On-U Sound / May '94 / Jet Star / SRD

New Bad Things

ENNUI GO
CD POP 005
Pop Secret / Apr '97 / Cargo
CD DRL 039
Darla / May '97 / Cargo

SOCIETY
CD LISS 13CD
Lissy's / Apr '96 / SRD

New Black Eagle Jazz Band

CHRISTMAS WITH THE NEW BLACK EAGLE JAZZ BAND
Tannenbaum / Blue Christmas / Let it snow / Santa Claus is coming to town / O holy night / God rest ye merry gentlemen / All I want for Christmas is my two front teeth / Jingle bell rock / It came upon a midnight clear / Winter wonderland / White Christmas / Silent night / Jingle bells
CD DARINGCD 3025
Daring / Sep '96 / ADA / CM / Direct

New Bomb Turks

DESTROY OH BOY
CD E 11560D
Crypt / Apr '93 / Shellshock/Disc

INFORMATION HIGHWAY REVISITED
CD EFACD 115852
Crypt / Oct '94 / Shellshock/Disc

PISSING OUT THE POISON
CD EFA 115982
Crypt / Oct '95 / Shellshock/Disc

SCARED STRAIGHT
CD 64792
Epitaph / Aug '96 / Pinnacle / Plastic Head

New Bushberry Mountain ...

BUSHBERRY MOUNTAIN (New Bushberry Mountain Daredevils)
CD MM 010CD
Mountain Music / May '96 / ADA

URBAN HILLBILLY (New Bushberry Mountain Daredevils)
CD EN 1105CD
Enigma / Nov '96 / ADA

New Celeste

CELTIC CONNECTION, THE
Music for a found harmonium / I once loved a lass / Wiggly jig / When a man's in love / Don't think about me / Celtic connection suite / Julie / Fare thee well sweet Mally
CD LCOM 9036
Lismor / Oct '90 / ADA / Direct / Duncans / Lismor

IT'S A NEW DAY
Banks of Ayr / Stumblin' and stottin' / Lasher / Posie / Scottish brawl / Reconnected / It's a new day / 70 Years / Caber / Polkadotty / Davie and Jeannie / Dance of Los / Randan / Prove yourself, yourself
CD IRCD 033
Iona / Jul '96 / ADA / Direct / Duncans

New Cool Collective

SOUL JAZZ LATIN FLAVOURS NINETIES VIBE
CD AL 73087
Club 802 / Jun '97 / Direct

New Departures Quintet

NEW DEPARTURES QUINTET, THE
CD HHCD 1010
Hot House / Mar '95 / Cadillac / Harmonia Mundi / Wellard

New Dylans

AMERICAN WAY, THE
CD RHRCD 75
Red House / Jul '95 / ADA / Koch

WARREN PIECE
CD RHRCD 61
Red House / Oct '95 / ADA / Koch

New Edition

CANDY GIRL
Gimme your love / She gives me a bang / Is this the end / Pass the beat / Popcorn love / Candy girl / Ooh baby / Should have never told me / Gotta have your lovin' / Jealous girl
CD 8101442
London / Sep '96 / PolyGram

HOME AGAIN
Oh, yeah, it feels so good / Hit me off / You don't have to worry / Tighten it up / Shop around / Hear me out / Something about you / Try again / How do you like you're love served / One more day / I'm still in love with you / Thankyou / Home again
CD MCD 11480
MCA / Aug '96 / BMG

New Electric Warriors

NEW ELECTRIC WARRIORS
Running / Battle torn heroes / She's no angel / Grind and heat / Feel the power / Hard man / Firing on all eight / If I were king / Rock and roll are four letter words / Chain reaction / Holding back your love / Workin' nights / Still on the outside / Hit / Bedtime
CD CDMETAL 13
Anagram / Sep '97 / Cargo / Pinnacle

New FADS

LOVE IT ALL
These foolish things / Life is an accident / Left right / Every once in a while / Why waste your love / Monday it is / Saxophone / What I feel / PSV / Kill my instincts / Souvenir
CD BIAS 285CD
Play It Again Sam / Jan '95 / Discovery / Plastic Head / Vital

PIGEONHOLE
CD BIAS 185CD
Play It Again Sam / Nov '90 / Discovery / Plastic Head / Vital

New Grass Revival

BARREN COUNTRY
CD FF 70083
Flying Fish / Mar '97 / ADA / CM / Direct / Roots

LIVE
CD SHCD 3771
Sugar Hill / Jan '97 / ADA / CM / Direct / Koch / Roots

ON THE BOULEVARD
CD SHCD 3745
Sugar Hill / Jan '97 / ADA / CM / Direct / Koch / Roots

WHEN THE STORM IS OVER/FLY THROUGH THE COUNTRY
Skippin' in the Mississippi dew / Good woman's love / Glory / All night train / Fly through the country / This heart of mine / Dancer / When she made laughter easy / Doin' my time / These days / Four days of rain / White freightliner blues / Sail to Australia / When the storm is over / And he says

"I love you" / Vamp in the middle / Like a child in the rain / Tennessee wagoner / Colly Davis / Crooked smile
CD ______ FF 032CD
Flying Fish / Feb '97 / ADA / CM / Direct / Roots

New Idol Son

REACH
CD ______ CDVEST 38
Bulletproof / Nov '94 / Pinnacle

New Islanders

CARIBBEAN DREAMS
CD ______ CNCD 5956
Disky / Jul '93 / Disky / THE

New Jazz Wizards

GOOD STUFF
CD ______ SOSCD 1244
Stomp Off / May '93 / Jazz Music / Wellard

New Jersey Kings

PARTY TO THE BUS STOP
CD ______ JAZIDCD 033
Acid Jazz / Jul '92 / Disc

STRATOSPHERE BREAKDOWN
CD ______ JAZIDCD 123
Acid Jazz / Nov '95 / Disc

New Kingdom

HEAVY LOAD
Good times / Headhunter / Frontman / Mad mad world / Mama and Papa / Cheap thrills / Mars / Are you alive / Half seas over / Mother nature / Calico cats / Mighty maverick / Lazy smoke
CD ______ GEECD 13
Gee Street / Nov '93 / PolyGram

PARADISE DON'T COME CHEAP
Mexico or bust / Horse latitudes / Infested / Unicorns were horses / Kickin' like Bruce Lee / Shining armour / Paradise don't come cheap / Co-pilot / Big 10 1/2 / Valhalla soothsayer / Animal / Half asleep / Terror mad visionary
CD ______ GEECD 18
Gee Street / Jul '96 / PolyGram

New London Consort

MUSIC FROM THE TIME
CD ______ CKHD 007
Linn / Aug '92 / PolyGram

New London School Of ...

DEEPEST CUT (New London School Of Electronics)
CD Set ______ RSNCD 19
Rising High / Jul '94 / 3mv/Sony

New Lost City Ramblers

NEW LOST CITY RAMBLERS 1958-1962, THE
Colored aristocracy / Hopalong Peter / Don't let your deal go down / When first into this country / Sales tax on the women / Rabbit chase / Leaving home / How can a poor man stand such times and live / Franklyn D Roosevelt's back again / I truly understand you love another man / Old fish song / Battleship of Maine / No depression in heaven / Dallas rag / Bill Morgan and his gal / Fly around my pretty little Miss / Lady from Carlisle / Brown's ferry blues / My long journey home / Talking hard luck / Teetotals / Sal got a meatskin / Railroad blues / On some foggy mountain top / My sweet farm girl / Crow black chicken
CD ______ SFCD 40036
Smithsonian Folkways / '91 / ADA / Cadillac / CM / Direct / Koch

NEW LOST CITY RAMBLERS 1963-1973, THE
John Brown's dream / Riding on that train / Titanic / Don't get trouble in your mind / Cowboy waltz / Shut up in the mines of coal creek / Private John Q / Old Johnny Brooker won't do / I've always been a rambler / Automobile trip through Alabama / Who killed poor Robin / My wife died on Saturday night / Little satchel / Black bottom strut / Cat's got the measles / Dog's got the whooping cough / Dear Okie / Smoketown strut / Little girl and the dreadful snake / Fishing creek blues / '31 depression blues / Black Jack daisy / Victory rag / Little carpenter / On our turpentine farm / Parlez - nous a' boire / Valse du bamboucheur / Old Joe bone
CD ______ SFCD 440040
Smithsonian Folkways / '92 / ADA / Cadillac / CM / Direct / Koch

OLD TIME MUSIC
Introduction / Leather britches / Free little bird / My name is John Johanna / Jesse James / Bow down / Stone's rag / Gold watch and chain / Worried man blues / Little darlin' pal of mine / Wildwood flower / Sally Johnson / Little birdie / Sail away ladies / Pretty little Miss out in the garden / Lost John / Chilly winds / Wish I was a single girl again / Waterbound / Needle case / Roll on Buddy / Bowling green / San Antonio rose / Old gospel ship / Train 45 / Oh death / Weapon of prayer / Black jack Davy / This world is not my home
CD ______ VCD 77011
Vanguard / Oct '95 / ADA / Pinnacle

OUT STANDING IN THE FIELD
CD ______ SF 40040CD
Smithsonian Folkways / Aug '93 / ADA / Cadillac / CM / Direct / Koch

New Mind

FORGE
CD ______ 08543442
Westcom / Mar '97 / Koch / Pinnacle

FRACTURED
CD ______ MA 442
Machinery / Nov '93 / Koch

New Model Army

B SIDES AND ABANDONED TRACKS
Heroin / Adrenalin / Nosense / Trust / Brave new world / RIP / Brave new world II / Ten commandments / Courage / Lights go out / Prison / Curse / Ghost of your father / Modern times / Drummy B / Marry the sea / Sleepwalking / Heroin (mix)
CD ______ CDEMC 3688
EMI / Sep '94 / EMI

GHOST OF CAIN, THE
Hunt / Lights go out / Fifty first State / All of this / Poison Street / Western dream / Love songs / Heroes / Ballad / Master race
CD ______ CDFA 3237
Fame / '94 / EMI

HISTORY
No rest / Better than them / Brave new world / Fifty first state / Poison street / White coats / Stupid questions / Vagabonds / Green and grey / Get me out / Purity / Space / Far better thing / Higher wall / Adrenalin / Luurstaap
CD ______ CDP 7989542
EMI / Sep '96 / EMI

IMPURITY
Get me out / Space / Innocence / Purity / Whirlwind / Marrakesh / Lust for power / Bury the hatchet / Eleven years / Lurhstap / Before I get old / Vanity
CD ______ CDFA 3273
Fame / Oct '92 / EMI

NO REST FOR THE WICKED
Frightened / Ambition / Grandmother's footsteps / Better than them / My country / There is no greater love / No rest / Young, gifted and skint / Drag it down / Shot 18 / Attack
CD ______ CDGOLD 1019
EMI Gold / Mar '96 / EMI

RAW MELODY MEN
Whirlwind / Charge / Space / Purity / White coats / Vagabonds / Get me out / Lib Ed / Better than them / Innocence / Love songs / lurhstap / Archway towers / Smalltown England / Green and grey / World
CD ______ CDFA 3296
Fame / May '93 / EMI

SMALL TOWN ENGLAND (2CD Set)
CD Set ______ SMDCD 129
Snapper / Jul '97 / Pinnacle

THUNDER AND CONSOLATION
I love the world / Stupid questions / 225 / Inheritance / Green and grey / Ballad of Bodmin Pill / Family life / Vagabonds / 125 mph / Archway towers / Charge / Chinese whispers / Nothing touches / White coats
CD ______ CDFA 3257
Fame / Aug '91 / EMI

New Musik

ANYWHERE
They all run after the carving knife / Areas / Churches / This world of walter / Luxury / While you wait / Changing minds / Peace / Design / Traps / Division / Back to room one
CD ______ 4746152
Epic / Jul '96 / Sony

FROM A TO B
Straight lines / Sanctuary / Map of you / Science / On islands / This world of water / Living by numbers / Dead fish (don't swim home) / Adventures / Safe side
CD ______ 4773532
GTO / Aug '94 / Sony

New Noakes

THROUGH GREEN AND PLEASANT LANDS
Second season / First season / Through green and pleasant lands / Easter ballad / Fourth season / Pax latinus / Anti-clockwise / Autumn (A piece for Charlotte)
CD ______ 33JAZZ 004CD
33 Jazz / May '95 / Cadillac / New Note/ Pinnacle

New Order

BEST OF NEW ORDER, THE
True faith '94 / Bizarre love triangle / 1963 / Regret / Fine time / Perfect kiss / Shellshock / Thieves like us / Vanishing point / Run / Round and round / World (price of love) / Ruined in a day / Touched by the hand of God / Blue Monday '88 / World in motion
CD ______ 8285802
Factory / Aug '95 / PolyGram

BLUE ORDER - A TRANCE TRIBUTE TO NEW ORDER (Various Artists)
CD ______ CLP 9985
Cleopatra / Jun '97 / Cargo / Greyhound / Plastic Head / RTM/Disc / SRD

NEWSPEAK (Interview)
CD ______ 3D 015
Network / Dec '96 / Total/BMG

REST OF NEW ORDER, THE
World / Blue Monday / True faith / Confusion / Touched by the hand of God / Bizarre love triangle / Everythings gone green / Ruined in a day / Regret / Temptation / Age of consent
CD ______ 8286612
CD ______ 8286572
Factory / Aug '95 / PolyGram

SUBSTANCE 1987 (2CD Set)
Ceremony / Everything's gone green / Temptation / Blue Monday / Confusion / Thieves like us / Perfect kiss / Subculture / Shellshock / State of the nation / Bizarre love triangle / True faith / Procession / Mesh / Hurt / In a lonely place / Beach / Confused / Murder / Lonesome tonight / Kiss of death / Shame of the nation / 1963
CD Set ______ 5200082
Factory / Jul '93 / PolyGram

New Order

DECLARATION OF WAR
CD ______ 422252FC031
Fan Club / Nov '94 / Direct

New Orleans Blue Serenaders

NEW ORLEANS BLUE SERENADERS
CD ______ BCD 221
GHB / Jan '93 / Jazz Music

New Orleans CAC Jazz ...

MOOD INDIGO (New Orleans CAC Jazz Orchestra)
Don't get around much anymore / New Orleans / Bye bye blackbird / Sometimes I'm happy / I'm just a lucky so and so / Spring can really hang you up the most / I love Paris / Lost mind / Let's get lost / Mood indigo / Everyday I have the blues / Stormy Monday / Not trustworthy
CD ______ ROUCD 2145
Rounder / Feb '97 / ADA / CM / Direct

New Orleans Classic Jazz ...

BLOWIN' OFF STEAM (New Orleans Classic Jazz Orchestra)
CD ______ SOSCD 1223
Stomp Off / Oct '92 / Jazz Music / Wellard

New Orleans Jazz Wizards

JAMBALAYA 1995
CD ______ 504CDS 55
504 / Jul '96 / Cadillac / Jazz Music / Target/BMG / Wellard

New Orleans Joymakers

NEW ORLEANS JOYMAKERS
CD ______ BCD 353
GHB / Nov '96 / Jazz Music

New Orleans Nightcrawlers

NEW ORLEANS NIGHTCRAWLERS
CD ______ ROUCD 2147
Rounder / Aug '96 / ADA / CM / Direct

New Orleans Ragtime ...

CREOLE BELLES (New Orleans Ragtime Orchestra)
Creole belles / Black and white rag / Purple rose of Cairo / War cloud / Maple leaf rag / High society / Entertainer / Ragtime dance / New Orleans hop scop blues / My Maryland / Chrysanthemum / Panama / Wall Street rag / Love will find a way / Rubber plant rag / You can have it, I don't want it / Tickled to death / Junk man rag / Winin' boy blues / St. Louis tickle / Hindustan / Ethiopia / Red pepper / Pickles and peppers
CD ______ ARHCD 420
Arhoolie / Apr '95 / ADA / Cadillac / Direct

New Orleans Rhythm Kings

NEW ORLEANS RHYTHM KINGS AND JELLY ROLL MORTON (New Orleans Rhythm Kings & Jelly Roll Morton)
Eccentric / Farewell blues / Discontented blues / Bugle call rag / Panama / Tiger rag / Livery stable blues / Oriental / Sweet lovin' man / That's a plenty / Shimmeshawabble / Weary blues / That Da DA strain / Wolverine blues / Maple leaf rag / Tin roof blues / Sobbin' blues / Marguerite / Angry / Clarinet / Marmalade / Mr. Jelly Lord / London blues / Milenberg joys / Mad
CD ______ MCD 47020
Milestone / Jan '93 / Cadillac / Complete/ Pinnacle / Jazz Music / Wellard

NEW ORLEANS RHYTHM KINGS VOL.1 1922-1923
CD ______ KJ 109FS
King Jazz / Oct '93 / Cadillac / Discovery / Jazz Music

NEW ORLEANS RHYTHM KINGS VOL.2
CD ______ VILCD 0132
Village Jazz / Aug '92 / Jazz Music / Target/BMG

NEW ORLEANS RHYTHM KINGS VOL.2 (1923-1924) (New Orleans Rhythm Kings & Bix Beiderbecke)
CD ______ KJ 110FS
King Jazz / Oct '93 / Cadillac / Discovery / Jazz Music

RARE RECORDINGS (The Golden Age of Jazz)
CD ______ JZCD 370
Suisa / Jun '92 / Jazz Music / THE

New Orleans Saxophone ...

NEW NEW ORLEANS MUSIC VOL.2 (New Orleans Saxophone Ensemble & Improvising Arts Quintet)
CD ______ ROUCD 2066
Rounder / '88 / ADA / CM / Direct

New Orleans Spiritualettes

I BELIEVE
CD ______ FA 418
Fremeaux / Feb '97 / ADA / Discovery

New Power Generation

EXODUS
CD ______ NPG 61032
New Power Generation / Mar '95 / EMI

New Riders Of The Purple ...

MARIN COUNTY LINE (New Riders Of The Purple Sage)
Till I met you / Llywelyn / Knights and queens / Green eyes a flashing / Oh what a night / Good woman likes to drink with the boys / Turkeys in a straw / Jasper / Echoes / Twenty good men / Little Miss Bad / Take a red
CD ______ MCAD 22107
One Way / Apr '94 / ADA / Direct / Greyhound

NEW RIDERS OF THE PURPLE SAGE (New Riders Of The Purple Sage)
I don't know you / What'cha gonna do / Portland woman / Henry / Dirty business / Glendale train / Garden of Eden / All I ever wanted / Last lonely eagle / Louisiana lady
CD ______ MCAD 22108
One Way / Apr '94 / ADA / Direct / Greyhound

WASTED TASTERS 1971-1975 (New Riders Of The Purple Sage)
Henry / Glendale train / Lousiana lady / I don't know you / Last lonely eagle / I don't need no doctor / Contract / Rainbow / Sweet lovin' one / Dim light thick smoke / She's no angel / Sutter's mill / Sailin' / Panama red / Lonesome LA cowboy / Kick in the head / Teradrops in my eyes / Hello mary lou / Dead flowers / You angel you / Singing cowboy / I heard you been layin' my old lady / Farewell Angelina
CD ______ RVCD 36
Raven / May '94 / ADA / Direct

WHO ARE THOSE GUYS (New Riders Of The Purple Sage)
CD ______ MCAD 22109
One Way / Apr '94 / ADA / Direct / Greyhound

New Scorpion Band

WHY, SOLDIER, WHY (Songs Of Battles Lost & Won)
Female drummer / On board a '98' / Jacky Tar / Lord Nelson's hornpipe / Why, soldier, why / Over the hills and far away / Gentleman soldier / High barbaree / Bony crossing the Rhine / Soldier's joy / Bold Nelson's praise / Balaclava / St. Helena march / Dark-eyed sailor / Dolphin / Tommy
CD ______ SAMPPCD 402
Soundalive / Aug '96 / Complete/Pinnacle

New Seekers

ANTHEMS (Their Greatest Hits)
You won't find another fool like me / Circles / Runaway / I get a little sentimental over you / Power of love / Forever in my mind / Never ending story of love / I'd like to teach the world to sing / What have they done to my song ma / Shambala / Beg steal or borrow / I wanna go back / Pinball wizard - see me, feel me / Stay / Come softly to me / Anthem
CD ______ 300682
Hallmark / Jul '96 / Carlton

COLLECTION, THE
CD ______ COL 037
Collection / Mar '95 / Target/BMG

GREATEST HITS
I'd like to teach the world to sing / Come softly to me / You won't find another fool like me / Morning has broken / What have they done to my song Ma / Circles / I get a

little sentimental over you / Your song / Beg, steal or borrow / Nevertheless (I'm in love with you) / Day by day / Georgy girl / Just an old fashioned love song / Goodbye is just another word / Pinball wizard / See me, feel me / Goin' back / Never ending song of love
CD 8453982
Polydor / May '91 / PolyGram

PERFECT HARMONY
I'd like to teach the world to sing / Beg, steal or borrow / Never ending song of love / Blowin' in the wind / Here, there and everywhere / Circles / Medley: Pinball wizard/See me feel me / You won't find another fool like me / Gentle on my mind / I get a little sentimental over you / Come softly to me / Your song / Unwithered rose / Sing hallelujah
CD 5500842
Spectrum / Oct '93 / PolyGram

WORLD OF THE NEW SEEKERS, THE
I'd like to teach the world to sing / Beg, steal or borrow / Come softly to me / You won't find another fool like me / Friends/ With a little help from my friends / Pinball wizard/See me, feel me / Nevertheless (I'm in love with you) / Brother Love's travelling salvation show / Circles / Beautiful people / One / Never ending song of love / Goodbye is just another word / Dance dance dance / What have they done to my song Ma / Melting pot / Something in the way he moves / Brand new song / Greatest song I've ever heard / I get a little sentimental over you
CD 5520802
Spectrum / May '96 / PolyGram

New Shtetl Band

JEWISH AND BALKAN MUSIC
CD GVM 121CD
Global Village / Jul '95 / ADA / Direct

New Sweet Breath

SHOTGUN DOWN AN AVALANCHE
CD BTO 005
Big Top / Jul '97 / Cargo

New Tradition

AR CAHAINS AR CEDL
CD CDLOC 1090
Lochshore / Jun '95 / ADA / Direct / Duncans

New Wet Kojak

NASTY INTERNATIONAL
CD TG 164CD
Touch & Go / Aug '97 / SRD

NEW WET KOJAK
CD TG 144CD
Touch & Go / Oct '95 / SRD

New Winds

DIGGING IT HARDER FROM AFAR
CD VICTOCD 028
Victo / Nov '94 / Harmonia Mundi / ReR Megacorp

New World

CHANGING TIMES
CD RTN 41208
Rock The Nation / Feb '95 / Plastic Head

TOM TOM TURN AROUND
Tom tom turn around / Kara kara / Sister Jane / But not afraid to dream / Sleep in the sun / Lord of the dance / Rooftop singing / Rose garden / Morning has broken / Sitting in the sun / Yesterday's gone / Old Shep / Sally's a lady / Killing me softly with her song / Something's wrong / If you could read my mind / Living next door to alice / Do you wanna dance
CD DC 865712
Disky / Mar '97 / Disky / THE

New York Allstars

COUNT BASIE REMEMBERED VOL.1
CD NHCD 031
Nagel Heyer / Mar '97 / Jazz Music

NEW YORK ALLSTARS PLAY THE MUSIC OF LOUIS ARMSTRONG, THE
When it's sleepy time down South: *Armstrong, Louis* / Mabel's dream: *Armstrong, Louis* / Sugar foot stomp: *Armstrong, Louis* / Big butter and egg man: *Armstrong, Louis* / Cornet chop suey: *Armstrong, Louis* / Wild man blues: *Armstrong, Louis* / Potato head blues: *Armstrong, Louis* / Muskrat ramble: *Armstrong, Louis* / Savoy blues: *Armstrong, Louis* / Struttin' with some barbecue: *Armstrong, Louis* / Basin street blues: *Armstrong, Louis* / Weather bird: *Armstrong, Louis* / Medley: *Armstrong, Louis* / Swing that music: *Armstrong, Louis* / If I could be with you: *Armstrong, Louis* / Mack the knife: *Armstrong, Louis* / Faithful hussar: *Armstrong, Louis* / Ole miss: *Armstrong, Louis* / Mabel's dream: *Armstrong, Louis* / When it's sleepy time down South: *Armstrong, Louis*
CD CD 029
Nagel Heyer / Jan '97 / Jazz Music

NEW YORK ALLSTARS VOL.1
CD CD 002
Nagel Heyer / May '96 / Jazz Music

NEW YORK ALLSTARS VOL.2
CD CD 003
Nagel Heyer / May '96 / Jazz Music

New York Band

GRANDES EXITOS
Si tu no estas / Maria / Y tu no estas / Ay Mama / El cibaeno / Dame Vida / Chim pun callao / Corazon de azucar / Que no me adivina / Mambo mix / Que beuno bvaila usted / Ponte el sombrero / Muevelo / El lloron / Pelotero / El caravine / Jala jala / Dancing mood / Nadie como tu
CD 66058069
RMM / Sep '95 / New Note/Pinnacle

New York City Gay Men's ...

LOVE LIVES ON (New York City Gay Men's Chorus)
CD VC 7596632
Virgin Classics / Jan '95 / EMI

New York Composers ...

FIRST PROGRAM IN STANDARD TIME (New York Composers Orchestra)
CD 804182
New World / Sep '92 / ADA / Cadillac / Harmonia Mundi

MUSIC BY EHRLICH, HOLCOMB, HOROVITZ & WIESELMAN (New York Composers Orchestra)
CD NW 397
New World / Aug '92 / ADA / Cadillac / Harmonia Mundi

New York Dolls

LIPSTICK KILLERS
Bad girl / Looking for a kiss / Don't start me talkin' / Don't mess with cupid / Human being / Personality crisis / Pills / Jet boy / Frankenstein
CD RE 104CD
ROIR / Nov '94 / Plastic Head / Shellshock/ Disc

NEW YORK TAPES 1972-1973
CD 622572
Skydog / Mar '96 / Discovery

PARIS BURNING
CD 622562
Skydog / Mar '96 / Discovery

RED PATENT LEATHER
Girls / Downtown / Pirate love / Personality crisis / Pills / Something else / Daddy rollin' stone / Dizzy Miss Lizzy
CD 422253
New Rose / May '94 / ADA / Direct / Discovery

ROCK 'N' ROLL
Courageous cat theme / Trash / Personality crisis / Babylon / Looking for a kiss / Lone star queen / Vietnamese baby / Lonely planet boy / Frankenstein / Private world / Chatterbox / Bad girl / Don't mess with cupid / Subway train / Who are the mystery girls / Stranded in the jungle / It's too late / Puss 'n' boots / Jet boy / Human being
CD 5221292
Mercury / Oct '94 / PolyGram

TOO MUCH TOO SOON
CD 8342302
Mercury / Jan '94 / PolyGram

New York Hardbop Quintet

ROKERMOTION
Rokermotion / Strike / More than you know / Hip Naz / El-Cee / Little Jake / Est of the sun / Wan
CD TCB 96352
TCB / Nov '96 / New Note/Pinnacle

New York Jazz Collective

I DON'T KNOW THIS WORLD WITHOUT DON CHERRY
CD 860032
Naxos Jazz / Jun '97 / Select

New York Jazz Ensemble

BUNK PROJECT, THE
In the sweet by 'n' by / Old rugged cross / Margie / Mecca flats blues / Over in gloryland / Algiers strut / What a friend we have in Jesus / Sobbin' blues / Bogalusa strut / Black cat blues / Red light blues / All whores like the way I ride / Burgundy Street Blues / Weary blues
CD 5149372
Limelight / Feb '93 / PolyGram

New York Loose

YEAR OF THE RAT
CD 1620492
Polydor / Sep '96 / PolyGram

New York School

NEW YORK SCHOOL, THE
CD ARTCD 6101
Hat Art / Sep '92 / Cadillac / Harmonia Mundi

New York Swing

PLAYS JEROME KERN
Song is you / I dream too much / Why do I love you / Smoke gets in your eyes / Can't help lovin' dat man / Sure thing / Pick yourself up / Bill / Yesterdays / Why was I born / I'm old fashioned / All the things you are / Remind me / Nobody else but me
CD CDC 9082
LRC / Apr '95 / Harmonia Mundi / New Note/Pinnacle

New Zealand Maori Chorale

NEW ZEALAND SINGS
CD VPS 488
Viking / Sep '96 / CM / Discovery / Harmonia Mundi

Newberry, Booker III

POWER PEOPLE
CD SCRCD 008
Scratch / Dec '96 / Koch / Scratch/BMG

Newborn, Phineas Jr.

HARLEM BLUES
Harlem blues / Sweet and lovely / Little girl blue / Ray's idea / Stella by starlight / Tenderly / Cookin' at the continental
CD OJCCD 662
Original Jazz Classics / Oct '96 / Complete/ Pinnacle / Jazz Music / Wellard

NEWBORN TOUCH, THE
Walkin' thing / Double play / Sermon / Diane / Blessing / Groove yard / Blue Daniel / Hard to find / Pazmuerte / Be deedle dee doo / Good lil' man
CD OJCCD 270
Original Jazz Classics / May '97 / Complete/ Pinnacle / Jazz Music / Wellard

SOLO
Stompin' at the Savoy / Easy living / How high the moon / Breeze and I / Nature boy / Days of wine and roses / Confirmation / Might as well be Spring / Love me or leave me / Temptation
CD CDLR 45020
L&R / Feb '91 / New Note/Pinnacle

WORLD OF PIANO, A
Cheryl / Manteca / Lush life / Daahoud / Oleo / Juicy Lucy / For Carl / Cabu
CD OJCCD 175
Original Jazz Classics / Apr '96 / Complete/ Pinnacle / Jazz Music / Wellard

Newcastle Utd FC

TOON ARMY TUNES (A Tribute To Newcastle United FC) (Various Artists)
Black 'n' white / We will follow united / Home Newcastle / Never been defeated / Harry Geordie medley / Blaydon races / Howay the lads 93 / Toon toon army / Andy Cole song / United, Newcastle united / Thank you mention from the team / Head over heals in love / Move on down / Fog on the Tyne / Geordie boys / Santa is a Geordie
CD CDGAFFER 3
Cherry Red / Nov '95 / Pinnacle

Newcomer, Carrie

ANGEL AT MY SHOULDER, AN
CD PH 1163CD
Philo / Apr '94 / ADA / CM / Direct

BIRD OR THE WING, THE
CD CDPH 1183
Philo / May '95 / ADA / CM / Direct

MY FATHER'S ONLY SON
Crazy in love / Tracks / These are the moments / You can choose / My father's only son / I'm not thinking of you / Up in the attic / Closer to you / Bearing witness / Madness you get used to / Rooms my mother made / Amelia almost
CD CDPH 1203
Philo / Oct '96 / ADA / CM / Direct

VISIONS AND DREAMS
CD CDPH 1193
Philo / Nov '95 / ADA / CM / Direct

Newell, Martin

BOX OF OLD HUMBUG, A (2CD Set)
CD Set BAH 33
Humbug / Sep '97 / Total/Pinnacle

GREATEST LIVING ENGLISHMAN, THE
Goodbye dreaming fields / Before the hurricane / We'll build a house / Greatest living Englishman / She rings the changes / Home counties boy / Street called prospect / Christmas in suburbia / Straight to you, boy / Jangling man / Green-gold girl of summer
CD BAH 10
Humbug / Feb '97 / Total/Pinnacle

OFF WHITE ALBUM
CD BAH 25
Humbug / Apr '96 / Total/Pinnacle

Newley, Anthony

VERY BEST OF ANTHONY NEWLEY, THE
Personally / Why / Do you mind / If she could come to you / Strawberry fair / And the Heaven's cried / Pop goes the weasel / Bee bom / What kind of fool am I / D-darling / That noise / My blue angel / Lifetime of happiness / I'll walk beside you / I've waited so long / I guess it couldn't happen to a nicer guy / Young only yesterday / Girls were made to love and kiss / You are too beautiful
CD 5520902
Spectrum / Jan '97 / PolyGram

WHAT KIND OF FOOL AM I
Candyman / Too much woman / Why / Rainbows / Do you mind / Way that I did / Bee bom / Nearly wonderful / Who can I turn to / White boy / Autumn / What kind of fool am I / Remember / Centrefold / If I were a rich man / Do you love me / Make 'em laugh / Puttin' on the ritz / They can't take that away from me / Thank heaven for little girls
CD 3036400122
Carlton / May '96 / Carlton

Newman, Colin

A - Z
I've waited for ages / And jury / Alone / Order for order / Image / Life on deck / Troisieme / S-S-S Star eyes / Seconds to last / Inventory / But no / B
CD BBL 20CD
Lowdown/Beggars Banquet / Sep '88 / RTM/Disc / Warner Music

BASTARD
Sticky / May / Slowfast (falling down the stairs with a drumkit) / Without / G-deep / Spaced in / Spiked / Orange house and the blue house / Turn
CD WM 3
Swim / Jul '97 / Kudos / RTM/Disc / SRD

COMMERCIAL SUICIDE
CD CRAM 045
Crammed Discs / Oct '86 / Grapevine/ PolyGram / New Note/Pinnacle / Prime / RTM/Disc

IT SEEMS
CD CRAM 058
Crammed Discs / May '88 / Grapevine/ PolyGram / New Note/Pinnacle / Prime / RTM/Disc

PROVISIONALLY ENTITLED THE SINGING FISH/NOT TO
CD CAD 108/201CD
4AD / Apr '88 / RTM/Disc

Newman, David

BLUE HEAD (Newman, David 'Fathead' Quintet)
Strike up the band / Blue head / Willow weep for me / Blues for David / What's new / Eyewitness blues
CD CCD 79041
Candid / Feb '97 / Cadillac / Direct / Jazz Music / Koch / Wellard

MR. GENTLE AND MR. COOL
Don't get around much anymore / Prelude to a kiss / Mr. Gentle and Mr.Cool / Almost cried / I let a song go out of my heart / Azure / What am I here for / Happy reunion / Come Sunday / Creole love call / Jeep's blues
CD KOKO 1300
Kokopelli / Oct '94 / New Note/Pinnacle

RETURN TO THE WIDE (Newman, David 'Fathead')
Buster's tune / Hard times / Thirteenth floor / Thing's ain't what they used to be / These foolish things / Two bones and a pick / City lights / Lush life / Night in Tunisia
CD CDMT 023
Magnum Music / Mar '93 / TKO Magnum

STILL HARD TIMES (Newman, David 'Fathead')
Shana / One for my baby (and one more for the road) / To love again / Still hard times / Please send me someone to love
CD MCD 5283
Muse / Sep '92 / New Note/Pinnacle

Newman, Denny

NOAH'S GREAT RAINBOW
CD NM 002
New Blue / Jul '95 / Hot Shot

Newman, Jackie

COMPLETE RECORDED WORKS
CD DOCD 5351
Document / Jun '95 / ADA / Hot Shot / Jazz Music

Newman, Jimmy C.

BOP A HULA/DIGGY LIGGY LO (2CD Set)
You didn't have to go / Cry cry darlin' / Can I be right / Your true and faithful one / What will I do / I'll always love you darlin' / Once again / Let me stay in your arms / Night time is cry time / Diggy liggy lo / You don't want

me to know / Do you feel like I feel about you / Daydreaming / Dream why do you hurt me so / Crying for a pastime / Angel have mercy / Blue darlin' / Let me stay in your arms / I thought I'd never fall in love again / God was so good / Let's stay together / What will I do (unissued) / I've got you on my mind / Seasons of my heart / Come back to me / I wanta tell all the world / Yesterday's dreams / Let the whole world talk / Honky tonk tears / Last night / No use to cry / Way you're living is breaking my heart / What a fool I was to fall for you / Fallen star / I can't go on this way / Need me (unissued) / Sweet kind of love / Need me / Cry cry darlin' / You're the idol of my dreams / Step aside shallow water / Bop a hula / Carry on / With tears in my eyes
CD Set _______ **BCD 15469**
Bear Family / Sep '90 / Direct / Rollercoaster / Swift

Newman, Joe

AT THE ATLANTIC
Summertime / Airmail special / I can't get started (with you) / When you're smiling / Caravan / Liza / Stardust
CD _______ **NCD 8810**
Phontastic / '93 / Cadillac / Jazz Music / Wellard

GOOD 'N' GROOVY (Newman, Joe Quintet)
AM romp / Li'l darlin' / Molasses / To rigmor / Just squeeze me / Loop-d-loop
CD _______ **OJCCD 185**
Original Jazz Classics / Jun '96 / Complete/ Pinnacle / Jazz Music / Wellard

GRAND NIGHT FOR SWINGING, A
CD _______ **NI 4012**
Natasha / Jan '93 / ADA / Cadillac / CM / Direct / Jazz Music

HANGIN' OUT (Newman, Joe & Joe Wilder)
Midgets / Here's that rainy day / Duet / Battle hymn of the Republic / Secret love / You've changed / Lypso mania / He was too good to me
CD _______ **CCD 4262**
Concord Jazz / Feb '92 / New Note/ Pinnacle

I FEEL LIKE A NEWMAN
CD _______ **BLCD 760905**
Black Lion / Jun '88 / Cadillac / Jazz Music / Koch / Wellard

Newman, June

WEST COAST BLUES (Newman, June & Gary Lee)
CD _______ **RQCD 1510**
Request / May '96 / Jazz Music / Wellard

Newman, Randy

BEST OF RANDY NEWMAN, THE (Lonely At The Top)
Love story / Living without you / I think it's going to rain today / Mama told me not to come / Sail away / Simon Smith and the amazing dancing bear / Political science / God's song (that's why I love mankind) / Rednecks / Birmingham / Louisiana 1927 / Marie / Baltimore / Jolly coppers of parade / Rider in the rain / Short people / I love LA / Lonely at the top / My life is good / In Germany before the war / Christmas in Capetown / My old Kentucky home
CD _______ **2411262**
WEA / Jun '87 / Warner Music

GOOD OLE BOYS
Rednecks / Marie / Guilty / Every man a king / Naked man / Back on my feet again / Birmingham / Mr. President (have a pity on the working man) / Louisiana 1927 / Kingfish / Wedding in Cherokee county / Rollin'
CD _______ **9272142**
WEA / Sep '89 / Warner Music

LITTLE CRIMINALS
Baltimore / I'll be home / In Germany before the war / Jolly coppers on parade / Kathleen / Old man on the farm / Rider in the rain / Short people / Sigmund Freud's impersonation of Albert Einstein In America / Texas girl at the funeral of her father / You can't fool the fat man
CD _______ **K 256404**
WEA / Jan '88 / Warner Music

TROUBLE IN PARADISE
CD _______ **7599237552**
Warner Bros. / May '94 / Warner Music

Newman, Todd

TEMPORARY SETBACK
CD _______ **BIR 037**
Barber's Itch / Jan '97 / Cargo

Newman, Tom

ASPECTS
CD _______ **NAGE 7CD**
Art Of Landscape / '86 / Sony

BAYOU MOON
CD _______ **NAGE 2CD**
Art Of Landscape / Feb '86 / Sony

FINE OLD TOM
Sad sing / Nursery rhyme / Song for SP / Will you be mine in the morning / Alison says / Day of the Percherons / Suzie / Poor Bill / Superman / Ma song / Penny's whistle boogie / She said she said / Ma song / Superman / Oh Susie / Poor Bill / She said she said
CD _______ **BP 166CD**
Blueprint / Jun '97 / Pinnacle

HOTEL SPLENDIDE
CD _______ **VP 195CD**
Voiceprint / Feb '97 / Pinnacle

LIVE AT THE ARGONAUT
Don't treat your woman bad / Kentucky / It don't come easy / Entropy / Gamblin' man / For the old times / Tales from Brendan's beard / Roving gambler / Draught guinnes / Paperback writer / Give a little take a little / Aeigough
CD _______ **VP 168CD**
Voiceprint / Feb '95 / Pinnacle

Newport Jazz Festival All ...

BERN CONCERT '89 (Newport Jazz Festival All Stars)
I want to be happy / Jeep's blues / Just a gigolo / I'm just a lucky so and so / Johnny come lately / Blue and sentimental / In a sentimental mood / Jumpin' at the woodside
CD _______ **CCD 4401**
Concord Jazz / Jan '90 / New Note/ Pinnacle

EUROPEAN TOUR (Newport Jazz Festival All Stars)
Tickle toe / Mood indigo / Love me or leave me / These foolish things / Take the 'A' train / Things ain't what they used to be / Through for the night
CD _______ **CCD 4343**
Concord Jazz / May '88 / New Note/ Pinnacle

Newport Rebels

JAZZ ARTISTS GUILD
Mysterious blues / Cliff walk / Wrap your troubles in dreams (and dream your troubles away) / Ain't nobody's business if I do / Me and you
CD _______ **CCD 79022**
Candid / Feb '97 / Cadillac / Direct / Jazz Music / Koch / Wellard

News From Babel

WORK RESUMED ON THE TOWER/ LETTERS HOME
CD _______ **RERNFBCD**
ReR/Recommended / Apr '97 / ReR Megacorp / RTM/Disc

Newsome, Sam

SAM I AM (Newsome, Sam Quintet)
CD _______ **CRISS 1056CD**
Criss Cross / May '92 / Cadillac / Direct / Vital/SAM

Newton, Adi

FILM
CD _______ **ARCD 007**
Anterior Research / Aug '97 / Cargo

Newton, Anney

NEW HORIZONS (Newton, Anney & The Relics)
CD _______ **REL 001CD**
Relic / Jul '95 / ADA

Newton, David

12TH OF THE 12TH (A Jazz Portrait Of Frank Sinatra)
My kind of town (Chicago is) / I've got the world on a string / I fall in love too easily / Witchcraft / Lady is a tramp / This is all I ask / It's nice to go trav'ling / Violets for your furs / All or nothing at all / You make me feel so young / All the way / Twelfth of the twelfth / Only the lonely / Saturday night is the loneliest night of the week / In the wee small hours of the morning
CD _______ **CCD 79728**
Candid / Feb '97 / Cadillac / Direct / Jazz Music / Koch / Wellard

EYE WITNESS
Ol' blues eyes / Bedroom eyes / Angel eyes / Eye witness / Soul eyes / Stars in my eyes / Eye of the hurricane / My mother's eyes
CD _______ **AKD 015**
Linn / Nov '91 / PolyGram

IN GOOD COMPANY (Newton, David Trio)
Get lost / Blessed land / Teach me tonight / June time / My romance / There's a small hotel / Sugar cake / Remark you made / Older and wiser / When will I see you
CD _______ **CCD 79714**
Candid / Feb '97 / Cadillac / Direct / Jazz Music / Koch / Wellard

RETURN JOURNEY
CD _______ **AKD 025**
Linn / Apr '94 / PolyGram

VICTIM OF CIRCUMSTANCE
Wishful thinking / Night we called it a day / Katy's song / It never entered my mind / Victim of circumstance / One and only / Please come home / Way you look tonight
CD _______ **AKD 013**
Linn / Feb '91 / PolyGram

Newton, Frankie

CLASSICS 1937-1939
CD _______ **CLASSICS 643**
Classics / Nov '92 / Discovery / Jazz Music

Newton, James

AFRICAN FLOWER
Black and tan fantasy / Virgin jungle / Strange feeling / Fleurette Africaine (the African flower) / Cotton tail / Sophisticated lady / Passion flower
CD _______ **CDP 7462922**
Blue Note / Feb '97 / EMI

ECHO CANYON
CD _______ **CDCEL 012**
Celestial Harmonies / May '87 / ADA / Select

IN VENICE
CD Set _______ **CDCEL 030/31**
Celestial Harmonies / Sep '88 / ADA / Select

ROMANCE AND REVOLUTION
Forever Charles / Meditation for integration / Peace / Evening leans towards you / Tenderly
CD _______ **BNZ 70**
Blue Note / Sep '87 / EMI

Newton, Juice

COUNTRY CLASSICS
It's a heartache / Let's keep it that way / Any way you want me / Sunshine / Angel of the morning / All I have to do is dream / Queen of hearts / Sweetest thing (I've ever known) / Heart of the night / I'm gonna be strong / Love's been a bit hard on me / Break it to me gently / Come to me: *Newton, Juice & Silver Spur* / Love like yours: *Newton, Juice & Silver Spur* / Hey baby: *Newton, Juice & Silver Spur*
CD _______ **CDMFP 6327**
Music For Pleasure / Apr '97 / EMI

Newton, Lauren

18 COLOURS (Newton, Lauren & Joelle Leandre)
CD _______ **CDLR 245**
Leo / May '97 / Cadillac / Impetus / Wellard

Newton-John, Olivia

BACK TO BASICS (The Essential Collection 1971-1992)
If not for you / Banks of the Ohio / What is life / Take me home country roads / I honestly love you / Have you never been mellow / Sam / You're the one that I want / Hopelessly devoted to you / Summer nights / Little more love / Xanadu / Magic / Suddenly / Physical / Rumour / Not gonna be the one / I need love / I want to be wanted / Deeper than a river
CD _______ **5126412**
Mercury / Jul '92 / PolyGram

EMI COUNTRY MASTERS (2CD Set)
Love song / Banks of the Ohio / Me and Bobby McGee / If not for you / Help me make it through the night / If you could read my mind / In a station / Where are you going to my love / Lullaby / No regrets / If I gotta leave / Would you follow me / If / It's so hard to say goodbye / Winterwood / What is life / Changes / Everything I own / I'm a small and lonely light / Just a little too much / Living in harmony / Why don't you write me / Angel of the morning / Mary Skeffington / If we only have love / My old man's got a gun / Maybe then I'll think of you / Amoureuse / Take me home country roads / I love you, I honestly love you / Music makes my day / Heartbreaker / Leaving / You ain't got the right / Feeling best / Rose water / Being on the losing end / If we try / Let me be there / Country girl / Loving you ain't easy / Have love will travel / Hands across the sea / Please Mr. please / Air that I breathe / Loving arms / If you love me (Let me know) / Have you never been mellow
CD Set _______ **CDEM 1503**
EMI / Aug '93 / EMI

GAIA (One Woman's Journey)
CD _______ **DSHCD 7017**
D-Sharp / Feb '95 / Pinnacle

RUMOUR, THE
Rumour / Can't we talk it over in bed / Get out / Walk through the fire / Love and let live / It's not heaven / Big and strong / Tutta la vita
CD _______ **8349572**
Mercury / Oct '88 / PolyGram

Newtown Neurotics

45 REVOLUTIONS PER MINUTE
CD _______ **FREUDCD 31**
Jungle / Feb '94 / RTM/Disc / SRD

PUNK SINGLES COLLECTION
Hypocrite / You said no / When the oil runs out / Oh no / Kick out the Tories / Mindless violence / Licensing hours / No sanctuary / Blitzreig bop / Hypocrite / I remember you / Suzi is a heartbreaker / Fools / Living with unemployment / Airstrip / My death / Never thought / Screaming / Stand by me / Mind of Valerie / Sect / Never thought
CD _______ **CDPUNK 91**
Anagram / Mar '97 / Cargo / Pinnacle

Nexus

WORLD PERCUSSION MUSIC (Nexus & Peter Sadlo)
CD _______ **315572**
Koch Classics / May '97 / Koch

NFL Horns Project

TRIANGLE BELOW CANAL STREET
CD _______ **IBCD 4**
Internal Bass / Feb '97 / Prime / Timewarp / Total/BMG

NG La Banda

BEST OF NG LA BANDA, THE
CD _______ **74321424392**
Milan / Jun '97 / Conifer/BMG / Silva Screen

Nganasan

SHAMANIC SONGS OF SIBERIAN ARCTIC
CD _______ **925642**
BUDA / Jun '93 / Discovery

Ni Bheaglaoich, Eilin

MILE DATH/A CLOAK OF MANY COLOURS
CD _______ **CIC 079CD**
Clo Iar-Chonnachta / Jan '92 / CM

Ni Bheaglaoich, Seosaimhin

UNDER THE SUN
CD _______ **CEFCD 170**
Gael Linn / Dec '95 / ADA / CM / Direct / Grapevine/PolyGram / Roots

Ni Bhrolchain, Deirbhile

SMAOINTE
CD _______ **CEFCD 147**
Gael Linn / Jan '94 / ADA / CM / Direct / Grapevine/PolyGram / Roots

Ni Chathasaigh, Maire

CAROLAN ALBUMS: THE MUSIC OF TURLOUGH O'CAROLAN (Ni Chathasaigh, Maire & Chris Newman)
Carolan's draught / John O'Connor / Colonel John Irwin (Planxty Irwin) / Hewlwtt / Maire Dhall / Lord Inchiquin / Morgan Magan / Si beag si mor / Princess Royal / John Drury (Planxty Drury) / Fanny Power / Carolan's concerto / Maurice O'Connor / Constantine Maguire / Mr. O'Connor / Robert Jordan / Bridget Cruise / Frank Palmer / Grace Nugent / George Brabazon / Kean O'Hara / Madam Judge / Eleanor Plunkett / Baptist Johnston
CD _______ **OBMCD 06**
Old Bridge / Apr '94 / ADA / Direct / Highlander

LIVE IN THE HIGHLANDS (Ni Chathasaigh, Maire & Chris Newman)
Turkey in the straw / Gander in the pratie hole/Donnybrook boy/Queen of the rushes / Thugamar fein an Samhradh linn / Unknown title/Wellington's reel / Eleanor Plunkett / Acrobat/Bonnie banchory/Millbrae / Roisin dubh / Humours of Ballyloughlin / A shaighdiuirin a chroi (Dear soldier of my heart)/Blackbird / Salt creek / Taimse I'm Chodladh / Sore point / Stroll on
CD _______ **OBMCD 08**
Old Bridge / Oct '95 / ADA / Direct / Highlander

LIVING WOOD, THE (Ni Chathasaigh, Maire & Chris Newman)
Caitlin ni aedha/The sport of the chase / Lady Dillon / Fiddler's dream/Whiskey before breakfast / Fare thee well lovely Mary / Walsh's hornpipe/The peacock's feather / Flax in bloom/Lough Allen/McAuliffe's / Beating around the bush / An paistin fionn/ La valse d'Hasperren / Charlie Hunter's/ Peggy's leg/Fogarty's jig / Cuach mo londubh bui/The Virginia / Mairead's mazurka / Bob McQuillan's/Sonny Brogan's / Moynihan's polkas
CD _______ **OBMCD 07**
Old Bridge / '95 / ADA / Direct / Highlander

OUT OF COURT (Ni Chathasaigh, Maire & Chris Newman)
Out of court / Harper's chair / Cherry blossom / Will you meet me tonight on the shore / Frieze breeches / Lady Gethin / Sore point / Graf spee / Tuirne mhaire / Eclipse/Hurricane / Old bridge / Wild geese / Lakes of Champlain / Stroll on
CD _______ **OBMCD 03**
Old Bridge / '91 / ADA / Direct / Highlander

Ni Dhomhnaill, Caitlin

SEAL MO CHUARTA
CD ____ **CIC 070CD**
Clo Iar-Chonnachta / Nov '93 / CM

Ni Dhomhnaill, Maighread

NO DOWRY
CD ____ **CEFCD 152**
Gael Linn / Jan '94 / ADA / CM / Direct / Grapevine/PolyGram / Roots

Ni Dhomhnaill, Triona

TRIONA
CD ____ **CEFCD 043**
Gael Linn / Jan '92 / ADA / CM / Direct / Grapevine/PolyGram / Roots

Ni Fhearraigh, Aoife

AOIFE
CD ____ **CEFCD 172**
Gael Linn / May '97 / ADA / CM / Direct / Grapevine/PolyGram / Roots

Ni Mhaonaigh, Mairead

CEOL ADUAIDH (Ni Mhaonaigh, Mairead & Frankie Kennedy)
CD ____ **CEFCD 102**
Gael Linn / Jan '94 / ADA / CM / Direct / Grapevine/PolyGram / Roots

Ni Riain, Noirin

CAOINEADH NA MAIGHDINE
CD ____ **CEFCD 084**
Gael Linn / Jan '94 / ADA / CM / Direct / Grapevine/PolyGram / Roots

STOR AMHRAN
CD ____ **OSS 7CD**
Ossian / Mar '95 / ADA / CM / Direct / Highlander

VOX DE NUBE (Ni Riain, Noirin & Monks Of Glenstal Abbey)
CD ____ **CEFCD 144**
Gael Linn / Jan '94 / ADA / CM / Direct / Grapevine/PolyGram / Roots

Ni Uallachain, Padraigin

BENEATH THE SURFACE
CD ____ **CEFCD 174**
Gael Linn / Feb '97 / ADA / CM / Direct / Grapevine/PolyGram / Roots

Niacin

NIACIN
No man's land / Clean-up crew / Do a little dirty work / I miss you (like I miss the sun) / One less worry / Three feet back / Bullet train blues / Hell to pay / Alone on my own little island / For crying out loud / Klaghorn / Spring rounds / Spring rounds squared / Pay dirt / Fudgesicle
CD ____ **SCD 90112**
Stretch / Feb '97 / New Note/Pinnacle

Niblock, Phill

YOUNG PERSON'S GUIDE TO PHILL NIBLOCK, A
CD ____ **BFFP 102CD**
Blast First / Jul '97 / RTM/Disc

Nice

AMERICA
CD ____ **CD 12334**
Laserlight / Apr '94 / Target/BMG

AMERICA - THE BBC SESSIONS
CD ____ **RRCD 224**
Receiver / Jul '96 / Grapevine/PolyGram

ARS LONGA VITA BREVIS
Daddy, where did I come from / Little Arabella / Happy Freuds / Intermezzo from Karelia suite / Don Edito el Gruva / Ars longa vita brevis
CD ____ **CLACD 120**
Castle / '86 / BMG

COLLECTION, THE
America / Happy Freuds / Cry of Eugene / Thoughts of Emerlist Davjak / Rondo / Daddy, where do I come from / Little Arabella / Intermezzo from Karelia Suite / Hang on to a dream / Diamond hard blue apples of the moon / Angel of death / Ars longa vita brevis
CD ____ **CCSCD 106**
Castle / Jan '93 / BMG

ELEGY
Third movement / America / Hang on to a dream / My back pages
CD ____ **CASCD 1030**
Charisma / Feb '91 / EMI

FIVE BRIDGES SUITE
Fantasia (1st bridge, 2nd bridge) / Chorale (3rd bridge) / High level fugue (4th bridge) / Finale / Intermezzo from Karelia suite / Pathetique (symphony no.6 3rd movement) / Country pie/Brandenburg concerto No. 6 / One of those people
CD ____ **CASCD 1014**
Charisma / Feb '91 / EMI

IMMEDIATE YEARS, THE (3CD Set)
Flower kings of flies / Thoughts of Ememrlist Davjack / Bonnie K / Rondo / War and peace / Tantalising Maggie / Dawn / Cry of Eugene / America / Diamond hard blue apples of the moon / Daddy / Where did I come from / Azrael / America 2nd ammendment / Little Arabella / Happy freuds / Intermezzo / Brandenburger / Don Edito El Gruva / First movement / Third movement (acceptance brandenburger) / Fourth movement (denial) / Coda / Extension to the big note: *Small Faces* / Azrael revisited / Hang on to a dream / Diary of an empty day / For example / Rondo (69) / She belongs to me / First movement (awakening) / Second movement (realization)
CD Set ____ **CDIMMBOX 2**
Charly / Aug '95 / Koch

THOUGHTS OF EMERLIST DAVJACK
Flower kings of flies / Thoughts of Emerlist Davjack / Bonnie K / Rondo / War and peace / Tantalising Maggie / Dawn / Cry of Eugene
CD ____ **CDIMM 010**
Charly / Feb '94 / Koch

Nice & Smooth

AIN'T A DAMN THING CHANGED
CD ____ **5234782**
RAL / Jan '96 / PolyGram

JEWEL OF THE NILE
Return of the hip hop freaks / Sky's the limit / Let's all get down / Doin' our own thang / Do whatcha gotta / Old to the new / Blunts / Get fucked up / Save the children / Cheri
CD ____ **5233362**
Island / Nov '94 / PolyGram

Nicholas, Albert

ALBERT NICHOLAS & ALAN ELSDON BAND VOL.1 (Nicholas, Albert & Alan Elsdon Band)
CD ____ **JCD 259**
Jazzology / Jul '96 / Jazz Music

ALBERT NICHOLAS & ALAN ELSDON BAND VOL.2 (Nicholas, Albert & Alan Elsdon Band)
CD ____ **JCD 269**
Jazzology / Nov '96 / Jazz Music

BADEN 1969 (Nicholas, Albert & Henri Chaix Trio)
CD ____ **SKCD 22045**
Sackville / Jan '97 / Cadillac / Jazz Music / Swift

NEW ORLEANS-CHICAGO CONNECTION (Nicholas, Albert & Art Hodes Quartet)
Digga digga do / Winin' boy blues / Song of the wanderer / Ain't misbehavin' / Blues my naughty sweetie gave to me / Anah's blues / Lover come back to me / Etta / I'm comin' Virginia / Rose room / Nick warms up / Rose room / I'm comin' Virginia / Lover come back to me / Winin' boy blues / Digga digga do / Careless love / Song of the wanderer / Ain't misbehavin' / Blues my naughty sweetie gave to me / Etta
CD ____ **DE 207**
Delmark / Jun '97 / ADA / Cadillac / CM / Direct / Hot Shot

Nicholas, John

THRILL ON THE HILL
CD ____ **ANTCD 0032**
Antones / Dec '94 / ADA / Hot Shot

Nicholas, Paul

THAT'S ENTERTAINMENT
Reggae like it used to be / Shufflin' shoes / Dancing with the captain / Sway / Sunday / If you were the only girl in the world / Grandma's party / Heaven on the 7th floor / Flat foot floyd / Doing it / Only for a minute / When you walk in the room / Mr. Mistoffelees / Old deuteronomy
CD ____ **5500132**
Spectrum / May '93 / PolyGram

Nicholls, Billy

UNDER ONE BANNER
CD ____ **EXPCD 3**
Expression / Nov '90 / Pinnacle

Nicholls, Gillie

SPIRIT TALK
CD ____ **SPINCD 152**
Spindrift / Jul '94 / CM / Roots

Nichols, Herbie

LOVE IS PROXIMITY (Nichols, Herbie Project)
CD ____ **1213132**
Soul Note / Mar '97 / Cadillac / Harmonia Mundi / Wellard

Nichols, Keith

SYNCOPATED JAMBOREE
CD ____ **SOSCD 1234**
Stomp Off / Oct '92 / Jazz Music / Wellard

Nichols, Nichelle

DOWN TO EARTH
CD ____ **CREV 045CD**
Rev-Ola / Feb '97 / 3mv/Vital

Nichols, Red

1929 RECORDINGS (Nichols, Red & Jack Teagarden)
Dinah / On the Alamo / Somebody to love me / Get happy / Smiles / They didn't believe / Rose of Washington Square / That da da strain / Sally won't you come back / New Yorkers
CD ____ **TAXS 52**
Tax / Aug '94 / Cadillac / Jazz Music / Wellard

BATTLE HYMN OF THE REPUBLIC (Nichols, Red & His Five Pennies)
CD ____ **JCD 90**
Jazzology / Mar '97 / Jazz Music

RADIO TRANSCRIPTIONS 1929-1930 (Nichols, Red & His Five Pennies)
CD ____ **CD 1011**
IAJRC / Nov '96 / Jazz Music / Wellard

RED NICHOLS 1936/WILL OSBORNE 1934 (Nichols, Red & Will Osborne)
CD ____ **CCD 110**
Circle / Apr '94 / Jazz Music / Swift / Wellard

RED NICHOLS AND MIFF MOLE (Nichols, Red & Miff Mole)
CD ____ **VILCD 0152**
Village Jazz / Aug '92 / Jazz Music / Target/BMG

RHYTHM OF THE DAY (Nichols, Red & His Five Pennies)
Rhythm of the day / Buddy's habit / Boneyard shuffle / Alexander's ragtime band / Alabama stomp / Hurricane / Cornfed / Mean dog blues / Riverboat shuffle / Eccentric / Feeling no pain / Original Dixieland one-step / Honolulu blues / There'll come a time / Harlem twist / Alice blue gown / Corine Corina / Oh Peter, you're so nice / Waiting for the evening mail / Sweet Sue, just you
CD ____ **CDAJA 5025**
Living Era / Feb '87 / Select

Nicholson, Gimmer

CHRISTOPHER IDYLLS
CD ____ **CD 9204**
Lucky Seven / Dec '94 / ADA / CM / Direct

Nick, Michael

DIS TANZ (Nick, Michael Trio & Dave Liebman)
CD ____ **TE 009**
BUDA / Jan '97 / Discovery

Nickel Bag

12 HITS AND A BUMP
CD ____ **USG 120092**
USG / Apr '97 / Cargo

Nicki

KLEINE WUNDER
Manchmoi glaubn's i war a star / Nur mit dir mit dir des war mei leben / Anders als die anderen / Doch wie's mal var vergiss i nie / Mehr von dir / Dann denk i du warst bei mir / Auf amoi / Einsam ohne di / I bin a bayriches cowgirl / Wenn teenager traumen / Des muss liebe sei
CD ____ **DC 868282**
Disky / Oct '96 / Disky / THE

WEIHNACHTEN MIT
Heilig abend is nimma weit / Weihnachtstraum d'liab is vom himmi kumma / Drobn im himmi herrscht hochbetried / Es wird scho glei dumpa / Winterwunderland / Heidschi bumbeidschi / leise rieselt der schnee / Weihnacht wie in der kinderzeit / Susse die glocken nie klinga / Mei schonster traum / Susser die glocken nie klinga
CD ____ **DC 868272**
Disky / Oct '96 / Disky / THE

Nicks, Stevie

BELLA DONNA
Belladonna / Kind of woman / Stop draggin' my heart around: *Nicks, Stevie & Tom Petty & The Heartbreakers* / Think about it / After the glitter fades / Edge of seventeen / How still my love / Leather and lace / Highwayman / Outside the rain
CD ____ **CZ 398**
EMI / Mar '91 / EMI

OTHER SIDE OF THE MIRROR
Rooms on fire / Long way to go / Two kinds of love / Oh my love / Ghosts / Whole lotta trouble / Fire burning / Cry wolf / Alice / Juliet / Doing the best I can (Escape from Berlin) / I still miss someone
CD ____ **CDEMD 1008**
EMI / Feb '94 / EMI

STREET ANGEL
Blue denim / Greta / Street angel / Docklands / Listen to the rain / Destiny / Unconditional love / Love is like a river / Rose garden / Maybe love / Just like a woman / Kick it / Jane
CD ____ **CDEMC 3671**
EMI / May '94 / EMI

TIMESPACE (The Best Of Stevie Nicks)
Sometimes it's a bitch / Stop draggin' my heart around: *Nicks, Stevie & Tom Petty & The Heartbreakers* / Whole lotta trouble / Talk to me / Stand back / Beauty and the beast / If anyone falls / Rooms on fire / Love's a hard game to play / Edge of seventeen / Leather and lace / I can't wait / Has anyone ever written anything for you / Desert angel
CD ____ **CDEMD 1024**
EMI / Aug '91 / EMI

WILD HEART
Stand back / I will run to you / Nothing ever changes / Sable on blond / Beauty and the beast / Wild heart / If anyone falls / Gate and garden / Night bird / Enchanted
CD ____ **CDGOLD 1017**
EMI Gold / Mar '96 / EMI

Nico

BLIND MELON
Pusher / Hell / Soup / No rain / Soul one / John Sinclair / All that I need / Glitch / Life ain't so shitty / Swallowed / Pull / St. Andrew's hall / Letters from a porcupine
CD ____ **CDEST 2291**
EMI / Feb '97 / EMI

CAMERA OBSCURA
Camera obscura / Tanaore / Win a few / My funny valentine / Das lied von einsanen madchens / Fearfully in danger / My heart is empty / Into the arena / Konig
CD ____ **BBL 63CD**
Beggars Banquet / Mar '96 / RTM/Disc / Warner Music

CHELSEA GIRL
Fairest of the seasons / These days / Little sister / Winter song / It was a pleasure then / Chelsea girl / I'll keep it with mine / Somewhere there's a feather / Wrap your troubles in dreams (and dream your troubles away) / Eulogy to Lenny Bruce
CD ____ **8352092**
Polydor / Apr '94 / PolyGram

CHELSEA GIRL LIVE
CD ____ **CLEO 61082**
Cleopatra / May '94 / Cargo / Greyhound / Plastic Head / RTM/Disc / SRD

CHELSEA LIVE
Tananore / One more chance / Procession / My heart is empty / Janitor of lunacy / Sphinx / You forget to answer / Fearfully in danger / Sixty forty / All tomorrow's parties / Purple lips / Femme fatale / Saeta / End
CD ____ **SEECD 461**
See For Miles/C5 / Oct '96 / Pinnacle

DO OR DIE
CD ____ **RE 117CD**
ROIR / Nov '94 / Plastic Head / Shellshock/Disc

DRAMA OF EXILE
Genghis Khan / Purple lips / One more chance / Henry Hudson / Heroes / Waiting for the man / Sixty forty / Sphinx / Orly flight
CD ____ **SEECD 449**
See For Miles/C5 / Aug '96 / Pinnacle

END, THE
It has not taken long / Secret side / You forgot to answer / Innocent and vain / Valley of the kings / We've got the gold / End / Das lied der Deutschen
CD ____ **IMCD 174**
Island / Mar '94 / PolyGram

FATA MORGANA 1988 (Nico's Last Concert) (Nico & The Faction)
CD ____ **SPV 08496202**
SPV / Sep '96 / Koch / Plastic Head

HEROINE
My heart is empty / Procession / All tomorrow's parties / Valley of the kings / Sphinx / We've got the gold / Mutterlein / Afraid / Innocent and vain / Frozen warnings / Fearfully in danger / Tananore / Femme fatale
CD ____ **CDMGRAM 85**
Anagram / Aug '94 / Cargo / Pinnacle

LIVE IN TOKYO
My heart is empty / Purple lips / Tananore / Janitor of lunacy / You forget to answer / 60-40 / My funny valentine / Sad lied von einsannen madchens / All tomorrow's parties / Femme fatale / End
CD ____ **DOJOCD 50**
Dojo / May '95 / Disc

MARBLE INDEX
Prelude / Lawns of dawns / No one is there / Ari's song / Facing the wind / Julius Caesar (memento hodie) / Frozen warnings / Evening of light / Roses in the snow / Nibelungen
CD ____ **7559610982**
WEA / Apr '91 / Warner Music

Nico Demus

DANCEHALL GIANT
CD ____ **49007 CD**
Positive Beat / Mar '97 / Jet Star

Nicol, Ken

LIVING IN A SPANISH TOWN
Midnight cowboy / Last night in Paris / Should've known better / Credit card blues / Living in a Spanish town / Last chances / I'd rather be with you / Down on the island / One more night / This time it's me / Jigs and reels / Back out of love / Same old lang syne
CD ______ **PLANCD 012**
Planet / Nov '96 / Direct

Nicolette

DJ KICKS (Various Artists)
It's yours: *Doc Scott* / Never not: *Katze, Nav* / Nightbreed: *Bolland, C.J.* / Java bass: *Shut Up & Dance* / Suicide: *Empire, Alec* / Migrant: *Palace Of Pleasure* / Phyzical: *Roni Size* / Ventolin: *Aphex Twin* / Pound your ironing board: *Mike Flowers Pops & Slang* / I woke up: *Nicolette* / Lash the 90ties: *Alec Empire* / Original nuttah: *UK Apachi & Shy FX* / Severe trauma: *Critical Mass* / Burning: *DJ Krust* / Pillow: *Ohm Square* / 70+ DF: *Horn* / Basses playin' loud: *TAGG* / Single ring: *Nicolette* / Sweat: *Shizuo* / Bastards: *Shut Up & Dance* / Too busy to live: *Oge* / You, them and maybe us: *Grammatix* / Angry dolphin: *Plaid* / Walhalla's gate: *Aquastep* / Bless to kill: *Mark NRG* / All day (DJ Kicks): *Nicolette*
CD ______ **K7 054CD**
Studio K7 / Mar '97 / Prime / RTM/Disc

LET NO-ONE LIVE RENT FREE IN YOUR HEAD
Don't be afriad / We never know / Song for Europe / Beautiful day / Always / Nervous / Where have all the flowers gone / No government / Nightmare / Judgement day / You are Heaven sent / Just to say peace and love / No government / Don't be ashamed (don't be afriad)
CD ______ **5326342**
Talkin' Loud / Oct '96 / PolyGram

NOW IS EARLY
CD ______ **SUADCD 1**
Shut Up & Dance / Apr '92 / SRD

Niebla, Eduardo

MEDITERRANEO (Niebla, Eduardo & Adel Salameh)
Mediterraneo / Andalucia / Gardens of the heart / Oasis
CD ______ **TUGCD 1012**
Riverboat / Apr '96 / New Note/Pinnacle / Stern's

POEMA (Niebla, Eduardo & Antonio Forcione)
CD ______ **CDJP 1035**
Jazz Point / Sep '93 / Cadillac / Harmonia Mundi

Niehaus, Lennie

LENNIE NIEHAUS QUINTET AND OCTET
I remember you / Bottoms up / I'll take romance / Day by day / Blue room / They say it's wonderful / My heart stood still / Star eyes / Just one of those things / Lens / Inside out / I can't believe that you're in love with me / Whose blues / More than the blues / Poinciana / You stepped out of a dream / I should care / Rose room / Nice work if you can get it / Cherokee
CD ______ **CD 53268**
Giants Of Jazz / Feb '97 / Cadillac / Jazz Music / Target/BMG

PATTERNS
CD ______ **FSCD 100**
Fresh Sound / Oct '90 / Discovery / Jazz Music

Niekku

NIEKKU
CD ______ **OMCD 11**
Olarin Musiiki Oy / Dec '93 / ADA / Direct

Nielson Chapman, Beth

YOU HOLD THE KEY
I don't know / You hold the key / Dance with me slow / Say it to me now / When I feel this way / Rage on rage / Only so many tears / In the time it takes / You say you will / Moment you were mine / Faithful heart / Dancer to the drum
CD ______ **93624523342**
Reprise / Sep '93 / Warner Music

Niemack, Judy

BLUE BOP
CD ______ **FRLCD 009**
Freelance / Oct '92 / Cadillac / Koch

HEARTS DESIRE (Niemack, Judy & Kenny Barron)
CD ______ **STCD 548**
Stash / '92 / ADA / Cadillac / CM / Direct / Jazz Music

LONG AS YOU'RE LIVING
CD ______ **FRLCD 014**
Freelance / Oct '92 / Cadillac / Koch

MINGUS, MONK & MAL (Niemack, Judy & Mal Waldron)
CD ______ **FRLCD 021**
Freelance / May '95 / Cadillac / Koch

STRAIGHT UP
CD ______ **FRLCD 0018**
Freelance / Apr '93 / Cadillac / Koch

Nieve, Steve

KEYBOARD JUNGLE ....PLUS
Ethnic Erithian / Hooligans and hula girls / Al Green / Spanish guitar / Man with a musical lighter / Outline of a hairdo / End of side one / Liquid looks / Thought of being Dad / Pink flamingoes on coffee pot boulevard / Mystery and majesty (of a banyan tree) / Couch potato rag / Page one of a dead girl's diary / End of an era / Pictures from a confiscated camera / Once upon a time in South America / Sword fight / Ghost town / Walk in Monet's back garden / Shadows of Paris / Loveboat / El rey de sol / 9/4 Rag / hands of Oriac / Birdcage walk / Divided heart
CD ______ **DIAB 814**
Diabolo / May '95 / Pinnacle

Nieves, Tito

ROMPECABEZA THE PUZZLE
Amores como tu / Vuelveme a querer / Desde que to tengo a ti / You bring me joy / Manias / Lo prometido es deuda / Can you stop the rain / Lo que son las cosa / Mi vida de ayer / Que no fracase este amor / Voy a arrancarte de mi / Mi corazon esta ocupado
CD ______ **66058027**
RMM / Nov '93 / New Note/Pinnacle

Night Ark

IN WONDERLAND
CD ______ **5344712**
EmArCy / Aug '97 / PolyGram

Night In Gales

TOWARDS THE TWILIGHT
CD ______ **NB 243CD**
Nuclear Blast / Jun '97 / Plastic Head

Night Sun

MOURNIN'
CD ______ **SB 041**
Second Battle / Jun '97 / Greyhound

Night Trains

CHECKMATE
Blow out / Takin' a stroll / Release the chain / Miles away / Take the cash / Hang on to that cove / On your toes / Hot and cool / Bongo breakdown / In the crowd / Checkmate / Street chase
CD ______ **CDBGP 1033**
Beat Goes Public / Feb '91 / Pinnacle

LOADED
CD ______ **JAZIDCD 018**
Acid Jazz / Jun '92 / Disc

SLEAZEBALL
Sure can't go to the moon / Hold on for the truth / Lonely road / On my own / Love is the teacher / Move on out together / What good is love / Smoky's clown / International way / Lovesick / Sleazeball
CD ______ **JAZIDCD 098**
Acid Jazz / Apr '94 / Disc

Nightblooms

24 DAYS AT CATASTROPHE CAFE
CD ______ **FIRECD 34**
Fire / Sep '93 / Pinnacle / RTM/Disc

NIGHTBLOOMS
CD ______ **FRIGHT 58CD**
Fierce / Mar '92 / RTM/Disc

Nightcrawlers

LET'S PUSH IT
Push the feeling on / Surrender your love / Don't let the feeling go / Should never (fall in love) / Just like before / Lift me up / World turns / Let's push it / I like it / All over the world
CD ______ **74321309702**
Arista / Sep '95 / BMG

LET'S PUSH IT FURTHER (The 12" Mixes) (Nightcrawlers & John Reid)
Push the feeling on / Keep on pushing our love / Surrender your love / Let's push it / Lift me up / Should I ever (fall in love) / Don't let the feeling go / Surrender your love (Wand's crunchy nut mix) / Let's push it (Motiv 8 bump 'n' boost vocal) / Push the feeling on (Argonaut's smokin' hot mix)
CD ______ **74321390432**
Arista / Aug '96 / BMG

Nightfall

ATHENIAN ECHOES
CD ______ **HOLY 014CD**
Holy / Oct '95 / Plastic Head

EONS AURA
CD ______ **HOLY 09CD**
Holy / Mar '95 / Plastic Head

MACABRE SUNSETS
CD ______ **HOLY 04CD**
Holy / Jun '94 / Plastic Head

PARADE INTO CENTURIES
CD ______ **HOLY 01CD**
Holy / Feb '95 / Plastic Head

Nighthawk, Robert

BLACK ANGEL BLUES
Down the line / Handsome lover / My sweet lovin' woman / Sweet black angel / Anna Lee blues / Return mail blues / Sugar papa / She knows how to love a man / Good news / Six three O / Prison bound / Jackson town gal / Sorry my angel / Someday
CD ______ **CDRED 29**
Charly / Sep '91 / Koch

MASTERS OF MODERN BLUES SERIES (Nighthawk, Robert & Houston Stackhouse)
CD ______ **TCD 5010**
Testament / Dec '94 / ADA / Koch

RARE CHICAGO BLUES RECORDINGS (From the Collection of Norman Dayron) (Nighthawk, Robert & His Flames Of Rhythm)
CD ______ **ROUCD 2022**
Rounder / Sep '91 / ADA / CM / Direct

Nighthawks

BACKTRACK
CD ______ **CDVR 036**
Varrick / '88 / ADA / CM / Direct / Roots

HARD LIVING
CD ______ **CDVR 022**
Varrick / '88 / ADA / CM / Direct / Roots

LIVE IN EUROPE
CD ______ **CCD 11014**
Crosscut / Nov '88 / ADA / CM / Direct

PAIN AND PARADISE
Trouble comin' every day / Shade tree mechanic / Same thing / Soul of a man / High temperature / Pain and paradise / Is love enough / Trouble on the way / I told you so / Snap it
CD ______ **BIGMO 1030**
Big Mo / Oct '96 / ADA / Direct

ROCK THIS HOUSE
CD ______ **BIGMO 1023**
Big Mo / Jul '94 / ADA / Direct

Nighthawks At The Diner

FOOL'S TANGO
King in yellow / Fool's tango / You invented me / Sunday afternoon / Dreamtime intermission / Killing sparrows / For better and for worse / Intel R inside / Won't say goodbye / Paul Wilson GR
CD ______ **AL 73092**
A / Jul '97 / Cadillac / Direct

Nightingale

BREATHING SHADOW
CD ______ **BMCD 66**
Black Mark / May '95 / Plastic Head

Nightingale, Mark

DESTINY
I'm old fashioned / My foolish heart / Song is you / Solitude / Don't mention the blues / Destiny / Whisper not / What is this thing called love
CD ______ **MR 874293**
Mons / Jun '97 / Montpellier

Nightingales

WHAT A SCREAM 1980-1986
Bristol road leads to Dachau / Hark my love / Nowhere to run / Blisters / Idiot strength / Seconds / Return journey / Crunch / Hedonists sigh / My brilliant career / Use your loaf / Which Hi-Fi / Paraffin brain / Only my opinion / Urban ospreys / This / Surplus and scarcity / Crafty fag / It's a cracker / Here we go now / Heroin / What a carry on / Faithful lump / At the end of the day
CD ______ **MAUCD 607**
Mau Mau / '91 / Pinnacle

Nightmare Lodge

NEGATIVE PLANET
CD ______ **MHCD 022**
Minus Habens / Jun '94 / Plastic Head

Nightmare Visions

SUFFERING FROM ECHOES
CD ______ **HNF 013CD**
Head Not Found / Feb '96 / Plastic Head

Nightmares On Wax

SMOKERS DELIGHT
CD ______ **WARPCD 36**
Warp / Sep '95 / Prime / RTM/Disc

WORD OF SCIENCE, A
CD ______ **WARPCD 4**
Warp / Apr '96 / Prime / RTM/Disc

Nightnoise

DIFFERENT SHORE, A
Call of the child / For Eamonn / Falling apples / Busker on the beach / Morning in Madrid / Another wee niece / Different shore / Mind the dresser / Clouds go by / Shuan
CD ______ **01934111662**
Windham Hill / Aug '95 / BMG

SHADOW OF TIME
One little nephew / March air / Shadow of time / Silky flanks / Water falls / Fionnghuala (mouth music) / Nigh in that land / This just in / For you / Sauvie island / Rose of Tralee / Three little nieces
CD ______ **01934111302**
Windham Hill / Nov '93 / BMG

SOMETHING OF TIME
CD ______ **01934110572**
Windham Hill / Jul '93 / BMG

WHITE HORSE SESSIONS
Silky flanks / Shadow of time / Jig of sorts / Shaun / Do we / Murrach na gealaich (Murdo of the moon) / Hugh / Moondance / Crickets wicket / Night in that land / At the races / Heartwood
CD ______ **01934111952**
Windham Hill / Mar '97 / BMG

WINDHAM HILL RETROSPECTIVE, A
19A / Toys not ties / Timewinds / Hugh / Cricket's wicker / Kid in the cot / Something of time / Swan / Bleu / At the races / Hourglass / End of the evening / Nollaig / Bridges / Bring me back a song
CD ______ **01934111112**
Windham Hill / Jan '95 / BMG

Nightsky Bequest

UNCOUNTED STARS, UNFOUNDED DREAMLANDS
CD ______ **POLYPH 004CD**
Polyphemus / Jul '96 / Plastic Head

Nightstick

BLOTTER
Workers of the world unite / Some boys / Set the controls for the heart of the sun / Mommy, what's a funkadelic / Blotter / Fellating the dying Christ
CD ______ **RR 69512**
Relapse / Mar '97 / Pinnacle / Plastic Head

Nightwing

MY KINGDOM COME
CD ______ **LIR 00123**
Long Island / Mar '97 / Cargo

NATURAL SURVIVORS
CD ______ **NM 009CD**
Neat Metal / May '96 / Pinnacle

Nigra Nebula

LIFE AFTER LIFE
CD ______ **EFA 125222**
Celtic Circle / Sep '95 / SRD

Nihilist

HERMIT
CD ______ **AFTERCD 6**
After 6am / Nov '95 / Plastic Head

SIBYL AND HERP
CD ______ **AFTERCD 5**
After 6am / Jan '95 / Plastic Head

Nihon No Oto Ensemble

TRADITIONAL JAPANESE
CD ______ **B 6784**
Auvidis/Ethnic / Oct '94 / ADA / Harmonia Mundi

Nika

STATE OF GRACE
CD ______ **110242**
Musidisc / Nov '93 / Discovery

Nikola

BALKAN TRADITIONAL (Nikola & Friends)
CD ______ **HMA 1903007CD**
Musique D'Abord / Aug '94 / Harmonia Mundi

Nil 8

HAL LE LUJAH
CD ______ **BOOK 2CD**
Worrybird / Nov '93 / SRD

Nile, Willie

ARCHIVE ALIVE
CD ______ **ACH 80009**
Archive / Jul '97 / Greyhound

Nilon Bombers

BIRD
CD ______ **ALMOCD 007**
Almo Sounds / Jul '96 / Pinnacle

Nilsson

VERY BEST OF NILSSON, THE
CD 74321486592
RCA / Aug '97 / BMG

Nilsson, Harry

ALL THE BEST
Without you / Everybody's talkin' / Mother nature's son / It's been so long / Good old desk / Without her / Mournin' glory story / Mr. Richland's favourite song / Mr. Bojangles / She's leaving home / Lullaby in ragtime / Makin' whoopee / Cuddly toy / River deep, mountain high / Little cowboy / As time goes by
CD MCCD 129
Music Club / Sep '93 / Disc / THE

AS TIME GOES BY (The Complete Schmilsson In The Night)
Intro / Lazy moon / For me and my gal / It had to be you / Always / Makin' whoopee / You made me love you / Lullaby in ragtime / I wonder who's kissing her now / What'll I do / Nevertheless (I'm in love with you) / This is all I ask / I'm always chasing rainbows / Make believe / Trust in me / It's only a paper moon / Thanks for the memory / Over the rainbow / As time goes by
CD 74321416362
Camden / Jan '97 / BMG

BEST OF NILSSON, THE
CD 74321223152
RCA / Aug '94 / BMG

EVERYBODY'S TALKIN' (The Very Best Of Harry Nilsson)
Everybody's talkin' / Without you / Me and my arrow / Without her / All I think about is you / Coconut / I guess the Lord must be in New York City / Mr. Bojangles / Spaceman / Little cowboy / Cuddly toy / Puppy song / Moonbeam song / Blanket for a sail / Mr. Richland's favourite song / Cowboy / Mucho mungo / Mother Nature's son / 1941 / Joy / I'll be home / Subterranean homesick blues
CD 74321476772
Camden / Apr '97 / BMG

LITTLE TOUCH OF SCHMILSSON IN THE NIGHT
For me and my gal / It had to be you / Lazy moon / Always / Makin' whoopee / You made me love you / Lullaby in ragtime / I wonder who's kissing her now / What'll I do / Nevertheless / This is all I ask / As time goes by
CD ND 90582
RCA / Aug '91 / BMG

NILSSON SCHMILSSON
Gotta get up / Driving along / Early in the morning / Moonbeam song / Down / Let the good times roll / Jump into the fire / Without you / I'll never leave you
CD ND 83464
RCA / Oct '87 / BMG

PUSSY CATS
Many rivers to cross / Subterranean homesick blues / Don't forget me / All my life / Old forgotten soldier / Save the last dance for me / Mucho mucho/Mt Elga / Loop de loop / Black sails (In the moonlight) / (We're gonna) Rock around the clock
CD 07863505702
RCA / Aug '96 / BMG

SIMPLY THE BEST
CD WMCD 5706
Disky / Oct '94 / Disky / THE

VERY BEST OF NILSSON VOL.1 (Without Her, Without You)
Over the rainbow / Without her / Cuddly toy / Wailing of the willow / Everybody's talkin' / I guess the Lord must be in New York City / Mother Nature's son / Puppy song / Mournin' glory story / Daddy's song / Maybe / Down to the valley / Life line / River deep, mountain high / Moonbeam song / Without you / Mucho mungo / Mount Elga / Subterranean homesick blues
CD ND 90520
RCA / Nov '90 / BMG

VERY BEST OF NILSSON VOL.2 (Lullaby In Ragtime)
Jesus Christ you're tall / Lullaby in ragtime / Something true / 1941 / Don't leave me / One / Sister Marie / Together / I will take you there / Think about your troubles / Me and my arrow / Buy my album / Cowboy / You can't do that / Remember (Christmas) / Daybreak / All I think about is you / Nevertheless (I'm in love with you) / Pretty soon there will be nothing left for everybody / Jesus Christ you're tall
CD ND 90659
RCA / Jan '94 / BMG

Nimal

VOIX DE SURFACE
CD RECDEC 31
Rec Rec / Oct '93 / Cadillac / Plastic Head / ReR Megacorp / SRD

Nimitz, Jack

CONFIRMATION (Nimitz, Jack Quartet)
CD FSR 5006CD
Fresh Sound / Jul '96 / Discovery / Jazz Music

Nimoy, Leonard

HIGHLY ILLOGICAL
CD CREV 017CD
Rev-Ola / Sep '93 / 3mv/Vital

Nimrod

NIMROD
CD SCRATCH 22
Scratch / Feb '97 / Cargo

Nimsgern, Frank

FRANK NIMSGERN (Nimsgern, Frank & Chaka Khan/Billy Cobham)
Last Summer / Just another way out / Catch the time / Take me away / Pretty secrets / Don't you think it's alright / Latin jokes / Pat's prelude / On the trip / Spring
CD 890012
Lipstick / Feb '91 / Vital/SAM

FUNKY SITE
CD INAK 9047
In Akustik / Apr '97 / Direct / TKO Magnum

TRUST
CD INAK 9031
In Akustik / Nov '95 / Direct / TKO Magnum

Nin, Khadja

SAMBOLERA
Sambolera mayi son / Sina mali, sina deni (free) / Wale watu / Mama Lusiya / Save us / Mwana wa mama / Leo Leya / M'barik fall / Soul le charme / Rosy / Bwana C
CD 74321360482
BMG / Jan '97 / BMG

Nine

CLOUD NINE
CD FILECD 469
Profile / Sep '96 / Pinnacle

NINE LIVEZ
CD FILECD 460
Profile / Mar '95 / Pinnacle

Nine Below Zero

BACK TO THE FUTURE
Soft touch / Bad town / Down in the dirt again / On the road again / Sweet little contessa / Mama talk to your daughter / Jump back baby / Another kinda love / One way street / Ain't coming back / Three times enough / Don't point your finger / Eleven plus eleven / Egg on my face / Sugar beet / Wipe away your kiss / Can't say yes, can't say no
CD WOLCD 1040
China / Feb '94 / Pinnacle

ICE STATION ZEBRO
CD 5404302
A&M / Mar '96 / PolyGram

LIVE IN LONDON
CD IGOCD 2023
Indigo / Jun '95 / ADA / Direct

OFF THE HOOK
CD WOLCD 1028
China / Sep '92 / Pinnacle

ON THE ROAD AGAIN
CD WOLCD 1014
China / Apr '91 / Pinnacle

WORKSHY
CD WOKCD 2027
China / Sep '92 / Pinnacle

Nine Inch Nails

BROKEN
Pinion / Wish / Last / Help me I am in hell / Happiness in slavery / Gave up / Physical / Suck
CD IMCD 8004
Island / Oct '92 / PolyGram

DISTURBED (Interview Disc)
CD DIST 001
Disturbed / Mar '96 / Total/BMG

DOWNWARD SPIRAL, THE
Mr. Self destruct / Piggy / Heresy / March of the pigs / Closer / Ruiner / Becoming / I do not want this / Big man with a gun / Warm place / Eraser / Reptile / Downward spiral / Hurt
CD CID 8012
Island / Mar '94 / PolyGram

FIXED
Gave up / Wish / Happiness in slavery / Throw this away / First fuck / Screaming slave
CD IMCD 8005
Island / Dec '92 / PolyGram

FURTHER DOWN THE SPIRAL
Piggy (Nothing can stop me now) / Art of destruction (part 1) / Self destruction / Heresy / Downward spiral / Hurt / At the heart of it all / Ruiner / Eraser (Denial, realization) / Self destruction, final
CD IMCD 8041
Island / May '95 / PolyGram

PRETTY HATE MACHINE
Head like a hole / Terrible lie / Down in it / Sanctified / Something I can never have / Kinda I want to / Sin / That's what I get / Only time / Ringfinger
CD CID 9973
Island / Sep '91 / PolyGram

Nine Lives

COMMON TRAP
CD BD 95001
Black Dog / Jul '96 / Nervous

Nine Pound Hammer

HAYSEED TIMEBOMB
CD EFA 11583 2
Crypt / Sep '94 / Shellshock/Disc

Ninefinger

NINEFINGERED
CD TDH 019
Too Damn Hype / Feb '97 / Cargo / SRD

Niney The Observer

FREAKS
CD HBCD 99
Heartbeat / Mar '95 / ADA / Direct / Greensleeves / Jet Star

HERE I COME AGAIN VOL.1
CD RN 7003
Rhino / Sep '96 / Grapevine/PolyGram / Jet Star

INTRODUCING
CD CB 6003
Caribbean / Jan '96 / TKO Magnum

NINEY THE OBSERVER
CD 14807
Spalax / Jun '97 / ADA / Cargo / Direct / Discovery / Greyhound

OBSERVER ATTACK DUB
CD RUSCD 8209
ROIR / Jul '95 / Plastic Head / Shellshock/ Disc

TURBO CHARGE
CD CDHB 85
Rounder / May '91 / ADA / CM / Direct

Ninjaman

BOOYAKKA BOOYAKKA
Disarm them / Go put it down / This girl is mine / Lighter / Education '94 / Gun fi bun / How master God world a run / Mi easy / Leff him / Reality (Part 2) / 'Pon mi mind / Woman a "U" ways / Matie / Sweeter ways
CD GRELCD 201
Greensleeves / Mar '94 / Jet Star / SRD

BOUNTY HUNTER
CD VYDCD 013
Vine Yard / Jul '96 / Grapevine/PolyGram

DON BAD MAN, THE
CD SONCD 0040
Sonic Sounds / Feb '93 / Jet Star

HARDCORE KILLING
CD GRELCD 191
Greensleeves / Sep '93 / Jet Star / SRD

HOLD ME (LIKE A M16)
Discipline child / Lou Lou / One black rat / Donkey mile / Lead me home / Walk that road / Vintage memories / Coming in hot / Kecke and kotch / On the road again
CD 113822
Musidisc / Jul '95 / Discovery

HOLLOW POINT BAD BOY
Bad boy nuh cub scout / Nuh badda trust dem / Tiger no dead / World dance / Write your will / Hold me / Whap dem bubba / Bad publicity
CD GRELCD 207
Greensleeves / Aug '94 / Jet Star / SRD

NOBODY'S BUSINESS BUT MY OWN
CD SHCD 45007
Shanachie / May '93 / ADA / Greensleeves / Koch

ORIGINAL FRONT TOOTH, GOLDTOOTH, GUN-PON-TOOTH DON GORGON
CD GRELCD 181
Greensleeves / Feb '93 / Jet Star / SRD

RUN COME TEST
CD RASCD 3118
Ras / Sep '93 / Direct / Greensleeves / Jet Star / SRD

TING A LING (SCHOOL PICKNEY)
CD GRELCD 176
Greensleeves / Nov '92 / Jet Star / SRD

WHAT A SHAME
What a shame / Warzone / New Jamaica / Two roads / Thank you Lord / Dem no like it / Bring dem all / Right hand / Bible a go through / Nice and slow
CD 119912
Musidisc UK / Sep '96 / Grapevine/ PolyGram

Nipa

GHANA A CAPELLA
CD 925692
BUDA / Jun '93 / Discovery

Nirvana

BARK AND THE BITE, THE (Interview Disc)
CD DIST 003
Disturbed / Mar '96 / Total/BMG

BLEACH
Blew / Floyd the barber / About a girl / School / Love Buzz / Paper cuts / Negative creep / Scoff / Swap meet / Mr. Moustache / Sifting / Big cheese / Downer
CD GFLD 19291
Geffen / Oct '95 / BMG

FROM THE MUDDY BANKS OF THE WISHKAH
Intro / School / Drain you / Aneurysm / Smeels like teen spirit / Been a son / Lithium / Sliver / Spank thru / Scentless apprentice / Heart-shaped box / Milk it / Negative creep / Polly / Breed / Tourette's / Blew
CD GED 25105
Geffen / Sep '96 / BMG

IN UTERO
Serve the servants / Scentless apprentice / Heart shaped box / Rape me / Frances Farmer will have her revenge on Seattle / Dumb / Very ape / Milk it / Pennyroyal tea / Radio friendly unit shifter / Tourette's / All apologies / Gallons of rubbing alcohol flow through the strip
CD GED 24536
Geffen / Sep '93 / BMG

INCESTICIDE
Dive / Sliver / Been a son / Turnaround / Molly's lips / Son of a gun / (New wave) Polly / Beeswax / Downer / Mexican seafood / Hairspray queen / Aero Zeppelin / Big long now / Aneurysm
CD GED 24504
Geffen / Dec '92 / BMG

INTERVIEW DISC
CD TELL 07
Network / Dec '96 / Total/BMG

INTERVIEW DISC
CD SAM 7008
Sound & Media / Nov '96 / Sound & Media

KURT COBAIN EXPOSE (2CD Set) (Cobain, Kurt)
CD Set OTR 1100039
Metro Independent / Jun '97 / Essential/ BMG

NEVERMIND
Smells like teen spirit / In bloom / Come as you are / Breed / Lithium / Polly / Territorial pissings / Drain you / Lounge act / Stay away / On a plain / Something in the way
CD DGCD 24425
Geffen / Aug '91 / BMG

SINGLE BOX SET (6CD Singles Set)
Smells like teen spirit / Drain you / Even in his youth / Aneurysm / Come as you are / Endless nameless / School / Drain you (live) / Lithium / Been a son / Curmudgeon / D7 / In bloom / Sliver / Polly / Heart shaped box / Milk it / Marigold / All apologies / Rape me / Moist vagina
CD Set GED 24901
Geffen / Nov '95 / BMG

TRIBUTE TO NIRVANA, A (Various Artists)
CD TR 002CD
Tribute / Jul '96 / Plastic Head

UNPLUGGED IN NEW YORK
About a girl / Come as you are / Jesus doesn't want me for a sunbeam / Man who sold the world / Pennyroyal tea / Dumb / Polly / On a plain / Something in the way / Plateau / Oh me / Lake of fire / All apologies / Where did you sleep last night
CD GED 24727
Geffen / Oct '94 / BMG

Nirvana

BLACK FLOWER
Black flower / I believe in magic / It happened two Sundays ago / Life ain't easy / Pentecost Hotel / World is cold without you / We can make it through / Satellite jockey / Excerpt from The blind and the beautiful / June / Tiny goddess / Illinois / Tres tres bien / Love suite
CD EDCD 378
Edsel / Oct '93 / Pinnacle

ORANGE & BLUE
CD EDCD 485
Edsel / Jun '96 / Pinnacle

SECRET THEATRE
CD EDCD 407
Edsel / Jan '95 / Pinnacle

TRAVELLING ON A CLOUD
Rainbow chaser / Pentecost hotel / Tiny Goddess / Girl in the park / Melanie blue / You can try it / Trapeze / Satellite jockey / Wings of love / Show must go on / Touch-

ables (All of us) / We can help you / Oh what a performance / Darling darlane
CD 5109742
Island / Jul '92 / PolyGram

Nissen, Peter

PETER NISSEN
CD BCD 348
GHB / Nov '96 / Jazz Music

Nite Life

AS THE NIGHT MOVES THE SINGING J
CD SUNCD 005
Sunvibe / May '93 / Jet Star

Nitrate

ACID STUKER
CD DBMLABCD 9
Labworks / Sep '96 / RTM/Disc / SRD

Nitrogen

INTOXICA (2CD Set)
CD Set ALPHACD 1
Alphaphone / Dec '96 / Kudos / Pinnacle

Nitschky, Morten

MUSIK TIL DIGTE (Nitschky, Morten Kvartet)
CD ASPCD 3502
Ambia / May '97 / Cadillac

Nitty Gritty

JAH IN THE FAMILY
CD BDCD 005
Greensleeves / Nov '92 / Jet Star / SRD

TRIALS AND CROSSES (Tribute To Nitty Gritty) (Various Artists)
CD VPCD 1304
VP / Aug '93 / Greensleeves / Jet Star / Total/BMG

TURBO CHARGED
Gimme some of you something / Turbo-charged / Ram up the dance / Key to your heart / Rub-a-dub a kill you / Amazing grace / Cry cry baby / Down in the ghetto / Don't want to lose you / Hog in a minty
CD GRELCD 514
Greensleeves / May '92 / Jet Star / SRD

Nitty Gritty Dirt Band

ALIVE/RARE JUNK
Crazy words crazy tune / Buy for me the rain / Candy man / Foggy mountain break-down / Rock me baby / Fat boys (can make it in Santa Monica) / Alligator man / Crazy words, crazy tune / Goodnight my love pleasant dreams / Reason to believe / End of your line / Willie the weeper / Hesitation blues / Sadie Green the vamp of New Orleans / Collegiana / Dr. Heckle and Mr. Jibe / Cornbread and lasses / Number and a name / Mournin' blues / These days
CD BGOCD 245
Beat Goes On / Mar '95 / Pinnacle

ALL THE GOOD TIMES
Sixteen tracks / Fish song / Jambalaya / Down in Texas / Creepin' round your back door / Daisy / Slim Carter / Hoping to say / Baltimore / Jamaica say you will / Do you feel it too / Civil war trilogy / Diggy liggy lo
CD BGOCD 93
Beat Goes On / Dec '90 / Pinnacle

COUNTRY CLASSICS
Battle of New Orleans / I have to do is dream / Bayou jubilee / Sally was a guddun / Rave on / Mr Bojangles / Honky tonkin' / House at pooh corner / Some of shelly's blues / Moon just turned blue / Make a little magic / American dream / Hey good lookin' / Slim carter / Diggy liggy id
CD CDMFP 6328
Music For Pleasure / Apr '97 / EMI

DREAM
CD BGOCD 311
Beat Goes On / Apr '96 / Pinnacle

HOLD ON
Fishin' in the dark / Joe knows how to live / Keepin' the road hot / Blue Ridge Mountain girl / Angelyne / Baby's got a hold on me / Dancing to the beat of a broken heart / Oh what a love / Oleanna / Tennessee
CD 7599255732
Warner Bros. / Feb '95 / Warner Music

PURE DIRT
Buy for me the rain / It's raining here in long beach / Dismal swamp / Tide of love / Holding / Call again / You're gonna' get it in the end / Shadow dream song / Song to Jutta / Teddy bears picnic / Truly right / Put a bar in my car / Candy man / I'll search the sky
CD BGOCD 243
Beat Goes On / Sep '94 / Pinnacle

RICOCHET
Teddy bears picnic / Happy fat annie / Coney island washboard / I'll never forget what's her name / Ooh po pi do girl / Put a bar in my car / It's raining here in long beach / Search the sky / Call again / Tide of love / Truly right / Shadow dream song
CD BGOCD 284
Beat Goes On / Oct '95 / Pinnacle

STARS AND STRIPES FOREVER
Jambalaya / Dirt band interview / Cosmic cowboy Part 1 / Aluminium record award / Fish song / Mr. Bojangles / Vassar Clements interview / Listen to the mockingbird / Sheikh of Araby / Resign yourself to me / Dixie hoedown / Cripple creek / Mountain whippoorwill / Honky tonkin' / House at Pooh corner / Buy for me the rain / Oh boy / Teardrops in my eyes / Glocoat blues / Stars and stripes forever / Battle of New Orleans / It came from the 50's / My true story / Diggy liggy lo
CD BGOCD 128
Beat Goes On / Jul '90 / Pinnacle

UNCLE CHARLIE AND HIS DOG TEDDY
Some of Shelly's blues / Rave on / Livin' without you / Uncle Charlie interview / Mr. Bojangles / Clinch Mountain breakdown / Propinquity / Cure / Opus 36 / Clementi / Chicken reel / Travellin' mood / Billy in the lowground / Swanee river / Randy Lynn rag / Santa Rosa / Prodigal's return / Yukon railroad / House at Pooh Corner / Jesse James / Uncle Charlie / Uncle Charlie interview / End / Spanish fandango
CD BGOCD 22
Beat Goes On / Apr '90 / Pinnacle

WILL THE CIRCLE BE UNBROKEN (2CD Set)
CD Set DC 870432
Disky / Aug '96 / Disky / THE

Nitzer Ebb

BELIEF, THE
CD CDSTUMM 61
Mute / Oct '88 / RTM/Disc

BIG HIT
CD CDSTUMM 118
Mute / Mar '95 / RTM/Disc

EBBHEAD
CD CDSTUMM 88
Mute / Sep '91 / RTM/Disc

SHOWTIME
CD CDSTUMM 72
Mute / Feb '90 / RTM/Disc

THAT TOTAL AGE
Fitness to purpose / Violent playground / Murderous / Smear body / Let your body learn / Let beauty loose / Into the large air / Join in the chant / Alarm / Join in the chant (metal mix) / Fitness to purpose ' / Murderous (instrumental)
CD CDSTUMM 45
Mute / May '87 / RTM/Disc

Nivens

SHAKE
CD DANCD 022
Danceteria / Jan '90 / ADA / Plastic Head / Shellshock/Disc

Nix, Bern

ALARMS AND EXCURSIONS (Nix, Bern Trio)
CD 804372
New World / Sep '93 / ADA / Cadillac / Harmonia Mundi

Nix, Don

GONE TOO LONG/SKYRIDER
Goin' thru another change / Feel a whole lot better / Gone too long / Backstreet girl / rollin' in my dreams / Yazoo city jail / Harpoon Arkansas turnaround / Forgotten town / Demain / Skyrider / Nobody else / Maverick woman blues / Do it again / Long tall Sally / I'll be in your dreams / On the town again / All for the love of a woman
CD DIAB 805
Diabolo / Feb '94 / Pinnacle

Nix, Rev. A.W.

REV. A.W. NIX VOL.1 1927-1928
CD DOCD 5328
Document / Mar '95 / ADA / Hot Shot / Jazz Music

REV. A.W. NIX/REV. EMMETT DICKINSON VOL.2 1928-1931 (Nix, Rev. A.W. & Rev. Emmett Dickinson)
CD DOCD 5490
Document / Nov '96 / ADA / Hot Shot / Jazz Music

Nixon, Mojo

HORNY HOLIDAYS (Nixon, Mojo & The Toadliquors)
CD 422427
New Rose / May '94 / ADA / Direct / Discovery

WHEREABOUTS UNKOWN
CD 422052
Last Call / May '95 / Cargo / Direct / Discovery

No Comment

EYES
CD SPV 07784712
SPV / Jul '94 / Koch / Plastic Head

No Doubt

BEACON STREET COLLECTION, THE
Open the gate / Total hate 95 / Stricken / Greener pastures / By the way / Snakes / That's just me / Squeal / Doghouse / Blue in the face
CD BS 03
Beacon Street / Apr '97 / Plastic Head

NO DOUBT
CD IND 92109
Interscope / Jul '96 / BMG

TRAGIC KINGDOM
Spiderwebs / Excuse me Mr. / Just a girl / Happy now / Different people / Hey you / Climb / Sixteen / Sunday morning / Don't speak / You can do it / World go 'round / End it on this / Tragic kingdom
CD IND 90003
Interscope / Jul '96 / BMG

No For An Answer

THOUGHT CRUSADE, A/FACE THE NATION (No For An Answer/Carry Nation)
CD FLY 002
Tackle Box / Oct '96 / Cargo

No Fraud

NO FRAUD
CD MIND 003CD
Nuclear Blast / Jul '91 / Plastic Head

No Fun At All

AND NOW FOR SOMETHING COMPLETELY DIFFERENT
CD JABSC 003CD
Burning Heart / Apr '97 / Plastic Head

NO STRAIGHT ANGLES
CD BHR 011CD
Burning Heart / Aug '95 / Plastic Head

OUT OF BOUNDS
CD BHR 013CD
Burning Heart / Oct '95 / Plastic Head

STRANDED
CD BHR 023CD
Burning Heart / May '95 / Plastic Head

VISIONS
CD BHR 003CD
Burning Heart / Aug '95 / Plastic Head

No Lesson Learned

ONE MORE SURRENDER
CD LF 269CD
Lost & Found / May '97 / Plastic Head

No Man

DAMAGE THE ENEMY
CD NAR 043CD
New Alliance / May '93 / Plastic Head

HOW THE WEST WAS WON
CD SST 281CD
SST / May '93 / Plastic Head

WHAMON EXPRESS
CD SST 267CD
SST / Sep '90 / Plastic Head

No Man

DRY CLEANING RAY
Dry cleaning Ray / Sweetside silver night / Jack the sax / Diet Mothers / Urban disco / Punished for being born / Kightlinger / Evelyn (The Song of slurs) / Sicknote
CD STONE 035CD
3rd Stone / Jun '97 / Plastic Head / Vital

FLOWERMIX
Angeldust / Faith in you / All I see / Natural neck / Heal the madness / You grow more / Beautiful (version) / Sample / Why the noise / Born simple
CD HIART 002
Hidden Art / Oct '96 / Pinnacle / Vital

FLOWERMOUTH
Angel gets caught in the beauty trap / You grow more beautiful / Animal ghost / Soft shoulders / Shell of a fighter / Teardrop fall / Watching over me / Simple / Things change
CD TPLP 67CD
One Little Indian / Jun '94 / Pinnacle

HEAVEN TASTE
Long day full / Babyship blue / Bleed / Road / Heaven taste
CD HIART 001
Hidden Art / Oct '96 / Pinnacle / Vital

LOVEBLOWS LOVECRIES
CD TPLP 57CD
One Little Indian / May '93 / Pinnacle

WILD OPERA
Radiant city / Pretty genius / Infant phenomenon / Sinister jazz / Housewives hooked on heroin / Librtino libretto / Taste my dream / Dry cleaning ray / Sheep loop / My rival Trevor / Time travel in Texas / My revenge on Seattle / Wild opera
CD STONE 027CD
3rd Stone / Sep '96 / Plastic Head / Vital

No Man Is Roger Miller

WIN INSTANTLY
CD SST 243CD
SST / Jul '89 / Plastic Head

No Means No

0+2=1
CD VIRUS 98CD
Alternative Tentacles / Oct '91 / Cargo / Greyhound / Pinnacle

DAY EVERYTHING BECAME ISOLATED AND DESTROYED, THE
CD Set VIRUS 62/63CD
Alternative Tentacles / Jan '89 / Cargo / Greyhound / Pinnacle

IN THE FISHTANK
CD FIRSTFISH 1CD
Konkurrent / May '97 / SRD

LIVE AND CUDDLY
CD Set VIRUS 97CD
Alternative Tentacles / '92 / Cargo / Greyhound / Pinnacle

MAMA
CD WRONG 001CD
Wrong / Nov '92 / SRD

NO MEANS NO PRESENTS: MR WRIGHT & MR WRONG
CD WRONG 13
Wrong / Oct '94 / SRD

SEX MAD
Sex mad / Dad / Obsessed / No fucking / She beast / Dead Bob / Long days / Metronome / Revenge / Self pity
CD VIRUS 56CD
Alternative Tentacles / '92 / Cargo / Greyhound / Pinnacle

SMALL PARTS ISOLATED AND DESTROYED
CD VIRUS 63CD
Alternative Tentacles / '88 / Cargo / Greyhound / Pinnacle

WHY DO THEY CALL ME MR. HAPPY
CD VIRUS 123CD
Alternative Tentacles / May '93 / Cargo / Greyhound / Pinnacle

WORLDHOOD OF THE WORLD AS SUCH
CD VIRUS 171CD
Alternative Tentacles / Nov '95 / Cargo / Greyhound / Pinnacle

WRONG
CD VIRUS 77CD
Alternative Tentacles / Oct '89 / Cargo / Greyhound / Pinnacle

No Mercy

MY PROMISE
Where do you go / Kiss you all over / Don't make me live without you / When I die / Please don't go / Bonita / My promise to you / D'yer mak R / Missing / This masquerade / In and out / Who do you love / How much I love you / Part of me / Where do you go
CD 74321466902
CD 74321481392
Arista / May '97 / BMG

No Neck Blues Band

LETTER FROM THE EARTH (2CD Set)
CD Set YODSOUND 1
Father Yod/Sound / Apr '97 / Cargo

No No Diet Bang

RAZZIA
CD 1991252
Brambus / Nov '93 / ADA

No One Is Innocent

UTOPIA
Black garden / Invisible / Chile / Nomenklatura / Radio 101 / Le poison / Women / Amere / Autobahn babies / Two people / Ce que nous savons / Inside / Pinecrest solution / Neuromatrix
CD 5243372
Island / Mar '97 / PolyGram

No Quarter

SURVIVORS (The Best Of No Quarter)
Seek 'til I find / No stopping it now / Illusions / Stand for glory / Fooled by your love / Ice cold / Now / Rise to the call / Surrender / Somewhere / What's going on / Survivors / Time and space / Racing for home
CD ETHEL 3
Vinyl Tap / Dec '94 / Cargo / Greyhound / Vinyl Tap

No Safety

LIVE AT THE KNITTING FACTORY
CD KFWCD 149
Knitting Factory / Feb '95 / Cargo / Plastic Head

SPILL
CD _____ KFWCD 127
Knitting Factory / Nov '94 / Cargo / Plastic Head

THIS LOST LEG
CD _____ RECDEC 25
Rec Rec / Oct '93 / Cadillac / Plastic Head / ReR Megacorp / SRD

No Secrets In The Family

PLAY AND STRANGE LAUGHTER
CD _____ RECDEC 23
Rec Rec / Oct '93 / Cadillac / Plastic Head / ReR Megacorp / SRD

No Security

WHEN THE GIST
CD _____ LF 063CD
Lost & Found / Aug '93 / Plastic Head

No Sports

KING SKA
CD _____ PHZCD 49
Unicorn / Jul '90 / Plastic Head

No Sweat

NO SWEAT
Heart and soul / Shake / Stay / On the edge / Waters Flow / Tear down the walls / Generation / Lean on me / Stranger / Mover
CD _____ 8282062
London / May '92 / PolyGram

No Use For A Name

DAILY GRIND, THE
CD _____ FATCD 507
Fatwreck Chords / Sep '93 / Plastic Head

LECHE CON CARNE
CD _____ FAT 522
Fatwreck Chords / Mar '95 / Plastic Head

No.1 De No.1

DAKAR SOUND VOL.6
CD _____ 2002969
Dakar Sound / Jan '97 / Stern's

Noa

CALLING
UNI / Too proud / By the light of the moon / Lama / Space / Too painful / Calling home / Mark of Cain / All is well / Camilla / Manhattan / Tel Aviv / Cascading / Savior
CD _____ GED 24965
Geffen / Jul '96 / BMG

Noakes, Rab

STANDING UP
I've hardly started / I wish I was in England / What do you want the girl to do / Solid gone / Love is a gamble / Downtown lights / Gently does it / Blue dream / Psycho killer / Deep water / Open all night / Niel gow's apprentice / Goodbye to all that / Lenny Bruce / When this bloody war is over / Remember my name / Absolutely sweet Marie
CD _____ MDMCD 003
Moidart / Oct '94 / Conifer/BMG

Noble, Liam

CLOSE YOUR EYES
CD _____ FMRCD 25
Future / Oct '95 / ADA / Harmonia Mundi

Noble, Ray

RAY NOBLE 1941 (Noble, Ray & His Orchestra)
CD _____ CCD 126
Circle / Aug '94 / Jazz Music / Swift / Wellard

VERY THOUGHT OF YOU, THE (Noble, Ray & Al Bowlly)
After all, you're all I'm after / Bugle call rag / By the fireside / Close your eyes / Dinah / Don't say goodbye / Double trouble / Down by the river / Goodnight sweetheart / I'll string along with you / Lazy day / Love is the sweetest thing / Love looked out / Mad about the boy / Maybe I love you too much / Oceans of time / Soon / Time on my hands / Very thought of you / Way down yonder in New Orleans / We've got the moon and sixpence / When you've got a little springtime in your heart / Where am I / You ought to see Sally on Sunday / You're more than all the world to me
CD _____ CDAJA 5115
Living Era / May '94 / Select

VERY THOUGHT OF YOU, THE
Very thought of you / Love is the sweetest thing / Spanish eyes / Dreaming a dream / Slumming on Park Avenue / By the fireside / Top hat, white tie and tails / I used to be colour blind / Medley / That's what life is made of / Let yourself go / Basin Street blues / Oh you nasty man / Change partners / Love locked out / Goodnight sweetheart / Medley / Medley
CD _____ PAR 2032
Parade / Oct '94 / Disc

Noble Rot

REAL LUST FOR LIFE
CD _____ BMCD 52
Black Mark / May '94 / Plastic Head

Noble, Steve

BUD MOON (Noble, Steve & Oren Marshall/Steve Buckley)
CD _____ PPPCD 002
Ping Pong / May '97 / Cadillac

Nobodys

SMELL OF VICTORY, THE
CD _____ HR 622CD
Hopeless / Jul '97 / Cargo / Greyhound

Nock, Mike

IN OUT AND AROUND (Nock, Mike Quartet)
Break time / Dark light / Shadows of forgotten love / Gift / Hadrian's wall / In, out and around
CD _____ CDSJP 119
Timeless Jazz / Jun '91 / New Note/ Pinnacle

NOT WE BUT ONE (Nock, Mike Trio)
CD _____ 860062
Naxos Jazz / Jun '97 / Select

ONDAS
Forgotten love / Ondas / Visionary / Land of the long white cloud / Doors
CD _____ 8291612
ECM / Aug '86 / New Note/Pinnacle

Nocturnal Emissions

BEFEHLOSNOTSTAND
CD _____ DV 22
Dark Vinyl / Nov '93 / Plastic Head / World Serpent

DROWNING IN A SEA OF BLISS
CD _____ TO 4
Touch / Oct '95 / Kudos / Pinnacle

MAGNETIZED LIGHT
CD _____ EEE 16CD
Audioglobe / Nov '94 / Plastic Head

SONGS OF LOVE AND REVOLUTION
CD _____ DVO 19CD
Dark Vinyl / May '95 / Plastic Head / World Serpent

VIRAL SHREDDING
CD _____ DV 011CD
Dark Vinyl / Sep '95 / Plastic Head / World Serpent

Nocturnal Rites

IN A TIME OF BLOOD AND FIRE
CD _____ MRRCD 032
Dark Age Music / Nov '96 / Plastic Head

Nocturne, Johnny

SHAKE 'EM UP (Nocturne, Johnny Band)
CD _____ BBCD 9553
Bullseye Blues / Nov '94 / Direct

WAILIN' DADDY (Nocturne, Johnny Band)
CD _____ BBCD 9526
Bullseye Blues / Jan '93 / Direct

Nocturnus

KEY, THE
CD _____ MOSH 023CD
Earache / Sep '90 / Vital

THRESHOLDS
CD _____ MOSH 055CD
Earache / Apr '92 / Vital

Node

NODE
Clock / Olivine / Slapback / Levy / Propane
CD _____ DVNT 005CD
Deviant / Oct '95 / Prime / Vital

Noferini, Stefano

FROM HERE TO THE MOON
CD _____ ACVCD 016
ACV / Jun '96 / Plastic Head / SRD

NOFX

I HEARD THEY SUCK...LIVE
CD _____ FATCD 528
Fatwreck Chords / Dec '96 / Plastic Head

LONGEST LINE
CD _____ FAT 503CD
Fatwreck Chords / Dec '96 / Plastic Head

MAXIMUM ROCK 'N' ROLL
CD _____ MYSTICCD 180
Mystic / Oct '94 / Cargo / Greyhound / Plastic Head

S & M AIRLINES
CD _____ E 86405CD
Epitaph / Nov '92 / Pinnacle / Plastic Head

Nogenja Jazz Soloist Ensemble

REGNI
CD _____ PSCD 93
Phono Suecia / May '97 / Cadillac / Impetus

Nogueras, Jose

TIEMPO NUEVO
CD _____ 66058077
RMM / Dec '95 / New Note/Pinnacle

Noirin Ni Riain

SOUNDINGS
CD _____ OSSCD 88
Ossian / Dec '94 / ADA / CM / Direct / Highlander

Noise & Paradox

NOISE & PARADOX
CD _____ NOZACD 8
Ninebar / Aug '97 / Kudos / Prime / RTM/ Disc

Noise Addict

MEET THE REAL YOU
CD _____ GR 024CD
Grand Royal / Apr '97 / Cargo / Plastic Head

YOUNG AND JADED
CD _____ GR 005CD
Grand Royal / Apr '97 / Cargo / Plastic Head

Noise Annoys

FIRST STEP
CD _____ EFA 11841CD
Vince Lombard / Jul '93 / SRD

Noise Box

BEGINNING, THE
CD _____ CLP 99272
Cleopatra / Jul '97 / Cargo / Greyhound / Plastic Head / RTM/Disc / SRD

Noise Unit

DECODER
CD _____ EFA 084662
Dossier / May '95 / Cargo / SRD

DRILL
CD _____ 08543372
Westcom / Feb '97 / Koch / Pinnacle

STRATEGY OF VIOLENCE
CD _____ CLEO 94752
Cleopatra / Aug '95 / Cargo / Greyhound / Plastic Head / RTM/Disc / SRD

Noiseaddict

YOUNG AND JADED
I wish I was him / My sarong / Meat / Pop queen / Back in your life / Don't leave
CD _____ WIJ 035CD
Wiiija / Apr '94 / RTM/Disc

Noisebox

MONKEY ASS
CD _____ SPV 08422202
SPV / Jun '95 / Koch / Plastic Head

Noitarega

NOITAREGA
CD _____ 40040CD
Sonifolk / Jun '94 / ADA / CM

Nolan, Anthony

CLASSIC IRISH MELODIES
CD _____ CHCD 040
Chart / Oct '96 / Direct / Koch

Nolan Irie

WORK SO HARD
People can you hear me / People's dub / Work so hard / Dub like nails / Irie feelings / Dub feelings / Because of dub / Turn it up / Dub it up / Never give it up / Just dub it up / Beware, the coming is nigh / Beware, the dub is nigh / Educated dub
CD _____ ARICD 81
Ariwa Sounds / Nov '93 / Jet Star / SRD

Noland, Patrick

PIANO GATHERING LIGHT
CD _____ NAIMCD 011
Naim Audio / May '97 / Koch

Noland, Terry

HYPNOTIZED
Hyopnotized / Ten little women / Come marry me / Oh baby look at me / Don't do me this way / Oh Judy / Sugar drop / Guess I'm gonna fall / There was a fungus among us / Everyone but one / One sweet kiss / Crazy dream / Let me be your hero / Puppy love / Patty baby / Teenage teardrops / Forever loving you / You and I / Leave me alone / My teenage heart / She's gone (master) / Ten little women / Hypnotized / World's a rockin' / Heartless woman / She's gone / That ain't right / Hound dog
CD _____ BCD 15428
Bear Family / Feb '90 / Direct / Rollercoaster / Swift

Nolans

BEST OF THE NOLANS, THE
In the mood for dancing / Attention to me / Don't love me too hard / Gotta pull myself together / Don't make waves / Sexy music / Thank you for the music / Every little thing / Simple case of loving you / I'm never gonna let you break my heart again / If it takes me all night / Let's make love / God knows / Dragon fly / Chemistry / Who's gonna rock you / Every home should have one / Touch me in the morning / Crashing down / Spirit, body and soul
CD _____ 4840442
Epic / May '96 / Sony

I'M IN THE MOOD FOR DANCING
I'm in the mood for dancing / Attention to me / Don't love me too hard / Chemistry / Dragonfly / Crashin' down / Sexy music / Gotta pull myself together / Every home should have one / Who's gonna rock you / Spirit, body and soul / Don't make waves
CD _____ QED 029
Tring / Nov '96 / Tring

I'M IN THE MOOD FOR DANCING
I'm in the mood for dancing / Attention to me / Don't love me too hard / Chemistry / Dragonfly / Crashin' down / Sexy music / Gotta pull myself together / Every home should have one / Who's gonna rock you / Spirit, body and soul / Don't make waves
CD _____ 101152
CMC / May '97 / BMG

VERY BEST OF THE NOLANS, THE
Somebody loves you / That's what friends are for / I'm in the mood for dancing / Who's gonna rock you / Dragonfly / Chemistry / Every home should have one / Gotta pull myself together / Out of control / Don't love me too hard / Attention to me / Don't make waves / Crashing down / Run to you / Sexy music / Spirit, body and soul / Almaz / Unchained melody
CD _____ SUMCD 4062
Summit / Nov '96 / Sound & Media

Nolet, Jim

WITH YOU
CD _____ KFWCD 150
Knitting Factory / Feb '95 / Cargo / Plastic Head

Nomad

QUATUOR VOCAL
CD _____ TE 011
EPM / Jun '97 / ADA / Discovery

Nomad, Naz

GIVE DADDY THE KNIFE, CINDY (Nomad, Naz & The Nightmares)
Nobody but me / Action woman / Wind blows your hair / Kicks / Cold turkey / She lied / I had too much to dream last night / Trip / I can only give you everything / I can't stand this love, goodbye / Do you know I know / Just call me Sky
CD _____ CDWIKM 21
Big Beat / Jun '88 / Pinnacle

Nomadix

ROAR TO THE MAX
CD _____ NDXCD 002
Roar / Aug '96 / Jet Star / Roots Collective / SRD

Nomads

POWERSTRIP
(I'm) out of it / Bad vibes / Better off dead / I don't know/I don't care / Sacred / Just lost / Kinda crime / Dig up the hatchet / Robert Johnsong / In the doghouse / Glad to be in your past / Blind spot
CD _____ RTD 1578082
World Service / Jun '94 / Vital

Nomicon

NOMICON/SARNATH (Split CD) (Nomicon/Sarnath)
CD _____ SHR 011CD
Shiver / Aug '95 / Plastic Head

Nomos

I WON'T BE AFRAID ANYMORE
CD _____ GRACD 205
Grapevine / Apr '95 / Grapevine/PolyGram

SET YOU FREE
CD _____ GRACD 230
Grapevine / Aug '97 / Grapevine/PolyGram

Non

BLOOD AND FAME
CD _____ CDSTUMM 32
Mute / Jan '87 / RTM/Disc

IN THE SHADOW OF THE SWORD
CD _______ CDSTUMM 113
Mute / Oct '92 / RTM/Disc

MIGHTI
CD _______ CDSTUMM 139
Mute / Oct '95 / RTM/Disc

Non-Fiction

IT'S A WONDERFUL LIE
CD _______ 085518242
SPV / Jan '96 / Koch / Plastic Head

Nonce

WORLD ULTIMATE
CD _______ 74321254522
RCA / Oct '95 / BMG

Nonchalant

UNTIL THE DAY
Intro / It's all over love / Crab rappers / 5 O'clock / Lookin' good to me / Kickin' it with non / Have a good time / Lights n' sirens / Non interlude / Until the day / Mr. Good Stuff / Thank you / Outro
CD _______ MCD 11265
MCA / Apr '96 / BMG

Nonet, Arnaud

KAMALA (Nonet, Arnaud Mattei)
CD _______ CDLLL 147
La Lichere / Aug '93 / ADA / Discovery

Nonoyesno

DEPSHIT ARKANSAS
CD _______ NB 0942
Nuclear Blast / Feb '94 / Plastic Head

Nonplace Urban Field

GOLDEN STAR
CD _______ INCCD 3315
Incoming / Apr '97 / Pinnacle

Nookie

SOUND OF MUSIC, THE
CD _______ RIVETCD 5
Reinforced / Mar '95 / SRD

Noonan, Carol

ABSOLUTION
CD _______ CDPH 1176
Philo / Sep '95 / ADA / CM / Direct

NOONAN BUILDING AND WRECKING (Noonan, Carol Band)
CD _______ PH 1196CD
Philo / Aug '96 / ADA / CM / Direct

Noone, Jimmie

APEX OF NEW ORLEANS JAZZ, THE (His 25 Greatest)
Play that thing: *Powers, Ollie Harmony Syncopators* / Messin' around: *Cookie's Gingersnaps* / Here comes the hot tamale man: *Cookie's Gingersnaps* / I know that you know: *Noone, Jimmie Apex Club Orchestra* / Four of five times: *Noone, Jimmie Apex Club Orchestra* / Every evening: *Noone, Jimmie Apex Club Orchestra* / Apex blues: *Noone, Jimmie Apex Club Orchestra* / Monday date: *Noone, Jimmie Apex Club Orchestra* / Blues my naughty sweetie gives to me: *Noone, Jimmie Apex Club Orchestra* / Oh sister ain't that hot: *Noone, Jimmie Apex Club Orchestra* / King Joe: *Noone, Jimmie Apex Club Orchestra* / Some rainy day: *Noone, Jimmie Apex Club Orchestra* / Chicago rhythm: *Noone, Jimmie Apex Club Orchestra* / I got a misery: *Noone, Jimmie Apex Club Orchestra* / I lost my gal from Memphis: *Noone, Jimmie New Orleans Band* / San: *Noone, Jimmie Apex Club Orchestra* / Way down yonder in New Orleans: *Noone, Jimmie New Orleans Band* / Blues jumped a rabbit: *Noone, Jimmie New Orleans Band* / Sweet Georgia Brown: *Noone, Jimmie New Orleans Band* / New Orleans hop scop blues: *Noone, Jimmie Orchestra* / Keystone blues: *Noone, Jimmie Orchestra* / Clambake in B flat: *Capitol Jazz Band* / Muskrat ramble: *Ory, Kid Creole Jazz Band* / Sugarfoot stomp: *Ory, Kid Creole Jazz Band*
CD _______ CDAJA 5235
Living Era / Apr '97 / Select

CLASSICS 1930-1934
CD _______ CLASSICS 641
Classics / Nov '92 / Discovery / Jazz Music

CLASSICS 1934-1940
CD _______ CLASSICS 651
Classics / Nov '92 / Discovery / Jazz Music

COLLECTION VOL.1, THE
CD _______ COCD 06
Collector's Classics / Nov '92 / Cadillac / Complete/Pinnacle / Jazz Music

COMPLETE RECORDINGS VOL.1 (3CD Set)
Lonesome and sorry / Baby o' mine / My blue heaven / Miss Annabelle Lee / I know that you know / Sweet Sue, just you / Four or five times / Every evening I miss you / Ready for the river / Forevermore / Oh sister ain't that hold / I ain't got nobody / Apex blues / Monday date / Blues my naughty sweetie gives to me / King Joe / Sweet Lorraine / Some rainy day / It's tight like that / Let's sow a wild oat / She's funny that way / St. Louis blues / Chicago rhythm / I got a misery / Wake up chill'un, wake up / Love me or leave me / Anything you want / Birmingham Bertha / Am I blue / My daddy's rock me / Ain't misbehavin' / That rhythm man / Off time / S'posin' / True blue / Through / Satisfied / I'm doin' what I'm doin' for love / He's a good man to have around / My melancholy baby / After you've gone / Love / El rado scuffle / Deep trouble / Crying for the Carolines / Have a little faith in me / Should I / I'm following you / When you're smiling / I lost my gal from Memphis / On revival day / I'm drifting back to dreamland / Virginia Lee / So sweet / San
CD Set _______ CDAFS 10273
Affinity / Oct '92 / Cadillac / Jazz Music / Koch

INTRODUCTION TO JIMMIE NOONE 1923-1940, AN
CD _______ 4034
Best Of Jazz / Jul '96 / Discovery

JIMMIE NOONE
CD _______ VILCD 0212
Village Jazz / Sep '92 / Jazz Music / Target/BMG

JIMMIE NOONE - 1930-1935 (Noone, Jimmie Apex Club Orchestra)
CD _______ SWAGGIECD 505
Swaggie / Jun '93 / Jazz Music

JIMMIE NOONE 1923-1928
CD _______ CLASSICS 604
Classics / Sep '91 / Discovery / Jazz Music

JIMMIE NOONE 1928-1929 (Noone, Jimmie & Friends)
CD _______ CLASSICS 611
Classics / Feb '92 / Discovery / Jazz Music

JIMMIE NOONE 1929-1930
CD _______ CLASSICS 632
Classics / Nov '92 / Discovery / Jazz Music

Noone, Peter

I'M INTO SOMETHING GOOD
CD _______ WMCD 5630
Disky / Oct '94 / Disky / THE

PETER NOONE SINGS HITS OF HERMAN'S HERMITS
CD _______ MU 5021
Musketeer / Oct '92 / Disc

Nooten, Pieter

SLEEPS WITH THE FISHES (Nooten, Pieter & Michael Brook)
CD _______ CAD 710 CD
4AD / Oct '87 / RTM/Disc

Nora

NORA
CD _______ HABITCD 002
Habit / Oct '95 / Plastic Head

Norbo, Soren

SOREN NORBO & JOAKIM MILDER (Norbo, Soren & Joakim Milder)
CD _______ MECCACD 2012
Music Mecca / May '97 / Cadillac / Jazz Music / Wellard

Nord Express

CENTRAL
CD _______ SLR 057CD
Slumberland / May '97 / Cargo

NORD EXPRESS
CD _______ SLR 051CD
Slumberland / Dec '96 / Cargo

Nord Rundfunk Bigband

BRAVISSIMO
Cat / Blue monk / Voodoo chile / Sagma / Night in Tunesia / Take the 'A' train / Superconductivity / Sister Sadie / Mood indigo / Django / Descent / Country roads
CD _______ 92322
Act / Jun '96 / New Note/Pinnacle

Nordenstam, Stina

AND SHE CLOSED HER EYES
CD _______ 4509938982
East West / Dec '96 / Warner Music

DYNAMITE
Under your command / Dynamite / Almost a smile / Mary Bell / Man with the gun / Until / This time John / CQD / Down desire avenue / Now that your leaving
CD _______ 0630182402
East West / Apr '97 / Warner Music

MEMORIES OF A COLOR
Memories of a color / Return of Alan Bean / Another story girl / His song / He watches her from behind / I'll be cryin' for you / Alone at night / Soon after Christmas / Walk in the dark
CD _______ 4509907672
East West / Dec '96 / Warner Music

Nordes

CRUZ DE PEDRA
CD _______ 20054CD
Sonifolk / Dec '94 / ADA / CM

Nordic All Women Big Band

SOMEWHERE IN TIME
CD _______ MECCACD 1048
Music Mecca / Nov '94 / Cadillac / Jazz Music / Wellard

Nordine, Ken

COLORS
CD _______ EFA 709542
Asphodel / Sep '96 / Cargo / SRD

DEVOUT CATALYST
CD _______ GDCD 4017
Grateful Dead / Feb '92 / Pinnacle

Nordstrom, Inger

I'LL LET YOU MAKE IT UP TO ME
CD _______ CDSGP 0145
Prestige / Jul '96 / Else / Total/BMG

Nordstrom, Nils

UR UPP LANDSKT (Nordstrom, Nils & Ann-Christine Granfors)
CD _______ AW 9CD
Tongang / Aug '96 / ADA

Noren, Fredrik

JAZZ IN SWEDEN 1980
CD _______ 1211
Caprice / Feb '87 / ADA / Cadillac / CM / Complete/Pinnacle

Noris, Gunter

DANCE WITH ME
Dirty mambo / Night dance / Tango negro / Corrida / Rainbow melody / Rock 'n' roll forever / Leipziger jive / Babloo you / Cha cha cubana / Viva la samba / Midnight in Munich / Animation / Brandenburger schwung / Furstenberg fantasie / Swinging Berlin / Frohliches meissen
CD _______ 12712
Laserlight / May '96 / Target/BMG

HOLIDAY DANCING (Noris, Gunter & His Gala Big Band)
CD _______ EDL 29172
Savoy / Dec '95 / Savoy / THE / TKO Magnum

TANZE MIT MIR IN DEN MORGEN (Noris, Gunter & His Gala Big Band)
CD _______ EDL 29142
Savoy / Dec '95 / Savoy / THE / TKO Magnum

WE PLAY REQUESTS VOL.1
CD _______ WRCD 5001
WRD / Oct '95 / Target/BMG

WE PLAY REQUESTS VOL.2
CD _______ WRCD 5002
WRD / Oct '95 / Target/BMG

Norman, Charlie

PAPA PIANO
CD _______ NCD 8830
Phontastic / Jun '94 / Cadillac / Jazz Music / Wellard

Norman, Chris

MIDNIGHT LADY (16 Original Hits)
CD _______ 12211
Laserlight / Nov '93 / Target/BMG

Norman, Jessye

CHRISTMAS ALBUM OF THE YEAR, THE (In The Spirit - Songs For Christmas)
Angels from the realms of glory / First Noel / It came upon a midnight clear / Away in a manger / O come little children / Of the Father's love begotten / Mary had a baby / Lo' how a rose e'er blooming / Puer natus / Ave Maria / Noel nouvelet / Christmas garland / Balade du Jesus-Christ / Silent night / Balm in Gilead / O come all ye faithful (adeste fidelis)
CD _______ 4549852
Philips / Nov '96 / PolyGram

Norman, Jim

TIME CHANGES
CD _______ DL 24005
Dark Light Music / Jun '96 / Grapevine/ PolyGram

Normand, Carla

JUST YOU (Normand, Carla & The New Deal Jazz Band)
CD _______ ACD 244
Audiophile / Apr '93 / Jazz Music

Norovbanzad, Namdzilin

URTIIN DUU
CD _______ JVC 53942
JVC World Library / Sep '96 / ADA / CM / Direct

Norris, Ken

MODERN FOLKLORE
CD _______ 829382
BUDA / Feb '97 / Discovery

Norris, Walter

HUES OF BLUES
Fontessa / Serenata / Hues of blues / I want to be happy / I can't get started (With you) / Backbone mode / Have you met Miss Jones / Spider web / Orchids in green / Afterthoughts
CD _______ CCD 4671
Concord Jazz / Nov '95 / New Note/ Pinnacle

LIVE AT MAYBECK RECITAL HALL VOL.4
Song is you / 'Round midnight / Waltz for Walt / Best thing for you / Darn that dream / Scrambled / Modus vivendi / It's always Spring / Body and soul
CD _______ CCD 4425
Concord Jazz / Aug '90 / New Note/ Pinnacle

SUNBURST (Norris, Walter Quartet)
Sunburst / What's new / Naima / Stella by starlight / Never should it ever end / So in love
CD _______ CCD 4486
Concord Jazz / Nov '91 / New Note/ Pinnacle

WINTER ROSE (Norris, Walter & Aladar Pege)
Playground / Winter rose / Elvesztetten paromat / For high notes / Child is born / Evening lights / Enkephalins
CD _______ ENJACD 30672
Enja / Oct '96 / New Note/Pinnacle / Vital/ SAM

Norrlatar

RAVN
Smaflamskan / En lohtua loyva / Lapp-Nilspolska / Ust Awarm / Nabbskotaget fran norr / Vals fran Alvik / Polska efter Fritz Sandberg / Sytamestani rakastan / Mikaels polska / Ravn
CD _______ XOUCD 105
Xource / May '97 / ADA / Direct

SIGN OF THE RAVEN
Ruts lilla / Silbaatno / Dans kring kuddens kudde / Shottis fran lulea / Karin och kalle / Sarisuando / Vackra norskan / Visa fran erkheikki / Algen / Ko over sarek / Sepan salli / Visa fran kieksiaisvaara / Tukkipoika / Sermiliik / Valurei / Na del twin
CD _______ RESCD 506
Resource / Jul '97 / ADA / Direct

Norte, Marisela

NORTE/WORD
CD _______ NAR 062CD
New Alliance / May '93 / Plastic Head

North Sea Gas

CALEDONIAN CONNECTION
CD _______ CDITV 483
Scotdisc / Jul '89 / Conifer/BMG / Duncans / Ross

KELTIC HERITAGE
CD _______ CDITV 541
Scotdisc / Sep '91 / Conifer/BMG / Duncans / Ross

POWER OF SCOTLAND, THE
CD _______ CDITV 607
Scotdisc / Oct '95 / Conifer/BMG / Duncans / Ross

Northeast Winds

IRELAND BY SAIL
CD _______ FE 2054
Folk Era / Dec '94 / ADA / CM

NORTHEAST WINDS ON TOUR
CD _______ FE 1403
Folk Era / Nov '94 / ADA / CM

Northern Cree Singers

COME & DANCE
CD _______ CRCD 6246
Canyon / Aug '96 / ADA

Northern Jazz Orchestra

GOOD NEWS
CD _______ LACD 38
Lake / Sep '94 / ADA / Cadillac / Direct / Jazz Music / Target/BMG

Northern Lights

CAN'T BUY YOUR WAY
Can't buy your way / My only love / Lighthouse / When the time had fully come / September's end / Rainmaker / City on a

hill / Take you back again / Heartache tonight / Shake this feeling / Jubilation / Anger and tears / On the edge
CD ______ FF 70593
Flying Fish / Mar '97 / ADA / CM / Direct / Roots

LIVING IN THE CITY
CD ______ RHRCD 94
Red House / Sep '96 / ADA / Koch

TAKE YOU TO THE SKY
Northern rain / Hold watcha got / Roseville fair / Early morning riser / Let it roll / T for Texas / Winterhawk / Home brew fever / April snow / Souvenirs / Back on my mind again / Bourree/Borealis blues
CD ______ FF 70533
Flying Fish / Nov '96 / ADA / CM / Direct / Roots

WRONG HIGHWAY BLUES
CD ______ FF 70632
Flying Fish / Nov '96 / ADA / CM / Direct / Roots

Northern Picture Library

ALASKA
Untitled / Into the ether / Catholic Easter colours / Glitter spheres / Insecure / Dreams and stars and sleep / Lucky / LSD icing / Truly madly deeply / Isn't it time you faced the truth / Untitled / Skylight / Of traffic and the ticking / Lucky (reprise) / Monotone
CD ______ ASKCD 023
Vinyl Japan / Oct '93 / Plastic Head / Vinyl Japan

Northrop, Kate

ROOTS & WINGS
CD ______ BRAM 1992342
Brambus / Nov '93 / ADA

Northup, Harry E.

HOMES
CD ______ NAR 120CD
New Alliance / Nov '95 / Plastic Head

Norton, Ricky

LITTLE SISTER
CD ______ ARN 001
Antea / Dec '96 / Nervous

Norvo, Red

DANCE OF THE OCTOPUS
Knockin' on wood / Honeysuckle rose / Blues in E flat / Gramercy square / Music goes 'round and around / I got rhythm / Oh Lady be good
CD ______ HEPCD 1044
Hep / Aug '95 / Cadillac / Jazz Music / New Note/Pinnacle / Wellard

FORWARD LOOK, THE (Norvo, Red Quintet)
Rhee waahnee / Forward look / Between the Devil and the deep blue sea / Room 608 / For Lena and Lennie / Cookin' at the Continental
CD ______ RR 8CD
Reference Recordings / Sep '91 / Jazz Music / May Audio

JIVIN' THE JEEP
CD ______ HEPCD 1019
Hep / Dec '87 / Cadillac / Jazz Music / New Note/Pinnacle / Wellard

LIVE FROM THE BLUE GARDENS: JANUARY 1942 (Norvo, Red & His Orchestra)
CD ______ MM 65090
Music Masters / Oct '94 / Nimbus

ON DIAL
Hallelujah / Get happy / Slam slam blues / Congo blues
CD ______ SPJCD 127
Spotlite / Apr '95 / Cadillac / Jazz Music / New Note/Pinnacle / Swift

RED NORVO VOL.1
CD ______ VJC 10052
Victorious Discs / Feb '91 / Jazz Music

RED NORVO WITH TAL FARLOW & CHARLES MINGUS VOL.2 (Norvo, Red/ Tal Farlow/Charles Mingus)
CD ______ VJC 10082
Vintage Jazz Classics / Oct '92 / ADA / Cadillac / CM / Direct

RED NORVO'S FABULOUS JAM SESSION
Hallelujah / Congo blues / Slam slam blues
CD ______ STB 2514
Stash / Sep '95 / ADA / Cadillac / CM / Direct / Jazz Music

ROCK IT FOR ME
Tears in my heart / Worried over you / Clap hands, here comes Charlie / Russian lullaby / Always and always / I was doing all right / 'S Wonderful / Our love is here to stay / Serenade to the stars / More than ever / Weekend of a private secretary / Please be kind / Jeannie, I dream of lilac time / Tea time / How can you forget / There's a boy in Harlem / Says my heart / Moonshine over Kentucky / Rock it for me / After dinner speech / If you were in my place (What would you do)
CD ______ HEPCD 1040
Hep / Sep '94 / Cadillac / Jazz Music / New Note/Pinnacle / Wellard

WIGWAMMIN'
Daydreaming (all night long) / Cigarette and a silhouette / (I've been) savin' myself for you / You leave me breathless / Put your heart in a song / Wigwammin' / Sunny side of things / How can I thank you / Garden of the moon / Just you, just me / Now it can be told / Jump jumps here / I haven't changed a thing / Love is where you find it / I used to be colour blind / Tisket-a-tasket / This is madness (to love like this) / Who blew out the flame / You're a sweet little headache / I have eyes / St Louis blues / You must have been a beautiful baby / Have you forgotten so soon
CD ______ HEPCD 1050
Hep / Jan '97 / Cadillac / Jazz Music / New Note/Pinnacle / Wellard

Nosferatu

LEGEND
CD ______ CLEO 10162
Cleopatra / Mar '94 / Cargo / Greyhound / Plastic Head / RTM/Disc / SRD

PRINCE OF DARKNESS
CD ______ HADCD 002
Hades / Aug '96 / RTM/Disc

RISE
Gathering / Rise / Dark angel / Her heaven / Lucy is red / Lament / Alone / Vampyres cry / Crysania / Siren / Away / Close
CD ______ POSSCD 006
Possession / May '93 / Vital

Nostramus

EARTHLIGHTS
CD ______ HEMP 5CD
Recordings Of Substance / Jun '97 / 3mv/ Vital / Kudos / Prime

Not Available

RESISTANCE IS FUTILE
CD ______ LF 268CD
Lost & Found / May '97 / Plastic Head

Not Even The TV

NOT EVEN THE TV
CD ______ ANA 001
Anathema / Oct '96 / Cargo

Not Sensibles

INSTANT PUNK CLASSICS
(I'm in love with) Margaret Thatcher / Little boxes / Garry Bushell's band of the week / Death to disco / Coronation Street hustle / Lying on the sofa / Instant classic / Girl with scruffy hair / Freedom / King Arthur / Ploppy / I am a clone / Sick of being normal / (Love is like) Banging my head against a brick wall / Because I'm mine / Wrong love / Blackpool rock / Daddy won't let me love you song / Don't wanna work anymore / I thought you were dead / I make a balls of everything I do / Teenage revolution / I am the bishop / Telephone rings again
CD ______ CDPUNK 38
Anagram / Aug '94 / Cargo / Pinnacle

Notes, Freddie

MONTEGO BAY (Notes, Freddie & The Rudies)
CD ______ CDTRL 349
Trojan / Sep '95 / Direct / Jet Star

Nothing Painted Blue

FUTURE OF COMMUNICATIONS, THE
Sorely tempted / Shaky start / Vengeful as hell / Lapped / I'm a haunted house / Future of communications
CD ______ SCT 0472
Scat / Sep '95 / Vital

PLACEHOLDERS
Couldn't be simpler / Weak / Drinking game / Career day / Spread your poison / In May / Masonic eye / Ballwalker / Travel well / Rightful heir / Houseguest / Kissing booth / Can't f
CD ______ SCT 0372
Scat / Oct '94 / Vital

POWER TRIPS DOWN LOVERS' LANE
White bicycles / Peace dividend / Block Colors / Officer Angel / Campaign Song / Register / Storefronts / Unscheduled Train / Epistemophelia / Smothered / Scapegoat / Few / Rock 'n' roll friend / Undeserving
CD ______ KOKOPOP 001CD
Kokopop / Aug '93 / Vital

Notorious BIG

LIFE AFTER DEATH (2CD Set)
Life after death / Somebody's gotta die / Hypnotize / Mad rapper / Kick in the door / Lovin' you tonight / Last day / Dice / I love the dough / What's beef / BIG / I'm coming out (more money) / Niggaz bleed / Story to tell / Notorious thugs / Interlude / Missing you / Another man / Cali (interlude) / Going back to Cali / 10 crack commandments / Playa hater / Interlude / Nasty boy / Interlude / Sky's the limit / World is filled / Interlude / My downfall / Long kiss goodnight / You're nobody
CD Set ______ 78612730112
Puff Daddy / Mar '97 / BMG

READY TO DIE
Intro / Things done changed / Gimmie the loot / Machine gun funk / Warning / Ready to die / One more change / Me (interlude) / What / Juicy / Everyday struggle / Me and my / Big poppa / Respect / Friend of mine / Unbelievable / Suicidal thoughts
CD ______ 78612730002
Arista / May '97 / BMG

Notre-Dame D'Argentan ...

REX PACIFICUS (Notre-Dame D'Argentan Benedictine Monks Choir)
CD ______ 74321333272
Milan / Sep '96 / Conifer/BMG / Silva Screen

Notre-Dame De Triors ...

GAUDE ET LAETARE (Notre-Dame De Triors Benedictine Monks Choir)
CD ______ 74321333262
Milan / Sep '96 / Conifer/BMG / Silva Screen

Notting Hillbillies

MISSING...PRESUMED HAVING A GOOD TIME
Railroad worksong / Bewildered / Your own sweet way / Run me down / One way gal / Blues stay away from me / Will you miss me / Please baby / Weapon of prayer / That's where I belong / I feel like going home
CD ______ 8426712
Vertigo / May '97 / PolyGram

Nottingham Forest FC

YOU REDS (20 Forest Favourites) (Various Artists)
We've got the whole world in our hands: *Nottingham Forrest & Paper Lace* / You can't win them all: *Clough, Brian & JJ. Barrie* / Brian: *Fat & Frantic* / Nottingham Forrest: *Blakwell, Vic & Supporters* / Marching to Munich: *Karl & the Heidelburgers* / You'll never walk alone: *Anderson, Viv & Trevor Francis* / Nottingham Forrest is my rock 'n' roll: *NJaal Helle* / Who'll win the European cup: *Medium Wave Band* / Magic in Madrid: *Shandy, Tristam* / Come on you forrest: *Fans* / Forest fire: *Strikers* / Nottingham forest is my soul: *NJaal Helle* / Do it cos you like it: *Fashanu, Justin* / We reign supreme: *Blott, Geoff & the Nottingham Boys* / You reds: *Resistance 77* / Psycho: *Merry Men* / Sorted for clough: *Give Us A Kiss* / Robin Hood: *Cortez, Hector & his Formation* / Road to Nottingham: *Richards, Josh* / It's only a game: *Clough, Brian & JJ Barrie & friends*
CD ______ CDGAFFER 8
Cherry Red / Aug '96 / Pinnacle

Nottingham Harmonic Choir

CHRISTMAS CAROLS
O little town of Bethlehem / O come all ye faithful (adeste fidelis) / God rest ye merry gentlemen / Silent night / Hark the herald angels sing / While shepherds watched their flocks / Good King Wenceslas / We wish you a Merry Christmas / Twelve days of Christmas / Torches / Christmas is coming / Of the Father's heart begotten / Personent hodie / O come, O come, Emmanuel / Holly and the ivy
CD ______ XMAS 001
Tring / Nov '96 / Tring

Notwist

12
CD ______ COM 10032162
Community / Jun '97 / Cargo

LIVE
CD ______ YCLS 021
Your Choice / Aug '94 / Plastic Head

Nouvelles Lectures ...

SPIRITUS REX (Nouvelles Lectures Cosmopolites)
CD ______ ETCD 12
Semantic / Apr '94 / Plastic Head

Nova Mob

NOVA MOB
Shoot your way to freedom / Puzzles / Buddy / See and feel and know / Little Miss Information / I won't be there anymore / Please don't ask / Sins of their sons / Beyond a reasonable doubt / If I was afraid/ Coda
CD ______ RTD 15717442
World Service / Apr '94 / Vital

Novak Seen

NOVAK SEEN
CD ______ SPV 08545832
SPV / Jun '96 / Koch / Plastic Head

Novalis

BANISHED BRIDGE
CD ______ RR 7050
Repertoire / Jun '97 / Greyhound

November's Doom

AMID ITS HALLOWED MIRTH
CD ______ AV 010
Avant Garde / Feb '95 / Plastic Head / RTM/Disc

Novembre

WISH IT WOULD
CD ______ POLYPH 001CD
Polyphemus / Jun '95 / Plastic Head

Novick, Billy

REMEMBERING YOU
CD ______ DARINGCD 3018
Daring / Oct '95 / ADA / CM / Direct

Novocaine

FRUSTRATION NO.10
CD ______ FIREMCD 61
Fire / Jan '97 / Pinnacle / RTM/Disc

NERVOUS DISPOSITION
Walls / Mother/father / Awake / Bittersoul / Stoneface / Frustration no.10 / Pondlife / Million miles / Sorry (scum like me) / Boring git / Waiting / Analyse / Horses / She knows nothing
CD ______ FIRECD 67
Fire / Aug '97 / Pinnacle / RTM/Disc

Now

ACME 143
CD ______ FO 26CD
Fearless / Apr '97 / Cargo / Plastic Head

Nowomowa

WASTED LANDS, THE
CD ______ NAGE 20 CD
Art Of Landscape / '88 / Sony

NRA

IS THIS FOR REAL
CD ______ BC 1708
Blitzcore / Oct '96 / Cargo

SURF CITY AMSTERDAM
CD ______ IGN 2H
Ignition / Mar '94 / Plastic Head

NRBQ

GOD BLESS US ALL
CD ______ ROUCD 3108
Rounder / '88 / ADA / CM / Direct

GROOVES IN ORBIT
Smackaroo / When things was cheap / Rain at the drive-in / How can I make you love me / Girl like that / Twelve bar blues / I like that girl / My girlfriend's pretty / Get rhythm / Daddy-O / Hit the hay
CD ______ C5CD 589
See For Miles/C5 / Aug '92 / Pinnacle

HONEST DOLLAR
CD ______ RCD 10240
Rykodisc / Jul '92 / ADA / Vital

MESSAGE FOR THE MESS AGE
Over your head / Don't bite the head / Designated driver / Everybody thinks I'm crazy / Spampinato / Advice for teenagers / Everybody's smokin' / Little bit of bad / Big dumb jukebox / Ramona / Nothin' wrong with me / Better word for love / Girl scout cookies
CD ______ RSFCD 800
Sequel / Oct '96 / BMG

TOKYO
I want you bad / Rain at the drive-in / Crazy girl / Just ain't fair / Ramona / Green lights / Ain't it all right / Everybody thinks I'm crazy / Blues stay away from me / Miracles / Little floater / I love her, she loves me / RC Cola and a Moon pie / If I don't have you / Me and the boys / You and I and George / Want you to feel good too
CD ______ ROUCD 3146
Rounder / Feb '97 / ADA / CM / Direct

UNCOMMON DENOMINATORS
CD ______ ROUCD 11506
Rounder / '88 / ADA / CM / Direct

WILD WEEKEND
It's a wild weekend / Little floater / Fire works / Boy's life / If I don't have you / Boozoo / That's who / Poppin' circumstance / One and only / Immortal for a while / Fraction of action / This love is true / Like a locomotive
CD ______ VUSCD 12
Virgin / Feb '90 / EMI

YOU'RE NICE PEOPLE YOU ARE
You're nice people you are / Encyclopedia / Always safety first / Music lesson / There's

a girl there's a boy / Next stop Brattleboro / Spider / Keep looking for tumbleweeds Danny / It's St. Patrick's day / We're walking / Plenty of somethin' / You're nice people you are / Sleep
CD ROUCD 8045
Rounder / Jul '97 / ADA / CM / Direct

NRG Ensemble

THIS IS MY HOUSE
Hyperspace / Cut flowers / Whirlwind / Bullseye witness / Bustanut / Burnt toast / Straight time / In the middle of Pennsylvania
CD DE 485
Delmark / Jun '97 / ADA / Cadillac / CM / Direct / Hot Shot

Nu Civilisation

NU CIVILISATION
CD STEAM 77CD
Vinyl Solution / Feb '94 / RTM/Disc

Nu Colours

NU COLOURS
Special kind of lover / Desire / Yes I will / Back together / Do you wanna go back (to when) / I pray / You gave me more / (You) Took me to heaven / Heart's a messenger / Don't mind waiting / Tomorrow love / Joy / Thinking about you / Special kind of lover (C&J RNB mix)
CD 5317512
Wild Card / Sep '96 / PolyGram

Nu Philly Groove

NU PHILLY GROOVE, THE
CD ITM 1494
ITM / Oct '95 / Koch / Tradelink

Nu Troops

MIGRATIONS
Transmigration / Goree island / Hamattan / Place to place / Asante / 741 / Ode to Ama / Incentricity / Papa Dayie / Pinocchio
CD DUNECD 01
Dune / Apr '97 / New Note/Pinnacle

Nu Yorican Soul

NU YORICAN SOUL
Runaway / MAW Latin blues / Gotta new life / It's alright I feel it / Jazzy Jeff's theme / Roy's scat / You can do it (baby) / Shoshana / I am the black gold of the sun / Nervous track / Nautilus (Mawtilus) / Mind fluid / Sweet tears / Habriendo El Dominate
CD 5344602
CD 5344512
Talkin' Loud / Feb '97 / PolyGram

Nu Yorican Symphony

NUYORICAN SYMPHONY LIVE AT THE KNITTING FACTORY
CD KFWCD 138
Knitting Factory / Feb '95 / Cargo / Plastic Head

Nua, Sean

OPEN DOOR, THE
CD SHAN 79082CD
Shanachie / May '93 / ADA / Greensleeves / Koch

Nuclear Assault

ASSAULT AND BATTERY
CD RRCD 244
Receiver / Sep '97 / Grapevine/PolyGram

OUT OF ORDER
CD CDFLAG 64
Under One Flag / Sep '91 / Pinnacle

SOMETHING WICKED
Something wicked / Another violent end / Behind glass walls / Chaos / Forge / No time / To serve man / Madness descends / Poetic justice / Art / Other end
CD ALTGOCD 003
Alter Ego / Apr '93 / Vital

SURVIVE
Brainwashed / Great depression / Equal rights / Good times, bad times / Survive / Wired / Technology
CD CDFLAG 21
Under One Flag / Jul '88 / Pinnacle

Nucleus

ELASTIC ROCK/WE'LL TALK ABOUT IT LATER
Elastic rock / Striation / Taranaki / Twisted track / Crude blues / Crude blues part two / 1916 (Battle of boogaloo) / Torrid zone / Stonescape / Earth mother / Speaking for myself, personally / Persephones jive / Song for the bearded lady / Sun child / Lullaby for a lonely child / We'll talk about it later / Oasis / Ballad of Joe Pimp / Easter 1916
CD BGOCD 47
Beat Goes On / Mar '94 / Pinnacle

Nuff Ruffness

NUFF RUFFNESS
CD WRA 81222CD
Wrap / May '94 / Koch

Nugent, Laurence

TRADITIONAL IRISH MUSIC ON FLUTE & TIN WHISTLE
CD SH 78001
Shanachie / Jun '96 / ADA / Greensleeves / Koch

Nugent, Ted

CALL OF THE WILD
Call of the wild / Sweet revenge / Pony express / Ain't it the truth / Renegade / Rot gut / Below the belt / cannonballs
CD EDCD 278
Edsel / Oct '89 / Pinnacle

GREAT GONZOS (The Best Of Ted Nugent)
Cat scratch fever / Just what the doctor ordered / Free for all / Dog eat dog / Motor city madness / Paralysed / Stranglehold / Baby, please don't go / Wango tango / Wang dang sweet poontang
CD 4712162
Epic / Feb '97 / Sony

LIVE AT HAMMERSMITH ODEON
Stormtroopin' / Just what the doctor ordered / Free for all / Dog eat dog / Cat scratch fever / Need you bad / Paralyzed / It don't matter / Wang dang sweet poontang / Stranglehold / Motor City madness / Gonzo
CD 4851052
Columbia / May '97 / Sony

ON THE EDGE
Dr. Slingshot / Night time / You talk sunshine, I breathe fire / Scottish tea / Good natured Emma / Prodigal man / Missionary Mary / St. Philip's friend / Journey to the centre of the mind / Flight of the byrd / Baby, please don't go / Inside the outside / Loaded for bear / On the edge
CD CDTB 097
Thunderbolt / '91 / TKO Magnum

OVER THE TOP
Down on Philips escalator / Surrender to your kings / Gimme love / For his namesake / I'll prove I'm right / Conclusion/Journey / To the centre of the mind / Migration / Lovely lady / Mississippi murderer / Let's go get stoned / It's not true / Ivory castles / Colours / Over the top
CD CDTB 120
Thunderbolt / May '91 / TKO Magnum

SPIRIT OF THE WILD
CD 7567826112
Atlantic / Jun '94 / Warner Music

TOOTH FANG AND CLAW
Lady luck / Living in the woods / Hibernation / Free flight / Maybellene / Great white buffalo / Sasha / No holds barred
CD EDCD 295
Edsel / Oct '89 / Pinnacle

Null

TERMINAL BEACH
CD MNF 13
Manifold / Feb '97 / Cargo

Numan, Gary

BERSERKER
CD NUMACD 1001
Numa / Dec '95 / Pinnacle

BEST OF GARY NUMAN 1978-1983, THE
CD BEGA 150CD
Beggars Banquet / Sep '93 / RTM/Disc / Warner Music

BEST OF GARY NUMAN 1984-1992, THE
I can't stop / Berserker / Skin game / I still remember / Machine and soul / Empty bed, empty heart / Are 'friends' electric / Your fascination / This disease / Miracles / Child with the ghost / Strange charm / London times / Time to die / America / My dying machine
CD EMPRCD 666
Emporio / Sep '96 / Disc

DANCE
Slow car to China / Night talk / Subway called you / Cry the clock said / She's got claws / Crash / Boys like me / Stories / My brother's time / You are, you are / Moral
CD BBL 28CD
Lowdown/Beggars Banquet / '88 / RTM/Disc / Warner Music

DARK LIGHT (2CD Set)
CD Set NUMACD 1012
Numa / Jun '95 / Pinnacle

DREAM CORROSION (2CD Set)
CD Set NUMACD 1010
Numa / Aug '94 / Pinnacle

EXHIBITION (2CD Set)
Me, I disconnect from you / That's too bad / My love is a liquid / Music for chameleons / We are glass / Bombers / Sister surprise / Are friends electric / I dream of wires / Complex / Noise noise / Warriors / Everyday I die / Cars / We take mystery to bed / I'm an agent / My centurion / Metal / You are in my vision / I die, you die / She's got claws / This wreckage / My shadow in vain / Down in the dark / Iceman comes
CD Set BEGA 88CD
Beggars Banquet / Sep '87 / RTM/Disc / Warner Music

EXILE
CD NUMACD 1014
Numa / Aug '97 / Pinnacle

FURY, THE
Call out the dogs / This disease / Your fascination / Miracles / Pleasure skin / Creatures / Tricks / God only knows / I still remember
CD NUMACD 1003
Numa / Oct '86 / Pinnacle

FURY, THE (Remixed)
CD NUMACDX 1003
Numa / Nov '96 / Pinnacle

GARY NUMAN ARCHIVE
Are friends electric / Me I disconnect from you / U got the look / Berserker / God film / We are glass / Poison / Creatures / Cars / Call out the dogs / God only knows / Down in the park / We take mystery to bed / My shadow in vain / Love isolation / Generator
CD RMCD 205
Rialto / Sep '96 / Disc / Total/BMG

GHOST
CD NUMACD 1007
Numa / Oct '92 / Pinnacle

GREATEST HITS (Numan, Gary & Tubeway Army)
Cars / I die: You die / Are 'friends' electric / Down in the park / We are glass / Bombers / We take mystery (to bed) / She's got claws / Complex / Music for chameleons / That's too bad / This wreckage / Warriors / Love needs no disguise / White boys and heroes / Sister surprise / Stormtrooper in drag
CD 5311492
PolyGram TV / Mar '96 / PolyGram

HUMAN
CD NUMACD 1013
Numa / Oct '95 / Pinnacle

ISOLATE
CD NUMACD 1008
Numa / Mar '92 / Pinnacle

MACHINE AND SOUL (Remixed)
CD NUMAXCD 1009
Numa / Sep '93 / Pinnacle

PEEL SESSIONS, THE (Gary Numan/ Tubeway Army - 29.5.79) (Numan, Gary & Tubeway Army)
Cars / Airlane / Films / Conversation / Me, I disconnect from you / Down in the park / I nearly married a human
CD SFPMCD 202
Strange Fruit / '89 / Pinnacle

PLEASURE PRINCIPLE/WARRIORS (2CD Set)
Airlane / Metal / Complex / Films / ME / Tracks / Observer / Conversation / Cars / Engineers / Sister surprise / Tick tock man / Love is like clock law / Rhythm of the evening / Warriors / Am render / Iceman comes / This prison moon / My centurion
CD Set BEGA 10CD
Beggars Banquet / Dec '87 / RTM/Disc / Warner Music

REPLICAS (Tubeway Army)
Me, I disconnect from you / Are friends electric / Machman / Praying to the aliens / Down in the park / You are in my vision / Replicas / It must have been years / I nearly married a human
CD MUSCD 509
MCI Original Masters / May '95 / Disc / THE

REPLICAS/THE PLAN (2CD Set)
Me, I disconnect from you / Are friends electric / Mach man / Praying to the aliens / Down in the park / You are in my vision / Replicas / It must have been years / When machines rock / I nearly married a human / This is my life / Critics / Monday troop / Mean street / Thoughts of No.2 / Basic J / Ice / Crime of passion / Check it / Out of sight
CD Set BEGA 7CD
Beggars Banquet / Dec '87 / RTM/Disc / Warner Music

SACRIFICE
CD NUMACD 1011
Numa / Oct '94 / Pinnacle

SACRIFICE (Remixed)
CD NUMACDX 1011
Numa / Mar '95 / Pinnacle

SELECTION
CD BBP 5CD
Beggars Banquet / Nov '89 / RTM/Disc / Warner Music

STORY SO FAR, THE (3CD Set)
CD Set RRXCD 505
Receiver / Jul '96 / Grapevine/PolyGram

STRANGE CHARM
CD NUMACD 1005
Numa / Oct '86 / Pinnacle

STRANGE CHARM (Remixed)
CD NUMACDX 1005
Numa / Nov '96 / Pinnacle

TELEKON/I ASSASSIN
This wreckage / Aircrash bureau / Telekon / Sleep by windows / I'm an agent / Remember I was vapour / Please push no more / Joy circuit / Wars songs / Dream of siam / Music for chameleons / This is my house / I, assassin / 1930's rust / We take mystery to bed
CD BEGA 19CD
Beggars Banquet / '88 / RTM/Disc / Warner Music

TUBEWAY ARMY/DANCE
Listen to the sirens / Life machines / Friends / Something's in the house / Everyday I die / Steel and you / Are you real / Dream police / Zero bars / Slowcar to China / Night talk / Subway called you / She's got claws / Crash / Boys like me / Stories / My brothers time / You are, you are
CD BEGA 4CD
Beggars Banquet / Dec '87 / RTM/Disc / Warner Music

WHITE NOISE
Intro / Berserker / Metal / Me I disconnect from you / Remind me to smile / Sister surprise / Music for chameleons / Iceman comes / Cold warning / Down in the park / This prison moon / I die you die / My dying machine / Cars / We take mystery to bed / We are glass / This new love / My shadow in vain / Are friends electric
CD NUMACD 1002
Numa / May '93 / Pinnacle

Numb

CHRISTMEISTER
CD KK 146
KK / Apr '96 / Plastic Head

FIXATE
CD KK 094
KK / Feb '94 / Plastic Head

WASTED SKY
CD KK 126CD
KK / Nov '94 / Plastic Head

Number One Cup

POSSUM TROT PLAN
CD FLY 012
Flydaddy / Mar '96 / Cargo / SRD

WRECKED BY LIONS
Ease back down / Backlit / Chisel / Paris / Bright orange / Fireball sun / Black choppers cry / Astronaut / Waiting on the lions / Maybe there's a thread / Tree song / Concordia / Malcolm's X-ray picnic / Flickers and flames / So inclined / Three miles from talent
CD BRRC 10132
Blue Rose / Jun '97 / 3mv/Pinnacle

Nuncira, Chuco

LA FUERZA MAYOR
CD TUMICD 019
Tumi / '92 / Discovery / Stern's

Nunes, Clara

CLARA NUNES COM... VIDA
Morena de Angola / Peixe com coco / Na linha do mar / Coisa da Antiga / Nacao / Viola de Penedo / Ijexa (Filhos de Gandhi) / Conto de Areia / Sem companhia / Coracao Leviano / A flor da Pele / As forcas da natureza / Amor perfeito / Menino Deus
CD CDEMC 3744
Hemisphere / Feb '96 / EMI

Nunez, Carlos

BROTHERHOOD OF STARS
Brotherhood of stars / Dawn / Two shores / Black shadow / Moonlight piper / Cantigueiras / Galician carol / Dancing with Rosina / Lela / Flight of the Earls / Rainmaker's air / Para Vigo me voy
CD 7432145375
RCA Victor / May '97 / BMG

Nunez, Joseito

CON LA ORQUESTA DE BELISARIO LOPEZ 1937-1940 (Nunez, Joseito & Belisario Lopez)
CD TCD 063
Tumbao Cuban Classics / Jul '96 / Discovery

Nuns

FOUR DAYS IN A HOTEL ROOM
CD EFA 122012
Musical Tragedies / Feb '94 / SRD

Nunu

KLEZMO-COPTER
Lomir sich iberbetn / Frejlechs / Djurdjevdan/Ederlezi / KalamatianosMoyde ani / Di lustign chossidn / Djelem djelem / Der hejser bulgar / Bavno pomasschko / Moja mala nema mane / Ale vasserlech flisn avek / Sto e ludo son sonilo / Baj mir bistu schejn / Ich hob dich zuvil lib / Bajtsche mir ois a finfunzwanziger

CD ______ TIP 8888282
Tiptoe / Sep '97 / New Note/Pinnacle

Nurse With Wound

150 MURDEROUS PASSIONS
CD ______ UD 009CD
United Dairies / Oct '96 / World Serpent

ACTS OF SENSELESS BEAUTY
Either open or unsound / Bloodclot / Window of possible organic development / Entertainer / Some magic powers
CD ______ UD 100CD
United Dairies / Jul '97 / World Serpent

CHANCE MEETING
CD ______ UD 001CD
United Dairies / Oct '96 / World Serpent

CRUMB DUCK (Nurse With Wound & Stereolab)
CD ______ UD 059CD
United Dairies / Oct '96 / World Serpent

HOMOTOPY FOR MARIE
CD ______ UD 013CD
United Dairies / Oct '96 / World Serpent

LARGE LADIES
CD ______ UD 038CD
United Dairies / Oct '96 / World Serpent

LIVE AT THE BAR MALDOROR
CD ______ UD 034CD
United Dairies / Oct '96 / World Serpent

MERZBILDSCHWET
CD ______ UD 004CD
United Dairies / Oct '96 / World Serpent

ROCK 'N' ROLL STATION
CD ______ UD 039CD
United Dairies / Oct '96 / World Serpent

SOLILOQUY FOR LILLITH (2CD Set)
CD Set ______ UD 035CD
United Dairies / Oct '96 / World Serpent

SPIRAL INSANA
Sea armchair / Migration to the head / Earthwork / Red period / This lady is for burning / Chasing the carrot / Sugarland / There's always another illusion / Stewing the red herring / Mourning smile / Pulse interplay / View from Lammas Tower / Swallowhead / Fitching / Wrong sucker / All that's left over / Forever chasing the carrot / Terminal song / Ship of the dead / Obituary obligations / Nihil
CD ______ UD 073CD
United Dairies / Mar '97 / World Serpent

SUCKED ORANGE, A
Paradise lost / Internal torment II / Autopsy / Stillborn / Deviated instinct / Resurrection encore / Doom / Means to an end / Confessor / Uncontrolled / Talion / Laws of retaliation / Electro hippies / Freddy's revenge / Toranaga / Dealers in death
CD ______ UD 032CD
United Dairies / Dec '89 / World Serpent

SUGAR FISH DRINK
CD ______ UD 036CD
United Dairies / Oct '96 / World Serpent

SYLVIA AND BABS
CD ______ UD 072CD
United Dairies / Oct '96 / World Serpent

THUNDER PERFECT MIND
CD ______ UD 040CD
United Dairies / Oct '96 / World Serpent

TO THE QUIET MEN...
CD ______ UD 003CD
United Dairies / Oct '96 / World Serpent

WHO CAN I TURN TO STEREO
CD ______ UD 049CD
United Dairies / Jan '97 / World Serpent

Nus

VERTICAL ANGELS, THE
CD ______ SR 102
Sub Rosa / May '96 / Direct / RTM/Disc / SRD / Vital

Nut

FANTANICITY
Brains / Scream / Sticky / Giant / Chunk / Fantanicity / Pleased / Crazy / Bitter / Burn / Bluegenes
CD ______ NUTCD 3P
Epic / Sep '96 / Sony

Nutley Brass

BEAT ON THE BRASS
CD ______ NTMCD 525
Nectar / Aug '96 / Pinnacle

Nutmeg

GHETTO'S CHILD
CD ______ 50571
Raging Bull / Jun '97 / Prime / Total/BMG

Nuttin' Nyce

DOWN FOR WHATEVER
CD ______ CHIP 160
Jive / Aug '95 / Pinnacle

Nuuk Posse

KAATAQ
CD ______ SR 108CD
Sub Rosa / Oct '96 / Direct / RTM/Disc / SRD / Vital

NWA

EFIL4ZAGGIN
Real niggaz don't die / Niggaz 4 life / Protest / Appetite for destruction / Don't drink that wine / Alwayz into something / To kill a hooker / One less bitch / Findum fuckum and flee / Automobile / She swallowed it / I'd rather fuck you / Approach to danger / 1-900 2 Compton / Dayz of wayback
CD ______ BRCD 562
4th & Broadway / Apr '91 / PolyGram

STRAIGHT OUTTA COMPTON
Straight outta Compton / Fuck tha police / Gangsta gangsta / If it ain't ruff / Parental discretion iz advised / Express yourself / I ain't tha 1 / Dopeman / Compton's 'n the house / 8 ball / Something like that / Quiet on tha set / Something 2 dance 2
CD ______ BRCD 534
4th & Broadway / Aug '89 / PolyGram

Ny'a

EMBRACE
CD ______ NAP 4220
Ichiban / Mar '96 / Direct / Koch

Nyah Fearties

GRANPA CREW
CD ______ NYAH 942
Danceteria / Feb '95 / ADA / Plastic Head / Shellshock/Disc

Nygaard

NO HURRY
CD ______ ROUCD 267
Rounder / Dec '90 / ADA / CM / Direct

Nygaard, Scott

DREAMER'S WALTZ
CD ______ ROUCD 0397
Rounder / Jun '96 / ADA / CM / Direct

Nyhus, Sven

BERGROSA
CD ______ MASTER 702CD
Master / Jul '93 / ADA

NYJO

ALGARHYTHMS (National Youth Jazz Orchestra)
Praia do vau / Bom dia, roseira / Quinto do lago / Faro way / Cartaz de rua / Portimao / Adeus tristeza / Cai fora / Montes de alvor / Holiday affair / East of the sun / Albufeira / Play off
CD ______ NYJCD 017
NYJO / Sep '96 / New Note/Pinnacle / TKO Magnum

BIG BAND CHRISTMAS (National Youth Jazz Orchestra)
Deck the halls with boughs of holly / Silent night / Christians awake / Maryland, my Christmas tree / In the bleak midwinter / At Christmas / I saw six ships / My dancing day / Wenceslas squared / Away in a manger / Thirst, The - No ale / O come all ye faithful (Adeste Fidelis) / Christmas blues / Take five kings / I left my heart in Royal David's City / Holly and the ivy / Hark the herald angels sing
CD ______ NYJCD 009
NYJO / Aug '94 / New Note/Pinnacle / TKO Magnum

COOKIN' WITH GAS (National Youth Jazz Orchestra)
Beyond the Hatfield Tunnel / Hot gospel / Step on the gas / Mr. B.G. / Be gentle / Behind the gasworks / Cookin' with gas / 'S Wonderful / We care for you / Big girl now / Gasanova / Afterburner / Water babies / Heat of the moment
CD ______ NYJCD 010
NYJO / Apr '95 / New Note/Pinnacle / TKO Magnum

COTTONING ON (National Youth Jazz Orchestra)
Sea island samba / Miss Malfatti, I presume / Cottoning on / Lady can tell / One for Oscar / Tenor each way / Blues for Duke / Be gentle / Night is a pup / Night slide / Gasbag blues
CD ______ NYJCD 016
NYJO / Dec '95 / New Note/Pinnacle / TKO Magnum

GIANTS OF, THE (National Youth Jazz Orchestra)
CD ______ NYJVC 901
NYJO / Apr '95 / New Note/Pinnacle / TKO Magnum

HALLMARK (National Youth Jazz Orchestra)
Hallmark / I have been here before / Blood orange / Adeus Tristeza / Samba for Cheryl / Have you seen them cakes / U-Turn / Suits me / While the cat's away / Reepicheep / Tara's Tuesday / Castle's in Spain
CD ______ NYJCD 015
NYJO / Apr '95 / New Note/Pinnacle / TKO Magnum

IN CONTROL (National Youth Jazz Orchestra)
CD ______ JHCD 037
Ronnie Scott's Jazz House / Mar '95 / Cadillac / Jazz Music / New Note/Pinnacle / TKO Magnum

LOOKING FORWARD, LOOKING BACK (National Youth Jazz Orchestra)
CD ______ NYJCD 012
NYJO / Apr '95 / New Note/Pinnacle / TKO Magnum

MALTESE CROSS (National Youth Jazz Orchestra)
CD ______ NYJCD 008
NYJO / Apr '95 / New Note/Pinnacle / TKO Magnum

MERRY CHRISTMAS AND A HAPPY NEW YEAR (National Youth Jazz Orchestra)
We wish you a Merry Christmas / O come, o come / Bethlehem lift off / While shepherds watched their flocks by night / Midnight clear / My gift to you / Noel nouvelet / OLTOB / Christmas song / Angels from the second storey / Childsotnes / Winter snow / It's Christmas / Twelve bars of Christmas / Auld land syne
CD ______ NYJCD 014
NYJO / Aug '94 / New Note/Pinnacle / TKO Magnum

PORTRAITS (National Youth Jazz Orchestra)
Blues at the bull / Woody / Basie / Dizzy / Duke / Bird / Quincy / Monk / Duke II / Kenton / Point of no return / Come on the blues / Royal flush / Southern horizons
CD ______ HHCD 1007
Hot House / May '95 / Cadillac / Harmonia Mundi / Wellard

REMEMBRANCE (National Youth Jazz Orchestra)
Remembrance (for Jim) / Remembrance (for Chrish and Eamonn) / Remembrance (for Kenny and Charlie) / Remembrance (for Valery) / I'll never forget / Half steps / Snakes and ladders / Long hot summer / Rodeo / Yessica / Take the CandA train / Almost there / Give up
CD ______ NYJCD 011
NYJO / Apr '95 / New Note/Pinnacle / TKO Magnum

THESE ARE THE JOKES (National Youth Jazz Orchestra)
Still doing the trick with the horse, Madam / First time I've seen dead people smoke (Smokey eyes) / Keep looking young-hang around with old people / Chef's rash has cleared up nicely / Much too much / No hair just a red head / Are we keeping you up sir / Roxy beaujolais / Audient was on its foot / Watching the traffic lights change / Don't go to her
CD ______ JHCD 024
Ronnie Scott's Jazz House / Jan '94 / Cadillac / Jazz Music / New Note/Pinnacle / TKO Magnum

THIS TIME LIVE AT THE CLUB (National Youth Jazz Orchestra)
CD ______ JHCD 049
Ronnie Scott's Jazz House / Jun '97 / Cadillac / Jazz Music / New Note/Pinnacle / TKO Magnum

UNISON IN ALL THINGS (National Youth Jazz Orchestra)
For starters / In a daze / You'd think I'd learn / Along came Benny / Dearly beloved / I wasn't looking for love / Unison in all things / Eyes down / Reprieve / Never the twain / How can you believe in love / Atropus / Blues for Mike / For starters
CD ______ NYJCD 018
NYJO / Feb '97 / New Note/Pinnacle / TKO Magnum

VIEW FROM THE HILL, A (National Youth Jazz Orchestra)
Marston Pedigree / Flight of the heart / View from the hill / Don't try and argue with me / Norwich Union / Riffin' the griffin / Ballad for Anne Boleyn / Fleet / Samba deeze, samba doze / Someone / Luton Hoo / Astra Brazilia
CD ______ JHCD 044
Ronnie Scott's Jazz House / Jan '96 / Cadillac / Jazz Music / New Note/Pinnacle / TKO Magnum

WITH AN OPEN MIND (National Youth Jazz Orchestra)
Cheese'n'Carrots / Revenge of the Amoebae / With an open mind / Remembrance for Jim / Aardvark / Syrup of Phiggs / Fly to me / Midnight oil / Going Dutch
CD ______ NYJCD 007
NYJO / Apr '95 / New Note/Pinnacle / TKO Magnum

Nylons

HAPPY TOGETHER
Happy together / Dance of love / Crazy in love / Touch of your hand / Kiss him goodbye / It's what they call magic / This island earth / Grown men cry / Chain gang / Face in the crowd
CD ______ RR 249623
Roadrunner / '89 / PolyGram

NYLONS, THE
CD ______ RR 349843
Roadrunner / '89 / PolyGram

ONE SIZE FITS ALL
CD ______ RR 349926
Roadrunner / '88 / PolyGram

ROCKAPELLA
CD ______ RR 9473 2
Roadrunner / '88 / PolyGram

SEAMLESS
CD ______ RR 349856
Roadrunner / '89 / PolyGram

Nyman, Michael

ESSENTIAL (Nyman, Michael Band)
CD ______ 4368202
Decca / Jan '93 / PolyGram

KISS AND OTHER MOVEMENTS, THE
Kiss / Nose list song / Tano between the lines / Images were introduced / Water dances (making a splash)-1 Stroking / Water dances (making a splash)-2 Gliding / Water dances (making a splash)-3 Synchronising
CD ______ EEGCD 40
EG / Jan '87 / EMI

LIVE
In Re Don Giovanni / Bird list / Queen of the night / Water dances - dipping / Water dances - stroking / Upside down violin - Slow/Faster/Faster still / Piano - concert suite
CD ______ CDVE 924
Virgin / Oct '94 / EMI

TIME WILL PRONOUNCE
Self-laudatory hymn of Inanna and her omnipotence / Time will pronounce / Convertability of lute strings / For John cage
CD ______ 4402822
Decca / Jun '93 / PolyGram

Nyman, Monica

SPRICKAN MELLAN VARLDARNA (Nyman, Monica Kvintett)
CD ______ IGCD 065
Imogena / May '97 / ADA / Cadillac

Nyolo, Sally

TRIBU
CD ______ 087952
Melodie / Nov '96 / ADA / Discovery / Grapevine/PolyGram / Greensleeves / Jet Star

Nyro, Laura

ELI AND THE THIRTEENTH CONFESSION
Luckie / Lu / Sweet blindness / Poverty train / Lonely women / Eli's comin' / Timer / Stoned soul picnic / Emma / Woman's blues / Once it was alright now (Farmer John) / December's boudoir / Confession
CD ______ 4872402
Columbia / Mar '97 / Sony

GONNA TAKE A MIRACLE
CD ______ BGOCD 27
Beat Goes On / Jul '91 / Pinnacle

STONED SOUL PICNIC (The Best Of Laura Nyro/2CD Set)
Wedding bell blues / Blowin' away / Billy's blues / Stoney end / And when I die / Lu / Eli's comin / Stoned soul picnic / Timer / Emmie / Confession / Capt. St. Lucifer / Gibsom Street / New York tendaberry / Save the country / Blackpatch / Upstairs by a chinese lamp / Beads of sweat / When I was a freeport and you were the main drag / I met him on a Sunday / Bells / Smile / Sweet blindness / Money / Mr. Blue / Wilderness / Mother's spiritual / Woman of the world / Louise's church / Broken rainbow / To a child / Lite a flame (the animal rights song) / And when I die / Save the country
CD Set ______ 4851092
Legacy / Feb '97 / Sony

TIME AND LOVE (The Music Of Laura Nyro) (Various Artists)
Time and love: *Snow, Phoebe* / Stoned soul picnic: *Sobule, Jill* / Buy and sell: *Vega, Suzanne* / When I think of Laura Nyro: *Siberry, Jane* / Stoney end: *Chapman, Beth Nielsen* / Eli's coming: *Germano, Lisa* / Wedding bell blues: *Roches* / And when I die: *Sweet Honey In The Rock* / Save the country: *Cash, Rosanne* / He's a runner: *Brooke, Jonathan* / Poverty train: *Larkin, Patty* / Sweet blindness: *Cole, Holly* / Upstairs by a chinese lamp: *Stern, Leni* / Woman's blue: *Bryant, Dana*
CD ______ TCD 4007
Astor Place / Jun '97 / New Note/Pinnacle

O

O

OLENTO
CD ______ EFA 501122
Sahko / Oct '96 / Plastic Head / SRD

TULKINTA
CD ______ EFA 501132
Sahko / May '97 / Plastic Head / SRD

O Yuki Conjugate

EQUATOR
CD ______ STCD 088
Staalplaat / May '95 / Vital/SAM

PEYOTE
CD ______ STCD 110
Staalplaat / Mar '95 / Vital/SAM

SUNCHEMICAL MIXES
CD ______ STCD 096
Staalplaat / Feb '96 / Vital/SAM

UNDERCURRENTS
CD ______ STCD 109
Staalplaat / Mar '95 / Vital/SAM

O-Level

DAY IN THE LIFE OF GILBERT & GEORGE, A
There's a cloud over Liverpool / I helped Patrick McGoohan escape / Odd man out / Apologise / We're not sorry / Sometimes good guys don't follow trends / Storybook beginnings / Sun never sets / Dressing up for the cameras / He's a professional / John Peel march / East Sheen revisited / Pseudo punk / O Level / We love Malcolm / Leave me / Everybody's on revolver tonight / Stairway to boredom / Many unhappy returns / I love to clean my polaris missile / Don't play God with my life / East Sheen
CD ______ CREV 005CD
Rev-Ola / Nov '92 / 3mv/Vital

O-Lieb

CONSTELLATION
Dimension X / Secret visitors / Spice diving / Subsonic interferences
CD ______ ROD 03
Recycle Or Die / Apr '96 / Kudos

Oakenfold, Paul

ALL STAR BREAKBEATS VOL.2 (Bust A Groove)
CD ______ MOLCD 34
Music Of Life / Jun '94 / Grapevine/ PolyGram

PAUL OAKENFOLD LIVE IN OSLO (2CD Set) (Various Artists)
CD Set ______ GU 004CD
Boxed / Jun '97 / SRD

PERFECTION - A PERFECTO COMPILATION (Mixed Live By Paul Oakenfold) (Various Artists)
Embracing the sunshine: *BT* / Tripping the light fantastic: *BT* / Loving you more: *BT* / I want to live: *Grace* / I dream: *Tilt* / Believe in me: *Quivver* / Not over yet: *Grace* / Passion: *Jon Of The Pleased Wimmin* / Dreams: *Wild Colour* / Sing it: *Mozaic* / Floor-essence: *Man With No Name* / Sun: *Virus* / Reach up: *Perfecto All Stars*
CD ______ 0630123482
Perfecto/East West / Oct '95 / Warner Music

Oakey, Philip

PHIL OAKEY/GIORGIO MORODER (Oakey, Philip & Giorgio Moroder)
Why must the show go on / In transit / Goodbye bad times / Brand new love (take a chance) / Valerie / Now / Together in electric dreams / Be my lover now / Shake it up
CD ______ CDV 2351
Virgin / Jun '88 / EMI

Oakley, Pete

GHOST IN THE CITY
CD ______ FE 103CD
Fellside / Mar '95 / ADA / Direct / Target/ BMG

Oasis

(WHAT'S THE STORY) MORNING GLORY
Hello / Roll with it / Wonderwall / Don't look back in anger / Hey now / Some might say / Cast no shadow / She's electric / Morning glory / Champagne supernova
CD ______ CRECD 189
Creation / Oct '95 / 3mv/Vital

(WHAT'S THE STORY) MORNING GLORY (4CD Singles/Interview Disc)
CD Set ______ CREMG 002
Creation / Nov '96 / 3mv/Vital

(WHAT'S THE STORY) MORNING GLORY (Interview)
CD ______ CREMG 001
Creation / Nov '96 / 3mv/Vital

BE HERE NOW
CD ______ CRECD 219
Creation / Aug '97 / 3mv/Vital

BROTHERHOOD (Interview Disc)
CD ______ BROS 2CD
CD ______ BROS 1CD
Shadows / Jun '97 / Total/BMG

DEFINITELY MAYBE
Rock 'n' roll star / Shakermaker / Live forever / Up in the sky / Columbia / Supersonic / Bring it on down / Cigarettes and alcohol / Digsy's dinner / Slide away / Married with children
CD ______ CRECD 169
Creation / Aug '94 / 3mv/Vital

DEFINITELY MAYBE SINGLES BOX (4CD Singles/Interview Disc)
CD Set ______ CREDM 002
Creation / Nov '96 / 3mv/Vital

GETTING HIGH (Interview Discs/2CD Set)
CD Set ______ CONV 001
Network / Feb '97 / Total/BMG

INTERVIEW DISC
CD ______ SAM 7023
Sound & Media / Nov '96 / Sound & Media

INTERVIEW DISC
CD ______ 94CD 1
CD ______ 94CD 2
Wax / Jan '97 / RTM/Disc / Total/BMG

MORNING GLORY (The Oasis Story/ 2CD Set)
CD Set ______ OTR 1100040
Metro Independent / Jun '97 / Essential/ BMG

OASIS INTERVIEW
CD ______ UFOMWW 11CD
UFO / Sep '96 / Pinnacle

SALLY CAN WAIT (Interview Discs/2CD Set)
CD Set ______ CONV 006
Network / Feb '97 / Total/BMG

Obadia, Hakki

IRAQI JEWISH/IRAQI MUSIC
CD ______ GV 147CD
Global Village / May '94 / ADA / Direct

O'Baoill, Sean

CEOLTA GAEL
CD ______ OSS 2CD
Ossian / Nov '90 / ADA / CM / Direct / Highlander

Oberlin, Russell

ENGLISH MEDIEVAL SONGS
CD ______ LEMS 8005
Lyrichord / Aug '94 / ADA / CM / Roots

ENGLISH POLYPHONY
CD ______ LEMS 8004
Lyrichord / Aug '94 / ADA / CM / Roots

FRENCH ARS ANTIQUA, THE
CD ______ LEMS 8007
Lyrichord / Aug '94 / ADA / CM / Roots

LAS CANTIGAS
CD ______ LEMS 8003
Lyrichord / Aug '94 / ADA / CM / Roots

NOTRE DAME ORGANA
CD ______ LEMS 8002
Lyrichord / Aug '94 / ADA / CM / Roots

TROUBADOUR/TROUVERE SONGS
CD ______ LEMS 8001
Lyrichord / Aug '94 / ADA / CM / Roots

Obermayer, Gilles

CONTRACTION
CD Set ______ G 004CD
Musikk Distribujson / Apr '95 / ADA

Obey, Ebenezer

GET YOUR JUJUS OUT
CD ______ RCD 20111
Rykodisc / Aug '91 / ADA / Vital

Obiedo, Ray

STICKS AND STONES
CD ______ 01934101422
Windham Hill / Jan '95 / BMG

ZULAYA
Flamingo / Castile / Zulaya / Midnight taboo / Santa Lucia intro / Aquinas / La samba / Another place / Forever / Santa Lucia
CD ______ 01934111622
Windham Hill / Apr '95 / BMG

Obituary

BACK FROM THE DEAD
Threatening skies / By the light / Inverted / Platonic disease / Download / Rewind / Feed on the weak / Lockdown / Pressure point / Back from the dead / Bullituary
CD ______ RR 88312
Roadrunner / Apr '97 / PolyGram

CAUSE OF DEATH
Infected / Chopped in half / Dying / Cause of death / Turned inside out / Bodybag / Circle of the tyrants / Find the arise / Memories remain
CD ______ RO 93702
Roadracer / Mar '96 / PolyGram

END COMPLETE, THE
CD ______ RC 92012
Roadrunner / Sep '96 / PolyGram

SLOWLY WE ROT
CD ______ RO 94892
Roadracer / Mar '96 / PolyGram

WORLD DEMISE
CD ______ RR 89952
Roadrunner / Sep '96 / PolyGram

Oblivians

PLAY 9 SONGS WITH MR. QUINTRON
CD ______ EFACD 12892
Crypt / Jun '97 / Shellshock/Disc

Oblivions

POPULAR FAVOURITES
CD ______ EFA 128762
Crypt / Jul '96 / Shellshock/Disc

SOUL FOOD
CD ______ EFA 115892
Crypt / Feb '95 / Shellshock/Disc

Obmana, Vidna

ECHOING DELIGHT
Winter monument / Crystal traveller / Empty night / Echoing delight / Glass splendour
CD ______ XCD 022
Extreme / Nov '96 / Vital/SAM

RIVER OF APPEARANCE, THE
CD ______ PRO 65
Projekt / Oct '96 / Cargo

SPIRITUAL BONDING
CD ______ XCD 027
Extreme / Feb '95 / Vital/SAM

WELL OF SOULS (2CD Set) (Obmana, Vidna & Steve Reich)
CD Set ______ PRO 60
Projekt / Oct '96 / Cargo

Obo

FUT VOL.1 & 2
CD ______ THCD 001
Tush / Oct '96 / Vital/SAM

O'Briain, Garry

SONGS FOR ALL AGES (O'Briain, Garry & Padraigin Ni Uallachain)
CD ______ CEFCD 166
Gael Linn / Jan '95 / ADA / CM / Direct / Grapevine/PolyGram / Roots

O'Brien, Dermot

BEST OF DERMOT O'BRIEN, THE (2CD Set)
Girl from Clare / Castlebar / Rare ould times / Nancy Spain / Donegal Danny / Waterford girls / Jock Stewart / County Mayo / Lisdoonvarna polka / Lakes of Sligo / Maggie / I will love you / Road to Malin Moor / Eileen / Old Claddagh ring / Boys of Killybegs / Slieve gallon braes / Nora / Connemara rose / Farewell to Galway / Katy Daly / Turfman from Ardee / Home boys home / Rocks of Bawn / Galway shawl
CD Set ______ PLSCD 218
Pulse / Feb '97 / BMG

WHERE THE THREE COUNTIES MEET
Farewell to Galway / Sailing home / Where the three counties meet / Ould claddagh ring / Home boys home / Come to the bower / I'm goin' home / Connemara rose / Slieve Gallion Braes / My ould tambourine / Boys of Killybegs / World goes round / Gypsy boy / County Leitrim Queen / Galway shawl / Nora / Holy ground / My Eileen / Road to Malinmore / Song of an Irish husband / Three leaf shamrock
CD ______ 3036001092
Carlton / Jun '97 / Carlton

O'Brien, Hod

OPALESSENCE
Opalessence / Touchstone / Bits and pieces / Joy road / Handful of dust / Blues walk / Detour ahead / Joy road (take 1)
CD ______ CRISS 1012CD
Criss Cross / Apr '92 / Cadillac / Direct / Vital/SAM

RIDIN' HIGH
CD ______ RSRCD 116
Reservoir Music / Nov '94 / Cadillac

O'Brien, Ian

DESERT SCORES
Mad Mike disease / Homeless / Dayride / Man from Del Monte (a fantasy theme) / Dark eye tango / Video games and data movements / Grandpa's drawers / Eurydice / Desrt scores and fusion daddies
CD ______ FERCD 003
Ferox / Feb '97 / Prime / SRD / Vital

O'Brien, Kelly

TRADITIONAL MUSIC OF IRELAND (O'Brien, Kelly & Sproule)
CD ______ SHAN 34014CD
Shanachie / Apr '95 / ADA / Greensleeves / Koch

O'Brien, Mick

MAY MORNING DEW, THE
CD ______ ACM 101CD
ACM / Nov '96 / ADA

O'Brien, Mollie

TELL IT TRUE
CD ______ SHCD 3846
Sugar Hill / Dec '96 / ADA / CM / Direct / Koch / Roots

O'Brien, Paddy

BANKS OF THE SHANNON (O'Brien, Paddy & Seamus Connolly)
CD ______ GLCD 3082
Green Linnet / Dec '93 / ADA / CM / Direct / Highlander / Roots

STRANGER AT THE GATE
CD ______ GLCD 1091
Green Linnet / Feb '90 / ADA / CM / Direct / Highlander / Roots

SUNNYSIDE
Keep on the sunny side / Loreena / Close to you / Little town on the Shannon / My wedding band (is a halo of gold) / My lovely Leitrim Shore / Devil woman / Will you think of you / Knock at my window love / She's mine / There goes my everything / Truck driving man / Everybody's reaching out for someone / Sweethearts in heaven / New attraction / She taught me how to yodel
CD ______ HM 051CD
Harmac / Mar '90 / I&B

O'Brien, Tim

AWAY OUT ON THE MOUNTAIN (O'Brien, Tim & Mollie)
CD ______ SHCD 3825
Sugar Hill / Oct '94 / ADA / CM / Direct / Koch / Roots

HARD YEAR BLUES
Good deal Lucille / Cora is gone / Land's end / Cabin in gloryland / High road / Cotton tail / Hard year blues / Honky tonk hardwood floor / Evening / Back up and push / Queen of hearts / Twelve gates to the city
CD ______ FF 70319
Flying Fish / Nov '96 / ADA / CM / Direct / Roots

ODD MAN IN
Fell in love (and I can't get out) / One way street / Circles around you / Handsome Molly / Lonely at the bottom too / Like I used to do / Lone tree standing / Love on hold / Flora, lily of the west / Hold to a dream / That's what I like about you / Every tear has a reason why / Hungry eyes / Romance is a slow dance
CD ______ SHCD 3790
Sugar Hill / Jul '91 / ADA / CM / Direct / Koch / Roots

OH BOY O'BOY (O'Brien, Tim & The O'Boys)
Church steeple / When I paint my masterpiece / Heartbreak game / Time to learn / Perfect place to hide / Run mountain / Good woman bad / Few are chosen / Shadows to light / Farmer's cused wife / Johnny don't get drunk/Rye straw / He had a long chain on
CD ______ SHCD 3808
Sugar Hill / May '93 / ADA / CM / Direct / Koch / Roots

RED ON BLONDE
Senor (Tales of Yankee power) / Tombstone blues / Farewell Angelina / Wicked messenger / Father of night / Subterranean homesick blues / Everything is broken / Man gave names to the animals / Masters of war / Oxford town / Maggie's farm / Forever young / Lay down your weary tune
CD ____ **SHCD 3853**
Sugar Hill / Dec '96 / ADA / CM / Direct / Koch / Roots

REMEMBER ME (O'Brien, Tim & Mollie)
Looking for the stone / If I had my way / Floods of south Dakota / Shut de do / Stagger lee / Remember me / Somebody the blues / Do right to me baby / That's the way to treat your woman / Motherless children / Pilgrim of sorrow / Hush while the little ones sleep / Out in the country
CD ____ **SHCD 3804**
Sugar Hill / Jul '92 / ADA / CM / Direct / Koch / Roots

ROCK IN MY SHOE
CD ____ **SHCD 3835**
Sugar Hill / Jul '95 / ADA / CM / Direct / Koch / Roots

TAKE ME BACK (O'Brien, Tim & Mollie)
Leave that liar alone / Sweet sunny South / I loved you a thousand ways / Just someone I used to know / Down to the valley to pray / Wave the ocean, wave the sea / Your long journey / When the roses bloom in Dixieland / Unwed fathers / Nobody's fault but mine / Papa's on the housetop / Dream of the miner's child / Christ was born in Bethlehem
CD ____ **SHCD 3766**
Sugar Hill / Aug '96 / ADA / CM / Direct / Koch / Roots

O'Brien-Moran, Jimmy

SEAN REID'S FAVOURITE
CD ____ **PPP 001CD**
Piping Pig / May '97 / ADA

O'Bryant, Jimmy

JIMMY O'BRYANT VOL.1 1924-1925
CD ____ **JPCD 1518**
Jazz Perspectives / May '95 / Hot Shot / Jazz Music

JIMMY O'BRYANT VOL.2 1923-1931 (O'Bryant, Jimmy & Vance Dixon)
CD ____ **JPCD 1519**
Jazz Perspectives / May '95 / Hot Shot / Jazz Music

Obsessed

LUNAR WOMB
CD ____ **H 00152**
Hellhound / Jan '92 / Koch

Obsession Quintet

BULGAROIDE TRIBU
CD ____ **DP 96013CD**
Mustradem / Aug '96 / ADA

OC

JEWELZ
CD ____ **5243992**
London / Aug '97 / PolyGram

Ocal, Burhan

OTTOMAN GARDEN
CD ____ **ED 13044**
L'Empreinte Digitale / Jan '97 / ADA / Harmonia Mundi

O'Canainn, Thomas

UILEANN PIPES AND SONG
CD ____ **PTICD 1035**
Pure Traditional Irish / Oct '95 / ADA / CM / Direct / Ross

Ocarina

SONG OF OCARINA
CD ____ **DSHLCD 7020**
D-Sharp / Aug '95 / Pinnacle

Ocasek, Ric

NEGATIVE THEATER
I still believe / Come alive / Quick change world / Ride with duce / What's on TV / Shake a little nervous / Hopped up / Take me silver / Telephone again / Race to nowhere / Help me find America / Who do I pay / Wait for fate / What is time / Fade away
CD ____ **9362452482**
WEA / Mar '93 / Warner Music

O'Cathain, Darach

DARACH O CATHAIN
CD ____ **SHCD 34005**
Claddagh / May '93 / ADA / CM / Direct

TRADITIONAL IRISH UNACCOMPANIED SINGING
CD ____ **CEFCD 040**
Gael Linn / Jan '94 / ADA / CM / Direct / Grapevine/PolyGram / Roots

Occasional Word

YEAR OF THE GREAT LEAP SIDEWAYS, THE
Open the box / Eternal truth, man / Thoroughly British affair / Clock clock / I'm so glad / Barnyard suite / Girl behind me / Missed my times / Evil venus tree / Eine steine knack muzak / Trixie's song / Train set / Sweet tea song / Nuts and bolts / Internal truth, woman / Playground that fought back / Skin diver / Mrs. Jones / Hortensia / Close the box
CD ____ **SEECD 420**
See For Miles/C5 / May '95 / Pinnacle

Occasionals

BACK IN STEP
Grand march / Boston two-step / Flying Scotsman / Hesitation waltz / Jacky tar two step / Circassion circle / Lombard waltz / Baden / Hullichan's jig / Duke of Perth / Russian ballet / Friendly waltz / Haymakers / Gypsy tap / Southern rose waltz / Drops of brandy / Call of the pipers / Orcadian strip the willow
CD ____ **CDTRAX 107**
Greentrax / Jul '96 / ADA / Direct / Duncans / Highlander

FOOTNOTES: THE COMPLETE SCOTTISH CEILIDH DANCE
Gay gordons / Eva three step / St. Bernard's waltz / Dashing white sergeant / Military two step / Canadian barn dance / Pride of Erin waltz / Strip the willow / Britannia two step / Waltz country dance / Cumberland square eight / Highland schottische / Swedish masquerade / Virginia reel / Foula reel / Veleta waltz / Eightsome reel / Last waltz
CD ____ **IRCD 021**
Lismor / Jan '93 / ADA / Direct / Duncans / Lismor

Occult

ENEMY WITHIN, THE
CD ____ **FDN 2011CD**
Foundation 2000 / Jun '96 / Plastic Head

PREPARE TO MEET THY DOOM
CD ____ **FDN 2010CD**
Foundation 2000 / Jun '94 / Plastic Head

Ocean

SILVER
CD ____ **DHR 1**
Doll's House / Mar '94 / Pinnacle

Ocean 11

GOOD, THE BAD AND THE UGLY, THE
CD ____ **ATY 003CD**
A To Y / Apr '97 / Plastic Head

Ocean, Billy

LOVE REALLY HURTS WITHOUT YOU
Love really hurts without you / Emotions in motion / On the run (the battle is over) / Whose little girl are you / He ain't as black as he is painted / What's gonna happen to our love / Wild beautiful woman / Light up the world with your sunshine / Can you feel it / Eye of a storm / Hungry for love / Super woman super lover
CD ____ **QED 114**
Tring / Nov '96 / Tring

LOVE REALLY HURTS WITHOUT YOU
Love really hurts without you / Emotions in motion / On the run (the battle is over) / Whose little girl is you / He ain't black as he's painted / On the run (battle is over) / What's gonna happen to our love / Wild beautiful woman / Light up the world with sunshine / Can you feel it / Eye of the storm / Hungry for love / Super woman, super lover / On the run (the battle is over)
CD ____ **100192**
CMC / May '97 / BMG

LOVER BOY
Loverboy / Let's get back together / Promise me / Without you / Long and winding road / It's never too late to try / Here's to you / Caribbean queen (no more love on the run) / Stand and deliver / Colour of love / There'll be sad songs (To make you cry) / If I should lose you / Showdown / Because of you
CD ____ **5501182**
Spectrum / Oct '93 / PolyGram

Ocean Blue

BENEATH THE RHYTHM AND SOUND
Peace of mind / Sublime / Listen it's gone / Either or / Bliss is unaware / Ice skating at night / Don't believe everything you hear / Crash / Cathedral bells / Relatives / Emotions ring
CD ____ **9362453692**
Sire / Sep '93 / Warner Music

Ocean Colour Scene

B SIDES SEASIDES AND FREE RIDES
Huckleberry grove / Day we caught the train (Acoustic) / Mrs Jones / Top of the world / Here in my heart / I wanna stay alive with you / Robin Hood / Chelsea walk / Outside of a circle / Clock struck 15 hours ago / Alibis / Chicken bones and stones / Cool cool water / Charlie Brown says / Day tripper / Beautiful losers
CD ____ **MCD 60034**
MCA / Mar '97 / BMG

MOSELEY SHOALS
Riverboat song / Day we caught the train / Circle lining your pockets / Fleeting mind / 40 past midnight / One for the road / It's my shadow / Policeman and pirates / Downstream / You've got it bad / Get away
CD ____ **MCD 60008**
MCA / Apr '96 / BMG

OCEAN COLOUR SCÈNE
Talk on / How about you / Giving it all away / Justine / Do yourself a favour / Third shade of green / Sway / Penny pinching rainy heaven days / One of those days / Is she coming home / Blue deep ocean / Reprise
CD ____ **5122692**
Fontana / Jan '96 / PolyGram

Oceanic

THAT ALBUM BY OCEANIC
Is this the end / Insanity / Heavenly feel / Wicked love / Ignorance / Controlling me / Strut / Using me / Give this love some meaning / Moments in time / Insanity / Wicked love
CD ____ **GOODCD 1**
Dead Dead Good / May '92 / Pinnacle

Ocho

TORNADO
Mamey Colorao / Tornado / Way we were / Sneakin' up behind you / Majnabuca / Mode 1 / Mode 2 / Mode 3 / Mode 4
CD ____ **USCDTOR 1**
Universal Sounds / Nov '96 / New Note/Pinnacle / Timewarp

Ochoa, Callixto

SALSA CUMBIA VALLENATO (Ochoa, Callixto & Las Vibraciones)
CD ____ **TUMICD 036**
Tumi / '94 / Discovery / Stern's

Ochoa, Rafael

HARPS OF VENUZUELA (Ochoa, Rafael & Rafael Aponte)
CD ____ **PS 65083**
PlayaSound / Mar '92 / ADA / Harmonia Mundi

Ochs, Phil

ALL THE NEWS THATS FIT TO SING
One more parade / Thresher / Talking Vietnam / Lou Marsh / Power and the glory / Celia / Bells / Automation song / Ballad of William Worthy / Knock on the door / Talking Cuban crisis / Bound for glory / Too many martyrs / What's that I hear
CD ____ **HNCD 4427**
Hannibal / Apr '94 / ADA / Vital

BROADSIDE TAPES VOL.1, THE
CD ____ **SFWCD 40008**
Smithsonian Folkways / Mar '95 / ADA / Cadillac / CM / Direct / Koch

GREATEST HITS
One way ticket home / Jim Dean of Indiana / My kingdom for a car / Boy in Ohio / Gas station women / Chords of fame / Ten cents a coup / Bach, Beethoven, Mozart and me / Basket in the pool / No more songs
CD ____ **EDCD 201**
Edsel / Jul '90 / Pinnacle

I AIN'T MARCHING ANYMORE
I ain't marching anymore / In the heat of the summer / Draft dodger rag / That's what I want to hear / That was The President / Iron lady / Highway man / Links on the chain / Hills of West Virginia / Men behind the guns / Talking Birmingham jam / Ballad of the carpenter / Days of decision / Here's to the state of Mississippi
CD ____ **HNCD 4422**
Hannibal / Apr '94 / ADA / Vital

LAST AMERICAN TROUBADOUR, THE (2CD Set)
Cross my heart / Flower lady / Outside of a small circle of friends / Pleasures of the harbor / Crucifixion / Tape from California / White boots marching in a yellow land / Half a century high / Joe Hill / War is over / William BYeates vists Lincoln Park and escapes unscathed / Here's to the state of Richard Nixon / Scorpion departs but never returns / Doesn't Lenny live here anymore / Rehearsals for retirement / I kill therefore I am / Bells / Highwayman / Another age / There but for fortune / One way ticket home / Jim Dean of Indiana / My kingdom for a car / Gas station women / Chords of fame / No more songs / Mona Lisa / I ain't marchin' anymore / School days / Power and the glory / Kansas City bomber / Bwatue / Niko Mchumba Ngombe / Changes
CD Set ____ **5407282**
A&M / Aug '97 / PolyGram

TOAST TO THOSE WHO ARE GONE, A
Do what I have to do / Ballad of Billie Sol / Coloured town / AMA Song / William Moore / Paul Crump / Going down to Mississippi / I'll be there / Ballad of Oxford / No Christmas in Kentucky / Toast to those who are gone / I'm tired
CD ____ **DIAB 813**
Diabolo / Oct '94 / Pinnacle

O'Connell, Bill

LOST VOICES
Lost voices / Yellowtail / Good enough / Chega de saudade / Cosat verde / Sidestep / Sand stones / Sophie rose / In time
CD ____ **ESJCD 235**
Essential Jazz / Oct '94 / BMG

O'Connell, Helen

SWEETEST SOUNDS, THE
CD ____ **HCD 251**
Hindsight / Aug '94 / Jazz Music / Target/BMG

O'Connell, Maura

ALWAYS
CD ____ **TFCB 5011CD**
Third Floor / Oct '94 / ADA / Direct / Total/BMG

BLUE IS THE COLOUR OF HOPE
CD ____ **9362450632**
WEA / Jan '95 / Warner Music

JUST IN TIME
Scholar / If you love me / Feet of a dancer / Isle of Malachy / New Orleans / Water is wide / Leaving Neidin / Crazy dreams / Love's old sweet song / Another morning / I will / Just in time
CD ____ **CDPH 1124**
Philo / '90 / ADA / CM / Direct

MAURA O'CONNELL
Living in these troubled times / God only knows / Send this whisper / Lovers at last / Till the right one comes along / I don't know how you do it / Saw you running / All of me / Love is on a roll / Spend the night with you / My Lagan love
CD ____ **TFCB 5007CD**
Third Floor / Oct '94 / ADA / Direct / Total/BMG

STORIES
Blue chalk / Hit the ground running / Love divine / Poetic justice / Stories / Half moon bay / This town can't get over you / Rainmaker / Shotgun down the avalanche / An ordinary day / If I fell / Wall around you heart
CD ____ **HNCD 1389**
Hannibal / Oct '95 / ADA / Vital

WANDERING HOME
West coast of Clare / I hear you calling / Down the moor / Teddy O'Neill / Shades of Gloria / Irish blues / Down where the drunkards roll / A Stor Ma Chroi / Down by the Sally Gardens / Dun Do Shuil / Singer's house
CD ____ **HNCD 1410**
Hannibal / Jun '97 / ADA / Vital

O'Connell, Moloney

KILKELLY (O'Connell, Moloney & Keane)
CD ____ **GLCD 1072**
Green Linnet / Feb '92 / ADA / CM / Direct / Highlander / Roots

O'Connell, Robbie

CLOSE TO THE BONE
Gay old hag / William Hollander / Week before Easter / Earl of Murray / Waterford waltz / With Kitty I'll go for a waltz / Torn petticoat/The rambling pitchfork / I know where I'm going / Bobby's britches / Sliabh na mBan / Ferrybank piper / Ham Sunday
CD ____ **GLCD 1038**
Green Linnet / Oct '88 / ADA / CM / Direct / Highlander / Roots

LOVE OF THE LAND, THE
Love of the land / Keg of brandy / Early riser / Full moon over Managua / Land of Liberty / Road to Dunmore / Two nations / Last of the Gleemen / You're not Irish
CD ____ **GLCD 1097**
Green Linnet / Nov '92 / ADA / CM / Direct / Highlander / Roots

NEVER LEARNED TO DANCE
Love knows no bounds / American lives / Galileo / Winning side / Turning of the tide / Hard to say goodbye / Man from Connemara / When the moon is full / Old man of the mountain / Mistress / So near / Singer
CD ____ **GLCD 1124**
Green Linnet / May '93 / ADA / CM / Direct / Highlander / Roots

O'Connor, Cavan

SMILIN' THROUGH
Rose of tralee / One alone / Danny boy / In the still of the night / Vagabond song / Hear my song Violetta / Could you be true to eyes of blue / God will remember / Little village green / Marie / My heart is always calling you / Put a little springtime / Shannon river / Smilin' through / Star and the rose / Star of County Down / Take me back to dear old Ireland / There's something in your eyes / When it's springtime in old Ire-

land / Without you / Would you take me back again / You, me and love
CD CDAJA 5085
Living Era / Mar '97 / Select

VAGABOND OF SONG, THE
CD PLATCD 35
Platinum / Mar '95 / Prism

VERY BEST OF THE SINGING VAGABOND, THE
CD SWNCD 001
Sound Waves / May '95 / Target/BMG

O'Connor, Charles

ANGEL ON THE MANTLEPIECE
CD ALZO 1CD
Ritual / Jul '95 / ADA

O'Connor, Des

LOVE COLLECTION, THE
CD CDSR 124
Telstar / Apr '97 / BMG

LOVE SONGS
CD CDSR 073
Telstar / May '96 / BMG

LOVIN' FEELING
CD CDSR 072
Telstar / May '96 / BMG

TO ALL THE GIRLS I'VE LOVED BEFORE
CD CDSR 071
Telstar / May '96 / BMG

VERY BEST OF DES O'CONNOR, THE
Careless hands / One two three O'Leary / When you're smiling / Everybody's talkin' / Raindrops keep fallin' on my head / For the good times / You always hurt the one you love / Your cheatin' heart / Didn't we / I pretend / Dream a little dream of me / With love / Anytime / Dick-a-dum-dum / Tips of my fingers / I'll go hopping / Lonliness (No sono Maddelena) / Something / All I need is you / Heartaches / Try to remember / Red roses for a blue lady / My thanks to you
CD CDMFP 6248
Music For Pleasure / Aug '96 / EMI

O'Connor, Gerry

LA LUGH (O'Connor, Gerry & Eithne Ni Uallachain)
Mal bhan ni Chilleannain/Destitution / Sterling Tom/Tommy Bhetty's hornmmpipe / One morning in May / Wedding jig/Aunt Lizzie's jig / Liostail me le Sairsint / Shetland bus / Donellan set / Road to Clady / Mummer's march/The Water Ouzel / Rosebuds in summer / Launching the boat / Draw near my wayward Darling / On Brigid's eve / Boy in his pants/Big John's jig / Emigrant's farewell / Drogheda lassies/The Donegal traveller/Lisa Ornstein's reel
CD CCF 29CD
Claddagh / Jun '93 / ADA / CM / Direct

TIME TO TIME
CD CLUNCD 051
Mulligan / Sep '86 / ADA / CM

O'Connor, Hazel

COVER PLUS
We're all grown up / Hanging around / Ee-i-adio / Not for you / Hold on / So you're born / Dawn chorus / Animal farm / Runaway / Do what you gotta do / Men of good fortune / That's life
CD MSCD 23
Music De-Luxe / Jul '95 / TKO Magnum

LIVE IN BERLIN
D-days / Runaway / Blackman / Spancil Hill / Tell me why / Hanging around / Will you / Eighth day / Calls the tune / If only / Reach / Driftwood
CD SRH 804
Start / Feb '97 / Disc

O'Connor, Mark

CHAMPIONSHIP YEARS 1975-1984, THE
Grey eagle / Clarinet polka / Dusty Miller / I don't love nobody / Wednesday night waltz / Herman's rag / Sally Goodin / Sally Johnson / Yellow rose waltz / Tom and Jerry / Billy in the lowground / Herman's rag / Allentown polka / Brilliancy / Black and white rag / Tom and Jerry / Clarinet polka / Dill pickle rag / Grey eagle / Leather britches / Don't let the deal go down / Golden eagle hornpipe / I don't love nobody / Brilliancy / Tug boat / Grey eagle / Beaumont rag / Hell among the yearlings / Bill Cheatham / Sally Goodin / Herman's rag / Choctaw / Westphalia waltz / Black and white rag / Herman's hornpipe / Dill pickle rag / Sally Ann / Clarinet polka / Arkansas traveller / Jesse polka
CD CMFCD 015
Country Music Foundation / Jan '93 / ADA / Direct

HEROES
CD 9362452572
WEA / Feb '94 / Warner Music

MARKOLOGY
Dixie breakdown / Markology / Kit's waltz / Fluid drive / Blackberry blossom / Pickin' the wind / Banks of the Ohio / Berserkeley / On top of the world
CD ROUCD 009
Rounder / Aug '93 / ADA / CM / Direct

NEW NASHVILLE CATS, THE
Bowtie / Restless / Nashville shuffle boogie / Pick it apart / Traveller's ridge / Granny White special / Cat in the bag / Ballad of Sally Anne / Swang / Dance of the ol' swamp rat / Bowl of bula / Lime rock / Sweet Suzanne / Orange blossom special / Now it belongs to you
CD 7599265092
Warner Bros. / Jun '92 / Warner Music

RETROSPECTIVE
CD ROUCD 11507
Rounder / '88 / ADA / CM / Direct

SOPPIN' THE GRAVY
Soppin' the gravy / Misty moonlight waltz / College hornpipe / Calgary polka / Morning star waltz / Tennessee Wagoner / Yellow rose waltz / Medley / Jesse polka / Dawn waltz / Wild fiddler's rag / Over the rainbow
CD ROUCD 0137
Rounder / '92 / ADA / CM / Direct

O'Connor, Martin

CHATTERBOX
CD DARACD 052
Dara / Oct '93 / ADA / CM / Direct / Else / Grapevine/PolyGram

CONNACHTMAN'S RAMBLES
CD LUNCD 027
Mulligan / Feb '95 / ADA / CM

PERPETUAL MOTION
Fandango / Rags to rock'n'roll / Happy hours / Carnival of Venice / Perpetual motion / Ebra polka / Emerald blues / Cajun medley / Beau St. Waltzes / Bulgarian jig / Sophie for Sofia / Midnight on the water / Hound dog
CD CCF 26CD
Claddagh / '90 / ADA / CM / Direct

O'Connor, Sinead

AM I NOT YOUR GIRL
Why don't you do right / Bewitched, bothered and bewildered / Secret love / Black coffee / Success has made a failure of our home / Don't cry for me Argentina / I wanna be loved by you / Gloomy Sunday / Love Letters / How insensitive / Don't cry for me Argentina (Inst)
CD CCD 1952
Ensign / Sep '92 / EMI

I DO NOT WANT WHAT I HAVEN'T GOT
Feel so different / I am stretched on your grave / Three babies / Emperor's new clothes / Black boys on mopeds / Nothing compares 2 U / Jump in the river / You cause as much sorrow / Last day of our acquaintance / I do not want what I haven't got
CD CCD 1759
Ensign / Mar '90 / EMI

LION AND THE COBRA, THE
Jackie / Mandinka / Jerusalem / Just like u said it would b / Never get old / Troy / I want your (hands on me) / Drink before the war / Just call me Joe
CD CCD 1612
Ensign / Oct '87 / EMI

UNIVERSAL MOTHER
Speech extract / Fire on Babylon / John I love you / My darling child / Am I a human / Red football / All apologies / Perfect Indian / Scorn not his simplicity / All babies / In this heart / Tiny grief song / Famine / Thank you for hearing me
CD CDCHEN 34
Ensign / Sep '94 / EMI

Octagon Man

EXCITING WORLD OF...
CD TRONCD 5X
Electron Industries / Nov '95 / RTM/Disc

October Faction

OCTOBER FACTION
CD SST 036CD
SST / May '93 / Plastic Head

SECOND FACTIIONALISATION
CD SST 056CD
SST / May '93 / Plastic Head

Octopus

RESTLESS NIGHT...PLUS
River / Summer / Council plans / Restless night / Thief / Queen and the pauper / I say / John's rock / Rainchild / Tide / Girlfriend / Laugh at the poor man
CD SEECD 328
See For Miles/C5 / Aug '97 / Pinnacle

Octopus

FROM A TO B
Your smile / Everyday kiss / If you want to give me more / King for a day / Adrenalina / Instrumental 1 / Jealousy / Magazine / From A to B / Instrumental 2 / Saved / Wait & see / Theme from Joy Pop / Night song / In this world
CD FOODCD 18
Food / Sep '96 / EMI

Octoscope

OCTOPHOBIC
CD CLP 9968
Cleopatra / Apr '97 / Cargo / Greyhound / Plastic Head / RTM/Disc / SRD

O'Day, Anita

ANITA O'DAY & HER QUARTET LIVE
CD SLCD 9004
Starline / Feb '94 / Jazz Music

ANITA O'DAY 1975
CD STCD 4147
Storyville / Feb '90 / Cadillac / Jazz Music / Wellard

ANITA O'DAY SINGS THE WINNERS
Take the 'A' train / Tenderly / Night in Tunisia / Four / Early Autumn / Four brothers / Sing sing sing / My funny valentine / Frenesi / Body and soul / What's your story Morning Glory / Peanut vendor / Whisper not / Blue champagne / Stompin' at the Savoy / Hershey Bar / Don't be that way / Peel me grape / Star eyes
CD 8379392
Verve / Apr '90 / PolyGram

ANITA O'DAY SWINGS COLE PORTER
Just one of those things / Love for sale / You'd be so nice to come home to / Easy to love / I get a kick out of you / All of you / Get out of town / I got you under my skin / Night and day / It's de-lovely / I love you / What is this thing called love / You're the top / My heart belongs to Daddy / Why shouldn't I / From this moment on / Love for sale / Just one of those things
CD 8492662
Verve / Mar '91 / PolyGram

BIG BAND YEARS, THE
Georgia on my mind / Just a little bit south of North Carolina / Slow down / Green eyes / Let me off uptown / Kick it / Stop the red light's on / Walls keep talking / Skylark / Bolero at the Savoy / Thanks for the boogie ride / That's what you think / Massachusetts / Murder he says / I'm going mad for a pad / And her tears flowed like wine / I want a grown up man / Memories of you / Opus 1 / Did you ever get that feeling in the moonlight / Boogie blues / Chickery chick / In the middle of May / Tea for two / Harriet
CD PLCD 547
President / Aug '96 / Grapevine/PolyGram / President / Target/BMG

HIGH STANDARDS
CD CDSL 5209
DRG / Jan '89 / Discovery / New Note/ Pinnacle

I GET A KICK OUT OF YOU
Song for you / Undecided / What are you doing the rest of your life / Exactly like you / When Sunny gets blue / It had to be you / Opus one / Gone with the wind
CD ECD 22054
Evidence / Jul '93 / ADA / Cadillac / Harmonia Mundi

JAZZ MASTERS
CD 5276532
Verve / Mar '96 / PolyGram

L'ART VOCAL 1941-1945
CD 700192
L'Art Vocal / Jul '97 / Discovery

LET ME OFF UPTOWN
Georgia on my mind / Just a little bit South of North Carolina / Slow down / Green eyes / Let me off uptown / Kick it / Stop, the red light's on / Watch the birdie / Walls keep talking / Skylark / Bolero at the Savoy / Thanks for the boogie ride / Pass the bounce / Harlem on parade / That's what you think / Massachusetts / Murder he says / Opus one / Boogie blues / That feeling in the moonlight / Tea for two / Harriet
CD TPZ 1046
Topaz Jazz / Jul '96 / Cadillac / Pinnacle

MEETS THE BIG BANDS
CD MCD 0472
Moon / Nov '93 / Cadillac / Harmonia Mundi

ONCE UPON A SUMMERTIME
Sweet Georgia Brown / Love for sale / 'S Wonderful / Tea for two / Once upon a summertime / Night and day / Anita's blues / They can't take that away from me / Boogie blues / Girl from Ipanema / Is you is or is you ain't my baby / Nightingale sang in Berkeley Square
CD JASMCD 2531
Jasmine / Feb '95 / Conifer/BMG / Hot Shot / TKO Magnum

PICK YOURSELF UP
I'm with you / Don't be that way / Rock 'n' roll waltz / Let's face the music and dance / Getaway and the chase / I never had a chance / Stompin' at the Savoy / Your picture's hanging crooked on the wall / Pick yourself up / We laughed at love / I'm not lonely / Stars fell on Alabama / Sweet Georgia Brown / Let's face the music and dance / Stars fell on Alabama / I won't dance / Man with a horn / I used to be colour blind / There's a lull in my life / Let's begin
CD 5173292
Verve / Jun '93 / PolyGram

RULES OF THE ROAD
Rules of the road / Black coffee / Detour ahead / Shaking the blues away / Music that makes me dance / As long as there's music / Sooner or later / What is a man / Here's that rainy day / It's you or no one / I told ya I love ya, now get out
CD CD 2310950
Pablo / Apr '94 / Cadillac / Complete/ Pinnacle

WAVE (Live at Ronnie Scott's)
Wave / You'd be so nice to come home to / On Green Dolphin street / I can't get started (with you) / It don't mean a thing if it ain't got that swing / Street of dreams / 'S wonderful / They can't take that away from me / Is you is or is you ain't my baby / My funny valentine / I cried for you / Four brothers
CD CLACD 330
Castle / '93 / BMG

O'Day, Molly

MOLLY O'DAY AND THE CUMBERLAND MOUNTAIN FOLKS
Tramp on the street / When God comes and gathers his jewels / Black sheep returned to the fold / Put my rubber doll away / Drunken driver / Tear stained letter / Lonely mound of clay / Six more miles / Singing waterfall / At the first fall of snow / Matthew twenty four / I don't care if tomorrow never comes / Hero's death / I'll never see sunshine again / Too late, too late / Why do you weep dear willow / Don't forget the family prayer / I heard my mother weeping / Mother's gone but not forgotten / Evening train / This is the end / Fifteen years ago / Teardrops falling in the snow / With you on my mind / If you see my saviour / Heaven's radio / When my time comes to go / Don't sell Daddy anymore whiskey / Higher in my prayers / Travelling the highway home / It's different now / When the angels rolled the stone away / It's all coming true / When we see our Redeemer's face
CD BCD 15565
Bear Family / Jun '92 / Direct / Rollercoaster / Swift

Odd Toot

BAMPOT
CD HEMP 8CD
Recordings Of Substance / Jul '97 / 3mv/ Vital / Kudos / Prime

Oden, Jimmy

JIMMY ODEN 1932-1948
CD SOB 35082CD
Story Of The Blues / Apr '95 / ADA / Koch

ST. LOUIS JIMMY ODEN VOL.1 1932-1944
CD DOCD 5234
Document / May '94 / ADA / Hot Shot / Jazz Music

ST. LOUIS JIMMY ODEN VOL.2 1944-1955
CD DOCD 5235
Document / May '94 / ADA / Hot Shot / Jazz Music

Odessa Balalaikas

ART OF THE BALALAIKA, THE
CD 7559790342
Nonesuch / Jan '95 / Warner Music

Odessa Express

BABEL
CD SYNCD 159
Syncoop / Jun '94 / ADA / Direct

Odetta

CHRISTMAS SPIRITUALS
Rise up shepherd and follow / What month was Jesus born in / Mary had a baby, yes Lord / Somebody talking 'bout Jesus / Virgin Mary had one son / Go tell it on the mountain / Shout for joy / Poor little Jesus / O Jerusalem / Ain't that a-rockin' / If anybody asks you / Beautiful star / Children go where I send thee
CD VMD 79079
Vanguard / Oct '96 / ADA / Pinnacle

ODETTA AND THE BLUES
Hard, oh Lord / Believe I'll go / Oh papa / How long blues / Hogan's alley / Leavin' this morning / Oh, my babe / Yonder come the blues / Make me a pallet on the floor / Weeping willow blues / Go down sunshine / Nobody knows you (when you're down and out)
CD OBCCD 509
Original Blues Classics / Nov '92 / Complete/Pinnacle / Wellard

ODETTA AT THE TOWN HALL
CD VMD 2109
Vanguard / Jan '96 / ADA / Pinnacle

SINGS BALLADS AND BLUES
CD _______________ TCD 1004
Tradition / Feb '96 / ADA / Vital

TIN ANGEL (Odetta & Larry Mohr)
CD _______________ OBCCD 565
Original Blues Classics / Jul '94 / Complete/Pinnacle / Wellard

WOMEN IN (E)MOTION FESTIVAL
CD _______________ T&M 101
Tradition & Moderne / Nov '94 / ADA / Direct

Odom, Andrew

FEEL SO GOOD (Odom, Andrew 'Big Voice' & Magic Slim/Lucky Peterson)
Feel so good / I made up my mind / Mother In Law Blues / Woke up this morning / Memo blues / Bad feeling / You say that you love me baby / Reconsider baby
CD _______________ ECD 260272
Evidence / Feb '93 / ADA / Cadillac / Harmonia Mundi

O'Donnell, Daniel

BOY FROM DONEGAL, THE
Donegal shore / Old rustic bridge / Galway bay / Forty shades of green / My side of the road / 5000 miles from Sligo / Old bog road / Slievenamon / Noreen Bawn / Ballyhoe
CD _______________ IHCD 04
Irish Heritage / Oct '89 / Prism

CHRISTMAS WITH DANIEL
Silent night / Memory of an old Christmas card / Silver bells / C-H-R-I-S-T-M-A-S / White Christmas / When a child is born / Rockin' around the Christmas tree / Christmas song / Christmas long ago / Gift / Christmas time in Inisfree / Snowflake / I saw Mommy kissing Santa Claus / Pretty paper
CD _______________ RITZBCD 704
Ritz / Nov '94 / Pinnacle

CLASSIC COLLECTION
CD _______________ RITZBCD 705
Ritz / Oct '95 / Pinnacle

DANIEL O'DONNELL IRISH COLLECTION
CD _______________ RITZCD 0080
Ritz / Jul '96 / Pinnacle

DATE WITH DANIEL O'DONNELL - LIVE, A
I just wanna dance with you / Whatever happened to old fashioned love / Somewhere between / Follow your dream / You're the reason / Love in your eyes / Minute you're gone / Little things / My Irish country home / Isle of Innisfree / I need you / Never ending song of love / Wedding song / My Donegal shore / Stand beside me / Old rugged cross / How great thou art / Pretty little girl from Omagh / My shoes keep walking back to you / Rose of Tralee / Our house is a home / Mountains of Mourne / Roses are red/Moonlight and roses
CD _______________ RITZBCD 702
Ritz / Oct '93 / Pinnacle

DON'T FORGET TO REMEMBER
I don't care / Old loves never die / I wonder where you are tonight / Don't be angry / Roses are red / Before I'm over you / Take good care of her / Pretty little girl from Omagh / Green willow / Don't let me cross over / Good old days / Pat Murphy's meadow / I just can't make it on my own
CD _______________ RITZCD 105
Ritz / Dec '87 / Pinnacle

ESPECIALLY FOR YOU
Singin' the blues / Lover's chain / You're the first thing I think of / Someday / There'll never be anyone else / Travelling light / Old broken hearts / Leaving is easy / She goes walking through my mind / Come back paddy reilly to Ballyjamesduff / Sweet forget me not / Silver threads among the gold / It comes and goes / Guilty / Happy years
CD _______________ RITBCD 703
Ritz / Oct '94 / Pinnacle

FAVOURITES
Bed of roses / Excuse me / Geisha girl / Home sweet home / Home is where the heart is / Forever you'll be mine / Streets of Baltimore / Bringing Mary home / Banks of my own lovely Lee / Green hills of Sligo
CD _______________ RITZCD 0052
Ritz / Apr '90 / Pinnacle

FOLLOW YOUR DREAM
I need you (intro) / Stand Beside Me / Eileen / Pretty Little Girl From Omagh / Destination Donegal / Medley / Medley / Wedding song (Ave Maria) / Irish country home / Ramblin' Rose / I just want to dance with you / Medley / Medley / White River stomp / Our House Is A Home / Never Ending Song Of Love / Rockin' alone in an old rocking chair / Standing Room Only / Welcome home / Love in your eyes / You send me your love / Turkey In The Straw / I Need You / Medley / Reprise / How Great Thou Art
CD _______________ RITZBCD 701
Ritz / Nov '92 / Pinnacle

I NEED YOU
Sing me an old Irish song / I need you / From a jack to a king / Lovely rose of Clare / Stand beside me / Irish eyes / Dear old Galway town / Three leaf shamrock / Veil of white lace / Kickin' each others hearts around / Medals for mothers / Wedding bells / Snowflake / Your friendly Irish way / Lough Melvin's rocky shore / I love you because
CD _______________ RITZCD 104
Ritz / Jun '87 / Pinnacle

LAST WALTZ, THE
Here I am in love again / We could / Last waltz of the evening / When only the sky was blue / Heaven with you / You know I still love you / Talk back trembling lips / Shelter of your eyes / When we get together / Ring of gold / Fool such as I / Memory number one / Look both ways / Little patch of blue / Marianne
CD _______________ RITZCD 0058
Ritz / Oct '90 / Pinnacle

SONGS OF INSPIRATION
CD _______________ RITZBCD 709
Ritz / Oct '96 / Pinnacle

THOUGHTS OF HOME
My shoes keep walking back to you / Mountains of Mourne / London leaves / Blue eyes cryin' in the rain / Old days remembered / Send me the pillow that you dream on / Moonlight and roses / Little piece of Heaven / Far far from home / Isle of Innisfree / My heart skips / I know one / I'll take you home again Kathleen / Second fiddle / My favourite memory / Forty shades of green
CD _______________ TCD 2372
Telstar / Oct '89 / BMG

TIMELESS (O'Donnell, Daniel & Mary Duff)
CD _______________ RITZBCD 707
Ritz / Mar '96 / Pinnacle

TWO SIDES OF DANIEL O'DONNELL, THE
Green glens of Antrim / Blue hills of Breffni / Any Tipperary town / Latchyco / Home town on the Foyle / These are my mountains / My Donegal shore / Crying my heart out over you / My old pal / Our house is a home / Your old love letters / Twenty one years / Highway 40 blues / I wouldn't change you if I could
CD _______________ RITZCD 500
Ritz / '91 / Pinnacle

VERY BEST OF DANIEL O'DONNELL, THE
I need you / Never ending song of love / Don't forget to remember / Country boy like me / She's no angel / Stand beside me / Eileen / Pretty little girl from Omagh / Danny boy / Wedding song / My Donegal shore / Letter from the postman's bag / Three bells / Our house is a home / Loved ones goodbye / Home is where the heart is / Old rugged cross / You send me your love / Take good care of her / Standing room only
CD _______________ RITZBCD 700
Ritz / Oct '91 / Pinnacle

O'Donnell, Eugene

FOGGY DEW, THE (O'Donnell, Eugene & James MacCafferty)
CD _______________ GLCD 1084
Green Linnet / Feb '91 / ADA / CM / Direct / Highlander / Roots

SLOW AIRS & SET DANCES
Downfall of Paris / Scotsman over the border / Lodge Road / Da auld resting chair/ Derry hornpipe / Barney Brallaghan/Ride a mile / Celtic lament / Planxty O'Donnell / Jockey to the fair / Hunt / I won't see you anymore, my dear / Three sea captains / Bonny lass o'Bon Accord / Hurry the jug / Humours of Bandon/Planxty Maggie Brown / Planxty Drury
CD _______________ GLCD 1015
Green Linnet / Oct '88 / ADA / CM / Direct / Highlander / Roots

O'Donnell, Peter

SHAKESPEARE BLUES
CD _______________ QMCD 001
Bareface / Jun '94 / Sony

O'Dowda, Brendan

IRISH FAVOURITES
CD _______________ CDMFP 6346
Music For Pleasure / May '97 / EMI

Odyssey

GREATEST HITS
Going back to my roots / Inside out / Magic touch / Oh no not my baby / Weekend lover / Don't tell me, tell her / Use it up and wear it out / Hang together / It will be alright / Follow me (play follow the leader) / Easy come, easy go / When you love somebody / If you're looking for a way out / Native New Yorker
CD _______________ ND 90436
RCA / Mar '90 / BMG

ROOTS
Joy (I know it) / You can't take it away / Going back to my roots / Before we say hello / Laughing and smiling / Sing / Joy (I know it)
CD _______________ 307312
Hallmark / Jun '97 / Carlton

Odyssey

ODYSSEY
CD _______________ TB 103
Tim's Brain / Jul '97 / Greyhound

Oedipussy

DIVAN
CD _______________ HANCD 1
Hansome / Mar '95 / Pinnacle

O'Farrell, Chico

CUBAN BLUES (The Chico O'Farrell Sessions/2CD Set)
CD Set _______________ 5332562
Verve / Jan '97 / PolyGram

O'Farrell, Sean

ALWAYS
Way love ought to be / Eighteen yellow roses / She's good at loving me / I'd love you to want me / Those brown eyes / Soldier's tale / Every road leads back to you / Judy / Champion of 403 Mulberry Drive / Baby don't you know / Always / Do you know how much I love you / Longing to hold you again / Still
CD _______________ RCD 535
Ritz / Oct '93 / Pinnacle

SONGS JUST FOR YOU
When the girl in your arms (is the girl in your heart) / This song is just for you / Love without end, Amen / Galway shawl / Walk on by / Nobody's child / Wanted / Billy can't read / Two loves / Straight and narrow / You would do the same for me / Hey pretty lady / Crystal chandeliers / Missing him
CD _______________ RCD 541
Ritz / Jun '94 / Pinnacle

Ofcro Tribe

SPORADIC SPIRO GYRA
CD _______________ EBSCD 125
Emergency Broadcast System / Nov '96 / BMG

Off & Gone

EVEREST
Gods have gone / Everest / Kopli / Sprinkle / Shasta / My God / Sigma receptor / Europia / Phosphanes
CD _______________ EYEUKCD 010
Eye Q / Sep '96 / Vital

Offer, Cullen

FEATHER MERCHANT
CD _______________ PCD 7091
Progressive / Jun '93 / Jazz Music

STRIKE UP THE BAND (Offer, Cullen Quartet)
CD _______________ PCD 7104
Progressive / Jun '96 / Jazz Music

SWINGIN' TEXAS TENOR, THE
CD _______________ PCD 7086
Progressive / Jun '93 / Jazz Music

Offermans, Wil

DAILY SENSIBILITIES
CD _______________ BVHAASTCD 9206
Bvhaast / Oct '87 / Cadillac

Offspring

IXMAY ON THE HOMBRE
CD _______________ 64872
Epitaph / Feb '97 / Pinnacle / Plastic Head

NITRO
CD _______________ 158032
Epitaph / Oct '95 / Pinnacle / Plastic Head

OFFSPRING
Jennifer lost the war / Elders / Out on patrol / Crossroads / Demons / Beheaded / Tehran / Thousand days / Blackball / I'll be waiting / Kill the president
CD _______________ 864602
Epitaph / Nov '95 / Pinnacle / Plastic Head

SMASH
CD _______________ 864322
Epitaph / May '94 / Pinnacle / Plastic Head

Offworld

ANOTHER PLANET
CD _______________ CRECD 203
Creation / Jul '96 / 3mv/Vital

Oficina De Cordas

PERNAMBUCO'S MUSIC
CD _______________ NI 5396
Nimbus / Oct '94 / Nimbus

O'Flaharta, John Beag

AN LOCHAN
CD _______________ CIC 084CD
Clo Iar-Chonnachta / Nov '93 / CM

AN TANCAIRE - FICHE AMHRAN 1980-1990
CD _______________ CIC 025CD
Clo Iar-Chonnachta / Jan '91 / CM

TA AN WORKHOUSE LAN
CD _______________ CICD 093
Clo Iar-Chonnachta / Dec '93 / CM

WINDS OF FREEDOM
CD _______________ CICD 106
CICD / Jan '95 / ADA

O'Flynn, Liam

BRENDAN VOYAGE (O'Flynn, Liam & Orchestra)
CD _______________ TARACD 3006
Tara / Oct '89 / ADA / CM / Conifer/BMG / Direct

GIVEN NOTE, THE
O'Farrell's welcome to Limerick / O'Rourke's/The Merry sisters/Colonel Fraser / Come with me over the mountain / Smile in the dark / Farewell to Govan / Joyce's tune / Green island/Spellan the fiddler / Foliada de Elvina / Ag taisteal na Blarnan / Rambler / Aherlow jig / Smith's a gallant fireman / Romeo's exile / Rocks of Bawn / Cailin na gruage doinne / Teno un amor na / Alborada - Unha noite no Santo Cristo
CD _______________ TARACD 3034
Tara / Oct '95 / ADA / CM / Conifer/BMG / Direct

OUT TO ANOTHER SIDE
Foxchase / Wild geese / Dean's pamphlet / Gynt at the gate / Winter's end / After Aughrim's great disaster / Blackwells / Ar Bhruach na laoi / Lady Dillon / Dollards and The Harlequin hornpipes / Sean O Duibhir a Ghleanna
CD _______________ TARACD 3031
Tara / Aug '93 / ADA / CM / Conifer/BMG / Direct

OG Funk

OUT OF THE DARK
Me and my folks / Funk is in the house / Funkadelic groupie / Music for my brother / I've been alone / I wanna know / Don't take your love from me / Outta the dark / Angie
CD _______________ RCD 10303
Black Arc / Jun '94 / Vital

Ogada, Ayub

EM MANA KUOYO
Obiero / Dala / Wa Winjigo Ero / Thum Nyatiti / Kronkrohino / 10% / Ondiek / Kothbiro / En Mana Kuoyo
CD _______________ CDRW 42
Realworld / May '93 / EMI

Ogden, Nigel

DOWN WITH THE CURTAIN
Down with the curtain / Selection / Call me madam / Westminster waltz / Legend of the Glass Mountain / April in Portugal / Portuguese washerwomen / My prayer / Tampico / On my own / I dreamed a dream / Lingering lovers / Ballet Egyptian themes / How deep is your love / 'S wonderful / Lady is a tramp / Who / Moving South / Moving out / I'm getting sentimental over you / Deed I do / Georgia on my mind / Coronation Scot / Valse triste / New era
CD _______________ OS 225
OS Digital / Dec '96 / Conifer/BMG

MUSIC FOR ALL
When the saints go marching in / Border ballad / Mulligan musketeers / Tritsch tratsch polka / Sweet and low / Kalinka / Liberty bell / Going home / Dam busters march / Bobby Shaftoe / Sailing / Storm at sea / Strawberry fair / Bells of St. Mary's / Tydi a roddiast / Jerusalem / Finlandia / Morte criste
CD _______________ OS 211
OS Digital / Jan '95 / Conifer/BMG

SENTIMENTAL JOURNEY/TRIBUTE TO REGINALD DIXON
Royal Air Force march past / I'll string along with you / You'll never know / Polly / Smile smile smile / Certain smile / Morning, Noon and night / I can't tell a waltz from a tango / Val suzon / Under the linden tree / I kiss your hand, Madame / Spitfire prelude / Cole Porter classics / Sentimental journey / Somebody stole my gal / Why did she fall for the leader of the band / Solitude / Saddle your blues to a wild mustang / Rosalie / I double dare you / Oh ma ma / I love to whistle / You're an education / I won't dance / Lovely to look at / Smoke gets in your eyes / Little girl / As time goes by / When I take my sugar to tea / Happy feet / Manhattan / Boo hoo / Marching with the organ
CD _______________ OS 214
OS Digital / Aug '95 / Conifer/BMG

SUNDAY CELEBRATION, A
Fanfare / March in A / Jesu joy of man's desiring / Prelude in classic style / Steal away / Faith / Prelude / Pie Jesu / I'll walk with God / O for the wings of a dove / Sanctuary of the heart / Scherzetto on St. George / St. George's Day / Big blue planet / Star of God / Elegy / Intermezzo/Easter

Hymn / Chorale prelude on Crimond / Lost chord
CD OS 221
OS Digital / Jul '96 / Conifer/BMG

WURLITZER CELEBRATION
Beyond the blue horizon / Valse romantique / Pizzicato polka / Celebration march / How are things in Glocca Morra / Art deco / Three piece suite / Duo / In a clock store / Shadow waltz / At the sign of the swingin' cymbal / Love everlasting / Minuet / Paean / Whistler and his dog / Dusk / Waterloo march / Tell me I'm forgiven / Gymnopedie / Eric coates fantasia
CD OS 206
OS Digital / Mar '94 / Conifer/BMG

Ogeret, Marc

CHANTS DE MARINS
CD 983772
EPM / Mar '96 / ADA / Discovery

O'Grada, Conal

TOP OF COOM, THE
CD CCF 27CD
Claddagh / Jan '91 / ADA / CM / Direct

O'Hagan, Sean

HIGH LLAMAS
Perry Como / Edge of the sun / Pretty boy / Hoping you would change your mind / C'mon let's go / Paint and pets / Doggy / Half face cat / Trees / Have you heard the latest news
CD FIENDCD 192
Demon / Jul '95 / Pinnacle

O'Hara, Betty

HORNS APLENTY
Euphonics / Stardust / My heart stood still / Pigeon toed Joad / It don't mean a thing (if it ain't got that swing) / You stepped out of a dream / Alligator crawl / Sleeping bee / Medley from 'On the town' / If dreams come true
CD DD 482
Delmark / Jun '97 / ADA / Cadillac / CM / Direct / Hot Shot

O'Hara, Mary

BEAUTIFUL MUSIC OF MARY O'HARA, THE
Lord of the dance / Danny boy / Last rose of summer / In an english country garden / Bunch of thyme / My lagan / Going home / Perhaps love / She moved through the fair / Messenger / One day at a time / Willie's gane to Melville castle / Roisin dubh / Scent of the roses / Scarborough Fair / Never saw the roses / Memory / Quiet land of Erin
CD MCCD 070
Music Club / Jun '92 / Disc / THE

COLLECTION, THE
CD COL 072
Collection / Mar '95 / Target/BMG

DOWN BY THE GLENSIDE (The Songs Of Ireland)
CD TCD 1055
Tradition / Jul '97 / ADA / Vital

INSTRUMENTAL COLLECTION, THE
Way we were / Londonderry air / Skye boat song / Pamela Brown / Bunch of thyme / Scarborough Fair / For the good times / Bright eyes / Walking in the air / Three times a lady / Going home / Greensleeves / In an English country garden / Memory / Annie's song / One day at a time
CD VALD 8059
Valentine / Jul '88 / Conifer/BMG

IRISH-SCOTTISH RECITAL VOCALS & HARP
An crann ubhall (the apple tree) / She lived beside the anner / Cucuin a chuauchin / Kitty of Coleraine / Roisin dubh / Down by the Sally gardens / Luibin o luth / I will walk with my love / Seothin seo / Parting / Is ar eirinn ni-n eosfhainn ce h-i / Last rose of summer / Sean sa bhriste leathair (John and his leather brecches) / Young Brigid O'Malley / Deus Meus (my God) / I know my love / Sliabh geal gcua / Trotting to the fair / Willie's gane to Melville castle / Song of the waterhouse / Annie Laurie / Laird of cockpen / Cro cheann t saile / Shetland lullaby / Fhideag airgid (silver whistle) / Elfin knight / Shetland spinning song / Bonnie Earl O'Moray / Iarla nam bratcha bana (earl fo the white banners) / Willie's drowned in yarrow / Afton water / Hebridean waulking song / TWA Corbies / Lord Randal / Lark in the clear air / Ae fond kiss / Oaken ashes / Pedlar's song / Una bhan (fair una) / Eros / Face to face / Lord of the dance / Among silence / Prayer of the butterfly / New year carol / Come lord
CD MAGPIE 6
See For Miles/C5 / Sep '95 / Pinnacle

ISN'T IT A LOVELY DAY
CD CDSR 074
Telstar / May '96 / BMG

LIVE AT CARNEGIE HALL
Rainy day people / Spanish lady / Ulst castle croon / Chanson pour les petits enfants / Perhaps love / Kitty of Coleraine / Oaken ashes / Judas and Mary / In an English country garden / Rose / Song of Glendun / Willie's gane to Melville castle / Scent of roses / Riddle song / Face to face / Snail / Say that I'll be sure to find you / 'Tis a gift (to be simple) / Lord of the dance / Greensleeves
CD VALD 8056
Valentine / Nov '88 / Conifer/BMG

RECITAL
Lark in the clear air / Oaken ashes / Una bhan (fair una) / Among silence / New year carol / Ae fond kiss / Pedlar's song / Eros / Face to face / Prayer of the butterfly / Come Lord
CD C5MCD 583
See For Miles/C5 / Apr '92 / Pinnacle

SONG FOR IRELAND, A
My Lagan love / Kitty of Coleraine / Soft day / Danny boy / Spanish lady / She moved through the fair / Gartan mothers lullaby / Down by the Sally gardens / Song of Glendun / Quiet land of Erin
CD VALD 8053
Valentine / '91 / Conifer/BMG

O'Hara, Mary Margaret

MISS AMERICA
To cry about / Year in song / Body's in trouble / Dear darling / New day / When you know why you're happy / My friends have / Help me lift you up / Keeping you in mind / Not be alright / You will be loved again
CD 379192
Koch International / Sep '96 / Koch

O'Heanai, Seasamh

O' MO DHUCHAS (From My Tradition)
CD CEFCD 051
Gael Linn / Jul '97 / ADA / CM / Direct / Grapevine/PolyGram / Roots

O'Hearn, Patrick

BETWEEN TWO WORLDS
Rainmaker / Sky juice / Cape perpetual / Gentle was the night / Fire ritual / Eighty seven dreams of a lifetime / Dimension D / Forever the optimist / Journey to Yoroba / Between two worlds
CD 259963
Private Music / Nov '89 / BMG

ELDORADO
Amazon waltz / Nepalese tango / Black Delilah / Chattahoochee field day / Illusionist / One eyed jacks / Hear our prayer / Delicate / Eldorado / There's always tomorrow
CD 260102
Private Music / Nov '89 / BMG

METAPHOR
CD DCR 10022
Deep Cave / Jun '96 / Vital/SAM

TRUST
CD DCR 10012
Deep Cave / Mar '97 / Vital/SAM

Ohia

SONGS
CD SC 04CD
Secretly Canadian / May '97 / Cargo

O'Higgins, Dave

BEATS WORKING FOR A LIVING
CD EFZ 1009
EFZ / Nov '94 / Vital/SAM

SECRET INGREDIENT, THE
Chelsea bridge / Icarus / Dedicated to you / Diddihuff / Naima / You are too beautiful / Somewhere near here / Secret ingredient / Girl talk / Moby Dick / Angel eyes
CD EFZ 1020
EFZ / Nov '96 / Vital/SAM

UNDER THE STONE
CD EFZ 1016
EFZ / Feb '96 / Vital/SAM

Ohio Players

ECSTASY
Ecstasy / You and me / (Not so) sad and lonely / (I wanna know) do you feel it / Black cat / Food stamps y'all / Spinning / Sleep talk / Silly Billy / Short change
CD CDSEW 026
Westbound / Feb '90 / Pinnacle

OBSERVATIONS IN TIME
Here today and gone tomorrow / Mother In Law / Stop lying to yourself / Over the rainbow / Find someone to love / Cold cold world / Summertime / Bad bargain / Man I am / Lonely street / Street party
CD EDCD 429
Edsel / Feb '96 / Pinnacle

OHIO PLAYERS
Over the rainbow / Lonely street / Street party / Summertime / Bad bargain / Man that I am / Find someone to love / Cold, cold world / Here today and gone tomorrow / Mother in law / Stop lying to yourself / Tell me why / You don't mean it / Trespassing / I've got to hold on / It's a crying shame / Soupbone / Soul party / Thing called love / My neighbours / I gotta get away / Love slips through my fingers / Being the man that I am / Lonely streets at midnight
CD GRF 045
Tring / Apr '93 / Tring

OL' SCHOOL
Skin tight / Ol' school / Pain / Skin tight / Sweet sticky thing / Thank you / I wanna be free / Love rollercoaster / Fire / Megamix
CD ESMCD 443
Essential / Oct '96 / BMG

ORGASM
Pain / Pleasure / Ecstasy / Climax / Funky worm / Player's balling (players doin' their own thing) / Varee is love / Sleep talk / Walt's first trip / Laid it / What's going on / Singing in the morning / Food stamps y'all / I want to hear / ain't that lovin' you
CD CDSEWD 062
Westbound / Jun '93 / Pinnacle

Ohlman, Christine

HARD WAY, THE (Ohlman, Christine & Rebel Montez)
CD DELD 3011
Deluge / Dec '95 / ADA / Direct / Koch

OHM

GROUNDED TO THE INNER CURRENT
CD WSCD 011
Word Sound Recordings / Feb '97 / Cargo / SRD

Ohman, Kjell

HAMMOND CONNECTION, THE (Ohman, Kjell & Arne Domnerus)
CD OPUS3CD 19402
Opus 3 / Nov '95 / Direct / Jazz Music

HYMNS FROM HOME
Abide with me / Blott en dag, ogonblick i sander / Psalm 23 / On a hill far away (old rugged cross) / How great thou art (o store gud) / In heavenly love abiding / Den blomstertid nu kommer (now blossom time is coming) / Eternal father / Summer psalm / Dear Lord and father of mankind / My second home / Mood indigo / God be in my head
CD TLW 002
Three Line Whip / Apr '96 / New Note/ Pinnacle

Oi Polloi

TOTAL ANARCHOI
CD REM 017
Released Emotions / Apr '92 / RTM/Disc

Oige

BANG ON
CD CDLDL 1241
Lochshore / Jun '96 / ADA / Direct / Duncans

LIVE
CD LDLCD 1225
Lochshore / Jan '95 / ADA / Direct / Duncans

Oil Seed Rape

SIX STEPS TO WOMANHOOD
CD JAKCD 2
Jackass / Aug '93 / Pinnacle

Oisin

BEALOIDEAS
CD OSS 38CD
Ossian / Jul '95 / ADA / CM / Direct / Highlander

CELTIC DREAM
CD OSS 85CD
Ossian / Aug '94 / ADA / CM / Direct / Highlander

JEANNIE C, THE
CD EUCD 1215
ARC / Sep '93 / ADA / ARC Music

OISIN
CD OSS 37CD
Ossian / Jul '95 / ADA / CM / Direct / Highlander

OVER THE MOOR TO MAGGIE
CD OSS 39CD
Ossian / Jul '95 / ADA / CM / Direct / Highlander

WINDS OF CHANGE
CD EUCD 1069
ARC / '91 / ADA / ARC Music

O'Jays

IN BED WITH THE O'JAYS (Their Greatest Love Songs)
Lovin' you / Keep on lovin' me / Cry together / Help (somebody please) / Serious hold on me / Sing my heart out / Let me touch you / What a woman / Darlin' darlin' baby (sweet, tender love) / If you find love again: *O'Jays & Najee* / Use ta be my girl / Emotionally yours / Just another lonely night / Cause I want you back again
CD CTMCD 301
EMI / Feb '97 / EMI

LOVE TRAIN (The Best Of The O'Jays)
Love train / Back stabbers / 992 Arguments / Survival / For the love of money / Put your hands together / Time to get down / Sunshine / Living for the weekend / I love music
CD 4805052
Epic / May '95 / Sony

Ojorojo

OJOROJO
CD EBM 008
East Bay Menace / Jun '97 / Cargo

Okafor, Ben

GENERATION
She said / Shadows / Love train / Sanctify my soul / Call me / Living in a suitcase / Generation / Go see / Be my brother / Susan / Sweet lady / Hear this voice
CD PCDN 137
Plankton / Aug '92 / Plankton

Okasili, Martin

INVISIBLE HISTORY OF THE BLACK CELT, THE
CD 0630141312
WEA / Jul '97 / Warner Music

O'Keefe, Danny

BREEZY STORIES
CD 7567814272
Atlantic / Jan '96 / Warner Music

O'Keeffe, Maire

HOUSE PARTY
CD CEFCD 165
Gael Linn / Oct '94 / ADA / CM / Direct / Grapevine/PolyGram / Roots

O'Keeffe, Padraig

KERRY FIDDLES (O'Keeffe, Padraig & Denis Murphy/Julia Clifford)
CD TSCD 309
Topic / May '94 / ADA / CM / Direct

SLIABH LUACHRA FIDDLE MASTER
CD RTECD 174
RTE / Dec '93 / ADA / Koch

Okeh Wranglers

BENEATH THE WESTERN SKIES
CD FCD 3038
Fury / Apr '96 / Nervous / TKO Magnum

Okin, Earl

MANGO & OTHER DELIGHTS
CD RGFCD 014
Road Goes On Forever / Oct '93 / Direct

Okolokolo

LA LEGENDE DES INDIENS
CD 992291
Wotre Music / Feb '97 / Discovery / New Note/Pinnacle

Okoshi, Tiger

FACE TO FACE
Face to face / Summertime / When the moon goes deep / Sentimental journey / Bubble dance / Fisherman's song / One note samba / Man with 20 faces / Don't tell me now / Who can I turn to / Eyes / Over the rainbow
CD JD 3318
JVC / Sep '89 / Direct / New Note/Pinnacle / Vital/SAM

Okossun, Sonny

AFRICAN SOLDIERS
CD FILERCD 414
Profile / Jul '91 / Pinnacle

ULTIMATE COLLECTION, THE
CD AVCCD 003
AVC/Ivory / Jan '97 / Stern's

Okoudjava, Boulat

LE SOLDAT EN PAPIER
CD LDX 274743
La Chant Du Monde / Jan '94 / ADA / Harmonia Mundi

Okuta Percussion

OKUTA PERCUSSION
CD SM 15042
Wergo / Aug '92 / ADA / Cadillac / Harmonia Mundi

OSIKA
CD EUCD 1343
ARC / Apr '96 / ADA / ARC Music

Ol' Dirty Bastard

RETURN TO THE 36 CHAMBERS
Intro / Shimmy shimmy ya / Baby c'mon / Brooklyn zoo / Hippa to da hoppa / Rawhide / Damage / Don't u know / Stomp / Goin' down / Drunk game / Snakes / Brooklyn zoo / Proteck ya neck / Cuttin' headz / Dirty dancin' / Harlem world

CD 7559616592
Warner Bros. / Mar '95 / Warner Music

Olatunji, Baba

DROP THE BEAT
CD RCD 10107
Rykodisc / Nov '91 / ADA / Vital

Old

FORMULA
Last look / Break (you) / Devolve / Under glass / Thug / Rid / Amoeba
CD MOSH 131CD
Earache / Oct '95 / Vital

HOLD ON TO YOUR FACE
What's the point / Two of me / Scrape remix 1 / Glitch / Scrape remix 2 / To ebb is to drift / Outlive tape edit / Total hag turntable action
CD MOSH 105CD
Earache / Nov '93 / Vital

Old & In The Way

OLD AND IN THE WAY
Pig in the pen / Old and in the way / Hobo song / Wild horses / White dove / Midnight moonlight / Knockin' on your door / Panama red / Kissimmee kid / Land of the Navajo
CD GDCD 4014
Grateful Dead / May '89 / Pinnacle

Old & New Dreams

PLAYING
Happy house / Mopti / New dream / Rush hour / Broken shadows / Playing
CD 8291232
ECM / Jun '86 / New Note/Pinnacle

Old Blind Dogs

CLOSE TO THE BONE
CD LDLCD 1209
Lochshore / Oct '93 / ADA / Direct / Duncans

LEGACY
CD CDLDL 1233
Lochshore / Oct '95 / ADA / Direct / Duncans

NEW TRICKS
CD LOC 1068CD
Lochshore / Jul '94 / ADA / Direct / Duncans

TALL TAILS
CD CDLDL 1220
Klub / Oct '94 / ADA / CM / Direct / Duncans / Ross

Old Hat Band

OLD HAT DANCE BAND
CD VT/OH 2CD
Veteran Tapes / Jun '93 / ADA / Direct

Old Man Stone

SPORK
CD REVXD 211
Revolver / Aug '97 / Revolver / Sony

Old Man's Child

BORN OF THE FLICKERING
CD CM 77147CD
Century Media / Dec '96 / Plastic Head

IN THE SHADES OF LIFE
CD SHAGRATH 005CD
Hot / Oct '96 / Plastic Head

Old Rope String Band

ROPERAMA DING DONG
CD ORSB 1CD
Old Rope / Aug '96 / ADA

Old Swan Band

STILL SWANNING AFTER ALL THESE YEARS
CD FRCD 31
Free Reed / Jul '95 / ADA / CM / Direct

Older Than Dirt

NO MORE EXCUSES
CD FNGCD 02
FNG / Sep '94 / Plastic Head

Oldfield, Mike

AMAROK
CD CDV 2640
Virgin / Jun '90 / EMI

COMPLETE MIKE OLDFIELD, THE (2CD Set)
Arrival / In dulci jubilo / Portsmouth / Jungle gardenia / Guilty / Blue Peter / Waldberg (the peak) / Etude / Wonderful land / Moonlight shadow / Family man / Mistake / Five miles out / Crime of passion / To France / Shadow on the wall / Excerpt from Tubular bells / Sheba / Mirage / Platinum / Mount Teide / Excerpt from Ommadawn / Excerpt from Hergest Ridge / Excerpt from Incantations / Excerpt from The killing fields
CD Set CDMOC 1
Virgin / Oct '85 / EMI

CRISES
Crises / Moonlight shadow / In high places / Foreign affair / Taurus three / Shadow on the wall
CD CDVIP 118
Virgin VIP / Mar '94 / EMI

DISCOVERY
To France / Poison arrows / Crystal gazing / Tricks of the light / Discovery / Talk about your life / Saved by a bell / Lake
CD CDV 2308
Virgin / Apr '92 / EMI

EARTH MOVING
Holy / Far country / Runaway son / Earth moving / Nothing but / Hostage / Innocent / See the light / Blue night / Bridge to paradise
CD CDVIP 169
Virgin VIP / Apr '97 / EMI

ELEMENTS (The Best Of Mike Oldfield)
Tubular bells / Family man / Moonlight shadow / Heaven's open / Five miles out / To France / Foreign affair / In Dulci jubilo / Shadow on the wall / Islands / Etude / Sentinel / Ommadawn (excerpt) / Incantations / Amarok / Portsmouth
CD VTCD 18
Virgin / Aug '93 / EMI

ELEMENTS 1973-1991 (4CD Set)
Tubular bells (part one) / Tubular bells (part two) / Hergest ridge / In dulci jubilo / Portsmouth / Vivaldi concerto in C / Ommadawn (part one) / On horseback / William Tell overture / Argiers / First excursion / Sailor's hornpipe / Incantations / I'm guilty / Path / Blue Peter / Woodhenge / Punkadiddle (live) / Polka (live) / Platinum 3 and 4 / Arrival / Taurus 1 / QE2 / Wonderful land / Sheba / Five miles out / Taurus II / Family man / Mount Teidi / Peak / Crises / Moonlight shadow / Foreign affair / Shadow on the wall / Taurus III / Crime of passion / Jungle gardenia / To France / Afghan / Tricks of the light (instrumental) / Etude / Evacuation / Legend / Islands / Wind chimes / Flying start / Magic touch / Earth moving / Far country / Holy / Amarok / Heaven's open
CD Set CDBOX 2
Virgin / Oct '93 / EMI

EXPOSED (2CD Set)
Incantations / Tubular bells / Guilty
CD Set CDVD 2511
Virgin / Jul '86 / EMI

FIVE MILES OUT
Taurus II / Family man / Orabidoo / Mount Teidi / Five miles out
CD CDVIP 114
Virgin / Jun '94 / EMI

HEAVEN'S OPEN
Make make / No dream / Mr. Shame / Gimme back / Heaven's open / Music from the balcony
CD CDVIP 153
Virgin VIP / Oct '96 / EMI

HERGEST RIDGE
Hergest ridge
CD CDV 2013
Virgin / Apr '86 / EMI

INCANTATIONS
Incantations / Guilty
CD CDVDT 101
Virgin / Apr '92 / EMI

ISLANDS
Wind chimes (part 1) / Wind chimes / Islands / Flying start / Northpoint / Magic touch / Time has come / When the night's on fire
CD CDV 2466
Virgin / Apr '92 / EMI

OMMADAWN
Ommadawn (parts 1 and 2)
CD CDVIP 185
Virgin VIP / Apr '97 / EMI

ORCHESTRAL TUBULAR BELLS
CD CDVIP 101
Virgin VIP / Nov '93 / EMI

ORCHESTRAL TUBULAR BELLS/ OMMADAWN/HERGEST RIDGE (Compact Collection Vol.1/3CD Set)
CD Set TPAK 15
Virgin / Oct '90 / EMI

QE2
QE2 / Taurus / Sheba / Conflict / Arrival / Wonderful land / Mirage / Celt / Molly / QE2 Finale
CD CDV 2181
Virgin / Oct '83 / EMI

QE2/PLATINUM/FIVE MILES OUT (Compact Collection Vol.2/3CD Set)
CD Set TPAK 16
Virgin / Oct '90 / EMI

SONGS OF THE DISTANT EARTH
CD 4509985812
WEA / Nov '94 / Warner Music

TUBULAR BELLS VOL.1
Tubular Bells (Part 1) / Tubular Bells (Part 2)
CD CDV 2001
Virgin / '83 / EMI

TUBULAR BELLS VOL.2
Sentinel / Dark star / Clear light / Blue saloon / Sunjammer / Red dawn / Bell / Weightless / Great plain / Sunset door / Tattoo / Altered state / Maya gold / Moonshine
CD 4509906182
WEA / Aug '92 / Warner Music

TUBULAR BELLS/HERGEST RIDGE/ OMMADAWN (Remixes/3CD Set)
Tubular bells / Hergest ridge / Ommadawn / Phaeacian games / Star's end / Rio Grande / First excursion / Algiers / Portsmouth / In dulci jubilo / Speak (tho you only say farewell)
CD Set CDBOX 1
Virgin / Dec '89 / EMI

VOYAGER
Song of the sun / Women of Ireland / She moves through the fair / Wild goose flaps its wings / Mont St. Michel / Flowers of the forest / Dark island / Voyager / Celtic rain / Hero
CD 0630158962
WEA / Aug '96 / Warner Music

Oldfield, Sally

CELEBRATION
Mandela / Morning of my life / Woman of the night / Celebration / Blue water / My damsel heart / Love is everywhere
CD CLACD 103
Castle / Apr '86 / BMG

EASY
Sun is in my eyes / You set my gypsy blood free / Answering you / Boulevard song / Easy / Sons of the free / Hide and seek / First born of the earth / Man of storm
CD CLACD 102
Castle / Apr '86 / BMG

MIRRORS
Mirrors / Mandala / Water bearer / Boulevard song / You set my gypsy blood free / Sun in my eyes / Easy / Morning of my life / Love is everywhere / Love of a lifetime / Broken Mona Lisa / Path with a heart / Let it all go / She talk's like a lady / Man child / Never knew love could get so strong
CD 5507262
Spectrum / Jan '95 / PolyGram

MORNING OF MY LIFE (2CD Set)
Mirrors / Night of the hunters moon / You set my gypsy blood free / Sun in my eyes / Easy / Booulevard song / I sing for you / Mandala / Morning of my life / Blue water / Celebration / Song of the lamp / Playing in the flame / Broken Mona Lisa / Man I love / Path with a heart / Water bearer / Weaver / Fire and honey / First born of the earth / Woman of the night / Love of a lifetime / River of my childhood / It's a long time a million light years away from home / Strange day in Berlin / Meet me in Verona / Never knew love could be so strong / Nenya / Song of the healer
CD Set SMDCD 198
Snapper / May '97 / Pinnacle

PLAYING IN THE FLAME
Playing in the flame / Love of a lifetime / River of my childhood / Let it all go / Song of the lamp / Rare lightning / Manchild / It's a long time / Song of the being
CD CLACD 215
Castle / Feb '91 / BMG

STRANGE DAY IN BERLIN
Path with a heart / Million light years away from home / She talks like a lady / Meet me in Verona / Strange day in Berlin / Never knew love could get so strong / This could be a lover / There's a miracle going on
CD CLACD 216
Castle / Feb '91 / BMG

WATER BEARER
Water bearer / Songs of the quendi / Weaver / Mirrors / Night of the hunter's moon / Child of Allah / Song of the bow / Fire and honey / Song of the healer
CD CLACD 101
Castle / Apr '90 / BMG

Oldfield, Terry

SPIRAL WAVES
CD VP 117CD
Voiceprint / Mar '93 / Pinnacle

Oldham, Andrew Loog

RARITIES (Oldham, Andrew Loog Orchestra & Chorus)
Da doo ron ron / Memphis, Tennessee / I wanna be your man / La Bamba / Funky and fleopatra / 365 rolling stones / Maggie Maggie May (parts 1 and 2) / Oh I do like to be on the B side / There are but five rolling stones / Rise of the Brighton surf / You better move on / Theme for a rolling stone / Tell 'em (you're coming back) / Last time / Needles and pins / Want to hold your hand / Right of way / Satisfaction / Carry on
CD SEECD 394
See For Miles/C5 / Oct '93 / Pinnacle

Oldland, Misty

SUPERNATURAL
I wrote you a song / Fair affair (Je T'Aime) / Got me a feeling / Imprison me / Why do I trust you / Caroline / Kissing the planet / One world / You are the one / Like I need / I often wonder / Groove eternity
CD 47595882
Columbia / Apr '94 / Sony

O'Leary, Christy

NORTHERN BRIDGE
Trip over the mountain / Norwegian wedding march / Banks of Sullane / O'Keef's/ I'd rather be married than left alone/Bill the weav / Young Reilly the fisherman / Peigin Leitir Mor / Rocking the cradle/Chesnut tree / Moorlough Mary / Summer waltz / Bellman's polka / Jimmy mo mhile stor / Groves of Donaghmore
CD OBMCD 09
Old Bridge / Jan '97 / ADA / Direct / Highlander

O'Leary, Diarmuid

CLASSIC IRISH BALLADS (O'Leary, Diarmuid & The Bards)
Isle of Innisfree / Come back Paddy Reilly / Spancil hill / Green fields of France / Follow me up to carlow / Fields of Athenry / Ferryman / Curragh of Kildare / Dublin in the rare old times / Down by the Sally gardens / Nancy spain / Band played waltzing Matilda / Cliffs of Dooneen / Whiskey in the jar / Bunch of thyme
CD TARACD 3018
Tara / Nov '94 / ADA / CM / Conifer/BMG / Direct

O'Leary, Johnny

DANCE MUSIC FROM THE CORK-KERRY BORDER
CD CR 01CD
CR / Aug '96 / ADA

TROOPER, THE
CD CEFCD 132
Gael Linn / Jan '94 / ADA / CM / Direct / Grapevine/PolyGram / Roots

Oliva, Sandro

WHO THE FUCK IS SANDRO OLIVA
CD EFA 034092
Muffin / Nov '94 / SRD

Olive

EXTRA VIRGIN (2CD Set)
Miracle / This time / Safer hands / Killing / You're not alone / Falling / Outlaw / Blood red tears / Curious / You are nothing / Muted / I don't think so / You're not alone
CD 74321481142
CD Set 743214886872
RCA / May '97 / BMG

Oliveira, Joao Pedro

ELECTRONIC AND COMPUTER COMPOSITIONS
CD NUM 01
Numerica / Jun '97 / ReR Megacorp

Oliveira, Valdeci

MACARENA (Latin Summer Hits) (Oliveira, Valdeca Y Banda Tropical)
Kizomba / Macarena / Sambolera mayi son / Brasil penta Brasil / Latin medley / Malaguena / Latin medley II / Tempo / Conga - Oye micanto / Latin medley III
CD 12861
Laserlight / Aug '96 / Target/BMG

Oliver

STANDING STONE
CD WHCD 001
Wooden Hill / Mar '97 / Wooden Hill

Oliver, Bob

BOB OLIVER & HIS HOT SEVEN (Oliver, Bob Hot Seven)
CD SOSCD 1312
Stomp Off / Nov '96 / Jazz Music / Wellard

Oliver, Frankie

LOOKING FOR THE TWIST
She lied to me / Give her what she wants / Love what you do for me / Who's gonna do it / Look how long / Live as one / Love and satisfaction / Melt into you / Show me / What is life / Looking for the twist / Down by the riverside
CD IJCD 3010
Island Jamaica / Jul '97 / Jet Star / PolyGram

Oliver, Joe 'King'

CLASSICS 1923
CD CLASSICS 650
Classics / Nov '92 / Discovery / Jazz Music

CLASSICS 1923-1926
CD CLASSICS 639
Classics / Nov '92 / Discovery / Jazz Music

CLASSICS 1926-1928 (Oliver, Joe 'King' & His Dixie Syncopators)
CD CLASSICS 618
Classics / Nov '92 / Discovery / Jazz Music

CLASSICS 1928-1930 (Oliver, Joe 'King' Orchestra)
CD CLASSICS 607
Classics / Oct '92 / Discovery / Jazz Music

CLASSICS 1930-1931
CD CLASSICS 594
Classics / Sep '91 / Discovery / Jazz Music

COMPLETE VOCALION & BRUNSWICK RECORDINGS (2CD Set)
Too bad / Snag it / Georgia man / Deep henderson / Jackass blues / Home town blues / Sorrow valley blues / Sugarfoot stomp / Wa wa wa / Tack Annie / Someday sweetheart / Dead man blues / New wang-wang blues / Dr. Jazz / Showboat shuffle / Every tub / Willie the weeper / Black snake blues / Farewell blues / Sobbin' blues / Tin roof blues / West End blues / Sweet Emmalina / Lazy mama / Got everything / Four or five times / Speakeasy blues / Aunt Hagar's blues / I'm watching the clock / Slow and steady / Papa de da da / Who's blue / Stop crying / Sugar blues / I'm crazy 'bout my baby / Loveless love / One more time / When I take my sugar to tea
CD CDAFS 10252
Affinity / Oct '92 / Cadillac / Jazz Music / Koch

DIPPERMOUTH BLUES (His 25 Greatest Hits)
Chimes Blues: *Oliver, Joe 'King' & His Creole Jazz Band* / Canal street blues: *Oliver, Joe 'King' & His Creole Jazz Band* / Dippermouth blues: *Oliver, Joe 'King' & His Creole Jazz Band* / Snake rag: *Oliver, Joe 'King' & His Creole Jazz Band* / Chattanooga stomp: *Oliver, Joe 'King' & His Creole Jazz Band* / Riverside blues: *Oliver, Joe 'King' & His Creole Jazz Band* / Snag it: *Oliver, Joe 'King' & His Creole Jazz Band* / Deep Henderson: *Oliver, Joe 'King' & His Dixie Syncopators* / Wa wa wa: *Oliver, Joe 'King' & His Dixie Syncopators* / Someday sweetheart: *Oliver, Joe 'King' & His Dixie Syncopators* / Showboat shuffle: *Oliver, Joe 'King' & His Dixie Syncopators* / Willie the weeper: *Oliver, Joe 'King' & His Dixie Syncopators* / Black snake blues: *Oliver, Joe 'King' & His Dixie Syncopators* / Farewell blues: *Oliver, Joe 'King' & His Dixie Syncopators* / Sobbin' blues: *Oliver, Joe 'King' & His Dixie Syncopators* / Tin roof blues: *Oliver, Joe 'King' & His Dixie Syncopators* / West End blues: *Oliver, Joe 'King' & His Dixie Syncopators* / Speakeasy blues: *Oliver, Joe 'King' & His Dixie Syncopators* / Aunt hagar's blues: *Oliver, Joe 'King' & His Dixie Syncopators* / I'm watchin the clock: *Oliver, Joe 'King' & His Dixie Syncopators* / New Orleans shout: *Oliver, Joe 'King' Orchestra* / Everybody does it in Hawaii: *Oliver, Joe 'King' Orchestra* / Rhythm club stomp: *Oliver, Joe 'King' Orchestra* / Struggle buggy: *Oliver, Joe 'King' Orchestra* / Shake it and break it: *Oliver, Joe 'King' Orchestra*
CD CDAJA 5218
Living Era / Dec '96 / Select

KING OF NEW ORLEANS, THE
CD CD 14547
Jazz Portraits / Jan '94 / Jazz Music

KING OLIVER & HIS ORCHESTRA 1929-30
West End blues / I've got that thing / Call of the freaks / Trumpet's prayer / Freakish light blues / Can I tell you / My good man Sam / What you want me to do / Sweet like this / Too late / I'm lonesome, sweetheart / I want you just myself / I can't stop loving you / Everybody does it in Hawaii / Frankie and Johnny / New Orleans shout / St. James Infirmary / I must have it / Rhythm club stomp / You're just my type / Edna / Boogie woogie / Mule face blues / Struggle buggy / Don't you think I love you / Olga / Shake it and break it / Stingaree blues / What's the use of living without you / You were only passing time with me / Nelson stomp / Stealing
CD Set ND 89770
Jazz Tribune / May '94 / BMG

KING OLIVER 1927-1931
CD TPZ 1009
Topaz Jazz / Oct '94 / Cadillac / Pinnacle

KING OLIVER 1928-1929
CD VILCD 0052
Village Jazz / Sep '92 / Jazz Music / Target/BMG

KING OLIVER VOL.3 1926-1928
CD KJ 135FS
King Jazz / Oct '93 / Cadillac / Discovery / Jazz Music

KING OLIVER VOL.4 1928
CD KJ 136FS
King Jazz / Oct '93 / Cadillac / Discovery / Jazz Music

KING OLIVER VOL.5 1928-1929
CD KJ 137FS
King Jazz / Oct '93 / Cadillac / Discovery / Jazz Music

KING OLIVER VOL.6 1929-1931
CD KJ 138FS
King Jazz / Oct '93 / Cadillac / Discovery / Jazz Music

KING OLIVER'S CREOLE JAZZBAND 1923-1924 (2CD Set) (Oliver, Joe 'King' & His Creole Jazz Band)
Just gone / Canal Street blues / Mandy Lee blues / I'm going away to wear you off my mind / Chimes blues / Weather bird rag / Dippermouth blues / Froggie moore / Snake rag / Sweet lovin' man / High society rag / Sobbin' blues / Where did you stay last night / Jazzin' baby blues / Alligator hop / Zulu's ball / Working man blues / Krooked blues / Chattanooga stomp / London cafe blues / Camp meeting blues / New Orleans stomp / Buddy's habits / Tears / I ain't gonna tell nobody / Room rent blues / Riverside blues / Sweet baby doll / Mabel's dream / Southern stomp / Kiss me sweet / Construction song / King Porter stomp / Tom cat
CD Set RTR 79007
Retrieval / Nov '96 / Cadillac / Direct / Jazz Music / Swift / Wellard

QUINTESSENCE, THE (1923-1928/2CD Set)
Just gone / Canal street blues / Mandy Lee blues / Weather bird rag / Dippermouth blues / Froggie Moore / Snake rag / Sweet lovin' man / High society rag / Sobbin' blues / Dipper mouth blues / Jazzin' babies blues / Alligator hop / Buddy's habit / I ain't gonna tell nobody / Riverside blues / Working man blues / Mabel's dream / Chattanooga stomp / London cafe blues / Camp meeting blues / Tom cat blues / Too bad / Snag it / Deep Henderson / Jackass blues / Sugar foot stomp / Wa wa wa / Showboat shuffle / Tin roof blues / You are such a cruel papa to me / My dif'rent kind of man / Tell me woman blues / Frisco train blues / In the bottle blues / What ya want me to do
CD Set FA 220
Fremeaux / Oct '96 / ADA / Discovery

RARE RECORDINGS AND ALTERNATES (The Golden Age Of Jazz)
CD JZCD 367
Suisa / Jun '92 / Jazz Music / THE

SHAKE IT AND BREAK IT
CD JHR 73536
Jazz Hour / May '93 / Cadillac / Jazz Music / Target/BMG

Oliver, Sy

YES INDEED
CD BB 8722
Black & Blue / Sep '96 / Discovery / Koch / Wellard

Olivia Tremor Control

DUSK AT CUBIST CASTLE (2CD Set)
Opera house / Frosted ambassador / Jumping fences / Define a transparent dream / No growing / Holiday surprise / Courtyard / Memories of Jacqueline 1906 / Tropical bells / Can you come down with us / Marking time / Green typewriters / Spring succeeds / Theme for a very delicious grand piano / I can smell the leaves / Dusk at cubist castle / Gravity car / NYC 25
CD Set BRRC 10082
Blue Rose / Jun '97 / 3mv/Pinnacle

EXPLANATION VOL.2 (Instrumental Themes And Sequences)
CD FLY 017X
Flydaddy / May '97 / Cargo / SRD

Ollie & The Nightingales

OLLIE & THE NIGHTINGALES
You'll never do wrong / Don't make the good suffer / Don't do what I did / I've got a feeling / You're leaving me / Broke in love / ABCD / Mellow way you treat your man / Girl you make my heart sing / I've never found a girl / Showered with love
CD CDSXE 068
Stax / Nov '92 / Pinnacle

Olney, David

DEEPER ME
CD CDPH 1117
Philo / Feb '95 / ADA / CM / Direct

EYE OF THE STORM
CD CDPH 1199
Philo / Sep '96 / ADA / CM / Direct

LIVE IN HOLLAND
CD SCR 35
Strictly Country / Dec '94 / ADA / Direct

REAL LIES
CD CDPH 1204
Philo / Aug '97 / ADA / CM / Direct

TOP TO BOTTOM
CD APCD 080
Appaloosa / '92 / ADA / Direct / TKO Magnum

Olneyville Sound System

BECAUSE WERE ALL IN THIS TOGETHER
CD LOAD 015CD
Load / Jun '97 / Cargo

Olodum

EGITO MADAGASCAR
CD 404325CD
Continental / Apr '97 / Cargo

Olomide, Koffi

N'DJOLI/BA LA JOIE 1978-1979 (Olomide, Koffi/Ba La Joie)
CD NG 028
Ngoyarto / Jan '97 / Stern's

TCHA TCHO
Tcha tcho du sorcier / Elle et moi / VIP / Mannequin / Henriquet / Mal aime / Experience / La ruta
CD STCD 1031
Stern's / Jul '90 / ADA / CM / Stern's

Olsen, Kristina

HURRY ON HOME
CD CDPH 1175
Philo / Aug '95 / ADA / CM / Direct

LIVE FROM AROUND THE WORLD
Walking blues / Love Kristina / Folding bicycle / Hurry on home / Roomates / Kind of mood I'm in / jane / Cry you a waterfall / Gila national forest / Better than TV / TV Free America / Come on in my kitchen / Alaska / Maria / Prop / Power of loving you / Gay friends / Your little brother sure can dance / Guitar camp / Something to despise / Live man in the dead of night / Proposal / In my arms / Dangerous / If I could tell you
CD CDPH 1195
Philo / Mar '97 / ADA / CM / Direct

LOVE, KRISTINA
CD PH 1157CD
Philo / Oct '93 / ADA / CM / Direct

Olson, Carla

WAVE OF THE HAND (The Best Of Carla Olson)
CD WMCD 1046
Watermelon / Mar '96 / ADA / Direct

Olympic Death Squad

BLUE
This is riot gear / Maple leaf / Show your age / Newfoundland / Sometimes I can breathe / Ski lump / Wakefield Street / Shortsleeve / Anti-kidnapping song / Yeah, uh-huh
CD TB 2002
Teenbeat / May '96 / Cargo / SRD / Vital

Olympics

DOIN' THE HULLY GULLY
Big boy Pete / Little Pedro / Stay away from Joe / Big Chief, Little Puss / Stay where you are / What'd I say / Private eye / Baby it's hot / Dooley / Baby hully gully / Dodge City / I'll never fall in love again / Working hard
CD CDCHD 324
Ace / Jul '91 / Pinnacle

O'Malley, Tony

NAKED FLAME, THE
Good times / Love of mine / I can understand it / My Buddy / For the children / Tell me why / Mr. Operator / Still crazy after all these years / Naked flame / Moody's mood / I'm in trouble
CD JHCD 040
Ronnie Scott's Jazz House / May '95 / Cadillac / Jazz Music / New Note/Pinnacle / TKO Magnum

SUNSHINE EVERY DAY
Sunshine
CD MMCD 001
Millenium / Jul '97 / Total/BMG

Omar

MUSIC
Music / You've got to move / Get to know you better / Tomorrow / Tasty morsel / Winner / Your loss, my gain / Don't sell yourself short / Who chooses the seasons / Last request / Walk in the park / In the midst of it
CD 5124012
Talkin' Loud / Nov '92 / PolyGram

THERE'S NOTHING LIKE THIS
There's nothing like this / Don't mean a thing / You and me / Positive / I'm in love / Meaning of life / Stop messing around / Serious style / I don't mind the waiting / Fine (acapella)
CD 5100212
Talkin' Loud / Jul '91 / PolyGram

THIS IS NOT A LOVE SONG
CD 74321496262
RCA / Aug '97 / BMG

Omar & The Howlers

BLUES BAG
CD PRLD 70281
Provogue / Aug '91 / Pinnacle

COURTS OF LULU
CD PRD 70452
Provogue / Mar '93 / Pinnacle

I TOLD YOU SO
Border girl / Give me a chance / Shake for me / Magic man / Rocket to nowhere / I told you so / Ice cold woman / I'm wish to you baby / East side blues
CD DFG 8417 CD
Dixie Frog / Oct '93 / Direct / TKO Magnum

LIVE AT THE PARADISO
CD PRD 70352
Provogue / Apr '92 / Pinnacle

LIVE AT THE PARADISO
CD BB 9529CD
Bullseye Blues / May '93 / Direct

MONKEY LAND
Monkey land / Big town shakedown / Night shadows / She's a woman / Dirty people / Next big thing / Tonight I think of you / Fire in the jungle / Modern man / Loud mouth woman / Ding dong clock
CD ANTCD 0011
Antones / Jan '93 / ADA / Hot Shot

SOUTHERN STYLE
Ton of blues / I want you / Snake rhythm rock / Bessie Mae / Full moon on Main Street / Pot of gold / You keep watchin' me / Run for the levee / Burn it off the ground / Judgement day / Angel blues / I think it's time to go
CD PRD 70952
Provogue / Sep '96 / Pinnacle

O'Mara, Peter

STAIRWAY
Abertura / Stairway / Round and round / Crescent / Mr. Lucky / For Emily / Weather or not / Change of wind / Continuity / Irish
CD ENJACD 70772
Enja / Jun '93 / New Note/Pinnacle / Vital/ SAM

OMC

HOW BIZARRE
CD 5334352
Polydor / Oct '96 / PolyGram

OMD

ARCHITECTURE AND MORALITY
New Stone Age / She's leaving / Souvenir / Sealand / Joan of Arc / Architecture and morality / Georgia / Beginning and the end
CD CDIDX 12
Virgin / Jan '95 / EMI

CRUSH
So in love / Secret / Bloc bloc bloc / Women 111 / Crush / Eighty eight seconds in Greensboro' / Native daughters of the Golden West / La femme accident / Hold you / Lights are going out
CD CDVIP 155
Virgin VIP / Oct '96 / EMI

DAZZLE SHIPS
Radio Prague / Genetic engineering / ABC auto indistry / Telegraph / This is Helena / International / Romance of the telescope / Silent running / Dazzle ships / Radio waves / Time zones / Of all the things we've made
CD CDVIP 170
Virgin VIP / Apr '97 / EMI

JUNK CULTURE
Junk culture / Tesla girls / Locomotion / Apollo / Never turn away / Love and violence / Hard day / All wrapped up / White trash / Talking loud and clear
CD CDV 2310
Virgin / '86 / EMI

LIBERATOR
Stand above me / Everyday / King of stone / Dollar girl / Dream of me / Sunday morning / Agnus dei / Love and hate you / Heaven is / Best years of our lives / Christine / Only tears
CD CDV 2715
Virgin / Jun '93 / EMI

ORCHESTRAL MANOEUVRES IN THE DARK
Bunker soldiers / Almost / Mysterreality / Electricity / Messerschmit twins / Messages / Julia's song / Red frame/White light / Dancing / Pretending to see the future
CD DIDCD 2
Virgin / '87 / EMI

ORGANISATION
Enola Gay / Second thought / VCL X1 / Motion and heart / Statues / Misunderstanding / More I see you / Promise / Stanlow
CD DIDCD 6
Virgin / Jul '87 / EMI

ORGANISATION/OMD/ARCHITECTURE & MORALITY (3CD Set)
CD Set TPAK 7
Virgin / Oct '90 / EMI

PACIFIC AGE
Stay (The black rose and the universal wheel) / (Forever) live and die / Pacific age / Dead girls / Shame / Southern / Flame of hope / Goddess of love / We love you / Watch us fall
CD CDV 2398
Virgin / Jun '93 / EMI

SUGAR TAX
Sailing on the seven seas / Pandora's box / Then you turn away / Speed of light / Was it something I said / Big town / Call my name / Apollo XI / Walking on air / Walk tall / Neon lights / All that matters
CD CDV 2648
Virgin / Apr '91 / EMI

UNIVERSAL
Universal / Walking on the Milky Way / Very close to far away / Boy from the chemist is here to see you / Too late / New head / Moon and the sun / Gospel of St. Jude / Black Sea / That was then / If you're still in love with me / Victory waltz
CD CDV 2807
Virgin / Sep '96 / EMI

Omega

TRANSCENDENT
CD HICD 08554002
SPV / Apr '96 / Koch / Plastic Head

Omen

BATTLE CRY
CD 398414215CD
Metal Blade / Nov '96 / Pinnacle / Plastic Head

CURSE
CD 398414216CD
Metal Blade / Nov '96 / Pinnacle / Plastic Head

ESCAPE TO NOWHERE
It's not easy / Radar love / Escape to nowhere / Cry for the morning / Thorn in your flesh / Poisoned / Nomads / King of the hill / No way out
CD RR 95442
Roadrunner / Nov '88 / PolyGram

REOPENING THE GATES
CD MASSCD 124
Massacre / Jun '97 / Plastic Head

TEETH
CD 398414206CD
Metal Blade / Nov '96 / Pinnacle / Plastic Head

Ominus

3RD ALBUM
CD KRLP 003CD
Koyote / Jun '97 / Arabesque / Koyote / Prime

Omlo Vent

MILD LANDING
CD CHILLUM 000
Chill Um / Jan '96 / Plastic Head

Omni Trio

DEEPEST CUT
CD ASHADOW 1CD
Moving Shadow / Feb '95 / SRD

HAUNTED SCIENCE
CD ASHADOW 6CD
Moving Shadow / Aug '96 / SRD

SKELETON KEYS
Skeleton keys / Silver / Fire island / Ocean driver / Sanctuary / Atomic state / Red rain / Twin town karaoke / Trippin' VIP / Twin town karaoke
CD ASHADOW 10CD
Moving Shadow / Aug '97 / SRD

Omnia Opera

OMNIA OPERA
Space bastard / Disbelief / Awakening / Floating settee / Each day / Brighter the sun / Bright sun / Freeze out
CD DELECCD 011
Delerium / May '93 / Cargo / Pinnacle / Vital

Omnibus Wind Ensemble

MUSIC BY FRANK ZAPPA
CD CD 19403
Opus 3 / Jun '96 / Direct / Jazz Music

Omnicron

GENERATION AND MOTION OF A PULSE, THE
CD IAE 003CD
Instinct Ambient Europe / May '95 / Plastic Head

Omnivore

ONE GIANT LEAP
CD ACTIVE 005D
Interactive / Sep '94 / 3mv/Sony

ONE SMALL STEP
Omnivorous / On the tip of my tongue / Munchies / Ethereal memorial / 9/10ths submerged / At elegant memorial
CD ACTIVE 002CD
Interactive / Feb '94 / 3mv/Sony

Omoumi, Hossein

NEY (Persian Classical Music)
CD ALCD 181
Al Sur / Sep '96 / ADA / Discovery

PERSIAN CLASSICAL MUSIC
CD NI 5359
Nimbus / Sep '94 / Nimbus

OMU

COOL BEAUTY
CD 99 1601
Ninetynine / Jul '96 / Timewarp

OMU
CD 99 2139
Ninetynine / Jul '96 / Timewarp

On Thorns I Lay

SOUNDS OF BEAUTIFUL EXPERIENCE
CD HOLY 012CD
Holy / Jun '95 / Plastic Head

Ondekoza

DEVILS ON DRUMS
CD 68917
Tropical / Apr '97 / Discovery

KAGURA
CD 68939
Tropical / Apr '97 / Discovery

LEGEND
CD 68965
Tropical / Apr '97 / Discovery

One & One

HOW LOW CAN I GO
CD PFP 42042
PFP / Apr '95 / Koch

One Hit Wonder

OUTFALL
Stay away / Powertrip / Floorlord / Go back to bed / 20 min / Corporate rock rules / Keep it together / Billy'd to the hilt / Saddle up / Useless / Kill (all the violent people) / Splitsville / All wrecked at z-man's / Bowl of cherries / Gorby doll / Head lights
CD 158102
Nitro / Mar '97 / Pinnacle / Plastic Head

WHERE'S THE WORLD
CD CDGRUBM 31
Food For Thought / Jan '95 / Pinnacle

One Inch Punch

TAO OF THE ONE INCH PUNCH
Just enough / Gemini / Latitudes / Represent / Bu / Take it in stride / Metaphysics / Wallflower / Orson Welles' martians / If
CD CDHUT 39
Hut / Sep '96 / EMI

One Style MDV

RIGHT TO SAY
CD CRAICD 034
Crai / Oct '93 / ADA / Direct

One Way System

BEST OF ONE WAY SYSTEM
Stab the judge / Give us a future / Just another hero / Jerusalem / Jackie was a junkie / Ain't no answers / No return / One way system / Gutter boy / Forgotten generation / Cum on feel the noize / Breakin' in / This is the age / Into the fires / Corrupted world / One day soon / Reason why / Children of the night / Shine again
CD CDPUNK 50
Anagram / Mar '95 / Cargo / Pinnacle

RETURN TO BREIZH
CD OWS 4CD
Visionary/Jettisoundz / Jun '97 / Cargo / Pinnacle / RTM/Disc / THE

WRITING ON THE WALL
Corrupted world / This is the age / One day soon / Nightmare / Neurotix / Reason why / Into the fires / Days are numbered / On the line / Life on the outside
CD AHOY 21
Captain Oi / Nov '94 / Plastic Head

O'Neal, Alexander

LOVE MAKES NO SENSE
In the middle / If you let it / Aphrodisia / Love makes no sense / Home is where the heart is / Change of heart / Lady / All that matters to me / Since I've been loving you / What a wonderful world
CD 549502
A&M / Feb '93 / PolyGram

O'Neal, Johnny

ON THE MONTREAL SCENE
Let me off uptown / Homeboy blues / While the blood is running warm / Come Sunday / Over joyed / Just loving you / Happy days are here again / Why try to change me now / Easy walker
CD JUST 852
Justin Time / May '96 / Cadillac / New Note/ Pinnacle

SOULFUL SWINGING (O'Neal, Johnny & Dave Young)
You're looking at me / One by one / Too late now / Night mist blues / Close your eyes / Ain't misbehavin' / Masquerade is over / What's bop
CD JAM 91282
Just A Memory / Jun '97 / New Note/ Pinnacle

O'Neal, Shaq

RETURN, THE
CD CHIP 154
Jive / Jan '95 / Pinnacle

SHAQ DIESEL
CD CHIP 146
Jive / Jan '94 / Pinnacle

YOU CAN'T STOP THE REIGN
Shaquille (interlude) / Still can't stop the reign / DIVA radio (interlude) / It was all a dream / No love lost / Strait playin' / Best to worst / Legal money / Edge of night / SHE (interlude) / Just be good to me / More to life / Big dog stomp / Game of death / Outro (interlude) / Player / Don't want to be alone
CD IND 90087
Interscope / Nov '96 / BMG

O'Neill, Sean

50 IRISH SINGALONG FAVOURITES (O'Neill, Sean Band)
CD ECD 3136
K-Tel / Jan '95 / K-Tel

IRISH PARTY SONGS (O'Neill, Sean Band)
At McCarthy's party / O'Hara from Tara / Blarney stone / Up the kingdom / Rakes of mallow / My beauty of Limerick / Kitty of Coleraine / Sweet Rosie O'Grady / O'Brien has no place to go / Galway races / Paddy works on the railway / Let Mr. Maguire sit down / Oul' lammas fair / Moonlight in Mayo / My Donegal shore / Any Tipperary Town / Bonny boy / When you were sweet sixteen / Mush mush toorali / Quare bungle rye / Cushy butterfield / Shamus O'Brien / Star of the county down / My Irish Molly O / Are you there Moriarty / Mick McGilligan's ball / Rose of Castlerae / Pretty little girl from Omagh / Where the grass grows the greenest / Ferry man / Gentle Mother / Old rustic bridge / One day at a time / Phil the fluter's ball / Harvest home / Little beggarman / Paddy McGinty's goat / Town of Ballybay / Slievenamon / Come back Paddy Reilly / Mountains of mourne / Doonaree / Cliffs of Dooneen / Banks of my own lovely Lee / Nightingale / Moonshine / My Bonnie lies over the ocean / Sing Irishman sing / Mick McGilligan's daughter / Old woman from Wexford / All for me grog / Famous Shamus / Dingle regatta
CD ECD 3342
K-Tel / May '97 / K-Tel

IRISH PUB SONGS (O'Neill, Sean Band)
If you're Irish/Bold O'Donoghue/I'll tell me Ma / Courtin' in the kitchen / Wild Rover/ Molly Malone/I belong to Glasgow / Loch Lomond/When Irish eyes are smiling / Irish rover/Brennan on the moor/Wild colonial boy/Muirsheen / Rose of Aranmore/Where the Counties meet / Where my Eileen is waiting / Danny boy/Galway Bay/Rose of Tralee / Goodbye Johnny dear/Old Bog Road/Farewell to Galway / Whiskey in the jar/Waxies' dargle / Dicey Reilly/Whiskey you're the Devil / Holy ground/It's a long way to Tipperary / Hello Patsy Fagan/Come down the mountain Katie Daley / When I was single/Love is teasing/Never wed an old man / Boys of Killybegs/Tim Finnegan's wake / Old maid in a garret/Goodbye Mick / Dublin O'Shea/Moonshiner/Juice of Barley/Rosin the bow / Maggie/Silver threads among the gold / Fiddler's green/Black Velvet band / Boul' Thady Quill/Boys from the County Armagh / Garden where the praties grow/Dan O'Hara / Home, boys, home/ Tongs by the fire
CD KCD 435
Celtic Collections / Jan '97 / Target/BMG

Ongala, Remmy

KERSHAW SESSIONS
CD ROOTCD 004
Strange Fruit / Mar '95 / Pinnacle

REMMY ONGALA & ORCHESTRE SUPER MATIMLIA (Ongala, Remmy & Orchestra)
Dodoma / One world / I want to go home / Inchi yetu (our country) / What can I say? (niseme nini) / No money, no life / Living together (tupendane) / Mrema / Kidogo kidogo (little by little)
CD CDRW 22
Realworld / Mar '92 / EMI

SONGS FOR THE POOR MAN (Ongala, Remmy & Orchestra)
Nasikitka / Karola / Kependa roho / Sauti ya mnyonge / Usingizi / Pamella / Muziki asili yake wapi / Mariam wangu / Kifo / Muziki asili yake wapi (version)
CD CDRW 6
Realworld / '90 / EMI

Ongley, Mark

SONG FOR ROS
CD HVRCD 0040
Hunter Valley / Sep '93 / Harmonia Mundi

Only Living Witness

INNOCENTS
CD CM 77017CD
Century Media / Feb '96 / Plastic Head

PRONE MORTAL FORM
CD CM 770722
Century Media / Jun '94 / Plastic Head

Only Love From Now

ULTRA
CD MAD 005CD
Mad / '95 / Plastic Head

Only Ones

BABY'S GOT A GUN
Happy pilgrim / Why don't you kill yourself / Me and my shadow / Deadly nightshade / Strange mouth / Big sleep / Oh Lucinda / Re-union / Trouble in the world / Castle built on sand / Fools / My way out of here
CD 4836622
Columbia / Mar '96 / Sony

BIG SLEEP
CD FREUDCD 045
Jungle / Sep '96 / RTM/Disc / SRD

EVEN SERPENTS SHINE
From here to eternity / Flaming torch / You've got to pay / No solution / In betweens / Out there in the night / Curtains for you / Programme / Someone who cares / Miles from nowhere / Instrumental
CD 4785032
Columbia / Feb '95 / Sony

IMMORTAL STORY, THE
Lovers of today / Peter and the pets / Whole of the law / Another girl another planet / Special view (aka telescopic love) / Beast / It's the truth / No peace for the wicked / Immortal story / From here to eternity / In betweens / No solution / Curtains for you / Someone who cares / Miles from nowhere / Your chosen life / Baby's got a gun / Why don't you kill yourself / Oh Lucinda (love becomes a habit) / Big sleep
CD 4712672
Columbia / Feb '92 / Sony

ONLY ONES LIVE, THE
Trouble in the world / Beast / Lovers of today / Why don't you kill yourself / As my wife says / Big sleep / City of fun / Programme / Happy pilgrim / Strange mouth / No peace for the wicked / Miles from nowhere / Another girl another planet / Me and my shadow
CD MAUCD 603
Mau Mau / Jul '89 / Pinnacle

ONLY ONES, THE
Whole of the law / Another girl another planet / Breaking down / City of fun / Beast / Creature of doom / It's the truth / Language problem / No place for the wicked / Immortal story
CD 4773792
Columbia / Aug '94 / Sony

REMAINS
Prisoner / Watch you drown / Flowers die / Devon song / My rejection / Baby's got a gun / Hope valley blues / Counterfeit woman / River of no return / I only wanna be your friend / Oh no / Don't hold your breath / Silent night / Don't feel too good
CD CDMGRAM 67
Anagram / Sep '96 / Cargo / Pinnacle

Ono, Seigen

NEKONOTOPIA NEKONOMANIA
Apple in the freezer / Enishie / Nekontopia nekonomania / My first wish / It's Denise / Person in the photography / 1989 / I think of you / Planador / Caramba / Berliner Nachte part 1 / Berliner Nachte part 2 / Berliner Nachte part 3 / Berliner Nachte part 4
CD MTM 29
Made To Measure / Apr '96 / New Note/ Pinnacle

Ono, Yoko

APPROXIMATELY INFINITE UNIVERSE (2CD Set)
CD Set RCD 10417/18
Rykodisc / Aug '97 / ADA / Vital

FEELING THE SPACE
CD RCD 10419
Rykodisc / Aug '97 / ADA / Vital

FLY (2CD Set)
CD Set RCD 10415/16
Rykodisc / Aug '97 / ADA / Vital

ONOBOX (6CD Set)
CD Set RCD 1022429
Rykodisc / Mar '92 / ADA / Vital

RISING
Warzone / Wouldnit / Ask the dragon / New York woman / Talking to the universe / Turn the corner / I'm dying / Where do we go from here / Kurushi / Will I / Rising / Goodbye my love / Revelations
CD CDEST 2276
Capitol / Jan '96 / EMI

RISING MIXES
Talking to the Universe / Source / Ask the dragon / Where do we go from here / Rising / Franklin summer
CD CDP 8372680
Capitol / Jun '96 / EMI

STORY, A
CD RCD 10420
Rykodisc / Aug '97 / ADA / Vital

WALKING ON THIN ICE
CD RCD 20230
Rykodisc / Mar '97 / ADA / Vital

Onset

POOL OF LIFE REVISITED, THE
Rakin' em down / Taker (2nd take) / Cowboy and his wife / Precious love / Talkin' space travel blues / Too proud to start / Trees and plants / Glad rag (instrumental) / Mansion on the hill / Pool of life (instrumental) / For you / Two times forgotten man / Poor and lonely girl / Starlight tuneful 9 / Another man's crime / Let's go home
CD PROBE 040CD
Probe Plus / Oct '94 / SRD

Onslaught

POWER FROM HELL
Damnation / Onslaught (Power from hell) / Thermo neuclear devastation / Skullcrusher / Lord of evil / Death metal / Angels of death / Devil's legion / Street meets steel / Skullcrusher / Witch hunt / Mighty empress
CD PRAGE 001CD
Powerage / Oct '96 / Plastic Head

Onyas

GET SHIT FACED WITH THE ONYAS
CD ANDA 196
Au-Go-Go / Jan '97 / Cargo / Greyhound / Plastic Head

Onyx

ALL WE GOT IZ US
Life or death / Last dayz / All we got iz us (Evil streets) / Purse snatchaz / Shout / I murder u / Betta off dead / Live niguz / Funkmotherfukaz / Most def / Act up / Getto mentalitee / Wrongs / Maintain / Walk in New York
CD 5292652
Def Jam / Oct '95 / PolyGram

BACDAFUCUP
CD 5234472
Def Jam / Jan '96 / PolyGram

Oofotr

OOFOTR
CD EKG 11CD
Norske Gram / Aug '96 / ADA

Oomph

FOOLS NEVER FAIL
CD DY 152
Dynamica / Jun '95 / Koch

SPERM
Suck-taste-spit / Sex / War / Dickhead / Schisma / Feiert das kreuz / Love / Das ist freiheit / Kismet / Bresathtaker / Ich bin der weg / U-said (live)
CD DY 62
Dynamica / Apr '94 / Koch

WUNSCHKIND
CD DY 00212
Dynamica / Nov '96 / Koch

Oomph

BETWEEN TWO WORLDS
CD GV 135CD
Global Village / May '94 / ADA / Direct

Oosh

VIEW, THE
Chat up / Missing lover / Spliff culture / Yard has no dandelion / Cloud / View / Charlie / No soul / I got this / Storm
CD 4509962862
Magnet / Sep '94 / Warner Music

OP8

SLUSH (OP8 & Lisa Germano)
Slush
CD VVR 1000332
V2 / Jun '97 / 3mv/Pinnacle

Opal

HAPPY NIGHTMARE BABY
CD SST 103CD
SST / May '93 / Plastic Head

Opaz

BACK FROM THE RAGGEDY EDGE (Opaz/Ray Hayden)
CD OPH 003CD
Opaz / Aug '95 / Jet Star / Pinnacle

Open House

SECOND STORY
CD GLCD 1144
Green Linnet / Oct '94 / ADA / CM / Direct / Highlander / Roots

Opera 1X

CALL OF THE WILD
CD MS 005CD
Nosferatu / Apr '95 / Plastic Head

Operating Strategies

DIFFICULTY OF BEING
CD EFA 11214
Danse Macabre / Apr '93 / SRD

Operating Theatre

RAPID EYE MOVEMENTS
CD UD 011CD
United Dairies / Oct '96 / World Serpent

Operation Ivy

OPERATION IVY
CD LOOKOUT 10CD
Lookout / Dec '96 / Cargo / Greyhound / Shellshock/Disc

Operator

ZERO DIVIDE
CD SOS 011CD
North South / Nov '96 / Pinnacle

Opeth

MORNINGRISE
CD CANDLE 015CD
Candlelight / Jul '96 / Plastic Head

ORCHID
CD CANDLE 010CD
Candlelight / Sep '95 / Plastic Head

Ophthalamia

JOURNEY INTO DARKNESS, A
CD AV 003
Avant Garde / May '94 / Plastic Head / RTM/Disc

VIA DOLOROSA
CD AV 013
Avant Garde / Jul '95 / Plastic Head / RTM/Disc

Opie, Alan

IN PRAISE OF GOD
CD DIONO 01
Revelation / Oct '92 / Plastic Head

Opik

OPIK
CD HARDCD 4
Concrete / Jun '95 / 3mv/Pinnacle / Prime / RTM/Disc / Total/BMG

Opium Den

DIARY OF A DRUNKEN SUN
CD 001AF2
Southern / Jun '93 / SRD

Oppermann, Rudiger

SAME SUN SAME MOON
CD SHAM 017CD
Shamrock / Feb '93 / ADA / Wellard

Oppressed

BEST OF THE OPPRESSED, THE
CD DOJOCD 227
Dojo / Jan '96 / Disc

OI OI MUSIC
CD AHOYCD 5
Captain Oi / Jul '93 / Plastic Head

Oppressor

AGONY
CD RRS 958CD
Diehard / Jan '97 / Plastic Head

Opthalamia

TO ELISHIA
CD NR 013CD
Necropolis / Jun '97 / Plastic Head

Optic Eye

LIGHT SIDE OF THE SUN
Sunburst (extended mix) / Brain of Morbius / Listening (Aural sculpture) / Chain reaction / Wobbling in space / Guitar man / Slaves of the crystal brain / On the other side / Far out race / Acid drops
CD CDTOT 17
Jumpin' & Pumpin' / Oct '94 / 3mv/Sony / Mo's Music Machine

Optic Nerve

CHILDREN OF THE UNIVERSE
CD 77021921
Omnisonus / Jun '97 / Cargo

FOREVER AND A DAY
CD SCACD 104
Screaming Apple / Jun '97 / Cargo / Greyhound

Optica

ALL THE COLOURS OF THE RAINBOW
CD KINXCD 2
Kinetix / Apr '95 / Pinnacle

FUZZ
Plasma eruption / Evolute / Dueterum / Mercury / Spacetime / Magnatron phz / Circular cube / Fuzz / Spaced bong baby
CD KINXCD 6
Kinetix / Apr '97 / Pinnacle

Optical 8

BUG
CD DSA 54048
CDSA / Dec '96 / Harmonia Mundi / ReR Megacorp

Optiganally Yours

SPOTLIGHT ON
CD HED 065CD
Headhunter / Jun '97 / Cargo

Optimum Wound Profile

ASPHYXIA
CD WB 1120CD
We Bite / May '95 / Plastic Head

Opus III

GURU MOTHER
CD HFCD 33
PWL / Sep '94 / Warner Music

MIND FRUIT
CD HFCD 24
PWL / Jul '92 / Warner Music

Ora

ORA
CD HBG 122/14
Background / Apr '94 / Background / Greyhound

Oracle

TREE
CD WM 2
Swim / Jun '94 / Kudos / RTM/Disc / SRD

Oral Groove

COLLISIONVILLE
CD CR 810952
Cross / Jul '97 / Greyhound

Orang

FIELDS AND WAVES
Barren / Jalap / P53 / Moider / Seizure / Moratorium / Superculture / Quondam / Forest / Hoo / Boreades / Fields and waves / Kuising
CD ECHCD 010
Echo / Jan '97 / EMI / Vital

HERD OF INSTINCT
CD ECHCD 002
Echo / Jul '94 / EMI / Vital

Orange 9mm

DRIVER NOT INCLUDED
CD 7567617462
Atlantic / May '95 / Warner Music

TRAGIC
Fire in the hole / Stick shift / Crowd control / Method / Dead in the water / Kiss it goodbye / Feel it / Failure / Take it away / Muted / Gun to your head / Tragic / Seven
CD 7567829022
Atlantic / Feb '97 / Warner Music

Orange Cakemix

BLUE ISLAND SOUND
CD ER 1034
Elefant / Aug '97 / Greyhound / SRD

FLUFFY PILLOW
CD DRL 029
Fuzzy Box/Darla / Jan '97 / Cargo

GRAPEFRUIT
CD BBPTC 24CD
Black Bean & Placenta Tape Club / Mar '97 / Cargo

LOVECLOUD AND SECRET TAPE
CD BBPTC 83
Black Bean & Placenta Tape Club / Jul '97 / Cargo

SILVER LINING UNDER WATER
CD DRL 031
Darla / Feb '97 / Cargo

Orange Deluxe

NECKING
CD GOODCD 4
Dead Dead Good / Jul '96 / Pinnacle

VODKA, DOUGHNUTS & DOLE
CD GOODCD 10
Dead Dead Good / Aug '96 / Pinnacle

Orange Juice

HEATHER'S ON FIRE, THE
Falling and laughing / Moscow / Moscow olympics / Blue boy / Lovesick / Simply thrilled honey / Breakfast time / Poor old soul / Poor old soul Pt.2 / Felicity / Upwards and onwards / Dying day / Holiday hymn
CD DUBH 955CD
Postcard / Oct '95 / Vital

ORANGE JUICE/YOU CAN'T HIDE YOUR LOVE FOREVER
Lean period / I guess I'm just a little bit too sensitive / Burning desire / Scaremonger / Artisans / What presence / Out for the count / Get while the gettings good / All that ever mattered / Salmon fishing in New York / Falling and laughing / Untitled melody / Wan light / Tender objects / Dying day / LOVE Love / Intuition told me / Upwards and onwards / Satellite city / Three cheers for our side / Consolation prize / Felicity / In a nutshell
CD 8477272
Polydor / Jan '91 / PolyGram

OSTRICH CHURCHYARD
Louise Louise / Three cheers for our side / (To put it in a) nutshell / Satellite city / Consolation prize / Holiday hymn / Intuition told me / Wan light / Dying day / Texas fever / Tender object / Falling and laughing / Lovesick / Poor old soul / You old eccentric
CD DUBH 954CD
Postcard / Oct '95 / Vital

RIP IT UP
Rip it up / Mud in your eye / Breakfast time / Flesh of my flesh / Hokoyo / Million pleading faces / Turn away / I can't help myself / Louise Louise / Tenterhook
CD 8397682
Polydor / Apr '92 / PolyGram

VERY BEST OF ORANGE JUICE, THE
Falling and laughing / Consolation prize / You old eccentric / LOVE love / Felicity / In a nutshell / Rip it up / I can't help myself / Flesh of my flesh / Tenterhooks / Bridge / Day I went down to Texas / Punch drunk / Place in my heart / Sad lament / Lean period / I guess I'm just a little too sensitive / Scaremonger / Artisans / Salmon fishing in New York / What presence / Out for the count
CD 5136182
Polydor / Apr '92 / PolyGram

Orange Sector

FAITH
CD CDZOT 18
Zoth Ommog / Aug '93 / Cargo / Plastic Head

KIDS IN AMERICA
CD CDZOT 126
Zoth Ommog / Nov '94 / Cargo / Plastic Head

Oranj Symphonette

ORANJ SYMPHONETTE PLAYS MANCINI
Shot in the dark / Experiment in terror / Pink Panther / Lujon / Inspector Clouseau / Moon River / Charade / Days of wine and roses / Mr. Yunioshi / Mr. Lucky / March of the cue balls / Baby elephant gun
CD GCD 79515
Gramavision / Oct '96 / Vital/SAM

Orb

ADVENTURES BEYOND THE ULTRAWORLD (2CD Set)
Little fluffy clouds / Earth (gala) / Supernova at the end of the universe / Back side of the moon / Spanish castles in space / Perpetual dawn / Into the fourth dimension / Outlands / Star 6 and 7 8 9 / Huge ever growing pulsating brain that rules from the centre
CD Set IMCD 234
Island / Sep '96 / PolyGram

AUNTIE AUBREY'S EXCURSIONS BEYOND THE CALL OF DUTY (2CD Set) (Various Artists)
Praying mantra: *Material* / Democracy: *Killing Joke* / Satellite serenade: *Suzuki, Keiichi* / Fast forward the future: *Zodiac Youth* /

Higher than the sun: *Primal Scream* / Ambient state: *Ready Made* / So and slow it grows: *Wir* / Secret squirrel: *Shimizu, Yasuki* / You gotta say yes to another excess: *Yello* / Out of body: *Innersphere* / Happiest girl: *Depeche Mode* / Ship of fools: *Erasure* / O'locco: *Sun Electric* / Ploy: *Maurizio* / Men of wadodem: *Time Unlimited* / 2 Much: *Paradise X* / Home: *Pop Will Eat Itself* / What goes on: *Love Kittens*
CD Set ______ **DVNT 012CD**
Deviant / Jul '96 / Prime / Vital

LIVE 1993 (2CD Set)
Huge ever growing pulsating brain that rules from the centre / Plateau / OOBE / Little fluffy clouds / Star 6 and 7 8 9 / Towers of dub / Blue room / Valley / Perpetual dawn / Assassin / Outlands / Spanish castles in space
CD Set ______ **IMCD 245**
Island / Mar '97 / PolyGram

ORBLIVION
Delta mkII / Ubiquity / Asylum / Bedouin / Molten love / Pi / SALT / Toxygene / Log of deadwood / Secrets / Passing of time / 72
CD ______ **CID 8055**
Island / Feb '97 / PolyGram

ORBSTORY (Interview Disc)
CD ______ **ORBK 1**
Sonic Book / Feb '97 / Cargo

ORBUS TERRARUM
Valley / Plateau / Oxbow Lakes / Montagne D'Or / Orbus terrarum / Occidental / Slug dub
CD ______ **CID 8037**
CD ______ **CIDX 8037**
Island / Mar '95 / PolyGram

UF.ORB
OOBE / UF Orb / Blue room / Towers of dub / Close encounters / Majestic / Sticky end
CD ______ **IMCD 219**
Island / Mar '96 / PolyGram

Orbestra

TRANSDANUBIAN SWINEHERDS
CD ______ **HNCD 1367**
Hannibal / Apr '92 / ADA / Vital

Orbison, Roy

ALL TIME GREATEST HITS
Only the lonely / Leah / In dreams / Uptown / It's over / Crying / Dream baby / Blue angel / Working for the man / Candy man / Running scared / Falling / Claudette / Ooby dooby / I'm hurtin' / Mean woman blues / Lana / Blue bayou / Oh pretty woman
CD ______ **CD 67290**
Monument / Jan '89 / Sony

BEST OF ROY ORBISON, THE
Oh pretty woman / Mean woman blues / Candy man / In dreams / Blue bayou / Pretty paper / Distant drums / I can't stop loving you / All I have to do is dream / It's over / Crying / Blue angel / Dream baby (how long must I dream) / Running scared / Only the the lonely (know the way I feel)
CD ______ **4633502**
Columbia / Feb '96 / Sony

BLACK & WHITE NIGHT (Orbison, Roy & Friends)
Oh pretty woman / Only the lonely / In dreams / Dream baby / Leah / Move on down the line / Crying / Mean woman blues / Running scared / Blue bayou / Candy man / Uptown / Ooby dooby / Comedians / (All I can do is) Dream of you / It's over
CD ______ **CDV 2601**
Virgin / Aug '91 / EMI

COLLECTION, THE
Trying to get to you / Ooby dooby / Go go go / You're my baby / Domino / Sweet and easy to love / Devil doll / Cause of it all / Fools hall of fame / True love goodbye / Chicken hearted / I like love / Mean little mama / Problem child / This kind of love / It's too late / I never knew / You're gonna cry / One more time / Lovestruck / Clown / Claudette
CD ______ **CCSCD 147**
Castle / Feb '93 / BMG

COLLECTION, THE
CD ______ **COL 027**
Collection / Mar '95 / Target/BMG

GOLDEN DAYS
Oh pretty woman / Running scared / Falling / Love hurts / Mean woman blues / I can't stop loving you / Crowd / Blue bayou / Borne on the wind / Lana / Only the lonely (know the way I feel) / It's over / Crying / Pretty paper / All I have to do is dream / Dream baby / Blue angel / Working for the man / Candy man / In dreams
CD ______ **4715552**
Monument / Apr '92 / Sony

GOLDEN DECADE 1960-1969, THE
Only the lonely / Bye bye love / I'm hurtin' / Love hurts / Here comes that song again / Double date / Legend in my time / Uptown / I can't stop loving you / Candy man / Darkness / Today's teardrops / Twenty two days / Cry / Blue angel / Running scared / Lana / Party heart / Dance / Crying / Dream baby / Beautiful dreamer / Crowd / Leah / Love star / Workin' for the man / Distant drums / Mama / Falling / In dreams / Blue bayou / She wears my ring / How are things in paradise / (They call you) Gigolette / Almost / San Fernando / Mean woman blues / Pretty paper / Borne on the wind / It's over / Oh pretty woman / Let the good times roll / (Say) you're my girl / Yes / Goodnight Claudette / Breakin' up is breakin' my heart / Ride away / Crawling back / Communication breakdown / There won't be many coming home / Too soon to know / Twinkle toes / So good / Cry softly lonely one / Lonesome number one / Walk on / Heartache / My friend / Penny arcade
CD ______ **NXTCD 246**
Sequel / May '93 / BMG

IN DREAMS/ORBISONGS
In dreams / Lonely wine / Shahdaroba / No one will ever know / Sunset / House without windows / Dream / Blue bayou / (They call you) Gigolette / All I have to do is dream / Beautiful dreamer / My prayer / Oh pretty woman / Dance / (Say) you're my girl / Goodnight / Nightlife / Let the good times roll / (I get so) Sentimental / Yo te amo Maria / Wedding day / Sleepy hollow / Twenty two Days / Legend in my time
CD ______ **4749572**
Monument / Feb '94 / Sony

KING OF HEARTS
You're the one / Heartbreak radio / We'll take the night / Crying / After the love has gone / Love in time / I drove all night / Wild hearts run out of time / Coming home / Careless heart
CD ______ **CDVUS 58**
Virgin / Nov '92 / EMI

LEGEND IN HIS TIME
Lonesome number one / Oh such a stranger / Legend in my time / I'm a Southern man / Belinda / Under suspicion / No chain at all / Can't wait / I'm hurtin' / Same street / Blue blue day / Too soon to know / I don't really want you / Old love song / Born to love you / Big hearted me / What about me
CD ______ **CDMF 079**
Magnum Force / '91 / TKO Magnum

LEGENDS IN MUSIC
CD ______ **LECD 069**
Wisepack / Jul '94 / Conifer/BMG / THE

LONELY & BLUE/CRYING
Only the lonely (Know the way I feel) / Bye bye love / Cry / Blue avenue / I can't stop loving you / Come back to me my love / Blue angel / Raindrops / Legend in my time / I'm hurtin' / Twenty two days / I'll say it's my fault / Crying / Great pretender / Love hurts / She wears my ring / Wedding day / Summer song / Dance / Lana / Loneliness / Let's make a memory / Nite life / Running scared
CD ______ **4749562**
Monument / Feb '94 / Sony

MAGIC OF ROY ORBISON, THE
CD ______ **CD 322696**
Koch Presents / Jul '97 / Koch

MYSTERY GIRL
You got it / Real world / Dream you / Love so beautiful / California blue / She's a mystery to me / Comedians / Windsurfer / Careless heart
CD ______ **CDV 2576**
Virgin / Apr '92 / EMI

ONLY THE LONELY
Only the lonely / In dreams / Crying / Dream baby / Working for the man / Candy man / Running scared / I'm hurtin' / Oh pretty woman / Ooby dooby / Lana / Blue bayou
CD ______ **CDVIP 113**
Virgin VIP / Nov '93 / EMI

OOBY DOOBY
CD ______ **MSCD 028**
Music De-Luxe / Apr '96 / TKO Magnum

RCA SESSIONS, THE (Orbison, Roy & Sonny James)
Almost eighteen: *Orbison, Roy* / Bug: *Orbison, Roy* / I'll never tell: *Orbison, Roy* / Jolie: *Orbison, Roy* / Paper boy: *Orbison, Roy* / Sweet and innocent: *Orbison, Roy* / Seems to me: *Orbison, Roy* / Apache: *James, Sonny* / Magnetism: *James, Sonny* / Young love: *James, Sonny* / Lana: *James, Sonny* / Legend of the brown mountain light: *James, Sonny* / Listen to my heart: *James, Sonny* / Hey little ducky: *James, Sonny* / Innocent angel: *James, Sonny* / Broken wings: *James, Sonny* / Day's not over yet: *James, Sonny* / Dance her by me (one more time): *James, Sonny* / Time's running backwards for me: *James, Sonny*
CD ______ **BCD 15407**
Bear Family / Jul '87 / Direct / Rollercoaster / Swift

ROCKER
Ooby dooby / Go go go / Trying to get to you / You're my baby / Rockhouse / Domino / Sweet and easy to love / Devil doll / Cause of it all / Fools hall of fame / True love goodbye / Chicken hearted / I like love / Mean little lover / Problem child / You tell me / I give up / One more time / Love struck / Clown / Claudette / This kind of love / It's too late / I never knew / You're gonna cry / I was a fool: *Orbison, Roy & Ken Cook* / Find my baby for me: *Orbison, Roy & Sonny Burgess* / Rockbilly gal: *Orbison, Roy & Hayden Thompson*
CD ______ **CPCD 8180**
Charly / Jun '96 / Koch

ROCKHOUSE
Ooby dooby / I like love / Clown / Cause of it all / Domino / Chicken hearted / Go go go / This kind of love / You're my baby / Claudette / Rockhouse / It's too late / Mean little mama / Fools' hall of fame / You're gonna cry / True love goodbye / Devil doll / Sweet and easy to love / Problem child / Tryin' to get to you
CD ______ **305912**
Hallmark / Jan '97 / Carlton

ROY ORBISON
CD ______ **12330**
Laserlight / May '94 / Target/BMG

ROY ORBISON (3CD Set)
CD Set ______ **KBOX 344**
Collection / Oct '95 / Target/BMG / TKO Magnum

ROY ORBISON SONGBOOK (Various Artists)
In dreams: *Jones, Tom* / Dream baby: *Shannon, Del* / Oh pretty woman: *Green, Al* / It's over: *Campbell, Glen* / Crying: *McLean, Don* / Only the lonely: *Wells, Kitty* / Down the line: *Hollies* / Blue Bayou: *Whitman, Slim* / Claudette: *Everly Brothers* / Best friend: *Cash, Johnny* / You've got love: *Holly, Buddy* / Uptown: *Gordon, Robert* / Lookin' for love: *Vee, Bobby* / Leah: *Higgins, Bertie* / Crowd: *Jennings, Waylon* / Lana: *Velvets* / Careless heart: *Tyler, Bonnie* / Running scared: *Shannon, Del* / California blue: *Humperdinck, Engelbert* / Lovin' man: *Francis, Connie*
CD ______ **VSOPCD 215**
Connoisseur Collection / Apr '95 / Pinnacle

SUN YEARS, THE
Ooby dooby / Trying to get to you / Go go go / You're my baby / Rock house / Domino / Sweet and easy / Devil doll / Cause of it all / Fools' hall of fame / True love goodbye / Chicken hearted / I like love / Mean little mama / Problem child / I was a fool / This kind of love / It's too late / I never knew / You're gonna cry / You tell me / I give up / One more time / Lovestruck / Clown / Claudette / Jenny / Find my baby for me
CD ______ **BCD 15461**
Bear Family / Apr '89 / Direct / Rollercoaster / Swift

VERY BEST OF ROY ORBISON, THE
Only the lonely / You got it / Oh pretty woman / In dreams / Crying: *Orbison, Roy & KD Lang* / Blue angel / Working for the man / Running scared / She's a mystery to me / Blue bayou / It's over / California blue / Claudette / Mean woman blues / Ooby dooby / Too soon to know / Falling / Dream baby / I drove all night / Pretty paper / Goodnight
CD ______ **CDV 2804**
Virgin / Nov '96 / EMI

Orbit, William

BEST OF STRANGE CARGOS
Water from a vine leaf / Dark eyed kid / Gringatcho Demento / Fire and mercy / Via Calente / Time to get wize / Ruby Heart (transmogrified) / Atom dream / Harry Flowers / Love my way / Riding to Rio / Story of light / Silent signals / Painted rock / Water babies
CD ______ **EIRSCD 1079**
IRS/EMI / Jun '96 / EMI

STRANGE CARGO VOL.1 (Hinterland)
CD ______ **4509992952**
N-Gram / Dec '96 / Warner Music

STRANGE CARGO VOL.3
Water from a vine leaf / Into the paradise / Time to get wize / Harry flowers / Touch of the night / Story of light / Gringatcho demento / Hazy shade of random / Best friend paranoia / Monkey king / Deus ex machina / Water babies
CD ______ **CDV 2707**
Virgin / Mar '93 / EMI

Orbital

EVENT HORIZON
CD ______ **8289392**
Internal / Aug '97 / Pinnacle / PolyGram

IN SIDES
Girl with the sun in her hair / Petrol / Box / Dwr budr / Adnans / Out there somewhere
CD ______ **8287632**
Internal / Apr '96 / Pinnacle / PolyGram

IN SIDES
Girl with the sun in her hair / Petrol / Box / Dwr budr / Adnans / Out there somewhere / Saint
CD ______ **TRCDR 10**
Internal / Apr '97 / Pinnacle / PolyGram

IN SIDES
CD ______ **123129CD**
Dutch East India / Apr '97 / Plastic Head / SRD

ORBITAL
Moebius / Speed freak / Oolaa / Desert storm / Fahrenheit 303 / Steel cube idolatory / High rise / Chime / Midnight / Belfast / Untitled / Macro head
CD ______ **TRUCD 9**
Internal / Apr '97 / Pinnacle / PolyGram

ORBITAL II
Time becomes / Planet of the shapes / Lush 31 / Lush 32 / Impact (the Earth is burning) / Remind / Walk now / Monday / Halcyon and on and on / Input out
CD ______ **TRUCD 2**
Internal / Apr '97 / Pinnacle / PolyGram

SNIVILISATION
Forever / I wish I had duck feet / Sad but true / Crash and carry / Science friction / Philosophy by numbers / Quality seconds / Are we here / Kein trink wasser / Attached
CD ______ **TRUCD 5**
Internal / Apr '97 / Pinnacle / PolyGram

Orchestra

NOT AS SOFTLY AS
CD ______ **MECCACD 1043**
Music Mecca / Nov '94 / Cadillac / Jazz Music / Wellard

Orchestra Baobab

PIRATE'S CHOICE
CD ______ **WCD 014**
World Circuit / May '90 / ADA / Cadillac / Direct / New Note/Pinnacle

Orchestra Jazz Siciliana

PLAYS THE MUSIC OF CARLA BLEY
440 / Lone arranger / Dreams so real / Baby baby / Joyful noise / Egyptian / Blunt object
CD ______ **843 207 2**
ECM / Nov '90 / New Note/Pinnacle

Orchestra Klezmer

ORIENT EXPRESS MOVING SHNORERS
CD ______ **TE 010**
EPM / Feb '97 / ADA / Discovery

Orchestra Marrabenta

INDEPENDENCE
CD ______ **CD PIR 12**
World Circuit / Apr '89 / ADA / Cadillac / Direct / New Note/Pinnacle

Orchestra Super Mazembe

MALOBA D'AMOR
Kassongo / Shauri yako / Salima (parts 1 and 2) / Mwana nyiau (parts 1 and 2) / Nabinakate / Maloba d'amor / Samba (parts 1 and 2)
CD ______ **AFRIZZ 007**
Disc Afrique / May '90 / CM / Roots

Orchestra Tango Cafe

TANGO ARGENTINO
CD ______ **SSCD 001**
Sounds Sensational / Jun '97 / Discovery

Orchestre Contrebasses

BASS, BASS, BASS, BASS, BASS & BASS
CD ______ **86232**
Melodie / Oct '93 / ADA / Discovery / Grapevine/PolyGram / Greensleeves / Jet Star

Orchestre De Tanger

AL-ALA ANTHOLOGY VOL.7
CD ______ **W 260030**
Inedit / Oct '96 / ADA / Discovery / Harmonia Mundi

Orchestre National

A PLUS TARD (Orchestre National De Jazz)
CD ______ **LBLC 6554**
Label Bleu / Nov '92 / New Note/Pinnacle

Orchestre National De Jazz

IN TEMPO
CD ______ **5324382**
Verve / Jul '96 / PolyGram

MERCI MERCI MERCI
CD ______ **5349452**
Verve / Aug '97 / PolyGram

REMINISCING
CD ______ **5324372**
Verve / Jul '96 / PolyGram

Orchid Airburst

SIXTY CYCLE STORIES
CD ______ **ORCH 1202**
Guitar Tree / Oct '95 / Plastic Head

Orchidee

TRADITIONAL CHINESE ZHENG AND QIN MUSIC
CD ______ **SM 16032**
Wergo / Jan '93 / ADA / Cadillac / Harmonia Mundi

Orchids

STRIVING FOR THE LAZY PERFECTION
Obsession no.1 / Striving for the lazy perfection / Searching / Welcome to my curious heart / Avignon / Living Ken and Barbie / Beautiful liar / Kind of Eden / Prayers to St. Jude / Lovechild / Give a little honey / I've got to wake up / Perfect reprise
CD _____ SARAH 617CD
Sarah / Jan '94 / Vital

Orchis

4000 WINTERS
Horsemen / Blood of bone / Blackwaterside / Hare / Jennet / Gallows man / Arcadia / Horn / He walks in winter / Megaera / Winter / Risen / From the iron wood
CD _____ CYT 03CD
Cryptanthus / Jan '97 / World Serpent

Order From Chaos

DAWN BRINGER
CD _____ SR 9507CD
Shiadarshana / Sep '95 / Plastic Head

STILLBIRTH MACHINE
CD _____ DEC 006
Decapitated / Apr '94 / Plastic Head

Order Odonata

EXPERIMENTS THAT IDENTIFY CHANGE
CD _____ BFLCD 18
Big Life / Feb '96 / Mo's Music Machine / Pinnacle / Prime

TECHNICAL USE OF SOUND IN MAGICK
CD _____ BFLCD 19
Dragonfly / Aug '96 / Mo's Music Machine / Pinnacle

Ordinaires

ONE
CD _____ BND 7CD
One Little Indian / May '90 / Pinnacle

Ordo Equitum Solis

HECATE
CD _____ EFA 112822
Glasnost / May '95 / SRD

OES
CD _____ EEE 015
Musica Maxima Magnetica / Nov '93 / Cargo / Plastic Head

PARASKENIA
CD _____ EEE 18
Musica Maxima Magnetica / Aug '94 / Cargo / Plastic Head

SOLSTITII TEMPORIS SENSUS
CD _____ EEE 07
Zoth Ommog / Nov '93 / Cargo / Plastic Head

O'Reagan, Brendan

WIND OF CHANGE, A
CD _____ CLUNCD 056
Mulligan / Jun '89 / ADA / CM

Orealis

NIGHT VISIONS
CD _____ GL 1152CD
Green Linnet / Nov '95 / ADA / CM / Direct / Highlander / Roots

OREALIS
CD _____ GLCD 1106
Green Linnet / Nov '92 / ADA / CM / Direct / Highlander / Roots

Orefiche, Armando

ARMANDO OREFICHE & HIS HAVANA CUBAN BOYS
CD _____ HQCD 59
Harlequin / Dec '95 / Hot Shot / Jazz Music / Swift / Wellard

Oregon

45TH PARALLEL
CD _____ VBR 20482
Vera Bra / Dec '90 / New Note/Pinnacle / Pinnacle

ALWAYS, NEVER AND FOREVER
CD _____ VBR 20732
Vera Bra / Sep '91 / New Note/Pinnacle / Pinnacle

CROSSING
Queen of Sydney / Pepe Linque / Alpenbridge / Travel by day / Kronach waltz / Glidj / Amaryllis / Looking glass / Crossing
CD _____ 8253232
ECM / New Note/Pinnacle

ECOTOPIA
Twice around the sun / Innocente / WBAI / Zephyr / Ecotopia / Leather cats / Redial / Song of the morrow
CD _____ 8331202
ECM / Oct '87 / New Note/Pinnacle

OREGON
Rapids / Beacon / Toast / Beside a brook / Ariana / There was no Moon that night / Skyline / Impending bloom
CD _____ 8117112
ECM / Oct '83 / New Note/Pinnacle

TROIKA
Charlotte's tangle / Gekko / Prelude / Mariella / Spanish stairs / Arctic turn/Land rover / Mexico for sure / Pale sun / I said OK / Tower / Minaret / Celeste
CD _____ VBR 20782
Vera Bra / Feb '95 / New Note/Pinnacle / Pinnacle

O'Reilly, Marie

IRISH TREASURES AND ORIGINALS VOL.2
CD _____ CIC 083CD
Clo Iar-Chonnachta / Nov '93 / CM

O'Reilly, Melanie

SEA KINGDOM, THE
CD _____ CMBCD 015
Cross Border Media / May '96 / ADA / Direct / Grapevine/PolyGram

TIR NA MARA
CD _____ CBM 015CD
Cross Border Media / Jul '95 / ADA / Direct / Grapevine/PolyGram

Organisation

FREE BURNING
CD _____ CDVEST 23
Bulletproof / Jul '94 / Pinnacle

SAVOR THE FLAVOR
CD _____ CDVEST 50
Bulletproof / May '95 / Pinnacle

Orgy Of Pigs

WHERE FEELINGS DIE
CD _____ DOMCD 016
Dominator / Apr '95 / Plastic Head

O'Riada, Sean

MISE EIRE
CD _____ CEFCD 080
Gael Linn / Jan '94 / ADA / CM / Direct / Grapevine/PolyGram / Roots

O'RIADA
CD _____ CEFCD 032
Gael Linn / Jan '94 / ADA / CM / Direct / Grapevine/PolyGram / Roots

O'RIADA SA GAIETY
CD _____ CEFCD 027
Gael Linn / Jan '94 / ADA / CM / Direct / Grapevine/PolyGram / Roots

PLAYBOY OF THE WESTERN WORLD, THE
CD _____ CEFCD 012
Gael Linn / Jan '91 / ADA / CM / Direct / Grapevine/PolyGram / Roots

Orichalcum

ORICHALCUM AND THE DEVIANT (Orichalcum & The Deviant)
CD _____ TIPCD 111
Tip / Apr '97 / Arabesque / Mo's Music Machine / Pinnacle / Prime

Orient Express

ORIENT EXPRESS, THE
CD _____ 2796
Head / Jun '97 / Greyhound

Oriental Brothers

NWA ADA DI NMA
CD _____ FLTRCD 527
Flame Tree / Apr '96 / Pinnacle

Orientation

BOSPORUS BRIDGE
CD _____ EFA 129732
Pantongue / Jun '97 / SRD

Orientexpressen

BALKANICA
Afrodites kullar / Uzni me sevdo / Trilliseste / Hora din voltine / Kucevacko kolo / Havanna club / Verbunk from Szatmar / Hora de la Goicea / Sokol mi leta visoko / Uskub / Kosmos / Regnet / Marice kolo repa/Maricas dans rovan / Bergets dans / Morgondans / Ciganski orijent / Starino stara planino / Savsat bari ve samasi / Joc din dracineti / Geamparalele / Novalukolo / Snosti si vidjach mila mamo / Slivova/Supernova / Dennes vals
CD _____ RESCD 510
Resource / Jul '97 / ADA / Direct

KARA TEN
CD _____ PAN 143CD
Pan / Jan '94 / ADA / CM / Direct

Original Danish Polcalypso ...

LIVE (Original Danish Polcalypso Orchestra)
CD _____ CCRCD 97002
Copenhagen Calypso / May '97 / Cadillac

Original Dixieland Jazz Band

75TH ANNIVERSARY, THE
Livery stable blues / Dixieland jazz band one-step / At the jazz band ball / Ostrich walk / Skeleton jangle / Tiger rag / Bluin' the blues / Fidgety feet / Sensation rag / Mourning blues / Clarinet marmalade / Lazy daddy / Margie Palesteena / Broadway rose / Sweet mama / Home again blues / Crazy blues / Jazz me blues / St. Louis blues / Royal garden blues / Dangerous blues / Bow wow blues
CD _____ ND 90650
Bluebird / May '92 / BMG

COMPLETE ORIGINAL DIXIELAND JAZZ BAND, THE
Livery stable blues / Dixie jass band one-step / At the Jazz Band Ball / Ostrich / Skeleton jangle / Tiger rag / Bluin' the blues / Fidgety feet / Sensation rag / Mournin' blues / Clarinet marmalade / Lazy daddy / Margie / Palesteena / Broadway rose / Sweet Mama / Home again blues / Crazy blues / Jazz me blues / St. Louis blues / Royal Garden blues / Dangerous blues / Bow wow blues (My Mama treats me like a dog) / Skeeton jangle / Clarinet marmalade / Bluin' the blues / Tiger rag / Barn yard blues / Original Dixieland one-step / Bluin' the blues / Tiger rag / Ostrich walk / Original Dixieland one-step / Satanic blues / Toddlin' blues / Who loves you / Fidgety feet (War cloud)
CD _____ ND 90026
Jazz Tribune / Jun '94 / BMG

DIXIELAND (Original Dixieland Stompers)
CD _____ 11012
Laserlight / '86 / Target/BMG

FIRST JAZZ BAND, THE (The Golden Age of Jazz)
CD _____ JZCD 369
Suisa / Jun '92 / Jazz Music / THE

FIRST JAZZ RECORDINGS 1917-1923
CD _____ 158492
Jazz Archives / Nov '95 / Discovery

SENSATION
Livery stable blues / Sensation rag / Dixie jass band one-step / That teasin' rag / Tiger rag / Bluein' the blues / Fidgety feet / Clarinet marmalade / Lazy daddy / At the Jazz Band Ball / Look at 'em doing it now / Ostrich walk / Satanic blues / Lasses candy / Tell me / I've got a captain working for me now / Mammy o'mine / I've lost my heart in Dixieland / Margie / Singin' the blues
CD _____ CDAJA 5023
Living Era / Oct '88 / Select

Original Gospel Harmonettes

LOVE LIFTED ME
Is you all on the altar / I won't let go / Righteous on the march / Step by step / After a while / Camp meeting / Count your blessings / Healer / Thy will / He's so real to me / In my heart / Love lifted me / He died / Heaven is a beautiful place / You've been good to me / I must tell Jesus / Don't forget about me / Now I'm ready / Royal telephone / Hymn
CD _____ CPCD 8115
Charly / Jul '95 / Koch

Original Hi-Fi

CHILI DUBS
CD _____ ZD 12CD
Zip Dog / Jun '97 / Grapevine/PolyGram / SRD / Vital

Original Killing Floor

ROCK THE BLUES
Woman you need love / Come home baby / Sunday morning / My mind can ride easy / Keep on walking / Lou's blues / Nobody by my side / Bedtime blues / Try to understand / Wet / Forget it / People change your mind
CD _____ SEECD 355
See For Miles/C5 / Sep '92 / Pinnacle

Original Mirrors

HEARTBEAT (The Best Of The Original Mirrors)
Sharp words / Refelections / Boys, the boys / Flying / Chains of love / Could this be heaven / Boys cry / Night of the angels / Panic in the night / Feel like a train / Heart, twango & rawbeat / Dancing with the rebels / Teenbeat / When you're young / Things to come / Darling in London / Don't cry baby / Don't wear red / Swing together / Time has come
CD _____ 5325942
Mercury / Jun '96 / PolyGram

Original Rockers

ROCKERS TO ROCKERS
CD _____ CDG 001
Different Drummer / Oct '93 / Pinnacle

Original Salt City Six

PLAY THE CLASSICS
CD _____ JCD 78
Jazzology / Jul '93 / Jazz Music

Original Salty Dogs

JOY JOY JOY
CD _____ SOSCD 1233
Stomp Off / May '93 / Jazz Music / Wellard

Originals

ANOTHER TIME, ANOTHER PLACE/ COME AWAY WITH ME
Fantasy interlude / Don't put me on / I've loved, I've lost, I've learned / Temporarily out of order / Ladies (we need you) / Take this love / It's alright / Jezebel / JEALOUS means I love you / While the cat's away / Come away with me / Stay with me / Blue moon / Thanks for your love (Happiness is you)
CD _____ CDSEWD 084
Southbound / Jul '93 / Pinnacle

Originoo Gunn Clappaz

DA STORM
Intro / Calm before da storm / No fear / Boom...boom...fucking prick / Gunn clapp / Emergency broadcast system / Hurricane starang / Danjer / Elements of da storm / Da storm / Wild cowboys in Bucktown / God don't like ugly / X-unknown / Elite fleet / Flappin'
CD _____ CDPTY 140
Priority/Virgin / Nov '96 / EMI

Orioles

JUBILEE JIVE ROCKIN' WITH THE ORIOLES
I may be wrong / It ain't gonna be like that / I cross my fingers / Shrimp boats / Baby I love you so / Don't stop / I'm just a fool in love / Along about sundown / Yes indeed / There's no one but you / Hold me, squeeze me / Wanted / Don't cry baby / Happy go lucky local / Longing / Once upon a time / My baby's gonna get it / Good looking baby / So much / How blind can you be / Don't keep it to yourself / My loved one / Bring that money home / Waiting / CC rider / I miss you so / Baby please don't go / Barbara Lee
CD _____ NEMCD 766
Sequel / Jun '96 / BMG

JUBILEE RECORDINGS, THE (6CD Set)
At night / Barbara Lee / It's too soon to know / Tell me so (Version 1) / I cover the waterfront / To be you / It seems so long ago / Lonely Christmas / Deacon Jones / Please give my heart a break / Tell me so (Version 2) / Dare to dream / Moonlight / Every dog-gone time / You're gone / Donkey serenade / It's a cold summer / Is my heart wasting time / I challenge your kiss / Kiss and a rose / So much / Forgive and forget / What are you doing New Year's Eve / Would you still be the one in my heart / Would you still be the one in my heart / You are my first love / If it's to be / I wonder when / Everything they said came true / I'd rather have you under the moon / We're supposed to be through / I need you so / Goodnight Irene / I cross my fingers / I cross my fingers / I can't seem to laugh anymore / Walking by the river / I miss you so / Lord's prayer / Oh holy night / I had to leave town / My prayer / I never knew / Pal of mine / Pal of mine / Happy go lucky local blues / Would I love you (Love you, love you) / Would I love you (Love you, love you) / When you're a long way from home / I'm just a fool in love / Barfly / Hold me squeeze me / Baby, please don't go / Don't tell her what happened to me / I may be wrong, but I think you're wonderful / Fool's world / You never cared for me / For all we know / Blame it on yourself / How blind can you be / When you're not around / Waiting / My loved one / Shrimp boats / Trust in me / Scandal / It's over because we're through / It ain't gonna be like that / Gettin' tired, tired, tired / Pretty, pretty rain / Why did you go / This I'll do my darling / Proud of you / No other love / Night has come / Don't stop / I promise you / My baby's gonna get it / Baby, I love you so / Once upon a time / I don't want to take a chance / Wanted / I'm beginning to think you care for me / Yes indeed / Don't keep it to yourself / I only have eyes for you / Once in a while / Good / Piccadilly / That's how I feel without you / Love birds / Don't cry baby / CC rider / Till then / Till then / Feeling Lo / Good looking baby / Along about sundown / You belong to me / Hold me, thrill me, kiss me / Teardrops on my pillow / Congratulations to someone / (Danger) Soft shoulders / Have you heard / Lonely wine / bad little girl / Dem days (Are gone forever) / One more time / Crying in the chapel / Crying in the chapel / Don't you think I out to know / Maybe you'll be there / Drowning every hope I ever had / In the Mission of St. Augustine / (Please) Write and tell me why (Version 1) / (Please) Write and tell me why (Version 2) / Robe of Cavalry / There's no one but you / Don't go to strangers / Secret love / In the chapel in the moonlight / Thank

the Lord, Thank the lord / Longing / If you believe / That's when the good Lord will smile / That's when the good Lord will smile / runaround / Count your blessings / Fair exchange / I love you mostly / I need you baby / Moody over you / Please sing my blues tonight / Cigareetos / Sitting here / Bring the money home / Angel / Don't cry / Sure fire / Danger / Crying in the chapel / Tell me so / At night / Forgive and forget / Come on home / First of summer / Panama Joe / Night and day / Shimmy time / So long
CD Set ______ BCD 15682
Bear Family / Mar '93 / Direct / Rollercoaster / Swift

SO MUCH FEELING
CD ______ BMCD 3054
Blue Moon / Jul '97 / Cadillac / Discovery / Greensleeves / Jazz Music / Jet Star / TKO Magnum

Orion

SOME THINK HE MIGHT BE KING ELVIS
That's alright Mama / Blue moon of Kentucky / Rockabilly rebel / See you later alligator / Suzie Q / I'm gonna be a wheel someday / Rockin' little angel / Crazy little thing called love / Long tall Sally / Memphis sun / Peggy Sue / Matchbox / There's no easy way / Baby please say yes / Born / If I can't have you / Ain't no good / Some you win, some you lose / Look me up (and lay it one me) / Old Mexico / Rainbow maker / Anybody out there / Midnight rendevous / Maybe tomorrow / She hates to be wrong / What now my love / Me and Bobby McGee
CD ______ BCD 15548
Bear Family / May '91 / Direct / Rollercoaster / Swift

Orion

1990
CD ______ RSCD 218
Keltia Musique / Feb '96 / ADA / Discovery

BLUE ROOM
CD ______ KMRS 207CD
Keltia Musique / Feb '94 / ADA / Discovery

Orlando, Johnny

LET'S GIVE LOVE A TRY
CD ______ ORCD 003
Orlando / Jan '96 / Jet Star

Orlando, Tony

KNOCK THREE TIMES (20 Greatest Hits)
Candida / Knock three times / I play and sing / Summer sand / What are you doing Sunday / Runaway / Happy together / Vaya con dios / You're a lady / Tie a yellow ribbon round the ole oak tree / Say, has anybody seen my sweet gypsy rose / Who's in the strawberry patch with Sally / Steppin' out (gonna boogie tonight) / Look in my eyes pretty woman / Love in your eyes / Up on the roof / Country / Look at you / You say the sweetest things / Cupid / He don't love you (like I love you)
CD ______ RMB 75085
Remember / Jan '96 / Total/BMG

Orleans

LET THERE BE MUSIC
Fresh wind / Dance with me / Time passes on / Your life my friend / Let there be music / Business as usual / Cold spell / Ending of a song / Give one heart / You've given me something
CD ______ 7559610282
Elektra / Jan '97 / Warner Music

WALKING AND DREAMING
CD ______ 7559610272
Elektra / Mar '97 / Warner Music

Orleans, Joan

AMAZING GRACE
CD ______ CD 321510
Koch International / Jul '97 / Koch

Ornberg, Tomas

THOMAS ORNBERG'S BLUE FIVE (Ornbergs, Tomas Blue Five)
CD ______ OP 8003CD
Opus 3 / Sep '91 / Direct / Jazz Music

Ornicar Big Band

JAZZ CARTOON
CD ______ BBRC 8902
Big Blue / Jun '92 / Harmonia Mundi

L'INCROYABLE HUCK
CD ______ BBRC 9106
Big Blue / Nov '92 / Harmonia Mundi

MAIS OU EST DONC ORNICAR
CD ______ BBRC 9208
Big Blue / Nov '92 / Harmonia Mundi

O'Rourke, Jim

DISENGAGE (2CD Set)
CD ______ STCD 048
Staalplaat / Feb '96 / Vital/SAM

Orphan Newsboys

LIVE AT LA
CD ______ JCD 250
Jazzology / Oct '93 / Jazz Music

Orphanage

AT THE MOUNTAINS OF MADNESS
CD ______ DSFA 1008CD
DSFA / Apr '97 / Plastic Head

BY TIME ALONE
CD ______ DSFA 1004CD
DSFA / Nov '96 / Plastic Head

OBLIVION
CD ______ DFSA 001CD
DSFA / Mar '96 / Plastic Head

ORPHANAGE
CD ______ DFSA 1001CD
DSFA / Jan '96 / Plastic Head

Orphaned Land

EL NORRA ALILA
CD ______ HOLY 018CD
Holy / Sep '96 / Plastic Head

SAHARA
CD ______ HOLY 7CD
Holy / Nov '94 / Plastic Head

Orpheus

BEST OF ORPHEUS, THE
Congress alley / Anatomy of I've never seen love like this / I've never seen love like this / Door knob / Can't find time to tell you / Can't find the time / Music machine / I'll stay with you / Never in my life / Dream / I'll fly / Just got back / Mine's yours / So far away in love / Borneo / She's not there / Love over there / Just a little bit / Walk away Renee / Roses / Magic air / Lovin' you / May I look at you / Brown arms in Houston / Me about you / I can make the sun rise / To touch our love again / By the size of my shoes / As they all fall / Joyful / Of enlightenment / I'll be there / Tomorrow man
CD ______ CDWIK 2
Big Beat / Aug '95 / Pinnacle

Orpheus Boys Choir

FAVOURITE CHRISTMAS (2CD Set)
CD Set ______ DCDCD 221
Castle / Nov '95 / BMG

Orquesta Almendra

MI ESCORPION 1946-1955
CD ______ TCD 065
Tumbao Cuban Classics / Jul '96 / Discovery

Orquesta Aragon

CHA CHA CHARANGA
CD ______ CD 071
Tumi / Apr '97 / Discovery / Stern's

LA CUBANISSIMA ORQUESTA ARAGON
CD ______ CD 0015
Egrem / Mar '96 / Discovery

LA INSUPERABLE
caserita villarena / Guajira con tumbao / Charlas del momento / Para bailar lo mismo me da / Baila carola / Si sabes bailar mi son / Pare cochero / Muy junto al corazon / Que tenga sabor / Un real de hielo / Busca los lentes / Aprende muchacho
CD ______ PSCCD 1001
Pure Sounds From Cuba / Feb '95 / Henry Hadaway / THE

Orquesta Casino De La Playa

ORQUESTA CASINO DE LA PLAYA
CD ______ HQCD 51
Harlequin / Aug '95 / Hot Shot / Jazz Music / Swift / Wellard

Orquesta Cuerdas Latinas

TANGOS INOLVIDABLES
A media luz / Sentimiento gaucho / El dia que me quieras / Quejas de bandoneon / Uno / Cuesta abajo / Yira yira / Mi noche triste / Volver / Cafetin de Buenos Aires / Vida mio / Confesion / Nostalgia / Jurame / Celos / El choclo
CD ______ CD 12546
Music Of The World / May '97 / ADA / Target/BMG

Orquesta Hasta Domingo

AMOR PURO
Amor puro y verdadero / Ay, mi amor / La necedad / Sediento de ti / Duende / Ya veras / Remedio no tengo / Ga met me mee / Spit spet / El compay
CD ______ AL 73023
A / Nov '96 / Cadillac / Direct

Orquesta Reve

LA EXPLOSION DEL MOMENTO
Rundera (son) / La gente no se puede aguantar (changui son) / De mayo / Changui clave / Mas viejo que ayer, mas joven que manana / El palo de anon / Que te importa a ti / Espero que pase el tiempo / You no quiero que seas celosa / El ron pa despue / Que cuento es ese / Que lastima me da contigo mi amor
CD ______ RWCD 4
Realworld / Jun '89 / EMI

Orquesta Romeu

BOCA LINDA
CD ______ TCD 076
Tumbao / Feb '97 / Discovery

Orquesta Tipica Victor

ORQUESTA TIPICA VICTOR 1926-1931
CD ______ HQCD 90
Harlequin / Jan '97 / Hot Shot / Jazz Music / Swift / Wellard

ORQUESTA TIPICA VICTOR 1926-1940
CD ______ EBCD 85
El Bandoneon / Jan '97 / Discovery

Orquestra Was

FOREVER'S A LONG, LONG TIME
CD ______ 5339152
Verve / Mar '97 / PolyGram

Orta, Paulo

GOOD NIGHT, BUENO NOCHE, BONNE NUIT
CD ______ 422493
New Rose / Nov '94 / ADA / Direct / Discovery

Ortega, Anthony

ANTHONY ORTEGA ON EVIDENCE
CD ______ EVCD 213
Evidence / Jan '94 / ADA / Cadillac / Harmonia Mundi

Ortega, Ginesa

SIENTO
CD ______ HMI 987011
Harmonia Mundi / May '97 / Cadillac / Harmonia Mundi

Orter, Hasan Cihat

INSPIRATION - TURKEY (Anatolian Folk Music)
CD ______ CDM 5658822
EMI Classics / Mar '96 / EMI

Ortolan

TRADITIONAL BRETON MUSIC
CD ______ KMCD 71
Keltia Musique / May '97 / ADA / Discovery

Orton, Beth

TRAILER PARK
She cries your name / Tangent / Don't need a reason / Live as you dream / Sugar boy / Touch me with your love / How far / Someone's daughter / I wish I never saw the sunshine / Galaxy of emptiness
CD ______ HVNLP 17CD
Heavenly / Oct '96 / 3mv/Pinnacle / BMG / Vital

Ory, Kid

CREOLE JAZZ BAND
Savoy blues / Good man is hard to find / Closer walk with thee / Shake that thing / Copenhagen / Royal garden blues / Mississippi mud / Roof blues / Indianaj
CD ______ GTCD 12008
Good Time Jazz / Oct '93 / Complete/ Pinnacle

ECHOES FROM NEW ORLEANS (Ory, Kid Creole Jazz Band)
CD ______ CD 53037
Giants Of Jazz / Sep '88 / Cadillac / Jazz Music / Target/BMG

INTRODUCTION TO KID ORY 1922-1944, AN
CD ______ 4023
Best Of Jazz / Sep '95 / Discovery

KID ORY 1944-1946
CD ______ AMCD 19
American Music / Jan '93 / Jazz Music

KID ORY AT THE CRYSTAL PIER 1947
CD ______ AMCD 90
American Music / Mar '97 / Jazz Music

KID ORY FAVOURITES
CD ______ FCD 60009
Fantasy / May '95 / Jazz Music / Pinnacle / Wellard

KID ORY PLAYS THE BLUES
CD ______ STCD 6035
Storyville / May '97 / Cadillac / Jazz Music / Wellard

KID ORY'S CREOLE JAZZ BAND (Ory, Kid Creole Jazz Band)
CD ______ DOCD 1002
Document / Nov '96 / ADA / Hot Shot / Jazz Music

KID ORY'S CREOLE JAZZ BAND 1944-1945
Creole song / Get out of here / Blue for Jimmie Noone / South / Panama / Under the bamboo tree / Careless love / Do what Ory say / Maryland my Maryland / Down home rag / 1919 Rag / Oh didn't he ramble / Ory's creole trombone / Weary blues / Maple leaf rag / Original dixieland one-step
CD ______ GTCD 12022
Good Time Jazz / Jul '94 / Complete/ Pinnacle

KID ORY'S CREOLE JAZZ BAND 1944-1946 (Ory, Kid Creole Jazz Band)
CD ______ 158872
Jazz Archives / Apr '97 / Discovery

LEGENDARY KID, THE
CD ______ GTCD 12016
Good Time Jazz / Oct '93 / Complete/ Pinnacle

RARE RECORDINGS (The Golden Age of Jazz)
CD ______ JZCD 368
Suisa / Jun '92 / Jazz Music / THE

THIS KID'S THE GREATEST (Ory, Kid Creole Jazz Band)
South Rampart street parade / Girls go crazy / How come you do me like you do / Four or five times / St. James infirmary / Bill Bailey, won't you please come home / Milneberg joys / Creole song / Bucket's got a hole in it / Creole love call / Ballin' the Jack / Aunt Hagar's blues
CD ______ GTCD 12045
Good Time Jazz / Oct '93 / Complete/ Pinnacle

O'Ryan

SOMETHING STRONG
CD ______ CDPAR 001
Parachute Music / Nov '95 / THE

Oryema, Geoffrey

BEAT THE BORDER
River / Kel kweyo / Market day / Lapwony / Umoja / Gang deyo / Hard labour / Payira wind / Lajok / Nomad
CD ______ CDRW 37
Realworld / Oct '93 / EMI

EXILE
Piny runa woko / Land of Anaka / Piri wango iya / Ye ye ye / Lacan woto kumu / Makambo / Jok omako nyako / Solitude / Lubanga / Exile
CD ______ CDRW 14
Realworld / Sep '90 / EMI

NIGHT TO NIGHT
Sardinia memories / Medieval dream / At my window / Careless world / Miracle man / Naa dream / LPJ Christine / Dancing steps / To the Metro / Gari Moshi / Passage at dusk / Sardinia memories (early evening) / On this night / Bye Bye Lady Dame
CD ______ CDRW 58
Realworld / Nov '96 / EMI

Os Ingenuos

CHOROS FROM BRAZIL
CD ______ NI 5338
Nimbus / Sep '94 / Nimbus

Osadebe, Chief Stephen Osita

KEDU AMERICA
CD ______ XENO 4044CD
Xenophile / Jun '96 / ADA / Direct

Osborne Brothers

BLUEGRASS 1956-1968 (4CD Set)
Who done it / Ruby are you mad / My aching heart / Teardrops in my eyes / Wild mountain honey / Down in the willow garden / Ho, honey ho / Della Mae / She's no angel (is this) / My destiny once more / Two lonely hearts / Lost highway / Love pains / It hurts to know / If you don't, somebody else will / Give this message to your heart / You'll never know / I love you only / It's just the idea / Lonely, lonely me / Sweethearts again / Blame me / There's a woman behind every man / Fair and tender ladies / Each season changes you / Black sheep returned to the fold / First fall of snow / Old hickory / Old Joe Clark / Big Ben / Billy in the lowground / John Henry / Banjo boy chrimes / Walking cane / Red wing / Seeing Nellie home / Jesse James / Cumberland gap / Lost indian / Poor old cora / Five days of heaven / Ain't gonna rain no mo / Banjo boys / Send me the pillow that you dream on / Worried man blues / May you never be alone / New partner / How's the world treating you / Night train to Memphis / Mule skinner blues / White lightning / Bluegrass music's really gone to town / Lovey told me goodbye / Ballad of Jed Clampett / Memories never die / Mule train / Are you mad / Sourwood mountain / Sweet thing / Take this hammer / Don't even look at me / Cuckoo bird / Bluegrass express / Me and

my old banjo / Pathway of teardrops / Gotta travel on / Salty dog blues / Kentucky / Bugle on the banjo (bugle call rag) / Cotton fields / Faded love / This heart of mine (can never say goodbye) / Charlie Cotton / I'll be alright tomorrow / Cut the cornbread / Hey hey bartender / Lonesome day / Big spike hammer / Memories / I know what it means to be lonesome / Up this hill and down in the pines / One tear / Making plans / Yesterday's gone / Footprints in the snow / Sure fire / Lonesome feeling / World of unwanted / Hard times / I'm leavin' / Kind of woman I got / One kiss away from loneliness / Let's say goodbye / Like we said hello / Someone before me / Walking the floor over you / Roll Muddy river / My favourite memory / Gal, you got a job to do / Rudy are you mad / Rocky top / When you wind down / Foggy mountain breakdown / Sisters (Billie Jean and Bonnie) / A-model / Lonesome road blues / Jessie James / Maiden's prayer / John Hardy / Little Willie / Hand me down my walking cane
CD Set **BCD 15598**
Bear Family / Mar '95 / Direct / Rollercoaster / Swift

BLUEGRASS 1968-1974 (4CD Set)
I'll never love another / I'll go steppin' too / Will you be lovin' another man / I'll never shed another tear / My little girl in Tenessee / Molly and Tenbrokks / Drivin' nails in my coffin / World of forgotten people / Cut the cornbread, mama / If I could count on you / I bowed on my knees and cried holy / Steal away and pray / Will you meet me over yonder / Where we'll never grow old / Medals for mother / Hide me O blest rock of ages / I pray my way out of trouble / How great thou art / What a friend we have in Jesus / Jesus sure changed me / Light at the river / That was yesterday / Working man / Banjo ringing Saturday night / Thanks for all the yesterdays / Midnight angel / Son of a sawmill man / No good sun of a gun / There'll be teardrops tonight / You win again / Blue moon of Kentucky / Where does the good times go / Put it off until tomorrow / Flyin' south / Will you visit me on Sundays / Nine pound hammer / When the grass grows over me / Tennessee hound dog / Somebody's back in town / Beneath still waters / Ruby are you mad / Siempre / Searching for yesterday / Listening to the rain / Georgia piney woods / Fightin' side of me / Let me be the first to know / Windy city / Kaw-Liga / My sweet love ain't around / You're running wild / My old Kentucky home / Tennesse stud / My heart would know / Muddy bottom / Colour me lonely / Take me home country roads / Tears are no strangers / Oh, the pain of loving you / Unfaithful one / Ballad of forty dollars / Tomorrow never comes / Sometimes you just can't win / Shelly's winter love / I wonder why you said goodbye / Tunnel of your mind / Eight more miles to Louisville / Love lifted me / Stand beside me, behind me / Miss you Mississippi / Teardrops will kiss the morning dew / Long lanky woman / Knoxville girl / Wash my face in the morning dew / Love's gonna live here / Today I started loving you again / Arkansas / Fireball mail / Midnight flyer / How long does it take (to be a stranger) / Blue heartache / Wabash cannonball / Try me one more time / Back to the country roads / Condition of Samuel Wilder's will / Tears / You're heavy on my mind / Checkin' her over / Lizzie Lou / Side saddle / High on a hill top / Sleep ridin' / Walk softly on the bridges / 7th of December / Fastest grass alive / Bluegrass melodies / We're holding on (to what we used to be) / Heartache looking for a home / MA special / I'm not that good at goodbye / Grandpa John / Little trouble / Born ramblin' man / Here today and gone tomorrow / El randa / In case you ever change your mind / Don't let the smokey mountains smoke get in / Summertime is past and gone / Highway headin' south
CD Set **BCD 15748**
Bear Family / Nov '95 / Direct / Rollercoaster / Swift

ONCE MORE VOL.1 & 2
CD **SHCD 2203**
Sugar Hill / Jan '97 / ADA / CM / Direct / Koch / Roots

Osborne, Jeffrey

JEFFREY OSBORNE
New love / Eeny meeny / I really don't need no light / On the wings of love / Ready for your love / Who you talkin' to / You were made to love / Ain't nothin' missin' baby / Congratulations
CD **CDMID 125**
A&M / Oct '92 / PolyGram

Osborne, Mary

MEMORIAL, A
CD **STCD 550**
Stash / '92 / ADA / Cadillac / CM / Direct / Jazz Music

Osborne, Mike

CASE FOR THE BLUES, A
CD **CCD 11037**
Crosscut / Jul '93 / ADA / CM / Direct

OUTBACK
CD **FMRCD 07**
Future / Oct '94 / ADA / Harmonia Mundi

SHAPES
CD **FMRCD 10**
Future / Mar '95 / ADA / Harmonia Mundi

Osbourne, Anders

WHICH WAY TO HERE
Pleasin' you / Favourite son / Burning on the inside / Limestone bay / What's going on here (Big lies) / Blame it on a few / Don't leave me / Brother, brother / Nothin' on / Place called home
CD **4616892**
Okeh/Epic / Jul '96 / Sony

Osbourne, Joan

EARLY RECORDINGS
Flyaway / Dreamin' about the day / His eyes are a blue million miles / Fingerprints / 4 camels / What you gonna do / Match burn twice / Billie listens / Wild world / Son of a preacher man / Get up Jack
CD **5342352**
Mercury / Nov '96 / PolyGram

RELISH
CD **5266922**
Mercury / Feb '96 / PolyGram

Osbourne, Johnny

BAD MAMA JAMA
CD **RNCD 2059**
Rhino / Jun '94 / Grapevine/PolyGram / Jet Star

DANCING TIME
CD **LG 21099**
Lagoon / May '94 / Grapevine/PolyGram

MR. BUDDY BYE
CD **VPCD 1446**
VP / Nov '95 / Greensleeves / Jet Star / Total/BMG

ROUGHER THAN THEM
CD **VYDCD 08**
Vine Yard / Sep '95 / Grapevine/PolyGram

SEXY THING
CD **LG 21092**
Lagoon / Apr '94 / Grapevine/PolyGram

SINGS ROOTS AND CULTURE (2CD Set) (Osbourne, Johnny & Bobby Melody)
Bring the sensie come: *Osbourne, Johnny* / Rub a dub session: *Osbourne, Johnny* / Bad ma ma jamma: *Osbourne, Johnny* / Can't buy my love: *Osbourne, Johnny* / Never ending love: *Osbourne, Johnny* / Let him go: *Osbourne, Johnny* / Going your way: *Osbourne, Johnny* / Looking at you: *Osbourne, Johnny* / Little girl come home: *Osbourne, Johnny* / Roots man music: *Bobby Melody* / Ram the session: *Bobby Melody* / Low the sensie man: *Bobby Melody* / Get up and dance: *Bobby Melody* / Come home: *Bobby Melody* / Carol say she love me: *Bobby Melody* / Your mine: *Bobby Melody* / Rock it a ready: *Bobby Melody* / Too fussy fussy: *Bobby Melody*
CD Set **MRCD 5**
Midnight Rock / Aug '97 / Grapevine/PolyGram / Jet Star

TRUTHS AND RIGHTS
CD **CDHB 3513**
Heartbeat / Jul '92 / ADA / Direct / Greensleeves / Jet Star

Osbourne, Ozzy

BARK AT THE MOON
Rock 'n' roll rebel / Bark at the moon / You're no different / Now you see it, now you don't / Forever / So tired / Waiting for darkness / Spiders
CD **4816782**
Epic / Nov '95 / Sony

BARK AT THE MOON/BLIZZARD OF OZ (2CD Set)
Rock 'n' roll rebel / Bark at the moon / You're no different / Now you see it (now you don't) / Forever / So tired / Waiting for darkness / Spiders / I don't know / Crazy train / Goodbye to romance / Dee / Suicide solution / Mr. Crowley / No bone movies / Revelation (Mother Earth) / Steal away (the night)
CD Set **4652112**
Epic / Oct '95 / Sony

BLIZZARD OF OZ
I don't know / Crazy train / Goodbye to romance / Dee / Suicide solution / Mr. Crowley / No bone movies / Revelation (mother earth) / Steal away (the night)
CD **4816742**
Epic / Nov '95 / Sony

DIARY OF A MADMAN
Over the mountain / Flying high again / You can't kill rock and roll / Believer / Little dolls / Tonight / SATO / Diary of a madman
CD **4816772**
Epic / Nov '95 / Sony

LIVE AND LOUD (2CD Set)
Intro / Paranoid / I don't want to change the world / Desire / Mr. Crowley / I don't know / Road to nowhere / Flying high again / Guitar solo / Suicide solution / Goodbye to romance / Shot in the dark / No more tears / Miracle man / Drum solo / War pigs / Bark at the moon / Mama I'm coming home / Crazy train / Black Sabbath / Changes
CD Set **4816762**
Epic / Nov '95 / Sony

NO MORE TEARS
Mr. Tinkertrain / I don't want to change the world / Mama I'm coming home / Desire / No more tears / SIN / Hellraiser / Time after time / Zombie stomp / AVH / Road to nowhere
CD **4816752**
Epic / Nov '95 / Sony

NO REST FOR THE WICKED
Miracle man / Devil's daughter (Holy war) / Crazy babies / Breakin' all the rules / Bloodbath in paradise / Fire in the sky / Tattooed dancer / Demon alcohol
CD **4816812**
Epic / Nov '95 / Sony

OZZ FEST LIVE, THE (Various Artists)
Loco: *Coal Chamber* / Ride thy neighbour: *Cellophane* / Broken foundation: *Earth Crisis* / Organized: *Powerman 5000* / Locust star: *Neurosis* / Replica: *Fear Factory* / These eyes: *Biohazard* / Attitude: *Sepultura* / Angel of death: *Slayer* / Perry Mason: *Osbourne, Ozzy*
CD **RAACD 001**
Red Ant / May '97 / Pinnacle

OZZMOSIS
Tomorrow / Dental / My little man / Mr. Jekyll doesn't hide / Old la / Tonight / Perry Mason / I just want you / Ghost behind my eyes / Thunder tonight / See you on the other side
CD **4810222**
Epic / Oct '95 / Sony

SPEAK OF THE DEVIL
Sympton of the universe / Snow blind / Black Sabbath / Fairies wear boots / War pigs / Wizard / Never say die / Sabbath bloody Sabbath / Iron man/Children of the grave / Paranoid
CD **4816792**
Epic / Nov '95 / Sony

TRIBUTE
I don't know / Crazy train / Believer / Mr. Crowley / Flying high again / Revelation (mother earth) / Steal away (the night) / Suicide solution / Iron man / Children of the grave / Paranoid / Goodbye to romance / No bone movies / Dee
CD **4815162**
Epic / Nov '95 / Sony

TRUST ME THE INTERVIEW
CD **CBAK 4062**
Baktabak / Feb '94 / Arabesque

ULTIMATE SIN
Ultimate sin / Secret loser / Never know why / Thank God for the bomb / Never / Lightning strikes / Killer of giants / Fool like you / Shot in the dark
CD **4816802**
Epic / Nov '95 / Sony

Osby, Greg

ART FORUM
Miss D'meena / Mood for thought / I didn't know about you / 2nd born to freedom / Dialectical interchange / Art forum / Don't explain / Half moon step / Perpetuity
CD **CDP 8373192**
Blue Note / Aug '96 / EMI

BLACK BOOK
Pillars / Mr. Freeman / Rocking chair / Buried alive / Poetry in motion / Black book / Smokescreen / Brewing poetry / Intuition / Fade to black medley
CD **CDP 8292662**
Blue Note / Oct '95 / EMI

GREG OSBY & SOUND THEATRE (Osby, Greg & Sound Theatre)
You big / Daigoro / Return to now / Shohachi bushi / Calculated risk / For real moments / Gyrhthmitoid / Knigrobade
CD **8344112**
jMT / Mar '93 / PolyGram

MINDGAMES
Dolemite / Mindgames / Thinking inside you / This is not a test / Excuse not / Mirror mirror / Silent attitude / Altered ego / All that matters / Chin lang
CD **8344222**
jMT / Feb '89 / PolyGram

SEASON OF RENEWAL
Sapphire / Enchantment / For the cause / Life's truth / Dialogue x / Season of renewal / Mischief makers / Word / Constant structure / Eye witness / Spirit hour
CD **8434352**
jMT / Apr '90 / PolyGram

Oscar, John

JOHN OSCAR, EDDIE MILLER & GEORGE NOBLE (Oscar, John & Eddie Miller/George Noble)
CD **DOCD 5191**
Document / Oct '93 / ADA / Hot Shot / Jazz Music

Oscar's Not Wild

WINDOW IN TIME, A
CD **ONW 1995**
Oscar's Not Wild / May '95 / Else

O'Shamrock, Barney

EVERGREEN ACCORDIAN
CD **MACCD 318**
Autograph / Aug '96 / BMG

FORTY SHADES OF GREEN
CD **MACCD 204**
Autograph / Aug '96 / BMG

IRISH ACCORDION, THE
Slievenamon / Old flames / Doonaree / Rose of Tralee / Rose of Mooncoin / Wild colonial boy / Irish American (medley) / How can you buy Killarney / Maggie / Fields of Athenry / Galway Bay / Molly Malone / Bunch of thyme / Danny boy / Hannigan's hooley / Banks of my own lovely Lee / When Irish eyes are smiling / Did your mother come from Ireland / Old bog road / Forty shades of green / Irish medley
CD **PLATCD 11**
Platinum / Jul '89 / Prism

O'Shea, Steve

IRISH PUB SONGS (47 Traditional Favourites)
Bould O'Donohue / Home boys home / Old woman from Wexford / Jug of punch / Brennan on the moor / Irish rover / Holy ground / Three lovely lassies / Charladies ball / Biddy Mulligan / Pride of Coombe / Harrigan / It's a long way to Tipperary / Dear ol'Donegal / Phil the fluter's ball / If you're Irish / Hannigan's hooley / Garden where the praties grow / Courtin' in the kitchen / Golden jubilee / It's a great day for the Irish / Stone outside Dan Murphy's door / Eileen O'Grady / Boys from County Armagh / Mick McGilligan's ball / Waxies dargle / Dicey Reilly / Down by the liffey side / My wild Irish rose / Nelly Kelly / Peggy O'Neill / Sweet Rosie O'Grady / Cockles and mussels / When Irish eyes are smiling / Danny Doogan's jubilee / Eileen Og / Star of CoDown / East-side west-side / Take me out to the ball game / Mary (a grand old name) / Who threw the overalls in Mrs Murphey's chowder / Boys from CoMayo / Lovely Leitrim / Homes of Donelgal / Where the three counties meet
CD **305722**
Hallmark / May '97 / Carlton

O'Shea, Tessie

I'M READY, I'M WILLING
CD **PASTCD 7078**
Flapper / Sep '95 / Pinnacle

Osibisa

AFRICAN FLIGHT
Time is right / Get up / Gumbe / Soldier boy / Jumbo / Abele / Kyrie Eleison / We gogo / Lost fisherman / Sakura
CD **AIM 1057**
Aim / Jun '96 / ADA / Direct / Jazz Music

CELEBRATION (The Best Of Osibisa)
CD **AIM 1036CD**
Aim / Oct '93 / ADA / Direct / Jazz Music

HEADS
Kokoroko / Wango wango / So so mi la so / Sweet America / Ye tie wo / Che che Kule / Mentumi / Sweet sounds / Do you know
CD **AIM 1047**
Aim / Apr '95 / ADA / Direct / Jazz Music

MONSORE
CD **RMCCD 0203**
Red Steel / Aug '96 / Pinnacle

MOVEMENTS
Ko ko Rio ko / Pata pata / Lion's walk / Inkosi sikeleli Africa / Movements / Drums 2001 carnival / Jambo / Life / Happy feeling rhymes
CD **INAK 8902CD**
In Akustik / Jul '97 / Direct / TKO Magnum

MYSTIC ENERGY
Meeting point / Celebration / Africa we go go / Orebo (magic people) / Moving on / Mama (I will be back) / Pata pata / Fatima / Obinkabimame
CD **MAUCD 614**
Mau Mau / Feb '92 / Pinnacle

OJAH AWAKE
Coffee song / Warrior / Flying bird / Cherry field / Dance the body music / Ojah awake / Keep on trying / Hamattan / Sakabo
CD **AIM 1056**
Aim / Jun '96 / ADA / Direct / Jazz Music

OSIBISA
Dawn / Music for Gong Gong / Ayiko Bia / Akwaaba / Oranges / Phallus C / Think about the people
CD **AIM 1045**
Aim / Apr '95 / ADA / Direct / Jazz Music

SUNSHINE DAY (Their Greatest Hits)
Sunshine day / Do it / Right now / Time is right / Coffee song / Sakura / Gumbe / Get up / Dance the body music / Densu / Warrior / Kolomashie / Ojah awake / Sakabo / Soldier / Keep on trying

CD 3036001122
Carlton / Jun '97 / Carlton

SUPERFLY TNT
CD RMCCD 0196
Red Steel / Aug '96 / Pinnacle

UNLEASHED IN INDIA
CD RMCCD 0200
Red Steel / May '96 / Pinnacle

WELCOME HOME
CD AIM 1055
Aim / Jun '96 / ADA / Direct / Jazz Music

WOYAYA
Beautiful seven / Y sharp / Spirits up above / Survival / Move on / Rabiatu / Woyaya
CD AIM 1046
Aim / Sep '96 / ADA / Direct / Jazz Music

Osiris

FUTURITY AND HUMAN DEPRESSIONS
CD SHARK 027CD
Shark / Jan '92 / Plastic Head

Oskar, Lee

BEST OF LEE OSKAR, THE
Promised land / Sunshine Kerl / San Francisco bay / Before the rain / More than words can say / Song for my son / Document / Feeling happy / My road
CD 74321305292
Avenue / Sep '95 / BMG

Oskorri

25 - KANTU URTE
CD KD 453CD
Elkar / May '97 / ADA

LANDALAN
CD KD 414CD
Elkar / Nov '96 / ADA

Osland, Miles

MY OL' KENTUCKY HOME (Osland, Miles Little Big Band)
CD SBCD 3015
Sea Breeze / Jun '96 / Jazz Music

Oslin, K.T.

MY ROOTS ARE SHOWING
Silver tongue and goldplated lies / Sand mountain blues / Hold watcha got / Tear time / (I'll see you in) Cuba / My baby comes back / Pathway of teardrops / Miss the Mississippi and you / Heart needs a home / Down in the valley
CD 07863669202
BNA / Sep '96 / BMG

Osmium

RISE UP
CD DMCD 1032
Demi-Monde / Feb '92 / RTM/Disc / TKO Magnum

Osmonds

VERY BEST OF THE OSMONDS
Crazy horses / Proud one / Make the world go away: *Osmond, Donny & Marie* / Love me for a reason / Young love: *Osmond, Donny* / When I fall in love: *Osmond, Donny* / Puppy love: *Osmond, Donny* / Down by the lazy river / Twelfth of never: *Osmond, Donny* / I'm leaving it (all) up to you: *Osmond, Donny & Marie* / Why: *Osmond, Donny* / One bad apple / Deep purple: *Osmond, Donny & Marie* / Too young: *Osmond, Donny* / Goin' home / Paper roses: *Osmond, Marie* / Morning side of the mountain: *Osmond, Donny & Marie* / Having a party / Let me in / I'm still gonna need you / I can't live a dream / Long haired lover from Liverpool: *Osmond, Jimmy* / Where did all the good times go: *Osmond, Donny* / Crazy horses
CD 5270722
Polydor / Apr '96 / PolyGram

Ossian

BEST OF OSSIAN, THE
St. Kilda wedding/Perrie werrie reel/Honourable Mrs. Moll's / 'S gann gunn d'irich mi chaoidh / Road to Drumleman / Sound of sleat/Aandowin' at the bow/Old reel / Will ye go to Flanders/Lord Lovat's lament / Duncan Johnstone/The duck/The curlew / Drunk at night, dry in the morning / I will set my ship in order / Rory Dall's sister's lament / Johnny Todd/Far from home / Jamie Raeburn/Broomielaw / Mrs. Stewart of Grantully/Be sud an'gille truagh/Harris danc
CD IRCD 023
Iona / Mar '94 / ADA / Direct / Duncans

BORDERS
Troy's wedding / Biddy from sligo / Rory Dall's sisters / Lament / Chairlie, oh Chairlie / I will set my ship in order / John Macdonald's / Sandpit / Bide ye yet / 'Neath the gloamin / Star at e'en / New house in St Peter's / Ewe wi' the crookit horn / Willie Murray's
CD IRCD 007
Iona / Aug '91 / ADA / Direct / Duncans

DOVE ACROSS THE WATER
Duck / Duncan Johnstone / Curlew / Braw sailin' on the sea / Drunk at night, dry in the morning / Will ye go to Flanders / Take the beggin / Mile Marbhaisg / Dove across the water / Iona theme / March: The cunning workmen / Columbia / Iona theme (reprise)
CD IRCD 004
Iona / Aug '91 / ADA / Direct / Duncans

LIGHT ON A DISTANT SHORE
Johnny Todd / Far from home / It was a' for our rightful king / Le chanson des livrees / Sun rises bright in France / Mrs. Stewart of Grantully / Be sud an' gille truagh / Calum Johnston's harris dance / Jamie Raeburn/ Broomielaw / Light on a distant shore / Arrival / New York harbour / At work on the land / In the new world
CD IRCD 009
Iona / Sep '91 / ADA / Direct / Duncans

OSSIAN
Corncrake / I hae a wife o'ma ain / Sitting in the stern of the boat / Ma rovin' eye / O mo dhuthaich (Oh my country) / Ossian's lament / Seventy second Highlanders' farewell to Aberdeen / Favourite dram / Ae fond kiss / Brose and butter / Monaghan jig / Jackson's bottle of brandy / Music of Spey / Let me in this ae night / Spoot O'Skerry / Willow Kishie / Simon's wart / Oidhche mhath leibh (goodnight to you)
CD SPRCD 1004
Springthyme / Apr '97 / ADA / CM / Direct / Duncans / Highlander / Roots

SEAL SONG
Sound of sleat / Aandowin' at the bow / Old reel / To pad the road wi, me / Coilsfield house / Heilandmen cam doon the hill / Thornton jig / Aye waukin' o / Corn rigs / Lude's supper / Road to Drumleman / Fisherman's song for attracting seals / Lieutenant / Maguire walking / Floor / Mull of the mountains
CD IRCD 002
Iona / Aug '91 / ADA / Direct / Duncans

ST. KILDA WEDDING
St Kilda wedding / Perrie werrie (reel) / Honourable Mr's Moll's reel / Give me a lass wi a lump o'land / Iomramh eadar il' a's uist / Dean cadalan samhach / Gala water David Manson / 'S gann gunn d'irich mi chaoidh / Farewell to whiskey / My love is the fair lad / Fourth bridge / Pretty peg / Braes o'strathblane / More grog coming / Tilley plump, DA / Foostra
CD IRCD 001
Iona / Aug '91 / ADA / Direct / Duncans

Ostanek, Walter

GERMAN BEER DRINKING SONGS
CD HADCD 191
Javelin / Nov '95 / Henry Hadaway / THE

Ostertag, Bob

TWINS (Ostertag, Bob & Otomo Yoshihide)
CD CMDD 00030
Creative Man / Jun '97 / ReR Megacorp

Ostroushko, Peter

HEART OF THE HEARTLAND
CD RHRCD 70
Red House / Oct '95 / ADA / Koch

PILGRIMS ON THE HEART ROAD
CD RHRCD 90
Red House / Jun '97 / ADA / Koch

SIUZ DUZ MUSIC
CD ROUC 0204
Rounder / Aug '95 / ADA / CM / Direct

O'Suilleabhain, Micheal

BETWEEN WORLDS
Oiche nollag/Christmas Eve / An tseangh liath/The old grey goose / An cailin deas cruite na mbo/The pretty milkmaid / Casadh na graige/The turning of the road / An mhaigdean cheansa/The gentle maiden / Fiach an mhada rua/The fox chase / Brian Boru / Idir eatarthu/Between worlds / Woodbrook / Ah, sweet dancer / Eleanor Plunkett / Heartwork / (Must be more) Crispy / River of sound / Lumen
CD CDVE 926
Venture / Aug '95 / EMI

CASADH/TURNING
By golly / Wexford carol / Brian Boru / Londubh agus an cheirseach / Blackbird and the thrush / Rolling wave / Casadh na graige / Turning of the road / King of the blind / Fairy queen / Planxty Irwin / Fanny power / Cearc agus coileach / Hen and the cock / Lady Maisterton
CD CDVE 904
Venture / Jun '91 / EMI

DOLPHIN WAY, THE
Christmas Eve / Plains of Boyle / Gentle fair Elly (Eiblhi gheal chiuin) / Old grey goose / Pretty milkmaid / Snowy breasted pearl / Carolan's concerto / Merrily kiss the quaker / Little fair haired child / Fox chase / Molly Halpin (Mollai ni ailpin) / Planxty Irwin / Gentle maiden
CD CDVE 1
Venture / '88 / EMI

GAISEADH / FLOWING
Woodbrook / Flowansionnamare / Eleanor Plunkett / (Must be more) Crispy / Through an eye of stone / At the still point of the turning world
CD CDVE 915
Venture / Nov '92 / EMI

MICHEAL O'SUILLEABHAIN
CD CEFCD 046
Gael Linn / Jan '92 / ADA / CM / Direct / Grapevine/PolyGram / Roots

OILEAN/ISLAND
Heartwork / Ah sweet dancer / Idir eatarthu / Between worlds / Carolan's farewell to music / Oilean/island / First movement / Second movement / Third movement / Ah sweet dancer (version)
CD CDVE 40
Venture / May '89 / EMI

O'Sullivan, Bernard

CLARE CONCERTINAS (O'Sullivan, Bernard & Tommy McMahon)
Babes in the wood / Cooraclare polka / Clare dragoons / Sandy groves of Piedmont / Humours of Ennistymon / Old torn petticoat / Tommy People's favourite / Mount Fabus hunt / Ollie Conway's selection / Kilrush races / Clogher reel / Burren reel / Bonaparte's retreat / Bonaparte's march / Barron's jig / Jackson's jig / Miltown jig / Rodney's glory / Tommy McMahon's reel / Over the waves / Girl I left behind me / Maggie in the wood / Martin Taltry's jig / Thomas Friel's jig / Joe Cunnean's jig / Sean Ryan's hornpipe / Danganella hornpipe / Job of journeywork / Ash plant / Maid of Mount Cisco
CD GL 3092CD
Green Linnet / Sep '94 / ADA / CM / Direct / Highlander / Roots

O'Sullivan, Gilbert

BY LARRY
CD PRKCD 25
Park / Mar '94 / Pinnacle

EVERY SONG HAS ITS PLAY
Overture / Showbiz / Dear dream / I wish I could cry / Nothing to fear / Pretty Polly / Can't find my way home / Dishonourable profession / You don't own me/If I know you / Nobody wants to know / Young at heart (we'll always remain) / I've never been short of a smile / Showbiz (reprise) / If you commence before the start
CD PRKCD 30
Park / Jun '95 / Pinnacle

HIMSELF
CD PRKCD 14
Park / May '94 / Pinnacle

I'M A WRITER NOT A FIGHTER
CD PRKCD 13
Park / May '94 / Pinnacle

LIVE IN JAPAN '93
CD BX 4232
BR Music / Mar '94 / Target/BMG

SOUNDS OF THE LOOP
Are you happy / Not that it bothers me / Sometimes / It's easy to see when you're blind / Having said that / Can't think straight / Best love I ever had / Divorce Irish style / Came and went / I'm not too young / I can give you / Can't think straight (Japanese version)
CD PRKCD 19
Park / Mar '93 / Pinnacle

O'Sullivan, Jerry

INVASION, THE
CD GLCD 1074
Green Linnet / Feb '92 / ADA / CM / Direct / Highlander / Roots

O'Sullivan, Maire

FROM THERE TO HERE
CD CIC 076CD
Clo Iar-Chonnachta / Nov '93 / CM

Oswald, John

DISCOSPHERE
CD RERJOCD
ReR/Recommended / Oct '96 / ReR Megacorp / RTM/Disc

PLEXURE
CD AVAN 016
Avant / Sep '93 / Cadillac / Harmonia Mundi

Other

OTHER, THE
CD DON 005CD
Honest Don's / Apr '97 / Greyhound / Plastic Head

Other Half

MR. PHARMACIST & THE LOST SINGLES
CD 842093
EVA / May '94 / ADA / Direct

Other Two

OTHER TWO AND YOU, THE
Tasty fish / Greatest thing / Selfish / Movin' on / Ninth configuration / Feel this love / Spirit level / Night voice / Innocence / Loved it (The other track)
CD 5200282
Factory / Nov '93 / PolyGram

Otherside

BURN BABY BURN
CD JRVCD 101
Vous / Oct '95 / Jet Star

Otis

ELECTRIC LANDLADY
CD CDVEST 73
Bulletproof / Jul '96 / Pinnacle

Otis, Johnny

JOHNNY OTIS SHOW/CREEPING WITH THE CATS (Otis, Johnny Show)
Midnight creeper (part 1) / Driftin' blues / Ali Baba's boogie / Let the sunshine in my life (once more) / Hey hey hey hey / Dog face (part 1) / Dog face (part 2) / Show me the way to go home / Sleepy shines butt shuffle / Organ grinder swing / Someday / Sadie / Butterball / Wa wa (part 1) / My eyes are full of tears / Turtle dove / Groove juice / Trouble on my mind / Number 69/ number 21 / Creeper returns / Stop, look and love me / Night is young (and you're so fine)
CD CDCHD 325
Ace / Jul '91 / Pinnacle

LET'S LIVE IT UP
Let's rock (let's surf awhile) / Hand jive one more time / It must be love / I say I love you / She's alright / Baby I got news for you / California mash (the hash) / Darling / I'll be true / Let's live it up / That's the chance you've got to take / Hey hey song / Somebody call the station / Early in the morning blues / You better love me / Queen of the twist / Oh my soul / Wilted rose buds / I know my love is true / Cold cold heart / Bye bye baby (I'm leaving you) / Yes / In the evening
CD CDCHARLY 269
Charly / Nov '92 / Koch

LIVE AT MONTEREY (Otis, Johnny Show)
Willie and the hand jive / Cry me a river / Cleanheads blues / I got a gal / Baby you don't know / Preacher's blues / Good rockin' tonight / Time machine / Margie's boogie / Little Esther's blues / Blowtop blues / T-Bone blues / Jelly jelly / Kidney stew / Things I used to do / RM blues / Shuggie's blues / You better look out / Goin' back to LA / Plastic man / Boogie woogie bye bye
CD EDCD 266
Edsel / May '88 / Pinnacle

NEW JOHNNY OTIS SHOW, THE
Drinkin' wine spo-dee-o-dee / Every beat of my heart / Jonella and Jack / What else can I do / Half steppin' woman / Why don't you do right / Big time scoop / I never felt this way before / Don't deceive me / So fine
CD ALCD 4726
Alligator / May '93 / ADA / CM / Direct

OTISOLOGY
Hand jive '85 / Roll with me Henry / Let's go Johnny / I'm ready for love / I'm scared of you / Fonkitup / I can't help myself / I wanna come over / Nut pony
CD CDMF 095
Magnum Force / Jan '96 / TKO Magnum

SPIRIT OF THE BLACK TERRITORY BANDS
CD ARHCD 384
Arhoolie / Apr '95 / ADA / Cadillac / Direct

Otis, Jon

SAND, THE MOON AND THE STARS, THE
CD LAKE 3060
Lakeside / Aug '95 / TKO Magnum

Otraslab

OTRASLAB
CD AS 017CD
Alley Sweeper / Mar '97 / Cargo

Ottawan

GREATEST HITS
CD DC 869792
Disky / Aug '96 / Disky / THE

VERY BEST OF OTTAWAN, THE
CD KWEST 5407
Kenwest / Feb '93 / THE

Otto, Hans

DAS BUCH DER KLANGE
CD Set CDKUCK 069/070
Kuckuck / '86 / ADA / CM

Ottopasuuna

SUOKAASUA
CD TEXCD 002
Texicalli / Nov '96 / Direct

SWAMP GAS
CD AMF 202
Amigo / Mar '96 / ADA / Cadillac / CM / Wellard

Otway, John

ALL BALLS AND NO WILLY/WHERE DID I GO RIGHT
In dreams / Too much air not enough oxygen / Telex / Montreal / Baby, it's the real thing / Middle of winter / Nothing's gone / Halloween / House is burning / Mass communication / Turn off your dream / Make good music / It's a pain / Blue eyes of the belle / Best dream / What a woman / Frightened and scared / Waiting / Hurting her more / Highwayman
CD TMC 9605
Music Corporation / Apr '96 / Pinnacle

COR, BABY THAT'S REALLY ME
Misty mountain / Gypsy / Murder man / Louisa on a horse / Really free / Geneve / Cheryl's going home / Beware of the flowers 'cause I'm sure they're going to get y / Baby's in the club / Best dream / Frightened and scared / DK 50/80 / Green grass of home / Turning point / Headbutts / Montreal / In dreams / Middle of winter / Jerusalem / Last of the mochicans / Racing cars (jet spotter of the track)
CD SBR 004CD
Strike Back / Oct '95 / Grapevine/PolyGram / Vital

LIVE
In dreams / Misty mountain / Cor baby that's really free / Bluey green / Racing cars / Beware of the flowers / Josephine / Louisa on a horse / Baby it's real thing / Two little boys / Best dream / Frightened and scared / Cheryl's goin' home / House of the rising sun / Geneve
CD OTCD 4001
Amazing Feet / Apr '95 / Grapevine/ PolyGram / Pinnacle / Vital

OTWAY & BARRETT/DEEP AND MEANINGLESS (Otway, John & Wild Willy Barrett)
CD TMC 9302
Music Corporation / Jan '96 / Pinnacle

TWO LITTLE BOYS
CD OTWAYS 1
Music Of Life / Sep '92 / Grapevine/ PolyGram

UNDER THE COVERS & OVER THE TOP
CD OTWAY 1CD
Music Of Life / Oct '92 / Grapevine/ PolyGram

Out Of Body Experience

ILLEGAL STATE OF MIND, AN
CD VP 17
Spinefarm / Feb '94 / Plastic Head

Out Of Darkness

CELEBRATION CLUB SESSION, THE
Walk on the water / Love to love / Worldpool / Cocaine / Valley (I'm gonna follow) / Child of the universe
CD PCDN 138
Plankton / Aug '93 / Plankton

Out Of My Hair

DROP THE ROOF
In the groove again / Safe boy / Wide together / Drop the roof / I'd rather be / Why it doesn't snow / Mary / Gracie's social please me's / Thieves in the fanclub / That's all / Mr. Jones / Wendy / Judas flip
CD 74321348372
RCA / Jun '97 / BMG

Out Ov Kontrol

OUT OV CONTROL
CD WRA 8121CD
Wrap / Apr '94 / Koch

Outback

BAKA
Air play / Baka / An dro nevez / Other side / Hold on / On the streets / Buenaventura / Dingo go
CD HNCD 1357
Hannibal / Apr '90 / ADA / Vital

DANCE THE DEVIL AWAY
CD HNCD 1369
Hannibal / Sep '91 / ADA / Vital

Outcast

OUT OF TUNE
CD TPLP 74CD
One Little Indian / Sep '96 / Pinnacle

Outcasts

BLOOD AND THUNDER
CD ROSE 16CD
New Rose / '84 / ADA / Direct / Discovery

OUTCASTS PUNK SINGLES COLLECTION
You're a disease / Don't want to be no adult / Frustration / Just another teenage rebel / Love is for sops / Cops are comin' / Self conscious over you / Love you for ever / Cyborg / Magnum force / Gangland warfare / Programme love / Beating and screaming part 1 / Beating and screaming part 2 / Mania / Angel face / Gangland warfare (version 2) / Nowhere left to run / Running's over, time to pray / Ruby / Seven deadly sins / Swamp fever / 1969 / Psychotic shakedown / Blue murder
CD CDPUNK 62
Anagram / Sep '95 / Cargo / Pinnacle

SELF CONSCIOUS OVER YOU
Self conscious over you / Clinical love / One day / Love is for sops / You're a disease / Love you for never / Princess grew up a frog / Cyborg / School teacher / Spiteful Sue / Cops are comin' / Just another teenage rebel
CD DOJOCD 182
Dojo / Feb '94 / Disc

Outhere Brothers

PARTY ALBUM
CD 0630127812
Eternal / Dec '95 / Warner Music

Outkast

ATLIENS
U may die / Two dope boyz in a cadillac / Atliens / Wheelz of steel / Jazzybelle / Elevators / Ova da woods / Babylon / Wailin' / Mainstream / Decatur psalm / Millenium / ET / 13th floor/growin' old / Elevators
CD 73008260322
Arista / Sep '96 / BMG

SOUTHERN PLAYALISTI CADILLACHMUSIZ
Peaches (Intro) / Myintrotoletuknow / Ain't no thang / Welcome to Atlanta / Southernplayalisticadillacchmusiz / Call of the wild / Player's ball (Original) / Claimin' true / Club donkey ass / Funky ride / Git up, git out / Dat true / Crumblin' erb / Hootie hoo / DEEP Player's ball (Reprise) / Flim flam
CD 73008260102
Arista / Jul '94 / BMG

Outlaws

DREAM OF THE WEST
Dream of the West / Outlaws / Husky team / Rodeo / Smoke signals / Ambush / Barbecue / Spring is near / Indian brave / Homeward bound / Western sunset / Tune for short cowboys
CD BGOCD 118
Beat Goes On / Sep '91 / Pinnacle

RIDE AGAIN (Singles A's & B's)
Swingin' low / Spring is near / Ambush / Indian brave / Valley of the Sioux / Crazy drums / Last Stage West / Ku-Pow / Sioux serenade / Fort Knox / Return of the outlaws / Texan spiritual / That set the Wild West free / Hobo / Law & order / Do-da-day / Keep a knockin' / Shake with me
CD SEECD 303
See For Miles/C5 / Oct '96 / Pinnacle

Outlaws

14 GREAT COUNTRY SONGS
CD PT 618001
Part / Jun '96 / Nervous

Outlines

BLIND ALLEY
CD L 8909302
Danceteria / Jan '90 / ADA / Plastic Head / Shellshock/Disc

Outrage

SPIT
Mr. Rightman / Faith / To you / Smoke / How bad / Key / Never make the same / Live my life / Inner strength / Eagle
CD 4509943082
WEA / Feb '94 / Warner Music

Outrageous Cherry

NOTHING'S GONNA CHEER YOU UP
CD 3G 18
Third Gear / Jun '97 / Cargo / Greyhound

Outrider

NO WAY OUT
Mourning rain / Turn away / Life's ballad / Love is killing me / Baby get back / I've been gifted by your love / My love will never die / There's no way out / Bigger than blue
CD CDSGP 001
Prestige / Aug '91 / Else / Total/BMG

Outside

ALMOST IN
CD DOR 18CD
Dorado / Dec '93 / Pinnacle

DISCOVERIES
First discovery / Sketchbook of a voyage / Moon after the fall / Parallel universe / Piano-scape / Finding ALH840001,65 / From here to infinity / Return
CD DOR 60CD
Dorado / Jun '97 / Pinnacle

ROUGH AND THE SMOOTH
CD DOR 43CD
Dorado / Jul '95 / Pinnacle

Outsiders

RIPPED SHIRT
CD PLAN 004CD
Planet / Mar '94 / Direct

Outsiders

CQ SESSIONS
CD CDP 1010DD
Pseudonym / Jun '97 / Greyhound

OUTSIDERS, THE
CD CDP 1021DD
Pseudonym / Jun '97 / Greyhound

Outskirts Of Infinity

INCIDENT AT PILATUS
CD DSKCD 002
Dark Skies / Aug '94 / RTM/Disc

STONE CRAZY
CD CDINF 002
Infinity / May '90 / Pinnacle

Oval

94 DISKONT
CD EFA 006632
Mille Plateau / May '95 / SRD

DISKONT
CD THRILL 036CD
Thrill Jockey / Dec '96 / Cargo / Greyhound

SYSTEMISCH
CD EFA 006592
Mille Plateau / Nov '94 / SRD

Ovans, Tom

DEAD SOUTH
Killing me / James Dean coming over the hill / 1945 / Here she comes / Folksinger / Rita, Memphis and the blues / Exile / Better off a lone / Real television / Pray for me / In the rain / Drowning man
CD FIENDCD 797
Demon / Jun '97 / Pinnacle

NUCLEAR SKY
CD FIENDCD 783
Demon / Jun '96 / Pinnacle

TALES FROM THE UNDERGROUND
Let it rain / Mr. Blue / Uncle Joe / Dance with me girl / Sailor / Angelou / Echoes of the fall / Lucky to be alive / Brakeman's blues / Real bono / Nine below zero / Waiting on you
CD SUR437CD
Survival / May '95 / ADA / Pinnacle

Overdose

PROGRESS OF DECADENCE
CD CDFLAG 83
Under One Flag / Nov '94 / Pinnacle

SCARS
CD CDMFN 213
Music For Nations / Nov '96 / Pinnacle

Overkill

FUCK YOU AND THEN SOME
Fuck you / Rotten to the core / Hammerhead / Use your head / Electro violence / Fuck you / Hole in the sky / Evil never dies / Rotten to the core / Fatal if swallowed / Answer / Overkill
CD SPV 08518722
SPV / May '97 / Koch / Plastic Head

HORRORSCOPE
Coma / Infectious / Blood money / Thanx for nothin' / Bare bones / Horrorscope / New machine / Frankenstein / Live young die free / Nice day... for a funeral / Solitude
CD 7567822832
Atlantic / Aug '91 / Warner Music

I HEAR BLACK
Dreaming in Columbian / I hear black / World of hurt / Feed my head / Shades of grey / Spiritual void / Ghost dance / Weight of the world / Ignorance and innocence / Undying / Just like you
CD 7567824762
Atlantic / Apr '93 / Warner Music

TRIUMPH OF WILL
CD SST 038CD
SST / Oct '93 / Plastic Head

Overli, Marit Haetta

OHCAME
CD ICD 942
Idut / Mar '96 / ADA

Overwhelming Colorfast

MOONLIGHT AND CASTANETS
CD HED 052
Headhunter / Oct '96 / Cargo

Owen, Mark

GREEN MAN
Green man / Clementine / Child / Are you with me / Naturally / Ask him to / Backpocket and me / Move on / Secondhand wonderland / My love / I am what I am / Is that what it's all about
CD 74321435142
RCA / Dec '96 / BMG

Owen Money

MADE IN WALES
Made in Wales: *Money, Owen* / Keep on running: *Money, Owen* / Wide eyed and legless: *Money, Owen* / Thank you: *Money, Owen* / No matter what: *Money, Owen* / Please send me daffodils: *Money, Owen* / Kiss: *Money, Owen* / My special angel: *Money, Owen* / Home again: *Money, Owen* / Working man: *Money, Owen* / No matter how hard it gets: *Money, Owen* / Myfanwy: *Money, Owen*
CD CDWM 111
Westmoor / Apr '97 / Target/BMG

Owens, Buck

BLUE LOVE
House down the block / You're for me / Down on the corner of love / Blue love / It don't show on me / Three dimension love / Why don't Mommy stay with Daddy and me / When I hold you / Country girl / I will love you always / Right after the dance / I'm gonna blow / Higher and higher and higher / Honeysuckle / Learnin' dirty tracks
CD CDSD 055
Sundown / Jan '93 / TKO Magnum

BUCK OWENS
CD DS 010
Desperado / Jun '97 / TKO Magnum

BUCK OWENS STORY VOL.1 1956-1964
CD PRS 23017
Personality / Feb '95 / Target/BMG

BUCK OWENS STORY VOL.2 1964-1968
CD PRS 23018
Personality / Feb '95 / Target/BMG

BUCK OWENS STORY VOL.3 1969-1989
CD PRS 23019
Personality / May '95 / Target/BMG

LIVE AT CARNEGIE HALL 1966 (Owens, Buck & The Buckaroos)
Act naturally / Together again / Love's gonna live here / Medley / Medley / Waitin' in your welfare line / Buckaroo / Streets of Laredo / I've got a tiger by the tail / Fun 'n' games / Twist and shout / Medley
CD CMFCD 012
Country Music Foundation / Jan '93 / ADA / Direct

Owens, Calvin

THAT'S YOUR BOOTY
CD CTC 203
Coast To Coast / Mar '96 / Grapevine/ PolyGram

TRUE BLUE
True blue / Hot burning fever / Don't you want a man like me / Texas stomp / Sitting here / Sweet meat / Cherry red / Woke up screaming / Lick or split / Deviation / Don't you want a woman like me / Dreams come true
CD IMP 707
Top Cat / Sep '95 / Discovery

Owens, Jack

IT MUST HAVE BEEN THE DEVIL (Owens, Jack & Bud Spires)
CD TCD 5016
Testament / Mar '95 / ADA / Koch

Owens, Jay

BLUES SOUL OF JAY OWENS
Come to my house / Steppin' stone / Bottom line / Chasing my dreams / Lake city, fla / Wishing well / Back row / Why do you treat me this way / Can't do the same thing again / Crosstown love / Missing you blues / My kind of woman / We're human
CD 4509965962
WEA / Jan '95 / Warner Music

Owens, Tex

CATTLE CALL
Cattle call / Pride of the prairie / Dude ranch party (part 1) / Dude ranch party (part 2) / Rockin' alone in an old rocking chair / Two sweethearts / By the rushing waterfall / Give me the plains at night / Let me ride the range / Porcupine serenade / Lost indian call / Grandpa and the lovebug / Daddy's old rocking chair / I'll be happy / Lonesome for you / Red roses bring memories of you / Yesterday's roses / Lonely for you, oh so long / Cowboy call / While I'm nearly home / Don't hide your tears darling / Cattle call (theme song)
CD BCD 15777
Bear Family / Nov '94 / Direct / Rollercoaster / Swift

Oxbow

LET ME BE A WOMAN
CD ____ **EFA 127201**
Crippled Dick Hot Wax / Apr '95 / SRD

Oxford Pro Musica Singers

AMONG THE LEAVES SO GREEN
Among the leaves so green / Bushes and briars / Black sheep / Bobby Shaftoe / Dashing away / Early one morning / Greensleeves / Londonderry air / My sweetheart's like Venus / O waly, waly / She's like the swallow / Sourwood mountain / Afton water / Brigg fair / Ca' the yowes / Faithful Johnny / I love my love / Strawberry fair / Swansea Town / Keel row / Oak and the ash / Sailor and young Nancy / Three ravens / Turtle dove / Yarmouth fair
CD ____ **PROUCD 137**
Proudsound / Apr '95 / Conifer/BMG

IN THE MOOD
Ain't misbehavin' / Autumn leaves / Begin the beguine / Blue moon / Continental / Deep purple / I got rhythm / Laura / Let's do it / Over the rainbow / She was beautiful / Smoke gets in your eyes / Summertime / 'S wonderful / Tea for two / Night and day / In the mood
CD ____ **PROUCD 141**
Proudsound / May '96 / Conifer/BMG

Oxford, Vernon

KEEPER OF THE FLAME (5CD Set)
Watermelon time in Georgia / Roll big wheels roll / Woman let me sing you a song / Move to town in the fall / Nashville women / Goin' home / Let's take a cold shower / Field of flowers / Hide / Stone by stone / Behind every good man there's a woman / Forgetfulness for sale / Baby sister / Goin' home / Honky tonk girls / Babies, stop your crying / Blues come in / Treat yourself right / Little sister throw your red shoes away / Old folk's home / That's the way I talk / Touch of God's hands / Come back and see us / This woman is mine / Mansion on the hill / Wedding bells / Don't let a little thing like that / You win again / Touch of God's hands / Come back and see us / Nashville women / What will I live on tomorrow / Wine, women and songs / I'd rather see you wave goodbye / This is where I came in / What color is wind / Hazard County Saturday night / Rise of Seymour Simmons / How high does the cotton grow mama / I've got to get Peter off your mind / We came awfully close to sin / Love and Pearl and me / She's always there / I wish you would leave me alone / We sure danced us some goodn's / Woman you've got a hold of me / Soft and warm / Surprise birthday party / Shadows of my mind / Country singer / Anymore / God keeps the wild flowers blooming / Giving the pill / Beautiful junk / Mowing the lawn / Wait a little longer please Jesus / Clean your own tables / Your waiting me is gone / Don't be late / Leave me alone with the blues / One more night to spare / Only the shadows know / Redneck / Good old fashioned Saturday night honky / Midnight memories / Red hot women (and ice cold beer) / Backslider's wine / Redneck roots / Songs that losers choose / Images / Brother jukebox / Kaw-Liga / Your cheatin' heart / Hey good lookin' / When God comes and gathers his jewels / Baby we're really in love / Wedding bells / Cold cold heart / I saw the light / Settin' the woods on fire / I can't help it / You win again / Jambalaya / I'm so lonesome I could cry / Mansion on the hill / Funeral / Nobody's child / Who were Ann and Louis Adams / There's a better place / Joanna / Mommy do you think I'll get to heaven / State of depression / Woman / Maggie the baby is crying / If I had my wife to love over / I'll forgive you for the last time / If there was no country music / Cattle call / I love to sing / Walkin' my blues away / If kisses could talk / Gonna ease my worried mind / No one else is listening / Turn the record over / I think living is sweet / Blanket of stars / Great Stoneface / Rainy day / Somebody to love me / Let your light shine / Bringing Mary home / Bad moon risin' / Letters have no arms / Mother's not dead, she's only sleeping / Honky tonk troubles / Daughter of the vine / They'll never take her love from me / Angel band / Have you loved your woman today / Lonesome rainin' city / Veil of white lace / Sweeter than the flowers / Busiest memory in town / Wings of a dove / This world holds nothin' since you're gone / Family bible / Always true / Where the soul of man never dies / Lord, I've tried everything but you / Better way of life / Uncloudy day / His and hers / House of gold / Baby sister / Sad situation / Dust on the bible / Early morning rain / Last letter / You're the reason / Are they gonna make us outlaws again / Long black veil / I feel chained
CD Set ____ **BCD 15774**
Bear Family / Oct '95 / Direct / Rollercoaster / Swift

Oxley, Pete

EAST COAST JOYS
Prelude / Feel free to fast forward / Sun at night / Being there / Hazelwaltz / Alchemie / Step inside love / Jutta and Ina's delightful discourse / Hercule, j'avance / Without a map / East coast joys
CD ____ **33JAZZ 034**
33 Jazz / Apr '97 / Cadillac / New Note/ Pinnacle

Oxley, Tony

ENCHANTED MESSENGER, THE (Oxley, Tony Celebration Orchestra)
CD ____ **1212842**
Soul Note / Dec '96 / Cadillac / Harmonia Mundi / Wellard

Oxymoron

PACK IS BACK, THE
CD ____ **KOCD 085**
Knock Out / Jun '97 / Cargo

O'Yaba

GAME IS NOT OVER, THE
CD ____ **SHCD 45005**
Greensleeves / Apr '93 / Jet Star / SRD

ONE FOUNDATION
CD ____ **FLTRCD 523**
Flame Tree / Feb '94 / Pinnacle

Oyewole, Abiodun

25 YEARS
When the revolution comes / 25 Years / Brothers working / Son's rising / Festival / Dread brother / Brown sugar / Sample this
CD ____ **RCD 10335**
Black Arc / Feb '96 / Vital

Oyster Band

DEEP DARK OCEAN
Sail on by / Little brother / Only when you call / Native son / Not like Jordan / North star / Milford haven / Tory / Be my luck / No reason to cry / Drunkard's waltz
CD ____ **COOKCD 128**
Cooking Vinyl / Aug '97 / Vital

DESERTERS
CD ____ **COOKCD 041**
Cooking Vinyl / Mar '92 / Vital

HOLY BANDITS
When I'm up I can't get down / Road to Santiago / I look for you / Gone west / We shall come home / Cry cry / Here's to you / Moving on / Ramblin' Irishman / Fire is burning / Blood wedding
CD ____ **COOKCD 058**
Cooking Vinyl / Feb '95 / Vital

LITTLE ROCK TO LEIPZIG
Jail song two / Gonna do what I have to do / Galopede / I fought the law / New York girls / Oxford girl / Too late now / Red barn stomp / Coal not dole / Johnny Mickey Barry's
CD ____ **COOKCD 032**
Cooking Vinyl / Apr '90 / Vital

RIDE
Too late now / Polish plain / Heaven to Calcutta / Tincans / This year, next year / New York girls / Gamblers / Take me down / Cheekbone City / Love vigilantes / My dog / Sins of a family
CD ____ **COOKCD 020**
Cooking Vinyl / Feb '95 / Vital

SHOUTING END OF LIFE, THE
We'll be there / Blood red roses / Jam tomorrow / By northern lights / Shouting end of life / Long dark street / Our lady of the battle / Everywhere I go / Put out the lights / Voices / Don't slit your wrists / World turned upside down
CD ____ **COOKCD 091**
Cooking Vinyl / Jul '97 / Vital

STEP OUTSIDE
Hal-an-Tow / Flatlands / Another quiet night in England / Milly Bond / Bully in the alley / Day that the ship goes down / Gaol song / Old dance / Bold Riley / Ashes to ashes
CD ____ **BAKECD 001**
Cooking Vinyl / May '90 / Vital
CD ____ **COOKCD 001**
Cooking Vinyl / Jun '97 / Vital

TRAWLER
Hal-an-tow / Another quiet night in England / We could leave right now / Blood wedding / Oxford girl / Granite years / Ramblin' Irishman / Love vigilantes / Polish plain / 20th April / Lost and found / One green hill / Coal not dole / Bells of rhymney
CD ____ **COOKCD 078**
Cooking Vinyl / Oct '94 / Vital

WIDE BLUE YONDER
Generals are born again / Pigsty Billy / Oxford girl / Following in father's footsteps / Lost and found / Coal creek mine / Rose of England / Careless life / Early days of a better nation / Lakes of Coolfin / Between the wars / Hal-an-tow / Flatlands / Another quiet night in England
CD ____ **COOKCD 006**
Cooking Vinyl / Aug '87 / Vital

Oz

ROLL THE DICE
CD ____ **BMCD 11**
Black Mark / '92 / Plastic Head

Ozark Mountain Daredevils

ARCHIVE ALIVE
CD ____ **ACH 80007**
Archive / Jul '97 / Greyhound

MODERN HISTORY
Everywhere she goes / Love is calling / I'm still dreaming / Turn it up / True love / Lonely knight / Over again / Heating up / River / Heart of the country / Wild the days
CD ____ **CDRR 303**
Request / Jan '90 / Jazz Music / Wellard

Ozkan, Talip

ART OF THE TANBUR, THE
CD ____ **C 560042**
Ocora / May '94 / ADA / Harmonia Mundi

MYSTERIES OF TURKEY
CD ____ **CDT 115**
Topic / Apr '93 / ADA / CM / Direct

Ozone, Makoto

NATURE BOYS
CD ____ **5312702**
Verve / Jun '96 / PolyGram

STARLIGHT
Starlight / Riverside expressway / Night spark / 03 / I love to be face to face (Malta) / Sky / Spring stream / Chega de saudade / Moonstone / Tenderly
CD ____ **JD 3323**
JVC / Nov '90 / Direct / New Note/Pinnacle / Vital/SAM

Ozric Tentacles

ARBORESCENCE
CD ____ **DOVECD 7**
Dovetail / Jun '94 / Pinnacle

BECOME THE OTHER
CD ____ **DOVECD 8**
Dovetail / Oct '95 / Pinnacle

BITS BETWEEN THE BITS
CD ____ **OTCD 6**
Dovetail / Feb '94 / Pinnacle

EROLAND
CD ____ **DMCD 1024**
Demi-Monde / Feb '92 / RTM/Disc / TKO Magnum

ERPLAND
CD ____ **DOVECD 1**
Dovetail / Jul '90 / Pinnacle

ERPSONGS
CD ____ **OTCD 1**
Dovetail / Feb '94 / Pinnacle

JURASSIC SHIFT
CD ____ **DOVECD 6**
Dovetail / Apr '93 / Pinnacle

LIVE ETHEREAL CEREAL
CD ____ **OTCD 3**
Dovetail / Feb '94 / Pinnacle

LIVE UNDERSLUNKY
CD ____ **DOVECD 5**
Dovetail / Apr '92 / Pinnacle

SLIDING GLIDING WORLDS
CD ____ **OTCD 5**
Dovetail / Feb '94 / Pinnacle

STRANGEITUDE
CD ____ **DOVECD 3**
Dovetail / Sep '91 / Pinnacle

TANTRIC OBSTACLES
CD ____ **OTCD 2**
Dovetail / Feb '94 / Pinnacle

THERE IS NOTHING
CD ____ **OTCD 4**
Dovetail / Feb '94 / Pinnacle

P

P

P
I save cigarette butts / Zing splash / Michael Stipe / Oklahoma / Dancing queen / John Glenn / Mr. Officer / White man sings the blues / Die Anne / Scrapings from ring / Deal
CD ______ **CDPCS 7379**
Capitol / Feb '96 / EMI

P-Hux

DELUXE
CD ______ **95022**
Black Olive / Jul '97 / Greyhound

Pablo All Stars

MONTREUX 1977
Cote D'Azur / Pennies from heaven / Camba de orfue / God bless the child / Sweethearts on parade
CD ______ **OJCCD 380**
Original Jazz Classics / Apr '93 / Complete/ Pinnacle / Jazz Music / Wellard

Pablo, Augustus

AUGUSTUS PABLO PRESENTS ROCKERS INTERNATIONAL VOL.1 (Various Artists)
El Rockers: *Jah Iny* / El rockers: *Pablo, Augustus* / El Rockers: *Pablo, Augustus* / El rockers: *Rockers All Stars* / Three men in a truck back: *Williams, Delroy* / Free Jah Jah children: *Jah Bull* / Cool melody: *Pablo, Augustus* / Rastaman: *Earl 16* / Peaceful man dub: *Rockers All Stars* / Protect them: *Reid, Norris* / Give a little bit: *Te Track* / Destiny: *Pablo, Augustus* / People of the world: *Sisters Jam*
CD ______ **GRELCD 145**
Greensleeves / Nov '92 / Jet Star / SRD

AUGUSTUS PABLO PRESENTS ROCKERS INTERNATIONAL VOL.2 (Various Artists)
Away with your fussing and fighting: *Delgado, Junior* / Selassi i veranda: *Jah Levi* / Zion a fe lion: *Jah Levi* / King David's melody: *Pablo, Augustus* / Cassava piece: *Pablo, Augustus* / 555 Crown Street: *Pablo, Augustus* / Solomon dub: *Pablo All Stars* / Rutland close: *Pablo All Stars* / False rasta: *Miller, Jacob* / Each one teach one: *Miller, Jacob* / Black force: *Reid, Norris* / Straight a yard: *Rockers All Stars* / Zimbian style: *Rockers All Stars* / Changing world version: *Rockers All Stars* / Changing world: *Earl 16*
CD ______ **GRELCD 168**
Greensleeves / Nov '92 / Jet Star / SRD

AUTHENTIC GOLDEN MELODIES
CD ______ **CDRP 002**
Rockers International / Oct '92 / Greensleeves / Jet Star

BLOWING WITH THE WIND
Blowing with the wind / Twinkling star / Ancient harmonies / Creation blues / Zion UFO / Eastern code / Twenty one years later / First world call / This song / Drums to the king
CD ______ **GRELCD 149**
Greensleeves / Sep '90 / Jet Star / SRD

DUBBING IN AFRICA
CD ______ **CRCD 68**
Charm / Jun '97 / Jet Star

EAST MAN DUB
Only Jah Jah dub / Eastman dub / Look within dub / Isn't it time / It up to Jah dub / Big yard connection / African step / Original scientist / Corner stone
CD ______ **GRELCD 109**
Greensleeves / '88 / Jet Star / SRD

HEALER DUB
CD ______ **CDRP 015**
Rockers Productions / Oct '96 / Greensleeves / Jet Star

HEARTICAL CHART
CD ______ **CDRP 004**
Rockers Productions / May '93 / Greensleeves / Jet Star

ITAL DUB
Big rip off / Roadblock / Curly dub / Well red / Gun trade / Shake up / Hillside airstrip / Barbwire disaster / Mr. Big / Ell's move / House raid / Shake down
CD ______ **TRCD 805**
A&A Productions / Jun '95 / Jet Star

KING DAVID'S MELODY
King David's melody / Zion high / Mr. Bassie / West Abyssinia / Israel in harmony / Rockers mood / Sufferer's trod / Revelation time / Selfish youth / Corner stone dub / Kent Road
CD ______ **GRELCD 170**
Greensleeves / Apr '92 / Jet Star / SRD

ONE STEP DUB
In the red dub / Hanging dub / Riot dub / One step dub / Zion way dub / Sunshine dub / Dubbing King James / Rastaman dub / Good looking dub / Night patrol dub
CD ______ **GRELCD 157**
Greensleeves / Apr '96 / Jet Star / SRD

ORIGINAL ROCKERS VOL.1
Rockers dub / Up Warrikka Hill / Cassava piece / Tubby's dub song / Jah dread / Brace a boy / Thunder clap / Park Lane special / New style / AP special
CD ______ **GRELCD 8**
Greensleeves / Aug '97 / Jet Star / SRD

PABLO & FRIENDS
CD ______ **RASCD 3220**
Ras / Nov '92 / Direct / Greensleeves / Jet Star / SRD

PRESENTS AUTHENTIC GOLDEN MELODIES
CD ______ **CDRP 003**
Rockers Productions / Nov '92 / Greensleeves / Jet Star

PRESENTS CULTURAL SHOWCASE
CD ______ **CDRP 001**
Rockers Productions / Nov '92 / Greensleeves / Jet Star

PRESENTS KING TUBBY
CD ______ **RNCD 2082**
Rhino / Dec '94 / Grapevine/PolyGram / Jet Star

PRESENTS ROOTS DJ'S FROM THE 1970'S AND 1980'S
Take it easy / Dub / El rocker / Rocking dub / False rumour / Real rock / Zion a fe lion / Bob shuffle lion dub / Guide I Jah / Lion of Judah dub / Let Jah be praised / Braces a boy
CD ______ **ABB 131CD**
Big Cat / Jun '97 / 3mv/Pinnacle

REBEL ROCK RADIO
CD ______ **CDHB 34**
Heartbeat / Aug '88 / ADA / Direct / Greensleeves / Jet Star

RISING SUN
Dub wiser / Hopi land / Rising sun / Fire red / Jah wind / Pipers of Zion / Day before the riot / African frontline / Melchesedec (the high priest) / Signs and wonders
CD ______ **SHCD 44009**
Shanachie / Jun '91 / ADA / Greensleeves / Koch

ROCKERS MEET KING TUBBY IN A FIRE HOUSE
CD ______ **SHANCD 43001**
Shanachie / Apr '88 / ADA / Greensleeves / Koch

THIS IS AUGUSTUS PABLO (Rebel Rock Reggae)
CD ______ **HBCD 34**
Heartbeat / '88 / ADA / Direct / Greensleeves / Jet Star
CD ______ **ARM 2001**
Above Rock / Jul '95 / SRD

THRILLER
Pablo nah jester / Fat girl Jean / Marcus Garvey / Rocky road / Skibo road / Thriller / Pablo in red / Everything I own / Last of the jestering / Striker / Always dub / Cultural dub / Rough dub / Gamblin' dub / Sleng teng in dub
CD ______ **PRCD 605**
President / Sep '96 / Grapevine/PolyGram / President / Target/BMG

Pablo's Eyes

YOU LOVE CHINESE FOOD
CD ______ **XCD 031**
Extreme / May '95 / Vital/SAM

Pace Bend

LIKE A DRINK
CD ______ **CMR 2012**
Blue Rose / Nov '95 / 3mv/Pinnacle

Pacheco, Johnny

PACHECO'S PARTY
Dile / Los compadres seguiran / La esencia del guaguanco / Latin gravy / Noche buena (Christmas eve) / Son del Callejon / Tengo uncarinito / Samrose como el guarapo / Tu barriga / El polverete / Amor en el arena / Danza del cocoye / Como cambian los tiempos / Anoranzas / Asi son bonco
CD ______ **CDHOT 512**
Charly / Sep '94 / Koch

Pacheco, Tom

BLUE FIELDS
CD ______ **FJ 2007**
Fjording / Aug '96 / ADA

EAGLE IN THE RAIN
CD ______ **TPCD 1**
Round Tower / Feb '94 / Avid/BMG

SUNFLOWERS AND SCARECROWS
CD ______ **RTMCD 30**
Round Tower / Apr '91 / Avid/BMG

TALES FROM THE RED LAKE
CD ______ **RTMCD 42**
Round Tower / Feb '93 / Avid/BMG

Pacher, Yves

MUSIQUE BUISSONNIERE
CD ______ **Y 225210CD**
Silex / Oct '93 / ADA / Harmonia Mundi

Pachinko

BEHIND THE GREEN PACHINKO
CD ______ **VIRUS 190CD**
Alternative Tentacles / Dec '96 / Cargo / Greyhound / Pinnacle

Packes, Jimmy

AXXE TO GRIND
CD ______ **AZJ 0012**
Azimuth Jag / Feb '94 / Plastic Head

Pacou

SYMBOLIC WARFARE
CD ______ **EFA 292692**
Tresor / Jul '97 / 3mv/BMG / Prime / SRD

Paczynski, Georges

8 YEARS OLD (Paczynski/Levinson/ Jenny-Clark)
CD ______ **BBRC 9209**
Big Blue / Jan '93 / Harmonia Mundi

Padilla, Pedro

VUELVA EN ALAS DEL PLACER (Padilla, Pedro Y Su Conjunto)
Llevame al cielo / En mi suelo Borincano / Dolores / Donde tu iras / Ay Maria / El dia que yo muera / Juramento / Triste y olvidado / La arboleda / Volver volver / Si yo tuviera un millon / Atardecer jibaro
CD ______ **ROUCD 5003**
Rounder / Jun '97 / ADA / CM / Direct

Padmanabhan, Raajeswari

MUSIC OF THE VEENA VOL.2
CD ______ **VICG 50382**
JVC World Library / Mar '96 / ADA / CM / Direct

Padre, Miguel

BRAZIL PERCUSSIONS
CD ______ **KAR 978**
Kardum / May '96 / Discovery

Paduart, Ivan

WHITE NIGHTS
Ecoline / White nights / Steps in the snow / Fairy tale / Heartsong / Between us / Guignolet kirsch / Closed eyes
CD ______ **AL 73061**
A / Nov '96 / Cadillac / Direct

Page 12

REVENGE AND MORE
Revenge and more
CD ______ **EFA 125342**
Celtic Circle / Dec '95 / SRD

Page, Betty

BETTY PAGE, DANGER GIRL (Burlesque Music)
Teledrama / Killer / Mood one / Sweet and sour / Agent who / Path of crime / Sidewalk blues / Driving drums / Dark room / Johnny's dive / Big strip / Tearaway brass / Bass designs / Riviera chase / Danger girl / Ton up / Three crimes / Crime action / Something cool / Depression / Fall out / Top secret
CD ______ **QDKCD 012**
QDK Media / Oct '96 / Direct

TRIBUTE TO BETTY PAGE (Various Artists)
CD ______ **CLP 99642**
Cleopatra / Jul '97 / Cargo / Greyhound / Plastic Head / RTM/Disc / SRD

Page, Hot Lips

CLASSICS 1938-1940
CD ______ **CLASSICS 561**
Classics / Oct '91 / Discovery / Jazz Music

CLASSICS 1940-1944
CD ______ **CLASSICS 809**
Classics / Apr '95 / Discovery / Jazz Music

DOCTOR JAZZ VOL.6
CD ______ **STCD 6046**
Storyville / Jul '96 / Cadillac / Jazz Music / Wellard

HOT LIPS PAGE
CD ______ **CD 14558**
Jazz Portraits / Jul '94 / Jazz Music

HOT LIPS PAGE STORY, THE
CD ______ **158892**
Jazz Archives / Jun '97 / Discovery

Page, Jimmy

NO INTRODUCTION NECESSARY (Page, Jimmy & Friends)
Lovin' up a storm / Everything I do is wrong / Think it over / Boll weevil song / Livin' lovin' wreck / One long kiss / Dixie fried / Down the line / Fabulous / Breathless / Rave on / Lonely weekends / Burn up
CD ______ **CDTB 007**
Magnum Music / Apr '93 / TKO Magnum

NO QUARTER (Page, Jimmy & Robert Plant)
Nobody's fault but mine / Thank you / No quarter / Friends / Yallah / City don't cry / Since I've been loving you / Battle of Evermore / Wonderful one / Wah wah / That's the way / Gallows pole / Four sticks / Kashmir
CD ______ **5263622**
Fontana / Oct '94 / PolyGram

OUTRIDER
Wasting my time / Wanna make love / Writes of winter / Only one / Liquid mercury / Hummingbird / Emerald eyes / Prison blues / Blues anthem
CD ______ **GED 24188**
Geffen / Nov '96 / BMG

SESSION MAN VOL.1
CD ______ **AIPCD 1041**
AIP / Jun '97 / Greyhound / RTM/Disc / Shellshock/Disc

SESSION MAN VOL.2
CD ______ **AIPCD 1053**
AIP / Jun '97 / Greyhound / RTM/Disc / Shellshock/Disc

SMOKE AND FIRE
Wailing sounds / Because I love you / Flashing lights / Gutty guitar / Would you believe / Smoke and fire / Thumping beat / Union Jack car / One for you baby / LONDON / Brightest lights / Baby come back
CD ______ **CDTB 2022**
Thunderbolt / '86 / TKO Magnum

Page, Larry

KINKY MUSIC (Page, Larry Orchestra)
Tired of waiting / Come on now / Something better beginning / You really got me / Don't ever change / Got my feet on the ground / All day and all of the night / One fine day / I go to sleep / Just can't go to sleep / Revenge / I took my baby home / Everybody's gonna be happy
CD ______ **MONDE 17CD**
Cherry Red / Oct '93 / Pinnacle

MUSIC FOR NIGHT PEOPLE (Page, Larry Orchestra)
CD ______ **MCCD 246**
Music Club / Jun '96 / Disc / THE

UP, UP AND AWAY (Page, Larry Orchestra)
I say a little prayer / Les bicyclettes de Belsize / Up, up and away / Music for night people / From Larry with love / Zabadak / Light my fire / Girl on a string / We can work it out / Erotic soul / House of the rising sun / Venus / Slinky thighs / Tired of waiting for you
CD ______ **SUMCD 4127**
Sound & Media / Jun '97 / Sound & Media

Page, Patti

WOULD I LOVE YOU
Now that I'm in love / Would I love you / Send my baby back to me / This is my song / Breeze / My lonely world / (How much is that) doggie in the window / I let a song go out of my heart / Whole world is singing my song / What a dream / Don't get around much anymore / Cross over the bridge / Steam heat / It's a wonderful world / I cried
CD ______ **JASCD 315**
Jasmine / May '94 / Conifer/BMG / Hot Shot / TKO Magnum

Page, Stu

CAN'T SING THE BLUES (Page, Stu Band)

CD MTNCD 001
Milltown / Sep '96 / Grapevine/PolyGram / PolyGram

Page, Tommy

FROM THE HEART
Whenever you close your eyes / Under the rainbow / Madly in love / You are my heaven / I still believe (prelude) / I still believe in you and me / Written all over my heart / My shining star / Can't get you outta my mind / I'll never forget you / Never gonna fall in love again
CD 7599265832
WEA / Jul '91 / Warner Music

Pahinui Brothers

PAHINUI BROTHERS, THE
Mele of my tutu e / Isa lei / Jealous guy / O kamawailua lani / My old friend the blues / Do you love me / Kowali / Waimamalo blues / Panin pua kea / Come go with me / Henehene ko aka
CD 01005820982
Private Music / Aug '92 / BMG

Pahinui, Cyril

6 & 12 STRING SLACK KEY GUITAR
CD DCT 38010CD
Dancing Cat / Mar '96 / ADA

Pahinui, Gabby

GABBY PAHINUI HAWAIIAN BAND
Alhoa ka manini / Ku 'U pua lei mokihana / Pu' uanahulu / Moani ke'ala / Blue Hawaiian moonlight / Moonlight lady / E nihi ka hele / Hawaiian love / Wahini U'I / Oli komo - chant / Ipo lei manu
CD EDCD 241
Edsel / Sep '91 / Pinnacle

Paice, Ashton, Lord

BBC RADIO 1 IN CONCERT
CD SFRSCD 030
Strange Fruit / Jul '97 / Pinnacle

Paich, Marty

ARRANGER, CONDUCTER, PIANO
It don't mean a thing if it ain't got that swing / Just in time / Moanin' / I've grown accustomed to her face / It's alright with me / Things ain't what they used to be / Move / I love Paris / No more / Love for sale / Warm valley / Groovin' high / Four brothers / Walkin' / Doggin' around / Swingin' the blues / All the things you are / Marty's blues
CD CD 53251
Giants Of Jazz / Jan '96 / Cadillac / Jazz Music / Target/BMG

PICASSO OF BIG BAND JAZZ, THE
From now on / Walkin' on home / Black rose / Tommy's toon / New soft shoe / What's new / Easy listnin' / Martyni time / Nice and easy
CD CCD 79031
Candid / Feb '97 / Cadillac / Direct / Jazz Music / Koch / Wellard

Paige, Elaine

CHRISTMAS
Walking in the air / Peace on Earth / Father Christmas eyes / Ave Maria / Wishing on a star / Santa Claus is coming to town / Coventry carol / Coldest night of the year / Light of the stable / I believe in Father Christmas / Thirty two feet and eight little tails / Winter's tale
CD 2292420402
WEA / Jul '95 / Warner Music

CINEMA
Windmills of your mind / Out here on my own / Prisoner / Sometimes / Do you know where you're going to / Up where we belong / Unchained melody / Bright eyes / Alfie / Missing / Way we were / Rose
CD 2292405112
WEA / Jul '95 / Warner Music

ELAINE PAIGE
If you don't want my love for you / Far side of the bay / So sad (to watch good love go bad) / Secrets / I want to marry you / Second time / Falling down to earth / Hot as sun / Last one to leave / How the heart approaches what it yearns / Miss my love today
CD 2292462042
WEA / Jul '95 / Warner Music

ENCORE
As if we never said goodbye / Perfect year / Memories / I know him so well / Another suitcase in another hall / I don't know how to love him / On my own / I dreamed a dream / Mon dieu / Hymne a l'amour / Non je ne regrette rien / With one look / Don't cry for me Argentina
CD 0630104762
East West / Nov '95 / Warner Music

LOVE CAN DO THAT
Love can do that / Oxygen / Heart don't change my mind / Same train / You don't own me / I only have eyes for you / Well almost / True colours / If I loved you / He's out of my life / Only the very best / Grow young
CD 74321228802
RCA / Sep '94 / BMG

PERFORMANCE
I have dreamed / Anything goes / Heart don't change my mind / Another suitcase in another hall / Rose / Love hurts / What'll I do/Who / I only have eyes for you / He's out of my life / I know him so well / Don't cry for me Argentina / Memory / Memory (reprise)
CD 74321446802
Camden / Feb '97 / BMG

PIAF
La vie en rose / La goualante du pauvre jean / Hymne a l'amour / C'est a hambourg / Les trois cloches / Mon dieu / Les amants d'un jour / La belle histoire d'amour / Je sais comment / Non, je ne regrette rien / L'accordeoniste
CD 4509946412
WEA / Dec '96 / Warner Music

QUEEN ALBUM, THE
Bohemian rhapsody / Kind of magic / Love of my life / Who wants to live forever / My melancholy blues / You take my breath away / Las palabras de amor (the words of love) / One year of love / Is this the world we created / Radio ga ga
CD CDVIP 106
Virgin VIP / Nov '93 / EMI

ROMANCE AND THE STAGE
They say it's wonderful / I got lost in his arms / As time goes by / Feeling good / More than you know / With every breath I take / Mad about the boy / I gaze in your eyes / Kismet suite / Stranger in paradise / He's in love / This is my beloved / Long before I knew you / How long has this been going on / Smoke gets in your eyes / September song / Song of a summer night
CD 74321136152
RCA / Sep '94 / BMG

STAGES
Memory / Be on your own / Another suitcase in another hall / Send in the clowns / Running back for more / Good morning starshine / Don't cry for me Argentina / I don't know how to love him / What I did for love / One night only / Losing my mind / Tomorrow
CD K 2402282
WEA / Jul '95 / Warner Music

Pain

PAIN
CD NB 223CD
Nuclear Blast / Jun '97 / Plastic Head

Pain Jerk

SNAKECHARMER'S BEAUTIFUL DAUGHTER (Pain Jerk & Dogliveroil)
CD BWCD 1
Bentley Welcomes Careful Drivers / May '97 / Cargo

Pain Teens

BEAST OF DREAMS
CD TR 41CD
Trance / Nov '95 / SRD

DESTROY THE LOVER
CD TR 17CD
Trance / Jun '93 / SRD

STIMULATION FESTIVAL
CD TR 10CD
Trance / Jul '92 / SRD

Paine Brothers

HONKY HELL
CD ROSECD 291
New Rose / Sep '92 / ADA / Direct / Discovery

Paingod

PAINGOD
CD CM 77163CD
Century Media / Apr '97 / Plastic Head

Painkiller

BURIED SECRETS
CD MOSH 062CD
Earache / Oct '92 / Vital

Paintin' By Numbers

BREAKBEAT SESSIONS VOL.1
CD 343722
Koch Dance Force / Mar '96 / Koch

Paisley Abbey Choir

SINGALONG CAROLS
Hark the herald angels sing / First noel / Ding dong merrily on high / On high / Away in a manger / See in yonder manger low / Holly and the ivy / Child in a manger / Good King Wenceslas / I saw three ships / O little town of Bethlehem / Once in Royal David's City / Unto us a boy is born / Angels from the realms of glory / Deck the halls with boughs of holly / Silent night / O come all ye faithful (adeste fidelis)
CD RECD 500
REL / Oct '96 / CM / Duncans / Highlander

Pajama Slave Dancers

FULL METAL UNDERPANTS
CD ROSE 271CD
New Rose / Dec '91 / ADA / Direct / Discovery

Pajeaud, Willie

WILLIE PAJEAUD AND HIS NO. BAND '55 (Pajeaud, Willie & His No. Band '55)
CD 504CD 31
504 / Feb '92 / Cadillac / Jazz Music / Target/BMG / Wellard

Pakkos, Gustaf

PAKKOS AND HJORT (Pakkos, Gustaf & Ole Hjort)
CD GCD 28
Grappa / May '96 / ADA

Pal, Asit

RHYTHMICALLY YOURS
CD CDJP 1038
Jazz Point / Jan '94 / Cadillac / Harmonia Mundi

Palace

ARISE THEREFORE
CD WIGCD 24
CD WIGCD 24X
Domino / Apr '96 / Vital

LOST BLUES AND OTHER SONGS (Palace Music)
Ohio river boat song / Riding / Valentine's day / Trudy dies / Come in / Little blue eyes / Horses / Stable will / Untitled / O how I enjoy the light / Marriage / West palm beach / Gulf shores / (End of) travelling / Lost blues
CD WIGCD 33
Domino / Apr '97 / Vital

PALACE BROTHERS (Palace Brothers)
CD WIGCD 14
Domino / Sep '94 / Vital

THERE IS NO ONE WHAT WILL TAKE CARE OF YOU (Palace Brothers)
CD ABBCD 050
Big Cat / Aug '95 / 3mv/Pinnacle

VIVA LAST BLUES (Palace Brothers)
More brother rides / Viva ultra / Brute choir / Mountain low / It's I who have left them / Work hard, play hard / New partner / Cat's blues / We all will ride / Old Jerusalem
CD WIG CD21
Domino / Aug '95 / Vital

Palace Songs

HOPE
CD WIGCD 18
Domino / Nov '94 / Vital

Palacio, Andy

KEIMOUN
Raga puriyan kalyan
CD INT 31712
Intuition / Jul '97 / New Note/Pinnacle

Paladin

PALADIN/CHARGE (2CD Set)
CD Set RMCCD 0202
Red Steel / Jul '96 / Pinnacle

Paladins

LET'S BUZZ
CD ALCD 4782
Alligator / May '93 / ADA / CM / Direct

MILLION MILE CLUB
Follow your heart / Everytime I see her / Lets buzz / 15 Days / Keep lovin' me / Kiddeo / Years since yesterday / Big Mary's / What side o' the door / One step
CD CAD 6015CD
4AD / Oct '96 / RTM/Disc

PALADINS
Hold on / Make it / Honky tonk all night / Let's go / Lucky man / Lover's rock / Daddy yar / Come on home / Bad case of love / Let 'er roll / Slow down
CD CDWIK 64
Big Beat / Apr '88 / Pinnacle

TICKET HOME
CD SECT2 10003
Sector 2 / Jul '94 / Cargo / Direct

YEARS SINCE YESTERDAY
CD ALCD 4762
Alligator / Apr '93 / ADA / CM / Direct

Palata Singers

SWING LOW (The 20th Anniversary)
CD FA 415
Fremeaux / Nov '96 / ADA / Discovery

Palatino

PALATINO
Dawn / Aleas / Calabrian nights / Variazione tre / Animal love / Interlude / Truncs e petulunta / Glenn's walk / 20 Small cigars / Lulu is back in town
CD LBLC 6585
Label Bleu / Jul '96 / New Note/Pinnacle

Pale Fountains

FROM ACROSS THE KITCHEN TABLE
Shelter / Stole the love / Jean's not happening / Bicycle thieves / Limit / Twenty seven ways to get back home / Bruised arcade / These are the things / It's only hard / From across the kitchen table / Hey / September sting
CD CDV 2333
Virgin / Jul '89 / EMI

PACIFIC STREET
Reach / Something on my mind / Unless / Southbound excursion / Natural / Faithful pillow (part 1) / You'll start a war / Beyond Friday's field / Abergele next time / Crazier / Faithful pillow (part 2)
CD CDV 2274
Virgin / Nov '89 / EMI

Pale Saints

COMFORTS OF MADNESS
Way the world is / Sea of sound / Little hammer / Deep sleep for Steven / Fell from the sun / Time thief / You tear the world in two / True coming dream / Insubstantial / Language of flowers / Sight of you
CD CAD 0002CD
4AD / Feb '90 / RTM/Disc

IN RIBBONS
CD CAD 2004CD
4AD / Mar '92 / RTM/Disc

SLOW BUILDINGS
King Fade / Angel (Will you be my) / One blue hill / Henry / Under your nose / Little gestures / Song of Solomon / Fine friend / Gesture of a fear / Always I / Suggestion
CD CAD 4014CD
4AD / Aug '94 / RTM/Disc

Paley's Watch

NOVEMBER
CD PCDN 144
Plankton / Aug '94 / Plankton

Palinckx

BORDER (Live In Zurich)
CD INTAKTCD 043
Intakt / May '97 / Cadillac

Palladinos

TRAVELLING DARK
In this place here / Northern flashes / I'll keep you in mind / Rocking the black road / Down at the station / I won't be going South (for a while) / Boom town / Saturday night / In my city heart / Moon on the motorway
CD 5402442
A&M / May '94 / PolyGram

Pallas

KNIGHTMOVES TO WEDGE
Stranger / Throwing stones at the wind / Win or lose / Imagination / Ratracing / Sanctuary / Just a memory / Dance through the fire
CD CENCD 002
Centaur / Oct '93 / Pinnacle

SENTINEL
Shock treatment / Cut and run / Arrive alive / Rise and fall (part one) / East west / March on Atlantis / Rise and fall (part two) / Heart attack / Atlantis / Ark of infinity
CD CENCD 001
Centaur / Oct '93 / Pinnacle

Palm, Anna

ARRIVING AND CAUGHT UP
Lake / Limbs / She's alive / Mumma / Air for Sharon / Masquerade / In need / Bloom / I can
CD PALMCD 1
Voiceprint / Feb '97 / Pinnacle

Palm Court Orchestra

MUSIC FOR TEA DANCING (20 Strict Tempo Favourites)
Tea for two / Wunderbar / It's a lovely day today / El choclo / Always true to my fashion / Getting to know you / Why do I love you / Can't help lovin' dat man / Hey there / Surrey with the fringe on top / You'll never walk alone / Mon amour / You can't get a man with a gun / Anything you can do / Best thing for you / Minette / Sheik of Araby / Kansas City / Breeze and I / Dinah
CD 306912
Hallmark / Jun '97 / Carlton

Palm Court Theatre Orchestra

PICNIC PARTY, THE
There's a ring around the Moon / Black eyes / Grasshoppers dance / Silver bird / Fiddlesticks rag / I'm forever blowing bubbles / Petite tonkinoise / Whistle for me / In the shadows / Polly / Down in Zanzibar / Ragtime bass player / Two little sausages / In a Persian market
CD ______ CHAN 8437
Chandos / Mar '87 / Chandos

Palm Skin Productions

REMILIXIR
Condition Red / Fair seven / How the West was won / Osaka / Trouble rides a fast horse / Flipper / Introduction to falling / New love games for your monkey / Meantime / Kitty's adventures in meat / Walking through water / Beethoven Street
CD ______ CDHUT 37
Hut / Oct '96 / EMI

Palma, Triston

TRISTON PALMA MEETS MICHAEL PALMER (2CD Set) (Palma, Triston & Michael Palmer)
Joker smoker: *Palma, Triston* / Babylon: *Palma, Triston* / Sad news: *Palma, Triston* / Peace and love in the ghetto: *Palma, Triston* / Ghetto living: *Palma, Triston* / Please stop your lying: *Palma, Triston* / Sing along: *Palma, Triston* / First time girl: *Palma, Triston* / Lover man: *Palma, Triston* / Ghetto dance: *Palmer, Michael* / Jamaica land: *Palmer, Michael* / Robbery: *Palmer, Michael* / She afe get it: *Palmer, Michael* / Cool nugh: *Palmer, Michael* / I want to dance with you: *Palmer, Michael* / Come natural: *Palmer, Michael* / Wha dis a guan: *Palmer, Michael* / Happy merry Christmas: *Palmer, Michael*
CD Set ______ MRCD 3
Midnight Rock / Jun '97 / Grapevine/PolyGram / Jet Star

Palmer, Holly

HOLLY PALMER
CD ______ 9362462812
Warner Bros. / Sep '96 / Warner Music

Palmer, John

BEYOND THE BRIDGE
CD ______ SCD 28023
Sargasso / Mar '97 / SRD

Palmer, Lillie

BUTTERFLY ZONE
CD ______ FIENDCD 778
Demon / Jun '96 / Pinnacle

Palmer, Michael

JOINT FAVOURITES (Palmer, Michael & Half Pint)
Crazy girl: *Half Pint* / What's going down: *Half Pint* / Tell me this tell me that: *Half Pint* / Day I can't forget: *Half Pint* / Freedom fighters: *Half Pint* / You're safe: *Palmer, Michael* / Belly lick: *Palmer, Michael* / Read your Bible: *Palmer, Michael* / I don't know why: *Palmer, Michael* / Saw you at the dance: *Palmer, Michael*
CD ______ GRELCD 89
Greensleeves / Mar '95 / Jet Star / SRD

Palmer, Robert

ADDICTIONS VOL.1
Bad case of lovin' you (Doctor Doctor) / Pride / Addicted to love / Sweet lies / Woke up laughing / Looking for clues / Some guys have all the luck / Some like it hot / What's it take / Every kinda people / Johnny and Mary / Simply irresistable / Style kills
CD ______ CID 9944
Island / Oct '89 / PolyGram

ADDICTIONS VOL.1/VOL.2 (2CD Set)
Bad case of lovin' you / Pride / Addicted to love / Sweet lies / Woke up laughing / Looking for clues / Some guys have all the luck / Some like it hot / What's it take / Every kinda people / Johnny and Mary / Simply irresistible / Style kills / Remember to remember / Sneakin' Sally through the alley / Maybe it's you / You are in my system / I didn't mean to turn you on / Can we still be friends / Men smart, women smarter / Too good to be true / Every kinda people / She makes my day / Best of both worlds / Give me an inch / You're gonna get what's coming / I dream of wires / Silver gun
CD Set ______ ISDCD 2
Island / Nov '95 / PolyGram

ADDICTIONS VOL.2
Remember to remember / Sneakin' Sally through the alley / Maybe it's you / You are in my system / I didn't mean to turn you on / Can we still be friends / Man smart, woman smarter / Too good to be true / Every kinda people / She makes my day / Best of both worlds / Give me an inch / You're gonna get what's coming / I dream of wires / Silver gun
CD ______ IMCD 246
Island / Mar '97 / PolyGram

CLUES
Looking for clues / Sulky girl / Johnny and Mary / What do you care / I dream of wires / Woke up laughing / Not a second time / Found you now
CD ______ IMCD 21
Island / Jun '89 / PolyGram

DON'T EXPLAIN
Your mother should have told you / Light years / You can't get enough of a good thing / Dreams to remember / You're amazing / Mess around / Happiness / History / I'll be your baby tonight / Housework / Mercy mercy me/I want you / Don't explain / Aeroplane / People will say we're in love / Not a word / Top 40 / You're so desirable / You're my thrill
CD ______ CDGOLD 1054
EMI Gold / Oct '96 / EMI

DOUBLE FUN
Every kinda people / Best of both worlds / Where can it go / Night people / Love can run faster / You overwhelm me / You really got me / Your gonna get what's coming
CD ______ IMCD 23
Island / Jun '89 / PolyGram

HEAVY NOVA
Simply irresistable / More than ever / Change his ways / Disturbing behaviour / Early in the morning / It could happen to you / She makes my day / Between us / Casting a spell / Tell me I'm not dreaming
CD ______ CDEMD 1007
EMI / Feb '94 / EMI

HONEY
Honey A / Honey B / You're mine / Know by now / Nobody but you / Love takes time / Honeymoon / You blow me away / Close to the edge / Closer to the edge / Girl u want / Wham bam boogie / Big trouble / Dreams come true
CD ______ CDEMD 1069
EMI / Sep '94 / EMI

PRESSURE DROP
Give me an inch / Work to make it work / Back in my arms / Riverboat / Pressure drop / Here with you tonight / Trouble / Fine time / Which of us is the fool
CD ______ IMCD 24
Island / Aug '89 / PolyGram

PRIDE
Pride / Deadline / Want you more / Dance for me / You are in my system / It's not difficult / Say you will / You can have it (take my heart) / What you waiting for / Silver gun
CD ______ IMCD 22
Island / Jun '89 / PolyGram

RIDIN' HIGH
Love me or leave me / Tender trap / You're my thrill / Want you more / Baby, it's cold outside / Aeroplane / Witchcraft / What a little moonlight can do / Don't explain / Chance / Good goody / Do nothin' 'til you hear from me / Honeysuckle rose / No not much / Riding high / Hard head
CD ______ CDEMD 1038
EMI / Sep '92 / EMI

RIPTIDE
Riptide / Hyperactive / Addicted to love / Trick bag / Get it through your heart / I didn't mean to turn you on / Flesh wound / Discipline of love / Riptide (reprise)
CD ______ IMCD 25
Island / Jun '89 / PolyGram

SECRETS
Bad case of lovin' you (Doctor Doctor) / Too good to be true / Can we still be friends / In walks love again / Mean ol' world / Love stop / Jealous / Under suspicion / Woman you're wonderful / What's it take / Remember to remember
CD ______ IMCD 26
Island / Aug '89 / PolyGram

SNEAKIN' SALLY THROUGH THE ALLEY
Sailing shoes / Hey Julia / Sneakin' Sally through the alley / Get outside / How much fun / From a whisper to a scream / Through it all there's you
CD ______ IMCD 20
Island / Aug '89 / PolyGram

SOME PEOPLE CAN DO WHAT THEY LIKE
One last look / Keep in touch / Man smart, woman smarter / Spanish moon / Have mercy / Gotta get a grip on you (part 2) / What can you bring me / Hard head / Off the bone / Some people can do what they like
CD ______ IMCD 69
Island / Nov '89 / PolyGram

VERY BEST OF ROBERT PALMER, THE
Addicted to love / Bad case of loving you / Simple irresistable / Get it on / Some guys have all the luck / I didn't mean to turn you on / Looking for clues / U R in my system / Some like it hot / Respect yourself / I'll be your baby tonight / Johnny & Mary / She makes my day / Know by now / Every kinda people / Mercy mercy me/I want you
CD ______ CDEMD 1088
EMI / Oct '95 / EMI

Palmer, Tom

LIVING WITH THE FLAWS
CD ______ TP 2CD
Tap / Aug '96 / ADA

Palmer, Tristan

IN DISCO STYLE ENTERTAINMENT (Palmer, Triston & Jah Thomas)
CD ______ MRCD 1003
Majestic Reggae / Feb '97 / Direct

Palmieri, Charlie

MONTUNO SESSION, THE
Tema de maria cerantes / Tumba palo / Descarga charanson / 6-8 Modal latin jazz / Talking about the Danzon / Paracachero / Que no muera / Son de mi vida / Oriente
CD ______ MRBCD 004
Mr. Bongo / Oct '95 / New Note/Pinnacle / RTM/Disc / SRD

Palmieri, Eddie

LA VERDAD (The Truth)
El cuarto / Congo yambumba / La verdad / Lisa / Noble cruise / Buscandote
CD ______ CDCHARLY 147
Charly / Nov '88 / Koch

PACHANGA TO JAZZ
El molestoso / Muneca / Mi mujer spiritual / Pa los congos / Bomba de corazon / Pensando en ti / La verdad / Lisa / Conga yumbambo / Buscandote
CD ______ CDHOT 519
Charly / Apr '95 / Koch

PALMAS
CD ______ 7559616492
Nonesuch / Dec '94 / Warner Music

SALSA BRAVA
Palo pa rumba / 1983 / Bomba de corazon / Bajo con tumbao / Pensando en ti / Venezuela / Solito / Lindo Yambu
CD ______ CDHOT 505
Charly / Oct '93 / Koch

SALSA MEETS JAZZ
Vamanos pa'l monte / Prohibition de salida / Que lindo llambu / Sabroso guaguanco / Diecisiete punto uno / Azucar / Justicia / Yo no soy guapo / Cara vez que te veo / El cuarto / Noble cruise
CD ______ CDHOT 511
Charly / Sep '94 / Koch

SUENO
Variations on a given theme / Azucar / Just a little dream / Covarde / Humpty Dumpty / La liberatad
CD ______ INT 30082
Intuition / Apr '90 / New Note/Pinnacle

SUENO
Variations on a given theme / Azucar / Just a little dream / Covarde / Humpty dumpty / Verdict on Judge Street / La libertad/ Comparsa
CD ______ INT 30112
Intuition / Sep '96 / New Note/Pinnacle

Palostine, Charlemange

FOUR MANIFESTATIONS ON SIX ELEMENTS
CD ______ BAR 014
Staalplaat / Jun '96 / Vital/SAM

Palusha

ISOLATION
Isolation / Isolation
CD ______ EV 0035CD
Universal Language / May '97 / Prime / RTM/Disc

Pameijer, Pam

PAM PAMEIJER & HIS NEW JAZZ WIZARDS
CD ______ SOSCD 1281
Stomp Off / Mar '95 / Jazz Music / Wellard

Pan

OLOLY
CD ______ ABBCD 049
Big Cat / Jun '93 / 3mv/Pinnacle

Pan African Orchestra

OPUS 1
Wia concerto no. 1 / Yaa yaa kole / Mmenson / Explorations - high life structures / Akan drumming / Sisala sebrew / Explorations - ewe 6/8 rhythms / Box dream / Adawura kasa
CD ______ CDRW 48
Realworld / Apr '95 / EMI

Pan Assembly

ROMANCE
CD ______ CD 01C
Carotte / May '97 / Jet Star

SO HOT SO SWEET
CD ______ CD 04C
Carotte / May '97 / Jet Star

Pan Head

TRIBUTE TO PAN HEAD
CD ______ CRCD 29
Charm / Mar '94 / Jet Star

Pan Ram

RATS
CD ______ SPV 08460072
SPV / Apr '96 / Koch / Plastic Head

Pan Thy Monium

DREAM 11
CD ______ AV 008
Avant Garde / May '95 / Plastic Head / RTM/Disc

KHAOOHS
CD ______ OPCD 14
Osmose / Oct '93 / Plastic Head

Panacea

LOW PROFILE DARKNESS
Low profile darkness
CD ______ CHROME 9CD
Chrome / Mar '97 / SRD

Panache Culture

TRAVEL IN A DREAM
CD ______ RN 0038
Runn / Oct '95 / Grapevine/PolyGram / Jet Star / SRD

Panama Jazz Band

ORIGINAL DIXIELAND ONE STEP
CD ______ BCD 275
GHB / Oct '92 / Jazz Music

Panamar Reed

REMOTE SOUL MODULATION
CD ______ IBCD 9
Internal Bass / Jul '97 / Prime / Timewarp / Total/BMG

Panasonic

KULMA
Teurastamo / Luotain / Vapina / Puhdistus / Jakso / Murto neste / Kylma massa / Hahmo / Aines / 25 / Saato / Kurnutus / Rutina / Moottori
CD ______ BFFP 132CD
Blast First / Jan '97 / RTM/Disc

VAKIO
CD ______ BFFP 118CD
Blast First / Sep '95 / RTM/Disc

Panatella, Slim

SLIM PANATELLA & THE MELLOW VIRGINIANS (Panatella, Slim & The Mellow Virginians)
Blues for Dixie / Looking after business / Heat of the moment / Lime rock / Sweet Lorraine / Cow cow boogie / Blue skies / Miles and miles of Texas / When you say you love me / Peach pickin' time / Texas hambone blues / Stay a little longer / Fool about a cigrette / Dill pickle rag
CD ______ CDACS 024
Acoustics / Oct '94 / ADA / Koch

Pandit, Korla

ODYSSEY
Kartikeya / Love song of the Nile / Harem bells / Kumar / Tale of the underwater worshippers / Misirlou / Kashmiri love song / Song of India / Espana / No me quiero tanto / Festival of the flowers / Orchids in the moonlight / Estrellita / Granada / La comparsita / It happened in Monterey / Las mananitas / Besame mucho / Maria bonita / Joyful tango
CD ______ FCD 24746
Fantasy / Jan '97 / Jazz Music / Pinnacle / Wellard

Pandoras

IT'S ABOUT TIME
CD ______ VOXXCD 2021
Voxx / Jan '94 / Else / RTM/Disc

Panegyris

GREEK FOLK FAVOURITES (Panegyris & Dora Stratou)
CD ______ TCD 1042
Tradition / Mar '97 / ADA / Vital

Panic

EPIDEMIC
CD ______ CDZORRO 24
Metal Blade / Jul '91 / Pinnacle / Plastic Head

FACT
Die tryin' / Close my eyes and jump / Burn one / Nonchalance / Two things (XYZ) / Hit and dragged / Rotator / Gone bad / Hell no fuck yes / Think about it
CD ______ CDZORRO 60
Metal Blade / May '93 / Pinnacle / Plastic Head

Pankow

FREIHEIT FUR DIE SKLAVEN
Gimme more (dub) / Girls and boys / In Heaven / Sickness takin' over / Freiheit fur die sklaven / Gimme more / She's gotta be mine / Nice bottom (schoener arsch) / Touch (I'm your bastard)
CD ______ **CONTECD 113**
Contempo / Jun '88 / Plastic Head

GISELA
CD ______ **CONTECD 131**
Contempo / '89 / Plastic Head

OMNE ANIMAL TRISTE POST COITUM
CD ______ **CONTECD 161**
Contempo / Oct '90 / Plastic Head

PANKOW
CD ______ **BYM 004CD**
Blank Your Mind / Oct '96 / Plastic Head

TREUE HUNDE
CD ______ **CONTECD 171**
Contempo / Jun '92 / Plastic Head

Pansy Division

DEFLOWERED
CD ______ **LOOKOUT 87CD**
Lookout / Oct '94 / Cargo / Greyhound / Shellshock/Disc

PILE UP
CD ______ **DAMGOOD 60CD**
Damaged Goods / Mar '95 / Shellshock/ Disc

UNDRESSED
CD ______ **LOOKOUT 70CD**
Lookout / Oct '94 / Cargo / Greyhound / Shellshock/Disc

WISH I'D TAKEN PICTURES
CD ______ **LOOKOUT 133CD**
Lookout / Feb '96 / Cargo / Greyhound / Shellshock/Disc

Panta Rhei

HOPA
CD ______ **829312**
BUDA / Nov '96 / Discovery

Pantera

COWBOYS FROM HELL
Cowboys from hell / Primal concrete sledge / Psycho holiday / Cemetery gates / Shattered / Medicine man / Sleep / Heresy / Domination / Clash with reality / Message in blood / Art of shredding
CD ______ **7567913722**
Atco / Jul '90 / Warner Music

FAR BEYOND DRIVEN
Strength beyond strength / Becoming / Five minutes alone / I'm broken / Good friends and a bottle of Pils / Hard lines, sunken cheeks / Slaughtered / Twenty five years / Shedding skin / Use my third arm / Throes of rejection / Planet caravan
CD ______ **7567923022**
Atco / Mar '94 / Warner Music

GREAT SOUTHERN TREND KILLERS, THE
Drag the waters / War nerve / It can't destroy my body / 13 steps to nowhere / Sandblasted skin / Underground in America / Suicide note part 1 / Suicide note part 2
CD ______ **7559619082**
Atco / May '96 / Warner Music

OFFICIAL LIVE: 101 PROOF
New level / Walk / Becoming / 5 minutes alone / Sandblasted skin / Suicide note part 2 / War nerve / This love / Dom/Hollow / Strength beyond strength / I'm broken / Cowboys from hell / Cemetery gates / Fuckin' hostile / Where you come from / I can't hide
CD ______ **7559620682**
East West / Aug '97 / Warner Music

VULGAR DISPLAY OF POWER, A
Mouth for war / New level / Walk / Fucking hostile / This love / Rise / No good for no one / Live in a hole / Regular people / By demons be driven / Hollow
CD ______ **7567917582**
Atco / Feb '92 / Warner Music

Pantoja, Antonio

SONGS OF THE ANDES
CD ______ **VICG 53392**
JVC World Library / Mar '96 / ADA / CM / Direct

Pants

PANTS, THE
CD ______ **HIPCD 006**
Hipster / Feb '97 / SRD

Papa Brittle

OBEY, CONSUME, MARRY & REPRODUCE
Trailer / Status Quo / Greed is good / Global intensified Nationalism / Heist your mind / Jesus in a limo / Crackdown 80's, 90's / Unsafe / Twenty seconds of noise / Enemy of the Brotherhood / Dissection of the great British public / Klan in the neighbourhood / Subconscious distortion of perception and sensation / Twisted and feckless
CD ______ **NET 055CD**
Nettwerk / Apr '94 / Greyhound / Pinnacle / Vital

POLEMIC BEAT POETRY
Fear on the airwaves / Economic warzone / Stress killer on the loose / Fear on the airwaves / Westminster Babylon / White tension / Genocide express / Expand demand / Maintain the system / Counter information / On with the polemic / I am mulatto
CD ______ **NET 060CD**
Nettwerk / Mar '96 / Greyhound / Pinnacle / Vital

Papa Elegua

REV'E Y SU CHARANGON
CD ______ **CD 0078**
Egrem / Mar '96 / Discovery

Papa Joe's All-Stars

HOT AND HAPPY
CD ______ **BCD 346**
GHB / Jul '96 / Jazz Music

Papa Ladji

LES BALLET AFRICAINS
CD ______ **LYRCD 7419**
Lyrichord / Aug '93 / ADA / CM / Roots

Papa Levi

BACK TO BASICS
Jah rastafari selassie I / Nuff black / One night stand / Jah mi fear / Back to basics / Can't impress / Pretty she pretty / Narcotic
CD ______ **ARICD 103**
Ariwa Sounds / Apr '94 / Jet Star / SRD

CODE OF PRACTICE
CD ______ **ARICD 060**
Ariwa Sounds / Sep '90 / Jet Star / SRD

Papa San

DJ RULE - 3 THE HARD WAY (Papa San/Tulloch T/Double Ugly)
CD ______ **RNCD 2029**
Rhino / Oct '93 / Grapevine/PolyGram / Jet Star

GI MI DI LOVING
CD ______ **794512**
Melodie / Dec '95 / ADA / Discovery / Grapevine/PolyGram / Greensleeves / Jet Star

HARD ROAD
Remedy / Nah fight no religion / Hard road to travel / Believe in love / Another life / Kill anything / Good, bad and ugly / Waan hold me down / Road jungle / Freedom
CD ______ **119892**
Musidisc UK / Jun '97 / Grapevine/ PolyGram

PRAY FI DEM
CD ______ **RASCD 3115**
Ras / Apr '93 / Direct / Greensleeves / Jet Star / SRD

SISTEM, THE
CD ______ **PWD 7415**
Pow Wow / Jul '93 / Jet Star

Papa Wemba

CLAN LANG LANGA - ZEA
CD ______ **CDS 6921**
Sonodisc / Jan '97 / Stern's

EMOTION
Yolele / Mandola / Show me the way / Fa fa fa fa fa (Sad song) / Rail on / Shofele / Image / Sala keba (Be careful) / Away y' okeyi (If you go away) / Epelo / Ah ouais (Oh yes)
CD ______ **CDRW 52**
Realworld / Mar '95 / EMI

LE VOYAGEUR
Maria Valencia / Lingo lingo / Le voyageur / Ombela / Jamais kolonga / Matinda / Yoko / Madilamba / Zero
CD ______ **CDRW 20**
Realworld / Apr '92 / EMI

PAPA WEMBA
CD ______ **STCD 1026**
Stern's / Mar '89 / ADA / CM / Stern's

VIVA LA MUSICA 1978-1979 (Papa Wemba & Koffi Olomide)
CD ______ **NG 027**
Ngoyarto / Jan '97 / Stern's

Papadimitriou, Sakis

PIANO ORACLES
CD ______ **CDLR 163**
Leo / Oct '94 / Cadillac / Impetus / Wellard

Papaila, Dan

POSITIVELY
Lover man / Prisms / Things ain't what they used to be / When a man loves a woman / Rush hour / Positively / That's the way of the world
CD ______ **CDSJP 403**
Timeless Jazz / Sep '93 / New Note/ Pinnacle

Papalote

CHISELLED IN STONE
CD ______ **LARRCD 283**
Larrikin / Jun '94 / ADA / CM / Direct / Roots

Papa's Culture

PAPA'S CULTURE BUT...
Swim / It's me / Time fekill 1 / Muffin man / Toes / Sometimes / Top 40 / Put me down / (Who is) Mack daddy love / Bronze / Time fekill 2 / Fire
CD ______ **7559614322**
Elektra / Dec '93 / Warner Music

Papas Fritas

HELIOSELF
CD ______ **MF 22**
Minty Fresh / Apr '97 / Pinnacle / SRD

Papasov, Ivo

BALKANOLOY
Miladeshki dance / Hristianova kopanitsa / Istoria na edna / Ivo's ruchenitsa / Song for Baba Nedelya / Ergenski dance / Mominsko horo / Tziganska ballada / Veseli Zborni / Proleten dance / Kasapsko horo
CD ______ **HNCD 1363**
Hannibal / May '91 / ADA / Vital

ORPHEUS ASCENDING (Papasov, Ivo & His Bulgarian Wedding Band)
CD ______ **HNCD 1347**
Hannibal / May '89 / ADA / Vital

Paper Bags

MUSIC TO TRASH
CD ______ **SST 200CD**
SST / May '93 / Plastic Head

Paperboy

CITY TO CITY
CD ______ **NP 54992**
Next Plateau / Jun '97 / PolyGram

Paperclip People

SECRET TAPES OF DOCTOR EICH
Welcome center / Oscillator / Paperclip man / Throw / Climax / Clear & present / Floor / Steam / Country bay goes dub / Slam dance / Parking garage politics / My neighbourhood
CD ______ **OPENCD 003**
Open / May '97 / Amato Disco / Pinnacle / Prime / Vital

Papete

BERIMBAU E PERCUSSAO (Music & Rhythms Of Brasil)
Cavalacanga / Processao dos mortos / Domingo no parque / Ponteio / O bonde / Promessa de pescador / Agua de coco / Se num samba / A ova / Berimba / E assim que eu sou / Ponto de caboclo / Iguape / Bomba meu bol / Cachimbo / Maraca
CD ______ **USCD 7**
Universal Sounds / May '97 / New Note/ Pinnacle / Timewarp

Paphiti, Savvas

GREEK POPULAR SONGS (Paphiti, Savvas & George Gregoriou)
CD ______ **EUCD 1236**
ARC / Nov '93 / ADA / ARC Music

Papy Tex

WASIWA (Papy Tex & Empire Bakuba)
CD ______ **CDS 7006**
Sonodisc / Jan '97 / Stern's

Paquette, David

OUTRAGEOUS
CD ______ **SACD 105**
Solo Art / Apr '94 / Jazz Music

Paquin, Anna

MAGNIFICENT NOSE, THE
CD ______ **74321237022**
RCA / Jul '96 / BMG

Paquito D'Rivera

CARIBBEAN JAZZ PROJECT, THE
CD ______ **INAK 9038**
In Akustik / Oct '95 / Direct / TKO Magnum

NIGHT IN ENGLEWOOD, A (Paquito D' Rivera & United Nations Orchestra)
CD ______ **MES 158292**
Messidor / Jul '94 / ADA / Koch

Parachute Men

EARTH, DOGS AND EGGSHELLS
CD ______ **FIRE 33024**
Fire / Oct '91 / Pinnacle / RTM/Disc

INNOCENTS, THE
CD ______ **FIRE 33014**
Fire / Oct '91 / Pinnacle / RTM/Disc

Parachute Regiment

PARAS, THE (Massed Bands Of The Parachute Regiment)
Green light / Airborne warrior / Red beret / Arnhem / Paras / Bruneval raid / Longest day / Sailing / Mount longdon / Marche des parachutist / Belges / Screaming eagles / Red devils / Aslo ran / Pomp and circumstance march No.4 / Ride of the valkyries / Delta wing / Three para songs / Songs of World War Two / American patrol / Elvis Presley, his greatest hits / Out of the sky / Echoes of an era / Space medley
CD ______ **BNA 5039**
Bandleader / '91 / Conifer/BMG

RIDE OF THE VALKYRIES (Band Of The Parachute Regiment)
Ride of the Valkyries / 3Dgs / Nibelungen march / Dutch tragedy / Bridge too far / Airborne advance / Festive fanfare and interlude / Stage centre / Oregon / Going home / Dave Brubeck - a portrait in time / Beauty and the beast / Armenian dances
CD ______ **BNA 5126**
Bandleader / Jul '96 / Conifer/BMG

Paracumbe

TAMBO
CD ______ **ASHECD 2005**
Ashe / Aug '97 / Direct

Paradis, Vanessa

VANESSA PARADIS
Natural high / Waiting for the man / Silver and gold / Be my baby / Lonely rainbows / Sunday mornings / Your love has got a handle on my mind / Future song / Paradise / Just as long as you are there / Lenny Kravitz
CD ______ **5139542**
Polydor / Sep '92 / PolyGram

VANESSA PARADIS LIVE
CD ______ **5216932**
Polydor / Mar '94 / PolyGram

Paradise Jazz Band

BLOWIN' THE BLUES AWAY
CD ______ **JCD 229**
Jazzology / Jan '94 / Jazz Music

Paradise Lost

GOTHIC
CD ______ **CDVILE 26**
Peaceville / Mar '95 / Pinnacle

ICON
CD ______ **CDMFN 152**
Music For Nations / Sep '93 / Pinnacle

ONE SECOND
One second / Another day / Sane / Say just words / Sufferer / Take me down / Lydia / This cold life / I despair / Mercy / Blood of another / Soul courageous / Disappear
CD ______ **CDMFNX 222**
CD ______ **CDMFN 222**
Music For Nations / Jul '97 / Pinnacle

PARADISE LOST
Intro / Deadly inner sense / Paradise lost / Our saviour / Rotting misery / Frozen illusion / Breeding fear / Lost paradise
CD ______ **CDVILE 17**
Peaceville / Apr '95 / Pinnacle

SHADES OF GOD
CD ______ **CDMFN 135**
Music For Nations / Jun '92 / Pinnacle

Paradogs

HERE COMES JOEY
CD ______ **PRD 70312**
Provogue / Nov '91 / Pinnacle

Paradox

BROKEN BARRICADE
Diagram 776 / Beyond the dream / Broken barricade / Mr. Davis / Inner secrets / Fantasia / Infinite moment / Rain song
CD ______ **5216872**
Verve / Mar '94 / PolyGram

Paragons

25 YEARS OF THE PARAGONS
CD ______ **RNCD 2099**
Rhino / Mar '95 / Grapevine/PolyGram / Jet Star

GOLDEN HITS
CD ______ **LG 21028**
Lagoon / Jun '93 / Grapevine/PolyGram

HEAVEN & EARTH
CD ______ **CDSGP 075**
Prestige / May '94 / Else / Total/BMG

MY BEST GIRL WEARS MY CROWN
Happy go lucky girl / I want to go back / When the lights are low / On the beach / Island in the sun / Riding on a high and windy day / Silver bird / Same song / Tide is high / I wanna be with you / Mercy mercy mercy / Wear you to the ball / I'm a worried

man / My best girl / You mean the world to me / Only a smile / Paragons medley
CD _____ CDTRL 299
Trojan / Mar '94 / Direct / Jet Star

RIDING HIGH
CD _____ RNCD 2085
Rhino / Dec '94 / Grapevine/PolyGram / Jet Star

Paralysed Age

BLOODSUCKER
CD _____ EFA 112702
Glasnost / Dec '94 / SRD

Paramaecium

WITHIN THE ANCIENT FOREST
CD _____ PGD 6950CD
Pleitegier / Sep '96 / Plastic Head

Paramount Jazzband Of ...

AIN'T CHA GLAD (Paramount Jazzband Of Boston)
CD _____ SOSCD 1205
Stomp Off / Aug '90 / Jazz Music / Wellard

PARAMOUNT JAZZ BAND, THE (Paramount Jazzband Of Boston)
Dans la rue d'antibes / Jelly roll / Joint is jumpin' / What a difference a day makes / On a slow boat to China / Old fashioned love / Come back sweet Papa / More I see you / Until the real thing comes along / It's a sin to tell a lie / I would do 'most anything for your love / Nevertheless (I'm in love with you) / Some of these days
CD _____ CDTTD 596
Timeless Jazz / Aug '95 / New Note/ Pinnacle

Paramount Singers

WORK & PRAY ON
CD _____ ARHCD 382
Arhoolie / Apr '95 / ADA / Cadillac / Direct

Paramounts

WHITER SHADES OF R & B
Poison Ivy / I feel good all over / Little bitty pretty one / Certain girl / I'm the one who loves you / It won't be long / Bad blood / Do I / Blue ribbons / Cuttin' in / You never had it so good / Don't ya like my love / Draw me closer / Turn on your love light / You've got what I want / Freedom
CD _____ EDCD 112
Edsel / Aug '91 / Pinnacle

Paranoid Visions

AFTER THE FACTION
CD _____ AXSO 1CD
AX-S / Aug '96 / SRD

Paranoise

START A NEW RACE
CD _____ OZ 003CD
Ozone / Jul '93 / Mo's Music Machine / Pinnacle / SRD

Paranonia

PARANONIA
CD _____ NZCD 021
Nova Zembla / Sep '95 / Plastic Head

Paranza Di Somma Vesuviana

SCENNENNO D'A MUNTAGNA
CD _____ NT 6719
Robi Droli / Jan '94 / ADA / Direct

Paras, Fabio

BIRTH OF SHIVA SHANTI, THE
CD _____ SHANTI 1CD
Junk Rock / Oct '93 / RTM/Disc

Pardesi Music Machine

SHAKE YOUR PANTS
CD _____ CDST 015
Star / May '90 / Pinnacle / Stern's

Parenti, Tony

STRUT YO' STUFF (Tony Parenti & Bands 1925-1929)
That's plenty / Cabaret echoes / Dizzy Lizzie / French market blues / La vida medley / Be yourself / 12th street blues / Creole blues / Strut yo' stuff / Midnight Papa / I need some lovin' / Cabaret echoes / Up jumped the devil / Weary blues / New crazy blues #1/#2 / African echoes / In the dungeon / When you and I were pals / Gumbo / You made me like it baby / Old man rhythm
CD _____ DGF 4
Frog / May '95 / Cadillac / Jazz Music / Wellard

TONY PARENTI & HIS NEW ORLENIANS
CD _____ JCD 1
Jazzology / Oct '92 / Jazz Music

Parga, Mario

MAGICIAN, THE
CD _____ PCOM 1116
President / Sep '91 / Grapevine/PolyGram / President / Target/BMG

Parham, Tiny

CLASSICS 1926-1929
CD _____ CLASSICS 661
Classics / Nov '92 / Discovery / Jazz Music

CLASSICS 1929-1940 (Parham, Tiny & His Musicians)
CD _____ CLASSICS 691
Classics / May '93 / Discovery / Jazz Music

TINY PARHAM 1926-1928
CD _____ DOCD 5341
Document / May '95 / ADA / Hot Shot / Jazz Music

TINY PARHAM 1928-1930 (2CD Set)
CD Set _____ CBC 1022
Timeless/Chris Barber Collection / Feb '97 / New Note/Pinnacle

Pariah

BLAZE OF OBSCURITY
Missionary of mercy / Puppet regime / Canary / Retaliate / Hypochondriac / Enemy within
CD _____ 857595
Steamhammer / Jun '89 / Pinnacle / Plastic Head

KINDRED, THE
CD _____ 857528
Steamhammer / '89 / Pinnacle / Plastic Head

Paris

GUERRILLA FUNK
Prelude / It's real / One time fo' ya mind / Guerrilla funk / Blacks and blues / Bring it to ya / Outta my life / What'cha see / Forty ounces and a fool / Back in the days / Guerrilla funk (Deep fo' real mix) / It's real (Mix) / Shots out
CD _____ CDPTY 108
Priority/Virgin / Nov '94 / EMI

Paris Africans

AFRICAN BICYCLETTE
CD _____ 829422
BUDA / Jun '97 / Discovery

Paris, Jackie

JACKIE PARIS/CARLOS FRANZETTI/ MARC JOHNSON
CD _____ ACD 158
Audiophile / Jan '94 / Jazz Music

NOBODY ELSE BUT ME
CD _____ ACD 245
Audiophile / Mar '95 / Jazz Music

Paris, Jeff

LUCKY THIS TIME
CD _____ NTHEN 6
Now & Then / Sep '95 / Plastic Head

Paris, Mica

CONTRIBUTION
Contribution / South of the river / If I love u 2 nite / Just to be with you / Take me away / Truth and honesty / Deep Afrika / More love / You can make a wish / Just make me the one / I've been watching you / Who can we blame / One world
CD _____ IMCD 184
Island / Mar '94 / PolyGram

SO GOOD
Where is the love: *Paris, Mica & Will Downing* / My one temptation / Like dreamers do / Breathe life into me / Nothing hits your heart like soul music / Sway / Don't give me up / I'd hate to love you / Great impersonation / So good
CD _____ IMCD 209
Island / Apr '95 / PolyGram

WHISPER A PRAYER
I never felt like this before / I wanna hold on to you / You put a move on my heart / We were made for love / Whisper a prayer / Too far apart / I bless the day / Two in a million / Positivity / Can't seem to make up my mind / You got a special way / Love keeps coming back
CD _____ IMCD 221
Island / Mar '96 / PolyGram

Paris Washboard

LOVE NEST
CD _____ SOSCD 1308
Stomp Off / Sep '96 / Jazz Music / Wellard

TRUCKIN'
CD _____ SOSCD 1293
Stomp Off / Nov '95 / Jazz Music / Wellard

Parisa

PARISA AT THE ROYAL FESTIVAL HALL (Persian Classical Music)
CD _____ PS 65155
PlayaSound / Oct '95 / ADA / Harmonia Mundi

Parisa, Fatemer V.

CLASSICAL VOCAL ART OF PERSIA, THE (Parisa, Fatemer V. & Seyyed N. Razavi)
CD _____ VICG 5269
JVC World Library / Jun '96 / ADA / CM / Direct

Parish, John

DANCE HALL AT LOUSE POINT (Parish, John & Polly Jean Harvey)
Girl / Rope bridge crossing / City of no sun / That was my veil / Urn with dead flowers in a drained pool / Civil war correspondent / Taut / Un cercle autour du soleil / Heela / Is that all there is / Dance hall at Louse Point / Lost fun zone
CD _____ CID 8051
CD _____ CIDX 8051
Island / Sep '96 / PolyGram

Park, Graeme

EAU DE HOUSE VOL.1
CD _____ FRSHCD 2
Fresh / Oct '96 / 3mv/Sony / Mo's Music Machine / Prime

Parker, Billy

BILLY PARKER AND FRIENDS
Something old, something new: *Parker, Billy & Jack Greene* / Memory number one: *Parker, Billy & Webb Pierce* / Too many irons in the fire: *Parker, Billy & Cal Smith* / Who said love was fair: *Parker, Billy & Jimmy Payne* / I believe I'm entitled to you: *Parker, Billy & Bill Carlisle* / Milk cow blues / Tomorrow never comes: *Parker, Billy & Ernest Tubb* / When I need love bad / Honky tonk girls: *Parker, Billy & Cal Smith* / Love don't know a lady: *Parker, Billy & Darrell McCall* / Take me back to Tulsa / Last country song: *Parker, Billy & Darrell McCall* / It's not me / If I ever need a lady / I see an angel every day / I'll drink to that / Why do I keep calling you honey, honey / Can I have what's left / What's a nice girl like you / One more last time / Hello out there
CD _____ BCD 15521
Bear Family / Oct '90 / Direct / Rollercoaster / Swift

Parker, Bobby

BENT OUT OF SHAPE
CD _____ BT 1086CD
Black Top / May '93 / ADA / CM / Direct

SHINE ME UP
CD _____ BT 1119CD
Black Top / Aug '95 / ADA / CM / Direct

Parker, Charlie

'ROUND MIDNIGHT
Night in Tunisia / Dizzy atmosphere / Groovin' high / Ko ko / Gypsy / Little Willie leaps in/52nd Street theme / Carvin' the bird / Charlie's wig / Barbados / Bird feathers / Charlie's theme / Be bop / Hot house / Ornithology / How high the moon
CD _____ SUMCD 4053
Summit / Nov '96 / Sound & Media

1949 CONCERT AND ALLSTARS 1950-51
CD _____ UCD 19009
Forlane / Jun '95 / Target/BMG

AUDIO ARCHIVE
Chasin' the bird / Crazeology / Yardbird suite / My old flame / Be bop a lula / Rocker / Bird of paradise / Don't blame me / Moose the mooche / Marmaduke / Street beat / Parker's mood / Theme / Bluebird / Relaxin' at Camarillo / 'Round midnight / Constellation / Slow boat to China
CD _____ CDAA 021
Tring / Jun '92 / Tring

AUTUMN IN NEW YORK
CD _____ LEJAZZCD 3
Le Jazz / Mar '93 / Cadillac / Koch

BEST OF CHARLIE PARKER, THE
CD _____ DLCD 4021
Dixie Live / Mar '95 / TKO Magnum

BEST OF THE BIRD, THE
CD _____ 17020
Laserlight / May '94 / Target/BMG

BIRD
CD _____ CD 53069
Giants Of Jazz / Mar '90 / Cadillac / Jazz Music / Target/BMG

BIRD (The Complete Charlie Parker On Verve/10CD Set)
Sweet Georgia Brown / Blues for Norman / I can't get started / Oh lady be good / After you've gone / I got rhythm / Introduction / Jazz at the Philharmonic blues / Bird / Repetition / No noise / Mango mangue / Okiedokie / Cardboard visa / Segment / Diverse / Passport / Opener / Lester leaps in / Embraceable you / Closer / Introduction / Flyin' home / How high the moon / Perdido / Just friends / Everything happens to me / April in Paris / Summertime / I didn't know what time it was / If I should lose you / Star eyes / Blues / I'm in the mood for love / Bloomdido / Oscar for treadwell / Mohawk / Melancholy baby / Leap frog / Relaxing with Lee / Dancing in the dark / Out of nowhere / Laura / East of the sun and West of the moon / They can't take that away from me / Easy to love / I'm in the mood for love / I'll remember April / What is this thing called love / April in Paris / Repetition / Easy to love / Rocker / Celebrity / Ballade / Afro Cuban jazz suite / Au private / She rote / KC blues / Star eyes / My little suede shoes / Un poquito de tu amor / Tico tico / Fiesta / Why do I love you / Blues for Alice / Si si / Swedish schnapps / Back home blues / Lover man / Temptation / Lover / Autumn in New York / Stella by starlight / Mama Inez / La cucaracha / Estrellita / Begin the beguine / La palome / Night and day / Almost like being in love / I can't get started / What is this thing called love / Jam blues / What is this thing called love / All the things you are / Dearly beloved / Nearness of you / I'll get by / Everything happens to me / Isn't it romantic / Funky blues / Song is you / Laird baird / Kim / Cosmic rays / In the still of the night / Old folks / If I love again / Chi chi / I remember you / Now's the time / Confirmation / I get a kick out of you / Just one of those things / My heart belongs to Daddy / I've got you under my skin / I love Paris
CD Set _____ 8371412
Verve / Dec '88 / PolyGram

BIRD (The Original Recordings Of Charlie Parker)
Now's the time / Laura / Mohawk / Kim / Blues for Alice / Laird baird / KC Blues / Lover man / Just friends / Bird / April in Paris / Lester leaps in
CD _____ 8371762
Verve / Nov '88 / PolyGram

BIRD AND DIZ (Parker, Charlie & Dizzy Gillespie)
Bloomdido / Oscar for treadwell / Mohawk / My melancholy baby / Leap frog / Relaxin' with Lee
CD _____ 8311332
Verve / Oct '88 / PolyGram

BIRD AT BIRDLAND (4CD Set)
CD Set _____ CDDIG 16
Charly / Jun '95 / Koch

BIRD AT ST. NICK'S
CD _____ OJCCD 41
Original Jazz Classics / Jun '95 / Complete/Pinnacle / Jazz Music / Wellard

BIRD IN CONCERT 1946-1952
CD Set _____ CDB 1215
Giants Of Jazz / Jul '92 / Cadillac / Jazz Music / Target/BMG

BIRD LIVES (Various Artists)
Yardbird suite: *Pepper, Art* / Confirmation: *Ammons, Gene* / Ornithology: *Evans, Bill* / Parker's mood (bless my soul): *Jefferson, Eddie* / Scrapple from the apple: *Mitchell, Blue* / Au privave: *Moody, James* / Repitition: *Montgomery, Wes* / Billie's bounce: *Griffin, Johnny* / Steeplechase: *Hawes, Hampton* / Now's the time: *Morgan, Frank* / Relaxin' at Camarillo: *Henderson, Joe*
CD _____ MCD 91662
Milestone / Apr '94 / Cadillac / Complete/ Pinnacle / Jazz Music / Wellard

BIRD MEETS DIZ (Parker, Charlie & Dizzy Gillespie)
CD _____ LEJAZZCD 21
Le Jazz / Feb '94 / Cadillac / Koch

BIRD OF PARADISE
CD _____ JHR 73531
Jazz Hour / Sep '93 / Cadillac / Jazz Music / Target/BMG

BIRD OF PARADISE BE-BOP GENIUS 1947
CD _____ CD 56029
Jazz Roots / Nov '94 / Target/BMG

BIRD SYMBOLS
Moose the mooche / Yardbird suite / Ornithology / Night in Tunisia / Bird's nest / Cool blues / Bird of paradise / Embraceable you / My old flame / Scrapple from the apple / Out of nowhere / Don't blame me
CD _____ RHCD 5
Rhapsody / Jul '91 / Jazz Music / President / Wellard

BIRD YOU NEVER HEARD, THE
CD _____ STCD 582
Stash / Jun '94 / ADA / Cadillac / CM / Direct / Jazz Music

BIRD'S BEST
CD _____ 5274522
Verve / Oct '95 / PolyGram

BIRD'S EYES VOL.10
CD _____ W 2002
Philology / Sep '93 / Cadillac / Harmonia Mundi

BIRD'S EYES VOL.11
CD _____ W 6222
Philology / Apr '94 / Cadillac / Harmonia Mundi

BIRD'S EYES VOL.12
CD ______ W 8422
Philology / Apr '94 / Cadillac / Harmonia Mundi

BIRD'S EYES VOL.13
CD ______ W 8432
Philology / May '94 / Cadillac / Harmonia Mundi

BIRD'S EYES VOL.14
CD ______ W 8442CD
Philology / Jul '94 / Cadillac / Harmonia Mundi

BIRD'S EYES VOL.15
CD ______ PHIL 8452
Philology / Oct '94 / Cadillac / Harmonia Mundi

BIRD'S EYES VOL.16
CD ______ PHIL 8462
Philology / Oct '94 / Cadillac / Harmonia Mundi

BIRD'S EYES VOL.19
CD ______ W 8492
Philology / Apr '95 / Cadillac / Harmonia Mundi

BIRD'S EYES VOL.20
CD ______ W 8502
Philology / Apr '95 / Cadillac / Harmonia Mundi

BIRD'S EYES VOL.21
CD ______ W 8512
Philology / Feb '96 / Cadillac / Harmonia Mundi

BIRD'S EYES VOL.22
CD ______ W 8522
Philology / Feb '96 / Cadillac / Harmonia Mundi

BIRD'S EYES VOL.7
CD ______ 214 W572
Philology / Aug '91 / Cadillac / Harmonia Mundi

BIRD'S EYES VOL.8
CD ______ CD 241 W802
Philology / May '92 / Cadillac / Harmonia Mundi

BIRD'S EYES VOL.9
CD ______ W 1202
Philology / Sep '93 / Cadillac / Harmonia Mundi

BIRD'S THE WORD 1944-1952 (2CD Set)
CD Set ______ JWD 102308
JWD / Oct '94 / Target/BMG

BLUEBIRD
CD ______ JHR 73532
Jazz Hour / Sep '93 / Cadillac / Jazz Music / Target/BMG

BOSTON 1952
CD ______ UPCD 2742
Uptown / Apr '97 / Cadillac / Harmonia Mundi

BROADCAST PEFORMANCES
CD ______ ESP 30012
ESP / Jan '93 / Jazz Music

CARNEGIE HALL CHRISTMAS 1949
CD ______ JASSCD 16
Jass / '88 / ADA / Cadillac / CM / Direct / Jazz Music

CARNEGIE HALL CONCERTS 1949-1950
CD ______ CD 53111
Giants Of Jazz / Jun '92 / Cadillac / Jazz Music / Target/BMG

CHARLIE PARKER (2CD Set)
CD Set ______ R2CD 4016
Deja Vu / Jan '96 / THE

CHARLIE PARKER
Bird's nest / How high the moon / Ko Ko / Moose the Mooch / Lover man (oh where can you be) / Klact-Oveeseds-Tene / Quasimodo / Cool blues / Stupendous / Red cross / Donna Lee / Move / Street beat / Relaxin' in Carmarillo / Bird of paradise / Carvin' the bird / Confirmations / Congo blues
CD ______ BN 031
Blue Nite / Feb '97 / Target/BMG

CHARLIE PARKER & JAY MCSHANN 1940-1944 (Parker, Charlie & Jay McShann Orchestra)
CD ______ STCD 542
Stash / Feb '91 / ADA / Cadillac / CM / Direct / Jazz Music

CHARLIE PARKER 1944-1946
CD ______ 158802
Jazz Archives / Feb '97 / Discovery

CHARLIE PARKER 1945-1953
CD ______ CD 53051
Giants Of Jazz / Mar '92 / Cadillac / Jazz Music / Target/BMG

CHARLIE PARKER 1947-1950
CD ______ CD 14549
Jazz Portraits / Jul '94 / Jazz Music

CHARLIE PARKER AT BIRDLAND & CAFE SOCIETY
CD ______ C&BCD 108
Cool & Blue / Oct '93 / Discovery / Jazz Music

CHARLIE PARKER COLLECTION
CD ______ COL 028
Collection / Jun '95 / Target/BMG

CHARLIE PARKER GOLD (2CD Set)
CD Set ______ D2CD 4016
Deja Vu / Jun '95 / THE

CHARLIE PARKER MEMORIAL BAND, THE (Charlie Parker Memorial Band)
Marmaduke / Out of nowhere / Don't blame me / Sweet Rosa / Little Willie leaps / Max the invincible roach / Star eyes / Laird baird / Bird of paradise / Visa
CD ______ CDSJP 373
Timeless Jazz / Nov '93 / New Note/ Pinnacle

CHARLIE PARKER ON DIAL (The Complete Sessions) (4CD Set)
Diggin' diz / Moose and mooche / Yardbird suite / Ornithology / Night in Tunisia / Max making wax / Lover man / Gypsy / Be bop / Home cooking / Lullaby in rhythm / Blues on the sofa / Kopely plaza blues / This is always / Dark shadows / Bird's nest / Cool blues / Relaxin' at Camarillo / Cheers / Carvin' the bird / Stupendous / Dexterity / Bongo bop / Dewey Square / Hymn / Bird of paradise / Embraceable you / Bird feathers / Klactoveesedstein / Scrapple from the apple / My old flame / Out of nowhere / Don't blame me / Drifting on a reed / Quasimado / Charlie's wig / Bongo beep / Crazeology / How deep is the ocean
CD Set ______ SPJCD 1014
Spotlite / May '93 / Cadillac / Jazz Music / New Note/Pinnacle / Swift

CHARLIE PARKER ON DIAL (Original Choice Takes - 2CD Set)
Diggin' diz / Moose the mooche / Yardbird suite / Ornithology / Night in Tunisia / Max making wax / Loveman / Gypsy / Be bop / This is always / Dark shadows / Bird's nest / Hot blues / Cool blues / Relaxin' at Camarillo / Cheers / Carvin' the bird / Stupendous / Dexterity / Bongo bop / Dewey Square / Hymn / Bird of paradise / Embraceable you / Bird feathers / Klactoveesedstein / Scrappel from the apple / My old flame / Out of nowhere / Don't blame me / Drifting on a reed / Quasimado / Charlie's wig / Bongo beep / Carazeology / How deep is the ocean
CD Set ______ SPJCD 1092
Spotlite / May '95 / Cadillac / Jazz Music / New Note/Pinnacle / Swift

CHARLIE PARKER STORY VOL.1, THE
CD ______ STBCD 2602
Stash / Aug '95 / ADA / Cadillac / CM / Direct / Jazz Music

CHARLIE PARKER STORY VOL.2, THE
CD ______ STBCD 2603
Stash / Aug '95 / ADA / Cadillac / CM / Direct / Jazz Music

CHARLIE PARKER WITH MILES DAVIS
CD ______ 30017
Giants Of Jazz / Sep '92 / Cadillac / Jazz Music / Target/BMG

CHASIN' THE BIRD
How high the moon / Moose the mooch / Be bop a lula / Yardbird suite / Crazeology / Slow boat to China / Riff raff / Scrapple from the apple / Star eyes / Sly mongoose / 'Round midnight / Theme / Rocker / Don't blame me / Relaxin' at Camarillo / Constellation / Bluebird / Parker's mood / Marmaduke / Bird of paradise / My old flame / Chasin' the Bird
CD ______ GRF 063
Tring / '93 / Tring

COLE PORTER SONGBOOK, THE
Easy to love / Begin the beguine / Night and day / What is this thing called love / In the still of the night / I get a kick out of you / Just one of those things / My heart belongs to daddy / I've got you under my skin / Love for sale / I love Paris
CD ______ 8232502
Verve / Feb '91 / PolyGram

COMPLETE BIRD AT BIRDLAND 1950-1951, THE (4CD Set)
Hot house / Out of nowhere / Visa / Anthropology / Wee / What's new / Little willie leaps / Yesterdays / 52nd street theme III / Dizzy atmosphere / Wahoo / I can't get started / Wee / 52nd street theme IV / Slow boat to china / Night in tunisia / 52nd street theme V / 52nd street theme inc / Wahoo / 'Round midnight / This time the dream's on me / Dizzy atmosphere / Night in Tunisia / 52nd street theme / Street beat / Out of nowhere inc / Little willie leaps / 52nd street theme / Ornithology / I'll remember April / 52nd street theme / Slow 52nd street theme / Embraceable you / Cool blues / 52nd street theme / Conception / Deception / Jumpin' with Symphony Sid / Anthropology / Embraceable you / Cheryl / Salt peanuts / Jumpin' with Symphony Sid / Easy to love / Rocker / Jumpin' with Symphony Sid / Just friends / Everything happens to me / East of the sun / Laura / Dancing in the dark / Jumpin' with Symphony Sid / Introduction / Blue 'n' boogie / Anthropology / Round midnight / Night in Tunisia / Jumpin' with Symphony Sid / What is this thing called love / Laura / Repetition / Interview / They can't take that away from me / Easy to love / Hot house / Embraceable you / How high the moon
CD Set ______ FBB 901
Ember / Nov '96 / TKO Magnum

COMPLETE BIRTH OF BEBOP 1940-1942
CD ______ STCD 535
Stash / Oct '91 / ADA / Cadillac / CM / Direct / Jazz Music

EARLY BIRD (The Best Of The 1945 Studio Recordings)
CD ______ LEJAZZCD 55
Le Jazz / Aug '96 / Cadillac / Koch

EARLY BIRD 1940-1945
CD ______ 158572
Jazz Archives / Jul '96 / Discovery

FROM DIZZY TO MILES
CD ______ CD 53052
Giants Of Jazz / Mar '90 / Cadillac / Jazz Music / Target/BMG

GITANES - JAZZ 'ROUND MIDNIGHT
Why do I love you / Tico tico / My little suede shoes / Un poquito de tu amor / Estrellita / I'm in the mood for love / Begin the beguine / Temptation / Easy to love / East of the sun and West of the moon / I didn't know what time it was / If I should lose you / Out of nowhere / I'll remember April / Autumn in New York / Laura / Ballade / Lover
CD ______ 5109112
Verve / Oct '91 / PolyGram

HIGHEST FLYING BIRD (14 Of His Classic Recordings)
Moose the mooche / Yardbird smile / Ornithology / Scrapple from the apple / Rocker / Sly mongoose / Star eyes / This time the dream's on me / Cool blues / My little suede shoes / Lester leaps in / Laura
CD ______ PAR 2002
Parade / May '90 / Disc

HOMAGE TO CHARLIE PARKER (Paris All-Stars)
Birks works / Warm valley / Third eye/Billy The Kid/Drum also waltzes / Old folks yardbird suite / Con alma / Cherokee / Night in Tunisia / Ooh-poo-pah-doo
CD ______ 3953002
A&M / Jan '91 / PolyGram

IMMORTAL SESSIONS VOL.1 1945-1948 (5CD Set)
Dream of you / Seventh Avenue / Groovin' high / All the things you are / Dizzy atmosphere / Salt peanuts / Shaw nuff / Lover man / Hot house / Hallelujah / Get happy / Slam slam blues / Congo blues / Moose the mouche / Yardbird suite / Ornithology / Night in Tunisia / Moose the mouche / Yardbird suite / Max making wax / Lover man / Gypsy / Be bop / This is always / Dark shadows / Dark shadows / Hot blues / Blow top blues / Cool blues / Cool blues / Relaxin' at Camarillo / Cheers / Carvin' the bird / Stupendous / Stupendous / Relaxin' at Camarillo / Cheers / Carvin' the bird / Dexterity / Bongo bop / Bongo bop / Dewey Square / Dewey Square / Bird of paradise / Embraceable you / Klactoveesedstein / Scrapple from the apple / My old flame / Out of nowhere / Don't blame me / Drifting on a reed / Quasimodo / Quasimodo / Charlie's wig / Bird feathers / Crazeology / Ko ko / Groovin' high / Big foot / Ornithology / Hot house / Salt peanuts / Out of nowhere / How high the moon / White Christmas
CD Set ______ EC 33252
Saga Jazz / Nov '96 / Complete/Pinnacle

IMMORTAL SESSIONS VOL.2 1949-1953 (5CD Set)
Slow boat to China / Cheryl / Scrapple from the apple / Be bop / Hot house / Oop bop sh'bam / Barbados / Salt peanuts / Groovin' high / Perdido / 'Round midnight / Move / Street beat / Ornithology / Cool blues / 52nd Street theme / Conversation / Blue 'n' boogie / Conversation / Anthropology / Conversation / Round Midnight / Conversation / Night in Tunisia / Jumpin' with symphony Sid / Repetition / April in Paris / What is this thing called love / April in Paris / Out of nowhere / East of the sun / Easy to love / Rocker / Sly mongoose / Moose the mouche / Star eyes / This time the dream's on me / Cool blues / My little suede shoes / Lester leaps in / Perdido / Salt peanuts / All the things you are / Hot house / Night in Tunisia
CD Set ______ EC 33192
Saga Jazz / Nov '96 / Complete/Pinnacle

IN A SOULFUL MOOD
CD ______ MCCD 205
Music Club / Jul '95 / Disc / THE

IN SWEDEN 1950
CD ______ STCD 4031
Storyville / Oct '87 / Cadillac / Jazz Music / Wellard

JAM SESSION
Jam blues / What is this thing called love / All the things you are / Dearly beloved / Nearness of you / I'll get by / Everything happens to me / Man I love / What's new / Soeone to watch over me / Isn't it romantic / Funky blues
CD ______ 8335642
Verve / Mar '90 / PolyGram

JAM SESSION 1952
CD ______ CD 53120
Giants Of Jazz / Jan '94 / Cadillac / Jazz Music / Target/BMG

JAZZ AT THE PHILHARMONIC
CD ______ CD 53107
Giants Of Jazz / May '92 / Cadillac / Jazz Music / Target/BMG

JAZZ AT THE PHILHARMONIC 1946
Sweet Georgia Brown / Blues for Norman / I can't get started / Oh lady be good / After you've gone / I got rhythm / Jazz at the Philharmonic blues
CD ______ 5137562
Verve / Mar '93 / PolyGram

JAZZ AT THE PHILHARMONIC 1949
Opener / Lester leaps in / Embraceable you / Closer / Flying home / How high the moon / Perdido
CD ______ 5198032
Verve / Feb '94 / PolyGram

JAZZ MASTERS
Confirmation / Oscar for treadwell / Dancing in the dark / Segment / Star eyes / Mango mangue / Repetition / Bird / KC blues / Melancholy baby / Blues for Alice / I can't get started / Kim / Just friends / She rote / Lover man
CD ______ 5198272
Verve / Feb '94 / PolyGram

JAZZ MASTERS (Charlie Parker Plays Standards)
Love for sale / If I should lose you / Almost like being in love / Why do I love you / I remember you / Easy to love / Old folks / I got rhythm / Laura / Estrellita / What is this thing called love / Embraceable you / I love Paris / How high the moon
CD ______ 5218542
Verve / Feb '95 / PolyGram

JAZZ PORTRAITS
Dizzy atmosphere / Hot house / Billie's bounce / Koko / Moose the mooche / Yardbird suite / Ornithology / Night in Tunisia / Lover man / Gypsy / Be bop / Bird's nest / Cool blues / Relaxin' at Camarillo / Cheers / Carvin' the bird / Stupendous / Donna Lee
CD ______ CD 14504
Jazz Portraits / May '94 / Jazz Music

LIVE AT ST. NICKS
CD ______ OJCCD 41
Original Jazz Classics / Jun '95 / Complete/Pinnacle / Jazz Music / Wellard

LIVE AT TRADE WINGS
CD ______ LEJAZZCD 48
Le Jazz / Nov '95 / Cadillac / Koch

LIVE IN LOS ANGELES 1947
CD ______ 550082
Jazz Anthology / Jan '94 / Cadillac / Discovery / Harmonia Mundi

LIVE PERFORMANCES
CD ______ ESP 30002
ESP / Jan '93 / Jazz Music

MASTERWORKS 1946-1947
Bird of paradise / Embraceable you / Crazeology / Dewey Square / My old flame / Relaxin' at Camarillo / Hymn / Klactoveesedstein / Don't blame me / Scrapple from the apple / Quasimodo / Dexterity / Night in Tunisia / Ornithology / Lover man / Yardbird suite / Moose the mooche / Gypsy / Be bop / Bird's nest / Out of nowhere / Cheers
CD ______ CD 53007
Giants Of Jazz / Mar '92 / Cadillac / Jazz Music / Target/BMG

MONTREAL 1953
CD ______ UPCD 2736
Uptown / Apr '97 / Cadillac / Harmonia Mundi

NOW'S THE TIME (Parker, Charlie Quartet)
Song is you / Laird baird / Kim / Cosmic rays / Chi chi / I remember you / Now's the time / Confirmation
CD ______ 8256712
Verve / May '87 / PolyGram

PARKER'S MOOD 1947-1950
CD ______ CD 56036
Jazz Roots / Jul '95 / Target/BMG

RARITIES FROM THE PRIVATE COLLECTION 1947-1950
CD ______ JZCD 311
Suisa / Feb '91 / Jazz Music / THE

RARITIES FROM THE PRIVATE COLLECTION 1950-1953
CD ______ JZCD 312
Suisa / Feb '91 / Jazz Music / THE

ROCKLAND PALACE CONCERT 1952 VOL.1
East of the sun / What is this thing called love / Stardust / Ornithology / Easy to love / Just friends / Dancing in the dark / Gold rush / Don't blame me / April in Paris / Repitition / Everything happens to me / Sly mongoose / Sly mongoose / Rocker / Laura / Lester leaps in
CD ______ JZCL 6010
Jazz Classics / Nov '96 / Cadillac / Direct / Jazz Music

ROCKLAND PALACE CONCERT 1952, THE (Complete Concert/2CD Set)
East of the sun / What is this thing called love / Stardust / Ornithology / Easy to love / Just friends / Dancing in the dark / Gold rush / Don't blame me / April in Paris / Repitition / Everything happens to me / Sly mongoose / Sly mongoose / Rocker / Laura / Lester leaps in / Out of nowhere / I didn't know what time it was / I'll remember April / Cool blues / East of the sun / Just friends / My little suede shoes / What is this thing called love / Repitition / This time's the dreams on me / Moose the moche / Star eyes / Rocker
CD Set ______ JZCL 5014
Jazz Classics / Nov '96 / Cadillac / Direct / Jazz Music

SAVOY RECORDINGS VOL.1
CD ______ VGCD 650107
Vogue / Jan '93 / BMG

SAVOY RECORDINGS VOL.2
CD ______ VGCD 650108
Vogue / Jan '93 / BMG

STREET BEAT
CD ______ CDSGP 088
Prestige / May '94 / Else / Total/BMG

SWEDISH SCHNAPPS (& The Great Quintet Sessions 1949-1951)
Si si / Swedish schnapps / Back home blues / Lover man / Blues for Alice / Au privave / She rote / KC blues / Star eyes / Segment diverse / Passport
CD ______ 8493932
Verve / Mar '92 / PolyGram

TRIUMPH OF CHARLIE PARKER
CD ______ CDCH 380
Milan / Jan '89 / Conifer/BMG / Silva Screen

UNHEARD CHARLIE PARKER: BIRDSEED VOL.1 1947-1950
CD ______ STB 2500
Stash / Apr '95 / ADA / Cadillac / CM / Direct / Jazz Music

WITH STRINGS (The Master Takes)
CD ______ 5239842
Verve / Feb '95 / PolyGram
CD ______ BMCD 3023
Blue Moon / Mar '96 / Cadillac / Discovery / Greensleeves / Jazz Music / Jet Star / TKO Magnum

YARDBIRD SUITE
CD ______ CD 56011
Jazz Roots / Aug '94 / Target/BMG

YARDBIRD SUITE
Confirmation / Scrapple from the apple / Out of nowhere / Hallelujah / Get happy / Moose the moochie / Bird of paradise / Night in Tunisia / Dizzy atmosphere / Groovin' high / Ko ko / Gypsy / Carvin' the bird / Bird feathers / Be bop / Yardbird suite
CD ______ CDMT 030
Meteor / Jul '97 / TKO Magnum

Parker, Elaine

'S WONDERFUL
Some of my best friends / Touch of your lips / In a sentimental mood / 'S Wonderful / Stardust / I did it all for you / Little girl blue / Carioca / They can't take that away from me / We could be flying / They say it's wonderful / Ol' man river / There's a small hotel / Joy / My foolish heart / Like a lover / Love for sale
CD ______ JHCD 027
Ronnie Scott's Jazz House / Jan '94 / Cadillac / Jazz Music / New Note/Pinnacle / TKO Magnum

Parker, Evan

50TH BIRTHDAY CONCERT
CD ______ CDLR 212/3
Leo / Jan '95 / Cadillac / Impetus / Wellard

CONIC SECTIONS
Conic section 1 / Conic section 2 / Conic section 3 / Conic section 4 / Conic section 5
CD ______ AHUM 015
Ah-Um / Jul '93 / Cadillac / New Note/ Pinnacle

CORNER TO CORNER (Parker, Evan & John Stevens)
CD ______ OGCD 005
Ogun / May '94 / Cadillac / Jazz Music / Wellard

IMAGINARY VALUES (Parker, Evan Trio)
CD ______ MCD 9401
Maya / Oct '94 / Complete/Pinnacle

NATIVES AND ALIENS (Parker, Evan & Paul Lytton/Barry Guy)
CD ______ CDLR 243
Leo / May '97 / Cadillac / Impetus / Wellard

PROCESS & REALITY
CD ______ FMPCD 37
FMP / Oct '87 / Cadillac

SAXOPHONE SOLOS
CD ______ CPE 20022
Chronoscope / Jun '95 / Cadillac / Harmonia Mundi / Wellard

TOWARD THE MARGINS
CD ______ 4535142
ECM / Jun '97 / New Note/Pinnacle

TWO OCTOBERS (Parker, Evan & Paul Lytton)
CD ______ EM 4009
Emanem / Sep '96 / Cadillac / Harmonia Mundi

Parker, Fess

GREAT AMERICAN HEROES
Daniel Boone / Little Nathan / Jim Bowie / Abraham Lincoln (the tall American) / George Washington / Patrick Henry (the Patriot) / Ballad of Davy Crockett / Andrew Jackson (Old Hickory) / Ben Franklin / Lewis & Clark / Johnny Clem / Ole Kit Carson
CD ______ BCD 16113
Bear Family / Nov '96 / Direct / Rollercoaster / Swift

Parker, Graham

12 HAUNTED EPISODES
CD ______ GRACD 204
Grapevine / Apr '95 / Grapevine/PolyGram

ACID BUBBLE GUM
CD ______ WENCD 015
When / Mar '97 / Pinnacle

ACID BUBBLEGUM
Turn it into hate / Sharpening axes / Get over it and move on / Bubblegum cancer / Impenetrable / She never let me down / Obsessed with Aretha / Beancounter / Girl at the end of the pier / Baggage / Milk train / Character assassination / They got it wrong as usual
CD ______ ESSCD 583
Essential / Jul '97 / BMG

ALONE IN AMERICA LIVE
White honey / Black honey / Soul corruption / Gypsy blood / Back in time / Change is gonna come / Watch the moon come down / Protection / Back to schooldays / Durban poison / You can't be too strong / Don't let it break you down
CD ______ FIENDCD 141
Demon / Apr '89 / Pinnacle

ALONE IN JAPAN LIVE
That's what they all say / Platinum blonde / Mercury poisoning / Sweet sixteen / No woman, no cry / Lunatic fringe / Long stem rose / Discovering Japan / Don't ask me questions / Watch the moon come down (revisited) / Just like Hermann Hesse / Too many knots to untangle / Chopsticks / Short memories
CD ______ FIENDCD 735
Demon / Aug '93 / Pinnacle

BBC LIVE IN CONCERT
CD ______ WINCD 083
Windsong / Jun '96 / Pinnacle

BURNING QUESTIONS
Release me / Too many knots to untangle / Just like Joe Meek's blues / Love is a burning question / Platinum blonde / Long stem rose / Short memories / Here it comes again / Mr. Tender / Just like Hermann Hesse / Yesterdays's cloud / Oasis / Worthy of your love / Substitute
CD ______ FIENDCD 721
Demon / Aug '92 / Pinnacle

CHRISTMAS CRACKER
Christmas is for mugs / New Year's revolution / Soul Christmas / Christmas is for mugs / New Year's revolution / Soul Christmas
CD ______ GPCD 3
Demon / Nov '94 / Pinnacle

EPISODES
CD ______ NTMCD 518
Nectar / May '96 / Pinnacle

HOWLING WIND/HEAT TREATMENT (2CD Set)
White honey / Nothing's gonna pull us apart / Silly thing / Gypsy blood / Between you and me / Back to schooldays / Soul shoes / Lady doctor / You've got to be kidding / Howling wind / Not if it pleases me / Don't ask me questions / Heat treatment / That's what they all say / Turned up too late / Black honey / Hotel chambermaid / Pourin' it all out / Back door love / Something you're goin' thru / Help me shake it / Fools' gold
CD Set ______ 5286032
Vertigo / Aug '95 / PolyGram

HUMAN SOUL
Little Miss Understanding / My love's strong / Dancing for money / Call me your doctor / Big man on paper / Soultime / Everything goes / Sugar gives you energy / Daddy's a postman / Green monkeys / I was wrong / You got the word (right where you want it) / Slash and burn
CD ______ FIENDCD 163
Demon / Oct '89 / Pinnacle

MONA LISA'S SISTER
Don't let it break you down / Under the mask of happiness / Back in time / I'm just your man / OK Heironymous / Get started, start a fire / Girl isn't ready / Blue highway / Success / I don't know / Cupid
CD ______ FIENDCD 122
Demon / Jul '88 / Pinnacle

MONA LISA'S SISTER/HUMAN SOUL/ ALONE IN USA/THE UP ESCALATOR (4CD Set)
CD Set ______ GRAHAM 1
Demon / '91 / Pinnacle

NO HOLDING BACK (3CD Set)
No holding back / Stupefaction / Empty lives / Manoeuvres / Love without greed / Don't let it break you down / Under the mask of happiness / I'm just your man / OK Hieronymus / Get started, start a fire / Cupid / Little misunderstanding / My love's strong / Dancing for money / Big man on paper / Everything goes / Daddy's a postman / You got the world (right where you want it) / She wants so many things / Strong winds / Kid with the butterfly net / Wrapping paper / Brand new book / Weeping statues / When I was king / Sun is gonna shine again / Release me / Just like Joe Meek's blues / Love is a burning question / Long stem rose / Here it comes again / Yesterday's cloud / Substitute / White honey / Black honey / Gypsy blood / Durban poison / Three Martini lunch / Hotel chambermaid / That's what they all say / Platinum blonde / Mercury poisoning / No woman no cry / Discovering Japan / Watch the moon come down / Chopsticks / Short memories / Christmas is for mugs / New York revolution / Soul Christmas / Protection
CD Set ______ FBOOK 15
Demon / Feb '97 / Pinnacle

PARKERILLA
CD ______ 8422632
Vertigo / Jan '94 / PolyGram

STRUCK BY LIGHTNING
She wants so many things / They murdered the clown / Strong winds / Kid with the butterfly net / And it shook me / Wrapping paper / That's where she ends up / Brand new book / Weeping statues / Guardian angels / Children and dogs / Over the border (to America) / When I was King / Ten girls ago / Sun is gonna shine again
CD ______ FIENDCD 201
Demon / Jan '91 / Pinnacle

TEMPORARY BEAUTY
Temporary beauty / Another grey area / No more excuses / Dark side of the bright lights / Can't waste a minute / Big fat zero / You hit the spot / It's all worth nothing alone / Crying for attention / Thankless task / Fear not / You can't take your love for granted / Glass jaw / Passive resistance / Sound like chains / Just like a man / Life gets better / Last couple on the dance floor / Miracle a minute / Habit worth forming
CD ______ 74321487282
RCA / May '97 / BMG

UP ESCALATOR, THE
No holding back / Devil's sidewalk / Stupefaction / Love without greed / Julie Julie / Endless night / Paralysed / Manoeuvres / Empty lives / Beating of another heart
CD ______ FIENDCD 121
Demon / Jun '90 / Pinnacle
CD ______ RE 1980
Razor & Tie / Jun '96 / Koch

VERTIGO (2CD Set) (Parker, Graham & The Rumour)
Between you and me / I'm gonna use it now / You've got to be kidding / Howlin' wind / Back to schooldays / White honey / That's what they all say / Back door love / Back to school days / Silly thing / Chain of fools / Don't ask me questions / You can't hurry love / Soul shoes / Kansas City / Heat treatment / Hotel chambermaid / Black honey / Fools' gold / Hold back the night / (let me get) sweet on you / New York shuffle / Watch the moon come down / Raid / Lady doctor / I'm gonna tear your playhouse down / Heat in Harlem / Gypsy blood / Discovering Japan / Local girls / Nobody hurts you / You can't be too strong / Passion is no ordinary word / Saturday nite is dead / Love gets you twisted / Protection / Waiting for the UFO's / Don't get excited / Mercury poisoning / I want you back
CD Set ______ 5341002
Mercury / Oct '96 / PolyGram

Parker, Junior

LITTLE JUNIOR PARKER
CD ______ CDC 9002
LRC / Oct '90 / Harmonia Mundi / New Note/Pinnacle

Parker, Kenny

RAISE THE DEAD
Too hot for me / Your girl's gone bad / Take it easy on a fool / She's the one for me / Shake hands with the devil / Baby cakes bop / Cryin' for help / You're so sharp / Blues for Mr. Bo / Crazy 'bout my baby / Brunoise / Afterglow
CD ______ JSPCD 275
JSP / Nov '96 / ADA / Cadillac / Direct / Hot Shot / Target/BMG

Parker, Kim

BEAUTIFUL FRIENDSHIP, A (Parker, Kim & Hakan Rydin)
CD ______ FLCCD 146
Four Leaf Clover / May '97 / Cadillac / Wellard

SOMETIMES I'M BLUE
CD ______ SN 1133
Soul Note / '86 / Cadillac / Harmonia Mundi / Wellard

Parker, Knocky

KNOCKY PARKER & GALVANISED WASHBOARD BAND
CD ______ BCD 1
GHB / Jan '94 / Jazz Music

Parker, Leon

ABOVE AND BELOW
Body movement / Bemsha swing / You don't know what love is / All my life / Above and below / Celebration / Epistrophy / BBBB / Evy / It's only a paper moon / Body movement II
CD ______ 4781982
Epicure / Feb '95 / Sony

BELIEF
Ray of light / Village song / Africa / Close your eyes / Calling out / Belief / Horizon Azul / Wide open / First child / In a sentimental mood / Belief (reprise)
CD ______ 4851382
Sony Jazz / Sep '96 / Sony

Parker, Maceo

DOING THEIR OWN THING (Parker, Maceo & All The Kings Men)
Maceo / Got to getcha / Southwick / Funky woman / Shake it baby / Better half / Don't waste this world away / (I remember) Mr. Banks / Thank you for letting me be myself again
CD ______ CPCD 8041
Charly / Jun '94 / Koch

FUNKY MUSIC MACHINE (Parker, Maceo & All The Kings Men)
Funky music machine / I want to sing / Dreams / Feeling alright / Something / Born to wander / TSU / For no one / Make it with you / Funky tale to tell
CD ______ CDSEWM 087
Southbound / Nov '93 / Pinnacle

SOUNDTRACK
CD ______ MM 801046
Minor Music / Feb '95 / Vital/SAM

Parker, Ray Jr.

BEST OF RAY PARKER JNR (Parker, Ray Jr. & Raydio)
Ghostbusters: *Parker, Ray Jr.* / You can't change that: *Raydio* / Woman needs love (just like you do): *Raydio* / More than one way to love a woman: *Raydio* / Stay the night: *Parker, Ray Jr.* / Let me go: *Parker, Ray Jr.* / Betcha can't love me just once: *Raydio* / Jack and Jill: *Raydio* / Other woman: *Parker, Ray Jr.* / Two places at the same time: *Parker, Ray Jr.* / Loving you: *Parker, Ray Jr.* / Girls are more fun: *Parker, Ray Jr.* / Is this a love thing: *Raydio* / For those who like to groove: *Raydio*
CD ______ 260365
Ariola / Dec '89 / BMG

COLLECTION, THE
Jack and Jill / You can't change that / Girls are more fun / Other woman / Is this a love thing / Still in the groove / Loving you / Bad boy / It's time to party now / Honey I'm rich / Two places at the same time / That old song / Let me go / Jamie / People next door / Ghostbusters
CD ______ 74321139862
Arista / Jul '93 / BMG

Parker, Robert

BAREFOOTIN'
Barefootin' / Let's go baby (where the action is) / Little bit of something / Sneakin' Sally through the alley / Better luck in the summertime / You see me / Give me the country side of life / Get right down / Get ta steppin' / Hiccup / Hot and cold / Skinny dippin' / I like what you do to me / Disco doctor
CD ______ CPCD 8013
Charly / Feb '94 / Koch

Parker, Rupert

CLASSICAL WORKS
CD ______ MSPCD 9601
Mabley St. / Sep '96 / Grapevine/ PolyGram

DOUBLE HARP (2CD Set)
CD Set ______ MSPCD 9301
Mabley St. / Sep '93 / Grapevine/ PolyGram

ELECTRIC HARP - ORIGINAL WORKS
CD ______ MSPCD 9504
Mabley St. / Sep '95 / Grapevine/ PolyGram

HARPBEAT
Earth song / How deep is your love / Tears in heaven / Unchained melody / You are not alone / Ironoco flow / Yesterday / Think twice / Free as a bird / Search for the hero / Kiss from a rose / I want to know what love is / Love is all around / Smile / Circle of life / Have you ever really loved a woman / Amazing grace
CD ________ HARPCD 1
Focus / Apr '96 / Total/BMG

SOLO
CD ________ MSPCD 9401
Mabley St. / Feb '94 / Grapevine/ PolyGram

SONGS FROM THE HARP (2CD Set)
Bridge over troubled water / Lady in red / Saving all my love / Daniel / Jealous guy / Careless whisper / Jameela / Moondance / Without you / Can't help falling in love with you / Stay with me 'til dawn / Music of the night / Throwing it all away / Wonderful tonight / Could it be magic / Up where we belong / He was beautiful / Since I don't have you / Long and winding road / Nobody does it better / Annie's song / Bright eyes / Weather with you / Vincent / Variation on a dream / Hello / I heard it through the grapevine / Power of love
CD Set ________ MSPCD 9404
Mabley St. / Nov '94 / Grapevine/PolyGram

WELL PLUCKED/WITH THE FLOW
Everything I do (I do it for you) / Sacrifice / Unchained Melody / Always A Woman / Three Times A Lady / She's not there / More Than Words / Wonder Why / One Day I'll Fly Away / Albatross / Eternal Flame / Best of my love / Oxygene / Miss You Nights
CD ________ VCD 3078
Victory Disques / Nov '92 / Grapevine/ PolyGram

Parker, Sonny

COMPLETE SONNY PARKER 1948-1953, THE
CD ________ BMCD 6003
Blue Moon / Jul '96 / Cadillac / Discovery / Greensleeves / Jazz Music / Jet Star / TKO Magnum

Parker, Teddy

NACHTEXPRESS NACH ST. TROPEZ
Nachtexpress nach St. Tropez / Hey little Lucy / Hatt ich ein weisses sportcoupe / Ich sah dich vorubergeh'n / Und dafur hast du nur ein Lacheln / Unser geheimnis / Geh' vorbei / Oh wie ist dah schon: *Parker, Teddy & Heidi Fischer* / Baby ich hol dich von der schule ab / Keine zeit / Wunderschones fremdes Madchen / Valentina / Heute bring' ich dich nach haus / So mussen teenager sein: *Parker, Teddy & Heidi Fischer* / Dream girl / Angela / Oh ja, oh yes, oh yeah / Baby muss das sein / Ein schones madchen so wie du / Oh Renata / Bossa nova in Panama / Holiday twist / In Copacabana / Liebe kalter als eis / Memphis Tennessee / das madchen mit dem taurigen blick / Leider leider / Sieben tage ohne Susi / Das siehst du nur bei mir / Alles wird gut: *Parker, Teddy & Leonie Bruckner* / Bist du einsam heut' nacht: *Parker, Teddy & Leonie Bruckner*
CD ________ BCD 15965
Bear Family / Dec '96 / Direct / Rollercoaster / Swift

Parker, Terence

TRAGEDIES OF A PLASTIC SOUL
CD ________ K7R 007CD
Studio K7 / Oct '96 / Prime / RTM/Disc

Parker, William

IN ORDER TO SURVIVE
CD ________ 1201592
Black Saint / Jan '96 / Cadillac / Harmonia Mundi

Parkin, Eric

MARIGOLD (Piano Impressions Of Billy Mayer)
Legends of King Arthur / Almond blossom / April's fool / Harp of the winds / Marigold / Railroad rhythm / Shallow waters / From a Spanish lattice / Song of the fir tree / Nimble fingered gentleman / Evening primrose / Ace of diamonds / Ace of hearts / Joker
CD ________ CHAN 8560
Chandos / '89 / Chandos

Parkins, Andrea

CAST IRON FACT
CD ________ KFWCD 184
Knitting Factory / Oct '96 / Cargo / Plastic Head

Parkins, Zeena

SHARK (Parkins, Zeena & Chris Cutler)
CD ________ RERCZ 1
ReR/Recommended / Oct '96 / ReR Megacorp / RTM/Disc

URSA'A DOOR
CD ________ VICTOCD 018
Victo / Nov '94 / Harmonia Mundi / ReR Megacorp

Parkinson, Chris

OUT OF HIS TREE
CD ________ PAN 147CD
Pan / Apr '94 / ADA / CM / Direct

Parkinson, Doug

IN AND OUT OF FOCUS 1966-1975
Sally go 'round the roses / Hey Gyp (dig the slowness) / And things unsaid / I had a dream / Advice / Dear Prudence / Without you / This must be the end / Hair / Baby blue eyes / Then I run / Today I feel no pain / Purple curtains / Pour out all you've got / Got to get a message to you / Do not go gentle / Caroline / Gotta get a groove / Love gun / Love is like a cloudy day / Everlasting love
CD ________ RVCD 58
Raven / Feb '97 / ADA / Direct

Parks, Van Dyke

CLANG OF THE YANKEE REAPER
Clang of the Yankee reaper / City on the hill / Pass that stage / Another dream / You're a real sweetheart / Love is the answer / Iron man / Tribute to Spree / Soul Train / Cannon in D
CD ________ 7599261852
Warner Bros. / Jan '96 / Warner Music

DISCOVER AMERICA
Jack Palance / Introduction / Bing Crosby / Steelband music / Four Mills brothers / Be careful / John Jones / FDR in Trinidad / Sweet Trinidad / Occapella / Sailin' shoes / Riverboat / Ode to Tobago / Your own comes first / G man hoover / Stars and stripes forever
CD ________ 7599261452
Warner Bros. / Jan '96 / Warner Music

IDIOSYNCRATIC PATH
Donovan's colours / John Jones / Pass that stage / Ode to Tobago / Attic / Clang of the Yankee reaper / Four mills brothers / You're a real sweetheart / Sailin' shoes / Vine street / Palm desert / Tribute to spree / Iron man / Sweet Trinidad / Be careful / Bing Crosby / Steelband music / Your own comes first / Stars and stripes forever
CD ________ DIAB 807
Diabolo / Oct '95 / Pinnacle

JUMP
Jump / Opportunity for two / Come along / I ain't going home / Many a mile to go / Taps / Invitation to sin, An / Home / After the ball / Look away / Hominy grove
CD ________ 7599238292
Warner Bros. / Jan '96 / Warner Music

SONG CYCLE
Vine Street / Palm desert / Widow's walk / Laurel Canyon Boulevard / All golden / Van Dyke Parks / Public domain / Donovan's colours / Attic / By the people / Potpourri
CD ________ EDCD 207
Edsel / Jul '88 / Pinnacle

Parlan, Horace

JOE VAN ENKHUIZEN MEETS THE RHYTHM SECTION
CD ________ CDSJP 249
Timeless Jazz / '88 / New Note/Pinnacle

US THREE
Us three / I want to be loved / Come rain or shine / Wadin' / Lady is a tramp / Walkin' / Return engagement
CD ________ CDP 8565812
Blue Note / Jun '97 / EMI

Parliament

CLONES OF DR. FUNKENSTEIN, THE
Prelude / Gamin' on ya / Dr. Funkenstein / Children of production / Gettin' to know you / Do that stuff / Everybody is on the one / I've been watching you / Funkin' for fun
CD ________ 8426202
Casablanca / Feb '91 / PolyGram

EARLY YEARS, THE
Red hot Mama / Come in out of the rain / Fantasy is reality / Breakdown / Loose booty / Unfinished instrumental / I call my baby pussycat / Put love in your life / Little old country boy / Moonshine heather (takin' care of business) / Oh Lord, why Lord/ Prayer / My automobile / There is nothing before me but thang / Funky woman / Livin' the life / Silent boatman
CD ________ DEEPM 023
Deep Beats / Jun '97 / BMG

GIVE UP THE FUNK (The Best Of Parliament)
CD ________ 5269952
Mercury / Sep '95 / PolyGram

Parmley, David

I KNOW A GOOD THING
I know a good thing when I feel it / Grandpa's radio / Have you come to say goodbye / She keeps hanging on / Someone took my place with you / Morristown / Excuse me / Down home / Someone on her mind / Sometimes silence says it all / Live and let live / From cotton to satin
CD ________ SHCD 3777
Sugar Hill / Jan '89 / ADA / CM / Direct / Koch / Roots

Parnell, Geoff

BRITPOP YEARS, THE
Alright / Wonderwall / Disco 2000 / High & dry / Girl like you / Changingman / Morning comes / Country house / Spaceman / Whatever / Venus as a boy / Two princes
CD ________ CDMFP 6226
Music For Pleasure / Aug '96 / EMI

Parnell, Jack

LIVE FROM RONNIE'S
Jamfs are coming / Autumn leaves / Whisper not / El Cahon / Airigin / Tenor madness / Alone together / Fried bananas / You don't know what love is / Whee
CD ________ CDSIV 1142
Horatio Nelson / Jul '95 / Disc

MEMORIES
Memories / Stardust / Touch of your lips / Shadow of your smile / I can't get started (with you) / Very thought of you / Serenade / I'll never smile again / Yesterdays / I had the craziest dream / Serenata / All the things you are / Remember / Way we were / Laura / Street of dreams
CD ________ 2MEM 1
Berkeley / Jan '89 / Jazz Music

Parnell, Lee Roy

EVERY NIGHT'S A SATURDAY NIGHT
Lucky me, lucky you / You can't get there from here / One foot in front of the other / All that matters anymore / Every night's a Saturday night / Tender touch / Better word for love / Honky tonk night time man / Baton rouge / Mama screw your wig on tight
CD ________ 7822188412
RCA / Jul '97 / BMG

LOVE WITHOUT MERCY
What kind of fool do you think I am / Back in my arms again / Rock / Ain't no short way home / Love without mercy / Road scholar / Night after night / Done deal / Tender moment / Rollercoaster
CD ________ 07822186842
Arista / Jan '94 / BMG

ON THE ROAD
CD ________ 07822187392
Arista / Jun '94 / BMG

WE ALL GET LUCKY SOMETIMES
Little bit of you / Knock yourself out / Heart's desire / When a woman loves a man / If the house is rockin' / We all get lucky sometimes / Saved by the grace of your love / Givin' water to a drowning man / I had to let it go / Squeeze me in / Catwalk
CD ________ 07822187902
Arista / Aug '95 / BMG

Parov, Nikola

KILIM
Anonym / Trance Danubius / Diva's smile / Mayo woman / Satyr's night / Tsami / Ritual / Passio
CD ________ HNCD 1408
Hannibal / Mar '97 / ADA / Vital

Parr, John

JOHN PARR
Magical / Naughty naughty / Love grammar / Treat me a like an animal / She's gonna love you to death / Revenge / Heartbreaker / Somebody stole my thunder / Don't leave your mark on me / St. Elmo's fire
CD ________ 8263842
London / Oct '85 / PolyGram

RUNNING THE ENDLESS MILE
Two hearts / Don't worry 'bout me / King of lies / Running the endless mile / Don't leave your mark on me / Scratch / Do it again / Blame it on the radio / Story still remains the same / Steal you away
CD ________ 8304012
London / Oct '86 / PolyGram

Parra, Violeta

PAROLES ET MUSIQUES
CD ________ 3020782
Last Call / Jun '97 / Cargo / Direct / Discovery

Parris, Rebecca

SPRING
Alone at night / It's you / Tell me on a Ferris wheel / You look so good / Save your love for me / He comes to me for comfort / You'll finally understand / Not like this / Spring
CD ________ 8443132
Limelight / Apr '94 / PolyGram

Parrondo, Jose

RECITAL DE CANTE FLAMENCO (Parrondo, Jose & Miguel Iven)
Malaguenas / Tientos y tangos / Solea / Tonas / Peteneras / Seguiriyas / Bulerias
CD ________ 93052
Emocion / Jul '95 / New Note/Pinnacle

Parry, Dylan & Neil

GOREUON (20 Welsh Country Songs) (Parry, Dylan & Neil/Traed Wadin)
Hen wlad llyn: *Parry, Dylan & Neil* / Eiddo i arall: *Parry, Dylan & Neil* / Cydio'n dy law: *Parry, Dylan & Neil* / Waunfawr: *Parry, Dylan & Neil* / Ei gwen yn y gwin: *Parry, Dylan & Neil* / Yr hen rebel: *Parry, Dylan & Neil* / Heli'n fy ngwaed: *Parry, Dylan & Neil* / Dyri i mi: *Parry, Dylan & Neil* / O mor braf fydd bod yn ol: *Parry, Dylan & Neil* / Ffrind: *Parry, Dylan & Neil* / Lliwiau: *Parry, Dylan & Neil* / Nid yw'r hen bentre fel y bu: *Parry, Dylan & Neil* / Troi'r cloc yn ol: *Parry, Dylan & Neil* / Blodau gwyn: *Parry, Dylan & Neil* / Potel fach o win: *Traed Wadin* / Mynd fel bom: *Traed Wadin* / Pys: *Traed Wadin* / Galilea: *Traed Wadin* / Hitio'r botel: *Traed Wadin* / 'Fory heb ei gyffwrdd: *Traed Wadin*
CD ________ SCD 2161
Sain / May '97 / ADA / Direct / Greyhound

Parry, Harry

GONE WITH THE WIND
Basin Street ball / Crazy rhythm / Sophisticated lady / Mr. Five by Five / If I had you / I can't dance / Don't you know I care (or don't you care to) / Who's sorry now / Someone's in the kitchen with Dinah / Stardust / I never knew / Boogie rides to Yorke / Onm the sunny side of the street / Don't be that way / Angry / Darktown strutters ball / Blues around my bed / Champagne / My favourite dream / Blue Lou / Bounce me brother with a solid four / Honeysuckle rose / Gone with the wind / Parry party
CD ________ RAJCD 840
Empress / Feb '95 / Koch

Parsons, Alan

ALAN PARSONS ON AIR
Blue blue sky / Too close to the sun / Blown by the wind / Cloudbreak / I can't look down / Brother up in Heaven / Fall free / Apollo / So far away / One day to fly / Blue blue sky
CD ________ TOTCD 6
Total / Mar '97 / Total/BMG

AMMONIA AVENUE (Parsons, Alan Project)
Prime time / Let me go home / One good reason / Since the last goodbye / Don't answer me / Dancing on a high wire / You don't believe / Pipeline / Ammonia Avenue
CD ________ 258885
Arista / '88 / BMG

BEST OF ALAN PARSONS PROJECT, THE (Parsons, Alan Project)
I wouldn't want to be like you / Eye in the sky / Games people play / Time / Pyramania / You wouldn't believe / Lucifer / Psychobabble / Damned if I do / Don't let it show / Can't take it with you / Old and wise
CD ________ 610052
Arista / Aug '95 / BMG

EVE (Parsons, Alan Project)
Lucifer / You lie down with the dogs / I'd rather be a man / You won't be there / Winding me up / Damned if I do / Don't hold back / Secret garden / If I could change your mind
CD ________ 258981
Arista / '88 / BMG

EYE IN THE SKY (Parsons, Alan Project)
Syrius / Eye in the sky / Children of the moon / Gemini / Silence and I / You're gonna get your fingers burned / Psychobabble / Mammagamma / Step by step / Old and wise
CD ________ 258718
Arista / Aug '95 / BMG

GREATEST HITS LIVE
CD ________ TOTCD 7
Total / Jul '97 / Total/BMG

I ROBOT (Parsons, Alan Project)
I wouldn't want to be like you / Some other time / Breakdown / Don't let it show / Voice / Nucleus / Day after day / Total eclipse / Genesis ch.1 vs.32 / I robot
CD ________ 259651
Arista / Mar '89 / BMG

PLAYS THE ALAN PARSONS PROJECT (Powell, Andrew)
Lucifer (Mamma Gamma) / Time / Games people play / Robot suite / Damned if I do / Pavane / What goes up / Eye in the sky / Old and wise
CD ________ DC 876742
Disky / May '97 / Disky / THE

PYRAMID (Parsons, Alan Project)
Voyager / What goes up... / Eagle will rise again / One more river / Can't take it with you / In the lap of the gods / Pyramania / Hyper gamma spaces / Shadow of a lonely man
CD ________ 258983
Arista / Apr '88 / BMG

TALES OF MYSTERY (Parsons, Alan Project)
Dream within a dream / Raven / Tell-tale heart / Cask of Amontillado / Dr. Tarr and

Professor Fether / Fall of the House of Usher / To one in Paradise
CD 8328202
London / Jun '92 / PolyGram

TRY ANYTHING ONCE (Parsons, Alan Project)
Three of me / Turn it up / Wine from the water / Breakaway / Jigue / Mr. Time / Siren song / Back against the wall / Re-jigue / Oh life (there must be more) / I'm talking to you / Dreamscape
CD 74321167302
Arista / Sep '96 / BMG

TURN OF A FRIENDLY CARD (Parsons, Alan Project)
Turn of a friendly card / Gold bug / Time / Games people play / I don't wanna go home / Nothing left to lose / May be a price to pay
CD 258982
Arista / May '88 / BMG

VERY BEST OF ALAN PARSONS PROJECT LIVE, THE (Parsons, Alan Project)
Sirius / Eye in the sky / Psychobabble / Raven / Time / Luciferama / Old and wise / You're gonna get your fingers burned / Prime time / Limelight / Don't answer me / Standing on higher ground / When / Take the money and run / You're the voice
CD 09026682292
RCA Victor / Jan '96 / BMG

VULTURE CULTURE (Parsons, Alan Project)
Let's talk about me / Separate lives / Days are numbers (The traveller) / Sooner or later / Vulture culture / Hawkeye / Somebody out there / Same old song and dance
CD 258884
Arista / '88 / BMG

Parsons, Dave

RECONCILE
CD AICD 002
A+I / Sep '96 / Koch / Scratch/BMG

Parsons, Gram

COSMIC AMERICAN MUSIC (The Grech Tapes 1972)
Song for you / Kentucky blues / Streets of Baltimore / Folsom prison blues / Lovesick blues / New soft shoe / How much I've lied / Still feeling blue / Ain't no Beatle, ain't no Rolling Stone / How can I forget you/Cry one more time / Song for you / Streets of Baltimore / That's all it took / Somebody's back in town / More and more / Teaching Emmy to sweep out the ashes / Daddy's fiddle / We'll sweep out the ashes in the morning / Cold cold heart / That's all it took / Song for you
CD CDSD 077
Sundown / Aug '96 / TKO Magnum

GP/GRIEVOUS ANGEL
Still feeling blue / We'll sweep out the ashes in the morning / Song for you / Streets of Baltimore / She / That's all it took / New soft shoe / Kiss the children / Cry one more time / How much I've lied / Big mouth blues / Return of the grievous angel / Hearts on fire / I can't dance / Brass buttons / Thousand dollar wedding / Cash on the barrelhead / Hickory wind / Love hurts / Ooh Las Vegas / In my hour of darkness
CD 7599261082
WEA / Jan '94 / Warner Music

LIVE 1973 (Parsons, Gram & Fallen Angels)
We'll sweep out the ashes / Country baptizing / Drug store truck drivin' man / Big mouth blues / New soft shoe / Cry one more time / Streets of Baltimore / That's all it took / Love hurts / California cottonfields / Encore medley
CD 8122727262
Rhino / Mar '97 / Warner Music

SAFE AT HOME (Parsons, Gram International Submarine Band)
Blue eyes / I must have been somebody else / You've known a satisfied mind / Folsom Prison blues / That's alright Mama / Millers cave / I still miss someone / Luxury liner / Strong boy / Do you know how it feels to be lonesome
CD CDSD 071
Sundown / Aug '97 / TKO Magnum

WARM EVENINGS, PALE MORNINGS AND BOTTLED BLUES 1963-1973
Zah's blues: *Shilohs* / Blue eyes: *International Submarine Band* / Strong boy: *International Submarine Band* / Truck driving man: *International Submarine Band* / Hot burrito: *Flying Burrito Brothers* / Christine's tune: *Flying Burrito Brothers* / Sin City: *Flying Burrito Brothers* / Dark end of the street: *Flying Burrito Brothers* / Wild horses: *Flying Burrito Brothers* / She: *Parsons, Gram & Emmylou Harris* / New soft shoe: *Parsons, Gram & Emmylou Harris* / We'll sweep out the ashes in the morning: *Parsons, Gram & Emmylou Harris* / Brass buttons: *Parsons, Gram & Emmylou Harris* / Return of the grievous angel: *Parsons, Gram & Emmylou Harris* / Drug store truck drivin' man: *Parsons, Gram & Emmylou Harris* / Brand new heartache: *Parsons, Gram & Emmylou Harris* / Love hurts: *Parsons, Gram & Emmylou Harris* / I'm your toy
CD RVCD 24
Raven / Jun '92 / ADA / Direct

Parsons, Niamh

LOOSELY CONNECTED
Katie Campbell's rambles / Streets of Forbes / Tinkerman's daughter / Little big time / Lover's ghost / Man of Arran / North Amerikay / We two people / One morning in May / Play a merry jig / Where are you (tonight I wonder) / Don't give your heart away
CD CDTRAX 052
Greentrax / May '92 / ADA / Direct / Duncans / Highlander

LOOSEN UP
Big bad wolf / Seeing things / Fancy waistcoat / Clohinne winds / Gently born/Micky Dans / Closer to you / Briar and the rose / I know my faith (is worth much more than me) / Heartbound express / Loosen up
CD GLCD 1167
Green Linnet / Jul '97 / ADA / CM / Direct / Highlander / Roots

Partisans

POLICE STORY
CD GET 15CD
Get Back / May '97 / Cargo / Pinnacle

Parton, Dolly

BEST OF DOLLY PARTON, THE
Jolene / I will always love you / Lonely comin' down / It's my time / Harper Valley PTA / Mama say a prayer / DIVORCE / We used to / Bobby's arms / Seeker / Hold me / Here you come again / Lovin' you / Sweet music man / I really got the feeling / Baby I'm burnin' / Two doors down / 9 to 5 / Me and little Andy / Love is like a butterfly / Do I ever cross your mind
CD 74321476802
Camden / Apr '97 / BMG

COLLECTION, THE
Save the last dance for me / I walk the line / Turn, turn, turn / Downtown / We had it all / She don't love you (like I love you) / We'll sing in the sunshine / I can't help myself / Elusive butterfly / Great pretender / Harper Valley PTA / DIVORCE / I will always love you / Jolene / Nine to Five / Here you come again
CD 74321139872
RCA / Jul '93 / BMG

COUNTRY GIRL
Jolene / My Tennessee mountain home / Bargain store / Love is like a butterfly / Just the two of us: *Parton, Dolly & Porter Wagoner* / I will always love you / Touch your woman / Seeker / Travelling man / Daddy come and get me / My blue tears / Coat of many colours / Joshua / Washday blues / Mule skinner blues (Blue yodel #8) / Coming for to carry me home / Afraid to love again: *Parton, Dolly & Porter Wagoner* / I washed my face in the morning dew: *Parton, Dolly & Porter Wagoner*
CD CDMFP 5914
Music For Pleasure / Apr '91 / EMI

ESSENTIAL DOLLY PARTON VOL.1, THE (I Will Always Love You)
Nine to five / Simple woman / Think about love / But you know I love you / Do I ever cross your mind / Real love / You're the only one / Sweet summer lovin' / Heartbreak Express / Tie our love (in a double knot) / Islands in the stream: *Rogers, Kenny & Dolly Parton* / Two doors down / God won't get you / Don't call it love / To Daddy / Starting over again / Tennessee homesick blues / Save the last dance for me / Old flames (can't hold a candle to you) / I will always love you
CD 74321665332
RCA / Feb '96 / BMG

ESSENTIAL DOLLY PARTON VOL.2, THE
Muleskinner blues / Touch your woman / Bargain store / Coat of many colours / My Tennessee mountain home / Joshua / Just because I'm a woman / Jolene / I will always love you / Light of a clear blue morning / Here you come again / Love is like a butterfly / We used to / Me and little Andy / It's all wrong but it's all right / All I can do / Heartbreaker / I really got the feeling / Seeker / Wings of a dove
CD 7863669332
RCA / May '97 / BMG

GREATEST HITS
Here you come again / Think about love / Baby I'm burning / Love is like a butterfly / Save the last dance for me / Heartbreaker / But you know I love you / Nine to Five / Islands in the stream / Don't call it love / Old flames (can't hold a candle to you) / Bargain store / Real love / Potential new boyfriend / Jolene / I will always love you / I really got the feeling / Starting over again / We had it all / You're the only one
CD PD 90407
RCA / Dec '89 / BMG

I WILL ALWAYS LOVE YOU (And Other Greatest Hits)
Why'd you come in here looking like that / Yellow roses / White limozeen / Eagle when she flies / Romeo / Rockin' years / To Daddy / Silver and gold / He's alive / I will always love you
CD 4838572
Columbia / Apr '96 / Sony

JOLENE
Jolene / When someone wants to leave / River of happiness / Early morning breeze / Highlight of my life / I will always love you / Randy / Living on memories of you / Lonely comin' down / It must be you
CD WMCD 5638
Disky / May '94 / Disky / THE

LOVE ALBUM VOL.1, THE
You are / Heartbreaker / Bargain store / I will always love you / Love is like a butterfly / Coat of many colours / Islands in the stream / Here you come again / Send me the pillow that you dream on / It's all wrong but it's all right / Jolene / One of those days
CD ND 90307
RCA / Feb '89 / BMG

LOVE ALBUM VOL.2, THE
We used to / You're the only one / But you know I love you / We had it all / Sweet music man / My girl (my love) / Almost in love / Sandy's song / I really don't want to know: *Parton, Dolly/Willie Nelson/Kris Kristofferson* / Sweet summer lovin' / Love I used to call mine / Starting over again
CD ND 90455
RCA / Nov '90 / BMG

SOMETHING SPECIAL
Crippled bird / Something special / Change / I will always love you / Green eyed boy / Speakin' of the Devil / Jolene / No good way of saying goodbye / Seeker / Teach me to trust
CD 4807542
Columbia / Sep '95 / Sony

TREASURES
Peace train / Today I started loving you again / Just when I need you most / Something's burning / Before the next teardrop falls / After the goldrush / Walking on sunshine / Behind closed doors / Don't let me cross over / Satin sheets / For the good times
CD RTD 80326
Rising Tide / Oct '96 / BMG

TRIO (Parton, Dolly/Linda Ronstadt/ Emmylou Harris)
Pain of loving you / Making plans / To know him is to love him / Hobo's meditation / Wildflowers / Telling me lies / My dear companion / Those memories of you / I've had enough / Rose wood casket / Farther along
CD 9254912
WEA / Feb '95 / Warner Music

Partridge, Andy

THROUGH THE HILL (Partridge, Andy & Harold Budd)
Hand 19 / Through the hill / Great valley of gongs / Western island of apples / Anima mundi / Hand 20 / Place of odd glances / Well for the sweat of the moon / Tenochtitlan's numberless bridges / Ceramic avenue / Hand 21 / Missing pieces in the game of salt and onyx / Mantle of peacock bones / Bronze coins showing genitals / Bearded aphrodite / Hand 22
CD ASCD 021
All Saints / Jan '95 / Discovery / Vital

Party Animals

GOOD VIBRATIONS
CD DB 47862
Deep Blue / Oct '96 / PolyGram

Party Boppers

SINGALONG ROCK 'N' ROLL PARTY
(We're gonna) rock around the clock / Shake, rattle and roll / See you later alligator / Shake, rattle and roll (reprise) / Bye bye love / Wake up little Susie / All I have to do is dream / Bird dog / Everyday / Heartbeat / Oh boy / That'll be the day / Peggy Sue / Rave on / Raining in my heart / It's my party / Locomotion / Stupid cupid / Sweet nothin's / Lipstick on your collar / Ma, he's making eyes at me / Ain't that a shame / Blueberry hill / Great balls of fire / Tutti frutti / Long tall Sally / Good golly Miss Molly / Whole lotta shakin' goin' on / C'mon everybody / Weekend / Summertime blues / Three steps to heaven / Hound dog / All shook up / Let me be your teddy bear / Blue suede shoes / Jailhouse rock / Return to sender / Wooden heart / Love me tender / Wonder of you
CD CDMFP 5834
Music For Pleasure / Oct '93 / EMI

Party Diktator

WORLDWIDE
CD DEP 003CD
Dead Eye / Nov '92 / SRD

Party Poppers

40 SING-ALONG FAVOURITES
Down at the old Bull And Bush / Daisy bell / Two lovely black eyes / Joshua / Oh oh Antonio / I'm forever blowing bubbles / Hello hello, who's your lady friend / You must have been a beautiful baby / Daddy wouldn't buy me a bow-wow / Waiting at the church / It's a long way to Tipperary / Pack up your troubles in your old kit back / Goodbye Dolly Gray / Bless 'em all / Hold your hand out, naughty boy / I do like to be beside the seaside / Lilly of Laguna / Tip toe tho' the tulips with me / Honeysuckle and the bee / Roamin' in the gloamin' / On mother Kelly's doorstep / Roll out the barrel / Who were you with last night / Don't dilly dally on the way / When you're smiling / Ma, he's making eyes at me / Side by side / (In) a shanty in old Shanty Town / On a slow boat to China / Bye bye blackbird / I'm shy, Mary Ellen, I'm shy / Let me call you sweetheart / When I grow too old to dream / On moonlight bay / By the light of the silvery moon / If you were the only girl in the world / You were meant for me / Ain't she sweet / Nellie Dean / Show me the way to go home
CD CDMFP 6105
Music For Pleasure / Jan '94 / EMI

ALL TOGETHER NOW (20 Sing-Along Anthems)
Three lions / We are the champions / Simply the best / We all stand together/All you need is love/Give peace a chan / On Ilkely Moor / We shall not be moved / When the Saints go marching in / Glory glory hallelujah / I'm forever blowing bubbles / Three lions / In my Liverpool home / He's got the whole world in his hands / Swing low, sweet chariot / Scotland the Brave / End of the road / Men of Harlech / I love you love me love / You'll never walk alone / Rule Britannia / Land of hope and glory / 'Ere we go
CD CDMFP 6278
Music For Pleasure / Nov '96 / EMI

LET'S HAVE A PARTY
Let's have a party / Agadoo / Let's twist again / March of the Mods / Birdie song / Simon says / Lambeth walk / Boomps a daisy / Y viva Espana / Paloma blanca / La Bamba / I came, I saw, I conga'd / Scotland the brave / Hokey cokey dance / Knees up Mother Brown / Can can / Hi ho silver lining / Last waltz / Auld lang syne
CD CDMFP 5948
Music For Pleasure / Oct '92 / EMI

SINGALONG 60'S PARTY
Sergeant Pepper's lonely hearts club band / Mighty Quinn / Downtown / Summer holiday / When I'm sixty four / little lovin' / With a little help from my friends / King of the road / I want to hold your hand / Winchester Cathedral / Sugar sugar / Hard day's night / Ob-la-di ob-la-da / World without love / Ferry 'cross the Mersey / Yellow submarine / Can't buy me love / Carnival is over / Hey Jude / Have I the right / Baby, now that I've found you / Oh pretty woman / Release me / Green green grass of home / I can't stop loving you / Crying in the chapel / Young ones / I like it / There's a kind of hush / I only want to be with you / How do you do it / Bachelor boy / Delilah / You'll never walk alone / Are you lonesome tonight / Last waltz
CD CDMFP 5892
Music For Pleasure / Sep '90 / EMI

SINGALONG CHRISTMAS PARTY VOL.1
White Christmas / I saw Mommy kissing Santa Claus / Let it snow, let it snow, let it snow / Frosty the snowman / Happy holiday / That's what I'd like for Christmas / When Santa got stuck up the chimney / It's the most wonderful time of the year / We three kings of Orient are / Jingle bells / Good King Wenceslas / Kings' horses / Santa Claus is coming to town / Rudolph the red nosed reindeer / Holiday season / Mary's boy child / When a child is born / Silent night / Deck the halls with boughs of holly / Stop the cavalry / Have yourself a merry little Christmas / Christmas song / Do you hear what I hear / Christmas dreaming / Little donkey / Winter wonderland / It's beginning to look like Christmas / I saw three ships / All I want for Christmas (is my two front teeth) / Silver bells / Sleigh ride / Joy to the world / I wish it could be Christmas every day / Merry Christmas everybody / We wish you a Merry Christmas / Auld lang syne / Christmas alphabet / Fairy on the Christmas tree / Jolly old St. Nicholas / Mr. Santa / Mistletoe and wine / Little drummer boy / O little town of Bethlehem / It came upon a midnight clear / God rest ye merry gentlemen
CD CDMFP 5795
Music For Pleasure / Dec '94 / EMI

SINGALONG CHRISTMAS PARTY VOL.2
Good Christian men rejoice / Here we come a-wassailing / I believe in Father Christmas / Rockin' around the Christmas tree / Mary had a baby boy / Jingle bell rock / Baby it's cold outside / Go tell it on the mountain / Twelve days of Christmas / Hark the herald angels sing / O come all ye faithful (adeste fidelis) / One in royal David's city / See amid the winter's snow / Angels from the realms of Glory / Saviour's day / Wonderful Christmas time / Ding dong merrily on high / On

Christmas night all Christians sing / O Christmas tree / First Noel / Away in a manger / Happy Christmas (war is over) / Do they know it's Christmas / Scarlet ribbons / Coventry carol / While shepherds watched their flocks by night / Rocking carol / Rise up shepherd and follow / Last Christmas / Merry Christmas everyone / Rockin' around the Christmas tree (reprise)
CD CDMFP 6180
Music For Pleasure / Oct '96 / EMI

Parveen, Abida

BEST OF ABIDA PARVEEN, THE
CD SHCD 64086
Shanachie / May '97 / ADA / Greensleeves / Koch

Pasadena Roof Orchestra

BEST OF THE PASADENA ROOF ORCHESTRA, THE
CD MATCD 313
Castle / Jun '95 / BMG

BEST OF THE PASADENA ROOF ORCHESTRA, THE
CD TRTCD 199
TrueTrax / Jun '95 / THE

BREAKAWAY
Breakaway / Jeepers creepers / Piccolo Pete / Very thought of you / Continental / Temptation rag / Sweet Georgia Brown / Ain't misbehavin' / Play that hot guitar / Rockin' chair / That's a plenty / Zing went the strings of my heart / Tom Thumb's drum / Love is good for anything that ails you / Stompin' at the Savoy / Just one more chance / Man from the South
CD CD PRO 3
Pasadena Roof Orchestra / Oct '91 / New Note/Pinnacle

COLLECTION, THE
It don't mean a thing if it ain't got that swing / Bye bye blackbird / Black bottom / Charleston / Temptation rag / Blue skies / What is this thing called love / Lullaby of Broadway / Nobody's sweetheart / You're the cream in my coffee / Singin' in the rain / Top hat, white tie and tails / I won't dance / Three little words / Stormy weather / Don't be that way / I'll see you again / Pasadena / Georgia / Whispering / Paddlin' Madelin' home / Varsity drag / Here's to the next time / Cheek to cheek
CD CCSCD 189
Castle / Jul '88 / BMG

GREATEST HITS
CD CD 845006
Bluebird / Jan '94 / BMG

HOME IN PASADENA
CD PDSCD 527
Pulse / Aug '96 / BMG

PASADENA - THE 25TH ANNIVERSARY
You ought to see Sally on sunday / Lullaby of broadway / Ol' man river / By the fireside / Puttin' on the ritz / Kansas city kitty / Old man blues / Happy days are here again / Home in Pasadena / You're my everything / Me and Jane in a plane / I want to be happy / Maple leaf ray / Some of these days / As time goes by / St. Louis blues
CD CDPRO 4
Pasadena Roof Orchestra / Mar '94 / New Note/Pinnacle

RHYTHM IS OUR BUSINESS
CD CDPRO 5
Pasadena Roof Orchestra / Oct '96 / New Note/Pinnacle

SENTIMENTAL JOURNEY
CD MCCD 110
Music Club / Jun '93 / Disc / THE

STEPPING OUT
Who walks in / My melancholy baby / How 'm doin / Creole love call / Sahara / Skirts / Pennies from Heaven / Latin from Manhattan / Business in 'F' / I can't get started (with you) / Louisiana / Golden wedding / I only have eyes for you / Minnie the moocher / Stepping out / Pasadena
CD CDPRO 2
Pasadena Roof Orchestra / Jan '90 / New Note/Pinnacle

TAKE ME BACK (Pasadena Roof Orchestra & The Swing Sisters)
When the midnight choo choo / Leaves for Alabam / Old yazoo / Dinah / Heebie jeebies / Nightinggale sang in Berkeley Square / It don't mean a thing if it ain't got that swing / Everybody loves my baby / Mood indigo / Civilization / Can't help lovin' that man / Sentimental gentleman fron Georgia / I'm sorry for myself / When I take my sugar to tea / Shoo shoo baby
CD EMPRCD 627
Emporio / Jun '96 / Disc

Pascoal, Hermeto

FESTA DOS DEUSES (Pascoal, Hermeto Group)
O galo do airan / Rainha da pedra azull / Viajando pelo Brasil / O farol que nos guia / Pensamento positivo / Peneirando agua / Cancao no paiol em curitiba aula de natacao / Tres coisas irmaos Latinos / Depois do baile / Quando as aves se encontram / Nasce o som / 'Round midnight / Fazenda nova / Ginga carioca / Chapeu de baeta
CD 5104072
Philips / May '93 / PolyGram

MUSICA LIVRE DE HERMETO PASCOAL, A (The Free Music Of Hermeto Pascoal)
Bebe / Carinhoso / Pin / Sereiarei / Asa branca / Gaio de roseira
CD 8246212
Verve / Apr '94 / PolyGram

Pass, Joe

APPASSIONATO
Relaxin' at Camarillo / Grooveyard / Body and soul / Nica's dream / Tenderly / When it's sleepy time down South / Red door / Gee baby ain't I good to you / Li'l darlin' / That's Earl brother / Stuffy / You're driving me crazy
CD CD 2310946
Pablo / Apr '94 / Cadillac / Complete/ Pinnacle

AT AKRON UNIVERSITY
It's a wonderful world / Body and soul / Bridgework / Tarde / Time in / Duke Ellington medley / Joy spring / I'm glad there is you
CD CD 2308249
Pablo / May '94 / Cadillac / Complete/ Pinnacle

BETTER DAYS
CD EFA 120682
Hotwire / May '95 / SRD

BLUES FOR FRED
Cheek to cheek / Night and day / Blues for Fred / Oh lady be good / Foggy day / Be myself / They can't take that away from me / Dancing in the dark / I concentrate on you / Way you look tonight
CD CD 2310931
Pablo / Apr '94 / Cadillac / Complete/ Pinnacle

CHECKMATE (Pass, Joe & Jimmy Rowles)
What's your story Morning Glory / So rare / As long as I live / Marquita / Stardust / We'll be together again / Can't we be friends / 'Deed I do / 'Tis Autumn / God bless the child
CD CD 2310865
Pablo / May '94 / Cadillac / Complete/ Pinnacle

CHOPS (Pass, Joe & Niels Pederson)
Have you met Miss Jones / Oleo / Lover man / Five pound blues / Come rain or come shine / Quiet nights / Tricrotism / Old folks / Yardbird suite / Your own sweet way
CD OJCCD 786
Original Jazz Classics / Jun '94 / Complete/ Pinnacle / Jazz Music / Wellard

DUETS (Pass, Joe & John Pisano)
Alone together / Baileywick / S'il vous plait / Lonely woman / Nina's birthday song / You were meant for me / Satie / Blues for the wee folk / For him H / Back to back
CD 23109592
Pablo / Dec '96 / Cadillac / Complete/ Pinnacle

EXIMIOUS (Pass, Joe Trio)
Foxy chick and a cool cat / Robbin's nest / Lush life / Serenata / We'll be together again / You to me are everything / Love for sale / Everything I got belongs to you / Night and day / Speak low
CD CD 2310877
Pablo / Apr '87 / Cadillac / Complete/ Pinnacle

FINALLY (Live In Stockholm) (Pass, Joe & Red Mitchell)
Shadow of your smile / Have you met Miss Jones / I thought about you / Doxy / All the things you are / These foolish things / Blue moon / For Django / Finally / Pennies from Heaven / Softly as in a morning sunrise
CD 5126032
EmArCy / Apr '93 / PolyGram

I REMEMBER CHARLIE PARKER
Just friends / Easy to love / Summertime / April in Paris / Everything happens to me / Laura / They can't take that away from me / I didn't know what time it was / If I should lose you / Out of nowhere (concept 1) / Out of nowhere (concept 2)
CD OJCCD 602
Original Jazz Classics / Nov '95 / Complete/ Pinnacle / Jazz Music / Wellard

IRA, GEORGE AND JOE (Joe Pass Loves Gershwin)
Bidin' my time / How long has this been going on / Soon / Oh lady be good / But not for me / Foggy day / It ain't necessarily so / Our love is here to stay / 'S wonderful / Nice work if you can get it / Embraceable you
CD OJCCD 828
Original Jazz Classics / Jun '95 / Complete/ Pinnacle / Jazz Music / Wellard

JOE PASS IN HAMBURG
On a clear day / Polka For Nina / dots and moonbeams / Love for sale / Indian summer / Sweet bossa / Fragments of blues / I'll know / Summer night / Waltz for Django / More than you know / Star eyes / Lullabye of the leaves / Soft winds / Sister Sadie
CD ACT 91002
Act / Sep '97 / New Note/Pinnacle

JOY SPRING
Joy spring / Some time ago / Night that has a thousand eyes / Relaxin' at Camarillo / There is no greater love
CD CDP 8352222
Pacific Jazz / Jan '96 / EMI

LIVE AT DONTE'S (Pass, Joe Trio)
What have they done to my song Ma / You stepped out of a dream / Time for love / Donte's inferno / You are the sunshine of my life / Secret love / Sweet Georgia Brown / Stompin' at the Savoy / Darn that dream / Milestones / Lullaby of the leaves / What are you doing the rest of your life / Blues for Pam
CD CD 2620114
Pablo / Apr '87 / Cadillac / Complete/ Pinnacle

LIVE AT LONG BEACH COLLEGE
Wave / Blues in G / All the things you are / 'Round midnight / Here's that rainy day / Duke Ellington's sophisticated lady melange / Blues dues / Bluesette / Honeysuckle rose
CD CD 2308239
Pablo / Apr '87 / Cadillac / Complete/ Pinnacle

MY SONG
CD CD 83326
Telarc / Aug '93 / Conifer/BMG

ONE FOR MY BABY
Bluesology / One for my baby (and one more for the road) / JP blues / Poinciana / I don't stand a ghost of a chance with you / I remember you / Bay city blues / Song is you
CD CD 2310936
Pablo / May '94 / Cadillac / Complete/ Pinnacle

PORTRAITS OF DUKE ELLINGTON
Satin doll / I let a song go out of my heart / Sophisticated lady / I got it bad and that ain't good / In a mellow tone / Solitude / Don't get around much anymore / Do nothin' 'til you hear from me / Caravan
CD CD 2310716
Pablo / May '86 / Cadillac / Complete/ Pinnacle

SUMMER NIGHTS
Summer nights / Anouman / Douce ambience / For Django / D-Joe / I got rhythm / E blue eyes / Belleville / In my solitude / Tears / In a sentimental mood / Them there eyes
CD CD 2310939
Pablo / Apr '94 / Cadillac / Complete/ Pinnacle

VIRTUOSO
Night and day / Stella by starlight / Here's that rainy day / My old flame / How high the moon / Cherokee / Sweet Lorraine / Have you met Miss Jones / 'Round midnight / All the things you are / Blues for Alican / Song is you
CD CD 2310708
Pablo / May '94 / Cadillac / Complete/ Pinnacle

VIRTUOSO LIVE
Stompin' at the Savoy / Just the way you are / Eric's smoozies blues / Beautiful love / Daquilo que eu sei / In the wee small hours of the morning / Love for sale / Mack the knife / So what's new / (Back home again in) Indiana
CD CD 2310948
Pablo / Jul '94 / Cadillac / Complete/ Pinnacle

WHITESTONE
Light in your eyes / Shuffle city / Estate / Daquilo que eu sei / Whitestone / Lovin' eyes / Amancer / I can't help it / Tarde / Fleeting moments
CD CD 2310912
Pablo / May '94 / Cadillac / Complete/ Pinnacle

Passage

SEEDY (The Best Of The Passage)
Xoyo / Carnal / Sharp tongue / Devils and angels / Horseplay / Man of war / Armour / Fear / Good and useful life / Drugface / Love is as / Angleland / Certain way to go / Time will tell / 2711 / Wave / Taboos
CD CDMRED 146
Cherry Red / Sep '97 / Pinnacle

Passaggio

PASSAGGIO (QUINTET CELEA COUTURIER)
L'Ibere / Lucculus / Arno / Ole rafafa / Gala / Norvegian flamenco / Hip / Warm canto / Hep / My foolish heart / Tabato / L'autre
CD LBLC 6567
Label Bleu / Nov '95 / New Note/Pinnacle

Passion Fodder

FAT TUESDAY
Extra extra / IOU / So this is love / My world is empty without you / I want it to be real / Dream / Move / Luz blanca / St. Helens / Heart hunters / Mardi gras / Skin poetry / In the echo / Hot waltz away / In the moodswing / Hard work / As you dig your hole / Tomorrow is a long time / Paname song / Violations / Dirt / God couldn't fight his way out of a wet brown bag
CD BBL 83CD
Beggars Banquet / Feb '90 / RTM/Disc / Warner Music

LOVE, WALTZES AND ANARCHY
Polished off / Pascal's waltz / Kill me Hannah / Hunger burns / Orwell cooks / Spokane / Struggle for love / Pray, anarchist / Girl that I marry
CD BBL 94CD
Beggars Banquet / '92 / RTM/Disc / Warner Music

WOKE UP THIS MORNING
Little wolf / My body betrays me she said / Happy new year / Letter from '38 / Man is a man / Love burns / Los Cuatro / Between ten and noon / Ventoline blues / I'd sell my soul to God
CD BBL 105CD
Beggars Banquet / '92 / RTM/Disc / Warner Music

Passion Play

TIME STANDS STILL
CD NTHEN 033CD
Now & Then / Apr '97 / Plastic Head

Passions

PASSION PLAYS
I'm in love with a German film star / Runaway / Swimmer / Someone special / Bachelor girls / Skin deep / African mine / Jump for joy / Letter / Love is essential / Your friend / Sanctuary
CD 5298602
Polydor / Jul '96 / PolyGram

Passos, Monica

CASAMENTO
CD EPC 100
EMP / Nov '93 / Harmonia Mundi

Pastels

MOBILE SAFARI
CD WIGCD 17
Domino / Feb '95 / Vital

SUCK ON THE PASTELS
CD CRECD 031
Creation / Jul '88 / 3mv/Vital

TRUCKLOAD OF TROUBLE
CD PAPCD 008
Paperhouse / Jun '93 / RTM/Disc

Pastor, Tony

CONFESSIN' 1940-1949 (Pastor, Tony & His Orchestra)
CD RACD 7114
Aerospace / May '96 / Jazz Music / Montpellier

TONY PASTOR ORCHESTRA 1941-1945
CD CCD 31
Circle / Aug '95 / Jazz Music / Swift / Wellard

TONY PASTOR ORCHESTRA 1945-1950
CD CCD 121
Circle / Aug '95 / Jazz Music / Swift / Wellard

Pastorius, Jaco

GOLDEN ROADS
CD SSCD 8074
Sound Hills / Apr '97 / Cadillac / Harmonia Mundi

HOLIDAY FOR PANS
CD SSCD 8001
Sound Hills / Feb '94 / Cadillac / Harmonia Mundi

HONESTLY
CD CDJP 1032
Jazz Point / Nov '91 / Cadillac / Harmonia Mundi

JACO (Pastorius, Jaco/Metheney/ Ditmas/Bley)
CD 1238462
IAI / Feb '93 / Cadillac / Harmonia Mundi

JACO PASTORIUS
Donna Lee / Come on come over / Continuum / Kuru/Speak like a child / Portrait of Tracy / Opus pocus / Okonkole y trompa / (Used to be a) cha-cha / Forgotten love
CD CD 81453
Sony Jazz / Jan '95 / Sony

JAZZ STREET (Pastorius, Jaco & Brian Melvin)
No clack / Miles modes / Wedding waltz / Drums of Yadzarah / Jazz Street / May day / Out of the night
CD CDSJP 258
Timeless Jazz / Jun '89 / New Note/ Pinnacle

LIVE IN ITALY
CD _______ **CDJP 1031**
Jazz Point / Nov '91 / Cadillac / Harmonia Mundi

Pat Kelly

BUTTERFLIES
CD _______ **SONCD 0076**
Sonic Sounds / May '95 / Jet Star

CLASSIC HITS
CD _______ **RNCD 2113**
Rhino / Jul '95 / Grapevine/PolyGram / Jet Star

PORTRAIT OF A LEGEND
CD _______ **ANGCD 21**
Angela / Oct '93 / Jet Star

Patato

RITMO Y CANDELA
CD _______ **RWCD 9702**
Night & Day / Feb '97 / ADA / Direct / Discovery

Pate, Johnny

AT THE BLUE NOTE
CD _______ **PS 008CD**
P&S / Sep '95 / Discovery

Paterson, Rod

SONGS FROM THE BOTTOM DRAWER (Rod Paterson Sings Burns)
Mary Morrison / Ye banks and braes / Wert thou in the cauld blast / Waukrife Minnie / Gray Twins / Parcel of rogues in a nation / Gae bring tae me a pint o'wine / Guidwife coont the lawin'/The coggie's revenge / Red red rose / Gloomy December / Man's a man / Ochone for somebody / Auld lang syne
CD _______ **CDTRAX 117**
Greentrax / Nov '96 / ADA / Direct / Duncans / Highlander

Pathologist

GRINDING OPUS OF FORENSIC MEDICAL PROBLEMS
CD _______ **MAB 008**
MAB / May '95 / Plastic Head

PUTREFACTIVE AND CADAVEROUS ODES ABOUT NECROTICISM
CD _______ **MABCD 002**
Plastic Head / Jun '93 / Plastic Head

Patinkin, Mandy

DRESS CASUAL
Doodle doodle doo (medley) / On the Atchison, Topeka and the Santa Fe / Bein' green / Triplets / I'm always chasing rainbows / Evening primrose / Pal Joey (suite) / Sorry grateful / Being alive / Ya got trouble (in River City) / Giants in the sky / Mr. Arthur's place / Yossel, yossel / Hollywood (medley)
CD _______ **CD 45998**
Columbia / May '91 / Sony

EXPERIMENT
CD _______ **7559793302**
Nonesuch / Jul '95 / Warner Music

MANDY PATINKIN
Over the rainbow / Coffee in a cardboard cup / Pretty lady / Brother can you spare a dime / Love unrequited / No more / Me and my shadow / No one is alone / Sonny boy / Rock-a-bye your baby with a Dixie melody / Casey (medley) / And the band played on / Marie / Once upon a time / Anyone can whistle / Soliloquy / I'll be seeing you / There's a rainbow 'round my shoulder / Top hat, white tie and tails / Puttin' on the ritz / Alexander's ragtime band / Swanee / My mammy / Handful of keys / Pennies from Heaven
CD _______ **CD 44943**
CBS / Apr '89 / Sony

Patino, Deborah

NOCTURNAL
CD _______ **NAR 081CD**
New Alliance / Mar '95 / Plastic Head

Patitucci, John

ANOTHER WORLD
Ivory coast / Ivory coast / Another world / My summer vacation / Soho steel / I saw you / Hold that thought / Norwegian sun / Griot / Showtime / Peace prayer / Shanachie / Till then / Ivory coast / Ivory coast
CD _______ **GRP 97252**
GRP / Aug '93 / New Note/BMG

HEART OF THE BASS
Concerto for jazz bass and orchestra / Heart of the bass / Four hands / Mullagh / Bach prelude in G major / Miniatures for solo bass
CD _______ **SCD 90012**
Stretch / Mar '97 / New Note/Pinnacle

MISTURA FINA
Mistura fina / Bate balaio / Puccini / Samba nova / Four loves / Assim nao da / Joys and sorrows / Aqua mae agua / Soul song / Varadero / love story / Barra da Tijuca (Tijuca bay) / Samba school
CD _______ **GRP 98022**
GRP / Mar '95 / New Note/BMG

ONE MORE ANGEL
Quasimodo / Arrival / On the Hudson / Sachi's eyes / San Michele / One more angel / Romance / Snowbound / Notre dame / Beloved
CD _______ **CCD 47532**
Concord Jazz / Jun '97 / New Note/ Pinnacle

SKETCHBOOK
Spaceships / Joab / If you don't mind / Scophile / Greatest gift / From a rainy night / Junk man / Two worlds / Backwoods / They heard it twice / Trane / Through the clouds
CD _______ **GRP 96172**
GRP / Aug '90 / New Note/BMG

Pato Banton

COLLECTIONS
Baby come back / Bubbling hot / Don't sniff coke / Tudo de bom / Wize up / One world (not three) / Roots, rock, reggae / Gwarn / Go Pato / Bad man and woman / Never give in / Save your soul / All drugs out / Pato's opinion pt.2
CD _______ **CDVX 2765**
Virgin / May '95 / EMI

MAD PROFESSOR RECAPTURES PATO BANTON (Pato Banton & Mad Professor)
CD _______ **ARICD 043**
Ariwa Sounds / Oct '94 / Jet Star / SRD

NEVER GIVE IN
Absolute perfection / My opinion / Don't Worry / Handsworth riot / Gwarn / Pato and Roger come again / Never give in / Don't sniff coke / Sattle Satan / King step / Hello Tosh
CD _______ **GRELCD 108**
Greensleeves / Feb '95 / Jet Star / SRD

Paton, Dave

FRAGMENTS
CD _______ **CDLDL 1257**
Lochshore / May '97 / ADA / Direct / Duncans

Patra

QUEEN OF THE PACK
Hardcore side / Hardcore / Think (about it) / Queen of the pack / Poor people's song / Wok the money / Romantic call / Cool-running side / Worker man / Sexual feeling / Be protected / Whining skill / Knock knock / In the mood
CD _______ **4741842**
Epic / Oct '93 / Sony

SCENT OF ATTRACTION
Pull up to the bumper / Dip and fall back / Hot stuff / Banana / Mek me hot / Scent of attraction / Goin' 2 the chapel / Time fi wine / Undercover lover / You want it / Deep inside
CD _______ **4807052**
Epic / Oct '95 / Sony

Patriarca, Ildo

VERANO PORTENO
CD _______ **KAR 996**
IMP / Apr '97 / ADA / Discovery

Patric C

HORRIBLE PLANS OF FLEX BUSTERMAN, THE
Intro (flex busterman) / Title / Enter your name / Fight the guards / Find the office / Crack the safe / Drive to the shaker house / Watch out for Zad / Set your weapons / Sex with annemone / Injection for life / Gingoos burgerstation / CALM / Now you know / Mental hangover / Hero / You failed / Everything has changed on LSD / You made it (perfect)
CD _______ **DHRCD 005**
Digital Hardcore / Mar '97 / Vital

Patrick Street

ALL IN GOOD TIME
Walsh's polkas / Prince among men (Only a miner) / Frank Quinn's reel / Lintheads / Pride of the Springfield Road / Lawrence Common / Goodbye Monday blues / Light and airy/All in good time / Mouth of Tobique/Billy Wilson / Girls along the road / Thames hornpipe / Fairy Queen / Dennis Murphy's reel/Bag of spuds/MacFarley's reel / Carrowclare / Lynch's barndances
CD _______ **SPDCD 1049**
Special Delivery / Apr '93 / ADA / CM / Direct

ALL IN GOOD TIME
CD _______ **GLCD 1125**
Green Linnet / May '95 / ADA / CM / Direct / Highlander / Roots

BEST OF PATRICK STREET, THE
CD _______ **NTMCD 503**
Nectar / Jun '95 / Pinnacle

CORNERBOYS
CD _______ **GLCD 1160**
Green Linnet / Feb '96 / ADA / CM / Direct / Highlander / Roots

IRISH TIMES
CD _______ **SPCD 1033**
Special Delivery / Mar '90 / ADA / CM / Direct

IRISH TIMES
CD _______ **GLCD 1105**
Green Linnet / May '95 / ADA / CM / Direct / Highlander / Roots

NO.2 PATRICK STREET
John McKenna's jigs / Braes of Moneymore / Hard by Seifin/Woodcock Hill / Tom Joad / Benton's jig/Benton's dream / William Taylor / Caherlistrane/Gallowglass/Kanturk jigs / Facing the chair / Sweeney's reel
CD _______ **GLCD 1088**
Green Linnet / Feb '90 / ADA / CM / Direct / Highlander / Roots

PATRICK STREET
CD _______ **GLCD 1071**
Green Linnet / Apr '88 / ADA / CM / Direct / Highlander / Roots

PATRICK STREET/ALL IN GOOD TIME
CD _______ **5016272104921**
Special Delivery / Apr '93 / ADA / CM / Direct

Patrick, David M.

GREAT EUROPEAN ORGANS (David Patrick Plays The Blackburn Cathedral Organ)
CD _______ **PRCD 371**
Priory / Jul '92 / Priory

Patrick, Johnny

GIRL FROM IPANEMA, THE
CD _______ **MATCD 243**
Castle / Nov '93 / BMG

HAMMOND ORGAN HITS
CD _______ **MATCD 243**
Castle / Mar '93 / BMG

HAMMOND ORGAN HITS
CD _______ **PLSCD 231**
Pulse / Jul '97 / BMG

Patriot

CADENCE FROM THE STREET
CD _______ **GMM 103**
GMM / Jun '97 / Cargo

Patry, Stefan

BAM BAM BAM
CD _______ **BB 898**
Black & Blue / Apr '97 / Discovery / Koch / Wellard

Patterson, Bobby

I GET MY GROOVE FROM YOU
I get my groove from you / Make sure you can handle it / If you took a survey / Everything good to you (don't have to be good for you) / How do you spell love / Recipe for peace / She don't have to see you (to see through you) / Right on Jody / Quiet, do not disturb / I just love you because I wanted to / One ounce of prevention / Whole funky world is a ghetto / What goes around comes around / It takes two to do wrong / Take time to know the truth / I'm in the wrong / If love can't do it (it can't be done) / I got a suspicion / Right place, wrong time
CD _______ **CPCD 8123**
Charly / Oct '95 / Koch

TAKING CARE OF BUSINESS
Till you give in / You just got to understand / What's your problem baby / If I didn't have you / Long ago / Soul is our music / Let them talk / Sock some lovin' at me / I'm Leroy, I'll take her / Broadway ain't funky no more / I met my match / Don't be so mean / Good ol' days / Busy busy bee / Sweet taste of love / TCB or TYA / What a wonderful night for love / My thing is your thing / Keeping it in the family / My baby's coming back to me / Guess who / Knockout power of love / Trial of Mary McGuire / If a man ever loved a woman / You taught me how to love / I'm in love with you / Married lady / If I didn't know better / Who wants to fall in love
CD _______ **CDKEND 098**
Kent / Apr '91 / Pinnacle

Patterson, Don

LEGENDS OF ACID JAZZ, THE (Patterson, Don/Booker Ervin)
CD _______ **PRCD 24178**
Prestige / Apr '97 / Cadillac / Complete/ Pinnacle

Patterson, Jordan

GIVE ME A CHANCE
Funky thang / Those pretty eyes / Life of misery / No educated woman / Thing I do for you / Blues hotel / Give me a chance / Your love is killing me / Fast lane / Natural
CD _______ **JSPCD 263**
JSP / Nov '95 / ADA / Cadillac / Direct / Hot Shot / Target/BMG

Patterson, Kellee

KELLEE
I'm gonna love you just a little more, baby / What you don't know / Mister magic / You are so beautiful / I love music / Stop, look and listen to your heart / Jolene / Time to space / Once not long ago
CD _______ **HUBCD 3**
Hubbub / Oct '95 / Beechwood/BMG / SRD / Timewarp

Patterson, Ottilie

BACK IN THE OLD DAYS (Patterson, Ottilie & Chris Barber)
Hot time in the old town tonight / Lordy Lord / Basin Street blues / T'ain't what you do (it's the way that you do it) / Bad spell blues / Squeeze me
CD _______ **CBJBCD 4001**
Chris Barber Collection / Apr '88 / Cadillac / New Note/Pinnacle

OTTILIE PATTERSON & CHRIS BARBER JAZZBAND 1955-1958
CD _______ **LA 30CD**
Lake / Oct '93 / ADA / Cadillac / Direct / Jazz Music / Target/BMG

Patterson, Rashsaan

RASHSAAN PATTERSON
Stop by / Spend the night / Where you are / So fine / Stay awhile / Come over / Can't we wait a minute / Joy / My sweetheart / Soul free / Ain't no way / Tears ago / Don't wanna lose it / One more night
CD _______ **MCAD 11559**
MCA / Feb '97 / BMG

Patti

PARIS TENU
CD _______ **3020362**
Arcade / Jun '97 / Discovery

Patto

ROLL 'EM SMOKE 'EM
Flat footed woman / Singing the blues on reds / Mummy / Loud green song / Turn turtle / I got rhythm / Peter Abraham / Can 'n 'P' and the attos (sea biscuits parts 1 and 2)
CD _______ **EDCD 510**
Edsel / Nov '96 / Pinnacle

SENSE OF THE ABSURD
Hold your fire / You, you point your finger / How's your Father / See you at the dance tonight / Give it all away / Air raid shelter / Tell me where you've been / Magic door / Beat the drum / Bad news / Man / Hold me back / Time to die / San Antone / Red glow / Government man / Money bag / Sittin' back easy / Hanging rope
CD _______ **5286962**
Mercury / Oct '95 / PolyGram

Patton, 'Big' John

ACCENT ON THE BLUES
Rakin' and scrapin' / Freedom jazz dance / Captain nasty / Village lee / Lite nit / Don't let me lose this dream / Village lee / Buddy boy / 2J / Sweet pea
CD _______ **CDP 8539242**
Blue Note / Jan '97 / EMI

MEMPHIS TO NEW YORK SPIRIT
Memphis / Footprints / Mandingo / Bloodyun / Steno / Man from the Tanganyika / Cissy Strut / Dragon slayer
CD _______ **CDP 8352212**
Blue Note / Mar '96 / EMI

ORGANISATION (The Best Of Big John Patton)
Along came John / Silver meter / Bermuda clay house / Hot sauce / Fat Judy / Amanda / Turnaround / Latona / Footprints / Jerry / Chitlins con carne / Freedom jazz dance / Ain't that peculiar / Barefootin' / Boogaloo boogie / Sissy strut / Dirty fingers / Man from Tanganyika / Memphis
CD _______ **CDP 8307282**
Blue Note / Sep '94 / EMI

THIS ONE'S FOR JA (Patton, 'Big' John Quintet)
CD _______ **DIW 919**
DIW / Jan '97 / Cadillac / Harmonia Mundi

Patton, Charlie

ALL TIME BLUES CLASSICS
CD _______ **8420302**
Music Memoria / Oct '96 / ADA / Discovery

CHARLIE PATTON VOL.1 1929
CD _______ **DOCD 5009**
Document / Feb '92 / ADA / Hot Shot / Jazz Music

CHARLIE PATTON VOL.2 1929
CD _______ **DOCD 5010**
Document / Feb '92 / ADA / Hot Shot / Jazz Music

CHARLIE PATTON VOL.3 1929-1934
CD DOCD 5011
Document / Feb '92 / ADA / Hot Shot / Jazz Music

FOUNDER OF DELTA BLUES
CD YAZCD 2010
Yazoo / Apr '95 / ADA / CM / Koch

REMAINING TITLES 1929-1934
CD WSECD 103
Wolf / Nov '90 / Hot Shot / Jazz Music / Swift

Patton, Mike

FRANZO OLTRANZISTA
CD TZA 7022
Tzadik / Feb '97 / Cargo

Pattullo, Gordon

GOLDEN SOUND OF SCOTTISH MUSIC FROM STARS PAST AND PRESENT
CD CDGR 149
Ross / Jun '95 / CM / Duncans / Highlander / Ross

SCOTTISH ACCORDION HITS
Sailor's hornpipe / College hornpipe / Lowe's hornpipe / Chester hornpipe / Trumpet hornpipe / Cuckoo waltz / Painter's choice / Para handy / Miss Suzanne Barbour / Jean's fancy / Boys of the Lough / Tony Reid of Balnakilly / Mist covered mountains of home / Alpine holiday / New ashludie rant / Elizabeth Adair / Princess Margaret's jig / Jimmy Stephen / Lochanside / Battle's o'er / Heather bells / Happy hours polka / Dashing white sergeant / Lord Saltoun / Catchin' rabbits / Inchmickery / Misty islands of the highlands / Crossing the minch / Banjo breakdown / Les triolets / Dark island / Pigeon pie / Moors of Perth / Shufflin' Samuel/Whistling Rufus / Memories of Willie snaith of Hexham / Dancing fingers
CD GRCD 57
Grasmere / Jun '93 / Highlander / Savoy / Target/BMG

SCOTTISH CELEBRATION, A
CD CDGR 160
Ross / Jun '97 / CM / Duncans / Highlander / Ross

Pau Brasil

BABEL
Ka ka / Fabula / Tres segredos / Olho d'agua / Babel / Uluri / Cordiheira / Tocaia / Festa na rua
CD ACT 50092
Act / Jun '97 / New Note/Pinnacle

Paul

PAUL
CD GRAVITYCD 2
Sugar / Sep '95 / RTM/Disc

Paul & Margie

TWENTY BEST FOLK SONGS OF AMERICA
CD EUCD 1202
ARC / Sep '93 / ADA / ARC Music

Paul, Billy

FIRST CLASS
CD KWEST 5405
Kenwest / Mar '93 / THE

Paul, Billy

TEXAS ROSE
Texas rose / Buckshot buck / Strange dream / Little girl / Still water runs the deepest / Rodeo Queen / Rollin' / Blue water / 501 / Bottom dollar / Real thing / Pretty girl / '57 Fairlane / Farm / Nothin' can stop me / My house is your honky tonk / Hillbilly hula gal
CD BCD 16155
Bear Family / Apr '97 / Direct / Rollercoaster / Swift

Paul, Bollenback

ORIGINAL VISIONS
CD CHR 70022
Challenge / Sep '95 / ADA / Direct / Jazz Music / Wellard

Paul, Daniel

RHYTHMS OF PARADISE
CD SP 7165CD
Soundings / Aug '96 / ADA / Else

Paul, Frankie

20 MASSIVE HITS
CD SONCD 0008
Sonic Sounds / Oct '90 / Jet Star

A WE RULE
A we rule / Rub a dub market / Run off him mouth / Free Jah children / Rastafari winner: *Paul, Frankie & Prince Jazzbo* / Stick a sensi / Give me time / Touch me all over / Missing you / Agony / Call the brigade / Shine on / We a don
CD RAS 3235
Ras / May '97 / Direct / Greensleeves / Jet Star / SRD

BACK TO THE ROOTS
Down in the ghetto / Bigger than jumbo / Heathen / Steady skanking / We rule the border / Don man (we rule the island) / Jah Jah children / Mystery lady / I just wanna love you / Miss your love / I can't say goodbye / Endless dreams / One in a million / Merry Christmas
CD RNCD 2043
Rhino / Apr '94 / Grapevine/PolyGram / Jet Star

CAN'T GET YOU OUT OF MY MIND
CD RRTGCD 7780
Rohit / Jul '90 / Jet Star

DANCE HALL DUO (Paul, Frankie & Pinchers)
CD RASCD 3237
Ras / Aug '88 / Direct / Greensleeves / Jet Star / SRD

DISTINCTIVE KINDA SINGER, A
CD GR 007CD
Graylan / Mar '96 / Grapevine/PolyGram / Jet Star

DON MAN
Ram dancehall / How I care for you / All out of my mind / Sexy thing (you got the body) / End of the road / You remind me / Row the boat / It feels so real / Recession / Here I go again / Let's stay together
CD HBCD 146
Greensleeves / Sep '93 / Jet Star / SRD

EVERY NIGGER IS A STAR
Things you say / I wanna sex you up / Every nigger is a star / Lonely baby / Hey girl / Dismal / Let's chill / Let me show you / I'll take you up girl / Next to you / Ram dancehall / Dry your eyes
CD GRELCD 165
Greensleeves / Sep '91 / Jet Star / SRD

FIRE DEH A MUS MUS TAIL
CD BDCD 001
Greensleeves / Nov '92 / Jet Star / SRD

FOREVER
CD RNCD 2128
Rhino / Nov '95 / Grapevine/PolyGram / Jet Star

FOREVER
CD WRCD 016
World / Jun '97 / Jet Star / TKO Magnum

FP THE GREATEST
CD FADCD 025
Fashion / Sep '92 / Jet Star / SRD

FREEDOM
CD CRCD 46
Charm / Nov '95 / Jet Star

HEARTICAL DON
Don't take it personal / Heartical Don / Let's be friends / Forever: *Paul, Frankie & Bobby Womack* / Last night / Hypocrite / I've got to fight / I want to rock / Nothing in the world / Idle jubee
CD SPCD 104
Super Power / Jun '91 / Jet Star

I'M READY
CD SAXCD 006
Saxon Studio / Mar '97 / Jet Star

I'VE GOT THE VIBES
CD DBTXCD 3
Digital B / Nov '95 / Jet Star

IF YOU WANT ME GIRL
Nasty / Oh baby / Baby don't leave me alone / Special love / Move if you're moving / If you want me girl / Written all over your face / Mr. Paul come back / Have mercy oh Jah / Lay your head / I can see your face / You are the sun
CD CDTRL 354
Trojan / Jun '95 / Direct / Jet Star

LOVE LINE
My love stand for you / Solid as a rock / Crackle theme bone / I wanna dance / New stylee dismissal / Love line / Medley song / Apple on stick / Dry your eyes / So long
CD GGCD 003
Glory Gold / Jan '89 / Jet Star

PASS THE TU-SHENG-PENG/TIDAL WAVE
Pass the tu-sheng-peng / War is in the dance / Jump no fence / Hot number / Hooligan / Only you / Don't worry yourself / Prophet / Them a talk about / If you / Dem a go feel it / Beat down the fence / Baby come home / Music is the staff of life / She's got style / Tidal wave / Your love is amazing / King champion / You too greedy / Hold me
CD GRELCD 502
Greensleeves / '88 / Jet Star / SRD

RAS PORTRAITS
Keep the faith / Songs of freedom / Don't pressure me / Rub-a-dub market / Dance hall nice / Tato / Children of Israel / A we rule / Give me what we want / Work hard / Gimme that potion / Stick of sensi
CD RAS 3316
Ras / Jun '97 / Direct / Greensleeves / Jet Star / SRD

REGGAE MAX
CD JSRNCD 10
Jet Star / Apr '97 / Jet Star

REJOICE
CD UPTCD 22
Uptempo / Mar '97 / Jet Star

SARA
CD FMCD 005
Fatman / Jan '97 / Jet Star / SRD

SHOULD I
CD CDHB 113
Heartbeat / Feb '92 / ADA / Direct / Greensleeves / Jet Star

SLOW DOWN
CD VPCD 1034
VP / Apr '89 / Greensleeves / Jet Star / Total/BMG

TALK ALL YOU WANT
CD VPCD 1363
VP / Aug '94 / Greensleeves / Jet Star / Total/BMG

TIMELESS
CD TYCD 003
Tan Yah / Oct '92 / Jet Star

TURBO CHARGE (Paul, Frankie & Pinchers)
I need you: *Paul, Frankie* / Kuff (don't mess with me): *Paul, Frankie* / Chat mi back: *Paul, Frankie* / Life is a gamble: *Pinchers* / Traveller: *Paul, Frankie* / I'm in love again: *Paul, Frankie* / Musical calamity: *Pinchers* / Memories of love: *Pinchers*
CD SUPCD 1
Super Supreme / Mar '89 / Jet Star

WARNING
Tato / Tickle me / Don't pressure me / Ragamuffin / Hungry belly / Warning / She's a maniac / Give me what we want / Rock you / Lady love
CD RASCD 3027
Ras / Nov '87 / Direct / Greensleeves / Jet Star / SRD

YOU TURN ME ON
CD RFCD 004
Record Factory / Nov '96 / Jet Star

Paul K

LOVE IS A GAS (Paul K & The Weathermen)
Apple in my eye / Another night on this earth / Slow it down / David Ruffin's tears / Everything that glitters / Lavender door / Deep freeze / Jesus children of America / Liars prayer / To see if you fall / Manna / Love is a gas / You're my best friend
CD A 109D
Alias / Feb '97 / Vital

Paul, Les

CAPITOL YEARS, THE (Paul, Les & Mary Ford)
Whispering / World is waiting for the sunrise / Lover / Mockin' Bird Hill / Nola / That old feeling / Little Rock getaway / Bye bye blues / Twelfth St. rag / I'm sitting on top of the world / Chicken reel / How high the moon / Walkin' and whistlin' blues / How deep is the ocean / Tico-tico / Vaya con dios
CD CDEMS 1309
Capitol / Jan '89 / EMI

WORLD IS WAITING FOR THE SUNRISE, THE (Paul, Les & Mary Ford)
CD 15436
Laserlight / Jan '93 / Target/BMG

Paulsen, Ralf

JUBILAUMS AUSGABE
CD 15126
Laserlight / Aug '91 / Target/BMG

Paulson, Bruce

MINNESOTA (Paulson, Bruce Quartet)
CD SBCD 3017
Sea Breeze / Jun '96 / Jazz Music

Pauly, Danielle

FLEUR DU JURA
Reve gourmand / L'epatante / Ballade matinale / Delice Catalan / Rapide digitale / Carte postale / Ballade Vosgienne / Clin d'oeil / File Indienne / Piccolo rag / Fleur du Jura / Exotic samba / Souffle Andalou / Matin tonique / Eclats de rire / Melody bolero / Valse des lucioles
CD CDSDL 353
Saydisc / Mar '94 / ADA / Direct / Harmonia Mundi

Pausini, Laura

LAURA PAUSINI
CD 4509998852
East West / Jun '95 / Warner Music

LE CHOSE CHE VIVE
CD 0630155552
East West / Feb '97 / Warner Music

Pauvros, Jean-Francois

MANG O
CD 14896
Spalax / Jun '97 / ADA / Cargo / Direct / Discovery / Greyhound

Pavarotti, Luciano

PAVAROTTI AND FRIENDS (For War Child) (Various Artists)
Holy mother: *Clapton, Eric & Luciano Pavarotti/East London Gospel Choir* / St. Teresa: *Osbourne, Joan* / I guess that's why they call it the blues: *John, Elton* / New York, New York: *Minnelli, Liza & Luciano Pavarotti* / My love (il volo): *Zucchero* / Run, baby, run: *Crow, Sheryl & Eric Clapton* / Certe notti: *Ligabue & Luciano Pavarotti* / Angel: *Secada, Jon* / Spirito: *Litfiba* / Third degree: *Clapton, Eric* / La ci darem la mano: *Crow, Sheryl & Luciano Pavarotti* / Le ragazze fanno grandi sogni: *Bennato, Edoardo & Solis Quartet* / Granada: *Secada, Jon & Luciano Pavarotti* / Mediterranean sundance: *De Lucia, Paco & Al Di Meola/ John McLaughlin* / Gesu bambino: *Osbourne, Joan & Luciano Pavarotti/East London Gospel Choir* / Live like horses: *John, Elton & Luciano Pavarotti*
CD 4529002
Decca / Dec '96 / PolyGram

TOGETHER FOR THE CHILDREN OF BOSNIA (Pavarotti, Luciano & Friends)
Per colpa di chi / Serenta rap/Mattinata / Can we go higher / Ordinary world / Clap clap / Miss Sarajevo / Cosi celeste / Linger / Come back to Sorrento / Penso positivo / Vesti la giubba / Heaven can wait / Ave Maria / One / Long black veil / Funiculi, funicula / Nessun dorma
CD 4521002
Decca / Mar '96 / PolyGram

Pavement

BRIGHTEN THE CORNERS
CD WIGCD 31
Domino / Feb '97 / Vital

CROOKED RAIN, CROOKED RAIN
CD ABB 56CD
Big Cat / Aug '95 / 3mv/Pinnacle

SLANTED AND ENCHANTED
CD ABB 34CD
Big Cat / Aug '95 / 3mv/Pinnacle

WESTING (BY MUSKET AND SEXTANT)
CD ABB 40CD
Big Cat / Aug '95 / 3mv/Pinnacle

WOWEE ZOWEE
We dance / Rattled by the rush / Black out / Brinks job / Grounded / Serpentine pal / Motion suggest itself / Lovermont / Extradition / Best friends arm / Grve architecture / At and T / Flux rad / Fight this generation / Kennel district / Spanos country rag / Half a canyon / Western homes
CD ABB 84CD
Big Cat / Apr '95 / 3mv/Pinnacle

Pavlov's Dog

PAMPERED MENIAL
Julia / Late November / Song dance / Fast gun / Natchez trace / Subway Sue / Episode / Preludin / Of once and future kings
CD 4690852
Columbia / Feb '95 / Sony

Pavone, Mario

DANCER'S TALES
CD KFWCD 205
Knitting Factory / Jun '97 / Cargo / Plastic Head

TOULON DAYS
CD 804202
New World / Sep '92 / ADA / Cadillac / Harmonia Mundi

Paw

DEATH TO TRAITORS
CD 5403912
A&M / Aug '95 / PolyGram

DRAGLINE
Gasoline / Sleeping bag / Jessie / Bridge / Couldn't know / Pansy / Lolita / Dragline / Veronica / One more bottle / Sugarcane / Hard pig
CD 5400652
A&M / Mar '94 / PolyGram

Pawar, Satya Dev

SATYA DEV PAWAR (Music Of North India)
CD C 560092
Ocora / Jun '97 / ADA / Harmonia Mundi

Pax

MAY GOD...
CD HBG 123/4
Background / Apr '94 / Background / Greyhound

Paxarino, Javier

TEMURA - THE MYSTERY OF SILENCE
Conductus mundi / Cortesanos / Preludio y danza / Canto del viento / Suspiro del moro / Reuda de juglar / Tierra baja / Reyes y reinas / Temura / Mater aurea
CD _______ 892172
Act / Oct '94 / New Note/Pinnacle

Paxton, Tom

AND LOVING YOU
Last hobo / Nothing but time / Home to me / Love changes the world / Missing you / You are love / And lovin' you / Every time / Bad old days / Panhandle wind / When we were good / All coming together
CD _______ FF 70414
Flying Fish / Jul '95 / ADA / CM / Direct / Roots

EVEN A GREY DAY
Even a grey day / I give you the morning / Love of loving you / When Annie took me home / Dance in the shadows / Annie's going to sing her song / Corrymeela / Outward bound / Wish I had a troubador / Hold on to me babe / Last thing on my mind
CD _______ FF 70280
Flying Fish / Jul '95 / ADA / CM / Direct / Roots

IT AIN'T EASY
CD _______ FF 70574
Flying Fish / Jul '95 / ADA / CM / Direct / Roots

LIVE FOR THE RECORD
Packwood / I don't want a bunny-wunny / Let's go to Michael Jackson's house / Michael and Lisa Marie / They call me 'Joey / Lament for a lost election / Tonya Harding / What did you learn in school today / Rambling boy / Last thing on my mind / Little girl / Names of the trees / Long way from your mountain / Dance in the kitchen / Modern maturity / I can't help but wonder where I'm bound / My favourite spring / Spin and turn
CD _______ SHCD 1053
Sugar Hill / Dec '96 / ADA / CM / Direct / Koch / Roots

NEW SONGS FROM THE BRIAR PATCH
Did you hear John Hurt / Pandora's box / Bring back the chair / Birds on the table / Talking Watergate / There goes the mountain / Cotton eyed Joe / You can eat dog food / You're so beautiful / Mr. Blue/White bones of Allende / Born on the fourth of July
CD _______ VMD 79395
Vanguard / Jan '96 / ADA / Pinnacle

ONE MILLION LAWYERS AND OTHER DISASTERS
CD _______ FF 70356
Flying Fish / Jul '95 / ADA / CM / Direct / Roots

POLITICS - LIVE
CD _______ FF 70486
Flying Fish / Jul '95 / ADA / CM / Direct / Roots

VERY BEST OF TOM PAXTON, THE
CD _______ FF 70519
Flying Fish / Jul '95 / ADA / CM / Direct / Roots

WEARING THE TIME
CD _______ SHCD 1045
Sugar Hill / Sep '96 / ADA / CM / Direct / Koch / Roots

Paycheck, Johnny

GREATEST HITS
Take this job and shove it / Slide off your satin sheets / Somebody loves me / Motel time again / In memory of memory / Mr. Love maker / A11 / She's all I got / For a minute there / Only hell my mama ever raised / Loving you beats all I ever seen / Song and dance man / Keep on lovin' me / Jukebox Charlie / Something about you I love / Someone to give my love to / Green green grass of home / Don't monkey with another monkey's monkey / Heaven's almost as big as Texas / Close all the honky tonks / Almost persuaded / Release me / All the time / Crazy arms / Heartaches by the number / Apartment no. 9
CD _______ GRF 070
Tring / Feb '93 / Tring

SURVIVOR
Buried treasures / He left it all / IQ blues / I can't quit drinkin' / Everything is changing / Ol pay ain't checked out yet / Palimony / You're every step I take / I never got over you / I'm a survivor
CD _______ VD 102
Dixie Frog / Sep '90 / Direct / TKO Magnum

TAKE THIS JOB AND SHOVE IT
CD _______ 15483
Laserlight / May '93 / Target/BMG

Payne, Cecil

CASBAH
CD _______ STCD 572
Stash / Mar '94 / ADA / Cadillac / CM / Direct / Jazz Music

CERUPA
Opening / Bolambo / I should care / Cerupa / Be wee / Cuba / Bosco / Brookfield andante
CD _______ DE 478
Delmark / Mar '97 / ADA / Cadillac / CM / Direct / Hot Shot

SCOTCH AND MILK
Scotch and milk / Wilhelmenia / I'm goin' in / If I should lose you / Que pasaning / Cit sac / Lady Nia / Et vous too Cecil
CD _______ DE 494
Delmark / Jul '97 / ADA / Cadillac / CM / Direct / Hot Shot

Payne, Freda

BEST OF FREDA PAYNE, THE
CD _______ CCSCD 811
Renaissance Collector Series / Mar '97 / BMG

DEEPER AND DEEPER (The Very Best Of Freda Payne)
Unhooked generation / I left some dreams back there / Rock me in the cradle of love / Cherish what is dear to you / Mama's gone goodbye / Bring the boys home / You brought the joy / I'm not getting any better / You've got to love somebody / Road we didn't take / He's my life / Band of gold / Deeper and deeper / Easiest way to fall / Now is the time to say goodbye / Just a woman / Through the memory of my mind / World don't owe you a thing / Suddenly it's yesterday / How can I live without my life / Odds and ends / You're the only bargain I've got
CD _______ HDH CD 005
HDH / Aug '89 / Pinnacle

Payne, Jimmy

NEW YORK FUNK VOL.1
Streets of New York / She's a reptile / Bathtub club / Love letters / Bone dance / Talking chicken / Off the Walrath / Waiting for you / Bottom line / Planet X / Far from home / Last chance
CD _______ GCD 79489
Gramavision / Dec '95 / Vital/SAM

NEW YORK FUNK VOL.2
CD _______ GCD 79504
Gramavision / Sep '95 / Vital/SAM

Payton, Nicholas

FROM THIS MOMENT
CD _______ 5270732
Verve / May '95 / PolyGram

GUMBO NOUVEAU
CD _______ 5311992
Verve / May '96 / PolyGram

Payvar, Faramarz

PERSIAN HERITAGE, A (Classical Music Of Iran) (Payvar, Faramarz Ensemble & Khatereh Parvaneh)
CD _______ 7559720602
Nonesuch / Jan '95 / Warner Music

Paz

BEST OF PAZ, THE
AC-DC-3 / Time stood still / Laying eggs / Yours is the light / Crotales / Iron works / Bell tree / Buddha
CD _______ SPJCD 554
Spotlite / Oct '95 / Cadillac / Jazz Music / New Note/Pinnacle / Swift

DANCING IN THE PARK
CD _______ FORT 2
Turret / Mar '96 / Cadillac / Turret / Wellard

LOVE IN PEACE
CD _______ CHECD 00102
Master Mix / Jan '92 / Jazz Music / New Note/Pinnacle / Wellard

MESSAGE, THE
Xenon / Message / Party / Citron presse / Slide time / Nylon stockings
CD _______ CDCHE 6
Master Mix / Aug '89 / Jazz Music / New Note/Pinnacle / Wellard

PEACE IS LOVE
Kandeen love song / Look inside / Amour em Paz / Dream sequence / Singing bowl / I can't remember / Bags
CD _______ CDCHE 102
Master Mix / Dec '91 / Jazz Music / New Note/Pinnacle / Wellard

Paz, Eduardo

NOMADEO
CD _______ 21086
Lyricon / May '96 / ADA

Paz, Suarez

MILONGA DEL ANGEL (Paz, Suarez Quinteto)
Calambre / Revirado / Caliente / Balada para mi muerte / Oblivion / Milonga del angel / Muerte del angel / Resurrection del angel / Primavera portena / Decarissimo / La comorra
CD _______ 74321491362
Milan / Jul '97 / Conifer/BMG / Silva Screen

Pazuzu

AND ALL WAS SILENT
CD _______ HNF 004CD
Head Not Found / Oct '95 / Plastic Head

Peabody, Dave

DOWN IN CAROLINA
CD _______ APCD 127
Appaloosa / Sep '96 / ADA / Direct / TKO Magnum

Peace Bureau

PEACE BUREAU
CD _______ EBCD 37
Eightball / Jan '95 / Vital

Peace, Love & Pitbulls

PEACE LOVE AND PITBULLS
(I'm the) Radio king kong / Dog church / Be my TV / Reverberation nation / Elektrik '93 / What's wrong / Nutopia / Futurehead / This is trash / Psycho / Hitch hike to Mars
CD _______ BIAS 238CD
Play It Again Sam / Apr '93 / Discovery / Plastic Head / Vital

RED SONIC UNDERWEAR
Itch / Das neue konzept / Warzaw / 2000 Ways of gettin' drunk / GOD (on vacation) / Animals / His head is spinnin' off / Good morning / War in my livin' room / Discussing the artist in pain / Pig machine / Skinny and white / Other life form / Complete guide (imitating a bulldozer) / Endless masturbation
CD _______ BIAS 291CD
Play It Again Sam / Oct '94 / Discovery / Plastic Head / Vital

Peace Of Mind

JOURNEY TO THE FORE
Things we do / Spirit of the juju / Strollin' / On the sly / Free fall / Times gone by / Peace of mind / Por que sera
CD _______ IBCD 6
Internal Bass / Feb '97 / Prime / Timewarp / Total/BMG

Peach

GIVING BIRTH TO A STONE
CD _______ MADMIN 009CD
Mad Minute / May '94 / Pinnacle / RTM/ Disc

Peaches & Herb

LOVE IS STRANGE
Love is strange / Two little kids / Rockin' good way (to mess around and fall in love) / Let's fall in love / Close your eyes / True love / Let's make a promise / My life / For your love / We belong together / I want to stay here / Time after time / When he touches me (nothing else matters) / Door is still open to my heart / Ten commandments of love
CD _______ EK 64842
Epic / Jun '96 / Sony

Peachey, Roland

RHYTHM OF THE ISLANDS (Peachey, Roland & His Royal Hawaiians)
World is waiting for sunrise / Sing me a song of the Islands / Who's sorry now / South sea lullabies / Indian love call / Cherokee / Queja tamper / Tango of roses / Julian / Siboney / Brazil / Chez moi / My gal Sal / Serenade of the Islands / Goodbye Hawaii / Alohe Oe / Wabash blues / Blue Tahitian moon / Sweet Leilani / South Sea Island / Hawaiian paradise / J'Attendrai (au revoir) / Rhythm of the Islands / One rose / I'll see you again / One kiss / Honolulu / Hawaiian war chant / Sophisticated hula / Moonlight and roses
CD _______ RAJCD 872
Empress / Mar '96 / Koch

Peacock, Annette

ABSTRACT CONTACT
CD _______ IRONIC 5CD
Ironic / Aug '88 / Cadillac

I HAVE NO FEELINGS
Nothing ever was, anyway / Butterflies / I'm not perfect / I have no feelings / Cynic / Carousel / You've left me / Sincereless / Freefall / This almost spring / Feeling's free / Personal revolution / Not enough
CD _______ IRONIC 4CD
Ironic / Feb '86 / Cadillac

PERFECT RELEASE, THE
Love's out to lunch / Solar systems / American sport / Loss of consciousness / Rubber hunger / Succubus / Survival
CD _______ SEECD 460
See For Miles/C5 / Oct '96 / Pinnacle

SKY-SKATING
CD _______ IRONIC 2CD
Ironic / Jul '89 / Cadillac

X-DREAMS
My mama never taught me how to cook / Real and defined androgens / Dear Bela / This feeling within' / Too much in the skies / Don't be cruel / Questions
CD _______ SEECD 451
See For Miles/C5 / Aug '96 / Pinnacle

Peacock, Gary

DECEMBER POEMS
Snow dance / Winterlude / Northern tale / December greenwings / Flower crystals / Celebrations
CD _______ 5310292
ECM / Feb '96 / New Note/Pinnacle

GUAMBA
Guamba / Requiem / Celina / Thyme time / Lila / Introending / Gardenia
CD _______ 8330392
ECM / Oct '87 / New Note/Pinnacle

ORACLE (Peacock, Gary & Ralph Towner)
Gaya / Flutter step / Empty carrousel / Inside inside / St. Helens / Oracle / Burly hello / Palermo ballad
CD _______ 5213502
ECM / Feb '94 / New Note/Pinnacle

SHIFT IN THE WIND
So green / Fractions / Last first / Shift in the wind centers / Caverns beneath the zoth / Valentine
CD _______ 8201592
ECM / Aug '86 / New Note/Pinnacle

TALES OF ANOTHER
Vignette / Tone field / Major / Trilogy / Trilogy (II) / Trilogy (III)
CD _______ 8274182
ECM / Feb '86 / New Note/Pinnacle

VOICE FROM THE PAST - PARADIGM
Voice from the past / Legends / Moor / Allegory / Paradigm / Ode from tomten
CD _______ 5177682
ECM / Feb '94 / New Note/Pinnacle

Pearce, Alison

MY LAGAN LOVE (AND OTHER SONGS OF IRELAND) (Pearce, Alison & Susan Drake)
Castle of Dromore / She moved through the fair / Next market day / Gartan mothers lullaby / I have a bonnet trimmed with blue / Little boats / I will walk with my love / Star of County Down
CD _______ CDH 88023
Helios / May '89 / Select

SONGS OF THE HEBRIDES (Pearce, Alison & Susan Drake)
Isle of my heart / Leaping galley / Spinning song / Sea longing / Crone's reel / Caristiona / Ullapool sailor's song / Eriskay lullaby / Reiving ships / O heartling of my heart / Birlinn of the white shoulders / Islay reapers' song / Ailein Duinn / Ship at sea / Loch Broom love song / Kirsteen / Sea wandering / Uncanny mannikin of the cattlefold / Death farewell
CD _______ CDH 88024
Helios / Feb '89 / Select

Pearce, Bob

KEEP ON KEEPIN' ON
CD _______ TRCD 9913
Tramp / Apr '93 / ADA / CM / Direct

Pearce, Dick

BIG HIT
CD _______ FMRCD 17
Future / Aug '95 / ADA / Harmonia Mundi

Pearce, Ian

IAN PEARCE/PAUL FURNISS/S. GRANT
CD _______ TLACD 03
Tasmanian Jazz Composers / Mar '95 / Jazz Music

Pearce, Monty

COUNTRY STYLE MIX
Blanket on the ground/'57 chevrolet / Seven lonely days/Anytime/Quicksilver / There goes my everything/Are you lonesome tonight / Hasta luego/Marcheta / I love you because/Just out of reach / Stand by your man / I'm a fool to care/I can't stop loving you / Distant drums/Nobody's darlin' but mine / Help me make it through the night/Make the world go away / South of the border (Down Mexico way)/Mexicali rose / Angelo / Tango dorado / San Antonio rose / Brush those tears from your eyes / Anna Marie/Oh How I miss you tonight / If the world stopped loving/Love me tender / Room full of roses/Someday (You'll want me to want you) / My grandfather's clock / Sioux City Sue/You are my sunshine / Pistol packin' mama/The yellow rose of Texas / Blue bayou / Rosanna
CD _______ SAV 176CD
Savoy / Jul '92 / Savoy / THE / TKO Magnum

EASY DANCING
CD _______ SAV 186CD
Savoy / May '93 / Savoy / THE / TKO Magnum

EASY DANCING VOL.5
CD SAV 237CD
Savoy / Dec '95 / Savoy / THE / TKO Magnum

KING OF THE ROAD
Heartaches by the number / Shades of gold / Crystal chandeliers / Welcome to my world / King of the road / One has my name (the other has my heart) / Hello Mary Lou / Oh Lonesome me / I love you so much it hurts / After all these years / From a Jack to a King / Candy kisses / Take these chains from my heart
CD SAV 182CD
Savoy / Feb '93 / Savoy / THE / TKO Magnum

Pearl Jam

NO CODE
Sometimes / Hail hail / Who you are / In my tree / Smile / Off he goes / Habit / Red mosquito / Lukin / Present tense / Mankind / I'm open / Around the bend
CD 4844482
Epic / Aug '96 / Sony

TELLTALES (Interview Disc)
CD TELL 10
Network / Jun '97 / Total/BMG

TEN
Once / Even flow / Alive / Why go / Black / Jeremy / Oceans / Porch / Garden / Deep / Release / Master/Slave
CD 4688842
Epic / Feb '92 / Sony

VITALOGY
Last exit / Spin the black circle / Not for you / Tremor Christ / Nothingman / Whipping / Pry, To / Corduroy / Bugs / Satan's bed / Better man / Ave davanita / Immortality / Stupid mop
CD 4778612
Epic / Nov '94 / Sony

VS
Go / Animal / Daughter / Glorified G / Dissident / WMA / Blood / Rear view mirror / Rats / Elderly woman behind the counter in a small town / Leash / Indifference
CD 4745492
Epic / Oct '93 / Sony

Pearlfishers

STRANGE UNDERWORLD OF THE TALL POPPIES, THE
CD MA 25
Marina / Apr '97 / SRD

Pearson, Duke

BAG'S GROOVE
CD BLC 760149
Black Lion / Jul '91 / Cadillac / Jazz Music / Koch / Wellard

I DON'T CARE WHO KNOWS IT
I don't care who knows it / Bloos / Beautiful friendship / Horn in / Canto Ossanha / Xibaba / I don't know / One I loved / Upa Neguinho / Captain Bicardi / Theme from Rosemary's baby
CD CDP 8352202
Blue Note / Mar '96 / EMI

Pearson, John

BUSY BOOTIN' (Pearson, John & Roger Hubbard)
Busy bootin' / As I went down the railroad track / Write me a few lines / Wort Worth and Dallas blues / Barrelhouse woman / Streamline train / Jesus on the mainline / Jitterbug swing / East St. Louis fare thee well / Cigarette blues / Don't take everybody to be your friend / Stealin' / Walkin' blues
CD TX 1007CD
Taxim / Jan '94 / ADA

GRASSHOPPERS IN MY PILLOW
CD LDR 92
Last Days / Apr '97 / Hot Shot / Last Days

Pearson, Johnny

SLEEPY SHORES
Sleepy shores / Nadia's theme / Heather / Concerto d'aranjuez / Feelings / Annie's song / All creatures great and small / Vincent / Just the way you are / Misty sunset / You don't bring me flowers / What's another year / Theme from the deerhunter / First time ever I saw your face / Killing me softly with his song / Winner takes it all / If
CD BR 1322
BR Music / Dec '95 / Target/BMG

SLEEPY SHORES (The Best Of Johnny Pearson)
Sleepy shores / All creatures great and small / One day in your life / Misty sunset / Chi mai / Sing / If / What's another year / Sorry seems to be the hardest word / For your eyes only / Concerto de Aranjuez / Love story / People / Also sprach zarathustra / You needed me / I honestly love you / Winner takes it all / Don't cry for me Argentina
CD MCCD 304
Music Club / Jun '97 / Disc / THE

THEMES AND DREAMS (Pearson, Johnny Orchestra)
Godfather / House of Caradus (theme) / All creatures great and small / Love dream / Chi mai / First love / Triangle (love theme and intro) / Chariots of fire / You are the one / Seduction / Love dreamer / Cavatina / I wish I knew (how it would feel to be free) / Love story
CD PRCD 132
President / Jun '89 / Grapevine/PolyGram / President / Target/BMG

Pearson, Ralph

ROMANTIC FLUTE
From a distance / Feel like making love / Baby come back to me / Close to you / Ben / Kiss from a rose / Don't want to lose you / Julia says / End of the road / Rainy days and Mondays / Smooth operator / I've had the time of my life / Woman in love / Saving all my love for you / That's what friends are for / Annie's song / Hello again / Make it with you
CD QED 220
Tring / Nov '96 / Tring

Peaston, David

INTRODUCING DAVID PEASTON
Two wrongs / Take me now / We're all in this together / Eyes of love / Thank you for the moment / God bless the child / Tonight / Can I / Don't say no
CD GFLD 19339
Geffen / Oct '96 / BMG

Peatbog Faeries

MELLOWOSITY
Lexy MacAskill / Eiggman / Manili beetle / Macedonian woman's rant / Angus Mackinnon / Leaving the road / Weary we've been/Dancing feet / Maids of mount Cisco / Mellowosity
CD CDTRAX 124
Greentrax / Dec '96 / ADA / Direct / Duncans / Highlander

Peddlers

PART ONE
Time after time / Girl talk / Who can I turn to / Stormy weather / Smile / Empty club blues / You're the reason I'm living / It ain't no big thing / Sneaking up on you / Pentathlon / What now my love / Lover / Comin' home baby / On a clear day you can see forever / Basin Street blues / Nobody likes me / I'm a boy in love
CD 4728352
Sony Jazz / Jun '97 / Sony

Pedersen, Herb

LONESOME FEELING
Last thing on my mind / Childish love / Fields have turned brown / Homecoming / Easy ride / Lonesome feeling / Willow garden / It's worth believing / Even the worst of us / Your love is like a flower
CD SHCD 3738
Sugar Hill / Jul '95 / ADA / CM / Direct / Koch / Roots

Pedersen, Leonardo

I WANT A ROOF (Pedersen, Leonardo Jazzkapel)
CD MECCACD 1047
Music Mecca / Nov '94 / Cadillac / Jazz Music / Wellard

Pedersen, Niels-Henning ...

ETERNAL TRAVELLER, THE (Pedersen, Niels-Henning Orsted)
Moto perpetu / En elefant kom marcherende / Jeg gik mig ud en Sommerday / Det haver sa nyeligen regnet / Hist hvor vejen slar en bugt / Jeg ved en Laerkerede / Sig manen langsomt haever / Dawn / Eternal traveller / Skul gammel venskab rejn forgo / Moto perpetu
CD CD 2310910
Pablo / Mar '97 / Cadillac / Complete/ Pinnacle

FRIENDS FOREVER (Pedersen, Niels-Henning Orsted Trio)
Hushaby / Kenny / Someday my prince will come / Elvira Madigan / Lullaby of the leaves / Shadow of your smile / Sometime ago / Days of wine and roses / Future child - friends forever
CD MCD 9269
Milestone / Jun '97 / Cadillac / Complete/ Pinnacle / Jazz Music / Wellard

HOMMAGE (Once Upon A Time) (Pedersen, Niels-Henning Orsted & Palle Mikkelborg)
Cream / Tango jalousi / Lullabye-bye / Sporge-Jorgen / Det haver sa nyeligen regnet / Lost in the stars / JP / That ol' black magic / September song
CD 5131892
EmArCy / Apr '93 / PolyGram

THOSE WHO WERE (Pedersen, Niels-Henning Orsted)
CD 5332322
Verve / Nov '96 / PolyGram

Pedicin, Michael Jr.

BECAUSE OF LOVE
Something you said / Extraordinary love / Some other time / Just a little taste of your love: *Pedicin, Michael Jr. & Carla Benson* / Round town / Dr. B / Joy of life / Because we love: *Pedicin, Michael Jr. & Carla Benson* / 12th Street licks / Can't leave yet / Somehting you said / Just a little taste of your life / Because of love
CD CDPJA 1
Passion / May '97 / 3mv/Pinnacle

Pedicin, Mike

JIVE MEDICIN (Pedicin, Mike Quintet)
Mambo rock / I want to hug you, kiss you, squeeze you / Rock-a-bye / I'm hip / Large, large house / Jackpot / Fe-fi-fo-fum / Hot barcarolle / You gotta go / When the cats come marching in / Banjo rock / Large, large house / Rock-a-bye / Hotter than a pistol / Teenage fairy tale / Beat / Save us, Preacher Davis / Close all the doors / Td's boogie / Hucklebuck / Calypso rock / Hi'yo Silver / Tiger rag / Ain't that a shame / Crazy ball / I want you to be my baby / Night train / Sweet Georgia Brown / Rock-a-bye / Hotter than a pistol (live)
CD BCD 15738
Bear Family / Oct '93 / Direct / Rollercoaster / Swift

Pee Dee Jazzband

JUBILEE CONCERT, THE (2CD Set) (Pee Dee Jazzband & Monty Sunshine)
CD Set MECCACD 2103
Music Mecca / May '97 / Cadillac / Jazz Music / Wellard

JUBILEE TOUR 1996
CD MECCACD 1094
Music Mecca / May '97 / Cadillac / Jazz Music / Wellard

Peebles, Ann

FILL THIS WORLD WITH LOVE
CD CDBB 9564
Bullseye Blues / Jun '96 / Direct

FLIPSIDE
CD HIUKCD 144
Hi / Aug '93 / Pinnacle

GREATEST HITS
Ninety nine pounds / Walk away / Give me some credit / Heartaches, heartaches / Somebody's on your case / I still love you / Part time love / Generation gap between us / Slipped, tripped and fell in love / Trouble heartaches and sadness / I feel like breaking up somebody's home / I pity the fool / Do I need you / One way street / I can't stand the rain / Beware / Love vibration / Dr. Love Power / It was jealousy / Being here with you / I'm gonna tear your playhouse down / When in your arms / Good day for lovin' / Come to Mama / Old man with young ideas / If this is heaven
CD HIUKCD 100
Hi / Apr '88 / Pinnacle

LOOKIN' FOR A LOVIN'
Respect / Make me yours / It's your thing / Won't you try me / My man (mon homme) / I'll get along / What you laid on me / You keep me hangin' on / Love played a game / I needed somebody / You're gonna make me cry / Bip bam thank you Mam / Handwriting on the wall / Livin' in lovin' out / Lookin' for a lovin' / You've got the papers (I've got the man) / I didn't take your man / Heartaches / Be for me / Mon belle amour / I'd rather leave while I'm in love
CD HIUKCD 105
Hi / Aug '90 / Pinnacle

ST. LOUIS WOMAN/MEMPHIS SOUL (3CD Set)
Beware / Crazy about you baby / I'll get along / Heartaches / Rescue me / 99lbs / Dr. Love Power / What you laid on me / Let your lovelight shine / Part time love / Love played a game / Old man with young ideas / Chain of fools / I didn't take your man / My man, he's a lovin' man / Somebody's on your case / It's your thing / Slipped, tripped and fell in love / It must be love / Respect / How strong is a woman / I don't lend my man / I pity the fool / You've got the papers / Breaking up somebody's home / Bip bam thank you Mam / I can't stand the rain / Being here with you / Come to Mama / Games / Handwriting on the wall / Do I need you / Livin' in lovin' out / You've got to feed the fire / I'm gonna tear your playhouse down / Make me yours / If this is Heaven / If we can't trust each other / Fill this world with love / Stand by your woman / Boy I gotta have you / You're more than I can stand / Mon belle amour / I still love you / Steal away / I needed somebody / You keep me hanging on / Walk away / Until you came into my life / Heartaches heartaches / You can't hold a man / Troubles, heartaches and sadness / It was jealousy / Put yourself in my place / I've been there before / Won't you try me / One way street / Love vibration / Lovin' you without love / I'm leaving you / I'm so thankful / I'd rather leave while I'm in love / You're gonna make me cry
CD Set HIBOOK 13
Hi / Feb '97 / Pinnacle

STRAIGHT FROM THE HEART/I CAN'T STAND THE RAIN
Slipped, tripped and fell in love / Trouble, heartaches and sadness / What you laid on me / How strong is a woman / Somebody's on your case / I feel like breaking up somebody's home / I've been there before / I pity the fool / Ninety nine pounds / I take what I want / I can't stand the rain / Do I need you / Until you came into my life / You keep me hangin' on / Run run run / If we can't trust each other / Love vibration / You got to feed the fire / I'm gonna tear your playhouse down / One way street
CD HIUKCD 137
Hi / Jan '93 / Pinnacle

TELLIN' IT/IF THIS IS HEAVEN
Come to Mama / I don't lend my man / I needed somebody / Stand by woman / It was jealousy / Dr. Love Power / You can't hold a man / Beware / Put yourself in my place / Love played a game / If this is heaven / Good day for lovin' / I'm so thankful / Being here with you / Boy I gotta have you / When I'm in your arms / You're gonna make me cry / Games / Lovin' you wihtout love / It must be love
CD HIUKCD 138
Hi / Jan '93 / Pinnacle

THIS IS ANN PEEBLES
CD HIUKCD 139
Hi / Jun '93 / Pinnacle

US R&B CHARTS HITS
CD HILOCD 13
Hi / Jan '95 / Pinnacle

Peeping Tom

EYES HAVE IT, THE
Room in the loft / Meeting of the waters / First of May / French polka / Be minor baby / Steamboat quickstep / Mote and beam / Beamish Mary / Tower green / Salty dog pokas / Annie's hornpipe / Liquor hornpipe / Highland hunt 1 / Highland hunt 2 / Duke of Grafton / Treat / Oscar Wood's jig / Serpent dance / Knockabower No.2 / Cobbler / Paddy and dandy / Wellington's advance / Connaught man's rambles / Lullaby waltzes / Prowed C / Mystery jig / Breach of Killiecrankie / Britches full of stitches / Showman's fancy / Alexander's favourite / Gaspe reel / Malarky / Redcar reel / Johnny comes marching home / Swallow's nest / Istanbull / Gighouse shuffle
CD FSCD 26
Folksound / Aug '94 / CM / Roots

LOOKING GOOD
CD FSCD 40
Folksound / Jun '97 / CM / Roots

SIGHT FOR SORE EYES, A
Camels are coming / Lizzie Lichine / Abbeyfield / Woolaton park / Charlie Stewart / Victors return / Routier 66 / Whirlpool / Les filles de St. Nicolas / MacMahon's march / Night on the gin / Bedbreaker / Rag on reels / Jolly Geordies / Ranting Ross / Catchgate crapshooter / Buttonhole / Rig-a-jig / Mother's ruin / Chateau / Enrico / Tuxedo junction / Boanupstekker / Jackanory jig / Scottish de lea / Miss Sayers Allemande
CD FSCD 21
Folksound / Aug '92 / CM / Roots

Peers, Donald

IN A SHADY NOOK
In a shady nook / Don't sweetheart me / You're in love / It's love love love / By the river of roses / You fascinating you / London pride / I met her on a Monday / Isabel loves a soldier / I'm all right / Johnny and Mary / Lights out till reveille / Forever and a day / Just a little cottage / Russian rose / St. Mary's in the twilight / Tangerine / Moonlight cocktail / Three little sisters / Hey little hen / Nevada / Sing everybody sing / Marie Elena
CD RAJCD 846
Empress / Feb '95 / Koch

VERY BEST OF DONALD PEERS, THE
CD SOW 907
Sound Waves / May '93 / Target/BMG

Pegboy

EARWIG
CD QS 28CD
Quarter Stick / Nov '94 / Cargo / SRD

STRONG REACTION
CD QS 007CD
Quarter Stick / '94 / Cargo / SRD

Pege, Aladar

SOLO BASS, JAZZ AND CLASSIC
CD RST 91532
RST / Feb '91 / Hot Shot / Jazz Music

Pegg, Bob

LAST WOLF
Dram for the singer / Lament for the farmer's young wife / Man from Luddenden Dean / Instructions to a young Lark man / Stone head / Last dance / Poet, the Priest

and the dancer / Adam and Evie / Wildwood song / Mermaid / Last wolf / Fiddler's cross
CD RHYD 5009
Rhiannon / Nov '96 / ADA / Direct / Vital

Peggio

ALTERAZIONE DELLA STRUTTURA
CD WD 012CD
Plastic Head / Jun '92 / Plastic Head

Pegram, George

GEORGE PEGRAM
CD ROUCD 0001
Rounder / Feb '95 / ADA / CM / Direct

Peguri, Charles

COMPOSITIONS 1907-30
CD FA 021CD
Fremeaux / Nov '95 / ADA / Discovery

Peking Opera Troupe

MONKEY KING, THE
CD VICG 50162
JVC World Library / Mar '96 / ADA / CM / Direct

Pekka Pohjola

KATKAVAARAN LOHIKAARME
CD 450996415
F-Music / Dec '94 / Direct

KEESOJEN LEHTO
CD LRCD 219
Love / Dec '94 / ADA / Direct / Greyhound

Pele

A-LIVE-A-LIVE-O
Don't worship me / Fair blows the wind for France / Swinging from a tree / Oh Lord part II / Chosen one / Mairas wedding / King's ransom / Fireworks / In the beginning
CD MAGCD 1049
M&G / Jun '94 / 3mv/Sony

SPORT OF KINGS, THE
CD MAGCD 1043
M&G / Dec '93 / 3mv/Sony

Pelican Daughters

BLISS
CD SR 9456
Silent / Jul '94 / Cargo / Plastic Head

Peligro

PELIGRO
Coffee shop / King of the road / Love hate war / Hellations from hell / Spazztic nerve / Cat burglar / Cornfed knuckle head / Black bean chili thing / I spy / Hellnation / Beloved infidels / No TV show / Dirty / No way / Cat swing / Mystery
CD VIRUS 165CD
Alternative Tentacles / May '95 / Cargo / Greyhound / Pinnacle

Pell, Axel Rudi

BALLADS, THE
CD SPV 08476642
Steamhammer / Jul '93 / Pinnacle / Plastic Head

BETWEEN THE WALLS
CD SPV 08476822
Nosferatu / Jun '94 / Plastic Head

BLACK MOON PYRAMID
CD SPV 08518282
SPV / May '96 / Koch / Plastic Head

LIVE IN GERMANY
CD SPV 08576972
SPV / May '95 / Koch / Plastic Head

MAGIC
Swamp Castle overture / Nightmare / Playing with fire / Magic / Turned to stone / Clown is dead / Prisoners of the sea / Light in the sky / Eyes of the lost
CD CD 08518362
Steamhammer / Jun '97 / Pinnacle / Plastic Head

Pell, Dave

PLAYS AGAIN (Pell, Dave Octet)
CD FSRCD 5009
Fresh Sound / Nov '96 / Discovery / Jazz Music

Pell Mell

BUMPER CROP
CD SST 158CD
SST / May '93 / Plastic Head

INTERSTATE
CD FNCD 337
Flying Nun / Feb '96 / RTM/Disc

Pelland, Paul

PAUL PELLAND & BOB PILSBURY (Pelland, Paul & Bob Pilsbury)
CD SOSCD 1212
Stomp Off / Oct '92 / Jazz Music / Wellard

Pellegrino, Antonio

CELESTIAL CHRISTMAS VOL.2
CD CDCEL 13038
Celestial Harmonies / Oct '91 / ADA / Select

Pellen, Jaques

CELTIC PROCESSION
CD Y225028
Silex / Jun '93 / ADA / Harmonia Mundi

PELLEN & DEL FRA/GRITZ/WHEELER
CD DSC 250152
Diffusion Breizh / Apr '94 / ADA

SORSEREZ
CD GWP 011
Gwerz / May '96 / ADA / Discovery

Pelt

BROWN CYCLOPAEDIA
CD VHF 25
VHF / Dec '96 / Cargo

MAX MEADOWS
CD VHF 28
VHF / Mar '97 / Cargo

Pelzl, Stefan

TALES OF SISYPHOS (Pelzl, Stefan 'Ju Ju' & Idris Muhammad)
CD RST 91580
RST / Mar '95 / Hot Shot / Jazz Music

Pemarwan, Gender Wayang

MUSIC FOR THE BALINESE SHADOW PLAY
Gending petegak "Sekar Gendontan" / Gending pemungkah / Gending angkat - Angkatan / Gending mesem / Gending angkat-angkatan, Batel / Gending delem, Batle / Gending rebong / Gending langiang
CD CMPCD 3014
CMP / Oct '94 / Cargo / Grapevine/PolyGram / Vital/SAM

Pembroke, Jim

PIGWORM
Do the pigworm / Just my situation / Sweet Marie / Time to make a stand / No new games to play / Another telephone call / Resigned to surrender / Sweet revelation / That's the way it goes / No more terra firma
CD LRCD 103
Love / May '97 / ADA / Direct / Greyhound

Pena, Miles

MILES PENA
Un sueno prohibido / Es mi culpa / Corazon partido / Dame tu perdon / Un sentimental / Aire no viciado en mi existir / Habale / Cuenta conmigo
CD 66058066
RMM / Jul '95 / New Note/Pinnacle

Pena, Paco

ART OF PACO PENA
CD NI 7011
Nimbus / Sep '94 / Nimbus

AZAHARA
CD NI 5116
Nimbus / Sep '94 / Nimbus

ENCUENTROS (Pena, Paco & Eduardo Falu)
CD NI 5196
Nimbus / Sep '94 / Nimbus

FABULOUS FLAMENCO (Nice 'N' Easy Series)
CD 8206922
Eclipse / Mar '92 / PolyGram

FLAMENCO PURO
Llanto gitano / La piedra escrita / Giralda del Sevilla / De badajoz a Madrid / Agua viento nieve y frio / Ay mi romera / El bordon y la prima / Feria de Sevilla / Fiesta de traina y jerez
CD 4439022
Decca / Oct '96 / PolyGram

MISA FLAMENCA
CD NI 5288
Nimbus / Sep '94 / Nimbus

Penal Colony

PUT YOUR HANDS DOWN
CD CLEO 10942
Cleopatra / Jun '94 / Cargo / Greyhound / Plastic Head / RTM/Disc / SRD

Penance

PARALLEL CORNERS
CD CM 77077CD
Century Media / Oct '94 / Plastic Head

ROAD LESS TRAVELLED, THE
CD RISE 007CD
Rise Above / Jul '92 / Plastic Head / Vital

Pencil

SKANTRON
CD GROW 0192
Grass / Jun '94 / Pinnacle / SRD

Pencil Tin

GENTLE HAND TO GUIDE YOU ALONG, A
CD BUS 10102
Bus Stop / Mar '97 / Cargo / Vital

Pendergrass, Teddy

JOY
Joy / 2 a.m. / Good to you / I'm ready / Love is the power / This is the last time / Through the falling rain / Can we be lovers
CD 7559607752
Elektra / Oct '94 / Warner Music

STAR COLLECTION
CD STCD 1004
Disky / Jun '93 / Disky / THE

TOUCH OF CLASS, A
Can't we try / Love TKO / Let me love you / Come and go with me / Only you / Close the door / I don't love you anymore / Whole town's laughing at me / I can't live without your love / Nine times out of ten / You can't hide from yourself / Be sure / More I get the more I want / Life is a song worth singing / When somebody loves you back / Turn off the lights / You're my latest, greatest inspiration
CD TC 878022
Disky / May '97 / Disky / THE

YOU AND I
CD EAGCD 004
Eagle / Aug '97 / BMG

Pendragon

9.15 LIVE
Victims of life / Circus / Leviathan / Red shoes / Alaska / Black Knight / Please / Fly high fall far / Higher circles
CD PEND 3CD
Pendragon/Toff / '91 / Pinnacle

AS GOOD AS GOLD
CD NOB 4CD
Pendragon/Toff / Nov '96 / Pinnacle

FALLEN DREAMS AND ANGELS
Third World in the UK / Dune / Sister Bluebird / Fallen dreams and angels
CD MOB 2CD
Pendragon/Toff / Mar '95 / Pinnacle

JEWEL
Higher circles / Pleasure of hope / Leviathan / At home with the earth / Snowfall / Circus / Oh Divineo / Black night / Fly high fall far / Victims of life
CD PEND 2CD
Pendragon/Toff / '91 / Pinnacle

KOWTOW
I walk the rope / Solid heart / AM / Time for a change / Total recall / Haunting / Kowtow
CD PEND 1CD
Pendragon/Toff / Nov '88 / Pinnacle

MASQUERADE OVERTURE
Masquerade overture / As good as gold / Paintbox / Pursuit of excellence / Guardian of my soul / Shadow / Masters of illusion
CD PEND 7CD
CD PEND 7CDL
Pendragon/Toff / Mar '96 / Pinnacle

REST OF PENDRAGON, THE
CD PEND 4CD
Pendragon/Toff / Jun '91 / Pinnacle

UTRECHT - THE FINAL FRONTIER
CD NOB 3CD
Pendragon/Toff / Oct '96 / Pinnacle

VERY VERY BOOTLEG, THE (Live In Lille)
Excalibur / Totall recall / Queen of hearts / We'll go hunting deer / Solid heart
CD MOB 1CD
Pendragon/Toff / Feb '94 / Pinnacle

WINDOW OF LIFE
CD PEND 6CD
Pendragon/Toff / Oct '93 / Pinnacle

WORLD, THE
CD PEND 5CD
Pendragon/Toff / Oct '91 / Pinnacle

Pendulum Floors

KICKING GOOD TIME WITH THE PENDULUM FLOORS
CD VVK 10
Villa Villakula / Feb '97 / Cargo

Pene, Omar

DIRECT FROM DAKAR (Pene, Omar & Super Diamono)
Aral sa doom / Mouride / Rer / Soweto / Niane / Coumba / Xaliss / Gainde / Xamlene / Yaye boye / Banna / Diaraf / Douweye
CD WSCD 102
Womad Select / Jul '97 / ADA / Direct

Penetration

DON'T DICTATE (The Best Of Penetration)
Come into the open / Lifeline / Firing squad / Never / Life's a gamble / VIP / Danger signs / Stone heroes / Don't dictate / Free money / Shout above the noise / She is the slave / Party's over / Future daze
CD CDOVD 450
Virgin / Feb '95 / EMI

MOVING TARGETS
Future daze / Life's a gamble / Lovers of outrage / Vision / Silent community / Stone heroes / Movement / Too many friends / Reunion / Nostalgia / Freemoney
CD CDV 2109
Virgin / '89 / EMI

PENETRATION
Duty free technology / Firing squad / Race against time / In the future / Free money/ Never / VIP / Don't dictate / Silent community / She is the slave / Danger signs / Last saving grace / Movement / Stone heroes / Vision / Future daze / Come into the open / Lovers of outrage / Too many friends / Killed in the rush
CD PILOT 001
Burning Airlines / Sep '93 / Total/Pinnacle

Penguin Cafe Orchestra

BROADCASTING FROM HOME
Music for a found harmonium / Prelude and yodel / More milk / Sheep dip / White mischief / In the back of a taxi / Music by numbers / Another one from the colonies / Air / Heartwind / Isle of view (music for helicopter pilots) / Now nothing
CD EEGCD 38
EG / Apr '92 / EMI

CONCERT PROGRAMME
CD Set ZOPFD 002
Zopf / Jul '95 / PolyGram

MUSIC FROM THE PENGUIN CAFE
Chartered flight / Hugebaby / Penguin Cafe single / Sound of someone you love / Zopf (from the colonies)
CD EEGCD 27
EG / Apr '92 / EMI

PENGUIN CAFE ORCHESTRA
Air a danser / Number 1-4 / Salty bean fumble / Yodel 1 / Telephone and rubber band / Cutting branches for a temporary shelter / Pythagoras' trousers / Yodel 2 / Paul's dance / Ecstasy of dancing fleas / Walk don't run / Flux / Simon's dream / Harmonic necklace / Steady state
CD EEGCD 11
EG / Apr '92 / EMI

PRELUDES, AIRS AND YODELS (A Penguin Cafe Primer)
CD AMBT 15
Virgin / Aug '96 / EMI

SIGNS OF LIFE
Bean fields / Southern jukebox music / Horns of the bull / Oscar tango / Snake and the lotus / Rosasolis / Sketch / Perpetuum mobile / Swing the cat / Wildlife / Dirt
CD EEGCD 50
EG / '87 / EMI

UNION CAFE
CD ZOPFD 001
Zopf / Jun '96 / Grapevine/PolyGram

WHEN IN ROME - LIVE
Air a danser / Yodel 1 / From the colonies / Southern jukebox music / Numbers 1-4 / Bean fields / Paul's dance / Oscar tango / Music for a found harmonium / Isle of view (music for helicopter pilots) / Prelude and yodel / Giles Farnaby's dream / Air / Dirt / Cutting branches for a temporary shelter / Telephone and rubber band
CD EEGCD 56
EG / Sep '88 / EMI

Penguins

EARTH ANGEL
Earth angel / Hey Senorita / Kiss a fool goodbye / Ookey ook / Love will make your mind go wild / Baby let's make some love / Lover or fool / Do not pretend / If you're mine / Be my lovin' baby / Cold heart / Sweet love / Let me make up your mind / Butterball / Money talks / Heart of a fool / Want me / That's how much I need you / I ain't gonna cry no more / No there ain't no news today / You're an angel
CD CDCH 249
Ace / Nov '90 / Pinnacle

Peniston, Ce Ce

FINALLY
We got a love thang / Finally / Inside that I cried / Lifeline / It should have been you / Keep on walkin' / Crazy love / I see love / You win, I win, we lose / Virtue
CD 3971822
A&M / Apr '95 / PolyGram

THOUGHT 'YA KNEW
Searchin' / I'm in the mood / Hit by love / Whatever it is / Forever in my heart / I'm not over you / Anyway you wanna go / Give what I'm givin' / Through those doors / Let my love surround you / Keep givin' me your

love / If you love me, I will love you / Maybe it's the way
CD 5401382
A&M / Jan '94 / PolyGram

Penn, Dan

DO RIGHT MAN
CD 9362455192
Warner Bros. / Oct '94 / Warner Music

Penn, Dawn

COME AGAIN
CD CDTRL 370
Trojan / Jul '96 / Direct / Jet Star

NO NO NO
I want a love I can see / I'm sorry / You don't love me (no no no) / Night and day / My love takes over / First cut is the deepest / I'll do it again / Hurt / Samfi boy / Keep in touch / My man / Blue yes blue
CD 7567923652
Warner Bros. / Jun '94 / Warner Music

Penn, Michael

FREE FOR ALL
Long way down (look what the cat drug in) / Free time / Coal / Seen the doctor / By the book / Drained / Slipping my mind / Strange season / Bunker hill / Now we're even
CD 07863611132
RCA / Nov '93 / BMG

Penniless People

VELOCITY
CD CDVEST 67
Bulletproof / Feb '96 / Pinnacle

Pennou Skoulm

PENNOU SKOULM
CD CD 854
Diffusion Breizh / Jan '95 / ADA

Penny Dreadfuls

PENNY DREADFULS
CD 7729122
Restless / Nov '96 / Vital

Pennywise

FULL CIRCLE
Fight till you die / Date with destiny / Get a life / Society / Final day / Broken / Running out of time / You'll never make it / Every time / Nowhere fast / What if I / Go away / Did you really / Bro hymn tribute
CD 64892
Epitaph / Apr '97 / Pinnacle / Plastic Head

UNKNOWN ROAD
CD E 864292
Epitaph / Aug '93 / Pinnacle / Plastic Head

WILD CARD (A Word From The Wise)
CD TS 003CD
Semaphore / May '95 / Plastic Head

Pensyl, Kim

UNDER THE INFLUENCE
CD SH 5019
Shanachie / Jun '96 / ADA / Greensleeves / Koch

WHEN YOU WERE MINE
CD SH 5010
Shanachie / Dec '94 / ADA / Greensleeves / Koch

Pentagram

BE FOREWARNED
Live free and burn / Too late / Ask no more / World will love again / Vamypyre love / Life blood / Wolf's blood / Frustration / Bride of evil / Nightmare gown / Petrified / Timeless heart / Be forewarned
CD CDVILE 42
Peaceville / Mar '95 / Pinnacle

DAY OF RECKONING
Day of reckoning / Broken vows / Madman / When the screams come / Burning saviour / Evil seed / Wartime
CD CDVILE 40
Peaceville / Aug '93 / Pinnacle

RELENTLESS
Death row / All your sins / Sign of the wolf / Ghoul / Relentless / Run my course / Sinister / Deist / You're lost, I'm free / Dying world / Twenty buck spin
CD CDVILE 38
Peaceville / Apr '93 / Pinnacle

RELENTLESS/DAY OF RECKONING
CD CDVILE 40
Peaceville / May '95 / Pinnacle

TRAIL BLAZER
CD SULH 70178
Nuclear Blast / Jan '95 / Plastic Head

Pentangle

ANNIVERSARY
CD HY 200122CD
Hypertension / Sep '93 / ADA / CM / Direct / Total/BMG

BASKET OF LIGHT
Light flight / Once I had a sweetheart / Springtime promises / Lyke wyke dirge / Train song / Hunting song / Sally go round the roses / Cuckoo / House carpenter
CD ESMCD 406
Essential / Jun '96 / BMG

CRUEL SISTER
Maid that's deep in love / When I was in my prime / Lord Franklin / Cruel sister / Jack Orion
CD ESMCD 458
Essential / Jan '97 / BMG

IN YOUR MIND
CD 295942
Ariola / Oct '94 / BMG

LIGHT FLIGHT (2CD Set)
CD Set SMDCD 154
Snapper / Jul '97 / Pinnacle

MAID THAT'S DEEP IN LOVE, A
CD SH 79066
Shanachie / Jul '90 / ADA / Greensleeves / Koch

PENTANGLE, THE
Let no man steal your thyme / Bells / Hear my call / Pentangling / Mirage / Way behind the sun / Bruton Town / Waltz / Travelling song
CD HILLCD 7
Wooded Hill / Nov '96 / Direct / World Serpent

SO EARLY IN THE SPRING
So early in the Spring / Blacksmith / Reynardine / Eministra / Lucky black cat / Bramble briar / Lassie gathering nuts / Gaia / Baron of Brackley
CD PRKCD 35
Park / Jun '96 / Pinnacle

SWEET CHILD
Market song / No more my lord / Turn your money green / Haitian fight song / Woman like you / Goodbye Pork Pie Hat / Three dances (Brentzel Gay/La Rotta/The Earle of Salisbury) / Watch the stars / So early in the Spring / No exit / Time has come / Bruton Town / Sweet child / I loved a lass / Three part thing / Sovay / In time / In your mind / I've got a feeling / Trees they do grow high / Moon dog / Hole in the coal
CD ESMCD 354
Essential / Jan '96 / BMG

Pentatonik

PENTATONIK (2CD Set)
Movements / About that / La verite / Solution / Create / Sleeper / Part 4 live / Detox / Real / Green / Passion / Prophesy / Pantatonik melody
CD Set DVNT 001CD
Deviant / Sep '95 / Prime / Vital

Penthouse

GUTTER EROTICA
Voyeur's blues / Gus' neck / la grotte d'amour / Road rash / Beauty in the beast / Deviant soiree / Harmonic surf spastic / Widow's chagrin / Mare Ingram's lament / Gin waltz / White coal / Lap dog shuffle / Face down
CD WDOM 34CD
World Domination / May '97 / Pinnacle / RTM/Disc

Pentti Rasankangas

ANKKAPAALLIKKO
CD OMCD 52
Olarin Musiiki Oy / Dec '93 / ADA / Direct

Penuela, Antonita

LA ESPABILA
CD 9154
Divucsa / Oct '96 / Discovery

People Like Us

BEWARE THE WHIM REAPER
CD STCD 101
Staalplaat / Feb '96 / Vital/SAM

GUIDE TO BROADCASTING
CD STCDMCD 002
Staalplaat / Sep '95 / Vital/SAM

NO...REALLY
CD CD 378142
Koch Jazz / Jul '97 / Koch

PEOPLE LIKE US/ABRAXAS (People Like Us/Abraxas)
CD GBCD 001
GB / Oct '96 / World Serpent

People Without Shoes

THOUGHTS OF AN OPTIMIST
CD RGE 1022
Enemy / Nov '94 / Grapevine/PolyGram

People's Temple Choir

HE'S ABLE
CD GM 04CD
Grey Matter / Jan '97 / Cargo

Peoples, Tommy

HIGH PART OF THE ROAD (Peoples, Tommy & Paul Brady)
CD SHANCD 34007
Shanachie / Jan '95 / ADA / Greensleeves / Koch

IRON MAN, THE
CD SHCD 79044
Shanachie / May '95 / ADA / Greensleeves / Koch

TRANQUIL IRISH MUSIC PLAYED ON THE FIDDLE
CD TRADCD 008
GTD / Mar '91 / ADA / Else

Peoplespeak

PEOPLESPEAK
Agitate the gravel / Rain / Wanawaki / Say it, do it / Others / Sometime / Burma / January
CD PS 1001
PS / Sep '92 / New Note/Pinnacle

Pep Rally

DEADLINE
CD 35520072
Onefoot / Oct '96 / Cargo

Pepgirlz

DOWN 'N' DIRTY
CD ALIVECD 27
Alive / Feb '97 / RTM/Disc / Shellshock/ Disc

Pepl, Harry

CRACKED MIRRORS (Pepl, Harry & Herbert Joos/Jon Christensen)
Wolkenbilder 1 / Reflections in a cracked mirror / Schikaneder delight / Die alte mar und das mann / More far out than east / Wolkenbilder 2 / Tintenfisch inki / Purple light
CD 8334722
ECM / Jul '88 / New Note/Pinnacle

Peplowski, Ken

CONCORD DUO SERIES...
Blue room / Why / Changes / Chasin' the Bird / Deep purple / You're my everything / s'posin' / Two not one / If I should lose you / In the dark / Just one of those things
CD CCD 4556
Concord Jazz / Jun '93 / New Note/ Pinnacle

DOUBLE EXPOSURE
(I would do) anything for you / There's no you / Lava / Blame it on my youth / Segment / High and flighty / Don't you know I care (or don't you care to) / Jubilee / Careless love / Imagination
CD CCD 4344
Concord Jazz / Jul '88 / New Note/Pinnacle

GOOD REED
Luck be a lady / Dream theme / Homage concerto for clarinet and jazz orchestra / Deep / I've never been in love before / Purple gazelle / Royal garden blues
CD CCD 47672
Concord Jazz / Jul '97 / New Note/Pinnacle

ILLUMINATIONS
June night / Trubbel / Panama / Between the Devil and the deep blue sea / How long has this been going on / Jim Dawg / Smada / Alone together / Did I remember / Nancy with the laughing face / Best things in life are free / If we never meet again
CD CCD 4449
Concord Jazz / Mar '91 / New Note/ Pinnacle

IT'S A LONESOME OLD TOWN
More than ever / They can't take that away from me / It's a lonesome old town / These foolish things / Supposin' / Bonicrates de muletas / It never entered my mind / In my life / Last night when we were young / Eternal triangle / Zingaro / Crimehouse
CD CCD 4673
Concord Jazz / Nov '95 / New Note/ Pinnacle

LIVE AT AMBASSADOR AUDITORIUM
Kirk's works / Nuts / I don't stand a ghost of a chance with you / Best things in life are free / At long last love / Menina flor / I brung you finjans for your zarf / Why try to change me now / Exactly like you
CD CCD 4610
Concord Jazz / Sep '94 / New Note/ Pinnacle

MR. GENTLE AND MR. COOL (Peplowski, Ken Quintet)
Mr. Gentle and Mr. Cool / Please be kind / You do something to me / Body and soul / Makin' whoopee / Stray horn / Follow your heart / On a misty night / Syeeda's song flute / There'll be some changes made / Count your blessings instead of sheep / When day is done
CD CCD 4419
Concord Jazz / Jul '90 / New Note/Pinnacle

NATURAL TOUCH (Peplowski, Ken Quintet)
I'll close my eyes / One I love (belongs to someone else) / Guess I'll hang my tears out to dry / Evidence / Evening / You never know / You must believe in spring / Flunk blues / Circles of threes / My buddy / How deep is the ocean / Say it isn't so / I thought about you
CD CCD 4517
Concord Jazz / Aug '92 / New Note/ Pinnacle

OTHER PORTRAIT, THE
Milestones/Anthropology / Dance preludes / Single petal of a rose / Concerto for clarinet and orchestra / Cadenza / Lonely woman / Duet
CD CCD 42043
Concord Concerto / Nov '96 / New Note/ Pinnacle

SONNY SIDE (Peplowski, Ken Quintet)
CD CCD 4376
Concord Jazz / May '89 / New Note/ Pinnacle

STEPPIN' WITH PEPS
Steppin' / Courtship / Among my souvenirs / Lotus blossom / No problems / Johnny come lately / Blue mood / Antigua / Lady's in love with you / Pretend / Huggles / Turn around
CD CCD 4569
Concord Jazz / Sep '93 / New Note/ Pinnacle

THREE CLARINETS (Peplowski, Ken & Antti Sarpila/Allan Vache)
CD NHCD 027
Nagel Heyer / Jul '96 / Jazz Music

Pepper, Art

AMONG FRIENDS
What is this thing called love / 'Round midnight / What's new / I'll remember April / Among friends: *Pepper, Art Quartet* / I'm getting sentimental over you: *Pepper, Art Quartet* / Blue bossa: *Pepper, Art Quartet* / Besame mucho: *Pepper, Art Quartet*
CD STCD 4167
Storyville / Feb '90 / Cadillac / Jazz Music / Wellard

ART 'N' ZOOT (Pepper, Art & Zoot Sims)
CD CD 23109572
Pablo / Apr '96 / Cadillac / Complete/ Pinnacle

ART PEPPER MEETS THE RHYTHM SECTION
You'd be so nice to come home to / Red pepper blues / Imagination / Waltz me blues / Straight life / Jazz me blues / Tin tin deo / Star eyes / Birk's works
CD OJCCD 338
Original Jazz Classics / Sep '93 / Complete/ Pinnacle / Jazz Music / Wellard

ARTHUR'S BLUES
Donna Lee / Road waltz / For Freddie / But beautiful / Arthur's blues
CD OJCCD 680
Original Jazz Classics / May '93 / Complete/ Pinnacle / Jazz Music / Wellard

COMPLETE GALAXY RECORDINGS 1978-1982, THE (16CD Set)
Miss who / Mambo koyama / Lover come back to me / Patricia / These foolish things / Chris's blues / Over the rainbow / Yardbrd suite / Ilove you / Pepper pot / These foolish things / Straight no chaser / Yesterdays / Night in Tunisia / Night in Tunisia / Diane / My friend John / Duo blues / Blues for Blanche / Landscape / Stardust / Donna Lee / Donna Lee / Blues for Blanche / So in love / Lover man / Body and soul / You go to my head / Tin tin deo / Stardust / Anthropology / In a mellow tone / Desafinado / My friend John / My friend John / True blues / Avalon / Trip / Landscape / Sometime / Mambo de la pinta / Red car / Over the rainbow / Mambo koyama / Straight life / Besame mucho / True blues / Avalon / Shadow of your smile / Landscape / Sometime / Mambo de la pinta / Over the rainbow / Mambo koyama / Straight life / Besame mucho / But beautiful / When you're smiling / Surf ride / Nature boy / Straight life #32 / September song / Make a list / Long ago and far away / Nature boy / Our song / Here's that rainy day / That's love / Winter moon / When the sun comes out / Blues in the night / Prisoner / Ol' man river / Here's that rainy day / Winter moon / When the song comes out / Our song / Prisoner of love / Mr. Big falls his JG hand / Close to you alone / There will never be another you / There will never be another you / Melolev / Goodbye again / Brazil / There will never be another you / Melolev / Goodbye again / Donna Lee / What's new / Landscape / Valse triste / Thank you blues / Road waltz / For Freddie / But beautiful / Mambo koyama / Landscape / Roadgame / Mambo koyama / Everything happens to me / Wee Allen's alley / Road waltz / Samba mom mom / When you're smiling / But beautiful / Roadgame / For Freddie / Arthur's blues / Over the rainbow / Tete a tete / Darn that dream / Body and soul / Way you look tonight / 'Round midnight / Night in Tunisia / Samba mom mom / Last thing blues / Over

the rainbow / Body and soul / Goin' home / Samba mom mom / Mellow tone / Don't let the sun catch you cryin' / Isn't she lovely / Billie's bounce / Lover man / Sweetest sounds / You go to my head / Stardust / Don't let the sun catch you cryin' / Darn that dream / Don't let the sun catch you cryin'
CD Set GCD 1016
Galaxy / Nov '96 / Pinnacle

COMPLETE VILLAGE VANGUARD SESSIONS, THE (Live 28-30th July 1977 - 9CD Set)
Blues for heard / Scrapple from the apple / But beautiful / My friend John / Cherokee / Blues for Heard / Over the rainbow / Trip / Blues for Les / Night in Tunisia / No limit / Valse triste / My friend John / You go to my head / Cherokee / Blues for Heard / Blues for Heard / Anthropology / These foolish things / For Freddie / Blues for Heard / Las cuevas de Mario / Stella by starlight / Goodbye / Vanguard max / Blues for Heard / Vanguard max / Las cuevas de Mario / Goodbye / For Freddie / Blues for Heard / My friend John / More for Les / Cherokee / Blues for Heard / For Freddie / More for Les / Caravan / Labyrinth / My friend John
CD Set 9CCD 44172
Contemporary / Nov '96 / Cadillac / Complete/Pinnacle / Jazz Music / Wellard

FRIDAY NIGHT AT THE VILLAGE VANGUARD
CD OJCCD 695
Original Jazz Classics / Nov '95 / Complete/Pinnacle / Jazz Music / Wellard

GETTIN' TOGETHER (Pepper, Art & Conte Candoli)
CD OJCCD 169
Original Jazz Classics / May '93 / Complete/Pinnacle / Jazz Music / Wellard

IN COPENHAGEN 1981 (2CD Set) (Pepper, Art & Duke Jordan)
Blues Montmartre / What is this thing called love / Over the rainbow / Caravan / Rhythm-a-ning / You go to my head / Basame mucho / Cherokee / Radio blues / Good bait / All the things you are
CD Set 2GCD 82012
Galaxy / Dec '96 / Pinnacle

INTENSITY
I can't believe that you're in love with me / I love you / Come rain or come shine / Long ago and far away / Gone with the wind / I wished on the moon / Too close for comfort
CD OJCCD 387
Original Jazz Classics / Feb '92 / Complete/ Pinnacle / Jazz Music / Wellard

LAURIE'S CHOICE
CD 17012
Laserlight / Aug '93 / Target/BMG

LIVE AT DONTE'S 1968 (2CD Set) (Pepper, Art Quintet)
CD Set FSCD 1039
Fresh Sound / Nov '95 / Discovery / Jazz Music

LIVING LEGEND
Orphelia / Here's that rainy day / What Laurie likes / Mr. Yohe / Lost life / Samba mom-mom
CD OJCCD 408
Original Jazz Classics / Apr '93 / Complete/ Pinnacle / Jazz Music / Wellard

MEMORIAL COLLECTION VOL.1
CD STCD 4128
Storyville / Feb '90 / Cadillac / Jazz Music / Wellard

MEMORIAL COLLECTION VOL.2
CD STCD 4129
Storyville / Feb '90 / Cadillac / Jazz Music / Wellard

MEMORIAL COLLECTION VOL.3
CD STCD 4130
Storyville / Feb '90 / Cadillac / Jazz Music / Wellard

MEMORIAL COLLECTION VOL.4
CD STCD 4146
Storyville / Feb '90 / Cadillac / Jazz Music / Wellard

MODERN JAZZ CLASSICS (Pepper, Art + Eleven)
Move / Groovin' high / Opus de funk / 'Round midnight / Four brothers / Shaw nuff / Bernie's tune / Walkin' shoes / Anthropology / Airegin / Walkin' / Donna Lee
CD OJCCD 341
Original Jazz Classics / Jun '94 / Complete/ Pinnacle / Jazz Music / Wellard

NO LIMIT
CD OJCCD 411
Original Jazz Classics / Nov '95 / Complete/Pinnacle / Jazz Music / Wellard

PEPPER RETURNS
Pepper returns / Broadway / I surrender dear / Art's opus / What is this thing called love / Foggy day / I can't give you anything but love / You go to my head / You and the night and the music / Abstract art / Val's pal / Pepper pot / Blues at twilight / Angel wings / Minority / Walkin' out blues
CD CD 53237
Giants Of Jazz / Jan '96 / Cadillac / Jazz Music / Target/BMG

ROADGAME
Roadgame / Road waltz / When you're smiling / Everything happens to me
CD OJCCD 774
Original Jazz Classics / Sep '93 / Complete/ Pinnacle / Jazz Music / Wellard

SATURDAY NIGHT AT THE VILLAGE VANGUARD
CD OJCCD 696
Original Jazz Classics / Nov '95 / Complete/Pinnacle / Jazz Music / Wellard

STRAIGHT LIFE
Surf ride / Nature boy / Straight life / September song / Make a list (make a wish) / Long ago and far away
CD OJCCD 475
Original Jazz Classics / Jun '96 / Complete/ Pinnacle / Jazz Music / Wellard

THURSDAY NIGHT AT THE VILLAGE VANGUARD
CD OJCCD 694
Original Jazz Classics / Nov '95 / Complete/Pinnacle / Jazz Music / Wellard

TRIP, THE
Trip / Song for Richard / Sweet love of mine / Junior cat / Summer knows / Red car
CD OJCCD 410
Original Jazz Classics / Mar '93 / Complete/ Pinnacle / Jazz Music / Wellard

WINTER MOON
Our song / Here's that rainy day / That's love / Winter moon / When the sun comes out / Blues in the night / Prisoner (love theme from 'Eyes of Laura Mars')
CD OJCCD 677
Original Jazz Classics / Nov '95 / Complete/ Pinnacle / Jazz Music / Wellard

Pepsi & Shirlie

HEARTACHE
Goodbye stranger / Can't give me love / What's going on inside your head / All right now / Lover's revolution / High time / Heartache / It's a shame / Surrender / Feels like the first time / Crime of passion / Someday
CD 5500092
Spectrum / May '93 / PolyGram

Percy X

SPYX
CD SOMACD 4
Soma / Feb '96 / RTM/Disc

Pere Ubu

DATAPANIK IN THE YEAR ZERO (5CD Set)
30 seconds over Tokyo / Heart of darkness / Final solution / Cloud 149 / Untitled / My dark ages / Heaven / Nonalignment pact / Modern dance / Laughing / Street waves / Chinese radiation / Life stinks / Real world / Over my head / Sentimental journey / Humor me / Book is on the table / Navvy / On the surface / Dub housing / Caligaris mirror / Thriller / I will wait / Drinking wine spodyody / Ubu dance party / Blow daddy o / Codex / Fabulous sequel / 49 guitars and one girl / A small dark cloud / Small was fast / All the dogs are barking / One less worry / Make hay / Goodbye / Voice of the sand / Kingdom come / Rhapsody in pink / Arabia / Young Miles in the basement / Misery goats / Loop / Rounder / Birdies / Lost in art / Horses / Crush this horn / Long walk home / Petrified / Stormy weather / West side story / Thoughts that go by steam / Big Ed's used farms / A day such as this / Vulgar boatman / My hat / Horns are a dilemma / Real world / Laughing / Streetwaves / Humor me / Over my head / Sentimental journey / Life stinks / My dark ages / Modern dance / Codex / Ubu dance party / Big Ed's used farms / Real world / Birdies / Incredible truth / It's in imagination / Never again / Sunset in the Antipodes / Fix my horn / Baking bread / Atom mind / Autumn leaves / Dear Richard / You're gonna watch me / Amphetamine / She smiled wild / Jaguar ride / Steve Canyon blues / Home life / 30 seconds over Tokyo / Heart of darkness / Pushin too hard
CD Set COOKCD 098
Cooking Vinyl / Aug '96 / Vital

FOLLY OF YOUTH
Folly of youth / Ball 'n' chain / Down by the river II / Memphis
CD FRYCD 043
Cooking Vinyl / Oct '95 / Vital

MODERN DANCE, THE/TERMINAL TOWER (2CD Set)
Non-alignment pact / Modern dance / Laughing / Street waves / Chinese radiation / Life stinks / Real world / Over my head / Sentimental journey / Humor me / Heart of darkness / 30 seconds over Tokyo / Final solution / Cloud 149 / Untitled / My dark ages / Heaven / Humor me (live) / Book is on the table / Not happy / Lonesome Cowboy Dave
CD Set MPG 74178
Movieplay Gold / Nov '95 / Target/BMG

RAY GUN SUITCASE
Folly of youth / Electricity / Beach boys / Turquoise fins / Vaccum in my head / Memphis / Three things / Horse / Don't worry / Ray gun suitcase / Surfer girl / Red sky / Montana / My friend is a stooge of the media priests / Down by the river
CD COOKCD089
Cooking Vinyl / Jul '95 / Vital

Peregoyo Y Su Combo Vacana

TROPICALISMO (A Colombian Salsa Recording)
Rio De Juaji / La palma de chontaduro / Asi es mi tierra / Mi buenaventura / Descarga vacana / La pluma / Ola de agua / Chenchudino / Martha Cecilia / El canalete / Sabor de vacana / Descarga vacana / Che pachanga
CD WCD 015
World Circuit / Dec '89 / ADA / Cadillac / Direct / New Note/Pinnacle

Perelman, Ivo

CAMA DE TERRA (Perelman, Ivo & Matthew Shipp/William Parker)
CD HMS 2372
Homestead / Dec '96 / Cargo / SRD

Perera, Roberto

HARP AND SOUL
Romantica / Place in the sun / Don't say goodbye / Hotel California / Maybe this time / Breathe again / Love dance / Malambo / Harp beat / Siesta
CD INAK 3036
In Akustik / Jul '97 / Direct / TKO Magnum

SEDUCTION
CD INAK 3030
In Akustik / Oct '96 / Direct / TKO Magnum

Peress, Cindy

WORLD IS WATCHING, THE
CD SHAM 1013CD
Shamrock / May '93 / ADA / Wellard

Perez, Carlos Jose

NOSTALGIAS 1936-1954
CD EBCD 77
El Bandoneon / Jul '96 / Discovery

Perez, Danilo

JOURNEY, THE
Capture / Morning / Forest / Taking chains / Voyage / Arrival / Awakening / New vision / Panama 2000 / Reminisce / Flight to freedom / Anticipation / Flight / African wave / Libre spirits
CD 01241631662
Novus / Jul '94 / BMG

PANAMONK
Monk's mood / Panamonk / Bright Mississippi / Think of one / Mercedes' mood / Hot bean strut / Reflections / September in Rio / Everything happens to me / 'Round midnight / Evidence and four in one / Monk's mood 2
CD IMP 11902
Impulse Jazz / Jun '96 / New Note/BMG

Perez, Pocho

EL NEGRITO
CD TUMICD 034
Tumi / '92 / Discovery / Stern's

Perfect

WHEN SQUIRRELS PLAY CHICKEN
Makes me happy / Sometimes / Alternative monkey / Miss self-esteem / Don't need to know where
CD 893152
Medium Cool / Aug '96 / Vital

Perfect Disaster

HEAVEN SCENT
CD FIRE 33027
Fire / Oct '90 / Pinnacle / RTM/Disc

UP
CD FIRE 33018
Fire / Oct '91 / Pinnacle / RTM/Disc

Perfect Houseplants

CLEC
CD EFZ 1011
EFZ / Jan '95 / Vital/SAM

PERFECT HOUSEPLANTS
These foolish times / Somewhere in England / Salvadors / Knees / Last summer / With hindsight / Fedora / When/Starry eyed / Going home
CD AHUM 014
Ah-Um / Jul '93 / Cadillac / New Note/ Pinnacle

SNAP CLATTER
Strictly for dancing / Curiosity threatens / Rag / Emerald / Gentle life / New day / Damp dog / Tango for stalling / Hush / Salome / EE
CD AKD 063
Linn / Apr '97 / PolyGram

PErFect ThYroID

MUSICAL BARNACLES
CD SHCD 5724
Shanachie / May '97 / ADA / Greensleeves / Koch

Perfume

ONE
I'm alive / Lover / Watch me bleed / You and I / As I go blind / Carving your name / Your life is now / One / Haven't seen you / I'm no saint / Changes / Fallen / Things that I love / Wild honey
CD STARC 104
Big Star / Mar '97 / Grapevine/PolyGram

Perfume Tree

DUST
CD ZULU 006CD
Zulu / Oct '95 / Plastic Head

Peril

MULTIVERSE
CD SFCD 015
Sound Factory / Jun '97 / ReR Megacorp

Peris, Phillip

DIDGERIDOO
Gone walkabout / Rainbow heartbeat / Bunyip calling / Down by the billabong / Under the shade of a coolabah tree
CD CP 10296
Cinq Planetes / May '97 / Harmonia Mundi

Perkins, Bill

FRONT LINE, THE (Perkins, Bill & Pepper Adams)
CD STCD 4166
Storyville / Feb '90 / Cadillac / Jazz Music / Wellard

I WISHED ON THE MOON
I wished on the moon / Remember / Beautiful love / Besame mucho / Opals / No more / Last port of call / Rockin' chair / Summer knows / Caravan
CD CCD 79524
Candid / Feb '97 / Cadillac / Direct / Jazz Music / Koch / Wellard

PERK PLAYS PREZ
CD FSR 5010CD
Fresh Sound / Apr '97 / Discovery / Jazz Music

QUIETLY THERE (Perkins, Bill & Victor Felder)
Quietly there / Emily / Groover wailin' / Time for love / Sure as you're born / Just a child / Keester parade / Shining sea / Something different / Shadow of your smile
CD OJCCD 1766
Original Jazz Classics / Jun '96 / Complete/ Pinnacle / Jazz Music / Wellard

REMEMBERANCE OF DINO'S
CD IPCD 8606
Interplay / Apr '94 / Jazz Music

TENORS HEAD ON (Perkins, Bill & Richie Kamuca)
Cotton tail / I want a little girl / Blues for two / Indian summer / Don't be that way / Oh look at me now / Spain / Pick a dilly / Solid De Sylvia / Just friends / All of me / Limehouse blues / Sweet and lovely
CD CDP 7971952
Blue Note / Feb '97 / EMI

WARM MOODS (Perkins, Bill & Frank Strazzeri)
CD FSRCD 191
Fresh Sound / Dec '92 / Discovery / Jazz Music

Perkins, Carl

BEST OF AND THE REST OF, THE
(We're gonna) Rock around the clock / That's alright mama / Kaw-liga / Tutti frutti / Yes it's me and I'm in love again / Blue suede shoes / Be bop a lula / Maybellene / Whole lotta shakin' goin' on / Hang up my rock 'n' roll shoes / shake, rattle and roll
CD CDAR 1025
Action Replay / Mar '91 / Tring

BEST OF CARL PERKINS, THE
CD MATCD 324
Castle / Feb '95 / BMG

BEST OF CARL PERKINS, THE
CD PLSCD 125
Pulse / Jul '96 / BMG

BLUE SUEDE SHOES
CD CDSGP 0164
Prestige / Aug '95 / Else / Total/BMG

BLUE SUEDE SHOES
CD MACCD 225
Autograph / Aug '96 / BMG

BLUE SUEDE SHOES
Blue suede shoes / Honky tonk gal / Movie Mag / Boppin' the blues / Honey don't / Let the jukebox keep on playing / Put your cat clothes on / Roll over Beethoven / Matchbox / Dixie fried / Pink pedal pushers / That's right / Turn around / All Mama's

children / Everybody's trying to be my baby / I'm sorry I'm not sorry
CD ____ SUMCD 4016
Summit / Nov '96 / Sound & Media

BLUE SUEDE SHOES (His Original Greatest Hits)
Matchbox / Pink pedal pushers / Blue suede shoes / Turn around / Boppin' the blues / That's right / Let the jukebox keep on playing / All mama's children / Honky tonk girl / Dixie fried / Everybody's trying to be my baby / I'm sorry, I'm not sorry / Put your cat cloths on / Roll over Beethoven / Sure to fall / Honey don't / Movie magg / Your true love / Gone, gone, gone / Glad all over
CD ____ 305692
Hallmark / Oct '96 / Carlton

BOPPIN' BLUE SUEDE SHOES
Movie magg / Let the jukebox keep on playing / Sure to fall / Honey don't / Blue suede shoes / Boppin' the blues / Dixie fried / Put your cat clothes on / Right string baby, but the wrong yo-yo / Everybody's tryin' to be my baby / That don't move me / Caldonia / Sweethearts or strangers / I'm so sorry, I'm not sorry / Matchbox / Roll over Beethoven / That's right / Forever yours / Your true love / YOU / Pink pedal pushers / I care / Lend me your comb / Look at that moon / Glad all over
CD ____ CPCD 8102
Charly / Jun '95 / Koch

CLASSIC CARL PERKINS (5CD Set)
Honky tonk babe / Movie Magg / Honky tonk gal / runaround / Turn around / Let the jukebox keep on playing / What you doin' when you're cryin' / You can't make love to somebody / Gone gone gone / Dixie bop / Perkin's wiggle / Blue suede shoes (take 1) / Blue suede shoes (take 2) / Blue suede shoes (take 3) / Honey don't / Tennessee / Sure to fall / All Mama's children / Everybody's tryin' to be my baby / Boppin' the blues / Put your cat clothes on / Only you / Right string baby, but the wrong yo-yo / All mama's children (false start) / Dixie fried / Dixie fried (false start) / I'm sorry I'm not sorry / That don't move me / Lonely street / Drink up and go home / Pink pedal pushers / Way you're living is breaking my heart / Take back my love / Somebody tell me / Instrumental / Red wing / Down by the riverside / Her love rubbed off / Caldonia / You can do no wrong / Sweethearts or strangers / Be honest with me / Your true love / Matchbox / Your true love (original tempo) / Keeper of the key / Roll over Beethoven / Try my heart out / That's right / Forever yours / YOU / I care / Lend me your comb / Look at the moon / Glad all over / Tutti frutti / Whole lotta shakin' goin' on / That's alright / Where the Rio de Rosa flows / Shake, rattle and roll / Long tall Sally / I got a woman / Hey good lookin' / Sittin' on top of the world / Good rockin' tonight / Jive after five / Rockin' record hop / Just tonight I'd call / Ready Teddy / Jenny Jenny / You were there / Because you're mine / Pop, let me have the car / Levi jacket and a longtail shirt / When the moon comes over the mountain / Sister twister / Ham bone / This life I live / Please say you'll be mine / Honey 'cause I love you / I don't see me in your eyes anymore / Highway of love / Pointed toe shoes / One-way ticket to lonliness / Drifter / Too much for a man to understand / LOVEVILLE / Big bad blues / Say when / Lonely heart / Love I'll never win / Let my baby be / Monkey shine / Mama of my song / One of these days / I wouldn't have you / Help me find my baby / After sundown / For a little while / Just for you / When the right time comes along / Fool I used to be / Forget me (next time around) / Hollywood city / I've just got back from there / Unhappy girls / Someday, somewhere someone waits for me / Anyway the wind blows
CD Set ____ BCD 15494
Bear Family / Feb '90 / Direct / Rollercoaster / Swift

COUNTRY BOY'S DREAM (The Dollie Masters)
Country boy's dream / If I could come back / Star of the show / Poor boy blues / Detroit city / Dream on little dreamer / Stateside / Sweet misery / Unmitigated gall / Shine shine shine / Without you / You can take the boy out of the... / Almost love / Old fashioned singalong / Old number one / My old hometown / Back to Tennessee / It's you / I'll go wrong again / Dear Abby / Lake country, cotton country / All you need to know / Quite like you / Just as long / Just as long / Baby I'm hung on you / Tom and Mary Jane / Mama and Daddy / Valda
CD ____ BCD 15593
Bear Family / Apr '92 / Direct / Rollercoaster / Swift

DIXIE FRIED
Honey don't / Boppin' the blues / Blue suede shoes / Put your cat clothes on / Dixie fried / Matchbox / Pink pedal pushers / That's right / I'm sorry I'm not sorry / Roll over Beethoven / Glad all over / Right string baby, but the wrong yo-yo / Everybody's tryin' to be my baby / Gone gone gone / Lend me your comb / All Mama's children / Sweet hearts or strangers / Your true love / Movie Magg / Tennessee / Sure to fall / Honky tonk gal / Turn around / Let the jukebox keep on playing
CD ____ CDCHARLY 2
Charly / Mar '86 / Koch

FIRST KING OF ROCK 'N' ROLL, THE
Blue suede shoes / Honey don't / I'm walkin' / Matchbox / Suzie Q / Memphis / Maybellene / Slippin' and slidin' / Be bop a lula / Roll over Beethoven / Hound dog / Whole lotta shakin' goin' on / Lucille / Jailhouse rock / All shook up / That's alright mama / Bird dog / Rock Island line
CD ____ ECD 3107
K-Tel / Jan '95 / K-Tel

FRIENDS FAMILY & LEGENDS
CD ____ CDMF 084
DRG / Jan '93 / Discovery / New Note/ Pinnacle

HOUND DOG
CD ____ MU 5062
Musketeer / Oct '92 / Disc

MAN AND THE LEGEND, THE
Blue suede shoes / Honey don't / I'm walkin' / Matchbox / Suzie Q / Memphis / Maybellene / Slippin' and slidin' / Be bop a lula / Roll over Beethoven / Hound dog / Whole lotta shakin' goin' on / Lucille / Jailhouse rock / All shook up / That's alright mama / Bird dog / Rock Island line / Singin' the blues / Got my mojo working
CD ____ CDMF 039
Magnum Force / May '95 / TKO Magnum

RARE TRACKS
CD ____ MCG 200014
Vampirella / Jun '97 / Nervous

SUN SESSIONS, THE
CD ____ MCCD 191
Music Club / Nov '94 / Disc / THE

UNISSUED CARL PERKINS, THE
CD ____ CPCD 8301
Charly / May '97 / Koch

UP COUNTRY VOL.2
CD ____ SOV 021CD
Sovereign / Sep '93 / Target/BMG

UP THROUGH THE YEARS 1954-1957
Honky tonk gal / Movie magg / Turn around / Gone gone gone / Let the jukebox keep on playing / You can't make love to somebody / Blue suede shoes / Honey don't / Tennessee / Boppin' the blues / All Mama's children / Everybody's tryin' to be my baby / Dixie fried / I'm sorry I'm not sorry / You can do no wrong / Matchbox / Your true love / Put your cat clothes on / Only you / Pink pedal pushers / That's right / Lend me your comb / Glad all over / Right string baby, but the wrong yo-yo
CD ____ BCD 15246
Bear Family / Nov '86 / Direct / Rollercoaster / Swift

Perkins, Carl

INTRODUCING CARL PERKINS
Way cross town / You don't know what love is / Lady is a tramp / Marble head / Woody 'n' you / West Side aka Mia / Just friends / It could happen to you / Why do I care / Lilacs in the rain / Carl's blues
CD ____ CDBOP 008
Boplicity / Jul '96 / Pinnacle

Perkins, Roy

RAM RECORDS STORY VOL.3 (Perkins, Roy 'Boogie Boy')
Drop top / That's what the mailman had to say / Hey lawdy Mama / Just another lie / Tell me you love me (And give me the reason why) / Am I the one / Ba da / Please be true / Cooking catfish / Tired of hanging around: *Page, Bobby & The Riff Raffs* / Drop top (Alt) / Ginning: *Patin, Scatman & The Ram Rods* / Girl next door: *Page, Bobby & The Riff Raffs* / I love my baby: *Page, Bobby & The Riff Raffs* / Red beans and rice: *Patin, Scatman & The Ram Rods* / Hey lawdy Mama (Take 1) / It's all over / These blues are here to stay / Anything your heart desires: *Simoneaux, Harry & The Riff Raffs* / Hippt ti yo: *Page, Bobby & The Riff Raffs* / This time: *Page, Bobby & The Riff Raffs* / Like twist: *Page, Bobby & The Riff Raffs* / Loneliness: *Page, Bobby & The Riff Raffs* / True love / Sweet Lily
CD ____ CDCHD 619
Ace / Mar '96 / Pinnacle

Perkins, Willie

BLUES LEGEND (Perkins, Willie 'Pinetop')
CD ____ CDSGP 0292
Prestige / Sep '96 / Else / Total/BMG

Perkins, Willie 'Pinetop'

AFTER HOURS
CD ____ CD 73088
Blind Pig / Mar '90 / ADA / CM / Direct / Hot Shot

BOOGIE WOOGIE KING
CD ____ ECD 260112
Evidence / Jan '92 / ADA / Cadillac / Harmonia Mundi

BORN IN THE DELTA
Everyday I have the blues: *Pinetop Perkins* / For you my love: *Pinetop Perkins* / Love on yonder wall: *Pinetop Perkins* / Blues after hours: *Pinetop Perkins* / Murmur low: *Pinetop Perkins* / How long how long blues: *Pinetop Perkins* / Baby what do you want me to do: *Pinetop Perkins* / Blues oh blues: *Pinetop Perkins*
CD ____ CD 83418
Telarc Blues / Sep '97 / Conifer/BMG

LIVE TOP
CD ____ DELD 3010
Deluge / Dec '95 / ADA / Direct / Koch

ON TOP
CD ____ DELCD 3002
Deluge / Jan '96 / ADA / Direct / Koch

PINETOP'S BOOGIE WOOGIE
CD ____ ANTCD 0020
Antones / Nov '93 / ADA / Hot Shot

Perko, Jukka

GARDEN OF TIME (Perko, Jukka & Severi Pyysalo)
CD ____ ODE 4012
Ondine / Feb '94 / ADA / Koch

Perlinpinpin Folc

MUSIC FROM GASCONY
CD ____ B 6834CD
Auvidis/Ethnic / Aug '96 / ADA / Harmonia Mundi

Perlman, Itzhak

KLEZMER VOL.1 (In The Fiddler's House) (Various Artists)
CD ____ CDC 5555552
EMI Classics / Mar '96 / EMI

KLEZMER VOL.2 (Live At The Fiddler's House) (Various Artists)
Doina: *Brave Old World* / A hora mit branfin: *Brave Old World* / Bukovina 212: *Brave Old World* / Lekho neraneo: *Brave Old World* / Healthy baby girl hora: *Klezmatics* / Golem dance: *Klezmatics* / Honga encore: *Klezmatics* / Nign: *Klezmatics* / Bulgars/The kiss: *Klezmatics* / Meron nigun/In the sukke: *Statman, Andy Klezmer Orchestra* / Sholem aleichem: *Statman, Andy Klezmer Orchestra* / Khaiterma: *Statman, Andy Klezmer Orchestra* / Andy's ride: *Statman, Andy Klezmer Orchestra* / A heymischer bulgar/Wedding dance: *Klezmer Conservatory Band* / Kale bazetsn/Khusidl: *Klezmer Conservatory Band* / Fun tashlikh: *Klezmer Conservatory Band* / A yingele fun poyln/Di mame is gegangen: *Klezmer Conservatory Band* / Processional / Klezmer suite / Ale brider
CD ____ CDC 5562092
EMI Classics / Feb '97 / EMI

Perlman, Ken

DEVIL IN THE KITCHEN
CD ____ MAR 6502CD
Marimac / Aug '96 / ADA

Pernice, Laurent

AXIDENT
CD ____ PER 018
Semantic / Feb '94 / Plastic Head

EXIT TO THE CITY
CD ____ PPP 113
PDCD / Oct '93 / Plastic Head

Pernick, Karen

APARTMENT 12
CD ____ SH 8021
Shanachie / Nov '96 / ADA / Greensleeves / Koch

Peron, Carlos

IMPERSONATOR VOL.2
CD ____ BIASCD 116
Play It Again Sam / Aug '89 / Discovery / Plastic Head / Vital

IMPERSONATOR VOL.3
CD ____ EFA 02852CD
ALL / Nov '92 / SRD

Perpetual Demise

ARTIC
CD ____ DSFA 1005CD
DSFA / Nov '96 / Plastic Head

Perplexa

PERPLEXA
CD ____ SS 007
Small Stone / May '97 / Cargo

Perrett, Peter

WOKE UP STICKY
CD ____ FIENDCD 773
Demon / Jun '96 / Pinnacle

Perrey, Jean Jacques

AMAZING NEW ELECTRONIC POP SOUNDS
CD ____ VMD 79286
Vanguard / Oct '96 / ADA / Pinnacle

BEST OF THE LATER YEARS
CD ____ CDBGPM 109
Beat Goes Public / Aug '97 / Pinnacle

ESSENTIAL PERREY & KINGSLEY
CD ____ VCD 71
Vanguard / Oct '96 / ADA / Pinnacle

MOOG INDIGO
Soul city / EVA / Rose and the cross / Cat in the night / Flight of the bumble bee / Moog indigo / Gossipo perpetuo / Country rock polka / Elephant never forgets / 18th century puppet / Hello Dolly / Passport to the future
CD ____ CDBGPM 103
Beat Goes Public / Apr '96 / Pinnacle

Perri, Joel

EL CONDOR DEL INDIO
CD ____ EUCD 1067
ARC / '89 / ADA / ARC Music

EL CONDOR PASA (Magic Of The Indian Flute)
CD ____ EUCD 1173
ARC / '91 / ADA / ARC Music

EL CONDOR PASA
CD ____ EUCD 1055
ARC / '89 / ADA / ARC Music

MANDOLINE
CD ____ EUCD 1047
ARC / '89 / ADA / ARC Music

MASTER OF THE INDIAN FLUTES
CD ____ EUCD 1329
ARC / Nov '95 / ADA / ARC Music

SOUFFLE DE VENTE
CD ____ EUCD 1029
ARC / '89 / ADA / ARC Music

TARANTELLA DEL DIAVOLO
CD ____ EUCD 1077
ARC / '89 / ADA / ARC Music

Perry, Al

RETRONUEVO (Perry, Al & Dan Stuart)
CD ____ NORM 169CD
Normal / Dec '94 / ADA / Direct

Perry, Bill

LOVE SCARS
Love scars / Lost in the blues / Fade to blue / Down / Darkness of your love / Boogie blues / Settle down, Fred / Smokey Joe / I'm leaving you / In my lonely room / 80 West / Fade to blue (reprise)
CD ____ VPBCD 31
Pointblank / Jan '96 / EMI

Perry, Frank

BELOVODYE - LAND OF THE WHITE WATERS
CD ____ IS 03CD
Isis / Apr '94 / ADA / Direct

Perry, James

PEACE LIKE A RIVER (Perry, James & Co.)
CD ____ WCL 110242
White Cloud / Jul '97 / Select

Perry, John G.

UNCLE SEABIRD
CD ____ VP 169CD
Voiceprint / Feb '95 / Pinnacle

Perry, Lazar

TANGODELIC
CD ____ IMP 945
IMP / Nov '96 / ADA / Discovery

Perry, Lee 'Scratch'

AFRICA'S BLOOD (Various Artists)
Do your thing: *Barker, Dave* / Dreamland: *Upsetters* / Long sentence: *Upsetters* / Not guilty: *Upsetters* / Cool and easy: *Upsetters* / Well dread: *Addis Ababa Children* / My girl: *Upsetters* / Sawdust: *Upsetters* / Place called Africa: *Prince, Winston* / Isn't it wrong: *Hurricanes* / Go slow/Bad luck/ Move me/Surplus: *Upsetters*
CD ____ CDTBL 166
Trojan / Sep '96 / Direct / Jet Star

ARKOLOGY (3CD Set)
Dub revolution (part 1): *Perry, Lee 'Scratch' & The Upsetters* / One step forward: *Romeo, Max* / One step dub: *Upsetters* / Vampire: *Devon Irons* / Vamp a dub: *Upsetters* / Sufferer's time: *Heptones* / Sufferer's dub: *Upsetters* / Sufferer's heights: *Junior Dread* / Don't blame on I: *Congos* / Much smarter: *Meditations* / Much smarter dub: *Upsetters* / Life is not easy: *Meditations* / Life is not easy dub: *Upsetters* / Tedious: *Junior Murvin* / War in a Babylon: *Romeo, Max* / Revelation dub: *Upsetters* / Mr. President: *Heptones & Jah Lion* / Chase the devil: *Romeo, Max* / Dreadlocks in moolight / Dread at the mantrols: *Mikey Dread* / In these times: *Walker, Errol* / In these times dub: *Upsetters* / Norman: *Romeo, Max & The Upsetters* /

Police and thieves: *Junior Murvin* / Magic touch: *DaCosta, Glen* / Soldier and police war: *Jah Lion* / Grumblin' dub: *Upsetters* / Bad weed: *Junior Murvin* / John public: *Walker, Errol* / John public (version): *Walker, Errol & Enos Barnes* / Roots train: *Junior Murvin & Dillinger* / No peace: *Meditations* / No peace dub: *Meditations* / Rasta train: *Green, Raphael & Dr.Alimantado* / Party time (part 2): *Upsetters* / Vibrate on: *Pablo, Augustus & The Upsetters* / Vibrators: *Upsetters* / Bird in hand: *Upsetters* / Congoman: *Congos* / Dyon anasawa: *Upsetters & Full Experience* / Rastaman shuffle: *Upsetters* / Why must I (version): *Heptones & Lee Perry* / Make up your mind: *Heptones* / Closer together: *Upsetter Revue & Junior Murvin* / Groovy situation: *Rowe, Keith* / Groovy dub: *Rowe, Keith* / To be a lover (have some mercy): *Faith, George* / Soul fire / Curly locks / Feast of the Passover: *Congos* / Roast fish and cornbread / Corn fish dub
CD Set ______ **CRNCD 6**
Island Jamaica / Jul '97 / Jet Star / PolyGram

AT THE BLACKHEART STUDIO (Perry, Lee 'Scratch' & The Scientist)
CD ______ **RN 7005**
Rhino / Sep '96 / Grapevine/PolyGram / Jet Star

BATTLE AXE (Various Artists)
Battle axe: *Upsetters* / Place called Africa: *Byles, Junior* / Cheerio: *Upsetters* / Picture on my wall: *Ras Darkins* / Cool operator: *Wilson, Delroy* / Knock three times: *Upsetters* / Pop a pop: *Andy Capp* / Earthquake: *Upsetters* / Don't cross the nation: *Mark & Luke* / Dark moon: *Upsetters* / Rough and smooth: *Upsetters* / Groove me: *Upsetters* / Easy snapping: *Upsetters* / I'm yours: *Wilson, Delroy*
CD ______ **CDTBL 167**
Trojan / Sep '96 / Direct / Jet Star

BEST OF LEE 'SCRATCH' PERRY, THE
CD ______ **UPCD 002**
Upsetter / Jul '97 / SRD

BLACK ARK EXPERRYMENTS (Perry, Lee 'Scratch' & Mad Professor)
Thank you / Super ape in good shape / Jungle safari / From heaven above / Heads of government / Open door / Black ark experryments / Poop song / Come back
CD ______ **ARICD 114**
Ariwa Sounds / Jun '95 / Jet Star / SRD

BLOOD VAPOUR
CD ______ **LACD 007**
La / May '94 / Plastic Head

BUILD THE ARK (2CD Set) (Perry, Lee 'Scratch' & The Upsetters)
My little Sandra: *Graham, Leo* / Dubbing Sandra: *Upsetters* / Long long time: *Heywood, Winston* / White belly rat: *Upsetter* / Freedom street: *Donaldson, Eric* / Land of love: *Sons Of Light* / Crossover: *Murvin, Junior* / Travelling: *Keese, Debra & The Black Five* / Green Bay incident: *Lord Sassafrass* / Thanks and praise: *Ainsworth, Junior* / Feelings: *Isaacs, Sharon* / A wah dat: *Junior Dread* / White belly rat: *Perry, Lee 'Scratch'* / Peace and love: *Shaumark & Robinson* / Think so: *Meditations* / At the feast: *Congos* / Ethiopian land: *Lewis, Peter & Paul* / Brother Noah: *Shadows* / Mr. Money Man: *Hensworth, Danny* / Feelings version: *Upsetters* / Dub dat: *Upsetter* / Judas de white belly rat: *Upsetters* / Freedom dub: *Upsetters* / Peace a dub: *Upsetters* / Land of dub: *Upsetters* / Dub so: *Upsetters* / Nyambie dub: *Upsetters* / Landmark dub: *Upsetters* / Green Bay version: *Upsetters* / Noah dub: *Upsetters* / Dub money: *Upsetters*
CD Set ______ **CDPRY 003**
Trojan / Mar '94 / Direct / Jet Star

DOUBLE SEVEN (Upsetters)
Kentucky skank / Double six: *U-Roy* / Just enough to keep me hanging on: *Isaacs, David* / In the laah / Jungle lion / We are neighbours: *Isaacs, David* / Soul man / Stick together: *U-Roy* / High fashion: *I-Roy* / Long sentence / Hail stones / Iron side / Cold weather / Waap you waa
CD ______ **CDTRL 70**
Trojan / Jul '96 / Direct / Jet Star

DUB AROUND THE WORLD
CD ______ **SFCD 5**
Sprint / Nov '95 / SRD

DUB CONFRONTATION VOL.2 (Perry, Lee 'Scratch' & King Tubby)
CD ______ **LG 21107**
Lagoon / Apr '95 / Grapevine/PolyGram

DUB TAKE THE VOODOO OUT OF REGGAE (Perry, Lee 'Scratch' & Mad Professor)
CD ______ **ARICD 131**
Ariwa Sounds / Sep '96 / Jet Star / SRD

EASTWOOD RIDES AGAIN (Upsetters)
Eastwood rides again / Hit me / Knock on wood / Popcorn / Catch this / You are adorable / Capsol / Power pack / Dollar in the teeth / Baby baby / Django / Red hot / Salt and pepper / Tight spot
CD ______ **CDTBL 125**
Trojan / Sep '96 / Direct / Jet Star

EXCALIBURMAN
CD ______ **SLCD 6**
Seven Leaves / Sep '93 / Greensleeves / Roots Collective / SRD

EXPERRYMENTS AT THE GRASS ROOTS OF DUB (Perry, Lee 'Scratch' & Mad Professor)
Jungle roots dub / Dubbing with the super ape / Alien in out a space / Sky high dub / Nucleus dub / Dub it wide open / Dub wise experryments / Pooping dub song / Black Ark come again
CD ______ **ARICD 115**
Ariwa Sounds / Oct '95 / Jet Star / SRD

FROM THE HEART OF THE CONGO
CD ______ **RN 0029CD**
Runn / Apr '94 / Grapevine/PolyGram / Jet Star / SRD

FROM THE SECRET LABORATORY
Secret laboratory / Inspector gadget / (I got the) Groove / Vibrate on / African hitchiker / You thought I was dead / Too much money / Push, push / African headcharge in the Hackney Empire / Party time / Seven devils dead
CD ______ **RRCD 55**
Reggae Refreshers / Aug '97 / PolyGram / Vital

GIVE ME POWER (Perry, Lee 'Scratch' & Friends)
Sick and tired: *Grant, Neville* / Rasta no pickpocket: *Byles, Junior* / Don't cross the nation: *Little Roy* / Give me power: *Stingers* / News flash: *Graham, Leo & The Upsetters* / Justice to the people: *Perry, Lee 'Scratch' & The Upsetters* / Babylon burning / Ring of fire: *Upsetters* / Dig the grave: *Upsetters* / Thanks we get: *Upsetters* / Public enemy no.1: *Max Romeo* / Mid East rock: *Dillinger & The Upsetters* / Forward up: *Stingers* / Hot tip: *Prince Django* / To be a lover: *Duffus, Shenley* / Give me power: *King Wah* / Flashing echo: *Graham, Leo & The Upsetters*
CD ______ **CDTRL 254**
Trojan / Sep '96 / Direct / Jet Star

GLORY DUB
CD ______ **RB 3015**
Reggae Best / Oct '95 / Grapevine/ PolyGram

GOOD, THE BAD AND THE UPSETTERS, THE (Perry, Lee 'Scratch' & The Upsetters)
CD ______ **LG 21083**
Lagoon / Aug '93 / Grapevine/PolyGram

GREAT KING OF DUB, THE
CD ______ **HS 2CD**
Hit Squad / Jun '97 / Jet Star

GUITAR BOOGIE DUB
CD ______ **RNCD 2057**
Rhino / May '94 / Grapevine/PolyGram / Jet Star

HEART OF THE ARK
CD ______ **SLCD 1**
Seven Leaves / Jul '94 / Greensleeves / Roots Collective / SRD

HEAVY MANNERS (Perry, Lee 'Scratch' & The Upsetters)
CD ______ **RB 3001**
Reggae Best / May '94 / Grapevine/ PolyGram

HOLD OF DEATH
CD ______ **RNCD 2007**
Rhino / May '93 / Grapevine/PolyGram / Jet Star

IN DUB AROUND (Upsetters)
CD ______ **SFCD 005**
Sprint / Jan '96 / SRD

INTRODUCING LEE PERRY
CD ______ **CB 6007**
Blue Silver / May '96 / Jet Star

KING OF DUB, THE
CD ______ **HS 3CD**
Hit Squad / Jun '97 / Jet Star

KUNG FU MEETS THE DRAGON (Perry, Lee 'Scratch' & The Upsetters)
CD ______ **LG 21112**
Lagoon / Aug '95 / Grapevine/PolyGram
CD ______ **JLCD 5000**
Justice League / Jul '97 / SRD

LARKS FROM THE ARK
Conscious man: *Jolly Brothers* / Nuh fe run down / Freedom / Brotherly love: *Jolly Brothers* / Groovy situation: *Rowe, Keith* / Them don't know love: *Rightious Vibes* / Rastafari: *Sibb[illegible] eroy* / Forward with love: *Mystic Eyes* / Such is life: *Lord Creator* / Elaine: *Mystic Eyes* / School girl dub / Don't be afraid: *Faith, George* / Cool down: *Jolly Brothers* / I've never had it so good: *Scott, Bunny* / Four & twenty dreadlock: *Prodical* / What's the use: *Scott, Bunny* / African freedom: *Brother Hood* / Colour: *Jolly Brothers*
CD ______ **NTMCD 511**
Nectar / Sep '95 / Pinnacle

LORD GOD MUZIK
CD ______ **ZSCDII0**
Heartbeat / Sep '91 / ADA / Direct / Greensleeves / Jet Star

MEET AT KING TUBBY'S (Perry, Lee 'Scratch' & The Upsetters)
CD ______ **RNCD 2027**
Rhino / Dec '93 / Grapevine/PolyGram / Jet Star

MEET SCIENTIST AT BLACK ART STUDIO (Perry, Lee 'Scratch' & The Upsetters)
CD ______ **GRCD 008**
Graylan / Jun '96 / Grapevine/PolyGram / Jet Star

MEETS BULLWACKIE IN SATANS DUB
CD ______ **RE 178CD**
ROIR / Nov '94 / Plastic Head / Shellshock/Disc

MEETS MAFIA & FLUXY IN JAMAICA (Perry, Lee 'Scratch' & The Upsetters)
CD ______ **LG 21025**
Lagoon / Jul '93 / Grapevine/PolyGram

MEETS THE MAD PROFESSOR IN DUB VOL.1 & 2 (Perry, Lee 'Scratch' & Mad Professor)
CD ______ **ANGCD 8/9**
Angella / Jan '91 / Jet Star

MEETS THE MAD PROFESSOR VOL.1
CD ______ **LG 21068**
Lagoon / Feb '93 / Grapevine/PolyGram

MEETS THE MAD PROFESSOR VOL.2
CD ______ **LG 21069**
Lagoon / Feb '93 / Grapevine/PolyGram

MILLIONAIRE LIQUIDATOR (Perry, Lee 'Scratch' & The Upsetters)
Introducing myself / Drum song / Grooving / All things are possible / Show me that river / I'm a madman / Joker / Happy birthday / Sexy lady / Time marches on
CD ______ **CDTRL 227**
Trojan / Mar '94 / Direct / Jet Star

MYSTIC WARRIOR
CD ______ **AROCD 054**
Ariwa Sounds / Aug '90 / Jet Star / SRD

ON THE WIRE
CD ______ **CDTRL 348**
Trojan / Apr '95 / Direct / Jet Star

OPEN THE GATES (2CD Set) (Perry, Lee 'Scratch' & Friends)
CD Set ______ **CDPRY 2**
Trojan / Mar '94 / Direct / Jet Star

ORIGINAL BLACK BOARD JUNGLE DUB
CD ______ **ORCHCD 1**
Red Honey / May '94 / RTM/Disc

ORIGINAL SUPER APE, THE (Perry, Lee 'Scratch' & The Upsetters)
CD ______ **CRCD 67**
Charm / Jun '97 / Jet Star

OUT OF MANY - THE UPSETTER (Various Artists)
Introducing myself: *Perry, Lee 'Scratch' & The Upsetters* / Small axe: *Marley, Bob & The Wailers* / Place called Africa: *Prince, Winston* / Don't rock my boat: *Marley, Bob & The Wailers* / Feeling is right: *Cadogan, Susan* / Be thankful: *Clarke, Bunny* / Kuchy skank: *Upsetters* / Garden of life: *Sibbles, Leroy* / Kentucky skank: *Perry, Lee 'Scratch' & The Upsetters* / Reaction: *Marley, Bob & The Wailers* / Public jestering: *Judge Winchester* / Long way: *Byles, Junior* / Mr. Brown: *Marley, Bob & The Wailers* / Stick together: *U-Roy* / Freak out skank: *Upsetters* / Justice to the people: *Perry, Lee 'Scratch' & The Upsetters* / Travelling Debra: *Keese, Debra & The Black Five*
CD ______ **CDTRL 297**
Trojan / Sep '96 / Direct / Jet Star

PEOPLE FUNNY BOY (The Early Upsetter) (Various Artists)
Honey love: *Walters, Burt* / Evol yenoh: *Walters, Burt* / Popeye on the shore: *Bennett, Val* / Nonesuch busted me bet: *Mellotones* / Handy cap: *Upsetters* / People funny boy: *Perry, Lee 'Scratch'* / Blowing in the wind: *Walters, Burt* / Spanish Harlem: *Bennett, Val* / Uncle Charlie: *Mellotones* / Tighten up: *Inspirations* / Place in the sun: *Isaacs, David*
CD ______ **CDTRL 339**
Trojan / Sep '96 / Direct / Jet Star

PRESENTS BLACK ARK ALMIGHTY DUB
CD ______ **BCD 403**
Black Ark / Dec '94 / Jet Star

REGGAE EMPEROR
CD ______ **RNCD 2137**
Rhino / Apr '96 / Grapevine/PolyGram / Jet Star

REGGAE GREATS (Various Artists)
Party time: *Heptones* / Police and thieves: *Murvin, Junior* / Groovy situation: *Rowe, Keith* / Soul fire: *Perry, Lee 'Scratch'* / War in a Babylon: *Max Romeo* / Wisdom: *Jah Lion* / To be a lover: *Faith, George* / Roast fish and cornbread: *Perry, Lee 'Scratch'* / Croaking lizard: *Prince Jazzbo* / Dreadlocks in moonlight: *Perry, Lee 'Scratch'*
CD ______ **RRCD 10**
Reggae Refreshers / Aug '97 / PolyGram / Vital

REMINAH DUB (Perry, Lee 'Scratch' & The Upsetters)
CD ______ **OMCD 11**
Original Music / Mar '96 / Jet Star / SRD

RETURN OF DJANGO (Upsetters)
Return of Django / Touch of fire / Cold sweat / Drugs and poison / Soulful I / Night doctor / One punch / Eight for eight / Live injection / Man for MI5 / Ten to twelve / Medical operation
CD ______ **CDTRL 19**
Trojan / Sep '96 / Direct / Jet Star

REVOLUTION DUB
CD ______ **RNCD 2120**
Rhino / Sep '95 / Grapevine/PolyGram / Jet Star

SCRATCH THE UPSETTERS AGAIN (Perry, Lee 'Scratch' & The Upsetters)
Bad tooth / Dentist / Out of space / One punch / Will you still love me tomorrow / Take one / Soul walk / I want to thank you / Mule train / Touch of fire / She is gone again / Result / Eastwood rides again / Hit me / Knock on wood / Popcorn / Catch this / You are adorable / Capsol / Power pack / Dollar in my teeth / Baby baby / Django / Red hot / Salt and pepper / Tight spot
CD ______ **CDTRL 352**
Trojan / Sep '96 / Direct / Jet Star

SENSI DUB VOL.2 (Perry, Lee 'Scratch' & King Tubby)
CD ______ **OMCD 15**
Original Music / Jul '93 / Jet Star / SRD

SENSI DUB VOL.2 & 3 (Perry, Lee 'Scratch' & King Tubby)
CD Set ______ **OMCD 015/16**
Original Music / Sep '90 / Jet Star / SRD

SOME OF THE BEST (Perry, Lee 'Scratch' & The Upsetters)
CD ______ **HBCD 37**
Heartbeat / Jul '88 / ADA / Direct / Greensleeves / Jet Star

SOUNDS FROM THE HOTLINE
CD ______ **CDHB 76**
Heartbeat / Aug '96 / ADA / Direct / Greensleeves / Jet Star

SUPER APE (Perry, Lee 'Scratch' & The Upsetters)
Zion's blood / Croaking lizard / Black vest / Underground / Curly dub / Dread lion / Three in one / Patience / Dub along / Super ape in good shape
CD ______ **RRCD 13**
Reggae Refreshers / Aug '97 / PolyGram / Vital

SUPER APE IN THE JUNGLE
CD ______ **ARICD 112**
Ariwa Sounds / Jul '95 / Jet Star / SRD

TECHNOMAJIKAL (Perry, Lee 'Scratch' & Dieter Meier)
CD ______ **RUSCD 8232**
ROIR / Jul '97 / Plastic Head / Shellshock/ Disc

TIME BOOM
CD ______ **ONUCD 43**
On-U Sound / Mar '94 / Jet Star / SRD

UPSETTER COLLECTION, THE (Upsetters)
Cold sweat / Return of Django / Check him out: *Bleechers* / Django shoots first / Kill them all: *Perry, Lee 'Scratch' & The Upsetters* / Vampire / Drugs and poison / Sipreano / Black IPA / Bucky skank: *Perry, Lee 'Scratch'* / Words of my mouth: *Gatherers* / Tipper special / Cow thief skank: *Perry, Lee 'Scratch' & Charlie Ace* / French connection / Better days: *Carlton & His Shoes* / Freak out skank
CD ______ **CDTRL 195**
Trojan / Sep '96 / Direct / Jet Star

UPSETTER IN DUB
Noah sugar pan / Ketch a dub / Version train / Rootically dub / Son of the Black Ark / Lorna Skank / If the cap fits / Dub a come / Tedious dub / Rejoice in skank / Babylon thief dub / Foundation solid / Bagman / Better reach / Dub in time / Fun and games / Sipple dub / Bionic rat dub
CD ______ **CDHB 77**
Heartbeat / May '97 / ADA / Direct / Greensleeves / Jet Star

UPSETTER PRESENTING DUB
CD ______ **RN 7010**
Rhino / Sep '96 / Grapevine/PolyGram / Jet Star

UPSETTER, THE (Upsetters)
Tide wave / Heat proof / To love somebody: *Brown, Buster* / Night doctor / Soulful one / Big noise / Man from MI5 / Dread luck / Kiddy-o: *Muskyteers* / Wolfman / Crying about you / Thunderball
CD ______ **CDTTL 13**
Trojan / Sep '96 / Direct / Jet Star

UPSETTERS A GO GO (Upsetters)
CD ______ **CDHB 136**
Heartbeat / Nov '95 / ADA / Direct / Greensleeves / Jet Star

UPSETTING THE NATION 1969-1970 (Upsetters & Friends)
Eight for eight: *Upsetters* / Outer space: *Upsetters* / To love somebody: *Brown, Buster* / Soulful I: *Upsetters* / Man from MI5: *Up-*

setters / I'll be waiting: *Termites* / Ten to twelve: *Upsetters* / Kiddy O: *Muskyteers* / Medical operation: *Upsetters* / Night Doctor: *Upsetters* / Self control: *Upsetters* / Crying about you: *Brown, Buster* / Thunderball: *Upsetters* / One punch: *Upsetters* / Vampire: *Upsetters* / Build my whole world around you: *Barker, Dave* / Prisoner of love: *Barker, Dave* / I was wrong: *Barker, Dave*
CD ______ **CDTRL 330**
Trojan / Sep '96 / Direct / Jet Star

VERSION LIKE RAIN (Upsetters & Friends)
I want a wine: *Graham, Leo* / Double wine: *Upsetters* / Hot and cold: *Pablo, Augustus & The Upsetters* / Fever: *Cadogan, Susan* / Beat down Babylon: *Byles, Junior* / Outformer: *Upsetters* / Beat down babylon: *Upsetters* / Iron wolf: *Upsetters* / Stick together: *U-Roy* / This world: *Milton, Henry* / Influenza: *Upsetters* / Informer man: *Byles, Junior & Jah-T* / Babylon burning: *Maxie* / Freedom fighter: *Bunny & Ricky* / Bet you don't know: *Duffus, Shenley*
CD ______ **CDTRL 278**
Trojan / Sep '96 / Direct / Jet Star

VOODOOISM (Various Artists)
Psalms 20: *Booms, James* / Proverbs of dub: *Upsetter* / Better future: *Walker, Errol* / Future dub: *Upsetter* / River: *Zap Pow* / Freedom: *Earl 16* / Africa: *Hombres* / Foundation dub: *Upsetter* / Voodooism: *Graham, Leo* / Dubism: *Upsetter* / African style: *Black Notes* / Wolf out deh: *Lloyd & Devon* / Shepherd Rod: *Upsetter*
CD ______ **PSCD 009**
Pressure Sounds / Aug '97 / Jet Star / SRD

WHO PUT THE VOODOO PON REGGAE
CD ______ **ARICD 130**
Ariwa Sounds / Sep '96 / Jet Star / SRD

WORDS OF MY MOUTH (The Producer Series) (Various Artists)
Words of my mouth: *Gatherers* / Words of my mouth: *Upsetters* / Kuchy skank: *Upsetters* / Rejoice in Jah Jah children: *Upsetters* / Rejoicing skank: *Silvertones* / Bushweed corntrash: *Bunny & Ricky* / Calling butt: *Upsetters* / Da ba day: *Upsetters* / Kiss me neck: *Upsetters* / Curly locks: *Byles, Junior* / Dreader locks: *Lee & Junior* / Many a call: *Unforgettables* / Too bad bull: *Bunny & Ricky* / Too bad cow: *Upsetters* / Fist of fury: *Perry, Lee 'Scratch'* / Herb vendor: *Horsemouth* / Cane river rock: *Upsetters* / Stay dead: *Perry, Lee 'Scratch'* / Kentucky skank: *Perry, Lee 'Scratch'* / Bathroom skank: *Perry, Lee 'Scratch'* / Spiritual whip: *Jah Lloyd*
CD ______ **CDTRL 374**
Trojan / Oct '96 / Direct / Jet Star

Perry, Linda

IN FLIGHT
In my dreams / Freeway / Uninvited / Success / Life in a bottle / Fill me up / Knock me out / Too deep / Taken / Fruitloop / Daydream / Machine man / In flight
CD ______ **IND 90061**
Interscope / Sep '96 / BMG

Perry, Phil

PURE PLEASURE
One touch / Way that I want U / After the love has gone / If only you knew / I love it, I love it / When it comes to love / Heaven / You say, I say / Angel of the night / Love don't love nobody
CD ______ **GRM 40272**
GRP / Oct '94 / New Note/BMG

Perry, Rich

BEAUTIFUL LOVE
CD ______ **SCCD 31360**
Steeplechase / May '95 / Discovery / Impetus

WHAT IS THIS (Perry, Rich Quartet)
CD ______ **SCCD 31374**
Steeplechase / Feb '96 / Discovery / Impetus

Perry, Steve

STREET TALK
Oh Sherrie / I believe / Go away / Foolish heart / It's only love / She's mine / You should be happy / Running alone / Captured by the moment / Strung out
CD ______ **4866602**
Columbia / Nov '96 / Sony

Persip, Charlie

CHARLIE PERSIP & SUPERBAND
CD ______ **NI 4028**
Natasha / Jun '94 / ADA / Cadillac / CM / Direct / Jazz Music

Person, Eric

ARRIVAL
CD ______ **1212372**
Soul Note / Apr '93 / Cadillac / Harmonia Mundi / Wellard

PROPHECY
CD ______ **1212872**
Soul Note / May '94 / Cadillac / Harmonia Mundi / Wellard

Person, Houston

GOODNESS
CD ______ **OJCCD 332**
Original Jazz Classics / Dec '95 / Complete/Pinnacle / Jazz Music / Wellard

LEGENDS OF ACID JAZZ, THE
CD ______ **PRCD 24179**
Prestige / Apr '97 / Cadillac / Complete/ Pinnacle

PERSON-IFIED
You're my everything / There's a small hotel / Stranger on the shore / Isn't it romantic / Detour ahead / Gentle rain / In the wee small hours of the morning / Blue jug / May the good Lord bless and keep you
CD ______ **HCD 7004**
High Note / Apr '97 / New Note/Pinnacle

PERSONALITY
Kittitian carnival / Funky sunday afternoon / Pain / Shotgun / Touch of the bad stuff / He'll fight my battles / All in love is fair / Mayola / Until it's time for you to go / You are the sunshine of my life / Don't go to strangers / Easy walker
CD ______ **CDBGPD 070**
Beat Goes Public / Mar '93 / Pinnacle

SOMETHING IN COMMON (Person, Houston & Ron Carter)
Blue seven / I thought about you / Mack the knife / Joy Spring / Good morning heartache / Anthropology / Once in a while / Blues for two
CD ______ **MCD 5376**
Muse / Apr '91 / New Note/Pinnacle

TALK OF THE TOWN
CD ______ **MCD 5331**
Muse / Sep '92 / New Note/Pinnacle

Persson, Bent

I REMEMBER CLIFFORD (Persson, Bent & Ludwigsson/Lundgren Quintet)
CD ______ **PACD 94081**
Pama / Dec '94 / Cadillac / Jazz Music

LOUIS ARMSTRONG'S 50 HOT CORNET CHORUSES VOL.1 & 2
CD ______ **CKS 3411**
Kenneth / Jun '96 / Cadillac / Jazz Music / Wellard

LOUIS ARMSTRONG'S 50 HOT CORNET CHORUSES VOL.3 & 4
Copenhagen / Someday sweetheart / Sidewalk blues / Jackass blues / Easy rider / Chant / Sugarfoot stomp / Grandpa's spells / Dixieland blues / Chicago breakdown / 29th and dearborn / Chattanooga stomp / Mr. Jelly Lord / Darktown shuffle / Panama blues / Dallas stomp / Stomp your stuff / Tampeekoe
CD ______ **CKS 3413**
Kenneth / Apr '94 / Cadillac / Jazz Music / Wellard

SWINGING STRAIGHT (Persson, Bent Sextet)
CD ______ **SITCD 9218**
Sittel / Jun '96 / Cadillac / Jazz Music

Persuaders

THIN LINE BETWEEN LOVE AND HATE
Thin line between love and hate / Let's go down together / Blood brothers / You musta put something in your love / Thanks for loving me / Love gonna pack up / If this is what you call love / Mr. Sunshine / Thigh spy / Can't go no further and do no better
CD ______ **7567804142**
Atlantic / Jan '96 / Warner Music

Persuasions

COMIN' AT YA
Return to sender / Don't let him take you love / Besame mucho / One mint julep / Let them talk / Mortal man / I'll be forever loving you / Just because / Drip drop / Crying in the chapel / Love me like a rock
CD ______ **FF 70093**
Flying Fish / Nov '96 / ADA / CM / Direct / Roots

MAN, OH MAN
Man, oh man / Don't make it what you want to go home / I could never love another after loving you / People get ready / When I leave these prison walls / Hymn no.9 / TA Thompson / Three angels / Good times / Buffalo soldier / Tempts jam / Don't look back/Runaway child/Running wild/Cloud nine / Gyspy woman / Sun / When Jesus comes
CD ______ **CTMCD 328**
EMI / Jul '97 / EMI

NO FRILLS
You can have her / Under the boardwalk / Sand in my shoes / I was wrong / I woke up in love this morning / I wonder do you love the Lord like I do / Still ain't got no band / Victim / Treasure of love / Sweet was the wine / What are you doing New Year's Eve / Slip slidin' away
CD ______ **ROUCD 3083**
Rounder / Aug '88 / ADA / CM / Direct

RIGHT AROUND THE CORNER
CD ______ **BBCD 9556**
Bullseye Blues / Oct '94 / Direct

SINCERELY
CD ______ **CDBB 9576**
Bullseye Blues / Aug '96 / Direct

Peruna Jazzmen

PERUNA JAZZMEN VOL.1 & 2
CD ______ **SOSCD 1003**
Stomp Off / Dec '94 / Jazz Music / Wellard

Perverted

POETIC TERRORISM IN AN ERA OF GRIEF
CD ______ **GAP 028**
Gap Recordings / Jun '95 / SRD

Pessary

INWARD COLLAPSE
CD ______ **DPROMCD 2**
Dirter Promotions / Oct '96 / Cargo / Pinnacle / World Serpent

LAID TO REST
CD ______ **DPROMCD 7**
Dirter Promotions / Oct '96 / Cargo / Pinnacle / World Serpent

Pestilence

SPHERES
Mind reflections / Multiple beings / Level of perception / Aurian eyes / Soul search / Personal energy / Voices from within / Spheres / Changing perspective / Phileas / Demise of time
CD ______ **CD RR 9081 2**
Roadrunner / Aug '93 / PolyGram

Pet Shop Boys

ACTUALLY
One more chance / Shopping / Rent / Hit music / What have I done to deserve this / It couldn't happen here / It's a sin / I want to wake up / Heart / King's Cross
CD ______ **CDPCSD 104**
Parlophone / Sep '87 / EMI

ALTERNATIVE
In the night / Man could get arrested / That's my impression / Was that what is was / Paninaro / Jack the lad / You know where you went wrong / New life / I want a dog / Do I have to / I get excited (you get excited to) / Don Juan / Sound of the atom splitting / One of the crowd / You funny uncle / It must be obvious / We all feel better in the dark / Bet she's not your girlfriend / Losing my mind / Music for boys / Miserabilsm / Hey headmaster / What keeps mankind alive / Shameless / Too many people / Violence / Decadence / If love were all / Euroboy / Some speculation
CD ______ **CDPCSDS 166**
CD Set ______ **CDPSCD 166**
Parlophone / Aug '95 / EMI

BEHAVIOUR
Being boring / This must be the place I waited years to leave / To face the truth / How can you expect to be taken seriously / Only the wind / My October symphony / So hard / Nervously / End of the world / Jealousy
CD ______ **CDPCSD 113**
Parlophone / Oct '90 / EMI

BILINGUAL
Discoteca / Single / Metamorphosis / Electricity / Se a vida e (that's the way life is) / It always comes as a surprise / Red letter day / Up against it / Survivors / Before / To step aside / Saturday night forever
CD ______ **CDPCSD 170**
Parlophone / Sep '96 / EMI

BILINGUAL (Limited Edition 2CD Set)
Discoteca / Single / Metamorphosis / Electricity / Se a vida e (that's the way life is) / It always comes as a surprise / Red letter day / Up against it / Survivors / Before / To step aside / Saturday night forever / Somewhere / Red letter day / To step aside / Before / Boy who couldn't keep his clothes on / Se a vida e (that's the way life is) / Discoteca
CD Set ______ **CDPCSDX 170**
Parlophone / Jul '97 / EMI

DISCO VOL.2
Absolutely fabulous / I wouldn't normally do this kind of thing / Go West / Liberation / So hard / Can you forgive her / Yesterday, when I was mad / We all feel better in the dark
CD ______ **CDPCSD 159**
Parlophone / Sep '94 / EMI

DISCOGRAPHY - THE COMPLETE SINGLES COLLECTION
West End girls / Love comes quickly / Opportunities (let's make lots of money) / Suburbia / It's a sin / What have I done to deserve this / Always on my mind / Heart / Domino dancing / Left to my own devices / It's alright / So hard / Being boring / Where the streets have no name / Jealousy / DJ culture / Was it worth it
CD ______ **CDPMTV 3**
Parlophone / Oct '91 / EMI

HITS OF THE PET SHOP BOYS, THE (PS Orchestra/Synthesizers)
Being boring / What have I done to deserve this / How can you expect to be taken seriously / So hard / It's a sin / Rent / Heart / I want a dog / Opportunities (let's make lots of money) / Love comes quickly / Suburbia / I'm not scared / Jealousy / Always on my mind / West end girls
CD ______ **QED 052**
Tring / Nov '96 / Tring

INTROSPECTIVE
Left to my own devices / I want a dog / Domino dancing / I'm not scared / Always on my mind / It's alright / In my house
CD ______ **CDPCS 7325**
Parlophone / Feb '94 / EMI

PET SHOP BOYS: INTERVIEW COMPACT DISC
CD ______ **CBAK 4021**
Baktabak / Nov '89 / Arabesque

PLEASE
Two divide by zero / West End girls / Opportunities (Lets make lots of money) / Love comes quickly / Suburbia / Tonight is forever / Violence / I want a lover / Later tonight / Why don't we live together
CD ______ **CDP 7462712**
Parlophone / Jun '86 / EMI

PLEASE/ACTUALLY/BEHAVIOUR (The Originals/3CD Set)
Two divided by zero / West end girls / Opportunities (lets make lots of money) / Love comes quickly / Suburbia / Tonight is forever / Violence / I want a lover / Later tonight / Why don't we live together / One more chance / Shopping / Rent / Hit music / What have I done to deserve this / It couldn't happen here / It's a sin / I want to wake up / Heart / King's Cross / Being boring / This must be the place I waited years to leave / To face the truth / How can you expect to be taken seriously / Only the wind / My October symphony / So hard / Nervously / End of the world / Jealousy
CD Set ______ **CDOMB 023**
EMI / Apr '97 / EMI

VERY
Can you forgive her / I wouldn't normally do this kind of thing / Liberation / Different point of view / Dreaming of the Queen / Yesterday, when I was mad / Theatre / One and one make five / To speak is a sin / Young offender / One in a million / Go west
CD ______ **CDPCSD 143**
Parlophone / Sep '93 / EMI

Peter & Gordon

EP COLLECTION, THE
Leave my woman alone / Hurtin' is loving / Long time gone / Lady Godiva / I got to pieces / Woman / Flower lady / Night in rusty armour / Sunday for tea / Start trying someone else / Love me baby / Lucille / If I were you / Pretty Mary / World without love / Tell me how / You don't have to tell me / Tears don't stop / Soft as the dawn / Leave me alone / Roving rambler / I don't want to see you again / Devant toi je suis sans voix (in front of you I am without a / True love ways / Ne me plains pas (don't feel sorry for me) / Le temps va le temps court (time is going, time is running) / L'unconnue (the unknown)
CD ______ **SEECD 426**
See For Miles/C5 / May '95 / Pinnacle

Peter & The Test Tube Babies

CRINGE
CD ______ **SPV 08430012**
SPV / Mar '96 / Koch / Plastic Head

JOURNEY TO THE CENTRE OF JOHNNY CLARKE'S HEAD
CD ______ **WB 3124CD**
We Bite / May '95 / Plastic Head

LOUD BLARING PUNK ROCK CD, THE
Oral Annie / We're too drunk / Pick yer nose (And eat it) / Vicars / Snakebite / I lust for the disgusting things in life / Tupperware party / Breast cancer / TQBBJ's / Student wankers / Big mouth / Child molester / Porno queen / Being sick / Excuses / Beat up the mods / Get 'em in (and get 'em off) / Rock 'n' roll is shit
CD ______ **WB 3125CD**
We Bite / May '95 / Plastic Head

MATING SOUNDS OF THE SOUTH AMERICAN FROG, THE
September part 1 / Guest list / One night stand / Let's burn / Jinx / Blown out again / Wimpeez / Easter bank holiday '83 / No invitation / Pissed punks (go for it) / Never made it / September part 2
CD ______ **WB 3123CD**
We Bite / May '95 / Plastic Head

PISSED AND PROUD
Moped lads / Banned from the pubs / Elvis is dead / Up yer bum / Smash and grab / Run like hell / Shit stirrer / Intensive care / Keep Britain untidy / Transvestite / Maniac / Disco / I'm the leader of the gang (I am)

CD ____ CDPUNK 3
Anagram / Apr '95 / Cargo / Pinnacle

PUNK SINGLES COLLECTION, THE
Banned from the pubs / Moped lads / Peacehaven wild kids / Run like hell / Up yer bum / Zombie creeping flesh / No invitation / Smash and grab / Jinx / Trapper ain't got a bird / Wimpeez / Never made it / Blown out again / Rotting in the fart sack / Ten deadly sins / Spirit of Keith Moon / Boozanza / Alchohol / Key to the city / Vicar's wank too
CD ____ CDPUNK 64
Anagram / Oct '95 / Cargo / Pinnacle

SOBERPHOBIA
Keys to the city / Louise / Spirit of keith moon / Allergic to life / All about love / He's on the whiskey / Boozanza / Every time I see her / Ghost in my bedsit / Every second counts
CD ____ WB 3128CD
We Bite / May '95 / Plastic Head

SUPERMODELS
CD ____ WB 1139CD
We Bite / Nov '95 / Plastic Head

TEN DEADLY SINS
CD ____ WB 3127CD
We Bite / May '95 / Plastic Head

TOTALLY TEST TUBED
Banned from the pubs / Moped lads / Peacehaven wild kids / Maniac / Transvestite / Elvis is dead / I lust for the disgusting things / TQGGBJ / Run like hell / Up yer bum / Vicar's wank too / Jinx / Trapper ain't got a bird / Blown out again / Never made it / Pissed punks (Go for it) / Spirit of Keith Moon / Zombie creeping flesh / Keys to the city / Louise wouldn't like it / Every second counts / All about love / September part 2
CD ____ WB 3126CD
We Bite / May '95 / Plastic Head

Peter & The Wolf

PETER & THE WOLF
CD ____ ZCDPW 011
Zok / Nov '96 / Grapevine/PolyGram / Total/BMG

Peter, John

JOHN PETER & RED HOT SEVEN (Peter, John & Red Hot Seven)
CD ____ JCD 176
Jazzology / Oct '91 / Jazz Music

Peter, Paul & Mary

C'MON FOLKS
CD ____ TC 022
That's Country / Mar '94 / BMG

PETER, PAUL & MARY
CD ____ 7599271572
WEA / Jan '96 / Warner Music

Peters & Lee

PETERS AND LEE
CD ____ PCOM 1098
President / Jun '89 / Grapevine/PolyGram / President / Target/BMG

WORLD OF PETERS & LEE, THE
Welcome home / By your side / Vincent / Don't stay away too long / So sad (to watch a good love go bad) / Crying game / Hey Mr. Music Man / Wonderful baby / Last happy song / Rainbow / When somebody thinks you're wonderful / If I fell / Only you / Come to me / Song from Moulin Rouge (where your heart is) / You belong to me / Don't blame me / Guess you'll never know
CD ____ 5515392
Spectrum / May '96 / PolyGram

Peters, Brian

CLEAR THE ROAD (Peters, Brian & Gordon Tyrrall)
CD ____ HARCD 031
Harbour Town / Jun '96 / ADA / CM / Direct / Roots

SEEDS OF TIME, THE
Manchester jig - welcome home / History lesson / Living in the past that never was / Cropper lads / Killy Fisher / My lad's ower bonny for the coal trade / Coffee and tea / Lowlands of Holland / Box in the attic / Northern Nanny / Low flier / Servant of the company / Sir William Stanier's favourite / Lovely Joan / Oyster girl / Lad with the trousers on / Mad Moll / False foudrage / Old holle hornpipe / Padlocks / Ruins by the shore / Dark island / Arran boat
CD ____ HARCD 021
Harbour Town / May '92 / ADA / CM / Direct / Roots

SHARPER THAN THE THORN
CD ____ PUGCD 002
Pugwash / Nov '96 / ADA / Direct

SQUEEZING OUT SPARKS
CD ____ PUG 001CD
Pugwash / Apr '94 / ADA / Direct

Peters, Hal

FIREBALL MAIL
CD ____ GRCD 6038
Goofin' / Feb '97 / Nervous / TKO Magnum

Peters, Mike

AER (Welsh Language Version Of 'Breathe') (Peters, Mike & The Poets)
CD ____ CRAICD 047
Crai / Dec '94 / ADA / Direct

BREATHE (Peters, Mike & The Poets)
Poetic justice / All I wanted / If I can't have you / Breathe / Love is a revolution / Who's gonna make the peace / Spiritual / What the world can't give me / Levis and bibles / Beautiful thing / Into the 21st century / This is war / Message / Back into the system / It just don't get any better than this / Train a comin' / New chapter (reprise)
CD ____ CRAI 042CD
Crai / Oct '94 / ADA / Direct

FEEL FREE
Shine on (13th dream) / Message / Feel free / All is forgiven / My calling / Regeneration / RIP / What is it for / Psychological combat zone / Love we made / Breathe / Broken silence
CD ____ TRACD 233
Transatlantic / Aug '96 / Pinnacle

Petersen, Pete

PLAYIN' IN THE PARK (Petersen, Pete & Collection Jazz Orchestra)
CD ____ CMD 8109
CMJ / Aug '89 / Jazz Music / Wellard

STRAIGHT AHEAD (Petersen, Pete & Collection Jazz Orchestra)
CD ____ CMCD 8020
CMJ / '88 / Jazz Music / Wellard

Peterson, Edward

UPWARD SPIRAL
Probably / Upward spiral / Elliott Ness / Objects in the mirror are closer than they appear / Poem for tortured spirits / Onus B / Dan's idea / For Dan / I didn't know what time it was
CD ____ DE 445
Delmark / Mar '97 / ADA / Cadillac / CM / Direct / Hot Shot

Peterson, James

TOO MANY KNOTS
Fish ain't bitin' / Flip floppin' my love / Call before you come home / Long handled spoon / Slob on the knob / Too many knots / Jacksonville / Every goodbye ain't gone / More than one way to skin a cat / Blind can't lead the blind / Killer rock
CD ____ ICH 1130CD
Ichiban / Oct '93 / Direct / Koch

Peterson, Lucky

I'M READY
I'm ready / It ain't right / You shook me / Junkyard / Who's been talkin' / I lost my faith last night / Tribute to the King / On the sea of love / Nothing but smoke / Spankin' Leroy / Don't cloud up on me / Precious Lord / Take my hand
CD ____ 5175132
EmArCy / Mar '94 / PolyGram

LUCKY STRIKES
Over my head / Can't get no loving on the telephone / Lucky strikes / Bad feeling / Earlene / Pounding of my heart / She spread her wings / Dead cat on the line / Heart attack
CD ____ ALCD 4770
Alligator / May '93 / ADA / CM / Direct

RIDIN'
Ridin' / Don't answer the door / Farther up the road / Kinda easy like / Baby, what you want me to do / Green onions / Little red rooster / You don't have to go
CD ____ ECD 260332
Evidence / Sep '93 / ADA / Cadillac / Harmonia Mundi
CD ____ IS 9192
Isabel / Mar '96 / Discovery

TRIPLE PLAY
Let the chips fall where they may / Your lies / Six o'clock blues / Repo man / I found a love / Jammin' in the jungle / Locked out of love / I'm free / Don't cloud up on me / Funky Ray
CD ____ ALCD 4789
Alligator / May '93 / ADA / CM / Direct

Peterson, Master Joe

MASTER JOE PETERSEN (The Phenomenal Boy Singer)
Smilin' through / My ain folk / No souvenirs / Rainbow valley / It's a sin to tell a lie / Sweetheart let's grow old together / Old rugged cross / Memories of childhood days / When they sound the last All Clear / You don't have to tell me / Two little tears / Badge from your coat / Perfect day / Little grey home in the West / My heart's in Old Killarney / Broken hearted clown / Choir boy / Goodnight my love
CD ____ LCOM 5233
Lismor / May '94 / ADA / Direct / Duncans / Lismor

Peterson, Oscar

1959 (Peterson, Oscar Trio)
CD ____ CD 53190
Giants Of Jazz / Sep '94 / Cadillac / Jazz Music / Target/BMG

BURSTING OUT WITH THE ALL STAR BIG BAND/SWINGING BRASS
CD ____ 5296992
Verve / Mar '96 / PolyGram

COMPLETE PABLO CD COLLECTION, THE (10CD Set)
CD Set ____ PACD 0012
Pablo / Nov '96 / Cadillac / Complete/ Pinnacle

DIGITAL AT MONTREUX
Old folks / Soft winds / (Back home again in) Indiana / That's all / Younger than Springtime / Caravan / Rockin' in rhythm / C jam blues / Solitude / Satin doll / Caravan (reprise) / On the trail
CD ____ CD 2308224
Pablo / May '94 / Cadillac / Complete/ Pinnacle

ENCORE AT THE BLUE NOTE (Peterson, Oscar Trio)
CD ____ CD 83356
Telarc / Oct '93 / Conifer/BMG

EXCLUSIVELY FOR MY FRIENDS (4CD Set)
At long last love / Easy walker / Tin tin deo / I've got a crush on you / Foggy day / Like someone in love / On a clear day / I'm in the mood for love / Girl talk / Robbins' nest / I concentrate on you/Moon river / Waltzing is hip/Satin doll / Love is here to stay / Sandy's blues / Alice in wonderland / Noreen's nocturne / In a mellotone / Nica's dream / On Green Dolphin Street / Summertime / Sometime's I'm happy / Who can I turn to / Emily / Quiet nights / Sax no end / When lights are low / Someone to watch over me / Perdido / Body and soul / Who can I turn to / Bye bye blackbird / I should care / Lulu's back in town / Little girl blues / Take the 'A' train
CD Set ____ 5138302
MPS Jazz / Apr '92 / PolyGram

GERSHWIN SONGBOOK, THE
Man I love / Fascinating rhythm / It ain't necessarily so / Somebody loves me / Strike up the band / I've got a crush on you / I was doing all right / 'S wonderful / Oh lady be good / I got rhythm / Foggy day / Love walked in
CD ____ 5296982
Verve / Apr '96 / PolyGram

GIRL TALK
On a clear day you can see forever / I'm in the mood for love / Girl talk / I concentrate on you / Moon river / Robbin's nest
CD ____ 8218422
MPS Jazz / Mar '93 / PolyGram

GITANES - JAZZ 'ROUND MIDNIGHT
Laura / It ain't necessarily so / These foolish things / You go to my head / I loves you Porgy / Angel eyes / On the sunny side of the street / Heartstrings / Bag's groove / Blues of the prairies / Little right foot / When I fall in love / Just a gigolo
CD ____ 5110362
Verve / Apr '92 / PolyGram

GOOD LIFE, THE
CD ____ OJCCD 627
Original Jazz Classics / Feb '92 / Complete/Pinnacle / Jazz Music / Wellard

HALLELUJAH TIME
CD ____ MCD 0502
Moon / Nov '93 / Cadillac / Harmonia Mundi

HELLO HERBIE (Peterson, Oscar Trio & Herb Ellis)
Naptown blues / Exactly like you / Day by day / Hamp's blues / Blues for HG / Lovely day to spend an evening / Seven come eleven
CD ____ 8218462
MPS Jazz / Jul '90 / PolyGram

HISTORY OF AN ARTIST
RB blues / I wished on the moon / You can depend on me / This is where it's at / Okie blues / I want to be happy / Texas blues / Main stem / Don't get around much anymore / Swamp fire / In a sentimental mood / Greasy blues / Sweetie blues / Gay's blues / Good life / Richard's round / Lady of the lavender mist
CD ____ CD 2310895
Pablo / Oct '92 / Cadillac / Complete/ Pinnacle

JAM AT MONTREUX '77
CD ____ OJCCD 378
Original Jazz Classics / Feb '92 / Complete/Pinnacle / Jazz Music / Wellard

JAZZ MASTERS
Night train / Woody 'n' you / Willow weep for me / Younger than Springtime / West Coast blues / Love for sale / Noreen's nocturne / OP / Blues etude / Gal in Calico / D & E blues / Bossa beguine / Evrev / Honey dripper / Someday my Prince will come
CD ____ 5163202
Verve / Apr '93 / PolyGram

JAZZ PORTRAIT OF FRANK SINATRA, A (Peterson, Oscar Trio)
You make me feel so young / Come dance with me / Learnin' the blues / Witchcraft / Tender trap / Saturday night is the loneliest night of the week / Just in time / It happened in Monterey / I get a kick out of you / All of me / Birth of the blues / How about you
CD ____ 8257692
Verve / Mar '93 / PolyGram

JAZZ SOUL OF OSCAR PETERSON, THE/AFFINITY (Peterson, Oscar Trio)
CD ____ 5331002
Verve / Dec '96 / PolyGram

LAST CALL AT THE BLUE NOTE (Peterson, Oscar Trio)
CD ____ CD 83314
Telarc / Sep '92 / Conifer/BMG

LIKE SOMEONE IN LOVE (Peterson, Oscar Trio)
CD ____ JHR 73570
Jazz Hour / Nov '93 / Cadillac / Jazz Music / Target/BMG

LIVE (Peterson, Oscar Trio)
CD ____ CD 2310940
Pablo / Apr '94 / Cadillac / Complete/ Pinnacle

LIVE AT THE NORTH SEA JAZZ FESTIVAL, 1980
Caravan / Straight no chaser / Like someone in love / There is no you / You stepped out of a dream / City lights / I'm old fashioned / Time for love / Bluesology / Goodbye / There is no greater love
CD ____ CD 2620115
Pablo / Apr '94 / Cadillac / Complete/ Pinnacle

LIVE IN 1953 (Peterson, Oscar Quartet & Buddy De Franco)
CD ____ EBCD 21112
Flyright / Feb '94 / Hot Shot / Jazz Music / Wellard

LLUBJANA 1964
CD ____ CD 53203
Giants Of Jazz / May '95 / Cadillac / Jazz Music / Target/BMG

LLUBJANA 1964 VOL.2
CD ____ CD 53204
Giants Of Jazz / May '95 / Cadillac / Jazz Music / Target/BMG

LOUIS ARMSTRONG MEETS OSCAR PETERSON (The Silver Collection) (Peterson, Oscar & Louis Armstrong)
That old feeling: *Armstrong, Louis & Oscar Peterson* / I'll never be the same: *Armstrong, Louis & Oscar Peterson* / How long has this been going on: *Armstrong, Louis & Oscar Peterson* / I was doing all right: *Armstrong, Louis & Oscar Peterson* / Moon song: *Armstrong, Louis & Oscar Peterson* / There's no you: *Armstrong, Louis & Oscar Peterson* / Sweet Lorraine: *Armstrong, Louis & Oscar Peterson* / Let's fall in love: *Armstrong, Louis & Oscar Peterson* / Blues in the night: *Armstrong, Louis & Oscar Peterson* / What's new: *Armstrong, Louis & Oscar Peterson* / Just one of those things: *Armstrong, Louis & Oscar Peterson* / You go to my head: *Armstrong, Louis & Oscar Peterson* / I get a kick out of you: *Armstrong, Louis & Oscar Peterson* / Makin' whoopee: *Armstrong, Louis & Oscar Peterson* / Willow weep for me: *Armstrong, Louis & Oscar Peterson* / Let's do it: *Armstrong, Louis & Oscar Peterson*
CD ____ 8257132
Verve / Mar '92 / PolyGram

MEETS DIZZY GILLESPIE
Caravan / Mozambique / Autumn leaves / Close your eyes / Blues for Bird / Dizzy atmosphere / Alone together / Con Alma
CD ____ J33J 20015
Pablo / Jul '86 / Cadillac / Complete/ Pinnacle

MORE I SEE YOU, THE
In a mellow tone / Gee baby ain't I good to you / Squatty Roo / More I see you / When my dreamboat comes home / Ron's blues / For all we know / On the trail / Blues for LSA
CD ____ CD 83370
Telarc / Jul '95 / Conifer/BMG

MOTIONS & EMOTIONS
Sally's tomato / Sunny / By the time I get to Phoenix / Wanderin' / This guy's in love with you / Wave / Dreamsville / Yesterday / Eleanor Rigby / Ode to Billy Joe
CD ____ 8212892
MPS Jazz / Jul '90 / PolyGram

MOTIONS & EMOTIONS/TRISTEZA ON PIANO/HELLO HERBIE (Three Originals/ 2CD Set) (Peterson, Oscar Trio)
Sally's tomato / Sunny / By the time I get to Phoenix / Wandering / This guy's in love with you / Wave / Dreamsville / Yesterday / Eleanor Rigby / Ode to Billy Joe / Tristeza / Nightingale / Porgy / Triste / You stepped out of a dream / Watch what happens / Down here on the ground / Fly me to the moon / Naptown blues / Exactly like you / Day by day / Hamp's blues / Blues for HG / Lovely way to spend an evening / Seven come eleven

CD Set 5210592
MPS Jazz / Apr '93 / PolyGram

NIGERIAN MARKETPLACE (Peterson, Oscar Trio)
Nigerian marketplace / Au privave / Nancy with the laughing face / Misty / Waltz for Debby / Cake walk / You look good to me
CD CD 2308231
Pablo / Jun '93 / Cadillac / Complete/ Pinnacle

NIGHT TRAIN (Peterson, Oscar Trio)
Night Train / C jam blues / Georgia on my mind / Bag's groove / Moten swing / Easy does it / Honeydripper / Things ain't what they used to be / I got it bad and that ain't good / Band call / Hymn to freedom
CD 8217242
Verve / Sep '84 / PolyGram

OSCAR PETERSON & STEPHANE GRAPPELLI (Peterson, Oscar & Stephane Grappelli Quartet)
Them there eyes / Blues for musidisc / Makin' whoopee / Thou swell / Walkin' my baby back home / Autumn leaves / Looking at you / Folks who live on the hill / I won't dance / Time after time / My one and only love / My heart stood still / Flamingo / If I had you / Let's fall in love
CD 403292
Accord / Mar '96 / Cadillac / Discovery

OSCAR PETERSON 1945-1950 (Peterson, Oscar Trio)
At sundown / Fine and dandy / Somebody loves me / Oscar's blues / Rockin' in rhythm / Poor butterfly / I surrender dear / Margie / Back home again in Indiana / Sweet Georgia Brown / Time on my hands / China boy / In a little Spanish town / Sweet Lorraine / Honeydripper / East of the sun (west of the moon) / My blue heaven / Flying home / Humoresque / I got rhythm / Sheik of Araby
CD CD 53181
Giants Of Jazz / Jul '97 / Cadillac / Jazz Music / Target/BMG

OSCAR PETERSON 1951
CD JAS 9501
Just A Memory / Dec '95 / New Note/ Pinnacle

OSCAR PETERSON AND HARRY EDISON (Peterson, Oscar & Harry Edison)
Easy living / Days of wine and roses / Gee baby ain't I good to you / Basie / Mean to me / Signify / Willow weep for me / Man I love / You go to my head
CD OJCCD 738
Original Jazz Classics / May '93 / Complete/ Pinnacle / Jazz Music / Wellard

OSCAR PETERSON AND ROY ELDRIDGE (Peterson, Oscar & Roy Eldridge)
Little Jazz / She's funny that way / Way you look tonight / Sunday / Bad hat blues / Between the Devil and the deep blue sea / Blues for Chu
CD OJCCD 727
Original Jazz Classics / Nov '95 / Complete/ Pinnacle / Jazz Music / Wellard

OSCAR PETERSON CHRISTMAS, AN
Winter wonderland / Santa Claus is coming to town / Let it snow, let it snow, let it snow / Silent night / Jingle bells / White Christmas / Have yourself a merry little Christmas / Christmas waltz / I'll be home for Christmas / Away in a manger / O Christmas tree / O little town of Bethlehem / God rest ye merry gentlemen / What child is this
CD CD 83372
Telarc / Nov '95 / Conifer/BMG

OSCAR PETERSON IN CONCERT
Bag's groove / I've got the world on a string / Daahoud / Gai / Sweet Georgia Brown / Tenderly / C jam blues / Pompton turnpike / Seven come eleven / Love for sale / Lollobrigida / Swingin' 'til the girls come home / Nuages / Avalon / Come to the Mardi Gras / Baby, baby, all the time / Easy does it / Sunday / Falling in love with love / Noreen's nocturne / Gypsy in my soul / Flamingo / Love you madly / 52nd Street
CD RTE 10022
RTE / Apr '95 / ADA / Koch

OSCAR PETERSON IN CONCERT
CD Set 710443CD
RTE / Apr '95 / ADA / Koch

OSCAR PETERSON IN RUSSIA (2CD Set)
I got it bad and that ain't good / I concentrate on you / Place St. Henri / Hogtown blues / On Green Dolphin Street / You stepped out of a dream / Wave / On the trail / Take the 'A' train / Summertime / Just friends / Do you know what it means to miss New Orleans / I loves you Porgy / Georgia on my mind / Li'l darlin' / Watch what happens / Hallelujah trail / Someone to watch over me
CD Set 2CD 2625711
Pablo / Dec '96 / Cadillac / Complete/ Pinnacle

OSCAR PETERSON MEETS ROY HARGROVE & RALPH MOORE (Peterson, Oscar & Roy Hargrove/Ralph Moore)
Tin tin deo / Rob Roy / Blues for Stephane / My foolish heart / Cool walk / Ecstasy / Just friends / Truffles / She has gone North York
CD CD 83399
Telarc Jazz / Nov '96 / Conifer/BMG

OSCAR PETERSON PLAYS BROADWAY
CD 5168932
Verve / Apr '94 / PolyGram

OSCAR PETERSON PLAYS COUNT BASIE
Lester leaps in / Easy does it / 9.20 special / Jumpin' at the woodside / Blues for Basie / Broadway / Blue and sentimental / Topsy / One o'clock jump / Jump at five
CD 5198112
Verve / Apr '93 / PolyGram

OSCAR PETERSON PLAYS MY FAIR LADY & FIORELLO (Peterson, Oscar Trio)
I've grown accustomed to her face / Get me to the church on time / Show me / I could have danced all night / On the street where you live / Wouldn't it be lovely / Rain in Spain / When did I fall in love / Little tin box / Home again / Til tomorrow / Politics and poker / Gentleman Jimmy / Unfair / On the side of the angels / Where do I go from here
CD 5216772
Verve / Mar '94 / PolyGram

OSCAR PETERSON PLAYS PORGY & BESS
I got plenty o' nuttin' / I wants to stay here / Summertime / Oh dey's so fresh and fine / Oh lawd I'm on my way / It ain't necessarily so / There's a boat that's leavin' soon for New York / Oh Bess, oh where's my Bess / Here come de honey man / Bess you is my woman now
CD 5198072
Verve / Apr '93 / PolyGram

OSCAR PETERSON PLAYS THE COLE PORTER SONGBOOK (Peterson, Oscar)
In the still of the night / It's alright with me / Love for sale / Just one of those things / I've got you under my skin / Everytime we say goodbye / Night and day / Easy to love / Why can't you behave / I love Paris / I concentrate on you / It's de-lovely
CD 8219872
Verve / Jul '97 / PolyGram

OSCAR PETERSON TRIO + ONE CLARK TERRY (Peterson, Oscar Trio & Clark Terry)
Brotherhood of man / Jim / Blues for Smedley / Roundalay / Mumbles / Mack the knife / They didn't believe me / Squeaky's blues / I want a little girl / Incoherent blues
CD 8188402
EmArCy / Jun '85 / PolyGram

OSCAR PETERSON TRIO AT STRATFORD SHAKESPEAREAN FESTIVAL, THE (Peterson, Oscar Trio)
Falling in love with love / How about you / Flamingo / Swinging on a star / Noreen Nocturne / Gypsy in my soul / Nuages / How high the moon / Love you madly / 52nd Street / Daisy's dream
CD 5137522
Verve / Jul '93 / PolyGram

OSCAR PETERSON TRIO AT THE CONCERTGEBOUW (Peterson, Oscar Trio)
Lady is a tramp / We'll be together again / Bluesology / Budo / I've got the world on a string / Daahoud / When lights are low / Evrev / Should I / Big fat Mama / Indiana / Joy spring / Elevation
CD 5216492
Verve / Mar '94 / PolyGram

OSCAR PETERSON, HARRY EDISON & EDDIE 'CLEANHEAD' VINSON (Peterson, Oscar & Harry Edison/Eddie 'Cleanhead' Vinson)
Stuffy / This one's for jaws / Everything happens to me / Broadway / Slooo drag / What's new / Satin doll
CD CD 2310927
Pablo / Apr '94 / Cadillac / Complete/ Pinnacle

PETERSON
CD OJCCD 383
Original Jazz Classics / Feb '92 / Complete/Pinnacle / Jazz Music / Wellard

PORGY AND BESS (Peterson, Oscar & Joe Pass)
Summertime / Bess you is my woman now / My man's gone now / It ain't necessarily so / I got plenty o' nuttin' / Oh, Bess, oh where's my Bess / I loves you Porgy / They pass by singin' / There's a boat that's leavin' soon for New York / Strawberry woman
CD CD 2310779
Pablo / Apr '94 / Cadillac / Complete/ Pinnacle

SATCH AND JOSH (Peterson, Oscar & Count Basie)
Bun's blues / These foolish things / RB burning / Exactly like you / Jumpin' at the woodside / Louis B / Lester leaps in / Big stockings / S and J blues
CD CD 2310722
Pablo / Apr '94 / Cadillac / Complete/ Pinnacle

SATURDAY NIGHT AT BLUE NOTE (Peterson, Oscar Trio)
CD CD 83306
Telarc / Sep '91 / Conifer/BMG

SIDE BY SIDE (Peterson, Oscar & Itzhak Perlman)
Dark eyes / Stormy weather / Georgia on my mind / Blue skies / Misty / Mack the knife / Night time / I loves you Porgy / On the trail / Yours is my heart alone / Makin' whoopee / Why think about tomorrow
CD CD 83341
Telarc / Oct '94 / Conifer/BMG

SILVER COLLECTION, THE
My foolish heart / 'Round midnight / Someday my Prince will come / Come Sunday / Nightingale / My ship / Sleepin' bee / Portrait of Jennie / Goodbye / Con Alma / Maidens of Cadiz / My heart stood still / Woody 'n' you
CD 8234472
Verve / Feb '92 / PolyGram

SKOL (Peterson, Oscar & Stephane Grappelli/Joe Pass)
Nuages / How about you / Someone to watch over me / Makin' whoopee / That's all / Skol blues
CD OJCCD 496
Original Jazz Classics / Feb '92 / Complete/ Pinnacle / Jazz Music / Wellard

SONG IS YOU, THE (2CD Set)
CD Set 5315582
Verve / Aug '96 / PolyGram

STRATFORD, ONTARIO, CANADA
CD CD 53209
Giants Of Jazz / Nov '95 / Cadillac / Jazz Music / Target/BMG

TIME AFTER TIME
Cool walk / Love ballade / Soft winds / Who can I turn to / Without a song / Time after time
CD CD 2310947
Pablo / May '94 / Cadillac / Complete/ Pinnacle

TIMEKEEPERS (Peterson, Oscar & Count Basie)
I'm confessin' that I love you / Soft winds / Rent party / (Back home again in) Indiana / Hey Raymond / After you've gone / That's the one
CD OJCCD 790
Original Jazz Classics / Sep '93 / Complete/ Pinnacle / Jazz Music / Wellard

TRIBUTE TO MY FRIENDS, A
Blueberry Hill / Sometimes I'm happy / Stuffy / Birk's works / Cotton tail / Lover man / Tisket-a-tasket / Rockin' chair / Now's the time
CD CD 2310902
Pablo / May '94 / Cadillac / Complete/ Pinnacle

TRIBUTE TO OSCAR PETERSON, A (Live At The Town Hall) (Peterson, Oscar & Friends)
Anything goes / Reunion blues / If you only knew / Bag's groove / Mumbles / Can't face the music / Here's to life / In a mellow tone / My foolish heart / Way you look tonight / Duke of Dubuque / Route 66 / Mack the knife
CD CD 83401
Telarc Jazz / Jun '97 / Conifer/BMG

TRIO, THE
Blues etude / Chicago blues / Easy listening blues / Come Sunday / Secret love
CD CD 2310701
Pablo / May '94 / Cadillac / Complete/ Pinnacle

TRIO, THE (Live From Chicago) (Peterson, Oscar Trio)
I've never been in love before / In the wee small hours of the morning / Chicago / Night we called it a day / Sometimes I'm happy / Whisper not / Billy boy
CD 8230082
Verve / Feb '94 / PolyGram

TRISTEZA ON PIANO (Peterson, Oscar Trio)
Tristeza / Nightingale / Porgy / Triste / You stepped out of a dream / Watch what happens / Down here on the ground / Fly me to the moon
CD 8174892
MPS Jazz / Mar '93 / PolyGram

TRUMPET SUMMIT MEETS THE OSCAR PETERSON BIG FOUR (Peterson, Oscar Big Four)
Daahoud / Chicken wings / Just friends / Champ
CD OJCCD 603
Original Jazz Classics / Mar '92 / Complete/ Pinnacle / Jazz Music / Wellard

VERY TALL (Peterson, Oscar Trio & Milt Jackson)
On Green Dolphin Street / Work song / Heartstrings / John Brown's body / Wonderful guy / Reunion blues
CD 8278212
Verve / Sep '93 / PolyGram

VIENNA CONCERT 1968
CD W 342CD
Philology / Apr '94 / Cadillac / Harmonia Mundi

WALKING THE LINE/ANOTHER DAY
I love you / Rock of ages / Once upon a summertime / Teach me tonight / Windmills of your mind / I didn't know what time it was / All of you / Blues for Martha / Greensleeves / I'm old fashioned / All the things you are / Too close for comfort / JAMF's are coming / It never entered my mind / Carolina shout
CD 5335492
MPS Jazz / Nov '96 / PolyGram

WE GET REQUESTS (Peterson, Oscar Trio)
Quiet nights of quiet stars / Days of wine and roses / My one and only love / People / Have you met Miss Jones / You look good to me / Girl from Ipanema / D and E blues / Time and again / Goodbye JD
CD 8100472
Verve / Mar '90 / PolyGram

WEST SIDE STORY (Peterson, Oscar Trio)
Something's coming / Somewhere / Jet song / Tonight / Maria / I feel pretty / Reprise
CD 8215752
Verve / Mar '88 / PolyGram

WILL TO SWING, THE (2CD Set)
Fine and dandy / Tenderly / Facsinating rhythm / Swingin' till the girls come home / Gypsy in my soul / When lights are low / Con alma / Ill wind / In the wee small hours of the morning / Daahoud / C Jam blues / Nightingale / Place St. Henri / I've got a crush on you / Lulu's back in town / Wave / Child is born / Younger than springtime
CD Set 8472032
Verve / May '91 / PolyGram

Peterson, Ralph

FO'TET PLAYS MONK, THE (Peterson, Ralph Fo'tet)
Jackie-ing / Skippy / Epistrophy / Played twice / Light blue / Criss cross / Four in one / Monkin' around / Spherically speaking / Well you needn't / Brillinat corners
CD ECD 22174
Evidence / Feb '97 / ADA / Cadillac / Harmonia Mundi

RECLAMATION PROJECT, THE
Further fo / Song of serenity / Long journey home / Insanity / Bottom / Turn it over / Just for today / Acceptance / For all my tomorrows / Keep it simple
CD ECD 22113
Evidence / Jun '95 / ADA / Cadillac / Harmonia Mundi

Peterson, Ricky

SMILE BLUE
CD GOJ 60042
Go Jazz / Sep '95 / Vital/SAM

TEAR CAN TELL, A
CD GOJ 60162
Go Jazz / Oct '95 / Vital/SAM

Petri, Michala

MOONCHILD'S DREAM
CD 09026625432
RCA / Jul '95 / BMG

Petrie, Robin

CONTINENTAL DRIFT (Petrie, Robin & Danny Carnahan)
CD FF 70442
Flying Fish / '88 / ADA / CM / Direct / Roots

Petrucciani, Michel

AU THEATRE DES CHAMPS-ELYEES
Medley of my favourite songs / Night sun in Blois / Radio dial / I mean you/Round about midnight / Even mice dance / Caravan / Love letter / Besame mucho
CD Set FDM 365702
Dreyfus / Mar '95 / ADA / Direct / New Note/ Pinnacle

BLUE NOTE YEARS, THE (The Best Of Michel Petrucciani)
Looking up / September song / Miles Davis licks / Play me / Home / Lullaby / La champagne / She did it again / Our tune / Bimini / Brazilian suite / O nana oye
CD CDP 7899162
Blue Note / Nov '93 / EMI

CONFRENCE DE PRESSE VOL.2 (Petrucciani, Michel & Eddy Louiss)
Autumn leaves / Hub art / Caravan / Naissance / Rachid / Caraibes / Au p'tit jour / Summertime
CD FDM 365732
Dreyfus / Dec '95 / ADA / Direct / New Note/ Pinnacle

DARN THAT DREAM (Petrucciani, Michel Trio)
CD 667722
Melodie / Apr '96 / ADA / Discovery / Grapevine/PolyGram / Greensleeves / Jet Star

LIVE
CD CCD 43006
Concord Jazz / '88 / New Note/Pinnacle

LIVE
Black magic / Miles Davis licks / Contradictions / Bite / Rachid / Looking up / Thank you note / Estate
CD CDP 7805892
Blue Note / Oct '94 / EMI

MARVELLOUS
Manhattan / Charlie Brown / Even mice dance / Why / Hidden joy / Shooting stars / You are my waltz / Dumb breaks / 92's Last / Besame mucho
CD FDM 365642
Dreyfus / Mar '94 / ADA / Direct / New Note/ Pinnacle

PROMENADE WITH DUKE
Caravan / Lush life / Take the 'A' train / African flower / In a sentimental mood / Hidden joy / One night in a hotel / Satin doll / C jam blues
CD CDP 7805902
Blue Note / Feb '93 / EMI

Petters, John

BOOGIE WOOGIE & ALL THAT JAZZ (Petters, John & His Rhythm)
CD RRCD 003
Roots / Apr '93 / Pinnacle

JOHN PETTERS & HIS RHYTHM WITH NEVILLE DICKIE (Petters, John & Neville Dickie)
CD RRCD 1002
Rose / May '96 / Jazz Music

SPIRITUAL (Petters, John New Orleans Allstars/Creole Jazzband)
CD RRCD 1007
Rose / Jun '96 / Jazz Music

Pettersson, Andreas

JOYRIDER
CD SITCD 9219
Sittel / Jun '96 / Cadillac / Jazz Music

LIVE IN FINLAND
CD DRCD 238
Dragon / Jan '87 / ADA / Cadillac / CM / Roots / Wellard

Petteway, Al

WATERS & THE WILD, THE
CD MMCD 205
Maggie's Music / Dec '94 / ADA / CM

WHISPERING STONES
CD MMCD 206
Maggie's Music / Dec '94 / ADA / CM

Pettiford, Oscar

MONTMARTRE BLUES
CD BLC 760124
Black Lion / Feb '89 / Cadillac / Jazz Music / Koch / Wellard

OSCAR PETTIFORD
CD BET 6017
Bethlehem / Jan '95 / ADA / ZYX

VIENNA BLUES
CD BLC 760104
Black Lion / Oct '94 / Cadillac / Jazz Music / Koch / Wellard

VIENNA BLUES -- THE COMPLETE SESSION
Cohn's limit / Gentle art of love / All the things you are / Stalag 414 / Vienna blues / Oscar's blues / Stardust / There will never be another you / Blues in the closet
CD BLCD 760104
Black Lion / Jun '88 / Cadillac / Jazz Music / Koch / Wellard

Pettis, Jack

HIS PETS, BAND AND ORCHESTRA (2CD Set)
CD Set KCM 0056
Kings Cross Music / Apr '97 / Cadillac / Harmonia Mundi / Wellard

Petty, Norman

15 CLASSIC MEMORIES VOL.1
Mood indigo / Jambalaya / If you see me crying / Pretty's little polka / I'll string along with you / Oh you pretty woman / Hey good lookin' / Gimme a little kiss, will ya, huh / Jax boogie / It's been a long, long time / Little black samba / Half as much / Echo polka / Dream is a wish your heart makes / My blue heaven
CD CDCHM 443
Ace / Jul '94 / Pinnacle

ORIGINAL NORMAN PETTY TRIO/ ENSEMBLE VOL.2 (15 More Classic Memories)
On the Alamo / Dirty Dum / Three little kisses / It's no sin / Bring your heart / Tennessee waltz / Walkin' to Missouri / Find me a golden street / China nights / Undecided / Mr. Tap-Toe / Candy and cake / As time goes by / Caravan / Kiss me goodnight
CD CDCHM 624
Ace / Jul '96 / Pinnacle

Petty, Tom

DAMN THE TORPEDOES
Refugee / Here comes the girl / Even the losers / Century city / Don't do me like that / What are you doin' in my life / Louisiana rain
CD MCLD 19014
MCA / Apr '92 / BMG

FULL MOON FEVER
Free fallin' / I won't back down / Love is a long road / Face in the crowd / Runnin' down a dream / Feel a whole lot better / Yer so bad / Depending on you / Apartment song / Alright for now / Mind with a heart of it's own / Zombie zoo
CD DMCG 6034
MCA / May '89 / BMG

GREATEST HITS (Petty, Tom & The Heartbreakers)
American girl / Breakdown / Anything that's rock 'n' roll / Listen to her heart / I need to know / Refugee / Don't do me like that / Even the losers / Here comes my girl / Waiting / You got lucky / Don't come around here no more / I won't back down / Runnin' down a dream / Free fallin' / Learning to fly / Into the great wide open / Mary Jane's last dance / Something in the air
CD MCD 10964
MCA / Oct '93 / BMG

HARD PROMISES
Waiting / Woman in love / Nightwatchman / Something big / Kings Road / Letting you go / Thing about you / Insider / Criminal kind / You can still change your mind
CD MCLD 19077
MCA / Nov '91 / BMG

INTO THE GREAT WIDE OPEN
CD MCAD 10317
MCA / Jul '91 / BMG

LET ME UP (I'VE HAD ENOUGH) (Petty, Tom & The Heartbreakers)
Jammin' me / Runaway train / Damage you've done / It'll all work out / My life / Think about me / All mixed up / Self made man / Ain't love strange / How many more days / Your world / Let me up (I've had enough)
CD MCLD 19141
MCA / Nov '92 / BMG

LONG AFTER DARK
One story town / You got lucky / Deliver me / Change of heart / Finding out / We stand a chance / Straight into darkness / Same old you / Between two worlds / Wasted life
CD MCLD 19078
MCA / Jun '92 / BMG

PACK UP THE PLANTATION
CD MCLD 19142
MCA / Nov '91 / BMG

PLAYBACK (6CD Set)
Big jangle / Breakdown / American girl / Hometown blues / Anything that's rock 'n' roll / I need to know / Listen to her heart / When the time comes / Too much ain't enough / No second thoughts / Baby's a rock 'n' roller / Refugee / Here comes my girl / Even the losers / Shadow of a doubt / Don't do me like that / Waiting / Woman in love / Something big / Thing about you / Insider / You can still change your mind / Spoiled and mistreated / You got lucky / Change of heart / Straight into darkness / Same old you / Rebels / Don't come around here no more / Southern accents / Make it better (forget about me) / Best of everything / So you want to be a rock 'n' roll star / Don't bring me down / Jammin' me / It'll all work out / Mikes life, Mikes world / Think about me / Self made man / Good booty / Free fallin' / I won't back down / Love is a long road / Runnin' down a dream / Yer so bad / Alright for now / Learning to fly / Into the great wide open / All or nothin' / Out in the cold / Built to last / Mary Jane's last dance / Christmas all over again / Outer sides / Casa dega / Heartbreaker's beach party / Trailer / Cracking up / Psychotic reactions / I'm tired Joey boy / Lonely weekends / Gator on the lawn / Make that connection / Down the line / Peace in LA / It's raining again / Somethin' else / I don't know what to say to you / Kings highway / Through the cracks / On the street / Depot street / Cry to me / I can't fight it / Since you said you loved me / Louisiana rain / Keeping me alive / Turning point / Stop draggin' my heart around / Apartment song / Big boss man / Image of me / Moon pie / Damage you've done / Nobody's children / Got my mind made up / Ways to be wicked / Can't get her out / Waiting for tonight / Travellin' / baby, let's play house / Wooden heart / God's gift to man / You get me high / Come on down to my house / You come through / Up in Mississipi tonight
CD Set MCAD 611375
MCA / Nov '95 / BMG

SHE'S THE ONE (Original Soundtrack)
CD 9362462852
Warner Bros. / Aug '96 / Warner Music

SOUTHERN ACCENTS
Rebels / It ain't nothin' to me / Don't come around here no more / Southern accents / Make it better / Spike / Dogs on the run / Mary's new car / Best of everything
CD MCLD 19079
MCA / Nov '90 / BMG

TOM PETTY & THE HEARTBREAKERS (Petty, Tom & The Heartbreakers)
Rockin' around (with you) / American girl / Luna / Mystery man / Fooled again (I don't like it) / Stranger in the night / Anything that's rock 'n' roll / Forever / Wild one / Home town blues / Breakdown
CD MCLD 19012
MCA / Apr '92 / BMG

WILDFLOWERS
CD 9362457592
WEA / Oct '94 / Warner Music

YOU'RE GONNA GET IT (Petty, Tom & The Heartbreakers)
When the time comes / You're gonna get it / Hurt / Magnolia / Too much ain't enough / I need to know / Listen to her heart / No second thoughts / Restless / Baby's a rock'n'roller
CD MCLD 19013
MCA / Apr '92 / BMG

Peyroux, Madeline

DREAMLAND
Walkin' after midnight / Hey sweet man / I'm gonna sit right down / (Getting some) Fun out of life / La vie en rose / Always a use / Prayer / Muddy water / Was I / Lovesick blues / Reckless blues / Dreamland
CD 7567829462
Warner Bros. / May '97 / Warner Music

PEZ

WAITING
Into nothing / Downtown / Play this round / Slave fire / Nice present / Down forever / Makeshift / Shame / Up to you / Glass globe / 5 A.M. / Love = death / Waiting / Plaid rock
CD R 3582
Rough Trade / Oct '94 / Pinnacle

PFM

ULISSE
CD RTI 11462
RTI / May '97 / Greyhound

PGR

CHEMICAL BRIDE, THE
CD SR 9218
Silent / Jul '94 / Cargo / Plastic Head

GRAVE (PGR/Merzbow/Asmus Tietchens)
CD SR 9114
Silent / Jul '94 / Cargo / Plastic Head

Phair, Liz

EXILE IN GUYVILLE
Six foot one / Help me Mary / Glory / Dance of the seven veils / Never said / Soap star Joe / Explain it to me / Canary / Mesmerizing / Fuck and run / Girls, girls, girls / Divorce song / Shatter / Flatter / Flower / Johnny sunshine / Gunshy / Stratford-on-Guy / Strange loop
CD OLE 0512
Matador / Aug '93 / Vital

JUVENILIA
Jealousy / Turning Japanese / Animal girl / California / South Dakota / Batmobile / Dead shark / Easy
CD OLE 1292
Matador / Jul '95 / Vital

WHIPSMART
Chopsticks / Supernova / Support system / X-ray man / Shane / Nashville / Go west / Cinco de mayo / Dogs of LA / Whipsmart / Jealousy / Crater lake / Alice springs / May Queen
CD 7567924292
Warner Bros. / Sep '94 / Warner Music

Phallus Dei

CYBERFLESH
CD PA 002CD
Paragoric / Sep '93 / Cargo / Plastic Head

LUXURIA
CD PA 008CD
Paragoric / May '95 / Cargo / Plastic Head

ORPHEUS AND EURYDICE
CD PA 017CD
Resurrection / Jan '96 / Plastic Head

PORNOCRATES
CD PA 006CD
Paragoric / Mar '95 / Cargo / Plastic Head

Phantom

PHANTOM
CD SHARK 023CD
Shark / Jan '92 / Plastic Head

Phantom 309

SINISTER ALPHABET, A
CD TUPCD 003
Tupelo / Jul '89 / RTM/Disc

Phantom Blue

BUILT TO PERFORM
CD RR 90272
Roadrunner / Mar '96 / PolyGram

PHANTOM BLUE
CD RR 94692
Roadrunner / Jun '89 / PolyGram

Phantom City

SHIVA RECOIL
Black data 1 / Black data 2
CD AMBT 21
Virgin / Apr '97 / EMI

Phantom Payn Act

BAD VIBES, ANYONE
CD GRCD 329
Glitterhouse / Sep '94 / Avid/BMG

TROUBLE WITH GHOSTS
CD GRCD 221
Glitterhouse / Sep '94 / Avid/BMG

Phantom Rockers

BORN TO BE WILD
CD TBCD 2002
Nervous / Mar '93 / Nervous / TKO Magnum

Phantom Surfers

EXCITING SOUNDS OF MODEL ROAD RACING
CD LK 183LPCD
Lookout / Aug '97 / Cargo / Greyhound / Shellshock/Disc

GREAT SURF CRASH OF '97, THE
CD LOOKOUT 155CD
Lookout / Sep '96 / Cargo / Greyhound / Shellshock/Disc

Pharaohs

AWAKENING
CD LHCD 025
Luv n' Haight / Jul '96 / Timewarp

IN THE BASEMENT (Unreleased)
CD LHCD 026
Luv n' Haight / Nov '96 / Timewarp

Pharcyde

BIZARRE RIDE II THE PHARCYDE
4 better or 4 worse (interlude) / Oh shit / It's jigaboo time / 4 better or 4 worse / I'm that type of nigga / If I were President / Soul flower / On the DL / Pack the pipe (interlude) / Officer / Ya mama / Passing me by / Otha fish / Quinton's on the way / Pack the pipe / Return of the B-Boy
CD 8287492
Go Beat / Aug '96 / PolyGram

LABCABINCALIFORNIA
Bullshit / Pharcyde / Groupie therapy / Runnin' / She said / Splattitorium / Somethin' that means somethin' / All live / Moment in time / It's all good / Hey you / Drop / Hustle / Little D / Devil music / End / Emerald butterfly / Just don't matter
CD 8287332
Go Beat / Apr '96 / PolyGram

Phase 5

MENTALE VERWANDLUNG
CD EFA 120562
Rap Nation / Apr '94 / SRD

Phauss

GOD T PHAUSS
CD SR 9459
Silent / Aug '94 / Cargo / Plastic Head

PHAUSS, KARKOWSKI & BILTING (Phauss, Karkowski & Bilting)
CD SR 9217
Silent / Jul '94 / Cargo / Plastic Head

Phelps, Kelly Joe

LEAD ME ON
CD BCD 00152
Burnside / Sep '96 / Koch

Phemales

LOVE DON'T LIVE HERE ANYMORE
CD RATTI 01
Ratti / May '97 / Jet Star

Phenobaridols

FISH LOUNGE
CD SFTRI 348CD
Sympathy For The Record Industry / Oct '95 / Cargo / Greyhound / Plastic Head

Phenonema 3

INNER VISION
CD CDPAR 002
Parachute Music / Nov '92 / THE

Phew

HIMITSU NO KNIFE
CD CMDD 00010
Creative Man / Jun '97 / ReR Megacorp

PHEW
CD DSA 54016
God Mountain / Jun '97 / ReR Megacorp

VIEW
CD DSA 54021
God Mountain / Jun '97 / ReR Megacorp

PHI

SOUND IS SOUND
CD NZ 008CD
Nova Zembla / Jan '95 / Plastic Head

Philadelphia Bluntz

BLUNTED AT BIRTH
Blunt chronicles / Hostility / Mosquito / I like that / Shaky shaky / Slidehead / Transformer / Jugs / Dum dum dum
CD ZEN 005CD
Indochina / Jul '95 / Pinnacle

Philadelphia International All ...

LET'S CLEAN UP THE GHETTO (Philadelphia International All Stars)
Trade winds / Let's clean up the ghetto / Ooh child / Now is the time to do it / Year of decision / Big gangster / New day / New world comin' / Old people / Save the children / Everybody's here
CD 12218
Laserlight / May '94 / Target/BMG

Philharmonic Chamber Choir

ALL IN THE APRIL EVENING
All in the April evening / Isle of Mull / Steal away / Dashing white sergeant / Were you there / Banks o'Doon / Peat fire / Smooring prayer / Loch Lomond / King Arthur / Belmont / Iona boat song / Herdmaiden's song / Bluebird / Faery song from "The Immortal Hour" / An eriskay love lilt
CD CDH 88008
Helios / May '88 / Select

Philharmonic Pop Orchestra

CLASSIC LOVE SONGS
CD TRTCD 178
TrueTrax / Feb '96 / THE

DOUBLE IMAGES
CD ISCD 111
Intersound / Jun '95 / Jazz Music

PHILHARMONIC POP ORCHESTRA
CD ISCD 118
Intersound / '91 / Jazz Music

POP CLASSICS
CD DCD 5303
Disky / Dec '93 / Disky / THE

POP TO THE PAST
CD ISCD 106
Intersound / Jun '95 / Jazz Music

Philip & Lloyd

BLUES BUSTERS, THE
CD RNCD 2122
Rhino / Nov '95 / Grapevine/PolyGram / Jet Star

Philip, Michael

AT THE RIVERSIDE (Philip, Michael Ceilidh Band)
CD SP 1035CD
Springthyme / May '93 / ADA / CM / Direct / Duncans / Highlander / Roots

Philippe, Louis

APPOINTMENT WITH VENUS
La pluie fait des claquettes / Man down the stairs / When I'm an astronaut / We live on an island / Orchard / Heaven is above me / Rescue the Titanic / Touch of evil / Ballad of Sophie Soloil / Angelica my love / I will / Exporado tales / Apertivo / Fires rise and die
CD ACME 5CD
El / Jul '89 / Pinnacle

CLARET
You Mary you / Domenica / What if a day / Monsieur Leduc / Man down the stairs / Red shoes ballet suite / Anna / Anna s'en va / With you and without you / Aperitivo / La pluie fait des claquettes / Telephone box / I collect stamps / Guess I'm dumb / Ruben's room / All stands still / Did you say her name was Peg / Night talk / Fires and rise and die / Yuri Gagarin
CD MONDE 4CD
Richmond / May '92 / Pinnacle

SUNSHINE
CD BAH 23
Humbug / Sep '97 / Total/Pinnacle

YURI GAGARIN
Diamond / Did you say her name was Peg / She's great / Endless September / Vision / Goodbye again / Anna s'en va / Jean and me / I collect stamps / Sunday morning Camden Town / Another boy / Yuri Gagarin
CD ACME 23CD
El / Oct '89 / Pinnacle

Philips, Flip

SPANISH EYES
Spanish eyes / Nature boy / Fat Tessie's ass / Nancy (With the laughing face) / Makin' whoopee / Everything happens to me / Love story / Jeannie / This is all I ask
CD CHCD 71013
Candid / Mar '97 / Cadillac / Direct / Jazz Music / Koch / Wellard

Philips, Glen

ELEVATOR
Micro / Sex messiah / Inca silver metallic / Ario / John Marshall / Vista cruiser / DNA I ran / Rememory / Tower of babel / Rain tonight / Death ship
CD SST 136CD
SST / May '93 / Plastic Head

Philips, Steve

JUST PICKIN' (Philips, Steve & Mark Knopfler)
CD TROV 2
Buried Treasure / Oct '96 / Total/BMG

Philistines Jr.

SINKING OF THE SS DANEHOWER, THE
CD DOT 9CD
Dot / Nov '95 / EMI

Phillips, Anthony

1984
Prelude 84 / 1984 / Anthem 1984
CD CDOVD 321
Virgin / '89 / EMI

ANTHOLOGY
Women were watching / Prelude '84 / Anthem from Tarka / Lucy will / Tregenna afternoons / Unheard cry / Catch at the tables / Lights on the hill / Now what / Um and aargh / Slow dance / Tears on a rainy day / God if I saw her now / Nightmare / Last goodbyes / Collections / Sleepfall: The geese fly west
CD BP 201CD
Blueprint / Oct '95 / Pinnacle

FINGER PAINTING
CD BP 209CD
Blueprint / Oct '95 / Pinnacle

GEESE AND THE GHOST, THE
CD CDOVD 315
Virgin / Nov '90 / EMI

GYPSY SUITE (Phillips, Anthony & Harry Williamson)
Gypsy suite / Tarka
CD BP 189CD
Blueprint / Sep '97 / Pinnacle

INVISIBLE MEN
Sally / Golden bodies / Going for broke / It's not easy / Traces / Guru / My time has come / Love in a hot air balloon / I want your heart / Falling for love / Women were watching
CD BP 211CD
Blueprint / Mar '96 / Pinnacle

LIVING ROOM CONCERT
CD BP 218CD
Blueprint / May '96 / Pinnacle

MEADOWS OF ENGLEWOOD, THE (Phillips, Anthony & Guillermo Cazenave)
Peggy in the sky without diamonds / Meadows of Englewood / Lucy: an illusion / Agent Mulder never resolves a single case / Sortilege / She'll be waiting / Circle / Picaesca / Ocho pomelos con pimienta...prestame un mango pibe
CD CD 30
Astral / Aug '97 / Pinnacle

MISSING LINKS VOL.1
CD PRO 012
Progress / Jul '92 / Vital

MISSING LINKS VOL.2 (The Sky Road)
Exile / Lifeboat suite / Bitter suite / Across the river Styx / Flock of souls / Along the towpath / Sky road / Tears on a rainy day / Tiwai: Island of the apes / Wild voices, quiet water / Suite / Serenita / Timepiece / Field of eternity / Beggar and the thief
CD BWKD 212
Brainworks / May '94 / Pinnacle

PRIVATE PARTS AND PIECES VOL.1
CD BP 202CD
Blueprint / Oct '95 / Pinnacle

PRIVATE PARTS AND PIECES VOL.2 (Back To The Pavilion)
CD BP 203CD
Blueprint / Oct '95 / Pinnacle

PRIVATE PARTS AND PIECES VOL.3 (Antiques)
CD BP 204CD
Blueprint / Mar '96 / Pinnacle

PRIVATE PARTS AND PIECES VOL.4 (A Catch At The Tables)
CD BP 205CD
Blueprint / Apr '96 / Pinnacle

PRIVATE PARTS AND PIECES VOL.5 (Twelve)
January / February / March / April / May / June / July / August / September / October / November / December
CD BP 206CD
Blueprint / Apr '96 / Pinnacle

PRIVATE PARTS AND PIECES VOL.6 (Ivory Moon)
Sunrise over Sienna / Basking shark - sea dog's air / Safe havens / Tara's theme / Winter's thaw / Old house / Moonfall / Rapids / Let us now make love
CD BP 207CD
Blueprint / Apr '96 / Pinnacle

PRIVATE PARTS AND PIECES VOL.7
CD BP 208CD
Blueprint / May '96 / Pinnacle

PRIVATE PARTS AND PIECES VOL.8
Aubade / Infra dig / Santuary / La dolorosa / New England suite / New England suite (II) / New England suite (III) / Last goodbyes / Sunrise and sea monsters / Iona / Cathedral woods / If I could tell you / Jaunty roads / Spirals / Pieces of eight (I) Pressgang / Pieces of eight (II) Sargasso / Pieces of eight (III) Sea-shanty / In the maze / Unheard cry / Now they're all gone
CD BP 212CD
Blueprint / May '96 / Pinnacle

PRIVATE PARTS AND PIECES VOL.9
CD BP 229CD
Blueprint / Nov '96 / Pinnacle

SAIL THE WORLD (Music From The Whitbread Race 1994)
Opening theme / Fast work / Dark seas / Cool sailing / Wildlife choir / I wish this would never end / Salsa / Roaring forties / Lonely whales / Icebergs / Majestic whales / In the Southern ocean / Freemantle doctor / Long way from home / Wildlife flotilla / Big combers / Cool sailing II / Cape horn / Amongst mythical birds / Salsa II / Into the tropics / In the doldrums / Heading for home and victory
CD RES 102CD
Resurgence / Apr '97 / Pinnacle

SIDES
CD BP 210CD
Blueprint / Apr '96 / Pinnacle

SLOW DANCE
CD BP 213CD
Blueprint / Mar '96 / Pinnacle

WISE AFTER THE EVENT
CD CDOVD 322
Virgin / '89 / EMI

Phillips, Barre

AQUARIAN RAIN
Bridging / Flow / Ripples edge / Inbetween I and E / Ebb / Promenade de Memoire / Eddies / Early tide / Water shed / Aquarian rain
CD 5115132
ECM / Mar '92 / New Note/Pinnacle

CAMOUFLAGE
CD VICTOCD 08
Victo / Nov '94 / Harmonia Mundi / ReR Megacorp

JOURNAL VIOLONE VOL.2
CD 8473282
ECM / Mar '94 / New Note/Pinnacle

THREE DAY MOON
A-i-a / Ms. P. / La folle / BRD / Ingul-Buz / SC and W
CD 8473262
ECM / Jun '92 / New Note/Pinnacle

Phillips, Brewer

HOME BREW
You don't have to go / For you my love / You're so cold / Hen house boogie / Lunchbucket blues / Don't you want to go home with me / Blue shadows / My baby don't love me no more / Laundromat blues / Looking for a woman / Cross examination / Homebrew / Right now / Tore down / Let the good times roll / Do what you will or may
CD DE 686
Delmark / Jun '97 / ADA / Cadillac / CM / Direct / Hot Shot

Phillips, Chynna

NAKED AND SACRED
Naked and sacred / When 2000 comes / Remember me / I live for you / This close / Till the end / Turn around / Just to hear you say that you love me / Follow love down / Jewel in my crown / Will you
CD CDEMC 3741
EMI / Feb '96 / EMI

Phillips, Eddie

RIFFMASTER OF THE WESTERN WORLD
CD PL 102152
Promised Land / Oct '90 / Direct / Kingdom

Phillips, Esther

BAD BAD GIRL
Ring-a-ding doo / I'm a bad bad girl / Deacon moves in / Looking for a man / Hound dog / Cherry wine / Turn the lamps down low / Flesh blood and bones / Last laugh blues / You took my love too fast / Saturday night daddy / Mainliner / Hollerin' and screamin' / Storm / Ramblin' blues / Aged and mellow blues
CD CDCHARLY 47
Charly / Jan '87 / Koch

CONFESSIN' THE BLUES
I'm gettin' 'long alright / Ronettes / Confessin' the blues / Romance in the dark / CC rider / Cherry red / In the evening / I love Paris / It could happen to you / Bye bye blackbird / Blow top blues / Jelly jelly blues / Long John blues
CD 7567906702
Atlantic / Jul '93 / Warner Music

CONFESSIN' THE BLUES
CD RSACD 807
Sequel / Oct '94 / BMG

LIVE AT THE RISING SUN
CD RS 0007CD
Rising Sun / Jul '95 / ADA

WAY TO SAY GOODBYE, A
It's all in the game / Mama said / Going in circles / Nowhere to run / We are through / Fa fa fa fa fa (sad song) / Mr. Bojangles / Shake this off / Way to say goodbye
CD MCD 5302
Muse / Feb '87 / New Note/Pinnacle

Phillips, Flip

AT THE HELM
CD CRD 327
Chiaroscuro / Mar '96 / Jazz Music

FLIP PHILLIPS AND SCOTT HAMILTON (Phillips, Flip & Scott Hamilton)
CD CCD 4334
Concord Jazz / Dec '87 / New Note/ Pinnacle

FLIP PHILLIPS AT THE HELM 1993
CD CRD 127
Chiaroscuro / Feb '95 / Jazz Music

FLIP WAILS - THE BEST OF THE VERVE YEARS
Zharg blues / Milano / Lover come back to me / Don't take your love from me / Blue room / Flippin' the blues / Dream a little / Dream of me / Funky blues / Cheek to cheek / Salute to Pres / Singin' in the rain / If I had you / Blues for the midgets / I didn't know what time it was / Three little words / Singin' the blues / Lady's in love / You'll never be the same / Music for a stripteaser / Topsy
CD 5216452
Verve / Jun '94 / PolyGram

LIVE AT THE 1986 FLOATING JAZZ FESTIVAL
CD CRD 314
Chiaroscuro / Mar '96 / Jazz Music

TRY A LITTLE TENDERNESS
CD CRD 321
Chiaroscuro / Mar '96 / Jazz Music

Phillips, John

JOHN THE WOLF KING OF LA
CD EDCD 372
Edsel / Nov '92 / Pinnacle

Phillips, Simon

PROTOCOL
Street wise / Protocol / V8 / Red rocks / Slofunk / Wall Street
CD CDGRUB 10
Food For Thought / Dec '88 / Pinnacle

Phillips, Sonny

SURE NUFF/ BLACK MAGIC
Sure nuff sure nuff / Be yourself / Oleo / Mobile to Chicago / Other blues / Make it plain / Wakin' up / Over the rainbow / Bean pie / I'm an old cowhand (from the Rio Grande) / Brotherhood
CD CDBGPD 063
Beat Goes Public / Jun '93 / Pinnacle

Phillips, Steve

BEEN A LONG TIME GONE (Phillips, Steve & The Famous Five)
CD CL 001CD
Clarion / Jul '95 / ADA / Hot Shot

STEEL RAIL BLUES
CD UACD 102
Unamerican Activities / Jan '97 / Hot Shot

Phillips, Stu

JOURNEY THROUGH THE PROVINCES, A
Village blacksmith / Champlain and St. Lawrence line / En roulant ma boule / Donkey riding / Legend of Perce rock / Horse trader / Canadee-i-o / Phantom priest / Dollard les ormeaux / Madelaine De Vecheres / Winter camp / Priest who slept one hundred years / Riverboat captain / Okanagan valley / Simon gun-a-noot / Mountain boy / Bill miner / Cartherine O'Hare Schubert / When the iceworms nest again / Legend of the fernie fire / Grand hotel / Bill Barker's party / Alexander Mackensie / Moon over the rockies / Fraser's valley / Star child / Almighty voice / Albert Johnson / Chief's lament / Ernest Cashel / White stallion legend / Nigger John / Bull train / Banff cave / Fireworks
CD _______________ **BCD 15721**
Bear Family / Aug '93 / Direct / Rollercoaster / Swift

Phillips, Utah

GOOD THOUGH
Cannonball blues / Queen of the rails / Going away / Frisco road / Starlight on the rails / Calling trains / Daddy what's a train / Moose turd pie / Old buddy goodnight / Phoebe Snow / Nickel plate road no.759 / Wabash cannonball/Tolono
CD _______________ **CDPH 1004**
Philo / Feb '97 / ADA / CM / Direct

PAST DIDN'T GO ANYWHERE, THE (Phillips, Utah & Ani Di Franco)
Bridges / Nevada city, California / Korea / Anarchy / Candidacy / Bum on the road / Enormously wealthy / Mess with people / Natural resources / Heroes / Half a ghost town / Holding on
CD _______________ **RBR 009CD**
Righteous Babe / Nov '96 / ADA
CD _______________ **COOKCD 124**
Cooking Vinyl / Apr '97 / Vital

WE HAVE FED YOU ALL A THOUSAND YEARS
Boss / We have fed you all a thousand years / Sheep and goats / Timberbeast's lament / Dump the bosses off your back / Lumberjack's prayer / Mr. Block / Preacher and the slave / Popular wobbly / Casey Jones - the union scab / Where the fraser river flows / Bread and roses / Joe Hill / Union burying ground / Two bums / Hallelujah / I'm a bum / Solidarity forever / There's power in a union
CD _______________ **PHCD 1076**
Philo / May '93 / ADA / CM / Direct

Phillips, Washington

I AM BORN TO PREACH THE GOSPEL
CD _______________ **CD 2003**
Yazoo / Sep '92 / ADA / CM / Koch

Philly Groove Orchestra

SOUNDS OF PHILLY
CD _______________ **HADCD 186**
Javelin / Nov '95 / Henry Hadaway / THE

Philosopher's Stone

PREPERATION
CD _______________ **KRANK 019CD**
Kranky / Jul '97 / Cargo / Greyhound

Phippen, Peter

BOOK OF DREAMS
CD _______________ **CR 7031CD**
Canyon / Nov '96 / ADA

Phish

BILLY BREATHES
CD _______________ **7559619712**
Elektra / Feb '97 / Warner Music

HOIST
CD _______________ **7559616282**
Elektra / Jun '97 / Warner Music

LAWN BOY
CD _______________ **7559612752**
Elektra / Jun '97 / Warner Music

LIVE ONE, A (2CD Set)
CD Set _______________ **7559617772**
Elektra / Jun '97 / Warner Music

PICTURE OF NECTAR, A
Llama / Eliza / Cavern / Poor heart / Stash / Manteca / Guelah papyrus / Magilla / Landlady / Glide / Tweezer / Mango song / Chalk dust torture / Faht / Catapult / Tweezer reprise
CD _______________ **7559612742**
Elektra / Jun '97 / Warner Music

RIFT
CD _______________ **7559614332**
Elektra / Jun '97 / Warner Music

STASH
Stash / Scent of a mule / Maze / Bouncing around the room / Gumbo / Sample in a jar / Split open and melt / Fast enough for you / Down with disease / You enjoy myself / If I could
CD _______________ **7559619332**
Elektra / Jul '96 / Warner Music

Phlebotomized

IMMENSE INTENSE SUSPENSE
CD _______________ **CYBERCD 12**
Cyber / Jan '95 / Amato Disco / Arabesque / Plastic Head

SKYCONTACT
CD _______________ **CYBERCD 20**
Cyber / Apr '97 / Amato Disco / Arabesque / Plastic Head

Phluide

BIFIDUS ACIDOPHILUS
CD _______________ **NRCD 1065**
Nation / May '96 / RTM/Disc

Phobia

RETURN TO DESOLATION
CD _______________ **RR 60932**
Relapse / Oct '94 / Pinnacle / Plastic Head

Phoenix Jig

ST
CD _______________ **SOHO 15CD**
Suburbs Of Hell / Aug '94 / Kudos / Pinnacle / Plastic Head

Phoenix Sax Quartet

RETURN OF BULGY GOGO
Two cod pieces / Dance variations / In memoriam Scott Fitzgerald / Pantomine / In memoriam Django Reinhardt / Patterns / Flying birds / Fugue in G minor / Saxe blue / What then is love / Mock Joplin / Three musical mishaps / Quincey's rag / Return of the pink panther
CD _______________ **URCD 106**
Upbeat / Apr '92 / Cadillac / Target/BMG

Phono Comb

FRESH GASOLINE
CD _______________ **QS 43CD**
Quarter Stick / Oct '96 / Cargo / SRD

Phunk Junkees

INJECTED
CD _______________ **6544925562**
WEA / Sep '95 / Warner Music

Phychodrama

ILLUSION, THE
CD _______________ **MASSCD 079**
Massacre / Nov '95 / Plastic Head

Piaf, Edith

ANTHOLOGIE
CD _______________ **EN 523**
Fremeaux / Feb '96 / ADA / Discovery

CHANSOPHONE 1936-1942
CD _______________ **701272**
Chansophone / Jun '93 / Discovery

DIAMOND COLLECTION, THE
CD _______________ **3004522**
Arcade / Feb '97 / Discovery

EARLY YEARS VOL.1 1936, THE
Hobo girls / Cezigue waltz / Stranger / My aperitif / Stay / Owls / Le fille et le chien / J'uis mordue / Pretty Julie / Even so / Take me for a spin / Go and dance / My lover in the colonial army / Sun was shining / He's not very sophisticated / Two musicians / Smuggler / Songs of the clothes / Little shop
CD _______________ **DRGCD 5561**
DRG / Aug '96 / Discovery / New Note/ Pinnacle

EARLY YEARS VOL.2 1937, THE
CD _______________ **DRGCD 5563**
DRG / Oct '96 / Discovery / New Note/ Pinnacle

EARLY YEARS VOL.3 1938-1945, THE
CD _______________ **DRGCD 5565**
DRG / Nov '96 / Discovery / New Note/ Pinnacle

EARLY YEARS VOL.4 1947-1948, THE
CD _______________ **DRGCD 5569**
DRG / Feb '97 / Discovery / New Note/ Pinnacle

EDITH PIAF AT THE PARIS OLYMPIA
Milord / Heureuse / Avec ce soleil / C'est a Hambourg / Legende / Enfin le printemps / Padam padam / Hymne a l'amour / L'accordeoniste / Mon manege a moi / Bravo pour le clown / Les mots d'amour / Les flons flons du bal / T'es l'homme qu'il me faut / Mon dieu / Mon vieux Lucien / Non, je ne regrette rien / La ville inconnue / La belle histoire d'amour / Les blouses blanches
CD _______________ **CZ 315**
EMI / Jun '90 / EMI

EDITH PIAF IN CONCERT
CD _______________ **3456001**
RTE / Oct '95 / ADA / Koch

EDITH PIAF TRIBUTE (Various Artists)
La vie en rose: *Summer, Donna* / Hymn to love: *Hart, Corey* / Jezebel: *Wilson, Ann* / When I see her: *Scheff, Jason* / Effect you have on me: *Benatar, Pat* / Lovers of one day: *Newton, Juice* / Carousel for two: *Lins, Ivan* / No regret: *Harris, Emmylou* / Three bells: *Russell, Leon* / My legionnaire: *Oslin, K.T.* / Black denim and motorcycle boots: *Spedding, Chris* / In memory
CD _______________ **DSHCD 7014**
D-Sharp / May '94 / Pinnacle

EMBRASSE MOI
Histoire de Coeur / J'ai Qui a L'Regarder / Un Monsieur Me Suit Dans La Rue / Coup de Grisou / Jimmy c'est Lui / Le Java de Cezigue / C'est toi le plus fort / Embrasse moi / On danse sur ma chanson / Entre Saint-Ouen et Clignancourt / Il Riait / Les Marins ca fait des voyages / Dans un Bouge du Vieux Port / C'est un Monsieur tres distingue / C'est Toujours le Meme Histoire / Le disque use / De L'Autre Cote De La Rue / 'Y a Pas D'Printemps / Quand Meme / 'Chand D'Habits
CD _______________ **MDF 102603**
Mudisque / Nov '96 / Target/BMG

ETOILES DE LA CHANSON VOL.1 1935-1942
CD _______________ **878162**
Music Memoria / Jun '93 / ADA / Discovery

ETOILES DE LA CHANSON VOL.2
CD _______________ **8414762**
Music Memoria / Sep '96 / ADA / Discovery

HER GREATEST RECORDINGS 1935-1942
Mon legionnaire / Un coin tout bleu / Mon coeur est au coin d'une rue / Le grand voyage du pauvre negre / Ballade de Mr. Browning / D'etait une histoire d'amour / On danse sur ma chanson / De l'autre cote de la rue / C'est toi le plus fort / Fais-moi valser / Paris - Mediterranee / Mon apero / Le fanion de la legion / Mon amant de la coloniale / Entre se ouen et clignancourt / L'etranger / C'etait un jour de fete / Les momes de la cloche / Elle frequentait la rue pigalle / C'est lui que mon coeur a choisi / L'accordeoniste
CD _______________ **CDAJA 5165**
Living Era / Apr '95 / Select

HYMN TO LOVE (Greatest Hits In English)
Hymn to love / One little man / La vie en rose / Chante moi / Simply a waltz / My God / Don't cry / Autumn leaves / I shouldn't care / Three bells / 'Cause I love you / My lost melody / Heaven have mercy / No regrets / Lovers for a day / Heureuse
CD _______________ **PRMCD 4**
Premier/EMI / May '96 / EMI

L'IMMORTELLE
La vie en rose / Les trois cloches / Hymne a l'amour / Mon dieu / Jezebel / Le noel de la rue / Padam padam / La chanson de Catherine / Bravo pour le clown / Johnny tu n'es pas un ange / Heureuse / La goualante du pauvre Jean / Enfin le printemps / L'accordeoniste / Le chant d'amour / C'est a Hambourg / Les amants d'un jour / La foule / Mon manege a moi / Milord / La ville inconnue / A quoi ca sert l'amour / Le diable de la Bastille / Non, je ne regrette rien
CD _______________ **CDEMC 3674**
EMI / Sep '96 / EMI

LA BELLE HISTOIRE D'AMOUR
Non, je ne regrette rien / Quoi ca sert l'amour / La vie en rose / Les amants d'un jour / La foule / Heureuse / Mon dieu / Milord / Mon manege a moi / Les mots d'amour / C'est a Hambourg / Comme moi / Le droit d'aimer / Les feuilles mortes / Bravo pour le clown / AU bal de la chance / Je t'ai dans la peau / Monsieur et madam / Padam..padam / Soeur Anne / Johnny tu n'es pas un ange / Hymne a l'amour / La fete continue / Dany / Il pleut / Les flons flons du bal (live) / La goualante du pauvre Jean / L'accordeoniste / Un refrain courait dans le rue / Bal dans ma rue / La rue aux chansons / Le noel de la rue / Notre dame de Paris / Sous le ciel de Paris / Serenade du pave / Marie trottoir / Les orges de barbarie / Kiosque a journaux / La ville inconnue / Boulevard du crime / Le bruit des ville / Les gens
CD Set _______________ **SA 872742**
Disky / Sep '96 / Disky / THE

LA MOME EARLY RECORDINGS 1936-44
CD _______________ **PASTCD 7068**
Flapper / Apr '95 / Pinnacle

LA MOME PIAF
CD _______________ **105012**
Musidisc / Mar '90 / Discovery

LA MOME PIAF VOL.1
Les momes de la cloche / L'etranger / Reste / La fille et le chien / La julie jolie / Moi valser / Mon amant de la coloniale / Il n'est pas distingue / La java de cezique / Mon apero / Les hiboux / Je suis mordue / Fais / Va danser / Y avaid du soleil / Les deux menetriers
CD _______________ **104 552**
Musidisc / Mar '90 / Discovery

LA MOME PIAF VOL.2
Mon legionnaire / Chants d'habits / Entre saint - queen et clingnancourt / Browning / Un jeune homme chantait / Le fanion de la legion / Tout fout le camp le chacal / Madeleine qu'avait du coeur / Le contrebandier / La petite boutique / Correcq et reguyer / Paris mediterranee / C'est toi le plus fort / Ding din dong / Le chacal
CD _______________ **104 562**
Musidisc / Mar '90 / Discovery

LA MOME PIAF VOL.3
CD _______________ **104 572**
Musidisc / Mar '90 / Discovery

LA RUE PIGALLE
Ne m'ecris pas / Le Petit Monsieur Triste / Elle frequentait la Rue Pigalle / Correqu' et Reguyer / Le Contrebandier / Browning / Ding din don / Le Chacal / Le Grand Voyage du Pauvre Negre / Je n'en connais pas la Fin / Les Deux Copains / L'Accordeoniste / J'ai Danse avec l'Amour / Ou sont-ils Mes Petits Copains / C'es la Moindre des Choses / C'etait un Jour de Fete / Simple comme Bonjour / Un Coin Tout Blue / Le Vagabond / C'etait une Histoire d'Amour
CD _______________ **MDF 102606**
Mudisque / Nov '96 / Target/BMG

LA VIE EN ROSE 1940-1946
CD _______________ **PASTCD 7820**
Flapper / Sep '97 / Pinnacle

LEGENDARY EDITH PIAF, THE
Heureuse / Non, Je ne regrette rien / La goualante du pauvre Jean / Padam padam / L'accordeoniste / La vie en rose / Les amants d'un jour / A quoi ca sert l'amour / Mon manege a moi / La foule / Les mots d'amour / Comme moi / Le droit d'aimer / Les feuilles mortes / Les flons flons du bal / Enfin le printemps / Mon dieu / C'est a Hambourg / Milord / Hymne a l'amour
CD _______________ **CDMFP 6071**
Music For Pleasure / Jun '89 / EMI

LITTLE SPARROW OF FRANCE
L'accoreoniste / Y'a pas d'printemps / Tu es partout / Le disque use / De L'autre cote de la rue / Le vagabond / C'etait une histoire d'amour / C'etait un jour de fete / J'ai danse avec l'amour / Jen'en connais pas le fin / Le petit monsieur triste / Elle frequentait la rue Pigalle / C'est lui que mon coeur a choisi / Le grand voyage du pouvre negre / Mon legonnaire / Paris Mediterrannee / Les mames de la cloche
CD _______________ **995762**
EPM / Apr '97 / ADA / Discovery

MON LEGIONNAIRE
Fas-Moi Vaiser / La Julie Jolie / Mon Amant de la Coloniale / Les deux Menetriers / Les Momes de la Cloche / L'Etranger / Mon Apero / Les Hiboux / Reste / J'suis Mordue / Va Danser / Le Fille et le Chien / 'Y avit du Soleil / Il n'est pas Distingue / Mon Legionnaire / Un Jeune Homme Chantait / Paris-Mediterranee / C'est Lui que mon Coeur a Choisi / Le Fanion de la Legion / Le Mauvais Matelot
CD _______________ **MDF 102605**
Mudisque / Nov '96 / Target/BMG

NON JE NE REGRETTE RIEN
CD _______________ **CD 0201**
Entertainers / Mar '92 / Target/BMG

SUCCES ET RARETES 1936-1945
CD _______________ **701602**
Chansophone / Nov '96 / Discovery

Piano Red

ATLANTA BOUNCE
CD _______________ **ARHCD 379**
Arhoolie / Apr '95 / ADA / Cadillac / Direct

BLUES BLUES BLUES
CD _______________ **BLCD 760181**
Black Lion / Apr '93 / Cadillac / Jazz Music / Koch / Wellard

DOCTOR IS IN, THE (4CD Set)
Jumpin' the boogie / Rockin' with Red / Let's have a time tonight / Red's boogie / Right string baby, but the wrong yo-yo / My gal Jo / Baby, what's wrong / Well, well baby / Just right bounce / Diggin' the boogie / Layin' the boogie / Bouncin' with Red / It makes no difference now / Hey good lookin' / Count the days I'm gone / My boogie / Sales tax boogie / Voo doopee doo / Daybreak / She walks right in / I'm gonna tell everybody / I'm gonna rock some more / She's dynamite / Everybody's boogie / Your mouth's got a hole in it / Right and ready / Taxi, taxi 6963 / Decatur Street boogie / Sober / She knocks me out / Going away baby / Chitlin' hop / Decatur Street blues / I ain't fattenin' frogs for snakes / Big rock Joe from Kokomo / Play it no mind / Jump man jump / Do she love me / Peach tree parade / Red's blues / Six o'clock bounce / Jumpin' with daddy / Gordy's rock / Real good thing / Goodbye/Please tell me baby / You were mine for a while / Sweetest little something / Since I fell for you / Wooee / Rock baby / Teach me to forget / Wild fire / Please don't talk about me when I'm gone / South / Coo cha / Dixie roll / Boston scored / One glimpse of heaven / Blues blues / Work with it / Eighter from Decatur / Please come back home / Comin' on / Ain't nobody's fool / Don't get around much

anymore / Umph-umph-umph / Got you on my mind / It's time to boogie / That's my desire / Teen-age bounce / Pay it no mind / Get up mare / 1-2-3 / My baby / Rock 'n' roll boogie / Nighttime / So worried / Blues, blues / Boogie re-bop / This old world / I feel good / Talk to me / Believe in me / Guitar walk / I've been rockin' / So shook up / Dr. Feelgood / Mr. Moonlight / Swabble / I'll be home one day / Sea breeze / I ain't gonna be a lowdown log no more / Don't let me catch you wrong / What's up doc / I'll give anything / Love is amazing / Bald headed Lena / It's a sin to tell a lie / Same old things keep happening / My gal Joe / Blang dong / I don't mind / Doctor's boogie / Let the house rock on / Doctor of love / It's sin to tell a lie / Good guys / Goodbye (I can't forget) / Don't tell me no dirty / Where did you go
CD Set BCD 15685
Bear Family / Nov '93 / Direct / Rollercoaster / Swift

PIANO 'C' RED
CD 422399
Last Call / Feb '97 / Cargo / Direct / Discovery

Pianorama

CHRISTMAS CRACKER, A
Jingle bells medley / Sleigh ride / Home for the holidays / It's beginning to look like Christmas / Snowy white snow and jingle bells / Hark the herald angels sing / Silent night / Winter wonderland / I saw Mommy kissing Santa Claus / Mistletoe and holly medley / Christmas song / Does Santa Claus sleep with his whiskers / Once upon a wintertime/Mary's boy child / White Christmas / God rest ye merry gentlemen
CD DLCD 112
Dulcima / Nov '95 / Savoy / THE

LET YOURSELF GO
Let's face the music and dance / Is it true what they say about dixie / You brought a new kind of love / Swinging down the lane
CD DLCD 111
Dulcima / Sep '91 / Savoy / THE

SENSATIONAL SIXTIES, THE
CD DLCD 108
Dulcima / Sep '90 / Savoy / THE

SHOW TIME IN DANCE TIME
Put me on a happy face/Me and my girl / Lambeth walk / On the street where you live/Dancing on the ceiling/If I rul / Mr. Snow/If I loved you/When the children are asleep / There's a small hotel / I'm gonna wash that man right outa my hair / I whistle a happy tune/Shall we dance/I want to be happy / Glamorous night/Waltz of my heart / Someday I'll find you/I'll see you again / Anything you can do / Surrey with the fringe on top / There's no business like shoe business / Best of times/June is bustin' out all over / We kiss in a shadow/I have dreamed / Bewitched, bothered and bewildered / Wonderful guy/Wunderbar / They say it's wonderful/I won't send roses/Younger than spri / Edelweiss/This nearly was mine / Why do I love you/People will say we're in love/ Doi' what co
CD DLCD 114
Dulcima / May '94 / Savoy / THE

WARTIME FAVOURITES
We're gonna hang out the washing on the Siegfried line / Run rabbit run / Hey little hen / Let the people sing / I've got sixpence / Roll out the barrel / Praise the lord and pass the ammunition / Mairzy doats and dozy doats / In the quartermaster's stores / I left my heart at the stage door canteen / If I had my way / I don't want to set the world on fire / You are my sunshine / Sgt Major's serenade / Don't sit under the apple tree / Dearly beloved / I'll be seeing you / Something to remember you by / Sailor with the navy blue eyes / Coming in on a wing and a prayer / I'm gonna get lit up (when the lights go on in London) / Fleet's in / That lovely weekend / Room 504 / Nightingale sang in Berkeley Square / It's foolish but it's fun / Elmer's tune / Lili Marlene / Yours / Jingle jangle / Deep in the heart of Texas / Oh Johnny oh / Wishing (will make it so) / Tangerine / Long ago and far away / Our love affair / It's a lovely day tomorrow / Wish me good luck as you wave goodbye / Kiss me goodnight, Sergeant Major / Nursie nursie / Ma, I miss your apple pie / You'll never know / Beneath the lights of home / Silver wings in the moonlight / Moonlight becomes you / When the lights go on again / All over the place / Down forget-me-not lane / White cliffs of Dover / We'll meet again
CD DLCD 106
Dulcima / Apr '95 / Savoy / THE

Pianosauras

GROOVY NEIGHBOURHOOD
CD ROUCD 9010
Rounder / '88 / ADA / CM / Direct

Piazza, Rod

BLUES IN THE DARK (Piazza, Rod & The Mighty Flyers)
CD BT 1062CD
Black Top / '92 / ADA / CM / Direct

CALIFORNIA BLUES
Chicken shack boogie / Bad bad boy / No more pretty presents / California blues / One mint julep / Worried life blues / Deep fried / Can't get that stuff no more / 4811 Wadsworth (aka blues for George) / It's too late brother / Low down dog
CD CDBTEL 7001
Black Top / Mar '97 / ADA / CM / Direct

HARPBURN
CD BT 1087CD
Black Top / Apr '93 / ADA / CM / Direct

LIVE AT BB KING'S, MEMPHIS (Piazza, Rod & The Mighty Flyers)
CD BIGMO 1026
Big Mo / Jul '94 / ADA / Direct

TOUGH AND TENDER (Piazza, Rod & The Mighty Flyers)
Power of the blues / Quicksand / Tough and tender / Sea of fools / She can't say no / Teaser / Blues and trouble / Under the big top / Scary boogie / Hang ten boogie / Searchin' for a fortune
CD CDTC 1165
Tonecool / Jul '97 / ADA / Direct

Piazzolla, Astor

5 TANGO SENSATIONS (Piazzolla, Astor & Kronos Quartet)
CD 7599792542
Nonesuch / Jan '95 / Warner Music

57 MINUTOS CON LA REALIDAD
Images / Milonga paras tres / Buenos Aires Huha Cero / Pasajes obscuras dos estellas / Tres minutus con la realidad / Mumuki / Sexteto / Adios nunino / Prelude to the cynical night (part 2)
CD INT 30792
Intuition / May '96 / New Note/Pinnacle

ADIOS NONINO
CD CD 12508
Music Of The World / Nov '92 / ADA / Target/BMG

ASTOR PIAZZOLLA
CD Set 74321342672
Milan / Jul '96 / Conifer/BMG / Silva Screen

ASTOR PIAZZOLLA - A FLUTE AND PIANO TRIBUTE (De La Vega & Franzetti)
CD 74321333282
Milan / Jun '96 / Conifer/BMG / Silva Screen

BALADA PARA UN LOCO AMELITA
CD CD 3508
Cameo / Nov '95 / Target/BMG

BANDONEON SINFONICO
CD 74321342682
Milan / Jul '96 / Conifer/BMG / Silva Screen

CONCERTO FOR BANDONEON & ORCHESTRA
CD 7559791742
Nonesuch / Jan '95 / Warner Music

EL NUEVO TANGO DE BUENOS AIRES
CD 74321342702
Milan Sur / Feb '97 / Conifer/BMG

G-STRING QUARTET PLAYS ASTOR PIAZZOLLA (G-String Quartet)
Michelangelo '70 / Milonga for three / Butcher's death / Marejadilla / Tango apasionado / La camorra II / Milonga del angel / Fugo 9 / Verano del '79 / Coral
CD CD 364232
Koch Schwann / Aug '96 / Koch

LA CAMORRA
La Camorra 1 / La Camorra 2 / La Camorra 3 / Soledad / Fugata / Sur: Los Suenos / Sur: Regresso al amor
CD AMCL 1021CD
American Clave / Jan '94 / ADA / Direct / New Note/Pinnacle

LATE MASTERPIECES (Tango-Zero Hour/Rough Dancer/La Camorra 3CD Set)
Tanguedia III / Milonga del angel / Concierto para quinteto / Milonga loca / Michelangelo '70 / Contrabajissimo / Mumuki / Prologue tango apasionado / Milonga for three / Street tango / Milonga picaresque / Knife fight / Leonara's song / Butcher's death / Leijia's game / Milonga for three (reprise) / Bailongo / Leonora's love theme / Finale (tango apasionada) / Prelude to the cyclical night part 2 / Soledad / Camorra / Camorra II / Camorra III / Fugata / Sur - los Suenos / Sur - regresso al amor
CD Set AMCL 10222
American Clave / Feb '97 / ADA / Direct / New Note/Pinnacle

LIBERTANGO
Libertango / Meditango / Undertango / Adios nonino / Violentango / Novi tango / Amelitango / Tristango
CD CD 62037
Saludos Amigos / Nov '93 / Target/BMG

LIBERTANGO
CD 68904
Tropical / May '97 / Discovery

LIVE IN VIENNA
Fracanapa / Verano Porteno / Caliente / Decarisimo / Libertango / Revirado / Invierno porteno / Adois nonino
CD 159222
Ronnie Scott's Jazz House / Jun '89 / Cadillac / Jazz Music / New Note/Pinnacle / TKO Magnum

LOS TANGUEROS (The Tangos Of Astor Piazzolla) (Ax, Emanuel & Pablo Ziegler)
Michelangelo / Milonga del angel / Tangata / Revirado / Verano portano / Soledad / Libertango / La muerta del angel / Decarissimo / Fuga y misterio / Adios nonino / Buenos Aires hors o
CD SK 62728
Sony Classical / Jan '97 / Sony

LUMIERE
Solitude / Mort / Lumiere / L'evasion / Bandoneon / Zita / Whisky / Escolaso
CD 68942
Tropical / May '97 / Discovery

LUNA (Piazzolla, Astor & The New Tango Sextet)
Hora cero / Tanguedia 3 / Milonga del angel / Camorra 3 / Preludio y fuga / Sex-tet / Luna
CD CDEMC 3723
Hemisphere / Oct '95 / EMI

MILONGA DEL ANGEL
CD CD 62036
Saludos Amigos / Oct '93 / Target/BMG

PARIS 1955
CD 3017742
Arcade / Feb '97 / Discovery

PERSEUCTA AND BIYUYA
CD 68943
Tropical / May '97 / Discovery

PIAZZOLLA AND BORGES (Piazzolla, Astor & Jorge Luis Borges)
El Tango / Jacinto Chiclana / Alquien le Dice al Tango / El Titere Milonga / A Don Nicanor Paredes / Oda Intima a Buenos Aires / El Hombre de la Esquina Rosada
CD 74321459712
Milan / Apr '97 / Conifer/BMG / Silva Screen

PIAZZOLLISSIMO 1974-1983
CD Set JAM 9103/52
Just A Memory / Mar '92 / New Note/ Pinnacle

ROUGH DANCER AND THE CYCLICAL NIGHT
CD AMCL 1019CD
American Clave / Jan '94 / ADA / Direct / New Note/Pinnacle

SADNESS OF A DOUBLE A, THE
CD 15970
Messidor / Apr '89 / ADA / Koch

SPIRIT OF BUENOS AIRES, THE
CD MAN 4891
Mandala / Dec '96 / ADA / Harmonia Mundi / Mandala

TANGAMENTE
CD Set JAM 9107/92
Just A Memory / Sep '93 / New Note/ Pinnacle

TANGO CATOLICO
CD ARNR 0894
Amiata / Jul '97 / Harmonia Mundi

TANGO PIAZZOLLA
CD MCCD 165
Music Club / Jul '94 / Disc / THE

TANGO: ZERO HOUR
Tanguedia III / Milonga del angel / Concierto para quinteto / Milonga loca / Michelangelo '70 / Countrabajissimo / Mumuki
CD AMCL 1013CD
American Clave / Jan '94 / ADA / Direct / New Note/Pinnacle

TANGOS FOR FLUTE AND GUITAR (Gallois, Patrick & Goran Sollscher)
Histoire du tango for flute and guitar / 4 estaciones portens for guitar / 6 tango etudes for flute / Tango no.2
CD 4491852
Deutsche Grammophon / May '97 / PolyGram

TANGUEDIA
CD CD 62010
Saludos Amigos / Oct '93 / Target/BMG

TRIDEZAS DE UN DOBLE A (Piazzolla, Astor Quinteto)
CD MES 159702
Messidor / Dec '92 / ADA / Koch

VERANO PORTENO
CD ENTCD 286
Entertainers / Mar '92 / Target/BMG

VIENNA CONCERT
CD MES 159222
Messidor / Jan '92 / ADA / Koch

Piazzolla, Daniel

DANIEL PIAZZOLLA Y SU OCTETO (Piazzolla, Daniel Y Su Octeto)
Violentango / El Diego / Romance del diablo / Mi viejo Piazzolla / Verano porteno / Tanti anni prima / Libertango / Los amantes / Lalla / Adios nonino
CD 74321383422
Milan / Aug '96 / Conifer/BMG / Silva Screen

Pic & Bill

TAKING UP THE SLACK
CD BAN 4109CD
Haven / Sep '91 / Pinnacle / Shellshock/ Disc

Picasso Trigger

BIPOLAR COWBOY
Serve this / Jack rabbit / Hod rod luvr / Towel song / Narcon milk shakes on sale today / Fried fish and cole slaw / Coco w / Skimmed milk / OCS / Reverend Money Waters / Club joiner / T-rash soundtrack for a t-rash heart / Jiminy slim / Riot girls taste like chicken / Let you down / Jerry bomber / City slut slander / You are / Carteret country castes / Buckshot goodbyes
CD A 081D
Alias / Aug '95 / Vital

FIRE IN THE HOLE
Rub a dub / Expect / Valentine / Get up / Matarcher / Beanpole / Sheltie / We're going down / Man's fault / Remind us / Queenie / TV mind / Mi lapizes muy grande / Colossal man / Count to ten
CD A 056D
Alias / Mar '94 / Vital

T'AIN'T
Lo-fi Tennesse mountain angel / 455 / Infinite belching boy / Red headed retard / Kiss me where it counts / Anti'd
CD A 077D
Alias / Jan '95 / Vital

Piccadilly Dance Orchestra

HAPPY DAYS ARE HERE AGAIN
CD MCCD 240
Music Club / Mar '96 / Disc / THE

SHALL WE DANCE
CD VIRCD 8326
TER / Mar '94 / Koch

Piccolo, Greg

HEAVY JUICE
Hammer / Baby I'm gone / Bolo blues / Freeze / It's obdacious / Mushmouth / Brother Jug's sermon / Plaid laces / Count your blessings / Highballin' daddy / Hawk's barrel house / Pic's gospel groove / Big boss man
CD FIENDCD 202
Demon / Oct '90 / Pinnacle

Pickens, Jo Ann

PRAISE HIM LIVE (Pickens, Jo Ann & M. Boungou)
CD FA 416
Fremeaux / Feb '97 / ADA / Discovery

Pickett, Dan

DAN PICKETT/SLIM TARHEEL 1949 (Pickett, Dan & Slim Tarheel)
Baby how long: *Pickett, Dan* / You got to do better: *Pickett, Dan* / Ride to funeral: *Pickett, Dan* / Decoration day: *Pickett, Dan* / Drivin' that thing: *Pickett, Dan* / That's grieving me: *Pickett, Dan* / Chicago blues: *Pickett, Dan* / Somebody changed the lock: *Tarheel Slim* / You're a little too slow: *Tarheel Slim* / Get on the road to glory: *Tarheel Slim*
CD FLYCD 25
Flyright / Oct '90 / Hot Shot / Jazz Music / Wellard

Pickett, Lenny

LENNY PICKETT & THE BORNEO HORNS (Pickett, Lenny & The Borneo Horns)
Dance music for Borneo Horns (1-5) / Solo for saxaphone / Septer / Dance suite / Landscape
CD HNCD 1321
Hannibal / May '89 / ADA / Vital

Pickett, Wilson

BEST OF WILSON PICKETT, THE
In the midnight hour / 634 5789 / I found a love / Mustang Sally / Ninety nine and a half (won't do) / Everybody needs somebody to love / Don't fight it / I'm a midnight mover / Funky Broadway / Soul dance number three / I'm in love / Land of a 1000 dances
CD 7567812832
Atlantic / Sep '94 / Warner Music

GREATEST HITS
CD 7567817372
Atlantic / Mar '93 / Warner Music

HEY JUDE
Save me / Hey Jude / Back in your arms / Toe hold / Night owl / My own style of loving / Man and a half / Sit down and talk this over / Search your heart / Born to be wild / People make the world
CD 7567803752
Atlantic / Jan '96 / Warner Music

I'M IN LOVE
Jealous love / Stagger Lee / That kind of love / I'm in love / Hello sunshine / Don't cry no more / We've got to have love / Bring it on home / She is looking good / I've come a long way
CD 8122722182
Atlantic / Jan '96 / Warner Music

IF YOU NEED ME
Baby don't weep no more for me / Down to my last heartbreak / I can't stop / Baby call on me / If you need me / Peace breaker / RB Special / I'm gonna love you / I'll never be the same / Give your lovin' right now
CD CWNCD 2018
Javelin / Jul '96 / Henry Hadaway / THE

IN PHILADELPHIA
CD 8122722192
Atlantic / Jan '96 / Warner Music

IN THE MIDNIGHT HOUR
In the midnight hour / Terdrops will fall / Take a little love / For better or worse / I found a love / That's a man's way / I'm gonna cry / Don't fight it / Take this love I've got / Come home baby / I'm not tired / Let's kiss and make up
CD 8122712752
Atlantic / Jul '94 / Warner Music

MAN AND A HALF, A (The Best Of Wilson Pickett/2CD Set)
I found a love / Let me be your boy / If you need me / It's too late / I'm gonna cry / Come home baby / In the midnight hour / Don't fight it / I'm not tired / That's a man's way / 634 5789 / Ninety nine and a half (won't do) / Land of 1000 dances / Mustang Sally / Three time loser / Everybody needs somebody to love / Soul dance number three / You can't stand alone / Funky broadway / Fire and water / Call my name, I'll be there / Don't let the green grass fool you / Get me back on time / Cole, Cooke and Redding / She said yes / You keep me hangin' on / Hey Joe / Toe hold / Mini skirt Minnie / Hey Jude / Man and a half / She's looking good / I found a true love / I'm a midnight mover / I've come a long way / Jealous love / Stagger / I'm in love
CD Set 8122702872
Atlantic / Jul '93 / Warner Music

VERY BEST OF WILSON PICKETT, THE
In the midnight hour / 634 5789 / Land of 1000 dances / Mustang Sally / Funky broadway / I'm in love / She's looking good / Hey Jude / Sugar sugar / Engine No.9 / Don't let the green grass fool you / Don't knock my love / Fire and water / I'm a midnight mover / I found a love / Everybody needs somebody to love
CD 8122712122
Atlantic / Jun '93 / Warner Music

Picketts

EUPHONIUM
Good good wife / Action speaks louder than words / Just passin' through / Baba O'Riley / Night fell / House made from cards / Should I stay or should I go / Seven / Overworked overloaded underpaid / I can't close my eyes / Same town, same planet (different world)
CD ROUCD 9056
Rounder / Oct '96 / ADA / CM / Direct

WICKED PICKETTS, THE
CD ROUCD 9046
Rounder / Aug '95 / ADA / CM / Direct

Pickford, Andy

DYSTOPIA
Cephalostral / Dreifarbig bomber / Angstrom / Girl from planet X / Overlander / May / Furnace / Last sundown / Chase / Belvedere / Sundance / Sayonara
CD CENCD 014
Centaur / May '97 / Pinnacle

MAELSTROM
Voyager / Cathedral / Blue world / Tetsuo / Synbiosis / Raumfahre / Oblivion / Hell's gate
CD CENCD 010
Centaur / Apr '95 / Pinnacle

REPLICANT
Relicant / Blonde is a suitcase / Questions / No one can hear you / Adios amigos / Wasted / Zweifarbig bomber / Cloudwatching / Sayonara
CD CENCD 004
Centaur / Oct '93 / Pinnacle

TERRAFORMER
Terraformer / Mesmereyes / Summers past / Akira / Djangotron / Out of the darkness / Get dyson / Darklands (don't be afraid) / Asgard / Twilight in Valhalla / Furnace / Still waters (run deep)
CD CENCD 008
Centaur / Jun '94 / Pinnacle

XENOMORPH
CD SER 010
Something Else / Jun '96 / Pinnacle

Picture House

SHINE BOX
Heavenly day / Somebody somewhere / Do I believe you / Fear of flying / Don't believe me / World and his dog / Fan club / 15th Time / Moments like these / Worldwide TV / I know better now / Empty nest
CD 336112
Koch International / Nov '96 / Koch

Pictures Of Tom

RIDICULOUS POSITIONS
CD BAH 19
Humbug / Aug '94 / Total/Pinnacle

Pidgeon, Rebecca

NY GIRL'S CLUB
CD CHECD 141
Chesky / Mar '96 / Discovery / Goldring

Pie Finger

DALI SURPRISE, A
CD CRELPCD 122
Creation / Apr '92 / 3mv/Vital

Piece Dogs

EYES FOR EYES
CD RR 90582
Roadrunner / May '93 / PolyGram

Pieces Of A Dream

BEST OF PIECES OF A DREAM, THE
Intro / Club jazz / Keep it smooth / Baby it's your turn now / Cool side / My love / For you / Mt Airy Groove / Rising to the top / Fo-fi-fo / Warm weather / 'Round midnight / Shadow of your smile / Si Lala
CD CDP 8358002
Blue Note / Apr '96 / EMI

Pied Pipers

GOOD DEAL MACNEAL 1944-1946
Gotta be this or that / I'll buy that dream / Come rain or come shine / Easy street / There's good blues tonight / Linger in my arms / Aren't you glad you're you / It's only a paper moon / Route 66 / Sentimental journey / Just a-sittin' and a-rockin' / Doin' what comes natur'lly
CD HEPCD 33
Hep / Aug '96 / Cadillac / Jazz Music / New Note/Pinnacle / Wellard

Pied Pipers

SCOTTISH & IRISH MUSIC
CD EUCD 1009
ARC / Sep '93 / ADA / ARC Music

Pieranunzi, Enrico

ISIS (Pieranunzi, Enrico Quartet & Quintet)
CD 1210212
Soul Note / Jan '94 / Cadillac / Harmonia Mundi / Wellard

NO MAN'S LAND (Pieranunzi, Enrico Trio)
CD 1212212
Soul Note / Oct '90 / Cadillac / Harmonia Mundi / Wellard

Pierce, Billie

NEW ORLEANS-THE LIVING LEGENDS (Pierce, Billie & Joseph 'De De')
CD OBCCD 534
Original Blues Classics / Nov '92 / Complete/Pinnacle / Wellard

ONE FOR CHUCK
CD SSC 1053D
Sunnyside / Nov '91 / Discovery

Pierce, Dede

DEDE & BILLIE PIERCE VOL.1 (Pierce, Dede & Billie)
CD AMCD 79
American Music / Nov '96 / Jazz Music

DEDE & BILLIE PIERCE VOL.2 (Pierce, Dede & Billie)
CD AMCD 80
American Music / Nov '96 / Jazz Music

DEDE PIERCE STOMPERS VOL.1
CD AMCD 81
American Music / Feb '95 / Jazz Music

DEDE PIERCE STOMPERS VOL.2
CD AMCD 82
American Music / Feb '95 / Jazz Music

Pierce, Hubbell

HUBBELL PIERCE & WILLIAM ROY SING AND PLAY COLE PORTER (Pierce, Hubbell & William Roy)
CD ACD 110
Audiophile / Nov '96 / Jazz Music

Pierce, Jeffrey Lee

RAMBLIN' JEFFREY LEE & CYPRESS GROVE
CD 527901220
Solid / Jun '93 / Plastic Head / Vital

Pierce, Joshua

PORTRAIT OF BROADWAY, A (Pierce, Joshua & Dorothy Jonas)
CD CDPC 5003
Prestige / Aug '90 / Else / Total/BMG

Pierce, Nat

5400 NORTH (Pierce, Nat Quintet)
5400 north / Pee Wee's blues / Loverman if I had you / Detour ahead / Love begins / Sweet Lorraine / Sweet and lovely / Blue Lou / There will never be another you / Foggy day (in London town) / Sign off
CD HEPCD 2004
Hep / Sep '96 / Cadillac / Jazz Music / New Note/Pinnacle / Wellard

BALLAD OF JAZZ STREET, THE
Pretty little girl / Melancholy baby / Black Jack / Soulville / Sister Sade / Ballad of Jazz Street
CD HEPCD 2009
Hep / Apr '97 / Cadillac / Jazz Music / New Note/Pinnacle / Wellard

BOSTON BUST OUT, THE
What can I say (after I'm sorry) / You were meant for me / King Edward the flatted fifth / That's the kinda girl / What's new / Paradise / Pat / Sheba
CD HEPCD 13
Hep / Nov '95 / Cadillac / Jazz Music / New Note/Pinnacle / Wellard

Pierce, Webb

HONKY TONK SONG
CD CTS 55423
Country Stars / Jun '94 / Target/BMG

KING OF THE HONKY-TONK
CD CMFCD 019
Country Music Foundation / Sep '94 / ADA / Direct

WONDERING BOY 1951-1958, THE (4CD Set)
Drifting Texas sand / If crying would make you care / California blues / You scared the love right out of me / New silver bells / Wondering / You know I'm still in love with you / I'm gonna see my baby / That heart belongs to me / I just can't be true / So used to loving you / I haven't got the heart / I'll always take care of you / Backstreet affair / I'm only wishin' / Slowly / Last waltz / Bow thy head / Country church / I'll go on alone / That's me without you / Broken engagement / We'll find a way / It's been so long / Don't throw your life away / Too late to worry now / There stands the glass / There's a better home / Mother call my name in prayer / I'm walking the dog / You just can't be true / Slowly / Broken engagement / Slowly / Even tho' / Sparkling brown eyes / Bugle call from Heaven / Thank you dear Lord / Kneel at the cross / Leaning on the everlasting arms / You're not mine anymore / I'm gonna fall out of love with you / Your good for nothing heart / Just imagination / I love you dear / More and more / I found someone that's true / Waltz you saved for me / One day later / In the jailhouse now / Sneakin' all around / I don't care / Just how long / Why baby why / Yes I know why / I found a true love / Because I love you / Little Rosa / Let forgiveness in / Any old time / You make love to everyone / Teenage boogie / I'm really glad you hurt me / Teenage boogie / Oh so many years / One week later / When I'm with you / Can I find it in your heart / Crying over you / I'm tired / It's my way / Someday / Honky tonk song / I care no more / Bye bye love / Missing you / Let forgiveness in / Who wouldn't love you / New panhandle rag / I know it was you / Don't do it darlin' / Holiday for love / How long / New raunchy / I'll get by somehow / English sweetheart / Down Panama way / Foreign love / You'll come back / New love affair / Falling back to me / Sittin' alone / I'm letting you go / Tupelo County jail / Waiting a lifetime / True love never dies / I think of you / I won't be cryin' anymore / I owe it to my heart / Violet and a rose / After the boy gets the girl / You make me live again / Crazy arms / Pick me up on your way down / Life to go / My shoes keep walking back to you
CD Set BCD 15522
Bear Family / Sep '90 / Direct / Rollercoaster / Swift

Pierre, Cameron

ABOUT TIME (IT HAPPENED)
Friday night / Rejoicing / Didi's groove / Linstead market / God's gift / If only / Time / Kayas la / Never be lonely
CD OKCD 01
Okou / Oct '96 / New Note/Pinnacle

Pierre, Marie

LOVE AFFAIR
Choose me / Can't go through (with life) / I believe / Somebody else's man / Nothing gained (for loving you) / Humanity / Rowing / My best friend / Walk away / Over reacting
CD CDTRL 177
Trojan / Nov '95 / Direct / Jet Star

Pierron, Gerard

GASTON COUTE
CD LDX 274947
La Chant Du Monde / Nov '92 / ADA / Harmonia Mundi

Pierrot Premier

ORANGE CLOUDS
CD HE 007
Home Entertainment / Dec '96 / Cargo

Pietro, Dave

FORGOTTEN DREAMS
Forgotten dreams / Winter of discontent / Pheonix rising / Lighthouse / Mutability / If I should lose you / Vortex / Karuna
CD AL 73049
A / Nov '96 / Cadillac / Direct

Pig

POKE IN THE EYE, A
CD EFA 2228CD
Yellow / Feb '89 / SRD

PRAISE THE LARD
CD CLP 9980
Cleopatra / Apr '97 / Cargo / Greyhound / Plastic Head / RTM/Disc / SRD

STROLL IN THE PORK, A
Death rattle 'n' roll / Hello hooray / Sondero luminoso / Gravy train / Watts
CD CONTECD 202
Contempo / Jan '97 / Plastic Head

Pigbag

BEST OF PIGBAG, THE
Papa's got a brand new pigbag / Weak at the knees / Hit the O deck / Getting up / Brazil nuts / Jump the line / Another orangutango / Sunny day / Big bean / Can't see for looking / Six of one / Big bag / Listen listen little man
CD KAZCD 3
Kaz / Nov '87 / BMG

Pigeonhed

FULL SENTENCE, THE
It's like the man said / Full sentence / Marry me / Keep on keepin' on / Battle flag / Glory bound / P-Street / Phunpurephun / Who's to blame / 31st of July / More than just a girl / Fire's comin' down / For those gone on / Honor
CD SPCD 373
Sub Pop / Apr '97 / Cargo / Greyhound / Shellshock/Disc
CD 9878702242
Warner Bros. / Aug '97 / Warner Music

PIGEONHEAD
CD SPCD 101/273
Sub Pop / Jul '93 / Cargo / Greyhound / Shellshock/Disc

Pigface

FEELS LIKE HEAVEN SOUNDS LIKE SHIT
CD INV 034CD
Invisible / Nov '95 / Plastic Head

GUB
Tapeworm / Bushmaster / Cylinder head world / Point blank / Suck / Symphony for taps / Greenhouse / Little sisters / Tailor made / War ich nicht immer ein guter junge / Blood and sand / Weightless
CD CDDVN 2
Devotion / Sep '91 / Pinnacle
CD INV 009CD
Invisible / Mar '96 / Plastic Head

LEAN JUICY PORK
CD INV 0122
Invisible / Jul '93 / Plastic Head

NOTES FROM THEE UNDERGROUND
Ashole / Divebomber / Your own you own / Fuck it up / Hagseed / Chickasaw / Empathy / Magazine / Think / Trivial scene / Slut/ Blood/Pain / Psalm springs eternal / Steamroller / Your music is garbage
CD CDDVN 29
Devotion / May '94 / Pinnacle

TRUTH WILL OUT
CD CDDVN 25
Devotion / Jan '94 / Pinnacle
CD INV 026CD
Invisible / Mar '96 / Plastic Head

WASHING MACHINE MOUTH
CD INV 021CD
Invisible / Mar '96 / Plastic Head

WELCOME TO MEXICO
CD INV 011CD
Invisible / Mar '96 / Plastic Head

WELCOME TO MEXICO...ASSHOLE
CD CDDVN 3
Devotion / Nov '91 / Pinnacle

Piggott, Mavis

LATE BLOOM
CD FLY 009
Blue Rose / Jan '96 / 3mv/Pinnacle

YOU CAN BE LOW
CD _______ FLY 015CD
Flydaddy/Blue Rose / Jul '96 / 3mv/Vital

Piirpauke

METAMORPHOSIS LIVE 1977-1995
CD _______ ZEN 2045CD
Rockadillo / Apr '96 / ADA / Direct

Pike, Dave

DAVE PIKE AND CHARLES MCPHERSON (Pike, Dave & Charles McPherson)
Scrapple from the apple / Off minor / Piano trio medley / Embraceable you / Up jumped Spring / Big foot
CD _______ CDSJP 302
Timeless Jazz / Jun '89 / New Note/ Pinnacle

MASTERPIECES
CD _______ 5318482
MPS Jazz / Dec '96 / PolyGram

PIKE'S GROOVE (Pike, Dave & Cedar Walton Trio)
CD _______ CRISS 1021CD
Criss Cross / Oct '92 / Cadillac / Direct / Vital/SAM

TIMES OUT OF MIND
Dance of the Grebes / Wee / Times out of mind / Djalama / Morning in the park / I love my cigar
CD _______ MCD 5446
Muse / May '92 / New Note/Pinnacle

Pilc, Jean Michel

BIG ONE
CD _______ EPC 890
European Music Production / Jan '94 / Harmonia Mundi

Piledriver

MOUTHFUL OF VENUS' SODA, A
CD _______ HEAD 4
Machinehead / Feb '97 / Cargo

Pilgrim Jubilee Singers

BEST OF THE PILGRIM JUBILEE SINGERS, THE
CD _______ NASH 4510
Nashboro / Feb '96 / Pinnacle

Pilgrim Travellers

BEST OF THE PILGRIM TRAVELLERS VOL.1 & 2, THE
I was there when the spirit came / Blessed be the name / Standing on the highway / Jesus hits like the atom bomb / I've got a mother gone home / Jesus I'm thankful / Straight street / Mother bowed / Old rugged cross / Something within me / Soldier's plea / Satisfied with Jesus / My old home / Jesus met the woman at the well / What a blessing in Jesus I've found / I want my crown / God shall wipe all tears away / Weary traveller / I'll tell it wherever I go / He will remember me / Lord help me carry on / Now Lord (yes, my Lord) / Lord hold my hand
CD _______ CDCHD 342
Ace / May '91 / Pinnacle

BETTER THAN THAT
I could do better than that / Please watch over me / Long ago (wooden church) / I never knew joy before / Leaning on the everlasting arms / I'm going through / How about you / I'll be there (in that number) / All the way (I'm willing to run) / Your mother is your friend / Gonna walk right out / Move up to heaven / What a friend we have in Jesus / Hard road to travel / Look down that lonesome road / Go ahead / In my heart / I love Jesus / He's my friend / Life you save may be your own (the safety song) / Troubles in my home will have to end / Every prayer will find it's answer / Close to thee / Troubled in mind / Bless us today / Hold on / After while
CD _______ CDCHD 564
Ace / Mar '94 / Pinnacle

WALKING RHYTHM
What are they doing (my lord) / Stretch out / My prayer / Good news / Dig a little deeper / Everybody's gonna have a wonderful time up there / Nothing can change me (since I found the lord) / Jesus / Thank you jesus / What a friend we have in Jesus / It's a blessing / Not a one / He's pleading in glory / Jesus gave me water / Jesus he's the one / King jesus will roll all burdens away / My eternal-home / Pass me not, o gentle saviour / Footprints of Jesus / When i join the jubilee / Call him by his name / Welcome home / My road's so rough and rocky / I love the lord / Deliver me from evil / Jesus is the first line of defence / Peace of mind / Angels tell mother / WDIA plug
CD _______ CDCHD 463
Ace / Mar '93 / Pinnacle

Pilgrim, Billy

BILLY PILGRIM
Get me out of here / Insomniac / Try / Here we go again / Halfway home / Hula hoop / Hurricane season / Lost and found in tinseltown / Too many people / Mama says
CD _______ 7567825152
Warner Bros. / May '94 / Warner Music

Pilkington, Mark

MARK PILKINGTON
CD _______ SCOTT 2CD
Mary Anne Scott / Mar '97 / Plastic Head

Pilot

FROM THE ALBUM OF THE SAME NAME
CD _______ C5CD 567
See For Miles/C5 / Jun '91 / Pinnacle

MAGIC
Sooner or later / January / Girl next door / Auntie Iris / Just a smile / You're my no.1 / Call me round / High into the sky / Magic / Passion piece / Penny in my pocket / Canada / Never give up / Over the moon / Don't speak loudly / Lovely lady smiles / Trembling
CD _______ DC 865792
Disky / Mar '97 / Disky / THE

MORIN HEIGHTS
CD _______ C5CD 569
See For Miles/C5 / Jun '91 / Pinnacle

SECOND FLIGHT
CD _______ C5CD 568
See For Miles/C5 / Jun '91 / Pinnacle

Pilotcan

SOCIALLY INEPT DISCO
CD _______ EVOL 2CD
Evol / May '97 / SRD

Pin Group

RETROSPECTIVE, A
CD _______ SB 68
Siltbreeze / Mar '97 / Cargo / Vital

Pinchers

BANDELERO
Si mi ya / On the attack / Bandelero / Bigger gun / My heart is booked / Pretending / Let's make a deal / Dreams and illusions / Don't change on me / Brotherly love
CD _______ JAMCD 8
Jammy's / Sep '91 / Jet Star

HOTTER
Play mate / Head back no careless / Hotter Mr. Pinchers / When (jive) / Border line / Be my friend / Nuff man / Have to die / Send another one come / Killer / Harder they come
CD _______ VYDCD 014
Vine Yard / Jul '96 / Grapevine/PolyGram

Pincock, Dougie

SOMETHING BLEW
Gem so small / Piper's piper / Eric Bigstones' leaky boat / Douglas Adams' fancy / Fastest gasman / Video kid / Miss Cara Spencer / Return to Kashmagiro / Balnain household / Tanks for the memory / Macrmmon's sweetheart / Rest / Unrest / Twins / January girl / Handyman's legacy / Rogart refusal / Songs for Chris
CD _______ CDTRAX 080
Greentrax / Nov '94 / ADA / Direct / Duncans / Highlander

Pinder, Michael

AMONG THE STARS
Power of love (can survive) / You can't take love away / Best things in life / Hurry on home / When you're sleeping / Fantasy flight / Among the stars / Upside down / Waters beneath the bridge / World today
CD _______ OSR 0432
One Step / Jul '97 / Pinnacle

PROMISE, THE
Free as a dove / You'll make it through / I only want to love you / Someone to believe in / Carry on / Message / Seed / Promise
CD _______ OSR 0433
One Step / Aug '97 / Pinnacle

Pine, Courtney

DESTINY'S SONG & THE IMAGE OF PURSUANCE
Beyond the thought of my last reckoning / In pursuance / Vision / Guardian of the flame / 'Round midnight / Sacrifice / Prismic omnipotence / Alone / Raggamuffin's tale / Mark of the time
CD _______ IMCD 114
Island / May '91 / PolyGram

JOURNEY TO THE URGE WITHIN
Mis-interpret / I believe / Peace / Delores St. S.F / As we would say / Children of the ghetto / When, where, how and why / CGC / Seen / Sunday song
CD _______ IMCD 112
Island / May '91 / PolyGram

MODERN DAY JAZZ STORIES
Prelude - The water of life / 37th chamber / Don't Xplain / Dah blessing / In the garden of Eden / Creation stepper / After the damaja / Absolution / Each one (must) teach one / Unknown warrior (Song for my forefathers) / I've known rivers / Outro - guiding light / Prince of peace
CD _______ 5290282
Talkin' Loud / Jan '96 / PolyGram

TO THE EYES OF CREATION
Healing song / Zaire (Interlude) / Country dance / Psalm / Eastern standard time / X-calibur (Interlude) / Meditation of contemplation / Life goes round / Ark of Mark (Interlude) / Children hold on / Cleopatra's needle / Redemption song / Holy grail
CD _______ IMCD 210
Island / Mar '95 / PolyGram

UNDERGROUND
CD _______ 5377452
Mercury / Sep '97 / PolyGram

VISION'S TALE, THE
Introduction / In a mellow tone / Just you, just me / Raggamuffin's stance / There is no greater love / Skylark / I'm an old cowhand (from the Rio Grande) / God bless the child / And then (a warrior's tale) / Our descendants' descendants / CP's theme
CD _______ IMCD 192
Island / Mar '94 / PolyGram

WITHIN THE REALMS OF OUR DREAMS
Sepia love song / Una muy bonita / Donna Lee / Up behind the beat / Time to go home / Delfeayo's dilemma / Raggamuffin and his lance / Slave's tale
CD _______ IMCD 193
Island / Jul '94 / PolyGram

Pingxin, Xu

ART OF THE CHINESE DULCIMER, THE
CD _______ EUCD 1293
ARC / Nov '95 / ADA / ARC Music

Pinhead Gunpowder

GOODBYE ELLSTON AVENUE
CD _______ LOOKOUT 168CD
Lookout / Feb '97 / Cargo / Greyhound / Shellshock/Disc

JUMP SALTY
CD _______ LOOKOUT 105
Lookout / '94 / Cargo / Greyhound / Shellshock/Disc

Pink, Celinda

UNCHAINED
I don't need no lover boy / You ain't leaving me without you / Hound dog / Pack your lies and go / I've changed since I've been unchained / Love her right off your mind / Taking my freedom / Found me a backdoor man / You better quit it / Sneakin' up your backdoor / Love you till the cows come home / Me and Bobby McGee / I've earned the right to sing the blues
CD _______ SORCD 0085
D-Sharp / Aug '95 / Pinnacle

Pink Fairies

KILL 'EM AND EAT 'EM
Broken statue / Fear of love / Undercover of confusion / Waiting for the ice cream to melt / Taking LSD / White girls on amphetamine / Seeing double / Fool about you / Bad attitude / I might be lying
CD _______ VEXCD 16
Demon / May '97 / Pinnacle

KILL EM 'N EAT' EM
Broken statue / Fear of love / Undercover of confusion / Waiting for the ice cream to melt / Taking LSD / White girls on amphetamine / Seeing double / Fool about you / Bad attitude / I might be lying
CD _______ FIENDCD 105
Demon / Oct '90 / Pinnacle

LIVE AT THE ROUNDHOUSE
City kids / Waiting for the man / Lucille / Uncle Harry's last freakout / Going down
CD _______ CDWIK 965
Big Beat / Jul '91 / Pinnacle

OUT OF THE BLUES AND INTO THE PINK
CD _______ HTDCD 46
HTD / Jan '96 / CM / Pinnacle

Pink Floyd

ANIMALS
Pigs on the wing 1 / Dogs / Pigs (three different ones) / Sheep / Pigs on the wing 2
CD _______ CDEMD 1060
EMI / Aug '94 / EMI

ATOM HEART MOTHER
Atom heart mother / If / Summer '68 / Fat old sun / Alan's psychedelic breakfast
CD _______ CDEMD 1072
EMI / Oct '94 / EMI

COLLECTION OF GREAT DANCE SONGS, A
One of these days / Money / Another brick in the wall pt 2 / Wish you were here / Shine on you crazy diamond / Sheep
CD _______ CDP 790 732 2
EMI / Nov '88 / EMI

DARK SIDE OF THE MOON
Speak to me / Breathe / On the run / Time / Great gig in the sky / Money / Us and them / Any colour you like / Brain damage / Eclipse
CD _______ CDEMD 1064
EMI / Aug '94 / EMI

DELICATE SOUND OF THUNDER (2CD Set)
Shine on you crazy diamond / Learning to fly / Yet another movie / Round and around / Sorrow / Dogs of war / On the turning away / One of these days / Time / Wish you were here / Us and them / Money / Another brick in the wall pt 2 / Comfortably numb / Run like hell
CD Set _______ CDEQ 5009
EMI / Nov '88 / EMI

DIVISION BELL, THE
Cluster one / What do you want from me / Poles apart / Marooned / Great day for freedom / Wearing the inside out / Take it back / Coming back to life / Keep talking / Lost for words / High hopes
CD _______ CDEMD 1055
EMI / Apr '94 / EMI

FINAL CUT, THE
Post war dream / Your possible pasts / One of the few / Hero's return / Gunner's dream / Paranoid eyes / Get your filthy hands off my desert / Fletcher memorial home / Southampton dock / Final cut / Not now John / Two suns in the sunset / Hero's return (part 2)
CD _______ CDEMD 1070
EMI / Oct '94 / EMI

FULL OF SECRETS (Interviews)
CD _______ 3D 014
Network / Dec '96 / Total/BMG

INTERVIEW DISC
CD _______ SAM 7005
Sound & Media / Nov '96 / Sound & Media

LONDON 1966-1967
Interstellar overdrive / Nick's boogie
CD _______ SFMDP 3
See For Miles/C5 / Sep '95 / Pinnacle

MEDDLE
One of these days / Pillow of winds / Fearless / San Tropez / Seamus / Echoes
CD _______ CDEMD 1061
EMI / Aug '94 / EMI

MOMENTARY LAPSE OF REASON, A
Signs of life / Learning to fly / Dogs of war / One slip / On the turning away / Yet another movie / Round and around / New machine (part 1) / Terminal frost / New machine (part 2) / Sorrow
CD _______ CDEMD 1003
EMI / Sep '87 / EMI

MOON REVISITED, THE (Tribute To Dark Side Of The Moon) (Various Artists)
Speak to me: *Cairo* / Breathe: *Cairo* / On the run: *La Vague, Rob* / Time: *Shadow Gallery* / Great gig in the sky: *Dark Side Of The Moon* / Money: *Magellan* / Us and them: *Enchant* / Any colour you like: *World Trade* / Brain Damage: *Berry, Robert* / Eclipse
CD _______ RR 89162
Roadrunner / Oct '95 / PolyGram

MORE
Cirrus minor / Nile song / Crying song / Up the Khyber / Green is the colour / Cymbaline / Party sequence / Main theme / Ibiza bar / More blues / Quicksilver / Spanish piece / Dramatic theme
CD _______ CDEMD 1084
EMI / Feb '96 / EMI

OBSCURED BY CLOUDS
Obscured by clouds / When you're in / Burning bridges / Gold it's in the... / Wot's... uh the deal / Mudmen / Childhood's end / Free four / Stay / Absolutely curtains
CD _______ CDEMD 1083
EMI / Feb '96 / EMI

ORCHESTRAL WORKS, THE (The Music Of Pink Floyd) (Royal Philharmonic Orchestra/David Palmer)
CD _______ 07863579602
RCA Victor / Nov '95 / BMG

PINK FLOYD: INTERVIEW PICTURE DISC
CD _______ CBAK 4013
Baktabak / Apr '88 / Arabesque

PIPER AT THE GATES OF DAWN, THE
Astronomy domine / Lucifer Sam / Matilda mother / Flaming / Pow R Toc H / Take up thy stethoscope and walk / Interstellar overdrive / Gnome / Chapter 24 / Scarecrow / Bike
CD _______ CDEMD 1073
EMI / Oct '94 / EMI

PIPER AT THE GATES OF DAWN, THE (30th Anniversary Remastered)
Astronomy Domine / Lucifer Sam / Matilda mother / Flaming / Pow R Toc H / Take up thy stethoscope and walk / Interstellar overdrive / Gnome / Chapter 24 / Scarecrow / Bike
CD _______ CDEMD 1110
EMI / Aug '97 / EMI

PLAYS THE HITS OF PINK FLOYD (Royal Philharmonic Orchestra)
Shine on you crazy diamond / Money / Us and them / Hey you / Another brick in the wall pt 2 / Wish you were here / Time / Great gig in the sky / In the flesh
CD _______ EDL 28382
Edel / Dec '94 / Pinnacle

PULSE (2CD Set)
Shine on you crazy diamond / Astronomy domine / What do you want from me / Learning to fly / Keep talking / Coming back to life / Hey you / Great day for freedom / Sorrow / High hopes / Another brick in the wall pt 2 / One of these days / Speak to me / Breathe / On the run / Time / Great gig in the sky / Money / Us and them / Any colour you like / Brain damage / Eclipse / Wish you were here / Comfortably numb / Run like hell
CD Set _______ CDEMD 1078
EMI / Jun '95 / EMI

RELICS
Arnold Layne / Interstellar overdrive / See Emily play / Remember a day / Paintbox / Julia dream / Careful with that axe, Eugene / Cirrus minor / Nile song / Biding my time / Bike
CD _______ CDEMD 1082
EMI / Feb '96 / EMI

ROCK AND POP REVIVAL PLAYS PINK FLOYD (Rock & Pop Revival)
CD _______ RPR 9402
Scratch / Mar '95 / Koch / Scratch/BMG

SAUCERFUL OF PINK, A (A Tribute To Pink Floyd) (Various Artists)
Set the controls for the heart of the sun: *Psychic TV* / Another brick in the wall: *Controlled Bleeding* / One of these days: *Spahn Ranch* / Wot's... uh the deal: *Sky Cries Mary* / Interstellar overdrive: *Spiral Realms* / Learning to fly: *Leather Strip* / To Roger Waters, wherever you are: *Geesin, Ron* / Jugband blues: *Eden* / On the run: *Din* / Hey you: *Alien Sex Fiend* / Careful with that axe Eugene / Lucifer Sam: *Electric Hellfire Club* / Pigs on the wing 1: *Helios Creed* / Let there be more light: *Pressurehead* / Young lust: *Penal Colony* / Saucerful of secrets: *Exp* / Point me at the sky: *Melting Euphoria* / Nile song: *Far Flung*
CD _______ CDBRED 120
Anagram / Sep '97 / Cargo / Pinnacle

SAUCERFUL OF SECRETS, A
Let there be more light / Remember a day / Set the controls for the heart of the sun / Corporal Clegg / Saucerful of secrets / See saw / Jugband blues
CD _______ CDEMD 1063
EMI / Aug '94 / EMI

SHINE ON (9CD Set)
Arnold Layne / Candy and a currant bun / See Emily play / Scarecrow / Apples and oranges / Paintbox / It would be so nice / Julia dream / Point me at the sky / Careful with that axe, Eugene / Let there be more light / Remember a day / Set the controls for the heart of the sun / Corporal Clegg / Saucerful of secrets / See saw / Jugband blues / One of these days / Pillow of winds / Fearless / San Tropez / Seamus / Echoes / Speak to me / Breathe / On the run / Time / Great gig in the sky / Money / Us and them / Any colour you like / Brain damage / Eclipse / Shine on you crazy diamond / Welcome to the machine / Have a cigar / Wish you were here / Pigs on the wing 1 / Dogs / Pigs (three different ones) / Sheep / Pigs on the wing 2 / In the flesh / Thin ice / Another brick in the wall pt 1 / Happiest days of our lives / Another brick in the wall pt 2 / Mother / Goodbye blue sky / Empty spaces / Young lust / One of my turns / Don't leave me now / Another brick in the wall pt 3 / Goodbye cruel world / Hey you / Is there anybody out there / Nobody home / Vera / Bring the boys back home / Comfortably numb / Show must go on / In the flesh / Run like hell / Waiting for the worms / Trial / Outside the wall / Signs of life / Learning to fly / Dogs of war / One slip / On the turning away / Yet another movie / Round and around / New machine 1 / Terminal frost / New machine 2 / Sorrow
CD Set _______ PFBOX 1
EMI / Nov '92 / EMI

THERE IS NO DARK SIDE (Interview Discs/2CD Set)
CD Set _______ CONV 005
Network / Feb '97 / Total/BMG

UMMAGUMMA (2CD Set)
Astronomy domine / Careful with that axe, Eugene / Set the controls for the heart of the sun / Saucerful of secrets / Sysyphus / Grantchester meadows / Several species of small furry animals gathered together... / Narrow way / Grand Vizier's garden party
CD Set _______ CDEMD 1074
EMI / Oct '94 / EMI

WALL, THE (2CD Set)
In the flesh / Thin ice / Another brick in the wall pt 1 / Happiest days of our lives / Another brick in the wall pt 2 / Mother / Goodbye blue sky / Empty spaces / Young lust / One of my turns / Don't leave me now / Another brick in the wall pt 3 / Goodbye cruel world / Hey you / Is there anybody out there / Nobody home / Vera / Bring the boys back home / Comfortably numb / Show must go on / In the flesh / Run like hell / Waiting for the worms / Trial / Outside the wall
CD Set _______ CDEMD 1071
EMI / Oct '94 / EMI

WISH YOU WERE HERE
Shine on you crazy diamond / Welcome to the machine / Have a cigar / Wish you were here
CD _______ CDEMD 1062
EMI / Aug '94 / EMI

WISHING (Interview Discs/2CD Set)
CD Set _______ CONV 008
Network / Mar '97 / Total/BMG

Pink Lincolns

PURE SWANK
CD _______ DSR 53
Dr. Strange / May '97 / Cargo / Greyhound / Plastic Head

Pink Turns Blue

MUZAK
CD _______ RTD 19519452
Our Choice / Jul '95 / Pinnacle

PERFECT SEX
CD Set _______ RTD 19519032
Our Choice / Apr '94 / Pinnacle

Pinky & Perky

TOP POP PARTY
Moving on up / Mysterious girl / You're gorgeous / Ooh aah (just a little bit) / Macarena / Freedom / That's the way I like it / Walking on sunshine / Blockbuster / Leader of the gang / Bridget the midget / Octopus's garden / You to me are everything / Kissing in the back row of the movies / Baby love / That's living alright
CD _______ CDMFP 6369
Music For Pleasure / May '97 / EMI

Pinnacle

CYBORG ASSASSIN
CD _______ KSCD 9409
Kissing Spell / Jun '97 / Greyhound

Pinski Zoo

DE-ICER
Bubble fun / Dust bowl / Fridge / Ben Hur / White out / Bouncing mirror / Nathan's song / Nightjar / De-icer / Slab
CD _______ SLAMCD 206
Slam / Oct '96 / Cadillac

Pinter, Judith

AT LAST THE WIND
CD _______ CD 158
Narada / Nov '92 / ADA / New Note/ Pinnacle

Piolot, Maxime

BRETON QUAND MEME
CD _______ RSCD 212
Keltia Musique / Apr '95 / ADA / Discovery

Pioneers

20 ORIGINAL FAMOUS HITS
CD _______ TPCD 001
Pioneer / Apr '92 / Jet Star

KICK DE BUCKET
CD _______ RNCD 2064
Rhino / Jun '94 / Grapevine/PolyGram / Jet Star

LONG SHOT KICK DE BUCKET (The Best Of The Pioneers)
Shake it up / Give me a little loving / Long shot kick de bucket / Jackpot / Pan ya machete / No dope me pony / Run come walla / Catch the beat / Things got to change / Reggae beat / Easy come easy go / Long shot / Black bud / Poor remeses / Samfie man / Simmer down quashie / Battle of the giants / Money day / Cherri cherri / Twice round the daffodils / Starvation / Story book children / I need your sweet inspiration / Let your yeah be yeah / Give and take / Time hard
CD _______ CDTRL 347
Trojan / Mar '97 / Direct / Jet Star

Pipe

SLOWBOY
CD _______ MRG 123CD
Merge / Jul '97 / Cargo / Greyhound / SRD

Piquet

FAULTY CARESS, THE
CD _______ CDPSST 2
Mute / May '96 / RTM/Disc

Piranhas

PIRANHAS, THE
Boyfriend / Love game / Green don't suit me / Fiddling while Babylon burns / Coffee / Something / Tension / Pleasure / Solo sex for two / Getting beaten up / Saxaphone / Final straw / Jilly / Coloured music / Yap yap yap / Happy families / Tension / Virginity / I don't want my body
CD _______ CDMGRAM 115
Anagram / Sep '97 / Cargo / Pinnacle

Pirates

DON'T MUNCHEN IT-LIVE IN EUROPE
CD _______ RPM 110
RPM / Jul '93 / Pinnacle

FISTFUL OF DUBLOONS, A
Linda Lou / Honey hush / Put your cat clothes on / Sweet love on my mind / Lonesome train (on a lonesome track) / Milk cow blues / Casting my spell / Tricky Dicky / Tear it up / Kaw-Liga
CD _______ EDCD 102
Edsel / Aug '92 / Pinnacle

FROM CALYPSO TO COLLAPSO
Jezebel / Good drink / Bad woman / Armageddon / Burning rubber / Turn up the heat / Lost and found / Slow down / Don't munchen it / Down to the bone / Friends for life
CD _______ CDTB 156
Thunderbolt / Nov '94 / TKO Magnum

HOME AND AWAY (Live In The 1990's)
I can tell / Lindy Lou / Don't munchen it / Do the dog / Friends for life/Shakin' all over / All in together / Jezebel / Good drink, bad woman / Talkin' 'bout you / Lost and found
CD _______ SJPCD 003
Angel Air / Jan '97 / Pinnacle

LIVE IN JAPAN
All by myself / Ain't got no money / I can tell / Lonesome train (on a lonesome track) / Money honey / Don't munchen it / Can't believe you wanna leave / Goin' back home / Please don't touch / Honey hush / Peggy Sue / Burnin' rubber / Shakin' all over / All in it together
CD _______ CDTB 143
Thunderbolt / Apr '93 / TKO Magnum

SAILING THROUGH FRANCE
CD _______ 422265
New Rose / May '94 / ADA / Direct / Discovery

WE'VE BEEN THINKING
Please don't touch / Good drink bad woman / Goin' back home / Better get better / Don't fool around with love / I am a man / Burnin' rubber / Armageddon / Rock bottom / Gibson martin fender / Blue suede shoes / Suenska Flicka
CD _______ BMAC 0317S
BMA / Sep '97 / Pinnacle

Pirchner, Werner

EU
Sonate vom rauhen leben / Streichquartett fur blaserquintett / Good news from the Ziller family / Kammer-symphonie 'Soiree Tyrolienne' / Do you know Emperor Joe / Two war and peace choirs / Kleine mes um 'c' fur den lieben gott / Solo sonata for bass-vibes
CD _______ 8294632
ECM / '86 / New Note/Pinnacle

Pirin Folk Ensemble

BULGARIAN VOICES
CD _______ EUCD 1340
ARC / Apr '96 / ADA / ARC Music

Pirnales

AQUAS
CD _______ KICD 27
Digelius / Jun '93 / Direct

BEST BEFORE
CD _______ OMCD 60
Olarin Musiiki Oy / Dec '94 / ADA / Direct

Piron, A.J.

DECEMBER ISSUE (Piron, A.J. New Orleans Orchestra)
Bouncin' around / Kiss me sweet / New Orleans wiggle / West Indies blues / Sud bustin' blues / West Indies blues / Do doodle oom / West Indies blues / Ghost of the blues / Bright star blues / Lou'siana swing / Sitting on the curbstone blues / Southern woman blues / Seawall special blues / Jailhouse blues / Kiss me sweet / Red man blues / Red man blues / Do just as I say / Bad bad mama / Willie Jackson's blues / She keeps it up all the time / Old New Orleans blues / Mama's gone goodbye
CD _______ AZCD 13
Azure / Nov '93 / Azure / Cadillac / Jazz Music / Swift / Wellard

Piss Drunks

URINE IDIOT
CD _______ RNR 001CD
Ransom Note / Oct '95 / Plastic Head

Pist.On

NUMBER ONE
Parole / Turbulent / Grey flap / Shoplifters of the world unite / I am no one / Eight sides / Afraid of life / Electra complex / Down and out / Mix me with blood / My feet / Exit wound
CD _______ CDMFN 211
Music For Nations / Nov '96 / Pinnacle

Pita

SEVEN TONS FOR FREE
CD _______ MEGO 009CD
Mego / Nov '96 / Plastic Head

Pitbull

CASUALTY
CD _______ LF 049CD
Lost & Found / Aug '93 / Plastic Head

NEW ALL TIME LOW
CD _______ LF 128CD
Lost & Found / May '95 / Plastic Head

PITBULL
CD _______ LF 093CD
Lost & Found / May '94 / Plastic Head

Pitch Shifter

DESENSITIZED
Lesson one / Diable / Ephemerol / Triad / To die is to gain / (A higher form of) killing / Lesson two / Cathode / N/A / Gatherer of data / NCM / Routine
CD _______ MOSH 075CD
Earache / Sep '97 / Vital

INDUSTRIAL
CD _______ CDVILE 56
Peaceville / Mar '95 / Pinnacle

INFOTAINMENT
Self replicating PSI / Introductory disclaimer / Underachiever / (We're behaving like) Insects / Virus / Product placement / (Harmless) Interlude / Bloodsweatsaliva / Hangar 84 / Whiteout / Phoenixology / Pitch sampler vol.1 / Pitch sampler vol.2
CD _______ MOSH 137CD
Earache / May '96 / Vital

SUBMIT
CD _______ MOSH 066CD
Earache / Apr '92 / Vital

Pitchblende

AU JUS
Nine volt / Your own arturo / Ambient noise / Karoshi / Cupcake Jones / Tourniquet / X's for I's / Human lie / Detector / Showroom / Practice song / Short term / Talking / Psychic power control
CD _______ OLE 1022
Matador / Feb '95 / Vital

GYGAX
Squeezing from the mole / New decadence / Burning man / Pertraining to the champ / Kevorkian / Mercator projection / Crumbs of affection / Sideling hill / Romanesque buttox
CD _______ OLE 1902
Matador / Feb '96 / Vital

Pitchford, Lonnie

ALL AROUND MAN
Elvira / All around man / If I had posession over judgement day / Real rock music/ Crawling King Snake / My babe / 55 blues / Bring it on home / This is the blues / Ghetto / CC rider / My sunny / Water in my gas tank / Louisiana blues / Lonesome blues / Sweet home Chicago / Don't you do that no more / If I had possession over judgement day / All around man / Drinkin' antiseptic
CD _______ R 2629
Rooster / Feb '97 / Direct

Pitney, Gene

20 GREATEST HITS
I wanna love my life away / Town without Pity / Man who shot Liberty Valance / Only love can break a heart / Twenty four hours from Tulsa / That girl belongs to yesterday / It hurts to be in love / I'm gonna be strong / I must be seeing things / Looking through the eyes of love / Princess in rags / Backstage (I'm lonely) / Nobody needs your love more than I do / Just one smile / Something's gotten hold of my heart / Somewhere in the country / Yours until tomorrow / Maria Elena / 24 Sycamore / Hello Mary Lou
CD _______ PLATCD 3904
Platinum / Dec '88 / Prism

24 HOURS FROM TULSA
Twenty four hours from Tulsa / Something's gotten hold of my heart / (I wanna) Love my life away / Town without pity / That girl belongs to yesterday / I'm gonna be strong / I must be seeing things / Looking through the eyes of love / Princess in rags / Backstage / It hurts to be in love / 24 Sycamore / Maria Elena / Yours until tomorrow / Somewhere in the country / Cold light of day / Just one smile / Nobody needs your love
CD _______ MUCD 9021
Musketeer / Apr '95 / Disc

AT HIS BEST
CD _______ PLSCD 190
Pulse / Apr '97 / BMG

BLUE GENE/MEETS THE FAIR YOUNG LADIES OF FOLKLAND
Twenty four hours from Tulsa / Autumn leaves / Half the laughter, twice the tears / I'll be seeing you / Lonely night dreams (of faraway arms) / Answer me, my love / Blue Gene / Yesterday's hero / Maybe you'll be there / Keep tellin' yourself / I can't runaway / House without windows / Take it like a man / Those eyes of Liza Jane / Laurie / Brandy is my true love's name / My suli-ram / Little Nell / Melissa and me / Oh Annie oh / Lyda Sue, Wh'dya do / Carrie / Hey pretty little black eyed Suzie / Song of Lorena / Darlin' Corey, ain't ya comin' down town / Ballad of Laura Mae / That girl belongs to yesterday
CD ____ NEMCD 890
Sequel / Nov '96 / BMG

DEFINITIVE COLLECTION, THE (2CD Set)
(I wanna) love my life away / I laughed so hard I cried / Louisiana Mama / Town without pity / Every breath I take / (The man who shot) Liberty Valance / Only love can break a heart / If I didn't have a dime (to play the jukebox) / Half heaven, half heartache / Tower tall / Mecca / Teardrop by teardrop / True love never runs smooth / Donna means heartache / 24 hours from Tulsa / That girl belongs to yesterday / Yesterday's hero / Nobody needs your love more than I do / It hurts to be in love / Hawaii / I'm gonna be strong / Aladdin's lamp / I must be seeing things / Last chance to turn around / Looking through the eyes of love / Princess in rags / Baby ain't that fine / Everybody knows but you and me / It's not that I don't love you / Gene are you there / Backstage / (In the) cold light of day / Boss's daughter / Just one smile / Nessuni mi puo guidicare / Something's gotten hold of my heart / She's a heartbreaker / Conquistador / Somewhere in the country / Billy you're my friend / Maria Elena / Street called hope / Shady lady / 24 sycamores / Yours until tomorrow / Baby I need your lovin' / Hello Mary Lou / Angelica / Little Betty falling star / Half the laughter, twice the tears / If I were / June is as cold as December / Cry your eyes out / Not responsible / You've lost that lovin' feelin' / Pretty Annabelle / She lets her hair down (early in the morning) / Marianne
CD Set ____ CPCD 81962
Charly / Oct '96 / Koch

EP COLLECTION, THE
CD ____ SEECD 313
See For Miles/C5 / Apr '91 / Pinnacle

ESSENTIAL COLLECTION, THE
CD Set ____ LECD 611
Wisepack / Apr '95 / Conifer/BMG / THE

GENE PITNEY SINGS BACHARACH, DAVID AND OTHERS /PITNEY TODAY
CD ____ NEMCD 896
Sequel / Jun '97 / BMG

GOLD COLLECTION, THE
Something's gotten hold of my heart / I'm gonna be strong / Looking through the eyes of love / That girl belongs to yesterday / 24 Sycamore / It hurts to be in love / Princess in rags / Backstage (I'm lonely) / (I wanna) love my life away / Maria Elena / Town without pity / I must be seeing things / Just one smile / Shady lady / 24 hours from Tulsa
CD ____ SUMCD 4014
Summit / Nov '96 / Sound & Media

GREATEST HITS
CD ____ CDGFR 052
Tring / Jun '92 / Tring

GREATEST HITS
Man who shot Liberty Valance / It hurts to be in love / I'm gonna be strong / Mecca / Town without pity / 24 Hours from Tulsa / Backstage (I'm lonely) / Looking through the eyes of love / (I wanna) love my life away / Every breath I take / Something's gotten hold of my heart / True love never runs smooth / I must be seeing things / Princess in rags / Only love can break a heart / Half heaven, half heartache / Last chance to turn around / She's a heartbreaker / Just one smile / If I didn't have a dime (to play the jukebox) / Yesterday's hero
CD ____ QED 087
Tring / Nov '96 / Tring

GREATEST HITS OF GENE PITNEY
CD ____ MACCD 124
Autograph / Aug '96 / BMG

HITS & MISSES
Man who shot Liberty Valance / Twenty four hours from Tulsa / Town without pity / Hello Mary Lou / Today's teardrops / Surefire bet / Donna means heartbreak / If I didn't have a dime / (I wanna) Love my life away / Every breath I take / Mecca / True love never runs smoothly / Teardrop by teardrop / Dream for sale / Half heaven, half heartache / Only love can break a heart / Bleibe bei mir (Town without pity) / I'll find you / Cradle of my arms / Please come back, baby / I'm going back to my love / Classical rock 'n' roll / Snuggle up baby / Strolling (through the park) / Faithful our love / Make believe lover (demo)
CD ____ BCD 15724
Bear Family / Feb '95 / Direct / Rollercoaster / Swift

I'M GONNA BE STRONG/LOOKING THROUGH THE EYES OF LOVE
I'm gonna be strong / Walk / I love you more today / Who needs it / Follow the sun / Lips are redder on you / It hurts to be in love / Last two people on Earth / That girl belongs to yesterday / E se domani / Hawaii / I'm gonna find myself a girl / I must be seeing things / Marianne / Save your love / Down in the subway / If Mary's there / Don't take candy from a stranger / One day / She's still there / Just one smile / I lost tomorrow (yesterday) / Looking thru' the eyes of love / There's no living without your loving / I'll never get to love you / Last chance to turn around / Rising tide of love
CD ____ NEMCD 891
Sequel / Nov '96 / BMG

LEGENDS IN MUSIC
CD ____ LECD 078
Wisepack / Jul '94 / Conifer/BMG / THE

LOOKING THROUGH THE EYES OF LOVE
CD ____ PDSCD 526
Pulse / Aug '96 / BMG

MANY SIDES OF GENE PITNEY/ONLY LOVE CAN BREAK A HEART
CD ____ NEMCD 888
Sequel / Jun '97 / BMG

PEARLS FROM THE PAST
CD ____ KLMCD 007
BAM / Nov '93 / Koch / Scratch/BMG

SINGS THE GREAT SONGS OF OUR TIME/NOBODY NEEDS YOUR LOVE
Tonight / Misty / Unchained melody / Rags to riches / Anywhere I wander / As long as she needs me / Maria / Close to my heart / More / On the street where you live / All the way / Time and the river / Looking thru' the eyes of love / Blue colour / Angelica / River street / Eyes talk / No matter what you do / California / Backstage / Conquistador / Turn around / Dream world / Pretty flamingo / Nobody needs your love / Princess in rags / Amore mio / In love again
CD ____ NEMCD 893
Sequel / Nov '96 / BMG

TWENTY FOUR HOURS FROM TULSA
Twenty four hours from Tulsa / Nobody needs your love / 24 sycamore / Princess in rags / Half heaven, half heartache / Shady lady / I must be seeing things / Looking through the eyes of love / It hurts to be in love / Somewhere in the country / Something's gotten hold of my heart / Man who shot liberty valance / Maria Elena / Backstage (I'm lonely) / I'm gonna be strong / Last chance to turn around / Just one smile / Yours until tomorrow / Only love can break a heart / Town without pity
CD ____ TRTCD 157
TrueTrax / Oct '94 / THE

VERY BEST OF GENE PITNEY, THE
Twenty four hours from Tulsa / Something's gotten hold of my heart / Cold light of day / Yours until tomorrow / Backstage (I'm lonely) / Somewhere in the country / Town without pity / Looking through the eyes of love / Girl belongs to yesterday / I'm gonna be strong / Princess in rags / Nobody needs your love / Shady lady / I must be seeing things / Maria Elena / Street called hope / Just one smile / (I wanna) Love my life away / It hurts to be in love / Man who shot liberty valance
CD ____ MCCD 155
Music Club / May '94 / Disc / THE

VERY BEST OF GENE PITNEY, THE
24 hours from Tulsa / Town without pity / I'm gonna be strong / Something's gotten hold of my heart / Looking through the eyes of love / Man who shot Liberty Valance / Mecca / It hurts to be in love / Backstage / I wanna love my life away / Every breath I take / If I didn't have a dime / Yesterday's hero / Just one smile / Last chance to turn around / She's a heartbreaker / Half heaven, half heartache / Only love can break a heart / I must be seeing things / Princess in rags / True love never runs smooth
CD ____ GFS 049
Going For A Song / May '97 / Else / TKO Magnum

YOUNG AND WARM AND WONDERFUL/JUST ONE SMILE
CD ____ NEMCD 895
Sequel / Jun '97 / BMG

Pitre, Austin

OPELOUSAS WALTZ
CD ____ ARHCD 452
Arhoolie / Feb '97 / ADA / Cadillac / Direct

Pixies

BOSSANOVA
Cecilia Ann / Velouria / Is she weird / All over the world / Down to the well / Blown away / Stormy weather / Rock music / Allison / Ana / Dig for fire / Happening / Hang wire / Havalina
CD ____ CADCD 0010
4AD / Aug '90 / RTM/Disc

DOOLITTLE
Debaser / Wave of mutilation / Dead / Mr. Grieves / La la I love you / There goes my gun / Silver / Tame / Here comes your man / Monkey gone to heaven / Crackity Jones / Number 13 baby / Hey / Gouge away
CD ____ CADCD 905
4AD / Feb '89 / RTM/Disc

SURFER ROSA
Bone machine / Something against you / Gigantic / Where is my mind / Tony's theme / Vamos / Brick is red / Break my body / Broken face / River Euphrates / Cactus / Oh my golly / I'm amazed / Caribou / Vamos / Isla de Incanta / Ed is dead / Holiday song / Nimrod's song / I've been tired / Levitate me
CD ____ CAD 803CD
4AD / Mar '88 / RTM/Disc

TROMPE LE MONDE
Trompe le monde / Planet of sound / Alec Eiffel / Sad punk / Head on / U-mass / Palace of the Brine / Letter to Memphis / Bird dream of the Olympus Mons / Space (I believe in) / Subbacultcha / Distance equals rate times time / Lovely day / Motorway to Roswell / Navajo know
CD ____ CADCD 1014
4AD / Sep '91 / RTM/Disc

Pizzaman

PIZZAMANIA
CD ____ RODE 05CD
Cowboy / Oct '96 / 3mv/Pinnacle

Pizzarelli, Bucky

BUCKY PLAYS BIX
CD Set ____ DAPCD 238
Audiophile / Apr '89 / Jazz Music

MEMORIAL, A
CD ____ STCD 551
Stash / '92 / ADA / Cadillac / CM / Direct / Jazz Music

SOLO FLIGHT 1981/86
CD ____ STCD 573
Stash / Feb '94 / ADA / Cadillac / CM / Direct / Jazz Music

SOLOS AND DUETS (2CD Set) (Pizzarelli, Bucky & John)
You must believe in spring / Fols who live on the hill / Bad and the beautiful / Last night when we were young / Medley / Smoke gets in your eyes / One morning in May / Medley/Autumn leaves/Autumn in New York / Flashes / Spring can really hang you up the most / Concerto for guitar / Guess I'll have to change my plan / Out of this world / End of a love affair / Ill wind / Bewitched / 'Round midnight / Solo flight / Blah blah blah / Candlelights / All this and heaven too / Medley/My wonderful one/My best girl / Love for sale / Pretty women / Nuages / Sutton mutton / Close enough for love / Undecided / All through the night / This nearly was mine / Come rain or come shine / Nikki / Stems / In a mellow tone / Soon / Why did I chose you / Romanza & in the dark / Come rain or shine / (There is) no greater love / In a mist / Four brothers / Lush life / Sleeping bee / Blame it on my youth / Goodbye
CD ____ JZCL 5007
Jazz Classics / Nov '96 / Cadillac / Direct / Jazz Music

Pizzarelli, John

DEAR MR. COLE
Style is coming back in style / What can I say after I say I'm sorry / Little girl / You must be blind / Sweet Georgia Brown / It's only a paper moon / September song / On the sunny side of the street / Nature boy / This way out / Too marvellous for words / Route 66 / Sweet Lorraine / Straighten up and fly right / LOVE / Unforgettable / Portrait of Jenny / Honeysuckle rose
CD ____ 01241631822
Novus / Apr '95 / BMG

HIT THAT JIVE, JACK
CD ____ STB 2508
Stash / Sep '95 / ADA / Cadillac / CM / Direct / Jazz Music

I LIKE JERSEY BEST
CD ____ STB 2501
Stash / Apr '95 / ADA / Cadillac / CM / Direct / Jazz Music

NATURALLY
Splendid splinter / I'm confessin' that I love you / Oh lady be good / When I grow too old to dream / Gee baby ain't I good to you / Baby, baby, all the time / Midnight blue / Seven on Charlie / Slappin' the cakes on me / Nuage / I cried for you / Naturally / You stepped out of a dream / Headed out to Vera's / Your song is with me
CD ____ 01241631512
Novus / Mar '93 / BMG

NEW STANDARDS
Fools fall in love / Oh how my heart beats for you (Swing) / Beautiful moons ago / I'm your guy / Come on-a-my house / Beautiful Maria of my soul / I only want some / I'm alright now / Just a skosh / Why do people fall in love / Hearts like mine are broken every day / Better run before it's spring / Give me your heart / Look at us / Oh how my heart beats for you
CD ____ 01241631722
Novus / Jul '94 / BMG

ONE NIGHT WITH YOU
CD ____ JD 153
Chesky / May '97 / Discovery / Goldring

Pizzicato 5

5 X 5
Pizzicatomania / Twiggy, Twiggy / Baby love child / Me Japanese boy / This years girl # 2
CD ____ OLE 0962
Matador / Aug '94 / Vital

HAPPY END OF THE WORLD
World is spinning at 45 rpm / Trailer music / It's a beautiful day / Love's prelude / Love's theme / My baby portable player sound / Mon amour Tokyo / Collision and improvisation / Porno 3003 / Arigato we love you / Ma vie l'ete de vie / Happy ending / Earth goes around
CD ____ OLE 1982
Matador / Sep '97 / Vital

MADE IN USA
I / Sweet soul revue / Magic carpet ride / Readymade FM / Baby love child / Twiggy twiggy/Twiggy Vs. James Bond / This year's girl / I wanna be like you / Go go dancer / Catchy / Peace music
CD ____ OLE 0992
Matador / Aug '94 / Vital

SOUND OF MUSIC BY PIZZICATO 5, THE
We love pizzicato five / Rock 'n' roll / Night is still young / Happy sad / Groovy is my name / Sophisticated catchy / Strawberry sleighride / If I were a groupie / Sweet Thursday / CJD / Fortune cookie / Airplane / Number five / Young / Night is still / Good / Peace music / CDJ
CD ____ OLE 1662
Matador / Jun '96 / Vital

PJ & Duncan

PSYCHE
CD ____ TCD 2746
Telstar / Nov '94 / BMG

TOP KATZ
CD ____ TCD 2793
Telstar / Nov '95 / BMG

PJ Harvey

4 TRACK DEMOS
Rid of me / Legs / Reeling / Snake / Hook / Fifty foot Queenie / Driving / Ecstasy / Hardly wait / Rub 'til it bleeds / Easy / M Bike / Yuri-G / Goodnight
CD ____ IMCD 170
Island / Oct '93 / PolyGram

DRY
Oh my lover / O Stella / Dress / Victory / Happy and bleeding / Sheela na gig / Hair / Joe / Plants and rags / Fountain / Water
CD ____ PURECD 010
Too Pure / Mar '92 / Vital

RID OF ME
Rid of me / Missed / Legs / Rub 'til it bleeds / Hook / Man size sextet / Highway 61 revisited / Fifty foot queenie / Yuri-G / Man size / Dry / Me Jane / Snake / Ecstasy
CD ____ CID 8002
Island / Apr '93 / PolyGram

TO BRING YOU MY LOVE
To bring you my love / Meet ze monsta / Working for the man / C'mon Billy / Teclo / Long snake moan / Down by the water / I think I'm a mother / Send his love to me / Dancer
CD ____ CID 8035
Island / Feb '95 / PolyGram

TO BRING YOU MY LOVE/THE B-SIDES ALBUM
To bring you my love / Meet ze monsta / Working for the man / C'mon Billy / Teclo / Long snake moan / Down by the water / I think I'm a mother / Send his love to me / Dancer / Reeling / Daddy / Lying in the sun / Somebody's down, somebody's name / Darling be there / Maniac / One time too many / Harder / Goodnight
CD ____ CIDZ 8035
Island / Nov '95 / PolyGram

Pla, Roberto

ROBERTO PLA'S LATIN JAZZ ENSEMBLE
CD ____ TUMICD 051
Tumi / Feb '96 / Discovery / Stern's

Plaatjies, Dizu

ETHNO TRANCE LIVE (Plaatjies, Dizu & Mzwandile Qotoyi)
Emva emakhaya / Xa ndigoduka / Samora machel / Qash qash / Jembe on the mountain / Long live shangran / Weh mama yho / Yenzeka / Senyuk intabe / Engcobo
CD ____ BNETCD 0012
Bootleg.Net / Feb '97 / Vital/SAM

Placebo

PLACEBO
Come home / Teenage angst / Bionic / 36 degrees / Hang on to your IQ / Nancy boy / I know / Bruise pristine / Lady of the flowers / Swallow
CD ____ **CDFLOOR 002**
Elevator / Jan '97 / Vital

Placebo Effect

GALLERIES OF PAIN
CD ____ **EFA 11204**
Danse Macabre / Apr '93 / SRD

MANIPULATED MIND CONTROL
CD ____ **EFA 053242**
Ausfahrt / Oct '94 / SRD

PAST...PRESENT 1989-1995
CD ____ **EFACD 6330**
Ausfahrt / Jul '96 / SRD

Placid Angles

CRY, THE
Scarlet season / Ocean / Fate / Casting shadows (on warm Sundays) / Now and always / Lavinia / Everything under the sun / Her elements / December tragedy (revisited)
CD ____ **PF 069CD**
Peacefrog / Jul '97 / Mo's Music Machine / Prime / RTM/Disc / Vital

Plainsong

AND WHAT'S THAT
CD ____ **TX 2002CD**
Taxim / Dec '93 / ADA

SISTER FLUTE
Pilgrims / Spirits / I love this town / People's Park / Reality / Can't explain / 53 miles from Spanish town / Roll away the stone / Freedom of the highway / Mount Shannon / Baby's calling me home / Falling stars / Loser's lounge
CD ____ **LICD 901327**
Line / Dec '96 / CM / Direct

Planet

SPLITTING THE HUMIDITY
CD ____ **FOCUS 6CD**
Focus / Oct '95 / Pinnacle

Planet Rockers

26 CLASSIC TRACKS
CD ____ **SPINCD 003**
Spinout / Jun '97 / Cargo

COMING IN PERSON
CD ____ **NOHITCD 005**
No Hit / Jan '94 / Cargo / SRD

INVASION OF THE PLANET ROCKERS
CD ____ **NOHITCD 007**
No Hit / Jan '94 / Cargo / SRD

Planetary Assault Systems

ARCHIVES
In from the night / Twilight / Trek / Flightdrop / Manipulator / Gated / Booster / Electric / Starway ritual
CD ____ **PF 039CD**
Peacefrog / Feb '96 / Mo's Music Machine / Prime / RTM/Disc / Vital

ELECTRIC FUNK MACHINE
Searchin' / Menace / Exploration of the ravish / Return / Dream / Battle / Signal / Shaken / Parting
CD ____ **PF 063CD**
Peacefrog / Mar '97 / Mo's Music Machine / Prime / RTM/Disc / Vital

Plant, Robert

FATE OF NATIONS
Calling to you / Down to the sea / Come into my life / I believe / Twenty nine palms / Memory song (Hello, hello) / If I were a carpenter / Colours of a shade / Promised land / Greatest gift / Great spirit / Network news
CD ____ **5148672**
Fontana / May '93 / PolyGram

MANIC NIRVANA
Hurting kind (I've got my eyes on you) / SSS and Q / Nirvana / Your ma said you cried in your sleep last night / Liars dance / Big love / I cried / Tie dye on the highway / Anniversary / Watching you
CD ____ **7567913362**
Atlantic / Aug '96 / Warner Music

PICTURES AT ELEVEN
Burning down one side / Moonlight in Samosa / Pledge pin / Slow dancer / Worse than Detroit / Fat lip / Like I've never been gone / Mystery title
CD ____ **SK 259418**
Swansong / '86 / Warner Music

Planxty

AFTER THE BREAK
CD ____ **TARACD 3001**
Tara / Oct '89 / ADA / CM / Conifer/BMG / Direct

COLD BLOW AND THE RAINY NIGHT
Johnny Cope / Reels / Cold blow and the rainy night / P stands for Paddy, I suppose / Polkas / Bansea's green glade / Nominsko horo / Little drummer / Lakes of Ponchartrain / Jigs / Green fields of Canada
CD ____ **SH 79011CD**
Shanachie / '90 / ADA / Greensleeves / Koch

WELL BELOW THE VALLEY, THE
CD ____ **SH 79010CD**
Shanachie / '88 / ADA / Greensleeves / Koch

WOMAN I LOVED SO WELL, THE
True love knows no season / Out on the ocean/Tiocfaidh tu abhaile liom / Roger O'Hehir / Tailor's twist / Kellswater / Johnny of Brady's lea / Woman I never forgot/Pullet/Ladies pantalettes / Little musgrave
CD ____ **TARACD 3005**
Tara / Jan '92 / ADA / CM / Conifer/BMG / Direct

Plasmatics

NEW HOPE FOR THE WRETCHED
Tight black pants / Monkey suit / Living dead / Test tube babies / Won't you / Concrete shoes / Squirm (live) / Want you baby / Dream lover / Sometimes / Corruption / Butcher baby
CD ____ **DOJOCD 79**
Dojo / Feb '94 / Disc
CD ____ **STIFFCD 16**
Disky / Jan '94 / Disky / THE

Plass, Wesley

I'LL BE THERE
CD ____ **ISCD 120**
Intersound / '91 / Jazz Music

KEEP GOING
CD ____ **ISCD 162**
Intersound / Sep '96 / Jazz Music

Plastic Venus

HELVEN PARK
CD ____ **WM 5**
Swim / Apr '96 / Kudos / RTM/Disc / SRD

Plasticland

DAPPER SNAPPINGS
CD ____ **EFA 156602**
Repulsion / Feb '95 / SRD

Plastico

PLASTICO
CD ____ **97522ULT**
Edel / May '96 / Pinnacle

Plastikman

MUSIK
CD ____ **CDNOMU 37**
Nova Mute / Nov '94 / Prime / RTM/Disc

SHEET ONE
CD ____ **NOMU 22CD**
Mute / Oct '93 / RTM/Disc

Plateau

MUSIC FOR GRASS BARS
CD ____ **CLP 9966**
Cleopatra / Jun '97 / Cargo / Greyhound / Plastic Head / RTM/Disc / SRD

Platinum Dance Orchestra

STRICT TEMPO (64 Great Dance Melodies)
Quickstep medley / Slow fox-trot medley / Samba medley / Barn dance medley / Tango medley / Palma waltz medley / Gypsy tap medley / Old time waltz medley / Rumba medley / Pride of Erin / Cha cha medley
CD ____ **PLATCD 03**
Platinum / Dec '88 / Prism

Platters

19 HITS
CD ____ **KCD 5002**
King / Apr '97 / Avid/BMG

20 CLASSIC TRACKS
CD ____ **MACCD 232**
Autograph / Aug '96 / BMG

ALL THE HITS AND MORE (2CD Set)
CD Set ____ **DBG 53041**
Double Gold / Apr '95 / Target/BMG

AUDIO ARCHIVE
Great pretender / Smoke gets in your eyes / Magic touch / Only you / Twilight time / Wonder of you / I get the sweetest feeling / I'm sorry / I love you 1000 times / Red sails in the sunset / Sweet sweet lovin' / Delilah / Harbour lights / My prayer / Washed ashore / Heaven on earth / I love you yes I do / All my love belongs to you / More I see you / Sayonara
CD ____ **CDAA 007**
Tring / Jan '92 / Tring

BEST OF THE PLATTERS, THE
Smoke gets in your eyes / Great pretender / My dream / Twilight time / You'll never never know / (You've got) The magic touch / One in a million / Enchanted / I'm sorry / Only you / Harbour lights / Red sails in the sunset / I wish / Sleepy lagoon / Ebb tide / Heaven on Earth / Remember when / My prayer
CD ____ **5517312**
Spectrum / Nov '95 / PolyGram

ENCHANTED
Great pretender / Enchanted / You'll never never know / Little things mean a lot / I'll never smile again / Magic touch / Sixteen tons / I'm sorry / September song / Where / You're making a mistake / My dream / Trees / Winner takes all
CD ____ **5500922**
Spectrum / Oct '93 / PolyGram

ESSENTIAL COLLECTION, THE (2CD Set)
CD Set ____ **LECD 619**
Wisepack / Apr '95 / Conifer/BMG / THE

FOUR PLATTERS AND ONE LOVELY DISH (9CD Set)
Bark, battle and ball / I wanna / Why should I / Only you (and you alone) / Great pretender / I'm just a dancing partner / Winner takes all / Magic touch / My prayer / Someone to watch over me / I'm sorry / At your beck and call / Heaven on earth / Bewitched, bothered and bewildered / On my word of honor / Glory of love / Have mercy / Remember when / You'll never, never know / One in a million / I give you my word / It isn't right / You've changed / He's mine / I'll get by / I don't know why / Heart of stone / I'd climb the highest mountain / Temptation / In the still of the night / September in the rain / Wagon wheels / You can depend on me / Take me in your arms / You're making a mistake / My dream / Lie low / Darktown strutters ball / Mean to me / You are too beautiful / No power on earth / I'm gonna sit right down and write myself a letter / Time and tide / Love you funny thing / In the middle of nowhere / When you return / Let's start all over again / Oh promise me / Don't forget / Only because / Sweet sixteen / Mystery of you / Indif'rent / Sixteen tons / Goodnight sweetheart, it's time to go / My serenade / Try a little tenderness / My old flame / Sleepy time gal / Don't blame me / Wish me love / Helpless / I wish / No matter what you are / Twilight time / Twilight time / That old feeling / I'll take you home again Kathleen / It's raining outside / For the first time / Whispering wind / But not like you / Out of my mind / Don't let go / You don't say / Are you sincere / If I didn't care / Smoke gets in your eyes / Thanks for the memory / I can't get started (with you) / Somebody loves me / My blue heaven / Love in bloom / Prisoner of love / Until the real thing comes along / I'll never smile again / Tisket-a-tasket / Hula hop / Wish it were me / Enchanted / Where / Love of a lifetime / Sound and the fury / To each his own / Harbor lights / By the sleepy lagoon / By the river Sainte Marie / Rainbow on the river / Sad river / Ebb tide / Reflections in the water / My secret / What does it matter / Whispering grass / I'll be with you in apple blossom time / Lullaby of the leaves / Jeannine / Tumbling tumbleweeds / Trees / Orchids in the moonlight / Little white gardenia / Honeysuckle rose / Life is just a bowl of cherries / When you wore a tulip / Roses of picardy / Movin' in / One love / Immortal love / Love, your magic spell is everywhere / Love is just around the corner / Love me or leave me / It's love love love / Let's fall in love / Advertise it / Who wouldn't love you / (I'm afraid) the masquerade is over / Nearness of you / You'll never know / It's magic / I love you truly / Love is / Love is the sweetest thing / Love is a many splendoured thing / Don't let me fall in love / True lover / Rear view mirror / I miss you so / I just got rid of a heartache / Reaching for a star / All the things you are / Song for the lonely / Say a prayer / How will I know / Keep me in love / If only you knew / Summertime / Embraceable you / People will say we're in love / Poor butterfly / Stormy weather / Every little movement / More than you know / September song / That old black magic / My heart belongs to daddy / Sometimes I'm happy / But not for me / Heartbreak / Memories / Moon over Miami / On the top of my mind / In a little Spanish town / Shine on harvest moon / OH how I miss you tonight / I'll see you in my dreams / Moonlight memories / Moonlight and roses / My reverie / Full moon and empty arms / Once in a while / Sentimental journey / It might as well be spring / But beautiful / I only have eyes for you / Pennies from heaven / Singin' in the rain / Blues in the night / As time goes by / My romance / Moonlight and shadows / Sweet Leilani / Stay as sweet as you are / Here comes heaven again / Viva jujuy / Cuando calienta el sol / Maria Elena / Solamente tu / Siboney / Amor / Aquellos ojos verdes / Aquarela do Brazil / Tu dolce voz / La hora del crepusculo / Besame mucho / Malaguena salerosa / Strangers / Winter wonderland / White Christmas / Silent night / Santa Claus is coming to town / I'll be home for Christmas / For Auld Lang Syne / Rudolph the red nosed reindeer / All I want for Christmas (is my two front teeth) / Come home for Christmas / Jingle bell rock / Jingle bells jingle / Blue Christmas / Christmas time / Sincerely / PS I love you / Hut sut song / Banana boat song (Day O) / Mississippi mud / False hearted lover / Michael, row the boat ashore / Crying in the chapel / Java jive / Three coins in the fountain / Way down yonder in New Orleans / Three bells / Song from Moulin Rouge / Little things mean a lot / (We're gonna) Rock around the clock / Don't be cruel / Tammy / Volare / Mack the knife / Summer place / Exodus song / Twist / Love me tender / Anniversary song / Gypsy / When I fall in love / Big forget / Soothe me / Easy street / It could happen to you / Blues serenade / These foolish things / Somewhere along the way / Lover / House of the rising sun / Hard hearted Hannah
CD Set ____ **BCD 15741**
Bear Family / Jan '94 / Direct / Rollercoaster / Swift

GOLDEN HITS COLLECTION
CD ____ **PWK 071**
Carlton / Sep '88 / Carlton

GOLDEN HITS, THE
Only you / Twilight time / Smoke gets in your eyes / You'll never know / Sixteen tons / My prayer / Great pretender / You've got the magic touch / September song / Ebb tide / Harbour lights / Red sails in the sunset / On a slow boat to China / Sleepy lagoon / Lazy river / Moonlight on the Colorado / Crying in the chapel / Summertime
CD ____ **8264472**
Mercury / '86 / PolyGram

GREAT PRETENDER, THE
Only you / Great pretender / Pledging my love / Twilight time / Harbour lights / Smoke gets in your eyes / With this ring / Sweet inspiration / Magic touch / Love you a thousand times / I believe / Put your hand in my hand / Red sails in the sunset / Shake it up mambo / Headin' home / My prayer
CD ____ **SUMCD 4013**
Summit / Nov '96 / Sound & Media

GREATEST HITS
CD ____ **GRF 215**
Tring / Mar '93 / Tring

GREATEST HITS
CD ____ **CDSGP 014**
Prestige / Oct '92 / Else / Total/BMG

GREATEST HITS
CD ____ **MACCD 126**
Autograph / Aug '96 / BMG

HITS COLLECTION, THE
Smoke gets in your eyes / Great pretender / My prayer / Only you / Twilight time / Harbour lights / Remember when / I'm sorry / I love you 1000 times / (You've got) that magic touch / With this ring / He's mine / I'll be home / Red sails in the sunset / Sweet sweet lovin' / Washed ashore
CD ____ **100432**
CMC / May '97 / BMG

MUSICOR YEARS, THE
With this ring / I love you 1000 times / I can't get used to sharing you / Don't hear, speak, see no evil / Washed ashore / Doesn't it ring a bell / Devri / Why do you wanna make me blue / Think before you walk / So many tears / Alone in the night / How beautiful our love is / Hard to get thing called love / Sweet sweet lovin' / Going back to Detroit / Run while it's dark / Fear of losing you / Not my girl / Get a hold of yourself / Shing-a-ling-a-loo / Baby baby / Love must go on / I'll be home / If I had a love / What name shall I give you my love / Magic touch / Sonata / Why
CD ____ **CDKEND 116**
Kent / Jul '94 / Pinnacle

ONLY YOU
CD ____ **15077**
Laserlight / Aug '92 / Target/BMG

PACKET OF THREE VOL.6 (3CD Set) (Platters/Canned Heat/Bob Marley & The Wailers)
Only you: *Platters* / I love you a thousand times: *Platters* / Unchained melody: *Platters* / I love you because: *Platters* / My prayer: *Platters* / Red sails in the sunset: *Platters* / Magic touch: *Platters* / Smoke gets in your eyes: *Platters* / Great pretender: *Platters* / Alone in the night: *Platters* / With this ring: *Platters* / Why: *Platters* / Harbour lights: *Platters* / Doesn't it ring a bell: *Platters* / I'm sorry: *Platters* / Twilight time: *Platters* / Remember when: *Platters* / Sayonara: *Platters* / Love letters: *Platters* / Spoonful: *Canned Heat* / Big road blues: *Canned Heat* / Rollin' and tumblin': *Canned Heat* / Got my mojo working: *Canned Heat* / Pretty thing: *Canned Heat* / Louise: *Canned Heat* / Dimples: *Canned Heat* / Don't hold on: *Canned Heat* / Straight ahead: *Canned Heat* / Rollin' and tumblin': *Canned Heat* / I'd rather be a devil: *Canned Heat* / Wish you would: *Canned Heat* / When things go wrong: *Canned Heat* / Sweet sixteen: *Canned Heat* / Bullfrog blues: *Canned Heat* / Dust my broom: *Canned Heat* / Chances are: *Marley, Bob & The Wailers* / Hammer: *Marley, Bob & The Wailers* / Touch me: *Marley, Bob & The Wailers* / How many times: *Marley, Bob & The Wailers* / Soul almighty: *Marley, Bob & The Wailers* / Kaya: *Marley, Bob & The Wailers* / Trench town rock: *Marley, Bob & The Wailers* / 400 years: *Marley, Bob & The*

Wailers / Lively up yourself: *Marley, Bob & The Wailers* / Soul captives: *Marley, Bob & The Wailers* / Back out: *Marley, Bob & The Wailers* / Soon come: *Marley, Bob & The Wailers* / Riding high: *Marley, Bob & The Wailers* / Soul shakedown party: *Marley, Bob & The Wailers* / Do it twice: *Marley, Bob & The Wailers* / Stop the train: *Marley, Bob & The Wailers* / Natural mystic: *Marley, Bob & The Wailers* / Rainbow country: *Marley, Bob & The Wailers* / Cheer up: *Marley, Bob & The Wailers* / Don't rock my boat: *Marley, Bob & The Wailers*
CD Set ________ **KLMCD 306**
BAM / Nov '96 / Koch / Scratch/BMG

PLATTERS
CD ________ **LECD 040**
Dynamite / May '94 / THE

PLATTERS (CD/CD Rom Set)
CD Set ________ **WWCDR 005**
Magnum Music / Apr '97 / TKO Magnum

PLATTERS COLLECTION
Great pretender / Smoke gets in your eyes / (You've got) the magic touch / Only you / Twilight time / Wonder of you / I get the sweetest feeling / I'm sorry / I love you 1,000 times / Red sails in the sunset / Harbour lights / My prayer / Washed ashore (on a lonely island in the sea) / Heaven on earth / I love you yes I do / All my love belongs to you / More I see you
CD ________ **QED 012**
Tring / Nov '96 / Tring

PLATTERS, THE
CD ________ **KLMCD 043**
BAM / Apr '95 / Koch / Scratch/BMG

PLATTERS, THE
Great pretender / I love you 1000 times / One in a million / With this ring / Pledging my love / Devri / Harbour lights / Sweet, sweet lovin' / Unchained melody / Only because / Twilight time / Doesn't it ring a bell / My prayer / Smoke gets in your eyes / Only you (and you alone) / I'm sorry / You'll never know / (You've got) the magic touch / Red sails in the sunset / If I had you / Washed ashore (on a lonely island in the sea)
CD ________ **399525**
Koch Presents / Jun '97 / Koch

PLATTERS, THE
CD ________ **HM 018**
Harmony / Jun '97 / TKO Magnum

PLATTERS/DRIFTERS ESSENTIALS (Platters & Drifters)
CD ________ **LECDD 626**
Wisepack / Aug '95 / Conifer/BMG / THE

REMEMBER WHEN
CD ________ **AIM 1026CD**
Aim / Oct '93 / ADA / Direct / Jazz Music

SINCERELY
Only you (And you alone) / Smoke gets in your eyes / Thanks for the memory / Red sails in teh sunset / I wish / I wanna / I only have eyes for you / On a slow boat to China / To each his own / Heaven on earth / I wish it were me / Glory of love / Lazy river / Sincerely
CD ________ **5500522**
Spectrum / May '93 / PolyGram

SIXTIES PLATTERS (2CD Set)
Only you (and you alone) / Great pretender / (You've got) The magic touch / My prayer / Heaven on Earth / I'm sorry / Twilight time / Smoke gets in your eyes / Harbour lights / I love you a thousand times / I'll be home / With this ring / Washed ashore (on a lonely island in the sea) / Sweet, sweet lovin' / If I had you / Lovely / I love you because / Baby, baby / Sonata / If I had a love / Going back to Detroit / Get a hold of yourself / Shing-a-ling-a-loo / Love must go on / I can't get used to sharing you / Why do you wanna make me feel blue / Run while it's dark / Devri / On the top of my mind / We ain't what we was / Doesn't it ring a bell / Fear of losing you / Not my girl / Don't hear, speak, see no evil / What name shall I give you / My love / Why / Think before you walk away / Hard to get a thing called love / How beautiful our love is / So many tears / Alone in the night (without you)
CD Set ________ **CPCD 82512**
Charly / Jan '97 / Koch

SMOKE GETS IN YOUR EYES
Great pretender / Only you / Harbour lights / Pledging my love / With this ring / My prayer / Smoke gets in your eyes / Twilight time / I'm sorry / If I had you / Red sails in the sunset / I'll be home / I love you 1000 times / Sweet sweet lovin' / Delilah / Washed ashore / Magic touch / Heaven on earth / I love you, yes I do / All my love belongs to you
CD ________ **CDINS 5045**
Charly / Sep '91 / Koch

SMOKE GETS IN YOUR EYES
CD ________ **MU 5071**
Musketeer / Oct '92 / Disc

SMOKE GETS IN YOUR EYES (20 Greatest Hits)
Great pretender / Only you / My prayer / Twilight time / Smoke gets in your eyes / I'm sorry / With this ring / Harbour lights / He's mine / Magic touch / One in a million / Red sails in the sunset / Platters mix / Heading home / Sweet inspiration / Riding in the mainline / Cheer up brother / Put your hand / God saw the blood / How great thou art
CD ________ **PLATCD 144**
Platinum / Mar '96 / Prism

Plaxico, Lonnie

SHORT TAKES
CD ________ **MCD 5477**
Muse / Mar '93 / New Note/Pinnacle

WITH ALL YOUR HEART
With all your heart / When you went away / Ray / Basement jammin' / Sixteenth Movement / Avonelle / Southside soul / As I gaze / Since we parted
CD ________ **MCD 5525**
Muse / Jul '95 / New Note/Pinnacle

Play Dead

COMPANY OF JUSTICE
CD ________ **FREUDCD 41**
Jungle / Sep '93 / RTM/Disc / SRD

FIRST FLOWER
CD ________ **CLEO 7519CD**
Cleopatra / Jan '94 / Cargo / Greyhound / Plastic Head / RTM/Disc / SRD

Playboys

EASY ROCKIN'
Shake your hips / Little Miss Pancake / Baby treat me right / Ritchie's rumba / Rakin' 'n' scrapin' / 24 hour girl / She sure can rock me / Revenge / Easy rockin' / Dizzy Miss Lizzy / Don't start cryin' now / Caldonia / Get on the right track / Rock-a-bye baby blues
CD ________ **JRCD 26**
Jappin' & Rockin' / Mar '97 / Swift / TKO Magnum

INVITATION TO DEATH
CD ________ **FCD 3008**
Fury / Mar '97 / Nervous / TKO Magnum

Players

CHRISTMAS
CD ________ **EXPALCD 6**
Expression / Nov '91 / Pinnacle

CHRISTMAS
CD ________ **EXVP 8CD**
Expression / Dec '96 / Pinnacle

Players Association

BORN TO DANCE
CD ________ **VMD 79398**
Vanguard / Oct '96 / ADA / Pinnacle

Playground

BENT, LOST OR BROKEN
CD ________ **HABITCD 001**
IFA / Oct '95 / Plastic Head

RESILIENCE
CD ________ **DPROMCD 5**
Dirter Promotions / Nov '91 / Cargo / Pinnacle / World Serpent

Playgroup

EPIC SOUND BATTLES VOL.1 & 2
Bombs scare / Epic sound battles / Crunch / Slither / Burn up / Deep and mintyful / Silent mover / Epic one drop / Shock absorbers / No speed limit / Boggs might fly / Ballroom control / Going overdrawn / Going for a song / Haphazard / Squeek squawk / Shoot out / Lost in LA
CD ________ **CDBRED 28**
Cherry Red / Aug '97 / Pinnacle

Playle, Jerry

BEYOND SILENCE
Another time / Riders on the storm / Toys / Nice pair / Senorina latina / World suite / Praying for rain / Mirage / Managua tormenta / Aries rising / Beyond silence
CD ________ **33JAZZ 022**
33 Jazz / Apr '95 / Cadillac / New Note/Pinnacle

Pleasant Gehman

RUINED
CD ________ **NAR 086CD**
New Alliance / Aug '93 / Plastic Head

Pleasers

THAMESBEAT
CD ________ **LMCD 052**
Lost Moment / Jan '97 / Else / Shellshock/Disc

Pleasure

BEST OF PLEASURE, THE
Bouncy lady / Straight ahead / Sassafras girl / Let me be the one / Two for one / Tune in / Foxy lady / Ghettos of the mind / Joyous / Glide / Strong love / Ladies night out / Pleasure for your pleasure / No matter what / Selim
CD ________ **CDBGPD 036**
Beat Goes Public / Jun '92 / Pinnacle

Pleasure Barons

LIVE IN LAS VEGAS
CD ________ **HCD 8044**
Hightone / Jul '94 / ADA / Koch

Pleasure Elite

BAD JUJU
CD ________ **CDVEST 13**
Bulletproof / Jun '94 / Pinnacle

Pleasure Fuckers

FOR YOUR PLEASURE
CD ________ **GRITA 35127CD**
Grita / Jun '96 / Plastic Head

Plecid

PLECID
CD ________ **ANJ 001CD**
Misanthropy / Apr '97 / Plastic Head

Pleiadians

IFO
CD ________ **BFLCD 24**
Dragonfly / Aug '97 / Mo's Music Machine / Pinnacle

Plethyn

BLAS Y PRIDD/GOLAU TAN GWMWL
Y gwlliaid / Ffarwel i blwy Llangywer / Ifan Pant y Fedwen / Can y cathreiniwr / Y morwr / Y sgythan / Helyntion caru / Lluen / Merch o blwy Penderyn / Cystal gen i swlt / Marwnad yr ehedydd / Pentre Llanfihangel / Hwlio'r heli / Twll bach y clo / Golau tan gwmwl / Y deryn du a'i blufyn sidan / Lodes lan / Gwaed ar eu dwylo / Un peth rwy'n ei garu / Y cryman bach / Pelydrau / Adar man y mynydd / Ye ferch yn ffair Llanidloes / Gwenno Penygelli / Deio bach / Tan yn Llyn
CD ________ **SAIN 6045CD**
Sain / Aug '94 / ADA / Direct / Greyhound

DRWS AGORED
Cwm y coed / Myn Mair / Breuddwyd Glyndwr / Rho wen yn dy gwsg / La Rochelle / Philomela / Hon yw fy Olwen i / Y ceidwad / Ffarwel i Aberystweth / Wylaf dros Iwerddon / Y deryn pur / Cysga di fy mhlentyn tlws / Tafarn fach glyd ar y cei
CD ________ **SAIN 4033CD**
Sain / Aug '94 / ADA / Direct / Greyhound

SEIDIR DDOE
CD ________ **SCD 2083**
Sain / Dec '94 / ADA / Direct / Greyhound

Plews, Steve

ANYWHERE (Plews, Steve Ensemble)
Anywhere / Thick withins / St. Magnus / 3675 Alta Brea / St. Magnus / Your territory / St. Magnus / Isthmus / Submantle / Tumuli / Cart low
CD ________ **ASSCD 15**
ASC / Jun '97 / Cadillac / New Note/Pinnacle

LIVE 1995 - MADE IN MANCHESTER
Idsong / God's mates / Riley's death / Sleepwalker / An idle person in love / Too much apple pie
CD ________ **ASCCD 6**
ASC / Jan '96 / Cadillac / New Note/Pinnacle

SECRET SPACES
Idsong / Humorists / Secret spaces / Fanfare for a pit pony / Free fantasia / Ivov / 188 / Pavanne for JW
CD ________ **ASCCD 3**
ASC / Sep '95 / Cadillac / New Note/Pinnacle

Plexi

CD EP
CD ________ **IFACD 003**
IFA / Nov '95 / Plastic Head

CHEER UP
CD ________ **SPCD 360**
Sub Pop / Oct '96 / Cargo / Greyhound / Shellshock/Disc

Pliers

I WANNA BE YOUR MAN
CD ________ **RNCD 2066**
Rhino / Aug '94 / Grapevine/PolyGram / Jet Star

Plimley, Paul

DENSITY OF LOVESTRUCK DEMONS (Plimley, Paul & Lisle Ellis/Donald Robinson)
CD ________ **CD 906**
Music & Arts / Feb '96 / Cadillac / Harmonia Mundi

Plimsouls

ONE NIGHT IN AMERICA
Hush hush / How long will it take / I want what you got / In this town / Help yourself / I'll get lucky / Now / Million miles away / Time won't let me / One more heartache / Dizzy Miss Lizzy / Come on now
CD ________ **422266**
New Rose / May '94 / ADA / Direct / Discovery

Plotkin, James

AURORA (Plotkin, James & Kazuyuki Null)
CD ________ **RKS 1113**
Rawkus / Feb '97 / Cargo / Greyhound

Plow United

GOODNIGHT SELLOUT
Plow 2 / You can't kill me casue I'm already dead / Header / Fuck up / Rock city / King / Burn up / Sell out / Lighters / Runaway / Confrontation / Go home / Father / I don't want to die tonight / Tour guide at the Alamo / Spindle / Reason / Plow / That girl / Martin / St. Patrick's day / Poison berries / You are here / Prince / World according to me
CD ________ **BLK 5002ECD**
Blackout / Oct '96 / Plastic Head / Vital

Plug

DRUM 'N' BASS FOR PAPA
CD ________ **ANGEL 1CD**
Blue Angel/Rising High / Jul '96 / 3mv/Sony

VISIBLE CRATER FUNK (Plug 1)
CD ________ **ANGEL 6CD**
Blue Angel / May '96 / 3mv/Sony / Prime / RTM/Disc

Plummer, Tonya

I'M READY
CD ________ **JBR 001**
Johnny Boy / Oct '94 / Else

Plunk

SWELL
CD ________ **GAP 026**
Gap Recordings / Jun '95 / SRD

Pluramon

PICK UP CANYON
CD ________ **EFA 006762**
Mille Plateau / Jul '96 / SRD

Pluto

PLUTO...PLUS
I really want it / Crossfire / And my old rocking horse / Down and out / She's innocent / Road to glory / Stealing my thunder / Beauty Queen / Mr. Westwood / Something that you loved / Rag a bone Joe / Bare lady
CD ________ **SEECD 265**
See For Miles/C5 / Oct '89 / Pinnacle

Pluto

RISING
CD ________ **ITPAL 002CD**
ITP / Jul '95 / Jumpstart / Kudos / Pinnacle

PM Dawn

BLISS ALBUM, THE
CD ________ **IMCD 222**
Gee Street / Mar '96 / PolyGram

JESUS WEPT
CD ________ **GEECD 16**
Gee Street / Oct '95 / PolyGram

OF THE HEART, OF THE SOUL, OF THE CROSS
Intro / Reality used to be a friend of mine / Paper doll / To serenade a rainbow (Tony Love mix) / Comatose / Watchers point of view (7" youth mix) / Even after I die / Ode to a forgetful mind (The more than words mix) / Twisted mellow / Paper doll (Flute mix) / In the presence of mirrors / Set adrift on memory bliss / Shake / If I wuz U
CD ________ **IMCD 235**
Island / Sep '96 / PolyGram

PMD

BUSINESS IS BUSINESS
Intro / Business is business / Leave your style cramped / Rugged 'n' raw / What cha gonna do: *PMD & Das EFX* / Never watered down: *PMD & Nocturnal* / It's the pee / Kool dat / Interlude / Its the one: *PMD & MOP* / Nuttin move: *PMD & Das EFX* / I'm a B-Boy / Rugged 'n' raw: *PMD & Das EFX*
CD ________ **4867362**
Relativity / Nov '96 / Sony

Po

DUCKS & DRAKES
CD ________ **RUTCD 001**
Rutland / Oct '93 / RTM/Disc

NOT MARKED ON THE ORDNANCE
CD ________ **RUTCD 004**
Rutland / Feb '96 / RTM/Disc

Poachers Pocket

FAIR GAME
CD WGSCD 267
Wild Goose / Feb '96 / ADA

Pocket Fishermen

FUTURE GODS OF ROCK
CD SECT2 10016
Sector 2 / Aug '95 / Cargo / Direct

Poco

BLUE AND GREY
CD MCAD 22068
One Way / Apr '94 / ADA / Direct / Greyhound

COWBOYS AND ENGLISHMEN
CD MCAD 22067
One Way / Apr '94 / ADA / Direct / Greyhound

CRAZY EYES
Blue water / Fool's gold / Here we go again / Brass buttons / Right along / Crazy eyes / Magnolia / Let's dance tonight
CD EK 66968
Epic / Jul '95 / Sony

ESSENTIAL COLLECTION, THE
CD HMNCD 008
Half Moon / Jun '97 / BMG

FORGOTTEN TRAIL (2CD Set)
Pickin' up the pieces / Grand junction / Consequently so long / First love / Calico lady / My kind of love / Hard luck / Last call (cold enchilada) / Honky tonk downstairs / Hurry up / You better think twice / Anyway bye bye / I guess you made it / C'mon / Hear that music / Kind woman / Just for me and you / Bad weather / Lullaby in September / You are the one / From the inside / Good feelin' to know / I can see everything / And settlin' down / Blue water / Fool's gold / Nothin's still the same / Skunk Creek / Here we go again / Crazy eyes / Get in the wind / Believe me / Rocky Mountain breakdown / Faith in the families / Western Waterloo / Whatever happened to your smile / Sagebrush serenade
CD Set 4874832
Epic / Jun '97 / Sony

FROM THE INSIDE/GOOD FEELIN' TO KNOW
From the inside / Bad weather / What am I gonna do / You are the one / Railroad days / Do you feel it to / Ol' forgiver / What if I should say I love you / Just for me and you / And settlin' down / Ride the country / I can see everything / Go and say goodbye / Keeper of the fire / Early times / Good feelin' to know / Restrain / Sweet lovin'
CD BGOCD 359
Beat Goes On / Jun '97 / Pinnacle

PICKIN' UP THE PIECES
Foreward / What a day / Nobody's fool / Calico lady / First love / Make me a smile / Short changed / Pickin' up the pieces / Grand junction / Oh yeah / Just in case it happens / Yes indeed / Tomorrow / Consequently so long / Do you feel it
CD EK 66227
Epic / Jul '95 / Sony

ROSE OF CIMARRON
Stealaway / Just like me / Rose of Cimarron / Company's coming / Slow poke / Too many nights too long / When you come around / Starin' at the sky / All alone together / Tulsa turnaround
CD MCAD 22076
One Way / Apr '94 / ADA / Direct / Greyhound

SEVEN
Drivin' wheel / Rocky mountain breakdown / Just call my name / Skatin' / Faith in the families / Krikkit's song / Angel / You've got your reasons
CD EK 66985
Epic / Jul '95 / Sony

Podewell, Polly

POLLY PODEWELL
CD ACD 276
Audiophile / Aug '95 / Jazz Music

Poem Rocket

FELIX CULPA
Eject / Deus absconditus / Animal planter / Contrail de l'avion / Small white animal / Flaw / Milky white entropy / Period / Pretty baby / Blue chevy impala
CD PCP 0292
PCP / Nov '95 / Vital

Poets

IN YOUR TOWER
CD STRIKE 901
Strike / Jun '97 / Greyhound

Pogatschar, Helga

MARS REQUIEM
CD EFA 155892
Gymnastic / Dec '95 / SRD

Pogues

BEST OF THE POGUES, THE
Fairytale of New York / Sally Maclennane / Dirty old town / Irish rover / Pair of brown eyes / Streams of whiskey / Rainy night in Soho / Fiesta / Rain street / Misty morning Albert Bridge / White City / Thousands are sailing / Broad majestic Shannon / Body of an American
CD 9031754052
WEA / Oct '91 / Warner Music

HELL'S DITCH
Sunny side of the street / Sayonara / Ghost of a smile / Hell's ditch / Lorca's novena / Summer in Siam / Rain street / Rainbow man / Wake of the Medusa / House of the Gods / Five green Queens and Jean / Maidrin rua / Six to go
CD 9031725542
WEA / Mar '94 / Warner Music

IF I SHOULD FALL FROM GRACE WITH GOD
If I should fall from grace with God / Turkish song of the damned / Bottle of smoke / Fairytale of New York / Metropolis / Thousands are sailing / South Australia* / Fiesta / Recruiting sergeant / Rocky road to Dublin / Galway races (medley) / Streets of sorrow/Birmingham six / Lullaby of London / Battle march / Sit down by the fire / Broad majestic Shannon / Worms
CD K 2444932
WEA / Mar '94 / Warner Music

PEACE AND LOVE
Gridlock / Young Ned of the hill / Cotton fields / Down all days / Lorelei / Boat train / Night train to Lorca / White City / Misty morning Albert Bridge / Blue heaven / USA / Gartioney rats / Tombstone / London you're a lady
CD K 2460862
WEA / Mar '94 / Warner Music

POGUE MAHONE
How come / Living in a world without her / When the ship comes in / Anniversary / Amadie / Love you till the end / Bright lights / Oretown / Pont Mirabeau / Tosspint / 4 o'clock in the morning / Where that love's been gone / Sun and the moon
CD 0630112102
WEA / Dec '96 / Warner Music

RED ROSES FOR ME
Transmetropolitan / Battle of Brisbane / Auld triangle / Waxie's dargle / Sea shanty / Dark streets of London / Streams of whiskey / Poor Paddy / Dingle regatta / Greenland whale fisheries / Down in the ground where the dead men go / Kitty
CD K 2444942
WEA / Mar '94 / Warner Music

REST OF THE BEST, THE
If I should fall from grace with God / Sick bed of Cuchulainn / Old main drag / Boys from the county hell / Young Ned of the hill / Dark streets of London / Repeal of the licensing laws / Yeah yeah yeah yeah yeah / London girl / Honky tonk women / Summer in siam / Turkish song of the damned / Sunny side of the street / Hell's ditch
CD 9031773412
WEA / Mar '94 / Warner Music

RUM, SODOMY AND THE LASH
Sick bed of Cuchulainn / Old main drag / Wild cats of Kilkenny / Man you don't meet every day / Pair of brown eyes / Sally Maclennane / Dirty old town / Jesse James / Navigator / Billy's bones / Gentleman soldier / And the band played waltzing Matilda / Pistol for Paddy Garcia
CD K 2444952
WEA / Mar '94 / Warner Music

WAITING FOR HERB
Tuesday morning / Smell of petroleum / Haunting / Once upon a time / Sittin' on top of the world / Drunken boat / Big city / Girl from the Wadi Hammamat / Modern world / Pachinko / My baby's gone / Small hours
CD 4509934632
WEA / Sep '93 / Warner Music

Pohjola, Pekka

HEAVY JAZZ
CD PELPCD 7
Pohjola / Feb '96 / Direct

Poindexter, Pony

PLAYS 'THE BIG ONES'/GUMBO
Midnight in Moscow / Moon river / Twistin' USA / Poinciana / Love me tender / Green eyes / Fly me to the moon / San Antonio rose / Front o' town / Happy strut / Creole girl / 4-11-44 / Back o' town / Muddy dust / French market / Gumbo fillet
CD CDBGPD 077
Beat Goes Public / Sep '93 / Pinnacle

Poindexter, Steve

MAN AT WORK
CD ACVCD 104
ACV / Dec '95 / Plastic Head / SRD

Pointed Sticks

PART OF THE NOISE
CD ZULU 015CD
Zulu / Oct '95 / Plastic Head

Pointer Sisters

BREAK OUT
Jump / Automatic / I'm so excited / I need you / Dance electric / Neutron dance / Easy persuasion / Baby come and get it / Telegraph your love / Operator
CD ND 90206
RCA / Aug '88 / BMG

COLLECTION, THE
Yes we can-can / Fairytale / Fire / Happiness / He's so shy / Slow hand / I'm so excited / American music / Should I do it / If you wanna get back / Your lady / I need you / Jump / Automatic / Neutron dance / Baby come and get it / Dare me / Twist my arm / Goldmine
CD 74321139572
RCA / Jul '93 / BMG

DARE ME
Automatic / Neutron dance / I'm so excited / Slowhand / Jump (for my love) / Heartbeat / Someday we'll be together / Dare me / Should I do it / I need you / I feel for you / American music / Baby come and get it / Heart to heart / Goldmine / See how the love goes / Everybody is a star / Fire
CD 74321487332
Camden / May '97 / BMG

JUMP (Best Of The Pointer Sisters)
Jump / Someday we'll be together / Automatic / He's so shy / Should I do it / Slow hand / Heart to heart / Telegraph your love / I'm so excited / Goldmine / Back in my arms / I need you / Neutron dance / Dare me / See how the love goes / Overnight success: *Pointer, Anita* / I'm ready for love: *Pointer, June* / Fire
CD 74321289862
RCA / Aug '95 / BMG

Pointer, Noel

NEVER LOSE YOUR HEART
CD SHCD 5007
Shanachie / Dec '93 / ADA / Greensleeves / Koch

Poison

FLESH AND BLOOD
Strange days of uncle Jack / Valley of lost souls / (Flesh and blood) sacrifice / Swamp juice (soul-o) / Unskinny bop / Let it play / Life goes on / Come hell or high water / Ride the wind / Don't give up an inch / Something to believe in / Ball and chain / Life loves a tragedy / Poor boy blues
CD CDEST 2126
Capitol / Jul '90 / EMI

GREATEST HITS 1986-1996
Nothin' but a good time / Talk dirty to me / Unskinny bop / Every rose has its thorn / Fallen angel / I won't forget you / Stand / Ride the wind / Look what the cat dragged in / I want action / Life goes on / (Flesh and blood) sacrifice / Cry tough / Your mama don't dance / So tell me why / Something to believe in / Sexual thing / Lay your body down
CD CTMCD 312
Capitol / Feb '97 / EMI

LOOK WHAT THE CAT DRAGGED IN
Cry tough / I want action / I won't forget you / Play dirty / Look what the cat dragged in / Talk dirty to me / Want some, need some / Blame it on you / No. 1 bad boy / Let me go to the show
CD CDGOLD 1027
EMI Gold / May '96 / EMI

OPEN UP AND SAY AHH
Love on the rocks / Nothin' but a good time / Back to the rocking horse / Good love / Tearin' down the walls / Look but you can't touch / Fallen angel / Every rose has its thorn / Your mama don't dance / Bad to be good
CD CDEST 2059
Capitol / Feb '94 / EMI

Poison 13

WINE IS RED POISON IS BLUE
CD SP 273B
Sub Pop / Nov '94 / Cargo / Greyhound / Shellshock/Disc

Poison Chang

FROM JA TO UK - MC CLASH VOL.3 (Poison Chang & Top Cat)
CD FADCD 027
Fashion / Jul '93 / Jet Star / SRD

RUMBLE IN THE JUNGLE VOL.2 (Poison Chang & Cutty Ranks)
CD JFCD 02
Fashion / Aug '95 / Jet Star / SRD

Poison Girls

STATEMENT (The Complete Recordings 1977-1989/2CD Set)
Revenge / Cat's eye / Piano lessons / Closed shop / I wanted the moon / Old tarts song / Crisis / Ideologically unsound / Bremen song / Political love / Jump Mama jump / Under the doctor / Reality attack / Persons unkown / State control / Bully boys / Tension / SS Snoopers / Promenade immortelle / Another hero / Hole in the wall / Underbitch / Alienation / Pretty Polly / Good time / Other / Daughters and sons / Tender love / Dirty work / Statement / Don't go home tonight / Fuckin' Mother / Where's the pleasure / Lovers are they worth it / Done it all before / Whiskey voice / Menage abbatoir / Take the toys / Soft touch / Toys / Velvet launderette / Rio disco stink / Cry no more / Mandy is having a baby / Fear is freedom / Happy now / Cinnamon garden / Offending article / Perfect crime / Tell the children / Cream dream / Real woman / Hot for love / Riot in my mind / Feeling the pinch / Desperate days / Voodoo pappadollar / Too close for comfort / Rockface / No more lies / Too proud / Price of grain / Stonehenge / Jenny / Girls over there / Let it go / Cupid / Mirror and glass / Abort the system / All the waystate banjo
CD Set COOKCD 087
Cooking Vinyl / Aug '97 / Vital

THEIR FINEST MOMENTS
CD NTMCD 541
Nectar / Mar '97 / Pinnacle

Poison Idea

FEEL THE DARKNESS
CD 64632
Epitaph / Jan '97 / Pinnacle / Plastic Head

KINGS OF PUNK
CD TG 92842
Roadrunner / Sep '91 / PolyGram

PAJAMA PARTY
Kick out the jams / Vietnamese baby / We got the beat / Motorhead / Endless sleep / Laudy Miss Clawdy / Jailhouse rock / Flamethrower love / New rose / Doctor doctor / Up front / Harder they come / Green onions
CD SOLO 34CD
Vinyl Solution / Aug '92 / RTM/Disc

PIG'S LAST STAND
CD SP 343
Sub Pop / Apr '96 / Cargo / Greyhound / Shellshock/Disc

RECORD COLLECTORS ARE PRETENTIOUS ASSHOLES
CD TG 92992
Roadrunner / Sep '91 / PolyGram

WAR ALL THE TIME
Temple / Romantic self destruction / Push the button / Ritual chicken / Nothing is final / Motorhead / Hot time / Steel rule / Typical / Murderer / Marked for life
CD SOL 40CD
Vinyl Solution / Sep '94 / RTM/Disc

Poisoned Electrick Head

BIG EYE AM
CD ABT 098CD
Abstract / Apr '94 / Cargo / Pinnacle / Total/BMG

HANGED MAN
CD BP 236CD
Blueprint / Nov '96 / Pinnacle

POISONED ELECTRICK HEAD
Immortal / Unborn / What ya gonna be son / Garden of Eden / Creature feature / Twentieth Century man/President's reply / Mortal
CD BP 237CD
Blueprint / Sep '97 / Pinnacle

Pojat, Pinnin

PINNIN POJAT & ERKKI RANKAVIITA (Pojat, Pinnin & Erkki Rankaviita)
CD KICD 44
Kansanmusiikki Instituutti / Nov '96 / ADA / Direct

Pokerface

LIFE'S A GAMBLE
CD ESM 008
Escape / Nov '96 / Cargo

Pokkela, Martti

OLD AND NEW KANTELE
CD EUCD 1040
ARC / '89 / ADA / ARC Music

Pokrovsky, Dmitri

LES NOCES
CD 7559793352
Nonesuch / Jan '95 / Warner Music

Poland, Chris

RETURN TO METALOPOLIS
CD RR 93482
Roadrunner / Sep '90 / PolyGram

Polar

LIVING INCINERATOR
Come in and take it all / Summer / Final hour / Fact isn't fiction / Just like you said / Golden gate / Two can live cheaper than one / In the same world / Last years me / Words / Broken home / City life
CD __________ CDC 002
Christel Deesk / May '97 / Vital

Polar Bear

POLAR BEAR
CD __________ DH 021
Dry Hump / Jun '97 / Cargo

Polara

POLARA
CD __________ 892762
Clean Up / Feb '95 / Amato Disco / Prime / Vital

Polcer, Ed

COAST TO COAST SWINGIN' JAZZ (Polcer, Ed & His All Stars)
CD __________ JCD 198
Jazzology / '91 / Jazz Music

SALUTE TO EDDIE CONDON (Polcer, Ed Allstars)
CD __________ CD 004
Nagel Heyer / May '96 / Jazz Music

Polecat, Tim

VIRTUAL ROCKABILLY
Thunder and lightnin' / Tornado / Jigsaw-man / Lady Medusa / Rockin' bones / Cat-man returns / Panic / Boys are back in town / Head on / Guardian angel / Shiver shiver / Rock until you drop / Pit / Jungle of the bass
CD __________ NERCD 078
Nervous / Aug '94 / Nervous / TKO Magnum

Polecats

CULT HEROES
CD __________ NERCD 001
Nervous / Oct '91 / Nervous / TKO Magnum

LIVE AND ROCKIN'
Pink and black / Blue jean bop / Rock Billy Boogie / Hip hip baby / We say yeah / Run-nin back / Miss Bobby Sox
CD __________ DOJOCD 172
Dojo / Jun '94 / Disc

Poletti, Jean-Paul

CORSICAN POLYPHONY (Poletti, Jean-Paul & Sartene Male Voice Choir)
CD __________ B 6841
Auvidis/Ethnic / Oct '96 / ADA / Harmonia Mundi

Police

GHOST IN THE MACHINE
Spirits in the material world / Every little thing she does is magic / Invisible sun / Hungry for you / Demolition man / Too much information / Rehumanise yourself / One world / Omega man / Secret journey / Darkness
CD __________ CDMID 162
A&M / Oct '92 / PolyGram

GREATEST HITS
Roxanne / Can't stand losing you / So lonely / Message in a bottle / Walking on the moon / Bed's too big without you / Don't stand so close to me / De Do Do Do De Da Da Da / Every little thing she does is magic / Invisible Sun / Spirits in the material world / Synchronicity II / Every breath you take / King of pain / Wrapped around your finger / Tea In The Sahara
CD __________ 5400302
A&M / Sep '92 / PolyGram

MESSAGE IN A BOX (4CD Set)
Nothing achieving / Fallout / Dead end job / Next to you / So lonely / Roxanne / Hole in my life / Peanuts / Can't stand losing you / Truth hits everybody / Born in the 50s / Be my girl Sally / Masoko tanga / Landlord / Message in a bottle / Regatta de blanc / It's alright for you / Bring on the night / Deathwish / Walking on the moon / On any other day / Bed's too big without you / Contact / Does everyone stare / No time this time / Visions of the night / Friends / Don't stand so close to me / Driven to tears / When the world is running down / Canary in a coalmine / Voices inside my head / Bombs away / De do do do de da da da / Behind my camel / Man in a suitcase / Shadows in the rain / Other way of stopping / Sermon / Shamelle / Spirits in the material world / Every little thing she does is magic / Invisible sun / Hungry for you / Demolition man / Too much information / Rehumanise yourself / One world / Omega man / Secret journey / Darkness / Flexible strategies / Low life / How stupid Mr. Bates / Kind of loving / Synchronicity / Walking in your footsteps / O my God / Mother / Miss Gradenko / Synchronicity II / Every breath you take / King of pain / Wrapped around your finger / Tea in the Sahara / Murder by numbers / Someone to talk to / Don't stand so close to me '86 / Once upon a daydream / I burn for you
CD Set __________ 5401502
A&M / Nov '93 / PolyGram

OUTLANDOS D'AMOUR
Next to you / So lonely / Hole in my life / Roxanne / Peanuts / Can't stand losing you / Truth hits everybody / Born in the 50s / Be my girl Sally / Masoko Tango
CD __________ CDMID 126
A&M / Aug '91 / PolyGram

POLICE LIVE, THE (2CD Set)
Next to you / So lonely / Truth hits every-body / Walking on the moon / Hole in my life / Fall out / Bring on the night / Message in a bottle / Bed's too big without you / Pea-nuts / Roxanne / Can't stand losing you / Landlord / Born in the 50's / Be my girl Sally / Synchronicity I / Synchronicity II / Walking in your footsteps / Message in a bottle / O my God / De do do do de da da da / Wrapped around your finger / Tea in the Sa-hara / Spirits in the material world / King of pain / Don't stand so close to me / Every breath you take / Roxanne / Can't stand losing you
CD Set __________ 5402222
A&M / May '95 / PolyGram

REGATTA DE BLANC
Message in a bottle / Regatta de blanc / It's alright for you / Bring on the night / Death-wish / Walking on the moon / On any other day / Bed's too big without you / Contact / Does everyone stare / No time this time
CD __________ CDMID 127
A&M / Oct '92 / PolyGram

REGATTA MONDATTA (Various Artists)
Every little thing she does is magic: *Chaka Demus & Pliers* / Roxanne: *Aswad* / Spirits in the material world: *Pato Banton & Sting* / Jamaican in New York: *Shinehead* / Every breath you take: *Wright, Betty* / One world (not three): *Marley, Ziggy & Sting* / Message in a bottle: *Priest, Maxi* / Can't stand losing you: *Steel Pulse* / Darkness: *Los Pericos* / Walking on the moon: *Sly & Robbie* / Bed's too big without you: *Hilton, Sheila* / Wrapped around your finger: *Jazz Jamaica*
CD __________ VTCD 147
Virgin / Aug '97 / EMI

ROYAL PHILHARMONIC ORCHESTRA PERFORM CLASSIC POLICE (Royal Philharmonic Orchestra)
Overture / De do do do de da da da / Re-leased / Every little thing she does is magic / Roxanne / Truth hits everybody / Arrested / Message in a bottle / Invisible sun / Walk-ing on the moon / Finale
CD __________ QED 036
Tring / Nov '96 / Tring

RPO PLAYS THE POLICE (Royal Philharmonic Orchestra)
Overture / Regatta de blanc / Spirits in the material world / Be my girl / Sally / De do do do de da da da / Released / Every little thing she does is magic / Roxanne / Trruth hits everybody / Arrested / Message in a bottle / Invisible sun / Walking on the moon / Don't stand so close to me / Finale
CD __________ EMPRCD 588
Emporio / Oct '95 / Disc

SYNCHRONICITY
Synchronicity / Walking in your footsteps / Oh my God / Mother / Miss Gradenko / Synchronicity II / Every breath you take / King of pain / Wrapped around your finger / Tea in the Sahara
CD __________ CDMID 186
A&M / Mar '93 / PolyGram

ZENYATTA MONDATTA
Don't stand so close to me / Driven to tears / When the world is running down / Canary in a coalmine / Voices inside my head / Bombs away / De do do do De da da da / Behind my camel / Man in a suitcase / Shadows in the rain / Other way of stopping
CD __________ CDMID 128
A&M / Oct '92 / PolyGram

Polish Nightingales

MOST BEAUTIFUL CHRISTMAS CAROLS, THE
CD __________ DCD 5231
Disky / Nov '92 / Disky / THE

Polite Force

CANTERBURY KNIGHTS
Birdworld / Childsplay / Mr. Sax speaks / Solitude / Food of the Gods/Gruel for the slobs / Arabadnaz / Extension / They shoot Indians (in Brazil) / Hey diddle diddle / For pleasure / Ritual/Dance no.2 / Man from Mars
CD __________ VP 187CD
Voiceprint / Feb '97 / Pinnacle

Polka Dogs

ENTERTAINERS, THE
CD __________ CDPAN 137
Pan / Apr '93 / ADA / CM / Direct

Polkemmet Grorud Pipe Band

PIPE BANDS OF DISTINCTION
CD __________ CD MON 808
Monarch / Jul '90 / ADA / CM / Direct / Duncans

Pollack, Ben

BEN POLLACK & HIS PICK-A-RIB BOYS
CD __________ JCD 224
Jazzology / Oct '93 / Jazz Music

Pollard, Lisa

I SEE YOUR FACE BEFORE ME
Stuffy / Nightingale sang in Berkley Square / Stalking / I let a song go our of my heart / Things we did last summer / Namely you / Old folks / All blues / Sometimes I'm happy / I see your face before me
CD __________ CCD 4681
Concord Jazz / Feb '96 / New Note/ Pinnacle

Pollard, Robert

NOT IN MY AIRFORCE
Maggie turns to flies / Quicksilver / Girl named Captain / Get under it / Release the sunbird / John strange school / Parakeet troopers / One clear minute / Chance to buy an island / I've owned you for centuries / Ash gray proclamation / Flat beauty / King of Arthur Avenue / Roofer's union fight song / Psychic pilot clocks out / Prom is coming
CD __________ OLE 2152
Matador / Sep '96 / Vital

Pollen

BLUETTE
CD __________ GROW 252
Grass / Sep '94 / Pinnacle / SRD

COLOURS AND MAKE BELIEVE
CD __________ DANCD 028
Danceteria / Feb '90 / ADA / Plastic Head / Shellshock/Disc

Pollier & Manchon

REEDS AND HAMMERS
CD __________ 870CD
Escalibur / May '97 / ADA / Discovery / Roots

Pollution Project

KRASNOJARSK
CD __________ EIDEXCD 1
Eidechse / May '97 / Essential/BMG / Prime

Polonsky, Jonny

HI MY NAME IS JONNY
Love lovely love / Truly ugly and dead too / In my mind / Evil scurvy love / Gone away / Downlow / Half mind / It's good to sleep / I didn't know what to dream at night / Uh-oh
CD __________ 74321300962
American / May '96 / BMG

Poltergeist

BEHIND THE MASK
CD __________ 8497152
Century Media / Feb '91 / Plastic Head

Polvo

CELEBRATE THE NEW DARK AGE
CD __________ TG 133CD
Touch & Go / May '94 / SRD

EXPLODED DRAWING
CD __________ TG 162CD
Touch & Go / May '96 / SRD

THIS ECLIPSE
CD __________ TG 156CD
Touch & Go / Nov '95 / SRD

TODAYS ACTIVE LIFESTYLES
CD __________ TG 114CD
Touch & Go / Apr '93 / SRD

Polygon

REFUGE
CD __________ EFA 112852
Glasnost / Jan '96 / SRD

Polygon Window

SURFING ON SINE WAVES
CD __________ WARPCD 7
Warp / Apr '96 / Prime / RTM/Disc

Polyphemus

SCRAPBOOK OF MADNESS
CD __________ BBQCD 134
Beggars Banquet / May '93 / RTM/Disc / Warner Music

STONEHOUSE
CD __________ BBQCD 171
Beggars Banquet / Sep '95 / RTM/Disc / Warner Music

Polyphonic Size

OVERNIGHT DAY, THE
CD __________ ROSE 150CD
New Rose / Aug '88 / ADA / Direct / Discovery

Polyploid

TOUCH PROOF
CD __________ INTRUCD 001
Intruder / Mar '97 / Essential/BMG / Prime

Polyyanka Russian Gypsy ...

PLAY BALALAIKA PLAY (Polyyanka Russian Gypsy Ensemble)
CD __________ MCD 71371
Monitor / Jun '93 / CM

Pomus, Doc

'TIL THE NIGHT IS GONE (A Doc Pomus Tribute) (Various Artists)
CD __________ 8122718782
Warner Bros. / Apr '95 / Warner Music

Pond

POND
CD __________ SPCD 66/233
Sub Pop / Feb '93 / Cargo / Greyhound / Shellshock/Disc

PRACTICE OF JOY BEFORE DEATH, THE
CD __________ SPCD 143357
Sub Pop / Feb '95 / Cargo / Greyhound / Shellshock/Disc

Pond Life

POND LIFE
CD __________ POND 001
Pond Life / May '96 / Wellard

Ponder, Jimmy

JUMP
CD __________ MCD 5347
Muse / Sep '92 / New Note/Pinnacle

MEAN STREETS
CD __________ MCD 5324
Muse / Sep '92 / New Note/Pinnacle

SOUL EYES
Kansas city / Soul eyes / All blues / Sun song / I didn't know what time it was / You are too beautiful / Love can be a lonley place / You don't have to go
CD __________ MCD 5514
Muse / Apr '95 / New Note/Pinnacle

Ponomarev, Valery

LIVE AT SWEET BASIL
CD __________ RSRCD 131
Reservoir Music / Oct '94 / Cadillac

MEANS OF IDENTIFICATION
CD __________ RSRCD 101
Reservoir Music / Dec '94 / Cadillac

PROFILE
CD __________ RSRCD 119
Reservoir Music / Nov '94 / Cadillac

TRIP TO MOSCOW
CD __________ RSRCD 107
Reservoir Music / Oct '89 / Cadillac

Ponsford, Jan

VOCAL CHORDS
View / When the birds start to sing / Univ-erasal love / Turn your whole world / Are we there yet / Your eyes / Clip-clop song / Prejudice groove / Prejudice
CD __________ ASCCD 5
ASC / Oct '95 / Cadillac / New Note/ Pinnacle

Pontarddulais Male Voice ...

SING SONGS OF ENGLAND, SCOTLAND, IRELAND & WALES (Pontarddulais Male Voice Choir)
Down among the dead men / Tom bowling / Linden lea / Golden slumbers / Annie Lau-rie / Flow gently sweet afton / Ye banks and braes / Will ye no come back again / Oft in the still of the night / Londonderry air / She moved through the fair / Cockles and mus-sels / March of the men of Harlech / All through the night / Davis of the white rock / Watching the wheat
CD __________ WMCD 2002
Westmoor / Oct '96 / Target/BMG

SOFTLY AS I LEAVE YOU (Pontarddulais Male Voice Choir)
Softly as I leave you / Ride the chariot / Doilch I'r 'or / Finnish forest / Windmills of your mind / Thanks be to God / Evening's pastorale / Bryn myrddin / Christus re-demptor (hyfrydol) / My Lord, what a morn-ing / Memory / Lord's prayer / Bywyd y bu-gail / Mil harddach wyt na'r rhosyn gwyn / Comrades in arms
CD __________ GRCD 8
Grasmere / May '94 / Highlander / Savoy / Target/BMG

WELSH MALE VOICES SING GERSHWIN (Pontarddulais Male Voice Choir)
Swanee / I got rhythm / Foggy day / Someone to watch over me / They can't take that away from me / I got plenty o' nuttin' / Nice work if you can get it / Embraceable you / How long has this been going on / 'S wonderful / Love is here to stay / But not for me / Somebody loves me / Oh lady be good / Summertime
CD ______ **3036000882**
Carlton / Jul '97 / Carlton

Pontier, Francini

TANGO (Pontier, Francini Orquesta)
CD ______ **VICG 53422**
JVC World Library / Mar '96 / ADA / CM / Direct

Ponty, Jean-Luc

ANTHOLOGY (2CD Set)
Question with no answer / Bowing-bowing / Echoes of the future / Aurora part 2 / Waking dream / REnaissance / New country / Enigmatic part 2 / Enigmatic ocean part 3 / Mirage / Egocentric molecules / Cosmic messanger / Ethereal mood / I only feel good with you / No strings attached / Stay with me / Taste for passion / Once a blue planet / Forms of life / Rhythms of hope / Mystical adventures (suite) part 4 / Mystical adventures (suite) part 5 / Jig / Final truth part 1 / Computer incantations for world peace / Individual choice / Nostalgia / Eulogy to Oscar Romeo / Infinite pursuit / In the kingdom of peace / Carcas / Forever together
CD Set ______ **8122721552**
Atlantic / Mar '96 / Warner Music

AURORA
Is once enough / Renaissance / Aurora / Passenger of the dark / Lost forest / Between you and me / Waking dream
CD ______ **7567815432**
Atlantic / Jun '93 / Warner Music

COSMIC MESSENGER
Cosmic messenger / Art of happiness / Don't let the world pass you by / I only feel good with you / Puppets' dance / Fake paradise / Ethereal mood / Egocentric molecules
CD ______ **7567815502**
Atlantic / Mar '93 / Warner Music

ENIGMATIC OCEAN
Overture / Trans love express / Mirage / Enigmatic ocean / Nostalgic lady / Struggle of the turtle to the sea
CD ______ **7567815122**
Atlantic / Mar '93 / Warner Music

FABLES
Infinite pursuit / Elephants in love / Radioactive legacy / Cats' tales / Perpetual rondo / In the kingdom of peace / Plastic idols
CD ______ **7567812762**
Atlantic / Mar '93 / Warner Music

GIFT OF TIME, THE
Prologue / New resolutions / Faith in you / No more doubts / Between sea and sky / Metamorphosis / Introspective / Perceptions / Gift of time
CD ______ **CK 40983**
Sony Jazz / Aug '97 / Sony

IMAGINARY VOYAGE
New country / Gardens of Babylon / Wandering on the milky way / Once upon a dream / Tarantula / Imaginary voyage
CD ______ **7567815352**
Atlantic / Jun '93 / Warner Music

LIVE AT CHENE PARK
Intro / Infinite pursuit / Tender memories / Between seal and sky / Caracas / Faith in you / After the storm / Gift of time / Eulogy for Oscar Romero / Amazon forest / Story teller / Elephant's in love / Journey's end
CD ______ **7567829642**
Atlantic / Apr '97 / Warner Music

LIVE AT DONTE'S
Hypomode de sol / People / California / Eight-one / Foosh / Sara's theme / Pamukkale / Cantaloupe island
CD ______ **CDP 8356352**
Pacific Jazz / Jan '96 / EMI

NO ABSOLUTE TIME
No absolute time / Savannah / Lost illusions / Dance of the spirits / Forever together / Caracas / African spirits / Speak out / Blue mambo / Child in you
CD ______ **592213**
FNAC / May '94 / Discovery

TCHOKOLA
CD ______ **4685222**
Sony Jazz / Jan '95 / Sony

Pony

COSMOVALIDATOR
CD ______ **FIRECD 41**
Fire / Aug '94 / Pinnacle / RTM/Disc

EL DORADO
CD ______ **HMS 2352**
Homestead / Mar '97 / Cargo / SRD

Pooh Sticks

FORMULA ONE GENERATION
CD ______ **SFTRI 58**
Sympathy For The Record Industry / Oct '96 / Cargo / Greyhound / Plastic Head

GREAT WHITE WONDER, THE
CD ______ **CHEREE 18CD**
Cheree / May '91 / SRD

MULTIPLE ORGASM
CD ______ **FRIGHT 047CD**
Fierce / Mar '92 / RTM/Disc

OPTIMISTIC FOOL
Opening night / Cool in a crisis / Starfishing / Optimistic fool / Who was it / Bad morning girl / Miss me / Working on a beautiful thing / Up on the roof / Prayer for my demo / All things must pass / Song cycle / First of a million love songs
CD ______ **925132**
Seed / May '95 / Vital

TRADEMARK OF QUALITY
CD ______ **FRIGHT 048CD**
Fierce / Jun '97 / RTM/Disc

Pook, Jocelyn

DELUGE
Requiem aeternam / Indigo dream / Oppenheimer / Thousand year dream / Forever without end / Blow the wind, pie jesu / Migrations / Goya's nightmare / Backwards priests / Forever without end / La blanche traversee / Flood
CD ______ **CDVE 933**
Venture / Feb '97 / EMI

Pooka

POOKA
City sick / Bluebell / Car / Graham Robert Wood / Breeze / Nothing in particular / Dream / Boomerang / Demon / Rollin' stone / Between my knees / Sleepwalking
CD ______ **4509935152**
WEA / Sep '93 / Warner Music

SPINNING
Mean girl / Higher / God sir / Shine / Lubrication / Rubber arms / Sweet butterfly / She is a rainbow / Insect / Spinning / This river / Ocean
CD ______ **TRDCD 1003**
Trade 2 / Sep '97 / PolyGram / RTM/Disc / Vital

Pool, Hamilton

RETURN TO ZERO
CD ______ **WMCD 1031**
Watermelon / Apr '95 / ADA / Direct

Poole

LATE ENGAGEMENT, THE
CD ______ **SPART 55CD**
Spin Art / Jun '97 / Cargo

Pooley, Ian

TIMES, THE
CD ______ **FIM 019CD**
Force Inc. / Apr '96 / Amato Disco / Arabesque / SRD

Pooley, Rod

TECHNORAMA (Keyboard Series)
Apache / Wind beneath my wings / Chi mai / One o'clock jump / Blanket on the ground / Amazing grace / Everything I do (I do it for you) / Hustle / It had to be you / Tijuana taxi / It's only a paper moon / Elizabethan serenade / Medley / April in Paris / Chariots of fire
CD ______ **CDGRS 1293**
Grosvenor / Dec '96 / Grosvenor

Poor Righteous Teachers

BLACK BUSINESS
144 K / Da rill shit / Nobody move / Ni fresh / Here we go again / Selah / Black business / Get off the crack / None can test / Ghetto we love / Rich mon time / Lick shots
CD ______ **FILECD 443**
Profile / Aug '93 / Pinnacle

NEW WORLD ORDER
CD ______ **FILECD 471**
Profile / Oct '96 / Pinnacle

Poorboys

POORBOYS
CD ______ **APCD 057**
Appaloosa / '92 / ADA / Direct / TKO Magnum

Poors Of Reign

WRECKED
CD ______ **FUCTCD 1**
Fat Terry / Sep '91 / Pinnacle

Poozies

CHANTOOZIES
We built fires / Mountaineer's sect / Les femmes chaussees / Willie's old trousers / Honesty / Foggy mountain top / Crazy raven / Waking up in wonderful wark / Dheanainn sugradh / Love on a farmboy's wages / Another train
CD ______ **HY 200132CD**
Hypertension / Mar '95 / ADA / CM / Direct / Total/BMG

Pop Du Monde Orchestra

ESSENTIAL PAN FLUTES
Everything I do / I will always love you / Cuts both ways / CAreless whisper / End of the road / I'll be there / Another day in paradise / First time / Promise me / I can't stop loving you / Tears in heaven / When a man loves a woman / When you tell me that you love me / Right here waiting / Lady in red / Unchained melody / Sacrifice / Why
CD ______ **DCA 865472**
Disky / Sep '96 / Disky / THE

GREAT INSTRUMENTAL LOVE SONGS
Under the bridge / Praying for a time / Soul provider / All woman / Show me heaven / I'm easy / Hold on / Another sad lovesong / Without you / Fields of gold / Your love is king / Everything I do / I will always love you / Most beautiful girl in the world / Love is all around / Dreams / Eternal flame / Nothing compares to you
CD ______ **DC 872012**
Disky / Sep '96 / Disky / THE

Pop Group

Y
Thief of fire / Snowgirl / Blood money / Savage sea / We are time / Words disobey me / Don't call me pain / Boys from Brazil / Don't sell your dreams
CD ______ **SCANCD 14**
Radarscope / May '96 / Pinnacle

Pop Will Eat Itself

BBC RADIO 1 SESSIONS 1986-1987
Black Country chainstore massacre / Demolition girl / Oh grebo I think I love you / Sweet sweet pie / Love missile / Ugly / Ha ha empty head / Picnic in the sky / Illusion of love / There is no love between us anymore / Evelyn
CD ______ **SFRSCD 005**
Strange Fruit / Apr '97 / Pinnacle

CURE FOR SANITY
Incredible PWEI vs the moral majority / Dance of the mad bastards / Eighty eight seconds and still counting / X, Y and Zee / City Zen Radio 1990/2000 FM / Dr. Nightmare's medication time / Touched by the hand of Cicciolina / 1000 times no / Psychosexual / Axe of men / Another man's rhubarb / Medicine man speaked with forked tongue / Nightmare at 20,000 feet / Very metal noise pollution / 92 degrees F (the 3rd degree) / Lived in splendour, died in chaos / Beat that refused to die
CD ______ **74321157912**
RCA / Nov '93 / BMG

DOS DEDOS MIS AMIGOS
CD ______ **INFECT 10CD**
CD ______ **INFECT 10CDX**
Infectious / Sep '94 / RTM/Disc

LOOKS OR THE LIFESTYLE
England's finest / Eat me, drink me, love me, kill me / Mother / Get the girl, kill the baddies / Always been a coward baby / Token drug song / Karmadrome / Urban futuristic / Pretty, pretty / I was a teenage grandad / Harry Dean Stanton
CD ______ **74321157902**
RCA / Nov '93 / BMG

SIXTEEN DIFFERENT FLAVOURS OF HELL
Urban futuristic / Get the girl, kill the baddies / Wise up sucker / Inject me / Axe of men / Can U dig it / Always been a coward baby / Karmadrome / Dance of the mad bastards / Another man's rhubarb / X, Y and Zee / 92 F / Touched by the hand of Cicciolina / Bullet proof / Def con one / Wake up, time to die / Pweization / Eat me, drink me, love me, kill me / Preaching to the perverted
CD ______ **74321153172**
RCA / Oct '93 / BMG

THIS IS THE DAY, THIS IS THE HOUR
PWEI is a four letter word / Preaching to the perverted / Wise up sucker / Sixteen different flavours of hell / Inject me / Can U dig it / Fuses have been lit / Poison to the mind / Def con one / Radio PWEI / Shortwave transmission on up to the minuteman / Satellite ecstatica / Now now James we're busy / Wake up, time to die / Wise up sucker (remix)
CD ______ **74321157922**
RCA / Nov '93 / BMG

TWO FINGERS MY FRIEND
CD ______ **INFECT 10CDR**
Infectious / Feb '95 / RTM/Disc

WISE UP SUCKERS
England's finest / Eat me, drink me, love me, kill me / X, Y, & Zee / 92 degrees F / Wise up sucker / Can u dig it / Def con one / Pweization / Karmadrome / Get the girl, kill the baddies / Now now James, we're busy / Preaching to the perverted / Cicciolina / Wake up, time to die / Harry Dean Stanton / Inject me / Dance of the mad / Very metal noise pollution
CD ______ **74321393392**
Camden / Jan '97 / BMG

Pope, Mal

COPPER KINGDOM
Copper kingdom / Fire and ice / Listen to me / Waiting for the heartaches / Soon you will be a man / You don't own me / Soul survivor / Life's a bitch / (You were a) friend of mine / Please don't go / Cover me
CD ______ **CDWM 112**
Westmoor / Oct '96 / Target/BMG

Pope, Odean

EPITOME (Pope, Odean Saxophone Choir)
CD ______ **1212792**
Soul Note / Nov '94 / Cadillac / Harmonia Mundi / Wellard

Pope, Sister Lucy

BEST OF SISTER LUCY POPE & THE PEARLY GATES, THE (Pope, Sister Lucy & The Pearly Gates)
CD ______ **NASH 4511**
Nashboro / Feb '96 / Pinnacle

Popek, Krzysztof

LETTERS AND LEAVES
CD ______ **PB 00139**
Power Bros. / Apr '97 / Harmonia Mundi

Popeluc

BLUE DOOR
CD ______ **MATS 013CD**
Steel Carpet / Aug '96 / ADA

Popguns

A PLUS DE CENT
Harley Davidson / Star / Get out / Stay alive / So amazing / Crushed / What are you waiting for / Day break / Can I kick it / Crazy / Gesture
CD ______ **POP 001CD**
Tall Pop / May '96 / Vital

ANOTHER YEAR ANOTHER ADDRESS
CD ______ **CDMRED 135**
Cherry Red / Oct '96 / Pinnacle

LOVE JUNKY
I'll take you down / Get out / Star / Second time around / Someone to dream of / Under starlight / Miserable boy / How to face it / Here in heaven / Over your head / So cold
CD ______ **STONE 016CD**
3rd Stone / Feb '95 / Plastic Head / Vital

PLUS DE CENT
CD ______ **ZYX 204252**
ZYX / Dec '96 / ZYX

Popinjays

BANG UP TO DATE WITH THE POPINJAYS
CD ______ **TPLP 28CD**
One Little Indian / Apr '90 / Pinnacle

TALES FROM THE URBAN PRAIRIE
Queen of the parking lot / Feelin' / When I believed in you / Moonheart / Slowly I reach / Hurricane / Kentish Town / Buffalo / Down / Drive the train
CD ______ **TPLP 48CD**
One Little Indian / May '94 / Pinnacle

Popol Vuh

CITY RAGA
CD ______ **239752**
Milan / Oct '95 / Conifer/BMG / Silva Screen

IN DEN GARTEN PHARAOS
CD ______ **14875**
Spalax / Oct '96 / ADA / Cargo / Direct / Discovery / Greyhound

SHEPHERD'S SYMPHONY
Shepherds of the future / Short visit to the great sorcerer / Wild vine / Shepherd's dream / Eternal love / Dance of the menads / Yes
CD ______ **MYSCD 114**
Mystic / Aug '97 / Pinnacle

SING FOR SONG DRIVES AWAY THE WOLVES
CD ______ **139142**
Milan / May '93 / Conifer/BMG / Silva Screen

Poppies

HONEYBEE
She is revolution / That's what we'll do / Love trippin' / Hello Saturday / Without freedom / All tomorrow's parties / Friends for life / La de da (a trilogy) / Wonderdrug / Soulflower / Mother groove / Love amplifier / Everyone's song
CD ______ **4509930682**
East West / Jul '93 / Warner Music

Poppy, Andrew

ALPHABED (A Mystery Dance)
Forty five is / Goodbye Mr. G / Amusement
CD ____ 4509947522
ZTT / Mar '94 / Warner Music

Popsicle

ABSTINENCE
CD ____ 4509956792
WEA / Feb '95 / Warner Music

POPSICLE
Not forever / Sadly missing / Use my name / Soft / Song ago / Dusty roads / American poet / Good with us / Speed it up / Please don't ask / Third opinion
CD ____ 0630169892
WEA / Jan '97 / Warner Music

Porch

PORCH
Damn I'm lazy / Little white cracker / My ragin' ragged / Booty / Expectorant / Your hair / Dip / Bum holy / Iceberg / Bulbous head / Tattoed love boys / Palm hair
CD ____ MR 0942
Mammoth / Feb '95 / Vital

Porcupine Tree

ON THE SUNDAY OF LIFE
CD ____ DELECCD 008
Delerium / May '92 / Cargo / Pinnacle / Vital

SKY MOVES SIDEWAYS, THE
Sky moves sideways (part one) / Dislocated day / Moon touches your shoulder / Prepare yourself / Moonloop / Sky moves sideways (part two)
CD ____ DELECCD 028
Delerium / Jan '95 / Cargo / Pinnacle / Vital

STAIRCASE INFINITIES
Cloud zero / Jokes on you / Navigator / Rainy taxi / Yellow hedgerow / Dreamscape
CD ____ BP 217CD
Blueprint / Oct '95 / Pinnacle

UP THE DOWNSTAIR
CD ____ DELECCD 020
Delerium / Jun '93 / Cargo / Pinnacle / Vital

YELLOW HEDGEROW DREAMSCAPE
Mute / Landscare / Prayer / Daughter in excess / Delightful suicide / Split image / No reason to live, no reason to die / Wastecoat / Towel / Execution of the will of The Marquis De Sade / Track eleven / Radioactive toy / Am empty box / Cross/Yellow hedgerow dreamscape / Music for the head
CD ____ MG 4291325
Metrognome / Aug '94 / Vital

Pore

NOTATION
CD ____ CDPPP 117
PDCD / Feb '94 / Plastic Head

Pork

SLOP
CD ____ EJO 7CD
Emperor Jones / Oct '96 / SRD

Pork Pie

OPERANOIA
Arthur Rainbow / Hippie / Merci Afrique / Candy lip / Get down / Ballade / Lazy day / Operanoia / Zulu stomp / Quiet American
CD ____ INT 31582
Intuition / Feb '97 / New Note/Pinnacle

Porn Orchard

URGES AND ANGERS
CD ____ CZ 039CD
C/Z / Jan '92 / Plastic Head

Porno For Pyros

GOOD GOD'S URGE
CD ____ 9362460522
Warner Bros. / May '96 / Warner Music

PORNO FOR PYROS
Sadness / Porno for pyros / Meija / Cursed female / Cursed male / Pets / Bad shit / Packin' 25 / Black girlfriend / Blood rag / Orgasm
CD ____ 9362452282
Warner Bros. / Apr '93 / Warner Music

Port Friendly

WELCOME TO PORT FRIENDLY
CD ____ RAIN 016CD
Cloudland / Aug '97 / Plastic Head / SRD

Portabales, Guillermo

AL VAIVEN DE MI CARRETA
CD ____ TCD 084
Tumbao Cuban Classics / Apr '97 / Discovery

EL CARRETERO
El carretero / Cumbiamba / Junto a un canaveral / Nostalgia guarjira / Tristeza guajira / Yo te canto puerto rico / Lamento cubano / Guateque campesino / Oye mi son / Al vaiven de mi carreta / Voy a santiago a mo / Flor de amor / Cuando sali de cuba / El arroyo que murmura / El amor de mi boohio / Romance guajiro
CD ____ WCD 043
World Circuit / Apr '96 / ADA / Cadillac / Direct / New Note/Pinnacle

Portal, Michel

CINEMAS
Histoire de vent / Max mon amour / Yeelen / Droit de response / Docteur petiot / Champ d'honneur / Yvan Ivanovitch
CD ____ LBLC 6574
Label Bleu / Jun '96 / New Note/Pinnacle

Portastatic

I HOPE YOUR HEART IS NOT BRITTLE
CD ____ ELM 17CD
Elemental / Feb '94 / RTM/Disc

NATURE OF SAP, THE
CD ____ MRG 120CD
Merge / Mar '97 / Cargo / Greyhound / SRD

Porteous, Wyckham

LOOKING FOR GROUND
CD ____ BBEA 6
Bohemia Beat / Feb '96 / ADA / CM / Direct

Porter, Art

POCKET CITY
Pocket city / Inside myself / Unending / Passion sunrise / Texas hump / Close to you / Little people / KGB / Broken promises / Meltdown / LA
CD ____ 5118772
Verve/Forecast / Feb '92 / PolyGram

STRAIGHT TO THE POINT
Straight to the point / Someone like you / Autumn in Europe / Free spirit / We should stay in love / Day without you / Skirt chaser / Second time around / It's been awhile / It's your move / Unconditional love
CD ____ 5179972
Verve/Forecast / Feb '93 / PolyGram

Porter, Cole

BEGIN THE BEGUINE (Various Artists)
CD ____ MACCD 244
Autograph / Aug '96 / BMG

COLE PORTER
CD ____ DVX 08082
Deja Vu / May '95 / THE

COLE PORTER COLLECTION, A (Various Artists)
CD ____ JASSCD 632
Jass / Feb '92 / ADA / Cadillac / CM / Direct / Jazz Music

COLE PORTER SONGBOOK (20 Instrumental Greats)
Another opening another show / Begin the beguine / C'est magnifique / From this moment on / I love Paris / It's all right with me / It's de-lovely / My heart belongs to daddy / Night and day / So in love / True love / What is this thing called love / Wunderbar / Allez-vous en / Why can't you behave / Can can / Where is the life that late I led / If I loved you truly / Were thine that special face / Well did you evah
CD ____ GRF 109
Tring / '93 / Tring

FIFTY MILLION FRENCHMEN
CD ____ 804172
New World / Aug '92 / ADA / Cadillac / Harmonia Mundi

FOREVER - COLE PORTER (Various Artists)
Anything goes: *Bennett, Tony & Count Basie Orchestra* / Begin the beguine: *Shaw, Artie* / I love you Samantha: *Crosby, Bing* / I've got you under my skin: *Bassey, Shirley* / It's alright with me: *Shore, Dinah* / Just one of those things: *Riddle, Nelson & Orchestra* / Do I love you: *Lee, Peggy & George Shearing* / Love for sale: *London, Julie* / Miss Otis regrets: *Wilson, Nancy* / Night and day: *Getz, Stan* / True love: *Martin, Dean* / All of you: *Darin, Bobby* / I love Paris: *Starr, Kay* / High society calypso: *Armstrong, Louis* / I am in love: *Lee, Peggy* / I get a kick out of you: *Cole, Nat 'King'* / Ev'ry time we say goodbye: *Vaughan, Sarah* / My heart belongs to Daddy: *London, Julie* / Let's do it (let's fall in love): *Riddle, Nelson & Orchestra* / Now you has jazz: *Crosby, Bing & Louis Armstrong*
CD ____ CDMFP 6263
Music For Pleasure / Nov '96 / EMI

WHO KNOWS
CD ____ AMSC 571
Avid / Jun '96 / Avid/BMG / Koch / THE

Porter, Larry

MARCH BLUES
CD ____ ENJACD 80922
Enja / Sep '95 / New Note/Pinnacle / Vital/ SAM

Porter Ricks

BIOKINETICS
CD ____ EFA 503012
Chain Reaction / Dec '96 / SRD / Vital

Porter, Willy

DOG EARED DREAM
Angry words / Rita / Jesus on the grille / Boab tree / Watercolour / Cool water / Be here now / Flying / Glow / Cold wind / Out of the blue
CD ____ 01005821342
Private Music / Feb '96 / BMG

Portion Control

MAN WHO DID BACKWARDS SOMERSAULTS
CD ____ TEQM 94003
TEQ / Jun '97 / Cargo / Plastic Head

Portishead

DUMMY
Mysterons / Sour times / Strangers / It could be sweet / Wandering star / Numb / Roads / Pedestal / Biscuit / Glory box
CD ____ 8285222
Go Discs / Aug '94 / PolyGram

Portmann, Mark

NO TRUER WORDS
No truer words / Slink / First time ever I saw your face / Walla, walla / Canyons / Come as you are / Last song / Michi / Here I go again / Summer in Trujillo / Destinations
CD ____ ZD 44001
Zebra / Apr '97 / New Note/Pinnacle

Portnoy, Jerry

HOME RUN HITTER (Portnoy, Jerry & The Streamliners)
CD ____ IGOCD 2026
Indigo / Jul '95 / ADA / Direct

POISON KISSES (Portnoy, Jerry & The Streamliners)
CD ____ MBCD 1202
Modern Blues / Sep '94 / ADA / Direct

Portrait

ALL THAT MATTERS
Here's a kiss / I can call you / All that matters / All natural girl / Friday night / Hold me close / Lovin' u is ah-ight / How deep is your love / Me oh my / Lay you down / Heartstrings / Much too much
CD ____ CDEST 2251
Capitol / Apr '95 / EMI

Portuondo, Omara

PALABRAS
Ausencia / Palabras / Juguete / Descame suerte / Si me comprendieras / Drume negrita / Y tal vez / Tardes grises / La vida es un sueno / Si me pudieras querer / Mi ayer / Abre tus ojos
CD ____ INT 31852
Intuition / Aug '97 / New Note/Pinnacle

Poser, Florian

REUNION (Poser, Florian & Klaus Ignatzek)
CD ____ BEST 1084CD
Acoustic Music / Apr '96 / ADA

Posey, Sandy

18 ORIGINAL COUNTRY CLASSICS
Born a woman / Single girl / What a woman in love won't do / I take it back / Are you ever coming home / Sunglasses / Twelfth of never / Here comes my baby back again / Just out of reach / It's all in the game / Don't touch me / I've been loving you too long / Will you love me tomorrow / Deep in Kentucky / It's not easy / Satin pillows / Arms full of sin / Hey mister
CD ____ 5525552
Spectrum / Sep '96 / PolyGram

VERY BEST OF SANDY POSEY, THE
Single girl / I take it back / What a woman in love won't do / Just out of reach / It's all in the game / Hey mister / Don't touch me / I've been loving you too long / Born a woman / Sunglasses / Twelfth of never / Satin pillows / Arms full of sin / Here comes my baby back again / Blue is my best color / Are you never coming home
CD ____ SOWCD 705
Sound Waves / May '93 / Target/BMG

Posies

AMAZING DISGRACE
Daily mutation / Ontario / Throwaway / Please return it / Hate song / Precious moments / Fight it (if you want it) / Everybody is a fucking liar / World / Grant Hart / Broken record / Certainty / Song # 1 / Will you ever ease your mind
CD ____ GED 24910
Geffen / Apr '96 / BMG

DEAR 23
My big mouth / Apology / You avoid parties / Help yourself / Everyone moves away / Golden blunders / Any other way / Suddenly Mary / Mrs. Green / Flood of sunshine
CD ____ GED 24305
Geffen / Nov '96 / BMG

FROSTING ON THE BEATER
Dream all day / Solar sister / Flavor of the month / Love letter boxes / Definite door / Burn and shine / Earlier than expected / Twenty Questions / When mute tongues can speak / Lights out / She lied by living / Coming right along
CD ____ GFLD 19298
Geffen / Oct '95 / BMG

Position Alpha

GREETINGS FROM THE RATS
CD ____ DRCD 199
Dragon / Jan '88 / ADA / Cadillac / CM / Roots / Wellard

TITBITS
CD ____ DRCD 252
Dragon / Oct '94 / ADA / Cadillac / CM / Roots / Wellard

Positive Dub

TRIBULATION VOL.3
CD ____ WSPCD 007
WSP / Aug '95 / Jet Star

Positive K

SKILLS DAT PAY DA BILLS, THE
Intro (Pos K theme) / Pass the mic / One 2 the head / Shakin' / How the fuck would you know / Carhoppers / Nightshift / Intro (Back the fuck up) / I got a man / Ain't no crime / Shout out / Friends / Minnie the moocher / Nightshift (Remix) / Flower grows in Brooklyn / It's all over
CD ____ BRCD 598
4th & Broadway / Apr '93 / PolyGram

Possum Dixon

POSSUM DIXON
Nerves / In buildings / Watch the girl destroy me / She drives / We're all happy / Invisible / Pharmaceutical itch / Executive slacks / Regina / John struck lucky / Elevators
CD ____ IND 92291
Interscope / Jul '96 / BMG

STAR MAPS
CD ____ IND 92625
Interscope / Jul '96 / BMG

Poster Children

DAISYCHAIN REACTION
CD ____ CRECD 131
Creation / Jul '92 / 3mv/Vital

JUNIOR CITIZEN
CD ____ 9362457372
Warner Bros. / Mar '95 / Warner Music

Potato Five

FIVE ALIVE
Shuttle disaster / Spit 'n' polish / Call me master / Live up / Jail me / Stop that train / Harvest in the east / Hi-Jacked / Stopped by a cop / Do the jerk / Western special / Got to go
CD ____ DOJOCD 181
Dojo / Jun '94 / Disc

Pothead

DESSICATED SOUP
CD ____ EFA 127592
Orangehaus / Jul '95 / SRD

RUMELY OIL PULL
CD ____ EFA 11973 2
Orangehaus / Sep '94 / SRD

Potlach

ALBUM BY POTLACH, AN
CD ____ DOL 028CD
Dolores / Mar '96 / Plastic Head

Potlatch

GRINGO
CD ____ DOLCD 015
Delores / Feb '95 / Plastic Head

Potter, Chris

CONCENTRIC CIRCLES
El Morocco / Klee / Blues in concentric circles / Dusk / Lonely moon / You and the night and the music / Mortal coils / In a sentimental mood / Aurora
CD ____ CCD 4595
Concord Jazz / May '94 / New Note/ Pinnacle

CONCORD DUO SERIES VOL.10
Hibiscus / Boulevard of broken time / Istanbul / Sail away / Tala / September song / New left (and we have our own talk show host) / Epistrophy / Hey Reggie / Giant steps
CD ____ CCD 4695
Concord Jazz / May '96 / New Note/ Pinnacle

MOVING IN
Nero's fiddle / Book of kells / Moving in / Kiss to build a dream on / Rhubarb / South for the winter / Forest / Pelog / Chorale / Old faithful
CD _______________ CCD 4723
Concord Jazz / Sep '96 / New Note/ Pinnacle

PURE
Salome's dance / Checking out / Resonance / Bad guys / Boogie stop shuffle / Second thoughts / That's what I said / Fool on the hill / Bonnie rose / Easy to love / Distant present / Every time we say goodbye
CD _______________ CCD 4637
Concord Jazz / Apr '95 / New Note/ Pinnacle

SUNDIATA
CD _______________ CRISS 1107
Criss Cross / Dec '95 / Cadillac / Direct / Vital/SAM

UNSPOKEN
Wistful / Seven eleven / Hieroglyph / Amsterdam blues / Et tu brute / Unspoken / No cigar / Time zone / New vision
CD _______________ CCD 47752
Concord Jazz / Sep '97 / New Note/ Pinnacle

Potter, Gary

FRIENDS (Potter, Gary Quartet)
Yesterdays / Sandu / Bernie's tune / Nearness of you / Crazeology / Autumn leaves / Scrapple from the apple / All the things you are / Steffani / Nica's dream / Nuages / Friends
CD _______________ HHR 0001
Hi-Hat / Oct '96 / New Note/Pinnacle

Potter, Nic

BLUE ZONE, THE
CD _______________ VP 103CD
Voiceprint / Dec '90 / Pinnacle

Pottoka

LE MYSTERE DU PEUPLE BASQUE
CD _______________ 992397
Wotre Music / Sep '96 / Discovery / New Note/Pinnacle

Potts, Bill

JAZZ SOUL OF PORGY & BESS, THE
Summertime / Woman is a sometime thing / My man's gone now / It takes a long pull to get here / I got plenty o' nuttin' / Bess you is my woman now / It ain't necessarily so / Prayer / Strawberry woman's call, honey man / Crab man / I love your Porgy / Clara Clara / There's a boat that's leavin' soon for New York / Oh Bess, oh where's my Bess / Oh lawd, i'm on my way
CD _______________ CDP 7951322
Blue Note / Feb '97 / EMI

Potts, Tommy

LIFFEY BANKS, THE
CD _______________ CC 13CD
Claddagh / Jun '95 / ADA / CM / Direct

Pound & Koch

ELECTRONIC DUB
CD _______________ RSNCD 21
Rising High / Aug '94 / 3mv/Sony

Pounder

E6
CD _______________ INV 087CD
Invisible / May '97 / Plastic Head

Pousseur, Henri

ACOUSMATRIX VOL.4
CD _______________ BVHAASTCD 9010
Bvhaast / Dec '89 / Cadillac

POV

HANDIN' OUT BEATDOWNS
Nuff of the ruff stuff / U got what I want / Anutha luv / Good lovin' / Tell me / Summer nights / Never believe / Let me do u / U R the only 1 / Sitting here waiting / Settle down / All thru the nite / Ball ya fist
CD _______________ 74321159462
Giant / Feb '94 / BMG

Poverty Stinks

ANOTHER WORLD
You're going away / Another World / Only One / You can't give enough / There Must Be / Hitch hiker / She / Take Me Home / Man Like Anyone Else / Don't Follow Me / Getting deeper / One Love / Waltz / Poverty Stinks
CD _______________ SNAP 004
Soap / Nov '92 / Vital

Poverty's No Crime

AUTUMN YEARS, THE
Ghost of a stone / Future in my hands / Rain of gods / Beat it when it hurts / Autumn years / Seconds / Lead me to the door / Enter nowhere / Heroes return
CD _______________ TT 00242
T&T / Jul '96 / Koch

Powder

BIFF BANG POWDER
CD _______________ DR 1015
Distortions / Jun '97 / Greyhound

Powder Monkeys

TIME WOUNDS ALL HEELS
CD _______________ ANDA 219CD
Au-Go-Go / Jun '97 / Cargo / Greyhound / Plastic Head

Powell, Baden

BADEN POWELL
CD _______________ 330352
Musidisc / Mar '96 / Discovery

BADEN POWELL & FILHOS
CD _______________ KAR 982
IMP / Sep '96 / ADA / Discovery

BADEN POWELL LIVE IN HAMBURG
CD _______________ BEST 1037CD
Acoustic Music / Nov '93 / ADA

CANTO ON GUITAR
Samba em preludio / Tres themas de fe Afro-Brasileira / Marcha Escocesa / Tributo a um amigo / Qua quara qua qua / Cegos do Nordeste
CD _______________ 8218662
MPS Jazz / Apr '94 / PolyGram

FRANKFURT OPERA CONCERT 1975 (Powell, Baden & Trio)
CD _______________ 68958
Tropical / Apr '97 / Discovery

LIVE AT MONTREUX 1995
CD _______________ FA 410
Fremeaux / Jul '96 / ADA / Discovery

MELANCOLIE
CD _______________ 139 213
Accord / '86 / Cadillac / Discovery

TRISTEZA ON GUITAR/POEMA ON GUITAR/APASSIANADO (Three Originals/2CD Set)
Tristeza / Canto de Xango / 'Round midnight / Sarava / Canto de / Ossanha / Manha de carnaval / Invencao em 7/12 / Das rosas / Som do carnaval / O astronauta / Fetinha pro poeta / Dindi / Consolacao / Tristeza e solidao / Samba triste / Euridice / All the things you are / Reza / Casa velha / Alcantra / Waltzing / Lembrancas / Abstrato / As flores / Balantofe / Brisa do mar
CD Set _______________ 5192162
MPS Jazz / Apr '94 / PolyGram

VIVO NO TEATRO SANTA ROSA
CD _______________ HE 30CD
Rare Brazil / Apr '97 / Cargo

Powell, Bud

'ROUND ABOUT MIDNIGHT AT THE BLUE NIGHT
Shawnuff / Lover man / There will never be another you / Monk's mood / Night in Tunisia / 'Round midnight / Thelonious / 52nd Street
CD _______________ FDM 365002
Dreyfus / Oct '93 / ADA / Direct / New Note/ Pinnacle

1953 - AUTUMN BROADCASTS
CD _______________ ESP 30242
ESP / Jan '93 / Jazz Music

1953 - SPRING BROADCASTS
CD _______________ ESP 30222
ESP / Jan '93 / Jazz Music

1953 - SUMMER BROADCASTS
CD _______________ ESP 30232
ESP / Jan '93 / Jazz Music

1953 - WINTER BROADCASTS
CD _______________ ESP 30212
ESP / Jan '93 / Jazz Music

AMAZING BUD POWELL VOL.1, THE
Un poco loco (first take) / Un poco loco (second take) / Dance of the infidels / 52nd Street / It could happen to you / Night in Tunisia / Wail / Ornithology / Bouncing with Bud / Parisian thoroughfare / Wail (alt. take) / Dance of the infidels (alt. take) / You go to my head / Ornithology (alt. master) / Un poco loco (alt. take 2) / Over the rainbow
CD _______________ CDP 7815032
Blue Note / Mar '95 / EMI

BEST OF BUD POWELL ON VERVE, THE
CD _______________ 5233922
Verve / Mar '94 / PolyGram

BIRDLAND, NEW YORK 1956
Tea for two / Lover come back to me / I want to be happy / I've got you under my skin / Hallelujah / It could happen to you / Lullaby of Birdland / Embraceable you / Ornithology / How high the moon
CD _______________ 550202
Jazz Anthology / Feb '94 / Cadillac / Discovery / Harmonia Mundi

BLUE NOTE CAFE PARIS 1961
CD _______________ ESP 10662
ESP / Jan '93 / Jazz Music

BLUES FOR BOUFFEMONT
In the mood for a classic / Una noche con frances / Relaxin' at Camarillo / Moose the mooche / Blues for Bouffemont / Little Willie leaps / My old flame / Star eyes / There will never be another you
CD _______________ BLCD 760135
Black Lion / Apr '90 / Cadillac / Jazz Music / Koch / Wellard

BOUNCING WITH BUD (Powell, Bud Trio)
CD _______________ DD 406
Delmark / Nov '89 / ADA / Cadillac / CM / Direct / Hot Shot

BUD PLAYS BIRD
Big foot / Shaw 'nuff / Buzzy / Yardbird suite / Relaxin' at Camarillo / Confirmation / Billie's bounce / Ko Ko / Barbados / Dewey Square / Moose the Mooch / Ornithology / Scrapple from the apple / Salt peanuts / Big foot (short version)
CD _______________ CDP 8371372
Roulette / Apr '96 / EMI

BUD POWELL TRIO PLAYS, THE (Powell, Bud Trio)
I'll remember April / (Back home again in) Indiana / Somebody loves me / I should care / Bud's bubble / Off minor / Nice work if you can get it / Everything happens to me / Embraceable you / Burt covers Bud / My heart stood still / You'd be so nice to come home to / Bag's groove / My devotion / Stella by starlight / Woody 'n' you
CD _______________ CDROU 1011
Roulette / Feb '90 / EMI

CELIA 1947-1957
CD _______________ CD 53075
Giants Of Jazz / Mar '92 / Cadillac / Jazz Music / Target/BMG

COMPLETE BLUE NOTE & ROOST RECORDINGS, THE (4CD Set)
I'll remember April / (Back home again in) Indiana / Somebody loves me / I should care / Bud's bubble / Off minor / Nice work if you can get it / Everything happens to me / Bouncing with Bud (alt. take 1) / Bouncing with Bud (alt. take 2) / Bouncing with Bud / Wail (alt. take) / Wail / Dance of the infidels (alt. take) / Dance of the infidels / 52nd Street / You go to my head / Ornithology / Ornithology (alt. take) / Un poco loco (alt. take 1) / Un poco loco (alt. take 2) / Un poco loco / Over the rainbow / Night in Tunisia / Night in Tunisia (alt. take) / It could happen to you / It could happen to you (alt. take) / Parisian thoroughfare / Autumn in New York / Reets and I / Reets and I (alt. take) / Sure thing / Collard greens and black eyed peas (alt. take) / Collard greens and black eyed peas / Polka dots and moonbeams / I want to be happy / Audrey / Glass enclosure / Embraceable you / Burt covers Bud / My heart stood still / You'd be so nice to come home to / Bag's groove / My devotion / Stella by straight / Woody 'n' you / Blue pearl / Blue pearl (alt. take) / Keepin' in the groove / Some soul / Frantic fancies / Bud on Bach / Idaho / Don't blame me / Moose the mooche / John's abbey (alt. take) / Sub City (alt. take) / Sub City / John's abbey / Buster rides again / Like someone in love / Dry soul / Marma lade / Monopoly / Time waits / Scene changes / Down with it / Comin' up (alt. take) / Comin' up / Duid deed / Cleopatra's dream / Gettin' there / Crossin' the channel / Danceland / Borderick
CD Set _______________ CDP 8300832
Blue Note / Oct '94 / EMI

COMPLETE ESSENTIAL JAZZ FESTIVAL CONCERT, THE
Shaw 'nuff / Blues in the closet / Willow weep for me / John's abbey / Salt peanuts / All the things you are / Just you, just me / Yesterdays / Stuffy
CD _______________ BLCD 760105
Black Lion / Jul '88 / Cadillac / Jazz Music / Koch / Wellard

COMPLETE VERVE RECORDINGS, THE
CD _______________ 5216692
Verve / Nov '94 / PolyGram

EARLY BUDS
Floogie boo / I don't know / Gotta do some war work / My old flame / Sweet Lorraine / Honeysuckle rose / Blue garden blues / Long tall Dexter / Dexter digs in / I can make you love me / Ray's idea / Serenade to a square / Good kick / Seven up / Blues in be bop / Epistrophy / Oop bop sh'bam / Rue Chaptal / Boppin' a riff / Fat boy / Webb City
CD _______________ TPZ 1059
Topaz Jazz / Mar '97 / Cadillac / Pinnacle

GENIUS OF BUD POWELL, THE
Tea for two / Hallelujah / Parisian thoroughfare / Oblivion / Dusk in sandi / Hallucinations / Fruit / Nightingale sang in Berkeley Square / Just one of those things / Last time I saw Paris
CD _______________ 8279012
Verve / Feb '92 / PolyGram

JAZZ PROFILE
Indiana / Bud's bubble / Wail / Dance of the infidels / Night in Tunisia / Burt covers Bud / Autumn in New York / Collard greens and black eyed peas / I want to be happy / Time waits / Comin' up / Bud on Bach
CD _______________ CDP 8549062
Blue Note / May '97 / EMI

PIANOLOGY (Powell, Bud & Thelonious Monk)
CD _______________ MCD 0552
Moon / Apr '94 / Cadillac / Harmonia Mundi

SALT PEANUTS
CD _______________ BLCD 760121
Black Lion / Aug '89 / Cadillac / Jazz Music / Koch / Wellard

STRICTLY CONFIDENTIAL
CD _______________ BLCD 760196
Koch / Nov '94 / Koch

Powell, Cozy

VERY BEST OF COZY POWELL, THE
CD _______________ 5377242
Polydor / Aug '97 / PolyGram

Powell, Dirk

IF I GO TEN THOUSAND MILES
CD _______________ ROUCD 0384
Rounder / May '96 / ADA / CM / Direct

Powell, Jesse

JESSE POWELL
Looking for love / All I need / Spend the night / I like / You don't know / You / Gloria, it's you that I need / Ooh I like it / Let go / If you like what you see / All alone / I will be loving you / Is it over
CD _______________ LSJD 11287
MCA / Mar '96 / BMG

Powell, Jimmy

MANDOLIN MOMENTS
Lara's theme / Sealed with a kiss / Spanish eyes / Godfather / Milanese waltz / Skye boat song / Certain smile / Serenata / Autumn leaves / LA paloma / Song for the seashore / Forever and ever / O sole mio / Breeze and I
CD _______________ PLATCD 32
Platinum / Jul '92 / Prism

R & B SENSATION
Sugar man / House of the rising sun / Captain Man / Nine live wire / Witness to a war / Progressive talking blues / I'm a rocker / On the beach / I can go down / Sugar baby / Slow down / Gonna find a cave / Strangers on a train / Slow lovin' man / Back in the USSR / Out of time / Ivory / Real cool / Hipster / Hold on / Rosavelt and Iralee / Do you really have a heart
CD _______________ SEECD 337
See For Miles/C5 / Feb '92 / Pinnacle

Powell, Keith

KEITH POWELL STORY, THE
Come and join the party / Answer is no / Tore up / You better let him go / I should know better / Too much monkey business / Walkin' and cryin' / New Orleans / People get ready / Paradise / Beyond the hill / Come home baby / Goodbye girl / It was easier to hurt her / When you move you lose: *Powell, Keith & Billie Davis* / Tastes sour don't it: *Powell, Keith & Billie Davis* / Victory / Some people only / Two little people: *Powell, Keith & Billie Davis* / You don't know like I know: *Powell, Keith & Billie Davis* / Swinging tight: *Powell, Keith & Billie Davis* / That's really some good: *Powell, Keith & Billie Davis* / Song of the moon / It keeps rainin'
CD _______________ NEMCD 717
Sequel / Nov '94 / BMG

Powell, Marilyn

SEEDS
Seeds / Hurt / No one's gonna be a fool forever / Time for peace / Tonight / Why didn't I think of that / Old lover / Once upon a time / Up in the world / Crazy / For you / Like no one else / Music / If you're looking for a heartache / Star
CD _______________ PCOM 1130
President / Oct '93 / Grapevine/PolyGram / President / Target/BMG

Powell, Mel

RETURN OF MEL POWELL, THE
CD _______________ CRD 301
Chiaroscuro / Mar '96 / Jazz Music

POWER

DEDICATED TO WORLD REVOLUTION
Revolution / Power to the people / Racemixer / Modern day slavery / Guerilla warfare / Tribute to the native Americans / Death machine / Future shock / US Peace plan / Legally insane / United snakes / Mayday / Out of control / Potential criminals / Class war / Let's kill 'em
CD _______________ NET 050CD

Nettwerk / Apr '94 / Greyhound / Pinnacle / Vital

Power

JUSTICE OF FIRE
CD RTN 41206
Rock The Nation / Feb '95 / Plastic Head

Power, Brendan

BLOW IN
CD HBCD 0008
Hummingbird / Apr '96 / ADA / Direct / Grapevine/PolyGram

JIG-JAZZ
CD PKCD 001
PK / Mar '96 / ADA

NEW IRISH HARMONICA
CD PM 002CD
Punch Music / Jan '96 / ADA / Roots

RIVERDANCE DISTILLED (Brendan Power Plays The Music From Riverdance)
Countess Cathleen / Reel around the sun / Slip into Spring / American wake / Lift the wings / Riverdance / Caoineadh chu chulainn / Firedance/Andalucia / Riverdance/ Women of Sidhe / Marta's dance/Russian dervish
CD CDTRAX 135
Greentrax / Jun '97 / ADA / Direct / Duncans / Highlander

STATE OF THE HARP
CD TCJAY 335
Jayrem / Jul '94 / CM / Jet Star

Power, Duffy

BLUES POWER
Hell hound / Mary open the door / Holiday / Little boy blue / Open the door / I need you / Midnight special / Gin house blues / Fox and geese / Exactly like you / Fixing a hole / Roll over Beethoven / I've been lonely baby / Lawdy Miss Clawdy / Lily / Little man you've had a busy day / City woman / Halfway / Louisiana blues / One night / Leaving blues
CD SEECD 356
See For Miles/C5 / Sep '92 / Pinnacle

JUST STAY BLUE
Love's gonna go / There's no living without your loving / I'm so glad you're mine / Dollar Mamie / Little boy blue / Little girl / Mary open the door / Hound dog / Rags and old iron / Just stay blue / Lilly / Hell hound / Love is shelter / Lawdy Miss Clawdy / Love's prescription / Halfway / Corine / Songs about Jesus / Lover's prayer / Swansong / River
CD RETRO 802
RPM / Jun '95 / Pinnacle

LITTLE BOY BLUE
Rosie / Leaving blues / It's funny / God bless the child / Coming round no more / Give me one / Mary open the door / Help me / Louisiana blues / Little boy blue / Exactly like you / One night / There you go / Red, white and blue
CD EDCD 356
Edsel / Sep '92 / Pinnacle

Power Mad

ABSOLUTE POWER
Slaughterhouse / Nice dreams / Test the steel (Powermad) / BNR / Brainstorms / Absolute power / Return from the fear / Plastic town / Failsafe / Final frontier
CD VSD 5808
Varese Sarabande / May '97 / Pinnacle

Power Of Dreams

IMMIGRANTS, EMIGRANTS AND ME
Jokes on me / Does it matter / Had you listened / Never told you / Never been to Texas / Maire I don't love you / Mothers eyes / Talk / Much too much / Stay / Bring you down / Where is the love / 100 ways to kill a man / My average day
CD 8432582
Polydor / Jul '90 / PolyGram

Power Of Expression

POWER OF EXPRESSION, THE
CD LF 107CD
Lost & Found / Oct '94 / Plastic Head

X-TERRITORIAL
CD CM 77120CD
Century Media / Feb '96 / Plastic Head

Power Pack Orchestra

YOUR 40 ALL-TIME DANCE HITS
In the mood / Opus one / Don't get around much anymore / I'm beginning to see the light / American patrol / Touch of your lips / Spanish harlem / My cherie amour / Shadow of your smile / Guitar boogie shuffle / Nut rocker / Goody goody / Deep in the heart of Texas / Hoots mon / Lara's theme / Moon river / Green leaves of summer / You made me love you / Limehouse blues / St. Louis Blues / Body and soul / Stranger on the shore / Moonlight serenade / Mood indigo / Tuxedo Junction / It happened in Monterey / String of pearls / Brazil / Sucu sucu / Caravan / Copacabana / Lipstick on your collar / Let there be drums / Never on a Sunday / Spanish flea / Hernando's hideaway / New fangled tangle / Get happy / Continental / Last waltz
CD CDMFP 6083
Music For Pleasure / Mar '90 / EMI

Power Rangers

POWER RANGERS
Go go Power Rangers (Long version) / Fight / Lord Zedd / Hey Rita / We need a hero / Combat / Go green ranger go / 5-4-1 / Zords / I will win / Go go Power Rangers (TV version) / White ranger tiger power / Power Rangers
CD 74321252982
RCA / Dec '94 / BMG

Power Station

POWER STATION
Some like it hot / Murderess / Lonely tonight / Communication / Get it on / Go to zero / Harvest for the world / Still in your heart
CD CDPRG 1011
Parlophone / Aug '93 / EMI

Power Steppers

BASS ENFORCEMENT
CD WWCD 15
Wibbly Wobbly / Nov '95 / SRD

BASS RE-ENFORCEMENT
CD WWCD 20
Universal Egg / Oct '96 / SRD

Powerhouse

NIGHTLIFE/LOVIN' MACHINE
CD PRD 70182
Provogue / Nov '90 / Pinnacle

NO REGRETS
Hypocrite / Revolt / Nothing sacred / Ignorant one / Numb / Do it for yourself / I shou-ld've known / Blind sided / Struggle / Choke hold / Fear of falling / Something ain't right / No regrets / Power trip
CD BLK 037ECD
Blackout / Jul '97 / Plastic Head / Vital

Powerhouse

FIVE PLUS FOUR
CD YP 020CD
Yellow / Mar '97 / Timewarp

Powerlord

AWAKENING, THE
Masters of death / Malice / Silent terror / Invasion of the Lords / Merciless Titans / Powerlord
CD SHARK 008 CD
Shark / Jun '88 / Plastic Head

Powers, Johnny

NEW SPARK (FOR AN OLD FLAME), A
Rattled / Rock you around the world / Something about you / Rocker Billy / Bigger heartaches / Trouble / Please please do / It'll be me / Honky tonkin' Saturday night / You win again / Singin' the blues / Stuck on you / Love to burn / New spark (for an old flame) / Love business / Say it / Help me I'm in need
CD NEXCD 259
Sequel / Oct '93 / BMG

Powersurge

POWERSURGE
CD RR 93112
Roadrunner / Jul '91 / PolyGram

Powertwang

SURFIN' DEAD
CD MADCD 017
Mental Disorder / Dec '96 / Nervous

Powrie, Glenna

ASHA
CD MCD 5392
Muse / Sep '92 / New Note/Pinnacle

Powrie, Ian

LEGEND OF THE FIDDLE
Ainsworth march/Laird of thrums/Andy Renwick's ferret / Banks of the Locheil/ Duncan Johnstone / Provost of Forgandenny/Jimmy's aye diggin'/Sands of Murness / Billy Thom's reel / Lady Elizabeth / Willie Atkinson/Leila's garden/Captain Keeler / Dark island / Memories of Bobby Macleod/Christina McNair Caskie / Margaret's waltz/Heather blossom special / Alex MacArthur of Biggar/Lady Charlotte Campbell/Peerie Will / Our Highland Queen / Cambridge hornpipe/Hoo dinnae ye play mair/Moray players / Laird of Corrieburn / Briony / David John Powrie/Calum John Builder / Will Powrie, the Angus ploughman / Back to the hills/Catching rabbits / Lament for Will Starr/Auchterarder VIP / Rural jig/ Margaret Cook's fancy/Ainster fisherman
CD CDLOC 1096
Lochshore / Oct '96 / ADA / Direct / Duncans

Poza

ODESSA
CD PS 65181
PlayaSound / Apr '97 / ADA / Harmonia Mundi

Pozo, Chano

LEGENDARY SESSIONS (Pozo, Chano & Arsenio Rodriguez/Machito & Orchestra)
CD TCD 017
Fresh Sound / Dec '92 / Discovery / Jazz Music

Prado, Perez

BESAME MUCHO
CD CD 62034
Saludos Amigos / Apr '94 / Target/BMG

CILIEGI ROSA
CD CD 62004
Saludos Amigos / Apr '94 / Target/BMG

EL REY DEL MAMBO
CD BM 514
Blue Moon / Jan '97 / Cadillac / Discovery / Greensleeves / Jazz Music / Jet Star / TKO Magnum

GO GO MAMBO (Prado, Perez & His Orchestra)
CD TCD 013
Fresh Sound / Dec '92 / Discovery / Jazz Music

KING OF MAMBO (Prado, Perez 'Prez')
Patricia / Ruletero / Mambo no.8 / Guaglione / Mambo no.5 / Paris / Cherry pink and apple blossom white / Caballo negro (mambo batri) / In a little Spanish town / My Roberta / Why wait / Mambo jambo / Rockambo baby / La rubia / San Remo / One night / Adios pampa mia
CD ND 90424
RCA / May '95 / BMG

LATINO
Jumbo jumbo / Ni hablar / Muchachita / La rubia / Martinica / Mama Y tata / Mambo del 65 / Latino / Jing a ling, jing a lang / Al compas del mambo / La nina popof / Paso bakan / Mi gallo / Ole mambo / Peanut vendor / Ritmo de chunga / Gateando / Oh Caballo
CD CD 62079
Saludos Amigos / Jan '96 / Target/BMG

MAMBO JAMBO
CD CD 62001
Saludos Amigos / Apr '94 / Target/BMG

MAMBO MANIA/HAVANA 3 AM
Cherry pink and apple blossom white / Ballin' the Jack / Tomcat mambo / April in Portugal / Mambo a la Kenton / High and mighty / Marilyn Monroe mambo / St. Louis blues mambo / Skokiaan / Mambo a la Billy May / Mambo de chattanooga / Mambo en sax / La comparsa / Desconfianza / La faraona / Besame mucho / Freeway mambo / Granada / Almendra / Bacoa / Peanut vendor / Baia / Historia de un amor / Mosaico cubano
CD BCD 15462
Bear Family / Feb '90 / Direct / Rollercoaster / Swift

MAMBOS (Prado, Perez & Benny More)
CD CD 62051
Saludos Amigos / May '94 / Target/BMG

POPS & PRADO
You're driving me crazy / Manhattan / Isle of Capri / Three little words / Carolina in the morning / Yes Sir, that's my baby / Ciribirbin / Ida, sweet as apple cider / If you knew Susie (Like I knew Susie) / Paper doll / Taking a chance on love / Heigh ho (The dwarfs marching song) / Millionaire / Catalania / Olga conga / Clap hands / Tic toc polly woc
CD 74321357432
RCA / Jun '96 / BMG

PREZ (Prado, Perez 'Prez')
Maria Bonita/Cu-cu-rru-cu-cu-Paloma / La borrachita (I'll never love again) / Machaca / Adios mi chaparrita (goodbye my little angel) / Marta / Lullaby of Birdland / Flight of the bumblebee / Leo's special / Come back to Sorrento / Fireworks / Estrellita del Sur / Beautiful Margaret / OK Joe Calypso / Leyenda Mexicana / Mama teach me to dance
CD 74321260522
RCA / Jun '97 / BMG

VOODOO SUITE/EXOTIC SUITE OF THE AMERICAS
Voodoo suite: *Prado, Perez & Shorty Rogers* / St. James Infirmary / In the mood / I can't get started (with you) / Jumpin' at the woodside / Stompin' at the Savoy / Music makers / Exotic suite of the Americas / Midnight in Jamaica / Mama yo quiero / Son of a gun / Jacqueline and Caroline / El relicario / I could have danced all night
CD BCD 15463
Bear Family / Feb '90 / Direct / Rollercoaster / Swift

Prague Castle Guard & ...

VIVAT FUCIK (Prague Castle Guard & Police Wind Orchestra)
Florentinsky pochod / Marinarella / Bosanska zora (koracnica) / Zimni boure / Kanizsi / Svaty Hubert / Sempre avanti / Dvorni intendant / Zvuky fanfar / Stary brucoun / Vjezd gladiatoru
CD 4101072431
Edit / Jun '97 / Czech Music Enterprises

Praise Space Electric

2 LEAVING DEMONS
Doc's groove / Sinnerman / Rhythm rhythm / Singing the same song / Diggin' at the dig in / Freedom / 300,000 million years / Waves of joy / Drain your wobbles away / Cybergenetic experiment X / Pebbles
CD DELECCD 015
Delerium / Apr '94 / Cargo / Pinnacle / Vital

Prajini, Zece

PEASANT BRASS BAND
CD 926552
BUDA / Sep '96 / Discovery

Pram

SARGASSO SEA
Loose threads / Little scars / Earthling and protection / Cotton candy / Three wild Georges / Serpentine / Crystal tips / Crooked tiles / Eels / Sea swells and distant squalls
CD PURECD 046
Too Pure / Sep '95 / Vital

STARS ARE SO BIG, THE EARTH IS SO SMALL
CD PURECD 026
Too Pure / Sep '93 / Vital

Prana

GEOMANTIK
CD MPCD 5
Matsuri / Jul '97 / Amato Disco / SRD

Prasit Thawon Ensemble

THAI CLASSICAL MUSIC
CD NI 5412CD
Nimbus / Oct '94 / Nimbus

Pratt, Andy

RESOLUTION (Pratt, Andy Collection)
CD RE 21162
Razor & Tie / Oct '96 / Koch

Praxis

TRANSMUTATION
Blast/War machine dub / Interface/Stimulation loop / Crash victim/Black science navigator / Animal behaviour / Dead man walking / Seven laws of woo / Interworld and the new innocence / Giant robot/Machines in the modern city / After shock (Chaos never died)
CD ADC 5
Douglas Music / May '97 / Cadillac / New Note/Pinnacle

TRANSMUTATION LIVE
CD GR 101011
Gravity / Mar '97 / Cargo / Greyhound / Plastic Head

Praying For The Rain

SANCTUARY
CD TWIN 103
Twin Arrows / Jul '97 / Grapevine/ PolyGram

Praying Mantis

CRY FOR THE NEW WORLD, A
CD CDFLAG 80
Under One Flag / Sep '93 / Pinnacle

PREDATOR IN DISGUISE
Can't see the angels / She's hot / This time girl / Time slipping away / Listen what your heart says / Still want you / Horn / Battle royal / Only you / Borderline / Can't wait forever
CD CDFLAG 77
Under One Flag / Feb '93 / Pinnacle

Preacher Boy

GUTTERS AND PEWS
Down and out in this town / Catfish / Ugly / Cold mountain music / I won't be there / Something is wrong / Buckshot / Railroad / New Orleans / In the darkened night / Back then we only cared for hell / 2 o'clock
CD BPCD 5034
Blind Pig / Nov '96 / ADA / CM / Direct / Hot Shot

PREACHER BOY & THE NATURAL BLUES
CD BPCD 5017
Blind Pig / Feb '95 / ADA / CM / Direct / Hot Shot

Preacher Jack

NON STOP BOOGIE
CD _______ SACD 097
Solo Art / Nov '96 / Jazz Music

RETURN OF THE BOOGIE MAN
All by myself / Say you'll stay until tomorrow / Break up / Yancey's bugle call / Public is my family, music is my life / Go tell it on the mountain / Mystery train / Jessie's boogie woogie / I'll be your baby / Who will buy the wine / Lovin' up a storm / Teardrop on a rose / Rounder boogie / May you never be alone like me / Be careful of stones that you throw / Just a closer walk with thee
CD _______ ROUCD 3145
Rounder / Feb '97 / ADA / CM / Direct

Preager, Lou

CRUISING DOWN THE RIVER
Saturday night / Sophisticated lady / Dodging around / Bring on the drums / Remember me / Don't take your love / I'll always be with you / I'd rather be me / Too bad / I close my eyes / Let's keep it that way / Cruising down the river / Did you ever get that feeling / Trees in / Good good good / Ashby De La Zouch / Let bygones be bygones / By that dream / Who could love / I'll get you alone / Sweet dreams / No one but you / Wonder of you / Down in the valley / Pretending
CD _______ CDEA 6000
Vocalion / Aug '97 / Complete/Pinnacle

DANCING AT THE HAMMERSMITH PALAIS (Preager, Lou & His Orchestra)
Saturday night / I'd rather be me / I'm beginning to see the light / In a little while / Bring on the drums / No one else will do / Too bad / I've got a heart filled with love / Trolley song / Waiting in Sweetheart Valley / I'll always be with you / Sophisticated lady / If I told a lie / Let's keep it that way / Doggin' around / I'll close my eyes / Lonely footsteps / Last waltz of the evening / Coming home / Remember me / Morning train / Don't take your love from me / Choc'late soldier from the USA
CD _______ RAJCD 866
Empress / Apr '96 / Koch

Prefab Sprout

ANDROMEDA HEIGHTS
Electric guitars / Prisoner of the past / Mystery of love / Life's a miracle / Anne Marie / Whoever you are / Steal your thunder / Avenue of stars / Swans / Fifth horseman / Weightless / Andromeda Heights
CD _______ KWCD 30
Kitchenware / May '97 / Sony

FROM LANGLEY PARK TO MEMPHIS
King of rock 'n' roll / Cars and girls / I remember that / Enchanted / Nightingales / Hey Manhattan / Knock on wood / Golden calf / Nancy let your hair down for me / Venus of the soup kitchen
CD _______ 4601242
Columbia / May '97 / Sony

FROM LANGLEY PARK TO MEMPHIS/ JORDAN: THE COMEBACK
King of rock 'n' roll / Cars and girls / I remember that / Enchanted / Nightingales / Hey Manhattan / Knock on wood / Golden calf / Nancy (Let your hair down for me) / Venus of the soup kitchen / Looking for Atlantis / Wild horses / Machine gun Ibiza / We let the stars go / Carnival 2000 / Jordan: The comeback / Jesse James symphony / Jesse James Bolero / Moon dog / All the world loves lovers / All boys believe anything / Ice maiden / Paris Smith / Wedding march / One of the broken / Michael / Mercy / Scarlet nights / Doo wop in Harlem
CD _______ PS 22CD
Columbia / May '97 / Sony

JORDAN - THE COMEBACK
Looking for Atlantis / Wild horses / Machine gun Ibiza / We let the stars go / Carnival 2000 / Jordan: The comeback / Jesse James symphony / Jesse James bolero / Moon dog / All the world loves lovers / All boys believe anything / Ice maiden / Paris Smith / Wedding march / One of the broken / Michael / Mercy / Scarlet nights / Doo wop in Harlem
CD _______ 4671612
Columbia / May '97 / Sony

LIFE OF SURPIRISES, A/STEVE MCQUEEN
CD Set _______ 4718862D
Columbia / Feb '93 / Sony

LIFE OF SURPRISES, A
King of rock 'n' roll / When love breaks down / Sound of crying / Faron Young / Carnival 2000 / Goodbye Lucille / Cruel / I remember that / Cars and girls / We let the stars go / Life of surprises / Appetite / If you don't love me / Wild horses / Hey Manhattan / All the world loves lovers
CD _______ 4718862
Columbia / Jun '92 / Sony

PROTEST SONGS
World awake / Life of surprises / Horsechimes / Wicked things / Dublin / Tiffanys / Talkin' scarlet / Till the cows come home / Pearly gates
CD _______ 4651182
Columbia / Feb '97 / Sony

STEVE MCQUEEN
Faron young / Bonny / Appetite / When love breaks down / Goodbye Lucille / Hallelujah / Moving the river / Horsin' around / Desire as / Blueberry pies / When the angels
CD _______ 4663362
Columbia / May '97 / Sony

STEVE MCQUEEN/FROM LANGLEY PARK TO MEMPHIS
Faron Young / Bonny / When love breaks down / Goodbye Lucille / No. 1 / Hallelujah / Appetite / Moving the river / Horsin' around / Desire as / Blueberry pies / When the angels / King of rock 'n' roll / Cars and girls / I remember that / Enchanted / Nightingales / Hey Manhattan / Knock on wood / Golden calf / Nancy (let your hair down for me) / Venus of the soup kitchen
CD Set _______ 4784822
Columbia / Mar '95 / Sony

SWOON
Don't sing / Cue fanfare / Green Isaac / Here on the eerie / Cruel / Couldn't bear to be special / I never play basketball now / Ghost town blues / Elegance / Technique
CD _______ 4609082
Columbia / May '97 / Sony

SWOON/STEVE MCQUEEN
Don't sing / Cue fanfare / Green Isaac / Here on the eerie / Cruel / Couldn't bear to be special / I never play basketball now / Ghost town blues / Elegance / Technique / Faron Young / Bonny appetite / When love breaks down / Goodbye Lucille / Hallelujah / Moving the river / Horsin' around / Desire as / Blueberry pies / When the angels
CD _______ PS 21CD
Columbia / May '97 / Sony

Pregnant

UNUSUAL LOVER
CD _______ SF 018CD
Swarf Finger / May '97 / Cargo

Prego

MOCHA EXPRESS
Mocha Express / Norbert's/Turn of the wheel / Grandjean/Laurel / Doigts de Carmen/Trois / Ami / Chasse a la Becasse / Madame Nuds Tarantella / Georgian twist / Littel green hat / Bailiffs bouree/Marijean/ Jeanmari / Trois matelots/Chemin du village / Adeles / Mexican hatstand/Winter sunshine / Boeing 747/Berceuse
CD _______ FSCD 24
Folksound / Jun '97 / CM / Roots

Prelude

AFTER THE GOLDRUSH
CD _______ PACD 7015
Disky / Sep '93 / Disky / THE

Prelude To Cycle 6

PRELUDE TO CYCLE 6 VOL.2
CD _______ JFR 007CD
Jazz Fudge / Jun '97 / Pinnacle

Prema

DRIVAL
CD _______ EVR 027CD
Equal Vision / Apr '97 / Plastic Head

Premature Ejaculation

ANESTHESIA
CD _______ DV 018CD
Dark Vinyl / Sep '93 / Plastic Head / World Serpent

ASSERTIVE DISCIPLINE
CD _______ DV 023CD
Dark Vinyl / Jan '95 / Plastic Head / World Serpent

NECESSARY DISCOMFORTS
CD _______ CLEO 75932
Cleopatra / Mar '94 / Cargo / Greyhound / Plastic Head / RTM/Disc / SRD

Premi

10 YEARS ON
CD _______ DMUT 1212
Multitone / Aug '93 / BMG

Premier Accordian Band

GO COUNTRY
CD _______ PLATCD 3924
Platinum / May '94 / Prism

GO HAWAIIAN
Clap clap sound / Aloha oe / Highland hulu / Beyond the reef / Now is the hour
CD _______ PLATCD 3925
Platinum / May '94 / Prism

GO SCOTTISH
CD _______ PLATCD 3926
Platinum / May '94 / Prism

Presencer, Alain

SINGING BOWLS OF TIBET
Invocation / Bowl voices / Shepherd's song / Lullaby / Bon-po chant / Lamentation / Symphony of the bowls
CD _______ CDSDL 326
Saydisc / Mar '94 / ADA / Direct / Harmonia Mundi

Presidents Of The USA

II
Ladies and gentlemen part 1 / Lunatic to love / Volcano / March 5 / Twig / Bug City / Bath of fire / Tiki God / LIP / Froggie / Toob amplifier / Supermodel / Puffy little shoes / Ladies and gentlemen part 2 / Basketball dream
CD _______ 4850922
Columbia / Nov '96 / Sony

PRESIDENTS OF THE USA
Kitty / Feather pluckin' / Lump / Stranger / Boll weevil / Peaches / Dune buggy / We are not going to make it / Kick out the jams / Body / Back porch / Candy / Naked and famous / Wake up / Twig in the wind
CD _______ 4810392
Columbia / Oct '95 / Sony
CD _______ 4843342
Columbia / Jul '96 / Sony

Presley

AFRICAN SWIM
CD _______ SHCD 6018
Sky High / Jul '95 / Direct / Jet Star

Presley, Elvis

AFTERNOON IN THE GARDEN, AN
Also sprach Zarathustra / That's alright / Proud Mary / Never been to Spain / You don't have to say you love me / Until it's time for you to go / You've lost that lovin' feelin' / Polk salad Annie / Love me / All shook up / Heartbreak hotel / (Let me be your) teddy bear / Don't be cruel / Love me tender / Blue suede shoes / Reconsider baby / Hound dog / I'll remember you / Suspicious minds / Introductions by Elvis / For the good times / An American trilogy / Funny how time slips away / I can't stop loving you / Can't help falling in love
CD _______ 07863674572
RCA / Mar '97 / BMG

ALL TIME GREATEST HITS, THE (2CD Set)
Heartbreak hotel / Blue suede shoes / Hound dog / Love me tender / Too much / All shook up / Teddy bear / Paralysed / Party / Jailhouse rock / Don't / Wear my ring around your neck / Hard headed woman / King Creole / One night / Fool such as I / Big hunk o' love / Stuck on you / Girl of my best friend / It's now or never / Are you lonesome tonight / Wooden heart / Surrender / His latest flame / Can't help falling in love / Good luck charm / She's not you / Return to sender / Devil in disguise / Crying in the chapel / Love letters / If I can dream / In the ghetto / Suspicious minds / Don't cry Daddy / Wonder of you / I just can't help believin' / American trilogy / Burning love / Always on my mind / My boy / Suspicion / Moody blue / Way down / It's only love
CD Set _______ PD 90100
RCA / Apr '97 / BMG

ALOHA FROM HAWAII
What now my love / Fever / Welcome to my world / Suspicious minds / CC rider / Burning love / Hound dog / I'll remember you / Long tall Sally / Whole lotta shakin' goin' on / American trilogy / Big hunk o' love / Can't help falling in love / Something / You gave me a mountain / Steamroller blues / My way / Love me / Johnny B Goode / It's over / Blue suede shoes / I'm so lonesome I could cry / I can't stop loving you
CD _______ 74321289872
RCA / Aug '95 / BMG

ALTERNATIVE ALOHA
Also sprach Zarathustra / CC rider / Burning love / Something / You gave me a mountain / Steamroller blues / My way / It's over / Blue suede shoes / I'm so lonesome I could cry / What now my love / Fever / Welcome to my world / Suspicious minds / I'll remember you / American trilogy / Big hunk o' love / Can't help falling in love / Blue Hawaii / Hound dog / Hawaiian wedding song / Ku-u-i-po
CD _______ PD 86985
RCA / Aug '88 / BMG

ALWAYS ON MY MIND
CD _______ 74321489842
RCA / May '97 / BMG

AMAZING GRACE (His Greatest Sacred Performances)
I believe / peace in the valley / Take my hand precious Lord / It is no secret / Milky white way / His hand in mine / I believe in the man in the sky / He knows just what I need / Mansion over the hilltop / In my father's house / Joshua fit de Battle of Jericho / Swing low, sweet chariot / I'm gonna walk dem golden stairs / If we never meet again / Known only to him / Working on the building / Crying in the chapel / Run on / How great thou art / Stand by me / Where no one stands alone / So high / Farther along / By and by / In the garden / Somebody bigger than you and I / Without him / If the Lord wasn't walking by my side / Where could I go but to the Lord / We call on him / You'll never walk alone / Only believe / Amazing grace / Miracle of the rosary / Lead me, guide me / He touched me / I've got confidence / Evening prayer / Seeing is believing / Thing called love / Put your hand in the hand / Reach out to Jesus / He is my everything / There is no God but God / I, John / Bosom of Abraham / Help me / If that isn't love / Why me Lord / You better run / Lead me / Nearer my God to thee
CD _______ 07863 664212
RCA / Oct '94 / BMG

AT THE WORLD'S FAIR/FUN IN ACAPULCO
Beyond the bend / Relax / Take me to the fair / They remind me too much of you / One broken heart for sale (Film version) / I'm falling in love tonight / Cotton candy land / World of our own / How would you like to be / Happy ending / One broken heart for sale / Fun in Acapulco / Vino, dinero y amor / Mexico / El toro / Marguerita / Bullfighter was a lady / No room to rhumba in a sports car / I think I'm gonna like it here / Bossa nova baby / You can't say no in Acapulco / Guadalajara
CD _______ 74321134312
RCA / Mar '93 / BMG

BACK IN MEMPHIS
Inherit the wind / This is the story / Stranger in my own hometown / Little bit of green / And the grass won't pay no mind / Do you know who I am / From a jack to a king / Fair's moving on / You'll think of me / Without love (there is nothing)
CD _______ ND 90599
RCA / Oct '91 / BMG

BLUE HAWAII (Original Soundtrack)
Blue Hawaii / Almost always true / Aloha oe / No more / Can't help falling in love / Rock-a-hula baby / Moonlight swim / Ku-u-I-pu / Ito eats / Slicin' sand / Hawaiian sunset / Beach boy blues / Island of love / Hawaiian wedding song / Steppin' out of line / Can't help falling in love / Slicin' sand / No more / Rock-a-hula baby / Beach boy blues / Blue Hawaii
CD _______ 07863674592
CD _______ 07863669592
RCA / Apr '97 / BMG

CLASSIC ELVIS
Blue suede shoes / Hound dog / All shook up / I got a woman / Lawdy Miss Clawdy / Wear my ring around your neck / Big hunk o' love / Mean woman blues / It's now or never / Fever / Return to sender / That's alright Mama / Treat me nice / My baby left me / Hard headed woman / Mystery train
CD _______ 74321476822
Camden / Apr '97 / BMG

COLLECTION VOL.1, THE
That's alright / Heartbreak hotel / I was the one / Blue suede shoes / My baby left me / Hound dog / Don't be cruel / Peace in the valley / One night / Loving you / I want you, I need you, I love you / Love me tender / Love me / All shook up / That's when your heartache begins
CD _______ 74321289882
RCA / Oct '96 / BMG

COLLECTION VOL.2, THE
Teddy bear / Party / Jailhouse rock / Don't / Wear my ring around your neck / I got stung / It's now or never / Stuck on you / Girl of my best friend / Mess of blues / Are you lonesome tonight / Big hunk o' love / Fool such as I / My wish came true
CD _______ 74321330172
RCA / Oct '96 / BMG

COLLECTION VOL.3, THE
Wooden heart / Surrender / Wild in the country / Can't help falling in love / Rock-a-hula baby / His latest flame / Follow that dream / Good luck charm / She's not you / Return to sender / Devil in disguise / Bossa nova baby / Such a night / Crying in the chapel / Love letters
CD _______ 74321400532
RCA / Aug '96 / BMG

COMMAND PERFORMANCES (The Essential 1960's Masters Vol.2 - 2CD Set)
GI blues / Wooden heart / Shoppin' around / Doin' the best I can / Flaming star / Wild in the country / Lonely man / Blue Hawaii / Rock-a-hula baby / Can't help falling in love / Beach boy blues / Hawaiian wedding song / Follow that dream / Angel / King of the whole wide world / I got lucky / Girls, girls, girls / Because of love / Return to sender / One broken heart for sale / I'm falling in love tonight / They remind me too much of you / Fun in Acapulco / Bossa Nova baby / Marguerita / Mexico / Kissin' cousins / One boy two little girls / Once is enough / Viva Las Vegas / What'd I say / Roustabout / Poison Ivy League / Little Egypt / There's a brand new day on the horizon / Girl happy / Puppet on a string / Do the clam / Harem holiday / So close, yet so far / Frankie and Johnny / Please don't stop loving me / Paradise Hawaiian style / This is my heaven / Spinout / All that I am / I'll be back / Easy come, easy go / Double trouble / Long leg-

ged girl with the short dress on / Clambake / You don't know me / Stay away / Joe / Speedway / Your time hasn't come yet, baby / Let yourself go / Almost in love / Little less conversation / Edge of reality / Charrol / Clean up your own backyard
CD Set ________ **07863666012**
RCA / Jun '95 / BMG

COMPLETE SUN SESSIONS, THE
That's alright mama / Blue moon of Kentucky / Good rockin' tonight / I don't care if the sun don't shine / Milkcow blues boogie / You're a heartbreaker / Baby let's play house / I'm left, you're right, she's gone / Mystery train / I forgot to remember to forget / I love you because / Blue moon / Tomorrow's night / I'll never let you go / Just because / Trying to get to you / Harbour lights / When it rains it really pours
CD ________ **PD 86414**
RCA / Jul '87 / BMG

DATE WITH ELVIS, A
Blue moon of Kentucky / Young and beautiful / Baby I don't care / Milk cow blue boogie / Baby let's play house / Good rockin' tonight / Is it so strange / I forgot to remember to forget
CD ________ **ND 90360**
RCA / Sep '89 / BMG

EASY COME, EASY GO/SPEEDWAY (Double Feature/Original Soundtracks)
Easy come, easy go / Love machine / Yoga is as yoga does / You gotta stop / Sing you children / I'll take love / She's a machine / Love machine (alternate take) / Sing you children (alternate take) / She's a machine (alternate take 13) / Suppose (alternate master) / Speedway / There ain't nothing like a song / Your time hasn't come yet, baby / Who are you, who am I / He's your uncle, not your dad / Let yourself go / Five sleepy heads / Suppose / Your groovy self
CD ________ **07863665582**
RCA / Mar '95 / BMG

ELVIS - A PORTRAIT (In Performance/ Interviews & Musical Tributes - 2CD Set)
Hound dog / Are you lonesone tonight: *Davis, John* / Interview / There's good rockin' tonight / Interview / I just can't help believing: *Davis, John* / Heartbreak hotel / In the ghetto: *Davis, John* / Interview / I got a woman / Jailhouse rock: *Davis, John* / Maybellene / Return to sender: *Davis, John* / Interview / I was the one / Until it's time for you to go: *Davis, John* / Blue suede shoes / Lawdy Miss Clawdy: *Davis, John* / Interview / Tweedle Dee / When my blue moon turns to gold: *Davis, John* / Interview / Money honey / That's alright Mama: *Davis, John* / Interview / Blue moon of Kentucky / Don't be cruel: *Davis, John* / Long tall Sally / His latest flame: *Davis, John* / Baby let's play house / Wooden heart: *Davis, John* / Love me tender: *Davis, John*
CD Set ________ **MUCD 9517**
Musketeer / May '96 / Disc

ELVIS - THE ALBUM
CD ________ **SGCD 001**
Dynamite / Nov '94 / THE

ELVIS 1956
Heartbreak hotel / My baby left me / Blue suede shoes / Glad you're mine / Tutti frutti / One sided love affair / Love me / Any place is paradise / Paralyzed / Ready Teddy / Too much / Hound dog / Any way you want me / Don't be cruel / Lawdy Miss Clawdy / Shake, rattle & roll / I want you, I need you / Rip it up / Heartbreak hotel / I got a woman / I was the one / Money honey
CD ________ **07863668172**
CD ________ **07863668562**
RCA / Jun '96 / BMG

ELVIS ELVIS ELVIS
That's alright mama / Blue moon of Kentucky / Heartbreak hotel / Long tall Sally / I was the one / Money, honey / I've got a woman / Blue suede shoes / Hound dog / Baby let's play house / Maybellene / Good rockin' tonight / Tweedle dee
CD ________ **MUCD 9017**
Musketeer / Apr '95 / Disc

ELVIS FOR EVERYONE
Your cheatin' heart / Summer kisses, Winter tears / Finders keepers / In my way / Tomorrow night / Memphis, Tennessee / For the millionth and the last time / Forget me never / Sound advise Santa Lucia / Met her today / When it rains it really pours
CD ________ **7863534502**
RCA / Apr '95 / BMG

ELVIS GOSPEL 1957-1971
Peace in the valley / Take my hand / Precious Lord / I'm gonna walk dem golden stairs / I believe in the man in the sky / Joshua fit de Battle of Jericho / Swing low, sweet chariot / Stand by me / Run on / Where could I go but to the Lord / So high / We call on him / Who am I / Lead me, guide me / Known only to him
CD ________ **74321187532**
RCA / Feb '94 / BMG

ELVIS IN CONCERT
Elvis fans comment / Opening riff / 2001 / CC rider / That's alright / Are you lonesome tonight / You gave me a mountain / Jailhouse rock / How great thou art / I really don't want to know / Elvis introduces his father / Hurt
CD ________ **74321146932**
RCA / Jul '93 / BMG

ELVIS IN PERSON
Blue suede shoes / Johnny B Goode / All shook up / Are you lonesome tonight / Hound dog / I can't stop loving you / My babe / Mystery train tiger man / Words / In the ghetto / Suspicious minds / Can't help falling in love
CD ________ **ND 83892**
RCA / Oct '91 / BMG

ELVIS IS BACK
Make me know it / Fever / Girl of my best friend / I will be home again / Dirty, dirty feeling / Thrill of your love / Soldier boy / Such a night / It feels so right / Girl next door / Like a baby / Reconsider baby
CD ________ **ND 89013**
RCA / Feb '89 / BMG

ELVIS IS STILL ALIVE (Various Artists)
CD ________ **MCG 20008**
Vampirella / Jun '97 / Nervous

ELVIS LIVE AT MADISON SQUARE GARDEN
2001 / That's alright mama / Proud Mary / Never been to Spain / You don't have to say you love me / You've lost that lovin' feelin' / Polk salad Annie / Love me / All shook up / Heartbreak hotel / Impossible dream / Hound dog / Suspicious minds / For the good times / American trilogy / Funny how time slips away / I can't stop loving you / Can't help falling in love / Why me Lord / How great thou art / Blueberry Hill / Can't stop loving you / Help me / Let me be there / My baby left me / Lawdy Miss Clawdy / Closing vamp
CD ________ **ND 90663**
RCA / Apr '92 / BMG

ELVIS NBC SPECIAL (TV soundtrack)
Trouble / Guitar man / Lawdy Miss Clawdy / Baby, what you want me to do / Heartbreak hotel / Hound dog / All shook up / Can't help falling in love / Jailhouse rock / Love me tender / Where could I go but to the Lord / Up above my head / Saved / Blue Christmas / One night / Memories / Nothingville / Big boss man / Little Egypt / If I can dream
CD ________ **ND 83894**
RCA / Mar '91 / BMG

ELVIS NOW
Help me make it through the night / Miracle of the rosary / Hey Jude / Put your hand in the hand / Until it's time for you to go / We can make the morning / Early morning rain / Sylvia / Fools rush in / I was born ten thousand years ago
CD ________ **74321148312**
RCA / Jul '93 / BMG

ELVIS PRESLEY
Blue suede shoes / I love you because / Tutti frutti / I'll never let you go / Money honey / I'm counting on you / I got a woman / One-sided love affair / Just because / Trying to get to you / I'm gonna sit right down and cry over you / Blue moon
CD ________ **ND 89046**
RCA / Oct '88 / BMG

ELVIS PRESLEY (Historic Live Recordings & Interviews/2CD Set)
Heartbreak hotel / Long tall Sally / I was the one / Money honey / I've got a woman / Blue suede shoes / Hound dog / Baby let's play house / Maybellene / That's alright Mama / Blue moon of Kentucky / There's good rockin' tonight / Tweedle dee
CD Set ________ **SAV 001**
Tring / Apr '96 / Tring

ELVIS PRESLEY COLLECTION VOL.4
Guitar man / US male / If I can dream / In the ghetto / Suspicious minds / Don't cry daddy / Wonder of you / You don't have to say you love me / There goes my everything / Rags to riches / I just can't help believing / An American trilogy / Burning love / Always on my mind / It's only love
CD ________ **74321422662**
RCA / Feb '97 / BMG

ELVIS PRESLEY INTERVIEWS, THE (3CD Set)
CD Set ________ **55581**
Laserlight / Mar '97 / Target/BMG

ELVIS PRESLEY LIVE
Heartbreak hotel / Long tall Sally / I was the one / Money honey / I've got a woman / Blue suede shoes / Hound dog / Baby let's play house / Maybellene / That's alright Mama / Blue moon of Kentucky / There's good rockin' tonight
CD ________ **JHD 068**
Tring / Apr '93 / Tring

ELVIS PRESLEY LIVE ON STAGE IN MEMPHIS
CC rider / I got a woman / Love me / Trying to get to you / Long tall Sally / Flip flop and fly / Jailhouse rock / Hound dog / Why me Lord / How great Thou art / Blueberry Hill / Help me / American trilogy / Let me be there / My baby left me / Lawdy Miss Clawdy / Can't help falling in love / Closing vamp
CD ________ **07863506062**
RCA / Feb '94 / BMG

ELVIS PRESLEY SONGBOOK, THE (A Tribute To The King) (Various Artists)
Heartbreak hotel: *D'Arby, Terence Trent* / Jailhouse rock: *King, Albert* / Mess o'blues: *Status Quo* / That's alright mama: *Stewart, Rod* / Suspicious mind: *Fine Young Cannibals* / I'm left you're right she's gone: *Lewis, Jerry Lee* / Devil in disguise: *Flying Burrito Brothers* / TROUBLE: *Gillan* / Teddy bear: *Youngblood, Sydney* / All shook up: *Beck, Jeff* / Too much: *Richard, Cliff* / Don't: *McLean, Don* / In the ghetto: *Cave, Nick* / Mean woman blues: *Orbison, Roy* / Burning love: *Spector, Ronnie* / Polk salad Annie: *White, Tony Joe* / Don't be cruel: *Swan, Billy* / Crawfish: *Thunders, Johnny & Patti Palladin*
CD ________ **VSOPCD 223**
Connoisseur Collection / May '96 / Pinnacle

ELVIS SINGS THE WONDERFUL WORLD OF CHRISTMAS
O come all ye faithful (Adeste Fidelis) / First Noel / On a snowy Christmas night / Winter wonderland / Wonderful world of Christmas / It won't seem like Christmas (without you) / I'll be home on Christmas day / If I get home on Christmas day / Holly leaves and Christmas trees / Merry Christmas baby / Silver bells
CD ________ **ND 81936**
RCA / Nov '93 / BMG

ELVIS TAPES, THE
CD ________ **CDRD 001**
Ace / Jul '91 / Pinnacle

ELVIS TODAY
T-R-O-U-B-L-E / And I love you so / Susan when she tried / Woman without love / Shake a hand / Pieces of my life / Fairytale / I can help / Bringing it back / Green green grass of home
CD ________ **ND 90660**
RCA / Apr '92 / BMG

ELVIS' CHRISTMAS ALBUM
Santa Claus is back in town / White Christmas / Here comes Santa Claus / I'll be home for Christmas / Blue Christmas / Santa bring my baby back to me / O little town of Bethlehem / Silent night / Peace in the valley / I believe / Take my hand, precious Lord / It is no secret
CD ________ **ND 90300**
RCA / Nov '96 / BMG

ELVIS' GOLDEN RECORDS VOL.1
Hound dog / Loving you / All shook up / Heartbreak hotel / Jailhouse rock / Love me / Too much / Don't be cruel / That's when your heartache begins / Teddy bear / Love me tender / Treat me nice / Anyway you want me (that's how I will be) / I want you, I need you, I love you
CD ________ **07863674622**
RCA / Jul '97 / BMG

ELVIS' GOLDEN RECORDS VOL.2 (50,000 Elvis Fans Can't Be Wrong)
I need your love tonight / Wear my ring around your neck / My wish came true / I got stung / Loving you / Teddy bear / One night / Hunk o' love / I beg of you / Fool such as I / Don't cha think it's time / Jailhouse rock / Treat me nice / Don't
CD ________ **07863674632**
RCA / Jul '97 / BMG

ELVIS' GOLDEN RECORDS VOL.3
It's now or never / Stuck on you / Fame and fortune / I gotta know / Surrender / I feel so bad / Are you lonesome tonight / His latest flame / Little sister / Good luck charm / Anything that's part of you / She's not you
CD ________ **07863674642**
RCA / Jul '97 / BMG

ELVIS' GOLDEN RECORDS VOL.4
Love letters / It hurts me / What I'd say / Please don't drag that string around / Indescribably blue / Devil in disguise / Lonely man / Mess of blues / Ask me / Ain't that lovin' you baby / Just tell her Jim said hello / Witchcraft
CD ________ **07863674652**
RCA / Jul '97 / BMG

ELVIS' GOLDEN RECORDS VOL.5
Suspicious minds / Kentucky rain / In the ghetto / Clean up your own backyard / If I can dream / Burning love / If you talk in your sleep / For the heart / Moody blue / Way down
CD ________ **07863674662**
RCA / Jul '97 / BMG

ESSENTIAL COLLECTION, THE
Heartbreak hotel / Blue suede shoes / Hound dog / Don't be cruel / Love me tender / All shook up / Teddy bear / Jailhouse rock / King Creole / Girl of my best friend / It's now or never / Are you lonesome tonight / Wooden heart / His latest flame / Can't help falling in love / Good luck charm / She's not you / Return to sender / Devil in disguise / Crying in the chapel / In the ghetto / Suspicious minds / Wonder of you / I just can't help believin' / American trilogy / Burning love / Always on my mind / Moody blue
CD ________ **74321228712**
RCA / Aug '94 / BMG

ESSENTIAL ELVIS VOL.1
Teddy bear / Loving you / Mean woman blues / Got a lot of livin' to do / Lonesome cowboy / Jailhouse rock / Treat me nice / Young and beautiful / Don't leave me now / I want to be free / Baby I don't care / Love me tender / Let me / Poor boy / We're gonna move / Party / Hot dog
CD ________ **PD 89980**
RCA / Jan '87 / BMG

ESSENTIAL ELVIS VOL.2 (Stereo 57)
I beg of you / Have I told you lately that I love you / Blueberry Hill / Peace in the valley / Is it so strange / It is no secret / Mean woman blues / That's when your heartache begins
CD ________ **PD 90250**
RCA / Jan '89 / BMG

ESSENTIAL ELVIS VOL.3 (Hits Like Never Before)
King Creole / Fool such as I / Your cheatin' heart / Don't cha think it's time / Lover doll / Danny / Crawfish / Ain't that lovin' you baby / I need your love tonight / I got stung / As long as I have you / Wear my ring around your neck / Big hunk o' love / Steadfast, loyal and true / King Creole (instrumental)
CD ________ **PD 90486**
RCA / May '90 / BMG

ESSENTIAL ELVIS VOL.4 (A Hundred Years From Now)
I didn't make it on playing guitar / I washed my hands in muddy water / Little cabin on the hill / Hundred years from now / I've lost you / Got my mojo working/Keep your hands off of it / You don't have to say you love me / It ain't no big thing (but it's growing) / Cindy, Cindy / Faded love / Fool / Rags to riches / Just pretend / If I were you / Faded love / Where did they go Lord / It's only love / Until it's time for you to go / Patch it up / Whole lotta shakin' goin' on / Bridge over troubled water / Lord's prayer
CD ________ **07863668662**
RCA / Jul '96 / BMG

FIFTIES INTERVIEWS, THE
Truth about me / Jacksonville, Florida / WMPS, Memphis / Witchita Falls, Texas / LaCrosse, Wisconsin / Little Rock, Arkansas / KLAC-TV, Memphis / New Orleans / New Orleans / St. Petersburg, Florida
CD ________ **CDMF 074**
Magnum Force / Feb '91 / TKO Magnum

FLAMING STAR/WILD IN THE COUNTRY/FOLLOW THAT DREAM (Double Feature/Original Soundtracks)
Flaming star / Summer kisses, winter tears / Britches a cane and a high starched collar / Black star / Flaming star (end title version) / Wild in the country / I slipped, I stumbled, I fell / Lonely man / In my way / Forget me never / Lonely man (solo) / I slipped, I stumbled, I fell (Alternate master) / Follow that dream / Angel / What a wonderful life / I'm not the marrying kind / Whistling tune / Sound advice
CD ________ **07863665572**
RCA / Mar '95 / BMG

FOR LP FANS ONLY
That's alright Mama / Lawdy Miss Clawdy / Mystery train / Playing for keeps / Poor boy / Money honey / I'm counting on you / My baby left me / I was the one / shake, rattle and roll / I'm left, you're right, she's gone / You're a heartbreaker / Tryin' to get to you / Blue suede shoes
CD ________ **ND 90359**
RCA / Sep '89 / BMG

FRANKIE AND JOHNNY/PARADISE, HAWAIIAN STYLE (Double Feature/ Original Soundtracks)
Frankie and Johnny / Come along / Petunia, the gardener's daughter / Chesay / What every woman lives for / Look out, Broadway / I've got beginner's luck / Down by the riverside/When the saints go marching in / Shout it out / Hard luck / Please don't stop loving me / Everybody come aboard / Paradise, Hawaiian style / Queenie Wahine's papaya / Scratch my back / Drums of the islands / Datin' / Dog's life / House of sand / Stop where you are / This is my heaven / Sand castles
CD ________ **07863663602**
RCA / Jun '94 / BMG

FROM ELVIS IN MEMPHIS
Wearin' that loved on look / Only the strong survive / I'll hold you in my heart / Long black limousine / It keeps right on a-hurtin' / I'm movin' on / Power of my love / Gentle on my mind / After loving you / True love travels on a gravel road / Any day now / In the ghetto
CD ________ **ND 90548**
RCA / Mar '91 / BMG

FROM ELVIS PRESLEY BOULEVARD, MEMPHIS, TENNESSEE
Hurt / Never again / Blue eyes cryin' in the rain / Danny boy / Last farewell / For the heart / Bitter they are / Solitaire / Love coming down / I'll never fall in love again
CD ________ **74321146912**
RCA / Jul '93 / BMG

FROM NASHVILLE TO MEMPHIS (The Essential 1960's Masters Vol.1 - 5CD Set)
Make me know it / Soldier boy / Stuck on you / Fame and fortune / Mess of blues / It feels so right / Fever / Like a baby / It's now or never / Girl of my best friend / Dirty, dirty feeling / Thrill of your love / I gotta know /

Such a night / Are you lonesome tonight / Girl next door went a'walking / I will be home again / Reconsider baby / Surrender / I'm coming home / Gently / In your arms / Give me the right / I feel so bad / It's a sin / I want you with me / There's always me / Starting today / Sentimental me / Judy / Put the blame on me / Kiss me quick / That's someone you never forget / I'm yours / His latest flame / Little sister / For the millionth and last time / Good luck charm / Anything that's part of you / I met her today / Night rider / Something blue / Gonna get back home somehow / (Such an) Easy question / Fountain of love / Just for old times sake / You'll be gone / I feel that I've known you forever / Just tell her Jim said hello / Suspicion / She's not you / Echoes of love / Please don't drag that string around / Devil in disguise / Never ending / What now, what next, where to / Witchcraft / Finders keepers / Love me tonight / (It's a) Long lonely highway / Western Union / Slowly but surely / Blue river / Memphis, Tennessee / Ask me / It hurts me / Down the alley / Tomorrow is a long time / Love letters / Beyond the reef / Come what may / Fools fall in love / Indescribably you / I'll remember you / If every day was like Christmas / Suppose / Guitar man/What'd I say (Original unedited master) / Big boss man / Mine / Just call me lonesome / Hi-heel sneakers / You don't know me / Singing trees / Too much monkey business / US male / Long black limousine / This is the story / Wearin' that loved on look / You'll think of me / Little bit of green / Gentle on my mind / I'm movin' on / Don't cry daddy / Inherit the wind / Mama liked the roses / My little friend / In the ghetto / Rubberneckin' / From a Jack to a King / Hey Jude / Without love (there is nothing) / I'll hold you in my heart / I'll be there / Suspicious minds / True love travels on a gravel road / Stranger in my own hometown / And the grass won't pay no mind / Power of my love / After loving you / Do you know who I am / Kentucky rain / Only the strong survive / It keep right on hurtin' / Any day now / If I'm a fool (For loving you) / Rain is moving on / Who am I / This time/I can't stop loving you (Informal recording) / In the ghetto (alt. take) / Suspicious minds (Alternate take 6) / Kentucky rain (Alt Take) / Big boss man / Down the alley (Alternate take 1) / Memphis, Tennessee (Alternate take) / I'm yours (alt. take) / His latest flame (Alternate take 4) / That's someone you never forget (alternate take) / Surrender (Alternate take 1) / It's now or never (Original undubbed master) / Love me tender/Witchcraft (From the 'Frank Sinatra Timex Spe
CD Set ________ **74321154302**
RCA / Oct '93 / BMG

GI BLUES (Original Soundtrack)
Tonight is so right for love / What's she really like / Frankfurt special / Wooden heart / GI blues / Pocketful of rainbows / Shopping around / Big boots / Didja ever / Blue suede shoes / Doin' the best I can / Big boots / Shoppin' around / Frankfurt special / Pocketful of rainbows / Didja ever / Big boots / What's she really like / Doin' the best I can
CD ________ **07863674602**
CD ________ **07863669602**
RCA / Apr '97 / BMG

GOOD ROCKIN' (Live In 1955)
Interview with Bill Collie / There's good rockin' tonight / Baby let's play house / Blue moon of Kentucky / I got a woman / That's alright Mama / Interview with Elvis / Tweedlee Dee / Baby let's play house / Maybellene / That's alright Mama / Blue moon of Kentucky / There's good rockin' tonight / I got a woman
CD ________ **307622**
Hallmark / Jul '97 / Carlton

GOOD ROCKIN' TONIGHT (Original Hayride Recordings January 1955)
That's alright Mama / Blue moon of Kentucky / Heartbreak hotel / Long tall Sally / I was the one / Money honey / I got a woman / Blue suede shoes / Hound dog / Baby let's play house / Maybellene / Good rockin' tonight / Tweedle Dee Tweedle Dum / Interview
CD ________ **PLATCD 146**
Platinum / Mar '96 / Prism

GOOD TIMES
Take good care of her / Loving arms / I got a feelin' in my body / If that isn't love / She wears my ring / I got a thing about you baby / My boy / Spanish eyes / Talk about the good times / Good time Charlie's got the blues
CD ________ **07863 504752**
RCA / Feb '94 / BMG

GREAT COUNTRY SONGS
I forgot to remember to forget / Blue moon of Kentucky / When my blue moon turns to gold again / Old Shep / Your cheatin' heart / (Now and then there's) A fool such as I / Just call me lonesome / There goes my everything / Kentucky rain / From a Jack to a King / I'll hold you in my heart (till I can hold you in my arms) / I really don't want to know / It keeps right on a hurtin' / Green green grass of home / Fairytale / Gentle on my mind / Make the world go away / You asked me to / Funny how time slips away / Help me make it through the night / Susan when she tried / He'll have to go / Always on my mind / Guitar man
CD ________ **07863668802**
RCA / Oct '96 / BMG

GREAT PERFORMANCES
My happiness / That's alright Mama / Shake, rattle and roll / Flip flop and fly / Heartbreak hotel / Blue suede shoes / Ready teddy / Don't be cruel / Got a lot of livin' to do / Jailhouse rock / Treat me nice / King Creole / Trouble / Fame and fortune / Return to sender / Always on my mind / American trilogy / If I can dream / Unchained melody / Memories
CD ________ **74321436022**
RCA / Feb '97 / BMG

HARUM SCARUM/GIRL HAPPY (Double Feature/Original Soundtracks)
Harem holiday / My desert serenade / Go eat young man / Mirage / Kismet / Shake that tambourine / Hey little girl / Golden coins / So close, yet so far / Animal instinct / Wisdom of the ages / Girl happy / Spring fever / Fort Lauderdale chamber of commerce / Startin' tonight / Wolf call / Do not disturb / Cross my heart and hope to die / Meanest girl in town / Do the clam / Puppet on a string / I've got to find my baby
CD ________ **74321134332**
RCA / Mar '93 / BMG

HE TOUCHED ME
He touched me / I've got confidence / Amazing grace / Seeing is believing / He is my everything / Bosom of Abraham / Evening prayer / Lead me, guide me / There is no God but God / Thing called love / I, John / Reach out to Jesus
CD ________ **ND 90661**
RCA / Apr '92 / BMG

HEARTBREAK HOTEL
Heartbreak hotel / Long tall Sally / I was the one / Money honey / I got a woman (I got a sweety) / Blue suede shoes / Hound dog / Baby let's play house / Maybellene / That's all right / Blue moon of Kentucky / Therre's good rockin' tonight / I got a woman (I got a sweety) / Tweedle dee
CD ________ **RM 1521**
BR Music / Jun '97 / Target/BMG

HIS HAND IN MINE
His hand in mine / I'm gonna walk dem golden stairs / My father's house / Milky white way / Known only to him / I believe / Joshua fit de battle of Jericho / Jesus knows what I need / Swing low, sweet chariot / Mansion over the hilltop / If we never meet again / Working on the building
CD ________ **ND 83935**
RCA / Oct '88 / BMG

HOLLYWOOD ALBUM/NASHVILLE ALBUM/LIVE IN LAS VEGAS 1969 (Collector's Gold - 3CD Set)
GI blues / Pocket full of rainbows / Big boots / Black star / Summer kisses, winter tears / I slipped, I stumbled, I fell / Lonely man / What a wonderful life / Whistling tune / Beyond the bend / One broken heart for sale / You're the boss / Roustabout / Girl happy / So close, yet so far / Stop, look and listen / Am I ready / How can you lose what you never had / Like a baby / There's always me / I want you with me / Gently / Give me the right / I met her today / Night rider / Just tell her Jim said hello / Ask me / Memphis, Tennessee / Love me tonight / Witchcraft / Come what may / Love letters / Going home / Blue suede shoes / I got a woman / Heartbreak hotel / Love me tender / Baby, what you want me to do / Runaway / Surrender/Are you lonesome tonight / Rubber neckin' / Memories / Introduction by Elvis Presley / Jailhouse rock/Don't be cruel / Inherit the wind/This is the story / Mystery train / Tiger man / Funny how time slips away / Loving you/Reconsider baby / What I'd say
CD Set ________ **PD 90574**
RCA / Aug '91 / BMG

HOW GREAT THOU ART
How great Thou art / In the garden / Somebody bigger than you and I / Farther along / Stand by me / Without him / So high / Where could I go but to the Lord / By and by / If the Lord wasn't walking by my side / Run on / Where no one stands alone / Crying in the chapel
CD ________ **ND 83758**
RCA / Apr '88 / BMG

I WISH YOU A MERRY CHRISTMAS
O come all ye faithful (Adeste Fidelis) / First Noel / On a snowy Christmas night / Winter wonderland / Wonderful world of Christmas / It won't seem like Christmas (without you) / I'll be home on Christmas Day / If I get home on Christmas Day / Holly leaves and Christmas trees / Merry Christmas baby / Silver bells / Santa Claus is back in town / White Christmas / Here comes Santa Claus / I'll be home for Christmas / Blue Christmas / Santa bring my baby back to me / O little town of Bethlehem / Silent night / Peace in the valley / I believe / Take my hand, precious Lord / It is no secret
CD ________ **ND 89474**
RCA / '87 / BMG

I'M 10,000 YEARS OLD (Elvis Country)
Snowbird / Tomorrow never comes / Little cabin home on the hill / Whole lotta shakin' goin' on / Funny how time slips away / I really don't want to know / There goes my everything / It's your baby / Fool / Faded love / I washed my hands in muddy water / Make the world go away / I was born ten thousand years ago
CD ________ **74321146922**
RCA / Jul '93 / BMG

IF EVERY DAY WAS LIKE CHRISTMAS
If every day was like Christmas / Blue Christmas / Here comes Santa Claus / White Christmas / Santa bring my baby back to me / I'll be home for Christmas / O little town of Bethlehem / Santa Claus is back in town / It won't seem like Christmas (without you) / If I get home on Christmas day / Holly leaves and Christmas trees / Merry Christmas baby / Silver bells / I'll be home on Christmas day (alternate version) / On a snowy Christmas night / Winter wonderland / Wonderful world of Christmas / O come all ye faithful (Adeste Fidelis) / First Noel / It won't seem like Christmas (without you) (alt. take) / If I get home on Christmas day (unreleased alternate take) / I'll be home on Christmas day / Christmas message from Elvis / Silent night / Holly leaves and Christmas trees (unreleased alternate take)
CD ________ **07863665062**
CD ________ **07863664822**
RCA / Nov '95 / BMG

INTERVIEWS, THE (Outstanding Rare Insights Into The King Of Rock 'n' Roll)
CD ________ **PLATCD 145**
Platinum / Mar '96 / Prism

JAILHOUSE ROCK (Original Soundtrack)
Jailhouse rock / Treat me nice / I want to be free / Don't leave me now / Young and beautiful / (You're so square) baby I don't care / Jailhouse rock / Treat me nice / I want to be free / Young and beautiful / Love me tender / Let me / Poor boy / We're gonna move / Don't leave me now / Treat me nice / Let me / We're gonna move / Poor boy / Love me tender
CD ________ **07863674532**
RCA / Apr '97 / BMG

KID GALAHAD/GIRLS GIRLS GIRLS (Double Feature/Original Soundtracks)
King of the whole wide world / This is living / Riding the rainbow / Home is where the heart is / I got lucky / Whistling tune / Girls, girls, girls - girls, girls, girls / I don't wanna be tied / Where do you come from / I don't want to / We'll be together / Boy like me, a girl like you / Return to sender / Because of love / Thanks to the rolling sea / Song of the shrimp / Walls have ears / We're coming in loaded / Mama / Plantation rock / Dainty little moonbeams / Girls, girls, girls
CD ________ **74321134302**
RCA / Mar '93 / BMG

KING CREOLE (Original Soundtrack)
King Creole / As long as I have you / Hard headed woman / Trouble / Dixieland rock / Don't ask me why / Lover doll / Crawfish / Young dreams / Steadfast, loyal and true / New Orleans / King Creole / As long as I have you / Danny / Lover doll / Steadfast, loyal and true / As long as I have you / King Creole
CD ________ **07863674542**
RCA / Apr '97 / BMG

KING OF ROCK 'N' ROLL, THE (The Complete 1950's Masters - 5CD Set)
My happiness / That's alright / I love you because / Harbour lights / Blue moon of Kentucky / Blue moon / Tomorrow night / I'll never let you go / I don't care if the sun don't shine / Just because / Good rockin' tonight / Milkcow blue boogie / You're a heartbreaker / Baby let's play house / I'm left, you're right, she's gone / Mystery train / I forgot to remember to forget / Trying to get to you / When it rains it really pours / I got a woman / Heartbreak hotel / Money honey / I'm counting on you / I was the one / Blue suede shoes / My baby left me / One sided love affair / So glad you're mine / I'm gonna sit right down and cry over you / Tutti frutti / Lawdy Miss Clawdy / Shake, rattle and roll / I want you, I need you, I love you / Hound dog / Don't be cruel / Any way you want me (that's how I will be) / We're gonna move / Love me tender / Poor boy / Let me / Playing for keeps / Love me / Paralyzed / How do you think I feel / How's the world treating you / When my blue moon turns to gold again / Long tall Sally / Old Shep / Too much / Anyplace is paradise / Ready Teddy / First in line / Rip it up / I believe / Tell me why / Got a lot o' livin' to do / All shook up / Mean woman blues / Peace in the valley / That's when your heartaches begin / Take my hand precious Lord / It's no secret what God can do / Blueberry Hill / Have I told you lately that I love you / Is it so strange / Party / Lonesome cowboy / Hot dog / One night of sin / (Let me be your) teddy bear / Don't leave me now / I beg of you / One night / True love / I need you so / Loving you / When it rains, it really pours / Jailhouse rock / Young and beautiful / I want to be free / (You're so square) baby I don't care / Don't leave me now / Blue Christmas / Here comes Santa Claus (right down Santa Claus Lane) / Silent night / O little town of Bethlehem / Santa bring my baby back / Santa Claus is back in town / I'll be home for Christmas / Treat me nice / My wish came true / Don't Danny / Hard headed woman / Trouble / New Orleans / Crawfish / Dixieland rock / Lover doll / Don't ask me why / As long as I have you / King Creole / Young dreams / Steadfast, loyal and true / Don'tcha think it's time / Your cheatin' heart / Wear my ring around your neck / I need your love tonight / Big hunk o' love / Ain't that loving you baby / Fool such as I / I got stung / Fool fool fool / Tweedle dee / Maybellene / Shake, rattle and roll / Heartbreak hotel / Long tall Sally / Blue suede shoes / Money honey / We're gonna move / Old Shep / I beg of you / Loving you / Young and beautiful / I want to be free / King Creole / As long as I have you / Ain't that loving you baby
CD Set ________ **PD 90689**
RCA / Jul '92 / BMG

KING OF ROCK 'N' ROLL, THE (Documentary & Music/2CD Set)
CD Set ________ **OTR 1100051**
Metro Independent / Jun '97 / Essential/BMG

KISSIN' COUSINS/CLAMBAKE/STAY AWAY, JOE (Double Feature/Original Soundtracks)
Kissin' cousins / Smoky mountain bay / There's gold in the mountains / One boy two little girls / Catchin' on fast / Tender feeling / Anyone (could fall in love with you) / Barefoot ballad / Once is enough / Kissin' cousins / Clambake / Who needs money / House that has everything / Confidence / Hey hey hey / You don't know me / Girl I never loved / How can you lose what you never had / Clambake (Reprise) / Stay away, Joe / Dominic / All I needed was the rain / Goin' home / Stay away
CD ________ **07863663622**
RCA / Jun '94 / BMG

LEGEND BEGINS, THE (Elvis Live)
That's alright mama / Blue moon of Kentucky / Tweedle Dee / Good rockin' tonight / Baby let's play house / I got a woman / Maybellene / Hound dog / Blue suede shoes / Money honey / I was the one / Long tall Sally / Heartbreak hotel
CD ________ **PWKS 4262**
Carlton / Mar '96 / Carlton

LIVE A LITTLE.../TROUBLE WITH GIRLS/CHANGE OF HEART/CHARRO (Double Feature/Original Soundtracks)
Almost in love / Little less conversation / Wonderful world / Edge of reality / Little less conversation (album version) / Charro / Let's forget about the stars / Clean up your own backyard / Swing low, sweet chariot / Swing low, sweet chariot / Signs of the zodiac / Almost / Whiffenpoof song / Violet / Clean up your own backyard (undubbed version) / Almost (undubbed version) / Have a happy / Let's be friends / Change of habit / Let us pray / Rubberneckin'
CD ________ **07863665592**
RCA / Mar '95 / BMG

LOVE LETTERS FROM ELVIS
Love letters / When I'm over you / If I were you / Get my mojo working / Heart of Rome / Only believe / This is our dance / Cindy Cindy / I'll never know / It ain't no big thing (but it's growing) / Life
CD ________ **ND 89011**
RCA / Jun '88 / BMG

LOVE ME TENDER
CD ________ **295 052**
RCA / May '95 / BMG

LOVING YOU (Original Soundtrack)
Mean woman blues / Teddy bear / Got a lot of livin' to do / Lonesome cowboy / Hot dog / Party / Blueberry Hill / True love / Don't leave me now / Have I told you lately that I love you / One night of sin / Loving you / Tell me why / Is it so strange / When it rains it really pours / I beg of you / Loving you / Party / Got a lot of livin' to do
CD ________ **07863674522**
RCA / Apr '97 / BMG

MEMPHIS RECORD, THE
Stranger in my own hometown / Power of love / Only the strong survive / Any day now / Suspicious minds / Long black limousine / Wearin' that loved on look / I'll hold you in my heart / After loving you / Rubberneckin' / I'm movin' on / Gentle on my mind / True love travels on a gravel road / It keeps right on a-hurtin' / You'll think of me / Mama like the roses / Don't cry daddy / In the ghetto / Fair is movin' on / Inherit the wind / Kentucky rain / Without love (there is nothing) / Who am I
CD ________ **74321187542**
RCA / Feb '94 / BMG

MOODY BLUE
Unchained melody / If you love me (let me know) / Little darlin' / He'll have to go / Let me be there / Way down / Pledging my love / Moody blue / She thinks I still care
CD ________ **ND 90252**
RCA / Apr '88 / BMG

ON STAGE (February 1970)
See rider blues / Release me / Sweet Caroline / Runaway / Wonder of you / Polk

salad Annie / Yesterday / Proud Mary / Walk a mile in my shoes / Let it be me
CD _______________ ND 90549
RCA / Mar '91 / BMG

ONE AND ONLY, THE
Heartbreak hotel / Long tall Sally / I was the one / Money honey / I got a woman / Blue suede shoes / Hound dog / Interviews (Arkansas 1965) / Baby let's play house / Maybellene / That's alright mama / Blue moon of Kentucky / Good rockin' tonight / I got a woman / Tweedle dee
CD _______________ HADCD 151
Javelin / May '94 / Henry Hadaway / THE

PLATINUM - A LIFE IN MUSIC (4CD Set)
I'll never stand in your way / That's alright / Blue moon / Good rockin' tonight / Mystery train / I got a woman / Heartbreak hotel / I'm counting on you / Shake, rattle and roll/ Flip, flop and fly / Lawdy, Miss Clawdy / I want you, I need you, I love you / Hound dog / Don't be cruel / Rip it up / Love me tender / When the saints go marching in / All shook up / Peace in the valley / Blueberry hill / Teddy bear / Jailhouse rock / New Orleans / I need your love tonight / Big hunk o'love / Bad Nauheim medley / Stuck on you / Fame and fortune / It's now or never / It feels so right / Mess of blues / Are you lonesome tonight / Reconsider baby / Tonight is so right for love / His hand in mine / Milky white way / I'm comin' home / I feel so bad / Can't help falling in love / Something blue / Return to sender / Bossa nova baby / How great thou art / Guitar man / You'll never walk alone / Oh how I love Jesus / Tennessee waltz / Blowin' in the wind / I can't help it / I'm beginning to forget you / After loving you / I got a woman / Tiger man / When my blue moon turns to gold again / Trying to get to you / If I can dream / In the ghetto / Suspicious minds / Power of my love / Baby what you want me do / Words / Johnny B Goode / Release me / CC rider / Wonder of you / Sound of your cry / You don't have to say you love me / Funny how time slips away / I washed my hands in muddy water / I was the one / Cattle call / Baby, let's play house / Don't / Money honey / What I'd say / Bridge over troubled water / Miracle of the rosary / He touched me / Bosom of Abraham / I'll be home on Christmas day / For the good times / Burning love / Separate ways / Always on my mind / American trilogy / Take good care of her / I've got a thing about you baby / Are you sincere / It's midnight / Promised land / Steamroller blues / And I love you so / TROUBLE / Danny boy / Moody blue / Hurt / For the heart / Pledging my way / Way down / My way / Jaycess speech
CD Set _______________ 07863674692
RCA / Jul '97 / BMG

POT LUCK WITH ELVIS
Kiss me quick / Just for old times sake / Gonna get back home somehow / (Such an) Easy question / Steppin' out of line / I'm yours / Something blue / Suspicion / I feel I've known you forever / Night rider / Fountain of love / That's someone you never forget
CD _______________ ND 89098
RCA / Apr '88 / BMG

PROMISED LAND
Promised land / There's a honky tonk angel (who will take me) / Help me / Mr. Songman / Love song of the year / It's midnight / Your love's been a long time coming / If you talk in your sleep / Thinking about you / You ask me to
CD _______________ ND 90598
RCA / Oct '91 / BMG

RAISED ON ROCK
Raised on rock / Are you sincere / Find out what's happening / I miss you / Girl of mine / For ol' times sake / If you don't come back / Just a little bit / Sweet Angeline / Three corn patches
CD _______________ 07863 503882
RCA / Feb '94 / BMG

RECONSIDER BABY
Reconsider baby / Tomorrow night / So glad you're mine / When it rains it really pours / My baby left me / Ain't that lovin' you baby / I feel so bad / Down in the alley / Hi-heel sneakers / Stranger in my own hometown / Merry Christmas baby
CD _______________ AFL1 5418
RCA / Jan '86 / BMG

SOMETHING FOR EVERYBODY
There's always me / Give me the right / It's a sin / Sentimental me / Starting today I'm yours / Gently / I'm coming home / In your arms / Put the blame on me / Judy / I want you with me / I slipped, I stumbled, I fell
CD _______________ ND 84116
RCA / Nov '90 / BMG

SOUNDS OF ELVIS, THE (Various Artists)
CD _______________ MACCD 294
Autograph / Aug '96 / BMG

SPINOUT/DOUBLE TROUBLE (Double Feature/Original Soundtracks)
Stop, look and listen / Adam and evil / All that I am / Never say yes / Am I ready / Beach shack / Spinout / Smorgasbord / I'll be back / Double trouble / Baby, if you'll give me all your love / Could I fall in love / Long legged girl with the short dress on / City by night / Old MacDonald / I love only one girl / There's so much world to see / It won't be long
CD _______________ 07863663612
RCA / Jun '94 / BMG

SUN SESSIONS, THE
That's alright mama / Blue moon of Kentucky / I don't care if the sun don't shine / Good rockin' tonight / Milk cow blues boogie / You're a heartbreaker / I'm left, you're right, she's gone / Baby let's play house / Mystery train / I forgot to remember to forget / I love you because / Trying to get to you / Blue moon / Just because / I'll never let you go
CD _______________ ND 89107
RCA / '88 / BMG

SYMPHONIC ELVIS (Moore, Scotty & Memphis Symphony Orchestra/Ettore Stratta)
CD _______________ 4509945732
Teldec Classics / Aug '96 / Warner Music

THAT'S THE WAY IT IS
I just can't help believin' / Twenty days and twenty nights / How the web was woven / Patch it up / Mary in the morning / You don't have to say you love me / You've lost that lovin' feelin' / I've lost you / Just pretend / Stranger in the crowd / Next step is love / Bridge over troubled water
CD _______________ 74321146902
RCA / Jul '93 / BMG

VIVA LAS VEGAS/ROUSTABOUT (Double Feature/Original Soundtracks)
Viva Las Vegas / If you think I don't need you / If you need somebody to lean on / You're the boss / What I'd say / Do the Vega / C'mon everybody / Lady love me (With Ann Margaret) / Night life / Today, tomorrow and forever / Yellow rose of Texas/ The eyes of Texas / Santa Lucia / Roustabout / Little Egypt / Poison ivy league / Hard knocks / It's a wonderful world / Big love, big heartache / One track heart / It's carnival time / Carmy town / There's a brand new day on the horizon / Wheels on my heels
CD _______________ 74321134322
RCA / Mar '93 / BMG

WALK A MILE IN MY SHOES (The Essential 1970's Masters - 5CD Set)
Wonder of you / I've lost you / Next step is love / You don't have to say you love me / Patch it up / I really don't want to know / There goes everything / Rags to riches / Where did they go / Life / I'm leavin' / Heart of Rome / It's only love / Sound of your cry / I just can't help believin' / How the web was woven / Until it's time for you to go / We can make the morning / An American trilogy / First time ever I saw your face / Burning love / It's a matter of time / Separate ways / Always on my mind / Fool / Steamroller blues / Raised on rock / For ol' times sake / I've got a thing about you baby / Take good care of her / If you talk in your sleep / Promised land / It's midnight / Loving arms / T-R-O-U-B-L-E / Mr. Songman / Bringing it back / Pieces of my life / Green, green grass of home / Thinking about you / Hurt / For the heart / Moody blue / She thinks I still care / Way down / Pledging my love / Twenty days and twenty nights / I was born about ten thousand years ago / Fool / Hundred years from now / Little cabin on the hill / Cindy Cindy / Bridge over troubled water / Got my mojo working / Keep your hands off it / It's your baby, you rock it / Stranger in the crowd / Mary in the morning / It ain't no big thing (but it's growing) / Just pretend / Faded love / Tomorrow never comes / Make the world go away / Funny how time slips away / I wash my hands in muddy water / Snowbird / Whole lotta shakin' goin' on / Amazing Grace / (That's what you get) For lovin' me / Lady Madonna / Merry Christmas baby / I shall be released / Don't think it's alright / It's still here / I'll take you home Kathleen / I will be true / My way / For the good times / Just a little bit / It's different now / Are you sincere / I got a feelin' in my body / You asked me to / Good time Charlie's got the blues / Talk about the good times / Tiger man / She thinks I still care / Danny boy / Love coming down / He'll have to go / CC rider / Men with broken hearts / Walk a mile in my shoes / Polk salad Annie / Let it be me / Proud Mary / Something / You've lost that lovin' feelin' / Heartbreak hotel / I was the one / One night / Never been to Spain / You gave me a mountain / It's impossible / Big hunk o'love / It's over / Impossible dream / Reconsider baby / I'll remember you / I'm so lonesome I could cry / Suspicious minds / Unchained melody / Twelfth of never / Softly as I leave you / Alla' en el Rancho Grande / Froggie went a-courtin' / Stranger in my home town
CD Set _______________ 74321303312
RCA / Sep '95 / BMG

Press Gang

BURNING BOATS
CD _______________ PUSS 0002CD
Cat / Apr '94 / ADA

FIRE
CD _______________ EFA 611012
Twah / Jan '96 / SRD

Pressure

PRESSURE FEATURING RONNIE LAWS (Pressure & Ronnie Laws)
That's the thing to do / Hold on / Fantastic dreams / Can you feel it / Shove it in the oven / Peaceful stream / Stay together / I promise
CD _______________ 74321305272
Avenue / Sep '96 / BMG

Pressure Of Speech

ART OF THE STATE
CD _______________ POS 100CD
North South / May '94 / Pinnacle

OUR COMMON PAST OUR COMMON FUTURE
CD _______________ POS 200CD
North South / Mar '96 / Pinnacle

Pressurehed

EXPLAINING THE UNEXPLAINED
CD _______________ CLP 9910
Cleopatra / Mar '97 / Cargo / Greyhound / Plastic Head / RTM/Disc / SRD

Preston Orpheus Choir

SONGS SACRED AND SECULAR
CD _______________ CDCA 928
SCS Music / Oct '93 / Conifer/BMG

Preston, Billy

ENCOURAGING WORDS
Right now / Little girl / Use what you got / My sweet Lord / Let the music play / Same thing again / I've got a feeling / Sing one for the Lord / When you are mine / I don't want you to pretend / Encouraging words / All things must pass / You've been acting strange / As long as I got my baby / All that I've got (I'm gonna give to you)
CD _______________ CDP 7812792
Apple / Mar '93 / EMI

Preston, Jimmy

JIMMY PRESTON 1948-1950
Messin' with Preston / Chop Suey Louie / Hucklebuck Daddy / Rock the joint / Early morning blues
CD _______________ FLYCD 33
Flyright / Apr '91 / Hot Shot / Jazz Music / Wellard

Preston, Johnny

BEST OF JOHNNY PRESTON, THE
Do what you did / Feel so fine / Running bear / Hearts of stone / Cradle of love / That's all I want / I want a rock 'n' roll guitar / Charming Billy / I'm startin' to go steady with the blues / Leave my kitten alone / Chief heartbreak / New baby for Christmas / Madre de dios / Chosen few / You'll never walk alone / Little boy blue / Broken hearts anonymous / Four letter word / Dream / Sitting here crying / City of tears / Kissin' tree
CD _______________ STCD 6
Stomper Time / Oct '96 / TKO Magnum

RUNNING BEAR
Charming Billy / Running bear / Cradle of love / Chief heartbreak / My heart knows / That's all I want / Just little boy blue / Leave my kitten alone / Sitting here crying / I want a rock and roll guitar / Hearts of stone / Do what you did / I played around with my love / Chosen few / Up in the air / Kissin' tree / Four letter word / Feel so fine / She once belonged to me / New baby for christmas / City of tears / I'm startin' to go steady with the blues / Dream / Madre de dios / You'll never walk alone / Danny Boy / Broken heart anonymous
CD _______________ BCD 15473
Bear Family / '88 / Direct / Rollercoaster / Swift

Pretenders

GET CLOSE
My baby / When I change my life / Light of the moon / Dance / Tradition of love / Don't get me wrong / I remember you / How much did you get for your soul / Chill factor / Hymn to her / Room full of mirrors
CD _______________ 2409762
WEA / Oct '86 / Warner Music

LAST OF THE INDEPENDENTS
Hollywood perfume / Night in my veins / Money talk / 977 / Revolution / All my dreams / I'll stand by you / I'm a mother / Tequila / Every mother's son / Rebel rock me / Colours / Forever young
CD _______________ 4509958222
WEA / May '94 / Warner Music

LEARNING TO CRAWL
Middle of the road / Back on the chain gang / Time the avenger / Show me / Watching the clothes / Thumbelina / My city was gone / Thin line between love and hate / I hurt you / 2000 miles
CD _______________ 9239802
WEA / Jan '84 / Warner Music

LIVE AT THE ISLE OF VIEW
CD _______________ 0630120592
WEA / Oct '95 / Warner Music

PRETENDERS II
Adultress / Bad boys get spanked / Message of love / I go to sleep / Birds of paradise / Talk of the town / Pack it up / Waste not, want not / Day after day / Jealous dogs / English rose / Louie Louie
CD _______________ 256924
WEA / Jul '93 / Warner Music

PRETENDERS, THE
Precious / Phone call / Up to the neck / Tattooed love boys / Space invaders / Wait / Stop your sobbing / Kid / Private life / Lovers of today / Brass in pocket / Mystery achievement
CD _______________ 256774
WEA / '83 / Warner Music

SINGLES, THE
Stop your sobbing / Kid / Brass in pocket / Talk of the town / I go to sleep / Day after day / Message of love / Back on the chain gang / Middle of the road / 2000 miles / Show me / Thin line between love and hate / Don't get me wrong / Hymn to her / My baby / I got you babe / What you gonna do about it
CD _______________ 2422292
WEA / Dec '87 / Warner Music

Pretty Maids

SCREAM
CD _______________ MASSCD 0472
Massacre / Mar '95 / Plastic Head

SCREAMIN' LIVE
CD _______________ MASSCD 081
Massacre / Nov '95 / Plastic Head

SPOOKED
CD _______________ MASSDP 119
Massacre / May '97 / Plastic Head

Pretty Things

CHICAGO BLUES JAM - 1991 (Pretty Things & Yardbird Blues Band)
You can't judge a book by the cover / Down in the bottom / Hush hush / Can't hold out / Spoonful / She fooled me / Time is on my side / Long tall shorty / Diddley daddy / Ain't got you / Caress me baby / Here's my picture / Chain of fools / Don't start cryin' now
CD _______________ FIENDCD 708
Demon / Oct '91 / Pinnacle

EP COLLECTION, THE
Don't bring me down / Rosalyn / Big boss man / We'll be together / I can never say / Honey I need / Rainin' in my heart / Sittin' all alone / Midnight to six man / LSD / Come see me / Buzz the jerk / Progress / We'll play house / Get the picture / Gonna find a substitute / Get a buzz / London town / Can't stand the pain / Me needing you / Roadrunner / Big city / Mama keep your big mouth shut / Judgement day / Cry to me / House in the country
CD _______________ SEECD 476
See For Miles/C5 / Jun '97 / Pinnacle

FALLEN ANGELS (Fallen Angels)
Fallen angels / California / Thirteenth floor suicide / Dance again / Shine on baby / My good Friday / Cold wind / I keep on / Dogs of war / Girl like you / When the Russians came back / Chance / Lazy days
CD _______________ SRH 801
Start / Feb '97 / Disc

MIDNIGHT TO 6
Don't bring me down / Children / Cry to me / Judgement day / We'll be together / Moon is rising / Progress / Midnight to six man / Get the picture / Roadrunner / I can never say / Mama keep your big mouth shut / I want your love / Raining in my heart
CD _______________ 5501862
Spectrum / Mar '94 / PolyGram

ON AIR
Don't bring me down / Hey mamma / Midnight to six man / Buzz the jerks / LSD / Big boss man / Defecting grey / Cold stone / Sickle clowns / She's a lover
CD _______________ BOJCD 3
Band Of Joy / Mar '92 / Pinnacle

OUT OF THE ISLAND
Cry to me / Baby doll / She's fine she's mine / Get the picture / Havana bound / Can't stop / Loneliest person/LSD / Private sorrow / Moon is rising / Big city / Cause and effect / Well known blues / You don't believe me / Judgement day
CD _______________ INAK 8708
In Akustik / Jul '97 / Direct / TKO Magnum

PRETTY THINGS 1967-1971 - THE SINGLES A'S & B'S
Defecting Grey / Mr. Evasion / Talkin' about the good times / Walking through my dreams / Private sorrow / Balloon burning / Good Mr. Square / Blue serge blues / October 26 / Cold stone / Summertime / Circus mind / Stone hearted mama
CD _______________ SEECD 103
See For Miles/C5 / Jun '96 / Pinnacle

PRETTY THINGS, THE
Roadrunner / Judgement day / 13 Chester Street / Big city / Unknown blues / Mama

keep your big mouth shut / Honey I need / Oh baby doll / She's fine, she's mine / Don't you lie to me / Moon is rising / Pretty thing
CD 8460542
Fontana / Jul '90 / PolyGram

UNREPENTANT - BLOODY BUT UNBOWED (2CD Set)
Rosalyn / Don't bring me down / Get yourself home / Roadrunner / Judgement day / Honey, I need / You don't believe me / Buzz the jerk / Cry to me / Midnight to six man / LSD / Death of a socialite / Growing in my mind / Defecting grey / SF sorrow is born / Private sorrow / Balloon burning / Old man going / Loneliest person / Scene one / In the square / Letter / Rain / Grass / Parachute / October 26 (Revolution) / Summertime / Peter / Rip off train / Havana bound / Dream/Joey / Bridge of God / Is it only love / Singapore silk torpedo / Under the volcano / Sad eye / Remember that boy / It's been so long / I'm calling / Office love / She don't / No future / God give me the strength (to carry on)
CD Set FRA 005D
Fragile / Oct '95 / Grapevine/PolyGram

WHITER SHADE OF DIRTY WATER, A (Pretty Things 'Mates)
He's waitin': *Pretty Things* / Strychnine: *Pretty Things* / Pushin' too hard: *Pretty Things* / Kicks: *Pretty Things* / Candy: *Pretty Things* / Louie Louie: *Pretty Things* / 96 tears: *Pretty Things* / Let's talk about girls: *Pretty Things* / Sometimes good guys don't wear white: *Pretty Things* / I'm a man: *Pretty Things* / Red River rock: *Pretty Things* / Midnight to 6 man: *Pretty Things*
CD CDKVL 9031
Kingdom / May '94 / Kingdom

WINE, WOMEN & WHISKEY (Pretty Things & Yardbird Blues Band)
Wine, women and whiskey / Sure look good to me / No questions / Amble / It's all over now / Bad boy / Spoonful / French champagne / My back scratcher / Can't hold out / Diddley daddy / I'm cryin' / Gettin' all wet
CD FIENDCD 748
Demon / Jan '94 / Pinnacle

Previn, Andre

ANDRE PREVIN & FRIENDS PLAY SHOWBOAT
CD 4476392
Deutsche Grammophon / May '95 / PolyGram

JAZZ AT THE MUSIKVEREIN
CD 5377042
Verve / Aug '97 / PolyGram

KING SIZE (Previn, Andre Jazz Trio)
CD OJCCD 691
Original Jazz Classics / Nov '95 / Complete/Pinnacle / Jazz Music / Wellard

PLAY A CLASSIC AMERICAN SONGBOOK (Previn, Andre & Thomas Stevens)
It might as well be spring / My funny valentine / Slowly/Laura / Bewitched, bothered and bewildered / I could write a book / It could happen to you/Here's that rainy day / You go to my head / Cabin in the sky/ Takin' a chance on love / I didn't know what time it was/Little girl blue / Easy living
CD DRGCD 5222
DRG / Apr '94 / Discovery / New Note/ Pinnacle

PREVIN AT SUNSET
I got it bad and that ain't good / Body and soul / Sunset in blue / All the things you are / Something to live for / Good enough to keep / That old blue magic / Blue skies / I found a new baby / Variations on a theme / Mulholland Drive
CD BLCD 760189
Black Lion / Jun '94 / Cadillac / Jazz Music / Koch / Wellard

Previn, Dory

IN SEARCH OF MYTHICAL KINGS (THE UA YEARS)
Mythical Kings and Iguanas / Ester's first communion / When a man wants a woman / Yada yada la scala / Lady with the braid / Beware of young girls / Angels and devils that following day / Don't put him down / Doppleganger / Left hand lost / New enzyme detergent demise of Ali McGraw / Twenty mile zone / Midget's lament / Michael Michael / I ain't his child / Stone for Bessie Smith / Starlet starlet on the screen who will follow Norma Jean / Mary C Brown and the Hollywood sign / King Kong / Play it again Sam / Going home
CD CDGO 2045
EMI / Feb '93 / EMI

Previte, Bobby

CLAUDE'S LATE MORNING (Previte, Bobby 'Weather Clear')
CD GCD 79447
Gramavision / Sep '95 / Vital/SAM

DULL BANG, GUSHING SOUND, HUMAN SHRIEK (Bought & Sold) (Previte, Bobby 'Weather Clear')
CD 378212
Koch Jazz / Aug '96 / Koch

HUE & CRY (Previte, Bobby 'Weather Clear')
Hubbub / Smack dab / More heaven and earth / 700 Camels / Valerie / Hue and cry / For John Laughlan and all that we stood for
CD ENJ 80642
Enja / Nov '94 / New Note/Pinnacle / Vital/ SAM

MOSCOW CIRCUS (Previte, Bobby 'Weather Clear')
CD GCD 79466
Gramavision / Sep '95 / Vital/SAM

PUSHING THE ENVELOPE (Previte, Bobby 'Weather Clear')
CD GCD 79509
Gramavision / Jun '96 / Vital/SAM

TOO CLOSE TO THE POLE
Too close to the pole / 3 minute heels / Countess' bedroom / Save the cups / Eleventh hour / Too close to the pole (reprise)
CD ENJ 93062
Enja / Nov '96 / New Note/Pinnacle / Vital/ SAM

Prevost, Eddie

LOCUS OF CHANGE
CD MRCD 32
Matchless / Jun '97 / Cadillac / ReR Megacorp

SUPER SESSION (Prevost, Eddie, Parker, Guy & Rowe)
CD MR 17
Matchless / '90 / Cadillac / ReR Megacorp

Prewitt, Archer

IN THE SUN
CD SAK 1015
Hi-Ball / Jun '97 / Cargo

Prezident Brown

BIG BAD AND TALENTED
CD RN 0032
X-Rated / Jun '95 / Jet Star

PREZIDENT BROWN
CD RNCD 0043
Runn / Apr '97 / Grapevine/PolyGram / Jet Star / SRD

PREZIDENT SELECTION
CD RN 0043
Runn / Apr '96 / Grapevine/PolyGram / Jet Star / SRD

Price, Alan

1960'S FRENCH EPS COLLECTION, THE (Price, Alan Set)
CD 525742
Magic / Jul '97 / Greyhound

ALAN PRICE ARCHIVE
Jarrow song / Please don't stop the carnival / House of the rising sun / I'm coming back / Hi-li-hi-lo / I just got love / Simon Smith and his amazing dancing bear / Mama divine / I put a spell on you / Don't try / Shame / House that Jack built / Love that I needed / Don't make me suffer / Frozen moments / Just for you / I have tried / Music in the city / Mr. Sunbeam
CD RMCD 209
Rialto / Sep '96 / Disc / Total/BMG

ANTHOLOGY (2CD Set)
CD Set SMDCD 204
Snapper / Jul '97 / Pinnacle

BEST OF ALAN PRICE, THE
CD MCCD 109
Music Club / Jun '93 / Disc / THE

GIGSTER'S LIFE FOR ME, A (Price, Alan & Electric Blues Company)
CD IGOCD 2048
Indigo / Nov '95 / ADA / Direct

GREATEST HITS IN CONCERT
CD CDRIA 2000
Rialto / Sep '96 / Disc / Total/BMG

LIVE IN CONCERT
CD GRF 209
Tring / Mar '93 / Tring

O LUCKY MAN (Original Soundtrack)
O lucky man / Poor people / Pastoral / Arrival / Look over your shoulder / Justice / My home town / Changes
CD 9362461372
Warner Bros. / Oct '96 / Warner Music

PRICE IS RIGHT, THE
Barefootin' / Angel eyes / Jump children / Don't try / Slow down / I just got love / Simon Smith and his amazing dancing bears / Mercy mercy / If I could / Shame / Fifty pence / Please / Mama divine / Don't do that again
CD 303492
Hallmark / Jul '97 / Carlton

PRICE OF FAME, THE (Price, Alan & Georgie Fame)
Yeh yeh: *Fame, Georgie & The Blue Flames* / Simon Smith and his amazing dancing bear / Get away / Hi-li hi-lo / Sitting in the park / Barefootin' / Let the sun shine in / Shame / Ride your pony / Jarrow song / Papa's got a brand new bag / I put a spell on you / In the meantime: *Fame, Georgie & The Blue Flames* / House that Jack built / Sunny / Falling in love again / My girl / Baby of mine / Let the good times roll / Don't stop the carnival
CD 5509312
Spectrum / Oct '95 / PolyGram

PRICELESS
Don't stop the carnival / House that Jack built / People are talking / I put a spell on you / Slow down / Hi-lili-hi-lo / Shame / Don't slam that door / Travellin' man / In times like these / Guess who / Nobody can / Papers / Cherie / If I could / Too much
CD EMPRCD 593
Emporio / Oct '95 / Disc

Price, Darren

UNDER THE FLIGHTPATH
Airspace / Lose no time / Things change / Blueprints / Counterpoint / Intermission / Long haul / Phizz / Over and out
CD NOMU 48CD
Nova Mute / Jun '97 / Prime / RTM/Disc

Price, Kate

DEEP HEARTS CORE
CD AMLCD 500
Priceless / Mar '96 / ADA

TIME BETWEEN, THE
CD PPCD 402
Priceless / Mar '96 / ADA

Price, Leontyne

CHRISTMAS SONGS (Price, Leontyne & Vienna Philharmonic/Herbert Von Karajan)
Silent night / Hark the herald angels sing / We three Kings of Orient are / Angels we have heard on high / God rest ye merry gentlemen / It came upon the midnight clear / Von himmel hoch, da komm ich her / Sweet li'l Jesus / Ave Maria / O holy night / Ave Maria / O holy night / Ave Maria / Alleluja
CD 4489982
Decca / Nov '96 / PolyGram

Price, Lloyd

HEAVY DREAMS
Chee-koo baby / Coo-ee baby / Oooh-oooh-oooh / Restless heart / Tell me pretty baby / They say / I'm too young / Ain't it a shame / Jimmie Lee / Baby, don't turn your back on me / Old echo song / Too late for tears / Carry me home / Little Bea / Night and day / Oh love / Woe ho ho / Breaking my heart (All over again) / Iyi yi gomen-a-sai / Country boy rock / Heavy dreams / Why / I'm goin' back
CD CDCHD 512
Ace / Jan '94 / Pinnacle

LAWDY
Lawdy Miss Clawdy / Mailman blues / Chee koo baby / Oo-ee baby / So long / Operator / Laurelle / What's the matter now / If crying was murder / Walkin' the track / Where you at / Lord, lord, amen / Carry me home / Frog legs / I wish your picture was you / Let me come home baby / Tryin' to find someone to love / Night and day blues / All alone / What a fire / Rock 'n' roll dance / I'm glad, glad / Baby please come home / Forgive me Clawdy
CD CDCHD 360
Ace / Nov '91 / Pinnacle

Price, Maryann

ETCHED IN SWING
CD WM 1014CD
Watermelon / May '94 / ADA / Direct

Price, Ray

HONKY TONK YEARS 1950-1966, THE (10CD Set) (Price, Ray & The Cherokee Cowboys)
Jealous lies / Your wedding corsage / If you're ever lonely darling / I saw my castles fall today / You've got my troubles now / I get the short end every time / Hey la la / Answer to The Last Letter / Till death do us part / Beyond the last mile / Heart aching blues / Weary blues (from waiting) / I made a mistake and I'm sorry / We crossed our heart / Your heart is too crowded / I lost the only one I knew / I've got to hurry hurry hurry / Talk to your heart / I know I'll never win your love again / Road of no return / You're under arrest (for stealing my heart) / Move on in and stay / I can't escape from you / Won't you please be mine / Don't let the stars get in your eyes / My old scrapbook / Price of loving you / That's what I get for loving you / Cold shoulder / You weren't ashamed to kiss me last night / Wrong side of town / Time / Start the music / Gone again / Way you've treated me / Wrong side of town / Who stole that train / Let your heart decide / You always get by / Leave her alone / Wall around your heart / Release me / I'll be there (if you ever want me) / Last letter / Much too young to die / I love you so much I let you go / I could love you more / What if he don't love you / If you don't somebody else will / I'm alone because I love you / Oh yes darling / One broken heart (don't mean a thing) / Sweet little Miss Blue Eyes / Way she got away / Let me talk to you / Call the Lord and he'll be there / Man called Peter / As strange as it seems (I still love you) / I can't go home like this / Don't you know me anymore / I don't want it on my conscience / Run boy / You never will be true / Don't tempt me / Slowly dying / Crazy arms / You done me wrong / Wild and wicked world / Crazy / Are you wasting my time / Fallin' fallin' fallin' / Wasted words / I've got a new heartache / Don't do this to me / Letters have no arms / I'll sail my ship alone / Mansion on the hill / I can't help it / Remember me (I'm the one who loves you) / I saw my castles fall today / Let me talk to you / Please don't leave me / Blues stay away from me / Pins and needles (in my heart) / I love you because / Many tears ago / I'll be there (when you get lonely) / It's all your fault / My shoes keep walking back to you / Faded love / Gone / Bye bye love / Four walls / Fallen star / Don't do this to me / Walls of tears / Curtain in the window / Talk to your conscience / There'll be no teardrops tonight / Driftwood on the river / Deep water / I'll keep on loving you / I love you so much it hurts / I told you so / Ice cold heart / I've gotta have my baby back / Please don't leave me / Talk to your heart / I'm tired / Wondering / Walkin' the floor / Invitation to the blues / I've got to know / Heartaches must be your name / City lights / Kissing your picture (is so cold) / That's what it's like to be lonesome / Punish me tomorrow / Heartaches by the number / Wild and wicked world / Beyond the last mile / Same old me / Under your spell again / Broken hearts will haunt your soul / One more time / Who'll be the first / City lights / Old rugged cross / In the garden / How big is God / Until then / Help through my unbelief / When I take my vacation in heaven / Faith / Rock of ages / Softly and tenderly / When the roll is called up yonder / Just as I am / Where he leads me (I will follow) / Now the day is over / I can't run away from myself / I wish I could fall in love today / Heart over mind / Twenty-fourth hour / Walkin' slow (and thinking 'bout her) / Soft rain / Here we are again / You're stranger than me / This cold war with you / Imagiantion's wonderful thing / Walkin' slow (and thinking about her) / Soft rain / San Antonio Rose / Maiden's prayer / My confession / Whose heart are you breaking now / Roly poly / Bubbles in my beer / Home in San Antone / You don't love me (but I'll always care) / You don't care what happens to me / Time changes everything / Kinda love I can't forget / Hang your head in shame / Night life / Lonely street / Wild side of life / Sittin' and thinkin' / Girl in the night / There's no fool like a young fool / If she could see me now / Bright lights and blonde haired women / Are you sure / Let me talk to you / This cold war with you / I've just destroyed the world / Walkin' slow (and thinking 'bout her) / Pride / Big shoes / Walk me to the door / You took her off my hands / Be a good girl / Make the world go away / I'll find a way (to free myself of you) / Let me talk to you / I've still got room (for one more heartache) / That's all that matters / Burning memories / Each time / Way to free myself / How long is forever / This cold war with you / Take me as I am (or let me go) / All right (I'll sign the papers) / I fall to pieces / Please talk to my heart / Cold cold heart / Still / I don't know why (I keep loving you) / Same old memories / Here comes my baby back again / Together again / Thing called sadness / Soft rain / Release me / Devil's dream / Linda Lou / Crazy arms / Lil' Liza Jane / Rubber dolly / Burnt fingers / Twinkle, twinkle little star / Maiden's prayer / Your old loveletters / Spanish two step / Liberty bells / Sing a sad song / Other woman / Tearful earful / Last letter / Born to lose / Just call me lonesome / Don't you ever get tired of hurting me / Funny how time slips away / Rose coloured glasses / Unloved, unwanted / Eye for an eye / Too much love is spoiling you / After effects (from loving you) / I'm not crazy yet / Way to survive / Another bridge to burn / Legend in my time / Take these chains in my heart / Don't touch me / Go away / I'd fight the world / I want to hear it from you / It should be easier now / Don't you believe her / Healing hands of time / Too late / Each time / Touch my heart / There goes my everything / It's only love / I lie a lot / Enough to lie / Swinging doors / Am I that easy to forget / Same two lips / Just for the record / I'm still not over you / I let my mind wander / Danny Boy
CD Set BCD 15843
Bear Family / Nov '95 / Direct / Rollercoaster / Swift

NIGHT LIFE
CD 379282
Koch International / Dec '96 / Koch

SAN ANTONIO ROSE (Sings A Tribute To Bob Wills)
CD 379172
Koch International / Aug '96 / Koch

Price, Sammy

1944 WORLD JAM SESSION (Price, Sammy & His Bluesicians)

CD ______ **PCD 7074**
Progressive / Nov '96 / Jazz Music

BARRELHOUSE & BLUES
Honey Grove Blues / Rosetta / St. James Infirmary / West End boogie / In the evening / Keepin' out of mischief now / Struttin' with Georgia
CD ______ **BLCD 760159**
Black Lion / Oct '92 / Cadillac / Jazz Music / Koch / Wellard

CLASSICS 1929-1941
CD ______ **CLASSICS 696**
Classics / Jul '93 / Discovery / Jazz Music

KINGS OF BOOGIE WOOGIE, THE (Price, Sammy Trio)
King Boogie parts 1 and 2 / Makin' whoopee / Keepin' out of mischief now / Bass and piano talking / Please don't talk about me when I'm gone / My blue heaven / Saint James infirmary / Boogie woogie French style / Baby, won't you please come home / Trouble in mind / Blues in my heart
CD ______ **STCD 5011**
Storyville / Dec '94 / Cadillac / Jazz Music / Wellard

Prichard, Peter

HARMONIC PIANO
CD ______ **WCL 11001**
White Cloud / May '94 / Select

Pricks

UNTITLED
CD ______ **IND 92395**
Interscope / Jul '96 / BMG

Pride & Glory

PRIDE AND GLORY
Losin' your mind / Horse called war / Shine on / Lovin' woman / Harvester of pain / Chosen one / Sweet Jesus / Troubled wine / Machine gun man / Cry me a river / Toe'n the line / Found a friend / Fadin' away / Hate your guts
CD ______ **GFLD 19342**
Geffen / Oct '96 / BMG

Pride, Charley

AMY'S EYES
White houses / Moody woman / Amy's eyes / After me, after you / I made love to you in my mind / Whole lotta love on the line / Nickles and dimes and love / Look who's looking / I wrote the songs that broke her heart / You hold my world together / Right one / Plenty good lovin'
CD ______ **RITZRCD 525**
Ritz / Apr '93 / Pinnacle

BEST OF CHARLEY PRIDE, THE
CD ______ **MATCD 330**
Castle / Feb '95 / BMG

CLASSIC COUNTRY
CD ______ **CDSR 070**
Telstar / May '95 / BMG

CLASSICS WITH PRIDE
Most beautiful girl in the world / Always on my mind / You've got to stand for something / After all these years / I don't know why I love you but I do / If tomorrow never comes / Ramblin' rose / You'll never walk alone / Please help me, I'm falling / Here in the real world / Walk on by / I love you because / Four in the morning / It's just a matter of time / Ramona / What's another year
CD ______ **CD 0064**
Ritz / Feb '92 / Pinnacle

CONCERT COLLECTION
Kaw-Liga / I'm so afraid of losing you again / Oklahoma morning / It's gonna take a little bit longer / Crystal chandeliers / Medley / Shutters and boards / Happiness of having you / My eyes can only see as far / Kiss an angel good morning / Let me live in the light of His love / Mississippi cotton picking delta town / Help me make it through the night / Louisiana man / Medley
CD ______ **PLATCD 165**
Platinum / Mar '96 / Prism

CRYSTAL CHANDELIERS
CD ______ **MUCD 3009**
Musketeer / Oct '94 / Disc

CRYSTAL CHANDELIERS
Crystal chandeliers / Kaw-liga / (I'm so) Afraid of losing you again / Oklahoma morning / It's gonna take a little bit longer / Does my ring hurt your finger / Too good to be true / I'd rather love you / All I have to offer you is me / Wonder could I live there anymore / Is anybody goin' to San Antone / I'm just me / Shutters and boards / Happiness of having you / My eyes can only see as far as you / Kiss an angel good morning / Let me live in the light of his love / Mississippi cotton pickin' Delta Town / Help me make it through the night / Louisiana man / There goes my everything / Lovesick blues / Me and Bobby McGee
CD ______ **CD 6016**
Music / Apr '96 / Target/BMG

CRYSTAL CHANDELIERS (The Best Of Charley Pride)
CD ______ **PLSCD 145**
Pulse / Apr '97 / BMG

ESSENTIAL CHARLEY PRIDE, THE
Just between you and me / Does my ring hurt your finger / Please help me I'm falling / All I have to offer you (is me) / Kaw-Liga / Is anybody going to San Antone / I'd rather love you / Wonder could I live there anymore / I can't believe that you've stopped loving me / She's too good to be true / Kiss an angel good mornin' / It's gonna take a little bit longer / I'm just me / Shoulder to cry on / Amazing love / My eyes can only see as far as you / I'll be leaving alone / Someone loves you honey / Burgers and fries / You're my Jamaica
CD ______ **7863674282**
RCA / May '97 / BMG

GREATEST HITS
Kaw-liga / I'm so afraid of losing you again / Oklahoma morning / It's going to take a little bit longer / Crystals chandeliers / Does my ring hurt your finger / Too good to be true / I'd rather love you / All I have to offer you is me / I wonder could I live there anymore / Is anybody going to San Antone / I'm just me / Shutters and boards / Happiness of having you / My eyes can only see as far as you / Kiss an angel good morning / Let me live in the light of his light / Mississippi cotton picking Delta town / Help me make it through the night / Louisanna man / There goes my everything / Lovesick blues / Me and Bobby McGee
CD ______ **MU 5070**
Musketeer / Oct '92 / Disc

JUST FOR THE LOVE OF IT
Just for the love of it / Walk on by / For today / Me and Bobby McGee / Lonestar lonely / I've been there / Lovesick blues / I'll be leaving alone / Sea of heartbreak / Burnin' down the tavern / In the midnight hour / Walls / Hello love / I don't think she's in love anymore / I came straight to you / Where do I put her memory / Burnin' down the tarvern
CD ______ **RITZRCD 559**
Ritz / Jun '96 / Pinnacle

KISS AN ANGEL GOOD MORNING
CD ______ **WMCD 5699**
Disky / Oct '94 / Disky / THE

VERY BEST OF CHARLEY PRIDE, THE
I'd rather love you / Is anybody going to San Antone / I'm so afraid of losing you again / Kiss an angel good morning / Just between you and me / All I have to offer you is me / Wonder could I live there anymore / I can't believe that you've stopped loving me / I'm just me / Crystal chandeliers / Amazing love / Happiness of having you / Easy part's over / I know one / Does my ring hurt your finger / For the good times / Kaw-liga / My eyes can only see as far as you / She's just an old love turned memory / Someone loves you honey
CD ______ **74321272142**
RCA / May '95 / BMG

Pride, Dickie

SHEIK OF SHAKE, THE
Don't make me love you / You're singin' our love song to somebody else / Fabulous cure / Betty Betty (go steady with me) / Primrose Lane / Anything goes / Isn't this a lovely day (to be caught in the rain) / You turned the tables on me / Loch Lomond / Falling in love / Give the simple life / Slippin' and slidin' / Bye bye blackbird / Midnight oil / No John / Frantic / It's only a paper moon / I could write a book / Too close for comfort / There's a small hotel / They can't take that away from me / Lulu's back in town
CD ______ **SEECD 344**
See For Miles/C5 / Mar '92 / Pinnacle

Pride Of Murray Pipe Band

BEST OF SCOTTISH PIPES AND DRUMS, THE
CD ______ **EUCD 1164**
ARC / Jun '91 / ADA / ARC Music

Pride, Steve

HAINT
CD ______ **SPURCD 001**
Spur / Jun '97 / Cargo

Pridebowl

DRIPPINGS OF THE PAST
CD ______ **BTR 007CD**
Bad Taste / Apr '96 / Plastic Head

SOFT SONG EP
CD ______ **BTR 008CD**
Bad Taste / Jul '96 / Plastic Head

Priest, Maxi

BEST OF ME, THE
Wild world / In the Springtime / Should I / How can we ease the pain: *Priest, Maxi & Beres Hammond* / Let me know / Housecall: *Priest, Maxi & Shabba Ranks* / Just a little bit longer / Caution / Some guys have all the luck / I know love: *Priest, Maxi & Tiger* / Strollin' on / Best of me / Crazy love / Woman in you / Peace throughout the world: *Priest, Maxi & Jazzie B* / Close to you
CD ______ **DIXCD 111**
10 / Oct '91 / EMI

BONAFIDE
Just a little bit longer / Close to you / Never did say goodbye / Best of me / Space in my heart / Human work of art / Temptress / Peace throughout the world / You / Sure fire love / Life / Prayer for the world
CD ______ **DIXCD 92**
10 / Jun '90 / EMI

COLLECTION, A
Strollin' on / Some guys have all the luck / How can we ease the pain / Groovin' in the midnight / Love don't come easy / Just a little bit longer / One more chance / Pretty little girl / Should I (put my trust in you) / Human work of art / Sure fire love / Fatty fatty
CD ______ **CDVIP 138**
Virgin VIP / Sep '95 / EMI

FE REAL
Can't turn away / Promises / Just wanna know / Groovin' in the midnight / Make my day / Ten to midnight / Careless whispers: *Priest, Maxi & Carla Marshall* / One more chance / Sublime / Amazed are we / Hard to get
CD ______ **CDVIP 156**
Virgin VIP / Oct '96 / EMI

INTENTIONS
Love train / Woman in you / Crazy love / Jehovah / Cry me a river / Strollin' on / Pretty little girl / Let me know / Festival time / Must be a way
CD ______ **DIXCD 32**
10 / '88 / EMI

MAN WITH THE FUN
That girl / Man with the fun / Watching the world go by / Message in a bottle / Heartbreak lover / Love will cross over / All kinds of people / Happy days / Golden teardrops / Are you ready for me / Ain't it enough / Human cry / Frienenemy / Won't let it slip away
CD ______ **CDVUS 110**
Virgin / Jul '96 / EMI

MAXI
Wild world / Suzie - you are / Goodbye to love again / You're only human / Same old story / Marcus / How can we ease the pain / It ain't easy / Some guys have all the luck / Problems / Reasons
CD ______ **OVEDC 347**
10 / Mar '91 / EMI

YOU'RE SAFE
Should I / Hey little girl / Dancing mood / Sensi / Caution / Stand up and fight / In the Springtime / Fatty fatty / You're safe / Throw me corn
CD ______ **CDVIP 172**
Virgin VIP / Apr '97 / EMI

Priestley, Brian

SALUTES 15 JAZZ PIANO GREATS
CD ______ **CD 90995**
FMR/Spirit Of Jazz / Dec '95 / Harmonia Mundi

YOU TAUGHT MY HEART TO SING
CD ______ **SOJCD 9**
FMR/Spirit Of Jazz / Dec '95 / Harmonia Mundi

Prima, Louis

BUONA SERA
CD ______ **RMB 75076**
Remember / Oct '95 / Total/BMG

CAPITOL COLLECTORS SERIES: LOUIS PRIMA
Just a gigolo/I ain't got nobody / Oh Marie / Buona sera / Jump, jive and wail / Basin Street blues/ When it's sleepy time down South / Lip / Whistle stop / Five months, two weeks, two days / Banana split for my baby / There'll be no next time / When you're smiling/ The sheik of Araby / Baby, won't you please come home / I've got the world on a string / Pennies from Heaven / Angelina/Zooma zooma / Beep beep / Embraceable you/I got it bad and that ain't good / Sing sing sing / That old black magic / Music goes 'round and around / Hey boy, hey girl / Lazy river / I've got you under my skin / You're just in love / Twist all night / St. Louis blues
CD ______ **CDP 7940722**
Premier/EMI / Jul '96 / EMI

CAPITOL RECORDINGS, THE (8CD Set)
Buona sera / Oh Marie / Just a gigolo / I ain't got nobody / Body and soul / Jump, jive and wail / Nothing's too good for my baby / (I'll be glad when you're dead) you rascal you / Basin Street blues / When it's sleepy time down South / Night train / Lip / Whistle stop / Five months, two weeks, two days / Banana split for my baby / Be mine (little baby) / When you're smiling / Sheikh of araby / Birth of the blues / Blow red blow / When the saints go marching in / Sentimental journey / There'll be no next time / Closer to the bone / I've got the world on a string / Much too young to lose my mind / Don't let a memory / Pennies from heaven / Baby, won't you please come home / Autumn leaves / Pump song / Boulevard of broken dreams / Natural guy / Beep beep / If you were the only girl in the world / Bourbon street blues / Sing sing sing / That old black magic / Judy / Felicia no capacia / That's my home / Moonglow / Gotta see baby tonight / Fee fie foo / Music goes 'round and around / Fever / Don't you take your love from me / Hey boy, hey girl / Lazy river / Hey boy, hey girl (reprise) / Nothing's too good for my baby / Oh Marie (alternate take) / I've got you under my skin / Don't take your love from me / You're just in love / Harlem nocturne / Glow worm / Just one of those things / All night long / Lover come back to me / Everybody knows / Ain't misbehavin' / Way down yonder in New Orleans / Three handed woman / St. Louis blues / Twist all night / John ping pong / Ooh look what you've done to me / Big Daddy / Sunday lover / Little girl blue / Scuba diver / I want you to be my baby / Shadrack / Next time / Lady of Spain / Hello lover, goodbye tears / Undecided / Come rain or come shine / Go back where you stayed last night / On the sunny side of the street / Exactly like you / Foggy day / How high the moon / Angelina / Zooma somma (medley) / Don't worry bout me / In the mood for love / Come back to sorrento / I gotta right to sing the blues / Robin Hood / Oh babe / Them there eyes / Honeysuckle rose / Tiger rag / Just because / Embraceable you / I got it bad and that ain't good / Should I / I can't believe that you're in love with me / White cliffs of Dover / Holiday / Greenback dollar bill / Love of my life (o sole mio) / Too marvellous for words / I wish you love / I would do most anything for you / Shy / Rock-a-doodle-doo / Young and in love / Someone to watch over me / Nearness of you / Indian love call / Just as much / Sometimes / You are my love / Whip-poor-will / I understand / If we never meet again / Mr. Wonderful / When day is done / All the things you are / When your lover has gone / You go to my head / Imagination / Fools rush in / As you desire me / You better go now / Good behaviour / You'll never know / Man I love / It's magic / What is this thing called love / Stormy weather / There'll never be another you / It's been a long, long time / You're driving me crazy / Stardust / What can I say after I say I'm sorry / Nitey nite / Hurt me / I keep forgetting / High school affair / Nothing in common / How are you fixed for love / s'posin' / Song is you / I'll get by / Never knew / I'll never smile again / Sweet and lovely / All the way / Lullaby of the leaves / East of the sun and west of the moon / I can't get started (with you) / Cocktails for two / Bim bam / Twinkle in your eye / Ten little women / Equator / Seven out / Kiss your hand madame / Love charm / Love nest / Put your mind at ease / It's better than nothing at all / Hold out for love / Good gracious baby / Handle with care / Dig that crazy chick / Hey there / I love Paris / On the street where you live / Song from Moulin Rouge / Three coins in the fountain / Too young / Rock-a-bye your baby with a Dixie melody / Love is a many splendoured thing / Around the world / La vie en rose / Bugs / Tennessee waltz / French poodle / Chantilly lace / Up jumped a rabbit / Just say I love her / Easy rockin' / Honey love / Street scene / Perdido / Kansas city / Love of my life (o sole mio 2nd version) / Ol' man river / Smilin' Billy / Skinny Minnie / Better twist now baby / Twistin' the blues / Continental twist / Tag that twistin' dolly / Come and do the twist / O ma-ma twist / I feel good all over / Later, baby, later / Ol man river
CD Set ______ **BCD 15776**
Bear Family / Sep '94 / Direct / Rollercoaster / Swift

GREATEST HITS
Lady in red / Music goes 'round and around / I'm an old cowhand (from the Rio Grande) / I'll be seeing you / I'll walk alone / My dreams are getting better all the time / Josephine please no lean on my bell / Hey ba ba re bop / Brooklyn boogie / Civilisation / Thousand island song / My cucuzza
CD ______ **JASCD 327**
Jasmine / Oct '94 / Conifer/BMG / Hot Shot / TKO Magnum

LOUIS & KEELY (Prima, Louis & Keely Smith)
Night and day / All I do is dream of you / Make love to me / I don't know why / Tea for two / And the angels sing / I'm confessin' that I love you / Why do I love you / You're my everything / Cheek to cheek / I've grown accustomed to her face / Bei mir bist du schon
CD ______ **JASCD 326**
Jasmine / Jan '95 / Conifer/BMG / Hot Shot / TKO Magnum

LOUIS PRIMA AND KEELY SMITH (Prima, Louis & Keely Smith)
When the saints go marching in / Hey, boy, hey, girl / That old black magic / I've got you under my skin / Five months, two weeks, two days / That's my home / Felicia no capicia / Moonglow / Fee fie foo / Bourbon street blues / It's magic / If you were the only girl / I wish you love / Judy / Night train / White cliffs of Dover / Should / I can't believe that you're in love with me / Love of my life (o sole mio) / Too marvellous for words
CD ______ **CD 392**
Entertainers / May '96 / Target/BMG

ON STAGE (Prima, Louis & Keely Smith)
CD ________ **JASCD 331**
Jasmine / Nov '95 / Conifer/BMG / Hot Shot / TKO Magnum

REMEMBER (Prima, Louis & His Orchestra)
Robin Hood / St. Louis blues / I'll walk alone / Angeline / Some Sunday morning / I don't wanna be loved / You gotta see baby tonight / White cliffs of Dover / Just a gigolo / I ain't got nobody
CD ________ **DAWE 12**
Magic / Nov '93 / Cadillac / Harmonia Mundi / Jazz Music / Swift / Wellard

RETURN OF THE WILD WEST (Prima, Louis & Keely Smith)
South of the border (Down Mexico way) / Come back to Sorrento / South Rampart street parade / I love you / For you / After you've gone / Grasshopper / Lonesome for you / Absent minded lover / I have but one heart / Ol' man mose / Chinatown, my Chinatown
CD ________ **JASCD 330**
Jasmine / Oct '94 / Conifer/BMG / Hot Shot / TKO Magnum

TOGETHER (Prima, Louis & Keely Smith)
Together / Paradise / Teach me tonight / Nyow nyoy nyow (the pussycat song) / They can't take that away from me / I can't give you anything but love / When my baby smiles at me / Let's get away from it all / Mashuga / Let's call the whole thing off / Mutual admiration society / Begin the beguine
CD ________ **JASCD 325**
Jasmine / Feb '94 / Conifer/BMG / Hot Shot / TKO Magnum

VERY BEST OF LOUIS PRIMA, THE
That's where the South begins / Stardust / Let's have a jubilee / (Looks like I'm) breaking the ice / It's the rhythm in me / Put on an old pair of shoes / Bright eyes / Swing me with rhythm / Chinatown, my Chinatown / Chasing shadows / Sugar is sweeter and so are you / In a little gypsy tea room / I'm living in a great big way / House rent party day / Jamaica shout / Let's swing it
CD ________ **SUMCD 4114**
Sound & Media / May '97 / Sound & Media

Prima Materia

ALBERT AYLER'S BELLS (Prima Materia & Rashied Ali)
CD ________ **KFWCD 190**
Knitting Factory / Mar '97 / Cargo / Plastic Head

MEDITATIONS (Prima Materia & Rashied Ali)
CD ________ **KFWCD 180**
Knitting Factory / Oct '96 / Cargo / Plastic Head

MUSIC OF JOHN COLTRANE
CD ________ **KFWCD 158**
Knitting Factory / Feb '95 / Cargo / Plastic Head

Primal Scream

GIVE OUT, BUT DON'T GIVE UP
Jailbird / Rocks / (I'm gonna) Cry myself blind / Funky jam / Big jet plane / Free / Call on me / Struttin' / Sad and blue / Give out but don't give up / I'll be there
CD ________ **CRECD 146**
Creation / Mar '94 / 3mv/Vital

PRIMAL SCREAM
Ivy Ivy Ivy / You're just dead skin to me / She power / You're just too dark to care / I'm losing more than I'll ever have / Gimme gimme teenage head / Kill the King / Lone Star girl
CD ________ **CRECD 054**
Creation / Sep '89 / 3mv/Vital

SCREAMADELICA
Movin' on up / Slip inside this house / Don't fight it, feel it / Higher than the sun / Come together / Damaged / Loaded / Shine like stars / Inner flight / I'm coming down
CD ________ **CRELPCD 076**
Creation / Sep '91 / 3mv/Vital

SONIC FLOWER GROOVE
Gentle Tuesday / Treasure trip / May the sun shine bright for you / Sonic sister love / Silent spring / Imperial / Love you / Leaves / Aftermath / We go down slowly rising
CD ________ **2292421822**
WEA / Jun '91 / Warner Music

VANISHING POINT
Burning wheel / Kowalski / Stuka / Star / Get Duffy / Motorhead / Out of the void / Trainspotting / Medication / If they move, kill 'em / Long life
CD ________ **CRECD 178**
Creation / Jul '97 / 3mv/Vital

Prime Movers

ARC
Immortal / Interloper / Sheep / Crystalline / Revelation / Obsession / Rollercoaster / Sublime / Aural sea / Misled / Prelude: Dawn of love / Mandrake root / Breed 'n' burn
CD ________ **CND 005CD**
Cyanide / Mar '93 / Vital

Prime Time Victim Show

PRIME TIME VICTIM SHOW
CD ________ **35540052**
Dig It All / Jun '97 / Cargo

Primer, John

KEEP ON LOVIN' THE BLUES
Keep on lovin' the blues / Axe to grind / My pencil won't write no more / One minute / Oh yeah / When I reach out for your love / Close to you / You can't stop doing what you're doin' / Like a ship / I've been travellin' / Pay the price / Meet me at the crossroads
CD ________ **0630183832**
Code Blue / May '97 / Warner Music

REAL DEAL, THE
CD ________ **0630108382**
Code Blue / Nov '95 / Warner Music

Primevals

LIVE A LITTLE
St. Jack / Justify / Cotton head / Fertile mind / Prairie chain / Heya / Sister
CD ________ **ROSE 123CD**
New Rose / Sep '87 / ADA / Direct / Discovery

Primich, Gary

COMPANY MAN
Company man / Turn your damper down / My home / Briar patch / What's it gonna be / Ain't you trouble / Big Daddy's coming home / Dry country blues / Hook, line and sinker / Varmint / Cold hand in mine / Jailbird
CD ________ **CDBT 1136**
Black Top / Mar '97 / ADA / CM / Direct

MR. FREEZE
Bad poker hand / I'm the one / Route 90 / Mr. Freeze / Go on fool / Dummy on your knee / Dallas Texas / Slap you silly / Jenny Brown / You came a long way from St. Louis / Red top / Easy ridin' mama / Let me go home whiskey
CD ________ **FF 70649**
Flying Fish / Oct '96 / ADA / CM / Direct / Roots

TRAVELLIN' MOOD
House rockin' party / Intro / Ding dong Daddy / Shake the boogie / Beer drinkin' woman / Triple trouble / Wild cat tamer / Caravan / Travellin' mood / She was a dreamer / School of hard knocks / Put the hammer down / Poodle bites / Knock me a kiss
CD ________ **FF 70635**
Flying Fish / May '97 / ADA / CM / Direct / Roots

Primitive Instinct

FLOATING TANGIBILITY
Heaven / 11-11 / Circles / Keep on running / Friend / Hypnotic / Slaves / One way man / Shame / Triludan
CD ________ **CYCL 003**
Cyclops / Jul '97 / Pinnacle

Primitive Radio Gods

ROCKET
Women / Motherfucker / Standing outside a broken phone booth with money in my hand / Who say / Rise and fall of the ooo man / Wherer the monkey meets the man / Are you happy / Chain reaction / Skin turns blue / Rocket
CD ________ **4836952**
Columbia / Dec '96 / Sony

Primitives

BEST OF THE PRIMITIVES, THE
Crash / Spacehead / Shadow / Thru the flowers / Nothing left / Out of reach / Summer rain / Sick of it / All the way down / Secrets / Can't bring me down / Way behind me / Noose / I almost touched you / You are the way / Lead me astray / Slip away / Give this world to you / Empathise / Earth thing / All the way down (beat version)
CD ________ **74321393432**
Camden / Jun '96 / BMG

BOMBSHELL
Crash / Stop killing me / Sick of it / Way behind me / Thru the flowers / Lead me astray / Secrets / Out of reach / You are the way / Empathise / Earth thing / All the way down / Don't want anything to change / Way behind me (Acoustic) / Stop killing me (Acoustic) / As tears go by / Secrets (Demo) / Crash (Demo)
CD ________ **74321226352**
RCA / Sep '94 / BMG

Primordia

GLEAMING EYE, THE
CD ________ **WSCD 003**
World Serpent / Oct '96 / World Serpent

Primrose, Christine

AITE MO GHAOIL (PLACE OF MY HEART)
CD ________ **COMD 1006**
Temple / Feb '94 / ADA / CM / Direct / Duncans / Highlander

STU NAM CHUMHNE
CD ________ **COMD 2024**
Temple / Apr '95 / ADA / CM / Direct / Duncans / Highlander

Primus

BROWN ALBUM, THE
CD ________ **IND 90126**
Interscope / Jul '97 / BMG

FRIZZLE FRY
To defy the laws of tradition / Too many puppies / Frizzle fry / You can't kill Michael Malloy / Pudding time / Spaghetti western / To defy / Ground hog's day / Mr. Know it all / John the fisherman / Toys go winding down / Sathington Willoby / Harold of the rocks
CD ________ **CAROLCD 1619**
Caroline / Jun '97 / Cargo / Vital

PORK SODA
Pork chop's little ditty / My name is mud / Welcome to this world / Bob / DMV / Ol' diamond back sturgeon / Nature boy / Wounded knee / Pork soda / Pressman / Mr. Krinkle / Air is getting slippery / Hamburger train / Hail santa
CD ________ **IND 92257**
Interscope / Jul '96 / BMG

SAILING THE SEAS OF CHEESE
Seas of cheese / Here come the bastards / Sgt. Baker / American life / Jerry was a race car driver / Eleven / Is it luck / Grandad's little ditty / Tommy the cat / Sathington waltz / Those damned blue-collar tweekers / Fish on (fisherman chronicles, chapter II) / Los bastardos
CD ________ **IND 91659**
Interscope / Aug '96 / BMG

SUCK ON THIS
John the fisherman / Ground hog's day / Heckler / Pressman / Jellikit / Tommy the cat / Pudding time / Harold of the rocks / Frizzle fry
CD ________ **CAROLCD 1620**
Caroline / Jun '97 / Cargo / Vital

TALES FROM THE PUNCH BOWL
Professor nutbutter's house of treats / Mrs. Blaileen / Wynona's big brown beaver / Southbound pachyderm / Space farm / Year of the parrot / Hellbound 17&1/2 / Glass sandwich / Del davis tree farm / De anza jig / On the tweek again / Over the electric grapevine / Captain shiner
CD ________ **IND 92553**
Interscope / Aug '96 / BMG
CD ________ **IND 92665**
Interscope / Jul '96 / BMG

Prince

1999
1999 / Little red corvette / Delirious / Let's pretend we're married / DMSR / Automatic / Something in the water (does not compute) / Free / Lady cab driver / All the critics love U in New York / International lover
CD ________ **9237202**
WEA / Nov '84 / Warner Music

AROUND THE WORLD IN A DAY
Around the world in a day / Paisley Park / Condition of the heart / Raspberry beret / Tambourine / America / Pop life / Ladder / Temptation
CD ________ **9252862**
Paisley Park / May '85 / Warner Music

BATMAN (Original Soundtrack)
Future / Electric chair / Arms of Orion / Partyman / Vicki waiting / Trust / Lemon crush / Scandalous / Batdance
CD ________ **9259362**
WEA / Feb '95 / Warner Music

CHAOS AND DISORDER
Chaos and disorder / I like it there / Dinner with Dolores / Same December / Right the wrong / Zannalee / I rock therefore I am / Into the light / I will / Dig u better dead / Had u
CD ________ **9362463172**
WEA / Jul '96 / Warner Music

COME
Come / Space / Pheromone / Loose / Papa / Race / Dark / Solo / Letitgo / Orgasm
CD ________ **9362457002**
WEA / Dec '96 / Warner Music

CONTROVERSY
Private joy / Ronnie talk to Russia / Let's work / Annie Christian / Jack U off / Sexuality / Controversy / Do me baby
CD ________ **256950**
WEA / '84 / Warner Music

DIAMONDS AND PEARLS (Prince & The New Power Generation)
Thunder / Daddy pop / Diamonds and pearls / Cream / Strollin' / Willing and able / Gett off / Walk don't walk / Jughead / Money don't matter 2 night / Push / Insatiable / Live 4 love
CD ________ **7599253792**
Paisley Park / Feb '95 / Warner Music

DIRTY MIND
Dirty mind / When you were mine / Do it all night / Gotta broken heart again / Uptown / Head / Sister / Party up
CD ________ **256862**
WEA / Jan '86 / Warner Music

EMANCIPATION (3CD Set)
Jam of the year / Right back here in my arms / Somebody's somebody / Get yo groove on / Courtin' time / Betcha by golly wow / We gets up / White mansion / Darned if I do / I can't make U love me / Mr. Happy / In this bed I scream / Sex in the summer / One kiss at a time / Soul sanctuary / Emale / Curious child / Dreamin' about U / Joint 2 joint / Holy River / Let's have a baby / Saviour / Plan / Friend lover sister mother wife / Slave / New world / Human body / Face down / La la la means I love you / Style / Sleep around / DA DA DA / My computer / One of us / Love we make / Emancipation
CD Set ________ **CDEMD 1102**
New Power Generation / Nov '96 / EMI

FOR YOU
For you / In love / Soft and wet / Crazy you / Just as long as we're together / Baby / My love is forever / So blue / I'm yours
CD ________ **256989**
WEA / Oct '87 / Warner Music

GIRL 6 (Original Soundtrack)
CD ________ **9362462392**
WEA / Mar '96 / Warner Music

GOLD EXPERIENCE, THE
Pussy control / Endorphinmachine / Shhh / We march / Most beautiful girl in the world / Dolphin / Now / 319 / Shy / Billy Jack Bitch / I hate U / Gold
CD ________ **9362459992**
WEA / Oct '95 / Warner Music

GRAFFITI BRIDGE
Can't stop this feeling I got / Question of U / Round and round: *Campbell, Tevin* / Joy in repetition / Tick tick bang / Thieves in the temple / Melody cool / Graffiti bridge / Release it: *Time* / Elephants and flowers / We can funk / Love machine / Shake: *Time* / Latest fashion / Still would stand all time / New power generation
CD ________ **7599274932**
WEA / Aug '90 / Warner Music

HITS AND B-SIDES, THE (3CD Set)
When doves cry / Pop life / Soft and wet / I feel for you / Why you wanna treat me so bad / When you were mine / Uptown / Let's go crazy / 1999 / I could never take the place of your man / Nothing compares 2 U / Adore / Pink cashmere / Alphabet Street / Sign o' the times / Thieves in the temple / Diamonds and pearls / 7 / Controversy / Dirty mind / I wanna be your lover / Head / Do me baby / Delirious / Little red corvette / I would die 4 U / Raspberry beret / If I was your girlfriend / Kiss / Peach / U got the look / Sexy MF / Gett off / Cream / Pope / Purple rain / Hello / 200 Balloons / Escape / Gotta stop (messin' about) / Horny toad / Feel U up / Girl / I love U in me / Erotic city / Shockadelica / Irresistible bitch / Scarlet pussy / La la la he he hee / She's always in my hair / Seventeen days / How come U don't call me anymore / Another lonely Christmas / God / 4 The tears in your eyes / Power fantastic
CD Set ________ **9362454402**
Paisley Park / Sep '93 / Warner Music

HITS VOL.1, THE
When doves cry / Pop life / Soft and wet / I feel for you / Why you wanna treat me so bad / When you were mine / Uptown / Let's go crazy / 1999 / I could never take the place of your man / Nothing compares 2 U / Adore / Pink cashmere / Alphabet Street / Sign o' the times / Thieves in the temple / Diamonds and pearls / 7
CD ________ **9362454312**
Paisley Park / Sep '93 / Warner Music

HITS VOL.2, THE
Controversy / Dirty mind / I wanna be your lover / Head / Do me baby / Delirious / Little red corvette / I would die 4 U / Raspberry beret / If I was your girlfriend / Kiss / Peach / U got the look / Sexy MF / Gett off / Cream / Pope / Purple rain
CD ________ **9362454352**
Paisley Park / Sep '93 / Warner Music

INTERVIEW DISC
CD ________ **SAM 7009**
Sound & Media / Nov '96 / Sound & Media

LOVESEXY
I no / Alphabet Street / Glam slam / Anna Stesia / Dance on / Lovesexy / When 2 R in love / I wish U heaven / Positivity
CD ________ **9257202**
Paisley Park / May '88 / Warner Music

METROPOLITAN ORCHESTRA PLAYS PRINCE, THE (Metropolitan Orchestra)
CD ________ **EMPRCD 705**
Emporio / Mar '97 / Disc

PARADE (Original Soundtrack - Under The Cherry Moon) (Prince & The Revolution)
Christopher Tracy's parade / New position / I wonder U / Under the cherry moon / Girls and boys / Life can be so nice / Venus de Milo / Mountains / Do U lie / Kiss / Anotherloverholenyohead / Sometimes it snows in April
CD 9253952
WEA / Apr '86 / Warner Music

PRINCE
I wanna be your lover / Why you wanna treat me so bad / Sexy dancer / When we're dancing close and slow / With you / Bambi / Still waiting / I feel for you / It's gonna be lonely
CD 256772
WEA / '86 / Warner Music

PRINCE: INTERVIEW COMPACT DISC
CD CBAK 4018
Baktabak / Nov '89 / Arabesque

PURPLE RAIN (Original Soundtrack) (Prince & The Revolution)
Let's go crazy / Take me with U / Beautiful ones / Computer blue / Darling Nikki / When doves cry / I would die 4 U / Baby I'm a star / Purple rain
CD 9251102
WEA / Feb '95 / Warner Music

SIGN O' THE TIMES (2CD Set)
Play in the sunshine / Housequake / Ballad of Dorothy Parker / It / Starfish and coffee / Slow love / Hot thing / Forever in my life / U got the look / If I was your girlfriend / Strange relationship / I could never take the place of your man / Cross / It's gonna be a beautiful night / Adore / Sign o' the times
CD Set 9255772
Paisley Park / Apr '87 / Warner Music

SYMBOL
My name is Prince / Sexy MF / Love 2 the 9s / Morning papers / Max / Segue / Blue light / I wanna melt with U / Sweet baby / Continental / Damn U / Arrogance / Flow / 7 / And God created woman / Three chains o' gold / Sacrifice of Victor
CD 9362450372
Paisley Park / Oct '92 / Warner Music

SYMBOLIC BEGINNINGS (2CD Set) (94 East)
CD Set CPCD 81042
Charly / Jul '95 / Koch

Prince Alla

ONLY LOVE CAN CONQUER (Prince Alla 1976-1979)
CD BAFCD 14
Blood & Fire / Mar '97 / Vital

Prince Buster

FABULOUS GREATEST HITS (Remastered)
Madness / Al Capone / Wash wash / God son / It's Burke's law / Ten commandments / Blackhead Chinaman / Thirty pieces of silver / Hard man fe dead / Earthquake / Judge Dread / Ghost dance / Take it easy / Too hot / My girl / This is a hold up / Shaking up Orange Street / Big 5 / Rough rider / Wreck a pum pum / Julie on my mind / Pharoah house crash / Tie the donkey's tail / Finger
CD NEXCD 253
Sequel / Oct '93 / BMG

ORIGINAL GOLDEN OLDIES VOL.1
CD PBCD 9
Prince Buster / Feb '89 / Jet Star

ORIGINAL GOLDEN OLDIES VOL.2
CD PBCD 10
Prince Buster / May '93 / Jet Star

PROPHET, THE
CD LG 21100
Lagoon / Sep '94 / Grapevine/PolyGram

Prince Charles

DEAD IN THE PROJECTS, DEAD IN AMERICA (Prince Charles & The City Beat Band)
CD RE 096CD
ROIR / Jun '97 / Plastic Head / Shellshock/Disc

GREATEST HITZ (Prince Charles & The City Beat Band)
CD RE 115CD
ROIR / Jun '97 / Plastic Head / Shellshock/Disc

Prince Charming Presents

PSYCHOTROPICAL HEATWAVE
CD WSCD 013
Word Sound Recordings / Dec '96 / Cargo / SRD

Prince Far-I

BLACKMAN LAND
Message from the king / Dream / Reggae music moving / Black man land / Marble stone / Wish I have a wing / Armageddon / Commandment of drugs / Badda card / Moses Moses / Some with roof / Foggy road / Put it out / King of kings / Ghetto living / River of Jordan
CD CDFL 9005
Frontline / Sep '90 / EMI / Jet Star

CRY TUFF DUB ENCOUNTER VOL.1
Message / Visitor / Right Way / Long Life / Encounter / Ghardaia Dub / Mansion of the almighty / Mozabites / Prince Of Peace / Abderrahmane
CD PSCD 13
Pressure Sounds / Apr '97 / Jet Star / SRD

CRY TUFF DUB ENCOUNTER VOL.3 (Prince Far-I & The Arabs)
CD PSCD 007
Pressure Sounds / Jan '96 / Jet Star / SRD

DUB TO AFRICA (Prince Far-I & The Arabs)
CD PSCD 002
Pressure Sounds / Apr '95 / Jet Star / SRD

DUBWISE
Throw away your gun / Love divine dub / If you want to do ya dub / Jah do that dub / No more war / Suru lere dub / Anambra dub / Kaduna dub / Oyo dub / Borno dub / Bendel dub / Ondo dub / Ogun dub
CD CDFL 9019
Frontline / Jun '91 / EMI / Jet Star

MUSICAL REVUE (Prince Far-I & Suns Of Arqa)
CD RE 161CD
ROIR / Jun '97 / Plastic Head / Shellshock/Disc

SPEAR OF THE NATION (Umkhonto We Sizwe)
Survival / Ask ask / African queen / Stop the war / Jerry doghead / Special request
CD TWCD 1013
Tamoki Wambesi / Jul '93 / Greensleeves / Jet Star / Roots Collective / SRD

VOICE OF THUNDER
Ten commandments / Tribute to Bob Marley / Hold the fort / Everytime I hear the word / Head of the Buccaneer / Shall not dwell in wickedness / Give I strength / Kingdom of God / Coming from the rock / Skinhead
CD CDTRLS 204
Trojan / May '90 / Direct / Jet Star

Prince Hammer

RESPECT I MAN
CD TWCD 1026
Tamoki Wambesi / Oct '95 / Greensleeves / Jet Star / Roots Collective / SRD

Prince Ital Joe

LIFE ON THE STREETS (Prince Ital Joe & Marky Mark)
Life in the streets (intro) / United / Rastaman vibration / Happy people / To be important / In love / Babylon / Love of a mother / Into the light / In the 90's / Prankster / Life in the streets
CD 4509963182
East West / Mar '95 / Warner Music

Prince Jammy

DANCEHALL KILLERS VOL.1
CD 792062
Greensleeves / Nov '92 / Jet Star / SRD

HIS MAJESTY'S DUB (Prince Jammy & King Tubby)
CD SJCD 003
Sky Juice / Apr '93 / Jet Star / SRD

KAMIKAZI DUB
Throne of blood / Brothers of the blade / Shoalin temple / Kamikaze / Oragami black belt / Fist of fury / Opium den / Swords of vengeance / Downtown Shangai rock / Waterfront gang war
CD CDTRL 174
Trojan / Feb '97 / Direct / Jet Star

SLENG TENG EXTRAVAGANZA
CD 792042
Greensleeves / Nov '92 / Jet Star / SRD

UHURU IN DUB (Prince Jammy Presents Black Uhuru In Dub) (Prince Jammy/Sly & Robbie)
Eden dub / Mystic mix / His imperial majesty / Weeping willow / Bad girls dub / Tonight is the night / Firehouse special / African culture / Crisis dub / Sound man style
CD CPCD 8281
Charly / May '97 / Koch

Prince Jazzbo

HEAD TO HEAD CLASH (Prince Jazzbo & I-Roy)
CD RASCD 3039
Ras / May '89 / Direct / Greensleeves / Jet Star / SRD

STRAIGHT TO PRINCE JAZZBO'S HEAD (Various Artists)
CD CC 2718
Crocodisc / Apr '95 / Grapevine/PolyGram

Prince Lincoln

21ST CENTURY (Prince Lincoln & Royal Rasses)
CD 15STHCDA 01
1-5 South / Apr '97 / Essential/BMG / Jet Star

Prince Paul

PSYCHO ANALYSIS - WHAT IS IT
CD EFA 012102
Word Sound Recordings / Aug '96 / Cargo / SRD

PSYCHOANALYSIS
CD WSCD 010
Word Sound Recordings / Feb '97 / Cargo / SRD

Princes Of Time

PRINCES OF TIME
CD MAS 004
Mas I Mas / Mar '96 / Discovery

Princess Sharifa

HERITAGE
CD ARICD 093
Ariwa Sounds / Jan '94 / Jet Star / SRD

Principal Edwards Magic ...

SOUNDTRACK & ASMOTO RUNNING BAND (Principal Edwards Magic Theatre)
Enigmatic insomniac machine / Sacrifice / Death of Don Quixote / Third sonnet to sundry notes of music / To a broken guitar / Pinky / McAlpine's dream / McAlpine verses the asmoto / Asmoto running band / Asmoto celebration / Further asmoto celebration / Total glycerol esther / Freef (R') all / Autumn lady dancing / Kettering song / Weirdsong of breaking through at last
CD SEECD 412
See For Miles/C5 / Oct '94 / Pinnacle

Principato, Tom

BLUE LICKS AND VOODOO THINGS
CD VDCD 111
Voodoo / Jun '96 / Direct

REALLY BLUE
Every minute, every hour / Sweet little woman / One for Danny / Stranger's eyes / Walkin' blues / Really blue / Standing at the crossroads again / In orbit / Kansas City blues / Baby please / In another dream / Here in my heart
CD VDCD 115
Voodoo / May '97 / Direct

Principle

DAMNED, THE (Principle & Silent Eclipse)
CD HAUS 2
Tribehaus Recordings / Jan '94 / Plastic Head

Principle, Peter

REVAUX AU BONGO
CD MTM 2
Made To Measure / Nov '88 / New Note/ Pinnacle

SEDIMENTAL JOURNEY
CD MTM 4
Made To Measure / May '93 / New Note/ Pinnacle

TONE POEMS
CD MTM 18
Made To Measure / Nov '88 / New Note/ Pinnacle

Principles Of Soul

PRINCIPLES OF SOUL
Strange land / Easy / Sammy / Blues for star eyes / People / Live and love / Nine to five / Bad reputation / POS / Mr. Comeback Man
CD URG 002CD
Urban Groove / Jul '95 / Vital

Prine, John

GERMAN AFTERNOONS
I just want you to dance with me / Love love love / Bad boys / They'll never take her love from me / Paradise / Lulu walls / Speed of the sound of loneliness / Sailin' around / If she were you / Linda goes to Mars
CD FIENDCD 103
Demon / Aug '87 / Pinnacle

GREAT DAYS (The John Prine Anthology/2CD Set)
Illegal smile / Spanish pipedream / Hello in there / Sam Stone / Paradise / Donald and Lydia / Late John Garfield blues / Yes I guess they should name a drink after me / Great compromise / Sweet revenge / Please don't bury me / Christmas in prison / Dear Abby / Blue umbrella / Common sense / Come back to us Barbara Lewis Hare Krishna Beauregard / Saddle in the rain / He was in heaven before he died / Fish anad whistle / That's the way that the world goes round / Bruised orange (chain of sorrow) / Sabu visits the twin cities alone / Automobile / Killing the blues / Down by the side of the road / Living in the future / It's happening to you / Storm windows / One red rose / Souvenirs / Aimless love / Oldest baby in the world / People putting people down / Unwed Fathers / Angel from montgomery / Linda goes to Mars / Bad boy / Speed of the sound of loneliness / It's a big old goofy world / Sins of Memphisto / All the best
CD Set 8122714002
Atlantic / Feb '94 / Warner Music

LIVE ON TOUR
Picture show / Quit hollerin' at me / You got gold / Unwed fathers / Space monkey / Late John Garfield blues / Storm windows / Jesus the missing years / Humidity built the snowman / Illegal smile / Daddy's little pumpkin / lake Marie / If I could / Stick a needle in my eye / You mean so much to me
CD OBR 015
Oh Boy / May '97 / ADA / CM / Direct

LOST DOGS AND MIXED BLESSINGS
New train / Ain't hurtin' nobody / All the way with you / We are the lonely / Lake Marie / Humidity built the snowman / Day is done / Quit hollerin' at me / Big fat love / Same thing happend to me / This love is real / Leave the lights on / He forgot that it was Sunday / I love you so much it hurts
CD RCD 10333
Rykodisc / Mar '97 / ADA / Vital

MISSING YEARS, THE
Picture show / All the best / Sins of Memphisto / Everybody wants to feel like you / It's a big old goofy world / I want to be with you always / Daddy's like pumpkin / Take a look at my heart / Great run / Way back then / Unlonely / You got cold / Everything is cool / Jesus the missing years
CD 5127742
This Way Up / '92 / PolyGram / SRD

PRIME PRINE
CD 7567815042
WEA / Feb '95 / Warner Music

Prinknash Abbey Monks

CHRISTMAS CHANT (Prinknash Abbey Monks & Stanbrook Abbey Nuns)
Laetundebus / Christus factus est / Christe Redemptor / Dominus dixit / Isiah ch9, vv1-6 / Verbum Caro / Alma Redemptoris Mater / Dominus dixit / Kyrie eleison / Gloria in excelsis / Omnes de Saba / Alleluia / Laetentur / Sanctus (and Benedictus) / Agnus Dei / In splendoribus / Angelus ad Virginem / Ecce Nomen / Quem Vidistis / Angelus ad pastores / Hodie Christus natus est / Puer natus
CD CDSDL 369
Saydisc / Oct '88 / ADA / Direct / Harmonia Mundi

Prins, Patrick

MOVIN' MELODIES (2CD Set)
CD Set 5406782
A&M / Mar '97 / PolyGram

Printed At Bismark's Death

TEN MOVEMENTS
CD EFA 112252
Danse Macabre / Jan '94 / SRD

Printup, Marcus

UNVEILED
Eclipse / When forever is over / Dig / Say it again / Leave your name and number / Unveiled / Stablemates / Soulful J / M and M / Yes or no / Amazing grace
CD CDP 8373022
Blue Note / Aug '96 / EMI

Prior, Andy

ALRIGHT, OK YOU WIN
Alright, OK you win / Nevertheless (I'm in love with you) / I've got you under my skin / I'm a fool to want you / Beware the man with love in his eyes / Love changes everything / Our summer of love / You make me feel so young / All the things you are / Lover / In this world with you / Almost like being in love / Yeh yeh / Dream is a wish
CD CDG 10
DG / Nov '94 / 3mv/Sony / Portland

AT LAST
At last / If I should lose you / Laura / Recipe for love / Very thought of you / Tangerine / Time for love / Why bother with love / Nearness of you / Sweet Georgia Brown / Moonlight in Vermont / West Side Stroy
CD CDG 6
DG / May '96 / 3mv/Sony / Portland

SHOT IN THE DARK, A (Prior, Andy & His Night Owls)
River stay 'way from my door / Hot toddy / Nightingale sang in Berkeley Square / Naked gun / I wish I were in love again / South Rampart street parade / That old black magic / Too little time / Peter Gunn / Puttin' on the ritz / Dragnet / Where or when / Warm breeze / Mack the knife / Victor and Hugo / Serenade in blue / Pennsylvania 6-5000 / Learning the blues

CD ______ CDG 7
DG / '93 / 3mv/Sony / Portland

Prior, Maddy

CAROLS AND CAPERS (Prior, Maddy & The Carnival Band)
Boar's head / Away in a manger / My dancing day / Monsieur Charpentier's Christmas stomp / See amid the winter's snow / Boy was born / Poor little Jesus / Turkey in the straw/Whiskey before breakfast / Wassail / Joy to the world / Cradle song / Shepherds rejoice / Old Joe Clark
CD ______ PRK CD9
Park / Nov '95 / Pinnacle

CHANGING WINDS
To have and to hold / Pity the poor / Night porter / Bloomers / Acappella Stella / Canals / Sovereign prince / Ali Baba / Mountain / In fighting / Another drink
CD ______ BGOCD 213
Beat Goes On / Dec '93 / Pinnacle

FLESH AND BLOOD
Sheath & knife / Rolling english road / Honest work / Finlandia / Hind horn / Bitty withy / Who am I / Cruel Mother / Boy on a horse / Jade / Brother Lawrence / Laugh and the kiss / Point / Heart of stone
CD ______ PRKCD 38
Park / Apr '97 / Pinnacle

HANG UP SORROW AND CARE
Prodigal's resolution / Playford tunes / World is turned upside down / Jovial begger / Leathern bottel / Iantha / An thou were my Ain Thing / Oh that I had but a fine man / Now O now I needs must part / Man is for the woman made / Northern catch/Little Barley Corne / Granny's delight/My Lady Foster's delight / Round of three country dances in one / Youth's the season made for joys / In the days of my youth / Never weatherbeaten saile / Old Simon the king
CD ______ PRKCD 31
Park / Oct '95 / Pinnacle

HAPPY FAMILIES (Prior, Maddy & Rick Kemp)
CD ______ PRKCD 4
Park / Aug '91 / Pinnacle

MEMENTO (The Best Of Maddy Prior)
After the death / Long shadows / Grey funnel line / Baggy pants / Rose / Commit the crime / Newcastle / Mater dolorosa / Woman in the wings / Face to face / Doffin' mistress / Mother and child / Accappella Stella / Sovereign Prince / Deep in the darkest night / Alex / Paternoster / Hallelujah
CD ______ PRKCD 028
Park / May '96 / Pinnacle

SING LUSTILY AND WITH GOOD COURAGE (Prior, Maddy & The Carnival Band)
Who would true valour see / As pants the hart / How firm a foundation / Light of the world / O worship the king / O for a thousand tongues / Lo he comes
CD ______ CDSDL 383
Saydisc / Mar '94 / ADA / Direct / Harmonia Mundi

TAPESTRY OF CAROLS, A (Prior, Maddy & The Carnival Band)
Sans Day carol / In dulci jubilo / God rest ye merry Gentlemen / It came upon a midnight clear / Holly and the ivy / Coventry carol / Ding dong merrily on high / Angel Gabriel / Angels from the realms of glory / Infant Holy / Virgin most pure / Unto us a boy is born / Rejoice and be merry / Joseph dearest / Personent Hodie / On Christmas night
CD ______ CDSDL 366
Saydisc / Mar '94 / ADA / Direct / Harmonia Mundi

WOMAN IN THE WINGS
Woman in the wings / Cold flame / Mother and child / Gutter geese / Rollercoaster / Deep water / Long shadows / I told you so / Rosettes / Cats' eyes / Baggy pants
CD ______ BGOCD 215
Beat Goes On / Mar '94 / Pinnacle

YEAR
Snowdrops/Birth / Swimming song / Marigold/Harvest home / Red and green / Long shadows / Somewhere along the road / What had you for supper / Saucy sailor / Fabled hare / Deep in the darkest night / Boys of bedlam / Twa corbies
CD ______ PRKCD 20
Park / Oct '93 / Pinnacle

YEAR/HAPPY FAMILIES (2CD Set)
CD Set ______ PRKCD 33
Park / Dec '95 / Pinnacle

Prior, Snooky

IN THIS MESS UP TO MY CHEST
CD ______ ANT 0028CD
Antones / Sep '94 / ADA / Hot Shot

Prism

LIVE 1975-1977
CD ______ SP 97002
Shroom / Aug '97 / Greyhound

METRONOME MELODY
Sunday brunch / Aurora mind / Gemini / Prominence / Where / Sweet memory / Pianissimo / Crystal edge / Velvet nymph / Global communication / Ocean blue
CD ______ SBLCD 5007
Sublime / Apr '96 / Vital

Prison

DISCIPLINE
CD ______ LF 163CD
Lost & Found / Jul '95 / Plastic Head

Prisonaires

JUST WALKIN' IN THE RAIN
Just walking in the rain / Baby please / Dreaming of you / That chick's too young to fry / Softly and tenderly / My god is real / Prisoner's prayer / No more tears / I know / If I were king / I wish / Don't say tomorrow / What'll you do next / Two strangers / What about Frank Clemen / Friends call me a fool / Lucille / I want you / Surleen / All alone and lonely / Rockin' horse
CD ______ BCD 15523
Bear Family / Aug '91 / Direct / Rollercoaster / Swift

JUST WALKIN' IN THE RAIN
CD ______ CPCD 8120
Charly / Aug '95 / Koch

Prisoners

WISERMISERDEMELZA, THE
Go go / Hurricane / Somewhere / Think of me / Love me lies / Tonight / Here come the misunderstood / Dream is gone / For now and forever / Unbeliever / Far away
CD ______ CDWIKD 937
Big Beat / May '90 / Pinnacle

Prisonshake

FAILED TO MENACE
Last time I looked / Either way evil eye / Brilliant idea / Ever and ever / Some chick you fucked / Stumble / Asiento / Cigarette day / (Not without) Grace / Nothing has to hurt / Humor
CD ______ OLE 0852
Matador / Jul '94 / Vital

Pritchard, Bill

DEATH OF BILL POSTERS
CD ______ TMCD 004
Third Mind / Aug '88 / Pinnacle / Third Mind

Pritchard, Peter

STUDIES FOR NEW ZEALAND HARMONIC PIANO VOL.2
CD ______ WCL 11017
White Cloud / Feb '96 / Select

Privat, Jo

MA BOITE A FRISSONS
CD ______ MDCD 321
Media 7 / Nov '96 / Cadillac / Discovery

MANOUCHE PARTIE
CD ______ NTCD 308
Nocturne / Nov '96 / Discovery

Pro Arte Guitar Trio

AMERICA
CD ______ WHL 2099
White Line / Apr '96 / Koch

Pro-Pain

CONTENTS UNDER PRESSURE
CD ______ 86622CIR
CD ______ 86632CIR
Edel / Jun '96 / Pinnacle

FOUL TASTE OF FREEDOM
CD ______ RR 90682
Roadrunner / Aug '96 / PolyGram

TRUTH HURTS
Make war (Not love) / Bad blood / Truth hurts / Put the lights out / Denial / Let sleeping dogs lie / One man army / Down in the dumps / Beast is back / Switchblade knife / Death on the dancefloor / Pound for pound / Foul taste of freedom
CD ______ RR 89852
Roadrunner / Sep '96 / PolyGram

Proby, P.J.

CALIFORNIA LICENSE (Jett Powers)
Bop ting a ling / Blue moon/Cherry pie/Silhouettes / Linda tu / Stranded in the jungle / Tomorrow night / Stagger Lee / Caledonia / Mia amore / Hound dog / Forever my darling / Daddy's home / Rockin' pneumonia and the boogie woogie flu
CD ______ SEECD 390
See For Miles/C5 / Jan '97 / Pinnacle

EP COLLECTION, THE
Hold me / Tips of my fingers / Together / Sweet and tender romance / Somewhere / That means a lot / Lonely teardrop / She cried / Maria / My prayer / Wicked woman / Rockin' pneumonia / It's no good for me / I can't make it alone / Good things are coming my way / Nicky Hoeki / If I ruled the world / Christmas song / Silent night / White Christmas / Try to forget her / Linda Lu / Answer me / Stagger Lee / I love, therefore I am / Whatever will be will be (Que sera sera)
CD ______ SEECD 440
See For Miles/C5 / Jun '96 / Pinnacle

LEGEND
Overture - I'm coming back / Yesterday has gone: *Proby, P.J. & Marc Almond* / Pain in your heart / Devil in red velvet / If I can dream / Rainbow road / Child of clay: *Proby, P.J. & Marc Almond* / Don't / If you love me (really love me) / Crawling back / Suburban opera / When
CD ______ PRMDCD 27
Premier/EMI / Mar '97 / EMI

ROUGH VELVET
Maria / I will / My prayer / To make a big man cry / What kind of fool am I / No other love / I apologise / When I fall in love / With these hands / I will come to you / Some enchanted evening / If I loved you / Rain on snow / I'm coming home / Turn her away / Somewhere / I can't make it alone / Per questo voglio te / What's wrong with my world / When love has passed you by / If I ruled the world / You've come back / We kiss in a shadow / It's your day today / Hold me / I'll go crazy / Just call and I'll be there / Linda Lou / Glory of love / Together / Question / Rockin' pneumonia and the boogie woogie flu / Stagger lee / Zing went the strings of my heart / (I'm afraid) The masquerade is over / Whatever will be will be (Que sera sera) / Hold what you've got / Cuttin' in / Let the water run down / That means a lot / Niki hoeky / I wanna thank you baby / That's the tune / Butterfly high / Day that Lorraine came down / Honey hush / Pretty girls everywhere / She's looking good / You can't come home again (if you leave me now) / Stranded in the jungle / Mary Hopkins never had days like this
CD ______ CDEM 1464
EMI / Oct '92 / EMI

THREE WEEK HERO
Three week hero / Day that Lorraine came down / Little friend / Empty bottles / Reflections (of your face) / Won't be long / Sugar Mama / I have a dream / It's too good to last / New directions / Today I killed a man / Medley
CD ______ BGOCD 87
Beat Goes On / Oct '90 / Pinnacle

Process

WORLD OF FIRE
CD ______ CR 014CD
Conversion / Jul '96 / Plastic Head

Proclaimers

HIT THE HIGHWAY
Let's get married / More I believe / What makes you cry / Follow the money / These arms of mine / Shout shout / Light / Hit the highway / Long long time ago / I want to be a christian / Your childhood / Don't turn out like your mother
CD ______ CDCHR 6066
Chrysalis / Feb '94 / EMI

SUNSHINE ON LEITH
I'm gonna be (500 miles) / Cap in hand / Then I met you / My old friend the blues / Sean / Sunshine on leith / Come on nature / I'm on my way / What do you do / It's Saturday night / Teardrops / Oh Jean
CD ______ CD25CR 18
Chrysalis / Mar '94 / EMI

THIS IS THE STORY
Throw the 'r' away / Over and done with / Misty blue / Part that really matters / (I'm gonna) burn your playhouse down / Letter from America / Sky takes the soul / It broke my heart / First attack / Make my heart fly / Beautiful truth / Joyful Kilmarnock blues
CD ______ CCD 1602
Chrysalis / Mar '93 / EMI

Proctor, Chris

ONLY NOW
Adrenaline / Tap room / Dialogues / Rambler/Kitty's wedding/Langstom's pony / Slickrock lament / Hotspot / Only now / October's window / Anymore
CD ______ CDFF 665
Flying Fish / Mar '97 / ADA / CM / Direct / Roots

STEEL STRING STORIES
CD ______ FF 554CD
Flying Fish / '92 / ADA / CM / Direct / Roots

TRAVELOGUE
CD ______ FF 70633CD
Flying Fish / Apr '94 / ADA / CM / Direct / Roots

Procul Harum

BEST OF PROCUL HARUM, THE
CD ______ BRCD 106
BR Music / Jan '95 / Target/BMG

EXOTIC BIRDS AND FRUIT
Nothing but the truth / Beyond the pale / As strong as Samson / Idol / Thin end of the wedge / Monsieur RMonde / Fresh fruit / Butterfly boys / New lamps for old
CD ______ ESMCD 291
Essential / Oct '95 / BMG

GRAND HOTEL
Grand hotel / Roberts box / Fires (which burn brightly) / For liquorice John / Bring home the bacon / Souvenir of London / TV Caesar / Rum tale / Toujours l'amour
CD ______ ESMCD 290
Essential / Oct '95 / BMG

HOMBURG AND OTHER HATS (The Best Of Procul Harum)
CD ______ ESSCD 295
Essential / Oct '95 / BMG

LONG GOODBYE, THE (The Symphonic Procul Harum) (Various Artists)
Conquistador: *London Symphony Orchestra* / Homburg: *London Symphony Orchestra* / Grand hotel: *London Symphony Orchestra* / Pandora's box: *London Symphony Orchestra* / Repent walpurgis: *London Symphony Orchestra* / Strangers in space: *London Symphony Orchestra* / Simple sister: *London Philharmonic Orchestra* / (You can't) Turn back the page: *London Philharmonic Orchestra* / Butterfly boys: *London Philharmonic Orchestra* / Salty dog: *London Symphony Orchestra* / Whiter shade of pale: *London Symphony Orchestra* / Long goodbye: *Sinfonia Of London*
CD ______ 09026680292
RCA Victor / Feb '96 / BMG

PROCUL HARUM
Whiter shade of pale / Salty dog / Shine on brightly / Wreck of the Hesperus / Long gone geek / Whaling stories / Homburg / Conquistador / Whisky train / Good Captain Clack / Barnyard story / Kaleidoscope
CD ______ CUCD 05
Disky / Oct '94 / Disky / THE

PROCUL'S NINTH
Taking the time / Pandora's box / Fools gold / Uniquiet zone / Final thrust / I keep forgetting / Without a doubt / Piper's tune / Typewriter torment
CD ______ ESMCD 292
Essential / Oct '95 / BMG

SHINE ON BRIGHTLY
Quite rightly so / Shine on brightly / Skip softly my moonbeams / Wish me well / Rambling on / Magdalena / In held 'twas in I / Glimpses of Nirvana / 'Twas tea time at the circus / In the Autumn of my madness / Look to your soul / Grand finale / Whisky train / Dead man's dreams / Still there'll be more / Nothing that I didn't know / About to die / Barnyard story / Piggy pig pig / Whaling stories / Your own choice
CD ______ RR 4667
Repertoire / Jun '97 / Greyhound

SOMETHING MAGIC
Something magic / Skating on thin ice / Wizard man / Mark of the claw / Strangers in space / Worm and the tree (1 to 3)
CD ______ ESMCD 293
Essential / Oct '95 / BMG

WHITER SHADE OF PALE, A
CD ______ RR 4666
Repertoire / Jun '97 / Greyhound

Prodigy

EXPERIENCE
CD ______ XLCD 110
XL / Nov '92 / Warner Music

FAT OF THE LAND
Smack my bitch up / Breathe / Diesel power / Funky shit / Serial thriller / Mindfields / Naraya / Firestarter / Climbatize / Fuel my fire
CD ______ XLCD 121
XL / Jul '97 / Warner Music

MUSIC FOR THE JILTED GENERATION
Intro / Break and enter / Their law / Full throttle / Voodoo people / Speedway / Heat / Poison / No good / One love / 3 kilos / Skylined / Claustrophobic sting
CD ______ XLCD 114
XL / Jul '94 / Warner Music

Product Of Society

SCHIZOPHRENAGENIC
CD ______ M 7020CD
Mascot / Jul '96 / Plastic Head

Product, Clive

FINANCIAL SUICIDE
CD ______ UTIL 002 CD
Utility / Jun '90 / Grapevine/PolyGram

Professionals

PROFESSIONALS
Little boys in blue / Mad house / Just another dream / Kamikaze / 1-2-3 / Crescendo / Mods skins punks / Join the professionals / Has anybody got an alibi / All the way with you / Kick down the doors
CD ______ CDOVD 459
Virgin / Jun '97 / EMI

Professor Frisky

ROUGHER
CD RN 0041
X-Rated / Apr '95 / Jet Star

Professor Longhair

BIG CHIEF
Big chief / Hey little girl / How long has that train been gone / I'm movin' on / Mess around / Medley / Tipitina / Little blues / Her mind is gone / Stagger Lee / Got my mojo working / Rum and coca cola / Mardi gras in New Orleans / Doin' it
CD CPCD 8231
Charly / Nov '96 / Koch

BIG EASY, THE
Big chief / Tipitina / Gone so long / How long has that train been gone / Messin' around / She ain't got no hair / Going to the mardi gras / Big chief (Alt.) / Her mind is gone / Baldhead
CD CDBM 094
Blue Moon / Feb '94 / Cadillac / Discovery / Greensleeves / Jazz Music / Jet Star / TKO Magnum

COMPLETE LONDON CONCERT, THE
Mess around / Hey now baby / Whole lotta lovin' / Go to the Mardi Gras / Bald head / Tipitna / Big chief / Every day I have the blues / Hey little girl / Rockin' pneumonia and the boogie woogie flu
CD JSPCD 202
JSP / Jul '87 / ADA / Cadillac / Direct / Hot Shot / Target/BMG

CRAWFISH FIESTA
CD ALCD 4718
Alligator / May '93 / ADA / CM / Direct

GO TO THE MARDI GRAS
CD WCD 120609
Wolf / Jun '97 / Hot Shot / Jazz Music / Swift

HOUSEPARTY NEW ORLEANS STYLE (The Lost Sessions 1971-1972)
No buts and maybes / Gone so long / She walked right in / Thank you pretty baby / 501 boogie / Tipitina / Gonna leave this town / Cabbagehead / Hey little girl / Big chief / Cherry pie / Junco partner / Everyday I have the blues / G jam / Dr. Professor Longhair
CD ROUCD 2057
Rounder / Jun '95 / ADA / CM / Direct

LAST MARDI GRAS
CD 7567814062
Atlantic / Jun '95 / Warner Music

LIVE IN GERMANY
Stompin' with Fess / Mess around / Big chief / Everyday I have the blues / How long has that train been gone / Bald head (she ain't got no hair) / Whole lotta lovin' / Tipitina / Go to the Mardi Gras / Hey little girl / Got my mojo working
CD 422379
Last Call / Feb '97 / Cargo / Direct / Discovery

LIVE ON THE QUEEN MARY
Tell me pretty baby / Mess around / Everyday I have the blues / Tipitina / I'm movin' on / Mardi Gras in New Orleans / Cry to me / Gone so long / Stagger Lee
CD S21 56844
One Way / Apr '94 / ADA / Direct / Greyhound

NEW ORLEANS PIANO
CD RSACD 808
Sequel / Oct '94 / BMG

NEW ORLEANS PIANO BLUES VOL.2
CD 7567814192
Atlantic / Jun '93 / Warner Music

ROCK 'N ROLL GUMBO
Junco partner / Meet me tomorrow night / Doin' it / How long has that train been gone / Tipitina / Rockin' pnuemonia and the boogie woogie flu / Jambalaya / Mean ol' world / Stagger Lee / Mess around / Hey now baby / (They call me) Professor Longhair
CD 5197462
Verve / Apr '93 / PolyGram

ROCK 'N' ROLL GUMBO
CD DD 3006CD
Dancing Cat / Feb '96 / ADA

RUM AND COKE
Everyday I have the blues / Jambalaya / Rum and coca cola / She walks right in / Shake, rattle and roll / Roberta / Mardi gras in New Orleans / Whole lotta lovin' / Gone so long / Doin' it / How long has that train been gone / Hey now baby / 501 boogie / Junco partner / She ain't got no hair / Gone so long (second conversation)
CD 598109230
Tomato / Aug '93 / Vital

Professor Shehab

EBN E SYNC (Professor Shehab & Loop)
CD WSCD 016
Word Sound Recordings / Feb '97 / Cargo / SRD

Professor's Blues Revue

PROFESSOR STRUT (Professor's Blues Revue & Karen Carroll)
Come on down to the blues bar / I wanna be with you / Professor Strut / You're leaving me / Everything is you / They call it Stormy Monday / Jealous kind of woman / This little light of mine
CD DD 650
Delmark / Mar '97 / ADA / Cadillac / CM / Direct / Hot Shot

Profit, Clarence

SOLO & TRIO SIDES
Don't leave me / There'll be some changes made / I got rhythm / Down home / Tropical nights / Tea for two / Body and soul / Blues / I didn't know what time it was / Dark eyes / Times Square blues / Hot and bothered / Azure / Kazoo moan: *Washboard Serenaders* / Washboards get together: *Washboard Serenaders* / In the middle of a kiss: *Georgia Washboard Stompers* / Every little moment: *Georgia Washboard Stompers*
CD CDMOIR 504
Memoir / Aug '93 / Jazz Music / Target/BMG

Profondo Rosso

TO LIVE AND DIE IN THE UK
CD NEATD 1057
Neat / Apr '97 / Pinnacle

Profound Effect

LASHING OUT
CD LF 156CD
Lost & Found / Aug '95 / Plastic Head

Prohibition

NOBODINSIDE
CD 059012
Distortion / Jun '94 / Plastic Head

Project

FROM ACROSS THIS GRAY LAND NO.3
CD HY 3910033CD
Hyperium / Nov '92 / Cargo / Plastic Head

Project 23

23
CD DOR 54CD
Dorado / Oct '96 / Pinnacle

Project G-7

TRIBUTE TO WES MONTGOMERY VOL.1, A
Impressions / Remembering Wes / Groove yard / Canadian sunset / Fried pies / Road song / Some rain or come shine / Serena / Yesterdays
CD ECD 22049
Evidence / Jul '93 / ADA / Cadillac / Harmonia Mundi

TRIBUTE TO WES MONTGOMERY VOL.2, A
More blues for Wes / Bock to bock / For heaven's sake / Montgomery blue / Finger pickin' / Never again / Polka dots and moonbeams / Samba Wes / West coast blues - three quarters of the house
CD ECD 22051
Evidence / Jul '93 / ADA / Cadillac / Harmonia Mundi

Project Kate

WAY BIRDS FLY
CD EVR 028CD
Equal Vision / May '97 / Plastic Head

Project Pitchfork

CHAKRA: RED
Human crossing / 2069 AD / Malicious delight / Alien crossing / Time / God wrote / Rush / December sadness / Temptation / Tower of lust / Celeste / I'll find my way home
CD SPV 8525942
SPV / Mar '97 / Koch / Plastic Head

EARLY YEARS 1989-1993, THE
CD CD 99943182
SPV / Sep '96 / Koch / Plastic Head

LAM BRAS
CD HY 21030
Hypertension / Nov '92 / ADA / CM / Direct / Total/BMG

RENASCENCE
CD SPV 05522063
SPV / Oct '94 / Koch / Plastic Head

SOULS ISLAND
CD HY 210519
Hypertension / Jul '93 / ADA / CM / Direct / Total/BMG

Project X

STRAIGHT EDGE REVENGE
CD LF 072
Lost & Found / Feb '94 / Plastic Head

Prolapse

BACK SATURDAY
CD LISSCD 8
Lissy's / Nov '95 / SRD

POINTLESS WALKS TO DISMAL PLACES
Serpico / Headless in a beat motel / Surreal Madrid / Doorstop rhythmic bloc / Burgundy spine / Black death ambulance / Chill blown / Hungarian suicide song / Tina this is Matthew stone
CD CDBRED 116
Cherry Red / Oct '94 / Pinnacle

Promise

PROMISE, THE
CD NTHEN 14
Now & Then / Sep '95 / Plastic Head

Promise Ring

HORSE LATITUDES
CD JT 1031
Jade Tree / Feb '97 / Cargo / Greyhound / Plastic Head

Prong

CLEANSING
Another worldly device / Whose fist is this anyway / Snap your fingers, snap your neck / Cut rate / Broken peace / One outnumbered / Out of this misery / No question / Not of this earth / Home rule / Sublime / Test
CD 4747962
Epic / Feb '94 / Sony

FORCE FED/THIRD FROM SUN EP
CD 185422
Southern / Apr '97 / SRD

PRIMITIVE ORIGINS
Disbelief / Watching / Cling to life / Denial / Dreams like that / In my view / Climate control / Persecution
CD 185412
Southern / Apr '97 / SRD

RUDE AWAKENING
Controller / Caprice / Rude awakening / Unfortunately / Face value / Avenue of the finest / Slicing / Without hope / Mansruin / Innocence gone / Dark signs / Close the door / Proud division
CD 4836512
Epic / Jun '96 / Sony

Propaganda

1,2,3,4
Vicious circle / Heaven give me words / Your wildlife / Only one word / How much love / Vicious / Ministry of fear / Wound in my heart / La carne, la morte e il diavolo
CD CDV 2625
Virgin / Apr '92 / EMI

SECRET WISH, A
Dream within a dream / Murder of love / Jewel duel / P machinery / Power force push drive / Dr. Mabuse / Sorry for laughing
CD 4509947492
ZTT / Mar '94 / Warner Music

WISHFUL THINKING (DISTURB DANCES)
Dr. Mabuse / P Machinery / Sorry for laughing / Jewelled / Murder of love
CD 4509947482
ZTT / Mar '94 / Warner Music

Propaghandi

HOW TO CLEAN EVERYTHING
CD FAT 506CD
Fatwreck Chords / Aug '93 / Plastic Head

LESS TALK, MORE ROCK
CD FAT 666CD
Fatwreck Chords / May '96 / Plastic Head

PROPAGANDI/I-SPY (Split CD) (Propagandi & I-Spy)
CD FAT 666CD
Fatwreck Chords / Jul '95 / Plastic Head

Proper Grounds

DOWNTOWN CIRCUS GANG
Black noize / Mind tempest / Joker E double / Jezebel / Money in the depths of a plagueless man / Downtown circus gang / 2 Kill a clown / Backwards mass/Black noize / I'm drowning / D-views man / Nature song / Fuck the blues / Purgatory / Seventh House on the bank / Black noize (reprise)
CD 9362452562
Sire / Mar '93 / Warner Music

Prophecy Of Doom

MATRIX
CD CORE 11CD
Metalcore / Jun '92 / Plastic Head

Prophet, Chuck

BALINESE DANCER
CD WOLCD 1031
China / Feb '93 / Pinnacle

BROTHER ALDO
CD FIRE 33022
Fire / Oct '91 / Pinnacle / RTM/Disc

FEAST OF HEARTS
CD WOLCD 1061
China / May '95 / Pinnacle

HOMEMADE BLOOD
Credit / You been gone / Inside track / Ooh wee / New Year's day / 22 Fillmore / Homemade blood / Whole lot more / Textbook case / K Mart family portrait / 'Til you came along / Parting song
CD COOKCD 114
Cooking Vinyl / Mar '97 / Vital

Prophet, Michael

BULL TALK
CD GRELCD 178
Greensleeves / Nov '92 / Jet Star / SRD

GUNMAN
CD GRELCD 509
Greensleeves / Apr '91 / Jet Star / SRD

LOVE IS AN EARTHLY THING
Rich man, poor man / Instructions / Never fall in love / Baby baby / Reggae music all right / Love is an earthly thing / It's a girl / Pretty face / Fussing and fighting
CD CPCD 8136
Charly / Oct '95 / Koch

SERIOUS REASONING
Fight to the top / Hear I prayer / Turn me loose / Gates of Zion / Praise you jah jah / Love and unity / Warn them / Conscious man / Give thanks / Serious reasoning
CD RRCD 48
Reggae Refreshers / Jul '94 / PolyGram / Vital

Prophets Of Da City

UNIVERSAL SOULJAZ
CD NATCD 54
Nation / Jun '95 / RTM/Disc

Propositions

AFRICANO
CD LHCD 002
Luv n' Haight / Jul '96 / Timewarp

Prosser, Alan

HALL PLACE
Sheepscar beck / Melancholy way / Harry Edward / Leaves of life / Two crows / Cromwell I / Something has got to change / Cromwell II / He feels no pain / Elham valley / Cold winter's night / By Lagan streams / Think of you / Money and love / Raise me up / Empire building
CD RD 001
Rafting Dog / Feb '97 / Direct

Protector

HERITAGE, THE
CD CC 020462CD
Major / Jan '94 / Plastic Head

LOST IN ETERNITY
CD CC 030057CD
Major / Aug '95 / Plastic Head

Proust, Jean-Michel

HARLEM NOCTURNE
CD BB 899
Black & Blue / Apr '97 / Discovery / Koch / Wellard

Prud'Homme, Emile

INOUBLIABLES DE L'ACCORDEON
CD 882422
Music Memoria / Aug '93 / ADA / Discovery

Pryor, Snooky

COUNTRY BLUES
Miss Mattie Mae / Stop teasing me / Mr. Charlie's mule / Mighty long time / Can I be your friend / Break it on down / Dirty news / Wrapped in sin / Time waits on no one / Call the doctor
CD NEBCD 926
Sequel / Jul '97 / BMG

TOO COOL TO MOVE
Keyhole in your door / Can I be your friend / Bottle it up and go / Hold me in your arms / Don't you want to know / Cheatin' and lyin' / Walkin' with Snooky / Fire, Fire / Coal black mare / Lovin' you is killin' me / Boogie twist / My baby been gone / Please be careful
CD ANTCD 0017
Antones / Nov '91 / ADA / Hot Shot

Psyched Up Janis

SWELL
Vanity / I died in my teens / Shudder / Modest us / Subsonic why / Swirl like you / Chandelier / dead green summer / Reddening star / New 5 / They / Fragments
CD 5320312
This Way Up / Apr '96 / PolyGram / SRD

Psychedelic Furs

ALL OF THIS AND NOTHING
President gas / All that money wants / Imitation of Christ / Sister Europe / Love my way / Highwire days / Dumb waiters / Pretty in pink / Ghost in you / Heaven / Heartbreak beat / All of this and nothing
CD ____ 4611102
CBS / Apr '91 / Sony

BBC SESSIONS
CD ____ SFRSCD 003
Strange Fruit / Feb '97 / Pinnacle

COLLECTION, THE
India / Sister Europe / We love you / Flowers / Dumb waiters / Sleep comes down / Mr. Jones / Love my way / Forever now / Danger / Shadow / Pretty in pink / Mack the knife / Heaven / Heartbeat / No release / Angels don't cry
CD ____ CCSCD 308
Castle / Oct '91 / BMG

MIRROR MOVES
Ghost in you / Here come cowboys / Heaven / Heartbeat / My time / Like a stranger / Alice's house / Only a game / Highwire days
CD ____ 4503562
Columbia / May '94 / Sony

TALK, TALK, TALK
Dumb waiters / Pretty in pink / I wanna sleep with you / No tears / Mr. Jones / Into you like a train / It goes on / So run down / All of this and nothing / She is mine
CD ____ 4836632
Columbia / Mar '96 / Sony

Psychedelic Warriors

WHITE ZONE
Frenzzy / Am I fooling / Pipe dreams / Heart attack / Time and space / White zone / Bay of Bengal / Moonbeam / Pulsating pussy / Love in space
CD ____ EBSSCD 113
Emergency Broadcast System / Nov '96 / BMG

Psychic Acoustic Sound Clash

PSYCHO ACOUSTIC SOUND CLASH VOL.1 (Sikorsky & Spooky Manilow)
Hello, greetings and welcome / Rise above the situation / Oskodelidali / Descent (into a permamaze) / Arooga / Zippotrancer / Biopsychic detonator / Glasnost muzak for kosmonauts / Biopsychic resonator / Open f biz niz / Cruisin' through / Psychoterrorist weapon no.2 / Rotordub / Altair 8800 / Corporate love number / Resistance of the sellout / Interlude / Transmission fault / Hypnotic city / Permanent maze / Warm jets / Abandon skip
CD ____ KIP 009
Staalplaat / Feb '97 / Vital/SAM

Psychic TV

AL OR AL
CD ____ DCD 9054
Dossier / Jan '97 / Cargo / SRD

ALLEGORY AND SELF
CD ____ TOPY 038CD
Temple / Aug '91 / Pinnacle / Plastic Head

BEAUTY FROM THEE BEAST
Roman P / Good vibrations / Hex sex / Godstar / Je t'aime / United 94 / Ev ov destruction / SMILE / IC Water / Horror house / Back to reality
CD ____ VICD 006
Visionary/Jettisoundz / Sep '95 / Cargo / Pinnacle / RTM/Disc / THE

BEYOND THEE INFINITE BEAT
Money for E / SMILE / Bliss / Horror house / IC water / Stick insect
CD ____ TOPY 049CD
Temple / Jul '90 / Pinnacle / Plastic Head
CD ____ VICD 004
Visionary/Jettisoundz / Oct '94 / Cargo / Pinnacle / RTM/Disc / THE

CATHEDRAL ENGINE
CD ____ EFA 084672
Dossier / Mar '95 / Cargo / SRD

COLD BLUE TORCH
CD ____ CLP 97112
Cleopatra / Jul '96 / Cargo / Greyhound / Plastic Head / RTM/Disc / SRD

DESCENDING
CD ____ SSCD 001
Semantic / Jan '94 / Plastic Head

ELECTRIC NEWSPAPER VOL.1
CD ____ DCD 9059
Dossier / Jan '97 / Cargo / SRD

ELECTRIC NEWSPAPER VOL.2
CD ____ DCD 9070
Dossier / Jan '97 / Cargo / SRD

FORCE THE HAND OF CHANCE
Just drifting / Terminus / Stolen kisses / Caresse / Guiltless / No go go / Ov power / Message from the temple
CD ____ CLEO 95952
Cleopatra / Jan '97 / Cargo / Greyhound / Plastic Head / RTM/Disc / SRD

HOLLOW COST, A
CD ____ VICD 003
Visionary/Jettisoundz / Sep '97 / Cargo / Pinnacle / RTM/Disc / THE

KONDOLE
CD ____ SR 9332
Silent / Jan '94 / Cargo / Plastic Head

KONDOLE/COPYCAT
CD ____ TOPYCD 46
Temple / Jul '89 / Pinnacle / Plastic Head

LISTEN TODAY
CD ____ SSCDV 01
Semantic / Jan '94 / Plastic Head

LIVE AT THEE BERLIN WALL VOL.1
CD ____ TOPYCD 052 CD
Temple / Sep '90 / Pinnacle / Plastic Head

LIVE AT THEE BERLIN WALL VOL.2
CD ____ TOPYCD 053 CD
Temple / Sep '90 / Pinnacle / Plastic Head

LIVE IN BREGENZ
CD ____ TOPY 020CD
Temple / Jan '91 / Pinnacle / Plastic Head

MEIN GOETTINGEN
CD ____ DCD 9046
Dossier / Jan '97 / Cargo / SRD

MOUTH OF THE NIGHT
Dawn / Ordeal of innocence / Wedding / Rebis / Separation and undressing / Discopravity / Immune zone / Climax
CD ____ VAULT 23
NMC / Oct '96 / Total/Pinnacle

PAGAN DAY
Catalogue / W kiss / Opium / Cold steel / Los Angeles / Iceland / Translucent carriages / Paris / Baby's gone away / Alice / New sexuality / Farewell
CD ____ CLEO 94692
Cleopatra / Jun '94 / Cargo / Greyhound / Plastic Head / RTM/Disc / SRD

PEAK HOUR
CD ____ TOPY 068CD
Temple / Apr '95 / Pinnacle / Plastic Head

RARE AND ALIVE
CD ____ TIBCD 10
NMC / Aug '93 / Total/Pinnacle

SINGLES VOL.1, THE (Hex Sex)
CD ____ CLEO 65082
Cleopatra / Mar '94 / Cargo / Greyhound / Plastic Head / RTM/Disc / SRD

SINGLES VOL.2, THE (Godstar)
CD ____ CLEO 95182
Cleopatra / Apr '95 / Cargo / Greyhound / Plastic Head / RTM/Disc / SRD

SIRENS
Stargods / Skreemer / Reunited / Sirens
CD ____ VICD 005
Cherry Red / Mar '95 / Pinnacle

THEE TRANSMUTION OV MERCURY
CD ____ EFA 084542
Dossier / Mar '94 / Cargo / SRD

THOSE WHO DO NOT
CD ____ CSR 10CD
Cold Spring / May '96 / Plastic Head / RTM/Disc

TOWARDS THEE INFINITE BEAT
Infinite beat / Bliss / Drone zone / SMILE / ICWater / Black rainbow / Short sharp taste ov mistress mix / Horror house / Jigsaw / Alien be-in / Stick insect / Money for E
CD ____ VICD 002
Visionary/Jettisoundz / Sep '94 / Cargo / Pinnacle / RTM/Disc / THE

TRIP RESET
CD ____ CLEO 9665
Cleopatra / Apr '96 / Cargo / Greyhound / Plastic Head / RTM/Disc / SRD

ULTRADRUG
Scoring / Tempted / Swallow / Bloodstream / B on E / Constant high / Back to reality / Eagle has landed / SUCK or know / Tempter / Still B on E / Gone paranoid / Loose nuts
CD ____ VICD 001
Visionary/Jettisoundz / Sep '97 / Cargo / Pinnacle / RTM/Disc / THE

Psychik Warriors Ov Gaia

KRAAK (Remixes)
Kraak
CD ____ KK 131CD
KK / Feb '96 / Plastic Head

OBSIDIAN
Obsidian / Challenge / Patience
CD ____ KK 090CD
KK / Dec '92 / Plastic Head

OV BIOSPHERES AND SACRED GROOVES (A Document Ov New Edge Folk Classics)
Obsidian / Challenge / Key / Linkage / Tides (they turn)
CD ____ KK 065CD
KK / '91 / Plastic Head
CD ____ KK 65CDD
KK / Apr '94 / Plastic Head

RECORD OF BREAKS, A
CD ____ KK 118CD
KK / Oct '95 / Plastic Head

Psycho Bunnies

VAMPIRE MISTRESS
And it hurts / Outsiders / Vampire mistress / Searchin' / I don't want you / Jolene / Fallen angels / Rock against romance / Not with you / He's 17 / Hey big Daddy / Blood and roses
CD ____ RAGECD 110
Rage / Feb '93 / Nervous / TKO Magnum

Psycho Motel

STATE OF MIND
CD ____ RAWCD 108
Raw Power / Apr '96 / Pinnacle

Psychograss

LIKE MINDS
CD ____ SHCD 3851
Sugar Hill / Jul '96 / ADA / CM / Direct / Koch / Roots

PSYCHOGRASS
Love on three levels / Little Jaco / Pleasant pheasant / Whiter shade of pale / Real dragon / Frogs on ice / Song for Kaila / Flanders rock / Dawn chorus / Wedges
CD ____ 01934111322
Windham Hill / Nov '93 / BMG

Psychomuzak

EXSTASIE, THE
Exstasie / Diamond zombie / Far in / Concentrate (over concentration) / Concentration
CD ____ DELECCD 018
Delerium / Feb '95 / Cargo / Pinnacle / Vital

SEND
CD ____ DELECCD 054
Delerium / Jun '97 / Cargo / Pinnacle / Vital

Psychopomps

IN THE SKIN
CD ____ HY 859210595
Hyperium / Jun '94 / Cargo / Plastic Head

Psychosis

SQUIRM
CD ____ MASSCD 018
Massacre / Nov '93 / Plastic Head

Psychotic Waltz

BLEEDING
CD ____ CDVEST 74
Bulletproof / Jul '96 / Pinnacle

INTO THE EVERFLOW
CD ____ CDMVEST 80
Music For Nations / Feb '97 / Pinnacle

MOSQUITO
CD ____ CDVEST 27
Bulletproof / Sep '94 / Pinnacle

SOCIAL GRACE, A
CD ____ CDMVEST 79
Music For Nations / Feb '97 / Pinnacle

Psychotic Youth

BAMBOOZLE
CD ____ SPV 08056922
SPV / May '95 / Koch / Plastic Head

BE IN THE SUN
CD ____ RA 91792
Roadrunner / Mar '92 / PolyGram

Psychotica

PSYCHOTICA
Ice planet hell / Worship / Starfucker love / Little Prince / Stop / Call / Freedom of choice / 180 / Sleep / Flesh and bone / Blue fear / What is God / La chocha / Barcelona / Future cybernation / New man / Awakening
CD ____ 74321384832
American / Sep '96 / BMG

Psychrist

ABYSMAL FIEND
CD ____ WHCD 004
Modern Invasion / Apr '95 / Plastic Head

Psyclone Rangers

BEATIN' ON THE BAT POLE
CD ____ WDO 0362
World Domination / Jul '96 / Pinnacle / RTM/Disc

DEVIL MAY CARE
CD ____ WDOM 015CD
World Domination / Mar '95 / Pinnacle / RTM/Disc

FEEL NICE
I wanna be Jack Kennedy / Spinnin' my head / Christie indecision / I feel nice / Hate noise / Stephen / Heaven / Riot girl / Bigger than a gun / Devil's down there / Perfect engine / You're not Edie Sedgwick
CD ____ WDOM 005CD
World Domination / May '94 / Pinnacle / RTM/Disc

Psyko Disko

PSYKO DISKO
CD ____ AFRCD 5
Flying Rhino / May '97 / Mo's Music Machine / Prime / SRD

Ptacek, Rainer

WORRIED SPIRITS
CD ____ FIENDCD 723
Demon / Oct '93 / Pinnacle

Pterodactyl

SNARE PRESSURE VOL.1
CD ____ DBASSCD 01
Dreambase / Nov '95 / Plastic Head

PTS

CAMPAIGN
Whistle / Firing line / Shadows / Green / Blood / Red fields / Walk with me / Campaign / Sweet dreams / Blue / Again / Restless / Last campaign
CD ____ PTSCD 03
P&C PTS / Jul '97 / Pinnacle

Public Enemy

APOCALYPSE '91 (The Enemy Strikes Black)
Lost at birth / Rebirth / Can't truss it / I don't wanna be called yo niga / How to kill a radio consultant / By the time I get to Arizona / Move / One million bottlebags / More news at 11 / Shut 'em down / Letter to the New York Post / Get the fuck outta Dodge / Bring the noise / Nightrain
CD ____ 5234792
Def Jam / Jul '95 / PolyGram

FEAR OF A BLACK PLANET
Contract on the world love jam / Brothers gonna work it out / 911 is a joke / Incident at 666 FM / Welcome to the terrordome / Meet the G that killed me / Pollywanacraka / Anti-nigger machine / Burn Hollywood burn / Power to the people / Who stole the soul / Fear of a black planet / Revolutionary generation / Can't do nuttin' for ya man / Reggie Jax / Leave this off your fuckin' charts / B side wins again / War at 33 1/3 / Final count of the collision between us and them / Fight the power
CD ____ 5234462
Def Jam / Jul '95 / PolyGram

GREATEST MISSES
Tie goes to the runner / Hit da road Jack / Gett off my back / Gotta do what I gotta do / Air hoodlum / Hazy shade of criminal / Megablast / Louder than a bomb / You're gonna get yours / How to kill a radio consultant / Who stole the soul / Party for your right to fight / Shut 'em down
CD ____ 5234872
Def Jam / Jul '95 / PolyGram

IT TAKES A NATION OF MILLIONS TO HOLD US BACK
Countdown to Armageddon / Bring the noise / Don't believe the hype / Cold lampin' wit' Flavor / Terminator X to the edge of panic / Mind terrorist / Louder than a bomb / Caught, can we get a witness / Show 'em whatcha got / She watch Channel Zero / Night of the living baseheads / Black steel in the hour of chaos / Security of the first world / Rebel without a pause / Prophets of rage / Party for your right to fight
CD ____ 5273582
Def Jam / Jul '95 / PolyGram

MUSE SICK-N-HOUR MESS AGE
Whole lotta love goin' on in the middle of hell / Theater part intro / Give it up / What side you on / Bedlam 13:13 / Stop in the name / What kind of power we got / So what'cha gonna do now / White heaven/ Black hell / Race against time / They used to call it dope / Ain'tnuttinbuttersong / Live and undrugged / Thin line between law and rape / I ain't madd at all / Death of a carjacka / I stand accused / Godd complexx / Hitler day / Harry Allen's interactive super highway phone call to Chuck / Livin' in a zoo
CD ____ 5233622
Def Jam / Aug '94 / PolyGram

YO, BUM RUSH THE SHOW
You're gonna get yours / Sophisticated bitch / Miuzi weighs a ton / Time bomb / Too much posse / Rightstarter (message to a black man) / Public enemy no.1 / MPE / Yo, bum rush the show / Raise the roof / Megablast / Terminator X speaks with his hands
CD ____ 5274412
Def Jam / Jul '95 / PolyGram

Public Image Ltd

ALBUM
FFF / Rise / Fishing / Round / Bags / Home / Ease
CD ____ CDV 2366
Virgin / Feb '86 / EMI

FLOWERS OF ROMANCE
Four enclosed walls / Track 8 / Phenagen / Flowers of romance / Under the house / Hy-

mies him / Banging the door / Go back / Francis massacre
CD CDV 2189
Virgin / Apr '90 / EMI

GREATEST HITS... SO FAR, THE
Public image / Death disco / Memories / Careering / Flowers of romance / This is not a love song / Rise / Home / Seattle / Body / Rules and regulations / Disappointed / Warrior / Don't ask me
CD CDV 2644
Virgin / Oct '90 / EMI

LIVE IN TOKYO
Annalisa / Religion / Low life / Flowers of romance / Death Disco / Solitaire / This is not a love song / Bad life / Banging the door / Under the house
CD VGDCD 3508
Virgin / Apr '92 / EMI

METAL BOX
Albatross / Memories / Swan lake / Poptones / Careering / No birds / Graveyard / Suit / Bad baby / Socialist / Chant / Radio 4
CD MTLCD 1
Virgin / Sep '96 / EMI

PARIS AU PRINTEMPS (PARIS IN SPRING)
Theme / Chant / Careering / Bad baby / Attack / Poptones / Lowlife
CD CDV 2183
Virgin / Apr '90 / EMI

PUBLIC IMAGE
Theme / Religion 1 / Religion 2 / Annalisa / Fodderstompf / Low life / Public image / Attack
CD CDV 2114
Virgin / Jun '88 / EMI

SECOND EDITION
Albatross / Memories / Swan lake / Pop tones / Careering / Socialist / Graveyard / Suit / Bad baby / No birds do sing / Chant / Radio 4
CD CDVD 2512
Virgin / Apr '92 / EMI

THAT WHAT IS NOT
Acid drops / Luck's up / Cruel / God / Covered / Love hope / Unfairground / Think tank / Emperor / Good things
CD CDV 2681
Virgin / Feb '92 / EMI

THIS IS WHAT YOU WANT... THIS IS WHAT YOU GET
Bad life / This is not a love song / Solitaire / Tie me to the length of that / Pardon / Where are you / 1981 / Order of death
CD CDV 2309
Virgin / Apr '90 / EMI

PUC

RECORDED THROUGH WALLS
CD P 0004
Staalplaat / Feb '96 / Vital/SAM

Pucho

BEST OF PUCHO, THE (Pucho & His Latin Soul Brothers)
Cantaloupe island / Vietnam mambo / Soul yamie / Something black / Shuckin' and jivin' / Got myself a good man / Maiden voyage / Strange thing mambo / Groover / Psychedelic pucho / Let love find you / Yambo / Swamp people / Dateline / Cloud 9 / Swing thing / Big stick
CD CDBGPD 069
Beat Goes Public / Feb '93 / Pinnacle

HEAT/JUNGLE FIRE (Pucho & His Latin Soul Brothers)
Heat / Georgia on my mind / Presence of your heart / Psychedelic Pucho / I can't stop loving you / Wanderin' rose / Let love find you / Candied yam / Payin' dues / Friendship train / Got myself a good man / Spokerman / Cloud 9 / Jamilah
CD CDBGPD 047
Beat Goes Public / Nov '92 / Pinnacle

LEGENDS OF ACID JAZZ, THE (Pucho & His Latin Soul Brothers)
CD PRCD 24175
Prestige / Apr '97 / Cadillac / Complete/ Pinnacle

RIP A DIP (Pucho & His Latin Soul Brothers)
Sex machine / Trouble man / Caravan / Slippin' into darkness / Zebula / Pucho's Descarga II / Greasy greens / Milestones / Mambo with me / Hot barbecue / Rip a dip / Good news blues / Guaguanco / Ritmo Nueva York
CD CDBGPD 102
Beat Goes Public / Feb '96 / Pinnacle

Pudding Maker

BOWIE, 72 AND OTHER STUFF
CD ORE 7
Wabana / Jan '97 / Cargo

Puente, Tito

BARBARABATIRI
CD CD 62053
Saludos Amigos / May '94 / Target/BMG

BLUE GARDENIA NEW YORK 1958 (Puente, Tito & Woody Herman)
CD 17031
Laserlight / May '94 / Target/BMG

EL REY (Puente, Tito & His Latin Ensemble)
Oye como va / Autumn leaves / Ran kan kan / Rainfall / Giant steps / Linda Chicana / Medley: Stella by starlight / Delirio / Equinoxe / El rey del timbal
CD CCD 4250
Concord Jazz / Jan '87 / New Note/ Pinnacle

EL REY DE LA SALSA
CD BM 522
Blue Moon / Jan '97 / Cadillac / Discovery / Greensleeves / Jazz Music / Jet Star / TKO Magnum

GOLDEN LATIN JAZZ ALL STARS (Live At The Village Gate)
Intro / New arrival / Sunflower / Afro blue / Skin jam / I loves you Porgy / Oye como va / Milestones
CD 66058021
RMM / Aug '93 / New Note/Pinnacle

GOZA MI TIMBAL
Airegin / Cha cha cha / Pent-up house / Picadillo a lo Puente / All blues / Ode to Cachao / Straight no chaser / Lambada timbales
CD CCD 4399
Concord Picante / Jan '90 / New Note/ Pinnacle

IN SESSION
Teach me tonight / Flight to Jordan / In a heart beat / Un poco mas / Thunderbird / Miami girl / Obsession / Tigimo + 2 / Tritone / Mood's mood for love
CD 66058037
RMM / Jul '94 / New Note/Pinnacle

MAMBO DIABLO (Puente, Tito & His Latin Ensemble)
Mambo diablo / Take five / Lush life / Pick yourself up / Lullaby of Birdland / No pienses asi / China / Eastern joy dance
CD CCD 4283
Concord Picante / Sep '86 / New Note/ Pinnacle

MAMBO GOZON
CD CD 62008
Saludos Amigos / Oct '93 / Target/BMG

MAMBO OF THE TIMES
Things to come / Jitterbug waltz / Mambo king / Passion flower / Baqueteo / Japan mambo / Mambo of the times / If you could see me now / Best is yet to come / El Titan
CD CCD 4499
Concord Jazz / Mar '92 / New Note/ Pinnacle

MAMBURAMA (Puente, Tito & His Orchestra)
Mambo tipico / Mambo Inn / Mambolino / Mambo rumbon / Mambo rama / Mambo lenko / Ran kan kan / Mambo with memambo gallego / Que lindo el mambo / Mambiando / Titoro / La guira / Este tumbao / Mambo suavecito / Bamaram bam bam / Penjamo / El ray del timbal / Esto es coco camina camaron / Tatalibaba / Guajeo en dominate / Picao y tostao / Coco seco
CD CDCHARLY 253
Charly / Oct '91 / Koch

MASTER TIMBALERO (Puente, Tito & His Latin Ensemble)
Old arrival / Enchantment / Sakura / Azu ki ki / Espresso por favor / Nostalgia in Times Square / Chow mein / Creme de menthe / Sun goddess / Vaya puente / Master Timbaleo / Bloomdido
CD CCD 4594
Concord Picante / May '94 / New Note/ Pinnacle

NIGHT BEAT/MUCHO PUENTE
Live a little (let's face it) / Late late scene / Midnight lament (minor moods) / Night hawk (minor moods) / Night hawk (coconut and rice) / Malibu beat / Mambo beat / Night ritual / Floozie / Poor butterfly / Lullaby of the leaves / Duerme (time was) / Noche de ronda (be mine tonight) / Ecstasy / Tea for two / Son de la loma / Tito's guajira / Almendra / La ola marina / Un poquito de tu amor / What a difference a day makes / Night beat (mono) / Emerald beach / Carioca (mono)
CD BCD 15686
Bear Family / May '93 / Direct / Rollercoaster / Swift

ON BROADWAY (Puente, Tito & His Latin Ensemble)
TP's special / Sophisticated lady / Bluesette / Soul song / On Broadway / Maria Cervantes / Jo je ti / First light
CD CCD 4193
Concord Picante / Sep '88 / New Note/ Pinnacle

PARE COCHERO
CD CCD 508
Caney / Nov '95 / ADA / Discovery

PUENTE GOES JAZZ
Whats this thing called love / Tiny-not Ghengis / What are you doin' honey / Lotus land / Lucky dog / Birdland after dark / That's a Puente / Yesterdays / Terry cloth / Tito'in
CD 07863661482
Bluebird / Apr '93 / BMG

ROYAL'T
Donna Lee / Tokyo blues / Virgo / Moanin' / Stompin' at the Savoy / Enquentro / Mambo gallego / Second wind / Royal't / Slam bam
CD CCD 4553
Concord Picante / Jun '93 / New Note/ Pinnacle

SALSA MEETS JAZZ
CD CCD 4354
Concord Jazz / Sep '88 / New Note/ Pinnacle

SENSATION
Fiesta a la king / Guajira for cal / 'Round midnight / Que sensacion / Jordu / Cantigo en la distancia / Morning / Spain
CD CCD 4301
Concord Picante / Apr '87 / New Note/ Pinnacle

SPECIAL DELIVERY
Be bop / Misterioso / Point East memories / Stablemates / On Green Dolphin Street / Autumn in Rome / Venus de Milo / Tito's colada / Barbara / Where you at / Flying home
CD CCD 4732
Concord Picante / Nov '96 / New Note/ Pinnacle

TITO MEETS MACHITO - THE MAMBO KINGS (Puente, Tito & Machito)
Mamboscope: *Machito & His Afro-Cubans* / Relax and mambo: *Machito & His Afro-Cubans* / Te he venido a buscar: *Machito & His Afro-Cubans/Graciela* / Sentimental mambo: *Machito & His Afro-Cubans* / Que bonito es Puerto Rico: *Machito & His Afro-Cubans/Graciela* / Feeding the chickens: *Machito & His Afro-Cubans* / Consternacion: *Machito & His Afro-Cubans* / Adivinanza: *Machito & His Afro-Cubans/Graciela* / El jamaiquino: *Machito & His Afro-Cubans* / Me miraste ye te mire: *Machito & His Afro-Cubans/Graciela* / Arollando: *Puente, Tito & Vicentico Valdes* / Pito Joe: *Puente, Tito* / Friquilandia: *Puente, Tito* / El yoyo: *Puente, Tito & Graciela* / Por tu amor: *Puente, Tito* / Caravan: *Puente, Tito* / Donkey serenade: *Puente, Tito* / Ricci Ricci: *Puente, Tito* / Undecided: *Puente, Tito* / Plaza stomp: *Puente, Tito*
CD CDHOT 612
Charly / Dec '96 / Koch

TOP PERCUSSION/DANCE MANIA
Elequana / Bragada / Obatala yeza / Alaumba chemache / Oguere madeo / Obraricosu / Four by two, part 1 / Conga alegre / Ti mon bo / Mon-ti / Hot timbales / El cayuco / Complication / Mambo gozon / Saca tu mujer / Liego mijan / Agua limpia todo / Cuando te vea / Mi chiquita quiere bembe / 3-D mambo / Varsity drag / Hong Kong mambo / Estoy siempre junto a ti
CD BCD 15687
Bear Family / May '93 / Direct / Rollercoaster / Swift

UN POCO LOCO (Puente, Tito & His Latin Ensemble)
Un poco loco / Swingin' shepherd blues / Alma con alma / El timbalon / Chang / Machito forever / Prelude to a kiss / Killer Joe / Triton
CD CCD 4329
Concord Picante / Oct '87 / New Note/ Pinnacle

YAMBEQUE
Yambeque / Guataca / Suave asi / Esperame / Delisse / Estoy siempre junto a ti / Plaza stomp / El yoyo / Oye lo que tiene el mambo / Ricci Ricci / Friquilandia / Arrollando / Cuban mambo / Guaguanco en tropicana / Preparen candela / Mambo en blues
CD CD 62081
Saludos Amigos / Jan '96 / Target/BMG

Puff Daddy

NO WAY OUT
CD 8612730122
Puff Daddy / Jul '97 / BMG

Puffball

SIX PACK TO GO
CD BHR 058CD
Burning Heart / Jun '97 / Plastic Head

Pugliese, Osvaldo

LA YUMBA
CD BMT 010
Blue Moon / Jul '97 / Cadillac / Discovery / Greensleeves / Jazz Music / Jet Star / TKO Magnum

Pui-Yeun, Lui

MUSIC OF THE PIPA
CD 7559720852
Nonesuch / Jan '95 / Warner Music

Puig, Cheo Belen

ME HAN DICHO 1937-1940
CD TCD 078
Tumbao Cuban Classics / Jan '97 / Discovery

Puissance

LET US LEAD
CD CMI 42
Cold Meat Industry / Jun '96 / Plastic Head / RTM/Disc

Pukwana, Dudu

COSMICS CHAPTER 90
Mra khali / Hamba (go away) / Big apple / Cosmics / Blues for Nick / Zwelistsha
CD AHUM 005
Ah-Um / Aug '90 / Cadillac / New Note/ Pinnacle

IN THE TOWNSHIPS (Pukwana, Dudu & Spear)
Baloyi / Ezilalini / Zukude / Sonia / Angel Nemali / Nobomyu / Sekela khuluma
CD CDEWV 5
Earthworks / '87 / EMI

Pulindo, Roberto

ROBERTO PULINDO Y LOS CLASICOS
Cuanto te debo / De garza a la palmita / Estoy sufriendo por ti / Sonia / Mi pequenito / Schottische / Mejor me voy / Una rosa para mi chica / Senorita cantinera / Los pollos
CD EDCD 7040
Easydisc / Jul '97 / Direct

Pullen, Don

CAPRICORN RISING
CD 1200042
Black Saint / Oct '90 / Cadillac / Harmonia Mundi

LIFE LINE (Pullen, Don Quartet)
Great escape, or run John Henry run / Seriously speaking / Soft seas / Nature's children / Protection / Newcomer; seven years later
CD CDSJP 154
Timeless Jazz / Jan '92 / New Note/ Pinnacle

RESOLUTION (Pullen, Don & H. Bluiett)
CD 1200142
Black Saint / Oct '90 / Cadillac / Harmonia Mundi

SIXTH SENSE, THE (Pullen, Don Quintet)
CD BSR 0088
Black Saint / '86 / Cadillac / Harmonia Mundi

Pullen, Stacey

DJ KICKS (Various Artists)
CD K7 049CD
Studio K7 / Oct '96 / Prime / RTM/Disc

Pulley

ESTEEM DRIVEN ENGINE
CD 64702
Epitaph / Oct '96 / Pinnacle / Plastic Head

Pulp

COUNTDOWN 1992-1983 (2CD Set)
CD Set NTMCDD 521
Nectar / Mar '96 / Pinnacle

DIFFERENT CLASS
Mis-shapes / Pencil skirt / Common people / I-spy / Disco 2000 / Live bed show / Something changed / Sorted for E's and wizz / FEELINGCALLEDLOVE / Underwear / Monday morning / Bar Italia
CD CID 8041
Island / Oct '95 / PolyGram

FREAKS
CD FIRECD 5
Fire / Apr '93 / Pinnacle / RTM/Disc

HIS 'N' HERS
Joyriders / Lipgloss / Acrylic afternoons / Have you seen her lately / She's a lady / Happy endings / Do you remember the first time / Pink glove / Someone like the moon / David's last summer
CD CID 8025
Island / Apr '94 / PolyGram

INTRO - THE GIFT RECORDINGS
Space / OU (12" Mix) / Babies / Styloroc (Nites of suburbia) / Razzamatazz / Sheffield: Sex city / Inside Susan: A story in 3 songs
CD IMCD 159
Island / Oct '93 / PolyGram

IT
My lighthouse / Wishful thinking / Joking aside / Boats and trains / Blue girls / Love love / In many ways / Looking for life / Everybody's problem / There was
CD REFIRECD 15
Fire / Nov '94 / Pinnacle / RTM/Disc

MASTERS OF THE UNIVERSE
CD ________ **FIRECD 36**
Fire / Jun '94 / Pinnacle / RTM/Disc

SEPARATIONS
CD ________ **FIRE 33026**
Fire / Oct '91 / Pinnacle / RTM/Disc

Pulse

SURFACE TENSIONS
CD ________ **HHCD 007**
Harthouse / Aug '94 / Mo's Music Machine / Prime / Vital

Pulsinger, Patrick

PORNO
CD ________ **EFA 122752**
Disko B / May '95 / SRD

Punaruu, Tamarii

KAINA MUSIC TRADITION
CD ________ **S 65812**
Manuiti / Feb '93 / Harmonia Mundi

Puncture

PUNCTURE
CD ________ **CDVEST 29**
Bulletproof / Aug '94 / Pinnacle

Pungent Stench

BEEN CAUGHT BUTTERING
CD ________ **NB 052CD**
Nuclear Blast / Jan '92 / Plastic Head

CLUB MONDO BIZARRE
CD ________ **NB 079CD**
Nuclear Blast / Mar '94 / Plastic Head

DIRTY RHYMES AND PYSCOTRONIC
CD ________ **NB 078CD**
Nuclear Blast / Jun '93 / Plastic Head

FOR GOD YOUR SOUL
CD ________ **842973**
Nuclear Blast / Aug '90 / Plastic Head

Punishable Act

INFECT
CD ________ **N 02462**
Noise / Sep '94 / Koch

PUNISHABLE ACT
PA / Running man / Scum / With what right / I don't need no / Two faces / Full of hate / Have a gun will shoot / More than a word / Why / Sign of a dead fellow / Hardcore preacher
CD ________ **N 02672**
Noise / Jun '96 / Koch

Punishers

BEAT ME
CD ________ **RUMBCD 015**
Rumble / Aug '92 / Nervous / Pinnacle

Punishment Of Luxury

LAUGHING ACADEMY
Puppet life / Funk me / Message / All white jack / Obsession / Radar bug/Metropolis / British baboon / Babalon / Excess bleeding heart / Laughing academy / Secrets / Brain bomb / Engine of excess / Jellyfish
CD ________ **DOJOCD 147**
Dojo / Sep '93 / Disc

REVOLUTION BY NUMBERS
CD ________ **OVER 66CD**
Overground / Aug '97 / Shellshock/Disc / SRD

Pura Fe & Ulali

CAUTION TO THE WIND
CD ________ **SHCD 5013**
Shanachie / May '95 / ADA / Greensleeves / Koch

Purdie, Bernard

MASTER DRUMMERS VOL.1
CD ________ **URCD 002**
Ubiquity / Jul '96 / Cargo / Timewarp

MASTER DRUMMERS VOL.2
CD ________ **URCD 010**
Ubiquity / Jul '96 / Cargo / Timewarp

PURDIE GOOD/SHAFT
Cold sweat / Montego bay / Purdie good / Wasteland / Everybody's talkin' / You turn me on / Shaft / Way back home / Attica / Them changes / Summer melody / Butterfingers
CD ________ **CDBGPD 050**
Beat Goes Public / Mar '93 / Pinnacle

SOUL TO JAZZ (Purdie, Bernard & WDR Big Band)
Moanin' / Superstition / Iko Iko / Senor blues / When a man loves a woman / Freedom jazz dance / Sidewinder / Brother where are you / Wade in the water / Work song / Land of 1000 dances / Gimme some lovin' / Moanin'
CD ________ **92422**
Act / Oct '96 / New Note/Pinnacle

SOUL TO JAZZ VOL.2
Motherless child / New Orlean's strutt / La Place Street / Nobody knows / Jubilation / Joshua / Mr. Magic / Theme from 'Shaft' / Amen
CD ________ **ACT 92532**
Act / Sep '97 / New Note/Pinnacle

Pure Gold

PURE GOLD
CD ________ **MAUCD 635**
Mau Mau / Apr '93 / Pinnacle

YOU LIGHT UP MY LIFE
CD ________ **GBCD 001**
Pure Gold / Nov '95 / Jet Star

Pure Morning

2 INCH HELIUM BUDDHA
CD ________ **SCANCD 21**
Radarscope / Jun '96 / Pinnacle

Purejoy

UNSUNG
CD ________ **FLY 0022**
Flydaddy/Blue Rose / Jun '96 / 3mv/Vital

Puressence

PURESSENCE
Near distance / I suppose / Mr. Brown / Understanding / Fire / Traffic jam in Memory Lane / Casting lazy shadows / You're only trying to twist my arm / Every house on every street / India
CD ________ **CID 8046**
Island / Apr '96 / PolyGram

Puricelli, Marc

MELTING POINT
Plunge / Prelude / So far away / Melting point / Notturno / Island chain / Zambito / St. Louise / So sweet is you / Brave moon / UC / Nothing changes too
CD ________ **5220582**
Limelight / Mar '94 / PolyGram

Purim, Flora

BUTTERFLY DREAMS
CD ________ **OJCCD 315**
Original Jazz Classics / Feb '92 / Complete/Pinnacle / Jazz Music / Wellard

FLIGHT, THE
Aviao / Perfume de cebola / My song for you / Maca / Branco e preto / Meu mestre coracao / Rainha da noite / Tarde / Radio experiencia / Dois irmaos / Dona olympia / Finale
CD ________ **BW 048**
B&W / Nov '96 / New Note/Pinnacle / SRD / Vital/SAM

LOVE REBORN
CD ________ **FCD 6209095**
Fantasy / Nov '86 / Jazz Music / Pinnacle / Wellard

MILESTONE MEMORIES
Moon Dreams / Vera Cruz / Windows / Cravo E Canela / What can I say / Casa Forte / Samba Michel / Open your eyes you can fly / Overture
CD ________ **CDBGP 1008**
Beat Goes Public / Mar '93 / Pinnacle

SPEED OF LIGHT
Secret from the sea / Wings / Portal da cor / Rhythm runner / Light as my flo' / Mojave crossing / O canto da sereira / This world is mine / Overture / Goddess of thunder / What you see / Maiasta
CD ________ **BW 044**
B&W / Nov '96 / New Note/Pinnacle / SRD / Vital/SAM

STORIES TO TELL
CD ________ **OJCCD 619**
Original Jazz Classics / Feb '92 / Complete/Pinnacle / Jazz Music / Wellard

Purna Das Baul

BAULS OF BENGAL
CD ________ **CRAW 11**
Crammed World / Jan '96 / New Note/ Pinnacle

Purnell, Alton

ALTON PURNELL/KEITH SMITH'S CLIMAX JAZZ BAND (Purnell, Alton & Keith Smith)
CD ________ **BCD 264**
GHB / Aug '95 / Jazz Music

Purple Helmets

RIDE AGAIN
Brand new Cadillac / I'm crying / Rosalyn / She's not there / First I look at the purse / Get yourself home / Oh pretty woman / Homework / Don't you like what I do / Money / Under the sun / Baby let me take you home / She la la / Baby / Everything's alright
CD ________ **422283**
New Rose / Jan '95 / ADA / Direct / Discovery

Purple Outside

MYSTERY LANE
CD ________ **NAR 052CD**
New Alliance / Sep '90 / Plastic Head

Purple Penguin

DE-TUNED
Tombstone / Only you / Mountain / Tribhuwan / No action / New Harlem / Mute noise / Razor / Passion / So high / Pressure / Memphis / End theme
CD ________ **COTCD 004**
Cup Of Tea / Feb '97 / Vital

Purrone, Tony

IN THE HEATH ZONE (Purrone, Tony Quartet)
CD ________ **SCCD 31410**
Steeplechase / Apr '97 / Discovery / Impetus

Pursey, Jimmy

CODE BLACK
CD ________ **AICD 003**
A+I / May '97 / Koch / Scratch/BMG

REVENGE IS NOT THE PASSWORD
CD ________ **3012832**
Arcade / Jul '97 / Discovery

Pursuit Of Happiness

WONDERFUL WORLD OF...
CD ________ **51010**
Iron / May '97 / Greyhound

Purtenance

MEMBER OF IMMORTAL DAMNATION
CD ________ **DL 011CD**
Drowned / Jun '93 / Plastic Head

Puschnig, Wolfgang

ALPINE ASPECTS
Root march / Little stars dancing and jumping / We reach for the sky / First meeting / Strange march / March of the lost illusion / Like a song, like a dance / Loony tune
CD ________ **5112042**
Amadeo / Feb '92 / PolyGram

PIECES OF A DREAM
Long way from home / Second Heaven / In another time / Far horizon / Long gone / I wish to be there / Fourth man / Fremd bin ich eingezogen / Little suite / Balsam project / Long remembered / It's quiet around the lake
CD ________ **8373222**
Amadeo / Oct '94 / PolyGram

Push

CAN'T FIGHT IT
CD ________ **PRCD 001**
Push / Jul '96 / Timewarp

Push

DROWNING
Drowning / Divided / Purity / Betrayed / Killing me / Die for you / Suicide ride / Worthless / Choked / Alone
CD ________ **SCCD 2**
Street Culture / Jun '97 / Else

Push Pull

PUSH PULL
CD ________ **SONG 1001**
Active / Jun '97 / ReR Megacorp

Pusherman

FLOORED
CD ________ **IGNCD 1**
Ignition / Sep '96 / 3mv/Vital

Pushmipulyu

TWO HANDS
CD ________ **WM 1**
Wolly Mammoth / Jun '97 / Timewarp

Pussy

PUSSY
CD ________ **HBG 123/5**
Background / Apr '94 / Background / Greyhound

Pussy Crush

TORMENTING THE EMOTIONALLY FRAIL
Mindless / Postcard / She ain't the one / Kill you / Do it / Beat your heart out / Witch bitch / Ghost of am empty bottle / Irrespectable / Fun, fun, fun / Loop / Come back to me / Grunk / Mainline / That girl / Roof surfing
CD ________ **LADIDA 039CD**
La-Di-Da / Nov '94 / Vital

Pussy Galore

CORPSE LOVE
CD ________ **HUT 013CD**
Hut / Feb '92 / EMI

RIGHT NOW
CD ________ **PRODCD 19**
Product Inc. / Feb '88 / Vital

Pussycat

STAR PORTRAIT: PUSSYCAT
CD ________ **16028**
Laserlight / '93 / Target/BMG

Pussycat Trash

NON-STOP HIP ACTION
CD ________ **SLAMPT 25CD**
Slampt Underground / Mar '95 / Shellshock/Disc

Pustit Musis

PUSTIT MUSIS
CD ________ **R 0007**
Rachot / Jun '97 / ReR Megacorp

Putrefy Factor 7

TOTAL MIND COLLAPSE
CD ________ **EFA 125232**
Celtic Circle / Aug '95 / SRD

Putrid Offal

EXULCERATION
CD ________ **CDAB 002**
Adipocre / Feb '94 / Plastic Head

PVC

PVC AFFAIR
CD ________ **DIVINE 006CD**
Taste / Nov '95 / Plastic Head / SRD

PVH

WHITE
CD ________ **CDCB 0201**
Carbon Base / Jun '95 / Plastic Head

Pyewackett

MAN IN THE MOON DRINKS CLARET, THE
CD ________ **MWCD 4007**
Music & Words / Jan '95 / ADA / Direct

Pygmy Archers Chorus

POLYPHONY OF THE DEEP RAIN FOREST (Music Of The Ituri Pygmies)
CD ________ **VICG 50152**
JVC World Library / Mar '96 / ADA / CM / Direct

Pylon

CHAIN
CD ________ **SKYCD 2020**
Sky / Sep '94 / Greyhound / Koch / Vital/ SAM

Pylon King

CITIZEN Z COUNTDOWN TO THE CONTINUUM
CD ________ **FIRECD 050**
Fire / Jul '95 / Pinnacle / RTM/Disc

Pyogenesis

LOVE NATION SUGARHEAD
CD ________ **NB 205CD**
Nuclear Blast / Nov '96 / Plastic Head

SWEET X RATED NOTHINGS/WAVES OF EROTICA
CD ________ **NB 240CD**
Nuclear Blast / Apr '97 / Plastic Head

SWEET X-RATED NOTHINGS
CD ________ **NB 1132**
Nuclear Blast / Oct '94 / Plastic Head

TWINALEBLEBLOOD
CD ________ **NB 136CD**
Nuclear Blast / Nov '95 / Plastic Head

Pyramid

OUT OF CONTROL
Star / Wasted time / Good time gals / Ambition / Out of control / Wiseman / Is this life / Call of the Gods / Hells bells
CD ________ **PYRA 01**
Scorpion / Jul '96 / Scorpion

Pyrexia

SERMON OF MOCKERY
CD ________ **DC 017**
Drowned / Apr '94 / Plastic Head

Pyrolator

WUNDERLAND
CD ________ **EFA 037632**
Atatak / Feb '94 / SRD

Q65

AFGHANISTAN
CD ______ CDP 1002DD
Pseudonym / Jun '97 / Greyhound

Q-Moog

ARC OF BLUENESS (2CD Set)
CD Set ______ SSR 191
Crammed Discs / Aug '97 / Grapevine/ PolyGram / New Note/Pinnacle / Prime / RTM/Disc

Q-Squad

PSYCHED
CD ______ N 02562
Noise / Jul '95 / Koch

Q-Tex

INTO THE LIGHT
Do you want me / Natural high / Heart of Asia / Lies / Deliverance / Water of life / Power of love / Symphonic / Believe / Promised me / Let the love / Pressure / To-night / Dreams / Into the light
CD ______ THIRD 11CD
23rd Precinct / Jul '97 / Pinnacle / Prime

Q-Tips

LIVE AT LAST (Q-Tips & Paul Young)
CD ______ RPM 102
RPM / Oct '92 / Pinnacle

Qasimov, Alim

MUGHAM OF AZERBAIDJAN, THE
CD ______ C 560013
Ocora / Sep '93 / ADA / Harmonia Mundi

QFX

ALIEN CHILD
CD ______ EPICD 9
Epidemic / Feb '97 / Grapevine/PolyGram / Mo's Music Machine

FREEDOM
CD ______ EPICD 3
Epidemic / Apr '95 / Grapevine/PolyGram / Mo's Music Machine

Qkumba Zoo

WAKE UP AND DREAM
CD ______ 07822189312
RCA / Feb '97 / BMG

Qntal

QNTAL 3
CD ______ EFA 155912
Gymnastic / Dec '95 / SRD

Quakes

LIVE IN TOKYO
CD ______ NERCD 084
Nervous / Feb '96 / Nervous / TKO Magnum

NEW GENERATION
New generation / How brave are you / Stranded in the streets / Anonymous / Sub-urbia / Dateless night / Wonderin' / Behind the wheel / It's gone / Your castle / Gothic girl / Now I wanna / Lover's curse
CD ______ NERCD 073
Nervous / Sep '93 / Nervous / TKO Magnum

VOICE OF AMERICA
CD ______ NERDCD 058
Nervous / Aug '90 / Nervous / TKO Magnum

Quarterman, Sir Joe

FREE SOUL
CD ______ CPCD 8079
Charly / Mar '95 / Koch

Quarteto Em Cy

SING VINICIUS DE MORAES
CD ______ KAR 984
IMP / Oct '96 / ADA / Discovery

Quartette

QUARTETTE
CD ______ RTMCD 79
Round Tower / Nov '96 / Avid/BMG

Quartette Indigo

QUARTETTE INDIGO
Ragtime dance / Naima / Andromeda / Footprints / Efua / Staurday night on Beale Street / Come Sunday / Ladies blues / Ruby my dear / Lift every voice and sing
CD ______ LCD 15362
Landmark / Sep '94 / New Note/Pinnacle

Quartette Slavei

BULGARIAN POLYPHONY VOL.4
CD ______ VICG 53442
JVC World Library / Mar '96 / ADA / CM / Direct

Quartz

RESURRECTION
CD ______ NM 012CD
Neat Metal / Oct '96 / Pinnacle

Quatre

EARTHCAKE
CD ______ LBLC 6539
Label Bleu / Jan '92 / New Note/Pinnacle

Quatro, Suzi

GOLD COLLECTION, THE
Can the can / 48 crash / Devil Gate Drive / Daytona demon / All shook up / Keep a knockin' / I may be too young / I bit off a bit more than I could chew / Wake up little Susie / Heartbreak hotel / Love hurts / Don't break my heart / I've never been in love / Mama's boy / Race is on / If you can't give me love
CD ______ CDGOLD 1004
EMI Gold / Mar '96 / EMI

IF YOU KNEW SUZI
Don't change my luck / Tired of waiting / Suicide / Evie / Race is on / If you can't give me love / Breakdown / Non citizen / Rock 'n' roll hoochie coo / Wiser than you
CD ______ 16159
Laserlight / Apr '96 / Target/BMG

ROCK HARD
Rock Hard / Glad all over / Love is ready / State of mind / Woman cry / Lipstick / Hard headed / Ego in the night / Lonely is the hardest / Lay me down / Wish upon me
CD ______ CSAPCD 102
Connoisseur Collection / Jun '90 / Pinnacle

WILD ONE (The Greatest Hits)
Can the can / 48 crash / Daytona demon / Devil gate drive / Too big / Wild one / Your mama won't like me / I bit off more than I could chew / I may be too young / Tear me apart / Roxy roller / If you can't give me love / Race is on / She's in love with you / Mama's boy / I've never been in love / Rollin' stone / All shook up / Keep a knockin' / Wake up little Susie
CD ______ CZ 281
EMI / Apr '90 / EMI

WILD ONE, THE (Classic Quatro)
CD ______ RE 21022
Razor & Tie / Jul '96 / Koch

Quays, Ronan

EBBING WINGS OF WISDOM
CD ______ DNDC 008CD
De Nova Da Capo / Oct '96 / World Serpent

Quazar

ZODIAC TRAX
Sunflower / Wanderlight / Khedan / Moonflower / Time / Gemini / Arrow / Rhythm dog / Zodiac trax / USA / Deeper and higher / 110
CD ______ STAR 006CD
Seven Stars / Jun '95 / Vital

Qubism

QUBISM
CD ______ EMIT 2294
Time Recordings / Sep '94 / Pinnacle

Que

GOOD LOVE (Que & Ruby Turner)
CD ______ BCQCD 1001
Black Current / Oct '92 / Grapevine/ PolyGram

Quebec, Ike

BALLADS
Nacy with the laughing face / Born to be blue / Man love / Lover man / Willow weep for me / If I could be one hour with you / Everything happens to me / Imagination / There is no greater love
CD ______ CDP 8566902
Blue Note / Jul '97 / EMI

BLUE AND SENTIMENTAL
Blue and sentimental / Minor impulse / Don't take your love from me / Blues for Charlie / Like / Count every star / That old black magic / It's all right with me
CD ______ CDP 7840982
Blue Note / Mar '95 / EMI

Quebec Pure Laine

MUSIQUE TRADITIONELLE
CD ______ PEML 0012CD
Peml / Apr '96 / ADA

Queen

BRIAN MAY TALKS
CD ______ BMTALK 1
UFO / Nov '96 / Pinnacle

DAY AT THE RACES, A
Long away / Millionaire waltz / You and I / Somebody to love / White man / Good old fashioned lover boy / Drowse / Teo torriate / Tie your mother down / You take my breath away
CD ______ CDPCSD 131
Parlophone / Sep '93 / EMI

DRAGON ATTACK (A Tribute To Queen) (Various Artists)
Another one bites the dust / Tie your Mother down / Sheer heart attack / We are the champions / We will rock you / I want it all / Kep yourself alive / Get down, make love / One vision / Save me / It's late / I'm in love with my car
CD ______ REVXD 209
Revolver / Dec '96 / Revolver / Sony
CD ______ DERCD 091
Cargo / Nov '96 / Cargo

FREDDIE MERCURY TALKS
CD ______ FMTALK 1
UFO / Nov '96 / Pinnacle

GAME, THE
Play the game / Dragon attack / Another one bites the dust / Need your loving tonight / Crazy little thing called love / Rock it (prime jive) / Don't try suicide / Sweet sister / Coming soon / Save me
CD ______ CDPCSD 134
Parlophone / Feb '94 / EMI

GREATEST HITS VOL.1
Bohemian rhapsody / Another one bites the dust / Killer queen / Fat bottomed girls / Bicycle race / You're my best friend / Don't stop me now / Save me / Crazy little thing called love / Now I'm here / Good old fashioned lover boy / Play the game / Flash / Seven seas of Rhye / We will rock you / We are the champions / Somebody to love
CD ______ CDPCSD 141
Parlophone / Jun '94 / EMI

GREATEST HITS VOL.1 & 2
Bohemian rhapsody / Another one bites the dust / Killer queen / Fat bottomed girls / Bicycle race / You're my best friend / Don't stop me now / Save me / Crazy little thing called love / Somebody to love / Now I'm here / Good old fashioned lover boy / Play the game / Flash / Seven seas of Rhye / We will rock you / We are the champions / Kind of magic / Under pressure: *Queen & David Bowie* / Radio gaga / I want it all / I want to break free / Innuendo / It's a hard life / Breakthru' / Who wants to live forever / Headlong / Miracle / I'm going slightly mad / Invisible man / Hammer to fall / Friends will be friends / Show must go on / One vision
CD Set ______ CDPCSD 161
Parlophone / Oct '94 / EMI

GREATEST HITS VOL.2
Kind of magic / Under pressure: *Queen & David Bowie* / I want it all / I want to break free / Innuendo / Breakthru' / Who wants to live forever / Headlong / Miracle / I'm going slightly mad / Invisible man / Hammer to fall / Friends will be friends / Show must go on
CD ______ CDPMTV 2
Parlophone / Oct '91 / EMI

HOT SPACE
Staying power / Dancer / Back chat / Body language / Action this day / Put out the fire / Life is real (song for Lennon) / Calling all girls / Las palabras de amor (the words of love) / Cool cat / Under pressure: *Queen & David Bowie*
CD ______ CDPCSD 135
Parlophone / Feb '94 / EMI

INNUENDO
Innuendo / I'm going slightly mad (edit) / I'm going slightly mad / Headlong / I can't live with you / Ride the wild wind / All God's people / These are the days of our lives / Delilah / Don't try so hard (edit) / Don't try so hard / Hitman (edit) / Hitman / Bijou (edit) / Bijou / Show must go on
CD ______ CDPCSD 115
Parlophone / Feb '91 / EMI

INTERVIEW AND PRESS CONFRENCES
CD ______ DISSCD 5
Wax / Apr '96 / RTM/Disc / Total/BMG

INTERVIEW COLLECTION, THE
CD ______ CBAK 4957
Baktabak / Feb '94 / Arabesque

INTERVIEW DISC
CD ______ SAM 7002
Sound & Media / Nov '96 / Sound & Media

JAZZ
Mustapha / Fat bottomed girls / Jealousy / Bicycle race / If you can't beat them / Let me entertain you / Dead on time / In only seven days / Dreamers ball / Fun it / Leaving home ain't easy / Don't stop me now / More of that jazz
CD ______ CDPCSD 133
Parlophone / Feb '94 / EMI

JOHN DEACON TALKS
CD ______ JDTALK 1
UFO / Nov '96 / Pinnacle

KIND OF MAGIC, A
Princes of the universe / Kind of magic / One year of love / Pain is so close to pleasure / Friends will be friends / Who wants to live forever / Gimme the prize / Don't lose your head / One vision / Friends will be friends / Forever
CD ______ CDP 7462672
EMI / Jun '88 / EMI

LIVE AT WEMBLEY '86 (2CD Set)
One vision / Tie your mother down / In the lap of the Gods / Seven seas of Rhye / Tear it up / Kind of magic / Under pressure / Another one bites the dust / Who wants to live forever / I want to break free / Impromptu / Brighton rock solo / Now I'm here / Love of my life / Is this the world we created / Baby I don't care / Hello Mary Lou / Tutti frutti / Gimme some lovin' / Bohemian rhapsody / Hammer to fall / Crazy little thing called love / Big spender / Radio ga ga / We will rock you / Friends will be friends / We are the champions / God save the Queen
CD Set ______ CDPCSP 7251
Parlophone / Jun '92 / EMI

LIVE KILLERS (2CD Set)
We will rock you / Let me entertain you / Death on two legs / Killer queen / Bicycle race / I'm in love with my car / Get down make love / You're my best friend / Now I'm here / Dreamers ball / Love of my life / '39 / Keep yourself alive / Don't stop me now / Spread your wings / Brighton rock / Bohemian rhapsody / Tie your mother down / Sheer heart attack / We are the champions / God save the Queen
CD Set ______ CDPCSD 138
Parlophone / Apr '94 / EMI

LIVE MAGIC
One vision / Tie your mother down / Seven seas of Rhye / Another one bites the dust / I want to break free / Is this the world we created / Bohemian rhapsody / Hammer to fall / Radio ga ga / We will rock you / Friends will be friends / We are the champions / God save the Queen / Kind of magic / Under pressure
CD ______ CDP 746 413 2
Parlophone / Jan '87 / EMI

MADE IN HEAVEN
It's a beautiful day / Made in Heaven / Let me live / Mother love / My life has been saved / I was born to love you / Heaven for everyone / Too much love will kill you / You don't fool me / Winter's tale
CD ______ CDPCSD 167
Parlophone / Nov '95 / EMI

MIRACLE, THE
Party / Khashoggi's ship / Miracle / I want it all / Invisible man / Breakthru' / Rain must fall / Scandal / My baby does me / Was it all worth it / Hang on in there / Chinese torture
CD ______ CDPCSD 107
Parlophone / May '89 / EMI

NEWS OF THE WORLD
We will rock you / We are the champions / Sheer heart attack / All dead all dead / Spread your wings / Fight from the inside / Get down make love / Sleeping on the side-walk / Who needs you / It's late / My melancholy blues
CD ______ CDPCSD 132
Parlophone / Sep '93 / EMI

NIGHT AT THE OPERA, A
Death on two legs / Lazing on a Sunday afternoon / You're my best friend / I'm in love with my car / Sweet lady / Seaside rendezvous / Good company / '39 / Prophet's song / Love of my life / Bohemian rhapsody / God save the Queen
CD ______ CDPCSD 130
Parlophone / Jul '93 / EMI

PASSING OPEN WINDOWS (A Symphonic Tribute To Queen) (Palmer, David & Royal Philharmonic Orchestra)
Bicycle race / Somebody to love / Killer Queen / Who wants to live forever / Death on two legs / Now I'm here / Innuendo / Love of my life / We are the champions / Keep passing open windows
CD ______ SK 62851
Sony Classical / Apr '97 / Sony

PHOTO SESSION (2CD Set)
CD Set ______ QU 2
UFO / Nov '92 / Pinnacle

QUEEN
Keep yourself alive / Doing alright / Great King Rat / My fairy King / Liar / Night comes down / Modern times rock 'n' roll / Son and daughter / Jesus / Seven seas of Rhye
CD ______ CDPCSD 139
Parlophone / Apr '94 / EMI

QUEEN II
Procession / Father to son / White Queen (as it began) / Some day one day / Loser in the end / Ogre battle / Fairy feller's master-stroke / Nevermore / March of the black Queen / Funny how love is / Seven seas of Rhye
CD ______ CDPCSD 140
Parlophone / Apr '94 / EMI

QUEEN'S RHAPSODY (Royal Philharmonic Orchestra)
CD ______ EDLCD 2560
Silva Screen / Oct '94 / Koch / Silva Screen

QUEEN: INTERVIEW COMPACT DISC
CD ______ CBAK 4022
Baktabak / Nov '89 / Arabesque

ROGER TAYLOR TALKS
CD ______ RTTALK 1
UFO / Nov '96 / Pinnacle

ROYAL PHILHARMONIC ORCHESTRA PLAY QUEEN (Royal Philharmonic Orchestra)
Flash / Play the game / We are the champions / Don't stop me now / Love of my life / Killer queen / You're my best friend / Teo torriate / Under pressure / Crazy little thing called love / Bohemian rhapsody
CD ______ CDMFP 5945
Music For Pleasure / Oct '92 / EMI

RPO PLAYS THE MUSIC OF QUEEN, THE (Royal Philharmonic Orchestra)
Barcelona / Flash / I want it all / Kind of magic / Great pretender / Bohemian rhapsody / Innuendo / Save me / Killer queen / I want to break free / Radio ga ga / We are the champions
CD ______ EMPRCD 675
Emporio / Apr '97 / Disc

SHEER HEART ATTACK
Brighton rock / Tenement funster / Flick of the wrist / Lily of the valley / Now I'm here / In the lap of the gods / Stone cold crazy / Bring back that Leroy Brown / She makes me (stormtrooper in stilettos) / In the lap of the gods...revisited / Killer queen / Dear friends / Misfire
CD ______ CDPCSD 129
Parlophone / Jul '93 / EMI

ULTIMATE QUEEN (20CD Box Set - From Queen To Made In Heaven)
CD Set ______ QUEENBOX 20
Parlophone / Nov '95 / EMI

WORKS, THE
Radio ga ga / Tear it up / It's a hard life / Man on the prowl / Machines (or Back to humans) / I want to break free / Keep passing the open windows / Hammer to fall / Is this the world we created
CD ______ CDPCSD 136
Parlophone / Feb '94 / EMI

Queen, B.B.

IN THE MOOD (FOR SOMETHING GOOD)
I'm in the mood (for something good) / Now love me / Blueshouse / Try to find me back / No time to hesitate / We gonna rock this house / Love you nights / I wanna be next to you / Soultrain / Hey BB be careful out there in the jungle / Blueshouse ballad
CD ______ CDEMC 3591
EMI / May '91 / EMI

Queen Elizabeth

QUEEN ELIZABETH
CD ______ ESPCD 2
Echo / Nov '94 / EMI / Vital

Queen Ida

COOKIN' WITH QUEEN IDA
Zydeco / Gator man / C'est moi / Love is the answer / La bas two step / 1-10 express / Dancing on the bayou / Ranger's waltz / Hard headed woman / Lady be mine
CD ______ GNPD 2197
GNP Crescendo / Sep '95 / ZYX

MARDI GRAS
Comment ca va / Oh, what can you do / Home on the bayou / Since you been gone / Louisiana / Where are you now / Mardi Gras / Object of my affection / Cajun cookin' / Mr. Fine / Papa on the fiddle / Molina / New kid on the bayou / I can see clearly now
CD ______ GNPD 2227
GNP Crescendo / Sep '95 / ZYX

Queen Latifah

NATURE OF A SISTA
Latifah's had it up 2 here / Nuff of the ruff stuff / One mo time / Give your love to me / Love again / Bad as a mutha / Fly girl / Sexy fancy / Nature of a sista / That's the way we flow / If you don't know / How do I love thee
CD ______ GEECD 8
Gee Street / Sep '91 / PolyGram

Queen Majeeda

CONSCIOUS
CD ______ HBCD 90
Heartbeat / Jun '93 / ADA / Direct / Greensleeves / Jet Star

Queen Sylvia

MIDNIGHT BABY
I'm hurtin' / Life and troubles / New York bound / Baby, What do I do / Midnight baby / Party / Can't get along / Why wonder / You treat me so mean / I love you
CD ______ ECD 260572
Evidence / Sep '94 / ADA / Cadillac / Harmonia Mundi

Queen Victoria School

TUNES OF SCOTLAND
CD ______ CDITV 611
Scotdisc / May '96 / Conifer/BMG / Duncans / Ross

Queen's College Choir

ORGAN OF QUEEN'S COLLEGE, OXFORD, THE (Queen's College Choir, Oxford)
CD ______ CDCA 925
Alpha / '91 / Abbey Recording

Queen's Division

ARRIVAL (Minden Band Of The Queen's Division)
Fanfare / Princess of Wales' Royal Regiment / Royal Regiment of Fusiliers / Royal Anglian Regiment / Pride on parade / Queen's Division / Bells / Red Square Review / Bridges over the River Cam / Prelude to comedy / Solemn occasion / Musical snuff box / Grasshoppers dance / Rondon grottesco / Gypsy trumpeter / Reverie / Big band swing / Tin Pan Alley / Symphonic Gershwin / Spirit of pageantry
CD ______ BNA 5124
Bandleader / Jul '96 / Conifer/BMG

Queen's Royal Scots Pipers

QUEEN'S ROYAL SCOTS PIPERS, THE
CD ______ EUCD 1312
ARC / Jul '95 / ADA / ARC Music

Queensryche

EMPIRE
Best I can / Thin line / Jet city woman / Della Brown / Another rainy night / Empire / Resistgance / Silent lucidity / Hand on heart / One and only / Anybody listening
CD ______ CDMTL 1058
EMI Manhattan / Sep '90 / EMI

HEAR IN THE NOW
Sign of the times / Cuckoo's nest / Get a life / Voice inside / Some people fly / Saved / You / Miles away / Reach / All I want / Hit the black / Anytime/Anywhere / Spool
CD ______ CDEMC 3764
EMI / Mar '97 / EMI

PROMISED LAND
9.28 a.m. / I am I / Damaged / Out of mind / Bridge / Promised land / Disconnected / Lady Jane / My global mind / One more time / Someone else
CD ______ CDMTL 1081
EMI Manhattan / Oct '94 / EMI

RAGE FOR ORDER
Walk in the shadows / I dream in infrared / Whisper / Gonna get close to you / Killing words / Surgical strike / Neue regal / Chemical youth (We are rebellion) / London / Screaming in digital / I will remember
CD ______ CDAML 3105
EMI Manhattan / Aug '91 / EMI

WARNING, THE
Warning / En force / Deliverance / No sanctuary / NM 156 / Take hold of the flame / Before the storm / Child of fire / Roads to madness
CD ______ CDP 7465572
EMI Manhattan / Feb '87 / EMI

Queers

BEAT OFF
CD ______ LOOKOUT 81CD
Lookout / Jun '97 / Cargo / Greyhound / Shellshock/Disc

DON'T BACK DOWN
CD ______ LOOKOUT 140CD
Lookout / Aug '96 / Cargo / Greyhound / Shellshock/Disc

GROW UP
CD ______ LOOKOUT 9CD
Lookout / Jul '95 / Cargo / Greyhound / Shellshock/Disc

LOVE SONGS
CD ______ LOOKOUT 66CD
Lookout / Jul '95 / Cargo / Greyhound / Shellshock/Disc

MOVE BACK HOME
CD ______ LOOKOUT 114CD
Lookout / Jun '97 / Cargo / Greyhound / Shellshock/Disc

Quench

SEQUENCHAL
CD ______ INFECT 20CD
Infectious / Nov '94 / RTM/Disc

Quest

LIVE AT THE MONTMARTRE
CD ______ STCD 4121
Storyville / Feb '90 / Cadillac / Jazz Music / Wellard

NATURAL SELECTION
As always / Natural selection / Nocturnal / Amethyst suite / Fahamivu / Michiyo / Moody time / Nighty-nite
CD ______ ECD 220822
Evidence / Feb '94 / ADA / Cadillac / Harmonia Mundi

OF ONE MIND
CD ______ CMPCD 047
CMP / '95 / Cargo / Grapevine/PolyGram / Vital/SAM

QUEST
CD ______ STCD 4158
Storyville / Feb '90 / Cadillac / Jazz Music / Wellard

Quest

CHANGE
CD ______ NTHEN 31CD
Now & Then / Oct '96 / Plastic Head

DO YOU BELIEVE
CD ______ NTHEN 5
Now & Then / Sep '95 / Plastic Head

Question Mark

96 TEARS (Question Mark & The Mysterians)
CD ______ RE 137CD
ROIR / Nov '94 / Plastic Head / Shellshock/Disc

ACTION (Question Mark & The Mysterians)
CD ______ MOVE 3001
Move / Jun '97 / Greyhound

Quick Change

CIRCUS OF DEATH
Will you die / Show no mercy / Sea witch / Circus of death / Injected / What's next / Sludge / ATL / Leave it to the beaver / Battle your fear / Death games / Plowed
CD ______ RR 95032
Roadrunner / Feb '89 / PolyGram

Quicksilver Messenger Service

ANTHOLOGY
Pride of man / Dino's song / Fool / Bears / Mona / Edward, the mad shirt grinder / Three or four feet from home / Fresh air / Just for love / Spindrifter / Local color / What about me / Don't cry my lady love / Hope / Fire brothers / I found love
CD ______ BGOCD 270
Beat Goes On / Mar '95 / Pinnacle

COMIN' THRU
Doin' time in the USA / Chicken / Changes / California state correctional facility blues / Forty days / Mojo / Don't lose it
CD ______ BGOCD 88
Beat Goes On / Jul '91 / Pinnacle

HAPPY TRAILS
Who do you love (part one) / When you love / Where you love / How do you love / Which do you love / Who do you love (part two) / Mona / Maiden of the cancer moon / Calvary / Happy trails
CD ______ BGOCD 151
Beat Goes On / Sep '92 / Pinnacle

JUST FOR YOU
CD ______ BGOCD 141
Beat Goes On / Jun '92 / Pinnacle

QUICKSILVER
CD ______ BGOCD 217
Beat Goes On / Jan '94 / Pinnacle

QUICKSILVER MESSENGER SERVICE
Pride of man / Light your windows / Dino's song / Gold and silver / It's been too long / Fool
CD ______ EDCD 200
Edsel / May '92 / Pinnacle

SHADY GROVE
Shady grove / Flute song / Three or four feet from home / Too far / Holy moly / Joseph's coat / Flashing lonesome / Words can't say / Edward, the mad shirt grinder
CD ______ EDCD 208
Edsel / Sep '90 / Pinnacle

SOLID SILVER
CD ______ EDCD 376
Edsel / Aug '93 / Pinnacle

ULTIMATE JOURNEY
Who do you love / Pride of man / Codine / Dino's song / Gold and silver / Joseph's coat / Shady grove / Fresh air / Too far / Stand by me / What about me / Mona
CD ______ SEECD 61
See For Miles/C5 / Apr '93 / Pinnacle

WHAT ABOUT ME
CD ______ BGOCD 58
Beat Goes On / Oct '90 / Pinnacle

Quickspace

QUICKSPACE
Swisher / Song for someone / Quasi-brau / Mouse tail / Winona / Docile I / Docile II
CD ______ CHOOSY 006CD
Kitty Kitty Corporation / Nov '96 / Vital

SUPO-SPOT
Happy song no.1 / Unique slippy / Extra plus / Found a way / Do it my own way / Whiff and spoof song / Exemplary swishy / Friend / Where have all the good times gone / Song for NME
CD ______ CHOOSY 008CD
Kitty Kitty Corporation / Jun '97 / Vital

Quiet Boys

BOSH
Righteous / Take four / Deeper / Blue 4 royal T / Inner sense / Prayer mat / Boshin' around / Conguero wronguero / Ghetto life / Never change / Love will find a way / Astral space
CD ______ JAZIDCD 121
Acid Jazz / Apr '95 / Disc

CAN'T HOLD THE VIBE
Inside your mind / Let it go / Give it all u got / Make me say it again girl / Roaring fast / Long way from me / Sim ting / Att etude / Modal / Can't hold the vibe / Mellow blow
CD ______ JAZIDCD 045
Acid Jazz / Mar '92 / Disc

DAZZLE
Guiding light / Dazzle / Everybody loves the sunshine / Chance for peace / Bosh tres bien / Way up there / Always be the one / State of mind / Play to win / Watuzi strut / Late exit / Future cliche
CD ______ TKCD 61
2 Kool / Mar '97 / Pinnacle / SRD

Quiet City

QUIET CITY
CD ______ CD 59002
Salt / Aug '96 / Else

Quiet Elegance

YOU GOT MY MIND MESSED UP
After you / Mama said / Do you love me / Something you got / I'm afraid of losing you / You brought the sun back into my life / I need love / Tired of being alone / Will you be my man (in the morning) / You got my mind messed up / Your love is strange / Roots of love / Love will make you feel better / Have you been making out OK / Set the record straight / How's your love life baby
CD ______ HIUKCD 109
Hi / Dec '89 / Pinnacle

Quiet Riot

RANDY RHOADS YEARS, THE
Trouble / Laughing gas / Afterglow of your love / Killer girls / Picking up the pieces / Last call for rock 'n' roll / Breaking up is a heartache / Force of habit / It's not so funny / Look in any window
CD ______ 8122714452
Atlantic / Feb '94 / Warner Music

Quigg, Stephen

VOICE OF MY ISLAND
Steal away / Gallant Murray / Voice of my island / Almost every circumstance / Strong women rule us with their tears / Freewheeling now / Work o' the weavers / Come by the hills / Whatever you say say nothing / Annie McKelvie / Willie's gane tae Melville Castle / Last leviathan
CD ______ CDTRAX 066
Greentrax / Jul '93 / ADA / Direct / Duncans / Highlander

Quine, Robert

BASIC (Quine, Robert & Fred Maher)
Pick up / Bluffer / Fala / Stray / Summer storm / Sixty five / Dark place / Despair / Village / Bandage bait
CD ______ CDOVD 470
Virgin / Jul '96 / EMI

Quinichette, Paul

KID FROM DENVER, THE
CD ______ **BCD 136**
Biograph / Aug '95 / ADA / Cadillac / Direct / Hot Shot / Jazz Music / Wellard

ON THE SUNNY SIDE
Blue dots / Circles / On the sunny side of the street / Cool-lypso
CD ______ **OJCCD 762**
Original Jazz Classics / Feb '97 / Complete/ Pinnacle / Jazz Music / Wellard

Quink Vocal Ensemble

INVISIBLE CITIES
Missa brevis / Priere / En begheeft myniet / Egidius waer besta bleven / Het visschertje / Trionfo di bacco e d'arianna / Madrigal / Psaume 121 / Due canti / Als ghys van de doodt sult zijn verbeten / Les mortels
CD ______ **CD 80384**
Telarc / Apr '96 / Conifer/BMG

Quinn

QUINN
Crown of life / Sacred revelation / In a perfect world / Prophecy / These four walls / In reverie / Autonomous / All alone / Lotus / Lavender moonlight / Red sky / Bardo thodol
CD ______ **SR 4001**
PLR / Jun '95 / Pinnacle

Quinn, Bill

TRIBUTE TO JIM REEVES, A
Whispering hope / Scarlet ribbons / Mexicali rose / Am I losing you / Just out of reach / Adios amigo / If only I had you / It hurts so much / Is it really over / You're free to go / This world is not my home / Four walls / I love you because / No one to cry to / (Not until) the next time / Anna Marie / Distant drums / He'll have to go / You're the only good thing / I won't forget you / Oh, how I miss you tonight
CD ______ **305132**
Hallmark / Jun '97 / Carlton

Quinn, Brendan

MELODIES AND MEDLEYS
My lady from Glenfarne / Lovely leitrim / My lovely rose of Clare / My heart skips a beat / Turn out the lights and love me tonight / Some broken hearts never mend / I recall a gypsy woman / Dublin in the rare old times / Any tipperary town / Among the Wicklow hills / He'll have to go / I won't forget you / I love you because
CD ______ **RITZRCD 515**
Ritz / Apr '92 / Pinnacle

MYSTERY, THE
CD ______ **CBMCD 019**
Cross Border Media / Jul '96 / ADA / Direct / Grapevine/PolyGram

Quinn, Eimaer

WINTER FIRE AND SNOW
CD ______ **PEACH 001**
Peach / Mar '97 / CM

Quinn, Frank

IF YOU ARE IRISH
If you are Irish / Rafferty's reel / Paddy McGinty's goat / Rakes of drummlish / Molly in the woods / Tan yard side / West port chorus / Shan van vough / Paddy Doyle / Leg of the duck / Eddie Dunn's favourite reel / Going to the fair / Donovan's reel / Goodbye Mike goodbye Pat / Old tea kettle / Green grow the rushes oh / Four courts / Far away in Australia / Peeler and the goat / New found reel / One night I came home to my Kitty / Jersey lightning / Emerald medley / Bunch of rushes / An Irish farewell
CD ______ **ARHCD 7033**
Arhoolie / May '97 / ADA / Cadillac / Direct

Quinn, Freddy

FREDDY QUINN 1956-1965
Sie hiess Mary Ann / Heimweh / Bel sante / Cigarettes and whisky / Junge komme bald wieder / So geht das jede nacht / Don't forbid me / At the hop / Stood up / Lonesome star / Heimatlos / Ein armer mulero / Ich bin bald wieder hier / Die gitarre und das meer / Unter fremden sternen / Guitar playing Joe / La guitarra Brasiliana / Der boss ist nicht hier / Ein schiff voll whiskey / You, you, you / Blue mirage / I'll hold you in my heart / By the way / Spanish eyes
CD ______ **BCD 15403**
Bear Family / Jul '87 / Direct / Rollercoaster / Swift

Quinn, Paul

PHANTOMS AND THE ARCHETYPES (Quinn, Paul & The Independent Group)
Phantoms and the Archetypes / Born on the wrong side of town / What can you do to me now / Should've known by now / Punk Rock Hotel / Superstar / Call my name / Damage Is Done / Darling I Can't Fight / Hangin' On
CD ______ **DUBH 921CD**
Postcard / Sep '92 / Vital

WILL I EVER BE INSIDE OF YOU (Quinn, Paul & The Independent Group)
Will I ever be inside of you / Have you been seen / Lover that's you all over / Mooreeffoc (misty thought) / Passing thought / Outre / Misty blue / Stupid thing / At the end of the night
CD ______ **DUBH 945CD**
Postcard / Oct '94 / Vital

Quintana, Alfonsin

VAMOS PA' LA RUMBA 1951-1953
CD ______ **TCD 082**
Tumbao Cuban Classics / Jul '96 / Discovery

Quintessence

SELF/INDWELLER
Cosmic surfer / Wonders of the universe / Hari om / Vishnu narain / Hallelujah / Celestrial procession / Self / Freedom / Water Goddess / Jesus is my life / Butterfly / It's all the same / Indweller / Portable realm / Holy roller / On the other side of the wall / Dedication / Bliss trip / Mother of the universe
CD ______ **DOCD 1982**
Drop Out / May '95 / Pinnacle

Quinteto Da Paraiba

MUSICA ARMORIAL (String Quartets From NE Brazil)
CD ______ **NI 5483**
Nimbus / Aug '96 / Nimbus

Quintetto Vocale Italiano

FREEDOM JAZZ DANCE
CD ______ **1212472**
Soul Note / Nov '92 / Cadillac / Harmonia Mundi / Wellard

Quintetto X

NOVO ESQUEMA DA BOSSA
CD ______ **RTCD 402**
Right Tempo / Jul '96 / New Note/ Pinnacle / Timewarp

Quipildor, Zamba

PUESTA DE SOL
CD ______ **BMF 004**
Blue Moon / Jul '97 / Cadillac / Discovery / Greensleeves / Jazz Music / Jet Star / TKO Magnum

Quireboys

BIT OF WHAT YOU FANCY, A/BITTER SWEET AND TWISTED (Remastered/ 2CD Set)
7 o'clock man / Man on the loose / Whippin' boy / Sex party / Sweet Mary Ann / I don't love you anymore / Hey you / Misled / Long time comin' / Roses and rings / There she goes again / Take me home tonight / Heartbreaker / How do you feel / Mayfair / Misled / 7 o'clock / Long time comin' / Pretty girls / I don't love you anymore / Stop right there / Please me / Tramps and thieves / White trash blues / Can't park here / King of New York / Don't bite the hand that feeds you / Last time / Debbie / Brother Louie / Ode to you (baby just walk) / Hates to please / My Saint Jude / Take no revenge / Wild wild wild / Ain't love blind / Tramps and thieves / Don't bite the hand that feeds / Ode to you (baby just walk) / Sweet little girl
CD Set ______ **CTMCD 200**
EMI / Feb '97 / EMI

FROM TOOTING TO BARKING
7 O'Clock / Hey you / Man on the loose / Mayfair / Where've you been to / Whipping boy / Devil of a man / Hates to please / I don't love you again / Roses and rings
CD ______ **ESMCD 400**
Essential / Jul '96 / BMG

MINI CD
CD ______ **SURCD 014**
Survival / Sep '91 / ADA / Pinnacle

Quoite

LOUNGE
CD ______ **DOSS 1201CD**
Possible / Sep '96 / Plastic Head

Quorthon

QUORTHON
CD ______ **BMCD 6669**
Black Mark / May '94 / Plastic Head

R

R Kelly

12 PLAY
Your body's callin' / Bump 'n' grind / Homie lover friend / It seems like your ready / Freak dat body / I like the crotch on you / Summer bunnies / For you / Back to the mood of things / Sadie / Sex me (parts 1 and 2) / 12 play
CD __________ CHIP 144
Jive / Mar '97 / Pinnacle

BORN INTO THE 90'S (R Kelly & Public Announcement)
She's loving me / She's got that vibe / Definition of a hotti / I know what you need / Keep it street / Born into the 90's / Slow dance / Dedicated / Honey love / Hangin' out / Hey love (can I have a word with you)
CD __________ CHIP 123
Jive / Mar '97 / Pinnacle

R. KELLY
CD __________ CHIP 166
Jive / Dec '95 / Pinnacle

Rabbit's Hat

OPTIC MANSION
CD __________ DMCD 1034
Demi-Monde / Oct '96 / RTM/Disc / TKO Magnum

Rabin, Oscar

TWO IN LOVE
No souvenirs / I understand / Moonlight avenue / I'd know you anywhere / I ain't got nobody / Deep in the heart of Texas / Sometimes / You again / Tica-ti, tica-ta / Angeline / At the woodchopper's ball / Bluebirds in the moonlight / I fall in love wiht you every day / My wubba dolly / Starlight serenade / Predigree on pomander walk / Daddy / Down Argentina way / My sisters and I / Two in love / Sweet madness / Who's taking you home tonight
CD __________ RAJCD 871
Empress / Oct '95 / Koch

Rabson, Ann

MUSIC MAKIN' MAMA
CD __________ ALCD 4848
Alligator / Mar '97 / ADA / CM / Direct

RAC

DIVERSIONS
CD __________ WARPCD 22
Warp / Apr '94 / Prime / RTM/Disc

Raca Negra

RACA NEGRA
CD __________ 1918192
EPM / Jul '97 / ADA / Discovery

Race, Hugo

EARLS WORLD (Race, Hugo & The True Spirit)
CD __________ NORMAL 125CD
Normal / May '94 / ADA / Direct

RUE MORGUE BLUES (Race, Hugo & The True Spirit)
CD __________ NORMAL 118CD
Normal / May '94 / ADA / Direct

SECOND REVELATOR (Race, Hugo & The True Spirit)
CD __________ NORMAL 135CD
Normal / May '94 / ADA / Direct

SPIRITUAL THIRST (Race, Hugo & The True Spirit)
CD __________ NORMAL 155CD
Normal / May '94 / ADA / Direct

VALLEY OF LIGHT
CD __________ PANNCD 10
Pandemonium / Mar '96 / RTM/Disc / Vital

Racer Ten

MELODIES AND MEMORIES
CD __________ SEMAPHORE 35862
Onefoot / Nov '96 / Cargo

Racer X

SECOND HEAT
CD __________ RR 349601
Roadrunner / Dec '87 / PolyGram

Rachel Z

ROOM OF ONE'S OWN
Artemisia / Trail of her blood in the snow / Room of one's own / Dane of the lioness cub / Feel the power / Gently sleeps the pear tree / Set her free / For her concubine / Talking and electrons / Ship of tears
CD __________ NYC 60232
NYC / Jun '96 / New Note/Pinnacle

Rachell, Yank

CHICAGO STYLE
CD __________ DD 649
Delmark / Nov '93 / ADA / Cadillac / CM / Direct / Hot Shot

Rachels

HANDWRITING
CD __________ QS 30CD
Quarter Stick / May '95 / Cargo / SRD

MUSIC FOR EGON SCHIELE
CD __________ Q 35CD
Quarter Stick / Feb '96 / Cargo / SRD

Racial Abuse

CLIMB
CD __________ LF 264CD
Lost & Found / Dec '96 / Plastic Head

Radakka

MALICE OF TRANQUILITY
CD __________ CM 77111CD
Century Media / Jan '96 / Plastic Head

Radar Bros.

RADAR BROS.
Lose your face again / Capital gain / Wise mistake of you / Stay / Supermarket pharmacy / On the floor / We're over here / Distant mine / Underwater culprits / This drive / Take stuff / Goddess
CD __________ 729272
Restless / Oct '96 / Vital

Radcliff, Bobby

LIVE AT THE RYNBORN
Improvisations on Honky Tonk / Please have mercy / Tramp / Early in the morning / Introject / Been around the world / Kool And The Gang / Honeydripper / Ten years ago / Twist
CD __________ CDBT 1141
Black Top / May '97 / ADA / CM / Direct

THERE'S A COLD GRAVE IN YOUR WAY
CD __________ BT 1110CD
Black Top / Nov '94 / ADA / CM / Direct

Radha Krishna Temple

RADHA KRISHNA TEMPLE
Govinda / Sri Guruvastak / Bhaja Bhakata/ Arotrika / Hare Krsna mantra / Sri Isopanisad / Bhaja Hure Mana / Govinda Jai Jai / Prayer to the spiritual masters
CD __________ CDP 7812552
Apple / Mar '93 / EMI

Radial Blend

ABANDON TIME
CD __________ SOHO 19CD
Suburbs Of Hell / Jan '95 / Kudos / Pinnacle / Plastic Head

ENOUGH ROADS
CD __________ SOH 021CD
Suburbs Of Hell / Jul '95 / Kudos / Pinnacle / Plastic Head

Radial Spangle

ICE CREAM HEADACHE
CD __________ MINTCD 8
Mint Tea / Jun '93 / RTM/Disc

SYRUP MACRANE
CD __________ BBQCD 163
Beggars Banquet / Aug '94 / RTM/Disc / Warner Music

Radiators

ALIVE-ALIVE-O (Live In London 1978/ Rare Studio Tracks)
Contact / Sunday world / Roxy girl / Electric shares / Press gang / Prison bars / Million dollar hero / Television screen / Walking home alone again / Psychotic reaction / Blitzin' at the Ritz / Enemies / Teenager in love / Hucklebuck / Teenage head / Shake some action / 1970 (I feel alright) / Private world / Strangers in fiction / Take my heart and run / Buying gold in heaven / Gold diggers of 1981 (Hits for the blitz) / Ballad of the faithful departed
CD __________ CDWIKD 164
Chiswick / Jun '96 / Pinnacle

COCKLES AND MUSSELS (The Best Of The Radiators)
Television screen / Love detective / Sunday world / Prison bars / Party line / Roxy girl / Enemies / Try and stop me / Million dollar hero / Let's talk about the weather / Johnny Jukebox / Confidential / They're looting in the town / Who are the strangers / Kitty Ricketts / Ballad of the faithful departed / Walking home alone again / Dead the beast, dead the poison / Stranger than fiction / Dancing years / Under Cleary's clock / Plura Belle
CD __________ CDWIKS 156
Chiswick / Oct '95 / Pinnacle

Radical Dance Faction

BORDERLINE CASES
Surplus people / Borderline / Four chuck chant / Riverwise / Sorepoint for a sickman / Chinese poem / Rogue trooper (live mix) / Back in the same place / Hot on the wire / Firepower
CD __________ EZ 001CD
Earthzone / Jul '94 / SRD

RAGGAMUFFIN STATEMENT
CD __________ CD4DS 4A
Inna State / May '95 / SRD

Radical Retard

ONCE I WOKE UP
CD __________ C 6201CD
R / Mar '94 / Plastic Head

Radio Big Band

SPECIAL EDITION
Chicago / Auf wiedersehen sweetheart / I remember Clifford / Body and soul / For you, for me, for evermore / Broadway / Easy living / Oh I do like to be beside the seaside / Imagination / Big band treasure chest
CD __________ RBB 002
Radio Big Band / Feb '95 / New Note/ Pinnacle

Radio Birdman

RITUALISM (CD/Book Set)
CD __________ CSREC 001
Citadel / Jun '97 / Greyhound

Radio Four

THERE'S GONNA BE JOY
Earnest prayer / If you miss me from praying / How much I owe / Building a home / I feel the spirit / Road's rocky / There's gonna be joy / That's all I need / Road's rough and rocky / How about you / When he calls / Whisper to Jesus / I received my blessings / One more river / What's he done for me / Walk around my bedside / Jesus never left me alone / What kind of man Jesus is / In my father's house / Believe every word he says / On my journey now / One day / Heaven is my goal / Jesus is my friend
CD __________ CDCHD 448
Ace / Jun '93 / Pinnacle

Radio Massacre International

FROZEN NORTH (2CD Set)
Wrecks / What's the point of going to Crete / Small frozen north / Rosemary's baby / Drown / Frozen north 1 / Frozen north 2
CD __________ CENCD 012
Centaur / Nov '95 / Pinnacle

REPUBLIC
Raw cane approach / Republic / Send off
CD __________ CENCD 018
Centaur / Apr '97 / Pinnacle

Radio Moscow

GET A NEW LIFE
CD __________ RMCD 104
Status / May '93 / PolyGram

Radio Stars

SOMEWHERE (THERE'S A PLACE FOR US)
CD __________ CDWIKD 107
Chiswick / May '92 / Pinnacle

Radio Sweethearts

NEW MEMORIES
Lonely footsteps / Every other song / Beer and whiskey / Is anybody going to San Antone / House of gold / I saw the light / New memories / Headin' on down the highway / Red Cadillac and a blck moustache / Don't make me wait / We've fallen out of love again / Out in the darkness
CD __________ SR 10032
St. Roch / Jul '97 / Cargo / Direct

Radio Tarifa

RUMBA ANGELINA
Rumba argelina / Oye china / Lamma bada / Manana / La canal / El baile de la bola / Soledad / La mosca / Tangos del argujero / Nu alrest / La pastora / Ronda de sanabria / Bulerias turcas / Nina
CD __________ WCD 042
World Circuit / May '96 / ADA / Cadillac / Direct / New Note/Pinnacle

TEMPORAL
La tarara / Las cuenvas / Canion sefardi / Baile de almut / Tangos de la condicion / Conductus / Temporal / El mandil de Carolina / Vestido de flores
CD __________ WCD 048
World Circuit / Jun '97 / ADA / Cadillac / Direct / New Note/Pinnacle

Radio Waves

RADIO WAVES
CD __________ RSNCD 32
Rising High / Apr '95 / 3mv/Sony

Radiohead

BENDS, THE
Planet Telex / Bends / High and dry / Fake plastic trees / Bones / Nice dream / Just / My iron lung / Bullet proof... I wish I was / Black star / Sulk / Street spirit (fade out)
CD __________ CDPCS 7372
Parlophone / Mar '95 / EMI

INTERVIEW DISC
CD __________ SAM 7029
Sound & Media / Mar '97 / Sound & Media

OK COMPUTER
Airbag / Paranoid android / Subterranean homesick alien / Exit music (for a film) / Let down / Karma police / Fitter, happier / Electioneering / Climbing up the walls / No surprises / Lucky / Tourist
CD __________ CDNODATA 02
Parlophone / May '97 / EMI

PABLO HONEY
You / Creep / How do you / Stop whispering / Thinking about you / Anyone can play guitar / Ripcord / Vegetable / Prove yourself / I can't / Lurgee / Blow out
CD __________ CDPCS 7360
Parlophone / Mar '93 / EMI

Radish

RESTRAINING BOLT
CD __________ 5346442
Mercury / Sep '97 / PolyGram

Radium Cats

OTHER WORLDS
Martian hop / Six foot down / Freak / Mygirl islike uranium / Idol with the golden head / Great shakin' fever / Return of the mystery train / Well I knocked (bim bam) / Strange, baby strange / Eraserhead / Let it rot / Zuvembi stroll / Pink hearse / Surfin' DOA
CD __________ NERCD 068
Nervous / May '92 / Nervous / TKO Magnum

Radu, Dinu

ROMANTIC PAN PIPES (Radu, Dinu & GSO)
I have a dream / Strawberry fields forever / Dark side of the moon / Scarborough fair / Sailing / Unchained melody / Amazing grace / If you leave me now / Something / Feelings / Here comes the sun / Sara / Yesterday / MacArthur park / Bird of paradise / House of the rising sun / Don't cry for me Argentina / Banks of the Ohio / Autumn dream / Let it be
CD __________ CD 6002
It's Music / Nov '95 / Total/BMG

Rae, Dashiell

SONG WITHOUT WORDS
CD __________ NAGE 4CD
Art Of Landscape / Feb '86 / Sony

Rae, Jesse

COMPRESSION
CD __________ EB 007
Echo Beach / Oct '96 / Cargo / Shellshock/Disc

Raeburn, Boyd

BOYD RAEBURN 1944
CD __________ CCD 22
Circle / Mar '95 / Jazz Music / Swift / Wellard

BOYD RAEBURN 1944-1945 (Raeburn, Boyd Orchestra)
CD __________ CCD 113
Circle / Mar '95 / Jazz Music / Swift / Wellard

JUBILEE PERFORMANCES 1946 (Raeburn, Boyd & His Orchestra)
Tonsillectomy / Rip Van Winkle / Caravan / How deep is the ocean / Boyd meets Stravinsky / Dalvatore Sally / Night in Tunisia / Hep boyds
CD __________ HEPCD 1

Hep / Oct '95 / Cadillac / Jazz Music / New Note/Pinnacle / Wellard

TRANSCRIPTION PERFORMANCES 1946
Boyd's nest / Blue prelude / High tide / Picnic in the wintertime / Are you livin' old man / Tush / Concerto for Duke / Where you at / Out of this world / Boyd meets Stravinsky / Personality / Dalvatore Sally / Blue echoes / I only have eyes for you / Two spoos in an igloo / Temptation / I can't believe that you're in love with me / I don't know why / More than you know / Amnesia / Cartaphilius / Night in Tunisia / I cover the waterfront / Foolish little boy
CD ____ **HEPCD 42**
Hep / Nov '93 / Cadillac / Jazz Music / New Note/Pinnacle / Wellard

Raekwon The Chef

ONLY BUILT 4 CUBAN LINX
Striving for perfection / Knuckleheadz / Knowledge God / Criminology / Incarcerated scarfaces / Rainy dayz / Guillotine / Can it be all so simple / Shark niggaz / Ice water / Glaciers of ice / Verbal intercourse / Wisdom body / Spot rusherz / Ice cream / Wu gambinos / Heaven G hell / North star
CD ____ **07863666632**
RCA / Jul '95 / BMG

RAF

ODE TO A TRACTOR
Pork / Stay where you are / Freezing dessert / Land of the dead and dying / Suburb of hell / Head of a monk / Ode to a tractor / Buchlain in Australia / Chant / Konkret
CD ____ **DEMCD 030**
Day Eight Music / Jun '93 / New Note/ Pinnacle

Rafferty, Gerry

CAN I HAVE MY MONEY BACK
New street blues / Didn't I / Mr. Universe / Mary Skeffington / Long way round / Can I have my money back / Sign on the dotted line / Make you break you / To each and everyone / One drink down / Don't count me out / Half a chance / Where I belong
CD ____ **HILLCD 3**
Wooded Hill / Sep '96 / Direct / World Serpent

CITY TO CITY
Ark / Baker Street / Right down the line / City to city / Sealin' time / Mattie's rag / Whatever's written in your heart / Home and dry / Island / Waiting for the day
CD ____ **CDFA 3119**
Fame / Jul '89 / EMI

EARLY YEARS, THE
CD ____ **TRTCD 196**
TrueTrax / Feb '96 / THE

NIGHT OWL
Days gone down / Night owl / Way that you do it / Why won't you talk to me / Get it right next time / Take the money and run / Family tree / Already gone / Tourist / It's gonna be a long night
CD ____ **CDFA 3147**
Fame / Jul '89 / EMI

ON A WING AND A PRAYER
Time's caught up on you / I see red / It's easy to talk / I could be wrong / Don't speak of my heart / Get out of my life woman / Don't give up on me / Hang on / Love and affection / Does he know what he's taken on / Light of love / Life goes on
CD ____ **5174952**
A&M / Feb '93 / PolyGram

ONE MORE DREAM
CD ____ **5292792**
PolyGram TV / Oct '95 / PolyGram

OVER MY HEAD
CD ____ **5235992**
A&M / Jul '95 / PolyGram

RIGHT DOWN THE LINE (The Best Of Gerry Rafferty)
Baker Street / Whatever's written in your heart / Bring it all home / Right down the line / Get it right next time / Way that you do it / Tired of talking / Garden of England / Sleepwalking / Night owl / As wise as a serpent / Dangerous age / Family tree / Shipyard town / Right moment / Look at the moon
CD ____ **CDUAG 330333**
United Artists / Oct '89 / EMI

TRANSATLANTIC YEARS, THE
CD ____ **CCSCD 428**
Castle / Mar '95 / BMG

Rafferty, Mike & Mark

DANGEROUS REEL, THE
CD ____ **AVL 95151CD**
Rapparee / Nov '96 / ADA

Rag Pickers Of Tokyo

RAG PICKERS OF TOKYO IN NEW ORLEANS
CD ____ **BCD 349**
GHB / Jun '96 / Jazz Music

Rage

END OF ALL DAYS
CD ____ **GUN 101CD**
Gun / Oct '96 / Plastic Head

MISSING LINK
CD ____ **N 02172**
Noise / Aug '93 / Koch

TEN YEARS IN RAGE
CD ____ **N 02912**
Noise / Sep '94 / Koch

Rage

SAVIOUR
CD ____ **PULSECD 9**
Pulse 8 / Mar '93 / BMG

Rage Against The Machine

EVIL EMPIRE
People of the sun / Bulls on parade / Vietnow / Revolver / Snakecharmer / Tire me / Rollin' down Rodeo / Wind below / Without a face / Roll right / Year of tha boomerang
CD ____ **4810262**
Epic / Apr '96 / Sony

RAGE AGAINST THE MACHINE
Bombtrack / Killing in the name / Take the power back / Settle for nothing / Bullet in the head / Know your enemy / Wake up / Fistful of steel / Township rebelion / Freedom
CD ____ **4722242**
Epic / Mar '93 / Sony

Ragermann

DELICIOUS FRUIT
Delicious fruit / Gayonnah / Legend / Agaravinthia / Agion oros / Mother's aha / Grenadine / Daskallah / In the bush / Elevato / Hinne ma tov
CD ____ **INAK 9045CD**
In Akustik / Jul '97 / Direct / TKO Magnum

Ragga Jam

HOT RAGGA, COOL REGGAE
Shine / Compliments on your kiss / Dedicated to the one I love / You don't love me / Sweets for my sweet / Twist and shout / Family affair / Baby I love your way / Red red wine / I can see clearly now / Sign / On a ragga tip / She don't let nobody / Dub be good to me
CD ____ **QED 045**
Tring / Nov '96 / Tring

RAGGA
Oh Carolina / Iron lion Zion / Sweat (alalalalalong) / Flex / All that she wants / Rock with you / Mr. Loverman / (I can't help) Falling in love with you / Bad boys / Deep / Girl, I've been hurt / Slow and sexy / Informer / Wheel of fortune
CD ____ **QED 129**
Tring / Nov '96 / Tring

Ragga Twins

FREEDOM TRAIN
CD ____ **SUADCD 006**
Shut Up & Dance / Feb '93 / SRD

REGGAE OWES ME MONEY
CD ____ **SUADCD 002**
Shut Up & Dance / Mar '91 / SRD

Raging Slab

DYNAMITE MONSTER BOOGIE CONCERT
Anywhere but here / Weatherman / Pearly / So help me / What have you done / Take a hold / Laughin' and cryin' / Don't worry about the bomb / Lynne / Lord have mercy / National dust / Ain't ugly non
CD ____ **74321287592**
American / Jun '95 / BMG

SING MONKEY SING
Shoulda known / Encounter / Never comin' down / Nobodies / Lay down / Gracious / C'mon and on / She like to / Better than what I did / Wrong / Gravity / Checkered demon / Skulls ending
CD ____ **74321359902**
American / Oct '96 / BMG

Ragnarok

ARISING REALM
CD ____ **HNF 028CD**
Voices Of Wonder / Jun '97 / Plastic Head

NATTFERD
CD ____ **HNF 012CD**
Head Not Found / Feb '96 / Plastic Head

TO MEND THE OAKEN HEART
Haeled under heofenum / Rekindling an old flame / ...And the Earth shall be Holy / Arose by another name / Passion to a golden dawn / Where once ravens... / Fortuna imperatix mundi / Heartfire and forge / To mend the oaken heart
CD ____ **NM 018**
Neat Metal / Apr '97 / Pinnacle

Ragnarok

RAGNAROK
CD ____ **SRS 3613CD**
Silence / Jul '95 / ADA / Direct

Ragtime Millionaires

LIFE IS GOOD SOMETIMES
Life is good sometimes / Jesus on the mainline / Two bridges / No fool like an old fool / Mr. Jelly Roll Baker / Spanish strings / My old clock / Strenuous life / Whatever you can get / Brother can you spare a dime / Andru's easy rdier / Hard hearted Hannah / Come back baby / Blues for Betty / Marbella blues / One way girl / When the dust settles
CD ____ **FECD 109**
Fellside / Nov '96 / ADA / Direct / Target/ BMG

MAKING A MILLION
National seven / B flattened by the blues / Dark road blues / Snowy morning blues / Stone cold sober / Buckets of rain / Making a million / Rivers of beer / Corine Corina / Diddy wah diddy / Everywhere I go / Hi-heel sneakers / Warm summer rain / Old man's bike / Things we do / Highway robbery / Over the river / Ragtime millionaire / Where does all the money go
CD ____ **FE 095CD**
Fellside / Jan '94 / ADA / Direct / Target/ BMG

Rah Band

BEST OF THE RAH BAND, THE
CD ____ **MCCD 217**
Music Club / Oct '95 / Disc / THE

Raheem The Dream

TIGHT 2 DEF
CD ____ **THUMP 009**
MBA / May '97 / Grapevine/PolyGram

Railroad Jerk

ONE TRACK MIND
Gun problem / Bang the drum / Pollerkoaster / Riverboat / What did you expect / Home = hang / Forty minutes / Ballad of Railroad Jerk / Big white lady / Help yourself / Zero blues / Some girls waved / You better go now
CD ____ **OLE 1272**
Matador / Mar '95 / Vital

THIRD RAIL
Clean shirt / Objectify me / You forgot / Natalie / You bet / Well / Dusty knuckle / Middle child / This is not to say I still miss you / Another nite at the bar / (I can't get no) Sleep / Sweet librarian
CD ____ **OLE 1992**
Matador / Oct '96 / Vital

Railway Children

LISTEN ON (The Best Of The Railway Children)
Every beat of the heart / Everybody / Give it away / Music stop / What she wants / Something so good / Hours go by / After the rain / You're young / Collide / Somewhere south / Listen on / Over and over / Gentle sound / Monica's light / So right / In the meantime
CD ____ **CDOVD 451**
Virgin / Feb '95 / EMI

Rain

TASTE OF RAIN
All I want / Going / Beat goes on / Lemonstone desired / Hold on / Here they are / Taste of rain / She's on fire / Mother earth / Inside out / Outback blues
CD ____ **4684422**
Columbia / Mar '97 / Sony

Rain

SEDIMENT
CD ____ **MET 001CD**
Metonymic / Jan '97 / Cargo

Rain, Billy

SALAD DAYS
CD ____ **4509961892**
Oval 2 / Oct '94 / Warner Music

Rain Parade

EMERGENCY THIRD RAIL POWER TRIP/EXPLOSIONS IN GLASS PLACE
CD ____ **MAUCD 611**
Mau Mau / Apr '92 / Pinnacle

Rainbow

BEST OF RAINBOW, THE (2CD Set)
All night long / Man on the silver mountain / Can't happen here / Lost in Hollywood / Since you've been gone / Stargazer / Catch the rainbow / Kill the king / Sixteenth century greensleeves / I surrender / Long live rock 'n' roll / Eyes of the world / Starstruck / Light in the black / Mistreated
CD Set ____ **8000742**
Polydor / '83 / PolyGram

DIFFICULT TO CURE
I surrender / Spotlight kid / No release / Magic / Vielleicht das nachster zeit / Can't happen here / Freedom fighter / Midtown tunnel vision / Difficult to cure
CD ____ **8000182**
Polydor / Aug '84 / PolyGram

DOWN TO EARTH
All night long / Eyes of the world / No time to lose / Making love / Since you've been gone / Love's no friend / Danger zone / Lost in Hollywood
CD ____ **8237052**
Polydor / Dec '86 / PolyGram

LIVE IN GERMANY 1976 (2CD Set)
Kill the king / Mistreated / Sixteenth century greensleeves / Catch the rainbow / Man on the silver mountain / Stargazer / Still I'm sad / Do you close your eyes
CD Set ____ **DPVSOPCD 155**
Connoisseur Collection / Oct '90 / Pinnacle

LONG LIVE ROCK 'N' ROLL
Long live rock 'n' roll / Lady of the lake / LA connection / Gates of Babylon / Sensitive to light / Kill the King / Shed / Rainbow eyes
CD ____ **8250902**
Polydor / Jan '93 / PolyGram

ON STAGE
Kill the king / Man on the silver mountain / Blues / Starstruck / Catch the Rainbow / Mistreated / Sixteenth century Greensleeves / Still I'm sad
CD ____ **8236562**
Polydor / Nov '86 / PolyGram

RAINBOW FAMILY ALBUM, THE (Various Artists)
CD ____ **VSOPCD 195**
Connoisseur Collection / Apr '94 / Pinnacle

RAINBOW RISING
Tarot woman / Run with the wolf / Starstruck / Do you close your eyes / Stargazer / Light in the black
CD ____ **8236552**
Polydor / Nov '86 / PolyGram

RITCHIE BLACKMORE'S RAINBOW
Man on the silver mountain / Self portrait / Black sheep of the family / Catch the rainbow / Snake charmer / Temple of the king / If you don't like rock'n'roll / Sixteenth century greensleeves / Still I'm sad
CD ____ **8250892**
Polydor / Jan '93 / PolyGram

STRAIGHT BETWEEN THE EYES
Death Alley driver / Stone cold / Bring on the night / Tite squeeze / Tearin' out my heart / Power / Miss Mistreated / Rock fever / Eyes on fire
CD ____ **5217092**
Polydor / Apr '94 / PolyGram

STRANGER IN US ALL
Wolf to the moon / Cold hearted woman / Hunting humans (insatiable) / Stand and fight / Ariel / Too late for tears / Black masquerade / Silence / Hall of the mountain king / Still I'm sad
CD ____ **74321303372**
Arista / Sep '95 / BMG

VERY BEST OF RAINBOW, THE
CD ____ **5376872**
Polydor / Aug '97 / PolyGram

Rainbow, Tucker

PUSH ME TO WAR
CD ____ **ARICD 094**
Ariwa Sounds / Dec '94 / Jet Star / SRD

Raincoats

LOOKING IN THE SHADOWS
CD ____ **R 4032**
Rough Trade / Jun '96 / Pinnacle

MOVING
No-one's little girl / Ooh ooh la la la / Dance of hopping mad / Balloon / Mouth of a story / I saw a hill / Overheard / Rainstorm / Body / Animal rhapsody
CD ____ **R 3062**
Rough Trade / Feb '94 / Pinnacle

ODY SHAPE
Shouting out loud / Family treat / Only loved at night / Dancing in my head / Ody shape / And then it's OK / Baby song / Red shoes / Go away
CD ____ **R 3042**
Rough Trade / Jan '94 / Pinnacle

RAINCOATS, THE
Fairytale in the supermarket / No side to fall in / Adventures close to home / Off duty trip / Lola / Void / Life on the line / You're a million / In love / No looking
CD ____ **R 3022**
Rough Trade / Sep '93 / Pinnacle

Raindrops

COMPLETE RAINDROPS, THE
What a guy / Hanky panky / I won't cry / It's so wonderful / Da doo ron ron / When the boy's happy (the girl's happy too) / Kind of boy you can't forget / Isn't that love / Every little beat / Even though you can't dance / That boy's messin' up my mind / Not too young to get married / That boy

John / Book of love / Let's go together / You got what I like / One more tear / Another boy like mine / Don't let go / Do wah diddy diddy / More than a man / Talk about me / Can't hide the hurtin'
CD _______________ NEMCD 713
Sequel / Nov '94 / BMG

Rainer & Das Combo

BAREFOOT ROCK
Mellow down easy / Unseen enemy / Life is fine / Barefoot rock / Sleepwalk / Around and around / That's how things get done / Broken promises / I am a sinner / If I had posession over judgement day / Where's that at / Last fair deal / How I wanted you / I wish you would
CD _______________ FIEND 756
Demon / Oct '94 / Pinnacle
CD _______________ GRCD 346
Glitterhouse / Aug '97 / Avid/BMG

NOCTURNES
CD _______________ GRCD 363
Glitterhouse / Apr '97 / Avid/BMG

POWDERKEG
CD _______________ TEX 1
Demon / Jul '93 / Pinnacle

TEXAS TAPES, THE
Power of delight / One man crusade / It's a matter of taste / Merciful God / (Making the) trains (run on time) / What's wrong romeo / Powder keg / Mush mind blues / Drive drive drive / Another man / That's how things get done / I am a sinner
CD _______________ FIENDCD 734
Demon / Jun '93 / Pinnacle

Rainey, Ma

MA RAINEY (Rainey, Gertrude 'Ma')
Jealous hearted blues / CC rider / Jelly bean blues / Countin' the blues / Slave to the blues / Chain gang blues / Bessemer bound blues / Wringin' and twistin' blues / Mountain Jack blues / Trust no man / Morning hour blues / Ma Rainey's black bottom / New boweavil blues / Black cat - Hoot owl blues / Hear me / Talking to you / Prove it on me blues / Victim of the blues / Sleep talking blues / Blame it on the blues / Daddy - Goodbye blues / Sweet rough man / Black eye blues / Leavin' this morning / Runaway blues
CD _______________ MCD 47021
Milestone / Jan '93 / Cadillac / Complete/ Pinnacle / Jazz Music / Wellard

MA RAINEY'S BLACK BOTTOM (Rainey, Gertrude 'Ma')
Ma rainey's black bottom / Don't fish in my sea / Booze and blues / Farewell Daddy blues / Oh papa blues / Blues oh blues / Shave 'em dry / Lucky rock blues / Screetch owl blues / Georgia cake walk / Sleep talking blues / Yonder come the blues
CD _______________ YAZCD 1071
Yazoo / Apr '91 / ADA / CM / Koch

PARAMOUNT SESSIONS VOL.1 (Rainey, Gertrude 'Ma')
CD _______________ HCD 12001
Black Swan / Oct '92 / Jazz Music

PARAMOUNT SESSIONS VOL.5 (Rainey, Gertrude 'Ma')
CD _______________ HCD 12005
Black Swan / May '95 / Jazz Music

Rainfall Years

33RD MARCH
CD _______________ WSCD 007
World Serpent / Oct '96 / World Serpent

Rainravens

RAINRAVENS
CD _______________ FIENDCD 785
Demon / Sep '96 / Pinnacle

Rainwater, Marvin

CLASSIC MARVIN RAINWATER (4CD Set)
I gotta go get my baby / Daddy's glad you came home / Albino pink-eyed stallion / Sticks and stones / Tea bag Romeo / Tennessee houn' dog yodel / Dem low down blues / Where do we go from here / Hot and cold / Mr. Blues / Get off the stool / What am I supposed to do / I feel like leaving town (sometimes) / Why did you have to go and leave me / Gonna find me a bluebird / Because I'm a dreamer / So you think you've got troubles / Look for me (I'll be waiting for you) / Wayward angel / My brand of blues / My love is real / Lucky star / Majesty of love / You my darling you / Whole lotta woman (undubbed version) / Whole lotta woman / That's the way I feel / Baby don't go / Two fools in love / Because I'm a dreamer / Down in the cellar / Crazy love / Moanin' the blues / Gamblin' man / I dig you baby / Dance me daddy / Nothin' needs nothin' (like I need you) / Need for love (there's always) / No good runaround / Late for love (don't be) / Last time / Can I count on your love / Let me live again / Lonely island / Born to be lonesome / Love me baby (like there's no tomorrow) / That's when I'll stop loving you / Song of new love / Half breed / Valley of the moon / Young girls / Pale faced Indian (lament of the Cherokee) / Hard luck blues / She's gone / Yesterday's kisses / You're not happy / I can't forget / Boo hoo / Tough top cat / Honky tonk in your heart (There's a) / Hey good lookin' / Do it now / It wasn't enough / That little house / Part time lover / That aching heart / Love's prison / Bad girl / I saw your new love today / My old home town / Branded / Sing the girls a song / Indian burial / Black sheep / Troubles my little boy had / Sorrow brings a good man down / I want your heart / Talk to me / Run for your life boy / Old gang's gone / Cold woman / Oklahoma hills / Wedding rings / I love my country / Burning bridges / Black Jack McClain / Heart's hall of fame / Hit and run lover / Korea's mountain northland / Tainted gold / Don't tell my boy (in prison living a lie) / Don't try to change your little woman / Do you want to know / Engineer's song (the boy and the engineer) / Freight train blues / Key / Let's go on a picnic / Moment's of love / So long / Teardrops / Wanderer in me / What you got, you don't want / Would your mother be proud of you / You can't keep a secret
CD Set _______________ BCD 15600
Bear Family / Nov '93 / Direct / Rollercoaster / Swift

ROCKIN' ROLLIN' RAINWATER
Hot and cold / Mr. Blues / Get off the stool / There's a honky tonk in your heart / My brand of blues / Whole lotta woman / That's the way I feel / Baby don't go / Down in the cellar / Crazy love / Moanin' the blues / Gamblin' man / I dig you baby / Dance me Daddy / (There's always) A need for love / Don't be Late for love / Last time / Love me baby (like there's no tomorrow) / Valley of the moon / Young girls / Hard luck blues / I can't forget / Boo hoo / Tough top cat / Oklahoma Hills / Henryetta, Oklahoma
CD _______________ BCD 15182
Bear Family / Jun '94 / Direct / Rollercoaster / Swift

WHOLE LOTTA WOMAN
I dig you baby / Whole lotta woman / Baby don't go / Moanin' the blues / Crazy love / Mr. Blues / Hot and cold / Get off the stool / Down in the cellar / That's the way I feel / Dance me Daddy / Love me baby (like there's no tomorrow) / (There's always) A need for love / (Don't be late) For love / Last time / Young girls / Boo hoo / Tough top cat / (There's a honky tonk) In your heart / I can't forget / Gamblin' man / My brand of blues / Valley of the Moon / Hard luck blues / Oklahoma Hills / Henryetta, Oklahoma / Oklahoma
CD _______________ BCD 15812
Bear Family / Jul '94 / Direct / Rollercoaster / Swift

Raised Fist

STRONGER THAN EVER
CD _______________ BHR 046CD
Burning Heart / Mar '97 / Plastic Head

YOUR NOT LIKE ME
CD _______________ BHR 017CD
Burning Heart / Feb '95 / Plastic Head

Raism

VERY BEST OF PAIN
CD _______________ KRONH 04CD
Osmose / Jul '96 / Plastic Head

Raissa

MEANTIME
Worm / Green as sea / Meantime / Murky / We are nowhere / Space where you were / Storm / Silver wind / Meantime (part two) / Forgive me / Time I can touch / Your summertime / Piccadilly / Meantime (part three)
CD _______________ 5310372
Polydor / Oct '96 / PolyGram

Raitt, Bonnie

COLLECTION, THE
Finest lovin' man / Women be wise / Love me like a man / I feel the same / Angel from Montgomery / My first night alone without you / Louise / Runaway / Wild for you baby / True love is hard to find / Give it up or let me go / Under the falling sky / Love has no pride / Guilty / What is success / Sugar mama / About to make me leave home / Glow / Willya wontcha / No way to treat a lady
CD _______________ 7599262422
WEA / Dec '96 / Warner Music

GIVE IT UP
Give it up or let me go / Nothing seems to matter / I know / If you gotta make a fool of somebody / Love me like a man / Stayed too long at the fair / Under the falling sky / You got to know how / You told me baby / Love has no pride
CD _______________ 7599272642
WEA / Feb '93 / Warner Music

LONGING IN THEIR HEARTS
Love sneakin' up on you / Longing in their hearts / You / Cool clear water / Circle dance / I sho do / Dimming of the day / Feeling of falling / Steal your heart away / Storm warning / Hell to pay / Shadow of doubt
CD _______________ CDEST 2227
Capitol / Apr '94 / EMI

LUCK OF THE DRAW
Something to talk about / Good man, good woman / I can't make you love me / Tangled and dark / Come to me / No business / One part be my lover / Not the only one / Papa come quick (Jody and Chico) / Slow ride / Luck of the draw / All at once
CD _______________ CDEST 2145
Capitol / Jun '91 / EMI

NICK OF TIME
Nick of time / Thing called love / Love letters / Cry on my shoulder / Real man / Nobody's girl / Have a heart / Too soon to tell / I will not be denied / I ain't gonna let you break my heart again / Road's my middle name
CD _______________ CDEST 2095
Capitol / Apr '89 / EMI

ROAD TESTED
Thing called love / Something to talk about / Never make your move too soon / Shake a little / Matters of the heart / Love me like a man / Kokomo medley / My opening farewell / Dimming of the day / Longing in their hearts / Love sneakin' up on you / Burning down the house / I can't make you love me / I believe I'm in love with you / Rock steady / Angel from Montgomery
CD _______________ CDEST 2274
Capitol / Nov '95 / EMI

Raiz De Pedra

DIARIO DE BORDO
Q quem tai / Sao sepe / Linha azul / Amigos de longe / As historias de domingos / Munique / Levando a vida / Tempos de minuano / O Navio
CD _______________ 8888222
Tiptoe / Apr '96 / New Note/Pinnacle

Raja-Nee

HOT AND READY
Quick / Turn it up / Taunted / Walking away with it / Who's been givin' it up / Sex in a jeep / Hot and ready / Give it to me / Take your time / Dance hall druglord / I wanna get next to you / Bitchism
CD _______________ 5490142
Perspective / Feb '95 / PolyGram

Rakasha Mancham

PHYIDAR
CD _______________ EEE 013CD
Musica Maxima Magnetica / Sep '93 / Cargo / Plastic Head

Rake's Progress

CHEESE FOOD PROSTITUTE
CD _______________ ALMOCD 001
Almo Sounds / May '95 / Pinnacle

Rakha, Ustad Alla

TABLA DUET (Rakha, Usted Alla & Zakir Hussain)
CD _______________ MR 1001
Moment / Apr '95 / ADA / Koch

Rakotozafy

MADAGASIKARA VOL.4 (Valihala Malazi - Historical Recordings From The 1960's)
Salama 'nareo tompoko o / Ramanjareo / O zaza ny fandeha diasa / Botofetsy / Tonga teto lala / Hitako o / Mandrosoa lahy mahaeva / Isa, roa, telo / Rey lahy, rey lahy / Varavarankely / Sega vaovao valiha malaza / Mandihiza raha manan' eratra / Iadiavan janako aho rafozako / Ny fitiavana raho vao miaraka / Miasa tsara raha manambady / Tangalamena / Lekatseka / Samy faly / Fisaorana
CD _______________ CDORBD 028
Globestyle / Jul '95 / Pinnacle

Raksha Mancham

CHOS KHOR
CD _______________ EEE 17
Musica Maxima Magnetica / Aug '94 / Cargo / Plastic Head

Ramalho, Elba

ENCANTO
Caminhoneiro solitairo / Sao Joao na estrada / Flora / Alegria real / Que nem vem nem / Duvida / Caminhos do coracao / Miragem do Porto / Cidadao na hora H / Noites olindenses / Amor de Indio / Encanto / Eu vou te amar
CD _______________ 5124162
Philips / Mar '93 / PolyGram

Ramani, Dr. N.

MUSIC IN THE RAGAS...
CD _______________ NI 5257
Nimbus / Sep '94 / Nimbus

Ramazzotti, Eros

DOVE C'E MUSICA
Dove c'e musica / Stella Gemella / Piu bella cosa / L'aurora / Lettera al futuro / Lo amero / Questo immenso show / Quasi amore / Yo sin tin / Lei pero / L'uragano meri / Buona vita
CD _______________ 74321354412
Arista / Aug '96 / BMG

MUSICA E
CD _______________ 259174
Arista / Aug '95 / BMG

TUTTE STORIE
Cose della vita / A mezza via / Un altra te / Memorie / In compagnia / Un grosso no / Favola / Non c'e piu fantasia / Nostalsong / Niente di male / Esodi / L'ulti ma rivoluzione / Silver e missie
CD _______________ 74321143292
Arista / Jan '94 / BMG

Ramblers Dance Band

HIT SOUND OF THE RAMBLERS DANCE BAND
CD _______________ FLTRCD 526
Flame Tree / Oct '95 / Pinnacle

Ramey, Troy

BEST OF TROY RAMEY & THE SOUL SEARCHERS, THE (Ramey, Troy & The Soul Searchers)
CD _______________ NASH 4505
Nashboro / Feb '96 / Pinnacle

Ramirez, Humberto

ASPECTS
Aspects / Chapter 27 / Rumbero siempre / At peace / El ministro / Amanda / Golden view / Camino azul / Touch of beauty
CD _______________ 66058039
RMM / Jul '94 / New Note/Pinnacle

PORTRAIT OF A STRANGER
El principe / Sanjuanero / Cuando estoy contigo (madrigal) / Catalina / Sonando con puerto rico / Un tipo con suerte / Ball players / My funny valentine / To the king / Portrait of a stranger / Cristina / Atmospheres
CD _______________ 66058091
Tropi / Feb '96 / New Note/Pinnacle

Ramirez, Louie

OTRA NOCHE CALIENTE (Ramirez, Louie & Ray De La Paz)
Otra noche caliente / El / Suddenly / Definitivamente / Soy feliz / Yo soy la rumba / Medley: Noche caliente hits
CD _______________ 66058008
RMM / Sep '93 / New Note/Pinnacle

Ramleh

ADIEU ALL YOU JUDGES (Ramleh/ Skullflower)
CD _______________ BF 78
Broken Flag / Oct '96 / Cargo / SRD

BE CAREFUL WHAT YOU WISH FOR
CD _______________ SFTRI 397CD
Sympathy For The Record Industry / Jan '96 / Cargo / Greyhound / Plastic Head

HOMELESS
CD _______________ FRR 006
Freek / Jul '94 / RTM/Disc / SRD

WORKS VOL.3 (2CD Set)
CD Set _______________ DPROMCD 40
Dirter Promotions / Oct '96 / Cargo / Pinnacle / World Serpent

Ramlosa Kvallar

NIGHTS WITHOUT FRAMES
Sega / Magnus Ladulaten / Bogdan dansar / Castaneda / Vallaten / Den maskulina mystiken / Ide och lardomshistoria / Areskutan / Sista Mars / Esten / Ramlosa blues / Grekisk sorgmarsch
CD _______________ RESCD 507
Resource / Jul '97 / ADA / Direct

Ramones

ALL THE STUFF (AND MORE) VOL.1 (2CD Set)
Blitzkrieg bop / Beat on the brat / Judy is a punk / Now I wanna sniff some glue / Don't go down the basement / Loudmouth / Havana affair / 53rd and 3rd / I don't wanna walk around with you / I wanna be sedated / Glad to see you go / I remember you / Sheena is a punk rocker / Pinhead / Swallow my pride / California sun / I wanna be your boyfriend / You're gonna kill that girl / Babysitter / Listen to my heart / Let's dance / Today your love, tomorrow the world / I can't be / Gimme gimme shock treatment / Oh oh I love her so / Suzy is a headbanger / Now I wanna be a good boy / What's your game / Commando / Chainsaw / You should never have opened that door / California sun (live)
CD _______________ 7599262202
Sire / Aug '90 / Warner Music

BRAIN DRAIN
I believe in miracles / Punishment fits the crime / Pet Semetary / Merry Christmas / Learn to listen / Zero zero UFO / All screwed up / Can't get you outta my mind / Ignorance is bliss
CD _______________ CCD 1725
Chrysalis / Jul '89 / EMI

END OF THE CENTURY
Do you remember rock 'n' roll radio / I'm affected / Danny says / Chinese rocks / Return of Jackie and Judy / Let's go baby / Baby I love you / I can't make it on time / This ain't Havanna
CD _______ **E599274292**
Sire / Mar '94 / Warner Music

HALFWAY TO SANITY
Wanna live / Bop 'til you drop / Garden of serenity / Weasel face / Go lil' Camaro go / I know better now / Death of me / I lost my mind / Real cool time / I'm not Jesus / Bye bye baby / Worm man
CD _______ **BEGA 89CD**
Beggars Banquet / Dec '87 / RTM/Disc / Warner Music

IT'S ALIVE
Rockaway beach / Teenage labotomy / Blitzkrieg bop / I wanna be well / Glad to see you go / Gimme gimme shock treatment / You're gonna kill that girl / I don't care / Sheena is a punk rocker / Havana affair / Commando / Here today, gone tomorrow / Surfin' bird / Cretin hop / Listen to my heart / California sun / I don't wanna walk around with you / Pinhead / Suzy is a headbanger / Let's dance / Oh oh I lover her so / Now I wanna sniff some glue / We're a happy family
CD _______ **9362460452**
Sire / Jan '96 / Warner Music

MARKY RAMONE & THE INTRUDERS (Marky Ramone & The Intruders)
Can't take it with you / I wants my beer / Coward with a gun / Telephone love / Good luck you're gonna need it / Three cheers for you / Oh no not again / Maybe tomorrow / Anxiety / Holding a grudge / Man of God / Back off / Better things
CD _______ **BLK 5005ECD**
Blackout / Nov '96 / Plastic Head / Vital

RAMONES MANIA (2CD Set)
I wanna be sedated / Teenage lobotomy / Do you remember rock 'n' roll radio / Gimme gimme shock treatment / Beat on the brat / Sheena is a punk rocker / I wanna live / Pinhead / Blitzkrieg bop / Cretin hop / Rockaway beach / Commando / I wanna be your boyfriend / Mama's boy / Bop 'till you drop / We're a happy family / Bonzo goes to Bitburg / Outsider / Psychotherapy / Wart hog / Animal boy / Needles and pins / Howling at the moon (sha la la) / Somebody put something in my drink / We want the airwaves / Chinese rocks / I just want to have something to do / KKK took my baby away / Indian giver / Rock 'n' roll high school
CD _______ **9257092**
Sire / Jun '88 / Warner Music

Ramos, Kid

TWO HANDS, ONE HEART
CD _______ **BM 9031**
Black Magic / Jul '95 / ADA / Cadillac / Direct / Hot Shot

Rampage

PRIORITY 1
CD _______ **ALMOCD 005**
Almo Sounds / Nov '95 / Pinnacle

SCOUTS HONOR...BY WAY OF BLOOD
Intro / Flipmode is da squad / Da night B4 my shit / Talk of the town / Get da money and dip / Set up / Wild for da night / Flipmode enemy no.1 / Take it to the streets / Conquer da world / Hall of fame / Niggaz is bad / We getz down / Rampage outro
CD _______ **7559620222**
Elektra / Jul '97 / Warner Music

Rampling, Danny

IN THE MIX (2CD Set) (Various Artists)
CD Set _______ **DRCD 1**
Metropole / Nov '95 / 3mv/Sony / Prime

LOVE GROOVE DANCE PARTY VOL.1 & 2, THE (2CD Set) (Various Artists)
CD Set _______ **LGCD 1**
CD Set _______ **LGCDSP 1**
Metropole / May '96 / 3mv/Sony / Prime

LOVE GROOVE DANCE PARTY VOL.3 & 4 (2CD Set) (Various Artists)
CD Set _______ **LGCDSP 2**
CD Set _______ **LGCD 2**
Metropole / Nov '96 / 3mv/Sony / Prime

LOVE GROOVE DANCE PARTY VOL.5 & 6 (3CD Set) (Various Artists)
CD Set _______ **LGCD 3**
Metropole / May '97 / 3mv/Sony / Prime

Rampolokeng, Lesego

END BEGINNINGS (Rampolokeng, Lesego & Kalahari Surfers)
CD _______ **RERLRSCD 1**
ReR/Recommended / Jul '93 / ReR Megacorp / RTM/Disc

Ramsey, Bill

SOUVENIRS
Wumba tumba schokoladeneisverkaufer / Casa bambu / Erwar vom Konstantinopolitanischen / Gesangverein / Cecilia / Mach keinen heck meck / Go man go / Souvenirs / Hier konn matrosen vor anker gehn / Telefon aus Paris / Gina, Gina / Jeden tag 'ne andre party / Die welt ist rund / Pigalle (die gross mausefalle) / Care oriental / Das madchen mit dem aufregenden gang / Zuckerpuppe (aus der Bauchtanz truppe) / Mach ein foto davon / Weit weg von hier: *Ramsey, Bill & Chris Howland* / Missouri cowboy: *Ramsey, Bill & Peter Alexander* / Yes, fanny, ich tu das: *Ramsey, Bill & Margret Furer* / So ein stroll in tirol: *Ramsey, Bill & Margret Furer* / Nichts gegen die weiber: *Ramsey, Bill & Bibi Johns* / Got a call from Paris / Rockin' mountain / Gina Gina / Pigalle / Telefon fra Paris
CD _______ **BCD 15672**
Bear Family / Jun '92 / Direct / Rollercoaster / Swift

Ramsey, Bill

WHEN I SEE YOU (Ramsey, Bill & Toots Thielemans)
CD _______ **BLR 84 022**
L&R / May '91 / New Note/Pinnacle

Ramsey, Bo

BO RAMSEY & THE BACKSLIDERS (Ramsey, Bo & The Backsliders)
CD _______ **DFGCD 8443**
Dixie Frog / Jun '96 / Direct / TKO Magnum

IN THE WEEDS
In the weeds / Desert flower / Precious / Everything is comin' down / Big Bill / Sidetrack lounge / King of clubs / Trapped again / Ain't it hard / Forget you / Living in a cornfield
CD _______ **DFGCD 8461**
Dixie Frog / May '97 / Direct / TKO Magnum

Ramsey, Jack

FULL COURT PRESS
CD _______ **ISS 004CD**
Issues / Sep '94 / Plastic Head

Ramshackle

CHIN ON THE CURB
CD _______ **0098602WHE**
Edel / Jul '97 / Pinnacle

DEPTHOLOGY
CD _______ **BLRCD 30**
Big Life / Nov '95 / Mo's Music Machine / Pinnacle / Prime

Ramzy, Hossam

BALADI PLUS
CD _______ **EUCD 1083**
ARC / '91 / ADA / ARC Music

BEST OF ABDUL HALIM HAFIZ, THE (Ramzy, Hossam & His Egyptian Ensemble)
CD _______ **EUCD 1195**
ARC / Apr '92 / ADA / ARC Music

BEST OF OM KOLTHOUM, THE (Ramzy, Hossam & His Egyptian Ensemble)
CD _______ **EUCD 1194**
ARC / Apr '92 / ADA / ARC Music

EGYPTIAN RAI (Ramzy, Hossam & Ensemble)
CD _______ **EUCD 1132**
ARC / '91 / ADA / ARC Music

EL SULTAAN
CD _______ **EUCD 1122**
ARC / '91 / ADA / ARC Music

ESHTA
CD _______ **EUCD 1121**
ARC / '91 / ADA / ARC Music

GAMAAL RAWHANY
CD _______ **EUCD 1368**
ARC / Nov '96 / ADA / ARC Music

INTRODUCTION TO EGYPTIAN DANCE RHYTHMS, AN
CD _______ **EUCD 1081**
ARC / '91 / ADA / ARC Music

KOUHAIL
CD _______ **EUCD 1120**
ARC / '91 / ADA / ARC Music

LATIN AMERICAN HITS FOR BELLYDANCE
CD _______ **EUCD 1259**
ARC / Mar '94 / ADA / ARC Music

RHYTHMS OF THE NILE
CD _______ **EUCD 1104**
ARC / '91 / ADA / ARC Music

RO HE (Classical Egyptian Bellydance)
CD _______ **EUCD 1082**
ARC / '91 / ADA / ARC Music

SAMYA (The Best Of Farid Al Atrash)
CD _______ **EUCD 1232**
ARC / Nov '93 / ADA / ARC Music

SOURCE OF FIRE
CD _______ **EUCD 1305**
ARC / Jul '95 / ADA / ARC Music

ZEINA (The Best Of Mohammed Abdul Wahab)
CD _______ **EUCD 1231**
ARC / Nov '93 / ADA / ARC Music

Ranaldo, Lee

FROM HERE TO INFINITY
CD _______ **SST 113CD**
SST / May '93 / Plastic Head

Ranch Girls

HILLBILLY HARMONY
CD _______ **GRCD 6071**
Goofin' / Dec '96 / Nervous / TKO Magnum

Ranch Hands

SWITCHED ON COUNTRY
Hello I love you / Sundown / Woman, beautiful woman / Ruby don't take your love to town / Gentle on my mind / Jolene / Let your love flow / Rhinestone cowboy / Oh lonesome me / Half the way / If I said you had a beautiful body / Detroit city / Down the Mississippi / Mississippi / Some days are diamonds / Slow hand / I don't wanna play house / Your cheatin' heart / Listen to the radio / You never gave up on me / Always on my mind / Love me tender / Honey / Sweetest things / Only love / Annie's song / Me and Bobby McGee / Help me make it through the night / When you were sweet sixteen / Love hurts / You needed me / Blue eyes crying in the rain / I will always love you / Wolverton Mountain / Coward of the county / Some broken hearts never mend / Take me home country roads / All I ever need is you / Heaven is my woman's love / You asked me to / Before the next teardrop falls / Banks of the Ohio / If you love me let me know / You're my best friend / I recall a gypsy woman / Shelter of your eyes / Silver threads and golden needles / Honey come back / Most beautiful girl in the world / Have I told you lately / I walk the line / Take me back
CD _______ **QED 121**
Tring / Nov '96 / Tring

Ranch Romance

BLUE BLAZES
Heartaches / What's wrong with you / Blue blazes / 'Deed I do / Arizona moon / Racin' / Burnin' bridges / Buckaroo / Lost heart / Cuttin' a rug / Trouble / Baby doll / Lucky one
CD _______ **SHCD 3794**
Sugar Hill / Sep '91 / ADA / CM / Direct / Koch / Roots

FLIP CITY
CD _______ **SHCD 3813**
Sugar Hill / Jan '94 / ADA / CM / Direct / Koch / Roots

WESTERN DREAM
When the bloom is on the sage / Lovesick blues / Baby's on the town / St. Louis blues / Cowboys and indians / St. James Avenue / Gotta lot of rhythm in my soul / Ain't no ash will burn / Why don't you love me (Like you used to) / Birmingham fling / Last one to know / Western dream
CD _______ **SHCD 3799**
Sugar Hill / Mar '92 / ADA / CM / Direct / Koch / Roots

Rancho Diablo

CHICKEN WORLD
CD _______ **THIRTEENCD 1**
Thirteenth Hour / Feb '95 / RTM/Disc

Rancho Relaxo Allstars

RANCHO RELAXO ALLSTARS VOL.1
CD _______ **EFA 122812**
Disko B / Sep '96 / SRD

Rancid Hell Spawn

AXE HERO
CD _______ **STUNCH 6**
Wrench / Sep '93 / Shellshock/Disc / SRD

Randall, Jon

WHAT YOU DON'T KNOW
This heart / If blue tears were silver / I came straight to you / If I hadn't reached for the stars / To pieces / Tennessee blues / What if you don't know / Only game in town / They're gonna miss when I'm gone / Just like you
CD _______ **74321272972**
RCA / Mar '95 / BMG

Randles, Philip

HEAR MY SONG
CD _______ **CDTS 040**
Maestro / Nov '93 / Savoy

ORGAN DANCE BONANZA
CD _______ **CDTS 052**
Maestro / Dec '95 / Savoy

PARTY DANCE BONANZA
CD _______ **CDTS 055**
Maestro / Dec '95 / Savoy

Randolph, Boots

YAKETY SAX
Percolator / Yakety sax (mono) / Hey Elvis / Difficult / I'm getting the message baby / Little big horn / Big daddy / Blue guitar / Greenback dollar / Sweet talk / Red light / La golondrina / Temptation / Battle of New Orleans / Sleepwalk / After you've gone / Little big horn / Sleep / So rare / Teach me tonight / Happy whistler / Estrellita / Big daddy / Bongo band / Yakety sax (stereo) / Hey Elvis
CD _______ **BCD 15459**
Bear Family / Apr '89 / Direct / Rollercoaster / Swift

Random Damage

RANDOM DAMAGE
CD _______ **M 7014CD**
Mascot / Oct '95 / Vital

Random Killing

RANDOM KILLING
CD _______ **BMCD 078**
Black Mark / Nov '95 / Plastic Head

THOUGHTS OF AGGRESSION
CD _______ **BMCD 074**
Black Mark / Jun '95 / Plastic Head

Randy

NO CARROTS FOR THE REHABILITATED
CD _______ **DOLCD 011**
Delores / Feb '95 / Plastic Head

REST IS SILENCE, THE
CD _______ **DOL 037CD**
Dolores / Oct '96 / Plastic Head

THERE'S NO WAY
CD _______ **DOL 016CD**
Dolores / Aug '95 / Plastic Head

THERE'S NO WAY WE'RE GONNA FIT IN
CD _______ **DOLCD 016**
Delores / Feb '95 / Plastic Head

Raney, Doug

BACK IN NEW YORK
CD _______ **SCCD 31409**
Steeplechase / Jul '97 / Discovery / Impetus

GUITAR, GUITAR, GUITAR
CD _______ **SCCD 31212**
Steeplechase / Jul '88 / Discovery / Impetus

MEETING THE TENORS (Raney, Doug Sextet)
CD _______ **CRISS 1006CD**
Criss Cross / Feb '94 / Cadillac / Direct / Vital/SAM

Raney, Jimmy

BUT BEAUTIFUL (Raney, Jimmy Trio)
CD _______ **CRISS 1065CD**
Criss Cross / Oct '92 / Cadillac / Direct / Vital/SAM

JAZZ GUITAR RARITIES
CD _______ **JZCD 377**
Suisa / Jun '93 / Jazz Music / THE

MASTER, THE (Raney, Jimmy Quartet)
CD _______ **CRISS 1009CD**
Criss Cross / Nov '90 / Cadillac / Direct / Vital/SAM

STOLEN MOMENTS (Raney, Jimmy & Doug Raney Quartet)
CD _______ **SCCD 31118**
Steeplechase / Jul '88 / Discovery / Impetus

VISITS PARIS
CD _______ **74321429252**
RCA / Apr '97 / BMG

WISTARIA (Raney, Jimmy Trio)
CD _______ **CRISS 1019CD**
Criss Cross / Nov '91 / Cadillac / Direct / Vital/SAM

Rangell, Nelson

DESTINY
Road ahead / Grace / Street wise / House is not a home / Going all the way / Rainbow shadows / Little dream girl / (On the) Phone / Sonora / Joie de vivre / Destiny
CD _______ **GRP 98142**
GRP / Apr '95 / New Note/BMG

TO BEGIN AGAIN
CD _______ **1390072**
Gaia / May '89 / New Note/Pinnacle

TURNING NIGHT INTO DAY
Starting now / Turning night into day / Journey / All for you / For the rest of my life / Romantique / Godzilla / From spark to flame / April snow / All hearts, one heart / Today's top story / La repuesta (The answer)
CD _______ **GRP 98642**
GRP / Apr '97 / New Note/BMG

YES THEN YES
Yes then yes / Looking forward / Never forgotten / Love is / Star stream / Swingin' for the fence / One heart calling / Runaround / Child's play / Time will tell

CD GRP 97552
GRP / Jan '94 / New Note/BMG

Ranglin, Alvin

HOLY GROUND
CD CDHB 62
Heartbeat / Sep '90 / ADA / Direct / Greensleeves / Jet Star

Ranglin, Ernest

BELOW THE BASSLINE
Congo man / Surfin' / King Tubby meets the rockers / Satta a masagana / 54-56 (was my number) / Ball of fire / Black disciples / Bourbon street skank / None shall escape the judgment / Nana's chalk pipe / Below the bass line
CD IJCD 4002
Island Jamaica Jazz / May '96 / PolyGram

MEMORIES OF BARBER MACK
Papa's bag juice / Fade away / For Juni / Undecided / Memories of Baber Mack / Stop that train / Blue mountains / Lovebird / Dancehall fever / Five thirty
CD IJCD 4004
Island Jamaica Jazz / May '97 / PolyGram

PLAY THE TIME AWAY
CD GM 001
Runn / May '96 / Grapevine/PolyGram / Jet Star / SRD

SOUL D'ERN
CD JHAS 611
Ronnie Scott's Jazz House / Aug '97 / Cadillac / Jazz Music / New Note/Pinnacle / TKO Magnum

SOUNDS & POWER
CD SOCD 50152
Studio One / Oct '96 / Jet Star

Rankin Family

ENDLESS SEASONS
As I roved out / River / Natives / Oganaich an or-fhuilt Bhulde/Am braighe / Forty days and nights / Eyes of Margaret / You feel the same way too / Endless seasons / Padstow / Blue eyed Suzie / Your boat's lost at sea
CD GRACD 217
Grapevine / Jul '96 / Grapevine/PolyGram

FARE THEE WELL LOVE
CD GRMCD 002
Grapevine / Jul '96 / Grapevine/PolyGram

NORTH COUNTRY
Fare thee well love / North Country / Oich u agus h-iuraibh eile (love song) / Borders and time / Mull river shuffle / Golden rod jig / Lisa Brown / Ho ro my nut brown maiden / Tramp miner / Rise again / Boat song / Christy Campbell medley / Betty Lou's reel / Turn that boat around
CD GRMCD 216
Grapevine / Jul '96 / Grapevine/PolyGram

RANKIN FAMILY
CD CDEST 2185
Capitol / Oct '92 / EMI

RANKIN FAMILY, THE
CD GRMCD 001
Grapevine / Jul '96 / Grapevine/PolyGram

Rankin File

FOR THE RECORD
Call on me / Sense of kind / Words and wisdom / Canadian trilogy / Leaving home / Whispy / Leaving is the story of my life / Carefully / Lost it on the road / Met her on the shap / Drank his son to death / Circle turns again / Mrs. Mann and me / Mr. Sax
CD CDTRAX 057
Greentrax / Dec '92 / ADA / Direct / Duncans / Highlander

Rankin, Iain

OUT OF THE BLUE
Teardrop on the ocean / Thirty storeys high / We're still here / Out of nowhere / Go to hell but turn right / Daddy was a miner / McGingle's violin / Make love to me / One step forward and two steps back / Next time you talk to heaven / Wild horses / Let's do it all over again
CD CDTRAX 069
Greentrax / Dec '93 / ADA / Direct / Duncans / Highlander

Rankin, Rita

LANTERN BURN (Rankin, Rita & Mary)
Tiree love song / Hi horo na horo eile / Western highway / Chi mi 'n geamhradh / Eilidh / Medley / Fair love of my heart / Long for the sea / Medley / Greenwood side / Brown haired maiden of the smooth tresses / Darkest winter / Fear a' bhata / Sarah / Lantern burn
CD IRCD 053
Iona / May '97 / ADA / Direct / Duncans

Ranking Joe

FAST FORWARD TO AFRICA
CD ARICD 107
Ariwa Sounds / May '96 / Jet Star / SRD

Rannenberg, Christian

LONG WAY FROM HOME (Rannenberg, Christian & Pink Piano Allstars)
CD BEST 1006CD
Acoustic Music / Nov '93 / ADA

Rant

MIXING IT
CD CMCD 074
Celtic Music / Jul '94 / CM

Raped

COMPLETE RAPED PUNK COLLECTION, THE
Moving target / Raped / Escalator hater / Normal / BIC / ECT / Foreplay playground / Cheap night out / Babysitting / Shit / LONDON / Slits / Cheap trash / Knock on wood
CD CDPUNK 35
Anagram / Jun '94 / Cargo / Pinnacle

Rapeman

TWO NUNS AND A PACK MULE
CD BFFP 33CD
Blast First / Nov '88 / RTM/Disc

Rapiers

BACK TO THE POINT
CD FCD 3034
Fury / Aug '94 / Nervous / TKO Magnum

Rapone, Al

PLAYS TRIBUTE TO CLIFTON CHENIER
Accordian man / Zydeco man / Oh Momon / Comin' home / Et 'tite fille / Rock me baby / Tu le ton son ton / Zydeco ils sont pas sale / Sa m'appel fou / Chere catin / You used to call me / Key to the highway / Hey Negress / Rosa Lee / It's my soul
CD ATM 1133
Atomic Theory / May '97 / ADA / Direct

Rapoon

FALLEN GODS
CD STCD 086
Staalplaat / May '95 / Vital/SAM

KIRGHIZ LIGHT, THE (2CD Set)
CD Set STCD 097
Staalplaat / Dec '95 / Vital/SAM

Rappin' 4-Tay

DON'T FIGHT THE FEELIN'
Back again / Dank season / Keep one in the chambra / Can u buckem / Just 'cause I called you a bitch / Playaz club / She's a sell out / I'll be around / Tear the roof off / Sucka free / Call it what you want / I got cha back / This is what I know / Gift / Out 4000 / Playaz club (sucka 3 remix) / I'll be around (wicked mix) / I'll be around (Al's brother 2 brother mix)
CD CTCD 45
Cooltempo / Jul '95 / EMI

Rapscallion

CHAMELEON DROOL
CD CDZORRO 41
Metal Blade / Jul '90 / Pinnacle / Plastic Head

Rara Machine

VOUDOU NOU
CD SHCD 64054
Shanachie / Oct '94 / ADA / Greensleeves / Koch

Rare Air

HARD TO BEAT
CD GLCD 1073
Green Linnet / Feb '93 / ADA / CM / Direct / Highlander / Roots

PRIMEVAL
CD GLCD 1104
Green Linnet / Feb '91 / ADA / CM / Direct / Highlander / Roots

SPACE PIPER
CD GLCD 1115
Green Linnet / '92 / ADA / CM / Direct / Highlander / Roots

Rare Bird

SYMPATHY
Sympathy / You went away / Nature's fruit / Bird on a wing / What you want to know / Beautiful scarlet / Hammerhead / I'm thinking / As your mind flies by
CD CDOVD 280
Charisma / Apr '90 / EMI

Rare Earth

DIFFERENT WORLD
CD 341002
Koch / Feb '93 / Koch

PACKET OF THREE VOL.7 (3CD Set) (Rare Earth/Chubby Checker/Doobie Brothers)
I know I'm losing you: *Rare Earth* / Get ready: *Rare Earth* / Born to wander: *Rare Earth* / I just want to celebrate: *Rare Earth* / Hey big brother: *Rare Earth* / Good time Sally: *Rare Earth* / Warm ride: *Rare Earth* / Here comes the night: *Rare Earth* / I can feel my love rising: *Rare Earth* / We're gonna have a good time: *Rare Earth* / Twist: *Checker, Chubby* / Dancin' party: *Checker, Chubby* / Popeye the hitchiker: *Checker, Chubby* / Fly: *Checker, Chubby* / Pony time: *Checker, Chubby* / Slow twistin': *Checker, Chubby* / Hucklebuck: *Checker, Chubby* / Limbo rock: *Checker, Chubby* / Birdland: *Checker, Chubby* / Hey bobba needle: *Checker, Chubby* / Twenty miles: *Checker, Chubby* / Let's twist again: *Checker, Chubby* / Rosie: *Checker, Chubby* / Hooka tooka: *Checker, Chubby* / Mary Ann limbo: *Checker, Chubby* / Let's limbo soul more: *Checker, Chubby* / Twist it up: *Checker, Chubby* / Loady lo: *Checker, Chubby* / Let's do the Freddie: *Checker, Chubby* / Dance the mess around: *Checker, Chubby* / By yourself: *Doobie Brothers* / Make it easy: *Doobie Brothers* / Quicksilver Princess: *Doobie Brothers* / Blue jay: *Doobie Brothers* / Coke can changes: *Doobie Brothers* / Runaround ways: *Doobie Brothers* / Pauper's diary: *Doobie Brothers* / I'll keep on givin': *Doobie Brothers* / Excitement: *Doobie Brothers* / Another way: *Doobie Brothers* / Song to JC: *Doobie Brothers* / On our way up: *Doobie Brothers* / Tilted park crud munchery: *Doobie Brothers*
CD Set KLMCD 307
BAM / Nov '96 / Koch / Scratch/BMG

Ras Iley

KING OF THE STAGE
CD WCD 395
JW / Feb '94 / Jet Star

Ras Ivi

ARK OF COVENANT (Ras Ivi & The Family Of Rastafari)
CD SZCD 003
Surr Zema Musik / Apr '95 / Jet Star

Ras Michael

FREEDOM SOUND (Ras Michael & The Sons Of Negus)
CD RNCD 2015
Rhino / Sep '93 / Grapevine/PolyGram / Jet Star

KIBIR AM LAK (Ras Michael & The Sons Of Negus)
CD CC 2712
Crocodisc / Jul '94 / Grapevine/PolyGram

KNOW NOW (Ras Michael & The Sons Of Negus)
CD SHANCD 64019
Shanachie / May '90 / ADA / Greensleeves / Koch

LOVE THY NEIGHBOUR (Ras Michael & The Sons Of Negus)
CD LLCD 001
Live & Learn / Mar '93 / Greensleeves / Jet Star

NEW NAME (Ras Michael & The Sons Of Negus)
CD RB 3007
Reggae Best / May '94 / Grapevine/ PolyGram

NYAHBINGHI (Ras Michael & The Sons Of Negus)
CD CC 2710
Crocodisc / Apr '94 / Grapevine/PolyGram

RAS MICHAEL-ZION TRAIN (Ras Michael & Zion Train)
CD SST 168CD
SST / May '93 / Plastic Head

RASTAFARI (Ras Michael & The Sons Of Negus)
CD GRELCD 153
Greensleeves / Feb '91 / Jet Star / SRD

RASTAFARI DUB (Ras Michael & The Sons Of Negus)
CD RE 162CD
ROIR / Nov '94 / Plastic Head / Shellshock/Disc

Ras Midas

STAND UP WISE UP
CD 14806
Spalax / Jun '97 / ADA / Cargo / Direct / Discovery / Greyhound

Rascoe, Moses

BLUES LIVE
CD FF 454CD
Flying Fish / May '93 / ADA / CM / Direct / Roots

Rashid, Xalid

MUSIC FROM KURDISTAN, THE
CD 926682
BUDA / Jun '97 / Discovery

Raskinen, Minna

REVELATIONS
CD OMCD 64
Olarin Musiiki Oy / Nov '95 / ADA / Direct

Rasle, Jean-Pierre

CORNERMUSIQUE
CD CMCD 058
Celtic Music / Mar '94 / CM

Rasmussen, Valdemar

DEN SIGNEDE DAG
CD MECCACD 1017
Music Mecca / Nov '94 / Cadillac / Jazz Music / Wellard

ET YNDIGT LAND
CD MECCACD 1029
Music Mecca / Nov '94 / Cadillac / Jazz Music / Wellard

KOERLIGHED AF GOLD QUINTET
CD MECCACD 1078
Music Mecca / May '97 / Cadillac / Jazz Music / Wellard

SONDERJYSK KAFFEBORD
CD MECCACD 1016
Music Mecca / Nov '94 / Cadillac / Jazz Music / Wellard

VELKOMMEN IGEN
CD MECCACD 1004
Music Mecca / Nov '94 / Cadillac / Jazz Music / Wellard

Raspberries

POWER POP VOL.1
CD RPM 162
RPM / Jun '96 / Pinnacle

POWER POP VOL.2
CD RPM 163
RPM / Jun '96 / Pinnacle

RASPBERRIES PRESERVED (Various Artists)
CD PR 6317
Ginger / Oct '96 / Cargo / Greyhound

Ratos De Paraos

ANARKOPHOBIA
CD RO 93262
Roadrunner / Apr '91 / PolyGram

Rattle 'N' Reel

OUTRAGEOUS
CD RNR 001CD
RNR / Oct '94 / ADA

Rattlers

SCARE ME TO DEATH
Scare me to death / Little red / Mine all mine / Cat crept in / Blue zoot / Hey baby / Always yours / You're my baby / Rattlin' boogie / Knife edge baby
CD NERCD 047
Nervous / Sep '93 / Nervous / TKO Magnum

Rattlers

PLEASURES IN MISADVENTURE
Born to grow old / Pedlar of York / Ten years from now / Long way down / Pawn in a blind man's game / Frog 'n' swan / Walter Doorplacket / Traveller's dance / You really don't care / Roll away the blues / Justice and the law / Liar / Out to lunch / Two for the road
CD PMRCD 10
Pagan Media / '96 / Pagan Media / Pinnacle

Rattlesnake Kiss

RATTLESNAKE KISS
Railroad / Sad Suzie / Angel / Alright by me / Nothing this good (could be real) / Wake up / Taste it / Don't make it right / All to me (that I was to you) / Kiss this
CD SOV 106CD
Sovereign / '92 / Target/BMG

Rattray, Mark

MUSICAL MAGIC (Rattray, Mark & Maggie Moon)
CD PLSCD 238
Pulse / Jul '97 / BMG

Rattus

RATTUS 1981-1984
CD RATCD 1
Poko / Nov '93 / Plastic Head

Ratzer, Karl

SATURN RETURNING
Just what you need / Finger snappin' good / Farmer's charm / Saturn returning / Main squeeze / Silent rain / Holy Mother song / Lobied
CD ENJ 93152
Enja / May '97 / New Note/Pinnacle / Vital/ SAM

Raun Fur Notizen

NON PLACE URBAN FIELD
CD INCCD 3312
Incoming / Sep '96 / Pinnacle

Raux, Richard

UNDER THE MAGNOLIAS (Raux, Richard Quartet)
CD _______ **CDLLL 27**
La Lichere / Aug '93 / ADA / Discovery

Rava, Enrico

ANIMALS (Rava, Enrico 4uartet)
Animals / Bellflower / Bella / Spider blues / Clown / Moon revisited / Infant / High castle
CD _______ **INAK 8801CD**
In Akustik / Jul '97 / Direct / TKO Magnum

NOIR (CD/Book Set)
3.17 am / Tango for Vasquez / Garbage can blues / Jazz at the club club / Amnesia / Papaya bar / Theme for Jessica Tatum / Trial / Diva / Life is great (anyway)
CD Set _______ **LBLC 6595**
Label Bleu / Feb '97 / New Note/Pinnacle

PILGRIM AND THE STAIRS, THE
Pilgrim and the stars / Parks / Bella / Pesce naufrago / Surprise hotel / By the sea / Blancasnow
CD _______ **8473222**
ECM / Jul '95 / New Note/Pinnacle

PLOT, THE
Tribe / On the red side of the street / Amici / Dr. Ra and Mr. Va / Foto di famiglia / Plot
CD _______ **5232822**
ECM / Jul '95 / New Note/Pinnacle

QUARTET
Lavari casalinghi / Fearless five / Tramps / 'Round midnight / Blackmail
CD _______ **5232832**
ECM / Jul '95 / New Note/Pinnacle

VOLVER (Rava, Enrico & Dino Saluzzi Quintet)
Bout de souffle / Minguito / Luna-volver / Tiempos de ausencias / Ballantine for valentine visions
CD _______ **8313952**
ECM / Feb '88 / New Note/Pinnacle

Ravana

COMMON DAZE
Good grief / Urban child / When they cry / Words in a rhyme / Wounded / Reasons to live / Who'll run your mind / Passing / Wherever you are
CD _______ **PNCD 001**
Prognetik / Jul '97 / Pinnacle

Raven

ALL FOR ONE
Take control / Mind over metal / Sledgehammer rock / All for one / Run silent, run deep / Hung drawn and quartered / Break the chain / Take it away / Seek and destroy / Athletic rock
CD _______ **NEATCD 1011**
Neat / '85 / Pinnacle

EVERYTHING LOUDER
Blind eye / No pain, no gain / Sweet Jane / Holy grail / Hungry / Insane / Everything louder / Between the wheels / Losing my mind / Get your fingers out / Wilderness of broken glass / Fingers do the walking / Bonus
CD _______ **08512162**
SPV / May '97 / Koch / Plastic Head

GLOW
CD _______ **SPV 08412092**
SPV / Jun '95 / Koch / Plastic Head

Raven, Jon

FRAGILE LIFE
CD _______ **BROCD 137**
Broadside / Aug '96 / Broadside / CM

Raven, Michael

FLOWERS OF PICARDY (Raven, Michael & Joan Mills)
Flowers of Picardy / Sicilian waltz / Epitaph on an Army of Mercenaries / La Russe waltz / Paris polka / Dancing lady / Green fields of England / Robin Hood's dance / Maid of Provence / Stafford County fair / Trecynon polka / Over the wall / New tenpenny bit / My last farewell to Stirling / Carrickfergus / Bentley canal / With measured sound/Adson's Sarabande / Cluster of nuts / Mallorca / Oh, fair enough / Cypress curtain / Mrs. Anne Harecourt's galliard / Robin Hood and the tanner / Rhododendron/The singer/The old soldier / Backwoodsman / March to Kandahar / Unknown grave
CD _______ **MR 73**
Michael Raven / Jun '97 / Michael Raven

HALLIARD, THE - JON RAVEN/THE JOLLY MACHINE (Raven, Michael & Nic Jones)
Calico printer's clerk / Unquiet grave / Ladies don't go a-thievin' / Midsummer fair / To the weavers gin ye / Long Lankin / Going for a soldier Jenny / Workhouse boy / Row bullies row / Lancashire lads / Thousand miles away / Love and murder / Last farewell / Jolly Joe / Rambling sailor / Chartists anthem / Nailmakers' lament / Charlie's song / Redditch needlemakers' lament / Landlord don't you cry / Freedom and reform / Potter's chant / Waiting for wages / Wednesbury town / Jolly machine / Collier's rant / John Whitehouse / Tommy Note / Dudley canal song
CD _______ **MR 77**
Michael Raven / Jun '97 / Michael Raven

RECITAL (Raven, Michael & Joan Mills)
Lass from the low country / Queen's marsh / Ruth Ellis / Fortune my foe / Brink of the white rock / Blackbird wilt thou go / Green bushes / Lark's elegy / Dancing Delilah / Cafe Cantrell / Hampton lullaby / Black is the colour / Brisk young widow / Come live with me / Minuet de la Cour / Charlie's song / Zambra mora / Hednesford town / Chattering magpie / Moorlough shore / Pennsylvanian song/Captain Heapy / Biker's song / Dove / Illic jacet / Alman / Raglan Road
CD _______ **MR 70**
Michael Raven / Jun '97 / Michael Raven

RETROSPECTIVE
Dark eyes/Farruca / Three Renaissance dances / Soleares / Guido's rag / Melancholy Pavan / Willow rag / Lichfield Bower processional / Vals by Aguado / Rhumba Cubana / Lady Mary/Argent / Going with David to Towyn / Three Iberian dances / Over the stone/Rakes of Mallow/Tanguillio/Prelude/Warrior's welcome home / Comical fellow / Bushes and briars / Two butcher's sirtos / Suite in E / Helston furry dance / Midnights of November / Jigg ashling / Ladies go dancing at Whitsun / Beatrice Hill's reel/Morpeth Rant / Dowland's Alman / Please to see the King / Off to California / Poor murdered woman/Clee Hill reel
CD _______ **MR 75**
Michael Raven / Jun '97 / Michael Raven

REYNARDINE TAPES, THE (Raven, Michael & Joan Mills)
Brewer's lady / December day dance / Queen of the night / Star of Belle Isle / Greek Street / Old Dublin fireman / Lichfield Greenhill Bower Processional / Three hearty young poachers / Tulla reel/The castle / Stafford pageant song / White copper alley / Trent waters/Marion's rambles / Johnny Gallagher / Eternal father / Lord Thomas / Lakes of Pontchartrain / Poor law Bill / Hungarian hat / Crafty maid's policy / Maid on the shore/Black Mountain/Gaunt man / Sally Gardens / Tarantos
CD _______ **CDMR 72**
Michael Raven / Jun '97 / Michael Raven

SHROPSHIRE LAD, A (Raven, Michael & Joan Mills)
On Wenlock Edge the wood's in trouble / Megan's daughter / Bredon Hill / Rhoslan reel / Half moon / White rose of summer / New mistress / Galaru/The blackbird / Along the fields / Is my team ploughing / Bard's dream / Ludlow recruit / Megan who lost her garter / Come pipe a tune / Lady mine/Gogerddan / Midnights of November / Long live Mary / Rising of the lark/Weep not for me / True lover / Beside the seashore/Good ale / Goldcup flowers / Where are you going / Deserter / Clover / Loitering with a vacant eye / Lady Owen's delight / Farewell to barn and stack and tree / My lady is more fair / Wenlock edge / Snowdon / When I was one and twenty / Farewell to Llangyfelach / Shrewsbury jail
CD _______ **MR 69**
Michael Raven / Jun '97 / Michael Raven

SONGS AND DANCES OF HEREFORDSHIRE (Raven, Michael & Joan Mills)
Lowlands of Holland / Jack Gore's galliard / Dives and Lazarus / Mr. Baskerville's volt / Foolish boy / Hunting the squirrel / Banks of sweet primroses / Ledbury timber-teams / Orange in bloom / Rich old lady / Holywell / Trees they do grow high / John Locke's polka / My mother bid me / Barbara Ellen / Milkmaid's song / Restless road / Speed the plough / Sheffield Park / Jack of the green / Thundermanshire / Moon shines bright / Blacksmith / Leaves of life / London town / Sheepskins / Rose in June / Blue-eyed stranger / Oh who is that / Cider Annie / Piers ploughman / Herefordshire lasses / Ledbury parson
CD _______ **MR 76**
Michael Raven / Jun '97 / Michael Raven

SONGS AND SOLOS (Raven, Michael & Joan Mills)
For Alan Green / Flowers in her hair / Nottingham swing/Bushes and briars / Octopus dancing / Winifred's dream/Winifred's jig / Lament for Owain Glyndwr / Slender boy/Waterloo dance / Irish girl / Bunch of rushes / Land of lost content / Vyrnwy waters / Mirror of my mind / Prelude in G/Mishca's restaurant / Pretty ploughboy / Lament for Peter Bellamy/Fred Jordan's galliard / Waiting for wages / Mainstone hornpipe/Byrne's hornpipe / Song of the fox / Gisburn lament/John of Paris/Bird on the wing / Midnight city / Lion cafe/Seth Brown's polkas / Lazy Jane / Kirton Grove/Dr. Fauster's tumblers / Schoon lief / Newcastle/A trip to Scarborough / Widow woman's daughter
CD _______ **MR 68**
Michael Raven / Jun '97 / Michael Raven

TAMING THE DRAGON'S STRINGS
Prelude / Dark lane/Now all is still/Raven's nest / Soulton Hall suite / Foxy's flying/Almost slain/Dead of Rajistan / Angelsey suite / You must come to Kilpeck / Stained glass/Food for dogs / Sarah Collins / Road to Lisdoonvarna/Road to Towyn / West / Linhope suite / Pell Well Hall/Wild bird weeping/Little dog sleeping / Midsummer Hill / Polly Gale's Tarantella / I can remember/Cidery wine/Dark-haired daughters / Singing bird/The bard's love / Lovliest of trees / Captain's apprentice/Tobago bound / Dark invader (a dog called Bruno) / Dead elm / Teapot time / My lady's suite / But he would/Before I come again/Summer's end / My last farewell
CD _______ **CDMR 71**
Michael Raven / Jun '97 / Michael Raven

WELSH GUITAR
Grey cuckoo / Sailor's grave/You carefree young lads / Honied kiss/Glwysen / Sweet Richard / Rhaeadr Falls / Rising of the sun / Harp / Rheged/Lady Treffael's conceit / Miller's song/Over the stone / Honied lip / Men of Wrexham's hornpipe / Glanbargoed / Farewell Marian / Machynlleth / Judgement/Old year passing / Spanish minuet/Maids of Montgomery / Tretower Waltz / John Francis / Llanberis Pass / Flowers of the thorn / Maltraeth / Watching the wheat/Gwenllian / Captain Morgan's march/Lady Sker / Gwenllian's repose / Come what may/Glandyfi / Fanny blooming fair / Weep not for me / Ap Siencyn/Abergynolwen / Blackbird / Llangoffen / My love is a Venus / Springtime is returning / Welsh rabbit/Llyn Gwernan / Missing boat / Cornthresher hornpipe / Clover of Merioneth / Once a farmer
CD _______ **MR 74**
Michael Raven / Jun '97 / Michael Raven

Raw Breed

LUNE TUNZ
CD _______ **CDCTUM 5**
Continuum / Oct '93 / Pinnacle

Raw Deal

LOVE'S OKAY
CD _______ **ARMCD 001**
Raw Deal / Mar '97 / Jet Star

Raw Material

RAW MATERIAL
CD _______ **HBG 123/2**
Background / Apr '94 / Background / Greyhound

Raw Power

FIGHT
CD _______ **GOD 014CD**
Godhead / Jul '95 / Plastic Head

LIVE FROM THE GUTTER
CD _______ **GOD 023CD**
Godhead / Jan '97 / Plastic Head

TOO TOUGH TO BURN
CD _______ **BABECD 7**
Rosemary's Baby / Sep '93 / Plastic Head

Raw Stylus

PUSHING AGAINST THE FLOW
CD _______ **WIRED 226**
Wired / Mar '96 / 3mv/Sony / Mo's Music Machine / Prime

Raw To The Core

IN THE MOOD VOL.2
CD _______ **ITM 001CD**
KGR / Oct '95 / Jet Star

Rawfrucht

RAWFRUCHT
CD _______ **SR 113**
Sub Rosa / Mar '97 / Direct / RTM/Disc / SRD / Vital

Rawhead, Jason

BACKFIRE
CD _______ **KKUK 005CD**
KK / '90 / Plastic Head

COLLISION HYPE
CD _______ **KK 061CD**
KK / Jul '91 / Plastic Head

JASON RAWHEAD
CD _______ **KK 024CD**
KK / '89 / Plastic Head

Rawicz & Landauer

THEIR GREAT PIANO HITS
CD _______ **PASTCD 7040**
Flapper / May '94 / Pinnacle

Rawls, Johnny

CAN'T SLEEP AT NIGHT (Rawls, Johnny & L.C. Luckett)
CD _______ **R 2630**
Rooster / Feb '97 / Direct

HERE WE GO
Here we go / Old flame / I would be nothing / Don't worry about it / Working my way back to you / Sweet woman / What a night / I got a problem / Gonna put you down / Candy man / I feel so good
CD _______ **JSPCD 271**
JSP / Oct '96 / ADA / Cadillac / Direct / Hot Shot / Target/BMG

Rawls, Lou

BALLADS
At last / I wonder where our love has gone / If I were a magician / I'm still in love with you / Sweet slumber / Good morning blues / This bitter Earth / Save your love for me / One more time / Chains of love / Oh what a night / Good night love
CD _______ **CDP 8566892**
Blue Note / Jul '97 / EMI

LOU RAWLS
Lady love / Stay a while with me / Groovy people / Dead end street / Tobacco Road / Love is a natural thing / (You make me feel like) A natural man / Let me be good to you / Tomorrow / Unforgettable / Send in the clowns / You'll never find another love like mine / These are the songs I sing
CD _______ **EXP 026**
Experience / May '97 / TKO Magnum

LOU RAWLS IN THE HEART
CD _______ **8479482**
Polydor / May '91 / PolyGram

LOVE IS A HURTIN' THING
Red top / Just squeeze me (don't tease me) / You're the one / Dead end street / Love is a hurtin' thing / Bring it on home / Another Saturday night / Righteous woman (monologue) / I wanna little girl / Tobacco road / How long, how long blues / Your good thing is about to end / I wonder / Whole lotta woman
CD _______ **CTMCD 329**
EMI / Jul '97 / EMI

SPOTLIGHT ON LOU RAWLS (Great Gentlemen Of Song)
Nobody but me / Street of dreams / God bless the child / Rockin' chair / St. James Infirmary / I wonder where our love has gone / Blues for the weepers / Stormy weather / Willow weep for me / Don't explain / Georgia on my mind / Ain't nobody's business if I do / When it's sleepy time down South / Just squeeze me / How long blues / Summertime / If it's the last thing I do / One for my baby (and one more for the road)
CD _______ **CZ 570**
Premier/EMI / Mar '96 / EMI

STAR COLLECTION
CD _______ **STCD 1002**
Disky / Jun '93 / Disky / THE

TOUCH OF CLASS, A
You'll never find another love like mine / This song will last forever / Time will take care of everything / Show business / Tomorrow / Sit down and talk to me / You can bring me all your heartaches / Tabacco road / Love is a hurtin' thing / See you when I git there / Your good thing (is about to end) / Dead end street / Lady love / Fine brown frame
CD _______ **TC 868752**
Disky / May '97 / Disky / THE

YOU'LL NEVER FIND
CD _______ **WMCD 5700**
Disky / Oct '94 / Disky / THE

Rawside

POLICE TERROR
CD _______ **WB 1133CD**
We Bite / Nov '95 / Plastic Head

Ray & Glover

PICTURE HAS FADED
Tell me Mama / Jimmy Bell / Can't see your face / Downtown blues / Sittin' on top of the world / Long haired donkey / Ice blue / Going away blues / Afraid to trust 'em / Mellow chick swing / Saturday blues / New Buddy Brown / If it looks like jelly / As the years go passing by
CD _______ **TK 92CD036**
T/K / Aug '94 / Pinnacle

Ray, Anthony

REVELATION
CD _______ **ARC 1000**
Active / Aug '96 / Else

Ray, Danny

BEST OF DANNY RAY, THE
CD _______ **BJCD 07**
Blackjack / Nov '96 / Jet Star

Ray J

EVERYTHING YOU WANT
Feel the funk intro / Let it go / Everything you want / Good thangs / Promise / Changes / Thank you / Let it go / Can't run can't hide / Rock with me / Love you from my heart / High on you / Because of you / Feel the funk outro
CD _______ **7559620172**
East West / Jun '97 / Warner Music

Ray, James

DIOS ESTA DE NUESTRO LADO (Ray, James Gangwar)

Rev rev lowrider / Heart surgery / 35,000 times / Badlands / Hardwar / Cadillac coming / Bad gin / Santa Susana / Coo ca choo
CD _______________ MRAY 341 CD
Merciful Release / Apr '92 / Warner Music

NEW KIND OF ASSASSIN, A (Ray, James Gangwar)
Mexico sundown blues / Texas / Mountain voices (remix) / Dust boat / Edie Sedgwick / Mexico sundown blues (edit)
CD _______________ MRAY 089 CD
Merciful Release / Aug '92 / Warner Music

THIRD GENERATION (Ray, James Gangwar)
Cobalt blue / Sinner / Fuelled up / Take it / Third generation / Blue lover / Strange / Luxury / Ridge
CD _______________ SURG 001CD
Surgury / Jun '93 / Vital

Ray, Johnnie

16 MOST REQUESTED SONGS
Cry / Walkin' my baby back home / All of me / Whiskey and gin / Let's walk that way / Don't blame me / Little cloud that cried / Just walking in the rain / Tell the lady I said goodbye / Why should I be sorry / Glad rag doll / Hey there / Please Mr. Sun / Such a night / As time goes by
CD _______________ 4720492
Columbia / Jul '92 / Sony

AT THE PALLADIUM
Please don't talk about me / Glad / Rag doll / Hundred years from now / Somebody stole my gal / With these hands / Walkin' my baby back home / As time goes by / Such a night
CD _______________ BCD 15666
Bear Family / Jun '92 / Direct / Rollercoaster / Swift

BEST OF JOHNNIE RAY, THE
Just walkin' in the rain / Hey there / Cry / Such a night / Little white cloud that cried / Faith can move mountains / Let's walk that-a-way / Paths of paradise / (Here I am) Broken hearted / Who's sorry now / Somebody stole my gal / Herando's hideaway / All of me / You don't owe me a thing / Build your love / Ain't misbehavin' / I'll never fall in love again / Please Mr. Sun / Yes tonight Josephine / If you believe / Look homeward angel / Song of the dreamer / As time goes by / Walkin' my baby back home
CD _______________ 4840402
Epic / May '96 / Sony

BEST OF JOHNNIE RAY/FRANKIE LAINE (Ray, Johnnie & Frankie Laine)
CD _______________ BTBCD 001
Sound Waves / Jun '93 / Target/BMG

CRY
Yes tonight Josephine / Just walking in the rain / I've got so many million years / Johnnie's comin' home / Look homeward angel / Up above my head / Good evening friends / Up until now / How long blues / You don't owe me a thing / No wedding today / Build your love / Streets of memories / Miss me, just a little / Texas tambourine / Pink sweater angel / Soliloquy of a fool / Endlessly / Plant a little seed / I'll make you mine / Papa loves mambo / Ooo aah oh / Flip flop and fly / Alexander's ragtime band / Little white cloud that cried / Cry / Ma sez, Pa sez / Full time job / Such a night / Hernando's hideaway
CD _______________ BCD 15450
Bear Family / May '90 / Direct / Rollercoaster / Swift

Ray, Kenny 'Blue'

IN ALL OF MY LIFE
I can't take it / No time to waste / In all of my life / Listen to me baby / '56 Eldorado / Can't do this to me / Bayou boogie / You got me nervous / Blues for the iceman / Bluesman for life / For Jannie Ray / Bailin' on the gator / What's on your mind / Throw me the whiskey
CD _______________ JSPCD 289
JSP / May '97 / ADA / Cadillac / Direct / Hot Shot / Target/BMG

Ray, Lucy

WHEN I GROW UP
When I grow up / Devil / Written in the stars / Calm / Life is a mess / I hate to lose / Where will I find my love / Mean to me / Love her / All those days / We will never parted
CD _______________ CYCLECD 004
Cycle / Feb '97 / CM / Direct

Ray, Michael

MICHAEL RAY & THE COSMIC KREWE (Ray, Michael & The Cosmic Krewe)
Rhythm and muse / Discipline / Carefree / Champions / Charlie B's / 3-22-93 / Pathology / Beans and rice / Island in space / Echoes of boat people
CD _______________ ECD 220842
Evidence / May '94 / ADA / Cadillac / Harmonia Mundi

Ray, Sugar

KNOCKOUT (Ray, Sugar & The Bluetones)
CD _______________ VRCD 037
Varrick / Sep '94 / ADA / CM / Direct / Roots

Ray, Will

INVISIBLE BIRDS
CD _______________ DFGCD 8449
Dixie Frog / Jun '96 / Direct / TKO Magnum
CD _______________ RTMCD 84
Round Tower / Feb '97 / Avid/BMG

Raye, Collin

IN THIS LIFE
What they don't know / In this life / Big river / Somebody else's Moon / You can't take it with you / That was a river / I want you bad (And that ain't good) / Latter day cowboy / Many a mile / Let it be me
CD _______________ 4723142
Epic / Feb '93 / Sony

Raye, Sol

MONA LISA
CD _______________ FECD 17
First Edition / Jun '97 / Jet Star

Raymen

REBEL YEARS 1985-1987, THE
CD _______________ SPV 07645762
SPV / Mar '96 / Koch / Plastic Head

Raymond, Clem

LOST CLARINET OF CLEM RAYMOND (Raymond, Clem & Dick Oxtot/Golden Age Jazz Band)
Boogaloosa strut / Pontchartrain blues / Wolverine blues / I can't give you anything but love / Tell me your dreams / When you wore a tulip / Clem's blues / Just a little while to stay here / Reep du dah / Piedmont blues / B-flat blues / Shine / Haunted blues / Boogaloosa strut
CD _______________ DE 208
Delmark / Mar '97 / ADA / Cadillac / CM / Direct / Hot Shot

Raymonde, Simon

BLAME SOMEONE ELSE
It's a family thing / Love undone / Seventh day / In my place / Supernatural / If I knew myself / It's raining today / Muscle and want / Worship me / Fault of mine / Days / Tired twilight
CD _______________ BELLACD 001
Bella Union / Sep '97 / Vital

Razed In Black

OVERFLOW
CD _______________ CLP 9956
Cleopatra / Mar '97 / Cargo / Greyhound / Plastic Head / RTM/Disc / SRD

Razor

SHOTGUN JUSTICE
CD _______________ FPD 3094
Fringe / Mar '95 / Plastic Head

VIOLENT RESTITUTION
CD _______________ 857 571
Steamhammer / '89 / Pinnacle / Plastic Head

Razor Baby

TOO HOT TO HANDLE
Danger / Rock this place / Downtown / Outta hand sister / Move me / Too hot to handle / Got me running / Low down and dirty
CD _______________ HMAXD 102
Heavy Metal / Aug '89 / Revolver / Sony

Razor Skyline

JOURNAL OF TRAUMA
CD _______________ COPCD 025
Cop International / Nov '96 / Cargo

Razorbacks

GO TO TOWN
CD _______________ OPM 2101CD
Other People's Music / Mar '97 / Greyhound / Plastic Head

I'M ON FIRE
CD _______________ FCD 3026
Fury / Aug '93 / Nervous / TKO Magnum

Razorcuts

WORLD KEEPS TURNING, THE
CD _______________ CRECD 045
Creation / Feb '89 / 3mv/Vital

Razzia

LABYRINTH
CD _______________ IRC 032
Impact / Mar '97 / Cargo

Re-Animator

CONDEMNED TO ETERNITY
Don't eat the yellow snow / St. Alphonzo's pancake breakfast / Cosmik debris / Apostrophe / Stink foot / I'm the slime / 50/50 / Dinah-Moe Humm / Nanook rubs it / Father O'Blivion / Excentrifugal forz / Uncle Remus / Camarillo brillo / Dirty love / Zomby woof / Montana
CD _______________ CDFLAG 37
Under One Flag / Oct '89 / Pinnacle

LAUGHING
CD _______________ CDFLAG 53
Under One Flag / Feb '91 / Pinnacle

THAT WAS THEN, THIS IS NOW
Take me away / 2 CV / Cold sweat / Hope / Last laugh / Kick back / Listen up / Sunshine times / That was then..This is now / DUAF
CD _______________ CDFLAG 67
Under One Flag / Oct '92 / Pinnacle

Rea, Chris

AUBERGE
Auberge / Gone fishing / You're not a number / Heaven / Set me free / Red shoes / Sing a song of love to me / Every second counts / Looking for the summer / And you my love / Mention of your name
CD _______________ 9031756932
Magnet / Feb '91 / Warner Music

ESPRESSO LOGIC
Espresso logic / Red / Soup of the day / Johnny needs a fast car / Between the devil and the deep blue sea / Julia / Summer love / New way / Stop / She closed her eyes
CD _______________ 4509943112
Magnet / Oct '93 / Warner Music

GOD'S GREAT BANANA SKIN
Nothing to fear / Miles is a cigarette / God's great banana skin / Nineties blues / Too much pride / Boom boom / I ain't the fool / There she goes / I'm ready / Black dog / Soft top, hard shoulder
CD _______________ 4509909952
Magnet / Nov '92 / Warner Music

LA PASSIONE (Original Soundtrack)
La Passione / Dov'e il signore / Le mans / Dov'e il signore part two / Disco la passione / You must follow / Shirley do you own a Ferrari / Girl in a sports car / When the grey skies turn to blue / Horses / Olive oil / Only to fly
CD _______________ 0630166952
East West / May '97 / Warner Music

NEW LIGHT THROUGH OLD WINDOWS (The Best Of Chris Rea)
Let's dance / Working on it / Ace of hearts / Josephine / Candles / On the beach / Fool (if you think it's over) / I can hear your heartbeat / Shamrock diaries / Stainsby girls / Windy town / Driving home for Christmas / Steel river
CD _______________ 2438412
Magnet / Oct '88 / Warner Music

ROAD TO HELL
Road to hell / Road to hell / You must be evil / Texas / Looking for a rainbow / Your warm and tender love / Daytona / That's what they always say / I just wanna be with you / Tell me there's a heaven
CD _______________ 2462852
Magnet / Feb '95 / Warner Music

VERY BEST OF CHRIS REA, THE
Road to hell / Josephine / Let's dance / Fool if you think it's over / Auberge / Julia / Stainsby girls / If you were me / On the beach / Looking for the summer / Giverney / Go your own way / God's great banana skin / Wintersong / Gone fishing / Tell me there's a heaven
CD _______________ 4509980402
Magnet / Oct '94 / Warner Music

WHATEVER HAPPENED TO BENNY SANTINI
Whatever happened to Benny Santini / Closer you get / Because of you / Dancing with Charlie / Bows and bangles / Fool (if you think it's over) / Three angels / Just one of those days / Standing in your doorway / Fires of spring
CD _______________ 2292423682
Magnet / Jan '93 / Warner Music

React 2 Rhythm

WHATEVER YOU DREAM
CD _______________ GRCD 002
Guerilla / Mar '92 / Pinnacle

Reactor

REVELATION
CD _______________ 1MF 37700332
Invisible / Jul '93 / Plastic Head

Reactor Outside

REACTOR OUTSIDE VOL.1
CD _______________ BR 001CD
Blue Room Released / Mar '97 / Essential/ BMG / SRD

Read, Jaime

END OF THE BEGINNING, THE
After the rains / Timewave / On the surface of the 9th moon / Collective consciousness / Harry runs out / Outwardly inward / Itty bitty pieces / Still LIFE / LHAS part one / Swans and elephants / Tribute to a gallop / Da breaks
CD _______________ FMDCD 001
Fragmented / Aug '97 / Prime / SRD

Reader, Eddi

CANDYFLOSS AND MEDICINE
CD _______________ 0630151202
Blanco Y Negro / Jul '96 / Warner Music

HUSH
Right place / Patience of angels / Dear John / Scarecrow / East of us / Joke (I'm laughing) / Exception / Red face big sky / Howling in ojai / When I watch you sleeping / Wonderful lie / Siren
CD _______________ 4509961772
Warner Bros. / Dec '96 / Warner Music

MIRMAMA
What you do with what you've got / Honeychild / All or nothing / Hello in there / Dolphins / Blacksmith / That's fair / Cinderellas downfall / Pay no mind / Swimming song / My old friend the blues
CD _______________ 74321158652
RCA / Sep '94 / BMG

Reading, Bertice

TED EASTON'S JAZZBAND & QUARTET
CD _______________ ACD 80
Audiophile / Apr '93 / Jazz Music

Reagon, Bernice Johnson

RIVER OF LIFE
Come and go with me to that land / We are climbing Jacob's ladder / Guide my feet, while I run this race / Hallelu / Land on the shore / Running / Easy street / River of life / Since I laid my burden down / Buses are a coming freedom song / There is more love somewhere / I am a lady
CD _______________ FF 70411
Flying Fish / Sep '96 / ADA / CM / Direct / Roots

Reagon, Toshi

KINDNESS
CD _______________ SFWCD 40095
Smithsonian Folkways / Jun '97 / ADA / Cadillac / CM / Direct / Koch

Real Cool Killers

ILLUSIONS
Just for fun / Knife / Daddy's footsteps / Judgement day / Myrtle Gordon / Bitter end / Much more than a hero / Illusion / Stupid lines / Open the night
CD _______________ SUR 453CD
Survival / Jun '94 / ADA / Pinnacle

Real Kids

GROWN UP WRONG
CD _______________ CED 231
Norton / Jun '97 / Greyhound

Real Life

HEARTLAND
CD _______________ INT 847 710
Interchord / '88 / CM

LITTLE PIECE OF HEAVEN, A
CD _______________ CANDRCD 80101
Candor / Nov '94 / Else

Real Live

TURNAROUND, THE
Pop the trunk / Ain't no love / Iceberg Slick / They got me / Gimmicks / Larry-O meets Iceberg Slick / Turnaround / All I ask of you (comin' through) / Real live shit / Trilogy of error / Money shows / Crime is money / Day you die
CD _______________ 7567926682
Atlantic / Oct '96 / Warner Music

Real People

LIVERPOOL - THE CALM BEFORE THE STORM (Real People & Rain)
Window pane: *Real People* / Truth: *Real People* / Everyday's the same: *Real People* / She: *Real People* / Believer: *Real People* / Seen the light: *Real People* / Some things must change: *Real People* / What u want: *Real People* / I don't belong: *Real People* / Run & hide: *Real People* / Car outside: *Real People* / Too much too young: *Real People* / All I want: *Rain* / Lemonstone desired: *Rain* / Here they are: *Rain* / Taste of rain: *Rain* / Inside out: *Rain* / Slippin' & slidin': *Rain*
CD _______________ 4836602
Columbia / Feb '96 / Sony

REAL PEOPLE, THE
Window pane / I can't wait / For you / Truth / Everyday's the same / Wonderful / Open up your mind (let me in) / She / In your

hands / Looking at you / Words / Another day
CD _______ 4680842
Columbia / Mar '97 / Sony

WHAT'S ON THE OUTSIDE
CD _______ MGGRCD 19
Granite / Nov '96 / Pinnacle

Real Thing

FEEL THE FORCE (2CD Set)
CD Set _______ SMDCD 175
Snapper / Jul '97 / Pinnacle

REAL THING
Real Thing / Can you feel the force / Get back on the right track / Move on up / Whenever you want my love / Rainin' through my sunshine / You'll never know what you're missing / Can't get by without you / Can't get by without you / I love music / (Livin' on the) frontline / Baby don't go / Children of the ghetto / You to me are everything / You to me are everything / Can you feel the force
CD _______ JHD 119
Tring / Apr '93 / Tring

YOU TO ME ARE EVERYTHING
You to me are everything / What'cha say, what'cha do / Can't get by without you / Love's such a wonderful thing / I want you back / Can you feel the force / Lady I love you all the time / Whenever you want my love / Love is a playground / Lightning strikes again / Boogie down / She's a groovy freak / You can't force the funk / He's just a moneymaker / You'll never know what you're missing / Dance with me / Watch out Carolina / Rainin' through my sunshine / Children of the ghetto
CD _______ 5507402
Spectrum / Sep '94 / PolyGram

Real TV

NOW WASH YOUR HANDS
CD _______ KNEK 1
Kuro Neko / Mar '97 / Total/Pinnacle

Reality

REGGAE BEAT
Stand up and be counted / Donna / Set me free / Peaceful man / Rasta man / Singer man / Tell me what's going on in your mind / Revolution / All my life / Make a move / OK / Gonna live my life / Steppin' out
CD _______ QED 137
Tring / Nov '96 / Tring

REGGAE, REGGAE, REGGAE
Stand up and be counted / Donna / Set me free / Peaceful man / Rasta man / Singer man / Tell me what's goin' on in your mind / Revolution / All my life / Make a move / OK / Gonna live my life / Steppin' out
CD _______ SOV 008CD
Sovereign / '92 / Target/BMG

Rebello, Jason

KEEPING TIME
Swings and roundabouts / Coral beads / Close your eyes / Silver surfer / Wind in the willows / Wind in the willows (piano) / Eraserhead (old piano) / Eraserhead (new piano) / Keeping time / Spider / Silver surfer (no sax) / Permanent love (full) / Permanent (edited) / Little man / Tic toc / Future / Untitled / Solo piece 1 / Solo piece 2
CD _______ 74321129042
Novus / Feb '93 / BMG

LAST DANCE (Rebello, Jason & Roy Rose)
Wind in the willows / Every little thing / Life is her friend / Play piano play / Last dance / Soul eyes / I am what you see / Tears / What is this thing called love / Foggy day / Adrian's wall / God bless the child
CD _______ ATJR 001
All That / May '95 / New Note/Pinnacle

Rebello, Simone

FASCINATING RHYTHM
CD _______ DOYCD 024
Doyen / Aug '93 / Conifer/BMG

SECRET PLACE, A
Secret place / Leyenda / Saturday's child / Ensemble / Jupiter's dance / Marimba spiritual
CD _______ DOYCD 040
Doyen / Jun '95 / Conifer/BMG

Rebelo, Nuno

SABADO 2 - MINIMAL SHOW
CD _______ GGG 001
Ananana / Jun '97 / ReR Megacorp

Rebirth Brass Band

REBIRTH KICKIN' IT LIVE
CD _______ ROUCD 2106
Rounder / Dec '94 / ADA / CM / Direct

ROLLIN'
CD _______ ROUCD 2132
Rounder / Oct '94 / ADA / CM / Direct

WE COME TO PARTY
CD _______ SH 6018
Shanachie / Jun '97 / ADA / Greensleeves / Koch

Rebo, Max

LIVING MAXISM
CD _______ GBMR 27
GBM / Apr '97 / Timewarp

Rebroff, Ivan

KALINKA MALINKA
CD _______ WMCD 5692
Disky / May '94 / Disky / THE

VERY BEST OF IVAN REBROFF VOL.1, THE
Evening chimes / Song of the Volga boatmen / Hava nagila / Im tiefen keller / Two white doves / Perestroika / Grosser alter don / Dark eyes / Schto nam gorje / Poj zyganka / Somewhere my love / Ol' man river / Kalinka malinka / La calunnia / Ach natascha / On the way from Petersburgh to Nowgorod / Cossack patrol
CD _______ MDMCD 001
Moidart / Jun '93 / Conifer/BMG

VERY BEST OF IVAN REBROFF VOL.2, THE
Mutterchen Russland / Hej Andrushka / If I were a rich man / My yiddishe momme / Lonely chimes / Barcarolle / Sah ein Knabein / Rosen steh'n / Elizabethan serenade / Moscow nights / Ach varmaeland / Mit der troike in die grosse Stadt / Ech dorogi / Ave Maria - plaisir d'amour / Cossacks must ride / Ode to joy
CD _______ MDMCD 002
Moidart / Jun '94 / Conifer/BMG

Recoil

BLOODLINE
CD _______ CDSTUMM 94
Mute / Apr '92 / RTM/Disc

Records

SMASHES, CRASHES AND NEAR MISSES
Starry eyes / Girl in golden disc / Teenarama / Up all night / I don't remember your name / Girls that don't exist / Hearts will be broken / All messed up and ready to go / Hearts in her eyes / Girl / Spent a week with you last night / Held up high / Rumour sets the woods alight / Same mistakes / Selfish love / Not so much the time / Affection rejected / Paint her face / Imitation jewellery / Rock 'n' roll love letter
CD _______ CDOVD 456
Virgin / Feb '95 / EMI

Recycle Or Die

SILK
Dimension X / Inner peace / Desert bean / Passion and hope / Oceans of infinity
CD _______ 4509940612
WEA / Oct '93 / Warner Music

Recyclers

VISIT
CD _______ BDV 9716
Babel / Mar '97 / ADA / Cadillac / Diverse / Harmonia Mundi

Red Alert

BLOOD, SWEAT AND BEERS
CD _______ KONCD 006
Knock Out / Mar '97 / Cargo

WE'VE GOT THE POWER
We've got the power / They came in force / Crisis / You've got nothing / SPG / Art of brutality / Industrial slide
CD _______ AHOYCD 12
Captain Oi / Jan '94 / Plastic Head

Red Army Choir

RED ARMY CHOIR VOL.4
CD _______ 242073
Planett / Feb '97 / Discovery

RED ARMY CHOIR, THE
CD _______ LDX 274768
La Chant Du Monde / Jan '94 / ADA / Harmonia Mundi

Red Aunts

NO.1 CHICKEN
CD _______ E 86446
Epitaph / Mar '95 / Pinnacle / Plastic Head

SALTBOX
CD _______ 64732
Epitaph / Aug '96 / Pinnacle / Plastic Head

Red Chair Fade Away

MESMERIZED
CD _______ ENG 1012
English Garden / Apr '94 / Background

Red Clay Ramblers

FAR NORTH (Original Soundtrack)
CD _______ SHCD 8502
Sugar Hill / Jan '97 / ADA / CM / Direct / Koch / Roots

LIE OF THE MIND, A (Original Soundtrack)
Run Sister run / South of the border (Down Mexico way)/In the pines / Honey babe / I love you a thousand ways / Home is where the heart is / Seeing it now / Blue Jay/The gal I left behind / Light years away / Cumberland mountain deer chase / Red rocking chair / Montana underscoring / Killing floor / I can't live without 'em blues / Folding the flag/Hard times
CD _______ SHCD 8501
Sugar Hill / Mar '89 / ADA / CM / Direct / Koch / Roots

RAMBLER
Cotton eyed Joe / Cajun Billy / Black smoke train / Saro Jane / Annie Oakley / Queen of Skye / Ninety and Nine / Mile long medley / Darlin' say/Pony cart / Hiawatha's lullaby / What does the deep sea say / Ryan's/Jordan reel / Barbeque / One rose/Hot buttered rum / Olkas
CD _______ SHCD 3798
Sugar Hill / Jan '92 / ADA / CM / Direct / Koch / Roots

Red Crayola

3 SONGS ON A TRIP TO THE UNITED STATES
CD _______ DC 105CD
Drag City / Jun '97 / Cargo / Greyhound

BLACK SNAKES
CD _______ DC 104CD
Drag City / Jun '97 / Cargo / Greyhound

COCONUT HOTEL (Red Krayola)
CD _______ DC 62
Drag City / Dec '96 / Cargo / Greyhound

GOD BLESS THE RED KRAYOLA AND ALL WHO SAIL IN IT (Red Krayola)
Say hello to Jamie Jones / Music / Shirt / Listen to this / Save the house / Victory garden / Coconut hotel / Sheriff Jack / Free piece / Ravi Shankar / Parachutist / Dairy maids lament / Big / Leejol / Sherlock Holmes / Dirth of tilth / Tina's gone to have a baby / Jewels of the Madonna / Green of my pants / Night song
CD _______ 14898
Spalax / Nov '96 / ADA / Cargo / Direct / Discovery / Greyhound

HAZEL (Red Krayola)
CD _______ DCD 98
Drag City / Jan '97 / Cargo / Greyhound

KANGAROO (Red Krayola)
CD _______ DC 80
Drag City / Dec '96 / Cargo / Greyhound

PARABLE OF ARABLE LAND, THE
Free form freakout / Hurricane fighter plane / Transparent radiation / War sucks / Pink stainless tail / Parable of arable land / Former reflections enduring doubt
CD _______ 14887
Spalax / Nov '96 / ADA / Cargo / Direct / Discovery / Greyhound

PARABLE OF ARABLE LAND, THE/GOD BLESS THE RED CRAYOLA
Free form freak out / Hurricane fighter plane / Transparent radiation / War sucks / Pink stainless tail / Parable of arable land / Former reflections enduring doubt / Say hello to Jamie Jones / Music / Shirt / Listen to this / Save the house / Victory garden / Coconut hotel / Sheriff Jack / Free piece / Ravi Shankar / Parachutist / Place for piano and electric bass guitar / Dairymaid's lament / Big / Leejol / Sherlock Holmes / Dirth of tilth / Tina's gone to have a baby / Jewels of the madonna / Green of my pants / Night song
CD _______ CDCRH 112
Charly / Jan '97 / Koch

RED KRAYOLA (Red Krayola)
CD _______ DC 52
Drag City / Dec '96 / Cargo / Greyhound

Red, Danny

RIDDIMWIZE
Can't live it up / Be grateful / Mystic lady / Don't cry soundboy / Rollin' stone / Rise up / Riddimwize / Teaser / Cool bad boy / Tell me why / Riddimwize / Can't live it dub / Rise up dub / Be dubful
CD _______ 4777742
Columbia / Sep '94 / Sony

Red Dawn

NEVER SAY SURRENDER
CD _______ NTHEN 10
Now & Then / Sep '95 / Plastic Head

Red Devils

KING KING
CD _______ 5144922
Phonogram / Jan '94 / PolyGram

Red Dragon

BUN THEM
CD _______ VPCD 1350
VP / Mar '94 / Greensleeves / Jet Star / Total/BMG

Red Eye

TIME FRAME ANARCHY
CD _______ AFTER CD4
After 6am / Dec '94 / Plastic Head

Red Fox

AS A MATTER OF FOX
Born again black man / Dry head shakira Pt 1 / Good body runs in ya family / No condom, no fun / Girl's vineyard (all fruits ripe) / I'm gonna take you home / Ghetto gospel / Pressure dem / Golden axe / Dry head shakira Pt 2 / Dem a murderer / Hey Mr. Rude bwoy / Dance hall scenario / Ya can't test me again
CD _______ 7559615312
Warner Bros. / Sep '93 / Warner Music

FACE THE FOX
CD _______ VPCD 2047
VP / May '96 / Greensleeves / Jet Star / Total/BMG

Red Fun

RED FUN
CD _______ CDMFN 173
Music For Nations / Dec '94 / Pinnacle

Red Guitars

SEVEN TYPES OF AMBIQUITY
CD _______ RPM 109
RPM / Jul '93 / Pinnacle

Red Harvest

HYBREED
CD _______ VOW 052CD
Voices Of Wonder / Oct '96 / Plastic Head

MASTER NATION
CD _______ VOW 046CD
Voices Of Wonder / Jul '95 / Plastic Head

NOMANSLAND
Cure / Righteous majority / Acid / No next generation / Machines way / (Live and pay) The holy way / Crackman / Face the fact / Wrong arm of the law
CD _______ BMCD 019
Black Mark / Apr '92 / Plastic Head

THERE'S BEAUTY IN THE PURITY OF SADNESS
CD _______ VOW 39C
Voices Of Wonder / Apr '94 / Plastic Head

Red Hot 'n' Blue

HAVIN' A BALL
CD _______ FCD 3033
Fury / '94 / Nervous / TKO Magnum

Red Hot Chili Peppers

BLOOD SUGAR SEX MAGIK
Power of equality / If you have to ask / Breaking the girl / Funky monks / Suck my kiss / I could have lied / Mellowship slinky in B major / Righteous and the wicked / Give it away / Blood sugar sex magik / Under the bridge / Naked in the rain / Apache rose peacock / Greeting song / My lovely man / Sir psycho sexy / They're red hot
CD _______ 7599266812
Warner Bros. / Oct '91 / Warner Music

FREAKY STYLEY
Jungle man / Hollywood (Africa) / American ghost dance / If you want me to stay / Nevermind / Freaky styley / Blackeyed blonde / Brothers cup / Battle ship / Lovin' and touchin' / Catholic school girls rule / Sex rap / Thirty dirty birds / Yertle the turtle
CD _______ CDFA 3309
Fame / Nov '94 / EMI

INTERVIEW DISC
CD _______ SAM 7028
Sound & Media / Mar '97 / Sound & Media

MOTHER'S MILK
Good time boys / Higher ground / Subway to Venus / Magic Johnson / Nobody weird like me / Knock me down / Taste the pain / Stone cold bush / Fire / Pretty little ditty / Punk rock classic / Sexy Mexican maid / Johnny kick a hole in the sky
CD _______ CDMTL 1046
EMI / Aug '89 / EMI

ONE HOT MINUTE
Warped / Aeroplane / Deep kick / My friends / Coffee shop / Pea / One big mob / Walkabout / Tear jerker / One hot minute / Transcending
CD _______ 9362457332
Warner Bros. / Sep '95 / Warner Music

OUT IN LA
Higher ground / Hollywood (Africa) / If you want me to stay / Behind the sun / Castles made of sand / Special secret song inside / FU / Get up and jump / Out in LA / Green heaven / Police helicopter / Nevermind / Sex rap / Blues for meister / You always

sing the same / Stranded / Flea fly / What it is / Deck the halls with boughs of holly
CD _______________ CDMTL 1082
EMI / Sep '97 / EMI

RED HOT CHILI PEPPERS
True men don't kill coyotes / Baby appeal / Buckle down / Get up and jump / Why don't you love me / Green heaven / Mommy, where's daddy / Out in LA / Police helicopter / You always sing / Grand pappy du plenty
CD _______________ CDFA 3297
Fame / May '93 / EMI

RED HOT CHILI PEPPERS/FREAKY STYLEY/UPLIFT MOFO PARTY PLAN (The Originals/3CD Set)
True men don't kill coyotes / Baby appeal / Buckle down / Get up and jump / Why don't you love me / Green heaven / Mommy where's daddy / Out in LA / Police helicopter / You always sing the same / Grand Pappy du plenty / Jungleman / Hollywood (Africa) / American ghost dance / If you want me to stay / Never mind / Freaky styley / Blackeyed blonde / Brother's cup / Battleship / Lovin' and touchin' / Catholic schoolgirls rule / Sex rap / 30 dirty birds / Yertle the turtle / Fight like a brave / Funky crime / Me & my friends / Backwoods / Skinny sweaty man / Behind the sun / Subterranean homesick blues / Special secret song inside / No chump love sucker / Walkin' on down the road / Love trilogy / Organic anti-beatbox band
CD Set _______________ CDOMB 004
EMI / Mar '97 / EMI

UPLIFT MOFO PARTY PLAN, THE
Fight like a brave / Funky crime / Me and my friends / Backwoods / Skinny sweaty man / Behind the sun / Subterranean homesick blues / Special secret song inside / No chump love sucker / Walkin' on down the road / Love trilogy / Organic anti-beat box band
CD _______________ CDAML 3125
EMI / Aug '90 / EMI

WHAT HITS
Higher ground / Fight like a brave / Behind the sun / Me and my friends / Backwoods / True men don't kill coyotes / Fire / Get up and jump / Knock me down / Under the bridge / Show me your soul / If you want me to stay / Hollywood (Africa) / Jungle man / Brothers cup / Taste the pain / Catholic school girls rule / Johnny kick a hole in the sky
CD _______________ CDMTL 1071
EMI / Oct '92 / EMI

Red House Painters

DOWN COLORFUL HILL
Twenty four / Medicine bottle / Down colorful hill / Japanese to English / Lord kill the pain / Michael
CD _______________ CAD 2014CD
4AD / Aug '92 / RTM/Disc

OCEAN BEACH
Cabezon / Summer dress / San Geronimo / Shadows / Over my head / Long distance runaround / Red carpet / Brockwell park / Moments / Drop
CD _______________ CAD 5005CD
4AD / Mar '95 / RTM/Disc

RED HOUSE PAINTERS
Grace Cathedral Park / Down through / Katy song / Mistress / Things mean a lot / Fun house / Take me out / Rollercoaster / New Jersey / Dragonflies / Mistress (piano version] / Mother / Strawberry Hill / Brown eyes
CD _______________ DAD 3008CD
4AD / May '93 / RTM/Disc

RED HOUSE PAINTERS
Evil / Bubble / I am a rock / Helicopter / New Jersey / Uncle Joe / Blindfold / Star spangled banner
CD _______________ CAD 3016CD
4AD / Oct '93 / RTM/Disc

SONGS FOR A BLUE GUITAR
Have you forgotten / Song for a blue guitar / Make like paper / Priest alley song / Trailways / Feel the rain fall / Long distance runaround / All mixed up / Revelation big sur / Silly love songs / Another song for a blue guitar
CD _______________ CID 8050
Island / Jul '96 / PolyGram

Red Jasper

ACTION REPLAY
CD _______________ HTDDWCD 9
HTD / Nov '92 / CM / Pinnacle

STING IN THE TALE
Faceless people / Guy Fawkes / TV screen / Second coming / Old Jack / Company director / Secret society / Magpie / I can hew
CD _______________ HTD CD 3
HTD / Dec '90 / CM / Pinnacle

Red London

LAST ORDERS PLEASE
CD _______________ KONCD 013
Knock Out / Mar '97 / Cargo

Red Lorry Yellow Lorry

BEST OF RED LORRY YELLOW LORRY, THE
CD _______________ CLEO 9404
Cleopatra / Jun '94 / Cargo / Greyhound / Plastic Head / RTM/Disc / SRD

BLASTING OFF
CD _______________ DW 23556CD
Deathwish / Nov '92 / Plastic Head

NOTHING WRONG
Nothing wrong / Do you understand / Calling / Big stick / Hands off me / She said / Sayonara / World around / Hard-away / Only dreaming / Never know / Pushing on / Time is tight
CD _______________ SITU 20 CD
Situation 2 / May '88 / Pinnacle

SINGLES 1982-1987, THE
Beating my head / I'm still waiting / Take it all away / Happy / He's red / See the fire / Monkey's on juice / Push / Silence / Hollow eyes / Feel a piece / Chance / Generation / Spinning around / Hold yourself down / Regenerate / Walking on your hands / Which side / Jipp (instrumental mix) / Cut down / Burning fever / Pushed me / Crawling mantra / Hangman / All the same / Shout at the sky
CD _______________ CDMRED 109
Cherry Red / Feb '94 / Pinnacle

SMASHED HITS
Beating my head / He's red / Monkeys on juice / Spinning round / Cut down / Take it all / Hollow eyes / Generation / Hold yourself down / Chance
CD _______________ DOJOCD 210
Dojo / May '95 / Disc

TALK ABOUT THE WEATHER/PAINT YOUR WAGON
CD _______________ CDMRED 115
Cherry Red / Jun '94 / Pinnacle

Red Moon Joe

ARMS OF SORROW
CD _______________ RRACD 013
Haven / Oct '91 / Pinnacle / Shellshock/Disc

Red Onion Jazzband

CREOLE RHAPSODY
CD _______________ BCD 309
GHB / Jul '93 / Jazz Music

Red Plastic Bag

ONE MORE (Red Plastic Bag & Mac Fingall)
CD _______________ WCD 499
JW / Oct '96 / Jet Star

Red Red Meat

RED RED MEAT
CD _______________ RRM 001
Sub Pop / Feb '95 / Cargo / Greyhound / Shellshock/Disc

THERE'S A STAR ABOVE THE MANGER TONIGHT
CD _______________ SPCD 387
Sub Pop / Feb '97 / Cargo / Greyhound / Shellshock/Disc

Red River

TEXAS ADVICE
Ride ride ride / Comin' to you live / Eight chrome and wings / Come on over / Dry country blues / Ain't workin' no more / Broke again / Lucky tonight / Cheap thrills / Texas advice / At the roadhouse tonite / I'll drink your booze / Talkin' to me / Something's gotta give / Goin' down / Mercury / Fools paradise / City doesn't weep
CD _______________ ROSE 210CD
New Rose / Aug '90 / ADA / Direct / Discovery

Red Rodney

BIRD LIVES
CD _______________ MCD 5371
Muse / Sep '92 / New Note/Pinnacle

RED GIANT
CD _______________ SCCD 31233
Steeplechase / '88 / Discovery / Impetus

SOCIETY RED (Red Rodney & The Danish Jazz Army)
CD _______________ MECCACD 1003
Music Mecca / Oct '89 / Cadillac / Jazz Music / Wellard

Red Rooster

STRAIGHT FROM THE HEART
CD _______________ MAPCD 93005
Music & Words / Aug '94 / ADA / Direct

Red Sekta

ANODIZE
CD _______________ EFA 125102
Celtic Circle / May '95 / SRD

Red Shoe Diaries

RED SHOE DIARIES
CD _______________ WWRCD 6001
Wienerworld / Jun '95 / THE

Red Snapper

PRINCE BLIMEY
CD _______________ WARPCD 45
Warp / Sep '96 / Prime / RTM/Disc

REELED AND SKINNED
CD _______________ WARPCD 33
Warp / Jun '95 / Prime / RTM/Disc

Red Stripe Ebony Steel Band

BEST OF STEELDRUMS
CD _______________ EUCD 1110
ARC / '91 / ADA / ARC Music

PRESENTS: POPULAR BEATLES SONGS
CD _______________ EUCD 1152
ARC / '91 / ADA / ARC Music

Red Sun

RED SUN & SAMULNORI (Red Sun & SamulNori)
More than ever / Far horizon / Ho ho / Kut / Golden bird / O-lim / No secrets
CD _______________ 8412222
Amadeo / Feb '93 / PolyGram

THEN COMES THE WHITE TIGER (Red Sun & SamulNori)
CD _______________ 5217342
ECM / Oct '94 / New Note/Pinnacle

Red Tail Chasing Hawks

BROTHER HAWK
CD _______________ CR 7029CD
Canyon / Nov '96 / ADA

Red Thunder

MAKOCE WAKAN
CD _______________ 379162
Koch International / Dec '95 / Koch

Red Velvet Trio

MILLION TEARS
CD _______________ TBCD 2007
Nervous / Mar '93 / Nervous / TKO Magnum

Redbone, Leon

CHRISTMAS ISLAND
White Christmas / Winter wonderland / Frosty the snowman / Blue Christmas / There's no place like home for the holidays / Toyland / Christmas Island / That old Christmas moon / I'll be home for Christmas / Let it snow, let it snow, let it snow / Christmas ball blues
CD _______________ AS 8890CD
August / Jan '94 / Direct

NO REGRETS
CD _______________ SHCD 3761
Sugar Hill / Jan '97 / ADA / CM / Direct / Koch / Roots

RED TO BLUE
CD _______________ SHCD 3840
Sugar Hill / Aug '95 / ADA / CM / Direct / Koch / Roots

SUGAR
Ghost of the Saint Louis blues / Roll along Kentucky moon / Right or wrong / Laughing blues / Breeze / Whistling colonel / Sugar / Pretty baby / When I take my sugar to tea / What you want me to do / Messin' around / So relax / 14th Street blues
CD _______________ 260555
Private Music / Mar '90 / BMG

UP A LAZY RIVER
Play gypsy play / At the chocolate bon bon ball / Lazy river / When Dixie stars are playing peek-a-boo / Mr. Jelly Roll Baker / Gotta shake that thing / You're a heartbreaker / Bittersweet waltz / Goodbye Charlie blues / That old familiar blues / Dreamer's holiday / I'm going home
CD _______________ 262666
Private Music / Apr '92 / BMG

WHISTLING IN THE WIND
Dancin' on Daddy's shoes / When I kissed that girl goodbye / Bouquet of roses / Truckin' 101 / Sittin' by the fire / Crazy over Dixie / Little grass shack / Love letters in the sand / You're gonna lose your gal / If I could be with you one hour tonight / Crazy about my baby / I ain't got nobody
CD _______________ 01005821172
Private Music / Apr '94 / BMG

Redcell

ESOTERIK/BLUE BINARY (Redcell/Cmetric)
CD _______________ B12CD 2
B12 / Jan '96 / Kudos / Pinnacle

Redd, Freddie

CONNECTION, THE
Who killed Cock Robin / Music forever / Wigglin' / OD / Jim Dunn's dilemma / Time to smile / Sister salvation (theme)
CD _______________ CDBOP 019
Boplicity / Jan '97 / Pinnacle

Redd Kross

PHASESHIFTER
CD _______________ 5181672
Phonogram / Jan '94 / PolyGram

SHOW WORLD
Pretty please me / Stoned / You lied again / Girl god / Mess around / One chord progression / Teen competition / Follow the leader / Vanity mirror / My secret life / Ugly town / Get out of myself / Kiss the goat
CD _______________ 5242752
This Way Up / Feb '97 / PolyGram / SRD

Redd, Sharon

SHARON REDD COLLECTION
CD _______________ CCSCD 388
Castle / Oct '93 / BMG

SHARON REDD/REDD HOT
You got my love / Can you handle it / It's a lie / Try my love on for size / Leaving you is easier said than done / Love is gonna get ya / You stayed on my mind / Never give you up / You're the one / Send your love / Beat the street / In the name of love / Takin' a chance on love / We're friends again
CD _______________ DEEPM 009
Deep Beats / Jan '97 / BMG

Redding, Noel

MISSING ALBUM, THE (Redding, Noel Band)
CD _______________ MSCD 005
Mouse / Feb '95 / Grapevine/PolyGram

Redding, Otis

DOCK OF THE BAY (The Definitive Collection)
Shake / Mr. Pitiful / Respect / Love man / Satisfaction / I can't turn you loose / Hard to handle / Fa fa fa fa fa (sad song) / My girl / I've been loving you too long / Try a little tenderness / My lover's prayer / That's how strong my love is / Pain in my heart / Change is gonna come / (Sittin' on the) dock of the bay / Cigarettes and coffee / These arms of mine / Tramp
CD _______________ 9548317092
Atlantic / Nov '92 / Warner Music

I'VE BEEN LOVIN' YOU TOO LONG
CD _______________ TS 022
That's Soul / Mar '94 / BMG

IMMORTAL OTIS REDDING, THE
I've got dreams to remember / You made a man out of me / Nobody's fault but mine / Thousand miles away / Happy song / Think about it / Waste of time / Champagne and wine / Fool for you / Amen
CD _______________ 7567802702
Atlantic / Mar '95 / Warner Music

IT'S NOT JUST SENTIMENTAL
Trick or treat / Loving by the pound 1 / There goes my baby / Remember me / Send me some lovin' / She's alright / Cupid / Boston monkey / Don't be afraid of love / Little ol' me / Loving by the pound 2 / You got good lovin' / Gone again / I'm coming home / (Sittin' on the) dock of the bay / Respect / Open the door / I've got dreams to remember / Come to me / Try a little tenderness / Stay in school
CD _______________ CDSXD 041
Stax / Jan '92 / Pinnacle

KING AND QUEEN (Redding, Otis & Carla Thomas)
Knock on wood / Let me be good to you / Tramp / Tell it like it is / When something is wrong with my baby / Lovey dovey / New year's resolution / It takes two / Are you lonely for me baby / Bring it on home to me / Ooh Carla ooh Otis
CD _______________ 7567822562
Atlantic / Nov '92 / Warner Music

LIVE AT THE WHISKEY-A-GO-GO VOL.1
I can't turn you loose / Pain in my heart / Just one more day / Mr. Pitiful / Satisfaction / I'm depending on you / Any ole way / These arms of mine / Papa's got a brand new bag / Respect
CD _______________ 8122703802
Atlantic / Oct '94 / Warner Music

LIVE AT THE WHISKEY-A-GO-GO VOL.2 (Good To Me)
Introduction / I'm depending on you / Your one and only man / Good to me / Chained and bound / Ol' man trouble / Pain in my heart / These arms of mine / I can't turn you loose / I've been loving you too long / Security / Hard day's night
CD _______________ CDSX 089
Stax / Apr '93 / Pinnacle

LOVE MAN
I'm a changed man / (Your love has lifted me) Higher and higher / That's a good idea / I'll let nothing separate us / Direct me / Love man / Groovin' time / Your feeling is

mine / Got to get myself together / Free me / Lover's question / Look at that girl
CD _______________ 8122702942
Atlantic / Nov '92 / Warner Music

OTIS (The Definitive Otis Redding/4CD Set)
CD Set _______________ 8122714392
Atlantic / Oct '93 / Warner Music

OTIS BLUE
Ole man trouble / Respect / Change is gonna come / Down in the valley / I've been loving you too long / Shake / My girl / Wonderful world / Rock me baby / Satisfaction / You don't miss your water
CD _______________ 7567803182
Atlantic / Nov '92 / Warner Music

OTIS REDDING DICTIONARY OF SOUL
Fa fa fa fa fa (sad song) / I'm sick y'all / Tennessee waltz / My sweet Lorene / Try a little tenderness / Day tripper / My lover's prayer / She put the hurt on me / Ton of joy / You're still my baby / Hawg for you / Love have mercy
CD _______________ 7567917072
Atlantic / Nov '92 / Warner Music

OTIS REDDING STORY, THE (3CD Set)
These arms of mine / That's what my heart needs / Mary's little lamb / Pain in my heart / Something is worrying me / Security / Come to me / I've been loving you too long / Change is gonna come / Shake / Rock me baby / Respect / You don't miss your water / Satisfaction / Chain gang / My lover's prayer / It's growing / Fa fa fa fa fa (sad song) / I'm sick y'all / Sweet Lorene / Try a little tenderness / Day tripper / Stay in school / You left the water running / Happy song / Hard to handle / Amen / I've got dreams to remember / Champagne and wine / Direct me / Your one and only man / Chained and bound / That's how strong my love is / Mr. Pitiful / Keep your arms around me / For your precious love / Woman, a lover, a friend / Home in your heart / Ole man trouble / Down in the valley / I can't turn you loose / Just one more day / Papa's got a brand new bag / Good to me / Cigarettes and coffee / Ton of joy / Hawg for you / Tramp / Knock on wood / Lovey dovey / New year's resolution / Ooh Carla ooh Otis / Merry Christmas baby / White Christmas / Love man / Free me / Look at that girl / Match game / Tell the truth / (Sittin' on the) dock of the bay
CD Set _______________ 7567817622
Atlantic / Mar '93 / Warner Music

PAIN IN MY HEART
Pain in my heart / Dog / Stand by me / Hey hey baby / You send me / I need your lovin' / These arms of mine / Louie Louie / Something is worrying me / Security / That's what my heart needs / Lucille
CD _______________ 7567802532
Atlantic / Jun '93 / Warner Music

SOUL ALBUM, THE
Just one more day / It's growing / Cigarettes and coffee / Chain gang / Nobody knows you (when you're down and out) / Good to me / Scratch my back / Treat her right / Everybody makes a mistake / Any ole way / 634 5789
CD _______________ 7567917052
Atlantic / Nov '92 / Warner Music

SOUL BALLADS
That's how strong my love is / Chained and bound / Woman, a lover, a friend / Your one and only man / Nothing can change this love / It's too late for your precious love / I want to thank you / Come to me / Home in your heart / Keep your arms around me / Mr. Pitiful
CD _______________ 7567917062
Atlantic / Nov '92 / Warner Music

TELL THE TRUTH
Demonstration / Tell the truth / Out of sight / Give away none of my love / Wholesale love / I got the will / Johnny's heartbreak / Snatch a little piece / Slippin' and slidin' / Match game / Little time / Swingin' on a string
CD _______________ 8122702962
Atlantic / Nov '92 / Warner Music

TRIBUTE TO OTIS REDDING, A (Various Artists)
I can't turn you loose / (Sittin' on the) dock of the bay / These arms of mine / Respect / I've been loving you too long / Good to me / Let me come on home / Tribute to a king
CD _______________ JD 3320
JVC / Jun '90 / Direct / New Note/Pinnacle / Vital/SAM

Reddog

AFTER THE RAIN
CD _______________ TX 1006CD
Taxim / Jan '94 / ADA

Reddy, Helen

BASIC ORIGINAL HITS
CD _______________ BA 860932
Disky / Mar '96 / Disky / THE

FEEL SO YOUNG (The Helen Reddy Collection)
Angie baby / You make me feel so young / Let's go up / I am woman / That's all / Ain't no way to treat a lady / Lost in the shuffle / Looks like love / Here in my arms / You and me against the world
CD _______________ CDSGP 0124
Prestige / Apr '95 / Else / Total/BMG

LOVE SONGS
CD _______________ CDGOLD 1073
EMI Gold / Apr '97 / EMI

VERY BEST OF HELEN REDDY, THE
Angie baby / Raised on rock / Leave me alone (ruby red dress) / Delta dawn / Peaceful / Our house / Emotion / I don't know how to love him / Crazy love / How / Lady of the night / Keep on singing / Somewhere in the night / Bluebird / Come on John / Don't mess with a woman / Candle on the water (live) / You're my world / I can't hear you no more / You and me against the world / Ain't no way to treat a lady / I am woman
CD _______________ CDGO 2044
Capitol / Sep '92 / EMI

Redell, Teddy

ROCKIN' TEDDY REDELL
CD _______________ CLCD 4406
Collector/White Label / Oct '96 / TKO Magnum

Redemption '87

REDEMPTION '87
CD _______________ NA 031CD
New Age / Jul '96 / Plastic Head

Redman

DARE IZ A DARKSIDE
CD _______________ 5238462
RAL / Dec '94 / PolyGram

MUDDY WATERS
Intro / Iz he 4 real / Rock da spot / Welcome (Interlude) / Case closed / Pick it up / Smoke Buddah / Whateva man / On fire / What do ya feel / Skit / Creepin' / It's like that (My big brother) / Da bump / Sheshall / What U lookin' 4 / Rollin' / Soopaman luva 3
CD _______________ 5334702
Mercury / Dec '96 / PolyGram

WHUT THEE ALBUM
Psycho ward / Time 4 sum aksion / Da funk / News break / So ruff / Rated R / Watch yo nuggets / Psycho dub / Jam 4 U / Blow your mind / Hardcore / Funky uncles / Redman meets Reggie Noble / Tonight's da night / Blow your mind (remix) / I'm a bad / Sessed one night / How to roll a blunt / Sooper lover interview / Day of sooperman lover / Encore
CD _______________ 5235182
Def Jam / Jul '97 / PolyGram

Redman, Dewey

AFRICAN VENUS
African Venus / Venus and Mars / Mr. Sandman / Echo prayer / Satin doll / Take the 'A' train / Turnaround
CD _______________ ECD 220932
Evidence / Jul '94 / ADA / Cadillac / Harmonia Mundi

CHOICES
Le cut / Everything happens to me / O'besso / Imagination / For mo
CD _______________ ENJACD 70732
Enja / Jan '95 / New Note/Pinnacle / Vital/SAM

LIVING ON THE EDGE (Redman, Dewey Quartet)
CD _______________ 1201232
Black Saint / Oct '90 / Cadillac / Harmonia Mundi

Redman, Don

CHANT OF THE WEED
Milenberg joys / Cherry / Some sweet day / Shim-me-sha-wabble / Save it pretty / Gee baby ain't I good to you / I'd love it / Way I feel today / Miss Hannah / Peggy / Talk to me / Rocky road / Chant of the weed / Shakin' the African / How'm I doin' (hey, hey) / Hot and anxious / I got rhythm / Underneath the Harlem moon / Nagasaki / How ya feelin' / Sophisticated lady / That blue eyed baby from Memphis / I got ya / Down home rag
CD _______________ TPZ 1043
Topaz Jazz / Apr '96 / Cadillac / Pinnacle

CLASSICS 1931-1933
CD _______________ CLASSICS 543
Classics / Dec '90 / Discovery / Jazz Music

CLASSICS 1933-1936
CD _______________ CLASSICS 553
Classics / Dec '90 / Discovery / Jazz Music

CLASSICS 1936-1939 (Redman, Don & His Orchestra)
Moonrise on the lowlands / I gotcha / Who wants to sing my love song / Too bad / We don't know from nuthin' / Bugle call rag / Stormy weather / Exactly like you / Man on the flying trapeze / On the sunny side of the street / Swingin' with the fat man / Sweet Sue, just you
CD _______________ CLASSICS 574
Classics / Oct '91 / Discovery / Jazz Music

DOIN' WHAT I PLEASE
Beau Koo Jack / Bugle call rag / Cherry / Chant of the weed / Doin' what I please / Gee baby ain't I good to you / Got the jitters / Henderson stomp / Hot and anxious / Hot mustard / How'm I doin' / I got rhythm / Miss Hannah / Nagasaki / Paducah / Rocky Road / Save it pretty Mama / Shakin' the African / Sophisticated lady / Sugarfoot stomp / Sweet Leilani / Sweet Sue, just you / Swingin' with the fat man / That's how I feel today / Whiteman stomp
CD _______________ CDAJA 5110
Living Era / Sep '93 / Select

FOR EUROPEANS ONLY
CD _______________ SCCD 36020
Steeplechase / Apr '97 / Discovery / Impetus

MUSIC OF DON REDMAN, THE (Various Artists)
CD _______________ NI 4027
Natasha / Feb '94 / ADA / Cadillac / CM / Direct / Jazz Music

Redman, Joshua

MOOD SWING
CD _______________ 9362456432
Warner Bros. / Sep '94 / Warner Music

SPIRIT OF THE MOMENT (Live At The Village Vanguard)
CD _______________ 9362459232
Warner Bros. / Aug '95 / Warner Music

WISH
Turnaround / Soul dance / Make sure you're sure / Deserving many / We had a sister / Moose the mooche / Tears in heaven / Whittlin' / Wish / Blues for Pat
CD _______________ 9362453652
Warner Bros. / Dec '93 / Warner Music

Rednex

SEX AND VIOLINS
Cotton eyed Joe / Hittin' the hay / Riding alone / Wish you were here / Mary Lou / Old pop in an oak / Nowhere in Idaho / Sad but true story of Ray Mingus / Fat Sally Lee / Shooter / McKenzie brothers / Rolling home / Wild and free
CD _______________ KGBD 502
Internal Affairs / Mar '97 / Pinnacle

Redolfi, Michel

DETOURS
CD _______________ MM 303
Sargasso / Oct '96 / SRD

Redouane, Aicha

EGYPTE
CD _______________ C 560020
Ocora / Jan '94 / ADA / Harmonia Mundi

Redpath, Jean

FINE SONG FOR SINGING, A
I will make you brooches / Up the Noran water / Captive song of Mary Stuart / Wild geese / Capernaum / Now the die is cast / South wind / Song of wandering aengus / Rohallion / Tryst / John O'Dreams / Broom o'the Cowdenknowes / Annie Laurie / Broken brook
CD _______________ CDPH 1110
Philo / '88 / ADA / CM / Direct

FIRST FLIGHT
CD _______________ ROUCD 11556
Rounder / Jul '90 / ADA / CM / Direct

JEAN REDPATH
CD _______________ CDPH 2015
Philo / '90 / ADA / CM / Direct

LEAVING THE LAND
Leaving the land / Miss Admiral Gordon's Strathspey / Scarborough settler's lament / Un Canadien errant / Last minstrel show / Snow goose / Next time round / Sonny's dream / Maggie / Halloween / Leaving Lerwick harbour / Now I'm easy / Wild lass
CD _______________ CDTRAX 029
Greentrax / Nov '90 / ADA / Direct / Duncans / Highlander

LOWLANDS
CD _______________ PH 1066CD
Philo / Aug '94 / ADA / CM / Direct

MUSIC AND SONGS OF THE SCOTTISH FIDDLE
Cradle song / Gow's lamentation for Abercarny / Lowlands of Holland / Through the wood laddie / Gow's lament for the death of his brother / Willie Duncan / Mrs. Dundas of Arniston / Birks o' Aberfeldy / I'm a doun for lack o' Johnnie / Caledonia's wail for Niel Gow / Heiress / Wee bird cam' to our ha' door / Highland Harry / Flower o' the Quern / Gow's lament for the death of his second wife
CD _______________ LCOM 7009
Lismor / Feb '97 / ADA / Direct / Duncans / Lismor

SONGS OF ROBERT BURNS VOL.1 & 2, THE
Cauld kail in Aberdeen / To the Weavers gin ye go / Wantonness / My Tocher's the jewel / Charlie he's my darling / Lady Mary Ann / Amang the trees / Country lassie / De'il's awa' wi' tha exciseman / Johnnie Blunt / Winter it is past / Red, red rose / Logan water / Corn rigs / Had I the wyte / Nine inch will please a lady / Beware o' Bonie Ann / Cooper o' Cuddy / Sweetest May / Parcel o' rogues in a nation / Auld lang syne / Hey how Johnnie lad / Mary Morrison / Dusty miller / It was a' for our rightfu' King / Sae flaxen were her ringlets
CD _______________ CDTRAX 114
Greentrax / Mar '96 / ADA / Direct / Duncans / Highlander

SONGS OF ROBERT BURNS VOL.3 & 4, THE
Lass o' Ecclefechan / Banks o' Doon / Slave's lament / O fare ye weel my auld wife / Belles of Mauchline / Duncan Davison / Ploughman / Phillis the fair / Deuk's dang o'er my Daddie / Will ye go to the Indies / My Mary / Song, composed in August / Reel o' Stumpie / Green grow the rashes / O can yea labour lea / Wha is that at my bower door / Address to the woodlark / Long winter night / There grows a bonny brier bush / Taylor fell thro' the bed / Here's his health in water / Behold my love / Rattlin' roarin' Willie / Tam Glen / Thou hast left me ever / Jamie / I'll ay ca' in by yon town
CD _______________ CDTRAX 115
Greentrax / Mar '96 / ADA / Direct / Duncans / Highlander

SONGS OF ROBERT BURNS VOL.5 & 6, THE
Lea rig / My collier laddie / O this is no my ain lassie / My Nanie / Fragment / Posie / Mill, Mill O / O, were I on Parnassus Hill / German Lairdie / Battle of Sherramoor / Lament of Mary Queen of Scots / You're welcome, Willie Stewart / Killiecrankie / Galloway Tam / Strathallan's lament / Fornicator / Here's to thy health / Last may a braw wooer / Gloomy December / Jamie, come try me / White cockade / Cardin O't / Sandy & Jockie / Hey ca' thro'
CD _______________ CDTRAX 116
Greentrax / Mar '96 / ADA / Direct / Duncans / Highlander

SONGS OF ROBERT BURNS VOL.7, THE
Mauchline lady / O merry hae I been / Gallant weaver / Young highland rover / Cauld is the e'enin blast / My father was a farmer / My love / She's but a lassie yet / Ode to Spring / O' guid ale comes / Bonnie lass o'Albanie / O, for ane-and-twenty, Tam / Where are the joys
CD _______________ CDTRAX 039
Greentrax / Nov '90 / ADA / Direct / Duncans / Highlander

SONGS OF THE SEAS
CD _______________ PHCD 1054
Philo / Aug '94 / ADA / CM / Direct

Redskins

NEITHER WASHINGTON NOR MOSCOW
CD _______________ 8288642
London / Jan '97 / PolyGram

Redway, Mike

MOONLIGHT AND LOVE SONGS
CD _______________ RKD 14
Redrock / Dec '94 / Target/BMG / THE

THOSE BEAUTIFUL BALLAD YEARS
Lark in the clear air / Rose of Killarney / Passing by / On the banks of the Wabash / I love the moon / Barbara Allen / I dream of Jeannie with the light brown hair / Just awearyin' for you / I'll be your sweetheart / When you and I were young Maggie / Mighty like a rose
CD _______________ RKD 7
Redrock / Dec '94 / Target/BMG / THE

Reece, Alex

AL'S RECORDS VOL.1 (Various Artists)
Touch me: *Reece, Alex & Paul Saunders* / Nu era: *Reece, Alex & Pim Aldridge* / Street player: *Reece, Alex & Ashley Brown* / Rough cut: *Reece, Alex & Ashley Brown* / Double edge: *DJ Pulse & The Jazz Cartel* / FVR: *Reece, Alex* / Nag: *Reece, Alex* / New York: *Reece, Alex* / Reactivate: *DJ Pulse & The Jazz Cartel* / Bounce: *Reece, Alex & Ashley Brown* / Skatta: *Reece, Alex* / Jazz shaker: *Reece, Alex*
CD _______________ ALSCD 1001
Al's Records / Apr '97 / PolyGram / Vital

SO FAR
Feel the sunshine / Jazz master / Intro / Acid lab / Pulp friction / Candles / Ibiza / Intro / Out of time / U R
CD _______________ BRCD 621
4th & Broadway / Aug '96 / PolyGram

Reece, Dizzy

ASIA MINOR
CD _______________ OJCCD 1806
Original Jazz Classics / Jul '94 / Complete/Pinnacle / Jazz Music / Wellard

Reed, A.C.

I GOT MONEY (Reed, A.C. & M. Vaughn)
CD ________ **BLE 597272**
Black & Blue / Oct '94 / Discovery / Koch / Wellard

I'M IN THE WRONG BUSINESS
I'm in the wrong business / I can't go on this way / Fast food Annie / This little voice / My buddy buddy friends / She's fine / These blues is killing me / Miami strut / Things I want you to do / Don't drive drunk / Hard times / Going to New York / Moving out of the ghetto
CD ________ **ALCD 4757**
Alligator / May '93 / ADA / CM / Direct

Reed, Dalton

LOUISIANA SOUL MAN
Read me my rights / Blues of the month club / Keep on loving me / Last to understand / Heavy love / Full moon / Keep the spirit / I'm only guilty of loving you / Party on the farm / Chained and bound
CD ________ **CDBB 9517**
Bullseye Blues / Sep '92 / Direct

WILLING AND ABLE
CD ________ **BB 9547**
Bullseye Blues / Apr '94 / Direct

Reed, Eric

IT'S ALL RIGHT TO SWING
Wade in the water / In a lonely place / You don't know what it is to love / Boo Boo strikes again / Undecided / Blues for Akmad / Third degree / He cares / Pineus coneus / Come Sunday
CD ________ **5302552**
MoJazz / Feb '94 / PolyGram

MUSICALE
Black, as in buhaina / Longhair's rumba / Cosa Nostra (our thing) / Frog's legs / Scandal I / Pete and repete / Love Devine / Baby sis / Scandal II / Shug / Upper wess side / Scandal III / No sadness, no pain / Blues to come
CD ________ **IMP 11962**
Impulse Jazz / Oct '96 / New Note/BMG

SOLDIER'S HYMN
Soldier's hymn / Greatest thing in all my life / Soft winds / Things hoped for / Coup de cone / Walk with me / Bee's knees / Miss Inferno / I didn't know what time it was / Sweet Lorraine / Mood indigo / Soldier's hymn
CD ________ **CCD 79511**
Candid / Feb '97 / Cadillac / Direct / Jazz Music / Koch / Wellard

SWING AND I, THE
CD ________ **5304682**
MoJazz / May '95 / PolyGram

Reed, Francine

CAN'T MAKE IT ON MY OWN
CD ________ **D 2248862**
Ichiban / Oct '96 / Direct / Koch

Reed, Hugh

TAKE A WALK ON THE CLYDE SIDE (Reed, Hugh & The Velvet Underpants)
CD ________ **ECLCD 9615**
Eclectic / Feb '96 / ADA / New Note/ Pinnacle

Reed, Jerry

ESSENTIAL JERRY REED, THE
Guitar man / Alabama jubilee / Amos Moses / Thing called love / When you're hot, you're hot / Smell the flowers / Koko Joe / You think all the ramblin' out of me / Uptown poker club / Claw / Lord, Mr. Ford / Good woman's love / Eastbound and down / Let's sing our song / Crude oil blues / I love you, what can I say / Bird / Texas bound and flyin' / She got the goldmine (I got the shaft) / Another puff
CD ________ **74321665922**
RCA / Feb '96 / BMG

GUITAR MAN
Guitar man / Folsom Prison blues / Devil went down to Georgia / Down on the corner / Thing called love / US male / Honkin' / Wabash cannonball / Tupelo Mississippi flash / 500 miles away from home / Struttin' / Amos Moses / Sweet memories / Sixteen tons / When you're hot you're hot / Blue moon of Kentucky / Don't it make you wanna go home / Promises / Bad bad Leroy Brown / Patches / Mule skinner blues / Ruby, don't take your love to town
CD ________ **74321415002**
Camden [illegible] BMG

[illegible] / Go on to school / [illegible]'m nervous / Caress [illegible]o sweet / Little rain [illegible]ne, shame, shame
________ **CWNCD 2029**
[illegible]Hadaway / THE

BIG BOSS MAN/DOWN IN VIRGINIA
Sugar sugar woman / Don't light my fire / Slow walking Mama / Jump and shout / Down in Virginia / Check yourself / I show an arrow to the sky / Ghetto woman blues / Big boss lady / I need you so / Judge should know / Give up and let me go / I'm leavin' / Shame, shame, shame / Run here to me baby / Life is funny / Two in one blues / My baby told me / Five years of good lovin' / When two people are in love / I've got to keep on rollin' / When I woke up this morning
CD ________ **SEECD 469**
See For Miles/C5 / Jan '97 / Pinnacle

BRIGHT LIGHTS, BIG CITY (Charly Blues Masterworks Vol.17)
You don't have to go / I don't go for that / Ain't that lovin' you baby / Can't stand to see you go / I love you baby / You've got me dizzy / Honey / Where you going / Little rain / Sun is shining / Honest I do / Down in Virginia / I'm gonna get my baby / Baby, what you want me to do / Found love / Hush hush / Big boss man / Bright lights big city / Aw shucks hush your mouth / Good lover / Shame, shame, shame
CD ________ **CDBM 17**
Charly / Apr '92 / Koch

CARESS ME BABY
Honest I do / Found love / Ain't that lovin' you baby / Little rain / Hush hush / Boogie in the dark / Cold and lonesome / Close together / Caress me baby / I'm nervous / Oh, John / Shame, shame, shame / You're something else / I ain't got you / Going fishing
CD ________ **CDSGP 086**
Prestige / Oct '93 / Else / Total/BMG

GUITAR, HARMONICA AND FEELING
High and lonesome / Jimmie's boogie / You don't have to go / Boogie in the dark / You upset my mind / She don't want me no more / I don't go for that / Ain't that lovin' you baby / You got for that / You got me dizzy / Honest I do / Sun is shining / End and odds / My bitter seed / Going to New York / Take out some insurance / Baby, what you want me to do / Hush hush / Found love / You gonna need my help / Found joy / Kind of lonesome / Blue Carnagie / Big boss man / Sugar sugar / Jimmy's rock / Bright lights big city / I'm going upside your head
CD ________ **CD 52012**
Blues Encore / '92 / Target/BMG

JIMMY REED - THE VEE JAY RECORDS (6CD Set)
High and lonesome / Jimmie's boogie / I found my baby / Roll and rhumba / You don't have to go / Boogie in the dark / Shoot my baby / Rockin' with Reed / You upset my mind / I'm gonna ruin you / Pretty thing / I ain't got you / She don't want me no more / Come on baby / I don't go for that / Baby, don't say that no more / Ain't that lovin' you baby / Can't stand to see you go / When you left me / I love you baby / My first plea / You got me dizzy / Honey don't let me go / Untitled instrumental / It's you baby / Honey, where you going / Do the thing / Little rain / Signals of love / Sun is shining / Baby, what's on your mind / Honest I do / State street boogie / Odds and ends / My baby (Down in Virginia) / You're something else / String to your heart / Go on to school / You got me crying / Moon is rising / Down in Virginia / I'm gonna get my baby / I wanna be loved / Caress me baby / I know it's a sin / You'n that sack / Going to New york / I told you baby / take out some insurance / I'm nervous / You know I love you / Baby, what you want me to do / Goin' by the river / Goin' by the river / Where can you be / Hush hush / I was so wrong / Blue blue water / Please don't / Found love / You gonna need my help / Hold me close / Come love / Big boss man / Meet me / I got the blues / Sugar sugar / Got me chasing you / Down the road / Want to be with you baby / Jimmy's rock / Tell the world I do / You're my baby / Ain't gonna cry no more / Close together / You know you're looking good / Laughing at the blues / I'm a love you / Kind of lonesome / Found joy / Tell me you love me / Bright lights / Baby what's wrong / Aw shucks / Hush your mouth / I'm Mr. Luck / Blue Carnegie / Take it slow / Good lover / Down in Mississippi / Too much / I'll change my style / Let's get together / In the morning / You can't hide / Back home at noon / Lookin' for you baby / Kansas city baby / Oh John / Shame, shame, shame / Cold and lonesome / There'll be a day / Ain't no big deal / Mary Mary / Upside the wall / Baby's so sweet / I'm gonna help you / Up tight / Mixed up / I'm trying to please you / Five long years / CC rider / Outskirts of town / Trouble in mind / Comebacks / How long blues / Roll 'em Pete / Cherry red / Wee wee baby / St. Louis blues / Worried life blues / Blues for 12 strings / New Chicago blues / Wear something green / Help yourself / Heading for a fall / Going fishing / Left handed woman / I wanna be loved (Crazy love) / Fifteen years / New leaf / When you're doing alright / I'm going upside your head / Devil's shoestring 2 / You've got me waiting / I'm the man down there / When girls do it / Don't think I'm through
CD Set ________ **CDREDBOX 9**
Charly / Feb '94 / Koch

LIVE AT LIBERTY HALL, HOUSTON 1972 (Reed, Jimmy & Johnny Winter)
Big boss man / Stop light / Down the road I go / Bright lights, big city
CD ________ **422349**
Last Call / Feb '97 / Cargo / Direct / Discovery

NEW JIMMY REED ALBUM, THE/ SOULIN'
Big boss man / I wanna know / Got nowhere / Two ways to skin a cat / Heartaches and trouble / Tell me what you want me to do / Honey I'll make two / You don't have to go / Don't play me cheap / Two sides to every story / I'm just trying to cop a plea / Two heads are better than one / Buy me a hound dog / Feel like I want to ramble / I wake up at daybreak / Peepin' and hidin' / Don't press your luck woman / I'm not going to let you down / I'm knocking on your door / Crazy about Oklahoma / Cousin Peaches / Ain't no time for fussin' / Dedication to Sonny
CD ________ **SEECD 468**
See For Miles/C5 / Jan '97 / Pinnacle

TAKE OUT SOME INSURANCE
CD ________ **CDRB 13**
Charly / Jul '93 / Koch

VERY BEST OF JIMMY REED, THE (& Roots Of The Blues Vol.5 Compilation/ 3CD Set)
I found my baby / You don't have to go / I'm gonna ruin you / She don't want me no more / I don't go for that / Ain't that lovin' you baby / Can't stand to see you go / Love you baby / You got me dizzy / Honey, where you going / Do the thing / Little rain / Sun is shining / Odds and ends / Honest I do / My bitter seed / Moon is rising / Down in Virginia / I'm gonna get my baby / I wanna be loved / Take out some insurance / What do you want me to do / Hush-hush / Found love / Come love / Big boss man / Close together / Tell me you love me / Bright lights / Big city / Baby / What's wrong / Aw shucks / Hush your mouth / Good lover / Too much / I'll change my style / Let's get together / Shame, shame, shame / When you're doing alright / I'm going upside your head / I'm the man down there / St Louis Blues: *Smith, Bessie* / Matchbox: *Jefferson, Blind Lemon* / Big road blues: *Johnson, Tommy* / Got the blues can't be satisfied: *Hurt, 'Mississippi' John* / Going up the country: *Barbecue Bob* / Spoonful blues: *Patton, Charlie* / Dupree blues: *Walker, Willie* / Sugar Mama blues: *Tampa Red* / Honky tonk train blue: *Lewis, Meade 'Lux'* / Lead pencil blues: *Temple, Johnny* / Sweet home Chicago: *Johnson, Robert* / Just a dream: *Broonzy, 'Big' Bill* / Harmonica stomp: *Terry, Sonny* / Good morning blues: *Leadbelly* / Country jail blues: *Big Maceo* / country blues: *Waters, Muddy*
CD Set ________ **VBCD 305**
Charly / Jul '95 / Koch

VERY BEST OF JIMMY REED, THE (2CD Set)
I found my baby / You don't have to go / I'm gonna ruin you / She don't want me no more / I don't go for that / Ain't that lovin' you baby / Can't stand to see you go / I love you baby / You got me dizzy / Honey, where you going / Do the thing / Little rain / Sun is shining / Odds and ends / Honest I do / My bitter seed / Moon is rising / Down in Virginia / I'm gonna get my baby / I wanna be loved / I told you baby / Take out some insurance / Baby, what you want me to do / Hush hush / Found love / Come love / Big boss man / Close together / Tell me you love me / Bright lights, big city / Baby, what's wrong / Aw shucks / Hush your mouth / Good lover / Too much / I'll change my style / Let's get together / Shame, shame, shame / When you're doing alright / I'm going upside your head / I'm the man down there
CD Set ________ **CPCD 82522**
Charly / Oct '96 / Koch

Reed, Kay

WE ARE ONE
CD ________ **GBW 006**
GBW / Jan '93 / Harmonia Mundi

Reed, Lou

BELLS, THE
CD ________ **262918**
Arista / Aug '92 / BMG

BERLIN
Berlin / Lady Day / Men of good fortune / Caroline says / How do you think it feels / Oh Jim / Caroline says II / Kids / Bed / Sad song
CD ________ **ND 84388**
RCA / Jun '86 / BMG

BETWEEN THOUGHT AND EXPRESSION (Lou Reed Anthology Box Set/3CD Set)
I can't stand it / Lisa says / Ocean / Walk on the wild side / Satellite of love / Vicious / Caroline says / How do you think it feels / Oh Jim / Caroline says / Kids / Sad song / Sweet Jane / Kill your sons / Coney Island baby / Nowhere at all / Kicks / Downtown dirt / Rock 'n' roll heart / Vicious circle / Temporary thing / Real good time together / Leave me alone / Heroin / Here comes the bride / Street hassle / Metal machine music / Bells / America / Think it over / Teach the gifted children / Gun / Blue mask / My house / Waves of fear / Little sister / Legendary hearts / Last shot / New sensations / My friend George / Doin' the things that we want to / Original wrapper / Video violence / Tell it to your heart / Voices of freedom
CD Set ________ **PD 90621**
RCA / Mar '92 / BMG

CONEY ISLAND BABY
Crazy feeling / Charley's girl / She's my best friend / Kicks / Gift / Oooh baby / Ain't nobody's business if I do / Coney Island baby
CD ________ **ND 83807**
RCA / Dec '86 / BMG

DIFFERENT TIMES (Lou Reed In The 70's)
I can't stand it / Love makes you feel / Lisa says / Walk on the wild side / Perfect day / Satellite of love / Vicious / Berlin / Caroline says / Sad song / Caroline says / Sweet Jane / Kill yor sons / Sally can't dance / Gift / She's my best friend / Coney Island baby
CD ________ **07863668642**
RCA / Aug '96 / BMG

GROWING UP IN PUBLIC
How do you speak to an angel / My old man / Keep away / Standing on ceremony / So alone / Our love is here to stay / Power of positive drinking / Smiles / Think it over / Teach the gifted children
CD ________ **262917**
Arista / Aug '92 / BMG

LEGENDARY HEARTS
Legendary hearts / Don't talk to me about work / Make up / Martial law / Last shot / Turn out the light / Pow wow / Betrayed / Bottoming out / Home of the brave / Rooftop garden
CD ________ **ND 89843**
RCA / Apr '91 / BMG

LOU REED & VELVET UNDERGROUND (Reed, Lou/Velvet Underground)
Sunday morning: *Reed, Lou* / I'm waiting for the man: *Reed, Lou* / Venus in furs: *Reed, Lou* / Candy says: *Velvet Underground* / Pale blue eyes: *Velvet Underground* / Beginning to see the light: *Velvet Underground* / Satellite of love: *Reed, Lou* / Nowhere at all: *Reed, Lou* / Vicious: *Reed, Lou* / Perfect day: *Reed, Lou* / Walk on the wild side: *Reed, Lou* / How do you think it feels: *Reed, Lou* / Sweet Jane: *Reed, Lou* / White light/ white heat: *Reed, Lou* / Sally can't dance: *Reed, Lou* / Wild child: *Reed, Lou* / I love you: *Reed, Lou* / Berlin: *Reed, Lou* / Coney Island baby: *Reed, Lou* / I love you, Suzanne: *Reed, Lou*
CD ________ **RADCD 21**
Global TV / Oct '95 / BMG

LOU REED LIVE IN CONCERT
Sweet Jane / I'm waiting for the man / Martial law / Satellite of love / Kill your sons / Betrayed / Sally can't dance / Wages of fear / Average guy / White light, white heat / Some kinda love / Sister Ray / Walk on the wild side / Heroin / Rock 'n' roll
CD ________ **74321431572**
Camden / Oct '96 / BMG

MAGIC AND LOSS
Dorita / What's good / Power and glory / Magician / Sword of damocles / Goodby mass / Cremation / Dreamin' / No change / Warrior king / Harry's circumcision / Gassed and stoked / Power and glory part II / Magic and loss
CD ________ **7599266622**
Sire / Jan '92 / Warner Music

NEW YORK
Romeo and Juliet / Halloween parade / Dirty boulevard / Endless cycle / There is no time / Last great American whale / Beginning of a great mystery / Busload of faith / Sick of you / Hold on / Good evening Mr. Waldheim / Christmas in February / Strawman / Dime store mystery
CD ________ **7599258292**
Sire / Feb '95 / Warner Music

ROCK 'N' ROLL HEART
I believe in love / Banging on my drum / Follow the leader / You wear it so well / Ladies pay / Rock 'n' roll heart / Temporary thing
CD ________ **262271**
Arista / Feb '93 / BMG

SALLY CAN'T DANCE
Ride Sally ride / Animal language / Baby face / NY stars / Kill your sons / Billy / Sally can't dance / Ennui
CD ________ **ND 90308**
RCA / Feb '89 / BMG

SET THE TWILIGHT REELING
CD ________ **9362461592**
Sire / Feb '96 / Warner Music

SONGS FOR DRELLA (Reed, Lou & John Cale)
Smalltown / Open house / Style it takes / Work / Trouble with classicists / Starlight / Faces and names / Images / Slip away / It wasn't me / I believe / Nobody but you / Dream / Forever changed / Hello it's me

CD 7599261402
WEA / Apr '90 / Warner Music

STREET HASSLE
Gimme some good times / Dirt / Street hassle / I wanna be black / Real good time together / Shooting star
CD 262270
Arista / Feb '93 / BMG

STREET HASSLE/THE BELLS (2CD Set)
CD Set 74321292092
RCA / Jan '95 / BMG

TRANSFORMER
Vicious / Andy's chest / Perfect day / Hangin' around / Walk on the wild side / Make up / Satellite of love / Wagon wheel / New York telephone conversation / I'm so free / Goodnight ladies
CD ND 83806
RCA / Aug '95 / BMG

TRANSFORMER/BERLIN (2CD Set)
CD Set 74321292102
RCA / Jan '95 / BMG

WALK ON THE WILD SIDE (The Best Of Lou Reed)
Satellite of love / Wild child / I love you / How do you think it feels / New York telephone conversation / Walk on the wild side / Sweet Jane / White light, white heat / Sally can't dance / Nowhere at all / Coney Island baby / Vicious
CD ND 83753
RCA / Oct '91 / BMG

Reed, Lucy

BASIC REEDING
CD ACD 273
Audiophile / Apr '93 / Jazz Music

Reed, Preston

ROAD LESS TRAVELLED, THE
CD FF 70423
Flying Fish / Oct '89 / ADA / CM / Direct / Roots

Reedstorm Saxophone Quartet

JAZZ STANDARDS
CD BEST 1075CD
Acoustic Music / Nov '95 / ADA

Reedy, Winston

GOLD
CD RNCD 2049
Rhino / Mar '94 / Grapevine/PolyGram / Jet Star

Reef

GLOW
Place your hands / I would have left you / Summer's in bloom / Lately stomping / Consideration / Don't you like it / Come back brighter / Higher vibration / I'm not scared / Robot riff / You're old / Lullaby
CD 4869402
Sony Soho2 / Jan '97 / Sony

REPLENISH
Feed me / Naked / Good feeling / Repulsive / Mellow / Together / Replenish / Choose to live / Comfort / Loose / End
CD 4806982
Sony Soho2 / Jun '95 / Sony

Reefa

LOVE LIFE LIVE LOVE
CD STRSCD 4
Stress / Oct '94 / Mo's Music Machine / Pinnacle / Prime

Reel 2 Real

ARE YOU READY FOR SOME MORE
Are you ready for some more / Jazz it up / Life's funny / Pick your choice / Mueve la cadera (move your body) / Ouhhh baby baby / Do not panic / Love hurts / Now that we found love / Jump around / Wicked and wild / I like it like that / Are you ready for some more (remix) / Jazz it up (remix)
CD CDTIVA 1012
Positiva / Jul '96 / EMI

MOVE IT (Reel 2 Real & The Mad Stuntman)
I like to move it / Can you feel it / Raise your hands / One life to live / Stuntman's anthem / Erick More's anthem (Can you feel it) / Conway / Wine your body / REX / Toety / Go on move
CD CDTIVA 1003
Positiva / Oct '94 / EMI

REEL 2 REMIXED (Reel 2 Real & The Mad Stuntman)
Go on move / Can you feel it / I like to move it / Conway / Raise your hands / Stuntman's anthem
CD CDTIVA 1007
Positiva / Aug '95 / EMI

Reel Union

BROKEN HEARTED I'LL WANDER
CD CLUNCD 033
Mulligan / Nov '86 / ADA / CM

Reeltime

REELTIME
CD GL 1154CD
Green Linnet / Jul '95 / ADA / CM / Direct / Highlander / Roots

Reese, Della

BEST THING FOR YOU, THE
What is there to say: *Reese, Della & Dick Stabile Orchestra* / You came a long way from St. Louis: *Reese, Della & Dick Stabile Orchestra* / If I ever should leave you: *Reese, Della & Dick Stabile Orchestra* / Be my love: *Reese, Della & Dick Stabile Orchestra* / Lamp is low/After the lights go down: *Reese, Della & Dick Stabile Orchestra* / Fly me to the moon: *Reese, Della & Dick Stabile Orchestra* / I could have danced all night: *Reese, Della & Dick Stabile Orchestra* / Swing low, sweet chariot: *Reese, Della & Dick Stabile Orchestra* / Best thing for you: *Reese, Della & John Cotter Orchestra* / Don't you know: *Reese, Della & John Cotter Orchestra* / Keep smiling at trouble: *Reese, Della & John Cotter Orchestra* / Don't cry Joe: *Reese, Della & John Cotter Orchestra* / I'm always chasing rainbows: *Reese, Della & John Cotter Orchestra* / Bill Bailey, won't you please come home: *Reese, Della & John Cotter Orchestra* / Put on a happy face/I want to be happy: *Reese, Della & John Cotter Orchestra* / But not for me: *Reese, Della & John Cotter Orchestra* / See what the boys in the backroom will have: *Reese, Della & John Cotter Orchestra* / Anything goes: *Reese, Della & John Cotter Orchestra* / My man: *Reese, Della & John Cotter Orchestra* / Nobody's sweetheart: *Reese, Della & John Cotter Orchestra*
CD JASCD 332
Jasmine / May '97 / Conifer/BMG / Hot Shot / TKO Magnum

DELLA
Lady is a tramp / You're driving me crazy / If I could be with you one hour tonight / Three o'clock in the morning / Until the real thing comes along / Thou swell / You made me love you / I'm beginning to see the light / I'm always chasing rainbows / What's the reason (I'm not pleasin') / Softly my love / You're nobody 'til somebody loves you / Baby won't you please come home / Moon love / Blue skies / Have you ever been lonely / Someday / I'll get by till the end of time / Please don't talk about me when I'm gone / Don't you know / Someday sweetheart
CD 74321415012
Camden / Oct '96 / BMG

HITS AND RARITIES
CD MAR 032
Marginal / Jun '97 / Greyhound

LIVE 1963 GAURD SESSIONS (Reese, Della & Duke Wellington)
CD EBCD 21102
Flyright / Feb '94 / Hot Shot / Jazz Music / Wellard

Reese Project

FAITH, HOPE & CLARITY
CD TRPCD 1
Network / Nov '92 / 3mv/Sony / Pinnacle

Reet Petite & Gone

USING THAT THING
Somebody's been using that thing / That's no way to get along / Waiting for a runaway train / Bring it on home / Dixie fried / Go ahead buddy / Battle of New Orleans / Good time flat blues / Looking for the heart of Saturday night / Goodbye lonesome, hello baby doll / Steady rolling man / Little red hen / Moonshine madness / Reet petite and gone / It mek / Canned heat
CD TERRCD 004
Terra Nova / Feb '97 / Direct

Reeves, Dianne

GRAND ENCOUNTER
Old country / Cherokee / Besame mucho / Let me love you / Tenderly / After hours / Ha / Some other Spring / Side by side / I'm okay
CD CDP 8382682
Blue Note / Nov '96 / EMI

QUIET AFTER THE STORM
Hello haven't I seen you before / Comes love / Smile / Jive samba / Country preacher / Detour ahead / Vermonja / Sargaco mar / Nine / In a sentimental mood / When morning comes / Both sides now / Sing my heart
CD CDP 8295112
Blue Note / Jun '95 / EMI

Reeves, Goebel

HOBO'S LULLABY
Tramp's mother / I learned about women from her / Drifter (part 1) / Drifter (part 2) / When the clock struck seventeen / Blue undertaker's blues (part 1) / Blue undertaker's blues (part 2) / Fortunes galore / My mountain gal / Song of the sea / In the land of never was / Texas drifter's warning / Cowboy's lullaby / Hobo's lullaby / Drifter's buddy (drifter's prayer) / Cowboy's prayer / Happy days (I'll never leave old Dixieland) / Wayward son / Reckless Tex / Soldier's return / Miss Jackson, Tennessee / My mountain gal / Cold and hungry / Meet me at the crossroads, pal / Yodeling teacher / Kidnapped baby
CD BCD 15680
Bear Family / Nov '94 / Direct / Rollercoaster / Swift

Reeves, Jim

18 VERY SPECIAL LOVE SONGS (Live From The Grand Ole Opry 1959)
I'd like to be / I know me / Anna Marie / Have I told you lately that I love you / Your old love letters / Till the end of the world / Making believe / Four walls / According to my heart / Just call me lonesome / Blue boy / I missed me / Am I losing you / I love you more / If you were only mine / How's the world treating you / I'm beginning to forget you / If heartaches are the fashion
CD PLATCD 163
Platinum / Mar '96 / Prism

ACCORDING TO MY HEART (At His Best)
CD PLSCD 215
Pulse / Apr '97 / BMG

BEST OF JIM REEVES, THE
CD MATCD 317
Castle / Dec '94 / BMG

BEST OF JIM REEVES, THE
CD 74321378412
RCA / Jul '96 / BMG

BEST OF JIM REEVES, THE
He'll have to go / Billy Bayou / According to my heart / Distant drums / Welcome to my world / I won't come in while he's there / Yonder comes a sucker / Four walls / Blue boy / I love you because / Anna Marie / Home / Am I losing you / Blue side of lonesome / Adios amigo / I won't forget you / I'm gonna change everything / I missed me / Partners / Losing your love / Waiting for a train / Is it really over
CD 74321446842
Camden / Feb '97 / BMG

CLASSIC COUNTRY
CD CDSR 068
Telstar / May '95 / BMG

DEAR HEARTS AND GENTLE PEOPLE
Have I told you lately that I love you / Just call me lonesome / How's the world treating you / If heartaches are the fashion / Home / Dear hearts and gentle people / I'm beginning to forget you / Roly poly / Wind up doll / Sweet evening breeze / Your old love letters / Till the end of the world / Making believe / Oaklahoma hills
CD CDSD 073
Sundown / Jun '92 / TKO Magnum

DISTANT DRUMS
Distant drums / I won't forget you / Is it really over / I missed me / Snowflake / Letter to my heart / Losing your love / This is it / Not until the next time / Good morning self / Where does a broken heart go / Overnight / Gods were angry with me
CD WMCD 5635
Disky / May '94 / Disky / THE

ESSENTIAL JIM REEVES, THE
Four walls / Blue boy / He'll have to go / Home / Am I losing you / Blizzard / I'm gettin' better / I know one / Adios amigos / I love you because / I'm gonna change everything / Welcome to my world / Is this me / I guess I'm crazy / This is it / Is it really over / Distant drums / I won't forget you / Blue side of lonesome / Suppertime
CD 74321665892
RCA / Feb '96 / BMG

GENTLEMAN JIM (4CD Set)
I'm hurtin' inside / If you were mine / That's a sad affair / Yonder comes a sucker / Jimbo Jenkins / I've lived a lot in my time / Ichabod crane / My lips are sealed / Your old love letters / Waltzing on top of the world / Beyond a shadow of a doubt / Love me a little bit more / According to my heart / Each time you leave / Highway to nowhere / Breeze (blow my baby back to me) / Roly poly / Tweedle o'twill / Have I told you lately that I love you / Oklahoma hills / Pickin' a chicken / I've got just the thing for you / I'm the mother of a honky tonk girl: *Reeves, Jim & Carol Johnson* / Am I losing you / Don't tell me / I can't fly / Don't ask me why / Waiting for a train / Look behind you / Four walls / Honey, won't you please come home / Gods were angry with me / I know (and you know) / Young hearts / I heard my heart break last night / Image of me / Anna Marie / Sea breeze / Blue without my baby / I love you more / Theme of love (I love to say I love you) / Wishful thinking / Two shadows on your window / Everywhere you go (single version) / Teardrops in my heart / Yours / I don't see me in your eyes anymore / I get the blues when it rains / I care no more / Final affair / You belong to me / My happiness / Everywhere you go / Blues in my heart / Need me / That's my desire / He'll have to go / In a mansion stands my love / Billy Bayou / I'd like to be partners / I'm beginning to forget you / If heartaches are the fashion / Home after awhile / Overnight blue boy / Charmaine / Mona Lisa / Marie / Goodnight Irene / Linda / Maria Elena / My Mary Ramona / Margie / My Juanita / Sweet Sue, just you / Just you / Snowflake / But you love me daddy: *Reeves, Jim & Steve Moore* / But you love me daddy: *Reeves, Jim & Dorothy Dillard* / Throw another log on the fire / Making believe / Till the end of the world / How's the world treating you / Someday (you'll want me to want you) / Just call me lonesome / Fool such as I / May the good Lord bless and keep you / Dear hearts and gentle people / Satan can't hold me / Scarlet ribbons / How long has it been / Teach me how to pray / Evening prayer / Padre of old San Antone / Suppertime / It is no secret / God be with you / Beautiful life / In the garden / Precious memories / Whispering hope / Flowers / Sunset, the trees
CD Set BCD 15439
Bear Family / Jun '89 / Direct / Rollercoaster / Swift

GENTLEMAN JIM (2CD Set)
CD Set DBG 53031
Double Gold / Apr '94 / Target/BMG

GENTLEMAN JIM
He'll have to go / Have I told you lately that I love you / I know one / Am I losing you / Your old love letters / Anna Marie / I'm beginning to forget you / I love you more / Waiting for a train / Mexican Joe / I missed me / According to my heart / Four walls / Bimbo / When God dips his love in my heart / Billy Bayou / Heartaches are the fashion / I'd like to be / Peace in the valley / Dear hearts and gentle people / I'm gettin' better / Yonder comes a sucker / Blue boy / Just call me lonesome / In a mansion stands my love
CD CD 6015
Music / Apr '96 / Target/BMG

HAVE I TOLD YOU LATELY
CD MU 5046
Musketeer / Oct '92 / Disc

HAVE I TOLD YOU LATELY
Am I losing you / He'll have to go / Have I told you lately that I love you / How's the world treating you / I love you more / Til the end of the world / I've lived a lot in my time / Oklahoma hills / I'm getting better / Bimbo / Anna Marie / Billy Bayou / Blue boy / Waiting for a train / When god dips his love in my heart / Just call me lonesome / If heartaches are in fashion / Your old love letters
CD 300072
Hallmark / Jul '96 / Carlton

HE'LL HAVE TO GO
He'll have to go / Bimbo / I'd like to be / Billy Bayou / In a mansion stands my love / I'm getting better / I know one / I missed me / Yonder comes a sucker / Waiting for a train / Am I losing you / According to my heart / Four walls / Mexican Joe / Anna Marie / Blue boy / Softly and tenderly / Peace in the valley
CD MUCD 9022
Musketeer / Apr '95 / Disc

I LOVE YOU MORE (Live)
If you were only mine / I love you more / Have I told you lately that I love you / Everywhere you go / Sweet evening breeze / Oklahoma hills where I was born / Evening prayer / Dear hearts and gentle people / I've lived a lot in my time / If heartaches are the fashion / Home / How's the world treating you / I'm beginning to forget you / Roly poly / Wind up / Your old love letters / Till the end of the world / Making believe / Just call me lonesome / Highway to nowhere / Beyond the shadow of a doubt
CD DATOM 3
A Touch Of Magic / Apr '94 / Harmonia Mundi

I LOVE YOU MORE
CD CTS 55433
Country Stars / Oct '95 / Target/BMG

IMMORTAL JIM REEVES, THE (2CD Set)
Four walls / Mexican Joe / Anna Marie / Blue boy / Softly and tenderly / He'll have to go / Bimbo / I'd like to be / Peace in the valley / Billy Bayou / In a mansion stands my love / I'm getting better / (Gimme that) Old tyme religion / I know one / I missed me / Yonder comes a sucker / Am I losing you / According to my heart / Beyond the shadow of a doubt / Evening prayer / Have I told you lately that I love you / Just call me lonesome / How's the world treating you / If heartaches are the fashion / Home / Dear hearts and gentle people / I'm beginning to forget you / Roly poly / Wind up / Sweet evening breeze / Your old love letters / Til the end of the world / Making believe / Oklahoma hills / Highway to nowhere / If you were mine / Everywhere you go / I love you more / I've lived a lot in my time / Waiting for a train
CD Set MUCD 9513
Musketeer / May '96 / Disc

JIM REEVES
Peace in the valley / Till the end of the world / Your old love letters / He'll have to go / According to my heart / Just call me lonesome / Four walls / If heartaches are the fashion / I'm beginning to forget y[illegible] / How's the world treating you / Mak[illegible] lieve / I love you more / I've liv[illegible]

my time / Dear hearts and gentle people / Blue boy / Am I losing you / Roly poly / In a mansion stands my love / I missed me / Have I told you lately that I love you
CD SUMCD 4028
Summit / Nov '96 / Sound & Media

JIM REEVES
CD DS 011
Desperado / Jun '97 / TKO Magnum

JIM REEVES
CD GFS 064
Going For A Song / Jul '97 / Else / TKO Magnum

JIM REEVES IN CONCERT
Yonder comes a sucker / Blue boy / Just call me lonesome / In a mansion stands my love / He'll have to go / Have I told you lately that I love you / I know one / Am I losing you / Your old love letters / Anna Marie / I'm beginning to forget you / I love you more / Waiting for a train / Mexican Joe / I missed me / According to my heart / Four walls / Bimbo / When God dips his love in my heart / Billy Bayou / If heartaches are the fashion / Peace in the valley
CD TRTCD 128
TrueTrax / Dec '94 / THE

JIM REEVES LIVE AT THE OPRY
CD SSLCD 208
Savanna / Jun '95 / THE

LEGENDS IN MUSIC
CD LECD 060
Wisepack / Jul '94 / Conifer/BMG / THE

LIVE AT THE OPRY
Yonder comes a sucker / Waiting for a train / Am I losing you / When God dips his love in my heart / According to my heart / Four walls / Mexican Joe / Anna Marie / Blue boy / Softly and tenderly Jesus is calling / He'll have to go / Bimbo / I'd like to be / Peace in the valley / Billy bayou / In a mansion stands my love / I'm getting better / Give me that old time religion / I know one / I missed me
CD CMFCD 008
Country Music Foundation / Oct '94 / ADA / Direct

LIVE ON AIR
Have I told you lately that I love you / Just call me lonesome / How's the world treating you / If heartaches are the fashion / Home / Dear hearts and gentle people / I'm beginning to forget you / Roly poly / Wind up / Sweet evening breeze (bring my baby back to me) / Your old love letters / 'Til the end of the world / Making believe / Oklahoma hills / Highway to nowhere / If you were mine / Everywhere you go / I love you more
CD QED 044
Tring / Nov '96 / Tring

MEXICAN JOE
CD CTS 55420
Country Stars / Jun '94 / Target/BMG

SPOTLIGHT ON JIM REEVES
Have I told you lately that I love you / Just call me lonesome / How's the world treating you / If heartaches are the fashion / Home / Dear hearts and gentle people / I'm beginning to forget you / Roly poly / Wind up doll / Sweet evening breeze / Your old love letters / Till the end of the world / Making believe / Oklahoma hills / Highway to nowhere / If you were mine
CD HADCD 126
Javelin / Feb '94 / Henry Hadaway / THE

TWELVE SONGS OF CHRISTMAS
Jingle bells / Blue Christmas / Senor Santa Claus / Old Christmas card, An / Merry Christmas polka / White Christmas / Silver bells / C-H-R-I-S-T-M-A-S / O little town of Bethlehem / Mary's boy child / O come all ye faithful (Adeste Fidelis) / Silent night
CD ND 82758
RCA / Oct '94 / BMG

ULTIMATE COLLECTION, THE (2CD Set)
I love you because / Welcome to my world / Have you ever been lonely: *Reeves, Jim & Patsy Cline* / Have I told you lately that I love you / He'll have to go / Make the world go away / Moon river / I won't forget you / When 2 worlds collide / Memories are made of this / You'll never know / Mona Lisa / Oh, how I miss you tonight: *Reeves, Jim & Deborah Allen* / Mexican Joe / It hurts so much to see you go / There's a heartache following me / Am I losing you / Blue side of lonesome / Four walls / Adios amigo / Distant drums / I can't stop loving you / From a Jack to a King / Roses are red (my love) / Moonlight and roses / You're the only good thing / Am I that easy to forget / You're free to go / Not until the next time / Don't let me cross over: *Reeves, Jim & Deborah Allen* / Anna Marie: *Reeves, Jim & Deborah Allen* / Trying to forget: *Reeves, Jim & Deborah Allen* / I won't come in while he's there: *Reeves, Jim & Deborah Allen* / This world is not my home: *Reeves, Jim & Deborah Allen* / Billy Bayou: *Reeves, Jim & Deborah Allen* / Is it really over: *Reeves, Jim & Deborah Allen* / White cliffs of Dover: *Reeves, Jim & Deborah Allen* / Blue boy: *Reeves, Jim & Deborah Allen* / Golden memories and silver tears: *Reeves, Jim & Deborah Allen* / Danny Boy: *Reeves, Jim & Deborah Allen*
CD Set 74321410872
RCA Victor / Sep '96 / BMG

WAITING FOR A TRAIN
CD MACCD 142
Autograph / Aug '96 / BMG

WELCOME TO MY WORLD (14CD Set)
My heart's like a welcome mat / Teardrops of regret / Chicken hearted / I've never been so blue / What were you doing last night / Wagon load of love / I could cry / Mexican Joe / Butterfly love / Let me love you just a little / El rancho del rio / It's hard to love just one / Bimbo / Gypsy heart / Echo bonita / Then I'll stop loving you / Beatin' on a ding dong / My rambling heart / Padre of old San Antone / Mother went a-walkin / I love you (and Ginny Wright) / I'll follow you / Penny candy / Where does a broken heart go / Wilder your heart beats (False start) / Wilder your heart beats / Drinking tequila / Red eyed and rowdy / Tahiti / Give me one more kiss / Are you the one / How many / Hillbilly waltz / Let me remember (Things I can't forget) / Spanish violins / Woman's love / Whispering willow / If you love me don't leave me / Each beat of my heart / Let me love you just a little (Alternative) / Then I'll stop loving you (Alternative) / Hillbilly waltz (Alternative) / Mexican Joe (Alternative) / Marriage of Mexican Joe / You're the sweetest thing / I've forgotten you / Sand in my shoes / There's someone who loves you / Heartbreaking baby / Did you darling / Standby / I'll always love you / never take no for an answer / Please leave my darling alone / You're slipping away from me / I'm hurtin' inside / If you were mine / That's a sad affair / Jimbo Jenkins / I've lived a lot in my time / Ichabod Crane / My lips are sealed / Your old love letters / Waltzing on top of the world / Beyond a shadow of a doubt / Love me a little bit more / According to my heart / Each time you leave / Highway to nowhere / Breeze (Blow my baby back to me) / Roly poly / Tweedle o'twill / Have I told you lately that I love you / Oklahoma hills / Pickin' a chicken / I've got just the thing for you / Mother of a honky tonk girl / Am I losing you / Don't tell me / I can't fly / Don't ask me why / Waiting for a train / Look behind you / Four walls / Honey, won't you please come home / Gods were angry with me / I know (And you know) / Please come home / Young hearts / Image of me / Two shadows on your window / Teardrops in my heart / Yours / I don't see me in your eyes anymore / I get the blues when it rains / I care no more / Final affair / You belong to me / My happiness / Everywhere you go (LP master) / Everywhere you go (Single master) / Blues in my heart / Need me / That's my desire / Anna Marie / Sea breeze / Blue without my baby / I love you more / Theme of love (I love to say I love you) / Wishful thinking / Charmaine / Mona Lisa / Marie / Goodnight Irene / Linda / Maria Elena / My Mary / Ramona / Margie / My Juanita / Sweet Sue, just you / Overnight / Blue boy / How long has it been / Teach me how to pray / Evening prayer / Suppertime / It is no secret / God be with you / Beautiful life / In the garden / Precious memories / Whispering hope / Flowers, the sunset, the trees / I'd like to be / Billy Bayou / Throw another log on the fire / Making believe / Till the end of the world / How's the world treating you / Someday (you'll want me to want you) / Just call me lonesome / Fool such as I / May the good lord bless and keep you / Dear hearts and gentle people / Satan can't hold me / Scarlet ribbons / If heartaches are the fashion / Home / Partners / I'm beginning to forget you / He'll have to go / In a mansion stands my love / After a while / Snowflake / But you love me Daddy / You'll never be mine again / Stand at your window / What would you do / Don't you want to be my girl (Poor little doll) / Dark moon / You're free to go / You're the only good thing (that's happened to me) / No one to cry to / OH how I miss you tonight / I'm getting better / Have I stayed away too long / Room full of roses / I was just walking out the door / We could / Take me in your arms and hold me / Almost / I missed me / I know one / Fool's paradise / Blizzard / Wreck of number nine / Letter edged in black / Tie that binds / Danny boy / Streets of Laredo / Rodger Young / Mighty everglades / It's nothing to me / That silver haired Daddy of mine / Wild rose / It hurts so much / Trouble in the amen corner / I'm waiting for ships that never come in / Farmer and the Lord / Gun / Spell of the Yukon / Shifting whispering sands / Seven days / Old tige / Annabel Lee / Why do I love you / Too many parties and too many pals / Men with broken hearts / Somewhere along the line / Missing angel / How can I write on paper (what I feel in my heart) / I never pass there anymore / Losing your love / Railroad bum / When two worlds collide / Fallen star / Most of the time / Blue side of lonesome / I won't forget you / Have you ever been lonely / There's always me / All dressed up and lonely / Welcome to my world / Be honest / I fall to pieces / Just walking in the rain / Blue skies / I'm a fool to care / It's no sin / Am I that easy to forget / Adios amigo / I'll fly away / Where do I go from here / This world is not my home / Oh gentle shepherd / Where we'll never grow old / I'd rather have Jesus / Have thine own way / Night watch / Across the bridge / My cathedral / Take my hands precious Lord / We thank thee / I catch myself crying / (That's when I see the blues) In your pretty brown eyes / Where do I go to throw a picture away / Letter to my heart / Pride goes before a fall / Little ole you / I'm gonna change everything / Bolandse nooientjie / Ek verlang na jou / Die ou kalahari / Roses are red / Just out of reach / Memories are made of this / Stand in / After loving you / One that got away / I'd fight the world / When you are gone / Once upon a time / O little town of Bethlehem / Old Christmas card / Silent night / Mary's boy child / O come all ye faithful (Adeste fidelis) / White Christmas / Jingle bells / Merry Christmas polka / Blue Christmas / Senor Santa Claus / C-H-R-I-S-T-M-A-S / Daar doer in die bosveld / Ding dong / Draf maar aan ou ryperd / Die blonde matroos / JY is my liefling / Indie skadu van ou tafelberg / Sarie Marais / Geboorteplasie / Net 'n stille uurtjie / Nooientjie van die ou transvaal / Verre land / My blinde hart / Good morning self / Is this me / Teardrops on the rocks / Heartbreak in silhouette / Auf wiedersehen sweetheart / Golden memories and silver tears / Blue canadian rockies / White cliffs of Dover / Guilty / Hawaiian wedding song / True / Old Kalahari / I'm crying again / You are my love / Lonely music / There's a heartache following me / You kept me awake last night / Talking walls / Before I died / Little ole dime / Bottle take effect / World you left behind / I've enjoyed as much of this as I can stand / Don't let me cross over / From a Jack to a King / Silver bells / Born to be lucky / Kimberly Jim / Could I be falling in love / Search is ended / Strike it rich / I grew up / Diamonds in the sand / Stranger's just a friend / Roving gambler / Dolly with the dimpled knees / Nickel piece of candy / Love is no excuse / Look who's talking / Mexicali Rose / Carolina moon / Moon river / When I lost you / It's only a paper moon / Roses / There's a new moon over my shoulder / One dozen roses / Moonlight and roses / What's in it for me / Rosa Rio / Oh what it seemed to be / I guess I'm crazy / Angels dont' lie / Not until the next time / I won't come in while he's there / This is it / Make the world go away / There's that smile again / You'll never know / Is it really you / I can't stop loving you / In the misty moonlight / Missing you / Maureen / Distant drums / Storm / Trying to forget / I heard my heart break last night / Nobody's fool / Gypsy feet / Writing's on the wall / I love you because / It's nothing to me / Jim Reeves medley / When did you leave Heaven / Christmas alone / ence upon a time / Jesus is calling / Wagon load of love / Wagon load of love / I'll tell the world I love you / Girl I left behind / Chitlin' blues / Dissatisfied / Penny for your thoughts / Near the cross / Humpty Dumpty heart / Naughty Angeline / Got you on my mind / Tjuana / Yonder comes a sucker / Mary Carter paint / Mary Carter paint / Mary Carter paint / Mary Carter paint / I'm glad you're better / Please forgive / Right words / You darling you / One little Rose / I'd rather not know / Ballad of 96 / Lonesome waltz / Your wedding / Read this letter / I let the world pass me by / Send me back my love / My hands are clean / Crying in my sleep / Deep dark water / Before you came along / Crying is my favourite mood / He will / Make me wonderful in her eyes / Beyond the clouds
CD Set BCD 15656
Bear Family / Jul '94 / Direct / Rollercoaster / Swift

YOUR OLD LOVE LETTERS
Have I told you lately that I love you / Just call me lonesome / How's the world treating you / If heartaches are the fashion / Home / Dear hearts and gentle people / I'm beginning to forget you / Roly poly / Wind up / Sweet evening breeze / Your old love letters / Till the end of the world / Making believe / Oklahoma blues / Highway to nowhere / If you were mine / Everywhere you go / I love you more / I've lived a lot in my time
CD GRF 199
Tring / Jan '93 / Tring

Reeves, Martha

24 GREATEST HITS (Reeves, Martha & The Vandellas)
CD 5300402
Motown / Jan '92 / PolyGram

DANCING IN THE STREET
Dancing in the street / Nowhere to run / In the midnight hour / It's the same old song / Come see about mee / I want you back / Jimmy mack / Heatwave / I say a little prayer / Gotta see Jane / Spooky / Get ready / I heard it through the grapevine
CD 305442
Hallmark / Oct '96 / Carlton

DANCING IN THE STREETS (Reeves, Martha & The Vandellas)
Dancing in the street / Nowhere to run / Heatwave / I'm ready for love / Third finger left hand / Jimmy Mack / Motoring / You've been in love too long / My baby loves me / I gotta let you go / Come and get these memories / Love like yours (Don't come knocking everyday) / Forget me not / Quicksand
CD 5302302
Motown / Jan '92 / PolyGram

HITS AND RARITIES (Martha & The Vandellas)
CD MAR 037
Marginal / Jun '97 / Greyhound

MOTOWN EARLY CLASSICS (Reeves, Martha & The Vandellas)
Dancing in the street / Third finger, left hand / Jimmy Mack / I'll have to let him go / There he is (at my door) / Hitch hike / Moments (to remember) / Heatwave / Hello stranger / In my lonely room / Wait till my Bobby gets home / Jerk / Dance party / Motoring / Dancing slow / Wild one / Nowhere to run / Never leave your baby's side
CD 5521172
Spectrum / Jul '96 / PolyGram

WE MEET AGAIN/GOTTA KEEP MOVING
Free again / You're like sunshine / I feel like magic / One line from every love song / Love don't come no stranger / What are you doing the rest of your life / Dedicated to be your woman / Special to me / Skating in the streets / That's what I want / Really like your rap / Gotta keep moving / Then you came / If it wasn't for my baby
CD CDSEWD 083
Southbound / Jul '93 / Pinnacle

Reeves, Reuben

COMPLETE VOCALIONS 1928-1933, THE
Dixie stomp / Drifting and dreaming / River blues / Parson blues / Papa skag stomp / Bugle call blues / Low down rhythm / Gotta feelin' for you / Blue sweets / Texas special blues / Black and blue / Moanin' low / Head low / Have you ever felt that way / Do I know what I'm doing / Shoo shoo boogie boo / Bigger and better than ever / Yellow five / Zuddan / MazeiScrews nuts and bolts
CD CBC 1039
Timeless Historical / Sep '97 / New Note/ Pinnacle

REUBEN REEVES & OMER SIMEON 1929-1933 (Reeves, Reuben 'River' & Omer Simeon)
CD JPCD 1516
Jazz Perspectives / May '95 / Hot Shot / Jazz Music

Reeves, Vic

I WILL CURE YOU
CD IMCD 242
Island / Mar '97 / PolyGram

Reflection

ERROMOMOUS WORLD
Night music in the sculptured air / Simple end to the beginning / Cold wind in the bright sun / Cold wind in a bright sun / Transparent / Errornormous bit / Flowers for the moon / Flowers for the moonlight / Journey around the unnamed border / Wall with paintings / Water/Blind/exhibition / Vertigo / Spiral bits / Many colours / Another sun / Beginning
CD CLR 432CD
Clear / Jul '97 / Prime / RTM/Disc

Refrigerator

ANCHORS OF BLOOD
CD COMM 040CD
Communion / Dec '96 / Cargo

Refused

EVERLASTING
CD EVRCD 033
Equal Vision / Mar '97 / Plastic Head

THIS IS THE NEW DEAL
CD BHR 002CD
Burning Heart / Oct '94 / Plastic Head

THIS JUST MIGHT BE...
CD WB 3116CD
We Bite / Jan '95 / Plastic Head

Regan, Joan

REMEMBER I LOVE YOU
Remember I love you / Send in the clowns / Come in from the rain / Let it be me / Wind beneath my wings / If you love me / Heartaches / You needed me / Together again / For the good times / Words / My way
CD NRCD 103
Nectar / Nov '96 / BMG

Regan Youth

REGAN YOUTH
CD NRA 13CD
New Red Archives / Apr '92 / Cargo / Plastic Head

Regenerator

REGENERATOR
CD HY 39100902
Hyperium / Jun '94 / Cargo / Plastic Head

Regenesis

LIVE
Watchers of the skies / Carpet crawlers / I know what I like / Supper's ready / In the

cage / Broadway melody of 1974 / Fly on a windshield / Lamb lies down on broadway
CD _______ MYSCD 112
Mystic / Jul '97 / Pinnacle

Reggio, Felice

I REMEMBER CHET
CD _______ CD 214W1112
Philology / Mar '92 / Cadillac / Harmonia Mundi

Regina, Elis

AQUARELA DO BRASIL (Regina, Elis & Toots Thielemans)
Wave / Aquarela do Brasil / Visao / Corrida de jangada / Wilsamba / Voce barquinho / O sonho / Five for Elis / Canto do Ossanha / Honeysuckle rose / Volta
CD _______ 8303912
Philips / Mar '92 / PolyGram

BOSSA MAIOR
CD _______ ELENCO 826621CD
Rare Brazil / Apr '97 / Cargo

FASCINACAO (The Best Of Elis Regina)
Menino das laranjas / Upa neguinho / Madalena / Lapinha / Corrida de jangada / Canto de Ossanha / Como nossos pais / O mestre sala dos mares / Vou deitar e rolar / O morro nao tem vez / Feio nao e bonito / Samba do carioca / Esse mundo a meu / Felicidade / Samba de negro / Vou andar por ai / Acender as velas / A voz de morro / O morro nao tem vez / Arrastao / Romaria / Mucuripe / Caso no campo / Fascinacao / Me dexias louca / Atras de porta / Cartomante / Dois pra la, drois pra ca / O rancho da goiabada
CD _______ 8368442
Verve / Mar '94 / PolyGram

NADA SERA COMO ANTES (Elis Interprets Milton Nascimento)
Nada sera como antes / Morro velho / Cais / Credo / Conversando no bar / Travessia / Caxanga / Vera Cruz / Cancao do sal / Ponta de areia
CD _______ 8228272
Verve / Apr '93 / PolyGram

Regina Regina

REGINA REGINA
More than I wanted to know / Big bad broken heart / Asking for the moon / Far cry from him / Ticket out of Kansas / Border town road / I should be laughing / Right plan, wrong man / Before I know about you / She'll let that telephone ring
CD _______ 74321409712
Giant / Apr '97 / BMG

Regis

GYMNASTICS
CD _______ DNCD 002
Downwards / Jan '97 / Plastic Head

Regredior

FORBIDDEN TEARS
CD _______ SHR 010CD
Shiver / Aug '95 / Plastic Head

Regulators

CONSIDER IT DONE
CD _______ STINGCD 040
Blue Sting / Jul '97 / CM / Hot Shot / Jazz Music / Swift

Rehberg & Bauer

FABT
CD _______ TO 32
Touch / Jun '97 / Kudos / Pinnacle

Rei, Panta

DANCE CONTINUES, THE
CD _______ DRCD 185
Dragon / Jan '88 / ADA / Cadillac / CM / Roots / Wellard

Reich, Max

SWEDISH WORKOUT
CD _______ MILL 044CD
Millenium / Mar '97 / Plastic Head / Prime / SRD

Reich, Steve

CAVE, THE
CD _______ 7559791012
Nonesuch / Mar '96 / Warner Music

CITY LIFE (Reich, Steve Ensemble)
Proverb / Nagoya marimbas / City life
CD _______ 7559794302
Nonesuch / Oct '96 / Warner Music

DESERT MUSIC, THE
CD _______ 9791012
Nonesuch / '86 / Warner Music

DESERT MUSIC/DIFFERENT TRAINS/ SIX MARIMBAS/TEHILLIM (4CD Set)
CD Set _______ 7559793762
Nonesuch / Jan '95 / Warner Music

DIFFERENT TRAINS (Reich, Steve & The Kronos Quartet)
Different trains / Electric counterpoint
CD _______ 9791762
Nonesuch / Jun '89 / Warner Music

DRUMMING
Part 1 / Part 2 / Part 3 / Part 4
CD _______ 9191702
Nonesuch / Mar '88 / Warner Music

EARLY WORKS
Come out 1966 / Piano phrase / Clapping music / It's gonna rain
CD _______ 7559791692
Nonesuch / Jan '95 / Warner Music

FOUR ORGANS - PHASE PATTERNS
CD _______ 642090MAN90
Mantra / Nov '94 / Cargo / Direct / Discovery

MUSIC FOR 18 MUSICIANS
CD _______ 8214172
ECM / '84 / New Note/Pinnacle

OCTET MUSIC FOR A LARGE ENSEMBLE
Music for a large ensemble / Violin phase / Octet
CD _______ 8272872
ECM / '85 / New Note/Pinnacle

SIX MARIMBAS
CD _______ 9791382
Nonesuch / Jan '87 / Warner Music

TEHILLIM
Parts I and II / Parts III and IV
CD _______ 8274112
ECM / '86 / New Note/Pinnacle

WORKS 1965-1995 (10CD Set)
CD Set _______ 7559794512
Erato / Jun '97 / Warner Music

Reicha, Anton

ANTON REICHA
CD _______ 999 0612
CPO / Jul '92 / Select

Reichel, Hans

ANGEL CARVER (Reichel, Hans & Tom Cora)
CD _______ FMPCD 15
FMP / Dec '87 / Cadillac

DAWN OF THE DACHSMAN...PLUS
CD _______ FMPCD 60
FMP / Oct '94 / Cadillac

SHANGHAIED ON TOR ROAD
CD _______ FMPCD 46
FMP / Aug '86 / Cadillac

SOLO - COCO BOLO NIGHTS
CD _______ FMPCD 10
FMP / Feb '85 / Cadillac

STOP COMPLAINING
CD _______ FMPCD 36
FMP / Nov '87 / Cadillac

Reid, Duke

BA BA BOOM (Various Artists)
Ba ba boom: *Jamaicans* / Only a smile: *Paragons* / Do it right: *Three Tops* / Carry go bring come: *Hinds, Justin & The Dominoes* / I'm in the mood for love: *Techniques* / Willow tree: *Ellis, Alton* / My best girl: *Paragons* / Sweet soul music: *Gladiators* / Breaking up: *Ellis, Alton* / Hopeful village: *Tennors* / Love up kiss up: *Termites* / Botheration: *Hinds, Justin & The Dominoes* / I'll be lonely: *Holt, John & Joya Landis* / Midnight confession: *Dillon, Phyllis* / Weather report: *Tennors* / Passion love: *Melodians*
CD _______ CDTRL 265
Trojan / Nov '94 / Direct / Jet Star

DUKE REID'S BOOM SHAKA LAKA (Various Artists)
CD _______ RNCD 2095
Rhino / Mar '95 / Grapevine/PolyGram / Jet Star

DUKE REID'S KINGS OF SKA (Various Artists)
CD _______ RNCD 2098
Rhino / Mar '95 / Grapevine/PolyGram / Jet Star

DUKE REID'S ROCKING STEADY (Various Artists)
CD _______ RNCD 2100
Rhino / Mar '95 / Grapevine/PolyGram / Jet Star

DUKE REID'S TREASURE ISLE (Various Artists)
CD _______ CDHB 095/096
Heartbeat / Aug '92 / ADA / Direct / Greensleeves / Jet Star

FROM BOOGIE TO NYAMBINGHI
CD _______ LG 21082
Lagoon / Jun '93 / Grapevine/PolyGram

IT'S ROCKIN' TIME
CD _______ CDTRL 279
Trojan / Mar '92 / Direct / Jet Star

JAMAICAN BEAT
CD _______ LG 21038
Lagoon / Jul '93 / Grapevine/PolyGram

MIDNIGHT CONFESSION
CD _______ LG 21084
Lagoon / Aug '93 / Grapevine/PolyGram

TRIBUTES TO SKATALITES
CD _______ LG 21015
Lagoon / Jun '93 / Grapevine/PolyGram

VERSION AFFAIR VOL.1
CD _______ LG 21062
Lagoon / Nov '92 / Grapevine/PolyGram

VERSION AFFAIR VOL.2
CD _______ LG 21066
Lagoon / Mar '93 / Grapevine/PolyGram

Reid, Jim

FREEWHEELING NOW (Reid, Jim & John Huband)
Hey Donald / Whar the dichty rins / Queer fowk / Cruachan Ben / O Gin I were a Baron's heir / Great storm is over / Music on his mind / Back in Scotland / Balaena / An t-eilean muileach / Lassie o' the morning / Moothie man / Oh dear me / Scattered / There's no indispensable man / Auld beech tree / Freewheeling now
CD _______ SPRCD 1030
Springthyme / Dec '93 / ADA / CM / Direct / Duncans / Highlander / Roots

I SAW THE WILD GEESE FLEE
Wild geese/Norland wind / Lassie wi the yellow coatie / Shearin's no for you / Stobbie parliament picnic / Upon the moss o' Burreldale / Up the Noran water / Bogie's Bonnie Belle / Flower of Northumberland / Foundry bar / Busk busk bonnie lassie / Spark among the heather / Rowan tree / Bogheid / Vinney den / Rohallion
CD _______ SPRCD 1015
Springthyme / Feb '97 / ADA / CM / Direct / Duncans / Highlander / Roots

Reid, Junior

BOOM SHACK A LACK
Cross over the border / Mother move / Big timer / Row your boat / There will be no darkness / Boom shak-a-lak / Drink out me royalty / Strange things / Sitting in the park / False rumours
CD _______ GRELCD 78
Greensleeves / Sep '89 / Jet Star / SRD

DOUBLE TOP (Reid, Junior & Cornell Campbell)
CD _______ TWCD 1033
Tamoki Wambesi / Jun '94 / Greensleeves / Jet Star / Roots Collective / SRD

JUNIOR REID & THE BLOODS (Reid, Junior & The Bloods)
CD _______ RASCD 3154
Ras / Jul '95 / Direct / Greensleeves / Jet Star / SRD

ONE BLOOD
One blood / Nuh so / Who done it / When it shows / Searching for better / Married life / Eleanor Rigby / Gruppie Diana / Sound / Dominant
CD _______ JRCD 1
Big Life / Feb '90 / Mo's Music Machine / Pinnacle / Prime

RAS PORTRAITS
All fruits ripe / Grammy / Rasta world dance / Anthem / Cry now / Listen to the voices / Dance na keep again / Gun court / Showers of blessing / Dread locks in the White House / Not a one man thing
CD _______ RAS 3327
Ras / Jun '97 / Direct / Greensleeves / Jet Star / SRD

VISA
Me have the view / Mr. Talkabout / Gun court / Him a touch it again / Friend enemy / Free that little tree / It's not a one man thing / Dreadlocks in the White House / No loafting / Cry now / Hospital, Cemetary or Jail / All fruits ripe / Youth man / Dance nah keep
CD _______ GRELCD 194
Greensleeves / Sep '93 / Jet Star / SRD

Reid, Loretto

CELTIC METTLE (Reid, Loretto & Brian Taheny)
Plantxy Cowan / Youngest daughter / Fleur de Quebec / Brian's favourite / Rakish Paddy / Planxty Robinson / Celtic mettle / Turlough Carolan's tribute / Dill pickle rag / Canuck set / Wedding promise/Johnny's dream / That's lovely, that is / Nios mo na aisling / Banks / Mason's apron / Prayer for the children / Strum 301
CD _______ IRCD 049
Iona / May '97 / ADA / Direct / Duncans

Reid, Lou

UNTITLED
CD _______ REB 1728CD
Rebel / Apr '96 / ADA / Direct

WHEN IT RAINS
Ain't it funny / Cry cry darlin' / Hand of the higher power / You better hold onto your heart / Red, white and blue / Callin' your name / Mom's old picture book / One track man / Absence makes the heart grow fonder / First step to heaven / Nobody's loves like mine
CD _______ SHCD 3788
Sugar Hill / Jul '91 / ADA / CM / Direct / Koch / Roots

Reid, Steve

MYSTERIES (Reid, Steve Bamboo Forest)
Mysteries / Sunrise celebration / Prelude to Mr. Mystery / Mr. Mystery / Soul mates / Hideaway of love / Ancient profiles / Spirit path / Pyramid of the sun / Look to the sky / Atlantis / City of gold / Guardian of the falls
CD _______ CD 83415
Telarc Jazz / Aug '97 / Conifer/BMG

WATER SIGN
Warm Summer rain / Dolphin ride / Tell til tease / Treasures of the heart / Waterfall / Special thanks / Peruvian Princess / Aruba moon / Candle dance / Secret of the Himalayas / Water sign
CD _______ CD 83396
Telarc Jazz / Sep '96 / Conifer/BMG

Reid, Terry

BANG BANG YOU'RE
CD _______ BGOCD 164
Beat Goes On / Dec '92 / Pinnacle

ROGUE WAVES
Ain't no shadow / Baby I love you / Stop and think it over / Rogue wave / Walk away Renee / Believe in the magic / Then I kissed her / Bowangi / All I have to do is dream
CD _______ BGOCD 140
Beat Goes On / Apr '92 / Pinnacle

SEED OF MEMORY
Faith to arise / Seed of memory / Brave awakening / To be treated right / Ooh baby (makes me feels so young) / Way you walk / Frame / Fooling you
CD _______ EDCD 425
Edsel / May '95 / Pinnacle

TERRY REID
Superlungs my supergirl / Silver white light / July / Marking time / Stay with me baby / Highway 61 revisited/Friends / May fly / Speak now or forever hold your peace / Rich kids blues / Hand don't fit the glove / This time / Better by far / Fire's alive
CD _______ BGOCD 168
Beat Goes On / Dec '92 / Pinnacle

Reid, Vernon

MISTAKEN IDENTITY
CP time / Mistaken identity / You say he's just a psychic friend / Who are you / Lightnin' / Projects / Uptown drifter / Saint Cobain / Important safety instructions / What's my name / Signed fictitious / Call waiting to exhale / My last nerve / Freshwater coconut / Mysterious power / Unborne embrace / Who invited you
CD _______ 4839212
Epic / Jul '96 / Sony

Reiersrud, Knut

HIMMELSKIP (Reiersrud, Knut & Iver Kleive)
CD _______ FX 163
Kirkelig Kultuverksted / Aug '96 / ADA

TRAMP
CD _______ FX 129CD
Kirkelig Kultuverksted / Apr '95 / ADA

Reign

EMBRACE
CD _______ 9040162
Mausoleum / Mar '95 / Grapevine/ PolyGram

Reigndance

PROBLEM FACTORY
Second time around / Temporarily an eternity / No room / Why divide / I'd tell you / Lazybones / You're wrong / Things will be different now / Luxury / Out of the question / Open arms / Better than I
CD _______ RTD 15717602
World Service / Jun '94 / Vital

Reilly, Paddy

16 EMERALD CLASSICS VOL.1
CD _______ DOCDX 9020
Dolphin / Jun '96 / CM / Else / Grapevine/ PolyGram / Koch

16 EMERALD CLASSICS VOL.2
CD _______ DOCDX 9021
Dolphin / Aug '96 / CM / Else / Grapevine/ PolyGram / Koch

20 GOLDEN IRISH BALLADS
Fields of Athenry / Bunch of thyme / Spancil hill / Galway races / Lark in the morning / Peggy Gordon / Joe Hill / Four green fields / Come out ye black and tans / Cliffs of Dooneen / Hills of Kerry / Arthur McBride / Matt Hyland / Galtee Mountain boy / Bunclody / Crack was ninety in the Isle Of Man / Sweet Carnlough Bay / Jim Larkin / Nation once again
CD _______ DOCDX 9006
Dolphin / May '96 / CM / Else / Grapevine/ PolyGram / Koch

FIELDS OF ATHENRY
Town I loved so well / Farewell to Nova Scotia / Galtee mountain boy / Farewell to the Rhonda / John O'Dreams / Scorn not his simplicity / Crack was ninety in the Isle of Man / Dancing at Whitsun / Mulligan and me / Jim Larkin / Bunch of thyme
CD ____ DOCDX 9002
Dolphin / Jun '96 / CM / Else / Grapevine/ PolyGram / Koch

PADDY REILLY
Flight of the Earls / Black Velvet Band / Pat Murphy's meadow / Little grey home in the West / Star of County Down / Grace / Rose of Mooncoin / Emigrant's letter / Slievenamon / Wild rover / Fields of Athenry / Dublin minstrel / Heaven around Galway bay / Long before your time
CD ____ KCD 480
Celtic Collections / Jan '97 / Target/BMG

PADDY REILLY'S GREATEST HITS LIVE
CD ____ CDIRISH 015
Outlet / Apr '97 / ADA / CM / Direct / Duncans / Koch / Ross

Reilly, Robert

TEMPTATION
Half a chance / Gone too long / Praying for rain / Long distance / North wind / Temptation / Towns like mine / Save me / After all these years / All I want
CD ____ SCARTCD 3
Scarlett Recordings / Jul '90 / Pinnacle

Reilly, Tommy

THANKS FOR THE MEMORY (Reilly, Tommy & James Moody)
CD ____ CHAN 8645
Chandos / Oct '88 / Chandos

Reimer, Jan

POINT OF NO RETURN, THE
CD ____ BEST 1020CD
Acoustic Music / Nov '93 / ADA

Rein Sanction

MARIPOSA
CD ____ SP 43/208CD
Sub Pop / Sep '92 / Cargo / Greyhound / Shellshock/Disc

Reincarnation

SEED OF HATE
CD ____ RPS 008MCD
Repulse / Oct '95 / Plastic Head

Reinders, Ge

AS'T D'R OP AAN KUMP
CD ____ MWCD 1005
Music & Words / Aug '94 / ADA / Direct

Reinhardt, Babik

ALL LOVE
CD ____ 400012
Melodie / Aug '94 / ADA / Discovery / Grapevine/PolyGram / Greensleeves / Jet Star

LIVE
CD ____ CDSW 8431
DRG / Sep '91 / Discovery / New Note/ Pinnacle

LIVE
CD ____ 400032
Melodie / Aug '94 / ADA / Discovery / Grapevine/PolyGram / Greensleeves / Jet Star

VIBRATION
CD ____ 400452
Melodie / Sep '95 / ADA / Discovery / Grapevine/PolyGram / Greensleeves / Jet Star

Reinhardt, Django

ART OF DJANGO, THE/THE UNFORGETTABLE
Mystery Pacific / little love, a little kiss / Running wild / Body and soul / Hot lips / Solitude / When day is gone / Tears / Rose room / Sheikh of Araby / Liebestraum no. 3 / Exactly like you / Miss Annabelle Lee / Ain't misbehavin' / Sweet Georgia Brown / Minor swing / Double scotch / Artillerie Lourde / St. James Infirmary / C Jam blues / Honeysuckle Rose / Dream of you / Begin the beguine / How high the moon / Nuages / I can't get started (with you) / I can't give you anything but love / Manoir de mes reves
CD ____ BGOCD 198
Beat Goes On / Jul '93 / Pinnacle

ATC BIG BAND LIVE 1945
CD ____ JCD 628
Jass / Mar '87 / ADA / Cadillac / CM / Direct / Jazz Music

AUDIO ARCHIVE
Dinah / Oh lady be good / Tiger rag / I saw stars / Avalon / Smoke rings / I've found a new baby / Djangology / Crazy rhythm / Lily belle May June / Sweet Sue, just you / Confessin' / Continental / Sheikh of Araby / Blue drag / Swanee river / Ton doux sourire / Chasing shadows / I've had my moments / Some of these days
CD ____ CDAA 024
Tring / Oct '91 / Tring

BEST OF DJANGO REINHARDT, THE
Limehouse blues / When day is done / St. Louis blues / Minor swing / My serenade / (I'll be glad when you're dead) you rascal you / Montimartre / I'll see you in my dreams / Naguine / Nuages / Blues Clair / Place de Brouckere / Manoir des mes reves / Django's tiger / Ol' man river / Diminishing / Oh lady be good / To each his own symphony
CD ____ CDP 8371382
Blue Note / Apr '96 / EMI

BRUSSELS AND PARIS
Porto cabello / Duke and Dukie / Songs d'automne / Babik / Del Salle / Just one of those things / Double whiskey / Dream of you / Impromptu / Vamp / Keep cool / Fleche d'or / Troublant bolero / Nuits de Saint Germain des pres / Crazy rhythm / Anouman / DR Blues / Fine and Dandy / Le soir / Chez moi / I cover the waterfront / Deccaphonie
CD ____ DRGCD 8473
DRG / Jul '96 / Discovery / New Note/ Pinnacle

CLASSICS 1934-1935
CD ____ CLASSICS 703
Classics / Jul '93 / Discovery / Jazz Music

CLASSICS 1935
CD ____ CLASSICS 727
Classics / Dec '93 / Discovery / Jazz Music

CLASSICS 1935-1936
CD ____ CLASSICS 739
Classics / Feb '94 / Discovery / Jazz Music

CLASSICS 1937 VOL.1
CD ____ CLASSICS 748
Classics / Aug '94 / Discovery / Jazz Music

CLASSICS 1937 VOL.2
CD ____ CLASSICS 762
Classics / Jun '94 / Discovery / Jazz Music

CLASSICS 1937-1939
CD ____ CLASSICS 777
Classics / Mar '95 / Discovery / Jazz Music

CLASSICS 1938-1939
CD ____ CLASSICS 793
Classics / Jan '95 / Discovery / Jazz Music

CLASSICS 1939-1940
CD ____ CLASSICS 813
Classics / May '95 / Discovery / Jazz Music

CLASSICS 1940-1941
CD ____ CLASSICS 852
Classics / Feb '96 / Discovery / Jazz Music

CLASSICS 1941-1942
CD ____ CLASSICS 877
Classics / Apr '96 / Discovery / Jazz Music

CLASSICS 1942-1943
CD ____ CLASSICS 905
Classics / Nov '96 / Discovery / Jazz Music

COMPLETE DJANGO REINHARDT VOL.2 1934-1935, THE (2CD Set)
CD ____ FA 302
Fremeaux / Jul '96 / ADA / Discovery

COMPLETE DJANGO REINHARDT VOL.3, THE (2CD Set)
CD ____ FA 303
Fremeaux / Oct '96 / ADA / Discovery

COMPLETE DJANGO REINHARDT VOL.4 1935-1936, THE (2CD Set)
CD Set ____ FA 304
Fremeaux / Nov '96 / ADA / Discovery

COMPLETE DJANGO REINHARDT VOL.5 1936-1937, THE (2CD Set)
CD Set ____ FA 305
Fremeaux / Feb '97 / ADA / Discovery

COMPLETE DJANGO REINHARDT VOL.6 1937, THE (2CD Set)
CD Set ____ FA 306
Fremeaux / Jun '97 / ADA / Discovery

CRAZY RHYTHM
Crazy rhythm 1937 / Dinah / Tiger rag / Smoke rings / I've found a new baby / Djangology / After you've gone / Limehouse blues / Nagasaki / Georgia on my mind / Honeysuckle Rose / Out of nowhere / Sweet Georgia Brown / Bugle call rag / Between the devil and the deep blue sea / I got rhythm / Japanese sandman / St. Louis blues / Oh lady be good / Crazy rhythm 1935
CD ____ CD 6048
Music / Oct '96 / Target/BMG

DEFINITIVE DJANGO REINHARDT VOL.1 (First Original Hot Club Recordings 1934-1935)
CD ____ JSPCD 341
JSP / Feb '93 / ADA / Cadillac / Direct / Hot Shot / Target/BMG

DEFINITIVE DJANGO REINHARDT VOL.2 (London Decca Recordings 1938-1939)
Honeysuckle rose / Sweet Georgia Brown / Night and day / My sweet / Souvenirs / Daphne / Black and white / Stompin' at the Decca / Tornerai / If I had you / It had to be you / Nocturne / Flat foot floogie / Lambeth walk / Why shouldn't I / I've got my love to keep me warm / Please be kind / Louise / Improvisation no.2 / Undecided / HCQ strut / Don't worry 'bout me / Man I love
CD ____ JSPCD 342
JSP / Jan '94 / ADA / Cadillac / Direct / Hot Shot / Target/BMG

DEFINITIVE DJANGO REINHARDT VOL.3
Billets doux / Swing from Paris / Them there eyes / Three little words / Appel direct / Hungaria / Jeepers creepers / Swing '39 / Japanese sandman / I wonder were my baby is tonight / Tea for two / My melancholy baby / Time on my hands / Twelfth year
CD ____ JSPCD 343
JSP / Apr '94 / ADA / Cadillac / Direct / Hot Shot / Target/BMG

DEFINITIVE DJANGO REINHARDT VOL.4
CD ____ JSPCD 344
JSP / Oct '94 / ADA / Cadillac / Direct / Hot Shot / Target/BMG

DEFINITIVE DJANGO REINHARDT VOL.5
CD ____ JSPCD 349
JSP / May '95 / ADA / Cadillac / Direct / Hot Shot / Target/BMG

DJANGO
CD ____ CDHD 234
Happy Days / Feb '97 / Conifer/BMG

DJANGO AND HIS AMERICAN FRIENDS VOL.1 & 2
Avalon / Rosetta / Honeysuckle rose / Sweet Georgia Brown / I got rhythm / Japanese sandman / I ain't got nobody / Bill Coleman blues / I'm coming Virginia / Montmartre / I know that you know me / What a difference a day makes / Stardust / Crazy rhythm / Bugle call rag / Sweet Sue, just you / Eddie's blues / Baby, won't you please come home / Somebody loves me / Farewell blues / Low cotton / Solid old man / Object of my affection / Out of nowhere / Between the devil and the deep blue sea / Hangin' around Boulden / Big Boy Blues / I can't believe that you're in love with me / Blue light blues / Finesse
CD ____ BGOCD 249
Beat Goes On / Dec '94 / Pinnacle

DJANGO REINHARDT
Chicago / Shine / Bugle call rag / I got rhythm / Honeysuckle rose / Crazy rhythm / Exactly like you / Charleston / You're driving me crazy / Nuages / Rose room / Swing guitars / I know that you know / Nagasaki / Japanese sandman / Ain't misbehavin' / Minor swing / Georgia on my mind / Sweet Georgia Brown / Limehouse blues / After you've gone
CD ____ 399533
Koch Presents / Jun '97 / Koch

DJANGO REINHARDT & HIS AMERICAN SWING BAND
CD ____ JASSCD 628
Jass / Oct '92 / ADA / Cadillac / CM / Direct / Jazz Music

DJANGO REINHARDT 1935
CD ____ OJCCD 772
Original Jazz Classics / Dec '93 / Complete/Pinnacle / Jazz Music / Wellard

DJANGO REINHARDT 1935-1939
CD ____ CD 14555
Jazz Portraits / Jul '94 / Jazz Music

DJANGO REINHARDT 1935-1939
CD ____ CD 56061
Jazz Roots / Jul '95 / Target/BMG

DJANGO REINHARDT 1938-1939
CD ____ JSP 343
JSP / Jun '94 / ADA / Cadillac / Direct / Hot Shot / Target/BMG

DJANGO REINHARDT AND FRIENDS
(I'll be glad when you're dead) you rascal you / Stephen's blues / Sugar / Sweet Georgia Brown / Tea for two / Younger generation / I'll see you in my dreams / Echoes of Spain / Naguine / What a difference a day makes / Tears / Limehouse blues / Daphne / At Jimmy's bar / Rosetta / Nuages / Pour vous (exactly like you) / Vendredi 13 / Petits mesonges (little white lies) / Stardust / Sweet Sue, just you / Swing de Paris
CD ____ PASTCD 9792
Flapper / Jun '92 / Pinnacle

DJANGO REINHARDT AND STEPHANE GRAPPELLI (Reinhardt, Django & Stephane Grappelli)
CD ____ CD 14580
Complete / Nov '95 / THE

DJANGO REINHARDT ET SON QUINTETTE DU HOT CLUB DE FRANCE (Quintette Du Hot Club De France)
CD ____ 403222
Musidisc / Nov '93 / Discovery

DJANGO REINHARDT PLAYS THE STANDARDS
You're driving me crazy / Solitude / Ain't misbehavin' / Shine / Exactly like you / Body and soul / Nagasaki / When day is done / Running wild / Crazy rhythm / Honeysuckle rose / Out of nowhere / St. Louis blues / Georgia on my mind / Oh lady be good / After you've gone / Limehouse blues / Sweet Georgia brown / Begin the beguine / I can't give you anything but love / Sweet Sue, just you / All of me
CD ____ RAJCD 808
Empress / Nov '93 / Koch

DJANGO REINHARDT/STEPHANE GRAPPELLI (Reinhardt, Django & Stephane Grappelli)
CD ____ PASTCD 9738
Flapper / Sep '91 / Pinnacle

DJANGO'S MUSIC
Tears / Limehouse blues / Daphne / At the Jimmy's bar / Festival swing '41 / Stockholm / Nympheas / Feerie / Seul ce soir / Bei dir war es immer so schoen / Nuages / Djangologie / Eclats de culvres / Django rag / Dynamisme / Tons' D ebene / Chez moi a six heures / Bellville / Oubli / Zuiderzee blues / ABC / Galement / Melodie au crepescule / Blues d'autrefois / Place de brouckere
CD ____ HEPCD 1041
Hep / Oct '94 / Cadillac / Jazz Music / New Note/Pinnacle / Wellard

DJANGOLOGY
CD ____ CD 53002
Giants Of Jazz / Mar '92 / Cadillac / Jazz Music / Target/BMG

DJANGOLOGY
Dinah / Tiger rag / Oh lady be good / I saw stars / Lily Belle May June / Sweet Sue just you / Confessin' / Continental / Blue drag / Swanee river / Ton doux sourire / Ultrafox / Avalon / Smoke rings / Clouds / Believe it beloved / I've found a new baby / St. Louis blues / Crazy rhythm / Sheik of Araby / Chasing shadows / I've had my moment / Some of these days / Djangology
CD ____ QED 071
Tring / Nov '96 / Tring

DJANGOLOGY 49
World is waiting for the sunrise / Hallelujah / I'll never be the same / Honeysuckle rose / All the things you are / Djangology / Daphne / Beyond the sea / Lover man / Marie / Minor swing / Ou est tu mon amour / Swing '42 / After you've gone / I got rhythm / I saw stars / Heavy artillery (artillerie lourde) / It's only a paper moon / Bricktop
CD ____ ND 90448
Bluebird / Apr '90 / BMG

GIPSY GENIUS, THE
CD ____ ENTCD 219
Entertainers / '89 / Target/BMG

I GOT RHYTHM
I got rhythm / Crazy rhythm / My melancholy baby / Jeepers creepers / Sweet Georgia Brown / Honeysuckle rose / Liza / Nauges / Nuits de St. Germain des pres / Just one of those things / I cover the waterfront / I wonder where my baby is tonight
CD ____ CDSGP 0106
Prestige / Jun '94 / Else / Total/BMG

I GOT RHYTHM (Reinhardt, Django & Stephane Grappelli)
Dinah / I'm confessin' that I love you / Swanee river / Sunshine of your smile / Believe it, beloved / Chasing shadows / I've had my moments / Some of these days / I got rhythm / Sheikh of araby / It don't mean a thing if it ain't got that swing / Viper's dream / Running wild / Ain't misbehavin' / Tears / Miss Annabelle Lee / Djangology / Daphne / Billets doux / Swing '39 / Tea for two / My melancholy baby / Younger generation / HCQ strut
CD ____ PPCD 78110
Past Perfect / Feb '95 / Glass Gramophone Co.

IN PARIS 1935-1936
Nagasaki / Oriental shuffle / After you've gone / Moong low / In the still of the night / Shine / Chasing shadows / It was so beautiful / I've had my moments
CD ____ DOLD 12
Old Bean / Dec '90 / Jazz Music / Wellard

INDISPENSABLE DJANGO REINHARDT 1949-1950, THE
Minor swing / Beyond the sea / World is waiting for the sunrise / Django's castle / Dream of you / Menilmontant / It's only a paper moon / I saw stars / Nuages / Swing guitars / All the things you are / Tisket-a-tasket / September song / Heavy artillery (Artillerie lourde) / Improvisation / Djangology / Daphne / I'll never be the same / Marie / Jersey bounce / I surrender dear / Hallelujah / Anniversary song / After you've gone / Swing '42 / Stormy weather / Brick top / Lover man / I got rhythm / Honeysuckle rose / St. Louis blues

CD ND 70929
RCA / Mar '94 / BMG

INTRODUCTION TO DJANGO REINHARDT 1934-1942, AN
CD 4036
Best Of Jazz / Sep '96 / Discovery

JAZZ MASTERS
CD 5169312
Verve / Apr '94 / PolyGram

JAZZ PORTRAITS
Limehouse blues / Nagasaki / After you've gone / You're driving me crazy / Ain't misbehavin' / Chicago / Georgia on my mind / Shine / Exactly like you / Charleston / Rose room / When day is done / Running wild (course movementee) / Swing guitars / Minor swing / Oriental shuffle / I can't give you anything but love / Sweet chorus
CD CD 14509
Jazz Portraits / May '94 / Jazz Music

KING OF THE GYPSIES
Swing guitars / Georgia on my mind / Charleston / Ain't misbehavin' / Limehouse blues / Hot lips
CD BSTCD 9101
Best Compact Discs / May '92 / Complete/ Pinnacle

LE QUINTETTE DU HOT CLUB DE FRANCE (Quintette Du Hot Club De France)
CD CD 56020
Jazz Roots / Aug '94 / Target/BMG

LE QUINTETTE DU HOT CLUB DE FRANCE (Quintette Du Hot Club De France)
CD CWNCD 2010
Javelin / Jun '95 / Henry Hadaway / THE

LONDRES 1938, PARIS 1938 (Reinhardt, Django & Stephane Grappelli)
CD 879482
Music Memoria / Jun '93 / ADA / Discovery

MUSIC OF DJANGO REINHARDT, THE
CD NI 4029
Natasha / Jun '94 / ADA / Cadillac / CM / Direct / Jazz Music

NUAGES (Reinhardt, Django & Stephane Grappelli)
Avalon / Blue drag / Confessin' / Continental / Dinah / Djangology / I saw stars / Improvisation / I've had my moments / Jive bomber / Low cotton / Nagasaki / Nocturne / Nuages / Oh Lady be good / Rose room / Smoke rings / Solid old man / Swanee river / Sweet chorus / Tiger rag / Ultrafox / When day is done
CD CDAJA 5138
Living Era / Aug '94 / Select

PARIS 1939, LONDRES 1939 (Reinhardt, Django & Stephane Grappelli)
CD 879492
Music Memoria / Jun '93 / ADA / Discovery

PECHE A LA MOUCHE (The Great Blue Star Sessions 1927-1953/2CD Set)
Peche a la mouche / Minor blues / (I love you) for sentimental reasons / Danse Norvegienne / Blues for Barclay / Folie a amphion / Vette / Anniversary song / Swing 48 / September song / Brazil / I'll never smile again / New York City / Django's blues / Love's mood / I love you / Nuages / Moppin' the bride / Insensiblement / Mano blues / Primitif / Gypsy with a song / Night and day / Confessin' (that I love you) / Blues for Ike / September song / Night and day / Insensiblement / Manoir des mes reves / Nuages / Confessin' (that I love you)
CD 8354182
Verve / Mar '94 / PolyGram

PRESENTATION STOMP 1928-1934 (2CD Set)
CD Set FA 301
Fremeaux / Apr '96 / ADA / Discovery

QUINTESSENCE, THE (1934-1943/2CD Set)
CD Set FA 205
Fremeaux / Oct '96 / ADA / Discovery

RARE DJANGO
CD CDSW 8119
DRG / Aug '91 / Discovery / New Note/ Pinnacle

RARE RECORDINGS
CD JZCD 376
Suisa / Jun '93 / Jazz Music / THE

ROME SESSIONS VOL.1 1949-1950
Waiting for the sunrise / Hallelujah / I'll never be the same / Honeysuckle rose / All the things you are / Daphne / La mer / Lover man / Marie / Anniversary song / Stormy weather / Russian songs medley / Jersey bounce / Sophisticated lady / Dream of you / At the Darktown strutter's ball / Royal Garden blues
CD 8274472
Jazztime / Jan '95 / Discovery

SOUVENIRS (Jazz Recollections) (Reinhardt, Django & Stephane Grappelli)
Honeysuckle Rose / Night and day / Sweet Georgia Brown / Souvenirs / My sweet / Liza / Stomping at Decca / Love's melody / Daphne / Lambeth walk / Nuages / HCQ Strut / Man I love / Improvisation no.2 / Undecided / Please be kind / Nocturne / I've got my love to keep me warm / Louise / Don't worry 'bout me
CD 8205912
London / Jun '88 / PolyGram

SWING DE PARIS (4CD Set)
CD Set CDDIG 12
Charly / Apr '95 / Koch

SWING FROM PARIS (Reinhardt, Django & Stephane Grappelli)
I got rhythm / St. Louis blues / Appel direct / Honeysuckle rose / Black and white / Limehouse blues / Moonglow / Billets doux / Daphne / China boy / Night and day / My sweet / It don't mean a thing if it ain't got that swing / Sweet Georgia Brown / Swing from Paris / I've found a new baby / Lambeth walk / Them there eyes / It was so beautiful / Three little words / HCQ strut / Swing '39
CD CDAJA 5070
Living Era / Apr '90 / Select

SWINGIN' WITH DJANGO (Reinhardt, Django & Stephane Grappelli)
CD CDHD 206
Happy Days / Feb '97 / Conifer/BMG

UNFORGETTABLE DJANGO REINHARDT, THE
China boy / Tornerai / My sweet / Souvenirs / Honeysuckle rose / Stompin' at Decca / I've found a new baby / Night and day / I've got my love to keep me warm / Improvisation / Limehouse blues / Them there eyes / Man I love / My melancholy baby / Hungaria / Appel direct / Three little words / Daphne / Tea for two / Billets doux / Ultrafox / I've had my moments
CD RHCD 6
Rhapsody / Dec '93 / Jazz Music / President / Wellard

Reininger, Blaine

BRUSSELS/USA (The Best Of Blaine Reininger Vol.1)
Night air / Gigolo grasiento / Mystery and confusion / Ash and bone / Teenage theatre / Tombee de la nuit / Zeb znd Lulu / Software pancake house / To the green door / Cafe au lait / Come the spring / Ralf and Florian go Hawaiian / Right mind / Letter from home / Broken fingers / One-way man / El mensajero divino
CD TWI 9642
Les Disques Du Crepuscule / May '96 / Discovery

COLORADO SUITE (Reininger, Blaine & Mikel Rouse)
CD MTM 3CD
Made To Measure / Nov '88 / New Note/ Pinnacle

Reischman, John

NORTH OF THE BORDER
CD ROUCD 315
Rounder / Jan '94 / ADA / CM / Direct

Reisel, Jacqueline

SONGS IN YIDDISH & LADINO VOL.2
CD YILADI 8803
Yiladi / Sep '94 / Direct

Reiter, Jorg

CAN'T STOP IT
CD ISCD 102
Intersound / '88 / Jazz Music

ON A DAY LIKE THIS
CD ISCD 165
Intersound / Jul '96 / Jazz Music

Rejano, Jimenez

GRITAR POR MI ANDALUCIA
CD 9172
Divucsa / Oct '96 / Discovery

Rejuvenate

MOMENT OF TRUTH
CD LF 082CD
Lost & Found / Sep '94 / Plastic Head

Rejuvination

INTRODUCTION
CD SOMACD 2
Soma / May '95 / RTM/Disc

Relativity

GATHERING PACE
Blackwell court / Gathering pace / Rose catha na mumhan / Miss Tara Macadam / Ma theid tu unaonaigh / Siun ni dhuibhir / When she sleeps / Monday morning reel / Ceol Anna
CD GLCD 1076
Green Linnet / May '88 / ADA / CM / Direct / Highlander / Roots

REM

AUTOMATIC FOR THE PEOPLE
Drive / Try not to breathe / Sidewinder sleeps tonite / Everybody hurts / New Orleans Instrumental No.1 / Sweetness follows / Monty got a raw deal / Ignoreland / Star me kitten / Man on the moon / Nightswimming / Find the river
CD 9362450552
WEA / Sep '92 / Warner Music

BEST OF REM, THE
Carnival of sorts / Radio free Europe / Perfect circle / Talk about the passion / So Central rain / (Don't go back to) Rockville / Pretty persuasion / Green grow the rushes / Can't get there from here / Driver 8 / Fall on me / I believe / Cuyahoga / One I love / Finest worksong / It's the end of the world as we know it (and I feel fine)
CD DMIRH 1
MCA / Aug '91 / BMG

BIRTH OF A MONSTER - INTERVIEW
CD VP 001
RPM / Oct '94 / Pinnacle

DEAD LETTER OFFICE
Crazy / There she goes again / Burning down / Voice of Harold / Burning hell / White Tornado / Toys in the attic / Windout / Ages of you / Pale blue eyes / Rotary ten / Bandwagon / Femme fatale / Walter's theme / King of the road / Wolves, lower / Gardening at night / Carnival of sorts (boxcars) / 1,000,000 / Stumble
CD CDMID 195
A&M / '94 / PolyGram

DOCUMENT
Finest worksong / Welcome to the occupation / Exhuming McCarthy / Disturbance at the Heron House / Strange / It's the end of the world as we know it (and I feel fine) / One I love / Fireplace / Lightnin' Hopkins / King of birds / Oddfellows local 151
CD IRLD 19144
MCA / Oct '92 / BMG
CD CTMCD 337
EMI / Sep '97 / EMI

EPONYMOUS
Gardening at night / So Central rain / Driver 8 / Fall on me / Finest worksong / Talk about the passion / Can't get there from here / Romance / One I love / It's the end of the world as we know it (and I feel fine) / Radio free Europe / (Don't go back to) Rockville
CD DMIRG 1038
MCA / Aug '93 / BMG

FABLES OF THE RECONSTRUCTION
Feeling gravity's pull / Maps and legends / Driver 8 / Life and how to live it / Old man Kensey / Can't get there from here / Green grow the rushes / Kohoutek / Auctioneer (another engine) / Good advice / Wendell Gee
CD IRLD 19016
MCA / Apr '92 / BMG
CD CTMCD 338
EMI / Sep '97 / EMI

GREEN
Pop song '89 / Get up / You are the everything / Stand / World leader pretend / Wrong child / Orange crush / Turn you inside out / Hairshirt / I remember California / Untitled
CD 9257952
WEA / Nov '88 / Warner Music

INTERVIEW DISC
CD SAM 7014
Sound & Media / Nov '96 / Sound & Media

LIFE'S RICH PAGEANT
Begin the begin / These days / Fall on me / Cuyahoga / Hyena / Underneath the bunker / Flowers of Guatemala / I believe / What if we give it away / Just a touch / Swan swan H / Superman
CD IRLD 19080
MCA / Nov '92 / BMG
CD CTMCD 339
EMI / Sep '97 / EMI

MONSTER
What's the frequency, Kenneth / Crush with eyeliner / King of comedy / I don't sleep, I dream / Star 69 / Strange currencies / Tongue / Bang and blame / I took your name / Let me in / Circus envy / You
CD 9362457402
WEA / Sep '94 / Warner Music

MURMUR
Radio free Europe / Pilgrimage / Laughing / Talk about the Passion / Moral kiosk / Perfect circle / Catapult / Sitting still / 9-9 / Shaking through / We walk / West of the fields
CD CDMID 129
A&M / Oct '92 / PolyGram

NEW ADVENTURES IN HI FI
How the west was won and where it got us / Wake up bomb / New test leper / Undertow / E-bow the letter / Leave / Departure / Bittersweet me / Be mine / Binky the doormat / Zither / So fast, so numb / Low desert / Electrolite
CD 9362463212
CD 9362463202
Warner Bros. / Sep '96 / Warner Music

OUT OF TIME
Radio song / Losing my religion / Low / Near wild Heaven / Endgame / Shiny happy people / Belong / Half a world away / Texarkana / Country feedback / Me in honey
CD 7599264962
WEA / Mar '91 / Warner Music

RECKONING
Harborcoat / Seven Chinese brothers / So central rain (I'm sorry) / Pretty persuasion / Time after time / Second guessing / Letter never sent / Camera / (Don't go back to) Rockville / Little America
CD CDMID 194
A&M / Oct '94 / PolyGram

SHINY CHATTY PEOPLE - INTERVIEW
CD CBAK 4041
Baktabak / Jan '92 / Arabesque

SURPRISE YOUR PIG (A Tribute To REM) (Various Artists)
CD SG 001
Plastic Head / Jul '92 / Plastic Head

Rembetika

TALKING TO CHAROS
CD EUCD 1169
ARC / '91 / ADA / ARC Music

Rembrandts

LP
End of the beginning / Easy to forget / My own way / Don't hide your love / Drowning in your tears / This house is not a home / April 29 / Lovin' me insane / There goes Lucy / As long as I am breathing / Call me / Comin' home / What will it take / Other side of night / I'll be there for you
CD 7559617522
Atlantic / Sep '95 / Warner Music

REMBRANDTS, THE
Just the way it is / Baby / Save me / Someone / Show me your love / New King / Every secret thing / If not for misery / Moonlight on Mt Hood / Goodnight / Burning timber / Confidential information / Everyday people / Follow you down
CD 7567914122
Atlantic / Jun '91 / Warner Music

UNTITLED
CD 7567922002
Atlantic / Jan '96 / Warner Music

Reminiscence Quartet

PSYCODELICO
CD YP 009ACD
Yellow / Jul '96 / Timewarp

RITMO BRASILIERO
CD YP 006CD
Yellow / Jul '96 / Timewarp

Remler, Emily

EAST TO WEST
Daahoud / Sweet Georgie Fame / East to West / Snowfall / Hot house / Softly as in a morning sunrise
CD CCD 4356
Concord Jazz / Sep '88 / New Note/ Pinnacle

FIREFLY
Strollin' / Look to the sky / Perk's blues / Firefly / Movin' along / Taste of honey / Inception / In a sentimental mood
CD CCD 4162
Concord Jazz / Sep '92 / New Note/ Pinnacle

JUST FRIENDS VOL.2 (A Gathering In Tribute To Emily Remler) (Various Artists)
CD JR 005032
Justice / Dec '92 / Koch

RETROSPECTIVE VOL.1 (Standards)
Daahoud / How insensitive / Strollin' / Hot house / In your own sweet way / Joy Spring / Softly as in a morning sunrise / Afro blue / Del sasser / In a sentimental mood
CD CCD 4453
Concord Jazz / Mar '91 / New Note/ Pinnacle

RETROSPECTIVE VOL.2 (Compositions)
Macha spice / Nunca mais / Waltz for my grandfather / Catwalk / Blues for herb / Transitions / Firefly / East to West / Antonio / Mozambique
CD CCD 4463
Concord Jazz / May '91 / New Note/ Pinnacle

TAKE TWO (Remler, Emily Quartet)
Cannonball / In your own sweet way / For regulars only / Search for peace / Pocket west / Waltz for my grandfather / Afro blue / Eleuthra
CD CCD 4195
Concord Jazz / Sep '92 / New Note/ Pinnacle

THIS IS ME
CD JR 005012
Justice / Sep '92 / Koch

Rena Rama

INSIDE - OUTSIDE
CD 1182
Caprice / Oct '90 / ADA / Cadillac / CM / Complete/Pinnacle

JAZZ IN SWEDEN 1973
CD 1049
Caprice / Mar '90 / ADA / Cadillac / CM / Complete/Pinnacle

Renaissance

BLESSING IN DISGUISE (Haslam, Annie Renaissance)
Blessing in disguise / Pool of tears / Love lies, love dies / Can't turn the night off / In another life / Raindrops and leaves / Whisper from Marseilles / I light this candle / What he seeks / See this through your eyes / Sweetest kiss / Children (Of Medellin) / New life / After the oceans are gone
CD CDTB 151
Thunderbolt / Jul '95 / TKO Magnum

CAMERA CAMERA
CD HTDCD 43
HTD / Oct '95 / CM / Pinnacle

DEATH OF ART
CD SHR 006CD
Shiver / Aug '95 / Plastic Head

NOVELLA
Can you hear me / Sisters / Midas man / Captive heart / Touching once (is so hard to keep)
CD 7599265162
WEA / Jan '96 / Warner Music

OCEAN GYPSY
Ocean gypsy / Things I don't understand / Young prince and princess / Carpet of the sun / At the harbour / I think of you / Star of the show / Trip to the fair / Great highway
CD HTDCD 71
HTD / Jun '97 / CM / Pinnacle

OTHER WOMAN, THE
Northern lights / Love / Other woman / So blase / Love lies / Somewhere west of here / Lock in on love / Deja vu / Don't talk / Quicksilver
CD HTDCD 27
HTD / Jan '95 / CM / Pinnacle

SCHEHERAZADE AND OTHER STORIES
Tip to the fair / Vultures fly high / Ocean gypsy / Song of Scheherazade / Fanfare / Betrayal / Sultan / Love theme / Young prince and princess / Festival preparations / Fugue for the Sultan / Festival / Finale
CD HTDCD 59
HTD / May '96 / CM / Pinnacle

SONG FOR ALL SEASONS, A
Opening out / Day of the dreamer / Closer than yesterday / Kindness (at the end) / Back home once again / She is love / Northern lights / Song for all seasons
CD 7599259592
WEA / Jan '96 / Warner Music

TIME LINE
Flight / Missing persons / Chagrin Boulevard / Richard IX / Entertainer / Electric avenue / Majik / Distant horizons / Orient express / Auto tech
CD HTDCD 42
HTD / Oct '95 / CM / Pinnacle
CD REP 4655WY
Repertoire / Jun '97 / Greyhound

TURN OF THE CARDS
Running hard / I think of you / Things I don't understand / Black flame / Cold is being / Mother Russia
CD HTDCD 51
HTD / Jan '96 / CM / Pinnacle

Renault, Philippe

BOSSA POUR SEPTEMBRE (Renault, Philippe Nonet)
CD BBRC 9105
Big Blue / Dec '91 / Harmonia Mundi

Renbourn, John

BEST OF JOHN RENBOURN, THE
CD PLSCD 147
Pulse / Feb '97 / BMG

BLACK BALLOON, THE
Moon shines bright / English dance / Bouree / Mist covered mountains of home / Orphan / Tarboulton / Pelican / Black balloon
CD PENT 001CD
Pentangle / Oct '93 / ADA
CD EDCD 527
Edsel / Jun '97 / Pinnacle

COLLECTION, THE
CD CCSCD 429
Castle / Mar '95 / BMG

JOHN BARLEYCORN (Renbourn, John Group)
CD EDCD 472
Edsel / Feb '96 / Pinnacle

JOHN RENBOURN/ANOTHER MONDAY
CD ESMCD 408
Essential / Jun '96 / BMG

LADY AND THE UNICORN, THE
Lady and the unicorn / Trotto / Saltrarello / Lamento di tristan / La rotta / Veri floris / Triple ballade / Bransie gay / Bransie de bourgogne / Alman / Melancholy galliard / Sarabande / My Johnny was a shoemaker / Westron wynde / Scarborough Fair
CD SHANCD 97022
Shanachie / '92 / ADA / Greensleeves / Koch

LADY AND THE UNICORN, THE/THE HERMIT
Trotto / Saltarello / Lamento di Tristan / La rotta / Veri floris / Bransle gay / Bransle de Bourgogne / Alman / Melancholy Galliard / Sarabande / Lady and the unicorn / My Johnny was a shoemaker / Westeron Wynde / Scarborough fair / Hermit / Old Mac Bladgitt / Caroline's tune / Three pieces by O'Carolan / Princess and the puddings / Pavanna (Anna Bannana) / Toy for two lutes / Lord Willoughby's welcome home
CD ESMCD 436
Essential / Oct '96 / BMG

LIVE IN AMERICA (Renbourn, John Group)
Lindsay / English dance / Cruel mother / Breton dances / Trees they grow high / Farewell nancy / Van Diemen's land / High Germany / Sidi Brahim / Month of May is past/Night orgies / John Dory / So early in the spring / Fair flower / John Barleycorn is dead
CD FF 7013
Flying Fish / Sep '96 / ADA / CM / Direct / Roots

LOST SESSIONS
CD EDCD 490
Edsel / Jul '96 / Pinnacle

NINE MAIDENS, THE
New nothynge / Fish in the well / Pavan d'Aragon / Variations on my Lady Carey's dompe / Circle dance / Nine maidens
CD FF 70378
Flying Fish / Nov '96 / ADA / CM / Direct / Roots

SHIP OF FOOLS
CD FF 70466
Flying Fish / Nov '96 / ADA / CM / Direct / Roots

SIR JOHN ALOT OF
Earle of Salisbury / Trees they do grow high / Lady goes to church / Morgana / Transfusion / Forty eight / My dear boy / White fishes / Sweet potato / Seven up
CD HILLCD 1
Wooded Hill / Sep '96 / Direct / World Serpent

SO CLEAR (2CD Set)
Lucky thirteen / Sally go round the roses / Forty-eight / Tic-tocative / Lord Franklin / Lady Nothing's toye puffe / Hermit / Shake shake mama / Waltz / Faro Annie / White house blues / Can't keep from crying / My sweet potato / Kokokmo blues / So clear / Lady and the unicorn / Will the circle be unbroken / Bicycle tune / Judy / I know my babe / Lost lover blues / One for William / Jack Orion / Trees they do grow high / Goat island / Maid that's deep in love / Back on the road again / Bransle gay/Bransle de Bourgogne / Earle of Salisbury / Come on in my kitchen / Willy O'Winsbury / Old Mac Bladgitt / In time / Alman/Melancholy galliard / Blues run the game
CD Set SMDCD 152
Snapper / May '97 / Pinnacle

WHEEL OF FORTUNE (Renbourn, John Group & Robin Williamson)
CD FIENDCD 746
Demon / Nov '93 / Pinnacle

Rendell, Don

IF I SHOULD LOSE YOU (Rendell, Don & His Big Eight)
If I should lose you / Calas vinas / All too soon / I can dream, can't I / Out of my window / Under pressure blues / Blues house effect / Hard knott pass / Relaxing at Loweswater / Jumpin' at the lakeside
CD SPJCD 546
Spotlite / May '93 / Cadillac / Jazz Music / New Note/Pinnacle / Swift

WHAT AM I HERE FOR (Rendell, Don Five)
This time the dream's on me / For minor's only / What am I here for / Honest Injun / Lament / Goodbye pork pie hat / My romance / This I dig of you / Bluesroom / Antibes / Shades of blue / Parisian thoroughfare
CD SPJCD 551
Spotlite / Sep '96 / Cadillac / Jazz Music / New Note/Pinnacle / Swift

Rene & Angela

BEST OF RENE & ANGELA, THE (Come My Way)
My first love / Come my way / Imaginary playmates / Love's alright / I love you more / Bangin' the boogie / Turn it out / Everything we do / Do you really love me / Free and easy / Secret rendezvous / Wanna be close to you / Wall to wall / Strangers again
CD CTMCD 305
EMI / Feb '97 / EMI

Renegade

LOST ANGELS
CD 15392
Laserlight / Aug '91 / Target/BMG

Renegade Soundwave

NEXT CHAPTER OF DUB, THE
CD CDSTUMM 90
Mute / Apr '95 / RTM/Disc

RENEGADE SOUNDWAVE 1987-1995 (2CD Set)
CD Set CDSTUMM 152
Mute / Jul '96 / RTM/Disc

RENEGADE SOUNDWAVE IN DUB
CD CDSTUMM 85
Mute / Oct '90 / RTM/Disc

SOUNDCLASH
CD CDSTUMM 63
Mute / Feb '90 / RTM/Disc

Renegades Steel Orchestra

BUMP AND WINE
CD 795872
Melodie / Dec '95 / ADA / Discovery / Grapevine/PolyGram / Greensleeves / Jet Star

Rent

CAST ALBUM
Tune up / Voice mail / Tune up / Rent / You okay honey / Tune up / One song glory / Light my candle / Voice mail / Today 4 U / You'll see / Tango - Maureen / Life support / Out tonight / Another day / Will I / On the street / Santa Fe / I'll cover you / We're okay / Christmas bells / Over the moon / La vie boheme / I should tell you / La vie boheme B / Seasons of love / Happy New Year / Voice mail / Happy new year B / Take me or leave me / Seasons of love B / Without you / Voice mail / Contact / I'll cover you - reprise / Halloween / Goodbye love / What you own / Voice mail / Finale / Your eyes / Finale B / Seasons of love
CD DRD 50003
Dreamworks / Sep '96 / BMG

Rent Party

PIC NIC
CD 422495
New Rose / Nov '94 / ADA / Direct / Discovery

Rent Party Revellers

SHE WAS JUST A SAILOR'S SWEETHEART
CD SOSCD 1220
Stomp Off / Oct '92 / Jazz Music / Wellard

Rentals

RETURN OF THE RENTALS
CD 9362460932
Warner Bros. / Jan '96 / Warner Music

Renzi, Mike

PROVIDENCE JAM (A Beautiful Friendship)
CD STB 2506
Stash / Sep '95 / ADA / Cadillac / CM / Direct / Jazz Music

REO Speedwagon

BEST FOOT FORWARD
Roll with the changes / Take it on the run / Don't let him go / Live every moment / Keep on loving you / Back on the road again / Wherever you're goin' (it's alright) / Can't fight this feeling / Shakin' it loose / Time for me to fly / Keep pushin' / I wish you were there
CD 4686032
Epic / Oct '91 / Sony

HI-INFIDELITY
Don't let him go / Keep on loving you / Follow my heart / In your letter / Take it on the run / Tough guys / Out of season / Shakin' it loose / Someone tonight / I wish you were there
CD CD 84700
Epic / '88 / Sony
CD EK 66233
Epic / May '95 / Sony

HITS, THE
I don't want to lose you / Here with me / Roll with the changes / Keep on loving you / That ain't love / Take it on the run / Don't let him go / Can't fight this feeling / Keep pushin' / In my dreams / Time for me to fly / Ridin' the storm out
CD 4655952
Epic / Jan '95 / Sony

Rep, Mike

TREE STUMP NAMED DESIRE (Rep, Mike & The Quotas)
CD AW 037
Anyway / Dec '96 / Cargo

Repercussions

EARTH AND HEAVEN
CD 9362456442
Warner Bros. / Feb '95 / Warner Music

Replacements

ALL SHOOK DOWN
Merry go round / Nobody / Sadly beautiful / When it began / Attitude / Torture / Last / One wink at a time / Bent out of shape / Someone take the wheel / All shook down / Happy town / My little problem
CD 7599262982
Sire / Feb '95 / Warner Music

DON'T TELL A SOUL
Talent show / Back to back / We'll inherit the earth / Achin' to be / They're blind / Anywhere's better than here / Asking me lies / I'll be you / I won't / Rock 'n' roll ghost / Darlin' one
CD 7599258312
Sire / Mar '94 / Warner Music

HOOTENANNY
Hootenanny / Run it / Color me impressed / Will power / Take me down to the hospital / Mr. Whirly / Whitin your reach / Buck hill / Love lines / You lose / Hayday / Treatment bound
CD TTR 83322
Twin Tone / Feb '95 / PolyGram

LET IT BE
I will dare / Favourite thing / We're comin' out / Tommy gets his tonsils out / Androgynous / Black diamond / Unsatisfied / Seen your video / Gary's got a boner / Sixteen blue / Answering machine
CD TTR 84412
Twin Tone / Feb '95 / PolyGram

PLEASED TO MEET ME
IOU / Alex Chilton / I don't know / Nightclub jitters / Ledge / Never mind / Valentine / Shooting dirty pool / Red red wine / Skyway / Can't hardly wait
CD 7599255572
Sire / Jul '93 / Warner Music

SORRY MA FORGOT TO TAKE OUT THE TRASH
Takin' a ride / Careless / Customer / Hanging downtown / Kick your door down / Otto / I bought a headache / Rattlesnakes / I hate music / Johnny's gonna die / Shiftless when idle / More cigarettes / Don't ask why / Somethin' to du / I'm in trouble / Love you till Friday / Shutup / Raised in the city
CD TTR 81232
Twin Tone / Feb '95 / PolyGram

STINK
Kids don't follow / Fuck school / Stuck in the middle / God damn job / White and lazy / Dope smokin' moran / Go / Gimme noise
CD TTR 82282
Twin Tone / Feb '95 / PolyGram

TIM
Hold my life / I'll buy / Kiss me on the bus / Dose of thunder / Waitress in the sky / Swingin' party / Bastards of young / Lay it down clown / Left of the dial / Little mascara / Here comes a regular
CD 7599253302
Sire / Jul '93 / Warner Music

Replicants

REPLICANTS
Just what I needed / Silly love songs / Life's a gas / Cinnamon girl / How do you sleep / Destination unknown / No good trying / Are friends electric / Dirty work / Bewlay brothers / Ibiza bar
CD 7244511172
Zoo Entertainment / May '96 / BMG

Repo, Teppo

HERDSMAN'S MUSIC FROM INGRIA
CD KICD 7
Kansanmusiikki Instituutti / Dec '94 / ADA / Direct

Reptilicus

CRUSHER OF BONES
CD PRCD 001
Product / Oct '96 / World Serpent

Republica

REPUBLICA
Ready to go / Bloke / Bitch / Get off / Picture me / Drop dead gorgeous / Out of the darkness / Wrapp / Don't you ever / Holly / Ready to go
CD 74321410522
De-Construction / Mar '97 / BMG

Repulsa

SEXPIG
CD SPV 084160522
SPV / May '96 / Koch / Plastic Head

Repulsion

HORRIFIED
Stench of burning death / Acid bath / Radiation sickness / Splattered cadavers / Festering boils / Eaten alive / Slaughter of

the innocent / Pestilent decay / Decomposed
CD ____ RR 6063CD
Relapse / Jun '93 / Pinnacle / Plastic Head

REQ

REQ ONE
CD ____ BRASSIC 3CD
Skint / Feb '97 / 3mv/Vital / Mo's Music Machine / Prime

Requiem

SOUL MACHINE
CD ____ SHARK 105CD
Shark / May '95 / Plastic Head

Requiem In White

OF THE WANT INFINITE
CD ____ EFA 01557CD
Apocalyptic Vision / Sep '96 / Cargo / Plastic Head / SRD

Resa

HAPPY NIGHTMARE
CD ____ 1213
Caprice / Oct '91 / ADA / Cadillac / CM / Complete/Pinnacle

Reshma

LEGEND, THE
CD ____ DMUT 1280
Multitone / Mar '96 / BMG

Residents

25TH ANNIVERSARY BOX SET (4CD Set)
Jambalaya / Don't be cruel / From the plains to Mexico / Double shot / Harry the head / Kaw-Liga / Jailhouse rock / It's a man's man's man's world / Satisfaction / World versus flying saucers / Flying / For Elsie / Let me be your teddy bear / Hit the road Jack / Have a bad day / Hunters / Gingerbread / Freak show / Cube E lite / God in three persons lite / God in three persons / Mole trilogy / Eskimo / Fingerprince / Third Reich 'n' roll / Not available / Meet the residents / Tryin' to beat it / Sad love song / Angry love song / Anganok / Teddy / I tried to cry / Struggle / Spaghetti sunday / Love me / Hallowed by thy ween / America
CD Set ____ RESBOX 1
Cargo / May '97 / Cargo

COMMERCIAL ALBUM
CD ____ INDIGO 21302
Indigo / Dec '96 / Cargo

DUCK STAB
CD ____ TORSOCD 406
Torso / Oct '87 / SRD

DUCK STAB/BUSTER AND GLEN (2CD Set)
CD Set ____ INDIGO 21272
Indigo / Dec '96 / Cargo

ESKIMO
CD ____ INDIGO 21362
Euro Ralph / Dec '96 / Cargo

EYE SORE (A Stab At The Residents) (Various Artists)
CD ____ INDIGO 21352
Euro Ralph / Dec '96 / Cargo

FINGERPRINCE
CD ____ TORSOCD 407
Torso / Dec '87 / SRD

FINGERPRINCE/BABY FINGERS (2CD Set)
CD Set ____ INDIGO 21312
Indigo / Dec '96 / Cargo

GEORGE AND JAMES
Rhapsody in blue / I got rhythm / Summertime / I'll go crazy / Try me / Think / I don't mind / Lost someone / Please please please / Night train
CD ____ INDIGO 21222
Indigo / Dec '96 / Cargo

GINGER BREAD MAN
CD ____ INDIGO 21292
Indigo / Dec '96 / Cargo

GOD IN THREE PERSONS
Hard and tenderly / Devotion / Thing about them / Their early years / Loss of a loved one / Touch / Service / Confused / Fine fat flies / Time / Silver sharp / Kiss of flesh / Pain and pleasure
CD ____ TORSOCD 055
Torso / '88 / SRD

HAVE A BAD DAY
CD ____ INDIGO 21332
Indigo / Dec '96 / Cargo

LIVE IN HOLLAND
CD ____ CD 018
Torso / Jul '87 / SRD

MEET THE RESIDENTS
CD ____ CD 416
Torso / Dec '88 / SRD

OUR FINEST FLOWERS
CD ____ INDIGO 21212
Indigo / Dec '96 / Cargo

OUR TIRED, OUR POOR, OUR HUDDLED MASSES (25th Anniversary/ 4CD Set)
Have a bad day concentrate / Hunters concentate / Gingerbreadman concentrate / Six amber things / He also serves / Ship of fools / Freak show concentrate / Cube E concentrate / God in three persons concentrate / Mole trilogy concentrate / Easter women / Amber / Red rider / Floyd / Nameless soul / Love leaks out / Simple song / Moisture / Loneliness / When we were young / Eskimo concentrate / Constantinople / Blue rosebuds / Lizard lady / Fingerprince concentrate / Third reich 'n' roll concentrate / Not available concentrate / Meet the residents concentrate / Aircraft damage / Jambalaya / Don't be cruel / From the plains to Mexico / Double shot / Harry the head / Don't / Gingerbread man / Kawliga / Where is she / Jailhouse rock / This is a man's world / Jingle bells / Satisfaction / Loser weed / Earth vs. flying saucer / Beatles play the Residents and the Residents play the beatle / For Elsie / Teddy bear / Surrender / Hit the road Jack / Tryin to beat it / Sirensong / Ugly beauty / Anganok / Teddy / I tired to cry / Cry of a crow / Struggle / Spaghetti Sunday / Love me / Hallowed by thy ween / America
CD Set ____ INDIGO 21372
Euro Ralph / Jul '97 / Cargo

POOR KAW-LIGA'S PAIN
CD ____ INDIGO 21242
Euro Ralph / Dec '96 / Cargo

THIRD REICH AND ROLL
CD ____ INDIGO 21232
Indigo / Dec '96 / Cargo

Resin Scraper

HEARD MENTALITY
CD ____ MAG 016
Mag Wheel / Dec '96 / Cargo

Resistance D

INEXHAUSTIBILITY
CD ____ HHSP 005CD
Harthouse / Nov '94 / Mo's Music Machine / Prime / Vital

ZTRING 2 OF LIFE
CD ____ HHCD 004
Harthouse / Mar '94 / Mo's Music Machine / Prime / Vital

Resolution

SEATTLE BROTHERHOOD
CD ____ LF 147CD
Lost & Found / Jun '95 / Plastic Head

Resonance Vox

PANDORA
Pandora / Peking doll / Vega / Ashita tenki ni / Passy home / Dr. Mambo X / Fire cracker / Kumpoo manman / Arashi no yoru kimi ni tsugu / Django 1953
CD ____ 5131232
Polydor / Mar '93 / PolyGram

RESONANCE VOX
Ame no suiyohbi / Barong / Partido forte / No money, no girl, no business (but we still have music) / Pona pela / Karula / Glory's stomp / On the beach / Iron claw / Merci brice / Flor
CD ____ 5218792
Verve / May '95 / PolyGram

Resonator

TELHARMONIUM
CD ____ NOZACD 04
Ninebar / Dec '96 / Kudos / Prime / RTM/ Disc

Respectable Groove

TELL TALE DUCKS
Tell tale ducks / In no mood / Air / No calypso / Rocky road to Dublin / She moves through the fair / Think of the other things / Local aesthetic / Folia and friends / Lucky with the weather
CD ____ FMRCD 29
Future / Jun '97 / ADA / Harmonia Mundi

Rest In Pieces

MY RAGE
CD ____ LF 081CD
Lost & Found / May '94 / Plastic Head

Resting Place Of The Mists

NEW VALIHA AND MAROVANY MUSIC FROM MADAGASCAR
CD ____ SH 64075
Shanachie / Dec '96 / ADA / Greensleeves / Koch

Restless

BEAT MY DRUM
CD ____ NUTACD 001
Madhouse / Dec '88 / Nervous

DO YOU FEEL RESTLESS
CD ____ NERCD 015
Nervous / '90 / Nervous / TKO Magnum

EARLY YEARS 1981-83, THE
CD ____ NERCD 026
Nervous / '90 / Nervous / TKO Magnum

FIGURE IT OUT
Road to paradise / Guitar man / Nowhere to go / Just an echo / Empty hands / Better than nothing / Still waiting / I go wild / Shopping around / Going back / His latest flame / Memoir blue
CD ____ NERCD 072
Nervous / Jun '93 / Nervous / TKO Magnum

NO.7
CD ____ NUTACD 6
Madhouse / Oct '91 / Nervous

S'OK S'ALRIGHT (Harmony Brothers)
CD ____ BSR 01
Blood Sucking / Jul '97 / Nervous

VERY BEST OF RESTLESS, THE
CD ____ NERCD 087
Nervous / Sep '96 / Nervous / TKO Magnum

WHY DON'T YOU JUST ROCK
CD ____ NERCD 004
Nervous / Jan '92 / Nervous / TKO Magnum

Restless Heart

BEST OF RESTLESS HEART, THE
You can depend on me / Fast movin' train / Tender lie / Bluest eyes in Texas / Familiar pain / Wheels / That rock won't roll / Till I loved you / Why does it have to (wrong or right) / I'll still be loving you
CD ____ PD 90608
RCA / Feb '92 / BMG

BIG IRON HORSES
Mending fences / We got the love / As far as I can tell / When she cries / Meet on the other side / Tell me what you dream / Blame it on love / Born in a high wind / Just in time / Big iron horses
CD ____ 74321138992
RCA / Apr '93 / BMG

MATTERS OF THE HEART
In this little town / Love train / Mind over matters of the heart / Baby needs new shoes / Hold you now / She's still in love / You're a stronger man than I am / Hometown boys / Sweet whiskey lies / I'd cross the line
CD ____ 07863663972
RCA / Jun '94 / BMG

Resurrection

I REFUSE
CD ____ NA 019CD
New Age / Jul '96 / Plastic Head

Retsin

EGG FUSION
CD ____ SMR 46CD
Simple Machines / May '96 / SRD

Return To Khafji

RETURN TO KHAFJI
CD ____ ABCD 004
Resurrection / Jan '96 / Plastic Head

Return To Sender

FESTIVAL TOUR
CD ____ NORMAL 175
Normal / Dec '94 / ADA / Direct

Return To Zero

RETURN TO ZERO
Face the music / There's another side / All you've got / This is my life / Rain down on me / Every door is open / Devil to pay / Until your love comes back around / Livin' for the rock 'n' roll / Hard time (in the big house) / Return to zero
CD ____ 07599244222
Giant / Apr '92 / BMG

Rev Brown

BARE IN CHANGE
CD ____ PRD 70742
Provogue / Mar '95 / Pinnacle

PSYCHOMACHIA
There's a rumour going round / Nobody loves me / All I want / Happy face blues / Come 'ere babe / Big city ley bus / Voodoo chile (Slight return) / Sunset on time / Sad sad day / Dreamland / Hypnotised / Certified
CD ____ PRD 70872
Provogue / Feb '96 / Pinnacle

Rev Hammer

BISHOP OF BUFFALO
Lamb / Tranquility of solitude / Etain / Ellan vannin / Circular blues / (Worse and worse) like the son of a goat / Every step of the way / Drunkard's waltz / Blood whisky / Spanish lullaby / Shanty / Chase
CD ____ COOKCD 063
Cooking Vinyl / Feb '94 / Vital

INDUSTRIAL SOUNDS AND MAGIC
CD ____ COOKCD 046
Cooking Vinyl / Jun '92 / Vital

Rev, Martin

CHEYENNE
CD ____ FM 1006CD
Marilyn / Jul '92 / Pinnacle

CLOUDS OF GLORY
CD ____ MAUCD 648
Mau Mau / Jul '96 / Pinnacle

SEE ME RIDIN'
CD ____ RUSCD 8220
ROIR / Feb '96 / Plastic Head / Shellshock/Disc

Revelation

ADDICTED
Jack's in the box / Addiction / Jack the lad / Wicked woman / Witches and wizards / Freewheeling
CD ____ CDR 108
Red Hot / Jun '95 / THE

Revelation

NEVER COMES SILENCE
CD ____ HELL 020CD
Hellhound / Dec '92 / Koch

SALVATION'S ANSWER
CD ____ RISE 006CD
Rise / Mar '92 / Pinnacle

YET SO FAR
Soul barer / Eternal search / Little faith / Grasping the nettle / Morning sun / Fallen / Alone / Natural steps / Yet so far
CD ____ H 00362
Hellhound / Feb '95 / Koch

Revelators

AMAZING STORIES
What does it take (to win your love) / Oh darlin' / Do right woman, do right man / Caribbean wind / El Salvador / Hot Burrito / Louisiana blues / I've got to find a way to win Maria back / If I could be there / Tupelo honey / Walk that line
CD ____ FIENDCD 729
Demon / Jun '93 / Pinnacle

WE TOLD YOU NOT TO CROSS US
CD ____ EFA 128842
Crypt / Apr '97 / Shellshock/Disc

Revelino

BROADCASTER
Radio speaks / Step on high / Down the streets / This song / All hope is fading / Rollercoaster / Close / Sixth sense / Statue of pride / Stay down / Dance again / Been and gone
CD ____ 120522
Musidisc / Oct '96 / Discovery

REVELINO
Happiness is mine / My bones / Hello / Don't lead me down / Taking turns / Libertine / World going down / That's what Emily says / No forever girl / I feel so tired / She's got the face / Slave / Tonight
CD ____ 119242
Musidisc UK / Mar '96 / Grapevine/ PolyGram

Revenants

HORSE OF A DIFFERENT COLOUR
CD ____ LONCD 931
Hunter / Sep '93 / Grapevine/PolyGram

Reverberation

BLUE STEREO MUSIC
Cross your sky / Fancy swim / Blue ensemble / Let it blow on / When the ships come down / It's all over now / Roses celeste / Big ship / Autogyre / Been tumbling down / So glad to go / Doctor doctor / Nite time (slight return) / Oscillations astrales / Just a little bit scared / Turning back to blue
CD ____ STONE 022CD
3rd Stone / Oct '96 / Plastic Head / Vital

Revere, Paul

ESSENTIAL RIDE 1963-1967, THE (The Best Of Paul Revere & The Raiders) (Revere, Paul & The Raiders)
Loule, Loule / Mojo workout / Over you / Crisco party / Walking the dog / Steppin' out / Just like me / Stepping stone / Kicks / Ballad of a useless man / Loule, go home / Take a look at yourself / Hungry / (You're a) Bad girl / Louise / Great airplane strike / In my community / Good thing / Why why why (is it so hard) / Ups and downs / Him or me, who's it gonna be
CD ____ CD 48949
Columbia / Jul '95 / Sony

LIKE LONG HAIR (Revere, Paul & The Raiders)
CD ____ FLASH 40
Flash / Jul '97 / Greyhound

REVOLUTION (Revere, Paul & The Raiders)
CD ______ SC 6096
Sundazed / Nov '96 / Cargo / Greyhound / Rollercoaster

SOMETHING HAPPENING (Revere, Paul & The Raiders)
CD ______ SC 6097
Sundazed / Nov '96 / Cargo / Greyhound / Rollercoaster

SPIRIT OF '67, THE (Revere, Paul & The Raiders)
CD ______ SC 6095
Sundazed / Nov '96 / Cargo / Greyhound / Rollercoaster

Rev. Horton Heat

FULL CUSTOM, THE
CD ______ SPCD 248
Sub Pop / Apr '93 / Cargo / Greyhound / Shellshock/Disc

LIQUOR TO THE FRONT
Big sky / Baddest of the bad / One time for me / Five-o-ford / In your wildest dreams / Entertainer / Rockin' dog / Jezebel / I can't surf / Liquor, beer and wine / I could get used to it / Cruisin' for a bruisin' / Yeah right
CD ______ IND 92364
Interscope / Jul '96 / BMG

SMOKE 'EM IF YOU GOT 'EM
Bullet / I'm mad / Bad reputation / It's a dark day / Big dwarf rodeo / Psychobilly freakout / Put it to me straight / Marijuana / Baby, you know who / Eat steak / D for Dangerous / Love whip
CD ______ SPCD 25/177
Sub Pop / '90 / Cargo / Greyhound / Shellshock/Disc

Revhead

SHE
CD ______ PEN 001
Music Of Life / Feb '97 / Grapevine/ PolyGram

Revolting Cocks

BEERS, STEERS AND QUEERS
CD ______ CDDVN 4
Devotion / Feb '92 / Pinnacle

BIG SEXY LAND
CD ______ CDDVN 6
Devotion / Mar '92 / Pinnacle

LINGER FICK'EM GOOD
CD ______ CDDVN 22
Devotion / Sep '93 / Pinnacle

YOU GODDAMNED SON OF A BITCH
CD ______ CDDVN 8
Devotion / Apr '92 / Pinnacle

Revolution 9

YOU MIGHT AS WELL LIVE
You don't know what love is / Giving up the ghost / Now that your lover has gone / Winter song / You broke my heart / Damaged goods / Jessica / Jealousy / Amen to that / Song noir / Living with you / Patron Saint of lonliness / Shining guiding star
CD ______ HABCD 1
Habana / Jul '95 / Pinnacle

Revolutionaries

BLACK ASH DUB
Marijuana / Herb / Collie / Lambs bread / Rizla / LSD / Acapulco / Cocaine
CD ______ CDTRL 186
Trojan / Jun '95 / Direct / Jet Star

MACCA POSTMAN DUB
CD ______ JMC 200218
Jamaican Gold / Apr '95 / Grapevine/ PolyGram / Jet Star

TOP RANKING DUB
CD ______ DR 001CD
Duke Reid / Sep '96 / SRD

Revolutionary Army Of The ...

GIFT OF TEARS (Revolutionary Army Of The Infant Jesus)
CD ______ PROBECD 012
Probe Plus / Dec '93 / SRD

GIFT OF TEARS/MIRROR/LITURGIE (Revolutionary Army Of The Infant Jesus)
CD ______ EFA 015512
Apocalyptic Vision / Oct '95 / Cargo / Plastic Head / SRD

PARADIS (Revolutionary Army Of The Infant Jesus)
CD ______ EFA 015632
Apocalyptic Vision / Feb '96 / Cargo / Plastic Head / SRD

Revolutionary Dub Warriors

RE-ACTION DUB VOL.1 (Deliverence)
CD ______ ONUCD 68
On-U Sound / Oct '94 / Jet Star / SRD

Revolver

BABY'S ANGRY
CD ______ HUTCD 015
Hut / Apr '92 / EMI

COLD WATER FLAT
Cool blue / Shakesdown / Cradle snatch / I wear your chain / Nothing without you / Bottled out / Coming back / Cold water flat / Makes no difference all the same / Wave
CD ______ CDHUT 8
Hut / Apr '93 / EMI

Revolving Paint Dream

MOTHER WATCH ME BURN
CD ______ CRECD 039
Creation / May '94 / 3mv/Vital

Revs

REVS, THE
Just ask why / We're so modern / Stay with me / Julie got a raise / Selfish / Making time / Joyrider / Ten seconds of temptation
CD ______ MASKCD 018
Vinyl Japan / Jan '93 / Plastic Head / Vinyl Japan

REX

REX
CD ______ 185302
Southern / Apr '95 / SRD

Rex

C
CD ______ 185322
Southern / Oct '96 / SRD

Rey, Alvino

BY REQUEST
CD ______ HCD 249
Hindsight / Jan '95 / Jazz Music / Target/ BMG

Reyes, Jorge

EK TUNKUL
CD ______ 7542977
Spalax / Feb '97 / ADA / Cargo / Direct / Discovery / Greyhound

FLAYED GOD, THE
CD ______ STCD 069
Staalplaat / May '95 / Vital/SAM

NIERIKA
CD ______ PS 9326
Silent / Oct '93 / Cargo / Plastic Head

Reyes, Lucha

CANCION MEXICANA
CD ______ ALCD 019
Alma Latina / Jul '96 / Discovery

Reyes, Marcial

PUERTO RICO IN WASHINGTON (Reyes, Marcial & Sus Pleneros De Bayamon)
CD ______ SFWCD 40460
Smithsonian Folkways / Dec '96 / ADA / Cadillac / CM / Direct / Koch

Reykjavik Jazz Quartet

REYKJAVIK JAZZ QUARTET
Changing weather / Alone together / So young / Flight 622 / Dark thoughts / Tongue in cheek / All the time / Hot house
CD ______ JHCD 032
Ronnie Scott's Jazz House / Jul '94 / Cadillac / Jazz Music / New Note/Pinnacle / TKO Magnum

Reynolds, Barry

I SCARE MYSELF
I scare myself / Irony / Guilt / More money / Till the doctor gets back / Broken English / Times Square / Over here (no time for justice) / Give me love / Bold Fenian men
CD ______ EDCD 511
Edsel / Feb '97 / Pinnacle

Reynolds, Debbie

DEBBIE/AM I THAT EASY TO FORGET
Love is a simple thing / S'posin' / You won't be satisfied / Moonglow / Hooray for love / Ev'ry time / You couldn't be cuter / Mean to me / Blue room / Here I am in love again / I like the likes of you / Time after time / Am I that easy to forget / Ask me to go steady / Summer romance / Aba daba honeymoon / I love you a thousand ways / Why not me / Just for a touch of your love / City lights / Too young to love / I can't love you anymore / Love is a thing
CD ______ JASCD 604
Jasmine / Oct '96 / Conifer/BMG / Hot Shot / TKO Magnum

Reynoso, Juan

PLAYS SONES AND GUSTOS
CD ______ CO 105
Corason / Jan '94 / ADA / CM / Direct

Rez Band

SILENCE SCREAMS
CD ______ OCE D 8123
Nelson Word / Jan '89 / Nelson Word

Rezillos

ATTACK OF THE GIANT REVILLOS (Revillos)
CD ______ RRCD 204
Receiver / Aug '95 / Grapevine/PolyGram

CAN'T STAND THE REZILLOS
Flying saucer attack / No / Someone's gonna get their head kicked in tonight / Top of the pops / 2000 AD / It gets me / Can't stand my baby / Glad all over / My baby does good sculptures / I like it / Gettin' me down / Cold wars / Bad guy reaction
CD ______ 7599269422
Sire / Jan '96 / Warner Music

FROM THE FREEZER (Revillos)
CD ______ DAMGOOD 97CD
Damaged Goods / Sep '96 / Shellshock/ Disc

LIVE AND ON FIRE IN JAPAN (Revillos)
Secret of the shadow / Bongo brain / Rock-a-boom / She's fallen in love with a monster man / Where's the boy for me / Rev up / Bitten by a lovebug / Mad from birth to death / Bobby come back to me / Fiend / Scuba scuba / My baby does good / Sculptures / Do the mutilation / Somebody's gonna get their head kicked in tonight / Yeah yeah
CD ______ ASKCD 046
Vinyl Japan / May '95 / Plastic Head / Vinyl Japan

MOTORBIKE BEAT (Revillos)
Motorbike / Where's the boy for me / Fiend / Rev up / Rock-a-boom / Bobby come back to me / Yeah yeah / On the beach / Bitten by a love bug / Cat call / Midnight / Z-X-7
CD ______ MAUCD 643
Mau Mau / Jul '95 / Pinnacle

RF7

ALL YOU CAN EAT
CD ______ GTA 001CD
Grand Theft Auto / Aug '95 / Cargo / Plastic Head

Rhabstallion

DAY TO DAY
Hard luck man / Chain reaction / Breadline / Day to day / I could not believe my eyes / Times ain't so bad / Runaway / Driving seat / Stranger stranger / Shock 'n' roll / Day go disco / Sioux child / You're to blame / Stranger stranger (Live)
CD ______ ETHEL 1
Vinyl Tap / Dec '94 / Cargo / Greyhound / Vinyl Tap

Rhatigan

LATE DEVELOPER
CD ______ ORGAN 018CD
Org / Jan '96 / Pinnacle

Rheinhallt H. Rowlands

BUKOWSKI
CD ______ ANKST 071CD
Ankst / Jun '97 / Shellshock/Disc

Rheostatics

BLUE HYSTERIA
CD ______ CARD 10392
Cargo / Dec '96 / Cargo

INTRODUCING HAPPINESS '94
CD ______ 9362456702
Warner Bros. / Aug '94 / Warner Music

Rhodes, Kimmie

WEST TEXAS HEAVEN
CD ______ 422505
New Rose / Feb '97 / ADA / Direct / Discovery

Rhodes, Sonny

BLUES IS MY BEST FRIEND
CD ______ KS 022
Flying Fish / Nov '94 / ADA / CM / Direct / Roots

I DON'T WANT MY BLUES COLOURED BRIGHT
CD ______ BM 9029
Black Magic / May '94 / ADA / Cadillac / Direct / Hot Shot

IN EUROPE
CD ______ APCD 023
Appaloosa / Mar '97 / ADA / Direct / TKO Magnum

JUST BLUES
I can't lose / Things I used to do / Please love me / House without love / Think / Cigarette blues / Strange things happening / It hurts me too / East Oakland stomp
CD ______ ECD 26060
Evidence / Mar '95 / ADA / Cadillac / Harmonia Mundi

Rhody, Alan

DREAMER'S WORLD
CD ______ TX 3005CD
Taxim / Jan '94 / ADA

Rhos Male Voice Choir

WITH A VOICE OF SINGING
CD ______ BNA 5083
Bandleader / Aug '93 / Conifer/BMG

Rhyne, Melvin

BOSS ORGAN (Rhyne, Melvin Quartet)
CD ______ CRISS 1080CD
Criss Cross / May '94 / Cadillac / Direct / Vital/SAM

LEGEND, THE
CD ______ CRISS 1059CD
Criss Cross / May '92 / Cadillac / Direct / Vital/SAM

TELL IT LIKE IT IS (Rhyne, Melvin & The Tenor Triangle)
CD ______ 1089CD
Criss Cross / Mar '95 / Cadillac / Direct / Vital/SAM

Rhythm & Noise

CHASM'S ACCORD
CD ______ ASP 0965
Asphodel / Nov '96 / Cargo / SRD

Rhythm Cadillacs

SHAKE THIS SHAK
CD ______ ROCK CD 8808
Rockhouse / Oct '88 / Nervous

Rhythm Collision

CLOBBER
CD ______ DSR 039
Dr. Strange / Nov '95 / Cargo / Greyhound / Plastic Head

COLLISION COURSE
CD ______ DSR 53CD
Dr. Strange / May '97 / Cargo / Greyhound / Plastic Head

UNSAFE DRIVING IN 19 EASY STEPS
CD ______ DSR 053CD
Dr. Strange / May '97 / Cargo / Greyhound / Plastic Head

Rhythm Devils

APOCALYPSE NOW (Sessions)
Compound / Trenches / Street gang / Beast / Steps / Tar / Lance / Cave / Hell's bells / Kurtz / Napalm for breakfast
CD ______ RCD 10109
Rykodisc / Sep '91 / ADA / Vital

Rhythm Invention

INVENTURES IN WONDERLAND
CD ______ WARPCD 15
Warp / Aug '93 / Prime / RTM/Disc

Rhythm Orchids

COMPLETE ROULETTE RECORDINGS (2CD Set)
Party doll / Don't make me cry / Hula love / Mary Lou / Maybellene / Cause I'm in love with you / Devil woman / Rock you little baby to sleep / Rockabilly walk / Rock-house / (We're gonna) rock around the clock / Whenever I'm lonely / Swingin' Daddy / C'mon baby / Somebody touched me / Teasable, pleasable you / That's why I cry / Girl with the golden hair / All for you / I think I'm gonna kill myself / Just to be with you / Taste of the blues / I ain't sharin' Sharon / Long lonely nights / Storm clouds / Something's got me going / You'll be glad / Eenie meenie minie moe / You made me love you / I'm stickin' with you / Everlovin' fingers / My baby's gone / Warm up to me baby / I trusted you / It's shameful / Cross over / Ever since that night / Aching hearts / Money honey / Raggedy Anne / Way back home / Last night / Stop wasting my time / Don't tell me your troubles / Can she kiss / I'm keeping you / Two step / By the light of the silvery moon / Stick with me / Whenever I'm lonely / My kind of woman / Blue moon / Always faithful / Wish I were tied to you / Walkin' on air / You're just wasting your time / (I need) your lovin' arms / Oh yeah, oh yeah, oh yeah / Mm mm / Just lookin'
CD Set ______ NEDCD 278
Sequel / May '96 / BMG

Rhythm Pigs

BABY FALCON GETAWAY
CD ______ WW 01
Werk Works / Mar '96 / SRD

Rhythm Trip

BRING DA RUCKUS
CD ______ CDVEST 70
Bulletproof / Apr '96 / Pinnacle

Rhythmaires

10TH ANNIVERSARY
CD RAUCD 006
Raucous / May '93 / Nervous / RTM/Disc / TKO Magnum

Rhythmakers

RHYTHMAKERS 1932, THE
Bugle call rag / Oh Peter / Margie / Spider crawl / Who's sorry now / Take it slow and easy / Bald headed mama / (I would do) anything for you / Mean old bedbug blues / Yellow dog blues / Yes suh / Who stole the lock / Shine on your shoes / It's gonna be you / Somebody stole Gabriel's horn
CD 158842
Jazz Archives / Feb '97 / Discovery

Rhythmatic

SPLAT, WHAT A BEAUTIFUL MESS
CD SPLATCD 1
Network / Nov '91 / 3mv/Sony / Pinnacle

Rhythmic State Crew

STATE CREW JAM (2CD Set)
Do your own thing / Funky MC / Power people / Get it together / Way it goes / Punks gonna pay / Now or never / Popped up / In the music / Keepin' on / Groove on / Move those feet / State crew jam / Feels good / Time 2 get sweeter / Just when you want / No DS allowed / Get real / Can I get a yes / Bad MF / Creator / Rock with me / Soap on a rope / 3rd sound / 14th message / Critical mass
CD Set DCSR 013
Clubscene / Apr '97 / Clubscene / Grapevine/PolyGram / Mo's Music Machine / Prime

Rias Orchestra

ORCHESTRAL COLOURS
CD ISCD 119
Intersound / '91 / Jazz Music

Ribeiro, Thomas

JET SET SOIREE
My love ain't the kind / Contrast / Fool for you / Rocket ship / Rudy / Midnight rain / Shadows / Heartaches / Honey shampoo / Don't let me be / If it takes all night
CD BRCD 622
4th & Broadway / Oct '96 / PolyGram

Ribot, Marc

DON'T BLAME ME
CD DIW 902
DIW / Dec '95 / Cadillac / Harmonia Mundi

PLAYS SOLO GUITAR WORKS OF FRANTZ CASSEUS
CD TWI 9792
Les Disques Du Crepuscule / May '96 / Discovery

REQUIEM FOR WHAT'S-HIS-NAME
CD TWI 9692
Les Disques Du Crepuscule / May '96 / Discovery

SHOE STRING SYMPHONETTES
CD TZA 7504
Tzadik / Feb '97 / Cargo

SHREK
CD AVAN 033CD
Avant / Jul '94 / Cadillac / Harmonia Mundi

RIC

DISTANCE
CD EFA 006552
Mille Plateau / Sep '94 / SRD

Ricardos Jazzmen

OLE MISS
CD MECCACD 1022
Music Mecca / Nov '94 / Cadillac / Jazz Music / Wellard

Ricchizzi, Gianni

RAGA YAMAN/RAGA BHUPALI
CD NI 5431
Nimbus / Apr '95 / Nimbus

Ricci, George

BIG HONK, A (Ricci, George & The Improverts/Lol Coxhill)
Big honk / Beyond the bell / Wave / Six fifty / Lost and found / Little mystery / Autumn leaves / Three songs for Dudu / I can't get started
CD SLAMCD 202
Slam / Oct '96 / Cadillac

Rice

FUCK YOU, THIS IS RICE
CD LOOKOUT 93CD
Lookout / Nov '94 / Cargo / Greyhound / Shellshock/Disc

Rice, Boyd

BOYD RICE PRESENTS LEGIONARI
CD H330 3CD
Hierarchy / Oct '96 / World Serpent

EASY LISTENING FOR THE HARD OF HEARING (Rice, Boyd & Frank Tovey)
CD CDSTUMM 20
Mute / May '96 / RTM/Disc

HATESVILLE
CD H330 1CD
Hierarchy / Oct '96 / World Serpent

MUSIC, MARTINIS...
CD BADVCCD 1969
New European / Oct '96 / World Serpent

RAGNAROK RUNE
CD WSB 13
World Serpent / Oct '96 / World Serpent

Rice Brothers

RICE BROTHERS VOL.1, THE
Grapes on the vine / This ole house / Original unlimited / Teardrops in my eyes / You're drifting away / Don't think twice, it's alright / Let it ride / Keep the light on Sadie / Soldier's joy / Whisper my name / Life is like a mountain railroad
CD ROUCD 0256
Rounder / '89 / ADA / CM / Direct

RICE BROTHERS VOL.2, THE
CD ROUCD 0286
Rounder / Nov '94 / ADA / CM / Direct

Rice, Daryle

FROM NOW ON
CD APCD 100
Appaloosa / Jun '94 / ADA / Direct / TKO Magnum

Rice, Larry

NOTIONS AND NOVELTIES
CD REB 1734CD
Rebel / Dec '96 / ADA / Direct

Rice, Tony

ACOUSTICS
CD ROUCD 0317
Rounder / Jul '94 / ADA / CM / Direct

BACKWATERS (Rice, Tony Unit)
CD ROUCD 0167
Rounder / Aug '88 / ADA / CM / Direct

CHURCH STREET BLUES
Church Street blues / Cattle in the cane / Streets of London / One more night / Gold rush / Any old time / Orphan Annie / House carpenter / Jerusalem Ridge / Last thing on my mind / Pride of man
CD SHCD 3732
Sugar Hill / Jan '97 / ADA / CM / Direct / Koch / Roots

COLD ON THE SHOULDER
Cold on the shoulder / Wayfaring stranger / John Hardy / Fare thee well / Bitter green / Mule skinner blues / Song for life / Why don't you tell me so / If you only knew / Likes of me / I think it's going to rain today
CD ROUCD 0183
Rounder / Dec '86 / ADA / CM / Direct

DEVLIN (Rice, Tony Unit)
CD ROUCD 11531
Rounder / '88 / ADA / CM / Direct

MANZANITA
CD ROUCD 0092
Rounder / '88 / ADA / CM / Direct

ME AND MY GUITAR
CD ROUCD 0201
Rounder / Aug '88 / ADA / CM / Direct

NATIVE AMERICAN
Shadows / St. James hospital / Night flyer / Why you been so long / Urge for going / Go my way / Nothin' like a hundred miles / Changes / Brother to the wind / John Wilkes Booth / Summer wages
CD ROUCD 0248
Rounder / Aug '88 / ADA / CM / Direct

PLAYS & SINGS BLUEGRASS
CD ROUCD 253
Rounder / Jan '94 / ADA / CM / Direct

RIVER SUITE FOR TWO GUITARS (Rice, Tony & John Carlini)
CD SHCD 3837
Sugar Hill / May '95 / ADA / CM / Direct / Koch / Roots

TONY RICE
CD ROUCD 0085
Rounder / '88 / ADA / CM / Direct

TONY RICE SINGS GORDON LIGHTFOOT
CD ROUCD 0370
Rounder / Aug '96 / ADA / CM / Direct

Rice, Wyatt

NEW MARKET GAP
CD ROUCD 272
Rounder / Dec '90 / ADA / CM / Direct

PICTURE IN A TEAR (Rice, Wyatt & Santa Cruz)
Picture in a tear / Molly / Santa Cruz breakdown / Sweetest rose / He died a Rounder at 21 / Separate ways / Katy did / Someone's telling lies / It's goodbye and so long to you / Can't help but wonder where I'm bound / I just don't know what I'll do / In his love I'll abide
CD ROUCD 0372
Rounder / Oct '96 / ADA / CM / Direct

Rich, Buddy

BIG SWING FACE
Norwegian wood / Big swing face / Monitor theme / Wack wack / Love for sale / Mexicali rose / Willowcrest / Beat goes on / Bugle call rag / Standing up in a hammock / Chicago / Lament for Lester / Machine / Silver threads among the blue / New blues / Od timey / Loose / Apples
CD CDP 8379892
Pacific Jazz / Jul '96 / EMI

BUDDY AND SOUL
Love and peace / St. Petersburg race / Soul lady / Street kiddie / Greensleeves / Soul kitchen / Hello I love you / Comin' home baby / Meaning of the blues / Ruth
CD BGOCD 23
Beat Goes On / Jun '94 / Pinnacle

BUDDY RICH AND HIS ORCHESTRA (Rich, Buddy & His Orchestra)
CD 15758
Laserlight / Aug '92 / Target/BMG

EASE ON DOWN THE ROAD (Rich, Buddy & His Big Band)
Time check / Backwoods sideman / Nuttville / Playhouse / Senator Sam / Big Mac / Three day sucker / Ease on down the road / Tommy (medley) / Pieces of dreams / Lush life / Nik-nik / Layin' it down
CD CDC 8511
LRC / Sep '93 / Harmonia Mundi / New Note/Pinnacle
CD 17095
Laserlight / Mar '97 / Target/BMG

EUROPE 77 (Rich, Buddy & His Orchestra)
CD DAWE 60
Magic / Nov '93 / Cadillac / Harmonia Mundi / Jazz Music / Swift / Wellard

HIS LEGENDARY 1947-1948 ORCHESTRA
I've got news for you / Man could be a wonderful thing / Good bait / Blue skies / Just you, just me / I believe / What is this thing called love / Daily double / Nellie's nightmare / Little white lies / You go to my head / Queer Street / Fine and dandy / That's rich / I may be wrong, but I think you're wonderful / Robbin's nest / Four rich brothers / Carioca
CD HEPCD 12
Hep / Aug '91 / Cadillac / Jazz Music / New Note/Pinnacle / Wellard

LIONEL HAMPTON PRESENTS BUDDY RICH (Rich, Buddy & Lionel Hampton)
Moment's notice / Giant steps / Buddy's Cherokee / Take the 'A' train / I'll never be the same / Latin silk / Buddy's rock / My funny valentine
CD CDGATE 7011
Kingdom Jazz / Jun '87 / Kingdom

MASTER OF DRUMS
Moment's notice / Giant steps / Buddy's cherokee / Take the 'A' train / I'll never be the same / Latin silk
CD 722 005
Scorpio / May '93 / Complete/Pinnacle

MERCY MERCY (Rich, Buddy & His Big Band)
Mercy mercy mercy / Preach and teach / Channel 1 suite / Big Mama Cass / Goodbye yesterday / Acid truth / Alfie / Ode to Billie Joe / Chavala / Mr. Lucky / Chelsea Bridge / Get happy
CD CDP 8543312
Pacific Jazz / Mar '97 / EMI

NO JIVE
You gotta try / Tales of Rhoda Rat / No jive / Lush life / Party time / Medley / Piece of the road suite
CD 01241660612
Novus / Oct '92 / BMG

RICH AND FAMOUS
Red snapper / Time will tell / Ballad of the matador / Dancing man / Cotton tail / One and only love / Manhattan - the city / Manhattan - central park
CD CDMT 004
Meteor / Jul '95 / TKO Magnum

SELECTIONS FROM WEST SIDE STORY (AND OTHER DELIGHTS) (Rich, Buddy & Maynard Ferguson)
West Side Story / Kilimanjaro cookout / Prelude to a kiss / Waltz of the mushroom hunters / Pilatus / Foggy night / Maria / Got the spirit / At the sound of the trumpet
CD 17092
Laserlight / Jan '97 / Target/BMG

SWINGIN NEW BIG BAND/KEEP THE CUSTOMERS SATISFIED
Readymix / Basically blues / Critic's choice / My mans gone now / Up tight / Sister Sadie / More soul / West side story Medley: / Keep the customer satisfied / Long days journey / Midnight cowboy medley / Celebration / Groovin' hard / Juicer is wild / Winning the west
CD BGOCD 169
Beat Goes On / Feb '93 / Pinnacle

SWINGIN' NEW BIG BAND
Readymix / Basically blues / Critic's choice / My man's gone now / Up tight (everything's alright) / Sister Sadie / More soul / West Side Story medley / What'd I say / Step right up / Apples / In a mellotone / Lament for Lester / Naptown blues / Hoe down
CD CDP 8352322
Pacific Jazz / Jan '96 / EMI

TAKE IT AWAY (Rich, Buddy & His Big Band)
CD BGOCD 210
Beat Goes On / Oct '93 / Pinnacle

Rich, Charlie

BEHIND CLOSED DOORS
CD PLSCD 110
Pulse / Apr '96 / BMG

BOSS MAN
CD 340502
Koch / Aug '95 / Koch

CHARLIE RICH
CD DS 012
Desperado / Jun '97 / TKO Magnum

FABULOUS CHARLIE RICH, THE
CD 340492
Koch / May '95 / Koch

GREATEST HITS
Most beautiful girl / Very special love song / Since I fell for you / My elusive dreams / Every time you touch me (I get high) / Behind closed doors / Life has its little ups and downs / All over me / I love my friend / We love each other / Daddy don't you walk so fast / She / Sunday kind of woman / Rollin' with the flow / Almost persuaded / Spanish eyes
CD 4721242
Epic / Sep '95 / Sony

MOST BEAUTIFUL GIRL IN THE WORLD
CD CTS 55426
Country Stars / Jun '94 / Target/BMG

REBOUND
Rebound / Whirlwind / Break up / Philadelphia baby / Big man / Everything I do is wrong / Lonely weekends / You never know about love / School days / There won't be anymore / Juanita / Little woman friend of mine / CC rider / Easy money / Gonna be waitin' / There's another place I can't go / Who will the next fool be / Sittin' and thinkin' / Midnight blues / Unchained melody / You finally found out / Stay / My baby done left me / Charlie's boogie
CD CDCHARLY 52
Charly / Feb '87 / Koch

SET ME FREE
CD 340482
Koch / May '95 / Koch

SINGS HANK WILLIAMS
My heart would know / Take these chains from my heart / Half as much / You win again / I can't help it / Hey good lookin' / Your cheatin' heart / Cold cold heart / Nobody's lonesome for me / I'm so lonesome I could cry / Wedding bells / They'll never take her love from me / Love is after me / Pass on by / Hurry up freight train / Only me / When something is wrong with my baby / Don't tear me down / Can't get it right / I'll shed no tears / To fool a fool / Who will the next fool be / Big time operator / Renee / Motels, hotels
CD DIAB 810
Diabolo / Oct '95 / Pinnacle

THAT'S RICH
CD CPCD 8146
Charly / Nov '95 / Koch

VERY BEST OF CHARLIE RICH, THE
Most beautiful girl / Big boss man / Rollin' with the flow / Life has it's little ups and downs / Mohair Sam / Sittin' and thinkin' / My elusive dreams / Lonely weekends / You don't know me / Mountain dew / Behind closed doors / Take it on home / Break up / There won't be any more / On my knees / Pass on by / Good time Charlie's got the blues / Who will the next fool be
CD PLATCD 218
Platinum / Feb '97 / Prism

Rich, Dave

AIN'T IT FINE
Your pretty blue eyes / Ain't it fine / I'm glad / Didn't work out did it / I'm sorry goodbye / Darling I'm lonesome / Tuggin' on my heart strings / I love 'em all / I forgot / I think I'm gonna die / Lonely street / Our last night together / City lights / Rosie let's get cozy / Burn on love fire / Red sweater / I've learned / Red beads / School blues / Sunshine in my heart / Chicken house / That's what this whole world needs / Saved from sin / Brand new feeling / Where else would I want to be / Key to my heart / I've thought it over / Just like mine
CD BCD 15763

Bear Family / Nov '94 / Direct / Rollercoaster / Swift

Rich Kids On LSD

RICHES TO RAGS
CD E 864452
Epitaph / Jan '95 / Pinnacle / Plastic Head

ROCK 'N' ROLL
CD E 864262
Epitaph / Jun '92 / Pinnacle / Plastic Head

Rich, Robert

TRANCES/DRONES
CD XLTD 001
Extreme / May '95 / Vital/SAM

Rich, Tony

WORDS (Rich, Tony Project)
Hey blue / Nobody knows / Like a woman / Grass is green / Ghost / Leavin' / Billy goat / Under her spell / Little ones / Missin' you
CD 73008260222
Arista / May '96 / BMG

Richard S

COOL SHOES (Richard S & The Vibe Tribe)
CD LIP 890372
Lipstick / Feb '96 / Vital/SAM

Richard, Cliff

32 MINUTES AND 17 SECONDS/WHEN IN SPAIN
It'll be me / So I've been told / How long is forever / I'm walking the blues / Turn around / Blueberry Hill / Let's make a memory / When my dreamboat comes home / I'm on my way / Spanish harlem / You don't know / Falling in love with love / Who are we to say / I wake up cryin' / Perfidia / Amor amor amor / Frenesi / Solamente una vez: *Vaya Con Dios* / Me lo dijo adela / Maria no mas / Tus besos / Quizas quizas quizas / Te quiero dijiste / Cancion de orfeo / Quien sera
CD CDEMC 3630
EMI / Oct '92 / EMI

40 GOLDEN GREATS (2CD Set)
Move it / Living doll / Travellin' light / Fall in love with you / Please don't tease / Nine times out of ten / Theme for a dream / Gee whiz it's you / When the girl in your arms (is the girl in your heart) / Girl like you / Young ones / Do you wanna dance / I'm lookin' out the window / It'll be me / Bachelor boy / Next time / Summer holiday / Lucky lips / It's all in the game / Don't talk to him / Constantly / On the beach / I could easily fall / Minute you're gone / Wind me up (let me go) / Visions / Blue turns to grey / In the country / Day I met Marie / All my love / Congratulations / Throw down a line / Goodbye Sam, hello Samantha / Sing a song of freedom / Power to all our friends / You keep me hangin' on / Miss you nights / Devil woman / I can't ask for anymore than you / My kinda life / Thief in the night
CD Set CDS 7924252
EMI / Jun '89 / EMI

ALWAYS GUARANTEED
One night / Once upon a time / Some people / Forever / Two hearts / Under your spell / This time now / My pretty one / Remember me / Always guaranteed
CD CDP 7467052
EMI / '89 / EMI

CAROLS
Saviour's day / Silent night / Little town / In the bleak mid-Winter / Sweet little Jesus boy / While shepherds watched their flocks by night / Mary / What you gonna name that pretty little baby / Joseph / God rest ye merry gentlemen / Unto us a child is born / Can it be true / O little town of Bethlehem
CD ALD 025
Alliance Music / Oct '95 / EMI

CLIFF RICHARD AND THE SHADOWS BOX SET (3CD Set) (Richard, Cliff & The Shadows)
Omoide no nagisa: *Shadows* / Giniro no michi: *Shadows* / Londonderry air: *Shadows* / Kimi to itsumademo: *Shadows* / Boys: *Shadows* / Boys: *Shadows* / Foot tapper: *Shadows* / Round and round: *Shadows* / Les girls: *Shadows* / Friends: *Shadows* / Shazam: *Shadows* / Guitar boogie: *Shadows* / Sleepwalk: *Shadows* / FBI: *Shadows* / Bongo blues: *Shadows* / Ranka chank: *Shadows* / Flyder and the spy: *Shadows* / Autumn: *Shadows* / Chinchilla: *Shadows* / Walkin': *Shadows* / Look in my eyes, Maria: *Richard, Cliff* / If I give my heart to you: *Richard, Cliff* / Maria: *Richard, Cliff* / Secret love: *Richard, Cliff* / Love letters: *Richard, Cliff* / I only have eyes for you: *Richard, Cliff* / All I do is dream of you: *Richard, Cliff* / When I grow too old to dream: *Richard, Cliff* / My heart is an open book: *Richard, Cliff* / Boom boom (that's how my heart beats): *Richard, Cliff* / Moonlight bay: *Richard, Cliff* / Forever kind of love: *Richard, Cliff* / La mer: *Richard, Cliff* / J'attendrai: *Richard, Cliff* / Shrine on the second floor: *Richard, Cliff* / Where the four winds blow: *Richard, Cliff* / Solitary man: *Richard, Cliff* / Things we said today: *Richard, Cliff* / Carnival (from Black Orpheus): *Richard, Cliff* / Little rag doll: *Richard, Cliff* / Pefidia: *Shadows* / 36-24-36: *Shadows* / All day: *Shadows* / My grandfather's clock: *Shadows* / Lady Penelope: *Shadows* / Zero X theme: *Shadows* / Thunderbirds theme: *Shadows* / Finders keepers: *Shadows* / Shane: *Shadows* / Giant (theme from): *Shadows* / Shotgun: *Shadows* / Las tres carabelas: *Shadows* / Adios muchachos: *Shadows* / Valencia: *Shadows* / Granada: *Shadows* / Tonight: *Shadows* / Fandango: *Shadows* / Little princess: *Shadows* / Gonzales: *Shadows* / Jet black: *Shadows* / Driftin' (live): *Shadows*
CD Set MAGPIE 1
See For Miles/C5 / Apr '92 / Pinnacle

CLIFF RICHARD AT THE MOVIES 1959-1974 (2CD Set)
No turning back / Living doll / Mad about you / Love / Voices in the wilderness / Shrine on the second floor / Friday night / Got a funny feeling / Nothing is impossible / Young ones / Lessons in love / When the girl in your arms / We say yeah (it's wonderful to be young) / Outsider / Seven days to a holiday / Summer holiday / Let us take you for a ride / Stranger in town / Bachelor boy / Swingin' affair / Dancing shoes / Next time / Big news / Wonderful life / Girl in every port / Little imagination / On the beach / Do you remember / Look don't touch / In the stars / What've I gotta do / Matter of moments / Shooting star / Finders keepers / Time drags by / Washerwoman / La la la song / Oh senorita / This day / Paella / Two a penny / Twist and shout / I'll love you forever today / Questions / It's only money / Midnight blue / Game / Brumburger duet / Take me high / Anti-brotherhood of man / Winning
CD Set CDEMD 1096
EMI / Jul '96 / EMI

CLIFF RICHARD THE ALBUM
Peace in our time / Love is the strongest emotion / I still believe in you / Love's salvation / Only angel / Handle my heart with love / Little mistreater / You move heaven / I need love / Hold us together / Human work of art / Never let go / Healing love / Brother to brother
CD CDEMD 1043
EMI / Apr '93 / EMI

DRESSED FOR THE OCCASION (Richard, Cliff & Philharmonic Orchestra)
Green light / We don't talk anymore / True love ways / Softly as I leave / Carrie / Miss you nights / Galadriel (spirit of starlight) / Maybe someday / Thief in the night / Up in the world / Treasure of love / Evil woman (reprise)
CD CZ 187
EMI / May '89 / EMI

FROM A DISTANCE (The Event)
Zing went the strings of my heart / Always / When / Glory of love / Hoots mon / Don't look now / Girl can't help it / Sea cruise / From a distance / Some people / We don't talk anymore / Shake, rattle and roll / Silhouettes / Move it / Summer holiday / Young ones / In the country / Good golly Miss Molly / Fighter/ Thief in the night / Share a dream / All the time you need / Saviour's day
CD CDP 7951872
EMI / Nov '90 / EMI

I'M NO HERO
Take another look / Anything I can do / Little in love / Here (so doggone blue) / Give a little bit more / In the night / I'm no hero / Dreamin' / Heart will break / Everyman
CD CDFA 3148
Fame / Jul '88 / EMI

LOVE SONGS
Miss you nights / Constantly / Up in the world / Carrie / Voice in the wilderness / Twelfth of never / I could easily fall / Day I met Marie / Can't take the hurt anymore / Little in love / Minute you're gone / Visions / When two worlds drift apart / Next time / It's all in the game / Don't talk to him / When the girl in your arms (is the girl in your heart) / Theme for a dream / Fall in love with you / We don't talk anymore
CD CDEMTV 27
EMI / Mar '88 / EMI

MY KINDA LIFE
Born to rock 'n' roll / Hotshot / Devil woman / Remember (when two worlds drift apart) / Carrie / Lean on you / We don't talk anymore / Monduy thru' Friday / Lucille / You've got wondering / Never even thought / Two hearts / Language of love / My kinda life
CD CDEMD 1034
EMI / Jun '92 / EMI

NOW YOU SEE ME, NOW YOU DON'T
Only way out / First date / Thief in the night / Where do we go from here / Son of thunder / Little town / It has to be you / Water is wide / Now you see me, now you don't / Be in my heart / Discovering
CD CZ 2
EMI / Oct '87 / EMI

PRIVATE COLLECTION (His Personal Best 1979-1988)
Some people / Wired for sound / All I ask of you: *Richard, Cliff & Sarah Brightman* / Carrie / Remember me / True love ways / Dreamin' / Green light / She means nothing to me: *Richard, Cliff & Phil Everly* / Heart user / Little in love / Daddy's home / We don't talk anymore / Never say die (give a little bit more) / Only way out / Suddenly: *Richard, Cliff & Olivia Newton-John* / Slow rivers: *Richard, Cliff & Elton John* / Please don't fall in love / Little town / My pretty one / Ocean deep / She's so beautiful / Two hearts / Mistletoe and wine
CD CDCRTV 30
EMI / Nov '88 / EMI

ROCK 'N' ROLL YEARS, THE
Lawdy Miss Clawdy / Move it / 20 flight rock / High class baby / My feet hit the ground / Livin' lovin' doll / Blue suede shoes / We say yeah / Mean streak / Nine times out of ten / That'll be the day / Choppin' and changin' / Do you wanna dance / Dancing shoes / Dynamite / What'd I say / Without you / Mean woman blues / Oh boy medley / Don't bug me baby / No turning back / Whole lotta shakin' goin' on / Living doll / I'm walking / Willie and the hand jive / Blueberry Hill / Please don't tease
CD CDEMD 1109
EMI / Jul '97 / EMI

ROCK ON WITH CLIFF RICHARD
Move it / High class baby / My feet hit the ground / Living doll / Mean streak / Never mind / Apron strings / Dynamite / Blue suede shoes / Twenty flight rock / Mean woman blues / Willie and the hand jive / Please don't tease / Nine times out of ten / D in love / Mumblin' Mosie / Gee whiz it's you / What'd I say / Got a funny feeling / Forty days / Tough enough / We say yeah / Do you wanna dance / It'll be me / Dancing shoes
CD CDMFP 6005
Music For Pleasure / Oct '87 / EMI

SUMMER HOLIDAY (Richard, Cliff & The Shadows)
Seven days to a holiday / Summer holiday / Let us take you for a ride / Les girls / Foot tapper / Round and round / Stranger in town / Orlando's mime / Bachelor boy / Swingin' affair / Really waltzing / All at once / Dancing shoes / Yugoslav wedding / Next time / Big news
CD CDMFP 6021
Music For Pleasure / Apr '88 / EMI

TOGETHER WITH CLIFF
Have yourself a merry little Christmas / O come all ye faithful (Adeste Fidelis) / We should be together / Mistletoe and wine / Christmas never comes / Christmas alphabet / Saviour's day / Christmas song / Scarlet ribbons / Silent night / White Christmas / This New Year
CD CDEMD 1028
EMI / Oct '91 / EMI

WINNER, THE
Winner / Wild geese / Such is the mystery / Reunion of the heart / Discovering / There's more to life / Peace in our time / Under the gun / Yesterday, today, forever / Where you are / Be in my heart / Fighter / Thief in my heart / From a distance
CD ALD 020
Alliance Music / May '95 / EMI

WIRED FOR SOUND
Wired for sound / Once in a while / Better than I know myself / Oh no don't let me go / 'Cos I love that rock 'n' roll / Broken doll / Lost in a lonely world / Summer rain / Young love / Say you don't mind / Daddy's home
CD CDFA 3159
Fame / Oct '87 / EMI

YOUNG ONES, THE (Richard, Cliff & The Shadows)
Friday night / Got a funny feeling / Peace pipe / Nothing's impossible / Young ones / All for one / Lessons in love / No one for me but Nicky / What d'you know, we've got a show / Vaudeville routine / Mambo / Savage / We say yeah
CD CDMFP 6020
Music For Pleasure / Apr '88 / EMI

Richard, Gary

ONCE UPON FOREVER
CD M 38D
World Disc / Aug '96 / Gallant

Richards, Ann

I'M SHOOTING HIGH
I'm shooting high / Moanin' low / Nightingale / Blues in my heart / I've got to pass your house to get to my house / Deep night / Poor little rich girl / Should I / I'm in the market for you / Absence makes the heart grow fonder / Lullaby of Broadway / Will you still be mine
CD JASCD 310
Jasmine / Jun '97 / Conifer/BMG / Hot Shot / TKO Magnum

Richards, Goff

GOFF RICHARDS & THE BRITISH NUCLEAR FUEL BAND (Richards, Goff & BNFL Band)
CD QPRL 055D
Polyphonic / Apr '93 / Complete/Pinnacle

Richards, Johnny

LIVE IN HI-FI STEREO 1957-58 (Richards, Johnny Big Band)
CD JH 1010
Jazz Hour / '91 / Cadillac / Jazz Music / Target/BMG

Richards, Keith

LIVE AT THE HOLLYWOOD PALLADIUM '88 (Richards, Keith & The X-Pensive Winos)
Take it so hard / How I wish / I could have stood you up / Too rude / Make no mistake / Time is on my side / Big enough / Whip it up / Locked away / Struggle / Happy / Connection / Rockawhile
CD CDVUS 45
Virgin / Feb '92 / EMI

MAIN OFFENDER
999 / Wicked as it seems / Eileen / Words of wonder / Yap yap / Bodytalks / Hate it when you leave / Runnin' too deep / Will but you won't / Demon
CD CDVUS 59
Virgin / Oct '92 / EMI

TALK IS CHEAP
Big enough / Take it so hard / Struggle / I could have stood you up / Make no mistake / You don't move me / How I wish / Rockawhile / Whip it up / Locked away / It means a lot
CD CDV 2554
Virgin / '88 / EMI

Richards, Red

DREAMY
CD SKCD 23053
Sackville / Aug '94 / Cadillac / Jazz Music / Swift

GROOVE MOVE (Richards, Red & George Kelly Sextet)
CD JP 1045
Jazz Point / May '95 / Cadillac / Harmonia Mundi

LULLABY IN RHYTHM
CD SKCD 23044
Sackville / Jun '93 / Cadillac / Jazz Music / Swift

MY ROMANCE
CD CDJP 1042
Jazz Point / May '94 / Cadillac / Harmonia Mundi

SWING TIME
CD CDJP 1041
Jazz Point / May '94 / Cadillac / Harmonia Mundi

Richards, Sue

GREY EYED MORN
CD MMCD 201
Maggie's Music / Dec '94 / ADA / CM

MORNING AIRE
CD MMCD 204
Maggie's Music / Dec '94 / ADA / CM

Richards, Terrie

I CRIED FOR YOU (Richards, Terrie & Harry Allen/Howard Alden)
CD CHECD 00107
Master Mix / Oct '93 / Jazz Music / New Note/Pinnacle / Wellard

Richards, Trevor

TREVOR RICHARDS NEW ORLEANS TRIO
CD SOSCD 1222
Stomp Off / Oct '92 / Jazz Music / Wellard

Richardson, Geoffrey

VIOLA MON AMOUR
Rhapsodic uke / Blossomville / Borrowed kalimba / On the beech / Life drawing / Blossomville (reprise) / Viola mon amour / Diogenes and Alexander / Well tempered ukelele / Fifty four homes / Rhapsodic uke (reprise) / Diogenes and Alexander (reprise)
CD VP 132CD
Voiceprint / Jun '93 / Pinnacle

Richardson, Jim

REVISITED (Richardson, Jim 'Pogo')
Mellow D / Three in one / Hackensack / Beatrice / Improvisation no.2 / Tricotism / Oscar rides again / Pettiford / Two little pearls / Samba / Ease it / Margarine / Laverne Walk / Bossa nouveau
CD SPJCD 541
Spotlite / Feb '97 / Cadillac / Jazz Music / New Note/Pinnacle / Swift

Richey, Kim

BITTER SWEET
CD 5342552
Mercury / Mar '97 / PolyGram

Richie, Lionel

BACK TO FRONT
Do it to me / My destiny / Love oh love / All night long / Easy / Still / Endless love: *Richie, Lionel & Diana Ross* / Running with the night / Dancing on the ceiling / Sail on / Hello / Truly / Penny lover / Stuck on you / Say you, say me / Three times a lady
CD _____ 5300182
Motown / May '92 / PolyGram

CAN'T SLOW DOWN
All night long / Stuck on you / Penny lover / Hello / Love will find a way / Running with the night / Only one / Can't slow down
CD _____ 5300232
Motown / Jan '92 / PolyGram

DANCING ON THE CEILING
Sela / Ballerina girl / Don't stop / Deep river woman / Love will conquer all / Tonight will be alright / Say you, say me / Night train (Smooth alligator) / Dancing on the ceiling / Love will find a way
CD _____ 5300242
Motown / Jan '92 / PolyGram

LIONEL RICHIE
Serves you right / Wandering stranger / Tell me / My love / Round and round / Truly / You are / You mean more to me / Just put some love in your heart
CD _____ 5300262
Motown / Jan '92 / PolyGram

LOUDER THAN WORDS
CD _____ 5322412
Mercury / Apr '96 / PolyGram

Richie Rich

SEASONED VETERAN
Intro / Funk / It's on / Let's ride / 30 minutes / Real pimp / Guess who's back / Fresh out / Niggas done changed: *Richie Rich & 2Pac* / Pillow / Check 'em / Real shit / Questions / It's not about you / Do G's get to go to heaven / Touch myself: *Richie Rich & T-Boz*
CD _____ 5334712
Def Jam / Nov '96 / PolyGram

Richies

PET SUMMER
CD _____ WB 1106CD
We Bite / Dec '93 / Plastic Head

WINTER WONDERLAND
CD _____ WB 065CD
We Bite / Jul '90 / Plastic Head

Richman, Jeff

LAST ARRIVAL
CD _____ LIP 890422
Lipstick / Jun '96 / Vital/SAM

Richman, Jonathan

BACK IN YOUR LIFE (Richman, Jonathan & Modern Lovers)
I'm a little airplane / Hey there little insect / Egyptian reggae / Ice cream man / I'm a little dinosaur / My little kookenhaken / South American folk song / New England / Morning of our lives
CD _____ HILLCD 15
Wooded Hill / Apr '97 / Direct / World Serpent

COLLECTION, THE
CD _____ CCSCD 397
Castle / Apr '94 / BMG

I, JONATHAN
CD _____ ROUCD 9036
Rounder / Jan '94 / ADA / CM / Direct

JONATHAN RICHMAN
Malaguena de Jojo / Everyday clothes / Blue moon / I eat with gusto, damn you bet / Sleepwalk / Mistake today for me / Action packed / Fender Statocaster / Closer / Miracles will start to happen / Que reste t'il de nos amours / Cerco
CD _____ ROUCD 9021
Special Delivery / Sep '94 / ADA / CM / Direct

JONATHAN RICHMAN & BARRENCE WHITFIELD (Richman, Jonathan & Barrence Whitfield)
CD _____ CDS 1
Rounder / '88 / ADA / CM / Direct

JONATHAN RICHMAN & THE MODERN LOVERS (Richman, Jonathan & Modern Lovers)
Rockin' shopping centre / Back in the USA / Important in your life / New England / Lonely financial zone / Hi dear / Abominable snowman in the market / Hey there little insect / Here come the Martian Martians / Springtime / Amazing grace
CD _____ CREV 008CD
Rev-Ola / Jan '93 / 3mv/Vital

JONATHAN, TE VAS A EMOCIONAR
CD _____ ROUCD 9040
Rounder / Apr '94 / ADA / CM / Direct

LIVE AT THE LONGBRANCH SALOON (Modern Lovers)
CD _____ 422439
New Rose / May '94 / ADA / Direct / Discovery

MODERN LOVERS (Modern Lovers)
Roadrunner / Astral plane / Old world / Pablo picasso / I'm straight / She cracked / Hospital / Someone I care about / Girlfriend / Modern world / Dignified and old / Government centre
CD _____ CREV 007CD
Rev-Ola / Nov '92 / 3mv/Vital

MODERN LOVERS LIVE (Modern Lovers)
Abdul and Cleopatra / She's gonna respect me / Love please / Affection / Buzz buzz buzz / Back in your life / Party in the woods tonight / My love is a flower (just beginning to bloom) / I'm nature's mosquito / Emaline / Lydia / I hear you calling me
CD _____ HILLCD 14
Wooded Hill / Apr '97 / Direct / World Serpent

PLEA FOR TENDERNESS, A
CD _____ NTMCD 506
Nectar / Jun '95 / Pinnacle

PRECISE MODERN LOVERS ORDER (Modern Lovers)
CD _____ ROUCD 9042
Rounder / Apr '95 / ADA / CM / Direct

RADIO ON/STOP AND SHOP (2CD Set)
CD Set _____ SMDCD 115
Snapper / Jul '97 / Pinnacle

ROCK 'N' ROLL WITH THE MODERN LOVERS (Richman, Jonathan & Modern Lovers)
Sweeping wind / Ice cream man / Rockin' rockin' leprechauns / Summer morning / Afternoon / Fly into the mystery / South American folk song / Rollercoaster by the sea / Dodge Veg-O-matic / Egyptian reggae / Coomyah / Wheels on the bus / Angels watching over me
CD _____ CREV 009CD
Rev-Ola / Feb '93 / 3mv/Vital

SURRENDER TO JONATHAN
CD _____ 9362462962
Vapour / Sep '96 / Warner Music

YOU MUST ASK THE HEART
CD _____ ROUCD 9047
Rounder / May '95 / ADA / CM / Direct

Richmond, Kim

PASSAGES
Passages / Old acquaintances / Passcaglia/ My funny valentine / Melon bells / Street of dreams / Soft feelings / Chic-a-brac / Images and likeness / Indian summer / Nardis
CD _____ SBCD 2043
Sea Breeze / Jul '92 / Jazz Music

Richthofen

SEELENWALZER
CD _____ GUN 132CD
Gun / Jun '97 / Plastic Head

Richthofen & Brown ...

FILM MUSIC OF HUGO FRIEDHOFER (Richthofen & Brown Symphonic Suite)
CD _____ 8105
Facet / May '97 / Conifer/BMG

Ricketts, Glen

I FOUND A LOVE
CD _____ DKCD 7773
DK / Apr '96 / Jet Star / Total/BMG

Ricks, Glen

FALL IN LOVE
CD _____ VYDCD 015
Vine Yard / Jul '96 / Grapevine/PolyGram

OH CAROLINA
CD _____ LG 21089
Lagoon / Mar '96 / Grapevine/PolyGram

Ricks, Jerry

DEEP IN THE WELL (Ricks, 'Philadelphia' Jerry)
CD _____ R 2636
Rooster / Aug '97 / Direct

Rico

BLOW YOUR HORN (Rico & The Rudies)
CD _____ CDTTL 12
Trojan / Aug '96 / Direct / Jet Star

BLOW YOUR HORN/BRIXTON CAT (Rico & The Rudies)
CD _____ CDTRL 361
Trojan / Jan '96 / Direct / Jet Star

RICO'S MESSAGE - JAMAICAN JAZZ (Rodriguez, Rico All Stars)
CD _____ 444102
Rhino / Jun '97 / Grapevine/PolyGram / Jet Star

RISING IN THE EAST
CD _____ JOVECD 3
Jove Music / Sep '94 / Jet Star / SRD

ROOTS TO THE BONE
Children of Sanchez / Midnight in Ethiopia / Free ganja / Take five / Far East / No politician / Firestick / Matches Lane / This day / Ramble / Lumumba / Africa / Man from Wareika / Over the mountain / Dial Africa
CD _____ RRCD 54
Reggae Refreshers / Apr '95 / PolyGram / Vital

TRIBUTE TO DON DRUMMOND, A
CD _____ TRRCD 01
Trybute / Jun '97 / SRD

Ricochets

MADE IN THE SHADE
Witchcraft / Migraine / Hey, girl / Yomping / I'm a loser / Crazy dream / King rocker / Black magic baby / Runnin' wild / Hit man / Worried 'bout you baby / Brand new Cadillac / Night ship / Everybody's rockin' / Don't blame me / Mama don't allow / Mad man / Worried 'bout you baby / Hit man
CD _____ NERDCD 005
Nervous / May '97 / Nervous / TKO Magnum

Riddle, Leslie

STEP BY STEP
Little school girl / Frisco blues / Broke and weary blues / Hilltop blues / Motherless children / Titanic / I'm out on the ocean a-sailing / I'm working on a building / I know what it means to be lonesome / Red river blues / One kind favor / If you see my saviour / Cannonball / Step by step
CD _____ ROUCD 0299
Rounder / May '93 / ADA / CM / Direct

Riddle, Nelson

CAPITOL YEARS, THE
Let's face the music and dance / You are the night and the music / Younger than springtime / You leave me breathless / You're an old smoothie / Then I'll be happy / I get along without you very well / I can't escape from you / Have you got any castles, baby / Darn that dream / Let yourself go / Jeannine / Without a song / September in the rain / S'posin' / Am I blue / Rain / I'll get by / Diga diga doo / For all we know / Time was / Something to remember you by / Get happy
CD _____ CDEMS 1489
Capitol / Apr '93 / EMI

JOY OF LIVING/LOVE IS A GAME OF POKER
Life is a bowl of cherries / You make me feel so young / Makin' whoopee / Bye bye blues / It's so peaceful in the country / Joy of living / It's a big wide wonderful world / June in January / Isn't this a lovely day / Floatin' like a feather / Thrill is gone / I love you / Time on my hands / I'll see you in my dreams / Lies / Dream / Blue moon / Linger awhile / All by myself / Sometimes I'm happy / Street of dreams
CD _____ CTMCD 117
EMI / Jun '97 / EMI

Ride

CARNIVAL OF LIGHT
CD _____ CRECD 147
Creation / Jun '94 / 3mv/Vital

GOING BLANK AGAIN
CD _____ CRECD 124
Creation / Jan '92 / 3mv/Vital

LIVE LIGHT
CD _____ 800022
Mutiny / Jul '97 / Cargo

NOWHERE
Seagull / Kaleidoscope / In a different place / Polar bear / Dreams burn down / Decay / Paralysed / Vapour trail / Taste / Here and now / Nowhere
CD _____ CRECD 074
Creation / Oct '90 / 3mv/Vital

SMILE
Chelsea Girl / Drive Blind / All I can see / Close my eyes / Like A Daydream / Silver / Furthest Sense / Perfect time
CD _____ CRECD 126
Creation / May '94 / 3mv/Vital

TARANTULA
CD _____ CRECD 180
Creation / Mar '96 / 3mv/Vital

Rideout, Bonnie

KINDRED SPIRITS
CD _____ MMCD 214
Maggie's Music / Apr '96 / ADA / CM

Riders In The Sky

ALWAYS DRINK UPSTREAM FROM THE HERD
CD _____ ROUCD 0360
Rounder / Jan '96 / ADA / CM / Direct

BEST OF THE WEST
CD _____ ROUCD 11517
Rounder / '88 / ADA / CM / Direct

BEST OF THE WEST RIDERS AGAIN
CD _____ ROUCD 11524
Rounder / '88 / ADA / CM / Direct

COWBOY SONGS
Jingle jangle jingle / Tumbling tumbleweeds / Don't fence me in / Cattle call / Ghost riders in the sky / Streets of Laredo / I ride an old paint / Red River Valley / Rawhide / Chasin' the sun / Back in the saddle again / Home on the range
CD _____ EDCD 7005
Easydisc / Oct '96 / Direct

PUBLIC COWBOY NO.1 (The Music Of Gene Autry)
Back in the saddle again / Sioux City Sue / Mexicali rose / You are my sunshine / Have I told you lately that I love you / Can't shake the sands of Texas from my shoes / Silver haired Daddy of mine / Be honest with me / Blue Canadian Rockies / Lonely river / South of the border / Ridin' down the canyon
CD _____ ROUCD 0410
Rounder / Nov '96 / ADA / CM / Direct

SADDIE PAIS
CD _____ ROUCD 8011
Rounder / '88 / ADA / CM / Direct

Ridge Racer

ALBUM, THE
CD _____ JVC 90022
JVC / Jul '96 / Direct / New Note/Pinnacle / Vital/SAM

Ridgley, Tommy

NEW ORLEANS KING OF THE STROLL, THE
New Orleans king of the stroll / Double eyed whammy / Is it true / Should I ever love again / My ordinary girl / I've heard that story before / Heavenly / Girl from Kooka Monga / In the same old way / Three times / Only girl for me / I love you yes I do / Please hurry home
CD _____ ROUCD 2079
Rounder / ADA / CM / Direct

SHE TURNS ME ON
CD _____ MBCD 1203
Modern Blues / Jun '93 / ADA / Direct

SINCE THE BLUES BEGAN
CD _____ BT 1115CD
Black Top / May '95 / ADA / CM / Direct

Ridout, Bonnie

CELTIC CIRCLES
CD _____ MMCD 209
Maggie's Music / Dec '94 / ADA / CM

SOFT MAY MORN
CD _____ MMCD 208
Maggie's Music / Dec '94 / ADA / CM

Riedel, Georg

KIRBITZ
CD _____ PHONTCD 9311
Phontastic / Jul '96 / Cadillac / Jazz Music / Wellard

Riessler, Michael

HELOISE
CD _____ WER 80082
Wergo / Nov '93 / ADA / Cadillac / Harmonia Mundi

MOMENTUM MOBILE
Anekdoten / La rage / Ein itllige sprag / Luigi / Marathon / Ba binga / Marsch der ketzer / Ost - west / Old Orleans, New Orleans / Song mecanique
CD _____ ENJ 90032
Enja / Mar '95 / New Note/Pinnacle / Vital/ SAM

TENTATIONS D'ABELARD
CD _____ WER 8010
Wergo / Dec '95 / ADA / Cadillac / Harmonia Mundi

Riff, Nick

CLOAK OF IMMORTALITY
Cloak of immortality / Creature feature / Way out / Staring into space / Like a zen stray / Something indside / Temple of dreams / Ghost / Tribal elders / From beyond they speak / Go far go wide
CD _____ DELECCD 017
Delerium / Apr '95 / Cargo / Pinnacle / Vital

FREAK ELEMENT
CD _____ DELECCD 001
Delerium / Jun '92 / Cargo / Pinnacle / Vital

Rig

BELLY TO THE GROUND
CD _____ CRZ 035CD
Cruz / Feb '94 / Plastic Head

Rigai, Amiram

AMIRAM RIGAI PLAYS LOUIS MOREAU GOTTSCHALK
CD _____ CDSF 40803
Smithsonian Folkways / Oct '93 / ADA / Cadillac / CM / Direct / Koch

Rigby, Amy

DIARY OF A MOD HOUSEWIFE
CD 379222
Koch International / Oct '96 / Koch

Rigby, Eleanor

BEST OF ELEANOR RIGBY VOL.1, THE (The Singles Collection)
CD FLEGCD 3
Future Legend / Mar '95 / Future Legend / Pinnacle

BEST OF ELEANOR RIGBY VOL.2, THE
I'm not like everybody else / She's got everything / Play with fire / Getting thru the day / Mod girls / Gotta move / For the video / Till the end of the day / Censorship / My Christmas card to you / More than the truth / Don't ask me what I say / All or nothing
CD FLEGCD 7
Future Legend / Jul '96 / Future Legend / Pinnacle

Riggan, Tracey

FRIENDS
Amazing grace / Challenge / Arms of the Father / Special friend / Never gonna look back / Security / Free / Dance of fire / Hide no more / Celebration
CD MYRCD 1283
Myrrh / Jan '92 / Nelson Word

Right Direction

ALL OF A SUDDEN
CD LF 133CD
Lost & Found / May '95 / Plastic Head

Right Said Fred

UP
CD SNOGCD 1
Gut / Mar '92 / Total/BMG

Righteous Brothers

GREATEST HITS
CD JHD 024
Tring / Jun '92 / Tring

INSPIRATIONS
Soul and inspiration / What now my love / Ebb tide / White cliffs of Dover / Go ahead and cry / Just once in my life / Stranded in the middle of no place / Great pretender / He will break your heart / Island in the sun / (I love you) for sentimental reasons / That lucky old sun / My darling Clementine / Georgia on my mind
CD 5501972
Spectrum / Mar '94 / PolyGram

ORIGINAL ALBUMS
CD DCD 5285
Disky / Dec '93 / Disky / THE

UNCHAINED MELODY
CD AVC 513
Avid / Dec '92 / Avid/BMG / Koch / THE

YOU'VE LOST THAT LOVIN' FEELING
You've lost that lovin' feeling / He / Along came Jones / Harlem shuffle / Hold on I'm coming / I who have nothing / Save the last dance for me / Will you love me tomorrow / Bring it on home to me / I'm leaving it up to you / In the midnight hour / Come rain or come shine / Secret love / Somewhere / You'll never walk alone / Drown in my own tears / I believe / Let it be me
CD 5512682
Spectrum / Mar '96 / PolyGram

Rights Of The Accused

KICK-HAPPY, THRILL-HUNGRY, RECKLESS AND WILLING
CD N 01672
Noise / '91 / Koch

Rigid Containers Band

ENGLISH LANDSCAPES
CD HARCD 1125
Harlequin / Jul '95 / TKO Magnum

Rigo, Sandor Buffo

BEST OF TRADITIONAL, THE (Rigo, Sandor Buffo & His Hungarian Gypsy Band)
CD SYNCD 148
Topic / Apr '93 / ADA / CM / Direct

Riisnaes, Knut

GEMINI TWINS
CD GMCD 175
Gemini / Oct '89 / Cadillac

Riley, Billy Lee

CLASSIC RECORDINGS 1956-1960 (2CD Set)
Rock with me baby / Troublebound / Flyin' saucer rock 'n' roll / I want you baby / Red hot / Pearly Lee / Wouldn't you / Baby, please don't go / Rockin' on the moon / Is that all to the ball, Mr Hall / Itchy / Thunderbird / Down by the riverside / No name girl / Come back baby / Got the water boiling / Open the door Richard: *Riley, Billy & Ernie Barton* / Dark muddy bottom / Repossession blues / That's what I want to do / Too much woman for me / Flyin' saucer rock 'n' roll / I want you / She's my baby / Pearly Lee (unissued) / Red hot (unissued) / That's right / Searchin' / Chatter and college man / Your cash ain't nothin' but trash / Swanee river rock / Betty and Dupree / Let's talk about us / Got the water boiling (unissued) / Saturday night fish fry / Folsom prison blues / Billy's blues / When a man gets the blues / Sweet William / Red hot (version) / Mud Island / My baby's got love
CD Set BCD 15444
Bear Family / Jul '90 / Direct / Rollercoaster / Swift

RED HOT
CD CPCD 8138
Charly / Mar '96 / Koch

ROCKIN' WITH BILLY (3CD Set)
CD Set CDSUNBOX 3
Charly / Feb '93 / Koch

Riley, Howard

BERNE CONCERT, THE (Riley, Howard & Keith Tippett)
CD FMRCD 08
Future / Mar '95 / ADA / Harmonia Mundi

CLASSICS (Riley, Howard & Art Themen Quartet)
Straight no chaser / Body and soul / All blues / 'Round midnight / Softly as in a morning sunrise
CD SLAMCD 222
Slam / Feb '97 / Cadillac

FEATHERS WITH JAKI (Riley, Howard & Jaki Byard)
'Round midnight / Straight no chaser / Swigger swagger / Feathers / Subway one / Sweet but short / Yesterdays / Subway two / Clochard
CD SLAMCD 215
Slam / Oct '96 / Cadillac

FLIGHT
CD FMRCD 26
Future / Dec '95 / ADA / Harmonia Mundi

INNER MINOR
Fast forward / Icon no more / Things / Wired / Dreaming / Inner minor / Home at last / Deflection / Glass / Au contraire / Starstruck / Walkway
CD ASCCD 16
ASC / Aug '97 / Cadillac / New Note/ Pinnacle

WISHING ON THE MOON
CD FMRCD 14
Future / Aug '95 / ADA / Harmonia Mundi

Riley, Jimmy

20 CLASSIC HITS
CD SONCD 0053
Sonic Sounds / Aug '93 / Jet Star

ATTENTION
CD PCD 0003
Blue Mountain / Jul '96 / Jet Star

Riley, Paul

WANDERER, THE
CD KMCD 44
KM / Feb '96 / ADA

Riley, Philip

PATTERN OF LANDS
CD WCL 110182
White Cloud / Sep '96 / Select

VISIONS AND VOICES
CD WCL 110122
White Cloud / May '95 / Select

Riley, Steve

'TIT GALOP POUR MAMA (Riley, Steve & Mamou Playboys)
CD ROUCD 6048
Rounder / Dec '90 / ADA / CM / Direct

LA TOUSSAINT (Riley, Steve & Mamou Playboys)
CD ROUCD 6068
Rounder / Jan '96 / ADA / CM / Direct

LIVE (Riley, Steve & Mamou Playboys)
CD ROUCD 6058
Rounder / May '94 / ADA / CM / Direct

TRACE OF TIME (Riley, Steve & Mamou Playboys)
Bayou noir / Mon vieux wagon / Old home waltz / Church point breakdown / Parleznous a boire / Lover's waltz / Sur le courtableau / La valse du regret / La Point-au-pic / Corner post / Zarico est pas sale
CD ROUCD 6053
Rounder / Jul '93 / ADA / CM / Direct

Riley, Terry

CADENZA ON THE NIGHT PLAIN (Riley, Terry & The Kronos Quartet)
CD GCD 79444
Gramavision / Sep '95 / Vital/SAM

LAZY AFTERNOON AMONG THE CROCODILES (Riley, Terry & Stefano Scodanibbio)
CD AI 008
Pierrot Lun / Jun '97 / ReR Megacorp

LISBON CONCERT
CD NA 087
New Albion / Oct '96 / Cadillac / Harmonia Mundi

PERSIAN SURGERY DERVISHES
CD NT 6715
Robi Droli / Jan '94 / ADA / Direct

POPPY NOGOOD AND THE PHANTOM BAND - ALL NIGHT FLIGHT
CD CORTI 04
Cortical / Jul '97 / Harmonia Mundi

RAINBOW IN CURVED AIR
CD 4778492
Columbia / Oct '94 / Sony

Rimes, Leann

BLUE
CD CURCD 028
Curb / Aug '96 / Grapevine/PolyGram

EARLY YEARS
CD CURCD 038
Curb / Feb '97 / Grapevine/PolyGram

YOU LIGHT UP MY LIFE (Inspirational Songs)
You light up my life / Rose / Bridge over troubled water / I beleive / Ten thousand angels cried / Clinging to a saving hand / On the side of angels / I know who holds tomorrow / God bless America / How do I live / Amazing Grace / National Anthem
CD CURCD 046
Curb / Sep '97 / Grapevine/PolyGram

Rimitti

CHEIKHA
CD ABSOLCD 5
Absolute / Jan '97 / Discovery / Koch

SIDI MANSOUR
CD ABSOLCD 2
Absolute / Apr '96 / Discovery / Koch

Rimmington, Sammy

CHRISTMAS IN NEW ORLEANS
CD BCD 209
GHB / Jan '94 / Jazz Music

GINGER PIG NEW ORLEANS JAZZ BAND
CD BCD 232
GHB / Oct '92 / Jazz Music

ON TOUR (Rimmington, Sammy & His Band)
CD BCD 211
GHB / Jun '95 / Jazz Music

ONE SWISS NIGHT
CD MECCACD 1021
Music Mecca / Jun '93 / Cadillac / Jazz Music / Wellard

SAMMY RIMMINGTON & HIS BAND (Rimmington, Sammy & His Band)
CD BCD 288
GHB / Aug '94 / Jazz Music

SAMMY RIMMINGTON & KEN PYE'S CREOLE SERENADERS (Rimmington, Sammy & Ken Pye Creole Serenaders)
CD PKCD 071
PEK / Mar '97 / Cadillac / Jazz Music / Wellard

Rimshots

EVERYBODY BOP NOW
CD JRCD 23
Jappin' & Rockin' / Oct '96 / Swift / TKO Magnum

SENTIMENTAL FOOLS
Honky tonk hardwood floor / Cattin' around / Sentimental fool / Won or lost / I had better times / Rock cat rock / Planet bop / Rust free / So tired of cryin' / I got a gal / I love the life I'm livin' / I fell in love / Don't come knocking at my door / Rock all night / Big river / Four minute warning / Shut up and drink your beer / Scratch on my record
CD JRCD 29
Vinyl Japan / Jul '97 / Plastic Head / Vinyl Japan

Rinaldi, Susana

EL TANGO RESPLANDECIENTE
CD 74321453302
Milan Sur / Feb '97 / Conifer/BMG

Rincon Surfside Band

SURFING SONGBOOK
CD VSD 5481
Varese Sarabande / Jan '95 / Pinnacle

Riney, Sam

DARK HERO
It is written / Nightwind / Everything reminds me of you / Chaco canyon / Choices / Too many steps / Until that time / Here we go / Dark hero / Live and let die / Whisper / Giverny
CD KOKO 1312
Kokopelli / Sep '96 / New Note/Pinnacle

Ringer, Jim

BAND OF JESSE JAMES, THE (Best Of Jim Ringer)
CD CDPH 1202
Philo / Aug '96 / ADA / CM / Direct

GOOD TO GET HOME
CD CIC 069CD
Clo Iar-Chonnachta / Nov '93 / CM

Ringo

EYEWITNESS
CD LG 21102
Lagoon / Apr '95 / Grapevine/PolyGram

Ringtailed Snorter

SEXUAL CHILD ABUSE
CD CDZOT 19
Zoth Ommog / Aug '93 / Cargo / Plastic Head

Ringworm

FLATLINE, THE
CD LF 135CD
Lost & Found / Mar '95 / Plastic Head

Rinne Radio

FINNISH AMBIENT TECHNO CHANT (Rinne Radio & Wimme)
Aromaa alt too / Vedet / In nera / Amen / Blue drift / 5 am / Eeva's panka / Teo teo / Freepop birds / Texas / This / Ecstacy / Boaimmas / Aromaa
CD 09026687522
Catalyst / Aug '97 / BMG

JOIK
Freepop birds / Helisma / Hot winters / Blue in purple / Aalloilla / Radio Soi - Freehop / This / Rohtasan / Vedet / Is / Villinraskas / Forest donk / Heaven
CD AAX 007
AAX / May '97 / Direct

UNIK
Aatto / Saloma / Teo Teo / Aalloilla II / Aromaa / Eeva's Panka / Family man / D# / Fear of the unknown / Mp
CD AAX 005
AAX / May '97 / Direct

Rinneradio

ROK
CD ZEN 2047CD
Rockadillo / Nov '96 / ADA / Direct

Rinpoche, Chogyal

CHOD: CUTTING THROUGH DUALISM
CD ARNR 0193
Amiata / Sep '93 / Harmonia Mundi

Rio

RIO
CD BLIPCD 102
Urban London / Mar '94 / Jet Star / Pinnacle

Riot

FIRE DOWN BELOW
CD 7559605762
Elektra / Jan '96 / Warner Music

LIVE
CD 7559679692
Elektra / Jan '96 / Warner Music

NIGHTBREAKER
CD SPV 084 62222
Rising Sun / Jun '94 / Cargo / Plastic Head

RESTLESS BREED
Restless breed / Hard lovin' man / CIA / When I was young / Loved by you / Loneshark / Over to you / Showdown / Dream away / Violent crimes
CD 7559601342
Elektra / Jan '96 / Warner Music

RIOT LIVE
CD CDZORRO 55
Metal Blade / Jul '92 / Pinnacle / Plastic Head
CD 398414011CD
Metal Blade / Jun '96 / Pinnacle / Plastic Head

ROCK CITY
Desperation / Warrior / Rock city / Overdrive / Angel / Tokyo rose / Heart of fire / Gypsy queen / This is what I get
CD 398414009CD
Metal Blade / Jun '96 / Pinnacle / Plastic Head

Riot City

RIOT CITY PUNK SINGLES COLLECTION
Fuck the tories / We are the Riot Squad / Civil destruction / Riots in the city / Why

should we / Religion doesn't mean a thing / Lost cause / Suspicion / Unite and fight / Police power / Society's fodder / In the future / Friday night hero / There ain't no solution / Government schemes / No potential threat / Ten years time / Hate the law / Hidden in fear / Lost cause (demo) / Unite and fight (demo)
CD _______________ CDPUNK 41
Anagram / Jan '95 / Cargo / Pinnacle

Riot Clone

STILL NO GOVERNMENT
CD _______________ RCR 005CD
Riot Clone / Aug '95 / Plastic Head

Riou

EXHIBITION OF THE SAMPLES
CD _______________ KK 137CD
KK / Sep '95 / Plastic Head

Rip, Jimmy

WAY PAST BLUE
It's going round / Close to you / Cold comfort / Snake eyes / Detroit jewel / Walk / Mojo / Insanity please / Layin' in the cut / State of mind / Way past blue
CD _______________ HBSCD 87004
House Of Blues / Apr '96 / ADA / BMG
CD _______________ 70010870042
House Of Blues / Jun '96 / ADA / BMG

Rip Masters

DON'T TREAD ON ME
CD _______________ MSECD 18
Mouse / Jul '96 / Grapevine/PolyGram

Ripe

PLASTIC HASSLE
CD _______________ BBQCD 149
Beggars Banquet / Apr '94 / RTM/Disc / Warner Music

Riperton, Minnie

BEST OF MINNIE RIPERTON, THE
Perfect angel / Lover and friend (Single version) / Memory lane / Woman of heart and mind / Loving you / Young willing and able / Can you feel what I'm saying / Stick together / Wouldn't matter where you are / Stay in love / Inside my love / Here we go / Give me time (Single version) / You take my breath away / Adventures in paradise / Simple things / Light my fire
CD _______________ CDP 7805162
Capitol / Aug '93 / EMI

COME TO MY GARDEN
Les fleurs / Completeness / Come to my garden / Memory band / Rainy day in centerville / Close your eyes and remember / Oh by the way / Expecting / Only when I'm dreaming / Wherever we are
CD _______________ CDBM 080
Blue Moon / Aug '97 / Cadillac / Discovery / Greensleeves / Jazz Music / Jet Star / TKO Magnum
CD _______________ AIM 1060
Aim / May '97 / ADA / Direct / Jazz Music

Rippingtons

LIVE IN LA
Indian summer / Aspen / Curves ahead / Weekend in Monaco / One summer night in Brazil / High roller / Dream of sirens / Once in a lifetime love / Tourists in paradise
CD _______________ GRP 97182
GRP / Jul '93 / New Note/BMG

WEEKEND IN MONACO
Weekend in Monaco / St. Tropez / Vienna / Indian summer / Place for lovers / Carnival / Moka java / High roller / Where the road will lead us
CD _______________ GRP 96812
GRP / Aug '92 / New Note/BMG

WELCOME TO THE ST. JAMES' CLUB
Welcome to The St James Club / Soul mates / I watched her walk away / Affair in San Miguel / Who's holding her now / Kenya / Wednesday's child / Tropic of Capricorn / Passion fruit / Victoria's secret
CD _______________ GRP 96182
GRP / Aug '90 / New Note/BMG

Ripple

BUT IT SURE IS FUNKY
I don't know what it is but it sure is funky / See the light in the window / You were right on time / Hell of a man / This ain't no time to be giving up / Funky song / Be my friend / Willie pass the water / Get off / Hey lady / Sweet lady / Get ready for a biggie / I'll be right there trying / I can't see you loving nobody but me / Maybe it's you / Dance lady dance / Complain to the clouds but you can't change the weather / If the music can't do it (nobody can) / Break song / Cross collaterization / Ripplin'
CD _______________ CDSEWD 098
Southbound / Feb '97 / Pinnacle

RIPPLE
You were right on time / Be my friend / I don't know what it is but it sure is funky / I'll be right there trying / Get off / See the light in the window / Funky song / Wilie pass the water / Dance lady dance / Ripplin'
CD _______________ CPCD 8093
Charly / Apr '95 / Koch

Riqueni, Rafael

MAESTROS
El bohio / Noches de cadix / Inspiration / Con salero y garbo / De chiclana a cai / Nostalgia flamenco / Recuerdo a sevilla / Sentir del sacromonte / Perfil flamenco / Mantilla e feria / Estrella amargura
CD _______________ EMO 93062
Act / Oct '95 / New Note/Pinnacle

Rishell, Paul

BLUES ON A HOLIDAY
CD _______________ CDTC 1144
Tonecool / May '94 / ADA / Direct

I WANT YOU TO KNOW (Rishell, Paul & Annie Raines)
CD _______________ CDTC 1156
Tonecool / Sep '96 / ADA / Direct

SWEAR TO TELL THE TRUTH
CD _______________ CDTC 1148
Tonecool / May '94 / ADA / Direct

Rising Sons

RISING SONS, THE
Statesboro blues / If the river was whiskey / By and by (poor me) / Candy man / Let the good times roll / 44 blues / 11th street overcrossing / Corine Corina / Tulsa county / Walkin' down the line / Girl with green eyes / Sunny's dream / Spanish lace blues / Devil's got my woman / Take a giant step / Flyin' so high / Dust my broom / Last fair deal gone down / Baby, what you want me to do / I got a little
CD _______________ 4728652
Columbia / May '93 / Sony

Rising Storm

CALM BEFORE THE STORM
CD _______________ AA 034
Arf Arf / Jul '97 / Greyhound

Risk

DIRTY SURFACES
CD _______________ 0876234
Steamhammer / Aug '90 / Pinnacle / Plastic Head

HELL'S ANIMALS
Monkey business / Perfect kill / Dead or alive / Secret of our destiny / Sicilian showdown / Torture and pain / Mindshock / Megalomania / Russian nights / Epilogue
CD _______________ 857593
Steamhammer / Jun '89 / Pinnacle / Plastic Head

Risk, Laura

JOURNEY BEGUN (Risk, Laura & Athena Tergis)
CD _______________ CUL 105CD
Culburnie / Oct '95 / ADA / CM / Direct / Duncans / Highlander / Ross

Ritchie, Jean

MOST DULCIMER, THE
CD _______________ GR 70714
Greenhays / Dec '94 / ADA / CM / Direct / Duncans / Jazz Music / Roots

MOUNTAIN BORN (Ritchie, Jean & Sons)
Mountain born / Loving Hannah / Love somebody, yes I do / Cuckoo / You are my dearest dear / Barley-Bright / Abigail / Deep shady groves / When sorrows encompass me round / Come all you fair and tender leadies / May Day / My dear companion / Come let us sing / One more mile / Our meeting is over
CD _______________ GR 70725
Greenhays / Oct '96 / ADA / CM / Direct / Duncans / Jazz Music / Roots

NONE BUT ONE/HIGH HILLS & MOUNTAINS
CD _______________ GR 70708
Greenhays / Dec '94 / ADA / CM / Direct / Duncans / Jazz Music / Roots

Rite Of Strings

RITE OF STRINGS
Indigo / Renaissance / Song to John / Chilean pipe song / Topanga / Morocco / Change of life / LA cancion de sofia / Memory canyon
CD _______________ CDP 8341672
IRS/EMI / Aug '95 / EMI

Ritenour, Lee

ALIVE IN LA
Little bumpin' / Night rhythms / Boss city / San Juan sunset / Uptown / Waltz for Carmen / Wes bound / Pacific nights / Rio funk / Four on six
CD _______________ GRP 98822
GRP / Jun '97 / New Note/BMG

BEST OF LEE RITENOUR, THE
Sun song / Captain fingers / Caterpillar / Three days of the condor / Fly by night / Little bit of this and a little bit of that / Wild rice / Isn't she lovely
CD _______________ EK 36527
Sony Jazz / Jul '95 / Sony

FRIENDSHIP
Sea dance / Woody creek / Crystal morning / It's a natural thing / Samurai night fever / Life is the song we sing
CD _______________ JMI 20092
JVC / Nov '93 / Direct / New Note/Pinnacle / Vital/SAM

GENTLE THOUGHTS
Captain caribe/Getaway / Chanson / Meiso / Captain fingers / Feel like makin' love / Gentle thoughts
CD _______________ JMI 20072
JVC / Apr '94 / Direct / New Note/Pinnacle / Vital/SAM

LARRY & LEE (Ritenour, Lee & Larry Carlton)
Crosstown kids / Low steppin' / LA Underground / Closed door jam / After the rain / Remembering JP / Fun in the dark / Lota about nothin' / Take that / Up and adam / Reflections of a guitar player
CD _______________ GRP 98172
GRP / Apr '95 / New Note/BMG

STOLEN MOMENTS
Uptown / Stolen moments / 24th Street blues / Haunted heart / Waltz for Carmen / St. Bart's / Blue in green / Sometime ago
CD _______________ GRP 96152
GRP / Apr '90 / New Note/BMG

WEST BOUND
West bound / Boss city / Four on six / Little bumpin' / Waiting in vain / Goin' on to Detroit / New day / Ocean Ave / Road song / West coast blues / NY Times
CD _______________ GRP 97052
GRP / Mar '93 / New Note/BMG

Ritmo Oriental

RITMO ORIENTAL IS CALLING YOU
Nena, asi no se vale / Yo traigo panatela / Que rico bailo yo / Martiza / La ritmo suena a areito / La ritmo te esta llamando / Maria baila el son / El que no sabe, sabe / Advertencia para todos / Si no hay posibilidad me voy
CD _______________ CDORB 034
Globestyle / Jan '89 / Pinnacle

Ritta, Canzoniere Della

MALEVENTO
CD _______________ NT 6734CD
Robi Droli / Apr '95 7 ADA / Direct

Ritter, Julie

MEDICINE SHOW
CD _______________ NAR 122CD
New Alliance / Jul '95 / Plastic Head

Ritter, Tex

HIGH NOON
High noon / Boogie woogie cowboy / Pecos Bill / Dallas darling / Eyes of Texas / Night Herding song / Pony express / High noon / He's a cowboy auctioneer / Billy the kid / Texas rangers / Cattle call / Goodbye my little cherokee / There's a goldstar in her window / In case you change your mind / I was out of my mind / Dark days in Dallas
CD _______________ BCD 15634
Bear Family / Feb '92 / Direct / Rollercoaster / Swift

Ritual Device

HENGE
CD _______________ RED 92
Redemption / Jun '93 / SRD

Rivas, Antonio

LA PERLA DE ARSEGUEL
CD _______________ MWCD 3002
Music & Words / Jun '92 / ADA / Direct

River Band

MUKAREL
CD _______________ MECCACD 2002
Music Mecca / May '97 / Cadillac / Jazz Music / Wellard

River City Brass Band

CONCERT IN THE PARK
El capitan / Daisy bell / Sweet and low / Belle of chicago / Maple leaf rage / Whirlwind polka / Grand dutchess / Semper fidelis / Fireman's polka / On with the motley / William Tell overture / Love's old sweet song / Lassus trombone / Washington post / Lost chord / Believe me if / All those endearing / Young charms / Liberty bell / 12th Street rag / Stars and stripes forever
CD _______________ QMPR 604D
Polyphonic / Mar '94 / Complete/Pinnacle

River City People

SAY SOMETHING GOOD
What's wrong with dreaming / Walking on ice / Under the rainbow / Carry the blame / Say something good / Thirsty / When I was young / No doubt / I'm still waiting / Home and dry / Huskisson St. / Find a reason
CD _______________ CDFA 3295
Fame / May '93 / EMI

Rivera, Hector

AT THE PARTY WITH HECTOR RIVERA
At the party / Shingaling baby / My foolsih heart / Pra voz wilma / I got my eye on you / Got to make up your mind / Playing it cool / Crown my heart / Calypso number 10 / Do it to me / Asia minor / I want a chance for romance / Hueso E Pellenjo / Angue tu mamino querra (aka Lily)
CD _______________ CDBGPD 082
Beat Goes Public / Jan '94 / Pinnacle

Rivera, Willie

EL DIA QE ME DEJES
El amor corre por mi cuenta / Puerto querido / Amiga mia / No podras escaparte / Dejate querer / Todo por quererte / El dia que me dejas / Ella quiere volver
CD _______________ 66058068
RMM / Dec '95 / New Note/Pinnacle

Riverdales

RIVERDALES, THE
CD _______________ LOOKOUT 120
Lookout / Sep '95 / Cargo / Greyhound / Shellshock/Disc

Rivers, Blue

BLUE BEAT IN MY SOUL (Rivers, Blue & The Maroons)
Guns of Navarone / Too much / Mercy mercy mercy / Phoenix city / Witchcraft man / Searching for you baby / I've been pushed around
CD _______________ SEECD 318
See For Miles/C5 / May '91 / Pinnacle

FROM SKA TO REGGAE (Rivers, Blue & The Maroons)
CD _______________ LG 21078
Lagoon / May '93 / Grapevine/PolyGram

Rivers, James

BEST OF NEW ORLEANS RHYTHM & BLUES VOL.3
CD _______________ MG 9009
Mardi Gras / Feb '95 / Jazz Music

Rivers, Johnny

JOHNNY RIVERS IN ACTION/CHANGES
Mountain of love / Promised land / I should have known better / I'm in love again / Rhythm of the rain / He don't love you like I love you / Cupid / Oh pretty woman / It's all over now / What am I doin' here with you / Moody river / Keep-a-knockin' / By the timer I get to Phoenix / Taste of honey / Days of wine and roses / California dreamin' / Do you want to dance / Cast your fate to the wind / Poor side of town / If I were a carpenter / Softly as I leave you / Shadow of your smile / Strangers in the night / Getting ready for tomorrow
CD _______________ BGOCD 355
Beat Goes On / Jul '97 / Pinnacle

LIVE AT THE WHISKY A GO GO/HERE WE A GO GO AGAIN
Memphis / It won't happen with me / Oh lonesome me / Lawdy Miss Clawdy / Whisky A Go Go / Walking the dog / Brown eyed handsome man / You can have her / Multiplication / Medley: La Bamba/Twist and shout / Maybellene / Dang me / Hello Josephine / Hi-heel sneakers / Can't buy me love / I've got a woman / Baby, what you want me to do / Midnight special / Roll over Beethoven / Walk myself on home / Johnny B Goode / Whole lotta shakin' goin' on
CD _______________ BGOCD 241
Beat Goes On / Feb '95 / Pinnacle

ROCKS THE FOLK/MEANWHILE BACK AT THE WHISKY A GO GO
Tom Dooley / Long time man / Michael (row the boat ashore) / Blowin' in the wind / Green green / Where have all the flowers gone / If I had a hammer / Tall oak tree / Catch the wind / 500 miles / Mr. Tambourine man / Jailer bring me water / Seventh son / Greenback dollar / Stop in the name of love / Un-Square dance / Silver threads and golden needles / Land of 1000 dances / Parchment Farm / I'll cry instead / Break up / Work song / Stagger Lee / Suzie Q
CD _______________ BGOCD 299
Beat Goes On / Oct '95 / Pinnacle

Rivers, Red

HILLBILLY HEART
Lorraine / Outside man / Before I go / Hillbilly heart / Hold on to your love / In the end / Twenty five years / What kind of fool / Drifting boy / Natural born lover / Since I left you

CD FIENDCD 795
Demon / May '97 / Pinnacle

Rivers, Sam

PORTRAIT - LIVE
CD FMPCD 82
FMP / May '97 / Cadillac

STREAMS
CD MVCZ 123
MCA / Apr '97 / BMG

Riverside Ceilidh Band

FIRST FOOTING
Gay Gordons / Gay Gordons (encore) / Strip the willow / Strip the willow (encore) / Dashing white sergeant / Dashing white sergeant (encore) / Song / Military two step / Pride of Erin waltz / Pride of Erin waltz (encore) / Eightsome reel / Highland schottische / Highland schottische (encore) / St. Bernard's waltz / St. Bernard's waltz (encore) / Canadian barn dance / Canadian barn dance encore
CD LISMOR 5241
Lismor / Jan '95 / ADA / Direct / Duncans / Lismor

HORSES FOR COURSES
CD LCOM 9035
Lismor / Apr '91 / ADA / Direct / Duncans / Lismor

Riverside Reunion Band

MOSTLY MONK
Bemsha swing / West coast blues / 'Round midnight / Well you needn't / Gemini / Ruby my dear / In walked bud / Four on six / Work song
CD MCD 9216
Milestone / Aug '94 / Cadillac / Complete/ Pinnacle / Jazz Music / Wellard

Rizzetta, Sam

SEVEN VALLEYS - HAMMERED DULCIMER
CD FF 70489
Flying Fish / Jan '90 / ADA / CM / Direct / Roots

RLW

PULLOVER
CD 32-GERANIUM
Table Of The Elements / Dec '96 / Cargo

RNC Chapel Choir

20 FAVOURITE HYMNS
Lead us heavenly father, lead us / All people that on earth do dwell / Immortal love for ever full / When I survey the wondrous cross / Ye holy angels bright / Alleluia, sing to Jesus / Christ is made the sure foundation / There is a green hill far away / Just as I am / Love divine, all love excelling / O God, our help in ages past / Guide me O thou great redeemer / O worship the king / Holy holy holy / Lord enthroned in heavenly splendour / Eternal father strong to save / Praise to the holiest / Now thank we all our God / Dear lord and father of mankind / Day thou gavest Lord is ended
CD CDMVP 826
SCS Music / Apr '94 / Conifer/BMG

RNC Wind Orchestra

EDWARD GREGSON WIND MUSIC (RNC Wind Orchestra/Manchester Boys Choir)
Celebration / Metamorphoses / Missa brevis pacem / Sword and the crown / Festivo
CD DOYCD 043
Doyen / Sep '95 / Conifer/BMG

GALLIMANFRY
Illyrian dances / SPQR / Suite Francaise / Mockbeggar variations / Deo gracias / Full fathom five / Galliman
CD DOYCD 042
Doyen / Sep '95 / Conifer/BMG

Roach, Archie

CHARCOAL LANE/JAMU DREAMING (2CD Set)
CD Set D 30851
Mushroom / Nov '96 / 3mv/Pinnacle

Roach, Max

DEEDS, NOT WORDS
CD OJCCD 304
Original Jazz Classics / Feb '93 / Complete/Pinnacle / Jazz Music / Wellard

DRUMS UNLIMITED
Drum also waltzes / Nommo / Drums unlimited / St. Louis blues / For big Sid / In the red
CD 7567813612
Atlantic / Apr '95 / Warner Music

EASY WINNERS (Roach, Max Double Quartet)
Bird says / Sis / Little booker / Easy winners
CD SNCD 1109
Soul Note / '86 / Cadillac / Harmonia Mundi / Wellard

FREEDOM NOW SUITE
CD CCD 79002
Candid / Feb '97 / Cadillac / Direct / Jazz Music / Koch / Wellard

HISTORIC CONCERTS (2CD Set) (Roach, Max & Cecil Taylor)
CD Set 121100/12
Soul Note / Nov '93 / Cadillac / Harmonia Mundi / Wellard

IN THE LIGHT (Roach, Max Quartet)
CD SNCD 1053
Soul Note / '86 / Cadillac / Harmonia Mundi / Wellard

IT'S CHRISTMAS AGAIN
CD 1211532
Soul Note / May '95 / Cadillac / Harmonia Mundi / Wellard

IT'S TIME
It's time / Another valley / Sunday afternoon / Living room / Profit / Lonesome lover
CD IMP 11852
Impulse Jazz / Mar '96 / New Note/BMG

MAX & DIZZY PARIS 1989 (2CD Set) (Roach, Max & Dizzy Gillespie)
In the beginning / Arrival / Versailles / Place de la concorde / Georges Cinq / Struttin' on the champs / Brother K / South Africa goddamn / Salt peanuts / Word / Fountain blues / Bastille day / Underground / Antilles / 'Round midnight / Messin' around / Metamorphosis / Just dreaming / Nairobi / Allen's Alley / Theme / Smoke that thunders / Oo pa pa da / Interview
CD Set 3964042
A&M / Apr '90 / PolyGram

MAX ROACH AND FRIENDS VOL.1
CD COD 018
Jazz View / Mar '92 / Harmonia Mundi

MAX ROACH AND FRIENDS VOL.2
CD COD 019
Jazz View / Aug '92 / Harmonia Mundi

MAX ROACH TRIO (Roach, Max Trio & The Legendary Hassan)
CD 7567822732
Atlantic / Apr '95 / Warner Music

MOP MOP
Kardouba / Stop motion / Night mountain / Cecillana / Mop mop / Jordu / Sophisticated lady / Who will buy / Love for sale / Long as you're living
CD LEJAZZCD 44
Le Jazz / Jun '95 / Cadillac / Koch

PLUS 4
Ezza thetic / Dr. Free-Zee / Just one of those things / Mr. X / Body and soul / Woody 'n' you / It don't mean a thing if it ain't got that swing / Love letters / Minor trouble
CD 8226732
EmArCy / Jul '90 / PolyGram

SCOTT FREE
Scott free (part 1) / Scott free (part II)
CD SNCD 1103
Soul Note / '86 / Cadillac / Harmonia Mundi / Wellard

SPEAK, BROTHER, SPEAK
CD OJCCD 646
Original Jazz Classics / Nov '95 / Complete/Pinnacle / Jazz Music / Wellard

SURVIVORS
Survivors / Third eye / Billy the kid / Jasme / Drum also waltzes / Sassy Max (self portrait) / Smoke that thunders
CD SNCD 1093
Soul Note / May '85 / Cadillac / Harmonia Mundi / Wellard

Roach, Michael

AIN'T GOT ME NO HOME
CD ST 001CD
Stella / Mar '94 / ADA

Roach, Nancy

DOUBLE SCOTCH
CD CIC 066CD
Clo lar-Chonnachta / Nov '93 / CM

Roachford

GET READY
Get ready / Survival / Funkee chile / Stone city / Wanna be loved / Bayou / Innocent eyes / Hand of fate / Takin' it easy / Higher / Vision of the future / Get ready (reprise)
CD 4681362
Columbia / Apr '95 / Sony

PERMANENT SHADE OF BLUE
Only to be with you / Johnny / Emergency / Lay your love on me / Ride the storm / This generation / I know you don't love me / Gus's blues (Intro) / Do we wanna live together / Cry for me / Guess I must be crazy / Higher love
CD 4758422
Columbia / Apr '94 / Sony

ROACHFORD
Give it up / Family man / Cuddly toy / Find me another love / No way / Kathleen / Beautiful morning / Lying again / Since / Nobody but you
CD 4606302
Columbia / Apr '92 / Sony

Road Runners

JUMP CHILDREN
CD APCD 124
Appaloosa / Jun '96 / ADA / Direct / TKO Magnum

Roadrunners

CATCH US IF YOU CAN
CD SFAX 001
SFAX / Jan '97 / Nervous

Roadside Picnic

LA FAMILLE
La famille / Precious metal / New travelling tune / Quazar / Truth in you / Frozen light / La famille / Promise / Hymn
CD BW 067
B&W / Nov '96 / New Note/Pinnacle / SRD / Vital/SAM

Rob Base

BREAK OF DAWN (Rob Base & DJ E-Z Rock)
CD 60802CLU
Edel / Jul '95 / Pinnacle

Robb, Terry

ACOUSTIC BLUES TRIO
CD BCD 00192
Burnside / May '96 / Koch

Robbins, Marty

BEST OF MARTY ROBBINS, THE (2CD Set)
Story of my life / Unchained melody / El Paso / Hawaiian wedding song / Singin' the blues / Big iron / Love me tender / White sports coat (and a pink carnation) / Devil woman / Can't help falling in love / Ruby Ann / Riders in the sky / 18 yellow roses / Am I that easy to forget / Streets of Loredo / Summertime / I did what I did for Maria / By the time I get to Phoenix / La Paloma / You gave me a mountain
CD Set 4851282
Columbia / Aug '96 / Sony

CONCERT COLLECTION
El Paso / Big iron on his hip / Jambalaya / Foggy mountain breakdown / Touch me with magic / Chime bells / Among my souvenirs / Jenny / Devil woman / Big boss man / That's alright Mama / Love me / Don't worry 'bout me / Ribbon of darkness / My woman my woman my wife / White sport coat and a pink carnation
CD PLATCD 162
Platinum / Mar '96 / Prism

COUNTRY 1951-1958 (5CD Set)
Tomorrow you'll be gone / I wish somebody else loves me / Love me or leave me alone / Cryin' 'cause I love you / I'll go on alone / Pretty words / You're breaking my heart / I can get along / I couldn't keep from crying / Just in time / Crazy little heart / After you leave / Lorelei / Castle in the sky / Your hearts turn to break / Why keep wishing / Half way chance with you / Sing me something sentimental / At the end of a long lonely day / Blessed Jesus, Should I fall don't let me lay / Kneel and let the Lord take your load / Don't make me ashamed / It's a long, long ride / It looks like I'm just in your way / I'm happy 'cause you're hurtin' / My isle of golden dreams / Have thine own way / God understands / Aloha oe / What made you change your mind / Way of a hopeless love / Pain and misery / Juarez / I'm too big to cry / Call me up / It's a pity what money can do / Time goes by / This broken heart of mine / I'll love you 'til the day I die / Don't let me hang around / Pray for me mother of mine / Daddy loves you / That's alright Mama / Gossip / Maybellene / Pretty mama / Mean mama blues / Long gone lonesome blues / I can't quit (I've gone too far) / Singin' the blues / Tennessee toddy / Baby I need you / Long tall Sally / Mr. Teardrop / Respectfully Miss Brooks / You don't owe me a thing / I'll know your gone / How long will it be / Where d'ya go / Most of the time / Same two lips / Your heart of blue is showing through / Knee deep in the blues / Little rosewood casket / Letter edged in black / Twenty one years / Convict and the rose / Bus stop song / Dream the miner's child / Little box of pine in the 7:29 / Wreck of number nine / Sad lover / Little shirt my mother made for me / My mother was a lady / When it's lamplighting time in the valley / Wreck of the 12:56 / It's too late now / I never let you cross my mind / I'll step aside / Bouquet of roses / I'm so lonesome I could cry / Lovesick blues / Moanin' the blues / Rose of ol' Pawnee / I hang my head and cry / Have I told you lately that I love you / All the world is lonely now / You only want me when you're lonely / Crying steel guitar waltz / Beautiful Ohio / Now is the hour / Down where the tradewinds blow / Sweet leilani / Beyond the reef / Constancy / Don't sing aloha when I go / Song of the Islands / Moonland / Island echoes / Faded petal from a beautiful bouquet / When I turned and slowly walked away / Jody / House with everything but love / Nothing but sweet lies / Baby I need you / Kaw-liga / Paper / Face / Many tears ago / Address unknown / Waltz of the wind / Hands you're holding now / Wedding bells / Shackles and chains / Oh how I miss you / Footprints in the snow / It's driving me crazy
CD Set BCD 15570
Bear Family / Aug '91 / Direct / Rollercoaster / Swift

COUNTRY 1960-1966 (5CD Set)
Devil woman / It's your world / Lonely too long / Over high mountain / Fly, buterfly, fly / Because it's wrong / Like all other times / Little Robin / It kinda reminds me / Address unkown / Yesterday's roses / Each night at nine / People's valley / No one will ever know / I'm not ready yet / I feel another heartbeat coming on / Ribbin of darkness / Robing gambler / Foggy foggy river / Lolene / Just before the battle Mother / Beautiful dreamer / Long, long ago / Melba from Melbourne / Change that dial / Only a picture stops time / Southern Dixie flyer / Everybody's darling plus mine / She means nothing to me now / Making excuses / Rainbow / I've lived a lifetime in a day / You won't have her long / Things I don't know / Urgently needed / I'll have to make some changes / Nine tenth of the law / Sorting memories / Hello heartache / One window, four walls / Working my way through a heartache / Would you take me back again / Do me a favor / Sixteen weeks / Seconds to remember / Another lost weekend / Last night about this time / This song / Hello baby / Don't worry / Time and a place for everything / Sixtytwo's most promising fool / Too far gone / April fool's day / Rich man, rich man / I've got a woman's love / Never look back / I'm beginning to forget you / Progressive love / Hands your holding now / Ain't life a crying shame / Kinda halfway feel / Little rich girl / Will the circle be unbroken / Little spot in heaven / Evening prayer / With his hands on my shoulder / There's power in the blood / When the roll is called up yonder / Where should I go (but to the lord) / Almost persuaded / What God has done / You gotta climb / Great speckled bird / Who at my door is standing / Have thine own way, Lord / Cigarettes and coffe blues / No tears milady / Wine flowed freely / Shoe goes on the other foot tonight / Not so long ago / I hope you learn a lot / Begging to you / In the ashes of an old love affair / Love's a hurtin game / Worried / Time can't make me forget / Baby talk to me / Pieces of your heart / It kinda reminds me of my own native land / Private Wilson White / Ain't it right / You gave me a mountain / To be in love with her / Matilda / It finally happend / They'll never take her love from me
CD Set BCD 15655
Bear Family / Nov '95 / Direct / Rollercoaster / Swift

DRIFTER, THE
CD 379342
Koch International / Jun '97 / Koch

ESSENTIAL MARTY ROBBINS, THE (2CD Set)
Tomorrow you'll be gone / I'll go on alone / Maybellene / Tennessee Toddy / I can't quit / Singin' the blues / Knee deep in the blues / Mister Teardrop / Story of my life / White sport coat (and a pink carnation) / She was only seventeen (He was one year more) / Just married / Ain't I the lucky one / Kaw-liga / Hanging tree / El Paso / Big iron / Song of the bandit / Cool water / Little sentimental / September in the rain / All the way / Unchained melody / Don't worry / Devil woman / Ruby Ann / Smokin' cigarettes and drinkin' coffee blues / I'm gonna be a cowboy / (Ghost) Riders in the sky / San Angelo / Man walks among us / Beautiful dreamer / Beyond the reef / Hawaiian wedding song / Yours (Quiereme mucho) / Tonight Carmen / Ribbon of darkness / Feleene (from El Paso) / Hello heartache / Begging to you / I walk alone / You gave me a mountain / My woman, my woman, my wife / Among my souvenirs / Return to me / Some memories just won't die / El Paso city
CD Set 4689092
Columbia / Jun '96 / Sony

GUNFIGHTER BALLADS AND TRAIL SONGS/MORE GUNFIGHTER BALLADS
Big iron / Cool water / Billy the kids / Hundred and sixty acres / They're hanging me tonight / Strawberry roan / El paso / In the valley / Master's calll / Running gun / Little green valley / Utah Carol / San Angelo / Prairie fire / Streets of Laredo / Song of the bandit / I've got no use for the woman / Five brothers / Little Joe the wrangler / Ride cowboy ride / This peaceful sod / She was young and she was pretty / My love
CD 4840332
Columbia / Jun '96 / Sony

HAWAII'S CALLING ME
Lovely Hula hands / Sea and me / Night I came to shore / Echo island / Kuu ipo Lani (my sweetheart Lani) / Beyond the reef / Hawaiian wedding song / Drowsy waters / Hawaiian bells / My wonderful one / Blue sand / Hawaii's calling me / Ku lu a (love song of kalua) / Drowsy waters (Wailana) / Song of the Islands / Don't sing aloha when

i go / Crying steel guitar waltz / My isle of golden dreams / Now is the hours (Maori Farewell song) / Sweet leilani / Down where the tradewinds blow / Aloha oe / Island echoes / Moonland / Constancy
CD _______________ BCD 15568
Bear Family / May '91 / Direct / Rollercoaster / Swift

MARTY AFTER MIDNIGHT
I'm in the mood for love / Misty / Looking back / September in the rain / Don't throw me away / Pennies from Heaven / Summertime / It had to be you / All the way / I'm having a ball / If I could cry / On the sunny side of the street
CD _______________ 379332
Koch International / Jun '97 / Koch

MUSICAL JOURNEY TO THE CARIBBEAN AND MEXICO
Girl from Spanish Town / Kingston girl / Sweet bird of paradise / Jamaica farewell / Calypso girl / Back to Montego Bay / Girl from Spanish Town / Kingston girl / Woman gets her way / Mango song / Calypso vacation / Blue sea / Bahama Mama / Tahitian boy / Native girl / Girl from Spanish Town / Yours / You belong to my heart / La Borachita / La paloma / Quiereme me mucho / Adios mariquita Llinda / Amor / Camellia
CD _______________ BCD 15571
Bear Family / May '91 / Direct / Rollercoaster / Swift

ROCK 'N' ROLL 'N' ROBBINS
That's all right / Long tall Sally / Long gone lonesome blues / Tennessee Toddy / Respectfully Miss Brooks / Mean Mama blues / Pretty Mama / Baby's gone / Teenager's Dad / Grown up tears / Mabelline / Ruby Ann
CD _______________ 379322
Koch / Jun '97 / Koch

ROCKIN' ROLLIN' ROBBINS VOL.1
That's alright Mama / Maybellene / Pretty mama / Mean mama blues / Tenessee Toddy / Singin' the blues / I can't quit (I've gone too far) / Long tall sally / Mr. Teardrop / Respectfully Miss Brooks / You don't owe me a thing / Baby I need you / Pain and misery / Footprints in the snow / It's driving me crazy / It's a long, long ride / Call me up (and I'll come calling on you)
CD _______________ BCD 15566
Bear Family / May '91 / Direct / Rollercoaster / Swift

ROCKIN' ROLLIN' ROBBINS VOL.2
White sports coat and a pink carnation / Grown up tears / Please don't blame me / Teenage dream / Story of my life / Once a week date / Just married / Stairway of love / She was only seventeen / Sittin' in a tree house / Ain't I the lucky one / Last time I saw my heart / Hanging tree / Blues country style / Jeannie and Johnnie / Foolish decision
CD _______________ BCD 15567
Bear Family / May '91 / Direct / Rollercoaster / Swift

ROCKIN' ROLLIN' ROBBINS VOL.3
Ruby Ann (chart version) / Sometimes I'm tempted / No signs of loneliness here / While you're dancing / Teenager's Dad / Ruby Ann / Cap and gown (fast) / Last night about this time / I hope you learn a lot / Love can't wait / Cigarettes and coffee / Little rich girl / Hello baby (goodbye baby) / Baby's gone / Cap and gown (slow) / Whole lot easier / She was young and she was pretty / Cap and gown (New york recording) / Sweet cora / Ain't live a cryin' shame / Silence and tears / You've been so busy baby
CD _______________ BCD 15569
Bear Family / Nov '93 / Direct / Rollercoaster / Swift

UNDER WESTERN SKIES (4CD Set)
El Paso / Cool water / In the valley / Running gun / Big iron / Master's call / Little green valley / Hundred and sixty acres / Billy the kid / Strawberry roan / They're hanging me tonight / Utah Carol / Saddle tramp / She was young and she was pretty / Streets of Laredo / Little Joe / Wrangler / I've got no use for the woman / Billy Venero / This peaceful sod / Five brothers / San Angelo / Ballad of the alamo (thirteen days of glory) / Hanging tree / Jimmy Martinez / Ghost train / Song of the bandit / Wind / Prairie fire / My love / Ride cowboy ride / Red river valley / Bend in the river / When the work's all done this fall / Abilene rose / Dusty winds / Old red / Doggone cowboy / Small man / Red hill of Utah / Tall handsome stranger / Fastest gun around / Man walks among us / Johnny Fedavo / Cowboy in the continental suit / I'm gonna be a cowboy / Cry stampede / Oh, Virginia / Meet me tonight in Loredo / Take me to the prairie / Wind goes / An old pal / Real pal / Feleena (from El Paso) / Never tie me down / Lonley old bunkhouse / Night time on the desert / Cottonwood tree / Mister shorty / When it's lamplighting time in the valley / Is there anything else I can say / Tonight Carmen / Waiting in Reno / Mission in Guadalajaro / Love's gone away / Bound for Old Mexico / Chaple bell chime / Don't go away Senor / In the valley of the Rio Grand / (Girl with) Gardenias in her hair / Spanish lullaby / That silver haired daddy of mine / Chant of the wanderer / (Ghost) Riders in the sky / South of the border (Down Mexico way) / Sundown (ballad of Bill Thaxton) / Queen of the big rodeo / Ava Maria Morales / Outlaws / El Paso city / I'm kin to the wind / Trail dreamin' / She's just a drifter / Way out there / Tumbling tumbleweeds / Pride and the badge / All around cowboy / Restless cattle / Dreamer / Lonely old bunkhouse / Shotgun rider
CD Set _______________ BCD 15646
Bear Family / Nov '95 / Direct / Rollercoaster / Swift

Robbins, Richard

VIA CRUCIS
CD _______________ 4540552
Point Music / Jun '96 / PolyGram

Robert & Johnny

WE BELONG TOGETHER
We belong together / Broken hearted man / I don't stand a ghost of a chance with you / Baby come home / You're mine / Eternity with you / Dream girl / Oh my love / Million dollar bills / I got you / Give me the key to your heart / Wear this ring / Gosh oh gee / Don't do it / I believe in you / God knows / Bad Dan / Indian marriage / Your kisses / Baby baby / I hear my heartbeat / Togetherness / I'm truly truly yours / Please me please / Try me pretty baby / Baby girl of mine / Train to paradise
CD _______________ CDCHD 384
Ace / Apr '93 / Pinnacle

Robert, George

LIVE AT THE CHORUS
Jeanine / Dolphin dance / Remembering Henri / Voyage / Village / Upper Manhattan Medical Group UMMG / Sandu
CD _______________ TCB 95102
TCB / Sep '95 / New Note/Pinnacle

TRIBUTE (Robert, George Quintet)
CD _______________ JFCD 004
Jazz Focus / Dec '94 / Cadillac

Robert, Jocelyn

FOLIE/CULTURE
CD _______________ RERJORCD
ReR/Recommended / Oct '96 / ReR Megacorp / RTM/Disc

Robert, Yves

TOUT COURT
CD _______________ ZZ 84103
Deux Z / Jan '94 / Cadillac / Harmonia Mundi

Roberts, Al Jr.

HELLO, IT'S REALLY ME (The Al Roberts Jr. Memorial Album)
Telephone rock / Les Paul / Spider in the bath / Too n-n-nervous to rock / You fell asleep on our wedding night / There oughta be a law / Electric chair rock 'n' roll / Too wrecked to rock / I'll be your hamburger king / Haunted house rock / Fatter by the hour / My gran 'pappy don' smoke no grass / Motorway food / 2% of 90% of 1% / Jailbait / Someone's torn out the very last page / Walkin' the cat / Another spot / She put the hurt on me / Don't give up your day job / Mother In Law / UFO rock and roll / Mama threw out my rock 'n' roll shoes / Little Lucy / He ate too many burgers / Rockabilly guitar man
CD _______________ NEMCD 928
Sequel / May '97 / BMG

Roberts, Hank

BIRDS OF PREY
Comin' home / Seven generations / Scream / Hear me / Pretty boy Tom / Angels and mud / Touch
CD _______________ 8344372
jMT / May '90 / PolyGram

BLACK PASTELS
Black pastels / Jamil / Mountain speaks / Rain village / Choqueno / This quietness / Granpappy's barn dance / Death dance / Scarecrow shakedown / Lucky's lament
CD _______________ 8344162
jMT / Feb '94 / PolyGram

LITTLE MOTOR PEOPLE
Saturday Sunday / Day dram dance/Beer hall commentary/On the job/Dark house / Sunday / Somewhere over the rainbow / Only minutes left / My favourite things / Little motor people / Donna Lee / Black as a sunny day / Autumn leaves / 30's picnic
CD _______________ 5140052
jMT / Jan '93 / PolyGram

Roberts, Howard

REAL HOWARD ROBERTS, THE
Dolphin dance / Darn that dream / Lady wants to know / Gone with the wind / Serenata / Angel eyes / All blues
CD _______________ CCD 4053
Concord Jazz / Apr '94 / New Note/ Pinnacle

Roberts, Kenny

JUMPIN' AND YODELIN'
I never see Maggie alone / Broken teenage heart / Newsboy / I'm looking for the bully of the town / Arizona yodeler / Wedding bells / Boogie woogie yodel song / One way ticket / I believe I'm entitled to you / I miss my swiss / I'd like to kiss Susie again / Mighty pretty waltz / Yodel polka / Ding dong bells are ringing agian / When I'd yoo hoo in the valley / Choo choo ch' boogie / She taught me how to yodel / FOB Tennessee / Billy and Nanny goat / Same ol' tune / Hillbilly style / Cry baby blues / River of tears / I've got the blues / Choc'late ice cream cone / Honky tonk sweetheart / Hillbilly fever / Just a yodel for me / Dream little cowboy / I wouldn't hurt you for the world / I finally got Maggie alone
CD _______________ BCD 15908
Bear Family / Feb '96 / Direct / Rollercoaster / Swift

Roberts, Marcus

AS SERENITY APPROACHES
Cherokee / Slippin' and slidin' / Blues in the evening time / First come, first serve / Nigh eve / As serenity approaches / Jitterbug waltz / St. Louis blues / I remember you / Preach, Reverend preach / Tint of blue / When the morning comes / Where or when / King Porter stomp / Creole blues / Broadway / Angel
CD _______________ PD 90624
Novus / Apr '92 / BMG

GERSHWIN FOR LOVERS
Foggy day / Man I love / Our love is here to stay / Summertime / Someone to watch over me / It ain't necessarily so / Nice work if you cna get it / They can't take that away from me / How long has this been going on / But not for me
CD _______________ 4777522
Columbia / Oct '94 / Sony

IF I COULD BE WITH YOU
Just a closer walk with thee / Maple leaf rag / Arkansas blues / Carolina shout / Embraceable you / Moonlight in Vermont / Keep off the grass / Rippling waters / Sweet repose / Country blues / If I could be with you one hour tonight / Let's call this / Every time we say goodbye / What is this thing called love / Mood indigo / Preach / Reverend preach / Snowy morning blues / Fascination / In a southern sense
CD _______________ 01241631492
Novus / Apr '93 / BMG

PORTRAITS IN BLUE (Roberts, Marcus & Orchestra Of St. Luke's/Robert Sadin)
Rhapsody in blue / I got rhythm / Yamekraw
CD _______________ SK 68488
Sony Classical / Aug '96 / Sony

TIME AND CIRCUMSTANCE
Soul mates / Exploration / Reflecting mirrors / Imperfect balance / Two rocks by the shore / Harvest time / Alone / Time and circumstance / Memories of one / Eternal dialogue / In retrospect / Optimism / When fire meets moonlight / Renewed vision
CD _______________ 4844512
Sony Jazz / Jul '96 / Sony

Roberts, Paul Dudley

FROM RAGS TO RICHES
CD _______________ DLD 1034
Dance & Listen / May '93 / Savoy / Target/BMG

I GOT RHYTHM
CD _______________ DLD 1035
Dance & Listen / Mar '93 / Savoy / Target/ BMG

Roberts, Roy

EVERY SHADE OF BLUE
CD _______________ KS 042CD
Kingsnake / Jul '97 / Hot Shot

Robertson, Herb

CERTIFIED
Friendly fire / Cosmic child / Don't be afraid we're not like the others / Eastawesta / Seeking seeds in the blues bazaar / Condensed version / Ghostsongs
CD _______________ 8491502
jMT / Oct '91 / PolyGram

Robertson, Jeannie

JEANNIE ROBERTSON
Bonnie wee lassie who never said no / What a voice / My plaidie's awa' / Gypsy laddie / When I was no' but sweet sixteen / MacCrimmon's lament / Roy's wife of Aldivalloch / Lord Lovat
CD _______________ OSS 92CD
Ossian / Aug '94 / ADA / CM / Direct / Highlander

Robertson, Justin

JOURNEYS BY DJ VOL.11 (2CD Set) (Various Artists)
CD Set _______________ JDJCD 11
JDJ / Jul '96 / 3mv/Pinnacle / SRD

Robertson, Kim

TREASURES OF THE CELTIC HARP
CD _______________ DMCD 114
Dara / Feb '96 / ADA / CM / Direct / Else / Grapevine/PolyGram

WOOD, FIRE AND GOLD
CD _______________ DM 119CD
Dargason Music / Aug '96 / ADA

Robertson, Lonnie

LONNIE'S BREAKDOWN
Lonnie's breakdown / Ozark mountain waltz / Mountain reel / Old Parnell / Untitled reel in B flat / Old time breakdown in A / Lady on a steamboat / Fiddler's blues / Lonnie's hornpipe / Big sandy river / Jump fingers / Saddle old Kate / Rock all the babies to sleep / Speed the plough / Caney Mountain hornpipe / Hazy hills waltz / Taney County breakdown / Lantern in the ditch / Lonesome Polly Ann / Kaiser waltz / Old Joe / Johnny, bring the jug around the hill / Cincinnati hornpipe / Natural bridge blues / Untitled reel in D / Wink the other eye / Malindy / Unnamed B flat waltz / Rag in C / Rosebud reel / A and E rag / Bluebird waltz / Arkansas stomp / Katy Hill/Darky's dream/Brown leaf rag
CD _______________ ROUCD 0375
Rounder / Nov '96 / ADA / CM / Direct

Robertson, Robbie

NATIVE AMERICANS
Coyote dance / Mahk tchi (Heart of the people) / Ghost dance / Vanishing breed / It's a good day to die / Golden feather / Akua Tutu / Words of fire, deeds of blood / Cherokee morning song / Skinwalker / Ancestor song / Twisted hair
CD _______________ CDEST 2238
EMI / Oct '94 / EMI

ROBBIE ROBERTSON
Fallen angel / Showdown at big sky / Broken arrow / Sweet fire of love / American roulette / Somewhere down the crazy river / Hell's half acre / Sonny got caught in the moonlight / Testimony
CD _______________ GFLD 19294
Geffen / Oct '95 / BMG

STORYVILLE
CD _______________ GFLD 19295
Geffen / Oct '95 / BMG

Robeson, Paul

BIG FELLA
Lazybones / Scarecrow / Fat li'l feller with his Mammy's eyes / Wagon wheels / Deep river / My curly headed baby / Carry me back to green pastures / Old folks at home (Swanee river) / High water / My heart is where the mohawk flows tonight / So early in the morning / Carry me back to old Virginny / Goodnight ladies / Way down South in Dixie / Poor old Joe / Oh Susanna / My old Kentucky home / River stay 'way from my door / Hail the crown / Love song / Killing song / Black emperor / I don't know what's wrong / Lazin' / You didn't oughta do such things / Ecantadora Maria / David of the white rock / Thora / Love at my heart / Ebenezer / King Joe / Little black boy / Little piccaninny's gone to sleep / When it's sleepy time down South
CD _______________ CDHD 245
Happy Days / Feb '97 / Conifer/BMG

GLORIOUS VOICE OF PAUL ROBESON, THE
Lonesome road / River stay 'way from my door / Mighty like a rose / My curly headed baby / Ol' man river / Round the bend of the road / Lazybones / Waterboy / Song of freedom / Sleepy river: *Robeson, Paul & Elisabeth Welch* / Carry me back to green pastures / Canoe song / I still suits me: *Robeson, Paul & Elisabeth Welch* / Lonely road / Passing by / My way / Summertime / It ain't necessarily so / All through the night / Just a wearyin' for you / Perfect day / Deep river
CD _______________ CZ 310
EMI / May '90 / EMI

GREAT VOICES OF THE CENTURY VOL.1, THE
Love song / Mighty like a rose / I'm goin' to tell God all o' my troubles: *Robeson, Paul & Lawrence Brown* / Song of freedom / St. Louis blues / Honey (dat's all) / Killing song / Oh no John: *Robeson, Paul & Lawrence Brown* / Carry me back to green pastures / Trees / Sylvia / At dawning / Songs my Mother taught me / Down lovers' lane / Cobbler's song / Swing low, sweet chariot / That's why darkies where born / Joshua fit de battle of Jericho: *Robeson, Paul & Lawrence Brown* / Black emperor / Ol' man river
CD _______________ CDMOIR 415
Memoir / Nov '94 / Jazz Music / Target/ BMG

GREAT VOICES OF THE CENTURY VOL.2, THE
Round the bend of the road / Take me away from the river / By and by / Were you there / Song of the fatherland / Mammy's little kinky headed boy / Wagon wheels / Canoe song / Just a wearyin' for you / Ballad for

Americans / Deep river / Just dreaming / Little man you've had a busy day / Old ark's a' movering / Ezekiel saw the wheel / Solitude / Mood indigo / Eriskay love lilt / Song of the Volga boatmen / Lonely road / Scarecrow / So shy
CD CDMOIR 426
Memoir / Nov '94 / Jazz Music / Target/ BMG

GREEN PASTURES
St. Louis blues / Rockin' chair / Mary had a baby, yes Lord / Love song / All God's chillun got wings / Banjo song / Bear the burden / When it's sleepy time down South / Killing song / High water / Lazybones / Carry me back to green pastures / Congo lullaby / Shortnin' bread / Snowball / Fat li'l feller with his mammy's eyes / Canoe song / River stay 'way from my door
CD CDAJA 5047
Living Era / Oct '88 / Select

INIMITABLE PAUL ROBESON, THE
Carry me back to green pastures / Lonesome road / Hush-a-bye-lullaby / All through the night / Little man you've had a busy day / Wagon wheels / I ain't lazy, I'm just dreaming / Shenandoah / Song of the Volga boatmen / Roll away clouds / So shy / Dear old Southland / Blue prelude / Round the bend of the road / King Joe - Part one / King Joe - Part two / Rockin' chair / Solitude / Nothin' / Got something in my soul / St. Louis blues / Perfect day / Ma curly-headed baby / All God's chillun got wings / Lazybones
CD PAR 2065
Parade / Jul '96 / Disc

LONESOME ROAD, A
Ol' man river / My curly headed baby / Waterboy / I'm goin' to tell God all o' my troubles / Oh didn't it rain / There's no hiding place / Poor old Joe / Scandalise my name / Ezekiel saw de wheel / Sinner please doan' let this harves' pass / Just keepin' on / My Lindy Lou / Steal away / Mighty like a rose / Deep river / Hear the lambs a-cryin' / Git on board, li'l chilun / Old folks at home (Swanee river) / Witness / Oh rock me Julie / Li'l gal / I got a home in that rock / Lonesome road / Little Pal
CD CDAJA 5027
Living Era / Oct '88 / Select

OL' MAN RIVER
Ol' man river / My old Kentucky home / Lazybones / My Lindy Lou / Poor old Joe / Old folks at home (Swanee river) / Just keepin' on / Little pal / Water boy / Joshua fit de battle of Jericho / Swing low, sweet chariot / Shenandoah / Wagon wheels / Got the South in my soul / St. Louis blues / Rockin' chair / River stay 'way from my door / Canoe song / Congo lullaby / Love song
CD RMB 75024
Remember / Nov '93 / Total/BMG

OL' MAN RIVER
CD 8418582
Music Memoria / Sep '96 / ADA / Discovery

OL' MAN RIVER
Love song / St. Louis blues / All God's chillun got wings / Rockin' chair / Mary had a baby, yes Lord / Killing song / Lazybones / Carry me back to green pastures / High water / Snowball / When it's sleepy time down South / Fat li'l feller with his Mammy's eyes / Congo lullaby / Shortnin' bread / Canoe song / Banjo song / River stay 'way from my door / Ol' man river
CD CD 12519
Music Of The World / Feb '95 / ADA / Target/BMG

PAUL ROBESON
Lazybones / It ain't necessarily so / Sleepy river / My way / I don't know what's wrong / Song of the Volga boatmen / Canoe song / Roll up sailorman / That's why darkies were born / Swing low, Sweet chariot / Mammy's little kinky headed boy / Roll away clouds / Just a wearyin' for you / Deep river / Sea fever / Absent / Mighty like a rose / On ma journey / Just keepin' on / Woman is a sometime thing / You didn't oughta do such things / Lazin' / Ol' man river
CD PASTCD 7009
Flapper / May '93 / Pinnacle

PAUL ROBESON
Ol' man river / Woman is a sometime thing / Summertime / Song of freedom / Black emperor / Fat li'l feller wid his mammy's eyes / Ma Lindy Lou / Love song / At dawning / Sleepy river / Lonely road / Mighty like a rose / Ma curley-headed baby / Canoe song / Honey / It ain't necessarily so / It takes a long pull to get there / All through the night / Cobbler's song / My way / No John no / St. Louis blues / Passing by / Eriskay love / Swing low sweet chariot
CD CDMFP 6352
Music For Pleasure / Jun '97 / EMI

PAUL ROBESON VOL.1
Sonny boy / It takes a long pull to get there / Summertime / Woman is a sometime thing / It ain't necessarily so / Congo lullaby / Canoe song / Mood indigo / Solitude / At dawning / All through the night / Lazybones / St. Louis blues / Old folks at home (Swanee River) / My old Kentucky home / My curly headed baby / Mighty like a rose / Waterboy / Deep river / Hammer song: *Robeson, Paul & Lawrence Brown* / Li'l David: *Robeson, Paul & Lawrence Brown* / Swing low, sweet chariot / Just a wearyin' for you / Ol' man river
CD GEMMCD 9356
Pearl / '89 / Harmonia Mundi

PAUL ROBESON VOL.2
Down in lovers' lane / Swing along / Bear the burden / All God's chillun got wings / Joshua fit de battle of Jericho / Old ark's a' movering / Ezekiel saw de wheel / Scandalise my name / Sinner please doan' let this harves' pass / Work all de summer / Didn't my Lord deliver Daniel / Dere's a man goin' roun' takin' names / Shenandoah / Little pal / Lonesome Road / Roll away clouds / Ho Ho / Climbing up / Song of freedom / Sleepy river / Trees / No John no / Song of the Volga boatmen / There is a green hill / Nearer, my God to thee / Fat li'l feller with his mammy's eyes / Mama's little baby love
CD GEMMCD 9382
Pearl / '90 / Harmonia Mundi

SONGS FOR FREE MEN
CD GEMMCD 9264
Pearl / Jan '97 / Harmonia Mundi

Robi Rob's Clubworld

ROBI ROB'S CLUBWORLD
Robi Rob's boriqua anthem / Shake that body / Love and happiness / Get funky / Make that money / Robi Rob's Clubworld / I live / Reach / Mi gente latina / Goodbye
CD 4854802
Columbia / Oct '96 / Sony

Robic, Ivo

MIT SIE BZEHN FANGT DAS LEBEN ERST AN
Morgen / Mit siebzehn fangt das leben erst an / Rot ist der Wein / Muli song / Rhondaly / Ay ay ay Paloma / Endlich / Auf der sonnenseite der welt / So allein / In einer bar in buffalo / Liebeleer / Du bist niemand, wenn niemand dich lieb hat / Traume vom Gluck / Schau dich night um / Ich denk nuran's wiedersehn / Wenn ich in deine augen schau / Tiefes blaues meer / Glaub daran (das leben ist schon) / Jezebel / Lass dein little girl nie weinen / Geh zu ihm / Ein ganzes leben lang / Fremde in der nacht / Mond guter freund / Happy muleteer / So alone / Endless / On the sunny side of the world
CD BCD 15671
Bear Family / Jun '92 / Direct / Rollercoaster / Swift

Robichaud Brothers

SLIPPERY STICK, THE
Grand Lake reel/Silver wedding reel / Coal branch reel/Emile Arsenault's / Moccasin shuffle/Brae reel / Fred's tuna/Money musk / Bunkhouse jig / Cousin Bill/Fiddlin' Phil / Island ferry/Herring reel / Herring brook/The High level hornpipe / Father Legere's marches / Constitution breakdown/Dragger's reel / Atlantic polkas / Tullybardine/La Disputeuse / March from my mother / Dancing hornpipe / Slippery stick / Leprechaun jig / Miramichi fire / Bouctouche reel/ Saint Anne's reel / Watch City hornpipe / Traditional New Brunswick jig / Abegweit breakdown
CD ROUCD 7016
Rounder / Oct '96 / ADA / CM / Direct

Robicheaux, Coco

SPIRITLAND
CD 8413862
Sky Ranch / Sep '96 / Discovery

Robillard, Duke

AFTER HOURS SWING SESSION
Trouble with me is you / Shivers / I can't believe that you're in love with me / Sweet Georgia Brown / Twist top / I'll never be the same / Tiny's tempo / Albi ain't here
CD NETCD 0033
Network / May '92 / Direct / Greensleeves / SRD

DANGEROUS PLACE
Had to be your man / Going straight / Dangerous place / Don't get me shook up / Take my word for it / Can't remember to forget / Duke's advice / Nothing like you (where I come from) / I may be ugly (but I sure know how to cook) / All over but the paying / No time / Black negligee
CD VPBCD 41
Pointblank / May '97 / EMI

DUKE'S BLUES (Robillard, Duke Band)
Midnight cannon ball / Glamour girl / I still love you baby / Texas hop / Don't leave me baby / Tell me why / Something to remember you by / Love slipped in / Information blues / Don't treat me like that / Never let you go / Gee I wish / My heart is cryin' / Red's riff / Dyin' flu
CD VPBCD 29
Pointblank / Jan '96 / EMI

ROCKIN' BLUES (Robillard, Duke & The Pleasure Kings)
CD ROUCD 11548
Rounder / '88 / ADA / CM / Direct

SWING
Cadillac Slim / Jumpin' blues / Exactly like you / Glide on / Zot / I'll always be in love with you / Shuffin' with some barbeque / Durn tottin' / You'd better change your ways / Jim jam
CD ROUCD 3103
Rounder / Jun '96 / ADA / CM / Direct

TEMPTATION
Rule the world / (You got my love) Sewed up / Live to give / Change is on / Life's funny / When my love comes down / This dream (still coming true) / Temptation / Never been satisfied / Born to love you / What's wrong
CD VPBCD 20
Virgin / Sep '94 / EMI

TURN IT AROUND (Robillard, Duke Band & Susan Forrest)
Down by the delta / Passionate kiss / Don't look at my girl like that / Just a human / Turn it around / Shoulda coulda woulda / High cost of loving / Sweets for my sweet / Tell me how / I think you know
CD ROUCD 3116
Rounder / Aug '96 / ADA / CM / Direct

YOU GOT ME (Robillard, Duke & Guests)
CD ROUCD 3100
Rounder / '88 / ADA / CM / Direct

Robin, Roger

REFLECTIONS
CD LOVCD 005
Love Injection / Apr '95 / Jet Star

UNDILUTED
CD LOVCD 004
Spider Ranks / Nov '93 / Jet Star

Robin, Ruggero

BIG ONE
CD CDSGP 0189
Prestige / Mar '96 / Else / Total/BMG

Robin S

FROM NOW ON
It must be love / Been so long / You know how to love me / Midnight / There is a need / Givin' u all that I've got / Shine on me / It's not enough / 24 hour love / All I do / We're in this together / It must be love / It must be love
CD 7567927162
Big Beat/Atlantic / Jun '97 / Warner Music

SHOW ME LOVE
Show me love / Luv 4 luv / I'm gonna love you right (tonight) / If we could just be friends / What I do best / My kind of man / I want to thank you / Once in a lifetime love / Back it up / Back and forth / Brighter day / Who's gonna raise the child
CD CHAMCD 1028
Champion / Mar '97 / 3mv/BMG

Robin, Thierry

GITANS
CD Y 225035CD
Silex / Mar '94 / ADA / Harmonia Mundi

LE REGARD NU
CD Y 225059
Silex / May '96 / ADA / Harmonia Mundi

Robine, Marc

LES TEMPS DES CERISES
CD 983462
EPM / Jul '95 / ADA / Discovery

Robinson, Carson

HOME SWEET HOME ON THE PRAIRIE (25 Cowboy Classics)
Clementine / Annie Laurie / Camptown races / Ain't ya comin' out tonight / Happy-go-lucky / Goin' to have a big time tonight / Little green valley / Leave the purty girls alone / When your hair has turned to silver / Missouri valley / Strawberry roan / In the Cumberland mountains / Ev'rybody's goin' but me / Oh Susannah / Tree top serenade / I was born in old Wyoming / Smoky mountain Bill / Swanee kitchen door / Sweet Virginia / Darling Nellie Gray / There's a bridle hangin' on the wall / I'm leavin' on that blue river train / Ramblin' cowboy / I'm an old cow hand / Texas Dan / With a banjo on my knee / Home sweet home on the prairie
CD CDAJA 5187
Living Era / Jun '96 / Select

Robinson, David

NEVER STOP LOVIN'
CD RYTCD 4188
Ichiban / Jun '94 / Direct / Koch

Robinson, Elzadie

ELZADIE ROBINSON VOL.1 1926-1928
CD DOCD 5248
Document / May '94 / ADA / Hot Shot / Jazz Music

ELZADIE ROBINSON VOL.2 1928-1929
CD DOCD 5249
Document / May '94 / ADA / Hot Shot / Jazz Music

Robinson, Fenton

I HEAR SOME BLUES DOWNSTAIRS
I hear some blues downstairs / Just a little bit / West side baby / I'm so tired / I wish for you / Tell me what's the reason / Going west / Killing floor / As the years go passing by
CD ALCD 4710
Alligator / May '93 / ADA / CM / Direct

MELLOW FELLOW (Charly Blues Masterworks Vol.41)
CD CDBM 41
Charly / Jun '93 / Koch

NIGHTFLIGHT
CD ALCD 4736
Alligator / May '93 / ADA / CM / Direct

SOMEBODY LOAN ME A DIME
CD ALCD 4705
Alligator / May '93 / ADA / CM / Direct

SPECIAL ROAD
7-11 Blues / Love is just a gamble / Special road / Too many drivers / Baby, please don't go / Crying the blues / Find a way / RM blues / Slick and greasy / Blue Monday / Money problem / Nothing but a fool / Little torch
CD ECD 260252
Evidence / Feb '93 / ADA / Cadillac / Harmonia Mundi

Robinson, Frank

EAST COAST TEXAS BLUES (Robinson, Frank & 'Guitar' Curtis)
CD BMCD 9028
Black Magic / Aug '96 / ADA / Cadillac / Direct / Hot Shot

Robinson, Jim

CLASSIC NEW ORLEANS JAZZ VOL.2
CD BCD 128
Biograph / Oct '93 / ADA / Cadillac / Direct / Hot Shot / Jazz Music / Wellard

Robinson, Jimmie Lee

LONELY TRAVELLER (Robinson, Jimmie Lee & The Ice Cream Men)
Lonely traveller / Easy baby / Can't be successful / Twist it baby / Leave my woman alone / I'll be your slave / Triflin' on you / All my life / 44 blues / Key to the highway / Times are getting harder / Lonely man / Robinson's rang tangle
CD DE 665
Delmark / Mar '97 / ADA / Cadillac / CM / Direct / Hot Shot

Robinson, Justin

JUSTIN TIME
CD 5132542
Verve / Mar '92 / PolyGram

Robinson, L.C.

MOJO IN MY HAND (Robinson, L.C. 'Good Rockin')
Mojo in my hand / Up and downs / Pinetop's boogie woogie / Across the bay blues / LC's shuffle / Can't be a winner / I've got to go / Stop and jump / She got it from the start / Thing's so bad in California / New train time / I'm just a country boy / LC's theme / Jesus did I know / I don't know what I would do without the Lord / Something mighty sweet about the Lord / Ida red / LC's blues / Sweet Jesus
CD ARHCD 453
Arhoolie / Nov '96 / ADA / Cadillac / Direct

Robinson, Orphy

VIBES DESCRIBES, THE
Once upon a time / Annavas / Fore to the power of M / Loneliest monk / Chunky but funky / For time to time / Monica / Make a change / Where's Winston / Eternal spirit / An and Vas / Juxtafusician / Golden brown / Krossover point / Savannah
CD CDBLT 1009
Blue Note / May '94 / EMI

WHEN TOMORROW COMES
All at sixes and sevens: *Orbison, Roy* / Bass of bad intentions - Part 1 - Deep: *Orbison, Roy* / Bass of bad intentions - Part 2 - Dark: *Orbison, Roy* / Bass of bad intentions - Part 3 - Dirty: *Orbison, Roy* / Jigsaw: *Orbison, Roy* / Let's see what tomorrow brings - Part 1: *Orbison, Roy* / Let's see what tomorrow brings - Part 2: *Orbison, Roy* / Let's see what tomorrow brings - Part 3: *Orbison, Roy* / Let's see what tomorrow brings - Part 4: *Orbison, Roy* / Let's see what tomorrow brings - Part 5: *Orbison, Roy* / Bach to 1st bass: *Orbison, Roy* / Bads means beautiful: *Orbison, Roy* / Jigsaw (reprise): *Orbison, Roy*
CD CDBLT 1004
Blue Note / Jan '92 / EMI

Robinson, Perry

KUNDALINI (Robinson, Perry/Nana Vasconcelos/Badal Roy)
CD 1238562
IAI / Sep '93 / Cadillac / Harmonia Mundi

Robinson, Reginald R.

SOUNDS IN SILHOUETTE
Ragtime pauper / Masquerade ball / To Mimie / Lake St. / Dream Natasha / Conductor / Holly Hock march / Jack Johnson rag / Sounds in silhouette / Ventriloquist / Champ rags / Swampy Lee / Peacherine rag / Sedidus walk / Little Dave blues / Charles L Johnson medley / Honor'e Chester / Knuckle fingers / Lonely Mable
CD DE 670
Delmark / Mar '97 / ADA / Cadillac / CM / Direct / Hot Shot

STRONGMAN, THE
Maple leaf rag / Good times rag / Strong man / Troubador serenade / Spring rag / Portrait of Scott Joplin / Ebony Venus / Petunia rag / Ballerina figurine / Finesse / Boogie man creep / Just try and escape the devil / Show stopper / Hustler's two-step / Kid / Scamp / Poker face blues / Nile river ripples / Jester / Georgia Tom / Original slow drag / Honeymoon waltz
CD DD 662
Delmark / Mar '97 / ADA / Cadillac / CM / Direct / Hot Shot

Robinson, Rev. Cleophus

SOMEONE TO CARE
Get away Jordan / Before this time another year / Morning and evening / Someone to care / Let the church roll on / Near the cross / It won't hurt you to speak / Peace in the valley / When the sun goes down / Grace made a change / I know prayer changes things / Jesus met the woman at the well / Until I found the Lord / I'm going to leave you in the hands of the Lord / Going over yonder / Strange things happening / Consecrated / You've got to love everybody / No more than you can bear / I can't help it / We'll understand it better by and by / Farther along / Lord I'm in your care / When the saints go marching in / Sometimes I feel like a Motherless child / Waiting for Jesus
CD CDCHD 566
Ace / Mar '94 / Pinnacle

Robinson, Smokey

BEING WITH YOU
Being with you / Food for thought / If you wanna make love / Who's sad / Can't fight love / You are forever / As you do / I hear the children singing
CD 5302192
Motown / Sep '93 / PolyGram

CHRISTMAS WITH THE MIRACLES (Merry Christmas From Motown) (Robinson, Smokey & The Miracles)
Santa Claus is coming to town / Let it snow, let it snow, let it snow / Winter wonderland / Christmas everyday / I'll be home for Christmas / Christmas song / White Christmas / Silver bells / Noel / O holy night
CD 5504052
Spectrum / Nov '96 / PolyGram

GREATEST HITS (Robinson, Smokey & The Miracles)
Being with you / Tracks of my tears / I second that emotion / I'm the one you need / Mickey's monkey / Going to a go go / I don't blame you at all / If you can want / Just to see her / More love / Just my soul responding / Tears of a clown / Abraham, Martin and John / You've really got a hold on me / Shop around / What's so good about goodbye / Ooo baby baby / Love I saw in you was just a mirage / Quiet storm / One heartbeat / Baby, baby, don't cry / Cruisin'
CD 5301212
Motown / Mar '96 / PolyGram

MOTOWN EARLY CLASSICS
Tracks of my tears / You've really got a hold on me / Shop around / You never miss a good thing / Way over there / Determination / Everybody's gotta pay some dues / If your mother only knew / What's so good about goodbye / Since you won my heart / Such is love, such is life / Monkey time / Wahwatusi / I gotta dance to keep from crying / From head to toe / Would I love you / Let me have some / Going to a Go-Go
CD 5521252
Spectrum / Jul '96 / PolyGram

SMOKEY'S SONGBOOK (Various Artists)
Tears of a clown: *Monitors* / Tracks of my tears: *Contours* / Shop around: *Griffin, Billy* / My girl: *Stubbs, Joe* / More love: *5th Dimension* / Hunter gets captured by the game: *Marvelettes* / You beat me to the punch: *Wells, Mary* / You really got a hold on me: *Ward, Sammy* / Way you do the things you do: *Motor City Allstars* / Don't mess with the bill: *Marvelettes* / My guy: *Wells, Mary* / Since I lost my baby: *Crawford, Carolyn* / Going to a go go: *Monitors* / From head to toe: *Clark, Chris* / Whole lotta shakin' in my head: *Johnson, Marv* / Get ready: *Taylor, Bobby & The Vancouvers* / What's easy for two is so hard for one: *Wells, Mary* / Goodbye cruel love: *Griner, Linda* / My baby must be a magician: *Marvelettes* / My smile is just a frown: *Crawford, Carolyn*
CD 3035990042
Motor City / Oct '95 / Carlton

TRACKS OF MY TEARS (The Very Best Of Smokey Robinson)
CD DINCD 17
Dino / '93 / Pinnacle

WHAT EVER MAKES YOU HAPPY (More Best Of Smokey Robinson & The Miracles 1961-1971) (Robinson, Smokey & The Miracles)
Money / Won't you take me back / Mighty good lovin' / I need a change / From head to toe / More, more, more of your love / Swept for you baby / Beauty is only skin deep / Don't think it's me / Dancing's alright / You only build me up to tear me down / I'll take you any way that you come / My world is empty without you / Dreams dreams / Backfire / Flower girl / Faces
CD 8122711812
Atlantic / Jun '93 / Warner Music

Robinson, Spike

AT THE STABLES (Robinson, Spike & Gene DiNovi)
Indian love call / Quietly there / So do I / Only make believe / Maybe you'll be there / Laura / Theme from The Bad And The Beautiful / Stockholm LA / I can't get started / He loves she loves / I won't cry / All the things you are / Alan's song
CD HEPCD 2071
Hep / Aug '97 / Cadillac / Jazz Music / New Note/Pinnacle / Wellard

IN TOWN WITH ELAINE DELMAR
Too close for comfort / You've changed / Just one of those things / In a sentimental mood / 'S Wonderful / Get out of town / Little girl blue / Everything I love / Young and foolish / Will you still be mine
CD HEPCD 2035
Hep / Jun '93 / Cadillac / Jazz Music / New Note/Pinnacle / Wellard

JUSA BIT O' BLUES VOL.1 (Robinson, Spike & Harry Edison Quintet)
One I love / Autumn leaves / Elaine / Just in time / 'Tis Autumn / Slow boat to China / Jus' a bit o' blues / Stars fell on Alabama / Time after time
CD 74012
Capri / Nov '93 / Cadillac / Wellard

JUSA BIT O' BLUES VOL.2 (Robinson, Spike & Harry Edison Quintet)
CD 74013
Capri / Sep '89 / Cadillac / Wellard

ODD COUPLE, THE (Robinson, Spike & Rob Mullins)
CD 74008
Capri / Oct '90 / Cadillac / Wellard

PLAYS HARRY WARREN
This heart of mine / At last / Boulevard of broken dreams / There will never be another you / I had the craziest dream / Shadow waltz / Serenade in blue / This is always / More I see you / Chattanooga choo choo / Cheerful little earful / I only have eyes for you / Lulu's back in town / I wish I knew
CD HEPCD 2056
Hep / Oct '94 / Cadillac / Jazz Music / New Note/Pinnacle / Wellard

SPIKE ROBINSON & GEORGE MASSO PLAY ARLEN (Robinson, Spike & George Masso)
Let's fall in love / Right as rain / I gotta right to sing the blues / Taking a chance on love / This time the dream is on me / Happiness is a thing called Joe / When the sun comes out / Last night when we were young / My shining hour / As long as I live / Come rain or come shine / Between the Devil and the deep blue sea
CD HEPCD 2053
Hep / Oct '92 / Cadillac / Jazz Music / New Note/Pinnacle / Wellard

SPIKE ROBINSON'S TENOR MADNESS
Here we go again / T'ain't no use / Tickle toe / Pretty one / Take four / Travelin' light / You 'n' me / One good turn / Note / Tenor madness / Stockholm - LA / Just an old manuscript / Goof and I / Quick one
CD ESJCD 600
Essential Jazz / Jun '97 / BMG

STAIRCASE TO THE STARS
Gone with the wind / Beautiful love / Gypsy sweetheart / It's always you / It's a blue world / Summer thing / From here to eternity / Stairway to the stars / It should happen to you
CD HEPCD 2049
Hep / Oct '91 / Cadillac / Jazz Music / New Note/Pinnacle / Wellard

THREE FOR THE ROAD (Robinson, Spike & Louis Stewart)
They didn't believe me / Dearly beloved / If you were mine / Yes sir that's my baby / Only a rose / My buddy / Song is you / For Heaven's sake / They say that falling in love is wonderful
CD HEPCD 2045
Hep / Oct '90 / Cadillac / Jazz Music / New Note/Pinnacle / Wellard

Robinson, Tad

ONE TO INFINITY
Empty apartment blues / Coming home / At the end of the tunnel / Eight days, 1 week / Trouble in mind / Can't print it fast enough / One to infinity / Walking in the sunshine / Lonely man / Raining in New York / Little rascal / Give love a chance
CD DE 673
Delmark / Mar '97 / ADA / Cadillac / CM / Direct / Hot Shot

Robinson, Tom

BACK IN THE OLD COUNTRY
Listen to the radio: Atmospherics / Too good to be true / Up against the wall / Northern rain / I shall be released / Mary Lynne / 2-4-6-8 Motorway / Drive all night / Don't take no for an answer / Where can we go tonight / Back in the old country / Alright all night / War baby / Power in the darkness / Crossing over the road / Rikki don't lose that number / Bitterly disappointed / Looking for a bonfire / Hard cases / Still loving you / Not ready / Bully for you / Long hot summer
CD VSOPCD 138
Connoisseur Collection / Oct '89 / Pinnacle

BLOOD BROTHER (Robinson, Tom & Jakko)
We've never had it so good / Driving through the desert / Blood brother / What have I ever done to you / Baby rages on / Tomboy / Kiss and roll over / Hard cases / Can't stop / My own sweet way / Rigging it up, Duncannon / Happy in the homelands / Jonestown / War is over
CD CASVP 001CD
Castaway Northwest / Jun '97 / Pinnacle

GLAD TO BE GAY (Cabaret '79)
Pub hassle / Coldharbour Lane / Baby you're an angel / Glad to be gay / Stand together / Truce / Closing a door / 1967 (so long ago) / Even Steven / Sartorial eloquence / Mad about the boy / Easy Street / Good to be gay / Glad to be gay / Last rites / Gay switchboard jingle
CD CNWVP 004CD
Castaway Northwest / Jul '97 / Pinnacle

GOLD COLLECTION, THE
Don't take no for an answer / 2-4-6-8 Motorway / I shall be released / Long hot summer / Power in the darkness / Bully for you / Never going to fall in love (again) / Getting tighter / Our people / Martin / Right on sister / I'm all right Jack / All right all night / Law and order / Grey cortina / Glad to be gay
CD CDGOLD 1015
EMI Gold / Mar '96 / EMI

HAVING IT BOTH WAYS
Disrespect / One / Rum thunderbird / Cold cold ground / Fool to myself / Hot dog / Sorry / Raining in Connecticut / Congo blue / Castaway / Last word
CD COOKCD 097
Cooking Vinyl / May '96 / Vital

LAST TANGO/MIDNIGHT AT THE FRINGE
Stornoway / Atmospherics / Night tide / Nut rocker / Surabaya Johnny / Bonfire / Tango an der wand / Cabin boy / Back in the old country / Old friend / Never gonna fall in love again / Too good to be true / Glad to be gay / War baby / 2468 motorway
CD CNWVP 002CD
Castaway Northwest / Aug '97 / Pinnacle

LIVING IN A BOOM TIME
CD COOKCD 052
Cooking Vinyl / Feb '95 / Vital

LOVE OVER RAGE
Roaring / Hard / Loved / Days / Driving green / Green / DDR / Fifty / Silence / Chance
CD COOKCD 066
Cooking Vinyl / Jun '97 / Vital

MOTORWAY
Number one protection / Winter of '79 / You gotta survive / Too good to be true / Martin / We didn't know (what was going on) / Up against the wall / Glad to be gay / Power in the darkness / 2-4-6-8 Motorway / Atmospherics / Listen to the radio / War baby
CD MSCD 6
Magnum Music / May '95 / TKO Magnum

NORTH BY NORTH WEST
Now Martins gone / Atmospherics / Can't keep away (Part II) / Looking for a bonfire / Merrily up on high / Those days / In the cold / Night tide / Duncannon / Love comes / Tango an der wand / Now Richards gone / Airtraum tango dob / Any favours / Out to lunch
CD CNWVP 003CD
Castaway Northwest / Jun '97 / Pinnacle

POWER IN THE DARKNESS (Robinson, Tom Band)
Up against the wall / Grey Cortina / Too good to be true / Ain't gonna take it / Long hot summer / Winter of '79 / Man you never saw / Better decide which side you're on / You gotta survive / Power in the darkness
CD COOKCD 076
Cooking Vinyl / Oct '94 / Vital
CD RE 2018
Razor & Tie / Aug '96 / Koch

RISING FREE (The Best Of Tom Robinson)
2-4-6-8 Motorway / I shall be released / Don't take no for an answer / Glad to be gay / Martin / Right on sister / Alright Jack (live) / P against the wall / Grey cortina / Too good to be true / Long hot summer / Winter of '79 / Power in the darkness / Waiting for my man / Getting tighter / All right all night / Bully for you / Never gonna fall in love again
CD CDGOLD 1098
EMI Gold / Jun '97 / EMI

SECTOR 27 COMPLETE (Sector 27)
Can't keep away / Invitation: What have we got to lose / Not ready / Mary Lynne / Looking at you / Five 2 five / Totall recall / Where can we go tonight / Take it or leave it / Bitterly disappointed / Day after day / Dungannon / Stornoway / One fine day / Won't you tell me how I feel / Martin's gone / Christopher calling / Shutdown / Out in the cold again
CD 5326422
Fontana / Jun '96 / PolyGram

TRB TWO (Robinson, Tom Band)
Alright all night / Why should I mind / Black angel / Let my people be / Blue murder / Bully for you / Crossing over the road / Sorry Mr. Harris / Law and order / Days of rage / Hold out
CD COOKCD 77
Cooking Vinyl / Oct '94 / Vital
CD RE 2019
Razor & Tie / Aug '96 / Koch

Robson & Jerome

ROBSON & JEROME
Unchained melody / Daydream believer / I believe / Sun ain't gonna shine anymore / Up on the roof / Amazing grace / Danny boy / (There'll be bluebirds over) The white cliffs of Dover / This boy / Little latin Lupe Lu / Love you forever / I'll come running back to you / If I can dream
CD 74321323902
RCA / Feb '97 / BMG

TAKE TWO
True love ways / Pretty woman / Keep the customer satisfied / Something's gotten hold of my heart / Price of love / Bring it on home to me / What becomes of the broken hearted / Saturday night at the movies / You'll never walk alone
CD 74321426252
RCA / Nov '96 / BMG

Robson, Mark

IN SEARCH OF A SIMPLE LIFE
CD AGASCD 014
Gliss / Aug '97 / Pinnacle

Roby, Charlie

UTOPIA IS NOT HERE
CD MAL 0102CD
Maladrin Music / Aug '95 / ADA

ROC

ROC
Desert wind / Excised / God willing / Hey you chick / Balloon / Real time / Plastic Jesus / I want you I need you I miss you / Gold bug / La heredia / 13 Summers / Hey Nicky / Sylvia's thighs / Ascension / Clouds
CD SETCD 022
Setanta / Jan '96 / Vital

VIRGIN
Dada / (Dis)count us in / Mountain / Cheryl / Corner off I-25 / Dead pool / Ever since yesterday / 25 reasons to leave me / KC / Cold chill just lately / Said what I said / Ocean and England
CD CDV 2829
Virgin / Aug '97 / EMI

Rocchi, Riccardo

IT'S JUST A MELTING POT OF EMOTIONS
CD ACVD 011
ACV / Nov '95 / Plastic Head / SRD

Roccisano, Joe

SHAPE I'M IN, THE (Roccisano, Joe & His Orchestra)
Borderland / New beginning / Mornings glory's story / Synthesis / Prism / Isabel / Shape I'm in / Piece of the pie / Don't stop now / Earth day / Blue Lou
CD LCD 15352
Landmark / Nov '93 / New Note/Pinnacle

Roche, Ives

TAHITI COOL VOL.4
CD PS 65806
PlayaSound / Nov '91 / ADA / Harmonia Mundi

Roches

CAN WE GO HOME NOW
Great gaels / Move / You (make my life come true) / Christlike / Home away from home / Can we go home now / When you're ready / I'm someone who loves you / So / My winter coat / Holidays
CD ________ **RCD 10299**
Rykodisc / Mar '97 / ADA / Vital

ROCHES, THE
We / Hammond song / Mr. Sellack / Damned old dog / Troubles / Train / Married men / Runs in the family / Quitting time / Pretty and high
CD ________ **7599273902**
WEA / Jan '96 / Warner Music

Rock Bottom

TONE
CD ________ **TRICKNOLOGY 1**
Tricknology / Apr '97 / Hot Shot

Rock Goddess

YOUNG & FREE
Young and free / Hello / So much love / Jerry / Streets of the city / Party never ends / Love has passed me by / Raiders / Love is a bitch / Boys will be boys / Sexy eyes / Rumour / Turn me loose / Hey lover
CD ________ **CDTB 155**
Thunderbolt / Jul '94 / TKO Magnum

Rock Melons

STRONGER TOGETHER
CD ________ **TVD 93360**
Mushroom / Jan '95 / 3mv/Pinnacle

Rock, Pete

MAIN INGREDIENT, THE (Rock, Pete & C.L. Smooth)
In the house / Carmel city / Physical / Sun won't come out / I got a love / Escapism / Main ingredient / World wide / All the places / Tell me / Take you there / Searching / Chick it out / In the flesh / It's on you / Get on the mic
CD ________ **7559616612**
Elektra / Nov '94 / Warner Music

MECCA AND THE SOUL BROTHER (Rock, Pete & C.L. Smooth)
Return to the Mecca / For Pete's sake / Ghettos of the mind / Lots of lovin' / Act like you know / Straighten it out / Soul brother no 1 / Wig out / Anger in the nation / They reminisce over you (TROY) / On and on / It's like that / Can't front on me / Basement / If it ain't rough, it ain't right / Skinz
CD ________ **7559609482**
Elektra / May '92 / Warner Music

Rock, Salt & Nails

4,6,2,1
CD ________ **FORCD 39**
Fourth Recording Company / Jul '96 / Grapevine/PolyGram

MORE AND MORE
Don't know about you/Friday card school / Someday / Jack broke da prison door / Life / Lucy Bain / More and more / Uneasy ride / Tilly plump set / Grandmother's eyes / Forced to return/Spootiskerry / Lucy Bain reprise
CD ________ **IRCD 030**
Iona / May '95 / ADA / Direct / Duncans

WAVES
Man who ate mountains / Slockit light - Waiting for the Federals / Happy to be here / Jack broke da prison door / Faroe rum / Oliver Jack / Willafjord / Iron horse / Arkansas traveller / Welcome / Central house / Square da Mizzen / Doon hingin' tie / Waves / Hut on Staffin Island / Barmaid / Music for a found harmonium
CD ________ **IRCD 025**
Iona / Jan '94 / ADA / Direct / Duncans

Rock Shop

MR. LEE'S SWINGING AFFAIR PRESENTS
CD ________ **BA 115CD**
Bacchus Archives / Feb '97 / Cargo / Plastic Head

Rockabillies

WOODSTOCK VIA MEMPHIS
CD ________ **POCD 004**
Popcorn / Feb '96 / Nervous

Rockabilly Mafia

ANOTHER DRUNKEN NIGHT
CD ________ **RUMBCD 002**
Rumble / Aug '92 / Nervous / Pinnacle

Rockats

GOOD, THE BAD, THE ROCKIN', THE
CD ________ **DAGCD 6**
Fury / Feb '97 / Nervous / TKO Magnum

LAST CRUSADE
CD ________ **TBCD 2005**
Nervous / Mar '93 / Nervous / TKO Magnum

Rocker, Lee

ATOMIC BOOGIE HOUR (Rocker, Lee & Big Blue)
CD ________ **BT 1121CD**
Black Top / Sep '95 / ADA / CM / Direct

LEE ROCKER'S BIG BAND
CD ________ **BT 1105CD**
Black Top / Sep '94 / ADA / CM / Direct

NO CATS
Rumblin' bass / Miracle in Memphis / One way or another / Shaky town / Screaming hunger / Love me good / Little piece of your love / Memphis freeze / Mr. Newman / Into the viod / Movin' on / Hard rain / The naked bass
CD ________ **DFGCD 8465**
Dixie Frog / Jul '97 / Direct / TKO Magnum

Rockers Hi-Fi

DJ KICKS (The Black Album) (Various Artists)
Rockers intro: *Farda P* / Theme from kung fu: *Danna, Jeff* / He builds the world: *Small Fish With Spine* / Feel: *Kid Loops* / Candles and versions: *Wraparound Sounds* / Up through the down pipe: *Grizzly* / Dub angel: *Snooze & DJ Cam* / Varispeed: *Electric J* / Callacop: *Deep Space Network* / Long life: *Prince Far-I & The Arabs* / Com-unique-ation: *Cee Mix* / RhyNever tell you: *thm & Sound/Tikiman* / Twisted system: *Terminal Head & Mr. Spee* / G13: *T-Power* / Saidisyabruklimmon: *Dr. Israel & Loop* / Bad head day: *Husik, Lida* / Dis ya opne: *More Rockers* / Rockers outro: *Farda P* / Black single: *Farda P*
CD ________ **K7 056CD**
Studio K7 / Jun '97 / Prime / RTM/Disc

MISH MASH
8th shade / Theme from Mish Mash / Now I deliver / Uneasy skanking / Fling mi ting / Mish mash episode one / 90 degree fuzz-walk / Mish mash episode two / Going under / Paths of life / One with another / Mish mash episode three / Copycat
CD ________ **0630457952**
WEA / Aug '97 / Warner Music

Rocket From The Crypt

SCREAM DRACULA SCREAM
Middle / Born in '69 / On a rope / Young livers / Drop out / Used / Ball lightning / Fat lip / Suit city / Heater hands / Misbeaten / Come see, come saw / Salt future / Burnt alive
CD ________ **ELM 34CD**
Elemental / Jan '96 / RTM/Disc

STATE OF THE ART IS ON FIRE, THE
CD ________ **SFTRI 320CD**
Sympathy For The Record Industry / Nov '96 / Cargo / Greyhound / Plastic Head

Rocket Fuel Is The Key

CONSIDER IT CONTEMPT
Fake / So it grips / World class / Carnival / Fulltime apathy / Out of context / 6 dozen of 1, 2/3 of another / Armchair politician / Live head down / Your skin / Consolation
CD ________ **THI 570222**
Thirsty Ear / Feb '97 / Vital

Rockets

ROCKETS, THE
Hole in my pocket / Won't you say you'll stay / Mr. Chips / It's a mistake / Let me go / Try my patience / I won't always be around / Pill's blues / Stretch your skin / Eraser
CD ________ **EDCD 520**
Edsel / May '97 / Pinnacle

Rockin' Bandits

WATCH OUT...WE'RE GONNA 'JUMP BACK'
Jump back boogie / Gonna rock with ya baby / Ain't gonna be your crazy cat / Long black train / Pretty little baby / I'm in love with you baby / Cruisin' blues / Oakie boogie / Angel girl / Lonely country girl / Two lane black top / My little baby / Folsom prison blues / Rock-a-baby rock / Midnight shift / Rock 'n' roll Mama / I don't care / Everybody's tryin' to be my baby
CD ________ **FCD 3036**
Fury / Mar '95 / Nervous / TKO Magnum

Rockin' Berries

HE IS IN TOWN
CD ________ **HADCD 205**
Javelin / Jul '96 / Henry Hadaway / THE

Rockin' Dopsie

FEET DON'T FAIL ME NOW
CD ________ **AIMA 1**
Rounder / Oct '95 / ADA / CM / Direct

Rockin' Ramrods

BEST OF THE ROCKIN' RAMRODS
Jungle call / I wanna be your man / I'll be on my way / Don't fool with Fu Manchu / Tears melt the stones / Play it / Bright lit blue skies / Mr. Wind / Can't you see / Mary Mary / Flowers in my mind / Vacuum / Trees / Rainy days / Looking in my window / Who do you think you are / Of not being able to sleep / Dead thoughts of Alfred / I sure need you / When I wake up in the morning / Go with you / Changes / My vision has cleared / I don't want to, I will / Troubles
CD ________ **CDWIKD 151**
Big Beat / May '95 / Pinnacle

Rockin' Rebels

ROCKIN' REBELS
CD ________ **622442**
Skydog / Apr '97 / Discovery

Rockin' Sidney

LIVE WITH THE BLUES
CD ________ **JSPCD 213**
JSP / Mar '88 / ADA / Cadillac / Direct / Hot Shot / Target/BMG

MY TOOT TOOT
My toot toot / My zydeco shoes / Joy to the south / Don't be a wallflower / Alligator waltz / Rock 'n' roll me baby / Joe Pete is in the bed / You ain't nothing but fine / If it's good for the gander / Twist to the zydeco / Dance and show off / Let me take you to zydeco / I got the blues for my baby / Louisiana creole man / If I could I would / No good woman / Send me some lovin' / Past bedtime / No good man / You don't have to go / It really is a hurtin' thing / Something's wrong / My little girl / Wasted days and wasted nights / Ya ya / Jalapena lena / Sweet lil' woman / Once is not enough / Cochon de lait
CD ________ **CDCH 160**
Ace / Jun '93 / Pinnacle

Rockin' Vincent

ROCKIN' VINCENT
CD ________ **DSCD 9252**
Collector/White Label / Feb '97 / TKO Magnum

Rockingbirds

WHATEVER HAPPENED TO THE ROCKINGBIRDS
Roll on forever / I like winter / Everybody lives with us / Band of dreams / We had it all / I woke up one morning / High part / Bitter tear / Before we got to the end / Hell / Let me down slow
CD ________ **COOKCD 084**
Cooking Vinyl / Aug '97 / Vital

Rockpile

SECONDS OF PLEASURE
Teacher teacher / If sugar was as sweet as you / Heart / Now and always / Knife and fork / Play that fast thing / Wrong way / Pet you and hold you / Oh what a thrill you / When I write the book / Fool too long / You ain't nothing but fine
CD ________ **FIENDCD 28**
Demon / Oct '90 / Pinnacle

Rocks

COMBAT ZONE
CD ________ **KR 004CD**
Kangaroo / Aug '95 / Plastic Head

Rockwell, Bob

ON THE NATCH (Rockwell, Bob Quartet)
CD ________ **SCCD 31229**
Steeplechase / Jul '88 / Discovery / Impetus

RECONSTRUCTION
CD ________ **SCCD 31270**
Steeplechase / Nov '90 / Discovery / Impetus

Rodan

RUSTY
CD ________ **QS 24CD**
Quarter Stick / Apr '94 / Cargo / SRD

Roddy, Ted

FULL CIRCLE
CD ________ **HCD 8065**
Hightone / Oct '95 / ADA / Koch

Roden, Jess

JESS RODEN
Reason to change / I'm on your side / Feelin easy / Sad story / On broadway / Ferry cross / Trouble in the mind / What the hell
CD ________ **IMCD 143**
Island / Aug '91 / PolyGram

Rodgers Melnick, Peter

ARCTIC BLUE
Arctic blue / Tundra / Breakaway / Wolf / Take off / Dream / Dixie's revenge / Looking for trouble / Living and the dead / No man's land / Return to Devil's cauldron / Cut to the chase / Mitchell dies / Mine / Up in flames / Trappers and hunters / In the shadows / Viking Bob / Freeing the wolf
CD ________ **ND 63030**
Narada / Nov '94 / ADA / New Note/ Pinnacle

Rodgers, Clodagh

YOU ARE MY MUSIC (The Best Of Clodagh Rodgers)
Come back and shake me / Lady love bug / Carolina days / Let me be the one / I am a fantasy / Together / Goodnight midnight / It's different now / Nothing rhymed / I will / I'm gonna make you love me / Natural woman / One day / Betcha by golly wow / Everybody go home the party's over / Will you still love me tomorrow / What in the world / Together we will make it / Ease your pain / That's the way I've always heard it should be / Day by day / You are my music
CD ________ **74321415042**
Camden / Jan '97 / BMG

Rodgers, Jimmie

AMERICA'S BLUE YODELER, 1930-1931
Blue yodel No. 8 / Jimmie's mean mama blues / I'm lonesome too / Mystery of number five / One rose / In the jailhouse now No.2 / For the sake of days gone by / Blue yodel No. 9 / TB Blues / Travellin' blues / Why there's a tear in my eye / Jimmie the kid / Wonderful city / Let me be your sidetrack
CD ________ **ROUCD 1060**
Rounder / Sep '91 / ADA / CM / Direct

AMERICAN LEGENDS
Rock all our babies to sleep / Peach pickin' time down in Georgia / Pistol packin' papa / Nobody knows but me / Mississippi river blues / Blue yodel no.9 (standin' on the corner) / Drunkard's child / Blue yodel no.10 / Blue yodel no.11 / Moonlight and skies / Mother, the queen of my heart / Those gambler's blues
CD ________ **12746**
Laserlight / May '97 / Target/BMG

DOWN THE OLD ROAD 1931-1932
Looking for a new mama / When the cactus is in bloom / Jimmie Rodgers visits the Carter Family / Carter Family and Jimmie Rodgers in Texas / Gambling dot blues / Southern cannonball / Roll along Kentucky moon / What's it my time ain't long / Hobo's meditation / Ninety nine years blues / Mississippi moon / Down the old road to home
CD ________ **ROUCD 1061**
Rounder / Sep '91 / ADA / CM / Direct

FATHER OF COUNTRY MUSIC, THE
You and my old guitar / My little lady / Prairie lullaby / When the cactus is in bloom / Pistol packin' Papa / Peach picking time in Georgia / I've only loved three women / Any old time / I'm lonesome too / Dear sunny South by the sea / Blue yodel no.10 / Sleep baby sleep / Never no mo' blues / Looking for a new Mama / No hard times / Gambling bar room blues / Frankie and Johnny / My old pal / Jimmie the kid / Blue yodel / Old pal of my heart / Sweet Mama hurry home / Roll along Kentucky moon
CD ________ **PASTCD 7814**
Flapper / Apr '97 / Pinnacle

FIRST SESSIONS, 1927-1928
Blue yodel / Soldier's sweetheart / Ben Dewberry's final run / Sleep, baby sleep / Mother was a lady / Dear old sunny south by the sea / Away out on the mountain / Treasures untold / Blue yodel no. 11 / Sailor's plea / In the jailhouse now / Memphis yodel / Brakeman's blues / Blue yodel no. 3
CD ________ **ROUCD 1056**
Rounder / '90 / ADA / CM / Direct

LAST SESSIONS, 1933
Blue yodel No. 12 / Dreaming with tears in my eyes / Cowhand's last ride / I'm free from the chain gang now / Yodeling my way back home / Jimmie Rodgers' last blue yodel / Yodeling ranger / Old pal of my heart / Years ago / Somewhere below the Mason Dixon line / Old love letters / Mississippi delta blues
CD ________ **ROUCD 1063**
Rounder / Mar '92 / ADA / CM / Direct

MEMORIES OF JIMMIE RODGERS (Various Artists)
When Jimmie Rodgers said goodbye: *Butcher, Dwight* / Life of Jimmie Rodgers/ The death of Jimmie Rodgers: *Autry, Gene* / Good luck old pal (til we meet bye and bye): *Autry, Gene* / When Jimmie Rodgers said goodbye: *Autry, Gene* / Memories of Jimmie Rodgers: *O'Daniel, W. Lee* / Jimmie Rodgers' life: *Kincaid, Bradley* / Death of Jimmie Rodgers: *Kincaid, Bradley* / Mrs. Jimmie Rodgers' lament: *Kincaid, Bradley* / Little Jimmie's goodbye to Jimmie Rodgers: *Sizemore, Asher & Little Jimmie* / When Jimmie Rodgers said goodbye #2: *Houchins, Kenneth* / Good luck old pal (til we meet

bye and bye): *Houchins, Kenneth* / Life of Jimmie Rodgers: *Kincaid, Bradley* / Death of Jimmie Rodgers: *Kincaid, Bradley* / Last thoughts of Jimmie Rodgers: *Tubb, Ernest* / Passing of Jimmie Rodgers: *Tubb, Ernest* / We miss him when the evening shadow falls: *Rodgers, Mrs. Jimmie* / My rainbow trail keeps winding on: *Rodgers, Mrs. Jimmie* / Women made a fool out of me: *Tubb, Ernest* / Nothing at all: *Wilburn Brothers* / Mr. Love: *Tubb, Ernest & Wilburn Brothers* / Anniversary blue yodel: *Snow, Hank* / Waitin' for a train: *Reeves, Jim*
CD BCD 15938
Bear Family / May '97 / Direct / Rollercoaster / Swift

MY OLD PAL
Blue yodel no. 1 (T for Texas) / Away out on the mountain / Frankie and Johnny / Gamblin' bar room blues / When the cactus is in bloom / Sleep, baby, sleep / My old pal / Daddy and home / My Carolina sunshine girl / Why there's a tear in my eye / We miss him when the evening shadows fall / Never no no' blues / Blue yodel no. 3 / I'm sorry we met / Blue yodel no. 5 / Any old time / Lullaby yodel / Looking for a new mama
CD CDAJA 5058
Living Era / Mar '89 / Select

NO HARD TIMES 1932
Blue yodel No. 10 / Whippin' that old TB / Rock all our babies to sleep / Home call / Mother, the queen of my heart / No hard times / Peach pickin' time in Georgia / Long tall mama blues / Gamblin' bar room blues / I've only loved three women / In the hills of Tennessee / Prairie lullaby / Miss the Mississippi and you / Sweet Mama hurry home
CD ROUCD 1062
Rounder / Feb '92 / ADA / CM / Direct

ON THE WAY UP 1929
High powered Mama / Tuck away my lonesome blues / Frankie and Johnny / I'm sorry we met / Train whistle blues / Everybody does it in Hawaii / Jimmie's Texas blues / Home call / Blue yodel No. 6 / Yodeling cowboy / My rough and rowdy ways / Land of my boyhood dreams / Whisper your mother's name / I've ranged, I've roamed, I've travelled / Hobo Bill's last ride
CD ROUCD 1058
Rounder / '91 / ADA / CM / Direct

RIDING HIGH, 1929-1930
Anniversary blue yodel / That's why I'm blue / Mississippi river blues / She was happy till she met you / Blue yodel no. 11 / Drunkard's child / Nobody knows but me / Moonlight and the skies / Why did you give me your love / Pistol packin' papa / Why should I be lonely / Take me back again / Those gambler's blues / My blue eyed Jane
CD ROUCD 1059
Rounder / '91 / ADA / CM / Direct

SINGING BRAKEMAN, THE (6CD Set)
Soldier's sweetheart / Sleep, baby, sleep / Ben Dewberry's final run / Mother was a lady / Blue yodel / Away out on the mountain / Dear old sunny south by the sea / Treasures untold / Brakeman's blues / Sailor's plea / In the jailhouse now / Blue yodel No. 2 / Memphis yodel / Blue yodel No. 3 / My old pal / Mississippi moon / My little old home down in New Orleans / You and my old guitar / Daddy and home / My little lady / I'm lonely and blue / Lullaby yodel / Never mo' blues / My Carolina sunshine girl / Blue yodel No. 4 / Waiting for a train / Desert blues / Any old time / Blue yodel No. 5 / High powered mama / I'm sorry we met / Everybody does it in Hawaii / Tuck away my lonesome blues / Train whistle blues / Jimmie's Texas blues / Frankie and Johnny / Homecall / Whisper your mother's name / Land of my boyhood dreams / Blue yodel No. 6 / Yodeling cowboy / My rough and rowdy ways / I've ranged, I've roamed, I've travelled / Hobo Bill's last ride / Mississippi river blues / Nobody knows but me / Anniversary blue yodel / She was happy till she met you / Blue yodel No. 11 / Drunkard's child / That's why I'm blue / Why did you give me your love / My blue eyed Jane / Why should I be lonely / Moonlight and skies / Pistol packin' papa / Take me back again / Those gambler's blues / I'm lonesome too / One rose / For the sake of days gone by / Jimmie's mean mama blues / Mystery of number five / Blue yodel No. 8 / Blue yodel No. 9 / TB blues / Travellin' blues / Jimmie the kid / Why there's a tear in my eye / Wonderful city / Let me be your sidetrack / Jimmie Rodgers visits the Carter Family / Carter Family and Jimmie Rodgers in Texas / When the cactus is in bloom / Gambling polka dot blues / Looking for a new mama / What's it / My good gal's gone / Southern cannonball / Roll along Kentucky moon / Hobo's meditation / My time ain't long / Ninety nine year blues / Down the old road to home / Blue yodel No. 10 / Home call / Mother the queen of my heart / Rock all my babies to sleep / Whippin' that old TB / No hard times / Long tall mama blues / Peach pickin' time in Georgia / Gamblin' bar room blues / I've only loved three women / In the hills of Tennessee / Prairie lullaby / Miss the Mississippi and you / Sweet mama hurry home / Blue yodel No. 12 / Dreaming with tears in my eyes / Cowhand's last ride / I'm free from the chain gang now / Dream with tears in my eyes / Yodeling my way back home / Jimmie Rodgers' last blue yodel / Yodeling ranger / Old pal of my heart / Old love letters / Mississippi Delta blues / Somewhere below the Mason Dixon line / Years ago / Singing brakeman / Pullman porters / In the jailhouse now No.2 / Mule skinner blues / Mother, the queen of my heart / Never no mo' blues / Blue yodel No. 1
CD Set BCD 15540
Bear Family / Mar '92 / Direct / Rollercoaster / Swift

TRAIN WHISTLE BLUES
Jimmie's mean mama blues / Southern Cannonball / Jimmie the kid / Travellin' blues / Mystery of number five / Memphis yodel / Blue yodel no. 4 (California blues) / Hobo Bill's last ride / Waiting for a train / Ben Dewberry's final run / My rough and rowdy ways / Blue yodel no. 7 (Anniversary blue yodel) / Brakeman's blues / Let me be your sidetrack / Hobo's meditation / Train whistle blues
CD CDAJA 5042
Living Era / Jun '86 / Select

YODELLING RANGER, THE
Jimmie the kid / Roll along Kentucky moon / Looking for a new Mama / Round up time out West / Sleep, baby, sleep / Yodelling my way back home / Gamblin' bar room blues / in the hills of Tennessee / Old pal of my heart / My lovin' gal Lucille / Standin' on the corner / She was happy till she met you / Peach pickin' time in Georgia / I'm lonesome too / Jimmie Rodgers' last blue yodel / Yodelling ranger / Missisippi moon / Prairie lullaby / Down the old road to home / Jimmie Rodgers visits the Carter family / Carter family and Jimmie Rodgers
CD RAJCD 806
Empress / Oct '92 / Koch

Rodgers, Nile

B MOVIE MATINEE
Groove master / Let's go out tonight / Stay out of the light / Same wavelength / Plan number 9 / State your mind / Face in the window / Doll squad
CD 7599252902
Atlantic / Jan '96 / Warner Music

Rodgers, Paul

LIVE (The Loreley Tapes)
Little bit of love / Be my friend / Feel like making love / Louisiana blues / Muddy Waters blues / Rolling stone / I'm ready / Wishing well / Mister Big / Fire and water / Hunter / Can't get enough / Alright now
CD SPV 08544672
SPV / Mar '97 / Koch / Plastic Head

MUDDY WATER BLUES
CD 8284242
London / Jun '93 / PolyGram

NOW
Soul of love / Overloaded / Heart of fire / Saving grace / All I want is you / Chasing shadows / Love is all I need / Nights like this / Shadow of the sun / I lost it all / Holding back the storm
CD SPV 08544662
SPV / Feb '97 / Koch / Plastic Head

Roditi, Claudio

JAZZ TURNS SAMBA
Moody's samba / Birks works / Speak low / Without a song / Come rain or come shine / Giant steps / Moanin' / Moment's notice / Donna Lee / Inside out
CD 5216162
Groovin' High / Mar '94 / PolyGram

MILESTONES (Roditi, Claudio & Paquito D'Rivera)
Milestones / I'll remember April / But not for me / Pent-up house / Brussels in the rain / Mr. PC
CD CCD 79515
Candid / Feb '97 / Cadillac / Direct / Jazz Music / Koch / Wellard

TWO OF SWORDS
Two of swords / Rua dona margarida / Airegin / Portrait of art / Dom Joaquim braga / How I miss Rio / Secret love / Blues for HO / Pra him / Con alma / Thabo
CD CCD 790504
Candid / Feb '97 / Cadillac / Direct / Jazz Music / Koch / Wellard

Rodrigues, Amalia

AMALIA RODRIGUES
CD DRGCD 5571
DRG / Feb '97 / Discovery / New Note/ Pinnacle

BEST OF FADO, THE (2CD Set)
Triste sina / Ceu da minha rua / O namorico da rita / Conta errada / Fadista louco / As rosas do meu caminho / Fado marujo / Fado das tamanquinhas / Fado da adica / Raizes / Bailaricos / Fado alfachinha / Job / Anjo inutil / Quando os outros te batem, beijo-te eu / Fado final / Esquina do pecado / Chave da minha / Tentacao / Sem razao / Fria claridade / Campinos do ribatejo / Le porque tens cinco pedras / Ave Maria fadista / A minha cancao / Disse mal de ti / Fado amalia / Fado do ciume / Cansaco / Que deus me perdoe / Aquela rua / Fado lisboeta
CD Set DBG 53026
Double Gold / Aug '96 / Target/BMG

COIMBRA
CD CD 12502
Music Of The World / Nov '92 / ADA / Target/BMG

FIRST RECORDINGS, THE
CD 995782
EPM / Oct '96 / ADA / Discovery

LIVE AT THE OLYMPIA
CD MCD 71442
Monitor / Jun '93 / CM

QUEEN OF THE FADO
CD SOW 90107
Sounds Of The World / Sep '93 / Target/ BMG

Rodriguez

PROUD HEART
CD CSC 1002
Continental Song City / Oct '95 / Direct

Rodriguez, Alfredo

CUBA LINDA
Tumbao a peruchin / Cuba linda / Cuando vuelvo a tu lado / Canto de palo / Tumba, mi tumba (tumbao Francesa) / Mercedita ya me voy / Drume negrita / Para francia flores y para / Cuba tambien (Guaguanco)
CD HNCD 1399
Hannibal / Nov '96 / ADA / Vital

Rodriguez, David

LANDIN '92
CD BRAM 1992352
Brambus / Nov '93 / ADA

TRUE CROSS, THE
CD DJD 3202
Dejadisc / May '94 / ADA / Direct

Rodriguez, Johnny

YOU CAN SAY THAT AGAIN
CD HCD 8073
Hightone / Jul '96 / ADA / Koch

Rodriguez, Johnny

JOHNNY RODRIGUEZ 1936-1940
CD HQCD 76
Harlequin / Jul '96 / Hot Shot / Jazz Music / Swift / Wellard

Rodriguez, Tito

MAMBO MONA (Rodriguez, Tito y Los Lobos del Mamboa)
CD TCD 014
Fresh Sound / Dec '92 / Discovery / Jazz Music

MUCHO CHA CHA
Cha cha cha Para Ti / This is mambo / Baranga / Asi Asi / Sabroso mambo / Todo es cha cha cha / Rico Rica cha / Agua con Azucar / Piel canela / Sun sun babae / Ya soy Feliz / La rumba no se Acabo / La renta / El Rinconcito / El Guaguanco del Caramelero / Los Cacos del amor
CD CD 62093
Saludos Amigos / Mar '97 / Target/BMG

Roea, Jude

MYSTIC IN THE MAKING
CD CDSGP 082
Prestige / Oct '94 / Else / Total/BMG

Roedelius, Hans Joachim

AFTER THE HEAT
CD SKYCD 3021
Sky / Nov '94 / Greyhound / Koch / Vital/ SAM

AUF LEISEN SOHLEN
CD SKYCD 3048
Sky / Feb '95 / Greyhound / Koch / Vital/ SAM

DURCH DIE WUSTE
CD SKYCD 3051
Sky / May '95 / Greyhound / Koch / Vital/ SAM

GESCHENK DES AUGENBLICKS
Gesckenk des Augenblicks / Adieu Quichotte / Troubadour / Kleine blume irgendwo / Ohn' unterlass / Gefundene zeit / Sehnsucht ich will dich lassen / Das sanfte / Tag fur tag / Zu fussen der berge am ufer des sees / Wurzeln des glucks
CD CDOVD 483
EG / Jun '97 / EMI

LUSTWANDEL
CD SKYCD 3058
Sky / Feb '95 / Greyhound / Koch / Vital/ SAM

PINK, BLUE AND AMBER
CD CTCD 040
Captain Trip / Jul '97 / Greyhound

THEATRE WORKS
CD MRC 016
Staalplaat / May '95 / Vital/SAM

WEEN DER SUDWIND WEHT
CD SKYCD 3064
Sky / Feb '95 / Greyhound / Koch / Vital/ SAM

Roessingh, Karel

THINKING OF YOU
CD MCD 1762
Midsummer / Aug '96 / Else

Roger, Aldus

CAJUN LEGEND, A
CD LLCD 1007
La Louisianne / Feb '94 / Swift

Rogers, Billy

GUITAR ARTISTRY OF BILLY ROGERS, THE
CD STCD 566
Stash / May '93 / ADA / Cadillac / CM / Direct / Jazz Music

Rogers, D.J.

SAY YOU LOVE ME
CD SCL 21142
Ichiban Soul Classics / Jun '96 / Koch

Rogers, Jimmy

BILL'S BLUES (Rogers, Jimmy/Hubert Sumlin/Big Bill Hickey)
CD ATD 1112CD
Atomic Theory / Dec '94 / ADA / Direct

BLUES 1927-1933, THE (2CD Set)
CD Set FA 254
Fremeaux / Oct '96 / ADA / Discovery

BLUES FOLLOW ME ALL DAY LONG (The Complete Shelter Recordings Of Jimmy Rogers Vol.2)
Act like you love me / Broken hearted blues / Information please / Bad luck blues / Gold-tailed bird / Lonesome blues / Brown-skinned woman / That's alright Mama / You're sweet / Sloppy drunk / Live at Ma Bee's / House rocker / Pretty baby / You're the one / Blues (follow me all day long) / Slick chick / I lost a good woman / Dorcie Belle
CD CZ 566
Premier/EMI / Feb '96 / EMI

COMPLETE CHESS RECORDINGS, THE
CD MCD 09372
Chess/MCA / Jul '97 / BMG / New Note/ BMG

FEELIN' GOOD
CD BPCD 5018
Blind Pig / Feb '95 / ADA / CM / Direct / Hot Shot

HARD WORKING MAN (Charly Blues Masterworks Vol.3)
I used to have a woman / Hard working man / My little machine / Give love another chance / What's the matter / Blues leave me alone / Sloppy drunk / If it ain't me / One kiss / I can't believe / What have I done / Trace of you / Don't turn me down / Don't you know my baby
CD CD BM 3
Charly / Apr '92 / Koch

JIMMY ROGERS WITH RONNIE EARL & THE BROADCASTERS
CD CCD 11033
Crosscut / Jan '94 / ADA / CM / Direct

LUDELLA
CD 422294
New Rose / May '94 / ADA / Direct / Discovery

SLOPPY DRUNK
Sloppy drunk / I can't sleep for worrying / Mistreated baby / Slick chick / Pretty baby / Left me with a broken heart / I lost the good woman / You're so sweet / Last time / Shelby county / Tricky woman / Sloppy drunk / Gold tailed bird / Walking by myself / That's alright / Ludella
CD ECD 260362
Evidence / Sep '93 / ADA / Cadillac / Harmonia Mundi

THAT'S ALL RIGHT
That's alright Mama / Ludella / Goin' away baby / Today today blues / World's in a tangle / She loves another man / Money, marbles and chalk / Chance to love / Back door friend / Crying shame / Mistreated baby / Last time / Out on the road / Left me with a broken heart / Act like you love me / Chicago bound / You're the one / Walking by myself / My baby don't love me no more / This has never been / Rock this house / My last meal / You don't know / Can't keep from worrying
CD CDRED 16
Charly / Sep '89 / Koch

THAT'S ALL RIGHT
I'm in love / That's alright Mama / Ludella / Goin' away baby / Today today blues / World is in a tangle / Hard working man / Back door friend / Mistreated baby / Left me with a broken heart / Blues all day long

(leave me alone) / Chicago bound / Sloppy drunk / You're the one / Walking by myself / If it ain't me / I can't believe / What have I done / Don't turn me down / Rock this house / You don't know
CD _____ CD 52040
Blues Encore / Oct '96 / Target/BMG

Rogers, Kenny

BEST OF KENNY ROGERS, THE (Rogers, Kenny & The First Edition)
CD _____ CTS 55402
Country Stars / Jan '92 / Target/BMG

BEST OF KENNY ROGERS, THE
CD _____ TRTCD 175
TrueTrax / Jul '96 / THE

CHRISTMAS
Christmas everyday / Kentucky homemade Christmas / Carol of the bells / Kids / Sweet little Jesus boy / Christmas is my favourite time of year / White Christmas / My favourite things / O' holy night / When a child is born
CD _____ CDMFP 6242
Music For Pleasure / Oct '96 / EMI

COLLECTION, THE
CD _____ COL 031
Collection / Oct '95 / Target/BMG

COUNTRY CLASSICS
Lady / Don't fall in love with a dreamer / Ruby (don't take your love to town) / She believes in me / Lucille / You decorated my life / Every time two fools collide / All I ever need is you / You needed me / Together again / You've lost that loving feeling / Why don't we go somewhere and love / But you know I love you / Love lifted me / Love or something like it / Another somebody done somebody / My world begins and ends with you / Just the way you are / You and me / We love each other
CD _____ CDMFP 6322
Music For Pleasure / Apr '97 / EMI

COUNTRY COLLECTION (Rogers, Kenny & The First Edition)
For the good times / She even woke me up to say goodbye / Me and Bobby McGee / King of Oak Street / Ticket to nowhere / Tell it all brother / Way it used to be / Just dropped in / Heed the call / Church without a name / But you know I love you / Poem for my little lady / Hurry up love / Run thru your mind / Sleep comes easy / Always leaving, always gone / I believe in music / Ruby, don't take your love to town
CD _____ MUCD 9023
Musketeer / Apr '95 / Disc

DAYTIME FRIENDS (The Very Best Of Kenny Rogers)
Gambler / Daytime friends, nightime lovers / Lucille / Ruby, don't take your love to town / Don't fall in love with a dreamer / Coward of the county / You decorated my life / Reuben James / She believes in me / Long arm of the law / Till I make it on my own / Son of Hickory Holler's tramp / Sweet music man / Green green grass of home / We've got tonight / Something's burning / Desperado / Lady / Abraham, Martin and John / Everytime two fools collide
CD _____ CDEMTV 79
EMI / Sep '93 / EMI

DUETS (Rogers, Kenny & Dottie West)
All I ever need is you / Till I can make it on my own / Just the way you are / You needed me / Let it be me / Together again / Midnight flyer / You've lost that lovin' feelin' / Let's take the long way around the world / Hey won't you play another somebody done somebody wrong song / Every time two fools collide / You and me / What's wrong with us today / Beautiful lies / That's the way it could have been / Why don't we go somewhere and love / Baby I'm a want you / Anyone who isn't me tonight / Loving gift / We love each other
CD _____ CDMFP 6111
Music For Pleasure / Mar '94 / EMI

ESSENTIAL COLLECTION, THE
CD Set _____ LECD 615
Wisepack / Apr '95 / Conifer/BMG / THE

FOR THE GOOD TIMES
CD _____ PLSCD 109
Pulse / Mar '96 / BMG

FOR THE GOOD TIMES (2CD Set)
CD Set _____ 24051
Delta Doubles / Jun '96 / Target/BMG

GIFT, THE
CD _____ 7014711024
3 Chord / Nov '96 / Total/BMG

GOLD COLLECTION, THE
CD _____ D2CD 28
Deja Vu / May '94 / THE

HITS COLLECTION, THE (Rogers, Kenny & The First Edition)
Ruby don't take your love to town / Something's burning / What am I gonna do / If wishes were horses / Shine on Ruby Mountain / For the good times / Lay it down / Sunshine / Ticket to nowhere / Where does Rosie go / Tell it all brother / Always leaving, always gone / Loser / Tulsa turnaround / Me and Bobby McGee / All God's lonely children / Once again she's all alone
CD _____ 100352
CMC / May '97 / BMG

KENNY ROGERS
CD _____ 15342
Laserlight / Nov '92 / Target/BMG

KENNY ROGERS
CD _____ DS 013
Desperado / Jun '97 / TKO Magnum

KENNY ROGERS STORY, THE (20 Golden Greats)
Lucille / Lady / Long arm of the law / You decorated my life / Sweet music man / Ruby, don't take your love to town / Love or something like it / Through the years / You are so beautiful / Don't fall in love with a dreamer / Gambler / Daytime friends / We've got tonight / Love lifted me / Coward of the county / Reuben James / Desperado / She believes in me / Something's burning / Blaze of glory
CD _____ CDEMTV 39
Liberty / Dec '87 / EMI

KENNY ROGERS/WILLIE NELSON ESSENTIALS (Rogers, Kenny & Willie Nelson)
CD _____ LECD 637
Wisepack / Aug '95 / Conifer/BMG / THE

LEGENDS IN MUSIC
CD _____ LECD 106
Wisepack / Sep '94 / Conifer/BMG / THE

LOVE SONGS
Lady / Ruby, don't take your love to town / Lucille / She believed in me / Together again / Don't fall in love with a dreamer / You decorated my life / Every time two fools collide / All I ever need is you / You needed me / Why don't we go somewhere and love / Love or something like it / Hey won't you play another somebody done somebody wrong song / My world begins and ends with you / You and me / We love each other / You've lost that lovin' feelin' / But you know I love you / Love lifted me / Just the way you are
CD _____ CDMFP 5880
Music For Pleasure / Apr '90 / EMI

RUBEN JAMES
CD _____ WMCD 5663
Disky / May '94 / Disky / THE

RUBY DON'T TAKE YOUR LOVE TO TOWN
Ruby, don't take your love to town / Green green grass of home / Sweet music man / Love or something like it / You and me / King of Oak Street / Reuben James / Puttin' in overtime at home / Daytime friends / Let it be me / Buried treasure / Son of Hickory Holler's tramp / I wasn't man enough / Mother country music / Lay down beside me / Lucille
CD _____ CDMFP 6001
Music For Pleasure / Sep '88 / EMI

RUBY DON'T TAKE YOUR LOVE TO TOWN
Ticket to nowhere / Conditions (Just dropped in) / She even woke me up to say goodbye / My Washington woman / Run thru your mind / Sleep comes easy / After all / For the good times / Something's burning / Hurry up love / Trying just as hard / Ruby, don't take your love to town / Heed the call / we all got to help each other / Poem for my little lady / Where does Rosie go / Sunshine / Reuben James / Loser / Church without a name / Green green grass of home / Sweet music man / Daytime friends
CD _____ MU 5066
Musketeer / Oct '92 / Disc

RUBY DON'T TAKE YOUR LOVE TO TOWN
CD _____ CDGFR 027
Tring / Jun '92 / Tring

RUBY DON'T TAKE YOUR LOVE TO TOWN
Ruby, don't take your love to town / Reuben James / Shine on Ruby mountain / Ticket to nowhere / Conditions (just dropped in) / She even woke me up to say goodbye / My Washington woman / Run thru your mind / Sleep comes easy / After all / For the good times / Something's burning / Hurry up love / Trying just as hard / Heed the call / We all got to help each other / Poem for my little lady / Where does Rosie go / Sunshine / Loser / Church without a name / Me and Bobby McGee / Always leaving, always gone / Calico silver / Way it used to be / Goodtime liberator
CD _____ GRF 027
Tring / Feb '93 / Tring

RUBY DON'T TAKE YOUR LOVE TO TOWN
CD _____ 15075
Laserlight / Aug '91 / Target/BMG

RUBY DON'T TAKE YOUR LOVE TO TOWN (Rogers, Kenny & The First Edition)
Ruby don't take your love to town / Me and Bobby McGee / Poem for my little lady / For the good times / Good lady of Toronto / Where does Rosie go / What am I gonna do / All God's lonely children / Lay it down / Tulsa turnaround / Tell it all brother / Love woman / I'm gonna sing you a sad song Suzie / King of Oak Street / Shine on Ruby Mountain / Heed the call / Molly / Camptown ladies / We all got to help eachother / After all
CD _____ CDSGP 094
Prestige / Mar '94 / Else / Total/BMG

RUBY DON'T TAKE YOUR LOVE TO TOWN (Rogers, Kenny & The First Edition)
Ruby don't take your love to town / Reuben James / Shine on Ruby Mountain / Conditions (just dropped in) / She even woke me up to say goodbye / My Washington woman / For the good times / Something's burning / Heed the call / We all got to help each other / Poem for my little lady / Where does Rosie go / Sunshine / Me and Bobby McGee / Calico silver / Elvira
CD _____ QED 010
Tring / Nov '96 / Tring

SPOTLIGHT ON KENNY ROGERS
Ruby, don't take your love to town / Me and Bobby McGee / Poem for my lady / For the good times / Good lady of Toronto / Where does Rosie go / What am I going to do / All God's lovely children / Lay it down / Tulsa turn around / Tell it all brother / Love woman / I'm going to sing a sad song Suzie / King of Oak Street / Shine on Ruby Mountain / Heed the call / Molly / Camptown ladies / We all got to help each other / After all
CD _____ HADCD 104
Javelin / Feb '94 / Henry Hadaway / THE

VERY BEST OF KENNY ROGERS, THE
What I did for love / Ruby, don't take your love to town / Don't fall in love with a dreamer: *Rogers, Kenny & Kim Carnes* / Gambler / Daytime friends / Love is strange: *Rogers, Kenny & Dolly Parton* / She believes in me / Lucille / Lady / Coward of the county / You decorated my life / Love lifted me / Something's burning / Islands in the stream: *Rogers, Kenny & Dolly Parton*
CD _____ 7599264572
WEA / Nov '90 / Warner Music

Rogers, Richard

SOUL TALKING
Woop de woo / Something good inside / Soul talking / Keep giving me love / Give you my love / Underground / My own love / Waiting on a sign / Isn't it a shame / Everybody knows
CD _____ XECD 9
Expansion / Oct '96 / 3mv/Sony

Rogers, Roy

BLUES ON THE RANGE
CD _____ CCD 11026
Crosscut / '92 / ADA / CM / Direct

RHYTHM & GROOVE
Vida's place / My heart's desire / Call on me / Built for comfort / Feel my care / For the love of a woman / Shakin' hands with the devil / Your mind is on vacation / Proud man / Blues for Brazil / Love me or leave me / Ever since I lost you / Wrong number / Remembering you
CD _____ VPBCD 33
Pointblank / Mar '96 / EMI

SLIDE ZONE
Get back in line / Spent money / House of blue dreams / Lover's moon / Livin' on borrowed time / Ode to the Delta / Not fade away / Slide zone / Lookin' up at downside / Rough house / Still a long ways to go / Off the cuff
CD _____ CDP 8294172
Liberty / Sep '94 / EMI

TRAVELLIN' TRACKS (Rogers, Roy & Norton Buffalo)
CD _____ BPCD 5003
Blind Pig / Jan '93 / ADA / CM / Direct / Hot Shot

Rogers, Sally

CLOSING THE DISTANCE (Rogers, Sally & Claudia Schmidt)
CD _____ FF 425CD
Flying Fish / May '93 / ADA / CM / Direct / Roots

WE'LL PASS THEM ON
CD _____ RHRCD 71
Red House / Aug '95 / ADA / Koch

WHEN HOWIE MET SALLY (Rogers, Sally & Howie Bursen)
CD _____ FF 538CD
Flying Fish / '92 / ADA / CM / Direct / Roots

Rogers, Shorty

AMERICA THE BEAUTIFUL (Rogers, Shorty & Bud Shank)
America the beautiful / Less is more / New dreams / Casa de luz / Lotus bud / Un poco loco / Good news / Here's that old martian again / Trult truly / Fun
CD _____ CCD 79510
Candid / Feb '97 / Cadillac / Direct / Jazz Music / Koch / Wellard

BIG SHORTY ROGERS EXPRESS, THE
Blues express / Pink squirrel / Coop de graas / Infinity promenade / Short stop / Boar-jibu / Pay the piper / Home with sweets / Tales of an African lobster / Contours / Chiquito loco / Sweetheart of Sigmund Freud
CD _____ 74321185192
RCA / Jul '94 / BMG

EIGHT BROTHERS (Rogers, Shorty & Bud Shank/Lighthouse All Stars)
Back to the basie-ics / Yesterday, today & forever / Unfinished dream / Magic man / Eight horns / Stray horns / Like it is / Battle hymn of the Republic / Essence of tenderness / Double trouble / No additives, no preservatives
CD _____ CCD 79521
Candid / Feb '97 / Cadillac / Direct / Jazz Music / Koch / Wellard

JUST A FEW 1951-1956
Moten swing / Isn't it romantic / Four mothers / Dickie's dream / Over the rainbow / Lady in red / Just a few / My heart stood still / Blues way up there / Blues way down there / Easy / Not really the blues / Baklava Bridge / Clickin' with clax / Twelfth Street rag
CD _____ CD 53208
Giants Of Jazz / Oct '96 / Cadillac / Jazz Music / Target/BMG

Rogers, Stan

BETWEEN THE BREAKS - LIVE
CD _____ FOG 002CD
Fogerty's Cove / Jul '94 / ADA

FOGERTY'S COVE
CD _____ FOG 1001CD
Fogerty's Cove / Jul '94 / ADA

FOR THE FAMILY
CD _____ R 002CD
Folk Tradition Canada / Jul '95 / ADA

FROM FRESH WATER
CD _____ FOG 007CD
Fogerty's Cove / Jul '94 / ADA

NORTHWEST PASSAGE
CD _____ FOG 004CD
Fogerty's Cove / Jul '94 / ADA

TURNAROUND
CD _____ FOG 001CD
Fogerty's Cove / Jul '94 / ADA

Rogers, Tammy

IN THE RED (Rogers, Tammy & Don Heffington)
CD _____ DR 0002
Dead Reckoning / Feb '96 / Avid/BMG

TAMMY ROGERS
CD _____ DR 00052
Dead Reckoning / Jun '96 / Avid/BMG

Rogerson, Diana

BEASTINGS
CD _____ UD 041CD
United Dairies / Oct '96 / World Serpent

Rogie, S.E.

DEAD MEN DON'T SMOKE MARIJUANA
Kpindigbee / Time in my life / Nor weigh me lek dat / Jaimgba tutu / Koneh pelawoe / Jojo yalah jo / Nyalomei luange / African gospel / Nyalimagotee / Dieman noba smoke tafee
CD _____ CDRW 46
Realworld / May '94 / EMI

Rogoff, Jill

ACROSS THE NARROW SEAS
CD _____ ALC 129CD
Alcazar / May '97 / ADA

Rojitas

REGALAME TU ENCANTO
CD _____ 74321401342
Milan / Sep '96 / Conifer/BMG / Silva Screen

Roland, Paul

DANSE MACABRE
Witchfinder General / Madame Guillotine / Great Edwardian air raid / Hanging judge / Still falls the snow / Matilda mother / Gabrielle / Requiem / Buccaneers / In the opium den / Twilight of the rock
CD _____ 422296
New Rose / May '94 / ADA / Direct / Discovery

DUEL
CD _____ 422297
New Rose / May '94 / ADA / Direct / Discovery

GARGOYLES
CD _____ GASCD 703
Gaslight / Jul '97 / Cargo

HOUSE OF DARK SHADOWS
CD _____ 422299
New Rose / May '94 / ADA / Direct / Discovery

STRYCHNINE
CD _____ 422431
New Rose / May '94 / ADA / Direct / Discovery

Rolie, Gregg

GRINGO
CD ______ 100334
Point / Mar '97 / Cargo

Rollerskate Skinny

SHOULDER VOICES
CD ______ PILLCD 3
Placebo / Sep '93 / RTM/Disc

Rollinat, Maurice

LA MORT LUI RICANE
CD ______ 983872
EPM / Feb '97 / ADA / Discovery

Rolling Stones

12 X 5
Around and around / Confessin' the blues / Empty heart / Time is on my side / Good times, bad times / It's all over now / 2120 South Michigan Avenue / Under the boardwalk / Congratulations / Grown up wrong / If you need me / Suzie Q
CD ______ 8444612
London / Jun '95 / PolyGram

AFTERMATH
Mother's little helper / Stupid girl / Lady Jane / Under my thumb / Don't cha bother me / Goin' home / Flight 505 / High and dry / Out of time / It's not easy / I am waiting / Take it or leave it / Think / What to do
CD ______ 8444662
London / Jun '95 / PolyGram

BEGGARS BANQUET
Sympathy for the devil / No expectations / Dear Doctor / Parachute woman / Jigsaw puzzle blues / Street fighting man / Prodigal son / Stray cat blues / Factory girl / Salt of the Earth
CD ______ 8444712
London / Jun '95 / PolyGram

BETWEEN THE BUTTONS
Let's spend the night together / Yesterday's papers / Ruby Tuesday / Connection / She smiled sweetly / Cool calm and collected / All sold out / My obsession / Who's been sleeping here / Complicated / Miss Amanda Jones / Something happened to me yesterday
CD ______ 8444682
London / Jun '95 / PolyGram

BIG HITS VOL.1 (High Tide And Green Grass)
Have you seen your mother, baby, standing in the shadow / Paint it black / It's all over now / Last time / Heart of stone / Not fade away / Come on / Satisfaction / Get off my cloud / As tears go by / Nineteenth nervous breakdown / Lady Jane / Time is on my side / Little red rooster
CD ______ 8444652
London / Jun '95 / PolyGram

BIG HITS VOL.2 (Through The Past Darkly)
Paint it black / Ruby Tuesday / She's a rainbow / Jumpin' Jack Flash / Mother's little helper / Let's spend the night together / Honky tonk women / Dandelion / 2000 Light years from home / Have you seen your mother, baby, standing in the shadow / Street fighting man
CD ______ 8444722
London / Jun '95 / PolyGram

BLACK AND BLUE
Hot stuff / Hand of fate / Cherry oh baby / Memory motel / Hey Negrita / Fool to cry / Crazy mama / Melody (inspiration by Billy Preston)
CD ______ CDV 2736
Virgin / Aug '94 / EMI

BRIAN JONES INTERVIEW
CD ______ RSBJ 1
UFO / Aug '96 / Pinnacle

CHARLIE WATTS INTERVIEW
CD ______ RSCW 1
UFO / Aug '96 / Pinnacle

DECEMBER'S CHILDREN (AND EVERYBODY'S)
She said yeah / Talkin' 'bout you / You better move on / Look what you've done / Singer not the song / Route 66 / Get off my cloud / I'm free / As tears go by / Gotta get away / Blue turns to grey / I'm movin' on
CD ______ 8444642
London / Jun '95 / PolyGram

DIRTY WORK
One hit (to the body) / Fight / Harlem shuffle / Hold back / Too rude / Winning ugly / Back to zero / Dirty work / Had it with you / Sleep tonight
CD ______ CDV 2743
Virgin / Aug '94 / EMI

EMOTIONAL RESCUE
Summer romance / Send it to me / Let me go / Indian girl / Where the boys go / Down in the hole / Emotional rescue / She's so cold / All about you / Dance (part 1)
CD ______ CDV 2737
Virgin / Aug '94 / EMI

EXILE ON MAIN STREET
Rocks off / Rip this joint / Casino boogie / Tumbling dice / Sweet Virginia / Torn and frayed / Sweet black angel / Loving cup / Shake your hips / Happy / Turd on the run / Ventilator blues / I just want to see his face / Let it loose / All down the line / Stop breaking down / Shine a light / Soul survivor
CD ______ CDV 2731
Virgin / Aug '94 / EMI

FLOWERS
Ruby Tuesday / Have you seen your mother, baby, standing in the shadow / Let's spend the night together / Lady Jane / Out of time / My girl / Backstreet girl / Please go home / Mother's little helper / Take it or leave it / Ride on baby / Sittin' on a fence
CD ______ 8444692
London / Jun '95 / PolyGram

GET YER YA-YA'S OUT (Rolling Stones Live In Concert)
Jumpin' Jack Flash / Carol / Stray cat blues / Love in vain / Midnight rambler / Sympathy for the devil / Live with me / Little Queenie / Honky tonk women / Street fighting man
CD ______ 8444742
London / Jun '95 / PolyGram

GOATS HEAD SOUP
Dancing with Mr. D / 100 years ago / Coming down again / Doo doo doo doo (Heartbreaker) / Angie / Silver train / Hide your love / Winter / Can you hear the music / Star star
CD ______ CDV 2735
Virgin / Aug '94 / EMI

GOT LIVE IF YOU WANT IT
Under my thumb / Get off my cloud / Lady Jane / Not fade away / I've been loving you too long / Fortune teller / Last time / Nineteenth nervous breakdown / Time is on my side / I'm alright / Have you seen your mother, baby, standing in the shadow / Satisfaction
CD ______ 8444672
London / Jun '95 / PolyGram

HOT ROCKS 1964-1971 (2CD Set)
Satisfaction / Get off my cloud / Paint it black / Under my thumb / Ruby Tuesday / Let's spend the night together / Jumpin' Jack Flash / Sympathy for the devil / Honky tonk women / Gimme shelter / You can't always get what you want / Brown sugar / Time is on my side / Heart of stone / Play with fire / As tears go by / Mother's little helper / Nineteenth nervous breakdown / Street fighting man / Midnight rambler / Wild horses
CD Set ______ 8444752
London / Jun '95 / PolyGram

INTERVIEW DISC
CD ______ TELL 05
Network / Dec '96 / Total/BMG

INTERVIEW DISC
CD ______ SAM 7011
Sound & Media / Nov '96 / Sound & Media

IT'S ONLY ROCK 'N' ROLL
If you can't rock me / Ain't too proud to beg / It's only rock 'n' roll / Till the next goodbye / Luxury / Time waits for no one / Dance little sister / If you really want to / Short and curlies / Fingerprint file
CD ______ CDV 2733
Virgin / Aug '94 / EMI

JAGGER/RICHARD SONGBOOK (Various Artists)
Last time: *Who* / Nineteenth nervous breakdown: *Flamin' Groovies* / Street fighting man: *Stewart, Rod* / Heart of stone: *Mekons* / Mother's little helper: *Coughlan, Mary* / Ruby Tuesday: *Melanie* / Out of time: *Farlowe, Chris* / Congratulations: *West Five* / Wild horses: *Flying Burrito Brothers* / Tell me: *Webb, Cassell* / Silver train: *Naked Prey* / Sympathy for the devil: *Ferry, Bryan* / Lady Jane: *Merrick, Tony* / Take it or leave it: *Searchers* / Sleepy city: *Mighty Avengers* / That girl belongs to yesterday: *Pitney, Gene* / As tears go by: *Faithfull, Marianne* / Honky tonk women: *Turner, Ike & Tina* / So much in love: *Inmates* / Will you be my lover tonight: *Bean, George* / Sitting on a fence: *Twice As Much* / Satisfaction: *Redding, Otis* / Connection: *Montrose* / Sister Morphine: *Faithfull, Marianne*
CD ______ VSOPCD 159
Connoisseur Collection / Apr '91 / Pinnacle

JAMMING WITH EDWARD (Hopkins/Cooder/Jagger/Wyman/Watts)
Boudoir stomp / It hurts me too / Edward's thrump up / Blow with Ry / Interlude a la el hopo / Loveliest night of the year / Highland fling
CD ______ CDV 2779
Virgin / May '95 / EMI

JUMP BACK (The Best Of The Rolling Stones 1971-1993)
Harlem shuffle / Start me up / Brown sugar / It's only rock 'n' roll / Mixed emotions / Angie / Tumbling dice / Fool to cry / Rock and a hard place / Miss you / Hot stuff / Emotional rescue / Respectable / Beast of burden / Waiting on a friend / Wild horses / Bitch / Undercover of the night
CD ______ CDV 2726
Virgin / Dec '93 / EMI

KEITH RICHARDS INTERVIEW
CD ______ RSKR 1
UFO / Aug '96 / Pinnacle

LET IT BLEED
Gimme shelter / Love in vain / Country honk / Live with me / Let it bleed / Midnight rambler / You got the silver / Monkey man / You can't always get what you want
CD ______ 8444732
London / Jun '95 / PolyGram

LIFE AND TIMES (Documentary and Music)
CD ______ OTR 1100049
Metro Independent / Jun '97 / Essential/BMG

MICK JAGGER INTERVIEW
CD ______ RSMJ 1
UFO / Aug '96 / Pinnacle

MORE HOT ROCKS (Big Hits And Fazed Cookies/2CD Set)
Tell me / Not fade away / Last time / It's all over now / Good times, bad times / I'm free / Out of time / Lady Jane / Sittin' on a fence / Have you seen your mother, baby, standing in the shadow / Dandelion / We love you / She's a rainbow / 2000 light years from home / Child of the moon / No expectations / Let it bleed / What to do / Money / Come on / Fortune teller / Poison ivy / Bye bye Johnny / I can't be satisfied / Long long while
CD Set ______ 8444782
London / Jun '95 / PolyGram

OUT OF OUR HEADS
She said yeah / Mercy mercy / Hitch hike / That's how strong my love is / Good times / Gotta get away / Talkin bout you / Cry to me / Oh baby / Heart of stone / Under assistant West Coast promotion man / I'm free
CD ______ 8444632
London / Jun '95 / PolyGram

ROCK 'N' ROLL CIRCUS (December 11th 1968) (Various Artists)
Song for Jeffrey: *Jethro Tull* / Quick one while he's away: *Who* / Ain't that a lot of love: *Taj Mahal* / Something better: *Faithfull, Marianne* / Yer blues: *Dirty Mac* / Whole lotta Yoko: *Ono, Yoko & Ivry Gitlis/Dirty Mac* / Jumping Jack flash: *Rolling Stones* / Parachute woman: *Rolling Stones* / No expectations: *Rolling Stones* / You can't always get what you want: *Rolling Stones* / Sympathy for the devil: *Rolling Stones* / Salt of the Earth: *Rolling Stones*
CD ______ 5267712
London / Oct '96 / PolyGram

ROLLING STONES
Route 66 / I just want to make love to you / Honest I do / I need you baby / Now I've got a witness / Little by little / I'm a king bee / Carol / Tell me (you're coming back) / Can I get a witness / You can make it if you try / Walking the dog
CD ______ 8444602
London / Jun '95 / PolyGram

ROLLING STONES BOX SET
CD Set ______ RS 1
UFO / Oct '92 / Pinnacle

ROLLING STONES INTERVIEWS, THE (3CD Set)
CD Set ______ 55582
Laserlight / Mar '97 / Target/BMG

ROLLING STONES NOW, THE
Everybody needs somebody / Down home girl / You can't catch me / Heart of stone / What a shame / I need you baby / Down the road apiece / Off the hook / Pain in my heart / Oh baby (we got a good thing goin') / Little red rooster / Surprise surprise
CD ______ 8444622
London / Jun '95 / PolyGram

ROYAL PHILHARMONIC ORCHESTRA PLAY THE ROLLING STONES (Royal Philharmonic Orchestra)
CD ______ DCD 5296
Disky / Sep '93 / Disky / THE

SHARED VISION VOL.2 (The Songs Of The Rolling Stones) (Various Artists)
CD ______ 5358452
London / Oct '96 / PolyGram

SINGLES COLLECTION, THE (The London Years/2CD Set)
Come on / I want to be loved / I wanna be your man / Stoned / Not fade away / Little by little / It's all over now / Good times, bad times / Tell me / I just want to make love to you / Time is on my side / Congratulations / Little red rooster / Off the hook / Heart of stone / What a shame / Last time / Play with fire / Satisfaction / Under assistant West coast promotion man / Spider and the fly / Get off my cloud / I'm free / Singer not the song / As tears go by / Gotta get away / Nineteenth nervous breakdown / Sad day / Paint it black / Stupid girl / Long long while / Mother's little helper / Lady Jane / Have you seen your mother, baby, standing in the shadow / Who's driving your plane / Let's spend the night together / Ruby Tuesday / We love you / Dandelion / She's a rainbow / 2000 light years from home / In another land / Lantern / Jumpin' Jack Flash / Child of the moon / Street fighting man / No expectations / Surprise surprise / Honky tonk women / You can't always get what you want / Memo from Turner / Brown sugar / Wild horses / I don't know why / Try a little harder / Out of time / Jiving sister Fanny / Sympathy for the devil
CD Set ______ 8444812
London / Jun '95 / PolyGram

SOME GIRLS
Miss you / When the whip comes down / Just my imagination / Some girls / Lies / Faraway eyes / Respectable / Before they make me run / Beast of burden / Shattered
CD ______ CDV 2734
Virgin / Aug '94 / EMI

STEEL WHEELS
Sad, sad, sad / Mixed emotions / Terrifying / Hold on to your hat / Hearts for sale / Blinded by love / Rock and a hard place / Can't be seen / Almost hear you sigh / Continental drift / Break the spell / Slippin' away
CD ______ CDV 2742
Virgin / Aug '94 / EMI

STICKY FINGERS
Brown sugar / Sway / Wild horses / Can't you hear me knocking / You gotta move / Bitch / I got the blues / Sister Morphine / Dead flowers / Moonlight mile
CD ______ CDV 2730
Virgin / Aug '94 / EMI

STRIPPED
Street fighting man / Like a rolling stone / Not fade away / Shine a light / Spider and the fly / I'm free / Wild horses / Let it bleed / Dead flowers / Slipping away / Angie / Love in vain / Sweet Virginia / Little baby
CD ______ CDV 2801
Virgin / Nov '95 / EMI

SYMPHONIC MUSIC OF THE ROLLING STONES, THE (Featuring Mick Jagger/Marianne Faithfull/Michael Hutchence) (London Symphony Orchestra/Peter Scholes)
Street fighting man / Paint it black / Under my thumb / As tears go by / Sympathy for the devil / Dandelion / Ruby Tuesday / Angie / She's a rainbow / Gimme shelter / Jumpin' Jack Flash
CD ______ 09026625262
RCA Victor / Jun '94 / BMG

SYMPHONIC ROLLING STONES (Hanover Radio Philharmonic Orchestra)
Satisfaction / Last time / Paint it black / Emotional rescue / As tears go by / Out of time / Angie / 19th nervous breakdown / Lady Jane / Fool to cry
CD ______ QED 227
Tring / Nov '96 / Tring

TALK (Interview)
CD ______ DISSCD 4
Wax / Apr '96 / RTM/Disc / Total/BMG

TATTOO YOU
Start me up / Hang fire / Slave / Little T and A / Black limousine / No use in crying / Neighbours / Worried about you / Tops / Heaven / Waiting on a friend
CD ______ CDV 2732
Virgin / Aug '94 / EMI

THEIR SATANIC MAJESTIES REQUEST
Citadel / In another land / Sing this all together (see what happens) / She's a rainbow / Lantern / Gomper / 2000 light years from home / On with the show / 2000 man
CD ______ 8444702
London / Jun '95 / PolyGram

UNDER COVER
Too much blood / Pretty beat up / Too tough / All the way down / It must be hell / Undercover of the night / She was hot / Tie you up (The pain of love) / Wanna hold you / Feel on baby
CD ______ CDV 2741
Virgin / Aug '94 / EMI

VOODOO LOUNGE
Love is strong / You got me rocking / Worst / Out of tears / I go wild / Brand new car / Sweethearts together / Suck on the jugular / Blinded by rainbows / Baby break it down / Thru and thru / Mean disposition / New faces / Moon is up / Sparks will fly
CD ______ CDV 2750
Virgin / Jul '94 / EMI

WHO ARE THE STONES (Interview Disc)
CD ______ CBAK 4008
Baktabak / Apr '88 / Arabesque

Rollinghead

LONG BLACK FEELING
CD ______ GROW 0072
Grass / Apr '94 / Pinnacle / SRD

Rollini, Adrian

ADRIAN ROLLINI GROUPS 1924-1927
CD ______ VILCD 0232
Village Jazz / Sep '92 / Jazz Music / Target/BMG

BOUNCIN' IN RHYTHM
CD ______ TPZ 1027
Topaz Jazz / Sep '95 / Cadillac / Pinnacle

Rollins, Henry

BIG UGLY MOUTH
CD QS 9CD
Quarter Stick / Jul '92 / Cargo / SRD

BLACK COFFEE BLUES
CD 213CD 021
2.13.61 / May '97 / Pinnacle

BOXED LIFE, THE (Spoken Word Performances Parts 1 & 2)
Bone tired / Airplanes / Airport courtesy phone / Jet lag / Hating someone's guts, part 1 / Funny guy / Love in Venice / Strength, part 1 / Strength, part 2 / Odd ball / Hating someone's guts, part 2 / Blues / Big knowledge / Good advice / Vacation in England / Condos / Trade secrets / I know you / Odd ball gets a big laugh
CD 72787210092
Imago / Jan '93 / BMG

COME IN AND BURN
Shame / Starve / All I want / End of something / On my way to the cage / Thursday afternoon / During a city / Neon / Spilling over the side / Inhale exhale / Saying goodbye again / Rejection / Disappearing act
CD DRD 50011
Dreamworks / Mar '97 / BMG

DEEP THROAT BOX SET
CD Set QS 13CD
Quarter Stick / Jul '92 / Cargo / SRD

DO IT (Rollins Band)
CD 986978
Intercord / Jan '94 / Plastic Head

GET IN THE VAN
CD Set 74321242382
Imago / Nov '94 / BMG

HARD VOLUME
CD 986979
Intercord / Jan '94 / Plastic Head

HOT ANIMAL MACHINE
CD 986976
Intercord / Jan '94 / Plastic Head

HUMAN BUTT
CD QS 12CD
Quarter Stick / Jul '92 / Cargo / SRD

LIFE TIME (Rollins Band)
Burned beyond recognition / What am I doing here / 1000 times beyond / Lovely / Wreckage / Gun in mouth blues / You look at you / If you're alive / Turned out
CD 986977
Intercord / Jan '94 / Plastic Head

LIVE AT MCCABES
CD QS 11CD
Quarter Stick / Jul '92 / Cargo / SRD

SWEAT BOX
CD QS 10CD
Quarter Stick / Jul '92 / Cargo / SRD

TURNED ON (Rollins Band)
Lonely / Do it / What have I got / Tearing / Out there / You didn't need / Hard / Followed around / Mask / Down and away / Turned inside out / Deitmar song / Black and white / What do you do / Crazy lover
CD QS 02CD
Quarter Stick / Dec '90 / Cargo / SRD

Rollins, Sonny

+3
What a difference a day made / Biji / They say it's wonderful / Mona Lisa / Cabin in the sky / HS / I've never been in love
CD MCD 92502
Milestone / Apr '96 / Cadillac / Complete/ Pinnacle / Jazz Music / Wellard

AIREGIN 1951-1956
CD CD 53060
Giants Of Jazz / Mar '92 / Cadillac / Jazz Music / Target/BMG

ALFIE
Alfie's theme / He's younger than you are / Street runner with child / Transition theme for minor blues or little Malcolm loves his / On impulse / Alfie's theme differently
CD IMP 12242
Impulse Jazz / Apr '97 / New Note/BMG

ALL THE THINGS YOU ARE
Yesterdays / Summertime / Lover man / 'Round midnight / Afternoon in Paris / It could happen to you / All the things you are / Just friends / At McKies / Now's the time / My one and only love / Travellin' light
CD ND 82179
Bluebird / Jul '90 / BMG

BEST OF SONNY ROLLINS, THE
Decision / Poor butterfly / Why don't I / Misterioso / Tune up / How are things in Glocca Morra / Sonnymoon for two / Softly as in a morning sunrise / Striver's row
CD CDP 7932032
Blue Note / Jan '96 / EMI

BRIDGE, THE
Without a song / Where are you / John S / Bridge / God bless the child / You do something to me
CD 09026685182
RCA Victor / Oct '96 / BMG

COMPLETE PRESTIGE RECORDINGS, THE (7CD Set)
Elysee / Opus V / Hilo / Fox hunt / Morpheus down / Blue room / Whispering / I know / Conception / Out of the blue / Denial / Bluing / Dig / My old flame / It's only a paper moon / Time on my hands / Mambo bounce / This love of mine / Shadrack / On a slow boat to China / With a song in my heart / Scoops / Newk's fadeaway / Compulsion / Serpent's tooth / 'Round midnight / In a sentimental mood / Stopper / Almost like being love / No Moe / Think of one / Let's call this / Friday the 13th / Soft shoe / Confab in tempo / I'll take romance / Airegin / Oleo / But not for me / Doxy / Movin' out / Swingin' for Bumsy / Silk 'n' satin / Solid / I want to be happy / Way you look tonight / More than you know / There's no business like show business / Paradox / Raincheck / There are such things / It's all right with me / In your own sweet way / No line / Vierd blues / I feel a song coming on / Pent-up house / Valse hot / Kiss and run / Count your blessings / My reverie / Most beautiful girl in the world / Paul's pal / When your lover has gone / Tenor madness / You don't know what love is / St. Thomas / Strode rode / Blue 7 / Moritat / I've grown accustomed to her face / Kids know / House I live in / Bird medley / B swift / My ideal / Sonny boy / Two different worlds / Ee-ah / B quick
CD Set 7PCD 4407
Prestige / Nov '96 / Cadillac / Complete/ Pinnacle

CUTTING EDGE, THE
CD OJCCD 468
Original Jazz Classics / Nov '95 / Complete/Pinnacle / Jazz Music / Wellard

DANCING IN THE DARK
Just Once / O T Y O G / Promise / I'll String Along With You / Allison
CD MCD 9155
Milestone / Oct '93 / Cadillac / Complete/ Pinnacle / Jazz Music / Wellard

DON'T ASK
Harlem boys / File / Disco Monk / My ideal / Don't ask / Tai-chi / And then my love I found you
CD OJCCD 915
Original Jazz Classics / May '97 / Complete/ Pinnacle / Jazz Music / Wellard

EAST BROADWAY RUN DOWN
East Broadway run down / Blessings in disguise / We kiss in a shadow
CD IMP 11612
GRP / Sep '95 / New Note/BMG

EASY LIVING
Isn't she lovely / Down the line / My one and only love / Arroz con pollo / Easy living / Hear what I'm saying
CD OJCCD 893
Original Jazz Classics / Nov '96 / Complete/ Pinnacle / Jazz Music / Wellard

ESSENTIAL, THE
Pannonica / La villa / Dearly beloved / Every time we say goodbye / Cutie / Last time I saw Paris / Happiness is a thing called Joe / Someday I'll find you / Freedom suite
CD FCD 60020
Fantasy / Oct '93 / Jazz Music / Pinnacle / Wellard

EUROPEAN CONCERTS
CD BS 18007
Bandstand / Jul '96 / Swift

FALLING IN LOVE WITH JAZZ
CD MCD 9179
Milestone / Oct '93 / Cadillac / Complete/ Pinnacle / Jazz Music / Wellard

FIRST RECORDINGS 1957
Sunny moon for two / Like someone in love / Theme from Tchaikovsky's symphony pathetic / Lust for life / I got it bad and that ain't good / Ballad medley: Flamingo
CD 550142
Jazz Anthology / Feb '94 / Cadillac / Discovery / Harmonia Mundi

FREEDOM SUITE
CD OJCCD 67
Original Jazz Classics / Oct '92 / Complete/Pinnacle / Jazz Music / Wellard

FREEDOM SUITE, THE (1956-1958)
CD CD 53062
Giants Of Jazz / Mar '92 / Cadillac / Jazz Music / Target/BMG

G-MAN
CD MCD 9150
Milestone / Oct '93 / Cadillac / Complete/ Pinnacle / Jazz Music / Wellard

HERE'S TO THE PEOPLE
Why was I born / I wish I knew / Here's to the people / Dr. Phil / Someone to watch over me / Young Roy / Lucky day / Long ago and far away
CD MCD 91942
Milestone / Mar '92 / Cadillac / Complete/ Pinnacle / Jazz Music / Wellard

HORN CULTURE
CD OJCCD 314
Original Jazz Classics / Sep '93 / Complete/Pinnacle / Jazz Music / Wellard

IN DENMARK VOL.1
CD MCD 0372
Moon / Aug '92 / Cadillac / Harmonia Mundi

IN DENMARK VOL.2
CD MCD 0382
Moon / Aug '92 / Cadillac / Harmonia Mundi

LIVE AT GREENWICH VILLAGE (Rollins, Sonny/Elvin Jones & Wilbur Ware)
CD CD 53044
Giants Of Jazz / Mar '90 / Cadillac / Jazz Music / Target/BMG

LIVE IN FRANCE
CD LS 2929
Landscape / Nov '92 / THE

LIVE MID 60'S
CD LS 2915
Landscape / Nov '92 / THE

LOVE AT FIRST SIGHT
Little lulu / Dream that we fell out of / Strode rode / Very thought of you / Caress / Double feature
CD OJCCD 753
Original Jazz Classics / Apr '93 / Complete/ Pinnacle / Jazz Music / Wellard

MOVING OUT
CD OJCCD 582
Original Jazz Classics / Feb '92 / Complete/Pinnacle / Jazz Music / Wellard

NEWK'S TIME
Tune up / Asiatic races / Wonderful, wonderful / Surrey with the fringe on top / Blues for Philly Joe / Namely you
CD CDP 7840012
Blue Note / Mar '95 / EMI

NEXT ALBUM
CD OJCCD 312
Original Jazz Classics / Apr '92 / Complete/Pinnacle / Jazz Music / Wellard

OLD FLAMES
Darn that dream / Where or when / My old flame / Time slimes / I see you face before me / Delia / Prelude to a kiss
CD MCD 9215
Milestone / Jan '94 / Cadillac / Complete/ Pinnacle / Jazz Music / Wellard

OLEO
CD JHR 73552
Jazz Hour / Jan '93 / Cadillac / Jazz Music / Target/BMG

PLUS FOUR
CD OJCCD 243
Original Jazz Classics / Feb '92 / Complete/Pinnacle / Jazz Music / Wellard

PRICELESS JAZZ
Three little words / Hold 'em Joe / Everything happens to me / Blue room / Alfie's theme / We kiss in a shadow / Blessing in disguise
CD GRP 98762
GRP / Jul '97 / New Note/BMG

QUARTETS, FEATURING JIM HALL
God bless the child / John S / You do something to me / Where are you / Without a song / Bridge / If ever I would leave you / Night has a thousand eyes
CD ND 85643
Bluebird / Apr '88 / BMG

ROLLINS MEETS CHERRY VOL.1
CD MCD 0532
Moon / May '94 / Cadillac / Harmonia Mundi

ROLLINS MEETS CHERRY VOL.2
CD MCD 0542
Moon / Apr '94 / Cadillac / Harmonia Mundi

ROLLINS PLAYS FOR BIRD (Rollins, Sonny Quintet)
CD OJCCD 214
Original Jazz Classics / Mar '93 / Complete/Pinnacle / Jazz Music / Wellard

ROLLINS ROUND MIDNIGHT
Yesterdays / Summertime / Without song / 'Round midnight / You do something to me / Lover man / There will never be another you / Where are you / God bless the child / Just friends / My one and only love / All the things you are
CD 74321393442
Camden / Jun '96 / BMG

SAXOPHONE COLOSSUS
CD OJCCD 291
Original Jazz Classics / Feb '92 / Complete/Pinnacle / Jazz Music / Wellard

SILVER CITY (A Celebration Of 25 Years On Milestone/2CD Set)
Autumn nocturne / Duke of iron / Cabin in the sky / Harlem boys / Where or when / To a wild rose / Tennessee waltz / G-man / McGhee / Someone to watch over me / I'm old fashioned / Just once / Lucky day / Darn that day / Darn that dream / Silver city / Skylark / Tell me you love me / Biji
CD Set MCD 25012
Milestone / Jan '97 / Cadillac / Complete/ Pinnacle / Jazz Music / Wellard

SONNY BOY
CD OJCCD 348
Original Jazz Classics / May '93 / Complete/Pinnacle / Jazz Music / Wellard

SONNY ROLLINS & CO 1964
Django / Afternoon in Paris / Now's the time / Four / Blue 'n' boogie / Night and day / Three little words / My ship / Love letters / Long ago and far away / Winter wonderland / When you wish upon a star / Autumn nocturne
CD 07863665302
Bluebird / Apr '95 / BMG

SONNY ROLLINS 1951-1958 (2CD Set)
CD Set CDB 1213
Giants Of Jazz / Jul '92 / Cadillac / Jazz Music / Target/BMG

SONNY ROLLINS AND THE CONTEMPORARY LEADERS PLUS
CD OJCCD 340
Original Jazz Classics / Apr '86 / Complete/Pinnacle / Jazz Music / Wellard

SONNY ROLLINS ON IMPULSE
On Green Dolphin Street / Everything happens to me / Hold 'em Joe / Blue room / Three little words
CD IMP 12232
Impulse Jazz / Apr '97 / New Note/BMG

SONNY ROLLINS WITH THE MODERN JAZZ QUARTET (Rollins, Sonny & Modern Jazz Quartet)
Stopper / Almost like being in love / No Moe / In a sentimental mood / Scoops / With a song in my heart / Newk's fadeaway / Time on my hands / This love of mine / Shadrack / On a slow boat to China / Mambo bounce / I know
CD OJCCD 11
Original Jazz Classics / Sep '93 / Complete/ Pinnacle / Jazz Music / Wellard

SONNY ROLLINS/VOL.2/NEWK'S TIME (3CD Set)
Decision / Bluesnote / Plain Jane / Sonnysphere / How are things in Giocca Morra / Why don't I / Wail march / Misterioso / Reflections / You stepped out of a dream / Poor butterfly / Tune up / Asiatic raes / Wonderful wonderful / Surrey with the fringe on top / Blues for Philly Joe / Namely you
CD Set CDOMB 008
Blue Note / Oct '95 / EMI

SOUND OF SONNY, THE
Last time I saw Paris / Toot toot tootsie / Dearly beloved / Cutie / Mangoes / Just in time / What is there to say / Every time we say goodbye / It could happen to you
CD OJCCD 292
Original Jazz Classics / Feb '92 / Complete/ Pinnacle / Jazz Music / Wellard

STOCKHOLM 1959
CD DRCD 229
Dragon / Jan '88 / ADA / Cadillac / CM / Roots / Wellard

TENOR MADNESS
CD OJCCD 124
Original Jazz Classics / Feb '92 / Complete/Pinnacle / Jazz Music / Wellard

TENOR MADNESS
CD CD 53061
Giants Of Jazz / Mar '92 / Cadillac / Jazz Music / Target/BMG

TENOR MADNESS AND SAXOPHONE COLOSSUS
Saxophone colossus - St Thomas / You don't know what love is / Strode rode / Moritat / Blue seven / Tenor madness, tenor madness / When your lover has gone / Paul's Pal / My reverie / Most beautiful girl in the world
CD CDJZD 002
Prestige / Jan '91 / Cadillac / Complete/ Pinnacle

THIS LOVE OF MINE
CD CDSGP 043
Prestige / Mar '93 / Else / Total/BMG

TOUR DE FORCE
CD OJCCD 95
Original Jazz Classics / Sep '93 / Complete/Pinnacle / Jazz Music / Wellard

WHAT'S NEW
CD 07863525722
Novus / Jul '93 / BMG

WORK TIME
CD OJCCD 72
Original Jazz Classics / Mar '93 / Complete/Pinnacle / Jazz Music / Wellard

Rolls Royce Brass Band

BEST OF BRASS, THE
Fanfare and flourishes / With one look / Twelfth street rag / We've only just begun / Oklahoma / Share my yoke / Ticket to ride / Love changes everything / Pop looks Bach / Trumpets wild / Swing low, sweet chariot / Solitaire / Pie Jesu / Magic flute / Star lake / Coronation march
CD QED 176
Tring / Nov '96 / Tring

PLAYS THE BEST OF BRASS
Men of Harlech / Coronation march / Pastime with good company / Fanfare and

flourishes / With one look / Twelfth Street rag / We've only just begun / Oklahoma / Share my yoke / Ticket to ride / Love changes everything / Pop looks Bach / Trumpets wild / Swing low, sweet chariot / Solitaire / Pie Jesu / Magic flute
CD WMCD 2003
Westmoor / Oct '96 / Target/BMG

Romance, Lance

FORTUNE AND FAME
Don't cheat lady / Fortune and fame / Headache / Concentrate on you / Treat you right / There you go again / Baby tonight / Ain't that a shame / On my mind
CD WRA 8101 CD
Wrap / Nov '91 / Koch

Romane

OMBRE (Gypsy Manouche A La Django)
CD IMP 943
IMP / Sep '96 / ADA / Discovery

QUINTET
CD JSL 023
JSL / Jan '95 / Discovery

SWING FOR NININE
CD BPE 127
Kardum / Nov '92 / Discovery

SWING IN NASHVILLE
CD IMP 949
IMP / Jun '97 / ADA / Discovery

Romano, Aldo

CANZONI
T'ho voluto bene / Romana non fare la stupida stasera / Munastario a Santa Chiara / Sapore di sale / Torna a surriente / O sole mio / Anima e core / Reginella / Come prima / Senza fina
CD ENJACD 91022
Enja / Jun '97 / New Note/Pinnacle / Vital/ SAM

CARNET DE ROUTES
Standing ovation / Vol / Daoulaged / Boroko dance / Annonbon / Les petits lits blancs / Flash memoire / Korokoro / Entrave
CD LBLC 6569
Label Bleu / Nov '95 / New Note/Pinnacle

NON DIMENTICAR
CD 5182642
Polydor / May '94 / PolyGram

Romanowski, Jeff

DREAMS
CD 55086CD
Strictly Rhythm / Jul '97 / Prime / RTM/ Disc / SRD / Vital

Romanthony

ROMANWORLD (2CD Set)
Romanworld / Make this love right / Now you want blues / Now you want me / Let me show you love / Come my way / Desire / Falling from grace / Testify / Soul on fire / Ministry of love / On the mix
CD Set AZCD 002
Azuli / Mar '97 / Amato Disco / Azuli / Mo's Music Machine / Prime / Vital

Romantics

MADE IN DETROIT
You and your folks, me and my folks / Love it up / I wanna know / Runaway / Leave her alone
CD CDSEWT 705
Westbound / Mar '93 / Pinnacle

Rome

ROME
I belong to you (every time I see your face) / Do you like this / Crazy love / Just once, once more, three times / I gotta be down / Do me right / That's the way I feel about cha / Real love / Feelin' kinda good / Let me come home / Never find another love like mine / Real joy / Heaven
CD 078636744124
RCA / May '97 / BMG

Romeo's Daughter

DELECTABLE
CD CDMFN 153
Music For Nations / Oct '93 / Pinnacle

Romer, Hanne

AKIJAVA (Romer, Hanne & Marietta Wandall Duo)
CD MECCACD 1012
Music Mecca / Nov '94 / Cadillac / Jazz Music / Wellard

Romero, Chan

FIFTIES FLASH BACK
CD RKCD 9501
Rockhouse / Mar '96 / Nervous

Romero, Pepe

FLAMENCO
Fiesta en Jerez / Fandangos por Verdiales / Garrotin / Tanguillos / Peteneras / Jota / Carabana Gitana / Farruca y rumba / Zorongo / Lamento Andaluz / Spanish dance: *Romero, Angel* / Recuerdos de la Alhambra / Vidalita: *Romero, Celedonio*
CD 4343612
Philips / Apr '96 / PolyGram

Romero, Rafael

MARIO BOIS COLLECTION VOL.18
CD LDX 2741027
Le Chant Du Monde / Dec '96 / Harmonia Mundi

Romeros

ROYAL FAMILY OF THE SPANISH GUITAR, THE (Traditional Spanish Folk & Guitar Music)
CD 4343852
Mercury Living Presence / May '97 / PolyGram

Romeu, Antonio

EL MAGO DE LAS TECLAS 1937-1940 (Romeu, Antonio Orquesta)
CD TCD 067
Tumbao Cuban Classics / Jul '96 / Discovery

ORIENTE Y OCCIDENTE (Romeu, Antonio Orquesta)
CD TCD 072
Tumbao Cuban Classics / Jul '96 / Discovery

Romiosini

PICTURES OF CRETE
CD EUCD 1049
ARC / '89 / ADA / ARC Music

SONGS AND DANCES FROM GREECE
CD EUCD 1163
ARC / '91 / ADA / ARC Music

Ron-E Was Another 1

SEXOCET
CD REVXD 182
FM / Mar '93 / Revolver / Sony

Rondat, Patrick

RAPE OF THE EARTH
CD CDGRUB 20
Food For Thought / Jun '91 / Pinnacle

Rondo Veneziano

CONCERTO PER MOZART
CD 261362
Private Music / Sep '96 / BMG

POESIA DI VENEZIA
CD 259826
Private Music / Aug '95 / BMG

VISIONI DI VENEZIA
CD 260213
Private Music / Aug '95 / BMG

Rondstadt, Linda

GREATEST HITS
You're no good / Silver threads and golden needles / Desperado / Love is a rose / That'll be the day / Long long time / Different drum / When will I be loved / Love has no pride / Heatwave / It doesn't matter anymore / Tracks of my tears
CD 253055
WEA / Jul '94 / Warner Music

Ronettes

BEST OF THE RONETTES, THE
Be my baby / Why don't they let us fall in love: *I Wonder* / Baby I love you: *I Wonder* / Best part of breaking up: *I Wonder* / So young / When I saw you / Do I love you / You baby / How does it feel / Born to be together / Is this what I get for loving you / Paradise / Here I sit / I wish I never saw the sunshine / Everything under the sun / You came, you saw, you conquered
CD CDP 7803162
EMI / Oct '92 / EMI

ULTIMATE
CD MAR 050
Marginal / Jun '97 / Greyhound

Roney, Antoine

TRAVELER, THE
Traveller / Cry of.... / Chief rahab / Mayan owl / Tempus fugit / On Green Dolphin street / Estate / Weaver of dreams / Bean and the boys
CD MCD 5469
Muse / Jul '94 / New Note/Pinnacle

WHIRLING
CD MCD 5546
Muse / Feb '96 / New Note/Pinnacle

Roney, Wallace

INTUITION
CD MCD 5346
Muse / Sep '92 / New Note/Pinnacle

SETH AIR
Melchizedek / Breath of Seth Air / Black people suffering / 28 rue pigalle / Lost / People / Gone / Wives and lovers
CD MCD 5441
Muse / Sep '92 / New Note/Pinnacle

STANDARD BEARER, THE
CD MCD 5372
Muse / Sep '92 / New Note/Pinnacle

VERSES
CD MCD 5335
Muse / Sep '92 / New Note/Pinnacle

Roni Size

NEW FORMS (2CD Set)
Railings: *Reprazent* / Brown paper bag: *Reprazent* / New forms: *Reprazent* / Let's get it on: *Reprazent* / Digital: *Reprazent* / Matter of fact: *Reprazent* / Mad cat: *Reprazent* / Heroes: *Reprazent* / Share the fall: *Reprazent* / Watching windows: *Reprazent* / Beatbox: *Reprazent* / Morse code: *Reprazent* / Destination: *Reprazent* / Intro: *Reprazent* / Hi potent: *Reprazent* / Trust me: *Reprazent* / Change my life: *Reprazent* / Share the fall: *Reprazent* / Down: *Reprazent* / Jazz: *Reprazent* / Ballet dance: *Reprazent*
CD Set 5349332
Talkin' Loud / Jun '97 / PolyGram

Ronny & The Daytonas

GTO (The Best Of Ronny & The Daytonas)
CD SC 11046
Sundazed / Feb '97 / Cargo / Greyhound / Rollercoaster

Ronson, Mick

ONLY AFTER DARK (2CD Set)
Love me tender / Growing up and I'm fine / Only after dark / Music is lethal / I'm the one / Pleasure man / Hey Ma get Papa / Slaughter on 10th Avenue / Leave my heart alone / Love me tender (live) / Slaughter on 10th Avenue (Live) / Billy Porter / Angel number nine / This is for you / White light, white heat / Play don't worry / Hazy days / Girl can't help it / Empty bed (lo me no andrei) / Woman / Seven days (B'side) / Stone love / I'd rather be me
CD Set GY 003SP
NMC / May '95 / Total/Pinnacle

Ronstadt, Linda

CRY LIKE A RAINSTORM, HOWL LIKE THE WIND
Still within the sound of my voice / Cry like a rainstorm / All my life: *Ronstadt, Linda & Aaron Neville* / Don't know much: *Ronstadt, Linda & Aaron Neville* / Adios / Trouble again / I keep it hid / So right, so wrong / Shattered / When something is wrong with my baby / Goodbye my friend
CD 9608722
Elektra / Oct '89 / Warner Music

DEDICATED TO THE ONE I LOVE
CD 7559619162
Elektra / Dec '95 / Warner Music

FOR SENTIMENTAL REASONS
When you wish upon a star / Bewitched, bothered and bewildered / You go to my head / But not for me / My funny valentine / I get along without you very well / Am I blue / (I love you) for sentimental reasons / Straighten up and fly right / Little girl blue / 'Round midnight
CD 9604742
Elektra / Sep '86 / Warner Music

GREATEST HITS VOL.1
You're no good / Silver threads and golden needles / Desperado / Love is a rose / That'll be the day / Long long time / Different drum / When will I be loved / Love has no pride / Heatwave / It doesn't matter anymore / Tracks of my tears
CD 253055
Asylum / '84 / Warner Music

GREATEST HITS VOL.2
It's so easy / I can't let go / Hurt so bad / Blue bayou / How do I make you / Back in the USA / Ooh baby baby / Poor, poor pitiful me / Tumbling dice / Just one look / Someone to lay down beside me
CD 252255
Elektra / Jul '94 / Warner Music

HASTEN DOWN THE WIND
Lose again / Tattler / If he's ever near / That'll be the day / Lo siento me vida / Hasten down the wind / Rivers of Babylon / Give one heart / Try me again / Crazy / Down so low / Someone to lay down beside me
CD K 9606102
Elektra / Sep '89 / Warner Music

ROUND MIDNIGHT
What's new / I've got a crush on you / Guess I'll hang my tears out to dry / Crazy he calls me / Someone to watch over me / I don't stand a ghost of a chance with you / What'll I do / Lover man / Goodbye / When I fall in love / Skylark / It never entered my mind / Mean to me / When your lover has gone / I'm a fool to want you / You took advantage of me / Sophisticated lady / Can't we be friends / My old flame / Falling in love again / Lush life / When you wish upon a star / Bewitched, bothered and bewildered / You go to my head / But not for me / My funny valentine / I get along without you very well / Am I blue / (I love you) for sentimental reasons / Straighten up and fly right / Little girl blue / 'Round midnight
CD 9604892
Elektra / Jul '94 / Warner Music

WHAT'S NEW
Skylark / Mean to me / My old flame / What's new / Lush life / Love man / Goodbye / (I love you) for sentimental reasons / Crazy he calls me / When I fall in love
CD 9602602
Elektra / Sep '83 / Warner Music

WINTER LIGHT
Heartbeats accelerating / Do what you gotta do / Anyone who had a heart / Don't talk (put your head on my shoulder) / Oh no, not my baby / It's too soon to know / I just don't know what to do with myself / River for him / Adonde voy / You can't treat the wrong man right / Winter light
CD 7559615452
Elektra / Dec '93 / Warner Music

Roof

UNTRACEABLE CIGAR, THE
CD RN 4
Konkurrent / Jun '96 / SRD

Rooks

CHIMES
CD NL 0036
Not Lame / Jul '97 / Cargo / Greyhound

DOUBLE DOSE OF POP, A (Rooks/20 Cent Crush)
CD NL 0033
Not Lame / Jul '97 / Cargo / Greyhound

Room

HALL OF MIRRORS
CD CD 700
Music & Arts / Sep '92 / Cadillac / Harmonia Mundi

Roomful Of Blues

DANCE ALL NIGHT
CD BBCD 9955
Bullseye Blues / Jul '94 / Direct

DRESSED UP TO GET MESSED UP
Money talks / What happened to the sugar / Let's ride / Yes indeed / Albi's boogie / Last time / Oh oh / Dressed up to get messed up / He knows the rules / Whiplash
CD CDVR 018
Varrick / '88 / ADA / CM / Direct / Roots

FIRST ALBUM, THE
CD CDVR 035
Varrick / '88 / ADA / CM / Direct / Roots

HOT LITTLE MAMA
Hot little mama / Big question / New Orleans shuffle / Sufferin' mind / Caravan / Loan me a helping hand / Long distance operator / Something to remember you by / Two bones and a pick / Little fine healthy thing / Sugar coated love / Jeep's blues
CD CDCHM 39
Ace / Jul '91 / Pinnacle

LIVE AT LUPO'S HEARTBREAK HOTEL
Gator's groove/Welcome to Lupo's / Coconut milk / Three hours past midnight / Three hundred pounds / House of joy / Pink champagne / Please don't leave / That's my life / Please don't leave me / Zydeco boogaloo
CD CDVR 024
Varrick / Nov '96 / ADA / CM / Direct / Roots

ROOMFUL OF BLUES
CD 32003CD
32 / May '96 / ADA

TURN IT ON, TURN IT UP
CD CDBB 66001
Bullseye Blues / Jun '96 / Direct

UNDER ONE ROOF
She'll be so fine / Running out of time / We b 3 / Standing here at the crossroads / Smack dab in the middle / Let me live / Still livin' in prison / Switchin' in the kitchen / From you / Q's blues / Easy baby / Farmer John / Baby, baby, baby / Rogue elephant
CD CDBB 9569
Bullseye Blues / Feb '97 / Direct

Rooney, Jim

BRAND NEW TENNESSEE WALTZ
Brand new Tennessee waltz / Be my friend tonight / Amanda / Heaven become a woman / We must believe in magic / Fish and whistle / Dreaming my dreams / Six white horses / Satisfied mind
CD APCD 067
Appaloosa / Jul '94 / ADA / Direct / TKO Magnum

Roos, Randy

PRIMALVISION
Ancestor / Black elk / Raven's light / Craftman's prelude / Chameleon's dance / Craftsman / Between states / Desert vision / Badlands / View from the summit / Ancestor's reprise
CD ND 62015
Narada / Oct '95 / ADA / New Note/ Pinnacle

Root Boy Slim

ROOT 6
Everybody's got a problem / Burger row / Hey Mr. President / I wanna be a businessman / Eight ball boogie / Sex with a capital X / You excite me / Our little mistake / Party at the Berlin Wall / Big yellow streetsweeper
CD CDNAK 6002
Naked Language / Feb '92 / Koch

Rootless

ROTTEN WOOD FOR SMOKING BEES
CD WALLCD 8
Wall Of Sound / May '95 / Prime / Soul Trader / Vital

Roots

SAYING SOMETHING (Roots & Blyth Davis Freeman)
CD IOR 770312
In & Out / Feb '96 / Vital/SAM

Roots

DO YOU WANT MORE
Intro / There's something goin' on / Proceed / Distortion to static / Mellow my man / I remain calm / Datskat / Lazy afternoon / vs Rahzel / Do you want more / What goes on part 7 / Essaywhuman / Swept away / You ain't fly / Silent treatment / Lesson part 1 / Unlocking
CD GED 24708
Geffen / Nov '94 / BMG

FROM THE GROUND UP
It's comin' / Distortion to static / Mellow my man / Dat scat / Worldwide / Do you want more
CD 5189412
Talkin' Loud / Jun '94 / PolyGram

ILLADELPH HALF LIFE
Intro / Respond/react / Section / Panic / It just don't stop / Episodes / Push up ya lighter / What they do / Vs. scratch / Concerto of the desperado / Clones / Universe at war / No alibi / Dave vs. us / No great pretender / Hypnotic / Ital (the universal side) / One shine / Adventures in wonderland / Outro
CD GED 24972
Geffen / Nov '96 / BMG

ORGANIX
Root is comin' / Pass the popcorn / Anticircle / Writers block / Good music (prelude) / Good music / Grits / Leonard I-V / I'm out deah
CD RRCD 001
Remedy / Jun '97 / Vital

Roots Control

DREAD WESTERN
CD WSCD 008
Word Sound Recordings / Feb '97 / Cargo / SRD

Roots Radics

FREELANCE
Earsay / Rainbow / I'm not a king / Too much fuss / Party time / Everywhere Natty go / Dance with me / Midnight / Mash it up / Reggae on Broadway
CD CDKVL 9021
Kingdom / Jan '87 / Kingdom

LIVE AT CHANNEL ONE
CD LAP 100CD
Live & Learn / Jul '95 / Greensleeves / Jet Star

RADICALLY RADICS
Radically radics / Dancehall massive / Nengeh nengeh / For you / Love thicker than blood / Give thanks and praise / Singing in the dancehall / Bingy Bunny medley / No bun it down / Watcha gonna do / Water more than flour (be my Queen) / Skettle / Siddling deh / Teach dem / Dancehall massive / Reggae for kids
CD RASCD 3234
Ras / Nov '96 / Direct / Greensleeves / Jet Star / SRD

Roots Syndicate

ROOTS OF DUB VOL.1 - GARVEY
CD DTCD 19
Disctex / Nov '93 / SRD

ROOTS OF DUB VOL.3 - MANDELA
CD DTCD 20
Discotex / May '94 / Jet Star

Rootsman

CITY OF DJINN (Rootsman & Muslimgauze)
CD TEMCD 009
Third Eye / Aug '97 / SRD

IN DUB WE TRUST
CD TEMCD 002
Third Eye / Jul '95 / SRD

INTERNATIONAL LANGUAGE OF DUB
CD TEMCD 004
Third Eye / Jan '96 / SRD

INTO THE LIGHT
CD TEMCD 05
Third Eye / Sep '96 / SRD

OUT OF THE DARKNESS (Rootsman Remixed)
CD TEMCD 006
Third Eye / May '97 / SRD

PRESENTS THIRD EYE DIMENSIONS
CD EB 011
Echo Beach / May '97 / Cargo / Shellshock/Disc

Rooyen, Jerry Van

AT 250 MILES PER HOUR
CD EFA 043792
Crippled Dick Hot Wax / Dec '96 / SRD

Roparz, Gwenola

BRETON MUSIC FOR THE CELTIC HARP
CD CD 130
Diffusion Breizh / Jan '95 / ADA

Ropers

WORLD IS FIRE, THE
CD TURN 33CD
Turntable Friend / Jun '97 / Cargo / SRD

Rorive, Jean-Pierre

ORGAN AND SAXOPHONE CONTEMPLATION (Rorive, Jean-Pierre & Andre Lamproye)
CD 74321452962
Jade / May '97 / Conifer/BMG

Ros, Edmundo

CELEBRATION
Cuban love song / South America take it away / Come closer to me / Amapola / Wedding samba / What a difference a day makes / Guantanamera / Brazil / I, yi, yi, yi / Alma llanera / Papa says / I've grown accustomed to her face / Girl from Ipanema / Mala Guena / Forbidden games / Peanut vendor / Laughing samba / How near is love / Colonel Bogey / Coffee song
CD 8440522
Eclipse / Jan '91 / PolyGram

COME WITH ME MY HONEY
Tico Tico / With me my honey / Linda Muier / Le Seguire (I'm so in love) / Brazil Moreno / Rum and Limonada / Jesusita en Chihuahua / Negra Consentida / Three caballeros / Los Hijos de Buda / Toku / Marie Elena / No te importe saber / La conga del amor / Nightingale / Soltero es mejor / Divina mujer / When I love I love / Conga boom / Te quiero dijis / Tropical magic
CD RAJCD 867
Empress / Jul '97 / Koch

EDMUNDO ROS & HIS RUMBA BAND VOL.3
CD HQCD 73
Harlequin / Jul '96 / Hot Shot / Jazz Music / Swift / Wellard

EDMUNDO ROS 1939-1941
CD HQCD 15
Harlequin / '92 / Hot Shot / Jazz Music / Swift / Wellard

TROPICAL MAGIC
CD HQCD 50
Harlequin / Mar '95 / Hot Shot / Jazz Music / Swift / Wellard

Ros, Lazaro

OLORUN
CD GLCD 4022
Green Linnet / Nov '94 / ADA / CM / Direct / Highlander / Roots

SONGS FOR ELEGUA (Ros, Lazaro & Olorun)
CD ASHECD 2001
Ashe / Nov '96 / Direct

Rosa Lee State

DUSTED CHOCOLATE ALMOND CROISSANT
CD PLANKCD 29
Plankton / May '97 / Cargo

Rosa Mota

BIONIC
From her to maternity / Shelf life / Victoria Falls / This grudge / Frostbitten / Pigeon / Space junk / Scenic layby / La chienne est dans l'arbre / Sometimes narcoleptic / Angel
CD 13THCD 3
Thirteenth Hour / Feb '97 / RTM/Disc

DRAG FOR A DRAG
CD PILLMCD 2
Placebo / Jun '93 / RTM/Disc

WISHFUL SINKING
CD 13THCD 2
Thirteenth Hour / Jan '95 / RTM/Disc

Rosales, Gerardo

VENEZUELA SONORA
La mano en el mono / De Venezuela para el mundo / Tumba y bongo / Chivo Venezolano / Chivo Cubano / Brujeria / Tremenda negra / Culo'e puya pa'l mundo / Quinta anauco / Popurri del tio Simon
CD AL 73053
A / Nov '96 / Cadillac / Direct

Rosana

LUNAS ROTAS
CD MCD 76015
MCA / Apr '97 / BMG

Rose, Alan

PAST AND PRESENT
CD FRCD 033
Foam / Oct '94 / CM

Rose Among Thorns

BUTTERFLY DREAMS
Plaids deep stained in red / Don't cry for me / Hero / Don't turn around / Journeys from afar / I'm going to get there / Run run run / Stepping stones / Butterfly dreams / My homelands calling me
CD HTDCD 31
HTD / Mar '95 / CM / Pinnacle

HIGHLITES
CD HTDCD 63
HTD / Jun '96 / CM / Pinnacle

ROSE AMONG THORNS
Prologue / Journey / Keep me warm / Dancing drum / Lady of Hay / Heart and Soul / So much to tell / Losers 'n' Dreamers / Lunar love / Hold on / Sail away / Take me home
CD HTDCD 6
HTD / May '91 / CM / Pinnacle
CD RME 0131CD
Renaissance / May '97 / ADA

THIS TIME IT'S REAL
CD HTDCD 8
HTD / Jul '92 / CM / Pinnacle
CD RME 0132CD
Renaissance / May '97 / ADA

Rose Chronicles

HAPPILY EVER AFTER
CD 067003010825
Nettwerk / Feb '97 / Greyhound / Pinnacle / Vital

SHIVER
Dwelling / Glide (free above) / Nothing's real / Deirdre / Brick and glue / Undertow / Bottle song / Visions / Shiver / Forgotten / Awaiting eternity
CD NET 051CD
Nettwerk / Mar '94 / Greyhound / Pinnacle / Vital

Rose, Dan

CONVERSATIONS
Fiber optic lover / Great harbour / Marcia / Conversations / Carla, Carla, Carla / Back burner / Designer in you / Across the divide / Shall we dance / Care and feeding
CD ENJACD 80062
Enja / Oct '93 / New Note/Pinnacle / Vital/ SAM

Rose, David

STRIPPER & OTHER FAVOURITES, THE (Rose, David & His Orchestra)
CD EMPRCD 501
Emporio / Apr '94 / Disc

Rose, Jon

BRAIN WEATHER
CD RERBJRCD 2
ReR/Recommended / Oct '96 / ReR Megacorp / RTM/Disc

VIOLIN MUSIC FOR RESTAURANTS
CD RERBJRCD
ReR/Recommended / Apr '90 / ReR Megacorp / RTM/Disc

Rose Marie

BEST OF ROSE MARIE, THE
CD MATCD 217
Castle / Dec '92 / BMG

DANNY BOY
When your old wedding ring was new / Make the world go away / Among my souvenirs / This is my Mother's day / Old rugged cross / When I leave the world behind / Pal of my cradle days / Sunshine of your smile / My mother's eyes / Answer to everything / Strollin' / Underneath the arches / Let the rest of the world go by / After all these years / Ave Maria / You'll never know / My blue heaven / Danny boy / We'll meet again / Wheel of fortune / When I grow too old to dream / Little one / Now is the hour / I apologise / Anniversary waltz
CD PLSCD 167
Pulse / Feb '97 / BMG

HEARTBREAKERS
It's a heartache / Sometimes when we touch / Crazy / Without you / Let the heartaches begin / Cry me a river / Heartbreaker / Heartaches / Crying / There's nothing in my life / You don't know me / I will always love you / She's got you / True love ways
CD CDDPR 121
Premier/MFP / May '94 / EMI

MY BLUE HEAVEN
CD DCDCD 223
Castle / Mar '96 / BMG

SONGS FROM THE HEART
CD MACCD 168
Autograph / Aug '96 / BMG

WHEN I LEAVE THE WORLD BEHIND
When I leave the world behind / Danny boy / Take it to the limit / It must be him / It comes from the heart / Too darn bad / It ain't easy bein' easy / Rock 'n' roll waltz / You can never stop me loving you / Looking for love / Right to sing it blue / It's a sin to tell a lie / You'll never walk alone / No regrets
CD MCCD 064
Music Club / '92 / Disc / THE

WHEN YOUR OLD WEDDING RING WAS NEW
When your old wedding ring was new / Make the world go away / This is my mother's day / Old rugged cross / When I leave the world behind / Wheel of fortune / When I grow too old to dream / We'll meet again / Legend in my time / Just for old times sake / Pal of my cradle days / Sunshine of youe smile / My mother's eyes / Answer to everything / Let the rest of the world go by / After all these years / Ave Maria / My blue heaven / Danny Boy / Now is the hour
CD TRTCD 152
TrueTrax / Oct '94 / THE

Rose, Michael

BE YOURSELF
CD CDHB 187
Heartbeat / Feb '96 / ADA / Direct / Greensleeves / Jet Star

BE YOURSELF DUB (Dubwize: Big Sound Frontline)
CD CDHB 192
Heartbeat / Jun '96 / ADA / Direct / Greensleeves / Jet Star

DANCE WICKED
Happiness / Dance wicked / Lion in the jungle: *Rose, Michael & Maxi Priest* / Run dem a run / Dreadlocks / Reality / Landlord / See and blind / I don't want to say goodbye / Mind made up / Never get me down / Life in the ghetto / Mind made up / Mind made up
CD CDHB 214
Heartbeat / Jun '97 / ADA / Direct / Greensleeves / Jet Star

DUB WICKED (Michael Rose Meets Mafia & Fluxy At The Grass Roots Of Dub)
Dub well happy / Wicked dub / Lion jungle dub / Gold mine / Dreadlocks in dub / Reality dub / Straight to landlord's head / Blinding version / Goodbye / Mind this yah dub / Dub up / Ghetto life
CD CDHB 215
Heartbeat / Jun '97 / ADA / Direct / Greensleeves / Jet Star

MICHAEL ROSE
CD CDHB 144
Heartbeat / Apr '95 / ADA / Direct / Greensleeves / Jet Star

NUH CARBON
CD GRELCD 227
Greensleeves / Jul '96 / Jet Star / SRD

RISING STAR
CD RFCD 003
Record Factory / Oct '95 / Jet Star

RUDE BOYS/SHORT TEMPER
CD CRCDM 4
Heartbeat / Aug '96 / ADA / Direct / Greensleeves / Jet Star

VOICE OF THE GHETTO
CD VPCD 1431
VP / Aug '95 / Greensleeves / Jet Star / Total/BMG

Rose, Ndiaye Doudou

DJABOTE
Ligue you ndeye / Cheikh anta diop / Rose rhythm / Sidati aidara / Baye kene ndiaye / Chants du burgam / Khine sine / Khine saloume / Walo / Tabala ganar / Diame / Ndiouk
CD CDRW 43
Realworld / Feb '94 / EMI

Rose Of Avalanche

ALWAYS THERE
CD ________ **FIRE 33007**
Fire / Oct '91 / Pinnacle / RTM/Disc

LA RAIN (The Singles Album)
LA rain / Rise to the groove / Conceal me / Goddess / Thousand landscapes / Gimme some lovin' / Too many castles in the sky / Dizzy Miss Lizzy / Assassin / Velveteen / Who cares / Just like yesterday / Always there / Waiting for the sun / Majesty
CD ________ **NTMCD 533**
Nectar / Feb '97 / Pinnacle

LIVE AT THE TOWN AND COUNTRY
Stick in the works / Just like yesterday / Mainline man / Velveteen / 1000 landscapes / Waiting for the sun / Always there / Dreamland / Too many castles / Gimme some lovin'
CD ________ **CONTECD 104**
Contempo / Nov '88 / Plastic Head

Rose Royce

GREATEST HITS LIVE
Carwash / I wanna get next to you / Wishing on a star / Love don't live here anymore / Do your dance / Is it love you're after / I love the feeling / Magic touch / Band in production
CD ________ **100282**
CMC / May '97 / BMG

LIVE
Is it love you're after / I'm in love / Wishing on a star / Magic touch / Do your dance / I wanna get next to you / Love don't live here anymore / Car wash
CD ________ **305662**
Hallmark / Oct '96 / Carlton

ROSE ROYCE
CD ________ **JHD 103**
Tring / Aug '93 / Tring

VERY BEST OF ROSE ROYCE LIVE, THE
Is it love you're after / I'm in love (and I love the feeling) / Wishing on a star / Magic touch / Do your dance / I wanna get next to you / Love don't live here anymore / Car wash
CD ________ **SUMCD 4079**
Summit / Nov '96 / Sound & Media

Rose, Sammy

FOOL'S GOLD
You're gonna miss me / One in the red dress / Destination heartbreak / Rose's lament / My heart can't take the beating / Jealous bone / Cold heart stare / Till I'm over you / Backside view / Sugar please / Fool's gold
CD ________ **BCD 15876**
Bear Family / Mar '95 / Direct / Rollercoaster / Swift

Rose, Tim

GAMBLER, THE
I just want to make love to you / He was born to be a lady / Dance on ma belle / It'll be alright on the night / Runaway / Moving targets / Gambler / Blow me back Santa Ana / So much to lose / Is there something 'bout the way I hold my gun / Bowery Avenue / Laurie
CD ________ **PCOM 1117**
President / Nov '91 / Grapevine/PolyGram / President / Target/BMG

Rose, Wally

RAGS, BLUES, JOYS
CD ________ **SACD 109**
Solo Art / Jul '93 / Jazz Music

Rosebud

ROSEBUD
My baby, your baby / Landslide / Eye of the hurricane / Fire / Fool for a broken heart / Dynamite / Too late now / Hot 'n' heavy / Love you till the day I die
CD ________ **MMT 3304 CD**
Shark / Jul '90 / Plastic Head

Rosenberg Trio

CARAVAN
Viajeiro / Melodie au crepuscle / Pent-up house / La promenade / Embraceable you / tears / Zebra / Chez moi / Stephaneske / Caravan / I surrender dear / Donna Lee / Night and day / Manoir de mes reves / Batida diferente / Manha de carnaval
CD ________ **5230302**
Verve / Aug '94 / PolyGram

GYPSY SWING
It don't mean a thing if it ain't got that swing / Django / Tequila / Miro tata Mimer (For my dad Mimer) / Do you know where you're going to / Cherokee / Bluesette / Guitar boogie / Rosemary's baby / Silk and steel / Cavatina / Hungaria / Children of Sanchez / Yours is my heart alone / Begin the beguine / Latscheben / How insensitive
CD ________ **5278062**
Verve / Mar '96 / PolyGram

ROSENBERG TRIO LIVE AT THE NORTH SEA JAZZ FESTIVAL 1992
For Sephora / Minor swing / Les yeux noirs / Chega de saudade / Be bop / Bossa dorada / Pent-up house / Sweet Georgia Brown / Nuages / Honeysuckle rose / Wasso's waltz / Armando's rumba / Blue bossa / Swing de Paris / Les feuilles mortes / Spain / Sweet Georgia Brown
CD ________ **5194462**
Verve / Feb '92 / PolyGram

Rosenberg, Susan

UPPA MARMORNS HOGA BERG
CD ________ **GCD 31**
Giga / May '97 / ADA / Total/BMG

Rosengren, Bernt

BIG BAND
CD ________ **1214**
Caprice / Jul '89 / ADA / Cadillac / CM / Complete/Pinnacle

PORGY AND BESS (Rosengren, Bernt & Carrl Frederik Orrje Trio)
CD ________ **LICD 3167**
Liphone / Jan '97 / Cadillac / Jazz Music

UG, THE
CD ________ **DRCD 211**
Dragon / Jan '88 / ADA / Cadillac / CM / Roots / Wellard

Rosenstein, Kimmel

RAMBLIN' AWAY
CD ________ **COPP 0149CD**
Copper Creek / Dec '96 / ADA

Rosenthal, Ted

LIVE AT MAYBECK RECITAL HALL VOL.38
It's all right with me / Long ago and far away / Lennie's pennies / Better you than me / You're a joy / Jesu joy of man's desiring / Drop me a line / 117th Street / Gone with the wind / Hallucinations / You've got to be modernistic
CD ________ **CCD 4648**
Concord Jazz / Jun '95 / New Note/ Pinnacle

NEW TUNES, NEW TRADITIONS (Rosenthal, Ted Trio)
San Francisco holiday / NTNT / Roll down, roll on / Valse desesperee / Rhythm-a-ning / 'Round midnight / Let's call this / Hackensack / New light / Straight beyond
CD ________ **66056003**
Ken Music / Jan '92 / New Note/Pinnacle

ROSENTHOLOGY
Love walked in / Snowscape / Slippin' and slidin' / Will you still be mine / Wow / Strike up the band / Primrose path / All the things you are / Scene is clean / Gig / Someone to watch over me / Over the bars
CD ________ **CCD 4702**
Concord Jazz / Jun '96 / New Note/ Pinnacle

Rosetta Stone

ADRENALINE
CD ________ **CLEO 12752**
Cleopatra / Feb '95 / Cargo / Greyhound / Plastic Head / RTM/Disc / SRD

EYE FOR THE MAIN CHANCE
CD ________ **MIN 01CD**
Minority/One / Aug '94 / Pinnacle

FOUNDATION STONES
CD ________ **CLEO 9323CD**
Cleopatra / Jan '94 / Cargo / Greyhound / Plastic Head / RTM/Disc / SRD

ON THE SIDE OF ANGELS
CD ________ **MIN 02CD**
Minority/One / Aug '94 / Pinnacle

TYRANNY OF INACTION
CD ________ **MIN 03CD**
Minority/One / Jan '95 / Pinnacle

URBAN DOGS
CD ________ **CLEO 93232**
Cleopatra / Feb '94 / Cargo / Greyhound / Plastic Head / RTM/Disc / SRD

Rosicrucian

NO CAUSE FOR CELEBRATION
CD ________ **BMCD 57**
Black Mark / Aug '94 / Plastic Head

SILENCE
Column of grey / Way of all flesh / Within the silence / Esoteric traditions / Autocratic faith / Nothing but something remains / Aren't you bored enough / Back in the habit / Defy the oppression / Do you know who you're crucifying
CD ________ **BMCD 025**
Black Mark / Oct '92 / Plastic Head

Rosolino, Frank

FOND MEMORIES OF
All the things you are / My funny valentine / I love you / Violets / Corcovado / Autumn leaves / Free for all
CD ________ **DTRCD 113**
Double Time / Nov '96 / Express Jazz

Ross, Andy

BEST OF THE DANSAN YEARS VOL.1, THE (Ross, Andy Orchestra & Victor Silvester Orchestra)
CD ________ **DACD 001**
Dansan / Jul '92 / Jazz Music / President / Target/BMG / Wellard

COME DANCING
You make me feel so young / Nice and easy does it / Day in, day out / Night and day / Jean / If this were the last song / Blue tango / Golden tango / Light Cavalry / September song / Feed the birds / Nice work if you can get it / Fascinatin' rhythm / Mr. Melody / Copacabana / Save the best for last / Speak softly love / Amparita Roca / Fat man boogie / Bill / Over the rainbow / Innuendo / Bohemian rhapsody / Radio Ga Ga / We are the champions
CD ________ **4756422**
Columbia / Jun '94 / Sony

COME DANCING (Ross, Andy & His Orchestra)
Let's face the music and dance / People will say we're in love / Flight of the foo birds / That old feeling / What now my love / Jesse / Weekend in New England / Guitar tango / Delilah / Hey daddy / On Broadway / September / Brazil / Copacabana / All in love is fair / History of love / El adorno / Leroy Brown / It had to be you / As if we never said goodbye
CD ________ **CDMFP 6183**
Music For Pleasure / Oct '95 / EMI

DANCE PARTY FAVOURITES (Ross, Andy & His Orchestra)
Disco medley / Salsa medley / Skip to me Lu/She'll be coming round the mountain / Killing me softly / Hill St. blues / Praterleben / You'd be so nice to come home to / Dancing in the dark / One love / Amazing Grace / Our love is here to stay / Manhattan / Typhoon / Feelings / Way we were / El Pico / Ain't misbehavin' / Something stupid / Love me tonight / Michael row the boat ashore
CD ________ **DACD 017**
Dansan / Nov '96 / Jazz Music / President / Target/BMG / Wellard

DANCING FEET (Ross, Andy Orchestra)
Dancing feet / I can't get started (with you) / Toujours l'amour toujours / It don't mean a thing if it ain't got that swing / Railway children / Spinning wheel / Embraceable you / How lucky you are / Thou swell / Portrait of you / Teach me tonight / (We're gonna) Rock around the clock / Time after time / May each day / Sing sing sing / White rose of Athens / Opportunity
CD ________ **PCOM 1107**
President / Jul '91 / Grapevine/PolyGram / President / Target/BMG

LIVE AT THE INTERNATIONAL (Ross, Andy & His Orchestra)
Strike up the band / South Rampart street parade / Thou swell / Bye bye blues / Danke schon / Golden tango / Jealousy / L'amour toujours l'amour / May each day / Belle of the ball / La ronde / Moonglow / Am I blue / La player / Portrait of my love / I only want to be with you / Winchester Cathedral / Lucretia Macevil / Happy birthday sweet sixteen / April in Portugal / Matrimony / Toreador / Baker Street / Battle of New Orleans / Go away little girl / Resurrection shuffle
CD ________ **PCOM 1123**
President / Jul '92 / Grapevine/PolyGram / President / Target/BMG

Ross, Annie

GASSER, A (Ross, Annie & Zoot Sims)
I'm just a lucky so and so / You're nearer / I'm nobody's baby / Lucky day / Invitation to the blues / You're driving me crazy / Invitation to the blues (instrumental) / Everything I've got / I didn't know about you / I was doing all right / You took advantage of me / I don't want to cry anymore / Bones for Zoot / Funky old bones / Brushes
CD ________ **CDP 7468542**
Blue Note / Feb '97 / EMI

MUSIC IS FOREVER
Coffee time / It had to be you / Going to Chicago blues / Twisted / I hadn't anyone till you / Marajuana / Jackie / That old feeling / It never entered my head / One meat ball / Farmer's market / Where do you start / Music is forever
CD ________ **DRGCD 91446**
DRG / Mar '96 / Discovery / New Note/ Pinnacle

SINGS A HANDFUL OF SONGS
CD ________ **FSCD 61**
Fresh Sound / Oct '90 / Discovery / Jazz Music

SKYLARK
Gypsy in my soul / I love Paris / I didn't know about you / Lady's in love with you / 'Tain't what you do / Don't let the sun catch you crying / Between the devil and the deep blue sea / Don't worry 'bout me / I've told every little star / Manhattan / Please don't talk about me when I'm gone / Skylark
CD ________ **DRGCD 8470**
DRG / Oct '96 / Discovery / New Note/ Pinnacle

Ross, Billy

BILLY ROSS & JOHN MARTIN (Ross, Billy & John Martin)
Hut on Staffin Island/Lone bush / Smith's a gallant fireman / Battle of Sheriffmuir / Dheanainn sugradh / Lass from Erin's Isle / Dr. MacInnes' fancy/Lexy MacAskill / Avondale / Scandinavian polkas / Bold navvy man / Braes of Lochel / Jenny Dang the weaver/Malcolm the tailor / Auld meal mill
CD ________ **SPRCD 1029**
Springthyme / Feb '94 / ADA / CM / Direct / Duncans / Highlander / Roots

Ross, Diana

ALL THE GREAT LOVE SONGS
I'm still waiting / My man (mon homme) / All of my life / Love me / After you / All night lover / Sparkle / It's my turn / Cryin' in my heart out for you / Endless love
CD ________ **5300562**
Motown / Mar '96 / PolyGram

ANTHOLOGY VOL.1 & 2
Reach out and touch / Ain't no mountain high enough / Remember me / Reach out, I'll be there / Surrender / I'm still waiting / Good morning heartache / Touch me in the morning / You're a special part of me: *Ross, Diana & Marvin Gaye* / Last time I saw him / My mistake (was to love you): *Ross, Diana & Marvin Gaye* / Sleepin' / Sorry doesn't always make it right / Do you know where you're going to / I thought it took a little time (but today I fell in love) / One love in my lifetime / Baby, I love your way / Young mothers / Brown baby/Save the children / Love hangover / Gettin' ready for love / Your love is so good for me / You got it / Top of the world / Lovin', livin' and givin' / What you gave me / Boss / It's my house / Upside down / I'm coming out / It's my turn / One more chance / Cryin' my heart out for you / My old piano / My man (mon homme) / Endless love: *Ross, Diana & Lionel Richie* / Imagine / Too shy to say
CD Set ________ **5301992**
Motown / Jan '93 / PolyGram

DIANA EXTENDED (The Remixes)
Boss / Love hangover / Upside down / Someday we'll be together / I'm coming out / Chain reaction / You're gonna love it
CD ________ **CDGOLD 1020**
EMI Gold / Apr '96 / EMI

EATEN ALIVE
Eaten alive / Oh teacher / Experience / Chain reaction / More and more / I'm watching you / Love on the line / I love being in love with you / Crime of passion / Don't give up on each other / Eaten alive (extended)
CD ________ **CDEMD 1051**
EMI / Nov '93 / EMI

FORCE BEHIND THE POWER
Change of heart / When you tell me that you love me / Battlefield / Blame it on the sun / You're gonna love it / Heavy weather / Force behind the power / Heart don't change my mind / Waiting in the wings / You and I / One shining moment / If we hold on together / No matter what you do
CD ________ **CDEMD 1023**
EMI / Feb '97 / EMI

FOREVER DIANA (4CD Set)
When the lovelight starts shining through his eyes / Breathtaking guy / Where did our love go / Baby love / Come see about me / Stop in the name of love / Back in my arms again / You send me / Nothing but heartaches / Put on a happy face / I hear a symphony / My world is empty without you / Love is like an itching in my heart / I hear a happy symphony / You can't hurry love / You keep me hangin' on / Love is here and now you're gone / Happening / Reflections / In and out of love / Forever came today / Love child / I'm gonna make you love me / Try it baby / I'm livin' in shame / Someday we'll be together / Reach out and touch / Ain't no mountain high enough / Remember me / Reach out, I'll be there / Surrender / I'm still waiting / Lady sings the blues / Good morning heartache / God bless the child / Touch me in the morning / Brown baby/Save the children / Last time I saw him / You are everything / My mistake (was to love you) / Do you know where you're going to / Love hangover / Confide in me / Come in from the rain / Gettin' ready for love / Home / Boss / It's my house / I ain't been licked / Upside down / I'm coming out / It's my turn / Endless love / My old piano / Why do fools fall in love / Mirror mirror / Work that body / Muscles / Missing you / Swept away / Eaten alive / Chain reaction / Family / Ninety nine and a half (Won't do) / What a wonderful world / Amazing Grace / If we hold on together / Workin' overtime / This house / Force behind the power / When you tell me that you love me / One shining moment / Waiting in the wings / Where did we go wrong / Back to the future / Let's make every moment count / Your love / It's a wonderful life / Best years of my life
CD Set ________ **DRBOX 1**
EMI / Oct '93 / EMI

MERRY CHRISTMAS
CD 5504032
Spectrum / Nov '94 / PolyGram

MOTOWN EARLY CLASSICS (Ross, Diana & The Supremes)
Stop in the name of love / You bring back memories / Come on boy / Time changes things / Run, run, run / Whisper you love me boy / Where did our love go / Ask any girl / Honey boy / Any girl in love (knows what I'm going through) / Come see about me / Mother dear / Baby love / (I'm so glad) Heartaches don't last always / You've really got a hold on me / Baby doll / Who could ever doubt my love / I'm in love again
CD 5521202
Spectrum / Jul '96 / PolyGram

MOTOWN'S GREATEST HITS: DIANA ROSS
Ain't no mountain high enough / Touch me in the morning / I'm still waiting / I'm gonna make you love me / Upside down / My old piano / You keep me hangin' on / Happening / Reflections / Baby love / You can't hurry love / Where did our love go / Stop in the name of love / All of my life
CD 5300132
Motown / Feb '92 / PolyGram

ONE WOMAN (The Ultimate Collection)
Where did our love go: *Supremes* / Baby love: *Supremes* / You can't hurry love: *Supremes* / Reflections: *Ross, Diana & The Supremes* / Reach out and touch / Ain't no mountain high enough / Touch me in the morning / Love hangover / I'm still waiting / Upside down / Do you know where you're going to / Endless love: *Ross, Diana & Lionel Richie* / Why do fools fall in love / Chain reaction / When you tell me that you love me / One shining moment / If we hold on together / Best years of my life / Your love / Let's make every moment count
CD CDONE 1
EMI / Oct '93 / EMI

SILK ELECTRIC
Muscles / So close / Still in love / Fool for your love / Turn me over / Who / Love's lies / In your arms / Anywhere you run to / I am me
CD CDEMD 1050
EMI / Nov '93 / EMI

STOLEN MOMENTS - THE LADY SINGS JAZZ & BLUES LIVE
Fine and mellow / Them there eyes / Don't explain / What a little moonlight can do / Mean to me / Lover man / Gimme a pigfoot and a bottle of beer / Little girl blue / There's a small hotel / I cried for you / God bless the child / Our love is here to stay / You've changed / Strange fruit / Good morning heartache / Ain't nobody's business if I do / My man (mon homme) / Fine and mellow (Reprise) / Where did we go wrong
CD CDEMD 1044
EMI / Apr '93 / EMI

STOP IN THE NAME OF LOVE
Baby love / Heatwave / Heartaches don't last always / Mother dear / Always in my heart / Get ready / Everything is good about you / Shake me, wake me (when it's over) / Who could ever doubt my love / Honey boy / Ask any girl / I'm in love again / Any girl in love (knows what I'm going through) / Stop in the name of love
CD 5500712
Spectrum / May '93 / PolyGram

TAKE ME HIGHER
If you're not gonna love me right / I never loved a man before / Swing it / Keep it right there / Don't stop / Gone / I thought that we were still in love / Voice of the heart / Only love can conquer all / I will survive
CD CDEMD 1085
EMI / Sep '97 / EMI

TOUCH (Supremes)
This is the story / Nathan Jones / Here comes the sunrise / Love it came to me this time / Johnny Raven / Have I lost you / Time and love / Touch / Happy (is a bumpy road) / It's so hard for me to say goodbye
CD 5302112
Motown / Jan '93 / PolyGram

TOUCH ME IN THE MORNING
Touch me in the morning / All of my life / We need you / Leave a little room / I won't last a day without you / Little girl blue / My baby / Imagine / Brown baby / Save the children
CD 5301652
Motown / Mar '96 / PolyGram

VERY SPECIAL SEASON, A
Winter wonderland / White Christmas / Wonderful Christmas time / What the world needs now / Happy Christmas (war is over) / Let it snow, let it snow, let it snow / Amazing grace / His eye is on the sparrow / Silent night / Overjoyed / O holy night / Someday at Christmas / Ave Maria / Christmas song
CD CDEMD 1075
EMI / Nov '94 / EMI

VOICES OF LOVE
Touch me in the morning / You're all I need to get by / Your love / So close / It's my turn / You are everything / When you tell me that you love me / Forever young / I am me / One shining moment / If we hold on together / Only love can conquer all / I'm still waiting / Missing you / Gone / In the ones you love / You are not alone / I hear (the voice of love)
CD CDEMD 1100
EMI / Nov '96 / EMI

WHERE DID OUR LOVE GO (Supremes)
Where did our love go / Stoned love / I still believe / Baby love / You're my driving wheel / Nathan Jones / Stop, I don't need no sympathy / You can't hurry love / If I love again / I hear a symphony / He's my man / Colours of love / Come see about me / I'm gonna let my heart do the walking / Stop in the name of love
CD ANT 001
Tring / Nov '96 / Tring

WHY DO FOOLS FALL IN LOVE
Why do fools fall in love / Sweet surrender / Mirror mirror / Endless love / It's never too late / Think I'm in love / Sweet nothin's / Two can make it / Work that body
CD CDGOLD 1044
EMI Gold / Jul '96 / EMI

Ross, Dr. Isiah

BOOGIE DISEASE
CD ARHCD 371
Arhoolie / Apr '95 / ADA / Cadillac / Direct

CALL THE DOCTOR
CD TCD 5009
Testament / Oct '94 / ADA / Koch

I WANT ALL MY FRIENDS TO KNOW
My little woman / Cat squirrel / I want all my friends to know / Boogie for the doctor / Hobo blues / Little school girl / That's alright mama
CD JSPCD 243
JSP / Apr '91 / ADA / Cadillac / Direct / Hot Shot / Target/BMG

Ross, Jerry

JERRY ROSS SYMPOSIUM, THE
Ma belle amie / Everything is beautiful / When love slips away / For the love of him / Let me love you one more time / Little green bag / But for love / Montego love theme / If you do believe in love / Venus / How can I be sure/Day by day / Take it out on me / I saw the light/Life and breath / Superwoman / If we only have love/Oh girl / It happened on a Sunday morning / Too late to turn back now/I wanna be where you are / Brandy (you're a fine girl) / It's the same old love / Too young / Duck you sucker
CD NEMCD 722
Sequel / May '95 / BMG

Ross, Malcolm

LOW SHOT
CD MA 14
Marina / Sep '95 / SRD

Ross, Richard

COMING FROM KANSAS CITY
Body and Fenderman / I wanna get funky / Comeback / God bless the child / I wanna make love to you / Jelly jelly / Just a dream / I'd rather drink muddy water / Since I fell for you / Gee baby ain't I good to you / Trick bag
CD AL 73072
A / Jul '97 / Cadillac / Direct

Ross, Ricky

WHAT YOU ARE
Good enening Philadelphia / Icarus / Cold easter / What you are / Radio on / When sinners fall / Jack singer / Lovers / Wake up and dream / Rosie Gordon lies so still / Promise you rain / Love isn't hard it's strong
CD 4839988
Epic / Jun '96 / Sony

Ross, Steve

CLOSE TO COLE PORTER
Close / Ev'rything I love / I've got a shooting box in Scotland / I'm throwing a ball tonight / Me and Marie / Begin the beguine / When the summer moon comes 'long / Get a kick out of you anything goes / Down in the depths / Picture of me without you / Night and day / What's this thing called love / Ev'ry time we say goodbye / They couldn't compare to you / Can-can / You don't know paree / I concentrate on you / Take me back to Manhattan / I happen to like New York / I've got you under my skin
CD SCATCD 1
Sophisticat / Jun '96 / New Note/Pinnacle

Rossbach, John

NEVER WAS PLUGGED
CD ALZCD 126
Alcazar / Feb '96 / ADA

Rosselson, Leon

GUESS WHAT THEY'RE SELLING AT THE HAPPINESS COUNTER
Hugga mugga chugga lugga humbugga boom chit / Story line / Barney's epic homer / Boys will be boys / My daughter, my son / Do you remember / Abiezer coppe / On her silver jubilee / Ugly ones / Susie / Invisible married breakfast blues / Years grow tall / Invisible man / Pills / Across the hills / Battle hymn of the new socialist party / World's police / Voices / Voice that lives inside you
CD CFCD 003
Fuse / Feb '88 / ADA / CM / Direct / Roots

INTRUDERS
CD CFCD 005
Fuse / Nov '95 / ADA / CM / Direct / Roots

PERSPECTIVES
Ant and the grasshopper / Perspectives / They're going to build a motorway / Plan / Man who puffs the big cigar / Garden of stone / History lesson / Ballad of a spycatcher / Song of the moderate man / Consider the majority / Saint / No cause for alarm / Experts / In the park / Last chance / Rules of the game / Somebody's stolen the end of my dream / Topside down party
CD CFCD 006
Fuse / Feb '97 / ADA / CM / Direct / Roots

ROSSELSONGS
Tim McGuire / Penny for the guy / Palaces of gold / We sell everything / Stand up for Judas / Sing a song to please us / She was crazy, he was mad / Not quite but nearly / Let your hair hang down / Don't get married, girls / I didn't mean it / No-one is responsible / Still is the memory green in my mind / Whoever invented the fishfinger / Who reaps the profits, who pays the price / It wasn't me, I didn't do it / Bringing the news from nowhere / World turned upside down
CD CFCD 001
Fuse / '88 / ADA / CM / Direct / Roots

WO SIND DIE ELEFANTEN
Neighbours' cat / Poet, the wife and the monkey / Wo sind die elefanten / Juggler / Whatever happened to Nannerl / Song of the old communist / Where's the enemy / William / General Lockjaw briefs the british media / Out of the fires and smoke of history
CD CFCD 002
Fuse / Feb '89 / ADA / CM / Direct / Roots

Rossendale Male Voice

VALLEY OF SONG, THE (Rossendale Male Voice Choir)
Ma belle marguerite / Donkey serenade / I gave my love a cherry / Phil the fluter's ball / Down in the valley / What shall we do with the drunken sailor / Hippopotamus song / Muss I denn / There is nothin' like a dame / I will give my love an apple / Ghost's high noon / Yesterday / Mad dogs and Englishmen / Cease thy affections / Lighthouse keeper and the mermaid / Blow the wind southerly / Old superb
CD CHAN 6602
Chandos / Jun '94 / Chandos

Rosser, Neil

GWYNFYD (Rosser, Neil A'i Bartneriaid)
CD CRAICD 043
Crai / Dec '94 / ADA / Direct

Rossi, Francis

KING OF THE DOGHOUSE
King of the doghouse / I don't know / Darling / Give myself to love / Isaac Ryan / Happy town / Wherever you go / Blue water / Fighter / Someone show me
CD CDV 2809
Virgin / Sep '96 / EMI

Rossi, Tino

EN CROISIERE AVEC LUI
Le chaland qui passe / Je voudrais un joli bateau / Amapola / Le bateau des Iles / Adieu Hawai / Le pousse-pousse / Tarantelle / Santa Lucia / O sole mio / Ecoutez les mandolines / Reginella / La chanson du voilier / Mon ile d'amour / Loin des guitares / Tant qu'ily aura des etoiles / Le joyeux bandit / Giovinella / Ma Ritournelle / Soirs D'Espagne / De Nice a Monte Carlo
CD UCD 19111
Forlane / Apr '96 / Target/BMG

ETOILES DE LA CHANSON
CD 8422092
Music Memoria / Nov '96 / ADA / Discovery

HISTOIRES D'AMOUR
Voulez-vous, madame / Rien qu'un chant d'amour / Pres du feu qui chante / Au bal de l'amour / Le chant du gardian / Toi que mon coeur appelle / Maria / Un soir, une nuit / Ce matin meme / J'ai deux mots dans mon coeur / Paquita / Donne moi ton sourire / Serenade sans espoir / J'attendrai / Tu etais la plus belle / Tristesse / Serenade pres de Mexico / Dites-lui de ma part / Soir de pluie / Ce soir
CD UCD 19110
Forlane / Nov '95 / Target/BMG

J'ATTENDRAI (The Best Of Tino Rossi)
J'attendrai / Vieni vieni / O corse, ile d'amour / Tant qu'il y aura des etoiles / Bella ragazzina / Reginella / Chant d'amour de Tahiti / Reviens / Tchi-tchi / Marinella / Tristesse (l'ambre s'enfuit) / Quand to reverras ton village / Le chant du gardian / Petit papa Noel / Serenade sur Paris / Mediterranee / Potpourri: Au pays du soleil / Ajaccio / Le tango nous invite / Cerisier rose et pommier blanc / Ma joie / La vie commence a 60 ans
CD CDEMS 1444
EMI / Apr '92 / EMI

J'ATTENDRAI
Tango de Marilou / Ou voulez vous aller / Aubade: Vainement, ma bien aimee / Reviens / Marinella / Serenade / Si tu le voulais / Bella Ragazzina / Romance de Maitre Pathelin / Catari, Catari (Core 'ngrato) / Amapola / Roses de Picardie / Le Paradis du reve / C'est a Capri / Chant d'amour de Tahiti / Pour t'avoir au clair de lune / Serenade Portugaise / Tant qu'il y aura des etoiles / Si vous l'aviez compris / Reginella / O Corse, ile d'amour / Vieni, vieni / J'attendrai
CD CDMOIR 520
Memoir / Mar '97 / Jazz Music / Target/BMG

L'INCOMPARABLE
CD UCD 19053
Forlane / Jun '95 / Target/BMG

PARIS VOICI PARIS
O corse ile d'amour / Catari / Vieni vieni / Ecris moi / O sole mio / Berceuse de Jocelyn / Tant qu'il y aura des etoiles / C'est a capri / Un jour je te dirai / O ciuciarella / Minuit chretiens / Chanson pour Nina / L'amour est une etoile / Paris voice Paris / Mia piccolina / Chanson pour ma brune / J'attendrai / Noel en mer / Tango de marilou / Pescadore / Credo / Guitare d'amour / Tchi tchi / Marinella
CD CDAJA 5168
Living Era / Dec '95 / Select

TINO ROSSI ANTHOLOGY
CD EN 524
Encyclopaedia / Sep '96 / Discovery

Rossy

ONE EYE ON THE FUTURE, ONE EYE ON THE PAST
CD SHCD 64046
Shanachie / May '93 / ADA / Greensleeves / Koch

Rostock Vampires

TRANSYLVANIAN DISEASE
CD NB 014CD
Nuclear Blast / Oct '89 / Plastic Head

Rosvett

FATAL
CD BIRD 045CD
Birdnest / Oct '94 / Cargo / Plastic Head

Roswells

ROSWELLS, THE
CD TDR 90940
TDR / Jul '97 / Greyhound

Roswoman, Michele

OCCASION TO RISE (Roswoman, Michele Trio)
Lazy bird / Sweet eye of hurricane Sally / Occasion to rise / Prelude to a kiss / Weird nightmare / First trip / We are / Nite flite / Eee-yaa / West Africa
CD ECD 22042
Evidence / Mar '93 / ADA / Cadillac / Harmonia Mundi

Rota, Nino

HARMONIA ENSEMBLE
CD JSL 015
JSL / Aug '93 / Discovery

Rotary Connection

SONGS
Respect / Weight / Sunshine of your love / Got my mojo working / Burning of the midnight lamp / Tales of brave Ulysses / This town / We're going wrong / Salt of the Earth
CD CDARC 520
Charly / Mar '95 / Koch

Roth, Arlen

GUITAR
CD ROUCD 11538
Rounder / '88 / ADA / CM / Direct

TOOLIN' AROUND
Tequila: *Roth, Arlen & Danny Gatton* / Let it slide: *Roth, Arlen & Jerry Douglas/Sam Bush* / Goin' back: *Roth, Arlen & Bill Lloyd* / Whiter shade of pale / Rollin' home: *Roth, Arlen & Albert Lee* / Black water: *Roth, Arlen & Duane Eddy* / I can't stop loving you / Housefire: *Roth, Arlen & Duke Robillard* / When a man loves a woman / Six days on the road: *Roth, Arlen & Brian Setzer* / No woman, no cry / '56 Buick Roadmasters from space
CD BPM 300CD
Blue Plate / May '97 / ADA / Direct / Greyhound

Roth, David

DIGGING THROUGH THE CLOSET
CD ____ FE 1414
Folk Era / Dec '94 / ADA / CM

RISISNG IN LOVE
CD ____ FE 1410
Folk Era / Dec '94 / ADA / CM

Roth, David Lee

CRAZY FROM THE HEAT
Easy Street / Just a gigolo / I ain't got nobody / California girls / Coconut grove
CD ____ 7599252222
WEA / Jul '92 / Warner Music

EAT 'EM AND SMILE
Yankee rose / Shy boy / I'm easy / Ladies nite in Buffalo / Goin' crazy / Tobacco Road / Elephant gun / Big trouble / Bump and grind / That's life
CD ____ 9254702
WEA / Aug '86 / Warner Music

SKYSCRAPER
Hot dog and a shake / Stand up / Hina / Perfect timing / Two fools a minute / Knucklebones / Just like paradise / Bottom line / Skyscraper / Damn good / California girls / Just a gigolo
CD ____ 9258242
WEA / Jan '89 / Warner Music

Rothberg, Patti

BETWEEN THE 1 AND THE 9
Flicker / Inside / This one's mine / Treat me like dirt / Looking for a girl / Forgive me / Up against the wall / Perfect stranger / Out of my mind / Change your ways / Remembering tonight / It's alright
CD ____ CDCHR 6114
Chrysalis / Sep '96 / EMI

Rothenberg, Ned

POWER LINES
CD ____ 804762
New World / Jan '96 / ADA / Cadillac / Harmonia Mundi

Rothenberg/Boone/Velez

ON THE CLIFFS OF THE HEART
CD ____ NT 6744
New Tone / Aug '96 / ADA / Impetus

Rotterdam Conservatory ...

CUBA - CONTRADANZAS & DANZONES (Rotterdam Conservatory Orquesta Tipica)
Las Alturas de Simpson / Los Ojos de Pepa / Ya esta el cafe, o me voy a la Aplandora / La Tedezco / Cadete constitucional / El Panuelo de Pepa / Almendra / Ayes del Alma / San Pascual Bailon / Yo no bailo mas Catalina / El Dedo de Landaluce / Three Rigadones from Le Grande Duchesse / El Sungambelo / El Bombin de Barreto / Pero por que / Milicianos en New York / Two danzas
CD ____ NI 5502
Nimbus / Nov '96 / Nimbus

Rotting Christ

PASSAGE TO ACTURO
CD ____ USRDEC 003CD
Unisound / Nov '95 / Plastic Head

PASSAGE TO ARCTURO
CD ____ DEC 003
Decapitated / Nov '93 / Plastic Head

SATANAS TEDEUM
CD ____ USR 015CD
Unisound / Nov '95 / Plastic Head

TRIARCHY OF THE LOST LOVERS
CD ____ CM 77128CD
Nuclear Blast / May '96 / Plastic Head

Rottrevore

INIQUITOUS
CD ____ DC 016
Drowned / Apr '94 / Plastic Head

Rotundo, Francisco

EL VIEJO VALS
CD ____ BMT 004
Blue Moon / Feb '97 / Cadillac / Discovery / Greensleeves / Jazz Music / Jet Star / TKO Magnum

Rough Cut

COME OUT
Almighty / Gun shot / Physically fit / Phoo jah / Ghetto livin' / Cool one / 100% pure love / Almighty space mix / Come out / Ghetto livin' / Bubble and wine / Cool one / Baby girl
CD ____ ZD 11CD
Zip Dog / Mar '97 / Grapevine/PolyGram / SRD / Vital

Rough 'n' Tumble

ROUGH 'N' ROLL
CD ____ PT 614001
Part / Jun '96 / Nervous

Rough Silk

CIRCLE OF PAIN
CD ____ MASSCD 115
Massacre / Jan '97 / Plastic Head

WALLS OF NEVER
CD ____ 9041032
Mausoleum / Mar '95 / Grapevine/ PolyGram

Rough Trade

ROUGHEST TRADE
Crimes of passion / All touch / Lie back and let me do everything / Weapons / Birds of a feather / Grade B movie / Baptism of fire / High school confidential / Shaking the foundations / Territorial / America bad and beautiful
CD ____ WKFMXD 43
FM / '86 / Revolver / Sony

Roulettes

STAKES AND CHIPS
CD ____ BGOCD 130
Beat Goes On / Apr '92 / Pinnacle

Roupe

ENTELCHY
CD ____ CDRE 02
Resource / Feb '97 / Kudos / Pinnacle

STROM
CD ____ INMCD 002
GPR / Mar '95 / 3mv/Vital

Rouse, Charlie

CINNAMON FLOWER
CD ____ RCD 10053
Rykodisc / '91 / ADA / Vital

EPISTROPHY
Nutty / Blue monk / Epistrophy / Ruby my dear / 'Round midnight
CD ____ LCD 15212
Landmark / Jun '89 / New Note/Pinnacle

LES JAZZ MODES
CD ____ BCD 134/135
Biograph / Aug '95 / ADA / Cadillac / Direct / Hot Shot / Jazz Music / Wellard

Rouse, Mikel

DENNIS CLEVELAND
CD ____ NW 80506
New World / Dec '96 / ADA / Cadillac / Harmonia Mundi

WALK IN THE WOODS (Rouse, Mikel & Broken Consort)
CD ____ MTM 6CD
Made To Measure / Sep '88 / New Note/ Pinnacle

Roussos, Demis

ADAGIO
Morning has broken / Tous les je vous aime / Oxygen / Too many dreams / Les mots qui font peur / Adagio / Italian song / Take me home / Spleen / Sergueii
CD ____ QED 222
Tring / Nov '96 / Tring

ADAGIO
Morning has broken / Tous les je vous aime / Oxygen / Too many dreams / Les mots qui font peu / Adagio / Italian song / Take me home / Spleen / Sergueii
CD ____ 100122
CMC / May '97 / BMG

DIAMOND COLLECTION, THE
CD ____ 602144
Arcade / Feb '97 / Discovery

FAVOURITE RARITIES
CD ____ RA 95012
BR Music / Sep '94 / Target/BMG

GREEK, THE
CD ____ BR 1292
BR Music / May '94 / Target/BMG

LES INOUBLIABLES DE...
CD ____ 472303
Flarenasch / Feb '97 / Discovery

LOST IN LOVE
Happy to be an island in the sun / Forever and ever / Can't say how much I love you / When forever has gone / Goodbye my love goodbye / My reason / Lost in love / I just don't know what to do with myself / Lost in a dream / Velvet mornings / Midnight is the time I need you / Gypsy lady / Senora (I need you) / Cancion de boda (The wedding song)
CD ____ 5500692
Spectrum / May '93 / PolyGram

MORNING HAS BROKEN
Morning has broken / Oxygen / Adagio / Les mots qui font peur / Italian song / Take me home / Tous lee 'je vous aime' / Spleen (Baudelaire) / Too many dreams / Sergueii
CD ____ 305582
Hallmark / Oct '96 / Carlton

MY FRIEND THE WIND
Rain and tears / We shall dance / Forever and ever (and ever) / My friend the wind / My reason / Goodbye my love goodbye / Follow me / Summer wine: *Roussos, Demis & Nancy Boyd* / Marie Jolie / Summer in her eyes / Greater love / Tropicana bay: *Roussos, Demis & Nancy Boyd* / Island of love / Lovely lady of Arcadia / I found you / Spring Summer Winter and Fall / I want to live / End of the world
CD ____ CDMFP 6074
Music For Pleasure / Aug '89 / EMI

TOO MANY DREAMS
Morning has broken / Tous les je vous aime / Oxygen / Too many dreams / Les mots qui font peur / Adagio / Italian song / Take me home / Spleen sergueii
CD ____ MSCD 5
Music De-Luxe / Jun '94 / TKO Magnum

Route 66

ROUTE 66
I'm moving out / You know I need you / It's not over / Black and white / I know it's not true / I'm not a punk / Keep on trying / Boys with mascara / You need affection / It's hard (a Trogg story) / It ain't nice / It's not over / I can tell / How do you feel right now / Did you / I like what I am / Give or fake / I just can't wait much longer / Cement garden / Give or fake / Always makin' time
CD ____ SPJCD 005
Angel Air / Mar '97 / Pinnacle

Routine

ROUTINE
CD ____ 99 2147
Ninetynine / Jul '96 / Timewarp

Routledge, Keith

PRAISE HIM ON THE PIANO
CD ____ SOPD 2049
Spirit Of Praise / May '92 / Nelson Word

Rova

JOHN COLTRANE'S ASCENSION
CD ____ 1201802
Black Saint / Mar '97 / Cadillac / Harmonia Mundi

WORKS VOL.1, THE
CD ____ 1201762
Black Saint / Sep '95 / Cadillac / Harmonia Mundi

WORKS VOL.2, THE
CD ____ 1201862
Black Saint / Aug '97 / Cadillac / Harmonia Mundi

Rova Saxophone Quartet

CHANTING THE LIGHT OF FORESIGHT
CD ____ NA 064
New Albion / May '94 / Cadillac / Harmonia Mundi

CROWD, THE (Rova)
CD ____ ARTCD 6098
Hat Art / Apr '92 / Cadillac / Harmonia Mundi

FROM THE BUREAU OF BOTH
CD ____ 1201352
Black Saint / Apr '93 / Cadillac / Harmonia Mundi

SAXOPHONE DIPLOMACY (Rova)
CD ____ ARTCD 6068
Hat Art / Nov '91 / Cadillac / Harmonia Mundi

THIS TIME WE ARE BOTH
CD ____ NA 041
New Albion / Aug '91 / Cadillac / Harmonia Mundi

Row, Porter

FREE 'N' EASY
CD ____ FRCD 032
Foam / Oct '94 / CM

Rowallan Consort

NOTES OF JOY
CD ____ COMD 2058
Temple / Feb '95 / ADA / CM / Direct / Duncans / Highlander

Rowan, Peter

ALL ON A RISING DAY
Midnight highway / Last train / Howlin' at the moon / Mr. Time clock / Behind these prison walls of love / Deal with the devil / Undying love / Wheel of fortune / All on a rising day / Freedom walkabout / Prayer of a homeless wanderer / John O'Dreams
CD ____ SHCD 3791
Sugar Hill / Oct '94 / ADA / CM / Direct / Koch / Roots

AWAKE ME IN THE NEW WORLD
Shaman's vision / Dreams of the sea / Pulcinella sails away / Caribbean woman / Dance with no shoes / Sugarcane / For Gods, for Kings and for gold / Awake me in the new world / All my relations / Remember that I love you / Maria de las Rosas / African banjo / Sailing home dance of Pulcinella
CD ____ SHCD 3807
Sugar Hill / May '93 / ADA / CM / Direct / Koch / Roots

BLUEGRASS BOY
CD ____ SHCD 3859
Sugar Hill / Oct '96 / ADA / CM / Direct / Koch / Roots

DUST BOWL CHILDREN
Dust bowl children / Before the streets were paved / Electric blanket / Little mother / Barefoot country road / Seeds my daddy sowed / Tumbleweed / Dream of a home / Rainmaker
CD ____ SHCD 3781
Sugar Hill / Jul '90 / ADA / CM / Direct / Koch / Roots

FIRST WHIPPOORWILL, THE
I'm on my way back to the old home / I'm just a used to be / I believed in you darling / Sweetheart you done me wrong / When the golden leaves begin to fall / I was left on the street / Goodbye old pal / When you are lonely / First whipperwill / Sitting alone in the moonlight / Boat of love / It's mighty dark to travel
CD ____ SHCD 3749
Sugar Hill / Jul '93 / ADA / CM / Direct / Koch / Roots

MEDICINE TRAIL
Riding high in Texas / My foolish pride / River of stone / Revelation / Lying on the line / Medicine trail / Blues come bother me / Dreaming I love you / Maui momma / Prairie lullabye
CD ____ FF 70205
Flying Fish / Sep '96 / ADA / CM / Direct / Roots

NEW MOON RISING (Rowan, Peter & The Nashville Bluegrass Band)
That high lonesome sound / Trail of tears / Memories of you / Moth to a flame / I'm gonna love you / One way / New moon rising / Jesus made the wine / Cabin of love / Meadow green
CD ____ SHCD 3762
Sugar Hill / Nov '94 / ADA / CM / Direct / Koch / Roots

PETER ROWAN AND RED HOT PICKERS (Rowan, Peter & The Red Hot Pickers)
Hobo song / Old old house / Willow garden / Jimmie Brown the newsboy / Wild Billy Jones / Hiroshima mon amour / Come ye tender hearted / Oh Susanna / Rosalie McFall / Good woman's love
CD ____ SHCD 3733
Sugar Hill / Dec '95 / ADA / CM / Direct / Koch / Roots

TREE ON A HILL (Rowan Brothers)
CD ____ SHCD 2823
Sugar Hill / Jun '94 / ADA / CM / Direct / Koch / Roots

WALLS OF TIME
Roving gambler / Lone pilgrim / Raglan Road / Going up the mountain / Casey's last ride / Moonshiner / Thirsty in the rain / Walls of time / Plains of waterloo / Hiroshima mon amour / Old old house / Willow garden
CD ____ SHCD 3722
Sugar Hill / Oct '96 / ADA / CM / Direct / Koch / Roots

WILD STALLIONS
CD ____ APCD 016
Appaloosa / Apr '94 / ADA / Direct / TKO Magnum

Rowe, Carlyle

DARLING
CD ____ DTCD 27
Discotex / Nov '96 / Jet Star

Rowe, Keith

DIMENSION OF PERFECTLY ORDINARY, A
CD ____ MR 19
Matchless / '90 / Cadillac / ReR Megacorp

Rowland, Dennis

GET HERE
Circle dance / Detour head / I don't care who knows (baby I'm yours) / Comeback / Autumn in New York / Get here / Don't you know I care / Things have got to change / I've grown accustomed to her face / Waiting for love / I think it's going to rain today
CD ____ CCD 4693
Concord Jazz / May '96 / New Note/ Pinnacle

NOW DIG THIS
All blues / My ship / I could write a book / Easy living / Someday my prince will come / 'Round midnight / You don't know love is / Pfrancing (no blues) / Meaning of the blues/Lament
CD ____ CCD 47512
Concord Jazz / Aug '97 / New Note/ Pinnacle

Rowles, Jimmy

LILAC TIME
Music music everywhere / Lullaby of the leaves / Theme from Arrest and Trial / Accent on youth / Night in Tunisia / Maury / I'm old fashioned / Morning lovely / Jeannine, I dream of lilac time / Belfast / Maurcie / After school / Time out / I wonder where love has gone / Chloe / Maids of Cadiz / Summer night
CD KOKO 1297
Kokopelli / Oct '94 / New Note/Pinnacle

PEACOCKS (Rowles, Jimmy & Michael Hashim)
CD STB 2511
Stash / Sep '95 / ADA / Cadillac / CM / Direct / Jazz Music

REMEMBER WHEN
Oh lady be good / Peacocks / Things are looking up / Outsity / Come Sunday / Let's fall in love / Remember when / Just like a butterfly / Grooveyard
CD CDCHE 11
Master Mix / Oct '91 / Jazz Music / New Note/Pinnacle / Wellard

TRIO (Rowles, Jimmy, Red Mitchell & Donald Bailey)
CD 740092
Capri / '90 / Cadillac / Wellard

Rowsome, Leo

CLASSICS OF IRISH PIPING VOL.1
Boil the breakfast early/Heather breeze / Savoureen deelish/Clare's dragoons / Blackbird / St. Patrick's day / Boolavogue/ Old Bog road / Boys of Wexford/Kelly the boy from Killane / Rights of man/Wexford/ Dunphy's hornpipe / Broom/Star of Munster/Milliner's daughter / Collier's reel/The maid of Tramore / Independent hornpipe/ The star hornpipe / Frieze breeches / Tomorrow morning/Cloone hornpipe / Cook in the kitchen/Rakes of kildare / Sweep's hornpipe/The friendly visit / Jockey to the fair / My darling asleep/Tongues of fire / Higgin's hornpipe/The queen of May / Fairie's revels/I won't be a nun / Shandon bells/ Haste, to the wedding / Rocky road to Dublin
CD TSCD 471
Topic / Sep '93 / ADA / CM / Direct

Rox Diamond

ROX DIAMOND
CD CDATV 25
Active / Jul '92 / Pinnacle

Roxette

CRASH, BOOM, BANG
Harleys and Indians (riders in the sky) / Crash boom bang / Fireworks / Run to you / Sleeping in my car / Vulnerable / First girl on the moon / Place your love / I love the sound of crashing guitars / What's she like / Do you wanna go the whole way / Lies / I'm sorry / Love is all (shine your light on me) / Go to sleep
CD CDEMD 1056
EMI / Apr '94 / EMI

DON'T BORE US, GET TO THE CHORUS
June afternoon / You don't understand me / Look / Dressed for success / Listen to your heart / Dangerous / It must have been love / Joyride / Fading like a flower / Big L / Spending my time / How do you do / Almost unreal / Sleeping in my car / Crash boom bang / Vulnerable / She doesn't live here anymore / I don't want to get hurt
CD CDEMTV 98
EMI / Oct '95 / EMI

JOYRIDE
Joyride / Hotblooded / Fading like a flower (every time you leave) / Knockin' on every door / Spending my time / I remember you / Watercolours in the rain / Big L / Soul deep / (Do you get) excited / Church of your heart / Small talk / Physical fascination / Things will never be the same / Perfect day
CD CDEMD 1019
EMI / Mar '91 / EMI

LOOK SHARP
Look / Dressed for success / Sleeping single / Paint / Dance away / Cry / Chances / Dangerous / Half a woman, half a shadow / View from a hill / I could never give you up / Shadow of a doubt / Listen to your heart
CD CDEMC 3557
EMI / Apr '89 / EMI

Roxxi

DRIVE IT TO YA HARD
CD RH 1491
FM / May '91 / Revolver / Sony

Roxy Music

AVALON
More than this / Space between / India / While my heart is still beating / Main thing / Take a chance with me / Avalon / To turn you on / True to life / Tara
CD EGCD 50
EG / Apr '92 / EMI

AVALON/FLESH AND BLOOD/ MANIFESTO (3CD Set)
CD Set TPAK 34
Virgin / Oct '94 / EMI

COUNTRY LIFE
Thrill of it all / Three and nine / All I want is you / Out of the blue / If it takes all night / Bittersweet / Triptych / Casanova / Really good time / Prairie rose
CD EGCD 16
EG / Jan '87 / EMI

FLESH AND BLOOD
In the midnight hour / Oh yeah / Same old scene / Flesh and blood / My only love / Over you / Eight miles high / Rain rain rain / Running wild / No strange delight
CD EGCD 46
EG / Sep '91 / EMI

FOR YOUR PLEASURE
Do the Strand / Beauty Queen / Strictly confidential / Editions of you / In every dream home a heartache / Bogus man / Grey lagoons / For your pleasure
CD EGCD 8
EG / Sep '91 / EMI

HEART STILL BEATING (LIVE)
India / Can't let go / While my heart is still beating / Out of the blue / Dance away / Impossible guitar / Song for Europe / Love is the drug / Like a hurricane / My only love / Both ends burning / Avalon / Editions of you / Jealous guy
CD EGCD 77
EG / Oct '90 / EMI

MANIFESTO
Ain't that so / Cry cry cry / Dance away / Manifesto / My little girl / Spin me round / Still falls the rain / Trash / Stronger through the years
CD EGCD 38
EG / Sep '91 / EMI

ROXY MUSIC
Bitters end / Bob / Chance meeting / If there is something / Ladytron / Re-make/Re-model / 2HB / Would you believe / Sea breezes
CD EGCD 6
EG / Sep '91 / EMI

ROXY MUSIC/FOR YOUR PLEASURE/ STRANDED (3CD Set)
CD Set TPAK 23
Virgin / Jan '93 / EMI

STRANDED
Street life / Just like you / Amazon / Psalm / Serenade / Song for Europe / Mother of pearl / Sunset
CD EGCD 10
EG / Sep '91 / EMI

THRILL OF IT ALL, THE (Roxy Music 1972-1982/4CD Set)
Re-make/Re-model / Ladytron / If there is something / 2HB / Chance meeting / Sea breezes / Do the Strand / Beauty Queen / Strictly confidential / Editions of you / In every dream home a heartache / Bogus man / For your pleasure / Street life / Just like you / Amazona / Song for Europe / Mother of pearl / Sunset / Thrill of it all / Three and nine / All I want is you / Out of the blue / Bitter sweet / Casanova / Really good time / Prairie Rose / Love is the drug / Sentimental fool / Could it happen to me / Both ends burning / Just another high / Manifesto / Trash / Angel eyes / Stronger through the years / Ain't that so / Dance away / Oh yeah / Same old scene / Flesh and blood / My only love / Over you / No strange delight / More than this / Avalon / While my heart is still beating / Take a chance with me / To turn you on / Tara / Virginia Plain / Numberer / Pyjamarama / Pride and the pain / Manifesto (remake) / Hula kula / Trash 2 / Your application's failed / Lover / Sultanesque / Dance away (remix) / South Downs / Always unknowing / Main thing / India / Jealous guy
CD Set CDBOX 5
Virgin / Nov '95 / EMI

VIVA ROXY MUSIC
Out of the blue / Pyjamarama / Bogus man / Chance meeting / If there is something / In every dream home a heartache / Do the Strand / Can't let go / My only love / Like a hurricane / Jealous guy
CD EGCD 25
EG / Sep '91 / EMI

Roy C

SHOTGUN WEDDING
Shotgun wedding / I'm gonna make it / I want to be where you are / She's gone (she took the TV and telephone) / Medley / To make you feel like a woman / Leaving on the morning train / I'm not going to eat a thing / I'm still in love with you / Love me til tomorrow / Second time around / I want to marry you / That's when I'll take you home / Rock me all night / Since I met you baby / Pick up the pieces / Love crazy / Somebody's right / Peepin' through the window / I keep holding on
CD NEMCD 764
Sequel / Jul '97 / BMG

Roy, Harry

GREETINGS FROM YOU
Tangerine / Hold your hats on / Oh the pity of it all / Humpty Dumpty heart / When I love I love / Was it love / Sentimental interlude / You bring the boogie woogie out in me / Greetings from you / Zoot suit / Do you care / When daddy comes home / Darling Daisy / Elmer's tune / Madelaine / Chattanooga choo choo / Tica ti tica ta / It's funny to everyone but me / In the middle of a dance / Blues in the night / Green eyes / Shrine of St. Cecilia
CD RAJCD 803
Empress / May '97 / Koch

HARRY ROY
Tiger rag / Canadian capers / Who walks in when I walk out / If I can't have Anna in Cuba / When I told the village belle / Campesina / Ever so quiet / Every time I look at you / Bugle call rag / Mr. Magician / My dog love's your dog / Nasty man / Harry Roy's new stage show / Valentina / Becky, play your violin / World is so small / Coconut oil (mama don't want)
CD PASTCD 9741
Flapper / Sep '91 / Pinnacle

HARRY ROY AND HIS ORCHESTRA (Roy, Harry & His Orchestra)
Bugle call rag / Alexander's ragtime band / 12th Street rag / Somebody stole my gal / Roy rag / Keep young and beautiful / Emaline / My last year's gal / Waiting for tomorrow and you / Tiger rag / Chinatown, my Chinatown / I've got my love to keep me warm / You've got me crying again / Snowball / Sing another line / When it's darkness on the delta / I was in the mood / Let's swing it / Me, myself and I / Back to back / You're a sweetheart / Here comes the sandman / This year's kisses / Bom di bom / Nobody's sweetheart / She had to go and lose it at the Astor
CD CDMFP 6361
Music For Pleasure / Jun '97 / EMI

KING OF HOT-CHA, THE (Roy, Harry & His Orchestra)
Bugle call rag / Chinatown my Chinatown / Cuban Pete / La Cucaracha / Goody goodbye / Goosey goosey / Heigh-ho / Hot time in town / I want the waiter with the water / King Porter stomp / Let's have a jubilee / Lullaby of Broadway / Maple leaf rag / My girl's a rhythm fan / No name rag / Red pepper / Roy rag / Sarawaki / That's a plenty / That's the way I like to hear you talk / What a difference a day made / Where did Robinson Crusoe go / You made me care
CD CDAJA 5225
Living Era / Aug '97 / Select

SHOOT THAT TIGER
Medley / Goody goody / Diddle dum dee / Man from Harlem / Chinatown my Chinatown / Limehouse blues / Casa loma stomp / Fox medley / Is it true what they say about Dixie / Cuban Pete / Nobody's sweetheart / Bugle call rag / Tiger rag / Canadian capers / Gershwin medley / Let's call the wole thing off / They can't take that away from me / Rita the rumba / Boo hoo / Sing baby sing / Bye bye baby / Where did Robinson Crusoe go with Friday on a Saturday night / Harry Roy stage show medley / Alone / Intro / Sarawacki / St. Louis blues / Piano madness / Somebody stole my gal
CD CDEA 6001
Vocalion / Aug '97 / Complete/Pinnacle

Roy, Larry

QUARTER TO THREE (Roy, Larry & Marilyn Lerner)
CD JTR 84372
Justin Time / Oct '92 / Cadillac / New Note/Pinnacle

Roy, Stephane

KALEIDOS
CD IMED 96
Diffunzioni Musicali / Jun '97 / ReR Megacorp

Roy, William

WHEN I SING ALONE
CD ACD 213
Audiophile / Nov '96 / Jazz Music

Royal Air Force

70 YEARS (Royal Air Force Central Band)
Brave defenders / Royal Air Force march past / Spitfire prelude and fugue / Lawrence of Arabia / Four caballeros / TV sports themes / Oor Wullie / Fanfare on the RAF call / March and dance of the comedians / Little light music / Viva musica / Introduction and march from the Battle Of Britain / Those magnificent men in their flying machines / Concert march- Cockleshell heroes / Elegy / March: Uxbridge
CD BNA 5009
Bandleader / Jun '87 / Conifer/BMG

AIRMEN, THE (Bands Of The Royal Air Force)
Fanfare on the RAF call / Royal Air Force march past / Dam busters / Keepers of the peace / Out of the blue / Holyrood / Those magnificent men in their flying machines / Songs of the early airmen / Grand March 'RAF' / Tiger squadron / Swing squadron / Cavalry of the clouds / Jolly airmen / Spitfire prelude and fuge / Tornado / Squadron / Battle of Britain march / When the squads go marching / Celebration march / Battle in the air
CD STACD 7003
Valentine / Jan '94 / Conifer/BMG

BIG BAND SPECTACULAR (Royal Air Force Squadronaires Band)
There's something in the air / Lover / Splanky / John Brown's other body / Stardust / Doin' Basie's thing / Autumn leaves / Sweet Georgia Brown / Glenn Miller Medley / In the mood / Little brown jug / String of pearls / Moonlight serenade / St. Louis blues march / Song of India / All the things you are / Captiva sound / That warm feeling / South Rampart street parade / Switch in time / Pennsylvania 6-5000 / Scott's place / Basie straight ahead / Bedtime for drums / Sounds familiar
CD BNA 5007
Bandleader / Jun '87 / Conifer/BMG

BRANDENBURG GATE (Band Of The RAF Germany)
Under the double eagle / Hoch und deutschmeister / Old comrades / Berliner luft / Celebration march / Colonel Bogey / Buck private / Bridge too far / Marche des parachutistes belges / BB and CF / Black adder / Entrance of the court / Auf der alm / Plaisir d'amour / Swiss miss / Suite Francaise / Brandenburg gate / Night flight to Madrid / Armenian dances
CD BNA 5046
Bandleader / '91 / Conifer/BMG

CELEBRATION (Staff Band Of WRAC)
ATS March / Preludium and fugue / Nimrod / Last past and reveille / Jubilant prelude / Crown imperial / Colonel Bogey / Twin eagle strut / Songs of World War Two / Auld lang syne / Furchtlos und treu / Clarinet carousel / Cornet carillon / Where no man has gone before / You needed me / Lassus trombone / Sabre dance / Tyrolean tuba / Living in the UK / Stage centre / WRAC March
CD BNA 5036
Bandleader / '91 / Conifer/BMG

FESTIVAL OF MUSIC 1987 (Massed Bands Of The Royal Air Force)
Fanfare and National Anthem / Jaguar / Marvin Hamlish showcase / Trumpet concerto-3rd movement (Hadyn) / Those magnificent men in their flying machines / Eleanor Rigby / Overture: Prince Igor / Marching with Sousa / Pines of the Appian Way (from 'The pines of Rome')
CD QPRM 112D
Polyphonic / '88 / Complete/Pinnacle

FESTIVAL OF MUSIC 1989 (Massed Bands Of The Royal Air Force)
Air crew on parade / Rhapsody in blue / Air of freedom / Phantom of the opera / Battle of Britain / Hampton Court / English dances / In the mood / Nightingale sang in Berkeley Square / After you've gone / To the few
CD QPRM 114D
Polyphonic / Jan '93 / Complete/Pinnacle

FESTIVAL OF MUSIC 1994 (Massed Bands Of The Royal Air Force)
Fanfare for the common man / March of friendship / Time piece / African symphony / Weber / Second concerto for clarinet / Travelogue / Big country / European excursion / Sahra omania / 1812 Overture
CD QPRM 122D
Polyphonic / Jan '95 / Complete/Pinnacle

FESTIVAL OF MUSIC 1995 (A Victory Salute) (Massed Bands Of The Royal Air Force)
633 Squadron / Dawn flight / Great escape / O mio babbino caro / Foggy day / My funny valentine / Armenian dance / Love changes everything / Global variations / Riverdance / Anthem / 76 trombones / Think of me / Malaguena / Songs of World War II / Dambusters march / Nimrod / Evening hymn and sunset / Royal Air Force march past
CD QPRM 123D
Polyphonic / Jan '96 / Complete/Pinnacle

GRAND PARADE (Royal Air Force Central Band)
Tiger squadron / Mad major / March of the bowmen / Pathfinder's march / Touchdown / March: The love of three oranges / Flight of the tees / Grand parade / Oak and the ash / Black Hole / March: Things to come / Spirals / Adagio / Detectives - Hill Street Blues / Kojak / Cagney and Lacey / Dempsey and makepeace
CD BNA 5028
Bandleader / '88 / Conifer/BMG

GREAT BRITISH MUSIC FOR WIND BAND (Western Band Of The RAF)
James Cook / Circumnavigator / Countdown / Theatre of music / Swiss festival overture / Christmas suite / All afoot / Music for a festival
CD QPRM 115D
Polyphonic / Jun '91 / Complete/Pinnacle

HEROES OF THE AIR (Royal Air Force Central Band)
Battle of Britain suite (Walton) / Spitfire prelude and fugue / Conquest of the air / Battle of Britain suite (Josephs) / Coastal command
CD CDPR 500
Premier/MFP / Jul '92 / EMI

MARCHES OF THE ROYAL AIR FORCE (Royal Air Force Central Band)
Royal Air Force March past / Jolly airman / Aircrew on parade / High flight / Skywatch / Flying review / With pomp and pride / Strike command march past / Tornado / Aces high / Royal air force college march / Songs of the early airmen / Acorn / Call to adventure / Royal Air Force Association march / Newcomers / Militant miss / Skywriter / Keepers of the peace / Radio / Jaguar / Holyrood / Per ardua ad astra / Grand march 'RAF'
CD BNA 5037
Bandleader / Apr '95 / Conifer/BMG

MARCHING THROUGH THE 20TH CENTURY (Band Of The Royal Air Force College Cranwell)
CD BNA 5103
Bandleader / Mar '94 / Conifer/BMG

MASSED BANDS OF THE RAF
Fantasy of RAF call / Knights of the air / Spitfire prelude / Bugler's holiday / Skyliner / Cheek to cheek / Conquest of the air / Flute concerto / Coastal command / Call of the trumpet / Dam busters march / Cavalry of the clouds / Colditz march / Clarinet candy / Battle for freedom / Salute to Britsh songs (medley) / Pathfinder's march / Reach for the sky / RAF march past
CD QPRM 121D
Polyphonic / Jan '94 / Complete/Pinnacle

RAF HQ BOMBER COMMAND SEXTET 1943-1944 (RAF HQ Bomber Command Sextet)
Clarinet marmalade / Rug cutter's swing / Washboard blues / Woo woo / At sundown / Squatty roo / Buddy's blues / Muskrat ramble / Christopher Columbus / Sweet Georgia Brown / 295 jump / Heartbreak blues / Jamboree jive / Low down empty railway station blues / King Porter stomp / Big noise from Winnetka / Ain't cha got music / Stevedore stomp / Ain't misbehavin' / One o'clock jump / It's the talk of the town / How am I to know / I wish I were twins / Soft winds
CD CYCD 74508
Celebrity / Feb '97 / Cadillac / Direct / Wellard

REACH FOR THE SKY (Bands Of The Royal Air Force)
CD MU 5007
Musketeer / Oct '92 / Disc

SALUTE TO HEROES (50th Anniversary Album) (Royal Air Force Central Band)
Royal Air Force march past / Pathfinder's march / Dambusters march / Those magnificent men in their flying machines / Reach for the sky / Out of the blue / Crown imperial / 633 squadron / Colditz march / Cavalry of the clouds / Secret army / Aces high / Spitfire prelude / Battle of Britain / We'll meet again / Valiant years / White cliffs of Dover / Run rabbit run
CD CDRAF 1
Premier/MFP / Jul '90 / EMI

SALUTE TO THE RAF (Royal Air Force Central Band)
Spitfire / Viscount Trenchard / Fanfare on the Royal Air Force call / Soldiers of the Queen / It's a long way to Tipperary / Pack up your troubles in your old kit bag / Goodbye-ee / Take me back to dear old Blighty / Gunfire / Army, Navy and Airforce / AVRO 540k / I don't want to join the Air Force / Bold aviator / Bless 'em all / AVRO Lancaster / Air raid warning siren / Winston Churchill / September 15th 1940 / BBC Announcement- "The Squadronaires" / Music in the air / We'll meet again / Big Ben / I'm gonna get lit up (when the lights go on in London) / Air raid / Coming in on a wing and a prayer / We're gonna hang out the washing on the Siegfried Line / nightingale sang in berkeley square / Run rabbit run / I've got sixpence / Kiss me goodnight / Sergeant Major / White cliffs of Dover / There'll always be an England / Lancaster returns / Dambusters march / Aerial combat / Reach for the sky / Aerial combat / Battle of Britain / Aerial combat / 633 Squadron / All clear siren / Speedbird salutes the few / RAF call / Evening hymn / Last Post sunset / March of the Royal Air Forces Association / Reveille / Ad Astra - An airman's hymn / Viscount Trenchard / Royal Air Force march past / Lightning
CD CDPR 105
Premier/MFP / Mar '93 / EMI

SWING SQUADRON (Royal Air Force Squadronaires Band)
There's something in the air / Opus 1 / Satin doll / Sheikh of Araby / Body and soul / Volando / String of pearls / When the squads go marching in / I've got my love to keep me warm / Beyond the bar / In the mood / Wind machine / Swing squadron / Here's that rainy day / Best blue / Bones away / Li'l darlin' / Flying home
CD BNA 5043
Bandleader / '91 / Conifer/BMG

SWORD AND THE CROWN, THE
CD QPRM 120D
Polyphonic / Aug '93 / Complete/Pinnacle

Royal Artillery

CALL FOR THE GUNS (Royal Artillery Band)
Call for the guns / Overture- The force of destiny / Nocturne / Blaze away / Lucy Long / Washington post / Festive overture / Gymnopedie No.1 / March: la pere la victoire / March: Rapier / Selections from Barnum / Regimental quick march / Regimental slow march
CD BNA 5054
Bandleader / Apr '91 / Conifer/BMG

MARCHES FOR EUROPE (Royal Artillery Band)
CD BNA 5080
Bandleader / Apr '93 / Conifer/BMG

Royal, Billy Joe

BILLY JOE ROYAL
CD 7567823272
Atlantic / Jan '96 / Warner Music

DOWN IN THE BOONDOCKS
CD MMCD 5741
Mammoth / Jun '92 / Vital

SPOTLIGHT ON BILLY JOE ROYAL
Down in the boondocks / Cherry Hill park / I knew you when / Up on the roof / On Broadway / Save the last dance for me / Stand by me / Hush / To love somebody / Tulsa / Campfire girls / I gotta be somebody / Raindrops keep falling on my head / Please come to Boston
CD HADCD 101
Javelin / Feb '94 / Henry Hadaway / THE

Royal Choral Society

CAROL COLLECTION
Once in Royal David's City / In dulci jubilo / I saw three ships / Fist nowell / Holly and the ivy / O little town of Bethlehem / God rest ye merry gentlemen / Silent night / While shepherds watched their flocks by night / Good King Wenceslas / Bethlehem down / Coventry carol / O come all ye faithful (adeste fidelis) / Hark the herald angels sing
CD 3036700022
Carlton / Oct '95 / Carlton

Royal Corps/Signals

SIGNALLER, THE (Band Of The Royal Corps Of Signals)
Regimental quick march / Begone dull care / Signaller / Swift and sure / Regimental slow march / HRH Princess Royal / On Richmond Hill bah'at / Donkey serenade / Lassus trombone / Vimy ridge / Master / Jubilee overture / Largo al factotum / Blandford suite / Nessun dorma / Rondo for horns / Carnival of Venice / Concerto for drum set / Farandole / History of the Royal Corps of Signals
CD BNA 5114
Bandleader / Aug '95 / Conifer/BMG

Royal Corps/Transport

CONCERT BANDSTAND (Band Of The Royal Corps Of Transport)
CD BNA 5071
Bandleader / Aug '92 / Conifer/BMG

MUSIC FROM THE GREAT HORSE SHOWS (Staff Band Of The Royal Corps Of Transport)
Fanfare / Tribute to next milton / Trotting medley / Television horse show themes / Music for heavy horses / Interval music / Another show / Cantering medley / Hunters, the judging music / Hunting medley / Quadrille time / Tribute to the horse / Finale
CD BNA 5035
Bandleader / '91 / Conifer/BMG

Royal Crescent Mob

GOOD LUCKY KILLER
CD EMY 1432
Enemy / Nov '94 / Grapevine/PolyGram

Royal Crown Revue

MUGZY'S MOVE
CD 9362461252
Warner Bros. / Oct '96 / Warner Music

Royal Doulton Band

HYMNS FOR BAND
Praise my soul the king of heaven / Onward christian soldiers / King of love my shepherd is / Day thou gavest Lord is ended / All things bright and beautiful / Lord's my shepherd / Amazing grace / Immortal, invisible, God only wise / Holy city / Now the day is over / He who would valiant be / All people that on earth do dwell / Old rugged cross / Now thank we all our God / Ave Maria / O praise ye the lord / Let us with a gladsome mind / Abide with me / Jerusalem / How sweet the name of Jesus sounds
CD BNA 5008
Bandleader / Jul '87 / Conifer/BMG

HYMNS FOR BAND VOL.2
Holy holy holy / Glorious things of thee are spoken / Therr is a green hill far away / Dear Lord and Father of mankind / I will sing the wondrous story / Thine is the glory / Pie Jesu / All the toil and sorrow done / Fill thou my life / Guide me o thou great Jehovah / Fight the good fight / Morning has broken / Jesus Christ is risen today / Be thou my guardian and my guide / Rejoice the Lord is King / Stand up, stand up for Jesus / Jesu joy of man's desiring / We plough the fields and scatter / Nearer my God to thee / I vow to thee my country
CD BNA 5034
Bandleader / '91 / Conifer/BMG

MARCHING FORWARD
CD BNA 5049
Bandleader / Feb '91 / Conifer/BMG

Royal Dragoon Guards

FAME AND RENOWN
CD BNA 5111
Bandleader / Oct '94 / Conifer/BMG

Royal Electrical/Mechanical ...

OPERATIC FESTIVAL, AN (Royal Electrical/Mechanical Engineers Corps Band)
Niblungen march / Le roi d'ys overture / Vissi d'arte / Easter hymn / Flower duet / Carmen suite / Marriage of Figaro overture / Deep inside the sacred temple / Impresario overture / Slaves chorus / Una voce poco fa / Coronation scene
CD BNA 5129
Bandleader / Dec '96 / Conifer/BMG

Royal Engineers

MUSIC FOR AN AMERICAN OCCASION
CD BNA 5125
Bandleader / Jul '96 / Conifer/BMG

Royal Family

STRAIGHT FROM THE UNDERGROUND
CD SPOCK 2CD
Music Of Life / Oct '90 / Grapevine/PolyGram

Royal Folkloric Troupe Of ...

COCO'S TAMAEVA (Royal Folkloric Troupe Of Tahiti)
CD S 65808
Manuiti / Mar '92 / Harmonia Mundi

COCO'S TEMAEVA VOL.2 (Royal Folkloric Troupe Of Tahiti)
CD S 65815
Manuiti / Feb '94 / Harmonia Mundi

Royal Highland Fusiliers

AFORE YE GO
Fanfare / March / Song for Suzanne / March: Birkenhead / Pipe dreams / March: Be ye also ready / Scottish serenade / Victory salute / Oft in the stilly night / Pipe set / Bays of Harris / Sunset salute / Seventy Ninth Farewell to Gibraltar / My own land / Tenth HLI crossing the Rhine / Misty morn / March: Assaye / Seventy Fourth Officers' mess call / Company marches (pipes) / Regimental marches (pipes) / Regimental slow march / Regimental quick march / March medley
CD BNA 5102
Bandleader / Jan '94 / Conifer/BMG

Royal Highland Regiment

PROUD HERITAGE
Reveille / Company marches / Headquarter company marches / Working day calls / Daily parade calls / Battalion parade tunes / Crimean long reveille / Retreat marches / Officer's mess blues night / Officer's mess guest night / March off parade / Lights out
CD LCOM 5221
Lismor / Sep '93 / ADA / Direct / Duncans / Lismor

Royal Hunt

CLOWN IN THE MIRROR
CD RRCD 90092
Rondel / Feb '97 / Cargo

Royal Hussars

SABRE AND SPURS (Royal Hussars Regiment Band)
Fanfare - Arrival / Princess of Wales march / Sabre and spurs / With sword and lance / Cavalry walk / Parade / March of the 18th Hussars / Golden spurs / Cavalry of the Steppes / Step lightly / New Colonial / Old Panama / Ca ira / Light of foot / Waveney namur / British eights / Rogue's march / Lincolnshire poacher / Regimental quick and slow marches
CD BNA 5033
Bandleader / Aug '89 / Conifer/BMG

Royal Liverpool Philharmonic ...

LIVERPOOL POPS (Royal Liverpool Philharmonic Orchestra)
You'll never walk alone / Educating Rita / Lancashire overture (medley) / Imagine / Hard day's night / Scaffold tribute (medley) / TV medley / Liverpool day (medley) / All together now (medley)
CD 3036801072
Carlton / May '97 / Carlton

Royal Logistic Corps

ON PARADE (Band Of the Royal Logistic Corps)
On parade / Wait for the wagon / Village blacksmith / Pioneer corps / Sugar and spice / First post / Sostenare / Oregon / Concerto for cornet / Flugelhorn and trumpet / Concerto for band / You'd be so nice to come home to / Concerto for clarinet / Power and glory / Forest of Arden
CD BNA 5117
Bandleader / Aug '95 / Conifer/BMG

Royal Marines

ASHOKAN FAREWELL, THE
Ashokan farewell / Rhapsody for trombone / Traumerei / Rhapsody for euphonium / Clarinet concerto in C / Gabriel's oboe / Trumpet concerto / Xylophonist's apprentice / Swan / Bach flute sonata no.4 in C / Evening breeze
CD CLCD 10595
Clovelly / Nov '95 / Target/BMG

BEATING RETREAT AND TATTOO
Fanfare / Salute to heroes / Soldiers to the sea / March and air / Silver bugles / Army of the Nile / Marines' walk / Sea solider / Montafortabeek / Top malo / Dunkirk veterans / Famous songs of the British Isles / Evening hymn and sunset / Britannic salute / God save the Queen / Heart of Oak / Fanfara alla danza / Admiral's regiment / Westering home / Per mare / Per terram / Wee Mac / Maranatha / Claymore / Semper / Supremus / Sussex by the sea / Commando patrol / At the close of the day / Lost post / Nimrod / Marines' hymn / Life on the ocean wave
CD GRCD 45
Grasmere / '91 / Highlander / Savoy / Target/BMG

BEST OF THE ROYAL MARINES, THE
CD MMCD 424
Music Masters / Jun '92 / Midland CD Club

BEST OF THE ROYAL MARINES, THE
Marche Lorraine / Pomp and circumstance march No.1 / El Capitan / Solid men to the front / Thunderer / King Cotton / Army and Marine / Le pere la Victoire / National emblem / Hands across the sea / Invincible eagle / Old comrades / Under the double eagle / L'entente cordiale / Semper fidelis / Bugler's holiday / Anchors aweigh / Colonel Bogey / On the quarterdeck / Derby day / Old Panama / Contemptibles
CD CDM 7699352
HMV / May '89 / EMI

BEST OF THE ROYAL MARINES, THE
Strike up the band / Radetsky march / Sailing / March: Things to come / March of youth / Anything goes / Thunderbirds / Gibraltar march / My way / Symphonic marches of John Williams / Hearts of oak/ A life on the ocean wave/Prelude and sunset / SSAFA march / Jerusalem / Navy day / Unchained melody / Holyrood / Cockleshell heroes / Here's a health unto her Majesty / Big country / On the quarterdeck
CD PWKS 4202
Carlton / May '94 / Carlton

BIG BAND SOUND, THE (Royal Marines Dance Band)
Stars and stripes forever / Makin' whoopee / Li'l darlin' / Samba de los gatos / Pink Panther / Frankie and Johnny / Route 66 / Drink tolly only / Yankee doodle dandy / Moonlight serenade / American patrol / Hot toddy / Georgia / Take the 'A' train / Stardust / Rabble rouser / Swing low / Cruisin' for a bluesin'
CD CLCD 10796
Clovelly / Jun '96 / Target/BMG

BY LAND AND SEA
National emblem / Preobrakensky march / Top malo / Concert march- Cockleshell heroes / Captain general / President elect / By land and sea / Anchors aweigh / Post horn gallop / Picconautical / In party mood / Falcon crest / Overture- Monte Carlo or bust / Barwick Green / Elizabeth Tudor
CD BNA 5030
Bandleader / '88 / Conifer/BMG

COMPLETE MARCHES OF KENNETH ALFORD
CD CLCD 102
Clovelly / Jan '94 / Target/BMG

GLOBE AND LAUREL
On parade / Globe and laurel / Officer of the day / Cavalry of the Steppes / Uncle Sammy / Dad's army march / Belphegor / Advance guard / My regiment / Brass buttons / Gladiator's farewell / Punjab / Contemptibles / Voice of the guns / Robinson's

grand entree / Dunedin / Vimy ridge / On the square
CD _______________ BNA 5023
Bandleader / Aug '89 / Conifer/BMG

KALEIDOSCOPE (Royal Marines Commando Forces Band)
March: Royal buglers / Jubilee overture / Londonderry air / Shepherd's hey / Valdres / March / Irish washerwoman / West Side story selection / Can't buy me love / Passion eyes / Time after time / All through the night / Kaleidoscope / Black is black / Lady in red / Blue rondo a la Turk / Whiter shade of pale
CD _______________ BNA 5064
Bandleader / May '92 / Conifer/BMG

LIFE ON THE OCEAN WAVE
Life on the ocean wave / Salute the sovereign / Portsmouth / Evening hymn - the day / Thou gavest Lord is ended/Sunset / By land and sea / Bugle fanfare / Drum display / Victory / On the quarterdeck / Greensleeves / Men of action / Cockleshell heroes / Hands across the sea / Warship / Anchors aweigh / Officers of the day / Picconautical / Troika / Post horn gallop / Salute to James Last / Nobilmente
CD _______________ MCCD 073
Music Club / Jun '92 / Disc / THE

MARCHES OF THE SEA
CD _______________ CLCD 101
Clovelly / Jan '94 / Target/BMG

MUSIC THAT STIRS THE NATION
CD _______________ MU 5008
Musketeer / Oct '92 / Disc

OLD COMRADES - NEW COMRADES
Old comrades / In the Bristol fashion / Lichfield / Cairo Road / Ventis secundis / Sea shanties / Parade of brass / Blue devils / New comrades / HM jollies / Broadlands / Little swiss piece / HMY Britannia / Nation / Up periscope / Glorious victory
CD _______________ GRACC 1
Grasmere / May '94 / Highlander / Savoy / Target/BMG

PORTSMOUTH
Heart of oak / Portsmouth / Warship / Splice the mainbrace / Nelson touch / Trafalgar / Viscount Nelson / Hands across the sea / Under the white ensign / Sea songs / Victory / Salute to the sovreign / Bugle fanfare / Drum display / Evening hymn / Sunset / Fantasia on British sea songs / Land of hope and glory
CD _______________ BNA 5020
Bandleader / Jun '93 / Conifer/BMG

ROYAL MARINES FOREVER (The Greatest Tunes From Their Greatest Bands/2CD Set)
Rule Brittania / March of youth / Aranuez mon amour / Birdland / Allegro deciso / Swing low, sweet chariot / Nautical suite / Splice the mainbrace / Sea Harriers / Huntsman / True and fair / Pineapple Poll / Drum display / Royal review / Nibelungen march / Drum and bugle display / Greensleeves / On parade / Skye boat song / Fugue and swing / SSAFA march / Battle of Trafalgar / Heart of oak / Life on the ocean wave / Prelude and sunset
CD Set _______________ 330462
Hallmark / Mar '97 / Carlton

SEA SOLDIER, THE
CD _______________ STACD 7002
Valentine / Nov '93 / Conifer/BMG

SPECTACULAR SOUNDS OF, THE (Royal Marines/Argyll & Sutherland Highlanders)
Fanfare royal occasion / Life on the ocean wave / Highland laddie / Famous songs of the British Isles medley / Fine old English gentleman / To be a farmer's boy / Here's a health unto His Majesty / British Grenadiers / Minstral boy / Annie Laurie / Men of Harlech / Pipe selection / Gordon boy (lang) / Barren rocks of Aden / Brown haired maiden / Marie's wedding / Major ACS Boswell / Captain D P Thomson / Lieutenant Colonel H L Clark / Sea shanties medley / What shall we do with the drunken sailor / Portsmouth / Rovin' / Hornpipe / Highland fling / Dornoch links / Marquis of Huntly / Man's a man for a' that / Arrival / Black bear / Fanfare no.1 / Royal salute / Drumbeatings / Time off / Argyll broadswords / Glendaurel highlanders / O'er the bows to Ballindalloch / Miss Ada Crawford / Because he was a bonny lad / Piper o'Drummond / Sleepy Maggie / All the blue bonnets are over the mountain / Soldiers return / Chariots of fire / Crown imperial / Day thou gavest Lord is ended / Sunset / Rule Britannia / Auld lang syne / Scotland the brave / Campbells are coming
CD _______________ CDMFP 6043
Music For Pleasure / Sep '88 / EMI
CD _______________ CDMFP 6315
EMI Gold / Feb '97 / EMI

VERY BEST OF THE ROYAL MARINES BAND, THE
Colonel Bogey / Standard of St. George / Great little army / El abanico / National Emblem / Anchors Aweigh / Semper fidelis / Cockershell heroes / Espana / Life on the ocean wave / Warship / On the square / This guy's in love with you / Sutherland's law theme / Shadow of your smile / Troika / Eye level / What the world needs now is love / On the track / When the saints go marching in
CD _______________ CDMFP 5789
Music For Pleasure / Jun '90 / EMI

Royal Military School Of Music

KNELLER HALL (Kneller Hall RMS Band)
Blow away the morning dew / Pinapple poll suite No.1 / Great little army / First suite in Eb for military band / Three humouresques / Tocatta mariale / HRH The Duke Of Cambridge / Sir Godfrey Kneller / Original suite / Serenade / Celebration
CD _______________ BNA 5109
Bandleader / Aug '94 / Conifer/BMG

SULLIVAN SALUTE (Kneller Hall RMS Band)
Procession March / Overture Iolanthe / Three little maids from school / Incidental music to Henry VIII / March / King Henry's song / Graceful dance / Danish march / Overture the yeomen of the guard / Absent Minded Beggar / Lost Chord / Battle of St.Gertrude / March of the Peers / Overture / Di Ballo
CD _______________ BNA 5067
Bandleader / Aug '92 / Conifer/BMG

Royal Philharmonic Orchestra

CHRISTMAS ALBUM, THE
Shepherd's pipe carol / Walking in the air / Nativity carol / Stable carol / Candlelight carol / Virgin Mary had a baby boy / Donkey carol / Holly and the ivy / Away in a manger / God rest ye merry gentlemen / First Noel / O come all ye faithful (adeste fidelis) / Once in Royal David's city / Unto us is born a son / O little town of Bethlehem / Good King Wenceslas / Hark the herald angels sing
CD _______________ TRP 083
Tring / Nov '96 / Tring

CLASSICS FOR THE MILLIONS (Royal Philharmonic Orchestra/Louis Clark)
CD _______________ SYCD 6320
Disky / May '94 / Disky / THE

CLASSICS OF LOVE
Three times a lady / If you leave me now / Up where we belong / You don't bring me flowers / Imagine / Weekend in New England / Miss you nights / One day I'll fly away / Memory / With you I'm born again / One day in your life / Sun ain't gonna shine anymore
CD _______________ CDMFP 5792
Music For Pleasure / Apr '90 / EMI

DREAMS
Unchained melody / Groovy kind of love / Everything I do (I do it for you) / Show me heaven / Take my breath away / My girl / Twin Peaks (Falling) / Second time (Bilitis) / Wind beneath my wings / It must have been love / Love changes everything / Music of the night / Any dream will do / Memory / Cavatina / Chariots of fire / Up where we belong / Hopelessly devoted to you / I've had the time of my life / Arthur's theme
CD _______________ MOCD 3003
More Music / Feb '95 / Sound & Media

HOOKED ON CLASSICS - THE ULTIMATE COLLECTION
Symphony of the seas / Hooked on Mendelssohn / Hooked on classics / Dance of the furies / Hooked on romance / Hooked on Rodgers and Hammerstein / Night at the opera / Also sprach Zarathustra / Hooked on Bach / Journey through the classics / Scotland the brave / Tales of the Vienna woods / Can't stop the classics / Hooked on romance (part 2) / Hooked on baroque
CD _______________ MCCD 003
Music Club / Feb '91 / Disc / THE

HOOKED ON CLASSICS - THE ULTIMATE PERFORMANCE (Royal Philharmonic Orchestra/Louis Clark)
Hooked on romance / Hooked on classics / Journey through the classics / Hooked on Baroque / Hooked on Mozart / Can't stop the classics / Hooked on Bach / Hooked on Rodgers and Hammerstein / Journey through America / Hooked on a song
CD _______________ 74321155582
Ariola Express / Sep '93 / BMG

LOVE SONGS
Time of my life / My girl / Stand by me / Show me heaven / Take a look at me now / Twin peaks / Hero / Arthur's theme / Look of love / Some enchanted evening / Secret love / Cavaleria rusticana / Hopelessly devoted to you / True love ways / Pachelbel canon / Someone to watch over me
CD _______________ 11910
Music / Feb '96 / Target/BMG

MEMORIES
Unchained melody / Groovy kind of love / Everything I do (I do it for you) / Up where we belong / Take my breath away / It must have been love / Lily was here / Chariots of fire / Speak softly love / Any dream will do / Love changes everything / Lara's theme / Second time / Send in the clowns / Memory / Cavatina
CD _______________ 11984
Music / Feb '96 / Target/BMG

RPO PLAYS ROCK CLASSICS
Simply the best / Time aftrer time / Eye of the tiger / Lost in France / Take my breath away / Another brick in the wall / Power of love / Good vibrations / I want to know what love is / House of the Rising Sun / Baker Street / Ruby Tuesday / Every breath you take / We don't need another hero / Wicked game / We are the champions
CD _______________ CD 6051
Music / Jan '97 / Target/BMG

VERY BEST OF HOOKED ON CLASSICS, THE (4CD Set)
Hooked on classics (Part 1 & 2) / Hooked on romance / Hooked on classics (Part 3) / Hooked on Bach / Hooked on Tchaikovsky / Hooked on a song / Hooked on Mozart / Hooked on Mendelssohn / Hooked on a can can / Also sprach zarathrustra (Excerpt) / Journey through the classics / Hooked on Haydn / Hooked on Romance(Opus 3) / Viva Vivaldi / Dance on the furies / Scotland the brave / Journey through the classics (part 2) / Journey through America / Hooked on marching / Symphony of the seas / Hooked on Rodgers and Hammerstein / Can't stop the classics / Hooked on America / Hooked on romance (part 2) / Night at the opera / Tales of the Vienna waltz / Hooked on Baroque / If you knew Sousa / If you knew Sousa (and friends) / Hooked on Baroque (part 2): *New World Ensemble* / Hooked on Adagio: *New World Ensemble* / Hooked on Gigue: *New World Ensemble* / Hooked on a Fugue: *New World Ensemble* / Hooked on Handel: *New World Ensemble* / Hooked on Vivaldi: *New World Ensemble* / Hooked on Scarlatti: *New World Ensemble* / Hooked on Baroque part 2 (reprise): *New World Ensemble*
CD Set _______________ ECD 3355
K-Tel / May '97 / K-Tel

Royal Scots Dragoon Guards

AMAZING GRACE
Amazing grace / Scotland the brave / Cornet carillon / Russian imperial anthem / Abide with me / Dark island / Ode 'An die Freude' (Song of joy) / Scottish soldier / Road to the isles / Drummer's call / Belmont (by cool Siloam's shady rill) / Bunessan / Banda / Little drummer boy / Standchen / Day is ended / Wooden heart / Going home
CD _______________ ND 74884
RCA / Jun '91 / BMG

AMAZING GRACE
CD _______________ MATCD 249
Castle / Dec '92 / BMG

AMAZING GRACE
Medley / Speed your journey (Song of the Hebrew slaves) / Moonliner rock march / Medley / Y viva Espana / Medley / Barock '75 / Medley / Brazil / Tribute to Duthart / Medley / Amazing grace / Una paloma blanca / 6/8 marches / Rock 'n' roll march / Largo / Theme in glory / Retreat airs / Rockout / 4/4 marches / Medley
CD _______________ TRTCD 134
TrueTrax / Dec '94 / THE

AMAZING GRACE
CD _______________ 74321292802
RCA / Jul '95 / BMG

AMAZING GRACE
CD _______________ PLSCD 185
Pulse / Apr '97 / BMG

IN THE FINEST TRADITION (Royal Scots Dragoon Guards Pipes & Drums)
Amazing grace / Three DG's / Send in the clowns / Symphonic marches of John Williams / Way old friends do / McPhedran's strathspey / Highland whiskey / Mermaid song / Troy's wedding / Mason's apron / Seventy Ninth farewell to Gibraltar / Highland cathedral / Scotland the brave / Black bear / Carillon / Going home / My home / Skye boat song / Irish air / Ballochmyle / Mrs. Lily Christie / Farewell to the creeks / Garb of old gaul / Moonstar
CD _______________ BNA 5017
Bandleader / Jul '88 / Conifer/BMG

ROYAL SCOTS DRAGOON GUARDS
Amazing grace / Gallowa' hills / Lili Marlene / Skye boat song / Black Watch polka / Battle of the Somme / Highland wedding / Mill in the Glen / Hills of home / Crossing the Rhine / Dovecote Park
CD _______________ MCCD 105
Music Club / May '93 / Disc / THE

SCOTTISH SALUTE
CD _______________ CDITV 455
Scotdisc / Jul '89 / Conifer/BMG / Duncans / Ross

SECOND TO NONE
CD _______________ LCOM 5248
Lismor / Aug '95 / ADA / Direct / Duncans / Lismor

TUNES OF GLORY
CD _______________ CDLOC 1069
Lochshore / Sep '94 / ADA / Direct / Duncans

VERY BEST OF THE ROYAL SCOTS DRAGOON GUARDS, THE
Amazing grace / Little drummer boy / Scotland the brave / Highland laddie / Morning has broken / Ode to joy (ode 'an die freude) / Day is ended / Reveille / Scottish waltz / Hayken's serenade / Russian imperial anthem / Going home
CD _______________ 74321339362
Camden / Jan '96 / BMG

Royal Scottish Orchestra

CHRISTMAS FANFARE, A
Jingle bells / Il est ne / Jesus ahatonia / We wish you a Merry Christmas / Ding dong merrily on high / Past 3 o'clock / O come, all ye faithful / Once in Royal David's City / Torches / Christmas fantasy / Hark the herald angels sing / Good King Wenceslas / Great and mighty wonder / Christmas piece / Schneewalzer / Two Christmas fanfares / Caribbean Christmas / Christmas song
CD _______________ CDCA 923
Alpha / Nov '91 / Abbey Recording

Royal Society Jazz Orchestra

ROYAL SOCIETY JAZZ ORCHESTRA
CD _______________ SOSCD 1208
Stomp Off / Jan '93 / Jazz Music / Wellard

Royal Tahitian Dance Co.

ROYAL TAHITIAN DANCE CO.
CD _______________ MCD 71758
Monitor / Jun '93 / CM

Royal, Teddy

ROYAL BLUE
CD _______________ SP 1003CD
Morning Groove / Apr '97 / New Note/ Pinnacle / Timewarp

Royal Trux

CATS AND DOGS
CD _______________ WIGCD 6
Domino / Jul '93 / Vital

ROYAL TRUX
CD _______________ WIGCD 5
Domino / Jun '93 / Vital
CD _______________ DC 5
Drag City / Dec '96 / Cargo / Greyhound

SWEET SIXTEEN
Don't try too hard / Morphic resident / Pickup / Cold joint / Golden rules / You'll be staying in room 323 / Can't have it both ways / 10 days 12 nights / Microwave made / Sweet sixteen / I'm looking through you / Roswell seeds and stems / Pol Pot pie
CD _______________ CDHUT 43
Hut / Apr '97 / EMI

THANK YOU
Night to remember / Sewers of Mars / Ray O Vac / Map of the city / Granny grunt / Lights on the levee / Fear strikes out / (Have you met) Horror James / You're gonna lose / Shadow of the wasp
CD _______________ CDHUT 23
Hut / Feb '95 / EMI

TWIN INFINITIVES
CD _______________ WIGCD 8
Domino / Jan '94 / Vital

Royal Ulster Constabulary

PIPE BANDS OF DISTINCTION
CD _______________ CDMON 814
Monarch / Jul '94 / ADA / CM / Direct / Duncans

Royal Welsh Fusiliers

TO THE BEAT OF A DRUM (Royal Welsh Fusiliers & Blaenavon Male Voice Choir)
Fanfare - the 300th / Men of Glamorgan / Lilliburlero / Grenadiers slow march / How stands the glass around / Quick march of the 23rd regiment / Marquis of Granby / Sospan fach / My Lord what a morning / Girl I left behind me / Lass of Richmond Hill / Calon lan / Soldiers of the Queen / Goodbye Dolly Gray / US Marine Corps hymn / Myfymwy / We'll keep a welcome / Vive la Canadienne / Keep the home fires burning / It's a long way to Tipperary / March of the Grenadiers / Royal Welch Fusiliers / Wish me luck as you wave me goodbye / Rachie / Cwm Rhondda / That astonishing infantry / British Grenadiers / Men of Harlech / Land of my fathers (Hen wlad fy nhadau) / God save the Queen
CD _______________ BNA 5026
Bandleader / Aug '89 / Conifer/BMG

Royal Yeomanry

MUSIC OF ERIC COATES, THE
Dam buster's march / Three bears suite / Youth of Britain / Man from the sea / Calling all workers / By the sleepy lagoon / London again suite / Oxford street / Langham place / Mayfair / Music everywhere
CD _______________ 302632
Hallmark / Jun '97 / Carlton

Royalettes

IT'S GONNA TAKE A MIRACLE (The MGM Sides)
CD _______________ SCL 21102
Ichiban Soul Classics / Mar '96 / Koch

Roza, Lita

SOMEWHERE, SOMEHOW, SOMEDAY
That's the beginning of the end / I've got my eyes on you / Oh dear what can the matter be / But beautiful / I'll never say Never Again again / End of a love affair / Not mine / As children do / There's nothing better than love / Allentown jail / Once in a while / Nel blu di pinto di blu / This is my town / Maybe you'll be there / Sorry, sorry, sorry / I could have danced all night / All alone / Other woman / Love can change the stars
CD ______ C5CD552
See For Miles/C5 / Jan '90 / Pinnacle

Rozalla

EVERYBODY'S FREE
CD ______ PULSECD 11
Pulse 8 / Oct '93 / BMG

LOOK NO FURTHER
I love music / You never love the same way twice / This time I found love / Baby / Look no further / Do you believe / Work me / If love is a dream / All that I need / Love work / I can't wait / Losing my religion / I love music (Mix) / Baby (Mix) / You never love the same way twice (Mix)
CD ______ 4779829
Epic / Mar '95 / Sony

RPB & Mac

BAJAN INVASION
CD ______ WCD 501
WIRL / Apr '97 / Jet Star

Rua

AO-TEA-ROA
Music from the jungles of Caledonia / Raider / Jeltic music / Moon & St. Christopher / Caribbean celts / Allelujah / HAyfever / College boy / Band on the run / Eleanor Rigby / Waltzurka / Winter's rage / Arrival in Auckland / Highland cream
CD ______ CDTRAX 103
Greentrax / Nov '95 / ADA / Direct / Duncans / Highlander

HOMELAND
CD ______ CDTRAX 061
Greentrax / Mar '93 / ADA / Direct / Duncans / Highlander

LIVE IN THE CATHEDRAL
CD ______ CDODE 1391
ODE / Jul '94 / CM / Discovery

Rub Ultra

LIQUID BOOTS AND BOILED SWEETS
Brown box nitro (dog's life) / Blasted freak / Health horror and the vitamin urge / Oily man eel / Your nasty hair / Generate / Whale boy / Free toy / Cat's gone underground / Suspend your belief / Castles / Voodoo accident
CD ______ FLATCD 21
Hi-Rise / Oct '95 / EMI / Pinnacle

Rubalcaba, Gonzala

BEST OF GONZALA RUBALCABA, THE
CD ______ 74321424352
Milan / Jun '97 / Conifer/BMG / Silva Screen

DIZ
Hot house / Woody 'n' you / I remember Clifford / Donna Lee / Bouncing with Bud / Smooch / Ah-leu-cha / Night in Tunisia / Con Alma
CD ______ CDP 8304902
Blue Note / Sep '95 / EMI

GIRALDILLA
Rumbero / Proyecto latino / Giraldilla / Campo finda / Encuentros / Presidente / Comienzo
CD ______ MES 158012
Messidor / Apr '93 / ADA / Koch

IMAGINE - LIVE IN AMERICA
Imagine / Contagio / First song / Woody 'n' you / Circuilo II / Perfidia / Mima
CD ______ CDP 8304912
Blue Note / Jan '96 / EMI

LIVE IN HAVANA 1986
CD ______ MES 158302
Messidor / May '95 / ADA / Koch

LIVE IN HAVANA VOL.1 & 2
CD ______ 15960
Ronnie Scott's Jazz House / Aug '89 / Cadillac / Jazz Music / New Note/Pinnacle / TKO Magnum

MI GRAN PASION
CD ______ 15999
Messidor / Apr '89 / ADA / Koch

Rubbersmell

INDIAN FLESH - INDIAN DOME
CD ______ CHILLUM 001
Chill Um / Jan '96 / Plastic Head

Rubella Ballet

AT THE END OF THE RAINBOW
CD ______ BND 2CD
One Little Indian / Feb '90 / Pinnacle

GREATEST TRIPS
CD ______ BND 3 CD
One Little Indian / Feb '90 / Pinnacle

Ruben & The Jets

CON SAFOS
CD ______ EDCD 405
Edsel / Jan '95 / Pinnacle

FOR REAL
CD ______ EDCD 406
Edsel / Nov '94 / Pinnacle

Rubettes

BEST OF THE RUBETTES, THE
Sugar baby love / Tonight / Under one roof / Judy run run / I'm just dreaming / I can do it / Jukebox jive / Little darlin' / Julia / Foe dee oh dee / You're the reason why / Sha na na song
CD ______ 8438962
Polydor / Sep '90 / PolyGram

JUKE BOX JIVE
CD ______ GRF 213
Tring / Mar '93 / Tring

Rubicon

ROOM 101
CD ______ BBQCD 170
Beggars Banquet / Apr '95 / RTM/Disc / Warner Music

Rubin, Joel

BEREGOVSKI'S KHASENE (Rubin, Joel Jewish Music Ensemble)
Tsu der khupe geyn / Volekhl / Baveynen di kale / Makonovetski's gas nign / Russian sher / Taksim / Sakhnovski's dobranotsh / Skotshne / Tish nigunim / Gershfeld's Bulgarish / Ahavo rabo / Zayt gezunt
CD ______ SM 16142
Wergo / Jun '97 / ADA / Cadillac / Harmonia Mundi

Rubin, Ruth

YIDDISH SONGS OF THE HOLOCAUST: A LECTURE/RECITAL
CD ______ GV 150CD
Global Village / May '94 / ADA / Direct

Rubin, Vanessa

PASTICHE
In a sentimental mood / Simone / I'm just a lucky so and so / When love is new / Black Nile / I only have eyes for you / Mosaic / Estoy siempre junto a ti / Weekend / Certain love / Arise and shine
CD ______ 01241631522
Novus / Apr '93 / BMG

Rubinoos

RUBINOOS, THE (Remastered)
I think we're alone now / Leave my heart alone / Hard to get / Peek-a-boo / Rock 'n' roll is dead / Memories / Nothing a little love won't cure / Wouldn't it be nice / Make it easy / I never thought it would happen / Fallin' in love / I wanna be your boyfriend / Lightning love affair / Drivin' music / Jennifer / 1,2,3 forever
CD ______ HILLCD 20
Wooded Hill / Jul '97 / Direct / World Serpent

Ruby

SALT PETER
CD ______ CRECD 166RL
CD ______ CRECD 166
Creation / Apr '96 / 3mv/Vital

Rucker, Vernis

STRANGER IN THE SHEETS
Fishin' for a man / You've been good for me / He's cheating on you / There must be someone for me / Fever / There's a hurt where my heart used to be / Put love first / Then came you / Stormy Monday / Dead to right / Strangers in the sheets
CD ______ CDCH 508
Ace / Jan '94 / Pinnacle

Ruckus

ALLEY PUNK ROCK
CD ______ LRR 023
Last Resort / Oct '96 / Cargo

Rud, Mike

WHYTE AVENUE
CD ______ JFCD 016
Jazz Focus / May '97 / Cadillac

Rudd, Roswell

FLEXIBLE FLYER
What are you doing the rest of your life / Maiden voyage / Suh blah buh sibi / Waltzing in the sagebrush / Moselle variations
CD ______ CDBLC 760215
Black Lion / Mar '96 / Cadillac / Jazz Music / Koch / Wellard

Rudder, David

GILDED COLLECTION 1986-1989
CD ______ CR 019CD
Lypsoland / May '97 / Jet Star

GILDED COLLECTION 1990-1993
CD ______ CR 024CD
Lypsoland / May '97 / Jet Star

LYRICS MAN
CD ______ CR 023CD
Lypsoland / May '97 / Jet Star

TALES FROM A STRANGE LAND
CD ______ CR 025CD
Lypsoland / May '97 / Jet Star

WRAPPED IN PLAIN BROWN
CD ______ CR 026CD
Lypsoland / May '97 / Jet Star

Rude Boys

RUDE AWAKENINGS
Come on let's do this / Written all over your face / I feel for you / Heaven / Pressure / I'm going thru / Are you lonely for me / Fool for you / Never get enough of it / I need you
CD ______ 7567821212
East West / Jul '91 / Warner Music

Rude Girls

MIXED MESSAGES
CD ______ FF 511CD
Flying Fish / '92 / ADA / CM / Direct / Roots

Rudi

BIG TIME (The Best Of Rudi)
Big time / Number one / Overcome by fumes / I spy / Genuine reply / Sometimes / Ripped in two / Who you / Time to be proud / Without you / Pressure's on / Yummy, yummy, yummy / Tigerland / When I was dead / Bewarewolf / Prince of pleasure / Love goes on / Crimson / 14 steps / Cops
CD ______ CDPUNK 77
Anagram / Aug '96 / Cargo / Pinnacle

Rudimentary Peni

DEATH CHURCH
CD ______ BOOB 004CD
Outer Himalayen / Apr '94 / SRD

EPS OF RP
CD ______ BOOB 003CD
Outer Himalayen / Sep '94 / SRD

POPE ADRIAN 37TH PSYCHRISTIATRIC
CD ______ BOOB 005CD
Outer Himalayen / Sep '95 / SRD

Rudiments

BITCH BITCH BITCH
CD ______ DILL 011
Dill / Jun '97 / Cargo / Greyhound

Rudolph, Adam

GIFT OF THE GNAWA
CD ______ FF 571CD
Flying Fish / May '93 / ADA / CM / Direct / Roots

MOVING PICTURES
CD ______ FF 612CD
Flying Fish / Feb '93 / ADA / CM / Direct / Roots

Ruf Der Heimat

RUF DER HEIMAT
CD ______ EFA 127652
Konnex / Aug '95 / SRD

Ruff 2 Da Smoove

RUFF 2 DA SMOOVE
CD ______ CDBR 10
Body Rock / Feb '95 / Jet Star

Ruffin, Jimmy

GREATEST MOTOWN HITS
What becomes of the broken hearted / Baby I've got it / I've passed this way before / Gonna give her all the love I've got / World so wide, nowhere to hide / Don't you miss me a little bit baby / Everybody needs love / It's wonderful (to be loved by you) / Gonna keep on tryin' till I win your love / This guy's in love with you / Farewell is a lonely sound / Stand by me: *Ruffin, Jimmy & David* / As long as there is l-o-v-e love / Sad and lonesome feeling / I'll say forever my love / Don't let him take your love from me / Maria / Living in a world I created for myself / Let's say goodbye tomorrow / He ain't heavy, he's my brother: *Ruffin, Jimmy & David*
CD ______ 5300572
Motown / Jan '93 / PolyGram

MOTOWN EARLY CLASSICS
What becomes of the broken hearted / Since I've lost you / How can I say I'm sorry / Baby I've got it / Gonna give her all the love I've got / 96 tears / You've got what it takes / Farewell is a lonely sound / I'll say forever my love / Stand by me: *Ruffin, David & Jimmy* / Set 'em up (move in for the thrill): *Ruffin, David & Jimmy* / Living in a world I created for myself / Lonely lonely man am I / I want her love / I'll never let you get away / Honey come back / Your love was worth waiting for: *Ruffin, David & Jimmy* / Turn back the hands of time: *Ruffin, David & Jimmy*
CD ______ 5521232
Spectrum / Jul '96 / PolyGram

Ruffins, Kermit

BIG BUTTER & EGG MAN, THE
CD ______ JR 11022
Justice / Jun '94 / Koch

WORLD ON A STRING
CD ______ JR 001101
Justice / Apr '93 / Koch

Ruffner, Mason

EVOLUTION
CD ______ PRD 70632
Provogue / May '94 / Pinnacle

Ruffnexx Sound System

RUFFNEXX
CD ______ 9362456052
Warner Bros. / Jul '95 / Warner Music

Rufus

RUFUSIZED/MASTERJAM (2CD Set)
CD Set ______ MCD 33006
MCA / Aug '96 / BMG

TELL ME SOMETHING GOOD
CD ______ HMNCD 003
Half Moon / Jun '97 / BMG

Ruhier, Eddie

PORTABLE HAMMOND
Della and the dealer / Travellin' light / Midnight in Mayfair / Go North / I dreamt I dwelt in marble halls / Georgia on my mind / Stand by your man / Beach baby / Flashback / Tiger rag / Rowan dance / Is Paris burning / Amazing grace / Medley / Earlswood / Watermelon man / Cavaquinho
CD ______ CDGRS 1292
Grosvenor / Dec '96 / Grosvenor

Ruiz, Floreal

MARIONETA
CD ______ BMT 008
Blue Moon / Jul '97 / Cadillac / Discovery / Greensleeves / Jazz Music / Jet Star / TKO Magnum

Ruiz, Hilton

HANDS ON PERCUSSION
Ornithology / Blues for cos / Mambo for vibes / 'Round midnight / Cotton tail / Jack's tune / Like Sonny / Maneguitos way / Salute to Eddie
CD ______ 66058061
RMM / May '95 / New Note/Pinnacle

HEROES
'Round midnight / Sonny mood / Guataca / Little suede shoes / Lover man / For Maz / Maiden voyage / Con alma / Tune up / Praise
CD ______ CD 83338
Telarc / May '94 / Conifer/BMG

LIVE AT BIRDLAND (Ruiz, Hilton Sextet)
Something grand / New arrival / Blues for two tenors / Mr. Kenyatta / Lisa / Night in Tunisia / I'll call you later / On green dolphin street / Footprints
CD ______ CCD 79532
Candid / Feb '97 / Cadillac / Direct / Jazz Music / Koch / Wellard

STRUT
Sidewinder / Going back to New Orleans / Bluz / Aged in soul / All my love is yours / Soca serenade / Why don't you steal my blues / Lush life
CD ______ PD 83053
RCA / May '89 / BMG

Ruiz, Jim

OH BROTHER WHERE ART THOU (Ruiz, Legendary Jim Group)
CD ______ MF 11
Minty Fresh / Jun '95 / Pinnacle / SRD

Rum & Black

WITHOUT ICE
CD ______ SUADCD 3
Shut Up & Dance / Sep '91 / SRD

Rumbata

ENCUENTROS
CD ______ CHR 70032
Challenge / Nov '95 / ADA / Direct / Jazz Music / Wellard

Rumbel, Nancy

NOTES FROM THE TREE OF LIFE
Tree of life / Lullaby / Night tribe / Anansi / Passing fancy / Song of hope / Dona nobis pacem / Coyote dance / Delicate balance / Satie
CD ND 61050
Narada / Dec '95 / ADA / New Note/ Pinnacle

Rumble

RAPED, KILLED AND LEFT
CD DE 06
Dead Elvis / Apr '96 / RTM/Disc

RUMBLE
Safe / Dontress / Suspect / Take me / Look at the kid / All I know / Serious ting / Crack song / Black man wagon / Follow me / Booyaka booyaka
CD GEECD 12
Gee Street / Nov '93 / PolyGram

Rumble Cats

WILD BLUE YONDER
CD RKCD 9701
Rockhouse / Feb '97 / Nervous

Rumillajta

CITY OF STONE
CD TUMICD 001
Tumi / '92 / Discovery / Stern's

HOJA DE COCA
CD TUMICD 002
Tumi / '92 / Discovery / Stern's

PACHAMAMA
CD TUMICD 003
Tumi / '92 / Discovery / Stern's

WIRACOCHA
CD RUM 1871CD
Rumillajta / Jan '90 / Stern's

Rumors Of The Big Wave

BURNING TIMES
Nightmare / Only green world / Needle full of dreams / Stranger to you / Burning times / I choose life / Love has a body / Tenderness / Echo of a scream / Spirit in the wasteland
CD 9362425352
Warner Bros. / Jun '93 / Warner Music

Rumour

RUMOUR
Frogs / Sprouts / Clogs / Krauts
CD STIFFCD 14
Disky / Jan '94 / Disky / THE

Rump

HATING BRENDA
CD CARCD 24
Caroline / Apr '94 / EMI

Rumsey, Howard

LIGHTHOUSE ALL STARS VOL.3 (Rumsey, Howard Lighthouse All Stars)
Swing shift / Out of somewhere / Mexican passport / Big girl / Vivi Zapata / No.1 / Mambo los feliz / Song is you / Jazz invention / Snap the whip / Love letters / Witch doctor no.1
CD OJCCD 266
Original Jazz Classics / Jan '97 / Complete/ Pinnacle / Jazz Music / Wellard

LIGHTHOUSE ALL STARS VOL.6
CD OJCCD 386
Original Jazz Classics / Jun '95 / Complete/Pinnacle / Jazz Music / Wellard

MUSIC FOR LIGHTHOUSEKEEPING (Rumsey, Howard Lighthouse All Stars)
CD OJCCD 636
Original Jazz Classics / Feb '92 / Complete/Pinnacle / Jazz Music / Wellard

OBOE/FLUTE
CD OJCCD 154
Original Jazz Classics / Jun '95 / Complete/Pinnacle / Jazz Music / Wellard

Run DMC

BACK FROM HELL
Sucker DJ's / What's it all about / Faces / Pause / Back from hell / Groove to the sound / Naughty / Not just another groove / Ave / Bob your head / Kick the frama lama lama / Word is born / Don't stop / P upon a tree / Livin' the city / Party time
CD FILECD 401
Profile / Nov '90 / Pinnacle

RUN DMC
Hard times / Rock box / Jam-master Jay / Hollis crew (Krush groove 2) / Sucker MC's (Krush-groove 1) / It's like that / Wake up / Thirty days / Jay's game
CD FILERCD 202
Profile / Apr '91 / Pinnacle

RUN DMC TOGETHER FOREVER (Greatest Hits 1983-1991)
CD FILERCD 419
Profile / Sep '91 / Pinnacle

Run Dog Run

BEAUTY SCHOOL DROPOUT
CD VOW 040CD
Voices Of Wonder / May '94 / Plastic Head

HOWLING SUCCESS, A
CD VOW 032C
Voices Of Wonder / Dec '93 / Plastic Head

Run On

NO WAY
Something sweet / Lab rats / As good as new / Look / Bring her blues / 1/2 of 1/2 / Anything you say / Road / Days away / Out for a walk / Ropa vieja / Sinnerman
CD OLE 2292
Matador / Feb '97 / Vital

START PACKING
Tried / Baap / Go there / A to Z / Miscalculation / In strength / Xmas trip / Doesn't anybody love the dark / Tell me / You said / Coffee together / Surprise
CD OLE 1532
Matador / Mar '96 / Vital

Run Westy Run

HARDLY, NOT EVEN
CD SST 192CD
SST / May '93 / Plastic Head

RUN WESTY RUN
CD SST 199CD
SST / Feb '89 / Plastic Head

Runaways

AND NOW...THE RUNAWAYS
Saturday night special / Eight days a week / Mama weer all crazee now / I'm a million / Right now / Take over / My buddy and me / Little lost girls / Black leather
CD CDMGRAM 63
Cherry Red / Mar '97 / Pinnacle

BORN TO BE BAD
CD FM 1004CD
Marilyn / Jul '92 / Pinnacle

Rundgren, Todd

ADVENTURES IN UTOPIA (Utopia)
Road to Utopia / You make me crazy / Second nature / Set me free / Caravan / Last of the new wave riders / Shot in the dark / Very last time / Love alone / Rock love
CD 8122708722
WEA / Mar '93 / Warner Music

ANOTHER LIVE (Utopia)
Another life / Wheel / Seven ray's / Intro (Mister Triscuits) / Something's coming / Heavy metal kids / Do ya / Just one victory
CD 8122708672
WEA / Jul '93 / Warner Music

ANTHOLOGY (Utopia)
CD 8122708922
WEA / May '95 / Warner Music

ANTHOLOGY
Open my eyes / We gotta get you a woman / Wailing wall / Be nice to me / Hello it's me / I saw the light / It wouldn't have made any difference / Couldn't I just tell you / Sometimes I don't know what to feel / Just one victory / Dream goes on forever / Last ride / Don't you ever learn / Real man / Black and white / Love of the common man / Cliches / All the children sing / Can we still be friends / You cried wolf / Time heals / Compassion / Hideaway / Bang the drum all day / Drive / Johnee jingo / Something to fall back on
CD 8122714912
WEA / Jul '93 / Warner Music

BACK TO THE BARS
Real man / Love of the common man / Verb: To love / Love in action / Dream goes on forever / Sometimes I don't know what to think / Range war / Black and white / Last ride / Cliches / Don't you ever learn / Never never land / Black Maria / Zen archer / I'm so proud / Oh baby baby / La la means I love you / I saw the light / It wouldn't have made any difference / Eastern intrigues / Initiation / Couldn't I just tell you / Hello it's me
CD 8122711092
WEA / Feb '93 / Warner Music

BALLAD OF TODD RUNDGREN
Long flowing robe / Ballad (Denny and Jean) / Bleeding / Wailing wall / Range war / Chain letter / Long time a long way to go / Boat on the Charles / Be nice to me / Hope I'm around / Parole / Remember me
CD 8122708632
WEA / Mar '93 / Warner Music

DEFACE THE MUSIC (Utopia)
I just want to touch you / Crystal ball / Where does the world to go hide / Silly boy / Alone / That's not right / Take it home / Hoi poloi / Life goes on / Feel too good / Always late / All smiles / Everybody else is wrong
CD 8122708732
WEA / Mar '93 / Warner Music

EVER POPULAR TORTURED ARTIST EFFECT, THE
Hideway / Influenza / Don't hurt yourself / There goes your baybay / Tin soldier / Emporer of the highway / Bang the drum all day / Drive / Chant
CD 8122708762
WEA / Mar '93 / Warner Music

FAITHFUL
Happenings ten years time ago / Good vibrations / Rain / Most likely you'll go your way and I'll go mine / If six was nine / Strawberry Fields forever / Black and white / Love of the common man / When I pray / Cliches / Verb: To love / Boogies (hamburger hell)
CD 8122708682
WEA / Mar '93 / Warner Music

HEALING
Healer / Pulse / Flesh / Golden goose / Compassion / Shine / Healing
CD 8122708742
WEA / Mar '93 / Warner Music

INITIATION, THE
Real man / Born to synthesize / Death of rock and roll / Eastern intrigues / Initiation / Fair warning / Treatise on cosmic fire / Fire of mind or solar fire / Fire of spirit or electric fire / Internal fire or fire by friction
CD 8122708662
WEA / Mar '93 / Warner Music

OOPS SORRY WRONG PLANET (Utopia)
Trapped / Windows / Love in action / Martyr / Abandon city / Gangreen / Crazy lady blue / Back on the street / Marriage of heaven and hell / Mount Angel / Rape of the young / Love is the answer
CD 8122708702
WEA / Mar '93 / Warner Music

PASSPORT COLLECTION, THE (Utopia)
Itch in my brain: *Rundgren, Todd* / Love with a thinker / Bring me my longbow / If I didn't try / Too much water / Maybe I could change / Crybaby / Welcome to my revolution / Winston Smith takes it on the jaw / I will wait / Fix your gaze / Play this game / Style / Stand for something / Secret society / Zen machine / Mated / Wildlife / Mimi gets mad / Mystified / More light / Man of action / Monument
CD 8122722872
WEA / Jul '96 / Warner Music

RA (Utopia)
Overture (inst) from journey to the centre of the / Communion with the sun / Magic dragon theatre / Jealousy / Eternal love / Sunburst finish / Hiroshima / Singring and the glass guitar
CD 8122708692
WEA / Mar '93 / Warner Music

REDUX 92: LIVE IN JAPAN (Utopia)
Fix your gaze / Zen machine / Trapped / Princess of the universe / Abandon city / Hammer in my heart / Swing to the right / Ikon / Hiroshima / Back on the street / Only human / Love in action / Caravan / Last of the new wave riders / One world / Love is the answer
CD 8122711852
WEA / Jun '93 / Warner Music

RUNT
Broke down and busted / Believe in me / We got to get you a woman / Who's that man / Once burned / Devil's bite / I'm in the clique / There are no words / Let's swing / Last thing you said / Don't tie my hands / Birthday carol
CD 8122708622
WEA / Mar '93 / Warner Music

SOMETHING ANYTHING
I saw the light / I wouldn't have made any difference / Wolfman Jack / Cold morning light / It takes two to tango / Sweeter memories / Intro / Breathless / Night the carousel burned down / Saving grace / Marlene / Song of the viking / I went to the mirror / Black Maria / One more day (no word) / Couldn't I just tell you / Torch song / Little red lights / Overture / Money: messin' with the kid / Dust in the wind / Piss Aaron / Hello it's me / Some folks is even whiter than me / You left me sore / Slut
CD 8122711072
WEA / Mar '93 / Warner Music

SWING TO THE RIGHT (Rundgren, Todd & Utopia)
Swing to the right / Lysistrata / Up / Junk rock (million monkey's) / Shinola / For the love of money / Last dollar on earth / Fahrenheit 451 / Only human / One world
CD 8122708752
WEA / Mar '93 / Warner Music

TODD
How about a little fanfare / I think you know / Spark of life / Elpee's worth of toons / Dream goes on forever / Lord Chancellor's nightmare / Drunken blue rooster / Last number 1 lowest common denomination / Useless begging / Sidewalk cafe / Izzat love / Heavy metal kids / In and out of the chakras we go / Don't you ever learn / Sons of 1984
CD 8122711082
WEA / Mar '93 / Warner Music

TODD RUNDGREN'S UTOPIA
Utopia theme: *Utopia* / Freak parade: *Utopia* / Freedom fighters: *Utopia* / Ikon: *Utopia*
CD 8122708652
WEA / Mar '93 / Warner Music

UTOPIA (Utopia)
Libertine / Bad little actress / Feet don't fail me now / Neck on up / Say yeah / Call it what you will / I'm looking at you but I'm talking to myself / Hammer in my heart / Burn three times / There goes my inspiration
CD 8122707132
WEA / Jul '93 / Warner Music

WIZARD, A TRUE STAR, A
International feel / Never never land / Tic tick tick it wears off / You / Need your head / Rock 'n' roll / Pussy / Dogfight giggle / You don't have to camp around / Flamingo / Zen archer / Just another onionhead / Da da dali / When the shit hits the fan / Sunset Boulevard / Le feel internacionale / Sometimes I don't know what to feel / Does anybody love you / I'm so proud / Ooo baby baby / La la means I love you / Cool jerk / Hungry for love / I don't want to tie you down / Is it my name / Just one victory
CD 8122708642
WEA / Mar '93 / Warner Music

Rundqvist, Gosta

GOSTA RUNDQVIST & KRISTER ANDERSON (Rundqvist, Gosta & Krister Andersin)
CD SITCD 9212
Sittel / Aug '94 / Cadillac / Jazz Music

Runners

PHONETIC
Secret world / Crooked man / Journeying / Funk talk / C Sands / Phonetic / Hours / Stomp
CD CDEYE 0010
i2i / Sep '95 / New Note/Pinnacle

Running Wild

BLACKHAND INN
CD NCD 007
Noise / Jan '96 / Koch

BLAZON STONE
CD NCD 005
Noise / Jan '96 / Koch

DEATH OR GLORY
Riding the storm / Renegade / Evilution / Running blood / Highland glory (the eternal flight) / Marooned / Bad to the bone / Tortuga bay / Death or glory / Battle of Waterloo / March on
CD NCD 004
Noise / Jan '96 / Koch

FIRST YEARS OF PIRACY, THE
CD N 01842
Noise / Jan '92 / Koch

MASQUERADE
CD N 02612
CD N 02619
Noise / Oct '95 / Koch

PILE OF SKULLS
CD NCD 006
Noise / Jan '96 / Koch

Runrig

AMAZING THINGS
Amazing things / Wonderful / Greatest flame / Move a mountain / Pog aon oidche earraich (One kiss one spring evening) / Dream fields / Song of the earth / Forever eyes of blue / Sraidean na roinn Eorpa (Streets of Europe) / Canada / Ard / On the edge
CD CDCHR 2000
Chrysalis / Mar '93 / EMI

BIG WHEEL, THE
Headlights / Healer in your heart / abhainn an t-aluaigh / Always the winner / This beautiful pain / An cuibhle mor/The big wheel / Edge of the world / Hearthammer / I'll keep coming home / Flower of the West
CD CCD 1858
Chrysalis / Jun '91 / EMI

CUTTER AND THE CLAN, THE
Alba / Cutter / Hearts of olden glory / Pride of the summer / Worker for the wind / Rocket to the moon / Only rose / Protect and survive / Our earth was once green / Aubhal as airds
CD CCD 1669
Chrysalis / May '95 / EMI

HEARTLAND
O cho mealt / This darkest winter / Lifeline / Air a' chuan / Dance called America / Everlasting gun / Skye / Cnoc na faille / Wire / An taireachd ard / Ferry / Tuireadh lain ruaidh
CD RRCD 005
Ridge / Feb '86 / ADA / CM / Direct / Duncans / Roots

HIGHLAND CONNECTION, THE
Gainhna gaella / Mairi / What time / Fichead bliadhna / Na luing air seoladh / Loch lomond / Na h-uain a's t-earrach / Foghar nan

eilean '78 / Twenty five pounder / Going home / Morning tide / Cearcal a chuain
CD RRCD 001
Ridge / Aug '89 / ADA / CM / Direct / Duncans / Roots

LONG DISTANCE (The Best Of Runrig)
(Stepping down the) glory road / Alba / Greatest flame / Rocket to the moon / Abhainn an t-sluaigh / Protect and survive / Rhythm of my heart / Hearthammer / An urbhal as airde (the highest apple) / Wonderful / Mighty Atlantic/Mara theme / Flower of the west / Every river / Siol ghoraidh / Hearts of olden glory / Skye / Loch Lomond
CD CDCHR 6116
Chrysalis / Oct '96 / EMI

MARA
Day in a boat / Nothing but the sun / Mighty Atlantic/Mara theme / Things that are / Road and the river / Meadhan oidche air on acairseid / Wedding / Dancing floor / Thairis air a ghleann / Lighthouse
CD CDCHR 6111
Chrysalis / Nov '95 / EMI

ONCE IN A LIFETIME
Dance called America / Protect and survive / Chiu mi'n geamradh / Rocket to the moon / Going home / Cnoc na feille / Nightfall on Marsco / S to mo leannan / Skye / Loch Lomond
CD CCD 1695
Chrysalis / Nov '88 / EMI

RECOVERY
'An toll dubh / Rubh nan cudeigean / 'Ic lain 'ic shaumais / Recovery / Instrumental / Nightfall on Marsco/'S tu mo leannan / Breaking the chains / Fuaim a bhlair / Tir an airm / Old boys / Dust
CD RRCD 002
Ridge / Aug '89 / ADA / CM / Direct / Duncans / Roots

SEARCHLIGHT
News from Heaven / Every river / City of lights / Eirinn / Tir a'mhurain / World appeal / Tear down these walls / Only the brave / Siol ghoraidh / That final mile / Smalltown / Precious years
CD CCD 1713
Chrysalis / Sep '89 / EMI

TRANSMITTING LIVE
Urlar / Ard / Edge of the world / Greatest flame / Harvest moon / Wire / Precious years / Every river / Flower of the West / Only the brave / Alba / Pog aon oidche earraich (one kiss one spring evening)
CD CDCHR 6090
Chrysalis / Nov '94 / EMI

Runswick, Daryl

HUMOURS OF DARYL RUNSWICK, THE
CD BML 014
British Music / Feb '96 / Forties Recording Company

VOICE THEATRE OF DARYL RUNSWICK, THE (Runswick, Daryl/ Electric Phoenix)
CD BML 015
British Music / Feb '96 / Forties Recording Company

Runt O' The Litter

KNOT THE METRONOME
Cricklewood set / Jock Stewart/The blackberry bush / Morrison's jig / Bowlegged tailor set / Coming down in the rain / Roving gambler off to California / Pipe on the hob / Nancy Spain / Summer sent you / Reconciliation set / Contradiction set / Twa Corbies/New mown hay / Ae fond kiss/Banish misfortune
CD IRCD 038
Iona / Aug '96 / ADA / Direct / Duncans

Rupaul

FOXY LADY
Happy / Party train / Little bit of love / Snapshot / Foxy lady / R u nasty / Falling / Dolores / Work that body / Celebrate / Snatched for the Gods / If you were a woman and I was a man
CD 8122722562
Rhino / Mar '97 / Warner Music

SUPERMODEL OF THE WORLD
Supermodel / Miss Lady DJ / Free your mind / Supernatural / House of love / Thinkin' bout you / Back to my roots / Prisoner of love / Stinky dinky / All of a sudden / Everybody dance / Shade shadey (now prance)
CD CDUCR 2
Union City / Jul '93 / EMI

Rupkina, Yanka

KALIMENKO DENKO
CD HNCD 1334
Hannibal / May '89 / ADA / Vital

Rurutu Choir

POLYNESIAN ODYSSEY
CD SHCD 64065
Shanachie / Sep '96 / ADA / Greensleeves / Koch

Rusby, Kate

HOURGLASS
CD PRCD 02
Pure / Mar '97 / CM / Direct

KATE RUSBY & KATHRYN ROBERTS (Rusby, Kate & Kathryn Roberts)
Recruited collier / Ned on the hill / Lorry ride / Queen and the soldier / Courting is a pleasure / Constant lovers / Dark eyed sailor / Hunting the hare / Plains of Waterloo / Exile
CD PRCD 01
Pure / May '95 / CM / Direct

Rush

2112
Lessons / Passage to Bangkok / Something for nothing / Tears / Twilight zone / 2112 overture / Temples of Syrinx / Discover / Presentation / Oracle / Dream / Soliloquy / Grand finale
CD 5346262
Mercury / Jul '97 / PolyGram

ALL THE WORLD'S A STAGE
Anthem / Bastille day / By-Tor and the snow dog / At the tobes of Hades / Across the Styx / Of the battle / Epilogue / Fly by night / In the mood / In the end / Lakeside park / Something for nothing / 2112 overture / Temples of syrinx / Presentation / Soliloquy / Grand finale / What you're doing / Working man / Finding my way
CD 8225522
Mercury / Apr '87 / PolyGram

CARESS OF STEEL
Bastille day / Fountain of Lamneth / In the valley / Didacts and narpets / No one at the bridge / Panacea / Bacchus plateau / Fountain / I think I'm going bald / Lakeside park / Necromancer / Into the darkness / Under the shadow / Return of the Prince
CD 8225432
Mercury / Apr '87 / PolyGram

CHRONICLES
Finding my way / Fly by night / Bastille day / 2112 overture / Temples of syrinx / Farewell to kings / Trees / Freewill / Tom Sawyer / Limelight / Subdivisions / Distant early warning / Big money / Force ten / Mystic rhythms / Working man / Anthem / Lakeside Park / What you're doing / Closer to the heart / La villa strangiato / Spirit of radio / Red Barchetta / Passage to Bangkok / New world man / Red sector A / Manhattan Project / Time stand still / Show don't tell
CD Set 8389362
Vertigo / Sep '90 / PolyGram

COUNTERPARTS
Animate / Stick it out / Cut to the chase / Nobody's hero / Between sun and moon / Alien shore / Speed of love / Double agent / Leave that thing alone / Cold fire / Everyday glory
CD 7567825282
WEA / Oct '93 / Warner Music

EXIT... STAGE LEFT
Spirit of radio / Red Barchetta / YYZ / Passage to Bangkok / Closer to the heart / Beneath, between and behind / Jacob's ladder / Broon's bane / Trees / Xanadu / Freewill / Tom Sawyer / La villa strangiato
CD 8225512
Mercury / Apr '87 / PolyGram

FAREWELL TO KINGS, A
Farewell to Kings / Xanadu / Closer to the heart / Cinderella man / Madrigal / Cygni X-1
CD 5346282
Mercury / Jul '97 / PolyGram

FLY BY NIGHT
Anthem / Beneath, between and behind / Best I can / By-Tor and the snow dog / At the tobes of Hades / Across the Styx / Of the battle / Epilogue / Fly by night / In the end / Making memories / Rivendell
CD 5346242
Mercury / Jul '97 / PolyGram

GRACE UNDER PRESSURE
Distant early warning / After image / Red sector A / Enemy within / Body electric / Kid gloves / Red lenses / Between the wheels
CD 5346342
Mercury / Jul '97 / PolyGram

HEMISPHERES
CD 5346292
Mercury / Jul '97 / PolyGram

HOLD YOUR FIRE
Force team / Time stand still / Open secrets / Prime mover / Lock and key / Tai Shan / High water
CD 8324642
Mercury / '88 / PolyGram

MOVING PICTURES
Tom Sawyer / Red Barchetta / YYZ / Limelight / Camera / Witch hunt / (Part III of Fear) / Vital signs
CD 5346312
Mercury / Jul '97 / PolyGram

PERMANENT WAVES
Spirit of radio / Freewill / Jacob's ladder / Entre nous / Different strings / Natural science
CD 5346302
Mercury / Jul '97 / PolyGram

POWER WINDOWS
Big money / Grand design / Manhattan Project / Marathon / Territories / Middletown dreams / Emotion detector / Mystic rhythms
CD 8260982
Mercury / Nov '85 / PolyGram

PRESTO
Show don't tell / Chain lightning / Pass / War paint / Scars / Presto / Super conductor / Anagram (for Mongo) / Red tide / Hand over fist / Available light
CD 7820402
WEA / Dec '89 / Warner Music

ROLL THE BONES
Dreamline / Bravado / Roll the bones / Face up / Where's my thing / Big wheel / Heresy / I don't stand a ghost of a chance with you / Neurotica / You bet your life
CD 7567822932
WEA / Sep '91 / Warner Music

RUSH
Before and after / Finding my way / Here again / In the mood / Need some love / Take a friend / What you're doing / Working man
CD 8225412
Mercury / Apr '87 / PolyGram

RUSH RETROSPECTIVE 1974-1980
CD 5349092
Mercury / Aug '97 / PolyGram

RUSH RETROSPECTIVE 1981-1987
CD 5439102
Mercury / Aug '97 / PolyGram

RUSH: INTERVIEW PICTURE DISC
CD CBAK 4055
Baktabak / Apr '92 / Arabesque

SHOW OF HANDS, A
Big money / Subdivisions / Marathon / Turn the page / Manhattan project / Mission / Distant early warning / Mystic rhythms / Witch hunt / Rhythm method / Force ten / Time stands still / Red sector A / Closer to the heart
CD 8463462
Mercury / Jan '89 / PolyGram

SIGNALS
Subdivisions / Analog kid / Chemistry / Digital man / Weapon / New world man / Losing it / Countdown
CD 5346332
Mercury / Jul '97 / PolyGram

TEST FOR ECHO
CD 7567829252
WEA / Aug '96 / Warner Music

WORKING MAN (A Tribute To Rush) (Various Artists)
CD RR 88712
Roadrunner / Sep '96 / PolyGram

Rush, Jennifer

JENNIFER RUSH
Madonna's eyes / Twenty five lovers / Come give me your hand / Nobody move / Never gonna turn back again / Ring of ice / Into my dreams / I see a shadow (not a fantasy) / Surrender / Power of love
CD 4609472
CBS / Oct '90 / Sony

POWER OF JENNIFER RUSH, THE
Destiny / Heart over mind / Ring of ice / Ave Maria (Survivors of a different kind) / Power of love / Higher ground / Flames of paradise: *Rush, Jennifer & Elton John* / Twenty five lovers / I come undone / Same heart: *Rush, Jennifer & Michael Bolton* / If you're ever gonna lose my love
CD 4691632
Columbia / Feb '92 / Sony

Rush, Otis

AIN'T ENOUGH COMIN' IN
Don't burn down the bridge / That will never do / Somebody have mercy / Fool for you / Homework / My jug and I / She's a good 'un / It's my own fault / Ain't enough comin' in / If I had any sense, I'd go back home / Ain't that good news / As the years go passing by
CD 5187692
This Way Up / Apr '94 / PolyGram / SRD

CLASSIC RECORDINGS
All your love / Three times a fool / She's a good 'un / It takes time / Double trouble / My love will never die / My baby is a good 'un / Checking on my baby / Jump sister Bessie / I can't quit you baby / If you were mine / Groaning the blues / Keep on loving me baby / Sit down baby / Love that woman / Violent love / So many roads, so many trains / I'm satisfied / So close / You know my love / I can't stop baby
CD CDCHARLY 217
Charly / Apr '90 / Koch

COLD DAY IN HELL
CD DD 638
Delmark / Jul '93 / ADA / Cadillac / CM / Direct / Hot Shot

DOUBLE TROUBLE (Charly Blues Masterworks Vol.24)
All your love / Three times a fool / She's a good 'un / It takes time / Double trouble / My love will never die / My baby is a good 'un / Checking on my baby / Jump sister Bessie / I can't quit you baby / If you were mine / Groaning the blues / Keep on loving me baby / Sit down baby / Love that woman / Violent love
CD CDBM 24
Charly / Apr '92 / Koch

DOUBLE TROUBLE - LIVE IN JAPAN 1986
Introduction/Tops / All your love / Please, please, please / Killing floor / Stand by me / Lonely man / Double trouble / Right place, wrong time / Got my mojo working / Gambler's blues
CD NEGCD 277
Sequel / Oct '95 / BMG

LIVE AND AWESOME
CD RBASE 30012
Red Base / May '97 / CM

LIVE IN EUROPE
Cut you loose / All your love / You're breaking my heart / I wonder why / Feel so bad / Society woman/Love is just a gamble / Crosscut saw / I can't quit you baby / I'm tore up / Looking back
CD ECD 260342
Evidence / Sep '93 / ADA / Cadillac / Harmonia Mundi
CD IS 9212
Isabel / Mar '96 / Discovery

LOST IN THE BLUES
Hold that train / You've been an angel / Little red rooster / Trouble, trouble / Please love me / You don't have to go / Got to be some changes made / You got me runnin' / I miss you so
CD ALCD 4797
Alligator / Aug '92 / ADA / CM / Direct

SCREAMIN' & CRYIN'
CD ECD 260142
Evidence / Jan '92 / ADA / Cadillac / Harmonia Mundi

SO MANY ROADS
CD DE 643
Blind Pig / Dec '95 / ADA / CM / Direct / Hot Shot

TOPS
Right place, wrong time / Crosscut saw / Tops / Feels so bad / Gambler's blues / Keep on loving me baby / I wonder why
CD BP 3188CD
Blind Pig / May '94 / ADA / CM / Direct / Hot Shot

Rush, Tom

BLUES, SONGS AND BALLADS
Duncan and Brady / I don't want your millions mister / San Francisco Bay blues / Mole's moan / Rye whiskey / Big fat woman / Nine pound hammer / Diamond Joe / Mobile Texas line / Joe Turner / Every day in the week / Alabamy bound / More pretty girls / I wish I could shimmy like my sister Kate / Original talking blues / Pallet on the floor / Drop down mama / Rag mama / Barb'ry Allen / Cocaine / Come back baby / Stagger Lee / Baby, please don't go
CD CDWIK 948
Big Beat / Aug '90 / Pinnacle

TOM RUSH/WRONG END OF THE RAINBOW
Driving wheel / Rainy day man / Drop down Mama / Old man song / Lullaby / These days / Wild child / Colors of the sun / Livin' in the country / Child's song / Wrong end of the rainbow / Biloxi / Merrimac County / Riding on a railroad / Came to see me yesterday in the merry month of May / Starlight / Sweet baby James / Rotunda / Jazzman / Gnostic serenade
CD BGOCD 361
Beat Goes On / Jul '97 / Pinnacle

Rushen, Patrice

HAVEN'T YOU HEARD (The Best Of Patrice Rushen)
Hang it up / When I found you / Haven't you heard / Settle for my love / Givin' it up is givin' up / Look up / Never gonna give you up / Forget me nots / Breakout / Remind me / Number one / Feels so real (won't let go) / Get off (you fascinate me)
CD 0349723882
Rhino / Aug '97 / Warner Music

STRAIGHT FROM THE HEART
Forget me nots / I was tired of being alone / All we need / Number one / Where there is love / Breakout / If only / Remind me / She will take you down to love
CD 8122735082
Elektra / Jul '96 / Warner Music

Rushing, Jimmy

BLUES SINGER 1929-1937, THE
CD JZCD 344
Suisa / Jan '93 / Jazz Music / THE

BLUES SINGER 1937-1938, THE
CD JZCD 345
Suisa / Jan '93 / Jazz Music / THE

JIMMY RUSHING WITH THE COUNT BASIE ORCHESTRA 1938-1945 (Rushing, Jimmy & Count Basie Orchestra)
Jimmy's blues / Take me back, baby / Harvard blues / Gee, baby ain't I good to you / One two three-o' Lairy / Rusty dusty blues / For the good of your country / Lost the blackout blues / Undecided blues / I'm gonna move to the outskirts of town / Goin' to Chicago blues / It's the same old South / I left my baby / I can't believe that you're in love with me / How long blues / You can depend on me / Baby, don't tell on me / Blues I like to hear / Do you wanna jump children / Evil blues
CD ______ CD 53298
Giants Of Jazz / Jul '97 / Cadillac / Jazz Music / Target/BMG

MR. FIVE BY FIVE
CD ______ TPZ 1019
Topaz Jazz / May '95 / Cadillac / Pinnacle

RUSHING LULLABIES
I'm coming Virginia / Knock me a kiss / Harvard blues / Mister five by five / Travellin' light / June night / It's a sin to tell a lie / Rosalie / Jimmy's blues / Someday sweetheart / When you're smiling / Somebody stole my gal / You can't run around blues / Say you don't mean it / 'Deed I do / Pink champagne / Did you ever / I cried for you / Three long years / I can't believe that you're in love with me / Good rockin' tonight / One evening / Russian lullaby / Travel the road of love
CD ______ CK 65118
Sony Jazz / Jun '97 / Sony

SWINGS THE BLUES
Sent for you yesterday and here you come today / Blue devil blues / Won't you be my baby / Boogie woogie / He ain't got rhythm / Listen my children and you shall hear / Good morning blues / Don't you miss your baby / Blues in the dark / Now will you be good / Do you wanna jump children / Evil blues / You can't run around / Undecided blues / Take me back, baby / Goin' to Chicago blues / I'm gonna move to the outskirts of town / Lazy lady blues / Jimmy's blues / Blues I like to hear
CD ______ RPCD 637
Robert Parker Jazz / Apr '97 / Conifer/BMG / New Note/Pinnacle

TWO SHADES OF BLUE (Rushing, Jimmy & Jack Dupree)
Way I feel / In the moonlight / She's mine, she's yours / You go get some more you fool / Somebody's spoiling these women / Walking the blues / Harelip blues / Overhead blues / Silent partner / Everybody's blues
CD ______ TKOCD 022
TKO / May '92 / TKO

WHO WAS IT SANG THAT SONG (Rushing, Jimmy Allstars)
Baby won't you please come home / 'C' Jam blues / I surrender dear / Deed I do / Almost home / Blue / Stormy Monday blues / Jelly jelly / Moten stomp / All of me
CD ______ 805102
New World / May '97 / ADA / Cadillac / Harmonia Mundi

YOU AND ME THAT USED TO BE, THE
You and me that used to be / Fine and mellow / When I grow too old to dream / I surrender dear / Linger awhile / Bei mir bist du schon / My last affair / All God's chillun got rhythm / More than you know / Home / Thanks a million
CD ______ ND 86460
Bluebird / Apr '89 / BMG

Russell & Hardin

EARLY YEARS
CD ______ EDCD 498
Edsel / Nov '96 / Pinnacle

Russell Family

OF DOOLIN, COUNTY CLARE
Campbell's reel / Heather breeze/The Traveller / St. Kevin of Glendalough / Potlick/The Peeler's jacket / Five mile chase / Russell's hornpipe/Fisher's hornpipe / Poor little fisher boy / Walls of Liscarroll/The battering ram / Garrett Barry's reel / Tommy glenny's reel / Connemara stockings/The Westmeath hunt / When Musheen went to Bunnan / Tatter Jack Walsh / De'il among the tailors / Roscrea cows / Fair haired boy/The black haired lass / Off to California / Give the girl her fourpence / Nora Daly
CD ______ GLCD 3079
Green Linnet / May '93 / ADA / CM / Direct / Highlander / Roots

RUSSELL FAMILY OF DOOLIN, CO. CLARE, THE
Campbell's reel / Heather breeze/The traveller / St. Kevin of Glendalough / Potlick/The peeler's jacket / Five mile chase / Russell's hornpipe/Fisher's hornpipe / Poor little fisher boy / Walls of Liscarroll/The battering ram / Garrett Barry's reel / Tommy Glenny's reel / Connemara stockings/The westmeath hunt / When Musheen went to Bunnan / Tatter Jack Walsh / De'il among the tailors / Roscrea cows / Fair haired boy/The black haired lass / Off to California / Give the girl her fourpence / Nora Daly
CD ______ OSS 8CD
Ossian / Jan '94 / ADA / CM / Direct / Highlander

Russell, Brenda

GREATEST HITS
Piano in the dark / So good, so right / Gravity / Kiss me with the wind / Get here / Dinner with Gershwin / Stop running away / In the thick of it / If only for one night / Way back when / Justice in truth / Le restaurant
CD ______ 5525402
Spectrum / Sep '96 / PolyGram

Russell, Calvin

CRACK IN TIME, A
Crack in time / Big brother / Nothin' / Behind the eight ball / Automated / North Austin slim / One step ahead / Living at the end of a gun / I should have been home / My way / This is my life / Little stars / Moments / Wagon to stars
CD ______ 422303
New Rose / May '94 / ADA / Direct / Discovery

DREAM OF THE DOG
CD ______ 422020
Last Call / Apr '95 / Cargo / Direct / Discovery

LE VOYAGEUR
CD ______ 422489
New Rose / Jan '95 / ADA / Direct / Discovery

SOLDIER
CD ______ 422422
New Rose / May '94 / ADA / Direct / Discovery

SOUNDS FROM THE FOURTH WORLD
CD ______ 422306
New Rose / Nov '94 / ADA / Direct / Discovery

Russell, Devon

MONEY SEX AND VIOLENCE
CD ______ RNCD 0010
RN / Jan '91 / Jet Star

Russell, George

AFRICAN GAME, THE
Event I: Organic life on earth begins / Event II: The Paleolithic game / Event III: Consciousness / Event IV: The survival game / Event V: The human sensing of unity with great / Event VI: African Empires / Event VII: Cartesian man / Event VIII: The mega-minimalist age / Event IX: The future
CD ______ CDP 7463352
Blue Note / Feb '97 / EMI

ELECTRONIC SONATA FOR SOULS LOVED BY NATURE (1968)
Part 1 / Part 2
CD ______ 1210342
Soul Note / Jan '94 / Cadillac / Harmonia Mundi / Wellard

EZZ-THETICS (Russell, George Sextet)
CD ______ OJCCD 70
Original Jazz Classics / Oct '92 / Complete/Pinnacle / Jazz Music / Wellard

IT'S ABOUT TIME (Russell, George Living Time Orchestra)
It's about time / Event
CD ______ LBLC 6587
Label Bleu / Mar '97 / New Note/Pinnacle

LIVE IN AN AMERICAN TIME SPIRAL (Russell, George New York Band)
CD ______ SNCD 1049
Soul Note / '86 / Cadillac / Harmonia Mundi / Wellard

LONDON CONCERT VOL.1 (Russell, George Living Time Orchestra)
CD ______ STCD 560
Stash / May '93 / ADA / Cadillac / CM / Direct / Jazz Music

LONDON CONCERT VOL.2 (Russell, George Living Time Orchestra)
CD ______ STCD 561
Stash / May '93 / ADA / Cadillac / CM / Direct / Jazz Music

LONDON CONCERT, THE (Live At Ronnie Scott's) (Russell, George Living Time Orchestra)
CD Set ______ LBLC 6527/8
Label Bleu / Nov '95 / New Note/Pinnacle

NEW YORK BIG BAND
CD ______ SNCD 1039
Soul Note / '86 / Cadillac / Harmonia Mundi / Wellard

OTHELLO BALLET SUITE/ELECTRONIC ORGAN SONATA 1
CD ______ 1210142
Soul Note / Oct '90 / Cadillac / Harmonia Mundi / Wellard

OUTER VIEW
CD ______ OJCCD 616
Original Jazz Classics / Jun '95 / Complete/Pinnacle / Jazz Music / Wellard

VERTICAL FORM VI
CD ______ 1210192
Soul Note / Nov '90 / Cadillac / Harmonia Mundi / Wellard

Russell, Hal

CONSERVING NRG (Russell, Hal & NRG Ensemble & Charles Tyler)
Rusty nails / Blue over you / OJN / Pontiac / Sine die / Overbite / Song singing to you / Swing sting / Linda's rock vamp
CD ______ PJP CD02
Principally Jazz / Feb '91 / Cadillac

FINISH SWISS TOUR, THE
Monica's having a baby / Aila/35 basic / Temporarily / Raining violets / For MC / Dance of the spider people / Ten letters of love / Hal the weenie / Linda's rock vamp / Mars theme
CD ______ 5112612
ECM / Oct '91 / New Note/Pinnacle

GENERATION (Russell, Hal & NRG Ensemble & Charles Tyler)
Sinus up / Poodle cut / Sponge / Tatwas / Cascade / Generation
CD ______ CHIEFCD 5
Chief / Jun '89 / Cadillac

HAL RUSSELL STORY
Intro and fanfare / Toy parade / Trumpet march / Riverside jump / Krupa / You're blase / Dark rapture / World class / Wood chips / My little grass shack / O and B / For M / Gloomy Sunday / Hair male / Bossa G / Mildred / Dope music / Two times two / Ayler song / Rehcabnettul / Steve's freedom principle / Lady in the lake / Oh well
CD ______ 5173642
ECM / Jun '93 / New Note/Pinnacle

Russell, Janet

BRIGHT SHINING MORNING
CD ______ HARCD 026
Harbour Town / Oct '93 / ADA / CM / Direct / Roots

DANCIN' CHANTIN' (Russell, Janet & Christine Kydd)
Rattlin' roarin' Willie / Fisherman's wife / Logan water / Les filles des forges / Maire Nighean Alastair / Up and awa' wi' the laverock / Duncan Gray / Lady Mary Anne / Reel o' stumpie / Tail toddle / Terror time / Strathmartine Braes / Clerk Saunders / La Caille / Pride's awa' / Bluebell polka / Parting glass / Jock since ever
CD ______ CDTRAX 077
Greentrax / Sep '94 / ADA / Direct / Duncans / Highlander

JANET RUSSELL AND CHRISTINE KYDD (Russell, Janet & Christine Kydd)
Buy broom besoms / Dainty Davie / Up wi' the Carls o'Dysart / De'il's awa' wi' tha exciseman / Deja mal Mariee / Bonnie at morn / Children of Africa / My Donald / Ode to big blue / Tae the weavers gin ye gang / Old and strong / Mountain song / Do you love an apple / Last carol / Stand up fight for your rights / Everyone 'neath a vine and fig tree
CD ______ CDTRAX 011
Greentrax / Aug '93 / ADA / Direct / Duncans / Highlander

Russell, John

BIRTHDAYS (Russell, John & Roger Turner)
CD ______ EM 4010
Emanem / Sep '96 / Cadillac / Harmonia Mundi

Russell, Luis

CLASSICS 1926-1929
CD ______ CLASSICS 588
Classics / Aug '91 / Discovery / Jazz Music

CLASSICS 1930-1934 (Russell, Luis & His Orchestra)
CD ______ CLASSICS 606
Classics / Oct '92 / Discovery / Jazz Music

COLLECTION 1926-1934, THE
CD ______ COCD 7
Collector's Classics / May '93 / Cadillac / Complete/Pinnacle / Jazz Music

LUIS RUSSELL & HIS ORCHESTRA (Russell, Luis & His Orchestra)
Savoy shout / Call of the freaks / Mahogany hall stomp / African jungle / Feelin' the spirit / Jersey lightning / Dalls blues / St Louis blues / Doctor blues / Saratoga shout / Song of the Swanee / Louisiana swing / On revival day / Muggin' lightly / Panama / High tension / Case on Dawn (ease on down) / At the Darktown strutter's ball / My blue heaven / Ghost of the freaks / Hokus pokus / Moods (primitive) / Ol' man river
CD ______ TPZ 1039
Topaz Jazz / Feb '96 / Cadillac / Pinnacle

LUIS RUSSELL AND HIS ORCHESTRA VOL.1 (Russell, Luis & His Orchestra)
CD ______ VILCD 0182
Village Jazz / Aug '92 / Jazz Music / Target/BMG

SAVOY SHOUT
CD ______ JSPCD 308
JSP / Aug '89 / ADA / Cadillac / Direct / Hot Shot / Target/BMG

Russell, Micho

LIMESTONE ROCK, THE
CD ______ GTDHCD 104
GTD / Jul '93 / ADA / Else

MAN FROM CLARE, THE
CD ______ TRADHCD 011
GTD / Jul '93 / ADA / Else

Russell, Pee Wee

JAZZ ORIGINAL
Love is just around the corner / Embraceable you / Serenade to a shylock / Serenade to a shylock / Sunday / I ain't gonna give nobody... / Georgia grind / Jig walk / Deuces wild / Last time I saw Chicago / About face / Don't leave me, Daddy / Rosetta / Squeeze me / Take me to the land of Jazz / Take me to the land of Jazz / Rose of Washington square / Rose of Washington square / Keepin' out of mischief now / DA blues / DA blues / Wailin' DA blues
CD ______ CMD 14042
Commodore Jazz / Feb '97 / New Note/ BMG

JAZZ REUNION (Russell, Pee Wee & Coleman Hawkins)
If I could be with you one hour tonight / Tin tin deo / Mariooch / All too soon / 28th and 8th / What am I here for
CD ______ CCD 79020
Candid / Feb '97 / Cadillac / Direct / Jazz Music / Koch / Wellard

LAND OF JAZZ
CD ______ TPZ 1018
Topaz Jazz / Apr '95 / Cadillac / Pinnacle

PORTRAIT OF PEE WEE
CD ______ FSCD 126
Fresh Sound / Jan '91 / Discovery / Jazz Music

WE'RE IN THE MONEY
CD ______ BLCD 760909
Black Lion / Jan '89 / Cadillac / Jazz Music / Koch / Wellard

Russell, Ray

CHILDSCAPE
Outland / Prelude / Pour me fish / Blue shoes no dance / Lundy Island / Pan piper / Childscape / Point perfect / Prelude / If only / Murmurs in reverse / Sketches of Gil
CD ______ BW 012
B&W / Nov '96 / New Note/Pinnacle / SRD / Vital/SAM

Russell, Tom

COWBOY REEL
El Liano / Bad half hour / Basque / Claude Dallas / Navajo rug / Indian cowboy / Gallo del cielo / Rayburn Crane / Sonora's death row / Zane grey / Roanie
CD ______ MRCD 161
Munich / '92 / ADA / CM / Direct / Greensleeves

HEART ON A SLEEVE
One and one / Heart on a sleeve / Blinded by the light of love / Touch of grey / Wild hearts / St. Olav's gate / Gallo del cielo / Mandarin oranges / Cropduster / Canadian whiskey / Chinese silver / Bowl of red
CD ______ BCD 15243
Bear Family / Aug '86 / Direct / Rollercoaster / Swift

HURRICANE SEASON (Russell, Tom Band)
Black pearl / Lord of the trains / Beyond the blues / Jack Johnson / Chocolate cigarette / Winnipeg / Evangeline hotel / Dollars worth of gasoline / Hurricane season / Haley's comet
CD ______ RTMCD 49
Round Tower / Jun '97 / Avid/BMG

OUT OF CALIFORNIA
CD ______ RTMS 9603CD
Round Tower / Sep '96 / Avid/BMG

POOR MAN'S DREAM (Russell, Tom Band)
Blue wing / Heart of the working man / Veteran's day / Walkin' on the moon / Outbound plane / Bergenfield / Spanish burgundy / Gallo del cielo / La frontera / Navajo rug / Under the gun / White trash song
CD ______ RTMCD 48
Round Tower / Feb '96 / Avid/BMG
CD ______ PHCD 1139
Philo / Sep '96 / ADA / CM / Direct

ROAD TO BAYAMON (Russell, Tom Band)
Home before dark / US Steel / Downtown train / Love makes a fool of the wise / Definition of a fool / As the crow flies / Road to Bayamon / Alkali / Wise blood / Joshua tree / Mexcal / William Faulkner in Hollywood / Fire
CD ______ PH 1116CD
Philo / '89 / ADA / CM / Direct

ROSE OF THE SAN JOAQUIN, THE
CD ____ **RTMCD 71**
Round Tower / Oct '95 / Avid/BMG

Russki Color

RUSSKI COLOR (Traditional Folk Melodies From Russia)
CD ____ **LDX 274955**
La Chant Du Monde / Jan '93 / ADA / Harmonia Mundi

Russo, Marc

WINDOW, THE
Southern tale / Shake / Intro / Window / Crooked numbers / Elizabeth / Whatever you want / Weekend / School / In the rain / Notes next to the notes
CD ____ **JVC 20352**
JVC / Jul '94 / Direct / New Note/Pinnacle / Vital/SAM

Rustavi Choir

GEORGIAN VOICES
CD ____ **7559792242**
Nonesuch / Jan '95 / Warner Music

Rusted Root

WHEN I WOKE
Drum trip / Ecstasy / Send me on my way / Cruel sun / Cat turned blue / Beautiful people / Martyr / Rain / Food and creative love / Lost in a crowd / Laugh as the sun / Infinite tamboura / Back to the Earth
CD ____ **5227132**
Mercury / Aug '95 / PolyGram

Rustichelli, Paolo

MYSTIC JAZZ
Femmes / Bold man / Capri / Merkel bokrug / Full moon / El topo / Bridge / Black plastic / Capri
CD ____ **5134152**
PolyGram Jazz / Apr '92 / PolyGram

Ruth Ruth

LAUGHING GALLERY
Uninvited / Uptight / All ready down / Bald Marie / Mission idiot / Amnesia / Neurotica / Don't shut me out / Pervert / I killed Meg the prom Queen / I grew up / GI youth
CD ____ **74321302772**
American / Nov '95 / BMG

LITTLE DEATH
CD ____ **64802**
Epitaph / Sep '96 / Pinnacle / Plastic Head

Rutherford, Mike

SMALLCREEPS DAY
Between the tick and the tock / Working in line / After hours / Cats and rats in this neighbourhood / Smallcreep alone / Out into the daylight / At the end of the day / Moonshine / Time and time again / Romani / Every road / Overnight job
CD ____ **CASCD 1149**
Charisma / Jun '89 / EMI

Rutherford, Paul

1989 AND ALL THAT (Rutherford, Paul & George Haslam)
1939 / Orion / 1977 / 1984 / Come Sunday / 1986 / Sigma / London lights / 1989
CD ____ **SLAMCD 301**
Slam / Oct '90 / Cadillac

Ruthless Rap Assassins

THINK - IT AIN'T ILLEGAL YET
What did you say your name was / Listen to the hit / Why me / Think / Hard and direct / I got no time / Radio / Down and dirty / No tale, no twist / Pick up the pace / (I try to) flow it out / Less mellow
CD ____ **CDEMC 3604**
Murdertone / Oct '91 / Pinnacle

Rutles

ARCHAEOLOGY
Major Happy's up & coming once upon a good time band / Rendezvous / Questionnaire / We've arrived (and to prove it we're here) / Lonely-phobia / Unfinished words / Hey Mister / Easy listening / Now she's left you / Knicker elastic King / I love you / Eine kleine middle klasse musik / Joe Public / Shangri-la / I don't know why / Back in '64
CD ____ **CDVUS 119**
CD ____ **CDVUSX 119**
Virgin / Oct '96 / EMI

Ruts

CRACK, THE
Babylon's burning / Dope for guns / SUS / Something that I said / You're just a... / It was cold / Savage circle / Jah war / Criminal mind / Backwater / Out of order / Human punk
CD ____ **CDV 2132**
Virgin / Jul '90 / EMI

DEMOLITION DANCING
CD ____ **RRCD 182**
Receiver / Apr '94 / Grapevine/PolyGram

RHYTHM COLLISION DUB VOL.1 (Ruts DC & Mad Professor)
CD ____ **RE 151CD**
ROIR / Nov '94 / Plastic Head / Shellshock/Disc

RULES
CD ____ **EFA 123032**
Vince Lombard / Jul '94 / SRD

SOMETHING THAT I SAID (The Best Of The Ruts)
In a rut / H-eyes / Babylon's burning / Dope for guns / SUS / Something that I said / You're just a... / It was cold / Savage circle / Jah war / Criminal mind / Backbiter / Out of order / Human punk / Staring at the rude boys / Love in vain / West one (Shine on me)
CD ____ **CDOVD 454**
Virgin / Feb '95 / EMI

Ruzicka, Karel

YOU'RE NEVER ALONE
CD ____ **CR 00122**
Czech Radio / Nov '95 / Czech Music Enterprises

Ryan, Barry

ELOISE
Love is love / Kitsch / Hunt / My mama / I'm sorry Susan / From my head to my toe / Can't let you go / Eloise / Colour of my love / We did it together / It is written / Caroline / Love always comes tomorrow / Goodbye
CD ____ **5503852**
Spectrum / Jan '95 / PolyGram

Ryan, Cathie

CATHIE RYAN
CD ____ **SH 78008**
Shanachie / Mar '97 / ADA / Greensleeves / Koch

Ryan, Marion

AT HER BEST
CD ____ **C5MCD 614**
See For Miles/C5 / Jun '94 / Pinnacle

Ryan, Sean

BACK HOME TO THE CLIFFS OF MOHIR
St Andrew's / Swallow / Reavey's / Brook / Slabh bloom / Frost is all over / Charlie Mulvihille's / McCollum's / Kiss me Kate / Sean Ryan's / Eel in the sink / Larry Redican's / Providence / Trip to Nenagh / Anne Sheehy's / Stage / Pipe on the hob / Coleman's / Tommy Coen's reels 1 and 2 / Thornton's / Tommy McGuire's / Fahy's jigs 1 and 2 / Bashful bachelor / McIntyre's / Star of munster / Paddy Kelly's / Killavil / Father Quinn's / McGreevey's
CD ____ **PTICD 1012**
Pure Traditional Irish / Mar '97 / ADA / CM / Direct / Ross

MINSTREL'S FANCY
CD ____ **CEFCD 169**
Gael Linn / Dec '95 / ADA / CM / Direct / Grapevine/PolyGram / Roots

TAKE THE AIR
CD ____ **CEFCD 142**
Gael Linn / Jan '94 / ADA / CM / Direct / Grapevine/PolyGram / Roots

Rybin Choir

SERBIAN AND BULGARIAN RELIGIOUS CHANTS
CD ____ **RUS 288087**
Saison Russe / May '96 / ADA

Ryce, Daryle

I WALK WITH... (Ryce, Daryle & Loonis McGlohon Trio/Quartet)
CD ____ **ACD 141**
Audiophile / Nov '96 / Jazz Music

UNLESS IT'S YOU
CD ____ **ACD 271**
Audiophile / Apr '93 / Jazz Music

Rydell, Bobby

BEST OF BOBBY RYDELL, THE
CD ____ **CDSGP 0156**
Prestige / Jul '95 / Else / Total/BMG

Ryder, Anna

EYE TO EYE
CD ____ **RM 01CD**
Rowdy / Oct '93 / ADA

Ryder, Mitch

BREAKOUT (Ryder, Mitch & The Detroit Wheels)
Walking the dog / I had it made / In the midnight hour / Ooh-poo-pah-doo / I like it like that / Little latin lupe lu / Medley / Shakin' with Linda / Stubborn kind of fellow / You get your kicks / I need help / Any day now / Breakout
CD ____ **CDSC 6008**
Sundazed / Jan '94 / Cargo / Greyhound / Rollercoaster

MITCH RYDER AND THE DETROIT WHEELS
CD ____ **CSAPCD 111**
Connoisseur Collection / Oct '92 / Pinnacle

SOCK IT TO ME (Ryder, Mitch & The Detroit Wheels)
Sock it to me baby / I can't hide it / Takin' all I can get / Slow fizz / Walk on by / I never had it better / Shakedown / Face in the crowd / I'd rather go to jail / Wild child / Medley / You are my sunshine / Ruby baby and peaches on a cherry tree
CD ____ **CDSC 6009**
Sundazed / Jan '94 / Cargo / Greyhound / Rollercoaster

TAKE A RIDE (Ryder, Mitch & The Detroit Wheels)
Shake a tail feather / Come see about me / Let your love light shine / Just a little bit / I hope / Jenny take a ride / Please please please / I'll go crazy / I got you / Sticks and stones / Bring it on home to me / Baby Jane (mo-mo Jane) / Joy
CD ____ **CDSC 6007**
Sundazed / Jan '94 / Cargo / Greyhound / Rollercoaster

Ryerson, Ali

BRASIL - QUIET DEVOTION
First Rita / Todos os sentidos / Send in the clowns / I'm not buying it / Double rainbow / Camila / Pensado bem / Stellar by midnight / Estate / Incantations / Praeludium II / Quiet devotion
CD ____ **CCD 47622**
Concord Picante / Jun '97 / New Note/ Pinnacle

IN HER OWN SWEET WAY
Preface / To start again / Everything changed / Parisagem cosmica / Martina / In your own sweet way / Sail away / Blue in green / Sometime ago / Chega de saudade / So remember me
CD ____ **CCD 4687**
Concord Jazz / Feb '96 / New Note/ Pinnacle

PORTRAIT IN SILVER
Windows / Beatrice / Ausencia / Shadowlight / Beautiful love / Zingaro / Very early / Jardin de la paresse / Lament / Summer knows
CD ____ **CCD 4638**
Concord Jazz / Apr '95 / New Note/ Pinnacle

Ryg, Jorgen

COLLECTION, THE (The Complete Recordings Of Jorgen Ryg/2CD Set)
CD Set ____ **MECCACD 2104**
Music Mecca / May '97 / Cadillac / Jazz Music / Wellard

Rykers

BROTHER AGAINST BROTHER
CD ____ **LF 102CD**
Lost & Found / Oct '94 / Plastic Head

FIRST BLOOD
CD ____ **LF 187CD**
Lost & Found / Oct '95 / Plastic Head

LESSON IN LOYALTY, A
Test of faith / As the laughter dies / Lesson in loyalty / Naturally / Still / Triggered / Cold/ lost/sick / 25 / Gutless / Sober / Shadowplay / Straight / Peak / Finally / Emergency / Who laughs at last
CD ____ **0630189282**
WEA / Aug '97 / Warner Music

PAYBACK TIME
CD ____ **LF 080CD**
Lost & Found / Jun '94 / Plastic Head

Ryman, John

ARTIFICE AND ARCHITECTURE
CD ____ **MILL 006MCD**
Millenium / Nov '94 / Plastic Head / Prime / SRD

Rymes With Orange

PEEL
CD ____ **RW 08882**
TKO / Sep '94 / TKO

Rypdal, Terje

AFRICA PEPPERBIRD (Rypdal, Terje & Jan Garbarek)
Sharabee / Mahjong / Beast of Kommodo / Blow away zone / MYB / Concentus / Africa pepperbird / Blupp
CD ____ **8434752**
ECM / Oct '90 / New Note/Pinnacle

AFTER THE RAIN
Autumn breeze / Air / Now and then / Wind / After the rain / Kjare maren / Little bell / Vintage year / Multer / Like a child, like a song
CD ____ **5231592**
ECM / Jul '95 / New Note/Pinnacle

BLUE (Rypdal, Terje & Chasers)
Curse / Kompet Gar / I disremember quite well / Og hva synes vi om det / Last nite / Blue / Tanga / Om bare
CD ____ **8315162**
ECM / Jul '87 / New Note/Pinnacle

CHASER
Ambiguity / Once upon a time / Geysir / Closer look / Orion / Chaser / Transition / Imagi (theme)
CD ____ **8272562**
ECM / Dec '85 / New Note/Pinnacle

DESCENDRE
Askjed / Circles / Innseiling / Men of mystery / Speil
CD ____ **8291182**
ECM / Jun '86 / New Note/Pinnacle

EOS (Rypdal, Terje & David Darling)
Eos / Bedtime story / Light years / Melody / Mirage / Adagietto / Laser
CD ____ **8153332**
ECM / Sep '88 / New Note/Pinnacle

IF MOUNTAINS COULD SING
Return of per ulv / It's in the air / But on the other hand / If mountains could sing / Private eye / Foran peisen / Dancing without reindeers / One for the roadrunner / Blue angel / Genie / Lonesome guitar
CD ____ **5239872**
ECM / Feb '95 / New Note/Pinnacle

ODYSSEY
CD ____ **8353552**
ECM / Sep '88 / New Note/Pinnacle

QED
Quod erat demonstradum opus 52 1st-5th movements / Largo Opus 55
CD ____ **5133742**
ECM / Jan '92 / New Note/Pinnacle

RYPDAL/VITOUS/DEJOHNETTE (Rypdal, Terje/Miroslav Vitous/Jack Dejohnette)
Sunrise / Den forste sne / Will / Believer / Flight / Seasons
CD ____ **8254702**
ECM / Aug '85 / New Note/Pinnacle

SART (Rypdal, Terje/Stenson/Jan Garbarek)
CD ____ **8393052**
ECM / Nov '89 / New Note/Pinnacle

SINGLES COLLECTION, THE
CD ____ **8377492**
ECM / Apr '89 / New Note/Pinnacle

SKYWARDS
Skywards / Into the wildness / It's not over until the fat lady sings / Pleasure is mine I'm sure / Out of this world / Shining / Remember to remember
CD ____ **5337682**
ECM / Mar '97 / New Note/Pinnacle

TERJE RYPDAL
Keep it like that tight / Rainbow / Electric fantasy / Lontano II / Tough enough
CD ____ **5276452**
ECM / Jul '95 / New Note/Pinnacle

TO BE CONTINUED (Rypdal, Terje/ Miroslav Vitous/Jack Dejohnette)
Maya / Mountains in the clouds / Morning-lake / To be continued / This morning / Topplue, vooter and skjerf / Uncomposed appendix
CD ____ **8473332**
ECM / Mar '92 / New Note/Pinnacle

UNDISONUS
CD ____ **837 755 2**
New Note / Mar '90 / Cadillac / New Note/ Pinnacle

WAVES
Per ulv / Karusell / Stenskoven / Waves / Dain curse / Charisma
CD ____ **8274192**
ECM / Feb '86 / New Note/Pinnacle

WHAT COMES AFTER
CD ____ **8393062**
ECM / Nov '89 / New Note/Pinnacle

WHENEVER I SEEM TO BE AWAY
Silver bird is heading for the sun / Hurt / Whenever I seem to be far away
CD ____ **8431662**
ECM / Jun '92 / New Note/Pinnacle

WORKS: TERJE RYPDAL
Waves / Den forste sne / Hung / Better off without you / Innseiling / Rainbow / Topplue, vooter and skjerf / Descendre
CD ____ **8254282**
ECM / Jun '89 / New Note/Pinnacle

Rzewski, Frederick

NIGHT CROSSING
CD ____ **CD 998**
Music & Arts / Aug '97 / Cadillac / Harmonia Mundi

NORTH AMERICAN BALLADS & SQUARES
CD ____ **ARTCD 6089**
Hat Art / Jan '92 / Cadillac / Harmonia Mundi

S

Saafi Bros.

MYSTIC CIGARETTES
CD _______________ BR 032CD
Blue Room Released / Sep '97 / Essential/ BMG / SRD

Sababougnouma

SABABOUGNOUMA (Balafons & Africans Drums)
CD _______________ PS 65156
PlayaSound / Oct '95 / ADA / Harmonia Mundi

Sabia

LIVE IN CULVER CITY
CD _______________ FF 70494
Flying Fish / Jul '89 / ADA / CM / Direct / Roots

Sablon, Jean

FRENCH SWINGING TROUBADOUR, THE
CD _______________ 995712
EPM / Jul '96 / ADA / Discovery

JE TIRE MA REVERENCE
Ce petit Chemin / Depuis que je suis a Paris / Jesais que vous etes Jolie / Miss Otis regrets / Melancolie / Il ne faut pas Briser en Reve / Seul / La Chanson Des Rues / Un seul couvert, please, James / Vous qui passez sans me voir / Sur les Quais du Vieux Paris / J'ai ta Main / Le Fiacre / J'Attendrai / Sur le Pont D'Avignon / Mon village au Clair de Lune / Je tire ma reverence / Ma Mie / Serenade Portugaise / Utrillo
CD _______________ MDF 102611
Mudisque / Nov '96 / Target/BMG

JEAN SABLON 1933-1946
CD _______________ FA 062
Fremeaux / Apr '97 / ADA / Discovery

JEAN SABLON IN PARIS
CD _______________ CDXP 606
DRG / Jan '89 / Discovery / New Note/ Pinnacle

SI TU MAINES
CD _______________ PASTCD 7058
Flapper / Apr '95 / Pinnacle

SUCCES ET RARETES 1932-1939
CD _______________ 701582
Chansophone / Sep '96 / Discovery

Sabot

VICE VERSA/SOMEHOW I DON'T THINK SO
CD _______________ SKIP 54
Broken / Mar '97 / Cargo / Greyhound

Sabot, Jean

HARMONICA FIDDLE (Sabot, Jean & Olivier Rozent)
CD _______________ HFCD 001
Diffusion Breizh / Mar '96 / ADA

Sabrejets

HELLBENT
Hellbent / Going down to Memphis / Born to boogie / In and out of love / Wild cat / Bang zoom / Long gone / Rooftop boogie / Midnight train / Wiggle
CD _______________ RAUCD 023
Raucous / Apr '97 / Nervous / RTM/Disc / TKO Magnum

Sabres Of Paradise

DEEP CUTS (Various Artists)
Ooh baby: *Secret Knowledge* / Roy revisited: *Waxworth Industries* / Musical science: *Musical Science* / Internal: *Blue* / Take the book: *Waxworth Industries* / X: *Corridor* / Vega God: *Jack Of Swords* / Sugar Daddy: *Secret Knowledge* / Smokebelch II: *Sabres Of Paradise*
CD _______________ SOP 001CD
Sabres Of Paradise / Oct '93 / Vital

HAUNTED DANCEHALL
Bubble and slide / Bubble and slide II / Duke of Earlsfield / Flight path estate / Planet D / Wilmot / Tow truck / Theme / Theme 4 / Return to Planet D / Ballad of Nicky McGuire / Jacob Street 7am / Chapel Street market 9am / Haunted dancehall
CD _______________ WARPCD 26
Warp / Nov '94 / Prime / RTM/Disc

PINK ME UP (A Sabrettes Compilation) (Various Artists)
Let's go to work: *Innersphere* / Vernal equinox: *Innersphere* / Altitude: *Voodoo People* / Spike it: *Sapiano* / Bunny new guinea pig: *Rabettes* / Through the floor: *Cause* / Quadrafunk: *Pyrex Detox* / Blacknuss: *Inky Blacknuss* / Guitarambience: *Pyrex Detox*
CD _______________ SBR 001CD
Sabres Of Paradise / Aug '94 / Vital

SABRESONIC VOL.2
CD _______________ WARPCD 34
Warp / Jul '95 / Prime / RTM/Disc

Sabri Brothers

GREATEST HITS
CD _______________ SH 64090
Shanachie / Jun '97 / ADA / Greensleeves / Koch

YA MUSTAPHA
Khwaja ka diwana / Tajdar-e-haram / Ya mustapha / La Ilaha Il-Allah
CD _______________ XENO 4041CD
Xenophile / Nov '96 / ADA / Direct

YAH HABIB
Saqia aur pila / Ya sahib ul jamal / Allah hi allah tan mein tar / Kal kamaliya wale
CD _______________ CDRW 12
Realworld / '89 / EMI

Sabri, Sarwar

MASTER DRUMMER OF INDIA
CD _______________ EUCD 1138
ARC / '91 / ADA / ARC Music

Sabrina

BOYS
Like a yo-yo / All of me / Doctor's orders / Boys (summertime love) / Funky girl / My Chico / Pirate of love / Sexy girl / Guys and dolls / Sex
CD _______________ QED 131
Tring / Nov '96 / Tring

BOYS
Like a yo yo / All of me / Doctor's orders / Funky girl / My Chico / Pirate of love / Sexy girl / Guys and dolls / Sex
CD _______________ 100052
CMC / May '97 / BMG

Sabu

HEARTBREAK
CD _______________ HMAXD 36
Heavy Metal / May '89 / Revolver / Sony

Sabu, Paul

IN DREAMS
CD _______________ NTHEN 18
Now & Then / Apr '95 / Plastic Head

Sacasas, Anselmo

ANSELMO SACASAS ORCHESTRA VOL.3 1942-1944
CD _______________ HQCD 77
Harlequin / Jan '97 / Hot Shot / Jazz Music / Swift / Wellard

SOL TROPICAL 1945-1949
CD _______________ TCD 079
Tumbao Cuban Classics / Jul '96 / Discovery

Saccharine Trust

PAST LIVES
CD _______________ SST 149CD
SST / May '93 / Plastic Head

Sachdev, G.S

LIVE IN CONCERT AT HAYWARD CA
CD _______________ LYRCD 7422
Lyrichord / Dec '94 / ADA / CM / Roots

SOLO BANSURI
CD _______________ LYRCD 7405
Lyrichord / '91 / ADA / CM / Roots

Sachse, Joe

SOLO - EUROPEAN HOUSE
CD _______________ FMPCD 41
FMP / Aug '87 / Cadillac

Sack

YOU ARE WHAT YOU EAT
CD _______________ LEMON 014CD
Lemon / Aug '94 / Pinnacle / Vital

Sackville

LOW EBB
CD _______________ CARTCD 2
Car Tunes / Dec '96 / Cargo

Sackville All Stars

CHRISTMAS RECORD
Santa Claus is coming to town / We three kings / At the Christmas ball / Winter wonderland / Go tell it on the mountain / Good King Wenceslas / Santa Claus came in the spring / Silent night / Let it snow, let it snow, let it snow / Old time religion
CD _______________ SKCD 23038
Sackville / Jun '93 / Cadillac / Jazz Music / Swift

SATURDAY NIGHT FUNCTION
John Hardy's wife / Trouble in mind / Jive at five / Russian lullaby / Good Queen Bess / Arkansas blues / Saturday night function / Rosalie
CD _______________ SKCD 23028
Sackville / Jun '93 / Cadillac / Jazz Music / Swift

TRIBUTE TO LOUIS ARMSTRONG, A
Song of the Islands / (I'll be glad when you're dead) you rascal you / Save it pretty Mama / On the sunny side of the street / Willie the weeper / I gotta right to sing the blues / Kiss to build a dream on / Big butter and eggman / Pennies from heaven / Keepin' out of mischief now / Sweethearts on parade
CD _______________ SKCD 23042
Sackville / Feb '89 / Cadillac / Jazz Music / Swift

Sacramento, Marcos

MODERNIDADE DA TRADICAO, A
CD _______________ 829202
BUDA / Mar '96 / Discovery

Sacramentum

FAR AWAY FROM THE SUN
CD _______________ CDAR 034
Fatwreck Chords / Dec '96 / Plastic Head

FINIS MALORUM
CD _______________ CDAR 023
Adipocre / Mar '95 / Plastic Head

Sacred Denial

SIFTING THROUGH THE WRECKAGE
Sifting through the wreckage / When I sleep / Brothers inventions / Some curiosity / Conquer / No way / Take a look around / Violent affection
CD _______________ 082955
Nuclear Blast / '90 / Plastic Head

Sacred Hearts

BROKEN DREAMS
CD _______________ TWISTBIG 3CD
Twist / Mar '94 / SRD

Sacred Mushroom

SACRED MUSHROOM, THE
CD _______________ EVA 852125B30
EVA / Nov '94 / ADA / Direct

Sacred Reich

AMERICAN WAY, THE
Love ..... hate / Crimes against humanity / I don't know / State of emergency / American way / Way it is / Flavors
CD _______________ RR 93925
Roadrunner / Jun '91 / PolyGram

HEAL
CD _______________ 398414106CD
Metal Blade / Feb '96 / Pinnacle / Plastic Head

IGNORANCE
Death squad / Victim of demise / Layed to rest / Ignorance / No believers / Violent solutions / Rest in peace / Sacred Reich / Administrative decisions
CD _______________ 398417008CD
Metal Blade / Mar '96 / Pinnacle / Plastic Head

SURF NICARAGUA
CD _______________ 398417009CD
Metal Blade / Mar '96 / Pinnacle / Plastic Head

Sacred Spirit

SACRED SPIRIT VOL.1 (Chants & Dances Of The Native Americans)
How the West was lost / Winter ceremony / Counterclockwise circle dance / Celebrate wild rice / Cradlesong / Advice for the young / Wishes of happiness and prosperity / Elevation / Intertribal song to stop the rain / Heal the soul / Brandishing the tomahawk
CD _______________ CDVX 2753
Virgin / Oct '95 / EMI

SACRED SPIRIT VOL.2 (Culture Clash)
Intro / Culture clash / Lay down / On the road / Legends / No more cotton / Interlude (to be a slave) / Sun won't talk no more / Black progress / Roots / Babes in the juke house / Brownsville, Tennesse / Interlude (to be a slave part 2) / Slow and easy / Sonnet xviii
CD _______________ CDV 2827
Virgin / Apr '97 / EMI

Sacrifice

APOCALYPSE INSIDE
My eyes see red / Apocalypse inside / Flesh / Salvation / Beneath what you see / Incarcerated / Ruins of the old / Lose / Freedom Slave
CD _______________ CDZORRO 62
Metal Blade / Jul '93 / Pinnacle / Plastic Head

Sacrilege

BEYOND THE REALMS OF MADNESS
Lifeline / At death's door / Sacred / Out of sight out of mind
CD _______________ CORECD 8
Metalcore / Nov '91 / Plastic Head

LOST IN THE BEAUTY YOU SLAY
CD _______________ BS 009CD
Burning Sun / Nov '96 / Plastic Head

TURN BACK TRILOBITE
CD _______________ CDFLAG 29
Under One Flag / Jan '89 / Pinnacle

Sacrosanct

TRAGIC INTENSE
CD _______________ 1MF 37700322
Invisible / Jul '93 / Plastic Head

Sad Cafe

EVERYDAY HURTS (The Best Of Sad Cafe)
Everyday hurts / Strange little girl / Hungry eyes / Black rose / Sail on / I'm in love again / La di da / My oh my / Nothing left Toulouse / I believe (love will survive) / Angel / Let love speak for itself / Losing you / Dreaming / Take me to the future / Crazy osyter
CD _______________ 74321500252
Camden / Jun '97 / BMG

Sad Lovers & Giants

E MAIL FROM ETERNITY
CD _______________ CDMGRAM 104
Cherry Red / Mar '96 / Pinnacle

Sad Whisperings

SENSITIVE TO AUTUMN
CD _______________ FDN 2007CD
Foundation 2000 / Dec '93 / Plastic Head

Sadana

MUSIC FROM CATALONIA
CD _______________ SYNCD 147
Topic / May '93 / ADA / CM / Direct

Sadat X

WILD COWBOYS
Lump lump / Wild cowboys / Sauce for birdheads / Open bar / Hang 'em high / Do it again / Game's sober / Smoking on the low / Pretty people / Interview / Stages and lights / Move on / Funkiest / Escape from New York / Hashout
CD _______________ 7863669222
RCA / Aug '96 / BMG

Saddar Bazaar

CONFERENCE OF THE BIRDS, THE
Sukoon / Arc of ascent (part 1) / Kiff riff / Garden of essence / Sukoon (reflection) / Shamsa (sunburst) / Baraka / Arc of ascent (part 2) / Freedom rider / Neelum blue
CD _______________ DELECCD 034
Delerium / Jul '97 / Cargo / Pinnacle / Vital

Sade

BEST OF SADE, THE
Your love is king / Hang on to your love / Smooth operator / Jezebel / Sweetest taboo / Is it a crime / Never as good as the first time / Love is stronger than pride / Paradise / Nothing can come between us / No ordinary love / Like a taboo / Kiss of life / Please send me someone to love / Cherish the day / Pearls
CD _______________ 4777932
Epic / Oct '94 / Sony

DIAMOND LIFE
Smooth operator / Your love is king / Hang on to your love / When am I gonna make a living / Frankie's first affair / Cherry pie / Sally / I will be your friend / Why can't we live together
CD _______________ 4811782
Epic / Oct '95 / Sony

LOVE DELUXE
No ordinary love / Feel no pain / I couldn't love you more / Like a tattoo / Kiss of life /

Cherish the day / Pearls / Bullet proof soul / Mermaid
CD 4726262
Epic / Oct '92 / Sony

PROMISE
Is it a crime / Sweetest taboo / War of the hearts / Jezebel / Mr. Wrong / Never as good as the first time / Fear / Tar baby / Maureen / You're not the man / Punch drunk
CD 4655752
Epic / Mar '90 / Sony

STRONGER THAN PRIDE
Love is stronger than pride / Paradise / Nothing can come between us / Haunt me / Turn my back on you / Keep looking / Clean heart / Give it up / I never thought I'd see the day / Siempre hay esperanza
CD 4604972
Epic / May '88 / Sony

Sadist

ABOVE THE LIGHT
CD NOSF 001CD
Nosferatu / Jun '95 / Plastic Head

Sadistik Exekution

WE ARE DEATH FUCK YOU
CD CD 022
Osmose / Oct '94 / Plastic Head

Sadness

DANTEFERNO
CD GOD 020CD
Godhead / Mar '96 / Plastic Head

Sadolikar, Shruti

RAGA MIYAN KI TODI/RAGA BIBHAS
CD NI 5346
Nimbus / Sep '94 / Nimbus

Saetas

SONGS FROM ANDALUZA
CD B 6785
Auvidis/Ethnic / Oct '94 / ADA / Harmonia Mundi

Saffire

BROADCASTING
CD ALCD 4811
Alligator / May '93 / ADA / CM / Direct

CLEANING HOUSE
CD ALCD 4840
Alligator / May '96 / ADA / CM / Direct

HOT FLASH (Saffire The Uppity Blues Woman)
Two in the bush is better than one in the hand / Sloppy drunk / One good man / Dirty sheets / Tom cat blues / Learn to settle for less / You'll never get me out of your mind / (Mr Insurance man) take out that thing / Hopin' it'll be alright / Little bit of your loving goes a very long way / Shopping for love / Elevator man / Torch song / Torch song (part 2) / Why don't you do right / Prove me wrong / (No need) Pissin' on a skunk
CD ALCD 4796
Alligator / May '93 / ADA / CM / Direct

OLD, BORROWED AND BLUE (The Uppity Blue Woman)
CD ALCD 4826
Alligator / Dec '94 / ADA / CM / Direct

UPPITY BLUES WOMAN, THE
CD ALCD 4780
Alligator / May '93 / ADA / CM / Direct

Saft, James

RAGGED JACK (Saft, James & Cuong Vu)
CD AVANT 68
Avant / May '97 / Cadillac / Harmonia Mundi

Saga

PLEASURE AND THE PAIN
CD BNA 0016
Bonaire / Jun '97 / Greyhound

Sage, Carson

FINAL KITCHEN BLOWOUT (Sage, Carson & The Black Riders)
CD EFA 11393D
Musical Tragedies / Jul '93 / SRD

Sage, Greg

14 SONGS FOR GREG SAGE & THE WIPERS (Various Artists)
CD TK 91CD010
T/K / May '94 / Pinnacle

SACRIFICE (FOR LOVE)
CD LS 92372
Roadrunner / Nov '91 / PolyGram

Sagittarius

PRESENT TENSE
CD SC 11053
Sundazed / Jun '97 / Cargo / Greyhound / Rollercoaster

SANITY OF MADNESS
CD VOW 049CD
Voices Of Wonder / Jul '95 / Plastic Head

Sagoo, Bally

BOLLYWOOD FLASHBACK
Chura liya / Yeh sama hai pyar ka / O saathi / Quarbani quarbani / Mehbooba mehbobba / Roop tera mastana / jab hum jawan honge / Waada na tod / Choli ke peeche
CD 4776972
Columbia / Sep '94 / Sony

RISING FROM THE EAST
Tum bin jiya / Ban mein aati thi / Nach malanga / Dil cheez / Tere nain / Jitna humne aaja ve maahi / Teri akhiyan / Laila / Milna julna / Dil cheez (remix)
CD 4850162
Columbia / Oct '96 / Sony

Sahm, Doug

BEST OF THE ATLANTIC SESSIONS, THE
CD RSACD 813
Sequel / Oct '94 / BMG

TEXAS TORNADO (The Best Of Doug Sahm)
CD 8122710322
WEA / Jul '93 / Warner Music

Sahraoui, Cheb

N'SEL FIK (Sahraoui, Cheb & Chaba Fadela)
N'sel fik / La verite / Hala la la / Rah galbi mrid / Ya eli nsitini / N'sel fik (Nouvelle version) / Ma andi zhar maak / Ana melit / Loukene ma nebghih / Mazal naachak
CD COOKCD 057
Cooking Vinyl / Oct '93 / Vital

Saigon Kick

LIZARD, THE
Cruelty / Hostile youth / Feel the same way / Freedom / God of 42nd Street / My dog / Peppermint tribe / Love is on the way / Lizard / All alright / Sleep / All I want / Body bags / Miss Jones / World goes round / Chanel
CD 7567921582
Atlantic / Jan '92 / Warner Music

WATER
One step closer / Space oddity / Water / Torture / Fields of rape / I love you / Sgt. Steve / My heart / On and on / Way / Sentimental girl / Close to you / Whne you were mine / Reprise
CD 7567923002
Atlantic / Jun '94 / Warner Music

Saih Pitu, Gamelan

HEAVENLY ORCHESTRA OF BALI, THE
CD CMP CD 3008
CMP / Jul '92 / Cargo / Grapevine/ PolyGram / Vital/SAM

Sailor

SAILOR
CD HM 019
Harmony / Jun '97 / TKO Magnum

Sain, Oliver

PARTY HEARTY (The Best Of Oliver Sain)
Booty bumpin' (double bump) / Soul serenade / Strollin' / 20-75 / Mr. King and Mr. Jordan / St. Louis breakdown / Comin' down soul / On the hill / Baby scratch my back / London express / Country funk / Night time / Harlem nocturne / Bus stop / Prayer / Just a lonely man / Going back to Memphis / Feel like dancin' / Apricot splash / Hey butterfly
CD CDSEWD 110
Southbound / Aug '96 / Pinnacle

Saindon, Ed

ON THE SUNNYSIDE
On the sunnyside of the street / Oh, lady be good / Love is here to stay / I can't give you anything but love / Ain't misbehavin / Back home in Indiana / Memories of you / Moonglow / Rosetta / When you wish upon a star / Limehouse blues / I found a new baby / It could happen to you / You brought a new kind of love to me / Sweet Lorraine / Sweet Georgia Brown
CD AL 73068
Challenge / Mar '97 / ADA / Direct / Jazz Music / Wellard

Sainkho

OUT OF TUVA
CD CRAW 6
Crammed World / Jan '96 / New Note/ Pinnacle

Saint & Campbell

TIME ON THE MOVE
CD COPCD 2
Copasetic / Feb '95 / BMG / Grapevine/ PolyGram / Jet Star / Pinnacle

Saint Preux

LA TERRA MONDO
CD WOLCD 1066
China / Jan '96 / Pinnacle

Saint Vitus

DIE HEALING
CD H 00352
Hellhound / Jan '95 / Koch

Saint-Paul, Lara

MAMMA
CD PCOM 1141
President / Nov '95 / Grapevine/PolyGram / President / Target/BMG

Saintcatee

MUSIC FOR
CD MASSCD 086
Massacre / Feb '96 / Plastic Head

Sainte-Marie, Buffy

COINCIDENCE (AND LIKELY STORIES)
Big ones get away / Fallen angels / Bad end / Emma Lee / Starwalker / Priests of the Golden Bull / Disinformation / Getting started / I'm going home / Bury my heart at Wounded Knee / Goodnight
CD CCD 1920
Ensign / Mar '92 / EMI

I'M GONNA BE A COUNTRY GIRL AGAIN
CD VMD 79280
Vanguard / Oct '96 / ADA / Pinnacle

QUIET PLACES
CD VMD 79330
Vanguard / Oct '96 / ADA / Pinnacle

SHE USED TO WANNA BE A BALLERINA
Rollin' mill man / Smack water jack / Sweet September morning / She used to wanna be a ballerina / Bells / Helpless / Moratorium / Surfer / Song of the French partisan / Soldier blue / Now you've been gone for a long time
CD VMD 79311
Vanguard / Oct '95 / ADA / Pinnacle

UP WHERE WE BELONG
Darling don't cry / Up where we belong / Piney Wood Hills / Cripple Creek / God is alive / Until it's time for you to go / Universal soldier / Goodnight / Dance me around / He's an Indian cowboy in the rodeo / Now that the buffalo's gone / Soldier blue / Eagle man/changing woman / Bury my heart at Wounded Knee / Starwalker
CD CDEMC 3745
Premier/EMI / Mar '96 / EMI

Saints

ETERNALLY YOURS
CD 422309
New Rose / May '94 / ADA / Direct / Discovery

HOWLING
Howling / Shadows / Something, somewhere, sometime / Something wicked / Only stone / Good Friday / Blown away / Last and laughing mile / You know I know / Only dreaming / Second coming / All for nothing
CD BLUCD 029
Blue Rose / Oct '96 / Direct

KNOW YOUR PRODUCT (The Best Of The Saints)
I'm stranded / (This) perfect day / Lipstick on your collar / River deep mountain high / Demolition girl / One way street / Story of love / Kissin' cousins / No time / Wild about you / Messin' with the kid / Nights in Venice / Do the robot / Know your product / Run down / Lost and found / Memories are made of this / Private affair / Minor aversion / No, your product / Swing for the crime / All times through paradise
CD CDGO 2069
EMI Gold / Oct '96 / EMI

PREHISTORIC SOUNDS
CD 422312
New Rose / May '94 / ADA / Direct / Discovery

Saisse, Philippe

NEXT VOYAGE
CD 5374162
Verve/Forecast / Aug '97 / PolyGram

Sakamoto, Ryuichi

1996
Day a gorilla gives a banana / Rain / Bibo no aozora / Last Emperor / 1919 / Merry Christmas Mr. Lawrence / May in the backyard / Sheltering sky / Tribute to NJP / High heels / Anoeko no torso / Wuthering heights / Parolibre / Acceptance / Little Buddha / Before long / Bring them home
CD 74321372422
Milan / Jun '96 / Conifer/BMG / Silva Screen

B-2 UNIT
CD SPALAX 14500
Spalax / Oct '96 / ADA / Cargo / Direct / Discovery / Greyhound

BEAUTY
You do me / Calling from Tokyo / Rose / Asadoya yunta / Futique / Amore / We love you / Diabaram / Pile of time / Romance / Chinsagu no hana
CD CDVUS 14
Virgin / Aug '91 / EMI

HEARTBEAT
Heartbeat / Rap the world / Triste / Lulu / High tide / Song lines / Nuages / Sayonara / Borom gal / Epilogue / Heartbeat (Tainai Kaiki) / Returning to the womb / Cloud
CD CDVUS 46
Virgin / Jun '92 / EMI

MUSICAL ENCYCLOPEDIA
Field work / Etude / Paradise lost / MAY in the backyard / Steppin' into Asia / Tibetan dance / Zen-gun / In a forest of feathers
CD DIXCD 34
10 / Jul '87 / EMI

SMOOCHY
CD 74321440072
Milan / Feb '97 / Conifer/BMG / Silva Screen

Sakhile

AFRICAN ECHOES
Maluti / Mshandira phamwe / Crossroads / Song for bra zakes / Phambili / Mantenga falls / Same time next year / Tears of joy
CD KAZ CD 17
Kaz / Oct '91 / BMG

Salad

ICECREAM
UV / Written by a man / Yeah yeah / Broken bird / Wanna be free / Size more woman than her / Cardboy King / Namedrops / Foreign cow / Terrible day / Wolves over Washington / Sky's our terminal
CD CID 8056
Island / May '97 / PolyGram

Salah, Sadaoui

ANTHOLOGY OF ARAB MUSIC VOL.1
CD AAA 106
Club Du Disque Arabe / Sep '95 / ADA / Harmonia Mundi

Salaryman

SALARYMAN
Rather / Inca picnic / Voids and superclusters / New centurions / Burning at the stake / I need a monkey / Hummous
CD EFA 049962
City Slang / Jul '97 / RTM/Disc

Salas Humara, Walter

LEAN
CD RTS 9
Normal / Jul '94 / ADA / Direct

Salas, Patricia

CHRISTMAS IN LATIN AMERICA
CD EUCD 1088
ARC / '91 / ADA / ARC Music

Salas, Steve

BACK FROM THE LIVING (Salas, Steve Colourcode)
CD USG 120072
USG / Apr '97 / Cargo

ELECTRIC POW WOW
CD Q 2572
Aquarius / Jul '97 / Greyhound

Salem

KADDISH
CD MRO 15CD
Morbid Sounds / Apr '95 / Plastic Head

Salem, Kevin

GLIMMER
CD RR 88772
Roadrunner / Sep '96 / PolyGram

SOMA CITY
CD RR 89792
Roadrunner / Oct '95 / PolyGram

Salgan, Horacio

MANO BRAVA (Salgan, Horacio & Ubaldo De Lio)
CD 74321453322
Milan Sur / Feb '97 / Conifer/BMG

TANGO VOL.1
CD MAN 4830
Mandala / May '94 / ADA / Harmonia Mundi / Mandala

Salim, Abdel Gadir

NUJUM AL-LAIL - STARS OF THE NIGHT
Gidraishinna / Al-lemoni / Nujum al-lail / Nitlaga nitlaga / Jeenaki / A'abir sikkah
CD CDORB 039
Globestyle / May '89 / Pinnacle

Salinas, Louis

SALINAS
La salsalinas / Santa Cruz / Funky tango / Rain (Lluvia) / Mob (la pesada) / Back to the place I love (salsa para volvar) / Mood (un clima) / Still (todavia) / For Ivan (para Ivan) / Cha cha rock / Count on me (cuenta conmigo) / Blue zamba (zamba triste) / Spike
CD GRP 98572
GRP / Feb '97 / New Note/BMG

Salisbury Cathedral Choir

HOW LOVELY ARE THY DWELLINGS
CD CDE 84288
Meridian / Aug '94 / Nimbus

Salma & Sabina

EK BAAR MILO HUMSE
CD IMUT 1023
Multitone / Mar '96 / BMG

Salmon, Kim

ESSENCE (Salmon, Kim & The Surrealists)
CD REDCD 21
Normal / May '94 / ADA / Direct

HELL IS WHERE MY HEART LIVES
CD REDCD 34
Red Eye / Jun '94 / Direct

HEY BELIEVER
CD GRCD 349
Glitterhouse / Nov '94 / Avid/BMG

HIT ME WITH THE SURREAL FEEL (Salmon, Kim & The Surrealists)
CD ITR 33CD
In The Red / Dec '96 / Cargo / Greyhound

JUST BECAUSE YOU CAN'T SEE IT (Salmon, Kim & The Surrealists)
CD BLACKCD 9
Black Eye / May '94 / Direct

KIM SALMON & THE SURREALISTS (Salmon, Kim & The Surrealists)
CD GRCD 381
Glitterhouse / Nov '95 / Avid/BMG

SIN FACTORY (Salmon, Kim & The Surrealists)
CD REDCD 33
Red Eye / Mar '94 / Direct

Salsa Blanca

MANUELA
CD TUMICD 035
Tumi / '93 / Discovery / Stern's

Salsa Celtica

MONSTRUOS Y DEMONIUS ANGELS AND LOVERS
Salsa celtica / La reina rumbera / Guajira del sol / Osain / Paisa / No hay olvido, pablito / La batea / Koukou / Frente a frente / El cometa bop / Escorpion / Loco y loco / Kulu
CD ECLCD 9717
Eclectic / Aug '97 / ADA / New Note/ Pinnacle

Salsoul Orchestra

NICE 'N' NAASTY
It's good for the soul / Nice 'n' naasty / It don't have to be funky (To be a groove) / Nightcrawler / Don't beat around the bush / Standing and waiting on love / Salsoul 3001 / We've only just begun/Feelings / Ritzy mambo / Jack and Jill
CD CPCD 8077
Charly / Mar '95 / Koch

SALSOUL ORCHESTRA, THE
CD CPCD 8059
Charly / Nov '94 / Koch

STREET SENSE
Zambesi / Burning spear / Somebody to love / Street sense / 212 North 12th / Sun after the rain
CD CPCD 8098
Charly / Apr '95 / Koch

Salt

AUSCULATE
Impro / Honour me / Beauty / God damn carneval / Obsession / Bluster / Lids / So / Witty / So I ached / Flutter / Sense / Undressed
CD CID 8045
Island / Mar '96 / PolyGram

Salt n' Pepa

BLACK'S MAGIC
Expression / Doper than dope / Negro wit' an ego / You showed me / Do you want me / Swift / I like to party / Black's magic / Start the party / Let's talk about sex / I don't know / Live and let die / Independent / Expression (Brixton bass mix)
CD 8281642
FFRR / Nov '91 / PolyGram

BLITZ OF SALT 'N' PEPA HITS, A (Remix)
Push it / Expression / Independent / Shake your thang (It's your thing) / Twist and shout / Let's talk about sex / Tramp / Do you want me / My mic sounds nice / I'll take your man / I gotcha / You showed me
CD 8282692
FFRR / Oct '91 / PolyGram

GREATEST HITS
Push it / Expression / Independent / Shake your thang (it's your thing) / Twist and shout / Let's talk about sex / I like it like that / Tramp / Do you want me / My mic sounds nice / I'll take your man / I gotcha / I am down / You showed me
CD 8282912
FFRR / Oct '91 / PolyGram

HOT COOL VICIOUS
Beauty and the beat / Tramp / I'll take your man / It's alright / Chick on the side / I desire / Showstopper / My mic sounds nice
CD 8282962
FFRR / Nov '91 / PolyGram

SALT WITH A DEADLY PEPA, A
Intro jam / Salt with a deadly pepa / I like it like that / Solo power / Shake your thang (it's your thing) / I gotcha / Let the rhythm run / Everybody get up / Spinderella's not a fella / Solo power (Syncopated soul) / Twist and shout / Hyped on the mic / Push it
CD 5500412
Spectrum / May '93 / PolyGram

VERY NECESSARY
Groove me / No one does it better / Somebody's gettin' on my nerves / Whatta man: *Salt n' Pepa & En Vogue* / None of your business / Step / Shoop / Heaven or hell / Big shot / Sexy noises turn me on / Somma time man / Break of dawn / PSA we talk / Shoop (radio mix) / Start me up
CD 8283772
FFRR / Oct '93 / PolyGram

Salt Tank

SCIENCE AND NATURE
Into the light of the shining path / Olympic 638 / Eugina (pacific diva) / Taj / Gaza strip / Isabella's dream / TT / Swell (Eden) / Final charge (D up) / Free lunch
CD TRUCD 11
Internal / May '96 / Pinnacle / PolyGram

WAVE BREAKS
Diamond halo / Da blues / Wave intruder / Cjax / Ritual / Badlands / Angels landing / Afterhours
CD 8289182
FFRR / Sep '97 / PolyGram

Salty Dogs Jazzband

LONG, DEEP & WIDE
CD BCD 237
GHB / Jan '93 / Jazz Music

Saluzzi, Dino

CITE DE LA MUSIQUE
Cite de la musique / Introduccion y Milonga del ausente / El Rio y el abuelo / Zurdo / Romance / Winter / How NY heart sings / Gorrion / Coral para mi pequeno y legano pueblo
CD 5333162
ECM / Mar '97 / New Note/Pinnacle

KULTRUM
Kultrum pampa / Gabriel kondor / Agua de paz / Pajaros Y ceibos / Ritmo arauca / El rio Y el abuelo / Pasos que quedan / Por el sol Y por la lluvia
CD 8214072
ECM / May '92 / New Note/Pinnacle

MOJOTORO (Saluzzi, Dino Group)
Mojotoro / Tango a mi padre / Mundos / Lustrin / Viernes santo / Milonga (la punalada) / El camino
CD 5119522
ECM / May '92 / New Note/Pinnacle

ONCE UPON A TIME - FAR AWAY IN THE SOUTH
Jose, Valeria and Matias / And the Father said... / Revelation / Silence / And he loved his brother, till the end / Far away in the south... / We are the children
CD 8277682
ECM / Apr '86 / New Note/Pinnacle

RIOS
Los them / Minguito / Fulano de tal / Sketch / He loved his brother 'til the end / Penta y uno / JAD / Lunch with pancho villa / My one and only love / Rios
CD VBR 21562
Intuition / Nov '95 / New Note/Pinnacle

SOLO BANDONEON (Saluzzi, Dino & Andina)
CD 8371862
ECM / Feb '89 / New Note/Pinnacle

Salvagnini, Massimo

VERY FOOL
Very fool / Bleeding shreds / Dream dram drum / Sigmund was here / Alcoholic baby / Sharps / Star guys / My favourite disease / Meat bubbles / Stupid question / Heretic ostrich / Twelve for two / Algoritmo / Old news / 'Tis autumn
CD CDSGP 095
Prestige / Jul '95 / Else / Total/BMG

Salvation Army Band/Choir

O COME ALL YE FAITHFUL
CD 74321435262
RCA / Oct '96 / BMG

ONWARD CHRISTIAN SOLDIERS
Onward christian soldiers / Fight the good fight / Love divine / What a friend we have in Jesus / O Worship the king / Rock of ages / He who would valiant be / When I survey the wonderous cross / How great thou art / Old rugged cross / Praise my soul / Lord's my shepherd / Abide with me / There is a green hill far away / Eternal Father strong to save / All things bright and beautiful / How sweet the name of Jesus sounds / Guide me, o thou great Jehovah / King of love / Goldcrest
CD 306932
Hallmark / May '97 / Carlton

Salvatore, Sergio

ALWAYS A BEGINNING
Always and beginning / Revolving door / What is this thing called love / Moon river / Darn that dream / Lullaby in time / Pink panther theme / Waltz / Isn't it romantic / After all / Note to Henry
CD CCD 4704
Concord Jazz / Jun '96 / New Note/ Pinnacle

Sam & Dave

GREATEST HITS
CD MU 5034
Musketeer / Feb '95 / Disc

HOLD ON I'M COMING
Hold on I'm comin' / If you got the loving / I take what I want / Ease me / I got everything I need / Don't make it so hard on me / It's a wonder / Don't help me out / Just me / You got it made / You don't know like I know / Blame me (don't blame my heart)
CD 7567802552
Atlantic / Jul '91 / Warner Music

I THANK YOU
I thank you / Everybody got to believe in somebody / These arms of mine / Wrap it up / If I didn't have a girl like you / You don't know what you mean to me / Don't turn your heater on / Talk to the man / Love is after me / Ain't that a lot of love / Don't waste that love / That lucky old sun
CD 8122710122
Atlantic / Mar '93 / Warner Music

LEGENDS IN MUSIC
CD LECD 063
Wisepack / Jul '94 / Conifer/BMG / THE

SAM & DAVE
It feels so nice / I got a thing going on / My love belongs to you / Listening for my name / No more pain / I found out / It was so nice while it lasted / You ain't no big thing baby / I need love / She's alright / Keep a walkin' / If she'll still have me / Garden of Earth / Azethoth / Queen Street gang / Clean innocent fun / Metempsychosis
CD EDCD 388
Edsel / Jun '94 / Pinnacle

SOUL MAN (The Best Of Sam & Dave)
You don't know like I know / Hold on I'm comin' / Said I wasn't gonna tell nobody / You got me hummin' / When something is wrong with my baby / Soul man / I thank you / Soul sister, brown sugar / Don't pull your love out / Can't you find another way / You don't know what you mean to me
CD AIM 2003CD
Aim / May '97 / ADA / Direct / Jazz Music

SOUL MEN
Soul man / May I baby / Broke down piece of man / Let it be me / Hold it baby / I'm with you / Don't knock it / Just keep holding on / Good runs the bad way / Rich kind of poverty / I've seen what loneliness can do
CD 8122702962
Atlantic / Jul '93 / Warner Music

SWEAT AND SOUL (The Anthology 1965-1971)
Place nobody can find / Goodnight baby / I take what I want / You don't know like I know / Hold on I'm comin' / I got everything I need / Don't make it so hard on me / Blame me (Don't blame my heart) / You got me hummin' / When something is wrong with my baby / Small portion of your love / I don't need nobody (to tell me bout my baby) / That's the way it's gotta be / Said I wasn't gonna tell nobody / Soothe me / I can't stand up for falling down / Toe hold / Soul man / May I baby / Just keep holding on / Good runs the bad way / Rich kind of poverty / I've seen what loneliness can do / My reason for living / I thank you / Wrap it up / Broke down piece of man / Shop around / Stop / Starting over again / Jody Ryder got killed / Don't pull your love / Knock it out the park / Standing in the safety zone / Baby baby don't stop now / One part love, two part pain / I'm not an indian giver / Holdin' on / You left the water running / Born again / Soul sister brown sugar / Don't turn your heater on / Ain't that a lot of love / Can't you find another way of doing it / Everybody got to believe in somebody / You don't know what you mean to me / This is your world / Come on in / Hold it baby
CD Set 8122712532
Atlantic / Dec '93 / Warner Music

SWEET SOUL MUSIC
CD 15076
Laserlight / Aug '91 / Target/BMG

SWEET SOUL MUSIC
Soul man / Hold on I'm comin' / Soul sister, brown sugar / Love the one you're with / Funky street / Mustang sally / Land of 1000 dances / How sweet it is (to be loved by you) / Respect / I thank you / Sweet soul music / I'll be doggone / Funky broadway / 634-5789 / Good lovin' / Satisfaction
CD ECD 3212
K-Tel / Mar '95 / K-Tel

TWO GREAT SOUL MEN
CD HADCD 208
Javelin / Jul '96 / Henry Hadaway / THE

Sam & Valley

MY FAVOURITE CLINIC
CD CAT 048CD
Rephlex / Jun '97 / Prime / RTM/Disc

Sam Black Church

LET IN LIFE
CD TAANG 77CD
Taang / Dec '93 / Cargo

SAM BLACK CHURCH
CD TAANG 76CD
Taang / Jun '93 / Cargo

Sam-ang Sam Ensemble

ECHOES FROM THE PALACE
CD CDT 140CD
Music Of The World / Apr '96 / ADA / Target/BMG

Samael

BLOOD RITUAL
CD 84 97374
Century Media / Dec '92 / Plastic Head

CEREMONY OF OPPOSITES
CD CM 77064CD
Century Media / Mar '94 / Plastic Head

PASSAGE
CD CM 77127CD
Century Media / Sep '96 / Plastic Head

SAMAEL 1987-1992
CD Set CM 7708522
Century Media / Jan '95 / Plastic Head

Samain

INDOMITUS
CD BLCR 7001CD
Destruktive Kommndoh / Dec '96 / Plastic Head

Samaroo Jets

QUINTESSENCE
Meditation / Tico tico / Everything I do (I do it for you) / Bee's melody / I'll be there / Alma llanera / Portrait of Trinidad / Coming in from the cold / O mere sona / Memory / Unforgettable / Two to go / Heal the world / One moment in time / Pan rising
CD DE 4024
Delos / Jul '94 / Nimbus

Sambalanco Trio

SAMBALANCO TRIO
CD 1501
Rare Brazil / Apr '97 / Cargo

Sambeat, Perico

DUAL FORCE
Body / Luso / Wonderful, wonderful / Lament / Dual force / Ask me now / Plot
CD JHCD 031
Ronnie Scott's Jazz House / Jun '94 / Cadillac / Jazz Music / New Note/Pinnacle / TKO Magnum

Sambora, Richie

STRANGER IN THIS TOWN
Rest in peace / Church of desire / Stranger in this town / Ballad of youth / One light burning / Mr. Bluesman / Rosie / River of love / Father time / Answer
CD 8488952
Phonogram / Sep '91 / PolyGram

Samer Band

MUSIC OF THE ROMANIES
CD 378182
Koch World / Sep '96 / Koch

Samiam

CLUMSY
As we're told / Time by the dime / Cradle / She's a part of me / No size that small / Simca / Routine / Tag along / Bad day / Capsized / Stepson
CD 7567826422
Atlantic / Aug '94 / Warner Music

YOU ARE FREAKING ME OUT
CD BHR 059CD
Burning Heart / Jun '97 / Plastic Head

Samite

SILINA MUSANGO
CD XENO 4047CD
Xenophile / Jun '96 / ADA / Direct

Samla Mammas Manna

MALTID
CD RESCD 505
Resource / Oct '93 / ADA / Direct

Sammes, Mike

IT HAD TO BE YOU
CD AVC 564
Avid / May '96 / Avid/BMG / Koch / THE

Sammy

DEBUT ALBUM
CD FIRECD 40
Fire / Jun '94 / Pinnacle / RTM/Disc

TALES OF GREAT NECK GLORY
CD FIRECD 58
Fire / Jun '96 / Pinnacle / RTM/Disc

Sammy Dread

ROADBLOCK
CD JJCD 068
Channel One / Sep '95 / Jet Star

STRONGER THAN BEFORE
CD RGCD 040
Rocky One / Apr '97 / Jet Star

WRAP UP A DRAW
CD SLCD 14
Seven Leaves / Mar '96 / Greensleeves / Roots Collective / SRD

Sample, Joe

COLLECTION, THE
Carmel / Woman you're driving me mad / Rainy day in Monterey / Sunrise / There are many stops alone the way / Rainbow seeker / Fly with the wings of love / Burning up the carnival / Night flight / Oasis
CD GRP 96582
GRP / Oct '91 / New Note/BMG

DID YOU FEEL THAT
CD 9362457292
East West / Aug '94 / Warner Music

OLD PLACES, OLD FACES
CD 9362461822
East West / Feb '96 / Warner Music

Sampou, Les

FALL FROM GRACE
Holy land / Alibis / Things I should've said / Home again / Ride the line / Flesh and blood / Weather vane / I already know / String of pearls / Fall from grace / Bull's-eye / Two strong arms
CD CDFF 657
Flying Fish / Nov '96 / ADA / CM / Direct / Roots

Sampson, Dave

SWEET DREAMS (The Complete Dave Sampson & The Hunters) (Sampson, Dave & The Hunters)
Sweet dreams / It's lonesome / If you need me / See you around / Why the chicken / 1999 / Goodbye twelve, hello teens / Talking in my sleep / Little girl of mine / Walking to heaven / Easy to dream / That's all / I've got a crush on you / Don't fool around / Why the chicken / Teenage dream / Wide wide world / Sandy Sandy moved away / My blue heaven / Sweet dreams
CD RPM 180
RPM / Jul '97 / Pinnacle

Sampson, Don Michael

COPPER MOON
CD APCD 110
Appaloosa / Jan '96 / ADA / Direct / TKO Magnum

CRIMSON WINDS
Cherokee river / Long black train / Six string healing wheel / Old black guitar case / Fighter / Song in the wind
CD R 103 CD
Red Horse / Aug '90 / BMG

Samson

BURNING EMOTION
Burning emotion / Tramp / Tell me / No turning back / Stranger / Don't turn away / Tomorrow / Silver screen / Too late / Don't close your eyes / Can't live without your love / Don't tell me it's over / Room 109 / Good to see you / Fight for your life
CD CDTB 169
Thunderbolt / Apr '95 / TKO Magnum

NINETEEN NINETY-THREE
Hey you / Dream / Back to you / Word
CD CDTB 159
Thunderbolt / Feb '96 / TKO Magnum

REFUGE
Good to see you / Can't live without your love / Turn on the lights / Love this time / Room 109 / Sate of emergency / Don't tell me it's over / Look to the future / Someone to turn to / Too late / Samurai sunset / Silver screen
CD CDTB 163
Thunderbolt / Sep '95 / TKO Magnum

SAMSON
CD CMGCD 008
Communique / Aug '93 / Plastic Head

THANK YOU AND GOODNIGHT
CD CDTB 160
Thunderbolt / Mar '95 / TKO Magnum

Samson, Paul

JOINT FORCES
Burning emotion / No turning back / Russians / Tales of the fury / Reach out to love / Chosen few / Tramp / Power of love / Tell me
CD CDTB 148
Magnum Music / Oct '94 / TKO Magnum

LIVE AT THE MARQUEE
Burning emotion / Stranger / Vice versa / Fighting man / Matter of time / Afraid of the light / Tell me / Turn on the lights / Earth Mother / Tomorrow / Don't turn away
CD CDTB 157
Thunderbolt / Nov '94 / TKO Magnum

Samsonov, Andrei

VOID IN
Void / CoH / Post M / Whispers / White
CD CDPSST 3
Mute / Feb '97 / RTM/Disc

San Francisco Starlight ...

CHEERFUL LITTLE EARFUL (San Francisco Starlight Orchestra)
CD SOSCD 1296
Stomp Off / Sep '96 / Jazz Music / Wellard

DOIN' THE RACOON (San Francisco Starlight Orchestra)
CD SOSCD 1271
Stomp Off / Apr '94 / Jazz Music / Wellard

San Miguel, Tomas

CON TXALAPARTA
CD 15641
Nuevos Medios / Jan '95 / ADA

LEZAO
Aleacion en danza / Una leyenda aurea / Akelarre / Kantico en flor de piedra / Devociones / El bertsolari / Latidos / Txalaparta mistica / El naciemiento de maritxu / Pleyades / Zalkdi dantza / Sintomas
CD ND 63034
Narada / Apr '96 / ADA / New Note/Pinnacle

Sanabria, Bobby

NEW YORK CITY ACHE (Sanabria, Bobby & Ascension)
CD FF 630CD
Flying Fish / Dec '93 / ADA / CM / Direct / Roots

Sanborn, David

BACKSTREET
I told U so / When you smile at me / Believer / Backstreet / Tear for crystal / Bums cathedral / Blue beach / Neither one of us
CD 9239062
WEA / Oct '87 / Warner Music

BEST OF DAVID SANBORN, THE
CD 9362457682
Warner Bros. / Nov '94 / Warner Music

LOVE SONGS
CD 9362460022
Warner Bros. / Nov '95 / Warner Music

PEARLS
CD 7559617592
Warner Bros. / Mar '95 / Warner Music

TAKING OFF
CD 7599272952
Warner Bros. / Oct '94 / Warner Music

UPFRONT
Snakes / Benny / Crossfire / Full house / Soul serenade / Hey / Bang bang / Ramblin'
CD 7559612722
Elektra / May '92 / Warner Music

VOYEUR
Let's just say goodbye / It's you / Wake me when it's over / One in a million / Run for cover / All I need is you / Just for you
CD 256900
Warner Bros. / Dec '81 / Warner Music

Sanchez

BOOM BOOM BYE BYE
CD GRELCD 186
Greensleeves / Jul '93 / Jet Star / SRD

BRING BACK THE LOVE
CD WRCD 001
World / Jun '97 / Jet Star / TKO Magnum

BROWN EYE GIRL
CD VPCD 1392
VP / Aug '95 / Greensleeves / Jet Star / Total/BMG

CAN WE TALK
CD GRELCD 211
Greensleeves / Dec '94 / Jet Star / SRD

FOREVER
CD CRCD 44
Charm / Oct '95 / Jet Star

GOLDEN VOICE OF REGGAE, THE
CD WRCD 018
World / Jun '97 / Jet Star / TKO Magnum

I CAN'T WAIT
CD VYDCD 3
Vine Yard / Sep '95 / Grapevine/PolyGram

MISSING YOU
CD NWSCD 8
New Sound / Mar '94 / Jet Star

NUMBER ONE DUB
CD RE 173CD
ROIR / Jun '97 / Plastic Head / Shellshock/Disc

ONE IN A MILLION
CD VPCD 1483
VP / Jul '97 / Greensleeves / Jet Star / Total/BMG

REGGAE MAX
CD JSRNCD 1
Jet Star / Mar '96 / Jet Star

SANCHEZ & FRIENDS
CD RNCD 2036
Rhino / Jan '94 / Grapevine/PolyGram / Jet Star

SANCHEZ MEETS COCOA T (Sanchez & Cocoa T)
CD SONCD 0051
Sonic Sounds / Jul '93 / Jet Star

SANCHEZ VOL.1
CD PHCD 2008
Penthouse / Aug '94 / Jet Star

SANCHEZ VOL.2
CD PHCD 2011
Penthouse / Aug '94 / Jet Star

SWEETEST GIRL, THE
CD RRTGCD 7708
Rohit / May '89 / Jet Star

Sanchez, David

DEPARTURE, THE
Ebony / Woody 'n' you / Interlude 1 / You got it diz / Santander / I'll be around / Departure / Nina's mood / Cara De Payaso / Interlude 2 / CJ / Postlude
CD 4765072
Columbia / Jul '94 / Sony

SKETCHES OF DREAMS
Africa Y Las Americas / Bomba blues / Falling in love / Extensions / Tu y mi cancion / Mal social / Sketches of dreams / Easy to remember / Little Melanie
CD 4803252
Sony Jazz / May '95 / Sony

STREET SCENES
Caras negras / Street scenes / Urban frequency / Dee like the breeze / Los cronopios / Four in one / Carmina / Soul of el barrio / Street scenes downtown / Elements
CD 4851372
Sony Jazz / Sep '96 / Sony

Sanchez, Poncho

BAILA MI GENTE - SALSA
Yumbambe / El conguero / Cuidate compai / Mama guela / Baila mi gente / Son son charari / Dichoso / Con migo / Sonando / Co co my my / Soul sauce (guachi guara) / Ven morena
CD CCD 4710
Concord Jazz / May '96 / New Note/ Pinnacle

BIEN SABROSO
Ahora / Bien sabroso / Nancy / Keeper of the flame / Brisa / Sin timbal / Una mas / Half and half / I can
CD CCD 4239
Concord Picante / Jul '88 / New Note/ Pinnacle

CONGA BLUE (A Tribute To Mongo Santamaria)
Black stockings / Besame Mama / Mambo de Cuca / Conga blue / Dulce amor / Manila / Watermelon man / Happy now / Mon pa mon po / Para ti
CD CCD 4726
Concord Picante / Oct '96 / New Note/ Pinnacle

EL CONGUERO
Siempre me va bien / Mi negra / Shiny stockings / Si no hay amor / Yumbambo / Agua dulce / Night walk / Tin tin deo / Cuidado
CD CCD 4286
Concord Picante / Jul '88 / New Note/ Pinnacle

EL MEJOR
Just a few / Son son charari / Suenos / Lip smacker / Angel / Monk / El jamaiquino / Dichoso / Suave cha / Typhoon
CD CCD 4519
Concord Picante / Sep '92 / New Note/ Pinnacle

FUERTE - STRONG
Fuerte / Baila mi gente / It could happen to you / Lo llores, mi corazon / Ixtapa / Co co my my / Siempre te amare / Alafia / Daahoud
CD CCD 4340
Concord Picante / May '88 / New Note/ Pinnacle

LA FAMILIA
CD CCD 4369
Concord Jazz / Feb '89 / New Note/ Pinnacle

NIGHT WITH PONCHO SANCHEZ, A
Siempre me va bien / Bien sabroso / Alafia / Time for love / Sonando / Tito medley / La familia
CD CCD 4558
Concord Picante / Jul '93 / New Note/ Pinnacle

PARA TODOS
Five brothers / Cold duck time / Ugetsu / Angue tu / Cha cha / Happy blues / Lament / Ven morena / Rapture / Meeker's blues / Afro blue
CD CCD 4600
Concord Picante / Jun '94 / New Note/ Pinnacle

SONANDO
Night in Tunisia / Sonando / Summer knows / Con tres tambores bata / Almendra / Sueno / Cals pals / Peruchin / Este san
CD CCD 4201
Concord Picante / Nov '89 / New Note/ Pinnacle

TRIBUTE TO CAL TJADER
Soul sauce / Tripocville / I showed them / Somewhere in the night / Song for Cal / Morning / Tu crees que / Leyte / Song for Pat / Liz-Anne / Poinciana cha cha / Oran
CD CCD 4662
Concord Jazz / Oct '95 / New Note/ Pinnacle

Sanchez, Roger

HARD TIMES (2CD Set)
CD Set NACD 002
Narcotic / Nov '95 / RTM/Disc / Vital

SECRET WEAPONS VOL.1
Spirit lift you up / Boom / Fill me / D-Day / Free your body / There it iz / Never give up / Rejoice / I need you
CD ORCD 013
One / Feb '94 / Vital

UNITED DJ'S OF AMERICA VOL.7/NEW YORK (Various Artists)
Flame: *Fine Young Cannibals* / Stalker: *Green Velvet* / Hindu lover: *D'Jaimin* / Mas groove: *Fisher, Cevin* / Studio 54: *Bones, Frankie* / C-lime woman: *TPM* / Release yo'-self: *Translantic Soul* / Problem child: *DPD* / Revival: *Hilmes, Braxton & Mark Grant* / Love commandments: *Jackson, Gisele* / Stand tall: *Department Of Soul* / Get up: *Stingily, Byron* / Can I get a witness: *Nesby, Ann*
CD UNDJACD 7
Stress / Apr '97 / Mo's Music Machine / Pinnacle / Prime

Sancton, Tommy

LOUISIANA FAIRYTALE (Sancton, Tommy & The Crescent Serenaders)
CD BCD 360
GHB / Nov '96 / Jazz Music

Sand

DYNAMIC CURVE
CD CRECD 089
Creation / May '94 / 3mv/Vital

FIVE GRAINS
CD CRECD 127
Creation / Nov '92 / 3mv/Vital

ULTRASONIC SERAPHIM (2CD Set)
CD Set UDORCD 2/3
United Durtro / Oct '96 / World Serpent

Sandals

CRACKED
Changed / Oscuriosso / Shake the brain / Joy / Arden's bud phase 3 / Cracked / Wake the brain / Open

CD 8285732
Open Toe / Oct '94 / PolyGram

RITE TO SILENCE
Feet / Nothing / No movement / Change / Arden's bud / We wanna live / We don't wanna be the ones to take the blame / Lovewood / Here comes the sign / Profound dub
CD 8284882
London / Apr '94 / PolyGram

Sandberg, Ulf

ULF SANDBERG QUARTET, THE (Sandberg, Ulf Quartet)
Bolivia / Blue reflections / I mean you / Manhattan transfusion / Driftin' / Samba for someone / Like a child / Carlton in and out / Bolivia (alternative version) / Tildess
CD JAZIDCD 074
Acid Jazz / Jun '93 / Disc

Sanders, John Lee

WORLD BLUE
CD HYCD 295155
Hypertension / Jul '95 / ADA / CM / Direct / Total/BMG

Sanders, Lisa

ISN'T LIFE FINE
CD EAR 011
Earth Music / Nov '96 / Cargo

Sanders, Pharoah

AFRICA
You've got to have freedom / Naima / Origin / Speak low / After the morning / Africa
CD CDSJP 253
Timeless Jazz / Feb '91 / New Note/ Pinnacle

AFRICA/MOON CHILD/WELCOME TO LOVE (Pharoah Sanders On Timeless/ 3CD Set)
You've got to have freedom / Naima / Origin / Speak low / After the morning / Africa / Heart to heart / Duo / Moon child / Moon rays / Night has a thousand eyes / All or nothing at all / Soon / Moniebah / You don't know what love is / Nearness of you / My one and only love / I want to talk about you / Soul eyes / Nancy / Polka dots and moonbeams / Sat it (over and over again) / Lament / Bird song
CD Set CDSJP 005
Timeless / Sep '96 / New Note/Pinnacle

BLACK UNITY
CD IMP 12192
Impulse Jazz / Apr '97 / New Note/BMG

ELEVATION
CD MVCZ 121
MCA / Apr '97 / BMG

HEART IS A MELODY
Ole / On a misty night / Heart is a melody of time (Hiroko's song) / Goin' to Africa / Naima / Rise 'n' shine
CD ECD 220632
Evidence / Nov '93 / ADA / Cadillac / Harmonia Mundi

JOURNEY TO THE ONE
Greetings to Idris / Doktor Pitt / Kazuko (peace child) / After the rain / Soledad / You've got to have freedom / Yemenja / Easy to remember / Think about the one / Bedria
CD ECD 220162
Evidence / Jul '92 / ADA / Cadillac / Harmonia Mundi

KARMA
Creator has a master plan / Creator has a master plan / Colours
CD IMP 11532
Impulse Jazz / Nov '95 / New Note/BMG

MESSAGE FROM HOME
CD 5295782
Verve / Mar '96 / PolyGram

MOONCHILD
Moon child / Moon rays / Night has a thousand eyes / All or nothing at all / Soon / Mananberg
CD CDSJP 326
Timeless Jazz / Aug '90 / New Note/ Pinnacle

PHAROAH
CD IN 1027CD
India Navigation / Jan '97 / Discovery / Impetus

PRAYER BEFORE DAWN, A
Light at the edge of the world / Dedication to James W Clark / Softly for Shyla / After the rain / Greatest love of all / Midnight at Yoshi's / Living space / In your own sweet way / Christmas song
CD ECD 22047
Evidence / Mar '93 / ADA / Cadillac / Harmonia Mundi

PRICELESS JAZZ
Astral traveling / Thembi / Naima / Bluesin' for John C / Japan / Upper Egypt and lower Egypt / Promise / Creator has a master plan
CD GRP 98802
GRP / Jul '97 / New Note/BMG

REJOICE
CD ECD 220202
Evidence / Jul '92 / ADA / Cadillac / Harmonia Mundi

SHUKURU
CD ECD 220222
Evidence / Aug '92 / ADA / Cadillac / Harmonia Mundi

WELCOME TO LOVE
You don't know what love is / Nearness of you / My one and only love / I want to talk about you / Soul eyes / Nancy / Polka dots and moonbeams / Say it (over and over again) / Lament / Bird song
CD CDSJP 358
Timeless Jazz / May '91 / New Note/ Pinnacle

Sanders, Ric

CARRIED AWAY (Sanders, Ric & Vikki Clayton & Fred T. Baker)
CD SVL 03CD
Speaking Volumes / Apr '95 / ADA

NEITHER TIME OR...
CD WRCD 017
Woodworm / Feb '92 / Pinnacle

WHENEVER
CD NP 001CD
Nico Polo / Aug '89 / ADA / Direct / Roots

Sanderson, Tommy

KEEP ON DANCING (Sanderson, Tommy & His Orchestra)
CD CDTS 003
Maestro / Aug '93 / Savoy

Sandira

ISHMAL DU BACH
CD INDO 002
Plastic Head / Jul '92 / Plastic Head

Sandke, Randy

BUCK CLAYTON LEGACY
CD CD 018
Nagel Heyer / May '96 / Jazz Music

BUCK CLAYTON REMEMBERED
CD CD 006
Nagel Heyer / May '96 / Jazz Music

CALLING ALL CATS
Calling all cats / Mr. Snow / I wished on the moon / Bad times at Bennington / Blues a' poppin' / Machaut / It's alright with me / In a metatone / Lida / I love you Samantha / What a beautiful yesterday / Blue room / Azalea
CD CCD 4717
Concord Jazz / Aug '96 / New Note/ Pinnacle

CHASE, THE
Lullaby of Broadway / Jordu / Ill wind / Booker / Chase / Folks who live on the hill / Primordial blooze / Oh miss Hannah / Hyde Park / So in love / Randy's Rolls Royce
CD CCD 4642
Concord Jazz / May '95 / New Note/ Pinnacle

GET HAPPY
Get happy / Tuscaloosa / Sicilienne / Humph / Sonata / Let me sing and I'm happy / You / Regret / Deception / Black beauty / Owl eyes / Boogie stop shuffle / Me and my shadow
CD CCD 4598
Concord Jazz / Jun '94 / New Note/ Pinnacle

I HEAR MUSIC
Wildfire / Thanks a million / Say it / Dream song / Muddy water / With a song in my heart / See you later / I gotta right to sing the blues / Domino / I hear music / I love Louis / Lullaby for Karen / BG postscript
CD CCD 4566
Concord Jazz / Aug '93 / New Note/ Pinnacle

NEW YORKERS
CD JCD 222
Jazzology / Oct '93 / Jazz Music

RANDY & JORDAN SANDKE & SANDKE BROTHERS
CD STCD 575
Stash / Feb '94 / ADA / Cadillac / CM / Direct / Jazz Music

Sandler, Albert

ALBERT SANDLER AND HIS ORCHESTRA (Sandler, Albert & His Orchestra)
Portrait of a toy soldier / Casino Tanze - Valse / Kisses in the dark / Faust - Selection / Rosa Mia - Tango serenade / Minuetto from Mozart's symphony (39) / Yvonne (waltz) / Allegro / Salut d'amour / From me to you / Folk tune and fiddle dance / By the sleepy lagoon / With you / Fairies' gavotte / Melody at dusk (Violin solo) / Souvenir d'Ukraine / Always in my heart / Boccherini's minuet in A / Japansy - Intermezzo / Biens Aimes - Waltz / King steps out

CD PASTCD 9732
Flapper / '90 / Pinnacle

Sandoval, Arturo

BEST OF ARTURO SANDOVAL, THE
CD 74321424382
Milan / Jun '97 / Conifer/BMG / Silva Screen

DAN-ZON
Conga / Africa / Groovin' high / A mis abuelos / Tres palabras / Dance on / Suavito / Conjunto / Guaguanco / Coconut groove / Conga (revisited) / Tres palabras (instrumental)
CD GRP 97642
GRP / May '94 / New Note/BMG

DREAM COME TRUE
CD GRP 97022
GRP / May '93 / New Note/BMG

FLIGHT TO FREEDOM
Flight to freedom / Last time I saw you / Caribeno / Samba de amore / Psalm / Rene's song / Body and soul / Tanga / Caprichosos de la habana / Marianela
CD GRP 96342
GRP / Mar '91 / New Note/BMG

I REMEMBER CLIFFORD
Daahoud / Joy spring / Parisian thoroughfare / Cherokee / I remember Clifford / Blues walk / Sandu / I get a kick out of you / Jordu / Caravan / I left this space for you
CD GRP 96682
GRP / Mar '92 / New Note/BMG

JUST MUSIC
El misterioso / Sambeando / Georgia on my mind / Libertao carnaval / Saving all my love / Al chicoy / My love
CD JHCD 008
Ronnie Scott's Jazz House / Jan '94 / Cadillac / Jazz Music / New Note/Pinnacle / TKO Magnum

LATIN TRAIN, THE
Be bop / La guarapachanga / Marte belona / Waheera / I can't get started (with you) / La PP / Royal poinciana / Latin train / Candela/Quimbombo / Drume negrita / Orula
CD GRP 98202
GRP / May '95 / New Note/BMG

NO PROBLEM
Nuestro blues / Los elefantes / Donna Lee / Rimsky / Campana / Fiesta mojo
CD JHCD 001
Ronnie Scott's Jazz House / Jan '94 / Cadillac / Jazz Music / New Note/Pinnacle / TKO Magnum

STRAIGHT AHEAD (Sandoval, Arturo & Chucho Valdes)
King Pete's heart / My funny valentine / Mambo influenciado / Claudia / Blues '88 / Blue monk
CD JHCD 007
Ronnie Scott's Jazz House / Feb '94 / Cadillac / Jazz Music / New Note/Pinnacle / TKO Magnum

SWINGIN'
Moontrane / Swingin' / Moment's notice / Streets of desire / Real Mcbop / Weirdfun / Dizzy's atmosphere / Reflection / Woody / It never gets old / Mack "The Knife"
CD GRP 98462
GRP / Jun '96 / New Note/BMG

TUMBAITO
CD MES 158742
Messidor / Apr '93 / ADA / Koch

Sandoval, Bernado

AURORA
CD 173232
Musidisc / Jan '97 / Discovery

VIDA (2CD Set)
CD Set 170952
Musidisc / Jan '97 / Discovery

Sandow

ANSCHLAG
CD FL 82
Fluxus / Nov '94 / Plastic Head

STATION EINER SUCHT
CD FLOO032
Fluxus / Jun '94 / Plastic Head

Sandoz

DARK CONTINENT
CD TONE 4CD
Touch / Jun '96 / Kudos / Pinnacle

DIGITAL LIFEFORMS
CD TO 21
Touch / Oct '95 / Kudos / Pinnacle

EVERY MAN GOT DREAMING
CD TO 28
Touch / Oct '95 / Kudos / Pinnacle

GOD BLESS THE CONSPIRACY
CD ALPHACD 2
Alphaphone / Jun '97 / Kudos / Pinnacle

INTENSELY RADIOACTIVE
CD TO 23
Touch / Jun '94 / Kudos / Pinnacle

Sandpipers

GUANTANAMERA
Guantanamera / Carmen / La bamba / La mer (beyond the sea) / Louie, Louie / Things we said today / Enamorado / What makes you dream, pretty girls / Stasera gli angeli non volano (for the last time) / Angelica
CD 5404152
A&M / Sep '95 / PolyGram

Sandra

CLOSE TO SEVEN
CD CDVIR 13
Virgin / Mar '92 / EMI

PAINTINGS IN YELLOW
Hiroshima / Life may be a big insanity / Johnny wanna live / Lovelight in your eyes / One more night / Skin I'm in / Paintings in yellow / Journey / Cold out here / I'm alive / Paintings / Come alive / End
CD CDV 2636
Virgin / Oct '90 / EMI

Sands, Colum

ALL MY WINDING JOURNEYS
CD SC 1035CD
Spring / Apr '96 / ADA / Direct

Sands Family

FOLK FROM THE MOURNES
Rathfriland on the hill / Mourne Maggie / We'll never go home / Land / Maid of Ballydoo / I wish I was single / Praties are dug / Rambling irishman / Children's medley / Mourne rambler / Rocks of Gibralter
CD PTICD 3001
Pure Traditional Irish / Mar '97 / ADA / CM / Direct / Ross

SANDS FAMILY COLLECTION
CD SC 1030CD
Spring / Jan '94 / ADA / Direct

Sands, Tommy

BEYOND THE SHADOWS
CD GLCD 3068
Green Linnet / Jun '93 / ADA / CM / Direct / Highlander / Roots

HEART'S A WONDER, THE
CD GLCD 1158
Green Linnet / Dec '95 / ADA / CM / Direct / Highlander / Roots

SINGING OF THE TIMES
CD GLCD 3044
Green Linnet / Oct '93 / ADA / CM / Direct / Highlander / Roots

Sands, Tommy

WORRYIN' KIND, THE (The Capitol Recordings)
Worryin' kind / Ring my phone / Blue ribbon baby / Man like wow / One day later / I ain't gettin' rid of you / Every little once in a while / I love you because / Ring-a-ding-ding / Rock light / Maybellene / Hearts of stone / Oop shoop / Hey Miss Fannie / Tweedle dee / Such a night / Honey love / Little mama / Chicken and the hawk / Big date / Soda pop pop / Sing boy sing / Teen age crush / Wicked woman / Is it ever gonna happen / Goin' steady / Bigger than Texas / Hawaiian rock / Jimmy's song / Wrong side of love
CD BCD 15643
Bear Family / Mar '92 / Direct / Rollercoaster / Swift

Sandunga

VALIO LA PENA ESPERAR
CD TUMICD 042
Tumi / '93 / Discovery / Stern's

Sandvik Small Band

SANDVIK SMALL BAND
CD SITCD 9217
Sittel / Feb '95 / Cadillac / Jazz Music

Sanford, Don

SAPPHIRE IN SEQUENCE VOL.2 (Sanford, Don & Tommy Sanderson)
CD CDTS 053
Maestro / Dec '95 / Savoy

Sangare, Oumou

KO SIRA
CD WCD 036
World Circuit / May '95 / ADA / Cadillac / Direct / New Note/Pinnacle

MOUSSOIOU
Djama kaissoumou / Diarabi / Woula bara diagna / Moussolou / Diya gneba / Ah ndiya
CD WCD 021
World Circuit / May '95 / ADA / Cadillac / Direct / New Note/Pinnacle

WOROTAN
Kun fe ko / N'guatu / Baba / Worotan / Denw / N'diya ni / Tiebaw / Sabu / Fantan ni mone / Djorolen
CD WCD 045

World Circuit / Jul '96 / ADA / Cadillac / Direct / New Note/Pinnacle

Sangeet, Apna

JAM TO THE BHANGRA VOL.1
CD _______ DMUT 1242
Multitone / Apr '96 / BMG

Sangkar Agung Ensemble

JEGOG
CD _______ VICG 50262
JVC World Library / Feb '96 / ADA / CM / Direct

JEGOG VOL.2
CD _______ VICG 52182
JVC World Library / Feb '96 / ADA / CM / Direct

Sangsters

BEGIN
Jesse / Feed the children / Heart like a wheel / Chorus song / Lea rig / White cockade / Sheath and knife / C-rap / Some kind of love / Will ye gang love / Steal away / Helen of Kirkconnel / Simple melody / Golden, golden / Silence and tears / Quiet comes in
CD _______ CDTRAX 065
Greentrax / Jul '93 / ADA / Direct / Duncans / Highlander

Sanity Assassins

RESISTANCE IS USELESS
CD _______ RRCD 011
Retch / Nov '96 / Cargo / Plastic Head

Sankey, Ira D.

JUST AS I AM
Count your blessings / Have you been to Jesus / I will sing the wonderous story / It is well / Just as I am / My Jesus, I love thee / O Happy day / Rock of ages / Shall we gather at the river / Stand up for Jesus / Trust and obey / We're marching to Zion / What a friend we have in Jesus / When the roll is called up yonder
CD _______ KMCD 987
Kingsway / Apr '97 / Complete/Pinnacle

Sanne

LANGUAGE OF THE HEART
CD _______ CDV 2744
Virgin / Jul '94 / EMI

Sansone, Jumpin' Johnny

CRESCENT CITY MOON
Give me a dollar / Anything anytime / Your kind of love / Popeyes and a hubigs part 2 / Sweet baby / Crawfish walk / Destination unknown / Crescent city moon / Uncle Joe / Just say yes / Talkin' is over (the walkin' has begun) / Please please me
CD _______ CDBB 9585
Bullseye Blues / Feb '97 / Direct

Sansone, Maggie

ANCIENT NOELS (Sansone, Maggie & Ensemble Galilei)
CD _______ MMCD 108
Maggie's Music / Dec '94 / ADA / CM

DANCE UPON THE SHORE
CD _______ MMCD 109
Maggie's Music / Dec '94 / ADA / CM

MIST AND STONE
CD _______ MMCD 106
Maggie's Music / Dec '94 / ADA / CM

MUSIC IN GREAT HALL (Sansone, Maggie & Ensemble Galilei)
CD _______ MMCD 107
Maggie's Music / Dec '94 / ADA / CM

TRADITIONS
CD _______ MMCD 104
Maggie's Music / Dec '94 / ADA / CM

Santamaria, Mongo

AFRO ROOTS
Afro blue / Che que re que che que / Rezo / Ayanye / Onyaye / Bata / Meta rumba / Chano pozo / Los Conquitos / Monte Adentro / Imaribayo / Mazacote / Yeye / Congobel / Macunsere / Timbales y bongo / Yambu / Bricamo / Longoito / Conga pa Gozar / Mi Guaguanco / Columbia
CD _______ PCD 24018
Pablo / Oct '93 / Cadillac / Complete/ Pinnacle

AT THE VILLAGE GATE
CD _______ OJCCD 490
Original Jazz Classics / Feb '92 / Complete/Pinnacle / Jazz Music / Wellard

BRAZILIAN SUNSET
Bonita / Costa del oro / Summertime / Gumbo man / Brazilian sunset / When love begins / Being here with you / Soca mi nice / Dawn's light / Breaking it in / Watermelon man / Sofrito
CD _______ CCD 79703
Candid / Mar '96 / Cadillac / Direct / Jazz Music / Koch / Wellard

JARRIBA
Quindimbia / Sabroso / Siempre en ti / Chombo chavada / A ti no mas / Mi novia / Antonio y Pedro / Quajira at the Blackhawk / Palo mayombe / Loco por ti / Come candela / Olga Pachanga / Mongo's theme / Entre amigos / Hilda melodia / Pay Joaquin / Lucy Cha / Manteco / Frederico / Eres tu / Esta melodia / Guaguanco flamenco
CD _______ FCD 24738
Fantasy / Aug '96 / Jazz Music / Pinnacle / Wellard

LIVE AT JAZZ ALLEY
Home / Bonita / Philadelphia / Para II / Manteca / Ponce / Come Candela / Iblano / Juan Jose / Afro blue
CD _______ CCD 4427
Concord Picante / Aug '90 / New Note/ Pinnacle

MAMBOMONGO
Mambomongo / Happy as a fat rat in a cheese factory / Gabrielle / Jelly belly / That's good / New one / Amancecer / Good Doctor / Little T / Manteca
CD _______ CDHOT 501
Charly / Oct '93 / Koch

MONGO EXPLODES/WATERMELON MAN
Skins / Fatback / Hammer head / Dot dot dot / Cornbread guajira / Dirty willie / Sweet potato pie / Bembe blue / Dulce amor / Tacos / Para ti / Watermelon man / Funny money / Cut that cane / Get the money / Boogie cha cha blues / Don't bother me no more / Love oh love / Yeh yeh / Peanut vendor / Bayou root / Suavito
CD _______ CDBGPD 062
Beat Goes Public / Apr '93 / Pinnacle

MONGO INTRODUCES LA LUPE (Santamaria, Mongo Orchestra)
Besito pa ti / Kiniqua / Canta bajo / Uncle Calypso / Montuneando / Que lindas son / Oye este guaguanco / Este mambo (this is my mambo) / Quiet stroll
CD _______ MCD 9210
Milestone / Apr '94 / Cadillac / Complete/ Pinnacle / Jazz Music / Wellard

MONGO RETURNS
CD _______ MCD 92452
Milestone / Feb '96 / Cadillac / Complete/ Pinnacle / Jazz Music / Wellard

MONGO'S MAGIC
Dr. Gasca / O mi shango / Lady Marmalade / Iberia / Naked / Funk up / Secret admirer / Song for you / Princess / What you don't know / Funk down / Leah
CD _______ CDHOT 516
Charly / Apr '95 / Koch

OLE OLA
CD _______ CCD 4387
Concord Picante / Aug '89 / New Note/ Pinnacle

OUR MAN IN HAVANA
CD _______ FCD 24729
Fantasy / Oct '93 / Jazz Music / Pinnacle / Wellard

PORTRAITS OF CUBA
CD _______ JD 145
Chesky / Jun '97 / Discovery / Goldring

SABROSO
Que maravilloso / En la felicidad / Pachanga pa ti / Tulibamba / Mambo de cuco / El bote / Pito pito / Guaguanco mania / Ja ja ja / Tula hula / Dimelo / La luna me voy / Para ti
CD _______ OJCCD 281
Original Jazz Classics / Sep '93 / Complete/ Pinnacle / Jazz Music / Wellard

SKINS
CD _______ MCD 47038
Milestone / Oct '93 / Cadillac / Complete/ Pinnacle / Jazz Music / Wellard

SOCA ME NICE
Con mi ritmo / Cookie / Cu-bop alert / Day tripper / Kathy's waltz / Quiet fire / Soca me nice / Tropical breeze
CD _______ CCD 4362
Concord Jazz / Nov '88 / New Note/ Pinnacle

SOY YO
La manzana (the apple) / Sweet love / Soy yo (that's me) / Salazar / Mayeya / Oasis / Smooth operator / Un dia de playa (a day at the beach)
CD _______ CCD 4327
Concord Picante / Oct '87 / New Note/ Pinnacle

WATERMELON MAN
Summertime / Gumbo man / Brazilian sunset / Where love begins / Being here with you / Soca mi nice / Dawn's light / Breaking it in / Watermelon man / Sofrito
CD _______ EMPRCD 569
Emporio / May '95 / Disc

Santana

ABRAXAS
Singing winds / Crying beasts / Black magic woman / Gypsy queen / Oye como va / Incident at Neshabur / Se acabo / Mother's daughter / Samba pa ti / Hope you're feeling better / El nicoya
CD _______ CD 32032
CBS / Mar '91 / Sony

ABRAXAS/AMIGOS/CARAVANSERAI (3CD Set)
Singing winds / Crying beasts / Black magic woman/Gypsy queen / Oye como va / Incident at Neshabur / Se a cabo / Mother's daughter / Samba pa ti / Hope you're feeling better / El Nicoya / Dance sister dance / Tell me you are tired / Let it shine / Gitano / Take me with you / Europa (earth's cry, heaven's smile) / Let me / Eternal caravan of reincarnation / Waves within / Look up (to see what's coming down) / Just in time to see the sun / Song of the wind / All the love of the universe / Future primitive / Stone flower / La fuente del ritmo / Every step of the way
CD Set _______ 4853232
Columbia / Oct '96 / Sony

ACAPULCO SUNRISE
Acapulco sunrise / Coconut grove / Hawaii / Hot tamales / El corazon manda / Studio jam No. 1 / Studio jam No. 2 / With a little help from my friends / Travellin' blues
CD _______ CDTB 087
Thunderbolt / '91 / TKO Magnum

ACAPULCO SUNRISE
Acapulco sunrise / Coconut grove / Hot tamales / With a little help from my friends / Every day I have the blues / Jam in E / Travellin' blues / Jammin' home / Latin tropical / Let's get ourselves together
CD _______ QED 117
Tring / Nov '96 / Tring

ACAPULCO SUNRISE
Jin-Go-La-Ba / Soul sacrifice / Acapulco sunrise / Coconut Grove / Hot Tamales / With a little help from my friends / Every day I have the blues / Jam in E / Let's get ourselves together
CD _______ 100182
CMC / May '97 / BMG

AS THE YEARS GO BY
Jin-go-lo-ba / El corazon manda / La puesta del sol / Persuasion / As the years go by / Soul sacrifice / Fried neckbones and home fries / Santana jam
CD _______ QED 056
Tring / Nov '96 / Tring

BEST OF SANTANA, THE
She's not there / Black magic woman/ Gypsy queen / Carnaval / Let the children play / Jugando / Vera Cruz / No one to depend on / Evil way / Oye como va / Jin-go-lo-ba / Soul sacrifice / Europa / Dealer / One chain (don't make no prison) / Samba pa ti / Dance, sister, dance / Hold on / Lightening in the sky / Aquamarine
CD _______ 4682672
Columbia / Jun '92 / Sony

BORBOLETTA
Spring manifestations / Cantos de los flores / Life is anew / Give and take / One with the sun / Aspirations / Practice what you preach / Mirage / Here and now / Flor de canela / Promise of a fisherman / Borboletta
CD _______ 4746852
Columbia / Feb '97 / Sony

CARAVANSERAI
Eternal caravan of reincarnation / Waves within / Look up (to see what's coming down) / Just in time to see the sun / Song of the wind / All the love of the universe / Future primitive / Stone flower / La fuente del ritmo / Every step of the way
CD _______ CD 65299
CBS / '88 / Sony

COLLECTION, THE
Jingo / Soul sacrifice / Persuasion / Every day I have the blues / La puesta del sol / As the years go by / Latin tropical (Short version) / Jam in E / Jam in G minor / With a little help from my friends / Santana jam
CD _______ COL 046
Collection / Jul '96 / Target/BMG

DANCE OF THE RAINBOW SERPENT (3CD Set)
Evil ways / Soul sacrifice / Black magic woman/Gypsy queen / Oye como va / Samba pa ti / Everybody's everything / Song of the wind / Toussaint l'overture / In a silent way / Waves within / Flame sky / Naima: *Santana, Carlos & John McLaughlin* / I love you too much / Blues for Salvador / Aqua marine / Bella / River / I'll be waiting / Love is you / Europa / Move on / Somewhere in Heaven / Open invitation / All I ever wanted / Hannibal / Brightest star / Wings of grace / Se eni a fe l'amo-kere kere / Mudbone / Healer / Chill out (things gonna change) / Sweet black cherry pie / Every now and then / This is this
CD Set _______ C3K 64605
Columbia / Sep '95 / Sony

EARLY YEARS, THE
CD _______ MU 5025
Musketeer / Oct '92 / Disc

EVOLUTION
Jingo / El corazon manda / La puesta del sol / Persuasion / As the years go by / Soul sacrafice / Fried neckbone and home fries / Latin tropical / Let's get ourselves together / Acapulco sunrise / Coconut grove / Hawaii / Hot tamales / Jam in E / Jammin' home / With a little help from my friends / Travellin' blues
CD _______ CDTB 502
Thunderbolt / Feb '94 / TKO Magnum

FIRST ALBUM, THE
CD _______ 8414102
Sky Ranch / May '96 / Discovery

GREATEST HITS
Evil ways / Jin-go-lo-ba / Hope you're feeling better / Samba pa ti / Persuasion / Black magic woman / Oye como va / Everything's coming up roses / Se acabo / Everybody's everything
CD _______ CD 32386
Columbia / Jun '92 / Sony

ILLUMINATIONS (Santana, Carlos & Alice Coltrane)
Guru Sri Chinmoy Aphorism / Angel of air / Angel of water / Bliss: The eternal now / Angel of sunlight / Illuminations
CD _______ 4838102
Columbia / Mar '96 / Sony

LATIN TROPICAL
Soul sacrifice / Fried neckbones and home fries / Santana jam / Latin tropical / Let's get ourselves together
CD _______ CDTB 079
Thunderbolt / Jun '95 / TKO Magnum

LIVE
Evil ways / Let's get ourselves together / Jin-Go-La-Ba / Rock me / Just ain't big enough / Funky piano / Way you do me
CD _______ 101182
CMC / May '97 / BMG

LIVE AT THE FILLMORE 1968 (2CD Set)
Jingo / Persuasion / Treat / Chunk a funk / Fried neckbones / Conquistadore rides again / Soul sacrifice / As the years go passing by / Freeway
CD Set _______ 4851062
Columbia / Mar '97 / Sony

LOTUS (2CD Set)
Meditation / Going home / A1 funk / Every step of the way / Black magic woman / Gypsy queen / Oye como va / Yours is the light / Batukada / Xibaba (she-ba-ba) / Stone flower / Waiting / Castillos de'arena / Se acabo / Samba pa ti / Savor / Toussaint l'overture / Incident at Neshabur / Lotus
CD Set _______ 4679432
Columbia / Jun '96 / Sony

MILAGRO
Introduction / Milagro / Somewhere in Heaven / Saja / Your touch / Life is for living / Red prophet / Agua que va caer / Make somebody happy / Free all the people / Gypsy / We don't have to wait / Adois
CD _______ 5131972
Polydor / Nov '93 / PolyGram

MOONFLOWER (2CD Set)
Dawn-go within / Carnaval / Let the children play / Jugando / I'll be waiting / Zulu / She's not there / Bahia / Black magic woman / Gypsy queen / Dance, sister, dance / Europa / Flor d'luna / Soul sacrifice / El Morocco / Transcendance / Savor / Toussaint l'overture
CD Set _______ 4633702
Columbia / Jun '96 / Sony

ODYSSEY
CD _______ CDTB 178
Thunderbolt / Jul '96 / TKO Magnum

ONENESS SILVER DREAMS GOLDEN REALITY
Chosen hour / Arise awake / Light versus darkness / Jim Jeannie / Transformation day / Victory / Silver dreams golden smiles / Cry of the wilderness / Guru's song / Oneness / Life is just a passing parade / Golden dawn / Free as the morning sun / I am free / Song for Devadip
CD _______ 4872382
Columbia / Mar '97 / Sony

PERSUASION
Jingo / El corazon manda / La puesta del sol / Persuasion / As the years go by
CD _______ CDTB 071
Thunderbolt / Jun '89 / TKO Magnum

SACRED FIRE (Live In South America)
Angels all around us / Viva la vida / Esperando / No one to depend on / Black magic woman/Gypsy queen / Oye como va / Samba pa ti / Guajira / Make somebody happy / Toussaint l'overture / Soul sacrifice/ Don't try this at home / Europa / Jingo
CD _______ 5210822
Polydor / Nov '93 / PolyGram

SAMBA PA TI
Earth's cry heaven's smile / Moonflower / I love you much too much / Guru's song / Illuminations / Transformation day / Samba pa ti / Aquamarine / Tales of Kilimanjaro / Life is a lady / Holiday / Revelations / Lightnin'
CD _______ 4625632
Columbia / Oct '95 / Sony

SANTANA
Waiting / Evil ways / Shades of time / Savor / Jin-go-lo-ba / Persuasion / Treat / You just don't care / Soul sacrifice
CD _______ CD 32003
Columbia / Feb '92 / Sony

CD CK 64212
Mastersound / Nov '94 / Sony

SANTANA
Acapulco sunrise / Jam in E / Everyday I have the blues / Coconut grove / Hot tamales / Jam in G minor / With a little help from my friends
CD 12568
Laserlight / Apr '96 / Target/BMG

SANTANA (2CD Set)
Acapulco sunrise / Soul sacrifice / Fried neckbones and some home fries / El corazon manda / Jam in E / Everyday I have the blues / Hot tamales / Santana jam / Persuasion / Jin-go-lo-ba / Coconut grove / Let's get ourselves together / Latin tropical / Jam in G minor / La puesta de sol / As the years go by
CD Set 24359
Laserlight / May '97 / Target/BMG

SANTANA BOX SET (3CD Set)
Jingo / El corazon manda / La puesta del sol / Persuasion / As the years go by / Soul sacrifice / Santana jam / Let's get ourselves together / Fried neckbones and some home fries / Latin tropical / Jam in E / Jam in G minor / With a little help from my friends / Travellin' blues / Everyday I have the blues / Jammin' home
CD Set KBOX 346
Collection / Nov '95 / Target/BMG / TKO Magnum

SANTANA LIVE
Evil ways / We've got to get together / Rock me / Just ain't good enough / Funky piano / Way you do to me
CD GRF 279
Tring / Apr '93 / Tring

SANTANA VOL.1
CD EXP 027
Experience / May '97 / TKO Magnum

SANTANA VOL.2
CD EXP 028
Experience / May '97 / TKO Magnum

SANTANA/ABRAXAS
Waiting / Evil ways / Shades of time / Savor / Jin-go-lo-ba / Persuasion / Treat / You just don't care / Soul sacrifice / Singing winds / Crying beasts / Black magic woman / Gypsy queen / Oye como va / Incident at Neshabur / Se acabo / Mother's daughter / Samba pa ti / Hope you're feeling better / El nicoya
CD Set 4652212
Columbia / Jun '93 / Sony

SWING OF DELIGHT, THE (Santana, Carlos)
Swapan tari / Spartacus love theme / Phuler matan / Song for my brother / Jharna Kala / Gardenia in llave / Golden hours / Shere Khan / Tiger
CD 4880022
Sony Jazz / Aug '97 / Sony

VERY BEST OF SANTANA, THE
Europa (earths cry, heavens smile) / Black magic woman / Oye como va / Samba pa ti / Carnaval / She's not there / Soul sacrifice / Let the children play / Jugando / No one to depend on / Evil ways / Dance sister dance (baila mi hermana) / Jingo-lo-ba / Everybody's everything / Hold on / One chain (don't make no prison) / Lightning in the sky / Aqua marine / Chill out (things gonna change)
CD CDX 32386
Columbia / Apr '97 / Sony

VIVA SANTANA (Live/2CD Set)
Everybody's everything / Black magic woman/Gypsy queen / Guajira / Jungle strut / Jingo / Ballin' / Bambara / Angel negro / Incident at Neshabur / Just let the music speak / Super boogie/Hong Kong blues / Song of the wind / Abi cama / Vilato / Paris finale / Brotherhood / Open invitation / Aquamarine / Dance, sister, dance / Europa / Peraza 1 / She's not there / Bambele / Evil ways / Daughter of the night / Peraza II / Black magic woman/Gypsy Queen (Live) / Oye como va / Persuasion / Soul sacrifice
CD Set 4625002
Columbia / Jun '97 / Sony

Santana

SUCH IS LIFE
Mr. President / Black European / Beware / Make a joyful noise / Call on me / Call on me dub / Signs of the times / Wonderful world / You're my woman / My woman dub / Such is life
CD NGCD 540
Twinkle / Feb '94 / Jet Star / Kingdom / SRD

Santana Brothers

BROTHERS
Transmutation / Industrial / Thoughts / Luz amor y vida / En aranjuez con tu amor / Contigo (with you) / Blues latino / La danza / Brujo / Trip / Reflections / Morning in Marin
CD CID 8034
Island / Sep '94 / PolyGram

Santasara

KING OF THE GYPSIES
Ilusion de abril / Amor sincero / Comprenderas / Soledad / Quierro verte / Felicidade / Libre soy / Fue asinaci gitano / Nuevo amor / Josefa
CD 3036400132
Carlton / Apr '96 / Carlton

Santos, John

HACIA EL AMOR (Santos, John & Coro Folklorico Kindembo)
Elegua-iroko / Merceditas / Chango / Tierra de mis suenos / Caridad / Guiro for oya / Toque for oya / Una carta abierta / Fiesta arara / Presidente Mandela / Siempre viviras / Dejame divertirme / Odudua / Hacia el amor
CD XENO 4034CD
Xenophile / Apr '96 / ADA / Direct

MACHETE (Santos, John & The Machete Ensemble)
CD XENO 4029
Xenophile / Mar '95 / ADA / Direct

Santos, Turibio

VALAS AND CHORUS
CD CDCH 574
Milan / Nov '91 / Conifer/BMG / Silva Screen

Santucci & Scopa

ON THE UNDERGROUND
CD RTCL 807CD
Right Tempo / Jul '96 / New Note/ Pinnacle / Timewarp

Sanvoisen

EXOTIC WAYS
CD N 02212
Noise / Jan '95 / Koch

SOUL SEASONS
Spirits / Mindwars / Behind my dreams / Difference / Soul seasons / Against the fears / Broken silence / Waiting for the rain / Somebody's stolen my name
CD N 02792
Noise / Feb '97 / Koch

Saoco

SIEMPRE SERE GUAJIRO
CD CDGR 155
Charly / May '97 / Koch

Sapphires

BEST OF THE SAPPHIRES, THE
Where is Johnny now / Your true love / Who do you love / Oh so soon / I found out too late / I've got mine you better get yours / Where is your heart (Moulin Rouge) / Gotta be more than friends / Wild child / Come on and love me / Baby you've got me / Hearts are made to be broken / Let's break up for a while / Our love is everything / Thank you for loving me / Gotta have your love / Gee I'm sorry baby / Evil one / How could I say goodbye / Gonna be a big thing / You'll never stop me from loving you / Slow fizz
CD NEMCD 676
Sequel / Aug '94 / BMG

Saprize

NO
CD RTD 19519162
Our Choice / Nov '94 / Pinnacle

Saquito, Nico

GOODBYE MR. CAT
Al vaiven de mi carreta / Me tenian amarrado con fe / Maria Cristina / Meneame la cuna, Ramon / A orillas del cauto / Estoy hecho tierra / Que lio company Andres / Adios company gato
CD WCD 035
World Circuit / Feb '94 / ADA / Cadillac / Direct / New Note/Pinnacle

Sara K

HOBO
Me misin' you / If I don't see you later / Brick house / I really do / Written in stone / You'll never walk alone / Oh well / Hobo / Oughtta be happy by now / I couldn't change your mind / Sizzlin' / Moving big picture
CD JD 155
Chesky / May '97 / Discovery / Goldring

Saraceno, Blues

PLAID
Last train out / Remember when / Elvis talking (you think it's over but it's not) / Never look back / Full tank / Scratch / Jaywalkin' / Friday's walk / Deliverance / Little more cream please / Shakes / Girth / Before the storm / Lighter shade of plaid / Funk 49 / Cat's squirrel / Jitter blast / LA Vignette / Frazzin' / Exit 21 / Tommy gun
CD 592228
Semetery / Nov '93 / New Note/Pinnacle

Sarasota Slim

BOURBON TO BEALE
CD APCD 069
Appaloosa / '92 / ADA / Direct / TKO Magnum

DEEP IN THE SOUTHERN TRENCHES (Live 1995)
CD AP 1302
Appaloosa / Nov '96 / ADA / Direct / TKO Magnum

Sarbib, Saheb

IT COULDN'T HAPPEN WITHOUT YOU
Conjunctions / It couldn't happen without you / Watchmacallit / You don't know what love is / East 11th Street / Sasa's groove / Crescent
CD SN 1210982
Soul Note / Oct '94 / Cadillac / Harmonia Mundi / Wellard

Sarcofago

LAWS OF SCOURGE
CD CDFLAG 66
Under One Flag / Apr '92 / Pinnacle

Sarcophagus

FOR WE ARE CONSUMED
CD RRS 957CD
Progress / Jul '96 / Cargo / Plastic Head

Sardaby, Michel

NIGHT CAP (Sardaby, Michel Trio)
CD SSCD 8004
Sound Hills / Nov '93 / Cadillac / Harmonia Mundi

Sardonica

GRINS AGAIN
CD MPL 008CD
Mutant Punk / Apr '97 / Cargo

Sarge

CHARCOAL
CD MUDCD 019
Mud / Nov '96 / Cargo

Sargent, Gray

SHADES OF GREY (Sargent, Gray Trio)
Let's get lost / Gray haze / Don't take your love from me / I know why / My foolish heart / AP in the PM / You don't know what love is / Nightingale sang / This time the dream's on me / My ideal / Long ago and far away / Love is a many splendoured thing
CD CCD 4571
Concord Jazz / Sep '93 / New Note/ Pinnacle

Sarkoma

INTERGRITY
CD CDVEST 16
Bulletproof / Jun '94 / Pinnacle

Sarnath

OVERSHINE
CD SHR 019CD
Shiver / Jul '96 / Plastic Head

Sarpila, Antti

HOT TIME IN UMEA (Tribute To Benny Goodman) (Sarpila, Antti/Ulf Johansson/ Ronnie Gardiner)
Body and soul / After you've gone / So rare / Running wild / Man I love / Exactly like you / I want to be happy / These foolish things / It had to be you / China boy / Indian summer / Sweet Sue, just you / Stealin' apples / I've found a new baby / Memories of you
CD NCD 8833
Phontastic / Aug '94 / Cadillac / Jazz Music / Wellard

ORIGINAL ANTTI SARPILA
CD ASCD 1
Hep / Oct '94 / Cadillac / Jazz Music / New Note/Pinnacle / Wellard

SWINGING ANTTI SARPILA
CD ASCD 4
Hep / Oct '94 / Cadillac / Jazz Music / New Note/Pinnacle / Wellard

TWO CLARINETS (Sarpila, Antti & Allan Vache)
CD NHCD 026
Nagel Heyer / Jul '96 / Jazz Music

Sarstedt, Peter

ASIA MINOR (Sarstedt, Peter & Clive)
Dream pilot / Teradactyl walk / Glider / India / River / Corigador / Vaguely connected
CD CMMR 923
Music Maker / May '93 / ADA / Grapevine/ PolyGram

PETER SARSTEDT/AS THOUGH IT WERE A MOVIE
I am a cathedral / Sons of Cain are Abel / No more lollipops / Stay within myself / You are my life / Sayonara / Where do you go to my lovely / Blagged / My Daddy is a millionaire / Once upon an everyday / Mary Jane / Time was leading us home / Many coloured semi precious Easter eggs / Time, love, hope, life / Overture / As though it were a movie / Open a tin / Step into the candlelight / Take off your clothes / Letter to a friend / Overture / Boulevard / Sunshine is expensive / Artist / Friendship song / Juan / I'm a good boy / National anthem / Frozen orange juice / Aretusa loser
CD BGOCD 274
Beat Goes On / May '95 / Pinnacle

Sash

IT'S MY LIFE
CD MULTYCD 1
Multiply / Jul '97 / Amato Disco / Prime / Total/BMG

Sash, Leon

I REMEMBER NEWPORT (Sash, Leon Trio)
Easy to remember / I remember Newport / Aren't you glad you're you / Pennies from Heaven / Polka dots and moonbeams / Misty / Our love is here to stay / There will never be another you / Lullaby of the leaves / I remember Newport / Aren't your glad you're you / Our love is here to stay
CD DD 416
Delmark / Jul '97 / ADA / Cadillac / CM / Direct / Hot Shot

Sasha

QAT COLLECTION VOL.2, THE
CD 74321223362
De-Construction / Aug '94 / BMG

Sasha

ALL OR NOTHING
CD DMUT 1270
Multitone / Nov '93 / BMG

CULTURAL VIBES
CD DMUT 1294
Multitone / Mar '96 / BMG

Satan

COURT IN THE ACT
Into the fire / Trial by fire / Blades of steel / No turning back / Broken treaties / Break free / Hunt you down / Ritual / Dark side of innocence / Alone in the dock / Dynamo / Pull the trigger / Break free
CD NM 019
Neat Metal / Apr '97 / Pinnacle

SUSPENDED SENTENCE/INTO THE FUTURE
CD 851 819
Steamhammer / '89 / Pinnacle / Plastic Head

Satan & Adam

MOTHER MOJO
Intro / Mother Mojo / Seventh avenue / Ain't nobody better than nobody / Heartbreak / Watermelon man / Funky thing / Silly little things / Freedom for my people / Crawdad hole / Mr. Contrell / Cry to me
CD FIENDCD 738
Demon / Aug '93 / Pinnacle

Satanic Surfers

666 MOTOR INN
CD BHR 053CD
Burning Heart / Feb '97 / Plastic Head

HERO OF OUR TIME
CD BHR 027CD
Burning Heart / Oct '95 / Plastic Head

KEEP OUT
CD BHR 018CD
Burning Heart / Feb '95 / Plastic Head

Satans Pilgrims

SOUL PILGRIMS
CD ES 1226CD
Estrus / Nov '95 / Cargo / Greyhound / Plastic Head

Satan's Rats

WHAT A BUNCH OF RODENTS
CD OVER 46CD
Overground / Feb '96 / Shellshock/Disc / SRD

Satchel

FAMILY
Isn't that right / Without love / Not too late / Criminal justice / Breathe deep / Time "O" the year / For so long / Some more trouble / Tomorrow / Roll on / Breathe deep (instrumental outro)
CD 4844282
Epic / Sep '96 / Sony

Satchmo Legacy Band

SALUTE TO POPS VOL.1
CD 1211162
Soul Note / Sep '89 / Cadillac / Harmonia Mundi / Wellard

SALUTE TO POPS VOL.2
CD _______ 1211662
Soul Note / Jan '93 / Cadillac / Harmonia Mundi / Wellard

Satisfact

SATISFACT
CD _______ KLP 65CD
K / Mar '97 / Cargo / Greyhound / SRD

Satriani, Joe

DREAMING II
Crush of love / Ice nine / Memories / Hordes of locusts
CD _______ 4736042
Relativity / May '93 / Sony

EXTREMIST, THE
Friends / Extremist / War / Cryin' / Rubina's blue sky happiness / Summer song / Tears in the rain / Why / Motorcycle driver / New blues
CD _______ 4716722
Relativity / Aug '92 / Sony

FLYING IN A BLUE DREAM
Flying in a blue dream / Mystical potato head groove thing / Can't slow down / Headless / Strange / I believe / One big rush / Big bad moon / Feeling / Phone call / Day at the beach / Back to Shalla-bal / Ride / Forgotten / Bells of Lal / Into the light
CD _______ 4659952
Relativity / May '93 / Sony

G3 LIVE IN CONCERT (Satriani, Joe/Eric Johnson/Steve Vai)
Going down: *Vai, Steve* / My guitar wants to kill: *Vai, Steve* / Red house: *Vai, Steve* / Cool no.9: *Satriani, Joe* / Flying in a blue dream: *Satriani, Joe* / Summer song: *Satriani, Joe* / Zap: *Johnson, Eric* / Manhattan: *Johnson, Eric* / Camel's night out: *Johnson, Eric* / Answers: *Vai, Steve* / For the love of God: *Vai, Steve* / Attitude song: *Vai, Steve*
CD _______ 4875392
Relativity / May '97 / Sony

JOE SATRIANI
Cool # 9 / Down, down, down / Luminous flesh giants / SMF / Look my way / Home / Moroccan sunset / Killer bee bop / Slow down blues / (You're) My world / Sittin' around
CD _______ 4811022
Relativity / Oct '95 / Sony

NOT OF THIS EARTH
Not of this Earth / Snake / Rubina / Memories / Brother John / Enigmatic / Driving at night / Hordes of locusts / New day / Headless horseman
CD _______ 4629722
Relativity / May '93 / Sony

NOT OF THIS EARTH/SURFING WITH THE.../FLYING IN A BLUE DREAM (3CD Set)
Not of this Earth / Snake / Rubina / Memories / Brother John / Enigmatic / Driving at night / Hordes of locusts / New day / Headless horseman / Surfing with the alien / Ice nine / Crushing day / Always with me, always with you / Satch boogie / Hill of the skulls / Circles / Lords of Karma / Midnight / Echo / Flying in a blue dream / Mystical potato head groove thing / Can't slow down / Headless / Strange / I believe / One big rush / Big bad moon / Feeling / Phone call / Day at the beach (New rays from the ancient sun) / Back to Shalla-bal / Ride / Forgotten Pt. 1 / Forgotten Pt. 2 / Bells of lal Pt. 1 / Bells of lal Pt. 2 / Into the light
CD Set _______ 4775192
Relativity / Oct '94 / Sony

SURFING WITH THE ALIEN
Surfing with the alien / Ice 9 / Crushing day / Always with me, always with you / Satch boogie / Hill of the skull / Circles / Lords of Karma / Midnight / Echo
CD _______ 4629732
Relativity / May '93 / Sony

TIME MACHINE
Time machine / Mighty turtle head / All alone / Banana mango / Thinking of you / Crazy / Speed of light / Baroque / Dweller on the threshold / Banana mango / Dreaming / I am become death / Saying goodbye / Woodstock jam / Satch boogie / Summer song / Flying in a blue dream / Cryin' / Crush of love / Tears in the rain / Always with me, always with you / Big bad moon / Surfing with the alien / Rubina / Circles / Drum solo / Lords of karma / Echo
CD _______ 4745152
Relativity / Oct '93 / Sony

Saturnine

FLAGS FOR UNKNOWN TERRITORIES
CD _______ DRT 031
Dirt / Nov '96 / Cargo / Greyhound

Saturn's Flea Collar

MONOSYLLABIC
CD _______ K 170CD
Konkurrel / Aug '96 / SRD

Satyricon

DARK MEDIEVAL TIMES
CD _______ FOG 001
Panorama / Sep '94 / Melcot Music

NEMESIS DIVINA
CD _______ FOG 012CD
Moonfog / Mar '96 / Plastic Head

SATYRICON/ENSLAVED (Satyricon/Enslaved)
CD _______ FOG 009CD
Moonfog / Feb '96 / Plastic Head

SHADOWTHRONE, THE
CD _______ FOG 003
Moonfog / Nov '94 / Plastic Head

Saunders, Merl

FIRE UP PLUS
CD _______ FCD 7711
Fantasy / Aug '97 / Jazz Music / Pinnacle / Wellard

Saunderson, Kevin

FACES & PHASES (2CD Set)
CD Set _______ SIXXCD 6
Six6 / Nov '96 / 3mv/Sony / Pinnacle

KEVIN SAUNDERS PRESENTS KMS
CD Set _______ KMSCD 1
Network / Oct '94 / 3mv/Sony / Pinnacle

Sausage

RIDDLES ARE ABOUND TONIGHT
Prelude to fear / Riddles are abound tonight / Here's to the man / Shattering song / Toyz 1988 / Temporary phase / Girls for single men / Recreating / Caution should be used while driving.........
CD _______ IND 92361
Interscope / Jul '96 / BMG

Sauter, Eddie

THAT'S ALL (Sauter-Finegan Orchestra)
CD _______ DAWE 80
Magic / Mar '97 / Cadillac / Harmonia Mundi / Jazz Music / Swift / Wellard

Savae

NATIVE ANGELS
CD _______ IAGO 204CD
Iago / Apr '96 / ADA

Savage

HOLY WARS
CD _______ NM 004CD
Neat Metal / Nov '95 / Pinnacle

HYPERACTIVE
We got the edge / Eye for an eye / Hard on your heels / Blind hunger / Gonna tear ya heart out / Running scared / Stevie's vengeance / Cardiac / All set to sing / Keep it on ice / She don't need you / We got the power
CD _______ CDMETAL 10
Anagram / Apr '97 / Cargo / Pinnacle

LOOSE 'N' LETHAL
Let it loose / Cry wolf / Berlin / Dirty money / Ain't no fit place / On the rocks / China run / White hot / No cause to kill / Devil take you / Back on the road
CD _______ NM 017
Neat Metal / Apr '97 / Pinnacle

Savage

AFRICAN ACHIEVEMENT
Africa / Rescue me / Curiosity / Give a little more / Oh Jah / Mr. President / Bad boy / Super power / I will be / Liberation / Love
CD _______ AADSAVCD 001
Celestial / Apr '97 / Celestial Global Entertainments

Savage, Alan

SONGS FROM THE WILDERNESS
Gone to Australia / Wounded / Who needs another love song / Tradition / Northern rain / I'm not angry / Psycho Michael / Wilderness road / Nothing's going to get me down / Comatose no.101 / Not so great escape
CD _______ NSKYCD 001
Northern Sky / Sep '97 / Direct / Pinnacle

Savage, Chantay

I WILL SURVIVE (DOIN' IT MY WAY)
Alright / I will survive / All night, all day / Baby...drive me crazy / Pillow talk / I'm willing / Love, need, want / All my love / 90's in the red / Turned away / Brown sugar / Let's do it right / Body / Calling / Do you my way / I will survive
CD _______ 74321381622
RCA / May '96 / BMG

Savage Young Beatles

CRY FOR A SHADOW
CD _______ SYB 1CD
Gecko / Jun '97 / Shellshock/Disc / Total/BMG

Savannah Jazzband

I CAN'T ESCAPE FROM YOU
CD _______ LACD 29
Le Jazz / Jul '93 / Cadillac / Koch

IT'S ONLY A BEAUTIFUL PICTURE
CD _______ LACD 51
Lake / Jun '95 / ADA / Cadillac / Direct / Jazz Music / Target/BMG

OUT IN THE COLD
Running wild / Yellow dog blues / Save your sorrow / Mama's gone goodbye / African queen / When my dreamboat comes home / Wabash blues / Nobody's fault but mine / Willie the weeper / Savoy blues / Ole Miss rag / Out in the cold / Tipi tipi tin / Yes, yes in your eyes / Out of nowhere / Original Dixieland one step
CD _______ LACD 82
Lake / Jun '97 / ADA / Cadillac / Direct / Jazz Music / Target/BMG

SAVANNAH JAZZ BAND
I can't escape / Kinklets / Sing on / I don't see me / All alone / Smiles / Gravier street / Shake it and break it / Miner's dream of homes / Lead me saviour / Buddy's habit / Curse of an aching heart / Trog's blues / At the cross / South Rampart Street parade
CD _______ LACD 99
Lake / Jun '93 / ADA / Cadillac / Direct / Jazz Music / Target/BMG

Savatage

DEAD WINTER DEAD
CD _______ 086202RAD
CD Set _______ 086252RAD
Edel / Oct '95 / Pinnacle

DUNGEONS ARE CALLING, THE
CD _______ 398414075CD
Metal Blade / Mar '97 / Pinnacle / Plastic Head

EDGE OF THORNS
Edge of thorns / He carves his stone / Lights out / Skraggy's tomb / Labyrinths / Follow me / Exit music / Degrees of sanity / Conversation piece / All that I bleed / Damien / Miles away / Sleep
CD _______ 7567824882
Atlantic / Mar '93 / Warner Music

GHOST IN THE RUINS (Tribute To Chris Oliva)
CD _______ SPV 08512142
SPV / Apr '96 / Koch / Plastic Head

HANDFUL OF RAIN
CD _______ CDVEST 32
Bulletproof / Aug '94 / Pinnacle

JAPAN LIVE '94
CD _______ IRSCD 993015
Hengest / Apr '97 / Grapevine/PolyGram

SIRENS
Sirens / Holocaust / I believe / Rage / On the run / Twisted little sister / Living for the night / Scream murder / Out on the streets
CD _______ 398414076CD
Metal Blade / Mar '97 / Pinnacle / Plastic Head

Savia Andina

SAVIA ANDINA
CD _______ TUMICD 040
Tumi / '93 / Discovery / Stern's

Saviour Machine

11
CD _______ MASSCD 094
Massacre / Mar '96 / Plastic Head

Savitt, Jan

FUTURISTIC SHUFFLE 1938-1941 (Savitt, Jan & His Orchestra)
CD _______ RACD 7113
Aerospace / May '96 / Jazz Music / Montpellier

LIVE IN HI-FI 1938 (Savitt, Jan & The Top Hatters)
CD _______ JH 1024
Jazz Hour / Feb '93 / Cadillac / Jazz Music / Target/BMG

Savolainen, Jarmo

TRUE IMAGE
True image / 80/81 / Sco-lastic / Down the line / Scene from above / Long ago and far away / Inky-pinky / Scenario / Things are the way they are / Inseperable / We don't know
CD _______ AL 73031
A / Nov '96 / Cadillac / Direct

Savoy Bearcats

NEW YORK VOL.3
CD _______ DGF 12
Frog / Mar '97 / Cadillac / Jazz Music / Wellard

Savoy Brown

BRING IT HOME
CD _______ CTC 0107
Coast To Coast / Jul '95 / Grapevine/PolyGram

LET IT RIDE
CD _______ CD 0848882
SPV / Mar '96 / Koch / Plastic Head

SAVAGE RETURN
CD _______ 8442432
Deram / Jan '96 / PolyGram

Savoy Jazzmen

30TH ANNIVERSARY (1962-1992)
CD _______ 322909
Koch / Feb '93 / Koch

Savoy, Marc

BENEATH A GREEN OAK TREE (Savoy, Marc & Dewey Balfa/D.L. Menard)
CD _______ ARHCD 312
Arhoolie / Apr '95 / ADA / Cadillac / Direct

HOME MUSIC WITH SPIRITS (Savoy-Doucet Cajun Band)
CD _______ ARHCD 389
Arhoolie / Apr '95 / ADA / Cadillac / Direct

LIVE AT THE DANCE (Savoy-Doucet Cajun Band)
CD _______ ARHCD 418
Arhoolie / Apr '95 / ADA / Cadillac / Direct

NOW AND THEN (Savoy-Smith Cajun Band)
Evangeline Playboys special / Rainbow waltz / Wee pee special / Old carpenter's waltz/Contredanse de Mamou / Blues de Basile / Walker special / C'est un pecher de dire un menterie / Le moulin casse / Savoy family waltz / Choupique / One step de McGees/O ma Josephine / Separation waltz / Baisse bas / Lovesick waltz / Two step de prairie soileau
CD _______ ARHCD 457
Arhoolie / Nov '96 / ADA / Cadillac / Direct

TWO-STEP D'AMEDE (Savoy-Doucet Cajun Band)
CD _______ ARHCD 316
Arhoolie / Apr '95 / ADA / Cadillac / Direct

Savoy Sultans

EVERYTHING SWINGS
Air mail special / Stolen sweets / Stomping at the Savoy / Sentimental journey / It don't mean a thing / In the mood / Just you, just me / Take the 'A' train / Funky Willie / Undecided
CD _______ VN 1005
Viper's Nest / Nov '96 / ADA / Cadillac / Direct / Jazz Music

Saw Doctors

ALL THE WAY FROM TUAM
Green and red of mayo / You got me on the run / Pied piper / My heart is livin' in the sixties still / Hay wrap / Wake up sleeping / Midnight express / Broke my heart / Exhilarating sadness / All the way from Tuam / FCA / Music I love / Yvonne / Never mind the strangers
CD _______ SAWDOC 002CD
Shamtown / Oct '94 / Pinnacle

IF THIS IS ROCK AND ROLL I WANT MY OLD JOB BACK
I useta lover / Only one girl / Why do I always want you / It won't be tonight / Irish post / Sing a powerful song / Freedom fighters / That's what she said last night / Red cortina / Presentation boarder / Don't let me down / Twenty five / What a day / n17 / I hope you meet again
CD _______ SAWDOC 001CD
Shamtown / Oct '94 / Pinnacle

SAME OUL TOWN
CD _______ SAWDOC 004CD
Shamtown / Feb '96 / Pinnacle

THAT'S WHAT SHE SAID LAST NIGHT
CD _______ ROKCD 751
Solid / Nov '91 / Grapevine/PolyGram

Sawai, Tadao

KOTO MUSIC
CD _______ PS 65180
PlayaSound / Apr '97 / ADA / Harmonia Mundi

Sawhney, Nitin

DISPLACING THE PRIEST
Oceans and rain / In the mind / Herccica latino / Saudades / Displacing the priest / Bengali song / Streets / Voices / Pieces of ten / Vidya
CD _______ CASTE 2CD
OutCaste / Oct '96 / 3mv/Sony

MIGRATION
CD _______ CASTE 1CD
OutCaste / Jan '96 / 3mv/Sony

SPIRIT DANCE
River pulse / Skylight / Taste / Pieces of ten / Wind and rain / Twilight daze / Chase the sun / Spirit dance
CD _______ SDCD 7001
Spirit Dance / Mar '94 / Direct / New Note/Pinnacle

Sax & Ivory

BEST OF SAX & IVORY, THE
CD PKCD 61194
K&K / Sep '94 / Jet Star

Sax Appeal

LET'S GO
Zoot suit / Wild river / Let's go / Makambo triangle / Longshore drift / One step further / Monkish / Rio / Stompin' on the saveloy / Midnight
CD JITCD 9401
Jazzizit / Jul '94 / New Note/Pinnacle

OUTSIDE IN
Outside in / Meek / Greens / Two of a kind / Waco Jaco / Gotta getta dep / Dimanche matin / Sonic samba / Whisperer / Outside in
CD JITCD 9606
Jazzizit / Mar '97 / New Note/Pinnacle

Sax, Mostafa

BEST OF EGYPTIAN BELLY DANCE MUSIC
CD EUCD 1131
ARC / '91 / ADA / ARC Music

Saxomania

SAXPAK
Portrait of a flirt / Sophisticated lady / Liza / Holberg prelude / I'll remember April / Twelfth Street rag / Candlelights / Holiday for strings / String of pearls / Saxophobia / Westminster waltz / I'm old fashioned / Four brothers / Promenade / Czardas / Perfidia / Marriage of Figaro overture / Lover man / Continental / Girl with the flaxen hair / Turkey in the straw / Shepherd's hey / Nola / Yankee doodle
CD CDWHL 216
White Line / Feb '97 / Koch

Saxon

BACK ON THE STREETS
Power and the glory / Backs to the wall / Watching the sky / Midnight rider / Never surrender / Princess of the night / Motorcycle man / 747 (Strangers in the night) / Wheels of steel / Nightmare / Back on the streets / Rock 'n' roll gypsy / Broken heroes / Devil rides out / Party 'til you puke / Rock the nations / Waiting for the night / Ride like the wind / I can't wait anymore / We are the strong
CD VSOPCD 147
Connoisseur Collection / Jan '90 / Pinnacle

BEST OF SAXON, THE
Eagle has landed / Ride like the wind / Crusader / Rainbow theme/Frozen rainbow / Midas touch / Denim and leather / Broken heroes / Dallas 1pm / 747 (strangers in the night) / Princess of the night / And the bands played on / Never surrender / This town rocks / Strong arm of the law / Heavy metal thunder
CD CDEMS 1390
EMI / Mar '91 / EMI

COLLECTION OF METAL, A
747 (Strangers in the night) / Rock 'n' roll gypsy / And the bands played on / Back on the streets / Ride like the wind / Big teaser / I can't wait anymore / Broken heroes / Raise some hell / Denim and leather / Rock the nations / Motorcycle man / Everybody up / Rock city / Set me free / Play it loud
CD CDGOLD 1055
EMI Gold / Oct '96 / EMI

DENIM AND LEATHER
Princess of the night / Never surrender / Out of control / Rough and ready / Play it loud / And the bands played on / Midnight rider / Fire in the sky / Denim and leather
CD CDGOLD 1011
EMI Gold / Mar '96 / EMI

DOGS OF WAR
Dogs of war / Burning wheels / Big tivin rolling / Dold on / Great white buffalo / Demolition alley / Walking through Tokyo / Give it all away / Yesterday's gone
CD 08576012
SPV / Nov '96 / Koch / Plastic Head

DONNINGTON
Motorcycle man / Still fit to boogie / Freeway mad / Backs to the wall / Wheels of steel / Bap shoo ap / 747 / Stallions of the highway / Machine gun
CD IRSCD 993011
Intercord / Apr '97 / Plastic Head

FOREVER FREE
CD WARCD 10
Warhammer / May '93 / Grapevine/ PolyGram

GREATEST HITS LIVE
Opening theme / Heavy metal thunder / Rock 'n' roll gypsy / And the bands played on / Twenty thousand feet / Ride like the wind / Motor cycle man / 747 (Strangers in the night) / See the light shining / Frozen rainbow / Princess of the night / Wheels of steel / Denim and leather / Crusader / Rockin' again / Back on the streets again
CD ESMCD 132
Essential / May '95 / BMG

LIVE AT THE MONSTERS OF ROCK
CD IRS 933011CD
Intercord / Jan '96 / Plastic Head

WHEELS OF STEEL/STRONG ARM OF THE LAW (Remastered/2CD Set)
Motorcycle man / Stand up and be counted / 747 (Strangers in the night) / Wheels of steel / Freeway mad / See the light shining / Street fighting man / Suzie hold on / Machine gun / Judgement day / Wheels of steel / See the light shining / Wheels of steel / 747 (Strangers in the night) / Stallions of the highway / Heavy metal thunder / To hell and back again / Strong arm of the law / Taking your chances / 20,000 feet / Hungry years / Sixth form girls / Dollars 1 PM / 20,000 feet / Hungry years / Strong arm of the law / Heavy metal thunder
CD Set CTMCD 201
EMI / Feb '97 / EMI

Saxon, Al

HOOKED ON THE '40'S (Saxon, Al '40s Band)
In the mood / Little white lies / Swinging on a star / Say something sweet to your sweetheart / Sentimental journey / I cried for you / I'll string along with you / Lullaby of broadway / 12th street rag / September in the rain / On the sunny side of the street / Dream / I've got my love to keep me warm / Lazy river / Paper doll / Sunday, Monday or always / That's my desire / There I've said it again / Blue moon / I've heard that song before / Baby face / April showers / Toot toot tootsie / Swanee skyliner / I can dream can't I
CD EMPRCD 515
Emporio / Jul '94 / Disc

Saxon, Sky

IN SEARCH OF BRIGHTER COLORS (Saxon, Sky & Fire Wall)
I hear the mountains crash / Lightning lightning / Put something sweet between your lips / Barbie doll look / Big screen / Baby baby / Come on pretty girl / Kick kick / Paisley rocker / Come a here right now
CD ROSE 155CD
New Rose / Dec '88 / ADA / Direct / Discovery

Saxtet

SAFER SAX
CD SERCD 8000
Serendipity / Aug '93 / Koch

Sayama, Masahiro

PLAY ME A LITTLE MUSIC
CD JD 3305
JVC / Jul '88 / Direct / New Note/Pinnacle / Vital/SAM

Sayer, Leo

ALL THE BEST
When I need you / Show must go on / One man band / Long tall glasses / Moonlighting / You make me feel like dancing / How much love / Thunder in my heart / I can't stop loving you (Though I try) / Raining in my heart / More than I can say / Have you ever been in love / Heart (Stop beating in time) / Orchard Road / Living in a fantasy / Giving it all away
CD CDCHR 1980
Chrysalis / Feb '93 / EMI

ENDLESS FLIGHT
Hold on to my love / You make me feel like dancing / Reflections / When I need you / No business like love business / I hear the laughter / Magdalena / How much love / I think we fell in love too fast / Endless flight
CD AHLCD 35
Hit / May '96 / Grapevine/PolyGram

HAVE YOU EVER BEEN IN LOVE
Until you come back to me / Sea of heartbreak / More than I can say / Darlin' / Don't wait until tomorrow / How beautiful you are / Orchard road / Aviation / Heart (Stop beating in time) / Your love still brings me to my knees / Have you ever been in love / Wounded heart / Love games / Never has a dream come true
CD AHLCD 37
Hit / May '96 / Grapevine/PolyGram

JUST A BOY
Telepathy / Train / Bells of St. Mary's / One man band / In my life / When I came home this morning / Long tall glasses / Another time / Solo / Giving it all away
CD AHLCD 36
Hit / May '96 / Grapevine/PolyGram

LEO SAYER
CD D 20010
Festival / Jun '97 / Greyhound

LOVE BALLADS
More than I can say / Orchard Road / When I need you / Till you come back to me / Bye bye now my sweet love / Darlin' / Don't wait until tomorrow / Have you ever been in love / Sea of heartbreak / Aviation / How beautiful you are / Heart (stop beating in time) / Your love still brings me to my knees / Love games / Wounded heart / Never had a dream come true
CD 12899
Laserlight / Feb '97 / Target/BMG

LOVE SONGS
CD MCCD 273
Music Club / Dec '96 / Disc / THE

SILVERBIRD
Innocent bystanders / Goodnight old friend / Drop back / Silver bird / Show must go on / Dancer / Tomorrow / Don't say it's over / Slow motion / Oh wot a life / Why is everybody going home
CD AHLCD 34
Hit / May '96 / Grapevine/PolyGram

Sayles, Charlie

I GOT SOMETHING TO SAY
CD JSPCD 261
JSP / Nov '95 / ADA / Cadillac / Direct / Hot Shot / Target/BMG

Sayles, Emmanuel

EMMANUEL SAYLES & THE BARRY MARTIN BAND (Sayles, Emmanuel & Barry Martyn Band)
CD BCD 359
GHB / Apr '97 / Jazz Music

Sayles Silverleaf Ragtimers

SAYLES SILVERLEAF RAGTIMERS
CD BCD 8
GHB / Aug '95 / Jazz Music

Sayyah, Emad

MODERN BELLY DANCE MUSIC FROM LEBANON
CD EUCD 1099
ARC / '91 / ADA / ARC Music

MODERN BELLY DANCE MUSIC FROM LEBANON VOL.2
CD EUCD 1226
ARC / Sep '93 / ADA / ARC Music

MODERN BELLY DANCE MUSIC FROM LEBANON VOL.4
CD EUCD 1332
ARC / Mar '96 / ADA / ARC Music

Scabs

SKINTIGHT
CD BIASCD 102
Play It Again Sam / '89 / Discovery / Plastic Head / Vital

Scaggiari, Stefan

STEFAN ITELY (Scaggiari Trio)
Just in time / I'm old fashioned / Icarus / All the way / Honeysuckle rose / Samba de bunda / Old folks / Where or when / Bittersweet / I've got the world on a string / Golden lady / Windswept high
CD CCD 4570
Concord Jazz / Sep '93 / New Note/ Pinnacle

STEFAN OUT
Love walked in / Felix / Love for sale / Make me a memory / Willow weep for me / Ill wind / Bolivia / When you're around / I am singing / If I could / Windows / For all we know
CD CCD 4659
Concord Jazz / Aug '95 / New Note/ Pinnacle

Scaggs, Boz

BOZ SCAGGS
I'm easy / I'll be long gone / Another day (another letter) / Now you're gone / Finding her / Look what I've got / Waiting for a train / Loan me a dime / Sweet release
CD 7567815452
Atlantic / May '93 / Warner Music

COME ON HOME
It all went down the drain / Ask me 'bout nothin' (but the blues) / Don't cry no more / Found love / Come on home / Pictures of a broken heart / Love letters / I've got your love / Early in the morning / Your good thing (is about to end) / T-Bone shuffle / Sick and tired / After hours / Goodnight Louise
CD CDVUS 124
Virgin / Apr '97 / EMI

SILK DEGREES
What can I say / Georgia / Jump street / What do you want the girl to do / Harbour lights / Lowdown / It's over / Love me tomorrow / Lido shuffle / We're all alone
CD 4719682
Columbia / Feb '97 / Sony

SOME CHANGE
You got my letter / Some change / I'll be the one / Call me / Fly like a bird / Sierra / Lost it / Time / Illusion / Follow that man
CD CDVUS 73
Virgin / Jun '94 / EMI

Scales Brothers

OUR HOUSE
Bamene bekon / All but one / Sambasara / Boneafield / Nsisim alouk / Province of China / Cascatas / Years later
CD ENJACD 91062
Enja / Jun '97 / New Note/Pinnacle / Vital/ SAM

Scan X

CHROMA
Dust / Grey lights / Secrets / Voodoo / Earthquake / Wood / Blackmoon / Turmoil / Blue 072c / Requiem / Red dogs / Wasteland
CD F 040CD
F-Communications / Jun '96 / Prime / Vital

Scanner

DELIVERY
Spirit of speech / Digital anchor / Treble spin / Fingerbug / Heidi / Barcode / Radio sprite / Throne of hives / Affaire / Vie one / My lost love hunting your lost face
CD MOSH 174CDL
CD MOSH 174CD
Earache / May '97 / Vital

MENTAL RESERVATION
CD MASSCD 058
Massacre / Oct '95 / Plastic Head

Scanner

MORT AUX VACHES
CD SAM 8001
Staalplaat / Oct '96 / Vital/SAM

NEW YORK SOUNDSCAPE (Scanner (2) & Shea/Nus)
CD QUANTUM 153
Sub Rosa / Jan '97 / Direct / RTM/Disc / SRD / Vital

PARIS SESSIONS (Scanner/Shea/Main)
CD QUANTUM 102
Sub Rosa / Nov '96 / Direct / RTM/Disc / SRD / Vital

SCANNER VOL.1
CD ASH 11
Ash International / Jan '95 / Kudos / Pinnacle

SULPHUR
CD SR 95
Sub Rosa / Feb '96 / Direct / RTM/Disc / SRD / Vital

Scarab

SECRETS OF THE PAST AND FUTURE
CD WSCD 019
Word Sound Recordings / Jun '97 / Cargo / SRD

Scarce

DEADSEXY
Honey simple / Freakshadow / Days like this / Stella / Glamourising / Cigarettes / Girl through me / Karona krome / All sideways / Thrill me / Sense of quickness / Given / Obviously midnight
CD PDOXCD 001
Paradox / Jul '95 / PolyGram / Vital

RED
CD ABB 79
Big Cat / Aug '95 / 3mv/Pinnacle

Scarecrow

TOUCH OF MADNESS, A
CD CDVEST 43
Bulletproof / Feb '95 / Pinnacle

Scarecrow's Shadow

SCARECROW'S SHADOW
CD NAK 6004CD
Naked Language / Sep '94 / Koch

Scared Of Chaka

MASONIC YOUTH
CD MTR 334CD
Empty / Oct '96 / Cargo / Greyhound / Plastic Head / SRD

Scarface

DIARY, THE
Intro / White sheet / No tears / Jesse James / G's / I seen a man die / One / Goin' down / One time / Hand of the dead body / Mind playin' tricks '94 / Diary / Outro
CD CDVUS 81
Virgin / Oct '94 / EMI

UNTOUCHABLE, THE
Intro / Untouchable / No warning / Southside / Sunshine: *Scarface & Lisa Crawford* / Money makes the world go round: *Scarface & Daz* / For real / Ya money or ya life / Mary Jane / Smile: *Scarface & 2Pac/Johnny P* / Smartz / Faith / Game over: *Scarface & Dr. Dre/Ice Cube/Too Short* / Outro: *Scarface & Dr. Dre/Ice Cube/Too Short*
CD CDVUS 125
Noo Trybe / Mar '97 / EMI

Scarfo

LUXURY PLANE CRASH
ELO / Jet samshed flat / Safecracker / Don't let go / Japanese cameras / Jazz cigarette / Cosmonaut no.7 / Pajo gear / Chomsky airport / Lifeline / Prison architect

CD BLUFF 045CD
Deceptive / Jul '97 / Vital

SCARFO
Eyesore / Coin op / Skinny / Backwater / Car chase / Thow it all / Wailing words
CD BLUFF 017CD
Deceptive / Oct '95 / Vital

Scarlet

CHEMISTRY
CD 0630146592
East West / Jul '96 / Warner Music

NAKED
CD 4509976432
WEA / Dec '96 / Warner Music

Scarlet Blue

CASTLES IN THE SAND
CD BLUE 1
Scarlet / Nov '96 / Cargo

Scarp

SCARP
CD BNQ 94CD
Arax Pan Global / Jul '94 / ADA / Direct

Scat Opera

ABOUT TIME
CD CDMFN 111
Music For Nations / Feb '91 / Pinnacle

FOUR GONE CONFUSION
CD CDMFN 140
Music For Nations / Oct '92 / Pinnacle

Scatman John

SCATMAN'S WORLD
Welcome to Scatland / Scatman's world / Only you / Quiet desperation / Scatman / Sing now / Popstar / Time (take your time) / Mambo jambo / Everything changes / Song of Scatland / Hi Louis / Scatman (remix)
CD 74321298792
RCA / Feb '97 / BMG

Scatterbrain

MINDUS INTELLECTUALIS
Write that hit / Beer muscles / Everybody does it / Funny thing / How could I love you / Dead man blues / Down with the ship
CD CDVEST 33
Bulletproof / Sep '94 / Pinnacle

Scelsi, Giacinto

BOT-BA (Scelsi, Giacinto & Marianne Schroeder)
CD ARTCD 6092
Hat Art / Oct '92 / Cadillac / Harmonia Mundi

Scenic

AQUATICA
CD WD 00382
World Domination / Sep '96 / Pinnacle / RTM/Disc

INCIDENT AT CIMA
CD IP 050CD
Independant Press / Nov '96 / Cargo
CD WD 00552
World Domination / Jul '97 / Pinnacle / RTM/Disc

Schaphorst, Ken

OVER THE RAINBOW (The Music Of Harold Arlen)
Out of this world / Man that got away / If I only had a brain / Lullaby / Ding dong, the witch is dead / Come rain or come shine / Accentuate the positive / Stormy weather / Get happy / Life's full of consequence / That old black magic / I've got the world on a string / Over the rainbow
CD AC 4204
Accurate / May '97 / Direct

Schatz, Lesley

BANJO PICKIN' GIRL
Winter it is past / Trouble in mind / Cruel sister / Barbara Allen / little Joe the wrangler / Zebra Dun / Streets of Laredo / Jesse James / Tom Dula / Banjo pickin' girl / Early one morning / Arthur McBride / Jack O'Hazlegreen / Great Silkie / Silver dagger / Rowan tree / White coral bells / Flor del pino / Tumbalalaika / Will the circle be unbroken
CD BCD 15729
Bear Family / May '93 / Direct / Rollercoaster / Swift

BRAVE WOLFE
Red river valley / Gypsy Davey / Oh Susanna / Brave Wolfe / Banks of the Ohio / I never will marry / Greensleeves / Greenpeace / I ride an old paint / Shady grove / Rising sun blues / Train that carried my man from town / Shortnin' bread / Cripple creek / Mole in the ground / Old Joe Clarke / Nine pound hammer / Turkey in the straw / Sinner man / Careless love / Pretty little horses
CD BCD 15735
Bear Family / May '93 / Direct / Rollercoaster / Swift

COYOTE MOON/ RUN TO THE WIND
It's about time / Alberta blue / Freight train bound / Way she would sing / Printed word / Coyote moon / Boppin' at the gamble / Going home / Old tin pot / Les' wish / Alberta waltz / Molly and tenbrooks / To each his own / I'll be on the road again / Run to the wind / Chinese silver / Slow dance / Wind (stay away) / Only sound you'll hear / Empty hands
CD BCD 15513
Bear Family / May '90 / Direct / Rollercoaster / Swift

HELLO STRANGER
Hello stranger / Shenandoah / Wayfaring stranger / Apple blossom time / Beautiful river valley / Sweetest gift / Water is wide / Somewhere in Tennessee / Froggie went acourtin' / Farewell to Nova Scotia / Home on the range / Down in the valley / Whiskey in the jar / Girl I left behind / Lily of the west / Did he mention my name / Spanish is a loving tongue / Cancion de cuna / La source / Brahms lullaby
CD BCD 15725
Bear Family / May '93 / Direct / Rollercoaster / Swift

WALLS, HEARTS AND HEROES
Walls and borders / Gotta go (Bremen Train) / Dry land / Lonely bird / Back to your arms / Girl gone wild / Old old doll / Take a stand (for the children) / I can hear ya callin' / Foothill's lullaby / My heart stands (at your door) / Gypsy blue / Wastin' the moon / Merlin and the cowboy / I can dance (like Arthur Murray) / New crescent moon / Once a dream / Way o' walkin' / Old Wooley / Christmas wish / In the cabin walls / Un Canadien errant
CD BCD 15674
Bear Family / Jun '92 / Direct / Rollercoaster / Swift

Schatz, Mark

BRAND NEW OLD TYME WAY
CD ROUCD 0342
Rounder / Jun '95 / ADA / CM / Direct

Schechter, Gregori

DER REBE ELIMELECH (Schechter, Gregori Klezmer Festival Band)
CD EUCD 1324
ARC / Nov '95 / ADA / ARC Music

Scheer

INFLICTION
Shea / Howling boy / Wish you were dead / In your hand / Demon / Babysize / Sad loved girl / Driven / Screaming / Goodbye
CD CAD 6006CD
4AD / May '96 / RTM/Disc

Scheetz, Jeff

WOODPECKER STOMP
CD RR 00012
Re-flexx / Nov '90 / Re-flexx

Schell, Daniel

IF WINDOWS THEY HAVE (Schell, Daniel & Kara)
Un celte / Remi sace an lacis dore / Vienna Carmen / Moustiquaries / If windows they have / Bigna zomer en ik loop altjid / Listen to short wave: Je suis dans / Tapi la nuit / Buches/logs/holz
CD MTM 13
Made To Measure / Sep '88 / New Note/ Pinnacle

Schenker, Michael

ANTHOLOGY (Schenker, Michael Group)
Rock bottom: *UFO* / Let it roll: *UFO* / Shoot shoot: *UFO* / Natural thing: *UFO* / Too hot to handle: *UFO* / Love to love: *UFO* / Doctor doctor: *UFO* / Only you can rock me: *UFO* / Armed and ready / Attack of the mad axeman / Are you ready to rock / Assault attack / Rock my nights away / Dogs of war / Rock will never die
CD VSOPCD 185
Connoisseur Collection / Apr '93 / Pinnacle

ASSAULT ATTACK (Schenker, Michael Group)
Assault attack / Rock you to the ground / Dancer / Samurai / Desert song / Broken promises / Searching for a reason / Ulcer
CD BGOCD 321
Beat Goes On / Aug '96 / Pinnacle

BEST OF MICHAEL SCHENKER GROUP, THE (Schenker, Michael Group)
Armed and ready / Cry for the nations / Victim of illusion / Into the arena / Are you ready to rock / Attack of the mad axeman / On and on / Assault attack / Dancer / Searching for a reason / Desert song / Rock my nights away / Captain Nemo / Let sleeping dogs lie / Bijou pleasurette / Lost horizons
CD MCCD 160
Music Club / May '94 / Disc / THE

BUILT TO DESTROY (Schenker, Michael Group)
Rock my nights away / I'm gonna make you mine / Dogs of war / Systems failing / Captain Nemo / Still love that little devil / Red sky / Time waits for no one / Walk the stage
CD BGOCD 344
Beat Goes On / Jan '97 / Pinnacle

CHAMPIONS OF ROCK (Schenker/ McAuley Group)
Save youself / Bad boys / Anytime / Get down to business / Shadow of the night / What we need / I am your radio / There has to be another way / This is my heart / Destiny / Take me back
CD CR 869932
Disky / Mar '97 / Disky / THE

COLLECTION, THE (Schenker, Michael Group)
Armed and ready / Lost horizons / Buou pleasurette / Ready to rock / Let sleeping dogs lie / But I want more / Into the arena / Attack of the mad axeman / Never trust a stranger / Dancer / Desert song / Broken promises / Rock my nights away / Captain Nemo / Walk the stage
CD CCSCD 294
Castle / Jul '91 / BMG

MICHAEL SCHENKER GROUP/MSG (Schenker, Michael Group)
CD BGOCD 316
Beat Goes On / Jul '96 / Pinnacle

ONE NIGHT AT BUDOKAN (Schenker, Michael Group)
Armed and ready / Cry from the nations / Attack of the mad axeman / Axeman / But I want more / Victim of illusion / Into the arena / On and on / Never trust a stranger / Let sleeping dogs lie / Courvoisier concerto / Lost horizons / Doctor doctor / Are you ready to rock
CD BGOCD 312
Beat Goes On / Jun '96 / Pinnacle

Scherer, Peter

CRONOLOGIA
CD TZ 7502
Tzadik / Oct '96 / Cargo

Schiano, Mario

SOCIAL SECURITY
CD VICTOCD 043
Victo / Mar '97 / Harmonia Mundi / ReR Megacorp

Schifrin, Lalo

MORE JAZZ MEETS THE SYMPHONY
Sketches of miles / Down here on the ground / Chano / Begin the beguine / Django / Old friends / Madrigal / Portrait of Louis Armstrong
CD 4509955892
Warner Bros. / Aug '94 / Warner Music

Schinjuku Thief

WITCH HAMMER, THE
CD DOROBO 003CD
Dorobo / Oct '95 / Plastic Head

Schizo

SOUNDS OF COMING
CD AVRCD 008
Nosferatu / Jun '94 / Plastic Head

Schleprock

AMERICA'S DIRTY LITTLE SECRET
CD 9362462772
Warner Bros. / Oct '96 / Warner Music

HIDE AND SEEK
CD LRR 004
Last Resort / Oct '96 / Cargo

Schlippenbach, Alexander

ELF BAGATELLEN (Schlippenbach Trio)
CD FMPCD 27
FMP / Aug '86 / Cadillac

PHYSICS (Schlippenbach Trio)
CD FMPCD 50
FMP / Dec '89 / Cadillac

Schlong

FISH BOOTY
CD BL 5
Bun Length / Dec '96 / Cargo

Schloss, Cynthia

SAD MOVIES
CD REVCD 3002
Revue / Feb '94 / Jet Star / THE / TKO Magnum

THIS IS LOVE
CD CRCD 26
Charm / Nov '93 / Jet Star

Schlott, Volker

DAY BEFORE, THE (Schlott, Volker Quartett)
CD BEST 1026CD
Acoustic Music / Nov '93 / ADA

WHY NOT (Schlott, Volker Quartett)
CD BEST 1083CD
Acoustic Music / Apr '96 / ADA

Schmid, Wolfgang

PARADOX (Schmid, Wolfgang & Billy Cobham/Bill Bickford)
Fonkey donkey / Four more years / Quadrant / Myohmyohyeoye / Walking in five / Jam O'James / Late nite / Shoes in seven / Five in
CD TIP 8888242
Tiptoe / Nov '96 / New Note/Pinnacle

Schmidt, Claudia

CLAUDIA SCHMIDT
CD FF 70066
Flying Fish / Mar '89 / ADA / CM / Direct / Roots

IT LOOKS FINE FROM HERE
CD RHRCD 64
Red House / Jul '95 / ADA / Koch

MIDWESTERN HEART
CD FF 241CD
Flying Fish / May '93 / ADA / CM / Direct / Roots

Schmidt, Irmin

ANTHOLOGY (3CD Set)
CD Set SPOONCD 32/33/34
The Grey Area / Oct '94 / RTM/Disc

IMPOSSIBLE HOLIDAYS
CD IRMIN 2CD
Mute / Jan '95 / RTM/Disc

MUSK AT DUSK
CD IRMIN 1CD
Mute / Jan '95 / RTM/Disc

Schmidt, Marie

SOPHISTICATED LADIES TO YOU (Schmidt, Marie & Benita Haastrup/Helle Marstrand)
CD MECCACD 1091
Music Mecca / May '97 / Cadillac / Jazz Music / Wellard

Schmitt, Timothy B.

PLAYIN' IT COOL
Playin' it cool / Lonely girl / So much in love / Something's wrong / Voice / Wrong number / Take a good look around you / Tell me what you dream / Gimme some money
CD 7559603592
WEA / Jul '96 / Warner Music

Schneider, Maria

COMING ABOUT (Schneider, Maria Jazz Orchestra)
El viento / Love theme from Spartacus / Bombshelter beast / Night watchmen / Coming about / Giant steps / Waxwing
CD ENJ 90692
Enja / Jul '96 / New Note/Pinnacle / Vital/ SAM

EVANESCENCE (Schneider, Maria Jazz Orchestra)
Wyrgly / Evanescence / Gumba blue / Some circles / Green piece / Gush / My lament / Dance you monster to my soft song / Last season
CD ENJ 80482
Enja / Apr '94 / New Note/Pinnacle / Vital/ SAM

Schneiderman, Rob

DARK BLUE
CD RSRCD 132
Reservoir Music / Oct '94 / Cadillac

NEW OUTLOOK
CD RSRCD 106
Reservoir Music / Oct '89 / Cadillac

RADIO WAVES
CD RSRCD 120
Reservoir Music / Nov '94 / Cadillac

SMOOTH SAILING
CD RSRCD 114
Reservoir Music / Nov '94 / Cadillac

STANDARDS
CD RSRCD 126
Reservoir Music / Nov '94 / Cadillac

Schnitt Acht

SLASH & BURN
CD CDDVN 23
Devotion / Sep '93 / Pinnacle

SUBURBAN MINDS
CD HY 391009CD
Hyperium / Nov '92 / Cargo / Plastic Head

Schnyder, Daniel

TARANTULA
With the devil on the backseat / Water / Samiel / Angst / Cairo / Caio cadenza / Mister / Wedding song / No smoking / Short life / Memoires / Tarantula / Cool sweets / Dolphy's dance / Homunculus / El cigaro
CD ENJ 93022

Enja / Nov '96 / New Note/Pinnacle / Vital/ SAM

Schoenberg, Loren

JUST A-SETTIN' AND A-ROCKIN'
CD ______ **MM 5039**
Music Masters / Oct '94 / Nimbus

TIME WAITS FOR NO ONE
CD ______ **MM 5032**
Music Masters / Aug '94 / Nimbus

Scholl, Bernd

SECRET GARDEN
CD ______ **SKYCD 3052**
Sky / Sep '95 / Greyhound / Koch / Vital/ SAM

Schonecker, Joachim

COMMON LANGUAGE
Blues and fashion / Bud's beaux arts / Snapshot / Contemplation / Ain't misbehavin' / Marie / Please talk after the beep / I hear a rhapsody / Back and forth / 'Round midnight / My shining hour
CD ______ **DTRCD 122**
Double Time / Mar '97 / Express Jazz

Schoolly D

ADVENTURES OF SCHOOLLY D
CD ______ **RCD 20050**
Rykodisc / May '92 / ADA / Vital

Schott, John

IN THESE GREAT TIMES
CD ______ **TZA 7115**
Tzadik / Feb '97 / Cargo

Schramm, Dave

VI
CD ______ **RTS 6**
Normal / Jul '94 / ADA / Direct

Schrammel & Slide

DEUX
CD ______ **BEST 9011CD**
Acoustic Music / Nov '95 / ADA

Schramms

LITTLE APOCALYPSE
CD ______ **OK 33022CD**
Okra / May '94 / ADA / Direct

ROCK, PAPER, SCISSORS, DYNAMITE
CD ______ **OKCD 33017**
Okra / Mar '94 / ADA / Direct

WALK TO DELPHI
CD ______ **OKRACD 007**
Okra / Nov '94 / ADA / Direct

Schroeder, Ingrid

BEE CHARMER
Bee charmer / Thing in the middle / Time passes / Move into the light / Waterbaby / Unforgiven / Not a day goes by / Average bear / Presence / Paint you blue
CD ______ **0630149822**
Magnet / Aug '96 / Warner Music

Schroeder, John

SPACE AGE SOUL (Schroeder, John Orchestra & Sounds Orchestral)
Hungry for love / Soul coaxin' / Ain't that peculiar / Soul trek / Agent double-o soul / Sweet soul talk / Soul destroyer / Soul for sale / Get out of my life woman / Where did our love go / Working in a coalmine / You've lost that loving feelin' / Sunny / Rescue me / Papa's got a brand new pig bag / You can't hurry love / Summertime / Lovin' you girl / How sweet it is (to be loved by you) / When a man loves a woman / Black is black
CD ______ **NEMCD 769**
Sequel / Jun '96 / BMG

Schroer, Oliver

JIGZUP
Victory of love / Toby's reel/The Job / Laughing in her sleep / Horseshoes and rainbows / Far away by the sea/Lady Diane Laundy/Seanaghan Kennedy's / Ansgar's jig/Kari's jig / Blow November wind/Sea of change / Devil and the little faces / Hub of the wheel / Jump up/Ghost dance / Roro / December 16th/Shooting star / If geese could sing / Bright eyes
CD ______ **IRCD 039**
Iona / Mar '97 / ADA / Direct / Duncans

Schubert

TOILET SONGS
CD ______ **9041542**
Mausoleum / Feb '95 / Grapevine/ PolyGram

Schubert, Matthias

BLUE AND GREY SUITE
Nichol's dime / La maitre / Blue and grey suite / Wariatka
CD ______ **ENJ 90452**
Enja / Oct '95 / New Note/Pinnacle / Vital/ SAM

Schuetz, Michael

JUST LIKE THAT
CD ______ **ISCD 163**
Intersound / Sep '96 / Jazz Music

Schuler, Manfred

SOUND OF AUSTRIA, A (Schuler, Manfred Zither & Folk Music Ensemble)
CD ______ **DIS 80116**
Dorian Discovery / Jan '94 / Conifer/BMG / Select

Schulkowsky, Robyn

HASTENING WESTWARD (Schulkowsky, Robyn & Nils Petter Molvaer)
CD ______ **4493712**
ECM / Nov '95 / New Note/Pinnacle

Schuller, Ed

ELEVENTH HOUR, THE (Schuller, Ed Band)
O zone / Eleventh hour / PM in the AM / Keeping still / Mountain / Love lite / Shamal / For dodo
CD ______ **TUTUCD 888124**
Tutu / May '92 / Vital/SAM

Schulz, Bob

TOGETHER AGAIN (Schulz, Bob & The Riverboat Ramblers)
CD ______ **BCD 279**
GHB / Jul '93 / Jazz Music

TRIBUTE TO TURK MURPHY (Schulz, Bob & His Frisco Band)
CD ______ **SOSCD 1288**
Stomp Off / Nov '95 / Jazz Music / Wellard

Schulze, Klaus

AUDENTITY
CD ______ **CDTB 505**
Thunderbolt / Mar '95 / TKO Magnum

BABEL
Nebuchadnezzar's dream / Foundation / Tower raises / First clouds / Communication problems / Gap of alienation / Immuring insanity / Heaven under feet / Deserted stones / Facing abandoned tools / Vanishing memories / Sinking into oblivion / Far from earth
CD ______ **CDVE 5**
Venture / May '94 / EMI

BEYOND RECALL
Grongo Nero / Trancess / Brave old sequence / Big fall / Airlight
CD ______ **CDVE 906**
Venture / Mar '93 / EMI

BODY LOVE
CD ______ **CDTB 123**
Thunderbolt / Jan '90 / TKO Magnum

DIG IT
CD ______ **CDTB 144**
Thunderbolt / Mar '94 / TKO Magnum

DOME EVENT, THE
Dome event / Andante / Nachtmusik Schattenhaft / Allegro / Energisch In gemesenem schritt / Sehr behaglich / Unbeschwert / Ohne hast / Scherzo: Un poco loco / Event: Rhythmisch uppig, Dann vergnugt Bewegt / Presto / Ubermutig, Sturmisch bewegt Heftig / Un poco loco (Reprise) / Crescendo / Finale: Tuttu synthi / After eleven
CD ______ **CDVE 918**
Venture / Mar '93 / EMI

DREAMS
Classical move / Five to four / Dreams / Klaustrophony
CD ______ **CDTB 039**
Thunderbolt / Aug '95 / TKO Magnum

DRESDEN PERFORMANCE/DRESDEN IMAGINARY SCENES
CD ______ **CDVED 903**
Venture / Nov '90 / EMI

DRIVE INN (Schulze, Klaus & Rainer Bloss)
Drive Inn / Sightseeing / Truckin' / Highway / Racing / Road to clear / Drive out
CD ______ **CDTB 028**
Thunderbolt / May '86 / TKO Magnum

DUNE
Dune / Shadows of ignorance
CD ______ **CDTB 145**
Thunderbolt / '86 / TKO Magnum

EN=TRANCE
En=trance / A-numerique / Fm delight / Velvet system
CD Set ______ **CDTB 061**
Thunderbolt / '89 / TKO Magnum

IRRLICHT
CD ______ **CDTB 133**
Thunderbolt / '86 / TKO Magnum

MIDITERRANEAN PADS
Decent changes / Miditerranean pads / Percussion / Planante
CD ______ **CDTB 081**
Thunderbolt / Jan '90 / TKO Magnum

MIRAGE
Aeronef / Eclipse / Exvasion / Lucidinterspace / Destinationvoid / Xylotones / Cromwaves / Willowdreams / Liquidmirrors / Springdance
CD ______ **CDTB 033**
Thunderbolt / Nov '86 / TKO Magnum

MOONDAWN
Floating / Mindphaser
CD ______ **CDTB 093**
Thunderbolt / Feb '91 / TKO Magnum

PICTURE MUSIC
Totem / Mental door
CD ______ **CDTB 098**
Thunderbolt / Jan '91 / TKO Magnum

POLAND LIVE 83
CD ______ **CDTB 504**
Thunderbolt / Nov '94 / TKO Magnum

ROYAL FESTIVAL HALL VOL.1
CD ______ **CDVE 916**
Venture / Nov '92 / EMI

ROYAL FESTIVAL HALL VOL.2
CD ______ **CDVE 917**
Venture / Nov '92 / EMI

TIMEWIND
Bayreuth return / Wahnfried 1883
CD ______ **CDCA 2006**
Virgin / Jun '88 / EMI

TRANCEFER
CD ______ **CDTB 146**
Thunderbolt / Jun '94 / TKO Magnum

X
CD ______ **CDTB 501**
Thunderbolt / Mar '96 / TKO Magnum

Schurch, Dorothea

INTERNI PENSIERI
CD ______ **INTAKTCD 046**
Intakt / May '97 / Cadillac

Schurr, Diane

BLUES FOR SCHURR
I'm not ashamed to sing the blues / When did you leave Heaven / Stormy Monday blues / These blues / Moonlight and shadows / Alright, OK you win / Who will the next fool be / Save your love for me / Someone to love / Toodle loo on down / You've got to hurt before you heal / I want to go home
CD ______ **GRP 98632**
GRP / Mar '97 / New Note/BMG

DIANE SCHUUR & THE COUNT BASIE ORCHESTRA (Schurr, Diane & Count Basie Orchestra)
CD ______ **GRP 95502**
GRP / Feb '92 / New Note/BMG

DIANE SCHUUR COLLECTION
CD ______ **GRP 95912**
GRP / Jun '89 / New Note/BMG

HEART TO HEART (Schurr, Diane & B.B. King)
No one ever tells you / I can't stop loving you / You don't know me / It had to be you / I'm putting all my eggs in one basket / Glory of love / Try a little tenderness / Spirit in the dark / Freedom / At last / They can't take that away from me
CD ______ **GRP 97722**
GRP / May '94 / New Note/BMG

LOVE WALKED IN
Love walked in / Time after time / Say it isn't so / Blue gardenia / Never let me go / Nothing ever changes my love for you / Sunday kind of love / How deep is the ocean / You're a sweetheart / I wanna be loved
CD ______ **GRP 98412**
GRP / Apr '96 / New Note/BMG

Schussler Du

SCHUSSLER DU
CD ______ **NV 47CD**
Nasty Vinyl / Oct '96 / Cargo

Schutz

SEVEN WORDS
CD ______ **0630176762**
Warner Bros. / Jul '97 / Warner Music

Schutz, Michael

DON'T LOOK BACK (Schutz, Michael & Marco Bronzini)
CD ______ **ISCD 115**
Intersound / Oct '91 / Jazz Music

Schutze, Paul

ABYSMAL EVENINGS
Red hand / Slow burning ghosts / Close heat of starlight / Font / Abysmal evenings / Lotus voltage / Delta haze / Night dissolved in the lakes of heaven
CD ______ **AMBT 19**
Virgin / Sep '96 / EMI

APART
Rivers of mercury / Skin of air and tears / Sleeping knife dance / Visions of a sand drinker / Coldest light / Eyeless and naked / Ghosts of animals / Taken (apart) / Consequence / Memory of water / Throat full of stars / Sleep
CD ______ **AMBT 6**
Virgin / Feb '95 / EMI

DEUS EX MACHINA
CD ______ **XCD 001**
Extreme / May '95 / Vital/SAM

ISABELLE EBRAHARDT: THE OBLIVION SEEKER
CD ______ **SDV 031CD**
SDV / Nov '94 / Plastic Head

NEW MAPS OF HELL
CD ______ **ABB 104CD**
Big Cat / Aug '96 / 3mv/Pinnacle

RAPTURE OF METALS
CD ______ **ABB 105CD**
Big Cat / Aug '96 / 3mv/Pinnacle

RAPTURES OF METALS, THE
CD ______ **SDV 027CD**
SDV / Oct '94 / Plastic Head

SITE ANUBIS
CD ______ **ABB 106CD**
Big Cat / Jun '96 / 3mv/Pinnacle

SURGERY OF TOUCH
CD ______ **SNTX 175**
Sentrax Corporation / Sep '94 / Plastic Head

Schwartz, Jonathan

ANYONE WOULD LOVE YOU
CD ______ **MCD 5325**
Muse / Sep '92 / New Note/Pinnacle

Schwarz, Rudy

SALMON DAVE
CD ______ **EFA 113882**
Musical Tragedies / May '94 / SRD

Schwehr, Cornelius

POCO A POCO SUBITO
CD ______ **ARTCD 6191**
Hat Art / Jan '97 / Cadillac / Harmonia Mundi

Schweizer, Irene

IRENE SCHWEIZER & ANDREW CYRILLE (Schweizer, Irene & Andrew Cyrille)
CD ______ **INTAKTCD 008**
Intakt / May '97 / Cadillac

IRENE SCHWEIZER & GUNTER SOMMER (Schweizer, Irene & Gunter Sommer)
CD ______ **INTAKTCD 007**
Intakt / May '97 / Cadillac

IRENE SCHWEIZER & HANS BENNINK (Schweizer, Irene & Hans Bennink)
CD ______ **INTAKTCD 010**
Intakt / May '97 / Cadillac

IRENE SCHWEIZER & LOUIS MOHOLO (Schweizer, Irene & Louis Moholo)
CD ______ **INTAKTCD 006**
Intakt / May '97 / Cadillac

LES DIABOLIQUES
CD ______ **INTAKTCD 033**
Intakt / Oct '94 / Cadillac

MANY AND ONE DIRECTION
CD ______ **INTAKTCD 044**
Intakt / May '97 / Cadillac

Schwitters, Kurt

URSONATE
CD ______ **ARTCD 6109**
Hat Art / May '92 / Cadillac / Harmonia Mundi

Sciaky, Carla

AWAKENING
CD ______ **GLCD 2115**
Green Linnet / Feb '95 / ADA / CM / Direct / Highlander / Roots

Scientist

AT CHANNEL ONE STUDIO (Scientist & The Mad Professor)
CD ______ **RN 7021**
Rhino / Jun '97 / Grapevine/PolyGram / Jet Star

DUB IN THE ROOTS TRADITION
CD ______ **BAFCD 12**
Blood & Fire / May '96 / Vital

HEAVYWEIGHT DUB CHAMPION
Seconds away / Straight left / Upper cut / Kidney punch / Saved by the bell / Right across / Jab / 1-2 / Below the belt / Knock out
CD ______ **GRELCD 13**
Greensleeves / Sep '92 / Jet Star / SRD

KING OF DUB
11 Guava Road dub / 13 Bread Lane dub / Burning Lane dub / 18 Drumalie Avenue / Gad man the prophet / Rise with version / Next door dub / Forgive them oh jah / Mass murder and corruption / King Tubby's hi-fi / Raw dub / Jack Ruby's hi power / Cultural

vibes / Everlasting version / Knockout version / King Sturgav
CD CDKVL 9029
Kingdom / Mar '87 / Kingdom

REPATRIATION DUB
CD TWCD 1058
Tamoki Wambesi / Nov '95 / Greensleeves / Jet Star / Roots Collective / SRD

SCIENTIST ENCOUNTERS PAC-MAN
Under surveillance / Price's wrath / Space invaders re-group / World cup squad lick their wounds / Vampire initiative / Malicious intent / Dark secret of the box / SOS / Man trap / Look out - behind you
CD GRELCD 46
Greensleeves / Mar '94 / Jet Star / SRD

SCIENTIST MEETS THE SPACE INVADERS
Beam down / Red shift / Time warp / Cloning process / Pulsar / Laser attack / Dematerialise / Fission / Supernova explosion / Quasar
CD GRELCD 19
Greensleeves / May '97 / Jet Star / SRD

SCIENTIST RIDS THE WORLD OF THE EVIL CURSE OF THE VAMPIRES
Voodoo curse / Dance of the vampires / Blood on his lips / Cry of the werewolf / Mummy's shroud / Corpse rises / Night of the living dead / Your teeth in my neck / Ghost of Frankenstein / Plague of zombies
CD GRELCD 25
Greensleeves / May '90 / Jet Star / SRD

SCIENTIST UPSET THE UPSETTER, THE (Scientist & The Upsetter)
CD HS 1CD
Hit Squad / Jun '97 / Jet Star

SCIENTIST WINS THE WORLD CUP
Five dangerous matches
CD GRELCD 37
Greensleeves / Feb '97 / Jet Star / SRD

Scientists

ABSOLUTE
CD REDCD 23
Red Eye / May '94 / Direct

Scientists Of Sound

1.4-4 OR BUST
CD DLCD 2
Downlow / Oct '96 / 3mv/Sony / Vital

Scissor Girls

WE PEOPLE SPACE WITH PHANTOM
CD ALP 63CD
Atavistic / Feb '97 / Cargo / SRD

Scissormen

MUMBO JUMBO
CD BACCYCD 003
Diversity / Sep '95 / 3mv/Vital

NITWIT
CD EVRCD 16
Eve / Nov '92 / Grapevine/PolyGram

Sclavis, Louis

ACCOUSTIC QUARTET
Sensible / Bafouee / Abrupto / Elke / Hop / Seconde / Beata / Rhinoceros
CD 5213492
ECM / Feb '94 / New Note/Pinnacle

CEUX QUI VEILLENT LA NUIT
Derniers regards / L'abstraite anglasie / L'aurore / Procession / L'ombre / Qumran / Ceux qui veillent la nuit / Manoir / Saro / Tenzin / Rapports certains
CD LBLC 6596
Label Bleu / Jul '96 / New Note/Pinnacle

LES VIOLENCES DE RAMEAU (Sclavis Sextet, Louis)
Le diable et son train / De ce trait enchante / Enez punir son injustice / Charmes / La torture d'Alphise / Usage de faux / Reponses a gavotte / Charmes / Pour vous...ces quelques fleurs / Ismenor / Post-mesotonique
CD 5331282
ECM / Oct '96 / New Note/Pinnacle

ROUGE (Sclavis, Louis Quintet)
One / Nacht / Kali la nuit / Reflet / Reeves / Les bouteilles / Moment donne / Face nord / Rouge / Yes love
CD 5119292
ECM / Mar '92 / New Note/Pinnacle

Scobey, Bob

BOB SCOBEY & HIS FRISCO BAND VOL.1
CD JCD 275
Jazzology / Mar '97 / Jazz Music

BOB SCOBEY'S FRISCO BAND
CD CD 53143
Giants Of Jazz / Jan '94 / Cadillac / Jazz Music / Target/BMG

DIRECT FROM SAN FRANCISCO
CD GTCD 12023
Good Time Jazz / Oct '93 / Complete/ Pinnacle

SCOBEY & CLANCY (Scobey, Bob & Clancy Hayes)
CD GTCD 12009
Good Time Jazz / Oct '93 / Complete/ Pinnacle

Scofield, John

BEST OF JOHN SCHOFIELD, THE
So sue me / Flower power / Big fan / Camp out / Call / You bet / Message to my friend / Tom Thumb / Do like Eddie / Kool
CD CDP 8533302
Blue Note / Nov '96 / EMI

BLUE MATTER
Blue matter / Trim / Heaven hill / So you say / Now she's blonde / Make me / Nag / Time marches on
CD GCD 79403
Gramavision / Sep '95 / Vital/SAM

ELECTRIC OUTLET
Big break / Best Western / Pick hits / Filibustero / Thanks again / King for a day / Phone home / Just my luck
CD GCD 79404
Gramavision / Sep '95 / Vital/SAM

FLAT OUT
Cissy strut / Secret love / All the things you are / In the cracks / Softly / Science and religion / Boss's car / Evansville / Rockin' pneumonia and the boogie woogie flu
CD GCD 79400
Gramavision / Sep '95 / Vital/SAM

GROOVE ELATION
Lazy / Peculiar / Let the cat out / Kool / Old soul / Groove elation / Carlos / Soft shoe / Let it shine / Bigtop
CD CDP 8328012
Blue Note / Nov '95 / EMI

HAND JIVE
I'll take Les / Dark blue / Do like Eddie / She's so lucky / Checkered past / Seventh Floor / Golden daze / Don't shoot the messenger / Whip the mule / Out of the city
CD CDP 8273272
Blue Note / Aug '94 / EMI

I CAN SEE YOUR HOUSE FROM HERE (Scofield, John & Pat Metheny)
I can see your house from here / Red one / No matter what / Everybody's party / Message to my friend / No way Jose / Say the brothers name / SCO / Quite rising / One way to be / You speak my language
CD CDP 8277652
Blue Note / Mar '94 / EMI

LIQUID FIRE
CD GCD 79501
Gramavision / May '95 / Vital/SAM

LIVE
CD ENJACD 30132
Enja / Nov '94 / New Note/Pinnacle / Vital/ SAM

LOUD JAZZ
Tell you what / Dance me home / Signature of Venus / Dirty rice / Wabash / Loud jazz / Otay / True love / Igetthepicture / Spy Vs. spy
CD GCD 79402
Gramavision / Sep '95 / Vital/SAM

MEANT TO BE (Scofield, John Quartet)
Big fan / Keep me in mind / Go blow / Chariots / Guinness spot / Mr. Coleman to you / Eisenhower / Meant to be / Some nerve / Lot in space / French flics
CD CDP 795 479 2
Blue Note / Mar '91 / EMI

OUT LIKE A LIGHT
CD ENJA 40382
Enja / Nov '94 / New Note/Pinnacle / Vital/ SAM

PICK HITS
CD GCD 79405
Gramavision / Sep '95 / Vital/SAM

PICK HITS LIVE
Picks and pans / Heaven will / Blue matter / Trim / Make me / Pick hits / Protocol / Thanks again / Georgia on my mind
CD GRV 88052
Gramavision / Feb '91 / Vital/SAM

ROUGH HOUSE
CD ENJA 30332
Enja / Nov '94 / New Note/Pinnacle / Vital/ SAM

SLO SCO
CD GV 794302
Gramavision / Dec '90 / Vital/SAM

SOLAR (Scofield, John & John Abercrombie)
CD CSAPCD 122
Connoisseur Collection / May '96 / Pinnacle

STILL WARM
Techno / Still warm / High and mighty / Protocol / Rule of thumb / Picks and pans / Gil b 643
CD GCD 79401
Gramavision / Sep '95 / Vital/SAM

WHO'S WHO
Looks like meringue / Cassidae / Beatles / Spoons / Who's who / How the west was won / Beckon call / New strings attached / How to marry a millionaire / Fat dancer
CD OW 34512
One Way / Jun '97 / ADA / Direct / Greyhound

Scooter Lee

HONKY TONK TWIST
CD SBDCD 3
Southbound / Jul '97 / Grapevine/ PolyGram

NEW ALBUM
CD SBDCD 2
Southbound / Jul '97 / Grapevine/ PolyGram

Scorn

COLOSSUS
Endless / Crimson seed / Blackout / Sky is loaded / Nothing hunger / Beyond / Little angel / White irises blind / Scorpionic / Night ash black / Sunstroke
CD MOSH 091CD
Earache / Jun '93 / Vital

DELIVERANCE
Deliverance / Deliverance through dub / Delivered / To high heaven / Black sun rising / Exodus
CD MOSH 176CD
Earache / Feb '97 / Vital

ELLIPSIS
Silver rain fell / Exodus / Dreamscape / Night ash black / Night tide / Falling / End / Automata / Light trap / Dreamscape 2
CD SCORNCD 001
Earache / Jun '95 / Vital

EVANESCENCE
Silver rain fell / Light trap / Falling / Automata / Days passed / Dreamspace / Exodus / Night tide / End / Slumber
CD MOSH 113CD
Earache / Jun '94 / Vital

GYRAL
Six hours one week / Time went slow / Far in out / Stairway / Forever turning / Black box / Hush / Trondheim - Gaule
CD SCORNCD 002
Earache / Nov '95 / Vital

LOGGHI BAROGGHI
Look at that / Do the geek / Next days / Spongie / Out of / It's on / Logghi barogghi / Black box 2 / Nut / Mission / Pithering twat / Fumble / Weakener / Go
CD MOSH 158CD
Earache / Aug '96 / Vital

VAE SOLIS
CD MOSH 054CD
Earache / Apr '92 / Vital

WHITE IRISES BLIND
White irises blind / Black ash dub / Drained / Host of scorpions / Lick forever dog / On ice / Heavy blood / Stairway
CD MOSH 175CD
Earache / Feb '97 / Vital

Scorpio Rising

PIG SYMPHONY
Talking backwards / Breathing underwater / Beautiful people / Watermelon girl / Oceanside / Silver surfing / Evelyn / Little pieces / Goofball / Sleeping sickness / Fountain of you
CD 9362452702
Warner Bros. / May '93 / Warner Music

Scorpions

ANIMAL MAGNETISM
Make it real / Don't make no promises (your body can't keep) / Hold me tight / Twentieth century man / Lady starlight / Falling in love / Only a man / Zoo / Animal magnetism
CD CDFA 3217
Fame / May '89 / EMI

BEST OF ROCKERS 'N' BALLADS, THE
Rock you like a hurricane / Can't explain / Rhythm of love / Big city nights / Lovedrive / Is there anybody there / Holiday / Still loving you / No one like you / Blackout / Another piece of meat / You give me all I need / Hey you / Zoo / China white
CD CDFA 3262
Fame / Oct '91 / EMI

BLACKOUT
Blackout / Can't live without you / You give me all I need / Now / Dynamite / Arizona / China white / When the smoke is going down
CD CDFA 3126
Fame / Nov '88 / EMI

CRAZY WORLD
Tease me please me / To be with you in heaven / Restless night / Kicks after six / Money and fame / Don't believe her / Wind of change / Lust or love / Hit between the eyes / Send me an angel
CD 8469082
Vertigo / Nov '90 / PolyGram

DEADLY STING
Coming home / Rock you like a hurricane / No one like you / Lovedrive / Bad boys running wild / I'm leaving you / Passion rules the game / China white / Walking on the edge / Coast to coast / Loving you Sunday morning / Another piece of meat / Dynamite / Can't live without you / Edge of time
CD CDEMC 3698
EMI / Feb '95 / EMI

LIVE BITES
CD 5269032
Mercury / Apr '95 / PolyGram

LOVE AT FIRST STING
Bad boys running wild / Rock you like a hurricane / I'm leaving you / Coming home / Same thrill / Big city nights / As soon as the good times roll / Crossfire / Still loving you
CD CDFA 3224
Fame / Aug '89 / EMI

LOVEDRIVE
Loving you Sunday morning / Another piece of meat / Always somewhere / Coast to coast / Can't get enough / Is there anybody there / Lovedrive / Holiday
CD CDFA 3080
Fame / Nov '88 / EMI

PURE INSTINCT
Wild child / Stone in my shoe / Where the river flows / Time will call your name / Are you the one / But the best for you / You and I
CD 0630145242
East West / Apr '96 / Warner Music

WORLDWIDE LIVE/SAVAGE AMUSEMENT/ROCKERS 'N' BALLADS (3CD Set)
Countdown / Coming home / Blackout / Bad boys running wild / Loving you Sunday morning / Make it real / Big city nights / Coast to coast / Holiday / Still loving you / Rock you like a hurricane / Can't live without you / Zoo / No one like you / Dynamite / Don't stop at the top / Rhythm of love / Passion rules the game / Media overkill / Walking on the edge / We let it rock (you let it roll) / Every minute of the day / Love on the run / Believe in love / Can't explain / Lovedrive / Is there anybody there / Another piece of meat / You give me all I need / Hey you / China white
CD Set CDS 7979632
EMI / Oct '91 / EMI

Scorpions

ANTHOLOGY 1959-1965
CD WHCD 004
Wooden Hill / Mar '97 / Wooden Hill

Scots Guards Bands

ON PARADE (Scots Guards Pipes & Drums Band)
CD CC 292
Music For Pleasure / Jun '93 / EMI

Scott, Bobby

FOR SENTIMENTAL REASONS
(I love you) for sentimental reasons / Night lights / Lovewise / More I see you / Gee baby ain't I good to you / I keep going back to Joe's / Mamselle / That's all / That Sunday that summer / Nature boy
CD MM 5025
Music Masters / Oct '94 / Nimbus

SLOWLY
CD MM 5053
Music Masters / Aug '94 / Nimbus

Scott, Bon

COMPLETE SESSIONS 1971-1972 (Scott, Bon & The Fraternity)
CD RVCD 56
Raven / Aug '97 / ADA / Direct

EARLY YEARS (Scott, Bon & The Valentines)
To know you is to love you / She said / Everyday I have to cry / I can't dance with you / Peculiar hole in the sky / Love makes sweet music / I can hear raindrops / Why me / Sookie sookie
CD C5CD520
See For Miles/C5 / Sep '91 / Pinnacle

HISTORICAL DOCUMENT (Scott, Bon & The Spectors)
CD SEACD 6
See For Miles/C5 / Oct '92 / Pinnacle

Scott, Buddy

BAD AVENUE
My babe / Big fat woman / Bad bad feeling / Big boss man / Rock me baby / Wake up baby / Today I started loving you again / Mother fur ya blues / With a feeling / Bring it on home to me / Wefare blues / Bad Avenue
CD 5175152
Verve / Feb '93 / PolyGram

Scott, Darrell

ALOHA FROM NASHVILLE
CD SHCD 3864
Sugar Hill / May '97 / ADA / CM / Direct / Koch / Roots

Scott, E.C.

COME GET YOUR LOVE
CD ____ BPCD 75019
Blind Pig / Jul '95 / ADA / CM / Direct / Hot Shot

Scott, Hector

BREATH OF JUNE (Scott, Hector & Neil McFarlane/Fiona Cameron)
CD ____ CDLOC 1102
Lochshore / Jun '97 / ADA / Direct / Duncans

Scott, Jack

CLASSIC SCOTT (5CD Set)
Greaseball / Baby she's gone / You can bet your bottom dollar / Two timin' woman / I need your love / My true love / Leroy / With your love / Indiana waltz / No one will ever know / I can't help it / I'm dreaming of you / Midgie / Save my soul / Geraldine / Goodbye baby / Way I walk / I never felt like this / Bella / Go wild little Sadie / What am I living for / There'll come a time / Baby Marie / Baby baby / What in the world's come over you / Goo deal Lucille / Oh little one / So used to loving you / Cruel world / Window shopping / Burning bridges / Your cheatin' heart / I can't escape from you / Cold cold heart / I could never be ashamed of you / They'll never take her love from me / Crazy heart / You win again / Half as much / I'm sorry for you my friend / Take these chains from my heart / My heart would know / May you never be alone / It's my way of loving you / My King / I'm satisfied with you / Am I the one / It only happened yesterday / True love is blind / Fancy meeting you again / Cool water / Take my hand, precious Lord / When the Saints go marching in / Swing low, sweet chariot / Ezekiel saw de wheel / Joshua fit de battle of Jericho / Little David play your harp / Roll Jordan roll / Down by the riverside / Old time religion / Gospel train / I want to be ready / Just a closer walk with thee / He'll understand and say Well Done / Lonesome Mary / Patsy / Is there something on your mind / Found a woman / Little feeling called love / Now that I / True true love / One of these days / Strange desire / My dream come true / Steps one and two / Sad story / You only see what you wanna see / I can't hold your letters (in my arms) / Cry cry cry / Grizzly bear / Part where I cried / Green green valley / Strangers / Laugh and the world laughs with you / Meo myo / All I see is blue / Jingle bell slide / There's trouble brewin' / Thou shalt not steal / I knew you first / I prayed for an angel / Blue skies (movin' in on me) / What a wonderful night out / Wiggle on out / Tall tales / Flakey John / Seperation's now granted / I don't believe in tea leaves / Standing on the outside looking in / Looking for Linda / I hope, I think, I wish / Gone again / Let's learn to live and love again / Don't hush the laughter / This is where I came in / Road keeps winding / With your love (stereo) / Indiana waltz (stereo) / No one will ever know (stereo) / I can't help it (stereo) / I'm dreaming of you (stereo) / Midgie (stereo) / Save my soul (stereo) / Geraldine (stereo) / Goodbye baby (stereo) / Way I walk (stereo) / If only / When the Saints go marching in (take 19) / Go away from here (crying in my beer) / Before the bird flies / Insane / My special angel / I keep changing my mind / Hard luck Joe / Billy Jack / Mary marry me / Face to the wall / I still love you enough / As you take a walk through my mind / You make it hard not to love you / You're just not gettin' better / Apple blossom time / Blues stay away from me / Stones / Bo's going to jail / Country witch
CD Set ____ BCD 15534
Bear Family / Aug '92 / Direct / Rollercoaster / Swift

JACK SCOTT/WHAT IN THE WORLD'S COME OVER YOU
Save my soul / With your love / Leroy / No one will ever know / Geraldine / I can't help it / Indiana waltz / Midgie / My true love / Way I walk / I'm dreaming of you / Goodbye baby / What in the world's come over you / Oh, little one / Am I the one / I'm satisfied with you / My King / It's my way of loving you / Burning bridges / Baby, baby / So used to loving you / Cruel world / Good deal Lucille / Window shopping
CD ____ BGOCD 303
Beat Goes On / Nov '95 / Pinnacle

SCOTT ON GROOVE
Flakey John / Jingle bell slide / There's trouble brewin' / Tall tales / Wiggle on out / I knew you first / Blue skies (moving in on me) / I prayed for an angel / Separation's now granted / Thou shalt not steal / Road keeps winding / Let's learn to live and love again / Don't hush the laughter / This is where I came in / Looking for Linda / I hope, I think, I wish / Standing on the outside looking in / Gone again / I don't believe in tea leaves / What a wonderful night out
CD ____ BCD 15445
Bear Family / '88 / Direct / Rollercoaster / Swift

WAY I WALK, THE
Leroy / Midgie / Way I walk / Goodbye baby / Go wild Little Sadie / Geraldine / Save my soul / Baby she's gone / Two timin' woman / I never felt like this / My true love / I'm dreaming of you / With your love / I can't help it / No one will ever know / Indiana waltz / Baby Marie / Bella / There comes a time / I need your love / You can bet your bottom dollar / What am I living for / There's trouble brewin' / Lonesome Mary / Greaseball
CD ____ RCCD 3002
Rollercoaster / Aug '90 / Rollercoaster / Swift

Scott, Jimmy

DREAM
Don't take you love from me / It shouldn't happen to a dream / I cried for you / So long / You never miss the water / It's the talk of the town / I'm through with love / Laughing on the outside / Dream
CD ____ 9362456292
Warner Bros. / Jul '94 / Warner Music

LIVE IN NEW ORLEANS (Scott, 'Little' Jimmy)
All of me / When your lover has gone / Everybody's somebody's fool / Lonliest house on the street / Anytime anyplace anywhere / Duelling tenors / Body and soul / Flying home
CD ____ CDCHM 664
Ace / Jul '97 / Pinnacle

LOST AND FOUND
I have dreamed / Stay with me / Folks who live on the hill / For once in my life / Dedicated to you / Day to day / Unchained melody / Sometimes I feel like a Motherless child / Exodus / I wish I knew
CD ____ RSACD 804
Sequel / Dec '94 / BMG

Scott, Linda

ULTIMATE
CD ____ MAR 048
Marginal / Jun '97 / Greyhound

Scott, Mike

BRING 'EM ALL IN
Bring 'em all in / Iona song / Edinburgh Castle / What do you want me to do / I know she's in the building / City full of ghosts (Dublin) / Wonderful disguise / Sensitive children / Learning to love him / She is so beautiful / Wonderful disguise (reprise) / Long way to the light / Building the city of light
CD ____ CDCHR 6108
Chrysalis / Sep '95 / EMI

Scott, Ossie

AT THEIR BEST (Scott, Ossie & Tan Tan)
CD ____ SPCD 05
Superpower / Nov '96 / Jet Star

Scott, Peggy

BEST OF PEGGY SCOTT AND JO JO BENSON, THE (Scott, Peggy & Jo Jo Benson)
CD ____ SCL 2103
Ichiban Soul Classics / Aug '95 / Koch

Scott, Ray

YOU DRIVE ME CRAZY
CD ____ CLCD 4412
Collector/White Label / Jan '97 / TKO Magnum

Scott, Raymond

POWERHOUSE VOL.1
CD ____ STCD 543
Stash / '92 / ADA / Cadillac / CM / Direct / Jazz Music

Scott, Ronnie

JAZZMAN (CD/Book Set)
CD ____ BKB 002
Elm Tree / Jun '95 / TKO Magnum

NEVER PAT A BURNING DOG (Scott, Ronnie Quintet)
Contemplation / I'm glad there is you / White caps / All the things you are / This love of mine / When love is new / Little sunflower
CD ____ JHCD 012
Ronnie Scott's Jazz House / Jan '94 / Cadillac / Jazz Music / New Note/Pinnacle / TKO Magnum

WHEN I WANT YOUR OPINION I'LL GIVE IT TO YOU
CD ____ JHAS 610
Ronnie Scott's Jazz House / Mar '97 / Cadillac / Jazz Music / New Note/Pinnacle / TKO Magnum

Scott, Shirley

BLUES EVERYWHERE
Autumn leaves / Blues everywhere / Oasis / Embraceable you / Triste / 'Round midnight / Theme
CD ____ CCD 79525
Candid / Feb '97 / Cadillac / Direct / Jazz Music / Koch / Wellard

OASIS
CD ____ MCD 5388
Muse / Sep '92 / New Note/Pinnacle

SKYLARK (Scott, Shirley Trio)
Skylark / I still want you/You are my heart's delight / All the things you are / Alone together / Peace / McGee and me / Party's over/Theme
CD ____ CCD 79536
Candid / Feb '97 / Cadillac / Direct / Jazz Music / Koch / Wellard

WALKIN' THING, A
Carnival / DT blues / Walkin' thing / When a man loves a woman / What makes Harold sing / Shades of Bu / How am I to know / Remember
CD ____ CCD 79719
Candid / Jan '97 / Cadillac / Direct / Jazz Music / Koch / Wellard

Scott, Sonny

COMPLETE RECORDINGS 1933
CD ____ SOB 035252
Story Of The Blues / Dec '92 / ADA / Koch

SONNY SCOTT
CD ____ DOCD 5450
Document / May '96 / ADA / Hot Shot / Jazz Music

Scott, Stephen

AMINAH'S DREAM
Aminah's dream / Behind the scenes / Young Confucius / Positive images / Pit and the pendulem / When God created woman / Lil bro'...life goes on / You are too beautiful / Moontrane / In the spur of the moment
CD ____ 5179962
Verve / Jul '93 / PolyGram

BEAUTIFUL THING, THE
CD ____ 5331862
Verve / Feb '97 / PolyGram

SOMETHING TO CONSIDER
In the beginning / Au private / Steps, paths and journeys / Everything I have is yours / Something to consider / Fact of the matter / Nubian chant / Pent-up house / No more misunderstandings / Ninth step / All the comforts of home
CD ____ 8495572
Verve / Jan '92 / PolyGram

Scott, Tom

BLOW IT OUT
CD ____ EK 46108
Sony Jazz / Aug '97 / Sony

BLUESTREAK
Tom cat / Gotta give it up / Love poem / Midtown rush / Only you / Maybe it's over / Sneakin' in the back / Dirty old man / Bluestreak / In your eyes
CD ____ GRP 98442
GRP / Jun '96 / New Note/BMG

DESIRE
Desire / Sure enough / Only one / Stride / Johnny B Badde / Meet somebody / Maybe I'm amazed / Chunk of funk
CD ____ 7599601622
Elektra / Mar '93 / Warner Music

FLASHPOINT
CD ____ GRP 95712
GRP / Oct '88 / New Note/BMG

NEW YORK CONNECTION
Dirty old man / Uptown and country / New York connection / Garden / Time and love / M8idtown rush / Looking out for number 7 / Appolonia (foxtrata) / You're gonna need me
CD ____ EK 64961
Sony Jazz / Aug '96 / Sony

NIGHT CREATURES
Night creatures / Don't get any better / Bhop / Anytime anyplace / We'll be together / Mazin' / Yeah / Refried / Daybreak / We'll be together (instrumental)
CD ____ GRP 98042
GRP / Feb '95 / New Note/BMG

RURAL STILL LIFE
CD ____ MVCZ 127
MCA / Apr '97 / BMG

TARGET
Target / Come back to me / Aerobia / He's too young / Got to get out of New York / Biggest part of me / Burindi bump
CD ____ 7567801062
Atlantic / Jun '93 / Warner Music

TOM CAT
Rock island pocket / Tom cat / Day way / Keep on doin' it / Love poem / Good morning Mr and Mrs America and all the ships / Backfence cattin' / Mondo / Refried
CD ____ EK 64960
Sony Jazz / Aug '96 / Sony

TOM SCOTT AND THE LA EXPRESS
Bless my soul / Sneakin in the back / King Cobra / Dahomey dance / Nunya / Easy life / Spindrift / Strut your stuff / LA expression / Vertigo
CD ____ EK 64959
Sony Jazz / Aug '96 / Sony

Scott, Tommy

COUNTRY HOLIDAY
I never loved no one but you / Does my ring hurt your finger / I'd rather love you / All I have to offer you / Rose Marie / Distant drums / This world is not my home / Cry / Any time / Someday you'll want me to want you / Crying time / Together again / But when I dream / Lovesick blues / Rock of ages / Kiss an angel good morning / There goes my everything / Pretty woman / Blanket on the ground / Stop / If I had my life to live over / Let me be there
CD ____ LCDITV 606
Scotdisc / Nov '95 / Conifer/BMG / Duncans / Ross

GOING HOME
CD ____ CDITV 564
Scotdisc / Oct '92 / Conifer/BMG / Duncans / Ross

HAIL HAIL CALEDONIA
CD ____ CDITV 597
Scotdisc / Nov '94 / Conifer/BMG / Duncans / Ross

HOLIDAY IN IRELAND
CD ____ CDITV 610
Scotdisc / Mar '96 / Conifer/BMG / Duncans / Ross

ORIGINAL HOPSCOTCH
CD ____ PLATCD 3923
Platinum / May '94 / Prism

PIPES AND STRINGS OF SCOTLAND VOL.1
Pride of bonnie Scotland / Ode to joy / Abide with me / Scottish banner / 'Tis a gift (to be simple) / Bonnie Mary of Argyle / Send in the clowns / Jesu joy of man's desiring / Rose of Kelvingrove / Song of the wind / Scott's choice / Light of the morning / Little drummer boy / Carnival is over
CD ____ CDITV 456
Scotdisc / Aug '89 / Conifer/BMG / Duncans / Ross

SCOTLAND FOREVER
CD ____ CDITV 545
Scotdisc / Sep '91 / Conifer/BMG / Duncans / Ross

TOMMY SCOTT AND HIS PIPES AND DIXIE BANDS
CD ____ CDITV 521
Scotdisc / Nov '90 / Conifer/BMG / Duncans / Ross

TOMMY SCOTT COLLECTION
Scotland forever / My ain folk / Going home / Old Scots mother mine / Glencoe / Rowan tree / Abide with me / Road to Dundee / Amazing grace / Flower of Scotland / Bonnie Mary of Argyle / Auld lang syne
CD ____ CDITV 431
Scotdisc / Nov '87 / Conifer/BMG / Duncans / Ross

TOMMY SCOTT'S COUNTRY HOP
CD ____ CDITV 569
Scotdisc / May '94 / Conifer/BMG / Duncans / Ross

TOMMY SCOTT'S HOPSCOTCH CEILIDH PARTY
CD ____ CDITV 528
Scotdisc / Dec '90 / Conifer/BMG / Duncans / Ross

TOMMY SCOTT'S ROYALE HIGHLAND SHOWBAND (Scott, Tommy's Royale Highland Showband)
Red river rose / March march march all the way / Morag of Dunvegan / Mingulay boat song / Maggie may / Day is ended / PK's salute / Pigeon on the gate / Pipes O'Drummond / De'il among the tailors / Kilt is my delight / Pipers patrol / Mount Fuji / Water is wide / Flute salad / Dark island / May kway o'may kway / High road to Linton
CD ____ CDITV 426
Scotdisc / Jun '87 / Conifer/BMG / Duncans / Ross

TOMMY SCOTT'S SCOTLAND
Annie Laurie / Dark Lochnagar / Great Glen / Skye boat song / Amazing grace / Flower of Scotland / Will ye no' come back again / Scotland forever / My love is like a red red rose / Flowers of the forest / Rowan tree / Green trees of Tyrol / My Ain folk / Auld lang syne
CD ____ CD ITV 411
Scotdisc / Dec '86 / Conifer/BMG / Duncans / Ross

TOMMY SCOTT'S STREET PARTY (Various Artists)
Scotland forever / Will ye come tae ma party / Goodnght Irene / Silver threads among the gold / Achy breaky heart / Auld lang syne / Bonnie wee Jeannie McColl / My ain folk / When your old wedding ring was new / Nobody's child
CD ____ CDITV 617
Scotdisc / Oct '96 / Conifer/BMG / Duncans / Ross

Scott, Tommy

TOMMY SCOTT
CD _____ **CLCD 2854**
Collector/White Label / Jul '97 / TKO Magnum

Scott, Toni

CHIEF, THE
CD _____ **CHAMPCD 1022**
Champion / Feb '90 / 3mv/BMG

Scott, Tony

CLARINET ALBUM, THE (Scott, Tony Quartet)
CD _____ **W 1132**
Philology / Nov '93 / Cadillac / Harmonia Mundi

DIALOGUE WITH MYSELF, LIKE A CHILD'S WHISPER
CD _____ **W 762**
Philology / Dec '95 / Cadillac / Harmonia Mundi

MEDITATION (Scott, Tony & Jan Akkerman)
Silmarillion / Offering / Blues, blues and then some more blues / Under the bo tree
CD _____ **8350702**
Verve / Jan '92 / PolyGram

MUSIC FOR YOGA MEDITATION AND OTHER JOYS
Prahna / Shiva / Samadhi / Hare krishna / Hatha / Kundalina / Sahasrarra / Treveni / Shanti
CD _____ **8353712**
Verve / Mar '94 / PolyGram

MUSIC FOR ZEN MEDITATION
Is not all one / Murmuring sound of the mountain / Quivering leaf, ask the wind / After the snow the fragrance / To drift like clouds / Za-zan (meditation) / Prajina paramita hridya sutra / Sanzan (moment of truth) / Satori (enlightenment)
CD _____ **8172092**
Verve / Jan '93 / PolyGram

SUNG HEROES
Misery (to lady day) / Portrait of Anne Frank / Remembrance of Art Tatum / Requiem for 'Hot Lips' Page / Blues for an African friend / For Stefan Wolpe / Israel / Memory of my father / Lament to manolete
CD _____ **SSC 1015D**
Sunnyside / Sep '86 / Discovery

TONY SCOTT & BILL EVANS 1957 (Scott, Tony & Bill Evans)
CD _____ **CD 53202**
Giants Of Jazz / May '95 / Cadillac / Jazz Music / Target/BMG

TONY SCOTT IN AFRICA
Mayibue Afrika Uhuuru (Long live Afrika freedom) / Calling the Gods / Freedom day / Rain prayer / Aaee-aaoo / Witch doctor / Voodoo
CD _____ **CD 12536**
Music Of The World / Jun '96 / ADA / Target/BMG

Scott-Adams, Peggy

HELP YOURSELF
CD _____ **BILLCD 100**
Secret Love / Mar '97 / 3mv/Sony

Scott-Heron, Gil

GLORY (The Gil Scott Heron Collection/ 2CD Set)
Johannesburg / Revolution will not be televised / Blue collar / New York City / Hello Sunday, hello road / We almost lost Detroit / Angel dust / Bottle / Winter in America / Delta man / South Carolina (Barnwell) / Inner city blues / Showbizness / B Movie / Lady Day and John Coltrane / I think I'll call it morning / You can depend on (the train from Washington) / Shut 'em down / Ain't no such thing as superman / Klan / Fast lane / Race track in France / Storm music / Save the children / Song for Bobby Smith / Beginnings / Legend in his own mind
CD Set _____ **353913**
Arista / Nov '90 / BMG

MINISTER OF INFORMATION
CD _____ **CCSCD 403**
Castle / Apr '94 / BMG

MOVING TARGET
Fast lane / Washington DC / No exit / Blue collar / Explanations / Ready or not / Black history of the world
CD _____ **254921**
Arista / Feb '97 / BMG

REFLECTIONS
Storm music / Grandma's hands / Is that jazz / Morning thoughts / Inner city blues / Siege of New Orleans / Gun / B Movie
CD _____ **254094**
Arista / Feb '97 / BMG

REVOLUTION WILL NOT BE TELEVISED, THE
Revolution will not be televised / Sex education - ghetto style / Get out of the ghetto blues / No knock / Lady Day and John Coltrane / Pieces of a man / Home is where the hatred is / Brother / Save the children / Whitey on the moon / Did you hear what they said / When you are who you are / I think I'll call it morning / Sign of the ages / Or down you fall / Needle's eye / Prisoner
CD _____ **ND 86994**
Bluebird / Apr '89 / BMG

SMALL TALK AT 125TH AND LENOX (A New Black Poet)
Introduction / Revolution will not be televised / Omen / Brother / Comment / Small talk at 125th and Lenox / Subject was faggots / Evolution (and flashbacks) / Plastic pattern people / Whitey on the moon / Vulture / Enough / Everyday / Paint it black / Who'll pay reparations on my soul
CD _____ **07863666112**
Flying Dutchman / Jun '97 / BMG

SPIRITS
Message to the messengers / Spirits / Give her a call / Lady's song / Spirits past / Other side (parts 1-3) / Work for peace / Don't give up
CD _____ **MUMCD 9415**
Mother / Aug '94 / PolyGram

Scottish Fiddle Orchestra

LEGENDARY SCOTTISH FIDDLE ORCHESTRA, THE (Scottish Fiddle Orchestra & John Mason)
CD _____ **RECD 498**
REL / Apr '95 / CM / Duncans / Highlander

SCOTTISH FIDDLE ORCHESTRA AT THE ROYAL ALBERT HALL, THE
Elizabeth's Royal Albert medley / Orkney two step / Scotland yet / Butterfly polka medley / Jigs from the Gow collection / Massacre of Glencoe / Old woolly jumper medley / Musical flea / Robert Wilson favourites medley / Irish fantasia medley / Western Isles medley / Crookit Bawbee / Eightsome reel medley / Auld lang syne
CD _____ **RECD 504**
REL / Jun '97 / CM / Duncans / Highlander

Scottish Gas Caledonia Pipe ...

OUT OF THE BLUE (Scottish Gas Caledonia Pipe Band)
2/4 marches / March / Strathspey and reel / Irish hornpipe rhythms / Pipe band medley / Irish set / Reels / Slow air / Hornpipes and reels / Jigs
CD _____ **CDTRAX 064**
Greentrax / Nov '93 / ADA / Direct / Duncans / Highlander

Scottish National Pipe & ...

SCOTLAND THE BRAVE (Scottish National Pipe & Drum Corps)
CD _____ **CNCD 5958**
Disky / Jul '93 / Disky / THE

Scottish Philharmonic Singers

PSALMS OF SCOTLAND
Psalm 23 Crimond / Psalm 100 Old 100th / Paraphrase 30 Kedron / Psalm 136 Crofts' 136th / Paraphrase 18 Glasgow / Psalm 43 Martyrs / Psalm 24 St George's, Edinburgh / Psalm 46 Stroudwater / Paraphrase 48 St Andrew / Paraphrase 65 Desert / Psalm 148 St John / Psalm 130 Martydrom / Psalm 124 Old 124th / Psalm 23 Orlington / Psalm 103 Coleshill / Psalm 36 London new / Psalm 95 Bon Accord / Paraphrase 2 Salzburg / Psalm 12 French / Psalm 72 Effingham
CD _____ **SCSCD 2830**
SCS Music / Apr '94 / Conifer/BMG

SCOTTISH PHILHARMONIC SINGERS
In praise of Islay / Rosebud by my early walk / Johnny Cope / Fairy lullaby / Scots wha hae / Island herdsmaid / Duncan Gray / Iona boat song / Ossianic processional / Flow gently sweet Afton / Charlie is my darling / Skye boat song / Fife fisher song / Ye banks and braes o' bonnie Doon / Ca' the Yowes / Loch Lomond / Island sheiling song / Eriskay love lilt / Flowers o' the forest / Donald Ewan's wedding
CD _____ **LCOM 9043**
Lismor / Apr '91 / ADA / Direct / Duncans / Lismor

Scottish Power Pipe Band

TARTAN WEAVE
CD _____ **CDMON 836**
Monarch / Aug '95 / ADA / CM / Direct / Duncans

Scottish Regiments

PIPES AND DRUMS OF THE SCOTTISH REGIMENT
CD _____ **CC 295**
EMI / May '93 / EMI

TUNES OF GLORY
CD _____ **MOICD 006**
Moidart / Jun '94 / Conifer/BMG

Scotto, Renata

GREAT VOICE
CD Set _____ **HR 4291/92**
New Note / Mar '91 / Cadillac / New Note/ Pinnacle

Scram C Baby

TASTE
CD _____ **GAP 018**
Gap Recordings / Feb '94 / SRD

Scrawl

BLOODSUCKER
CD _____ **SMR 17D**
Simple Machines / May '93 / SRD

Scream

FUMBLE/BANGING THE DRUM
CD _____ **DIS 82D**
Dischord / Jul '93 / SRD

SCREAM: LIVE
CD _____ **YCLS 010CD**
Your Choice / Jun '94 / Plastic Head

STILL SCREAMING/THIS SIDE UP
CD _____ **DIS 81D**
Dischord / Jul '93 / SRD

Scream

NO MORE CENSORSHIP
CD _____ **RASCD 4001**
Ras / Dec '88 / Direct / Greensleeves / Jet Star / SRD

Screamin' Cheetah Wheelies

SCREAMIN' CHEETAH WHEELIES
Shakin' the blues / Ride the tide / Something else / This is the time / Slow burn / Leave your pride (at the front door) / Jami / Sister mercy / Majestic / Moses brown / Let it flow
CD _____ **7567825072**
WEA / Mar '94 / Warner Music

Screaming Iguanas Of Love

GLAD YOU WEREN'T THERE
CD _____ **NAK 6003CD**
Naked Language / Sep '94 / Koch

WILD WILD WILD
Wild wild wild / Never let you fall / Hole in my soul / Girl stuff / Let it down / Back together / Punch it / Madison / Ain't a thing about it / Our gang / I think of you / Let me explain / Stone's throw away / Stuck to you
CD _____ **NAK 6001 CD**
Naked Language / Nov '91 / Koch

Screaming Lord Sutch

MURDER IN THE GRAVEYARD
CD _____ **FCD 3023**
Fury / Mar '95 / Nervous / TKO Magnum

RAVING LOONEY PARTY FAVOURITES
I'm a hog for you baby / Monster rock / Penny Penny / Jenny Jenny / Keep a knockin' / Long tall Sally / Jack The Ripper / Rockabilly madman / Murder in the graveyard / All black and hairy / London rocker / Rock and shock / Scream and scream
CD _____ **303042**
Hallmark / Jul '97 / Carlton

Screaming Trees

ANTHOLOGY (2CD Set)
CD Set _____ **SST 260CD**
SST / May '93 / Plastic Head

BUZZ FACTORY
Black sun morning / Flower web / End of the universe
CD _____ **SST 248CD**
SST / Mar '89 / Plastic Head

CHANGE HAS COME
Change has come / Days / Flashes / Time speaks her golden tongue / I've seen you before
CD _____ **SP 48B**
Sub Pop / Dec '96 / Cargo / Greyhound / Shellshock/Disc

DUST
Halo of ashes / Make my mind / Look at you / Dying days / Sworn and broken / All I know / Witness / Traveler / Dime western / Gospel plow
CD _____ **4839802**
Epic / Jul '96 / Sony

EVEN IF AND ESPECIALLY WHEN
Transfiguration / Straight out to any place / World painted / Don't look down / Girl behind the mask / Flying / Cold rain / Other days and different planets / Pathway / You know where it's at / Back together / In the forest
CD _____ **SST 132CD**
SST / May '93 / Plastic Head

INVISIBLE LANTERN
CD _____ **SST 188CD**
SST / Sep '88 / Plastic Head

OTHER WORLDS
CD _____ **SST 105CD**
SST / May '93 / Plastic Head

UNCLE ANESTHESIA
Beyond this horizon / Bed of roses / Uncle Anethesia / Story of her fate / Caught between / Lay your head down / Before we arise / Something about today / Alice said / Time for light / Disappearing / Ocean of confusion / Closer
CD _____ **4673072**
Epic / Feb '92 / Sony

Screaming Tribesmen

BONES AND FLOWERS
CD _____ **RCD 1007**
Rykodisc / Jun '92 / ADA / Vital

I'VE GOT A FEELING
CD _____ **RCD 1006**
Rykodisc / May '93 / ADA / Vital

Screams For Tina

SCREAMS FOR TINA
CD _____ **CDSATE 11**
Zoth Ommog / Nov '94 / Cargo / Plastic Head

Screeching Weasel

ANTHEM FOR A NEW TOMORROW
CD _____ **LOOKOUT 76CD**
Lookout / Jun '97 / Cargo / Greyhound / Shellshock/Disc

ANTHEM FOR THE NEW NATIONS
CD _____ **LOOKOUT 76CD**
Lookout / Jan '97 / Cargo / Greyhound / Shellshock/Disc

BARK LIKE A DOG
CD _____ **FAT 547CD**
Fatwreck Chords / Dec '96 / Plastic Head

BOOGARA
CD _____ **LOOKOUT 62CD**
Lookout / Jan '97 / Cargo / Greyhound / Shellshock/Disc

HOW TO MAKE ENEMIES
CD _____ **LOOKOUT 97CD**
Lookout / Jan '97 / Cargo / Greyhound / Shellshock/Disc

KILL THE MUSICIANS
CD _____ **LOOKOUT 95CD**
Lookout / Jan '97 / Cargo / Greyhound / Shellshock/Disc

MY BRAIN HURTS
CD _____ **LOOKOUT 50CD**
Lookout / Jun '97 / Cargo / Greyhound / Shellshock/Disc

WIGGLE
CD _____ **LOOKOUT 63CD**
Lookout / Jan '97 / Cargo / Greyhound / Shellshock/Disc

Screeper

GOLDEN BOY EP
CD _____ **MOUTHY 5CD**
Mouthy Production / Jun '97 / Shellshock/ Disc

Screw

BURNING IN WATER
CD _____ **398417015CD**
Metal Blade / Jun '96 / Pinnacle / Plastic Head

Screw Radio

TALK RADIO VIOLENCE
CD _____ **SST 324CD**
SST / Jan '96 / Plastic Head

Screwdriver

TEACH DEM
CD _____ **GS 70037 CD**
Greensleeves / Apr '92 / Jet Star / SRD

Script

21 SYNTHESIZER SPACE HITS
CD _____ **CDCH 076**
Milan / Feb '91 / Conifer/BMG / Silva Screen

Scritti Politti

CUPID AND PSYCHE '85
Word girl / Small talk / Absolute / Little knowledge / Don't work that hard / Perfect way / Lover to fall / Wood beez (pray like Aretha Franklin) / Hypnotize / Flesh and blood / Absolute (version) / Hypnotize (version) / Wood Beez (version)
CD _____ **CDV 2350**
Virgin / Jun '85 / EMI

PROVISION
Boom there she was / Overnite / First boy in this town (Lovesick) / All that we are / Best thing ever / Oh Patti (don't feel sorry for loverboy) / Bam salute / Sugar and spice / Philosophy now / Oh Patti (don't feel sorry for loverboy) (extended) / Boom there she was (dub)
CD _____ **CDV 2515**
Virgin / Aug '91 / EMI

Scuba

UNDERWATER SYMPHONIES
CD _____ **CRECD 136**
Creation / Oct '95 / 3mv/Vital

SCUD

EDWIN INCIDENT, THE
CD BGR 009
BGR / Mar '95 / Plastic Head

Scud Mountain Boys

EARLY YEAR, THE
CD SPCD 389
Sub Pop / Jun '97 / Cargo / Greyhound / Shellshock/Disc

MASSACHUSETTS
CD SPCD 342
Sub Pop / Mar '97 / Cargo / Greyhound / Shellshock/Disc

Scully & Bunny

LONG LONG TIME
CD SONCD 0092
Sonic Sounds / Jul '97 / Jet Star

Scum

MOTHER NATURE
CD BMCD 46
Black Mark / Aug '94 / Plastic Head

Scum Of Toytown

STRIKE
CD WOWCD 41
Words Of Warning / Mar '95 / SRD / Total/ BMG

Scum Rats

GO OUT
CD RUMBCD 001
Rumble / Aug '92 / Nervous / Pinnacle

LIVE AT THE BIG RUMBLE
CD RUMBCD 014
Rumble / Aug '92 / Nervous / Pinnacle

SDI

SIGN OF THE WICKED
CD 15390
Laserlight / Aug '91 / Target/BMG

SDL

SPACE AGE FRONTIER
CD DBMLABCD 5
Labworks / Oct '95 / RTM/Disc / SRD

SDR Big Band

EASY LIFE
CD ISCD 160
Intersound / Sep '96 / Jazz Music

Sea & Cake

BIZ
CD EFA 121152
Moll / Oct '95 / SRD

FAWN
CD THRILLCD 39UK
Thrill Jockey / Apr '97 / Cargo / Greyhound

NASSAU
CD EFA 121122
Moll / May '95 / SRD

SEA AND CAKE, THE
Jacking the ball / Polio / Bring my car I feel to smash it / Flat lay the waters / Choice blanket / Culabra cut / Bombay / Showboat angel / So long to the captain / Lost in autumn
CD R 3102
Rough Trade / Feb '94 / Pinnacle

Sea, David

GROOVE MISSION
CD JVC 90101
JVC / Mar '97 / Direct / New Note/ Pinnacle / Vital/SAM

Sea Horses

LISTEN
Asking heaven and heart / Salute to the sun / Exaltations / Angles of incidence / Pray / Satori / Kissing flowers / For our emotions / Open veins / Insufferance / Confession
CD SH 777
Mandala / Apr '91 / ADA / Harmonia Mundi / Mandala

Sea Nymphs

SEA NYMPHS, THE
CD ALPHCD 021
Alphabet Business Concern / May '95 / Plastic Head

Sea Train

MARBLEHEAD MESSENGER, THE
CD S21 57661
One Way / Apr '94 / ADA / Direct / Greyhound

Sea Urchins

LIVE FROM LONDON
CD FRIGHT 061
Fierce / Jun '97 / RTM/Disc

STARDUST
CD SARAH 609CD
Sarah / Mar '95 / Vital

Seabrook, Terry

CAN'T STOP NOW (Seabrook, Terry Cubana Bop)
Cubana bop / This nearly was mine / Moanin' / Autumn leaves / Myles from home / Can't stop now / For us / Peruchin / Cantaloupe island / Flight / Que caliente / Soundwaves / Festival mambo / One by one
CD CBCD 1
TSM / May '96 / Jet Star

Seaford College Chapel Choir

FOR THE BEAUTY OF THE EARTH
CD GRCD 71
Grasmere / Nov '95 / Highlander / Savoy / Target/BMG

Seahorses

DO IT YOURSELF
I want to know / Blinded by the sun / Love is the law / Boy in the picture / Love me and leave me / Suicide Drive / Happiness is egg shaped / Round the universe / Hello / 1999
CD GED 25134
Geffen / May '97 / BMG

Seal

SEAL
Beginning / Deep water / Crazy / Killer / Whirlpool / Future love paradise / Wild / Show me / Violet
CD ZTT 9CD
ZTT / May '91 / Warner Music

SEAL VOL.2
Bring it on / Prayer for the dying / Dreaming in metaphors / Don't cry / Fast changes / Kiss from a rose / People asking why / Newborn friend / If I could / I'm alive / Bring it on (reprise)
CD 4509962562
ZTT / May '94 / Warner Music

Seal, Joseph

MIGHTY WURLITZER
CD MACCD 151
Autograph / Aug '96 / BMG

WURLITZER
CD TRTCD 184
TrueTrax / May '95 / THE

Seals, Brady

TRUTH, THE
Natural born lovers / Truth / Another you, another me / Still standing tall / Kentucky boy / Boy oh boy (ain't that just like my girl) / She / You can have your own way with me / She doesn't love here anymore / Junkie for your love
CD 9362462582
Warner Bros. / Jun '97 / Warner Music

Seals, Dan

IN A QUIET ROOM
CD TDC 010
Tour Data Corporation / Mar '96 / Direct

Seals, Son

BAD AXE
Don't pick me for your fool / Going home (where women got meat on their bones) / Just about to lose your clown / Friday again / Cold blood / Out of my way / I think you're foolin' me / I can count on my blues / Can't stand to see her cry / Person to person
CD ALCD 4738
Alligator / May '93 / ADA / CM / Direct

CHICAGO FIRE
CD ALCD 4720
Alligator / May '93 / ADA / CM / Direct

LIVE AND BURNING
CD ALCD 4712
Alligator / May '93 / ADA / CM / Direct

LIVING IN THE DANGER ZONE
Frigidaire woman / I can't lose the blues / Woman in black / Tell it to another fool / Ain't that some shame / Arkansas woman / Danger zone / Last four nickels / My time now / Bad axe / My life
CD ALCD 4798
Alligator / May '93 / ADA / CM / Direct

MIDNIGHT SON
CD ALCD 4708
Alligator / May '93 / ADA / CM / Direct

NOTHING BUT THE TRUTH
CD ALCD 4822
Alligator / Sep '94 / ADA / CM / Direct

SON SEALS BLUES BAND (Seals, Son Blues Band)
Mother In Law Blues / Sitting at my window / Look now baby / Your love is a cancer / All you love / Cotton pickin' blues / Hot sauce / How could she leave me / Going home tomorrow / Now that I'm down
CD ALCD 4703
Alligator / Feb '94 / ADA / CM / Direct

SPONTANEOUS COMBUSTION (Son Seals Live)
Crying for my baby / Don't pick me for your fool / Mother blues / No no baby / Your love is like a cancer / I need my baby back / Sitting here thinking / Every goodbye ain't gone / Sun is shining / Landlord at my door / Trouble trouble / Don't lie to me
CD ALCD 4846
Alligator / Nov '96 / ADA / CM / Direct

Seam

ARE YOU DRIVING ME CRAZY
CD EFA 049602
City Slang / Jul '95 / RTM/Disc

HEADSPARKS
CD EFA 0407626
City Slang / Apr '92 / RTM/Disc

PROBLEM WITH ME
CD EFA 0492326
City Slang / Sep '93 / RTM/Disc

Seance

FORNEVER LAID TO REST
Who will not be dead / Reincarnage / Blessing of death / Sin / Haunted / Fornever laid to rest / Necronomicon / Wind of Gehenna / Inferna cabbala
CD BMCD 017
Black Mark / Jun '92 / Plastic Head

SALTRUBBED EYES
CD BMCD 44
Black Mark / Jan '94 / Plastic Head

Sear Bliss

PAGAN WINTER
CD TM 1202CD
Mascot / Mar '97 / Plastic Head

Search & Destroy

MUSIC FOR HAPP-E PARTIES
CD DB 47922
Deep Blue / Sep '96 / PolyGram

Searchers

30TH ANNIVERSARY COLLECTION 1962-1992, THE (3CD Set)
CD Set NEXCD 170
Sequel / Feb '92 / BMG

BEST OF THE SEARCHERS, THE
Needles and pins / Love potion no.9 / Sweets for my sweet / Listen to me / Hungry for love / Farmer John / Take it or leave it / Where have all the flowers gone / Someday we've gonna love again / Don't throw your love away / Some other guy / When you walk in the room / He's got no love / Ain't gonna kiss you / When I get home / WHat have they done to the rain / Have you ever loved somebody / Sugar and spice / Take me for what I'm worth / Goodbye my love
CD MCCD 291
Music Club / May '97 / Disc / THE

BRITISH 60'S, THE (Searchers/Gerry & The Pacemakers)
Sweets for my sweet: *Searchers* / Take it or leave it: *Searchers* / Goodbye my love: *Searchers* / When you walk in the room: *Searchers* / Don't throw your love away: *Searchers* / Take me for what I'm worth: *Searchers* / Needles and pins: *Searchers* / Sugar and spice: *Searchers* / What have they done to the rain: *Searchers* / Someday we're gonna love again: *Searchers* / How do you do it: *Gerry & The Pacemakers* / Ferry across the Mersey: *Gerry & The Pacemakers* / You'll never walk alone: *Gerry & The Pacemakers* / It's still rock'n'roll to me: *Gerry & The Pacemakers* / Roll over Beethoven: *Gerry & The Pacemakers* / Unchained melody: *Gerry & The Pacemakers* / Imagine: *Gerry & The Pacemakers* / Running man: *Gerry & The Pacemakers* / I want you just the way you are: *Gerry & The Pacemakers* / Don't let the sun catch you crying: *Gerry & The Pacemakers*
CD PLATCD 206
Platinum / Feb '97 / Prism

EP COLLECTION, THE
When you walk in the room / Missing you / Oh my lover / This empty place / No one else could love me / What have they done to the rain / Goodbye my love / Till I met you / Can't help forgiving you / I don't want to go on without you / Till you say you'll be mine / Sweets for my sweet / Since you broke my heart / Too many miles / Take me for what I'm worth / Take it or leave it / Someday we're gonna love again / Bumble bee / System / Love potion no.9 / Money / Alright / Just like me / Everything you do / If I could find someone / It's all been a dream / Hungry for love / Sea of heartbreak / Ain't gonna kiss ya / Don't cha know
CD SEECD 275
See For Miles/C5 / Jul '89 / Pinnacle

MIKE PENDER'S SEARCHERS
CD GRF 185
Tring / Jan '93 / Tring

NEEDLES AND PINS
Needles and pins: *Tyler, Bonnie* / When you walk in the room / I don't want to go on without you / What have they done to the rain / Farmer John / Someday we're gonna love again / Goodbye my love / All my sorrows / Sugar and spice / Take me for what I'm worth / Love potion no.9 / Don't throw your love away / Stand by me / Be my baby / Magic potion / Sweets for my sweet
CD 21020
Laserlight / Jul '97 / Target/BMG

SEARCHERS, THE
Sweets for my sweet / Sugar and spice / Needles and pins / Saints and sinners / Missing you / Goodbye my love / Glad all over / Have you ever loved somebody / Love potion no.9 / Take it or leave it / When you walk in the room / What have they done to the rain / It's all been a dream / Someday we're gonna love again / Don't throw your love away / He's got no love / Take me for what I'm worth / Alright / Money / When I get home
CD CDMFP 5922
EMI / Oct '91 / EMI

SWEETS FOR MY SWEET
Sweets for my sweet / He's got no love / Take me for what I'm worth / What have they done to the rain / Someday we're gonna love again / Take it or leave it / Needles and pins / Have you ever loved somebody / Don't throw your love away / When you walk in the room / Sugar and spice / Goodbye my love
CD 5507412
Spectrum / Sep '94 / PolyGram

Sears, Al

SEAR-IOUSLY
125th Street, New York / Shake hands / Tan skid lad / Brown boy / Huffin' and puffin' / Sear-iously / Mag's alley / Fo yah / In the good old summertime / Ivory cliffs / Easy Ernie / Vo sa / Goin' uptown / Tweedle dee / Come and dance with me / Come a runnin' / Tom, Dick 'n' Henry / Tina's canteen / Right now, right now / Midnight wail / Love call / Rock 'n' roll ball / Here's the beat / Great googa mooga / Fo ya
CD BCD 15668
Bear Family / Jun '92 / Direct / Rollercoaster / Swift

Seaton, B.B.

EVERYDAY PEOPLE
Now I know / Good to me / Just a little more time / Private lessons / Everyday people / Gimme little love / Tell me if you're ready / Still look sexy / Some day I'll be free / Photographs and souvenirs
CD RNCD 2012
Rhino / Jul '93 / Grapevine/PolyGram / Jet Star

GREATEST HITS
CD CDSBS 001
Soul Beat / Aug '96 / Jet Star / SRD

Seaweed

FOUR
CD SPCD 110/286
Sub Pop / Sep '93 / Cargo / Greyhound / Shellshock/Disc

SEAWEED
CD TUPCD 028
Tupelo / Oct '91 / RTM/Disc

SPANAWAY
CD EC2A 0034
Polydor / Nov '96 / PolyGram

Sebadoh

BAKESALE
CD WIGCD 11
Domino / Jun '95 / Vital

BUBBLE AND SCRAPE
CD WIGCD 4
Domino / Jun '95 / Vital

HARMACY
CD WIGCD 26
Domino / Aug '96 / Vital

MAGNET'S COIL
CD CORX 016CD
Cortex / Feb '97 / Cargo

ROCKING THE FOREST
CD WIGCD 2
Domino / Jun '95 / Vital

SEBADOH VOL.3
CD HMS 1682
Homestead / Jul '94 / Cargo / SRD

SEBADOH VS. HELMET
CD WIGCD 3
Domino / Jun '95 / Vital

WEED FORRESTIN
CD HMS 1582
Homestead / '94 / Cargo / SRD

Sebastian, John B.

JOHN B SEBASTIAN
Red eye express / She's a lady / What she thinks about / Magical connection / You're a big boy / Rainbows all over your blues / How have you been / Baby, don't ya get crazy / Room nobody lives in / Fa-fana-fa / I had a dream
CD _______ **EDCD 304**
Edsel / Jan '90 / Pinnacle

Sebestyen, Marta

APOCRYPHA
CD _______ **HNCD 1368**
Hannibal / Apr '97 / ADA / Vital

BEST OF MARTA SEBESTYEN, THE
En csak azt csodalom / Termetes / Szol a kakacs mar / Repulj madar, repulj / Da je visnya / Hindi lullabye / Istenem istenem / Shores of Loch Brann/Hazafele / Szeress egyet, s legyen szep / Tavasz, tavasz / Gold, silver or love / Szerelem, szerelem
CD _______ **HNCD 1412**
Hannibal / Mar '97 / ADA / Vital

KISMET
Devoika mome / Sino moi / Leaving Derry Quay / Eleni / Gold, silver or love / Hindu lullabye / Shores of loch brann / Hazafele / If I were a rose (ha en rozsa velnek) / Imam sluzhba (the conscript)
CD _______ **HNCD 1392**
Hannibal / Feb '96 / ADA / Vital

MARTA SEBESTYEN AND MUZIKAS (Sebestyen, Marta & Muzikas)
CD _______ **HNCD 1330**
Hannibal / Apr '97 / ADA / Vital

Sebo, Ferenc

HUNGARIAN FOLK MUSIC (Sebo, Ferenc Ensemble)
CD _______ **ROUCD 5005**
Rounder / Feb '93 / ADA / CM / Direct

Secada, Jon

HEART, SOUL & A VOICE
Whipped / Take me / If you go / Good feelings / Where do I go from you / Fat chance / Mental picture / Stay / La la la / Don't be silly / Eyes of a fool / Si te vas (If you go) / Tuyo (Take me)
CD _______ **SBKCD 29**
SBK / Feb '95 / EMI

JON SECADA
Just another day / Dreams that I carry / Angel / Do you believe in us / One of a kind / Time heals / Do you really want me / Misunderstood / Always something / I'm free / Otro dia mas sin verte / Angel (Spanish version)
CD _______ **SBKCD 19**
SBK / Aug '92 / EMI

SECADA
Too late too soon / Heaven is you / Believe / Get me over you / It's enough / Ready for love / I live for you / Who will take care of me / After all is said and done / Forever is as long as it lasts / Too late too soon / Amandolo
CD _______ **SBKCD 32**
SBK / Jun '97 / EMI

Seck, Mansour

N'DER FOUTA TOORA VOL.2
CD _______ **STCD 1073**
Stern's / Mar '96 / ADA / CM / Stern's

Seck, Thione

DAALY
CD _______ **STCD 1070**
Stern's / Jan '97 / ADA / CM / Stern's

DAKAR SOUND VOL.5
CD _______ **2002851**
Dakar Sound / Jan '97 / Stern's

Secola, Keith

CIRCLE
CD _______ **NORMAL 162CD**
Normal / Mar '94 / ADA / Direct

Secombe, Harry

COLLECTION, THE
On the street where you live / Where is love / Gigi / Speak softly to me / O Mimi Tu Piu Non Torni: *Secombe, Harry & Delme Bryn-Jones* / Au fond du Temple Saint: *Secombe, Harry & Delme Bryn-Jones* / Day by day / Send in the clowns / I've grown accustomed to her face / If ever I would leave you / Onward christian soldiers / It is no secret / Swing low, sweet chariot / Beautiful Isle of somewhere / All things bright and beautiful / How great thou art / Battle Hymn of the Republic / Desiderata / Whispering hope / Lord's my shepherd / Perfect day / God be in my head
CD _______ **3036000732**
Carlton / Feb '97 / Carlton

HIGHWAY FAVOURITES
Guide me thou great redeemer / Little understanding / O love that will not let me go / Jerusalem / Rock of ages / God be in my head / All things bright and beautiful / Who's the one / Onward Christian soldiers / Old rugged cross / 23rd Psalm / For the beauty of the earth / Cover me with love / There is a green hill / Prayer perfect / How great thou art / Song of joy / Abide with me
CD _______ **KMCD 832**
Kingsway / May '95 / Complete/Pinnacle

HIGHWAY OF LIFE
CD _______ **CDSR 021**
Telstar / Sep '93 / BMG

MY FAVOURITE CAROLS
Here we come a-wassailing / While shepherds watched their flocks by night / Good King Wenceslas / Silent night / First Noel / O come all ye faithful (Adeste Fidelis) / That's what I'd like for Christmas / Mary's boy child / Once in Royal David's City / Holly and the ivy / God rest ye merry gentlemen / White Christmas / Ave Maria / Nessun dorma
CD _______ **5509302**
Spectrum / Nov '96 / PolyGram

SIR HARRY
CD _______ **PRCD 143**
President / May '93 / Grapevine/PolyGram / President / Target/BMG

THIS IS MY SONG
This is my song / Younger than springtime / When you wish upon a star / Story of a starry night / Father of girls / Falling in love with love / September song / Three coins in the fountain / Impossible dream / Come back to Sorrento / Catari, catari / Some enchanted evening / O sole mio / Nessun dorma
CD _______ **5501882**
Spectrum / Mar '94 / PolyGram

VERY BEST OF HARRY SECOMBE, THE
If I ruled the world / Moulin rouge / Girls were made to love and kiss / Vienna, city of my dreams / Man without love / Lead kindly light / Falling in love with you / Santa Lucia / Summer song / Bless this house / This is my song / Grinzing / Love is a many splendoured thing / Funiculi funicula / I long to see the day / Il lamento de Federico / Stranger in paradise / Be my love / Here in my heart / Abide with me
CD _______ **5527192**
Spectrum / Jan '97 / PolyGram

VERY BEST OF SIR HARRY SECOMBE, THE
Onward Christian soldiers / Battle hymn of the Republic / Guide me o thou great / Jehovah / How sweet the name of Jesus sounds / When I survey / Somewhere / Jerusalem / I vow to thee my country / Holy city / Old rugged cross / How great thou art / Lord's prayer / When you look back / On your life / Cover me with love / You'll never walk alone
CD _______ **WSTCD 9724**
Nelson Word / Apr '92 / Nelson Word

YOURS SINCERELY
Love changes everything / Sunrise sunset / Amazing grace / Impossible dream / September song / Land for all seasons / If / I'll see you again / Nessun dorma / Colours of my life / Cover me with love / Right to sing / Father of girls / What kind of fool am I / We'll keep a welcome / If I loved you / What a wonderful world / And yet
CD _______ **5107322**
Philips / Nov '91 / PolyGram

Second Decay

TASTE
CD _______ **SPV 08484722**
Lost & Found / Oct '94 / Plastic Head

Second Hand

DEATH MAY BE YOUR SANTA CLAUS
Funeral / Hangin' on a eyelid / Lucifer and the egg / Somethin' you got / Cyclops / Sic transit gloria mundi / Revelations ch16 vs, 9-21 / Take to the skies / Death may be your santa claus / Baby you are another monster
CD _______ **SEECD 479**
See For Miles/C5 / Jul '97 / Pinnacle

Second Life

SECOND LIFE
CD _______ **SB 040**
Second Battle / Jun '97 / Greyhound

Second Voice

DAWN (2CD Set)
CD Set _______ **EFA 129062**
Kodex / May '96 / SRD

Secrecy

RAGING ROMANCE
CD _______ **N 01822**
Noise / '91 / Koch

Secret Affair

GLORY BOYS BEHIND CLOSED DOORS
Glory boys / Shake and shout / Going to a go go / Time for action / New dance / Days of change / Don't look down / One way world / Let your heart dance / I'm not free (but I'm cheap)
CD _______ **74321276182**
RCA / Jul '95 / BMG

VERY BEST OF SECRET AFFAIR, THE (Time For Action)
Time for action / Glory boys / My world / Sound of confusion / Do you know / Soho strut / Big beat / Hide and seek / So cool / Do you know / One way world / Let your heart dance / Streetlife parade / Looking through my eyes / Days of change / Going to a go-go / Lost in the night (Mack The Knife) / Shake and shout / New dance / I'm not free (but I'm cheap)
CD _______ **74321487322**
Camden / May '97 / BMG

Secret Goldfish

AQUA-PET
CD _______ **BENT 012CD**
Creeping Bent / Jun '96 / RTM/Disc

Secret Knowledge

SO HARD
Hard theme / Love me now / I dig your ass / Love beads / Sugar daddy / Dracula / Drac-drums / Escape to New York / Dirty low down dog / Dear Johnny / 2 much of nuthin' / Fire
CD _______ **74321342442**
De-Construction / Sep '96 / BMG

Secret Life

SOLE PURPOSE
CD _______ **PULSE 18CD**
Pulse 8 / Feb '95 / BMG

Secret Shine

UNTOUCHED
Suck me down / Temporal / Spellbound / So close I come / Into the ether / Toward the sky / Underworld / Sun warmed water
CD _______ **SARAH 615CD**
Sarah / Mar '95 / Vital

Secret Square

SECRET SQUARE
CD _______ **E6 003CD**
Elephant 6 / Feb '97 / Cargo

Secret Stars

SECRET STARS
CD _______ **SHR 80CD**
Shrimper / Dec '96 / Cargo

Section Brain

HOSPITAL OF DEATH
CD _______ **MABCD 005**
MAB / Jan '94 / Plastic Head

Sector

INDUSTRIAL COSMETICS
CD _______ **AT 01CD**
Atmosphere / Jun '95 / Plastic Head

ORANGE
CD _______ **AT 06CD**
Atmosphere / Jan '96 / Plastic Head

Sedaka, Neil

BEST OF NEIL SEDAKA, THE
CD _______ **74321113142**
RCA / Aug '94 / BMG

BREAKING UP IS HARD TO DO
CD _______ **WMCD 5698**
Disky / Oct '94 / Disky / THE

GREATEST HITS
Sing me / Standing on the inside / Laughter in the rain / Oh, Carol / Stairway to heaven / Hey little devil / Happy birthday sweet sixteen / Calendar girl / New York city blues / Love will keep us together / Solitaire / Lonely night (angel face) / Sad eyes / Bad blood / Immigrant / Breaking up is hard to do
CD _______ **PLATCD 365**
Platinum / '91 / Prism

GREATEST HITS
I go ape / Oh Carol / Stairway to heaven / Run Sampson run / You mean everything to me / Calendar girl / I must be dreaming / Little devil / Happy birthday sweet sixteen / Next door to an angel / Let's go steady again
CD _______ **ND 89171**
RCA / Apr '90 / BMG

GREATEST HITS IN CONCERT
CD _______ **JHD 015**
Tring / Jun '92 / Tring

GREATEST HITS LIVE
CD _______ **MU 5028**
Musketeer / Oct '92 / Disc

GREATEST HITS LIVE
I'm a song, sing me / Standing on the inside / Laughter in the rain / Oh Carol / Medley / Calender girl / New York City blues / Love will keep us together / Solitaire / Lonely night (angel face) / Sad eyes / Bad blood / Immigrant / Breaking up is hard to do
CD _______ **QED 186**
Tring / Nov '96 / Tring

HIS GREATEST HITS OF THE 60'S
Oh Carol / Little devil / I go ape / Happy birthday sweet sixteen / Breaking up is hard to do / Calendar girl / Stairway to heaven / Next door to an angel / King of clowns / You mean everything to me / One way ticket (to the blues) / Sweet little you
CD _______ **CDMFP 5819**
Music For Pleasure / Oct '91 / EMI

HOLLYWOOD CONCERT
CD _______ **CD 3504**
Cameo / Aug '94 / Target/BMG

IMMACULATE NEIL SEDAKA, THE
Sing me / Standing on the inside / Laughter in the rain / Oh carol / Stairway to Heaven / Little devil / Happy birthday sweet sixteen / Calendar girl / New York City blues / Love will keep us together / Solitaire / Lonely night (Angel face) / Sad eyes / Bad blood / Immigrant / Breaking up is hard to do
CD _______ **PLATCD 151**
Platinum / Mar '96 / Prism

IN PERSON
I am a song (sing me) / Standing on the inside / Laughter in the rain / Oh, Carol / Climb up (stairway to heaven) / Hey little devil / Happy birthday sweet sixteen / Calendar girl / New York City blues / Love will keep us together / Solitaire / Lonely night / Sad eyes / Bad book / Immigrant / Breaking up is hard to do
CD _______ **307102**
Hallmark / Jun '97 / Carlton

ITALIANO
CD _______ **CNR 1025**
Marginal / Jun '97 / Greyhound

LAUGHTER AND TEARS
Standing on the outside / Love will keep us together / Solitaire / Other side of me / little lovin' / Lonely nights / Brighton / I'm a song, sing me / Breaking up is hard to do / Laughter in the rain / Cardboard California / Bad blood / Queen of 1964 / Hungry years / Betty Grable / Beautiful you / That's when the music takes me / Our last song together
CD _______ **5500322**
Spectrum / May '93 / PolyGram

LAUGHTER IN THE RAIN
CD _______ **MACCD 234**
Autograph / Aug '96 / BMG

LEGENDS IN MUSIC
CD _______ **LECD 073**
Wisepack / Jul '94 / Conifer/BMG / THE

LOVE WILL KEEP US TOGETHER
Love will keep us together / Rainy day bells / My son and I / Clown time / When a love affair is through / My Athena / Desiree / Going nowhere / I'm a song, sing me / Little lovin' / Steppin' out / Betty Grable / I go ape / Stupid cupid / Number one with a heartache / You turn me on / Can't get you out of my mind / Blinded by your love / No getting over you
CD _______ **5173512**
Polydor / Oct '92 / PolyGram

NEIL SEDAKA
CD _______ **295054**
Ariola Express / Jul '92 / BMG

NEIL SEDAKA
CD _______ **GFS 063**
Going For A Song / Jul '97 / Else / TKO Magnum

OH CAROL
CD _______ **WMCD 5650**
Disky / May '94 / Disky / THE

SINGER & HIS SONGS, THE
Oh Carol / Breaking up is hard to do / Rainy day bells / Little devil / Can't get you out of my mind / Happy birthday sweet sixteen / No getting over you / I go ape / Betty grable / Calendar girl / When a love affair is through / Next door to an angel / Clown time / Stairway to heaven / One way ticket (to the blues) / You turn me on / My son and I / Miracle song
CD _______ **MCCD 148**
Music Club / Feb '94 / Disc / THE

SOLITAIRE
Prelude / Solitaire / Silent movies / Rosemary blues / Little song / God bless Joanna / Cardboard California / Gone with the morning / I wish I had a carousel / Adventures of a boy child wonder / Is anybody going to miss you / Better days are coming / What have they done to the moon / One more mountain to climb / Home / I'm a song / Don't let it mess your mind / Beautiful you / That's when the music takes me
CD _______ **MUCD 9024**
Musketeer / Apr '95 / Disc

SPOTLIGHT ON NEIL SEDAKA
Rosemary blue / One more mountain to climb / Silent movies / What have they done to the moon / Super bird / Cardboard California / God bless Joanna / Little song / Prelude / Gone with the morning / Ring-a-rock / While I dream
CD _______ **HADCD 118**
Javelin / Feb '94 / Henry Hadaway / THE

SWEET SIXTEEN
Happy birthday sweet sixteen / Standing on the inside / I'm a love song (sing me) / Laughter in the rain / Oh Carol / Stairway to heaven / Hey little devil / Calendar girl / New York City blues / Love will keep us together / Solitaire / Lonely night (angel face) / Sad eyes / Bad blood / Immigrant / Breaking up is hard to do
CD _______ CD 6013
Music / Apr '96 / Target/BMG

TIMELESS (The Very Best Of Neil Sedaka)
Happy birthday sweet sixteen / Breaking up is hard to do / Calender girl / Our last song together / Oh Carol / I go ape / One way ticket (to the blues) / Next door to an angel / Standing on the inside / Immigrant / Laughter in the rain / Hungry years / That when the music takes me (live) / Solitaire / Love will keep us together / Queen of 1964 / Little devil / Other side of me / Stairway to heaven / Miracle song
CD _______ 5114422
Polydor / Oct '91 / PolyGram

VERY BEST OF NEIL SEDAKA, THE
Calendar girl / Oh Carol / King of clowns / Next door to an angel / Let's go steady again / Breaking up is hard to do / Happy birthday sweet sixteen / Little devil / I go ape / Stairway to heaven / Diary / You mean everything to me
CD _______ 74321446812
Camden / Feb '97 / BMG

Seddiki, Sidi

SHOUFI
Shouffin qouna / Maliki / Liam / Haram aliq / Bent nass / Galbi / Zin / Melkoum / Qaoun allah / Lachir
CD _______ CDORB 063
Globestyle / Oct '90 / Pinnacle

Sedrenn

ON OUR WAY
CD _______ KMCD 62
Keltia Musique / Jul '96 / ADA / Discovery

See Me Suffer

CHEESE
CD _______ EFA 127082
Old World / Feb '96 / SRD

Seeds

BAD PART OF TOWN/LIVE ALBUM BEDTIME (Seeds/Sky Saxon)
CD _______ 842110
EVA / May '94 / ADA / Direct

EVIL HOODOO
March of the flower children / Wind blows your hair / Tripmaker / Try to understand / Evil hoodoo / Chocolate river / Pushin' too hard / Falling off the edge / Mr. Farmer / Up in her room / Can't seem to make you mine / Pictures and designs / Flower lady and her assistant / Rollin' machine / Out of the question / Satisfy you
CD _______ DOCD 1998
Drop Out / Jul '91 / Pinnacle

FADED PICTURE, A
CD _______ DOCD 1992
Drop Out / Sep '91 / Pinnacle

FLOWER PUNK (3CD Set)
Can't seem to make you mine / No escape / Evil hoodoo / Girl I want you / Pushin' too hard / Try to understand / Nobody spoil my fun / It's a hard life / You can't be trusted / Excuse excuse / Fallin' in love / Mr. Farmer / Pictures and designs / Tripmaker / I tell myself / Faded picture / Rollin' machine / Just let go / Up in her room / March of the flower children / Travel with your mnd / Out of the question / Painted doll / Flower lady and her assistant / Now a man / Thousand shadows / Two fingers pointing on you / Where is the entrance way to play / Six dreams / Fallin' / Pretty girl / Moth and the flame / I'll help you / Cry wolf / Plain spoken / Gardener / One more time / Creepin' about 20 / Buzzin' around / Mr. Farmer / No escape / Satisfy you / Night time girl / Up in her room / Gypsy plays his drums / Can't seem to make you mine / Mumble bumble / Forest outside your door / 900 million people daily all making love / Pushin' too hard / Wind blows your hair / Other place / She's wrong / Fallin' off the edge / Chocolate river / Daisy Mae / Wind blows your hair / Satisfy you / Wildblood / Sad and alone / Lose your mind / Thousand shadows
CD Set _______ FBOOK 16
Demon / Feb '97 / Pinnacle

Seefeel

CH-VOX
CD _______ CAT 038CD
Rephlex / Nov '96 / Prime / RTM/Disc

QUIQUE
CD _______ PURECD 028
Too Pure / Oct '93 / Vital

SUCCOUR
CD _______ WARPCD 28
Warp / Mar '95 / Prime / RTM/Disc

Seeger, Mike

3RD ANNUAL REUNION
CD _______ ROUCD 0313
Rounder / Jan '95 / ADA / CM / Direct

CLOSE TO HOME (Old Time Music From Mike Seeger's Collection 1952-1967)
CD _______ SFWCD 40097
Smithsonian Folkways / Jul '97 / ADA / Cadillac / CM / Direct / Koch

FRESH OLD TIME MUSIC
CD _______ ROUCD 0262
Rounder / Aug '88 / ADA / CM / Direct

THIRD ANNUAL FAREWELL REUNION
CD _______ ROUCD 0313
Rounder / Nov '94 / ADA / CM / Direct

WAY DOWN IN NORTH CAROLINA (Seeger, Mike & Paul Brown)
Wandering boy / I have no one to love me (but the sailor) / Down to Tampa / Rout / Trader boatman / Green icy mountain / Cacklin' hen / Make me a pallet / Goodbye, little Bonnie / What'll I do with the baby-o / Way down in North Carolina / Rabbit chase / New river train / Tee la lollee / Loving Emma / Little Maggie / Walking that pretty girl home / Cousin Sally Brown / Chilly winds / That girl I love / Let me fall
CD _______ ROUCD 0383
Rounder / Jun '96 / ADA / CM / Direct

Seeger, Peggy

AMERICAN FOLK SONGS FOR CHILDREN (Seeger, Peggy & Mike)
Yonder she comes / Down comes a lady / Who's that tapping at the window / Such a getting upstairs / Toodala / How old are you / Jimmy Rose he went to town / What shall we do when we all go out / Goodbye Julie / Goodbye old paint / Oh, oh, the sunshine / Sweet water rolling / Wind blow East / Rain, come wet me / It rained a mist / Rain or shine / One cold and frosty morning / By'm bye / Jim along Josie / There was a man and he was mad / Riding in the buggy, Miss Mary Jane / Billy Barlow / Juniper tree / Old Joe Clarke / Down by the Greenwood Sidey-O / Roll that brown jug down to town / As I walked out one holiday / She'll be coming round the mountain / Juba / Run, chillen run / All around the kitchen / I'm going to join the army / Scraping up sand in the bottom of the sea / Old Mister Rabbit / Old Molly Hare / Oh, John the rabbit / Little pig / Bought me a cat / Hop old squirrel / My horses ain't hungry / Did you go to the Barney / Have a little dog / Frog went a-courtin' / Little bird, little bird / Free little bird / Poor old crow / Ducks in the Millpond / Jim Crack Corn / Eency weency spider / Dog tick / Who built the ark: Noah, Noah / Mary wore her red dress / Pretty little girl with the red dress on / This lady she wears a dark green shawl / Walk along John / Do, do pity my case / Hanging out the linen clothes / Lula gal / Old Aunt Kate / What did you have for your supper / Baby dear / Johnny get your hair cut / I got a letter this morning / Rose, Rose and up she rises / What'll we do with the baby / Hush little baby / Pick a bale of cotton / This old hammer / Train is a-coming / Little black train / When the train comes along / John Henry / Every Monday morning / Going down to town / Sailing in the boat / Blow boys blow / Fire down below / Sally go round the sunshine / This old man / Skip to my Lou / When I was a young maid / Closet key / Built my lady a fine brick house / Where oh where is pretty little Susie / Jingle at the windows / Adam had seven sons / Here sits a monkey / Go to sleepy / Monday morning go to school / Hush 'n' bye / Turtle dove / Mary had a baby / Jesus born in Bethlea / Cherry tree carol
CD _______ ROUCD 8001
Rounder / Feb '97 / ADA / CM / Direct

AMERICAN FOLK SONGS FOR CHRISTMAS (Seeger, Peggy & Mike)
CD _______ ROUCD 0268/69
Rounder / '90 / ADA / CM / Direct

CLASSIC PEGGY SEEGER
Cumberland gap / Lady of Carlisle / Come all ye fair & tender maidens / Deer song / I never will marry / Devilish Mary / Fair maid by the shore / Three banjo tunes / Wife of Usher's well / Rambling gambler / Cruel war is raging / Trooper and the maid / When I was in my prime / So early, early in the Spring / Chickens they are crowing / Who's that knocking at my window / Lass of Roch Royal / Who's going to shoe your pretty foot / Englewood Mine / Just as the tide was flowing / Kicking mule / Heartless lady / Tittery Nan / Loving Reilly / If he'd be a buckaroo
CD _______ FE 105CD
Fellside / Mar '96 / ADA / Direct / Target/BMG

MIKE & PEGGY SEEGER (Seeger, Peggy & Mike)
CD _______ ROUCD 11543
Rounder / '88 / ADA / CM / Direct

ODD COLLECTION, AN
CD _______ ROUCD 4031
Rounder / May '96 / ADA / CM / Direct

SONGS OF LOVE AND POLITICS (The Folkways Years 1955-1992)
CD _______ SFWCD 40048
Smithsonian Folkways / Nov '94 / ADA / Cadillac / CM / Direct / Koch

Seeger, Pete

AMERICAN FOLK SONG, THE
CD _______ ENTCD 241
Entertainers / Mar '92 / Target/BMG

AMERICAN INDUSTRIAL BALLADS
CD _______ SF 40058CD
Smithsonian Folkways / Aug '94 / ADA / Cadillac / CM / Direct / Koch

DARLING COREY & GOOFING OFF SUITE
CD _______ SFCD 40018
Smithsonian Folkways / Jun '93 / ADA / Cadillac / CM / Direct / Koch

FEEDING THE FLAME
CD _______ FF 541CD
Flying Fish / '92 / ADA / CM / Direct / Roots

LINK IN THE CHAIN, A (2CD Set)
Living in the country / My Oklahoma home blowed away / Get up and go / Oh I had a golden thread / Never wed an old man / Queen Anne front / Cryderville jail / Waist deep in the Big Muddy / This land is your land / Draft dodger rag / Pill / Where have all the flowers gone / My name is Lisa Kalvelage / Turn, turn, turn / Guantanamera / Last train to Nuremberg / Keep your eyes on the prize / Oh freedom / We shall overcome / Coral Creek march / Pretty Boy Floyd / Hobo's lullaby / Aimee Semple McPherson / Cowboy's lament / Jesse James / Belle stars / Harry Sims / Mrs. McGrathe / Jay Gould's daughter / Nameless lick / What did you learn in school today / Henry my son / Put your finger in the air / Michael row the boat ashore / This old car / Be kind to your parents / Cumberland mountain bear chase / This land is your land
CD Set _______ 4851102
Columbia / Nov '96 / Sony

LIVE AT NEWPORT 1963-1965
Intro / Manyura manyah / Malaika / Oh Mary don't you weep / Foolish frog / Deep blue sea / Never wed an old man / Old Joe Clark/ Never wed an old man / Holy ground / Darlin' Corey/Skip to my Lou/Going across the mountains / Midnight special / It takes a worried man / Coral creek march / Where have all the flowers gone / Down by the riverside
CD _______ VCD 77008
Vanguard / Oct '94 / ADA / Pinnacle

TRADITIONAL CHRISTMAS CAROLS
CD _______ SFWCD 40024
Smithsonian Folkways / Dec '94 / ADA / Cadillac / CM / Direct / Koch

Seekers

CARNIVAL OF HITS (Durham, Judith & The Seekers)
Morningtown Ride / World of our own / Island of dreams / Red rubber ball / Colours of my life / Georgy girl / Land is your land / Carnival is over / When will the good apples fall / Someday one day / Kumbaya / 59th Street Bridge song / Walk with me / Leaving of Liverpool / I'll never find another you / Little light of mine / Times they are a-changin' / We shall not be moved / One world love / Keep a dream in your pocket
CD _______ CDEMTV 83
EMI / Apr '94 / EMI

LIVE IN CONCERT (25 Year Reunion Celebration) (Durham, Judith & The Seekers)
When the stars begin to fall / With my swag all on my shoulder / Plaisir d'amour / Morningtown ride / You're my spirit / Kumbaya / Gospel medley / Come the day / One world love / When will the good apples fall / Devoted to you / Colours of my life / Time and again / Red rubber ball / I am Australian / I'll never find another you / Georgy girl / World of our own / Carnival is over / Keep a dream in your pocket
CD _______ CDDPR 130
Premier/MFP / Mar '95 / EMI

SEEKERS, THE
I'll never find another you / World of our own / Carnival is over / Some day one day / Walk with me / Morningtown ride / Georgy girl / When will the good apples fall / Emerald City / We shall not be moved / Island of dreams / Open up them pearly gates / Kumbaya / Blowin' in the wind / Wreck of ol' 97 / Lemon tree / Whiskey in the jar / Five hundred miles / Gypsy Rover / South Australia / Danny boy / Waltzing Matilda / Water is wide
CD _______ CC 226
Music For Pleasure / Sep '88 / EMI

Seekers Of The Truth

OUT OF IGNORANCE
CD _______ LF 243CD
Lost & Found / Sep '96 / Plastic Head

Seelenwinter

IF SOUL TURNS INTO FLESH
CD _______ MASSCD 102
Massacre / Sep '96 / Plastic Head

SEELENWINTER
CD _______ MASSCD 048
Massacre / Mar '95 / Plastic Head

Seelos, Ambros

DANCE GALA '90 (Seelos, Ambros Orchestra)
CD _______ 322287
Koch / Dec '92 / Koch

DANCE GALA '91 (Seelos, Ambros Orchestra)
CD _______ 322462
Koch / Dec '92 / Koch

DANCE GALA '92 (Seelos, Ambros Orchestra)
CD _______ 322665
Koch / Dec '92 / Koch

DANCE GALA '93 (Seelos, Ambros Orchestra)
CD _______ 322863
Koch / Dec '92 / Koch

DANCE GALA VOL.1 : FORMAL BALLROOM DANCING (Seelos, Ambros Orchestra)
CD _______ 340052
Koch / Apr '93 / Koch

LET'S GO DANCING (Seelos, Ambros Orchestra)
Donde vas a Bailar / Spanish flamenco matadors / Hablando suave / Baby trumpets / Love is my life / Goofus / Festival de Corcovado / Drive in jive / Moonflight / Manzanillo / Irgendwann / We belong together / You and me / Girl / Quinto quinto / Pianowellen
CD _______ 323579
Koch International / May '96 / Koch

TANZ GALA (Seelos, Ambros Orchestra)
CD _______ CD 395703
Koch / Nov '93 / Koch

TYPICAL LATIN (Seelos, Ambros Orchestra)
CD _______ 340092
Koch / Aug '93 / Koch

Seely

JULIE ONLY
Bitsa Jane / Meteor shower / Sealskin / Red flume / Crystal Clara / Shine / Lucky penny / Bubblebath / Past Sap Street and go on / Exploring the planets / Inside / Bugles / Wind and would / How to live like a King's kid
CD _______ PURECD 061
Too Pure / Nov '96 / Vital

PARENTHA SEE
CD _______ TE 2007
Third Eye / Nov '96 / Cargo

Seelyhoo

FIRST CAUL, THE
Miss Sarah MacFadyen/Farewell to Rock o' Cleary / Mick's knitted triplets/Brumely brae/Jenny's chickens / Air sgiathan na h-oidhche / First leg/Last leg / Mhurchaidh bhig a chinn a chonnais/Dairmaid's reel / Sometimes it doesn't work/Lucky cap/Potato tree / Hoy's dark and lofty Isle / Superwasp/Along the coast of Norway/Neckbuster / Sean McGuire/Bear Island/Drever's reel / Cuin a chi mi thusa luaidh / Stornsay weaver/Trip to California / Dh'iomain mam bo / Lost job/Old copperplate/Diesel accordion / Walk/Miss Lyall's / Fly to Rousay/ Porto the rat/Dale's place
CD _______ CDTRAX 102
Greentrax / Jan '96 / ADA / Direct / Duncans / Highlander

Seers

PSYCH OUT
Wildman / Rub me out / One summer / Welcome to deadtown / I'll be there / You keep me praying / Walk / Sun is in the sky / Fly away / Breathless / Freedom trip / (All late nite) tequila drinking blues / Magic potion / Lightning strikes
CD _______ CDBRED 86
Cherry Red / Feb '90 / Pinnacle

Seersucker

PUSHING ROPE
CD _______ SKYCD 5010
Sky / Sep '94 / Greyhound / Koch / Vital/ SAM

Seffer, Debora

SILKY
CD _______ CDLLL 157
La Lichere / Aug '93 / ADA / Discovery

Segal, Misha

ZAMBOOKA
CD _______ MM 65068
Music Masters / Oct '94 / Nimbus

Segan

TO MY LORD
CD FA 408
Fremeaux / Jul '96 / ADA / Discovery

Seger, Bob

AGAINST THE WIND (Seger, Bob & The Silver Bullet Band)
Horizontal bop / You'll accompany me / Her strut / No man's land / Long man's land / Long twin silver line / Against the wind / Good for me / Betty Lou's gettin' out tonight / Fire lake / Shinin' brightly
CD CDP 7460602
Capitol / Feb '95 / EMI

DISTANCE, THE (Seger, Bob & The Silver Bullet Band)
Even now: *Seger, Bob* / Makin' Thunderbirds: *Seger, Bob* / Boomtown blues: *Seger, Bob* / Shame on the moon: *Seger, Bob* / Love's the last to know: *Seger, Bob* / Roll me away: *Seger, Bob* / House behind a house: *Seger, Bob* / Comin' home: *Seger, Bob* / Little victories: *Seger, Bob*
CD CZ 403
Capitol / Mar '91 / EMI

FIRE INSIDE, THE (Seger, Bob & The Silver Bullet Band)
Take a chance / Real love / Sightseeing / Always in my heart / Fire inside / Real at the time / Which way / Mountain / Blind love / She can't do anything wrong
CD CDEST 2149
Capitol / Feb '95 / EMI

GREATEST HITS
Roll me away / Night moves / Turn the page / You'll accomp'ny me / Hollywood nights / Still the same / Mainstreet / Old time rock 'nd' roll / We've got tonight / Against the wind / Fire inside / Like a rock C'est la vie / In your time
CD CDEST 2241
Capitol / Feb '95 / EMI

IT'S A MYSTERY (Seger, Bob & The Silver Bullet Band)
Rite of passage / Lock and load / By the river / Manhattan / I wonder / It's a mystery / Revisionism Street / Golden boy / I can't save you Angelene / Sixteen shells from a 30-6 / West of the moon / Hands in the air
CD CDEST 2271
Capitol / Feb '96 / EMI

LIVE BULLET
Nutbush City Limits / Travellin' man / Beautiful loser / Jody girl / Looking back / Get out of Denver / Let it rock / I've been working / Turn the page / UMC / Bo Diddley / Ramblin' gamblin' man / Heavy music / Katmandu
CD CDP 7460852
Capitol / Feb '95 / EMI

NIGHT MOVES
Rock 'n' roll never forgets / Night moves / Fire down below / Sunburst / Sunspot baby / Mainstreet / Come to poppa / Ship of fools / Mary Lou
CD CDP 7460752
Capitol / Feb '95 / EMI

NINE TONIGHT
Nine tonight / Trying to live my life without you / You'll accompany me / Hollywood nights / Night moves / Rock 'n' roll never forgets / Let it rock / Old time rock 'n' roll / Mainstreet / Against the wind / Fire down below / Her strut / Feel like a number / Fire lake / Betty Lou's gettin' out tonight / We've got tonight
CD CDP 7460862
Capitol / Feb '95 / EMI

STRANGER IN TOWN
Hollywood nights / Still the same / Old time rock 'n' roll / Till it shines / Feel like a number / Ain't got no money / We've got tonight / Brave strangers / Famous final scene
CD CDP 7460742
Capitol / Feb '95 / EMI

Segundo, Compay

YO VENDO AQUI
CD 0630194612
Warner Bros. / Jul '97 / Warner Music

Seiler, Peter

SENSITIVE TOUCH
Still the same sun / Reef moods / Journey to nowhere / I'm on my way / Mountain peaks / Her song / Sensitive touch
CD 710 069
Thunderbolt / '89 / TKO Magnum

Seis Del Solar

ALTERNATE ROOTS
CD MES 158312
Messidor / Apr '95 / ADA / Koch

DECISION
Sentimento de cancion / Island walk / Una sola casa / Un nuevo dia / Decision / Sea dance / Mirage / Entregate / Heart dues / Newtown
CD MES 158212
Messidor / Apr '96 / ADA / Koch

Seka

LOVES HYMN
CD TG 92972
Roadrunner / Jul '91 / PolyGram

Seka, Monique

OKAMAN
CD 503842
Declic / Apr '95 / Jet Star

Selah Jubilee Singers

SELAH JUBILEE SINGERS VOL.1 1939-1941
CD DOCD 5499
Document / Nov '96 / ADA / Hot Shot / Jazz Music

SELAH JUBILEE SINGERS VOL.2 1941-1944
CD DOCD 5500
Document / Nov '96 / ADA / Hot Shot / Jazz Music

Seldom Scene

15TH ANNIVERSARY CELEBRATION LIVE
Sittin' on top of the world / Big train from Memphis / Lorena / Dark as a dungeon / Blue Ridge / Raised by the railroad line / Don't know my mind / Drifting too far from the shore / Those memories of you / Keep me from blowing away / Wheels / Carolyn at the broken wheel inn / If I needed you / Rose of old Kentucky / I couldn't find my walkin' shoes / Workin' on a building / Say you lied / High on a hilltop / Sweetest gift / Take me on your life boat
CD SHCD 2202
Sugar Hill / Jul '88 / ADA / CM / Direct / Koch / Roots

ACT 4
CD SHCD 3709
Sugar Hill / Nov '95 / ADA / CM / Direct / Koch / Roots

AFTER MIDNIGHT
Lay down Sally / Hearts overflowing / Old hometown / Stompin' at the Savoy / Border incident / After midnight / If I had left it up to you / Heartsville Pike / Stolen love / Let old Mother Nature have her way
CD SHCD 3721
Sugar Hill / Dec '94 / ADA / CM / Direct / Koch / Roots

AT THE SCENE
Girl I know / Jamaica say you will / Open up the window, Noah / Winter wind / Heal it / Weary pilgrim / It turns inside out / Champion / Born of the wind / Peaceful dreams
CD SHCD 3736
Sugar Hill / Mar '92 / ADA / CM / Direct / Koch / Roots

BLUEGRASS - THE WORLD'S GREATEST SHOW (Various Artists)
When somebody wants to leave: *Seldom Scene* / House of the rising sun: *Seldom Scene* / Hickory wind: *Seldom Scene* / Wild Kentucky road: *Seldom Scene* / Alabama jubilee: *Seldom Scene* / Old train: *Seldom Scene* / Through the bottom of the glass: *Seldom Scene* / Out among the stars: *Seldom Scene* / Two little boys: *Country Gentlemen* / Today has been a lonesome day: *Country Gentlemen* / Bringing Mary home: *Country Gentlemen* / I'll stay around: *Original New South* / I'm not broke, but I'm badly bent: *Original New South* / Fireball: *Original New South* / Why don't you tell me so: *Original New South* / Freeborn man: *Original New South* / Train 45: *Original New South* / Fox on the run: *Country Gentlemen* / Waiting for the boys to come home: *Country Gentlemen* / Ages and ages ago: *Country Gentlemen* / Saturday night at the Opry: *Country Gentlemen* / Feel like my time ain't long: *Country Gentlemen*
CD SHCD 2201
Sugar Hill / Mar '89 / ADA / CM / Direct / Koch / Roots

CHANGE OF SCENERY, A
Breaking new ground / Casting a shadow in the road / Settin' me up / Alabama clay / I'll be a stranger there / West Texas wind / Satan's choir / In despair / What goes on / One way rider
CD SHCD 3763
Sugar Hill / Sep '88 / ADA / CM / Direct / Koch / Roots

DREAM SCENE
CD SHCD 3858
Sugar Hill / Oct '96 / ADA / CM / Direct / Koch / Roots

LIKE WE USED TO BE
CD SHCD 3822
Sugar Hill / Mar '94 / ADA / CM / Direct / Koch / Roots

SCENE 20 (20th Anniversary Concert/ 2CD Set)
Intro (Haven't I got the right to love you) / Gardens and memories / House of gold / Picture's of life's other side / Satan's jewelled crown / Will you ready to go home / Were you there / Weary pilgrim / Leavin' harlan / Take him in / Stompin' at the Savoy / Something in the wind / Muddy water / Open up the window / Breakin' new ground / Old train / Wait a minute / Blue ridge cabin home / Gypsy moon / In the pines / And on bass / Another lonesome day / Have mercy on my soul / House of the rising sun/Walk don't run / In the midnight hour
CD Set SHCD 2501
Sugar Hill / Sep '92 / ADA / CM / Direct / Koch / Roots

SCENIC ROOTS
If you ever change your mind / Lost in your memory / Wrath of God / Before I met you / Red Georgia Clay / I've cried my last tear / Not in my arms / Highway of heartache / Long black veil / Last call to glory / Distant train / How mountain girls can love
CD SHCD 3785
Sugar Hill / Jul '90 / ADA / CM / Direct / Koch / Roots

Selecter

GREATEST HITS
Three minute hero / Too much pressure / Celebrate the bullet / Bomb scare / Deep water / Time hard / They make me mad / Bristol and Miami / Missing words / James Bond / On my radio / Whisper / Carry go bring home / Murder / Washed up and left for dead / Last tango in dub
CD CDGOLD 1034
EMI Gold / May '96 / EMI

GREATEST HITS LIVE
Too much pressure / On my radio / Missing words / Murder / Three minute hero / Everyday (time hard) / Other side of love / Whisper / Street feeling / Selecter / Washed up and left for dead / Out on the streets again / Train to skaville / Trout / Whip them down / Ladders / Neurotica / California screaming / Orange street / My sweet collie
CD EMPRCD 663
Emporio / Oct '96 / Disc

HAIRSPRAY
CD TX 51214CD
Triple X / Oct '95 / Plastic Head

HAPPY ALBUM
CD FIENDCD 751
Demon / May '94 / Pinnacle

LIVE AT ROSKILDE
Three minute hero / California screaming / I want justice / Missing words / Neurotica / Selecter / Train to skaville / Hairspray / Carry go bring / Murder / Madness / Orange street / My sweet collie
CD CDBM 114
Blue Moon / Nov '96 / Cadillac / Discovery / Greensleeves / Jazz Music / Jet Star / TKO Magnum

LIVE INJECTION
Live injection / Whip them down / Three minute hero / California screaming / Everyday / I want justice / Missing words / Neurotica / Selector / James Bond / Train to Skaville / On my radio / Too much pressure / Murder / Orange street / My sweet collie / Madness
CD CDBM 108
Blue Moon / Jun '96 / Cadillac / Discovery / Greensleeves / Jazz Music / Jet Star / TKO Magnum

PRIME CUTS VOL.1
Something's burning / Coming up / Dial my number / Woke up laughing / Touissants children / Whisper of the rain / Nameless / Use me up / I really didn't have the time / Clear water / No regrets / On my radio
CD CDBM 103
Blue Moon / Nov '94 / Cadillac / Discovery / Greensleeves / Jazz Music / Jet Star / TKO Magnum

PRIME CUTS VOL.2
On my radio / Three minute hero / Whisper / Shoorah, shoorah / Celebrate the bullet / Missing words / Out on the streets / Tell me what the others do / Street feeling / Selecter / Best of both worlds / Too much pressure
CD CDBM 106
Blue Moon / Jun '96 / Cadillac / Discovery / Greensleeves / Jazz Music / Jet Star / TKO Magnum

RARE SELECTER VOL.3 (Versions)
CD DOJOCD 205
Dojo / May '95 / Disc

SELECTERIZED (The Best Of The Selecter 1991-1996)
On my radio / Whip them down / Hairspray / Three minute hero / Sugar town / Die happy / California screaming / Selecter / Madness / Ladders / Missing words / My perfect world / Too much pressure 96 / Whisper / Celebrate the bullet / On my radio 91
CD DOJOCD 270
Dojo / Oct '96 / Disc

TOO MUCH PRESSURE (2CD Set)
Madness / On my radio 1991 / Selecter / Deep water / Missing words / Three minute hero / Too much pressure / I can see clearly now / Best of both worlds / Shoorah shoorah / Coming up / Something's burning / Touissants children / Tell me what the others do / On my radio / Madness: *Selecter & Prince Buster* / Rough rider: *Selecter & Prince Buster* / James Bond / Train to Skaville / Orange street / Sweet dreams / Celebrate the bullet / Washed up and left for dead / Out on the streets / Carry go bring come / Murder / My collie not a dog / I want justice / Copasetic / Reggae beat
CD Set SMDCD 138
Snapper / May '97 / Pinnacle

Self, Ronnie

BOP A LENA
Bop a Lena / I ain't going nowhere / You're so right for me / Ain't I'm a dog / Too many lovers (unissued) / Date bait / Big blon' baby / Petrified / Flame of love / Big fool / Black night blues / Pretty bad blues / Three hearts later / Rocky Road blues / Do it now / Bless my broken heart / This must be the place / Big town / Some other world / Instant man / Oh me, oh my / Whistling words / Past, present and future / So high / I've been there / Moon burn (unissued) / Some things you can't change / Houdini / Go go cannibal (unissued) / Ugly stick (unissued)
CD BCD 15436
Bear Family / Jul '90 / Direct / Rollercoaster / Swift

Self Transforming Machine ...

BITONE (Self Transforming Machine Elves)
CD NZCD 025
Nova Zembla / Apr '95 / Plastic Head

Sellers Engineering Band

BRASS BAND CONCERT
Oklahoma / Love on the rocks / Black and white rag / Under the double eagle / Somewhere over the rainbow / Dem bones / Someone to watch over me / Hora stacato / Love changes everything / Raymonde overture / Teddy bears' picnic / Nightingale sang in Berkeley Square / Send in the clowns
CD 305072
Hallmark / Jun '97 / Carlton

WE LOVE A PARADE
Entry of the Gladiators / Seventy six Trombones / Royal trophy / Dam busters march / Toeador's march / Arromanches / Marche militaire / Parade of the tin soldiers / Marche slave / Punchinello / I love a parade / Gladiator's farewell / Musical joke / Shield of Liberty / Radetzky march / Rhapsody on Scottish marches / Coronation march
CD CHAN 4527
Chandos / Aug '93 / Chandos

Selvaggio, Pete

GALLERIA
CD 378302
Koch Jazz / Nov '96 / Koch

Sema 4

IN MEMORY OF...
CD DRCD 015
Detour / Feb '97 / Detour / Greyhound

Semantics

BONE OF CONTENTION
CD SST 167CD
SST / May '88 / Plastic Head

Semara Ratih Gamelan

GONG SEMARA DANA
Jagra parwata / Kindama / Catur angurit / Gora angurit / Gora merdawa / Lengker
CD VICG 54552
JVC / Oct '96 / Direct / New Note/Pinnacle / Vital/SAM

Semper, George

MAKIN' WAVES
CD HUBCD 14
Hubbub / Jan '97 / Beechwood/BMG / SRD / Timewarp

Sempiternal Death Reign

SPOOKY GLOOM, THE
CD FDN 8099CD
Plastic Head / Jan '92 / Plastic Head

Senator Flux

STORYKNIFE
CD EM 92632
Roadrunner / Oct '91 / PolyGram

Senators

LOVELY
Best friend / East of here / Forty nights / Hosing down the strand / Disbelieve it / Strange sound / Port in my storm / Late train home / Simple game / Stranger's house / Another love song / Girl I adore / End
CD 8283192
Go Discs / Apr '92 / PolyGram

Senders

JUMPIN' UPTOWN
CD BLUELOONCD 031
Blue Loon / Dec '96 / Hot Shot

Sene, Yande Coude

NIGHT SKY IN SINE SALOUM
CD _____ SH 64085
Shanachie / May '97 / ADA / Greensleeves / Koch

Senensky, Bernie

RHAPSODY
I hear a rhapsody / Come rain or come shine / Goodbye, Mr Evans / Winnibop / Together / Winnie's revenge / Yesterday's thoughts / Someday my prince will come
CD _____ CDSJP 434
Timeless Jazz / Sep '96 / New Note/ Pinnacle

Senghor, Sonar

LOST AFRICA (Senghor, Sonar Troupe)
CD _____ TCD 1044
Tradition / Mar '97 / ADA / Vital

Sensa Yuma

EVERY DAY'S YOUR LAST DAY
CD _____ RRCD 013
Retch / Jun '97 / Cargo / Plastic Head

Sensation

BORN TO LOVE YOU
CD _____ WRCD 36
Techniques / Nov '92 / Jet Star

Sensefield

BUILDING
CD _____ REG 8CD
Regal / Jun '96 / Prime / RTM/Disc

BUILDING
CD _____ REV 046CD
Revelation / Jan '97 / Plastic Head

KILLED FOR LESS
CD _____ REVEL 32CD
Revelation / May '94 / Plastic Head
CD _____ REG 9CD
Regal / Aug '96 / Prime / RTM/Disc

SENSEFIELD
CD _____ REVEL 033CD
Revelation / Oct '94 / Plastic Head

Senseless Things

EMPIRE OF THE SENSELESS
Homophobic asshole / Keepsake / Tempting Kate / Hold it down / Counting friends / Just one reason / Cruel moon / Primary instinct / Rise (Song for Dean and Gene) / Ice skating at the Milky Way / Say what you will / Runaways
CD _____ 4735252
Epic / Mar '93 / Sony

Senser

STACKED UP
CD _____ TOPPCD 008
Ultimate / Mar '94 / Pinnacle

Sensorama

WELCOME
CD _____ LADOCD 2022
Ladomat / Oct '95 / Plastic Head

Sensurreal

NEVER TO TELL A SOUL
CD Set _____ BMU 005CD
Beam Me Up / Feb '95 / Vital

OCCASIONAL SERIES
CD _____ BMU 013CD
North South / Jun '96 / Pinnacle

Sentenced

AMOK
CD _____ CM 77076CD
Century Media / Apr '95 / Plastic Head

DOWN
CD _____ CM 77146CD
Century Media / Nov '96 / Plastic Head

LOVE AND DEATH
CD _____ CM 77101CD
Century Media / Oct '95 / Plastic Head

SHADOWS OF THE PAST
CD _____ CM 7716CD
Century Media / Jan '96 / Plastic Head

Senter, Boyd

BOYD SENTER 1928-1930
'Tain't clean / Eniale blues / Just so-so / I wish I could shimmy / Mobile blues / Prickly heat / No more / Original Stackoo'Lee blues / Original chinese blues / Somebody's wrong / Wabash blues / Goin' back to Tennessee / Rich man, poor man, beggar man, thief / I'm in the jailhouse now / Doin' you good / Shine / Sweetheart blues / Beale street blues / Copenhagen (Stomp) / No one / Waterloo / Give it to me right away / Smiles
CD _____ CBC 1032
Timeless Jazz / Aug '96 / New Note/ Pinnacle

Sentridoh

COLLECTION OF PREVIOUSLY RELEASED SONGS, A (Barlow, Lou & His Sentridoh)
CD _____ EFA 049402
City Slang / May '94 / RTM/Disc

ORIGINAL LOSING LOSERS
CD _____ SHR 67CD
Shrimper / Dec '96 / Cargo

September 67

LUCKY SHOE
Busy building / Setting the old house on fire / Fire engine red / Lucky shoe / What's wrong with Alice / Giant / Mercy is the red bird / Don't break / Hazel Motes / Poor boy / Cassandra on the dance floor / Little lantern face / Bring back the weight
CD _____ CDVX 2828
Virgin / Mar '97 / EMI

September When

ONE EYE OPEN
No simple reason / Fish song / Can I trust you / Street jam / Let the rain fall / Comes around / Not my day / Nightflight / What you give is what you get / Pretty lonely star / Beauty of it
CD _____ 4509918142
East West / May '93 / Warner Music

Septeto Hananero

75 YEARS LATER
CD _____ CORA 126
Corason / Nov '95 / ADA / CM / Direct

Septic Flesh

MYSTIC PLACES OF DAWN
CD _____ HOLY 5CD
Holy / May '94 / Plastic Head

OPHIDIAN WHEEL
CD _____ HOLY 23CD
Holy / Mar '97 / Plastic Head

SEPTIC FLESH
CD _____ HOLY 12CD
Holy / Jun '95 / Plastic Head

Sepultura

ARISE
CD _____ RO 93282
Roadracer / Sep '96 / PolyGram

BENEATH THE REMAINS
CD _____ RO 95112
Roadracer / Sep '96 / PolyGram

BESTIAL DEVASTATION
CD _____ SBD 001
Bestial Productions / Mar '97 / Cargo

BLOOD ROOTED
Procreation (of the wicked) / Inhuman nature / Policia / War / Crucificados pelo sistema / Symptom of the universe / Mine / Lookaway / Dusted / Roots bloody roots / Drug me / Refuse resist / Slave new world / Propaganda / Beneath the remains/Escape to the void / Kaiowas / Clenched fist / Biotech is Godzilla
CD _____ RR 88212
Roadrunner / Aug '97 / PolyGram

CHAOS AD
Refuse/Resist / Territory / Slave new world / Amen / Kaiowas / Propaganda / Biotech is Godzilla / Nomad / We are not as others / Manifest / Hunt / Clenched fist / Policia / Inhuman nature
CD _____ RR 90002
Roadrunner / Dec '96 / PolyGram

CHAOS AD (US Edition)
CD _____ RR 88592
Roadrunner / Oct '96 / PolyGram

MORBID VISIONS
CD _____ RO 92762
Roadracer / Sep '96 / PolyGram

ROOTS
CD _____ RR 89002
CD _____ RR 89005
Roadrunner / Nov '96 / PolyGram

ROOTS OF SEPULTURA (2CD Set)
CD Set _____ RR 89008
Roadrunner / Nov '96 / PolyGram

SCHIZOPHRENIA
CD _____ RO 93602
Roadracer / Sep '96 / PolyGram

Sepulveda, Charlie

NEW ARRIVAL, THE
CD _____ ANCD 8767
Antilles/New Directions / Aug '91 / PolyGram

Sequence

SISTERS OF RAP, THE (The Best Of The Sequence)
Monster jam with Spoonie Gee / Funk you up / And you know that / Simon says / We don't rap the rap / Funky sound (tear the roof off) / I don't need your love / Love changes / Unaddressed letter / Sequence party / Fi-ya up that funk / Funk that you mothers
CD _____ DEEPM 002
Deep Beats / Nov '96 / BMG

Sequentia

DANTE AND THE TROUBADOURS
CD _____ 05472772272
BMG / Aug '95 / BMG

EL SABIO
CD _____ 05472771732
BMG / Nov '92 / BMG

VOICE OF THE BLOOD
CD _____ 05472773462
BMG / Nov '95 / BMG

VOX IBERICA BOX SET
CD Set _____ 05472773332
BMG / Feb '94 / BMG

Serban, Andrei

ROMANIAN FOLK MUSIC (Serban, Andrei & His Orchestra)
CD _____ SYN CD 150
Syncoop / Apr '93 / ADA / Direct

Sereba, Kouame Gerard

KILIMANDJARO
CD _____ KGS 004CD
Musikk Distribujson / Dec '94 / ADA

Serenata Mexicana

CANCIONES DE MEXICO
CD _____ MRM 004
Modern Blues / Feb '94 / ADA / Direct

Serenity

BREATHING DEMONS
CD _____ HOLY 020CD
Holy / Jan '97 / Plastic Head

THEN CAME SILENCE
CD _____ HOLY 010CD
Holy / Feb '95 / Plastic Head

Serenity

31 (Organic Technolo) (Serenity Dub)
CD _____ INCCD 3306
Incoming / Mar '96 / Pinnacle

41 (Digital Roots)
CD _____ INCCD 3307
Incoming / Mar '96 / Pinnacle

Sergeant Fury

TURN THE PAGE
CD _____ SPV 08412082
SPV / Apr '95 / Koch / Plastic Head

Sermon, Erick

DOUBLE OR NOTHING
Intro / Bomdigi / Freak out / In the heat / Tell 'em / In the studio / Boy meets world / Welcome / Live in the backyard / Set it off / Focus / Move on / Smooth thought / Do your thing / Man above / Message / Open fire
CD _____ 5292862
RAL / Nov '95 / PolyGram

NO PRESSURE
Payback II / Stay real / Imma gitz mine / Hostile / Do it up / Safe sex / Hittin' switches / Erick Sermon / Hype / Li'l grazy / Ill shit / Swing it over here / All in the mind / Female species
CD _____ 52335132
Def Jam / Jan '96 / PolyGram

Serpent

IN THE GARDEN OF THE SERPENT
CD _____ RAD 006CD
Radiation / Apr '96 / Plastic Head

Serpent Power

SERPENT POWER
CD _____ VMD 79252
Vanguard / Oct '96 / ADA / Pinnacle

Serpico

RUMBLE
CD _____ EVRCD 030
Equal Vision / Mar '97 / Plastic Head

Serrie, John

ENCHANTRESS
Dyt it / Seamless / Enchantress / As was / Precious / Free hand / Heartfelt / Dance one / Shortly / Image
CD _____ CD 83392
Telarc Jazz / Nov '96 / Conifer/BMG

PLANETARY CHRONICLES VOL.2
First night out / Vista range / Aftervisions / Continuum / On a frontier of fables
CD _____ MPCD 2006
Miramar / Oct '94 / New Note/Pinnacle

Sertl, Doug

JOY SPRING
CD _____ STCD 565
Stash / May '93 / ADA / Cadillac / CM / Direct / Jazz Music

Servat, Giles

A-RAOK MONT KUIT
CD _____ KM 45
Keltia Musique / Sep '94 / ADA / Discovery

Servotron

NO ROOM FOR HUMANS
CD _____ LOUDEST 19
One Louder / Jun '97 / Mo's Music Machine / Shellshock/Disc / SRD

SPARE PARTS
CD _____ LOUDEST 22
One Louder / Jun '97 / Mo's Music Machine / Shellshock/Disc / SRD

SETI

GEOMETRY OF NIGHT
CD _____ INCCD 3310
Incoming / Jul '96 / Pinnacle

KNOWLEDGE
CD _____ ASH 21CD
Ash International / Jan '95 / Kudos / Pinnacle

PHAROS
CD Set _____ IAE 001
Instinct Ambient Europe / Apr '95 / Plastic Head

Setters

SETTERS, THE
CD _____ WM 1020
Watermelon / Jul '94 / ADA / Direct

Setzer, Brian

BRIAN SETZER ORCHESTRA, THE (Setzer, Brian Orchestra)
Lady luck / Ball and chain / Sittin' on it all the time / Good rockin' Daddy / September skies / Brand new cadillac / There's a rainbow 'round my shoulder / Route 66 / Your true love / Nightingale sang in Berkeley Square / Straight up / Drink that bottle down
CD _____ 74321195772
Arista / Apr '94 / BMG

Sevag, Oystein

GLOBAL HOUSE
CD _____ 01934111482
Windham Hill / Sep '95 / BMG

LINK
CD _____ 01934111232
Windham Hill / Sep '95 / BMG

Seven Day Diary

SKIN AND BLISTER
CD _____ 9362458702
Warner Bros. / May '95 / Warner Music

Seven Dials Band

MUSIC OF DICKENS AND HIS TIME, THE
College hornpipe / Some folks who have grown old / Ratcatcher's daughter / Home, sweet home / Begone dull care / Ivy green / Young jolly waterman / Soldier's tear / Old towler / Fine old English gentleman / David Copperfield polkas / All's well / Country life / Shiverand Shakery (The man who couldn't get warm) / Mr. Wardle's carol / Christmas carol quadrilles / Believe me if all those endearing young charms / Workhouse boy / Child's hymn / Sir Roger de Coverley
CD _____ BEJOCD 9
Beautiful Jo / Feb '97 / ADA / Direct

Seven Grand Housing ...

NO WEAPONS FORMED AGAINST WE SHALL PROSPER (Seven Grand Housing Authority)
CD _____ EFA 063402
Ausfahrt / Aug '97 / SRD

Seven Little Sisters

COW TROUSERS
CD _____ RGB 5012
BGR / Mar '95 / Plastic Head

Seven Mary Three

ROCKCROWN
Lucky / Rockcrown / Needle can't burn / Honey of generation / Home stretch / People like new / Make up your mind / Gone away / Times like these / I could be wrong / Angry blue / Houdini's angels / This evening's great excuse / Player piano / Oven
CD _____ 7567830182
Warner Bros. / Jun '97 / Warner Music

Seven Seconds

MUSIC, THE MESSAGE, THE
Ghost / Such and such / Music / Message / Kinda future / My gravity / See you tomorrow / Get a different life / Talkbox / My

list / First ya told us / Born without a mind / Punk rock teeth / Girl song / I can remember / Even better plan / Kids are united
CD 481452
Epic / Dec '95 / Sony

OURSELVES
CD 722762
Restless / Feb '95 / Vital

SOUL FORCE REVOLUTION
CD 723442
Restless / Feb '95 / Vital

Seven Sioux

ANOTHER
CD XM 029CD
X-Mist / Apr '92 / Cargo / SRD

Sevenchurch

BLEAK INSIGHT
Perceptions / Low / Surreal wheel / Crawl line / Sanctum / Autobituary
CD N 02222
Noise / Sep '93 / Koch

Sevens

SEVENS
CD AK 2CD
Akashic / Apr '97 / Cargo / Greyhound / SRD

Severed Heads

CUISINE (WITH PISCATORIAL)
Pilot in hell / Seven of oceans / Finder / Estrogen / King of the sea / Host of quadrille / Life in the whale / Twister / Ugly twenties / Piggy smack / Golden height / I'm your antidote / Tingler (they shine within) / Goodbye / Her teeth the ally / Skippy roo kangaroo / Ottoman / Quest for oom pa pa / Wonder of all the world
CD NETCD 028
Nettwerk / Mar '92 / Greyhound / Pinnacle / Vital

Severin

ACID TO ASHES
CD DIS 72VCD
Dischord / Sep '92 / SRD

Severinsen, Doc

GOOD MEDICINE
Brass roots / Good medicine / Prelude 'Come sweet death'/ Love story / Liberia / Godfather waltz / Rhapsody for now / Medley
CD 07863660622
Bluebird / Oct '92 / BMG

UNFORGETTABLY DOC
What is this thing called love / Love / Unforgettable / Lush Life / Georgia On My Mind / Speak Low / Music Of The Night / Bad and the beautiful / Someone to watch over me / Misty / Wind beneath my wings / Memory
CD CD 80304
Telarc / Sep '92 / Conifer/BMG

Seward, Alec

LATE ONE SATURDAY EVENING
What has Annie got / Risin' sun shine on / Her ways are so sweet / CC rider / Goin' down slow / Rock me Darlin' / Late one Saturday evening / Blues all round my head / Feel so good / Blues all around my head / Trouble in mind / Creepin' blues / Cousin John / I wish I'd listened
CD TBA 13007
Blues Alliance / Aug '96 / New Note/ Pinnacle

Sewing Room

NICO
CD DEADELVIS 005
Dead Elvis / Nov '95 / RTM/Disc

Sex Gang Children

BLIND
CD CLEO 51222
Cleopatra / Jun '94 / Cargo / Greyhound / Plastic Head / RTM/Disc / SRD

ECSTASY AND VENDETTA OVER NEW YORK
CD CLEO 3833
Cleopatra / Aug '94 / Cargo / Greyhound / Plastic Head / RTM/Disc / SRD

MEDEA
CD CDSATE 07
Talitha / Dec '93 / Plastic Head

PLAY WITH CHILDREN
CD CLEO 6957
Cleopatra / May '94 / Cargo / Greyhound / Plastic Head / RTM/Disc / SRD

SHOUT AND SCREAM (2CD Set)
CD Set AOP 50
Dressed To Kill / Feb '97 / Total/BMG

Sex Love & Money

ERA
CD CDMFN 180
Music For Nations / Jan '95 / Pinnacle

Sex Pistols

AFTER THE ANARCHY (Various Artists)
Rich kids: *Rich Kids* / Marching men: *Rich Kids* / Ghosts of princes in towers: *Rich Kids* / Justifiable homicide: *Goodman, Dave & Friends* / Public image: *Public Image Ltd* / London boys: *Thunders, Johnny* / 1-2-3: *Professionals* / Stones: *Spectres* / Join the professionals: *Professionals* / This is not a love song: *Public Image Ltd* / Street full of soul: *London Cowboys* / Let's get crazy: *London Cowboys* / It ain't me girl: *Hot Club* / World gone wild: *Chequered Past* / Only the strong survive: *Chequered Past* / Animal speaks: *Golden Palominos* / World destruction: *Time Zone* / Mercy: *Jones, Steve*
CD VSOPCD 188
Connoisseur Collection / Jun '93 / Pinnacle

ALIVE
God save the Queen / Pretty vacant / Problems / EMI / Liar / New York / Anarchy in the UK / No feelings / Submission / I wanna be me / Seventeen / Satellite / Anarchy in the UK (live) / Did you no wrong (live) / I'm a lazy sod (live) / New York (live) / Stepping stone (live) / Liar (Live) / Pretty vacant (live) / Suburban kids (live) / Submission (live) / Substitute (live) / No feeling (live) / Problems (live) / Don't give me no lip, child (live) / No fun (live)
CD ESDCD 321
Essential / Oct '95 / BMG

FLOGGING A DEAD HORSE
Anarchy in the UK / I wanna be me / God save the Queen / Did you no wrong / Pretty vacant / Holidays in the sun / No fun / My way / Something else / Silly thing / C'mon everybody / Stepping stone / Great rock 'n' roll swindle / No one is innocent
CD CDV 2142
Virgin / Oct '86 / EMI

GREAT ROCK 'N' ROLL SWINDLE, THE (Highlights)
God save the Queen (Symphony) / Great rock 'n' roll swindle / You need hands: *McLaren, Malcolm* / Silly thing / Lonely boy / Something else / (We're gonna) Rock around the clock / C'mon everybody / Who killed Bambi / No one is innocent: *Biggs, Ronnie* / L'anarchie pour le UK / My way
CD CDVDX 2510
Virgin / Jan '92 / EMI

INTERVIEW DISC
CD SEX 1CD
Total / May '96 / Total/BMG

KISS THIS
Anarchy in the UK / God save the Queen / Pretty vacant / Holidays in the sun / I wanna be me / Did you no wrong / Satellite / Don't give me no lip child / Stepping stone / Bodies / No feelings / Liar / Problems / Seventeen / Submission / EMI / My way / Silly thing
CD CDV 2702
Virgin / Oct '92 / EMI

KISS THIS (Limited Edition With Live In Trondheim CD)
Anarchy in the UK / God save the Queen / Pretty vacant / Holidays in the sun / I wanna be me / Did you no wrong / Satellite / Don't give me no lip child / Stepping stone / Bodies / No feelings / Liar / Problems / Seventeen / Submission / EMI / My way / Silly thing / Anarchy in the UK (live) / I wanna be me (live) / Seventeen (live) / New York / EMI (live) / No fun / Problems (live) / God save the Queen (live)
CD Set CDVX 2702
Virgin / Oct '92 / EMI

LIVE AT CHELMSFORD PRISON
Lazy sod / New York / No lip / Stepping stone / Suburban kids / Submission / Liar / Anarchy in the UK / Did you no wrong / Substitute / No fun / Pretty vacant / Problems / I wanna be me
CD DOJOCD 66
Dojo / Mar '93 / Disc

LIVE AT WINTERLAND
God save the queen / I wanna be me / Seventeen / New York / EMI / Belsen was a gas / Bodies / Holidays in the sun / Liar / No feelings / Problems / Pretty vacant / Anarchy in the UK / No fun
CD WENCD 008
When / Nov '96 / Pinnacle

MINI ALBUM, THE
CD DOJOCD 265
Dojo / Jun '96 / Disc

NEVER MIND THE BOLLOCKS, HERE'S THE SEX PISTOLS
Holidays in the sun / Bodies / No feelings / Liar / God save the Queen / Problems / Seventeen / Anarchy in the UK / Submission / Pretty vacant / New York / EMI
CD CDVX 2086
Virgin / Oct '86 / EMI

NEVER MIND THE BOLLOCKS/SPUNK
Holidays in the sun / Bodies / No feelings / Liar / God save the queen / Problems / Seventeen / Anarchy in the UK / Submission / Pretty vacant / New York / EMI / Feelings / Just me / Nookie / No future / Lots of fun / Who was it / New York (Looking for a kiss) / EMI / Satellite
CD SPUNK 1
Virgin / Jun '96 / EMI

NO FUTURE UK
CD RRCD 117
Receiver / Jul '93 / Grapevine/PolyGram

ORIGINAL PISTOLS LIVE
No feelings / Anarchy in the UK / I'm a lazy sod / Liar / Dolls (New York) / Don't give me no lip child / Substitute / Pretty vacant / I wanna be me / Problems / Submission / No fun
CD CDFA 3149
Fame / Jul '89 / EMI

PIRATES OF DESTINY
CD DOJOCD 222
Dojo / Jan '96 / Disc

RAW
Pretty vacant / Submission / EMI / Anarchy in the UK / Don't give me no lip child / Liar / Seventeen / Dolls / No feelings / No fun / Problems / I wanna be me / Substitute
CD EMPRCD 716
Emporio / Jun '97 / Disc

SEX PISTOLS (Fully Illustrated Book & Interview Disc)
CD SAM 7033
Sound & Media / Jun '97 / Sound & Media

WANTED
CD DOJOCD 216
Dojo / Jun '95 / Disc

Sexepil

SUGAR FOR THE SOUL
CD 0630107692
East West / Feb '96 / Warner Music

Sexpod

HOME
CD PILLMCD 6
Placebo / Jan '95 / RTM/Disc

Sexsmith, Ron

OTHER SONGS
Thinking out loud / Strawberry blonde / Average Joe / Thinly veiled disguise / Nothing good / Pretty little cemetry / It never fails / Clown in broad daylight / At different times / Child star / Honest mistake / So young / While you're waiting / April after all
CD IND 90123
Interscope / Jul '97 / BMG

RON SEXSMITH
Secret heart / There's a rhythm / Words we never use / Summer blowin' town / Lebanon, Tennesse / Speaking with the angel / In place of you / Heart with no companion / Several miles / From a few streets over / First chance I get / Wastin' time / Galbraith street
CD IND 92485
Interscope / May '96 / BMG

Sexteto Habanero

SEXTETO HABANERO 1926-1931
CD HQCD 53
Harlequin / Aug '95 / Hot Shot / Jazz Music / Swift / Wellard

SEXTETO HABANERO 1926-1948
CD HQCD 82
Harlequin / Nov '96 / Hot Shot / Jazz Music / Swift / Wellard

Sexton, Ann

YOU'RE GONNA MISS ME
I had a fight with love (and I lost) / I'm his wife, you're just a friend / You got to use what you got / Color my world blue / I want to be loved / You've been doing me wrong for so long / Who's gonna love you / You can't win / Love love love / You're letting me down / You've been gone too long / Come back home / Keep on holding on / Loving you, loving me / You're gonna miss me / If I work my thing on you / You're losing me / Sugar Daddy / Be serious / Have a little mercy
CD CPCD 8012
Charly / Feb '94 / Koch

Sexton Ming

ROGUE MALE (Sexton Ming & Steady)
CD SWEE 007CD
Sweet / Aug '97 / Shellshock/Disc / SRD

Seymour, Daren

AUROBINDO: INVOLUTION (Seymour, Daren & Mark Van Hoen)
CD ASH 24CD
Ash International / Jan '95 / Kudos / Pinnacle

Seyoum, Betsat

URBAN AZMARIS OF ETHIOPIA (Seyoum, Betsat & Abbebe Fekade)
Enegenagnalen / Ambassel / Bati / Abeba abeba / Anteye / Tizita / Aysh ayshenna / Anteye / Endenesh gedawo / Yelewem abay / Enegenegnalen
CD 122166
Long Distance / Feb '96 / ADA / Discovery

SF Seals

NOWHERE
Back again / Don't underestimate me / 8's / Janine's dream / Still / Day 12 / Winter song / Baby blue / Demons on the corner / Missing
CD OLE 0892
Matador / Jun '94 / Vital

TRUTH WALKS IN SLEEPY SHADOWS
SF sorrow / Ladies of the sea / Ipecec / Locked out / Bold letters / Flashback caruso / Pulp / Soul of Patrick Lee / Kid's pirate ship / How did you know / Stellar lullabye
CD OLE 1622
Matador / Sep '95 / Vital

SFT

SCHWARMA
CD CDSTUMM 151
Mute / Sep '96 / RTM/Disc

SFX

SFX ALBUM, THE (SFX & Alan Murphy)
CD NAIMCD 004
Naim Audio / Apr '97 / Koch

Shabazz, Lakim

PURE RIGHTEOUSNESS
CD SDCD 1
Jet Star / Mar '89 / Jet Star

Shabba Ranks

A MI SHABBA
Ram dancehall / Shine eye gal / Spoil me appetite / Well done / Fattie fattie / Rough life / Let's get it on / Ice cream love / High seat / Gal nuh ready / Medal and certificate / Original woman
CD 4774822
Epic / Jun '95 / Sony

AS RAW AS EVER
Trailor load a girls / Where does slackness come from / Woman tangle / Gun pon me / Gone up / Ambi get scarce / Housecall: *Shabba Ranks & Maxi Priest* / Flesh axe / Mi di girls dem love / Fist a ris / Jame: *Shabba Ranks & KRS 1* / Park yu benz
CD 4681022
Epic / Apr '95 / Sony

BEST BABY FATHER/JUST REALITY
CD VYDCD 06
Vine Yard / Sep '95 / Grapevine/PolyGram

CAAN DUNN (The Best Of Shabba Ranks)
CD VPCD 1450
VP / Dec '95 / Greensleeves / Jet Star / Total/BMG

GOLDEN TOUCH
CD GRELCD 141
Greensleeves / Apr '90 / Jet Star / SRD

KING OF DANCEHALL
CD 080892
Melodie / Sep '94 / ADA / Discovery / Grapevine/PolyGram / Greensleeves / Jet Star

LOVE PUNANNY BAD
CD 080862
Jammy's / Apr '93 / Jet Star

MR. MAXIMUM
CD GRELCD 172
Greensleeves / Jun '92 / Jet Star / SRD

RAPPING WITH THE LADIES
CD GRELCD 150
Greensleeves / Aug '90 / Jet Star / SRD

ROUGH AND READY VOL.1
Mr. Loverman: *Shabba Ranks & Chevelle Franklin* / Pirate's anthem: *Shabba Ranks, Cocoa T & Home T* / Wicked in bed / Wootop / Gal yuh good / Just reality / Hard and stiff / Raggamuffin
CD 4714422
Epic / Aug '92 / Sony

ROUGH AND READY VOL.2
Housecall / Girls whine / Ting a ling a school pickney sing ting / Telephone love deh pon mi mind / Get up stand up and rock / Mr. Tek it back / Jam / Roots and culture / Twice my age / Pay down pon it / Respect / Ting-a-ling (the original)
CD 4742312
Epic / Nov '93 / Sony

VIP
Born as a Don / VIP / Best baby father / Woman mi run down / What a nite / No to coke / Shock out and have fun / Just reality / Whe you get it from / Gal yu good / Back and bellyrat / Roots and culture / Wicked inna bed / Rammer / Crab-louse a go round / Mandela free / Are you sure / Pay down pon it
CD SUMCD 4084
Summit / Nov '96 / Sound & Media

Shack

WATERPISTOL
CD ____ MA 16
Marina / Nov '95 / SRD

Shades Apart

SEEING THINGS
CD ____ REVCD 057
Revelation / Mar '97 / Plastic Head

Shades Of Kenton Jazz ...

ROUND MIDNIGHT (Shades Of Kenton Jazz Orchestra)
Here's that rainy day / Chiapas / Painted rhythm / Artistry in boogie / Intermission riff / Hey there / Stella by starlight / Stairway to the stars / Reuben's blues / Over the rainbow / Swinghouse / Artistry in rhythm
CD ____ HEPCD 2043
Hep / Feb '89 / Cadillac / Jazz Music / New Note/Pinnacle / Wellard

Shades Of Rhythm

SHADES
CD ____ 9031741042
ZTT / Dec '91 / Warner Music

SHADES OF RHYTHM
Exactly / Sweet sensation / Homicide / Everybody / Lonely days, lonely nights / Sound of eden / Lies / Armageddon / Exorcist / Summer of '89
CD ____ 9031762762
WEA / Jan '92 / Warner Music

Shadow

SHADOW MEETS NANNY GOAT (Shadow & Nanny Goat)
CD ____ VPCD 1236
VP / Jul '92 / Greensleeves / Jet Star / Total/BMG

Shadow Gallery

SHADOW GALLERY
Dance of Fools / Darktown / Mystified / Question at hand / Final hour / Sat goodbye to the morning / Queen of the city of ice
CD ____ RR 91442
Roadrunner / Sep '92 / PolyGram

Shadow Ring

WAXWORK ECHOES
CD ____ HERMES 019
Corpus Hermeticum / Nov '96 / Cargo

Shadowfax

ESPERANTO
CD ____ CDEB 2523
Earthbeat / May '93 / ADA / Direct

Shadowland

MAD AS A HATTER
USI (United states of insanity) / Mephisto bridge / Flatline / Seventh year / Father / Burning / Zuleika / Mad as a hatter / Salvation comes
CD ____ VGCD 003
Verglas Music / May '96 / Pinnacle

RING OF ROSES
Whistleblower / Jigsaw / Scared of the dark / Painting by numbers / Hall of mirrors / Kruhulick syndrome / Ring of roses / Dorian Gray / I, Judas
CD ____ VGCD 006
Verglas Music / Jul '97 / Pinnacle

Shadows

20 GOLDEN GREATS: SHADOWS
Apache / Frightened city / Guitar tango / Kon-Tiki / Genie with the light brown lamp / Warlord / Place in the sun / Atlantis / Wonderful land / FBI / Savage / Geronimo / Shindig / Stingray / Theme for young lovers / Rise and fall of Flingel Bunt / Maroc 7 / Dance on / Man of mystery / Foot tapper
CD ____ CDP 7462432
EMI / Aug '87 / EMI

ANOTHER STRING OF HOT HITS AND MORE
Wonderful land / Atlantis / Black is black / Goodbye yellow brick road / River deep, mountain high / Rise and fall of Flingel Bunt / Midnight cowboy / Pinball wizard / See me, feel me / Apache / God only knows / Stardust / Walk don't run / Most beautiful girl / Good vibrations / Something / Superstar / Trains and boats and planes / Honky tonk women / FBI / Kon-Tiki
CD ____ CDMFP 6002
Music For Pleasure / Oct '87 / EMI

APACHES PLAY THE HITS OF THE SHADOWS, THE (Apaches)
Apache / Kon Tiki / Man of mystery / Wonderful land / Atlantis / FBI / Dance on / Red river rock / Blue shadows / Guitar tango / War Lord / Maroc 7 / Mary Anne / Riders in the sky / Theme from The Deer Hunter (Cavatina) / Slaughter on tenth avenue / Don't cry for me Argentina / Sailing
CD ____ QED 041
Tring / Nov '96 / Tring

AT THEIR VERY BEST
Apache / Man of mystery / Shindig / Wonderful land / Rise and fall of flingel bunt / Deer hunter / Boys / Frightened city / Theme for young lovers / Dance on / Savage / FBI / Guitar tango / Genie with the light brown lamp / Atlantis / Foot tapper / Don't cry for me Argentina / Kon-Tiki / Geronimo / Stranger
CD ____ 8415202
Polydor / Apr '94 / PolyGram

BEST OF HANK MARVIN & THE SHADOWS, THE (Marvin, Hank & The Shadows)
Another day in paradise / Every breath you take / Jessica / Rise and fall of Flingel Bunt / Atlantis / I will always love you / Foot tapper / Cavatina / Heartbeat / Everything I do (I do it for you) / Riders in the sky / Dance on / Hot rox / Sylvia / Moonlight shadow / Apache / Mrs. Robinson / Walking in the air / Lady in red / Don't cry for me Argentina / Guitar tango / Wonderful land / Kon-Tiki / FBI
CD ____ 5238212
Polydor / Oct '94 / PolyGram

BEST OF THE SHADOWS, THE
FBI / Kon-Tiki / Guitar tango / Wonderful land / Atlantis / Savage / Frightened city / Lost city / Little bitty tear / Apache / Rise and fall of flingel bunt / Don't make my baby blue / Chattanooga choo choo / In the mood / Lonely bull / Dakota / Don't it make you feel good / Zambesi / Temptation
CD ____ DC 878662
Disky / Mar '97 / Disky / THE

DANCE ON
CD ____ 16090
Laserlight / Oct '95 / Target/BMG

DANCE WITH THE SHADOWS/SOUND OF THE SHADOWS
Chattanooga choo choo / Blue shadows / Tonight / That's the way it goes / Big B / In the mood / Lonely bull / Dakota / French dressing / High and mighty / Don't it make you feel good / Zambesi / Temptation / Brazil / Lost city / Little bitty tear / Blue sky, blue sea, blue me / Bossa roo / Five hundred miles / Cotton pickin' / Deep purple / Santa Anna / Windjammer / Dean's theme / Breakthru' / Let it be me / National provincial samba / Fandango
CD ____ CZ 379
EMI / Feb '91 / EMI

DREAMTIME
Medley: Imagine / Three times a lady / Just the way you are / I you leave me now / Up where we belong / Misty / Careless whisper / I guess that's why they call it the blues / I just called to say I love you / Always on my mind / Sealed with a kiss / Walking in the air / Going home / Skye boat song
CD ____ 5500942
Spectrum / Oct '93 / PolyGram

EARLY YEARS 1959-1966, THE (6CD Set)
CD Set ____ CDS 7971712
EMI / Sep '91 / EMI

EP COLLECTION VOL.2, THE
Omoide no nagisa / Londonderry air / Boys / Foot tapper / Les girls / Shazam / Sleepwalk / Bongo blues / Flyder and the spy / Chinchilla / Gin iro no michi / Kimi to itsumademo / Boys / Round and round / Friends / Guitar boogie / FBI / Ranka chank / Autumn / Walkin'
CD ____ SEECD 296
See For Miles/C5 / Sep '90 / Pinnacle

EP COLLECTION VOL.3, THE
Quartermaster's stores / It's been a blue day / I wish I could shimmy like my sister Arthur / Sweet dreams / Driftin' / Don't be a fool with love / Be bop a lula / Late night set / 1861 / Spring is nearly here / Back home / Some are lonely / Alice in Sunderland / Blue star / Jet black / Feelin' fine / Saturday dance / Perfidia / Chu chi / Find me a golden street / Bongo blues / It's a man's man's man's world
CD ____ SEECD 375
See For Miles/C5 / Oct '93 / Pinnacle

EP COLLECTION, THE
Perfidia / 36-24-36 / All day / My grandfather's clock / Lady Penelope / Zero X theme / Thunderbird / Finders keepers / Mustang / Shane / Giant (theme from) / Shotgun / Las tres carabelas / Adios muchachos / Valencia / Granada / Tonight / Fandango / Little princess / Gonzales / Jet black / Driftin' (live)
CD ____ SEECD 246
See For Miles/C5 / '88 / Pinnacle

FIRST 20 YEARS AT THE TOP (75 Classic Original Recordings 1959-1979)
Feelin' fine / Don't be a fool with love / Driftin' / Jet black / Saturday dance / Lonesome fella / Apache / Quartermaster's stores / Stranger / Man of mystery / FBI / Midnight / Frightened city / Back home / Kon-Tiki / 36-24-36 / Savage / Peace pipe / Wonderful land / Stars fell on Stockton / Guitar tango / What a lovely tune / Boys / Dance on / All day / Foot tapper / Breeze and I / Atlantis / I want you to want me / Shindig / It's been a blue day / Geronimo / Shazam / Theme for young lovers / This hammer / Rise and fall of Flingel bunt / It's a man's man's man's world / Rhythm and greens / Miracle / Genie with the light brown lamp / Little princess / Mary Anne / Chu chi / Stingray / Alice in Sunderland / Don't make my baby blue / My grandfather's clock / War lord / I wish I could shimmy like my sister Arthur / Arthur / I met a girl / Late night set / Place in the sun / Will you be there / Dreams I ddream / Scotch on the socks / Maroc 7 / Bombay duck / Tomorrow's cancelled / Somewhere / Running out of world / Dear old Mrs Bell / Trying to forget the one you love / Slaughter on 10th Avenue / Turn around and touch me / Jungle jam / Let me be the one / Run Billy run / It'll be me babe / Another night / Love deluxe / Don't cry for me Argentina / Cavatina / En aranjuez con tu amor / Heart of glass / Riders in the sky
CD Set ____ CDSHAD 2
EMI / May '95 / EMI

FROM HANK, BRIAN, BRUCE AND JOHN
Snap, crackle and how's your dad / Thing of beauty / Letter / Wild roses / Holy cow / Last train to Clarksville / Day I met Marie / Evening glow / Naughty nippon lights / San Francisco / Tokaido line / Alentjo / Let me take you there / Mister, you're a better man than I
CD ____ BGOCD 20
Beat Goes On / Apr '90 / Pinnacle

GOOD VIBRATIONS (3CD Set)
Dance on / Atlantis / Bandit / Guitar tango / Superstar / 36-24-36 / Stardust / Foottapper / Kon-tiki / God only knows / Peace pipe / Trains and boats and planes / Apache / Honky tonk woman / Bo Diddley / FBI / Theme from Deer Hunter (cavatina) / Something / Man of mystery / Geronimo / Classical gas / Midnight / Parisienne walkways / Don't make my baby blue / What a lovely tune / Don't cry for me Argentina / Frightened city / South of the border / Most beautiful girl / Baker street / Rodrigo's guitar concerto de aranjuez / Bright eyes / Walk don't run / Good vibrations / Rise & fall of Flingel Blunt / Shindig / Wonderful land / Mary Anne / Shazam / Perfida / Breeze and I / Midnight cowboy / Goodbye yellow brick road / Rumble / Savage / Black is black / Riders in the sky / Slaughter on 10th avenue
CD Set ____ SA 872782
Disky / Sep '96 / Disky / THE

GREATEST HITS
Apache / Man of mystery / FBI / Midnight / Frightened city / Kon-Tiki / 36-24-36 / Savage / Peace pipe / Wonderful land / Stars fell on Stockton / Guitar tango / Boys / Dance on / Stranger
CD ____ CZ 189
EMI / May '89 / EMI

HITS OF THE SHADOWS (Delta Guitars)
Apache / Man of mystery / FBI / Kon Tiki / Wonderful land / Quatermasters store / Guitar tango / Dnce on / Red river rock / Foot tapper / Atlantis / Shindig / Geronimo / Theme from young lovers / Blue shadows / Rise and fall of Flingel Bunt / Parisiene walkways / Riders in the sky
CD ____ CD 6079
Music / Jun '97 / Target/BMG

HITS RIGHT UP YOUR STREET
Telstar / Chi mai / We don't talk anymore / Imagine / Woman / Hats off to Wally / One day I'll fly away / Summer love / Misty / This ole house / Winner takes all / Sailing / Thing-me-jig / More than I can say / Cowboy cafe / Third man, Theme from / Nut rocker
CD ____ PWKS 4106
Carlton / Jul '96 / Carlton

JIGSAW
Jigsaw / Prelude in E major / Cathy's clown / Friday on my mind / Chelsea boot / With a hmm hmm on my knee / Tennessee waltz / Stardust / Semi-detached suburban Mr. James / Winchester cathedral / Maria Elena / Green eyes
CD ____ BGOCD 66
Beat Goes On / '89 / Pinnacle

MOONLIGHT SHADOWS
Moonlight shadow / Walk of life / I just called to say I love you / Every breath you take / Nights in white satin / Hello / Power of love / Three times a lady / Against all odds / Hey Jude / Dancing in the dark / I know him so well / Memory / Imagine / Sailing / Whiter shade of pale
CD ____ 5524162
Spectrum / Sep '96 / PolyGram

ORIGINAL CHART HITS 1960-1980, THE (2CD Set)
Apache / Man of mystery / Stranger / FBI / Midnight / Frightened city / Kon-Tiki / Savage / Peace pipe / Shadoogie / Wonderful land / Sleepwalk / Guitar tango / Boys / Dance on / Foot tapper / Atlantis / Shindig / Geronimo / Theme for young lovers / Perfidia / Mustang / Cosy / Nivram / Little B / Rise and fall of Flingel Bunt / Rhythm and greens / Genie with the light brown lamp / Mary Anne / Stringray / Don't make my baby blue / Warlord / I met a girl / Place in the sun / Dreams I dream / Maroc 7 / Bombay duck / Tomorrow's cancelled / Dear old Mrs Bell / Slaughter on 10th Avenue / Turn around and touch me / Let me be the one / Don't cry for me Argentina / Deer hunter / Riders in the sky / Thunderbirds theme / Little princess / Tonight / Flyder and the spy / Chatta nooka choo choo
CD Set ____ CDEM 1354
EMI / Feb '90 / EMI

REFLECTION
Eye of the tiger / Crockett's theme / Right here waiting / Every little thing she does is magic / Sealed with a kiss / Uptown girl / Strawberry Fields forever / Riders in the sky / Flashdance / Something's gotten hold of my heart / Love changes everything / Nothing's gonna stop us now / Bilitis / You'll never walk alone / Always on my mind
CD ____ 8471202
Polydor / Oct '90 / PolyGram

ROCKIN' WITH CURLY LEADS
Pinball wizard / See me feel me / Years away / Humbucker / Deep roots / Jungle jam / Gracie / Good vibrations / Turn around and touch me / Wide mouthed frog / Rockin' with curly leads / Gutbucket / Jumpin' Jack input
CD ____ BGOCD 84
Beat Goes On / Oct '90 / Pinnacle

SHADOW MUSIC/SHADES OF ROCK
I only want to be with you / Fourth street / Magic doll / Stay around / Maid marion's theme / Benno-san / Don't stop now / In the past / Fly me to the moon / Now that you're gone / One way to love / Razzamatazz / Sigh / March to Drina / Proud Mary / My babe / Lucille / Johnny B Goode / Paperback writer / Satisfaction / Bony Moronie / Get back / Something / River deep, mountain high / Memphis / What'd I say
CD ____ CZ 477
EMI / Feb '92 / EMI

SHADOWS AND FRIENDS, THE
CD ____ BR 1372
BR Music / May '94 / Target/BMG

SHADOWS ARE GO
CD ____ 9711
Scamp / Jul '97 / Cargo / Greyhound

SHADOWS COLLECTION, THE (3CD Set)
Saturday night / Chinchilla / Apache / Bongo blues / Man of mystery / Shadoogie / Sleepwalk / Nivram / Blue star / FBI / Savage / Rumble / Some are lonely / Wonderful land / Theme from The Boys / Foot tapper / Round & round / Shindig / I want you to want me / It's been a blue day / Rise & fall of Flingel Bunt / Rhythm & greens / Blue shadows / Ranka chank / Genie with the light brown lamp / Warlord / Dreams I dream / Scotch on the socks / Maroc 7 / Tomorrow's cancelled / Day I met Marie / Snap, crackle & how's your Dad / Tokaido line / Voyage to the bottom of the bath / Banana man / Poem / Slaughter on 10th Avenue / Sacha / Tokyo guitar / Sunday for seven days / Boogatoo / Break another dawn / Turn around and touch me / Humbucker / Honourable puff puff / Rose Rose / Let me be the one / It'll be me babe / Bermuda triangle / Creole nights / Flamingo / Syndicated / Love deluxe / Sweet Saturday night / Song for Duke / Baker Street / Theme from The Deerhunter / Rodrigo's guitar concerto Aranjuez / Rusk / Riders in the sky
CD Set ____ CDTRBOX 232
Trio / Jul '96 / EMI

SHADOWS IN THE 60'S, THE
Dance on / Foot tapper / Guitar tango / Man of mystery / Stranger / Midnight / 36-24-36 / Peace pipe / Stars fell on Stockton / Boys / Mary Anne / Don't make my baby blue / Frightened city / Savage / Shindig / Breeze and I / All day / What a lovely tune / Bo Diddley / Quartermaster's stores / Bandit / Little B / South of the border (Down Mexico way) / Shazam
CD ____ CDMFP 6076
Music For Pleasure / Sep '89 / EMI

SHADOWS IN THE NIGHT
Lady in red / Love changes everything / Power of love / Winner takes it all / Sealed with a kiss / All I ask of you / One moment in time / Careless whisper / I just called to say I love you / I want to know what love is / I guess that's why they call it the blues / Missing / Going home / Right here waiting / Chi Mai / Dancing in the dark
CD ____ 8437982
PolyGram TV / Apr '93 / PolyGram

SHADOWS, THE/OUT OF THE SHADOWS
Shadoogie / Blue star / Nivram / Baby my heart / See you in my drums / All my sorrows / Stand up and say that / Gonzales / Find me a golden street / Theme from a filleted place / That's my desire / My resistance is low / Sleepwalk / Big boy / Rumble / Bandit / Cosy / 1861 / Perfidia / Little B / Bo Diddley / South of the border (Down Mexico way) / Spring is nearly here / Are they all like you / Tales of a raggy tramline / Some are lonely / Kinda cool
CD ____ CZ 378
EMI / Feb '91 / EMI

SIMPLY SHADOWS
I know you were waiting (for me) / We don't need another hero / Walking in the air / Careless whisper / Don't give up / I guess that's why they call it the blues / Heart will break tonight / Lady in red / Pulaski / Take my breath away / Eastenders / I want to

know what love is / Skye boat song / Jealous guy / Chain reaction / Howard's Way
CD _______________ 8336822
Polydor / Oct '87 / PolyGram

SOUND OF THE SHADOWS, THE
Brazil / Lost city / Little bitty tear / Blue sky / Blue sea / Bossa roo / Five hundredd miles / Cotton pickin' / Deep purple / Five hundred miles / Santa ama / Windjammer / Dean's theme / Breakthru / Let it be me / National provincial samba
CD _______________ DORIG 105
EMI / Jul '97 / EMI

STEP FROM THE SHADOWS (Marvin, Welch & Farrar)
Marmaduke / Lady of the morning / Time to come / Lonesome mole / Black eyes / Brownie Kentucky / Skin deep / Faithful / You never can tell / Hard to live with / Music makes my day / Mistress fate and father time / Silvery rain / Wish you were here / Thousand conversations / Tiny Robin / Thank heavens I've got you / Please Mr. please
CD _______________ SEECD 78
See For Miles/C5 / Apr '93 / Pinnacle

STEPPIN' TO THE SHADOWS (16 Great Tracks As Only The Shadows Can Play Them)
You win again / I wanna dance with somebody (who loves me) / He ain't heavy, he's my brother / Candle in the wind / Farewell my lovely / Mountains of the moon / Nothings gonna change my love for you / Heaven is a place on earth / When the going gets tough / Alone / All I ask of you / Stack it / Shoba / You keep me hangin' on / Some people / One moment in time
CD _______________ 8393572
Polydor / May '89 / PolyGram

STRING OF HITS
Riders in the sky / Parisienne walkways / Classical gas / Deer hunter / Bridge over troubled water / You're the one that I want / Heart of glass / Don't cry for me Argentina / Song for Duke / Bright eyes / Rodrigo's guitar concerto de aranjuez / Baker Street
CD _______________ CDMFP 5724
Music For Pleasure / Nov '91 / EMI

THEMES AND DREAMS
Crockett's theme / Up where we belong / Take my breath away / Deer hunter / Walking in the air / If you leave me now / One day I'll fly away / Africa / Every breath you take / Memory / Nights in white satin / Candle in the wind / You win again / Sailing / Just the way you are / Moonlight shadow
CD _______________ 5113742
Polydor / Nov '91 / PolyGram

VOCALS
Bandit / Saturday dance / Feelin' fine / Don't be a fool (with love) / Baby my heart / Lonesome fella / All my sorrows / Mary Anne / My way / Will you be there / Little bitty tear / Me oh my / That's the way it goes / Stay around / One way to love / Day I met Marie / Dreams I dream / Don't make my baby blue / This hammer / Be bop a lula
CD _______________ SEECD 475
See For Miles/C5 / Feb '97 / Pinnacle

Shadows

DARK SIDE OF THE SHADOWS, THE
CD _______________ DOG 9109CD
Wild Dog / Aug '95 / Koch

IT AIN'T EASY BEIN' SLEAZY
CD _______________ DOG 9105CD
Wild Dog / Aug '95 / Koch

Shady

WORLD
CD _______________ BBQCD 166
Beggars Banquet / Nov '94 / RTM/Disc / Warner Music

Shady Grove Band

CHAPEL HILLBILLY WAY
CD _______________ FF 70639
Flying Fish / Feb '95 / ADA / CM / Direct / Roots

MULBERRY MOON
CD _______________ FF 544CD
Flying Fish / '92 / ADA / CM / Direct / Roots

Shafer, Robert

HILLBILLY FEVER
Dixie fried / Beam me up Scotty Moore / Just another ambush / Drink you off my mind / Every kind of music / Hillbilly fever / Haze over coal river / Will your lawer talk to God / Cadillac man / I want a lavender cadillac / Bumble boogie / Return of the flatwoods monster
CD _______________ UPSTART 028
Upstart / Feb '97 / ADA / Direct

Shafer, Ted

ORIGINAL JELLY BLUES (Shafer, Ted Jelly Roll Jazz Band)
CD _______________ SOSCD 1278
Stomp Off / May '95 / Jazz Music / Wellard

SAN FRANCISCO (Shafer, Ted Jelly Roll Jazz Band)
CD _______________ MMRCCD 1
Merry Makers / '93 / Jazz Music

TOE-TAPPING DIXIELAND (Shafer, Ted Jelly Roll Jazz Band)
CD _______________ MMRCCD 13
Merry Makers / Mar '97 / Jazz Music

Shaffer, Doreen

SUGAR SUGAR
CD _______________ JFCD 4648
Joe Frazier / Mar '95 / Jet Star

Shaftman

SHAFTMAN
CD _______________ EFA 115172
Crypt / Feb '96 / Shellshock/Disc

Shaggs

SHAGGS, THE
CD _______________ CREV 019CD
Rev-Ola / Nov '94 / 3mv/Vital

Shaggy

BOOMBASTIC
In the summertime / Boombastic / Something different / Forgive them father / Heartbreak Suzie / Finger Smith / Why you treat me so bad / Woman a pressure / Train is coming / Island lover / Day oh / Jenny / How much more / Gal you a pepper
CD _______________ CDV 2782
Virgin / Oct '95 / EMI

IN DUB
CD _______________ DOCD 003
Graylan / Jun '96 / Grapevine/PolyGram / Jet Star

MIDNITE LOVER
My dream / Perfect song / Warm and tender love / Geenie / Sexy body girls / Piece of my heart / Think ah so it go / Midnite lover / Mission / Way back home / John Doe / Thank you Lord
CD _______________ CDV 2838
Virgin / Aug '97 / EMI

ORIGINAL DOBERMAN
Kibbles and bits / Bullet proof buddy / Chow / Alimony / Wildfire / PHAT / Glamity power / Get down to it / Man a yard / Soldering / Lately / Jump and rock / We never danced to the rub-a-dub sound
CD _______________ GRELCD 208
Greensleeves / Jul '97 / Jet Star / SRD

PURE PLEASURE
Soon be done / Give thanks and praise / Lust / Oh Carolina / Tek set / Bedroom bounty hunter / Nice and lovely / Love how them flex / All virgins / Ah-e-a-oh / It bun me / Big up / Bow wow wow / Follow me / Mampie / Oh Carolina (Raas bumba claat version)
CD _______________ GRELCD 184
Greensleeves / Jul '97 / Jet Star / SRD

Shaheen, Simon

SALTANAH (Shaheen, Simon & Vishnwa Mohan Bhatt)
Dawn / Ghazal / Saltanah / Mists / Dusk
CD _______________ WLAES 51CD
Waterlilly Acoustics / Feb '97 / ADA

TURATH
CD _______________ CMP CD 3006
CMP / Jul '92 / Cargo / Grapevine/ PolyGram / Vital/SAM

Shai

IF I EVER FALL IN LOVE
Sexual interlude / Comforter / If I ever fall in love / Sexual / Together forever / If I ever fall in love (accapella) / Flava / Baby, I'm yours / Waiting for the day / Changes / Don't wanna play / Lord I've come
CD _______________ MCLD 19354
MCA / Apr '97 / BMG

Shaikh, Adham

DRIFT
CD _______________ AMB 60062
Instinct / Feb '97 / Cargo

JOURNEY TO THE SUN
CD _______________ IAE 006CD
Instinct Ambient Europe / Jul '95 / Plastic Head

Shaka Shamba

NAMEBRAND
CD _______________ GRELCD 203
Greensleeves / Apr '94 / Jet Star / SRD

Shaka, Tom

HIT FROM THE HEART
CD _______________ CCD 11025
Crosscut / '92 / ADA / CM / Direct

HOT 'N' SPICY
CD _______________ CCD 11036
Crosscut / Jan '94 / ADA / CM / Direct

TIMELESS IN BLUES
CD _______________ CDST 03
Stumble / Nov '95 / Direct

Shakatak

CHRISTMAS ALBUM, THE
Happy Christmas to ya / Winter wonderland / White Christmas / O little town of Bethlehem / Silent night / Christmas time again / Christmas in Rio / Good King Wenceslas / Let it snow, let it snow, let it snow / Sing (Little one) / God rest ye merry gentlemen / Lonely on Christmas day / Jingle bells / Christmas song / Away in a manger / Auld lang syne
CD _______________ CDINZ 3
Debut / Nov '96 / 3mv/Sony / Pinnacle

COLLECTION, THE
Down on the street / Day by day / Invitations / Dark is the night / You'll never know / Don't blame it on love / Lady (To Billie Holiday) / Holding on / Streetwalkin' / Night birds / Easier said than done / Out of this world / Dr. Dr / Bitter sweet / Something special / Light of my life / Turn the music up / Mr. Manic and Sister cool
CD _______________ 5520202
Spectrum / Mar '96 / PolyGram

FULL CIRCLE
Brazillian love affair / Catwalk / Out of my sight / Sweet Sunday / You are / Walk in the night / Haze / Diamond in the night / Midnight temptation / Havana express / Tonight's the night / Blue azure
CD _______________ CDINZ 4
Inside Out / Feb '95 / 3mv/Sony

JAZZ CONNECTIONS VOL.1
Deja vu'll see ya / L'aggio l'amour / Out of the blue / One for cara / Eyes of the sea / Dance like Fred Astaire/Jazz creepin'/bermuda rig / Blue note / Twilight time / Interlude
CD _______________ CDSHAK 1
Inside Out / Sep '96 / 3mv/Sony

JAZZ CONNECTIONS VOL.2
Damokani suite / Golden wings / Quiet storm / Paradise/prelude / Nights over Tokyo / One day, one night, one love / Only yesterday / Cavalcante/Island girl / One more
CD _______________ CDSHAK 2
Inside Out / Sep '96 / 3mv/Sony

JAZZ CONNECTIONS VOL.3
Heart to heart / China Bay / My utopia/Pastel shade/Climbing high/Perfect smile / Madinina / Disorder at the border / Whispers in the night / Lazy / This boy is mine / Silk emotion
CD _______________ CDSHAK 3
Inside Out / Sep '96 / 3mv/Sony

JAZZ CONNECTIONS VOL.4
Sunshiny day / High life / Open your eyes / Marie Louise / Sea dreamin' / No one knows/Why me / Runnin' away / Endurance / Nothing but a dream hideaway / Conquistador
CD _______________ CDSHAK 4
Inside Out / Sep '96 / 3mv/Sony

JAZZ CONNECTIONS VOL.5
First love/Hungry / Just the way we are / Kagape / Dreamtime / Chi-chi-castanengo racing / With the wind / Story of my life / Catch me if you can / After midnight / Please don't go / Undercurrent
CD _______________ CDSHAK 5
Inside Out / Sep '96 / 3mv/Sony

JAZZ CONNECTIONS VOL.6
Danceland / Runaway Bay / Coco kazu/One day soon / Midnight walkin' / Just the way it goes deadline / Run with the tide/Nocturne / Looking for rainbows / Two people (one love story) / When night falls
CD _______________ CDSHAK 6
Inside Out / Sep '96 / 3mv/Sony

ON THE STREET
Down on the street / Easier said than done / Invitations / Out of this world / Holding on / Lights on my life / Lady (To Billie Holiday) / Dark is the night / Doctor doctor / Something special / Mr. Manic and Sister cool / Turn the music up / Bittersweet / You'll never know
CD _______________ 5500082
Spectrum / May '93 / PolyGram

OUT OF THIS WORLD
Dark is the night / Don't say that again / Slip away / On nights like tonight / Out of this world / Let's get together / If you can see me now / Sanur
CD _______________ OW 30014
One Way / Sep '94 / ADA / Direct / Greyhound

STREET LEVEL
One day at a time / Street level / Sleepin' alone / Siberian breeze / Anyway you want it / Night ain't over yet / Watchin' the rain / Without you / Jump 'n' pump / Empty skies / Calm before the storm / Vibe tribe
CD _______________ CDINZ 1
Debut / Mar '93 / 3mv/Sony / Pinnacle

UNDER THE SUN
Soul destination / Don't walk away / Paradise island / Rest of your life / Crosstown / One for the boyz / Beyond the reach / Can't stop running / Sweat / It's over / Fly by night / Shine your light
CD _______________ CDINZ 2
Debut / Nov '92 / 3mv/Sony / Pinnacle

Shakedown Club

SHAKEDOWN CLUB, THE
CD _______________ BDV 9403CD
Babel / Jul '94 / ADA / Cadillac / Diverse / Harmonia Mundi

Shaker

KISS ME
CD _______________ TPLP 70CD
One Little Indian / May '96 / Pinnacle

Shakespears Sister

HORMONALLY YOURS
Goodbye cruel world / I don't care / My 16th apology / Are we in love yet / Emotional thing / Stay / Black sky / Trouble with Andre / Moonchild / Catwoman / Let me entertain you / Hello (turn your radio on)
CD _______________ 8282662
London / Feb '92 / PolyGram

SACRED HEART
Heroine / Run silent / Run deep / Dirty mind / Sacred heart / Heaven in your arms / You're history / Break my heart / Red rocket / Electric moon / Primitive love / Could you be loved / Twist the knife / You made me come to this
CD _______________ 8281312
London / May '92 / PolyGram

Shakta

SILICON TRIP
CD _______________ DFLCD 23
Dragonfly / Feb '97 / Mo's Music Machine / Pinnacle

Shakuhachi Surprise

SPACE STREAKINGS OVER MOUNT SHASTA
CD _______________ GR 35CD
Skingraft / Oct '96 / SRD

Shalamar

BIG FUN
Right time for us / Take me to the river / Right in the socket / Second time around / I owe you one / Let's find the time for love / Girl
CD _______________ NEBCD 791
Sequel / Jul '96 / BMG

FRIENDS
Night to remember / Don't try to change me / Help me / On top of the world / I don't wanna be the last to know / Friends / Playing to win / I just stopped by because I had to / There it is / I can make you feel good
CD _______________ NEBCD 789
Sequel / Jul '96 / BMG

LOOK, THE
Closer / Dead giveaway / You can count on me / Right here / No limits / Disappearing act / Over and over / You're the one for me / You won't miss love (Until it's gone) / Look
CD _______________ NEBCD 788
Sequel / Jul '96 / BMG

NIGHT TO REMEMBER, A
Night to remember / There it is / I can make you feel good / Over and over / My girl loves me / Amnesia / Leave it all up to love / Whenever you need me / Uptown festival / Second time around / Lovely lady / Work it out / Sweeter as the days go by / On top of the world / Don't try to change me / You won't miss love (until it's gone)
CD _______________ 5507542
Spectrum / Mar '95 / PolyGram

THREE FOR LOVE
Full of fire / Attention to my baby / Somewhere there's a love / Some things never change / Make that move / This is for the lover in you / Work it out / Pop along kid
CD _______________ NEBCD 790
Sequel / Jul '96 / BMG

VERY BEST OF SHALAMAR, THE
Friends / Take that to the bank / Second time around / There it is / Make that move / I can make you feel good / I owe you one / Uptown festival / Dancing in the sheets / Disappearing act / Night to remember / Dead giveaway / Amnesia / Deadline USA / My girl loves me / Over and over / Circumstantial evidence / Sweeter as the days go by
CD _______________ CCSCD 803
Renaissance Collector Series / Sep '95 / BMG

Shalawambe

SAMORA MACHEL
Mulemeleni / Abantu balafwa / Twansanswa / Umpele njibikile / Kambelenkete / Samora machel / Ifilamba / Icupo cha perm / Mulamu
CD _______________ DIAB 817CD
Diabolo / Nov '95 / Pinnacle

Shaljean, Bonnie

FAREWELL TO LOUGH NEAGH
Roslin Castle / Captain O'Neill / Colonel O'Hara / Sir Festus Burke / Foweles in the frith / Edi beo thu hevene quene / Summer is icumen in / Clocks back reel / Kilburn jig / Diarmuid's well / Wild Irishman / Her mantle so green / Planxty Drew / Mary O'Neill / Maid of Derry
CD _______ **CDSDL 372**
Saydisc / Mar '94 / ADA / Direct / Harmonia Mundi

Sham 69

A FILES, THE
CD _______ **AICD 004**
A+I / Apr '97 / Koch / Scratch/BMG
CD _______ **EFACD 12359**
Empty / Jul '97 / Cargo / Greyhound / Plastic Head / SRD

ADVENTURES OF THE HERSHAM BOYS, THE
Money / Fly dark angel / Joey's on the street again / Cold blue in the night / Mister, you're a better man than I / Lost on highway 46 / Voices / Questions and answers / What have we got / If the kids are united / Borstal breakout
CD _______ **ESMCD 515**
Essential / Jun '97 / BMG

BEST OF SHAM 69, THE (2CD Set)
Borstal breakout / Family life / Tell us the truth / Angels with dirty faces / Cockney kids are innocent / If the kids are united / Hurry up Harry / That's life / Questions and answers / Hersham boys / You're a better man than I / Money / Joey's on the street / Tell the children / Unite and win / Poor cow / Game / What have we got / Red London / I don't wanna / Rip off / I'm a man / Ulster boy / It's never to late / Hey little rich boy / They don't understand / What about the lonely / George Davis is innocent
CD Set _______ **ESDCD 350**
Essential / Nov '95 / BMG

BEST OF SHAM 69, THE
Borstal breakout / Family life / Tell us the truth / Angels with dirty faces / Cockney kids are innocent / If the kids are united / Hurry up Harry / That's life / Questions and answers / Hersham boys / You're a better man than I / Money / Joey's on the street / Tell the children / Unite and win / Poor cow / Game / What have we got
CD _______ **ESMCD 512**
Essential / Jun '97 / BMG

COMPLETE LIVE
Hurry up Harry / I don't wanna / If the kids are united / Borstal breakout / Angels with dirty faces / They don't understand / Rip and tear / Day tripper / That's life / Poor cow / Give a dog a bone / Questions and answers / Tell us the truth / Hersham boys / Vision and the power / White riot
CD _______ **CLACD 153**
Castle / Oct '89 / BMG

FIRST, THE BEST AND THE LAST
Borstal breakout / Hey little rich boy / Angels with dirty faces / Cockney kids are innocent / If the kids are united / Sunday morning nightmare / Hurry up Harry / Questions and answers / Give the dog a bone / Hersham boys / Tell the children / Unite and win
CD _______ **5134292**
Polydor / Apr '94 / PolyGram

GAME
Game / Lord of the flies / In and out / Human zoo / Give a dog a bone / Tell the children / Spray it on the wall / Simon / Poor cow / Dead or alive / Deja Vu / Run wild run free / Unite and win / Daytripper
CD _______ **ESMCD 516**
Essential / Jun '97 / BMG

INFORMATION LIBRE
Break on through / Uptown / Planet trash / Information libertaire / Caroline's suitcase / Feel it / King Kong drinks cocacola / Saturdays and strangeways / Breeding dinosaurs / Wild and wonderful
CD _______ **DOJOCD 236**
Dojo / Jan '96 / Disc

LIVE IN JAPAN
CD _______ **DOJOCD 105**
Dojo / Feb '94 / Disc

SHAM 69 LIVE
If the kids are united / Joey's on the street again / James Dean / Ulster boy / Rip off / They don't understand / Questions and answers / Day tripper / Who gives a damn / What have we got / That's life / Red London / Everybody's innocent / White riot / Borstal breakout / Tell us the truth
CD _______ **EMPRCD 582**
Emporio / Oct '95 / Disc

SOAPY WATER AND MR. MARMALADE
CD _______ **3012792**
Culture Press / Jun '97 / Cargo
CD _______ **AICD 001**
A+I / Mar '97 / Koch / Scratch/BMG

TELL US THE TRUTH
We got a fight / Rip off / Ulster / George Davis is innocent / They don't understand / Borstal breakout / Family life / Hey little rich boy / I'm a man I'm a boy / What about the lonely / Tell us the truth / It's never too late / Who's generation / What have we got
CD _______ **ESMCD 513**
Essential / Jun '97 / BMG

THAT'S LIFE
Leave me alone / Who gives a damn / Everybody's right, everybody's wrong / That's life / Win or lose / Hurry up Harry / Evil way / Reggae pick up part 1 / Sunday morning nightmare / Reggae pick up part 2 / Angels with dirty faces / Is this me or is this you
CD _______ **DOJOCD 257**
Dojo / Mar '96 / Disc

UNITED
If the kids are united / What have we got / Red lion / Voices / Angels with dirty faces / Questions and answers / That's life / Borstal breakout / Joey's on the street / They don't understand / Tell us the truth / Hersham boys
CD _______ **304462**
Hallmark / Jun '97 / Carlton

Shamaani Duo

HUNKA LUNKA
CD _______ **SNAP 355CD**
Snap / Nov '96 / ADA

Shamanic Tribes On Acid

303 TO INFINITY
Mandala moon / Starglider / Tantalus / Book of changes / Golden bell / Elastic psychedelic / Spiral 303 / Herbal meditation / Omega sunset / Acid punk
CD _______ **KINXCD 7**
Kinetix / Mar '97 / Pinnacle

Shame Idols

ROCKET CAT
CD _______ **310712**
Frontier / Jul '97 / Plastic Head / Vital

Shamen

AXIS MUTATIS
CD _______ **TPLP 52CDL**
CD _______ **TPLP 52CD**
One Little Indian / Oct '95 / Pinnacle

COLLECTION, THE
CD _______ **TPLP 72CD**
CD _______ **TPLP 72CDR**
One Little Indian / Jan '97 / Pinnacle

DIFFERENT DRUM
CD _______ **TPLP 42CDR**
One Little Indian / Nov '93 / Pinnacle

DROP
Something about you / Passing away / Young 'til yesterday / World theatre / Through with you / Where do you go / Do what you will / Happy days / Through my window / Velvet box / I don't like the way the world is / Other side / Four letter girl
CD _______ **MAUCD 613**
Mau Mau / Nov '91 / Pinnacle

EN-TACT
CD _______ **TPLP 22CD**
One Little Indian / Oct '90 / Pinnacle

HEMPTON MANOR
Freya / Urpflanze / Cannabeo / Khat / Bememe / Indica / Rausch / Kava / El-fin / Monoriff
CD _______ **TPLP 62CD**
One Little Indian / Oct '96 / Pinnacle

IN GORBACHEV WE TRUST
Synergy / Raspberry infundibulum / Adam strange / Transcendental / Raptyouare / Sweet young thing / War prayer / Jesus loves Amerika / Misinformation / In Gorbachev we trust
CD _______ **FIENDCD 666**
Demon / Jan '89 / Pinnacle

Shampoo

GIRL POWER
Girl power / News flash / I know what boys like / Bare knuckle girl / Zap pow / War paint / You love it / Boys are us / We play dumb / I'm gonna scream / Don't call me babe
CD _______ **FOODCD 16**
Food / Sep '96 / EMI

Shamrock Singers

WHEN IRISH EYES ARE SMILING
CD _______ **MACCD 202**
Autograph / Aug '96 / BMG

Shand, Jimmy

20 GOLDEN TRACKS
Shandon bells / Biddy the bowl wife / Frost is all over / Pet o' the pipers / George Harrison's reel / Come let us dance and sing / Davy Nick Nack / Soft lowland tongue / Annie Laurie / My Nannie's awa' / I lo'ed nae a lassie but ane / Stone court / Mrs. Jimmy Shand's fancy / Miss Maria Stewart / Black dance / Thurso wedding / Wandering drummer / Breadalbane reel / Aikey brae / Muckle Friday fair / St. Andrew's parade / Bobby Watson / Lord Lyndoch / Duke of Gordon / Laird o' Thrums / Lady Anne Hope / Muckin' o' Geordie's byre / Lady Nellie Wemyss / Braidleys house / Major Mackie / Queens bridge / Calton hill / Hopeful lover / Cailin mo Ruinsa / Leaving Barra / Morag of Dunvegan / Cock o' the North / Jeannie King / Brydie's polka / Standchen / Paddywhack / Dan the cobbler / Saddle the pony / Come o'er the stream Charlie / Rothesay Bay / Sound the Pibroch / My love is like a red red rose / O Gin I were a Baron's heir / Wonder hornpipe / Harvest home / Trumpet hornpipe / If you're Irish come into the parlour / With my shillelagh under my arm / Galloway House / Georgina Catherine MacDonald's fancy / Earl Gray
CD _______ **CDGR 154**
Ross / Feb '96 / CM / Duncans / Highlander / Ross

LAST TEN YEARS, THE (Shand, Jimmy & His Band)
Georgina Catherine MacDonald's fancy / Lord Randal's bride / Calton Hill reel / Lady Elgin of Broomhall / Lord Elgin of Broomhall / Green glens of Antrim / Come back to Erin / Bryce Laing's welcome to Auchtermuchty / John and Mary's Young's golden wedding anniversary / Threave Castle polka / Major Norman Orr Ewing / Crossing the new Forth Bridge / Seventy second Highlanders' farewell to Aberdeen / Jimmy Shand's 80th year / Now is the hour / At the end of a perfect day / MacKenzie highlanders / Glengarry quickstep / Teribus / Sweet maid of Glendaruel / Francis Wright's waltz / Suptd. Ian Thompson's farewell to the Fife police / Jimmy Shand's compliments to Willie Laird / Guardians of the Gulf / Royal Guard Regiment of HM Sultan Of Oman / Heather mixture twostep / Badge of Scotland / Fifty first Highland Division / Hills of Alva / MacNeils of Ugadale / John D Burgess / Hugh MacPherson / Piper's weird / Flower o' the Quern / Cradle song / Lochanside / Bill Dickman of Stonehouse / Woodlands polka / Scottish horse / Bugle horn / MacDonald's awa' tae the war / Gentle maiden / Believe me, if all those endearing young charms / Come back Paddy Reilly to Ballyjamesduff / James Duff / Rose of Tralee / Ian Powrie's welcome to Dunblane / Jimmy Shand's compliments to Ian Powrie / Whitley chapel barn dance / Miss Elder / John MacDonald of Glencoe / Maresland twostep
CD _______ **WGRCD 13**
Ross / Dec '89 / CM / Duncans / Highlander / Ross

LEGENDARY JIMMY SHAND MBE, THE
Newcastle reel medley / Grannie Heilan hame medley / Scotland the brave medley / Braes of Elchie medley / Agnes waltz / MacKenzie highlanders medley / Maggie and Jock / Cumberland reel medley / Strathspey medley / Royal Scots polka / Welcome home fisher lads / Ian and Bunty medley / Auld reekie / Lady Dorothea medley / L'entrainante / 6.20 two step / Brides of Erin medley / Pipe matches medley / Light and airy medley / Somebody stole my gal medley / Reel/Georgia medley
CD _______ **RECD 514**
REL / Jun '97 / CM / Duncans / Highlander

LEGENDARY JIMMY SHAND, THE
Linton ploughman / Marching with Jimmy Shand / Gaelic waltz selection / Gay Gordons / When you and I were young Maggie / Bluebell polka / Irish two step / Royal Scots polka / I'll take you home agin Kathleen / Highland schottische / Swilcan / Northern lights of Aberdeen / Black dance
CD _______ **CDSL 8284**
EMI Gold / Feb '97 / EMI

LEGENDARY JIMMY SHAND, THE
Muckin' o' Geordie's byre / Lady Nellie Wemyss / Braidley's house / Major Mackie / Scotland the brave / Thistle of Scotland / We're no awa' tae bide awa' / Cailin mo ruin-sa / Leaving barra / Morag of Dunvegan / Cock o' the North / Jeannie King / Bluebell polka / If you're Irish come into the parlour / With my shillelagh under me arm / Royal Scots polka / Lord Lyndoch / Duke of Gordon / Laird o' Thrums / Lady Anne Hope / Gordon B Cosh / Kinkell braes / Ythan bar / Northern lights of Aberdeen / Black dance / Thurso wedding / Wandering drummer / Breadalbane reel / Miss Bennetts jig / John Mearn's favourite / Balcomie House / Threave castle polka / Mrs. Cholmondely's reel / Lass o' paties mill / O Harveston Castle / Deveron reel / Blow the wind southerly / O hey ya seen the roses blow / Cushie butterfield / Cullercoats fish lass / Peter's peerie boat / Boonie doon / Jeanie's blue e'en / Neidpath castle / Tom's highland fling / Scotch mist / Lamb skinnet / John Grumlie / I lo'ed nae a lassie but Ane / Brinkie braes / Aunice Gillie's farewell to Loch Gilphead / John Bain Mackenzie / Galloway house reel / Georgina Catherine MacDonald's fancy
CD _______ **CC 248**
Music For Pleasure / Sep '89 / EMI

SCOTTISH FANCY, A (Shand, Jimmy & His Band)
White heather jig / Grosvenor House strathspey / Campbells are coming / Balmoral strathspey / Miss Hadden's reel / Quiet and snug strathspey / Hooper's jig / Waltz country dance / Galloway House reel / Express / La tempete / Marie's wedding / Road to the isles / Waverley
CD _______ **GRCD 37**
Grasmere / Sep '89 / Highlander / Savoy / Target/BMG

Shand, Jimmy Jr.

BEST OF JIMMY SHAND JR., THE
Auchtermuchty Gala march / Lass from Glasgow Town / Badenoch polka / Gay Gordons medley / Shamrock waltzes medley / Reels medley / Ring family two step / Rabbie Burns marches / Trip to Bavaria medley / Singalong waltz medley / Jigs medley / Medley / Gay Gordons medley #2 / Welcome Christmas morning / Eva three step medley
CD _______ **EMPRCD 721**
Emporio / Jun '97 / Disc

Shane, Mark

TREASURE ISLAND
CD _______ **JJZ 9603**
Jukebox / Nov '96 / Jazz Music

Shangaie

CHANSON MARINEES
CD _______ **CD 857**
Diffusion Breizh / Aug '95 / ADA

Shangoya

COLLECTION, THE
CD _______ **MPD 6006**
Flying Fish / Nov '94 / ADA / CM / Direct / Roots

Shangri-Las

BEST OF THE SHANGRI-LAS, THE
Remember (walkin' in the sand) / Leader of the pack / What is love / Give him a great big kiss / Maybe / Out in the streets / Give us your blessings / Heaven only knows / Never again / What's a girl supposed to do / Dum dum ditty / Right now and not later / Train from Kansas City / I can never go home anymore / Long live our love / Sophisticated boom boom / He cried / Dressed in black / Past, present and future / Paradise / Love you more than yesterday / Sweet sound of Summer / I'll never learn / Take the time / Footsteps on the roof
CD _______ **5527642**
Spectrum / Feb '97 / PolyGram

COLLECTION, THE
CD _______ **COL 043**
Collection / Mar '95 / Target/BMG

GOLD
CD _______ **GOLD 069**
Gold / Aug '96 / Else

HIT SINGLE COLLECTABLES
CD _______ **DISK 4512**
Disky / Apr '94 / Disky / THE

MYRMIDONES OF MELODRAMA
Remember (walkin' in the sand) / It's easier to cry / Leader of the pack / What is love / Give him a great big kiss / Maybe / Out in the streets / Boy / Give us your blessings / Heaven only knows / Right now and not later / Train from Kansas city / I can never go home anymore / Bulldog / Long live our love / Sophisticated boom boom / He cried / Dressed in black / Past, present and future / Love you more than yesterday / Paradise / Never again / I'm blue / What's a girl supposed to do / Dum dum ditty / You cheated, you lied / Give him a great big kiss (alt take) / Dating courtesy Pt 1 / Dating courtesy Pt 2 / Hate to say I told you so / Wishing well
CD _______ **RPM 136**
RPM / Apr '95 / Pinnacle

PEARLS FROM THE PAST
CD _______ **KLMCD 013**
BAM / May '94 / Koch / Scratch/BMG

Shank, Bud

BUD SHANK PLAYS CONCERTO FOR ALTO SAX AND ORCHESTRA (Shank, Bud & The Royal Philharmonic Orchestra)
Here's that rainy day: *Shank, Bud Quartet* / Body and soul / Concerto for jazz alto saxophone and orchestra
CD _______ **MOLECD 12**
Mole Jazz / Apr '87 / Cadillac / Impetus / Jazz Music / Wellard

CRYSTAL COMMENTS (Shank, Bud & Bill Mays, Alan Boradbent)
Scrapple from the apple / How are things in glocca morra / I'll take romance / Solar / Body and soul / On green dolphin street
CD _______ **CCD 4126**
Concord Jazz / Feb '94 / New Note/ Pinnacle

DOCTOR IS IN, THE
Doctor is in / Embraceable you / If I should lose you / JP'S afternoon / I can't get started / I'm old fashioned / Once I had a secret love / Sonatina for Melissa / Over the rainbow / Doctor is out
CD _______ **CCD 79520**
Candid / Feb '97 / Cadillac / Direct / Jazz Music / Koch / Wellard

DRIFTING TIMELESSLY
CD ____ 75001
Capri / Jun '87 / Cadillac / Wellard

I TOLD YOU SO
I told you so / My funny valentine / Continental / Emily / Dance of the little ones / My old flame / Limehouse blues
CD ____ CCD 79533
Candid / Feb '97 / Cadillac / Direct / Jazz Music / Koch / Wellard

LOST CATHEDRAL, THE
CD ____ ITMP 970087
ITM / Oct '95 / Koch / Tradelink

NEW GOLD (Shank, Bud Sextet)
Port Townsend / Alternate rout / Let me tell you why / Straight no chaser / Perkolater / Grizzly / Finger therapy (for Sherman) / Linda / Killer Joe / Funcused blues / Little rootie tootie
CD ____ CCD 79707
Candid / Feb '97 / Cadillac / Direct / Jazz Music / Koch / Wellard

SUNSHINE EXPRESS
CD ____ CCD 6020
Concord Jazz / Sep '91 / New Note/ Pinnacle

TALES OF THE PILOT
CD ____ CAPR 74025
Capri / Jan '89 / Cadillac / Wellard

Shankar, Lakshminarayana

LAKSHMI SHANKAR EVENING CONCERT
CD ____ RSMCD 102
Ravi Shankar Music Circle / Apr '94 / Conifer/BMG

MRCS
Adagio / March / All I care / Reasons / Back again / Al's hallucinations / Sally / White buffalo / Ocean waves
CD ____ 8416422
ECM / Jun '91 / New Note/Pinnacle

NOBODY TOLD ME
Chittham irangaayo / Chodhanai thanthu / Nadru dri dhom - tillana
CD ____ 8396232
ECM / Nov '89 / New Note/Pinnacle

PANCHA NADAI PALLAVI
Ragam tanam pallavi / Ragam: Sankarabharanam / Talam mahalakshmi tala / 9/12 beats / Pancha nadai pallavi
CD ____ 8416412
ECM / Jun '90 / New Note/Pinnacle

SONG FOR EVERYONE
CD ____ 8237952
ECM / Apr '85 / New Note/Pinnacle

WHO'S TO KNOW
Ragam tanam pallavi / Ananda nadamaadum tillai sankara
CD ____ 8272692
ECM / Dec '85 / New Note/Pinnacle

Shankar, Ravi

AT THE WOODSTOCK FESTIVAL
Raga puriya-Dhanashri / Gat in Sawarital / Tabla solo in Jhaptal / Raga manj-khama
CD ____ BGOCD 117
Beat Goes On / Jul '91 / Pinnacle

CHANTS OF INDIA
CD ____ CDC 8559482
EMI Classics / Sep '97 / EMI

CONCERT FOR PEACE LIVE AT THE ROYAL ALBERT HALL
CD Set ____ MRCD 1013
Moment / Oct '95 / ADA / Koch

FESTIVAL FROM INDIA
CD ____ BGOCD 301
Beat Goes On / Nov '95 / Pinnacle

FROM INDIA
CD ____ CD 12522
Music Of The World / Feb '95 / ADA / Target/BMG

IMPROVISATIONS
CD ____ BGOCD 115
Beat Goes On / Jul '91 / Pinnacle

IN CONCERT
CD ____ BGOCD 302
Beat Goes On / May '96 / Pinnacle

IN NEW YORK
CD ____ BGOCD 144
Beat Goes On / Jun '92 / Pinnacle

IN SAN FRANCISCO
CD ____ BGOCD 197
Beat Goes On / Dec '93 / Pinnacle

INDIA'S MASTER MUSICIAN
CD ____ BGOCD 218
Beat Goes On / Jan '94 / Pinnacle

INSIDE THE KREMLIN
Prarambh / Shanti mantra / Three ragas in D minor / Sandhya / Tarana / Bahu-rang
CD ____ 259620
Arista / Feb '89 / BMG

LIVE AT MONTEREY 1967
Raga todi / Rupak tal (7 beats) / Tabla solo in ektal (12 beats)
CD ____ RSMCD 101
Ravi Shankar Music Circle / Apr '94 / Conifer/BMG

LIVE AT THE MONTEREY FESTIVAL
Raga Bhimpalasi / Tabla solo in Ektal / Dhun
CD ____ BGOCD 147
Beat Goes On / Jul '93 / Pinnacle

PANDIT RAVI SHANKAR
CD ____ C558 674
Ocora / '88 / ADA / Harmonia Mundi

PORTRAIT OF A GENIUS
CD ____ BGOCD 99
Beat Goes On / '91 / Pinnacle

RAGAS (2CD Set)
Palas kafi / Bilashkani todi / Ramdas malhar / Malika
CD Set ____ FCD 247142
Fantasy / Mar '96 / Jazz Music / Pinnacle / Wellard

RAVI - IN CELEBRATION (4CD Set) (Shankar, Ravi/Various Artists)
Charukeshi / Bhatiyar / Adarini / Marwa / Dhun Kafi / V7 1/2 / Jait / Sandhya raga / Ghanashyam / Tilak shyam / Duet for sitar & violin / Sitar concertos 1&2 / Morning love / Indo Japan finale / Enchanted dawn / Vandana / Hey Nath / Pather Panchali / Supaney me aye / West eats meat / Oh bhagawan / Friar Park / Tana mana / I am missing you / Ta Na Tom / Fire night / Sanware Sanware / Dispute & violence / Shanti mantra
CD Set ____ CDS 5555772
Angel / Mar '96 / EMI

RAVI - IN CELEBRATION (Highlights) (Shankar, Ravi/Various Artists)
Dhun Kafi: *Shankar, Ravi* / Supaney mein aye: *Shankar, Ravi* / 2nd Movement Sitar Concerto: *Shankar, Ravi* / 3rd Movement Sitar Concerto no.1: *Shankar, Ravi* / West eats meat: *Shankar, Ravi* / Tilak Shyam: *Shankar, Ravi* / I am missing you: *Shankar, Ravi*
CD ____ CDC 5556172
Angel / Sep '96 / EMI

RAVI SHANKAR
CD ____ C 570000CD
Ocora / Jul '95 / ADA / Harmonia Mundi

RAVI SHANKAR & ALI AKBAR KHAN IN CONCERT 1972 (2CD Set) (Shankar, Ravi & Ali Akbar Khan)
Raga / Hem bihag / Manj Khamaj part 1 / Manj Khamaj part 2 / Sindhi Bhairavi
CD Set ____ CDSAPDO 1002
Apple / Feb '97 / EMI

RAVI SHANKAR IN VENICE
CD ____ ED 1031
Edelweiss / Mar '96 / Discovery / Planetarium

SOUND OF THE SITAR
Raga Malkauns / Tala Sawari (Tabla Solo) / Pahari Dhun
CD ____ BGOCD 171
Beat Goes On / Apr '93 / Pinnacle

TANA MANA (Shankar, Ravi Project)
Chase / Tana mana / Village dance / Seven and 10 1/2 / Friar park / Romantic voyage / Memory of Uday / West eats meat / Reunion / Supplication
CD ____ 259962
Private Music / Nov '89 / BMG

TOWARDS THE RISING SUN (Shankar, Ravi & Friends)
Padhasapa / Kaharwa / Rokudan / Namah shivaya / Tribute to Nippon / Homage to Baba Allauddin
CD ____ 4495992
Deutsche Grammophon / Jun '96 / PolyGram

TRANSMIGRATION MACABRE
Madness / Anxiety / Submission / Transmigration / Reflection / Fantasy / Torment / Death / Retribution
CD ____ C5CD 596
See For Miles/C5 / Mar '97 / Pinnacle

Shanks, Andy

DIAMONDS IN THE NIGHT (Shanks, Andy & Jim Russell)
Balgonie barn/Thirty year man / Ash pirates / Rags and days / Streets and dances / Money, guns and the green green forest / St. Andrew in the window / Compass heart / Road here / Diamonds in the night / Midnight city buses / Mogadishu / Fiddler / Wake
CD ____ CUL 112D
Culburnie / Jun '97 / ADA / CM / Direct / Duncans / Highlander / Ross

Shanley, Eleanor

DESERT HEART
CD ____ GRACD 225
Grapevine / Jul '97 / Grapevine/PolyGram

ELEANOR SHANLEY
CD ____ GRACD 206
Grapevine / Apr '95 / Grapevine/PolyGram

Shannon

COLLECTION, THE
CD ____ CCSCD 394
Castle / Apr '94 / BMG

Shannon Castle Singers

MEDIAEVAL BANQUET
CD ____ DOLCD 1007
Dolphin / Jul '96 / CM / Else / Grapevine/ PolyGram / Koch

Shannon Singers

60 SHADES OF GREEN
CD ____ CDIRISH 002
Outlet / Mar '96 / ADA / CM / Direct / Duncans / Koch / Ross

CHRISTMAS PARTY
CD ____ CCSCD 801
Outlet / Jan '95 / ADA / CM / Direct / Duncans / Koch / Ross

GOLDEN COLLECTION OF IRISH SONGS
CD ____ CDIRISH 008
Outlet / Oct '95 / ADA / CM / Direct / Duncans / Koch / Ross

Shannon, Del

ALL THE HITS AND MORE
Runaway / Hats off to Larry / Hey little girl / So long baby / Cry myself to sleep / Little town flirt / Two kinds of teardrops / Two silhouettes / Keep searchin' / Stranger in town / Broken promises / Swiss maid / From me to you / Handy man / Do you wanna dance / You never talked about me / Kelly / Give her lots of lovin' / Over you / Break up / Why don't you tell him / Jody / Sue's gotta be mine / Answer to everything
CD ____ QED 098
Tring / Nov '96 / Tring

BEST OF DEL SHANNON, THE
Runaway / Hats off to Harry / So long baby / Dream baby / Hey little girl / Break up / Cry myself to sleep / You never talked about me / Swiss maid / Little town flirt / Hey baby / Two kinds of teardrops / Kelly / Mary Jane / From me to you / Stranger in town / Keep searchin' (we'll follow the sun) / Do you wanna dance / Handy man / Runaround Sue / That's the way love is / Sues gotta be mine / Two silhouettes / World without love
CD ____ CD 6011
Music / Apr '96 / Target/BMG

GOLD
CD ____ GOLD 051
Gold / Aug '96 / Else

GREATEST HITS
Runaway / Hats off to Larry / Little town flirt / Swiss maid / Hey little girl / Two kinds of teardrops / So long baby / She's gotta be mine / From me to you / Handyman / Do you want to dance / Big hurt / Keep searchin' / Stranger in town / Break up / Cry myself to sleep / Two silouettes / Don't gild the lily / Lily / Ginny in the mirror / I go to pieces
CD ____ CPCD 8001
Charly / Oct '93 / Koch

GREATEST HITS
CD ____ MU 5017
Musketeer / Oct '92 / Disc

LIVE IN ENGLAND/AND THE MUSIC PLAYED ON
Hats off to Larry / Handyman / Swiss maid / Hey little girl / Little town flirt / Kelly / Crying / Two kinds of teardrops / Coopersville yodel / Answer to everything / Keep searchin' / What's the matter baby / So long baby / Runaway / It's my feeling / Mind over matter / Silently / Cut and come again / My love has gone / Led along / Life is nothing / Music plays on / Easy to say / Friendly with you / Raindrops / He cheated / Leaving you behind / Runaway '67
CD ____ BGOCD 280
Beat Goes On / Jun '95 / Pinnacle

LOOKING BACK
Runaway / Hats off to Larry / Don't gild the lily, Lily / So long baby / Answer to everything / Hey little girl / I don't care anymore / You never talked about me / I won't be there / Ginny in the mirror / Cry myself to sleep / Swiss maid / Little town flirt / Two kinds of teardrops / Kelly / Two silhouettes / From me to you / Sue's gonna be mine / That's the way love is / Mary Jane / Handyman / World without love / Do you wanna dance / Keep searchin' / Broken promises / I go to pieces / Stranger in town / Break up / Why don't you tell him / Move it on over
CD ____ VSOPCD 161
Connoisseur Collection / Apr '91 / Pinnacle

PACKET OF THREE VOL.2 (3CD Set) (Shannon, Del/Little Richard/Jerry Lee Lewis)
Runaway: *Shannon, Del* / Hats off to Larry: *Shannon, Del* / Hey little girl: *Shannon, Del* / Little town flirt: *Shannon, Del* / Two kinds of teardrops: *Shannon, Del* / Keep on searchin': *Shannon, Del* / Swiss maid: *Shannon, Del* / Handy man: *Shannon, Del* / Do you wanna dance: *Shannon, Del* / Misery: *Shannon, Del* / Dream baby: *Shannon, Del* / Broken promises: *Shannon, Del* / Two silhouettes: *Shannon, Del* / Wide wide world: *Shannon, Del* / Ginny in the mirror: *Shannon, Del* / You never talked about me: *Shannon, Del* / She thinks I still care: *Shannon, Del* / Why don't you tell him: *Shannon, Del* / Sue's gotta be mine: *Shannon, Del* / Kelly: *Shannon, Del* / Rip it up: *Little Richard* / Lucille: *Little Richard* / Jenny Jenny: *Little Richard* / Money honey: *Little Richard* / Hound dog: *Little Richard* / Good golly Miss Molly: *Little Richard* / Groovy little Suzy: *Little Richard* / Cherry red: *Little Richard* / Long tall Sally: *Little Richard* / Dancin' round the world: *Little Richard* / I'm trampin': *Little Richard* / Keep a knockin': *Little Richard* / Slippin' and slidin': *Little Richard* / Baby face: *Little Richard* / Without love: *Little Richard* / Talkin' bout soul: *Little Richard* / Ready Teddy: *Little Richard* / Ooh my soul: *Little Richard* / Belle stars: *Little Richard* / Funky dish rag: *Little Richard* / Who's sorry now: *Lewis, Jerry Lee* / Flip, flop and fly/Shake, rattle 'n' roll: *Lewis, Jerry Lee* / Chantilly lace: *Lewis, Jerry Lee* / Great balls of fire: *Lewis, Jerry Lee* / Whole lotta shakin' goin' on: *Lewis, Jerry Lee* / What'd I'd say: *Lewis, Jerry Lee* / Honky tonk angels: *Lewis, Jerry Lee* / Think about it darlin': *Lewis, Jerry Lee* / Help me make it through the night: *Lewis, Jerry Lee* / Middle age crazy: *Lewis, Jerry Lee* / Mona Lisa: *Lewis, Jerry Lee* / Little Queenie: *Lewis, Jerry Lee* / Brown eyed handsome man: *Lewis, Jerry Lee* / Good golly Miss Molly/ Tutti frutti: *Lewis, Jerry Lee* / I got a woman: *Lewis, Jerry Lee* / Please don't ask about me: *Lewis, Jerry Lee* / Boogie woogie country man: *Lewis, Jerry Lee* / Another place, another time: *Lewis, Jerry Lee* / Me and Bobby McGee: *Lewis, Jerry Lee* / Rockin' Jerry Lee: *Lewis, Jerry Lee*
CD Set ____ KLMCD 302
BAM / Nov '96 / Koch / Scratch/BMG

PEARLS FROM THE PAST
CD ____ KLMCD 002
BAM / Nov '93 / Koch / Scratch/BMG

RUNAWAY
CD ____ RMB 75027
Remember / Nov '93 / Total/BMG

RUNAWAY (The Ultimate Collection)
Runaway / Kelly / So long baby / Swiss maid / Hats off to Larry / Answer to everything / Cry myself to sleep / Two kinds of teardrops / Don't gild the lily, Lily / Jody / Keep searchin' (we'll follow the sun) / From me to you / Do you want to dance / Handy man / Little town flirt / You never talked about me / Two silhouettes / Hey little girl / I go to pieces / Sue's gotta be mine
CD ____ 3036000792
Carlton / Jul '97 / Carlton

RUNAWAY HITS
Little town flirt / Runaway / Jody / Hats off to Larry / So long baby / Swiss maid / Answer to everything / Hey little girl / Cry myself to sleep / Two kinds of teardrops / Kelly / Handyman / Two silouettes / Sue's gotta be mine / Keep searchin' / Stranger in town
CD ____ EDCD 121
Edsel / Nov '86 / Pinnacle

THIS IS MY BAG/TOTAL COMMITMENT
CD ____ BGOCD 307
Beat Goes On / Mar '96 / Pinnacle

Shannon, Hugh

SALOON SINGER (2CD Set)
CD Set ____ ACD 171/172
Audiophile / Jul '96 / Jazz Music

TRUE BLUE HUGH
CD ____ ACD 140
Audiophile / Apr '93 / Jazz Music

Shannon, Mem

MEM SHANNON'S 2ND BLUES ALBUM
Wrong people are in charge / Old men / Charity / Say that then (The parlez-vous francais song) / One thin dime / Mirror, mirror / My humble opinion / Down broke / Do you 'yuh' what I say / Mr. Blues / Blues is back
CD ____ HNCD 1409
Hannibal / Apr '97 / ADA / Vital

Shannon, Preston

BREAK THE ICE (Shannon, Preston Band)
CD ____ BB 9545CD
Bullseye Blues / Aug '94 / Direct

Shannon, Sharon

EACH LITTLE THING
CD ____ GRACD 226
Grapevine / Mar '97 / Grapevine/PolyGram

OUT THE GAP
CD ____ ROCDG 14
Grapevine / Jan '95 / Grapevine/PolyGram

SHARON SHANNON
Glentown / Blackbird / Queen of the West / Retour des hirondelles/Tune for a found harmonium / Miss Thomson and Derry reel / Munster hop / Tickle her leg / Marguerita suite / Coridinio / Anto's cajun cousins / Cornphiopa corafinne and skidoo / Marbhna luimni / Phil Cunningham sets / Woodchoppers/Reel des Voygeurs
CD ____ ROCDG 8
Grapevine / Jan '95 / Grapevine/PolyGram

Shannon, Tom

ROCKIN' REBELS
Tom Shannon show logo / Wild weekend / Rockin' crickets / Whole lotta shakin' goin' on / Another wild weekend / Rumble / Hully gully rock / Flibbity jibbitt / Honky tonk / Happy popcorn / Monday morning / Sweet little sixteen / Buffalo blues / Tequila / Wild rebel / Third man theme / Wild weekend cha cha / Ram-bunk-shush / Telstar / Donkey walk / Stripper / Coconuts / Loaded dice / Anyway you want me / Theme from the rebel / Wild weekend theme
CD _______ CDCHD 426
Ace / May '94 / Pinnacle

Shanti, Oliver

TAI CHI
CD _______ SKV 006CD
Sattva Art / Jul '95 / THE

Shanty Crew

SEA SHANTIES & SAILOR SONGS (Classics From The Great Days Of Sail 1840-1890)
Prologue: the leef fore brace / Old moke pickin' on the banjo / Can't ye hilo / Where am I to go, M'Johnnies / One more day / Rolling coal / Randy dandy o / Ranzo ray / Yankee john, stormalong / Frankie's trade / Bring em down / Do let me 'lone susan / General Taylor / Gals o'Dublin town / Paddy Doyle's boots / Bully in the alley / Heave away boys heave away / Johnny Bowker / Common Sailors / Spanish ladies / I'm bound away / Shallow brown / Fire down below / John Kanaka / Cheer'ly man / Hi-o, come roll me over / East Indiaman / Paddy lay back / Epilogue: d'ye mind
CD _______ BHCD 9601
Brewhouse / Dec '96 / ADA / Brewhouse Music

Shaolin Wooden Men

SHAOLIN WOODEN MEN
CD _______ NZ 013
Nova Zembla / Jul '94 / Plastic Head

Shapeshifter

MYSTERY OF BEING
CD _______ HY 85921054
Hyperium / Apr '94 / Cargo / Plastic Head

Shapiro, Helen

BEST OF THE EMI YEARS, THE
Tip toe through the tulips / Don't treat me like a child / You don't know / Walkin' back to happiness / Birth of the blues / Tell me what he said / Little Miss Lonely / St. Louis blues / Teenager in love / Keep away from other girls / Let's talk about love / Lipstick on your collar / Little devil / Queen for tonight / I want to be happy / Look who it is / Woe is me / All alone am I / Fever / Walk on by
CD _______ CDEMS 1398
EMI / May '91 / EMI

BOPPIN' HELEN HITS OUT
CD _______ MA 007
Marginal / Jun '97 / Greyhound

EP COLLECTION, THE
Little devil / I don't care / Don't treat me like a child / You don't know / Teenager in love / Lipstick on your collar / Beyond the sea / Little Miss Lonely / Day the rains came / Tell me what he said / Walkin' back to happiness / I apologise / Let's talk about love / When I'm with you / Because they're young / St. Louis blues / Goody goody / Birth of the blues / Keep away from other girls / After you've gone
CD _______ SEECD 272
See For Miles/C5 / Oct '89 / Pinnacle

HELEN IN NASHVILLE
Not responsible / I cried myself to sleep last night / Young stranger / Here today and gone tomorrow / It's my party / No trespassing / I'm tickled pink / I walked right in (with my eyes wide open) / Sweeter than sweet / You'd think he didn't know me / When you hurt me / I cry / Woe is me
CD _______ C5CD545
See For Miles/C5 / '89 / Pinnacle

HELEN SHAPIRO
Don't treat me like a child / You don't know / Walkin' back to happiness / Tell me what he said / Let's talk about love / Little Miss Lonely / Keep away from other girls / Queen for tonight / Woe is me / Look who it is / Fever / Look over your shoulder / Tomorrow is another day / Shop around / I wish I'd never loved you / When I'm with you / Marvellous lie / Kiss 'n' run / I apologise / Sometime yesterday / I don't care / Cry my heart out / Daddy couldn't get me one of those / Walking in my dreams / Ole Father Time / He knows how to love me / I walked right in (with my eyes wide open) / You won't come home / I was only kidding / It's so funny I could cry
CD _______ CC 259
Music For Pleasure / Oct '90 / EMI

IMMER DIE BOYS
Frag'mich nicht warum / Komm sei wieder gut / Den ton kenn'ich schon / Gestern nachmittag / Ich war der star heute nacht / Glaube mir, Jonny / Schlafen kann ich nie / Warum gerade ich / Immer die boys / Rote rosen und vergissmeinnicht / Sag dass es schonist / Ich such mir meinen brautigam alleine aus / Der weg zu de inem herzen / Das ist nicht die feine englische art / Walkin' back to happiness / Don't treat me like a child / Tout ce qu'il voudra / J'ai tant de remords / Parlons d'amour / Sans penser a rien
CD _______ BCD 15509
Bear Family / Jul '90 / Direct / Rollercoaster / Swift

KADOSH
CD _______ MANNACD 041
Manna Music / Sep '93 / BMG

NOTHING BUT THE BEST
We being many / Nothing but the best / Be thou my people / Water on stone / Jerusalem / Kings of kings / Search me and know me / Father in heaven / Oh Lord, our Lord / You are my salvation / God will provide a lamb / Fall upon us now / There is someone
CD _______ ICCD 13530
ICC / May '95 / Total/BMG

SENSATIONAL
Teenager sings the blues / Blues in the night / Are you lonesome tonight / Tearaway Johnny / Without your love / Aren't you the lucky one / Every one but the right one / It's alright without me / Lookin' for my heart / Basin Street blues / You must be readin' my mind / Till I hear the truth from you / Sensational / Easy come, easy go / Remember me / End of the world / It might as well rain until September / Here in your arms / Only once / Just a line / Forget about the bad things / Wait a little longer / In my calendar / Empty house
CD _______ RPM 151
RPM / Jul '95 / Pinnacle

Shapiro, Yaacov

BEST OF YIDDISH FOLK SONGS
Kinder jorn / Vu bistu geven / Aroiskumen zolstu main meidl / Shabes shabes / Unter boimer / Abisl zin abisl reign / Rebe elimelech / Shlof shoin main jankele / Idish gesl / Kadish / Di zun is fargangen / Skeshenever shtikele / Hobn mir a meidl / Hop maine humentashn
CD _______ EUCD 1216
ARC / Sep '93 / ADA / ARC Music

YIDDISH TRADITIONAL SONGS
CD _______ EU 1337CD
ARC / Mar '96 / ADA / ARC Music

Sharakan Early Music ...

MUSIC OF ARMENIA VOL.2, THE (Sharakan Early Music Ensemble)
CD _______ 131162
Celestial Harmonies / Aug '96 / ADA / Select

Shareh, Oku

TURTLE DANCE SONGS OF SAN JUAN PEBLO
CD _______ 803012
New World / Sep '92 / ADA / Cadillac / Harmonia Mundi

Sharif, Jamil

PORTRAITS OF NEW ORLEANS
CD _______ UKJ 128
Dalya / Oct '93 / Jazz Music

Shark Taboo

BLACK ROCK SANDS
CD _______ PLASCD 021
Plastic Head / Nov '89 / Plastic Head

Sharkboy

MATINEE
CD _______ NUDECD 2
Nude / Apr '94 / 3mv/Vital

VALENTINE TAPES
CD _______ NUDECD 4
Nude / Sep '95 / 3mv/Vital

Sharkey, Feargal

FEARGAL SHARKEY
Good heart / You little thief / Ghost train / Ashes and diamond / Made to measure / Someone to somebody / Don't leave it to nature / Love and hate / Bitter man / It's all over now
CD _______ CDVIP 166
Virgin VIP / Oct '96 / EMI

Sharks

COLOUR MY FLESH
Hanger 84 / Grave robber / Desire calls / Time bomb / Blue water, white death / Rat race / Man with the x-ray eyes / Jet boy / On the run / Too little, too late / Parasite / Sgt rock
CD _______ CDMPSYCHO 14
Anagram / Jun '97 / Cargo / Pinnacle

PHANTOM ROCKERS
CD _______ NERCD 008
Nervous / Oct '91 / Nervous / TKO Magnum

RECREATIONAL KILLER
Screw / Bye bye girl / Charlie (93 version) / Recreational killer / Dealer / Hooker / Surfcaster / Morphine daze / Publican gullican / Gettin' even with you / Something in my basement / Blockhouse / I'm hooked on you / Schizoid man / Charlie 2 / Scratchin' my way out
CD _______ CDMPSYCHO 13
Anagram / Jun '97 / Cargo / Pinnacle

Sharma, Pandit Shiv Kumar

RAGA PURIYA
CD _______ NRCD 0060
Navras / May '96 / New Note/Pinnacle

Sharma, Shivkumar

CALL OF THE VALLEY
Rag pahadi / Ghara dadra / Dhun mishra / Bageshwari / Rag piloo / Bhoop / Rag des
CD _______ CDEMC 3707
EMI / Apr '95 / EMI

RAG MADHUVANTI/RAG MISRA TILANG
CD _______ NI 5110
Nimbus / Sep '94 / Nimbus

Sharon, Ralph

MAGIC OF COLE PORTER, THE (Sharon, Ralph Trio)
You're the top / All through the night / Easy to love / Get out of town / You'd be so nice to come home to / I concentrate on you / I've got you under my skin / Down in the depths / So in love / Anything goes / Let's do it / From this moment on / What is this thing called love / Do I love you / Night and day / I love Paris / Love for sale / I love you / It's all right with me / All of you / I get a kick out of you / Why should I / Just one of those things / Long last love / Begin the beguine / Sorta Porter
CD _______ CDSIV 1123
Horatio Nelson / Jul '95 / Disc

MAGIC OF GEORGE GERSHWIN, THE (Sharon, Ralph Trio)
Fascinating rhythm / They all laughed / Somebody loves me / 'S Wonderful / But not for me / Soon / I loves you Porgy / I got rhythm / They can't take that away from me / Someone to watch over me / Man I love / Our love is here to stay / There's a boat that's leavin' soon for New York / Rhapsody in blue / Foggy day / Embraceable you / Liza / How long has this been going on / Swanee / Love walked in / Oh lady be good
CD _______ CDSIV 1116
Horatio Nelson / Jul '95 / Disc

MAGIC OF IRVING BERLIN, THE (Sharon, Ralph Trio)
CD _______ CDSIV 1134
Horatio Nelson / Jul '95 / Disc

MAGIC OF JEROME KERN, THE (Sharon, Ralph Trio)
CD _______ CDSIV 1138
Horatio Nelson / Oct '96 / Disc

MAGIC OF RODGERS & HART, THE (Sharon, Ralph Trio)
I didn't know what time it was / Falling in love with love / Most beautiful girl in the world / Lover / Wait till you see her / Slaughter on 10th Avenue / You are too beautiful / I wish I were in love again / Bewitched, bothered and bewildered / Ten cents a dance / Have you met Miss Jones / It's easy to remember / Where or when / Mountain greenery / I could write a book / Mimi / On your toes / Thou swell / My romance / This can't be love / My funny valentine / Lady is a tramp / There's a small hotel / Little girl blue / Isn't it romantic / Blue room / It never entered my mind / Blues for Rodgers and Hart
CD _______ CDSIV 1130
Horatio Nelson / Nov '96 / Disc

PORTRAIT OF HAROLD
My shining hour / Ill wind / Let's fall in love / This time the dream's on me / It's only a paper moon / Portrait of Harold / Come rain or come shine / It was written in the stars / Between the devil and the deep blue sea / Man that got away / I've got the world on a string / Out of this world / Sing my heart / Sleepin' bee / Hit the road to dreamland / Right as the rain / That old black magic
CD _______ DRGCD 91447
DRG / May '96 / Discovery / New Note/ Pinnacle

SWINGS THE SAMMY CAHN SONGBOOK (Sharon, Ralph Trio & Gerry Mulligan)
My king of town / Teach me tonight / Mario Lanza medley - Be my love / Guess I'll hang my tears out to dry / It's magic / It's you or no one / Call me irresponsible / Blues for Sammy / Things we did last summer / Autumn in Rome / I should care / All the way / Time after time / Tender trap
CD _______ DRGCD 5232
DRG / Feb '95 / Discovery / New Note/ Pinnacle

Sharp 9

UNTIMED
CD _______ 9041532
Mausoleum / Feb '95 / Grapevine/ PolyGram

Sharp, Brian

AMOR AMOR
CD _______ CDGRS 1247
Grosvenor / Feb '93 / Grosvenor

FREEWAY
CD _______ CDGRS 1212
Grosvenor / Feb '93 / Grosvenor

Sharp, Elliott

ABSTRACT REPRESSIONISM 1990-1999
CD _______ VICTOCD 019
Victo / Nov '94 / Harmonia Mundi / ReR Megacorp

ARC VOL.2 (The Seventies)
CD _______ ALP 92CD
Atavistic / Jun '97 / Cargo / SRD

BLACKBURST (Sharp, Elliot & Zeena Parkins)
CD _______ VICTOCD 044
Victo / Mar '97 / Harmonia Mundi / ReR Megacorp

DATACIDE
CD _______ EMY 1162
Enemy / Nov '92 / Grapevine/PolyGram

FIGURE GROUND
CD _______ TZA 7505
Tzadik / Feb '97 / Cargo

HAMMER, ANVIL, STIRRUP (Sharp, Elliott & The Soldier String Quartet)
CD _______ SST 232CD
SST / Dec '89 / Plastic Head

IN THE LAND OF THE YAHOOS
CD _______ SST 128CD
SST / Feb '88 / Plastic Head

INTERFERENCE (Sharp, Elliott & Carbon)
CD _______ ALP 50CD
Atavistic / Jun '97 / Cargo / SRD

ISM/ARC (Sharp, Elliott & Carbon)
CD _______ ALP 61CD
Atavistic / Jun '97 / Cargo / SRD

MONSTER CURVE
CD _______ SST 208CD
SST / May '93 / Plastic Head

PSYCHO-ACOUSTIC (Sharp, Elliot & Zeena Parkins)
CD _______ VICTOCD 026
Victo / Oct '94 / Harmonia Mundi / ReR Megacorp

TECTONICS VOL.1
CD _______ EFA 127622
Atonal / Jun '95 / SRD

TECTONICS VOL.2 (Field & Stream)
CD _______ EFA 129382
Atonal / Apr '97 / SRD

TOCSIN (Sharp, Elliott & Carbon)
CD _______ EMY 1342
Enemy / Nov '94 / Grapevine/PolyGram

Sharp, John

BETTER THAN DREAMS
CD _______ RR 54CD
Reference Recordings / May '96 / Jazz Music / May Audio

Sharpe, Jack

CATALYST (A Tribute To Tubby Hayes) (Sharpe, Jack Big Band)
Milestones / You know I care / Sharpe edge / Suddenly last Tuesday / Keith / Souriya / Allisamba
CD _______ CDFRG 716
Frog / Jun '89 / Cadillac / Jazz Music / Wellard

ROARIN' (Sharpe, Jack Big Band)
I'm beginning to see the light / Old folks / Mayfly / Wait and see / 100 degrees proof / Skylark / All the things you are / K and J / J and B
CD _______ JHCD 016
Ronnie Scott's Jazz House / Jan '94 / Cadillac / Jazz Music / New Note/Pinnacle / TKO Magnum

Sharpe, Ray

LINDA LU
Linda Lu / Monkey's uncle / Oh my baby's gone / That's the way I feel / Kewpie doll / Red sails in the sunset / Silly Dilly Millie / Bus song / TA blues / Long John / Gonna let it go this time / Bermuda / Give'n up / For you my love / Justine / On the street where you live / There'll come a day / Dallas / So sorry / Hey little girl / Thank you so much / New Linda Lu / TA blues / Long John / Kewpie doll / On the street where you live / Red sails in the sunset
CD _______ BCD 15888
Bear Family / Nov '95 / Direct / Rollercoaster / Swift

Sharpe, Rocky

FABULOUS ROCKY SHARPE & THE REPLAYS (Sharpe, Rocky & The Replays)
Rama lama ding dong / Imagination / Love will make you fail in school / Martian hop / Shout shout (knock yourself out) / Heart / Never / Come on let's go / Looking for an echo / Teenager in love / Never be anyone else but you / Get a job
CD ______ CDFAB 009
Ace / Oct '91 / Pinnacle

SO HARD TO LAUGH (Sharpe, Rocky & The Razors)
I wonder why / Drip drop / Daddy cool / Devil or angel / One summer night / So hard to laugh so easy to cry / What's your name / Mathilda / Poison ivy / That's my desire / Pretty little angel eyes / As long as I'm moving / Whole lotta shakin' goin' on / Splish splash
CD ______ CDWIKM 116
Chiswick / Mar '93 / Pinnacle

Sharpshooters

CHOKED UP
CD ______ SDW 0182
Shadow / Jan '97 / Cargo / Plastic Head

Sharriff, Imam Omar

RAVEN, THE
CD ______ ARHCD 365
Arhoolie / Apr '95 / ADA / Cadillac / Direct

Sharrock, Linda

LIKE A RIVER
CD ______ 5230152
Amadeo / Mar '95 / PolyGram

ON HOLIDAY
God bless the child / Ain't nobody's business if I do / Them there eyes / Lady blues / Lady sings the blues / Lover man / You go to my head / Good morning heartache
CD ______ 8433812
Polydor / Feb '94 / PolyGram

Sharrock, Sonny

GUITAR
CD ______ EMY 1022
Enemy / Nov '94 / Grapevine/PolyGram

SEIZE THE RAINBOW
CD ______ EMY 1042
Enemy / Nov '92 / Grapevine/PolyGram

SONNY SHARROCK: LIVE IN NEW YORK
CD ______ EMY 1082
Enemy / Nov '94 / Grapevine/PolyGram

Shaskeen

IRISH TRADITIONAL MUSIC AND SONG
CD ______ CDIRISH 010
Outlet / Oct '95 / ADA / CM / Direct / Duncans / Koch / Ross

SILVER JUBILEE COLLECTION
CD ______ FA 3509CD
GTD / Jul '95 / ADA / Else

TRADITIONAL MUSIC FROM BELFAST
CD ______ IRISHCD 10
Outlet / Jun '96 / ADA / CM / Direct / Duncans / Koch / Ross

Shatner, William

TRANSFORMED MAN, THE
King Henry The Fifth / Elegy For The Brave / Theme From Cyrana / Mr. Tambourine Man / Hamlet / It Was A Very Good Year / Romeo And Juliet / How Insensitive / Spleen / Lucy In The Sky With Diamonds / Transformed man
CD ______ CREV 004CD
Rev-Ola / Nov '92 / 3mv/Vital

Shava Shava

DIGGIN' THE ROOTS
CD ______ DMUT 1248
Multitone / Jan '94 / BMG

Shave The Monkey

DRAGONFLY
CD ______ APE 3002CD
Pecheron / Oct '94 / ADA

MAD ARTHUR
CD ______ APE 3003CD
Pecheron / Apr '96 / ADA

UNSEELIE COURT
CD ______ APE 3001CD
Pecheron / Oct '94 / ADA

Shaver

TRAMP ON YOUR STREET
Heart of Texas / Oklahoma wind / Georgia on a fast train / Live forever / If I give my soul / Tramp on your street / KAND Corsicana, Texas / Good ol' USA / Hottest thing in town / When the fallen angels fly / Take a chance on romance / Old chunk of coal / I want some more/Tenntex tear down
CD ______ DFGCD 8430
Dixie Frog / Jun '96 / Direct / TKO Magnum

Shaver, Billy Joe

OLD FIVE AND DIMERS LIKE ME
CD ______ 379382
Koch / Feb '97 / Koch

RESTLESS WIND
Texas uphear Tennessee / Good Lord knows / Ride me down easy / When I get my wings / Ain't no good in Mexico / Love you till the cows come home / Woman is the wonder of the world / When the word was thunderbird / America, you are my woman / Restless wind / Evergreen / Billy B Damned / We stayed too long at the fair / Honky tonk heroes / I'm going crazy in 3/4 time / Gypsy boy / Chicken on the ground / Everything, everywhere's / Slow rollin' low / Silver wings of time / Believer / You asked me to / Lately I've been leaning towards the blues / I couldn't be me without you / Music city USA
CD ______ BCD 15775
Bear Family / Jun '94 / Direct / Rollercoaster / Swift

Shaver, Eddy

BAPTISM OF FIRE
Pleasure and pain / Velvet chains / Lighting a torch / Call me a doctor / Drown in love / Hair of the dog / Prayer in paradise / King of fools / If it don't kill you / Good news blues / Baptism of fire
CD ______ DFGCD 8452
Dixie Frog / Oct '96 / Direct / TKO Magnum

Shavers, Charlie

BLUES SINGERS
Freight train blues / My Daddy rocks me / I am a woman / Low down dirty groundog / Jive is here / Downhearted blues
CD ______ CBC 1025
Timeless Jazz / Sep '95 / New Note/Pinnacle

CLASSICS 1944-1945
CD ______ CLASSICS 944
Classics / Jun '97 / Discovery / Jazz Music

MOST INTIMATE, THE (The Finest Of Charlie Shavers - The Bethlehem Years)
CD ______ BET 6019
Bethlehem / Jan '95 / ADA / ZYX

YOUNG SHAVERS
Havin' a ball / Margie / Undecided / It feels good / Sweet Georgia Brown / Front and centre / Royal Garden blues / Jumping in the pump room / Blues petite / Georgia cabin / Texas moaner blues / Tweed me / Comin' back / St. Louis blues / Step on it / Riding on 52nd Street / My man / El salon de gutbucket / Bottle's empty / For lovers only / Black market stuff / Laguna leap / I'll never be the same / Swingin' on Central / Kicks
CD ______ TPZ 1064
Topaz Jazz / Apr '97 / Cadillac / Pinnacle

Shaw, Adrian

TEA FOR THE HYDRA
CD ______ WO 27CD
Woronzow / Jun '96 / Pinnacle

Shaw, Artie

22 ORIGINAL BIG BAND RECORDINGS (Shaw, Artie Orchestra)
CD ______ HCD 401
Hindsight / Jun '95 / Jazz Music / Target/BMG

ARTIE SHAW
CD ______ 22705
Music / Nov '95 / Target/BMG

ARTIE SHAW
CD ______ 15713
Laserlight / Apr '94 / Target/BMG

ARTIE SHAW & HIS ORCHESTRA (Shaw, Artie Orchestra)
'S wonderful / Man and his dream / April in Paris / Summertime / I cover the waterfront / Blues / I could write a book / Don't take your love from me / Beyond the blue horizon / Maid with the flaccid air / Time on my hands / Deep purple / Prelude in C major
CD ______ 15757
Laserlight / Aug '92 / Target/BMG

ARTIE SHAW & HIS ORCHESTRA VOL.1 1938 (Shaw, Artie Orchestra)
April in my heart / Night over Shanghai / Small fry / Just a kid named Joe / When I go a-dreamin' / Leapin' at the Lincoln / What is this thing called love / Lambeth walk / They say / Shine on harvest moon / Out of nowhere / Simple and sweet / Blue interlude / Apple blossom time / Deep in a dream
CD ______ HCD 139
Hindsight / Sep '96 / Jazz Music / Target/BMG

ARTIE SHAW & HIS RHYTHM MAKERS 1938 (Shaw, Artie & Rhythm Makers)
Toy trumpet / Any old time / Powerhouse / Call of the freaks / Lost in the shuffle / If dreams come true / 'S wonderful / Meade Lux special / Sweet and low / Indian love call
CD ______ TAX 37092
Tax / Aug '94 / Cadillac / Jazz Music / Wellard

ARTIE SHAW 1940-1941
Frenesi / Alice blue gown / Temptation / Sweet Sue / King for a day / Out of nowhere / Jungle drums / Frenesi / Along the Santa Fe trail / Looking for yesterday / Everything's jumpin' / Concerto for clarinet / Frenesi / Whispers in the night / There I go / Prelude in C sharp / DR Livingstone I presume / Nobody knows the trouble I've seen / Blues in the night / There'll be some changes made / Little gates special
CD ______ HEPCD 19
Hep / Jun '97 / Cadillac / Jazz Music / New Note/Pinnacle / Wellard

ARTIE SHAW ORCHESTRA VOL.2 (Shaw, Artie Orchestra)
Stardust / They say / My heart stood still / Begin the beguine / Dancing in the dark / Serenade to a savage / Day in, day out / I don't want to walk without you / Rockin' chair / Temptation / Carioca / Out of nowhere / Softly as in a morning sunrise / Blues in the night / Back bay shuffle / Jungle drums / All the things you are / Someone's rocking my dreamboat / I poured my heart into a song / Rose room / Smoke gets in your eyes / My blue heaven
CD ______ PASTCD 7038
Flapper / Mar '94 / Pinnacle

ARTISTRY OF THE ARTIE SHAW ORCHESTRA 1949, THE (Shaw, Artie Orchestra)
CD ______ FSCD 2012
Fresh Sound / Sep '96 / Discovery / Jazz Music

ASTONISHING ARTIE SHAW, THE
Love and learn / Free wheeling / Rose room / Fee fi fo fum / Oh lady be good / I've a strange new rhythm in my heart / Just you, just me / I surrender Dear / Vilia / Let'er go / You can tell she comes from Dixie / It ain't right / Streamline / Cream puff / Non-stop flight / Sweet Adeline / Blues / I'll be with you in apple blossom time / Prosschai
CD ______ PAR 2027
Parade / Jul '94 / Disc

BEGIN THE BEGUINE
Nightmare / Indian love call / Back bay shuffle / Any old time / Traffic jam / Comes love / What is this thing called love / Begin the beguine / Oh lady be good / Frenesi / Serenade to a savage / Deep purple / Special delivery stomp / Summit Ridge Drive / Temptation / Stardust / Blues (parts 1 and 2) / Moonglow / Moon ray / Carioca
CD ______ ND 86274
Bluebird / Apr '88 / BMG

BEGIN THE BEGUINE
Any old time: *Shaw, Artie & Billie Holiday* / April in Paris / Back bay shuffle / Begin the beguine / Concerto for clarinet / Dancing in the dark / Deep purple / Donkey serenade / Frenesi / I surrender dear / Moonglow / Nightmare / Oh Lady be good / Rosalie / Special delivery stomp / St. James infirmary / Stardust / Summit Ridge Drive / Traffic jam / Yesterdays
CD ______ CDAJA 5113
Living Era / Aug '93 / Select

BIG BAND BASH (Shaw, Artie Orchestra)
CD ______ CD 53093
Giants Of Jazz / Mar '92 / Cadillac / Jazz Music / Target/BMG

CHANT
Streamline / Sweet Lorraine / Love is good for anything that ails you / No more tears moonlight and shadows / Was it rain / All alone / All God's chillun got rhythm / It goes to your feet / Because I love you / Night and day / I surrender dear / Blue skies / Someday sweetheart / Afraid to dream / If you should ever leave / Sweet Adeline / How dry I am / Am I in love / Fe, fi, fo, fum / Please pardon us, we're in love / Chant / Blues Pt.1
CD ______ HEPCD 1046
Hep / Jul '96 / Cadillac / Jazz Music / New Note/Pinnacle / Wellard

CLASSICS 1936
CD ______ CLASSICS 855
Classics / Feb '96 / Discovery / Jazz Music

CLASSICS 1936-1937
CD ______ CLASSICS 886
Classics / Jul '96 / Discovery / Jazz Music

CLASSICS 1937
CD ______ CLASSICS 929
Classics / Apr '97 / Discovery / Jazz Music

CONCERTO FOR CLARINET (Shaw, Artie Orchestra)
One night stand / Traffic jam / Summit ridge drive / Prosschai / I surrender Dear / Marinella / Oh lady be good / You can tell she comes from Dixie / Darling not without you / Moonlight and shadows / Concerto for clarinet / You're a sweet little headache / Sometimes I feel like a Motherless child / Monsoon / Non stop flight / I have eyes / You're giving me a song and a dance / Special delivery stomp / Why begin again / Serenade to a savage / Free for all
CD ______ RAJCD 830
Empress / Jul '94 / Koch

CREAM OF ARTIE SHAW & HIS ORCHESTRA, THE
Stardust / They say / My heart stood still / Begin the beguine / Dancing in the dark / Serenade to a savage / Day in, day out / I don't want to walk without you / Rockin' chair / Temptation / Carioca / Out of nowhere / Softly as in a morning sunrise / Blues in the night / Back bay shuffle / Jungle drums / All the things you are / Someone's rocking my dreamboat / I poured my heart into a song / Rose room / Smoke gets in your eyes / My blue heaven
CD ______ PASTCD 9779
Flapper / Nov '92 / Pinnacle

GLOOMY SUNDAY (Shaw, Artie Orchestra)
Begin the beguine / Moonglow / Oh lady be good / Gloomy Sunday / Man I love / Temptation / Night/Mare / Diga diga doo / Carioca / Donkey serenade / Frenesi / Serenade to a savage / Deep purple / I didn't know that time it was / Yesterdays / Rosalie / Indian love call / Jungle drums
CD ______ CD 56003
Jazz Roots / Aug '94 / Target/BMG

GREAT ARTIE SHAW & HIS ORCHESTRA, THE
CD ______ CWNCD 2001
Javelin / Jun '95 / Henry Hadaway / THE

IN THE BEGINNING - 1936
CD ______ HEPCD 1024
Hep / Dec '87 / Cadillac / Jazz Music / New Note/Pinnacle / Wellard

IN THE BLUE ROOM/IN THE CAFE ROUGE
Nightmare / Together / My reverie / Sobbin' blues / Jeepers creepers / In the mood / Non-stop flight / Begin the beguine / Old stamping ground / Chant / Stardust / Carioca / At sundown / I'm sorry for myself / Maria, my own / Diga diga doo / Moonray / Everything is jumpin' / St. Louis blues / I've got my eye on you / My blue heaven / El Rancho Grande / Sweet Sue, just you / Man from Mars
CD ______ 74321185272
RCA Victor / Oct '94 / BMG

INDIAN LOVE CALL (Shaw, Artie Orchestra)
CD ______ JHR 73535
Jazz Hour / May '93 / Cadillac / Jazz Music / Target/BMG

INTRODUCTION TO ARTIE SHAW 1937-1942, AN
CD ______ 4016
Best Of Jazz / Apr '95 / Discovery

JAZZ PORTRAITS (Shaw, Artie Orchestra)
Begin the beguine / Moonglow / Oh lady be good / Gloomy Sunday / Man I love / Temptation / Nightmare / Diga diga doo / Carioca / Donkey serenade / Frenesi / Serenade to a savage / Deep purple / I didn't know what time it was / Yesterdays / Rosalie / Indian love call / Jungle drums
CD ______ CD 14501
Jazz Portraits / May '93 / Jazz Music

LAST RECORDINGS, THE (Rare & Unreleased/2CD Set)
Pied piper theme / Love of my life / Rough ridin' / Yesterdays / Lyric / Bewitched, bothered and bewildered / Lugubrious / S'posin' / Tenderly / When the quail come back to San Quentin / Imagination / Besame mucho / My funny valentine / Too marvellous for words / I can't get started (with you) / Sad sack / Dancing on the ceiling / Someone to watch over me / Mysterioso / Chaser
CD Set ______ 8208472
Limelight / May '92 / PolyGram

LIVE IN 1938-1939 VOL.1
CD ______ PHONTCD 7609
Phontastic / Apr '94 / Cadillac / Jazz Music / Wellard

LIVE IN 1938-1939 VOL.2
CD ______ PHONTCD 7613
Phontastic / Apr '94 / Cadillac / Jazz Music / Wellard

LIVE IN 1938-1939 VOL.3
CD ______ PHONTCD 7628
Phontastic / Apr '94 / Cadillac / Jazz Music / Wellard

LIVE IN HI-FI
CD ______ JH 1031
Jazz Hour / Jul '93 / Cadillac / Jazz Music / Target/BMG

LIVE PERFORMANCES 1938-39 (Shaw, Artie Orchestra)
CD ______ HBCD 502
Hindsight / Nov '93 / Jazz Music / Target/BMG

MORE LAST RECORDINGS - THE FINAL SESSIONS
CD Set ______ MM 65101/2
Music Masters / Oct '94 / Nimbus

NON STOP FLIGHT
Blues (part 1) / Blues (part 2) / It's a long way to Tipperary / I've a strange new rhythm in my heart / If it's the last thing I do / Nightmare / Shoot the likker to me, John Boy / Free-wheeling / Let 'er go / Strange loneliness / Monsoon / I'm yours / Just you, just me / Free for all / Whistle while you work / One song / Goodnight, Angel / There's a new moon over the old mill / Non-stop flight / I'll be with you in apple blossom time
CD HEPCD 1048
Hep / Sep '96 / Cadillac / Jazz Music / New Note/Pinnacle / Wellard

OLD GOLD MELODY & MADNESS SHOWS
CD JH 1050
Jazz Hour / Jul '96 / Cadillac / Jazz Music / Target/BMG

OLD GOLD SHOWS - 1938-39 (Shaw, Artie Orchestra)
CD JH 1009
Jazz Hour / '91 / Cadillac / Jazz Music / Target/BMG

RADIO YEARS, THE (Vol.1 1938) (Shaw, Artie Orchestra)
Nightmare (theme) / Sobbin' blues / I can't believe that you're in love with me / They say / It had to be you / My revenue / Sweet Adeline / Who blew out the flame / Copenhagen / Nightmare (closing theme) / Nightmare (theme) / Begin the beguine / You're a sweet little headache / Old stamping ground / What is this thing called love / Jungle drums / It had to be you / Thanks for everything / Copenhagen / Nightmare (closing theme)
CD JUCD 2018
Jazz Unlimited / Nov '94 / Cadillac / Jazz Music / Wellard

STARDUST (20 Swing Band Classics)
Stardust / Jungle drums / Day in day out / April in Paris / St. James Infirmary / Yesterday / Gloomy Sunday / Smoke gets in your eyes / Keepin' myself for you / Deep in a dream / Deep purple / It had to be you / My blue Heaven / Concerto for clarinet / Any old time / All the things you are / Donkey serenade / Dancing in the dark / I don't want to walk without you / Don't take your love from me
CD 306672
Hallmark / Jul '97 / Carlton

TRAFFIC JAM
Man I love / Muchodenada / Love is the sweetest thing / Love walked in / You're mine / Oh you crazy moon / Serenade to a savage / Sweet little headache / What is this thing called love / Thanks for everything / Mood in question / Orinoco / Traffic jam / I'm coming Virginia / Last two weeks in July / Lilacs in the rain
CD NI 4013
Natasha / May '93 / ADA / Cadillac / CM / Direct / Jazz Music

TRAFFIC JAM (Live Broadcasts 1938-1939)
Nightmare (theme) / Begin the beguine / Deep in a dream / Back bay shuffle / Non-stop flight / I have eyes / Carioca / Better-than-average-girl / Jungle dreams / I cried for you / Back bay shuffle / My heart belongs to daddy / I want my share of love / Diga diga doo / Diga diga doo / It's all yours / Rosalie / Zigeuner / Copenhagen / Pastel blue / Traffic jam / I'm in love with the honorable Mr. So-And-So / Chant / Prosschai / Nightmare (theme)
CD VN 1008
Viper's Nest / Nov '96 / ADA / Cadillac / Direct / Jazz Music

WHAT IS THIS THING CALLED LOVE
Let's walk / Love of my life / How deep is the ocean / Glider / Hornet / They can't convince me / I got the sun in the morning / Along with me / You do something to me / In the still of the night / Begin the beguine / My heart belongs to Daddy / Night and day / What is this thing called love / I've got you under my skin / Get out of town / For you, for me, for evermore / Changing my tune / Love for sale / Guilty / And so to bed / Don't you believe it dear / It's the same old dream / I believe
CD PLCD 557
President / Feb '97 / Grapevine/PolyGram / President / Target/BMG

Shaw Brothers

COLLECTION, THE
CD FE 2041
Folk Era / Dec '94 / ADA / CM

Shaw, Eddie

CAN'T STOP NOW (Shaw, Eddie & The Wolf Gang)
Greedy man / Can't stop now / Casino blues / Howlin' for my darling / Stole my daughter / We're gonna make it / Rockin' with Eddie / Love me or leave me / Chicago man / Playing with the blues / Don't use me baby / Country boy / I gotta tell somebody
CD DE 698
Delmark / Jun '97 / ADA / Cadillac / CM / Direct / Hot Shot

IN THE LAND OF THE CROSSROADS
Delta bound / Tears are falling / Fannie Mae Jones / I got to go / She didn't tell me everything / My friend Rosco / Dunkin' donut woman / Take home pay / Wine head mole / Chicago man / Operator / Blues at the crossroads
CD R 2624
Rooster / Feb '97 / Direct

MOVIN' & GROOVIN' MAN
Highway bound / Blues dues / Blues for tomako / Dunkin' donut woman / Louisiana blues / Movin' and groovin' man / Sad and lonesome / Big leg woman / I've got to tell somebody / My baby and me
CD ECD 260282
Evidence / Feb '93 / ADA / Cadillac / Harmonia Mundi

Shaw, Ian

ECHO OF A SONG, THE
CD JHCD 048
Ronnie Scott's Jazz House / Oct '96 / Cadillac / Jazz Music / New Note/Pinnacle / TKO Magnum

FAMOUS RAINY DAY
CD EFZ 1017
EFZ / Feb '96 / Vital/SAM

GHOSTSONGS
Danny boy / Spinning wheel / When Sassy sings / Broken blue heart / Me, myself and I / Some other time/People will say we're in love / Lover man / Calling you / Sophisticated lady/I've got it bad and that ain't good / Somewhere / Goodbye Pork Pie Hat / Blame it on my youth
CD JHCD 025
Ronnie Scott's Jazz House / Jan '94 / Cadillac / Jazz Music / New Note/Pinnacle / TKO Magnum

TAKING IT TO HART
CD JHCD 036
Ronnie Scott's Jazz House / Mar '95 / Cadillac / Jazz Music / New Note/Pinnacle / TKO Magnum

Shaw, Marlena

DANGEROUS
Out of this world / Whisper not / Ooo-wee-baby you're the one for me / Blackberry winter / Close enough for love / Dangerous / Nearness of you / Dim the lights / You make me feel brand new / You're my everything / Beautiful friendship / Give me one more chance / Keep on trustin'
CD CCD 4707
Concord Crossover / Jul '96 / New Note/ Pinnacle

ELEMENTAL SOUL
Your mind is on vacation / Paint your pretty picture / How deep is the ocean / Where do you start / Once again we've begun to love / Handy man / Why oh why / Brothers / 'Round midnight / I'm alone again / My old flame / Our love is here to stay
CD CCD 47742
Concord Jazz / Aug '97 / New Note/ Pinnacle

FEEL THE SPIRIT (Shaw, Marlena & Joe Williams)
In the beginning / My Lord / Feel the spirit / Go down Moses / Wade in the water / Great camp meeting / Were you there / Walk with me / I couldn't hear nobody pray / In my heart / Little David / His eye is on the sparrow / Pass it on / Lord's prayer / Doxology
CD CD 83362
Telarc / Jun '95 / Conifer/BMG

Shaw, Pat

LIES & ALIBIS (Shaw, Pat & Julie Matthews)
CD FATCAT 001CD
Fat Cat / Jun '93 / ADA / CM / Direct

Shaw, Robert

MA GRINDER, THE
CD ARHCD 377
Arhoolie / Apr '95 / ADA / Cadillac / Direct

Shaw, Sandie

ALWAYS SOMETHING THERE TO REMIND ME
Always something there to remind me / Monsieur Dupont / You've not changed / Heaven knows I'm missing him now / Stop / Today / Think it all over / Words / You've been seeing her again / Those were the days / Tonight in Tokyo / Maple village / What now my love / Right to cry
CD QED 133
Tring / Nov '96 / Tring

ALWAYS SOMETHING THERE TO REMIND ME
Always something there to remind me / Maple Village / Voice in the crowd / Show me / Maybe I'm amazed / Scarborough fair / You've been seeing her again / Turn on the sunshine / That's why / Today / Ne me quitte pas / Time after time / What now my love / Words

CD WB 878602
Disky / Mar '97 / Disky / THE

CHOOSE LIFE
Dragon king's daughter / Mermaid / Let down your hair / East meets west / Bark back at dogs / Life is like a star / Moontalk / Sister sister / Wish I was
CD RETRO 801
RPM / Jun '95 / Pinnacle

CLASSIC ARTISTS
CD JHD 048
Tring / Jun '92 / Tring

COLLECTION, THE
CD COL 067
Collection / Jan '95 / Target/BMG

COMPLETE SANDIE SHAW, THE
As long as you're happy / Ya-Ya-Da-Da / Always something there to remind me / Don't you know / Girl don't you know / I'd be far better off without you / Everybody loves a lover / Gotta see my baby every day / Love letters / Stop feeling sorry for yourself / Always / Don't be that way / It's in his kiss (The shoop shoop song) / Downtown / You won't forget me / Lemon tree / Talk about love / I'll stop at nothing / You can't blame him / Long live love / I've heard about him / Message understood / Don't you count on it / You don't love me no more / I don't need that kind of lovin' / Down dismal ways / Oh no he don't / When he was a child / Do you mind / How glad am I / I know / Till the night begins to die / Too bad you don't want me / One day / When I fall in love / How can you tell / If ever you need me / Tomorrow / Hurting you / Nothing ever comes easy / Stop before start / Run / Long walk home / Think sometimes about me / Hide all emotion / I don't need anything / Keep in touch / Puppet on a string / Had a dream last night / Ask any woman / I don't think you want me anymore / No moon
CD Set NEDCD 230
Sequel / May '93 / BMG

COVER TO COVER
Scarborough fair / Lay lady lay / Satisfaction / Rose garden / Jeane / I get a kick out of you / Reviewing the situation / Walking the dog / Maybe I'm amazed / What now my love / Ne me quitte pas / Love me do / Homeward bound / Sympathy for the devil / (Get your rocks on) Route 66 / Those were the days
CD EMPRCD 625
Emporio / Jun '96 / Disc

EP COLLECTION, THE
CD SEECD 305
See For Miles/C5 / '90 / Pinnacle

GREATEST HITS
Puppet on a string / Message understood / Nothing comes easy / Had a dream last night / Long live love / Stop feeling sorry for yourself / Hide all emotion / Tomorrow / You won't forget me / (There's) Always something there to remind me / Tell the boys / I'd be better off without you / No moon / Girl don't come / Think sometimes about me / Love walk home / Don't you count on it / Don't you want me anymore
CD RM 1545
BR Music / Apr '97 / Target/BMG

GREATEST HITS OF SANDIE SHAW
CD MACCD 171
Autograph / Aug '96 / BMG

LONG LIVE LOVE
CD WMCD 5611
Disky / May '94 / Disky / THE

LONG LIVE LOVE (All Her Hits)
CD DC 869812
Disky / Aug '96 / Disky / THE

LOVE ME PLEASE LOVE ME
Love me please love me / One note samba / Smile / Yes my darling daughter / Ne me quitte pas / Every time we say goodbye / Way that I remember him / Hold 'im down / I get a kick out of you / Time after time / That's why / By myself / Tonight in Tokyo / You've been seeing her again / You've not changed / Don't make me cry / Today / London / Don't run away / Stop
CD RPM 124
RPM / Mar '94 / Pinnacle

NOTHING LESS THAN BRILLIANT (The Best Of Sandie Shaw)
Always something there to remind me / Long live love / Girl don't come / Message understood / Nothing less than brilliant / Hand in glove / Are you ready to be heart-broken / Girl called Johnny / I'll stop at nothing / Heaven knows I'm missing him now / You've not changed / Monsieur Dupont / I don't owe you anything / Anyone who had a heart: *Shaw, Sandie & BEF* / Comrade in arms / Hello angel / Strange bedfellows / Words / Every time we say goodbye / Your time is gonna come / Frederick / Please help the cause against loneliness / Tomorrow / Nothing comes easy / Puppet on a string
CD CDVIP 183
Virgin VIP / Apr '97 / EMI

PUPPET ON A STRING
Always something there to remind me / It's in his kiss (The shoop shoop song) / Always / Long live love / I've heard about him / When I fall in love / Do you mind / Baby I need your loving / Nothing comes easy / Love letters / Puppet on a string / Had a dream last night / Downtown / Run / You won't forget me / I don't need anything / Tell the boys / I'll cry myself to sleep / Tomorrow
CD 5507552
Spectrum / Sep '94 / PolyGram

REVIEWING THE SITUATION
CD RPM 101
RPM / Jul '93 / Pinnacle

SANDIE SHAW SUPPLEMENT, THE
Route 66 / Homeward bound / Scarborough Fair / Right to cry / Same things / Our song of love / Satisfaction / Words / Remember me / Change of heart / Aranjuez mon amour / What now my love / Show me / One more lie / Together / Turn on the sunshine / Those were the days / Make it go / Monsieur Dupont / Voice in the crowd
CD RPM 112
RPM / Oct '93 / Pinnacle

SANDIE/ME
Everybody loves a lover / Gotta see my baby everyday / Love letters / Stop feeling sorry for yourself / Always / Don't be that way / It's in his kiss (The shoop shoop song) / Downtown / You won't forget me / Lemon tree / Baby, I need your loving / Talk about love / You don't love me no more / I don't need that kind of lovin' / Down dismal ways / Oh no he don't / When I was a child / Do you mind / How glad I am / I know / Till the night begins to die / Too bad you don't want me / One day / When I fall in love
CD SEECD 436
See For Miles/C5 / Oct '95 / Pinnacle

Shaw, Thomas

BORN IN TEXAS
CD TCD 5027
Testament / Oct '95 / ADA / Koch

Shaw, Victoria

IN FULL VIEW
CD 9362455922
Warner Bros. / Mar '96 / Warner Music

VICTORIA SHAW
Just to say we did / Different drum / In spite of it all / Let's talk about me / For all the sake of love / Stuck on you / Wild rose / Don't move / One of those days / I say the grace
CD 9362466142
Reprise / May '97 / Warner Music

Shaw, Woody

IN MY OWN SWEET WAY
CD IOR 70032
In & Out / Sep '95 / Vital/SAM

LIVE/BEMSHA SWING (2CD Set)
Bemsha swing / Ginseng people / Well you needn't / Eric / United / Nutty / In a Capricornian way / Star eyes / Theloniously speaking
CD Set CDP 8290292
Blue Note / Aug '97 / EMI

TIME IS RIGHT, THE
CD 1231682
Red / Apr '93 / ADA / Cadillac / Harmonia Mundi

Shazar, Pal

THERE'S A WILD THING IN THE HOUSE
Falling is a form of flying / Penny for your thoughts / San Francisco Bay / Three sheets to the wind / Small talk with the ticket man / If it's you that I got here / Ain't nobody's mistress but my own / Then I met Anna / Scared / Wade went wild / Sentimental breakdown
CD TRACD 113
Transatlantic / Apr '96 / Pinnacle

She

PENANCE
Hallelujah / She / Marlene miles away / Stand by your bed / Blossom tear coloured blown / Kiss my arse / Betty Bucksuttle / Red, greens and blues / Pour no more / I'm going down / Baby blues / Panic attack
CD PROBE 042CD
Probe Plus / Mar '96 / SRD

Shea, David

DOWN RIVER, UP STREAM (Shea, David & DJ Grazhoppa)
CD DSL 003D
Downsall Plastics / Nov '96 / Cargo / SRD

LIVE SESSIONS (Shea, David & Scanner/Robert Jampson)
CD QUANTUM 051
Sub Rosa / Sep '96 / Direct / RTM/Disc / SRD / Vital

SATYRICON
CD SR 111
Sub Rosa / Apr '97 / Direct / RTM/Disc / SRD / Vital

SHOCK CORRIDOR
CD ____ AVAN 013
Avant / Nov '92 / Cadillac / Harmonia Mundi

TOWER OF MIRRORS, THE
CD ____ SR 94
Sub Rosa / Mar '96 / Direct / RTM/Disc / SRD / Vital

Shearing, George

ALONE TOGETHER (Shearing, George & Marian McPartland)
O grande amor / To Bill Evans / All through the night / Born to be blue / They say it's Spring / Alone together / There'll be other times / Nobody else but me / Chasing shadows / Improvisation on a theme
CD ____ CCD 4171
Concord Jazz / Feb '91 / New Note/ Pinnacle

BEST OF GEORGE SHEARING, THE
Midnight in the air / Have you met Miss Jones / Dancing on the ceiling / Cuban love song / Folks who live on the hill / Nothing ever changes my love for you / Friendly persuasion (thee I love) / Later / Cheek to cheek / Sand in my shoes / Kinda cute / September in the rain / East of the sun and West of the moon / Estampa Cubano / Ship without a sail / Laura / Bernie's tune / Canadian sunset
CD ____ CDP 8335702
Capitol Jazz / Nov '95 / EMI

BLUES ALLEY JAZZ
One for the woofer / Autumn in New York / (I'm afraid) the masquerade is over / Soon it's gonna rain / High and inside / For every man there's a woman / This couldn't be the real thing / Up a lazy river
CD ____ CCD 4110
Concord Jazz / Nov '89 / New Note/ Pinnacle

BREAKIN' OUT (Shearing, George Trio)
CD ____ CCD 4335
Concord Jazz / Dec '87 / New Note/ Pinnacle

BURNISHED BRASS/SATIN BRASS
Memories of you / Lulu's back in town / If you were mine / Burnished brass / These things you left me / Mine / Beautiful love / Cuckoo in the clock / Sometimes I feel like a motherless child / Cheek to cheek / Blame it on my youth / Basie's movement / Deep night / In the blue of evening / I could write a book / Sleepy Manhattan / If I had you / Just plain Bill / First floor please / Chelsea bridge / Ship without a sail / Stairway to the stars / You look like someone / Night flight
CD ____ CTMCD 120
EMI / Jun '97 / EMI

COCKTAILS FOR TWO (Shearing, George Quintet)
CD ____ JW 77016
JWD / May '93 / Target/BMG

COLLECTION, THE
Missouri scrambler / Overnight bop / How come you love me like you do / Stomp in F / Riff up them stairs / Boogie ride / Spookie woogie / Oh lady be good / You stepped out of a dream / Softly as a morning sunrise / Five flat flurry / Southern fried / Wednesday night hop / Pretty girl is like a melody / More than you know / Cymbal Simon / How could you / These foolish things / Blue boogie / Trunk call / Squeezin' the blues / Delayed action
CD ____ RAJCD 881
Empress / Nov '96 / Koch

DEXTERITY
Dexterity / You must believe in Spring / Sakura / Long ago and far away / Can't we be friends / As long as I live / Please send me someone to love / Duke Ellington medley
CD ____ CCD 4346
Concord Jazz / Jul '88 / New Note/Pinnacle

ELEGANT EVENING, AN (Shearing, George & Mel Torme)
I'll be seeing you / Love and the moon / Oh you crazy moon / No moon at all / After the waltz is over / This time the dream is on me / Last night when we were young / You changed my life / I had the craziest dream / Darn that dream / Brigg fair / My foolish heart / You're driving me crazy
CD ____ CCD 4294
Concord Jazz / Jul '87 / New Note/Pinnacle

EVENING AT CHARLIE'S, AN (Shearing, George & Mel Torme)
Just one of those things / On Green Dolphin Street / Dream dancing / I'm hip / Then I'll be tired of you / Caught in the middle of my years / Welcome to the club / Nica's dream / Chase me Charlie / Love is just around the corner
CD ____ CCD 4248
Concord Jazz / Sep '84 / New Note/ Pinnacle

EVENING WITH GEORGE SHEARING, AN (Shearing, George & Mel Torme)
All God's chillun got rhythm / Born to be blue / Give me the simple life / Good morning heartache / Manhattan hoedown / You'd be so nice to come home to / Nightingale sang in Berkeley Square / Love / It might as well be Spring / Lullaby of Birdland
CD ____ CCD 4190
Concord Jazz / Mar '87 / New Note/ Pinnacle

FAVOURITE THINGS
My favourite things / Angel eyes / Ina calm / Not you again / Taking a chance on love / Let me / Summer song / Anna's song / Anyone can whistle / Moonray / I'm getting off here / PS I love you / It amazes me
CD ____ CD 83398
Telarc Jazz / Mar '97 / Conifer/BMG

GEORGE SHEARING IN DIXIELAND (Shearing, George & Dixie Six)
Clap your hands / Truckin' / New Orleans / Take five / Blue monk / Alice in Dixieland / Mighty like the blues / Destination moon / Soon / Lullaby of Birdland / Desafinado
CD ____ CCD 4388
Concord Jazz / Sep '89 / New Note/ Pinnacle

GRAND PIANO
When a woman loves a man / It never entered my mind / Mack the knife / Nobody else but me / Imitations / Taking a chance on love / If I had you / How insensitive / Easy to love / While we're young
CD ____ CCD 4281
Concord Jazz / Sep '86 / New Note/ Pinnacle

HOW BEAUTIFUL IS THE NIGHT (Shearing, George & The Robert Farnon Orchestra)
CD ____ CD 83325
Telarc / May '93 / Conifer/BMG

I HEAR A RHAPSODY (Live At The Blue Note)
Bird feathers / Dreamsville / End Of A Love Affair / Zingaro / Duke / I hear a rhapsody / (I'm afraid) the masquerade is over / Horizon / Just a mood / Wail / Too Late Now
CD ____ CD 83310
Telarc / Sep '92 / Conifer/BMG

JAZZ MASTERS
CD ____ 5299002
Verve / Jun '96 / PolyGram

JAZZ MOMENTS
Makin' whoopee / What is this thing called love / What's new / Like someone in love / Heart of winter / Blues in 94 / Symphony / When Sunny gets blue / Wonder why / Mood is mellow / Gone with the wind / It could happen to you
CD ____ CDP 8320852
Capitol Jazz / Aug '95 / EMI

LIVE AT THE CAFE CARLYLE (Shearing, George & Don Thompson)
Pent-up house / Shadow of your smile / Teach me tonight / Cheryl / Blues for breakfast / PS I love you / I cover the waterfront / Tell me a bedtime story / Stratford stomp / Inside
CD ____ CCD 4246
Concord Jazz / '88 / New Note/Pinnacle

LONDON YEARS 1939-1943
How come you like me like you do / Stomp in F / Squeezing the blues / Southern fried / Missouri scrambler / Overnight hop / Delayed action / Beat me Daddy, eight to the bar / How could you / Pretty girl is like a melody / These foolish things / More than you know / Softly as in a morning sunrise / You stepped out of a dream / Spoodie woogie / Moon ray / Rosetta / I'll never let a day pass me by / Coquette / Out of nowhere / Can't we be friends / I don't stand a ghost of a chance with you / Guilty / I found a new boogie / Sweet Lorraine
CD ____ HEPCD 1042
Hep / Feb '95 / Cadillac / Jazz Music / New Note/Pinnacle / Wellard

MORE GRAND PIANO (Solo Piano)
My silent love / Change partners / My favourite things / You don't know what love is / Ramona / People / East of the sun and west of the moon / I can't get started (with you) / Dream / Wind in the willows
CD ____ CCD 4318
Concord Jazz / Jul '87 / New Note/Pinnacle

ON A CLEAR DAY (Shearing, George & Brian Torff)
Love for sale / On a clear day (You can see forever) / Brasil '79 / Don't explain / Happy days are here again / Have you met Miss Jones / Lullaby of Birdland
CD ____ CCD 4132
Concord Jazz / Dec '93 / New Note/ Pinnacle

ONCE AGAIN THAT SHEARING SOUND
East of the sun and west of the moon / I like to recognise the tune / I'll never smile again / I hear music / Girl talk / Autumn serenade / Consternation / Stars in my eyes / Strollin / Very early / Conception / Peace / Lullaby of birdland
CD ____ CD 83347
Telarc / Sep '94 / Conifer/BMG

PAPER MOON (The Songs Of Nat 'King' Cole) (Shearing, George Trio)
Straighten up and fly right / I'm lost / Sweet Lorraine / Nature boy / Homeward bound / I'm thru with love / It's only a paper moon / Gee baby ain't I good to you / Lost April / Peaches / You've changed / I'd love to make love to you / Could ja / I can't see for lookin'
CD ____ CD 83375
Telarc / May '96 / Conifer/BMG

PERFECT MATCH, A (Shearing, George & Ernestine Anderson)
CD ____ CCD 4357
Concord Jazz / Oct '88 / New Note/ Pinnacle

PIANO
It had to be you / Daisy / Thinking of you / Sweet and lovely / It's you or no one / Wendy / Am I blue / Miss Invisible / You're my everything / John O'Groats / Waltz for Claudia / For you / Children's waltz / Happiness is a thing called Joe
CD ____ CCD 4400
Concord Jazz / Jan '90 / New Note/ Pinnacle

SATIN AFFAIR/CONCERTO FOR MY LOVE
Early autumn / You were never lovelier / Stardust / Baubles, bangles and beads / It's not you / Party's over / Midnight sun / Here's what I'm here for / I like to recognise the tune / My own / My romance / Bolero no.3 / Portrait of Jennie / I'm in the mood for love / Answer me my love / I wish you love / Love letters / I fall in love too easily / Love is the sweetest thing / Portrait of my love / PS I love you / Lady love be mine / In love in vain / Love child
CD ____ BGOCD 269
Beat Goes On / Apr '95 / Pinnacle

SHEARING ON STAGE
September in the rain / On the street where you live / Roses of Picardy / Little Niles / Caravan / I'll remember April / Little white lies / East of the sun and west of the moon / Nothing be de best / Love is just around the corner / Walkin' / I cover the waterfront / Love walked in / Bel-Air
CD ____ CDREN 004
Renaissance / '89 / Jazz Music / Wellard

SWINGIN'S MUTUAL, THE (Shearing, George & Nancy Wilson)
Things we did last Summer / All night long / My gentleman friend / Born to be blue / I remember Clifford / On Green Dolphin Street / Let's live again / Whisper not / Nearness of you / Evansville / Don't call me / Inspiration / You are there / Wait till you see her / Blue Lou / Oh, look at me now / Lullaby of Birdland
CD ____ CDP 7991902
Blue Note / Mar '95 / EMI

TWO FOR THE ROAD (Shearing, George & Carmen McRae)
I don't stand a ghost of a chance with you / Gentleman friend / Cloudy morning / If I should lose you / What is there to say / You're all I need / More than you know / Too late now / Ghost of yesterday / Two for the road
CD ____ CCD 4128
Concord Jazz / '89 / New Note/Pinnacle

WALKIN'
That's earl, brother / My one and only love / Pensativa / Walkin' / When she makes music / Celia / Subconscious Lee / Suddenly / Bag's groove / Every time we say goodbye / Loot to boot
CD ____ CD 83333
Telarc / Apr '95 / Conifer/BMG

Shearing, Peter G.

VIKING DREAM
CD ____ CDSGP 9006
Prestige / Apr '95 / Else / Total/BMG

Shed Seven

CHANGE GIVER
Dirty soul / Speakeasy / Long time dead / Head and hands / Casino girl / Missing out / Dolphin / Stars in your eyes / Mark / Ocean pie / On an island with you
CD ____ 5236152
Polydor / Sep '96 / PolyGram

MAXIMUM HIGH, A
Getting better / Magic streets / Where have you been tonight / Going for gold / On standby / Out by my side / Lies / This day was ours / Ladyman / Falling from the sky / Bully boy / Parallel lines
CD ____ 5310392
Polydor / Apr '96 / PolyGram
CD ____ 5333772
Polydor / Sep '96 / PolyGram

MAXIMUM HIGH, A/THE B-SIDES (2CD Set)
Getting better / Magic streets / Where have you been tonight / Going for gold / On standby / Out by my side / Lies / This day was ours / Ladyman / Falling from the sky / Bully boy / Parallel lines / Long time dead / Around your house / Swing my wave / Out by my side / Immobilise / Killing time / This is my house / Barracuda / Mobile 10 / Stepping on hearts / Never again / Song seven / Making waves / Sleep easy / Only dreaming
CD Set ____ 5334162
Polydor / Sep '96 / PolyGram

Sheehan, Stephen

EYES OF THE WILDERNESS
CD ____ ROSE 199 CD
New Rose / Jun '90 / ADA / Direct / Discovery

Sheep On Drugs

DOUBLE TROUBLE
CD ____ INV 057CD
Invisible / Jun '96 / Plastic Head

GREATEST HITS
Uberman / Acid test / Fifteen minutes of fame / Track X / Suzie Q / Catch 22 / Mary Jane / Motorbike / TV USA / Chard / Cheep
CD ____ CID 8006
Island / Mar '93 / PolyGram

ON DRUGS
Intro / Chasing dreams / English rose / Let the good times roll / Beefcake / Segway / A2H / Clucking / Slap happy / Slim Jim / Lolita / Slow suicide / Hi-fi low-life / Dirtbox blues
CD ____ CID 8020
Island / Apr '94 / PolyGram

ONE FOR THE MONEY
CD ____ INV 061CD
Invisible / Feb '97 / Plastic Head

Sheer Taft

ABSOLUTELY SHEER
CD ____ CRELPCD 121
Creation / Jun '92 / 3mv/Vital

Sheer Terror

LOVE SONGS FOR THE UNLOVED
Love song for the unloved / Tale of moran / Jimmy's high life / Not waving, drowning / Rock bottom on the kitchen floor / Skinhead girl / Drunk, divorced and downhill fast / Broken / Outro / College boy / For Rudy the Kraut / Walnut St / Be still my heart / Walls / Everything's life / Goodbye farewell
CD ____ BLK 023ECD
Blackout / Jan '97 / Plastic Head / Vital

NO GROUNDS FOR PITY
Obsoletion / Smile For A Price / Howard Unruh / Not Giving Up / Burning Time / Owe You Nothing / Into My Life / Fashion Fighter / Ready To Halt / Owe You Nothing / Burning Time / Into My Life / Not Giving Up / Only 13 / Obsoletion / Howard Unruh / Rome Song / Ashes, Ashes / Walls / Ready To Halt / Only 13 / Into My Life / Burning Time / Smile For A Price / Everything & Nothing / Twisting & Turning / Burning Time
CD ____ BLK 033ECD
Blackout / Nov '96 / Plastic Head / Vital

Sheffield Harmony

BEST OF THE BARBERSHOP, THE
Wonderful day like today / Give me a barbershop song / Sing me that song again / Oh you beautiful doll / Tie me to your apron strings again / South Rampart street parade / Don't leave me mammy / Rock-a-bye your baby with a dixie melody / Hush / Nightingale sang in Berkeley Square / That great come and get it day / Crossing Jordan river / Fare thee well / Waiting for the Robert E Lee / April showers / Operator / Play a vaudeville song tonight / Little pal / There is nothin' like a dame / Love at home / Carolina in the morning / Only you / I'm sitting on top of the world / Wonderful day like today (reprise)
CD ____ CDMFP 5944
Music For Pleasure / Aug '92 / EMI

Sheik Chinna Moulana

NADHASWARAM
CD ____ SM 15072
Wergo / Nov '92 / ADA / Cadillac / Harmonia Mundi

Sheik, Duncan

DUNCAN SHEIK
CD ____ 7567828792
Atlantic / Sep '96 / Warner Music

Shelby, K. Alexi

FLAWLESS VICTORY
CD ____ ACVCD 015
ACV / Mar '96 / Plastic Head / SRD

Sheldon, Jack

HOLLYWOOD HEROES (Sheldon, Jack Quintet)
Joint is jumpin' / Pardon my southern accent / Poor butterfly / Lover / Rosetta / I thought about you / I want to be happy
CD ____ CCD 4339
Concord Jazz / May '88 / New Note/ Pinnacle

ON MY OWN (Sheldon, Jack & Ross Tomkins)
Accentuate the positive / Love of mine / Blues in the night / How about you / Day drama / Opus one / Losing my mind / I can't get started (with you) / New York medley / Laughing on the outside / Avalon / Over the rainbow

CD ______ CCD 4529
Concord Jazz / Oct '92 / New Note/ Pinnacle

Shellac

AT ACTION PARK
CD ______ TG 141CD
Touch & Go / Nov '94 / SRD

Shelley, Pete

HOMOSAPIEN
CD ______ RE 2126
Razor & Tie / Feb '97 / Koch

XL-1
CD ______ GRACD 202
Grapevine / Aug '94 / Grapevine/PolyGram

Shelleyan Orphan

BUMROOT
CD ______ R 2792
Rough Trade / Mar '92 / Pinnacle

Shelor, Sammy

LEADING ROLL
CD ______ SHCD 3865
Sugar Hill / Jul '97 / ADA / CM / Direct / Koch / Roots

Shelter

ATTAINING THE SUPREME
CD ______ EVR 007CD
Equal Vision / Apr '97 / Plastic Head

MANTRA
CD ______ RR 89382
Roadrunner / Oct '95 / PolyGram

PERFECTION
CD ______ REVEL 016CD
Revelation / Jan '96 / Plastic Head

Shelton, Anne

EARLY YEARS OF ANNE SHELTON, THE
CD ______ SWNCD 003
Sound Waves / Oct '95 / Target/BMG

HERE'S ANNE SHELTON
There goes that song again / Nightingale sang in Berkeley Square / We mustn't say goodbye / Where or when / Last time I saw Paris / Fools rush in / Lili marlene / At last / Blues in the night / I'll never smile again / You'll never know / Coming in on a wing and a prayer / Only forever / Begin the beguine / Taking a chance on love / My yiddish momme / Kiss the boys goodbye / Swingin' on a star
CD ______ 306282
Hallmark / Jan '97 / Carlton

LET THERE BE LOVE
While the music plays on / Daddy / Better not roll those blue blue eyes / Minnie from Trinidad / Russian rose / St. Louis blues / Yes my darling daughter / Until you fall in love / Little steeple pointing to a star / Let there be love / Amapola / Tomorrow's sunrise / Fools rush in / Always in my heart / How about you / How green was my valley / I don't want to walk without you / My devotion / Taxi driver's serenade / South wind / Only you / My yiddishe Momme
CD ______ RAJCD 815
Empress / Jul '94 / Koch

NIGHTINGALE SANG, A
I'll be with you in apple blossom time / Last time I saw Paris, Daddy, blues in the night / Kiss the boys goodbye / Begin the beguine / You'd be so nice to come home to
CD ______ PASTCD 7048
Flapper / Aug '94 / Pinnacle

NOW HEAR THIS
Now hear this / Hurry home / Where can I go / Great pretender / Souvenir d'italie / Too young to go steady / Carnival is closed today / Volare / Sail along silv'ry moon / Where were you when I needed you / It's you / Harbour lights / Dancing with tears in my eyes / Nein nein fraulein / Daydreams / My one and only love / Forever / Tonights my night / Tread softly (you're treading on my heart) / How green was my valley / Village of St. Bernadette / I hear that song again / You're not living in vain / Lay down your arms
CD ______ C5MCD 624
See For Miles/C5 / Jul '95 / Pinnacle

SENTIMENTAL JOURNEY
Crazy / Tangerine / Sentimental journey / Nightingale sang in Berkeley Square / Don't fence me in / I'll walk alone / Run rabbit run / When the lights go on again / White cliffs of Dover / You'll never know / After all / Don't sit under the apple tree / I left my heart at the stage door canteen / Roll out the barrel / I'll get by / Boogie woogie bugle boy / I'll be seeing you / Chattanooga choo choo / Lili Marlene / Just look around
CD ______ PLCD 537
President / Nov '94 / Grapevine/PolyGram / President / Target/BMG

SOLDIER'S SWEETHEART MEMORIAL ALBUM, THE
I'll never smile again / I'll be seeing you / There goes that song again / Yes my darling daughter / Fools rush in / I don't want to walk without you / You'd be so nice to come home to / Coming in on a wing and a prayer / Last time I saw paris / I don't want to set the world on fire / Nightingale sang in Berkeley Square / Taking a chance on love / Only you / Daddy / My yiddishe momme / Until you fall in love / Ampola / St. Louis blues / Kiss the boys goodbye / Lili Marlene
CD ______ PAR 2061
Parade / Mar '95 / Disc

Shelton, Roscoe

ROSCOE SHELTON SINGS
Are you sure / Think it over / Pleadin' for love / I was wrong, played with love / I've been faithful / Say you really care / It's my fault / Something's wrong / Baby look what your doin' to me / Miss you so / Is it too late babe / Let me believe in you / Crazy over you / We've been wrong / Baby it's true love / Fool wrapped up in love / Blue and miserably unhappy / I'm so ashamed but I didn't know / I'm tellin' you baby, that's all / Lonely heartaches / Why didn't you tell me (for so long) / Why do you worry me / There is nothing I can do / Save me want your lovin' sometime
CD ______ EXCD 3007
Ace / Dec '96 / Pinnacle

SHE'S THE ONE
CD ______ APCD 114
Appaloosa / Oct '95 / ADA / Direct / TKO Magnum

Shenasa, Mas'oud

SANTOUR, THE
CD ______ AAA 140
Club Du Disque Arabe / Dec '96 / ADA / Harmonia Mundi

Shepard, Jean

MELODY RANCH GIRL, THE (5CD Set)
Twice the lovin' (in half the time) / Crying steel guitar waltz / Keep it a secret / Nobody else can love you like I do / I'd rather die young / Dear John letter: *Shepard, Jean & Ferlin Husky* / My wedding ring / With all these memories / Forgive me John: *Shepard, Jean & Ferlin Husky* / Why did you wait / You'll come crawlin' / Mysteries of life / Let's kiss and try again: *Shepard, Jean & Ferlin Husky* / Glass that stands beside you / Two whoops and a holler / Don't fall in love with a married man / What'll you have: *Shepard, Jean & Ferlin Husky* / It tickles: *Shepard, Jean & Simon Crum* / Please don't divorce me / Did you tell her about me / Don't rush me / You sent her an orchid (you sent me a rose) / Take possession / Satisfied mind / Beautiful lies / I thought of you / You're calling me sweetheart again / He loved me once and he'll love me again / Girls in disgrace / This has been your life / Just give me love / Thank you just the same / Over and over / Tell me what I want to hear / Shadows on the wall / I'll thank you all my life / I learned it all from you / Hello old broken heart / Sad singin' and slow ridin' / It's hard to tell the married from the free / Did I turn down a better deal / Passing love affair / I married you for love / I'm thinking tonight of my blue eyes / Be honest with me / Under suspicion / I want you to go where no one knows me / Tomorrow I'll be gone / If you can walk away / Go on, go on / I lost you after all / It scares me half to death / You're just the kind of guy / Too late with the roses / Other woman / Act like a married man / I used to love you / Weak and the strong / You'd better go / Thief in the night / Memory / I love you because / You win again / You can't break the chains of love / Secret of life / Jealous heart / Sweet temptation / I'll take the blame / I'll never be free / I'll hold you in my heart / I hate myself / You're telling me sweet lies again / He's my baby / Just another girl / Jeopardy / Are you certain / Better love next time / Have heart, will love / Heartaches, teardrops and sorrow / I didn't mean to make you cry / Sweetheart don't come back / How do you tell it to a child / One you slip around with / Mysteries of life / Did I turn down a better deal / Root of all evil (is a man) / Where people go / Lonely little world / I don't apologise for loving you / Mockin' bird hill / Another / Blues stay away from me / If you haven't, you can't feel the way I do / Under your spell again / Waltz of the angels / One white rose / Big midnight special / You're the only good thing / Colour song / Got you on my mind / For the children's sake / Nobody but myself / No one knows / Would you be satisfied / If you were losing him to me / Second best / Two voices, two shadows, two faces / Go on with your dancing / I can't seem to say goodbye / So wrong, so fast / How long does it hurt (when a heart breaks) / I don't remember / Leave me alone / Biggest cry / I've got to talk to Mary / It's torture / Your conscience or your heart / I turned right around and went home / I've learned to live with you / Nobody like you / Lake Lonely / It's never too late / One less heartache / Tear dropped by / When your house is not a home / I can't cry him away / That's what lonesome is / Foggy river / When two world collide / Loose talk / I can't stop loving you / Big wheel / Born to lose / If you've got the money, I've got the time / Half a mind / Cigarettes and coffee blues / That's what it's like to be lonesome / Violet and a rose / Just call me lonesome / Two little boys / He plays the bongo (I play the banjo) / Second fiddle (to an old guitar) / Ain't nobody's business if I do: *Shepard, Jean & Cal Smith* / It was too late: *Shepard, Jean & Cal Smith* / Someone's gotta cry / Ain't you ashamed / Don't take advantage of me / Let me be the judge / More to love than this / Franklin County moonshine
CD Set ______ BCD 15905
Bear Family / Dec '96 / Direct / Rollercoaster / Swift

Shepard, Ollie

COMPLETE RECORDED WORKS VOL.1 1937-1939
CD ______ DOCD 5434
Document / May '96 / ADA / Hot Shot / Jazz Music

COMPLETE RECORDED WORKS VOL.2 1939-1941
CD ______ DOCD 5435
Document / May '96 / ADA / Hot Shot / Jazz Music

Shepherd, Cybill

MAD ABOUT THE BOY
CD ______ TWI 4702
Les Disques Du Crepuscule / Mar '96 / Discovery

Shepherd, Dave

GOOD ENOUGH TO KEEP
CD ______ BLCD 760514
Black Lion / Nov '95 / Cadillac / Jazz Music / Koch / Wellard

TRIBUTE TO BENNY GOODMAN (Shepherd, Dave Quintet)
CD ______ AVC 595
Avid / Jun '97 / Avid/BMG / Koch / THE

Shepherd, James

RHYTHM AND BLUES (Shepherd, James Versatile Brass)
Arrival of the Queen of Sheba / Moonlight in Vermont / Long John's hornpipe / Lazybone blues / Three English dances / Rhythm and blues / Little white donkey / Fantasy and vibrations / Three miniatures
CD ______ QPRL 035D
Polyphonic / '88 / Complete/Pinnacle

VERSATILE BRASS
CD ______ DOYCD 031
Doyen / Nov '93 / Conifer/BMG

Shepherd, Kenny Wayne

LEDBETTER HEIGHTS
Born with a broken heart / Deja voodoo / Aberdeen / Shame, shame, shame / One foot on the path / Everybody gets the blues / While we cry / I'm leaving you (commit a crime) / Riverside / What's goin' down / Ledbetter Heights
CD ______ 74321288292
Giant / Apr '96 / BMG

Shepherd, Meg

TRANSMUTATIONS (Shepherd, Meg & Alcides Lanza)
CD ______ ESP 9601CD
Shelan / Jun '97 / ReR Megacorp

Shepp, Archie

BLACK GYPSY
CD ______ 500792
Musidisc / Sep '96 / Discovery

BLASE
My angel / There is a balm in Gilead / Sophisticated lady / Touareg / Blase
CD ______ LEJAZZCD 26
Le Jazz / Aug '94 / Cadillac / Koch

FIFTH OF MAY (Shepp, Archie & Jasper Van't Hof)
CD ______ CDLR 45004
L&R / Jul '88 / New Note/Pinnacle

FIRE MUSIC
Ham bone / Malcolm Malcolm Semper Malcolm / Los Olvidados
CD ______ MCAD 39121
Impulse Jazz / Jun '89 / New Note/BMG

FOUR FOR TRANE
Syeeda's song flute / Mr. Syms / Cousin Mary / Niema / Rufus
CD ______ IMP 12182
Impulse Jazz / Apr '97 / New Note/BMG

FREEDOM (Shepp, Archie Quintet)
CD ______ JMY 10072
JMY / Aug '91 / Harmonia Mundi

GOIN' HOME (Shepp, Archie & Horace Parlan)
CD ______ SCCD 31079
Steeplechase / Jul '88 / Discovery / Impetus

I KNOW ABOUT THE LIFE
CD ______ SKCD 23026
Sackville / Jun '93 / Cadillac / Jazz Music / Swift

IN MEMORY OF ARCHIE SHEPP (Shepp, Archie & Chet Baker)
CD ______ CDLR 45006
L&R / Jul '88 / New Note/Pinnacle

KWANZA
CD ______ MVCZ 124
MCA / Apr '97 / BMG

LIVE IN PARIS (Shepp, Archie & Eric Le Lann)
CD ______ LOZ 10
Arcade / Apr '97 / Discovery

LOVER MAN
CD ______ CDSJP 287
Timeless Jazz / Jun '89 / New Note/ Pinnacle

MAMA ROSE
CD ______ SCCD 31169
Steeplechase / Jul '88 / Discovery / Impetus

MONTREUX VOL.1
Lush life / U-jamaa / Crucificado / Miss Toni
CD ______ FCD 741027
Freedom / Sep '88 / Cadillac / Jazz Music / Koch / Wellard

PARLAN DUO REUNION (Shepp, Archie & Horace Parlan)
CD ______ CDLR 45003
L&R / Oct '88 / New Note/Pinnacle

RISING SUN
CD ______ RS 0005
Just A Memory / Oct '94 / New Note/ Pinnacle

SEA OF FACES, A
CD ______ 1200022
Black Saint / Sep '95 / Cadillac / Harmonia Mundi

SOMETHING TO LIVE FOR
Flower is a lovesome thing / My foolish heart / Strange fruit / You're blase / Something to live for / Georgia on my mind / Hello, young lovers / California blues
CD ______ CDSJP 439
Timeless / Apr '97 / New Note/Pinnacle

SPLASHES (Shepp, Archie Quartet)
Arrival / Reflexions / Groovin' high / Steam / Manhattan
CD ______ CDLR 45005
L&R / Jul '88 / New Note/Pinnacle

STREAM
CD ______ JHR 73520
Jazz Hour / Sep '93 / Cadillac / Jazz Music / Target/BMG

THERE'S A TRUMPET IN MY SOUL
There's a trumpet in my soul suite (part 1) / Samba da rua / Zaid (part 1) / Down in Brazil / There's a trumpet in my soul suite (part 2) / Zaid (part 2) / It is the year of the rabbit / Zaid (part 3)
CD ______ FCD 41016
Freedom / Dec '87 / Cadillac / Jazz Music / Koch / Wellard

TRUMPET IN MY SOUL
CD ______ FCD 74106
Freedom / Oct '89 / Cadillac / Jazz Music / Koch / Wellard

YASMINA, A BLACK WOMAN
Yasmina, a black woman / Sonny's back / Body and soul
CD ______ LEJAZZCD 51
Le Jazz / Oct '95 / Cadillac / Koch

Sheppard, Andy

ANDY SHEPPARD
Java jive / Esme / Twee / Sol / Coming second / Want a toffee / Liquid
CD ______ IMCD 115
Antilles/New Directions / May '91 / PolyGram

ANDY SHEPPARD & INCLASSIFICABLE (Sheppard, Andy & Inclassificable)
Where we going / Slow boat / Hush hush / RCA / Ocean view / Is everything alright up there / Too close to the flame / Ships in the night / Sharp practice
CD ______ LBLC 6583
Label Bleu / Jul '95 / New Note/Pinnacle

IN-CO-MOTION
ASAP / Eargliding / Backstage passes / Movies / Upstate / Let's lounge / Pinky
CD ______ IMCD 195
Island / Jul '94 / PolyGram

INTRODUCTIONS IN THE DARK
Romantic / Rebecca's / Optics / Conversations / Forbidden fruit
CD ______ IMCD 116
Antilles/New Directions / May '91 / PolyGram

MOVING IMAGE (Sheppard, Andy & Steve Lodder)
CD ______ 5338752
Verve / Nov '96 / PolyGram

RHYTHM METHOD
Sofa safari / Undercovers / Access all areas / So / Well kept secret / Hop dreams

CD _______________ CDBLT 1007
Blue Note / Nov '93 / EMI

SOFT ON THE INSIDE
Soft on the inside / Rebecca's silk stockings / Carla, Carla, Carla / Adventures in the rave trade
CD _______________ IMCD 194
Island / Jul '94 / PolyGram

Sher, Oscar

CLASSICAL SPANISH GUITAR OF OSCAR SHER, THE
La fiesta / Que c'est triste / Love theme from 'romeo and juliet' / Aranjuez / Cancion del sur / El dia que me quieras / Gracias a la vida / Sur / Guajira / Esta tarde vi llover / Luz del amanecer / Que nadia sepami sufrir / Viva jujuy / La distancia tu / Adio nonino
CD _______________ QED 104
Tring / Nov '96 / Tring

Sherburn, Chris

LAST NIGHT'S FUN (Sherburn, Chris & Denny Bartley)
CD _______________ SOM 002
Sound Out Music / Oct '95 / ADA / Direct

Sheridan, Tony

FIRST (Sheridan, Tony & The Beatles)
Ain't she sweet / Cry for a shadow / When the saints go marching in / Why / If you love me baby / What'd I say / Sweet Georgia Brown / Let's dance / Ruby baby / My Bonnie / Nobody's child / Ready Teddy / Ya ya / Kansas city
CD _______________ 5500372
Spectrum / May '93 / PolyGram

LIVE AND DANGEROUS (Documentary/Live) (Sheridan, Tony & The Beat Brothers)
CD _______________ OTR 1100019
Metro Independent / Jun '97 / Essential/BMG

SHERIDAN IN CONTROL (Documentary/Live)
CD _______________ OTR 1100018
Metro Independent / Jun '97 / Essential/BMG

Sheriff, Dave

LOVE TO LINE DANCE
CD _______________ DS 004CD
Scratch / Dec '96 / Koch / Scratch/BMG

Sherman, Bim

CRAZY WORLD
CD _______________ CEND 1600
Century / Oct '96 / Shellshock/Disc

CRUCIAL CUTS VOL.1
CD _______________ CEND 400
Century / Sep '94 / Shellshock/Disc

IN A RUB A DUB STYLE
CD _______________ OMCD 013
Original Music / May '95 / Jet Star / SRD

IT MUST BE A DREAM
My woman / Just can't stand it / Can I be free from crying / Missing you / Lovers leap / Simple life / Solid as a rock / It must be a dream / Bewildered / Over the rainbow / Golden locks
CD _______________ MNTCD 1005
Mantra / Jun '97 / RTM/Disc

LION HEART DUB
CD _______________ CEND 1800
Century / Jan '97 / Shellshock/Disc

MIRACLE
CD _______________ MNTCD 1004
Mantra / Jun '96 / RTM/Disc

REALITY (Sherman, Bim & Dub Syndicate)
CD _______________ CEND 1700
Century / Nov '92 / Shellshock/Disc

TAKEN OFF
CD _______________ CEND 2001
Century / Nov '94 / Shellshock/Disc

Sherman, Daryl

CELEBRATING MILDRED BAILEY (Sherman, Daryl & John Cocuzzi)
CD _______________ ACD 295
Audiophile / Nov '96 / Jazz Music

Sherrys

POP POP POP-PIE
Pop Pop Pop-Pie / Your hand in mine / Dancin' the Strand / Double order mashed potatoes / Dance / Slop time / Fly / At the hop / Let's stomp again / Bristol twistin' Danny / New cha cha cha / Last dance / Last dance / Oh la la limbo / Saturday night / I've got no one / Society / My guy / Monk, monk, monkey / That boy of mine
CD _______________ BCD 16105
Bear Family / Nov '96 / Direct / Rollercoaster / Swift

Sherwood, Bobby

BOBBY SHERWOOD ORCHESTRA VOL.1 1944-1946 (Sherwood, Bobby Orchestra)
CD _______________ CCD 28
Circle / Nov '96 / Jazz Music / Swift / Wellard

BOBBY SHERWOOD ORCHESTRA VOL.2 1944-1946 (Sherwood, Bobby Orchestra)
CD _______________ CCD 115
Circle / Nov '96 / Jazz Music / Swift / Wellard

Shew, Bobby

TRIBUTE TO THE MASTERS
Nica's dream / Whisper not / Rhyhtm-a-ning / In your own sweet way / Confirmation / Tiny capers / In a sentimental mood / This I dig of you / Night in Tunisia
CD _______________ DTRCD 101
Double Time / Dec '96 / Express Jazz

TRUMPETS NO END (Shew, Bobby & Chuck Findley)
CD _______________ DCD 4003
Delos / Mar '90 / Nimbus

Shicheng, Lin

ART OF THE PIPA
CD _______________ C 560046
Ocora / Nov '93 / ADA / Harmonia Mundi

Shide & Acorn

LEGEND OF THE DREAMSTONES
CD _______________ KSCD 9310
Kissing Spell / Jun '97 / Greyhound

PRINCESS OF THE ISLAND
CD _______________ KSCD 9460
Kissing Spell / Jun '97 / Greyhound

Shield

VAMPIRESONGS
CD _______________ DFR 10
Desperate Flight / Feb '97 / Cargo

Shields, Chris

HAUNT ME
Haunt me / Fool / Talking 'bout that feeling / Never the same again / Gently fade away / In another time / Your tender touch / Things you do to me / Thousand dreams / Secret love / But the neighbours ain't / Mother love
CD _______________ CRAZCD 195
Go Crazy / Sep '93 / Go Crazy Music

Shields, Lonnie

TIRED OF WAITING
Woman is dangerous / Tears become my tears / If you want my loving (Come to me) / I got the blues / If you know Jesus / Full time loving / Coming of the lord / One more chance / Busy man / All I need is your love / Cheating on me / Full time lover
CD _______________ JSPCD 270
JSP / Oct '96 / ADA / Cadillac / Direct / Hot Shot / Target/BMG

Shift

SPACESUIT
CD _______________ EVR 025CD
Equal Vision / May '97 / Plastic Head

Shihab, Sahib

CONVERSATIONS
CD _______________ BLCD 760169
Black Lion / Oct '93 / Cadillac / Jazz Music / Koch / Wellard

Shihad

CHURN
Factory / Screwtop / Scacture / Stations / Clapper-loader / I only said / Derail / Bone orchard / Happy meal
CD _______________ N 02492
Noise / Jul '94 / Koch

KILLJOY
CD _______________ N 02542
Noise / Apr '95 / Koch

LA LA LAND
CD _______________ N 02693
Noise / Nov '96 / Koch

SHIHAD
CD _______________ N 02692
Noise / Mar '97 / Koch

Shijuku Thief

SCRIBBLER, THE
CD _______________ DOROBO 002CD
Dorobo / Sep '95 / Plastic Head

Shimita El Diego

MYSTIC (Shimita El Diego & Zaitoum)
CD _______________ CD 64002
Sonodisc / Jan '97 / Stern's

Shindell, Richard

BLUE DIVIDE
CD _______________ SH 8014
Shanachie / Dec '94 / ADA / Greensleeves / Koch

Shine, Brendan

ALWAYS A WELCOME
There's always a welcome / I'm your man from Strabane / Lovely Isle of Green / Gather up me bags / Loaugh key / Irish Elvis Presley / Bury me not on the lone prairie / I'm a savage for bacon and cabbage / My Galway Queen / Time marches on / David's dream / Meet me in Tralee / Old faithful / Big green Mercury / Joe come on home
CD _______________ CDPLAY 1031
Play / Dec '92 / Avid/BMG / Koch

BEST OF BRENDAN SHINE, THE
CD _______________ 3036300122
Carlton / May '97 / Carlton

COLLECTION, THE
CD _______________ PLACD 101
Play / Oct '94 / Avid/BMG / Koch

FAR FAR AWAY
CD _______________ APLCD 1039
Avid / Nov '96 / Avid/BMG / Koch / THE

I WANNA STAY WITH YOU
I wanna stay with you / Lay down beside me / When the lovin' is through / Hello Darlin' / One more chance / Saints and sinners / Drive me to drink / Walkin' on new grass / Squeeze box / Shoe the donkey / It dosen't matter anymore / Some broken hearts never mend / Dad / Goodbye / (There's) The door / If tomorrow never comes / Love bug / Rock 'n' roll kids / Not counting you / When two lovers meet
CD _______________ 3036000082
Carlton / Nov '95 / Carlton

I'LL SETTLE FOR OLD IRELAND (18 Country & Irish Favourites)
Are we making love / Dear hearts and gentle people / I will settle for old Ireland / When two lovers meet / Broken pledge / Jeannie Marie / Abbeyshrule / Soft sweet and warm / Woodlands of Loughlin / Time on my hands / By the devil / Down the wrong road again / Humours of Scariff / Ballinasloe fair / My Eileen is waiting for me / Ballinamona hat / Seasons of my heart / Faster horses
CD _______________ 306052
Hallmark / Jan '97 / Carlton

IF YOU EVER GO OVER TO IRELAND (2CD Set)
Forty miles from Poplar Bluff / Once a day / A bunch of violets blue / I'll do it all again / Coastline of Mayo / Lovin' you (so long now) / Say it again / Astoreen Bawn / Boy inside me / Mama tried / How much time / Bright city lights / Oul' Ballymoe / Spancil hill / Roving Galway boy / Sadie of my dreams / Low back car / What do I care / Woman to woman / Kikfenora jigs / Bonnish Jenny / Dear God / Girl who broke my heart / More than words can tell / Loving you / Hello Mr DJ / I like beer / Living with the shades pulled down / Geese in the bog / Make me dream / It's no secret / Goodnight Irene / King and queen of fools / Say it's not you / Yes I'm feeling better / If you ever go over to Ireland
CD Set _______________ 330132
Hallmark / Jul '96 / Carlton

WITH LOVE
Old Tralee / Thank god for kids / Good times / These are the sounds I love / Murphy's widow / Moon behind the hill / Old grey suit / Pipes of Donegal / My son / Diddling song / Only our rivers run free / Bunch of violets blue / Now I'm easy / Did you miss me
CD _______________ PLAYCD 1037
Play / Mar '96 / Avid/BMG / Koch

Shinehead

TRODDIN'
Troddin' thru / Buff bay / Accident / More than a feeling / Woman like you / Keep on singin' / Me and them / Sniper / Keep on / Good girls bad boys / Never been in love B4 / Reprimand / Boom bangin' / Best creation
CD _______________ 7559616672
Warner Bros. / Sep '94 / Warner Music

Shines, Johnny

JOHNNY SHINES
CD _______________ HCD 8028
Hightone / Jul '94 / ADA / Koch

JOHNNY SHINES WITH BIG WALTER HORTON (Shines, Johnny & Big Walter Horton)
CD _______________ TCD 5015
Testament / Mar '95 / ADA / Koch

MASTERS OF MODERN BLUES SERIES
CD _______________ TCD 5002
Testament / Aug '94 / ADA / Koch

MR. COVER SHAKER
CD _______________ BCD 125
Biograph / Jan '93 / ADA / Cadillac / Direct / Hot Shot / Jazz Music / Wellard

STANDING AT THE CROSSROADS
CD _______________ TCD 5022
Testament / May '95 / ADA / Koch

TRADITIONAL DELTA BLUES
CD _______________ BCD 121
Biograph / '92 / ADA / Cadillac / Direct / Hot Shot / Jazz Music / Wellard

Shiney Gnomes

MC CREATRIX
CD _______________ RTD 19519172
Our Choice / Feb '95 / Pinnacle

Shining Path

NO OTHER WORLD
Freedom / No other world / They may be blind / Kiss of death / It was my turn to lose / This is my punishment / Kill / Wrath of dog / End
CD _______________ DEMCD 029
Day Eight Music / Jun '93 / New Note/Pinnacle

Shinjuku Thief

BLOODY TOURIST
Komachi ruins / Feather woman of the jungle / Burdon of dreams / Sacrifice / Preacher's ghost / Hallucinations / Open wound / Nkoma / Year of silence / Graven image / Ba benzele
CD _______________ XCD 016
Extreme / Jun '97 / Vital/SAM

Ship Of Fools

CLOSE YOUR EYES (FORGET THE WORLD)
In the wake of / Where is here / Passage by night / L=SD2 / SOL93 / Starjumper / Western lands / Close your eyes (forget the world)
CD _______________ KTB 013CD
Dreamtime / Jun '93 / Kudos / Pinnacle

OUT THERE SOMEWHERE
Elevator / Diesel spaceship / First light / Guidance is internal / Out there somewhere / From time / Eternal guidance
CD _______________ CDKTB 18
Dreamtime / Apr '95 / Kudos / Pinnacle

Shipp, Matthew

BY THE LAW OF MUSIC (Shipp, Matthew Trio)
Signal / By the law of music / Implicit / Fair play / Grid / Whole movement / Game of control / Point to point / PX / Grid / Coo / XZU / Solitude
CD _______________ ARTCD 6200
Hat Art / Jun '97 / Cadillac / Harmonia Mundi

CIRCULAR TEMPLE (Shipp, Matthew Trio)
Circular temple
CD _______________ 74321327582
Infinite Zero / Mar '96 / BMG

CRITICAL MASS
CD _______________ 213CD 003
2.13.61 / Jun '96 / Pinnacle

FLOW OF X (Shipp, Matthew Quartet)
Flow of x / Flow of silence / Flow of y / Flow of M / Flow of U / Instinctive codes
CD _______________ 213CD 026
2.13.61 / Jun '97 / Pinnacle

PRISM (Shipp, Matthew Trio)
CD _______________ BKM 58CD
Brinkman / Nov '96 / Cargo
CD _______________ KFW 998CD
Knitting Factory/Ectoplasm / Feb '97 / Cargo

ZO (Shipp, Matthew Duo)
CD _______________ RR 1262
Rise / Dec '94 / Pinnacle

Shirelles

BABY IT'S YOU
Baby it's you / Irresistible you / Thing I want to hear (pretty words) / Big John / Same old story / Voice of experience / Soldier boy / Thing of the past / Twenty one / Make the night a little longer / Twisting in the USA / Putty in your hands
CD _______________ CDSC 6012
Sundazed / Jan '94 / Cargo / Greyhound / Rollercoaster

BEST OF THE SHIRELLES, THE
Dedicated to the one I love / Look a here baby / Tonight's the night / Will you still love me tomorrow / Boys / Mama said / Thing of the past / What a sweet thing that was / Big John / Putty in your hands / Baby it's you / Soldier boy / Welcome home baby / Mama here comes the bride / Stop the music / It's love that really counts / Everybody loves a lover / Foolish little girl / Abracadabra / Don't say goodnight and mean goodbye / What does a girl do / Don't let it happen to us / Girl is not a girl / Sha la la / His lips get in the way / Thank you baby / Doomsday / Maybe tonight / Shades of blue / Don't go home (My little darling) / Last minute miracle / Wait till I give the signal
CD _______________ CDCHD 356
Ace / Apr '92 / Pinnacle

DEFINITIVE COLLECTION, THE (2CD Set)
Dedicated to the one I love / Look-a-here baby / Teardrop and a lollipop / Doin' the ronde / Please be my boyfriend / I saw a tear / Tonight's the night / Dance is over / Will you love me tomorrow / Boys / Mama said / Blue holiday / Thing of the past / What a sweet thing that was / Big John / Twenty one / Baby it's you / Things I want to hear / Soldier boy / Love is a swingin' thing / Welcome home baby / Mama here comes the bride / Stop the music / It's love that really counts / Everybody loves a lover / I don't think so / Foolish little girl / Not for all the money in the world / Don't say goodnight and mean goodbye / I didn't mean to hurt you / Abra ka dabra / What does a girl do / Don't let it happen to us / Things go better with Coca Cola / It's a mad mad mad mad world / 31 flavours / Tonight you're gonna fall in love with me / 20th century rock 'n' roll / Sha la la / His lips get in the way / Thank you baby / Doomsday / Maybe tonight / Are you still my baby / Ssh I'm watching the movie / March / Everybody's goin' mad / My heart belongs to you / (Mama) my soldier boy is coming home / I met him on a Sunday / Till my baby comes home / Whatever will be will be (Que sera sera) / Shades of blue / When the boys talk about the girls / Teasin' me / Look away / Don't go home (my little darlin') / Nobody's baby after you / Bright shiny colours / Too much of a good thing / Last minute miracle / Wait until I give the signal / Hippie walk / Commercial
CD Set _____ CPCD 81902
Charly / Sep '96 / Koch

FABULOUS SHIRELLES
Will you still love me tomorrow / Soldier boy / Dedicated to the one I love / Foolish little girl / Mama said / Baby it's you / Big John / Welcome home baby / Everybody loves a lover / Don't say goodnight and mean goodbye / Tonight's the night / What does a girl do
CD _____ CDFAB 011
Ace / Oct '91 / Pinnacle

GIVE A TWIST PARTY (Shirelles & King Curtis)
Mama here comes the bride / Take the last train home (instr.) / Welcome home baby / I've got a woman / I still want you / Take the last train home (vocal) / Love is a swingin' thing / Ooh-poo-pah-doo / New Orleans / Mr. Twister / Potato chips
CD _____ CDSC 6013
Sundazed / Jan '94 / Cargo / Greyhound / Rollercoaster

LEGENDS IN MUSIC
CD _____ LECD 077
Wisepack / Sep '94 / Conifer/BMG / THE

LOST & FOUND
Good good time / Long day, short night / You'll know when the right boy comes along / Rocky / Go tell her / Remember me / For my sake / Celebrate your victory / Hands off, he's mine / Crossroads in your heart / He's the only guy I'll ever love / One of the flower people / I'm feeling it too / If I had you / There goes my heart / Shh, I'm watching the movie
CD _____ CDCHD 521
Ace / May '94 / Pinnacle

SHIRELLES, THE
CD _____ KLMCD 039
BAM / Nov '94 / Koch / Scratch/BMG

SHIRELLES, THE
CD _____ GOLD 070
Gold / Jul '96 / Else

ULTIMATE
CD _____ MAR 044
Marginal / Jun '97 / Greyhound

WILL YOU LOVE ME TOMORROW
Dedicated to the one I love / Tonight's the night / Will you still love me tomorrow / Boys / Mama said / Thing of the past / What a sweet thing that was / Big John / Baby it's you / Soldier boy / Welcome home baby / Stop the music / It's love that really counts / Everybody loves a lover / Foolish little girl / Don't say goodnight and mean goodbye / What does a girl do / Sha la la / Thank you baby / Maybe tonight
CD _____ CDCHARLY 173
Charly / Jan '89 / Koch

Shirley & Lee

SWEETHEARTS OF THE BLUES 1952-1963, THE (4CD Set)
Sweethearts / I'm gone / Real thing / Korea / Baby / Shirley, come back to me / Shirley's back / Shirley's back / Why did I / So in love / So in love / Reason why / Time has come / I love you so / Proposal / Two happy people / Lee goofed / Every fool has his day / Down in my heart / Keep on / Confessin' / When the sun goes down / Tryin' to fool me / Rumours blue / Comin' over / Takes money / I didn't want you / You'd be thinking of me / I'll thrill you / Feel so good / Lee's dream / I'll do it / Tell me so / That's what I'll do / Little world / Let the good times roll / Do you mean to hurt me so / Everything / We will be forever happy / I feel good / That's what I wanna do / Now that's over / I want to dance / Marry me / Before I go / Don't you know / Rock all night / Rockin' with the clock / Flirt / Love no one but you / Live on the farm / Everybody's rockin' / Don't leave me here to cry / Come on and have your fun / All I want to do is cry / True love never dies / When day is done / So tired / SHirley come back to me / Like you used to do / Bewildered / Who are we fooling / Keep loving me / You move me / Let's live it up / I've been loved before / I'll never be free / After last night / I love the way you love / Your love makes the difference / I was lucky / Lover's mistake / Everybody needs somebody / Your day is coming / Two peas in a pod / Good for nothing baby / Well-a well-a / Our kids / They've got to understand / Call me a fool / Hard to believe / Behind the make up / Keep the magic working / Girl you're married now / It's been so long / Joker / Together we stand / My last letter / I'm old enough / You wouldn't / Little thing / Engagement / Don't stop now / Hey little boy / Golden rule / Honky tonk music / Dancing world / Thank you / Wouldn't be here / Brink of disaster / Paper doll / When I fall in love / Don't marry too soon / Honey bee / When a girl meets a boy / Never let me go / Surf Heaven / Surfer's hangout / Somebody put a juke box in the study hall
CD Set _____ BCD 15960
Bear Family / Apr '97 / Direct / Rollercoaster / Swift

Shirley, Roy

BLACK LION NEGUS RASTAFARI
CD _____ CDLINC 011
Lion Inc. / Dec '95 / Jet Star / SRD

CONTROL THEM VOL.1
CD _____ GRCD 004
Sprint / Jul '96 / SRD

GET IN THE GROOVE (Shirley, Roy & Stranger Cole/Ken Parker)
CD _____ RGCD 0038
Rocky One / Apr '97 / Jet Star

Shiv

FLAYED AND ASHAMED
Unsatisfaction / Crazy cooter / Fruit pie / Coworker / QRXT65723 / Plumber / Leave now / Punk / Swazi spoon position / Emk / Long distance dedication / Bank it / Highneckin
CD _____ THI 570202
Thirsty Ear / Jan '97 / Vital

Shiv & Hari

YUGAL BANDI
Raga jhinjhoti / Raga msihra piloco
CD _____ RSMCD 104
Ravi Shankar Music Circle / May '94 / Conifer/BMG

Shiva

FIREDANCE
How can I / En cachent / Wild machine / Borderline / Stranger lands / Angel of monz / Rendezvous with death / User / Call me in the morning / Shiva / Rock lives on / Sympathy
CD _____ CDMETAL 8
Anagram / Jan '97 / Cargo / Pinnacle

Shiva Burlesque

MERCURY BLUES
CD _____ DRCD 7
Fundamental / Nov '96 / Cargo / Plastic Head / Shellshock/Disc

Shiver

WALPURGIS
CD _____ RF 601
Red Fox / Jun '97 / Greyhound

Shivers

BURIED LIFE, THE
CD _____ GRCD 398
Glitterhouse / May '97 / Avid/BMG

SHIVERS, THE
CD _____ GRCD 372
Glitterhouse / Aug '95 / Avid/BMG

Shizuo

SHIZUO VS. SHIZOR
Sweat / Punks / Braindead / New kick / Emptiness / Duty / Sexual high / Tight / Dr. LSD / Zen / Crack meets the hammer / Blondo / Making love / Chill
CD _____ DHRCD 007
Digital Hardcore / Jun '97 / Vital

Shizzoe, Hank

LOW BUDGET
CD _____ CCD 11046
Crosscut / Nov '94 / ADA / CM / Direct

Shlomit

SONGS IN HEBREW
CD _____ 340862
Koch International / Jun '96 / Koch

Sho

TROUBLE MAN (Sho & Willie D)
CD _____ WRA 8125CD
Wrap / Apr '94 / Koch

Sho Nuff

FROM THE GUT TO THE BUTT
Funkasize you / Steppin' out / You chose me / Thinking of you / Get it together / Watch me do it / I live across the street / Come on / Mix match man / Total answer
CD _____ CDSXE 092
Stax / Aug '93 / Pinnacle

Shoales, Ian

I GOTTA GO
CD _____ 213CD 016
2.13.61 / May '97 / Pinnacle

Shock Box

DROPPIN' THE BOMB
CD _____ RTN 41211CD
Rock The Nation / Jan '96 / Plastic Head

Shock Headed Peters

FEAR ENGINE, THE
CD _____ CP131 05CD
Cyclops / Oct '96 / World Serpent

NOT BORN BEAUTIFUL
CD _____ CP131 03CD
Cyclops / Oct '96 / World Serpent

SEVERAL HEADED ENEMY
CD _____ CP131 01CD
Cyclops / Oct '96 / World Serpent

TENDERCIDE
CD _____ CP131 07CD
Cyclops / Oct '96 / World Serpent

Shock Therapy

DARK YEARS, THE
CD _____ EFA 08440CD
Dossier / Oct '92 / Cargo / SRD

HATE IS A FOUR LETTER WORD
CD _____ SPV 08419572
SPV / May '95 / Koch / Plastic Head

HEAVEN AND EARTH
CD _____ EFA 084552
Dossier / Mar '94 / Cargo / SRD
CD _____ SPV 08419552
SPV / Jun '95 / Koch / Plastic Head

Shocked, Michelle

ARKANSAS TRAVELER
33 rpm Soul / Come a long way / Secret to a long life / Contest coming (Cripple creek) / Over the waterfall / Shaking hands (Soldier's joy) / Jump Jim crow / Hold me back (Frankie and Johnny) / Strawberry jam / Prodigal daughter (Cotton eyes Joe) / Blackberry blossom / Weaving way / Arkansas traveller / Woody's rag
CD _____ 5121892
London / Apr '92 / PolyGram

CAPTAIN SWING
Ged is a real estate developer / On the greener side / Silent ways / Sleep keeps me awake / Cement lament / (Don't you mess around with) my little sister / Looks like Mona Lisa / Too little, too late / Street corner ambassador / Must be luff
CD _____ 8388782
London / Jun '92 / PolyGram

KIND HEARTED WOMAN
Stillborn / Homestead / Winter wheat / Cold comfort / Eddie / Child like Grace / Fever breaks / Silver spoon / Hard way / No sign of rain
CD _____ 01005821452
Private Music / Nov '96 / BMG

MERCURY POISED
On the greener side / Anchorage / Come along way / Quality of mercy / Street corner ambassador / Too little too late / If love was a train / When love was a train / When I grow up / Prodigal daughter / Over the waterfall / Holy spirit / Stillborn
CD _____ 5329602
London / Nov '96 / PolyGram

TEXAS CAMPFIRE TAPES
5 a.m. in Amsterdam / Secret admirer / Incomplete image / Who cares / Down on Thomas St. Fogtown / Steppin' out / Hep cat / Necktie / (Don't you mess around with) my little sister / Ballad of patched eye and Meg / Secret to a long life / Chain smoker / Stranded in a limousine / Goodnight Irene
CD _____ COOKCD 002
Cooking Vinyl / Apr '88 / Vital

Shocking Blue

BEST OF SHOCKING BLUE, THE
CD _____ CSAPCD 114
Connoisseur Collection / Jan '94 / Pinnacle

Shoenfelt, Phil

BACKWOODS CRUCIFIXION
Garden of Eden / Light that surrounds you / Devil's hole / Walkaway / Marianne, I'm falling / Psyche / Hateful heart / Salvation Hotel
CD _____ PAPCD 002
Paperhouse / May '90 / RTM/Disc

GOD IS THE OTHER FACE OF THE DEVIL
Charlotte's room / Gambler / Alchemy / Hospital / Black rain / Only you / Martha's well / Killer inside / Well of souls / Pale light shining
CD _____ BAH 11
Humbug / Oct '93 / Total/Pinnacle

LIVE IN PRAGUE
CD _____ 7102692
NMC / May '96 / Total/Pinnacle

Shoes

AS IS (2CD Set)
CD Set _____ BV 105962
Black Vinyl / Jan '97 / Cargo

BLACK VINYL SHOES
Boys don't lie / Do you wanna get lucky / She'll disappear / Tragedy / Writing a postcard / Not me / Someone finer / Capital gain / Fatal running start / Okay it really hurts / Fire for a while / If you'd stay / Nowhere so fast
CD _____ CREV 016CD
Rev-Ola / Sep '93 / 3mv/Vital
CD _____ BV 100922
Black Vinyl / Nov '96 / Cargo

BOOMERANG/SHOES ON ICE
CD _____ BV 181902
Black Vinyl / Nov '96 / Cargo

FRET BUZZ
CD _____ BV 104952
Black Vinyl / Nov '96 / Cargo

PRESENT TENSE/TONGUE TWISTER
CD _____ BV 198882
Black Vinyl / Nov '96 / Cargo

PROPELLER
CD _____ BV 102942
Black Vinyl / Nov '96 / Cargo

SHOES BEST
CD _____ BV 197872
Black Vinyl / Nov '96 / Cargo

SILHOUETTE
Get my message / Will you spin for me / When push comes to shove / Shining / It's only you / Twist and bend it / I wanna give it to you / Turn around / Running wild / Oh, Angeline / Bound to fade / Suspicion
CD _____ BV 151912
Black Vinyl / Nov '96 / Cargo

STOLEN WISHES
CD _____ ROSE 202CD
New Rose / May '90 / ADA / Direct / Discovery
CD _____ BV 101892
Black Vinyl / Nov '96 / Cargo

Shoham, Jeremy

JUST EAST OF JAZZ (Shoham, Jeremy & James Woodrow)
CD _____ JEOJCD 1
Just East Of Jazz / May '97 / Cadillac

Sholle, Jon

CATFISH FOR SUPPER
Mississippi gal / Plum cake / Sweet kind of love / EBA / Bully samba / Catfish for supper / Bugle call rag / Triangle / Railroad blues / Oahu blues / You're there / I don't love nobody / Peach tree shuffle
CD _____ ROUCD 3026
Rounder / Nov '96 / ADA / CM / Direct

OUT OF THE FRYING PAN
Durham's bull / Jon's jump / Pike County breakdown / Golden slippers / Sweet Sue / Red wing / Farewell blues / Hunza guitar boogie / 8th of January / Woody's rag / Banks of the Ohio / Put on your old grey bonnet / D medley / Corrina
CD _____ ROUCD 0398
Rounder / Jun '97 / ADA / CM / Direct

Shonen Knife

LET'S KNIFE
Riding the rocket / Bear up bison / Twist Barbie / Tortoise theme 2 / Antonio baka guy / Ah Singapore / Flying jelly attack / Black bass / Cycling is fun / Watchin' girl / I am a cat / Tortoise theme 1 / Devil house / Insect collector / Burning farm
CD _____ RUST 001CD
August / Jan '93 / 3mv/Vital

ROCK ANIMALS
CD _____ RUST 009CD
August / Jan '94 / 3mv/Vital

WE ARE VERY HAPPY YOU CAME
Lazybone / Public bath / Goose steppin' mama / I wanna eat choco bars / Suzy is a headbanger / Boys / Red kross
CD _____ RUST 004CD
August / Apr '93 / 3mv/Vital

Shooglenifty

SHOOGLENIFTY LIVE AT SELWYN HALL

CD ________ WS 008CD
Womad Select / Aug '96 / ADA / Direct

VENUS IN TWEED
Pipe tunes / Horace / Point Road / Venus in tweeds / Waiting for Conrad / Two fifty to Vigo / Paranoia / Buying a blanket / Tammienorrie / Point Road (mix)
CD ________ CDTRAX 076
Greentrax / Aug '94 / ADA / Direct / Duncans / Highlander

WHISKY KISS, A
Da eye wifey / She's in the attic / Song for Susie / Whisky kiss / Good drying / Hoptsoi / Price of a pig / Farewell to Nigg
CD ________ CDTRAX 106
Greentrax / Jun '96 / ADA / Direct / Duncans / Highlander

Shootyz Groove

HIPNOSIS
Regardless / Manhole / Lilly Pad / POnce / Inter zone / Anchor / Fantasy no.5 / Triangle music / Groovyland / Nothing for you / Diamond mine / Other side / Reverse side / 8 million times
CD ________ RR 88292
Roadrunner / Jun '97 / PolyGram

JAMMIN IN VICIOUS ENVIRONMENTS
CD ________ ABT 101CD
Abstract / May '95 / Cargo / Pinnacle / Total/BMG

Shop Assistants

WILL ANYTHING HAPPEN
I don't wanna be friends with you / All day long / Before I wake / Caledonian Road / All that ever mattered / Fixed grin / Somewhere in China / Train from Kansas City / Home again / Seems to be / After dark / All of the time / What a way to die / Nature lover
CD ________ OVER 62CD
Overground / Jun '97 / Shellshock/Disc / SRD

Shopping Trolley

SHOPPING TROLLEY
CD ________ HNCD 1349
Hannibal / Jan '90 / ADA / Vital

Shore, Dinah

BLUES IN THE NIGHT
As we walk into the sunset / Blues in the night / Body and soul / Boy in khaki, a girl in lace / Chloe / Down Argentina way / He's my guy / Honeysuckle rose / Manhattan serenade / Memphis blues / Mocking Bird lament / Mood indigo / Murder he says / My man / Skylark / Smoke gets in your eyes / Somebody loves me / Something to remember you by / Sophisticated lady / Stardust / Three little sisters / Yes my darling daughter / You and I / You'd be so nice to come home to
CD ________ CDAJA 5136
Living Era / Jun '94 / Select

DINAH'S SHOW TIME 1944-47
You're a builder upper / Can't you read between the lines / Sometimes I'm happy / Linger in my arms a little longer / Rainy night in Rio / Laura / Just one of those things / Love me or leave me / Dreamer / Tallahassee / How high the moon / Night and day / Dixieland band: Button up your overcoat / I've got the world on a string / Way you look tonight / Smoke gets in your eyes / Shoo, shoo baby / Yesterdays / Man I love / Zing went the strings of my heart / I'll walk alone / Tess's torch song / Lover come back to me / Gotta be this or that
CD ________ HEPCD 45
Hep / Feb '95 / Cadillac / Jazz Music / New Note/Pinnacle / Wellard

EMI PRESENTS THE MAGIC OF DINAH SHORE
April in Paris / Blues in the night / One I love (belongs to somebody else) / Falling in love with love / Gypsy / I've got you under my skin / Love is here to stay / Man I love / My funny Valentine / Sentimental journey / Somebody loves me / My melancholy baby / It's all right with me / It had to be you / I'll walk alone / I only have eyes for you / Buttons and bows / Lover come back to me / Way down yonder in New Orleans / Song is ended
CD ________ CDMFP 6372
Music For Pleasure / May '97 / EMI

LIKE SOMEONE IN LOVE
I thought about you / Last night / Imagination / Say it / Jim / You can't brush me off / My man / Is it taboo / All I need is you / I don't want to walk without you / Maybe / Something to remember you by / Now I know / Night is young and your so beautiful / I'll walk alone / My romance / Like someone in love / I can't tell why I love you but I do / Sleigh ride in July
CD ________ ROYCD 201
Flare / Jul '96 / Target/BMG

MAD ABOUT YOU, SAD WITHOUT YOU
Thrill of a new romance / I like to recognise the tune / Darn that dream / Smoke gets in your eyes / Outside of that I love you / How come you do me like you do / Somebody loves me / Mocking bird lament / I'm through with love / Somebody nobody loves / All alone / Not mine / Skylark / One dozen roses / I can't give you anything but love / Mad about him, sad without him / Dearly beloved / Boy in khaki, a girl in lace / Murder, he says / You'd be so nice to come home to
CD ________ HQCD 43
Harlequin / Jun '94 / Hot Shot / Jazz Music / Swift / Wellard

RHAPSODY (18 Classic Superb Performances)
I've got my eyes on you / Just a whistlin' and whistlin' / Shake down the stars / Yes my darling daughter / Down Argentina way / I hear a rhapsody / I do, do you / Honeysuckle rose / If it's you / Daisy bell (On a bicycle made for two) / You and I / Is it taboo / Don't leave me Daddy / Happy in love / Sometimes / Blues in the night / Three little sisters / Manhattan serenade
CD ________ PLATCD 159
Platinum / Mar '96 / Prism

TAKING A CHANCE ON LOVE
Taking a chance on love / I only have eyes for you / One I love (belongs to somebody else) / Our love is here to stay / Falling in love / It's easy to remember / It all depends on you / Somebody loves me / I'm old fashioned / East of the sun and West of the moon / Sentimental journey / I hadn't anyone till you / Mad about him, sad without him, how can I be glad without him / I'll walk alone / Dear hearts and gentle people / Gypsy / Blues in the night / Man I love / Yes indeed
CD ________ CD 363
Entertainers / Mar '96 / Target/BMG

VERY BEST OF DINAH SHORE, THE
CD ________ SWNCD 006
Sound Waves / Oct '95 / Target/BMG

WHEN DINAH SHORE RULED THE EARTH
CD ________ VJCD 1052
Vintage Jazz Classics / Feb '94 / ADA / Cadillac / CM / Direct

YOU'D BE SO NICE TO COME HOME TO
CD ________ PASTCD 7821
Flapper / Jun '97 / Pinnacle

Short, Bobby

LIVE AT THE CARLYLE
Do I hear you saying I love you / Tea for two / Night and day / Too marvellous for words / Our love is here to stay / Drop me off in Harlem / Body and soul / I can't give you anything but love / I can dream, can't I / I get a kick out of you / Satin doll / Nearness of you / Paradise / Easy to love / After you, who / Every time we say goodbye
CD ________ CD 83311
Telarc / Mar '92 / Conifer/BMG

SONGS OF NEW YORK (Live At The Cafe Carlyle)
New York New York / Penthouse serenade / She's a latin from Manhattan / Autumn in New York / East side of heaven / When love beckoned (in fifty-second street) / Way out west on West End Avenue / Black butterfly/ Harlem butterfly medley / My personal property / Broadway / Sidewalks of New York / Take me back to Manhattan / Upper Madison Avenue blues
CD ________ CD 83346
Telarc / Feb '96 / Conifer/BMG

Short n' Curlies

BITTER 'N' TWISTED
CD ________ KONCD 019
Knock Out / Mar '97 / Cargo

Shorter, Wayne

ATLANTIS
Endangered species / Three Marias / Last silk hat / When you dream / Who goes there / Atlantis / Shere Khan / Criancas / On the eve of departure
CD ________ 4816172
Sony Jazz / Dec '95 / Sony

HIGH LIFE
Children of the night / At the fair / Maya / On the Milky Way Express / Pandora awakened / Virgo rising / High life / Midnight in Carlotta's hair / Black swan (in memory of Susan Portlynn Romeo)
CD ________ 5292242
Verve / Mar '96 / PolyGram

JUJU
Juju / Deluge / House of Jade / Mahjong / Yes or no / Twelve more bars to go / Juju / House of Jade
CD ________ CDP 8376442
Blue Note / Jun '96 / EMI

NATIVE DANCER
Ponta de Areia / Beauty and the beast / Tarde / Miracle of the fishes / Diana / Ana Maria / Lilia / Joanna's theme
CD ________ 4670952
Columbia / Jan '95 / Sony

SECOND GENESIS
Ruby and the pearl / Pay as you go / Second Genesis / Mr. Chairman / Tenderfoot / Albatross / Getting to know you / I didn't know what time it was
CD ________ LEJAZZCD 9
Le Jazz / Mar '93 / Cadillac / Koch

SPEAK NO EVIL
Fee fi fo fum / Dance cadaverous / Speak no evil / Infant eyes / Wild flower / Out to lunch / Straight up and down / Witch hunt
CD ________ CDP 7465092
Blue Note / Mar '95 / EMI

THIS IS JAZZ
Endangered species / Lusitanos / Port of entry / Three Marias / Eurydice / When it was now / Beauty and the beast / Mahogany bird / Diana
CD ________ CK 64973
Sony Jazz / Oct '96 / Sony

Shortino, Paul

BACK ON TRACK
Kid is back in town / Body and soul / Girls like you / Pieces / Bye bye to love / Everybody can fly / Give me love / Remember me / Rough life / Forgotten child / When there's a life
CD ________ CDVEST 3
Bulletproof / Mar '94 / Pinnacle

Shorty

FRESH BREATH
CD ________ GR 14CD
Skingraft / Jun '94 / SRD

THUMB DAYS
CD ________ GB 062
Gasoline Boost / Jul '93 / Plastic Head

Shotgun Messiah

SECOND COMING, THE
CD ________ RR 92392
Roadrunner / Nov '91 / PolyGram

Shotgun Rationale

ROLLERCOASTER
CD ________ EFA 11894 CD
Vince Lombard / Jun '93 / SRD

Shotgun Symphony

FORGET THE RAIN
Carousel of broken dream / Line / What if / Eyes of anger / Playing with fools / Yesterday's gone / Two songs / My escape / Waiting for the sun / XLV
CD ________ 410222
Sha-La / Mar '97 / Cargo

Shotmaker

MOUSE EAR
CD ________ TMU 013CD
Troubleman / Feb '97 / Cargo

Shotts & Dykehead ...

ANOTHER QUIET SUNDAY (Shotts & Dykehead Caledonia Pipe Band)
CD ________ COMD 2037
Temple / Feb '94 / ADA / CM / Direct / Duncans / Highlander

BY THE WATERS EDGE (Shotts & Dykehead Caledonia Pipe Band)
Hornpipe - The walrus / March, strathspey and reel / Slow air "By the waters edge" / Jigs and slow air / Slow air "Farewell to camraw" / Strathspey and reel / Medley / Slow air "Piper alpha" / Dance jigs / 6/8 Marches / Retreat marches
CD ________ LCOM 5229
Lismor / Aug '94 / ADA / Direct / Duncans / Lismor

Shoukichi, Kina

MUSIC POWER FROM OKINAWA (Shoukichi, Kina & Champroose)
Haisai ojisan / Uwaki bushi / Red ojisan / Bancho guwa / Agarizachi / Sukuchinamun / Ichimushiguwanu yuntaku / Bashaguwa suncha / Shimaguwa song / Tokyo sanbika
CD ________ CDORBD 072
Globestyle / Oct '91 / Pinnacle

Shoulders

TRASHMAN'S SHOES
Charm / On Sunday / Trashman shoes / Beckoning bells / Weatherman / I'll take what's left / Lula's bar and pool / Unle achin / whole way to the halfway house / All the nights to come / Fare thee well
CD ________ DJD 3208
Dejadisc / May '94 / ADA / Direct

Shout

IN YOUR FACE
Borderline / Give me an answer / Getting ready / Getting on with life / Ain't givin' up / When the love is gone / Faith hope and love / In your face / Moonlight sonata / Waiting on you
CD ________ CDMFN 92
Music For Nations / May '89 / Pinnacle

IT WON'T BE LONG
CD ________ CDMFN 88
Music For Nations / Aug '89 / Pinnacle

Show & AG

GOODFELLAS
Never less than ill / You know now / Check it out / Add on / Next level / Time for ... / Got the flava / Neighborhood sickness / All out / Medicine / Got ya back / Next level / You want it
CD ________ 8286412
FFRR / Oct '95 / PolyGram

Show Of Hands

BACKLOG 1987-1991
CD ________ CDIS 08
Isis / Mar '95 / ADA / Direct

BEAT ABOUT THE BUSH
Beat about the bush / Class of Seventy Three / Armadas / Nine hundred miles / Shadows in the dark / Galway farmer / White tribes / Day has come / Hook of love / Cars / Blue cockade / Mr. May's/Gloucester hornpipe / Oak
CD ________ CDIS 05
Isis / Mar '94 / ADA / Direct

COLUMBUS (DIDN'T FIND AMERICA)
Columbus (Didn't find America) / Exile / Breakfast for Altan / Scattering tears
CD ________ CDIS 07
Isis / Apr '94 / ADA / Direct

LIE OF THE LAND
Hunter / Unlock me / Well / Keeper / Captains / Weary / Ratcliffe highway / Safe as houses / Man in green / Preacher / M Ferguson / Exile
CD ________ HMCD 02
Hands On / May '97 / ADA / CM / Direct

LIVE AT THE ROYAL ALBERT HALL
Columbus (didn't find America) / Day has come / Preacher / Cuthroats, crooks and con men / Blue cockade / Soldiers joy / Exile / Man in green / Dove / Well / Hunter / Captains / Blind fiddler / Santiago / Galway farmer / Time after time
CD ________ HMCD 01
Hands On / May '97 / ADA / CM / Direct

SHOW OF HANDS 'LIVE'
Silver dagger / Blind fiddler / Don't it feel good / I still wait / Exile / Yankee clipper / Man of war / Bonnie Light Horseman / I'll put a stake through his heart / Low down in the broome / Six o'clock waltz / Sit you down / Wolf at the door / Caught in the rain / Santiago / It's all your fault
CD ________ CDIS 06
Isis / Mar '95 / ADA / Direct

Showaddywaddy

20 GREATEST HITS
CD ________ JHD 017
Tring / Jun '92 / Tring

HITS COLLECTION BOX (3CD Set)
CD Set ________ 10352
CMC / Jun '97 / BMG

HITS COLLECTION VOL.1
CD ________ 10052
CMC / Jun '97 / BMG

JUMP, BOOGIE AND JIVE
Hang up my rock 'n' roll boots / Red hot / Another sad and lonely night / Pretty little angel eyes / I'm walkin' / Tutti frutti
CD ________ PCOM 1112
President / Jul '91 / Grapevine/PolyGram / President / Target/BMG

VERY BEST OF SHOWADDYWADDY, THE
Hey rock 'n' roll / Rock 'n' roll lady / Sweet music / Three steps to Heaven / Heartbeat / Under the moon of love / When / You got what it takes / Dancin' party / I wonder why / Little bit of soap / Pretty little angel eyes / Remember then / Sweet little rock 'n' roller / Why do lovers break each others hearts / Blue moon
CD ________ SUMCD 4003
Summit / Nov '96 / Sound & Media

Showmen

SOME FOLKS DON'T UNDERSTAND IT
It will stand / Country fool / This misery / Wrong girl / Fate planned it this way / For you my darling / Valley of love / Owl sees you / Swish fish / I'm coming home / Strange girl / I love you, can't you see / Let her feel it in your kiss / True fine mama / 39-21-40 shape
CD ________ CDCHARLY 226
Charly / Jul '90 / Koch

Shozo

SOUNDS OF BREATH
CD ________ SYN 7
Knock On Wood / Apr '97 / Discovery

Shreeve, Mark

ASSASSIN
Assassin / Angel of fire / Tyrant / System six
CD ________ CENCD 005
Centaur / Jun '94 / Pinnacle

CRASH HEAD
Crash head / Darkness comes / Edge of darkness / Dead zone / Shrine / Angels of death / It / Night church / Hellraiser
CD CENCD 007
Centaur / Sep '94 / Pinnacle

LEGION
Legion / Storm column / Flags / Sybex factor / Domain 7 / Con / Stand
CD CENCD 006
Centaur / Sep '94 / Pinnacle

RED SHIFT
Red shift / Spin / Shine / Blue shift
CD CLPCD 002
Champagne Lake / Apr '97 / Pinnacle

Shri

DRUM THE BASS
CD CASTE 4CD
OutCaste / May '97 / 3mv/Sony

Shriekback

NATURAL HISTORY (The History Of Shriekback)
CD Set ESDCD 217
Essential / Sep '94 / BMG

PRIESTS AND KANIBALS (The Best Of Shriekback)
Nemesis (7") / Hammerheads / All lined up / My spine is a base line / Hand on my heart / Achtung / Mercy dash (7") / Suxck / Health and knowledge and wealth and power / Nerve / Only thing that shines / Coelacanth / Nemesis (Arch deviant) / Cloud of nails (Pimp up a storm) / Mercy dash (12" Extended version) / Fish below the ice
CD 74321226362
RCA / Sep '94 / BMG

SACRED CITY
CD SHRIEK 1CD
World Domination / Feb '94 / Pinnacle / RTM/Disc

Shrieve, Michael

FASCINATION
CD CD 67
CMP / May '95 / Cargo / Grapevine/ PolyGram / Vital/SAM

TWO DOORS
CD CMPCD 074
CMP / Jan '96 / Cargo / Grapevine/ PolyGram / Vital/SAM

Shrimp Boat

CAVALE
Pumpkin lover / Duende suite / Line song / Blue green song / What do you think of love / Swinging shell / Creme brulee / I'll name it Sue / Free love overdrive / Dollar bill / Apples / Smooth ass / Small wonder / Oranges / Henny penny
CD R 3002
Rough Trade / Jul '93 / Pinnacle

Shrivastav, Baluji

CLASSICAL INDIAN RAGAS
CD EUCD 1101
ARC / '91 / ADA / ARC Music

CLASSICAL INDIAN SITAR AND SURBAHAR RAGAS
CD EUCD 1139
ARC / '91 / ADA / ARC Music

Shrubs

VESSELS OF THE HEART
CD DOM 2CD
Public Domain / Nov '88 / RTM/Disc

Shu, Shomyo Shingon

BUDDHIST RITUAL "LIVE"
CD LDX 274976
La Chant Du Monde / May '94 / ADA / Harmonia Mundi

Shu-De

KONGUREY
CD NTCD 6745
Newtone / Mar '96 / ADA

VOICES FROM THE DISTANT STEPPE
Sygyt khoomei kargyraa / Aian dudal (Songs of devotion and praise) / Beezhinden (Coming back from Beijing) / Buura / Durgen chugaa (Tongue twisters) / Throat singing and igil / Yraazhy kys (The singing girl) / Shyngyr-shyngyr / Baian-dudai / Khomus solo / Meen khemchim / Opei yry (A lullaby) / Tyva-uruankhai / Chasphy-khem (The river chashby) / Kadarchynying / Kham
CD CDRW 41
Realworld / Jan '94 / EMI

Shudder To Think

50,000 BC
Call of the playground / Red house / Beauty strike / Saddest day of my life / Man who rolls / All eyes are different / Kissesmack of past action / Resident wine / She's a skull / Survival / You're gonna look fine / Love / Hop on one foot

CD 4869382
Epic / May '97 / Sony

FUNERAL AT THE MOVIES
CD DIS 54CD
Dischord / '94 / SRD

GET YOUR GOAT
CD DIS 67CD
Dischord / '94 / SRD

LIVE
CD YCLS 020
Your Choice / Aug '94 / Plastic Head

PONY EXPRESS RECORD
CD ABB 65CD
Big Cat / Aug '95 / 3mv/Pinnacle

Shuffle Demons

BOP RAP
CD SP 1124CD
Stony Plain / Oct '93 / ADA / CM / Direct

STREETNIKS
CD SP 1128CD
Stony Plain / Oct '93 / ADA / CM / Direct

WHAT DO YOU WANT
CD SP 1152CD
Stony Plain / Oct '93 / ADA / CM / Direct

Shufflin' Joe

AFRICAN JAZZ PIONEERS
CD 669882
Melodie / Nov '96 / ADA / Discovery / Grapevine/PolyGram / Greensleeves / Jet Star

Shugg

SHUGG VS. COCKPIT (2CD Set) (Shugg & Cockpit)
CD Set BSR 202CD
Bittersweet / Nov '96 / Cargo

Shull, Tad

DEEP PASSION
CD CRISS 1047CD
Criss Cross / May '91 / Cadillac / Direct / Vital/SAM

Shut Up & Dance

BLACK MEN UNITED
CD PULSE 22CD
Pulse 8 / Oct '95 / BMG

DEATH IS NOT THE END
CD SUADCD 005
Shut Up & Dance / Jun '92 / SRD

Shutdown

EMITS A REAL BRONZE CHEER
CD CDHOLE 003
Golf / Mar '95 / Plastic Head

Shy FX

FORMULA, THE (Various Artists)
CD EBONCD 001
Ebony / Sep '96 / SRD

JUST AN EXAMPLE
CD SOURCDLP 4
SOUR / Oct '95 / SRD

Shyheim

LOST GENERATION, THE
Shit iz real / Dear God / Jiggy comin' / 5 elements / Shaolin style / Real bad boys / What makes the world go round / Can you feel it / Life as a shorty / Don't front/Let's chill / Things happen / See what I see / Still there / Young godz
CD CDVUS 109
Virgin / Jun '96 / EMI

Si (Cut) Dub

BEHIND YOU
CD SOHSP 025
Sprawl / Mar '97 / SRD

Siam

LANGUAGE OF MENACE, THE
CD NTHEN 11
Now & Then / Sep '95 / Plastic Head

PRAYER
CD A2Z 85009CD
A-Z / Jul '96 / Plastic Head

Sibbles, Leroy

IT'S NOT OVER
CD VPCD 1452
VP / Dec '95 / Greensleeves / Jet Star / Total/BMG

Sibeba

HIJAS DEL SOL
Sibeba / People from here / Foreigners / Agreement between two sisters / Fertility rite / Moon / Daughters of the sun / Turn around / Aids / Traditional ways / Ship of man / Crow of the rooster / In the lap / Birds are sleeping / Tirso de molina

CD INT 31782
Intuition / Aug '96 / New Note/Pinnacle

Siberil, Soig

DIGOR
CD GWP 005CD
Gwerz / Aug '93 / ADA / Discovery

ENTRE ARDOISE ET GRANIT
CD GWP 013CD
Gwerz / Sep '96 / ADA / Discovery

Siberry, Jane

SUMMER IN THE YUKON
Life is the red wagon / Miss Punta Blanca / Calling all angels / Above the treeline / In the blue light / Seven steps to the wall / Mimi on the beach / Walking / Very large hat / Lobby / Red high heels / Map of the world / Taxi ride
CD 7599269362
Atlantic / Apr '92 / Warner Music

TEENAGER
CD SHEEB 1
Sheeba / Feb '97 / Pinnacle

WHEN I WAS A BOY
Temple / Calling all angels / Love is everything / Sail across the water / All the candles in the world / Sweet incarnadine / Gospel according to darkness / Angel stepped down / Vigil / At the beginning of time / Love is everything (version)
CD 7599268242
Atlantic / Jul '93 / Warner Music

Sick Of It All

LIVE IN A WORLD FULL OF HATE
CD LF 073CD
Lost & Found / Dec '93 / Plastic Head

REVELATION RECORDINGS 1987-89, THE
CD LF 083CD
Lost & Found / May '94 / Plastic Head

SCRATCH THE SURFACE
No cure / Insurrection / Consume / Goatless / Maladjusted / Free spirit / Desperate fool / Force my hand / Cease fire / Farm team / Return to reality / Scratch the surface / Step down / Who sets the rules
CD 7567924222
WEA / Nov '94 / Warner Music

SPREADING THE HARDCORE REALITY
CD LF 084MCD
Lost & Found / May '94 / Plastic Head

Sick On The Bus

SICK ON THE BUS
CD BUSCD 001
Bus Pop / Mar '96 / Plastic Head

Sickler, Don

MUSIC OF KENNY DORHAM (Sickler, Don/Jimmy Heath/Cedar Walton)
CD RSRCD 111
Reservoir Music / Nov '94 / Cadillac

Sicko

YOU CAN FEEL THE LOVE
CD EFA 123582
Empty / Mar '94 / Cargo / Greyhound / Plastic Head / SRD

Side By Side

YOU'RE ONLY YOUNG ONCE
CD LF 040CD
Lost & Found / Sep '95 / Plastic Head

Sidebottom, Frank

FRANK SIDEBOTTOM'S ABC AND D
Born in Timperley / Anarchy in Timperley / Timperley sunset / Wild thing in Timperley / Next train to Timperley / Oh Timperley / Surfin' Timperley / Xmas is really fantastic / O come all ye faithful (adeste fidelis) / I wish it could be xmas everyday / Xmas medley / Twist 'n' shout / Benefit of Mr. Kyte / Flying / It was nearly 20 years ago today / Mull of Timperley / Guess who's been on match of the day / Robbins aren't bobbins / Puff 'n' blow / Estudiantes (striped shirts/black panties) / Radio ga ga / Save me / We will rock you / Frank Gordon / I am the champion / Everybody loves Queen / I should be so lucky / Love poem for Kylie / Bohemian rapsody / Bros medley / What for from my mum / Firm favourite ads / Elvis medley / Hit the north / Electricity / Hey you riot policeman / Blackpool fool / Indie medley / Mr. Custard / Zoo scrapbook / Hey you street artist / Monopoly song
CD CDMRED 143
Cherry Red / Apr '97 / Pinnacle

Sideral

MIL PARSECS
CD PODUKCD 023
Pod England / Jan '96 / Plastic Head

Sideshow

SIDESHOW
CD FLY 011CD
Flydaddy/Blue Rose / Jun '96 / 3mv/Vital

Sidewinder

COLONIZED
Vodun conspiracy / Scarification dub / Total destruction of mind and body / Return to BC / Homosapien meets the microbe / Ballistic loop / Zero gravity / Ten ton ghetto blaster / Big bang theory / Photic driver / Infrasonic version / Psycho-acoustic dub / Cryonic suspension / Silicon based predator / Forbidden zone / Destination DNA / Drummer as mechanism / Concrete jungle probe / Enter the beast / White viper sound system / Termite colony / Omega bug
CD EFA 006782
Mille Plateau / Oct '96 / SRD
CD AMBT 17
Virgin / Sep '96 / EMI

Sidi Bou Said

BROOOCH
CD TOPPCD 005
Ultimate / Jul '94 / Pinnacle

OBSESSIVE
Obsessive / Like you / Stoppe / Funny body / Zazie / Mionotaur / Harold and Maude / 20,000 Horses / Seams undone / Rat king / Bella / Bridge song
CD TOPPCD 053
Ultimate / Apr '97 / Pinnacle

Sidibe, Sali

FROM TIBUKTU TO GAO
CD SHAN 65011CD
Shanachie / Oct '93 / ADA / Greensleeves / Koch

Sidney, Anthony

ANTHOLOGY
St. Patrick's Day / Snail stepper / Prologo / My classic soul / Changing shadow / April / Line of women in white / Wonder world / Peru / Little David
CD CONTECD 149
Contempo / Oct '90 / Plastic Head

Sidran, Ben

COOL PARADISE
She steps into a dream / Searching for a girl like you / If someone has to wreck your life / Lip service / Language of the blues / Cool paradise / Desire of love / Bye bye blackbird / Walking with the blues / So long
CD GOJ 60012
Go Jazz / Sep '95 / Vital/SAM

ENIVRE D'AMOUR
Shine a light on me / Enivre d'amour / Everything happens to me / Freedom jazz dance / On the sunny side of the street / Critics / Pepper / Too hot too touch / Longing for Bahia / I wanna be a bebopper
CD GOJ 60102
Go Jazz / Sep '95 / Vital/SAM

GOOD TRAVEL AGENT, A
Doctor's blues / Broad daylight / Piano players / Turn to the music / Good travel agent / There they go / Lover man / Mitsubishi boy / On the cool side / Space cowboy / Last dance
CD GOJ 60082
Go Jazz / Sep '95 / Vital/SAM

HEAT WAVE
Mitsubishi boy / Lover man / Lover man / Brown eyes / On the cool side / Old Hoagy / Heatwave / Take it easy greasy / Up a lazy river / That's what the note said / Lost in the stars
CD GOJ 60092
Go Jazz / Sep '95 / Vital/SAM

LIFE'S A LESSON
Eliyahu / Oseh shalom / Life's a lesson / Ani ma'amin / Avinu Malchenu / Tree of life / B'rosh hashana / Eli Eli / Shofar shogood / Y'did nefesh / Kol Nidre / Hashiveni / Hatikvah / Face your fears / Hine ma tov
CD GOJ 60132
Go Jazz / Sep '95 / Vital/SAM

MR. P'S SHUFFLE
CD GOJ 60192
Go Jazz / Jun '96 / Vital/SAM

Sie

RUBAN D'ALPHA
CD PUSSYCD 004
Pussy Foot / Nov '96 / RTM/Disc

Siebel, Paul

PAUL SIEBEL
CD CDPH 1161
Philo / Nov '95 / ADA / CM / Direct

Siebert, Budi

PYRAMID CALL
Life power / Sunrise / Feather of thruth / Third eye / Sphinx / Flight of the falcon / Voice of the heart / Cosmic soul / Golden kobra / Sunset / Illuminated pyramid / Ankh

of the earth / Life dream / Horus / Remember all
CD _______ CD 256
Narada / Jun '95 / ADA / New Note/ Pinnacle

WILD EARTH
Wild earth / Dancing with the bear / Beauty within / Black rain - Grey snow / Winds from the south / Silent earth / Phoenix rises / Round my way / On your shores / Gentle earth
CD _______ ND 63031
Narada / Mar '95 / ADA / New Note/ Pinnacle

Siegal Schwall

SIEGAL SCHWALL REUNION CONCERT, THE
You don't love me like that / Devil / Leaving / Hey, Billie Jean / I wanna love ya / I think it was the wine / I don't want you to be my girl / When I've been drinking / Hush hush
CD _______ ALCD 4760
Alligator / May '93 / ADA / CM / Direct

Siegel, Corky

CHAMBER BLUES
CD _______ ALCD 4824
Alligator / Nov '94 / ADA / CM / Direct

Siegel, Janis

SLOW HOT WIND
CD _______ VSD 5552
Varese Sarabande / May '95 / Pinnacle

Siegel, Julian

PARTISANS (Siegel, Julian & Phil Robson Quartet)
Partisans / Sudden shower / Like someone in love / Wigsworld / Wish shoes / Z car / Snarf / Bad peace / Time before / Leave it
CD _______ EFZ 1021
EFZ / Jun '97 / Vital/SAM

Sieger, Lucinda

I BELIEVE
CD _______ TIRCD 002
Totem / Mar '96 / Grapevine/PolyGram / THE

Sielwolf

V
CD _______ KK 124CD
KK / Apr '97 / Plastic Head

Sierra, Fredy

VALLENATO (Sierra, Fredy & Eglio Vega)
CD _______ TUMICD 041
Tumi / Jun '93 / Discovery / Stern's

Sierra Maestra

DUNDUNBANZA
Juana pena / Dundubanza / No me llores / Bururu barara / Change ta veni / Mi guajira son / Cangrejo fue a estudiar / Kila qique y chocolate / El gago / El reloj de pastora
CD _______ WCD 041
World Circuit / Oct '94 / ADA / Cadillac / Direct / New Note/Pinnacle

Sierra, Ruben

IMAGEN VIVA
Cuando la recuerdo / Eres mia / Imagen viva / Voy a dejarte lina cancion / Lo mismo que ayer / Esta es tru cama / Demliestame / Mi fanatica mayor / Eso eres tu
CD _______ 66058056
RMM / Feb '95 / New Note/Pinnacle

Siffre, Labi

IT MUST BE LOVE
CD _______ MCCD 141
Music Club / Nov '93 / Disc / THE

MAKE MY DAY
Make my day / Watch me / For the children / Prayer / Nothing in the world like love / Some say / Just a little more line / Words / Maybe tomorrow / I love you / Maybe / Talk about / Too late / My song / It must be love / Crying, laughing, loving, lying / If you have faith / Fool me a good night / Give love / Something on my mind / I don't know what's happened to... / Bless the telephone / Who do you see / Cannock Chase
CD _______ VSOPCD 137
Connoisseur Collection / Jul '89 / Pinnacle

MAN OF REASON
CD _______ WOLCD 1015
China / May '91 / Pinnacle

Sigh

GHASTLY FUNERAL THEATRE
Soushiki / Shingontachikawa / Doman seman / Imiuta / Shikigami / Higeki
CD _______ NIHIL 17CD
Cacophonous / Feb '97 / Plastic Head / RTM/Disc

INFIDEL ART
Izuna / Zombie terror / Desolation / Last elegy / Suicidogenic / Beyond centuries
CD _______ NIHIL 7CD
Cacophonous / Jun '97 / Plastic Head / RTM/Disc

SCORN DEFEAT
CD _______ ANTIMOSH 007CD
Deathlike Silence / Apr '94 / Plastic Head

Siglo XX

FEAR AND DESIRE
Fear and desire / Everything is on fire / Lost in violence / Sorrow and pain / Thirty five poems / On the third day / My sister called silence / Pain came
CD _______ CDBIAS 087
Play It Again Sam / '88 / Discovery / Plastic Head / Vital

FLOWERS FOR THE REBELS
Sister in the rain / Fear / No one is innocent / Afraid to tell / Sister suicide / Till the act is done / Shadows / Flesh and blood / Ride
CD _______ CDBIAS 051
Play It Again Sam / '88 / Discovery / Plastic Head / Vital

UNDER A PURPLE SKY
CD _______ CDBIAS 145
Play It Again Sam / Jan '90 / Discovery / Plastic Head / Vital

Signs Of Trouble

SIGNS OF TROUBLE
Shameless / Good love / Rainmaker / Till now / Take my hand / Signs of trouble / She's mine / Smiling / God knows / Harmony / Hour of need
CD _______ SOT 1997
Signs Of Trouble / Jun '97 / Else

Signs Ov Chaos

FRANKENSCIENCE
Thee devil's tongue / Kode ov thee future / Honey / Believe / Phunky dogg / Body suction / Pheel tha pulse / Praise / Comin' t'get ya / Discipline through fear / Phunky punctuation / Science ov love / Rhythm ov love / P-Phaze
CD _______ MOSH 162CD
Earache / Sep '96 / Vital

Sigue Sigue Sputnik

FIRST GENERATION 2ND EDITION, THE
CD _______ FREUDCD 55
Jungle / Jun '96 / RTM/Disc / SRD

FIRST GENERATION, THE
Rockit miss USA / Sex bomb boogie / 21st century boy / Teenage thunder / She's my man / Love missile F1-11 / Jayne Mansfield / Ultra violence / Krush groove girls / Rock-a-jet baby / Rebel rebel
CD _______ FREUDCD 35
Jungle / Dec '90 / RTM/Disc / SRD

Silberstein, Moshe

SHALOM ISRAEL
CD _______ CNCD 5953
Disky / Jul '93 / Disky / THE

Sileas

BEATING HARPS
Pipers / Silver whistle / Oh wee white rose of Scotland / Solos / Puirt a buel / Shore of Gruinard / Ca' The Yowes / Dogs / Beating harps
CD _______ GLCD 1089
Green Linnet / Oct '93 / ADA / CM / Direct / Highlander / Roots

PLAY ON LIGHT
Buain a'choirce / May Colvin / Cumba easbuig earraghaidbeal / Laill leatbag / Cameron MacFayden/Dr. Cameron's casebook / Miss Kirsten Lindsay Morrison / Mo dhombnullan fhein / Planxty crockery / Domhnall dubh / Pi li li liu / Dr. Florence Campbell of Jammalamadugu / Duncan Johnstone / Castlebay scrap/Stuarts rant / Ain't no sunshine/Flawless juggler / Miss Ann Cameron of Balvenie / Amy's rollerskates/Paddy's leather britches / Sior chaineadh
CD _______ CDTRAX 118
Greentrax / Oct '96 / ADA / Direct / Duncans / Highlander

Silencers

BLOOD AND RAIN (The Singles 1986-1996)
CD _______ SILENCD 1
JLP / Sep '96 / Total/BMG

BLUES FOR BUDDHA
Answer me / Scottish rain / Real McCoy / Blues for Buddha / Walk with the night / Razor blades of love / Skin games / Wayfaring stranger / Sacred child / Sand and stars / My love is like a wave
CD _______ PD 71859
RCA / Nov '88 / BMG

SECONDS OF PLEASURE
I can feel it / Cellar of dreams / Small mercy / It's only love / Misunderstood / Life can be fatal / Unhappiest man / Walkmans and magnums / Street walker song / My prayer / Unconcious
CD _______ 74321141132
RCA / May '93 / BMG

SILENCERS
CD _______ NER 3011
Total Energy / Jul '97 / Cargo / Greyhound

Silent Death

STONE COLD
CD _______ MASSCD 044
Massacre / Jan '95 / Plastic Head

Silent Partners

IF IT'S ALL RIGHT, IT'S ALL RIGHT
CD _______ ANTCD 0010
Antones / Jan '93 / ADA / Hot Shot

Silent Phase

THEORY OF SILENT PHASE, THE
Waterdance / Body rock / Air puzzle / Meditive fusion / Earth (interlude) / Spirit of sankofa / Spirit journey / Fire (prelude) / Psychotic funk / Electric relaxation / Love comes & goes / Forbidden dance
CD _______ TMT 001CD
R&S / Nov '95 / Vital

Silent Poets

FIRM ROOTS
CD _______ 992158CD
Ninetynine / Nov '96 / Timewarp

POTENTIAL MEETING
CD _______ 99 2123
Ninetynine / Jul '96 / Timewarp

Silk

LOSE CONTROL
Interlude / Happy days / Don't keep me waiting / Girl U for me / Freak me / When I think about you / Baby it's you / Lose control / It had to be you / I gave to you
CD _______ 7559613942
Keia/Elektra / Mar '93 / Warner Music

SILK
Hooked on you / Because of your love / It's so good / Don't rush / I can go deep / What kind of love is this / Don't go to bed mad / Don't cry for me / Now that I've lost you / How could you say you love me / Remember me
CD _______ 7559618492
Keia/Elektra / Nov '95 / Warner Music

Silk Saw

COME FREELY, GO SAFELY
CD _______ SR 107CD
Sub Rosa / May '96 / Direct / RTM/Disc / SRD / Vital

DYSTOPIA
CD _______ SR 116
Sub Rosa / Jul '97 / Direct / RTM/Disc / SRD / Vital

Silkscreen

RELIEF
Intro / Left right / Emotions / Don't / Mornings of today / They call / Oblivion / Fight me / Helping hands / Indifferently / Sore / No more / Bad love / Valium / Stay
CD _______ DEDCD 027
Dedicated / Apr '97 / BMG / Vital

Silkworm

DEVELOPER
Give me some skin / Never met a man I didn't like / City glows / Developer / Devil is beating his wife / Ice station zebra / Waiting on a train / Song with one part / Goodnight Mr. Maugham / It's too bad
CD _______ OLE 2202
Matador / Apr '97 / Vital

FIREWATER
Nerves / Drink / Wet firecracker / Slow hands / Cannibal, cannibal / Tarnished angel / Quicksand / Ticket tulane / Don't make plans this Friday / Caricature of a joke / Killing my ass / River / Miracle mile / Lure of beauty / Severence pay / Swings
CD _______ OLE 1582
Matador / Feb '96 / Vital

Sill, Gary

SATIE - THREE GYMNOPEDIES
CD _______ INVCD 090
Invincible / Aug '96 / Else

Silly Sisters

NO MORE TO THE DANCE
Blood and gold / Cake and ale / Fine horseman / How shall I / Hedger and ditcher / Agincourt Carol / Barring of the door / What'll we do / Almost every circumstance / Old miner
CD _______ TSCD 450
Topic / Aug '88 / ADA / CM / Direct

SILLY SISTERS
Burnin' o'Auchidoon / Lass of roch royal / Seven joys of Mary / My husband's got no courage in him / Singing the travels / Silver whistle / Grey funnel line / Geordie / Seven wonders / Four loom weaver / Game of cards / Dame Durden
CD _______ BGOCD 214
Beat Goes On / Jan '94 / Pinnacle

Silly Wizard

GLINT OF SILVER, A
CD _______ GLCD 1070
Green Linnet / Mar '87 / ADA / CM / Direct / Highlander / Roots

KISS THE TEARS AWAY
Queen of Argyl / Golden golden / Finlay M Macrae / Banks of the Lee / Sweet Dublin Bay / Mo nighean donn / Gradh mo chroidhe / Banks of the Bann / Greenfields of Glentown / Galtee reel / Bobby Casey's number two / Wing commander Donald MacKenzie's reel / Loch Tay boat song
CD _______ SHANCD 79037
Shanachie / Apr '88 / ADA / Greensleeves / Koch

LIVE AT CENTER STAGE
CD _______ GLV 1
Green Linnet / Mar '95 / ADA / CM / Direct / Highlander / Roots

LIVE WIZZARDRY
CD _______ GLCD 3036/37
Green Linnet / Oct '93 / ADA / CM / Direct / Highlander / Roots

Silos

ASK THE DUST
CD _______ NORMAL 166
Normal / Jun '95 / ADA / Direct

DIABLO
CD _______ NORMAL 163
Normal / May '94 / ADA / Direct

HASTA LA VICTORIA
CD _______ NORMAL 143
Normal / May '94 / ADA / Direct

Silva, Alan

ALAN SILVA
CD _______ ESP 10912
ESP / Jan '93 / Jazz Music

MY COUNTRY (Silva, Alan & Celestrial Communication Orchestra)
CD _______ CDLR 302
Leo / Apr '89 / Cadillac / Impetus / Wellard

Silva, Chelo

LA REINA TEJANA DEL BOLERO
CD _______ ARHCD 423
Arhoolie / Jan '96 / ADA / Cadillac / Direct

Silva, Maynard

HOWL AT THE MOON (Silva, Maynard & The New Hawks)
CD _______ WCD 12088
Wolf / Apr '97 / Hot Shot / Jazz Music / Swift

Silvadier, Pierre-Michel

D'AMOUR FOU D'AMOUR
CD _______ A XVI
Seventh / Dec '95 / Cadillac / Harmonia Mundi / ReR Megacorp

Silveira, Ricardo

STORYTELLER
Francesca / Upon a time / Storyteller / Island magic / Still think of you / Puzzle / Fountains / After the rain / Always there / That day in Tahiti
CD _______ KOKO 1307
Kokopelli / Nov '95 / New Note/Pinnacle

Silver Apples

ELECTRONIC EVOCATIONS (A Tribute To The Silver Apples) (Various Artists)
CD _______ RAPTCD 002
Enraptured / May '97 / Cargo

Silver Birch

SILVER BIRCH
CD _______ DORIS 3
Vinyl Tap / Jan '96 / Cargo / Greyhound / Vinyl Tap

Silver Convention

GREATEST HITS
Get up and boogie / Save me / Everybody's talking 'bout love / Fly Robin fly / Tiger baby / No no Joe / Play me like a yo yo / Thank you Mr. DJ / Love in a sleeper / San Francisco hustle / Telegram / Get it up / I like it / Blame it on the music / You've got what it takes / Spend the night with me / Breakfast in bed
CD _______ 100462
CMC / May '97 / BMG

Silver, Horace

BAGHDAD BLUES, THE
CD _______ CD 53138

Giants Of Jazz / Jan '95 / Cadillac / Jazz Music / Target/BMG

BEST OF HORACE SILVER (Blue Note Years)
Opus de funk / Doodlin' / Room 608 / Preacher / Senor blues / Cool eyes / Home cooking / Soulville / Cookin' at the continental / Peace / Sister Sadie / Blowin' the blues away
CD _____ CDP 7911432
Blue Note / Dec '95 / EMI

FURTHER EXPLORATIONS
Outlaw / Melancholy mood / Pyramid / Moon rays / Safari / Ill wind
CD _____ CDP 8565832
Blue Note / Jun '97 / EMI

HARDBOP GRANDPOP, THE
I want you / Hippest cat in Hollywood / Gratitude / Hawkin' / Diggin' on Dexter / We've got silver at six / Hardbop Grandpop / Lady from Johannesburg / Serenade to a teakettle
CD _____ IMP 11922
Impulse Jazz / Jun '96 / New Note/BMG

HORACE SILVER 1952-1954
CD _____ CD 53131
Giants Of Jazz / Sep '94 / Cadillac / Jazz Music / Target/BMG

SENOR BLUES
CD _____ CD 53134
Giants Of Jazz / Nov '92 / Cadillac / Jazz Music / Target/BMG

SILVER'S BLUE
Silver's blue / To beat or not to beat / How long has this been going on / I'll know / Shoutin' out / Hank's tune / Night has a thousand eyes
CD _____ 4765212
Sony Jazz / Dec '95 / Sony

SIX PIECES OF SILVER
Cool eyes / Shirl / Camouflage / Enchantment / Senor blues / Senor blues (45 version) / Virgo / For heaven's sake / Tippin' / Senor blues (vocal version)
CD _____ CDP 7815392
Blue Note / Feb '97 / EMI

SONG FOR MY FATHER (Cantiga Para Meu Pai) (Silver, Horace Quintet)
Song for my father / Natives are restless tonight / Calcutta cutie / Que pasa / Kicker / Lonely woman / Sanctimonious Sam / Sighin' and cryin' / Silver threads among the soul
CD _____ CDP 7841852
Blue Note / Mar '95 / EMI

TOKYO BLUES
Too much Sake / Sayonara blues / Tokyo blues / Cherry blossom / Ah so
CD _____ CDP 8533552
Blue Note / Nov '96 / EMI

Silver Jews

NATURAL BRIDGE
CD _____ WIGCD 28
Domino / Oct '96 / Vital

STARLITE WALKER
CD _____ WIGCD 15
Domino / Oct '94 / Vital

Silver King Band

LIVE AT THE DIVE
CD _____ DZCD 009
Danger Zone / Apr '97 / Hot Shot

Silver Leaf Jazz Band

STREETS & SCENES OF NEW ORLEANS
CD _____ GTCD 15001
Good Time Jazz / May '95 / Complete/ Pinnacle

Silver Leaf Quartette Of ...

COMPLETE RECORDED WORKS (Silver Leaf Quartette Of Norfolk)
CD _____ DOCD 5352
Document / Jun '95 / ADA / Hot Shot / Jazz Music

Silver, Mike

DEDICATION
CD _____ SR 0194CD
Silversound / Apr '95 / ADA / Roots

ROADWORKS (Live)
Too many lies / Angel in deep shadow / Pretoria / Heatwave / Somebody's angel / Old fashioned Saturday night / Where would you rather be tonight / Let it be so / Not that easy / NASA / Down South / Circle of stones / Nothing to do with me / Sailors all / Certain something / Time for leaving / Mine for ever more
CD _____ SR 0190CD
Silversound / Aug '90 / ADA / Roots

Silver Sun

SILVER SUN
Test / Golden skin / Dumb / Julia / Far out / Last day / Service / Yellow light / Lava / 2 digits / This 'n' that / Wonderful / Bad haircut / Nobody / Animals feets
CD _____ 5372082
Polydor / May '97 / PolyGram

Silverchair

FREAKSHOW
Slave / Freak / Abuse me / Lie to me / No association / Cemetry / Pop song for us rejects / Door / Learn to hate / Petrol and chlorine / Roses / Nobody came
CD _____ 4871032
Columbia / Feb '97 / Sony

FROGSTOMP
Israel's son / Tomorrow / Faultline / Pure massacre / Shade / Blind / Leave me out / Suicidal dream / Madman / Undecided / Cicada / Findaway
CD _____ 4803402
Murmur / Sep '95 / Sony

Silverfish

FAT AXL
CD _____ WIJ 006CD
Wiiija / Jan '91 / RTM/Disc

ORGAN FAN
CD _____ CRECD 118
Creation / May '92 / 3mv/Vital

Silverhead

16 AND SAVAGED
CD _____ REP 4646WY
Repertoire / Jun '97 / Greyhound

Silverheel

7000 DAYS 9000 SUNSETS
CD _____ FOCUSCD 9
Focus / Oct '95 / Pinnacle

Silvers, Jim

MUSIC MAKIN' MAMA FROM MEMPHIS
Cannonball yodel / Paul's saloon / My, my, my / Each season changes you / Goodbye California (Hello Illinois) / You gotta let all the girls know you're a cowboy / I wanna see Las Vegas / Waltz across Texas / Model 2017 / Old faithfull / Music makin' mama from Memphis / Last to get the news / Julie / Cash on the barrelhead / For your own good / I ate the whole damn hog / Call me a cab / Blue night / Cryin' my heart out over you / Ain't it strange / Last to get the news / Music makin' mama from Memphis / Losin' you (might be the best thing yet) / Scrap of paper and a 20 cent pen / Ocean of dreams
CD _____ BCD 15555
Bear Family / Jan '92 / Direct / Rollercoaster / Swift

Silverstate

GONDWANA RAIN
CD _____ CDSGP 0318
Prestige / Mar '97 / Else / Total/BMG

Silvertones

SILVER BULLETS
I'll take you home / Early in the morning / Sugar sugar / Souvenir of Mexico / Rejoice Jah Jah children / Rejoicing skank / That's when it hurts / Soul sister / Rock me in your soul / Sweet and loving baby / He'll break your heart / Are you sure
CD _____ CDTRL 69
Trojan / Nov '96 / Direct / Jet Star

Silvester, Victor

BALLROOM DANCING WITH THE VICTOR SILVESTER ORCHESTRA (Silvester, Victor & His Ballroom Orchestra)
CD _____ PLSCD 223
Pulse / Jul '97 / BMG

COME DANCE WITH ME - 20 BALLROOM FAVOURITES (Silvester, Victor & His Ballroom Orchestra)
I can dream, can't I / Come dance with me / C'est si bon / Always true to you in my fashion / Waltz of my heart / Autumn leaves / I wonder where my baby is tonight / C'est magnifique / Unforgettable / Tea for two / Whisper while you waltz / By candle light / Lady is a tramp / 'S Wonderful / Till there was you / Moonlight serenade / Charleston / Mr. Sandman / April in Paris / It happened in Monterey
CD _____ CC 8233
Music For Pleasure / Jan '94 / EMI

COME DANCING VOL.1
CD _____ MU 3007
Musketeer / Oct '92 / Disc

COME DANCING VOL.2
CD _____ MU 3008
Musketeer / Oct '92 / Disc

IN A DANCING MOOD (Silvester, Victor & His Ballroom Orchestra)
CD _____ MATCD 283
Castle / Sep '93 / BMG

LET'S DANCE (2CD Set) (Silvester, Victor & His Ballroom Orchestra)
On your toes / My blue heaven / Very thought of you / If I had you / It happened in Monterey / One night of love / I once had a heart Margarita / You know it all smarty / Kiss the boys goodbye / June in January / September song / Roses of Picardy / Ramona / Could be / Gotta be this or that / Apple for the teacher / Time on my hands / Stella by starlight / Love is my reason / Love everlasting / Nice work if you can get it / Moonlight and roses / You couldn't be cuter / Deep purple / Once in a while / Luna rossa / Goody goody / Zing went the strings of my heart
CD Set _____ CDDL 1197
EMI / Nov '92 / EMI

STRICT TEMPO DANCING (4CD Set) (Silvester, Victor & His Ballroom Orchestra)
CD Set _____ MBSCD 405
Castle / Nov '93 / BMG

STRICTLY BALLROOM (Silvester, Victor & His Ballroom Orchestra)
Too close for comfort / Lady's in love with you / Call me irresponsible / You're my everything / Amore baciami / I give my heart / Belle of the ball / Gotta be this or that / Old devil moon / My foolish heart / It can't be wrong / Foggy day / Boy next door / Around the world / At the jazz band ball / Cerveza / One / Al di la / Copacabana / La cumparsita / I'll go where your music takes me / You were never lovelier / One I love (Belongs to somebody else)
CD _____ TRTCD 150
TrueTrax / Dec '94 / THE

STRICTLY BALLROOM
CD _____ MACCD 143
Autograph / Aug '96 / BMG

TRULY GREAT DANCE MELODIES (Silvester, Victor & His Ballroom Orchestra)
CD _____ DCD 5365
Disky / Apr '94 / Disky / THE

Silvestri, Alan

SHATTERED
CD _____ 262208
Milan / Nov '91 / Conifer/BMG / Silva Screen

Simbi

KREOL
CD _____ IG 059
Imogena / Aug '96 / ADA / Cadillac

VODOU BEAT
CD _____ XENO 4038
Xenophile / Dec '95 / ADA / Direct

Simeon, Omer

OMER SIMEON 1926-29
CD _____ 157752
Hot 'n' Sweet / Jul '93 / Discovery

Simien, Terrance

THERE'S ROOM FOR US ALL
CD _____ BT 1096CD
Black Top / Jan '94 / ADA / CM / Direct

ZYDECO ON THE BAYOU
Zydeco on the bayou / Back in my baby's arms / Stop the train / Zydeco zambada / Don't cry no more / I'll do it all over again / Intro / Ta casse mon coeur / Love we shared / I'll say so long / Will the circle be unbroken / Moi su pas tracasser
CD _____ FIENDCD 715
Demon / Apr '92 / Pinnacle

SIMM

WELCOME
CD _____ DOSSCD 002
Possible / Mar '97 / Plastic Head

Simmons, 'Little' Mac

COME BACK TO ME BABY
CD _____ WCD 120884
Wolf / Nov '96 / Hot Shot / Jazz Music / Swift

Simmons, Patrick

ARCADE
Out on the streets / So wrong / Don't make me do it / Why you givin' up / Too long / Knocking at your door / If you want a little love / Have you seen her / Sue sad / Dream about me
CD _____ 7559602552
Elektra / Jan '97 / Warner Music

Simms, Ginny

GINNY SIMMS MEMORIAL ALBUM, THE
CD _____ VN 150
Viper's Nest / Nov '94 / ADA / Cadillac / Direct / Jazz Music

Simon & Garfunkel

BEST OF SIMON & GARFUNKEL, THE (RTE Concert Orchestra)
CD _____ 8990052
Naxos / Oct '95 / Select

BOOKENDS
Bookends / Save the life of my child / America / Overs / Voice of old people / Old friends / Fakin' it / Punky's dilemma / Hazy shade of winter / At the zoo / Mrs. Robinson
CD _____ CD 63101
CBS / Dec '85 / Sony

BRIDGE OVER TROUBLED WATER
Bridge over troubled water / El condor pasa / Cecilia / Keep the customer satisfied / So long, Frank Lloyd Wright / Boxer / Baby driver / Only living boy in New York / Why don't you write me / Bye bye love / Song for the asking
CD _____ 4624882
Columbia / Sep '93 / Sony
CD _____ 4804182
Mastersound / Jul '95 / Sony

BRIDGE OVER TROUBLED WATER/ SOUNDS OF SILENCE/THE GRADUATE (3CD Set)
Bridge over troubled water / El condor pasa / Cecilia / Keep the customer satisfied / So long, Frank Lloyd Wright / Boxer / Baby driver / Only living boy in New York / Why don't you write me / Bye bye love / Song for the asking / Sound of silence / Leaves that are green / Blessed / Kathy's song / Somewhere they can't find me / Anji / Homeward bound / Most peculiar man / April come she will / We've got a groovy thing goin' / I am a rock / Richard Cory / Sound of silence / Singleman party foxtrot / Mrs. Robinson / Sunporch cha-cha-cha / Scarborough fair/Canticle / On the strip / April come she will / Folks / Scarborough fair/Canticle / Great effect / Bright green pleasure machine / Whew / Mrs. Robinson / Sound of silence
CD Set _____ 4853242
Columbia / Oct '96 / Sony

DEFINITIVE SIMON AND GARFUNKEL, THE
Wednesday morning 3am / Sound of silence / Homeward bound / Kathy's song / I am a rock / For Emily, wherever I may find her / Scarborough Fair/Canticle / 59th Street Bridge song / Seven o'clock news/ Silent night / Hazy shade of winter / El condor pasa (If I could) / Mrs. Robinson / America / At the zoo / Old friends / Bookends theme / Cecilia / Boxer / Bridge over troubled water / Song for the asking
CD _____ MOODCD 21
Columbia / Nov '91 / Sony

GRADUATE, THE (Original Soundtrack)
Sound of silence / Singleman party foxtrot / Mrs. Robinson / Sunporch cha-cha-cha / Scarborough Fair/Canticle / On the strip / April come she will / Folks / Scarborough Fair/Canticle / Great effect / Big bright green pleasure machine / Whew
CD _____ CD 32359
Columbia / Feb '94 / Sony

GREATEST HITS
Mrs. Robinson / For Emily, wherever I may find her / Boxer / 59th Street Bridge song / Sound of silence / I am a rock / Scarborough Fair / Canticle / Homeward bound / Bridge over troubled water / America / Kathy's song / If I could / Bookends / Cecilia
CD _____ CD 69003
CBS / Mar '87 / Sony

PARSLEY, SAGE, ROSEMARY AND THYME
Scarborough Fair / Patterns / Cloudy / Big bright green pleasure machine / 59th Street Bridge song / Dangling conversation / Flowers never bend with the rainfall / Simple desultory philippic / For Emily, wherever I may find her / Poem on the underground wall / Seven o'clock news / Silent night
CD _____ CD 32031
CBS / Apr '89 / Sony

SIMON & GARFUNKEL COLLECTION, THE
I am a rock / Homeward bound / America / 59th Street Bridge song / Wednesday morning 3am / El condor pasa / At the zoo / Scarborough Fair / Boxer / Sound of silence / Mrs. Robinson / Keep the customer satisfied / Song for the asking / Hazy shade of Winter / Cecilia / Old friends / Bookends / Bridge over troubled water
CD _____ CD 24005
CBS / Apr '88 / Sony

SOUND OF SILENCE
Sound of silence / Leaves that are green / Blessed / Somewhere they can't find me / Kathy's song / Homeward bound / Most peculiar man / I am a rock / Richard Cory / April come she will
CD _____ CD 62690
CBS / Dec '85 / Sony

WEDNESDAY MORNING 3AM
You can tell the world / Last night I had the strangest dream / Bleecker Street / Sparrow / Benedictus / Sound of silence / He was my brother / Peggy O / Go tell it on the mountain / Sun is burning / Times they are a changin' / Wednesday morning 3 AM
CD _____ 4633752
Columbia / Feb '96 / Sony

Simon & The Bar Sinisters

LOOK AT ME I'M COOL
CD _____ CD 023
Upstart / Aug '95 / ADA / Direct

Simon, Arletty Michel

LA COMPILATION
CD ____ UCD 19087
Forlane / Jun '95 / Target/BMG

Simon, Carly

BEST OF CARLY SIMON, THE
That's the way I've always heard / Right thing to do / Mockingbird / Legend in your own time / Haven't got time for the pain / You're so vain / No secrets / Night owl / Anticipation / Attitude dancing
CD ____ 9548304602
WEA / May '91 / Warner Music

CLOUDS IN MY COFFEE (3CD Set)
Let the river run / You belong to me / Nobody does it better / Coming around again / Jesse / Stuff that dreams are made of / You're so vain / Touched by the sun / Haven't got time for the pain / Better not tell her / Legend in your own time / Mockingbird / That's the way I've always heard it should be / All I want is you / Right thing to do / Like a river / Anticipation / Give me all night / Angel from Montgomery / Raining / I'm all it takes to make you happy / Easy on the eyes / Turn of the tide / Libby / Have you seen me lately / My new boyfriend / Voulez-vous danser / Night before Christmas / Halfway 'round the world / Life is eternal / We have no secrets / Why / Take me out to the ballgame / Back the way / Itsy bitsy spider / Play with me / My luv is like a red, red rose / It happens every day / Boys in the trees / Julie through the glass / Orpheus / Never been gone / Happy birthday / Devoted to you / Davy / Do the walls come down / Danny boy / Dink's blues / We're so close / Someone waits for you / Born to break my heart / Time after time / What shall we do with the child / I've got a crush on you / Something wonderful / You're the love of my life / I get along without you very well / By myself / I see your face before me
CD Set ____ 07822187982
Arista / Mar '96 / BMG

COMING AROUND AGAIN
Itsy bitsy spider / If it wasn't love / Coming around again / Give me all night / As time goes by / Do the walls come down / It should have been me / Stuff that dreams are made of / Two hot girls / You have to hurt / All I want is you / Hold what you've got
CD ____ 261038
Arista / Nov '90 / BMG

GREATEST HITS LIVE
You're so vain / Nobody does it better / Coming around again / It happens every day / Anticipation / Right thing to do / Do the walls come down / You belong to me / Two hot girls / All i want is you / Never been gone
CD ____ 259196
Arista / Aug '95 / BMG

LETTERS NEVER SENT
Intro / Letter never sent / Lost in your love / Like a river / Time works on all the wild young men / Touched by the sun / Davy / Halfway 'round the world / What about a holiday / Reason / Private / Catch it like a fever / Born to break my heart / I'd rather it was you
CD ____ 07822187522
Arista / Nov '94 / BMG

MY ROMANCE
My romance / By myself / I see your face / When your lover is gone / In the wee small hours of the morning / My funny valentine / Something wonderful / Little girl blue / He was good to me / What has she got / Bewitched, bothered and bewildered / Danny boy / Time after time
CD ____ 262019
Arista / Jan '92 / BMG

NO SECRETS
Right thing to do / Carter family / You're so vain / His friends are more than fond of Robin / We have no secrets / Embrace me, you child / It was so easy / Waited so long / Night owl / When you close your eyes
CD ____ 7559606842
WEA / Jul '93 / Warner Music

Simon Chase

WITCH DOCTOR, THE
CD ____ 35700
Sphinx Ministry / Nov '96 / Cargo

Simon, Edward

BEAUTY WITHIN
Mastery of all situations / Beauty within / Rare days / In search of power / Reprise 1 / El Dia que me quieras / Homecoming / Calling / Reprise 2
CD ____ AQCD 1025
Audioquest / Sep '95 / ADA / New Note/Pinnacle

EDWARD SIMON
Colega / Alma llanera, part 1 / Alma llanera, part 2 / Caballo viejo / Slippin' and slidin' / Stop looking to find (it finds you) / Magic between us / Teen's romance
CD ____ KOKO 1305
Kokopelli / Nov '95 / New Note/Pinnacle

Simon, Joe

DROWNING IN THE SEA OF LOVE
Glad to be your lover / Something you can do today / I found my dad / Mirror don't lie / Ole night owl / You are everything / If / Let me be the one (the one who loves you) / Pool of bad luck
CD ____ CDSEW 021
Southbound / Apr '90 / Pinnacle

GREATEST HITS (The Spring Years 1970-1977)
Your time to cry / Help me make it through the night / You're the one for me / All my hard times / Georgia blue / Drowning in the sea of love / Pool of bad luck / Power of love / Trouble in my home / I found my Dad / Step by step / Cleopatra Jones / River / Carry me / Best time of my life / Get down get down (get on the floor) / Music in my bones / I need you, you need me / Come get to this / Easy to love / You didn't have to play no games / One step at a time / For your love love love
CD ____ CDSEWD 102
Southbound / May '97 / Pinnacle

LOOKING BACK (The Best Of Joe Simon)
Chokin' kind / My special prayer / No sad songs / San Francisco is a lonely town / Message from Maria / Looking back / Baby don't be looking in my mind / Teenagers' prayer / Nine pound steel / You keep me hangin' on / Put your trust in me / It's hard to get along / Misty blue / Farther on down the road / Yours love / That's the way I want our love
CD ____ CDCHARLY 144
Charly / Nov '88 / Koch

MOOD, HEART AND SOUL/ TODAY
Neither one of us / I would still be there / Good time Charlie's got the blues / Covering the same old ground / Walking down lonely street / Best time of my life / What we gonna do now / I'm in the mood for you / Carry me / Come back home / Let's spend the night forever / I just want to make love to you / Let the good times roll / Come get to this / What a wonderful world / I need you, you need me / I'll take care of you / Music for my lady
CD ____ CDSEWD 971
Southbound / Apr '91 / Pinnacle

MR. SHOUT
CD ____ CDCHD 663
Ace / Aug '97 / Pinnacle

MY ADORABLE ONE
CD ____ CDRB 28
Charly / Aug '95 / Koch

SOUNDS OF SIMON
To lay down beside you / I can't see nobody / Most of all / No more me / Your time to cry / Help me make it through the night / My woman, my woman, my wife / I love you more / Georgia blue / All my hard times
CD ____ CDSEWD 954
Southbound / Oct '90 / Pinnacle

SOUNDS OF SIMON/SIMON COUNTRY
To lay down beside you / I can't see nobody / Most of all / No more me / Your time to cry / Help me make it through the night / My woman, my woman, my wife / I love you more than anything / Georgia blue / All my hard times / Do you know what it's like to be lonesome / You don't know me / To get to you / Before the next teardrop falls / Someone to give my love to / Good things / Kiss an angel good morning
CD ____ CDSEW 954
Southbound / Oct '90 / Pinnacle

Simon, John

LEGACY
It's you or no one / Ceora / Strollin' / Nomis / Aries
CD ____ MCD 5566
Muse / Aug '96 / New Note/Pinnacle

Simon, Jona

PIANO AFTER MIDNIGHT (Simon, Jona Trio)
CD ____ CDSGP 0140
Prestige / Apr '95 / Else / Total/BMG

Simon, Paul

ANTHOLOGY
Sound of silence / Cecilia / El condor pasa / Boxer / Mrs. Robinson / Bridge over troubled water / Me and julio down by the schoolyard / Peace like a river / Mother and child reunion / American tune / Loves me like a rock / Kodachrome / Gone at last / Still crazy after all these years / Something so right / Fifty Ways to leave your lover / Slip slidin' away / Late in the evening / Hearts and bones / Rene and Georgette Magritte with their dog after the war
CD ____ 9362454082
WEA / Oct '93 / Warner Music

CONCERT THE PARK - AUGUST 15TH, 1991
Obvious child / Boy in the bubble / She moves on / Kodachrome / Born at the right time / Train in the distance / Me and Julio down by the schoolyard / I know what I know / Cool cool river / Bridge over troubled water / Proof / Coast / Graceland / You can call me Al / Still crazy after all these years / Loves me like a rock / Diamonds on the soles of her shoes / Hearts and bones / Late in the evening / America / Boxer / Cecelia / Sound of silence
CD ____ 7599267372
WEA / Nov '91 / Warner Music

GRACELAND
Boy in the bubble / Graceland / I know what I know / Gumboots / Diamonds on the soles of her shoes / You can call me Al / Under African skies / Homeless / Crazy love Vol 2 / All around the world or the myth of fingerprints
CD ____ 9254472
WEA / Sep '86 / Warner Music

HEARTS AND BONES
Think too much / Train in the distance / Cars are cars / Late great Johnny Ace / Allergies / Hearts and bones / When numbers get serious / Song about the moon / Rene and Georgette Magritte with their dog after the war
CD ____ 9239422
WEA / '83 / Warner Music

LIVE RHYMIN' - IN CONCERT
Me and Julio down by the schoolyard / Homeward bound / American tune / El condor pasa / Duncan / Boxer / Mother and child reunion / Sound of silence / Jesus is the answer / Bridge over troubled water / Loves me like a rock / America
CD ____ 9255902
WEA / Dec '87 / Warner Music

ONE TRICK PONY
Late in the evening / That's why God made the movies / One-trick pony / How the heart approaches what it yearns / Oh Marion / Ace in the hole / Nobody / Jonah / God bless the absentee / Long long day
CD ____ 256846
WEA / Feb '94 / Warner Music

PAUL SIMON
Mother and child reunion / Duncan / Everything put together falls apart / Run that body down / Armistice Day / Me and Julio down by the schoolyard / Peace like a river / Papa hobo / Hobo blues / Paranoia blues / Congratulations / Kodachrome / Tenderness / Take me to the Mardi Gras / Something so right / One man's ceiling is another man's floor / American tune / Was a sunny day / Learn how to fall / St. Judy's comet / Loves me like a rock
CD ____ 9255882
WEA / Dec '87 / Warner Music

PAUL SIMON SONGBOOK (Various Artists)
CD ____ VSOPCD 173
Connoisseur Collection / Jun '92 / Pinnacle

RHYTHM OF THE SAINTS
Obvious child / Boy in the bubble / She moves on / Kodachrome / Born at the right time / Train in the distance / Me and Julio down by the schoolyard / I know what I know / Cool cool river / Bridge over troubled water / Proof / Coast / Graceland / Further to fly
CD ____ 7599260982
WEA / Oct '90 / Warner Music

STILL CRAZY AFTER ALL THESE YEARS
Still crazy after all these years / My little town: *Simon, Paul & Art Garfunkel* / I do it for your love / Fifty ways to leave your lover / Night game / Gone at last: *Simon, Paul & Phoebe Snow/Jessie Dixon Singers* / Some folk's lives roll easy / Have a good time / You're kind / Silent eyes
CD ____ 9255912
WEA / Dec '87 / Warner Music

THERE GOES RHYMIN' SIMON
Kodachrome / Tenderness / Take me to the Mardi Gras / Something so right / One man's ceiling is another man's floor / American tune / Was a sunny day / Learn how to fall / St. Judy's comet / Loves me like a rock
CD ____ 9255892
WEA / Dec '87 / Warner Music

Simon, Tito

I CRIED A TEAR
I cried a tear / Every beat of my heart / I'd rather go blind / River of tears / That's where it's at / Tell it like it is / After loving you / Hold on to what you've got
CD ____ FECD 10
First Edition / Apr '93 / Jet Star

Simon, Vannessa

DEFINITIVE SOURCE
CD ____ KDCD 7
Congo / Jun '97 / SRD / Total/BMG

Simona, Tiziana

GIGOLO (Simona, Tiziana & Kenny Wheeler)
CD ____ ITM 0014CD
ITM / '89 / Koch / Tradelink

Simone, Nina

BALTIMORE
Baltimore / Everything must change / Family / My father / Music for lovers / Rich girl / That's all I want from you / Forget / Balm in Gilead / If you pray right
CD ____ 4769062
Sony Jazz / Jan '95 / Sony

BEST OF NINA SIMONE, THE
In the morning / I shall be released / Day and night / It be's that way sometimes / I want a little sugar in my bowl / My man's gone now / Why (the king of love is dead) / Compensation / I wish I knew (how it would feel to be free) / Go to hell / Do what you gotta do / Suzanne
CD ____ ND 90376
RCA / Sep '89 / BMG

BEST OF NINA SIMONE, THE
I loves you Porgy / Break down and let it all out / Four women / Pirate Jenny / Sinner man / Don't let me be misunderstood / I put a spell on you / Mississippi goddam / Other woman / Ne me quitte pas / See line woman / Wild is the wind
CD ____ 8228462
Philips / Mar '86 / PolyGram

BEST OF NINA SIMONE, THE (The Colpix Years)
Children go where I send you / It might as well be spring / Willow weep for me / Other woman / Fine and mellow / Wild is the wind / You can have him / I loves you Porgy / Forbidden fruit / Gin house blues / Work song / House of the rising sun / I got it bad and that ain't good / Solitude / It don't mean a thing if it ain't got that swing / Twelfth of never / Baubles, bangles and beads / Gimme a pigfoot / Every time we say goodbye
CD ____ CDROU 1048
Roulette / Mar '92 / EMI

BLUES, THE
Do I move you / Day and night / In the dark / Real real / My man's gone now / Backlash blues / I want a little sugar in my bowl / Buck / Since I fell for you / House of the rising sun / Blues for Mama / Pusher / Turn me on / Nobody's fault but mine / Go to hell / I shall be released / Gin house blues
CD ____ ND 83101
Novus / Apr '91 / BMG

BROADWAY, BLUES & BALLADS
Don't let me be misunderstood / Night song / Laziest girl in town / Something wonderful / Don't take all night / Nobody / I am blessed / Of this I'm sure / See line woman / Our love / How can I / Last rose of summer
CD ____ 5181902
Verve / Feb '94 / PolyGram

COLLECTION, THE
My way / House of the rising sun / Save me / Here comes the sun / I love you porgy / I wish I knew how it would feel to be free / Gin house blues / Seems I'm never tired lovin' you / My sweet Lord / Times they are a-changin' / I want a little sugar in my bowl / Mr Bojangles / I shall be released / Ain't got no / I got life to love somebody / Angel of the morning
CD ____ ND 90566
RCA / Feb '97 / BMG

DO NOTHIN' TILL YOU HEAR FROM ME
Just in time / House of the rising sun / It don't mean a thing if it ain't got that swing / I loves you Porgy / Gin house blues / Assingment song / Solitude / Sea lion woman / No opportunity necessary, no experience needed / Black is the colour of my true love's hair / Wild is the wind / Nobody / Don't let me be misunderstood / Do nothin' 'til you hear from me / I got it bad and that ain't good / Hey Buddy Bolden / My way
CD ____ GRF 022
Tring / '93 / Tring

DON'T LET ME BE MISUNDERSTOOD
Don't let me be misunderstood / Last rose of Summer / Ne me quitte pas / Work song / Little girl blue / Trouble in mind / Strange fruit / Love me or leave me / Come ye / I put a spell on you / Don't explain / Wild is the wind / What more can I say / Nobody knows you when you're down and out / I loves you Porgy / Mississippi Goddam
CD ____ 8343082
Mercury / Jan '93 / PolyGram

FEELING GOOD (The Very Best Of Nina Simone)
CD ____ 5226692
Verve / Jul '94 / PolyGram

IN CONCERT
CD ____ RMB 75011
Remember / Nov '93 / Total/BMG

JAZZ MASTERS
Black is the colour of my true love's hair / I put a spell on you / Love me or leave me / Little girl blue / My baby just cares for me / I loves you Porgy / Work song / Ne me quitte pas / Wild is the wind / See line woman / Strange fruit / Pirate Jenny / Four women / Mississippi goddam / Don't let me be misunderstood / I hold no grudge
CD ____ 5181982
Verve / Mar '93 / PolyGram

JAZZ MASTERS
Sugar in my bowl / Old Jim Crow / Go limp / Four women / Images / Come ye / Be my husband / Take me to the water / I'm going back home / If you pray right / Fodder on my wings / If you knew me/Let it be me / Last rose of Summer / Mississippi goddam
CD _______________ 5298672
Verve / Oct '96 / PolyGram

LADY BLUE (2CD Set)
My baby just cares for me / Don't smoke in bed / He's got the whole world in his hands / Mood indigo / He needs me / African mailman / Love me or leave me / I love you Porgy / Good bait / For all we know / Central Park blues / You'll never walk alone / Plain gold ring / Little girl blue / My baby just cares for me / House of the rising sun / Don't let me be misunderstood / Ain't got no/I got life / No opportunity necessary, no experience needed / Young, gifted and black / Ain't no use / After you've gone / Assignment song / Gin house blues / Do what you gotta do / Mississippi goddam / See line woman / Other woman / Four women / I just to know I'm alive
CD Set _______________ CPCD 82402
Charly / Oct '96 / Koch

LET IT BE ME (Live At Vine Street)
My baby just cares for me / Sugar in my bowl / Fodder on my wings / Be my husband / Just like a woman / Balm in Gilead / Stars / If you pray right (Heaven belongs to you) / If you knew / Let it be me / Baltimore / Four women / Mississippi Goddam
CD _______________ 8314372
Verve / May '87 / PolyGram

LITTLE GIRL BLUE (Jazz As Played In An Exclusive Side Street Club)
Mood indigo / Don't smoke in bed / Love me or leave me / He needs me / My baby just cares for me / Little girl blue / Central park blues / I loves you Porgy / Good bait / Plain gold ring / You'll never walk alone
CD _______________ BET 6021
Bethlehem / Jan '95 / ADA / ZYX

LIVE AND KICKIN'
CD _______________ FREUDCD 32
Jungle / Nov '89 / RTM/Disc / SRD

MOON OF ALABAMA (2CD Set)
CD Set _______________ JD 1214
Jazz Door / Oct '96 / Koch

MY BABY JUST CARES FOR ME
My baby just cares for me / Don't smoke in bed / Mood indigo / He needs me / Love me or leave me / I loves you Porgy / You'll never walk alone / Good bait / Central Park blues / Plain gold ring / Little girl blue / My baby just cares for me (Ext.version) / My baby just cares for me (mix)
CD _______________ CPCD 8002
Charly / Aug '96 / Koch

MY BABY JUST CARES FOR ME
CD _______________ ENTCD 266
Entertainers / Mar '92 / Target/BMG

MY BABY JUST CARES FOR ME (Live At Ronnie Scott's)
God, God, God / If you knew / Mr. Smith / fodder on her wings / Be my husband / I loves you Porgy / Other woman / Mississippi goddam / Moon over Alabama / For a while / My baby just cares for me / See live woman / I sing just to know that I'm alive
CD _______________ CLACD 331
Castle / Mar '94 / BMG

NINA SIMONE
CD _______________ 295055
Ariola / Feb '95 / BMG

NINA SIMONE
House of the rising sun / I loves you Porgy / Love me or leave me / You took my teeth / Do what you gotta do / Saratoga / Sea line woman / African mailman / After you've gone / Ain't no use / Don't smoke in bed / Four women / Fodder on her wings / Good bait / It's cold out here / Just in time / Central Park blues / You'll never walk alone
CD _______________ BN 034
Blue Nite / Feb '97 / Target/BMG

NINA SIMONE & HER FRIENDS (An Intimate Variety Of Vocal Charm)
CD _______________ BET 6020
Bethlehem / Jan '95 / ADA / ZYX

NINA SIMONE - THE 1960'S VOL.1 (Je Me Quitte Pas)
I loves you Porgy / Plain gold ring / Pirate Jenny / Old Jim Crow / Don't smoke in bed / Go limp / Mississippi Goddam / I put a spell on you / Tomorrow is my turn / Ne me quitte pas / Marriage is for old folks / July tree / Gimme some / Feeling good / One September day / Blues on purpose / Beautiful land / You've got to learn / Take care of business
CD _______________ 8385432
Mercury / Apr '94 / PolyGram

NINA SIMONE - THE 1960'S VOL.2 (Mood Indigo)
Be my husband / Nobody knows you when you're down and out / End of the line / Trouble in mind / Tell me more and more and then some / Chilly winds don't blow / Ain't no use / Strange fruit / Sinnerman / Mood indigo / Other woman / Love me or leave me / Don't explain / Little girl blue / Chauffeur / For myself / Ballad of Hollis Brown / This year's kisses / Images / Neared blessed Lord
CD _______________ 8385442
Mercury / Jan '90 / PolyGram

NINA SIMONE - THE 1960'S VOL.3 (Work Song)
I love your lovin' ways / Four women / What more can I say / Lilac wine / That's all I ask / Break down and let it all out / Why keep on breaking my heart / Wild is the wind / Black is the colour of my true love's hair / If I should lose you / Either way I lose / Don't pay them no mind / I'm gonna leave you / Brown eyed handsome man / Keeper of the flame / Gal from Joe's / Take me to the water / I'm going back home / I hold no grudge / Come ye / He ain't comin' home no more / Work song / I love my baby
CD _______________ 8385452
Mercury / Jan '90 / PolyGram

NINA SIMONE IN CONCERT/I PUT A SPELL ON YOU
I loves you Porgy / Plain gold ring / Pirate Jenny / Old Jim Crow / Don't smoke in bed / Go limp / Mississippi Goddam / I put a spell on you / Tomorrow is my turn / Ne me quitte pas / Marriage is for old folks / July tree / Gimme some / Feeling good / One September day / Blues on purpose / Beautiful land / You've got to learn / Take care of business
CD _______________ 8465432
Mercury / Feb '97 / PolyGram

NINA'S BACK
It's cold out here / Porgy / I sing just to know that I'm alive / For a while / Fodder on her wings / Touching and caring / Saratoga / You must have another lover
CD _______________ CDMT 019
Meteor / '85 / TKO Magnum
CD _______________ FREUDCD 28
Jungle / Jul '89 / RTM/Disc / SRD

RELEASED
Backlash blues / Blues for Mama / I shall be released / It be's that way sometimes / I want a little sugar in my bowl / My man's gone now / Why (the king of love is dead) / I wish I knew how it would feel to be free / Do what you gotta do / Do I move you / In the dark / Look of love / Since I fell for you / Mr. Bojangles / Just like a woman / Turn me on / Nobody's fault but mine / Ain't got no / I got life / I loves you Porgy / Gin House blues
CD _______________ 74321431552
Camden / Jan '97 / BMG

RISING SUN COLLECTION
CD _______________ RSCD 004
Just A Memory / Apr '94 / New Note/ Pinnacle

SINGLE WOMAN
Single woman / Lonesome cities / If I should lose you / Folks who live on the hill / Love's been good to me / Papa, can you hear me / Il n'y a pas d'amour / Just say I love him / More I see you / Marry me
CD _______________ 7559615032
Elektra / Aug '93 / Warner Music

SPOTLIGHT ON NINA SIMONE
Work song / Angel of the morning / Ain't got no...I got life / You can have him / Lovin' woman / Little Liza Jane / Here comes the sun / My way / Fine and mellow / Nina's blues / Porgy
CD _______________ HADCD 109
Javelin / Feb '94 / Henry Hadaway / THE

Simons, Tito

TAKE A LOOK
Without love / Only the lonely know / Lavenders blue / Oh Patricia / Boom biddi boom / Black pearls / Oh Leona / Count the hours / Take a look around / Lord's army / Cheating games / Reggae is a music from Jamaica
CD _______________ WSRCD 104
World Sound / Sep '96 / Jet Star

Simonsson, Simon

DRANGKAMMARLTAR (Simonsson, Simon & Olle Eriksson)
CD _______________ GCD 32
Giga / May '97 / ADA / Total/BMG

Simper, Nick

SLIPSTREAMING/FUTURE TIMES
Candice Larene / Rocky road blues / Independent man (Hey Mama) / Slipstreaming / Schoolhouse party / Sister / Mississippi lady / Time will tell / Pull out and start again / Get down, lay down / She was my friend / Future times / Undercover man / Something's burning / Hard drink and easy women
CD _______________ RPM 125
RPM / Jun '97 / Pinnacle

Simple Agression

FORMULATIONS IN BLACK
Quiddity / Formulation in black / Lost / Phychoradius / Sea of eternity / Of winter / Simple aggression / Frenzy / Madd / Spiritual voices / Jedi mind trick / Share your pain
CD _______________ CDVEST 1
Bulletproof / Mar '94 / Pinnacle

Simple Minds

CELEBRATION
Life in a day / Chelsea girl / Premonition / Factory / Calling your name / I travel / Changeling / Celebrate / Thirty frames a second / Kaleidoscope
CD _______________ CDV 2248
Virgin / Apr '90 / EMI

EMPIRES AND DANCE
I travel / Today I died again / This fear of Gods / Celebrate / Constantinople line / Twist, run, repulsion / Thirty frames a second / Kant-kino / Room / Capital city
CD _______________ CDV 2247
Virgin / Jun '88 / EMI

GLITTERING PRIZE (1981-1992)
Waterfront / Don't you forget about me / Alive and kicking / Sanctify yourself / Love Song / Someone, somewhere in summertime / See the lights / Belfast child / American / All the things she said / Promised you a miracle / Ghostdancing / Speed your love to me / Glittering prize / Let there be love / Mandela Day
CD _______________ SMTVD 1
Virgin / Oct '92 / EMI

GOOD NEWS FROM THE NEXT WORLD
She's a river / Night music / Hypnotised / Great leap forward / Seven deadly sins / And the band played on / My life / Criminal world / This time
CD _______________ CDV 2760
Virgin / Jan '95 / EMI

LIFE IN A DAY
Someone / Life in a day / Sad affair / All for you / Pleasantly disturbed / No cure / Chelsea girl / Wasteland / Destiny / Murder story
CD _______________ VMCD 6
Virgin / Jul '87 / EMI

LIFE IN A DAY/REAL TO REAL CACOPHONY/EMPIRES AND DANCE (3CD Set)
CD Set _______________ TPAK 2
Virgin / Oct '90 / EMI

LIVE - IN THE CITY OF LIGHT (2CD Set)
Ghostdancing / Big sleep / Waterfront / Promised you a miracle / Someone, somewhere in summertime / Oh jungleland / Alive and kicking / Don't you forget about me / Once upon a time / Book of brilliant things / East at Easter / Sanctify yourself / Love song / Sun city / Dance to the music / New gold dream
CD Set _______________ CDSM 1
Virgin / May '87 / EMI

NEW GOLD DREAM (81-82-83-84)
Someone, somewhere in summertime / Colours fly and catherine wheel / Promised you a miracle / Big sleep / Somebody up there likes you / New gold dream / Glittering prize / Hunter and the hunted / King is white and in the crowd
CD _______________ CDV 2230
Virgin / Apr '92 / EMI

ONCE UPON A TIME
Once upon a time / All the things she said / Ghostdancing / Alive and kicking / Oh jungleland / I wish you were here / Sanctify yourself / Come a long way
CD _______________ CDV 2364
Virgin / Oct '85 / EMI

REAL LIFE
Real life / See the lights / Let there be love / Woman / Stand by love / Let the children speak / African skies / Ghost rider / Banging on the door / Travelling man / Rivers of ice / When two worlds collide
CD _______________ CDVIP 175
Virgin VIP / Apr '97 / EMI

REAL TO REAL CACOPHONY
Real to real / Naked eye / Citizen (dance of youth) / Veldt / Carnival (shelter in a suitcase) / Factory / Cacophony / Premonition / Changeling / Film theme / Calling your name / Scar
CD _______________ CDVIP 157
Virgin VIP / Oct '96 / EMI

SONS AND FASCINATION
In trance as mission / Sweat in bullet / Seventy cities as love brings the fall / Boys from Brazil / Love song / This earth that you walk upon / Sons and fascination / Seeing out the angel / Theme for great cities / American / Twentieth century promised land / Wonderful in young life / Careful in career / League of nations / Sound in seventy cities
CD _______________ CDV 2207
Virgin / Apr '86 / EMI

SPARKLE IN THE RAIN
Up on the catwalk / Book of brilliant things / Speed your love to me / Waterfront / East at Easter / Street hassle / White hot day / C moon / Kick inside of me / Shake off the ghosts / Cry like a baby
CD _______________ CDV 2300
Virgin / Mar '92 / EMI

STREET FIGHTING YEARS
Street fighting years / Wall of love / Take a step back / Let it all come down / Belfast child / Soul crying out / This is your land / Kick it in / Mandela day / Biko
CD _______________ MINDD 1
Virgin / May '89 / EMI

Simpleton

HEAVEN ME REACH
CD _______________ WRCD 005
World / Jun '97 / Jet Star / TKO Magnum

QUARTER TO 12
CD _______________ GRELCD 226
Greensleeves / Jun '96 / Jet Star / SRD

Simply Red

HOLDING BACK THE YEARS (The Greatest Hits 1985-1996)
Holding back the years / Money's too tight to mention / Right thing / It's only love / New flame / You've got it / If you don't know me by now / Stars / Something got me started / Thrill me / Your mirror / For your babies / So beautiful / Angel / Fairground
CD _______________ 0630165522
East West / Oct '96 / Warner Music

LIFE
You make me believe / So many people / Lives and loves / Fairground / Never never love / So beautiful / Hillside Avenue / Remembering the first time / Out on the range / We're in this together
CD _______________ 0630120692
East West / Oct '95 / Warner Music

MEN AND WOMEN
Right thing / Infidelity / Suffer / I won't feel bad / Every time we say goodbye / Let me have it all / Love fire / Move on out / Shine / Maybe someday
CD _______________ 2420712
East West / Feb '95 / Warner Music

NEW FLAME, A
It's only love / New flame / You've got it / To be with you / More / Turn it up / Love lays its tune / She'll have to go / If you don't know me by now / Enough
CD _______________ 2446892
East West / Feb '89 / Warner Music

PICTURE BOOK
Come to my aid / Sad old red / Look at you now / Heaven / Jericho / Money's too tight to mention / Holding back the years / Open up the red box / No direction / Picture book
CD _______________ 9031769932
East West / Mar '92 / Warner Music

SIMPLY SAX (The Music Of Simply Red) (Kelles, Erwin & John Thirkel)
Sad old red / Holding back the years / Right thing / Everytime we say goodbye / It's only love / A new flame / You've got it / To be with you / She'll have to go / If you don't know me by now / Something got me started / Stars / Thrill me / For your babies / Your mirror / Fairground / Remembering the first time / Never never love / We're in this together
CD _______________ ANT 013
Tring / Nov '96 / Tring

STARS
Something got me started / Stars / Thrill me / Your mirror / She's got it bad / For your babies / Model / How could I fall / Freedom / Wonderland
CD _______________ 9031752842
East West / Oct '91 / Warner Music

Simpson, Carole

ALL ABOUT CAROLE
You make me feel so young / Listen little girl / You forgot your gloves / Sure thing / Gentleman friend / Your name is love / Everytime / Oh look at me now / Time / I'll be around / There will never be another you / Just because we're kids
CD _______________ JASCD 309
Jasmine / Jul '95 / Conifer/BMG / Hot Shot / TKO Magnum

Simpson, Martin

61 HIGHWAY
CD _______________ BEJ 012CD
Beautiful Jo / Aug '96 / ADA / Direct

BAND OF ANGELS (Simpson, Martin & Jessica)
CD _______________ RHRCD 96
Red House / Oct '96 / ADA / Koch

CLOSER WALK WITH THEE, A
Weary blues / Old rugged cross / Salutation march / Spinning wheel / Savoy blues / Moose march / If I had my life to live over / East coast trot / Just a closer walk with thee / Marie / Chimes blues / Wreck of ol' 97 / Does Jesus care / Dinah / Saratoga swing
CD _______________ FLE 1007CD
Fledg'ling / Jul '94 / ADA / CM / Direct

COLLECTION, THE
First cut is the deepest / Roving gambler / This war may last you for years / Masters of war / Reuben's train / Handsome Mollly / Moonshine / Green linnet/Grinning in your face / Shawnee town / Moth / For Jessica, sad or high kicking / No depression in heaven / Stillness in company / Lakes of Ponchartrain / Doney girl / Essequibo river / Keel row
CD _______________ SHCD 79089

Shanachie / Jun '94 / ADA / Greensleeves / Koch

MARTIN SIMPSON LIVE
CD _______ BEJOCD 011
Beautiful Jo / Apr '96 / ADA / Direct

MUSIC FOR THE MOTHERLESS CHILD (Simpson, Martin & Wu Man)
One more day / A minor blues / White snow in Spring / Dives and lazarus / Coo coo bird / Sometimes I feel like a Motherless child
CD _______ WLACS 49CD
Waterlilly Acoustics / Feb '97 / ADA

RED ROSES (Simpson, Martin & Jessica)
We were all the heroes / Dreamtime / Spare change/The gypsies / How I wanted to / Icarus / Company you keep / Mermaid / Seven sisters / Turtle and the asp / Gardeners child / Red roses
CD _______ RHYD 5001
Rhiannon / Jul '96 / ADA / Direct / Vital

SMOKE AND MIRRORS
Poormouth / See that my grave is kept clean / Broke down engine / New kitchen blues / Hard love / I want my crown / Will this house be blessed / Delia / Lock, stock and barrel / Spoonful / Me and my chauffeur / Big road blues / Road kill / Gone fishing
CD _______ RHYD 5011
Rhiannon / Oct '95 / ADA / Direct / Vital

SPECIAL AGENT
CD _______ FLED 3005
Fledg'ling / Nov '95 / ADA / CM / Direct

Simpsons

SIMPSONS SING THE BLUES, THE
School day / Born under a bad sign / Moanin' Lisa blues / Deep deep trouble / God bless the child / I love to see you smile / Springfield soul stew / Look at all those idiots / Sibling rivalry / Do the Bartman
CD _______ GED 24308
Geffen / Nov '96 / BMG

Sims, Frankie Lee

LUCY MAE BLUES
Lucy Mae blues / Don't take it out on me / Married woman / Wine and gin bounce / Boogie 'cross the country / Jelly roll baker / I'm so glad / Long gone / Raggedy and dirty / Yeh, baby / No good woman / Walking boogie / Frankie's blues / Crying won't help you / I done talked and I done talked / Lucy Mae blues (Part 2) / Rumba my boogie / I'll get along somehow / Hawk shuffle / Frankie Lee's 2 O' Clock jump
CD _______ CDCHD 423
Ace / Sep '92 / Pinnacle

Sims, Joyce

COME INTO MY LIFE
Come into my life / Love makes a woman / It wasn't easy / All and all / Lifetime love / Change in you / Walk away / All and all (the UK remix) / All and all (Megamix)
CD _______ 8280772
London / Dec '87 / PolyGram

Sims, Kym

TOO BLIND TO SEE IT
Too blind to see it / Take my advice / Little bit more / Take me to the groove / One look / I found love / Shoulda known better / In my eyes / Never shoulda let you go / I can't stop / Too blind to see it (soul mix)
CD _______ 7567921042
Atco / Apr '92 / Warner Music

Sims, Pete 'La Roca'

SWINGTIME
Drum town / Body and soul / Susan's waltz / Tomorrow's expectation / Candyman / Nihon Bashi / Candu Amanda's song
CD _______ CDP 8548762
Blue Note / Aug '97 / EMI

Sims, Willie

STORY TELLER
CD _______ NAR 113CD
New Alliance / Nov '94 / Plastic Head

Sims, Zoot

AT RONNIE SCOTTS '61 (Sims, Zoot Quartet)
CD _______ FSRCD 134
Fresh Sound / Dec '90 / Discovery / Jazz Music

BIG STAMPEDE, THE
You're my girl / Purple cow / Ill wind / Big stampede / Too close for comfort / Jerry's jaunt / How now blues / Bye ya
CD _______ CDMT 017
Meteor / Aug '89 / TKO Magnum

BLUES FOR TWO (Sims, Zoot & Joe Pass)
Blues for two / Dindi / Remember / Poor butterfly / Black and blue / Pennies from Heaven / I hadn't anyone till you / Take off
CD _______ OJCCD 635
Original Jazz Classics / Feb '92 / Complete/ Pinnacle / Jazz Music / Wellard

BOHEMIA AFTER DARK
CD _______ JHR 73578
Jazz Hour / May '94 / Cadillac / Jazz Music / Target/BMG

DOWN HOME (Sims, Zoot Quartet)
Jive at five / Doggin' around / Ascap / Avalon / I cried for you / Bill Bailey, won't you please come home / Goodnight sweetheart / There'll be some changes made / I've heard that blues before
CD _______ CDGR 122
Charly / Mar '97 / Koch

ELEGIAC (Sims, Zoot & Bucky Pizzarelli)
CD _______ STCD 8238
Storyville / May '96 / Cadillac / Jazz Music / Wellard

FOR LADY DAY
Easy living / That ole devil called love / Some other Spring / I cover the waterfront / You go to my head / I cried for you / Body and soul / Travellin' light / You're my thrill / No more / My man (mon homme)
CD _______ CD 2310942
Pablo / Jan '94 / Cadillac / Complete/ Pinnacle

GETTING SENTIMENTAL
I'm getting sentimental over you / Restless / Fred / Caravan / Dream dancing / Very thought of you / Love me
CD _______ CHCD 71006
Candid / Mar '97 / Cadillac / Direct / Jazz Music / Koch / Wellard

HAPPY OVER HOAGY (Sims, Zoot & Al Cohn Septet)
CD _______ JASSCD 5
Jass / '88 / ADA / Cadillac / CM / Direct / Jazz Music

HOAGY & COLE (Sims, Zoot & Al Cohn)
CD _______ JCD 5
Jass / Sep '87 / ADA / Cadillac / CM / Direct / Jazz Music

I HEAR A RHAPSODY
CD _______ ATJCD 5967
All That's Jazz / Aug '92 / Jazz Music / THE

IF I'M LUCKY (Sims, Zoot & Jimmy Rowles)
Where our love has gone / Legs / If I'm lucky / Shadow waltz / You're my everything / It's all right with me / Gypsy sweetheart / I hear a rhapsody
CD _______ OJCCD 683
Original Jazz Classics / Nov '95 / Complete/ Pinnacle / Jazz Music / Wellard

IN A MELLOW TONE (2CD Set)
Groovin' high / Emily / All things you are / Take the 'A' train / Lester leaps in / Girl from Ipanema / That ole devil called love / Caravan / I got it bad and that ain't good / In a mellow tone / Over the rainbow / Softly as in a morning sunrise / Jitterbug waltz
CD Set _______ JLR 103604
Live At EJ's / May '96 / Target/BMG

IN COPENHAGEN
CD _______ STCD 8244
Storyville / May '95 / Cadillac / Jazz Music / Wellard

ON THE KORNER
CD _______ 2310953
Pablo / Nov '95 / Cadillac / Complete/ Pinnacle

RARE DAWN SESSIONS
CD _______ BCD 131
Biograph / Oct '94 / ADA / Cadillac / Direct / Hot Shot / Jazz Music / Wellard

SOMEBODY LOVES ME
Summerset / Honeysuckle rose / Summer thing / Somebody loves me / Gee baby ain't I good to you / Nirvana / (Back home again in) Indiana / Memories of you / Come rain or come shine / Up a lazy river / Send in the clowns / Airmail special / Ham hock blues / Ring dem bells
CD _______ 17085
Laserlight / Mar '97 / Target/BMG

SUDDENLY IT'S SPRING
Brahm's...I think / I can't get started (with you) / MacGuffie's blues / In the middle of a kiss / So long / Never let me go / Suddenly it's spring / Emaline
CD _______ OJCCD 742
Original Jazz Classics / May '93 / Complete/ Pinnacle / Jazz Music / Wellard

SUMMER THING, A
CD _______ 15754
Laserlight / Aug '92 / Target/BMG

TONITE'S MUSIC TODAY (Sims, Zoot & Bob Brookmeyer)
CD _______ BLCD 760907
Black Lion / Jun '88 / Cadillac / Jazz Music / Koch / Wellard

ZOOT SIMS & THE GERSHWIN BROTHERS
Man I love / How long has this been going on / Oh lady be good / I've got a crush on you / I got rhythm / Embraceable you / 'S wonderful / Someone to watch over me / Isn't it a pity / Summertime
CD _______ OJCCD 444
Original Jazz Classics / Feb '93 / Complete/ Pinnacle / Jazz Music / Wellard

ZOOT SIMS AND BOB BROOKMEYER (Sims, Zoot & Bob Brookmeyer)
King / Lullaby of the leaves / I can't get started (with you) / Snake eyes / Morning fun / Whooeeeeee / Someone to watch over me / My old flame / Boxcars
CD _______ BLCD 760914
Black Lion / '88 / Cadillac / Jazz Music / Koch / Wellard

ZOOT SIMS IN PARIS
CD _______ CDSW 8417
DRG / Jan '89 / Discovery / New Note/ Pinnacle

Sin Alley

DETROIT 442
CD _______ DD 035CD
Demolition Derby / Jan '97 / Greyhound / Nervous

Sin E

SIN E
Freeze, bitches / Houmous of green lanes / Come and watch me / Estelle's peppers / Snows they melt the soonest / Barnsley abacus / Maid of Coolmore / Reels for Luke / Kama / Lust / Sh jigs
CD _______ RHYD 5006
Rhiannon / Feb '96 / ADA / Direct / Vital

Sinatra, Frank

16 MOST REQUESTED SONGS
All or nothing at all / You'll never know / Saturday night is the loneliest night of the week / Dream / Put your dreams away / Day by day / Nancy with the laughing face / Oh what it seemed to be / Soloqay (part 1 and 2) / Five minutes more / Things we did last summer / Coffe song (they've got a awful lot of coffee in Brazil) / Time after time / Ma'm'selle / Fools rush in / Birth of the blues
CD _______ 4805132
Columbia / May '95 / Sony

1949 LITE UP TIME SHOWS
CD _______ EBCD 21162
Flyright / Feb '94 / Hot Shot / Jazz Music / Wellard

20 CLASSIC TRACKS: FRANK SINATRA
Come fly with me / Around the world / French Foreign Legion / Moonlight in Vermont / Autumn in New York / Let's get away from it all / April in Paris / London by night / It's nice to go travellin' / Come dance with me / Something's gotta give / Just in time / Dancing in the dark / Too close for comfort / I could have danced all night / Saturday night is the loneliest night of the week / Cheek to cheek / Baubles, bangles and beads / Day in, day out
CD _______ CDMFP 50530
Music For Pleasure / Mar '92 / EMI

40 FAMOUS SONGS FROM THE MUSICALS (2CD Set)
You'll never walk alone / Girl that I marry / Begin the beguine / September song / Oh, what a beautiful morning / People will say we're in love / Song is you / You're lonely and I'm lonely / It's a lovely day tomorrow / Without a song / I'll be seeing you / World is in my arms / Just one of those things / You do something to me / Ol' man river / You are love / They didn't believe me / Love me or leave me / There's no business like show business / 'S wonderful / Embraceable you / Kiss me again / Where or when / All the things you are / If I loved you / Someone to watch over me / These foolish things (remind me of you) / Why shouldn't I / Bess, oh where's my bess / They say it's wonderful / Soliloquy / Lost in the stars / Falling in love with love / You make me feel so young / I'll string along with you / I've got my love to keep me warm / On the sunny side of the street / Who told you I cared / I don't why (I just do)
CD Set _______ DBG 53057
Double Gold / Jul '97 / Target/BMG

50 FAMOUS SONGS FROM THE MOVIES (2CD Set)
Too romantic / Say it / This is the beginning of the end / April played the fiddle / I haven't time to be a millionaire / Call of the canyon / I could make you care / Our love affair / I'd know you anywhere / Do you know why / Not so long ago / You lucky people, you / It's always you / Dolores / I'll never let a day pass by / Love me as I am / How about you / Poor you / I'll take Tallulah / Last call for love / Be careful, it's my heart / You'll never know / Night and day / You make me feel so young / I'm in the mood for love / Sunday, Monday or always / If you please / I couldn't sleep a wink last night / Lovely way to spend an evening / Music stopped / White christmas / I begged her / What makes the sunset / I fall in love too easily / Stormy weather / Charm of you / Embraceable you / I should care / Friend of yours / Over the rainbow / House I live in (that's America to me) / You are too beautiful / I only have eyes for you / Paradise / All through the day / Two hearts are better than one / That old black magic / Somewhere in the night / Five minutes more / Somebody loves me
CD Set _______ DBG 53056
Double Gold / Jul '97 / Target/BMG

ALL OF ME (50 Great Performances/ 2CD Set)
Blue skies / I don't stand a ghost of a chance / Music stopped / You make me feel so young / Just one of those things / You do something to me / Begin the beguine / Ol' man river / For you / Night and day / Nevertheless / Out of nowhere / You are love / I've got my love to keep me warm / On the sunny side of the street / Hundred years from today / I wonder who's kissing her now / I'm in the mood for love / Don't blame me / They didn't believe me / Tenderly / Love me or leave me / Somebody loves me / I'll string along with you / 'S wonderful / It might as well be spring / Day by day / Lily Belle / I'll be seeing you / Home on the range / All of me / Stars in your eyes / Ole buttermilk sky / I'll get by (as long as I have you) / Chickery chick / Sweet Lorraine / Gimme a little kiss, will ya huh / All the things you are / Put your dreams away (for another day) / It had to be you / San Fernando Valley / Long ago and far away / It could happen to you / Amor / I'll walk alone / With a song in my heart / Over the rainbow / Close to you / Saturday night (is the lonliest night of the week) / Nancy (with the laughing face)
CD Set _______ DBG 53055
Double Gold / Jul '97 / Target/BMG

AMONG MY SOUVENIRS
Five minutes more / Oh what it seemed to be / Begin the beguine / Full moon and empty arms / Someone to watch over me / You go to my head / These foolish things / I don't know why / Day by day / You are too beautiful / I only have eyes for you / I don't stand a ghost of a chance with you / Why shouldn't I / Try a little tenderness / All through the day / One love / How cute can you be / Bess, oh where's my Bess / They say it's wonderful / Somewhere in the night / Coffee song / Among my souvenirs / September song / Things we said last Summer
CD _______ CDGR 109
Charly / Jan '97 / Koch

AT THE MOVIES
From here to eternity / Three coins in the fountain / Young at heart / She's funny that way / Just one of those things / Someone to watch over me / Not as a stranger / Tender trap / Our town / Impatient years / Love and marriage / Look to your heart / Johnny Concho theme (Wait for me) / All the way / Chicago / Monique / They came to Cordura / High hopes / All my tomorrows
CD _______ CDP 7993742
Capitol / Apr '93 / EMI

AUDIO ARCHIVE
You make me feel so young / Night and day / 'S Wonderful / Somebody loves me / Begin the beguine / It all depends on you / Just one of those things / Ol' man river / Love me or leave me / They say it's wonderful / Nevertheless / Don't blame me / Out of nowhere / On the sunny side of the street / Blue skies / You are my love / Music stopped / I don't stand a ghost of a chance with you / They did not believe me / You do something to me
CD _______ CDAA 005
Tring / Jun '92 / Tring

BEGIN THE BEGUINE
CD _______ MU 5043
Musketeer / Oct '92 / Disc

BEST OF FRANK SINATRA, THE
CD _______ DLCD 4007
Dixie Live / Mar '95 / TKO Magnum

BLUE NOTE PLAYS SINATRA (Various Artists)
Come rain or come shine: *Blakey, Art & The Jazz Messengers* / All or nothing at all: *Hubbard, Freddie* / Guess I'll hang my tears out to dry: *Gordon, Dexter* / Dancing in the dark: *Adderley, Cannonball* / I've got you under my skin: *Rollins, Sonny* / Witchcraft: *Three Sounds* / I love Paris: *Terrasson, Jacky* / It never entered my mind: *Davis, Miles* / Nancy (with the laughing face): *Quebec, Ike* / This love of mine: *Green, Benny* / Angel eyes: *Lovano, Joe* / It was a very good year: *Three Sounds*
CD _______ CDP 8352822
Blue Note / Mar '96 / EMI

CAPITOL COLLECTORS SERIES: FRANK SINATRA
I'm walking behind you / I've got the world on a string / From here to eternity / South of the border (Down Mexico way) / Young at heart / Don't worry 'bout me / Three coins in the fountain / Melody of love: *Sinatra, Frank & Ray Anthony* / Learnin' the blues / Same old Saturday night / Love and marriage / Tender trap / How little it matters, how little we know / Hey jealous lover / Can I steal a little love / All the way / Chicago / Witchcraft / High hopes / Nice 'n' easy
CD _______ CZ 228
Capitol / Sep '89 / EMI

CAPITOL YEARS, THE (3CD Set)
I've got the world on a string / Lean baby / I love you / South of the border (Down Mexico way) / From here to eternity / They can't take that away from me / I get a kick out of you / Young at heart / Three coins in the fountain / All of me / Taking a chance on love / Someone to watch over me / What is this thing called love / In the wee small

hours of the morning / Learnin' the blues / Our town / Love and marriage / Tender trap / Weep they will / I thought about you / You make me feel so young / Memories of you / I've got you under my skin / Too marvellous for words / Don't like goodbyes / How little it matters, how little we know / Your sensational / Hey jealous lover / Close to you / Stars fell on Alabama / I got plenty o' nuttin' / I wish I were in love again / Lady is a tramp / Night and day / Lonesome road / If I had you / Where are you / I'm a fool to want you / Witchcraft / Something wonderful happens in summer / All the way / Chicago / Let's get away from it all / Autumn in New York / Come fly with me / Everybody loves somebody / It's the same old dream / Put your dreams away / Here goes / Angel eyes / Guess I'll hang my tears out to dry / Ebb tide / Only the lonely / One for my baby (and one more for the road) / To love and be loved (Single version) / I couldn't care less / Song is you / Just in time / Saturday night is the loneliest night of the week / Come dance with me / French Foreign Legion / One I love (Belongs to someone else) / Here's that rainy day / High hopes / When no one cares / I'll never smile again / I've got a crush on you / Embraceable you / Nice 'n' easy / I can't believe that you're in love with me / On the sunny side of the street / I've heard that song before / Almost like being in love / I'll be seeing you / I gotta right to sing the blues
CD Set ______ **CDS 7943172**
Capitol / Nov '90 / EMI

CHAIRMAN OF THE BORED (A Tribute To Frank Sinatra) (Various Artists)
CD ______ **GROW 12122**
Grass / Oct '93 / Pinnacle / SRD

CHRISTMAS SONGS
White Christmas / Silent night / Adeste fideles (O come all ye faithful) / Jingle bells / Have yourself a merrly little Christmas / Christmas dreaming (A little early this year) / It came upon the midnight clear / O little town of Bethlehem / Santa Claus is coming to town / Let it snow, let it snow, let it snow / Medley / Ave Maria / Winter wonderland / Lord's prayer
CD ______ **4782562**
Columbia / Nov '96 / Sony

CLASSIC YEARS VOL.1, THE
CD ______ **CDSGP 091**
Prestige / Nov '93 / Else / Total/BMG

CLASSIC YEARS VOL.2, THE
CD ______ **CDSGP 157**
Prestige / Mar '95 / Else / Total/BMG

CLOSE TO YOU
Close to you / PS I love you / Love locked out / Everything happens to me / It's easy to remember / Don't like goodbyes / With every breath I take / Blame it on my youth / It could happen to you / I've had my moments / I couldn't sleep a wink last night / End of a love affair / If it's the last thing I do / There's a flaw in my flute / Wait till you see her
CD ______ **BU 19**
Capitol / Mar '88 / EMI

COLLECTION, THE
CD ______ **COL 051**
Collection / Apr '95 / Target/BMG

COME DANCE WITH ME
Come dance with me / Something's gotta give / Just in time / Dancing in the dark / Too close for comfort / I could have danced all night / Saturday night is the loneliest night of the week / Day in, day out / Cheek to cheek / Baubles, bangles and beads / Song is you / Last dance
CD ______ **CDP 7484682**
Capitol / Nov '92 / EMI

COME FLY WITH ME
Come fly with me / Around the world / Isle of Capri / Moonlight in Vermont / Autumn in New York / On the road to Mandalay / Let's get away from it all / April in Paris / London by night / Brazil / Blue Hawaii / It's nice to go travellin'
CD ______ **CDP 7484692**
Capitol / Nov '92 / EMI

COME SWING WITH ME
Day by day / Sentimental journey / Almost like being in love / Five minutes more / American beauty rose / Yes indeed / On the sunny side of the street / Don't take your love from me / That old black magic / Lover / Paper doll / I've heard that song before / I love you / Why should I cry over you / How could you do a thing like that to me / River stay 'way from my door / I gotta right to sing the blues
CD ______ **CZ 391**
Capitol / Mar '91 / EMI

COMPLETE CAPITOL SINGLES COLLECTION, THE (4CD Set)
Lean baby / I'm walking behind you / I've got the world on a string / My one and only love / Anytime anywhere / From here to Eternity / I love you / South of the border / Take a chance / Young at heart / Don't worry 'bout me / I could have told you / Rain (falling from the skies) / Three coins in the fountain / Gal that got away / Half as lovely (twice as true) / It worries me / When I stop loving you / White Christmas / Christmas waltz / Someone to watch over me / You, my love / Melody of love / I'm gonna live till I die / Why should I cry over you / Don't change your mind about you / Two hearts two kisses / From the bottom to the top / If I had three wishes / Learnin' the Blues / Not as a stranger / How could you do a thing like that to me / Same old Saturday night / Fairy tale / Love and marriage / Impatient years / (Love is the) tender trap / Weep they will / You'll get yours / Flowers mean forgiveness / (How little it matters) how little we know / Five hundred guys / Johnny Concho theme (wait for me) / You're sensational / Well did you evah / Mind if I make love to you / Who wants to be a millionaire / You forgot all the words (while I still remember the tune) / Hey jealous lover / Your love for me / Can I steal a little love / So long my love / Crazy love / Something wonderful happens in summer / You're cheatin' yourself (if you're cheatin' on me) / All the way / Chicago / Witchcraft / Tell her you love her / Christmas waltz / Mistletoe and holly / Nothing in common / How are you fixed for love / Same old song and dance / Minique / Mr. Success / Sleep warm / No one ever tells you / To love and be loved / Time after time / French Foreign Legion / All my tomorrows / High hopes / They came to Cordura / Talk to me / River, stay 'way from my door / It's over, it's over, it's over / This was my love / Nice 'n' easy / You'll alwways be the one I love / Ol' McDonald / My blue heaven / Sentimental baby / Sentimental journey / American beauty Rose / Moon was yellow / I've heard that song before / Five minutes more / I'll remember April / I love Paris / Hidden Persuassion / Ya better stop / Sea song / Look to your heart / I believe / Love looks so well on you
CD Set ______ **CDFRANK 53**
Premier/EMI / Oct '96 / EMI

COMPLETE COLUMBIA RECORDINGS 1943-1952, THE (4CD Set)
Close to you / People will say we're in love / If you are but a dream / Saturday night (is the loneliest night in the week) / White Christmas / I fall in love too easily / Ol' man river / Stormy weather / Embraceable you / She's funny that way / My melancholy baby / Where or when / All the things you are / I should care / Dream / Put your dreams away / Over the rainbow / If I loved you / Someone to watch over me / You go to my head / These foolish things / House I live in / Nancy (with the laughing face) / Full moon and empty arms / Oh what it seemed to be / I don't stand a ghost of a chance with you / Why shouldn't I / Try a little tenderness / Begin the beguine / They say it's wonderful / That old black magic / How deep is the ocean (how blue is the sky) / Home on the range / Five minutes more / Things we did last summer / Among my souvenirs / September song / Blue skies / Guess I'll hang my tears out to dry / Lost in the stars / There's no business like show business / Time after time / Brooklyn bridge / Sweet Lorraine / Always / Mam'selle / Stella by starlight / My romance / If I had you / One for my baby (and one more for the road) / But beautiful / You're my girl / All of me / Night and day / S'posin' / Night we called it a day / Song is you / What'll I do / Music stopped / Fools rush in / I've got a crush on you / Body and soul / I'm glad there is you / Autumn in New York / Nature boy / Once in love with Amy / Some enchanted evening / Huckle-buck / Let's take an old fashioned walk / It all depends on you / Bye bye baby / Don't cry Joe (let her go, let her go, let her go) / That lucky old sun (just rolls around heaven all day) / Chattanoogie shoe shine boy / American beauty rose / Should I (reveal) / You do something to me / Lover / When you're smiling (the whole world smiles with you) / London by night / Meet me at the Copa / April in Paris / I guess I'll have to dream the rest / Nevertheless / Am I loved / Hello, young lovers / We kiss in a shadow / I'm s fool to want you / Love me / Deep night / I could write a book / I hear a rhapsody / My girl / Birth of the blues / Azure-te (Paris blues) / Why try to change me now
CD Set ______ **C4K 64681**
Columbia / Nov '95 / Sony

COMPLETE REPRISE STUDIO RECORDINGS, THE (20CD Set)
CD Set ______ **9362460132**
Reprise / Jan '96 / Warner Music

DANCE HALL DAYS, THE
Fools rush in / Hear my song Violetta / Over the rainbow / How about you / Blue skies / Sunshine of your smile / These foolish things remind me of you / Embraceable you / In blue of the evening / Stardust / Without a song / I haven't time to be a millionaire / Whispering / Nancy (with the laughing face) / Do I worry / Night we called it a day / Oh look at me now / Polka dots and moonbeams / You'll never walk alone / I'll be seeing you
CD ______ **ECD 3293**
K-Tel / Feb '97 / K-Tel

DANCING IN THE DARK
Lady is a tramp / I get a kick out of you / I've got you under my skin / Moonlight in Vermont / When your lover has gone / Bewitched / Imagination / At long last love / My funny valentine / My blue heaven / Come fly with me / Dancing in the dark / All the way / You make me feel so young / On the sunny side of the street / Love me or leave me / For you / Where or when / Moon was yellow / Just one of those things / I've got my love to keep me warm / Road to Mandalay / You are love / They didn't believe me / I could have danced all night
CD ______ **CD 6039**
Music / Sep '96 / Target/BMG

DUETS VOL.1
Lady is a tramp: *Sinatra, Frank & Luther Vandross* / What now my love: *Sinatra, Frank & Aretha Franklin* / I've got a crush on you: *Sinatra, Frank & Barbara Streisand* / Summer wind: *Sinatra, Frank & Julio Iglesias* / Come rain or come shine: *Sinatra, Frank & Gloria Estefan* / New York, New York: *Sinatra, Frank & Tony Bennett* / They can't take that away from me: *Sinatra, Frank & Natalie Cole* / You make me feel so young: *Sinatra, Frank & Charles Aznavour* / Guess I'll hang my tears out to dry: *Sinatra, Frank & Carly Simon* / In the wee small hours of the morning: *Sinatra, Frank & Carly Simon* / I've got the world on a string: *Sinatra, Frank & Liza Minnelli* / Witchcraft: *Sinatra, Frank & Anita Baker* / I've got you under my skin: *Sinatra, Frank & Bono* / All the way: *Sinatra, Frank & Kenny G* / One for my baby (and one more for the road): *Sinatra, Frank & Kenny G*
CD ______ **CDEST 2218**
Capitol / Nov '93 / EMI

DUETS VOL.2
For once in my life: *Sinatra, Frank/Stevie Wonder/Gladys Knight* / Moonlight in Vermont: *Sinatra, Frank & Linda Ronstadt* / Foggy day: *Sinatra, Frank & Willie Nelson* / Come fly with me: *Sinatra, Frank & Luis Miguel* / Fly me to the moon: *Sinatra, Frank & Jobim* / Embracable you: *Sinatra, Frank & Lena Horne* / House I live in: *Sinatra, Frank & Neil Diamond* / Luck be a lady: *Sinatra, Frank & Chrissie Hynde* / Bewitched, bothered and bewildered: *Sinatra, Frank & Pattie LaBelle* / Best it yet to come: *Sinatra, Frank & Jon Secada* / How do you keep the music playing: *Sinatra, Frank & Lorrie Morgan* / Funny Val: *Sinatra, Frank & Lorrie Morgan* / When or where: *Sinatra, Frank/Steve Lawrence/Edie Gorme* / My kind of town (Chicago is): *Sinatra, Frank & Frank Sinatra Jr.* / Mack the knife: *Sinatra, Frank & Jimmy Buffett* / Christmas song: *Sinatra, Frank & Nat 'King' Cole*
CD ______ **CDEST 2245**
Capitol / Nov '94 / EMI

EARLY YEARS, THE (2CD Set)
CD Set ______ **AVC 552**
Avid / Jan '96 / Avid/BMG / Koch / THE

EARLY YEARS, THE
Night and day / Hair of gold, eyes of blue / That's my affair / I don't believe in rumours / I've had this feeling before / Trolley song / Surrey with the fringe on top / Candy / Lullaby of Broadway / Blue skies / Just one of those things / I've got my love to keep me warm / On the sunny side of the street / Out of nowhere / Somebody loves me / Love me or leave me
CD ______ **SUMCD 4082**
Summit / Nov '96 / Sound & Media

ESSENTIAL COLLECTION, THE
CD Set ______ **LECD 606**
Wisepack / Apr '95 / Conifer/BMG / THE

FAMOUS CONCERTS, THE
CD ______ **15263**
Laserlight / Aug '91 / Target/BMG

FIRST DEFINITIVE PERFORMANCES, THE (2CD Set)
CD Set ______ **AMSC 566**
Avid / Jun '96 / Avid/BMG / Koch / THE

FOR YOU
CD ______ **3001042**
Scratch / Jul '95 / Koch / Scratch/BMG

FRANK SINATRA (2CD Set)
CD Set ______ **R2CD 4011**
Deja Vu / Jan '96 / THE

FRANK SINATRA (3CD Set)
Blue skies / Somebody loves me / Sweethearts on parade: *Sinatra, Frank & Louis Armstrong* / Be careful that's my heart / Fools rush in / I'll be seeing you / Imagination / It's always you / Everything happens to me / Begin the beguine / Sinner kissed an angel / I think of you / Ol' man river / Stardust / Whispering / Lamplighter's serenade / I've got my love to keep me warm / From the bottom of my heart / Night & day / Personality / Our love affair / On the sunny side of the street / Lover come back to me / There's no business like show business: *Sinatra, Frank & Doris Day* / How about you / Some enchanted evening / Take me / Tea for two: *Sinatra, Frank & Dinah Shore* / Oh look at me now / This is the beginning of the end / This love of mine / Song is you / One I love belongs to somebody else / You make me feel so young / Make believe / Street of dreams / Nancy with the laughing face / Come out come out wherever you are / Exactly like you: *Sinatra, Frank & Nat 'King' Cole* / Don't bring Lulu: *Sinatra, Frank & Jack Carson* / No can do: *Sinatra, Frank & Lena Romany* / Birth of the blues: *Sinatra, Frank & Louis Armstrong* / I saw you first: *Sinatra, Frank & Marcy McGuire* / This can't be love: *Sinatra, Frank & Margaret Whiting* / Yes indeed: *Sinatra, Frank & Sy Oliver* / Figaro: *Sinatra, Frank & Carlos Ramirez* / Together: *Sinatra, Frank & Eileen Barton* / Till we meet again: *Sinatra, Frank & Bing Crosby* / Meet me tonight in Dreamland: *Sinatra, Frank & Bing Crosby* / Thee's a long trail: *Sinatra, Frank & Bing Crosby* / (I don't stand) A ghost of a chance (With you) / I fall in love with you everyday / Laura / Love me or leave me / 'S wonderful / You do something to me
CD Set ______ **KBOX 364**
Collection / Nov '96 / Target/BMG / TKO Magnum

FRANK SINATRA
CD ______ **HM 020**
Harmony / Jun '97 / TKO Magnum

FRANK SINATRA COLLECTION, THE
Nice 'n' easy / Cheek to cheek / I'm gonna sit right down and write myself a letter / As time goes by / Witchcraft / I've got you under my skin / You make me feel so young / I can't get started (with you) / I get a kick out of you / Chicago / Come fly with me / Lady is a tramp / Tender trap / My funny valentine / Night and day / You'd be so nice to come home to / Dancing in the dark / Let's get away from it all / Nice work if you can get it / One for my baby (and one more for the road)
CD ______ **CDEMTV 41**
EMI / Dec '87 / EMI

FRANK SINATRA COLLECTION, THE
Night and day / Whispering / How about you / Our love affair / Begin the beguine / I've got my love to keep me warm / (I don't stand) A ghost of a chance / Blue skies / Out of nowhere / Somebody loves me / Love me or leave me / Tea for two / Stardust / You made me feel so young / On the sunny side of the street / Come fly with me / Just one of those things / I've got you under my skin / I get a kick out of you / Moonlight in Vermont / My funny valentine / I could have danced all night
CD ______ **PAR 2068**
Parade / Nov '96 / Disc

FRANK SINATRA COLLECTION, THE (A Tribute To A Legend - 4CD Set)
On the sunny side of the street / Begin the beguine / Don't blame me / It all depends on you / Somebody loves me / 'S wonderful / Love me or leave me / Tenderly / Nevertheless (I'm in love with you) / They didn't believe me / I've got my love to keep me warm / It only happens when I dance with you / My happiness / I wonder who's kissing her now / Hundred years from today / I don't know why / Little white lies / Between the devil and the deep blue sea / Fools rush in / Hear my song, Violetta / Over the rainbow / How about you / Blue skies / Sunshine of your smile / These foolish things (remind me of you) / Embraceable you / In the blue of the evening / Stardust / Without a song / I haven't time to be a millionaire / Whispering / Nancy (with the laughing face) / Do I worry / Night we called it a day / Oh, look at me now / Polka dots and moonbeams / You'll never walk alone / I'll be seeing you / There are such things / Night and day / This love of mine / Time after time / Too romantic / How do you do without me / Love lies / I think of you / I'll never smile again / Be careful, it's my heart / Last call for love / It's a lovely day for love / Our love affair / I'd know you anywhere / Love me as I am / I'll never let a day pass by / Violets for your furs / You're breaking my heart all over again / Say it / I could make you care / This is the beginning of the end / You lucky people, you / Sweet Lorraine / Lamplighter's serenade / Free for all / Poor you / Dolores / Call of the canyon / Not so long ago / Light a candle in the chapel / Imagination / April played the fiddle / Song is you / Dig down deep / Fable of the rose / Who / We three / Daybreak / East of the sun (and west of the moon) / One I love belongs to someone else / Somewhere a voice is calling / Looking for yesterday
CD Set ______ **ECD 3330**
K-Tel / Mar '97 / K-Tel

FRANK SINATRA COLLECTOR'S EDITION
CD ______ **DVX 08032**
Deja Vu / Apr '95 / THE

FRANK SINATRA ESSENTIALS
CD ______ **LECDD 606A**
Wisepack / Aug '95 / Conifer/BMG / THE

FRANK SINATRA GOLD (2CD Set)
CD Set ______ **D2CD 4011**
Deja Vu / Jun '95 / THE

FRANK SINATRA SINGS FOR ONLY THE LONELY
Only the lonely / Angel eyes / What's new / It's a lonesome old town / Willow weep for me / Goodbye / Blues in the night / Guess I'll hang my tears out to dry / Ebb tide / Spring is here / Gone with the wind / One for my baby (and one more for the road) / Sleep warm / Where or when
CD ______ **CDP 7484712**
Capitol / Feb '88 / EMI

FRANK SINATRA SINGS HIS GREATEST HITS
All of me / I could write a book / I've got a crush on you / Night and day / Saturday night (is the loneliest night in the week) / Brooklyn Bridge / Nancy / House I live in / Birth of the blues / Body and soul / April in Paris / I'm glad there is you / Sweet Lorraine / Time after time / Laura / Song is you / I'm a fool to want you / Put your dreams away
CD 4875062
Columbia / Jun '97 / Sony

FRANK SINATRA SINGS RODGERS & HAMMERSTEIN
Oh what a beautiful mornin' / People will say we're in love / Surrey with the fringe on top / If I loved you / You'll never walk alone / Soliloquy / It might as well be Spring / That's for me / A fellow needs a girl / So far / Younger than Springtime / Some enchanted evening / Bali ha i / Hello young lovers / We kiss in a shadow / I whistle a happy tune
CD 4814262
Columbia / Aug '96 / Sony

FRANK SINATRA SINGS THE GREATS VOL.1, THE
Just one of those things / 'S Wonderful / On the sunny side of the street / Ol' man river / Somebody loves me / Music stopped
CD BSTCD 9102
Best Compact Discs / May '92 / Complete/ Pinnacle

FRANK SINATRA SINGS THE GREATS VOL.2, THE
Swinging on a star / Lover come back to me / Girl that I marry / Come fly with me / I get a kick out of you / I've got you under my skin / Moonlight in Vermont / April in Paris / She's funny that way / Lady is a tramp / You make me feel so young / All the way / I could have danced all night / Just one of those things / Willow weep for me / Dancing in the dark / At long last love / All of me
CD BSTCD 9112
Best Compact Discs / Apr '94 / Complete/ Pinnacle

FRANK SINATRA SINGS THE SELECT COLE PORTER
I've got you under my skin / I concentrate on you / What is this thing called love / You do something to me / At long last love / Anything goes / Night and day / Just one of those things / I get a kick out of you / You'd be so nice to come home to / I love Paris / From this moment on / C'est magnifique / It's all right with me / Mind if I make love to you / You're sensational
CD CDP 7966112
Capitol / Aug '91 / EMI

FRANK SINATRA SINGS THE SELECT JOHNNY MERCER
Too marvellous for words / Day in, day out / Laura / Jeepers creepers / Blues in the night / Something's gotta give / Fools rush in / PS I love you / When the world was young / That old black magic / Autumn leaves / I thought about you / Dream / One for my baby (and one more for the road)
CD CDP 7803262
Capitol / Apr '95 / EMI

FRANK SINATRA SINGS THE SELECT RODGERS & HART
Lover / Glad to be unhappy / I din't know what time it was / Where or when / It's easy to remember / There's a small hotel / Wait till you see her / Little girl blue / My funny valentine / It never entered my mind / Blue moon / I could write a book / Dancing on the ceiling / Lady is a tramp / Spring is here / I wish I was in love again / Bewitched, bothered and bewildered
CD CDP 7803232
Capitol / Apr '95 / EMI

FRANK SINATRA SINGS THE SELECT SAMMY CAHN
Come fly with me / Time after time / (Love is) the tender trap / Guess I'll hang my tears out to dry / Love and marriage / Saturday night (is the loneliest night in the week) / All the way / I've heard that song before / All my tomorrows / It's the same old dream / Come dance with me / Three coins in the fountain / Day by day / To love and be loved / High hopes / It's the last thing I do / Five minutes more / Last dance
CD PRMCD 14
Premier/EMI / Oct '96 / EMI

FRANK SINATRA SINGS THE SONGS OF SAMMY CAHN AND JULE STYNE
CD VJC 1045
Vintage Jazz Classics / Feb '94 / ADA / Cadillac / CM / Direct

FRANK SINATRA STORY, THE (40 Swing & Ballad Classics From 1939 To 1953/2CD Set)
From the bottom of my heart / On a little street in Singapore / East of the sun / I'll never smile again / It started all over again / You'll never know / I couldn't sleep a wink last night / If you are but a dream / Saturday night (is the loneliest night in the week) / There's no you / White Christmas / I dream of you (more than you dream) / I fall in love too easily / Ol' man river / Embraceable you / All or nothing at all / Just as though you were here / Close to you / Shine / Our love / When your lover has gone / She's funny that way / My melancholy baby / All the things you are / I should care / Dream / Over the rainbow / If I loved you / Jesus is a rock / My shawl / Someone to watch over me / You go to my head / These foolish things / I don't know why / Nancy (with the laughin' face) / Long ago and far away / Guess I'll hang my tears out to dry / Yes indeed / Tenderly / This can't be love
CD Set 303272
Hallmark / Mar '97 / Carlton

FRANK SINATRA VOL.3 (Stardust) (Sinatra, Frank & Tommy Dorsey Orchestra)
Stardust / I'll be seeing you / Dolores / This love of mine / Everything happens to me / Without a song / You and I / Oh, look at me now / It's always you / I tried / You might have belonged to another / I guess I'll have to dream the rest / Do I worry / How do you do without me / I think of you / Love me as I am / I'll never let a day pass by / Pale moon / Two in love / Let's get away from it all (Parts 1 & 2)
CD CD 403
Entertainers / Jul '96 / Target/BMG

FRANK SINATRA VOL.4 (Blue Skies) (Sinatra, Frank & Tommy Dorsey Orchestra)
Blue skies / There are such things / In the blue of evening / Dig down deep / Sunshine of your smile / How about you / Sinner kissed an angel / Violets for your furs / Be careful it's my heart / You lucky people you / Snootie little cutie / Daybreak / It started all over again / Light a candle in the chapel / Somewhere a voice is calling / Last call for love / Just as though you were here / Street of dreams / Take me / I'll take Tallulah
CD CD 404
Entertainers / Jul '96 / Target/BMG

FRANK SINATRA, DEAN MARTIN & SAMMY DAVIS JR. VOL.1 (Sinatra, Frank & Dean Martin/Sammy Davis Jr.)
CD JH 1033
Jazz Hour / Oct '93 / Cadillac / Jazz Music / Target/BMG

FRANK SINATRA, DEAN MARTIN & SAMMY DAVIS JR. VOL.2 (Sinatra, Frank & Dean Martin/Sammy Davis Jr.)
CD JH 1034
Jazz Hour / Oct '93 / Cadillac / Jazz Music / Target/BMG

GOLD COLLECTION, THE
CD D2CD 11
Deja Vu / Dec '92 / THE

GOLDEN DAYS OF RADIO
CD PWKS 4225
Carlton / Nov '94 / Carlton

GOT THE WORLD ON A STRING
I've got the world on a string / Them there eyes / If I could be with you one hour tonight / Under a blanket of blue / Just you, just me / Let's fall in love / Hands across the table / You must have been a beautiful baby / Someone to watch over me / I'll string along with you / Thou swell / You took advantage of me / Where or when / This can't be love / Try a little tenderness / Platinum blues / I'm confessin' that I love you / Sometimes I'm happy / My funny valentine / That old black magic
CD CDSB 007
Starburst / Jan '96 / TKO Magnum

GREATEST HITS (The Early Years)
If you are but a dream / Nancy (with the laughing face) / Girl that I marry / House I live in / Saturday night (is the loneliest night in the week) / Five minutes more / I have but one heart (O Marenariello) / Time after time / People will say we're in love
CD 4625612
Columbia / Dec '95 / Sony

HELLO YOUNG LOVERS
Netherless / What can I say after I say I'm sorry / Hello, young lovers / Love me or leave me / You toook advantage of me / Let's fall in love / Them there eyes / Somebody loves me / On the sunny side of the street / 'S Wonderful / Under a blanket of blue / I don't know why / Thou swell / I'm confessin' that I love you / Out of nowhere / Hundred years from today / Between the devil and the deep blue sea / What is this thing called love / Night and day / Just you, just me
CD MUCD 9025
Musketeer / Apr '95 / Disc

HIT PARADE SHOWS MAY 1949
CD JH 1036
Jazz Hour / Aug '94 / Cadillac / Jazz Music / Target/BMG

HOUSE I LIVE IN 1943-1946, THE
CD VJC 10072
Victorious Discs / Aug '90 / Jazz Music

I GET A KICK OUT OF YOU
CD ENTCD 231
Entertainers / Mar '92 / Target/BMG

I'LL BE SEEING YOU (Sinatra, Frank & Tommy Dorsey)
I'll be seeing you / Fools rush in / It's a lovely day today / Tomorrow / World is in my arms / We three (my echo, my shadow and me) / Dolores / Everything happens to me / Let's get away from it all / Blue skies / There are such things / Daybreak / You're part of my heart
CD 07863664272
Bluebird / Oct '94 / BMG

I'M IN THE MOOD FOR LOVE
's wonderful / I've got my love to keep me warm / I'm in the mood for love / Begin the beguine / Somebody loves me / Tenderly / I don't know why / I'll string along with you / On the sunny side of the street / They didn't believe me / Lady from the 29 palms / Hair of gold eyes of blue / It only happens when I dance with you / Nevertheless I'm in love with you / Between the devil and the deep blue sea / My happiness
CD 300142
Hallmark / Jul '96 / Carlton

I'VE GOT YOU UNDER MY SKIN
CD ENTCD 229
Entertainers / '88 / Target/BMG

IMAGINATION
Imagination / I'll never smile again / Hear my song Violetta / Fool rush in (where angels fear to tread) / This is the beginning of the end / Sky fell down / Shake down the stars / Moments in the moonlight / Say it / Dable of the rose / Devil may care / Call of the canyon / Love lies / World is in my arms / Our love affair / Looking for yesterday / We three / When you awake / Anything / Your breaking my heart all over again
CD CD 401
Entertainers / Jun '96 / Target/BMG

IN CELEBRATION
CD EXC 101
Exclusive / Nov '95 / Target/BMG

IN THE WEE SMALL HOURS
In the wee small hours of the morning / Glad to be unhappy / I get along without you very well / Deep in a dream / I see your face before me / Can't we be friends / When your lover has gone / What is this thing called love / I'll be around / Ill wind / It never entered my mind / I'll never be the same / This love of mine / Last night when we were young / Dancing on the ceiling
CD CDP 7968262
Capitol / Nov '92 / EMI

INIMITABLE FRANK SINATRA, THE (18 Hit Songs)
Come fly with me / Dancing in the dark / All the way / You make me feel so young / Love me or leave me / On the sunny side of the street / Blue skies / Begin the beguine / I didn't stand a ghost of a chance / Night and day / Somebody loves me / Just one of those things / You are my love / They didn't believe me / Out of nowhere / I've got my love to keep me warm / For you / Road to Mandalay
CD PLATCD 157
Platinum / Mar '96 / Prism

INSTRUMENTAL MEMORIES (Various Artists)
Lady is a tramp / You make me feel so young / Something stupid / One for my baby / That old black magic / All the way / Come fly with me / My way / Chicago / Strangers in the night / Witchcraft / Nancy / Tender trap / I've got you under my skin / I get a kick out of you / New York, New York
CD 306942
Hallmark / Jun '97 / Carlton

KID FROM HOBOKEN, THE (4CD Set)
CD Set CDDIG 6
Charly / Feb '95 / Koch

LEGENDS IN MUSIC
CD LECD 055
Wisepack / Jul '94 / Conifer/BMG / THE

LIGHT UP TIME 1949
CD JRR 1492
JR / Jul '92 / THE

LIVE (Seattle 9/6/1957)
CD JH 3001
Jazz Hour / Jun '95 / Cadillac / Jazz Music / Target/BMG

LIVE DUETS 1943-1957
CD VCD 1101
Voice / Jun '94 / Direct

LIVE IN AUSTRALIA (Sinatra, Frank & Red Norvo)
Perdido / Between the devil and the deep blue sea / I could have danced all night / Just one of those things / I get a kick out of you / At long last love / Willow weep for me / I've got you under my skin / Moonlight in Vermont / Lady is a tramp / Brief monologue from Frank / Angel eyes / Come fly with me / All the way / Dancing in the dark / One for my baby / All of me / On the road to Mandalay / Night and day
CD CDP 8375132
Blue Note / Mar '97 / EMI

LIVE IN CONCERT
You are the sunshine of my life / What now my love / My heart stood still / What's new / For once in my life / If / In the still of the night / Soliloquy / Maybe this time / Where or when / You will be my music / Strangers in the night / Angel eyes / New York, New York / My way
CD CDEST 2272
Premier/EMI / Dec '95 / EMI

LONDON 1 JUNE 1962
CD JRR 1622
JR / Apr '94 / THE

LOVE SONGS (Sinatra, Frank & Tommy Dorsey)
I'll never smile again / Stardust / Dolores / Everything happens to me / This love of mine / I'll guess I'll have to dream the rest / Violets for your furs / There are such things / Daybreak / It started all over again / Only forever / Just as though you were here / Night we called it a day / Lamplighter's serenade / Song is you / Night and day
CD 09026687012
RCA Victor / Mar '97 / BMG

MELBOURNE 19 JANUARY 1955
CD JRR 1552
JR / Nov '93 / THE

MONTE CARLO 14 JUNE 1958
CD JRR 1582
JR / Jul '92 / THE

MY WAY (The Best Of Frank Sinatra/ 2CD Set)
CD 9362467102
CD Set 9362467122
Reprise / Aug '97 / Warner Music

NEW YORK, NEW YORK (His Greatest Hits)
I get a kick out of you / Something stupid / Moon river / What now my love / Summer wind / Mrs. Robinson / My way / Strangers in the night / For once in my life / Yesterday / That's life / Girl from Ipanema / Lady is a tramp / Bad, Bad Leroy Brown / Ol' man river
CD 9239272
Reprise / '87 / Warner Music

NIGHT AND DAY
CD RMB 75020
Remember / Nov '93 / Total/BMG

NIGHT AND DAY (20 Classics)
CD CWNCD 2017
Javelin / Jul '96 / Henry Hadaway / THE

NIGHT AND DAY
CD LOK 01CD
Night & Day / Jan '94 / ADA / Direct / Discovery

OLD GOLD SHOWS 1946
CD JH 1040
Jazz Hour / Feb '95 / Cadillac / Jazz Music / Target/BMG

PACKET OF THREE VOL.5 (3CD Set) (Sinatra, Frank/Ray Charles/Louis Armstrong)
Come fly with me: *Sinatra, Frank* / Dancing in the dark: *Sinatra, Frank* / All the way: *Sinatra, Frank* / You make me feel so young: *Sinatra, Frank* / Love me or leave me: *Sinatra, Frank* / On the sunny side of the street: *Sinatra, Frank* / Blue skies: *Sinatra, Frank* / Begin the beguine: *Sinatra, Frank* / I don't stand a ghost of a chance with you: *Sinatra, Frank* / Night and day: *Sinatra, Frank* / Somebody loves me: *Sinatra, Frank* / Just one of those things: *Sinatra, Frank* / You are love: *Sinatra, Frank* / They didn't believe me: *Sinatra, Frank* / Out of nowhere: *Sinatra, Frank* / I've got my love to keep me warm: *Sinatra, Frank* / For you: *Sinatra, Frank* / Road to Mandalay: *Sinatra, Frank* / What'd I'd say: *Charles, Ray* / Georgia on my mind: *Charles, Ray* / Hardhearted Hannah: *Charles, Ray* / Ruby: *Charles, Ray* / Sticks and stones: *Charles, Ray* / Them that got: *Charles, Ray* / One mint julep: *Charles, Ray* / Hit the road Jack: *Charles, Ray* / Unchain my heart: *Charles, Ray* / Hide nor hair: *Charles, Ray* / Baby it's cold outside: *Charles, Ray* / At the club: *Charles, Ray* / I can't stop loving you: *Charles, Ray* / Born to lose: *Charles, Ray* / Careless love: *Charles, Ray* / You don't know me: *Charles, Ray* / You are my sunshine: *Charles, Ray* / Your cheating heart: *Charles, Ray* / Don't set me free: *Charles, Ray* / Take these chains from my heart: *Charles, Ray* / No one: *Charles, Ray* / Mame: *Armstrong, Louis* / When the saints go marching in: *Armstrong, Louis* / Ain't misbehavin': *Armstrong, Louis* / Cabaret: *Armstrong, Louis* / Kiss to build a dream on: *Armstrong, Louis* / Please don't talk about me when I'm gone: *Armstrong, Louis* / Blueberry Hill: *Armstrong, Louis* / Hello Dolly: *Armstrong, Louis* / St. Louis blues: *Armstrong, Louis* / That's my desire: *Armstrong, Louis* / Mack the knife: *Armstrong, Louis* / Back ole town blues: *Armstrong, Louis* / Fly me to the moon: *Armstrong, Louis* / Indiana: *Armstrong, Louis* / Tiger rag: *Armstrong, Louis* / Black and blue: *Armstrong, Louis* / C'est si bon: *Armstrong, Louis* / St. James Infirmary: *Armstrong, Louis* / Someday you'll be sorry: *Armstrong, Louis* / Sweethearts on parade: *Armstrong, Louis* / Jelly roll blues: *Armstrong, Louis*
CD Set KLMCD 305
BAM / Nov '96 / Koch / Scratch/BMG

POINT OF NO RETURN, THE
When the world was young / I'll remember April / September song / Million dreams ago / I'll see you again / There will never be another you / Somewhere along the way / It's a blue world / These foolish things / As time goes by / I'll be seeing you / Memories of you

CD CDP 7483342
Capitol / Nov '92 / EMI

PORTRAIT OF FRANK SINATRA, A
CD GALE 411
Gallerie / May '97 / Disc / THE

PORTRAIT OF SINATRA (2CD Set)
All or nothing at all / If you are but a dream / Night and day / Sweet Lorraine / Guess I'll hang my tears out to dry / Nancy / House I live in / Blue skies / There's no you / When your lover has gone / Stormy weather / Nearness of you / These foolish things / Saturday night (is the loneliest night in the week) / Where or when / Someone to watch over me / Put your dreams away / All of me / There's no business like show business / Falling in love with love / You go to my head / Everybody loves somebody / I believe / Why was I born / I've got a crush on you / Body and soul / That old feeling / Almost like being in love / September song / It never entered my mind / I only have eyes for you / Song is you / Don't cry Joe / It all depends on you / Continental / I'm a fool to want you
CD Set 4874972
Columbia / Jul '97 / Sony

RADIO RARITIES 1943-1949
CD VJC 10302
Vintage Jazz Classics / '91 / ADA / Cadillac / CM / Direct

RADIO YEARS
CD CDSR 017
Telstar / Jun '93 / BMG

RADIO YEARS 1939-1955, THE (6CD Set)
All or nothing / After all / I've got my eyes on you / Polka dots and moonbeams / Deep night / Whispering / Sky fell down / On the isle of May / It's a blue world / Fable of the rose / Marie / I'll get by / Lover is blue / Careless / I'll never smile again / Our love affair / East of the sun and west of the moon / One I love / Shadow on the sand / That's how it goes / I get a kick out of you / Let's get lost / Embraceable you / Night and day / Close to you / I couldn't sleep a wink last night / Falling in love with you / Music stopped / My ideal / Speak low / People will say we're in love / Long ago and far away / Sweet Lorraine / Swinging on a star / These foolish things / Very thought of you / All the things you are / My melancholy baby / Homesick / That's all / Till the end of time / What makes the sunset / I fall in love too easily / I begged her / Don't forget tonight tomorrow / That's for me / I found a new baby / I'm always chasing rainbows / Aren't you glad you're you / It might as well be spring / Lily belle / If I loved you / Slowly / Great day / I only have eyes for you / Oh what it seemed to be / Full moon and empty arms / Exactly like you / Summertime/It ain't neccessarily so / Bess, oh where's my bess / I fall in love with you every day / It's a good day / My sugar is so refined / Ole buttermilk sky / Lullaby of broadway / I won't dance
CD Set CDMT 901
Meteor / Aug '95 / TKO Magnum

REHEARSALS AND BROADCASTS 1942-1946
CD VJC 10042
Victorious Discs / Aug '90 / Jazz Music

REPRISE COLLECTION, THE (4CD Set)
CD Set 7599263402
Reprise / Sep '95 / Warner Music

REPRISE YEARS, THE
All the way / Come rain or come shine / I get a kick out of you / Night and day / All or nothing at all / I've got you under my skin / Didn't we / Strangers in the night / It was a very good year / Call me irresponsible / One for my baby (and one more for the road) / My kind of town (Chicago is) / September of my years / Luck be a lady / Something stupid / New York, New York / My way
CD 7599265222
Reprise / Dec '93 / Warner Music

ROMANTIC FRANK SINATRA, THE (2CD Set)
From the bottom of my heart / Melancholy mood / My buddy / Here comes the night / All or nothing at all / Ciribiribin / Night we called it a day / Lamplighter's serenade / Song is you / Night and day / You'll never know / Close to you / Sunday, Monday or always / People will say we're in love / Oh what a beautiful morning / I couldn't sleep a wink last night / Lovely way to spend an evening / If you are but a dream / There's no you / I dream of you / What makes the sunset / I fall in love to easily / Saturday night (is the loneliest night in the week) / Charm of you / Ol' man River / Stormy weather / When your lover has gone / Embraceable you / Kiss me again / She's funny that way / Mighty lak' a rose / Cradle song / Friend of yours / Dream / Homesick, that's all / I should care / If I loved you / You'll never walk alone / Stars in your eyes / My shawl / House I live in / America the beautiful / Nancy (with the laughing face) / Put your dreams away
CD Set CPCD 82582
Charly / Jan '97 / Koch

SCREEN SINATRA
From here to eternity / Three coins in the fountain / Young at heart / Just one of those things / Someone to watch over me / Not as a stranger / Tender trap / Wait for me (Johnny Concho theme) / All the way / Chicago / Monique-Song from Kings Go Forth / They came to Cordura / To love and be loved / High hopes / All my tomorrows / It's all right with me / C'est magnifique / Dream
CD CDMFP 6052
Music For Pleasure / Mar '89 / EMI

SENTIMENTAL GENTLEMAN 1940-1942 (2CD Set)
I'll be seeing you / Polka dots and moonbeams / Fools rush in / Imagination / East of the sun (and west of the moon) / I'll never smile again / Whispering / One I love (belongs to somebody else) / Love lies / Our love affair / We three (my echo, my shadow and me) / Do you know why / Marie / 14. star dust / How am I to know / Oh look at me now / You might have belonged to another / It's always you / You lucky people / Without a song / Everything happens to me / Let's get away from it all / This love of mine / Free for all / I guess I'll have to dream the rest / Blue skies / Sinner kissed an angel / Violets for your furs / How about you / Snootie little cutie / Street of dreams / In the blue of evening / There are such things / It started all over again / Who / Song is you
CD Set FA 974
Fremeaux / Apr '97 / ADA / Discovery

SINATRA (Music From The CBS Mini-Series)
Where the blue of the night meets the gold of the day: *Crosby, Bing* / Temptation: *Crosby, Bing* / All or nothing at all / Shake down the stars / Without a song / Street of dreams / I'll be seeing you / I'll never smile again / Sing sing sing: *Goodman, Benny* / Where or when / Stormy weather / Our love affair / I fall in love too easily / Hucklebuck / Fairy tale / Lover man: *Holiday, Billie* / You go to my head / I'm a fool to want you / It was a very good year / Autumn in New York / It all depends on you / They can't take that away from me / Come fly with me / High hopes / One for my baby (and one more for the road) / You make me feel so young / That's life / All the way / New York, New York / My way
CD 9362450912
Reprise / Nov '92 / Warner Music

SINATRA 80TH ALL THE BEST (2CD Set)
Lean baby / I'm walking behind you / I've got the world on a string / From here to eternity / South of the border (Down Mexico way) / Young at heart / Three coins in the fountain / Come fly with me / Someone to watch over me / Melody of love / Night and day / Learnin' the blues / Same old Saturday night / Love and marriage / Impatient years / (Love is) the tender trap / (How little it matters) How little we know / Johnny Concho theme (wait for me) / Lady is a tramp / Well did you evah / Hey jealous lover / I've got you under my skin / All the way / Chicago / Witchcraft / How are ya fixed for love / No one ever tells you / Time after time / In the wee small hours of the morning / You make me feel so young / I get a kick out of you / All my tomorrows / High hopes / What is this thing called love / Moon was yellow (and the night was young) / I love Paris / Blues in the night / Guess I'll hang my tears out to dry / Nice 'n' easy / Thye Christmas song
CD Set CDESTD 2
Premier/EMI / Dec '95 / EMI

SINATRA ARCHIVES VOL.2
CD FAS 19402
JR / Jul '92 / THE

SINATRA AT THE SANDS (Sinatra, Frank & Count Basie)
Come fly with me / I've got a crush on you (vocal only) / I've got you under my skin / Shadow of your smile / Street of dreams / One for my baby (and one more for the road) / Fly me to the moon / One o'clock jump / You make me feel so young / All of me / September of my years / Get me to the church on time / It was a very good year / Don't worry 'bout me / Makin' whoopee / Where or when / Angel eyes / My kind of town (Chicago is)
CD 9010192
Reprise / Nov '86 / Warner Music

SINATRA CHRISTMAS ALBUM, THE
Jingle bells / Christmas song / Mistletoe and holly / I'll be home for Christmas / Have yourself a merry little Christmas / Christmas waltz / First Noel / Hark the herald angels sing / O little town of Bethlehem / O come all ye faithful (Adeste fidelis) / It came upon a midnight clear / Silent night / White Christmas / Christmas waltz (alternate)
CD CDMFP 5797
Music For Pleasure / Oct '96 / EMI

SINATRA'S SWINGIN' SESSION
When you're smiling / Blue moon / S'posin' / It all depends on you / It's only a paper moon / My blue Heaven / Should I / September in the rain / Always / I can't believe that you're in love with me / I concentrate on you / You do something to me / Sentimental baby / Ol' MacDonald / Hidden persuasion
CD BU 20
Capitol / Mar '88 / EMI

SONG IS YOU, THE (3CD Set) (Sinatra, Frank & Tommy Dorsey)
Sky fell down / Too romantic / Shake down the stars / Moments in the moonlight / I'll be seeing you / Say it / Polka dots and moonbeams / Fable of the rose / This is the beginning of the end / Hear my song Violetta / Fools rush in / Devil may care / April played the fiddle / I haven't time to be a millionaire / Imagination / Yours is my heart alone / You're lonely and I'm lonely / East of the sun and west of the moon / Head on my pillow / It's a lovely day tomorrow / I'll never smile again / All this and heaven too / Where do you keep your heart / Whispering / Trade winds / One I love (belongs to somebody else) / Call of the canyon / Love lies / I could make you care / World is in my arms / Our love affair / Looking for yesterday / Tell me at midnight / We three (my echo, my shadow and me) / When you awake / Anything / Shadows on the sand / You're breaking my heart all over again / I'd know you anywhere / Do you know why / Long ago / Stardust / Oh look at me now / You might have belonged to another / You lucky people / It's always you / I tried / Dolores / Without a song / Do I worry / Everything happens to me / Let's get away from it all / I'll never let a day pass me by / Love me as I am / This love of mine / I guess I'll have to dream the rest / You and I / Neiani / Free for all / Blue skies / Two in love / Pale moon / I think of you / How do you do without me / Sinner kissed an angel / Violets for your furs / Sunshine of your smile / How about you / Snootie little cutie / Poor you / I'll take Tallulah / Last call for love / Somewhere a voice is calling / Just as though you were here / Street of dreams / Take me / Be careful it's my heart / In the blue of evening / Dig down deep / There are such things / Daybreak / It started all over again / Light a candle in the chapel / Too romantic / Shake down the stars / Hear my song Violetta / You're lonely and I'm lonely / Our love affair / Violets for your fur / Night we called it a day / Lamplighter's serenade / Song is you / Night and day / I'm getting sentimental over you / Who / I hear a rhapsody / I'll never smile again / Half way down the street / Some of your sweetness (got into my heart) / Once in a while / Little love / It came to me / Only forever / Marie / Yearning / How am I to know / You're part of my heart / Announcements / You're stepping on my toes / You got the best of me / That's how it goes / When daylight dawns / When sleepy stars begin to fall / Goodbye lover, goodbye / One red rose / Things I love / In the blue of evening / Just as though you were here / Frank Sinatra's farewell to the Tommy Dorsey Orchestra / Song is you
CD Set 07863663532
Bluebird / Jan '97 / BMG

SONGBOOK (2CD Set)
You make me feel so young / All the way / On the sunny side of the street / On the road to Mandalay / Dancing in the dark / For you / Come fly with me / They don't believe me / Just one of those things / I've got you under my skin / I get a kick out of you / My funny valentine / Bewitched / Lady is a tramp / At long last love / Moonlight in Vermont / My blue heaven / When your lover has gone / Imagination / I could have danced all night / Begin the beguine / I've got my love to keep me warm / (I didn't stand a) Ghost of a chance / Blue skies / Out of nowhere / Somebody loves me / Love me or leave me / Tea for two / This love of mine / Stardust / Night and day / I think of you / Lamplighter's serenade / Street of dreams / Whispering / This is the beginning of the end / Be careful, it's my heart / Sinner kissed an angel / How about you / Our love affair
CD Set MUCD 9509
Musketeer / May '96 / Disc

SONGS BY SINATRA (2CD Set)
Introduction / Stars in your eyes / Talk / There's no you / Old Gold commercial / Gotta be this or that: *Pied Pipers* / If I loved you / Talk with music / Embraceable you: *Sinatra, Frank & The Crosby Kids* / Old Gold commercial #2 / Closing / On the atchison, Topeka and the Snata Fe / I'll buy that dream: *Pied Pipers* / Skit: *Pied Pipers* / Old commercial: *Pied Pipers* / My melancholy baby / You was right: *Lee, Peggy* / Surrey with fringe on top: *Pied Pipers* / I fall in love too easily / Old gold commercial / Talk / House I live in / You'll never know / As time goes by / Are you glad you're you / It might as welll be you / In the middle of May / Button up your overcoat / Day by day / Lily Belle / Ol' man river / There's no you / Paris aye, aye / It's been a long long time / It's only a paper moon / All the things you are / Skit with music / Two hearts are better than one / Let it snow let it snow let it snow
CD Set OTA 101976
BR Music / Jun '97 / Target/BMG

SONGS BY SINATRA - OLD GOLD SHOWS VOL.2 (2CD Set)
That's for me / Kiss goodnight: *Sinatra, Frank & Patty Andrews* / Old gold commercial: *Sinatra, Frank & Patty Andrews* / We'll be together again: *Sinatra, Frank & Patty Andrews* / How deep is the ocean: *Sinatra, Frank & Patty Andrews* / Begin the beguin: *Andrews Sisters* / At the paramount: *Andrews Sisters* / Old gold commercial: *Andrews Sisters* / Tampico: *Pied Pipers* / Without a song: *Pied Pipers* / I'll never smile again: *Sinatra, Frank & Tommy Dorsey/Pied Pipers* / I begged her / I fall in love with you every day / Great day / Good king Wenceslas/Wassail song / Embraceable you: *Pied Pipers* / Symphony / Father time / Lullaby / Let's start the new year right: *Sinatra, Frank & Bob Mitchell Boys Choir* / You'll never walk alone / America the beautiful / But I did: *Maxwell, Marilyn* / Stranger in town: *Pied Pipers* / Till the end of time: *Pied Pipers* / Felicia no capricia: *Prima, Louis* / Some Sunday morning: *Prima, Louis* / House I live in / You keep coming back like a song / This is always
CD Set OTA 101977
On The Air / Jun '97 / Target/BMG

SONGS FOR SWINGIN' LOVERS
Too marvellous for words / Old devil moon / Pennies from Heaven / Our love is here to stay / I've got you under my skin / I thought about you / We'll be together again / Makin' whoopee / Swingin' down the lane / Anything goes / How about you / You make me feel so young / It happened in Monterey / You're getting to be a habit with me / You brought a new kind of love to me
CD BU 17
Capitol / Mar '88 / EMI

SONGS FOR YOUNG LOVERS & SWING EASY
CD CDP 7484702
Capitol / Nov '92 / EMI

SPOTLIGHT ON FRANK SINATRA
I wonder who's kissing her now / I'll string along with you / Devil and the deep blue sea / Speak low / Mimi / At long last love / Lover is blue / Day by day / Five more minutes / After I say I'm sorry / Serenade of the bells / Long ago and far away / I wish I didn't love you so / You're the top / It's all up to you / Some other time
CD HADCD 131
Javelin / Feb '94 / Henry Hadaway / THE

STARS SALUTE SINATRA (Various Artists)
Night and day: *Astaire, Fred* / How about you: *Garland, Judy* / Sunday, Monday or always: *Crosby, Bing* / Fools rush in: *Miller, Glenn* / One for my baby (and one more for the road): *Horne, Lena* / They can't take that away from me: *Dorsey, Jimmy* / I get a kick out of you: *Merman, Ethel* / Sweet Lorraine: *Tatum, Art* / Yesterdays: *Holiday, Billie* / Jeepers creepers: *Armstrong, Louis* / Imagination: *Fitzgerald, Ella* / I'll follow my secret heart: *Coward, Noel* / Lady is a tramp: *Dorsey, Tommy* / All or nothing: *Haymes, Dick* / Glad to be unhappy: *Wiley, Lee* / I'll never smile again: *Shelton, Anne* / I didn't know what time was: *Shaw, Artie* / Where are you: *Bailey, Mildred* / Embraceable you: *Hackett, Bobby* / Blues in the night: *Shore, Dinah* / River stay 'way from my door: *Waters, Ethel* / When your love has gone: *Austin, Gene* / Always: *Durbin, Deanna* / Mood indigo: *Ellington, Duke*
CD CECD 4
Collector's Edition / Nov '95 / TKO Magnum

SUNDAY MORNING OR ALWAYS
CD CPCD 8157
Charly / Nov '95 / Koch

SWING & DANCE WITH FRANK SINATRA
Saturday night (is the loneliest night in the week) / All of me / I've got a crush on you / Huckle buck / It all depends on you / Bye bye baby / All of me / Should I / You do something to me / Lover / When you're smiling / It's only a paper moon / My blue heaven / Continental / Meet me at the Copa / Nevertheless / There's something missing / Farewell / Farewell to love
CD 4851882
Columbia / Aug '96 / Sony

SWING EASY
Jeepers creepers / Taking a chance on love / Wrap your troubles in dreams (and dream your troubles away) / Lean baby / I love you / I'm gonna sit right down and write myself a letter / Get happy / All of me / How could you do a thing like that to me / Why should I cry over you / Sunday / Just one of those things
CD CDMFP 5973
Music For Pleasure / Oct '92 / EMI

SWINGIN' AFFAIR, A
Night and day / I wish I were in love again / I got plenty o' nuttin' / I guess I'll have to change my plan / Nice work if you can get it / Stars fell on Alabama / No one ever tells you / I won't dance / Lonesome road / At long last love / You'd be so nice to come home to / I got it bad and that ain't good / From this moment on / If I had you / Oh, look at me now
CD CZ 393
Capitol / Mar '91 / EMI

THERE ARE SUCH THINGS (Sinatra, Frank & Tommy Dorsey)
Blue skies / Call of the canyon / Daybreak / East of the sun and west of the moon /

Everything happens to me / Fools rush in / Hear my song Violetta / How about you / I'll never smile again / Imagination / Let's get away from it all / One I love (belongs to somebody else) / Polka dots and moonbeams / Sinner kissed an angel / Somewhere a voice is calling / Stardust / There are such things / This love of mine / Too romantic / Violets for your furs / Whispering / Without a song / Yours is my heart alone
CD ______ CDAJA 5106
Living Era / Apr '93 / Select

THERE'LL BE SOME CHANGES MADE
CD ______ VCD 1102
Voice / Jun '94 / Direct

THIS IS FRANK SINATRA 1953-1957
I've got the world on a string / Three coins in the fountain / Love and marriage / From here to eternity / South of the border (Down Mexico way) / Rain / Gal that got away / Young at heart / Learnin' the blues / My one and only love / Tender trap / Don't worry 'bout me / Look to your heart / Anytime anywhere / Not as a stranger / Our town / You, my love / Same old Saturday night / Fairy tale / Impatient years / I could have told you / When I stop loving you / If I had three wishes / I'm gonna live till I die / Hey jealous lover / Everybody loves somebody / Something wonderful happens in summer / Half as lovely / You're cheating' yourself (if you're cheatin' on me) / You'll always be the one I love / You forgot all the words / How little it matters, how little we know / Time after time / Crazy love / Johnny Concho theme (wait for me) / If you are but a dream / So long, my love / It's the same old dream / I believe / Put your dreams away
CD Set ______ CDDL 1275
EMI / Nov '94 / EMI

THIS LOVE OF MINE
From the bottom of my heart / Melancholy mood / My buddy / It's funny to everyone but me / On a little street in Singapore / East of the Sun and West of the moon / Our love affair / This love of mine / Blue skies / How about you / There are such things / Night we called it a day / Lamplighter's serenade / Song is you / Night and day / Close to you / You'll never know / Sunday Monday or always / I begged her / If you are but a dream / People will say we're in love / Oh what a beautiful morning
CD ______ CDMOIR 511
Memoir / Sep '95 / Jazz Music / Target/ BMG

THIS ONE'S FOR TOMMY
CD ______ VCD 1103
Viper's Nest / May '95 / ADA / Cadillac / Direct / Jazz Music

TIME AFTER TIME
Time after time / Our love / All or nothing at all / On a little Street in Singapore / East of the sun and West of the moon / I'll never smile again / Everything happens to me / This love of mine / There are such things / Just as though you were there / People will say we're in love / Lovely way to spend an evening / I couldn't sleep a wink last night / Night and day / White Christmas / You'll never know / Long ago (and far away) / Guess I'll hang my tears out to dry / Saturday night / I'll walk alone / Exactly like you / I fall in love too easily / Body and soul / You'll be so nice to come home to / Our love is here to stay / I can't believe that you're in love with me / Day by day
CD ______ CECD 1
Collector's Edition / Oct '95 / TKO Magnum

TOUCH OF CLASS, A
As time goes by / You'll never know / How deep is the ocean / I only have eyes for you / People will say we're in love / Embraceable you / September song / Blue skies / They say it's wonderful / Begin the beguine / Fools rush in / Let's get away from it all / You'll never walk alone / There will never be another you / Things we did last summer / In the blue of the evening / Day by day / Too romantic
CD ______ TC 877042
Disky / May '97 / Disky / THE

TRIBUTE TO THE GUV'NOR, A
Saturday night is the loneliest night / You'll never know / Oh what a beautiful morning / Stormy weather / People will say we're in love / At long last love / Sunday morning or always / Day by day / Close to you / Night and day / Lovely way to spend an evening / White christmas / I dream of you (more than you dream of me) / Cradle song / What makes a sunset / Ol' man river / If you please / Embraceable you / Kiss me again / I fall in love too easily
CD ______ ALPCD 101
Alpha Entertainments / Mar '97 / Pinnacle

TWENTY GOLDEN GREATS
That old black magic / Love and marriage / Fools rush in / Lady is a tramp / Swingin' down the lane / All the way / Witchcraft / It happened in Monterey / You make me feel so young / Nice 'n' easy / Come fly with me / High hopes / Let's do it / I've got you under my skin / Chicago / Three coins in the fountain / It's nice to go trav'ling / Young at heart / In the wee small hours of the morning / Tender trap
CD ______ CDEMTV 10
Capitol / May '92 / EMI

UNHEARD FRANK SINATRA VOL.1 & 2, THE (2CD Set)
Your hit parade theme & opening announcements / I've heard that song before / As time goes by / As time goes by / Let's get lost / If you please / Pistol packin' mama / I'll be seeing you / I love you / Your hit parade end theme show closer excerpt / Everything I have is yours / I can't get out of this mood / Miss Annabelle Lee / Too much in love / Amor / As long as there is music / Dancing in the dark / It could happen to you / Come out wherever you are / It had to be you / If loveliness were music / More and More / More than you know / Easter parade / Candy / This is always / You keep coming back like a song / End theme put your dreams away / They say it's wonderful / Opening theme and D-Day announcement / They'll be a hot time in the town of Berlin / Song is you / Where or when / America the beautiful / Nancy with the laughing face / I've got a woman crazy for me / It could happen to you / I'll be seeing you / Begin the beguine / Speak low / Opening and announcements / It's only a paper moon / I fall in love too easily / Charm of you / Oh Bess where's my Bess / It might as well be Spring / House that I live in that's America to me / Coffee song (they've got an awful lot of coffee in Brazil) / Lost in the stars / Closing theme put your dreams away / I saw you first / Lovely way to spend an evening / I couldn't sleep a wink last night
CD Set ______ VOICE 1100
Voice / Aug '97 / Direct

UNHEARD FRANK SINATRA VOL.4 - I'LL BE SEEING YOU
CD ______ VJCD 1051
Vintage Jazz Classics / Feb '94 / ADA / Cadillac / CM / Direct

V DISCS - THE COLUMBIA YEARS, THE (1943-1952/2CD Set)
I only have eyes for you / Kiss me again / (There's gonna be a) Hot time in the town of Berlin / Music stopped / I couldn't sleep a wink last night / Way you look tonight / I'll be around / You've got a hold on me / Lovely way to spend an evening / She's funny that way / Speak low / Close to you / My shining hour / Long ago and far away / Some other time / Come out come out wherever you are / Put your dreams away / And then you kissed me / All the things you are / All of me / Nancy with the laughing face / Mighty like a rose / Falling in love with love / Cradle song / I'll follow my secret heart / There's no you / Someone to watch over me / Let me love you tonight / Just close your eyes / If you are but a dream / Strange music / Dick Haymes, Dick Todd and Como / None but the lonely heart / Ol' man river / Homesick, that's all / Night is young and you're so beautiful / Aren't you glad you're you / You brought a new kind of love to me / I'll never smile again / Without a song / Was the last time I saw you (the last time) / Don't forget tonight tomorrow / Oh - What it seemed to be / Over the rainbow / Where is my Bess / My romance / Song is you / Fall in love with you ev'ry day / They say it's wonderful / You are too beautiful / Come rain or come shine / Stormy weather
CD Set ______ C2K 66135
Legacy / Oct '94 / Sony

WASHINGTON DC APRIL 1973
CD ______ JRR 1732
JR / Oct '94 / THE

WHERE ARE YOU
Where are you / Night we called it a day / I cover the waterfront / Maybe you'll be there / Laura / Lonely town / Autumn leaves / I'm a fool to want you / I think of you / Where is the one / There's no you / Baby, won't you please come home / I can read between the lines / It worries me / Rain / Don't worry 'bout me
CD ______ CZ 390
Capitol / Mar '91 / EMI

WHISPERING
Whispering / East of the sun and west of the moon / Polka dots and moonbeams / I could make you care / Shadows in the sand / Tell me at midnight / I haven't time to be a millionaire / April played the fiddle / Yours is my heart alone / You're lonely and I'm lonely / Head on my pillow / It's a lovely day tomorrow / All this and heaven too / Where do you keep your heart / Trade winds / One I love / I'd know you anywhere / Do you know why / Not so long ago
CD ______ CD 402
Entertainers / Jun '96 / Target/BMG

YOU MAKE ME FEEL SO YOUNG
Night and day / Laura / Somebody loves me / Little white lies / This can't be love / You make me feel so young / Speak low / You do something to me / Begin the beguine / Tenderly / On the sunny side of the street / Love me or leave me / They didn't believe me / Out of nowhere / I've got my love to keep me warm / For you
CD ______ ENTCD 213
Entertainers / '88 / Target/BMG

YOU MAKE ME FEEL SO YOUNG
You make me feel so young / 'S wonderful / Love me or leave me / On the sunny side of the street / Blue skies / They say it's wonderful / Begin the beguine / Ol' man river / Don't blame me / It all depends on you / I fall in love with you / Music stopped / I don't stand a ghost of a chance with you / You do something to me / Night and day / Somebody loves me / Just one of those things / Nevertheless / You are love / They did not believe me / Out of nowhere / I've got my love to keep me warm / For you
CD ______ GRF 136
Tring / '93 / Tring

YOUNG BLUE EYES
CD ______ CDGR 107
Charly / Jan '96 / Koch

YOUNG SINATRA
Oh what a beautiful morning / If you please / Saturday night is the loneliest night of the week / Sunshine of your smile / East of the sun and west of the moon / Delores / I guess I'll have to dream the rest / Blue skies / I'll never smile again / Whispering / Take me / Be careful it's my heart / Without a song / This love of mine / Lamplighter's serenade / Night and day / If you are but a dream / Kiss me again / There's no you / I dream of you / I begged her / I fall in love too easily / Embraceable you / When your love has gone
CD ______ CDHD 263
Happy Days / Feb '97 / Conifer/BMG

YOUR HIT PARADE 1947
CD ______ JRR 1472
JR / Jul '92 / THE

YOUR HIT PARADE 1948
CD ______ JRR 1482
JR / Jul '92 / THE

YOUR HIT PARADE 1949
CD ______ JRR 2492
JR / Apr '94 / THE

Sinatra, Nancy

BOOTS
As tears go by / Day tripper / I move around / It ain't me babe / These boots are made for walking / In my room / Lies / So long babe / Flowers on the wall / If he'd leave me / Run for your life / City never sleeps at night / Leave my dog alone / In our time / These boots are made for walkin' (mono)
CD ______ NANCD 104
Nancy / Nov '96 / Grapevine/PolyGram

GREATEST HITS
Storybook children / These boots are made for walking / Sugar town / Something stupid / How does that grab you, darlin' / Summer wine / Sundown sundown / I've been down so long / Sand / Oh lonesome me / Ladybird / Jackson / You've lost that lovin' feelin' / Some velvet morning / Did you ever / Elusive dreams / Greenwich village folksong man / So long, babe
CD ______ PLATCD 3903
Platinum / Oct '88 / Prism

GREATEST HITS
CD ______ PA 7112
Paradiso / Apr '94 / Target/BMG

GREATEST HITS
CD ______ NANCD 102
Nancy / Jul '96 / Grapevine/PolyGram

HITS OF NANCY & LEE (Sinatra, Nancy & Lee Hazelwood)
CD ______ NANCD 101
Nancy / Jul '96 / Grapevine/PolyGram

HOW DOES THAT GRAB YOU
CD ______ NANCD 105
Nancy / Feb '97 / Grapevine/PolyGram

NANCY IN LONDON
On Broadway / End / Step aside / I can't grow peaches on a cherry tree / Summer wine / Wishin' and hopin' / This little bird / Shades / The more I see you / Hutchinson Jail / Friday's child / 100 years / You only live twice / Tony Rome / Life's a trippy thing
CD ______ NANCD 103
Nancy / Nov '96 / Grapevine/PolyGram

SUGAR
CD ______ NANCD 106
Nancy / Feb '97 / Grapevine/PolyGram

Sinclair, Dave

MOON OVER MAN
Wanderlust / Tropic island / Mallorcan dance / Make yourself at home / Harry / Moon over man / Where have I gone / Ice cream / Make a brand new start / Moving on / Lost in the woods / Reminiscermemoring / Honky dorry / Piano player / Back for tea / Here to stay
CD ______ BP 119CD
Blueprint / Aug '96 / Pinnacle

MOON OVER MOON
Wanderlust / Tropical island / Mallorcan dance / Make yourself at home / Harry / Where have I gone / Make a brand new start / Moving on / Lost in the woods / Reminiscermemoring / Honky dorry / Piano player / Back for tea / Here to stay
CD ______ VP 119CD
Voiceprint / May '93 / Pinnacle

Sinclair, Richard

CARAVAN OF DREAMS
Going for a song / Cruising / Only the brave / Plan it Earth / Heather / Keep on coming / Emily / Felafel shuffle / Five go wilde
CD ______ HTDCD 7
HTD / Sep '96 / CM / Pinnacle

EVENING OF MAGIC, AN
CD ______ HIDCD 17
HTD / Jan '94 / CM / Pinnacle

Sincola

CRASH LANDING IN TEEN HEAVEN
Rundown / Not 100% pure / Happy MF / One hit wonder / Nerd God / Legendary nowhere / Letterbomb / Star '79 / In the bone garden / Start/Stop / Canal / Red Danube
CD ______ CAROL 003CD
Caroline / Sep '96 / Cargo / Vital

SINCOLA
CD ______ RR 1232
Rise / Feb '94 / Pinnacle

Sindelfingen

ODGIPIG
CD ______ HBG 122/10
Background / Apr '94 / Background / Greyhound

Sindy Kills Me

SINDY KILLS ME
Clearblue / Snakeskin jacket
CD ______ PANNCD 14
Pandemonium / Jul '96 / RTM/Disc / Vital

Sine

VITAL SINES
Eaglesfield skyline / Stand up and be counted / Valentine / Good day for goodbyes / Anne-elise / Nirvana / Black sea rover / Go away / A better man
CD ______ MIN 07CD
Minority/One / Aug '97 / Pinnacle

Sinfield, Pete

STILLUSION
Can you forgive a fool / Night people / Will it be you / Hanging fire / House of hopes and dreams / Wholefood boogie / Piper / Under the sky / Envelopes of yesterday / Song of the sea goat / Still
CD ______ BP 152CD
Blueprint / Aug '96 / Pinnacle

Singabangqobi

GREATER IS HE
CD ______ FIFCD 1001
Friends In Fellowship / Oct '92 / Jet Star

Singers & Players

GOLDEN GREATS VOL.1
CD ______ ONUCD 4
On-U Sound / Sep '89 / Jet Star / SRD

GOLDEN GREATS VOL.2
CD ______ ONUCD 26
On-U Sound / Jul '95 / Jet Star / SRD

LEAPS AND BOUNDS
CD ______ CDBRED 58
Cherry Red / Sep '91 / Pinnacle

Singers Unlimited

CHRISTMAS
Deck the halls with boughs of holly / Ah bleak and chill the wintry wind / Bright, bright the hollly berries / Nigh Bethlehem / While by my sheep / It came upon a midnight clear / Silent night / Joy to the world / Wassailing song carol of the Russian children / Good King Wenceslas / O come all ye faithful (Adeste Fidelis) / Coventry carol / Have yourself a merry little Christmas / Jesu parvule / Caroling, caroling / What are the signs
CD ______ 8218592
MPS Jazz / Nov '84 / PolyGram

Singh, Talvin

ANOKHA (Talvin Singh Presents Soundz Of The Asian Underground) (Various Artists)
Jaan: *Singh, Talvin* / Flight IC 408: *State Of Bengal* / Kizmet: *Lelonek* / Shang high: *Future Soundz Of India* / Chitagong chill: *State Of Bengal* / Mumbai theme tune: *Rahman, A.R.* / Distant sun: *Singh, Talvin* / Heavy intro: *Amar* / Equation: *Equal I* / Spiritual masterkey: *Osmani Soundz* / Accepting tranquility: *Milky Bar Kid* / K-ascendant: *Biswas, Kingsuk*
CD ______ CIDM 1120
Omni / Feb '97 / PolyGram

Singing Kettle

GREATEST HITS VOL.1
CD ______ KOP 27CD
Kettle / Aug '95 / CM / Duncans / Roots / Ross

Singing Melody

SINGING MELODY
If I'm crazy / Send come call me / You bring me joy / Love thingI'm going down / Love thing / I'm going down / Give it all up / In the mood / Rock bottom / Nothing wrong / Brighter day / Turn the lights down / Cross dem border
CD ______ 119902
Musidisc UK / Jun '97 / Grapevine/ PolyGram

Singing Sweet

DON'T SAY NO
CD ______ CFCD 2
Colin Fat / Apr '93 / Jet Star

Single Cell Orchestra

DEAD VENT 7
CD ______ EFA 003182
Reflective / Jul '95 / RTM/Disc / SRD

KNOCKOUT DROPS
CD ______ EFA 709622
Asphodel / Sep '96 / Cargo / SRD

Single Gun Theory

EXORCISE THIS WASTELAND
CD ______ NTCD 039
Nettwerk / '88 / Greyhound / Pinnacle / Vital

FLOW RIVER OF MY SOUL
CD ______ W 230088
Edel / May '95 / Pinnacle

LIKE STARS IN MY HAND
CD ______ NETCD 020
Nettwerk / Nov '91 / Greyhound / Pinnacle / Vital

Singleton, T-Bone

WALKIN' THE FLOOR
Sunset blues / Walkin' the floor / Reconcile / Don't ever go / Boogie train / Light in a dark place / Gonna make me cry / Let me be your man / Tryna get along / Power up
CD ______ JSPCD 267
JSP / May '96 / ADA / Cadillac / Direct / Hot Shot / Target/BMG

Sinikka

HAR DU LYTTET TIL ELVENE OM NATTA
CD ______ GR 4017CD
Grappa / Mar '96 / ADA

Sinister

DIABOLICAL SUMMONING
CD ______ NB 081
Nuclear Blast / Aug '93 / Plastic Head

HATE
CD ______ NB 131
Nuclear Blast / Jul '95 / Plastic Head

Sinkadus

AURUM NOSTRUM
Snalblast / Manuel / Agren / Attestupan
CD ______ CYCL 048
Cyclops / Mar '97 / Pinnacle

Sinner

BOTTOM LINE
CD ______ 342612
No Bull / Oct '95 / Koch

DANGEROUS CHARM
CD ______ N 01013
Noise / Nov '87 / Koch

IN THE LINE OF FIRE
CD ______ 343472
Koch International / May '96 / Koch

NO MORE ALIBIS
CD ______ 343462
No Bull / Mar '96 / Koch

RESPECT
CD ______ 342702
No Bull / Dec '95 / Koch

Sinners

TURN IT UP
CD ______ MNWCD 213
MNW / Jan '92 / ADA / Vital

Sinoath

RESEARCH
CD ______ POLYPH 003CD
Polyphemus / Jul '96 / Plastic Head

STILL IN GREY DYING
CD ______ 1 STSINONCD
SPV / May '95 / Koch / Plastic Head

Sins Of The Flesh

1ST AID - BUTCHERED BEATS
CD ______ FILECD 7HZ
X-Communication / Nov '96 / RTM/Disc

Sinti

SINTI
Going to the USA / Que pasa / Dark eyes (Ojos negros) / Flintstones / Hi Pat / Isn't she lovely / For Wesley / Blues for Ike / Patchiena / My emotion / Chez moi / On my mind / For Hans / Fricha / Limehouse blues / Caravan / Dina
CD ______ 4837452
Sony Jazz / Mar '96 / Sony

Siouxsie & The Banshees

HYENA
Take me back / Running town / Pointing bone / Blow the house down / Dazzle / We hunger / Belladonna / Swimming horses / Bring me the head of the preacher man
CD ______ 8215102
Wonderland / Mar '95 / PolyGram

JOIN HANDS
Poppy day / Regal zone / Placebo effect / Icon / Premature burial / Playground twist / Mother / On mein papa / Lord's prayer
CD ______ 8390042
Wonderland / Mar '95 / PolyGram

JU JU
Spellbound / Into the light / Arabian knights / Halloween / Monitor night shift / Sin in my heart / Head cut / Voodoo dolly
CD ______ 8390052
Wonderland / Mar '95 / PolyGram

KALEIDOSCOPE
Happy house / Tenant / Trophy / Hybrid / Clockface / Lunar camel / Christine / Desert kisses / Red light / Paradise place / Skin
CD ______ 8390062
Wonderland / Mar '95 / PolyGram

KISS IN THE DREAMHOUSE, A
Cascade / Green fingers / Obsession / She's a carnival / Circle / Melt / Painted bird / Cacoon / Slowdive
CD ______ 8390072
Wonderland / Mar '95 / PolyGram

NOCTURNE
Intro (The rite of spring) / Israel / Dear Prudence / Paradise place / Melt / Cascade / Pulled to bits / Nightshift / Sin in my heart / Slowdive / Painted bird / Happy house / Switch / Spellbound / Helter skelter / Eve white, Eve black / Voodoo dolly
CD ______ 8390092
Wonderland / Mar '95 / PolyGram

PEEP SHOW
Peek-a-boo / Killing jar / Scarecrow / Carousel / Burn-up / Ornaments of gold / Turn to stone / Rawhead and bloody bones / Last beat of my heart / Rhapsody
CD ______ 8372402
Wonderland / Mar '95 / PolyGram

RAPTURE, THE
O Baby / Tearing apart / Stargazers / Fall from grace / Not forgotten / Sick child / Lonely one / Falling down / Forever / Rapture / Double life / Love out me
CD ______ 5237252
Wonderland / Oct '94 / PolyGram

SCREAM, THE
Pure / Jigsaw feeling / Overground / Carcass / Helter skelter / Mirage / Metal postcard / Nicotine stain / Surburban relapse / Switch
CD ______ 8390082
Wonderland / Mar '95 / PolyGram

STRAWBERRY GIRL (A Tribute To Siouxsie & The Banshees) (Various Artists)
CD ______ DOP 52
Doppelganger / Jul '97 / Total/BMG

SUPERSTITION
Kiss them for me / Fear (Of the unknown) / Cry / Drifter / Little sister / Shadowtime / Silly thing / Got to get up / Silver waterfalls / Softly / Ghost in you
CD ______ 8477312
Wonderland / Mar '95 / PolyGram

THROUGH THE LOOKING GLASS
Hall of mirrors / Trust in me / This wheel's on fire / Strange fruit / This town ain't big enough for the both of us / You're lost little girl / Passenger / Gun / Little Johnny Jewel
CD ______ 8314742
Wonderland / Mar '95 / PolyGram

TINDERBOX
Candy man / Sweetest chill / This unrest / Cities in dust / Cannons / Party's fall / 92 / Land's end / Quarterdrawing of the dog / Execution / Lullaby / Umbrella / Cities in dust (Extended version)
CD ______ 8291452
Wonderland / Mar '95 / PolyGram

TWICE UPON A TIME
CD ______ 5171602
Wonderland / Mar '95 / PolyGram

Sipahi, Nesrin

SHARKI LOVE SONGS FROM ISTANBUL (Sipahi, Nesrin & The Kudsi Erguner Ensemble)
CD ______ CMP CD 3009
CMP / Jul '92 / Cargo / Grapevine/ PolyGram / Vital/SAM

Siperkov

GIPSY MUSIC
CD ______ SYNCD 163
Syncoop / Jun '94 / ADA / Direct

Sir Bald Diddley

NITROGEN PEROXIDE
CD ______ WIGCD 013
Alopecia / Apr '97 / Plastic Head

Sir Doug & The Texans

TEXAS ROCK FOR COUNTRY ROLLERS
CD ______ EDCD 535
Edsel / Aug '97 / Pinnacle

Sir Douglas Quintet

COLLECTION, THE
CD ______ COL 060
Collection / Mar '95 / Target/BMG

Sir Galtfrid's Trombones

DON'T BE AFRAID
CD ______ LICD 3169
Liphone / Jan '97 / Cadillac / Jazz Music

Sir Lancelot

LEGENDARY SIR LANCELOT, THE
CD ______ LYRCD 7406
Lyrichord / '91 / ADA / CM / Roots

TRINIDAD IS CHANGING (1940's/1950's)
Century of the common man / Trinidad is changing / Donkey City / Neighbour neighbour leave me door / Night in Central Park / Ugly woman / Scandal in the family / Young girls today / Oken karange / Sweet like a honey bee / Pan American way / Gimme crab and callaloo / Mary Ann / Take me take me (to San Pedro) / Matilda Matilda / West Indian families
CD ______ FLYCD 942
Flyright / May '95 / Hot Shot / Jazz Music / Wellard

Sir Mix-A-Lot

CHIEF BOOT KNOCKA
Sleepin' with my fonk / Take my stash / Double my stash / Don't call me Da Da / Just da pimpin' in me / Let it beaounce / Brown shuga / Put 'em on the glass / Nast dog / I checks my bank / Ride / What's real / Chief boot knocka / Monsta' mack
CD ______ 74321243422
American / Aug '95 / BMG

MACK DADDY
One time's got no case / Mack Daddy / Baby got back / Swap meet lovie / Seattle ain't bullshit / Lock jaw / Boss is back / Testarossa / Rapper's reputation / Spring on the cat / Jack back / I'm your new God / No holds barred
CD ______ 74321248472
American / Jun '95 / BMG

RETURN OF THE BUMPASAURUS
You can have her / Da bomb / Buckin' my horse / Mob style / Top ten list / Man u luv ta hate / Bark like you want it / Bumpasaurus cometh / Bumpasaurus / Denial / Aunt Thomasina / Jump on it / Aintsta / Sag / Message to a drag artist / Lead yo horse / Playthang / Funk fo da bvld / Slide
CD ______ 74321372442
American / Sep '96 / BMG

SEMINAR
Seminar / Beepers / National anthem / My hooptie / Goretex / (peek-a-boo) Game / I got game / I'll roll you up / Something about my benzo / My bad side
CD ______ 74321248462
American / Jun '95 / BMG

SWASS
Buttermilk biscuits (keep on square dancin') / Posse on Broadway / Gold / Swass / Rippin' / Attack on the stars / Mail dropper / Hip hop solider / Iron man / Bremelo / Square dance rap / Romantic interlude / F the b's
CD ______ 74321248452
American / Jun '95 / BMG

Sircle Of Silence

SUICIDE CANDYMAN
CD ______ 342142
No Bull / Dec '95 / Koch

Siren

STRANGE LOCOMOTION/SIREN
Ze-ze-ze-ze / Get right church / Wake up my children / Wasting my time / Sixteen women / First time I saw your face / Gardener man / And I wonder / Asylum / Bertha Lee / I wonder where / Relaxing with Bonnie Lou / Some dark day / Hot potato / Soon / Gigolo / I'm all aching / Strange locomotion / Shake my hand / Lonesome ride / Fat moaning minnie / Squeeze me
CD ______ SEECD 413
See For Miles/C5 / Oct '94 / Pinnacle

Siren Circus

POEMS ON A GHOST OF A SUBJECT
CD ______ SCD 28024
Sargasso / Jun '97 / SRD

Sirkel

SIRKEL (Sirkel & Ric Sanders)
CD ______ BAJ 171549CD
Baj / May '97 / ADA

Sirota, Ted

REBEL ROOTS (Sirota, Ted Rebel Souls)
CD ______ NAIMCD 014
Naim Audio / Mar '97 / Koch

Sirrah

ACME
Acme / Passover 1944 / On the verge / AU tomb / Iridium / Pillbox impression / Panacea / Bitter seas / In the final moment
CD ______ CDMFN 025
Music For Nations / Sep '96 / Pinnacle

WILL TOMORROW COME
To bring order / For the sake of nothing / Patron / Lash / Will tomorrow come / High treason / Sepsis / Rhea / Madcap / Floor's embrace
CD ______ CDMFN 225
Music For Nations / Aug '97 / Pinnacle

Sirtos Ensemble

FOLK MUSIC OF GREECE
CD ______ HMP 3903060
HM Plus/Quintana / Oct '94 / Harmonia Mundi

Sissoko, Mama

AMOURS JARABI
CD ______ 829402
BUDA / Jun '97 / Discovery

Sista

4 ALL THE SISTAS AROUND THE WORLD
Hip hop / Hit u up / Sweat you down / Find my love / 125th Street / Secret admirer / I don't mind / Feel of your lips / Good thang / I wanna be wit u / Brand new
CD ______ 7559616532
East West / Aug '94 / Warner Music

Sister 7

THIS THE TRIP
This the trip / Bottle rocket / Know what you mean / Nobody's home / Flesh and bones / Perfect / Say good-bye / Tumblin down / Under the sun / Shelter / Some things are free
CD ______ 078221883528
RCA / Jul '97 / BMG

Sister Aaron

PURIFICATION
CD ______ E 113992
Musical Tragedies / Dec '93 / SRD

Sister Audrey

POPULATE
CD ______ ARICD 070
Ariwa Sounds / Nov '91 / Jet Star / SRD

Sister C.B.

SPIRIT OF THE ZITHER (Sister C.B. Of Carmel De Lucon)
CD ______ 74321340062
Milan / May '96 / Conifer/BMG / Silva Screen

Sister Carol

BLACK CINDERELLA
CD ______ CDHB 193
Heartbeat / Apr '97 / ADA / Direct / Greensleeves / Jet Star

CALL MI SISTER CAROL
CD ______ HBCD 93
Heartbeat / Nov '94 / ADA / Direct / Greensleeves / Jet Star

LYRICALLY POTENT
CD ______ CDHB 213
Heartbeat / Jun '96 / ADA / Direct / Greensleeves / Jet Star

Sister Double Happiness

HORSEY WATER
CD ______ SPCD 137337
Sub Pop / Nov '94 / Cargo / Greyhound / Shellshock/Disc

SISTER DOUBLE HAPPINESS
CD ______ SST 162CD
SST / May '93 / Plastic Head

UNCUT
San Diego / Will you come / Ashes / Whipping song / Doesn't make sense / Honey don't / Keep the city clean / Do what you gotta do / Where do we run / No good for you / Lightnin' / Louise
CD ______ SPCD 105277

Sub Pop / Jul '93 / Cargo / Greyhound / Shellshock/Disc

Sister George

DRAG KING
Sister George / Let's breed / Janey's block / Roccoco subversive / Handlebar / Krap / Virus envy / 100 times no
CD _______________ PUSS 003CD
Catcall / Feb '94 / Vital

Sister Grant

DOWN AT CROSS (Sister Grant & The Gospelettes)
CD _______________ KGC 107
Kangaroo / Apr '94 / ADA

HARBOUR IN JESUS (Sister Grant & The Gospelairs)
CD _______________ KGC 104
Kangaroo / Apr '94 / ADA

Sister Machine Gun

METROPOLIS
CD _______________ TVT 72442
TVT / Jul '97 / Cargo / Greyhound

Sister Morphine

SISTER MORPHINE
CD _______________ 789010792
Emerald City / Mar '97 / Cargo

Sister Psychic

SURRENDER, YOU FREAK
Surrender you freak / Part of love / Velvet dog / I can't breathe / Happiness / Kim the waitress / Little bird / Death by fascination / Sleepwalking / Clapper (wish I was blind) / Blue river / Eddie Mars / On the floor
CD _______________ 727442
Restless / Mar '94 / Vital

Sister Sledge

ALL AMERICAN GIRLS
All American girls / He's just a runaway / If you really want me / Next time you'll know / Happy feeling / Ooh you caught my heart / Make a move / Don't you let me lose it / Music makes me feel good / I don't want to say goodbye
CD _______________ 8122719142
Rhino / May '95 / Warner Music

AND NOW...SISTER SLEDGE...AGAIN
CD _______________ FMDXD 190
FM / Mar '93 / Revolver / Sony

GREATEST HITS LIVE
Everybody dance / Thinking of you / He's the greatest dancer / True love / Frankie / Brother, brother, stop / Love of the Lord / We are family / Lost in music/Melody is good to me / Everybody dance/We are family/Frankie/Thinking of you
CD _______________ MDCD 10
Music De-Luxe / Jun '95 / TKO Magnum

HITS OF SISTER SLEDGE
CD _______________ KLMCD 025
BAM / Apr '94 / Koch / Scratch/BMG

LIVE
Everybody dacne / Frankie / Lost in music / Thinking of you / We are family / True love / He's the greatest dancer / Love of the Lord / Brother, brother stop
CD _______________ EMPRCD 712
Emporio / Apr '97 / Disc

LOVE SOMEBODY TODAY
Got to love somebody / You fooled around / I'm a good girl / Easy street / Reach your peak / Pretty baby / How to love / Let's go on a vacation
CD _______________ 8122719132
Rhino / May '95 / Warner Music

SISTER SLEDGE LIVE
Everybody dance / Thinking of you / He's the greatest dancer / True love / Frankie / Brother brother stop / Love of the Lord / We are family / Medley
CD _______________ SUMCD 4077
Summit / Nov '96 / Sound & Media

VERY BEST OF SISTER SLEDGE, THE
We are family / He's the greatest dancer / All American girls / Pretty baby / Got to love somebody / Frankie / Lost in music / Thinking of you / Mama never told me / Reach your peak / Lost in music (mix)
CD _______________ 9548318132
WEA / Feb '93 / Warner Music

WE ARE FAMILY
He's the greatest dancer / Lost in music / Somebody loves me / Thinking of you / We are family / Easier to love / You're a friend to me / One more time
CD _______________ 8122715872
Rhino / Jun '95 / Warner Music

Sisters Of Glory

GOOD NEWS IN HARD TIMES
CD _______________ 9362459902
Warner Bros. / Aug '95 / Warner Music

Sisters Of Mercy

FIRST, LAST AND ALWAYS
Black planet / Walk away / No time to cry / Rock and a hard place / Marian (version) / First and last and always / Possession / Nine while nine / Amphetamine logic / Some kind of stranger
CD _______________ 9031773792
Merciful Release / Jun '92 / Warner Music

FIRST, LAST FOREVER
CD _______________ CLEO 6642CD
Cleopatra / Jan '94 / Cargo / Greyhound / Plastic Head / RTM/Disc / SRD

GIFT (Sisterhood)
Jihad / Colours / Giving ground / Finland red, Egypt white / Rain from heaven
CD _______________ 11316842
Merciful Release / Jun '94 / Warner Music

SISTERS OF MERCY: INTERVIEW PICTURE DISC
CD _______________ CBAK 4010
Baktabak / Apr '88 / Arabesque

SLIGHT CASE OF OVERBOMBING, A (Greatest Hits Vol.1)
Under the gun / Temple of love / Vision thing / Detonation Boulevard / Dr. Jeep / More / Lucretia my reflection / Dominion/ Mother Russia / This Corrosion / No time to cry / Walk away / Body and soul
CD _______________ 4509935792
Merciful Release / Aug '93 / Warner Music

SOME GIRLS WANDER BY MISTAKE
Alive / Floorshow / Phantom / 1969 / Kiss the carpet / Lights / Valentine / Fix / Burn / Kiss the carpet (reprise) / Temple of love / Heartland / Gimme shelter / Damage done / Watch / Home of the hit-men / Body electric / Adrenochrome / Anaconda
CD _______________ 9031764762
Merciful Release / Apr '91 / Warner Music

THOUGHTS AND PRAYERS
CD _______________ 3D 004
Network / Dec '96 / Total/BMG

Sisters Unlimited

NO BED OF ROSES
CD _______________ FE 104CD
Fellside / Jun '95 / ADA / Direct / Target/ BMG

NO LIMITS
No going back / Promises / Breastfeeding baby in the park / Tomorrow / Mouth music / My better years / Working girl blues / Dance / Old and strong / My true love once / When I was single / On children / No man's momma / Forgive and forget / We were there
CD _______________ HARCD 013
Harbour Town / Nov '91 / ADA / CM / Direct / Roots

Sit n' Spin

PAPPY'S CORN SQUEEZIN'
CD _______________ MRCD 116
Munster / Mar '97 / Cargo / Greyhound / Plastic Head

Sivann, Sylvie

TRADITIONAL JEWISH MUSIC
CD _______________ PS 65178
PlayaSound / Mar '97 / ADA / Harmonia Mundi

Sivertsen, Kenneth

REMEMBERING NORTH
Nimis (near but far) / Cock ones head / Remembering / Going home / Division / Sideblink / From Paris to Mosterhamn / Procession / Tony's rain / Journey / Rain
CD _______________ NYC 60072
NYC / Aug '94 / New Note/Pinnacle

Sivuca

NORTE FORTE
CD _______________ 68959
Tropical / Apr '97 / Discovery

Siwa, Tala Mena

SAE ENA
CD _______________ MWCD 5001
Music & Words / Aug '96 / ADA / Direct

Six & Violence

LETTUCE PREY
CD _______________ ANDCD 9
A New Day / Feb '97 / Direct

Six And A Half

NEW YORK, PARIS, NICE
Road 66 / Berimbau / Quand ca balance / Lush life / La javanaise / Looking up / Que reste t il de nos amours / Bluesette / Take the 'A' train / La valse des lilas / St Thomas / Je me suis fait tout petit
CD _______________ FDM 365842
Dreyfus / May '97 / ADA / Direct / New Note/Pinnacle

Six Feet Under

ALIVE AND DEAD
CD _______________ 398414118CD
Metal Blade / Oct '96 / Pinnacle / Plastic Head

HAUNTED
CD _______________ 398414093
Metal Blade / Oct '95 / Pinnacle / Plastic Head

Six Finger Satellite

PARANORMALIZED
CD _______________ SPCD 366
Sub Pop / Dec '96 / Cargo / Greyhound / Shellshock/Disc

PIGEON IS THE MOST POPULAR BIRD, THE
Untitled / Home for the holy day / Untitled / Laughing Larry / Untitled / Funny like a clown / Untitled / Deadpan / Untitled / Hi lo jerk / Untitled / (Love) via satellite / Untitled / Save the last dance for Larry / Untitled / Zeroes and ones / Untitled / Neuro-harmonic conspiracy / Untitled (10) / Takes one to know one / Symphony in A
CD _______________ SPCD 268
Sub Pop / Aug '93 / Cargo / Greyhound / Shellshock/Disc

SEVERE EXPOSURE
CD _______________ SP 299B
Sub Pop / Dec '96 / Cargo / Greyhound / Shellshock/Disc

Six Fingered People

TEMPTATIONS
CD _______________ BR 034CD
Blue Room / Jul '97 / Essential/BMG / Mo's Music Machine / Prime / SRD

Six Winds

ANGER DANCE
CD _______________ BVHAASTCD 9305
Bvhaast / Feb '86 / Cadillac

Six Yard Box

IMAGINATION IS GREATER THAN KNOWLEDGE
Sweet leaf / What's the point / K4R Part III / Cat is wiser / Pictures of matchstick men (12" mix) / Clutter up buttering / Spellbound / K4R Part IV / Pictures of matchstick men (Reggae mix)
CD _______________ MOSH 087CD
Earache / Apr '93 / Vital

Sixteen Deluxe

BACKFEED MAGNETBABE
CD _______________ TR 37CD
Trance / May '95 / SRD

Sixths

WASP'S NESTS
CD _______________ FACD 206
Factory Too / Jul '95 / Pinnacle / PolyGram

Sjosten, Lars

IN CONFIDENCE
CD _______________ DRCD 197
Dragon / Sep '88 / ADA / Cadillac / CM / Roots / Wellard

SELECT NOTES
CD _______________ CAPRICE 1216
Caprice / May '89 / ADA / Cadillac / CM / Complete/Pinnacle

Skaboosh

FREETOWN
Movin' up an' movin' on / Fanfare / Bareback ridin / Freedom / Time / Startin from scratch / Spain / Ain't got any money / I want to grow old with you by my side
CD _______________ BP 128CD
Blueprint / Aug '96 / Pinnacle

Skaff, Gregg

BLUES AND OTHER NEWS
Walk the walk / Johnny come lately / Red dirt / Ya-dig / My mans gone now / In walked bud / Knapton vibe / Comin at ya / Highway 70 / Jig saw
CD _______________ DTRCD 111
Double Time / Nov '96 / Express Jazz

Skagarak

BIG TIME
CD _______________ 10192
CMC / Jun '97 / BMG

Skaggs, Ricky

FAMILY AND FRIENDS
Lost and I'll never find the way / Two different worlds / River of memory / Talk about sufferin' / Think of what you've done / Toy heart / Hallelujah I'm ready / Say / Won't you be mine / Won't it be wonderful there / River of Jordan
CD _______________ ROUCD 0151
Rounder / Aug '88 / ADA / CM / Direct

ORIGINAL RECORDINGS
CD _______________ CDSD 015
Magnum Music / Sep '94 / TKO Magnum

SKAGGS & RICE (Skaggs, Ricky & Tony Rice)
Bury me beneath the willow / Mansions for me / There's more pretty girls than one / Memories of mother and dad / Where the soul of man never dies / Talk about sufferin' / Will the roses bloom / Tennessee blues / Old crossroads / Have you someone (in heaven waiting)
CD _______________ SHCD 3711
Sugar Hill / Jan '97 / ADA / CM / Direct / Koch / Roots

SWEET TEMPTATION
I'll take the blame / Cabin home on the hill / Baby I'm in love with you / I'll stay around / Could you love me one more time / Sweet temptation / Put it off until tomorrow / Baby girl / Forgive me / I know what it means to be lonesome
CD _______________ SHCD 3706
Sugar Hill / Aug '96 / ADA / CM / Direct / Koch / Roots

THAT'S IT
Red apple rag / At the Darktown strutter's ball / Florida blues / Bubble gum song / Whitesburg / Meeting house branch / Sweet Georgia Town / Hook and line / Southern moon / Twenty one fiddle salute / That's it / Evergreen shore
CD _______________ CDSD 040
Sundown / Dec '86 / TKO Magnum

Skandalous All Stars

HIT ME
CD _______________ SH 5720
Shanachie / Mar '97 / ADA / Greensleeves / Koch

Skankin' Pickle

GREEN ALBUM
CD _______________ DSR 042
Dr. Strange / Jun '97 / Cargo / Greyhound / Plastic Head

SKAFUNKRASTAPUNK
Road zombie / It's not too late / Doing something naughty / Hulk Hogan / Racist world / Burnt head / Asian man / Ska / Fight / How funk / Fakin' Jamaican / 24 second song / You shouldn't judge a man by the hair on his butt / Peter Piper and Mary
CD _______________ DILL 012CD
Dill / Jun '97 / Cargo / Greyhound

SKANKIN' PICKLE FEVER
Hussein skank / Pseudo punk / Silly willy / Ice Cube, Korea wants a word with you / Toothless and grey / Pass you by / Dub / Song 3 / Whatever happened / Anxiety attack / Skinless friend / Larry Smith / I missed the bus / Roland Alphonso's dub / Hand twister / David Duke is running for president / Hit my brain
CD _______________ DILL 014CD
Dill / Jun '97 / Cargo / Greyhound

Skaos

BACK TO LIVE
CD _______________ EFA 946252
Pork Pie / Dec '95 / SRD

Skatalites

BALL OF FIRE
CD _______________ IJCD 4005
Island Jamaica / Aug '97 / Jet Star / PolyGram

HI BOP SKA
CD _______________ SH 45019
Shanachie / Dec '94 / ADA / Greensleeves / Koch

HOG IN A COCOA (Skatalites & Friends)
CD _______________ LG 21016
Lagoon / May '93 / Grapevine/PolyGram

LIBERATION SKA
CD _______________ RNCD 2056
Rhino / May '94 / Grapevine/PolyGram / Jet Star

SKA AUTHENTIC VOL.1
CD _______________ SOCD 9006
Studio One / Mar '96 / Jet Star

SKAMANIA (2CD Set)
CD Set _______________ DOXOCD 266
Dojo / Jul '96 / Disc

SKATALITES, THE
CD _______________ 444112
Jet Set / Jun '97 / Grapevine/PolyGram

STRETCHING OUT
CD _______________ RE 141CD
ROIR / Nov '94 / Plastic Head / Shellshock/Disc

Skatenigs

OH WHAT A MANGLED WEB WE HAVE
CD _______________ CDVEST 14
Bulletproof / Jun '94 / Pinnacle

Skeaping, Lucie

RAISINS AND ALMONDS (Skeaping, Lucie & The Burning Bush)
Yoi m'enamori d'un aire (I fell in love with the charms) / Tum Balalaika (Play balalaika) / Chassidic melody No. 24 / Tsen kopikes (Ten kopeks) / Adio querida (Good bye my love) / Puncha, puncha (The perfumed rose) / Sha, Shtil (Shh, Quiet) / Una matica de ruda (a little bunch of rue) / Chassidic melody No. 13 / Di alte kashe (The eternal question) / Avrix mi galanica (Open, my sweet) / Gey ikh mir shpatsirn (As I went walking) / Una hija tiene el rey (The King has a daughter) / Di mezinke oysgegebn (My youngest daughter's married) / Mi padre era de Francia / Oyfn pripetchik (On the hearth) / Chassidic melody No. 10, La rose enflorece (The rose blooms) / Rozhinkes mit mandlen / Zog nit keynmol (Never say)
CD _______ CDSDL 395
Saydisc / Mar '94 / ADA / Direct / Harmonia Mundi

Skeduz

RAG AR PLINN
CD _______ KMCD 72
Keltia Musique / Jun '97 / ADA / Discovery

Skee Lo

I WISH
Superman / I wish / Never crossed my mind / Top of the stairs / Come back to me / Waitin' for you / Holdin' on / You ain't down / Crenshaw / This is how it sounds / Burger song / I wish (Street mix)
CD _______ 5297892
Wild Card / Dec '95 / PolyGram

Skeletal Earth

DE-EVOLUTION
CD _______ DAR 0172
Desperate Attempt / Mar '95 / SRD

EULOGY FOR A DYING FOETUS
CD _______ FDNCD 8215
Plastic Head / Jan '92 / Plastic Head

Skeletal Family

SINGLES PLUS
Trees / Just a friend / Night / Waiting here / She cries alone / Wind blows / Eternal / Waiting here (version) / Night (version) / So sure / Batman / Lies / Promised land / Stand by me / Puppet / Waltz / Guilt
CD _______ CDMGRAM 75
Cherry Red / Mar '94 / Pinnacle

Skeleton Crew

BLUE MANIA
Satisfaction guaranteed / Glory hunter / Watch your step / Can't buy love with money / Mother earth / Blues got me / Trail of tears / Chinese eyes / Mississippi burning / See me later / Walking in my sleep
CD _______ 109042
Musidisc / Mar '92 / Discovery

Skeletons

IN THE FLESH/ROCKIN' BONES
Trans am / Tell her I'm gone / Very last day / Blood surfin' / Sour snow / Gas money / She drives me out of my mind / B gas accord / Crazy country hop / Outta my way / Older guys / Laugh at me / Waitin' for a slow dance / Meaning of the blues / I'm a little but I'm loud / Thirty days in the workhouse / I play the drums / Primitive / For every heart
CD _______ FIENDCD 178
Demon / Aug '90 / Pinnacle

NOTHING TO LOSE
Nothin' to lose / Charming Billie / It's OK to be lonely / I'm goin' home/Mad old lady / Pay to play / Tubb's theme / World you grace / I ain't lyin' / Whiffle ball song / Downhearted / Cool summer / Educated fool / Country boys don't cry / Get what you need
CD _______ HCD 8080
Hightone / Jun '97 / ADA / Koch

WAITING
CD _______ A 030D
Alias / Nov '92 / Vital

Skellern, Peter

CHEEK TO CHEEK
Cheek to cheek / Continental / Puttin' on the Ritz / Top hat, white tie and tails / Stormy weather / All or nothing at all / Busy line / Love is the sweetest thing / Two sleepy people / Deep purple / Raining in my heart / Where do we go from here / They all laughed / Way you look tonight
CD _______ 74321152192
Ariola Express / Sep '93 / BMG

SENTIMENTALLY YOURS
Too much I'm in love / Raining in my heart / They can't take that away from me / Still magic / Love is the sweetest thing / Isn't this a lovely day / Where do we go from here / Continental / When somebody thinks you're wonderful / Skylark / Deep purple / Over her / Way you look tonight / Two sleepy people / You and I / Cheek to cheek / While I'm away / Sweet words / Put out the flame / Night and day
CD _______ 74321393332
Camden / Jan '97 / BMG

STARDUST MEMORIES
CD _______ 4509981322
Warner Bros. / Dec '96 / Warner Music

WORLD OF PETER SKELLERN, THE
Hold on to love / You're a lady / Tattooed lady / Too much, I'm in love / Society ladies / My lonely room / Our Jackie's getting married / Vicarious vestments / Skin and bone / Make it easy for me / Uncle Sam / No more Sunday papers / Sad affair / Piano rag / Up for the shoot / Big time Indian chief / Honey chil' / Sleepy guitar
CD _______ 5512722
Spectrum / May '96 / PolyGram

Skelton, John

ONE AT A TIME
CD _______ PAN 146CD
Pan / Oct '93 / ADA / CM / Direct

Sketch

COSMOSIS
CD _______ 33JAZZ 003CD
33 Jazz / Jun '93 / Cadillac / New Note/ Pinnacle

Skew Siskin

ELECTRIC CHAIR MUSIC
CD _______ GUN 110CD
Gun / Nov '96 / Plastic Head

SKEW SISKIN
If the walls could talk / Out of control / I wanna know / Livin' on the redline / In another world / I gotta go away / When the sun goes down / Sniffin' the dirt / Thank you for the time / All day and all of the night / Cheap trick / Shake down and roll
CD _______ 07599244592
Giant / Aug '92 / BMG

Skid Row

B SIDE OURSELVES
Psychotherapy / C'mon and love me / Delivering the goods / What you're doing / Little wing
CD _______ 7567824312
Atlantic / Oct '92 / Warner Music

SKID ROW
Big guns / Sweet little sister / Can't stand the heartache / Piece of me / Eighteen and life / Rattlesnake shake / Youth gone wild / Here I am / Makin' a mess / I remember you / Midnight tornado
CD _______ 7819362
Atlantic / Feb '95 / Warner Music

SLAVE TO THE GRIND
Monkey business / Slave to the grind / Threat / Quicksand Jesus / Psycho love / Get the fuck out / Livin' on a chain gang / Creepshow / In a darkened room / Riot act / Mudkicker / Wasted time
CD _______ 7567822422
Atlantic / Jun '91 / Warner Music

SUBHUMAN RACE
CD _______ 7567827302
Atlantic / Dec '96 / Warner Music

Skid Row

SKID ROW (Gary Moore, Brush Shiels and Noel Bridgeman)
Benedict's cherry wine / Saturday morning man / Crystal ball / Mr. Deluxe / Girl called Winter / Morning Star Avenue / Silver bird
CD _______ CLACD 343
Castle / Jun '94 / BMG

Skids

DUNFERMLINE
Into the valley / Charles / Saints are coming / Scared to dance / Sweet suburbia / Of one skin / Night and day / Animation / Working for the Yankee dollar / Charade / Masquerade / Circus games / Out of town / Goodbye civilian / Woman in Winter / Hurry on boys / Iona / Fields
CD _______ CDVM 9022
Virgin / Jul '93 / EMI

SCARED TO DANCE
Into the valley / Scared to dance / Of one skin / Dossier (of fallibility) / Melancholy soldiers / Hope and glory / Saints are coming / Six times / Calling the tune / Integral plot / Scale / Charles
CD _______ CDV 2116
Virgin / Jun '90 / EMI

SWEET SUBURBIA (The Best Of The Skids)
Into the valley / Charles / Saints are coming / Scared to dance / Sweet suburbia / Of one skin / Night and day / Animation / Working for the Yankee dollar / Charade / Masquerade / Circus games / Out of town / Goodbye civilian / Woman in winter / Hurry on boys / Iona / Fields
CD _______ CDOVD 457
Virgin / Feb '95 / EMI

Skillet Lickers

SKILLET LICKERS
CD _______ CUY 3509CD
County / Apr '96 / ADA / Direct

Skillz

PROMISE
CD _______ 50570
Raging Bull / Jun '97 / Prime / Total/BMG

Skin & Bones

NOT A PRETTY SIGHT
CD _______ EQNCD 2
Equinox / Jul '90 / Total/BMG

Skin

LUCKY
Spit on you / How lucky are you / Make it happen / Face to face / New religion / Escape from reality / Perfect day / Let love rule your heart / Juliet / No way out / Pray / One nation / I'm alive / Inside me inside you
CD _______ CDPCSD 168
Parlophone / Mar '96 / EMI

Skin

BLOOD, WOMAN, ROSES
CD _______ CDPROD 4
Product Inc. / '89 / Vital

SHAME, HUMILITY, REVENGE
CD _______ CDPROD 11
Product Inc. / Mar '88 / Vital

WORLD OF SKIN
CD _______ YGCD 002
Young God / Jul '95 / Vital

Skin Alley

TO PAGHAM AND BEYOND
CD _______ AACD 022
Audio Archive / Jun '97 / Greyhound

Skin Chamber

TRIAL
On a drunk / Throb / Ripping fist / Torturous world / Sloven / Glisten / Slowcrime / Trial / Swallowing scrap metal Pt 5
CD _______ RR 90752
Roadrunner / Apr '93 / PolyGram

WOUND
CD _______ RR 92742
Roadrunner / Oct '91 / PolyGram

Skin, Flesh & Bones

DUB IN BLOOD VOL.1
CD _______ SSCD 001
Sunshot / Oct '96 / SRD

DUB IN BLOOD VOL.2
CD _______ SSCD 002
Sunshot / Oct '96 / SRD

Skin Kandy

TAKE YOUR HABIT HOME
CD _______ BLK 5006ECD
Blackout / Mar '97 / Plastic Head / Vital

Skin Of Tears

SHIT HAPPENS
CD _______ LF 198CD
Lost & Found / Jan '96 / Plastic Head

Skin The Peeler

FRIENDS AND LOVERS
CD _______ STP 101CD
Skindependent / Mar '94 / CM

WORLD DANCE
CD _______ CDSTP 100
Skindependent / Dec '91 / CM

Skin Yard

1000 SMILING KNUCKLES
CD _______ CRZ 017CD
Cruz / May '93 / Plastic Head

FIST SIZED CHUNKS
CD _______ CRZ 009CD
Cruz / Apr '90 / Plastic Head

INSIDE THE EYE
CD _______ CRZ 027CD
Cruz / May '93 / Plastic Head

SKIN YARD
CD _______ CRZ 015CD
Cruz / May '93 / Plastic Head

Skink

DEAF TO SUGGESTION
Deadlock / Undercurrents / Enemy / Violator / Drug called religion / Blood eagle / Dark side / Real deep shit / Hand comes down
CD _______ BGR 006
BGR / Mar '95 / Plastic Head

Skinlab

BOUND, GAGGED AND BLINDFOLDED
CD _______ CM 77174
Century Media / Apr '97 / Plastic Head

Skinner, Billy

KOSEN RUFU
CD _______ AC 3333CD
Accurate / Nov '93 / Cadillac

Skinny Puppy

BACK AND FORTH SERIES TWO
Intro / Sleeping beast / K-9 / Monster radio man / Quiet solitude / Pit / Sore in a masterpiece/Dead of winter / Unovis on a stick / To a baser nature / AM/Meat flavour / My voice sounds like shit / Smothered hop / Explode the PA / Assimilate / Edge of insanity
CD _______ W230078
Nettwerk / Jan '93 / Greyhound / Pinnacle / Vital

BRAP (2CD Set)
CD Set _______ 08922402
Westcom / Apr '96 / Koch / Pinnacle

CLEANSE, FOLD AND MANIPULATE
First aid / Addiction / Shadow cast / Draining faces / Mourn / Second touch / Tear or beat / Trauma hounds / Anger / Epilogue
CD _______ NETCD 019
Nettwerk / Nov '90 / Greyhound / Pinnacle / Vital

LAST RIGHTS
Hinder / Killing game / Cancelled / Xception / Catbowl / Hurtful 2 / River's end / Fester / Premonition / Wrek / Epilogue 2
CD _______ NET 038CD
Nettwerk / Apr '92 / Greyhound / Pinnacle / Vital

MIND: THE PERPETUAL INTERCOURSE
One time one place / God's gift / Three blind mice / Love / Stairs and flowers / Antagonism / 200 years / Dig it / Burnt with water
CD _______ NTCD 037
Nettwerk / '88 / Greyhound / Pinnacle / Vital

PROCESS, THE
Jahya / Death / Candle / Hardest head / Cult process / Curcible / Blue serge / Morter / Amnesia / Cellar heart
CD _______ 74321310972
American / Feb '96 / BMG

RABIES
CD _______ NETCD 023
Nettwerk / Jul '90 / Greyhound / Pinnacle / Vital

REMISSION AND BITES
CD _______ BIAS 048
Play It Again Sam / Jan '87 / Discovery / Plastic Head / Vital

TESTURE
CD _______ CD315439
Nettwerk / '89 / Greyhound / Pinnacle / Vital

TOO DARK PARK
CD _______ NET 026CD
Nettwerk / Sep '93 / Greyhound / Pinnacle / Vital

VIVISECT VI
Dogshit / VS gas attack / Harsh stone white / Human disease (SKUMM) / Who's laughing now / Testure / State aid / Hospital waste / Fritter (Stella's home)
CD _______ NETCD 021
Nettwerk / Nov '90 / Greyhound / Pinnacle / Vital

WORLOCK (Twelve Inch Anthology)
CD _______ W230041
Nettwerk / '89 / Greyhound / Pinnacle / Vital

Skippies

WORLD UP
CD _______ NR 422455
New Rose / Jan '94 / ADA / Direct / Discovery

Skirt

CHOKING ON SUGAR
CD _______ SH 5715
Shanachie / Nov '96 / ADA / Greensleeves / Koch

Skitzo

SKITZO MANIA
Skitzo mania / Dr. Death / Shipwreck Island / Witching hour / Lonesome train (on a lonesome track) / Possessed / I'm going Skitzo / Caledonia / Poltergeist / Your cheatin' heart / Under pressure / House of the rising sun
CD _______ NERCD 028
Nervous / May '87 / Nervous / TKO Magnum

TERMINAL DAMAGE
CD _______ NERCD 039
Nervous / Sep '88 / Nervous / TKO Magnum

VERTIGO
CD _______ NERCD 090
Nervous / Jun '97 / Nervous / TKO Magnum

Skjelbred, Ray

CHICAGO SESSIONS (Skjelbred, Ray Quartet)
CD _______ SACD 98
Solo Art / Jul '93 / Jazz Music

Skjerveheim, Lars

HEIMLENGT
CD _______ BK 13
Buen / Mar '96 / ADA

Skolvan

SWING & TEARS
CD _______ KM 46
Keltia Musique / Oct '94 / ADA / Discovery

Skooby

HITCH A RIDE WITH SKOOBY
CD _______ ASSCD 004
Funky Ass / Jul '96 / Else / Timewarp

JUST COOKIN'
CD _______ ASSCD 001
Funky Ass / Jul '96 / Else / Timewarp

Skooshny

EVEN MY EYES
CD _______ MZR 3
Minus Zero / Feb '97 / Cargo / Greyhound

Skorr

POPULAR UKRAINIAN DANCES (Skorr & Ukrainian Ensemble)
CD _______ MCD 71446
Monitor / Jun '93 / CM

Skoubie Dubh Orchestra

SPIKE'S 23 COLLECTION
CD _______ LDL 1210CD
Lochshore / Jul '94 / ADA / Direct / Duncans

Skrapp Metal

SENSITIVE
CD _______ PAR 2008CD
PAR / Nov '92 / Koch

Skree

FAT MOUTH SHOUTS OUT
CD _______ FRR 020
Freek / May '96 / RTM/Disc / SRD

THERE IS A POP BONE IN MY BODY
I'm evil and I must be stopped / Fussy moon / Jink of an eye / Spool / History sick
CD _______ FRR 026
Freek / Apr '97 / RTM/Disc / SRD

Skrew

DUSTED
CD _______ CDDVN 28
Devotion / May '94 / Pinnacle

SHADOW OF DOUBT
CD _______ 398417025CD
Metal Blade / Apr '96 / Pinnacle / Plastic Head

Skud

BULLGATOR
CD _______ BGR 017CD
BGR / Oct '95 / Plastic Head

Skull

NO BONES ABOUT IT
CD _______ CDMFN 117
Music For Nations / Jun '91 / Pinnacle

Skull Snaps

SKULL SNAPS
My hang up is you / Having you around / Didn't I do it to you / All of a sudden / It's a new day / I'm your pimp / I turn my back on love / Trespassing / I'm falling out of love
CD _______ CPCD 8094
Charly / Apr '95 / Koch

Skullflower

ARGON
CD _______ FRR 012
Freek / May '95 / RTM/Disc / SRD

IIIRD GATEKEEPER
CD _______ HD 001
Headdirt / Nov '92 / SRD

RUINS
CD _______ SX 006
Shock / '89 / Cadillac / Pinnacle

TRANSFORMER
CD _______ SFTR 1325CD
Psychedelic Noise / Jan '96 / Plastic Head

Skunk Anansie

PARANOID AND SUNBURNT
CD _______ TPLP 55CD
One Little Indian / Oct '95 / Pinnacle

STOOSH
Yes it's fucking political / All I want / She's my heroine / Infidelity (only you) / Hedonism (just because you feel good) / Twisted (everyday hurts) / We love your apathy / Brazen (weep) / Pickin' on me / Milk is my sugar / Glorious pop song
CD _______ TPLP 85CD
One Little Indian / Oct '96 / Pinnacle

Skunkhour

SKUNKHOUR
Pullatickin / Cow and a pig / Horse / Booty full / Back to basics / Sheep of Sam / Free man / Do you like it / State / Echinda
CD _______ JAZIDCD 113
Acid Jazz / Jul '95 / Disc

Sky

BEST OF SKY, THE
Toccata / Westway / Sanara / Gymnopedie No.1 / Moonroof
CD _______ MCCD 172
Music Club / Sep '94 / Disc / THE

SKY (Sky 1/Sky 2/Sky 3 - 3CD Set)
CD Set _______ MCBX 001
Music Club / Sep '95 / Disc / THE

SKY VOL.1
Westway / Carrillon / Danza / Gymnopedie No.1 / Cannonball / Where opposites meet
CD _______ MCCD 077
Music Club / Jun '92 / Disc / THE

SKY VOL.1
CD _______ MER 008
Tring / Mar '93 / Tring

SKY VOL.2
Hotta / Dance of the little fairies / Sahara / Fifo / Vivaloi / Tuba smarties / Ballet-volta / Gavotte and variations / Andante / Tristan's magic garden / El cielo / Scipio (part 1 and 2) / Toccata
CD _______ MCCD 078
Music Club / Jun '92 / Disc / THE

SKY VOL.2
CD _______ MER 009
Tring / Mar '93 / Tring

SKY VOL.3
Grace / Chiropodie no.1 / Westwind / Sarabande / Connecting rooms / Moonroof / Sister Rose / Hello / Dance of the big fairies / Meheeco / Keep me safe and keep me warm / Shelter me from darkness
CD _______ MCCD 079
Music Club / Jun '92 / Disc / THE

SKY WRITING
Toccata / Westway / Gymnopedie / Vivaldi / Skylark / Hotta / Masquerade / Dance of the little fairies / Keep me safe and keep me warm / Meheeco / Grace / Chiropodie No.1 / El cielo / Moonroof / Carillon / Yelatso pedi / Ride of the valkyries
CD _______ MDCD 8
Music De-Luxe / '90 / TKO Magnum

Sky Cries Mary

RETURN TO THE INNER EXPERIENCE
Walla walla / Moving like water / Gone / 2000 Light years from home / When the fear stops / Lay down your head / Rain / Ocean which humanity is / Broken down / Rosaleen / Bus to gate / Joey's aria / We will fall
CD _______ WDOM 006CD
World Domination / May '94 / Pinnacle / RTM/Disc

THIS TIMELESS TURNING
CD _______ WDOM 011CD
World Domination / Oct '94 / Pinnacle / RTM/Disc

Sky High

AFRICAN VENGANCE (Sky High & The Mau Mau)
CD _______ CD 1004
Sky High / Sep '94 / Direct / Jet Star

LION JUNGLE (Sky High & The Mau Mau)
CD _______ SHCD 2001
Ras / Jan '95 / Direct / Greensleeves / Jet Star / SRD

MARCUS GARVEY CHANT (Sky High & The Mau Mau)
CD _______ RASCD 3107
Ras / Nov '92 / Direct / Greensleeves / Jet Star / SRD

SKYHIGH IN DUBLAND VOL.1 (Sky High & The Mau Mau)
CD _______ SH 2003
Skyhigh / Jun '96 / Jet Star

Sky Painter

LONG WINTER OF MARS
CD _______ RP 05CD
Red Planet / Jan '94 / Plastic Head

Skyclad

BURNT OFFERING FOR THE BONE IDOL, A
War and disorder / Broken promised land / Spinning Jenny / Salt on earth (another man's poison) / Karmageddon (the suffering silence) / Ring stone round / Men of straw / R'vannith / Declaration of indifference / Alone in death's shadow
CD _______ N 01862
Noise / Mar '92 / Koch

BURNT OFFERING, A
CD _______ N 01862
Noise / Nov '96 / Koch

IRRATIONAL ANTHEMS
CD _______ MASSCD 084
Massacre / Jan '96 / Plastic Head

JONAH'S ARK
CD _______ N 02092
Noise / Nov '96 / Koch

OLD ROPE
CD _______ N 02752
Noise / Nov '96 / Koch

PRINCE OF THE POVERTY LINE
CD _______ N 02392
Noise / Nov '96 / Koch

QUI AVANT GARDE A CHANCE
CD _______ MASSCD 104
Massacre / Nov '96 / Plastic Head

SILENT WHALES OF LUNAR SEA
CD _______ N 02282
Noise / Nov '96 / Koch

TRACKS FROM THE WILDERNESS
CD _______ N 01943
Noise / Nov '96 / Koch

Skylab

SKYLAB NO.1
River of bass / Seashell / Depart / Next / Ghost dance / Shhh / Indigo / Ah ee hu / Electric blue / Six nine / Tokyo 1 / Tokyo elevator
CD _______ LATCD 21
L'Attitude / Dec '95 / PolyGram / Vital

Skylark

ALL OF IT
Fair Jane/Townsend's jig/Captain White's jig / Pretty Susan / Tryst / Heel and toe / Siuil arun / Contradiction set / All of it / Ball and pin / In contempt / Teelin polkas / Braes of Balquhidder / Dewdrops on the corn/Pat McKenna's jig/Cook in the kitchen / For a new baby
CD _______ GLCD 3046
Green Linnet / Aug '92 / ADA / CM / Direct / Highlander / Roots

LIGHT AND SHADE
Mad French / Brown girl / Sunflower / Neil Mulligan's jig / Upon St. Nicholas boat / Cruel wars / O'Donnel's fancy/Get up old woman and shake yourself / Star above the garter / Little pack of tailors / Frank Quinn's and Peter McArdle's highlands / Factory girl / Up in smoke / Young and foolish / Munster bacon/The hawk/Paddy Kierce's jig / Boys of Mullaghbawn / Gypsy
CD _______ CC 57CD
Claddagh / Feb '92 / ADA / CM / Direct

RAINING BICYCLES
CD _______ CC 62CD
Claddagh / Aug '96 / ADA / CM / Direct

Skylarks

BEST OF THE SKYLARKS, THE
CD _______ NASH 4005
Nashboro / Feb '96 / Pinnacle

Skyliners

SINCE I DON'T HAVE YOU
Since I don't have you / This I swear / I'll be seeing you / Lonely way to be / If I loved you / Warm / When I fall in love / Tired of me / Pennies from Heaven / It happened today / Zing went the strings of my heart / One night, one night / Tomorrow / Lorraine from Spain / I can dream, can't I
CD _______ CDCH 78
Ace / May '91 / Pinnacle

Skyscraper

SUPERSTATE
CD _______ DSCD 001
Dynosupreme / Nov '95 / SRD

Slab

FREEKY SPEED
CD _______ DUKE 020CD
CD _______ DUKE 020CDL
Hydrogen Dukebox / Apr '96 / 3mv/Vital / Kudos / Prime

Slade

AMAZING KAMIKAZE SYNDROME, THE
My oh my / Run runaway / C'est la vie / Slam the hammer down / Cocky rock boys / In the doghouse / Ready to explode / Razzle dazzle man / Cheap 'n' nasty love / High and dry
CD _______ CLACD 419
Castle / Nov '96 / BMG

COLLECTION, THE
Run run away / Everyday / We'll bring the house down / Ruby red / (And now the waltz) c'est la vie / Do you believe in miracles / Still the same / My oh my / All join hands / Wheels ain't comin' down / 7 year bitch / Myzterious mizster Jones / Lock up your daughters / Me and the boys / Gudbye t' jane / Mama weer all crazee now / Love is like a rock
CD _______ CCSCD 444
Castle / Nov '96 / BMG

CRACKERS
Let's dance / Santa Claus is coming to town / Hi ho silver lining / We'll bring the house down / Cum on feel the noize / All join hands / Okey cokey / Merry Christmas everybody / Do you believe in miracles / Let's have a party / Get down and get with it / My oh my / Run runaway / Here's to (the New Year) / Do they know it's Christmas / Auld lang syne / You'll never walk alone / Mama weer all crazee now
CD _______ CCSCD 401
Castle / Nov '93 / BMG

FEEL THE NOIZE (The Very Best Of Slade)
Get down and get with it / Coz I love you / Look wot you dun / Take me bak 'ome / Mama weer all crazee now / Gudbuy t'Jane / Cum on feel the noize / Skweeze me, pleeze me / My friend Stan / Everyday / Bangin' man / Far far away / How does it feel / In for a penny / We'll bring the house down / Lock up your daughters / My oh my / Run run away / All join hands / Radio wall of sound / Merry xmas everybody
CD _______ 5371052
Polydor / Jan '97 / PolyGram

GENESIS OF SLADE, THE (Rare Recordings From 1964-1966) (Various Artists)
CD _______ TMC 9606
Music Corporation / Mar '97 / Pinnacle

NOBODY'S FOOL
CD _______ 8491832
Polydor / May '91 / PolyGram

OLD, NEW, BORROWED AND BLUE
CD _______ 8491812
Polydor / May '91 / PolyGram

PLAY IT LOUD
Raven / See us here / Dapple rose / Could I / One way hotel / Shape of things to come / Know who you are / I remember / Pouk hill / Angelina / Dirty joker / Sweet box
CD _______ 8491782
Polydor / May '91 / PolyGram

SLADE ALIVE VOL.1
Hear me calling / In like a shot from my gun / Darling be home soon / Know who you are / Keep on rocking / Get down with it / Born to be wild
CD _______ 8411142
Polydor / Apr '91 / PolyGram

SLADE ALIVE VOL.2
Get on up / Take me bak 'ome / My baby left me / Be / Mama weer all crazee now / Burning in the heat of love / Everyday / Gudbuy t'Jane / On eyed Jacks with moustaches / C'mon feel the noize
CD _______ 8491792
Polydor / May '93 / PolyGram

SLADE COLLECTION 1981-1987, THE
Run runaway / Everyday / We'll bring the house down / Ruby red / C'est la vie / Do you believe in miracles / Still the same / My oh my / All join hands / Wheels ain't coming down / Seven year bitch / Myzterious Mizter Jones / Lock up your daughters / Me and the boys / Gudbye t' Jane / Mama weer all crazee now / Love is like a rock
CD _______ ND 74926
RCA / Apr '91 / BMG

SLADE IN FLAME
How does it feel / Them kinda monkeys can't swing / So far, so good / Summer song / OK yesterday was yesterday / Far far away / This girl / Lay it down / Heaven knows / Standing on the corner
CD _______ 8491822
Polydor / May '91 / PolyGram

SLADE ON STAGE
Rock and roll / When I'm dancin' I ain't fightin' / Everyday / Lock up your daughters / We'll bring the house down / Night to remember / Gudbye to Jane / Mama weer all crazee now
CD _______ CLACD 420
Castle / Nov '96 / BMG

SLADEST
Cum on feel the noize / Look wot you dun / Gudbuy t' Jane / One way hotel / Skweeze me pleaze me / Pouk Hill / Shape of things to come / Take me back 'ome / Coz I luv you / Wild winds are blowing / Know who you are / Get down and get with it / Look at last nite / Mama weer all crazee now
CD _______ 8371032
Polydor / May '93 / PolyGram

SLAYED
How d'you ride / Whole world's goin' crazee / Look at last nite / I won't let it 'appen agen / Move over / Gudbuy t' Jane / Gudbuy gudbuy / Mama weer all crazee now / I don't mind / Let the good times roll
CD _______ 8491802
Polydor / May '91 / PolyGram

TILL DEAF DO US PART
Rock 'n' roll preacher / Lock up your daughters / Till deaf do us part / Ruby red / She brings out the devil in me / Night to remember / M'hat m'coat / It's your body not your mind / Let the rock roll out of control / That was no lady that was my wife / Knuckle sandwich Nancy / Till deaf resurrected
CD ____ CLACD 415
Castle / Nov '96 / BMG

WALL OF HITS
Radio wall of sound / Coz I luv you / Take me bak 'ome / Mama weer all crazee now / Cum on feel the noize / Skweeze me, pleeze me / Universe / Merry Christmas everybody / Get down and get with it / Look wot you dun / Gudbuy t' Jane / My friend Stan / Everyday / Bangin' man / Far far away / How does it feel / Thanks for the memory (wham bam thank you mam) / Let's call it quits / My oh my / Run run away
CD ____ 5116122
Polydor / Nov '91 / PolyGram

WE'LL BRING THE HOUSE DOWN
We'll bring the house down / Night starvation / Wheels ain't coming down / Hold on to your hats / My baby's got it / When I'm dancin' I ain't fightin' / Dizzy mama / Nuts, bolts and screw / Lemme love into ya / I'm a rocker
CD ____ CLACD 418
Castle / Nov '96 / BMG

WHATEVER HAPPENED TO SLADE
CD ____ 8491842
Polydor / May '93 / PolyGram

YOU BOYZ MAKE BIG NOIZE
Love is like a rock / That's what friends are for / Still the same / Fools go grazy / She's heavy / We won't give in / Won't you rock with me / Ooh la la in LA / Me and the boys / Sing shout (knock yourself out) / Roaring silence / It's hard having fun nowadays / You boyz make big noize / Boyz
CD ____ CLACD 417
Castle / Nov '96 / BMG

Slagle, Steve

OUR SOUND
I didn't know what time it was / Eve / Little rootie tootie / Theme for Ernie / Crazy she calls me / Haitian flight song / Lush life / All or nothing at all / Beautiful friendship
CD ____ DTRCD 107
Double Time / Dec '96 / Express Jazz

REINCARNATION
CD ____ SCCD 31367
Steeplechase / Apr '96 / Discovery / Impetus

SPREAD THE WORD
CD ____ SCCD 31354
Steeplechase / May '95 / Discovery / Impetus

SLAM

HEADSTATES
CD ____ SOMACD 5
Soma / May '96 / RTM/Disc

Slammer

NIGHTMARE SCENARIO
CD ____ HMRXD 170
Heavy Metal / Apr '91 / Revolver / Sony

Slant 6

INZOMBIA
CD ____ DIS 94CD
Dischord / May '95 / SRD

SODA POP RIP OFF
CD ____ DIS 91CD
Dischord / Mar '94 / SRD

Slapdash

ACTUAL REALITY
CD ____ NB 197CD
Nuclear Blast / Nov '96 / Plastic Head

Slapp Happy

ACNALBASAC NOOM
Casablanca moon / Me and Paravati / Mr. Rainbow / Michelangelo / Drum / Little something / Secret / Dawn / Half way there / Charlie 'n' Charlie / Slow moon's rose / Everybody's slimmin' / Blue eyed William / Karen / Messages
CD ____ RERSHCD
ReR/Recommended / Jul '96 / ReR Megacorp / RTM/Disc

CASABLANCA MOON/DESPERATE STRAIGHTS
Casablanca moon / Me and Paravati / Half way there / Michelangelo / Dawn / Mr. Rainbow / Secret / Little something / Drum / Haiku / Slow moon's rose / Some questions about hats / Owl / Worm is at work / Bad alchemy / Europa / Desperate straights / Riding tigers / Apes in capes / Strayed / Giants / Extracts from the Messiah / In the sickbay / Caucasian lullaby
CD ____ CDOVD 441
Virgin / Oct '93 / EMI

Slapshot

16 VALVE HATE
CD ____ LF 195CD
Lost & Found / Aug '95 / Plastic Head

BLAST FURNACE
CD ____ WB 2098CD
We Bite / Jun '93 / Plastic Head

LIVE AT THE SO36
CD ____ WB 2111CD
We Bite / May '94 / Plastic Head

OLDTYME HARDCORE
CD ____ CMCD 77129
Century Media / Jun '96 / Plastic Head

STEP ON IT
CD ____ TAANG 028 CD
Taang / Jan '89 / Cargo

STEP ON IT/BACK ON THE MAP
CD ____ TAANG 28CD
Taang / Nov '92 / Cargo

SUDDEN DEATH
CD ____ TAANG 40CD
Taang / Nov '92 / Cargo

UNCONSCIOUSNESS
CD ____ WB 21142
We Bite / Oct '94 / Plastic Head

Slapstick

LOOKIT
CD ____ AM 003
Asian Man / Feb '97 / Cargo / Greyhound / Plastic Head

SLAPSTICK
CD ____ AM 009
Asian Man / Jun '97 / Cargo / Greyhound / Plastic Head

Slash's Snake Pit

IT'S FIVE O'CLOCK SOMEWHERE
Neither can I / Dime store rock / Beggers and hangers on / Good to be alive / What do you want to be / Monkey chow / Back and forth again / I hate everybody (but you) / Be the ball / Doin' fine / Take it away / Jizz da pit lower / Some city ward
CD ____ GED 24730
Geffen / Feb '95 / BMG

Slater, Luke

FOUR CORNERED ROOM
CD ____ GPRCD 3
GPR / Feb '94 / 3mv/Vital

LUKE SLATER 1992-1994
CD ____ PF 068CD
Peacefrog / Aug '97 / Mo's Music Machine / Prime / RTM/Disc / Vital

MY YELLOW WISE RUG
CD ____ GPRCD 8
GPR / Sep '94 / 3mv/Vital

X FRONT VOL.2
CD ____ PF 11CD
Peacefrog / Oct '93 / Mo's Music Machine / Prime / RTM/Disc / Vital

Slatkin, Leonard

ANDERSON - THE TYPEWRITER
CD ____ 09026680482
RCA / Aug '95 / BMG

Slaton, Wendi

TURN AROUND AND LOOK
CD ____ JR 006012
Justice / Nov '92 / Koch

Slaughter

FEAR NO EVIL
CD ____ SPV 08576002
SPV / May '95 / Koch / Plastic Head

Slaughter Joe

PIED PIPER OF FEEDBACK
CD ____ CRECD 084
Creation / May '94 / 3mv/Vital

Slaughter, John

ALL THAT STUFF AIN'T REAL
Red tail light / Get some rest / Louisiana 1927 / I've got the proof / Something you got / Ready to fall / Lost and found / On my way to heaven / St James' infirmary / I can't swim / Don't fool yourself / Shame on you
CD ____ CDSJP 430
Timeless Jazz / Oct '95 / New Note/ Pinnacle

NEW COAT OF PAINT, A (Slaughter Blues Band)
Riding with the king / Walking on sunset / I believe to my soul / Paint my mailbox blue / Watch your step / Cold cold feeling / Woke up this morning / Help me / Don't go the strangers / New coat of paint
CD ____ CDSJP 313
Timeless Jazz / Jun '92 / New Note/ Pinnacle

Slava

KAGAN
CD ____ ORACD 1
AO / Dec '93 / Pinnacle

Slave

FUNK STRIKES BACK, THE
CD ____ ICH 1144CD
Ichiban / Feb '94 / Direct / Koch

MASTERS OF THE FUNGK
CD ____ D 2248622
Ichiban / Jan '96 / Direct / Koch

REBIRTH
Are you ready / Way you dance / My everything / Everybody's talkin' / Thrill me / Victim of circumstance / I love you / Andy's ways / Behind closed doors / How is this love
CD ____ ICH 1055CD
Ichiban / Oct '93 / Direct / Koch

STELLAR FUNK (The Best Of Slave)
Slide / Party song / Stellar funk / Are you ready for love / Way out / Feel so real / Dancin' in the key of life / Weak at the knees / Nobody can be you / Wait for me / Snap shot / Just a touch of love / Stolen jam
CD ____ 8122715922
Atlantic / Mar '94 / Warner Music

Slave Master

UNDER THE 6
Godless / Heal / Damnation / Come out / Day of requital / Final call / Walk the water / Down / Each one teach one / Freedom
CD ____ RCD 10302
Black Arc / Jun '94 / Vital

Slave One

REPULSOR
CD ____ FDN 2015CD
Mascot / Jun '97 / Plastic Head

Slaves

TALKING REGGAE
CD ____ 669122
Greensleeves / Nov '92 / Jet Star / SRD

Slawterhaus

LIVE
CD ____ VICTOCD 013
Victo / Nov '94 / Harmonia Mundi / ReR Megacorp

Slayan, Piter

MASTERS OF MINANGKABAU, THE (Music From Sumatra) (Slayan, Piter & M. Halim)
CD ____ CDMANU 1531
ODE / Jul '97 / CM / Discovery

Slayer

DECADE OF AGGRESSION
Hell awaits / Anti-christ / War ensemble / South of Heaven / Raining blood / Altar of sacrifice / Jesus saves / Captor of sin / Born of fire / Post mortem / Spirit in black / Dead skin mask / Seasons in the abyss / Mandatory suicide / Angel of death / Hallowed point / Blood red / Die by the sword / Expendable youth / Chemical warfare / Black magic
CD ____ 74321248512
American / Dec '94 / BMG

DIVINE INTERVENTION
Killing field / Sex murder act / Fictional reality / Ditto head / Divine intervention / Circle of beliefs / SS III / Serenity in murder / Two-thirteen / Mind control
CD ____ 74321236772
American / Oct '94 / BMG

HELL AWAITS
Hell awaits / At dawn they sleep / Praise of death / Captor of sin / Hardening of the arteries / Kill again / Haunting the chapel / Necrophiliac / Crypts of eternity
CD ____ 398414031CD
Metal Blade / Feb '96 / Pinnacle / Plastic Head

LIVE UNDEAD/HAUNTING THE CHAPEL
CD ____ 398414011CD
Metal Blade / Feb '96 / Pinnacle / Plastic Head

REIGN IN BLOOD
Angel of death / Piece by piece / Necrophobic / Altar of sacrifice / Jesus saves / Criminally insane / Reborn / Epidemic / Post mortem / Raining blood
CD ____ 74321248482
American / Dec '94 / BMG

SATANIC SLAUGHTER VOL.1 (A Tribute To Slayer) (Various Artists)
CD ____ BS 03CD
Black Sun / Nov '95 / Plastic Head

SATANIC SLAUGHTER VOL.2 (A Tribute To Slayer) (Various Artists)
CD ____ BS 006CD
Black Sun / Nov '96 / Plastic Head

SEASONS IN THE ABYSS
War ensemble / Blood red / Spirit in black / Expendable youth / Dead skin mask / Hallowed point / Skeletons of society / Temptation / Born of fire / Seasons in the abyss
CD ____ 74321248502
American / Dec '94 / BMG

SHOW NO MERCY
Evil has no boundaries / Die by the sword / Metal storm / Black magic / Final command / Show no mercy / Anti-christ / Fight till death / Aggressive perfector / Tormentor / Crionics / Face the Slayer
CD ____ 398414032CD
Metal Blade / Feb '96 / Pinnacle / Plastic Head

SOUTH OF HEAVEN
South of heaven / Silent scream / Live undead / Behind the crooked cross / Mandatory suicide / Ghosts of war / Read between the lies / Cleanse the soul / Dissident aggressor / Spill the blood
CD ____ 74321248492
American / Dec '94 / BMG

UNDISPUTED ATTITUDE
Disintegration / Leeches / Abolish government / Can't stand you / Drunk drivers against mad mothers / Guilty of being white / I hate you / Filler / I don't want to hear it / Spiritual law / Mr. Freeze / Violent pacification / Memories of tomorrow / Richard hung himself / I wanna be your dog / Gemini
CD ____ 74321357592
American / May '96 / BMG

Slazenger, Jake

DAS IST EIN GROOVY BEAT JA
CD ____ WARPCD 42
Warp / Jul '96 / Prime / RTM/Disc

MAKESARACKET
CD ____ CLR 410CD
Clear / Jun '95 / Prime / RTM/Disc

Sleater Kinney

CALL THE DOCTOR
CD ____ CHSW 13CD
Chainsaw / Dec '96 / Cargo

Sledge, Percy

20 GREATEST HITS
CD ____ MU 5016
Musketeer / Oct '92 / Disc

BEHIND CLOSED DOORS
When a man loves a woman / Sitting on the dock of the bay / My special prayer / Behind closed doors / Warm and tender love / Tell it like it is / Take time to know her / I've been loving you too long / It tears me up / Cover me / Bring it on home to me / Try a little tenderness / If loving you is wrong / You send me
CD ____ MSCD 026
Music De-Luxe / Feb '96 / TKO Magnum

BLUE NIGHT
You got away with love / Love come knockin' / Why did you stop / I wish it would rain / Blue night / These ain't raindrops / Your love will save the world / First you cry / Going home tomorrow / Grand blvd / I've got dreams to remember
CD ____ VPBCD 21
Pointblank / Nov '94 / EMI

GREATEST HITS
CD ____ CDSGP 044
Prestige / Apr '93 / Else / Total/BMG

IT TEARS ME UP (The Best Of Percy Sledge)
When a man loves a woman / I'm hanging up my heart for you / Put a little lovin' on me / Love me like you mean it / It tears me up / Warm and tender love / Love me tender / Dark end of the street / Take time to know her / Try a little tenderness / Bless your sweet little soul / True love travels on a gravel road / Sudden stop / Stop the world tonight / It's all wrong but it's all right / Drown in my own tears / Out of left field / Kind woman / Cover me / That's the way I want to live my life / Push Mr. Pride aside / It can't be stopped / Rainbow road
CD ____ 8122702852
Atlantic / Mar '93 / Warner Music

LEGENDS IN MUSIC
CD ____ LECD 065
Wisepack / Jul '94 / Conifer/BMG / THE

LITTLE TENDERNESS, A
When a man loves a woman / Cover me / Take time to know her / Try a little tenderness / I've been loving you too long / It tears me up / My special prayer / Bring it on home / If loving you is wrong / You send me / Walkin' in the sun / Behind closed doors / Love among people / Warm and tender love / I'll be your everything
CD ____ SUMCD 4009
Summit / Nov '96 / Sound & Media

OUT OF LEFT FIELD
My adorable one / Take time to know her / My special prayer / Thief in the night / Out of left field / It tears me up / When a man loves a woman / You're pouring water on a drowning man / Just out of reach / Cover me / Warm and tender love

CD TKOCD 008
TKO / '92 / TKO

PERCY
Bring your lovin' to me / You had to be there / All night train / She's too pretty to cry / I still miss someone / Faithful kind / Home type thing / Personality / I'd put angels around you / Hard lovin' woman / When a man loves a woman
CD CDCHARLY 95
Charly / Jul '87 / Koch

PERCY SLEDGE COLLECTION
CD COL 048
Collection / Jun '95 / Target/BMG

SPOTLIGHT ON PERCY SLEDGE
Warm and tender love / Cover me / You're pouring water on a drowning man / My special prayer / Take time to know her / My adorable one / Sudden stop / Good love / Walking in the sun / It tears me up / Make it good and make it last / Out of left field / Behind closed doors / Just out of reach / Thief in the night / When a man loves a woman
CD HADCD 125
Javelin / Feb '94 / Henry Hadaway / THE

WANTED AGAIN
Keep the fire burning / Kiss an angel good morning / If you've got the money honey / Today I started loving you again / Wabash cannonball / Wanted again / Hey good lookin' / He'll have to go / She thinks I still care / For the good times
CD FIENDCD 140
Demon / Jul '89 / Pinnacle

WHEN A MAN LOVES A WOMAN
When a man loves a woman / Warm and tender love / Bring it on home to me / Behind closed doors / Try a little tenderness / Tell it like it is / My special prayer / (Sittin' on the) dock of the bay / (If loving you is wrong) I don't want to be right / Take time to know her / It tears me up / I've been loving you too long / Cover me / You send me
CD ECD 3087
K-Tel / Jan '95 / K-Tel

WHEN A MAN LOVES A WOMAN (The Best Of Percy Sledge)
When a man loves a woman / Warm and tender love / It tears me up / Take time to know her / Just out of reach / My special prayer / Out of left field / Baby help me / Sudden stop / Cover me / Adorable one / Dark end of the street
CD AIM 2002CD
Aim / May '97 / ADA / Direct / Jazz Music

WHEN A MAN LOVES A WOMAN
When a man loves a woman / Warm and tender love / Just out of reach / Cover me / It tears me up / My special prayer / Take time to know her / You're all around me / Out of left field / Dark end of the street / Sudden stop / Adorable one
CD 100582
CMC / May '97 / BMG

WHEN A MAN LOVES A WOMAN
CD CD 322698
Koch Presents / Jul '97 / Koch

Sleep

SLEEP VOL.1
CD TUPCD 034
Tupelo / Feb '92 / RTM/Disc

SLEEPS HOLY MOUNTAIN
Dragonaut / Druid / Evil gypsy / Some grass / Aquarian / Holy mountain / Inside the sun / From beyond / Nain's baptism
CD MOSH 079CD
Earache / Mar '93 / Vital

Sleep Chamber

SECRETS OV 23
CD EEE 014CD
Musica Maxima Magnetica / Sep '93 / Cargo / Plastic Head

SOME GODZ DIE YOUNG
CD 45932E
Funfundvierz / Jun '97 / Cargo / Greyhound

Sleeper

IT GIRL, THE
Lie detector / Sale of the century / What do I do now / Good luck Mr. Gorsky / Feeling peaky / Shrinkwrapped / Dress like your Mother / Statuesque / Glue ears / Nice guy Eddie / Stop your crying / Factor 41 / Click off gone
CD SLEEPCD 012
Indolent / May '96 / 3mv/BMG / Vital

PREPARING FOR TOMORROW'S BREAKDOWN
CD EXC 0122
Excursion / Jun '94 / SRD

Sleeping Dogs Wake

HOLD ME UNDER THE STARS
CD 39101133
Hyperium / Jan '97 / Cargo / Plastic Head

SPIDERBILLY'S SNAKEDANCE
CD 39101263
Hyperium / Jan '97 / Cargo / Plastic Head

SUGAR KISSES
CD HY 39100832
Hyperium / Dec '93 / Cargo / Plastic Head

THRENODY
CD 39101202
Hyperium / Jan '97 / Cargo / Plastic Head

UNDER THE STARS
CD 39101262
Hyperium / Jan '97 / Cargo / Plastic Head

UNDERSTANDING
CD 39101192
Hyperium / Jan '97 / Cargo / Plastic Head

WALK ON
CD 39100793
Hyperium / Jan '97 / Cargo / Plastic Head

Sleepyhead

STAR DUSTER
CD HMS 2142
Homestead / Dec '94 / Cargo / SRD

Sleight Of Hand

SECEDE
CD HMRXD 196
Heavy Metal / Nov '95 / Revolver / Sony

Slick, Earl

IN YOUR FACE
CD CDZORRO 34
Metal Blade / Sep '91 / Pinnacle / Plastic Head

Slick Pelt

HELL FROM THE HILLS
CD SP 001
Slick Pelt / Aug '96 / Nervous

Slick Rick

BEHIND BARS
CD 5238472
Def Jam / Feb '95 / PolyGram

GREAT ADVENTURES OF SLICK RICK, THE
Treat her like a prostitute / Ruler's back / Children's story / Moment I feared / Let's get crazy / Indian girl / Teenage love / Mona Lisa / Kit (what's the scoop) / Hey young world / Teacher teacher / Lick the balls
CD 5273592
Def Jam / Jan '96 / PolyGram

RULER'S BACK, THE
CD 5234802
Def Jam / Jan '96 / PolyGram

Slickee Boys

FASHIONABLE LATE
CD ROSE 147CD
New Rose / May '88 / ADA / Direct / Discovery

LIVE AT LAST
Gotta tell my why / Dream lovers / Missing part / Sleepless nights / Disconnected / Droppin' off to sleep / Brain that refused to die / Death lane / Life of the party / Pictures of matchstick men / When I go to the beach / Jailbait Janet / This party sucks / Here to stay
CD ROSE 169CD
New Rose / Aug '89 / ADA / Direct / Discovery

Slide 5

RHODE TRIP
CD URCD 015
Ubiquity / Jul '96 / Cargo / Timewarp

Slightly Bewildered String ...

SLIGHTLY BEWILDERED (Slightly Bewildered String Band)
CD SC 1095CD
Starc / Aug '96 / ADA / Direct

Slim

SLIM
What it is / Abducted / Water / Triple threads / Your chair / My dangerous life / Idyll
CD EMIT 0097
Emit / Apr '97 / Pinnacle

Slimani, Abdel Ali

MRAYA
Laziza / Habibti / Zeyna / Mraya / Yasmin / Alger / Hadi / Ana guellile / Ana guellile (dub)
CD CDRW 55
Realworld / Jan '96 / EMI

Slingbacks

ALL POP, NO STAR
No way down / Wasted / Hey Douglas / Trashy broken heart / Sometimes I hate you / All pop, no star / Autumn teen sound / Boy who wanted a heroine / Insufferable / Better think hard / Whorehouse priest / Junkstruck / Stupid boyfriend
CD CDV 2816
Virgin / Oct '96 / EMI

Slinger, Cees

LIVE AT THE NORTH SEA JAZZ FESTIVAL
CD MCD 198244
Limetree / Oct '92 / New Note/Pinnacle

Slipmatt

DREAMSCAPE VOL.1 - EXTRA SENSORY PERCEPTION (Mixed By Slipmatt/DJ Sy & Randall - 3CD Set) (Various Artists)
CD Set DSRCD 001
Dreamscape / Jul '97 / Beechwood/BMG

HARDCORE HEAVEN VOL.1 (Mixed By Slipmatt/Dougal/Seduction/Sy - 2CD Set) (Various Artists)
CD Set HMLCD 101
Heaven / Mar '97 / Grapevine/PolyGram

SLIPMATT TAKES CONTROL (Various Artists)
CD KICKCD 29
Kickin' / Nov '95 / Prime / SRD

Slippers

CHANCE TO DANCE
CD GRCD 6049
Goofin' / Nov '96 / Nervous / TKO Magnum

Slipstream

SIDE EFFECTS
CD CHE 37CD
Che / Nov '95 / SRD

SLIPSTREAM
CD CHE 22CD
Che / Mar '95 / SRD

Slits

CUT
Instant hit / So tough / Spend spend spend / Shoplifting / FM / Ping pong affair / Newtown / Love and romance / Typical girls / Adventures close to home
CD IMCD 90
Island / Feb '90 / PolyGram

IN THE BEGINNING (An Anthology)
Vindictive / Boring life / Slime / New town / Love and romance / Shoplifting / Number one enemy / Number one enemy / In the beginning / New town / Man next door / I heard it through the grapevine / Typical girls / Fade away / In the beginning
CD FREUDCD 057
Jungle / Aug '97 / RTM/Disc / SRD

Sloan

ONE CHORD TO ANOTHER
CD MURSD 023
Murder / Apr '97 / Cargo

Sloane, Carol

HEART'S DESIRE
Secret love / Memories of you / Heart's desire / September in the rain / Devil may care / You must believe in Spring / Them there eyes / Never never land / My ship / He loves and she loves / Fairy tales / Robbin's nest / You'll see / For Susannah Kyle
CD CCD 4503
Concord Jazz / May '92 / New Note/ Pinnacle

OUT OF THE BLUE
Prelude to a kiss / More I see / Aren't you glad you're you / Deep purple / Little girl blue / Life is just a bowl of cherries / Who cares / My silent love / My ship / Will you still be mine / Night and day
CD 378102
Koch Jazz / May '96 / Koch

SONGS CARMEN SANG
I'm gonna lock my heart (and throw away the key) / What can I say after I say I'm sorry / If the moon turns green / Sunday / Suppertime / Just you, just me / It's like reaching for the moon / What a little moonlight can do / Cloudy morning / Autumn nocturne / That old black magic / Folks who live on the hill / I'm an errand girl for rhythm
CD CCD 4663
Concord Jazz / Sep '95 / New Note/ Pinnacle

SONGS SINATRA SANG, THE
I've got you under my skin / In the still of the night / One for my baby / At long last love / I'll be around / Fly me to the moon / In the wee small hours of the morning / You make me feel so young / Night we called it a day / You go to my head / I fail in love too easily / Best is yet to come / Young at heart
CD CCD 4725
Concord Jazz / Sep '96 / New Note/ Pinnacle

SWEET & SLOW
Sometime ago / One morning in May / I'm way ahead of the game / I'm getting sentimental over you / Until I met you / Sweet and slow / You're getting to be a habit / Woman's intuition / Baubles, bangles and beads / Older man / One hour / I got it bad and that ain't good
CD CCD 4564
Concord Jazz / Aug '93 / New Note/ Pinnacle

WHEN I LOOK IN YOUR EYES
Simple life / Isn't this a lovely day (to be caught in the rain) / Midnight sun / Take your shoes off, baby / I didn't know about you / Soon / Old devil moon / Let's face the music and dance / Something cool / Tulip or turnip / I was telling him about you / When I look in your eyes / Will you still be mine
CD CCD 4619
Concord Jazz / Nov '94 / New Note/ Pinnacle

Sloe Gin Joes

SLOE GIN JOES
Hot link / Fryin' pan / I can't go home like this / Gettin' a dog / Let's drive / Chicken stew / Club soda / She's my baby doll
CD EC 1003
Ever Cool / Apr '97 / Nervous

Sloman, John

DISAPPEARANCES CAN BE DECEPTIVE
Foolin' myself / Breathless / Jealous / In too deep / Save us / Now you say goodbye / Perfect strangers / She talks about you / Parting you / Hooked on a dream
CD WKFMXD 114
FM / Aug '88 / Revolver / Sony

Sloppy Seconds

DESTROYED
I don't wanna be a homosexual / Come back Traci / Take you home / Black roses / Runnin' from the CIA / Horror of party beach / Black mail / So fucked up / Germany / Janie is a nazi / I want 'em dead / If I had a woman / Veronica / Candy man / Steal your beer / Time bomb
CD CDZORRO 71
Metal Blade / Mar '94 / Pinnacle / Plastic Head

KNOCK YOUR BLOCK OFF
CD TAANG 71CD
Taang / Jun '93 / Cargo

LIVE - NO TIME FOR TUNING
CD SPV 08456982
SPV / Dec '96 / Koch / Plastic Head
CD TX 51231CD
Triple X / Oct '96 / Plastic Head

SLOPPY SECONDS
CD TAANG 059CD
Taang / Jun '92 / Cargo

WHERE THE EAGLES DARE
CD MA 113231CD
Musical Tragedies / Nov '92 / SRD

Slotek

7
CD EFA 012172
Word Sound Recordings / Apr '97 / Cargo / SRD

Slovenly

HIGHWAY TO HANNOS
CD SST 287CD
SST / May '93 / Plastic Head

RIPOSTE
Way untruths are / Old / new / On the surface / Prejudice / Emma / Enormous critics / Myer's dark / Not mobile / As if it always happens / Little resolve
CD SST 089CD
SST / May '93 / Plastic Head

WE SHOOT FOR THE MOON
CD SST 209CD
SST / Mar '89 / Plastic Head

Slow Burn

CANDY FROM A STRANGER
CD SPCD 04
Shadow Play / Nov '93 / Plastic Head

Slow Loris

10 COMMANDMENTS, THE
CD 185392
Southern / Oct '96 / SRD

Slowburn

BLISSED OUT BEATS
CD CDRAID 529
Rumour / Mar '96 / 3mv/Sony / Mo's Music Machine / Pinnacle

Slowdive

JUST FOR A DAY
CD CRECD 094
Creation / Aug '91 / 3mv/Vital

PYGMALION
Rutti / Crazy for you / Miranda / Trellisaze / Cello / Just heaven / Visions of la / Blue skied an' clear / All of us
CD ______ CRECD 168
Creation / Feb '95 / 3mv/Vital

SOUVLAKI
CD ______ CRECD 139
Creation / May '93 / 3mv/Vital

Slowly

MING
CD ______ CHILLCD 003
Chillout / Oct '94 / Kudos / Pinnacle / RTM/Disc
CD ______ CHILLXCD 003
Chillout / Apr '95 / Kudos / Pinnacle / RTM/Disc

Slowpoke

MADCHEN
CD ______ GROW 222
Grass / Oct '94 / Pinnacle / SRD

Sludge Nation

BLOW YOUR SPEAKERS
CD ______ LEFT 47CD
Rhythm King / Nov '96 / 3mv/Pinnacle / BMG

Sludgeworth

SLUDGEWORTH
CD ______ LOOKOUT 131CD
Lookout / Nov '95 / Cargo / Greyhound / Shellshock/Disc

Slug

3 MAN THEMES, THE
CD ______ PCP 0242
PCP / May '96 / Vital

OUT SOUND, THE
X-Chest / Aurora F / Here and now / Crawl / Sung II meat / King of ghosts / Symbol for snack / Lofthouse / Co-ordinate points / Kitty thai spice
CD ______ PCP 0132
Matador / Aug '94 / Vital

Slugbait

MEDIUM TO HEAVY FLOW
CD ______ DPROMCD 26
Dirter Promotions / Jul '95 / Cargo / Pinnacle / World Serpent

Slum Turkeys

COMMUNICATE
CD ______ COX 029CD
Meantime / Apr '92 / Cadillac / Vital

Slusser, David

DELIGHT AT THE END OF THE TUNNEL
CD ______ TZA 7024
Tzadik / Jul '97 / Cargo

Sluts n' Strings & 909

CARRERA
Intro / Put me on / It's a blast / Past the gates / Puta / Civilized / Dig this / Dear Trevor / Hard move / Crunchy custom
CD ______ CDCHEAP 003
Cheap / May '97 / Plastic Head / Vital

Slutt

MODEL YOUTH
Angel / Breaking all the rules / Twisted / Women of the night / Revolution / Atomic envelope / TKO / Thrill me / Shooting for love / Through the fire / Too far to run / Model youth / Blue suede shoes
CD ______ NEATCD 1043
Neat / '88 / Pinnacle

Sly & Robbie

BLAZING HORNS IN DUB
CD ______ RNCD 2097
Rhino / Mar '95 / Grapevine/PolyGram / Jet Star

CARIB SOUL (Various Artists)
CD ______ RASCD 3089
Ras / Apr '92 / Direct / Greensleeves / Jet Star / SRD

CRUCIAL REGGAE (Driven By Sly & Robbie) (Various Artists)
Music is my desire: *Moses, Pablo* / New age music: *Inner Circle* / Just like that: *Toots & The Maytals* / Saturday evening: *Third World* / Reggae fever: *Steel Pulse* / One love jamdown / Rainbow culture: *Aswad* / Jogging: *McGregor, Freddie* / Happiness: *Uhuru* / Some guys have all the luck: *Tucker, Junior*
CD ______ RRCD 37
Reggae Refreshers / Jul '92 / PolyGram / Vital

DUB ROCKERS DELIGHT
Leaving dub / Dub glory / Righteous dub / Dub to my woman / Night of dub / Dub softly / Doctor in dub / Bound in dub / Dub in government / Jah in dub
CD ______ CDBM 055
Blue Moon / '91 / Cadillac / Discovery / Greensleeves / Jazz Music / Jet Star / TKO Magnum

MAMBO TAXI
CD ______ DSR 19841
Taxi / Jun '97 / Jet Star

MAMBO TAXI (Taxi Gang)
Mission impossible: *Sly & Robbie/Neville Hinds* / Good, the bad and the ugly: *Sly & Robbie/Neville Hinds* / Fire in de oven: *Sly & Robbie* / La bamba: *Sly & Robbie/Ambelique & Chevelle* / Live it up: *Sly & Robbie/Ansil Collins* / Village caller: *Sly & Robbie/Robbie Lyn* / Sunny Sunday: *Sly & Robbie/Dean Fraser* / Mambo taxi: *Sly & Robbie/Nambo Robinson* / Alfred Hitchcock: *Sly & Robbie/Neville Hinds* / Apartment: *Sly & Robbie/Franklyn Bubbler Waul* / Rasta reggae: *Sly & Robbie/Nambo Robinson* / Far out: *Sly & Robbie/Robbie Lyn*
CD ______ 5244102
Island Jamaica / Aug '97 / Jet Star / PolyGram

MONEY DUB
CD ______ RNCD 2063
Rhino / Jun '94 / Grapevine/PolyGram / Jet Star

OVERDRIVE IN OVERDUB
CD ______ SONCD 0055
Sonic Sounds / Jan '94 / Jet Star

POWERMATIC DANCEHALL VOL.1 (Various Artists)
CD ______ RASCD 3111
Ras / Mar '93 / Direct / Greensleeves / Jet Star / SRD

REGGAE GREATS (A Dub Experience)
Destination unknown / Assault on Station 5 / Joyride / Demolition city / Computer malfunction / Jailbreak / Skull and crossbones / Back to base
CD ______ RRCD 29
Reggae Refreshers / Sep '91 / PolyGram / Vital

REMEMBER PRECIOUS TIMES
CD ______ RASCD 3109
Ras / Mar '93 / Direct / Greensleeves / Jet Star / SRD

RHYTHM KILLERS
Fire / Boops (Here to go) / Let's rock / Yes we can can / Rhythm killer / Bank job
CD ______ 8427852
Island / '90 / PolyGram

SLY & ROBBIE PRESENT JACKIE MITTOO (Sly & Robbie/Jackie Mittoo)
CD ______ RNCD 2108
Rhino / Jun '95 / Grapevine/PolyGram / Jet Star

SLY AND ROBBIE HITS 1987-1990
CD ______ SONCD 0010
Sonic Sounds / Jan '91 / Jet Star

SLY AND ROBBIE PRESENT THE PUNISHERS
CD ______ CIDM 1104
Mango / Nov '93 / PolyGram / Vital

TAXI CHRISTMAS, A (Taxi Gang)
CD ______ RASCD 3102
Ras / Dec '92 / Direct / Greensleeves / Jet Star / SRD

TAXI FARE
CD ______ HBCD 39
Heartbeat / Jul '87 / ADA / Direct / Greensleeves / Jet Star

Sly & The Revolutionaries

SENSI DUB VOL.1 & 7 (Sly & The Revolutionaries/Jah Power Band)
CD ______ OMCD 030
Original Music / Sep '95 / Jet Star / SRD

Small

CAKES
CD ______ ROCK 60782
Rockville / Mar '93 / Plastic Head / SRD

CHIN MUSIC
Mona skips breakfast / Shaken, not stirred / Weather king / Tumble dry / Pretty side down / Toastmaster / My head is full of chocolate / Pet rock / Could you be on my side / Scenic route / Start with the victim
CD ______ A 061D
Alias / Oct '94 / Vital

SILVER GLEAMING DEATH MACHINE
Steal some candy / Bert factor / Wind, the rain and the lava / Halter and flick / Vega and Boston / B is for bridge / Three-legged race / Do the math / Copping chords / Map of the stars / There's a hatchet buried around here somewhere / Shunned off, pissed off / Top of the hill
CD ______ A 089D
Alias / Oct '95 / Vital

TRUE ZERO HOOK
True zero hook: *Small 23* / Off balance: *Small 23* / Noodles: *Small 23* / Makes me high: *Small 23* / Red comes up: *Small 23* / Rechose: *Small 23* / Finding it hard: *Small 23* / Saturday: *Small 23* / Wall to paint on: *Small 23* / Before we forget: *Small 23* / Get used to it: *Small 23* / Chopsocky: *Small 23*
CD ______ A 050D
Alias / Nov '93 / Vital

Small Faces

AUTUMN STONE, THE (Remastered)
Here comes the nice / Autumn stone / Collibosher / All or nothing / Red balloon / Lazy Sunday / Call it something nice / I can't make it / Afterglow of your love / Sha la la la lee / Universal / If I were a carpenter / Every little bit hurts / My mind's eye / Tin soldier / Just passing / Itchycoo park / Hey girl / Wide-eyed girl on the wall / Whatcha gonna do about it / Wham bam thank you mam / Donkey rides penny a glass / All or nothing / Tin soldier / Rollin' over
CD ______ ESMCD 478
Essential / May '97 / BMG

BEST OF THE SMALL FACES, THE
Sha la la la lee / My mind's eye / Universal / Watcha gonna do about it / Hey girl / I can't make it / All or nothing / Here comes the nice / Afterglow of your love / Tin soldier / Autumn stone / Rollin' over / Lazy Sunday / Every little bit hurts / I feel much better / Itchycoo park
CD ______ SUMCD 4001
Summit / Nov '96 / Sound & Media

COMPLETE COLLECTION, THE
All or nothing / Don't burst my bubble / Journey / Afterglow of your love / Ogden's nut gone flake / Itchycoo Park / Tell me have you ever seen me / Wham bam thank you mam / Tin soldier / Universal / Every little bit hurts / Lazy Sunday / Call it something nice / Song of a baker / Happy days toy town / Collibosher / Autumn stone / Just passing / Red balloon / Rollin' over / Wide eyed girl on the wall / Here comes the nice / If I were a carpenter
CD ______ CCSCD 302
Castle / Nov '91 / BMG

DECCA ANTHOLOGY 1965-1967
Whatch'a gonna do about it / What's a matter baby / I've got mine / It's too late / Sha-la-la-la-lee / Grow your own / Hey girl / Almost grown / Shake / Come on children / You'd better believe it / One night stand / Sorry she's mine / Own up time / You need loving / Don't stop what you're doing / E too D / All or nothing / Understanding / My minds eye / I can't dance with you / Just passing / Patterns / Runaway / Yesterday, today and tomorrow / That man / My way of giving / (Tell me) Have you ever seen me / Take this hurt off me / Baby don't you do it / Plum Nellie / You've really got a hold on me / Give her my regards / Imaginary love / It's not what you do
CD ______ 8445832
London / Mar '96 / PolyGram

FROM THE BEGINNING
Runaway / My mind's eye / Yesterday, today and tomorrow / That man / My way of giving / Hey girl / Tell me, have you ever seen me / Come back and take this hurt off me / All or nothing / Baby don't do it / Plum Nellie / Sha la la la lee / You really got a hold on me / What'cha gonna do about it
CD ______ 8207662
London / May '91 / PolyGram

GREATEST HITS
Itchycoo Park / Wham bam thank you ma-'am / Universal / Son of a baker / Rene / Here comes the nice / Tin soldier / Autumn stone / Afterglow of your love / Red balloon / All or nothing / Lazy Sunday
CD ______ CLACD 146
Castle / Apr '89 / BMG

HIT SINGLE COLLECTABLES
CD ______ DISK 4504
Disky / Apr '94 / Disky / THE

IMMEDIATE YEARS, THE (4CD Set)
You really got me / Money money / What'cha gonna do about it / Sha la la la lee / Hey girl / My mind's eye / My mind's eye / All or nothing / Yesterday, today & tomorrow / I can't make it / Just passing / Here comes the nice / Itchycoo Park / I'm only dreaming / Tin soldier / I feel much better / Lazy Sunday / Rollin' over / Universal / Donkey rides, a penny, a glass / Afterglow of your love / Wham, bam, thank you Mam / I can't make it / Just passing / Here comes the nice / Itchycoo Park / I'm only dreaming / Tin soldier / I feel much better / Universal / Donkey rides, a penny, a glass / Wham, bam, thank you Mam / (Tell me) Have you ever seen me / Something I want to tell you / Feeling lonely / Happy boys happy / Things are going to get better / My way of giving / Green circles / Become like you / Get yourself together / All our yesterdays / Talk to you / Show me the way / Up the wooden hills to Bedfordshire / Eddie's dreaming / Ogden's nut gone flake / Afterglow of your love / Long agos and world's apart / Rene / Song of a baker / Lazy Sunday / Happiness Stan / Rollin' over / Hungry intruder / Journey / Happydaystoytown / Rollin' over (live) / If I were a carpenter / Every little bit hurts (live) / All or nothing (live) / Tin soldier (live) / Call it something nice / Autumn stone / Every little bit hurts / Collibosher / Red balloon / Don't burst my bubble / (Tell me) Have you ever seen me / Green circles / Picaninny / Pig trotters / War of the worlds / Wide-eyed girl on the wall / Tin soldier (instrumental) / Green circles / Wham, bam, thank you Mam / Collibosher / Hungry intruder / Red balloon / Autumn stone / Wide-eyed girl on the wall
CD Set ______ CDIMMBOX 1
Immediate / Oct '95 / Koch / Target/BMG

IT'S ALL OR NOTHING
Sha la la la lee / Sorry she's mine / All or nothing / Grow your own / Come on children / Don't stop what you're doing / Own up time / What's a matter baby / I've got mine / It's too late / Runaway / Almost grown / You better believe it / My minds eye
CD ______ 5500472
Spectrum / May '93 / PolyGram

ITCHYCOO PARK
CD ______ CD 12208
Laserlight / Aug '93 / Target/BMG

LONG AGOS AND WORLDS APART (A Tribute To The Small Faces) (Various Artists)
Understanding: *Primal Scream* / I can't make it: *Dodgy* / It's too late: *BLOW* / My mind's eye: *Northern Uproar* / I've got mine: *Mantaray* / Afterglow: *Changing Man* / Universal: *60ft Dolls* / Become like you: *Granny Takes A Trip* / Song of a baker: *Ocean Colour Scene* / Rollin' over: *Whiteout* / Reservoir mods: *Almost Grown* / Talk to you: *Hypergio* / Here come the nice: *Buzzcocks* / That man: *Ride* / Autumn stone: *Gene*
CD ______ NYCE 001CD
Nice / Sep '96 / Vital

OGDEN'S NUT GONE FLAKE
Ogden's nut gone flake / Afterglow of your love / Long agos and worlds apart / Rene / Son of a baker / Lazy Sunday / Happiness Stan / Rollin' over / Hungry intruder / Journey / Mad John / Happy days toy town / Tin soldier
CD ______ ESMCD 477
Essential / May '97 / BMG

SMALL FACES
(Tell me) Have you ever seen me / Something I want to tell you / Feeling lonely / Happy boys happy / Things are going to get better / My way of giving / Green circles / Become like you / Get yourself together / All our yesterdays / Talk to you / Show me the way / Up the wooden hills to Bedfordshire / Eddie's dreaming
CD ______ CDIMM 004
Charly / Feb '94 / Koch

SMALL FACES (Remastered)
Tell me have you seen her / Something I want to tell you / Feeling lonely / Happy boys happy / Things are going better / My way of giving / Green circles / Become like you / Get yourself together / All our yesterdays / Talk to you / Show me the way / Up the modern hill to bed / Eddie's dreaming / Itchycoo park / I'm only dreaming / I feel much better / Tin soldier / Here comes the nice
CD ______ ESMCD 476
Essential / May '97 / BMG

VERY BEST OF THE SMALL FACES, THE (2CD Set)
What'cha gonna do about it / Sha la la la lee / Hey girl / All or nothing / My mind's eye / I can't make it / Here come the Nice / Talk to you / Itchycoo park / I'm only dreaming / Tin soldier / I feel much better / Universal / Donkey rides, a penny, a glass / Wham, bam, thank you mam / (Tell me) have you ever seen me / Things are going to get better / My way of giving / Get yourself together / All our Sundays / Ogden's nut gone flake / Afterglow (of your love) / Long agos and worlds apart / Rene / Song of a baker / Lazy Sunday / Happiness Sam / Rollin' over / Hungry intruder / Journey / Mad John / Happydaystoytown / Picaninny / Green circles / Call it something nice / Autumn stone / Red balloon / If I were a carpenter / Every little bit hurts / Don't burst my bubble
CD Set ______ CPCD 82602
Charly / Nov '96 / Koch

Small Factory

FOR IF YOU CANNOT FLY
CD ______ QUIGD 6
Quigley / Feb '95 / EMI

Small, Fred

EVERYTHING POSSIBLE
CD ______ FF 70625CD
Flying Fish / Dec '93 / ADA / CM / Direct / Roots

I WILL STAND FAST
CD ______ FF 704941
Flying Fish / Oct '89 / ADA / CM / Direct / Roots

JAGUAR
CD ______ FF 570CD
Flying Fish / May '93 / ADA / CM / Direct / Roots

NO LIMIT
CD ______ ROUCD 4018
Rounder / Jan '94 / ADA / CM / Direct

Small, Judy

BEST OF - WORD OF MOUTH, THE
Alison and me / How many times / Mothers, daughters, wives / Manly ferry song / Walls and windows / Much too much trouble / Golden arches / Speaking hands, hearing eyes / One voice in the crowd / Song for Jacqueline / Alice Martin / Mary Parker's lament / Family maiden aunt / You don't speak for me / Women of our time / Futures exchange
CD ______ **CDTRAX 050**
Greentrax / Mar '92 / ADA / Direct / Duncans / Highlander

BEST OF THE 80'S
CD ______ **CMMCD 007**
Larrikin / Jun '94 / ADA / CM / Direct / Roots

SECOND WIND
CD ______ **CMM 008CD**
Larrikin / Jul '94 / ADA / CM / Direct / Roots

Small, Michael

MOBSTERS
CD ______ **VSD 5334**
Varese Sarabande / Aug '91 / Pinnacle

Smaller

BADLY BADLY
CD ______ **BETCD 003**
Better / Apr '97 / 3mv/Vital

Smart, Leroy

EVERY TIME
CD ______ **RASCD 3139**
Ras / Jun '94 / Direct / Greensleeves / Jet Star / SRD

IMPRESSIONS OF BURNING SOUNDS
CD ______ **CDBS 564**
Burning Sounds / Mar '97 / Grapevine/ PolyGram / Jet Star / Total/BMG

LEROY SMART & FRIENDS
CD ______ **LG 21113**
Lagoon / Aug '95 / Grapevine/PolyGram

LET EVERYONE SURVIVE
CD ______ **JMC 200207**
Jamaican Gold / May '89 / Grapevine/ PolyGram / Jet Star

PRIVATE MESSAGE
CD ______ **DGVCD 2024**
Dynamite & Grapevine / Sep '93 / Grapevine/PolyGram / Greensleeves / Jet Star

TALK'BOUT FRIEND
CD ______ **VYDCD 09**
Vine Yard / Sep '95 / Grapevine/PolyGram

Smart Went Crazy

NOW WE'RE EVEN
CD ______ **DISS 96CD**
Dischord / Jan '96 / SRD

Smarties

OPERATION THUNDERBUNNY
CD ______ **859 314**
Steamhammer / Jun '89 / Pinnacle / Plastic Head

SMASH

SELF ABUSED
Revisited no. 5 / Barrabas / Oh ovary / Altruism / Reflections of you (Remember me) / Self abused / Scream silent / Another love / Another shark in the deep end of my swimming pool / Real surreal / Dear Lou / Bang bang bang (Granta 25) / Time / ALLYC / Trainspotter
CD ______ **FLATCD 6**
Hi-Rise / Sep '94 / EMI / Pinnacle

Smashed Gladys

SMASHED GLADYS
CD ______ **HMUSA 49**
Heavy Metal / Nov '85 / Revolver / Sony

Smashers

LOUD, CONFIDENT AND WRONG
CD ______ **APCD 076**
Appaloosa / Jun '92 / ADA / Direct / TKO Magnum

Smashing Pumpkins

GISH
I am one / Siva / Rhinoceros / Bury me / Crush / Snail / Fristessa / Window paine / Daydream / Suffer
CD ______ **HUTCDX 2**
Hut / May '94 / EMI

GREAT PUMPKIN THAT NEVER ARRIVED, THE (Interview Disc)
CD ______ **DIST 004**
Disturbed / Mar '96 / Total/BMG

INTERVIEW DISC
CD ______ **SAM 7019**
Sound & Media / Nov '96 / Sound & Media

MELLON COLLIE AND THE INFINITE SADNESS (2CD Set)
Mellon Collie and the infinite sadness / Tonight tonight / Jellybelly / Zero / Here is no why / Bullet with butterfly wings / To forgive / Fuck you (an ode to no one) / Love / Cupid De Locke / Galapogos / Muzzle / Porcelina of the vast oceans / Take me down / Where boys fear to tread / Bodies / Thirty three / In the arms of sleep / 1979 / Tales of a scorched earth / Thru the eyes of Ruby / Stumbleine / XYU / We only come out at night / Beautiful / Lily (my one and only) / By starlight / Farewell and goodnight
CD Set ______ **CDHUTD 30**
Hut / Nov '95 / EMI

PISCES ISCARIOT
Soothe / Frail & bedazzled / Plume / Whir / Blew away / Pissant / Hello Kitty Kat / Obscured / Landslide / Starla / Blue / Girl named Sandoz / La Dolly Vita / Spaced
CD ______ **CDHUT 41**
Hut / Oct '96 / EMI

SIAMESE DREAM
Cherub rock / Quiet / Today / Hummer / Rocket / Disarm / Soma / Geek USA / Mayonaise / Spaceboy / Silverfuck / Sweet sweet / Luna
CD ______ **CDHUT 11**
Hut / Jun '93 / EMI

Smear, Pat

SO YOU FELL IN LOVE WITH A MUSICIAN
CD ______ **SST 294CD**
SST / May '93 / Plastic Head

Smersh

EMMANUELLE GOES TO BANGKOK
Touch of Venus / Great Ceasar's ghost / Burn / Titanic fantastic / Blonde devil / You remind me of summer / Armoured man / Under your hoop / Brown out / Riding with the Pharoahs / Discotes
CD ______ **KK 47CD**
KK / Apr '90 / Plastic Head

GREATEST STORY EVER DISTORTED, THE
Licorice rope / Jack your metal / Japanese princess / Bootie heaven / Spook house
CD ______ **KK 019CD**
KK / Mar '89 / Plastic Head

Smietana, Jarek

FLOWERS IN MIND
CD ______ **338502**
Koch Jazz / Sep '96 / Koch

JAREK SMIETANA QUARTET
CD ______ **338262**
Koch Jazz / Nov '96 / Koch

Smith & Mighty

BASS IS MATERNAL
CD ______ **ZCDKR 2**
More Rockers / Nov '95 / 3mv/Sony

Smith, Al

HEAR MY BLUES
Night time is the right time / Pledging my love / I've got a girl / I'll be alright / Come on pretty baby / Tears in my eyes / Never let me go / I've got the right kind of lovin'
CD ______ **OBCCD 514**
Original Blues Classics / Apr '94 / Complete/Pinnacle / Wellard

MIDNIGHT SPECIAL
Five long years / You're a sweetheart / Baby don't worry 'bout me / Ride on midnight special / Bells / Goin' to Alabama / I'll never let you go / I can't make it by myself
CD ______ **OBCCD 583**
Original Blues Classics / Oct '96 / Complete/Pinnacle / Wellard

Smith, Barkin' Bill

BLUEBIRD BLUES (Smith, Barkin' Bill & Dave Specter/Ronnie Earl)
Things I'd do for you / Tell me what's the reason / Bluebird blues / Wind chill / Get me while I'm free / Buzz me / Lie to me / Railroad station blues / Our course is run / Take a little walk with me
CD ______ **DD 652**
Delmark / Mar '97 / ADA / Cadillac / CM / Direct / Hot Shot

GOTCHA
Sufferin' mind / As long as I have you / Down the line / Someday after awhile / Too fine for cryin' / You're too much / Blue guitar / Get your kicks / I love to love you / One kiss / I got what I wanted / Hot tomato / No rollin' blues / What makes these things happen to me
CD ______ **DE 672**
Delmark / Mar '97 / ADA / Cadillac / CM / Direct / Hot Shot

Smith, Bessie

AMERICAN LEGENDS
T'aint nobody's business / Baby, won't you please come home / St. Louis blues / Reckless blues / Sobbin' hearted blues / Cold in hand blues / You've been a good old wagon / I ain't got nobody / Sing, sing prison blues / Follow the deal on down / Nobody can bake a sweet jelly roll like mine / I'm wild about that thing
CD ______ **12737**
Laserlight / May '97 / Target/BMG

AUDIO ARCHIVE
I'm down in the dumps / Take me for a buggy ride / Do your duty / He's got me goin' / Kitchen man / You've got to give me some / I used to be your sweet mama / Devil's gonna git you / Thinking blues / Send me to the 'lectric chair / Trombone cholly / Cake walkin' babies from home / Yellow dog blues / Soft pedal blues / Dixie flyer blues / Nashville woman blues / Careless love blues / JC Holmes blues / I ain't gonna play no second fiddle
CD ______ **CDAA 032**
Tring / Jan '91 / Tring

BESSIE SMITH
CD ______ **DVBC 9092**
Deja Vu / May '95 / THE

BESSIE SMITH 1925-1933
CD ______ **CD 53090**
Giants Of Jazz / Mar '92 / Cadillac / Jazz Music / Target/BMG

BLUE SPIRIT BLUES
I'm down in the dumps / Blue spirit blues / Kitchen man / Foolish man blues / Thinking blues / Devil's gonna git you / Send me to the 'lectric chair / I'm wild about that thing / You've got to give me some / Standing in the rain blues / He's got me goin' / Do your duty / Dyin' by the hour / Lock and key / Gimme a pigfoot / Take me for a buggy ride / I used to be your sweet mama / Trombone cholly / Alexander's ragtime band / Good man is hard to find
CD ______ **GRF 102**
Tring / '93 / Tring

CLASSICS 1923
CD ______ **CLASSICS 761**
Classics / Jun '94 / Discovery / Jazz Music

CLASSICS 1923-1924
CD ______ **CLASSICS 787**
Classics / Nov '94 / Discovery / Jazz Music

CLASSICS 1924-1925
CD ______ **CLASSICS 812**
Classics / May '95 / Discovery / Jazz Music

CLASSICS 1925-1927
CD ______ **CLASSICS 843**
Classics / Nov '95 / Discovery / Jazz Music

CLASSICS 1927-1928
CD ______ **CLASSICS 870**
Classics / Apr '96 / Discovery / Jazz Music

CLASSICS 1928-1929
CD ______ **CLASSICS 897**
Classics / Oct '96 / Discovery / Jazz Music

COMPLETE COLLECTION VOL.1, THE (2CD Set)
Downhearted blues / Gulf coast blues / Aggravatin' papa / Beale Street Mama / Baby, won't you please come home / Oh daddy blues / Ain't nobody's business if I do / Keeps on a rainin' / Mama's got the blues / Outside of that / Bleeding hearted blues / Lady luck blues / Yodling blues / Midnight blues / If you don't, I know who will / Nobody in town can bake a sweet jelly roll like man / Jailhouse blues / St. Louis gal / Sam Jones blues / Graveyard dream blues / Cemetery blues / Far away blues / I'm going back to my used to be / Whoa, Tillie, take your time / My sweetie went away / Any woman's blues / Chicago bound blues / Mistreating daddy / Frosty morning blues / Haunted house blues / Eavesdropper's blues / Easy come, easy go blues / Sorrowful blues / Pinchbacks - Take 'em away / Rcoking chair blues / Ticket agent / Ease your window down / Boweavil blues / Hateful blues
CD Set ______ **4678952**
Columbia / May '91 / Sony

COMPLETE COLLECTION VOL.2, THE (2CD Set)
Frankie blues / Moonshine blues / Lou'siana low-down blues / Mountain top blues / Work house blues / House rent blues / Salt water blues / Rainy weather blues / Weeping willow blues / Bye bye blues / Sing sing prison blues / Follow the deal on down / Sinful blues / Woman's trouble blues / Love me daddy blues / Dying gambler's blues / St. Louis blues / Reckless blues / Sobbin' hearted blues / Cold in hand blues / You've been a good ole wagon / Cake walkin' babies from home / Yellow dog blues / Soft pedal blues / Dixie flyer blues / Nashville women's blues / Careless love blues / JC Holmes blues / I ain't got nobody / My man blues / Nobody's blues but mine / New gulf coast blues / Florida bound blues / At the Christmas ball / I've been mistreated and I don't like it
CD Set ______ **4687672**
Columbia / May '93 / Sony

COMPLETE COLLECTION VOL.4, THE (2CD Set)
Standin' in the rain blues / It won't be you / Spider man blues / Empty bed blues (part 1) / Empty bed blues (part 2) / Put it right here (Or keep it out there) / Yes indeed he do / Devil's gonna git you / You ought to be ashamed / Washwoman's blues / Slow and easy man / Poor man's blues / Please help me to get him out of my mind / Me and my gin / I'm wild about that thing / You've got to give me some / Kitchen man / I've got what it takes / Nobody knows you (when you're down and out) / Take it right back / He's got me goin' / It makes my love come down / Wasted life blues / Dirty no-gooders blues / Blue spirit blues / Worn out Papa blues / You don't understand / Don't cry baby / Keep it to yourself / New Orleans hop skop blues / See if I'll care / Baby have pity on me / On revival day (A Rhythmic spiritual) / Moan you moaners / Hustlin' Dan / Black mountain blues / In the house blues / Long old road / Blue blues / Shipwreck blues
CD Set ______ **4729342**
Columbia / May '94 / Sony

COMPLETE RECORDINGS VOL.5, THE (2CD Set)
Need a little sugar in my bowl / Safety Mama / Do your duty / Gimme a pigfoot / Take me for a buggy ride / I'm down in the dumps / Yellow dog blues / Nashville woman's blues / Careless love blues / Muddy water (a mississippi moan) / Bessie and the ladies / Life on the road / Life on the road II / Life on the road III
CD Set ______ **4835852**
Columbia / Feb '96 / Sony

COMPLETE ST. LOUIS BLUES
CD ______ **JZCD 308**
Suisa / Feb '91 / Jazz Music / THE

DO YOUR DUTY
CD ______ **IGOCD 2008**
Indigo / Nov '94 / ADA / Direct

EMPRESS OF THE BLUES
Gimme a pigfoot and a bottle of beer / Downhearted blues / Yellow dog blues / Careless love / Good man is hard to find / St. Louis blues / Do your duty / Cold in hand blues / Send me to the 'lectric chair / Empty bed blues / Nobody's blues but mine / Alexander's ragtime band / Them's graveyard words / New Orleans hopscotch blues / One and two blues / Take me for a buggy ride / Squeeze me / Nobody knows you (When you're down and out)
CD ______ **CBCD 001**
Collector's Blues / Jan '96 / TKO Magnum

EMPRESS OF THE BLUES, THE (Charly Blues Masterworks Vol.31)
CD ______ **CDBM 31**
Charly / Jan '93 / Koch

EMPTY BED BLUES (Her 23 Greatest)
Downhearted blues / Keep on rainin' / St. Louis blues / Cold in hand blues / Cake walkin' babies / Yellow dog blues / At the Christmas ball / Jazzbo Brown from Memphis Town / Gin house blues / Baby doll / Lost your head blues / Backwater blues / Trombone cholly / Send me to the 'lectric chair / Dyin' by the hour / Empty bed blues / Put it right here / I'm wild about that thing / Kitchen man / Nobody knows you when you're down and out / New Orleans hop scoop blues / Do your duty / Gimme a pig foot and a bottle of beer
CD ______ **CDAJA 5213**
Living Era / Sep '96 / Select

GREATEST BLUES SINGER IN THE WORLD, THE
Downhearted blues / Gulf coast blues / Nobody in town can bake a sweet jelly roll like mine / Jailhouse blues / Graveyard dream blues / Cemetery blues / Frosty morning blues / Haunted house blues / Easy come, easy go blues / Follow the deal on down / Sinful blues / Lady luck blues / Reckless blues / Cold in hand blues / Mean old bedbug blues / Yellow dog blues / Sweet mistreater / Empty bed blues / Blue spirit blues / Black mountain blues / In the house blues / Nashville woman's blues
CD ______ **CD 52009**
Blues Encore / '92 / Target/BMG

INTRODUCTION TO BESSIE SMITH 1923-1933, AN
CD ______ **4030**
Best Of Jazz / Mar '96 / Discovery

MAMA'S GOT THE BLUES
CD ______ **TPZ 1002**
Topaz Jazz / Jul '94 / Cadillac / Pinnacle

RECKLESS BLUES
CD ______ **CD 14546**
Jazz Portraits / Jan '94 / Jazz Music

ST. LOUIS BESSIE & ALICE MOORE VOL.1 1927-1929
CD ______ **DOCD 5290**
Document / Dec '94 / ADA / Hot Shot / Jazz Music

ST. LOUIS BESSIE & ALICE MOORE VOL.2 1934-1941
CD DOCD 5291
Document / Dec '94 / ADA / Hot Shot / Jazz Music

Smith, Bob

VISIT
CD CD 1518
Virgo / Jul '97 / Greyhound

Smith, Bobby

THAT'S FOR SURE (Smith, Bobby & The Erskine Hawkins Alumni)
Bess's boogie / Desert night / Mopsticks / Blue keys / Wee Gee blues / Lazy Suzy / That's for sure / Sweet and lovely / Flip a coin / Poodgy / Skippin' and hoppin' / After hours / Disco / Smoothie / Better get right / Dash hound / Cinder bottom / Tippin' in / Swan / Station break / Helicopter / Buffalo nickel
CD DE 484
Delmark / Jun '97 / ADA / Cadillac / CM / Direct / Hot Shot

Smith, Brian

MOONLIGHT SAX
CD NELCD 104
Timbuktu / Aug '93 / Pinnacle

UNFORGETTABLE SAX
CD NELCD 105
Timbuktu / Aug '93 / Pinnacle

Smith, Bryan

BEST OF BRYAN SMITH VOL.1, THE (Smith, Bryan & His Piano)
CD CDTS 002
Maestro / Aug '93 / Savoy

BLUE ISLANDS (Smith, Bryan & New Hawaiians)
Jealous heart / Oh lonesome me / Don't stay away too long / Arrivederci Roma / Who's sorry now / My foolish heart / I talk to the trees / Pagan love song / Coming home
CD DACD 016
Dansan / Aug '96 / Jazz Music / President / Target/BMG / Wellard

BRYAN'S CHRISTMAS BOX
CD CDTS 017
Maestro / Dec '95 / Savoy

DANCING FOR PLEASURE (Smith, Bryan & His Festival Orchestra)
Horse guards blue / Stella d'Italia (Star of Italy) / Closer / Once in a while / Edwardians / Sobre las olas (Over the waves) / I'll never say Never Again again / That's a plenty / Blue Tahitian moon / Just for a while / Suzy / Tango 65 / Egerland march / Bandstand march / Make believe / It looks like rain in Cherry Blossom Lane / Kind regards / Pink Colombine / Rags and tatters / Stumbling / Student Prince waltz / Anytime's kissing time / Tango hacienda / Tango sombrero
CD CC 275
Music For Pleasure / Oct '91 / EMI

DANSAN SEQUENCE COLLECTION VOL.2, THE (Smith, Bryan & His Dixielanders)
CD DNSN 902
Dansan / Oct '93 / Jazz Music / President / Target/BMG / Wellard

FOR ME AND MY GAL
Robin's return / Keep your seats please / Chinese laundry blues / When I'm cleaning windows (The window cleaner) / How wonderful to know / I'm confessin' / If I could only make you care / Vilia / Wedding / Waltz of my heart / Fold your wings / Turkey in the straw / Waiting for the Robert E Lee / Alabama jubilee / For me and my gal / Whispering / Heart of my heart / Leaning on a lamp post / Echo of a serenade / Return to me / Addio / Harbour lights / Black and white rag / Temptation rag / Johnson rag / LOVE / Dream / I left my heart in San Francisco / Lovely way to spend an evening / Just one more chance / Forgotten dreams / Singing piano / Drigo's serenade / Anytime's kissing time / Perhaps, perhaps, perhaps / My blue heaven / Oh lady be good / Side by side / On the sunny side of the street / Enjoy yourself / Little brown jug / Diamonds are a girls best friend
CD DACD 014
Dansan / Jun '96 / Jazz Music / President / Target/BMG / Wellard

MARCHING AND WALTZING
CD DLCD 113
Dulcima / May '94 / Savoy / THE

MUSIC MUSIC MUSIC
Music music music / Stumbling / Crazy Otto rag / Careless hands / Song of my life / Cuban love song / El cumbanchero / Back in your own back yard / All of me / Play a simple melody / Put your arms around me honey / Ivory rag / Don't bring Lulu / Spanish eyes / Beautiful lover
CD DACD 015
Dansan / Aug '96 / Jazz Music / President / Target/BMG / Wellard

WHISTLING RUFUS
Whistling Rufus / Carolina / Abie my boy / Wheezy Anna / You're adorable / What more can I say / If I had my way / Hold me / Underneath the arches / Amazing grace / All through the night / Plaisir d'amour / El cumbanchero / Let him go let him Tarry / Tavern in the town / She'll be coming round the mountain / Tom Dooley / Blue ribbon gal / Clementine / My bonnie lies over the mountain / Bill Bailey / I'm in love with two sweethearts / Girl in the Alice blue gown / Let us be sweethearts over again / Miss you / Greatest mistake of my life / All by yourself in the moonlight / Heartbreaker / Sweet Sue just you / Red River valley / Down at the old bull and bush / Ash grove / Two lovely black eyes / One of those songs / Just loving you / Careless hands / I love you beacause / Years may come years may go / Matchstalk men and mathstalk cats and dogs / Melodie d'amour / Song of my life
CD DACD 013
Dansan / Jun '96 / Jazz Music / President / Target/BMG / Wellard

Smith, Byther

I'M A MAD MAN
CD BB 9527CD
Bullseye Blues / May '93 / Direct

MISSISSIPPI KID
Judge of honor / Don't hurt me no more / President's daughter / Living in pain / Ashamed of myself / I don't know where you go / Blues on the moon / Your daughter don't want me no more / Give me my white robe / Runnin' to New Orleans / Cora, you made a man out of me / Monticello lonely / Mississippi kid
CD DE 691
Delmark / Feb '97 / ADA / Cadillac / CM / Direct / Hot Shot

Smith, Carl

SATISFACTION GUARANTEED (5CD Set)
Guilty conscience / I just droppped in to say goodbye / My lonely heart's runnin' wild / Washing my dreams in tears / I overlooked an orchid / This side of heaven / I won't be at home / Mr. Moon / If teardrops were pennies / There's nothing as sweet as my baby / Let's live a little / Me and my broken heart / Don't just stand there / Please come back home / There'll never be another Mary / My lonely heart's runnin' wild / Let old Mother Nature have her way / Little girl in my home town / I just dropped in to say goodbye / Are you teasing me / That's the kind of love I'm looking for / Nail-scarred hand / We shall meet some day / How about you / Blood that stained the old rugged cross / Gethsemane / Softly and tenderly / Amazing Grace / I'll be list'ning / Our honeymoon / Sing her a love song / Lovin' is livin' / I want to take my baby home with me / Trademark / This orchid means goodbye / Just wait 'til I get you alone / Do I like it / Darlin' am I the one / Hey Joe / If you tried as hard to love me / Love oh crazy love / Time's a-wastin' / No second chance / Satisfaction guaranteed / House that love built / Who'll buy my hearraches / Oh no / What am I going to do with you / Doggone it baby, I'm in love / If I could hold back the dawn / Back up Buddy / Look what thought's done to me / I just dropped in to say goodbye / Lovin' is livin' / Go boy go / More than anything else in the world / If you saw her through my eyes / No I don't believe I will / Loose talk / Time changes everything / Baby I'm ready / Kisses don't lie / Wait a little longer please / Works of the Lord / Answers / My dream of the old rugged cross / I just don't care anymore / Oh stop / Baby I'm ready / There's a bottle where she used to be / Wicked lies / Old lonesome times / I've changed / There she goes / No second chance / Come back to me / Don't tease me / If you do dear / I just dropped in to say goodbye / I feel like cryin' / You're free to go / Outlaw / Snowdeer / Doorstep to heaven / You are the one / If you want it, I've got it / Before I met you / Mr. Moon / San Antonio Rose / Live and let live / You are my sunshine / Steel guitar rag / This world is not my home / Standing on promises / Old Camp meeting days / When the roll is called up yonder / You can't hurt me anymore / That's the way I like you best / I won't be mad I'll be glad / That's what you think / Pass me not / Glory land way / Anywhere is home / When they ring them golden bells / No trespassing / Try to take it like a man / Mr. Lost / Happy Street / Amazing Grace / Why, why / Emotions / You're so easy to love / You're name is beautiful / Dry your darling's eyes / Best years of your life / Slowly / More and more / I overlooked an orchid / Let's live a little / Mr. Moon / Night train to Memphis / Honky tonk man / Hang your head in shame / I love you a thousand ways / Sweet little Miss Blue Eyes / If teardrops were pennies / We're not going steady anymore / Guess I've been around too long / Goodnight Mister Sun / Walking the slow walk / Love was born / It's all my heartache / Lonely girl / I'll kiss the past goodbye / Be good to her / Ten thousand drums / Tall, tall gentleman / I'll walk with you / Tomorrow night / Make the waterwheel roll / Past / I betcha my heart I love you / It's a lovely lovely world
CD Set BCD 15849
Bear Family / May '96 / Direct / Rollercoaster / Swift

Smith, Carmelita

PEACE AND LOVE
CD IMCD 01
CIS / Jan '97 / Jet Star

Smith, Carrie

FINE AND MELLOW
CD ACD 164
Audiophile / May '95 / Jazz Music

Smith, Charlene

FEEL THE GOOD TIMES
Feel the good times / Count on me / Sometimes / I learned my lesson / Too much for me / Let it slide / I got what you need / World goes round / No more lies / What'cha do
CD WOLCD 1069
China / Jul '95 / Pinnacle

Smith, Cheikh M.

TOUBABOU
CD WCOA 203CD
World Circuit / May '93 / ADA / Cadillac / Direct / New Note/Pinnacle

TOUBABOU BALAFOLA
CD OA 203
PAM / Feb '94 / ADA / Direct

Smith, Clara

CLARA SMITH VOL.1 1923-1924
CD DOCD 5364
Document / Jul '95 / ADA / Hot Shot / Jazz Music

CLARA SMITH VOL.2 1924
CD DOCD 5365
Document / Jul '95 / ADA / Hot Shot / Jazz Music

CLARA SMITH VOL.3 1925
CD DOCD 5366
Document / Jul '95 / ADA / Hot Shot / Jazz Music

CLARA SMITH VOL.4 1926-1927
CD DOCD 5367
Document / Jul '95 / ADA / Hot Shot / Jazz Music

CLARA SMITH VOL.5 1927-1929
CD DOCD 5368
Document / Jul '95 / ADA / Hot Shot / Jazz Music

CLARA SMITH VOL.6 1930-1932
CD DOCD 5369
Document / Jul '95 / ADA / Hot Shot / Jazz Music

Smith, Connie

ESSENTIAL CONNIE SMITH, THE
Once a day / Nobody but a fool (would love you) / I can't remember / Cry cry cry / Then and only then / If I talk to him / Ain't had no lovin' / Hurtin's all over / I never once stopped loving you / You and your sweet love / Cincinatti Ohio / I'll come running / Burning a hole in my mind / Run away little tears / Ribbon of darkness / Just one time / Just for what I am / Love is the look you're looking for / If it ain't love (let's leave it alone) / How great Thou art
CD 07863668242
RCA Nashville / Aug '96 / BMG

Smith, Craig

CRAIG SMITH
Sandy river belle / Two long years / St. Louis blues / Charade / Curly headed woman / Humoresque / Memory of your smile / Girl I left behind me / Annie Laurie / Rose of Alabama / Clinch Mountain backstep / My old Kentucky home / Moscow nights
CD ROUCD 0357
Rounder / May '97 / ADA / CM / Direct

Smith, Darden

DEEP FANTASTIC BLUE
First day of the sun / Broken branches / Running kind / Skin / Silver and gold / Drowning man / Different train / Chariots / Stop talking / Hunger
CD FIENDCD 930
Demon / Jun '97 / Pinnacle

NATIVE SOIL
Bus stop bench / Red sky / Little Maggie / Veteran's day / Sticks and stones / Keep an open mind / Wild West show / Painter's song / Two dollar novels / God's will / Clatter and roll
CD WM 1009
Watermelon / Jun '93 / ADA / Direct

Smith, Derek

DARK EYES (Smith, Derek Trio)
CD PRSCDSP 204
Prestige / May '94 / Else / Total/BMG

DEREK SMITH PLAYS THE MUSIC OF JEROME KERN
Ol' man river / Fine romance / Folks who live on the hill / I'm old fashioned / Long ago and far away / Way you look tonight / I won't dance
CD PCD 7055
Progressive / Jun '93 / Jazz Music

PLAYS PASSIONATE PIANO
CD MICH 4526
Hindsight / Sep '92 / Jazz Music / Target/ BMG

TRIO 1994, THE (Smith, Derek & Milt Hinton/Bobby Rosengarden)
CD CRD 322
Chiaroscuro / Mar '96 / Jazz Music

Smith, Elliot

EITHER/OR
CD KRS 269CD
Kill Rock Stars / Mar '97 / Cargo / Greyhound / Plastic Head

Smith, Floyd

RELAXIN' WITH FLOYD
CD BB 8752
Black & Blue / Jan '97 / Discovery / Koch / Wellard

Smith, Gary

7 IMPROVISATIONS (Smith, Gary & John Stevens)
CD SOUL 9
Soul Static Sound / Jun '96 / SRD

RHYTHM GUITAR
CD IMPCD 18920
Impetus / Mar '92 / Cadillac / Impetus

STEREO
Chelsea / Brutal / Chelsea / Primitive No.2 / Chelsea / Trio / Glissandi/polyrhythms / Primitive No.3 / Musical interlude / HF / MMM / Primitive No.1 / MM / Slab / Chelsea
CD CPE 20032
Chronoscope / Jun '97 / Cadillac / Harmonia Mundi / Wellard

Smith, Geoff

15 WILD DECEMBERS
CD SK 66605
Sony Classical / Jan '97 / Sony

BLACKFLOWERS
CD SK 62686
Sony Classical / Jun '97 / Sony

Smith, Gregg

PARTY WARRIOR
CD CDSGP 013
Prestige / Mar '92 / Else / Total/BMG

Smith, Hal

CALIFORNIA HERE I COME
CD JCD 182
Jazzology / Feb '91 / Jazz Music

HAL SMITH & HIS CREOLE SUNSHINE JAZZ BAND
CD BCD 350
GHB / Jun '96 / Jazz Music

MILNEBURG JOYS
CD BCD 277
GHB / Oct '92 / Jazz Music

MUSIC FROM THE MAUVE DECADES (Smith, Hal & Keith Ingram/Bobby Gordon)
CD SKCD 22033
Sackville / Aug '94 / Cadillac / Jazz Music / Swift

SWING BROTHER SWING (Smith, Hal California Swing Cats)
CD JCD 255
Jazzology / Jul '96 / Jazz Music

Smith, Howie

SECOND DOOR ON THE LEFT (Smith, Howie Group)
CD SBCD 3019
Sea Breeze / Jun '96 / Jazz Music

Smith, Huey

PITTA PATTIN' (Smith, Huey 'Piano' & Friends)
Rockin' pneumonia and the boogie woogie flu / Through fooling around / It do me good / Don't you just know it / I'll never forget / Coo coo over you / Smile for me / You got to / We like mambo / Bury me dead / (I do things come) naturally / What'cha bet / I've got everything / Baby you hurt me / Blues '67 / High blood pressure
CD CDCHARLY 225
Charly / Dec '90 / Koch

Smith, Ivy

IVY SMITH & COW COW DAVENPORT 1927-1930 (Smith, Ivy & Cow Cow Davenport)
CD BDCD 6039
Blues Document / May '93 / ADA / Hot Shot / Jazz Music

Smith, Jabbo

CLASSICS 1929-1938
CD CLASSICS 669
Classics / Oct '92 / Discovery / Jazz Music

COMPLETE 1928-1938 SESSIONS, THE (2CD Set)
CD Set 158112
Jazz Archives / Dec '93 / Discovery

JABBO SMITH 1929-1938
Got butter on it / Ready hokum / Jazz battle / Little Willie blues / Sleepy time blues / Take your time / Sweet 'n' low blues / Take me to the river / Ace of rhythms / Let's get together / Sua sha stomp / Michigander blues / Decatur Street tutti / Till times get better / Lina blues / Weird and blue / Croonin' the blues / I got the stinger / Boston skuffle / Tanguay blues / Band box stomp / Moanful blues
CD RTR 79013
Retrieval / Nov '96 / Cadillac / Direct / Jazz Music / Swift / Wellard

Smith, Jack

ROCKABILLY PLANET
CD FF 70510
Flying Fish / Jul '89 / ADA / CM / Direct / Roots

Smith, Jimmy

ALL THE WAY LIVE (Smith, Jimmy & Eddie Harris)
You'll see / Autumn leaves / Child is born / 8 Counts for Rita / Old folks / Sermon
CD MCD 9251
Milestone / Jun '96 / Cadillac / Complete/ Pinnacle / Jazz Music / Wellard

ANGEL EYES
CD 5276322
Verve / Nov '96 / PolyGram

AT CLUB 'BABY GRAND' WILMINGTON, DELAWARE OCTOBER 1956
CD CD 53114
Giants Of Jazz / Jan '94 / Cadillac / Jazz Music / Target/BMG

BACK AT THE CHICKEN SHACK
Back at the Chicken Shack / When I grow too old to dream / Minor chant / Messy Bessy / On the sunny side of the street
CD CDP 7464022
Blue Note / Mar '95 / EMI

BEST OF JIMMY SMITH, THE (Blue Note Years)
Sermon / Fungi mama / When Johnny comes marching home / Jumpin' the blues / Back at the chicken shack / Champ / All day long
CD BNZ 147
Blue Note / Dec '88 / EMI

CAT, THE (The Incredible Jimmy Smith)
Joy house theme / Basin Street blues / Cat / Carpetbagger's theme / St. Louis blues / Chicago serenade / Delon's blues / Blues in the night / Love cage theme
CD 8100462
Verve / Apr '89 / PolyGram

CHRISTMAS COOKIN'
God rest ye merry gentlemen / Jingle bells / We three Kings / Christmas song / White Christmas / Santa Claus is comin' to town / Silent night / Baby it's cold outside / Greensleeves
CD 5137112
Verve / Apr '92 / PolyGram

FOURMOST
CD MCD 9184
Milestone / Oct '93 / Cadillac / Complete/ Pinnacle / Jazz Music / Wellard

FURTHER ADVENTURES OF JIMMY & WES (Smith, Jimmy & Wes Montgomery)
King of the road / Maybe September / OGD (road song) / Call me / Milestones / Mellow mood / 'Round midnight
CD 5198022
Verve / Feb '94 / PolyGram

HOME COOKIN'
CC rider / Sugar Hill / I got a woman / Messin' around / Gracie / Come on baby / Motorin' along / Since I fell for you / Apostrophe / Motorin' along / Since I fell for you
CD CDP 8533602
Blue Note / Nov '96 / EMI

I'M MOVIN' ON
I'm movin' on / Hotel happiness / Cherry / T'ain't no use / Back talk / What kind of fool am I / Organic greenery / Day in, day out
CD CDP 8327502
Blue Note / Jun '95 / EMI

JAZZ MASTERS
Organ grinder's swing / Preacher / Side mouthin' / I'll close my eyes / Blues and the abstract truth / OGD (road song) / Hobo flats / Bashin' / Meditation / Walk on the wild side / Johnny come lately / Maybe September / G'wan train
CD 5218552
Verve / Feb '94 / PolyGram

MIDNIGHT SPECIAL
Midnight special / Subtle one / Jumpin' the blues / Why was I born / One o'clock jump
CD BNZ 162
Blue Note / May '91 / EMI

NEW SOUND, A NEW STAR, A (2CD Set)
Way you look tonight / You get'cha / Midnight sun / Lady be good / High and the mighty / But not for me / Preacher / Tenderly / Joy / Champ / Bayou / Deep purple / Moonlight in Vermont / Ready 'n' able / Turquoise / Bubbis / Gone with the wind / Jamey / My funny Valentine / Slightly Monkish / I can't give you anything but love / Judo mambo / Willow weep for me / Lover come back to me / Well you needn't / Fiddlin' the minors / Autumn leaves / I cover the waterfront
CD Set CDP 8571912
Blue Note / Aug '97 / EMI

PRIME TIME
CD MCD 9176
Milestone / Oct '93 / Cadillac / Complete/ Pinnacle / Jazz Music / Wellard

SUM SERIOUS BLUES
Sum serious blues / Around the corner / Hurry change if you're comin' / Sermon / You've changed / Moof's blues / Open for business / I'd rather drink Muddy Water
CD MCD 9207
Milestone / Apr '94 / Cadillac / Complete/ Pinnacle / Jazz Music / Wellard

TALKIN' VERVE (The Roots Of Acid Jazz)
CD 5315632
Verve / Aug '96 / PolyGram

Smith, Johnny

LEGENDS (Smith, Johnny & George Van Eps)
I'm old fashioned / Macho's lullaby / 'Round midnight / Wally's waltz / Black black black / Golden earrings / Romance de los pinos / Nortena / Maid with the flaxen hair / Waltz / Old castle / Sevilla / Cheek to cheek / Foggy day / Tangerine / Sunny / Why was I born / I didn't know what time it was / Tea for two / Man I love / For you / I hadn't anyone till you / I could write a book
CD CCD 4616
Concord Jazz / Oct '94 / New Note/ Pinnacle

Smith, Johnny

GEARS (Smith, Johnny 'Hammond')
Tell me what to do / Los conquistadores chocolates / Lost on 23rd Street / Fantasy / Shifting gears / Can't we smile
CD OJCCD 914
Original Jazz Classics / May '97 / Complete/ Pinnacle / Jazz Music / Wellard

GEARS/FOREVER TAURUS (Smith, Johnny 'Hammond')
Tell me what to do / Los conquistadores chocolates / Lost on 23rd Street / Fantasy / Shifting gears / Can't we smile / Old devil moon / Countdown / Walk in sunshine / Ghetto samba / Cosmic voyager / My ship / Forever Taurus
CD CDBGPD 037
Beat Goes Public / Oct '92 / Pinnacle

LEGENDS OF ACID JAZZ, THE (Smith, Johnny 'Hammond')
CD PRCD 24177
Prestige / Apr '97 / Cadillac / Complete/ Pinnacle

THAT GOOD FEELING/TALK THAT TALK (Smith, Johnny 'Hammond')
That good feeling / Bye bye blackbird / Autumn leaves / I'll remember April / Billie's bounce / My funny valentine / Puddin' / Talk that talk / Affair to remember / End of a love affair / Minors allowed / Riptide / Misty / Benny's diggin' / Portrait of Jennie
CD CDBGPD 061
Beat Goes Public / Jun '93 / Pinnacle

Smith, Keely

BE MY LOVE
Be my love / You're nobody 'til somebody loves you / You made me love you / Smoke gets in your eyes / How deep is the ocean / Don't let the stars get in your eyes / I'd climb the highest mountain / Pretend / I'm gonna sit right down and write myself a letter / Fascination / My reverie / It's all in the game
CD JASCD 321
Jasmine / Feb '94 / Conifer/BMG / Hot Shot / TKO Magnum

BECAUSE YOU'RE MINE
Because you're mine / Canadian sunset / No other love / Memories are made of this / My special angel / Please Mr.Sun / Only you / Because / Tell me why / Moments to remember / Prisoner of love / Loveliest night of the year
CD JASCD 333
Jasmine / Dec '96 / Conifer/BMG / Hot Shot / TKO Magnum

CAPITOL YEARS, THE
Sweet and lovely / Cocktails for two / Song is you / I'll get by / Lullaby of the leaves / On the sunny side of the street / I can't get started (with you) / I'll never smile again / s'posin' / East of the sun and west of the moon / All the way / I never knew / I wish you love / You go to my head / When your lover has gone / Fools rush in / Don't take your love from me / Imagination
CD CZ 305
Capitol / Apr '90 / EMI

CHEROKEELY SWINGS
To each his own / Where is your heart (Moulin Rouge) / My heart cries for you / Yellow bird / That lucky old sun / Too young / True love / Secret love / Rags to riches / Young at heart / Stranger in paradise / My devotion
CD JASCD 323
Jasmine / Jan '95 / Conifer/BMG / Hot Shot / TKO Magnum

DEARLY BELOVED
CD JASCD 328
Jasmine / Nov '95 / Conifer/BMG / Hot Shot / TKO Magnum

KEELY CHRISTMAS
White Christmas / Christmas island / O little town of Bethlehem / Jingle bells / Here comes Santa Claus / O holy night / Silent night / Christmas song / Hark the herald angels sing / I'll be home for Christmas / Rudolph the red nosed reindeer / O come all ye faithful (Adeste fidelis) / Blue Christmas
CD JASCD 329
Jasmine / Oct '94 / Conifer/BMG / Hot Shot / TKO Magnum

SPOTLIGHT ON KEELY SMITH
It's magic / You go to my head / Stardust / I can't get started (with you) / When your lover had gone / Sweet and lovely / Stormy weather / Fools rush in / Song is you / Mr. Wonderful / It's been a long, long time / I'll never smile again / Someone to watch over me / I'll get by / Don't take your love from me / Lullaby of the leaves / There will never be another you / Imagination / On the sunny side of the street / I wish you love
CD CDP 7803272
Capitol / Apr '95 / EMI

SWING YOU LOVERS
Swing you lovers / I love to you / Misty / I love you / If I could be with you one hour tonight / Hello, young lovers / All or nothing at all / All night long / Talk to me / Everybody loves a lover / They say it's wonderful / At long last love
CD JASCD 322
Jasmine / Jul '94 / Conifer/BMG / Hot Shot / TKO Magnum

TWIST WITH KEELY SMITH/DOIN' THE TWIST WITH LOUIS PRIMA (Smith, Keely/Louis Prima)
Twist: *Smith, Keely* / I know: *Smith, Keely* / Peppermint twist: *Smith, Keely* / Ya ya twist: *Smith, Keely* / Sticks and stones: *Smith, Keely* / Twistin' the night away: *Smith, Keely* / Let's twist again: *Smith, Keely* / What I'd say: *Smith, Keely* / Twistin' cowboy Joe: *Smith, Keely* / Mother goose twist: *Smith, Keely* / Shout: *Smith, Keely* / When the saints go twistin' in: *Smith, Keely* / Twist: *Prima, Louis* / Continental twist: *Prima, Louis* / Tag that twistin' dolly: *Prima, Louis* / Marie: *Prima, Louis* / Alright, okay, you win: *Prima, Louis* / Doin' the twist: *Prima, Louis* / Let's twist again: *Prima, Louis* / Night train: *Prima, Louis* / Route 66: *Prima, Louis* / Glow worm: *Prima, Louis* / Honeydripper: *Prima, Louis* / Side by side: *Prima, Louis*
CD JASCD 334
Jasmine / Dec '96 / Conifer/BMG / Hot Shot / TKO Magnum

WHAT KIND OF FOOL AM I
What kind of fool am I / Fly me to the moon / More I see you / But not for me / What's new / Don't blame me / If I should lose you / Then I'll be tired of you / But beautiful / Love me tender / Nature boy / I love you so much it hurts
CD JASCD 324
Jasmine / Jun '94 / Conifer/BMG / Hot Shot / TKO Magnum

Smith, Keith

KEITH SMITH & HIS CLIMAX BLUES BAND (Smith, Keith & His Climax Blues Band)
CD BCD 27
GHB / Aug '94 / Jazz Music

PORTRAIT OF KEITH SMITH VOL.1, A (Mr. Hefty Jazz)
Thriller rag / Mrs. Noone's blues / Get out of here and go on home / Sorry to leave this city / I can't escape from you (you can't escape from me) / ODJB one step / Franklin Street blues / Weary blues / Ting-a-ling / Blues and booze / Georgia on my mind / Milenberg joys / Blues for Mr. Hefty / Sister Kate / Everybody loves somebody sometime / Royal garden blues / Goin' home now
CD LACD 67
Lake / Sep '96 / ADA / Cadillac / Direct / Jazz Music / Target/BMG

PORTRAIT OF KEITH SMITH VOL.3, A (The Swing Is Here Again) (Smith, Keith Hefty Jazz All Stars)
Chicken ain't nothin' but a bird / Patrol wagon blues / Just sittin' and a rockin' / Perdido Street blues / Sweet Marijuana Brown / Caldonia / Let's fly away / I love you / Medi two / You're a lucky guy / After you've gone / Red rides again / Gee baby ain't I good to you / Struttin' with some barbecue / 'S wonderful / Dippermouth blues
CD LACD 80
Lake / May '97 / ADA / Cadillac / Direct / Jazz Music / Target/BMG

Smith, Kendra

FIVE WAYS TO DISAPPEAR
Aurelia / Bohemian zebulon / Temporarily Lucy / In your head / Space unadorned / Maggots / Drunken boat / Dirigible / Valley of the morning sun / Judge not / Get there / Saturn / Bold marauder
CD CAD 5008CD
4AD / May '95 / RTM/Disc

GUILD OF TEMPORAL ADVENTURERS, THE
Stars are in your eyes / Earth same breath / Waiting in the rain / She brings in the rain / Iridescence 31 / Wheel of the law
CD FSC 001 CD
Fiasco / Aug '92 / RTM/Disc / Vital

Smith, Laura

LAURA SMITH VOL.1 (1924-1927)
CD DOCD 5429
Document / Jul '96 / ADA / Hot Shot / Jazz Music

Smith, Leo

DIVINE LOVE
CD 5291262
ECM / Jul '96 / New Note/Pinnacle

KULTURE JAZZ
Don't you remember / Kulture of jazz / Song of humanity / Fire-sticks, crysanthemums and moonlight / Seven rings of light in the Holy Trinity / Louis Armstrong counterpointing / Albert Ayler in a spiritual light / Kemet Omega reigns (for Billie Holiday) / Love supreme (for John Coltrane) / Mississippi delta sunrise (for Bobbie) / Mother: Sarah Brown-Smith-Wallace / Healer's voyage on the sacred river / Uprising
CD 5190742
ECM / Jun '93 / New Note/Pinnacle

PROCESSION OF THE GREAT ANCESTRY
Blues: Jah Jah is the greatest love / Procession of the great ancestry / Flower that seeds the earth / Third world, grainery of pure earth / Who killed David Walker / Celestial sparks in the sanctuary / Nuru light: The prince of peace
CD CHIEFCD 6
Chief / Jun '89 / Cadillac

Smith, Linda

PREFERENCE
CD SPY 7CD
Harriet / Jun '97 / Cargo

Smith, Little George

HARMONICA ACE
Rockin' / Telephone blues / Blues in the dark / Blues stay away / Have myself a ball / I found my baby / Oopin' doopin' doopin' / California blues / Hey Mr. Porter / Early one Monday morning (take 1) / Love life / Cross-eyed Suzie Lee / You don't love me / Early one Monday morning (take 2)
CD CDCHD 337
Ace / Jun '91 / Pinnacle

Smith, Lonnie Liston

COSMIC FUNK (Smith, Lonnie Liston & Cosmic Echoes)
Cosmic funk / Footprints / Beautiful woman / Sais (Egypt) / Peaceful ones / Naima
CD 7863505912
Flying Dutchman / Jun '97 / BMG

EXPANSIONS
Expansions / Dessert nights / Summer days / Voodoo woman / Peace / Shadows / My love
CD ND 80934
RCA / Mar '94 / BMG

FLAVOURS
CD 500802
Musidisc / Sep '96 / Discovery

MOVE YOUR HAND
Charlie Brown / Layin' in the cut / Move your hand / Sunshine superman / Dancin' / In an easy groove
CD CDP 8312492
Blue Note / Mar '96 / EMI

VERY BEST OF LONNIE LISTON SMITH, THE
Space princess / Get down everybody (it's time for world peace) / Desert nights / Voodoo woman / Chance for peace / Visions of a new world / Song for the children / Fruit music / Quiet moments / Quiet dawn / Sunbeams / Expansions / Prelude (live) / Expansions (live)
CD _____ 74321137612
RCA / Jul '93 / BMG

Smith, Mamie

MAMIE SMITH VOL.1 (1920-1921)
CD _____ DOCD 5357
Document / Jun '95 / ADA / Hot Shot / Jazz Music

MAMIE SMITH VOL.2 (Get Hot)
CD _____ DOCD 5358
Document / Jun '95 / ADA / Hot Shot / Jazz Music

MAMIE SMITH VOL.3 (1922-1923)
CD _____ DOCD 5359
Document / Jun '95 / ADA / Hot Shot / Jazz Music

MAMIE SMITH VOL.4 (First Lady Of The Blues)
CD _____ DOCD 5360
Document / Jun '95 / ADA / Hot Shot / Jazz Music

Smith, Marc

PAST PRESENT AND FUTURE
CD _____ DCSR 014
Clubscene / Jun '97 / Clubscene / Grapevine/PolyGram / Mo's Music Machine / Prime

PAST, PRESENT AND FUTURE
Procastinator / Taking over me / Kickstart / Oh no / Boom and pow / Pump up the noise / Nexus / Journey / Relax your mind / Do that to me / Echoplex
CD _____ CSR 014
Clubscene / Jun '97 / Clubscene / Grapevine/PolyGram / Mo's Music Machine / Prime

Smith, Marvin

KEEPER OF THE DRUMS
Just have fun / Miss Ann / Love will find a way / Song of joy / Creeper / Now I know / Thinking of you / Simple samba song
CD _____ CCD 4325
Concord Jazz / Sep '87 / New Note/ Pinnacle

ROAD LESS TRAVELLED, THE (Smith, Marvin 'Smitty')
Neighbourhood / Wish you were here with me part 1 / Gothic 17 / Road less travelled / I'll love you always / Salsa blue / Concerto in BG / Wish you were here with me part 2
CD _____ CCD 4379
Concord Jazz / Jul '89 / New Note/Pinnacle

Smith, Melvin

AT HIS BEST (2CD Set)
Up on the hill / School boy blues / Reliefin' blues / They ain't gonna tell it right / Rampaging Mama / Homesick blues / Come back my darlin' / Real true gal / Everybody's got the blues / I remember / California baby / Looped / Baby I'll be there / I'm out of my mind / Woman trainer / Business man's blues / Sarah Kelly (from Plumnelly) / Six times six / Call me darling, call me swetheart, dear / What's to become of me / Hot ziggety zag / Letter to my baby / I don't have to hunt no more / Every pound / Miss Brown / I feel like goin' home / It went down easy / Why do these things have to be / Things you oughta know / No baby / You can't stay here / Crazy baby
CD Set _____ BCD 15703
Bear Family / Nov '94 / Direct / Rollercoaster / Swift

Smith, Michael

TIME
CD _____ FF 70613
Flying Fish / Nov '94 / ADA / CM / Direct / Roots

Smith, Michael W.

CHRISTMAS (Smith, Michael W/ Hollywood Presby. Choir/American Boys Choir)
Sing, choirs of angels: *Smith, Michael W.* / Lux venit (The Light comes) / Arise, shine, for your light has come / Anthem for Christmas / First snowfall / Christ the Messiah / No eye had seen: *Smith, Michael W/Amy Grant/Hollywood Presby. Choir* / All is well / Memoirs / Gloria / Silent night
CD _____ RRACD 0052
Reunion / Dec '89 / Nelson Word

GO WEST YOUNG MAN
CD _____ RRACD 0063
Reunion / Jan '91 / Nelson Word

Smith, Mike

ON A COOL NIGHT (Smith, Mike Quintet & Ron Friedman)
Don't scare me none / Speak no evil / Jeanie / Stars fell on Alabama / Autumn leaves / Stu's blues / On a cool night / Big P
CD _____ DD 448
Delmark / Mar '97 / ADA / Cadillac / CM / Direct / Hot Shot

SINATRA SONGBOOK, THE
CD _____ DE 480
Delmark / Aug '95 / ADA / Cadillac / CM / Direct / Hot Shot

TRAVELER (Smith, Mike Quintet)
Traveller / Rosebud / Child's paradise / Chromatose / Nepotism / Monte Carlo / Witch hunt / If you never come to me / Angel eyes / Full tilt
CD _____ DE 462
Delmark / Mar '97 / ADA / Cadillac / CM / Direct / Hot Shot

TRAVELLER, THE (Smith, Mike Quintet)
CD _____ DDCD 462
Delmark / Nov '93 / ADA / Cadillac / CM / Direct / Hot Shot

UNIT 7 (A Tribute to Cannonball Adderley)
Unit 7 / Hi fly / La luz de la luna / Work song / Jeanine / Pisces / Dat dere / Little taste
CD _____ DD 444
Delmark / Mar '97 / ADA / Cadillac / CM / Direct / Hot Shot

Smith, Orville

WALKING ON A TIGHTROPE
CD _____ RIZ 00042
Riz / Oct '96 / Jet Star

Smith, Patti

BAREFOOT (A Tribute To Patti Smith) (Various Artists)
CD _____ DOP 50
Doppelganger / Jul '97 / Total/BMG

DREAM OF LIFE
People have the power / Going under / Up there, down there / Paths that cross / Dream of life / Where duty calls / Looking for you (I was) / Jackson song / As the night goes by / Wild leaves
CD _____ 07822188282
Arista / Jul '96 / BMG

EASTER
Till victory / Space monkey / Because the night / Ghost dance / Babelogue / Rock 'n' roll nigger / Privilege / We three / Twenty fifth floor / Easter / Break it up / High on rebellion / Godspeed
CD _____ 07822188262
Arista / Jul '96 / BMG

GONE AGAIN
Gone again / Beneath the Southern cross / About a boy / My madrigal / Summer cannibals / Dead to the world / Wing ravens / Wicked messenger / Fireflies / Farewell reel
CD _____ 07822187472
CD _____ 07822384742
Arista / Jul '96 / BMG

HORSES
Gloria / Redondo beach / Birdland / Free money / Kimberly / Break it up / Land / Horses / Land of a thousand dances / La mer / Elegie / My generation
CD _____ 07822188272
Arista / Jun '96 / BMG

RADIO ETHIOPIA
Ask the angels / Ain't it strange / Poppies / Pissing in the river / Pumping (my heart) / Distant fingers / Radio Ethiopia / Abyssinia
CD _____ 07822188252
Arista / Jul '96 / BMG

WAVE
Frederick / Dancing barefoot / Citizen ship / Hymn revenge / Seven ways of going / Broken flag / Wave / So you want to be a rock 'n' roll star
CD _____ 07822188292
Arista / Jul '96 / BMG

Smith, Paul

SOFTLY BABY (Smith, Paul Quartet)
Softly / Taking a chance on love / Easy to love / Long live Phineas / I didn't know what time it was / I'll remember April / Invitation / I got rhythm / Man I love / Blues a la PT
CD _____ JASCD 311
Jasmine / Jun '97 / Conifer/BMG / Hot Shot / TKO Magnum

Smith, 'Pigmeat' Pete

JAZZ WOODBINE (New Originals In Fingerpicking/Bottleneck Blues Tradition)
CD _____ PIGME 008
Pigme / Apr '97 / Hot Shot

Smith, Ray

SHAKE AROUND
CD _____ CPCD 8117
Charly / Aug '95 / Koch

Smith, Roger

MY COLORS
Miss Wiggle (so what) / Hopscotch / Can you stand the rain / Only we know / Fallin' behind / Just bacause / Hermosa / I'm ready / Elly Mae / Illusionary dreamer / Serenade you / R Y B W and others / Put your faith in me
CD _____ JVC 20632
JVC / Dec '96 / Direct / New Note/Pinnacle / Vital/SAM

UNEXPECTED TURNS
CD _____ EM 4014
Emanem / Dec '96 / Cadillac / Harmonia Mundi

Smith, Slim

20 RARE GROOVES
CD _____ RNCD 2050
Rhino / Mar '94 / Grapevine/PolyGram / Jet Star

20 SUPER HITS
CD _____ SONCD 0004
Sonic Sounds / Jan '91 / Jet Star

FOREVER (Smith, Slim & The Uniques)
Ain't too proud to beg / Everybody needs love / Slip away / Let me go girl / People get ready, do rock steady / Love and devotion / Watch this sound / Out of love / A-yuh / Just a miracle / That's the way love is / Run come / Precious love / Standing in / Freedom song / Sitting in the park / Send me some loving / Everybody needs love / Gypsy woman / Never let me go / Speak no evil / My conversation / Beatitude / I am lost / Girls like dirt / One fine day / Please stay / Version of love / Forever / My girl
CD _____ RN 7013
Rhino / Apr '97 / Grapevine/PolyGram / Jet Star

RAIN FROM THE SKIES
Love power / It's alright / Don't tell your mama / Love and affection / Sunny side of the sea / Money love / Travel on / Stand up and fight / Sitting in the park / Turning point / Time has come / Take me back / Will you still love me / Burning fire / This feeling / Rain from the skies / Just a dream / Send me some lovin' / Blinded by love / Where do I turn / My conversation
CD _____ CDTRL 303
Trojan / Mar '94 / Direct / Jet Star

Smith, Steve

VITALIVE
CD _____ VBR 20512
Vera Bra / Dec '90 / New Note/Pinnacle / Pinnacle

Smith, Stuff

CLASSICS 1936-1939
CD _____ CLASSICS 706
Classics / Jul '93 / Discovery / Jazz Music

LIVE AT MONTMARTRE
CD _____ STCD 4142
Storyville / Feb '90 / Cadillac / Jazz Music / Wellard

LIVE IN PARIS 1965
CD _____ FCD 120
France's Concert / Oct '88 / BMG / Jazz Music

MAD GENIUS OF VIOLIN VOL.1 1936-1944, THE
CD _____ 158912
Jazz Archives / Jun '97 / Discovery

ONYX CLUB SPREE
I hope Gabriel likes my music / I'm putting all my eggs in one basket / I don't want to make history (I just want to make love) / 'Taint no use / After you've gone / You're a viper / Robins and roses / It ain't right / Old Joe's hittin' the jug / Serenade for a wealthy widow / Twilight in Turkey / Where is the sun / Upstairs / Onyx club spree / My thoughts / My blue Heaven / It's up to you / I've got you under my skin / Crescendo in drums / Joshua / Is is / Time and again
CD _____ TPZ 1061
Topaz Jazz / Feb '97 / Cadillac / Pinnacle

STUFF SMITH TRIO WORLD JAM SESSIONS RECORDING 1943
CD _____ PCD 7053
Progressive / Jun '96 / Jazz Music

Smith, Tab

ACE HIGH
Cottage for sale / Sunny side of the street / Tis Autumn / Teddy's brannin' / Strange / These foolish things / Ace high / Auf wiedersehn / Cuban boogie / My mother's eyes / I've had the blues all day / You belong to me / Red hot and blue / Bit of blues / Pennies from heaven / Seven up / I live true to you / Cherry / My baby / Closin' time
CD _____ DD 455
Delmark / Mar '97 / ADA / Cadillac / CM / Direct / Hot Shot

BECAUSE OF YOU
CD _____ DD 429
Delmark / Dec '89 / ADA / Cadillac / CM / Direct / Hot Shot

JUMPTIME 1951-1952
Because of you / Slow motion / Dee Jay special / Sin / Under a blanket of blue / How can you say we're thru / Wig song / Hands across the table / One man dip / Down beat / Brown baby / Knotty-headed women / Boogie joogie / Can't we take a chance / All my life / Jump time / This love of mine / Ain't got nobody / Love is a wonderful thing / Nursery rhyme jump
CD _____ DD 447
Delmark / Mar '97 / ADA / Cadillac / CM / Direct / Hot Shot

Smith, Tim

EXTRA SPECIAL OCEANLAND WORLD
CD _____ ALPHCD 020
Alphabet Business Concern / Jun '96 / Plastic Head

Smith, Tommy

AZURE
Gold of the azure / Escape ladder / Siesta / Smile of flamboyant wings / Vowel song / Constellation - the morning star / Calculation / Dancer / Dialogue of the insects / Blue
CD _____ AKD 059
Linn / May '97 / PolyGram

MISTY MORNING AND NO TIME
CD _____ AKD 040
Linn / May '95 / PolyGram

PEEPING TOM
New road / Follow your heart / Merry go round / Slip of the tongue / Interval time / Simple pleasures / Peeping Tom / Quiet picnic / Affairs, please / Harlequin / Boats and boxes / Biting at the apple / Baked air
CD _____ CDBLT 1002
Blue Note / May '90 / EMI

REMINISCENCE (Smith, Tommy & Forward Motion)
CD _____ AKD 024
Linn / Feb '94 / PolyGram

Smith, Tony

BIG CAT
Renegade / Arabella / Botswana / Don't lose it / Dark bark / Cruisin' / Big cat / South wind / Angie
CD _____ JITCD 9502
Jazzizit / Sep '95 / New Note/Pinnacle

RUNNER
Talkback / Runner / Suspicious / Michelle's song / Horse / Sleepwalking / Phase phase / Githie manitou / Whirlpool
CD _____ JITCD 9708
Jazzizit / Jul '97 / New Note/Pinnacle

Smith, Trixie

TRIXIE SMITH VOL.1 1922-1924
CD _____ DOCD 5332
Document / May '95 / ADA / Hot Shot / Jazz Music

TRIXIE SMITH VOL.2 1925-1939
CD _____ DOCD 5333
Document / May '95 / ADA / Hot Shot / Jazz Music

Smith, TV

IMMORTAL RICH
CD _____ BAH 21
Humbug / Jan '95 / Total/Pinnacle

RIP
CD _____ BAH 5
Humbug / Mar '93 / Total/Pinnacle

Smith, Warren

CALL OF THE WILD
Cave in / I don't believe I'll fall in love today / After the boy gets the girl / Whole lot of nothin' / Odds and ends / Call of the wild (unissued) / Old lonesome feeling / Call of the wild / Book of broken hearts / I fall to pieces / Foolin' around / Take good care of her / Pick me up on your way down / Just call me lonesome / Heartbreak Hotel / I still miss someone / Kissing my pillow / I can't stop loving you / Why baby why: *Smith, Warren & Shirley Collie* / Why I'm walkin': *Smith, Warren & Shirley Collie* / Five minutes of the latest blues / Put me back together again / Bad news gets around / Hundred and sixty pounds of hurt / That's why I sing in a honky tonk / Big city ways / Blue smoke / Judge and jury / Future x / She likes attention
CD _____ BCD 15495
Bear Family / Apr '90 / Direct / Rollercoaster / Swift

CLASSIC SUN RECORDINGS
Rock 'n' roll Ruby / I'd rather be safe than sorry / Black Jack David / Ubangi stomp / Darkest cloud / So long I'm gone / Who took my baby / I couldn't take the chance / Miss Froggie / Red Cadillac and a black moustache / Stop the world (and let me off) / I fell in love / Got love if you want it / Old lonesome feeling (incomplete) / Tell me who / Tonight will be the last night / Dear John / Hank Snow medley / Do I love you / Uranium rock / Goodbye Mr. Love / Sweet sweet girl / I like your kind of love / My hanging day

CD BCD 15514
Bear Family / Apr '92 / Direct / Rollercoaster / Swift

ROCKABILLY LEGEND
CD CPCD 8119
Charly / Aug '95 / Koch

Smith, Wayne

SLENG TENG (Smith, Wayne & Prince Jammy's Computerised Dub)
Under me sleng teng / In thing / Love don't love me / My Lord my God / Icky all over / E 20 / Like a dragon / Hard to believe / Leave her for you / Walk like granny
CD GRELCD 513
Greensleeves / May '92 / Jet Star / SRD

WICKED IN A DANCE HALL
CD RRTGCD 7785
Rohit / Jul '90 / Jet Star

Smith, Whispering

WHISPERING SMITH
CD PASTCD 7074
Flapper / Oct '95 / Pinnacle

Smith, Willie

CLASSICS 1925-1937 (Smith, Willie 'The Lion')
CD CLASSICS 662
Classics / Nov '92 / Discovery / Jazz Music

CLASSICS 1937-1938 (Smith, Willie 'The Lion')
CD CLASSICS 677
Classics / Mar '93 / Discovery / Jazz Music

CLASSICS 1938-1940 (Smith, Willie 'The Lion')
CD CLASSICS 692
Classics / May '93 / Discovery / Jazz Music

HARLEM JOYS (Smith, Willie 'The Lion')
There's gonna be the devil to pay / Streamline girl / What can I do with a foolish girl like you / Harlem joys / Echo of spring / Breeze (blow my baby back to me) / Swing brother swing / Sittin' at the table (opposite you) / Swamp land (is calling me) / More than that / I'm all out of breath / I can see you all over the place / Get acquainted with yourself / Knock wood / Peace brother peace / Old stomping ground / Blues why don't you let me alone / I've got to think it over / Achin' hearted blues / Honeymoonin' on a dime
CD CDAFS 1032
Charly / Jun '93 / Koch

LION AND THE LAMB, THE (Smith, Willie 'The Lion' & His Cubs)
What can I do with a foolish little thing like you do / Harlem joys / Lost / Mutiny in the parlour / Swampland is calling / More than that / I can see you all over the place / Achin' hearted blues / Morning air / Echoes of Spring / Concentrating / Fading star / Passionette / Rippling waters / Breakaway / Between the devil and the deep blue sea / Tea for two / I'll follow you / Finger buster / Lion and the lamb / I'm coming Virginia / Limehouse blues / Strange fruit / You're the limit / 12th Street rag / Bugle call rag
CD TPZ 1057
Topaz Jazz / Nov '96 / Cadillac / Pinnacle

LION ROARS AGAIN (Smith, Willie 'The Lion')
CD CBC 1012
Bellaphon / Jun '93 / New Note/Pinnacle

LIVE 1945 (Smith, Willie & Harry James All Stars)
Introduction / Sweet Georgia brown / These foolish things (remind me of you) / Honeysuckle rose / Body and soul / Introduction / Sweet Georgia brown / It's the talk of the town / Tea for two
CD VN 1011
Viper's Nest / Aug '97 / ADA / Cadillac / Direct / Jazz Music

PORK AND BEANS (Smith, Willie 'The Lion')
Pork and beans / Moonlight cocktail / Spanish Venus / Junk man rag / Squeeze me / Love will find a way / I'm just wild about Harry / Memories of you / Alexander's ragtime band / All of me / Ain't misbehavin' / Man I love / Summertime / Ain't she sweet
CD BLCD 760144
Black Lion / Jan '85 / Cadillac / Jazz Music / Koch / Wellard

Smither, Chris

ANOTHER WAY TO FIND YOU
High heel sneakers/Big boss man / Another way to find you / Down in the flood / Lonely time / Lonesome Georgia Brown / Catfish / Every mother's son / I got mine / Don't it drag on / Love you like a man / I feel the same / Friend of the devil / Shake sugaree / Tulane / Have you seen my baby / Song for Susan / Homunculus
CD FF 70568
Flying Fish / Nov '96 / ADA / CM / Direct / Roots

HAPPIER BLUE
Happier blue / Memphis in the meantime / Devil's real / No more cane on the Brazos / Mail order mystics / No reward / Already gone / Killing the blues / Rock 'n' roll doctor / Magnolia / Honeysuckle dog / Take it all / Time to spend
CD FIENDCD 739
Demon / Mar '94 / Pinnacle

I'M A STRANGER TOO/DON'T DRAG IT ON
CD CLT 5838CD
Collectables / May '97 / Greyhound

SMALL REVELATIONS
CD HCD 8077
Hightone / Feb '97 / ADA / Koch

UP ON THE LOWDOWN
CD HCD 8060
Hightone / Apr '95 / ADA / Koch

Smiths

ASK ME, ASK ME, ASK ME (Interview)
CD 3D 008
Network / Jan '97 / Total/BMG

BEST OF THE SMITHS VOL.1, THE
This charming man / William, it was really nothing / What difference does it make / Stop me if you think you've heard this one before / Girlfriend in a coma / Half a person / Rubber ring / How soon is now / Hand in glove / Shoplifters of the world unite / Sheila take a bow / Some girls are bigger than others / Panic / Please please please let me get what I want
CD 4509900442
WEA / Aug '92 / Warner Music

BEST OF THE SMITHS VOL.2, THE
Boy with the thorn in his side / Headmaster ritual / Heaven knows I'm miserable now / Ask / Oscillate wildly / Nowhere fast / Still ill / That joke isn't funny anymore / Shakespeare's sister / Girl afraid / Reel around the fountain / Last night I dreamt somebody loved me / There is a light that never goes out
CD 4509904062
WEA / Nov '92 / Warner Music

HATFUL OF HOLLOW
William, it was really nothing / What difference does it make / These things take time / This charming man / How soon is now / Handsome devil / Hand in glove / Still ill / Heaven knows I'm miserable now / This night has opened my eyes / You've got everything now / Accept yourself / Girl afraid / Back to the old house / Reel around the fountain / Please, please, please let me get what I want
CD 4509918932
WEA / Feb '95 / Warner Music

LOUDER THAN BOMBS
Is it really so strange / Sheila take a bow / Shoplifters of the world unite / Sweet and tender hooligan / Half a person / London / Panic / Girl afraid / Shakespeare's sister / William, it was really nothing / You just haven't earned it yet baby / Heaven knows I'm miserable now / Ask / Golden lights / There is a light that never goes out
CD 4509938332
WEA / Feb '95 / Warner Music

MEAT IS MURDER
Headmaster ritual / Barbarism begins at home / Rusholme ruffians / I want the one I can't have / What she said / Nowhere fast / That joke isn't funny anymore / Well I wonder / Meat is murder
CD 4509918952
WEA / Feb '95 / Warner Music

QUEEN IS DEAD, THE
Frankly, Mr. Shankly / I know it's over / Never had no one ever / Cemetery gates / Big mouth strikes again / Vicar in a tutu / There is a light that never goes out / Some girls are bigger than others / Queen is dead / Boy with the thorn in his side
CD 4509918962
WEA / Feb '95 / Warner Music

RANK
Queen is dead / Panic / Vicar in a tutu / Ask / Rusholme ruffians / What she said / Cemetery gates / London / Big mouth strikes again / Draize Train / Boy with the thorn in his side / Is it really so strange / I know it's over / Still ill / His latest flame
CD 4509919002
WEA / Feb '95 / Warner Music

SMITHS IS DEAD, THE (Various Artists)
Queen is dead: *Boo Radleys* / Frankly Mr. Shankly: *High Llamas* / I know it's over: *Trash Can Sinatras* / Never had no one ever: *Bragg, Billy* / Cemetary gates: *Frank & Walters* / Bigmouth strikes again: *Placebo* / Boy with the thorn in his side: *Bis* / Vicar in a tutu: *Therapy* / There is a light that never goes out: *Divine Comedy* / Some girls are bigger than others: *Supergrass*
CD 4867452
Epic / Nov '96 / Sony

SMITHS SINGLES
CD 4509990902
WEA / Feb '95 / Warner Music

SMITHS, THE
Reel around the fountain / You've got everything now / Miserable lie / Pretty girls make graves / Hand that rocks the cradle / This charming man / Still ill / Hand in glove / What difference does it make / I don't owe you anything / Suffer little children
CD 4509918922
WEA / Feb '95 / Warner Music

SMITHS: INTERVIEW COMPACT DISC
CD CBAK 4025
Baktabak / Nov '89 / Arabesque

STRANGEWAYS HERE WE COME
Rush and a push and the land is ours / I started something I couldn't finish / Death of a disco dancer / Girlfriend in a coma / Stop me if you think you've heard this one before / Last night I dreamt somebody loved me / Unhappy birthday / Paint a vulgar picture / Death at one's elbow / I won't share you
CD 4509918992
WEA / Feb '95 / Warner Music

WORLD WON'T LISTEN, THE
Panic / Ask / London / Big mouth strikes again / Shakespeare's sister / There is a light that never goes out / Shoplifters of the world unite / Boy with the thorn in his side / Asleep / Unloveable / Half a person / Stretch out and wait / That joke isn't funny anymore / You haven't earned it yet baby / Rubber ring / Oscillate wildly / Money changes everything
CD 4509918982
WEA / Feb '95 / Warner Music

Smog

DOCTOR CAME AT DAWN
CD WIGCD 27
Domino / Sep '96 / Vital

JULIUS CAESAR
Strawberry rash / Your wedding / Thirty seven push-ups / Stalled on the tracks / One less star / Golden / When you talk / I am Star Wars / Connections / When the power goes out / Chosen one / What kind of angel / Stick in the mud
CD OLE 0972
Matador / Jul '94 / Vital

RED APPLE FALLS
Morning papers / Blood red bird / Red apples / I was a stranger / To be of use / Red apple falls / Ex-con / Inspirational / Finer days
CD WIGCD 35
Domino / May '97 / Vital

SEWN TO THE SKY
CD DC 74CD
Drag City / Dec '96 / Cargo / Greyhound

WILD LOVE
CD EFAD 49522
Skunk / Mar '95 / Pinnacle

Smoke No Bones

SMOKE NO BONES
CD ONER 006
One Drop / Apr '97 / Timewarp / Vital

Smokehouse

SWAMP JIVE
CD ICH 9017CD
Ichiban / Oct '93 / Direct / Koch

Smokie

ALICE (WHO THE X IS ALICE)
Who the fuck is Alice / Lay back in the arms of someone / If you think you know how to love me / Needles and pins / Don't play your rock 'n' roll to me / Oh Carol / I'll meet you at midnight / It's your life / Boulevard of broken dreams / I feel love / For a few dollars more / Take good care of my baby / This side of paradise / Something's been making me blue / Wild angels / Naked love / It's my heart / Living next door to Alice / Can't cry hard enough
CD WAGCD 247
Now / Nov '95 / Total/BMG

BEST OF SMOKIE, THE
Living next door to Alice / Needles and pins / Oh Carol / Lay back in the arms of someone / Something's been making me blue / Couldn't live / Talking her 'round / Train song / Loser / Miss you / Run to you / Here lies a man / Now you think you know / No-one could ever love you more / Goin' tomorrow / Will you love me / You took me by surprise / Stranger with you
CD 74321476832
Camden / Apr '97 / BMG

COLLECTION VOL.1, THE
Living next door to Alice / Mexican girl / Wild wild angels / Something's been making me blue / If you think you know how to love me / For a few dollars more / Don't play your rock 'n' roll to me / Needles and pins / It's your life / Baby it's you / Changing all the times / Lay back in the arms of someone / Oh Carol / I'll meet you at midnight
CD 262538
Arista / Jun '92 / BMG

COLLECTION VOL.2, THE (The Complete B-Sides 1975-1978)
Couldn't live / Talking her round / Train song / Loser / Miss you / Run to you / Here lies a man / Now you think you know / No one coul ever love you more / Going tomorrow / Will you love me / You took me by surprise / Stranger with you
CD 74321232942
Ariola / Nov '94 / BMG

HITS COLLECTION BOX (3CD Set)
CD Set 10332
CMC / Jun '97 / BMG

ROCK AWAY YOUR TEARDROPS
My heart is true / Cry in the night / Hold on for the night / Never fight again / Rock away your teardrops / Second choice / Hold on tight / Only love hurts / Looking daggers / Hot girls and summer nights / If you think you know how to love me
CD 100542
CMC / May '97 / BMG

SMOKIE
CD GFS 060
Going For A Song / Jul '97 / Else / TKO Magnum

SMOKIE GREATEST HITS LIVE
I'll meet you at midnight / Lay back in the arms of someone / Medley / Something's making me blue / Wild angels / If you think you know how to love me / Don't play myour rock 'n' roll to me / Rock away your teardrops / Cry in the night / Oh Carol / Needles and pins / Living next door to Alice / Whiskey in the jar
CD PLATCD 3916
Platinum / Apr '93 / Prism

Smoking Popes

BORN TO QUIT
Midnight moon / Rubella / Gotta know right now / Mrs. You and Me / Just broke up / My lucky day / Need you around / Can't help the teardrop / Adena / On the shoulder
CD CDEST 2277
Capitol / Mar '96 / EMI

Smooth

SMOOTH
Mind blowin' / It's Summertime / Way back when / Blowin' up my pager / PYT / Swing it to the left side / Good stuff / Love groove / Jeeps & Benzos / Ghetto style / Undercover lover / Let it go
CD CHIP 162
Jive / Aug '95 / Pinnacle

Smoothe Da Hustler

ONCE UPON A TIME IN AMERICA
CD FILECD 467
Profile / Apr '96 / Pinnacle

Smoothies

PICKLE
CD 185292
Southern / Sep '95 / SRD

Smothers, Smokey

BOSSMAN
CD BM 9022
Black Magic / Jun '93 / ADA / Cadillac / Direct / Hot Shot

SECOND TIME AROUND
Bluesman / Second time around / Soft winds / Crack head woman / I get evil / Clouds in my heart / Got to be some changes made / In the zone / Somebody / Let me in / My baby's gone / I better go now
CD CCD 11051
Crosscut / Feb '97 / ADA / CM / Direct

Smudge

HOT SMOKE AND SASSAFRAS
CD WIGCD 19
Domino / Feb '95 / Vital

MANILOW
CD WIGCD 7
Domino / Feb '94 / Vital

TEA, TOAST & TURMOIL
Spoilt brat / Straight face down / Outside / Make all our dreams come true / Pulp / Plug it up / Divan / Alison / Don't want to be Grant McLennan / Stranglehold / Dabble / Leroy de Foix / Tea, toast and turmoil / Foccacia / Steak and chips / Babaganouj
CD SALD 207
Shake / Oct '93 / Vital

Smugglers

SELLING THE SIZZLE
CD LOOKOUT 136CD
Lookout / Mar '96 / Cargo / Greyhound / Shellshock/Disc

Smulyan, Gary

LURE OF BEAUTY, THE (Smulyan, Gary Quintet)
CD CRISS 1049CD
Criss Cross / Nov '91 / Cadillac / Direct / Vital/SAM

SAXOPHONE MOSAIC (Smulyan, Gary Nonet)
CD 1092CD
Criss Cross / Jan '95 / Cadillac / Direct / Vital/SAM

WITH STRINGS
Bad and the beautiful / Lush life / Thanks for you / It happens quietly / Don't follow the crowd / We've got a sure thing / Beware my heart / Moment of truth / Yesterday's gardenias / Two for the seesaw
CD CRISS 1129CD
Criss Cross / Jul '97 / Cadillac / Direct / Vital/SAM

Smurfs

ALL STAR SHOW
CD 290344
Ariola Express / Sep '96 / BMG

GO POP AGAIN
True blue / So natural / Shout / Roller / Smurfin' alive / Shy smurf's in the ring / Hush hush / Dancing Queen / Smurf walk / Line dance smurf / 31524 / Yodelling smurfs / Papa smurfs / Grandpa we love you
CD CDEMTV 155
EMI / Aug '97 / EMI

MERRY CHRISTMAS WITH THE SMURFS
CD 290366
Column / Nov '96 / Total/BMG

SMURF'S CHRISTMAS PARTY, THE
Christmas with the Smurfs / Rockin' round the Christmas tree / Rudolph the red-nosed reindeer / Winter wonderland / Frosty the snowman / I wish it could be Christmas every day / I saw Smurfette kissing Santa Claus / Merry Christmas everybody / All I want for Christmas is my two front teeth / Wonderful Christmastime / Let it snow / Christmas with the Smurfs / Silent night / Mistletoe and wine / Smurfland Christmas song (Mary's boy child) / White Christmas / Last Christmas / Little boy (Smurf that Santa Claus forgot) / On this Smurfary day / Smurfs in the snow / Lonely this Christmas / Smurfland Christmas song / Your Christmas wish / We wish you a merry Christmas
CD CDEMTV 140
EMI / Nov '96 / EMI

SMURFS GO POP, THE
Smurfs are back / Mr. Smurftastic / I've got a little puppy / Noisy Smurf / Find the Smurf / Smurfland / Our Smurfing party / Don't stop Smurfing / Smurfhillbilly Joe / We're the Smurfs / Smurfland Olympics / Smurfing ways / Mr. Blobby & the Smurfs / Football forever / Smurfing world
CD CDEMTV 121
EMI / Jul '96 / EMI

SMURFS HITS 1997 VOL.1
Wannabe a smurf star / Smurfs get upside your head / Smurf it up / Smurfs are coming home / Keep on smurfing / Smurf drummer / Get yourself smurfing / Small talk / Laughter smurf / Ooh aah smurf a little bit / Smurfing down the highway / Smurfbilly rock / Smurf Macarena / Only way / Your first school
CD CDEMTV 150
EMI TV / Feb '97 / EMI

Smut

BLOOD, SMUT AND TEARS
Cave / Alone / Spirit / Symphony / No sacrifice / Women / Baby Jack / Emotional suicide / Take back the night / Object of intentions / Autumn storm / Goodness, no grief
CD 892402
Spanish Fly / Apr '94 / Vital

Smyth, Gilli

EVERY WITCHES WAY
Simple / Bold and brazen / Show is over / We who were raging / Beltaine / Four horsemen / Medicine woman / Animal / Magic / Lammas / I am witch / Lady wise / Simples
CD VP 139CD
Voiceprint / Jun '93 / Pinnacle

Smyth, Sean

BLUE FIDDLE, THE
CD LUNCD 060
Mulligan / Apr '94 / ADA / CM

Snagapuss

WHAP DEM MERLENE
CD SVCD 4
Shocking Vibes / Feb '94 / Jet Star

Snagga

LINE UP ALL THE GIRKS DEM
CD HCD 7007
Hightone / Aug '94 / ADA / Koch

Snail, Azalia

BLUE DANUBE
CD NORMAL 197CD
Normal / Jan '96 / ADA / Direct

Snake Corps

SPICE
Science kills / Nothing / This is seagull / Come the glorious day / House of man / Calling you / Strangers / Man in the mirror / More than the ocean / Yesterday with you / In flux / Colder than the kiss / Party's over / Sky in your eyes / Dreamland
CD CDMGRAM 97
Anagram / Oct '95 / Cargo / Pinnacle

Snake Finger

NIGHT OF DESIRABLE OBJECTS
CD AIM 1011CD
Aim / Oct '93 / ADA / Direct / Jazz Music

Snakepit Rebels

SNAKEPIT REBELS
CD FLCCCD 114
Tring / Jun '91 / Tring

Snap

SNAP ATTACK (The Best Of Snap)
Power / Ooops up / Cult of Snap / Mary had a little boy / Colour of love / Rhythm is a dancer / Exterminate / Do you see the light / Welcome to tomorrow / First last eternity / World in my hand / Rame
CD 74321384864
Arista / Aug '96 / BMG

SNAP ATTACK (The Remixes)
Power '96: *Snap & Einstein* / Exterminate / Rhythm is a dancer / Oops up / Colour of love / Do you see the light / Rame / Mary had a little boy / First last eternity / Power / Welcome to tomorrow / Cult of Snap / World in my dub/Oops up
CD 74321340792
CD 74321395192
Arista / Aug '96 / BMG

WELCOME TO TOMORROW
Green grass grows (earth follows) / It's a miracle (people need to love one another) / Rame / Dream on the moon / Welcome to tomorrow (are you ready) / World in my hands (we are one) / First last eternity (till the end) / Waves / Where are the boys, where are the girls / It's not over
CD 74321223842
Arista / Oct '94 / BMG

WORLD POWER
Power / Cult of snap / I'm gonna get you (to whom it may concern) / Mary had a little boy / Ooops up / Believe the hype / Witness the strength / Blase blase
CD 260682
Arista / Aug '95 / BMG

Snapcase

LOOKINGLASSELF
CD VR 013CD
Victory / Sep '96 / Plastic Head

PROGRESSION THROUGH UNLEARNING
CD VR 51CD
Victory / Apr '97 / Plastic Head

SNAPCASE
CD VR 132
Victory / Apr '94 / Plastic Head

Snapper

ADM
CD FNCD 294
Flying Nun / Mar '96 / RTM/Disc

Snatch

CORNBREAD & ALISON MEOWLY
CD FM 03
Fundamental / Nov '96 / Cargo / Plastic Head / Shellshock/Disc

Snatch It Back

DYNAMITE
CD TRCD 9904
Tramp / Nov '93 / ADA / CM / Direct

EVIL
CD TRCD 9907
Tramp / Nov '93 / ADA / CM / Direct

Sneaker Pimps

BECOMING X
Low place like home / Tesko suicide / 6 Underground / Becoming X / Spin spin sugar / Post-modern sleaze / Waterbaby / Roll on / Wasted early Sunday morning / Walking zero / How do
CD CUP 020CDX
Clean Up / Jun '97 / Amato Disco / Prime / Vital

Sneak's Noyse

CHRISTMAS NOW IS DRAWING NEAR
Good people all this Christmastide / Sweet was the song the virgin sang / Down in yon forest / Holly and the ivy / Joseph was an old man / Angelus ad Virginem / Hail Mary full of grace / Tomorrow shall be my dancing day / Furry day carol / Deck the halls with boughs of holly / God bless you merry gentlemen
CD CDSDL 371
Saydisc / Oct '86 / ADA / Direct / Harmonia Mundi

Sneetches

LIGHTS OUT WITH THE SNEETCHES
I need someone / In my car / Lonelei / Fifty four hours / I don't expect her for you / Home again / No one knows / Only for a moment
CD CRECD 077
Creation / Apr '91 / 3mv/Vital

OBSCUREYEARS
CD CREV 031CD
Rev-Ola / Nov '94 / 3mv/Vital

SOMETIMES THAT'S ALL WE HAVE
CD CRECD 043
Creation / May '94 / 3mv/Vital

STARFUCKER
CD BUS 10062
Bus Stop / May '95 / Cargo / Vital

Snell, Adrian

ALPHA AND OMEGA
CD MYRCD 1210
Myrrh / '86 / Nelson Word

Snell, Howard

JEUX D'ENFANTS (Snell, Howard Brass)
CD QPRZ 010D
Polyphonic / Feb '93 / Complete/Pinnacle

Snenska Hotkvinetten

SVENSKA HOTKVINETTEN
CD DRCD 223
Dragon / Jan '88 / ADA / Cadillac / CM / Roots / Wellard

Snetberger, Ferenc

BUDAPEST CONCERT, THE
Budapest mood / Springtime in winter / Song to the east / Brazil / Dolphin / Little bossa / Variation / Tangoa free / Bossa for Egberto / Manha de carnaval / Budapest encore
CD 8888232
Tiptoe / Jul '96 / New Note/Pinnacle

SIGNATURE
Toni's carnival II / Passages / Obsession / Tangoa free / Poems for my people / Surprise / Variation
CD ENJ 90172
Enja / May '95 / New Note/Pinnacle / Vital/SAM

SNFU

...AND NO ONE ELSE WANTED TO PLAY
CD BYO 009CD
Better Youth Organisation / Oct '96 / Cargo

BETTER THAN A STICK IN THE EYE
CD CAR 001CD
Cargo / Oct '96 / Cargo

FYULABA
CD 64722
Epitaph / Sep '96 / Pinnacle / Plastic Head

IF YOU SWEAR, YOU'LL CATCH NO FISH
CD BY 017CD
Better Youth Organisation / Oct '96 / Cargo

LAST OF THE BIG TIME SUSPENDERS, THE
CD CAR 011CD
Cargo / Oct '96 / Cargo

ONE VOTED MOST LIKELY TO SUCCEED, THE
CD E 864412
Epitaph / Mar '95 / Pinnacle / Plastic Head

SOMETHING GREEN AND LEAFY THIS WAY COMES
CD E 86430CD
Epitaph / Dec '93 / Pinnacle / Plastic Head

Snidero, Jim

SAN JUAN (Snidero, Jim Sextet)
CD 1232652
Red / Feb '97 / ADA / Cadillac / Harmonia Mundi

STORM RISING
Fast lane / Takin' it easy / Storm rising / Beatrice / Break away / Virgo / Reluctance / Depressions
CD 66056006
Ken Music / Mar '92 / New Note/Pinnacle

WHILE YOU'RE HERE (Snidero, Jim Quartet)
CD 1232412
Red / Mar '92 / ADA / Cadillac / Harmonia Mundi

Sniff 'n' The Tears

BEST OF SNIFF 'N' THE TEARS, A
Driver's seat / What can daddy do / Thrill of it all / Looking for you / One love / Driving beat / Night life / Snow White / Roll 'em blues / Poison pen mail / Hungry eyes / Steal my heart / Ride blue divide
CD CDWIK 102
Chiswick / Aug '91 / Pinnacle

FICKLE HEART
Driver's seat / New lines on love / Carve your name on my door / This side of the blue horizon / Sing / Rock 'n' roll music / Fight for love / Thrill of it all / Slide away / Last dance / Looking for you
CD CDWIKM 9
Chiswick / Aug '91 / Pinnacle

GAMES UP, THE
Game's up / Moment of weakness / What can daddy do / Night life / If I knew then / One love / Five and zero / Poison pen mail / Rodeo drive
CD CDWIKM 92
Chiswick / Aug '90 / Pinnacle

LOVE/ACTION
Driving beat / Put your money where your mouth is / Snow White / For what they promise / Without love / Steal my heart / That final love / Don't frighten me / Love action / Shame
CD CDWIKM 96
Chiswick / Feb '91 / Pinnacle

NO DAMAGE DONE
CD PRD 70482
Provogue / Jan '92 / Pinnacle

RIDE BLUE DIVIDE
Hand of fate / Hungry eyes / Roll the weight away / Like wildfire / Trouble is my business / You may find your heart / Gold / Ride blue divide / Company man
CD CDWIKM 97
Chiswick / Apr '91 / Pinnacle

Snoop Doggy Dogg

DOGGY STYLE
Bathtub / G funk intro / Gin and juice / Tha shiznit / Lodi Dodi / Murder was the case / Serial killa / Who am I (What's my name) / For all my niggaz and bitches / Ain't no fun / Doggy dogg world / Gz and hustlas / Pump pump
CD IND 92279
Interscope / Feb '97 / BMG

THA DOGGFATHER
Intro / Doggfather / Ride 4 me / Up jump tha boogie / Freestyle conversation / When I grow up / Snoop bounce / Gold rush / (Tear 'em off) me and my doggz / You thought / Vapors / Groupie / 2001 / Six minutes / (DJ) Wake up / Snoop's upside ya head / Blueberry / Traffic jam / Doggyland / Downtown assassins / Outro
CD IND 90038
Interscope / Feb '97 / BMG

Snooze

MAN IN THE SHADOW
Snooze theme / So close and yet so far / Your consciousness goes bip / Before sunrise / Tribute to Horace / Killer with a gun / Pretty good privacy / I wanna be with you / Middle class lady / Down for mine / Anais plot / Man in the shadow / Chase
CD SSR 172CD
SSR / Mar '97 / Amato Disco / Grapevine/ PolyGram / Prime / RTM/Disc

Snow

MURDER LOVE
CD 7567617372
East West / Mar '95 / Warner Music

Snow, Hank

ESSENTIAL HANK SNOW, THE
Rhumba boogie / I'm moving on / Golden rocket / Unwanted sign upon your heart / Music makin' Mama from Memphis / Goldrush is over / I don't hurt anymore / Fool such as I / Gal who invented kissin' / I went to your wedding / Would you mind / Lady's man / Yellow roses / Miller's cave / Beggar to a king / I've been everywhere / Ninety miles an hour (down a dead end street) / Let me go lover / Wishing well (down in the well) / Hello love
CD 7863669312
RCA / May '97 / BMG

SINGING RANGER VOL.1 (The Complete Early 50's Hank Snow/4CD Set)
I'm movin' on / With this ring / Rumba boogie / Paving the highway with tears / Golden rocket / Your locket has broken my heart / Unwanted sign upon my heart / (I wish upon) my little golden horseshoe / Confused with the blues / You pass me by / Love entered the iron door / I cried but my tears were too late / One more ride / Hobo Bill's last ride / Wreck of ol' 97 / Ben Dewberry's final run / Mystery of number five / Engineer's child / Law of love / Nobody's child / I wonder where you are tonight / Star spangled waltz / Blind boy's dog / Marriage vow / Only rose / Anniversary of my broken heart / Music makin' mama from Memphis

/ Highest bidder / Gold rush is over / Love's game of let's pretend / Bluebird Island: *Snow, Hank & Anita Carter* / Down the trail of aching hearts: *Snow, Hank & Anita Carter* / Lady's man / Fool such as I / Why do you punish me / Chattin' with a chick in Chattanooga / Greatest sin / Married by the Bible, divorced by the law / There wasn't an organ at our wedding / Zeb Turner's gal / Golden river / Moanin' / I knew that we'd meet again / Yodeling cowboy / On that old Hawaiian shore with you / On that old Hawaiian shore with you / I'm movin' on to glory / Jesus wept / Pray / These things shall pass / He'll understand and say well done / I just telephone upstairs / I'm in love with Jesus / Gal who invented kissin' / Spanish fireball / Honeymoon on a rocketship / Between fire and water / Boogie woogie flying cloud / I can't control my heart / For now and always / Message from the tradewinds / I traded love / Next voice you hear / When Mexican Joe met Jole Blon / I went to your wedding / Jimmie the kid / My blue eyed Jane / When Jimmie Rodgers said goodbye: *Snow, Hank & Jimmie Rodgers* / Southern Cannonball / Anniversary blue yodel / Why did you give me your love / Mississippi river blues / In daddy's footsteps / Gloryland march / Christmas roses / Reindeer boogie / Frosty the snowman / Silent night / My mother / Just keep a movin' / My sweet Conchita / Panamama / Unfaithful / Wabash blues / It's you, only you that I love: *Snow, Hank & Betty Cody* / Would you mind / In an old Dutch garden / Owl and I / I don't hurt anymore / Stolen moments / Hilo march / Act 1, act 2, act 3 / Yellow roses / No longer a prisoner / Sweet Marie / My Arabian baby / Bill is falling due / Blossoms in the springtime / I'm glad I'm on the inside (looking out) / When it's reveille time in Heaven / My religion's not old fashioned / Invisible hands / Little children / Alphabet / God's little candles / God's little candles

CD Set ________________ **BCD 15426**

Bear Family / Nov '88 / Direct / Rollercoaster / Swift

SINGING RANGER VOL.2 (4CD Set)

Love's call from the mountain (unissued) / I've forgotten you / That crazy mambo thing / Let me go, lover / Old spinning wheel: *Snow, Hank & Chet Atkins* / At the Darktown strutter's ball: *Snow, Hank & Chet Atkins* / Silver bell: *Snow, Hank & Chet Atkins* / Under the double eagle: *Snow, Hank & Chet Atkins* / It's you, only you that I love: *Snow, Hank & Anita Carter* / Keep your promise, Willie Thomas: *Snow, Hank & Anita Carter* / Crying, waiting, hoping / Someone mentioned your name / I'm glad to see you once again / Mainliner (the hawk of the West) / Cuba rhumba / Scale to measure love / Blue sea blues / Twelfth Street rag / Rainbow boogie / Vaya con dios / Madison madness / Can't have you blues / Dog bone (unissued) / Born to be happy / Golden rocket / Hobo Bill's last ride / Stolen moments / Pray / Nothing but sweet lies (unissued) / Conscience I'm guilty / Hula rock / Two won't care / Party of the second part (unissued) / These hands / Reminiscin': *Snow, Hank & Chet Atkins* / New Spanish two-step: *Snow, Hank & Chet Atkins* / In an 18th century drawing room / La cucaracha / Born to lose (unissued) / I'm movin' in / Sunshine serenade / El rancho grande / Grandfather's clock / Lover's farewell / Carnival of Venice / Old Doc Brown / That pioneer mother of mine / Blind boy's prayer / Lazybones / What do I know today / Trouble, trouble, trouble / First nighters / How to play the guitar / Little britches / What is father / Horse's prayer / Wedding bells / Loose talk / I almost lost my mind / Sing me a song of the islands / Memories are made of this / These tears are not for you / Singin' the blues / My life with you / Poison love / Among my souvenirs / Born to lose / It's been so long darling / La paloma / Oh wonderful world / Chant of the wanderer / I really don't want to know / Squid jiggin' ground / New blue velvet band / Calypso sweetheart / I'm hurtin' all over (unissued) / My memory (unissued) / Party of the second part marriage and divorce / Unfaithful (unissued) / Tangled mind / My arms are a house / Love's call from the mountain / On a Tennessee Saturday night (unissued) / Big wheels / Woman captured me / I heard my heart break last night / I wish I was the moon / My lucky friend / Whispering rain / I'm hurtin' all over / I'm here to get my baby out of jail / Don't make me go to bed and I'll be good / Convict and the rose / There's a little box of pine on the 729 / Put my little shoes away / Letter edged in black / Old Shep / Prisoner's prayer / Drunkard's child / Little Buddy / Nobody's child / Blue Danube / Waltz, Kitty waltz (unissued) / Brahms lullaby / Sleepy Rio Grande / Brahms lullaby

CD Set ________________ **BCD 15476**

Bear Family / Jul '90 / Direct / Rollercoaster / Swift

SINGING RANGER VOL.3 (12CD Set)

Casey Jones was his name / Southbound / Streamlined cannonball / (I heard that) Lonesome whistle / Waiting for a train / Wreck of the number nine / Pan American / Big wheels / Ghost trains / Chattanooga choo choo / Last ride / Crazy engineer / One more ride / Wreck of ol' 97 / Crazy little train of love / Any old time / Blue yodel no. 10 / Travellin' blues / Never no' mo' blues / Gambling polka dot blues / You and my old guitar / Roll along Kentucky moon / Moonlight and skies / One rose (that's left in my heart) / Tuck away my lonesome blues / Down the old road to home / I'm sorry we met / Chasin' a rainbow / Doggone that train / Father time and mother love / I heard my heart break last night / Walkin' and talkin' / Rockin' rollin' ocean / Miller's cave / Dreamer's island / Change of the tide / I'm movin' on / Golden rocket / My mother / I don't hurt anymore / Conscience I'm guilty / I'm asking for a friend / Bluebird Island / Fool such as I / Marriage vow / With this ring I thee wed / My Nova Scotia home / Tramp's story / Lifetime blues / Maple leaves / Casey's washerwoman boogie / Hawaiian sunset / Man who robbed the bank of Santa Fe / Man behind the gun / Restless one / Call of the wild / Laredo / Way out there / Patanio, the pride of the plains / Queen of Draw Poker Town / On the rhythm range / Chant of the wanderer / Wayward wind / Following the sun all day / Texas plains / Teardrops in my heart / Tumbling tumbleweeds / Heartbreak trail / Cool water / Riding home / At the rainbow's end / It's a little more like Heaven / I went to your wedding / Just a faded petal from a beautiful bouquet / Blue roses / Human / Breakfast with the blues / Down the trail of aching hearts / Let me go, lover / Tangled mind / Next voice you hear / Stolen moments / Gal who invented kissin' / Gold rush is over / Ninety miles an hour (down a dead end street) / My memories of you / Wishing well / I stepped over the line / Ninety days / Wedding picture / I've cried a mile / Listen / Friend / When today is a long time ago / Black diamond / Ancient history / You're losing your baby / You're the reason / Poor little Jimmie / Beggar to a king / Countdown / Down at the pawnshop / I know you / You take the future (and I'll take the past) / Dog bone / If I try hard enough / Poison love / Legend in my time / Bury me deep / Fraulein / Mansion on the hill / Send me the pillow that you dream on / On a petal from a faded rose / Return to me / Heart belongs to me / I'll go on alone / I care no more / I love you because / Address unknown / Rumba boogie / Music makin' Mama from Memphis / These hands / Letter from Vietnam to mother / Born for you / Late and great love of my heart / Promised to John: *Snow, Hank & Anita Carter* / If today were yesterday: *Snow, Hank & Anita Carter* / For sale: *Snow, Hank & Anita Carter* / Rose of old Monterey: *Snow, Hank & Anita Carter* / My adobe hacienda: *Snow, Hank & Anita Carter* / I never will marry: *Snow, Hank & Anita Carter* / Mockin' Bird Hill: *Snow, Hank & Anita Carter* / No letter today: *Snow, Hank & Anita Carter* / I dreamed of an old love affair: *Snow, Hank & Anita Carter* / If it's wrong to love you: *Snow, Hank & Anita Carter* / When my blue moon turns to gold again: *Snow, Hank & Anita Carter* / Let's pretend: *Snow, Hank & Anita Carter* / Pair of broken hearts: *Snow, Hank & Anita Carter* / I've been everywhere / Jamaica farewell / Blue Canadian Rockies / Geisha girl / When it's Springtime in Alaska / Galway Boy / My Filipino rose / Lili Marlene / Melba from Melbourne / Atlantic coastal line / Isle of Sicily / Gypsy and me / I ain't been anywhere / Sonny boy / Indian love call / Unchained melody / Beautiful dreamer / My isle of golden dreams / Brahms lullaby / Blue tango / Dark moon / Vaya con dios / In an old Dutch garden / By an old Dutch mill / I can't stop loving you / Convict and the rose / Limbo rock / Hold me tight / Tammy / Everybody does it in Hawaii / I saw the light / Green leaves of Summer / Difficult / Wheels / Tiptoeing / Waltz you saved for me / Lay my head beneath the rose / Whispering hope / Wabash blues / Sentimental journey / Am I losing you / I get the blues when it rains / Sweet Marie / Birth of the blues / White Christmas / Little stranger (in a manger) / Christmas roses / Silent night / C-H-R-I-S-T-M-A-S / Blue Christmas / Reindeer boogie / Frosty the snowman / Christmas wants / Rudolph the red nosed reindeer / God is my Santa Claus / Long eared Christmas donkey / Face on the ballroom floor / Dangerous Dan McGrew / Cremation of Sam McGee / Spell of the Yukon / Ballad of blasphemous Bill / Ballad of one eyed Mike / Ballad of hard luck Henry / My friends / He'll understand and say well done / I saw a man / Rich man am I / Jesus wept / I'm movin' on to glory / Gloryland march / Farther along / Invisible hands / Last mile of the way / Sweet hour of prayer / These things shall pass / His hands / What then / Lord's way of sayin' goodnight / Dear Lord / Remember me / I see Jesus / My religion's not old fashioned / I'm glad I'm on the inside (looking out) / Runt / How big is God / Shop worn / Man who is wise / This train / I'll go marching into glory / I'd rather be on the inside looking out / Lord it's me again / Lord I do believe / Learnin' a new way of life / Wildflower / Little Joe / Put your arms around me / Color song / Your little band of gold / Prisoner's dream / Answer to Little Blossom / There's a star spangled banner waving / Old Rover / Mother I thank you for the bible you gave / Prisoner's song / Walking the last mile / Rockin' alone in an old rocking chair / Lonesome / She wears my ring / White silver sands / Trouble in mind / Mary Ann regrets / Six days on the road / Bummin' around / From a Jack to a King / Handcuffed to love / What more can I say / I wish my heart could talk / Hula love / Cry my guitar, cry on / Beyond the reef / To you my sweetheart, aloha when I go / Hawaiian cowboy / My little grass shack in Kealakekua, Hawaii / On the beach in Waikiki / Tradewinds / Pearly shells / On that old Hawaiian shore with you / Now is the hour / Tears in the tradewinds / King's serenade / Whispering tradewinds / Spanish fireball / Cross the Brazos at Waco / El Paso / Caribbean / Senorita Rosalita / Cuba rhumba / Nuevo laredo / Blue rose of the Rio / Maria Elena / Adios amigo / Among my souvenirs / Miami snow / Springtime in the Rockies / Blossoms in the Springtime / At the first fall of snow / Snowbird / Seasons / Roses in the snow / Flying South / January / You're as welcome as the flowers in May / Peach pickin' time in Georgia / All nite cafe / Tip of my fingers / He dropped the world in my hands / Blue blue day / It kinda reminds me of me / All the time / Blue side of lonesome / There goes my everything / Once more you're mine again / Million and one / Green green grass of home / Wound time can't erase / I just wanted to know how the wind was blowin' / Who will answer / Cure for the blues / That's when the hurtin' sets in / Rome wasn't built in a day / Name of the game was love

CD Set ________________ **BCD 15502**

Bear Family / Jun '92 / Direct / Rollercoaster / Swift

SINGING RANGER VOL.4 (9CD Set)

If I ever get back to Georgia / Gentle on my mind / Honey / Sweet dreams / Break my mind / Where has all the love gone / Green green green / Oh lonesome me / Like a bird / I really don't want to know / (As love goes) so goes my heart / Vanishing breed / It's a hard wind that blows / Brand on my heart / Francesca / When today is a long time ago / Come the morning / I wish it was mine / Cure for the blues / Crying time / There's the chair / Snowbird / I threw away the rose / Me and Bobby McGee / Just bidin' my time / I'm moving / Silver rails / Go with my heart / Wabash cannonball / Engineer's child / Casey Jones was his name / Fire ball mail / Folsom prison blues / Lonely train / That same old dotted line / I'm movin' in / Train my woman's on / Durquesne, Pennyslvania / Canadian pacific / Crack in the box car door / North to Chicago / City of New Orleans / Texas silver zephyr / Get on my love train / My blue river rose / Blue velvet band / Wanderin' on / Old doc brown / Stolen moments / When that someone you love doesn't love you / My mother / Nobody's child / Little buddy / Hobo's meditation / My rough and rowdy ways / Frankie and Johnny / She was happy till she met you / Away out on the mountain / Cowhand's last ride / Everybody does it in Hawaii / I've ranged, I've roamed, I've travelled / Ninety nine year blues / Mother, the queen of my heart / Whisper your mother's name / Home call / My blue eyed Jane / Waiting for a train / Pistol packin' Papa / TB Blues / My little old home down in New Orleans / Why did you give me your love / In the jailhouse now / Gambling polka dot blues / One rose (that's left in my heart) / Hobo Bill's last ride / Nobody knows but me / Hello love / One minute past eternity / No one will ever know / For the good times / Sunday morning coming down / Everytime I love her / Seashores of old Mexico / Gypsy feet / Ribbon of darkness / My way / Bob / Friend / Governor's hand / Rolling thunder in my mind / I'm not at all sorry for you / My dreams tell it like it was / It's over, over nothing / Till the end of time / Four in the morning / I've got ot give it all to you / Daisy a day / Today I started loving you again / I have you and that's enough for me / I washed my hands in muddy water / It just happened that way / Last thing on my mind / Big silver screen at the Strand / Six string Tennessee flat top box / Somewhere my love / Why me Lord / Born to be with you / I keep dreaming of you all the time / Birth of the blues / Hijack / Come live with me / That's you and me / Paper roses / Why do you punish me / Mama tried / Prisoner's song / All I can hold to / You're easy to love / Just want you to know / Right or wrong / Colorado country morning / Top of the morning / She even woke me up to say goodbye / So good to be back with you / Follow me / Merry go round of love / Almost lost my mind / You're wondering why / Ninety miles an hour (down a dead end street) / Breakfst with the blues / Trying to get my baby off my mind / Trouble in mind / I'm gonna bid my blues goodbye / Love is so elusive / I've done at least one thing / Don't rock the boat / If you could just remember / That heart belongs to me / I'm still moving on / Inside out / Somewhere, someone is waiting for you / I put her on (and wore away her time) / Who's been here since I've been gone / That's when he dropped the world in my hands / Night I stole Sammy Morgan's gin / I wonder where you are tonight / I takes to long / Nevertheless / Forever and one day / Just one of a kind / My happiness / Mysterious lady from St.Martinique / Ramblin' rose / Good gal is good to find / Hula love / Things / Pain didn't show / Stop me from loving you / My first night alone / It was love / All I want to do is touch you / There is something about you / What we had is over / Stay a while / Hasn't it been good together / After the love has gone / Check / Forbidden lovers / Love takes two / It's too far gone / It's over, over nothing / First hurt / Golden rocket / I've been everywhere / I almost lost my mind / Caribbean / I'm movin' on / Send me the pillow that you dream on / I don't hurt anymore / Fools such as I / It makes no difference now / Spanish eyes / Sweetheart of sigma / Over the rainbow (instr) / Tradewinds over Mamala Bay (instr) / Indian love call / You belong to me / Wabash blues (instr) / King's serenade / Make the world go away (instr) / Oh wonderful world (instr) / My isle of golden dreams (instr) / Tuck away my lonesome blues (instr) / Tammy (instr) / Beautiful Ohio (Instr) / Song of India / Sunrise serenade (Inst) / Misty dawn (instr) / Vaya con dios / I remember you love in my prayers / I'm movin' on (live) / Send me the pillow you dream on / In the misty moonlight / Orange blossom special / Tammy / Black diamond / Whispering tradewinds (snow in Hawaii) / Hawaiian sunset

CD ________________ **BCD 15787**

Bear Family / Apr '94 / Direct / Rollercoaster / Swift

THESAURUS TRANSCRIPTIONS, THE (5CD Set)

Weary river / Bury me deep / Let's pretend / Address unknown / Golden river / Blue yodel no. 12 / I'm here to get my baby out of jail / Brand on my heart / With this ring I thee wed / I wonder where you are tonight / Fire on the mountain / Draggin' / Steel guitar rag / Wabash blues / I'm movin' on / Handcuffed to love / Convict and the rose / Anniversary blue yodel / Frankie and Johnny / Closed for repairs / End of the world / I wonder if you feel the way I do / Pins and needles / Where romance calls / Streamlined cannonball / Trouble in mind / Last letter / Headin' down the wrong highway / Lonely / Blue eyes cryin' in the rain / These tears are not for you / Jealous heart / Hawaiian cowboy / I'm thinking tonight of my blue eyes / Whispering hope / It is no secret / Molly darling / I'll remember you love in my prayers / Blue dreams / Blow yo' whistle freight train / Lonely river / I'll never let you go little darling / Texas plains / Born to lose / Too many tears / Travellin' blues / Faded rose, a broken heart / Yodeling ranger / Roll along Kentucky moon / Zeb Turner's gal / Sun has gone down on our love / I walk alone / Old Shep / Mississippi river blues / Linda Lou / My good gal's gone / Breeze / This cold war with you / I love you Nellie / Beautiful dreamer / 12th Street rag / Bye bye blues / Hilo march / Orange blossom special / Beaumont ride / Just when I needed you / Ninety nine years blues / My blue eyed Jane / Yodeling cowboy / Cannonball / It's been so long darling / Lover's farewell / You nearly lose your mind / Kentucky waltz / There's a pony standing in his stall / Among my souvenirs / Little old home down in New Orleans / Go on alone / Cowhand's last ride / I almost lost my mind / Patanio, the pride of the plains / That heart belongs to me / Peach pickin' time in Georgia / Alabama jubilee / Farewell blues / In an old dutch garden / Sally Goodin / Arkansas traveller / Petal from a faded rose / It's a sin / Wedding bells / At mail call today / Those blue eyes don't sparkle anymore / Have I stayed away too long / San Antonio rose / Each minute seems a million years / Blue steel blues / Then I turned and walked slowly away / Blue rose of the Rio / My wubba dolly / Tuck away my lonesome blues / Land of my childhood dreams / Wreck of ol' 97 / My life with you / One rose (that's left in my heart) / I'm coming home / Song of the saddle / Easter parade / Peter Cottontail / My rough and rowdy ways / Sing me a song of the Islands / Little Joe / White Christmas / Blue Christmas / Making believe / Any old time / Never no mo' blues / When my blue moon turns to gold again / Katy Hill / Put your arms around me / I was sorta wonderin' / Over the waves / Do right daddy blues / As long as I live / Loose talk / Waltz you saved for me / Memories are made of this / I really don't want to know / Wayward wind / Chant of the wanderer / Put on your old grey bonnet / When you and I were young Maggie / Sentimental journey / Birth of the blues

CD Set ________________ **BCD 15488**

Bear Family / Feb '91 / Direct / Rollercoaster / Swift

YODELLING RANGER, THE 1936-1947 (5CD Set)

Prisoned cowboy / Lonesome blue yodel / Blue for old Hawaii / We met down in the hills of old Wyoming / My San Antonio Mama / My little swiss maiden / Was there ever a pal like you / Blue velvet band / Someday you'll care / I'll ride back to lonesome valley / Bluer than blue / Yodelling back to you / There's a picture on Pinto's bridle / Texas cowboy / On the Mississippi shore / Under Hawaiian skies / She's a rose from the Garden of Prayer / Wanderin' on / Broken wedding ring / You didn't have to tell me / His message home / Answer to The Blue Velvet Band / I'll tell the world I love

you / Polka dot blues / Alphabet song / Galveston rose / Broken dreams / Let's pretend / Days are long, I'm weary / I traded my saddle for a rifle / When that someone you love doesn't love you / Rainbow's end / We'll never say goodbye, Just say so long / I'm sending you red roses / Goodnight litle buckaroos / When my blue moon turns to gold again / Dream tide / Seal our parting with a kiss / You'll regret those words my darling / You promised to love me to the end of the world / Just across the bridge of gold / There's a pony that's lonely tonight / Old moon of Kentucky / Rose of the Rio / Lonely and heartsick / Your last kiss has broken my heart / When it's over I'll be coming back to you / Mother is praying / Soldier's last letter / Riding along, singing a song / Don't hang around me anymore / Only a rose from my mother's grave / Too many tears / Your little band of gold / Sunny side of the mountain / You broke the chain that held our hearts / My blue river rose / You played love on the strings of my heart / How she could yodel / Headin' home / Dry those tears little girl and don't cry / In memory of you dear old pal / Can't have you blues / Just waiting for you / Just waiting for you / My kalua sweetheart / I'll not forget my mother's prayer / Darling I'll always love you / Blue ranger / Just a faded petal from a beautiful bouquet / My sweet Texas Bluebonnet Queen / I'm gonna bid my blues goodbye / Down where the dark waters flow / Answer to Galveston Rose / Brand on my heart / No golden tomorrow / On that old Hawaiian shore with you / You've broken my heart / Linda Lou / My mother / Drunkard's son / Within this broken heart of mine / My Filipino rose / Night I stole Sammy Morgan's gin / My two timin' woman / Wasted love / Broken hearted / You sad kiss goodbye / Somewhere along life's highway / Out on the open range / Little buddy / Journey my baby back home / I knew that we'd meet again / Within this broken heart of mine (Alt) / My two timin' woman (Alt) / Wasted love (Alt) / Life story, Part 1 / Life story, Part 2 / Marriage and divorce / I don't hurt anymore
CD Set ____ **BCD 15587**
Bear Family / Mar '93 / Direct / Rollercoaster / Swift

Snowboy

BEST OF SNOWBOY, THE (Snowboy & The Latin Section)
Night in Tunisia / Wild spirit / Mr. PC / Beyond the snowstorm / Mambito / Where's the one / Snow snow quick quick snow / In the wee small hours of the morning / Flintstones / 42nd and Broadway / Anarchy in the UK / Something's coming
CD ____ **JAZIDCD 102**
Acid Jazz / Nov '94 / Disc

DESCARGA MAMBITA (Snowboy & The Latin Section)
CD ____ **JAZIDCD 040**
Acid Jazz / Sep '91 / Disc

PIT BULL LATIN JAZZ (Snowboy & The Latin Section)
CD ____ **JAZIDCD 126**
Acid Jazz / Oct '95 / Disc

SOMETHING'S COMING
September rains / Salute to elegua / Flintstones / Dreamstate / Greeting from Southend / 42nd and Broadway / Interlude in son / Dilo como yo / Anarchy in the UK / Something's coming / Chant to aggayu / Somewhere
CD ____ **JAZIDCD 092**
Acid Jazz / Jan '94 / Disc

Snowmen

SOUNDPROOF
CD ____ **NORMAL 172CD**
Normal / Feb '95 / ADA / Direct

Snuff

CAUGHT IN SESSION
Win some / From both sides/I think we're alone now / Another girl / Now you don't remember me/No one home / Inst. jingle no.1 / Funny faces / Inst. jingle no.2 / Vikings on the tundra / B / Batten down the hedges / Short jingle
CD ____ **MASKCD 073**
Vinyl Japan / Sep '97 / Plastic Head / Vinyl Japan

DEMMAMUSSABEBONK
Martin / Defeat / Dick trois / Nick Northern / Look mum there's vikings on the Tundra again / Batten down the hatches / Gone to the dogs / Sunny places / Horse and cart / Squirrels / Cricklewood / B / Punchline / Who
CD ____ **BLUFF 023CD**
Deceptive / Jan '96 / Vital

KILBURN NATIONAL 27.11.90
Somehow / Porro / Hairy wombie / City crusty is attacked by soap / Damage is done / I see / What kind of love / Hazy shade of winter / Day of the PX's / Do nothing / Too late / Win some lose some
CD ____ **ASKCD 048**
Vinyl Japan / Jan '97 / Plastic Head / Vinyl Japan

POTATOES AND MELONS AT WHOLESALE PRICES (Direct To You The Public)
Come and gone / Ye olde folke twatte / Time dub / Magic moments / Russian fields / Rivers of Babylon / Theme from Whatever happened to the likely lads / Pink purple
CD ____ **BLUFF 042CD**
Deceptive / Jun '97 / Vital

REACH
CD ____ **KLP 12**
K / Jun '97 / Cargo / Greyhound / SRD

Snyder, Todd

STEP RIGHT UP
Elmo and Henry / I believe you / Side show blues / Enough / TV guide / Hey hey / Moon dawg's tavern / Prison walls / Horseshoe lake / It all adds up / Tension / Late last night / 24 hours a day / Better than ever / Blues part 2
CD ____ **MCD 11412**
MCA / Aug '96 / BMG

So Much Hate

LIES
CD ____ **XM 040**
X-Mist / Dec '93 / Cargo / SRD

Soap

DUMB FUNK RESISTANCE
CD ____ **HHUKCD 002**
Harthouse / Oct '95 / Mo's Music Machine / Prime / Vital

Soares, Fernando Machado

FADO FROM COIMBRA
CD ____ **C 559 041**
Ocora / Feb '89 / ADA / Harmonia Mundi

SOB

WHAT'S THE TRUTH
CD ____ **RISE 4 CD**
Rise / Dec '90 / Pinnacle

Sober

FIRST STEP
CD ____ **BIRD 049**
Birdnest / Jun '97 / Cargo / Plastic Head

YEAH YEAH YEAH
CD ____ **BIRD 98CD**
Birdnest / Feb '97 / Cargo / Plastic Head

Sobin A'r Smaeliaid

A RHAW
CD ____ **SCD 2017**
Sain / Feb '95 / ADA / Direct / Greyhound

Social Disorder

GOIN' THE DISTANCE
CD ____ **LF 153CD**
Lost & Found / Jul '95 / Plastic Head

Social Distortion

MAINLINER
CD ____ **0930435022**
RCA / Sep '96 / BMG
CD ____ **435022**
Time Bomb / Apr '97 / Cargo

MOMMY'S LITTLE MONSTER
CD ____ **0930435002**
RCA / Sep '96 / BMG
CD ____ **435002**
Time Bomb / Apr '97 / Cargo

PRISON BOUND
CD ____ **0930435012**
RCA / Sep '96 / BMG
CD ____ **435012**
Time Bomb / Apr '97 / Cargo

WHITE LIGHT, WHITE HEAT, WHITE TRASH
Dear lover / Don't drag me down / Intitled / I was wrong / Through these eyes / Down on the world again / When the angels sing / Gotta know the rules / Crown of thorns / Pleasure seeker / Down here / Under my thumb
CD ____ **4843742**
Epic / Sep '96 / Sony

Social Interiors

WORLD BEHIND YOU, THE
CD ____ **XCD 029**
Extreme / Feb '95 / Vital/SAM

Social Justice

UNITY IS STRENGTH
CD ____ **LF 136CD**
Lost & Found / May '95 / Plastic Head

Society Of Soul

BRAINCHILD
Geneses / EMBRACE / Changes / It only gets better / Interlude / Brainchild / Ghetto fuh life / Right tonight / Judas / Pushin' / Migratention / Sonja Marie / Wind / Blac mermaid / Peaches n' erb / No hard feelings
CD ____ **73008260232**
Arista / Jun '96 / BMG

Society Syncopators

REVOLUTIONARY BLUES
CD ____ **NEW 2022**
Australian Jazz / Jul '96 / Jazz Music

Sodom

AGENT ORANGE
Agent orange / Tired and red / Incest / Remember the fallen / Magic dragon / Exhibition bout / Ausgebombt / Baptism of fire
CD ____ **SPV 847597**
SPV / Feb '97 / Koch / Plastic Head

BETTER OFF DEAD
Eye for an eye / Saw is the law / Capture the flag / Never healing wound / Resurrection / Shellfire defense / Turn your head around / Bloodtrials / Better off dead / Stalinorgel
CD ____ **8476261**
Steamhammer / Nov '90 / Pinnacle / Plastic Head

GET WHAT YOU DESERVE
CD ____ **SPV 08476762**
CD ____ **SPV 08476542**
SPV / Feb '97 / Koch / Plastic Head

IN THE SIGN OF EVIL
Outbreak of evil / Blasphemer / Burst command 'til war / Sepulchral voice / Witching metal
CD ____ **SPV 0857533**
SPV / Feb '97 / Koch / Plastic Head

MAROONED - LIVE
CD ____ **SPV 08476852**
SPV / Feb '97 / Koch / Plastic Head

MASQUERADE IN BLOOD
CD ____ **SPV 08576962**
SPV / Feb '97 / Koch / Plastic Head

MORTAL WAY OF LIVE
CD ____ **SPV 857576**
SPV / Feb '97 / Koch / Plastic Head

OBSESSED BY CRUELTY
CD ____ **857 533**
Steamhammer / '88 / Pinnacle / Plastic Head

PERSECUTION MANIA
CD ____ **SPV 857509**
Steamhammer / Feb '97 / Pinnacle / Plastic Head

TEN BLACK YEARS (The Best Of Sodom/2CD Set)
Tired and red / Saw is the law / Agent orange / Wachturm/Erwachtet / Sodomy and lust / Remember the fallen / Nuclear winter / Outbreak of evil / Resurrection / Bombenhagel / Masquerade in blood / Bullet in the head / Stalinhagel / Shellshock / Angel dust / Hunting season / Abuse / 1000 days of Sodom / Gomorrah / Unwanted youth / Tarred and feathered / Iron fist / Jabba The Hut / Silence is consent / Incest / Shellfire defense / Gone to glory / Fratricide / Verrecke / One step over the line / My atonement / Sodomized / Aber bitte mit sahne / Die stumme ursel / Mantelmann
CD Set ____ **SPV 08618342**
SPV / Feb '97 / Koch / Plastic Head

THIS WAY OF LIFE
CD ____ **847576**
Steamhammer / '90 / Pinnacle / Plastic Head

TIL DEATH DO US PART
CD ____ **GUN 119CD**
Gun / Feb '97 / Plastic Head

Sodre, Raimundo

REAL
CD ____ **68972**
Tropical / Apr '97 / Discovery

Sod's Opera

COME ON LADS
I haven't seen old Hitler / D-Day dodgers / Ode to a Gezira lovely / Tins / Ballad of Wadi Maktilla / Dying soldier / Service police song / Kiss me goodnight, Sergeant Major / Thanks for the memory / Come on chaps / Firth of Forth / Down the mine / Sailor's wife / Longmoor / I don't want to join the army / Bloody Orkney / We are the boys / Africa star / Sinking of the Graf Spee / My bomber lies over the ocean / When this bloody war is over / Gay Caballero / Onward 15th Army group / Highland division's farewell to Sicily / Bless 'em all
CD ____ **BEJOCD 7**
Beautiful Jo / Jun '95 / ADA / Direct

Sofa Glue

SMILE
CD ____ **RNR 004CD**
Ransom Note / Oct '95 / Plastic Head

Sofa Head

PRE MARITAL PREDICAMENT
CD ____ **COXCD 001**
Meantime / Jan '91 / Cadillac / Vital

Sofia Singers

TRADITION SINGS ON
CD ____ **925992CD**
BUDA / Aug '94 / Discovery

Soft Boys

CAN OF BEES
CD ____ **RCD 20231**
Rykodisc / Nov '92 / ADA / Vital

INVISIBLE HITS
CD ____ **RCD 20233**
Rykodisc / Nov '92 / ADA / Vital

SOFT BOYS 1976-1981, THE
Wey wey hep uh hole / It's not just the size of a walnut / Ugly Nora / Yodelling hoover / Hear my Brane / Face of death / Wading through a ventilator / Give it to The Soft Boys / I want to be an angelpoise lamp / Fatman's son / Where are the prawns / Psychedelic love / Heartbreak hotel / Caroline says / We like bananas / Pigworker / Do the chisel / Return of the sacred crab / That's when your heartache begins / Book of love / Sandra's having her brain out / Leppo and the jooves / Rat's prayer / Have a heart, Betty (I'm not fireproof) / Mystery train / He's a reptile / Rock 'n' roll toilet / Insanely jealous / Underwater moonlight / I wanna destroy you / Queen of eyes / Kingdom of love / Positive vibrations / Gigolo aunt / Train around the bend / Only the stones remain
CD ____ **RCD 10234/35**
Rykodisc / Aug '93 / ADA / Vital

UNDERWATER MOONLIGHT
I wanna destroy you / Kingdom of love / Positive vibrations / I got the hob / Insanely jealous / Tonight / You'll have to go sideways / I'm an old pervert / Queen of eyes / Underwater moonlight
CD ____ **RCD 20232**
Rykodisc / Nov '92 / ADA / Vital

Soft Cell

ART OF FALLING APART, THE
Forever the same / Where the heart is / Numbers / Heat / Kitchen sink drama / Baby doll / Loving you hating me / Art of falling apart
CD ____ **5102962**
Some Bizarre/Mercury / Sep '92 / PolyGram

MEMORABILIA - THE SINGLES (Soft Cell & Marc Almond)
Memorabilia / Tainted love / Bedsitter / Say hello, wave goodbye / What / Torch / Soul inside / Where the heart is / I feel love / Tears run rings / Lover spurned / Something's gotten hold of my heart
CD ____ **8485122**
Some Bizarre/Mercury / Apr '91 / PolyGram

NON STOP ECSTATIC DANCING
Memorabilia / Where did our love go / What / Man could get lost / Chips on my shoulder / Sex dwarf
CD ____ **5102952**
Some Bizarre/Mercury / Sep '92 / PolyGram

NON STOP EROTIC CABARET (Remastered)
Frustration / Tainted love / Seedy films / Youth / Sex dwarf / Entertain me / Chips on my shoulder / Bedsitter / Secret life / Say hello, wave goodbye / Where did our love go / Memorabilia / Facility girls / Fun city / Torch / Insecure me / What / So
CD ____ **5325952**
Some Bizarre / Jun '96 / Pinnacle

SAY HELLO TO SOFT CELL
Bedsitter / Say hello wave goodbye / Man could get lost / Facility girls / Sex dwarf / Torch / It's a mug's game / Born to lose / Heat / Art of falling apart / You only live twice / Where was your heart (when you needed it most) / Mr. Self Destruct / Disease and desire / Numbers / Frustration
CD ____ **5520862**
Spectrum / Mar '96 / PolyGram

SINGLES 1981-1985, THE
Memorabilia / Tainted love / Bedsitter / Say hello, wave goodbye / Torch / What / Where the heart is / Numbers / Soul inside / Down in the subway
CD ____ **8307082**
Some Bizarre/Mercury / Nov '86 / PolyGram

Soft Machine

ALIVE AND WELL RECORDED IN PARIS
White kite / Eos / Odds bullets and blades, pt I / Odds bullets and blades, pt II / Song of the sunbird / Puffin' / Huffin / Number three / Nodder / Surrounding silence / Soft space
CD ____ **SEECD 290**
See For Miles/C5 / Jan '90 / Pinnacle

BUNDLES
Hazard profile / Gone sailing / Bundles / Land of the bag snake / Man who waved at trains / Peff / Four gongs two drums / Floating world
CD ____ **SEECD 283**
See For Miles/C5 / '89 / Pinnacle

HARVEST YEARS, THE (The Best Of Soft Machine)
Hazard profile / Gone sailing / Bundles / Land of the bag snake / Man who waved at trains / Peff / Four gongs, two drums / Songs of Aeolus / Kayoo / Aubade / Second bundle / Camden tandem / One over the eight / Number three / Nodder / Soft space
CD C5MCD 623
See For Miles/C5 / Apr '97 / Pinnacle

LIVE AT THE PARADISO
Hulloder / Dada was here / Tthank you Pierrot Lunaire / Have you ever bean green / Pataphysical introduction part 2 / As long as he lies perfectly still / Fire engine passing with bells clanging / Hibou, anemone & bear / Fire engine passing with bells clanging (reprise) / Pig / Orange skin food / Door opens and closes / 10.30 returns to the bedroom
CD BP 193CD
Blueprint / Oct '96 / Pinnacle

LIVE AT THE PROMS
Out-rageous / Facelift / Esther's nosejob / Pig / Orange skin food / Door opens and closes / Pigling bland / 10.30 returns to the bedroom
CD CDRECK 5
Reckless / Aug '88 / RTM/Disc

LONDON 1967 (Soft Machine/Mark Leeman/Davey Graham)
CD 14557
Spalax / Jun '97 / ADA / Cargo / Direct / Discovery / Greyhound

RUBBER RIFF
Crunch / Pavan / Jombles / Little floating music / Hi power / Little Miss B / Splot / Rubber riff / Sam's short shuffle / Melina / City steps / Gentle turn / Porky / Travelogue
CD BP 190CD
Blueprint / Sep '97 / Pinnacle

SOFT MACHINE VOL.1 & 2 (2CD Set)
Hope for happiness / Joy of a toy / Hope for happiness (reprise) / Why am I so short / So boot if at all / Certain kind / Save yourself / Priscilla / Lullaby letter / We did it again / Plus belle qu'une poubelle / Why are we sleeping / Box 25/4 / Pataphysical introduction Part 1 / Concise British alphabet Part 1 / Hibou, anenome and bear / Concise British alphabet Part 2 / Hulloder / Dada was here / Thank you Pierrot Lunaire / Have you ever bean green / Pataphysical introduction Part 2 / Out of tunes / As long as he lies perfectly still / Dedicated to you but you weren't listening / Fire engine passing with bells clanging / Pig / Orange skin food / Door opens and closes / 10.30 returns to the bedroom
CD Set CDWIKD 920
Big Beat / Sep '89 / Pinnacle

SOFTS
Aubade / Tale of taliesin / Ban ban caliban / Song of Aeolus / Out of season / Second bundle / Kayoo / Camden tandem / Nexus / One over the eight / Etika
CD SEECD 285
See For Miles/C5 / Jan '90 / Pinnacle

SPACED
CD RUNE 90
Cuneiform / Nov '96 / ReR Megacorp

THIRD
Facelift / Slightly all the time / Moon in June / Out bloody rageous
CD BGOCD 180
Beat Goes On / Mar '93 / Pinnacle
CD 4714072
Columbia / Jul '96 / Sony

Softballetforms

REMIX FOR ORDINARY PEOPLE
CD SSR 160CD
SSR / Feb '96 / Amato Disco / Grapevine/ PolyGram / Prime / RTM/Disc

Softies

IT'S LOVE
CD KLP 43CD
K / Oct '95 / Cargo / Greyhound / SRD

WINTER PAGEANT
CD KLP 61CD
K / Jan '97 / Cargo / Greyhound / SRD

Software

DIGITAL DANCE
Oceans breath / Magnificent shore / Waking voice / Island sunrise / Magic beach / Seagulls audience / Digital dance
CD 710 071
Thunderbolt / Mar '88 / TKO Magnum

LIVE
CD 710084
Magnum Music / Nov '89 / TKO Magnum

Soki Vangu

SOKI VANGU/BELLA BELLA VOL.3 1975-1980 (Soki Vangu & Bella Bella)
CD NG 031
Ngoyarto / Jan '97 / Stern's

Sol Invictus

BLACK EUROPE (Sol Invictus Live)
CD WSCDL 002
World Serpent / Oct '96 / World Serpent

BLADE, THE
Blade / In Heaven / Time flies / House above the world / Laws and crowns / Once upon a time / See how we fall / Gealdor / From the wreckage / Nothing here / Remember and forget
CD TURSA 014CD
Tursa / Apr '97 / World Serpent

CUPID AND DEATH
CD TURSA 011CD
Tursa / Oct '96 / World Serpent

DEATH OF THE WEST
CD TURSA 008CD
Tursa / Oct '96 / World Serpent

IN THE RAIN
CD TURSA 010CD
Tursa / Oct '96 / World Serpent

KILLING TIDE
CD TURSA 003CD
Tursa / Oct '96 / World Serpent

KING AND QUEEN
CD TURSA 006CD
Tursa / Oct '96 / World Serpent

LE CROIX
CD TURSA 007CD
Tursa / Oct '96 / World Serpent

LET US PRAY (Sol Invictus Live)
CD TURSA 005CD
Tursa / Oct '96 / World Serpent

LEX TALIONIS
CD TURSA 001CD
Tursa / Oct '96 / World Serpent

SOL VERITAS LUX
CD SVL 002CD
Tursa / Sep '90 / World Serpent

TREES IN WINTER
CD TURSA 002CD
Tursa / Oct '96 / World Serpent

Sol Y Canto

SANCOCHO
CD ROUCD 6055
Rounder / Dec '94 / ADA / CM / Direct

SENDERO DEL SOL
Tamboe y guitarra / Que bonita luna / Pregonero / Gracias a la vida / Ijexa (Filhos de Gandhi) / Zamba del grillo / En esta tarde gris / Sal a caminar / Bulerias del charco / En mi viejo San Juan / Alejandro's ghost
CD ROUCD 6063
Rounder / Sep '96 / ADA / CM / Direct

Sola, Payita

SONG OF ARGENTINA - THE PERCUSSIONISTS OF GUINEA
CD 825012
BUDA / Apr '91 / Discovery

Solal, Martial

A PIACERE - TRIPTYQUE (Solal, Martial & Francois Mechali)
CD 590067
Musidisc / Sep '96 / Discovery

BIG BAND
Tango et pretexte / Valse a trois temps / Tango / Suite
CD 84937812
Verve / Mar '93 / PolyGram

IMPROVISE POUR FRANCE MUSIQUE (2CD Set)
Just you, just me / Don't blame me / L'ami remy est effare / Ballade / Cheek to cheek / 'Round midnight / Ah non / Woodin' you / Cuivre a la mer / Tout va tres bien madame la marquise / Somebody loves me / Night in Tunisia / Hommage a tex a very / Tea for two / Lover man / Cumparsita / Darn that dream / Take the 'A' train / I can't get started (with you) / Corcovado
CD Set JMS 186382
JMS / Dec '95 / New Note/BMG

Solar Eclipse

FROM HERE
CD AFTERCD 003
After 6am / Jan '95 / Plastic Head

Solar Race

HOMESPUN
CD OREZCD 546
Silvertone / May '97 / Pinnacle

PEEL SESSIONS, THE
CD ORECD 542
Silvertone / Oct '96 / Pinnacle

Solar Systems

REMOTE VIEWERS
CD INTRUCD 2
Intruder / May '97 / Essential/BMG / Prime

Solarus

EMPTY NATURE
CD RR 69652
Relapse / Aug '97 / Pinnacle / Plastic Head

Solas

SOLAS
CD SH 78002
Shanachie / Jun '96 / ADA / Greensleeves / Koch

SUNNY SPELLS AND SCATTERED SHOWERS
CD SHCD 78010
Shanachie / Jun '97 / ADA / Greensleeves / Koch

Solberg, James

ONE OF THESE DAYS (Solberg, James Band)
Too damn much lovin' / One of these days / One false move / Still called the blues / Cheaper to keep her / There must be a better world somewhere / Can it be / Ringin' in my head / Litehouse keeper / Nobody to blame / Do you call that a buddy / Love made a fool out of me / Ain't no way / Everyday
CD ATM 1120
Atomic Theory / Aug '96 / ADA / Direct
CD DFGCD 8453
Dixie Frog / Sep '96 / Direct / TKO Magnum

Soley

SPECIAL SOUKOUSS
CD PS 66404
PlayaSound / Apr '97 / ADA / Harmonia Mundi

Solid Doctor

BEATS MEAN HIGHS
CD PORK 030
Pork / May '96 / Kudos / Pinnacle / Prime

Solid Gold Hell

BLOOD AND THE PITY
CD FNCD 346
Flying Nun / Oct '96 / RTM/Disc

SWINGIN' HOT MURDER
CD FNCD 298
Flying Nun / Sep '94 / RTM/Disc

Solid Senders

EVERYTHING'S GONNA BE ALRIGHT
CD TR 9920CD
Tramp / Aug '94 / ADA / CM / Direct

Solidor, Suzi

SUZI SOLIDOR 1933-1939
CD 121
Chansophone / Nov '92 / Discovery

Soling, Johnny

JOHNNY SOLING
CD GRD 27
Grappa / May '96 / ADA

Solis, Sebastian

EL GAUCHO, EL INKA
CD EUCD 1033
ARC / '89 / ADA / ARC Music

FESTIVAL LATINO (Solis, Sebastian, Patricia Salas & Pablo Carcamo)
CD EUCD 1074
ARC / '91 / ADA / ARC Music

FROM CUBA TO TIERRA DEL FUEGO
CD EUCD 1066
ARC / '89 / ADA / ARC Music

Solitaire

FEARLESS
CD ROD 08
Recycle Or Die / Apr '96 / Kudos

RITUAL GROUND
CD SR 9341
Silent / Jan '94 / Cargo / Plastic Head

Solitaires

WALKING ALONG WITH
Walking alone / Wedding / How long / I really love you so (honey babe) / Please remember my heart / Blue valentine / Later for you baby / Honeymoon / Angels sang / Girl is gone / I don't stand a ghost of a chance with you / Chances I've taken / Give me one more chance / Please kiss this letter / You've sinned / What did she say / Wonder why / South of the border (Down Mexico way) / Fine little girl / Nothing like a little girl / At night / When will the lights shine for me / Light a candle in the chapel / My dear / Come back my love / Stranger in paradise / Time is here
CD CDCHD 383
Ace / Oct '92 / Pinnacle

Solitude

FROM WITHIN
CD CDVEST 18
Bulletproof / Nov '94 / Pinnacle

Solitude Aeturnus

DOWNFALL
CD IRSCD 993022
Hengest / Jan '97 / Grapevine/PolyGram

THROUGH THE DARKEST HOUR
CD CDVEST 35
Bulletproof / Nov '94 / Pinnacle

Solo

SOLO
What a wonderful world / Back 2 da street / Blowin' my mind / Cupid / Heaven / Xxtra / It's such a shame / He's not good enough / Another Saturday night/Everybody loves to cha cha / Where do u want me to put it / Keep it right here / I'm sorry / Under the boardwalk / In bed / (Last night I made love) Like never before / Prince Street / Holdin' on / Change is gonna come / Solo strut
CD 5490172
Perspective / Dec '95 / PolyGram

Solo, Napoleon

SHOT
CD BBSCD 006
Blue Beat / Oct '89 / Grapevine/PolyGram

Solo, Ralph

CAR ACCIDENTS, GUITAR ACCIDENTS
CD BBPTC 6
Black Bean & Placenta Tape Club / Oct '96 / Cargo

Soloff, Lew

LITTLE WING
CD 66055015
Sweet Basil / Jul '92 / New Note/Pinnacle

Soloman Grundy

SOLOMAN GRUNDY
CD NAR 049CD
New Alliance / Sep '90 / Plastic Head

Solstice

LAMENTATIONS
CD CANDLE 007CD
Candlelight / Aug '94 / Plastic Head

Solstice

CIRCLES
CD ANDCD 13
A New Day / Feb '97 / Direct

HALCYON
CD GOD 026CD
Godhead / Jun '97 / Plastic Head

PRAY
CD SPV 08476902
SPV / May '95 / Koch / Plastic Head

Solution AD

HAPPILY EVER AFTER
CD 7567927082
Atlantic / Oct '96 / Warner Music

Solve, Gilda

MY SIMPLE SONG
CD BB 646
Black & Blue / Apr '97 / Discovery / Koch / Wellard

Solvent Drag

INSENTIENT
CD GBO4 CD
Gasoline Boost / Nov '92 / Plastic Head

Soma

ARCANE EP
CD XCS 036
Extreme / Jun '96 / Vital/SAM

HOLLOW EARTH
CD XCD 028
Extreme / Feb '95 / Vital/SAM

INNER CINEMA, THE
Stygian vista / Arcane / Golden dawn / Drunken Atlantean / Baal / Collector / Risen from agartha / Antediluvian / Alchemical nuptial / Shambhala / Endless
CD XCD 038
Extreme / Nov '96 / Vital/SAM

Some More Crime

ANOTHER DOMESTIC DRAMA
CD ZZ 009
Hyperium / Jul '93 / Cargo / Plastic Head

Somerville, Jimmy

DARE TO LOVE
Heartbeat / Hurt so good / Cry / Love thing / By your side / Dare to love / Someday we'll be together / Alright / Too much of a

good thing / Dream gone wrong / Come lately / Safe in these arms / Because of him
CD 8285402
London / Jun '95 / PolyGram

READ MY LIPS
Comment te dire adieu / You make me feel (mighty real) / Perfect day / Heaven here on earth (with your love) / Don't know what to do / Read my lips / My heart is in your hands / Control / And you never thought this could happen to you / Rain
CD 5500422
Spectrum / May '93 / PolyGram

SINGLES COLLECTION, THE
Smalltown boy / Don't leave me this way / It ain't necessarily so / Comment te dire adieu / Never can say goodbye / Why / You are my world / For a friend / I feel love / There's more to love / So cold the night / To love somebody / Run from love / Tomorrow / Disenchanted / Read my lips / You make me feel (Mighty real)
CD 8282682
London / Aug '91 / PolyGram

Somethin' For The People

SOMETHIN' FOR THE PEOPLE
CD 9362460602
Warner Bros. / Jul '96 / Warner Music

Something Happens

BEDLAM A GO-GO
CD CDV 2695
Virgin / Jul '92 / EMI

BEEN THERE, SEEN THAT, DONE THAT
Beach / Incoming / Take this with you / Forget Georgia / Way I feel / Both men crying / Burn clear / Give it away / Tall girls club / Shoulder high / Here comes the only one again / Be my love / Promised / Seven days 'til 4 am / Free and easy
CD CDV 2561
Virgin / Oct '88 / EMI

STUCK TOGETHER WITH GOD'S GLUE
What now / Hello hello hello hello hello (petrol) / Parachute / Esmerelda / I had a feeling / Kill the roses / Brand new God / Room 29 / Patience business / Devil in Miss Jones / Good time coming / Feel good / Skyrockets
CD CDV 2628
Virgin / May '90 / EMI

Something Pretty Beautiful

SOMETHING PRETTY BEAUTIFUL
CD CRECD 075
Creation / May '94 / 3mv/Vital

Somewhere In Europe

GESTURES
CD BADVCCD 45
New European / Oct '96 / World Serpent

IRON TREES ARE IN FULL BLOOM, THE
CD TSCD 1
These Silences / Oct '96 / World Serpent

SAVAGE DREAMS
CD TSCD 2
These Silences / Oct '96 / World Serpent

Sommerfolk

BEHAKLICHKEIT
CD BEST 1009CD
Acoustic Music / Nov '93 / ADA

Sommers, Joanie

HITS AND RARITIES
CD MAR 001
Marginal / Jun '97 / Greyhound

Son 14

CUBANIA (Son 14 & Tiburon)
CD CD 065
Tumi / Feb '97 / Discovery / Stern's

Son Of Crackpipe

BENEVOLENCE OF DOGS AND EVOLUTIONARY ACCIDENTS
CD BGRO 15CD
BGR / Oct '95 / Plastic Head

Son Of Noise

ACCESS DENIED - BULLSHIT AND POLITICS VOL.1
CD COM 102152
Tribehaus Recordings / Sep '95 / Plastic Head

Son Volt

STRAIGHTAWAYS
Caryatid easy / Back into your world / Picking up the signal / Left a slide / Creosote / Cemetery savior / Last minute shakedown / Been set back / No more parades / Way down Watson
CD 9362465182
Reprise / Aug '97 / Warner Music

Sonar Nation

CYLINDERS IN BLUE
CD ABT100CD
Abstract / May '95 / Cargo / Pinnacle / Total/BMG

Sondheim, Alan

RITUAL
CD ESP 10482
ESP / Jan '93 / Jazz Music

T'OTHER LITTLE TUNE
CD ESP 10822
ESP / Jan '93 / Jazz Music

Sonerien Du

REDER NOZ
CD EOG 005CD
EOG / Nov '96 / ADA

TREDAN
CD CD 829
Diffusion Breizh / Apr '95 / ADA

Song Of The Native Land ...

INSTRUMENTAL TEXTURES (Song Of The Native Land Ensemble)
Four generations / Lullaby of the South / Love song / River Lam and reminiscence / Market in spring / Festivities in the homeland mountains and rivers / Flowing water, golden sapeque, spring wind, dragon and tiger / Season for picking fruit / Morning on the terraced fields / Song of the black haired horse / Sakura
CD VICG 54542
JVC / Oct '96 / Direct / New Note/Pinnacle / Vital/SAM

Songrien Du

TRADITION VIBRANTE
CD KMCD 004
Keltia Musique / Jul '90 / ADA / Discovery

Songs: Ohia

SONGS: OHIA
CD SC 03
Secretly Canadian / May '97 / Cargo

Sonic Experience

DEF TILL DAWN
CD STUCD 2
Strictly Underground / Nov '93 / SRD

Sonic Sufi

SACRAMENTAL
CD PSY 018CD
PSY Harmonics / Oct '95 / Plastic Head

Sonic Violence

TRANSFIXION
CD KTB 004CD
Dreamtime / May '92 / Kudos / Pinnacle

Sonic Voyager

ENDLESS MISSION
CD APR 006CD
April / May '95 / Plastic Head / Shellshock/Disc

Sonic Walters

MEDICATION
CD RA 91782
Roadrunner / Apr '92 / PolyGram

Sonic Youth

ANAGRAMA
Anagrama / Improvisation ajout'e / Tremens / Mieux: de corrosion
CD SYR 1CD
SYR / Jun '97 / Cargo

BAD MOON RISING
CD BFFP 1 CD
Blast First / Nov '86 / RTM/Disc

CONFUSION IS SEX/KILL YOUR IDOLS
CD BFFP 113CD
Blast First / Mar '95 / RTM/Disc

DAYDREAM NATION
CD BFFP 34CD
Blast First / Oct '88 / RTM/Disc

DIRTY
100% / Swimsuit issue / Theresa's sound world / Drunken butterfly / Shoot / Wish fulfillment / Sugar kane / Orange rolls, angel's spit / Youth against facism / Nic fit / On the strip / Chapel hill / Stalker / JC / Purr creme brulee
CD GFLD 19296
Geffen / Oct '95 / BMG

EVOL
CD BFFP 4CD
Blast First / Nov '86 / RTM/Disc

EXPERIMENTAL JET SET, TRASH AND NO STAR
Winner's blues / Bull in the heather / Starfield road / Skink / Screaming skull / Self-obssessed and sexxee / Bone / Androgynous mind / Quest for the cup / Waist / Doctor's orders / Tokyo eye / In the mind of the bourgeois reader / Sweet shine
CD GFLD 19329
Geffen / Sep '96 / BMG

GOO
Dirty boots / Tunic (song for Karen) / Mary Christ / Kool thing / Mote / My friend Goo / Disappearer / Mildred Pierce / Cinderella's big score / Scooter and Jinx / Titanium expose
CD GFLD 19297
Geffen / Oct '95 / BMG

SCREAMING FIELDS OF SONIC LOVE
CD BFFP 119CD
Blast First / Apr '95 / RTM/Disc

SISTER
CD BFFP 20CD
Blast First / Jun '87 / RTM/Disc

SONIC DEATH (Early Sonic Youth/Live 1981-1983)
CD BFFP 32CD
Blast First / '89 / RTM/Disc

WASHING MACHINE
Becuz / Junkie's promise / Saucer-like / Washing machine / Unwind / Little trouble girl / No Queen blues / Panty lies / Skip tracer / Diamond sea
CD GED 24825
Geffen / Oct '95 / BMG
CD GED 24909
Geffen / Mar '96 / BMG

WHITEY ALBUM, THE (Ciccone Youth)
Needle gun / G force / Platform 11 / Me and Jill / Hi everybody / Children of Satan / Moby Dick / Into the groovy / March of the Ciccone robots / Macbeth / Burning up / Two cool rock chicks listening to Neu / Addicted to love / Making the nature scene / Tuff titty rap
CD BFFP 28CD
Blast First / Mar '88 / RTM/Disc

Sonics

FIRE AND ICE/THE LOST TAPES
CD JRCD 7009
Jerden / Oct '96 / Cargo

HERE ARE THE SONICS/BOOM
CD 422331
New Rose / May '94 / ADA / Direct / Discovery

MAINTAINING MY COOL
CD JRCD 7001
Jerden / Oct '96 / Cargo

PSYCHO-SONIC
Witch / Do you love me / Roll over beethoven / Boss hoss / Dirty robber / Have love will travel / Psycho / Money (that's what I want) / Walking the dog / Night time is the right time / Strychnine / Good golly Miss Molly / Hustler / Psycho (Live) / Cinderella / Don't be afraid of the dark / Skinny Minnie / Let the good times roll / Don't you just know it / Jenny Jenny / He's waiting / Louie Louie / Since I fell for you / Hitch hike / It's alright / Shot down / Keep on knockin' / Witch (Live) / Witch
CD CDWIKD 115
Big Beat / Feb '93 / Pinnacle

SINDERELLA
CD BCD 4011
Bomp / Jan '97 / Cargo / Greyhound / RTM/Disc / Shellshock/Disc

Sonnier, Jo El

CAJUN LIFE
Cajun life / Tes yeux bleu / Allons a Lafayette / Bayou teche / Les flames d'enfer / Lacassine special / Chere Alice / Louisiana blues / Les grande bois / Perrodin two step
CD ROUCD 3049
Rounder / Aug '88 / ADA / CM / Direct

CAJUN PRIDE
Lake Arthur special / Juste une affair / Pine Grove blues / Lawtell two step / La valse de grand mamou / French blues / Mamou two step / Midnight waltz / Step it fast / Jolie fille / Armede Ardoin / Johnnie fais bien
CD ROUCD 6069
Rounder / May '97 / ADA / CM / Direct

CAJUN ROOTS
CD ROUCD 6059
Rounder / Jul '94 / ADA / CM / Direct

CAJUN YOUNG BLOOD (Sonnier, Jo El & Sidney Brown/Robert Bertrand)
Jump little frog / Rolling pin / I'm leaving you / Durald waltz / Bean / I'd like to forget / Monkey on my back / Little petite / One I love / Johnny B Goode / Cafe sho / My blue letter / Fee fee poncho / Hurricane Audry / Auntie's peanuts / There's no goodbyes / Didn't come home / Tasso gumbo / Valse de Rose Marie / (Ship of) broken heart / My 50 cents / Legend ofiry LeJeune / Monkey played fiddle / We passed your door / I'd like to forget / Aye yeah / Last waltz / Big wheel rolling
CD CDCHD 596
Ace / Jul '96 / Pinnacle

Sonny & Cher

BEAT GOES ON, THE
CD 7567917962
Atlantic / Mar '93 / Warner Music

SONNY & CHER COLLECTION
Gypsies / Tramps and thieves / Dark lady / Way of love / I got you babe / Baby don't go / All I ever need is you / Laugh at me / Dead ringer for love / Beat goes on / Little man / Half breed / What now my love / But you're mine / Cowboy's work is never done
CD 9548301522
Atlantic / Dec '90 / Warner Music

Sonora Pine

SONORA PINE VOL.2, THE
CD QS 47CD
Quarter Stick / Aug '97 / Cargo / SRD

SONORA PINE, THE
CD QS 39CD
Quarter Stick / May '96 / Cargo / SRD

Sons Of Blues

LIVE 1982
Never make your move to soon / Did you ever love a woman / Eyesight to the blind / Sweet little angel / My kind of woman / Reconsider baby / Detroit, Michigan / Goin' on main street
CD ECD 260492
Evidence / Sep '94 / ADA / Cadillac / Harmonia Mundi

Sons Of Champlin

LOOSEN UP NATURALLY
1982-A / Thing to do / Misery isn't free / Rooftop / Everywhere / Don't fight it, do it / Get high / Black and blue rainbow / Hello sunlight / Things are gettin' better / Freedom
CD SEECD 441
See For Miles/C5 / Jun '96 / Pinnacle

Sons Of Geronimo

TWIST
CD REVXD207
Revolver / Aug '97 / Revolver / Sony

Sons Of Hercules

SONS OF HERCULES
Piece of mine / Crawlin' back / IOU Nothing / Damaged goods / Lost in space / Guttersnipe / Black and blue / Shakin' street / Angel on fire / Carving knife
CD 119432
Musidisc UK / Jun '96 / Grapevine/ PolyGram

Sons Of Selina

NOUR D'OUI
Climb / Life is but / Existing services / Gamato manopano / Of the first water / Once every so often / Four plus twenty / Growing bold / Anxiety / It's a boy / On a promise / Dreamshadow
CD DELECCD 025
Delerium / Aug '94 / Cargo / Pinnacle / Vital

Sons Of Silence

SILENCE FM
Yessiree / Going to fat / More bass, vicar / Ain't we grand / Larry addled / It's a bloodbath / Guilded step / Low speed chase / Cocktails at dawn / Oddball/highball / Cotterless crank / Going to fast / Spanish: Wolverhampton / Love and kisses / Silent key
CD BAY 1CD
Leaf / Jun '97 / RTM/Disc

SPOKE (Live In Nevers)
CD NM 009
Noise Museum / Apr '97 / RTM/Disc

Sons Of Soul

SONS OF SOUL
CD 50536
Raging Bull / Jun '97 / Prime / Total/BMG

Sons Of The Desert

GREEDY
Chop-a-nose day / All gone / Lambs' tidgerrs / Don't praise her / Greedy as I get / OKB / Bruno / Bear baiting / Tear-apart change bag / Beat the trees / Arrogant & ungrateful / Cornered (in a barn) / Holiday home / (I'm) Blind / Sperm jacket
CD LBLC 2527
Indigo / Nov '96 / New Note/Pinnacle

Sons Of The Pioneers

WAGON WEST (4CD Set)
Forgive and forget / Cool water / Timber trail / Stars and stripes on Iwo Jima / You're getting tired of me / Gold star mother with silvery hair / You'll be sorry when I'm gone / I wear your memory in my heart / Cowboy camp meetin' / Tumbling tumbleweeds / Out California way / Grievin' my heart out for you / No one to cry to / Everlasting hills of Oklahoma / Chant of the wanderer / Blue prairie / Trees / Letter marked unclaimed / Baby doll / Penny for your thoughts / Have

I told you lately that I love you / Let's pretend / Cigarettes, whiskey and wild, wild women / Teardrops in my heart / My best to you / Will there be sagebrush in Heaven / You don't know what lonesome is / You never miss the water / Lead me gently home father / Too high, too wide, too low / Out in pioneertown / Hundred and sixty acres / Seawalker / Read the bible every day / Last round-up / Two eyes, two lips but no heart / Cowboy country / Bar-none ranch (in the sky) / Where are you / Calico apron and a gingham gown / Happy birthday polka / Let me share your name / Wind / Whiffenpoof song / Old rugged cross / Power in the blood / Touch of God's hand / Rounded up in glory / Santa Fe, New Mexico / Down where the Rio flows / My feet takes me away / Red River valley / Serenade to a coyote / Missouri is a devil of a woman / No rodeo dough / Sentimental, worried and blue / Little grey home in the West / I still do / Riders in the sky / Room full of roses / No one here but you / Lie low little doggies (the cowboy's prayer) / Let's go west again / Love at the country fair / Wedding dolls (from your wedding cake) / Outlaws / Roses / Eagle's heart / Land beyond the sun / I told them all about you / Wagons west / Rollin' dust / Song of the wagonmaster / Chuckawalla swing / Old man atom / What this country needs / Baby, I ain't gonna cry no more / Little white cross / America forever / Daddy's little cowboy / Moonlight and roses / Bring your roses to her now / San Antonio rose / Mexican rose / Lonesome / Wonderous word / Resurrectus / Waltz of roses / Lord's prayer / Heartbreak hill / Holeo / Diesel smoke / Almost / Empty saddles / There's a goldmine in the sky / Old pioneer / Home on the range / If you would only be mine / Sierra Nevada / River of no return / Lilies grows high / Lonely little
CD Set ____ BCD 15640
Bear Family / Aug '93 / Direct / Rollercoaster / Swift

Sons Of The San Joaquin

GOSPEL TRAILS
CD ____ SHCD 6022
Shanachie / Jun '97 / ADA / Greensleeves / Koch

Sons Of The Subway

RUFF RUGGED AND REAL
CD ____ BETCD 004
Infonet / Aug '97 / Pinnacle / Prime / Vital

Sonz Of A Loop Da Loop Era

FLOWERS IN MY GARDEN
CD ____ SUBBASE 19 CD
Suburban Base / Mar '93 / Pinnacle / Prime

Sophia

FIXED WATER
CD ____ FLOWCD 004
Flower Shop / Nov '96 / SRD

Sopor Aeternus

ICH TOTE
CD ____ EFA 01552
Apocalyptic Vision / Dec '95 / Cargo / Plastic Head / SRD

INEXPERIENCED SPIRAL TRAVELLER
CD ____ AV 021CD
Apocalyptic Vision / Jun '97 / Cargo / Plastic Head / SRD

TODESWUNSCH
CD ____ EFA 015592
Apocalyptic Vision / Dec '95 / Cargo / Plastic Head / SRD

Sopwith Camel

HELLO HELLO AGAIN
CD ____ NEMCD 601
Sequel / Apr '90 / BMG

Sorabji/Marek/Buso

CATHEDRALS IN SOUND
CD ____ AIRCD 9043
New Note / Aug '92 / Cadillac / New Note/ Pinnacle

Soraya

ON NIGHTS LIKE THIS
CD ____ 5290002
London / Jun '97 / PolyGram

Sorbye, Lief

SPRINGDANCE
CD ____ EUCD 1056
ARC / '89 / ADA / ARC Music

Sorotan Belle

SOROTAN BELLE
CD ____ KDCD 349
Elkar / May '97 / ADA

Sorrels, Rosalie

ALWAYS A LADY
CD ____ GLCD 2110
Green Linnet / May '93 / ADA / CM / Direct / Highlander / Roots

BE CAREFUL THERE'S A BABY IN THE HOUSE
CD ____ GLCD 2100
Green Linnet / '92 / ADA / CM / Direct / Highlander / Roots

BORDERLINE HEART
CD ____ GLCD 2119
Green Linnet / Sep '95 / ADA / CM / Direct / Highlander / Roots

LONG MEMORY, THE (Sorrels, Rosalie & Utah Phillips)
CD ____ RHRCD 83
Red House / May '96 / ADA / Koch

MISCELLANEOUS RECORD VOL.1
CD ____ GLCD 1042
Green Linnet / Nov '88 / ADA / CM / Direct / Highlander / Roots

THEN CAME THE CHILDREN
CD ____ GLCD 2099
Green Linnet / '92 / ADA / CM / Direct / Highlander / Roots

TRAVELIN' LADY RIDES
CD ____ GLCD 2109
Green Linnet / May '93 / ADA / CM / Direct / Highlander / Roots

WHAT DOES IT MEAN TO LOVE
CD ____ GL 2113
Green Linnet / Feb '94 / ADA / CM / Direct / Highlander / Roots

Sorrow

FORGOTTEN SUNRISE
CD ____ R 09262
Roadrunner / Sep '91 / PolyGram

Sorrow

UNDER THE YEW POSSESSED
CD ____ PIX 001CD
Piskidisc / Oct '96 / World Serpent

Sort Of Quartet

PLANET MAMON
CD ____ SST 315CD
SST / Jul '95 / Plastic Head

Sortie

SORTIE
CD ____ JUST 472
Justin Time / Oct '92 / Cadillac / New Note/Pinnacle

SOS Band

DIAMOND IN THE RAW
CD ____ 4607352
Epic / Nov '89 / Sony

Sosa, Mercedes

SINO
Y dale alegria mi corazon / Honrar la vida / La solitaria / Caruso / Rio de camalotes / Luna / Sina / La ultima curda / Encuentros y despedidas / Palito de tola / La media pena / Cinco siglos igual
CD ____ 5142282
Verve World / Apr '93 / PolyGram

SINO
CD ____ 68961
Tropical / May '97 / Discovery

Soukous Express

SOUKOUS EXPRESS VOL.2 (Ambience Night)
CD ____ CDP 5238
Piros/Sonodisc / Jan '97 / Stern's

SOUL

WHAT IS IT/CAN YOU FEEL IT
Down in the ghetto / Get ready / Burning spear / Express yourself / Soul / Message from a black man / Memphis underground / Can you feel it / Tell it like it is / Do what ever you want to do / Peace of mind / My cherie amour / Love, peace and power / To mend a broken heart / Sleeping beauty
CD ____ CDBGPD 107
Beat Goes Public / Jul '96 / Pinnacle

Soul Asylum

AND THE HORSE THEY RODE IN ON
Spinnin / Bitter pill / Veil of tears / Nice guys (Don't get paid) / Something out of nothing / Gullible's travels / Brand new shine / Easy street / Grounded / Be on your way / We 3 / All the king's friend
CD ____ CDMID 190
A&M / Nov '93 / PolyGram

CLAM DIP & OTHER DELIGHTS
Just plain evil / Chains / Secret no more / Artificial heart / P-9 / Take it to the root
CD ____ TTR 881442
Twin Tone / Feb '95 / PolyGram

GRAVE DANCERS UNION
Somebody to shove / Black gold / Runaway train / Keep it up / Homesick / Get on out / New world / April fool / Without a trace / Growing into you / 99% / Sun maid
CD ____ 4722532
Columbia / Oct '92 / Sony

HANG TIME
Down on up to me / Little too clean / Sometime to return / Cartoon / Beggars and choosers / Endless farewell / Standing in the doorway / Marionette / Ode / Jack of all trades / Twiddly dee / Heavy rotation
CD ____ CDMID 189
A&M / Nov '93 / PolyGram

LET YOUR DIM LIGHT SHINE
Misery / To my own devices / Shut down / Hope up / Primises broken / Bittersweet / String of pearls / Crawl / Caged rat / Eyes of a child / Just like anyone / Tell me when / Nothing to write home about / I did my best
CD ____ 4803202
Columbia / Jun '95 / Sony

MADE TO BE BROKEN
Tied to the tracks / Ship of fools / Can't go back / Another world another day / Made to be broken / Never really been / Whoa / New feelings / Growing pains / Long way home / Lone rider / Ain't that tough / Don't it...
CD ____ TTR 86662
Twin Tone / Feb '95 / PolyGram

SAY WHAT YOU WILL, CLARENCE, KARL SOLD THE TRUCK
Draggin' me down / Long day / Money talks / Voodoo doll / Stranger / Do you know / Sick of that song / Religiavision / Spacehead / Walkin' / Broken glass / Masquerade / Happy / Black and blue
CD ____ TTR 84392
Twin Tone / Feb '95 / PolyGram

WHILE YOU WERE OUT
Freaks / Carry on / No man's land / Crashing down / Judge / Sun don't shine / Closer to the stars / Never too soon / Miracle mile / Lap of luxury / Passing sad daydream
CD ____ TTR 86912
Twin Tone / Feb '95 / PolyGram

Soul Bossa

COME INTO SOUL BOSSA
CD ____ DISHY 23CD
Dishy Recordings / Jun '97 / SRD

Soul Bossa Trio

ABSTRACT TRUTH
CD ____ BOM 05CD
Bomba / Jul '96 / Amato Disco / Mo's Music Machine / Prime / Timewarp

DANCING IN THE STREET
CD ____ BOM 02CD
Bomba / Jul '96 / Amato Disco / Mo's Music Machine / Prime / Timewarp

SOUL BOSSA TRIO
CD ____ CBCD 003
Cubop / Jul '96 / Timewarp

TASTE OF SOUL BOSSA
CD ____ BOM 01CD
Bomba / Jul '96 / Amato Disco / Mo's Music Machine / Prime / Timewarp

WILD JUMBO
CD ____ BOM 07CD
Bomba / Nov '96 / Amato Disco / Mo's Music Machine / Prime / Timewarp

Soul Brothers

SOUL OF SOWETO
Umlohla / Siyayi dudula / Indlada / Umlenze / Kuyeza nakuwe / Bazobuya / Uzongihumbula / Ngixolele / Inhlonipho / Umnandi / Uthando lwenu / Hamba ntombi
CD ____ MOU 40332
Mountain / Oct '95 / CM

Soul Cages

MOMENTS
CD ____ MASSCD 085
Massacre / Feb '96 / Plastic Head

SOUL CAGES
CD ____ MASSCD 032
Massacre / Jun '94 / Plastic Head

Soul Children

FRICTION/ BEST OF TWO WORLDS
I'll be the other woman / What's happening baby / Can't let you go / It's out of my hands / Just one moment / We're gettin' too close / Love makes it right / Bring it here / Thanks for a precious nothing / Put your world in my world (best of two worlds) / Give me one good reason / Got to get away from it all / Hang ups of holding on / Wrap it up tonight / Let's make a sweet thing sweeter / Finish me off / Don't break away
CD ____ CDSXD 056
Stax / Jun '93 / Pinnacle

SINGLES, THE/OPEN DOOR POLICY
Don't take my kindness for weakness / It ain't always what you do (it's who you let see you do it) / Hold on I'm comin' / Make it good / Ridin' on love's merry go-round / Love is a hurtin' thing / Poem on the school house door / Come back kind of love / Signed, sealed, delivered (I'm yours) / I don't know what this world is coming to / Hearsay / Stir up the boogie, Part II / Who you used to be / Strangers / Summer in the shade / Can't give up a good thing / Butt la rose / Hard living with a man / believing
CD ____ CDSXD 101
Stax / Jan '94 / Pinnacle

Soul Coughing

IRRESISTIBLE BLISS
Super bon bon / Soft serve / White girl / Soundtrack to Mary / Lazybones / 4 out of 5 / Paint / Disseminated / Collapse / Sleepless / Idiot kings / How many cans
CD ____ 8287592
Slash / Apr '97 / PolyGram

RUBY VROOM
Is Chicago, is not Chicago / Sugar free jazz / Casiotone nation / Blue eyed devil / Bus to Beelzebug / True dreams of Wichita / Screenwriter's blues / Moon Sammy / Supra genius / City of motors / Uh zoom zip / Down to this / Mr. Bitterness / Janine
CD ____ 8285552
Slash / Sep '94 / PolyGram

Soul, David

BEST OF DAVID SOUL, THE
Don't give up on us / Tattler / Silver lady / I wish I was / It sure brings out the love in your eyes / Seem to miss so much (coalminer's song) / Let's have a quiet night in / Going in with my eyes open / One more mountain to climb / Topanga / 1927 Kansas city / Landlord / Nobody but a fool or a preacher / Bird on the wire
CD ____ MCCD 152
Music Club / Feb '94 / Disc / THE

Soul Defenders

SOUL DEFENDERS AT STUDIO ONE
CD ____ CDHB 066
Heartbeat / Jun '91 / ADA / Direct / Greensleeves / Jet Star

Soul Family Sensation

BURGER HABIT
CD ____ TPLP 45CD
One Little Indian / Sep '93 / Pinnacle

NEW WAVE
CD ____ TPLP 35CD
One Little Indian / Sep '91 / Pinnacle

Soul For Real

CANDY RAIN
Candy rain / Every little thing I do / All in my mind / If you want it / I wanna be your friend / Ain't no sunshine / Spend the night / I don't know / I fonly you knew / Thinking of you / Piano interlude
CD ____ MCD 11125
MCA / Mar '95 / BMG

FOR LIFE
Stay / Never felt this way / You just don't know / Love you so / Let's stay together / Good to you / Being with you / Leavin' / Where do we go / I'm coming home / Your love is calling / I don't wanna say goodbye / Can't you tell
CD ____ UPTD 53012
Universal / Sep '96 / BMG

Soul Generation

BATTLE OF THE BANDS (Soul Generation/The Joneses)
That's the way it's gotta be (body and soul): *Soul Generation* / Ray of hope: *Soul Generation* / Super fine: *Soul Generation* / Praying for a miracle: *Soul Generation* / Million dollars: *Soul Generation* / In your way: *Soul Generation* / Wait so long: *Soul Generation* / Key to your heart: *Soul Generation* / Sweet thing: *Soul Generation* / I wonder what she's doing: *Soul Generation* / Baby (there is nothing you can do): *Joneses* / Pretty, pretty: *Joneses* / Pull my string: *Joneses* / Hold up: *Joneses* / I can't see what you see in me: *Joneses* / Mary Mary: *Joneses* / Lovin' you: *Joneses* / She loves you: *Joneses* / Sweet water boy: *Joneses* / Win your love: *Joneses*
CD ____ NEMCD 930
Sequel / Jul '97 / BMG

Soul II Soul

SOUL II SOUL VOL.1 - CLUB CLASSICS
Keep on movin' / Back to life / Feel free / Live rap / Dance / Jazzie's groove / Fairplay / Happiness / Holdin' on Bambelea / African dance / Acapella
CD ____ DIXCD 82
10 / Mar '89 / EMI

SOUL II SOUL VOL.2 - 1990 A NEW DECADE
Get a life / Jazzie B / Daddae Harvey / Love comes through / People / Missing you / Courtney blows / 1990 a new decade / Dreams a dream / Time (untitled) / In the heat of the night / Our time has now come / Nomsa caluza / Sonti mndebele

CD DIXCD 90
10 / Apr '92 / EMI

SOUL II SOUL VOL.3 - JUST RIGHT
Joy / Take me higher / Storm / Direction / Just right / Move me no mountain / Intelligence / Future / Mood / Everywhere
CD DIXCD 100
10 / Apr '92 / EMI

SOUL II SOUL VOL.4 - THE CLASSIC SINGLES 1988-1993
Back to life / Keep on movin' / Get a life / Dreams a dream / Missing you / Just right / Move me no mountain / People / Fairplay / Jazzie's groove / Wish / Joy / Keep on movin' (mixes) / Back to life (mixes)
CD CDV 2724
Virgin / Oct '93 / EMI

SOUL II SOUL VOL.5 - BELIEVE
Love enuff / Ride on / How long / Feeling / Universal love / Be a man / Zion / Don't you dream / Game dunn / Sunday / Pride / I care / B groove / Believe
CD CDV 2739
Virgin / Jul '95 / EMI

SOUL II SOUL VOL.6 - TIME TO CHANGE
CD CID 8060
Island / Sep '97 / PolyGram

Soul Immigrants

HEALTHY VIBE FOR A MOOD WORLDWIDE, A
Should I hold out / Tribe of love / Just another wasted live / Tension in the city / Transforming me / High on love / Keep on striving / Half the world / Warming up / Earl's tribute
CD LIP 89472
Lipstick / Feb '97 / Vital/SAM

Soul, Jimmy

IF YOU WANT TO BE HAPPY (The Very Best Of Jimmy Soul)
If you want to be happy / I can't hold out any longer / Some kinda nut / Twistin' Matilda (and the channel) / Take me to Los Angeles / Call me / When I get my car / Everybody's gone ape / Guess things happen that way / She's alright / Church street in the summertime / Church street in summertime / I want to know if you love me / You're nothin' / I hate you baby / My little room / You can't have your cake / I know why dreamers cry / Hands off / I love you so / Treat 'em rough / I need your love / Tell me why / Don't release me / When Matilda comes / Go 'way Christina
CD CDCHD 593
Ace / Jan '96 / Pinnacle

Soul Junk

1953
CD HMS 2362
Homestead / Nov '96 / Cargo / SRD

Soul Oddity

TONE CAPSULE
Mezzo modular / Welcome back to earth / Little alien / People party / Freq shift / Clipped / Soul communication / DJ Tokyo / Cruxx / Fugue
CD ASW 6173
Astralwerks / Jun '96 / Cargo / Vital

Soul Station

CUT'N THE GROOVE
CD YRB 004
Yardbird Suite / Jun '97 / Timewarp

Soul Stirrers

HEAVEN IS MY HOME
Christ is all / He's my rock (wait on Jesus) / In a few more days / Golden bells / Sinner run to Jesus / Heaven is my home (take 1) / Heaven is my home (Take 2) / Till then / Out on a hill / Swing low, sweet chariot / Loved ones are waiting / Love of God / When the gates swing open / Lord laid his hands on me / That's all I need to know / My life belongs to him / There's not a friend like Jesus / Heaven is my home
CD CDCHD 478
Ace / Jul '93 / Pinnacle

JESUS GAVE ME WATER
Jesus gave me water / Christ is all / Come let us go back to god / I'm on the firing line / How far am I from canaan / Jesus done just what he said / He's my rock (wait on jesus) / Joy joy to my soul / I'm gonna build on that shore / Until Jesus calls me home / Jesus will lead me to that promised land / It wont' be long / Let me go home / Someday somewhere / Jesus paid the debt / End of my journey / He's my friend / I have a friend above all others / I gave up everything to follow him / Come and go to that land / Any day now / Jesus I'll never forget / All right now / Pray / Come to go to that land / I'm so happy in the service of the lord
CD CDCHD 464
Ace / Mar '93 / Pinnacle

LAST MILE OF THE WAY, THE
Last mile of the way / Mean old way / That's heaven to me / Were you there (false starts) / Were you there / Lord remember me / Pilgrim of sorrow / He's my guide / He's my guide (incomplete) / Last mile of the way (incomplete) / All right now / He'll make a way / Jesus I'll never forget / Come and go to that land / Just as I am / He'll welcome me / He's my friend / Jesus paid the debt / Jesus will lead me to that promised land / Jesus will lead me to that promised land / It won't be very long / How far am I from Canaan (incomplete) / How far am I from Canaan / Let me go home
CD CDCHD 563
Ace / Mar '94 / Pinnacle

Soul Syndicate

MOODIE DUB VOL.1 (Soul Syndicate & Black Slate)
CD MMLP 952
Moodie / Mar '94 / Jet Star / SRD

MOODIE IN DUB VOL.3
CD MMCD 1032
Moodie / Sep '94 / Jet Star / SRD

Soul Train

JAZZ IN SWEDEN 1986
CD 1335
Caprice / Feb '90 / ADA / Cadillac / CM / Complete/Pinnacle

Soul Whirling Somewhere

EATING THE SEA
CD HY 39100892
Hyperium / Apr '94 / Cargo / Plastic Head

Souled American

FROZEN
CD EFA 121072
Moll / Dec '94 / SRD

NOTES CAMPFIRE
CD EFA 121192
Moll / Feb '97 / SRD

Souls At Zero

TASTE FOR THE PEVERSE, A
CD 086272CTR
Edel / Oct '95 / Pinnacle

Souls Of Mischief

93 TIL INFINITY
CD CHIP 138
Jive / Oct '93 / Pinnacle

NO MAN'S LAND
CD CHIP 163
Jive / Oct '95 / Pinnacle

Soulside

SOON COME HAPPY
CD DISCHORD 51
Dischord / Feb '91 / SRD

Soumah, Momo Wandel

GUINEE MATCHOWE
CD 926532
BUDA / Jul '96 / Discovery

Sound

SHOCK OF DAYLIGHT
CD RENCD 1
Warzone / Mar '96 / RTM/Disc

THUNDER UP
CD CDBIAS 053
Play It Again Sam / Apr '87 / Discovery / Plastic Head / Vital

Sound Factory

DANCE HITS FOR KIDS
Wannabe / Quit playing games / Freedom / Mysterious girl / Sexy eyes / Soldier soldier / Macarena / Where do you go / Who do you think you are / Be my lover / Ooh aah just a little bit / Ready or not / Little boy / 2 Become 1
CD KI 881312
Disky / Jul '97 / Disky / THE

Sound Information

COLLECTION, THE
CD EBSC 005
Echo Beach / Jan '97 / Cargo / Shellshock/Disc

Soundgarden

BADMOTORFINGER
Rusty cage / Outshined / Slaves and bulldozers / Jesus christ pose / Face pollution / Somewhere / Searching with my good eye closed / Room a thousand years wide / Mind riot / Drawing flies / Holy water / New damage
CD 3953742
A&M / Oct '91 / PolyGram

DOWN ON THE UPSIDE
Applebite / Never the machine forever / Tighter and tighter / No attention / Switch opens / Overfloater / Unkind / Boot camp / Rhinosaur / Zero chance / Dusty / Ty Cobb / Blow up the outside world / Burden in my hand / Never named
CD 5405262
A&M / May '96 / PolyGram

LOUDER THAN LOVE
Ugly truth / Hands all over / Gun / Power trip / Get on the snake / Full on Kevin's Mom / Loud love / I wake / Now wrong no right / Uncovered / Big dumb sex
CD CDA 5252
A&M / Sep '89 / PolyGram

LOUDER THAN LOVE/ BADMOTORFINGER (2CD Set)
CD CDA 24118
A&M / Oct '93 / PolyGram

SCREAMING LIFE
CD SPCD 12
Sub Pop / Dec '96 / Cargo / Greyhound / Shellshock/Disc

SCREAMING LIFE/FOPP
Hunted down / Entering / Tears to forget / Nothing to say / Little Joe / Hand of God / Kingdom of come / Swallow my pride / Fopp / Fopp (dub)
CD SPCD 12A/B
Sub Pop / Feb '94 / Cargo / Greyhound / Shellshock/Disc

SUPERUNKNOWN
Let me drown / My wave / Fell on black days / Mailman / Superunknown / Head down / Black hole sun / Spoonman / Limo wreck / Day I tried to live / Kickstand / Fresh tendrils / 4th of July / Half / Like suicide / She likes surprises
CD 5402152
A&M / Mar '94 / PolyGram

ULTRAMEGA OK
Flower / All your lies / 665 / Beyond the wheel / 667 / Mood for trouble / Circle of power / He didn't / Smokestack lightnin' / Nazi driver / Head injury / Incessant mace / One minute of silence
CD SST 201CD
SST / Nov '88 / Plastic Head

Sounds From The Ground

KIN
CD WWCD 14
Wibbly Wobbly / Nov '95 / SRD

Sounds Incorporated

SOUNDS INCORPORATED
Spartans / Detroit / Rinky dink / My little red book / Hall of the mountain king / One mint julep / Last night / Crane / Emily / Mogambo / Bullets / Spanish Harlem / Little bird / If we lived on top of a mountain / Old and the new / Grab this thing / Boil over / I'm comin' through / Fingertips / I'm in love again
CD SEECD 371
See For Miles/C5 / Feb '97 / Pinnacle

Sounds Of Blackness

AFRICA TO AMERICA: THE JOURNEY OF THE DRUM
Hold on (Part 1) / I'm going all the way / Ah been 'buked (Part 1) / I believe / Hold on (Part 2) / Everything's gonna be alright / Sun up to sundown / Lord will make a way / He took away all my pain / Place in my heart / Harder they are, the bigger they fall / Drum (Africa to America) / Royal Kingdoms/Rise/ My Native Land / Very special love / Strange fruit / Black butterfly / You've taken by blues and gone / Livin' the blues / Ah been 'buked (Part 2) / I'm going all the way (Brixton flavour)
CD 5490092
Perspective / Apr '94 / PolyGram

EVOLUTION OF GOSPEL
Chains / Optimistic / Ah been workin' / Pressure (pt.1) / Testify / Gonna be free one day / Stand / Pressure (pt.2) / Your wish is my command / Hallelujah Lord / We give you thanks / He holds the future / What shall I call him / Better watch your behaviour / Please take my hand / I'll fly away / Harambee
CD 3953612
Perspective / Oct '91 / PolyGram

NIGHT BEFORE CHRISTMAS, THE
Born in a manger / Soul holidays / It's Christmas time / Away in a manger / O come all ye faithful (Adeste Fidelis) / O' Holy night / Peace on earth for everyone / Children go / Santa's comin' to town / Dance, chitlins, dance / Holiday love / Santa won't you come by / Jolly one's here / Dash away all/ Reindeer revolt / Give us a chance / Santa watch yo' step / Why don't you believe in me / Merry Christmas to the world
CD 5490002
Perspective / Oct '92 / PolyGram

TIME FOR HEALING
Africana / Spirit / We are gonna make it through / Hold on (change is coming) / Love will never change / Love train / God cares / Hold on (don't let go) / Crisis / We are gonna make it through / You can make it if you try / Blackness blues / Spiritual medley / So far away / Familiar waters / Time for healing / We are gonna make it through / Kwanzaa-umoja-uhuru
CD 5490292
Perspective / May '97 / PolyGram

Sounds Of Christmas ...

SWINGING CHRISTMAS, A (Sounds Of Christmas Orchestra)
Jingle bells / Sleigh ride / Merry Christmas darling / It's the most wonderful time of the year / Johnny bring the pine tree in / Carol of the bells / I heard the bells on Christmas day / Caroling, caroling / Deck the halls / O Tannenbaum / We wish you a Merry Christmas / O come, O come Emmanuel / What child is this / Gentle Mary laid her child / Angels from the realms of Glory / Christmas is / Silver bells / Mistletoe & holly / Christmas is the warmest time of year / Toyland / Sleep well little children / We need a little Christmas / It's beginning to look a lot like Christmas / Christmas waltz / Joy to the world / God rest ye merry gentlemen / Angels we have heard on high / Silent night / Christmas song (chestnuts roasting on an open fire) / I'll be home for Christmas / White Christmas / Do you hear what I hear / It came upon a midnight clear / O little town of Bethlehem / First Noel / Hark the herald angels sing / Winter wonderland / Let it snow, let it snow, let it snow / Have yourself a merry little Christmas
CD CDVIP 141
Virgin VIP / Nov '96 / EMI

Sounds Of The Future

FEAR OF THE FUTURE EP
CD FORM 28
Formation / Sep '93 / SRD

Sounds Orchestral

BEST OF SOUNDS ORCHESTRAL, THE
CD PLSCD 225
Pulse / Jul '97 / BMG

CAST YOUR FATE TO THE WIND
CD NEMCD 617
Sequel / Nov '91 / BMG

EASY PROJECT VOL.5, THE (Sounds Rare)
Have faith in your love / Sounds like Jacques / Go home girl / Do nothin' 'til you hear from me / Porcelain / Ain't that peculiar / Boy and a girl / Fifth Avenue walkdown / Our love story / From Nashville with love / Image / Gloria Gloria / Blue tango / Blue bolero / West of Carnaby / Hopping dance / Black is black / I couldn't live without your love / Mas que nada / Baubles bangles and beads
CD NEMCD 992
Sequel / Aug '97 / BMG

SOUNDS ORCHESTRAL MEETS JAMES BOND
Thunderball / Solitaire / Goldfinger / Mr. Kiss Kiss Bang Bang / Blues for pussy / Mr. Oddjob / Moonshot / James Bond theme / Spectre / From Russia With Love / Kissy Suzuki / 007 theme
CD NEBCD 908
Sequel / Sep '96 / BMG

Soundtech Steel Orchestra

BANKS
CD CCD 0022
CRS / Apr '96 / ADA / Direct / Jet Star

Soup Dragons

HOTWIRED
CD BLRCD 15
Big Life / May '92 / Mo's Music Machine / Pinnacle / Prime

HYDROPHONIC
One way street / Don't get down (Get down) / Do you care / May the force be with you / Contact high / All messed up / Time is now / Freeway / Rest in peace / JF junkie / Automatic speed queen / Out of here / Motherfunker / Painkilla / Cruel lust / Black and blues / Hypersonic re-entry
CD 5227812
Mercury / Sep '94 / PolyGram

LOVEGOD
CD SOUPCD 2R
Big Life / Jul '90 / Mo's Music Machine / Pinnacle / Prime

Source

ORGANISED NOISE
Vagator / Eclipse / Neuromancer / Real thing / Squeeze / Analysis / Release it / Beyond time
CD RS 93005CD
R&S / May '93 / Vital

Source Experience

DIFFERENT JOURNEYS
Unkown territory / Gate 41 / Point zero / Pressure drop / Diatonic shift / Intruder / X-ray / Night shift / Voices of the spirit
CD RS 94056CD
R&S / Nov '94 / Vital

Souskay

SOUSKAY
CD CD 69812

Melodie / '91 / ADA / Discovery / Grapevine/PolyGram / Greensleeves / Jet Star

South African National ...

CLASSIC UNCHAINED MELODIES (South African National Symphony Orchestra)
CD _____ CDSGP 1098
Prestige / Sep '95 / Else / Total/BMG

South, Eddie

CLASSICS 1923-1937
CD _____ CLASSICS 707
Classics / Jul '93 / Discovery / Jazz Music

CLASSICS 1937-1941
CD _____ CLASSICS 737
Classics / Feb '94 / Discovery / Jazz Music

EDDIE SOUTH IN PARIS 1929 & 1937
Doin' the raccoon / Two guitars / Eddie's blues / Sweet Georgia Brown / Oh lady be good / Dinah / Daphne / Somebody loves me / I can't believe that you're in love with me / Swing interpretation of the first movement of the concerto / Fiddle blues / Improvisations on the first movement of the concerto
CD _____ DRGCD 8405
DRG / Sep '93 / Discovery / New Note/ Pinnacle

South 'Frisco Jazz Band

BIG BEAR STOMP
CD _____ SOSCD 1307
Stomp Off / Jul '96 / Jazz Music / Wellard

BROKEN PROMISES
CD _____ SOSCD 1180
Stomp Off / Aug '90 / Jazz Music / Wellard

GOT EVERYTHING, DON'T WANT ANYTHING
CD _____ SOSCD 1240
Stomp Off / Nov '92 / Jazz Music / Wellard

SAGE HEN STRUT
CD _____ SOSCD 1143
Stomp Off / Apr '94 / Jazz Music / Wellard

SOUTH 'FRISCO JAZZ BAND VOL.1
CD _____ MMRCCD 4
Merry Makers / Feb '94 / Jazz Music

SOUTH 'FRISCO JAZZ BAND VOL.1
CD _____ SOSCD 1027
Stomp Off / Dec '94 / Jazz Music / Wellard

SOUTH 'FRISCO JAZZ BAND VOL.2
CD _____ MMRCCD 7
Merry Makers / Feb '94 / Jazz Music

THESE CATS ARE DIGGIN' US
CD _____ SOSCD 1035
Stomp Off / Mar '95 / Jazz Music / Wellard

South, Svenn

SOUTH CONNECTION
CD _____ LAB 001
Lab / Sep '96 / Shellshock/Disc

Souther, Richard

ILLUMINATION
CD _____ SK 62853
Sony Classical / Jun '97 / Sony

Southern Culture On The Skids

DITCH DIGGIN'
CD _____ SH 21142
Safe House / Nov '96 / Cargo

FOR LOVERS ONLY
CD _____ SH 21082
Safe House / Nov '96 / Cargo

GIRL FIGHT
CD _____ SFTRI 266CD
Sympathy For The Record Industry / Dec '96 / Cargo / Greyhound / Plastic Head

Southern Exposure

SMALL TOWN
Little company / Walls of time / Wheel hoss / Gypsy breeze / African breeze / I'm just a used to be / Green light / Moonshine whiskey / Wild Bill Jones / Bonaparte's retreat / Small town
CD _____ GRP 002
Get Real Productions / Sep '93 / Get Real Productions

Southern Pacific

COUNTY LINE
CD _____ 7599258952
WEA / Jan '96 / Warner Music

ZUMA
Midnight highway / Honey I dare you / New shade of blue / Dream on / Invisible man / Wheels on the line / Just hang on / All is lost / Bail out / Trail of tears
CD _____ 7599256092
WEA / Jan '96 / Warner Music

Southern Sons

DEEP SOUTH GOSPEL
CD _____ ALCD 2802
Alligator / Oct '93 / ADA / CM / Direct

SOUTHERN SONS 1941-1944/ RICKMONDS HARMONISING QUARTET 1943 (Southern Sons/Rickmonds Harmonising Quartet)
CD _____ DOCD 5492
Document / Nov '96 / ADA / Hot Shot / Jazz Music

Southern, Jeri

MEETS COLE PORTER/AT THE CRESCENDO
Don't look at me that way / Get out of town / Looking at you / It's all right with me / Let's fly away / Why shouldn't I / You're the top / After you / Which / I concentrate on you / It's bad for me / Weren't we fools / I thought of you last night / I get a kick out of you / Dancing on the ceiling / Blame it on my youth / Remind me / You better go now / I'm just a woman / Something I dreamed last night / Nice work if you can get it / When I fall in love
CD _____ CTMCD 112
EMI / Mar '97 / EMI

SOUTHERN BREEZE
CD _____ FSRCD 104
Fresh Sound / Jan '93 / Discovery / Jazz Music

YOU BETTER GO NOW/WHEN YOUR HEART'S ON FIRE
You better go now / Give me time / Something I dreamed last night / Man that got away / When I fall love / Just got to have him around / Dancing on the ceiling / Speak softly to me / What good am I without you / I thought of you last night / That ole devil called love again / Remind me / Smoke gets in your eyes / Can I forget you / Little girl blue / I remember you / He was good to me / You're driving me crazy / You make me feel so young / Someone to watch over me / Autumn in New York / My ship / No more / Let me love you
CD _____ JASCD 602
Jasmine / Aug '96 / Conifer/BMG / Hot Shot / TKO Magnum

Southern, Sheila

WITH LOVE (Southern, Sheila & Royal Philharmonic Orchestra)
What are you doing the rest of your life / My funny valentine / My coloring book / How beautiful is night / Nearness of you / Losing my mind / Country girl / My one and only love / Memory / Touch me in the morning / She's out of my life
CD _____ CDSIV 1107
Horatio Nelson / Nov '96 / Disc

Southside Johnny

BEST OF SOUTHSIDE JOHNNY & THE ASBURY JUKES, THE (Southside Johnny & The Asbury Jukes)
I don't want to go home / Fever / This time it's for real / Love on the wrong side of town / Without love / Having a party / Got to get you off my mind / Snatchin' it back / Sweeter than honey / You mean so much to me / Little by little / Got to be a better way home / This time baby's gone for good / Hearts of stone / Take it inside / Talk to me / Next to you / Trapped again
CD _____ 4735882
Sony Music / '89 / Sony

SPITTIN' FIRE (2CD Set)
It's been a long time / Talk to me / Fever / Blue radio / Trapped again / We'll make the world stand still / Love on the wrong side of town / Day in and day out / Wild horses / Little Calcutta / Fade away / It's all over now / Hoochie coochie man / I played the fool / Lovey dovey / Coming back / All night long / I don't want to go home
CD Set _____ 120272
Musidisc UK / Feb '97 / Grapevine/ PolyGram

Souvenir, William

NA'F MI WANG
CD _____ MWCD 3012
Music & Words / Aug '96 / ADA / Direct

TIN TELE, A
CD _____ MWCD 3010
Music & Words / Jul '95 / ADA / Direct

Soviet Army Chorus

POPULAR SELECTIONS (Soviet Army Chorus & Band)
CD _____ MCD 71500
Monitor / Jun '93 / CM

SONG OF YOUTH (Soviet Army Chorus & Band)
Song of youth / Birch tree in a field did stand / Far away / Song of the Volga boatmen / You are always beautiful / Along Peter's street / Tipperary / Ah lovely night / Kamarinskaya / Annie Laurie / Song of the plains / Kalinka / Bandura / Oh no, John / Snow flakes / Ukrainian poem / Soldier's chorus
CD _____ CDC 747 833 2
Angel / Aug '87 / EMI

Soviet France

ELSTRE
CD _____ CHARRMCD 5
Charrm / Jul '90 / Plastic Head

IN.VERSION
CD _____ CHARRMCD 24
Charrm / Oct '96 / Plastic Head

MOHNOMISCHE
CD _____ CHARRMCD 4
Charrm / '84 / Plastic Head

POPULAR SOVIET SONGS AND YOUTH CULTURE
CD _____ STCD 024
Staalplaat / Sep '95 / Vital/SAM

Sovory

SOVORY
CD _____ 5277512
Polydor / Oct '96 / PolyGram

SOW

JE M'AIME
CD _____ 39100932
Hyperium / Jan '97 / Cargo / Plastic Head

Soweto String Quartet

ZEBRA CROSSING
Mbayi mbayi / Zebra crossing / Zulu lullaby / Kwela / Paul Simon 'Graceland' collection / Bossa baroque / Shut up and listen / St. Agnes and the burning train / Kadeni kwazulu / Nytilo nytilo / Where were you taking me to / Nkosi sikelel' iAfrica / Mbayi mbayi
CD _____ 74321268652
RCA Victor / May '96 / BMG

SPA

SPA
Made in heaven / It looks like rain / Fellow ship of man / I've had you all / Nice nice nice / Reprise / Just a ride / Chemical chance / DNA / Wing / Hog heaven / Well / Christians who kill
CD _____ NSKYCD 004
Northern Sky / Sep '97 / Direct / Pinnacle

Space

VERY BEST OF SPACE, THE
Magic fly / Carry on, turn me on / Air force / Save your love for me / Space media / Deeper zone / Baby's paradise / Let me know the wonder / Blue tears / Secret dreams
CD _____ QED 143
Tring / Nov '96 / Tring

Space

SPIDERS
Neighbourhood / Mister psycho / Female of the species / Money / Me and you vs the world / Lovechild of the queen / No-one understands / Voodoo roller / Drop dead / Dark clouds / Major pager / Kill me / Charlie M / Growler
CD _____ GUTCD 1
Gut / Sep '96 / Total/BMG

Space Cowboys

LOCKED 'N' LOADED
CD _____ RTD 19512672
Our Choice / Nov '92 / Pinnacle

Space Streakings

7-TOKU
CD _____ GR 18CD
Skingraft / Nov '94 / SRD

Spacebow

BIG WAVES
CD _____ NW 50012
Extreme / May '95 / Vital/SAM

Spacebox

KICK UP
CD _____ CTCD 025
Captain Trip / Jul '97 / Greyhound

Spaceheads

ROUND THE OUTSIDE (Live)
CD _____ DBC 208CD
Darkblue / Mar '97 / Cargo

Spacehog

RESIDENT ALIEN
Zeroes / To be a millionaire, was it likely / Spacehog / Starside / In the meantime / Candyman / Never coming down / Shipwrecked / Last dictator / Only a few / Never coming down / Cruel to be kind / Space is the place
CD _____ 7559618342
Elektra / Feb '97 / Warner Music

Spacemaid

SUPERCOOL
Baby come on / Supercool / Girl who sold the world / Beautiful boys beautiful girls / Boy racer / I see comets / Just a song / Do you remember rock 'n' roll radio / Fake fur $50 vamp / Bigger than life / Pink hotel
CD _____ STARC 108
Big Star / Sep '97 / Grapevine/PolyGram

Spacemen 3

1 + 1 = 3 (2CD Set)
CD Set _____ NTMCDD 534
Nectar / Mar '97 / Pinnacle

DREAM WEAPON
CD _____ ORBIT 001CD
Space Age / Oct '95 / Plastic Head

FOR ALL THE FUCKED UP CHILDREN OF THE WORLD
CD _____ SFTRI 1368CD
Sympathy For The Record Industry / May '95 / Cargo / Greyhound / Plastic Head

LIVE IN EUROPE
CD _____ ORBIT 002CD
Space Age / Oct '95 / Plastic Head

LOSING TOUCH
CD _____ MR 011CD
Munster / Apr '92 / Cargo / Greyhound / Plastic Head

PEFORMANCE
CD _____ REF 33011
Fire / Oct '91 / Pinnacle / RTM/Disc

PERFECT PRESCRIPTIONS
Take me to the other side / Walking with Jesus / Ode to street hassle / Ecstasy symphony / Transparent radiation / Feel so good / Things'll never be the same / Come down easy / Call the doctor
CD _____ REF 33006
Fire / Oct '91 / Pinnacle / RTM/Disc

PLAYING WITH FIRE
CD _____ FIRE 33016
Fire / Oct '91 / Pinnacle / RTM/Disc

RECURRING
Big City / Just to see you smile / I love you / Set me free/I've got the key / Set me free / Why couldn't I see / Just to see you smile / When tomorrow hits / Feel so sad / Hypnotised / Sometimes / Feeling just fine (head full of shit) / Billy Whizz/Blue 1 / Drive/ Feel so sad / Feeling just fine (alternative mix)
CD _____ FIRE 33023
Fire / Oct '91 / Pinnacle / RTM/Disc

REVOLUTION OR HEROIN
CD _____ FRIGHT 053
Fierce / Oct '95 / RTM/Disc

SOUND OF CONFUSION
CD _____ RED 33005
Fire / Oct '91 / Pinnacle / RTM/Disc

SPACEMEN ARE GO
CD _____ BCD 4044
Bomp / Jan '97 / Cargo / Greyhound / RTM/Disc / Shellshock/Disc

TAKING DRUGS TO MAKE MUSIC
CD _____ BCD 4047
Bomp / Jan '97 / Cargo / Greyhound / RTM/Disc / Shellshock/Disc

TRANSLUCENT FLASHBACKS (The Glass Singles)
CD _____ FLIPCD 003
Fire / Jun '95 / Pinnacle / RTM/Disc

Spacer

ATLAS EARTH
CD _____ PUSSYCD 002
Pussy Foot / Mar '96 / RTM/Disc

Spaceshits

WINTER DANCE PARTY
CD _____ SFTRI 488CD
Sympathy For The Record Industry / Jul '97 / Cargo / Greyhound / Plastic Head

Spacetime Continuum

EMIT ECAPS
Iform / Kairo / Simm City / Funkyar / Swing fantasy / Movement no.2 / Vertigo / Twister / Pod / String of pearls
CD _____ REFCD 7
Reflective / Jan '96 / RTM/Disc / SRD

REMIT RECAPS
CD _____ REFCD 9
CD _____ ASW 61002
Astralwerks / Nov '96 / Cargo / Vital

Spaceways

TRAD
Time changes space / At home with the snake / City / Charlie X / Pink panza / Rice / Requiem for Ra / Kurosawa meets slow Charlie / Crimes / Riding on the tip / Man who fell to Easton / Death of a silent planet / Pinhead plutonium / Better / Tyner
CD _____ COTCD 002
Cup Of Tea / Sep '96 / Vital

Spacewurm

ARMY OF GOD
CD VC 111CD
Vinyl Communication / Jun '97 / Cargo / Greyhound / Plastic Head

Spady, Clarence

NATURE OF THE BEAST
Baby baby baby / Answer to the man / Change my way of livin' / Nature of the beast / Bad axe / Built for comfort / Picture of love / Hi-heeled sneakers / Good fool is hard to find / Blues walk / Gospel blues
CD ECD 260802
Evidence / Sep '96 / ADA / Cadillac / Harmonia Mundi

Spahn Ranch

ARCHITECTURE
CD CLP 9977
Cleopatra / Apr '97 / Cargo / Greyhound / Plastic Head / RTM/Disc / SRD

BLACKMAIL STARTERS KIT
CD CLEO 94772
Cleopatra / Jun '94 / Cargo / Greyhound / Plastic Head / RTM/Disc / SRD

BREATH & TAXES
CD CDZOT 116
Zoth Ommog / Aug '94 / Cargo / Plastic Head

Spain

BLUE MOODS OF SPAIN
CD 729262
Restless / Sep '96 / Vital

BLUE MOODS OF SPAIN, THE
So it's true / Ten nights / Dreaming of love / Untitled / Her used-to-been / Ray of light / World of blue / I lied / Spiritual
CD 729102
Restless / Sep '95 / Vital

Spand, Charlie

CHARLIE SPAND 1929-1931
CD DOCD 5108
Document / Nov '92 / ADA / Hot Shot / Jazz Music

Spandau Ballet

BEST OF SPANDAU BALLET, THE
To cut a long story short / Freeze / Musclebound / Chant no.1 (I don't need this pressure on) / Paint me down / She loved like diamond / Instinction / Lifeline / True / Gold / Only when you leave / I'll fly for you / Highly strung / Round and round / Fight for ourselves / Through the barricades / How many lies / Raw / Be free with your love
CD CCD 1894
Chrysalis / Sep '91 / EMI

BEST OF SPANDAU BALLET, THE (18 Original Hits/3CD Set)
Only when you leave / Age of blows / Foundation / Coffee club / Nature of the beast / Glow / Musclebound / Pleasure / Heaven is a secret / Code of love / Pharaoh / Always in the back of my mind / Highly strung / Revenge for love / Mandolin / Missionary / Innocence and science / With the pride
CD Set LAD 873262
Disky / Nov '96 / Disky / THE

COLLECTION, THE
CD CDGOLD 1081
EMI Gold / Apr '97 / EMI

HEART LIKE A SKY
Be free with your love / Crashed into love / Big feeling / Matter of time / Motivator / Raw / Empty spaces / Windy town / Handful of dust
CD 4844722
Columbia / Jul '97 / Sony

JOURNEYS TO GLORY
To cut a long story short / Reformation / Mandolin / Muscle bound / Ages of blows / Freeze / Confused / Toys
CD CDGOLD 1046
EMI Gold / Jul '96 / EMI
CD DC 875512
Disky / May '97 / Disky / THE

PARADE
Only when you leave / Highly strung / I'll fly for you / Nature of the beast / Revenge for love / Always in the back of my mind / With the pride / Round and round
CD CDGOLD 1010
EMI Gold / Mar '96 / EMI

SINGLES COLLECTION, THE
Gold / Lifeline / Round and round / Only when you leave / Instinction / Highly strung / True / Communication / I'll fly for you / To cut a long story short / Chant no.1 (I don't need this pressure on) / She loved like diamond / Paint me down / Freeze / Musclebound
CD CCD 1498
Chrysalis / Apr '86 / EMI

THROUGH THE BARRICADES
Barricades - introduction / Cross the line / Man in chains / How many lies / Virgin / Fight for ourselves / Swept / Snakes and lovers / Through the barricades / With pride
CD 4502592
CBS / Feb '94 / Sony

TWELVE INCH MIXES
Gold / Lifeline / Round and round / Only when you leave / Instinction / Highly restrung / True / Communication / I'll fly for you / To cut a long story short / Chant no.1 (I don't need this pressure on) / She loved like diamond / Paint me down / Freeze / Musclebound
CD CCD 1574
Chrysalis / Feb '94 / EMI

Spaniels

GOODNITE SWEETHEART
CD CDGR 173
Charly / Jul '97 / Koch

Spanier, Herbie

ANTHOLOGY 1962-1993
CD JUST 552
Justin Time / Feb '94 / Cadillac / New Note/Pinnacle

Spanier, Muggsy

CLASSICS 1939-1942
CD CLASSICS 709
Classics / Jul '93 / Discovery / Jazz Music

CLASSICS 1939-1944
CD CD 14570
Jazz Portraits / May '95 / Jazz Music

CLASSICS 1944
CD CLASSICS 907
Classics / Nov '96 / Discovery / Jazz Music

GREAT 16 - MUGGSY SPANIER'S RAGTIME BAND
Relaxin' at the Touro / Mandy, make up your mind / Bluin' the blues / That da da strain / I wish I could shimmy like my sister Kate / At sundown / Lonesome road / Eccentric / At the jazz band ball / Dinah / Big butter and egg man / Livery stable blues / What did I do to be so black and blue / Riverboat shuffle / Someday sweetheart / Dippermouth blues
CD 74321130392
Bluebird / Sep '93 / BMG

MUGGSHOT
At Sundown / Baby, won't you please come home / Bluin' the blues / Bullfrog blues / Chicago / China boy / Dallas blues / Darktown strutters ball / Down to Steamboat Tennessee / Four or five times / Friars Point Shuffle / Hesitating blues / I wish I could shimmy like my sister Kate / I've found a new baby / Mobile blues / Nobody's sweetheart / Relaxin' at the Touro / Royal Garden blues / Sugar / That's a plenty / There'll be some changes made / Why can't it be poor little me / (I'll be glad when you're dead) you rascal you / You're bound to look like a monkey
CD CDAJA 5102
Living Era / Mar '93 / Select

MUGGSY SPANIER & TESCHEMACHER'S CHICAGOANS (Spanier, Muggsy & Frank Teschemaker)
CD VILCD 0012
Village Jazz / Nov '93 / Jazz Music / Target/BMG

MUGGSY SPANIER 1939 (The Ragtime Band Sessions)
Big butter and egg man / Someday sweetheart / Eccentric (That eccentric rag) / That da da strain / At the jazz band ball / I wish I could shimmy like my sister Kate / Dippermouth blues / Livery stable blues / Riverboat shuffle / Relaxin' at the Touro / At sundown / Bluin' the blues / Lonesome road / What did I do to be so black and blue / Mandy, make up your mind
CD 07863665502
Bluebird / Jun '95 / BMG

MUGGSY SPANIER ALL STARS (Spanier, Muggsy All Stars)
CD STCD 6033
Storyville / May '97 / Cadillac / Jazz Music / Wellard

MUGGSY SPANIER VOL.1 1924-1927
CD KJ 107FS
King Jazz / Oct '93 / Cadillac / Discovery / Jazz Music

MUGGSY SPANIER VOL.2 1928-1929
CD KJ 108FS
King Jazz / Oct '93 / Cadillac / Discovery / Jazz Music

MUGGSY, TESCH AND THE CHICAGOANS (Spanier, Muggsy & Frank Teschemaker)
CD VILCD 0142
Village Jazz / Aug '92 / Jazz Music / Target/BMG

Spanish Fly

ANYTHING YOU WANT
CD 9362459262
Warner Bros. / Jun '95 / Warner Music

FLY BY NIGHT (Original Ballet Soundtrack & Insert Tongue Here)
Movement no.1/Opening / Movement no.2/ Snake lady / Transition no.1 / Movement no.3/Sisters / Transition no.2 / Movement no.4/Pas De Deux / Movement no.5/End of the night / Some other sisters / Joshua prayer / Tongue insert/Tongue sandwich / Love song 110
CD AC 5024
Accurate / May '97 / Direct

RAGS TO BRITCHES
CD KFWCD 114
Knitting Factory / Feb '95 / Cargo / Plastic Head

Spanish Gipsy

CON AMOR
CD EUCD 1190
ARC / Apr '92 / ADA / ARC Music

Spann, Otis

BIGGEST THING SINCE COLOSSUS (Spann, Otis & Fleetwood Mac)
My love depends on you: *Spann, Otis* / Walkin': *Spann, Otis* / It was a big thing: *Spann, Otis* / Temperature is rising (1002 F): *Spann, Otis* / Dig you: *Spann, Otis* / No more doggin': *Spann, Otis* / Ain't nobody's business if I do: *Spann, Otis* / She needs some loving: *Spann, Otis* / I need some air: *Spann, Otis* / Someday baby: *Spann, Otis*
CD 4759722
Blue Horizon / Feb '95 / Sony

BLUES IS WHERE IT'S AT, THE
Popcorn man / Brand new house / Chicago blues / Steel mill blues / Down on Sarah street / Ain't nobody's business if I do / Nobody knows Chicago like I do / My home is on the Delta / Spann blues
CD BGOCD 221
Beat Goes On / Mar '94 / Pinnacle

BLUES NEVER DIE
Blues never die / I got a feeling / One more mile to go / Feeling good / After while / Dust my broom / Straighten up baby / Come on / Must have been the Devil / Lightning / I'm ready
CD OBCCD 530
Original Blues Classics / Nov '92 / Complete/Pinnacle / Wellard

BLUES OF OTIS SPANN, THE
Rock me Mama / Keep your hand out of my pocket / Sarah Street / Country boy / Meet me in the bottom / I got a feeling / You're gonna need my help / I came from Clarksdale / Spann's boogie / Blues don't like nobody / Pretty girls everywhere / Lost sheep in the fold / Jangle boogie / Natural days / Stirs me up
CD SEECD 369
See For Miles/C5 / Oct '93 / Pinnacle

BOTTOM OF THE BLUES, THE
Heart loaded with trouble / Diving duck / Shimmy baby / Looks like twins / I'm a fool / My man / Down to earth / Nobody knows / Dr. blues
CD BGOCD 92
Beat Goes On / Nov '90 / Pinnacle

CHICAGO BLUES
CD TCD 5005
Testament / Oct '94 / ADA / Koch

CRYIN' TIME
Home to Mississippi / Blues is a botheration / You said you'd be on time / Crying time / Blind man / Someday / Twisted snake / Green flowers / New boogaloo / Mule kicking in my stall
CD VMD 6514
Vanguard / Feb '96 / ADA / Pinnacle

GOOD MORNING MR. BLUES
CD APR 3016CD
Analogue Revival / Dec '96 / ADA

OTIS SPANN IS THE BLUES
Hard way / Take a little walk with me / Otis in the dark / Little boy blue / Country boy / Beat-up team / My daily wish / Great Northern stomp / I got rambling on my mind / Worried life blues
CD CCD 79001
Candid / Feb '97 / Cadillac / Direct / Jazz Music / Koch / Wellard

WALKING THE BLUES
It must have been the devil / Otis blues / Going down slow / Half ain't been told / Monkey face woman / This is the blues / Evil ways / Come day go day / Walking the blues / Bad condition / My home is on the delta
CD CCD 79025
Candid / Feb '97 / Cadillac / Direct / Jazz Music / Koch / Wellard

Spare Snare

LIVE AT HOME
Thorns (version 1) / Shine on now / Wired for sound / Super slinky / As a matter of fact / Skateboard punk rocker / Bugs / My better half / Call the birds / Thorns (version 2)
CD CHUTECD 005
Chute / May '95 / Vital

WESTFIELD LANE
CD ORE 8
Wabana / Feb '97 / Cargo

Sparklehorse

VIVA DIXIE SUBMARINE TRANSMISSIONPLOT
Homecoming queen / Weird sisters / 850 double pumper holley / Rainmaker / Spirit ditch / Tears on fresh fruit / Saturday / Cow / Little bastard choo choo / Hammering the cramps / Most beautiful widow in town / Heart of darkness / Ballad of a cold lost marble / Someday I will treat you good / Sad and beautiful world / Gasoline horseys
CD CDEST 2280
Capitol / May '96 / EMI

Sparkler

WICKER PARK
Hey long hair / I'll keep you warm / Discover / What are you waiting for / For you / Don't despair / Hey 17 / Motorcycle / You know who you are / Magic Lantern / Another star / Grand arrival
CD 74321441152
Revolution / May '97 / BMG

Sparkman, Steve

SMITH RIDGE (A Tribute To The Stanley Style)
CD COP 142CD
Copper Creek / Apr '96 / ADA

Sparkmarker

500 WATT BURNER
CD CRISIS 012
Crisis / Mar '97 / Plastic Head

Sparks

BIG BEAT
Big boy / I want to be like everybody else / Nothing to do / I bought Mississippi river / Fill-er up / Everybody's stupid / Thrown her away (and get a new one) / Confusion / Screwed up / White woman / I like girls / Tearing the place apart / Gone with the wind
CD IMCD 201
Island / Jul '94 / PolyGram

GRATUITOUS SAX AND SENSELESS VIOLINS
Gratuitous sax / When do I get to sing 'My Way' / (When I kiss you) I hear Charlie Parker playing / Frankly Scarlett I don't give a damn / I thought I told you to wait in the car / Hear no evil, see no evil, speak no evil / Now that I own the BBC / Tsui Hark / Ghost of Liberace / Let's go surfing / Senseless violins
CD 74321232672
Arista / Jun '97 / BMG

HALF NELSON
CD 8122713002
Atlantic / Jul '93 / Warner Music

IN THE SWING
This town ain't big enough for the both of us / Hasta manana Monsieur / Amateur hour / Lost and found / Never turn your back on mother earth / I like girls / I want to hold your hand / Get in the swing / Looks, looks, looks / England / Big boy / Something for the girl with everything / Marry me / Gone with the wind
CD 5500652
Spectrum / May '93 / PolyGram

INDISCREET
Hospitality on parade / Happy hunting ground / Without using hands / Get in the swing / Under the table with her / How are you getting home / Pineapple / Tits / This ain't 1918 / Lady is lingering / In the future / Looks, looks, looks / Miss the start, miss the end / Profile / I want to hold your hand / England
CD IMCD 200
Island / Jul '94 / PolyGram

INTERIOR DESIGN
So important / I just got back from heaven / Lots of reasons / You got a hold of my heart / Love-o-rama / Toughest girl in town / Let's make love / Stop me if you've heard this before / Walk down memory lane / Madonna / Big brass ring
CD CDTB 141
Thunderbolt / '88 / TKO Magnum

KIMONO MY HOUSE
This town ain't big enough for the both of us / Amateur hour / Falling in love with myself again / Here in heaven / Thank God it's not Christmas / Hasta manana Monsieur / Talent is an asset / Complaints / In my family / Equator / Barbecutie / Lost and found
CD IMCD 198
Island / Jul '94 / PolyGram

MAEL INTUITION (It's a Mael Mael Mael World/The Best Of The Sparks 1974-1976)
This town ain't big enough for the both of us / Hasta manana monsieur / Tearing the place apart / At home, at work, at play / Never turn your back on Mother Earth / Get in the swing / Amateur hour / Looks, looks, looks / Thanks but no thanks / Gone with

the wind / Something for the girl with everything / Thank God it's not Christmas
CD _______________ IMCD 88
Island / Feb '90 / PolyGram

PROPAGANDA
Propaganda / At home, at work, at play / Reinforcements / BC / Thanks but no thanks / Don't leave me alone with her / Never turn your back on Mother Earth / Something for the girl with everything / Achoo / Who don't like kids / Bon voyage / Alabamy right / Marry me
CD _______________ IMCD 199
Island / Jul '94 / PolyGram

SO IMPORTANT
CD _______________ 12571
Laserlight / Oct '95 / Target/BMG

Sparks Brothers

SPARKS BROTHERS 1932-1935
CD _______________ DOCD 5315
Document / Dec '94 / ADA / Hot Shot / Jazz Music

Sparks, Melvin

LEGENDS OF ACID JAZZ, THE
Thank you (Falettin' me be mice elf again) / I didn't know what time it was / Charlie Brown / Stinker / Spill the wine / Who's gonna take the weight / Spark plug / Conjunction Mars / Alone together / Dig dis
CD _______________ PRCD 24171
Prestige / Oct '96 / Cadillac / Complete/ Pinnacle

SPARKS/AKILAH
Thank you / I didn't know what time it was / Charlie Brown / Stinker / Spill the wine / Love the life you live / On the up / All wrapped up / Akilah / Blues for JB / Image of love
CD _______________ CDBGPD 064
Beat Goes Public / Jan '93 / Pinnacle

TEXAS TWISTER
Whip whop / Gathering together / Judy's groove / Texas twister / Ain't no woman (Like the one I got) / I want to talk about you / Star in the crescent / I've got to have you / Mocking bird / Looking for a love / Get ya some / Get down with the get down / Bump & stomp / In the morning / If you want my love
CD _______________ CDBGPD 092
Beat Goes Public / Aug '95 / Pinnacle

Sparks, Tim

NUTCRACKER SUITE
CD _______________ BEST 1028CD
Acoustic Music / Nov '93 / ADA

Sparrow

CARNIVAL JAMBACK SOCA BALLADS
CD _______________ BLS 1019CD
BLS / Aug '95 / Jet Star

SOCA LOVER
CD _______________ BLSCD 1020
BLS / Apr '97 / Jet Star

Sparrow

HATCHING OUT...PLUS
I'm coming back / Well I can tell you / Don't ask me / Nightmare / Many things are clear / Rollercoaster / Dream song / Rainsung song / Break my heart again / Round and round / Hiawatha / Hello goodbye
CD _______________ SEECD 434
See For Miles/C5 / Jan '97 / Pinnacle

Sparrow Dragon

AGAIN
CD _______________ RNCD 2011
Rhino / Jun '93 / Grapevine/PolyGram / Jet Star

Sparrow, Johnny

DANCIN' TIME VOL.3
CD _______________ SAV 240CD
Savoy / Dec '95 / Savoy / THE / TKO Magnum

Spasm

SPASM
CD _______________ INV 048CD
Invisible / Jan '96 / Plastic Head

Spaulding, James

BRILLIANT CORNERS
CD _______________ MCD 5369
Muse / Sep '92 / New Note/Pinnacle

GOTSTABE A BETTER WAY
CD _______________ MCD 5413
Muse / Sep '92 / New Note/Pinnacle

Spazz

SWEATIN' TO THE OLDIES
CD _______________ SAH 36
Slap A Ham / Jun '97 / Cargo / Greyhound / Plastic Head

Spdfgh

LEAVE ME LIKE THIS
CD _______________ DRT 030
Dirt / Nov '96 / Cargo / Greyhound

Speake, Martin

AMAZING GRACE
Iris / Quasimodo / I'll follow my secret heart / It's you / Subconscious Lee / Amazing grace / How about you / How my heart sings / Little girl I'll miss you / Topsy / Toxicology
CD _______________ SPJCD 558
Spotlite / Jun '97 / Cadillac / Jazz Music / New Note/Pinnacle / Swift

Speaking Canaries

SONGS FOR THE TERRESTRIALLY CHALLENGED
CD _______________ SCT 0392
Scat / Feb '95 / Vital

Spear Of Destiny

BBC LIVE IN CONCERT
Land of shame / Strangers in our town / Pumpkin man / Embassy song / Never take me alive / Outlands / Was that you / Miami Vice / Rocket ship / Once in her lifetime / All you young men / Mickey / Liberator
CD _______________ WINDCD 055
Windsong / Mar '94 / Pinnacle

COLLECTION, THE
CD _______________ CCSCD 297
Castle / Oct '91 / BMG

LIVE AT THE LYCEUM 22.12.85
Rainmaker / Rocket ship / Attica / Come back / Up all night / Mickey / Young men / World service / Playground of the rich / Grapes of wrath / I can see / Liberator / Prisoner of love / Incinerator / These days are gone / Do you believe in the westworld
CD _______________ MAUCD 638
Mau Mau / Jun '93 / Pinnacle

TIME OF OUR LIVES (The Best Of Spear Of Destiny)
Never take me alive / Outlands / Traveller / Strangers in our town / Miami Vice / Time of our lives / Man that never was / So in love with you / March or die / I remember / Radio radio / Life goes on / If the guns / Was that you
CD _______________ CDOVD 449
Virgin / Feb '95 / EMI

Spearhead

CHOCOLATE SUPA HIGHWAY
Africa on line / Chocolate supa highway / Keep me lifted / Food for tha masses / U can't sing R song / Payroll (stay strong) / Madness in tha hood (Free ride) / Rebel music (3 O'clock roadblock) / Why oh why / Comin' to gitcha / Life sentence / Ganja babe
CD _______________ CDEST 2293
Parlophone / Mar '97 / EMI

HOME
People in the middle / Love is da shit / Piece o' peace / Positive / Of course you can / Hole in the bucket / Home / Dream team / Runfayalifel crime to be broke in America / 100,000 miles / Red beans and rice / Caught without an umbrella
CD _______________ CDEST 2236
Capitol / Sep '94 / EMI

Spearman's Double Trio

SMOKEHOUSE
CD _______________ 1201572
Black Saint / Oct '94 / Cadillac / Harmonia Mundi

Spears, Billie Jo

BILLIE JO SPEARS
CD _______________ DS 014
Desperado / Jun '97 / TKO Magnum

COUNTRY CLASSICS
Blanket on the ground / What I've got in mind / Today I started loving you again / Don't ever let go of me / All I want is you / I've never loved anyone more / Say it again / I fall to pieces / True love / Love ain't the question / Every time I sing a love song / I've got to go / Since I fell for you / Come on home / What a love I have in you / There's more to a tear than meets the eye / What the world needs now is love / Love ain't gonna wait for us / I love you because / Put a little love in your heart
CD _______________ CDMFP 6320
Music For Pleasure / Apr '97 / EMI

EMI COUNTRY MASTERS (2CD Set)
I love you because / He's got more love in his little finger / Help me make it through the night / Marty Gray / I'll share my world with you / I stayed long enough / Today I started loving you again / It coulda been me / Snowbird / See the funny little clown / Harper Valley PTA / Blanket on the ground / Rose garden / Stay away from the apple tree / Lay down beside me / Silver wings and golden rings / Livin' in a house full of love / What I've got in mind / Apartment no. 9 / On the rebound / Faded love / Never did like whiskey / Your old love letters / I'm not easy / Yours love / If you want me / Heart over mind / Too much is not enough / Mr. walker, it's all over / Lonely hearts club / Tips and tables / Teardrops will kiss the morning dew / True love / I've got to go / Take me to your world / '57 Chevrolet / Stand by your man / Love ain't gonna wait for us / Price I pay to stay / Yesterday / I will survive / Livin' our love together / Games people play / Sing me an old fashioned song / Rainy days and rainy nights / Standing tall / Misty blue / Your good girl's gonna go bad / For the good times / What the world needs now is love
CD Set _______________ CDEM 1481
EMI / Apr '93 / EMI

GREATEST HITS
CD _______________ WMCD 5680
Disky / Nov '93 / Disky / THE

LOVE SONGS
Blanket on the ground / What I've got in mind / Today I started loving you again / Don't ever let go of me / All I want is you / I've never loved anyone before / Say it again / I fall to pieces / True love / Love ain't the question (love ain't the answer) / Every time I sing a love song / I've got to go / Since I fell for you / Come on home / What a love I have in you / There's more to a tear than meets the eye / What the world needs now is love / Love ain't gonna wait for us / I love you because / Put a little love in your heart
CD _______________ CDMFP 6112
Music For Pleasure / Mar '94 / EMI

MAGIC OF BILLIE JO SPEARS, THE
CD _______________ TKOCD 002
TKO / '92 / TKO

MISTY BLUE
CD _______________ 15476
Laserlight / Nov '92 / Target/BMG

OUTLAW WOMAN
Why must all goods times be memories / It's not easy / Outlaw woman / Come back (when you can stay forever) / Couldn't love have picked a better place to die / I'm gonna love lovin' you / Wisdom of a fool / Blue orleans / I don't want to talk about it / Something for your memory to do
CD _______________ 3036300092
Country Skyline / May '96 / Carlton

QUEEN OF COUNTRY MUSIC, THE
Cry / Country roads / Make the world go away / Slow hand / I believe / Love letters in the sand / You light up my life / Heartaches by the number / Always on my mind / Raindrops keep falling on my head / Misty / Paper roses / If you love me (let me know) / Amazing grace
CD _______________ CDMFP 6272
Music For Pleasure / Sep '96 / EMI

SINGS THE COUNTRY GREATS
'57 Chevrolet / Loving him was easier / Hey won't you play another somebody done somebody wrong song / Till something better comes along / Sing me an old fashioned song / Every time I sing a love song / See the funny little clown / That's what friends are for / Blanket on the ground / Ode to Billy Joe / Misty blue / I don't wanna play house / Hurt / Stand by your man / He's got more love in his little finger / Take me to your world
CD _______________ CDMFP 5784
Music For Pleasure / May '91 / EMI

UNMISTAKABLY
Every time I close my eyes / One smokey rose / Mutual aquaintance / I got this train to ride / If wishes were wings / We need to walk / Keep me from dreamin' / Star / We're over / It won't be long
CD _______________ ETCD 194
Etude / Sep '92 / Grapevine/PolyGram

Special A

SPECIAL A ENCOUNTERS MIXMAN
CD _______________ BLKMCD 008
Blakamix / Dec '94 / Jet Star / SRD

Special Ed

LEGAL
CD _______________ FILERCD 297
Profile / Sep '90 / Pinnacle

Special EFX

BODY LANGUAGE
Body heat / Seduction / Sunset / Night rhythm / Till we meet again / Spy vs spy / When love cries / Papa jinda / Mikes D / Free
CD _______________ JVC 20512
JVC / Nov '95 / Direct / New Note/Pinnacle / Vital/SAM

CATWALK
Nitty gritty / Mercy mercy me / Passions / Dancing cobra / Siana / George can't dance / So happy, so sad / Hip hop bop / Forever this love / Concrete jungle
CD _______________ JVC 20382
JVC / Oct '94 / Direct / New Note/Pinnacle / Vital/SAM

HERE TO STAY
Nine lives of the cat / Heavenly delight (Your face) / Here to stay / Since you've been away / Lights out / Unfinished business / Lucky seven / New passage / Who's smiling now / Real deal / Brave new world
CD _______________ JVC 90152
JVC / Apr '97 / Direct / New Note/Pinnacle / Vital/SAM

SPECIAL DELIVERY
Safari / Sambuca nights / Much too soon / Forever hold your peace / Foggy streets of London / Slug / Waiting / Katalin
CD _______________ FCD 0004
Limetree / Nov '95 / New Note/Pinnacle

Special Project

KID LOOPS VS. COOL BREEZE
CD _______________ FILT 012CD
Filter / Nov '96 / Pinnacle / Prime / RTM/ Disc

Specials

SPECIALS SINGLES, THE (The Best Of The Specials)
Gangsters / Message to you Rudy / Nite club / Too much too young / Guns of Navarone / Rat race / Rude boys outa jail / Stereotype / Internation jet set / Do nothing / Ghost town / Why / Friday night / Saturday morning / Racist friend / Free Nelson Mandela / What I like most about you is your girlfriend
CD _______________ CCD 5010
Chrysalis / Aug '91 / EMI

SPECIALS, THE
Message to you Rudy / Do the dog / It's up to you / Nite klub / Doesn't make it alright / Concrete jungle / Too hot / Monkey man / (Dawning of a) New era / Blank expression / Stupid marriage / Too much too young / Little bitch / You're wondering now
CD _______________ CCD 5001
Chrysalis / Nov '92 / EMI

TODAY'S SPECIALS
Take five / Pressure drop / Hypocrite / Goodbye girl / Little bit / Time has come / Somebody got murdered / 007 / Simmer down / Maga dog / Bad boys
CD _______________ KUFFCD 2
Kuff / Mar '96 / EMI

TOO MUCH TOO YOUNG
Too much too young / Enjoy yourself (it's later than you think) / Man at C&A / Rude boys outa jail / I can't stand it / Do the dog / Blank expression / (Dawning of a) New era / Monkey man / Hey little rich girl / Pearl's cafe / Little bitch / Rat race / Message to you Rudy / Do nothing / You're wondering now
CD _______________ CDGOLD 1022
EMI Gold / May '96 / EMI

Species Of Fish

SONGS OF A DUMB VOICE
CD _______________ KIP 006
Staalplaat / Dec '95 / Vital/SAM

Specimen

AZOIC
CD _______________ FREUDCD 054
Jungle / Jun '97 / RTM/Disc / SRD

Speckled Red

DIRTY DOZENS, THE
Dirty dozens / Right string but the wrong yo yo / If you've ever been down / Wilkins street stomp / Cow cow blues / Just blues / Red's boogie woogie / Going down slow / Highway 61 blues / After dinner blues / Cryin' in my sleep / Early in the morning / love is like a faucet / Speckled Red speaks / Delmar blues / Feel so good / Dirtier dozens / Dirtiest dozens
CD _______________ DE 601
Delmark / Nov '96 / ADA / Cadillac / CM / Direct / Hot Shot

SPECKLED RED 1929-1938
CD _______________ DOCD 5205
Document / Oct '93 / ADA / Hot Shot / Jazz Music

Speckmann

SPECKMANN
CD _______________ NB 056CD
Nuclear Blast / Feb '92 / Plastic Head

Specter, Dave

BLUEPLICITY (Specter, Dave & The Bluebirds)
CD _______________ DD 664
Delmark / May '94 / ADA / Cadillac / CM / Direct / Hot Shot

LEFT TURN ON BLUE
Get back home / Stop hold it / Killer Jack / Till the end of time / Party girl / Juice head baby / Left turn on blue / Unleavened soul / Hopeless / What's the matter / Tremble / Roll baby roll / When will the blues leave
CD _______________ DE 693
Delmark / Feb '97 / ADA / Cadillac / CM / Direct / Hot Shot

LIVE IN EUROPE (Specter, Dave & The Bluebirds)
CD _______________ CCD 11047
Crosscut / Nov '95 / ADA / CM / Direct

Spector, Phil

CHRISTMAS GIFT FOR YOU FROM PHIL SPECTOR, A (Various Artists)
White Christmas: *Love, Darlene* / Frosty the snowman: *Ronettes* / Bells of St. Mary's: *Soxx, Bob B. & The Blue Jeans* / Santa Claus is coming to town: *Crystals* / Sleigh ride: *Ronettes* / Marshmallow world: *Love, Darlene* / I saw Mommy kissing Santa Claus: *Ronettes* / Rudolph the red nosed reindeer: *Crystals* / Winter wonderland: *Love, Darlene* / Parade of the wooden soldiers: *Crystals* / Christmas (baby please come home): *Love, Darlene* / Here comes Santa Claus: *Soxx, Bob B. & The Blue Jeans* / Silent night: *Spector, Phil & Artists*
CD _______________ PSCD 1005
EMI / Dec '95 / EMI

PHIL SPECTOR - BACK TO MONO (1958-1969/4CD Set) (Various Artists)
To know him is to love him: *Teddy Bears* / Corine Corina: *Peterson, Ray* / Spanish harlem: *King, Ben E.* / Pretty little angel eyes: *Lee, Curtis* / Every breath I take: *Pitney, Gene* / I love how you love me: *Paris Sisters* / Under the moon of love: *Lee, Curtis* / There's no other (like my baby): *Crystals* / Uptown: *Crystals* / He hit me (and it felt like a kiss): *Crystals* / He's a rebel: *Crystals* / Zip a dee doo dah: *Soxx, Bob B. & The Blue Jeans* / Puddin' 'n' tain: *Alley Cats* / He's sure the boy I love: *Crystals* / Why do lovers break each others hearts: *Soxx, Bob B. & The Blue Jeans* / Today I met the boy I'm gonna marry: *Love, Darlene* / Da doo ron ron: *Crystals* / Heartbreaker: *Crystals* / Why don't they let us fall in love: *Veronica* / Chapel of love: *Love, Darlene* / Not too young to get married: *Soxx, Bob B. & The Blue Jeans* / Wait 'til my Bobby gets home: *Love, Darlene* / All grown up: *Crystals* / Be my baby: *Ronettes* / Then he kissed me: *Crystals* / Fine fine boy: *Love, Darlene* / Baby I love you: *Ronettes* / Ronettes: *Ronettes* / Girls can tell: *Crystals* / Little boy: *Crystals* / Hold me tight: *Treasures* / Best part of breaking up: *Ronettes* / Soldier baby of mine: *Ronettes* / Strange love: *Love, Darlene* / Stumble and fall: *Love, Darlene* / When I saw you: *Ronettes* / So young: *Veronica* / Do I love you: *Ronettes* / Keep on dancin': *Ronettes* / You baby: *Ronettes* / Woman in love (with you): *Ronettes* / Walking in the rain: *Ronettes* / You've lost that lovin' feelin': *Righteous Brothers* / Born to be together: *Ronettes* / Just once in my life: *Righteous Brothers* / Unchained melody: *Righteous Brothers* / Is this what I get for loving you: *Ronettes* / Long way to be happy: *Love, Darlene* / (I love you) for sentimental reasons: *Righteous Brothers* / Ebb tide: *Righteous Brothers* / This could be the night: *Modern Folk Quartet* / Paradise: *Ronettes* / River deep, mountain high: *Turner, Ike & Tina* / I'll never need more than this: *Turner, Ike & Tina* / Love like yours (don't come knockin' everyday): *Turner, Ike & Tina* / Save the last dance for me: *Turner, Ike & Tina* / I wish I never saw the sunshine: *Ronettes* / You came, you saw, you conquered: *Ronettes* / Black pearl: *Checkmates* / Love is all I have to give: *Checkmates* / White Christmas: *Love, Darlene* / Frosty the snowman: *Ronettes* / Bells of St. Mary's: *Soxx, Bob B. & The Blue Jeans* / Santa Claus is coming to town: *Crystals* / Sleigh ride: *Ronettes* / Marshmallow world: *Love, Darlene* / I saw Mommy kissing Santa Claus: *Ronettes* / Rudolph the red nosed reindeer: *Crystals* / Winter wonderland: *Love, Darlene* / Parade of the wooden soldiers: *Crystals* / Christmas (baby please come home): *Love, Darlene* / Here comes Santa Claus: *Soxx, Bob B. & The Blue Jeans* / Silent night: *Spector, Phil & Artists*
CD Set _______________ CDP 7980632
EMI / Nov '91 / EMI

Spector, Ronnie

DANGEROUS
CD _______________ RVCD 48
Raven / Dec '95 / ADA / Direct

Spectre

ILLNESS, THE
CD _______________ WSCD 006
Word Sound Recordings / Feb '96 / Cargo / SRD

MISSING TWO WEEKS, THE
Covert dub / Spectre overseas / Missing two weeks / Throw down spears / Spectre in the dance / Mad Frank lends a hand / Blow / Vibration version / Tribute to scratch / Errors / Prez / End games
CD _______________ 74321296552
Natural Response / Feb '96 / BMG

Spectrum

POX ON YOU, A (Spectrum & Jessamine)
CD _______________ ORBIT 003CD
Space Age / May '96 / Plastic Head

Specula

ERUPT
Desolation nightmare / She walks in sunshine / Hello pain / Forever loving you / Can't we all / Stand by / Rock stepper / Inertia / Steal your love / Dual
CD _______________ SCT 0422
Scat / Aug '95 / Vital

Spedding, Chris

CAFE DAYS
CD _______________ 422340
New Rose / Nov '94 / ADA / Direct / Discovery

ENEMY WITHIN
CD _______________ OPM 2103CD
Other People's Music / Mar '97 / Greyhound / Plastic Head

GUITAR GRAFITTI
Video life / Radio times / Time warp / Midnight boys / Bored, bored / Walkin' / Break-out / Frontal lobotomy / Hey Miss Betty / More lobotomy
CD _______________ 422342FC054
Fan Club / Nov '94 / Direct

GUITAR JAMBOREE
CD _______________ 422343FC
Fan Club / Nov '94 / Direct

I'M NOT LIKE EVERYBODY ELSE
I'm not like everybody else / Box number / I got a feeling / Crying game / Depravity / Musical press / Contract / Counterfeit / Shot of rhythm and blues / Mama coco
CD _______________ 422345FC055
Fan Club / Nov '94 / Direct

JUST PLUG HIM IN
CD _______________ 422346FC081
Fan Club / Nov '94 / Direct

MEAN AND MOODY
For what we are about to hear / Backwood progression / Only lick I know / Listen while I sing my song / Saw you yesterday / Hill / Don't leave me / White lady / She's my friend / London town / Dark end of the street / Please Mrs. Henery / Never carry mor than you can eat / Words don't come / Backwood theme
CD _______________ SEECD 372
See For Miles/C5 / Jan '97 / Pinnacle

Speech

SPEECH
Can you hear me / If you think the system's working / Filled with real / Why you gotta be feeling like this / If you was me / Impregnated tid bits of dope hits / Let's be hippies / Freestyle / Like Marvin Gaye said / Hopelessly / Insomnia song / Poor little music boy / Ghetto sex / Tell me something / Running wild
CD _______________ CTCD 52
Cooltempo / Sep '97 / EMI

Speed Queens

SPEED QUEENS
CD _______________ SFTRI 454CD
Sympathy For The Record Industry / Feb '97 / Cargo / Greyhound / Plastic Head

Speed The Plough

MARINA
Just a little / Written each day / Said and done / Once in a while / Late birds / Saint restored / High wire / Love song / Bayswater lane / Hard friend to keep / Hourglass / In the atmosphere / Marina
CD _______________ ESD 81102
East Side Digital / Jul '96 / Vital

Speedfreak

DESTRUCTION BY SPEED
CD _______________ EFA 007502
Shockwave / Sep '94 / SRD

FOR YOU
CD _______________ EFA 008762
Shockwave / Feb '96 / SRD

Speedy J

G SPOT
CD _______________ WARPCD 27
Warp / Mar '95 / Prime / RTM/Disc

G SPOT & LIVE (2CD Set)
CD Set _______________ 378462
Frantic / Nov '96 / Cargo

GINGER
CD _______________ WARPCD 14
Warp / Jun '93 / Prime / RTM/Disc

LIVE
CD _______________ HHCD 015
Harthouse / Nov '95 / Mo's Music Machine / Prime / Vital

PUBLIC ENERGY NO.1
Tuning in / Patterns / Melanor / In-formation / Pure energy / Haywire / Hayfever / Telsa / Drainpipe / Canola / As the bubble expands
CD _______________ NOMU 54CD
Nova Mute / Apr '97 / Prime / RTM/Disc

Speegle, David

DIM LIGHTS AND CANDLES
CD _______________ CDSGP 017
Prestige / Jan '93 / Else / Total/BMG

Spell

SEASONS IN THE SUN
CD _______________ CDSTUMM 126
Mute / Oct '93 / RTM/Disc

Spellbound

SPACE ROCKIN'
CD _______________ PT 603002
Part / Jun '96 / Nervous

Spelmansforbund, Blekinge

SONGS AND DANCES FROM SWEDEN
CD _______________ EUCD 1108
ARC / '91 / ADA / ARC Music

Spence, Bill

HAMMERED DULCIMER RETURNS, THE
CD _______________ FHR 041CD
Front Hall / Nov '95 / ADA

HAMMERED DULCIMER, THE
CD _______________ FHR 302CD
Front Hall / Nov '95 / ADA

Spence, Joseph

BAHAMIAN GUITARIST
CD _______________ ARHCD 349
Arhoolie / Apr '95 / ADA / Cadillac / Direct

OUT ON THE ROLLING SEA (A Tribute To Joseph Spence) (Various Artists)
CD _______________ HPR 2004CD
Hokey Pokey / Jul '94 / ADA / Direct

Spencer, Elvin

PICKING UP THE PIECES
CD _______________ GWX 42222
Ichiban / Aug '96 / Direct / Koch

Spencer, Joel

BRIGHTER SIDE, THE (Spencer, Joel & Kelly Sill)
Fear of flying / Rosebud / Greater fool / Additional dialogue / Naomi / Brighter side / Ironic line / Charlie's tonic
CD _______________ TJA 10026
Jazz Alliance / Feb '96 / New Note/Pinnacle

Spencer, John B.

BACK PAGES 1: THE LOUT'S LP
CD _______________ RTMCD 34
Round Tower / Nov '90 / Avid/BMG

BACK PAGES 2: BLUE SMARTIES
CD _______________ RTMCD 35
Round Tower / Nov '93 / Avid/BMG

BACK PAGES 4: JUDAS AND THE OBSCURE
CD _______________ RTMCD 37
Round Tower / Nov '93 / Avid/BMG

LEFT HAND OF LOVE, THE
CD _______________ RTMCD 82
Round Tower / May '97 / Avid/BMG

PARLOUR GAMES
Parlour games / Billy / Slow beers / Sweet Lucinda / Poor little rich boy / Drive-in movies / Behold the king is dead / Dead man's shoes / Alone together / Left hand of love / Count ten / London I knew / Going down South / Quiet nights
CD _______________ RTMCD 23
Round Tower / Feb '91 / Avid/BMG

SUNDAY BEST
CD _______________ RTMCD 39
Round Tower / May '92 / Avid/BMG

Spencer, Jon

CRYPT STYLE (Spencer, Jon Blues Explosion)
CD _______________ EFA 115022
Crypt / Jan '94 / Shellshock/Disc

EXTRA WIDTH (Spencer, Jon Blues Explosion)
Afro / History of lies / Back slider / Soul letter / Soul typecast / Pant leg / Hey mom / Big road / Train / Inside the world of the Blues Explosion / World of sex
CD _______________ OLE 0522
Matador / Aug '93 / Vital

JON SPENCER BLUES EXPLOSION (Spencer, Jon Blues Explosion)
Write a song / IEV / Exploder / Rachel / Chicken walk / White tail / 78 Style / Changed / What to do / Waterman / Biological / Intro A / Vacuum of loneliness / Feeling of love / Shoot it / Support a man / Comeback / History of sex / Eliza Jane / Eye to eye
CD _______________ CAROLCD 1719
Caroline / Jun '97 / Cargo / Vital

JON SPENCER BLUES EXPLOSION, THE
CD _______________ HUTCD 003
Hut / Apr '92 / EMI

MO' WIDTH (Spencer, Jon Blues Explosion)
CD _______________ ANDA 166CD
Augogo / Feb '97 / Cargo / Greyhound

NOW I GOT WORRY (Spencer, Jon Blues Explosion)
Skunk / Identity / Wail / Fuck shit up / 2 kindsa love / Love all of me / Chicken dog / Rocketship / Dynamite lover / Hot shot / Can't stop / Firefly child / Eyeballin' / RL got soul / Get over here / Sticky
CD _______________ CDSTUMM 132
Mute / May '97 / RTM/Disc

ORANGE (Spencer, Jon Blues Explosion)
Bell bottoms / Ditch / Dang / Very rare / Sweat / Cowboy / Orange / Brenda / Dissect / Blues X man / Full grown / Flavor / Greyhound
CD _______________ OLE 1052
Matador / Sep '94 / Vital

Spencer, Sarah

LAISSEZ LES BONS TEMPS ROULER (Spencer, Sarah Rue Conti Jazz Band)
Mardi Gras in New Orleans / My life will be sweeter / Somebody else is taking my place / In the garden / Whoopin' blues / Mama Inez / What a friend we have in Jesus / Junco partner / Bogalousa strut / Lead me saviour / Sweet fields
CD _______________ LACD 22
Lake / Jan '93 / ADA / Cadillac / Direct / Jazz Music / Target/BMG

Spendel, Christoph

CITY KIDS
If you were here / City kids / Just like a smile / Phat city / French girls / Modern jazz / Wild and wonderful / Night magic / Blue light / Ocean avenue / Moon over Florida / East-side song
CD _______________ TCB 01052
TCB / Jun '96 / New Note/Pinnacle

READY FOR TAKE OFF
Salsito / Carly / Ready for take off / Monday in July / Rain / Queen's plaza / Downtown / Tapsi strikes again
CD _______________ CDLR 45010
L&R / Dec '88 / New Note/Pinnacle

SPENDEL
White cars / New York PM / Mr. Cameo / Midnight / Columbus circle / Byton funk / Banana republic / Eilat / Otto's magic bus / Hugo update / Suite 11F / Piano graffity / Manhattan candlelight
CD _______________ CDLR 45014
L&R / Jan '90 / New Note/Pinnacle

Spermbirds

EATING GLASS
CD _______________ XM032CD
X-Mist / Apr '92 / Cargo / SRD

NOTHING IS EASY
CD _______________ WB 031CD
We Bite / '88 / Plastic Head

RICH MAN'S HIGH
CD _______________ IRS 5977055
Community / Feb '94 / Cargo

THANKS
CD _______________ DEP 02CD
Dead Eye / Jun '93 / SRD

Sphere

PUMPKIN'S DELIGHT
CD _______________ 1232072
Red / Apr '93 / ADA / Cadillac / Harmonia Mundi

Spice & Co

CAMOUFLAGE
CD _______________ CRSCD 007
CRS / Apr '96 / ADA / Direct / Jet Star

FIRST DECADE, THE
CD _______________ CRSCD 011
CRS / Apr '96 / ADA / Direct / Jet Star

IN DE CONGALINE
CD _______________ CRSCD 009
CRS / Apr '96 / ADA / Direct / Jet Star

WORLD DANCE, THE
CD _______________ CRSCD 003
CRS / Apr '96 / ADA / Direct / Jet Star

Spice

VARIO BEL AIR
CD _______________ SPV 08511182CD
SPV / Nov '96 / Koch / Plastic Head

Spice Girls

OLD SPICE - THE EARLY DAYS (2CD Set/Documentary & Music)
CD Set _______________ OTR 1100057
Metro Independent / Aug '97 / Essential/ BMG

SPICE
Wannabe / Say you'll be there / 2 become 1 / Love thing / Last time lover / Mama / Who do you think you are / Something kinda funny / Naked / If U can't dance

CD CDV 2812
Virgin / Oct '96 / EMI

Spicelab

DAY ON PLANET EARTH, A
CD HHCD 009
Harthouse / Oct '94 / Mo's Music Machine / Prime / Vital

LOST IN SPICE
CD HARTUKCD 2
Harthouse / Oct '93 / Mo's Music Machine / Prime / Vital

Spider Babies

ADVENTURES IN SEX AND VIOLENCE
CD GI 0132
GI Productions / Mar '97 / Cargo / Greyhound

Spiderfoot

SPIDERFOOT
CD SPID 1
Immigrant / May '97 / Cargo

Spiders

COMPLETE IMPERIAL RECORDINGS, THE (2CD Set)
I didn't want to do it / You're the one for a thrill / Mellow Mama / Lost and bewildered / Tears begin to flow / Why do I love you / Love's all I'm puttin' down / I'll stop crying / Mmm mmm baby (hey baby) / Walking around in circles / I'm searchin' / Real thing / She keeps me wondering / Three times seven equals twenty one / That's enough / Sukey Sukey Sukey / Bells in my heart / Am I the one / Don't knock / True (you don't love me) / Witchcraft / You played the part / Is it true / How I feel / That's the way to win my heart / Goodbye / I'll be free / Don't pity me / Dear Mary / A1 in my heart / Without love / Someday bye and bye / That's my desire / Better be on my way / Honey bee / I'm glad for your sake / Poor boy / Bells are ringing / I miss you times / You're the one / Tennessee Slim
CD Set BCD 15673
Bear Family / Jun '92 / Direct / Rollercoaster / Swift

Spiders

BACK
CD PECD 471
Ciruela El / Jun '97 / Greyhound

Spiegl, Steve

THEN AND NOW (Spiegl, Steve Big Band)
CD 710022
Capri / Oct '94 / Cadillac / Wellard

Spier, Bernd

OHNE EIN BESTIMMTES ZIEL
Memphis, Tennessee / Ohn ein bestimmtes Ziel / Hey Mr. Postman / Heut' bei mir-Und dann / Ein dufte party / Das kannst dur mir nicht verbieten / Was ich an dir am meis ten liebe / Das war mein schonster Tanz / Sag nicht goodbye / Chone Madchen muss man lieben / Keiner weiss, dass wir uns lieben / Ich bin nicht schuld daran / Du bist schoner als die ander'n / Einmal geht der Vorhang zu / Du bizt fur mich geboren / Der neue tag beginnt / Wenn erst der abend kommt / Danke schon / Julia / Mir geht es wunderbar: *Spier, Bernd & Uwe* / Komm zu mir: *Spier, Bernd & Uwe* / Two strangers / I only came to dance with you / Million and one times / Rose Marie / Pretty Belinda / Klopf dreimal / Lass dein little girl nie weinen
CD BCD 15591
Bear Family / Mar '92 / Direct / Rollercoaster / Swift

Spike & Tyla's Hotknive

FLAGRANTLY YOURS
CD CDBLEED 18
Bleeding Hearts / Jul '96 / Pinnacle

Spillane, Davy

ATLANTIC BRIDGE
Atlantic Bridge / Davie's reels / Daire's dream / Tribute to Johnny Doran / O'Neill's statement / Sliverish / By the river of gems / Pigeon on the gate / In my life / Lansdowne blues
CD COOKCD 009
Cooking Vinyl / Aug '88 / Vital

OUT OF THE AIR
Atlantic bridge / Daire's dream / Mystic seacliffs / Litton Lane / River of gems / Storm / Road to Ballyalla / One for Phil
CD COOKCD 016
Cooking Vinyl / Jun '97 / Vital

PIPEDREAMS
Shifting sands / Undertow / Shorelines / Call across the canyon / Midnight walker / Mistral / Rainmaker / Stepping in silence / Morning wings / Corcomroe
CD TARACD 3026
Tara / Oct '94 / ADA / CM / Conifer/BMG / Direct

PLACE AMONG THE STONES, A
Darklight / Promised rain / Place among the stones / Western whisper / Starry night / Elgeebar / Callow Lake / Forever frozen / Always travelling / Near the horizon
CD 4769302
Columbia / Oct '95 / Sony

SHADOW HUNTER, THE
Lucy's tune / Indiana drones / Carron streams / Watching the clock / Walker of the snow / Hidden ground / White crow / Moyasta junction / Journeys of a dreamer / One day in June / Equinox / Host of the air
CD COOKCD 030
Cooking Vinyl / Apr '90 / Vital

Spillane, John

WELLS OF THE WORLD
CD HBCD 0011
Hummingbird / Aug '97 / ADA / Direct / Grapevine/PolyGram

Spin Doctors

HOMEBELLY GROOVE
What time is it / Off my line / Freeway of the plains / Lady Kerosene / Yo baby / Little Miss can't be wrong / Shinbone Alley / Refrigerator car / Sweet widow / Stepped on a crack / Yo mama's a pajama / Rosetta stone
CD 4728962
Epic / Dec '93 / Sony

POCKET FULL OF KRYPTONITE
Jimmy Olsen's blues / What time is it / Little miss can't be wrong / Forty or fifty / Refrigerator car / More than she knows / Two princes / Off my line / How could you want him (When you know you could have me) / Shinbone Alley / Hard to exist
CD 4682502
Epic / Mar '93 / Sony

TURN IT UPSIDE DOWN
Big fat funky booty / You let your heart go too fast / Cleopatra's cat / Hungry Hamed's / Biscuit head / Indifference / Bags of dirt / Mary Jane / More than meets the ear / Laraby's gang / At this hour / Someday all this will be road / Beasts in the woods
CD 4768862
Epic / Jun '94 / Sony

Spina

LE MEILLEUR DES MONDES
CD 120962
Wowoka / Aug '97 / Grapevine/PolyGram

Spina Bifida

ZIYADHA
CD CDAR 010
Adipocre / Feb '94 / Plastic Head

Spinal Tap

THIS IS SPINAL TAP
Hell hole / Tonight I'm gonna rock you / Heavy duty / Rock 'n' roll creation / America / Cups and cakes / Big bottom / Sex farm / Stonehenge / Gimme some money / Flower people
CD 8178462
Polydor / Aug '90 / PolyGram

Spinanes

MANOS
CD SPCD 114292
Sub Pop / Nov '93 / Cargo / Greyhound / Shellshock/Disc

NOEL, JONAH AND ME
CD SPCD 328
Sub Pop / May '94 / Cargo / Greyhound / Shellshock/Disc

STRAND
CD SPCD 345
Sub Pop / Feb '96 / Cargo / Greyhound / Shellshock/Disc

Spine

TRANSITION
Ride my own spine / NAC / Irreversible / Sickness to insanity / Salt the sores / But now that I'm gone / We are theirs / Leave neveragaining
CD SST 302CD
SST / Mar '94 / Plastic Head

Spinners

BEST OF THE SPINNERS, THE
CD MATCD 228
Castle / Dec '92 / BMG

MAGGIE MAY
CD PLSCD 174
Pulse / Apr '97 / BMG

ONE AND ONLY, THE
Lord of the dance / All day singing / Blaydon races / Last thing on my mind / Amazing grace / We shall not be moved / Guantanamera / Jamaica farewell / To be a farmer's boy / Foggy dew / Greensleeves / Lovely Joan / North country maid / Liverpool hornpipes / Collier's rant / Dane the flora / Banks of the Ohio / Shepherd lad / Waters o' Tyne / Lamorna / Bucket of the mountain dew / When I first came to this land / So long (it's been good to know yuh)
CD CC 8239
EMI / Nov '94 / EMI

SPINNERS IN CONCERT, THE
All day singing / Moonshiner / William Brown / Bleacher lass o' Kelvinhaugh / Jane and Louisa / Tom Brown / Castles in the air / Calico printer's clerk / Guantanamera / Deep blue sea / Poverty knock / Lamorna / Cobbler's song / Ring of iron / Waltzing Matilda / Little boy / Mule skinner blues / So long, it's been good to know you
CD CC 212
Music For Pleasure / May '88 / EMI

Spiny Anteaters

ALL IS WELL
CD KRANK 004CD
Kranky / Mar '97 / Cargo / Greyhound

CURRENT
CD KRANK 011
Kranky / Mar '97 / Cargo / Greyhound

Spiral Jetty

BAND OF GOLD
Don't walk away / Tourists send postcards / Breathe / Queen bitch / Tongue-black pie / Drunken lies / Coat of hair / La / Cherry's lament / Social age
CD OUT 1102
Brake Out / Jan '93 / Direct

Spiral Tribe

SOUND OF TEKNIVAL, THE (Various Artists)
CD 3014772
Techno Import / Nov '96 / Cargo

Spirea X

FIREBLADE SKIES
CD CAD 1017CD
4AD / Oct '91 / RTM/Disc

Spires Of Oxford

SPIRES OF OXFORD
CD LOUD 013CD
Colourful Clouds / Jul '97 / Cargo

Spirit

CLEAR (Remastered)
Dark eyed woman / Apple orchard / So little time to fly / Ground hog / Policeman's ball / Ice / Give a life, take a life / I'm truckin' / Clear / Caught / New dope in town / 1984 / Sweet Stella baby / Fuller brush man / Coral
CD 4844162
Columbia / Nov '96 / Sony

COLLECTION, THE
CD CCSCD 319
Castle / Oct '91 / BMG

FAMILY THAT PLAYS TOGETHER, THE
I got a line on you / It shall be / Poor Richard / Sikly Sam / Drunkard / Darlin' if / All the same / Jewish / Dream within a dream / She smiled / Aren't you glad
CD 4773552
Epic / Aug '94 / Sony

FAMILY THAT PLAYS TOGETHER, THE (Remastered)
I got a line on you / It shall be / Poor Richard / Silky Sam / Drunkard / Darlin' if / It's all the same / Jewish / Dream within a dream / She smiles / Aren't you glad / Fog / So little to say / Mellow fellow / Now or anywhere / Space chile
CD 4851742
Columbia / Nov '96 / Sony

LIVE AT LA PALOMA
CD CREW 22003
Werc Crew / Jul '97 / Greyhound

MERCURY YEARS, THE
CD 5346022
Mercury / Jun '97 / PolyGram

SPIRIT
Fresh garbage / Uncle Jack / Mechanical world / Taurus / Girl in your eyes / Straight arrow / Topanga windows / Gramophone man / Water woman / Great canyon fire in general / Elijah
CD 4809652
Epic / Aug '95 / Sony

SPIRIT (Remastered)
Fresh garbage / Uncle Jack / Mechanical world / Taurus / Girl in your eye / Straight arrow / Topanga windows / Gramophone man / Water woman / Great canyon fire in general / Elijah / Veruska / Free spirit / If I had a woman / Elijah (alternate take)
CD 4851752
Columbia / Nov '96 / Sony

TIME CIRCLE (2CD Set)
Fresh garbage / Uncle Jack / Mechanical world / Taurus / Girl in your eye / Straight arrow / Topanga windows / Gramophone man / Great canyon fire in general / I got a line on you / It shall be / Poor Richard / Silky Sam / Sherozode / All the same / Dream within a dream / Aren't you glad / Eventide / Green gorilla / Rehearsal theme / Fog / Now or anywhere / Dark eyed woman / So little time to fly / Ground hog / Ice / I'm truckin' / New dope in town / 1984 / Sweet Stella baby / Nothin' to hide / Nature's way / Animal zoo / Love has found a way / Why can't I be free / Mr. Skin / When I touch you / Street worm / Morning will come / Turn to the right
CD Set 4712682
Legacy / Jun '96 / Sony

TWELVE DREAMS OF DR. SARDONICUS
Nothin' to hide / Nature's way / Animal zoo / Love has found a way / Why can't I be free / Mr. Skin / Space child / When I touch you / Street worm / Life has just begun / Morning will come / Soldier / We've got a lot to learn / Potatoland (theme) / Open up your heart / Morning light / Potatoland (prelude) / Potatoland (introduction) / Turn to the right / Donut house / Fish fry road / Information / My friend
CD 4766032
Epic / Apr '94 / Sony

TWELVE DREAMS OF DR. SARDONICUS (Remastered)
Prelude - Nothin' to hide / Nature's way / Animal zoo / Love has found a way / Why can't I be free / Mr. Skin / Space child / When I touch you / Street worm / Life has just begun / Morning will come / Soldier / Rougher road / Animal zoo (mono single version) / Morning will come (alternate mono mix) / Red light roll on
CD 4851732
Columbia / Nov '96 / Sony

Spirit Feel

SPIRIT FEEL
CD TPLP 77CD
One Little Indian / Mar '95 / Pinnacle

Spirit Level

KINDRED SPIRITS
CD URCD 009
Ubiquity / Jul '96 / Cargo / Timewarp

NEW YEAR
CD FMRCD 03
Future / Jan '89 / ADA / Harmonia Mundi

ON THE LEVEL
Over the moon / Spiral staircase / Seventh heaven / Tollbridge / Merhaba mustafa / Y ya la quiero / Sometime never / You and I / Looking on the bright side / La dolce vita
CD 33JAZZ 021
33 Jazz / Apr '95 / Cadillac / New Note/ Pinnacle

Spirit Of Science

SPIRIT OF SCIENCE (2CD Set)
Untitled tracks / Sunishta
CD Set NSKYCD 002
Northern Sky / Sep '97 / Direct / Pinnacle

Spirit Of The Day

LABOUR DAY
Darkhouse / Profiteers / Run boy / Expensive/Cinema of pain / Take it from the source / Political / Hounds that wait outside your door / Drinking man / Gottingen street
CD SP 1123CD
Stony Plain / Oct '93 / ADA / CM / Direct

Spirit Of The West

OLD MATERIAL 1984-1986
CD SP 1141CD
Stony Plain / Oct '93 / ADA / CM / Direct

TRIPPING UP THE STAIRS
CD CMCD 035
Celtic Music / Mar '94 / CM

Spirit Traveller

PLAYING HITS FROM MOTOR CITY
Signed, sealed, delivered (I'm yours) / Since I lost my baby / Ain't that peculiar / Ain't nothing like the real thing / You keep me hangin' on / OOO baby baby / Tracks of my tears / Ain't no mountain high enough / I love you / It's growing / You've really got a hold on me
CD JVC 20292
JVC / Feb '94 / Direct / New Note/Pinnacle / Vital/SAM

Spirits Of Rhythm

SPIRITS OF RHYTHM 1932-1934
Underneath the Harlem moon / How deep is the ocean / Nobody's sweetheart / I got rhythm / I've got the world on a string / Rhythm / I'll be ready when the great day comes / My old man / Way down yonder in New Orleans / From Monday on / As long as I live / Junk man / Dr. Watson and Mr. Holmes / That's what I hate about love / Shoutin' in that amen corner / It's a long way to Tipperary / I woke up with a teardrop in my eye / Exactly like you / I'm walking this town / We've got the blues
CD RTR 79004
Retrieval / Nov '96 / Cadillac / Direct / Jazz Music / Swift / Wellard

Spiritual Beggars

ANOTHER WAY TO SHINE
CD ____ **CDMFN 198**
Music For Nations / Mar '96 / Pinnacle

SPIRITUAL BEGGARS
CD ____ **WAR 002CD**
Wrong Again / Apr '96 / Plastic Head

Spiritualized

LADIES AND GENTLEMEN WE ARE FLOATING IN SPACE (12xCDS Set)
Ladies and gentlemen we are floating in space / Come together / I think I'm in love / All of my thoughts / Stay with me / Electricity / Home of the brave / Individual / Broken heart / No God only religion / Cool waves / Cop shoot cop
CD Set ____ **DEDCD 034S**
Dedicated / Jul '97 / BMG / Vital
CD ____ **DEDCD 034**
Dedicated / May '97 / BMG / Vital

LAZER GUIDED MELODIES
CD ____ **DEDCD 004**
Dedicated / Jul '97 / BMG / Vital

PURE PHASE (Spiritualized Electric Mainline)
CD ____ **DEDCD 017S**
Dedicated / Jan '95 / BMG / Vital
CD ____ **DEDCD 017**
Dedicated / Jul '97 / BMG / Vital

Spiro & Wix

MOTION
Tara's theme / Cloudscapes / Glory season / Days of honour / Race of champions / Save the robot / Slow motion / Airborne / Summits at zero / LBW / Deceptive bends
CD ____ **PRMDCD 8**
Premier/EMI / Aug '96 / EMI

Spiro, Mark

NOW IS THEN
CD ____ **WESTCD 5**
West Coast / Mar '97 / Cargo

Spiro, Michael

BATA KETU (Spiro, Michael & Mark Lamson)
Prelude / Elegua/Exu / Osain/Osanyin / Chango/Xango / Iroko / Ochosi/Oxossi / Ochun/Oxum
CD ____ **INT 32172**
Intuition / Jun '97 / New Note/Pinnacle

Spitfire

ELECTRIC COLOUR CLIMAX
CD ____ **FULL 2CD**
Lowlife / Aug '96 / 3mv/Vital

FEVERISH
CD ____ **DANCD 097**
Danceteria / Mar '95 / ADA / Plastic Head / Shellshock/Disc

SEX BOMB
CD ____ **PAPCD 21**
Paperhouse / Sep '93 / RTM/Disc

Spitfire Band

SPITFIRE BAND SWINGS FROM STAGE TO SCREEN
CD ____ **ACD 2500**
Attic / '88 / Swift

Spitnik Devils

FOR BUTTSUCKERS AND OTHER FUCKERS
CD ____ **PCD 037**
Progress / Nov '96 / Cargo / Plastic Head

Spitters

SUN TO SUN
Sun to sun / Days into a week / Cradle / Living things / Impasse / Swipe / Strange / Throat
CD ____ **PCP 0302**
PCP / Jan '96 / Vital

Spivak, Charlie

CHARLIE SPIVAK
CD ____ **CCD 017**
Circle / Oct '93 / Jazz Music / Swift / Wellard

FOR SENTIMENTAL REASONS (Spivak, Charlie & His Orchestra)
CD ____ **VJC 1041**
Vintage Jazz Classics / Feb '93 / ADA / Cadillac / CM / Direct

UNCOLLECTED, THE (1943-1946) (Spivak, Charlie & His Orchestra)
Stardreams / Mean to me / Serenade in blue / I used to love you / Cuddle up a little closer / Blue Lou / Laura / More than you know / Stardust / Accentuate the positive / Solitude / Travellin' light / Blue champagne / Let's go home / It's the same old dream / Saturday night
CD ____ **HCD 105**
Hindsight / Oct '95 / Jazz Music / Target/ BMG

Spivey, Victoria

VICTORIA SPIVEY VOL.1 1926-1927
CD ____ **DOCD 5316**
Document / Mar '95 / ADA / Hot Shot / Jazz Music

VICTORIA SPIVEY VOL.2 1927-1929
CD ____ **DOCD 5317**
Document / Mar '95 / ADA / Hot Shot / Jazz Music

VICTORIA SPIVEY VOL.3 1929-1936
CD ____ **DOCD 5318**
Document / Mar '95 / ADA / Hot Shot / Jazz Music

VICTORIA SPIVEY VOL.4 1936-1937
CD ____ **DOCD 5319**
Document / Mar '95 / ADA / Hot Shot / Jazz Music

WOMAN BLUES (Spivey, Victoria & Lonnie Johnson)
CD ____ **OBCCD 566**
Original Blues Classics / Jul '95 / Complete/Pinnacle / Wellard

Spizz

SPIZZ NOT DEAD SHOCK 1978-1988
CD ____ **CDMRED 130**
Cherry Red / May '96 / Pinnacle

UNHINGED (Spizz Energi)
CD ____ **DAMGOOD 36**
Damaged Goods / Mar '94 / Shellshock/ Disc

SPK

DIGITALIS AMBIGUA, GOLD AND POISON
CD ____ **NTCD 035**
Nettwerk / Feb '88 / Greyhound / Pinnacle / Vital

INFORMATION OVERLOAD UNIT
CD ____ **SPKCD 1**
The Grey Area / Sep '92 / RTM/Disc

LEICHENSCHREI (Sozialistisches Patienten Kollektiv)
Genetik transmission / Post mortem / Desolation / Napalm/Terminal patient / Cry from the sanatorium / Baby blue eyes / Israel / Internal bleeding / Chamber musik / Despair / Agony of the plasma / Day of pigs / Wars of Islam / Maladia Europa
CD ____ **SPKCD 2**
The Grey Area / Aug '92 / RTM/Disc

ZAMI LEHMANNI
CD ____ **SPKCD 3**
The Grey Area / Sep '92 / RTM/Disc

Splash 4

KICKS IN STYLE
CD ____ **ES 1235CD**
Estrus / Feb '97 / Cargo / Greyhound / Plastic Head

Splashband

RIDDIM A TON
CD ____ **CCD 0028**
CRS / Apr '96 / ADA / Direct / Jet Star

Splatcats

RIGHT ON
CD ____ **PRD 70092**
Provogue / May '90 / Pinnacle

Splatter

FROM HELL TO ETERNITY
CD ____ **SECT2 10010**
Sector 2 / Oct '96 / Cargo / Direct

Spleen

SOUNDTRACK TO SPLEEN
CD ____ **SF 006CD**
Swarf Finger / Jan '97 / Cargo

Splendora

IN THE GRASS
CD ____ **379122**
Koch International / Dec '95 / Koch

Splinter Test

SULPHUR - LOW SEED REPLICATION
Debris ov murder / Sulphur - low seed replication / Burned out but building
CD ____ **NERO 23**
Twilight Command / Apr '97 / World Serpent

Splintered

JUDAS CRADLE
CD ____ **DPROMCD 17**
Dirter Promotions / Dec '93 / Cargo / Pinnacle / World Serpent

RLW
CD ____ **BRCD 961005**
Black Rose / Nov '96 / Cargo

Split Enz

ANNIVERSARY
CD ____ **D 98010**
Mushroom / Apr '95 / 3mv/Pinnacle

BEST OF SPLIT ENZ, THE
Titus / Late last night / Matinee idyll 129 / Amy (darling) / Lovey dovey / Time for a change / Crossroads / Another great divide / Bold as brass / My mistake / I see red / I got you / One step ahead / History never repeats / Six months in a leaky boat / Message to my girl
CD ____ **CDCHR 6059**
Chrysalis / Jan '94 / EMI

HISTORY NEVER REPEATS (The Best Of Split Enz)
CD ____ **CDMID 175**
A&M / Oct '92 / PolyGram

TRUE COLOURS
Shark attack / I got you / Whats the matter with you / Double happy / I wouldn't dream of it / I hope I never / Nobody takes me seriously / Missing person / Poor boy / How can I resist her / Choral sea
CD ____ **CDMID 130**
A&M / Oct '92 / PolyGram

Split Up

FATES GOT A DRIVER
CD ____ **DOG 031CD**
Doghouse / Aug '95 / Plastic Head

Splitsville

ULTRASOUND
CD ____ **BDCD 9037**
Big Deal / Jul '97 / Greyhound

Splodgenessabounds

LIVE
CD ____ **RRCD 237**
Receiver / Aug '97 / Grapevine/PolyGram

Spock's Beard

BEWARE OF DARKNESS
Beware of darkness / Thoughts / Doorway / Chatauqua / Walking on the wind / Waste away / Time has come
CD ____ **GEPCD 1018**
Giant Electric Pea / Mar '97 / Pinnacle

LIGHT
CD ____ **GEPCD 1017**
Giant Electric Pea / Oct '96 / Pinnacle

Spolier

CRASHPAD
Something for nothing / Up above / Crashpad / Custom fit / Where to / Small stone / Prism 23 / Four walls / Moving in theory / Numero
CD ____ **PCP 0152**
Matador / Oct '94 / Vital

Sponge

ROTTING PINATA
Pennywheels / Rotting pinata / Giants / Neenah Menasha / Miles / Plowed / Drownin' / Molly / Fields / Rainin'
CD ____ **4769822**
Columbia / Sep '95 / Sony

WAX ECSTATIC
My purity / Got to be a bore / Wax ecstatic (to sell Angelina) / Drag Queens of Memphis / I am Anastasia / Silence is their drug / Have you seen Mary / My baby said / Death of a drag Queen / Velveteen
CD ____ **4841862**
Columbia / Sep '96 / Sony

Spongetones

BEAT AND TORN
CD ____ **BV 129932**
Black Vinyl / Nov '96 / Cargo

OH YEAH
CD ____ **BV 120642**
Black Vinyl / Nov '96 / Cargo

TEXTURAL DRONE THING
CD ____ **BV 122462**
Black Vinyl / Nov '96 / Cargo

Spontaani Vire

SPONTAANI VIRE
CD ____ **J 15CD**
JCD / Nov '96 / ADA

Spontaneous Combustion

SPONTANEOUS COMBUSTION/TRIAD
Speed of light / Listen to the wind / Leaving / 200 lives / Down with the moon / Reminder / Spaceship / Brainstorm / Child life / Love and laughter / Pan / Rainy day / Monolith
CD ____ **SEECD 472**
See For Miles/C5 / Feb '97 / Pinnacle

Spontaneous Music Ensemble

KARYOBIN
CD ____ **CPE 20012**
Chronoscope / Jan '94 / Cadillac / Harmonia Mundi / Wellard

QUINTESSENCE VOL.1
CD ____ **EM 4015**
Emanem / Jul '97 / Cadillac / Harmonia Mundi

QUINTESSENCE VOL.2
CD ____ **EM 4016**
Emanem / Jul '97 / Cadillac / Harmonia Mundi

SUMMER '67
CD ____ **EM 4005**
Emanem / Dec '95 / Cadillac / Harmonia Mundi

Spookey Ruben

MODES OF TRANSPORTATION
Terra magnifica / These days are old / Crydtal cradle / Running away / Welcome to te house of food / Wendy MacDonald / Size of you / It's not what you do it's you / Mars / Donate your heart to a stranger / Life insurance / Medley
CD ____ **CDEMC 3753**
EMI / Jul '97 / EMI

WENDY MCDONALD/LIVE IN JAPAN
CD ____ **TVT 54132**
TVT / Mar '97 / Cargo / Greyhound

Spooky

FOUND SOUND
Central heating / Miscellaneous / Onglon / Bamboo / Aphonia / Tungsten / Lowest common denominator / Relapse / Hypo-allergenic / Fingerbobs / Plan B / Concussion / Interim / Consume / Silver / Seneschal
CD ____ **GENRCD 1**
Generic / Jul '96 / PolyGram / Vital

GARGANTUAN
Don't panic / Schmoo / Aqualung / Little bullet part 1 / Little bullet part 2 / Land of Oz / Something's got to give / Orange coloured liquid / Schmoodub / Let go
CD ____ **GENRCD 2**
Generic / Oct '96 / PolyGram / Vital

Spooky Tooth

BEST OF SPOOKY TOOTH, THE
Tobacco Road / Better by you, better than me / It's all about a roundabout / Waitin' for the wind / Last puff / Evil woman / That was only yesterday / I am the walrus / Self seeking man / All sewn up / Times have changed / As long as the world keeps turning / Weight
CD ____ **IMCD 74**
Island / '89 / PolyGram

LAST PUFF
CD ____ **EDCD 468**
Edsel / Feb '96 / Pinnacle

Spoon

SOFT EFFECTS
Mountain to sound / Waiting for the kid to come out / I could see the dude / Get out the state / Loss leaders / Don't but the realistic / Government darling
CD ____ **OLE 2362**
Matador / Feb '97 / Vital

TELEPHONO
Don't buy the realistic / Not turning off / All the negatives have been destroyed / Cvantez / Nefarious / Claws tracking / Dismember / Idiot driver / Towner / Wanted to be your friend / Theme to Wendel / Stivers / Primary / Government darling / Plastic Mylar
CD ____ **OLE 2012**
Matador / May '96 / Vital

Spooned Hybrio

SPOONED HYBRIO
CD ____ **GU 5CD**
Guernica / Oct '93 / Pinnacle

Spore

FEAR GOD
CD ____ **TAANG 75CD**
Taang / Dec '93 / Cargo

GIANT
CD ____ **TANNG 81**
Taang / Aug '94 / Cargo

SPORE
CD ____ **TAANG 74CD**
Taang / Jun '93 / Cargo

Sports Guitar

MARRIED 3 KIDS
Very weird / Never waste / Help / Chords / So shy / Reliable / Hero / Dinner / Life's a plain / Doesn't matter / Get you out / Robocop / Wanna walk / Croonin'
CD ____ **OLE 2432**
Matador / Aug '97 / Vital

Sposito, John

VOYAGER IV
CD ____ **CDSGP 9017**
Prestige / Jun '95 / Else / Total/BMG

VOYAGER V
CD _____ **CDSGP 9027**
Prestige / Jun '95 / Else / Total/BMG

VOYAGER VI
CD _____ **CDSGP 9028**
Prestige / Jun '95 / Else / Total/BMG

Spotnicks

HIGHWAY BOOGIE
Highway boogie / Lost property / Could it be love / Mighty bump / Love is a symphony / Truck driver's dream / Just another boy / Dolly H / Let it roll roll roll / Besame mucho
CD _____ **CDMF 036**
Magnum Force / Jun '86 / TKO Magnum

Spragga Benz

TWO BADD DJ'S (Spragga Benz & Beenie Man)
CD _____ **VPMHCD 3105**
VP / May '97 / Greensleeves / Jet Star / Total/BMG

Sprague, Carl T.

CLASSIC COWBOY SONGS
Home on the range / It is no secret / Following the cowtrail / Girl I loved in sunny Tennessee / When the work's all done this fall / Kissing / Club meeting / Bad companions / Rounded up in glory / Red river valley / Roll on little dogies / Last great roundup / Last fierce charge / Gambler / Boston burglar / Orphan girl / Utah Carol / Just break the news to mother / Chicken / Cowman's prayer / Sarah Jane / My Carrie Lee / Zebra Dun / Mormon cowboy / Cowboy's meditation / Kicking mule
CD _____ **BCD 15456**
Bear Family / Dec '88 / Direct / Rollercoaster / Swift

Spriguns

JACK WITH A FEATHER (Spriguns Of Tolgus)
CD _____ **HBG 122/9**
Background / Apr '94 / Background / Greyhound

Spring Heel Jack

68 MILLION SHADES
Take one / Midwest / 60 Seconds / Pan / Plates / Bar / Eesti / Roger Tessier / Island / Suspensions / Take two / Take three
CD _____ **TRDCD 1000**
Trade 2 / Jul '96 / PolyGram / RTM/Disc / Vital

BUSY CURIOUS THIRSTY
Bells / Casino / Bank of America / Galapagos 3 / Halle bop / Happy baby / Sirens / Bells / Fresh kills landfill / Wrong guide
CD _____ **TRCD 1004**
Trade 2 / Sep '97 / PolyGram / RTM/Disc / Vital

THERE ARE STRINGS
Only you / Masquerade / Flying again / Oceola / Where do you fit in / Derek / There are strings / Colonades / Lee Perry part 1 / Day of the dead
CD _____ **R 3533**
Rough Trade / Aug '95 / Pinnacle

VERSIONS
60 Seconds dub / Suspensions dub / Pan Dub / Crash dub / Kino / Island version / Regal talkies
CD _____ **TRDCD 1001**
Trade 2 / Sep '96 / PolyGram / RTM/Disc / Vital

Springer, Mark

SWANS AND TURTLES (Springer, Mark & Sarah Sarhandi)
Torreador / Scattered gloves / Desire / Inner secret / Nothing serious / Swans and turtles / Yellow / Brown / Road into the forest
CD _____ **CDVE 902**
Venture / Feb '91 / EMI

Springfield, Dusty

AM I THE SAME GIRL
Son of a preacher man / Stay awhile / All I see is you / I close my eyes and count to ten / Take another little piece of my heart / This girl's in love with you / Second time around / Don't let me lose this dream / Sunny / They long to be close to you / Welcome home / Just one smile / Windmills of your mind / Breakfast in bed / Haunted / Give me time / Am I the same girl / Spooky
CD _____ **5520932**
Spectrum / Mar '96 / PolyGram

BLUE FOR YOU
I just don't know what to do with myself / Your hurtin' kinda love / Will you still love me tomorrow / Every day I have to cry / Some of your lovin' / No easy way down / If you go away / Goin' back / Morning please don't come / How can I be sure / What do you do when love dies / I can't make it alone / My colouring book / Yesterday when I was young
CD _____ **5500052**
Spectrum / May '93 / PolyGram

DUSTY - THE LEGEND OF DUSTY SPRINGFIELD (4CD Set)
How can I be sure / Stay awhile / I just don't know what to do with myself / Son of a preacher man / All cried out / I will come to you / Some of your lovin' / Give me time / I'm coming home again / What's it gonna be / Losing you / Nothing has been proved / Yesterday when I was young / Your hurtin' kinda love / I only want to be with you / All I see / I'll try anything / I close my eyes and count to ten / Brand new me / Your love still brings me to my knees / Magic garden / What good is I love you / You don't have to say you love me / Baby don't you know / Wishin' and hopin' / Corrupt ones / Tanto so che moi me passa / How can I learn to say goodbye / Summer is over / Where am I going / Something in your eyes / I only wanna laugh / Sweet lover no more / Meditation / Come for a dream / Once upon a time / Will you still love me tomorrow / Goodbye / Lose again / I want to be a free girl / Don't say it baby / Heartbeat / He's got something / What do you do when love dies / Time after time / Softcore / When the midnight train leaves for Alabam / La bamba / Love like yours / Go ahead on / What have I done to deserve this / In the middle of nowhere / Another night / Little by little / That's the kind of love I've got for you / In private / I just wanna be there / Mama's little girl / I can't give back the love I feel for you / Oh no not my baby / Donnez moi / Reputation / Mockingbird / Am I the same girl / When the lovelight starts shining / Take me for a little while / Bring him back / Every ounce of strength / Blind sheep / Goin' back / I think it's going to rain today / Tupelo honey / Chained to a memory / Who can I turn to / If you go away / What are you doing the rest of your life / Love me by name / No easy way down / Never love again / I just fall in love again / That's how heartaches are made / I don't want to hear it anymore / I wish I'd never loved you / Just a little lovin' / Who will take my place / I'd rather leave while I'm in love / Sandra / I've been wrong before / If it hadn't been for you / I had a talk with my man / Second time around / Close to you / Look of love
CD Set _____ **5222542**
Philips / Aug '94 / PolyGram

DUSTY IN MEMPHIS
Just a little lovin' / So much love / Son of a preacher man / I don't want to hear it anymore / Don't forget about me / Breakfast in bed / Just one smile / Windmills of your mind / In the land of make believe / No easy way down / I can't make it alone / Willie and Laura Mae Jones / That old sweet roll (Hi de ho) / What do you do when love dies
CD _____ **5286872**
Mercury / Sep '95 / PolyGram

EVERYTHING'S COMING UP DUSTY
CD _____ **BGOCD 74**
Beat Goes On / '89 / Pinnacle

GIRL CALLED DUSTY, A
Mama said / You don't own me / Do re mi / When the lovelight starts shining through his eyes / My colouring book / Mockingbird / Twenty four hours from Tulsa / Nothing / Anyone who had a heart / Will you love me tomorrow / Wishin' and hopin' / Don't you know / I only want to be with you / He's got something / Every day I have to cry / Can I get a witness / All cried out / I wish I'd never loved you / Once upon a time / Summer is over
CD _____ **5345202**
Mercury / Feb '97 / PolyGram

GOIN' BACK (The Best Of Dusty Springfield 1962-1994)
CD _____ **8487892**
Philips / May '94 / PolyGram

REPUTATION
Reputation / Send it to me / Arrested by you / Time waits for no one / I was born this way / In private / Daydreaming / Nothing has been proved / I want to stay here / Occupy your mind
CD _____ **CDFA 3320**
Fame / Apr '95 / EMI

SOMETHING SPECIAL (2CD Set)
Something special / Reste encore un instant / Je ne peux pas t'en vouloir / I'll love you for a while / Needle in a haystack / Tu che ne sai / Di fronte a l'amore / I will always want you / I'm gonna leave you / Small town girl / I've got a good thing / Don't forget about me / No stranger am I / Don't speak of love / Earthbound gypsy / Wasn't born to follow / Song for you / Haunted / I am your child / You set my dreams to music / Give me the night / Baby blue / Your love still brings me to my knees / It goes like it goes / Just one smile / Something in your eyes / I'd rather leave while I'm in love / Let me love you before you go / Tupelo honey / I just fall in love again / What are you doing the rest of your life / Who will take my place / Who can I turn to / Joe / Who could be lovin' you other than me / I've been wrong before / I can't make it alone / Close to you / My colouring book / If you go away / Sandra / No easy way down / Breakfast in bed / Long after tonight is all over / This girl's in love with you / I think it's gonna rain today / Love me by name / Look of love
CD Set _____ **5288182**
Mercury / Apr '96 / PolyGram

VERY FINE LOVE, A
Roll away / Very fine love / Wherever would I be / Go easy on me / You are the storm / I can't help the way I don't feel / All I have to offer you is love / Lovin' proof / Old habits die hard / Where is A
CD _____ **4785082**
Columbia / Sep '96 / Sony

Springfield, Rick

BEST OF RICK SPRINGFIELD, THE
CD _____ **74321431602**
RCA / Oct '96 / BMG

GREATEST HITS
Jessie's girl / I've done everything for you / Love is alright tonight / Don't talk to strangers / What kind of fool am I / Affair of the heart / Human touch / Love somebody / Bop 'till you drop / Celebrate youth / State of the heart / Rock of life
CD _____ **74321289892**
RCA / Aug '95 / BMG

Springfields

OVER THE HILLS AND FAR AWAY (2CD Set)
Dear John / I done what they told me / Breakawaway / Good news / Wimoweh mambo / Black hills of Dakota / Row row row / Green leaves of summer / Silver dollar / Allentown jail / Lonesome traveller / Dear hearts and gentle people / They took John away / Eso es el amor / Two brothers / Tzena tzena tzena / Bambino / Goodnight Irene / Frar away places / Silver threads and golden needles / Aunt Rhody / Swahili papa / Gotta travel on / Island of dreams / Johnson boys / Settle down / There's a big wheel / Greenback dollar / Midnight special / Wabash cannonball / Alone with you / Cottonfields / Foggy mountain top / Little by little / Maggie / Darling Allalee / Mountain boy / My baby's gone / Waf woof / Say I won't be there / Little boat / Come on home / Pit-a-pat / If I was down and out / Marcabamba / No sad songs for me / Where have all the flowers gone
CD Set _____ **5349302**
Mercury / Jun '97 / PolyGram

Springsteen, Bruce

BORN IN THE USA
Cover me / Born in the USA / Darlington County / Working on the highway / Downbound train / I'm on fire / No surrender / Bobby Jean / I'm goin' down / Glory days / Dancing in the dark / My hometown
CD _____ **CD 86304**
CBS / Aug '84 / Sony

BORN TO RUN
Spirit in the night / Because the night / 10th Avenue freeze out / Thunder road / Born to run / Back streets / She's the one / Meeting across the river / Jungleland / Night
CD _____ **CD 69170**
CBS / '83 / Sony
CD _____ **4804162**
Mastersound / Jul '95 / Sony

BRUCE SPRINGSTEEN SONGBOOK (Various Artists)
CD _____ **VSOPCD 224**
Connoisseur Collection / May '96 / Pinnacle

DARKNESS ON THE EDGE OF TOWN
Badlands / Adam raised a Cain / Something in the night / Candy's room / Racing in the street / Promised land / Factory / Streets of fire / Prove it all night / Darkness on the edge of town
CD _____ **CD 86061**
CBS / Jul '84 / Sony

DARKNESS ON THE EDGE OF TOWN/ NEBRASKA (2CD Set)
CD _____ **4716072**
Columbia / Jul '94 / Sony

DARKNESS ON THE EDGE.../ GREETINGS FROM ASBURY.../THE WILD... (3CD Set)
Badlands / Adam raise a cain / Something in the night / Candy's room / Racing in the street / Promised land / Factory / Streets of fire / Prove it all night / Darkness on the edge of town / E Street shuffle / Sandy / Kitty's back / Wild Billy's circus story / Incident on 57th Street / Rosalita (come out tonight) / New York City serenade / Blinded by the light / Growin' up / Mary Queen of Arkansas / Does this bus stop at 82nd Street / Lost in the flood / Angel / For you / Spirit in the night / It's hard to be a saint in the city
CD Set _____ **4853252**
Columbia / Oct '96 / Sony

GHOST OF TOM JOAD, THE
Ghost of Tom Joad / Straight time / Highway 29 / Youngstown / Sinola cowboys / Line / Balbo Park / Dry lightning / New timer / Across the border / Galveston Bay / Best was never enough
CD _____ **4816502**
Columbia / Nov '95 / Sony

GREATEST HITS
Born to run / Thunder road / Badlands / River / Hungry heart / Atlantic City / Dancing in the dark / Born in the USA / My hometown / Glory days / Brilliant disguise / Human touch / Better days / Streets of Philadelphia / Secret garden / Murder incorporated / Blood brothers / This hard land
CD _____ **4785552**
Columbia / Feb '95 / Sony

GREETINGS FROM ASBURY PARK NJ
Blinded by the light / Growing up / Mary Queen of Arkansas / Does this bus stop at 82nd Street / Lost in the flood / Angel for you / Spirit in the night / It's hard to be a saint in the city
CD _____ **CD 65480**
CBS / Nov '82 / Sony

HUMAN TOUCH
Human touch / Soul driver / Fifty seven channels (and nothin' on) / Cross my heart / Gloria's eyes / With every wish / Real world / All or nothing at all / Man's job / I wish I were blind / Long goodbye / Real man / Pony boy
CD _____ **4714232**
Columbia / Mar '92 / Sony

LIVE 1975-1985 (3CD Set) (Springsteen, Bruce & The E Street Band)
Thunder road: *Springsteen, Bruce* / Adam raised a Cain: *Springsteen, Bruce* / Spirit in the night: *Springsteen, Bruce* / 4th of July, Asbury Park (Sandy): *Springsteen, Bruce* / Paradise by the 'c': *Springsteen, Bruce* / Fire: *Springsteen, Bruce* / Growing up: *Springsteen, Bruce* / It's hard to be a saint in the city: *Springsteen, Bruce* / Backstreets: *Springsteen, Bruce* / Rosalita: *Springsteen, Bruce* / Raise your hand: *Springsteen, Bruce* / Hungry heart: *Springsteen, Bruce* / Two hearts: *Springsteen, Bruce* / Cadillac ranch: *Springsteen, Bruce* / You can look (but you'd better not touch): *Springsteen, Bruce* / Independence day: *Springsteen, Bruce* / Badlands: *Springsteen, Bruce* / Because the night: *Springsteen, Bruce* / Candy's room: *Springsteen, Bruce* / Darkness on the edge of town: *Springsteen, Bruce* / Racing in the street: *Springsteen, Bruce* / This land is your land: *Springsteen, Bruce* / Nebraska: *Springsteen, Bruce* / Johnny 99: *Springsteen, Bruce* / Reason to believe: *Springsteen, Bruce* / Born in the USA: *Springsteen, Bruce* / Seeds: *Springsteen, Bruce* / River: *Springsteen, Bruce* / War: *Springsteen, Bruce* / Darlington County: *Springsteen, Bruce* / Working on the highway: *Springsteen, Bruce* / Promised land: *Springsteen, Bruce* / Cover me: *Springsteen, Bruce* / I'm on fire: *Springsteen, Bruce* / Bobby Jean: *Springsteen, Bruce* / My home town: *Springsteen, Bruce* / Born to run: *Springsteen, Bruce* / No surrender: *Springsteen, Bruce* / 10th Avenue freeze out: *Springsteen, Bruce* / Jersey girl: *Springsteen, Bruce*
CD _____ **4502272**
CBS / Nov '86 / Sony

LUCKY TOWN
Better days / Lucky town / Local hero / If I should fall behind / Leap of faith / Big muddy / Living proof / Book of dreams / Souls of the departed / My beautiful reward
CD _____ **4714242**
Columbia / Mar '92 / Sony

NEBRASKA
Nebraska / Atlantic city / Mansion on the hill / Johnny 99 / Highway patrolman / State trooper / Used cars / Open all night / My father's house / Reason to believe
CD _____ **4633602**
CBS / Feb '89 / Sony

PLUGGED - MTV IN CONCERT
Red headed woman / Better days / Atlantic city / Darkness on the edge of town / Man's job / Human touch / Lucky town / I wish I were blind / Thunder road / Light of day / If I should fall behind / Living proof / My beautiful reward
CD _____ **4738602**
Columbia / Apr '93 / Sony

RIVER, THE (2CD Set)
Ties that bind / Sherry darling / Jackson Cage / Two hearts / Independence day / Hungry Heart / Out in the street / Crush on you / You can look (but you'd better not touch) / I wanna marry you / River / Point blank / Cadillac Ranch / I'm a rocker / Fade away / Stolen car / Ramrod / Price you pay / Wreck on the highway
CD Set _____ **4773762**
Columbia / Sep '94 / Sony

TUNNEL OF LOVE
Ain't got you / Tougher than the rest / All that heaven will allow / Spare parts / Cautious man / Walk like a man / Tunnel of love / Two faces / Brilliant disguise / One step up / When you're alone / Valentine's day
CD _____ **4602702**
CBS / Oct '87 / Sony

WILD, THE INNOCENT AND THE E STREET SHUFFLE, THE
E Street shuffle / 4th of July, Asbury Park (Sandy) / Kitty's back / Wild Billy's circus / Incident on 57th Street / Rosalita / New York City serenade

CD ______ CD 32363
CBS / Apr '89 / Sony

Sprinkler

MORE BOY, LESS FRIEND
CD ______ SP 211CD
Sub Pop / Nov '92 / Cargo / Greyhound / Shellshock/Disc

Sproton Layer

WITH MAGNETIC FIELDS DISRUPTED
CD ______ NAR 055CD
New Alliance / May '93 / Plastic Head

Sproule, Daithi

HEART MADE OF GLASS, A
Lonely Waterloo / Turkish revery / Gabham molta bride / Patty's tune / Bold Belfast shoemaker / Banks of Claudy / September / Gleanntain ghlas ghaoth dobhair / House carpenter / Beaver brig / Bonny bunch of roses / Cailin na gruaige doinne/Little star
CD ______ GLCD 1123
Green Linnet / May '93 / ADA / CM / Direct / Highlander / Roots

Sprouse, Blaine

INDIAN SPRINGS (Sprouse, Blaine & Kenny Baker)
Oh demi slippers / Molly darlin' / Owensboro / Avalon / September waltz / Three days in Dublin / Coker creek / K and W waltz / Cotton town breakdown / Indian springs
CD ______ ROUCD 0259
Rounder / '89 / ADA / CM / Direct

Sprout, Tobin

CARNIVAL BOY
Natural alarm / Cooler jocks / E's navy blue / Bone yard / Carnival boy / Martin's mounted head / Gas daddy gas / To my beloved Martha / White flyer / I didn't know / Gallant men / It's like soul man / Hermit stew / Last man well known to kingpin
CD ______ OLE 2162
Matador / Sep '96 / Vital

Spudmonsters

MOMENT OF TRUTH
CD ______ MASSCD 109
Massacre / Nov '96 / Plastic Head

STOP THE MADNESS
CD ______ MASSCD 017
Massacre / Jun '95 / Plastic Head

Spunk

SPUNK
CD ______ VIRION 101
Sound Virus / Sep '94 / Plastic Head

Spyra

PHONEHEAD
CD ______ PS 0666CD
Fax / Mar '97 / Plastic Head

Spyro Gyra

20/20
Unwritten letter / Ruled by Venus / 20/20 / Three sisters / Sweet baby James / Deep end / Together / Dark-eyed lady / South American Sojourn / Rockaway to sunset / Return of the pygmy
CD ______ GRP 98682
GRP / May '97 / New Note/BMG

CATCHING THE SUN
Catching the sun / Cockatoo / Autumn of our love / Laser material / Percolator / Philly / Lovin' you (interlude) lovin' you / Here again / Safari
CD ______ 74321202622
RCA / Feb '97 / BMG

DREAMS BEYOND CONTROL
Walk the walk / Patterns in the rain / Breakfast at Igor's / Waltz for Isabel / South beach / Send me one line / Bahia / Kindred spirit / Birk's law / Same difference / Delicate prey / Friendly fire
CD ______ GRP 97432
GRP / Sep '93 / New Note/BMG

HEART OF THE NIGHT
Heart of the night / De la luz / Westwood moon / Midnight / Playtime / Surrender / Valentino's / Believe / As we sleep / When evening falls / J squared / Best thing
CD ______ GRP 98492
GRP / Apr '96 / New Note/BMG

LOVE & OTHER OBSESSIONS
Lost and found / Ariana / Serengeti / Fine time to explain / Third street / Group therapy / Horizon's edge / Let's say goodbye / On liberty road (for South Africa) / Rockin' a heart place / Baby dreams / Open season
CD ______ GRP 98112
GRP / Mar '95 / New Note/BMG

MORNING DANCE
Morning dance / Jubilee / Rasul / Song for Lorraine / Starburst / It doesn't matter / Little Linda / End of Romanticism / Heliopolis
CD ______ 74321202612
MCA / May '94 / BMG

THREE WISHES
Pipo's song / Introduction to breathless / Breathless / Real time / Jennifer's lullaby / Whitewater / Inside your love / Nothing to lose / Three wishes / Gliding / Yemanja / Rollercoaster / Three wishes (reprise)
CD ______ GRP 96742
GRP / May '92 / New Note/BMG

Squadronaires

THERE'S SOMETHING IN THE AIR
There's something in the air / South Rampart Street parade / C jam blues / Pompton turnpike / Ringle dingle / Anchors aweigh / Commando patrol / Boston bounce / Rimg dem bells / Cow cow boogie / High society / Mistakes / Mission on Moscow / That's a plenty
CD ______ HEPCD 44
Hep / Dec '90 / Cadillac / Jazz Music / New Note/Pinnacle / Wellard

THERE'S SOMETHING IN THE AIR
Chattanooga choo choo / Beat me Daddy, eight to the bar / Blues in the night / Pennyslyania polka / Me and Melinda / Be careful it's my heart / Jersey bounce / Tropical magic / Jealous / Lover's lullaby / String of pearls / Cow cow boogie / Commando patrol / Drummin' man / Darktown strutters ball / Boogie woogie bugle boy / My mother would love you / (Back home again in) Indiana / Lament to love / All of me / There's something in the air
CD ______ RAJCD 816
Empress / Feb '94 / Koch

THERE'S SOMETHING IN THE AIR
All of me / Anchors aweigh / Blue Lou / Bounce me brother with a solid four / Chattanooga choo choo / Cherokee / Darktown strutters ball / Daybreak / Dolores / Drummin' man / Goodnight sweet neighbour / How sweet you are / (Back home again in) Indiana / Jazz me blues / Jersey bounce / Ringle dingle / Sinner kissed an angel / Some sunny day / South Rampart Street parade / String of pearls / That day it rained / That's a-plenty / There's something in the air / Way down yonder in New Orleans / You're my baby
CD ______ CDAJA 5128
Living Era / Mar '94 / Select

WARTIME MEMORIES
There's something in the air tonight / Skyliner / We're gonna hang out the washing on the Siegfried Line / Nightingale sang in Berkeley Square / White cliffs of Dover / Foggy day / South Rampart Street parade / Lili Marlene / I'll be seeing you / We'll meet again / Little brown jug / You'll never know / I'm gonna get lit up (when the lights go on in London) / News bulletins from throughout the war
CD ______ CDMFP 6123
Music For Pleasure / May '94 / EMI

Squarepusher

FEED ME WEIRD THINGS
CD ______ CAT 037CD
Rephlex / Jun '96 / Prime / RTM/Disc

HARD NORMAL DADDY
Coopers world / Beep street / Rustic raver / Airdog D9 / Chin hippy / Papalon / Ex boogie / Fat controller / Vic acid / Male pill part 13 / Rat/P's and Q's / Rebus
CD ______ WARPCD 50
Warp / Apr '97 / Prime / RTM/Disc

Squatweiler

NEW MOTHERSTAMPER
CD ______ SPART 56
Spin Art / Jun '97 / Cargo

Squeeze

BABYLON AND ON/EASTSIDE STORY
CD ______ CDA 24120
A&M / Jul '92 / PolyGram

COOL FOR CATS
Slap and tickle / Revue / Touching me touching you / It's not cricket / It's so dirty / Hop, skip and jump / Up the junction / Hard to find / Slightly drunk / Goodbye girl / Cool for cats / Up the junction (live)
CD ______ CDMID 131
A&M / Oct '92 / PolyGram

EAST SIDE STORY
In quintessence / Someone else's heart / Tempted / Piccadilly / There's no tomorrow / Woman's world / Is that Love / F-hole / Labelled with love / Someone else's bell / Mumbo Jumbo / Vanity fair / Messed around
CD ______ CDMID 132
A&M / Oct '92 / PolyGram

EXCESS MODERATION (2CD Set)
Take me I'm yours / Model / Revue / Christmas Day / Blood & guts / Going crazy / Knack / If I didn't love you / Separate beds / I think I'm go go / What the butler saw / Piccadilly / Trust / Tempted / Woman's world / Squabs on forty fab / Elephant ride / Tongue like a knife / His house her home / When the hangover strikes / Apple tree / Within these walls without you / On my mind tonight / Hope fell down / No place like home / What have they done / Tough love / Striking matches / Peyton Place / Dr. Jazz / Melody Motel / Slaughtered, gutted & heartbroken / Maidstone / House of love / Truth / Letting go / It's over / Loving you tonight / Cold shoulder / Some fantastic place
CD Set ______ 5406482
A&M / Nov '96 / PolyGram

GREATEST HITS
Take me I'm yours / Goodbye girl / Cool for cats / Up the junction / Slap and tickle / Another nail in my heart / Pulling mussels (from the shell) / Tempted / Labelled with love / Black coffee in bed / Annie get your gun / Last time forever / Hourglass / Trust me to open my mouth / Footprints / If it's love / Is that love / King George street / No place like home / Love circles
CD ______ 3971812
A&M / May '92 / PolyGram

PLAY
Satisfied / Crying in my sleep / Letting go / Day I get home / Truth / House of love / Cupid's toy / Gone to the dogs / Walk a straight line / Sunday street / Wicked and cruel / There is a voice
CD ______ 7599266442
Reprise / Sep '91 / Warner Music

RIDICULOUS
Electric trains / Heaven knows / Grouch of the day / Walk away / This summer / Got to me / Long face / I want you / Daphne / Lost for words / Great escape / Temptation for love / Sound asleep / Fingertips
CD ______ 5404402
A&M / Aug '96 / PolyGram

ROUND AND A BOUT, A
Footprints / Pulling mussels (from the shell) / Black coffee in bed / She doesn't have to shave / Is that love / Dr. Jazz / Up the junction / Slaughtered / Gutted and heartbroken / Is it too late / Cool for cats / Take me I'm yours / If it's love / Hourglass / Labelled with love / Annie get your gun / Boogie woogie country girl / Tempted
CD ______ EIRSCD 1084
IRS/EMI / Jun '96 / EMI

SOME FANTASTIC PLACE
Everything in the world / Some fantastic place / Third rail / Loving you tonight / It's over / Cold shoulder / Talk to him / Jolly comes home / Images of loving / True colours (the storm) / Pinocchio
CD ______ 5401402
A&M / Oct '93 / PolyGram

Squiban, Didier

BREST 1996 - PENN-AR-BRED
CD ______ L'OZ 08CD
L'Oz / Aug '96 / ADA

Squidboy

KIDS TALK TO KILLERS
CD ______ ALLIED 74CD
Allied / Sep '96 / Cargo / Greyhound / Plastic Head

Squip

WENN UBERHAUDT
CD ______ 9604CD
Verlag DS / May '97 / ADA

Squire

BIG SMASHES
CD ______ TANGCD 4
Tangerine / Aug '92 / RTM/Disc

GET READY TO GO
CD ______ TANGCD 7
Tangerine / Aug '94 / RTM/Disc

Squire, Chris

FISH OUT OF WATER
Hold out your hand / You by my side / Silently falling / Lucky seven / Safe (canon song)
CD ______ 7567815002
Atlantic / Jan '96 / Warner Music

Squires, Dorothy

BEST OF DOROTHY SQUIRES, THE
CD ______ SOW 713
Sound Waves / Nov '94 / Target/BMG

LIVE AT THE LONDON PALLADIUM (3CD Set)
My way / Back in your own backyard/Everything is beautiful / Do I worry / Swanee, Swanee river/Ol' man river/Lazy river / For once in my life / Autograph book / Why did I choose you / If you love me (Hymne a l'amour) / Man that got away / My way / 'S wonderful/They say it's wonderful/Wonderful one / Don't take your love from me / It's the talk of the town / It can't be done / Gibraltar anthem / Safe in my arms again / Didn't we / Say it with flowers / Mother's day/The gypsy/A tree in the meadow / I'm walking behind you / I can live again / I've gotta be me / My way / My way / Happy heart / There goes my heart / Shaking the blues away / Where do I begin / Bewitched / Till / Autograph book / What a wonderful world / As long as he needs me / On Mother Kelly's doorstep / Mother's day / Everything's coming up roses / My way / Life goes on / For once in my life / If he walked into my life / Where have all the flowers gone / When the world is ready / Glory hallelujah (Battle hymn of the Republic) / Pack up your troubles in your old kit bag / Goodbye Dolly Gray / It's a long way to Tipperary / Mama / When there's love in your heart / I've gotta be me / My way
CD Set ______ STE 7071
Sterndale / Mar '97 / Target/BMG

SAY IT WITH FLOWERS
Say it with flowers / And so to sleep again / Roses of Picady / Gypsy / Someone other than me / Do I worry / Secret that's never been told / Legend of the well / On the sunny side of the street / Song of the valley / Mother's day / Look around / Snowflakes / To be worthy of you / Bewitched / Old soft shoe / Two strangers meet / Our song
CD ______ CDMFP 6216
Music For Pleasure / Apr '96 / EMI

WITH ALL MY HEART
Gypsy / It's a pity to say goodnight / When you lose the one you love / I'll close my eyes / Changing partners / Danger ahead beware / Don't search for love / White wings / With all my heart / When I grow too old to dream / Yes I'll be here / Torremolinos / Tree in the meadow / I still believe / In all the world / Come home to my arms / Safe in my arms / Sorrento and you / Mother's day / Coming home / I'm walking behind you / Someone to love / Blue blue water / Reflections on the water
CD ______ C5CD 604
See For Miles/C5 / Mar '96 / Pinnacle

Squires, Rosemary

ELLA FITZGERALD SONGBOOK (Squires, Rosemary & Maxine Daniels & Babrbara Jay)
Tisket-a-tasket / It don't mean a thing if it ain't got that swing / But not for me / They all laughed / This cant' be love / Someone to watch over me / Soon / Every time we say goodbye / Foggy day / That old black magic / Miss Otis regrets / Love for sale / Take a chance on love / Cheek to cheek / Frim fram sauce / Ten cents a dance / Manhattan / Thou swell / Looking for a boy / Fine romance / How about you / Anything goes / They can't take that away from me / I concentrate on you / Dream dancing / You do something to me / Airmail special / Mack the knife
CD ______ SPJCD 556
Spotlite / Oct '94 / Cadillac / Jazz Music / New Note/Pinnacle / Swift

Squirrel Bait

SKAG HEAVEN
CD ______ DEX 11
Drag City / Feb '97 / Cargo / Greyhound

SQUIRREL BAIT
CD ______ DEX 10
Drag City / Feb '97 / Cargo / Greyhound

Squirrel Nut Zippers

INEVITABLE, THE
Lover's lane / Danny Diamond / I've found a new baby / Anything but love / Good enough for Grandad / Wished for you / Plenty more / You're driving me crazy / Wash Jones / Club limbo / Lugubrious whing whang / La grippe
CD ______ MR 1052
Mammoth / Apr '95 / Vital

Squirtgun

ANOTHER SUNNY AFTERNOON
CD ______ LOOKOUT 167CD
Lookout / Feb '97 / Cargo / Greyhound / Shellshock/Disc

SHENADIGANS
CD ______ LOOKOUT 118CD
Lookout / Oct '95 / Cargo / Greyhound / Shellshock/Disc

Srinivas, U.

DAWN RAGA
CD ______ WS 003CD
Womad Select / Aug '96 / ADA / Direct

DREAM (Srinivas, U. & Michael Brook)
Dance / Think / Run / Dream
CD ______ CDRW 47
Realworld / May '95 / EMI

MODERN MANDOLIN MAESTRO
Ghananayakam / Ninnvvina / Arulseya / Ragam madhyamavati / Thanam / Palinchu kamakshi / Saravana bhava / Malai pozudinile / Folk note
CD ______ CDORBD 068
Globestyle / Mar '91 / Pinnacle

RAMA SREERAMA
CD ______ CDRW 39
Realworld / Jul '94 / EMI

SSD

POWER
CD TAANG 050CD
Taang / Jun '92 / Cargo

St. Christopher

DIG DEEP BROTHER 1984-1990
Forevermore starts here / To the mountain / Charmelle / Who's next on Cupid's hit list / Climb on forever / If I could capture / My fond farewell / Even the sky seems blue / Rivers run dry / Awe / I wish I hadn't seen her / Remember me to her / Tell the world / Our secret / Crystal clear / Rollercoaster / Where in the world / Josephine why / All of a tremble / On the death of my son / Sinking ships / For one so weak / My fortune / How can you tell / Wanda
CD ASKCD 026
Vinyl Japan / Jun '93 / Plastic Head / Vinyl Japan

LIONESS
Loneliness is a friend of mine / Tangled up in blue / Jewels in your hair / Utopian / Hell / She looks like you / With her in mind / Where you are, everything is / As good as married / Flirtation / Loneliness is a friend of mine (reprise)
CD ASKCD 053
Vinyl Japan / Oct '96 / Plastic Head / Vinyl Japan

LOVE YOU TO PIECES
Away / Ladder / Crush / Baptise me baby / Wildest dreams / Everything now / Magic spell / Liberty / For the world to see / Dive / Stars belong to me / Pieces
CD ASKCD 027
Vinyl Japan / Feb '94 / Plastic Head / Vinyl Japan

MAN I COULD SCREAM
CD ASK 6CD
Vinyl Japan / '92 / Plastic Head / Vinyl Japan

St. Clair, Isla

INHERITANCE
Flowers of the forest / Ye Jacobites by name / Smile in your sleep / Farewell tae tarwathie / Fear a'bhata / MacCrimmon's lament / Fifty first highland division's farewell to Sicily / Come ye o'er frae france / Hush ye noo / Norland wind / Freedom come-all-ye / Hills of Ardmorn
CD MOICD 008
Moidart / May '93 / Conifer/BMG

SCENES OF SCOTLAND
Lest we forget / Queen Edinbro' / Couthy Cullen / Ballachuilish / Call tae arms / Lament for the commandos/Dunkirk / Lullin' the littlin' / Toast to Stornaway / Lifeboat / Spinning wheel / Glen Isla/Green ruby waltz / Glencoe / Bonnie boats o'Buckie / Poet & lover
CD CDTRAX 119
Greentrax / Oct '96 / ADA / Direct / Duncans / Highlander

St. Clement Danes Choir

MOST BEAUTIFUL CHRISTMAS SONGS, THE
CD DCD 5133
Disky / Nov '92 / Disky / THE

TRADITIONAL ENGLISH CHRISTMAS CAROLS
CD CNCD 5934
Disky / Nov '92 / Disky / THE

St. Domingo De Silos Monks ...

LIGHT OF SILOS, THE (St. Domingo De Silos Monks Choir)
CD Set 74321402892
Milan / Oct '96 / Conifer/BMG / Silva Screen

St. Eloi Juniors

PREMYE FWA
CD CDS 7327
Sonodisc / Jan '97 / Stern's

St. Etienne

CASINO CLASSICS (The Remix Album - 2CD Set)
Like a motorway / Join our club / Pale movie / Speedwell / Only love can break your heart / Who do you think you are / Avenue / Hug my soul / Like a motorway (David Holmes remix) / Angel / Filthy / People get real / Nothing can stop us / Sometimes in winter / Sea / Burnt out car / He's on the phone / Cool kids of death / Angel (Broadcast mix)
CD Set HVNLP 16CDL
CD Set HVNLP 16CD
Heavenly / Oct '96 / 3mv/Pinnacle / BMG / Vital

FOXBASE ALPHA
This is Radio Etienne / Only love can break your heart / Wilson / Can't sleep / Girl VII / Spring / She's the one / Stoned to say the least / Nothing can stop us / Etienne gonna die / London belongs to me / Like the swallow / Dilworth's theme
CD HVNCD 1
Heavenly / Sep '91 / 3mv/Pinnacle / BMG / Vital

SO TOUGH
Mario's cafe / Railway Jam / Date with spelman / Calico / Avenue / You're in a bad way / Memo to pricey / Hobart paving / Leafhound / Clock milk / Conichita matrinez / No rainbows for me / Here come clown feet / Junk the morgue / Chicken soup
CD HVNLP 6CD
Heavenly / Jan '93 / 3mv/Pinnacle / BMG / Vital

TIGER BAY
Urban clearway / Former lover / Hug my soul / Like a motorway / On the shore / Marble lions / Pale movie / Cool kids of death / Western wind / Tankerville / Boy scouts of America
CD HVNLP 8CD
Heavenly / Feb '94 / 3mv/Pinnacle / BMG / Vital

TOO YOUNG TO DIE (The Singles Collection 1991-1995)
CD HVNLP 10CD
CD HVNLP 10CDX
Heavenly / Nov '95 / 3mv/Pinnacle / BMG / Vital

YOU NEED A MESS OF HELP TO STAND ALONE
Who do you think you are / Archway people / California snow story / Kiss and make up / Duke duvet / Filthy / Join our club / Paper / People get real / Some place else / Speedwell
CD HVNLP 7CD
Heavenly / Nov '93 / 3mv/Pinnacle / BMG / Vital

St. Germain

BOULEVARD
Deep in it / Thank U Mum (4 everything you did) / Street scene / Easy to remember / Sentimental mood / What's new / Dub experience II / Forget it
CD F 002CD
F-Communications / Aug '96 / Prime / Vital

St. John's College ...

CAROLS FOR CHRISTMAS (St. John's College Cambridge Choir)
Ding dong merrily on high / O little town of Bethlehem / Born on Earth / Twelve days of Christmas / Up good Christen folk / Silent night / Good King Wenceslas / While shepherds watched their flocks by night / God rest ye merry gentlemen / Holly and the ivy / Away in a manger / Shepherd's pipe carol / First Noel / I saw three ships / Suo gan / Hark the herald angels sing
CD 4501112
Belart / Nov '96 / PolyGram

CHRISTMAS CAROLS (St. John's College Cambridge Choir)
God rest ye merry gentlemen / Ding dong merrily on high / O little town of Bethlehem / Unto us a boy is born / Good King Wenceslas / Holly and the ivy / I sing of a maiden / Two Welsh carols / Silent night / Hark the herald angels sing / Jesus Christ the apple tree / In the bleak midwinter / O come all ye faithful (Adeste Fidelis) / Shepherd's pipe carol / On Christmas night / Away in a manger / There is no rose / Balulalow
CD CHAN 8485
Chandos / '86 / Chandos

St. John, Bridget

ASK ME NO QUESTIONS/SONGS FOR THE GENTLEMEN
To B without a hitch / Autumn lullaby / Curl your toes / Like never before / Curious crystals of unusual purity / Barefeet and hot pavements / I like to be with you in the sun / Lizard-long-tongue-boy / Hello again (of course) / Many happy returns / Broken faith / Ask me no questions / Day a way / City crazy / Back to stay / Seagull Sunday / If you's been there / Song for the Laird of Connaught Hall (part 2) / Making losing better / Lady and the gentle man / Downderry daze / Pebble and the man / It seems very strange
CD SEECD 408
See For Miles/C5 / Sep '94 / Pinnacle

JUMBLEQUEEN
Sparrowpit / Song for the waterden widow / I don't know if I can take it / Some kind of beautiful / Last goodnight / Curious and woolly / Want to be with you / Jumblequeen / Sweet painted lady / Long long time
CD BGOCD 260
Beat Goes On / Feb '95 / Pinnacle

TAKE THE FIFTH
CD RGFCD 026
Road Goes On Forever / Oct '95 / Direct

THANK YOU FOR
Nice / Thank you for / Lazarus / Good baby goodbye / Love minus zero, no limit / Silver coin / Happy day / Fly high / To leave your cover / Every day / Song as long as it wants to go on
CD SEECD 428
See For Miles/C5 / Jul '95 / Pinnacle

St. John, Kate

INDESCRIBABLE NIGHT
There is sweet music here that softer falls / Paris skies / Now the night comes stealing in / Fireflies / Le premier bonheur du jour / Green park blues / Wherefore art thou / Variety lights / On the bridge / Indescribable night / Shadows of doubt / Chat voyeur / Mr. Goodbyes
CD ASCD 025
All Saints / Jun '95 / Discovery / Vital

SECOND SIGHT
Don't they know you've gone / Where the wind blows / Songs and silhouettes / Flicker of gold / My lonely love / Notti senza amore / J'attendrai / Fireworks / Foolish dance / Dark heavens / Colonel Sinnot's song of love
CD ASCD 034
All Saints / Sep '97 / Discovery / Vital

St. Johnny

HIGH AS A KITE
CD R 2966
Rough Trade / Feb '93 / Pinnacle

St. Louis Jimmy

GOIN' DOWN SLOW
Poor boy / Nothin' but the blues / Mother's day blues / Some sweet day / My heart is loaded with trouble / I'm St. Louis bound / Goin' down slow / Sweet as she can be / Monkey faced woman
CD OBCCD 584
Original Blues Classics / Oct '96 / Complete/Pinnacle / Wellard

St. Louis Ragtimers

ST. LOUIS RAGTIMERS
CD SOSCD 1267
Stomp Off / Oct '93 / Jazz Music / Wellard

ST. LOUIS RAGTIMERS VOL.2
CD BCD 362
GHB / Jun '96 / Jazz Music

St. Mark, Keverenn Brest

TU PE DU
CD KBSM 001CD
KBSM / Mar '96 / ADA

St. Michael Singers

YE SERVANTS OF GOD (St. Michael Singers, Coventry/Paul Leddington Wright)
Christ the Lord is risen today / Christ whose glory / Jesu lover of my soul / Jesus the name high over all / O for a heart to praise / Ye servants of God / Thou God of truth
CD KMCD 891
Kingsway / May '96 / Complete/Pinnacle

St. Paul's Cathedral Choir

CAROLS FROM ST. PAUL'S CATHEDERAL (St. Paul's Cathedral Choir/Life Guards)
O come all ye faithful (Adeste Fidelis) / Away in a manger / First Noel / Ding dong merrily on high / Holly and the ivy / O little town of Bethlehem / Joy to the world / In dulci jubilo / Once in Royal David's City / Sussex carol / See amid the winter's snow / In the bleak midwinter / Mary's lullaby / Silent night / Hark the herald angels sing
CD CDPR 124
Premier/MFP / Nov '94 / EMI

St. Vitus

BORN TOO LATE
CD SST 082CD
SST / Oct '87 / Plastic Head

HEAVIER THAN THOU
CD SST 266CD
SST / May '93 / Plastic Head

MOURNFUL CRIES
CD SST 161CD
SST / Sep '88 / Plastic Head

V
Living backwards / When emotion dies / Ice monkey / Angry man / I bleed black / Patra / Jack Frost / Mind food
CD H 00052
Hellhound / Apr '90 / Koch

Stackhouse, Houston

CRYIN' WON'T HELP YOU
CD EDCD 383
Edsel / Oct '94 / Pinnacle

Stackridge

BBC RADIO 1 IN CONCERT
God speed the plough / Lummy days / Tea time / Anyone for tennis / Amazing Agnes / She taught me how to yodel / 32 west mall / Syracuse the elephant / Volunteer / Whose that up there with Bill Stokes / No-one's more important than the earthworm / Dora the female explora
CD SFRSCD 032
Windsong / Jul '97 / Pinnacle

FRIENDLINESS
CD SIVCD 0010
Red Steel / Aug '96 / Pinnacle

FRIENDLINESS...PLUS
CD EDCD 487
Edsel / Aug '96 / Pinnacle

MAN IN THE BOWLER HAT
Fundamentally yours / Pinafore days / Last plimsoll / To the sun and the moon / Road to Venezuela / Galloping gaucho / Humiliation / Dangerous beacon / Indifferent hedgehog / God speed / Do the stanley / C'est la vie / Let there be lids
CD EDCD 488
Edsel / Jul '96 / Pinnacle

STACKRIDGE
Grande piano / Percy the penguin / Three legged table / Dora the female explorer / Essence of porphyry / Marigold conjunction / 32 West Mall / Marzo plod / Slark
CD SIVCD 0009
Red Steel / Nov '96 / Pinnacle
CD EDCD 518
Edsel / Mar '97 / Pinnacle

Stackwaddy

STACKWADDY/BUGGER OFF
Roadrunner / Bring it to Jerome / Mothballs / Sure nuff 'N' yes I do / Love story / Suzie Q / Country line special / Rollin' stone / Mystic eyes / Kentucky / Rosalyn / Willie the pimp / Hoochie coochie man / It's all over now / Several yards / You really got me / I'm a lover not a fighter / Meat pies 'ave come but band's not here yet / It ain't easy / Long tall shorty / Repossession boogie
CD SEECD 407
See For Miles/C5 / Sep '94 / Pinnacle

Stacy Cats

ROCKJIVE
CD RKCD 9312
Rockhouse / May '93 / Nervous

Stacy, Jess

EC-STACY
CD TPZ 1050
Topaz Jazz / Aug '96 / Cadillac / Pinnacle

JESS STACY (20 Great Piano Performances 1935-1945)
Barrelhouse / Rhythm rhythm (I got rhythm) / Take me to the land of jazz / Rose of Washington Square / I got rhythm / Blue room / Carnegie jump / Darktown strutters ball / Mad house / Roll 'em / Big John special / Opus 3/4 / Vultee special / Ec-Stacy / Spain / Down to steamboat Tennessee / Daybreak serenade / It's only a paper moon / In a mist / Candlelights / In the dark / I ain't got nobody / Blue fives / Ridin' easy / Sing sing sing
CD CDAJA 5172
Living Era / May '95 / Select

STACY JESS 1935-39
CD CLASSICS 795
Classics / Mar '95 / Discovery / Jazz Music

STACY STILL SWINGS
CD CRD 133
Chiaroscuro / Mar '96 / Jazz Music

Stadacona Band

ON THE QUARTER DECK
On the quarter deck / Parade of the tall ships / Helen Creighton folk songs / Vedette / Overture to an unwritten comedy / Concertino for flute / Seven seas overture / Les arrivals / Gladiator's farewell / You needed me / Shadows in the moonlight / I just fall in love again / Processions of the nobles / Nova scotia farewell / Barrett's privateers / HM Jollies / Heart of oak
CD BNA 5113
Bandleader / Jun '95 / Conifer/BMG

Stafford, Jo

CAPITOL COLLECTORS SERIES: JO STAFFORD
Old acquaintance / How sweet you are / Long ago and far away / I love you / It could happen to you / Trolley song: *Stafford, Jo & The Pied Pipers* / There's no you / That's for me / Symphony / Ridin' on the gravy train / This is always / Things we did last summer / Smoke dreams: *Stafford, Jo & Starlighters* / Temptation (Timtayshun) / I'm so right tonight / Serenade of the bells / I never love anyone / He's gone away / Congratulations / Once and for always / Some enchanted evening / Whispering hope: *Stafford, Jo & Gordon MacRae* / Ragtime cowboy Joe / Scarlet ribbons / It's great to be alive: *Stafford, Jo & Johny Mercer* / No other love
CD CZ 414
Capitol / Apr '91 / EMI

CAPITOL YEARS, THE
Best things in life are free / Long ago and far away / On the sunny side of the street / Boy next door / I'll be with you in apple blossom time: *Stafford, Jo & Nat 'King' Cole* / Ragtime cowboy Joe: *Stafford, Jo & Starlighters* / There's no you / diamonds are a girl's best friend: *Stafford, Jo & Starlighters*

/ Play a simple melody: *Stafford, Jo & Starlighters* / Let's take the long way home / Stanley Steamer: *Stafford, Jo & Starlighters* / You belong to me / Shrimp boats / Georgia on my mind / Jambalaya / Come rain or come shine / Day by day / Gentleman is a dope / I'll be seeing you / Trolley song
CD ____ CDEMS 1371
Capitol / Feb '91 / EMI

DRIFTING & DREAMING (Stafford, Jo & Dick Haynes)
CD ____ VJC 1040
Vintage Jazz Classics / Nov '92 / ADA / Cadillac / CM / Direct

FOR YOU
CD ____ CDMOIR 513
Memoir / Nov '95 / Jazz Music / Target/ BMG

JO STAFFORD 1940-1944
For you / Whatcha know Joe / Blues in the night / Swingin' on nothin' / Embraceable you / Yes indeed / Let's just pretend / It isn't a dream anymore / My my / Who can I turn to / What can I say after I say I'm sorry / Little man with a candy cigar / Margie / Manhattan serenade / Night we called it a day / Candy / Conversation while dancing / I'll be seeing you
CD ____ CD 420
Entertainers / Mar '97 / Target/BMG

JO STAFFORD STORY, THE
Old acquaintance / I remember you / Too marvellous for words / How sweet you are / It could happen to you / Trolley song / Boy next door / I love you / Long ago and far away / I didn't know about you / Walkin' my baby back home / There's no you / That's for me / Symphony / On the sunny side of the street / Candy / Over the rainbow / I'll be with you in apple blossom time / Let's take the long way home / Sometimes I'm happy / Fools rush in / Ridin' on the gravy train / This is always / Things we did last summer
CD ____ JASMCD 2544
Jasmine / Apr '97 / Conifer/BMG / Hot Shot / TKO Magnum

ONE AND ONLY, THE
I promise you / Friend of yours / Why can't you behave / This is the moment / Roses of Picardy / Smiling through / Last mile home / Red River Valley / If I ever love again / Happy times / On the out-going tide / If I loved you / Goodnight Irene / Autumn leaves / Some time / La vie en rose / Our very own / I hate men / Congratulations / Old rugged cross
CD ____ CDSL 8276
Music For Pleasure / Nov '95 / EMI

SOLDIERS' SWEETHEARTS (3CD Set) (Stafford, Jo/Vera Lynn/Anne Shelton)
You belong to me: *Stafford, Jo* / Allentown jail: *Stafford, Jo* / Come rain or come shine: *Stafford, Jo* / On London Bridge: *Stafford, Jo* / As I love you: *Stafford, Jo* / Make love to me: *Stafford, Jo* / Shrimp boats: *Stafford, Jo* / Tennessee waltz: *Stafford, Jo* / I'll be seeing you: *Stafford, Jo* / Whispering hope: *Stafford, Jo* / Teach me tonight: *Stafford, Jo* / Jambalaya: *Stafford, Jo* / Thank you for calling, goodbye: *Stafford, Jo* / Ay round the corner: *Stafford, Jo* / If: *Stafford, Jo* / Keep it secret: *Stafford, Jo* / Stardust: *Stafford, Jo* / Hawaiian war chant: *Stafford, Jo* / If you've got the money, I've got the time: *Stafford, Jo* / Embraceable you: *Stafford, Jo* / Every night when the sun goes in: *Stafford, Jo* / I should care: *Stafford, Jo* / It is no secret: *Stafford, Jo* / St. Louis blues: *Stafford, Jo* / We'll meet again: *Lynn, Vera* / Wishing (will make it so): *Lynn, Vera* / Mexicali Rose: *Lynn, Vera* / I paid for the lie that I told you: *Lynn, Vera* / I shall be waiting: *Lynn, Vera* / Little Sir Echo: *Lynn, Vera* / Little boy that Santa Claus forgot: *Lynn, Vera* / Goodnight children everywhere: *Lynn, Vera* / My own: *Lynn, Vera* / Who's taking you home tonight: *Lynn, Vera* / Bells of St. Mary's: *Lynn, Vera* / Harbour lights: *Lynn, Vera* / It's a sin to tell a lie: *Lynn, Vera* / Lonely sweetheart: *Lynn, Vera* / Memory of a rose: *Lynn, Vera* / It's a lovely day tomorrow: *Lynn, Vera* / I'll pray for you: *Lynn, Vera* / Nightingale sang in Berkeley Square: *Lynn, Vera* / Medley: *Lynn, Vera* / Wish me luck as you wave me goodbye: *Lynn, Vera* / I'll never smile again: *Shelton, Anne* / There goes that song again: *Shelton, Anne* / Yes my darling daughter: *Shelton, Anne* / Fools rush in: *Shelton, Anne* / I don't want to walk without you: *Shelton, Anne* / You'd be so nice to come home to: *Shelton, Anne* / Coming in on a wing and a prayer: *Shelton, Anne* / Last time I saw Paris: *Shelton, Anne* / I don't want to set the world on fire: *Shelton, Anne* / Nightingale sang in Berkeley Square: *Shelton, Anne* / Taking a chance on love: *Shelton, Anne* / Only you: *Shelton, Anne* / Daddy: *Shelton, Anne* / My Yiddishe Momme: *Shelton, Anne* / Until you fall in love: *Shelton, Anne* / Amapola: *Shelton, Anne* / Kiss the boys goodbye: *Shelton, Anne* / Lili Marlene: *Shelton, Anne* / I'll be seeing you: *Shelton, Anne*
CD Set ____ PAK 905
Parade / May '95 / Disc

SPOTLIGHT ON JO STAFFORD (Great Ladies Of Song)
It was just one of those things / I didn't know about you / Walking my baby back home / Too marvellous for words / In the still of the night / Autumn leaves / Sugar / Haunted heart / Best things in life are free / Boy next door / Sometimes I'm happy / Fools rush in / On the sunny side of the street / I remember you / Always true to you in my fashion / La vie en rose / Over the rainbow / I'll be with you in apple blossom time
CD ____ CZ 565
Premier/EMI / Mar '96 / EMI

VERY BEST OF JO STAFFORD, THE
You belong to me / Allentown jail / Come rain or come shine / On London Bridge / As I love you / Make love to me / Shrimp boats / Tennessee waltz / I'll be seeing you / Whispering hope / Teach me tonight / Jambalaya / Thank you for calling goodbye / Ayround the corner / If / Keep a secret / Keep it a secret / Stardust / Hawaiian war chant / St. Louis blues / It is no secret / I should care / Every night when the sun goes in / Embraceable you / If you've got the money, I've got the time / Hawaiina war chant
CD ____ PAR 2064
Parade / May '96 / Disc

Stafford, Terell

CENTRIPETAL FORCE
Addio / I'll wait / Skylark / Old devil moon / Child is born / Mia / For the broken hearted / My romance / Daahoud / Somebody bigger than you and I
CD ____ CCD 79718
Candid / Jul '97 / Cadillac / Direct / Jazz Music / Koch / Wellard

TIME TO LET GO
Time to let go / Was it meant to be / Polka dots and moonbeams / Qui qui / On the trail / Why / Soon / Send in the clowns / Just a closer walk with thee
CD ____ CACD 79702
Candid / Feb '97 / Cadillac / Direct / Jazz Music / Koch / Wellard

Stagg, Richard

JAPANESE BAMBOO FLUTE, THE
CD ____ EUCD 1103
ARC / '91 / ADA / ARC Music

Stahl, Jeanie

MYSTERIES
CD ____ DARINGCD 3017
Daring / Nov '95 / ADA / CM / Direct

Staines, Bill

GOING TO THE WEST
CD ____ RHRCD 56
Red House / Oct '95 / ADA / Koch

LOOKING FOR THE WIND
CD ____ RHRCD 79
Red House / Dec '95 / ADA / Koch

Stains

SONGS FOR SWINGING LOVERS
CD ____ DOXOCD 260
Dojo / Jul '96 / Disc

Stainsby, Trevor

RHYTHM OF RETURN, THE
CD ____ HWYLCD 3
Hwyl / May '89 / Hwyl

Stakka Bo

GREAT BLONDINO, THE
CD ____ 5316582
Polydor / Apr '96 / PolyGram

Stalag 13

IN CONTROL
CD ____ LF 058
Lost & Found / Aug '93 / Plastic Head

Stallings, Mary

I WAITED FOR YOU (Stallings, Mary & Gene Harris)
When or where / Love dance / I waited for you / Blues in my heart / Dedicated to you / It's crazy / Serenade in blue / But not for me / I wanna be loved / Only trust your heart / Ain't nobody's business if I do
CD ____ CCD 4620
Concord Jazz / Nov '94 / New Note/ Pinnacle

SPECTRUM
Black coffeee / Daydream / I just dropped by to say hello / If I had you / Just as though you were here / No love, no nothin' / Robbin's nest / Say it isn't so / Soft winds / Solitude / Some other time / Tears in heaven / Things are looking up
CD ____ CCD 4689
Concord Jazz / Apr '96 / New Note/ Pinnacle

Stallone, Frank

CLOSE YOUR EYES
I can't believe / Close your eyes / I got a ring to sing the blues / Saturday night / Exactly like you / By the river St. Marie / Gee baby ain't I good to you / I didn't know what time it was / Baby won't you please come here / Long ago and far away
CD ____ 30373 00022
Carlton / Mar '96 / Carlton

Stamford Bridge

COME UP AND SEE US SOMETIME/ THE FIRST DAY OF YOUR LIFE
Little boy blue / Roly poly / Johnny Rebel / Happiness and rainy days / Come up and see me sometime / Face in the crowd / Falling in and out of love / Chelsea / Molly Perkins / Wonder lady / Yours sincerely / Vicar's daughter / What do I care / Rise Sally rise / Mother of nature / Goodbye today, hello tomorrow / Let's go to San Francisco / Who knows what I need / Move out of town / First day of your life / Letter from America / Chaquita Maria / Tumbleweed town / Arizona lost and gone / Four letter word / Ossie / World of fantasy
CD ____ SEECD 478
See For Miles/C5 / Jun '97 / Pinnacle

Stamm, Marvin

BOP BOY
CD ____ MM 65065
Music Masters / Oct '94 / Nimbus

MYSTERY MAN
CD ____ MM 65085
Music Masters / Oct '94 / Nimbus

Stampin' Ground

DEMONS RUN AMOK
CD ____ WB 1169CD
We Bite / Jun '97 / Plastic Head

STAMPIN' GROUND
CD ____ WB 1148MCD
We Bite / Sep '96 / Plastic Head

Stanciu, Simon

MUSIQUE TZIGANE EN ROUMAINE
CD ____ ARN 64236
Arion / Aug '93 / ADA / Discovery

Stand Up

WORDS IN MOTION
CD ____ CI 0052
CI / Mar '93 / SRD

Standells

DIRTY WATER
Medication / Little Sally Tease / There is a storm comin' / Nineteenth nervous breakdown / Dirty water / Pride and devotion / Sometimes good guys don't wear white / Hey Joe / Why did you hurt me / Rari / Why pick on me / Paint it black / Mi hai fatto innamorare / Black hearted woman / Girl and the moon / Mr. Nobody / My little red book / Mainline / Have you ever spent the night in jail
CD ____ CDSC 6019
Sundazed / Apr '94 / Cargo / Greyhound / Rollercoaster

DIRTY WATER/THE HOT ONES
CD ____ EVA 842121B5
EVA / Nov '94 / ADA / Direct

HOT ONES, THE
Last train to Clarksville / Wild thing / Sunshine superman / Sunny afternoon / Li'l Red Riding Hood / Eleanor Rigby / Black is black / Summer in the city / You were the one / School girl / Ten o'clock scholar / When I was a cowboy / Don't ask me what to do / Misty lane / Standell's love them
CD ____ CDSC 6021
Sundazed / Apr '94 / Cargo / Greyhound / Rollercoaster

HOT ONES, THE/TRY IT
Last train to Clarksville / Wild thing / Sunshine superman / Sunny afternonn / Li'l Red Riding Hood / Eleanor rigby / Black is black / Summer in the city / Nineteenth nervous breakdown / Dirty water / Can't help but love you / Ninety nine and a half (won't do) / Trip to paradise / St. James infirmary / Try it / Barracuda / Did you ever have that feeling / All fall down / Poor shell of a man / Riot on sunset strip
CD ____ CDWIKD 112
Big Beat / Mar '93 / Pinnacle

IS THIS THE WAY YOU GET YOUR HIGH
Dirty water / Rari / Sometimes good guys don't wear white / Medication / There is a storm comin' / Nineteenth nervous breakdown / Why did you hurt me / Why pick on me / Paint it black / Black hearted woman / Mainline / Mr. Nobody / Wild thing / Riot on Sunset Strip / Try it / Barracuda / Poor shell of a man / Can't help but love you / Ninety nine and a half (won't do) / Animal girl / Soul drippin' / enimal girl
CD ____ CDWIKD 114
Big Beat / Jun '93 / Pinnacle

STANDELLS RARITIES (& Riot On Sunset Strip)
Riot on sunset strip / Sunset Sally: *Mugwumps* / Sunset theme: *Sidewalk Sounds* / Old country: *Travis, Debra* / Don't need your lovin': *Chocolate Watch Band* / Children of the night: *Mom's Boys* / Make the music pretty: *Sidewalk Sounds* / Get away from here / Like my baby: *Drew* / Sitting there standing: *Chocolate Watch Band* / Love me / Batman / Our candidate / Boy who is lost / It's all in your mind / School girl / I hate to leave you / Looking at tomorrow / Don't say nothing at all / Try it (Alternate vocal) / Rari (Extended version)
CD ____ CDWIKD 113
Big Beat / Jun '93 / Pinnacle

TRY IT
Can't help but love you / Ninety nine and a half (won't do) / Trip to paradise / St. James infirmary / Try it / Did it ever have the feeling / All fall down / Poor shell of a man / Riot on sunset strip / Get away from here / Animal girl / Soul drippin' / Can you dig it
CD ____ CDSC 6022
Sundazed / Apr '94 / Cargo / Greyhound / Rollercoaster

WHY PICK ON ME
Why pick on me / Paint it black / Mi hai fatto innamorare / I hate to leave / Black hearted woman / Sometimes good guys don't wear white / Girl and the moon / Looking at tomorrow / Mr. Nobody / My little red book / Mainline / Have you ever spent the night in jail / Our candidate / Don't say nothing at all / Boy who is lost
CD ____ CDSC 6020
Sundazed / Apr '94 / Cargo / Greyhound / Rollercoaster

Stanford Prison Experiment

GATO HUNCH
You're the Vulgarian / Repeat removal / (Very) Put out / Cansado / Flap / So far, so good / El nuevo / Accomplice / Harcord idiot / Swoon / Worst case scenario
CD ____ WDOM 020CD
World Domination / Aug '95 / Pinnacle / RTM/Disc

STANFORD PRISON EXPERIMENT
CD ____ WDOM 009CD
World Domination / Jun '94 / Pinnacle / RTM/Disc

Stanko, Tomasz

BALLADYNA
First song / Tale / Num / Duet / Balladyna / Last song / Nenaliina
CD ____ 51928922
ECM / Nov '93 / New Note/Pinnacle

LEOSIA
Morning heavy song / Die weisheit von le comte lautreamont / Farewell to Maria / Brace / Trinity / Forlorn walk / Hungry howl / No bass trio / Euforila / Leosia
CD ____ 5316932
ECM / Apr '97 / New Note/Pinnacle

LITANIA (Music Of Krzystof Komeda)
Svantatic / Sleep safe and warm / Nightime daytime requiem / Ballada / Litania / Sleep safe and warm / Repetition / Ballad for Bernt / Witch
CD ____ 5375512
ECM / Sep '97 / New Note/Pinnacle

MATKA JOANNA
CD ____ 5239862
ECM / Oct '95 / New Note/Pinnacle

TWET
CD ____ PBR 33860
Power Bros. / Aug '95 / Harmonia Mundi

Stanley & The Turbines

AFRICA
CD ____ LG 21117
Lagoon / Aug '96 / Grapevine/PolyGram

BIG BAMBOO
CD ____ JMC 200203
Jamaican Gold / Feb '93 / Grapevine/ PolyGram / Jet Star

Stanley Brothers

CLINCH MOUNTAIN BLUEGRASS
Introduction / Orange blossom special / How mountain girls can love / Model T / Man of constant sorrow / Gathering flowers for the Master's bouquet / Choo choo coming / All aboard for Baltimore / White dove / Hard times / Jordan / Rank stranger / Little birdie / Shout little Luly / Clinch Mountain backstep / Hard times / Little Maggie / How mountain girls can love / Man of constant sorrow / Little glass of wine / Big tildy / Orange blossom special
CD ____ VCD 77018
Vanguard / Jan '96 / ADA / Pinnacle

SHADOWS OF THE PAST
CD ____ COPCD 101
Copper Creek / May '96 / ADA

SONGS OF THE STANLEY BROTHERS (Various Artists)
Long journey home: *Jim & Jesse* / Say, won't you be mine: *Skaggs, Ricky* / Man of constant sorrow: *Furtado, Tony & Tim O'Brien* / Girl behind the bar: *Dry Branch Fire Squad* / If I lose: *Grisman, David* / Harbor of love: *Johnson Mountain Boys* / Clinch Mountain backstep: *Munde, Alan* / Vision of Mother: *Val, Joe & New England Bluegrass Boys* / Dream of a miner's child: *Boyens, Phyllis & Hazel Dickens* / White

dove: *Jim & Jesse/Ricky Scaggs* / You'd better get right: *Williams, Vern* / Rank strangers to me: *Hot Rize*
CD EDCD 7022
Easydisc / Feb '97 / Direct

STANLEY BROTHERS & THE CLINCH MOUNTAIN BOYS (2CD Set) (Stanley Brothers & The Clinch Mountain Boys)
Won't you be mine / This weary heart you stole away / I'm lonesome without you / Our last goodbye / Poison lies / Dickson County breakdown / I long to see the old folks / Voice from on high / Memories of mother / Could you love me (one more time) / Nobody's love is like mine / I just got wise / Blue moon of Kentucky / Close by / Calling from heaven / Harbor love / Hard times / Baby girl / Say you'll take me back / I worship you / You're still on my mind / I hear my saviour calling / Just a little talk with Jesus / So blue / You'd better get right / Tragic love / Lonesome and blue / Orange blossom special / Clinch mountain blues / Big Tilda / Will he wait a little longer / Angel Band / Cry from the cross / Who will call you sweetheart / I'm lost, I'll never find the way / Let me walk, Lord, by your side / Lonesome night / Flood / Fling ding / I'll never grow tired of you / Loving you too well / Daybreak in Dixie / If that's the way you feel / Life of sorrow / I'd rather be forgotten / No school bus in heaven / Meet me tonight / Ain't nobody's business if I do
CD Set BCD 15681
Bear Family / Oct '93 / Direct / Rollercoaster / Swift

STANLEY BROTHERS & THE CLINCH MOUNTAIN BOYS 1949-1952 (Stanley Brothers & The Clinch Mountain Boys)
Vision of mother / White dove / Gathering flowers for the master's bouquet / Angels are singing / It's never too late / Have you someone (in Heaven waiting) / Little glass of wine / Let me be your friend / We'll be sweethearts in Heaven / I love no one but you / Too late to cry / Old home / Drunkard's hell / Fields have turned brown / Hey hey hey / Lonesome river / I'm a man of constant sorrow / Pretty Polly / Life of sorrow / Sweetest love / Wandering boy / Let's part the best of friends
CD BCD 15564
Bear Family / Nov '93 / Direct / Rollercoaster / Swift

STANLEY SERIES VOL.3
CD COPCD 5511
Copper Creek / Feb '96 / ADA

Stanley, Michael

MISERY LOVES COMPANY (More Of The Best 1975-1983) (Stanley, Michael Band)
CD RE 2125
Razor & Tie / Feb '97 / Koch

Stanley, Ralph

MASTERS OF THE BANJO (Stanley, Ralph & Tony Ellis/Seleshe Damassae)
CD ARHCD 421
Arhoolie / Apr '95 / ADA / Cadillac / Direct

MY ALL AND ALL
Jesus on the mainline / He's my all and all / I hope to meet you in the morning / This old troublesome world / Loving grace of God / Uncloudy day / I'm not ashamed / We are drinking from the fountain / Take me home / While eternal ages roll / Two coats / I firmly promise you
CD REBCD 1740
Rebel / Jul '97 / ADA / Direct

RALPH STANLEY - SATURDAY NIGHT AND SUNDAY MORNING (2CD Set)
CD Set FRC 9001
Freeland Recording Company / Oct '93 / ADA / Direct

SHORT LIFE OF TROUBLE
CD REB 1735CD
Rebel / Dec '96 / ADA / Direct

Stansfield, Lisa

AFFECTION
This is the right time / Mighty love / Sincerity / Love in me / All around the world / What did I do to you / Live together / You can't deny it / Poison / When are you coming back / Affection / Wake up baby / Way you want it
CD 260379
Arista / Aug '95 / BMG

IN SESSION
Only way / Bitter sweet / Thought police / Walking on thin ice / Listen to your heart / Only love (can break your heart) / More than love / Don't stop me for the mailman / Boy you have known / Red lights / Make sure that the feelin's right / Spinning top / Take care, goodnight / Alibi's
CD SOV 016CD
Sovereign / Aug '96 / Target/BMG

LISA STANSFIELD
Never gonna fall / Real thing / I'm leavin' / Suzanne / Never, never gonna give you up / Don't cry for me / Line / Very thought of you / You know how to love me / I cried my last tear last night / Honest / Somewhere in time / Got me missing you / Footsteps / Real thing / People hold on
CD 74321458512
Arista / Mar '97 / BMG

REAL LOVE
Change / Real love / Set your loving free / I will be waiting / All woman / Soul deep / Make love to ya / Time to make you mine / Symptoms of loneliness and heartache / It's got to be real / First joy / Tenderly / Little more love
CD 262300
Arista / Jul '96 / BMG

Stanshall, Vivian

TEDDY BOYS DON'T KNIT
King Kripple / Slave valse / Gums / Biwilderbeeste / Calypso to calapso / Tube / Ginger geezer / Cracks are showing / Flung a dummy / Possibly an arm chair / Fresh faced boys / Terry keeps his clips on / Bass Macaw and broken bottles / Nose hymn / Everyday I have the blues / Smoke signals at night / Nouveau riffe
CD CASCD 1153
Charisma / Jun '91 / EMI

Stanton, Ian

ROLLIN' THUNDER
CD SRCD 003
Stream / Nov '96 / Stream / Vital

Staple Singers

BEALTITUDE: RESPECT YOURSELF
This world / Respect yourself / Name the missing word / I'll take you there / This old town / We the people / Are you sure / Who do you think you are / I'm just another soldier / Who
CD CDSXE 001
Stax / May '91 / Pinnacle

GREAT DAY
Gloryland / Everybody will be happy / Here me call, here / Nobody knows the trouble I've seen / I'm willin' / Great day / Do you know him / New-born soul / Dying man's plea / New home / Wish I had answered / Better home / Old time religion / Swing low, sweet chariot / Motherless children / Gamblin' man / I know I've been changed / Jesus is all / You got shoes / What are they doing (in heaven today) / Will the Lord rememeber me / My dying bed / Let Jesus lead you / Praying time / I can't help from cryin' sometime / Masters of war
CD CDCH 391
Ace / May '92 / Pinnacle

RESPECT YOURSELF (The Best Of The Staple Singers)
Heavy makes you happy / Long walk to DC / This world / Respect yourself / I see it / We'll get over / Take you there / Oh la de da / Are you sure / If you're ready (come go with me) / Touch a hand, make a friend / City in the sky / People come out of your shell / You've got to earn it / Love is plentiful / Got to be some changes made / Be what you are / This old town / Slow train / My main man
CD CDSX 006
Stax / Oct '87 / Pinnacle

SOUL FOLK IN ACTION/WE'LL GET OVER
We've got to get ourselves together / (Sittin' on the) dock of the bay / Top of the mountain / Slow train / Weight / Long walk to DC / Got to be some changes made / Ghetto / People, my people / I see it / This year / We'll get over / Give a damn / Everyday people / End of our road / Tend to your own business / Solon bushi / Challenge / God bless the children / Games people play / Wednesday in your garden / Gardener / When will be paid (For the work we did)
CD CDSXD 109
Stax / Jul '94 / Pinnacle

STAPLE SWINGERS
This is a perfect world / What's your thing / You've got to earn it / You're gonna make me cry / Little boy / How do you move a mountain / Almost / I'm a lover / Love is plentiful / Heavy makes you happy / I like the things about you / Give a hand take a hand
CD CDSXE 035
Stax / Feb '91 / Pinnacle

UNCLOUDY DAY
Uncloudy day / Let me ride / Help me Jesus / I'm coming home / God's wonderful love / Low is the way / Ain't that good news / This may be the last time / I had a dream / Going away / I know I got religion / Will the circle be unbroken / Stand by me / Come up in glory / Pray on / Somebody save me / Each day / So soon / Too close / Let's go home
CD CPCD 8087
Charly / Apr '95 / Koch

Staples, Mavis

DON'T CHANGE ME NOW
Ready for the heartbreak / Sweet things you do / Chokin' kind / House is not a home / Security / Good to me / You send me / I'm tired / Why can't it be like it used to be / You're the fool / You're all I need / I have learned to do without you / How many times / Endlessly / Since I fell for you / Since you became a part of my life / Don't change me now / You're driving me (to the arms of a stranger) / Pick up the pieces / Chains of love / What happened to the real me / It makes me wanna cry
CD CDSX 014
Stax / Aug '88 / Pinnacle

SPIRITUALS AND GOSPELS (Staples, Mavis & Lucky Peterson)
CD 5335622
Verve / Nov '96 / PolyGram

VOICE, THE
CD 0060542
Edel / May '95 / Pinnacle

Staples, Pops

FATHER FATHER
Father Father / Why am I treated so bad / Too big for your britches / Jesus is going to make up (My dying bed) / Downward road / People get ready / Hope in a hopeless world / You got to serve somebody / Waiting for my child / Simple man / Glory glory
CD VPBCD 19
Pointblank / May '94 / EMI

PEACE IN THE NEIGHBORHOOD
CD VPBCD 8
Pointblank / Mar '92 / EMI

Star Accordion Band

SCOTTISH FAVOURITES VOL.2
These are my mountains / Song of the Clyde / Dancing in Kyle / Sottish soldier / Donald, where's yer troosers / Crooked bawbee / There was a lad
CD CDSLP 606
Lochshore / May '97 / ADA / Direct / Duncans

Star Blanket Jr.

GET UP AND DANCE
CD CR 6268CD
Canyon / Nov '96 / ADA

Star Pimp

SERAPHIM 280Z
Slave girl / Size zero / Yoko Phono / Snowball / Little tattoo / Pee test / Greatest hits of love / Human dolphin / Palmolive / Vegan pussy / Gold / Titty / Vocal fader
CD TUP 0502
Tupelo / Jan '94 / RTM/Disc

Starclub

STARCLUB
Hard to get / Let your hair down / Call my name / Forever / All falls down / World keeps turning / Bad machine / We believe / Question / Answer / Pretty thing
CD CID 9995
Island / Mar '93 / PolyGram

Starclub

IHOJIN
CD INDIGO 35012
Pop Biz / Oct '96 / Cargo / Greyhound

Stardust, Alvin

HITS GO ON
CD STIFFCD 18
Disky / Nov '93 / Disky / THE

I'M A MOODY GUY (Fenton, Shane & The Fentones)
I'm a moody guy / Five foot two / Eyes of blue / Why little girl / It's all over now / It's gonna take magic / Cindy's birthday / Too young for sad memories / Fallen leaves on the ground / You're telling me / Walk away / Don't do that / I'll know / Fool's paradise / You need love / Somebody else not me / I ain't got nobody / Hey Miss Ruby / Hey Lulu / I do, do you / Breeze and I
CD SEECD 369
See For Miles/C5 / Feb '97 / Pinnacle

Starfish Enterprises

SONIC SYMPHONY NO.1
CD EL 112CD
Electrip / Nov '94 / Plastic Head

Starfish Pool

AMPLIFIED TONES
CD NZ 034
Nova Zembla / May '95 / Plastic Head

CHILL OUT N CONFUSED
CD NZ 016
Nova Zembla / Oct '94 / Plastic Head

Starfish TX

FRUSTRATED
CD TR 55CD
Trance Syndicate / Mar '97 / SRD

STELLAR SONIC SOLUTIONS
CD TR 40CD
Trance / Oct '95 / SRD

Stargazers

BACK IN ORBIT
Crazy but true / Loretta / It's only a paper moon / Baby, baby, baby / Got that beat / Walking beat / Sweet Georgia Brown / Dig that rock'n'roll / Stargazer's blues / Crazy man crazy / Every cloud has a silver lining / Feeling happy
CD CDCH 312
Ace / Mar '91 / Pinnacle

FROFFEE COFFEE
Froffee coffee / Fools fall in love / Swingin' on a star / Oh baby doll / County line / Milk-crate mania / What's the matter with music now / Just a gigolo / Willow weep / Where would we be tonight / Mack the knife / Song about a train / Sugar and spice
CD JRCD 27
Jappin' & Rockin' / Mar '97 / Swift / TKO Magnum

SPEAKING CLOCK SAYS...ROCK, THE
Lights out / Rockin' Robin / In a little Spanish town / See you later alligator / Pete's beat / Stop beatin' around the mulberry bush / Cat / Just go wild over rock 'n' roll / Lady killer / Florida twist / Shake, rattle and roll / Eat your heart out Annie
CD JRCD 004
Jappin' & Rockin' / Jan '93 / Swift / TKO Magnum

Starkweather

CROSSBEARER
CD TOODAMNHY 32
Too Damn Hype / May '94 / Cargo / SRD

INTO THE WIRE
CD EDISON 001
Edison / Jul '97 / Greyhound

Starlight Conspiracy

SOUNDS LIKE A SILVER HOLLER
CD CTA 009
Catapult / May '97 / Cargo / Greyhound

Starlight Orchestra

MUSIC FROM A FRENCH CAFE
Aubade d'oiseaux / Ca gaze / Reine de musette / Automne / La valse des as / Le denicheur / Sous les ponts de Paris / Retour des hirondelles / Bourrasque / Jongleur / Brise Napolitaine / Les triolets / Romance de la nuit / Vendredi treize / Reve d'accordeoniste / Les papillons de la nuit / Perles de cristal / A la bonheur / Bel oiseau / Princesse accordeon / Une partie de petanque / Mazurka fantaisie
CD QED 079
Tring / Nov '96 / Tring

SUMMER LOVING
Sealed with a kiss / Under the influence of love / Let your love flow / Daytime friends / Physical / Happening / Albatross / It never rains in southern California / Hard rock cafe / Isn't she lovely / Hopelessly devoted to you / You light up my life / Song sung blue / Blue bayou / Green onions / Rhapsody in white / Stranger on the shore / Hustle / Wipeout / Summer of '42
CD QED 099
Tring / Nov '96 / Tring

Starlights

SOLDERING
CD HBCD 102
Heartbeat / Jan '94 / ADA / Direct / Greensleeves / Jet Star

Starling, John

LONG TIME GONE
Long time gone / Turned you to stone / Half a man / Jordan / White line / Hobo on a freight train to heaven / Last thing I needed / Brother juke box / Carolyn at the Broken Wheel Inn / He rode all the way to Texas / Drifting too far from the shore / Dark hollow / (I heard that) Lonesome whistle / Roads and other reasons / Sin City
CD SHCD 3714
Sugar Hill / '88 / ADA / CM / Direct / Koch / Roots

WAITIN' ON A SOUTHERN TRAIN
New Delhi freight train / We know better / Carolina star / Other side of life / Waitin' on a southern train / Heart trouble / Homestead in my heart / Hey bottle of whisky / Those memories of you / Slow movin' freight train
CD SHCD 3724
Sugar Hill / Aug '95 / ADA / CM / Direct / Koch / Roots

Starlings

TOO MANY DOGS
CD 4509951952
Anxious / Apr '94 / Warner Music

VALID
Now take that / That's it you're in trouble / Unhealthy / Start again / Bad Dad / Right school / Shoot up hill / Sick puppy / Jack
CD 4509902852
Anxious / Aug '92 / Warner Music

Starmarket

CALENDER
CD ________ DOL 038CD
Dolores / Jul '96 / Plastic Head

STARMARKET
CD ________ DOL 022CD
Dolores / Jun '95 / Plastic Head

Starpimp

DOCUDRAMA
CD ________ KRS 265CD
Kill Rock Stars / Nov '96 / Cargo / Greyhound / Plastic Head

Starr, Andy

DIG THEM SQUEAKY SHOES
She's a going Jessie / One more time / Rockin' rollin' stone / Deacon Jones / No room for your kind / Round and round / I wanna go south / Give me a woman / Dig them squeaky shoes / Dirty bird song / Do it right / Rockin' reelin' country style / Tell me why / For the want of your love / Love is a simple thing / Me and the fool / Lover man / Knee shakin' / Evil Eve / Little bitty feeling / Lost in a dream / Pledge of love / Do it right now / I'm seeing things (I shouldn't see) / Somali Dolly / I waited for you to remember
CD ________ BCD 15890
Bear Family / Jun '95 / Direct / Rollercoaster / Swift

Starr, Edwin

20 GREATEST MOTOWN HITS
Stop her on sight (SOS) / Twenty five miles / Headline news / Agent double o soul / Backstreet / I want my baby back / Funky music sho nuff turns me on / Soul master / You've got my soul on fire / Who's right, who's wrong / War / Stop the war now / Way over there / Take me clear from here / Cloud 9 / There you go / Gonna keep on tryin' till I win your love / Time / My weakness is you / Harlem
CD ________ 5300642
Motown / Jan '93 / PolyGram

MOTOWN EARLY CLASSICS
Stop her on sight (SOS) / Agent Double-O Soul / Headline news / My weakness is you / If my heart could tell the story / Way over there / You beat me to the punch / Oh how happy / Love is my destination / Time is passin' by / Mighty good lovin' / I am the man for you baby / I'm glad you belong to me / I am your man / Backyard lovin' man / Twenty-five miles / She should have been home / We'll find a way
CD ________ 5521212
Spectrum / Jul '96 / PolyGram

STOP HER ON SIGHT (SOS)
Stop her on sight (SOS) / Headline news / Time is passin' by / I am the man for you baby / Love is my destination / We'll find a way / Oh how happy / You beat me to the punch / Twenty-five miles / Backyard lovin' man / Running back and forth / Mighty good lovin' / All around the world / I'm glad you belong to me / She should have been home / I am your man
CD ________ 5512862
Spectrum / Aug '95 / PolyGram

TIMELESS ENERGY
Smooth / Did I jump (or fall in love) / Dream big / On the boulevard of broken hearts / Bedtime story / Can't stop (thinking about you) / Give you back the loving / Just another fool in love / (Get up) Whirlpool of love / Rumours / Patch up / Wait for me / Old flame / Summer madness / Show you love / Long night / If it could only be
CD ________ 3036450012
Carlton / Mar '96 / Carlton

Starr, Frankie

ELEVATOR BOOGIE
Elevator boogie / That's the way the big ball bounces / Sky writin' airplane / I don't care what you used to be / I love you too much to leave you / I'm paying the price / Cross my heart (I'm not double crossing you) / There's a vacancy / Your kind wasn't meant for me / My heart can't stand another tear / I want someone to love / You broke your heart breaking mine / Your Daddy's looped again: *Starr, Frankie & Dot Allen* / My woman ain't pretty / Elevator baby / That crazy dream / Between you, me & the gatepost / Great fireball / Little Joe Weatherly / Tear stained bible / John 3-16 / Our love is at an end: *Starr, Frankie & Marty Robbins* / For a lifetime: *Starr, Frankie & Marty Robbins* / I've lost my love and you: *Starr, Frankie & Marty Robbins* / I want someone to love: *Starr, Frankie & Marty Robbins*
CD ________ BCD 15990
Bear Family / Nov '96 / Direct / Rollercoaster / Swift

Starr, Freddie

AFTER THE LAUGHTER
It's only make believe / Fever / I don't want to talk about it / Love hurts / Halfway to paradise / You got it / I will / Sun ain't gonna shine anymore / Teddy bear / I love how you love me / Run to my lovin' arms / I'm lost without you
CD ________ CDMFP 5909
Music For Pleasure / Apr '91 / EMI

Starr, Kay

CAPITOL COLLECTORS SERIES: KAY STARR
I'm the lonesomest gal in town / You've got to see mama ev'ry night / You were only fooling (while I was falling in love) / So tired / Bonaparte's retreat / Hoop dee doo / Mississippi / I'll never be free / I waited a little too long / Wheel of fortune / Fool, fool, fool / Kay's lament / Side by side / Comes a-long-a-love / When my dreamboat comes home / Half a photograph / Allez-vous en / Changing partners / If you love me (really love me) / Man upstairs / Toy or treasure / Lazy river / Foolin' around / Crazy / Rock 'n' roll waltz
CD ________ CZ 411
Capitol / Mar '91 / EMI

EMI PRESENTS THE MAGIC OF KAY STARR
Comes a-long a-love / Side by side / Changing partners / Am I a toy or a treasure / Crazy / Going to Chicago blues / Half a photograph / I love Paris / I'm the lonesomest gal in town / If you love me, really love me / It had to be you / Lazy river / Lovesick blues / More than you know / Nevertheless I'm in love with you / On a slowboat to China / PS I love you / Rock 'n' roll waltz / Singing the blues / Wheel of fortune / You're just in love / When a woman loves a man / I'll always be in love with you / Fool fool fool / Allez vous en (go away)
CD ________ CDMFP 6292
Music For Pleasure / May '97 / EMI

I CRY BY NIGHT/LOSERS WEEPERS
I'm alone because I love you / I cry by night / Baby, won't you please come home / More than you know / Lover man (oh where can you be) / My kinda love / It had to be you / Whispering grass / Nevertheless / What do you see in her / PS I love you / I'm still in love with you / You always hurt the one you love / I should care / I'm a fool to care / Don't take your love from me / When I lost you / Only forever / Gonna get a guy / Please don't talk about me when I'm gone / I miss you so / Faded summer love / When a man loves a woman / Into each life some rain must fall
CD ________ CTMCD 113
EMI / Mar '97 / EMI

KAY STARR
Wheel of fortune / I'll always be in love with you / If you love me (really love me) / Comes a-long-a-love / Two brothers / Lovesick blues / Side by side / You've got to see Mama ev'ry night / If I could be with you one hour tonight / Mississippi / Bonaparte's retreat / You broke your promise / Half a photograph / Come on a my house / I wanna love you / Three letters / I wish I had a wishbone / tell me how long the trains been gone / Mama goes where Papa goes / Tonight you belong to me / Changing partners / Dancing on my tears / Waiting at the end of the road / I forgot to forget / Rock 'n' roll waltz
CD ________ CC 8238
EMI / Nov '94 / EMI

KAY STARR 1947
CD ________ HCD 214
Hindsight / Jun '94 / Jazz Music / Target/BMG

MOONBEAMS AND STEAMY DREAMS
CD ________ STCD 534
Stash / Oct '91 / ADA / Cadillac / CM / Direct / Jazz Music

MOVIN'
On a slow boat to China / I cover the waterfront / Around the world / Sentimental journey / Night train / Riders in the sky / Goin' to Chicago blues / (Back home again in) Indiana / Song of the wanderer / Swingin' down the lane / Lazy river / Movin'
CD ________ JASCD 307
Jasmine / Mar '95 / Conifer/BMG / Hot Shot / TKO Magnum

WHAT A DIFFERENCE A DAY MADE
Dixieland band / There's a lull in my life / Ain't misbehavin' / What a difference a day made / What can I say dear after I say I'm sorry / Nobody knows the trouble I've seen / What goes up must come down / Honeysuckle rose / My future just passed / Betcha I getcha / You're always there / Don't do something to someone else / Blame my absentminded heart / It's a great feeling
CD ________ HCD 229
Hindsight / Mar '96 / Jazz Music / Target/BMG

Starr, Ringo

BEAUCOUPS OF BLUES
Beaucoups of blues / Love don't last long / Fastest growing heartache in the west / Coochy coochy / Silent homecoming / Waiting / Loser's lounge / I wouldn't have it any other way / Wine, women and loud happy songs / Without her / Woman of the night / I'd be talking all the time / Fifteen dollar draw
CD ________ CDPAS 10002
Apple / May '95 / EMI

LIVE FROM MONTREUX (Starr, Ringo & His All-Starr Band)
Really serious introduction / I'm the greatest / Don't go where the road don't go / Yellow submarine / Desperado / I can't tell you why / Girls talk / Weight of the world / Bang the drum all day / Walking nerve / Black Maria / In the city / American woman / Boys / With a little help from my friends
CD ________ RCD 20264
Rykodisc / Oct '93 / ADA / Vital

SENTIMENTAL JOURNEY
Sentimental journey / Night and day / Whispering grass / Bye bye blackbird / I'm a fool to care / Stardust / Blue turning grey over you / Love is a many splendoured thing / Dream / You always hurt the one you love / Have I told you lately that I love you / Let the rest of the world go by
CD ________ CDPCS 7101
Apple / May '95 / EMI

Stars Of Faith

FAMOUS SPIRITUALS, NEGRO SPIRITUALS
CD ________ BB 3222
Black & Blue / Sep '95 / Discovery / Koch / Wellard

LIVE AT MONTREUX
CD ________ BLE 591862
Black & Blue / Apr '92 / Discovery / Koch / Wellard

Stars Of The Lid

BALLASTED ORCHESTRA
CD ________ KRANK 015CD
Kranky / Jan '97 / Cargo / Greyhound

Starsound

BEST OF STARS ON 45
CD ________ MCCD 192
Music Club / Nov '94 / Disc / THE

STARS ON 45
Do you want to know a secret / Nowhere man / Eight days a week / My sweet lord / Hard day's night / Video killed the radio star / Cathy's clown / Bird dog / Sherry / Buona sera / At the hop
CD ________ CDMFP 6031
Music For Pleasure / Sep '88 / EMI

Starsound Orchestra

I'M IN THE MOOD FOR ROMANCE
CD ________ LPCD 1023
Disky / Apr '94 / Disky / THE

Starspeed Transmission

METAMORPHIC ILLUMINATION
CD ________ NZ 012CD
Nova Zembla / Aug '94 / Plastic Head

Starvation Army

MERCENARY POSITION
CD ________ RAVE 019CD
Rational / Sep '91 / Vital

Stasis

ALBUM
CD ________ OPCD 1
Op-Art / Apr '97 / Prime / RTM/Disc

INSPIRATION
Natural people / Sound files nos 68 / Inside / Exosphere / Sound files nos 13 / They shit chips don't they / Pork chop hill / Sound files nos 94 / World out of time / Inspiration / Sound files nos 7 / Welcome to the new age disco
CD ________ PF 028CD
Peacefrog / Aug '95 / Mo's Music Machine / Prime / RTM/Disc / Vital

State

CONTROL
CD ________ SOS 1CD
Sound Sound / Mar '94 / Plastic Head

SEARCHES FOR NAKED FORMS
CD ________ SOS 2CD
Sound Sound / Mar '94 / Plastic Head

State Of Grace

EVERYONE ELSE'S UNIVERSE
Conspiracy / Perfect and wild / Sea-saw / Hello (fall out the lions) / Rose II / Name of the game
CD ________ STONE 028CD
3rd Stone / Apr '97 / Plastic Head / Vital

JAMBOREEBOP
Whetherette / Smile / And love will fall / Flourescent sea / Hello / Mystery / Bitter sun / Different world / Rose / New fear / Truth / Jamboreebop
CD ________ STONE 014CD
3rd Stone / May '95 / Plastic Head / Vital

PACIFIC MOTION
Sooner or later / Miss you IV / Camden / Love pain and passion II / Bitter sun II / Ruby sky / Head / PS High / Miss you (Arizona mix)
CD ________ STONE 008CD
3rd Stone / Mar '94 / Plastic Head / Vital

State Of Mind

EXPOSE THE HIDEOUT
Driftin' / Secret affair / Waves / Raw elementz / Moments of pleasure / Don't know why / Way it is / Why / In ya brain / Everyday / Distance
CD ________ COTCD 006
Cup Of Tea / Mar '97 / Vital

State Of The Heart

CHRISTMAS MOODS
White Christmas / Spaceman came travelling / I believe in Father Christmas / Mistletoe & wine / Last Christmas / Wonderful Christmastime / Rockin' around the Christmas tree / Merry Christmas everybody / I wish it could be Christmas everyday / Another rock'n'roll Christmas / Frosty the snowman / Rudolph the red nosed reindeer / I saw Mommy kissing Santa Claus / Winter wonderland / Fairytale of New York / Santa Claus is coming to town / Please come home for Christmas / Lonely this Christmas / Happy Xmas (war is over) / Christmas song / Blue Christmas / Do they know it's Christmas / Let it snow, let it snow, let it snow / When a child is born / Stay another day / First Noel
CD ________ VTCD 105
Virgin / Nov '96 / EMI

PURE SAX
Love me for a reason / Careless whisper / Save the best for last / Can you feel the love tonight / Most beautiful girl in the world / Holding back the years / You are not alone / I wonder why / Crazy for you / After the love has gone / How am I supposed to live without you / True / Lily was here / End of the road / Goodnight girl / I want to know what love is / I believe / My funny valentine
CD ________ CDVIP 182
Virgin VIP / Apr '97 / EMI

SAX AT THE MOVIES
Unchained melody / Love is all around / Show me heaven / Because you loved me / How deep is your love / Kiss from a rose / Can you feel the love tonight / Somewhere out there / Everything I do (I do it for you) / Glory of love / Arthur's theme (Best that you can get) / (I've had) The time of my life / Up where we belong / When a man loves a woman / My funny valentine / Take my breath away / It must have been love / Gangasta's paradise (Pasttime paradise)
CD ________ CDVIP 181
Virgin VIP / Apr '97 / EMI

SAX COLLECTION, THE (2CD Set)
Love me for a reason / Careless whisper / Save the best for last / Girl from Ipanema / Most beautiful girl in the world / Holding back the years / You are not alone / I wonder why / Crazy for you / After the love has gone / How am I supposed to live without you / True / Lily was here / End of the road / Goodnight girl / I want to know what love is / I believe / Baker Street / Unchained melody / Love is all around / Show me heaven / Because you loved me / How deep is your love / Kiss from a rose / Can you feel the love tonight / Somewhere out there / Everything I do (I do it for you) / Glory of love / Arthur's theme (best that you can get) / (I've had) the time of my life / Up where we belong / When a man loves a woman / My funny valentine / I will always love you / Take my breath away / It must have been love / Waiting for a star to fall / Gangsta's paradise (pastime paradise)
CD Set ________ VTDCD 122
Virgin / Mar '97 / EMI

State Street Ramblers

STATE STREET RAMBLERS
CD ________ CJR 1003
Gannet / May '96 / Cadillac / Jazz Music

STATE STREET RAMBLERS VOL.1 1927-1931
CD ________ JPCD 1512
Jazz Perspectives / Dec '94 / Hot Shot / Jazz Music

STATE STREET RAMBLERS VOL.2 1931-1936
CD ________ JPCD 1513
Jazz Perspectives / Dec '94 / Hot Shot / Jazz Music

Statetrooper

STATETROOPER
Shape of things to come / Set fire to the night / Dreams of the faithful / Stand me up / Veni vidi vici / Last stop to heaven / She got the look / Too late / Armed and ready
CD ________ WKFMXD 91
FM / May '87 / Revolver / Sony

Static Icon

SIN MACHINE
CD ________ MA 672
Machinery / Apr '96 / Koch

SLAVE
It's a lifestyle / Taste the pain / Desire / Whip it / Unite / Krakow / Why do we believe / Overcome
CD MA 00682
Machinery / Mar '97 / Koch

Static Seekers

BODY AUTOMATIC
CD AXS 007CD
Axis / Sep '90 / Plastic Head

Statik

TEMPESTA
Free to choose what / So close / Essential times / Dr. Wheeler / Valentine / Dreams of mine / Sonar / Jack / Amazed by you / In our own dub / Jack laid bare
CD COTCD 003
Cup Of Tea / Oct '96 / Vital

Statik Sound System

TEMPESTA - THE REWORKINGS
Living in essential times / Sonar / Essential times / Dreams of mine / Amazed by you / Jack / Dr. Wheeler / Valentine / Amazed by you / Free to choose / Outside now
CD COTCD 009
Cup Of Tea / Jul '97 / Vital

Statis

FROM THE OLD TO THE NEW
From the old / Utopia planetia / Moon bong / Behind the smile / Beatings skins / Ale house blues / Samba de fat bloke / Moody old teacher / Gun
CD PF 046CD
Peacefrog / Jun '96 / Mo's Music Machine / Prime / RTM/Disc / Vital

Statman, Andy

ANDY'S RAMBLE
CD ROUCD 0244
Rounder / Dec '94 / ADA / CM / Direct

BETWEEN HEAVEN AND EARTH (Statman, Andy Quartet)
CD SH 64079
Shanachie / Feb '97 / ADA / Greensleeves / Koch

SONGS OF OUR FATHERS (Traditional Jewish Melodies) (Statman, Andy & David Grisman)
CD AC 014CD
Acoustic Disc / Apr '97 / ADA / Koch

Staton, Candi

BEST OF CANDI STATON, THE
CD 9362457302
Warner Bros. / Nov '95 / Warner Music

GLORIFY
Sing a song / He is Lord / To glorify your name / It's not easy / Have you tried God / First face / I want to see / God's got it / He's coming back
CD CDBM 075
Blue Moon / '91 / Cadillac / Discovery / Greensleeves / Jazz Music / Jet Star / TKO Magnum

GOSPEL ALBUM, THE
CD 3036450022
Carlton / May '97 / Carlton

STAND UP AND BE A WITNESS
Stand up / I'm depending on you / You don't know / He's always there / Advance / God's got an answer / Until you make it through / Glory of Jesus / Hallel
CD CDBM 077
Blue Moon / Apr '90 / Cadillac / Discovery / Greensleeves / Jazz Music / Jet Star / TKO Magnum

STANDING ON THE PROMISES
Blood rushes / No not one / There is the power in the word / Glory to his name / Living on the edge of time / Let not your heart be troubled / Oh I want to see him / When he reached down his hand for me / Finally, finally
CD CDBM 096
Blue Moon / Oct '93 / Cadillac / Discovery / Greensleeves / Jazz Music / Jet Star / TKO Magnum

Staton, Dakota

ISN'T THIS A LOVELY DAY
Isn't this a lovely day (to be caught in the rain) / I cover the waterfront / Gee baby ain't I good to you / My lean baby / If he walked into my life / I'll close my eyes / Close your eyes / (I'm afraid) the masquerade is over / Ain't no use
CD MCD 5502
Muse / Sep '95 / New Note/Pinnacle

LET ME OFF UPTOWN
When lights are low / Willow weep for me / But not for me / You don't know what love is / Best thing for you / Song is you / Avalon / Until the real thing comes along / If I should lose you / Gone with the wind / Let me off uptown / Anything goes / When Sunny gets blue / They all laughed / Too close for comfort / Cherokee / September in the rain / East of the sun and west of the moon / It's you or no one / Song is ended (but the melody lingers on) / Goodbye / Love walked in
CD CDREN 005
Renaissance / '89 / Jazz Music / Wellard

Statton, Alison

SHADY TREES, THE (Statton, Alison & Spike)
Where to start / Unspoken word / Rain / Blind faith / Pontymister / Time out / Stages / Corridors of blue / Dream monsters / Seed remains / Platfrom tickets / Sidings / Crucial timing / Point of view
CD ASKCD 68
Vinyl Japan / May '97 / Plastic Head / Vinyl Japan

TIDAL BLUES (Statton, Alison & Spike)
Greater notion / In this world / Empty hearth / Open eyes / Take heart / Lemming time / Mr. Morgan / Hidden combat / Seaport town / Find and seek / Tidal blues / Alternations
CD ASKCD 037
Vinyl Japan / Oct '94 / Plastic Head / Vinyl Japan

Status Quo

AIN'T COMPLAINING
CD 8346042
Vertigo / Feb '91 / PolyGram

B SIDES AND RARITIES
I who have nothing / Neighbour neighbour / Hurdy gurdy man / Laticia / (We ain't got) nothin' yet / I want it / Almost but not quite there / Wait just a minute / Gentleman Joe's sidewalk cafe / To be free / When my mind is not alive / Make me stay a little bit longer / Auntie Nellie / Price of love / Little Miss Nothing / Down the dustpipe / Face without a soul / In my chair / Gerdundula / Tune to the music / Good thinking Batman / Time to fly / Do you live in fire / Josie
CD CCSCD 271
Castle / Sep '90 / BMG

BACK TO THE BEGINNING (2CD Set)
CD Set CDLIK 81
Decal / Sep '91 / Koch

BEST OF STATUS QUO, THE
CD TRTCD 198
TrueTrax / Jul '96 / THE

COLLECTION, THE
Pictures of matchstick men / Green tambourine / Technicolour dreams / Sunny cellophane skies / Paradise flat / Clown / Antique Angelique / Ice in the sun / Lakky lady / Is it really me / Gerdundula / Neighbour neighbour / Paradise flat
CD CCSCD 114
Castle / '88 / BMG

DOG OF TWO HEAD
Umleitung / Nanana / Something's going on in my head / Railroad / Gerdundula / Mean girl / Someone's learning
CD CLACD 206
Castle / Sep '90 / BMG

DON'T STOP
Fun fun fun: *Status Quo & The Beach Boys* / When you walk in the room / I can hear the grass grow / You never can tell (it was a teenage wedding) / Get back / Safety dance / Raining in my heart / Don't stop / Sorrow / Proud Mary / Lucille / Johnny and Mary / Get out of Denver / Future's so bright (I gotta wear shades) / All around my hat: *Status Quo & Maddy Prior*
CD 5310352
PolyGram TV / Feb '96 / PolyGram

EARLY WORKS, THE (3CD Set)
I who have nothing: *Spectres* / Neighbour, neighbour: *Spectres* / Hurdy gurdy man: *Spectres* / Laticia: *Spectres* / (We ain't got) nothin' yet: *Spectres* / I want it: *Spectres* / Almost but not quite there: *Traffic Jam* / Wait just a minute: *Traffic Jam* / Pictures of matchstick men / Gentleman Joe's sidewalk cafe / Black veils of melancholy / To be free / Ice in the sun / When my mind is not alive / Elizabeth dreams / Paradise flat / Technicolour dreams / Spicks and specks / Sheila / Sunny cellophane skies / Green tambourine / Make me stay a little bit longer / Auntie Nellie / Are you growing tired of my love / So ends another life / Price of love / Face without a soul / You're just what I was looking for today / Antique Angelique / Poor old man / Mr. Mind Detector / Clown / Velvet curtains / Little Miss Nothing / When I awake / Nothing at all / Josie / Down the dustpipe / Time to fly / Do you live in fire / (April) Spring, Summer and Wednesdays / Daughter / Everything / Lazy poker blues / Is it really me / Gotta go home / Junior's waiting / Shy fly / Lakky lady / Need your love / Spinning wheel blue / In my chair / Gerdundula (original version) / Tune to the music / Good thinking batman / Umleitung / Nanana / Something going on in my head / Mean girl / Railroad / Someone's learning / Nanana / Nanana / Gerdundula
CD Set ESBCD 136
Essential / Dec '90 / BMG

FEW BARS MORE, A
Whatever you want / What you are proposing / Softer ride / Price of love / Drifting away / She don't fool me / Who gets the love / Let's work together / Bring it on home / Backwater / I saw the light / Don't stop me now / Come rock with me / Rockin' all over the world
CD 5500022
Spectrum / May '93 / PolyGram

HELLO
And it's better now / Blue eyed lady / Caroline / Claudie / Forty five hundred times / Reason for living / Roll over lay down / Softer ride
CD 8481722
Vertigo / Feb '91 / PolyGram

ICE IN THE SUN
CD SSLCD 204
Savanna / Jun '95 / THE

ICE IN THE SUN
CD PLSCD 206
Pulse / Apr '97 / BMG

INTROSPECTIVE: STATUS QUO
Mean girl / Ice in the sun / Pictures of matchstick men / Interview part one / Down the dustpipe / Little Miss Nothing / Is it really me / Interview part two
CD CINT 5003
Baktabak / Nov '90 / Arabesque

IT'S ONLY ROCK & ROLL
Wanderer / Don't waste my time / Something 'bout you baby I like / Blue eyed lady / Accident prone / Where am I / Little dreamer / Ain't complaining / Hard ride / Mess of blues / You don't own me / Your smiling face / Name of the game / Enough is enough
CD 5501902
Spectrum / Sep '94 / PolyGram

LIVE AT THE NEC
Caroline / Roll over lay down / Backwater / Little lady / Don' you drive my car / Whatever you want / Hold you back / Rockin' all over the world / Over the edge / Don't waste my time
CD 8189472
Vertigo / Feb '91 / PolyGram

MA KELLY'S GREASY SPOON
Spinning wheel blues / Daughter / Everything / Shy fly / Junior's wailing / Lakky lady / Need your love / Lazy poker blues / Is it really me / Gotta go home / April, Spring, Summer and Wednesdays
CD CLACD 169
Castle / Dec '89 / BMG

NEVER TOO LATE/BACK TO BACK
Never too late / Something bout you baby I like / Take me away / Falling in falling out / Carol / Long ago / Mountain lady / Don't stop me now / Enough is enough / Riverside / Mess of blues / Ol rag blues / Can't be done / Too close to the ground / No contract / Win or lose / Marguerita time / Your kind of love / Stay the night / Going down town tonight
CD 8480882
Vertigo / Feb '91 / PolyGram

ON THE LEVEL
Broken man / Bye bye Johnny / Down down / I saw the light / Most of the time / Night ride / Over and one / What to do / Where am I
CD 8481742
Vertigo / Feb '91 / PolyGram

OTHER SIDE OF STATUS QUO, THE
Magic / Power of rock / Don't give it up / Rotten to the bone / You lost the love / Heartburn / Perfect remedy / A B Blues / Keep me guessing / Joanne / Doing it all for you / Lonely / That's alright / I wonder why / Gerundula / Long legged girl with the short dress on / Forty five hundred times / Junior's wailing
CD VSOPCD 213
Connoisseur Collection / Feb '95 / Pinnacle

PICTURES OF MATCHSTICK MEN
Down the dustpipe / Mean girl / Gerundula / Price of love / Make me stay a little bit longer / Josie / Hurdy gurdy man / Something going on in my head / Green tambourine / Pictures of matchstick men / Ice in the sun / Black veils of melancholy / Laticia / I who have nothing / Tune to the music / Spicks and specks / Umleitung / Nanana
CD 5507272
Spectrum / Mar '95 / PolyGram

PICTURESQUE MATCHSTICKABLE MESSAGES FROM THE STATUS QUO
Black veils of melancholy / When my mind is not alive / Ice in the sun / Elizabeth dreams / Gentleman Joe's sidewalk cafe / Paradise flat / Technicolour dreams / Spicks and specks / Sheila / Sunny cellophane skies / Green tambourine / Pictures of matchstick men
CD CLACD 168
Castle / Dec '89 / BMG

PILEDRIVER
All the reasons / Big fat mama / Don't waste my time / O baby / Paper plane / Roadhouse blues / Unspoken words / Year
CD 8841712
Vertigo / Feb '91 / PolyGram

QUO/BLUE FOR YOU
Backwater / Just take me / Break the rules / Drifting away / Don't think it matters / Fine fine fine / Lonely man / Slow train / Is there a better way / Mad about the boy / Ring of a change / Blue for you / Rain / Rollin' home / That's a fact / Ease your mind / Mystery song
CD 8480892
Vertigo / Feb '91 / PolyGram

ROCK TIL YOU DROP
Like a zombie / All we really wanna do (Polly) / Fakin' the blues / One man band / Rock 'til you drop / Can't give you more / Warning whot / Let's work together / Bring it on home / No problems / Good sign / Tommy / Nothing comes easy / Fame or money / Price of love / Forty five hundred times
CD 5103412
Vertigo / Jan '93 / PolyGram

ROCKIN' ALL OVER THE WORLD
Baby boy / Can't give you more / Dirty water / For you / Hard time / Hold you back / Let's ride / Rockin' all over the world / Too far gone / Who am I / You don't own me / Rockers rollin'
CD 8481732
Vertigo / Feb '91 / PolyGram

ROCKING ALL OVER THE YEARS
Pictures of matchstick men / Ice in the sun / Paper plane / Caroline / Break the rules / Down down / Roll over lay down / Rain / Wild side of life / Rockin' all over the world / Whatever you want / What you're proposing / Something 'bout you baby I like / Rock 'n' roll / Dear John / Ol' rag blues / Marguerita time / Wanderer / Rollin' home / In the army now / Burning bridges (on and off and on again) / Anniversary waltz
CD 8467972
Vertigo / Oct '90 / PolyGram

SPARE PARTS
Face without a soul / You're just what I was looking for today / Are you growing tired of my love / Antique Angelique / So ends another life / Poor old man / Mr. Mind detector / Clown / Velvet curtains / Little Miss Nothing / When I awake / Nothing at all
CD CLACD 205
Castle / Sep '90 / BMG

STATUS QUO
CD MATCD 291
Castle / Mar '94 / BMG

THIRSTY WORK
Goin' nowhere / I didn't mean it / Confidence / Point of no return / Sail away / Like it or not / Soft in the head / Queenie / Lover of the human race / Sherri don't fail me now / Rude awakening time / Back on my feet / Restless / Ciao ciao / Tango / Sorry
CD 5236072
Vertigo / Aug '94 / PolyGram

TWELVE GOLD BARS VOL.1
Rockin' all over the world / Down down / Caroline / Paper plane / Break the rules / Again and again / Mystery song / Roll over lay down / Rain / Wild side of life / Whatever you want / Living on an island
CD 8000622
Vertigo / Nov '84 / PolyGram

WHATEVER YOU WANT/JUST SUPPOSIN'
Whatever you want / Shady lady / Who asked you / Your smiling face / Living on an island / Come rock with me / Rockin' on / Runaway / Breaking away
CD 8480872
Vertigo / Feb '91 / PolyGram

Stauber, Beverly

NAIL MY FEET TO THE KITCHEN FLOOR
CD NERCD 064
Nervous / '91 / Nervous / TKO Magnum

Stead, Joe

EXTRAVAGANT SCHEMES
CD APL 002CD
APL / Nov '96 / ADA

Steakknife

GODPILL
CD EFA 120112
X-Mist / Nov '95 / Cargo / SRD

Stealer's Wheel

BEST OF STEALER'S WHEEL, THE
Stuck in the middle with you / Nothing's gonna change my mind / Star / This morning / Steamboat row / Next to me / Right or wrong / Go as you please / Benediction / Waltz / Blind faith / Late again / Wheelin' / Jose
CD CSAPCD 106
Connoisseur Collection / Jun '90 / Pinnacle

STUCK IN THE MIDDLE
Stuck in the middle with you / Who cares / Benediction / Go as you please / Late again / Everything will turn out fine / Blind faith / Star / Outside looking in / Found my way to you / Right or wrong / You put something better inside of me
CD CDMID 151
A&M / Oct '92 / PolyGram

Steam Jenny

WELCOME BACK
CD _____ CDLOC 1082
Lochshore / Oct '94 / ADA / Direct / Duncans

Steamboat Band

RUMOURS & RIDERS
Got no tears / Died without sleeping / Everybody needs the morning rain / Fall from grace / Hit the bottle again / Take your hands off the wheel / Just like me / Running to Waycross / Goodbye Mary Jane / Take a little time (Off my hands) / Restless lullaby / She's coming my way / Let it pass me by
CD _____ 5274732
Polydor / Apr '95 / PolyGram

Steaming Jungle

RUPUNI SAFARI
CD _____ ARICD 111
Ariwa Sounds / Sep '95 / Jet Star / SRD

Steampacket

ROCK GENERATION
CD _____ 14555
Spalax / Jun '97 / ADA / Cargo / Direct / Discovery / Greyhound

Stecher, Jody

HEART SONGS (Stecher, Jody & Kate Brislin)
Orphan train / Walkin' through your town in the snow / Hood river roll on / Scofield mine disaster / Miner's lullaby / Rock salt and nails / Green rolling hills of West Virginia / Ragged old man / Jury set him free / Faded rose / John D. Lee / Golden mansion / I remember loving you
CD _____ ROUCD 0424
Rounder / Jul '97 / ADA / CM / Direct

STAY AWHILE (Stecher, Jody & Kate Brislin)
CD _____ ROUCD 0334
Rounder / Apr '95 / ADA / CM / Direct

Steckar, Marc

PACKWORK (Steckar, Marc Tubapack)
CD _____ BBRC 9310
Big Blue / Jan '94 / Harmonia Mundi

Steel

STEEL
CD _____ EFA 006662
Mille Plateau / Oct '95 / SRD

Steel Band Des Caraibes

STEEL MUSIC FROM THE CARIBBEAN
CD _____ 824552
BUDA / Nov '90 / Discovery

Steel, Eric

BACK FOR MORE
911 / Something for nothing / Low down / Crazy lady / Stray cat blues / Back for more / Meant to be / Material law / Insert gently
CD _____ KILCD 1003
Killerwatt / Oct '93 / Kingdom

Steel Fury

LESSER OF TWO EVILS
CD _____ 859 803
Steamhammer / '89 / Pinnacle / Plastic Head

Steel Pole Bath Tub

LIVE
CD _____ YCLS 019
Your Choice / Jun '94 / Plastic Head

LURCH
Christina / Hey you / Paranoid / I am Sam I am / Bee sting / Swerve / Heaven on dirt / Lime away / River / Time to die / Welcome aboard it's love / Hey Bo Diddley / Thru the windshield of love / Tear it apart
CD _____ TUPCD 16
Tupelo / Jul '90 / RTM/Disc

MIRACLE OF SOUND IN MOTION, THE
Pseudoephendrine hydrochloride / Train to Miami / Exhale / Thumbnail / Down all the days / Carbon / Bozeman / Borstal / 594 / Waxl
CD _____ TUP 472
Tupelo / Apr '93 / RTM/Disc

SOME COCKTAIL SUGGESTIONS
Ray / Living end / Slip / Hit it / Speaker phone / Wasp jar
CD _____ TUP 0512
Tupelo / Jan '94 / RTM/Disc

Steel Prophet

GODDESS PRINCIPLE, THE
CD _____ MASSE 001
Massacre / Aug '95 / Plastic Head

Steel Pulse

HANDSWORTH REVOLUTION
Handsworth revolution / Bad man / Soldiers / Sound check / Prodigal / Ku klux klan / Prediction / Macka splaff
CD _____ RRCD 24
Reggae Refreshers / Nov '90 / PolyGram / Vital

RASTANTHOLOGY (The Best Of Steel Pulse)
CD _____ WMDCD 3
Wise Man Doctrine / Oct '96 / Jet Star / Total/BMG

REGGAE GREATS
Sound system / Babylon makes the rules / Don't give in / Soldier / Prodigal son / Ku klux klan / Macka splaff / Drug squad / Reggae fever / Handsworth revolution
CD _____ 5528862
Spectrum / Jul '97 / PolyGram

SOUND SYSTEM (The Island Anthology/ 2CD Set)
CD Set _____ 5243232
Island Jamaica / Jul '97 / Jet Star / PolyGram

TRIBUTE TO THE MARTYRS
Unseen guest / Sound system / Jah Pickney / Biko's kindred lament / Tribute to the martyrs / Babylon makes the rules / Uncle George / Blasphemy
CD _____ RRCD 17
Reggae Refreshers / Sep '90 / PolyGram / Vital

VICTIMS
Taxi driver / Can't get you (out of my system) / Soul of my song / Grab a girlfriend / Feel the passion / Money / Victims / Gang warfare / To tutu / Free the land / We can do it / Stay with the rhythm / Evermore / Dudes / Taxi
CD _____ MCLD 19345
MCA / Oct '96 / BMG

Steele, Davy

CHASING SHADOWS
Kishmul's galley / Brand new day / Loch Tay boat song / Jimmy Waddell/Lochanside / Long hellos, short goodbyes / Tam glen/ Dancing in Dinan / Tibby Dunbar/The brothers reconciliation / Calton weaver / Leave her Johnny, leave her / Chasing shadows / Scotland yet
CD _____ HYCD 297171
Hypertension / May '97 / ADA / CM / Direct / Total/BMG

SUMMERTIME
CD _____ CMCD 046
Celtic Music / Apr '94 / CM

Steele, Jan

VOICES AND INSTRUMENTS (Steele, Jan & John Cage)
All day / Distant saxophones / Rhapsody spaniel / Experiences no.1 / Experiences no.2 / Wonderful widow of eighteen springs / Forever and sunsmell / In a landscape
CD _____ CDOVD 481
EG / Jul '97 / EMI

Steele, Jay

NATURAL GUITAR VOL.2, THE
CD _____ 2687
NorthSound / Aug '96 / Gallant

Steele, Jevetta

HERE IT IS
Say a little prayer for you / Baby are you / And how / You're gonna love me / Here it is / Calling you / In this man's world / Good foot / Skip 2 my u my darling / Where do we go from here / Love will follow
CD _____ 108772
Musidisc UK / Mar '92 / Grapevine/ PolyGram

Steele, Tommy

EP COLLECTION, THE
Rock with the caveman / Wedding bells / Doomsday rock / Singin' the blues / Take me back baby / Handful of songs / Rebel rock / Will it be you / Happy guitar / Knee deep in the blues / Put a ring on her finger / Young love / Come on let's go / Elevator rock / Only man on the island / Time to kill / Little white bull / Number twenty two across the way / You gotta go / Singin' time / Cannibal pot / Build up / Water, water
CD _____ SEECD 347
See For Miles/C5 / Oct '96 / Pinnacle

HANDFUL OF SONGS, A
Handful of songs / Singin' the blues / Young love / Water water / Cannibal pot / It's all happening / Where have all the flowers gone / Nairobi / I put the lightie on / Georgia on my mind / Where's the birdie / Rock with the caveman / Butterfingers / Shiralee / What a little darlin' / She's too far above me / Hey you / Flash bang wallop
CD _____ 5500182
Spectrum / May '93 / PolyGram

ROCK 'N' ROLL YEARS, THE (Steele, Tommy & The Steelemen)
Rock with the caveman / C'mon let's go / Butterfly / Give give give / Elevator rock / Rebel rock / You gotta go / Build up / Put a ring on her finger / You were mine / Swallow tail coat / Singin' the blues / Doomsday rock / Knee deep in the blues / Two eyes / Take me back baby / Writing on the wall / Hey you / Teenage party / Plant a kiss / Rock around the town / Drunken guitar / Tallahassee lassie
CD _____ SEECD 203
See For Miles/C5 / Oct '96 / Pinnacle

SINGING IN THE RAIN AND OTHER GREAT STANDARDS
Singing in the rain / Rambling rose / Tip toe through the tulips / When the red red robin / (I'd like to get you) on a slow boat to China / You made me love you / On mother kelly's doorstep / I'll be with you in apple blossom time / In a shanty in old shanty town / Underneath the arches / Carolina in the office / My mammy / April showers / Is it true what they say about Dixie / Baby face / I wonder who's kissing her now / Hey good lookin' / On the sunny side of the street / Zip-a-dee-doo-dah / When you're smiling / Bells are ringing for me and my girl / Me and my girl / My lucky star / You must have been a beautiful baby / Oh you beautiful doll / Boiled beef and carrots / Any old iron / Knocked 'em out in the old kent road / My old man's a dustman / My old man said follow the van / I've got a lovely bunch of coconuts / Consider yourself / I'm getting married in the morning / I'm Henery the eighth, I am / Knees up Mother Brown / Roll out the barrel
CD _____ 300742
Hallmark / Jul '96 / Carlton

WORLD OF TOMMY STEELE, THE
Singin' the blues / Little white bull / Handful of songs / Shiralee / Half a sixpence / Rock with the caveman / Water water / Come on let's go / Sweet Georgia Brown / Where's the birdie / Nairobi / What a mouth / If the rain's got to fall / Where have all the flowers gone / Only man on the island / Knee deep in the blues / Butterfingers / Number 22 across the way / She's too far above me / Happy guitar
CD _____ 5520162
Spectrum / May '96 / PolyGram

Steeler

STRIKE BACK
CD _____ 851 861
Steamhammer / '88 / Pinnacle / Plastic Head

UNDERCOVER
CD _____ 857 512
Steamhammer / '89 / Pinnacle / Plastic Head

Steeles

HEAVEN HELP US ALL
Heart in my hand / Tide keeps lifting me / Never get over you / Well done / I don't wanna be without U / Heaven help us all / It'll be alright / Oh what a gift / Those were the days / Big God
CD _____ 7559612902
Nonesuch / Aug '93 / Warner Music

Steeleye Span

ALL AROUND MY HAT
Black jack David / Hard times of old England / Cadwith anthem / All around my hat / Gamble gold (Robin Hood) / Wife of Usher's well / Sum wavves (Tunes) / Dance with me / Bachelors hall
CD _____ CDGOLD 1009
EMI Gold / Mar '96 / EMI

BACK IN LINE
CD _____ PRKCD 8
Park / Aug '91 / Pinnacle

BELOW THE SALT
Spotted cow / Rosebuds in June / Jigs / Sheepcrook and black dog / Royal forester / King Henry / Gaudete / John Barleycorn / Saucy sailor
CD _____ BGOCD 324
Beat Goes On / Sep '96 / Pinnacle

BEST OF AND THE REST OF STEELEYE SPAN, THE
CD _____ CDAR 1012
Action Replay / Oct '94 / Tring

BEST OF STEELEYE SPAN LIVE IN CONCERT, THE
CD _____ PRK 27CD
Park / Oct '94 / Pinnacle

BEST OF STEELEYE SPAN, THE
Gaudete / All around my hat / Thomas the rhymer / Alison Gross / Little Sir Hugh / Cam ye o'er frae France / Long lankin / Gone to America / Let her go down / Black jack David / Bach goes to Limerick
CD _____ CCD 1467
Chrysalis / '88 / EMI

COLLECTION IN CONCERT, THE
Blacksmith / Weaver / Spotted cow / One misty moisty morning / King Henry / Fox / Two butchers / Jack Hall / Canon / Shaking of the sheets / All around my hat / Tunes / Gaudete
CD _____ PRKCD 27
Park / Nov '94 / Pinnacle

COMMONERS CROWN
Little Sir Hugh / Bach goes to Limerick / Long lankin / Dogs and ferrets / Galtee farmer / Demon lover / Elf call / Weary cutters / New York girls
CD _____ BGOCD 315
Beat Goes On / Jul '96 / Pinnacle

EARLY YEARS, THE
Blacksmith / Marrowbones / Western wynde / All things are quite silent / Lovely on the water / Boys of Bedlam / My Johnny was a shoemaker / Cold haily windy night / Horn of the hunter / Jigs / Prince Charlie Stuart / Reels / Dark eyed sailor / Rave on / Brisk young butcher / Wee weaver / When I was on horseback / Ploughboy and the Cockney / One night as I lay on my bed
CD _____ VSOPCD 132
Connoisseur Collection / Apr '89 / Pinnacle

KING, THE (The Best Of The Early Years)
Calling song / Fisherman's wife / Copshawholme fair / All things are quite silent / My Johnny was a shoemaker / Fly up my cock / Twa corbies / One night as I lay on my bed / Cold haily, windy night / Prince Charlie Stewart / Lark in the morning / King / Rave on / Ploughboy and the cockney / Gower wassail / Paddy Clancy's jig / Willie clancy's fancy / Skewball
CD _____ CRESTCD 022
Mooncrest / Nov '96 / ADA / Direct

LIVE AT LAST
Athol highlanders / Walter Bulwer's polka / Saucy sailor / Black freighter / Maid and the palmer / Hunting the wren / Montrose / Bonnets so blue / False knight on the road
CD _____ BGOCD 342
Beat Goes On / Mar '97 / Pinnacle

NOW WE ARE SIX
Seven hundred elves / Edwin / Drink down the moon / Now we are six / Thomas the rhymer / Mooncoin jig / Long-a-growing / Two magicians / Twinkle twinkle little star / To know him is to love him
CD _____ BGOCD 157
Beat Goes On / Dec '92 / Pinnacle

ORIGINAL MASTERS
Sir James the rose / Black jack David / All around my hat / Wife of Usher's well / Fighting for strangers / Thomas the rhymer / Seven hundred elves / Long lankin / Elf call / Cam ye o'er frae France / Bonnie moorhen / Alison Gross / Mooncoin jig / Drink down the moon / Stewball / Lovely on the water / Jigs / Brides favourite / Tansey's fancy / One misty moisty morning / Saucy sailor / Gaudete
CD _____ BGOCD 322
Beat Goes On / Mar '97 / Pinnacle

PARCEL OF ROGUES, A
One misty moisty morning / Alison Gross / Bold poachers / Ups and down / Robbery with violins / Wee wee man / Weaver and the factory maid / Rogues in a nation / Can ye o'er frae France / Hares on the mountain
CD _____ BGOCD 323
Beat Goes On / Oct '96 / Pinnacle

ROCKET COTTAGE
London / Bosnian hornpipes / Ofreo / Nathan's reel / Twelve witches / Brown girl / Fighting for strangers / Silgo maid / Sir James the Rose / Drunkard
CD _____ BGOCD 318
Beat Goes On / Jul '96 / Pinnacle

SAILS OF SILVER
Sails of silver / My love / Barnet Fair / Senior service / Gone to America / Where are they now / Let her go down / Longbone / Marigold/Harvest home / Tell me why / Lark in the morning / Thomas / Johnny was a shoe maker
CD _____ PRKCD 40
Park / Jun '97 / Pinnacle

SPANNING THE YEARS (2CD Set)
Blacksmith / My Johnny was a shoe maker / King / Lovely on the water / Marrowbones / Rave on / Gaudette / John Barleycorn / Alison Gross / Robbery with violins / Rogues in a nation / Cam ye o'er frae France / Thomas the rhymer / To know him is to love him / New York girls / Long lankin / Black jack David / Hard times of Old England / All around my hat / London / Fighting for strangers / Black freighter / Victory / False knight on the road / Rag doll / Let her go down / Sails of silver / Gone to America / My love / Lady diamond / Blackleg miner / One misty moisty morning / Fox / Following me / Tam lin
CD Set _____ CDCHR 6093
Chrysalis / Apr '95 / EMI

STACK OF STEELEYE SPAN, A (Their Finest Folk Recordings 1973-1975)
Blacckleg miner / Dark-eyed sailor / Hills of Greenmore / Lowlands of Holland / Blacksmith / Bryan O'Lynn/Hag with the monkey / Boys of bedlam / False knight on the road / Female drummer / Lovely on the water / Four nights drunk / When I was on horseback / Marrowbones / Captain Coulston / Dowd's favourite/10 pound float/Morning dew / Wee weaver

CD ______ **EMPRCD 668**
Emporio / Oct '96 / Disc

STORM FORCE TEN
Awake awake / Sweep chimney sweep / Wife of the soldier / Victory / Black freighter / Some rival / Treadmill song / Seventeen come Sunday
CD ______ **BGOCD 337**
Beat Goes On / Dec '96 / Pinnacle

TIME
Prickly bush / Old maid in the Garrett / Harvest of the moon / Underneath her apron / Cutty Wren / Go from my window / Elf knight / Water is wide / You will burn / Corbies / Song will remain
CD ______ **PRKCD 34**
Park / Mar '96 / Pinnacle

Steely & Cleevie

PLAY STUDIO ONE VINTAGE
CD ______ **CDHB 116**
Heartbeat / May '92 / ADA / Direct / Greensleeves / Jet Star

STEELY & CLEEVIE PRESENTS HARDCORE
CD ______ **SCCD 2**
Steely & Cleevie / Oct '93 / Jet Star

Steely Dan

AJA
Black cow / Aja / Deacon blues / Peg / Home at last / I got the news / Josie
CD ______ **MCLD 19145**
MCA / Nov '90 / BMG

ASIA
CD ______ **DMCA 102**
MCA / Jan '85 / BMG

BEST OF STEELY DAN, THE (Remastered)
Reelin' in the years / Rikki don't lose that number / Peg / FM (no static at all) / Hey nineteen / Deacon blues / Black Friday / Bodhisattva / Do it again / Haitian divorce / My old school / Midnite cruiser / Babylon sisters / Kid Charlemagne / Dirty work / Josie
CD ______ **MCD 10967**
MCA / Nov '93 / BMG

CAN'T BUY A THRILL
Do it again / Dirty work / Kings / Midnite cruiser / Only a fool / Reelin' in the years / Fire in the hole / Brooklyn (owes the charmer and me) / Change of the guard / Turn that heartbeat over again
CD ______ **MCLD 19017**
MCA / Apr '92 / BMG

CATALYST
Sun mountain / Barrytown / Take it out on me / Cave's of Altamira / Charlie Freak / You go where I go / Any world (that I'm welcome to) / Little with sugar / Android warehouse / More to come / Parker's band / Oh wow it's you again / Stone piano / Yellow peril / Roaring of the lamb / This seat's been taken / Ida Lee / Undecided / Horse in town
CD ______ **CDTB 503**
Thunderbolt / Jun '94 / TKO Magnum

CITIZEN 1972-1980 (The Best Of Steely Dan/4CD Set)
Do it again / Dirty work / Kings / Midnite cruiser / Only a fool would say that / Reelin' in the years / Fire in the hole / Brooklyn (owes the charmer under me) / Change of the guard / Turn that heartbeat over again / Bodhisattva / Razor boy / Boston rag / Your gold teeth / Showbiz kid / My old school / King of the world / Pearl of the quarter / Rikki don't lose that number / Night by night / Any major dude will tell you / Barrytown / East St. Louis toodle-oo / Parker's band / Through with buzz / Pretzel logic / With a gun / Charlie Freak / Monkey in your soul / Bodhisattva (live) / Black Friday / Bad sneakers / Rose darling / Daddy don't live in that New York City no more / Dr. Wu / Everyone's gone to the movies / Chain lightning / Your gold teeth II / Any world (that I'm welcome to) / Throw back the little one / Kid Charlemagne / Caves of Altmira / Don't take me alive / Sign in stranger / Fez / Green earrings / Haitian divorce / Everything you did / Royal scam / Here at the western world / Black cow / Aja / Peg / Deacon blues / Home at last / I got the news / When Josie comes home / FM / Babylon sisters / Hey nineteen / Glamour profession / Gaucho / Time out of mind / My rival / Third world man / Everyone's gone to the movies (demo)
CD Set ______ **MCAD 410981**
MCA / Jan '94 / BMG

COUNTDOWN TO ECSTASY
Bodhisattva / Razor boy / Boston rag / Your gold teeth / Showbiz kid / My old school / Pearl of the quarter / King of the world
CD ______ **MCLD 19018**
MCA / Apr '92 / BMG

GAUCHO
Babylon sisters / Hey nineteen / Glamour profession / Gaucho / Time out of mind / My rival / Third world man
CD ______ **MCLD 19146**
MCA / Oct '92 / BMG

GOLD
Hey nineteen / Green earring / Deacon blues / Chain lightning / FM / Black cow / King of the world / Babylon sisters
CD ______ **MCAD 10387**
MCA / Aug '91 / BMG

KATHY LIED
Black Friday / Bad sneakers / Rose darling / Daddy don't live in that New York City no more / Dr. Wu / Everyone's gone to the movies / Your gold teeth II / Chain lightning / Any world (that I'm welcome to) / Throw back the little ones
CD ______ **MCLD 19082**
MCA / Nov '92 / BMG

OLD REGIME
Brain tap shuffle / Come back baby / Don't let me in / Old regime / Brooklyn / Mock turtle song / Soul rain / I can't function / Yellow peril / Let George do it
CD ______ **CDTB 040**
Thunderbolt / May '87 / TKO Magnum

PRETZEL LOGIC
Rikki don't lose that number / Night by night / Any major dude will tell you / Barrytown / East St. Louis toodle-oo / Parker's band / Thru with buzz / Pretzel logic / With a gun / Charlie freak / Monkey in your soul
CD ______ **MCLD 19081**
MCA / Nov '91 / BMG

REELIN' IN THE YEARS (The Very Best Of Steely Dan/2CD Set)
Do it again / Reelin' in the years / My old school / Bodhisattva / Showbiz kid / Rikki don't lose that number / Pretzel logic / Black Friday / Bad sneakers / Dr. Wu / Haitian divorce / Kid Charlemagne / Fez / Peg / Josie / Deacon blues / Hey nineteen / Babylon sisters
CD Set ______ **MCLDD 19147**
MCA / Dec '92 / BMG

ROYAL SCAM, THE
Kid Charlemagne / Sign in stranger / Fez / Caves of Altmira / Don't take me alive / Green earring / Haitian divorce / Everything you did / Royal scam
CD ______ **MCLD 19083**
MCA / Nov '92 / BMG

SPOTLIGHT ON STEELY DAN
Braintap shuffle / Come back baby / Don't let me in / Stone piano / Brooklyn / Mock turtle song / Soul ram / I can't function / Yellow peril / Let George do it / Parker's band / Any world (that I'm welcome to) / Barrytown / Ida Lee
CD ______ **HADCD 103**
Javelin / Feb '94 / Henry Hadaway / THE

STONE PIANO
Android warehouse / Horse in town / More to come / Parker's band / Ida Lee / Stone piano / Any world (that I'm welcome to) / Take it out on me / This seat's been taken / Barrytown
CD ______ **CDTB 054**
Thunderbolt / Apr '88 / TKO Magnum

SUN MOUNTAIN
Berry town / Android warehouse / More to come / Sun mountain / Ida Lee / Any world (that I'm welcome to) / Stone piano / Caves of Altmira / Horse in town / Roaring of the lamb / Parker's band / Oh wow it's you / You go where I go / This seat's been taken / Little with sugar / Take it out on me
CD ______ **CDTB 139**
Magnum Music / Nov '92 / TKO Magnum

Steffen, Bruno

CITY OF GLASS (Steffen/Althaus Quartet)
CD ______ **BRAM 1990132**
Brambus / Nov '93 / ADA

IN BETWEEN (Steffen, Bruno & Heiner Althaus)
CD ______ **BRAM 1992372**
Brambus / Nov '93 / ADA

Steffen, Peter

ALS ICH EIN KLEINER JUNGE WAR
Als ich ein kleiner junge war / Huh-a-ho / Zwei sommer long / Wenn morgen fruh die sonne / Es war an der riviera / Tag fur tag / Sag, warum willst du von mir gehen / Schau in meine augen / Auf meinen jungen kann ich / Eine himmelblaue kutsche / Der puppenspieler / Pepinos freund pasquale / Wie im September / Es liegt mir am herzen / Die kleine stadt will schlafen geh'n / Erst musst du mal zur schule geh'n / Dir, dir nur allein / Tabu / Twist / Ich bin dein, du bist mein / Sag' Papa / Hilo-Hulalei / Sie war ein kind der heide / Beim auseinandergeh'n / Hor mal mein junge / Drei zartliche kusse / Wer im November nicht liben kann / Goodbye, auf wiedersehn
CD ______ **BCD 15996**
Bear Family / Jul '96 / Direct / Rollercoaster / Swift

Steffens, Dirk

7TH STEP
CD ______ **SB 030**
Second Battle / Jun '97 / Greyhound

Stegall, Keith

PASSAGES
CD ______ **5284372**
Mercury / Feb '96 / PolyGram

Steidl, Bernd

PSYCHO ACOUSTIC OVERTURE
Irrlichter / Metamorphosis / Cobra Negra / Jeux D'eau / Death of Ludwig II / Eine Kleine Bassmusik / Walburg's night / Papillon / La campanella / Will-O-The-Wisp / In Venice
CD ______ **RR 9204 2**
Roadrunner / Oct '92 / PolyGram

Steig, Jeremy

ELEGANT HUMP
CD ______ **500812**
Musidisc / Sep '96 / Discovery

Stein

KONIGZUCKER
CD ______ **RTD 19516982**
Our Choice / Mar '95 / Pinnacle

Stein, Hal

CLASSIC SESSIONS (Stein, Hal & Warren Fitzgerald)
CD ______ **PCD 7050**
Progressive / Jun '93 / Jazz Music

Stein, Ira

SPUR OF THE MOMENT
Way back when / Fiddletown / Footsteps / Tributaries / Continuum II / La source / Spur of the moment / Winter wind / Pinnacles / Horseshoe hill / Dominique
CD ______ **ND 63029**
Narada / Jul '94 / ADA / New Note/Pinnacle

Steinman, Jim

BAD FOR GOOD
Bad for good / Lost boys and golden girls / Love and death and an American guitar / Stark raving love / Out of the frying pan (and into the fire) / Surf's up / Dance in my pants / Left in the dark
CD ______ **4720422**
Epic / Oct '92 / Sony

ORIGINAL SIN (Pandora's Box)
Invocation / Original sin (the natives are restless tonight) / Twentieth century fox / Safe sex (when it comes 2 loving U) / Good girls go to heaven (bad girls go everywhere) / Requiem metal / I've been dreaming up a storm lately / It's all coming back to me now / Opening of the box / Want ad / My little red book / It just won't quit / Pray lewd / Future ain't what it used to be
CD ______ **CDVIP 171**
Virgin VIP / Apr '97 / EMI

Stelin, Tena

SACRED SONGS
CD ______ **WRCD 008**
World / Jun '97 / Jet Star / TKO Magnum

SUN AND MOON (Stelin, Tena & Centry)
CD ______ **DUBVCD 010**
Dub Vintage / Dec '94 / Jet Star

TAKE A LOOK AT THE WORLD
CD ______ **DUBVCD 011**
Dub Vintage / Dec '94 / Jet Star

Steltch

RHYTHM OF BUST
CD ______ **SON 003 2**
Sonic Noise / Mar '93 / SRD

Stems

WEED OUT (Live At The Old Melbourne 1986)
CD ______ **HOWR 8**
House Of Wax / Jun '97 / Cargo / Greyhound

Stendal Blast

WAS VERDORRT
CD ______ **EFA 155842**
Gymnastic / May '95 / SRD

Stenson, Bobo

REFLECTIONS (Stenson, Bobo Trio)
Enlightener / My man's gone now / Not / Dorrmattan / Q / Reflections in D / 12 Tones old / Mindiatyr
CD ______ **5231602**
ECM / Feb '96 / New Note/Pinnacle

SOUNDS AROUND THE HOUSE, THE
CD ______ **1206**
Caprice / Jan '89 / ADA / Cadillac / CM / Complete/Pinnacle

Stensson, Ewan

PRESENT DIRECTIONS
CD ______ **DRCD 218**
Dragon / Aug '87 / ADA / Cadillac / CM / Roots / Wellard

Step Forward

IT DID MAKE A DIFFERENCE
CD ______ **DFR 14**
Desperate Flight / Jan '97 / Cargo

Stephanie

BEST OF STEPHANIE, THE
CD ______ **3020222**
Arcade / Jun '97 / Discovery

Stephen C

NATURAL PIANO VOL.2, THE
CD ______ **2898**
NorthSound / Aug '96 / Gallant

Stephens, Anne

TEDDY BEARS PICNIC
CD ______ **PASTCD 7067**
Flapper / Jun '95 / Pinnacle

Stephens, Richie

MIRACLES
CD ______ **VPCD 1457**
VP / Apr '96 / Greensleeves / Jet Star / Total/BMG
CD ______ **CRCD 48**
Charm / Jan '96 / Jet Star

SPECIAL WORK OF ART
CD ______ **PHCD 2062**
Penthouse / Mar '97 / Jet Star

Stephenson, Martin

SWEET MISDEMEANOUR (The Best Of Martin Stephenson & The Daintees)
CD ______ **FIEND 770CD**
Demon / Nov '95 / Pinnacle

THERE COMES A TIME (Stephenson, Martin & The Daintees)
CD ______ **8283982**
Kitchenware / Jul '93 / Sony

YOGI IN MY HOUSE
CD ______ **FIENDCD 762**
Demon / Feb '95 / Pinnacle

Steppenwolf

AT YOUR BIRTHDAY PARTY/ STEPPENWOLF
Don't cry / Chicken wolf / Lovely meter / Round and down / It's never too late / Sleeping dreaming / Jupiter child / She'll be better / Cat killer / Rock me / God fearing man / Mango juice / Happy birthday / Ball crusher / Forty days and forty nights / Fat Jack / Renegade / Foggy mental breakdown / Snow blind friend / Who needs ya / Earschplittenloudenboomer / Hippo stomp
CD ______ **BGOCD 336**
Beat Goes On / Dec '96 / Pinnacle

BORN TO BE WILD
CD ______ **MPG 74016**
Movieplay Gold / May '93 / Target/BMG

FIVE FINGERS DISCOUNT (Kay, John & Steppenwolf)
Five fingers discount / You / All I want is what you got / None of the above / Balance / Down to Earth / Hot night in a cold town / Hold your head up / For rock 'n' roll / Every man for himself
CD ______ **100452**
CMC / May '97 / BMG

MONSTER
CD ______ **BGOCD 126**
Beat Goes On / Sep '91 / Pinnacle

STEPPENWOLF
Born to be wild / Magic carpet ride / Monster / America / Power play / What would you do / Paymaster / Back home / Draft register / From here to eventually / Three stripes / Suicide
CD ______ **EXP 029**
Experience / May '97 / TKO Magnum

Steppes

ALIVE ALIVE OH
CD ______ **VOXXCD 2065**
Voxx / Feb '92 / Else / RTM/Disc

HARPS AND HAMMERS
CD ______ **VOXXCD 2064**
Voxx / Feb '91 / Else / RTM/Disc

Steps Ahead

LIVE IN TOKYO 1986
Beirut / Oops / Self portrait / Sumo / Cajun / Safari / In a sentimental mood / Trains
CD ______ **NYC 60062**
NYC / May '94 / New Note/Pinnacle

NYC
Well in that case / Lust for life / Red neon, go or give / Charanga / Get it / NYC / Stick jam / Absolutely maybe / Festival paradiso
CD ______ **INT 30072**
Intuition / Apr '90 / New Note/Pinnacle

VIBE
Buzz / From light to light / Penn station / Vibe / Green dolphin street / Miles away / Staircase / Renezvous / Crunch / Waxing and wanning / Miles away reprise (the gentle giant)

CD _______________ NYC 60122
NYC / Feb '95 / New Note/Pinnacle

YIN YANG
CD _______________ NYC 60012
NYC / Jul '92 / New Note/Pinnacle

Stereo Maximus

QUILOMBO
CD _______________ ABB 028CD
Big Cat / Oct '91 / 3mv/Pinnacle

Stereo MC's

33-45-78
On 33 / Use it / Gee street / Neighbourhood / Toe to toe / What is soul / Use it (part 2) / Outta touch / Sunday 19th March / This ain't a love song / Ancient concept / On the mike / Back to the future
CD _______________ IMCD 127
Island / Apr '91 / PolyGram

CONNECTED
Connected / Ground level / Everything / Sketch / Fade away / All night long / Step it up / Playing with fire / Pressure / Chicken shake / Creation / End
CD _______________ BRCD 589
4th & Broadway / Oct '92 / PolyGram

SUPERNATURAL
I'm a believer / Scene of the crime / Declaration / Elevate my mind / What'cha gonna do / Two horse town / Ain't got nobody / Goin' back to the wild / Lost in music / Life on the line / Other side / Set me loose / What's the word / Early one morning / Smokin' with the motherman / Relentless
CD _______________ IMCD 185
Island / Mar '94 / PolyGram

Stereolab

EMPEROR TOMATO KETCHUP
Metronomic underground / Cybele's revenge / Percolator / Les yper-sound / Spark plug / OLV 26 / Noise of carpet / Tomorrow is already here / Emperor tomato ketchup / Monstre sacre / Motoroller scalatron / Slow fast hazel / Anonymous collective
CD _______________ DUHFCD 11
Duophonic UHF Discs / Mar '96 / RTM/Disc

GROOP PLAYED SPACE AGE BACHELOR PAD MUSIC, THE
Avant garde (MOR) / Groop played chord X / Space age bachelor pad music / Ronco symphony / We're not adult orientated / UMF-MFP / We're not adult orientated
CD _______________ PURECD 019
Too Pure / Mar '93 / Vital

MARS AUDIAC QUINTET
CD _______________ DUHFCD 05
Duophonic UHF Discs / Aug '94 / RTM/ Disc

PENG
CD _______________ PURECD 011
Too Pure / May '92 / Vital

REFRIED ECTOPLASM
CD _______________ DUHFCD 09
Duophonic UHF Discs / Sep '95 / RTM/ Disc

TRANSIENT RANDOM NOISE BURSTS
CD _______________ DUHFCD 02
Duophonic UHF Discs / Sep '93 / RTM/ Disc

Stereophonic Space Sound ...

PLAYS LOST TV THEMES (Stereophonic Space Sound Unlimited)
CD _______________ DD 0126CD
Dr. Dream / Apr '97 / Cargo

Stereophonics

WORD GETS AROUND
CD _______________ VVR 1000432
CD _______________ VVR 1000438
Banana / Aug '97 / 3mv/Pinnacle

Stereotaxic Device

STEREOTAXIC DEVICE
CD _______________ KK 046CD
KK / Jan '91 / Plastic Head

Steril

VENUS TRAP
CD _______________ 08543292
Westcom / Feb '97 / Koch / Pinnacle

Sterling

MONSTERLINGO
Is this the time / Intravenous / Three hand man / Out of the sunlight / Shiver / Crawl Mary / Dream queen / 5x bigger / Addlestone rock / Headless / Good sun / Him
CD _______________ MNTCD 1006
Mantra / Apr '97 / RTM/Disc

Sterling Jubilee Singers

JESUS HITS LIKE THE ATOM BOMB
Jesus hits like the atom bomb / Devotional / Peace in the valley / God shall wipe all tears away / Little wooden church on the hill / Lord's prayer / Will he welcome me there / Job / I never heard a man / My Jesus knows / Every time I try to do my best / Operator / Testimony / Benediction
CD _______________ 805132
New World / Jun '97 / ADA / Cadillac / Harmonia Mundi

Sterling, Peter

GYPSY ROAD
CD _______________ M 44D
World Disc / Aug '96 / Gallant

Stern, Leni

SECRETS
CD _______________ ENJA 50932
Enja / Mar '92 / New Note/Pinnacle / Vital/ SAM

TEN SONGS
Miss V / Talk to me / Mary Ellen / If anything / Shooting star / Trouble / Our man's gone now / Sparrows / More trouble / Glass
CD _______________ LIP 890092
Lipstick / Feb '95 / Vital/SAM

WORDS
CD _______________ LIP 890282
Lipstick / May '95 / Vital/SAM

Stern, Peggy

PLEIADES (Stern, Peggy Trio)
CD _______________ W 822
Philology / Apr '94 / Cadillac / Harmonia Mundi

Sternklang

FREESTYLESPACEPHUNK
CD _______________ BSCD 014
BeatService / Jul '97 / Shellshock/Disc

Stetson Stompers

100% LINE DANCE MUSIC
Hillybilly rock, hillbilly roll / Honkytonk crowd / Cannibals / Any man of mine / Pick up the fiddle / All you ever do is bring me down / Dancin' cowboys / Perez prez / Baby come back / County auction / Whose bed has your boots been under / End of the line / Little bitty / Orange blossom special
CD _______________ RBCD 544
Sharpe / Apr '97 / Duncans / Target/BMG

COUNTRY LINE DANCING MUSIC
Chattahoochee / Not counting you / Streets of Bakersfield / Achey breaky heart / Sweet dream baby / Sheriff is a huntin' me a man / These boots are made for walking / Just call me lonesome / New way to light up an old flame / Mama knows the highway / Summertime blues / Guitars and cadillacs
CD _______________ RBCD 531
Sharpe / May '96 / Duncans / Target/BMG

Stevens, Beth & April

SISTERS
Wishful thinking / Sisters / Who's crying for you now / Tired old heart / What about me / My old friend the blues / In my time of dying / Jeanie and Tommy / Blue / Tomorrow is forever / Bed of roses / When we're gone long gone
CD _______________ ROUCD 0396
Rounder / Oct '96 / ADA / CM / Direct

Stevens, Cat

BUDDAH AND THE CHOCOLATE BOX
Music / Oh very young / Sun/C79 / Ghost town / Jesus / Ready to love / King of trees / Bad penny / Home in the sky
CD _______________ IMCD 70
Island / Nov '89 / PolyGram

CATCH BULL AT FOUR
Sitting / Boy with a moon and star on his head / Angelsea / Silent sunlight / Can't keep it in / 18th Avenue (Kansas City nightmare) / Freezing steel / O'Caritas / Sweet scarlet / Ruins
CD _______________ IMCD 34
Island / Jul '89 / PolyGram

EARLY TAPES
I love my dog / First cut is the deepest / Bad night / I'm so sleepy / Blackness of the night / School is out / Northern wind / View from the top / Come on and dance / Where are you / Granny / Moonstone / Ceylon city / Kitty
CD _______________ 5501082
Spectrum / Oct '93 / PolyGram

FOREIGNER
Foreigner suite / Hurt / How many times / Later / Hundred I dream
CD _______________ IMCD 72
Island / Nov '89 / PolyGram

GREATEST HITS
Wild world / Oh very young / Can't keep it in / Hard headed woman / Moonshadow / Two fine people / Peace train / Ready / Father and son / Sitting / Morning has broken / Another Saturday night
CD _______________ IMCD 168
Island / Mar '93 / PolyGram

LIFE OF THE LAST PROPHET, THE (Early Life/Prophethood/Migration/ Conquest Of Makkah) (Islam, Yusuf)
Tala'a al-badru' alayna / La iiaha illa allah / Muhammad al mustafa
CD _______________ MOL 7001CD3
Mountain Of Light / Mar '97 / Pinnacle

MONA BONE JAKON
Lady D'Arbanville / Maybe you're / Pop star / I think I see the light / Trouble / Mona bone jakon / I wish I wish / Katmandu / Fill my eyes / Timer / Time / Lillywhite
CD _______________ IMCD 35
Island / '89 / PolyGram

TEA FOR THE TILLERMAN
Where do the children play / Hard headed woman / Wild world / Sad Lisa / Miles from nowhere / But I might die tonight / Longer boats / Into white / On the road to find out / Father and son / Tea for the tillerman
CD _______________ IMCD 36
Island / '89 / PolyGram

TEASER AND THE FIRECAT
Wind / Ruby love / If I laugh / Changes IV / How can I tell you / Tuesday's dead / Morning has broken / Bitter blue / Moon shadow / Peace train
CD _______________ IMCD 104
Island / Mar '90 / PolyGram

VERY BEST OF CAT STEVENS, THE
Where do the children play / Wild world / Tuesday's dead / Lady D'Arbanville / First cut is the deepest / Oh very young / Ruby love / Morning has broken / Moonshadow / Matthew and son / Father and son / Can't keep it in / Hard headed woman / Old school yard / I love my dog / Another Saturday night / Sad Lisa / Peace train
CD _______________ 8401482
Island / Jun '95 / PolyGram

Stevens, Kenni

YOU
Who's been lovin' you / Hurt this way / Never gonna give you up / 24-7-365 / You don't know / I bleed for you / You / Didn't mean to hurt you / Work me up / Anne
CD _______________ CDDB 502
Debut / May '88 / 3mv/Sony / Pinnacle

Stevens, Meic

ER COF AM BLANT Y CWM
Er cof am blant y cwm / Yr eglwys ar y cei / Tafarn Elfed / Sabots Bernie / Morwen y medd / Yfory y plant / Angau opera ffug y clon / Mae gen i gariad / Bwda Bernie / Brenein y bop / Iraq
CD _______________ CRAICD 036
Crai / Mar '94 / ADA / Direct

WARE'N NOETH
CD _______________ SCD 4088
Sain / May '97 / ADA / Direct / Greyhound

Y BALEDL
CD _______________ SCD 2001
Sain / Feb '95 / ADA / Direct / Greyhound

Stevens, Mike

JOY
CD _______________ DOMECD 5
Dome / Oct '95 / 3mv/Sony

Stevens, Peter

TAKEN BY THE LIGHT (Stevens, Peter Band)
CD _______________ 35638
Sphinx Ministry / Nov '96 / Cargo

Stevens, Ray

BEST OF RAY STEVENS, THE
Everything is beautiful / Mr. Businessman / Unwind / Yakety yak / Bridget the Midget / Gitarzan / Along came Jones / Turn your radio on / Mama and a papa / Moonlight special / Streak / Time for us / She belongs to me / Young love / Raindrops keep falling on my head / Indian love call / Something / Leaving on a jet plane / Bye bye love / Misty
CD _______________ MOCD 3011
More Music / Feb '95 / Sound & Media

BIGGEST AND THE BEST, THE
Everything is beautiful / Gitarzan / All my trials / Mr. Businessman / Streak / Have a little talk with myself / Unwind / Along came Jones / Losin' streak / Bridget the midget / Turn your radio on / Ahab the Arab / Sunset strip / Misty / Sunday mornin' comin' down / Moonlight special / Young love / Mama and a Papa / America communicate with me / Indian love call
CD _______________ 3036000872
Carlton / Jul '97 / Carlton

HIT SINGLE COLLECTABLES
CD _______________ DISK 4510
Disky / Apr '94 / Disky / THE

Stevens, Shakin'

BEST OF SHAKIN' STEVENS, THE
This ole house / You drive me crazy / It's late / Green door / Teardrops / Oh Julie / Love worth waiting for / I'll be satisfied / Marie Marie / It's raining / Give me your heart tonight / Shirley / Cry just a little bit / Rockin' good way (to mess around and fall in love) / Letter to you / Why do you treat me this way
CD _______________ 4837292
Epic / Feb '96 / Sony

GREATEST HITS
This ole house / You drive me crazy / Letter to you / It's raining / Green door / Hot dog / Teardrops / Breaking up my heart / Oh Julie / Marie Marie / Love worth waiting for / It's late / Give me your heart tonight / Shirley / Blue Christmas / Cry just a little bit / Rockin' good way / I'll be satisfied
CD _______________ 4669932
Epic / Sep '93 / Sony

SHAKIN' STEVENS
CD _______________ GRF 234
Tring / Aug '93 / Tring

UNIQUE ROCK'N'ROLL CHRISTMAS, THE
Rockin' little Christmas / White Christmas / Sure won't seem like Christmas / I'll be home this Christmas / Merry Christmas everyone / Silent night / It's gonna be a lonely Christmas / Best Christmas of them all / Merry Christmas pretty baby / Christmas wish / Blue Christmas / So long Christmas
CD _______________ 4692602
Epic / Nov '91 / Sony

Stevens, T.M.

BOOM OUT OF CONTROL
CD _______________ USG 35829422
USG / Apr '97 / Cargo

Stevens, Tanya

BIG THINGS A GWAN
CD _______________ RNCD 0034
Runn / May '97 / Grapevine/PolyGram / Jet Star / SRD

Stevenson, Savourna

CUTTING THE CHORD
Aeolian / Basse Breton rhapsody / Cutting the chord / Harplands / Blues in 10
CD _______________ ECLCD 9308
Eclectic / Jan '96 / ADA / New Note/ Pinnacle

TUSITALA, TELLER OF TALES
CD _______________ ECLCD 9412
Eclectic / Jan '96 / ADA / New Note/ Pinnacle

TWEED JOURNEY
Source / Fording the tweed / Waulk from the tweed / Lost bells / Trows and Cowdieknowes / Percussion solo / Forest flowers / Tweed journey
CD _______________ ECLCD 9001
Eclectic / Jan '96 / ADA / New Note/ Pinnacle

Stewart Family

STEWARTS O'BLAIR (Stewart, Belle & Family)
Come a' you jolly Ploomen / Lakes of Shillin / Bonnie hoose o'Airlie / Moving on song / Nobleman / Jock Stewart / Inverness-shire / Banks of the Lee / Betsy belle / Dawning of the day / My dog and gun / Berryfields o'Blair / I'm no coming oot the noo / Mickey's warning / Hatton woods / Parting song / Canntaireachd
CD _______________ OSS 96CD
Ossian / Aug '94 / ADA / CM / Direct / Highlander

Stewart, Al

24 CARAT
Running man / Midnight rocks / Constantinople / Merlin's time / Mondo sinistro / Murmansk run/Ellis Island / Rocks in the ocean / Paint by numbers / Optical illusion / Here in Angola / Indian summer / Pandora / Delia's gone / Princess Olivia
CD _______________ CZ 512
EMI / Aug '92 / EMI

BEST OF AL STEWART, THE (Centenary Collection)
On the border / Song on the radio / Year of the cat / Time passages / Midnight rocks / Merlin's time / Broadway hotel / One stage before / Indian summer / Lori, don't go right now / Electric Los Angeles sunset / Running man / Paint by numbers / Mondo sinistro / Night train to Munich / Almost Lucy / Life between the wars
CD _______________ CTMCD 310
EMI / Feb '97 / EMI

BETWEEN THE WARS
Night train to Munich / Age of rhythm / Sampan / Lindy comes to town / Three mules / League of notions / Between the wars / Betty Boop's birthday / Marion the Chatelaine / Joe the Georgian / Always the cause / Laughing into 1939 / Black Danube
CD _______________ CDEMC 3710
EMI / Feb '97 / EMI

CHRONICLES (The Best Of Al Stewart)
Year of the cat / On the border / If it doesn't come naturally, leave it / Time passages / Almost Lucy / Song on the radio / Running man / Merlin's time / In Brooklyn / Soho (needless to say) / Small fruit song / Manu-

script / Roads to Moscow (live) / Nostradamus - Pt. 1 / World goes to Riyadh
CD ____ **CDEMC 3590**
EMI / Apr '91 / EMI

LAST DAYS OF THE CENTURY
Last days of the century / Real and unreal / King of Portugal / Where are they now / License to steal / Josephine Baker / Antarctica / Ghostly horses of the plain / Red toupee / Bad reputation / Fields of France
CD ____ **CDENV 505**
Enigma / Sep '88 / EMI

MODERN TIMES
CD ____ **BGOCD 156**
Beat Goes On / Nov '92 / Pinnacle

ORANGE
You don't even know me / Amsterdam / Songs out of the clay / News from Spain / I don't believe you / Once an orange, always an orange / I'm falling / Night of the 4th of May
CD ____ **BGOCD 154**
Beat Goes On / Nov '92 / Pinnacle
CD ____ **4844412**
Columbia / Jul '96 / Sony

PAST, PRESENT AND FUTURE
Old admirals / Warren Harding / Soho (needless to say) / Last day of June 1934 / Post World War Two blues / Roads to Moscow / Terminal blues / Nostradamus
CD ____ **BGOCD 155**
Beat Goes On / Sep '92 / Pinnacle

RHYMES IN ROOMS
Flying sorcery / Soho (needless to say) / Time passages / Josephine Baker / On the border / Nostradamus / Fields of France / Clifton in the rain / Small fruit song / Broadway hotel / Leave it / Year of the cat
CD ____ **CDFA 3315**
Fame / Feb '95 / EMI

RUSSIANS AND AMERICANS
Lori don't go right now / Don't go right now / Gypsy and the rose / Accident on 3rd street / Strange girl / Russians and Americans / Cafe society / 1-2-3 / Candidate
CD ____ **CZ 523**
EMI / Jul '93 / EMI

TIME PASSAGES
Valentina way / Life in dark water / Man for all seasons / Almost Lucy / Time passages / Palace of Versailles / Timeless skies / End of the day / Song on the radio
CD ____ **CDFA 3312**
Fame / Dec '94 / EMI

TIME PASSAGES/YEAR OF THE CAT/ RUSSIANS AND AMERICANS (The Originals/3CD Set)
Valentina way / Life in dark water / Man for all seasons / Almost Lucy / Time passages / Palace of Versailles / Timeless skies / End of the day / Song on the radio / Lord Grenville / On the border / Midas shadow / Sand in your shoes / If it doesn't come naturally, leave it / Flying sorcery / Broadway hotel / One stage before / Year of the cat / Lori don't go right now / Gypsy and the rose / Accident on 3rd Street / Strange girl / Russians and Americans / Cafe society / 1-2-3 / Candidate
CD Set ____ **CDOMB 020**
EMI / Mar '97 / EMI

TO WHOM IT MAY CONCERN (Al Stewart 1966-1970)
Elf / Turn into earth / Bedsitter images / Swiss Cottage manoeuvres / Carmichaels / Scandinavian girl / Pretty golden hair / Denise at sixteen / Samuel, oh how you've changed / Cleave to me / Long way down from Stephanie / Ivich / Belecka doodle day / Lover man / Clifton in the rain / In Brooklyn / Old Compton Street blues / Ballad of Mary Foster / Life and life only / You should have listened to Al / Love chronicles / My enemies have sweet voices / Small fruit song / Gethsemane, again / Burbling / Electric Los Angeles sunset / Manuscript / Black Hill / Anna / Room of roots / Zero she flies
CD ____ **CDEM 1511**
EMI / Nov '93 / EMI

YEAR OF THE CAT
Lord Grenville / On the border / Midas shadow / Sand in your shoes / If it doesn't come naturally, leave it / Flying sorcery / Broadway hotel / One stage before / Year of the cat
CD ____ **CDFA 3253**
Fame / Apr '91 / EMI

Stewart, Amii

BEST OF AMII STEWART, THE (2CD Set)
CD Set ____ **SMDCD 166**
Snapper / Jul '97 / Pinnacle

DESIRE
My heart and I / Desire / Hurry to me / Come sail away / Here's to you / Song for Elena / One love / Saharan dream / Sean Sean / Could heaven be
CD ____ **MSCD 16**
Music De-Luxe / Mar '95 / TKO Magnum

Stewart, Andy

ANDY STEWART COLLECTION, THE (20 Scottish Favourites)
Scottish soldier / Dr. Finlay / Cambeltown Loch / Battle's o'er / Highlandman's Umbrella / I'm off to Bonnie Scotland / Road to the Isles / Scotland yet / Farewell 51st farewell / Muckin' O' Geordie's byre / Donald, where's yer troosers / Girl from Glasgow town / Ho ro my nut brown maiden / Tunes of glory / Wild rover / Road and the miles to Dundee / Courtin' in the kitchen / Lassie come and dance with me / I love to wear a kilt / Going doon the water
CD ____ **CDMFP 5700**
EMI / Mar '93 / EMI

ANDY STEWART'S SCOTLAND
CD ____ **CDITV 563**
Scotdisc / May '93 / Conifer/BMG / Duncans / Ross

FOREVER IN SONG
Donald, where's yer troosers / Highlandman's umbrella / Lock Marie island / Lovely Stornoway / Dancing in kyle / Song of the Clyde / In praise of Islay / Rothesay bay / Joy of my heart / Loch Lomond / Stop your ticklin' jock / Roamin' in the gloamin' / Wee Deoch an' Doris / Keep right on to the end of the road / Away up in Clachan / Gordon for me / Jock McKay / My ain hoose / Westering home / Wild mountain thyme / Horee - horo / Wild rover / Waggle o' the kilt / It's nice to get up in the morning / Tobermoray / Safest o' the family / I' foo the noo / Wedding of Sandy McNab / Will ye no' come back again / Skye boat song / Come ower the stream, Charlie / Rise and follow Charlie / Take me back / Barren rocks of Aden / Farewell 51st farewell / Jock Cameron / bee baw babbity / Queen Mary / Height starvation song / Do re mi / Ye canny shove yer granny aff a bus / Andy where's yer kilt / Hiking song / Ho ro my nut brown maiden / Uist tramping song / Marching through the heather / I belong to Glasgow / Sailign up the Clyde / We've got a baby in the house / Ninety four this morning / Johnny Lad / Bonnie wee Jeannie McColl / Soor milk cairt / Wee toon clerk / Dashing white sergeant / Tartan ball / Lassie come and dance with me / Country dance / There was a lad / Polly Stewart / De'il's awa' wi' tha exciseman / Man's a man for a' that / Tartan / Campbells are coming / Johnny cope / Piper O'Dundee / Old Scottish waltz / Bonnie wells o'wearie / Back in bonnie Scotland / Bonnie Scotland / Haste ye back / Scotland the brave / We're no awa' tae bide awa' / Mairi's wedding / Thistle of Scotland / Muckin' O' Geordie's byre / Lass O'Fyvie / Nickie tams / Barnyards o'delgaty / Auld lang syne
CD ____ **PLATCD 3921**
Platinum / Nov '93 / Prism

VERY BEST OF ANDY STEWART, THE
Andy where's your kilt / I belong to Glasgow / Sailing up the Clyde / We've got a baby in the hoose / Ninety-four this morning / Mull of Kintyre / Bee baw babbity / Queen Mary / Height starvation song / Ye canny shove yer granny aff a bus / My ain house / Westering home / Wild mountain thyme / Horee-horoo / Wild rover / Scotland the brave / We're no awa'tae bide awa / Mairie's wedding / Thistle of Scotland / Rumour / Stop yer ticklin' Jock / Roamin' in the gloaming / Wee deoch'n'Doris / Keep right on to the end of the road / Will ye no come back again / Skye boat song / Come over the stream Charlie / Rise and follow Charlie / Green grow the rushes / My love she's but a lassie yet / Bonnie Jean / Donald where's your troosers / Highlandman's umbrella / Loch Marie islands / Lovely Stornoway / Dancing in Kyle / Song of Clyde / In praise of Isla / Rothesay bay / Joy of my heart / Granny's heilan hame / Johnny lad / Bonnie wee Jeannie McColl / Soor milk cairt / Wee toon clerk / Northern lights of Aberdeen / Rothesay bay / I belong to Glasgow / There was a lad / Polly Stewart / De'il's awa' wi' tha exciseman / Man's a man / When you and I were young Maggie / We're no awa 'tae bide awa' / Old Scottish waltz / Bonnie well o'wearie / Back to bonnie Scotland / Bonnie Scotland / Hast ye back / Auld lang syne
CD ____ **MCVD 30008**
Emerald Gem / Nov '96 / BMG

Stewart, Andy M.

AT IT AGAIN (Stewart, Andy M. & Manus Lunny)
CD ____ **GLCD 1107**
Green Linnet / Feb '92 / ADA / CM / Direct / Highlander / Roots

BY THE HUSH
CD ____ **GLCD 3030**
Green Linnet / Oct '93 / ADA / CM / Direct / Highlander / Roots

DUBLIN LADY (Stewart, Andy M. & Manus Lunny)
Take her in your arms / Where are you / Dublin Lady / Freedom is like gold / Bogie's bonnie belle / Dinny the piper / Heart of the home / Humours of whiskey / Tak' it man tak' it
CD ____ **GLCD 1083**
Green Linnet / Feb '92 / ADA / CM / Direct / Highlander / Roots

FIRE IN THE GLEN (Stewart, Andy M./ Phil Cunningham/Manus Lunny)
CD ____ **SHAN 79062 CD**
Shanachie / Oct '89 / ADA / Greensleeves / Koch

MAN IN THE MOON
CD ____ **GLCD 1140**
Green Linnet / Apr '94 / ADA / CM / Direct / Highlander / Roots

SONGS OF ROBERT BURNS
CD ____ **GLCD 3059**
Green Linnet / '92 / ADA / CM / Direct / Highlander / Roots

Stewart, Bob

WELCOME TO THE CLUB (Stewart, Bob & Hank Jones)
Day in, day out / I'll never be the same / Body and soul / September in the rain / Don't misunderstood / Fools rush in / Then I'll be tired of you / Just friends / Did I remember / When Sunny gets blue / What a little moonlight can do / Love look away / Every time we say goodbye / Very thought of you
CD ____ **CDLR 45017**
L&R / Aug '90 / New Note/Pinnacle

Stewart, Dave

AS FAR AS DREAMS CAN GO (Stewart, Dave & Barbara Gaskin)
Locomotion / Lenina Crowe / I'm losing you / Roads girdle the globe / Do I still figure in your life / When the guards are asleep / Make me promises / Do we see the light of day / As far as dreams can go
CD ____ **BRCD 9008940**
Broken / '88 / Broken

BIG IDEA, THE (Stewart, Dave & Barbara Gaskin)
Levi Stubbs' tears / My scene / Grey skies / Subterranean homesick blues / Heatwave / Crying game / Deep underground / Shadowland / Mr. Theremin / New Jerusalem
CD ____ **BRCD 9009330**
Broken / '90 / Broken

BROKEN RECORDS - THE SINGLES (Stewart, Dave & Barbara Gaskin)
I'm in a different world / Leipzig / It's my party / Johnny Rocco / Siamese cat song / Busy doing nothing / Rich for a day / Waiting in the wings / Emperor's new guitar / Hamburger song / Henry and James / World spins so slow
CD ____ **BRCD 9008900**
Broken / '87 / Broken

SELECTED TRACKS (Stewart, Dave & Barbara Gaskin)
CD ____ **STIFFCD 24**
Disky / Jan '94 / Disky / THE

SPIN (Stewart, Dave & Barbara Gaskin)
Walking the dog / Cloths of heaven / Eight miles high / Ameila / Trash planet / Golden rain / Your lucky star / Cast your fate to the wind / Louie Louie / Sixties never die / Star blind
CD ____ **BRCD 9011400**
Broken / Aug '92 / Broken

UP FROM THE DARK (Stewart, Dave & Barbara Gaskin)
I'm in a different world / Leipzig / It's my party / Lenina Crowe / Do I still figure in your life / Busy doing nothing / I'm losing you / Roads girdle the globe / When the guards are asleep / World spins so slow / Siamese cat song / Do we see the light of day / Henry and James / As far as dreams can go
CD ____ **BRCD 10011**
Broken / '86 / Broken

Stewart, David A.

GREETINGS FROM THE GUTTER
Heart of stone / Greeting from the gutter / Crazy sister / Chelsea lovers / Jealousy / St. Valentine's day / kinky sweetheart / Damien save me / Tragedy street / You talk a lot / Oh no, not you again
CD ____ **4509975462**
East West / Dec '96 / Warner Music

Stewart, Gary

GARY'S GREATEST
CD ____ **HCD 8030**
Hightone / Jun '94 / ADA / Koch

I'M A TEXAN
CD ____ **HCD 8050**
Hightone / Jul '94 / ADA / Koch

OUT OF HAND
Drinkin' thing / Honky tonkin' / I see the want to in your eyes / This old heart won't let go / Draggin' shackles / She's actin' single (I'm drinkin' doubles) / Back sliders' wine / Sweet country red / Out of hand / Williamson County
CD ____ **HCD 8026**
Hightone / Sep '94 / ADA / Koch

Stewart, Grant

DOWNTOWN SOUNDS (Stewart, Grant Quintet)
CD ____ **CRISS 1085CD**
Criss Cross / May '94 / Cadillac / Direct / Vital/SAM

MORE URBAN TONES
Nica's temple / I should care / You go to my head / Rabbitron / All through the night / You sweet and fancy lady / Manhattan Bridge / Pie eye blues
CD ____ **CRISS 1124CD**
Criss Cross / Feb '97 / Cadillac / Direct / Vital/SAM

Stewart, John

AIRDREAM BELIEVER
CD ____ **SHCD 8015**
Shanachie / Aug '95 / ADA / Greensleeves / Koch

CALIFORNIA BLOODLINES...PLUS
California bloodlines / Razor back woman / She believes in me / Omaha rainbow / Pirates of Stone County Road / Shackles and chains / Heart full of woman and a bellyful of Tenness / Willard / Big Joe / Mother country / Lonesome picker / You can't look back / Missouri birds / July you're a woman / Never goin' back / Friend of Jesus / Marshall wind
CD ____ **SEECD 87**
See For Miles/C5 / Jun '96 / Pinnacle

CALIFORNIA BLOODLINES/WILLARD MINUS TWO
California bloodlines / Razor back woman / She believes in me / Omaha rainbow / Pirates of Stone County Road / Shackles and chains / Mother Country / Some lonesome picker / You can't look back / Missouri birds / July you're a woman / Never goin' back / Big Joe / Julie / Judy angel rain / Belly full of Tennessee / Friend of Jesus / Clack clack / Hero from the war / Back in Pomona / Willard / Golden rollin' belly / All American girl / Oldest living son / Earth rider
CD ____ **BCD 15468**
Bear Family / Jul '89 / Direct / Rollercoaster / Swift

CANNONS IN THE RAIN/WINGLESS ANGELS
Durango / Chilly winds / Easy money / Anna on a memory / All time woman / Road away / Armstrong / Spirit / Wind dies down / Cannons in the rain / Lady and the outlaw / Hung on your heart / Rose water / Wingless / Angels / Some kind of love / Survivors / Summer child / Josie / Rise stone blind / Mazatlan / Let the big horse run
CD ____ **BCD 15519**
Bear Family / Oct '90 / Direct / Rollercoaster / Swift

CHILLY WINDS
CD ____ **FE 1401CD**
Folk Era / Dec '94 / ADA / CM

COMPLETE PHOENIX CONCERTS, THE
Wheatfield lady / Kansas rain / You can't look back / Pirates of Stone County Road / Runaway fool of love / Roll away the stone / July you're a woman / Last campaign trilogy / Oldest living son / Little road and a stone to roll / Kansas / Cody / California bloodlines / Mother country / Cops / Never goin' back / Freeway pleasure / Let the big horse run
CD ____ **BCD 15518**
Bear Family / Feb '91 / Direct / Rollercoaster / Swift

LIVE AT THE TURF INN SCOTLAND
CD ____ **FE 1428**
Folk Era / Aug '96 / ADA / CM

PUNCH THE BIG GUY
CD ____ **SHCD 08009**
Shanachie / Mar '94 / ADA / Greensleeves / Koch

ROUGH SKETCHES
CD ____ **FE 1437CD**
Folk Era / May '97 / ADA / CM

Stewart, Louis

OVERDRIVE
All the things you are / Oh lady be good / Polka dots and moonbeams / Oleo / Yesterdays / Stompin' at the savoy / Body and soul / Walkin' / My shining hour
CD ____ **HEPCD 2057**
Hep / Aug '94 / Cadillac / Jazz Music / New Note/Pinnacle / Wellard

Stewart, Mark

CONTROL DATA
CD ____ **CDSTUMM 93**
Mute / Mar '96 / RTM/Disc

MARK STEWART
Survival / Survivalist / Anger / Hell is empty / Stranger / Forbidden colour / Forbidden / Fatal / Attraction
CD ____ **CDSTUMM 43**
Mute / Oct '87 / RTM/Disc

METATRON
CD ____ **CDSTUMM 62**
Mute / Apr '90 / RTM/Disc

Stewart, Michael

BLUE PATCHES (Stewart, Michael 'Patches')

CD HIBD 8016
Hip Bop / May '97 / Koch / Silva Screen

Stewart, Priscilla

PRISCILLA STEWART 1924-1928
CD DOCD 5476
Document / Sep '96 / ADA / Hot Shot / Jazz Music

Stewart, Rex

CLASSICS 1934-1946
CD 931
Classics / Apr '97 / Discovery / Jazz Music

INTRODUCTION TO REX STEWART 1920-1941, AN
CD 4005
Best Of Jazz / Dec '93 / Discovery

REX STEWART STORY 1926-1945, THE
CD 158622
Jazz Archives / Oct '96 / Discovery

REXATIOUS (His Greatest Recordings 1926-1941)
Jackass blues / Old black Joe's blues / Rocky road / Do you believe in love at first sight / Stingaree / Baby ain't you satisfied / Rexatious / Lazy man's shuffle / Back room romp / Tea and trumpets / Monmartre / Low cotton / Finesse / I know that you know / Solid old man / Bugle call rag / Diga diga doo / Mobile bay / Subtle Slough / Show-boat shuffle / Kissin' my baby goodnight / Trumpet in spades / Morning glory / Boy meets horn
CD CDAJA 5200
Living Era / May '96 / Select

Stewart, Robert

JUDGEMENT
CD 1232682
Red / Aug '97 / ADA / Cadillac / Harmonia Mundi

Stewart, Rod

AMAZING GRACE (Stewart, Rod & The Faces)
Reason to believe / Dirty old town / That's alright / Handbags and gladrags / Street fighting man / Sweet little rock 'n' roller / Cut across shorty / Sailor / Old raincoat won't ever let you down / Pinball wizard / It's all over now / Jealous guy / Stay with me / Amazing grace
CD 5500262
Spectrum / May '93 / PolyGram

ATLANTIC CROSSING
Three times a loser / Alright for an hour / All in the name of rock 'n' roll / Drift away / Stone cold sober / I don't want to talk about it / It's not the spotlight / This old heart of mine / Still love you / Sailing
CD 256151
WEA / Feb '87 / Warner Music

BEST OF ROD STEWART, THE
Maggie May / You wear it well / Baby Jane / Do ya think I'm sexy / I was only joking / This old heart of mine / Sailing / I don't want to talk about it / You're in my heart / Young Turks / What am I gonna do (I'm so in love with you) / First cut is the deepest / Killing of Georgie / Tonight's the night / Every beat of my heart / Downtown train
CD 9260342
WEA / '89 / Warner Music

BLONDES HAVE MORE FUN
Do ya think I'm sexy / Dirty weekend / Ain't love a bitch / Best days of my life / Is that the thanks I get / Attractive female wanted / Blondes have more fun / Last summer / Standing in the shadows of love / Scarred and scared
CD 7599273762
WEA / Jan '91 / Warner Music

BODY WISHES
Dancin' alone / Baby Jane / Move me / Body wishes / Sweet surrender / What am I gonna do / Ghetto blaster / Ready now / Strangers / Again / Satisfied
CD 9238772
WEA / Jul '84 / Warner Music

CAMOUFLAGE
Infatuation / All right now / Some guys have all the luck / Can we still be friends / Bad for you / Heart is on the line / Camouflage / Trouble
CD 9250952
WEA / Jul '84 / Warner Music

COAST TO COAST - OVERTURES AND BEGINNERS (Live) (Stewart, Rod & The Faces)
It's all over now / Cut across shorty / Too bad / Angel / Stay with me / I wish it would rain / I'd rather go blind / Borstal boys / Jealous guy / Every picture tells a story / Amazing grace
CD 8321282
Mercury / Nov '87 / PolyGram

EARLY YEARS, THE
I just got some / Bright lights big city / Ain't that lovin' you baby / Mapper's blues / Why does it go on / Shake / Keep your hands off her / Don't you tell nobody / Just like I treat you / Day will come / Little Miss Understood / Come home baby
CD ECD 3109
K-Tel / Jan '95 / K-Tel

EVERY BEAT OF MY HEART
Who's gonna take me home / Another heartache / Night like this / Red hot in black / Here to eternity / Love touch / In my own crazy way / Every beat of my heart / Ten days of rain / In my life / Trouble
CD 9254462
WEA / Jul '86 / Warner Music

EVERY PICTURE TELLS A STORY
Every picture tells a story / Seems like a long time / That's alright / Amazing grace / Tomorrow is such a long time / Maggie May / Mandolin wind / I'm losing you / Reason to believe
CD 8223852
Mercury / Aug '95 / PolyGram

FOOTLOOSE AND FANCY FREE
Hot legs / You're insane / You're in my heart / Born loose / You keep me hangin' on / (If loving you is wrong) I don't want to be right / You gotta nerve / I was only joking
CD 9273232
WEA / Jun '89 / Warner Music

GASOLINE ALLEY
Gasoline alley / It's all over now / Only a hobo / My way of giving / Country comfort / Cut across shorty / Lady Day / Jo's lament / I don't want to discuss it
CD 8469982
Mercury / Aug '95 / PolyGram

HANDBAGS AND GLADRAGS (The Mercury Recordings 1970-1974/2CD Set)
Every picture tells a story / Interludings / You wear it well / You put something better inside / Only a hobo / Reason to believe / It's all over now / Cut across shorty / Los Paraguayos / Mandolin wind / Crying laughing loving lying / Street fighting man / Man of constant sorrow / I know I'm losing you / Lay Day / So tired / Oh no not my baby / What made Milwaukee famous (has made a loser out of me) / Maggie May / Gasoline alley / Dixie toot / Everytime we say goodbye / Twistin' the night away / True blue / Lochinvar farewell / Italian girls / Mama you've been on my mind / Country comfort / Sweet little rock 'n' roller / I wouldn't change a thing / I'd rather go blind / Angel / Missed you / Dirty old town
CD Set 5288232
Mercury / Oct '95 / PolyGram

IF WE FALL IN LOVE TONIGHT
CD 9362464672
Warner Bros. / Nov '96 / Warner Music

LEAD VOCALIST
I ain't superstitious: *Beck, Jeff Group* / Handbags and gladrags / Cindy incidentally: *Faces* / Stay with me: *Faces* / True Blue / Sweet lady Mary: *Faces* / Hot legs / Stand back / Ruby Tuesday / Shotgun wedding / First I look at the purse / Tom Traubert's blues
CD 9362452582
WEA / Feb '93 / Warner Music

MAGGIE MAY
Maggie May / Oh no not my baby / Twistin' the night away / Mandolin wind / Jodie / I'd rather go blind / Cindy's lament / Seems like a long time / Country comfort / (I know) I'm losing you / I wouldn't ever change a thing / Blind prayer / Hard road / I've grown accustomed to her face
CD 5511102
Spectrum / Jul '95 / PolyGram

NEVER A DULL MOMENT
True blue / Los Paraguayos / Mama you been on my mind / Italian girls / Angel / Interludings / You wear it well / I'd rather go blind / Twistin' the night away
CD 8262632
Mercury / Aug '95 / PolyGram

NIGHT ON THE TOWN, A
Ball trap / Pretty flamingo / Big bayou / Wild side of life / Trade winds / Tonight's the night / First cut is the deepest / Fool for you / Killing of Georgie
CD 7599273392
WEA / Jun '93 / Warner Music

OLD RAINCOAT WON'T LET YOU DOWN, AN
Street fighting man / Man of constant sorrow / Blind prayer / Handbags and gladrags / Old raincoat won't ever let you down, An / I wouldn't ever change a thing / Cindy's lament / Dirty old town
CD 8305722
Mercury / Aug '95 / PolyGram

ONCE IN A BLUE MOON
CD 9362451172
WEA / Nov '92 / Warner Music

ORIGINAL FACE, THE
I just got some bright lights / Big city / Ain't that lovin' you baby / Moppers blues / Why does it go on / Shake / Keep your hands off her / Don't you tell nobody / Just like I treat you / Day will come / Just a little misunderstood / Baby come home / Sparky rides / Can I get a witness / Baby take me
CD CDTB 085
Thunderbolt / Sep '90 / TKO Magnum

OUT OF ORDER
Lost in you / Wild horse / Lethal dose of love / Forever young / My heart can't tell you no / Dynamite / Nobody knows you (when you're down and out) / Crazy about her / Try a little tenderness / When I was your man
CD 9256842
WEA / Jul '92 / Warner Music

ROD STEWART
Just a little misunderstood / Shake / Can I get a witness / I just got some / Red balloon / Just like I treat you / Sparky riders / Don't you tell nobody / Ain't that loving you baby / Baby baby / Bright lights big city / Keep your hands off her / Baby take me / Moppers blues / Why does it go on
CD EXP 030
Experience / May '97 / TKO Magnum

ROD STEWART
CD GFS 061
Going For A Song / Jul '97 / Else / TKO Magnum

SMILER
Sweet little rock 'n' roller / Lochnagar / Farewell / Sailor / Bring it on home to me / Let me be your car / (You make me feel like) a natural man / Dixie toot / Hard road / I've grown accustomed to her face / Girl from the North Country / Mine for me
CD 8320562
Mercury / Aug '95 / PolyGram

SPANNER IN THE WORKS
Windy town / Downtown lights / Leave Virginia alone / Sweetheart / This / Lady Luck / You're the star / Muddy, Sam and Otis / Hang on St. Christopher / Delicious / Soothe me / Purple heather
CD 9362458672
Warner Bros. / May '95 / Warner Music

STORYTELLER (Complete Anthology 1964-1990/4CD Set)
Good morning little school girl / Can I get a witness / Shake / So much to say / Little Miss understood / I've been drinking / I ain't superstitious / Shapes of things / In a broken dream / Street fighting man / Handbags and gladrags / Gasoline alley / Cut across shorty / Country comforts / It's all over now / Sweet lady Mary / Had me a real good time / Maggie May / Mandolin wind / I'm losing you / Reason to believe / Every picture tells a story / Stay with me / True blue / Angel / You wear it well / I'd rather go blind / Twistin' the night away / What made Milwaukee famous (has made a loser out of me) / Oh no not my baby / Pinball wizard / Sweet little rock 'n' roller / Let me be your car / You can make me dance / Sing or anything / Sailing / I don't want to talk about it / Stone cold sober / To love somebody / Tonight's the night / First cut is the deepest / Killing of Georgie / Get back / Hot legs / I was only joking / You're in my heart / Do ya think I'm sexy / Passion / Oh God / I wish I was home tonight / Tonight I'm yours (don't hurt me) / Young turks / Baby Jane / What am I gonna do (I'm so in love with you) / People get ready / Some guys have all the luck / Infatuation / Love touch / Every beat of my heart / Lost in you / My heart can't tell you no / Dynamite / Crazy about her / Forever young / This old heart of mine / Downtown train
CD Set 9259872
WEA / Nov '89 / Warner Music

TONIGHT I'M YOURS
Tonight I'm yours / How long / Tora tora tora / Tear it up / Only a boy / Just like a woman / Jealous / Sonny / Young Turks / Never give up on a dream
CD 7599236022
WEA / Jun '93 / Warner Music

UNPLUGGED...AND SEATED
Hot legs / Tonight's the night / Handbags and gladrags / Cut across Shorty / Every picture tells a story / Maggie May / Reason to believe / People get ready / Have I told you lately that I love you / Tom Traubert's blues / First cut is the deepest / Mandolin wind / Highgate shuffle / Stay with me / Having a party
CD 9362452892
WEA / May '93 / Warner Music

UP ALL NIGHT
CD 9362458672
Warner Bros. / Apr '95 / Warner Music

VAGABOND HEART
Rhythm of my heart / Rebel heart / Broken arrow / It takes two / When a man's in love / You are everything / Motown song / Go out dancing / No holding back / Have I told you lately that I love you / Moment of glory / Downtown train / If only
CD 7599265982
WEA / Mar '91 / Warner Music

Stewart, Sandy

SONGS OF JEROME KERN (Stewart, Sandy & Dick Hyman)
CD ACD 205
Audiophile / Jun '95 / Jazz Music

Stewart, Slam

CLASSICS 1945-1946
CD CLASSICS 939
Classics / Jun '97 / Discovery / Jazz Music

SHUT YO' MOUTH
CD DE 1024
Delos / Mar '91 / Nimbus

SLAM BAM
CD BB 8612
Black & Blue / Feb '96 / Discovery / Koch / Wellard

SLAM STEWART MEMORIAL ALBUM (Stewart, Slam & Bucky Pizzarelli)
CD STB 2507
Stash / Sep '95 / ADA / Cadillac / CM / Direct / Jazz Music

TWO BIG NICE (Stewart, Slam & Major Holley)
CD BLE 591242
Black & Blue / Apr '91 / Discovery / Koch / Wellard

Stewart, Tinga

TINGA STEWART RETURNS WITH THE DANCEHALL DJS
Northless duci / Hip hop / Best that I can / Love can make you happy / We can dance / Moon / Gal over dehso / Out of your spell / Dreams / Play reggae music / Street side junkie / Have you ever been in love / Reggae down town
CD CY 78937
Nyam Up / Mar '95 / Conifer/BMG

Stewart, Wendy

ABOUT TIME VOL.1
Hip hip bouree / Pheasant feathers; Bonawe highlanders / Stirling castle / Rachel Rose / Harp song of the Dane women / Miss Gordon of Gight / St. Bride's coracle; The streams of Abernethy / Puinneagan Cail; William Joseph Guppy / King's house; Wild west waltz
CD CDTRAX 059
Greentrax / Jan '93 / ADA / Direct / Duncans / Highlander

ABOUT TIME VOL.2
MacLeod of Mull / Kitchen papaer / January man / Rachel Rae / Fish feis / Probabobably / Maggie's pancakes / Break yer bass drone / Fotheringay / Pavane / Barbara Grigor / Little cascade / Dances with friends / Dusty Miller / Love and whiskey / Bobbing Joan / An caiorac / Carolan's welcome / Drummond castle
CD CDTRAX 126
Greentrax / Mar '97 / ADA / Direct / Duncans / Highlander

Stex

SPIRITUAL DANCE
Chapter 22 / Take this feeling / If I were you / Not coming back / Moses / Still feel the rain / Inside out / Free this innocent soul / Pray / Never gonna see me
CD SBZCD 004
Some Bizarre / Sep '92 / Pinnacle

Stickman

MUSICA
CD K7 041CD
Studio K7 / Oct '96 / Prime / RTM/Disc

Stiefel, Christopher

ANCIENT LONGING
CD JL 111412
Lipstick / May '95 / Vital/SAM

Stiff Kittens

EAT THE PEANUT
CD PSYC 4
Psychic / Aug '94 / 3mv/Pinnacle

Stiff Little Fingers

ALL THE BEST (2CD Set)
Suspect device / Wasted life / Alternative Ulster / 78 rpm / Gotta get away / Bloody Sunday / Straw dogs / You can't say crap on the radio / At the edge / Running bear / White Christmas / Nobody's hero / Tin soldiers / Back to front / Mr. Fire coal man / Just fade away / Go for it / Doesn't make it alright / Silver lining / Safe as houses / Sad eyed people / Two guitars clash / Listen / That's when your blood bumps / Good for nothing / Talkback / Stands to reason / Bits of kids / Touch and go / Price of admission
CD Set CDEM 1428
EMI / Oct '91 / EMI

ALTERNATIVE CHARTBUSTERS
Suspect device / Alternative Ulster / Gotta getaway / At the edge / Nobody's heroes / Tin soldier / Just fade away / Silver lining / Johnny was / Last time / Mr. Fire Coalman / Two guitars clash
CD AOK 103
Plastic Head / Jan '92 / Plastic Head

FLY THE FLAGS
Long way to paradise / Roots, radicals, rockers and reggae / Nobody's hero / No surrender / Gotta getaway / Just fade away / Cosh / Johnny 7 / Barbed wire love / Stand up and shout / Johnny was / Wasted life / Beirut moon / Fly the flag / Suspect

device / Doesn't make it alright / Each dollar a bullet / Alternative Ulster
CD DOJOCD 75
Dojo / Nov '92 / Disc

GET A LIFE
Get a life / Can't believe in you / Road to kingdom come / Walk away / No laughing matter / Harp / Forensic evidence / Baby blue (What have they been telling you) / I want you / Night the wall came down / Cold / When the stars fall from the sky / What if I want more
CD ESMCD 488
Essential / Apr '97 / BMG

HANX
Nobody's hero / Gotta getaway / Wait and see / Barbed wire love / Fly the flag / Alternative Ulster / Johnny was / At the edge / Wasted life / Tin soldiers / Suspect device
CD CDFA 3215
Fame / Feb '89 / EMI

INFLAMMABLE MATERIAL
Suspect device / State of emergency / Here we are nowhere / Wasted life / No more of that / Barbed wire love / White noise / Breakout / Law and order / Johnny was / Alternative Ulster / Closed groove
CD CZ 165
EMI / Mar '89 / EMI

NOBODY'S HEROES
Gotta getaway / Wait and see / Fly the flag / At the edge / Nobody's hero / Bloody dub / Doesn't make it alright / I don't like you / No change / Suspect device / Tin soldiers
CD CZ 166
EMI / Mar '89 / EMI

NOW THEN
Falling down / Won't be told / Love of the common people / Price of admission / Touch and go / Bits of kids / Welcome to the whole week / Big city nights / Talkback / Is that what you fought the war for
CD CDGOLD 1090
EMI Gold / Apr '97 / EMI

STIFF LITTLE FINGERS
CD SFRCD 1
Strange Fruit / Nov '89 / Pinnacle

TINDERBOX
CD SLF 100CD
Spitfire / Jun '97 / Total/BMG

Stiffs

NIX NOT NOTHING
Chelsea / Sad song / 250624 / Space nothing / Fairy tales / Generation crap / Engineering / Blow away baby / Work / Quick Wotson / Mary Pickford / Die mother die / Fear in the night
CD 74321279692
American / Jul '95 / BMG

Stigers, Curtis

CURTIS STIGERS
Sleeping with the lights on / I wonder why / You're all that matters to me / Man you're gonna fall in love with / People like us / Never saw a miracle / I guess it wasn't mine / Nobody loves you like I do / I keep telling myself / Count my blessings / Last time I said goodbye
CD 261953
Arista / Jul '96 / BMG

Stigma A Go Go

IT'S ALL TRUE
CD GROW 0312
Grass / Feb '95 / Pinnacle / SRD

Stigmata

HYMNS FOR AN UNKNOWN GOD
CD TDH 017
Too Damn Hype / Feb '97 / Cargo / SRD

Stille Volk

HANTAOMA
CD HOLY 024CD
Holy / Apr '97 / Plastic Head

Stillpoint

MAPS WITH EDGES
CD RBADCD 16
Beyond / Jul '96 / Kudos / Pinnacle

Stills, Stephen

LONG MAY YOU RUN (Stills, Stephen & Neil Young)
Long may you run / Make love to you / Midnight on the bay / Black coral / Ocean girl / Let it shine / 12/8 blues / Fontaine bleau / Guardian angel
CD 7599272302
Reprise / Jun '93 / Warner Music

MANASSAS (Stills, Stephen Manassas)
Song of love / Crazies / Cuban bluegrass / Jet set / Anyway / Both of us (bound to lose) / Fallen eagle / Jesus gave love away for free / Colorado / So begins the task / Hide it so deep / Don't look at my shadow / It doesn't matter / Johnny's garden / Bound to fall / How far / Move around / Love gangster / What to do / Right now / Treasure (take one) / Blues man
CD 7567828082
Atlantic / Nov '95 / Warner Music

STEPHEN STILLS
Love the one you're with / Do for the others / Church (part of someone) / Old times, good times / Go back home / Sit yourself down / To a flame / Black Queen / Cherokee / We are not helpless
CD 7567828092
Atlantic / Nov '95 / Warner Music

Stillsuit

AT THE SPEED OF LIGHT
CD TVT 71002
TVT / Mar '97 / Cargo / Greyhound

Stilluppsteypa

ONE SIDE MONA LISA/THE FRONT SIDE ONLY
CD F 8
Fire Inc. / Jan '97 / Cargo

Stiltskin

MIND'S EYE, THE
CD WWD 1
White Water / Oct '94 / 3mv/Sony

Stimela

KHULULANI
Siyaya phambili / Never seem to learn / Song of hope / Song tells a story / Go on living your life / Part to play / Khululani / Confusion / Colours and shades / Take me to the top / Nothing matters / You're the one I love
CD FLTRCD 506
Flame Tree / Feb '93 / Pinnacle

Sting

BRING ON THE NIGHT
Bring on the night / Consider me gone / Low life / We work the black seam / Driven to tears / Dream of the blue turtles / Demolition man / One world / Love is the seventh wave / Moon over Bourbon Street / I burn for you / Another day / Children's crusade / I've been down so long / Tea in the Sahara
CD CDMID 192
A&M / May '94 / PolyGram

DREAM OF THE BLUE TURTLES, THE
If you love somebody set them free / Love is the seventh wave / We work the black seam / Russians / Children's crusade / Shadows in the rain / Consider me gone / Dream of the blue turtles / Moon over Bourbon Street / Fortress around your heart
CD DREMD 1
A&M / Jun '85 / PolyGram

FIELDS OF GOLD (The Best Of Sting 1984-1994)
When we dance / If you love somebody set them free / Fields of gold / They dance alone / If I ever lose my faith in you / We'll be together / Nothing 'bout me / Fragile / Englishman in New York / All this time / Seven days / Mad about you / Russians / Love is the seventh wave / It's probably me: *Sting & Eric Clapton* / Demolition man / This cowboy song
CD 5403072
A&M / Nov '94 / PolyGram

MERCURY FALLING
Hounds of winter / I hung my head / Let your soul be your pilot / I was brought to my senses / You still touch me / I'm so happy I cant' stop crying / All four seasons / Twenty five to midnight / La belle dame sans regrets / Valparaiso / Lithium sunset
CD 5404862
A&M / Mar '96 / PolyGram

MUSIC OF STING, THE (London Symphony Orchestra)
Russians / Moon over Bourbon Street / Synchronicity II / Fortress around your heart / King of pain / Invisible sun / Every breath you take / Why should I cry for you / Wrapped around your finger / They dance alone
CD EIRSCD 1081
IRS/EMI / Jun '96 / EMI

NOTHING LIKE THE SUN
Lazarus heart / Be still my beating heart / Englishman in New York / History will teach us nothing / They dance alone / Fragile / We'll be together / Straight to my heart / Rock steady / Sister Moon / Little wing / Secret marriage
CD CDA 6402
A&M / Oct '87 / PolyGram

PLAY THE MUSIC OF STING (London Symphony Orchestra)
Russians / Moon over Bourbon Street / Synchronicity II / Fortress around your heart / King of pain / Invisible sun / Every breath you take / Why should I cry for you / Wrapped around your finger / They dance alone
CD ALTGOCD 005
Alter Ego / Nov '96 / Vital

SOUL CAGES, THE
Island of souls / All this time / Mad about you / Jeremiah blues (Part 1) / Why should I cry for you / Saint Agnes and the burning train / Wild wild sea / Soul cages / When the angels fall
CD 3964052
A&M / Jan '91 / PolyGram

STING (Interview)
CD 3D 012
Network / Dec '96 / Total/BMG

TEN SUMMONER'S TALES
Prologue (If I ever lose my faith in you) / Love is stronger than justice (The magnificent seven) / Fields of gold / Heavy cloud no rain / She's too good for me / Seven days / St. Augustine in hell / It's probably me / Everybody laughed but you / Shape of my heart / Something the boy said / Epilogue (Nothing 'bout me)
CD 5400752
A&M / Mar '93 / PolyGram

Sting & The Radio AC

NUCLEAR WASTE
CD BP 181CD
Blueprint / Sep '96 / Pinnacle

Stinga, Paul

CHARMS OF THE ROMANIAN MUSIC (Stinga, Paul & His Orchestra)
Sirba de la seaca / Batrineasca / Taraneasca de la burau Jeni / Suite de Moldavie I / Suite de Moldavie II / Purtata de la bistrica / Suite de muntenie / Hora din rasomiresti / Joc din bihor / Suite de banat / Suite de Transilvanie
CD PV 787021
Disques Pierre Verany / May '87 / Kingdom

Stinkerbell

HISSEY FIT
CD LRR 016
Last Resort / Oct '96 / Cargo

Stitt, Sonny

AUTUMN IN NEW YORK
Stardust / Cherokee / Autumn in New York / Gypsy / Lover man / Matterhorns / Hello / Nightwork
CD BLCD 760130
Black Lion / Apr '90 / Cadillac / Jazz Music / Koch / Wellard

BACK IN MY OWN HOME TOWN
(I'm afraid) the masquerade is over / Duty free / I can't get started (with you) / My little suede shoes / Simon's blues / Streamline Stanley / There will never be another you
CD BLE 597542
Black & Blue / Dec '90 / Discovery / Koch / Wellard

BACK TO MY OWN HOME TOWN
CD BB 8772
Black & Blue / Feb '97 / Discovery / Koch / Wellard

BATTLE OF THE SAXES (Stitt, Sonny & Richie Cole)
CD AIM 1010CD
Aim / Oct '93 / ADA / Direct / Jazz Music

CONSTELLATION
Constellation / I don't stand a ghost of a chance with you / Webb City / By accident / Ray's idea / Casbah / It's magic / Topsy
CD MCD 5323
Muse / Sep '92 / New Note/Pinnacle

GOOD LIFE, THE (Stitt, Sonny & The Hank Jones Trio)
Deuces wild / Autumn leaves / Angel eyes / Bye bye blackbird / Polka dots and moonbeams / My funny valentine / As time goes by / Ain't misbehavin' / Good life / Body and soul
CD ECD 220882
Evidence / Jun '94 / ADA / Cadillac / Harmonia Mundi

JAZZ MASTERS
CD 5276512
Verve / Mar '96 / PolyGram

JUST FRIENDS (Stitt, Sonny & Red Holloway)
Way you look tonight / Forecast / You don't know what love is / Getting sentimental over you / Lester leaps in / Just friends / All God's chillun got rhythm
CD LEJAZZCD 40
Le Jazz / May '95 / Cadillac / Koch

LAST STITT SESSIONS VOL.1 & 2
CD MCD 6003
Muse / Sep '92 / New Note/Pinnacle

LEGENDS OF ACID JAZZ, THE
Turn it on / Bar-b-que man / Miss Riverside / Cry me a river / There are such things / Goin' to DC / Aires / Black vibrations / Calling card / Where is love / Them funky changes
CD PRCD 24169
Prestige / Oct '96 / Cadillac / Complete/ Pinnacle

MADE FOR EACH OTHER
Samba de orfeo / Funny / Glory of love / Very thought of you / Blues for JJ / Funny / Night has a thousand eyes / Honey / Night has a thousand eyes
CD DD 426
Delmark / Jul '97 / ADA / Cadillac / CM / Direct / Hot Shot

SALT AND PEPPER (Stitt, Sonny & Paul Gonsalves)
Salt and pepper / S'posin' / Theme from the Lord Of The Flies / Perdido / Star dust / Surfin' / Lester leaps in / Estrellita / Please don't talk about me / Touchy / Never..sh / My mother's eyes / I'm getting sentimental over you
CD IMP 12102
Impulse Jazz / Mar '97 / New Note/BMG

SONNY STITT SITS IN WITH THE OSCAR PETERSON TRIO (Stitt, Sonny & Oscar Peterson Trio)
I can't give you anything but love / Au private / Gypsy / I'll remember April / Scrapple from the apple / Moten swing / Blues for Pres, Sweets and Ben and all the other funky ones / I didn't know what time it was / I remember you / I know that you know
CD 8493962
Verve / Mar '91 / PolyGram

SONNY'S BLUES (Archive Series - Live At Ronnie Scott's)
Ernest's blues / Home sweet home / Mother / My Mother's eyes / Sonny's theme song / Blues with Dick and Harry / It could happen to you / Oh Lady be good
CD JHAS 603
Ronnie Scott's Jazz House / Jun '95 / Cadillac / Jazz Music / New Note/Pinnacle / TKO Magnum

SOUL CLASSICS
CD OJCCD 6003
Original Jazz Classics / Jul '94 / Complete/Pinnacle / Jazz Music / Wellard

STITT, EDISON & DAVIS (Stitt, Sonny & Harry 'Sweets' Edison/Eddie 'Lockjaw' Davis)
CD DM 15017
DMA Jazz / Jul '96 / Jazz Music

THERE IS NO GREATER LOVE (Stitt, Sonny, Harry 'Sweets' Edison & Eddie 'Lockjaw' Davis)
CD JHR 73557
Jazz Hour / Jan '93 / Cadillac / Jazz Music / Target/BMG

Stivell, Alan

A LANGONNET
CD FDM 36203
Dreyfus / Oct '94 / ADA / Direct / New Note/Pinnacle

AGAIN
CD FDM 361982
Dreyfus / Oct '93 / ADA / Direct / New Note/Pinnacle

BRIAN BORU
Brian Boru / Let the plinn / Mna na heireann / Ye banks and braes o' bonnie Doon / Mari's wedding / Ceasefire / De ha bla / Sword dance / Parlamant lament / Lands of my fathers
CD FDM 362082
Dreyfus / Jul '95 / ADA / Direct / New Note/ Pinnacle

CELTIC SYMPHONY (Tir Na Nog)
Journey to inner spaces / Nostalgia for the past and future / Song and profound lake that I interrogate / Dissolution in the great all / Regaining consciousness / Vibratory communion with the universe / In quest of the Isle / Landing on the isle of the pure world / First steps on the Isle / Discovery of the radiant city / March towards the city / Universal festival / Sudden return to the relative and interrogative world
CD ROUCD 11523
Rounder / '88 / ADA / CM / Direct

CHEMINS DE TERRE
CD FDM 36202
Dreyfus / Oct '94 / ADA / Direct / New Note/Pinnacle

HARPE CELTIQUE
CD FDM 36200
Dreyfus / Oct '94 / ADA / Direct / New Note/Pinnacle

HARPES DU NOUVEL AGE
CD FDM 36206
Dreyfus / Oct '94 / ADA / Direct / New Note/Pinnacle

JOURNEE A LA MAISON
CD DRYF 8343164 2
Dreyfus / Jan '93 / ADA / Direct / New Note/Pinnacle

LEGENDE
CD FDM 36205
Dreyfus / Oct '94 / ADA / Direct / New Note/Pinnacle

REFLETS
CD FDM 36201
Dreyfus / Oct '94 / ADA / Direct / New Note/Pinnacle

TERRE DES VIVANTS
CD _______________ **FDM 36204**
Dreyfus / Oct '94 / ADA / Direct / New Note/Pinnacle

TRO AR BED
Ar C'Hoant dimezin / Rouantelezh Vreizh / Dugelezh Vreizh / Stok Ouzh an Enez / Liegemen of the trembling slopes / We shall survive / Cailin og deas / O'Carolan's farewell/The musical priest / An nighean dubh / Fest hypnoz
CD _______________ **FDM 36187**
Dreyfus / Aug '97 / ADA / Direct / New Note/ Pinnacle

ZOOM (2CD Set)
Eliz iza / Suite des Montagnes / Marig ar Pollanton / Ys / Atrde cuan / Maro ma mestrez / Suzy McGuire / Kimiad / Jenovefa / Stok ouzh an enez / Negro song / Rory Dall's love tune / La dame du lac / An advod / Mna na heireann / Suite Irlandaise / Suite Sudarmoricaine / Tri martolod / Rouantelezh vreizh / Beg ar van / Raog mont d'ar skol / An alarch / Deliverance / Ne bado ket atao / An nighean dubh / Ar bale / Spred hollvedel / Da ewan / REturn / Brian Boru / Pop plinn / Ian Morrison Reel / Lands of my fathers
CD Set _______________ **FDM 361892**
Dreyfus / Jun '97 / ADA / Direct / New Note/ Pinnacle

Stoa

URTHONA
CD _______________ **HY 39100592**
Hyperium / Jul '93 / Cargo / Plastic Head

Stockhausen, Karlheinz

KONTAKTE
CD _______________ **E 87**
Ecstatic Peace / Jun '97 / Cargo / Greyhound

Stockhausen, Markus

COSI LONTANO...QUASI DENTRO (So Far Almost Inside)
CD _______________ **8371112**
ECM / Feb '89 / New Note/Pinnacle

POSSIBLE WORLDS
CD _______________ **CMPCD 68**
CMP / Sep '95 / Cargo / Grapevine/ PolyGram / Vital/SAM

SOL MESTIZO
Creation / Takirari / Emanacion / Reconciliation / Yemaye / La conquista / In your mind / Adentro / Davindad / Zampona / Canto indio / Refelxion / Loncanao / Queca / Desolacion / Asfalto
CD _______________ **92222**
Act / Feb '96 / New Note/Pinnacle

TAGTRAUM (Stockhausen, Markus & Simon)
Glocken / Kuche / Passacaglia / Himmel auf / Ungewitter / Gamelan / Weltraum / Ping pong / Klangduo / Feuerwerk / Yeah / Zwei Bruder / Gran finale / Tagtraum / Miles mute / Wustenwind / Esprit / Bumerang
CD _______________ **UBM 1139**
New Note / Dec '92 / Cadillac / New Note/ Pinnacle

Stockholm Jazz Orchestra

JIGSAW
CD _______________ **DRCD 213**
Dragon / Jan '88 / ADA / Cadillac / CM / Roots / Wellard

SOUNDBITES (Stockholm Jazz Orchestra & James McNeely)
CD _______________ **DRCD 311**
Dragon / May '97 / ADA / Cadillac / CM / Roots / Wellard

Stockton's Wing

CROOKED ROSE, THE
Master's daughter / Some fools cry / Aaron's key / When you smiled / Angel / Humours of Clonmult / Black Hill / Prince's feather / Chasing down a rainbow / Catalina / Lonesome road / Stars in the morning East
CD _______________ **TARACD 3028**
Tara / May '92 / ADA / CM / Conifer/BMG / Direct

LETTING GO
Letting go / Maids of Castlebar / Jig mayhem / Another day / All the time / Eastwood / Rossclogher jigs / I'll believe again / Anyone out there / Sliabh Lucan polkas / Hold you forever
CD _______________ **TARA 3036**
Tara / Nov '95 / ADA / CM / Conifer/BMG / Direct

STOCKTON'S WING
Master's daughter/Blessings/Denis O'Brien's reel / Some fools cry / Aaron's key/Rose in the heather/O'Dea's jig / When you smiled / Angel / Humours of Clonmult/ Lough Gowna/The congress / Black Hill / Prince's feather/Corner House / Chasing down a rainbow / Catalina / Lonesome Road / Stars in the morning East
CD _______________ **KCD 475**
Celtic Collections / Jan '97 / Target/BMG

Stoddart, Pipe Major

GREATEST PIPERS VOL.3
CD _______________ **LS 5151CD**
Lismor / Apr '95 / ADA / Direct / Duncans / Lismor

PIPERS OF DISTINCTION
CD _______________ **CDMON 806**
Monarch / Jul '90 / ADA / CM / Direct / Duncans

WORLD'S GREATEST PIPERS VOL.3, THE
CD _______________ **LCOM 5151**
Lismor / Sep '95 / ADA / Direct / Duncans / Lismor

Stojiljkovic, Jova

BLOW 'BESIR' BLOW
Sampionski cocek / Safetov cocek / Vranjsko / Izrael orijent / Cifteteli / Jovino kolo / Durak i srecko / Djokino cocek / Beogradska cocek / Ekstra cocek / Romski cocek
CD _______________ **CDORBD 038**
Globestyle / Feb '96 / Pinnacle

Stoker

SYNCOPATE
Straight no chaser / Killer Joe / Mood indigo / Side winder / Good morning heartache / Walk tall / St. Thomas / Sister Mamie / Jeannine / All blues / Ronnie's Bonnie / Blue in green
CD _______________ **ACD 6**
Douglas Music / May '97 / Cadillac / New Note/Pinnacle

Stokes, Frank

CREATOR OF THE MEMPHIS BLUES
CD _______________ **YAZCD 1056**
Yazoo / Jun '91 / ADA / CM / Koch

FRANK STOKES DREAM (Memphis Blues Anthology)
CD _______________ **YAZCD 1008**
Yazoo / Mar '92 / ADA / CM / Koch

VICTOR RECORDINGS - 1928-29, THE
CD _______________ **DOCD 5013**
Document / Feb '92 / ADA / Hot Shot / Jazz Music

Stoll, Steve

DAMN ANALOG TECHNOLOGY
CD _______________ **SM 80332**
Profile / Feb '97 / Pinnacle

Stoller, Rhet

EMBER LANE
Travelling song / Perpetual Summer / Sea breeze / Concerto for a rainbow / Lucky five / Ember lane / Tree top woman / Sandy's rave up / Ocean serenade / Down the line
CD _______________ **SEECD 348**
See For Miles/C5 / Jul '92 / Pinnacle

Stomp That Pussy

HATE IS THE MOVE
CD _______________ **LF 057**
Lost & Found / Jan '94 / Plastic Head

Stone

EMOTIONAL PLAYGROUND
Small tales / Home base / Last chance / Above the grey sky / Mad Hatter's den / Dead end / Adrift / Haven / Years after / Time dive / Missionary of charity / Emotional playground
CD _______________ **8410562**
Black Mark / Feb '92 / Plastic Head

Stone, Billy

WEST TEXAS SKY
Brand new shade of red / Into every life (A little love must fall) / When two people meet / Just like a diamond / West Texas sky / Was you / Pictures never lie / You just don't know what you've got / Holmes county home / Miz Leah / Family reunion / My heart jumped over the moon / All love needs / Love love love / That empty chair / Last Dallas cowboy / Walter petty / What in the world (Is this coming to) / This old / Grandma's old gas stove / Master electrician / Ain't no telling what a fool will do / What are we trying to prove / Sight for sore ears / Little brother
CD _______________ **BCD 15736**
Bear Family / May '93 / Direct / Rollercoaster / Swift

Stone Breath

SONGS OF MOONLIGHT RAIN
CD _______________ **CAM 001CD**
Camera Obscura / Mar '97 / Cargo

Stone By Stone

I PASS FOR HUMAN
CD _______________ **SST 247CD**
SST / Jul '89 / Plastic Head

Stone, Carl

CARL STONE
CD _______________ **EMIT 1196**
Time Recordings / Jul '96 / Pinnacle

MOM'S
CD _______________ **NA 049**
New Albion / Nov '92 / Cadillac / Harmonia Mundi

Stone, Cliffie

TRANSCRIPTIONS 1945-1949
Draggin' the bow / Beautiful brown eyes / Mine all mine / Mule skinner blues / Little cabin home on the hill / Blue steel blues / Stuck up blues / Mandolin boogie / Bill Cheatham / Red's boogie / Freight train blues / After you've gone / Flop eared mule / Sugar hill / Cactus set-up / Daughter of Jolie Blon / Steel guitar rag / Free little bird / Honky tonkin' / Oh lady be good / Sally Goodin / Little rock getaway
CD _______________ **RFDCD 08**
Country Routes / Oct '91 / Hot Shot / Jazz Music

Stone, Doug

FROM THE HEART
Warning labels / Made for lovin' you / Leave me the radio / This empty house / Why didn't I think of that / Ain't your memory got no pride at all / Workin' end of a hoe / Too busy being in love / She's got a future in the movies / Left, leaving, goin' or gone
CD _______________ **4721312**
Epic / Jan '93 / Sony

Stone Funkers

HARDER THAN KRYPTONITE
Here we go-go / Talk / Bassrace / Sucker 4 your love / Message from da falcon / STONEFUNK Theme / Rock city / Good time / We come to party / Slam da phunk / Massive party / Can U follow
CD _______________ **9031715022**
WEA / Jul '91 / Warner Music

Stone, Gordon

TOUCH AND GO
CD _______________ **ALZCD 124**
Alcazar / Feb '96 / ADA

Stone, Jesse

JESSE STONE ALIAS CHARLES CALHOUN
Ace in the hole / Mister jelly fingers / Hey, sister Lucy (what makes your lips so) / Donkey and the elephant / Keep your big mouth shut / Sneaky Pete / I came home unexpectedly / Who's zat / Bling a ling a ling / Don't let it get away / Get it while you can / Who killed 'er / Cole slaw (sirghum switch) / Do it now / Easy walkin' / Oh that'll be joyful / Runaway / Smack dab in the middle / (I don't know) Why the car won't go / Come and dance with me / Hey tiger / Night life / Barrelhouse / Rocket / My pigeon's gone / Jamboree / Stash / Tall and short / Crawfish / Tadpole wiggle
CD _______________ **BCD 15695**
Bear Family / Feb '96 / Direct / Rollercoaster / Swift

Stone, Lew

CREAM OF LEW STONE & HIS BAND, THE (Stone, Lew & His Band)
Undecided / Ups and downs / Coffee in the morning / Moon remembered, but you forgot / Shades of Hades / Flat foot floogie / Apple blossom time / Why waste your tears / Nine pins in the sky / Dark clouds / Serenade for a wealthy widow / There's something wrong with the weather / Frog on the water-lily / Get happy / I get along without you very well / I want the waiter (with the water) / Lonely / Beale Street blues / Louisiana hayride / My wubba Dolly / Music maestro please / St. Louis blues
CD _______________ **PASTCD 7041**
Flapper / Mar '94 / Pinnacle

RIGHT FROM THE HEART (Stone, Lew & His Orchestra)
CD _______________ **DOLD 3**
Old Bean / Sep '93 / Jazz Music / Wellard

Stone Love

GO GO WINE
CD _______________ **STONECD 1**
Stone Love / Mar '97 / Jet Star

STONE LOVE - CHAMPION SOUND (Various Artists)
CD _______________ **SGCD 17**
Sir George / Nov '94 / Jet Star / Pinnacle

STONE LOVE ON THE ROAD VOL.1 (Various Artists)
CD _______________ **SGCD 13**
Sir George / Mar '93 / Jet Star / Pinnacle

STONE LOVE ON THE ROAD VOL.3 (Various Artists)
CD _______________ **SGCD 18**
Sir George / Nov '94 / Jet Star / Pinnacle

STONE LOVE PRESENTS GO GO WINE (Various Artists)
CD _______________ **OPCD 2048**
Stone Love / Oct '96 / Jet Star

STONE LOVE VOL.3 (Various Artists)
CD _______________ **VPCD 1448**
VP / Nov '95 / Greensleeves / Jet Star / Total/BMG

Stone Roses

COMPLETE STONE ROSES, THE
So young / Tell me / Sally Cinnamon / All across the sands / Here it comes / Elephant stone / Full fathom five / Hardest thing in the world / Made of stone / Going down / She bangs the drum / Mersey paradise / Standing here / I wanna be adored / Waterfall / I am the resurrection / Where angels play / Fool's gold / What the world is waiting for / Something burning / One love
CD _______________ **ORECD 535**
Silvertone / Jul '96 / Pinnacle

GARAGE FLOWER
CD _______________ **GARAGECD 1**
Silvertone / Nov '96 / Pinnacle

SECOND COMING
Breaking into heaven / Driving South / Ten storey love song / Daybreak / Your star will shine / Straight to the man / Begging you / Tightrope / Good times / Tears / How do you sleep / Love spreads
CD _______________ **GED 24503**
Geffen / Dec '94 / BMG

STONE ROSES
I wanna be adored / Waterfall / She bangs the drum / Don't stop / Bye bye badman / Elizabeth my dear / (Song for my) Sugar spun sister / Made of stone / Shoot you down / This is the one / I am the resurrection
CD _______________ **ORECD 502**
Silvertone / Mar '97 / Pinnacle

TURNS INTO STONE
CD _______________ **ORECD 521**
Silvertone / Mar '97 / Pinnacle

WHAT A TRIP
CD _______________ **CBAK 4045**
Baktabak / Jan '91 / Arabesque

Stone, Sly

BEST OF SLY AND THE FAMILY STONE (Sly & The Family Stone)
Dance to the music / I want to take you higher / Thank you (falettinme be mice elf agin) / I get high on you / Stand / M'lady / Skin I'm in / Everyday people / Sing a simple song / Hot fun in the summertime / Don't call me nigger, whitey / Brave and strong / Life / Everybody is a star / If you want me to stay / (You caught me) smilin' / Whatever will be will be (Que sera sera) / Running away / Family affair
CD _______________ **4717582**
Epic / Jul '92 / Sony

COLLECTION, THE (Sly & The Family Stone)
CD _______________ **CCSCD 307**
Castle / Sep '91 / BMG

DANCE TO THE MUSIC (Sly & The Family Stone)
You're my only love / Heavenly angel / Oh what a night / You've forgotten me / Yellow moon / Honest / Nerves / Help me with my broken heart / Long time alone / Uncle Sam needs you my friend
CD _______________ **CDTB 1029**
Thunderbolt / Nov '87 / TKO Magnum

EVERY DOG HAS ITS DAY (Sly & The Family Stone)
CD _______________ **CDSGP 0125**
Prestige / Dec '94 / Else / Total/BMG

FAMILY AFFAIR (Sly & The Family Stone)
My woman's head / New breed / As I get older / Somethin' bad / Fire in my heart / She's my baby / Free as a bird / Girl won't you go / Everything I need / Why can't you stay / Off the hook / Dance your pants off / Under the influence of love / Crazy love song / Seventh son
CD _______________ **CDTB 119**
Thunderbolt / Apr '91 / TKO Magnum

FRESH (Sly & The Family Stone)
In time / If you want me to stay / Let me have it all / Frisky / Thankful 'n' thoughtful / Skin I'm in / I don't know / Keep on dancing / Whatever will be will be (Que sera sera) / If it were left up to me / Babies makin' blues
CD _______________ **4851702**
Epic / Sep '96 / Sony

GREATEST HITS (Sly & The Family Stone)
I want to take you higher / Everybody is a star / Stand / Life / Fun / You can make it if you try / Dance to the music / Everyday people / Hot fun in the summertime / M'lady / Sing a simple song / Thank you (falettinme be mice elf agin)
CD _______________ **4625242**
Epic / Sep '90 / Sony

IN THE STILL OF THE NIGHT (Sly & The Family Stone)
In the still of the night / Searchin' / Don't say I didn't warn you / Ain't that lovin' you baby / Swim / Every dog has his day / Suki suki / Seventh son / I can't turn you loose / Take my advice / Watermelon man / I ain't got nobody / I you were blue / Rock dirge / High love / Life of fortune and fame
CD _____ CDTB 129
Thunderbolt / Sep '91 / TKO Magnum

PEARLS FROM THE PAST
CD _____ KLMCD 005
BAM / Nov '93 / Koch / Scratch/BMG

PRECIOUS STONE (In The Studio With Sly Stone 1963-1965) (Various Artists)
Swim: *Sly & Rose* / Scat swim: *Stone, Sly* / I taught him: *Scott, Gloria* / Don't say I didn't warn you: *Scott, Gloria* / Help me with my broken heart: *Stone, Sly* / Out of sight: *Stone, Sly* / Nerve of you: *O'Connor, Emile* / Every dog has his day: *O'Connor, Emile* / On Broadway: *Stone, Sly* / Searchin': *Stone, Sly* / Lord, Lord: *Stone, Sly* / Seventh son: *Stone, Sly* / Jerk: *Sly & Sal* / That little old heartbreaker: *Freeman, Bobby* / I'll never fall in love again: *Freeman, Bobby* / Ain't that lovin' you baby: *Preston, Billy* / Buttermilk: *Stone, Sly* / Fake it: *George & Teddy* / Laugh: *George & Teddy* / Little Latin lupe lu: *Preston, Billy* / Dance all night: *Sly & Freddie* / Temptation walk: *Stone, Sly* / Underdog: *Stone, Sly* / Radio spot: *Stone, Sly* / Can't you tell I love her: *Preston, Billy* / Life of fortune and fame: *Preston, Billy* / Take my advice: *Preston, Billy* / As I get older: *Preston, Billy*
CD _____ CDCHD 539
Ace / Aug '94 / Pinnacle

SPOTLIGHT ON SLY & FAMILY STONE (Sly & The Family Stone)
Honest / Ain't that lovin' you baby / Watermelon man / Hi love / Life of fortune and fame / Don't say I didn't warn you / Take my advice / In the still of the night / If you were blue / Searchin' / Every dog has his day / I ain't got nobody / Seventh son / I can't turn you loose / Swim / Nerves
CD _____ HADCD 119
Javelin / Feb '94 / Henry Hadaway / THE

THERE'S A RIOT GOIN' ON (Sly & The Family Stone)
Luv 'n' Haight / Just like a baby / Poet / Family affair / Africa talks to you - 'The Asphalt Jungle' / There's a riot goin' on / Brave and strong / (You caught me) smilin' / Time / Spaced cowboy / Running away / Thank you for talking to me Africa
CD _____ 4670632
Epic / Apr '94 / Sony

WHOLE NEW THING, A (Sly & The Family Stone)
Underdog / If this room could talk / Run run run / Turn me loose / Let me hear it from you / Advice / I cannot make it / Trip to your heart / I hate to love her / Bad risk / That kind of person / Dog
CD _____ EK 66424
Epic / Jul '95 / Sony

Stone Soup

STONE SOUP
CD _____ MTMCD 199620
MTM / Apr '97 / Cargo

Stone Telling

STONE TELLING
CD _____ NS 001CD
Network Sound / Jul '96 / Plastic Head

Stone Temple Pilots

CORE
Dead and bloated / Sex type thing / Wicked garden / No memory / Sin / Naked Sunday / Creep / Piece of pie / Plush / Wet my bed / Crackerman / Where the river goes
CD _____ 7567824182
Atlantic / Nov '92 / Warner Music

PURPLE
Meat plow / Vasoline / Lounge fly / Interstate love song / Still remains / Pretty penny / Silvergun superman / Big empty / Unglued / Army ants / Kitchenware and candy bars
CD _____ 7567826072
Atlantic / Jun '94 / Warner Music

TINY MUSIC...SONGS FROM THE VATICAN GIFT SHOP
Press play / Big bang baby / And so I know / Art school girl / Trippin' on a hole in a paper heart / Seven caged tigers / Daisy / Ride the cliche / Adhesive / Lady picture show / Tumble in the rough / Pop's love suicide
CD _____ 7567828712
Atlantic / Mar '96 / Warner Music

Stone The Crows

STONE THE CROWS
Big Jim Salter / Love 74 / Touch of your loving hand / Sad Mary / Good time girl / On the highway / Mr. Wizard / Sunset cowboy / Raining in your heart / Seven lakes
CD _____ CDTB 070
Thunderbolt / Jun '89 / TKO Magnum

Stoned

ED'S DINER
CD _____ ASR 12
Ampersand / Jun '97 / Cargo

MUSIC FOR THE MORONS
CD _____ ASR 6
Ampersand / Oct '96 / Cargo

Stoneflow

SCULPTURE
CD _____ CC 027054CD
Shark / May '95 / Plastic Head

Stoneham, Harry

LIVE AT ABBEY ROAD (Stoneham, Harry Trio)
Oh lady be good / My foolish heart / Jersey bounce / East of the sun and west of the moon / I should care / Harlem nocturne / Strike up the band / Out of nowhere / Georgia on my mind / How high the moon / (Back home again in) Indiana / Moonlight in vermont / Now is the time
CD _____ GRCD 55
Grasmere / Oct '92 / Highlander / Savoy / Target/BMG

Stoneking, Fred

SADDLE OLD SPIKE (Fiddle Music From Missouri)
Birdie in a snowbank / Horse and buggy-o / Sugar Betty Ann / Evelyn's waltz / Honey Creek special / Burt County breakdown / Buzzard in a pea patch / Who's going to talk to Dinah / Blackberry waltz / Old Indiana / Old gray goose / Muddy weather / McCowan's waltz / Needle in a haystack / Cherry blossoms / Saddle old Spike / Green's waltz / Dance around Molly / Humansville / Blackberry one-step / Walk along, John / Willott's hornpipe / No little home to go to / Rye whiskey / Goodbye Liza Jane / Frisky Jim
CD _____ ROUCD 0381
Rounder / Nov '96 / ADA / CM / Direct

Stony Sleep

MUSIC FOR CHAMELEONS
CD _____ ABB 138CD
Big Cat / Jul '97 / 3mv/Pinnacle

Stop

NEVER
CD _____ FOR 0010
Backs / Feb '96 / RTM/Disc

Storey, Liz

SOLID COLORS
Wedding rain / Pacheco pass / Without you / Hymn / Things with wings / Solid colours / Bradley's dream / Water caves / Peace piece
CD _____ 01934110232
Windham Hill / Jan '95 / BMG

Storm & Stress

STORMANDSTRESS
CD _____ TG 173CD
Touch & Go / Jul '97 / SRD

Storm

STORM, THE
You keep me waiting / I've got a lot to learn about love / In the raw / You're gonna miss me / Call me / Show me the way / I want you back / Still loving you / Touch and go / Gimme love / Take me away / Can't live without love
CD _____ 7567917412
Atlantic / May '96 / Warner Music

Storm

NORDAVIND
CD _____ FOG 004CD
Moonfog / May '95 / Plastic Head

Stormclouds

NIGHTMARES IN THE SKY
CD _____ CLOUD 2CD
Rainfall / Jun '97 / Greyhound

Storming Heaven

LIFE IN PARADISE
CD _____ 199610
MTM / Oct '96 / Cargo

Stormwitch

BEAUTY AND THE BEAST
Call of the wicked / Beauty and the beast / Just for one night / Emerald eyes / Tears by the firelight / Tigers of the sea / Russia's on fire / Cheyenne / Welcome to Bedlam
CD _____ 15348
Laserlight / Aug '91 / Target/BMG

SHOGUN
CD _____ SPV 8476842
SPV / Oct '94 / Koch / Plastic Head

WALPURGIS NIGHT
CD _____ 15391
Laserlight / Aug '91 / Target/BMG

Stormy Monday Band

LIVE AT 55
CD _____ BLUE 10102
Blues Beacon / Nov '91 / New Note/ Pinnacle

Storvan

AN DEIZIOU KAER
CD _____ KMCD 65
Keltia Musique / Sep '96 / ADA / Discovery

Story

ANGEL IN THE HOUSE, THE
So much mine / Missing person afternoon / Gilded cage / When two and two are five / At the still point / Angel in the house / Mermaid / Barefoot ballroom / In the gloaming / Fatso / Love song / Amelia / Fatso, part 2
CD _____ 7559614712
Elektra / Aug '93 / Warner Music

GRACE IN GRAVITY
CD _____ 7559613212
Elektra / Jun '92 / Warner Music

Story Board

STORY BOARD
CD _____ PMC 1113
Pan Music / Jan '93 / Harmonia Mundi

Storyville

PIECE OF YOUR SOUL, A
Bitter rain / Good day for the blues / Blind side / Don't make me cry / What passes for love / Solid ground / Piece of your sole / Cynical / Luck runs out / Can't go there any more / Share that smile
CD _____ 0630152702
Code Blue / Apr '97 / Warner Music

Storyville New Orleans Jazz ...

MEMORIES FROM OLAND (Storyville New Orleans Jazz Band)
CD _____ MECCACD 2008
Music Mecca / May '97 / Cadillac / Jazz Music / Wellard

Stotzem, Jacques

CLEAR NIGHT
CD _____ BEST 1030CD
Acoustic Music / Nov '93 / ADA

STRAIGHT ON
CD _____ BEST 1013CD
Acoustic Music / Nov '93 / ADA

Stover, Don

THINGS IN LIFE
CD _____ ROUCD 0014
Rounder / Feb '95 / ADA / CM / Direct

Stradlin, Izzy

IZZY STRADLIN AND THE JU JU HOUNDS
Somebody knockin' / Pressure drop / Time gone by / Shuffle it all / Bucket o'trouble / Train tracks / How will it go / Cuttin' the rug / Take a look at the guy / Come on now inside
CD _____ GED 24490
Geffen / Jun '97 / BMG

Stradling, Rod

RHYTHMS OF THE WORLD
CD _____ FMSD 5021
Rogue / Oct '91 / Stern's

Strafe Feur Rebellion

LUFTHUNGER (Ten Catastrophes In The History Of The World & Music)
CD _____ TO 19
Touch / Mar '91 / Kudos / Pinnacle

PIANO GUITAR
CD _____ STCD 73
Staalplaat / Feb '96 / Vital/SAM

Straight Faced

BROKEN
CD _____ F 022CD
Fearless / Apr '97 / Cargo / Plastic Head

GUILTY
CD _____ F 024CD
Fearless / Apr '97 / Cargo / Plastic Head

Straijer, Horacio

STRAIJER-HURTADO (Straijer, Horacio & Horacio Hurtado)
Desde abajo / Leguero / So what / Someday my prince will come / TM / Pueblo sin nimbre / Vuelta de rocha / Little Hay Road / Un salto al vacio / Paseante / Orilla del cielo
CD _____ SLAMCD 503
Slam / Oct '96 / Cadillac

Strain

HERE AND NOW
CD _____ NA 032CD
New Age / Jul '96 / Plastic Head

Strait, George

BLUE CLEAR SKY
Blue clear sky / Carried away / Rockin' with arms of your memory / She knows when you're on my mind / I ain't never seen no on like you / I can still make Cheyenne / King of the mountain / Do the right thing / I'd just as soon go / Need I say more / Check yes or no
CD _____ MCD 11428
MCA / Apr '96 / BMG

CARRY YOUR LOVE WITH ME
Round about way / Carrying your love with me / One night at a time / She'll leave you with a smile / Won't you come home (and talk to a stranger) / Today my world slipped away / I've got a funny feeling / Nerve / That's me (every chance I get) / Real good place to start
CD _____ MCD 11584
MCA / Apr '97 / BMG

EASY COME EASY GO
Stay out of my arms / Just look at me / Easy come, easy go / I'd like to have that one back / Lovebug / I wasn't fooling around / Without me around / Man in love with you / That's where my baby feels at home / We must be loving right
CD _____ MCAD 10907
MCA / Mar '94 / BMG

HOLDING MY OWN
You're right I'm wrong / Holding my own / Gone as a girl can get / So much like my dad / Trains make me lonesome / All of me (loves all of you) / Wonderland of love / Faults and all / It's all right with me / Here we go again
CD _____ MCAD 10532
MCA / Jun '92 / BMG

LEAD ON
You can't make a heart love somebody / Adalida / I met a friend of yours today / Nobody has to get hurt / Down Louisiana way / Lead on / What am I waiting for / Big one / I'll always be loving you / No one but you
CD _____ MCAD 11092
MCA / Jan '95 / BMG

STRAIT OUT OF THE BOX (4CD Set)
I just can't let you go on dying like this / (That don't change) way I feel about you / I don't want to talk it over anymore / Unwound / Blame it on Mexico / Her goodbye hit me in the heart / If you're thinking you want a stranger (there's one coming h / Any old love won't do / Fool hearted memory / Marina Del Rey / I can't see Texas from here / Heartbroke / What would your memory do / Amarillo by morning / I thought I heard you calling my name / Fire I can't put out / You look so good in love / 80 Proof bottle of tear stopper / Right or wrong / Let's fall ot pieces together / Does Fort Worth / Ever cross your mind / Cowboy rides away / Fireman / Chair / You're something special to me / Haven't you heard / In too deep / Lefty's gone / Nobody in his right mind would've left her / It ain't cool to be crazy about you / Ocean front property / Rhythm of the road / Six pack to go / All me Ex's live in Texas / Am I blue / Famous last words of a fool / Baby blue / If you ain't lovin' (you ain't livin) / Baby's gotten good at goodbye / Bigger man than me / Hollywood squares / What's going on in my world / Ace in the hole / Love without end, amen / Drinking champagne / I've come expect it from you / You know me better than that / Chill of an early fall / Lovesick blues / Milk cow blues / Gone as a girl can get / So much like my Dad / Trains make me lonesome / Wonderland of love / I cross my heart / Heartland / When did you stop loving me / Overnight male / King of broken hearts / Where the sidewalk ends / Easy come, easy go / I'd like to have that one back / Lovebug / Man in love with you / Just look at me / Stay out of my arms / Big balls in Cowtown / Big one / Fly me to the moon / Check yes or no / I know she still loves me
CD Set _____ MCAD 411263
MCA / Nov '95 / BMG

Straitjacket Fits

BLOW
CD _____ FNCD 251
Flying Nun / Sep '93 / RTM/Disc

Strandberg, Paul

FUTURISTIC RHYTHM
CD _____ SITCD 9210
Sittel / Aug '94 / Cadillac / Jazz Music

Strange Brew

EARTH OUT
CD _____ CDROB 40
Rob's Records / Feb '96 / Pinnacle / RTM/Disc

Strange Nature

WORLD SONG
CD NATURECD 1
WEA / Jul '93 / Warner Music

Strange Parcels

DISCONNECTION
CD ONUCD 57
On-U Sound / Jul '94 / Jet Star / SRD

Strange, Billy

STRANGE COUNTRY
CD TCD 1032
Tradition / Nov '96 / ADA / Vital

Strangelove

LOVE AND OTHER DEMONS
Casualties / Spiders and flies / Living with the human machines / She's everywhere / Sway / Beautiful alone / Elin's photograph / 20th century cold / 1432 / Sea of black
CD FOODCD 15
Food / Jun '96 / EMI

TIME FOR THE REST OF YOUR LIFE
Sixer / Time for the rest of your life / Quiet day / Sand / I will burn / Low life / World outside / Return of the real me / All because of you / Fire (show me light) / Hopeful / Kite / Is there a place
CD FOODCD 11
Food / Sep '97 / EMI

Stranger

ROLLING THUNDER
CD ORCCD 2
Octopus / Jul '96 / Kudos / Pinnacle

Stranglers

ABOUT TIME
Golden boy / Money / Face / Sinister / Little blue lies / Still life / Paradise row / She gave it all / Lies and deception / Lucky finger / And the boat sailed by
CD WENCD 001
When / May '95 / Pinnacle

ALL TWELVE INCHES
Midnight Summer dream / Skin deep / No mercy / Let me down easy / Nice in Nice / Always the sun / Big in America / Shakin' like a leaf / All day and all of the night / Was it you / 96 tears / Sweet smell of success
CD 4714162
Epic / Sep '96 / Sony

AURAL SCULPTURE
Ice queen / Skin deep / Let me down easy / No mercy / North winds / Uptown / Punch and Judy / Spain / Laughing / Souls / Mad hatter
CD 4746762
Epic / Feb '97 / Sony

BLACK AND WHITE
Tank / Nice 'n' sleazy / Outside Tokyo / Mean to me / Sweden (all quiet on the eastern front) / Hey (rise of the robots) / Toiler on the sea / Curfew / Threatened / Do you wanna / In the shadows / Enough time / Death and night and blood (Yukio) / Tits / Walk on by
CD CZ 109
EMI / Aug '88 / EMI

COLLECTION 1977-1982, THE
(Get a) grip (on yourself) / Peaches / Hangin' around / No more heroes / Duchess / Walk on by / Waltzinblack / Something better change / Nice 'n' sleazy / Bear cage / Who wants the world / Golden brown / Strange little girl / La folie
CD CDFA 3230
Fame / Aug '89 / EMI

COLLECTION, THE
CD CDGOLD 1071
EMI Gold / Apr '97 / EMI

DEATH & NIGHT & BLOOD
CD RRCD 187
Receiver / May '94 / Grapevine/PolyGram

DREAMTIME
Always the sun / Dreamtime / Was it you / You'll always reap what you sow / Ghost train / Nice in Nice / Big in America / Shakin' like a leaf / Mayan skies / Too precious
CD CD 26648
Epic / Oct '86 / Sony

EARLY YEARS 1974-1976 (Rare, Live & Unreleased)
(Get a) Grip (on yourself) / Bitching / Go Buddy go / (Get a) grip (on yourself) (live) / Sometimes / Bitching (live) / Peasant in the big shitty / Hanging around / Peaches
CD CLACD 401
Castle / Jun '94 / BMG

FELINE
Midnight summer dream / It's a small world / Ships that pass in the night / European female / Let's tango in Paris / Paradise / All roads lead to Rome / Blue sister / Never say goodbye
CD 4844692
Epic / Jul '97 / Sony

GREATEST HITS (1977-1990)
Peaches / Something better change / No more heroes / Walk on by / Duchess / Golden brown / Strange little girl / European female / Skin deep / Nice in Nice / Always the sun / Big in America / All day and all of the night / 96 tears / No mercy
CD 4675412
Epic / Nov '90 / Sony

HIT MEN, THE (The Complete Singles 1977-1990)
Grip '89 (get a) grip (on yourself) / London lady / Peaches / Go buddy go / Hanging around / Choosey Susie / Something better change / Straighten out / No more heroes / English towns / 5 minutes / Nice 'n' sleazy / Toiler on the sea / Mean to me / Walk on by / Duchess / Nuclear device (wizard of aus) / Don't bring Harry / Raven / Bear cage / Who wants the world / Waltzinblack / Thrown away / Just like nothing on earth / Let me introduce you to the family / Golden brown / La folie / Tramp / Strange little girl / European female / Midnight summer dream / Paradise / Skin deep / No mercy / Let me down easy / Nice in nice / Always the sun / Big in America / Shakin like a leaf / Was it you / All day and all of the night / 96 tears / Sweet smell of success
CD CDEMC 3759
EMI / Jan '97 / EMI

LA FOLIE
Non-stop / Everybody loves you when you're dead / Tramp / Let me introduce you to the family / Ain't nothin' to it / Love to hate / Pin up / Two to tango / Golden brown / How to find true love and happiness in the present day / La folie
CD CDFA 3083
Fame / Nov '88 / EMI

LIVE (X-CERT)
(Get a) grip (on yourself) / Dagenham Dave / Burning up time / Dead ringer / Hangin' around / Feel like a wog / Straight out / Do you wanna / Five minutes / Go buddy go / Peasant in the big shitty / In the shadows
CD CDFA 3313
Fame / Dec '94 / EMI

LIVE AT THE HOPE & ANCHOR (The Requests Show - Nov 22 1977)
Tits / Choosey Susie / Goodbye Toulouse / Bitching / School Mam / Peasant in the big shitty / In the shadows / Walk on by / Princess of the streets / Go buddy go / No more heroes / Straighten out / Peaches / Hangin' around / Dagenham Dave / Sometimes / Bring on the nubiles / London lady
CD CDFA 3316
Fame / Feb '95 / EMI

MENINBLACK
Waltzinblack / Just like nothing on Earth / Second coming / Waiting for the meninblack / Turn the centuries turn / Two sunspots / Four horsemen / Thrown away / Manna machine / Hallo to our men / Top secret
CD CDFA 3208
Fame / Sep '88 / EMI

NO MORE HEROES
I feel like a wog / Bitching / Dead ringer / Dagenham Dave / Bring on the nubiles / Something better change / No more heroes / Peasant in the big shitty / Burning up time / English towns / School Mam / In the shadows / Straighten out / Five minutes / Rok it to the moon
CD PRDFCD 6
Premier/EMI / Jul '96 / EMI

OLD TESTAMENT, THE (The UA Studio Recordings 1977-1982/4CD Set)
Sometimes / Goodbye toulouse / London lady / Princess of the streets / Hangin' around / Peaches / (Get a) Grip (On yourself) / Ugly / Down in the sewer / Choosey Susie / Go Buddy go / I feel like a wog / Bitching / Dead ringer / Dagenham Dave / Bring on the nubiles / Something better change / No more heroes / Peasant in the big shitty / Burning up time / English towns / School Mam / Straighten out / Five minutes / Rok it to the moon / Tank / Nice 'n' sleazy / Outside Tokyo / Sweden (All quiet on the Eastern front) / Hey rise of the robots / Toiler of the sea / Curfew / Threatened / In the shadows / Do you wanna / Death and night and blood (yukio) / Enough time / Shut up / Walk on by / Mean to me / Old codger / Longships / Raven / Dead loss angeles / Ice / Baroque bordello / Nuclear device / Shah shah a go go / Don't bring Harry / Duchess / Meninblack / Genetix / Fools rush out / Yellowcake / Vietnamerica / Bear cage / Who wants the world / Waltzinblack / Just like nothing on Earth / Second coming / Waiting for the meninblack / Turn the centuries turn / Two sunspots / Four horsemen / Trown away / Manna machine / Hallow to our men / Top secret / Maninwhite / Non-stop / Everybody loves you when you're dead / Tramp / Let me introduce you to the family / Ain't nothin' to it / Man they love to hate / Pin up / It only takes two to tango / Golden brown / How to find true love and happiness in the present day / La Folie / Love 30 / Strange little girl / Cruel garden / (Get a) Grip (on yourself)
CD Set CDS 7999242
EMI / Sep '92 / EMI

RADIO ONE
CD ESSCD 283
Essential / Nov '95 / BMG

RATTUS NORVEGICUS (Stranglers IV)
Sometimes / Goodbye Toulouse / London lady / Princess of the streets / Hangin' around / Peaches / (Get a) Grip (on yourself) / Ugly / Down in the sewer: Falling / Down in the sewer: Trying to get out again / Rat's rally / Choosy Susie / Go Buddy go / Peasant in the big shitty
CD PRDFCD 5
Premier/EMI / Jul '96 / EMI

RAVEN, THE
Longships / Raven / Dead loss Angeles / Ice / Baroque bordello / Nuclear device / Shah shah a go go / Don't bring Harry / Duchess / Meninback / Genetix / Bear cage
CD CDFA 3131
Fame / Aug '88 / EMI

SINGLES (The UA Years)
(Get a) grip (on yourself) / Peaches / Go buddy go / Something better change / Straighten out / No more heroes / Five minutes / Nice 'n' sleazy / Walk on by / Duchess / Nuclear device / Don't bring Harry / Bear cage / Who wants the world / Thrown away / Just like nothing on Earth / Let me introduce you to the family / Golden brown / La folie / Strange little girl
CD CDEM 1314
Liberty / Feb '89 / EMI

WRITTEN IN RED
CD WENCD 009
CD WENPD 009
When / Jan '97 / Pinnacle

Strapping Fieldhands

GOBS ON THE MIDWAY
CD SB 53
Siltbreeze / Feb '97 / Cargo / Vital

Strapping Young Lad

HEAVY AS A REALLY HEAVY THING
CD CM 770922
Century Media / May '95 / Plastic Head

Strasser, Hugo

60'S, THE (Strasser, Hugo & His Dance Orchestra)
CD 16055
Laserlight / May '94 / Target/BMG

DANCES IN STRICT RHYTHM (2CD Set)
Popocatepetl twist / Yesterday man / Woolly bully / My boy lollipop / Letkiss / Memphis Tennessee / Hully gully firehouse / La bamba / C'mon and swim / Girl from Ipanema / Limbo rock / Viens danser la bostella / I get around / Knock knock who's there / El condor pasa / Save your kisses for me / Rivers of Babylon / Love story / Pariser tango / Raindrops keep falling on my head / Waterloo / Is this the way to Amarillo / Viva Espana / Yes sir, I can boogie / Paloma blanca / New York, New York / Ein bisschen frieden / Atlantis is calling / La isla bonita / Nikita / I just called to say I love you / Hey mambo / Copacabana / Midnight lady / Reet petite / Theater
CD Set 24339
Laserlight / Dec '96 / Target/BMG

HUGO STRASSER'S DANCE PARTY (Strasser, Hugo & His Dance Orchestra)
Crazy rhythm / Congratulations / Love story / I could have danced all night / Fascination / Ramona / Maria from Bahia / Samba cielito / Reet petite / Red roses for a blue lady / Moonlight and roses / Undecided / Frenesi / La cumparsita / Kiss of fire / Spanish gypsy dance / Y viva Espana / Wunderbar
CD GRCD 38
Grasmere / Nov '89 / Highlander / Savoy / Target/BMG

LATIN RHYTHMS
CD 16119
Laserlight / Jun '95 / Target/BMG

STRICTLY DANCING (Strasser, Hugo & His Dance Orchestra)
CD 26098
Laserlight / Nov '93 / Target/BMG

Strata Institute

CIPHERSYNTAX
Slang / Bed stuy / Turn of events / Decrepidus / Ihgnat down / Micro-move / Wild / Humantic / Abacus / Ihgnat
CD 8344252
jMT / Jan '92 / PolyGram

Strathclyde Police Pipers

CHAMPION OF CHAMPIONS
Marches / Jigs / Strathspey and reel / Polkas / Hornpipes / Slow air
CD LCDM 9028
Lismor / Aug '90 / ADA / Direct / Duncans / Lismor

SIX IN A ROW (1981-1986)
March, strathspey and reel / Marches / Slow air - Jigs and hornpipe / 9/8 marches / 2/4 marches / Solo pipe selection / Drum salute / Slow air, hornpipe and jigs / March, strathspey and reel / Slow air, hornpipe and jigs / March, strathspey and reel
CD LCOM 5165
Lismor / Aug '96 / ADA / Direct / Duncans / Lismor

STRATHCLYDE POLICE PIPERS, THE
CD LCOM 5201
Lismor / Jul '91 / ADA / Direct / Duncans / Lismor

Stratovarius

EPISODE
CD TT 0222
T&T / May '96 / Koch

FOURTH DIMENSION
Against the wind / Distant skies / Galaxies / Winter / Startovarious / Lord of the wasteland / 030366 / Nightfall / We hold the key / Twilight symphony / Call of the wilderness
CD TT 0142
T&T / Feb '95 / Koch

TWILIGHT TIME
CD TT 0022
T&T / '94 / Koch

VISIONS
Kiss of Judas / Black diamond / Forever free / Before the Winter / Legions / Abyss of your eyes / Holy light / Paradise / Coming home / Visions (Southern cross)
CD TT 00312
T&T / May '97 / Koch

Straume, Bjorgulv

FRA AETT TIL AETT
CD BS 96CD
BS / Nov '96 / ADA

Straus, Ste

STE REAL
Je suis prete / Met play - G mix / Yo boom / Trop dur pour un seul homme / Track cheul / Nee gangstaa / Met play - East coast mix
CD 122053
Plug It / Nov '94 / Vital

Stravaig

MOVIN' ON
Birkin tree / (Back home again in) Indiana / Song of the fishgutters / Terror time / Pressers / Dumfries hiring fair / Dundee weaver / Bonnie wee lassie's answer / My aim countrie / Miller tae ma trade / Davey fae / Bonnie lass come ower the buru / Another clearing time / Di nanina
CD CDTRAX 074
Greentrax / Jul '94 / ADA / Direct / Duncans / Highlander

Straw Dogs

COMPLETE DISCOGRAPHY, THE
CD LF 199CD
Lost & Found / Jan '96 / Plastic Head

OWN WORST NIGHTMARE
CD LF 034CD
Lost & Found / Apr '92 / Plastic Head

UNDER THE HAMMER
CD LF 030CD
Lost & Found / Apr '92 / Plastic Head

Straw, Syd

WAR AND PEACE
CD 5324572
Mercury / Oct '96 / PolyGram

Strawberry Alarm Clock

STRAWBERRIES MEAN LOVE
Incense and peppermints / Rainy day mushroom pillow / Sit with the guru / Tomorrow / Black butter - present / Love me again / Pretty song from psych out / World's on fire / Birds in my tree / Birdman of Alkatrash / Small package / They saw the fat one coming / Strawberries mean love
CD CDWIKD 56
Big Beat / Jan '92 / Pinnacle

Strawberry Story

CLAMMING FOR IT
Gone like summer / Pushbutton head / I still want you / Ashlands Road / Close my eyes / Kissamatic lovebubble / Chicken biscuit / Buttercups and daisys / Made of stone / Caroline / Twenty six / Shame about Alice / Behind this smile / Freight train / Midsummer's daydream / Tell me now
CD ASKCD 025
Vinyl Japan / Jun '93 / Plastic Head / Vinyl Japan

Strawbs

CHOICE SELECTION OF STRAWBS
Lay down / Lemon pie / Lady fuschia / Autumn / Glimpse of heaven / Hangman and the papist / New world / Round and round / I only want my love to grow in you / Benedictus / Hero and heroine / Song of a sad little girl / Tears and pavan / To be free / Part of the union / Down by the sea
CD CDMID 173
A&M / Oct '92 / PolyGram

DEEP CUTS/BURNING FOR YOU (2CD Set)
I only want my love to grow on you / Turn me around / Hard hard winter / My friend

peter / Soldier's tale / Simple visions / Charmer / (Wasting my time) thinking of you / Beside the Rio Grande / So close and yet so far away / Burning for me / Cut like a diamond / I feel your loving coming on / Barcarole (for the death of Venice) / Alexander the great / Keep on trying / Back in the old routine / Heartbreaker / Carry me home / Goodbye (is not an easy word to say)
CD Set RGFCD 027
Road Goes On Forever / Aug '96 / Direct

GREATEST HITS LIVE
CD RGFCD 015
Road Goes On Forever / Jul '95 / Direct

HALCYON DAYS (The Very Best Of The Strawbs/2CD Set)
Ghosts / On growing older / Man who called himself Jesus / Stormy down / I turned my face into the wind / Queen of dreams / Witchwood / Keep the devil outside / Hangman and the Papist / Benedictus / Golden salamander / Tokyo Rosie / Hero and heroine / Pick up the pieces / Lay down / Ciggy Barlust / Out in the cold / Round and round / Oh how she changed / Battle / Grace Darling / Blue angel / Here it comes / Shepherd's song / We'll meet again sometime / Martin Luther King's dream / Burn baby burn / Shine on silver sun / Why and wherefore / Floating in the wind / Absent friend / Part of the union / Will ye go / River / Down by the sea / Tell me what you see in me
CD Set 5406622
A&M / Feb '97 / PolyGram

HEARTBREAK HILL
CD RGFWC 024
Road Goes On Forever / Apr '95 / Direct

STRAWBS IN CONCERT, THE
CD WIN 069
Windsong / Apr '95 / Pinnacle

UNCANNED PRESERVES (2CD Set)
CD Set RGFCD 003
Road Goes On Forever / '92 / Direct

Strawhead

TIFFIN
CD DRCD 902
Dragon / '90 / ADA / Cadillac / CM / Roots / Wellard

VICTORIAN BALLADS
CD DRGNCD 941
Dragon / Mar '94 / ADA / Cadillac / CM / Roots / Wellard

Strawman

LOTTERY, THE
CD ALLIED 53
Allied / May '95 / Cargo / Greyhound / Plastic Head

Stray

ALIVE AND GIGGIN'
Leave it down to us / Fire and glass / After the storm / Take a life / Jericho / I believe it / Mr. Wind / Buying time / Running wild / All in your mind
CD MYSCD 108
Mystic / Jul '97 / Pinnacle

LIVE AT THE MARQUEE
CD MYS 104CD
Mystic / Jun '96 / Pinnacle

LOST AND FOUND (2CD Set)
CD Set SMDCD 125
Snapper / Jul '97 / Pinnacle

Stray Cats

BEST OF THE STRAY CATS, THE
Stray cat strut / Rock this town / Rebels rule / Built for speed / Little Miss Prissy / Too hip gotta go / My one desire / I won't stand in your way / C'mon everybody / Fishnet stockings / Runaway boys / (She's) Sexy & 17 / Baby blue eyes / Jeanie, Jeanie, Jeanie / You don't believe me / Ubangi stomp / Double talkin' baby / Storm the Embassy / Rumble in Brighton / Gonna ball
CD 74321446822
RCA / Jan '97 / BMG

CHOO CHOO HOT FISH
CD 9070147
Dino / May '92 / Pinnacle

CHOO CHOO HOT FISH
CD ESMCD 424
Essential / Aug '96 / BMG

ORIGINAL COOL
Somethin' else / Oh boy / Twenty-flight rock / I fought the law / Lonesome tears / Your true love / Be bop a lula / Blue jean cop / Can't help falling in love / Flying saucer rock 'n' roll / Chet ditty (hidden charms) / Trying to get to you / Let it rock / Stood up / Train kept a rollin'
CD ESMCD 395
Essential / Jul '96 / BMG

RUNAWAY BOYS (2CD Set)
Elvis on velvet / Cry baby / Please don't touch / Sleepwalk / Lust and love / Beautiful blues / Cross of love / My heart is a liar / Mystery train / Somethin' else / Twenty flight rock / I fought the law / Lonesome tears / Your true love / Bluejean bop / Can't help falling in love / Flying saucers rock 'n' roll / Stood up / Blast off / Runaway boys / Stray cat strutt / Rock this town / Sexy and seventeen / Built for speed / Look at the cadillac / Race is on / Bring it back again / Something's wrong with my radio / Double talking baby / Let's go faster / Too hip gotta go / Rumble in Brighton / Gene and Eddie / Elvis on velvet / Cry baby / Gina
CD Set SMDCD 182
Snapper / May '97 / Pinnacle

STRAY CATS ARCHIVE
Stray Cat strut / Runaway boys / Rockabilly rules OK / Built for speed / Tonight's the night / Summertime blues / Elvis on velvet / Foggy mountain breakdown / Tear it up / Bring it back again / Something's wrong with my radio / Stray Cat blues / Gene and Eddie / Fishnet stockings / Race is on / Cry baby / Gina / Too hip gotta go / I fought the law / Something else
CD RMCD 211
Rialto / Sep '96 / Disc / Total/BMG

Strayhorn, Billy

BILLY STRAYHORN PROJECT, THE
CD STCD 533
Stash / Feb '91 / ADA / Cadillac / CM / Direct / Jazz Music

LUSH LIFE
CD 4722062
Sony Jazz / Nov '92 / Sony

PEACEFUL SIDE OF BILLY STRAYHORN, THE
Lush life / Just a sittin' and a rockin' / Passion flower / Take the 'A' train / Strange feeling / Day dream / Chelsea bridge / Multi-coloured blue / Something to live for / Flower is a lovesome thing
CD CDP 8525632
Capitol Jazz / Oct '96 / EMI

Strazzeri, Frank

I REMEMBER YOU (Strazzeri, Frank Trio)
CD FSCD 123
Fresh Sound / Jan '91 / Discovery / Jazz Music

Stream

TAKE IT OR LEAVE IT
CD 342792
No Bull / Dec '95 / Koch

Street Called Straight

STREET CALLED STRAIGHT
Reconciled / All you Madonnas / Destination / Count-down to eternity / Mary's eyes / World without end / Think / Think (reprise) / Rose of Sharon / What a wonderful night / You will answer
CD FLD 9247
Frontline / Apr '92 / EMI / Jet Star

Street Troopers

TAKE THE BATTLE TO THE STREETS
CD KOCD 049
Knock Out / Apr '97 / Cargo

Streetwalkers

VICIOUS BUT FAIR...PLUS
Mama was mad / Chili con carne / Diceman / But you're beautiful / Can't come in / Belle star / Sam / Cross time woman / Downtown flyers / Gypsy moon / Crawfish / Raingame / Crazy charade / Shotgun messiah / Decadence code / Daddy rollin' stone
CD SEECD 352
See For Miles/C5 / Jun '92 / Pinnacle

Strehli, Angela

BLONDE & BLUE
CD ROUCD 3127
Rounder / Jan '94 / ADA / CM / Direct

Streisand, Barbra

BACK TO BROADWAY
Some enchanted evening / Everybody says don't / Music of the night / Speak low / As if we never said goodbye / Children will listen / I have a love / I've never been in love before / Luck be a lady / With one look / Man I love / Move on
CD 4738802
Columbia / Jun '93 / Sony

BARBRA STREISAND ALBUM, THE
Cry me a river / My honey's loving arms / I'll tell the man in the street / Taste of honey / Who's afraid of the big bad wolf / Soon it's gonna rain / Happy days are here again / Keepin' out of mischief now / Much more / Come to the supermarket / Sleepin' bee
CD 4749042
Columbia / Jan '94 / Sony

BARBRA STREISAND LIVE (2CD Set)
Overture / As if we never said goodbye / Opening remarks / I'm still here/Everybody says don't/Don't rain on my parade / Can't help lovin' dat man / I'll know / People / Lover man / Therapist dialogue 1 / Will he like me / Therapist dialogue 2 / He touched me / Evergreen / Therapist dialogue 3 / Man that got away / On a clear day (you can see forever) / Entr'acte / Way we were / You don't bring me flowers / Lazy afternoon / Disney medley / Not while I'm around / Ordinary miracles / Yentl medley / Happy days are here again / My man for all we know / Somewhere
CD Set 4775992
Columbia / Oct '94 / Sony

BROADWAY ALBUM
Putting it together / If I loved you / Something's coming / Not while I'm around / Being alive / I have dreamed / We kiss in a shadow / Something wonderful / Send in the clowns / Pretty women / Ladies who lunch / Can't help lovin' dat man / I loves you Porgy / Porgy, I's your woman now / Somewhere
CD CD 86322
CBS / Feb '86 / Sony

CHRISTMAS ALBUM
Christmas song / Jingle bells / Have yourself a merry little Christmas / White Christmas / My favourite things / Best of gifts / Silent night / Gounod's Ave Maria / O little town of Bethlehem / I wonder as I wander / Lord's prayer
CD 4605362
Columbia / Nov '96 / Sony

COLLECTION OF GREATEST HITS AND MORE, A
We're not makin' love anymore / Woman in love / All I ask of you / Comin' in and out of your life / What kind of fool / Main event/ Fight / Someone that I used to love / By the way / Guilty / Memory / Way he makes me feel / Somewhere
CD 4658452
CBS / Nov '89 / Sony

GREATEST HITS VOL.2
Evergreen / Prisoner / My heart belongs to me / Songbird / You don't bring me flowers: *Streisand, Barbra & Neil Diamond* / Way we were / Sweet inspiration / Where you lead / All in love is fair / Superman / Stoney end
CD CD 86079
CBS / '86 / Sony

GUILTY
Guilty / Woman in love / Run wild / Promises / Love inside / What kind of fool / Life story / Never give up / Make it like a memory
CD CD 86122
CBS / '83 / Sony

HIGHLIGHTS FROM JUST FOR THE RECORD
You'll never know / Sleepin' bee / Miss Marmelstein / I hate music / Nobody's heart (belongs to me) / Cry me a river / Judy Garland medley / Get happy / Happy days are here again / People / Second hand rose / My name is Barbra / Act II medley / Best things are life are free / You wanna bet / Come rain or come shine / Don Rickles (monologue) / Sweetest sounds / You're the top / What are you doing the rest of your life / Crying time / Medley / Quiet thing / There won't be trumpets / Evergreen / Between yesterday and tomorrow / You don't bring me flowers: *Streisand, Barbra & Neil Diamond* / Papa, can you hear me / I know him so well / Warm all over
CD 4716402
Columbia / Jul '92 / Sony

JUST FOR THE RECORD (4CD Set)
You'll never know / Jack Paar show / PM east, moon river / Miss Marmelstein / Happy days are here again / Bon soir, keepin' out of mischief now / I hate music / Nobody's heart (belongs to me) / Value / Cry me a river / Who's afraid of the big bad wolf / I had myself a true love / Lover come back to me / Spring can really hang you up the most / My honey's lovin' arms / Any place I hang my hat is home / When the sun comes out / Medley / Medley / I'm the greatest star / My man (mon homme) / Auld lang syne / People / Second hand rose / Medley from My Name is Barbra / Give me the simple life / Nobody knows you (when you're down and out) / Best things in life are free / He touched me / You wanna bet / House of flowers / Ding dong / Witch is dead / Too long at the fair / Look at that face / Starting here, starting now / Belle of 14th street / Good man is hard to find / Some of these days / I'm always chasing rainbows / Happening in Central Park / Silent night / Don't rain on my parade / Funny girl / Come rain or come shine / Hello Dolly / On a clear day (you can see forever) / When you gotta go / In the wee small hours of the morning / Singer / I can do it / Stoney end / Close to you / We've only just begun / Since I fell for you / What's up doc / You're the top / What are you doing the rest of your life / If I close my eyes / Between yesterday and tomorrow / Hatikvah / Can you tell the moment / Way we were / Crying time / God bless the child / Quiet thing / There won't be trumpets / Star is born / Lost inside of you / Evergreen / You don't bring me flowers / Way we were (live) / Guilty / Papa, can you hear me / Moon and I / Piece of sky / I know him so well / If I loved you / Putting it together / Voice / Over the rainbow / Theme from Nuts / Here we are at last / Back to Broadway / Warm all over
CD Set 4687342
Columbia / Oct '91 / Sony

LIVE CONCERT AT THE FORUM
Sing / Make your own kind of music / Starting here, starting now / Don't rain on my parade / Monologue / On a clear day (You can see forever) / Sweet inspiration / Where you lead / Didn't we / My man (mon homme) / Stoney end / Happy days are here again / People
CD 4879432
Columbia / Jul '97 / Sony

LOVE SONGS
Memory / You don't bring me flowers / My heart belongs to me / Wet / New York state of mind / Man I love / No more tears / Comin' in and out of your life / Evergreen / I don't break easily / Kiss me in the rain / Lost inside of you / Way we were / Love inside
CD CD 10031
CBS / Sep '84 / Sony

ON A CLEAR DAY YOU CAN SEE FOREVER
Hurry, it's lovely up here / Main title / On a clear day (you can see forever) / Love with all the trimmings / Melinda / Go to sleep / He isn't you / What did I have that I don't have / Come back to me
CD 4749072
Columbia / Jan '94 / Sony

ONE VOICE
Somewhere / Evergreen / Something's coming / People / Over the rainbow / Guilty / Papa, can you hear me / Way we were / It's a new world / Happy days are here again / America the beautiful
CD 4508912
CBS / May '87 / Sony

PEOPLE
Absent minded me / When in Rome / Fine and dandy / Suppertime / Will he like me / How does the wine taste / I'm all smiles / Autumn / My lord and master / Love is a bore / Don't like goodbyes
CD 4604982
Columbia / Oct '95 / Sony

SECOND BARBRA STREISAND ALBUM, THE
Any place I hang my hat is home / Right as the rain / Down with love / Who will buy / When the sun comes out / Gotta move / My colouring book / I don't care much / Lover come back to me / I stayed too long at the fair / Like a straw in the wind
CD 4749082
Columbia / Jan '94 / Sony

STAR IS BORN, A
Watch closely now / Queen Bee / Everything / Lost inside of you / Hellacious acres / Love theme / Woman in the moon / I believe in love / Crippled crow / With one more look at you
CD 4749052
Columbia / Jan '94 / Sony

THIRD ALBUM, THE
My melancholy baby / Just in time / Taking a chance on love / Bewitched, bothered and bewildered / Never will I marry / As time goes by / Draw me a circle / It had to be you / Make believe / I had myself a true love
CD 4749092
Columbia / Jan '94 / Sony

WHAT ABOUT TODAY
What about today / Ask yourself why / Honey pie / Punky's dilemma / Until it's time for you to go / That's a fine kind of freedom / Little tin soldier / With a little help from my friends / Alfie / Morning after / Goodnight
CD 4749012
Columbia / Jan '94 / Sony

Strength Through Joy

FORCE OF TRUTH AND LIES, THE
CD NERO 6CD
Twilight Command / Oct '96 / World Serpent

SALUTE TO LIGHT (2CD Set)
CD Set NERO 11CD
Twilight Command / Oct '96 / World Serpent

Stressball

STRESSBALL
CD IRSCD 981201
Intercord / Jan '94 / Plastic Head

Stribling, Simon

SIMON STRIBLING
CD JCD 257
Jazzology / Jul '96 / Jazz Music

Strictly Inc.

STRICTLY INC.
Don't turn your back on me / Walls of sound / Only seventeen / Serpent said / Never let me know / Charity balls / Something to live for / Piece of you / Island in the darkness / Strictly incognito
CD CDV 2790
Virgin / Sep '95 / EMI

Strife

IN THIS DEFIANCE
CD ____ **VR 054**
Victory / Apr '97 / Plastic Head

ONE TRUTH
CD ____ **VR 16CD**
Victory / Apr '95 / Plastic Head

Strike

I SAW THE FUTURE
Intro / I have peace / I saw the future / Morning after / Inspiration / Come with me / U sure do / Wrapped inside the rhythm / M y love is real / Shut it / My love is for real / No compromise / Live for today
CD ____ **FRSHCD 3**
Fresh / Jun '97 / 3mv/Sony / Mo's Music Machine / Prime

String A Longs

WHEELS
Wheels / Brass buttons / Should I / Scottie / Nearly sunrise / Sunday / My blue heaven / Mathilda / Skippin' / Mina bird / Happy melody / Panic button / Walk don't run / Summertime / Perfidia / Bulldog / Spinnin' my wheels / Red river twist / Take a minute / You don't have to go / Torquay / Harbour lights / Tell the world / Are you lonesome tonight / My babe / Heartaches / Replica
CD ____ **CDCHD 390**
Ace / Jan '93 / Pinnacle

String Driven Thing

MACHINE THAT CRIED, THE (The Band's Official Version)
Heartfeeder / To see you / Night club / Sold down the river / Two timin' rama / Travelling / People on the street / House / Machine that cried / River of sleep / If only the good / It's a game / Part of the city
CD ____ **OZITCD 0021**
Ozit / May '97 / Cargo / Direct

SUICIDE - LIVE IN BERLIN
Let me down / Nightclub / Two timin' rama / Suicide / To see you / Dreams into dust / My real hero / Circus / Park circus / You miss me / Road goes on
CD ____ **OZITCD 0018**
Ozit / May '97 / Cargo / Direct

String Quartet

WARM EVENINGS
CD ____ **CCD 4050**
Concord Jazz / Nov '89 / New Note/ Pinnacle

String Trio Of New York

AREA CODE 212
CD ____ **1200482**
Black Saint / Dec '96 / Cadillac / Harmonia Mundi

ASCENDANT
CD ____ **STCD 532**
Stash / Oct '91 / ADA / Cadillac / CM / Direct / Jazz Music

BLUES
CD ____ **1201482**
Black Saint / Sep '95 / Cadillac / Harmonia Mundi

OCTAGON
CD ____ **120131**
Black Saint / Apr '94 / Cadillac / Harmonia Mundi

REBIRTH OF A FEELING
CD ____ **1200682**
Black Saint / May '94 / Cadillac / Harmonia Mundi

Stringle, Julian

PATHFINDER
Pathfinder / Fortune green / Wendy blue / Catwalk / In sentimental mood / Samba for Liza / Paris / Softly as in a morning sunrise / Billie's bounce / Joker / Kia
CD ____ **MSPCD 9501**
Mabley St. / Apr '95 / Grapevine/PolyGram

Strings Of Paris

BALLROOM DANCE FESTIVAL
CD ____ **BMC 87117**
Beautiful Music Collection / Jun '95 / Target/BMG

PANFLUTE MEMORIES
CD ____ **BMC 87125**
Beautiful Music Collection / Jun '95 / Target/BMG

Stripling Brothers

STRIPLING BROTHERS VOL.1 1928-1934
CD ____ **DOCD 8007**
Document / Apr '97 / ADA / Hot Shot / Jazz Music

STRIPLING BROTHERS VOL.2 1934-1936
CD ____ **DOCD 8008**
Document / Apr '97 / ADA / Hot Shot / Jazz Music

Stritch, Elaine

STRITCH
Are you having any fun / You're getting to be a habit with me / That's the beginning of the end / Angels sing / Let it snow, let it snow, let it snow / That's my boy / I don't want to walk without you / Too many rings around Rosie / Object of my affection / Easy street / If / There's a lull in my life / You took avantage of me
CD ____ **DRGCD 91434**
DRG / Aug '95 / Discovery / New Note/ Pinnacle

Strobe

CIRCLE NEVER ENDS
CD ____ **BBA 11**
Big Cat / Mar '94 / 3mv/Pinnacle

Strobinell

BREIZH HUD
CD ____ **KMCD 66**
Keltia Musique / Jul '96 / ADA / Discovery

Strohm, John P.

CALEDONIA (Strohm, John P. & The Hello Strangers)
Slip away / Tangelo / Jennifer and Jean / Someone besides me / Geronimo's Cadillac / Fool / Backseat driver / Kill the lights / Freightliner / Powderkeg / Love theme / Thelma / See you around
CD ____ **FLT 106**
Flat Earth / Dec '96 / Cargo
CD ____ **FIENDCD 932**
Demon / Aug '97 / Pinnacle

Strong, Jon

FOLLOW ME
Follow me / In your dreams / Joined at the hip / Call my number / Same world / Killing fields of love / Bad news on the mountain / Diamond shine / Judas kiss / Gun metal grey
CD ____ **AKD 023**
Linn / Oct '93 / PolyGram

Strongheart

RITUAL
CD ____ **HNRCD 005**
Hengest / May '97 / Grapevine/PolyGram

Stroscio, Cesar

RIO DE LA PLATA
CD ____ **829052CD**
BUDA / Jul '95 / Discovery

Strung Out

ANOTHER DAY IN PARADISE
CD ____ **FAT 517CD**
Fatwreck Chords / Jan '97 / Plastic Head

SUBURBAN TEENAGE WASTELANDBLUES
CD ____ **FAT 537CD**
Fatwreck Chords / Jan '97 / Plastic Head

Strunz, Jorge

AMERICAS (Strunz, Jorge & Adeshir Farah)
Caracol / El jaguar / Candela / Alas del sur / Americas / Luna suave (soft moon) / Balada (for Heideh) / Gypsy earrings / Rayo / Selva
CD ____ **8122790412**
Atlantic / May '93 / Warner Music

FRONTERA (Strunz, Jorge & Adeshir Farah)
Quetzal / Zona liberada / Reng / Cassiopeia / Rio nuevo / Abrazo / Amritsar / Dervish
CD ____ **MCD 9123**
Milestone / Nov '95 / Cadillac / Complete/ Pinnacle / Jazz Music / Wellard

GUITARS (Strunz, Jorge & Adeshir Farah)
CD ____ **MCD 9136**
Milestone / Jun '95 / Cadillac / Complete/ Pinnacle / Jazz Music / Wellard

Stuart, Dan

CAN O' WORMS
CD ____ **NORMAL 189**
Normal / May '95 / ADA / Direct

RESTRONUEVO (Stuart, Dan & Al Perry)
CD ____ **NORMAL 169CD**
Normal / Aug '94 / ADA / Direct

Stuart, Marty

BUSY BEE CAFE
One more ride / Blue railroad train / I don't love nobody / Watson's blues / Busy bee cafe / Down the road / Hey porter / Boogie for Clarence / Get in line brother / Soldier's joy / Long train gone
CD ____ **SHCD 3726**
Sugar Hill / Jan '97 / ADA / CM / Direct / Koch / Roots

MARTY STUART
If it ain't got you / Whiskey ain't working / Hillibilly rock / Now that's country / Burn me down / Likes of me tempted / This one's gonna hurt you / Little things / Weight / Western girls / Don't be cruel
CD ____ **MCD 11237**
MCA / Mar '95 / BMG

THIS ONE'S GONNA HURT YOU
Me and Hank and Jumping Jack Flash / High on a mountain top / This one's gonna hurt you / Down home / Between you and me / Hey baby / Doin' my time / Now that's country / King of Dixie / Honky tonky crowd
CD ____ **MCAD 10596**
MCA / Mar '94 / BMG

Stubbert, Brenda

IN JIG TIME
CD ____ **CDTRAX 139**
Greentrax / Aug '97 / ADA / Direct / Duncans / Highlander

Stubblefield, John

MORNING SONG
Blues for the moment / King of harts / So what / Morning song / Blue moon / Night in Lisbon / Shaw of Newark / In a semtimental mood / Slick stud and sweet thang / Here and there / Here's one
CD ____ **ENJ 80362**
Enja / Feb '94 / New Note/Pinnacle / Vital/ SAM

Stubseid, Gunnar

STUBSEID AND MOLLER (Stubseid, Gunnar & Ale Moller)
CD ____ **HCD 7123**
Helio / May '97 / ADA

Stuck Mojo

PIGWALK
CD ____ **CM 77133CD**
Century Media / Sep '96 / Plastic Head

SNAPPIN' NECKS
CD ____ **CM 77088CD**
Century Media / Aug '95 / Plastic Head

VIOLATED
CD ____ **CM 77122CD**
Century Media / May '96 / Plastic Head

Studebaker John

OUTSIDE LOOKIN' IN (Studebaker John & The Hawks)
CD ____ **BPCD 75022**
Blind Pig / Jul '95 / ADA / CM / Direct / Hot Shot

TREMOLUXE (Studebaker John & The Hawks)
CD ____ **BPCD 5031**
Blind Pig / Apr '96 / ADA / CM / Direct / Hot Shot

Students Choir Utrecht

OFFICIUM TENEBRARUM
CD ____ **CDCEL 022**
Celestial Harmonies / Jul '88 / ADA / Select

Studer, Freddy

SEVEN SONGS
Sans titre / Ein blindenhund und ein / Belydance on a chessboard / Hajime / Soly sombra / I don't hear anything / SFK
CD ____ **VBR 20562**
Vera Bra / Jun '91 / New Note/Pinnacle / Pinnacle

Stunning

PARADISE IN THE PICTUREHOUSE
CD ____ **ROCD 005**
Solid / Oct '90 / Grapevine/PolyGram

Sturr, Jimmy

I LOVE TO POLKA
CD ____ **ROUCD 6067**
Rounder / Jun '95 / ADA / CM / Direct

LIVING ON POLKA TIME
CD ____ **ROUCD 6082**
Rounder / Aug '97 / ADA / CM / Direct

POLKA ALL NIGHT LONG
All night long / Swirl / Tavern in the town / Edelweiss / Alice / Krakow Bridge / Cajun fiddle / Big Ball's in Cowtown / Dizzy fingers / Green valley / My Sophie / Can't afford to be a star / Alice
CD ____ **ROUCD 6077**
Rounder / Nov '96 / ADA / CM / Direct

POLKA YOUR TROUBLES AWAY
CD ____ **ROUCD 6057**
Rounder / Oct '94 / ADA / CM / Direct

Stuve, Bill

BIG NOISE
CD ____ **TRCD 9906**
Tramp / Nov '93 / ADA / CM / Direct

Style Council

COST OF LIVING
It didn't matter / Right to go / Heavens above / Fairytales / Angel / Walking the night / Waiting / Cost of living / Woman's song
CD ____ **8314432**
Polydor / Jan '87 / PolyGram

ESSENTIAL COLLECTION, THE
Speak like a child / Headstart for happiness / Long hot Summer / Paris match / It just came to pieces in my hands / My ever changing moods / Whole point of no return / Ghosts of Dachau / You're the best thing / Big boss groove / Man of great promise / Homebreakers / Down in the Seine / Stones throw away / With everything to lose / Boy who cried wolf / Cost of loving / Changing of the guard / Why I went missing / It's a very deep sea
CD ____ **5294832**
Polydor / Feb '96 / PolyGram

HERE'S SOME THAT GOT AWAY
Love pains / Party chambers / Whole point of no return / Ghosts of dachau / Sweet loving ways / Casual affair / Woman's song / Mick's up / Waiting on a connection / Night after night / Piccadilly trail / When you call me / My very good friend / April's fool / In love for the first time / Big boss groove / Mick's company / Bloodsports / Who will buy / I ain't goin' under / I am leaving / Stone's throw away
CD ____ **5193722**
Polydor / Jun '93 / PolyGram

HOME AND ABROAD (LIVE)
My ever changing moods / Lodgers / Head start for happiness / When you call me / Whole point of no return / With everything to lose / Homebreaker / Shout to the top / Walls come tumbling down / Internationalists
CD ____ **8291432**
Polydor / Aug '86 / PolyGram

INTRODUCING THE STYLE COUNCIL
Long hot summer / Head start for happiness / Speak like a child / Long hot summer (Club mix) / Paris match / Mick's up / Money go round (Club mix)
CD ____ **8152772**
Polydor / PolyGram

OUR FAVOURITE SHOP
Homebreaker / All gone away / Come to Milton Keynes / Internationalists / Stones throw away / Stand up comics instructions / Boy who cried wolf / Man of great promise / Down in the Seine / Lodgers / Luck / With everything to lose / Our favourite shop / Walls come tumbling down / Shout to the top
CD ____ **8257002**
Polydor / Aug '90 / PolyGram

SINGULAR ADVENTURES OF THE STYLE COUNCIL, THE (Greatest Hits Vol.1)
You're the best thing / Have you ever had it blue / Money go round / My ever changing moods / Long hot summer / Lodgers / Walls come tumbling down / Shout to the top / Wanted / It didn't matter / Speak like a child / Solid bond in your heart / Life at a top peoples health farm / Promised land / How she threw it all away / Waiting / Have you ever had it blue (12" mix) / Long hot summer (12" mix)
CD ____ **8378962**
Polydor / Mar '89 / PolyGram

Styler, Glyn

LIVE AT THE MERMAID LOUNGE
CD ____ **TRUCK 03D**
Truckstop / Apr '97 / SRD

Stylistics

BEST OF THE STYLISTICS, THE
Can't give you anything (but my love) / Let's put it all together / I'm stone in love with you / You make me feel brand new / Sing baby sing / Na na is the saddest word / Sixteen bars / Star on a TV show / Funky weekend / Break up to make up / Can't help falling in love / Peek-a-boo / 7000 Dollars and you / You'll never go to heaven (if you break my heart)
CD ____ **8429362**
Mercury / May '90 / PolyGram

BEST OF THE STYLISTICS, THE
Can't give you anything (but my love) / You make me feel brand new / Let's put it all together / I'm stone in love with you / Funky weekend / You'll never get to heaven (if you break my heart) / Peek-a-boo / Stop, look, listen (to your heart) / Betcha by golly wow / Sing baby sing / Star on a TV show / Na na is the saddest word / 7000 Dollars and you / Break up to make up / Love at first sight / Only for the children / You're a big girl now / You are everything
CD ____ **5511142**
Spectrum / Mar '96 / PolyGram

SPOTLIGHT ON THE STYLISTICS
CD 8483392
Mercury / Jul '93 / PolyGram

Styx

BEST OF TIMES, THE (The Best Of Styx)
Best of times / Babe / Boat on the river / Mr. Roboto / Show me the way / Renegade / Borrowed time / Blue collar man (long nights) / AD 1928 / Rockin' the paradise / Sing for the day / Too much time on my hands / Don't let it end / Lady '95 / Little Suzie / It takes love
CD 5404652
A&M / Jul '97 / PolyGram

BOAT ON THE RIVER
CD 3969592
A&M / Mar '95 / PolyGram

PARADISE THEATRE
AD 1928 / Rockin' in paradise / Too much time on my hands / Nothing ever goes as planned / Best of times / Lonely people / She cares / Snowblind / Halfpenny, two penny / AD 1958 / State street Sadie
CD CDMID 154
A&M / Oct '92 / PolyGram

Sub Dub

DANCEHALL MALFUNCTION
CD EFA 709722
Asphodel / Jun '97 / Cargo / SRD

Sub Zero

HAPPINESS WITHOUT LOVE
CD TDH 0016
Too Damn Hype / Dec '96 / Cargo / SRD

HAPPINESS WITHOUT PEACE
CD CMCD 77157
Century Media / Mar '97 / Plastic Head

Subarachnoid Space

ALMOST INVISIBLE
CD RR 69592
Relapse / Aug '97 / Pinnacle / Plastic Head

EITHER OR
CD UC 041
Unit Circle / Jun '97 / Cargo

Subcircus

SUBCIRCUS
I want you like an accident / U love U / 20th century bitch / Shelly's on the telephone / Storm fly baby / 86'D / Gravity girl and analogue / Las zoot suit / Article 11 (early departure) / So strange
CD ECHCD 013
Echo / Sep '96 / EMI / Vital

Subdudes

ANNUNCIATION
(You'll be) satisfied / Why can't I forget about you / Angel to be / I know / Late at night / Miss Love / Poverty / Message man / Save me / Fountains flow / Cold nights / Sugar pie / It's so hard
CD 72902103232
High Street / Jun '94 / BMG

PRIMITIVE STREAK
All the time in the world / Carved in stone / Break down these walls / Why do you hurt me so / Faraway girl / Love somebody / Lonely soldier / Too soon to tell / Do me a favour / She / Don't let 'em / Sarita / Love o' love
CD 72902103442
High Street / Jun '96 / BMG

Subhumans

29-29 SPLIT VISION
CD FISH 16CD
Bluurg / Feb '92 / Shellshock/Disc

EPLP
CD FISH 14CD
Bluurg / Feb '92 / Shellshock/Disc

FROM THE CRADLE TO THE GRAVE
CD FISH 8CD
Bluurg / Feb '92 / Shellshock/Disc

PISSED OFF, WITH GOOD REASON
CD 417242
Frantic / Dec '96 / Cargo

WORLDS APART
CD FISH 12CD
Bluurg / Feb '92 / Shellshock/Disc

Subject 13

BLACK STEELE PROJECT, THE
CD SEL 20CD
Crammed Discs / Sep '97 / Grapevine/ PolyGram / New Note/Pinnacle / Prime / RTM/Disc

Submarine

KISS ME TILL YOUR EARS BURN OFF
CD FAN 1022
Fantastick / Mar '94 / SRD

SUBMARINE
CD TOPPCD 007
Ultimate / Mar '94 / Pinnacle

Submissives

ANVIL WILL WEAR OUT MANY A HAMMER, AN
CD DON 006CD
Honest Don's / Jun '97 / Greyhound / Plastic Head

Subotnick, Morton

AND THE BUTTERFLIES BEGIN TO SING
CD 805142
New World / Aug '97 / ADA / Cadillac / Harmonia Mundi

Subramaniam, Dr. L.

ELECTRIC MODES VOL.1 & 2
CD WLAES 4CD
Waterlilly Acoustics / Nov '95 / ADA

KALYANI
CD WLAES 19CD
Waterlilly Acoustics / Nov '95 / ADA

PACIFIC RENDEZVOUS
CD CDMANU 1508
Manu / Mar '96 / ADA / Discovery

RAGA DHARMAVATI
Ragam and Tanam / Pallavi and tabla solo / Ragamalika
CD RMSCD 106
Ravi Shankar Music Circle / May '94 / Conifer/BMG

RAGA HEMEVATI
CD NI 5227
Nimbus / Sep '94 / Nimbus

SARASVATI
CD WLAES 24CD
Waterlilly Acoustics / Nov '95 / ADA

THREE RAGAS FOR SOLO VIOLIN
CD NI 5323
Nimbus / Sep '94 / Nimbus

Subramanium, Karaikudi

MASTERS OF RAGA
CD SM 16082
Wergo / Sep '95 / ADA / Cadillac / Harmonia Mundi

SUNADA (Subramaniam, Karaikudi & Trichy Sankaran)
Sarasasamadana / Varanarada / Ramachandra bhavayami / Nidu charanamule: Ragam / Nidu charanamule: Tanam and kriti / Tiruppugar: Iyal Isaiyum / Mayatita svarupini
CD CDT 127
Topic / Apr '93 / ADA / CM / Direct

Subsurfing

FROZEN ANTS
Number readers / Face with corn / Frozen ants / Sleepless snake / Angel fish / She swims above the horizon / HSJ
CD AMB 5941CD
Apollo / Apr '95 / Vital

Subterfuge

SYNTHETIC DREAM
Last dimension / Pain everlasting / Enchantress / Unconscious world / Ninety seconds of homelessness / Shadows of reality / City / Journey to eternity / Liquid eternity / Cosmopolis / Death of love
CD PRIME 013CD
Prime / Nov '93 / Pinnacle / Vital

Subtle Plague

IMPLOSION
CD NORM 159CD
Normal / Mar '94 / ADA / Direct

Subtropic

HOMEBREW
CD REFCD 6
Subtropic / Dec '95 / RTM/Disc

Suburban Studs

COMPLETE STUDS COLLECTION
Suburban stud / Dissatisfied / Rumble / Resistor / I hate school / My generation / Traffic jam / Revenge / Questions / Necro / Razor blades / Two victims / Young power / Panda control / Bondage / Throbbing lust / No faith / Snipper / Hit and run / I hate school (live) / Sinkin down / Hudini charms / Savier of love / White light / All that jazz / Supernatural / Questions (sax version) / No faith (sax version)
CD CDPUNK 21
Anagram / Oct '93 / Cargo / Pinnacle

Subvert

SUBVERT
CD SFLS 282
Selfless / Dec '94 / SRD

Subway Sect

WE OPPOSE ALL ROCK 'N' ROLL
Nobody's scared / Don't split it / Parallel lines / Chain smoking / Rock 'n' roll even / Ambition / Double negative / Head held high / Stool pigeon / Watching the devil / Spring is grey / Stop that girl / Exit no return / Staying out of view / Parallel lines
CD OVER 53CD
Overground / Dec '96 / Shellshock/Disc / SRD

Success-n-Effect

BACK-N-EFFECT
Angel dust / Blueprint / Robo's housin' / Seven Gs I'll flow / Slick the slick / Real deal (Holyfield) / Mack of the year / Jump 2 it (house from the South) / Slow flow / So many faces / Nuthin' but success / 360
CD ICH 1108CD
Ichiban / Oct '93 / Direct / Koch

Succulent Blue Sway

SOUNDTRACK
CD DOROBO 006CD
Dorobo / Oct '95 / Plastic Head

Suchas

LOW LEVEL THERAPY
CD CDVEST 47
Bulletproof / Apr '95 / Pinnacle

Suck Pretty

3 HEADS
CD KFWCD 181
Knitting Factory / Oct '96 / Cargo / Plastic Head

Suckspeed

UNKNOWN GENDER
CD WB 10992CD
We Bite / Aug '93 / Plastic Head

Sudden, Nikki

7 LIVES LATER
CD GRCD 403
Glitterhouse / May '97 / Avid/BMG

BACK TO THE COAST
CD CRECD 083
Creation / May '94 / 3mv/Vital

DEAD MEN TELL NO TALES
When I cross the line / Before I leave you / Dog latin / Wooden leg / Dog rose / How many lies / Cup full of change / Kiss at dawn
CD CRECD 016
Creation / Feb '91 / 3mv/Vital

DEAD MEN TELL NO TALES/TEXAS (Sudden, Nikki & The Jacobites)
CD CRECD 018
Creation / Feb '91 / 3mv/Vital

GROOVE CREATION (Sudden, Nikki & The French Revolution)
CD CRECD 041
Creation / Apr '89 / 3mv/Vital

JEWEL THIEF
CD UFO 004CD
UFO / Oct '91 / Pinnacle

KISS YOU KIDNAPPED CHARABANC (Sudden, Nikki & Roland S. Howard)
Wedding hotel / Rebel grave / Sob story / Snowplough / Quick thing / Feather beds / French revolution blues / Crossroads / Don't explain / Hello wolf (little baby) / Better blood / Debutante blues / Girl without a name / Wedding hotel (The Moose)
CD CRECD 022
Creation / Nov '90 / 3mv/Vital

Suddenly Tammy

TAMMY
CD 9362455242
Warner Bros. / May '94 / Warner Music

WE GET THERE WHEN WE DO
Stacey's trip / Plant me / Way up / Pretty back / Bebee / No respect girl / Can't decide / Disease / Lamp / How me / Instrumental / Fearless / Ryan / Mount Rushmore
CD 9362458312
Warner Bros. / Mar '95 / Warner Music

Sudhalter, Dick

AFTER AWHILE
Dream a little dream of me / People will say we're in love / Tea for two / Blue room / My heart stood still / Love nest / Rose of Washington Square / After awhile
CD CHR 70014
Challenge / May '96 / ADA / Direct / Jazz Music / Wellard

FRIENDS WITH PLEASURE
CD ACD 159
Audiophile / Mar '95 / Jazz Music

Suede

COMING UP
Trash / Filmstar / Lazy / By the sea / She / Beautiful ones / Starcrazy / Picnic by the motorway / Chemistry between us / Saturday night
CD NUDE 6CD
Nude / Sep '96 / 3mv/Vital

DOG MAN STAR
Introducing the band / We are the pigs / Heroine / Wild ones / Daddy's speeding / Power / New generation / This Hollywood life / Two of us / Black or blue / Asphalt world / Still life
CD NUDE 3CD
Nude / Oct '94 / 3mv/Vital

INTERVIEW DISC
CD SAM 7031
Sound & Media / Mar '97 / Sound & Media

SUEDE
So young / Animal nitrate / She's not dead / Moving / Pantomine horse / Drowners / Sleeping pills / Breakdown / Metal Mickey / Animal lover / Next life
CD NUDE 1CD
Nude / Mar '93 / 3mv/Vital

Suesse, Diana

KEYBOARD WIZARDS OF THE GERSHWIN ERA VOL.2
CD GEMMCD 9202
Pearl / Dec '95 / Harmonia Mundi

Suffer

GLOBAL WARMING
CD NPR 002CD
Napalm / Mar '94 / RTM/Disc

Suffocation

BREEDING THE SPAWN
Beginning of sorrow / Breeding the spawn / Epitaph of the credulous / Marital decimation / Prelude to repulsion / Anomalistic offerings / Ornaments of decrepancy / Ignorant deprivation
CD RR 91132
Roadrunner / Mar '93 / PolyGram

HUMAN WASTE
CD NB 051CD
Nuclear Blast / Jul '91 / Plastic Head

Sufi

LIFE'S RISING
Bluesunslide / Lover / Into the blue / Chrysalids / Desert flower / From slow syrup silence rise time tilted glances / Lostaday / Still pool reflects a clear moon / Beloved / Soon
CD AMBT 9
Virgin / Jun '95 / EMI

LOVERS AND TRIPPERS
CD AGENT 4CD
Secret Agent / Jun '97 / SRD

Sufit, Alisha

ALISHA THROUGH THE LOOKING GLASS
CD SUFIT 010
Magic Carpet / Oct '96 / Greyhound

LOVE AND THE MAIDEN
CD MC 1002CD
Magic Carpet / Oct '96 / Greyhound

Sugar

BEASTER
Come around / Tilted / Judas cradle / JC auto / Feeling better / Walking away
CD CRECD 153
Creation / Apr '93 / 3mv/Vital

COPPER BLUE
Act we act / Good idea / Changes / Helpless / Hoover dam / Slim / If I can't change your mind / Fortune teller / Slick / Man on the moon
CD CRECD 129
Creation / Jul '92 / 3mv/Vital

FILE UNDER EASY LISTENING
Gift / Company book / Your favorite thing / What you want it to be / Gee Angel / Panama city motel / Can't help you anymore / Granny cool / Believe what you're saying / Explode and make up
CD CRECD 172
Creation / Sep '94 / 3mv/Vital

Sugar Blue

BLUE BLAZES
CD RRCD 901301
Ruf / Dec '94 / Pinnacle

FROM PARIS TO CHICAGO
CD 157562
Blues Collection / Feb '93 / Discovery

IN YOUR EYES
CD TRIP 7711
Ruf / Oct '95 / Pinnacle

Sugar Loaf Express

SUGAR LOAF EXPRESS (Sugar Loaf Express & Lee Ritenour)
Sugar loaf express / Morning glory / That's the way of the world / Slippin' in the back door / Tomorrow / Lady soul

FONDATION MAEGHT NIGHTS (Sun Ra & His Arkestra)
CD _______________ COD 006
Jazz View / Mar '92 / Harmonia Mundi

HOLIDAY FOR SOUL DANCE
CD _______________ ECD 220112
Evidence / May '92 / ADA / Cadillac / Harmonia Mundi

JAZZ IN SILHOUETTE
CD _______________ ECD 220122
Evidence / May '92 / ADA / Cadillac / Harmonia Mundi

LIVE AT THE HACKNEY EMPIRE (Sun Ra & The Year 2000 Myth Science Arkestra)
CD _______________ CDLR 214/5
Leo / Feb '95 / Cadillac / Impetus / Wellard

LIVE FROM SOUNDSCAPE (Sun Ra & His Arkestra)
CD _______________ DIW 388
DIW / Feb '94 / Cadillac / Harmonia Mundi

LIVE FROM SOUNDSCAPE/POSSIBILITY OF ALTERED DESTINY (Sun Ra & His Arkestra)
CD Set _______________ DIW 388/2
DIW / Feb '94 / Cadillac / Harmonia Mundi

LIVE IN LONDON
CD _______________ BFFP 60CD
Blast First / May '96 / RTM/Disc

LOVE IN OUTER SPACE (Sun Ra & His Arkestra)
CD _______________ CDLR 154
Leo / Sep '88 / Cadillac / Impetus / Wellard

MAGIC CITY, THE
Magic city / Shadow world / Abstract eye / Abstract 'I'
CD _______________ ECD 220692
Evidence / Nov '93 / ADA / Cadillac / Harmonia Mundi

MONORAILS AND SATELLITES
CD _______________ ECD 220132
Evidence / May '92 / ADA / Cadillac / Harmonia Mundi

MY BROTHER THE WIND VOL.2
CD _______________ ECD 220402
Evidence / Nov '92 / ADA / Cadillac / Harmonia Mundi

NIGHT IN EAST BERLIN, A (Sun Ra & His Cosmo Discipline Arkestra)
CD _______________ CDLR 149
Leo / Sep '87 / Cadillac / Impetus / Wellard

OTHER PLANES OF THERE
CD _______________ ECD 220372
Evidence / Nov '92 / ADA / Cadillac / Harmonia Mundi

OUT THERE A MINUTE
CD _______________ BFFP 42CD
Blast First / Mar '89 / RTM/Disc

PURPLE NIGHT
Journey towards stars / Friendly galaxy / Love in outer space / Stars fell on Alabama / Of invisible them / Neverness / Purple night blues
CD _______________ 3953242
A&M / Sep '90 / PolyGram

QUIET PLACE IN THE UNIVERSE, A
CD _______________ CDLR 198
Leo / Oct '94 / Cadillac / Impetus / Wellard

SECOND STAR TO THE RIGHT (Salute To Walt Disney)
CD _______________ CDLR 230
Leo / Oct '95 / Cadillac / Impetus / Wellard

SINGLES, THE (2CD Set)
Foggy day / Daddy's gonna tell you no lie / Bye bye / Somebody's in love / Medicine for a nightmare / Saturn / Dreaming / Supersonic jazz / Happy New Year to you / It's Christmas time / Muck muck (matt matt) / Hot skillet Mama / Great balls of fire / Hours after / Teenager's letter of promises / I'm so glad you love me / Sun one / Sun man speaks / October / Adventure in space / Message to Earthman / State Street / Blue set / Big city blues / Tell her to come on home / I'm making believe / Bridge / Rocket no.9 / Blues on planet Mars / Saturn moon / Sky is crying / She's my baby / I'm gonna unmask the batman / I want an easy woman / Perfect man / Journey to Saturn / Enlightenment / Love in outer space / Disco 2100 / Sky blues / Rough house blues / Cosmo extensions / Quest / Outer space plateau
CD Set _______________ ECD 221642
Evidence / Oct '96 / ADA / Cadillac / Harmonia Mundi

SOLO PIANO VOL.1
CD _______________ 1238502
IAI / Nov '92 / Cadillac / Harmonia Mundi

SOUND OF JOY (Sun Ra & His Arkestra)
CD _______________ DD 414
Delmark / Dec '94 / ADA / Cadillac / CM / Direct / Hot Shot

SOUND SUN PLEASURE
CD _______________ ECD 220142
Evidence / May '92 / ADA / Cadillac / Harmonia Mundi

SPACE IS THE PLACE
It's after the end of the world / Under different stars / Discipline / Watusa / Calling planet earth / I am the alter-destiny / Satelites are spinning / Cosmic forces / Outer spaceways incorporated / We travel the spaceways / Overseer / Blackman/Love in outer space / Mysterious crystal / I am the brother of the wind / We'll wait for you / Space is the place
CD _______________ ECD 220702
Evidence / Nov '93 / ADA / Cadillac / Harmonia Mundi

SPACEWAYS INCORPORATED
CD _______________ BLCD 760191
Black Lion / Feb '94 / Cadillac / Jazz Music / Koch / Wellard

ST. LOUIS BLUES
CD _______________ 1238582
IAI / Nov '93 / Cadillac / Harmonia Mundi

STARDUST FROM TOMORROW (2CD Set) (Sun Ra & His Intergalaxtic Arkestra)
CD Set _______________ CDLR 235/236
Leo / May '97 / Cadillac / Impetus / Wellard

SUN RA SEXTET AT THE VILLAGE VANGUARD
CD _______________ ROUCD 3124
Rounder / Jan '94 / ADA / CM / Direct

SUN SONG
CD _______________ DD 411
Delmark / '84 / ADA / Cadillac / CM / Direct / Hot Shot

SUNRISE IN DIFFERENT DIMENSIONS
CD _______________ ARTCD 6099
Hat Art / Dec '91 / Cadillac / Harmonia Mundi

SUPER SONIC JAZZ (3CD Set)
CD _______________ ECD 220152
Evidence / May '92 / ADA / Cadillac / Harmonia Mundi

VISITS PLANET EARTH/INTERSTELLAR LOW WAYS
CD _______________ ECD 220392
Evidence / Nov '92 / ADA / Cadillac / Harmonia Mundi

WE TRAVEL THE SPACE WAYS/BAD AND BEAUTIFUL
CD _______________ ECD 220382
Evidence / Nov '92 / ADA / Cadillac / Harmonia Mundi

Sun Rhythm Section

OLD TIME ROCK 'N' ROLL
Old time rock 'n' roll / Red hot / That's alright mama / Let it roll / Still rockin' / Don't send me no more drinks / You're a heartbreaker / Tutti frutti / Love my baby
CD _______________ CDMF 073
Magnum Force / Oct '89 / TKO Magnum

PIONEERS OF ROCK'N'ROLL
Pioneers of rock and roll / I'm so lonely / My love to remember / Hold you close / Greenback dollar / Rockabilly I back / Comin' back to Memphis / Boogie woogie rock 'n' roll / You're the reason / If I could write you a song / Jeannie Jeannie Jeannie / Ooh wee / Bye bye
CD _______________ CDMF 085
Magnum Force / Dec '92 / TKO Magnum

Sunamoto, Chiho

MAMBO JAMBO
CD _______________ CDGRS 1248
Grosvenor / Feb '93 / Grosvenor

NIGHT AND DAY
CD _______________ CDGRS 1271
Grosvenor / Feb '95 / Grosvenor

TUXEDO JUNCTION
CD _______________ CDGRS 1233
Grosvenor / Feb '93 / Grosvenor

WHAT'S NEW
Work song / When you wish upon a star / I'm beginning to see the light / What's new / One o'clock jump / Spring fairies / Colours of the wind / Do you know the way to San Jose / Speak low / Merry Christmas Mr. Lawrence / Alfie / Hard to say I'm sorry / Romeo and Juliet fantasy overture / Adagio / Warsaw concerto / Rhapsody on a theme by Paganini
CD _______________ CDGRS 1296
Grosvenor / May '97 / Grosvenor

Sunbeam

OUT OF REALITY
CD _______________ CLP 9916
Hypnotic / Mar '97 / Cargo / SRD

Sunbrain

GOOD SIDE
CD _______________ GROW 0142
Grass / Jun '94 / Pinnacle / SRD

Sunda

MUSIQUE ET CHANTS CLASSIQUE (Music From Java)
CD _______________ C 580064
Ocora / Dec '95 / ADA / Harmonia Mundi

Sunda Africa

NO RISK NO FUN
Tanpa rintangan tak ada kegembiran / Tarian bidadari / Pengembara orang jipsi / Perjalanan ke India / Semua bersama-sama / Mengenang ilham leluhur / Rahasia rembulan / Raja / Khayalan yang tak dikenal / Sweet pain of sadness
CD _______________ CDORBD 095
Globestyle / Apr '97 / Pinnacle

Sunday Club

UNDERGROUND CINEMA
CD _______________ FIREMCD 49
Fire / Jul '95 / Pinnacle / RTM/Disc

Sundays

BLIND
I feel / Goodbye / Life and soul / More / On earth / God made me / Love / What do you think / Twenty four hours / Blood on my hands / Medicine
CD _______________ CDPCSD 121
Parlophone / Feb '94 / EMI

READING, WRITING AND ARITHMETIC
Skin and bones / Here's where the story ends / Can't be sure / I won / Hideous towns / You're not the only one I know / Certain someone / I kicked a boy / My finest hour / Joy
CD _______________ CDPCS 7378
Parlophone / May '96 / EMI

Sunderland AFC

ROKER ROAR (A Tribute To Sunderland AFC & Supporters) (Various Artists)
Sunderland all the way: *Sunderland & Bobby Knoxall* / Gannin't Roker Park: *Ronnie Roker & The Black Cats* / Ticket fro the game: *Northeast* / Sunderland: *Fine Art* / Super Sunderland: *New City Sound* / Z Cars: *Rawlings, Brian Band* / Roker roar: *Hulme, Lloyd & The Supporters Squad* / Charley Hurley speaks: *Hurley, Charley* / Daydream believer: *Simply Red & White* / Ain't no stopping us now: *Sunderland AFC FA Cup Final Squad 1992* / Sunderland forever: *Universal* / Why can't you stay: *Shak Mad* / Dicky Ord song: *Simply Red & White* / We're the lads: *SR6* / Last roar at Roker: *ALS* / Twelve days of Sunderland: *Red & White Santas* / I left my heart in Roker Park: *Alfie*
CD _______________ CDGAFFER 18
Cherry Red / Jul '97 / Pinnacle

Sundial

ACID YANTRA
CD _______________ BBQCD 173
Sundial / Jun '95 / RTM/Disc

LIBERTINE
CD _______________ BBQCD 138
Beggars Banquet / Jun '93 / RTM/Disc / Warner Music

OTHER WAY OUT
CD _______________ UFO 1CD
UFO / Apr '91 / Pinnacle

OTHER WAY OUT
CD _______________ GAAS 2502
Clear Spot / Feb '97 / Cargo / SRD

REFLECTOR
CD _______________ UFO 008CD
UFO / Mar '92 / Pinnacle

RETURN JOURNEY
CD _______________ GAAS 2503
Clear Spot / Feb '97 / Cargo / SRD

Sundogs

TO THE BONE
CD _______________ ROUCD 9044
Rounder / Apr '94 / ADA / CM / Direct

Sundown

DESIGN 19
CD _______________ CMCD 77161
Century Media / Jun '97 / Plastic Head

Sundowners

BUSH TRACKS
CD _______________ 8145742
Fable / Mar '96 / Fable

Sunkings

HALL OF HEADS
CD _______________ GPRCD 7
GPR / Aug '94 / 3mv/Vital

Sunny

COUNTRY PASSION
When love finds you / Power of love / How am I supposed to live without you / I'm still dancin' with you / Don't let love slip by / Little bit more / It's a heartache / Only one road / You cheated / Help me make it through the night / I've got to stay away from you / When I need you / Mention of your name / I want you completely / Love hurts / Why did I fall in love with you / Everything I do (I do it for you)
CD _______________ QED 173
Tring / Nov '96 / Tring

Sunny Day Real Estate

DIARY
CD _______________ SPCD 121302
Sub Pop / May '94 / Cargo / Greyhound / Shellshock/Disc

SUNNY DAY REAL ESTATE
CD _______________ SPCD 316
Sub Pop / Nov '95 / Cargo / Greyhound / Shellshock/Disc

Sunnyland Blues Band

MEAN DOG
Run for cover / Big easy woman / Fall to pieces / Time to think gain / Carry me / Helpless / Can't fight what you can't see / Move along / Pull me under / Dust my broom / Little by little / Bang for the buck / Little eden
CD _______________ INAK 9044
In Akustik / Jul '97 / Direct / TKO Magnum

Sunnyland Slim

CHICAGO JUMP (Sunnyland Slim Blues Band)
You used to love me / Halsted Street jump / Cryin' for my baby / Give you all my money / Calling out / I feel so bad / Got to stop this mess / From afar / Never picked no cotton / Chicago jump / Jammin' with Sam
CD _______________ ECD 26067
Evidence / Jul '95 / ADA / Cadillac / Harmonia Mundi

DECORATION DAY (Sunnyland Slim Blues Band)
Sun is going down / Past life / Decoration day / Boogie 'n' the blues / Depression blues / Tired of travelling / Canadian walk / Patience like Job / Sunnyland jump / Rock little Daddy / Every time I get to drinking / Sunnyland's New Orleans boogie / One room country shack / Tin pan alley / Dust my broom
CD _______________ ECD 260532
Evidence / Sep '94 / ADA / Cadillac / Harmonia Mundi

HOUSE RENT PARTY
I'm just a lonesome man / Sad old Sunday (Mother's Day) / Boogie man / Hard time (when Mother's gone) / Chicago woman / I'm in love / Bad times (cost of living) / Nervous breakdown / It keeps rainin' / Brown skin woman / Old age has got me / That's alright Mama / Sad old Sunday / I'm just a lonesome man / Bad times
CD _______________ DD 655
Delmark / Mar '97 / ADA / Cadillac / CM / Direct / Hot Shot

SUNNYLAND TRAIN
Sunnyland train / Be my baby / Sometime I worry / Decoration day / All my life / Tin pan alley / Unlucky one / Pinetop's boogie woogie / Worried about my baby / Highway 61 / Backwater blues / Sad and lonesome / She used to love me / Sittin' here thinkin' / I feel so good / Patience like Job / Goin' down slow
CD _______________ ECD 26066
Evidence / Jul '95 / ADA / Cadillac / Harmonia Mundi

Suns Of Arqa

ALAP JOE JHALA
CD _______________ ARKA 2102CD
Arka Sound / Feb '92 / Vital

ANIMAN
CD _______________ ARKA 2110CD
Arka Sound / Mar '97 / Vital

ARQAOLOGY
CD _______________ ARKA 2105CD
Arka Sound / Jun '92 / Vital

CRADLE
CD _______________ CDEASM 004
Earthsounds / Aug '93 / Earthsounds

JAGGERNAUT WHIRLING DUB
Bilawal / Yaman kalyan / Misra pahvadi / Bhairavi / Bhupali
CD _______________ ARKA 2103CD
Arka Sound / Nov '94 / Vital

KOKOROMOGHI
CD _______________ ARKA 2104CD
Arka Sound / Jan '95 / Vital

LAND OF A THOUSAND CHURCHES
Truth lies / Govinda go / Open the door to your heart / La pucelle d'Orleans / Kalilotalove / Heavenly bodies / Govinda's house / Kyrie / Paradisum in dub / Give love / Truth lies there in / Libera me / Ark of the arquans / In paradisum / Sisters of wyrd / Govinda (I wait each day) / Les anciens mystiques / Erasmus meets the earthling / Deep journey
CD _______________ ARKA 2101CD
Arka Sound / Apr '93 / Vital

LIVE WITH PRINCE FAR-I
Hey Jagunath / Bhoopali / Steppin' to the music / Throw away your guns / Brujo magic / 83 struggle / Transcedance music / Foggy road / What you gonna do / No song for Allah / Shamanism skank / Nah myoho renge kyo / Thunder bolt dark void
CD ARKA 2100CD
Arka Sound / Mar '94 / Vital

SHABDA
Tomorrow never knows / There is no danger here / Bharavi alap / Through the gate we go / Bharavi live / Pure reality / Great invocation / Basant alap / Basant dhrupad / Beyond the beyond / Great unique / Waterloo / Fire of life / Hear the call
CD ARKA 2109CD
Arka Sound / Sep '95 / Vital

TOTAL ECLIPSE OF THE SUNS REMIXES 1979-1995
Durga dub / Juggernaut / Gavati / Govinda's dream / Beyond the beyond / Inca man / Tabla school / Acid tabla / Sully's reel
CD ARKA 2108CD
Arka Sound / Oct '95 / Vital

Sunscreem

03
Portal / Pressure / B / Doved up / Love u more / Perfect motion / Chasing dreams / Your hands / Idaho / Walk on / Broken English / Release me / Psycho
CD 4722182
Sony Soho2 / Sep '96 / Sony

CHANGE OR DIE
Exodus / Ice screems / Something / When / Syclick / For maddened prophets / Looking at you / No angel / Secrets / Cheng cheng / White skies / Be of good heart
CD 4813132
Sony Soho2 / Mar '96 / Sony

Sunset Dance Orchestra

DANCING YEARS PART 1, THE
Blue skies / I'm putting all my eggs in one basket / Dancing cheek to cheek / Chinatown, my chinatown / Bells of Saint Mary's / They can't take that away from me / After you've gone / White Christmas / Home on the range / Way you look tonight / Pretty baby / Pennies from heaven / Carolina in the morning / My mammy / Swingin' on a star / Pick yourself up / Let's face the music and dance / Anniversary song
CD WRCD 5003
WRD / Nov '95 / Target/BMG

DANCING YEARS PART 2, THE
Sunshine cake / Top hat, white tie and tails / I'm sittin' on top of the world / Toot toot tootsie goodbye / Moonlight becomes you / Smoke gets in your eyes / Swanee / Where the blue of the night meets the cold of the day / Fine romance / Back in your own back yard / Don't fence me in / Baby face / Wrap your troubles in dreams / Isn't this a lovely day (to be caught in the rain) / Continental / Sonny boy / Night and day / In the cool, cool, cool of the evening
CD WRCD 5004
WRD / Nov '95 / Target/BMG

Sunset Heights

TEXAX TEA
CD KGBCD 1
KGB / Oct '94 / Total/BMG

Sunset Stampede

SUNSET STAMPEDE
CD WWRCD 6003
Wienerworld / Jun '95 / THE

Sunset Yellow

AFTER SUNSET
CD CLP 9939
Hypnotic / Mar '97 / Cargo / SRD

Sunshine Kids

TUBED
CD VOW 054CD
Voices Of Wonder / Feb '96 / Plastic Head

Sunshine, Monty

GOTTA TRAVEL ON
You tell me your dream / Pretty baby / Sleep my little Prince / Down in Honky Tonk Town / Goin' home / Martha / Sheikh of Araby / Careless love / Wise guy / Pallet on the floor / Gotta travel on / Burgundy St. Blues / Joe Avery's blues
CD CDTTD 570
Timeless Traditional / Nov '91 / Jazz Music / New Note/Pinnacle

IN LONDON
CD BLCD 760508
Black Lion / Oct '93 / Cadillac / Jazz Music / Koch / Wellard

JUST A CLOSER WALK WITH THEE
CD CDTTD 592
Timeless Traditional / Aug '95 / Jazz Music / New Note/Pinnacle

JUST A LITTLE WHILE TO STAY HERE (Sunshine, Monty Jazz Band)
Just a little while to stay here / Postman's lament / South / Old stag-o-lee blues / Ole Miss rag / My old Kentucky home / Jambalaya / Lily of the valley / You always hurt the one you love / Ma, he's making eyes at me / When I move to the sky / Corinne Corinna / Black cat on a fence / There's yes yes in your eyes
CD LACD 70
Lake / Oct '96 / ADA / Cadillac / Direct / Jazz Music / Target/BMG

NEW ORLEANS HULA (Great British Traditional Jazzband Vol.3) (Sunshine, Monty Jazz Band)
CD LACD 47
Lake / May '95 / ADA / Cadillac / Direct / Jazz Music / Target/BMG

SOUTH (Sunshine, Monty Jazz Band)
It's tight like that / Memphis blues / Ice cream / Wabash blues / All the girls / South / Bill Bailey, won't you please come home / Bugle boy march / Ups and downs / Carry me back to old virginity / If I ever cease to love / Isle of Capri / When I grow too old to dream
CD CDTTD 583
Timeless Traditional / Jun '94 / Jazz Music / New Note/Pinnacle

Sunship

SUNSHIP
CD FILT 017CD
Filter / Apr '97 / Pinnacle / Prime / RTM/Disc

Sunshot

CAUGHT IN THE ACT OF ENJOYING OURSELVES
Nasties / She says / Big mistake / Stop me / Baby doll / Happy ever after / Play time / Twisting / Lose my grip / Brainstorm / Tank
CD DVAC 005 CD
Deva / Sep '92 / Vital

IRON BALL DIRECTION
Nasties / Baby doll / Kill or be killed / Big mistake / Tank / She says / Lose my grip / Sally's ladders / Play time / Happy ever after
CD DVAC 007
NMC / Jun '93 / Total/Pinnacle

Sunt

TWEEZ
CD TG 138D
Touch & Go / May '93 / SRD

Suonsaari, Klaus

REFLECTING TIMES (Suonsaari, Klaus Quintet)
CD STCD 4125
Storyville / Feb '89 / Cadillac / Jazz Music / Wellard

Supahead

CAULK
CD TOODAMNHY 42
Too Damn Hype / Feb '95 / Cargo / SRD

Super 5 Thor

FORD
CD ECHO 101
Echo Static / Apr '97 / Cargo

GAZELLE
CD ECHO 103
Echo Static / Jun '97 / Cargo

Super Cat

DON DADA
It fe done: *Super Cat & Josie Wales* / Ghetto red hot / Them no care / Dolly my baby / Don't test / Must be bright / Don dada / Think me come fi play / Big and ready / Coke Don / Nuff man a dead / Oh it's you / Fight fi power / Yush talk
CD 4715702
Columbia / Aug '92 / Sony

SI BOOPS DEH
CD WRCD 0021
Techniques / Nov '95 / Jet Star

STRUGGLE CONTINUES, THE
Dance / Girlstown / Turn / Warning / Forgive me Jah / My girl Josephine / 'A' Class rub-a-dub / Too greedy / South central / Ready back / Every nigger is a star / Settlement / I hear dem seh
CD 4772922
Columbia / Oct '95 / Sony

Super Deluxe

FAMOUS
Lizadrin / Famous / She came on / Love her madly / Flustered / Disappearing / Johnny's gone fishing / Holly's dream vacation / Smile / Suitcases / Sunshine for now
CD LUXCD 003
Luminous / Sep '96 / Vital

Super Discount

SUPER DISCOUNT (The Album) (Various Artists)
Le patron est devenu fou: *Minos Pour Main Basse (Sur La Ville)* / Prix choc: *De Crecy, Etienne* / Super disco: *Gopher, Alex* / Soldissimo: *Air* / Affaires a faire: *La Chatte Rouge* / Tout doit disparaitre: *Minos Pour Main Basse (Sur La Ville)* / Tout a 10 balles: *DJ Tall* / Liquidation totale: *De Crecy, Etienne* / Les 10 jours fous: *Mooloodjee* / Destoskage massif: *Gopher, Alex* / Fermeture definitive: *Mr. Learn*
CD DIF 002CD
Different / Mar '97 / PolyGram

Super Furry Animals

FUZZY LOGIC
God show me magic / Fuzzy birds / Something for the weekend / Frisbee / Hometown unicorn / Gathering moss / If you don't want me to destroy you / Bad behaviour / Mario man / Hangin' with Howard Marks / Long gone / For now and ever
CD CRECD 190
Creation / May '96 / 3mv/Vital

Super Rail Band

MANSA
Silanide / Mansa / Kamalimba / Niamatoutou kono / Tolonte sebessa / Dounia / Kanou sale / Fourou kilon
CD LBLC 2520
Indigo / May '96 / New Note/Pinnacle

NEW DIMENSIONS IN RAIL CULTURE (Super Rail Band of the Buffet de la Gare de Bamako, Mali)
Foliba / Bedianamogo / Tallassa / Konowale / Mali yo
CD CDORB 001
Globestyle / Jul '90 / Pinnacle

Super Star

GREATEST HITS VOL.1
CD CRECD 134
Creation / Jun '92 / 3mv/Vital

Superalmendrado

GOTTA GIVE IT UP
CD DEDD 003CD
Dedicated / Feb '95 / BMG / Vital

Supercharger

GOES WAY OUT
CD ES 127CD
Estrus / Jun '96 / Cargo / Greyhound / Plastic Head

WALL TO WALL MOUSTACHE
Supercharger / We rock / Jim'll fix it / Boomer / Spacemaker deluxe / Airport '77 / Bouffant idiots / Return of the red eye / Filters / Wall to wall
CD ZEN 012CD
Indochina / Jul '97 / Pinnacle

Superchunk

ALBUM
CD EFA 049662
City Slang / Oct '95 / RTM/Disc

FOOLISH
CD EFA 049382
City Slang / Apr '94 / RTM/Disc

INCIDENTAL MUSIC 1991-1995
CD EFA 049592
City Slang / Jul '95 / RTM/Disc

ON THE MOUTH
CD EFA 04915262
City Slang / Jan '93 / RTM/Disc

Superconductor

HIT SONGS FOR GIRLS
Scootin' / There goes Helen / For Kelly Freas / Nobody's cutie / Thorsen's eleven / Come on hot dog / E-Z bake oven / Lordy / I'm gonna knock your block off allstar / Feedbackin'
CD TUP 0482
Tupelo / Aug '93 / RTM/Disc

Superdrag

REGRETFULLY YOURS
Sucked out / Cynicality / Carried / Slot machine / Garmonbozia / Phaser / Rocket / Nothing good is real / What if you don't fly / Truest love / Whitey's theme / NA kicker / Destination Ursa Major
CD 7559619002
Elektra / Oct '96 / Warner Music

Supereal

ELIXIR
Body medusa / Aquaplane / Blue beyond belief / Mass motion / I almost love you / Terminal high rip / United state of love / One nation
CD GRCD 005
Guerilla / Nov '92 / Pinnacle

Supergrass

I SHOULD COCO
I'd like to know / Caught by the fuzz / Mansize rooster / Alright / Lose it / Lenny / Strange ones / Sitting up straight / She's so loose / We're not supposed to / Time / Sofa of my lethargy / Time to go
CD CDPCS 7373
Parlophone / May '95 / EMI

IN IT FOR THE MONEY
In it for the money / Richard III / Tonight / Late in the day / G-song / Sun hits the sky / Going out / It's not me / Cheapskate / You can see me / Hollow little reign / Sometimes I make you sad
CD CDPCS 7388
Parlophone / Jun '97 / EMI

Supergroove

TRACTION
CD 74321218462
RCA / Oct '95 / BMG

Superior

BEHIND
Truth ain't kind / Why / Tomorrow's eve / Nades / Escape from reality / Dreamtime / Tainted silence / Total void / Until the end
CD TT 00262
T&T / Nov '96 / Koch

Supermodel

CLUMBA MAR
CD FIRECD 56
Fire / Apr '96 / Pinnacle / RTM/Disc

Supermorris

MR. SLAM
CD RN 0030
Runn / Nov '93 / Grapevine/PolyGram / Jet Star / SRD

Supernaturals

IT DOESN'T MATTER ANYMORE
Please be gentle with me / Smile / Glimpse of the light / Lazy lover / Love has passed away / Dung beetle / Stammer / I don't think so / Pie in the sky / Day before yesterday's man / Prepeare to land / Trees
CD FOODCD 21
Food / Jun '97 / EMI

Supernova

AGES 3 AND UP
CD ARRCD 65008
Amphetamine Reptile / Nov '95 / Plastic Head

Superskill

SUPERIOR
CD OUT 002CD
Wonderbrain / May '94 / Plastic Head

Supersnazz

DEVIL YOUTH BLUES, THE
CD TBI 35CD
Time Bomb / May '97 / SRD

Superstar

18 CARAT
CD CFAB 001CD
Camp Fabulous / Mar '97 / 3mv/Vital

Supersuckers

LA MANO CORUNDA
CD SPCD 120301
Sub Pop / Apr '94 / Cargo / Greyhound / Shellshock/Disc

MUST'VE BEEN HIGH
CD SPCD 380
Sub Pop / Apr '97 / Cargo / Greyhound / Shellshock/Disc

SACRILICIOUS
CD SPCD 303
Sub Pop / Sep '95 / Cargo / Greyhound / Shellshock/Disc

SONGS ALL SOUND THE SAME, THE
CD EFA 11351
Musical Tragedies / Jul '92 / SRD

Supertouch

EARTH IS FLAT, THE
CD REVEL 021CD
Revelation / Apr '92 / Plastic Head

Supertramp

BREAKFAST IN AMERICA
Gone Hollywood / Logical song / Goodbye stranger / Breakfast in America / Oh darling / Take the long way home / Lord is it mine / Just another nervous wreck / Casual conversation / Child of vision
CD 3937082
A&M / May '97 / PolyGram

CRIME OF THE CENTURY
School / Bloody well right / Hide in your shell / Asylum / Dreamer / Rudy / If everyone was listening / Crime of the century
CD 3936472
A&M / May '97 / PolyGram

CRISIS, WHAT CRISIS
Easy does it / Sister moonshine / Ain't nobody but me / Soapbox opera / Another man's woman / Lady / Poor boy / Just a normal day / Meaning / Two of us
CD 3945602
A&M / May '97 / PolyGram

EVEN IN THE QUIETEST MOMENTS
Give a little bit / Loverboy / Even in the quietest moments / Downstream / Babaji / From now on / Fool's overture
CD 3946342
A&M / May '97 / PolyGram

FAMOUS LAST WORDS
Crazy / Put on your old brown shoes / It's raining again / Bonnie / Know who you are / My kind of lady / C'est le bon / Waiting so long / Don't leave me now
CD 3937322
A&M / May '97 / PolyGram

INDELIBLY STAMPED
Your poppa don't mind / Travelled / Rosie had everything planned / Remember / Forever / Potter / Coming home to see you / Times have changed / Friend in need / Aries
CD CDA 3149
A&M / '88 / PolyGram

PARIS LIVE (2CD Set)
School / Ain't nobody but me / Logical song / Bloody well right / Breakfast in America / You started laughing / Hide in your shell / From now on / Dreamer / Rudy / Soapbox opera / Asylum / Take the long way home / Fool's overture / Two of us / Crime of the century
CD Set CDD 6702
A&M / '88 / PolyGram

SUPERTRAMP
It's a long road / Aubade / And I am not like other birds of prey / Words unspoken / Maybe I'm a beggar / Home again / Nothing to show / Shadow song / Try again / Surely
CD CDA 3129
A&M / '88 / PolyGram

SUPERTRAMP SONGBOOK, THE
CD CCV 8919
Compact Club / Apr '94 / BMG

VERY BEST OF SUPERTRAMP, THE
School / Goodbye stranger / Logical song / Bloody well right / Breakfast in America / Rudy / Take the long way home / Crime of the century / Dreamer / Ain't nobody but me / Hide in your shell / From now on / It's raining again / Give a little bit / Cannonball
CD TRACD 1992
A&M / Jul '92 / PolyGram

Supor Aeternus

EHJEH ASCHER EHJEH
Ehjeh ascher ehjeh
CD EFA 015692
Apocalyptic Vision / Jun '96 / Cargo / Plastic Head / SRD

Supreme Chord Jesters

HUNGRY FOR THE WORD
CD SCAT 1CD
Scat / Jul '96 / Timewarp

PLAYGROUND
CD SCAT 3CD
Scat / Jul '96 / Timewarp

Supreme Dicks

WORKINGMAN'S DICK
CD FFR 002CD
Freek / Aug '94 / RTM/Disc / SRD

Supreme Love Gods

SUPREME LOVE GODS
CD DABCD 2
Beggars Banquet / Jun '93 / RTM/Disc / Warner Music

Supremes

HITS, THE
Stop in the name of love / Nathan Jones / Where did our love go / He's my man / Baby love / Love child / Someday we'll be together / Happening / Stoned love / Reflections / You can't hurry love / Automatically sunshine / I hear a symphony / Touch / Back in my arms again / Up the ladder to the roof / I guess I'll miss the man / My world is empty without you / I'm gonna let my heart do the walking / You keep me hangin' on
CD 307742
Hallmark / Jun '97 / Carlton

WITH LOVE FROM US TO YOU
CD MAR 024
Marginal / Jun '97 / Greyhound

Sureshot

UNDERGROUND SYMPHONY
CD NOZACD 02
Ninebar / Jun '96 / Kudos / Prime / RTM/ Disc

Surf Creatures

X-50
CD WIGCD 011
Alopecia / Nov '96 / Plastic Head

Surf Trio

CURSE OF THE SURF TRIO
CD CD 95030
Pin Up / Jun '97 / Greyhound

SAFARI IN A LIVING GRAVEYARD
CD BRCD 5002
Blood Red Discs / Mar '97 / Greyhound / Nervous

Surface

NICE TIME 4 LOVIN', A (The Best Of Surface)
Nice time 4 lovin' / Happy / Closer than friends / You are my everything / I missed (title song reprise) / Shower me with your love / First time / Never gonna let you down / World of own / Christmas time is here
CD 4690542
Columbia / Oct '95 / Sony

Surface Of The Earth

MUKWEP
CD HERMES 021
Corpus Hermeticum / Apr '97 / Cargo

Surfaris

SURF PARTY
Wipeout / Tequila / Shake n' stomp / Surfer Joe / Point panic / Pipeline / Summertime blues / Something else / Earthquake / Hiawatha / Louie Louie / Apache / Scatter shield / Let's go trippin' / Surfbeat / Misirolu
CD GNPD 2239
GNP Crescendo / Aug '95 / ZYX

Surge

EMERGENCE
CD BACCYCD 001
Diversity / May '96 / 3mv/Vital

Surgeon

BASIC TONAL VOCABULARY
CD 74321473142
Tresor / Jun '97 / 3mv/BMG / Prime / SRD

COMMUNICATIONS
CD DNCD 001
Downwards / Jun '97 / Plastic Head

Surgery

NATIONWIDE
CD TRR 89201CD
Twin Tone / Sep '90 / PolyGram

SHIMMER
Bootywhack / Off the A list / Shimmer / Vibe out / Mr. Scientist / Low cut blues / D-Nice / Gulf coast / Nilla waif / Didn't I know you once / No 1 pistola
CD 756782579
East West / '94 / Warner Music

TRIM, 9TH WARD HIGH ROLLER
CD ARRCD 35/225
Amphetamine Reptile / Jun '93 / Plastic Head

Surman, John

ADVENTURE PLAYGROUND
Only yesterday / Figfoot / Quadraphonic question / Twice said once / Just for now / As if we knew / Twisted roots / Duet for one / Seven
CD 5119812
ECM / Sep '92 / New Note/Pinnacle

AMAZING ADVENTURES OF SIMON SIMON
Nestor's saga (the tale of the ancient) / Buccaneers / Kentish hunting (Lady Margaret's air) / Pilgrim's way (to the seventeenth walls) / Within the halls of Neptune / Phoenix and the fire / Fide et amore (by faith and love) / Merry pranks (the jester's song) / Fitting epitaph
CD 8291602
ECM / Aug '86 / New Note/Pinnacle

BIOGRAPHY OF REV ABSALOM DAWE
First light / Countess journeys / Monastic calling / Druid's circle / 'Twas but piety / Three aspects / Long narrow road / Wayfarer / Far corners / An image
CD 5237492
ECM / Sep '95 / New Note/Pinnacle

BRASS PROJECT, THE
Returning exile / Coastline / New one two / Special motive / Wider vision / Silent lake / Mellstock quire tantrum clangley / All for a shadow
CD 5173622
ECM / May '93 / New Note/Pinnacle

ROAD TO SAINT IVES
Polperro / Tintagel / Trethevy quoit / Rame head / Mevagissey / Lostwithiel / Perranporth / Bodmin moor / Kelly Bray / Piperspool / Marazion / Bedruthan steps
CD 8438492
ECM / Oct '90 / New Note/Pinnacle

STORAAS NORDIC QUARTET
Traces / Unwritten letter / Offshore piper / Gone to the dogs / Double trouble / Ved sorevatn / Watching shadows / Illusions / Wild bird
CD 5271202
ECM / Mar '95 / New Note/Pinnacle

STRANGER THAN FICTION
CD 5218502
ECM / Sep '94 / New Note/Pinnacle

SURMAN FOR ALL SAINTS
Round the round / Twelve alone / Electric plunger / Cascadence / Walls / Satisfied air / Matador / Saints alive / Barcarolle
CD 8254072
ECM / Jan '89 / New Note/Pinnacle

UPON REFLECTION
Edges of illusion / Filigree / Caithness to Kerry / Beyond a shadow / Prelude and rustic dance / Lamp fighter / Following behind / Constellation
CD 8254722
ECM / '82 / New Note/Pinnacle

Surman, Martin

LIVE AT WOODSTOCK TOWN HALL (Martin, Stu & John Surman)
Harry Lovett - Man without a country / Are you positive you're negative / Wrested in mustard / Professor Goodly's implosion machine / Master of disaster / Don't leave me like this
CD BGOCD 290
Beat Goes On / Nov '95 / Pinnacle

Surrealists

HEY BELIEVER
CD GRCD 349
Glitterhouse / May '97 / Avid/BMG

Suryana, Ujang

INSTRUMENTALS VOL.1
CD FLTRCD 516
Flame Tree / Sep '93 / Pinnacle

Suso, Jali Nyama

ART OF THE KORA, THE
CD C 5580027
Ocora / Aug '96 / ADA / Harmonia Mundi

Suso, Salieu

GRIOT
CD LYRCD 7418
Lyrichord / Aug '93 / ADA / CM / Roots

Suspiral

GREAT AND SECRET SHOW, THE
CD NIGHTCD 007
Nightbreed / Nov '95 / Plastic Head

Sussed

ALL HAIL THE YOUNG ASSASSINS
CD GOODCD 13
Dead Dead Good / Sep '97 / Pinnacle

Sutch, Screaming Lord

LIVE MANIFESTO
CD JETCD 1004
Jet / Oct '92 / Total/Pinnacle

ROCK AND HORROR
Scream and scream / All black and hairy / Jack the ripper / Monster rock / Rock and shock / Murder in the graveyard / London rocker / Penny penny / Rockabilly madman / Oh well / Loonabilly / Go Berry go
CD CDCHM 65
Ace / Jul '91 / Pinnacle

Sutherland Brothers

REACH FOR THE SKY (Sutherland Brothers & Quiver)
When the train comes / Dirty city / Arms of Mary / Something special / Love on the moon / Ain't too proud / Dr. Dancer / Reach for the sky / Moonlight lady / Mad trail
CD 4805262
Columbia / May '95 / Sony

Sutherland, Madge

HOME FREE
CD CDJMI 2100
Jahmani / Dec '95 / Grapevine/PolyGram / Jet Star / THE

Sutton, Ralph

ALLIGATOR CRAWL
CD SACD 92
Solo Art / Feb '93 / Jazz Music

AT CAFE DES COPAINS
CD SKCD 22019
Sackville / Jun '93 / Cadillac / Jazz Music / Swift

EASY STREET (Sutton, Ralph & Bob Barnard)
CD SKCD 2040
Sackville / Jul '96 / Cadillac / Jazz Music / Swift

EYE OPENER
Rippling waters / Viper's drag / Memories of you / Gone with the wind / June night / Old fashioned love / Cottage for sale / When I grow too old to dream / Clothes line ballet
CD SACD 122
Solo Art / Mar '97 / Jazz Music

JAMMIN' AT RUDI'S (Sutton, Ralph & Pops Foster/Bob Wilber)
CD JCD 262
Jazzology / Jun '96 / Jazz Music

LIVE AT MAYBECK RECITAL HALL VOL.30
Honeysuckle rose / In a mist / Clothes line ballet / In the dark / Ain't misbehavin' / Echo of Spring / Dinah / Love lies / Russian lullaby / St. Louis blues / Viper's drag / After you've gone
CD CCD 4586
Concord Jazz / Dec '93 / New Note/ Pinnacle

LIVE AT SUNNIE'S RENDEZVOUS (Sutton, Ralph Trio)
CD STCD 8288
Storyville / May '97 / Cadillac / Jazz Music / Wellard

MORE SOLO PIANO
CD SKCD 22036
Sackville / Aug '94 / Cadillac / Jazz Music / Swift

PARTNERS IN CRIME (Sutton, Ralph & Bob & Len Barnard)
Swing that music / One morning in May / Old folks / Rain / I never knew / Slow boat to China / 'S wonderful / How can you face me / West End avenue blues / Diga diga doo
CD SKCD 22023
Sackville / Jun '93 / Cadillac / Jazz Music / Swift

RALPH SUTTON 1975 SOLO SIDES
Love lies / Eye opener / Echoes of spring / Morning air / In the dark / Viper's drag / Cottage for sale / Old folks / T'ain't so honey, t'ain't so / Honeysuckle rose / Handful of keys / Somebody stole my gal / Ain't misbehavin' / Keeping out of mischief / My fate is in your hands / Alligator crawl / I found a new baby
CD FLYCD 911
Flyright / Jul '96 / Hot Shot / Jazz Music / Wellard

RALPH SUTTON QUARTET, THE
CD STCD 8243
Storyville / Jan '97 / Cadillac / Jazz Music / Wellard

RALPH SUTTON QUARTET/TRIO
CD STCD 8210
Storyville / Jul '96 / Cadillac / Jazz Music / Wellard

SUNDAY SESSION (Sutton, Ralph & Milt Hinton/Butch Miles)
CD SKCD 2044
Sackville / Jul '96 / Cadillac / Jazz Music / Swift

Sutton-Curtis, Barbara

SOLO & DUETS (Sutton-Curtis, Barbara & Ralph Sutton)
CD SKCD 22027
Sackville / Jun '93 / Cadillac / Jazz Music / Swift

Suzuki, Yoshio Chin

MORNING PICTURE
CD JD 3306
JVC / Jul '88 / Direct / New Note/Pinnacle / Vital/SAM

Svart Parad

SVART PARAD 1984-1986
CD FINNREC 012
Distortion / Sep '96 / Plastic Head

Sven Gali

IN WIRE
What you give / Keeps me down / Worms / Make me / Red moon / Tired of listening / Shallow truth / Rocking chair / Helen / Who said
CD 74321282112
RCA / May '95 / BMG

SVEN GALI
Under the influence / Tie dyed skies / Sweet little gypsy in my garden / Freaxz / Love don't live here anymore / Stiff competition / Real thing / Whisper in the rain / Twenty five hours a day / Here today, gone tomorrow / Disgusteen
CD 74321114422
RCA / Mar '93 / BMG

Svuci, Kalsijki

BOSNIAN BREAKDOWN
Oho ho sto je liepo / Ja te cekam milice / Crven fesic / Komsinice mila moja / Frula svira kosu kujem / Ramino kolo / Ako zelis mene / Inoco moja krivdoco / Otimas se branis se / Sedam puta lola se ozenio / Sota
CD ____ CDORB 074
Globestyle / Jan '92 / Pinnacle

SWA

EVOLUTION 1985-1987
CD ____ SST 157CD
SST / Aug '88 / Plastic Head

VOLUME
CD ____ SST 282CD
SST / May '93 / Plastic Head

WINTER
CD ____ SST 238CD
SST / Mar '89 / Plastic Head

Swains

ELECTRIC SOUL
CD ____ KK 068CD
KK / Jun '92 / Plastic Head

SONIC MIND JUNCTION
CD ____ KK 097
KK / Nov '93 / Plastic Head

Swainson, Neil

FORTY NINTH PARALLEL (Swainson, Neil Quintet)
Forty ninth parallel / Port of Spain / Southern exposure / On the lam / Don't hurt yourself / Homestretch
CD ____ CCD 4396
Concord Jazz / Nov '89 / New Note/ Pinnacle

Swaleh, Zuhura

JINO LA PEMBE (Swaleh, Zuhura & Maulidi Musical Party)
Shani / bado basi / Safari / Singetema / Kisu chako / Humvui alovikwa / Parare / Jino la pembe / Nalia na jito / Mdudu
CD ____ CDORBD 075
Globestyle / Sep '92 / Pinnacle

Swallow

BLOW
Lovesleep / Tastes like honey / Sugar your mind / Mensurral / Peekaboo / Lacuna / Oceans and blue skies / Follow me down / Halo / Cherry stars collide / Head in a cave
CD ____ CAD 2010CD
4AD / Jul '92 / RTM/Disc

Swallow, Steve

CARLA (Swallow, Steve Sextet)
Deep trouble / Crab alley / Fred and Ethel / Read my lips / Afterglow / Hold it against me / Count the ways / Last night
CD ____ 8334922
Watt / Oct '87 / New Note/Pinnacle

DECONSTRUCTED
Running in the family / Babble on / Another fine mess / I think my wife is a hat / Bird world war / Bug in a rug / Lost in Boston / Name that tune / Viscous consistency / Deconstructed
CD ____ 5371192
Watt / May '97 / New Note/Pinnacle

REAL BOOK
Bite your Grandmother / Second hand motion / Wrong together / Outfits / Thinking out loud / Let's eat / Better times / Willow / Muddy in the bank / Ponytail
CD ____ 5216372
Watt / Jun '94 / New Note/Pinnacle

SWALLOW
Belles / Soca symphony / Slender thread / Thrills and spills / William and Mary / Doin' it slow / Thirty five / Ballroom / Playing with water
CD ____ 5119602
Watt / Mar '92 / New Note/Pinnacle

Swamp Terrorists

GROW - SPEED INJECTION
Ratskin / Hidden (crab) / Vault I / Skizzo pierce / Rebuff / Vault II / Green blood / Braintrash / Vault III / Rawhead / SSM / Drop the dig / Ratskin (floatmix) / Drip the dog
CD ____ MA 0092
Machinery / Mar '92 / Koch

Swamptrash

IT DON'T MAKE NO NEVER MIND
CD ____ FFUS 3301CD
Fast Forward / '88 / Fast Forward Records

Swampwalk

STRANGLED AT BIRTH
CD ____ CDBLEED 6
Bleeding Hearts / Oct '93 / Pinnacle

Swan, Billy

BILLY SWAN
CD ____ DS 015
Desperado / Jun '97 / TKO Magnum

BILLY SWAN/FOUR
I just want to taste your wine / Ms. Misery / I got it for you / Number one / Vanessa / Lucky / You're the one / Love you baby, to the bone / Your true love / Blue suede shoes / Swept away / Playing the game of love / Pardon me / Oliver Swan / Smokey places / Don't kill our love / Not everyone knows / Last call / California song (for Marlu) / Me and my honey
CD ____ SEECD 471
See For Miles/C5 / Jan '97 / Pinnacle

I CAN HELP
All shook up / Drivin' wheel / Rave on / When will I be loved / Hallelujah I love her so / Vanessa / Don't be cruel / My bucket's got a hole in it / I can help / Bright lights, big city / I'd rather go blind / Shake, rattle and roll / Lover please / Since I met you baby / Great balls of fire / Rock this joint / Me and Bobby McGee / Rockhouse
CD ____ 305082
Hallmark / Jun '97 / Carlton

I CAN HELP/ROCK 'N' ROLL MOON
Lover please / I can help / I'm her foot / I'd like to work for you / Shake, rattle and roll / Queen of my heart / Don't be cruel / Wedding bells / Ways of a woman in love / PMS / Everything's the same (ain't nothin' changed) / You're the pain (in my heart) / (You just) woman handled my mind / Stranger / Baby my heart / Got you on my mind / Come by / Ubangi stomp / Home of the blues / Overnight thing (usually) / Rock 'n' roll moon blues
CD ____ SEECD 470
See For Miles/C5 / Jan '97 / Pinnacle

Swan Death

BLACK WOLF
CD ____ 9227966CD
Nightbreed / Apr '97 / Plastic Head

Swan, Jimmy

HONKY TONKIN' IN MISSISSIPPI
I had a dream / Juke joint mama / I love you too much / Trifflin' on me / Last letter / Little church / Mark of shame / Losers weepers / One more time / Lonesome daddy blues / Frost on my roof / Why did you change your mind / Hey baby, baby / It's your turn to cry / Good and lonesome / Country cattin' / Way that you're livin' / Lonesome man / I love you too much / Don't conceal you're wedding ring / No one loves a broken heart / It takes a lonesome man / Rattlesnakin' Daddy / Asleep in the deep / Walkin' my dog / Good and lonesome / Why did you change your mind
CD ____ BCD 15758
Bear Family / Nov '93 / Direct / Rollercoaster / Swift

Swan Silvertones

HEAVENLY LIGHT
Jesus is all the world to me / Love lifted me / I'm sealed / How I got over / Have thine own way / Shine on me / Heavenly light shine on me / Jesus keep me near the cross / He won't deny me / Every day and every hour / Four and twenty elders / Shine on me medley / My rock / Lord's prayer / Medley / I'm coming home / After a while
CD ____ CDCHD 482
Ace / Jul '93 / Pinnacle

LOVE LIFTED ME AND MY ROCK
Trouble in my way / How I got over / After a while / Prayer in my mouth / Glory to his name / I'm a rollin' / Let's go / Jesus changed this heart of mine / I'm coming home / Love lifted me / Heavenly light shine on me / Day will surely come / My rock / Since Jesus came into my heart / I cried / What do you know about Jesus / Milky white way / He won't deny me / Jesus is a friend / Motherless child / Man in Jerusalem / Keep my heart / Oh how I love Jesus / This little light of mine
CD ____ CDCHD 340
Ace / May '91 / Pinnacle

SINGING IN MY SOUL
Oh Mary don't you weep / Great day in December / Singin' in my soul / At the cross / He saved my soul / Why I love him so / Jesus is alright with me / Lord is coming / Nobody but you / Love lifted me / Call him Jesus / Leave your burden there / Cross for me / I'll be satisfied / Send my child / I thank you Lord / Come to Jesus / Without a mother / Search me Lord / Bible days
CD ____ CPCD 8089
Charly / May '95 / Koch

Swana, John

FEELING'S MUTUAL, THE
CD ____ 1090CD
Criss Cross / Jan '95 / Cadillac / Direct / Vital/SAM

INTRODUCING JOHN SWANA
CD ____ CRISS 1045CD
Criss Cross / Apr '91 / Cadillac / Direct / Vital/SAM

JOHN SWANA AND FRIENDS
CD ____ CRISS 1055CD
Criss Cross / May '92 / Cadillac / Direct / Vital/SAM

Swanee Quintet

BEST OF THE SWANEE QUINTET, THE
CD ____ NASH 4503
Nashboro / Feb '96 / Pinnacle

Swans

BODY TO BODY JOB TO JOB
CD ____ YGCD 004
Young God / Jul '95 / Vital

CHILDREN OF GOD
New mind / In my garden / Sex God sex / Blood and honey / Like a drug / You're not real, girl / Beautiful child / Blackmail / Trust me / Real love / Blind love / Children of God
CD ____ PRODCD 17
Product Inc. / Nov '87 / Vital

CHILDREN OF GOD/WORLD OF SKIN (2CD Set)
New mind / In my garden / Over love lies / Sex, God, Sex / Blood and honey / Like a drug / You're not real girl / Beautiful child / Black mail / Trust me / Real love / Blind love / Children of God / Ill swallow you / 1000 years / Everything at once / Cry me a river / Breathing water / Blood on your hands / Nothing without you / We'll fall apart / I want to be your dog / My own hands / Turn to stone / Cold bed / 24 hours / Red rose / One small sacrifice / Still a sacrifice / Center of your heart
CD Set ____ YGCD 011
Young God / May '97 / Vital

COP/YOUNG GOD
Half Life / Job / Why Hide / Clayman / I Crawled / Raping A Slave / Your Property / Cop / Butcher / Thug / Young God / This Is Mine
CD ____ KCC 1CD
K422 / Aug '92 / Vital

DI TUR IST ZU
Ligeti's breath / Hilflos kind / Ich sehe die alle in einer reihe / YRP / You know everything / M/F / Sound section
CD ____ RTD 15731402
World Service / May '96 / Vital

FILTH
CD ____ YGCD 1
Young God / Jul '95 / Vital

GREAT ANNIHILATOR, THE
In / I am the sun / She lives / Celebrity lifestyle / Mother/Father / Blood promise / Mind, body, light, sound / My buried child / Warm / Alcohol the seed / Killing for company / Mothers milk / Where does a body end / Telepathy / Great annihilator / Out
CD ____ YGCD 009
Young God / Jan '95 / Vital

GREED
CD ____ KCC 2CD
K422 / Mar '86 / Vital

HOLY MONEY
CD ____ KCCD 3
Some Bizarre / Feb '88 / Pinnacle

LOVE OF LIFE
CD ____ YGCD 005
Young God / Jul '95 / Vital

OMNISCIENCE
Mother's milk / Pow r sac / Will serve / Her / Black eyed dog / Amnesia / Love of life / Other side of the world / Rutting / God loves America / Omnipotent
CD ____ YGCD 007
Young God / Jul '95 / Vital

REAL LOVE
CD ____ LOVETWOCD
Love / May '92

REAL LOVE
CD ____ ALP 58CD
Atavistic / Jan '97 / Cargo / SRD

SOUNDTRACKS FOR THE BLIND (2CD Set)
Red velvet corridor / I was a prisoner in your skull / Helpless child / Live through me / Yum-yab killers / Beautiful days / Volcano / Mellothumb / All lined up / Surrogate 2 / How they suffer / Animus / Red velvet wound / Sound / Her mouth is filled with honey / Bloodsection / Hypogirl / Minus something / Empathy / I love you this much / YRP / Fans lament / Secret friends / Final sac / YRP2 / Surogate drone
CD Set ____ YGCD 010
Young God / Oct '96 / Vital

WHITE LIGHT FROM THE MOUTH OF INFINITY
CD ____ YGCD 3
Young God / Jul '95 / Vital

Swans Of Avon

WHEN HEAVEN FALLS
CD ____ PANT 218CD
Nightbreed / Apr '97 / Plastic Head

Swap

SWAP
CD ____ AMCD 735
Amigo / May '97 / ADA / Cadillac / CM / Wellard

Swarbrick, Dave

50TH BIRTHDAY CONCERT (Various Artists)
Drowsy Maggie: *Swarbrick, Dave & Fairport Convention* / Heilanman: *Swarbrick, Dave & Fairport Convention* / 72nd's farewell to Aberdeen: *Marriot, Beryl Ceilidh Band* / 93rd's farewell to Gibraltar: *Marriot, Beryl Ceilidh Band* / Atholl highlanders: *Marriot, Beryl Ceilidh Band* / Hag with the money: *Marriot, Beryl Ceilidh Band* / Sleepy: *Marriot, Beryl Ceilidh Band* / Keech in the Creel: *Campbell, Ian Folk Group* / Viva la Quince Brigade: *Campbell, Ian Folk Group* / Oh dear oh: *Swarbrick, Dave & Martin Carthy* / Begging song: *Swarbrick, Dave & Martin Carthy* / Trip we took over the mountain: *Swarbrick, Dave & Martin Carthy* / Hens march: *Fairport Convention* / Four poster bed: *Fairport Convention* / Rosie: *Fairport Convention* / Hexamshire Lass: *Fairport Convention* / Dirty linen: *Fairport Convention*
CD ____ MASHCD 001
Cooking Vinyl / Jun '96 / Vital

LIVE AT JACKSONS LANE
CD ____ ATRAXCD 595
Bowsaw / Feb '96 / ADA

SMIDDYBURN/FLITTIN'
Wat ye wha I met the streen / Ribbons of the redheaded girl / Ril gan ainm / Sir Charles Coote / Smiths / I have a wife of my own / Lady Mary Haye's scotch measure / Wishing / Victor's return / Gravel walk / When the battle is over / Sword dance / Young black crow / Sean O'Dwyer of the glen / Hag with the money / Sleepy Maggie / It suits me well / Bride's march / Keelmans pertition / Show me the way to Sallingford / Sword dance / Parthenia / Pittnegardener's rant / Floggin / Grey daylight / Hawk / Ten pound fiddle / Jamaica / With all my heart / Nathaniel Gow's lament / Rory of the hills / Rakes of Sollohad / Dr. Isaacs Maggot / Cupids garden / Boadicea
CD ____ RVCD 54
Raven / Aug '96 / ADA / Direct
CD ____ ESMCD 434
Essential / Oct '96 / BMG

SWARBRICK/SWARBRICK VOL.2
Heilanman/Drowsy Maggie / Carthy's march / White cockade/Doc Boyd's jig/Durham Rangers / My singing bird / Nightingale / Once I loved a maiden fair / Byker Hill / Ace and deuce of Pipering / Hole in the wall / Ben Dorian / Hullichans/Chorus jig / 79th's farewell to Gibraltar / Arthur McBride/Snug in the blanket / Athole highlanders / Shannon bells/Fairy dance/Miss McLeod's reel / King of the fairies / Chief O'Neil's favourite/ Newcastle hornpipe / Sheebeg and Sheemore / Rocky road to Dublin/Sir Philip McHugh / Planxty Morgan Mawgan / Swallow's tail/Rakes of Kildare/Blackthorn stick / Sheagh of Rye/The friar's breeches / Derwentwaters farewell/The noble Squire Dacre / Teribus/Farewell to Aberdeen / Bonaparte's retreat / Coulin
CD ____ ESMCD 355
Essential / Jan '96 / BMG

Sward, Pierre

JAZZ 'N' SOUL
CD ____ FLCCD 147
Four Leaf Clover / May '97 / Cadillac / Wellard

Swarovski Musik Wattens

NATIONAL ANTHEMS OF THE WORLD (2CD Set)
CD Set ____ 340872
Koch International / Sep '96 / Koch

Swartz, Harvey

IT'S ABOUT TIME (Swartz, Harvey & Urban Earth)
CD ____ 1390112
Gaia / Feb '89 / New Note/Pinnacle

Swat

DEEP INSIDE A COPS MIND
CD ____ ARRCD 54334
Amphetamine Reptile / Aug '94 / Plastic Head

Sweat, Keith

GET UP ON IT
Interlude (how do you like it) / How do you like it / It gets better / Get up on it / Feels so good / How do you like it (part 2) / Intermission break / My whole world / Grind on you / When I give my love / Put your lovin' through the test / Telephone love /

Come into my bedroom / For you (you got everything)
CD 7559615502
Elektra / May '94 / Warner Music

I'LL GIVE ALL MY LOVE TO YOU
I'll give all my love to you / Make you sweat / Come back / Merry go round / Your love / Your love (part 2) / Just one of them thangs / I knew that you were cheatin / Love to love you
CD 7559608612
Elektra / Jun '90 / Warner Music

KEEP IT COMIN'
Keep it comin' / Spend a little time / Why me baby / I really love you / Let me love you / I want to love you down / I'm going for mine / (There you go) tellin' me no again / Give me what I want / Ten commandments of love / Keep it comin'
CD EKT 103CD
Elektra / Nov '91 / Warner Music

KEITH SWEAT
CD 7559617072
Elektra / Jun '96 / Warner Music

MAKE IT LAST FOREVER
Something just ain't right / Right and a wrong way / Tell me it's me you want / I want her / Make it last forever / In the rain / How deep is your love / Don't stop your love
CD 9607632
Elektra / Jul '88 / Warner Music

Sweaty Nipples

BUG HARVEST
CD CDVEST 37
Bulletproof / Jan '95 / Pinnacle

SWED

CROSSTALK
CD EFA 034072
Muffin / Oct '94 / SRD

Swedish String Quartet

LIVE AT SALSTA CASTLE
Poor butterfly / Avalon / Limehouse blues / I got rhythm / Tangerine / Have you met Miss Jones
CD NCD 8803
Phontastic / '93 / Cadillac / Jazz Music / Wellard

STOMPIN' AND FLYING
If I had you / Lover / Old folks / It could happen to you / Sweet Sue, just you / Flying home / Oh lady be good
CD NCD 8805
Phontastic / '93 / Cadillac / Jazz Music / Wellard

Swedish Swing Society

WHAT'S NEW
CD SITCD 9235
Sittel / May '97 / Cadillac / Jazz Music

WINTER SWING
CD SITCD 9213
Sittel / Mar '95 / Cadillac / Jazz Music

Sweeney's Men

SWEENEY'S MEN/THE TRACKS OF SWEENEY
Rattlin' roarin' Willy / Sullivan's John / Sally Brown / My dearest dear / Exile's jig / Handsome cabin boy / Dicey Reilley / Tom Dooley / Willy o' Winsbury / Dance to your Daddy / House carpenter / Johnston / Reynard the fox / Dreams for me / Pipe on the hob / Brain jam / Pretty Polly / Standing on the shore / Mistake no doubt / Go by brooks / When you don't care / Afterthoughts / Hiram Hubbard / Hall of mirrors
CD ESMCD 435
Essential / Oct '96 / BMG

Sweet

A
CD AIM 1048
Aim / Apr '95 / ADA / Direct / Jazz Music

ANSWER, THE (Scott, Andy/Sweet)
CD CDP 1029DD
Pseudonym / Jun '97 / Greyhound

BALLROOM HITZ (The Best Of The Sweet)
CD 5350012
PolyGram TV / Jan '96 / PolyGram

BEST OF SWEET, THE
Ballroom blitz / Blockbuster / Need a lot of lovin' / New York connection / Rock 'n' roll disgrace / Hellraiser / Burning / Done me wrong alright / Reflections / Little Willy / Funny funny / Co co / Chop chop / Alexander Graham Bell / Poppa Joe / Santa Monica sunshine / Tom Tom turnaround / Wig wam bam
CD 74321476792
Camden / Apr '97 / BMG

BLOCKBUSTER (Live On Stage)
Hell raiser / Burning / Someone else / Rock 'n' roll disgrace / Need a lot of loving / Done me wrong alright / You're not wrong for loving me / Man with the golden arm / Wig wam bam / Little Willy / Teenage rampage / Keep on knockin' / Shakin all over / Great balls of fire / Reelin' and rockin' / Ballroom blitz / Blockbuster / FBI
CD MDCD 013
Music De-Luxe / Jan '96 / TKO Magnum

BLOCKBUSTERS
Ballroom blitz / Hellraiser / New York connection / Little Willy / Burning / Need a lot of lovin' / Wig wam bam / Blockbuster / Rock 'n' roll disgrace / Chop chop / Alexander Graham Bell / Poppa Joe / Co co / Funny funny
CD ND 74313
RCA / Dec '89 / BMG

COLLECTION, THE
Teenage rampage / Rebel rouser / Solid gold brass / Stairway to the stars / Turn it down / Six teens / Into the night / No you don't / Fever of love / Lies in your eyes / Fox on the run / Restless / Set me free / AC/DC / Sweet fa / Action / Peppermint twist / Heartbreak today / Lost angels / Lady Starlight
CD CCSCD 230
Castle / Oct '89 / BMG

DESOLATION BOULEVARD
Six teens / Fox on the run / Turn it down / Medusa / Solid gold brass / Lady Starlight / Man with the golden arm / Breakdown / My generation
CD CLACD 170
Castle / Dec '89 / BMG

ELECTRIC LANDLADY
CD RRCD 241
Receiver / Apr '97 / Grapevine/PolyGram

GREATEST HITS
CD 290586
Ariola Express / Dec '92 / BMG

GREATEST HITS LIVE
CD AIM 1041
Aim / Apr '95 / ADA / Direct / Jazz Music

HANOVER SESSIONS (4CD Set) (Scott, Andy/Sweet)
CD Set CDP 1028DD
Pseudonym / Jun '97 / Greyhound

HARD CENTRES - THE ROCK YEARS
Set me free / Sweet FA / Restless / Yesterday's rain / White mice / Cockroach / Keep it in / Live for today / Windy city / Midnight to daylight
CD CDMZEB 11
Anagram / Sep '95 / Cargo / Pinnacle

HITZ, BLITZ, GLITZ (Andy Scott's Sweet)
Action / Blockbuster / Fox on the run / Teenage rampage / Love is like oxygen / Six teens / Ballraiser blitz / Hellraiser / Wig wam bam / Little Willy / Turn it down / Peppermint twist
CD CDEC 5
Out Of Time / Sep '96 / Direct / Total/BMG

LET'S GO (Connolly, Brian/Sweet)
CD KLMCD 054
BAM / Sep '96 / Koch / Scratch/BMG

LET'S GO
Ballroom blitz / Rock 'n' roll disgrace / AC/DC / Burn on the flame / Fox on the run / Action / Cockroach / Windy City / Laura Lee (show me the way) / Are you coming to see me / Hard times / 4th of July / Live for today / Solid gold brass / Lady starlight / Lies in your eyes
CD EMPRCD 717
Emporio / Jun '97 / Disc

LIVE AT THE MARQUEE
CD SPV 858826
SPV / Mar '96 / Koch / Plastic Head

LOVE IS LIKE OXYGEN (The Singles Collection 1978-1982)
CD CDP 1009DD
Pseudonym / Jun '97 / Greyhound

SOLID GOLD ACTION
CD RRCD 214
Receiver / Apr '96 / Grapevine/PolyGram

SWEET LIVE 1973, THE
Ballroom blitz / Little Willie / Rock 'n' roll disgrace / Done me wrong alright / Hellraiser / You're not wrong for loving me / Burning/Someone else will / Man with the golden arm / Need a lot of lovin' / Wig wam bam / Teenage rampage / Blockbuster / Keep on knockin' / Shakin' all over / Lucille / Great balls of fire / Reelin' and rockin' / Peppermint twist / Shout
CD DOJOCD 89
Dojo / Mar '93 / Disc

SWEET, THE
Blockbuster / Ballroom blitz / Little Willie / Fox on the run / Action / Hell raiser / Wig wam bam / Teenage rampage / Burn on the flame / Do it again / Wait till the morning comes / Let's go
CD EXP 031
Experience / May '97 / TKO Magnum

Sweet Baby

IT'S A GIRL
CD LOOKOUT 157CD
Lookout / Oct '96 / Cargo / Greyhound / Shellshock/Disc

SWEET BABY/BRENTS TV (Sweet Baby/ Brents TV)
CD LOOKOUT 102CD
Lookout / Sep '96 / Cargo / Greyhound / Shellshock/Disc

Sweet Daisy

SLUDGE
CD GOD 021MCD
Godhead / Sep '96 / Plastic Head

Sweet Diesel

KIDS ARE DEAD, THE
Empire strikes back / Supermarket / Morning breath / I hate the man / (I'm just a) Kid in this town / You want it / Gallon man / Kids are dead / Enemy / Workers comp / What happened to my anger
CD ENG 014ECD
Engine / Mar '97 / Vital

SEARCH AND ANNOY
CD GKCD 020
Go-Kart / Oct '96 / Greyhound / Pinnacle

Sweet Exorcist

CLONKS COMING
CD WARPCD 1
Warp / Apr '96 / Prime / RTM/Disc

SPIRIT GUIDE TO LOW TECH
CD T 3313
Touch / Oct '95 / Kudos / Pinnacle

Sweet Honey In The Rock

BREATHS (The Best Of Sweet Honey In The Rock)
Breaths / Stranger blues / Joanne little / Ella's song / More than a paycheck / Mandiacapella / Study war no more / Waters of Babylon (rivers of Babylon) / Oughta be a woman / On children / Chile your waters run red through Soweto / Azanian freedom song
CD COOKCD 008
Cooking Vinyl / Jan '97 / Vital

FEEL SOMETHING DRAWING ME ON
Waters of Babylon (rivers of Babylon) / In the upper room / Leaning and depending on the Lord / Try Jesus / Feel something drawing on me
CD COOKCD 082
Cooking Vinyl / Mar '95 / Vital

GOOD NEWS
Breaths / Chile your waters run red through Soweto / Good news / If you had lived / On children / Alla that's all right, but / Echo / Oh death / Biko / Oughta be a woman / Time on my hands / Sometime
CD COOKCD 027
Cooking Vinyl / Aug '89 / Vital

IN THIS LAND
CD CDEB 2522
Earthbeat / May '93 / ADA / Direct

LIVE AT CARNEGIE HALL
Beautitudes / Where are the keys to the kingdom / Emergency / Are my hands clean / Peace / My lament / Run run mourner run / Letter to Dr. Martin Luther King / Ode to the international debt / Your worries ain' like mine / Song of the exile / Denko / Drinking of the wine / Wade in the water / Our side won
CD BAKECD 003
Cooking Vinyl / May '90 / Vital
CD FF 70106
Flying Fish / Feb '97 / ADA / CM / Direct / Roots

OTHER SIDE, THE
Mandiacapella / Step by step / Deportees / Moving on / Stranger blues / Venceremos / Other side / No images / Gift of love / Mae Frances / Let us go back to the old landmark / Tomorrow
CD COOKCD 083
Cooking Vinyl / Mar '95 / Vital

SACRED GROUND
CD 9425802
Earthbeat / Jan '96 / ADA / Direct

SELECTIONS 1976-1988
CD CDFF 667668
Flying Fish / Aug '97 / ADA / CM / Direct / Roots

STILL ON THE JOURNEY
CD EBCD 942536
Earthbeat / Nov '93 / ADA / Direct

SWEET HONEY IN THE ROCK
Sweet honey in the rock / Sun will never go down / Dream variations / Let us all come together / Joanne Little / Jesus is my only friend / Are there any rights I'm entitled to / Going to see my baby / You make my day pretty / Hey mann / Doing things together / Travelling shoes / Sweet honey in the rock
CD COOKCD 080
Cooking Vinyl / Mar '95 / Vital

WE ALL EVERYONE OF US
Study war no more / What a friend we have in Jesus / Sweet bird of youth / How long / More than a paycheck / Azanian freedom song / Listen to the rhythm / Testimony / Oh Lord hold my hand / Battle for my life / Ella's song / I'm gon' stand / We all everyone of us
CD COOKCD 081
Cooking Vinyl / Mar '95 / Vital

Sweet Inspirations

BEST OF THE SWEET INSPIRATIONS, THE
CD SCL 2506
Ichiban Soul Classics / Mar '95 / Koch

ESTELLE, MYRNA AND SYLVIA
Wishes and dishes / You roam when you don't get it at home / Slipped and tripped / All it takes is you and me / Pity yourself / Emergency / Call me when all else fails / Whole world is out / Why marry / Sweet inspiration / Why am I treated so bad
CD CDSXE 062
Stax / Jul '92 / Pinnacle

Sweet, Matthew

100% FUN
Sick of myself / Not when I need it / We're the same / Giving it back / Everything changes / Lost my mind / Come to love / Walk out / I almost forgot / Super baby / Get older / Smog moon
CD 72445110812
Zoo Entertainment / Mar '95 / BMG

ALTERED BEAST
Dinosaur act / Devil with the green eyes / Ugly truth / Time capsule / Someone to pull the trigger / Knowing people / Life without you / Ugly truth rock / In too deep / Reaching out / Falling / What do you know / Evergreen
CD 72445110502
Zoo Entertainment / Jul '93 / BMG

BLUE SKY ON MARS
Come back to California / Back to you / Where you get love / Hollow / Behind the smile / Until you break / Over it / Heaven and Earth / All over my head / Into your drug / Make believe / Missing time
CD 614453113029
Zoo Entertainment / Apr '97 / BMG

GIRLFRIEND
CD PD 90644
Zoo Entertainment / Jun '92 / BMG

Sweet, Michael

MICHAEL SWEET
CD CD 02231
Way Hey / May '95 / Total/BMG

Sweet People

SUMMER DREAM
Et les oiseaux chantaient / Heartstring / Un ete avec toi / Elodie / Lake como / Santorini / Balladepoour tsi-co tsi co / Aria pour une voix / La foret enchantee / Barcarolle / Le grande large / Aria pour notre amour / Perce / Nuits blanche / Wonderful day
CD 8312132
Polydor / Apr '94 / PolyGram

Sweet, Rachel

PROTECT THE INNOCENT
CD STIFFCD 10
Disky / Jan '94 / Disky / THE

Sweet Sister

FLORA & FAUNA
CD CDFLAG 82
Under One Flag / Nov '94 / Pinnacle

Sweet Talks

HOLLYWOOD HIGHLIFE PARTY
CD ADC 301
PAM / Feb '94 / ADA / Direct

Sweet Tooth

CRASH LIVE
CD HD 002
PDCD / Apr '94 / Plastic Head

Sweet William

KIND OF STRANGEST DREAM
CD HY 39100282CD
Hyperium / Nov '92 / Cargo / Plastic Head

Sweetback

SWEETBACK
Gaze / Softly softly / Sensations / Au natural / Arabesque / You will rise / Chord / Walk of Ju / Hope she'll be happier / Come dubbing / Cloud people / Powder
CD 4853902
Epic / Nov '96 / Sony

Sweetbelly Freakdown

SWEETBELLY FREAKDOWN
CD JT 1032CD
Jade Tree / Apr '97 / Cargo / Greyhound / Plastic Head

Sweetest Ache

GRASS ROOTS
Love me gently / Something we can find / Carry me home / Good days gone / One more time / Jayne / Nothing ever ends / Never gonna say goodbye / Honey / Little angel
CD ASKCD 029
Vinyl Japan / Mar '94 / Plastic Head / Vinyl Japan

Sweethearts Of The Rodeo

BEAUTIFUL LIES
CD SHCD 3857
Sugar Hill / Sep '96 / ADA / CM / Direct / Koch / Roots

RODEO WALTZ
CD SHCD 3819
Sugar Hill / Aug '96 / ADA / CM / Direct / Koch / Roots

SWEETHEARTS OF THE RODEO
Midnight girl/Sunset town / Hey doll baby / Since I found you / Gotta get away / Chains of gold / Chosen few / Everywhere I turn / I can't resist
CD 4605312
CBS / Feb '88 / Sony

Sweetmouth

GOODBYE TO SONGTOWN
CD PD 74971
RCA / Apr '97 / BMG

Sweetpea

CHICKS HATE WES
CD TR 51CD
Trance / May '96 / SRD

Swell

41
CD ARBCD 6
Beggars Banquet / Apr '94 / RTM/Disc / Warner Music

TOO MANY DAYS WITHOUT THINKING
Throw the wine / What I always wanted / Make mine you / Fuck even flow / At Lennie's / When you come over / (I know) the trip / Going up (to Portand) / Bridgette, you love me / Sunshine everyday
CD BBQCD 187
Beggars Banquet / Mar '97 / RTM/Disc / Warner Music

WELL
Intro / At long last / Everything / Down / Turtle song / It's OK / Price / Showbiz / Tired / Wash your brain / Soda jerk fountain / Suicide fountain / Thank you, good evening
CD MEANCD 002
Mean / Jun '92 / Vital

Swell Maps

JANE FROM OCCUPIED EUROPE
Robot factory / Let's buy a fridge / Border country / Cake shop / Helicopter spies / Big maz in the desert / Big empty field / Mining villages / Collusion with a frogman / Mangrove delta plan / Secret island / Whatever happens next / Blenheim shots / Raining in my room / Let's build a car / Epic's trip / Uh / Secret island / Amphitheatres / Big empty field / Stairs are like an avalanche / Then Poland
CD MAPS 002CD
The Grey Area / Jul '89 / RTM/Disc

TRAIN OUT OF IT
CD MAPS 003CD
The Grey Area / Aug '91 / RTM/Disc

TRIP TO MARINEVILLE, A
HS art / Another song / Vertical slum / Spitfire parade / Harmony in your bathroom / Don't throw ashtrays at me / Midget submarines / Bridge head / Full moon in my pocket / Blam / Full moon reprise / Gunboats / Adventuring into basketry / My little shops / Ripped and torn / International rescue / Loin of the surf / Shoot the angels / Elephant flowers / Turn me on dead man / Bronze and baby shoes / Nevertoseeanotherway
CD MAPS 001CD
The Grey Area / Jul '89 / RTM/Disc

Swelling Meg

WELL
CD NGM 007
NGM / Jul '96 / SRD

Swerdlow, Tommy

PRISONER OF THE GIFTED SLEEP
CD NAR 074CD
New Alliance / Dec '93 / Plastic Head

Swervedriver

EJECTOR SEAT RESERVATIONS
CD CRECD 157
Creation / Aug '95 / 3mv/Vital

MEZCAL HEAD
For seeking heat / Duel / Blowin' cool / Mickey / Last train to Satansville / Harry and Maggie / Change is gonna come / Girl on a motorbike / Duress / You find it everywhere
CD CRECD 143
Creation / Sep '93 / 3mv/Vital

RAISE
CD CRECD 093
Creation / Oct '91 / 3mv/Vital

SWF Orchestra

VIVACE
CD ISCD 159
Intersound / Sep '96 / Jazz Music

Swift, Duncan

BROADWAY CONCERT, THE
CD ESSCD 258
Essential / Feb '95 / BMG

BROADWOOD CONCERT, THE
Frog-i-more / Ostrich walk / Sweet Lorraine / Man overboard / Creole bells / Very thought of you / Like someone in love / Just a closer walk with thee / Digah's stomp / One night in trinidad / Nettlebed stomp / Tell me why I'm feeling blue / Merry peasant / Russian rag / Cry me a river / Striding after fats / Guitar shuffle / You can't lose a broken heart / Ain't cha glad
CD ESJCD 543
Essential Jazz / Apr '97 / BMG

OUT LOOKING FOR THE LION
CD BEARCD 28
Big Bear / Jun '88 / BMG

Swift, Jude

COMMON GROUND
CD NOVA 9139
Nova / Jan '93 / New Note/Pinnacle

MUSIC FOR YOUR NEIGHBOURHOOD
CD NOVA 8917
Nova / Jan '93 / New Note/Pinnacle

Swimmer

PETITS POIS
CD SWEE 004CD
Sweet / Jun '96 / Shellshock/Disc / SRD

Swimwear Catalogue

FNOPRX BOUTIQUE
CD APR 013CD
April / Oct '96 / Plastic Head / Shellshock/ Disc

NTUNXUN
CD APR 005CD
April / Mar '95 / Plastic Head / Shellshock/ Disc

Swindle

WITHIN THESE WALLS
CD GRL 003CD
Grilled Cheese / Oct '96 / Cargo

Swing & Sway Orchestra

ABSOLUT LEVANDE DANSMUSIK (Swing & Sway Orchestra & Arne Domnerus)
CD NCD 8853
Phontastic / May '97 / Cadillac / Jazz Music / Wellard

Swing Out Sister

GET IN TOUCH WITH YOURSELF
Get in touch with yourself / Am I the same girl / Incomplete without you / Everyday crime / Circulate / Who let the love out / Understand / Not gonna change / Don't say a word / Love child / I can hear you but can't see you (Inst.) / Everyday crime (Instrumental)
CD 5122412
Fontana / May '92 / PolyGram

IT'S BETTER TO TRAVEL
Breakout / Twilight world (superb, superb mix) / After hours / Blue mood / Surrender / Fooled by a smile / Communion / It's not enough / It's better to travel / Breakout (Nad mix) / Surrender (Stuff gun mix) / Twilight world (Remix) / Communion (Instrumental)
CD 8322132
Fontana / Jul '93 / PolyGram

KALEIDOSCOPE WORLD
You on my mind / Where in the world / Forever blue / Heart for fire / Tainted / Waiting game / Precious game / Masquerade / Between strangers / Kaleidoscope affair
CD 8382932
Fontana / Jul '93 / PolyGram

LIVING RETURN, THE
Better make it better / Don't let yourself down / Ordinary people / Mama didn't raise no fool / Don't give up on a good thing / Making the right move / La la (Means I love you) / Feel free / Stop and think it over / That's the way it goes / All in your mind / O pesadelo dos autores / Low down dirty business
CD 5226502
Fontana / Jun '94 / PolyGram

Swingin' Haymakers

FOR RENT
CD CCD 907
Circle / Aug '95 / Jazz Music / Swift / Wellard

Swinging Blue Jeans

1960'S FRENCH EPS COLLECTION, THE
CD 519362
Magic / Jul '97 / Greyhound

ALL THE HITS PLUS MORE
CD CDPT 003
Prestige / Mar '94 / Else / Total/BMG

BEST OF THE SWINGING BLUE JEANS 1963-66, THE
Hippy hippy shake / It's too late now / Save the last dance for me / That's the way it goes / One of these days / Shakin' all over / Crazy about my baby / Shake, rattle and roll / Angie / Good golly Miss Molly / Don't worry 'bout me / Sandy / You're no good / Do you know / Long tall Sally / Don't make me over / Now the Summer's gone / Promise you'll tell her / It isn't there / Lawdy Miss Clawdy
CD CDSL 8254
EMI / Jul '95 / EMI

BLUE JEANS A' SWINGING
Ol' man Mose / Save the last dance for me / That's the way it goes / Around and around / It's all over now / Long tall Sally / Lawdy Miss Clawdy / Some sweet day / It's so right / Don't it make you feel good / All I want is you / Tutti Frutti / Ol' man Mose / Save the last dance for me / That's the way it goes / Around and around / It's all over now / Long tall Sally / Lawdy Miss Clawdy / Some sweet day / It's so right / Don't it make you feel good / All I want is you
CD DORIG 104
EMI / Aug '97 / EMI

BLUE JEANS ARE IN
CD MOGCD 007
Moggie / Dec '94 / Else

EMI YEARS, THE
Three little fishes / Now I must go / Hippy hippy shake / It's too late now / Shaking feeling / Good golly Miss Molly / Ol' man Mose / Don't it make you feel good / Lawdy Miss Clawdy / You're no good / Long tall Sally / Shakin' all over / Tutti frutti / Make me know you're mine / Ready Teddy / Crazy about my baby / I've got a girl / Chug-a-lug / You're welcome to my heart / I wanna be there / Sidney, gotta draw the line / I want love / Don't make me over / What can I do today / Tremblin' / Rumours, gossip, words untrue / One woman man / Something's coming along / Don't go out into the rain (you're gonna melt) / What have they done to Hazel / Now that you've got me (you don't seem to want me) / Summer somes Sunday / Hey Mrs. Housewife / Big city
CD CDEMS 1446
EMI / Apr '92 / EMI

LIVE SHARIN'
Tulane / My life / Again and again / Good golly Miss Molly / Don't stop / I saw her standing there / She loves you / Caroline / You're no good / Heatwave / Shakin' all over / It's so easy / When will I be loved / Hard day's night / Hippy hippy shake
CD CDPT 502
Prestige / Jul '90 / Else / Total/BMG

Swinging Ladies

TAKE TWO
CD INAK 9039
In Akustik / Oct '96 / Direct / TKO Magnum

Swinging Utters

JUVENILE PRODUCT OF THE WORKING CLASS, A
CD FAT 545CD
Fatwreck Chords / Sep '96 / Plastic Head

SOUNDS WRONG
CD IFACD 010
IFA / Oct '95 / Plastic Head

Swingle Singers

AROUND THE WORLD (A Folk Song Collection)
CD VC 7596162
Virgin Classics / Jan '95 / EMI

JAZZ SEBASTIAN BACH
Fugue en re mineur / Prelude pour choral d'orgue / Aria / Prelude en F majeur / Bourree / Fugue en D mineur / Fugue en re majeur / Prelude no.9 / Sinfonia / Prelude en D majeur / Canon / Invention en D majeur / Vivace / Prelude et fugue en mi mineur / Choral de la cantate / Gavotte / Prelude et fugue en D majeur / Fugue en sol majeur / Adagio / Prelude et fugue en do diese majeur / Prelude du choral / Fugue no.21 du prelude et fugue en si bemol majeur BWV 866
CD 8247032
Philips / Jan '88 / PolyGram

NOTHING BUT BLUE SKIES (The Irving Berlin Songbook)
Top hat, white tie and tails / How deep is the ocean / Isn't it a lovely day / Blue skies / Always / They say it's wonderful / No strings / Song is ended / Steppin' out with my baby / Let yourself go / Cheek to cheek/ Let's face the music and dance / Marrying for love/The girl that I marry / What'll I do / Puttin' on the ritz / Abraham / Change partners / Heatwave / I've got my love to keep me warm / Count your blessings / White Christmas
CD SUMCD 4054
Summit / Nov '96 / Sound & Media

PLACE VENDOME (Swingle Singers & Modern Jazz Quartet)
Little David's fugue / Air for G string / Vendome / Ricercare a 6 / When I am laid in Earth / Alexander's fugue / Three windows
CD 8245452
Philips / Oct '93 / PolyGram

Swingset Police

KADICKADEE
CD BV 161962
Black Vinyl / Nov '96 / Cargo

Swirl

PLUMPTUOUS
CD AMUSE 014CD
Playtime / May '92 / Pinnacle

Swirlies

WHAT TO DO ABOUT THEM
CD TAANG 65CD
Taang / Oct '92 / Cargo

Swish

SUPERMAX
Pretty box / Game / Klauss / Spin / Rockstar / Shell / Marjorie song
CD IMAY 001
Instant Mayhem / May '96 / Vital

Swiss Dixie Stompers

PETITE FLEUR
CD JCD 184
Jazzology / Oct '93 / Jazz Music

Swoons

YOUR ASS, EY
CD LRR 020
Last Resort / Oct '96 / Cargo

Swordmaster

POSTMORTEM TALES
CD OPCD 055
Osmose / Jun '97 / Plastic Head

SWV

IT'S ABOUT TIME
Anything / I'm so into you / Right here / Weak / You're always on my mind / Downtown / Coming home / Give it to me / Black pudd'n / It's about time / Think you're gonna like it / That's what I need / SWV (in the house) / Weak / Right here (Vibe mix)
CD 74321166112
Arista / Feb '97 / BMG

NEW BEGINNING
New beginning / You're the one / Whatcha need / On and on / It's all about U / Use your heart / Where is the love / Fine time / Love so amazin' / You are my love / I'm so in love / When this feeling / What's it gonna be / Tha's what I'm here for / Don't waste your time / Soul intact
CD 07863664872
Arista / Apr '96 / BMG

RELEASE SOME TENSION
CD 74321496162
RCA / Aug '97 / BMG

REMIXES, THE
CD 07863664012
Arista / Jun '94 / BMG

Sybil

GOOD 'N' READY
CD HFCD 28
PWL / May '93 / Warner Music

GREATEST HITS
When I'm good and ready / Love I lost / Don't make me over / Walk on by / Make it easy on me / Beyond your wildest dreams / Falling in love / Let yourself go / My love is guarenteed / Oh how I love you / You're the love of my life / Love's calling / Open up the door / Crazy 4 U / Let it rain / Guarantee of love / Stronger together / Didn't see the signs / When I'm good and ready
CD NP 54929
Next Plateau / Jun '97 / PolyGram

SYBILIZATION
CD HFCD 17
PWL / Nov '90 / Warner Music

WALK ON BY
CD HFCD 10
PWL / Feb '90 / Warner Music

Sykes, Roosevelt

ANN ARBOR JAZZ & BLUES FESTIVAL VOL.3 (Sykes, Roosevelt & Victoria Spivey)
Comments: *Sykes, Roosevelt* / Driving wheel: *Sykes, Roosevelt* / Night time is the right time: *Sykes, Roosevelt* / Run this bogie: *Sykes, Roosevelt* / St. James Infirmary: *Sykes, Roosevelt* / Dirty mother for you: *Sykes, Roosevelt* / Looka here (C'mon let's shake): *Sykes, Roosevelt* / Black snake blues: *Spivey, Victoria* / Detroit moan: *Spivey, Victoria* / Victoria Spivey comments: *Spivey, Victoria* / Low down man blues (you're a rank stud): *Spivey, Victoria* / Organ grinder blues: *Spivey, Victoria* / I'm tired: *Spivey, Victoria* / Brooklyn Bridge blues: *Spivey, Victoria*
CD NEXCD 284
Sequel / Aug '96 / BMG

BIG TIME WOMAN
CD IMP 311
IMP / Feb '97 / ADA / Discovery

BLUES BY ROOSEVELT 'HONEYDRIPPER' SYKES
CD SFWCD 40051
Smithsonian Folkways / Nov '95 / ADA / Cadillac / CM / Direct / Koch

FEEL LIKE BLOWING MY HORN
Feel like blowing my horn / My hamstring's poppin' / Blues will prank with your soul / Jubilee time / All days are good days / Sykes' gumboogie / Rock-a-bye birdie / Moving blues / Don't bat your eye / All days are good days / Eagle rock me baby / Jubilee time / Love the one you're with
CD DE 632
Delmark / Jul '97 / ADA / Cadillac / CM / Direct / Hot Shot

GOLD MINE
Big Ben / Boot that thing / Springfield blues / Henry Ford blues / I'm a dangerous man / True thing / You understand / Whole lot of children / Last laugh / Gold mine / 44 blues / Sugar cup
CD DD 616
Delmark / Mar '97 / ADA / Cadillac / CM / Direct / Hot Shot

HARD DRIVIN' BLUES
Kickin' motor scooter / Red-eye Jesse Bell / I like what you do (when you do what you did last night) / New fire detective blues / North Gulfport boogie / Watch your step (if you just can't be good) / Ho ho ho / Key to your heart / We gotta move / Dresser drawers / Living the right life / Run this boogie / Slidell blues / Mistake in life / You so small / Concentration blues / She's got me straddle a log
CD DD 607
Delmark / Mar '97 / ADA / Cadillac / CM / Direct / Hot Shot

HONEYDRIPPER, THE
CD SOB 35422
Story Of The Blues / Apr '93 / ADA / Koch

HONEYDRIPPER, THE (The Honeydripper's Duke's Mixture)
Goin' down slow / Ice cream freezer / Lost my boogie / Sweet Georgia Brown / St. James infirmary / Honeysuckle rose / Basin Street blues / Rock me / Woman is in demand / Dirty Mother for you
CD 5197272
Verve / Apr '93 / PolyGram

HONEYDRIPPER, THE
CD OBCCD 557
Original Blues Classics / Jul '95 / Complete/Pinnacle / Wellard

MUSIC IS MY BUSINESS
CD 157702
Blues Collection / Feb '93 / Discovery

MUSIC IS MY BUSINESS
Music is my business / Mistake in life / New York boogie / Dream woman / Stop stoppin' me / Look out for yourself / Some right, some wrong / Take time out / Hot pants / Good woman / Just smile / Last chance / Who's that pretty woman / How long
CD TBA 13010
Blues Alliance / Dec '96 / New Note/ Pinnacle

MUSIC IS MY BUSINESS
Music is my business / Mistake in life / New York boogie / Dream woman / Stop stoppin' me / Look out for yourself / Some right, some wrong / Take time out / Hot pants / Good woman / Just smile / Leavin' Chicago / Funky side / Last chance / Who's that pretty woman / How long
CD CPCD 8223
Charly / Oct '96 / Koch

RETURN OF ROOSEVELT SYKES, THE
CD OBCCD 546
Original Blues Classics / Nov '92 / Complete/Pinnacle / Wellard

ROOSEVELT SYKES VOL.1 1929-1930
CD DOCD 5116
Document / Oct '92 / ADA / Hot Shot / Jazz Music

ROOSEVELT SYKES VOL.10 1951-1957
CD BDCD 6050
Blues Document / Sep '94 / ADA / Hot Shot / Jazz Music

ROOSEVELT SYKES VOL.2 1930-1931
CD DOCD 5117
Document / Oct '92 / ADA / Hot Shot / Jazz Music

ROOSEVELT SYKES VOL.3 1931-1933
CD DOCD 5118
Document / Oct '92 / ADA / Hot Shot / Jazz Music

ROOSEVELT SYKES VOL.4 1934-1936
CD DOCD 5119
Document / Oct '92 / ADA / Hot Shot / Jazz Music

ROOSEVELT SYKES VOL.5 1937-1939
CD DOCD 5120
Document / Oct '92 / ADA / Hot Shot / Jazz Music

ROOSEVELT SYKES VOL.6 1939-1940
CD DOCD 5121
Document / Nov '92 / ADA / Hot Shot / Jazz Music

ROOSEVELT SYKES VOL.7 1941-1944
CD DOCD 5122
Document / Oct '92 / ADA / Hot Shot / Jazz Music

ROOSEVELT SYKES VOL.8 1945-1947
CD BDCD 6048
Blues Document / Sep '94 / ADA / Hot Shot / Jazz Music

ROOSEVELY SYKES VOL.9 1947-1951
CD BDCD 6049
Blues Document / Sep '94 / ADA / Hot Shot / Jazz Music

Sylla, Macire

MARIAMA (Sylla, Macire & Djembe-Fare)
CD 3019492
Arcade / Feb '97 / Discovery

Sylvester

COLLECTION, THE
CD CCSCD 393
Castle / May '94 / BMG

LIVING PROOF
Overture / Body strong / Blackbird / Could it be magic / Song or you / Happiness / Lover man (oh where can you be) / Sharing something perfect between ourselves / You are my friend / Dance (Disco heat) / You make me feel (Mighty real)
CD CDSEWD 107
Southbound / Nov '96 / Pinnacle

SELL MY SOUL/TOO HOT TO SLEEP
I need you / I'll dance to that / Change up / Sell my soul / Doin' it for the real thing / Cry me a river / My life is loving you / Fever / New beginings / Thinking right / Can't forget the love / Too hot to sleep / Give it up (Don't make me wait) / Here is my love / Can't you see / Ooo baby baby / I can't believe I'm in love / Ne beginnings
CD CDSEWD 106
Southbound / Jul '96 / Pinnacle

STAR (The Best Of Sylvester)
Stars (everybody is one) / Dance / Down down down / I need somebody to love tonight / I who have nothing / You make me feel (mighty real) / My life is loving you / Can't stop dancing / Body strong / Over and over / Disco international
CD CDSEW 007
Southbound / Jun '89 / Pinnacle

SYLVESTER/STEP VOL.2
Over and over / I tried to forget you / Changes / Tipsong / Down down down / Loving grows up slow / I been down / Never too late / You make me feel (Mighty real) / Dance (Disco heat) / You make me feel (Mighty real) / Grateful / I took my strength from you / Was it something that I said / Just you and me forever
CD CDSEWD 104
Southbound / Nov '95 / Pinnacle

Sylvestre, Anne

CHANTE...AU BORD DE LA FONTAINE
CD 984062
EPM / Apr '97 / ADA / Discovery

Sylvestre, Randafison

ART OF RANDAFISON SYLVESTRE, THE
CD VICG 50122
JVC World Library / Mar '96 / ADA / CM / Direct

Sylvia

VERY BEST OF SYLVIA, THE
CD DEEPMC 013
Deep Beats / Mar '97 / BMG

Sylvian, David

BRILLIANT TREES
Pulling punches / Ink in the well / Nostalgia / Red guitar / Weathered wall / Back waters / Brilliant trees
CD CDV 2290
Virgin / Jun '84 / EMI

DAMAGE (Sylvian, David & Robert Fripp)
Damage / God's monkey / Brightness falls / Every colour you are / Firepower / Gone to earth / Twentieth Century dreaming (a shaman's song) / Wave / River man / Darshan (the road to Graceland) / Blinding light of heaven / First day
CD DAMAGE 1
Virgin / Sep '94 / EMI

DARSHAN (Sylvian, David & Robert Fripp)
Darshan (The road to Graceland) / Darshan
CD SLYCD 1
Virgin / Feb '94 / EMI

FLUX AND MUTABILITY
Flux (a big bright colour world) / Mutability (a new beginning in the offing)
CD CDVE 43
Venture / Sep '89 / EMI

GONE TO EARTH
Taking the veil / Laughter and forgetting / Before the bullfight / Gone to Earth / Wave / River man / Silver moon / Healing place / Answered prayers / Where the railroad meets the sea / Wooden cross / Silver moon over sleeping steeples / Campfire coyote country / Bird of prey vanishes into a bright blue / Home / Sunlight seen through towering trees / Upon this earth
CD CDVDL 1
Virgin / Apr '92 / EMI

PLIGHT AND PREMONITION (Sylvian, David & Holger Czukay)
Plight (the spiralling of winter ghosts) / Premonition
CD CDVE 11
Venture / Mar '88 / EMI

SECRETS OF THE BEEHIVE
September / Boy with the gun / Maria / Orpheus / Devil's own / When poets dreamed of angels / Mother and child / Let the happiness in / Waterfront / Forbidden colours
CD CDV 2471
Virgin / Jul '91 / EMI

Symarip

SKINHEAD MOONSTOMP
Skinhead moonstomp / Phoenix city / Skinhead girl / Try me best / Skinhead jamboree / Chicken merry / These boots are made for walking / Must catch a train / Skin flint / Stay with him / Fung shu / You're mine
CD CDTRL 187
Trojan / Jan '95 / Direct / Jet Star

Symphonic Orchestra

ORCHESTRA ROCK VOL.3 (The Love Classics)
With you I'm born again / Up where we belong / One day in your life / Three times a lady / Cavatina / You don't bring me flowers / Memory / One day I'll fly away / Imagine / Sun ain't gonna shine anymore / Hard to say I'm sorry / Miss you nights / I wish it would rain down / My funny valentine / It's raining again / All you need is love
CD MCCD 075
Music Club / Jun '92 / Disc / THE

Symphony X

DAMNATION GAME, THE
CD SPV 08424402
SPV / May '96 / Koch / Plastic Head

SYMPHONY X
CD SPV 0844432
SPV / May '96 / Koch / Plastic Head

Syms, Sylvia

SYLVIA SYMS SINGS/SONGS OF LOVE
Then I'll be tired of you / I'm the girl / Lilac wine / I don't want to cry anymore / Honey in the honeycomb / Woman's intuition / Experiment / Let me love you / We just couldn't say goodbye / I'm so happy I could cry / Down with love / He loves and she loves / Can't we be friends / Hands across the table / Isn't it romantic / Dancing in the dark / So far / When a woman loves a man / Alone too long / What's the use of won'drin' / I am loved / Don't ever leave me / I'll be seeing you
CD JASCD 606
Jasmine / Oct '96 / Conifer/BMG / Hot Shot / TKO Magnum

Symtpom

TEMPORARY ALIEN RESIDENCE
CD LFCD 010
Little Fish / Jul '97 / Total/BMG

Synaesthesia

EPHEMERAL
CD CDZOT 180
Zoth Ommog / Jul '97 / Cargo / Plastic Head

Syncopace

SYNCOPACE
CD CROCD 228
Black Crow / Jul '91 / CM / Roots

Syndicate

SMILE SAYS IT ALL
CD SICD 255
Sticky / May '97 / Pinnacle / SRD / Total/ BMG

Syndicate Of Sound

LITTLE GIRL
CD SC 6120
Sundazed / May '97 / Cargo / Greyhound / Rollercoaster

Synetics

PURPLE UNIVERSE, THE
CD CAT 006CD
Rephlex / Mar '97 / Prime / RTM/Disc

Synopsis '77

LIVE IN MITTWEIDA
CD SYN 01
FMP / May '97 / Cadillac

Synthonic 2000

CHARIOTS OF FIRE (2CD Set)
Oxygene IV / Theme from Antarctica / Twin Peaks / L'Opera Sauvage / Crockett's theme / Chariots of fire / Sadness part 1 / Tubular bells / Autobahn / Dances with wolves / Rotations logic / Theme from Rain Man / Equinoxe / Fanfare for the common man / Miami Vice theme / Mammagamma / Eve of war / Black hole / China / Boat / Theme from Battlestar Galactica / L'Apocalypse des Animaux / Conquest of paradise / To the unknown man / Rockit / Aurora / Magic fly / Tubbs and Valerie / Lucifer / Vienna / Omen / Midnight express / Blade runner / Chi Mai / Magnetic fields / Terminator 2
CD Set RCACD 208
RCA / Jul '97 / BMG

SYPH

WIELEICHT
CD EFA 037622
Atatak / Apr '94 / SRD

Syrinx

KALEIDOSCOPE OF SYMPHONIC ROCK
CD CYBERCD 9
Cyber / Aug '94 / Amato Disco / Arabesque / Plastic Head

System 01

DRUGSWORK
CD 74321250592
Tresor / Feb '95 / 3mv/BMG / Prime / SRD

System 7

777
CD BFLCD 1
Big Life / Mar '93 / Mo's Music Machine / Pinnacle / Prime

GOLDEN SECTION
Rite of Spring / Don Corleone / Y2K / Ring of fire / Exdreamist / Wave bender / Sinom X files / Merkaba / Y2K (back to the future) / Borobudor
CD BFLCD 27
Butterfly / Jul '97 / Pinnacle / Prime / Vital

POINT 3: FIRE ALBUM
CD BFLCA 11
Big Life / Oct '94 / Mo's Music Machine / Pinnacle / Prime

POWER OF 7
CD BFLCD 16
Big Life / Feb '96 / Mo's Music Machine / Pinnacle / Prime

SYSTEM 7
Sunburst / Freedom fighters / Habibi / Altitude / Bon humeur / Fractal liaison / Dog / Thunderdog / Listen / Strange quotations / Miracle / Over and out
CD DIXCD 102
10 / Jun '91 / EMI

SYSTEM EXPRESS
CD BFLCD 21
CD BFLCD 21X
Big Life / Oct '96 / Mo's Music Machine / Pinnacle / Prime

Syzygy

MORPHIC RESONANCE
CD Set RSNCD 22
Rising High / Sep '94 / 3mv/Sony

Szabo, Gabor

SORCERER, THE
Beat goes on / Little boat / Lou-ise / What is this thing called love / Space / Stronger than us
CD MCAD 33117
Impulse Jazz / Apr '90 / New Note/BMG

SORCERER, THE
Beat goes on / Little boat / Louise / What is this thing called love / Space / Stronger

than us / Mizrab / Comin' back / Los matodoros / People / Corcovado
CD _______________ IMP 12112
Impulse Jazz / Apr '97 / New Note/BMG

Szabo, Sandor

SANCTIFIED LAND
Arrivers / Our presence and thirtyness / Equation of the existence / Ferdinandus / Miramare / Sikonda / Sanctified land / Departers
CD _______________ HWYLCD 6
Hwyl / Jun '91 / Hwyl

Szaszcsavas Band

FOLK MUSIC FROM TRANSYLVANIA
CD _______________ QUI 903072
Quintana / Mar '92 / Harmonia Mundi

Szelevenyi, Akosh

PANNONIA (Szelevenyi, Akosh Ensemble)
CD _______________ EPC 891
European Music Production / Jan '94 / Harmonia Mundi

T

T-Connection

MAGIC
Do what you wanna do / Disco magic / Go back home / Got to see my lady / Crazy mixed up world / Mother's love / Monday morning / Peace line
CD ________ **MUSCD 512**
MCI Original Masters / May '95 / Disc / THE

T-Model Ford

PEE-WEE GET MY GUN
Cut you loose / Been a long time / Turkey and the rabbit / Let me in / Sugar farm / Feels so bad / Where you been / T-model theme / I'm insane / Nobody gets me down / Can't be touched
CD ________ **03032**
Fat Possum / Jun '97 / Cargo / Pinnacle

T-Power

SELF EVIDENT TRUTH OF AN INTUITIVE MIND, THE
CD ________ **SOURCDLP 3**
SOUR / Oct '95 / SRD

WAVEFORM
CD ________ **TPOWCD 2**
Anti-Static / Oct '96 / Pinnacle / Vital

Ta Ixiar, Maixa

UHINEZ UHIN
CD ________ **KD 432CD**
Elkar / Nov '96 / ADA

Tab Two

FLAGMAN AHEAD
MBN Trumpet intro / No flagman ahead / Wanna lay (on your side) / Swingbridge / (There's) Not a lot / What'cha gonna do / Scubertplatz / Vraiment Paris / Tab jam / Curfew / Permanent protection
CD ________ **CDVIR 34**
Virgin / Aug '95 / EMI

Tabackin, Lew

I'LL BE SEEING YOU (Tabackin, Lew Quartet)
I surrender dear / Wise one / I'll be seeing you / Ruby my dear / Chic lady / Perhaps / Isfahan / Lost in meditation / In walked bud
CD ________ **CCD 4528**
Concord Jazz / Oct '92 / New Note/ Pinnacle

TENORITY
Soon / Autumn nocturne / Me and my shadow / Fashion's flower / Chasin' the carrot / Sentimental journey / Trinkel tinkle / Best thing for you / You stepped out of a dream / You don't know what love is
CD ________ **CCD 4733**
Concord Jazz / Nov '96 / New Note/ Pinnacle

WHAT A LITTLE MOONLIGHT CAN DO
What a little moonlight can do / Easy living / I wished on the moon / Love letters / Poinciana / This time the dream's on me / Broken dreams / Leaves of absinthe / Dig
CD ________ **CCD 4617**
Concord Jazz / Oct '94 / New Note/ Pinnacle

Tabane, Philip

UNH
CD ________ **7559792252**
Nonesuch / Jan '95 / Warner Music

Tabor, June

AGAINST THE STREAMS
Shameless love / I want to vanish / False, false / Pavanne / He fades away / Irish girl / Apples and potatoes / Beauty and the beast / Turn off the road / Windy city / Waiting for the lark
CD ________ **COOKCD 077**
Cooking Vinyl / Aug '94 / Vital

ALEYN
Great Valerio / I wonder what's keeping my true love tonight / No good at love / Bentley and Craig / Fiddler / April morning / Di nakht / Fair maid of Islington/Under the greenwood tree / Go from my window / Proper sort of gardener / Johnny O'Bredislee / Shallow brown
CD ________ **TSCD 490**
Topic / Jul '97 / ADA / CM / Direct

ANGEL TIGER
CD ________ **COOKCD 049**
Cooking Vinyl / Aug '97 / Vital

ANTHOLOGY
Mississippi summer / Verdi cries / Strange affair / She moves among men / Lay this body down / Band played waltzing Matilda / Night comes in / King of Rome / Lisbon / Month of January / Hard love / Dark eyed sailor / Heather down the moor / Cold and raw / Sudden waves / No man's land/Flowers of the forest
CD ________ **MCCD 126**
Music Club / Sep '93 / Disc / THE

ASHES AND DIAMONDS
Reynard the fox / Devil and bailiff McGlynn / Streets of forbes / Lord Maxwell's last goodnight / Now I'm easy / Clerk Saunders / Earl of Aboyne / Lisbon / Easter tree / Cold and raw / No man's land / Flowers of the forest
CD ________ **TSCD 360**
Topic / Oct '92 / ADA / CM / Direct

CUT ABOVE, A
CD ________ **TSCD 410**
Topic / Nov '90 / ADA / CM / Direct

FREEDOM AND RAIN (Tabor, June & The Oyster Band)
Mississippi summer / Lullaby of London / Night comes in / Valentine's day is over / All tomorrow's parties / Dives and Lazarus / Dark eyed sailor / Pain or paradise / Susie Clelland / Finisterre
CD ________ **COOKCD 031**
Cooking Vinyl / Feb '95 / Vital

SINGING THE STORM (Tabor, June & Danny Thompson/Savourna Stevenson)
Baker / Singing the storm / Dawn / Earth, wind, water / Witch of Fauldshope / Maybe then I'll be a rose / Gypsy Queen / Fleur de Lys / Broom of Cowdenknowes / Beyond ballad / Jean Gordon
CD ________ **COOKCD 102**
Cooking Vinyl / May '96 / Vital

SOME OTHER TIME
Some other time / Night and day / You don't know what love is / Body and soul / This is always / Pork pie hat / Solitude / I've got you under my skin / Man I love / Meditation / Sophisticated lady / 'Round midnight
CD ________ **HNCD 1346**
Hannibal / Sep '89 / ADA / Vital

Tabrizi-Zadeh, Mahmoud

SCENES
CD ________ **ALCD 194**
Al Sur / Sep '96 / ADA / Discovery

Tabuh Pacific

MUSIC FOR GAMELAN
CD ________ **CDMANU 1514**
Manu / Sep '96 / ADA / Discovery

Tabula Rasa

EKKEDIEN TANSSI
Ekkedien tanssi / Uskollinen / Aamukasteen laiva / Omantunnon rukous / Lasihelmipeli / Rakastaa / Kehto / Babylo rasa / Saasta mun paa / Rakastatko viela kun on ilta / Yksin
CD ________ **LRCD 170**
Love / May '97 / ADA / Direct / Greyhound

TABULA RASA
Lahto / Miks' ette vastaa vanhat puut / Tuho / Gryf / Tyhja on taulu / Nyt maalaan elamaa / Vuorellaistuja / Prinssi
CD ________ **LRCD 135**
Love / May '97 / ADA / Direct / Greyhound

Taburiente

A TIERRA
CD ________ **68976**
Tropical / Apr '97 / Discovery

Tackhead

FRIENDLY AS A HAND GRENADE
CD ________ **WRCD 013**
World / Nov '89 / SRD

POWER INC VOL.1
CD ________ **BLCCD 10**
Blanc / Jun '95 / Pinnacle / Shellshock/ Disc

TACKHEAD TAPE TIME
Mind at the end of tether / Half cut again / Reality / MOVE / Hard left / Get this / Man in a suitcase / What's my mission now
CD ________ **NTCD 036**
Nettwerk / Feb '88 / Greyhound / Pinnacle / Vital

Tacklebox

ON
CD ________ **ROCK 60982**
Rockville / Mar '93 / Plastic Head / SRD

Taco

VERY BEST OF TACO, THE
CD ________ **10232**
CMC / Jun '97 / BMG

Tacticos, Manos

MUSIC FROM THE GREEK ISLANDS (2CD Set) (Tacticos, Manos & His Bouzoukis)
O Andonis (theme from 'Z') / Lefteris / Delfini - Delfinaki / Natane to Ikosiena / San sfiriksis tries fores / Nostalgia / Athena / Vrehi O Theos / Epipoleos (impulsive) / Tist' anathema in 'afto / Ela agapi mou / Stou kosmou tin aniforia / Strose to stroma sou yia thio / Afto to agori (that boy) / Siko horepse kouli mou / Siko horepse sirtaki / Faliriotissa / Laikos horos / Ta pedia tou pirea / Pai-pai / Ftochologia / Varka sto yialo / Ta thakria mou eene kafta
CD Set ________ **CDDL 1029**
Music For Pleasure / Nov '91 / EMI

Tactile

INSCAPE
CD ________ **SNTX 3003CD**
Sentrax Corporation / May '96 / Plastic Head

Tacuma, Jamaaladeen

BOSS OF THE BRASS
CD ________ **GCD 79434**
Gramavision / Sep '95 / Vital/SAM

DREAMSCAPE
CD ________ **DIW 904**
DIW / Feb '96 / Cadillac / Harmonia Mundi

HOUSE OF BASS
CD ________ **GCD 79502**
Gramavision / Feb '95 / Vital/SAM

JUKE BOX
CD ________ **GCD 79436**
Gramavision / Sep '95 / Vital/SAM

MUSIC WORLD
Kimono queen / Tokyo cosmopolitaan / Matsuru / Rouge / Kismet / Creator has a master plan / Jamila's theme / One more night
CD ________ **GCD 79437**
Gramavision / Sep '95 / Vital/SAM

RENAISSANCE MAN
Renaissance man / Flashback / Let's have a good time / Next stop / Dancing in your head / There he stood / Battle of images / Sparkle
CD ________ **GCD 79438**
Gramavision / Sep '95 / Vital/SAM

SHOW STOPPER
Sunk in the funk / Rhythm box / From me to you / Animated creation / Bird of paradise / Show stopper / From the land of sand / Sophisticated us
CD ________ **GCD 79435**
Gramavision / Sep '95 / Vital/SAM

Tad

8-WAY SANTA
Jinx / Giant killer / Wired god / Delinquent / Hedge hog / Flame tavern / Trash truck / Stumblin' man / Jack Pepsi / Candi / 3-D witch hunt / Crane's cafe / Plague years
CD ________ **SPCD 8/122**
Sub Pop / '91 / Cargo / Greyhound / Shellshock/Disc

INFRARED RIDINGHOOD
Ictus / Emotional cockroach / Red eye angel / Dementia / Halcyon nights / Tool marks / Mystery copter / Particle accelerator / Weakling / Thistle suit / Bullhorn / Bludge
CD ________ **7559617892**
Warner Bros. / Apr '95 / Warner Music

LIVE ALIEN BROADCAST
CD ________ **CDMFN 181**
Music For Nations / Jan '95 / Pinnacle

SALT LICK
Axe to grind / High on the hog / Loser / Hibernation / Glue machine / Potlatch / Wood goblins / Cooking with gas / Daisy
CD ________ **GRCD 76**
Glitterhouse / Apr '90 / Avid/BMG

Tad Morose

LEAVING THE PAST BEHIND
CD ________ **BMCD 043**
Black Mark / May '94 / Plastic Head

PARADIGMA
CD ________ **BMCD 085**
Black Mark / Jan '96 / Plastic Head

SENDER OF...
CD ________ **BMCD 056**
Black Mark / Mar '95 / Plastic Head

Tafari, Judah Eskender

RASTAFARI TELL YOU
CD ________ **GPCD 007**
Gussie P / Sep '95 / Jet Star

Taff, Russ

WINDS OF CHANGE
CD ________ **9362456762**
Warner Bros. / Jun '95 / Warner Music

Tafolla, Joey

INFRA RED
CD ________ **RR 93422**
Roadrunner / Apr '91 / PolyGram

OUT OF THE SUN
CD ________ **RR 95732**
Roadrunner / '89 / PolyGram

Tag Team

WHOOMP (THERE IT IS)
Whoomp (There it is) / Funkey / Kick da flow / Get nasty / Bring it on / Wreck da set / Gettin' phat / Just call me DC / Bobyhead / Drop 'em / It's somethin' / You go girl / Free style
CD ________ **CLU 60062**
Club Tools / Feb '94 / Arabesque / Grapevine/PolyGram / Mo's Music Machine / Total/BMG

TAGC

BURNING WATER
CD ________ **DFX 17CD**
Dark Vinyl / Mar '95 / Plastic Head / World Serpent

Taggy Tones

HEARTBREAK HOTEL
CD ________ **CDS 10156**
Milkcow / Mar '96 / Nervous

LIVE AT EIGENS BALLROOM
CD ________ **EIGEN 38**
AGM / Jan '97 / Nervous

LOST IN THE DESERT
I miss you / Monster bop / Big machine / People are strange / Wild girl / Double trouble / Saturday night / Trouble boys / Everybody's rockin' / Keep on waiting / Nose pickin' Mama / Lonely tonight / baby I don't care / Champagne for breakfast / Blue train / My first guitar / Kinky Miss Pinky
CD ________ **NERCD 080**
Nervous / Apr '95 / Nervous / TKO Magnum

VIKING ATTACK
So fine, so kind / BC stomp / 501 / John and Mary / Pretty eyes / Rebel cat / To my Dad / Paris, Copenhagen / Crazy love / Viking attack / Crazy kid / From me to you / C'mon Johnny / Sound of guns / Letter to my baby / Myggen svermer
CD ________ **NERCD 070**
Nervous / Feb '93 / Nervous / TKO Magnum

Tah, Geggy

GRAND OPENING
Last word (one for her) / Go / LA Lulah / Giddy up / P Sluff / Tucked in / Fasterhan / Who's in a hurry / Intro / Ovary / Bomb fishing / Crack of dawn / Ghost of P Sluff / Welcome to the world (Birthday song)
CD ________ **9362452542**
Luaka Bop / Jul '94 / Warner Music

Tahitian Choir

RAPA ITI
Oparo e oparo e / Morotiri nei / Himene tatou / Tarema / Ei reka e / Tatou ki ota / Te vahine ororagni / Te matamua / I te fenua / Tamaki a te mau ariki / Oparo / Tevaitau / Va hiti / Tau matamua / Te parau o eri rama
CD ________ **SH 64055**
Shanachie / Dec '94 / ADA / Greensleeves / Koch

Tahitian Man Singers

TOP 20 "TANE"
CD ________ **S 65813**
Manuiti / Nov '93 / Harmonia Mundi

Tai Pan

SLOW DEATH
CD ________ **SHARK 108CD**
Shark / Jun '95 / Plastic Head

Taiko Drum Ensemble

SOH DAIKO
CD ________ **LYRCD 7410**
Lyrichord / '91 / ADA / CM / Roots

Tailgators

HIDE YOUR EYES
CD ________ **LS 93962**
Roadrunner / Mar '90 / PolyGram

IT'S A HOG GROOVE
CD ______ **UPSTART 019**
Upstart / Feb '96 / ADA / Direct

Taino, Joe

HOODOO MAN
Dozer for a dime / Junkyard dog / Wide glide / Cold pillow / Loiza Aldea / Goin' to Chicago / Odd blues / Pickin' the blues / Hoodoo man / Lorraine / Cry of the warrior / Take me now / Annalee / Fortune woman
CD ______ **PRD 70902**
Provogue / May '96 / Pinnacle

Taj Mahal

BIG BLUES (Live At Ronnie Scott's)
Big Blues / Mail box blues / Stagger Lee / Come on in my kitchen / Local local girl / Soothin' / Fishin' blues / Statesboro blues / Everybody is somebody
CD ______ **CLACD 328**
Castle / Apr '94 / BMG

DANCING THE BLUES
Blues ain't nothin' / Hardway / Strut / Goin' to the river / Mockingbird / Blue light boogie / Hoochie coochie coo / That's how strong my love is / Down home girl / Stranger in my own hometown / Sittin' on top of the world / I'm ready
CD ______ **01005821122**
Private Music / Mar '94 / BMG

EVENING OF ACOUSTIC MUSIC, AN
CD ______ **T&M 004**
Tradition & Moderne / Nov '94 / ADA / Direct

GIANT STEP
Linin' Track / Country blues / Wild ox man / Little Rain Blues / Little soulful tune / Candy man / Cluck old hen / Colored aristocracy / Blind boy rag / Stagger Lee / Cajun tune / Fishin' Blues / Annie's lover
CD ______ **EDCD 264**
Edsel / Apr '88 / Pinnacle

LIKE NEVER BEFORE
Don't call us / River of love / Scattered / Every wind (in the river) / Blues with a feeling / Squat that rabbit / Take all the time you need / Love up / Cake walk into town / Big legged mommas are back in style / Take a giant step
CD ______ **261679**
Private Music / Jun '91 / BMG

LIVE AND DIRECT
Jorge Ben / Reggae no. 1 / You're gonna need somebody / Little brown dog / Take a giant step / LOVE Love / And who / Suva serenade / Airplay
CD ______ **CDTB 121**
Thunderbolt / Aug '95 / TKO Magnum

MULEBONE
Jubilee / Graveyard mule (hambone rhyme) / Me and the mule / Song for a banjo dance / But I rode some / Hey hey blues / Shake that thing / Intermission blues / Crossing (lonely day) / Bound no'th blues / Final
CD ______ **GV 794322**
Gramavision / Mar '91 / Vital/SAM

NATCH'L BLUES, THE
Good morning Miss Brown / Corine Corina / I ain't gonna let nobody steal my mail... / Done changed my way of living / She caught the Katy / Cuckoo / You don't miss your water / Lot of love
CD ______ **4836792**
Columbia / Mar '96 / Sony

RISING SUN COLLECTION
CD ______ **RSCD 003**
Just A Memory / Apr '94 / New Note/ Pinnacle

SENOR BLUES
Queen Bee / Think / Iresistable you / Having a real bad day / Senor blues / Sophisticated / Oh Lord, things are getting crazy up here / I miss you baby / You rascal you / Mind your own business / 21st century gypsy singin' lover man / At last (I found a love) / Mr. Pitiful
CD ______ **1005821512**
Private Music / Jul '97 / BMG

TAJ
Everybody is somebody / Paradise / Do I love her / Light of the Pacific / 'Deed I do / Soothin' / Pillow talk / Local local girl / Kauai Kalypso / French letter
CD ______ **GCD 79433**
Gramavision / Sep '95 / Vital/SAM

TAJ MAHAL
Leaving trunk / Statesboro blues / Checkin' up on my baby / Everybody's got to change sometime / Ezy ryder / Dust my broom / Diving duck blues / Celebrated walkin' blues
CD ______ **4809682**
Columbia / Aug '95 / Sony

TAJ'S BLUES
Leaving trunk / Statesboro blues / Everybody's got to change / Sometime / Bound to love me some / Frankie and Albert / East Bay woman / Dust my broom / Corinna / Jelly roll / Fishin' blues / Needed time / Curiosity blues / Horse shoes / Country blues
CD ______ **4716602**
Columbia / Jul '92 / Sony

Tajes, Juan Carlos

TANGO CANCION (Tajes, Juan Carlos & Piet Capello)
La concion de Buenos Aires / Milonga de Albornoz / A Homero / Bailate un tango, Ricardo / Caseron de tejas / Milonga de la ganzua / Mil novecientos sesenta y cuatro / Los paraguas de Buenos Aires / Pequena nina mia / Oro y plata / Milonga en ay menor / Milonga de dos hermanos / Elegia / Y todavia te quiero / Pobre negra
CD ______ **AL 73029**
A / Nov '96 / Cadillac / Direct

Tajima, Tadashi

SHAKUHACHI
CD ______ **CDT 124CD**
Music Of The World / Jul '94 / ADA / Target/BMG

Takadja

DIYE
CD ______ **15025**
Black Sun / May '97 / ADA

Takahashi, Ayuo

PRIVATE TAPES
CD ______ **PSFD 64**
PSF / Dec '95 / Harmonia Mundi

Takahashi, Yukihiro

NEUROMANTIC
Glass / Grand espoir / Connection / New (red) roses / Extraordinary / Drip dry eyes / Curtains / Charge / Something in the air
CD ______ **SPALAX 14501**
Spalax / Oct '96 / ADA / Cargo / Direct / Discovery / Greyhound

WHAT, ME, WORRY
What...me worry / It's gonna work out / Sayonara / This strange obsession / Flashback / Real you / Disposable love / My highland home in Thailand / All you got to do / It's all too much
CD ______ **SPALAX 14502**
Spalax / Oct '96 / ADA / Cargo / Direct / Discovery / Greyhound

Takano, Max

NEW YORK, NEW YORK
CD ______ **CDGRS 1205**
Grosvenor / Feb '93 / Grosvenor

SPIRIT OF MUSIC
When you wish upon a star / Superman / Corner pocket / Carmina burana / Funeral march of a Marionette / April fools / Greensleeves / Air water music / Merry Christmas Mr. Lawrence / Stars and stripes / Moonlight serenade / Cross my heart / Hooker's hooker / Tap dance / Media luz, A (Medium Light)
CD ______ **CDGRS 1253**
Grosvenor / Feb '95 / Grosvenor

Takara

ETERNAL FAITH
CD ______ **NTHEN 7**
Now & Then / Sep '95 / Plastic Head

Takase, Aki

PERDIDO
CD ______ **ENJACD 40342**
Enja / Sep '95 / New Note/Pinnacle / Vital/ SAM

Takatina, He Toa

AUTHENTIC MAORI SONGS
CD ______ **CDODE 1007**
ODE / Feb '90 / CM / Discovery

Take 6

BROTHERS
CD ______ **9362462352**
Reprise / Feb '97 / Warner Music

JOIN THE BAND
Can't keep goin' on and on / All I need (is a chance) / My friend / It's gonna rain / You can never ask too much (of love) / I've got life / Stay tuned (interlude) / Biggest part of me / Badiyah (interlude) / Harmony / Four Miles (interlude) / Even though / Why I feel this way / Lullaby
CD ______ **9362454972**
Reprise / Jun '94 / Warner Music

Take That

EVERYTHING CHANGES
Everything changes / Pray / Wasting my time / Relight my fire / Love ain't here anymore / If this is love / Whatever you do to me / Meaning of love / Why can't I wake up with you / You are the one / Another crack in my heart / Broken your heart / Babe
CD ______ **74321169262**
RCA / Feb '97 / BMG

GREATEST HITS
How deep is your love / Never forget / Back for good / Sure / Love ain't here anymore / Everything changes / Babe / Relight my fire / Pray / Why can't I wake up with you / Could it be magic / Million love songs / I found heaven / It only takes a minute / Once you've tasted love / Promise / Do what u like
CD ______ **74321355582**
RCA / Mar '96 / BMG

INTERVIEW DISC
CD ______ **SAM 7007**
Sound & Media / Nov '96 / Sound & Media

TAKE THAT AND PARTY
I found heaven / Once you've tasted love / It only takes a minute / Million love songs / Satisfied / I can make it / Do what you like / Promises / Why can't I wake up with you / Never want to let you go / Give good feeling / Could it be magic / Take That and party
CD ______ **74321109232**
RCA / Feb '96 / BMG

Takemura, Nobukazu

CHILD'S VIEW
CD ______ **992157CD**
Ninetynine / Nov '96 / Timewarp

Takeshita, Kazuhira

FOLK SONGS OF AMAMI
CD ______ **VICG 53592**
JVC World Library / Feb '96 / ADA / CM / Direct

Takis & Anestos

GREEK FOLK DANCES
CD ______ **MCD 71722**
Monitor / Jun '93 / CM

Tala'i, Daryoush

TRADITION CLASSIQUE DE L'IRAN VOL.2 (Tala'i, Daryoush & Djamchid Chemirani)
CD ______ **HMA 1901031**
Musique D'Abord / Nov '93 / Harmonia Mundi

Talamh, Sean

TRADITIONAL IRISH MUSIC
CD ______ **EUCD 1252**
ARC / Mar '94 / ADA / ARC Music

Talbot, Mick

OFF THE BEATEN TRACK (Talbot, Mick & Steve White)
Are we on / Sticks and stones / 'Til the cows come home / Out of my box / Off the beaten track / Hopes and fears / Riding the rapids / Sonny's prayer / Three's a crowd / Under my skin
CD ______ **NNCD 1002**
New Note / Sep '96 / Cadillac / New Note/ Pinnacle

Tale

RIVERMAN VOL.1
CD ______ **VPCD 1**
Voyage Productions / Jun '94 / Plastic Head

Talila

PAPIROSSN
CD ______ **LDX 274956**
La Chant Du Monde / Jan '93 / ADA / Harmonia Mundi

Talisman

BEST OF TALISMAN, THE
CD ______ **ERCD 1031**
Empire / Feb '97 / Jet Star

LIFE
CD ______ **NTHEN 21**
Now & Then / Oct '95 / Plastic Head

Talk Talk

ASIDES AND BESIDES (2CD Set)
Talk talk / Today / My foolish friend / It's my life / Such a shame / Such a shame / Dum dum girl / Without you / Life's what you make it / Living in another world / Pictures of Bernadette / Happiness is easy / Talk talk / Mirror man / Candy / Strike up the band / Question mark / My foolish friend / Call in the night boys / Why is it so hard / Again a game...again... / Dum dum girl / It's getting late in the evening / For what it's worth / Pictures of Bernadette / Eden / John Cope
CD Set ______ **CDEMC 3670**
EMI / Nov '96 / EMI

COLOUR OF SPRING, THE
Happiness is easy / I don't believe in you / Life's what you make it / April 15th / Living in another world / Give it up / Chameleon day / Time it's time
CD ______ **CDFA 3291**
Fame / Apr '93 / EMI
CD ______ **RETALK 102**
EMI / Sep '97 / EMI

HISTORY REVISITED (The Remixes)
Living in another world / Such a shame / Happiness is easy / Today / Dum dum girl / Life's what you make it / Talk Talk / It's my life / Living in another world (Curious world dub mix)
CD ______ **CDPCS 7349**
Parlophone / Feb '91 / EMI

IT'S MY LIFE
Dum dum girl / Such a shame / Renee / It's my life / Tomorrow / Started / Last time / Call in the night boys / Does Caroline know / It's you
CD ______ **CDFA 3274**
Fame / Oct '92 / EMI
CD ______ **RETALK 101**
EMI / Sep '97 / EMI

LAUGHING STOCK
Myrrhman / Ascension day / After the flood / Tapehead / New grass / Rune
CD ______ **8477172**
Polydor / Sep '91 / PolyGram

NATURAL HISTORY (The Very Best Of Talk Talk)
Today / Talk talk / My foolish friend / Such a shame / Dum dum girl / It's my life / Give it up / Living in another world / Life's what you make it / Happiness is easy / I believe in you / Desire
CD ______ **CDPCSD 109**
Parlophone / May '90 / EMI

PARTY'S OVER, THE
Talk talk / It's so serious / Today / Party's over / Hate / Have you heard the news / Mirror man / Another word / Candy
CD ______ **CDFA 3187**
Fame / Apr '88 / EMI
CD ______ **RETALK 100**
EMI / Sep '97 / EMI

SPIRIT OF EDEN
Rainbow / Eden / Desire / Inheritance / I believe in you / Wealth
CD ______ **CDFA 3293**
Fame / Jun '93 / EMI
CD ______ **RETALK 103**
EMI / Sep '97 / EMI

VERY BEST OF TALK TALK, THE
It's my life / Talk talk / Today / Dum dum girl / Have you heard the news / Such a shame / For what it's worth / Life's what you make it / Eden / April 5th / Living in another world / I believe in you / Give it up / John Cope / Wealth / Time it's time
CD ______ **CDEMC 3763**
EMI / Jan '97 / EMI

Talking Heads

FEAR OF MUSIC
I Zimbra / Mind / Cities / Paper / Life during wartime / Memories can't wait / Air / Heaven / Animals / Electric guitar / Drugs
CD ______ **256707**
Sire / '94 / Warner Music

LITTLE CREATURES
And she was / Give me back my name / Creatures of love / Lady don't mind / Perfect world / Stay up late / Walk it down / Television man / Road to nowhere
CD ______ **CDFA 3301**
Fame / Nov '93 / EMI

MORE SONGS ABOUT BUILDINGS AND FOOD
Thank you for sending me an angel / With our love / Good thing / Warning sign / Girls want to be with the girls / Found a job / Artists only / I'm not in love / Stay hungry / Take me to the river / Big country
CD ______ **256531**
Sire / Jan '87 / Warner Music

NAKED
Blind / Mr. Jones / Totally nude / Ruby dear / Nothing but flowers / Democratic circus / Facts of life / Mommy, daddy / Big daddy / Cool water / Bill
CD ______ **CDFA 3300**
Fame / Nov '93 / EMI

NO TALKING, JUST HEADS (Heads)
Damage I've done / King is gone / No talking just head / Never mind / No big bang / Don't take my kindness for weakness / No more lonely nights / Indie hair / Punk lolita / Only the lonely / Papersnow / Blue blue moon
CD ______ **MCD 11504**
MCA / Nov '96 / BMG

ONCE IN A LIFETIME (The Best Of Talking Heads)
Psycho Killer / Take me to the river / Once in a lifetime / Burning down the house / This must be the place (Naive melody) / Life during wartime / And she was / Road to nowhere / Wild wild life / Nothing but flowers / Sax and violins / Lifetime piling up
CD ______ **CDEMD 1039**
EMI / Oct '92 / EMI

REMAIN IN LIGHT
Great curve / Cross-eyed and painless / Born under punches (heat goes on) / Houses in motion / Once in a lifetime / Listening wind / Seen and not seen / Overload
CD ______ **256867**
Sire / '83 / Warner Music

SAND IN THE VASELINE (2CD Set)
Sugar on my tongue / I want to live / Love building on fire / I wish you wouldn't say that / Psycho killer / Don't worry about the government / No compassion / Warning sign / Take me to the river / Heaven / Mem-

ories can't wait / I zimbra / Once in a lifetime / Cross-eyed and painless / Burning down the house / Swamp / This must be the place (Naive melody) / Life during wartime / Girlfriend is better / And she was / Stay up late / Road to nowhere / Wild wild life / Love for sale / City of dreams / Mr. Jones / Blind / Nothing but flowers / Sax and violins / Gangster of love / Lifetime piling up / Popsicle / Paris
CD Set ______ CDEQ 50101
EMI / Oct '92 / EMI

SPEAKING IN TONGUES
Burning down the house / Making flippy floppy / Swamp / Girlfriend is better / Slippery people / I get wild / Pull up the roots / Moon rocks / This must be the place (Naive melody)
CD ______ 9238832
Sire / '83 / Warner Music

STOP MAKING SENSE
Psycho Killer / Swamp / Slippery people / Burning down the house / Girlfriend is better / Once in a lifetime / What a day that was / Life during wartime / Take me to the river
CD ______ CDFA 3302
Fame / Nov '93 / EMI

STOP MAKING SENSE/LITTLE CREATURES/TRUE STORIES (The Originals/3CD Set)
Psycho killer / Swamp / Slippery people / Burning down the house / Girlfriend is better / Once in a lifetime / What a day that was / Life during wartime / Take me to the river / And she was / Give me back my name / Creatures of love / Lady don't mind / Perfect world / Stay up late / Walk it down / Television man / Road to nowhere / Love for sale / Puzzlin' evidence / Hey now / Papa Legba / Wild wild life / Radio head / Dream operator / People like us / City of dreams
CD Set ______ CDOMB 003
EMI / Mar '97 / EMI

TALKING HEADS '77
Uh-oh, love comes to town / New feeling / Tentative decisions / Happy day / Who is it / No compassion / Book I read / Don't worry about the government / First week / Last week... carefree / Psycho killer / Pulled up
CD ______ K 256647
Sire / Feb '87 / Warner Music

TRUE STORIES
Love for sale / Puzzlin' evidence / Hey now / Papa Legba / Wild wild life / Radio head / Dream operator / People like us / City of dreams / Wild wild life (remix)
CD ______ CDFA 3231
Fame / Sep '89 / EMI

Tall Dwarfs

STUMPY
Swan song / They like you, undone / The green, green grass of someone else's home / Severed head of Julio / Crocodile / Macrame / Song of a jealous lover / Honey, I'm home / Jesus the beast / Cruising with Cochran / Things / Mojave / Box of aroma / Ghost town / Deep-fried / Disorientated boogie / And that's not all / Pull the thread (and unravel me) / Dessicated / Albumen / Two minds / Up
CD ______ FNCD 384
Flying Nun / Feb '97 / RTM/Disc

Tallari

KOMMIAMMASTI
CD ______ KICD 45
Kansanmusiikki Instituutti / Nov '96 / ADA / Direct

KONSTA
CD ______ KICD 31
Kansanmusiikki Instituutti / Dec '94 / ADA / Direct

Talley, James

AMERICAN ORIGINALS
Find somebody and love them / Bury me in New Orleans / Baby she loves a rocker / Whiskey on the side / Are they gonna make us outlaws again / Way to say I love you / New York town / Open all night / Montana song / Ready to please / We're all one family
CD ______ BCD 15244
Bear Family / '86 / Direct / Rollercoaster / Swift

BLACKJACK CHOIR/ AIN'T IT SOMETHIN'
Bluesman / Alabama summertime / Everybody loves a love song / Magnolia boy / Mississippi river whistle town / Daddy just called it the blues / Up from Georgia / Migrant Jesse Sawyer / You know I've got to love her / When the fiddler packs his case / Ain't it somethin' / Only the best / We keep tryin' / Dixie blues / Not even when it's over / Nine pounds of hashbrowns / Richland, Washington / Middle C mama / Woman troubles / Old time religion / Poets of the West Virginia mines / What will there be for the children
CD ______ BCD 15435
Bear Family / Jul '89 / Direct / Rollercoaster / Swift

GOT NO BREAD/ TRYIN' LIKE THE DEVIL
WLee O'Daniel and the Light Crust Dough Boys / Got no bread, no milk, no money / Red river memory / Give him another bottle / Calico gypsy / To get back home / Big taters in the sandy land / No openers needed / Blue eyed Ruth and my Sunday suit / Mehan, Oklahoma / Daddy's song / Take me to the country / Red river reprise / Forty hours / Deep country blues / Give my love to Marie / Are they gonna make us outlaws again / She tries not to cry / Tryin' like the devil / She's the one / Sometimes I think about Suzanne / Nothin' but the blues / You can't ever tell
CD ______ BCD 15433
Bear Family / Nov '93 / Direct / Rollercoaster / Swift

LIVE
Tryin' like the devil / Woman trouble / Whiskey on the side / Dixie blues / W Lee O'Daniel and the light crust doughboys / Not even when it's over / Nothin' like love / Find somebody and love them / Survivors / Bluesman / I can't surrender / We keep tryin' / Are you gonna make us outlaws again / Give my love to Mary / Alabama summertime / Take me to the country / Take a whiff on me
CD ______ BCD 15704
Bear Family / Jun '94 / Direct / Rollercoaster / Swift

LOVE SONGS AND THE BLUES
Your sweet love / Whatever gets you through your life / I can't surrender / He went back to Texas / Working girl / Little child / Up from Georgia / All because of you / Collection of sorrows / 'Cause I'm in love with you / May your dreams come true
CD ______ BCD 15464
Bear Family / Jul '89 / Direct / Rollercoaster / Swift

ROAD TO TORREON
Maria / Ramon estevan / H John Tarragon / Demona / La rosa Montana / She was a flower / Rosary / Storm / Little child / Anna Maria / I had a love way out West
CD ______ BCD 15633
Bear Family / Jun '92 / Direct / Rollercoaster / Swift

Talulah Gosh

BACKWASH
CD ______ KLP 44CD
K / May '96 / Cargo / Greyhound / SRD

ROCK LEGENDS VOL.69
Beatnik boy / My best friend / Steaming train / Just a dream / Talulah gosh / Don't go away / Escalator over the hill / My boy says / Way of the world / Testcard girl / Bringing up baby / I can't get no satisfaction (Thank god) / Strawberry girl
CD ______ ONLYCD 011
Avalanche / May '91 / RTM/Disc

Tam Tam

DO IT TAM TAM
CD ______ CID 9983
Island / May '92 / PolyGram

Tamalin

RHYTHM AND RHYME
CD ______ GRACD 227
Grapevine / Jul '97 / Grapevine/PolyGram

Tamarack

FIELDS OF ROCK AND SNOW
CD ______ FE 1407
Folk Era / Nov '94 / ADA / CM

FROBISHER BAY
CD ______ FE 1409
Folk Era / Nov '94 / ADA / CM

Tambastics

TAMBASTICS
CD ______ CD 704
Music & Arts / Apr '93 / Cadillac / Harmonia Mundi

Tamia

SOLITUDES (Tamia & Pierre Favre)
CD ______ 8496454
ECM / Feb '92 / New Note/Pinnacle

Tammles

SANS BAGAGE
CD ______ BUR 832CD
Escalibur / '90 / ADA / Discovery / Roots

Tampa Red

BLUEBIRD RECORDINGS 1934-1936, THE (2CD Set)
I'll kill your soul (and dare your spirit to move) / If I let you get away with it (you'll do it all the time) / I'll find my way / You've got to do better / Kingfish blues / You don't want me blues / Nobody's sweetheart now / I'm just crazy 'bout you / I still got California on my mind / Grievin' and worryin' blues / Give it up Buddy and get goin' / Somebody's been usin' that thing / Mean mistreater blues / Happy Jack / I'm so disappointed in you / Worried devil blues / Christmas and New Years's blues / Sweet woman / I'll get a break someday / Witchin' hour blues / Stockyard fire / Worthy of you / If it ain't that gal of mine / Mean old Tom cat blues / Mean old Tom cat blues / Don't dog your woman / Singing and crying blues / Shake it up a little / My baby said yes / I'm betting on you / Rowdy woman blues / Keep on dealin' (play your hand) / (I could learn to love you) so good / When I take my vacation in Harlem / Drinkin' my blues away / Dark and stormy night / Good woman blues / You missed a good man / Wailing blues / When you were a gal of seven / Let's get drunk and truck / Maybe it's someone else you love / I wonder what's the matter / She don't know my mind / She don't know my mind
CD Set ______ 07863667212
Bluebird / Feb '97 / BMG

DON'T JIVE ME
CD ______ OBCCD 549
Original Blues Classics / Nov '92 / Complete/Pinnacle / Wellard

DON'T TAMPA WITH THE BLUES
CD ______ OBCCD 516
Original Blues Classics / Nov '92 / Complete/Pinnacle / Wellard

GUITAR WIZARD, THE
It's tight like that / Big fat Mama / No matter how she done it / Reckless man blues / Don't leave me here / Dead cat on the line / Things' bout comin' my way No.2 / You can't get that stuff no more / If you want me to love you / Turpentine blues / Western bound blues / That stuff is here / Sugar Mama blues / Sugar Mama blues No.2 / Black angel blues / Things 'bout coming my way / Denver blues
CD ______ 4757022
Columbia / May '94 / Sony

IT HURTS ME TOO
CD ______ IGOCD 2004
Indigo / Oct '94 / ADA / Direct

TAMPA RED VOL.1 1928-1929
CD ______ DOCD 5073
Document / '92 / ADA / Hot Shot / Jazz Music

TAMPA RED VOL.1 1934-1935
CD ______ BDCD 6044
Blues Document / May '93 / ADA / Hot Shot / Jazz Music

TAMPA RED VOL.10
CD ______ DOCD 5210
Document / Oct '93 / ADA / Hot Shot / Jazz Music

TAMPA RED VOL.11
CD ______ DOCD 5211
Document / Oct '93 / ADA / Hot Shot / Jazz Music

TAMPA RED VOL.12
CD ______ DOCD 5212
Document / Oct '93 / ADA / Hot Shot / Jazz Music

TAMPA RED VOL.13
CD ______ DOCD 5213
Document / Oct '93 / ADA / Hot Shot / Jazz Music

TAMPA RED VOL.14
CD ______ DOCD 5214
Document / Oct '93 / ADA / Hot Shot / Jazz Music

TAMPA RED VOL.15
CD ______ DOCD 5215
Document / Oct '93 / ADA / Hot Shot / Jazz Music

TAMPA RED VOL.2 1929
CD ______ DOCD 5074
Document / '92 / ADA / Hot Shot / Jazz Music

TAMPA RED VOL.2 1935-1936
CD ______ BDCD 6045
Blues Document / May '93 / ADA / Hot Shot / Jazz Music

TAMPA RED VOL.3 1929-1930
CD ______ DOCD 5075
Document / '92 / ADA / Hot Shot / Jazz Music

TAMPA RED VOL.4 1929-1930
CD ______ DOCD 5076
Document / '92 / ADA / Hot Shot / Jazz Music

TAMPA RED VOL.5 1931-1934
CD ______ DOCD 5077
Document / Oct '93 / ADA / Hot Shot / Jazz Music

TAMPA RED VOL.6
CD ______ DOCD 5206
Document / Oct '93 / ADA / Hot Shot / Jazz Music

TAMPA RED VOL.7
CD ______ DOCD 5207
Document / Oct '93 / ADA / Hot Shot / Jazz Music

TAMPA RED VOL.8
CD ______ DOCD 5208
Document / Oct '93 / ADA / Hot Shot / Jazz Music

TAMPA RED VOL.9
CD ______ DOCD 5209
Document / Oct '93 / ADA / Hot Shot / Jazz Music

Tamplin

IN THE WITNESS BOX
CD ______ NTHEN 024CD
Now & Then / Jan '96 / Plastic Head

Tamplin, Ken

WE THE PEOPLE
CD ______ A2Z 85006CD
A-Z / Jul '96 / Plastic Head

Tams

BEST OF THE TAMS, THE
I've been hurt / Go away little girl / Take away / Be young, be foolish, be happy / Hey girl don't bother me / You lied to your Daddy / Weep little girl / It's alright / Laugh it off / Shelter / What kind of fool / Letter / Greatest love / All my hard times
CD ______ BGOCD 266
Beat Goes On / Feb '95 / Pinnacle

BEST OF THE TAMS, THE
CD ______ CDSGP 0110
Prestige / Sep '94 / Else / Total/BMG

Tamson, Jock

JOCK TAMSON'S BAIRNS (Tamson, Jock Bairns)
Lasses fashion / Robin / Merry nicht under the Tummel Brig / Braes o' Balquhidder / Greig's strathspey / Miss Wharton Duff / Lady Keith's lament / Gates of Edinburgh / O'er Bogie / Mrs. Gordon of Uvie / Tibbie Fowler / Shetland fiddler's society / Grant's reel / Gladstone's reel / Laird o' Drum / Kempy Kaye / Donald Willie and his dog / Peter MacKinnon of Skeabost / Arthur Bignold of Lochrosque / Hugh MacDonald / Sandy Duff / Birkin tree / Hieland soldier / Mullindhu / Skye man's jig / Jenny Dang the weaver / Brave Lewie Roy / Wantonness / Cathkin Braes / Miss Grace Hay's delight / Sheperdess / In dispraise of whisky / Hills of Perth / Mrs. MacDougall
CD ______ CDTRAX 112
Greentrax / Apr '96 / ADA / Direct / Duncans / Highlander

Tamulevich, David

MUSTARD'S RETREAT (Tamulevich, David & Michael Hough)
CD ______ RHRCD 72
Red House / Aug '95 / ADA / Koch

Tamura, Natsuki

HOW MANY (Tamura, Natsuki & Satoka Fujii)
CD ______ LEOLABCD 029
Leo Lab / May '97 / Cadillac

Tananas

ORCHESTRA MUNDO
CD ______ 342602
Koch International / Dec '95 / Koch
CD ______ 669712
Melodie / Mar '96 / ADA / Discovery / Grapevine/PolyGram / Greensleeves / Jet Star

TanaReid

BLUE MOTION (Tana, Akira & Rufus Reid)
Day and night / Con alma / Blue motion / Tata's dance / It's the nights I like / I concentrate on you / Medley / With a song in my heart / Amy Marie / Elvinesque
CD ______ ECD 220752
Evidence / Feb '94 / ADA / Cadillac / Harmonia Mundi

LOOKING FORWARD (Tana, Akira & Rufus Reid)
Billy / Gold minor / Duke / Skyline / Falling in love / Bell / Third eye / Reminiscing / Love dreams / Looking forward
CD ______ ECD 22114
Evidence / Jun '95 / ADA / Cadillac / Harmonia Mundi

PASSING THOUGHTS (Tana, Akira & Rufus Reid)
Hotel le hot / City slicker / Heroes / Cheek to cheek / Sophisticated lady / Prelude to a kiss / Hope for now / Passing thoughts / Light blue / It's the magical look in your eyes / Scufflestyle
CD ______ CCD 4505
Concord Jazz / May '92 / New Note/Pinnacle

Tanenbaum, David

ASTOR PIAZZOLLA - EL PORTENO
CD ______ NA 065
New Albion / May '94 / Cadillac / Harmonia Mundi

Tangerine

TANGERINE
CD ____ CRECD 061
Creation / May '94 / 3mv/Vital

Tangerine Dream

ALPHA CENTAURI
CD ____ ESMCD 346
Essential / Feb '96 / BMG

ALPHA CENTAURI/ ATEM
Sunrise in the third system / Fly and collision of the comas sola / Alpha Centauri / Atem / Fauni-gena / Circulation of events / Wahn
CD ____ 8856180692
Relativity / Oct '87 / Pinnacle

ATEM
CD ____ ESMCD 348
Essential / Feb '96 / BMG

ATMOSPHERICS
CD ____ EMPRCD 564
Emporio / Mar '95 / Disc

COLLECTION, THE
Genesis / Circulation of events / Fauni-gena / Alpha Centauri / Fly and collision of the comas sola / Journey through a burning brain / Birth of liquid plejades / White clouds
CD ____ CCSCD 161
Castle / Jul '87 / BMG

CYCLONE
Bent cold sidewalk / Rising runner missed by endless sender / Madrigal meridian
CD ____ TAND 9
Virgin / Apr '95 / EMI

DREAM ROOTS COLLECTION, THE (5CD Set)
Birth of liquid plejades / Journey through a burning brain / Alpha centauri / Zeit / Wahn / Fauni-gena / Green desert / White clouds / Astral voyager / Origin of supernatural probabilities / Indian summer / Ride on a ray / Livemiles / Tangent / Smile / Livemiles / Vigour / Central Park / Zen garden / Livemiles / Le parc / 21st century common man / Underwater sunlight / Livemiles / London / Gaudi Park / Barbakane / Alchemy of my heart / Horizon / Song of the whale / Yellowstone Park / Tyger / Bois de Boulogne / Tiergarten / Poland / Barbakane / Livemiles / Rarebird / Song of the whale / London / Valley of the sun / Beach bay bunker / Vanishing blue / Red morpho
CD Set ____ ESFCD 420
Essential / Nov '96 / BMG

DREAM SEQUENCE (2CD Set)
Dream is always the same / Phaedra / Rubycon / Stratosfear / Choronzon / Cherokee Lane / Cinnamon Road / Kiew mission / Ricochet / Cloudburst flight / Force majeure / Tangram / Beach stone / Logos / White eagle / Dominion / Love on a real train
CD Set ____ CDTD 1
Virgin / Apr '92 / EMI
CD ____ TDI 001CD
TDI / Jul '96 / Pinnacle

ELECTRONIC MEDITATION
CD ____ ESMCD 345
Essential / Feb '96 / BMG

ENCORE (Live)
Cherokee lane / Monolight / Coldwater canyon / Desert dream
CD ____ TAND 1
Virgin / Apr '95 / EMI

FORCE MAJEURE
Force Majeure / Cloudburst flight / Thru Metamorphic rocks
CD ____ TAND 10
Virgin / Apr '95 / EMI

FROM DAWN TILL DUSK 1973-1988
Song of the whale (part 1: from dawn) / Song of the whale (part 2: from dusk) / Bois de Boulogne / Ride on the ray / Poland / London / Le parc / Live miles (extract) / Central Park / Zeit / Wahn
CD ____ MCCD 034
Music Club / Sep '91 / Disc / THE

GOBLINS CLUB
Towards the evening star / At Darwin's motel / On crane's passage / Rising haul in silence / United Goblins parade / Lamb with radar eyes / Elf June and the midnight patrol / Sad Merlin's Sunday
CD ____ WENCD 011
When / Sep '96 / Pinnacle

GREEN DESERT
CD ____ ESMCD 349
Essential / Feb '96 / BMG

HYPERBOREA
No man's land / Hyperborea / Cinnamon road / Sphinx lightning
CD ____ TAND 4
Virgin / Jul '95 / EMI

LE PARC
Bois de Boulogne / Central Park / Gaudi Park / Tiergarten / Zen garden / Le Parc / Hyde Park / Cliffs of Sydney / Yellowstone Park
CD ____ ESMCD 364
Essential / May '96 / BMG

LILY ON THE BEACH
Too hot for my chinchilla / Lily on the beach / Alaskan summer / Desert drive / Mount Shasta / Crystal curfew / Paradise cove / Twenty nine palms / Valley of the kings / Radio city / Blue Mango Cafe / Gecko / Long island sunset
CD ____ 260103
Private Music / Dec '89 / BMG

LIVE MILES
Live miles
CD ____ ESMCD 368
Essential / May '96 / BMG

LOGOS (Live At The Dominion, London 1982)
Logos / Dominion
CD ____ TAND 3
Virgin / Jul '95 / EMI

OASIS
Flashflood / Zion / Reflections / Cliff dwellers / Waterborne / Cedar breaks / Summer storm / Hopi mesa heart
CD ____ TDI 007CD
TDI / Jun '97 / Pinnacle

OPTICAL RACE
Marrakesh / Atlas eyes / Mothers of rain / Twin soul tribe / Optical race / Cat scan / Sun gate / Turning of the wheel / Midnight trail / Ghazal (Love song)
CD ____ 259557
Private Music / Aug '88 / BMG

PERGAMON
CD ____ ESMCD 413
Essential / May '96 / BMG

PHAEDRA
Phaedra / Mysterious semblance at the strand of nightmares / Movements of a visionary / Sequent C
CD ____ TAND 5
Virgin / Feb '95 / EMI

POLAND (The Warsaw Concert)
Poland / Tangent / Barbarkne / Horizon
CD ____ ESMCD 365
Essential / May '96 / BMG

PRIVATE MUSIC OF TANGERINE DREAM, THE
Melrose / Too hot for my chinchilla / Long Island sunset / Atlas eyes / Sun gate / Rolling down Cahuenga / Three bikes in the sky / After the call / Electric lion / Dolls in the shadow / Beaver town / Roaring of the bliss
CD ____ 01005821052
Private Music / Feb '93 / BMG

RICOCHET
Ricochet
CD ____ TAND 7
Virgin / Feb '95 / EMI

ROCKOON
Big city of dwarves / Red roadster / Touchwood / Graffiti Street / Funky Atlanta / Spanish love / Lifted veil / Penguin reference / Body corporate / Rockoon / Girls on Broadway
CD ____ ESMCD 403
Essential / Jul '96 / BMG

RUBYCON
Rubycon
CD ____ TAND 6
Virgin / Feb '95 / EMI

STRATOSFEAR
Stratosfear / Big sleep in search of Hades / 3 a.m. at the border of the marsh / Invisible limits
CD ____ TAND 8
Virgin / Feb '95 / EMI

TANGENTS 1973-1983 (5CD Set)
Mojave plan (Desert part) / No man's land / Kiew mission / Ricochet / Force majeure / Logos (blue part) / Stratosfear / Mysterious semblance at the strand of nightmares / Cinnamon road / Tangram (solution part) / White eagle / Phaedra / Logos (red part) / Sphinx lightning / Desert dream / Invisible limits / Exit / Mojave plan (canyon part) / Tangram (puzzle part) / Monolight / Rubycon (The Decision) / Cloudburst flight / Pilots of purple twilight / Logos (velvet part) / Monolight (yellow part) / Tangram (future part) / Rubycon (dice part) / Hyperborea / Rubycon (crossing part) / Dominion / Pergamon (piano part) / Going West / Dream is always the same / Alien goodbye / Call / Run / Betrayal (Sorceror theme) / Rainbirds move / Creation / Charly the kid / Journey / Scrap yard / Dirty cross roads / Search / Highway patrol / Grind / Risky business / Beach theme / Vulcano / Jogger / South Dakota / Coppercoast / Great barrier reef / Night at Ayers Rock / Afternoon on the Nile / Crane routing / Silver scale / Jamaican monk
CD Set ____ CDBOX 4
Virgin / Oct '94 / EMI

TANGERINE AMBIENCE (A Tribute To Tangerine Dream) (Various Artists)
CD ____ CLP 0048
Cleopatra / Aug '97 / Cargo / Greyhound / Plastic Head / RTM/Disc / SRD

TANGERINE DREAM
Phaedra / Mysterious semblance at the strand of nightmares / Movements of visionary / Sequent 'C' / Rubycon pt.1 / Stratosfear
CD ____ VI 873772
Disky / Oct '96 / Disky / THE

TANGRAM
CD ____ TAND 11
Virgin / Apr '95 / EMI

TOURNADO
Flashflood / 220 volt / Firetongues / Girls on Broadway / Little blond in the park of attractions / Rising haul in silence / Lamb with radar eyes / Touchwood / Towards the evening star
CD ____ TDI 008CD
TDI / Sep '97 / Pinnacle

TURN OF THE TIDES
CD ____ CTCZ 108
Coast To Coast / Nov '96 / Grapevine/ PolyGram

TYGER
Tyger / London / Alchemy of the heart / Smile / 21st century common man
CD ____ ESMCD 367
Essential / May '96 / BMG

TYRANNY OF BEAUTY
CD ____ TDI 002CD
TDI / Oct '96 / Pinnacle

UNDERWATER SUNLIGHT
Song of the whale / Song of the whale / Dolphin dance / Ride on the Ray / Scuba Scuba / Underwater twilight
CD ____ ESMCD 366
Essential / May '96 / BMG

WHITE EAGLE
Mojave plan / Midnight in Tula / Convention of the 24 / White Eagle
CD ____ TAND 2
Virgin / Jul '95 / EMI

ZEIT
Birth of liquid plejades / Nebulous dawn / Origin of supernatural possibilities / Zeit
CD ____ ESMCD 347
Essential / Feb '96 / BMG

Tangle Edge

EULOGY
CD ____ DMCD 1029
Demi-Monde / May '93 / RTM/Disc / TKO Magnum

IN SEARCH OF A NEW DAWN
CD ____ DMCD 1009
Demi-Monde / Mar '95 / RTM/Disc / TKO Magnum

TAKRA
CD ____ DELECCD 065
Delerium / Jun '97 / Cargo / Pinnacle / Vital

Tank, John

SO IN LOVE
So in love / Address this issue / Snow place / West of the moon / Suite - peace / We'll say hello again / Vengeance / Uptown lex / Whipmarks
CD ____ TCB 95602
TCB / Dec '95 / New Note/Pinnacle

Tankard

STONE COLD SOBER
Jurisdiction / Broken image / Mindwild / Ugly beauty / Centrefold / Behind the back / Stone cold sober / Blood guts and rock 'n' roll / Lost and found (tantrum part 2) / Sleeping with the past / Freibier / Of strange people talking under Arabian skies
CD ____ N 01902
Noise / Jun '92 / Koch

TWO-FACED
CD ____ N 02332
Noise / Feb '94 / Koch

Tannahill Weavers

BEST OF THE TANNAHILL WEAVERS 1979-1989, THE
Geese in the bog/Jig of slurs / Auld lang syne / Tranent muir / Highland laddie / Lucy Cassidy/Bletherskate/Smith of Chilliechassie / Farewell to Fiunary/Heather Island / Roddie MacDonald's favourite / Gypsy laddie / Jamie Raeburn's farewell / Johnny Cope/Atholl Highlanders / I once loved a lass / Turf lodge/Cape Breton's fiddlers' welcome to the Shetlands / Lady Margaret Stewart/Flaggon
CD ____ GLCD 1100
Green Linnet / Jul '92 / ADA / CM / Direct / Highlander / Roots

CAPERNAUM
CD ____ GLCD 1146
Green Linnet / Aug '94 / ADA / CM / Direct / Highlander / Roots

CULLEN BAY
CD ____ GLCD 1108
Green Linnet / Mar '91 / ADA / CM / Direct / Highlander / Roots

DANCING FEET
Turf lodge / Tranent Muir / Isabeaux S'y Promene / Fisher row / Wild mountain thyme / Maggie's pancakes / Mary Morrison / Campbeltown kiltie ball / Final trawl
CD ____ GLCD 1081
Green Linnet / Apr '92 / ADA / CM / Direct / Highlander / Roots

LAND OF LIGHT
Lucy Cassidy / Scottish settler's lament / Ronald Maclean's farewell to Oban / Dunrobin castle / Rovin' heilandman / Yellow haired laddie / Land of light / Queen amang the heather/Mairi Anne... / Bustles and bonnets / American stranger / Conon Bridge
CD ____ GLCD 1067
Green Linnet / Jun '88 / ADA / CM / Direct / Highlander / Roots

LEAVING ST. KILDA
Good drying set / Hieland Harry / Rigs o' rye / Athol gathering / St. Kilda set / Shearin's no for you / Three healths / Crann Tara set / Wars o' Germany / Islay charms set / Last May a braw wooer / Fareweel you silver darlin's
CD ____ GLCD 1176
Green Linnet / Nov '96 / ADA / CM / Direct / Highlander / Roots

MERMAID'S SONG
Greenwood side/Highland laddie/Pattie / Logie o' Buchan / Elspeth Campbell/Kenny Gilles of Portnalong/Skye/Malcolm Joh / Mermaid's song/Herra boys/Captain Horn/ Fourth floor / Are ye sleeping Maggie/ Noose and the ghillie / A Bruxa / Come under my plaidie / Campbell's farewell to Redcastle / Flashmarket close / MacArthur/ Colonel Fraser/Swallow's tale / Ass in the graveyard
CD ____ GLCD 1121
Green Linnet / Feb '89 / ADA / CM / Direct / Highlander / Roots

PASSAGE
Roddie MacDonald's favourite / Jamie Raeburn's farewell / Harris and the mare / Duntroon/Trip to Alaska / Highland laddie / At the end of a pointed gun / Lady Dysie / Coach house reel/Marie Christina / Phuktiphanno/John MacKenzie's fancy / Drink a round
CD ____ GLCD 3031
Green Linnet / Oct '93 / ADA / CM / Direct / Highlander / Roots

Tannas

HERITAGE
CD ____ CDLDL 1217
Lochshore / Nov '94 / ADA / Direct / Duncans

RU-RA
CD ____ CDLDL 1231
Lochshore / Oct '95 / ADA / Direct / Duncans

Tannehill, Frank

COMPLETE RECORDINGS 1932-1941
CD ____ SOB 035262
Story Of The Blues / Feb '93 / ADA / Koch

Tanner

(GERMO) PHOBIC
CD ____ HED 075
Headhunter / Jun '97 / Cargo

ILL-GOTTEN GAINS
Hey jigsaw / Computers that breathe / Wig / Still a rat / Man below dim moon / Seiner / Catalogue / Kid / Purma Park / Guard dog / Noose / Spastic art / Not a fitting niche
CD ____ CAROL 17892
Caroline / May '96 / Cargo / Vital

Tanrikorur, Cinucen

CINUCEN TANRIKORUR
CD ____ C 580045
Ocora / Feb '94 / ADA / Harmonia Mundi

Tans, J.C.

AROUND THE WORLD
CD ____ BVHAASTCD 8905
Bvhaast / Sep '92 / Cadillac

Tansads

DRAG DOWN THE MOON (Tansads Live)
CD ____ TRACD 118
Transatlantic / Apr '96 / Pinnacle

FLOCK
Band on a rainbow / Fear of falling / She's not gone / God on a string / Iron man / Waiting for the big one / Dance / Sunlight in the morning / G Man / Ship of fools / I know I can (but I won't) / Heading for the heart / Separate souls
CD ____ TRACD 1
Transatlantic / Apr '96 / Pinnacle

UP THE SHIRKERS
Eye of the average / Camelot / Brian Kant / Zig zag / Music down / Waste of space / Chip pan ocean / English rover / John John / Reason to be / Revolution / Turn on/tune up
CD ____ ESMCD 352
Essential / Nov '95 / BMG

Tansey, Seamus

BEST OF SEAMUS TANSEY, THE
CD ____ PTICD 1007

Pure Traditional Irish / Jun '96 / ADA / CM / Direct / Ross

EASTER SNOW
Josie McDermott's/Kitty gone a milking / Piper Anderson's delight / John Brennan's favourite/Ladd O'Beirne's favourite / Easter snow / Mick Flatley's delight/Ed Reavey's favourite / Dillon's favourite/The bag o'spuds / Tribute to Peggy McGrath/John McKenna's jig / Dunphy's hornpipe/Sean Ryan's favourite / May morning dew / Jimeen Gannon's delight/Dowd's no.9 / Lament for the death of Staker Wallace / Maid in the cherry tree/Farewell to Ireland / Famine requiem / Ah surely/Maud Miller / Seannie Davey's reel/Alfie Joe Denning's reel
CD ____ COMD 2063
Temple / Mar '97 / ADA / CM / Direct / Duncans / Highlander

Tanzmusik

SINCEKAI
CD ____ RSNCD 26
Rising High / Jan '95 / 3mv/Sony

Tao

ESOTERIC RED
Sleeping junk / Larvae / Esoteric red / Nocturnal / Kaleidoscope / Scarifice / Jinn and tonic / Radiance / Medium / Curvature/ Overture / Sacred swell / Pharmacos / Astral circle / Green material / Riot in Lagos
CD ____ WORDD 005
Language / Jul '97 / Grapevine/PolyGram / Prime / Vital

Tapajos, Sebastiao

AFFINITIES (Tapajos, Sebastiao & G. Peranzzetta)
CD ____ 68984
Tropical / Jul '97 / Discovery

BRASILIDADE
Vila rica / Rancheira / Cancao para marisa / Olinda medieval / Repentes / O bonde das seis / Brinquedo pra o junior / Criancas da minha terra / Perere / Pelourinho / Frevo
CD ____ 68945
Tropical / Apr '97 / Discovery

SAMBAS AND BOSSAS (Tapajos, Sebastiao & Friends)
Waves / Brasileiro and samba em Berlin / Cancao para marisa / Sertao / Ganga / viajeiro / Tristeza / Vale do amanihecer / Xingu / Lua joa igarapes / Tocata para Billy Blanco / Chega de saudade / Asa branca / Sorriso da tristeza
CD ____ 68930
Tropical / Jul '97 / Discovery

XINGU - GITARRE UND PERCUSSION
Xingu / Intoducao / Percutindo / Bacurau / Percussorongando / Odeon / Brasileiro and samba em Berlin / Escolado mar / Xadrez / Luz negra
CD ____ 68907
Tropical / Apr '97 / Discovery

Tapani Varis

MUNNIHAPPUUNA
CD ____ KICD 46
Kansanmusiikki Instituutti / Nov '96 / ADA / Direct

Tapia Eta Leturia Band

TAPIA ETA LETURIA BAND, THE
CD ____ KD 412CD
Elkar / Nov '96 / ADA

Tapia, Oscar Moreno

SONGS OF MEXICO VOL.2 (Tapia, Oscar Moreno & Los Mecateros)
CD ____ VICG 53362
JVC World Library / Mar '96 / ADA / CM / Direct

Tappa Zukie

DEEP ROOTS
CD ____ RASCD 3224
Ras / Sep '96 / Direct / Greensleeves / Jet Star / SRD

FROM THE ARCHIVES
CD ____ RASCD 3135
Ras / Jun '95 / Direct / Greensleeves / Jet Star / SRD

MASSIVE RESISTANCE (Various Artists)
CD ____ RASCD 3142
Ras / Jun '94 / Direct / Greensleeves / Jet Star / SRD

TAPPA ZUKIE IN DUB
CD ____ BAFCD 8
Blood & Fire / Sep '95 / Vital

Tapsi Turtles

I WANNA HEAR THE SUNSHINE
CD ____ TTT 001CD
We Bite / Sep '96 / Plastic Head

Tar

OVER AND OUT
CD ____ TGCD 145
Touch & Go / Oct '95 / SRD

Tar Babies

DEATH TRIP
CD ____ SON 0042
Sonic Noise / Jan '93 / SRD

HONEY BUBBLE
CD ____ SST 236CD
SST / Jul '89 / Plastic Head

Tara

BOYS IN THE LANE
CD ____ EUCD 1019
ARC / '89 / ADA / ARC Music

RIGS OF THE TIME
CD ____ EUCD 1006
ARC / '89 / ADA / ARC Music

Tara Key

EAR AND ECHO
CD ____ HMS 2222
Homestead / May '95 / Cargo / SRD

Taraf De Carancebes

MUSICIENS DU BANAT - ROUMANIA
CD ____ Y225208
Silex / Jun '93 / ADA / Harmonia Mundi

Taraf De Haidouks

HONOURABLE BRIGANDS MAGIC HORSES AND EVIL EYE
CD ____ CRAW 13
Crammed Discs / Apr '95 / Grapevine/ PolyGram / New Note/Pinnacle / Prime / RTM/Disc

MUSIQUE DES TZIGANES DE ROUMANIE
CD ____ CRAW 2
Crammed World / Jan '96 / New Note/ Pinnacle

Taran

MOD & MINI SPACE AGE
CD ____ COMP 026CD
Compost / Oct '96 / Plastic Head / SRD / Timewarp

Tardiff, Paul

POINTS OF DEPARTURE
CD ____ 378002
Koch Jazz / Oct '96 / Koch

Tarika

BALANCE
CD ____ FMSD 5028
Rogue / Jan '94 / Stern's

BIBIANGO
CD ____ GLCD 4028
Green Linnet / Jan '95 / ADA / CM / Direct / Highlander / Roots

FANAFODY
CD ____ FMSD 5024
Rogue / Oct '92 / Stern's

SON EGAL
Tsy kivy / Avelo / Voandalana / Zotra / Sonegaly / Rafrancois / Vavaka / Ady / Sento / Raha tiany / Forever / Diso be / Aza misy miteniteny
CD ____ XEN 04042CD
Xenophile / Feb '97 / ADA / Direct

Tarika Sammy

BENEATH SOUTHERN SKIES
CD ____ SHCD 64067
Shanachie / Jul '96 / ADA / Greensleeves / Koch

Tarmey, Bill

AFTER HOURS
It's too late / Love don't live here anymore / Almaz / Everything I own / Wonderful tonight / Funny how time slips away / She's out of my life / Fool if you think it's over / What'll I do / Love on the rocks / I'm not in love / Never thought / I'm all out of love / Sandman's coming
CD ____ PRMTVCD 2
Premier/EMI / Apr '96 / EMI

GIFT OF LOVE, A
Nobody loves me like you do / Somewhere out there / In your eyes / Tonight I celebrate my love / It might be you / That's all / Save the best for last / Everything I do (I do it for you) / She loves me / Right here waiting / Hundred ways / Weekend in New England / If we hold on together / Wind beneath my wings
CD ____ CDEMC 3665
EMI / Nov '93 / EMI

TIME FOR LOVE
Time for love / Don't it make my brown eyes blue / IOU / I'm the one / If I thought you'd ever change your mind / If this is what love can do / Don't know much / Dance of love / Some people / Perfect year / One shining moment / Belonging / You and I / As long as you are there
CD ____ CDEMTV 85
EMI / Oct '94 / EMI

Tarnation

GENTLE CREATURES
Game of broken hearts / Halfway to madness / Well / Big o motel / Tell me it's not so / Two wrongs / Lonely lights / Gentle creatures / Listen to the wind / Hand / Do you fancy me / Yellow birds / Burn again / Stranger in the mirror / It's not easy
CD ____ CAD 5010CD
4AD / Sep '95 / RTM/Disc

MIRADOR
An awful shade of blue / Wait / Place where I know / Is she lonesome now / Your thoughts and mine / Christine / Destiny / There's someone / Like a ghost / Idly / Little black egg / You'll understand
CD ____ CAD 7004CD
4AD / Apr '97 / RTM/Disc

Tarras, Dave

YIDDISH AMERICAN KLEZMER MUSIC
CD ____ YAZCD 7001
Shanachie / Apr '92 / ADA / Greensleeves / Koch

Tartan Amoebas

IMAGINARY TARTAN MENAGERIE
Ska reggae / Sub heaven / Penguin blues / Road rage / New pipe order / Brief case shuffle / Clavershouse / I close my eyes / Adios amoebas
CD ____ IRCD 034
Iona / Nov '95 / ADA / Direct / Duncans

TARTAN AMOEBAS
Pinch of snuff / Reels of Tulloch / Lark in the morning / Miss Stewart / Loch Leven Castle / Funky pipes / Dubh / Alex's reels / Johnnie Cope / Kwela
CD ____ CDTRAX 133
Greentrax / May '97 / ADA / Direct / Duncans / Highlander

Tartan Lads

TARTAN LADS OF BONNIE SCOTLAND
CD ____ CDITV 540
Scotdisc / May '91 / Conifer/BMG / Duncans / Ross

Tartaros

GRAND PSYCHOTIC CASTLE
CD ____ NR 6688CD
Necropolis / May '97 / Plastic Head

Tasavallan Presidentti

LAMBERT LAND
Lounge / Lambert Land / Celebration of the saved nine / Bargain / Dance / Last quarters
CD ____ LRCD 60
Love / May '97 / ADA / Direct / Greyhound

MILKY WAY MOSES
Milky way Moses / Caught from the air / Jelly: confusing the issue / How to start a day / Piece of mind
CD ____ LRCD 102
Love / Nov '96 / ADA / Direct / Greyhound

Tasby, Finis

PEOPLE DON'T CARE
CD ____ SHCD 9007
Shanachie / May '95 / ADA / Greensleeves / Koch

Tasha Killer Pussies

SHAKE & VAC
CD ____ 5503 BAG
Bag / Jan '97 / Total/BMG

Tashan

FOR THE SAKE OF LOVE
Tempted / Been a long time / Ecstatic / For the sake of love / Single and lonely / Still in love / Love is forever / Romantically inspired / Control of me / Insane / All I ever do / Love of my life
CD ____ 4724112
Columbia / Mar '94 / Sony

Tashian, Barry

HARMONY (Tashian, Barry & Holly)
It's too late to pray / I'll take my time / Don't kneel at my graveside / Wild wind / Power of love / Two ways to fall / Fools hall of fame / Blues for Dixie / Hello sorrow / Lonesome and blue / All I have to offer you is me / Love you give
CD ____ ROUCD 0412
Rounder / Mar '97 / ADA / CM / Direct

LIVE IN HOLLAND (Tashian, Barry & Holly)
CD ____ SCR 27
Strictly Country / Jul '95 / ADA / Direct

READY FOR LOVE (Tashian, Barry & Holly)
Ready for love / Let me see the light / Heaven with you / Heart full of memories / Hearts that break / Highway 86 / Price of pride / Diamond / Ring of gold / Memories remain / If I knew then / This old love
CD ____ ROUCD 0302
Rounder / May '93 / ADA / CM / Direct

STRAW INTO GOLD (Tashian, Barry & Holly)
CD ____ ROUCD 0332
Rounder / Nov '94 / ADA / CM / Direct

TRUST IN ME (Tashian, Barry & Holly)
Trust in me / Home / Blue eyes / Ramona / Making a change / You're running wild / Party doll / My favourite memory / Poor woman's epitaph / Look both ways / Boy who cried love / I can't dance
CD ____ CDRR 302
Request / Mar '92 / Jazz Music / Wellard

Tassilli Players

AT THE COWSHED
CD ____ FISHNO 3CD
Konkurrent / Jul '97 / SRD

OUTER SPACE
CD ____ WWCD 21
Universal Egg / Sep '96 / SRD

WONDERFUL WORLD OF WEED IN DUB, THE
CD ____ WWCD 11
Wibbly Wobbly / Sep '95 / SRD

Taste

LIVE AT THE ISLE OF WIGHT
What's going on / Sugar mama / Morning sun / Sinner boy / I feel so good / Catfish
CD ____ 8416022
Polydor / Apr '94 / PolyGram

ON THE BOARDS
What's going on / Railway and gun / It's happened before, it'll happen again / If the day was any longer / Morning sun / Eat my words / On the boards / If I don't sing I'll cry / See here / I'll remember
CD ____ 8415992
Polydor / Apr '94 / PolyGram

TASTE
Blister on the moon / Leaving blues / Sugar Mama / Hail / Born on the wrong side of time / Dual carriageway pain / Same old story / Catfish / I'm moving on
CD ____ 8416002
Polydor / Jul '94 / PolyGram

Taste Of Fear

TASTE OF FEAR
CD ____ LF 118CD
Lost & Found / Feb '95 / Plastic Head

Taste Of Honey

BEAUTY AND THE BOOGIE
Boogie oogie oogie / Rescue me / Disco dancin' / Sukiyaki / I'll try something new / Do it good / Midnight snack / Sayonara / Love me tonite / Never go wrong / If we loved / Don't you lead me on / We got the groove / Boogie oogie oogie
CD ____ CTMCD 330
EMI / Jul '97 / EMI

Taste Of Joy

TRIGGER FABLES
CD ____ W 230089
Nettwerk / Mar '96 / Greyhound / Pinnacle / Vital
CD ____ FAC 86442
Edel / May '96 / Pinnacle

Tate, Baby

SEE WHAT YOU DONE
CD ____ OBCCD 567
Original Blues Classics / Oct '95 / Complete/Pinnacle / Wellard

Tate, Buddy

BALLAD ARTISTRY OF BUDDY TATE, THE
CD ____ SKCD 23034
Sackville / Oct '92 / Cadillac / Jazz Music / Swift

BUDDY TATE AND HIS BUDDIES
CD ____ CRD 123
Chiaroscuro / Mar '96 / Jazz Music

BUDDY TATE, HUMPHREY LYTTELTON & RUBY BRAFF (Tate, Buddy & Humphrey Lyttelton/Ruby Braff)
Kansas City woman / One for me / Candyville / Outswinger / Steevos / Clarinet lemonade / Swinging scorpio / Mean to me / I surrender dear / My Monday date / Take the 'A' train / Pan Am blues
CD ____ 8747132
DA Music / Jul '96 / Conifer/BMG

GROOVIN' WITH TATE
Me 'n' you / Idling / Blow low / Moon dog / No kiddin' / Miss Ruby Jones / Blues for Trix / Salt mines / I'm just a lucky so and

so / East of the Sun and West of the moon / Makin' whoopee / Boardwalk / Overdrive
CD ________ PCD 24152
Prestige / Jun '96 / Cadillac / Complete/ Pinnacle

JUMPING ON THE WEST COAST (Tate, Buddy & Friends)
CD ________ BLCD 760175
Black Lion / Mar '93 / Cadillac / Jazz Music / Koch / Wellard

JUST JAZZ (Tate, Buddy & Al Grey)
CD ________ RSRCD 110
Reservoir Music / Dec '94 / Cadillac

SWINGING SCORPIO (Tate, Buddy & Humphrey Lyttelton)
CD ________ BLC 760165
Black Lion / '92 / Cadillac / Jazz Music / Koch / Wellard

TEXAS TWISTER, THE
CD ________ NW 352
New World / '88 / ADA / Cadillac / Harmonia Mundi

WHEN I'M BLUE
CD ________ BB 8662
Black & Blue / Apr '96 / Discovery / Koch / Wellard

Tate, Danny

DANNY TATE
CD ________ CDCUS 16
Charisma / Jan '92 / EMI

Tate, Grady

BODY AND SOUL
CD ________ MCD 9208
Milestone / Jun '95 / Cadillac / Complete/ Pinnacle / Jazz Music / Wellard

Tater Totz

TATER COMES ALIVE
CD ________ ROCK 60542
Rockville / Jul '93 / Plastic Head / SRD

Taters & Pie

NO MORE PUTTING OFF
Let the white moon shine / Heather island/ Catching flies / Where lies and land / Piskeflode / Sirens and screams / Fools never die out / Jamie foyers / East Anglian sunset / Sea fever / Chasing chickens / Highway to eternal night / Love is all he needs / Hands's have no tears to cry/Jonathan's hat / Farewell
CD ________ GFMSCDS 6
Green Fingers / Nov '93 / Green Fingers Music

Tathak, Pandit Ashok

COLOURFUL WORLD OF PANDIT ASHOK TATHAK, THE
CD ________ CD 3301
Saraswati / Aug '94 / Direct

Tati, Cheb

DANS LA VIE
Dans la vie / Sada / Bled / Labsa / La moda / President / Henini / La moda jungle / Dans la vie
CD ________ JVC 90072
JVC / Oct '96 / Direct / New Note/Pinnacle / Vital/SAM

Tattoo

BLOOD RED
CD ________ RR 94962
Roadrunner / Dec '88 / PolyGram

Tatum, Art

20TH CENTURY PIANO GENIUS (2CD Set)
CD Set ________ 5317632
Verve / Aug '96 / PolyGram

ART OF TATUM (25 Great Solo Performancs 1932-1944) (Various Artists)
Tiger rag / Sophisticated lady / (I would do) anything for you / After you've gone / Stardust / Shout / Liza / Gone with the wind / Stormy weather / Chloe / Sheikh of araby / Teas for two / Deep purple / Elegie / Humoresque / Get happy / Lullaby of the leaves / Moonglow / Love me / Cocktails for two / St. Louis blues / Begin the beguine / Rosetta / Sweet Lorraine
CD ________ AIA 5164
ASV / Apr '95 / Select

ART TATUM 1940-1941
CD ________ CLASSICS 800
Classics / Mar '95 / Discovery / Jazz Music

ART'S ART
(Back home again in) Indiana / Sheik of Araby / Sweet Lorraine / Get happy / St. Louis blues / Gone with the wind / Lullaby of the leaves / Elegie / Tiger rag / Chloe / Stormy weather / Humoresque / Moonglow / Cocktails for two / Rosetta / Tea for two / Love me / Begin the beguine / Emaline / Deep purple
CD ________ 305042
Hallmark / Jul '97 / Carlton

BODY AND SOUL
CD ________ JHR 73514
Jazz Hour / May '93 / Cadillac / Jazz Music / Target/BMG

CLASSICS 1932-1934
CD ________ CLASSICS 507
Classics / Apr '90 / Discovery / Jazz Music

CLASSICS 1934-1940
CD ________ CLASSICS 560
Classics / Oct '91 / Discovery / Jazz Music

CLASSICS 1940
CD ________ CLASSICS 831
Classics / Sep '95 / Discovery / Jazz Music

CLASSICS 1944
CD ________ CLASSICS 825
Classics / Sep '95 / Discovery / Jazz Music

COMPLETE BRUNSWICK & DECCA SESSIONS 1932-1941 (3CD Set)
Strange as it seems / I'll never be the same / You gave me everything but love / This time it's love / Tea for two / St. Louis blues / Tiger rag / Sophisticated lady / Moonglow / (I would do) anything for you / When a woman loves a man / Emaline / Love me / Cocktails for two / After you've gone / Stardust / Ill wind / Shout / Beautiful love / Liza / I ain't got nobody / Boots and saddle / Body and soul / With plenty of money and you / What will I tell my heart / I've got my love to keep me warm / Gone with the wind / Stormy weather / Chloe / Sheikh of araby / Deep purple / Elegie / Humoresque / Sweet Lorraine / Get happy / Lullaby of the leaves / Begin the beguine / Rosetta / (Back home again in) Indiana / Wee baby blues / Stompin' at the Savoy / Last goodbye blues / Battery bounce / Lucille / Rock me mama / Corine Corina / Lonesome graveyard blues
CD ________ CDAFS 10353
Affinity / Apr '93 / Cadillac / Jazz Music / Koch

COMPLETE CAPITOL RECORDINGS VOL.1
Willow weep for me / I cover the waterfront / Aunt Hagar's blues / Nice work if you can get it / Someone to watch over me / Dardanella / Time on my hands (you in my arms) / Sweet Lorraine / Somebody loves me / Don't blame me / September song / Melody in F / Tea for two / Out of nowhere
CD ________ CZ 278
Capitol / Jan '92 / EMI

COMPLETE PABLO GROUP MASTERPIECES 1954-1956, THE (6CD Set)
Blues in C / Undecided / Under a blanket of blue / Blues in B flat / Foggy day / Street of dreams / 'S wonderful / Makin' whoopee / Old fashioned love / Blues in my heart / My blue heaven / Hands across the table / You're mine you / Idaho / Night and day / I won't dance / In a sentimental mood / Moon is low / Moon song / You took advantage of me / This can't be love / I surrender dear / I won't dance / In a sentimental mood / What is this thing called love / I'll never be the same / Makin' whoopee / Hallelujah / Perdido / More than you know / How high the moon / This can't be love / Stars fell on Alabama / Lover man / Prisoner of love / Love for sale / Love for sale / Body and soul / Please be kind / This can't be love / Hallelujah / Verve blues / Plaid / Somebody loves me / September song / What is this thing called love / What is this thing called love / Just one of those things / More than you know / Some other Spring / If / Blue Lou / Love for sale / Isn't it romantic / I'll never be the same / I guess I'll have to change my plans / Trio blues / Deep night / This can't be love / Memories of you / Once in a while / Foggy day / Lover man / You're mine, you / Makin' whoopee / Deep night / Once in a while / This can't be love / Gone with the wind / All the things you are / Have you met Miss Jones / My one and only love / Night and day / My ideal / Where or when / Gone with the wind / Gone with the wind / Have you met Miss Jones
CD Set ________ 6PACD 4401
Pablo / Nov '96 / Cadillac / Complete/ Pinnacle

COMPLETE PABLO SOLO MASTERPIECES 1953-1956, THE (7CD Set)
Can't we be friends / This can't be love / Elegy / Memories of you / Over the rainbow / If you hadn't gone away / Body and soul / Man I love / Makin' whoopee / September song / Begin the beguine / Humouresque / Louise / Love for sale / Judy / I'm comin' Virginia / Wrap your troubles in dreams / Dixieland band / Embraceable you / Come rain or come shine / Just a-sittin' and a-rockin' / There will never be another you / Tenderly / What does it take / You took advantage of me / I've got the world on a string / Yesterdays / I hadn't anyone till you / Night and day / Jitterbug waltz / Someone to watch over me / Very thought of you / You're driving me crazy / I don't stand a ghost of a chance with you / I cover the waterfront / Where or when / Stay as sweet as you are / Fine and dandy / All the things you are / Have you met Miss Jones / In a sentimental mood / I'll see you again / I'll see you in my dreams / Ill wind / Isn't this a lovely day / Blue skies / Without a song / Stompin' at the Savoy / My last affair / I'm in the mood for love / Taboo / Would you like to take a walk / I've got a crush on you / Japanese sandman / Too marvellous for words / Aunt Hagar's blues / Just like a butterfly that's caught in the rain / Gone with the wind / Danny boy / They can't take that away from me / Tea for two / It's the talk of the town / Blue Lou / When a woman loves a man / Willow weep for me / Ain't misbehavin' / Smoke gets in your eyes / Mighty like a rose / Stars fell on Alabama / Blue moon / There's a small hotel / Caravan / Way you look tonight / You go to my head / Lover come back to me / Sophisticated lady / Dancing in the dark / Love me or leave me / Cherokee / These foolish things / Deep purple / After you've gone / I didn't know what time it was / Somebody loves me / What's new / Sweet Lorraine / Crazy rhythm / Isn't it romantic / You're blase / You're mine, you / Indiana / That old feeling / Heatwave / She's funny that way / I surrender dear / Happy feet / Mean to me / Boulevard of broken dreams / Moonlight on the Ganges / Moon song / When your lover has gone / Moon is low / If I had you / S'posin' / Don't worry 'bout me / Prisoner of love / Moonglow / I won't dance / I can't give you anything but love / Lullaby of rhythm / Out of nowhere / I gotta right to sing the blues / It's only a paper moon / Everything I have is yours / I only have eyes for you / On the sunny side of the street / Do nothin' 'til you hear from me / So beats my heart for you / If you hadn't gone away / Please be kind / Someone to watch over me / Begin the beguine / Willow weep for me / Humouresque
CD Set ________ 7PACD 44042
Pablo / Nov '96 / Cadillac / Complete/ Pinnacle

GENIUS OF KEYBOARD, THE
Blue Lou / Gone with the wind / Foggy day / September song / Love for sale / You took advantage of me / Makin' whoopee / Willow weep for me / Hallelujah / Once in a while / This can't be love / All the things you are / My blue Heaven / I cover the waterfront / Somebody loves me
CD ________ CD 53019
Giants Of Jazz / Jun '88 / Cadillac / Jazz Music / Target/BMG

IN PRIVATE
CD ________ FSCD 127
Fresh Sound / Jan '91 / Discovery / Jazz Music

INTRODUCTION TO ART TATUM 1933-1944, AN
CD ________ 4022
Best Of Jazz / Jul '95 / Discovery

JAZZ PORTRAITS
Tiger rag / St. Louis blues / Begin the beguine / (Back home again in) Indiana / Get happy / What will I tell my heart / Sheikh of Araby / Stormy weather / Tea for two / Sophisticated lady / I've got my love to keep me warm / Gone with the wind / Rosetta / Stompin' at the Savoy / Sweet Lorraine / I'll get by / Battery bounce / It had to be you
CD ________ CD 14523
Jazz Portraits / May '94 / Jazz Music

MASTERPIECES
CD ________ 158632
Jazz Archives / Oct '96 / Discovery

MASTERPIECES OF ART TATUM, THE
CD ________ 393502
Music Memoria / Aug '94 / ADA / Discovery

ON THE SUNNY SIDE 1944-1945
I know that you know / Man I love / Dark eyes / Body and soul / On the sunny side of the street / Flying home / Fine and dandy / It had to be you / Ja-da / Sweet and lovely / Boogie / If I had you / Topsy / Soft winds / Hallelujah / Poor butterfly / Song of the vagabonds / Lover / Memories of you / Runnin' wild / Yesterdays / Kerry dance
CD ________ TPZ 1066
Topaz Jazz / Jun '97 / Cadillac / Pinnacle

PIANO SOLO - PRIVATE SESSIONS (New York 1952)
CD ________ 550052
Jazz Anthology / Jan '94 / Cadillac / Discovery / Harmonia Mundi

PIANO STARTS HERE
CD ________ 4765462
Sony Jazz / May '94 / Sony

QUINTESSENCE, THE (1933-1945/2CD Set)
CD ________ FA 217
Fremeaux / Apr '96 / ADA / Discovery

RARE TEST PRESSINGS AND TRANSCRIPTIONS 1932-1951
CD ________ JZCD 360
Suisa / Feb '92 / Jazz Music / THE

ROCOCO PIANO OF ART TATUM, THE
Gone with the wind / Stormy weather / Sheikh of araby / Tea for two / Rosetta / Humoresque / Sweet Lorraine / Get happy / Lullaby of the leaves / Tiger rag / Sweet Emmalina / Emaline / Moon glow / Love me / Cocktails for two / St. Louis blues / Begin the beguine / (Back home again in) Indiana / Stompin' at the savoy / Battery bounce / Rock me Mama / Corine Corina
CD ________ PASTCD 7031
Flapper / Jan '94 / Pinnacle

SOLOS 1937/CLASSIC PIANO SOLOS
Fine and dandy / Emaline / I guess I'll have to change my plans / Limehouse blues / I gotta right to sing the blues / Indiana / I've got the world on a string / What is this thing called love / I'm comin' Virginia / Can't we be friends / You took advantage of me / All God's chillun got rhythm / Come rain or come shine / Begin the beguine / Body and soul / I know that you know / Honeysuckle rose / Introspection / Memories of you / Kerry Dance
CD ________ UCD 19010
Forlane / Sep '96 / Target/BMG

ST. LOUIS BLUES
Tiger rag / Tea for two / St. Louis blues / Strange as it seems / Sophisticated lady / It'll never be the same / When a woman loves a man / Shout / You gave me everything but love / This time it's love / Liza / (I would do) anything for you / After you've gone / Stardust / I ain't got nobody / Beautiful love
CD ________ GRF 085
Tring / '93 / Tring

STANDARD SESSIONS, THE
CD ________ CD 919
Music & Arts / Feb '96 / Cadillac / Harmonia Mundi

STANDARD TRANSCRIPTIONS, THE (2CD Set)
CD Set ________ CD 673
Music & Arts / Jul '91 / Cadillac / Harmonia Mundi

STANDARDS
CD ________ BLCD 760143
Black Lion / Nov '92 / Cadillac / Jazz Music / Koch / Wellard

TATUM GROUP MASTERPIECES VOL.1
What is this thing called love / I'll never be the same / Makin' whoopee / Hallelujah / Perdido / More than you know / How high the moon
CD ________ 24054182
Pablo / Oct '93 / Cadillac / Complete/ Pinnacle

TATUM GROUP MASTERPIECES VOL.2
Verve blues / Plaid / Somebody loves me / September song / Deep purple
CD ________ 24054242
Pablo / Oct '93 / Cadillac / Complete/ Pinnacle

TATUM GROUP MASTERPIECES VOL.3
Blues in C / Undecided / Under a blanket of blue / Blues in B flat / Foggy day / Street of dreams / 'S wonderful
CD ________ 24054252
Pablo / Oct '93 / Cadillac / Complete/ Pinnacle

TATUM GROUP MASTERPIECES VOL.4
Old-fashioned love / Blues in my heart / My blue Heaven / Hands across the table / You're mine / You / Idaho
CD ________ 24054272
Pablo / Oct '93 / Cadillac / Complete/ Pinnacle

TATUM GROUP MASTERPIECES VOL.5
Night and day / I won't dance / In a sentimental mood / Moon is low / Moon song / You took advantage of me / This can't be love / I surrender dear
CD ________ 24054282
Pablo / Oct '93 / Cadillac / Complete/ Pinnacle

TATUM GROUP MASTERPIECES VOL.6
Just one of those things / More than you know / Some other Spring / If / Blue Lou / Love for sale / Isn't it romantic / I'll never be the same / I guess I'll have to change my plan / Trio blues
CD ________ 2405429
Pablo / Oct '93 / Cadillac / Complete/ Pinnacle

TATUM GROUP MASTERPIECES VOL.7
Deep night / This can't be love / Memories of you / Once in a while / Foggy day / Lover man / You're mine / You / Makin' whoopee
CD ________ 24054302
Pablo / Nov '95 / Cadillac / Complete/ Pinnacle

TATUM GROUP MASTERPIECES VOL.8
Gone with the wind / All the things you are / Have you met Miss Jones / My one and only love / Night and day / My ideal / Where or when
CD ________ 24054312
Pablo / Jan '97 / Cadillac / Complete/ Pinnacle

TATUM SOLO MASTERPIECES VOL.1
Moonglow / Love for sale / Body and soul / Just a sittin' and a rockin' / it's only a paper moon / Have you met Miss Jones / Stay as sweet as you are / My last affair / Willow weep for me

CD 24054322
Pablo / Oct '93 / Cadillac / Complete/ Pinnacle

TATUM SOLO MASTERPIECES VOL.2
Elegy / This can't be love / There will never be another you / Gone with the wind / I don't stand a ghost of a chance with you / Lover come back to me / I'll see you in my dreams / Heatwave / September song
CD 24054332
Pablo / Oct '93 / Cadillac / Complete/ Pinnacle

TATUM SOLO MASTERPIECES VOL.3
Yesterdays / Tenderly / Jitterbug waltz / Love me or leave me / Deep purple / Begin the beguine / Dixieland band / All the things you are / Crazy rhythm / Prisoner of love
CD 24054342
Pablo / Oct '93 / Cadillac / Complete/ Pinnacle

TATUM SOLO MASTERPIECES VOL.4
Aunt Hagar's blues / Isn't this a lovely day (to be caught in the rain) / Ill wind / I've got the world on a string / Stardust / Man I love / What's new / They can't take that away from me
CD 24054352
Pablo / Oct '93 / Cadillac / Complete/ Pinnacle

TATUM SOLO MASTERPIECES VOL.5
Makin' whoopee / Don't worry 'bout me / That old feeling / Louise / Fine and dandy / Stompin' at the Savoy / Blue moon / I cover the waterfront / Stars fell on Alabama / You're driving me crazy
CD 24054362
Pablo / Oct '93 / Cadillac / Complete/ Pinnacle

TATUM SOLO MASTERPIECES VOL.6
I've got a crush on you / There's a small hotel / Night and day / Way you look tonight / Cherokee / I'm coming Virginia / Do nothin' 'til you hear from me / You're blase / Ain't misbehavin'
CD 24054372
Pablo / Oct '93 / Cadillac / Complete/ Pinnacle

TATUM SOLO MASTERPIECES VOL.7
Mighty like a rose / What does it take (to win your love) / Taboo / Humoresque / Smoke gets in your eyes / Moon song / Dancing in the dark / Japanese sandman / So beats my heart for you
CD 24054382
Pablo / Oct '93 / Cadillac / Complete/ Pinnacle

TATUM SOLO MASTERPIECES VOL.8
In a sentimental mood / Blue skies / These foolish things / She's funny that way / Sweet Lorraine / Sunny side of the street / I won't dance / You go to my head / Talk of the town
CD 24054392
Pablo / Oct '93 / Cadillac / Complete/ Pinnacle

TEA FOR TWO
CD BLCD 760192
Black Lion / Feb '94 / Cadillac / Jazz Music / Koch / Wellard

TEA FOR TWO 1933-1940
CD CD 56068
Jazz Roots / Jul '95 / Target/BMG

TRIO DAYS
I got rhythm / Cocktails for two / I ain't got nobody / After you've gone / Moonglow / Deep purple / (I would do) anything for you / Liza / Tea for two / Honeysuckle rose / Man I love / Dark eyes / Body and soul / I know that you know / On the sunny side of the street / Flying home / Boogie / If I had you / Topsy / Soft winds
CD LEJAZZCD 43
Le Jazz / Jun '95 / Cadillac / Koch

V DISC YEARS 1944-1946, THE
CD BLCD 760114
Black Lion / Apr '91 / Cadillac / Jazz Music / Koch / Wellard

Tauber, Richard

COLLECTION, A
Without a song / Indian summer / Lover come back to me / One day when we were young / One alone / Plaisir d'amour / My moonlight madonna / Dearly beloved / Can I forget you / Pedro, the fisherman / Blue Danube / Perfect day / Serenade / We'll gather lilacs / English rose / Someday we shall meet again / Once there lived a fair lady / Beneath my window / First love is best love / Long ago and far away
CD 307412
Hallmark / Jul '97 / Carlton

GERMAN FOLK SONGS
CD BLA 103002
Belage / Mar '95 / Target/BMG

GREAT ORIGINAL PERFORMANCES 1923-1929
Girls were made to love and kiss / Ich mocht einamal wieder / Bei einem tee 'a deux / Keiner schlafe / Can I forgive you / English rose / Ich kusse ihre hand madam / Nobody could love you more / On with the motley / Gruss mir mein wien / Flower song / O madchen, mein madcheni / Frohe botschaft / Di bist die welt fur mich / Wolgalied / Il mio tesoro / Vienna, city of my dreams / You are my heart's delight
CD RPCD 301
Robert Parker Jazz / Sep '96 / Conifer/BMG / New Note/Pinnacle

GREAT VOICES OF THE CENTURY
Prize song / Am stillen herd / Selig sind / Ach so fromm / Solo profugo / Ewig will lehdir gehoeren / Non plangere liu / Nessun dorma / Lug dursel lug / Addio fiorito asil / Lenski's aria / Adieu mignon / Di rigori armato / Flower song / Recondito armante / Lucevan le stelle
CD TKOCD 020
TKO / May '92 / TKO

MY LOVE FOR YOU
My love for you / English rose / Love everlasting / Can I forget you / World is waiting for sunrise / I know of two bright eyes / Sympathy / At the balalaika / Rosalie / Intermezzo / So deep is the night / Caprice Viennois / Liebestraum / Angels guard thee / Elegie / Love's last word is spoken / My heart & I / Jealousy / Little grey home in the West / Starlight serenade / Girls were made to love and kiss / Die Fledermaus
CD CDMOIR 433
Memoir / May '96 / Jazz Music / Target/ BMG

OLD CHELSEA
CD BLA 103003
Belage / Feb '95 / Target/BMG

ONLY A ROSE
CD CDMOIR 421
Memoir / Jun '93 / Jazz Music / Target/ BMG

VIENNA, CITY OF MY DREAMS
CD CDHD 189
Happy Days / Sep '92 / Conifer/BMG

YOU ARE MY HEART'S DELIGHT
CD PASTCD 7042
Flapper / May '94 / Pinnacle

Taudi Symphony

TAUDI SYMPHONY
Aujack swing / Africa soul / TODI / Caron style / Jam / Le lama el ritmo / Ludwig in the sunshine / Carcass / Royal Albert Hall / Loran's dance / Aktual / Africa soul (dub version)
CD FR 346CD
Big Cheese / Apr '95 / Vital

Tavares

BEST OF THE TAVARES ON TOUR, THE
Bad times / Never had a love like this before / Medley / I hope you'll be very unhappy without me / You are the words, you are the music / Turn your love around / More than a woman / Heaven must be missing an angel
CD SUMCD 4074
Summit / Nov '96 / Sound & Media

BEST OF THE TAVARES, THE
What can I do / Check it out / That's the sound that lonely makes / Remember what I told you to forget / Too late / She's gone / It only takes a minute / Love I never had / Heaven must be missing an angel / Don't take away the music / Whodunit / Goodbye my love (pleasant dreams) / More than a woman / Never had love like this before / Bad times / Loveline
CD C2 89380
Capitol / Aug '93 / EMI

DANCE HEAVEN
Whodunnit / Don't take away the music / It only takes a minute / I hope you'll be very unhappy without me / Bad times / Turn your love around / More than a woman / You are the words, you are the music / Check it out / Remember what I told you to forget / She's gone / Heaven must be missing an angel
CD 304152
Hallmark / Jun '97 / Carlton

GOLD COLLECTION, THE
It only takes a minute / Heaven must be missing an angel / Slow train to paradise / Never had a love like this before / Check it out / She's gone / My ship / Don't take away the music / Whodunit / Mighty power of love / One step away / Ghost of love / Love I never had / I wanna see you soon / Bein' with you / More than a woman
CD CDGOLD 1016
EMI Gold / Mar '96 / EMI

IT ONLY TAKES A MINUTE
Bad times / Games, games / Madam butterfly / Too late / Wonderful / Little girl / In this lovely world / Strangers in dark corners / It only takes a minute / Remember what I told you to forget / Heaven must be missing an angel / Paradise / Break down for love / Love uprising
CD CTMCD 314
EMI / Apr '97 / EMI

TAVARES LIVE IN CONCERT
CD JHD 104
Tring / Aug '93 / Tring

Tawney, Cyril

DOWN THE HATCH
Charlie Mopp's / Early one evening / Bluey brink / Jug of this / Boozing / Oh good ale / Pint of contraception / Down where the drunkards roll / Sucking cider through a straw / As soon as the pub closes / On a Monday morning / All through the beer / Drunken maidens / Parting glass / Old pubs / Sparrow in the tree top / Farewell to the whiskey / Jolly roving tar / Come to Australia / Reunion / I mean to get jolly well drunk / Fathom the bowl / Barley mow
CD NGL 101CD
Neptune / May '94 / ADA / Neptune

Taylor, Allan

FADED LIGHT
CD T 005CD
T / Nov '95 / ADA / CM

LINES
CD T 002CD
T / Aug '94 / ADA / CM

LOOKING FOR YOU
Traveller / So long / Looking for you / Win or lose / Veteran / Dove / Restless / Joseph / Misty on the water / Cold hard town / Crazy man / Hard to tell
CD RTD 35760132
Stockfish / Apr '97 / Roots Music

SO LONG
CD T 004CD
T / Aug '94 / ADA / CM

Taylor, Art

WAILIN' AT THE VANGUARD (Taylor, Art Wailers)
Street intro / AT's shout / Bridge theme/Mr. A.T. revisited / Band introductions / Dear old Stockholm / Stressed out / So sorry please / Bridge theme / Mr. A.T. revisited / Interchat / Sophisticated lady / In a sentimental mood / Chelsea Bridge / Harlem mardi gras / Bridge theme/Salt peanuts
CD 5196772
Verve / May '94 / PolyGram

Taylor, Billy

BILLY TAYLOR TRIO WITH CANDIDO (Taylor, Billy Trio & Candido)
Mambo Inn / Bit of Bedlam / Declivity / Love for sale / Live one / Different bells
CD OJCCD 152
Original Jazz Classics / May '97 / Complete/ Pinnacle / Jazz Music / Wellard

HOMAGE
Homage / Step into my dream / Billy and Dave / On this lean, mean street / Barbados beauty / Kim's song / Hope and hostility / Uncle Bob / Two shades of blue / Dave and Billy / Back to my dream plus / It happens all the time / One for fun
CD GRP 98062
GRP / Mar '95 / New Note/BMG

WHERE'VE YOU BEEN (Taylor, Billy Quartet & Joe Kennedy)
CD CCD 4145
Concord Jazz / Jul '96 / New Note/ Pinnacle

Taylor, Bram

FURTHER HORIZONS
CD FE 092CD
Fellside / Oct '93 / ADA / Direct / Target/ BMG

Taylor, Cecil

3 PHASIS
CD NW 303
New World / Aug '92 / ADA / Cadillac / Harmonia Mundi

AIR
Number one (take one) / Number one (take two) / Air (take nine) / Air (take 21) / Air (take 24) / Port of call (take 3)
CD CCD 79046
Candid / Feb '97 / Cadillac / Direct / Jazz Music / Koch / Wellard

ALMS/TIERGARTEN (SPREE) (Taylor, Cecil European Orchestra)
CD Set FMPCD 089
FMP / Oct '85 / Cadillac

CECIL TAYLOR 1955-1961
CD CD 53172
Giants Of Jazz / Sep '94 / Cadillac / Jazz Music / Target/BMG

CECIL TAYLOR UNIT
Idut / Serdab / Holiday en masque
CD NW 201
New World / '88 / ADA / Cadillac / Harmonia Mundi

CELEBRATED BLAZONS (Taylor, Cecil & Feel Trio)
CD FMPCD 58
FMP / Oct '94 / Cadillac

CELL WALK FOR CELESTE
Cell walk for Celeste / Davis / Section C / Jumpin' punkins / Jumpin' punkins / Davis / Cell walk for Celeste
CD CCD 9034
Candid / Feb '97 / Cadillac / Direct / Jazz Music / Koch / Wellard

CHINAMPAS
CD CDLR 153
Leo / Mar '88 / Cadillac / Impetus / Wellard

CROSSING
CD JHR 73505
Jazz Hour / Sep '93 / Cadillac / Jazz Music / Target/BMG

FONDATION MAEGHT NIGHTS
CD COD 001
Jazz View / Mar '92 / Harmonia Mundi

FONDATION MAEGHT NIGHTS VOL.2
CD COD 002
Jazz View / Jun '92 / Harmonia Mundi

FONDATION MAEGHT NIGHTS VOL.3
CD COD 003
Jazz View / Jul '92 / Harmonia Mundi

GARDEN VOL.1
CD ARTCD 6050
Hat Art / Nov '90 / Cadillac / Harmonia Mundi

GREAT PARIS CONCERT, THE
Student studies / Student studies / Amplitude / Niggle feuigle
CD BLCD 760201
Black Lion / Apr '95 / Cadillac / Jazz Music / Koch / Wellard

HEARTH, THE (Taylor, Cecil & Evan Parker/T. Tonsinger)
CD FMPCD 11
FMP / Nov '84 / Cadillac

IN EAST BERLIN (Taylor, Cecil & Gunter Sommer)
CD Set FMPCD 1314
FMP / Oct '86 / Cadillac

INDENT
Indent: first layer / Indent: second layer / Indent: third layer
CD FCD 41038
Freedom / Dec '87 / Cadillac / Jazz Music / Koch / Wellard

IWONTUNWONSI
CD SSCD 8065
Sound Hills / Jan '96 / Cadillac / Harmonia Mundi

JUMPIN' PUNKINS
Jumpin' punkins / OP / I forgot / Things ain't what they used to be
CD CCD 79013
Candid / Feb '97 / Cadillac / Direct / Jazz Music / Koch / Wellard

LEAF PLAM HAND (Taylor, Cecil & Tony Oxley)
CD FMPCD 06
FMP / Jul '88 / Cadillac

LIVE IN BOLOGNA (Taylor, Cecil Unit)
CD CDLR 100
Leo / Mar '88 / Cadillac / Impetus / Wellard

LOOKING
CD FMPCD 31
FMP / Dec '87 / Cadillac

LOOKING
CD FMPCD 28
FMP / Mar '85 / Cadillac

LOOKING - THE FEEL TRIO
CD FMPCD 25
FMP / Jun '85 / Cadillac

LOOKING AHEAD
Luyah, the glorious step / African violets / Of what / Wallering / Toll / Excursion on a wobbly rail
CD OJCCD 452
Original Jazz Classics / Oct '93 / Complete/ Pinnacle / Jazz Music / Wellard

NEW YORK CITY RHYTHM AND BLUES (Taylor, Cecil & Buell Neidlinger)
OP / Cell walk for Celeste / Cindy's main mood / Things ain't what they used to be
CD CCD 79017
Candid / Feb '97 / Cadillac / Direct / Jazz Music / Koch / Wellard

ONE TOO MANY SALTY SWIFT AND NOT GOODBYE
CD Set ARTCD 26090
Hat Art / Dec '91 / Cadillac / Harmonia Mundi

PLEISTOZAEN MIT WASSER (Taylor, Cecil & Derek Bailey)
CD FMPCD 16
FMP / Aug '88 / Cadillac

REGALIA (Taylor, Cecil & Paul Lovens)
CD FMPCD 03
FMP / May '89 / Cadillac

REMEMBRANCE (Taylor, Cecil & Louis Moholo)
CD FMPCD 04
FMP / Dec '87 / Cadillac

RIOBEC (Taylor, Cecil & Gunter Sommer)
CD FMPCD 02
FMP / May '89 / Cadillac

SILENT TONGUES
Abyss / Petals and filaments / Jitney / Taylor crossing part one / Crossing / After all / Jitney No. 2 / After all No. 2
CD FCD 41005
Freedom / Sep '87 / Cadillac / Jazz Music / Koch / Wellard

SOLO - ERZULIE MAKETH SCENT
CD FMPCD 18
FMP / Aug '89 / Cadillac

SPOTS, CIRCLES & FANTASY (Taylor, Cecil & Han Bennink)
CD FMPCD 05
FMP / Jan '88 / Cadillac

SPRING OF TWO BLUE J'S (Taylor, Cecil Unit)
CD COD 008
Jazz View / Aug '92 / Harmonia Mundi

TRANCE
CD BLCD 760220
Black Lion / Jun '97 / Cadillac / Jazz Music / Koch / Wellard

WINGED SERPENT (Taylor, Cecil Segments 11)
CD SNCD 1089
Soul Note / '86 / Cadillac / Harmonia Mundi / Wellard

WORLD OF CECIL TAYLOR, THE
Air / This nearly was mine / Port of call / EB / Lazy afternoon
CD CCD 9006
Candid / Feb '97 / Cadillac / Direct / Jazz Music / Koch / Wellard

Taylor, Dave

CADILLACS AND MOONLIGHT
CD MCD 705
Midnight Rock / Jun '97 / Nervous

Taylor, David

PAST TELLS
CD 804362
New World / Feb '94 / ADA / Cadillac / Harmonia Mundi

Taylor, Debbie

STILL COMIN' DOWN ON YA
No if's, and's or but's / (I just make believe) I'm touching you / Too sad to tell / Second to none / Romance without finance / Leaving him tomorrow / No deposit, no return / Eye doctor / Jeremiah
CD NEMCD 941
Sequel / Jul '97 / BMG

Taylor, Derek

MY KIND OF JOLSON
CD CDOK 3008
OK / Dec '89 / Ross

Taylor, Eddie

BAD BOY (Charly Blues - Masterworks Vol. 35)
Bad boy / ET blues / Ride 'em on down / Big town playboy / You'll always have a home / Don't knock at my door / I'm gonna love you / Lookin' for trouble / Find my baby / Stroll out west / I'm sitting here / Do you want me to cry / Train fare / Leave this neighborhood / Somethin' for nothin'
CD CDBM 35
Charly / Jan '93 / Koch

BAD BOY (Taylor, Eddie 'Big Town Playboy' & Vera Taylor)
CD WCD 120711
Wolf / Jul '95 / Hot Shot / Jazz Music / Swift

I FEEL SO BAD
CD HCD 8027
Hightone / Sep '94 / ADA / Koch

LONG WAY FROM HOME
CD BPCD 5025
Blind Pig / Dec '95 / ADA / CM / Direct / Hot Shot

MY HEART IS BLEEDING (Taylor, Eddie Blues Band)
My heart is bleeding / Going to Virginia / So bad / Lexington breakdown / Blow wind blow / Wreck on 83 Highway / Soul brother / There'll be a day / Lawndale blues / Gamblin' woman / I got a little thing they call it swing / One day I get lucky / Dust my broom
CD ECD 260542
Evidence / Sep '94 / ADA / Cadillac / Harmonia Mundi

Taylor, Eric

ERIC TAYLOR
CD WWMCD 1040
Watermelon / Nov '95 / ADA / Direct

Taylor, Eva

NOT JUST THE BLUES
Of all the wrongs you've done me / Everybody loves my baby / Mandy make up your mind / I'm a little blackbird / Cake-walking babies from home / Pickin' on your baby / Papa de da da / Just wait 'till you see my baby / Living high, sometimes / Coal cart blues / You can't shush Katie (the gabbiest girl in town) / Shake that thing / Get it fixed / I've found a new baby / Pile of logs and stone (called home) / When the red, red robin comes bob, bob, bobbin along / (There's a blue ridge in my heart) Virginia / Nobody but my baby is getting my love / Morocco blues / Candy lips (I'm stuck on you) / Scatter your smiles / Where that old man river flows / Shout sister shout
CD TPZ 1044
Topaz Jazz / May '96 / Cadillac / Pinnacle

Taylor, Gary

ONE DAY AT A TIME
In search of / Where do we go / Special / Think about me / Time has run out of time / Will you come back / One day at a time / I will be here / Who we are / Don't go there / Rest my lips
CD XECD 3
Expansion / Jun '95 / 3mv/Sony

REFLECTIONS
Restless / Blind to it all / In and out of love / After effect / One love, one people / Time after time / Take control / Eye to eye / I need / Don't be so distant / APB / Irresistible love / Never too blue / Sign my life away
CD EXCDP 8
Expansion / Nov '94 / 3mv/Sony

SQUARE ONE
Hold me accountable / Irresistible love / APB / Pieces / Square one / Read between the lines / Never too blue / I need you now / Eye to eye / One and only
CD EXCD 6
Expansion / Mar '93 / 3mv/Sony

TAKE CONTROL
Take control / Whatever / I need / In and out of love / Wishful thinking / Don't be so distant / I live 4 U / Sign my life away / Time after time
CD EXCDP 5
Expansion / Jun '90 / 3mv/Sony

Taylor, Hound Dog

BEWARE OF THE DOG (Taylor, Hound Dog & The House Rockers)
Give me back my wig / Sun is shining / Kitchen sink boogie / Dust my broom / Comin' around the mountain / Let's get funky / Rock me / It's alright / Freddie's blues
CD ALCD 4707
Alligator / May '93 / ADA / CM / Direct

GENUINE HOUSEROCKING MUSIC (Taylor, Hound Dog & The House Rockers)
Ain't got nobody / Gonna send you back to Georgia / Fender bender / My baby's coming home / Blue guitar / Sun is shining / Phillips goes bananas / What'd I say / Kansas City / Crossroads
CD ALCD 4727
Alligator / May '93 / ADA / CM / Direct

HOUND DOG TAYLOR AND THE HOUSE ROCKERS (Taylor, Hound Dog & The House Rockers)
She's gone / Walking the ceiling / Held my baby last night / Taylor's rock / It's alright / Phillip's theme / Wild about you baby / I just can't make it / It hurts me too / 44 blues / Give me back my wig / 55th Street boogie
CD ALCD 4701
Alligator / May '93 / ADA / CM / Direct

LIVE AT JOE'S PLACE
CD 422319
Last Call / Feb '92 / Cargo / Direct / Discovery

NATURAL BOOGIE (Taylor, Hound Dog & The House Rockers)
Take five / Hawaiian boogie / See me in the evening / You can't sit down / Sitting at home alone / One more time / Roll your moneymaker / Buster's boogie / Sadie / Talk to my baby / Goodnight boogie
CD ALCD 4704
Alligator / May '93 / ADA / CM / Direct

Taylor, James

BEST LIVE
Sweet baby James / Handyman / Your smiling face / Steamroller blues / Mexico / Walking man / Country road / Fire and rain / How sweet it is (to be loved by you) / Riding on a railroad / Something in the way she moves / Sun on the moon / Up on the roof / Copperline / Slap leather / You've got a friend / That lonesome road
CD 4766572
Columbia / Apr '94 / Sony

GREATEST HITS
Something in the way she moves / Carolina on my mind / Fire and rain / Sweet baby James / Country roads / You've got a friend / Don't let me be lonely tonight / Walking man / How sweet it is (to be loved by you) / Mexico / Shower the people / Steamroller
CD 7599273362
WEA / '94 / Warner Music

HOURGLASS
Line 'em up / Enough to be your way / Little more time with you / Gaia / Ananas / Jump up behind me / Another day / Up er mei / Up from your life / Yellow and rose / Boatman / Walking my baby back home / Hangnail
CD 4877482
Columbia / Jun '97 / Sony

JT
Your smiling face / There we are / Honey don't leave LA / Another grey morning / Bartender's blues / Secret o'life / Handyman / I was only telling a lie / Looking for love on Broadway / Terra nova / If I keep my heart out of sight / Traffic jam
CD 4746802
Columbia / Feb '97 / Sony

LIVE
Sweet baby James / Traffic jam / Handyman / Your smiling face / Secret of life / Shed a little light / Everybody has the blues / Steamroller blues / Mexico / Millworker / Country road / Fire and rain / Shower the people / How sweet it is (to be loved by you) / New hymn / Walking man / Riding on a railroad / Something / Sun on the moon / Up on the roof / Don't let me be lonely tonight / She thinks I still care / Copperline / Slap leather / Only one / You make it easy / Carolina on my mind / I will follow / You've got a friend / That lonesome road
CD 4742162
Columbia / Sep '93 / Sony

MUD SLIDE SLIM AND THE BLUE HORIZON
Love has brought me around / You got a friend / Places in my past / Riding on a railroad / Soldiers / Mud slide slim / Hey Mister, that's me upon the jukebox / Upon the jukebox / You can close your eyes / Machine gun Kelly / Long ago and far away / Let me ride / Highway song / Isn't it nice to be home again
CD 256004
WEA / '89 / Warner Music

SWEET BABY JAMES
Sweet baby James / Lo and behold / Sunny skies / Steam Roller / Country roads / Oh Susanna / Fire and rain blossom / Anywhere like heaven / Oh baby don't you lose your lip on me / Suite for 20G / Love has brought me around / You've got a friend / Places in my past / Riding on a railroad / Soldiers / Mud slide slim / Hey mister, that's me upon the jukebox / You can close your eyes / Machine gun Kelly / Long ago and far away / Let me ride / Highway song / Isn't it nice to be home again
CD 246043
WEA / Apr '84 / Warner Music

Taylor, James

DO YOUR OWN THING (Taylor, James Quartet)
Love the life / Killing time / Money / JTQ theme / Ted's asleep / Always there / Oscar / Samba for Bill and Ben / Valhalla / Fat / Peace song
CD 8437972
Polydor / Oct '90 / PolyGram

GET ORGANIZED (Taylor, James Quartet)
Grooving home / Electric boogaloo / Stretch / It doesn't matter / Riding high / Touchdown / Breakout / Brothers batucada / Bluebird / Bossa pilante
CD 8394052
Polydor / May '89 / PolyGram

IN THE HAND OF THE INEVITABLE (Taylor, James Quartet)
CD JAZIDCD 115
Acid Jazz / Feb '95 / Disc

LIVING UNDERGROUND (Taylor, James Quartet)
CD JAZIDCD 140
Acid Jazz / Jun '96 / Disc

Taylor, John

AMBLESIDE DAYS (Taylor, John & John Surman)
Lodore falls / Wandering / Ambleside days / Scale force / Coniston falls / Pathway / Clapperclowe / Dry stone
CD AHUM 013
Ah-Um / Oct '92 / Cadillac / New Note/ Pinnacle

BLUE GLASS (Taylor, John Trio)
Pure and simple / Spring is here / Q / Hermana guapa / Blue glass / How deep is the ocean / Fragment / Think before you think / Evansong / Clapperclowe
CD JHCD 020
Ronnie Scott's Jazz House / Jan '94 / Cadillac / Jazz Music / New Note/Pinnacle / TKO Magnum

PAUSE AND THINK AGAIN
CD FMRCD 24
Future / Dec '95 / ADA / Harmonia Mundi

Taylor, John

FEELINGS ARE GOOD AND OTHER LIES
CD B5 274747
B5 / Dec '96 / Cargo
CD REVXD 215
Revolver / Apr '97 / Revolver / Sony

Taylor, Johnnie

CHRONICLE
Who's making love / Take care of your homework / Testify / I could never be president / Love bones / Steal away / I am somebody / Jody's got your girl and gone / I don't wanna lose you / Hijackin' love / Standin' in for Jody / Doing my own thing (Part 2) / Doing my own thing / Stop doggin' me / I believe in you (You believe in me) / Cheaper to keep her / We're getting careless with our love / I've been born again / It's September / Try me tonight / Just keep on loving me
CD CDSXE 084
Stax / Jul '93 / Pinnacle

JOHNNIE TAYLOR PHILOSOPHY CONTINUES/ONE STEP BEYOND
Testify / Separation line / Love bones / Love is a hurtin' thing / I had a fight with love / I could never be president / It's amazing / Who can I turn to / Games people play / It's your thing / Time after time / Party life / Will you love me forever / I am somebody / I don't wanna lose you / Don't take my sunshine / Jody's got your girl and gone / Fool like me
CD Set CDSXD 108
Stax / Jul '94 / Pinnacle

RAW BLUES/LITTLE BLUEBIRD
Where there's smoke there's fire / Hello sundown / Pardon me lady / Where can a man go from here / That bone / That's where it's at / Part time love / If I had it to do all over / You're good for me / You can't keep a good man down / You can't win with a losing hand / Little bluebird / Toe hold / I've got to love somebody's baby / Just the one (I've been looking for) / Outside love / You can't get away from it / I had a dream / Somebody's sleeping in my bed / I ain't particular / Steal away / Stop dogging me / Jody's got your girl and gone
CD CDSXD 051
Stax / Jun '92 / Pinnacle

SOMEBODY'S GETTIN' IT
Disco lady / Somebody's gettin' it / Pick up the pieces / Running out of lines / Did he make love to you / Your love is rated X / I'm just a shoulder to cry on / Love is better in the am / Just a happy song / Right now
CD CDCHARLY 160
Charly / Mar '89 / Koch

WANTED: ONE SOUL SINGER
I got to love somebody's baby / Just the one I've been looking for / Watermelon man / Where can a man go from here / Toe hold / Outside love / ain't that lovin' you / Blues in the night / I had a dream / Sixteen tons / Little bluebird
CD 7567822532
Atlantic / Apr '95 / Warner Music

Taylor, Koko

AUDIENCE WITH THE QUEEN, AN (Live From Chicago)
Let the good times roll / I'm a woman / Going back to luka / Devil's gonna have a field day / Come to Mama / I'd rather go blind / Let me love you / Wang dang doodle
CD ALCD 4754
Alligator / May '93 / ADA / CM / Direct

EARTH SHAKER
CD ALCD 4711
Alligator / May '93 / ADA / CM / Direct

FORCE OF NATURE
CD ALCD 4817
Alligator / Feb '94 / ADA / CM / Direct

FROM THE HEART OF A WOMAN
Something strange is going on / I'd rather go blind / Keep your hands off him / Thanks but no thanks / If you got a heartache / Never trust a man / Sure had a wonderful time last night / Blow top blues / If walls could talk / It took a long time
CD ALCD 4724
Alligator / May '93 / ADA / CM / Direct

JUMP FOR JOY
CD ALCD 4784
Alligator / May '93 / ADA / CM / Direct

QUEEN OF THE BLUES
CD ALCD 4740
Alligator / Oct '93 / ADA / CM / Direct

SOUTH SIDE LADY
CD ECD 260072
Evidence / Jan '92 / ADA / Cadillac / Harmonia Mundi

WHAT IT TAKES
Got what it takes / Don't mess with the messer / Whatever I am you made me / I'm a little mixed up / Wang dang doodle / (I got) All you need / Love me / What came first the chicken or the hen / Insane asylum / Fire / I don't care who knows / Twenty nine ways (to my baby's door) / Blue prelude / I need more and more / Um huh my baby / Bills, bills and more bills / I got what it takes
CD MCD 09328
Chess/MCA / Apr '97 / BMG / New Note/ BMG

Taylor, Lewis

LEWIS TAYLOR
Lucky / Bittersweet / Whoever / Track / Song / Betterlove / How / Right / Damn / Spirit
CD CID 8049
Island / Aug '96 / PolyGram

Taylor, Little Johnny

GALAXY YEARS, THE
You'll need another favour / What you need is a ball / Part time love / Somewhere down the line / Since I found a new love / My heart is filled with pain / First class love / If you love me like you say / You win, I lose / Nightingale melody / I smell trouble / True love / For your precious love / I've never had a woman like you before / Somebody's got to pay / Help yourself / One more chance / Please come home for Christmas / All I want is you / Zig zag lightning / Things that I used to do / Big blue diamonds / I know you hear me calling / Drivin' wheel / Sometimey woman / Double or nothing
CD CDCHD 967
Ace / Apr '91 / Pinnacle

PART-TIME LOVE
You're the one / As quick as I can / What you need is a ball / You gotta go on / She tried to understand / Since I found a new love / Darling believe me / She's yours, she's mine / Stay sweet / Somewhere down the line / Part time love
CD CD 229
Wellard / Dec '87 / Wellard

UGLY MAN
Have you ever been to Kansas City / Never be lonely and blue / LJT / Ugly man / It's my fault, darlin' / I enjoy you / How can a broke man survive / King size souvenir / Have you ever been to Kansas City (Reprise)
CD ICH 1042CD
Ichiban / Oct '93 / Direct / Koch

Taylor, Lynn

I SEE YOUR FACE BEFORE ME
CD PS 0011CD
P&S / Sep '95 / Discovery

Taylor, Martin

ARTISTRY
Polka dots and moonbeams / Stella by starlight / Teach me tonight / Dolphin / Georgia on my mind / They can't take that away from me / Here, there and everywhere / Just squeeze me / Gentle rain / Cherokee / That certain smile
CD AKD 020
Linn / Mar '93 / PolyGram

CHANGE OF HEART
73 Berkeley street / Gypsy / You don't know me / After hours / Change of heart / I get along without you very well / Angels's camp
CD AKD 016
Linn / Nov '91 / PolyGram

DON'T FRET
I love you / Blue in green / I'm old fashioned / Laverne Walk / Moonlight in Vermont / Mugavero / Don't fret / You know it's true
CD AKD 014
Linn / Feb '91 / PolyGram

PORTRAITS
Shiny stockings / Like someone in love / Sweet Lorraine / I got rhythm / Why did I choose you / My funny valentine / Do you knwo what it means to Miss New Orleans / I remember Clifford / Ol'man river / Here, there and everywhere / In a mellow tone / My one and only love / Kiko / Very early
CD AKD 048
Linn / Mar '96 / PolyGram

SARABANDA
CD 1390182
Gaia / Feb '89 / New Note/Pinnacle

SPIRIT OF DJANGO
Chez Fernand / Minor swing / Night and day / Nuages / James / Django's dream / Swing '42 / Oh lady be good / Honeysuckle rose / Johnny and Mary
CD AKD 030
Linn / Oct '94 / PolyGram

Taylor, Matt

RADIO CITY BLUES
CD MSECD 009
Mouse / Jun '95 / Grapevine/PolyGram

TROUBLE IN THE WIND
CD AIM 1034CD
Aim / Oct '93 / ADA / Direct / Jazz Music

Taylor, Melvin

BLUES ON THE RUN
Travellin' man / Lowdown dirty shame / Escape / Cold cold feeling / Just like a woman / Chitlins con carne
CD ECD 260412
Evidence / Mar '94 / ADA / Cadillac / Harmonia Mundi

DIRTY POOL (Taylor, Melvin & The Slack Band)
Too sorry / Dirty pool / I ain't superstitious / Kansas City / Floodin' in California / Born under a bad sign / Right place, wrong time / Telephone song / Merry christmas baby
CD ECD 26088
Evidence / Aug '97 / ADA / Cadillac / Harmonia Mundi

MELVIN TAYLOR AND THE SLACK BAND (Taylor, Melvin & The Slack Band)
Texas flood / Depression blues / Grooving in New Orleans / Talking to Anna Mae / Tin pan alley / All your love / Don't throw your love on me so strong / T-bone shuffle / Voodoo chile (slight return) / Tequila
CD ECD 260732
Evidence / Oct '95 / ADA / Cadillac / Harmonia Mundi

PLAYS THE BLUES FOR YOU
Talking to Anna Mae, Part 1 / TV Mama / I'll play the blues for you / Born to lose / Tribute to Wes / Cadillac assembly line / Voodoo Daddy / Talking to Anna Mae, Part 2 / Groovin' in Paris
CD ECD 260292
Evidence / Feb '93 / ADA / Cadillac / Harmonia Mundi

Taylor, Mick

MICK TAYLOR
Leather jacket / Alabama / Slow blues / Baby I want you / Broken hands / Giddy up / SW5
CD 4778522
Columbia / Oct '94 / Sony

MICK TAYLOR AND CARLA OLSON LIVE (Taylor, Mick & Carla Olson)
Who put the sting in the honeybee / Slow rollin' train / Trying to hold on / Rubies and diamonds / See the light / You can't move in / Broken hands / Sway / Hartley quits / Midnight mission / Silver train
CD FIENDCD 197
Demon / Oct '90 / Pinnacle

WITHIN AN ACE (Taylor, Mick & Carla Olson)
Justice / Dark horses / Why did you stop / World of pain / Fortune / Within an ace / Man once loved / How many days / Rescue fantasy / Is the lady gone
CD FIENDCD 726
Demon / Jan '93 / Pinnacle

Taylor, Rod

LIBERATE
CD WSPCD 004
Word Sound & Power / Nov '93 / SRD

Taylor, Roger

FUN IN SPACE
Fun in space / No violins / Laugh or cry / Let's get crazy / Future management / My country / Good times are now / Magic is loose / Interlude in Constantinople / Airheads
CD CDPCS 7380
Parlophone / May '96 / EMI

HAPPINESS
Nazis 1994 / Happiness / Revelations / Touch the sky / Foreign sand / Freedom train / You had to be there / Key / Everybody hurts sometime / Loneliness / Dear Mr. Murdoch / Old friends
CD CDPCSD 157
Parlophone / Sep '94 / EMI

STRANGE FRONTIER
Strange frontier / Beautiful dreams / Man on fire / Racing in the street / Masters of war / Killing time / Abandonfire / Young love / It's an illusion / I cry for you
CD CDPCS 7381
Parlophone / May '96 / EMI

Taylor, Rusty

RUSTY TAYLOR & STEVE LANE'S RED HOT PEPPERS (Taylor, Rusty & Steve Lane's Red Hot Peppers)
Cake walkin' babies from home / Wrap your troubles in dreams (and dream your troubles away) / Trombone cholly / Just too bad / Do your duty / You've got to give me some / Baby, won't you please come home / Cheatin' on me / I've got what it takes / Alexander's ragtime band / There's a blue ridge 'round my heart, Virginia / Shine / I'm coming Virginia / Put it right here / Atlanta / Take me for a buggy ride / Spanish shawl / After you've gone
CD AZMC 17
Azure / Apr '93 / Azure / Cadillac / Jazz Music / Swift / Wellard

Taylor, Sam

BACK BEAT VOL.5 (The Rhythm Of The Blues) (Taylor, Sam 'The Man')
Big beat / Harlem nocturne / As time goes by / Hit the road / Taylor made / Oo wee / Look out / Fish roll / Let's ball / Sam's blues / Boss is home / Ride Sammy ride / Real gone / Blue suede shoes / O'ho oh yeah uh huh / To a wild rose
CD 5112702
Mercury / Oct '94 / PolyGram

Taylor, Simon

IRISH GUITAR, THE
CD OSS 1CD
Ossian / Jan '87 / ADA / CM / Direct / Highlander

Taylor, Steve

I PREDICT 1990
CD MYRCD 6873
Myrrh / Jan '88 / Nelson Word

Taylor, Tot

BOX OFFICE POISON
Australian / Arise Sir Tot / I was frank / Spoil her / Mr. Strings / Nevermore / Ballad of Jackie and Ivy / People will talk / I never rome / Babysitting / Mr. String's come back / My independant heart
CD TOTE 3
Soundcakes / Oct '88 / 3mv/Sony

INSIDE STORY, THE
CD TOTE 2
Soundcakes / Oct '88 / 3mv/Sony

MY BLUE PERIOD
Wrong idea / It must have been a craze / It's good for you / It's all a blur / Wild scene / I'll wait / Compromising life / Young world / I'll miss the lads / It's not a bad old place / Girl did this
CD TOTE 4
Soundcakes / Oct '88 / 3mv/Sony

PLAYTIME
CD TOTE 1
Soundcakes / Oct '88 / 3mv/Sony

Taylor, Tyrone

WAY TO PARADISE
CD VPCD 1378
VP / Jan '95 / Greensleeves / Jet Star / Total/BMG

Taylor, Vince

I'LL BE YOUR HERO
CD 842132
EVA / Jun '94 / ADA / Direct

Taylor, Will

TAYLOR MADE FOR SEQUENCE DANCERS
La golondrina/My thanks to you / Sometimes when we touch / Unforgettable/And I love you so / I won't send roses/A certain smile / Best of times / Nice people/Ready willing and able / Island of dreams/My ain folk / Things we did last summer/Count your blessings instead of sh / Cherry pink and apple blossom white/Like I do / I just want to dance with you / Softly as in the morning sunrise/Echo of a serenade / Kiss of fire/A woman in love / Just walking in the rain / On the sunny side of the street/Sonny boy / Slow boat to China/Black hills of Dakota / Mama Inez / Sweet muchacha / I've never been in love before/The gypsy / De corazon a corazon / Gentle maiden/Try to remember / Sweetest song in the world
CD CDVA 6
Tema / Mar '97 / Savoy / Target/BMG

TC Hug

PIE-MONDO
I'm doing fine / Go-go UFO / Greatest hour / Matters on the brain / So real / Hometruths / Find / Gunaway / Free lunch / Someone / Two heads / I will be well / Pie-mondo
CD AMUSE 34CD
Playtime / Mar '97 / Pinnacle

TC Islam

PLANET 2020 (TC Islam & The Phunky)
CD ANTICDLP 2
Anti-Static / Oct '96 / Pinnacle / Vital

Tchinar, Ashik Feyzullah

SACRED CHANTS OF ANATOLIA
CD C 580057
Ocora / Jan '96 / ADA / Harmonia Mundi

TDF

RETAIL THERAPY
Blue rock / Angelica / Pnom-sen / Sno-god / Sienna / Seven / Angelica's dream / What she wants / Donna / Rip stop / What else
CD 9362464892
Warner Bros. / Mar '97 / Warner Music

Te Kanawa, Kiri

CHRISTMAS SONGS (Te Kanawa, Kiri & Roberto Alagna/Thomas Hampson)
Toyland / I'll be home for Christmas / Silent night / Minuit / Chretiens (cantique de Noel) / O holy night / In dulci jubilo / Il est ne le divin enfant / Have yourself a merry little Christmas / Christmas song / Chestnuts roasting by an open fire / My Christmas song for you / Winter wonderland / O tannebaum / In the bleak mid-winter / Sleigh ride / Twelve days of Christmas / White Christmas
CD CDC 5661762
EMI Classics / Nov '96 / EMI

KIRI SIDETRACKS (The Jazz Album)
CD 4340922
Philips / May '92 / PolyGram

Te Track

LET'S GET STARTED/EASTMAN DUB (Te Track & Augustus Pablo)
CD GRELCD 505
Greensleeves / Apr '90 / Jet Star / SRD

Teagarden, Jack

ACCENT ON TROMBONE
CD FSRCD 138
Fresh Sound / Dec '90 / Discovery / Jazz Music

BEST OF JACK TEAGARDEN
CD DLCD 4022
Dixie Live / Mar '95 / TKO Magnum

BIG T
CD TPZ 1001
Topaz Jazz / Jul '94 / Cadillac / Pinnacle

BIG T JUMP 1944-1946
CD JCD 643
Jass / Aug '95 / ADA / Cadillac / CM / Direct / Jazz Music

BLUES SINGER 1931-1941, THE
CD JZCD 346
Suisa / Jan '93 / Jazz Music / THE

CLASSICS 1934-1939
CD CLASSICS 729
Classics / Dec '93 / Discovery / Jazz Music

CLASSICS 1939-1940
CD CLASSICS 758
Classics / Aug '94 / Discovery / Jazz Music

CLASSICS 1940-1941
CD CLASSICS 839
Classics / Sep '95 / Discovery / Jazz Music

CLASSICS 1941-1943
CD CLASSICS 874
Classics / Apr '96 / Discovery / Jazz Music

CLEVELAND, OHIO 1958 (Teagarden, Jack Allstars)
CD JCD 199
Jazzology / Oct '92 / Jazz Music

HAS ANYBODY SEEN JACKSON VOL.2
CD JCD 637
Jass / Jan '93 / ADA / Cadillac / CM / Direct / Jazz Music

I GOTTA RIGHT TO SING THE BLUES
That's a serious thing / I'm gonna stomp Mr. Henry Lee / Dinah / Never had a reason to believe in you / Tailspin blues / Dancing with tears in my eyes / Sheikh of Araby / Basin Street blues / (I'll be glad when you're dead) you rascal you / Two tickets to Georgia / I gotta right to sing the blues / Ain't cha glad / Texas tea party / Hundred years from today / Fare thee well to Harlem / Christmas night in Harlem / Davenport blues
CD CDAJA 5059
Living Era / Feb '89 / Select

INDISPENSABLE JACK TEAGARDEN, THE
She's a great, great girl / I'm gonna stomp Mr. Henry Lee / That's a serious thing / Tailspin blues / Never had a reason to believe in you / Buy buy for baby (or baby will bye bye you) / Sentimental baby / Futuristic rhythm / Louise / My kinda love / Sweetheart we need each other / From now on / Two tickets to Georgia / Fare thee well to Harlem / Christmas night in Harlem / Ain't misbehavin' / At the Darktown strutter's ball / Every now and then / Barrel house music / I'se a muggin' / St. Louis blues / Blues after hours / Jam session at Victor / Say it simple / There'll be some changes made / I cover the waterfront / You took advantage of me
CD Set ND 89613
RCA / Mar '94 / BMG

INTRODUCTION TO JACK TEAGARDEN 1928-1943, AN
CD 4025
Best Of Jazz / Sep '95 / Discovery

IT'S TIME FOR T VOL.1:1941/HAS ANYBODY SEEN JACKSON (2CD Set) (Teagarden, Jack Orchestra)
Frenesi / Here's my heart / Accident'ly on purpose / It all comes back to me / Prelude in c# minor / Nobody knows the trouble I've seen / Casey Jones / Made up my mind / Afternoon of a faun 12blue mist / Anitra's dance / Yankee doddle / Off to the races / These things you left me / Rhythm hymn / I can't get away from the blues / Deep river / Blow the man down / Harlem jump / Well, of course / It's time for T / Star told a story / Fort Knox jump / Sing a love song: *Teagarden, Jack & His Orchestra* / Has anybody here seen Jackson: *Teagarden, Jack & His Orchestra* / Mr. Jessie blues: *Teagarden, Jack & His Orchestra* / Impressions of Meade Lux Lewis: *Teagarden, Jack & His Orchestra* / Prelude on G minor: *Teagarden, Jack & His Orchestra* / Swing without words: *Teagarden, Jack & His Orchestra* /

Bashful baby blues: *Teagarden, Jack & His Orchestra* / Soft as spring: *Teagarden, Jack & His Orchestra* / Barcarolle: *Teagarden, Jack & His Orchestra* / Get off on a fugue: *Teagarden, Jack & His Orchestra* / Heaven is mine again: *Teagarden, Jack & His Orchestra* / No need to be sorry: *Teagarden, Jack & His Orchestra* / This is no laughing matter: *Teagarden, Jack & His Orchestra* / Funiculi, funicula: *Teagarden, Jack & His Orchestra* / Sherman shout: *Teagarden, Jack & His Orchestra* / Barracks blues: *Teagarden, Jack & His Orchestra* / Dig the groove: *Teagarden, Jack & His Orchestra* / Salt on a Devil's tail: *Teagarden, Jack & His Orchestra* / You know (just as well as I do): *Teagarden, Jack & His Orchestra* / Time out: *Teagarden, Jack & His Orchestra* / Pied Piper: *Teagarden, Jack & His Orchestra* / Octoroon: *Teagarden, Jack & His Orchestra* / Rompin' and stompin': *Teagarden, Jack & His Orchestra* / Glass blues: *Teagarden, Jack & His Orchestra*
CD _______ JZCL 5012
Jazz Classics / Nov '96 / Cadillac / Direct / Jazz Music

IT'S TIME FOR TEA VOL.1 1941
CD _______ JASSCD 624
Jass / '92 / ADA / Cadillac / CM / Direct / Jazz Music

JACK TEAGARDEN & PEE WEE RUSSELL (Teagarden, Jack & Pee Wee Russell)
CD _______ OJCCD 1708
Original Jazz Classics / Jun '95 / Complete/Pinnacle / Jazz Music / Wellard

JACK TEAGARDEN 1930-1934 (Teagarden, Jack & His Orchestra)
CD _______ CLASSICS 698
Classics / Jul '93 / Discovery / Jazz Music

JAZZ ORIGINAL
King Porter stomp / Eccentric / Davenport blues / Original dixieland one-step / Bad actin' woman / Mis'ry and the blues / High society / Music to love by / Meet me where they play the blues / Riverboat shuffle / Milenberg joys / Blue funk
CD _______ CDCHARLY 80
Charly / '87 / Koch

MASTERS OF JAZZ VOL.10
CD _______ STCD 4110
Storyville / Feb '89 / Cadillac / Jazz Music / Wellard

TEAGARDEN PARTY, A
Muddy river blues / Somewhere a voice calling / Swingin' on a teagarden gate / Wolverine blues / (I'll be glad when you're dead) you rascal you / Plantation moods / Shake your hips / Somebody stole Gabriel's horn / Love me / I just couldn't take it baby / Hundred years from today / Blue river / Ol' Pappy / Fare-thee well to Harlem / Stars fell on Alabama / Junk man / Gotta right to sing the blues / Ain't cha glad / Dr. Heckle and Mr. Jibe / Texas tea party
CD _______ PAR 2013
Parade / Apr '94 / Disc

TEXAS TROMBONE LIVE
CD _______ CDSG 403
Starline / Aug '89 / Jazz Music

Teallach Ceilidh Band

CATCHING THE SUN RISE
Stool of repentance / Letham smiddy / Athol highlanders / Mountains of Pomeroy / Irish soldier laddie / Yellow's on the broom / John Barleycorn / Martin the Stout / All the blue bonnets are over the border / MacDonald's awa' tae the war / Rocks of bawn / David Ross of Rosehall / Major Manson at Clachantrushal / Rainy day / Lark in the morning / Mysteries of knock / Barrowburn reel / Jack broke da prison door / Donald Blue / Sleep sound ida morning / Arthur McBride / Athol and Breadalbane / Cameron highlanders / Old skibbereen / Sean O'Dwyer of the Glen / Royal Scots / Sleepy Maggie / Bessie McIntyre / All the way to Galway / Chris O'Callaghan / Hunting the hare / Shiramee / Back to the Haggard / Mo Dhachaidh (my home)
CD _______ LCOM 5208
Lismor / '91 / ADA / Direct / Duncans / Lismor

DROPS OF BRANDY
CD _______ SPRCD 1028
Springthyme / Jan '90 / ADA / CM / Direct / Duncans / Highlander / Roots

Team Dresch

CAPTAIN MY CAPTAIN
CD _______ CHSW 18CD
Chainsaw / Dec '96 / Cargo

PERSONAL BEST
CD _______ CHSW 11CD
Chainsaw / Dec '96 / Cargo

Tear Ceremony

HOURGLASS OF OPALS, AN
CD _______ MA552
Machinery / Jun '94 / Koch

Tear Garden

BOUQUET OF BLACK ORCHIDS
Sheila liked the rodeo / Ophelia / Tear garden / My thorny thorny crown / Romulus and venus / White coats and haloes / Blobbo / Sybil the spider consumes himself / Ship named despair / Centre bullet / You and me and rainbows / Oo ee oo
CD _______ NET 047CD
Nettwerk / Jul '93 / Greyhound / Pinnacle / Vital

LAST MAN TO FLY, THE
Hipper form / Running man / Turn me on dead man / Romulus and Venus / Great lie / Empathy with the devil / Love notes and carnations / Ship named despair / White coats and haloes / Isis veiled / Last post / Thirty technicolour scrambled egg trip down the hellhole
CD _______ NET 027CD
Nettwerk / Apr '92 / Greyhound / Pinnacle / Vital

TIRED EYES SLOWLY BURNING
Deja vu / Room with a view / Coma / Valium / You and me and rainbows / Ooh ee oo ee
CD _______ NTCD 034
Nettwerk / Feb '88 / Greyhound / Pinnacle / Vital

TO BE AN ANGEL BLIND
CD _______ 067003010726
Nettwerk / Nov '96 / Greyhound / Pinnacle / Vital

Teardrop Explodes

EVERYBODY WANTS TO SHAG...THE TEARDROP EXPLODES
Ouch monkeys / Serious danger / Metranil Vavin / Count to ten and run for cover / Inpsychopedia / Soft enough for you / You disappear from view / Challenger / Not my only friend / Sex / Terrorist / Strange house in the snow
CD _______ 8424392
Mercury / Mar '90 / PolyGram

KILIMANJARO
Ha ha I'm drowning / Sleeping gas / Treason / Second head / Reward poppies / Went crazy / Brave boys keep their promises / Bouncing babies / Books / Thief of Baghdad / When I dream
CD _______ 8368972
Mercury / Jan '96 / PolyGram

WILDER
Bent out of shape / Colours fly away / Seven views of Jerusalem / Pure joy / Falling down around me / Culture bunker / Tiny children / Passionate friend / Like Leila Khaled said / Great dominions
CD _______ 8368962
Mercury / Jan '96 / PolyGram

WILDER/KILIMANJARO (2CD Set)
Ha ha I'm drowning / Sleeping gas / Treason / Second head / Reward / Poppies / Passionate friend / Tiny children / Like Leila Khaled said / And the fighting takes over / Great dominions / Bent out of shape / Colours fly away / Seven views of Jerusalem / Pure joy / Falling down around me / Culture bunker / Went crazy / Brave boys keep their promises / Bouncing babies / Books / Thief of Baghdad / When I dream
CD Set _______ 5286012
Mercury / Aug '95 / PolyGram

Tears For Fears

ELEMENTAL
CD _______ 5148752
Fontana / Jun '93 / PolyGram

HURTING, THE
Mad world / Pale shelter / Ideas as opiates / Memories fade / Suffer the children / Hurting / Watch me bleed / Change / Prisoner / Start of the breakdown
CD _______ 8110392
Fontana / Jan '88 / PolyGram

HURTING, THE/SONGS FROM THE BIG CHAIR (2CD Set)
Hurting / Mad world / Pale shelter / Ideas as opiates / Memories fade / Suffer the children / Watch me bleed / Change / Prisoner / Start of the breakdown / Change (new) / Shout / Working hour / Everybody wants to rule the world / Mother's talk / I believe / Broken / Head over heels / Broken (live) / Listen
CD Set _______ 5285992
Fontana / Aug '95 / PolyGram

RAOUL AND THE KINGS OF SPAIN
Raoul and the kings of Spain / Falling down / Secrets / God's mistake / Sketches of pain / Los reyes catalicos / Sorry / Humdrum and humble / I choose you / Me and my big ideas / Los reyes catalicos (reprise)
CD _______ 4809822
Epic / Oct '95 / Sony

SATURNINE, MARSHALL, LUNATIC
CD _______ 5281142
Fontana / Jun '96 / PolyGram

SEEDS OF LOVE, THE
Badman's song / Sowing the seeds of love / Advice for the young at heart / Standing on the corner of the third world / Swords and knives / Famous last words / Woman in chains
CD _______ 8387302
Fontana / Sep '89 / PolyGram

SONGS FROM THE BIG CHAIR
Shout / Working hour / Everybody wants to rule the world / Mother's talk / I believe / Broken / Head over heels / Broken (live) / Listen
CD _______ 8243002
Fontana / Mar '85 / PolyGram

TEARS ROLL DOWN (Greatest Hits 1982-1992)
Sowing the seeds of love / Everybody wants to rule the world / Woman in chains / Shout / Head over heels / Mad world / Pale shelter / I believe / Laid so low (tears roll down) / Mother's talk / Change / Advice for the young at heart
CD _______ 5109392
Fontana / Mar '92 / PolyGram

Tebar, Ximo

SON MEDITERRANEO
CD _______ 0630109932
East West / Apr '96 / Warner Music

Tebot Piws

Y GORE A'R GWAETHA
CD _______ SCD 2049
Sain / Dec '94 / ADA / Direct / Greyhound

Technical Jed

OSWALD CUP
CD _______ SPART 51CD
Spin Art / Jan '97 / Cargo

Techniques

CLASSIC VOL.2
CD _______ WRCD 0019
Techniques / Nov '95 / Jet Star

ROCK STEADY CLASSICS
CD _______ RNCD 2078
Rhino / Dec '94 / Grapevine/PolyGram / Jet Star

RUN COME CELEBRATE
CD _______ HBCD 121
Greensleeves / Jun '93 / Jet Star / SRD

TECHNIQUES IN DUB, THE
Born to love / Purify / Gambling / In the mood / I'll be waiting / Man of my word / Find a foll / Fish mouth / Marry me / Stalag / Stalag 18 / Ghetto / Once in my life / Warboat / Watch out / Black man / Who is the one / Top secret / Ready or not
CD _______ PSCD 15
Pressure Sounds / Sep '97 / Jet Star / SRD

Techno Animal

RE-ENTRY
Flight of the hermaphrodite / Mighty atom smasher / Mastadon Americanus / City heathen dub / Narco Agent vs The Medicine Man / Demodex invasion / Evil spirits/Angel dust / Catatonia / Needle Park / Red Sea / Cape Canaveral / Resuscitator
CD _______ AMBT 8
Virgin / May '95 / EMI

Techno Army

TECHNO ARMY
CD _______ WENCD 006
When / Apr '96 / Pinnacle

Technohead

HEADSEX
I wanna be a hippy / Headsex / Accelerator 2 / Passion / Get high / Mary Jane / Get stoned / Keep the party going / Sexhead / Gabba hop
CD _______ DB 47919
Deep Blue / Feb '96 / PolyGram

Technoise

TECHNOISE/HYWARE (Technoise/Hyware)
CD _______ IRE 1042
I / Oct '96 / SRD

Technossomy

SYNTHETIC FLESH
CD _______ AFRCD 2
Flying Rhino / Mar '97 / Mo's Music Machine / Prime / SRD

Technotronic

GREATEST HITS
CD _______ CCSCD 426
Castle / May '95 / BMG

THIS BEAT IS TECHNOTRONIC
This beat is technotronic / Pump up the jam / Get up (before the night is over) / Move this / Rockin' over the beat / Hey yoh here we go / Work / Turn it up / Move that body / Voices / One and one / Megamix
CD _______ MCCD 297
Music Club / May '97 / Disc / THE

Technova

ALBUM
Firehorse one / Waiting / Sativa / Stalker / Transcience / Pacific highways / Third party / Alwah / Water margin / Yeah sister / Relentless / Forgotten
CD _______ SOP 006CD
Emissions / Nov '95 / Amato Disco / Vital

TANTRIC STEPS
Fema / Delta / Tetra / Tantra / Hydra / Shinobo / Data / Irezume / Plateau
CD _______ SOPCD 002
Sabres Of Paradise / Oct '94 / Vital

Tecnogod

2000 BELOW ZERO
Get back: *Technogod* / Addition and subtraction: *Technogod* / In this day and age: *Technogod* / Kipple: *Technogod* / Technogod: *Technogod* / Wer Wo Was: *Technogod* / Come to: *Technogod* / Class thang: *Technogod* / (We don't need this) Facist groove thang: *Technogod* / Wild appetites: *Technogod* / Destiny manifesto: *Technogod* / Bone swing: *Technogod* / Rhythm of Pam: *Technogod* / Kaposi's last stand: *Technogod* / Silence=death: *Technogod* / Luthering: *Technogod*
CD _______ 119602
Musidisc UK / Nov '96 / Grapevine/PolyGram

Tedesco, Tommy

ROUMANIS JAZZ RHAPSODY
CD _______ 75002
Capri / Sep '89 / Cadillac / Wellard

Tedio Boys

OUTER SPACE SHIT
CD _______ ELM 018
Elevator / Feb '97 / Nervous

Tee Set

24 CARAT
Early in the morning / Believe what I say / Don't you leave / Please call me / Now's the time / What can I do / Tea is famous / Rose in my hand / Mr. Music man / Ma belle amie / Finally in love again / If you do believe in love / She likes weeds / In your eyes / Little lady / Sunny day in Greece / Shotguns / Mary Mary / Bandstand / Do it baby / Linda Linda / Red red wine / Magic lantern / Tribute to the Spencer Davis Group
CD _______ SJPCD 014
Angel Air / Aug '97 / Pinnacle

EMOTION
Just another hour / I go out of my mind / Don't you leave / Midnight hour / Nothing can ever change / Jet set / Willy nilly / Play that record / Can your monkey do the dog / So fine / For Miss Caulker / You better believe it / Early in the morning / Believe what I say / Don't go mess with Cupid / Long ago / Please call me / So I came back to you / Now's the time / Bring a little sunshine / What can I do / Colours of the rainbow / When I needed you so
CD _______ RPM 134
RPM / Aug '94 / Pinnacle

Teebrooke, Paul W.

CONNECTIONS
Almost upon us / Just a little groove / Loose connection / 121346 / Nova / Blackgold / Bush re-bushed / Hus / Blue light / Explanation unnecessary
CD _______ OP 6CD
Op-Art / Jun '97 / Prime / RTM/Disc

Teen Angels

DADDY
CD _______ SPCD 330
Sub Pop / Jan '96 / Cargo / Greyhound / Shellshock/Disc

Teen Generate

SMASH HITS
CD _______ ES 1222CD
Vermiform / Apr '96 / Cargo / Greyhound / Plastic Head

Teen Kings

ARE YOU READY (Unissued 1956 Recordings)
Ooby dooby / Racker tracker / Blue suede shoes / Brown eyed handsome man / St. Louis Blues / All by myself / Lawdy Miss Clawdy / Jam / Rock house / Singin' the blues / Pretend / Rip it up / Trying to get to you / TK Blues / Go go go / Bo Diddley / Do you remember
CD _______ RCCD 3012
Rollercoaster / Mar '95 / Rollercoaster / Swift

Teen Queens

EDDIE MY LOVE
Eddie my love / Red top / All my love / Billy boy / Zig zag / Till the day I die / Love sweet love / Just goofed / Rock everybody / Baby mine / So all alone / Teenage idol / Let's

kiss / Riding / No other / Two loves and two lives / I miss you / My heart's desire
CD CDCHD 581
Ace / Feb '95 / Pinnacle

Teenage Fanclub

BANDWAGONESQUE
Concept / Satan / December / What you do to me / I don't know / Star sign / Metal baby / Pet rock / Sidewinder / Alcoholiday / Guiding star / Is this music
CD CRECD 106
Creation / Oct '91 / 3mv/Vital

DEEP FRIED FAN CLUB
CD FLIPCD 002
Fire / Feb '95 / Pinnacle / RTM/Disc

FANDEMONIUM
CD NTMCD 543
Nectar / Apr '97 / Pinnacle

GRAND PRIX
About you / Sparky's dream / Mellow doubt / Don't look back / Verisimilitude / Neil Jung / Tears / Discolite / Say no / Going places / I'll make it clear / I gotta know / Hardcore/ Ballad
CD CRECD 173
Creation / May '95 / 3mv/Vital

KING, THE
CD CRECD 096
Creation / Aug '91 / 3mv/Vital

SONGS FROM NORTHERN BRITAIN
Start again / Ain't that enough / I can't feel my soul / I don't want control of you / Planets / Take the long way round / Mount Everest / I don't care / Can we find a place / It's a bad world / Your love is the place where I come from / Speed of light
CD CRECD 196
CD CRECD 196L
Creation / Jul '97 / 3mv/Vital

THIRTEEN
Hang on / Cabbage / Radio / Norman 3 / Song to the cynic / 120 mins / Escher / Commercial alternative / Fear of flying / Tears are cool / Ret Liv Dead / Get funky / Gene Clark
CD CRECD 144
Creation / Oct '93 / 3mv/Vital

Teenage Film Stars

STAR
CD CRECD 111
Creation / Jul '92 / 3mv/Vital

Teenagers In Trouble

TEENAGERS IN TROUBLE/FAT PAUL
CD SF 007CD
Swarf Finger / Jan '97 / Cargo

Teengenerate

GET ACTION
CD EFACD 11586
Crypt / Dec '94 / Shellshock/Disc

SAVAGE
CD SFTRI 257CD
Sympathy For The Record Industry / Nov '96 / Cargo / Greyhound / Plastic Head

Tees Valley Jazzmen

CREAM TEES
CD PKCD 069
PEK / Mar '97 / Cadillac / Jazz Music / Wellard

Tehom

DESPIRITUALISATION OF NATURE
CD NERO 10CD
Twilight Command / Oct '96 / World Serpent

Teitelbaum, Richard

SEA BETWEEN, THE (Teitelbaum, Richard & Carlos Zingaro)
CD VICTOCD 03
Victo / Nov '94 / Harmonia Mundi / ReR Megacorp

Tejakula Gamelan Ensemble

GAMELAN GONG KEBYAR VOL.3
CD VICG 53522
JVC World Library / Mar '96 / ADA / CM / Direct

Tek 9

IT'S NOT WHAT YOU THINK IT IS (The Oldies But Goodies 1991-1995 - 2CD Set)
CD Set SSR 161CD
SSR / Mar '96 / Amato Disco / Grapevine/ PolyGram / Prime / RTM/Disc

Tekbilek, Omar Faruk

MYTHICAL GARDEN
CD 130922
Celestial Harmonies / Aug '96 / ADA / Select

Tekken

ALBUM, THE
CD JVC 90032
JVC / May '96 / Direct / New Note/ Pinnacle / Vital/SAM

Tekno 2

NEVER ON TIME - THE LP
CD DANCECD 001
D-Zone / Jun '92 / Pinnacle

Tekton Motor Corporation

CHAMPIONS
CD CDKTB 19
Dreamtime / Nov '96 / Kudos / Pinnacle

HUMAN RACE IGNITION
Cognitive magnitude / Ignition / Dreams / Horizon / Interactive turbulence / Champion 1st part / Spiral emotions / Champion 2nd part / Turning wheel / Cyber transducing / Mechanical spirit / Alert on the victory ahead / Dromologic mind
CD CDKTB 11
Dreamtime / Apr '95 / Kudos / Pinnacle

Tele

PIECE OF MIND
Intro invitation / Twisted / Tired of Ballin / Strange / Success / Let it rain / Sho nuff / Time / Black haven / Suave house / (Interlude) cell call / U can't tell / (Interlude) all about money / Survival / Piece of mind
CD 4867352
Relativity / Nov '96 / Sony

Telefunken & Flying

DISTANT STATION
CD WIGCD 29
Domino / Dec '96 / Vital

Telescopes

TASTE
CD CHEREE 009CD
Cheree / Aug '90 / SRD

UNTITLED
CD CRECD 79
Creation / Mar '94 / 3mv/Vital

Television

ADVENTURE
Glory / Days / Foxhole / Careful / Carried away / Fire / Ain't that nothin' / Dream's dream
CD 7559605232
WEA / '92 / Warner Music

BLOW UP, THE
Blow up / See no evil / Prove it / Elevation / I don't care / Venus De Milo / Foxhole / Ain't that nothin' / Knockin' on Heaven's door / Little Johnny Jewel / Friction / Marquee moon / Satisfaction
CD RE 114CD
ROIR / Nov '94 / Plastic Head / Shellshock/ Disc

MARQUEE MOON
See no evil / Venus / Friction / Marquee moon / Elevation / Guiding light / Prove it / Torn curtain
CD 9606162
WEA / '89 / Warner Music

Tell Tale Hearts

HIGH TIDE ANTHOLOGY
CD VOXXCD 2027
Voxx / Oct '94 / Else / RTM/Disc

Tella, Sylvia

REGGAE MAX
CD JSRNCD 15
Jet Star / Jun '97 / Jet Star

SPELL
CD JASCD 2
Sarge / Apr '97 / Jet Star

Tellu

SUDEN AIKA
CD KICD 43
Kansanmusiikki Instituutti / Aug '96 / ADA / Direct

Telo

RITUAL DEBATE
CD NZ 0062
Nova Zembla / Apr '94 / Plastic Head

Telson, Bob

WARRIOR ANT (Telson, Bob & Little Village)
Juices / Glow of the likeness / O shadow / I am / Welcome to me / Contessa / In the pavillion / Each time she takes one / All wars are lost / Ant alone / More juices / Little village
CD GCD 79490
Gramavision / Sep '95 / Vital/SAM

Telstar Ponies

IN THE SPACE OF A FEW MINUTES
CD FIRECD 52
Fire / Oct '95 / Pinnacle / RTM/Disc

VOICES FROM THE NEW MUSIC
CD FIRECD 60
Fire / Oct '96 / Pinnacle / RTM/Disc

Tembang Sunda

MUSIC FROM WEST JAVA
CD CDCEL 13134
Celestial Harmonies / May '97 / ADA / Select

SUNDANESE TRADITIONAL SONGS
CD NI 5378CD
Nimbus / Oct '93 / Nimbus

Temiz, Okay

FIS FIS TZIGANES
CD CDLLL 107
La Lichere / Aug '93 / ADA / Discovery

ISTANBUL DA EYLUL
CD CDLLL 67
La Lichere / Aug '93 / ADA / Discovery

MAGNET DANCE
Mus mus, mis mis / Ayiras / Komsu / Din din dina / Gulhane / Exmar / Namor / Izimrik / Gelen esme
CD 8888192
Tiptoe / Aug '95 / New Note/Pinnacle

Tempchin, Jack

AFTER THE RAIN (Tempchin, Jack & The Seclusions)
CD TX 2009CD
Taxim / Jan '94 / ADA

Temperance Seven

33 NOT OUT
After you've gone / Home in Pasadena / Saratoga shout / Me and Jane in a plane / Cecelia / Mooche / Black bottom / Deep Henderson / Happy feet / Royal garden blues / Varsity drag / Seven and eleven / Borneo / Ziggy / Chili bom bom / Thirty three out not / Mary / Button up your overcoat / You, you're driving me crazy
CD URCD 103
Upbeat / Dec '90 / Cadillac / Target/BMG

PASADENA AND THE LOST CYLINDERS (Music From The Archives)
Charley my boy / You're driving me crazy / My baby just cares for me / Chilli bom bom / My Mama's in town / Words / China boy / Ukelele lady / My blue heaven / Oh, baby / I wonder what's become of Joe / Take me over / Carole / Mooche / Vo do do de o blues / Seven and eleven / East St.Louis toodle oo / Pleasant moments / Pasadena / Japanese dream / Deep Henderson / Ain't she sweet / Sugar / Sugar / Sugar / From Russia with love / Jimmy (Thompson) / Thoroughly modern Millie
CD LACD 77
Lake / Jun '97 / ADA / Cadillac / Direct / Jazz Music / Target/BMG

TEA FOR EIGHT
Waterloo Road / Charleston / Tea for two / Louisiana / Sahara / Running wild / Hard hearted Hannah / Charley my boy / My Momma's in town / Ukelele lady / Twelfth Street rag / 11.30 saturday night
CD URCD 101
Upbeat / Mar '90 / Cadillac / Target/BMG

WRITING ON THE WALL
Dog bottom / I can't sleep / From Monday On / Writing on the wall / Crying for the Carolines / Man I Love / Everybody loves my baby / San / Mornington Crescent / My baby just cares for me / Drum crazy / Mississippi Mud / Brown eyes / Ain't she sweet / There Ain't No Sweet man Worth the Salt Of My Tears / My Blue heaven / 'S Wonderful
CD RRCD 108
Upbeat / Sep '92 / Cadillac / Target/BMG

Temperley, Joe

CONCERTO FOR JOE
Hackensack / Snibor / Sentimental mood / Blues for Nat / East of the sun and west of the moon / Single petal of a rose / Cotton tail / Awright already / Blues / Slow for Joe / Day at a time / Sixes and sevens
CD HEPCD 2062
Hep / Mar '95 / Cadillac / Jazz Music / New Note/Pinnacle / Wellard

NIGHTINGALE
Raincheck / Body and soul / Indian summer / Sunset and a mocking bird / Petite fleur / Nightingale / It's you or no one / Creole love / Action / My love is like a red red rose
CD HEPCD 2052
Hep / Mar '92 / Cadillac / Jazz Music / New Note/Pinnacle / Wellard

Tempest

TEMPEST/LIVING IN FEAR
Gorgon / Foyers of fun / Dark house / Brothers / Up and on / Grey and black / Strange her / Upon tomorrow / Funeral empire / Paperback writer / Stargazer / Dance to my tune / Living in fear / Yeah yeah yeah / Waiting for a miracle / Turn around
CD NEXCD 159
Sequel / Dec '90 / BMG

Tempest

SUNKEN TREASURE (Unreleased Tracks 1989-1992)
CD FAM 10103CD
Firebird / Jul '95 / ADA

SURFING TO MECCA
CD FAM 10105CD
Firebird / Jul '95 / ADA

Temple, Johnny

BLUES 1935-1940, THE (2CD Set)
CD Set FA 256
Fremeaux / Feb '97 / ADA / Discovery

JOHNNY TEMPLE VOL.1 1935-1938
CD DOCD 5238
Document / May '94 / ADA / Hot Shot / Jazz Music

JOHNNY TEMPLE VOL.2 1938-1940
CD DOCD 5239
Document / May '94 / ADA / Hot Shot / Jazz Music

JOHNNY TEMPLE VOL.3 1940-1949
CD DOCD 5240
Document / May '94 / ADA / Hot Shot / Jazz Music

Temple Of The Dog

TEMPLE OF THE DOG
Say hello to heaven / Reach down / Hunger strike / Pushin' forward back / Call me a dog / Times of trouble / Wooden Jesus / Your savior / Four, walled world / All night thing
CD 3953502
A&M / Jun '92 / PolyGram

Temple Roy

DEAF AND DUMB
CD EB 012
Echo Beach / Mar '97 / Cargo / Shellshock/Disc

Temple, Shirley

ON THE GOOD SHIP LOLLIPOP
CD PLCD 541
President / Aug '95 / Grapevine/PolyGram / President / Target/BMG

SHIRLEY TEMPLE VOL.1 (America's Sweetheart)
On the good ship lollipop / Baby take a bow / On account-a I love you / Love's young dream / Lullaby to a doll / Animal crackers in my soup / When I grow up / Believe me, if all those endearing young charms / Song and dance / Polly wolly doddle / Early bird / At the codfish ball / Sextette from Lucia / Right somebody to love / Oh my goodness / Buy a bar of barry's/When I'm with you / But definitely / Peck's theme song / You've gotta each your spinach baby / I love a military man / Hey, what did the blue jay say / He was a dandy / Picture me without you / Get on board little children / Minstrel show introduction/Dixie-Anna
CD PASTCD 7096
Flapper / Sep '96 / Pinnacle

SHIRLEY TEMPLE VOL.2 (America's Sweetheart)
You've gotta S-M-I-L-E to be H-A-double-P-P-Y / Goodnight my love / That's what I want for Christmas / In our little wooden shoes / Hold God pray thy name / Silent night / Be optimistic and smile / How can I thank you / We should be together / If all the world were paper / When you were sweet sixteen / Courtroom scene / An old straw hat / Come and get your happiness / Rebecca's medley / Toy trumpet / This is a happy little ditty / I love to walk in the rain / Wot'cher (knock'd 'em in The Old Kent Road) / One, two, three / Lay-de-o / 5th Avenue / Young people / I wouldn't take a million / Tra-la-la-la / Leo is on the air / Kathleen
CD PASTCD 7097
Flapper / Sep '96 / Pinnacle

Templebeat

MEDIASICKNESS
CD CDWHIP 022
Sub/Mission / Dec '96 / Cargo

Templegate

INNOCENCE
Innocence / Never be / Deep / Anger overload / Give / Salvation / Better off dead / Killing time / What I need / Wherever I fall / Suffer / Bastard son
CD CDBLEED 13
Bleeding Hearts / Aug '95 / Pinnacle

Templeton, Alec

BACH GOES TO TOWN
Three little fishes / Blues in the night / Lost chord / Shortest Wagnerian opera / Tea for

two / Body and soul / Music goes 'round and around
CD PASTCD 7057
Flapper / Feb '95 / Pinnacle

Temptations

BEST OF THE TEMPTATIONS, THE
CD 31272
Scratch / Oct '94 / Koch / Scratch/BMG

CLOUD NINE
Cloud 9 / I heard it through the grapevine / Runaway child running wild / Love is a hurtin' thing / Hey girl (I like your style) / Why did she have to leave me (why did she have to go) / I need your lovin' / Don't let him take your love from me / I gotta find a way (to get you back) / Gonna keep on tryin' till I win your love
CD 5301532
Motown / Aug '93 / PolyGram

FOR LOVERS ONLY
CD 5305682
Motown / Sep '95 / PolyGram

GREATEST HITS
CD PA 7142
Paradiso / Mar '94 / Target/BMG

MASTERPIECE
Hey girl (I like your style) / Masterpiece / Ma / Law of the land / Plastic man / Hurry tomorrow
CD 5301002
Motown / Jan '93 / PolyGram

MILESTONE
Eeny meeny miney mo / Any old lovin' (just won't do) / Hoops of fire / We should be makin' love / Jones' / Get ready / Corner of my heart / Whenever you're ready / Do it easy / Wait a minute / Celebrate
CD 5300052
Motown / Jan '93 / PolyGram

MOTOWN EARLY CLASSICS
My girl / I'll be in trouble / (Girl) Why you wanna make me blue / Girl's alright with me / Get ready / (You're me dream) Come true / I couldn't cry If I wanted to / You're the one I need / You'll lose a precious love / Ain't too proud to beg / Who's lovin' you / Nobody but you / I gotta know now / Too busy thinking about my baby / You've got to earn it / Everybody needs love / It's growing / Don't look back
CD 5523232
Spectrum / Jul '96 / PolyGram

MOTOWNS GREATEST HITS: TEMPTATIONS
CD 5300152
Motown / Jan '93 / PolyGram

ONE BY ONE (The Best Of The Temptations/2CD Set)
My whole world ended (the moment you left me) / I've lost evrything I've ever loved / I'm so glad I fell for you / Which way to my baby / Double cross / It's so hard for me to say goodbye / This used to be the home of Johnnie Mae / Can I / If you left me / Girl you need a change of mind / Date with the rain / Eddie's love / Feel like givin' up / Once you had a heart / I miss you / Common man / Darling come back home / Keep on truckin' / Tell her love has felt the need / Boogie down / Shoeshine boy / Happy / Get the cream off the top / Walk away from love / Heavy love / Statue of a fool / He's a friend / When the lights come down on love / Everything's coming up love / Just let me hold you for a night / You're my peace of mind / Don't look any further / (You're my) Aphrodisiac / Coolin' out / Soulmate
CD Set 5306152
Motown / Jul '96 / PolyGram

ORIGINAL LEAD SINGERS
Get ready / My girl / I can't get next to you / Papa was a rolling stone / Superstar (remember how you got where you are) / Just my imagination (running away with me) / Masterpiece / Ain't too proud to beg / Ball of confusion / Cloud nine / Runaway child (running wild) / Beauty is only skin deep / Keep on truckin' / Way you do the things you do / I wish it would rain / I'm losing you / Psychedelic shack
CD 100212
CMC / May '97 / BMG

TEMPTATIONS, THE
CD EXP 032
Experience / May '97 / TKO Magnum

Temptones

TEMPTONES, THE
Girl I love you / Goodbye / Say these words of love / Something good / Baby, yes I do / Goodbye / Girl I love you / Say these words of love / I don't want to cry / I wish it would rain / I've been good to you / Meaning of existence / My girl / Voice your choice / I've been trying / So fine / Say it baby / I want a love I can see / So hard to be loved by you / Goodbye
CD BCD 15917
Bear Family / May '96 / Direct / Rollercoaster / Swift

Ten

TEN
CD NTHEN 027CD
Now & Then / Jun '96 / Plastic Head

Ten Foot Pole

TEN FOOT POLE/SATANIC SURFERS (Split CD) (Ten Foot Pole & Satanic Surfers)
CD BTR 003CD
Bad Taste / Nov '95 / Plastic Head

UNLEASHED
Fiction / John / It's not me / Denial / What you want / Daddy / Damage / Too late / Excuses / Pride and shame / Regret / Hey Pete / ADD
CD 64782
Epitaph / Mar '97 / Pinnacle / Plastic Head

Ten Years After

COLLECTION, THE
Hear me calling / No title / Spoonful / I can't keep from crying sometimes / Standing at the crossroads / Portable people / Rock your mama / Love like a man (long version) / I want to know / Speed kills / Boogie on / I may be wrong but I won't be wrong always / At the woodchoppers' ball / Spider in your web / Summertime / Shantung cabbage / I'm going home
CD CCSCD 293
Castle / Jul '91 / BMG

CRICKLEWOOD GREEN
Sugar the road / Working on the road / 50,000 miles beneath my brain / Year 3,000 blues / Me and my baby / Love like a man / Circles / As the sun still burns away
CD CDGOLD 1052
EMI Gold / Oct '96 / EMI

CRICKLEWOOD GREEN/WATT/A SPACE IN TIME (3CD Set)
Sugar the road / Working on the road / 50,000 miles beneath my brain / Year 3000 blues / Me & my baby / Love like a man / Circles / As the sun still burns away / I'm coming on / My baby left me / Think about the times / I say yeah / Band with no name / Gonna run / She lies in the morning / Sweet little sixteen / One of these days / Here they come / I'd love to change the world / Over the hill / Baby won't you let me rock 'n' roll you / Once there was a time / Let the sky fall / Hard monkeys / I've been there too / Uncle Jam
CD Set CDOMB 011
Chrysalis / Oct '95 / EMI

ESSENTIAL TEN YEARS AFTER
Rock 'n' roll music to the world / I'd Love to change the world / I'm going home / Choo choo mama / Tomorrow / I woke up this morning / Me and my baby / Good morning little school girl / Goin' back to Birmingham / 50,000 miles beneath my brain / Sweet little sixteen / I'm coming on / Love like a man / Baby won't you let me rock 'n' roll you
CD CDCHR 1857
Chrysalis / Oct '92 / EMI

I'M GOING HOME
I'm going home / I'd love to change the world / It's getting harder / Love like a man / Woodchoppers ball / Rock 'n' roll music to the world / Me and my baby / I woke up this morning / Stoned women / Cho cho mama / Slow blues in 'c' / 50,000 miles beneath my brain / Positive vibrations / Hear me calling
CD DC 868782
Disky / Nov '96 / Disky / THE

RECORDED LIVE
One of these days / You give me loving / Good morning little school girl / Hobbitt / Help me / Classical things / Scat thing / I can't keep from crying sometimes / Sometimes / Silly thing / Slow blues in 'C' / I'm going home / Choo choo Mama
CD BGOCD 341
Beat Goes On / Mar '97 / Pinnacle

ROCK 'N' ROLL MUSIC TO THE WORLD
You give me loving / Convention prevention / Turned off TV blues / Standing at the station / You can't win them all / Religion / Choo choo mama / Tomorrow I'll be out of town / Rock 'n' roll music to the world
CD BGOCD 348
Beat Goes On / May '97 / Pinnacle

SPACE IN TIME, A
One of these days / Here they come / I'd love to change the world / Over the hill / Baby won't you let me rock 'n' roll you / Once there was a time / Let the sky fall / Hard monkeys / I've been there too / Uncle Jam
CD BGOCD 351
Beat Goes On / Jul '97 / Pinnacle

SSSSH
Bad scene / Two time Mama / Stoned woman / Good morning little school girl / If you should love me / I don't know that you don't know my name / Stomp / I woke up this morning
CD BGOCD 338
Beat Goes On / Feb '97 / Pinnacle

STONEDHENGE
I can't live without you, Lydia / Woman trouble / Skoobly-oobly-doo-bob / Hear me calling / Sad song / Three blind mice / No title / Faro / Speed kills / Going to try
CD BGOCD 356
Beat Goes On / Jul '97 / Pinnacle

WATT
I'm coming on / My baby left me / Think about the times / Band with no name / Gonna run / She lies in the morning / Sweet little sixteen
CD BGOCD 345
Beat Goes On / Apr '97 / Pinnacle

Tenaglia, Danny

GAG ME WITH A TUNE (Various Artists)
Way we used to be: *Fisher, Cevin* / Happy: *Albanese, Judy* / Hipnotizing: *BOP & Buzz* / Check this out: *Fisher, Cevin* / I found it: *Daphne* / We kan never be satisfied: *Dunn, Mike* / Gonna luv: *McSpadden, C.J.* / Dedication: *Jones, Nick* / Werking: *Head Case* / Banji dance: *Cassanova's Revenge* / Where we at: *BOP & Buzz* / It doesn't matter: *Jones, Shay*
CD TWCD 90002
Twisted UK / Feb '97 / Amato Disco / BMG / Prime / RTM/Disc / Vital

Tendekist Wanganui Band

CHAMPION BRASS
CD CDODE 1306
ODE / Feb '90 / CM / Discovery

Tender Fury

IF ANGER WERE SOUL I'D BE JAMES BROWN
CD TX 92582
Roadrunner / Nov '91 / PolyGram

Tenebrae

DYSANCHELIUM
CD SPI 17CD
Spinefarm / Oct '94 / Plastic Head

Tenko

AT THE TOP OF MT BROCKEN
CD ACCDEC 48
ReR/Recommended / Mar '94 / ReR Megacorp / RTM/Disc

DRAGON BLUE
CD SFCD 004
Sound Factory / Jun '97 / ReR Megacorp

Tennessee Rhythm Riders

STEP IT UP AND GO
That's the way it's gonna be / Rockaway rock / Hillbilly baby / Little red caboose / You won't believe this / Step it up and go / Truck driver's rock / Woman in town / Hot rod girl / Tennessee special / Kiss me quick and go / Good gosh girl / Kaw-liga / Ranch hand boogie / Road of sadness / Pistol boogie / When your house is not your home / Juke box boogie
CD FCD 3048
Fury / May '97 / Nervous / TKO Magnum

Tenney, Gerry

LET'S SING A YIDDISH SONG (Tenney, Gerry & Betty Albert Schreck)
CD GV 134CD
Global Village / Nov '93 / ADA / Direct

Tenney, James

BRIDGE & FLOCKING
CD ARTCD 6193
Hat Art / Dec '96 / Cadillac / Harmonia Mundi

Tenor, Jimi

EUROPA
CD PUUCD 2
Still Bubbling / Sep '95 / Plastic Head

INTERVISION
Outta space / Downtown / Sugardaddy / Never say it aloud / Can't stay with you baby / Tesla / Caravan / Wiping put / Wiping out / Shore Hotel / Nobody's perfect / Atlantis
CD WARPCD 48
Warp / Mar '97 / Prime / RTM/Disc

Tenor Saw

TENOR SAW LIVES ON
CD CD 005
Sky High / Jan '93 / Direct / Jet Star

WITH LOTS OF SIGN (Tenor Saw & Nitty Gritty)
CD BR 002CD
Black Roots / Nov '94 / Jet Star

Tenores Di Bitti

AMMENTOS
CD NT 6746CD
Newtone / Mar '96 / ADA

S'AMORE 'E MAMA
Lamentu / Monte seris / Anghelos cantade / Sa ballarina / S'amore 'e mama / T'amo / Sos ojos largimosos / Su manxanile / Sos artigianos / Satiras / S'annunziata / Sardinia soundscape
CD CDRW 60
Realworld / Jul '96 / EMI

Tenpole Tudor

LET THE FOUR WINDS BLOW
Let the four winds blow / Throwing my baby out with the bath water / Trumpeters / It's easy to see / What you doing in Bombay / Local animal / Her fruit is forbidden / Tonight is the night / Unpaid debt / King of Siam / Sea of thunder
CD STIFFCD 12
Disky / Jan '94 / Disky / THE

SWORDS OF A THOUSAND MEN (2CD Set)
Swords of a thousand men / Go wilder / I wish / Header now / Here are the boys / Wunderbar / 3 bells in a row / Tell me more / Judy Annual / I can't sleep / Anticipation / What else can I do / Confessions / Love and food / There are the boys / Wunderbar / Let the four winds blow / Throwing my baby out with the bathwater / Trumpeters / It's easy to see / What you doing in Bombay / Local animal / Her fruit is forbidden / Tonight is the night / Unpaid debt / King of Siam / Sea of thunder / Conga tribe / Tenpole 45 / Fashion / Rock and roll music
CD Set SMDCD 144
Snapper / May '97 / Pinnacle

WUNDERBAR (The Best Of Tenpole Tudor)
Three bells in a row / Swords of a thousand men / Go wilder / Header now / Wunderbar / What else can I do / I can't sleep / Confessions / Tell me more / Throwing my baby out with the bath water / Let the four winds blow / Tonight is the night / What you doing in Bombay / Her fruit is forbidden / Sea of thunder / Hayrick song
CD DOJOCD 76
Dojo / Nov '92 / Disc

Tepper, Robert

NO REST FOR THE WOUNDED HEART
CD MTM 199611
MTM / Nov '96 / Cargo

Tequila Sisters

OUT OF THE SHADOWS
CD MSPCD 9403
Mabley St. / Jul '94 / Grapevine/PolyGram

Ter Veldhuis, Jacob

DIVERSO IL TEMPO
CD BVHAASTCD 9308
Bvhaast / Oct '94 / Cadillac

Terem Quartet

CLASSICAL
Eine kleine nachtmusik / Ave Maria / Concerto grosso in G-minor / Waltz / Chardash / Oginsky's polonaise / Funeral march / Nocturne 'Separation' / Flea waltz
CD CDRW 49
Realworld / Oct '94 / EMI

TEREM
Lyrical dance / Fantasy / Legend of the old mountain man / Cossack's farewell / Toccata / Variations on Swan Lake / Simfonia lubova / Old carousel / Two-step Nadya / Tsiganka / Letni Kanikuli / Country improvisation / Valenki / Baryni
CD CDRW 23
Realworld / Mar '92 / EMI

Terminal Cheesecake

KING OF ALL SPACEHEADS
CD JAKCD 8
CD JAKCDX 8
Jackass / Jul '94 / Pinnacle

PEARLESQUE
CD WSCD 001
World Serpent / Oct '96 / World Serpent

Terminals

TERMINALS LIVE
CD MED 001
Medication / Dec '96 / Cargo

Terminator X

TERMINATOR X AND THE VALLEY OF THE JEEP BEETS
Vendetta... the big getback / Buck whylin': *Chuck D & Sister Souljah* / Homey don't play dat: *Bonnie 'N' Clyde* / Juvenile delinquintz: *Juvenile Delinquintz* / Blues: *Andreas 13* / Back to the scene of the bass: *Interrogators* / Can't take my style: *Celo Of The Casino Brothers* / Wanna be dancin' / DJ is the selector: *Dub Master* / Run that go: *Spacey B Experience* / Power thang / No further: *Section 8* / High priest of turbulence: *Chief Groovy Loo* / Ain't got nuthin'
CD 5234822
RAL / Jan '96 / PolyGram

Termos, Paul

SHAKES & SOUNDS
CD ____ **GEESTCD 05**
Geest Gronden / Oct '87 / Cadillac

Ternent, Billy

UNMISTAKABLE SOUND OF BILLY TERNENT VOL.3, THE (Ternent, Billy & His Orchestra)
CD ____ **SAV 241CD**
Savoy / Dec '95 / Savoy / THE / TKO Magnum

UNMISTAKABLE SOUND OF BILLY TERNENT VOL.4 (Ternent, Billy & His Orchestra)
CD ____ **SAV 242CD**
Savoy / Dec '95 / Savoy / THE / TKO Magnum

Terra Ferma

TURTLE CROSSING
Lunar surprise / Fire / Scream / Visions / Poet / Floating / Snakecharmer / Planet Ogo / Crazy people
CD ____ **PLAT 30CD**
Platipus / May '97 / Prime / SRD

Terra Sul

KINDNESS OF STRANGERS
Lands / Kindness of strangers / Mestico / Matatlantica / Caminhando / Incognito / Deus dara / Meia luz / KYZ / Debra Ann / Heavenly bodies
CD ____ **5303162**
MoJazz / Oct '94 / PolyGram

Terrasson, Jacky

JACKY TERRASSON
I love Paris / Just a blues / My funny valentine / Hommage a lill boulanger / Bye bye blackbird / He goes on a trip / I fall in love too easily / Time after time / For once in my life / What a difference a day makes / Cumba's dance
CD ____ **CDP 8293512**
Blue Note / Feb '95 / EMI

REACH
I should care / Rat race / Baby Plum / I love you for sentimental reasons / Reach/ Smoke/Reach / Happy man / First affair / Just one of those things
CD ____ **CDP 8357932**
Blue Note / Jan '96 / EMI

Terre Thaemlitz

COUTURE COSMETIQUE
CD ____ **CAI 20022**
Caipirnha / May '97 / Cargo

Terrell

ANGRY SOUTHERN GENTLEMAN
Let's go for a ride / Straw dogs (Before the fall) / Dreamed I was the devil / Newhope / Angry southern gentleman / Piece of time / Toystore / Redneck gigolo / Broken man / Blacktop runaways / Long train / Come down to me
CD ____ **VPBCD 23**
Pointblank / Apr '95 / EMI

BEAUTIFUL SIDE OF MADNESS
Chant of faith / Hopeful sinner / Home / Convince myself / Hollywood drag / Pour our souls / Georgia O'Keefe / Black & white blues / Whitley Flats / Shotgun / Needle's kiss / Beautiful side of madness
CD ____ **VPBCD 37**
Pointblank / Oct '96 / EMI

Terremoto

COSA NATURAL
En tus suenos / Me dio risa en el alma / Que te peredone / Al tiempo le pregunte / Sonaba el canto del gallo / A la del desamparo / Sigue cantando gitano / Camino de los juncales / Entre triana y Jerez
CD ____ **B 6847**
Auvidis/Ethnic / Jul '97 / ADA / Harmonia Mundi

Territory Singers

TERRITORY SINGERS VOL.1 1922-1928
CD ____ **DOCD 5470**
Document / Jul '96 / ADA / Hot Shot / Jazz Music

TERRITORY SINGERS VOL.2 1928-1930
CD ____ **DOCD 5471**
Document / Jul '96 / ADA / Hot Shot / Jazz Music

Terror Against Terror

PSYCHOLIGICAL WARFARE
CD ____ **PA 001CD**
Paragoric / May '95 / Cargo / Plastic Head

Terror Fabulous

GLAMOROUS
CD ____ **NWSCD 7**
New Sound / Mar '94 / Jet Star

LYRICALLY ROUGH
CD ____ **GRELCD 221**
Greensleeves / Oct '95 / Jet Star / SRD

YAGA YAGA
Number 2 / Broke wine butterfly / Mr. Big Man / From birth / You must be a fool / Talk 'bout / If you know you're ready / You nuh kotch / Yaga yaga / Pretty teenager / Gangster's anthem / Action / Miss Goody Goody / Too bad / Water bed expert
CD ____ **7567923272**
Warner Bros. / Aug '94 / Warner Music

Terrorgruppe

UBER AMERIKA
CD ____ **BYO 042CD**
Better Youth Organisation / Feb '97 / Cargo

Terrorizer

WORLD DOWNFALL
After world obliteration / Tear of napalm / Corporation pull in / Resurrection / Need to live / Dead shall rise / Injustice / Storm of stress / Human prey / Condemned system / Enslaved by propaganda / Whirlwind struggle / World downfall / Ripped to shreds
CD ____ **MOSH 016CD**
Earache / Nov '89 / Vital

Terrorvision

FORMALDEHYDE
Problem solved / Ships that sink / American TV / New policy one / Jason / Killing time / Urban space crime / Hole for a soul / Don't shoot my dog / Desolation town / My house / Human being
CD ____ **VEGASCD 1**
Total Vegas / May '93 / EMI

HOW TO MAKE FRIENDS AND INFLUENCE PEOPLE
Alice, what's the matter / Oblivion / Stop the bus / Discotheque wreck / Middle man / Still the rhythm / Ten shades of grey / Stab in the back / Pretend best friend / Time o' the signs / What the doctor ordered / Some people say / What makes you tick
CD ____ **VEGASCD 2**
Total Vegas / Apr '94 / EMI
CD ____ **VEGASCDX 2**
EMI / Sep '97 / EMI

REGULAR URBAN SURVIVORS
Enteralterego / Superchronic / Perseverance / Easy / Hide the dead girl / Conspiracy / Didn't bleed red / Dog chewed the handle / Junior / Bad actress / If I was you / Celebrity hit list / Mugwump
CD ____ **VEGASCD 3**
Total Vegas / Mar '96 / EMI

Terry

SILVERADO TRAIL (Terry & The Pirates)
Wish I was your river / Sweet emotions / I can't dance / Heartbeatin' away / Silverado trail / Follow her around / Risin' of the moon / Mustang ride / Gun metal blues / Inlaws and outlaws / Nighthawkin' the dawn
CD ____ **CDWIK 89**
Big Beat / Jan '90 / Pinnacle

Terry & Gerry

BEST EVER TERRY AND GERRY ALBUM IN THE WORLD...EVER, THE
Hello / Joey / Ballad of a nasty man / CARS / Thousand towns / Butter's the bread of a rich man's life / Independent's day / Last bullet in the gun / Banking on Simon / Pizza pie and junk / Reservation / Fashion rodeo / Percy Crusoe / Good, the bad, and the usherette / Wolfman's request / Kennedy says / Clothes shop closed
CD ____ **CDMRED 144**
Cherry Red / Jun '97 / Pinnacle

Terry, Clark

ALTERNATE BLUES (Terry, Clark/ Freddie Hubbard/Dizzy Gillespie/Oscar Peterson)
Alternate one / Alternate two / Alternate three / Alternate four / Wrap your troubles in dreams (and dream your troubles away) / Here's that rainy day / Gypsy / If I should lose you
CD ____ **OJCCD 744**
Original Jazz Classics / May '93 / Complete/ Pinnacle / Jazz Music / Wellard

CLARK AFTER DARK
CD ____ **5290882**
MPS Jazz / Mar '96 / PolyGram

COLOUR CHANGES
CD ____ **CCD 9009**
Candid / Jul '87 / Cadillac / Direct / Jazz Music / Koch / Wellard

EXPRESS
CD ____ **RR 73CD**
Reference Recordings / Jul '96 / Jazz Music / May Audio

IN ORBIT (Terry, Clark Quartet & Thelonious Monk)
CD ____ **OJCCD 302**
Original Jazz Classics / Apr '92 / Complete/Pinnacle / Jazz Music / Wellard

LUCERNE 1978 (Terry, Clark & Chris Woods)
Hymn / Silly samba / I want a little girl / Straight no chaser / On the trail / Lemon drop / Somebody done stole my blues / God bless the child / Somewhere over the rainbow
CD ____ **TCB 02082**
TCB / Aug '97 / New Note/Pinnacle

MELLOW MOODS
CD ____ **PCD 24136**
Pablo / Jun '95 / Cadillac / Complete/ Pinnacle

OW (2CD Set)
My secret love / Ow / Just and old manuscript / Jingle bells / Georgia on my mind / Shaw 'nuff / Oh lady be good / Mack the knife / Rebecca / God bless the child / Straight, no chaser / On Green Dolphin Street / All blues / Take the 'A' train
CD Set ____ **JLR 103601**
Live At EJ's / May '96 / Target/BMG

SECOND SET, THE
One foot in the gutter / Opus ocean / Michelle / Serenade to a bus seat / Joonji / Ode to a flugelhorn / Funky Mama / Interview
CD ____ **JD 127**
Chesky / Mar '95 / Discovery / Goldring

SHADES OF BLUE
CD ____ **CHR 70007**
Challenge / Jun '95 / ADA / Direct / Jazz Music / Wellard

SPACEMEN, THE
CD ____ **CRD 309**
Chiaroscuro / Mar '96 / Jazz Music

TOP AND BOTTOM BRASS
Mili-Terry / Swinging Chemise / My heart belongs to Daddy / Blues for Etta / Top 'n' bottom / 127 / Sunday kind of love / Mardi Gras waltz
CD ____ **OJCCD 764**
Original Jazz Classics / Dec '96 / Complete/ Pinnacle / Jazz Music / Wellard

Terry, Gordon

LOTTA LOTTA WOMEN
Lotta lotta women / It ain't right / I had a talk with me / Queen of the seasons / Gonna go down the river / Lonely road / Honky tonk man / You remembered me / Revenooer man / Long black limousine / Wild desire / Little ole you / How my baby can love / Fortune of love / Slow down old world / For old time's sake / You'll regret / Hook, line and sinker / Maybe / Keep on talking / Then I heard the bad news / I don't hurt anymore / Saddest day / All by my lonesome / Battle of New Orleans / Fifty stars / When they ring these wedding bells / Almost alone
CD ____ **BCD 15881**
Bear Family / Nov '95 / Direct / Rollercoaster / Swift

Terry, Iain

ROCK TIL MIDNIGHT
CD ____ **PT 607001**
Part / Jun '96 / Nervous

Terry, Lillian

DREAM COMES TRUE, A (Terry, Lillian & Tommy Flanagan)
CD ____ **1210472**
Soul Note / Oct '90 / Cadillac / Harmonia Mundi / Wellard

OO-SHOO-BE-DOO-BE....OO,OO
CD ____ **SN 1147**
Soul Note / '86 / Cadillac / Harmonia Mundi / Wellard

Terry, Sonny

AT SUGAR HILL (Terry, Sonny & Brownie McGhee)
CD ____ **OBCCD 536**
Original Blues Classics / Nov '92 / Complete/Pinnacle / Wellard

BACK TO NEW ORLEANS (Terry, Sonny & Brownie McGhee)
Let me be your big dog / Pawn shop / You don't know / Betty and dupree / Back to New Orleans / Stranger here / Fox hunt / I'm prison bound / Louise Louise / Baby how long / Freight train / I got a woman / Hold me in your arms / CC and the O blues / Devil's gonna git you / Don't you lie to me / That's why I'm walking / Wrong track / Blue feeling / House lady / I know better
CD ____ **CDCH 372**
Ace / May '92 / Pinnacle

BLOWIN' THE FUSES (Terry, Sonny & Brownie McGhee)
CD ____ **TCD 1013**
Tradition / May '96 / ADA / Vital

BLUES BROTHERS (Terry, Sonny & Brownie McGhee)
CD ____ **PLSCD 186**
Pulse / Apr '97 / BMG

BROWNIE MCGEE & SONNY TERRY SING (Terry, Sonny & Brownie McGhee)
CD ____ **SFCD 40011**
Smithsonian Folkways / Sep '94 / ADA / Cadillac / CM / Direct / Koch

CALIFORNIA BLUES (Terry, Sonny & Brownie McGhee)
I got fooled / No need of running / I feel so good / Thinkin' and worrying / I love you baby / California blues / Walkin' and lyin' down / First and last love / Christine / I have had my fun / Whoppin' and Squalin' / Waterboy cry / Motherless child / Sportin' life / John Henry / I'm a stranger / Cornbread and peas / Louise / I done done / Meet you in the morning / Poor boy from home / Hudy Leadbelly / Something's wrong at home / Take this home / Take this hammer / Baby's gone / Lose your money
CD ____ **CDCHD 398**
Ace / May '93 / Pinnacle

DUO, THE (Terry, Sonny & Brownie McGhee)
CD ____ **CD 52032**
Blues Encore / May '94 / Target/BMG

FOLKWAYS YEARS 1944-1963, THE
CD ____ **SFWCD 40033**
Smithsonian Folkways / Dec '94 / ADA / Cadillac / CM / Direct / Koch

GOING IT ALONE (Terry, Sonny & Brownie McGhee)
Cold wind blowing / Feel like robbin' the grave / Keep on lovin' you / Mean old woman / Blues had a baby / Selling out / That train and my woman / Rainy day / Cut off from my baby / Chicken when I'm hungry / Mean and evil / Black night road / Playing with the thing / Ask myself a question
CD ____ **TBA 130122**
Blues Alliance / Jun '97 / New Note/ Pinnacle

HOMETOWN BLUES (Terry, Sonny & Brownie McGhee)
Mean ol' Frisco / Man ain't nothin' but a fool / Woman is killing me / Meet you in the morning / Stranger blues / Feel so good / Forgive me / Sittin' on top of the world / Crying the blues / Key to the highway / Ease my worried mind / Bulldog blues / CC rider / Going down slow / Bad blood / Lightnin's blues / Dissatisfied woman / Pawn shop blues
CD ____ **4744092**
Sony Jazz / Dec '93 / Sony

JUST A CLOSER WALK WITH THEE (Terry, Sonny & Brownie McGhee)
CD ____ **OBCCD 541**
Original Blues Classics / Nov '92 / Complete/Pinnacle / Wellard

LEGENDARY SONNY TERRY & BROWNIE MCGHEE, THE (Terry, Sonny & Brownie McGhee)
John Henry / Midnight special / Muddy water / Take this hammer whup / Sportin' life / Cornbread and peas / Louise, Louise / Hooray, hooray, this woman is killing me / Evil hearted me / Sonny's squall / Red river blues / Spread the news around / Just about crazy / Wholesale dealin' papa / Just a closer walk with thee / I shall not be moved / Back to New Orleans / Don't you lie to me / That's why I'm walking / Freight train
CD ____ **NTMCD 526**
Nectar / Aug '96 / Pinnacle

LONDON SESSIONS 1958, THE (Terry, Sonny & Brownie McGhee)
Just a dream / I've been treated wrong / Woman's lover blues / Climbing on top of the hill / Southern train / Black horse blues / Gone but not forgotten / I love you baby / Cornbread, peas and black molassas / You'd better mind / Brownie blues / Change the lock on my door / Auto-mechanics blues / Sonny's blues / Wholesale and retail / Fox chase / Way I feel / Hooray (this woman is killing me)
CD ____ **NEXCD 120**
Sequel / Apr '90 / BMG

MIDNIGHT SPECIAL (Terry, Sonny & Brownie McGhee)
Sonny's squall / Red river blues / Gone gal / Blues before sunrise / Blues of happiness / Understand me / Jealous man / Midnight special / East Coast blues / Muddy water / Beggin' and cryin'
CD ____ **CDCH 951**
Ace / Aug '90 / Pinnacle

ORIGINAL, THE (Terry, Sonny & Brownie McGhee)
What a beautiful city / Dirty mistreater / Don't dog your woman / Harmonica hop / Doggin' my heart around / Daisy / Blowin' the fuses / Right on that shore / Blues for the lowlands / Walk on / Down by the riverside / I'm a stranger here / Trouble in mind / Everybody's blues / Po' boy / Drinkin' in the blues
CD ____ **CDBM 122**
Blue Moon / Jun '97 / Cadillac / Discovery / Greensleeves / Jazz Music / Jet Star / TKO Magnum

PO' BOY (Terry, Sonny & Brownie McGhee)
CD ____ **IMP 306**
IMP / Sep '96 / ADA / Discovery

SONNY AND BROWNIE (Terry, Sonny & Brownie McGhee)
People get ready / Bring it on home to me / You bring out the boogie in me / Sail away

/ Sonny's thing / White boy / Lost in the blues / Battle is over (but the war goes on) / Walkin' my blues away / Big wind (is a' comin') / Jesus gonna make it alright / God and man / On the road again
CD 3972002
A&M / Oct '94 / PolyGram

SONNY IS KING
CD OBCCD 521
Original Blues Classics / Nov '92 / Complete/Pinnacle / Wellard

SONNY TERRY 1938-1945/ALONZO 1955 (Terry, Sonny & Alonzo Scales)
CD DOCD 5230
Document / Apr '94 / ADA / Hot Shot / Jazz Music

SONNY TERRY AND BROWNIE MCGHEE (Terry, Sonny & Brownie McGhee)
CD BGOCD 75
Beat Goes On / '89 / Pinnacle

SONNY'S STORY
I ain't gonna be your dog no more / My baby done gone / Worried blues / High powered woman / Pepperheaded woman / Sonny's story / I'm gonna get on my feet after a while / Four o'clock blues / Telephone blues / Great tall engine
CD OBCCD 503
Original Blues Classics / Nov '92 / Complete/Pinnacle / Wellard

WHOOPIN' (Terry, Sonny & Johnny Winter/Willie Dixon)
CD ALCD 4734
Alligator / May '93 / ADA / CM / Direct

WIZARD OF THE HARMONICA, THE
CD STCD 8018
Storyville / Jan '97 / Cadillac / Jazz Music / Wellard

Terry, Todd

BEST OF TODD TERRY'S UNRELEASED PROJECTS, THE
CD BB 042132CD
Broken Beat / Jan '96 / Plastic Head

DAY IN THE LIFE OF TODD TERRY
CD SOMCD 2
Ministry Of Sound / Jul '96 / 3mv/Sony / Mo's Music Machine / Warner Music

MINISTRY OF SOUND - SESSIONS VOL.8 (2CD Set) (Various Artists)
CD Set MINCD 8
Ministry Of Sound / Jul '97 / 3mv/Sony / Mo's Music Machine / Warner Music

READY FOR A NEW DAY
Preacher / Something's going on / I'm feelin' it / Ready for a new day / It's over love / Satisfaction guaranteed / Sax trac / Come on baby / Free yourself / Live without you / Keep on jumpin' / Rave / Something goin' on / Keep on jumpin'
CD 5360762
Manifesto / Jul '97 / PolyGram

TODD TERRY PROJECT (Terry, Todd Project)
Put your hands together / Bolla / I'm goin' insane / Holdin' on / Definition wild side / Take me / Dee intermission / Day in the life part 11 / Do what you want / Popular demand / Don't get carried away / Day in the groove
CD CHAMPCD 1027
Champion / May '92 / 3mv/BMG

Terveet Kadet

KUMIA JA VERTA 1987
CD AA 028
AA / Jul '97 / Cargo / Greyhound

SIGN OF THE CROSS
CD AA 025
AA / Jul '97 / Cargo / Greyhound

Terzis, Michalis

MAGIC OF THE GREEK BOUZOUKI
Dance of the dolphins / Near the sea / Dance of the fisherman / Trikimia / Olympus / Morning breeze / Trip with Alexandra / Nocturno / Flight of the seagull / South wind / Dance of Captain Michalis / Sea dream / Mermaid on the boat
CD EUCD 1206
ARC / Sep '93 / ADA / ARC Music

NOSTIMON IMAR
CD EUCD 1076
ARC / '89 / ADA / ARC Music

Tesi, Riccardo

COLLINE (Tesi, Riccardo & Patrick Vaillant)
CD Y 225048CD
Silex / Apr '95 / ADA / Harmonia Mundi

IL BALLO DELLA LEPRE
CD MWCD 4001
Music & Words / Apr '93 / ADA / Direct

UN BALLO LISCIO
CD Y 225056CD
Silex / Mar '96 / ADA / Harmonia Mundi

Tesla

FIVE MAN ACOUSTICAL JAM
CD GEFD 24311
Geffen / Feb '91 / BMG

PSYCHOTIC SUPPER
CD GEFD 24424
Geffen / Aug '91 / BMG

Test Department

BRITH GOF GODDIN
Sarff / Gwyr A Aeth Gatraeth / Arddyledog Ganu / Glasfedd Eu Hancwyn / Trichant Eurdochog / Yn Nydd Cadiawr / Truan Yw Gennyffi
CD MOP 004CD
Ministry Of Power / Aug '92 / RTM/Disc / Vital

ECSTASY UNDER DURESS
CD RUSCD 8213
ROIR / Oct '95 / Plastic Head / Shellshock/Disc

GOODNIGHT OUT, A
Goodnight / Milk of human kindness / Generous terms / Victory / We shall return no more / Demonomania / Voice of reason
CD MOP 003CD
Some Bizarre / Mar '94 / Pinnacle

LEGACY (1990-93)
CD FREUDCD 47
Jungle / Oct '94 / RTM/Disc / SRD

LIVE ATONAL
CD EFA 08438
Dossier / Jul '92 / Cargo / SRD

MATERIA PRIMA
CD DEPTCD 1
Jungle / Jan '95 / RTM/Disc / SRD

PAX BRITANNICA
CD MOP 006CD
Ministry Of Power / Sep '96 / RTM/Disc / Vital

PROVEN IN ACTION
CD DEPTCD 002
Sub Rosa / Apr '96 / Direct / RTM/Disc / SRD / Vital

TERRA FIRMA
Nadka / Siege / Current affairs / Dark eyes / Terra firma
CD SUBCD 00212
Sub Rosa / '88 / Direct / RTM/Disc / SRD / Vital

TOTALITY
CD KK 140CD
KK / Nov '95 / Plastic Head

Testa, Gianmaria

MONTGOLFIERES
Citta lunga / La traiettorie delle mongolfiere / Habanara / La donna del bar / Dento la tasca di un qualuque mattino / Un aeroplance a vela / Come le onde del mare / L'automobile / Senza titolo / La donne nelle stazione / Maria / Manacore / La terre delle colline
CD LBLC 2519
Indigo / Jun '96 / New Note/Pinnacle

Testament

DEMONIC
Demonic refusal / Burning times / Together as one / Jun-jun / John Doe / Murky waters / Hatred's rise / Distorted lives / New eyes of old / Ten thousand thrones / Nostrovia
CD CDMFN 221
CD CDMFNX 221
Music For Nations / Jun '97 / Pinnacle

LIVE AT THE FILLMORE
CD CDMFN 186
Music For Nations / Jul '95 / Pinnacle

LOW
CD 7567826452
Atlantic / May '95 / Warner Music

PRACTICE WHAT YOU PREACH
Practice what you preach / Perilous nation / Envy time / Time is coming / Blessed in contempt / Greenhouse effect / Sins of omission / Ballad, The (A song of hope) / Nightmare (coming back to you) / Confusion fusion
CD 7820092
Atlantic / Feb '95 / Warner Music

RITUAL, THE
Sermon / As the seasons grey / Electric crown return to serenity / Ritual / Deadline / So many lies / Let go of my world / Agony / Troubled dreams / Signs of chaos / Electric crown / Return to serenity
CD 7567823922
East West / May '92 / Warner Music

Testify

BALLROOM KILLER
CD RTD 19519192
Our Choice / Jul '95 / Pinnacle

TESTIFY
CD RTD 19516392
Our Choice / Oct '93 / Pinnacle

YOUR VISION
CD RTD 19515923
Our Choice / Jul '93 / Pinnacle

Testimony

SATISFACTION WARRANTED
CD MABCD 006
MAB / Jan '94 / Plastic Head

Tetes Noires

CLAY FOOT GODS
CD ROUCD 9008
Rounder / '88 / ADA / CM / Direct

Tew, Alan

STRINGS GO LATIN (Tew, Alan & Tony Hatch)
CD PLSCD 230
Pulse / Jul '97 / BMG

Tex, Joe

AIN'T GONNA BUMP NO MORE
Ain't gonna bump no more (With no big fat woman) / Be cool / Leaving you dinner / I mess eveything up / We held on / Music ain't got no colour / Loose caboose / Rub down / Congratulations / You can be my star / You might be diggin' the garden / Give the baby anything the baby wants / Takin' a chance / You're in too deep / God of love / Baby let me steal you / Woman cares / Love me right girl / I gotcha
CD CDSEWD 043
Southbound / Jun '93 / Pinnacle

BUMP TO THE FUNK
Papa was too / Men are getting scarce / You need me, baby / Anything you wanna know / We can't sit down now / I can't see you no more / You're right, Ray Charles / Give the baby anything the baby wants / I gotcha / You said a bad word / King Thaddeus / Cat's got her tongue / My body wants you / I'm goin' back again / I don't want you to love me / Ain't gonna bump no more (with no big fat women) / I mess up everything I get my hands on / Loose caboose / Who gave birth to the funk / Stick your key in (and start your car)
CD CPCD 8081
Charly / Mar '95 / Koch

DIFFERENT STROKES
Have you ever / My neighbours got the gimmes / Mrs. Wiggles / Baby it's rainin' / Under your powerful love / Don't play with me / Same things it took to get me / All a man needs is his woman's love / When a woman stops loving a man / I can see everybody's baby / She said yeah / Time brings about a change / I don't want you to love me / I'm gonna try love again / This time we'll make it all the way / It's ridiculous / We're killing ourselves / Back off / Does it run in your family / Living in the last days / I've seen enough
CD CDCHARLY 161
Charly / Jan '89 / Koch

GREATEST HITS (2CD Set)
Hold what you've got / Only girl I've ever loved / Meet me in church / Woman can change a man / Same things it took to get me / I want to (do everything with you) / Don't make your children pay (for your mistakes) / Sweet woman like you / Love you save (may be your own) / SYSLJFM (the letter song) / I believe I'm gonna make it / Papa was too / Show me / All a man needs (is his woman's love) / Woman like that, yeah / Woman's hands / Skinny legs and all / Men are gettin' scarce / I'll never do you wrong / You need me / Baby / Buying a book / Anything you wanna know / She said yeah / I can't see everybody's baby / I gotcha / Bad feet / Takin' a chance / Woman stealer / under your powerful love / I'm going back again / Have you ever / Baby it's raining / Time brings about a change / I don't want you to love me (if you're gonna talk about it) / Ain't gonna bump no more (with no big fat woman) / Hungry
CD Set CPCD 82662
Charly / Dec '96 / Koch

I GOTCHA (His Greatest Hits)
Hold what you've got / You got what it takes / Woman can change a man / One monkey don't stop no show / I want (to do everything for you) / Sweet woman like you / Love you save (may be your own) / SYSLJFM (The letter song) / I believe I'm gonna make it / I've got to do a little bit better / Papa was, too (Tramp) / Show me / Woman like that, yeah / Woman's hands / Skinny legs and all / Men are getting scarce / I'll never do you wrong / Keep the one you got / Buying a book / I gotcha
CD CPCD 8015
Charly / Feb '94 / Koch

SHOW ME THE HITS AND MORE
CD ICH 1149CD
Ichiban / Jan '94 / Direct / Koch

SKINNY LEGS AND ALL
SYSLJFM (The letter song) / Love you save (may be your own) / Show me / Hold what you've got / Heep see few know / Someone to take your place / One monkey don't stop no show / If sugar was as sweet as you / Meet me in church / You got what it takes / I had a good home but I left (part 1) / Don't let your left hand know / Woman can change a man / Skinny legs and all / I want to (do everything for you) / Sweet woman like you / I believe I'm gonna make it / Men are getting scarce / I'm a man / I've got to do a little bit better / Papa was too / Watch the one (that brings the bad news) / Truest woman in the world / Chicken crazy
CD CDKEND 114
Kent / Mar '94 / Pinnacle

STONE SOUL COUNTRY
Just out of reach / Detroit city / Set me free / Heartbreak Hotel / Together again / King of the road / Dark end of the street / I'll never do you wrong / Make the world go away / Funny how time slips away / Ode to Billy Joe / Release me / Skip a rope / Engine engine / Honey / By the time I get to Phoenix / Green green grass of home / Papa's dreams
CD CDCHARLY 184
Charly / Jun '89 / Koch

VERY BEST OF JOE TEX, THE
Hold what you've got / One monkey don't stop no show / Woman (can change a man) / I want (do everything for you) / Don't make your children pay (for your mistakes) / Sweet woman like you / Love you save / You better believe it baby / I've got to do a little bit better / SYSLJFM (The letter song) / I believe I'm gonna make it / Woman sees a hard time (when her man is gone) / Watch the one (that brings the bad news) / Papa was too / Truest woman in the world / Show me / Woman like that, yeah / Woman's hands / Skinny legs and all / Men are getting scarce / I'll never do you wrong / Keep the one you've got / You need me, baby / Buying a book / It ain't sanitary / You're right, Ray Charles / I gotcha
CD CDCHARLY 133
Charly / Jul '88 / Koch

YOU'RE RIGHT (King Of Downhome Soul)
You're right, Ray Charles / You need me, baby / Dark end of the street / Woman like that, yeah / Keep the one you got / Same things it took to get me / I'll never do you wrong / Take the fifth amendment / Sweet sweet woman / We can't sit down now / Buying a book / Sure is good / That's the way / Anything you wanna know / Only way / Grandma Mary / Take my baby a little love / I can see everybody's baby / She said yeah / When a woman stops loving a man / Woman stealer / Funny how time slips away
CD CDKEND 117
Kent / Jan '95 / Pinnacle

Texabilly Rockers

HONEY LET'S GO
Tennessee train / I'm gonna catch you baby / Feelin' blue / True love / Cadillac stomp / Who's that cat / Just because / Booze-a-billy bop / Honey let's go / Rockabilly boogie / Wrong yo yo / Mystery baby / I was the one
CD RNRCD 002
Metralha / May '97 / Nervous

Texas

SOUTHSIDE/RICK'S ROAD (2CD Set)
I don't want a lover / Tell me why / Everyday now / Southside / Prayer for you / Faith / Thrill has gone / Fight the feeling / Fool for love / One choice / Future is promises / So called friend / Fade away / Listen to me / You owe it all to me / Beautiful angel / So in love with you / You've got to give a little / I want to go to heaven / Hear me now / Fearing these days / I've been missing you / Winter's end
CD Set 5286042
Vertigo / Aug '95 / PolyGram

WHITE ON BLONDE
0.30 / Say what you want / Drawing crazy patterns / Halo / Put your arms around me / Insane / Blacke eyed boy / Polo mint city / White on blonde / Postcard / 0.25 / Ticket to lie / Good advice / Breathless
CD 5343152
Mercury / Feb '97 / PolyGram

Texas Is The Reason

DO YOU KNOW WHO YOU ARE
CD REVCD 051
Revelation / Apr '96 / Plastic Head

Texas Lone Star

DESPERADOS WAITING FOR A TRAIN
Good hearted woman / Here I am again / Friend of the devil / Desperados waiting for the train / Fast train / Me and my uncle / Wild horses / In my own way / Bluebirds are singing for you / Luckenbach, Texas (Back to the basics of love) / Painted ladies
CD BCD 15692
Bear Family / Aug '92 / Direct / Rollercoaster / Swift

Texas Red

WHAT KIND OF WOMAN IS THAT
CD BLRCD 034
Blue Loon / May '97 / Hot Shot

Texass

TEXASS
CD _______ IFACD 002
IFA / Oct '95 / Plastic Head

Texier, Henri

PARIS BATIGNOLLES (Texier, Henri Quartet)
CD _______ LBLC 6506
Label Bleu / May '92 / New Note/Pinnacle

RESPECT
Respect / Thingin / Too much, too often / Ladies waders / In the year of the dragon / Abacus / Lee and me / Idyll / Am(i)en / Marcello Mastroianni
CD _______ LBLC 6612
Label Bleu / Aug '97 / New Note/Pinnacle

SCENE IS CLEAN, THE (Texier, Henri Trio)
CD _______ LBLC 6540
Label Bleu / Jun '91 / New Note/Pinnacle

Tez Fa Siyon

P YOURNESS
CD _______ CDLINC 010
Lion Inc. / Dec '95 / Jet Star / SRD

Tezerdi

TEZERDI
CD _______ PAN 152
Pan / Oct '94 / ADA / CM / Direct

TGVT

TGVT
CD _______ HY 39100972
Hyperium / Jun '94 / Cargo / Plastic Head

TH(C) 3.2

FISH SEX
CD _______ PM 32001
Pretentious Moi / Jun '96 / RTM/Disc

Thackeray, Jimmy

EMPTY ARMS MOTEL
CD _______ BPCD 5001
Blind Pig / Jan '93 / ADA / CM / Direct / Hot Shot

SIDEWAYS IN PARADISE (Thackeray, Jimmy & John Mooney)
CD _______ BP 5006CD
Blind Pig / Mar '94 / ADA / CM / Direct / Hot Shot

WILD NIGHT OUT (Thackery, Jimmy & The Drivers)
CD _______ BPCD 75021
Blind Pig / Jul '95 / ADA / CM / Direct / Hot Shot

Thackery, Jimmy

DRIVE TO SURVIVE (Thackery, Jimmy & The Drivers)
Drive to survive / You got work to do / That's how I feel / All about my girl / Play to win / Cool guitars / Slow down baby / Long, lean and lanky / Bruford's bop / Rub on up / Apache
CD _______ BPCD 5035
Blind Pig / Nov '96 / ADA / CM / Direct / Hot Shot

PARTNERS IN CRIME (Thackery, Jimmy & Tom Principato/The Assassins)
CD _______ VDCD 112
Voodoo / Jun '96 / Direct

Thanatos

EMERGING FROM THE NETHERWORLDS
CD _______ SHARK 015 CD
Shark / Apr '90 / Plastic Head

REALM OF ECSTASY
CD _______ SHARKCD 025
Shark / Jan '92 / Plastic Head

Tharpe, Sister Rosetta

1938-1941 VOL.1
CD _______ DOCD 5334
Document / May '95 / ADA / Hot Shot / Jazz Music

1942-1944 VOL.2
CD _______ DOCD 5335
Document / May '95 / ADA / Hot Shot / Jazz Music

That Dog

THAT DOG
CD _______ GU 6CD
Guernica / Oct '93 / Pinnacle

That Kid Chris

LIVE AND DIRECT FROM THE DIGITAL DUNGEON VOL.1 (Various Artists)
Creation: *Brooklyn South* / Creation (club mix): *Brooklyn South* / You know I like it: *Ospina, Davidson Project* / Me hace sentir: *IZE 1* / Can U dig it: *That Kid Chris* / Tribal ridims: *Last Sounds Of Tribal* / Bounce: *Bionic Grooves* / Red hook groove: *Brooklyn South* / Let's go disco: *Southern Comfort* / Let's go disco (original): *Southern Comfort* / Let's go disco (Sneak's lethal mix): *Southern Comfort* / Music takes U higher: *Bionic Grooves* / Feel tha vibe: *That Kid Chris* / Pump: *Time Bomb* / Higher: *No Joke* / Mamba: *Latin Kings* / Suiteness: *Brooklyn South* / Jungle love: *Roc & Kato*
CD _______ 550922
Moonroof / Jul '97 / RTM/Disc

That Petrol Emotion

CHEMICRAZY
Hey venus / Blue to black / Mess of words / Sensitize / Another day / Gnaw mark / Scum surfin' / Compulsion / Tingle / Head staggered / Abandon / Sweet shiver burn
CD _______ CDV 2618
Virgin / Apr '90 / EMI

END OF THE MILLENNIUM PSYCHOSIS
Sooner or later / Every little bit / Cellophane / Candy love satellite / Here it is...take it / Price of my soul / Groove check / Bottom line / Tension / Tired shattered man / Goggle box / Under the sky
CD _______ CDV 2550
Virgin / Oct '88 / EMI

MANIC POP THRILL
Fleshprint / Can't stop / Lifeblood / Natural kind of joy / It's a good thing / Circusville / Mouth crazy / Tightlipped / Million miles away / Lettuce / Cheapskate / Blindspot / V2 / Jesus says / Deadbeat / Mine / Non-alignment pact
CD _______ DIAB 823
Diabolo / Mar '97 / Pinnacle

That Uncertain Feeling

500/600
CD _______ GOODCD 5
Dead Dead Good / May '95 / Pinnacle

Thatcher On Acid

CURDLED/MOONDANCE
CD _______ SKIP 55
Broken / Mar '97 / Cargo / Greyhound

PRESSING 1984-91
CD _______ DAR 013CD
Desperate Attempt / Nov '94 / SRD

Thau

UTAH
CD _______ FROG 0012
Pingo / Mar '95 / Plastic Head

THD

MECHANICAL ADVANTAGE
CD _______ HY 859210588
Hypnobeat / Jun '94 / Plastic Head

The The

BURNING BLUE SOUL
CD _______ HAD 113CD
4AD / Jun '84 / RTM/Disc

DUSK
True happiness this way lies / Love is stronger than death / Dogs of lust / This is the night / Slow emotion replay / Helpline operator / Sodium light baby / Lung shadows / Bluer than midnight / Lonely planet
CD _______ 4724682
Epic / Sep '96 / Sony

HANKY PANKY
Honky tonkin' / Six more miles / My heart would know / If you'll be a baby to me / I'm a long gone daddy / Weary blues from waiting / I saw the light / Your cheatin' heart / I can't get you off my mind / There's a tear in my beer / I can't escape from you
CD _______ 4781392
Epic / Feb '95 / Sony

INFECTED
Infected / Out of the blue (into the fire) / Heartland / Sweet bird of truth / Slow train to dawn / Twilight of a champion / Mercy beat / Angels of deception / Disturbed
CD _______ CD 26770
Epic / May '87 / Sony

MIND BOMB
Good morning beautiful / Armageddon days are here (again) / Violence of truth / Kingdom of rain / Beat(en) generation / August and September / Gravitate to me / Beyond love
CD _______ 4633192
Epic / Apr '94 / Sony

SOUL MINING
I've been waiting for tomorrow / This is the day / Sinking feeling / Uncertain smile / Twilight hour / Soul mining / Giant / Perfect / Three orange kisses from Kazan / Nature of virtue / Mental healing process / Waitin' for the upturn / Fruit of the heart
CD _______ 4663372
Epic / Mar '90 / Sony

Theard, Sam

LOVIN' SAM THEARD 1929-1934
CD _______ DOCD 5479
Document / Sep '96 / ADA / Hot Shot / Jazz Music

Theatre Of Hate

COMPLETE SINGLES COLLECTION
Original sin / Legion / Rebel without a brain / My own invention / Nero / Incinerator / Do you believe in the Westworld / Propaganda / Hop / Conquistador / Eastworld / Assegai / Poppies / Brave new soldiers / Heathen / King of kings / Number twelve / Thalidomide / St Teresa / Abbatoir
CD _______ CDMGRAM 93
Cherry Red / May '95 / Pinnacle

RETRIBUTION OVER THE WESTWORLD 1996
CD _______ RRCD 229
Receiver / Aug '96 / Grapevine/PolyGram

TEN YEARS AFTER
Hop / Americana / East world / Grapes of wrath / Solution / Omen / Aria / Murder of love / Black Madonna / Flying Scotsman / Man who tunes the drums
CD _______ MAUCD 637
Mau Mau / Jun '93 / Pinnacle

Theatre Of Tragedy

ROSE FOR THE DEAD
CD _______ MASSCD 130
Massacre / Apr '97 / Plastic Head

VELVET DARKNESS
CD _______ MASSCD 107
Massacre / Oct '96 / Plastic Head

Theatricum Chemicum

VERSO LA LUCE
CD _______ EFA 148242
Glasnost / Oct '95 / SRD

Thee Headcoatees

BALLAD OF THE INSOLENT PUP
What once was / This heart / Pretend / Ballad of the insolent pup / You'll be sorry now / All my feelings denied / It's bad / When you stop loving me / Two hearts beating / No respect / Again and again / Now is not the best time / I was led to believe / You'll never do it baby
CD _______ ASKCD 045
Vinyl Japan / Oct '94 / Plastic Head / Vinyl Japan

HAVE LOVE WILL TRAVEL
CD _______ ASKCD 011
Vinyl Japan / Oct '92 / Plastic Head / Vinyl Japan

PUNK GIRLS
CD _______ SFTRI 463CD
Sympathy For The Record Industry / Mar '97 / Cargo / Greyhound / Plastic Head

SOUND OF THE BASKERVILLES (Thee Headcoatees & Thee Headcoats)
CD _______ OVER 42CD
Overground / Dec '95 / Shellshock/Disc / SRD

Thee Headcoats

BEACH BUMS MUST DIE
CD _______ EFA 11563 D
Crypt / Apr '93 / Shellshock/Disc

CONUNDRUM
CD _______ SCRAG 2CD
Hangman's Daughter / Sep '94 / Shellshock/Disc / SRD

DEERSTALKING MEN (Thee Headcoat Sect)
CD _______ SCRAG 8CD
Hangman's Daughter / Sep '96 / Shellshock/Disc / SRD

HEAVENS TO MURGATROYD EVEN, IT'S THEE HEADCOATS
CD _______ SPCD 6119
Sub Pop / May '93 / Cargo / Greyhound / Shellshock/Disc

IN TWEED WE TRUST
CD _______ DAMGOOD 96CD
Damaged Goods / Jun '96 / Shellshock/ Disc

LIVE IN LONDON (Thee Headcoats & Thee Headcoatees)
CD _______ DAMGOOD 30CD
Damaged Goods / Mar '94 / Shellshock/ Disc

Thee Hypnotics

LIVER THAN GOD
All night long / Let's get naked / Revolution stone / Rock me baby / Justice in freedom
CD _______ SP 54B
Sub Pop / Jan '94 / Cargo / Greyhound / Shellshock/Disc

VERY CRYSTAL SPEED MACHINE, THE
Keep rollin' on / Heavy liquid / Phil's drum acropolis / Goodbye / If the good lord love ya / Ray's baudelaire / Caroline inside out / Tie it up / Down in the hole / Peasant song / Fragile / Look what you've done / Broken morning has
CD _______ 74321264512
American / Jun '95 / BMG

Thee Johanz

CONFIDENTIAL LP
CD _______ 53IRDTJ12CD
Irdial / Sep '95 / RTM/Disc

Thee Madkatt Courtship

BY DAWN'S EARLY LIGHT
Wet Wednesday / By dawn's early light / Tha' mental blowout / Panic 60466 / Lovetraxx 1990 / Who tha' critics / Revelation / Da mindfuck / Phuzon
CD _______ SLIKCD 001
Deep Distraxion/Profile / Oct '95 / Pinnacle

Thee Mighty Caesars

ACROPOLIS NOW
I've got everything indeed / When the night comes / (Miss America) got to get you outside my head / Ask the dust / I don't need no baby / Dictator of love / Now I know / I can judge a daughter / Li'l Red Riding Hood / Loathsome 'n' wild / Despite all this / I feel like giving in / I was led to believe
CD _______ SCRAG 9CD
Hangman's Daughter / Apr '97 / Shellshock/Disc / SRD

CAESAR'S PLEASURE
Wily cayote / Miss Ludella Black / Death of a mighty caesar / Why don't you try my love / It ain't no sin / You'll be sorry now / All of your love / Give it to me / Baby please / Little by little / What you've got / I've got everything indeed / When the night comes / You make me die / Loathsome 'n' wild / I don't need no baby / I was led to believe / Man taken from guts / Devious means / I've been waiting / True to you / I can't find pleasure / Come into my life / Double axe / Neat neat neat / She's just 15 years old / Everything I've got to give / Lie detector / Why can't you see / Cowboys are square
CD _______ CDWIKD 124
Big Beat / Feb '94 / Pinnacle

SURELY THEY WERE THE SONS OF GOD
Wiley coyote / (Miss America) Got to get you outside my head / I don't need no baby / Stay the same / Double axe / I was led to believe / You make me die / Now I know / I've been waiting / Loathsome 'n' wild / You'll be sorry now / I can't find pleasure / Kinds of women / Lie detector / Confusion / Baby who mutilated everybody's heart / Suck the dog / Beat on the brat / Career opportunities / Because just because / Headcoats on / Somebody like you / Searching high and low / Don't wanna be ruled by women and money no more / Don't break my laws / Strange words / Signals of love / I've got everything indeed / Devious means / Why don't you try my love / Wise blood / It's you I hate to lose / Miss Loudella Black
CD _______ CD 0141823
Crypt / Jul '93 / Shellshock/Disc

Thee Phantom Creeps

TEENAGE FINGERS
Sweetcorn / I love Lucy / Marty party / Prayer to overtaking / Do the dead / Churn it up / Long arm / Dirty love song / Head on backwards / Teenage fingers / Sign / Bad place / Strychnine / Teenage fingers / Bad place / Trance dance
CD _______ FART 1
Armed & Fat / Dec '96 / Cargo

Thee Rayguns

REBEL ROCKERS
CD _______ RAUCD 013
Raucous / Feb '95 / Nervous / RTM/Disc / TKO Magnum

Thee Waltons

DRUNK AGAIN
CD _______ RAUCD 69
Raucous / May '94 / Nervous / RTM/Disc / TKO Magnum

ESSENTIAL COUNTRY BULLSHIT
CD _______ SPV 08476802
Steamhammer / Jun '94 / Pinnacle / Plastic Head

GET OUT YER VEGETABLES
Get out yer vegetables / Rubber chicken / Kings of veg-a-billy / Barking up the wrong tree / Elvis P / Devil in disguise / Hound dog / Famous / Devil's music / Drunk son / Tear it up
CD _______ CDGRAM 90
Cherry Red / Feb '95 / Pinnacle

LIK MY TRAKTER
Colder than you / Sunshine / Water well and the farmer's hand / In the meantime / I could care less / Truth and beauty / Living room / Look at me / Naked rain / (Don't let it) Slide / Fine line / Like my tractor
CD _______ 4509919512
WEA / Mar '94 / Warner Music

LOCK UP YER LIVESTOCK
CD ___ RAUCD 007
Raucous / Aug '93 / Nervous / RTM/Disc / TKO Magnum

Theessink, Hans

BABY WANTS TO BOOGIE
CD ___ BG 1020CD
Blue Groove / Apr '94 / CM

CRAZY MOON
CD ___ MWCD 2018
Music & Words / Nov '95 / ADA / Direct

HARD ROAD BLUES-SOLO
CD ___ SPINCD 155
Making Waves / Dec '94 / CM

JOHNNY & THE DEVIL
CD ___ BG 2020CD
Blue Groove / Apr '94 / CM

TITANIC
CD ___ BG 3020CD
Blue Groove / Apr '94 / CM

Theis & Nyegaard Jazzband

THEIS/NYEGAARD JAZZBAND 1963/88 (The First 25 Years)
Chant / West End blues / Sidewalk blues / Sweet Georgia Brown / It don't mean a thing if it ain't got that swing / Blue turning grey over you / After you've gone / Someday you'll be sorry / Ain't misbehavin' / Willow weep for me / I found a new baby / Confessin' / Baby, won't you please come home / You can depend on me
CD ___ STCD 4174
Storyville / Feb '90 / Cadillac / Jazz Music / Wellard

TONIGHT LIVE
CD ___ MECCACD 2017
Music Mecca / May '97 / Cadillac / Jazz Music / Wellard

Thelin, Eje

POLYGLOT
CD ___ 1291
Caprice / Dec '92 / ADA / Cadillac / CM / Complete/Pinnacle

Them

THEM
Mystic eyes / If you and I could be as two / Little girl / Just a little bit / I gave my love a diamond / Gloria / You just can't win / Route 66 / My little baby / Bright lights big city / I'm gonna dress in black / Go on home baby / Don't look back / I like it like that
CD ___ 8205632
London / Feb '94 / PolyGram

Themis, John

ATMOSPHERIC CONDITIONS
Emily / Trick / Post-hypnotic suggestions / Cinderella's last waltz / Electric storm / Transition / Black mamba samba / Trouble
CD ___ NAGE 1CD
Art Of Landscape / Jan '86 / Sony

ENGLISH RENAISSANCE
Over the dark cloud / James I / Open Arms / Catrina / Cross crusader / English renaissance / Steed for a king / Don't wake the dragon George
CD ___ NAGE 11CD
Art Of Landscape / Jul '86 / Sony

Then Jerico

ELECTRIC
Big area / Word / Motive / Fault / Quiet place (apathy and sympathy) / Clank (countdown to oblivion) / Blessed days / Electric / Prairie rose / Reeling / You ought to know / Big sweep / One life / Darkest hour
CD ___ 5501932
Spectrum / Mar '94 / PolyGram

RADIO JERICO (2CD Set)
Let her fall / Muscle deep / Blessed days / Hitcher / Play dead / Quiet place / Electric / Searching / Big area / Muscle deep / Motive / Under fire / Reeling / Where you lie / What does it take / Sugarbox / Helpless / You ought to know / Blessed days / Hitcher / Where you lie / Sugarbox / What does it take / Reeling / Motive / Big area / Muscle deep
CD Set ___ MURD 001CD
Murder / Jul '97 / Pinnacle

Theo

SMOOTH LOVER
CD ___ STPCD 1
Keeling / May '96 / Jet Star

Theodorakis, Mikis

BALLAD OF MAUTHAUSEN
CD ___ CD 7
Sound / '86 / ADA

BIRTHDAY CONCERT 1995, THE
CD ___ 68974
Tropical / Apr '97 / Discovery

BOUZOUKIS OF MIKIS THEODORAKIS, THE
Sto parathiri stekoussoun / Myrtia / Tou mikou voria / Varka sto yialo / Marina / Yitonia ton anghelon / Balanda tou andrikou / To yelasto pedi / Apagoghi / To parathiro / Mana mou ke panayia
CD ___ 111 692
Musidisc / May '90 / Discovery

CANTO GENERAL
CD ___ INT 31142
Intuition / Jun '93 / New Note/Pinnacle

TOGETHER IN CONCERT (Theodorakis, Mikis & Z. Livaneli)
CD ___ 68987
Tropical / Jul '97 / Discovery

TROUBADOUR FROM GREECE, THE
CD ___ SOW 90104
Sounds Of The World / Sep '93 / Target/ BMG

ZORBS - THE BALLET
CD ___ INT 31032
Intuition / Jul '92 / New Note/Pinnacle

Therapy

BABYTEETH
CD ___ 185072
Southern / Mar '93 / SRD

HATS OFF TO THE INSANE
CD ___ 5401392
A&M / Sep '93 / PolyGram

INFERNAL LOVE
Epilepsy / Stories / Moment of clarity / Jude the obscene / Bowels of love / Misery / Bad mother / Me vs. you / Loose / Diane / Thirty seconds
CD ___ 5403792
A&M / Jun '95 / PolyGram

PLEASURE DEATH
CD ___ 185082
Southern / Apr '93 / SRD

TROUBLEGUM
Knives / Screamager / Hellbelly / Stop it you're killing me / Nowhere / Die laughing / Unbeliever / Trigger inside / Lunacy booth / Isolation / Turn / Femtex / Unrequited / Brainsaw / You are my sunshine
CD ___ 5401962
A&M / Nov '93 / PolyGram

Thergothon

STEAM FROM THE HEAVENS
CD ___ AV 001
Avant Garde / May '94 / Plastic Head / RTM/Disc

Therion

BEAUTY IN BLACK, THE
CD ___ NB 125CD
Nuclear Blast / Mar '95 / Plastic Head

BEYOND SANCTORIUM
CD ___ CDATV 23
Active / Jul '92 / Pinnacle

LEPACA KLIFFOTH
CD ___ NB 216CD
Nuclear Blast / Nov '96 / Plastic Head

SIREN OF THE WOODS
CD ___ NB 178CD
Nuclear Blast / Jul '96 / Plastic Head

THELI
CD ___ NB 179CD
Nuclear Blast / Sep '96 / Plastic Head

These Animal Men

ACCIDENT AND EMERGENCY
Life support machine / So sophisticated / When your hands are tied / Monumental moneymaker / Riverboat captain / New wave girl / 24 hours to live / Going native / Ambulance man / Light emitting electrical wave / April 7th
CD ___ CDHUT 40
Hut / Apr '97 / EMI

COME ON JOIN THE HIGH SOCIETY
Sharp kid / Empire building / Ambulance / This year's model / You're always right / Flawed is beautiful / This is the sound of youth / Sitting tenant / Too sussed / Come on join the high society / We are living / High society
CD ___ FLATCD 8
Hi-Rise / Sep '94 / EMI / Pinnacle

TAXI FOR THESE ANIMAL MEN
You're always right / Nowhere faces / My human remains / False identification / Wait for it
CD ___ FLATMCD 14
Hi-Rise / Mar '95 / EMI / Pinnacle

TOO SUSSED
CD ___ FLATMCD 4
Hi-Rise / Jun '94 / EMI / Pinnacle

These Immortal Souls

GET LOST (DON'T LIE)
Marry me (lie lie) / Hide / These immortal souls / Hey little child / I ate the knife / Blood and sand she said / One in shadow one in sun / Open up and bleed / Blood and sand she said (alternate) / I ate the knife (alternate) / These immortal souls (alternate)
CD ___ CD STUMM 48
Mute / Oct '87 / RTM/Disc

Thessalonians

SOULCRAFT
CD ___ PS 9334
Silent / Oct '93 / Cargo / Plastic Head

They Might Be Giants

APOLLO 18
Dig my grave / I palindrome I / She's actual size / My evil twin / Mammal / Statue got me high / Spider / Guitar (The lion sleeps tonight) / Dinner bell / Narrow eyes / Hall of heads / Which describes how you're feeling / See the constellation / If I wasn't shy / Turn around / Hypnotist of ladies / Fingertips / Space suit
CD ___ 7559612572
Elektra / Mar '92 / Warner Music

DON'T LET'S START
CD ___ TPCD 14
One Little Indian / Nov '89 / Pinnacle

FACTORY SHOWROOM
CD ___ 7559618622
Elektra / Feb '97 / Warner Music

FLOOD
Theme from flood / Lucky ball and chain / Dead / Particle man / We want a rock / Birdhouse in your soul / Istanbul (not Constantinople) / Your racist friend / Twisting
CD ___ 7559609072
Elektra / '89 / Warner Music

JOHN HENRY
Subliminal / Snail shell / Sleeping in the flowers / Unrelated thing AKA driver / I should be allowed to think / Extra savoir faire / Why must I be sad / Spy / O do not forsake me / No one knows my plan / Dirt bike / Destination moon / Self called nowhere / Meet James Ensor / Thermostat / Window out of jail / Stomp box / End of the tour
CD ___ 7559616542
Elektra / Sep '94 / Warner Music

LINCOLN
Ana ng / Cowtown / Lie still / Little bottle / Purple toupee / Cage and aquarium / Where your eyes don't go / Piece of dirt / MR. Me / Pencil rain / World's address / I've got a match / Santa's beard / You'll miss me / They'll need a crane / Shoehorn with teeth / Stand on your own head / Snowball in hell / Kiss me / Son of God
CD ___ 7559611452
Elektra / Jun '91 / Warner Music

THEY MIGHT BE GIANTS
Everything right is wrong again / Put your hand inside the puppet head / Number three / Don't let's start / Footsteps / Toddler hiway / Rabid child / Nothing's gonna change my clothes / She was a hotel detective / She's an angel / Youth culture killed / My dog / Boat of car / Absolutely Bill's mood chess piece face / I hope that I get old before I die / Alienation's for the rich / Day / Rhythm section want ad
CD ___ EKT 80 CD
Elektra / Nov '90 / Warner Music

Thielemans, 'Toots'

BLUESETTE (Thielemans, Jean 'Toots')
CD ___ CDCH 303
Milan / Feb '91 / Conifer/BMG / Silva Screen

BRASIL PROJECT, THE (Thielemans, Jean 'Toots')
Comecar de novo / Obi / Felicia and Bianca / O cantador / Joana Francesca / Coisa feita / Preciso aprender a so ser / Furta boa / Coracao vagabundo / Manha de carnaval / Casa forte / Moments / Bluesette
CD ___ 01005821012
Private Music / Jul '96 / BMG

CONCERTO FOR HARMONICA (Thielemans, Jean 'Toots')
Prelude to a new life / Toots / Mo blues / Song for Willy Graz / Ne me quitte pas / Passionement / Asco / You just forgot that I love you / Coda / Body and soul
CD ___ TCB 94802
TCB / Nov '94 / New Note/Pinnacle

EAST COAST, WEST COAST (Thielemans, Jean 'Toots')
CD ___ 01005821202
Private Music / Feb '95 / BMG

FOOTPRINTS (Thielemans, Jean 'Toots')
Footprints / Blues on time / Gymnopedie no.1 / Round midnight/Good evening Thelonious / If you could see me now / When I fall in love / What kind of fool am I / Laura / Windmills of your mind/Bonjour Michel / Sultry serenade / C to G jam blues
CD ___ 8466502
EmArCy / Mar '93 / PolyGram

FOR MY LADY (Thielemans, Jean 'Toots' & Shirley Horn Trio)
For my lady / How long has this been going on / Blues in the closet / Someone to watch over me / I'm beginning to see the light / More I see you / Mooche / Close your eyes / Blue and sentimental / Corcovado / Willow weep for me / Once in a while
CD ___ 5101332
EmArCy / Feb '92 / PolyGram

IMAGES
Days of wine and roses / I never told you / Dr.Pretty / Airegin / Images / Day dream / Giant steps / Snooze / Stella by starlight / Revol
CD ___ CHCD 71007
Candid / Jul '97 / Cadillac / Direct / Jazz Music / Koch / Wellard

JAZZ MASTERS (Thielemans, Jean 'Toots')
Undecided / Body and soul / Flirt / Soldier in the rain / Hummin' / Brown ballad / You're my blues machine / Bluesette / Big bossa / Tenor madness / Nocturne / Vai passar / Killer Joe / Peacocks / C to G jam blues / For my lady
CD ___ 5352712
Verve / Oct '96 / PolyGram

LIVE (Thielemans, Jean 'Toots')
Days of wine and roses / Lullaby / Tenor madness / Nice to be around / Strange boogie man / Dat mistige rooie beest / Dream girl / I do it for your love / You're my blues machine / Autumn leaves / My little Anna / C jam blues
CD ___ 8316942
Polydor / Feb '93 / PolyGram

LIVE IN THE NETHERLANDS (Thielemans, Jean 'Toots' & Joe Pass/ N.H. Orsted Pederson)
Blues in the closet / Mooche / Thriving on a riff / Autumn leaves / Someday my Prince will come
CD ___ CD 2308233
Pablo / Apr '94 / Cadillac / Complete/ Pinnacle

MAN BITES HARMONICA (Thielemans, Jean 'Toots')
CD ___ OJCCD 1738
Original Jazz Classics / Oct '92 / Complete/Pinnacle / Jazz Music / Wellard

ONLY TRUST YOUR HEART (Thielemans, Jean 'Toots')
CD ___ CCD 4355
Concord Jazz / Sep '88 / New Note/ Pinnacle

SILVER COLLECTION, THE (Thielemans, Jean 'Toots')
I do it for your love / My little suede shoes / You're my blues machine / Dirty old man / Summer of '42 / Bluesette / Muskrat ramble / Mooche / What are you doing the rest of your life / Gentle rain / First time ever I saw your face / Big bossa / Ben / You've got it bad girl / Love remembered / Old friend
CD ___ 8250862
Polydor / May '88 / PolyGram

TOOTS THIELEMANS (Thielemans, Jean 'Toots')
CD ___ CD 53238
Giants Of Jazz / Nov '95 / Cadillac / Jazz Music / Target/BMG

TWO GENERATIONS (Thielemans, Jean 'Toots')
Bluesette / Be be creole / Monologue / Two generations / Why did I choose you / Uncle Charlie / Friday night / T T / Inner journey / L'eternal mari
CD ___ FCD 0003
Limetree / Nov '95 / New Note/Pinnacle

Thierry, Jacques

HAWAIIAN GUITAR VOL.2, THE (Thierry, Jacques & Trio Kailus)
CD ___ PS 65081
PlayaSound / Nov '91 / ADA / Harmonia Mundi

Thievery Corporation

SOUNDS FROM THE THIEVERY HI-FI
CD ___ ESL 5CD
18th Street Lounge / Apr '97 / Cargo

Thieves

THIEVES
CD ___ CDHUT 12
Hut / May '94 / EMI

Thigpen, Ed

MR. TASTE (Thigpen, Ed Trio)
CD ___ JUST 432
Justin Time / Oct '92 / Cadillac / New Note/Pinnacle

YOUNG MEN AND OLD
Strike up the band / Yesterdays / Summertime / Night and day / Scramble / Shuffin' long / Oh my gosh / Dark before the dawn / I should care
CD ___ CDSJP 330
Timeless Jazz / Aug '90 / New Note/ Pinnacle

Thile, Chris

LEADING OFF...
CD ___ SHCD 3828

Sugar Hill / Nov '94 / ADA / CM / Direct / Koch / Roots

STEALING SECOND
CD ______ SHCD 3863
Sugar Hill / Apr '97 / ADA / CM / Direct / Koch / Roots

Thilo, Jesper

FLAT FOOT BOOGIE
CD ______ MECCACD 1010
Music Mecca / Nov '94 / Cadillac / Jazz Music / Wellard

HALF NELSON (Thilo, Jesper Quartet)
CD ______ MECCACD 1009
Music Mecca / Jul '93 / Cadillac / Jazz Music / Wellard

JESPER THILO & ANN FARHOLT/ THOMAS CLAUSEN (Thilo, Jesper & Ann Farholt/Thomas Clausen)
CD ______ MECCACD 2025
Music Mecca / May '97 / Cadillac / Jazz Music / Wellard

JESPER THILO PLAYS BASIE AND ELLINGTON
CD ______ MECCACD 2102
Music Mecca / May '97 / Cadillac / Jazz Music / Wellard

JESPER THILO QUARTET AND HARRY EDISON (Thilo, Jesper Quartet)
CD ______ STCD 4120
Storyville / Feb '89 / Cadillac / Jazz Music / Wellard

JESPER THILO/CLARK TERRY (Thilo, Jesper & Clark Terry)
Just one of those things / Sophisticated lady / Save your love for me / Rose room / Wave / Ballad for Lester / Cherokee / Sunday / Did you call her today / Stardust / Frog eyes / Body and soul
CD ______ STCD 8204
Storyville / Nov '94 / Cadillac / Jazz Music / Wellard

PLAYS BASIE
CD ______ MECCACD 1035
Music Mecca / Nov '94 / Cadillac / Jazz Music / Wellard

SHUFFLIN'
CD ______ MECCACD 1015
Music Mecca / Nov '94 / Cadillac / Jazz Music / Wellard

WE LOVE HIM MADLY (Thilo, Jesper Quintet)
CD ______ MECCACD 1025
Music Mecca / Jul '93 / Cadillac / Jazz Music / Wellard

Thin Lizzy

BAD REPUTATION
Bad reputation / Dancin' in the moonlight / Dear Lord / Downtown sundown / Killer without cause / Opium train / Soldier of fortune / Southbound / That woman's gonna break your heart
CD ______ 5322982
Mercury / Mar '96 / PolyGram

BLACK ROSE
Do anything you want to / Toughest street in town / S and M / Waiting for an alibi / Sarah / Got to give it up / Get out of here / With love / Roisin dubh
CD ______ 5322992
Mercury / Mar '96 / PolyGram

CHINATOWN
We will be strong / Chinatown / Sweetheart / Sugar blues / Killer on the loose / Havin' a good time / Genocide / Didn't I / Hey you
CD ______ 83033932
Vertigo / Jun '89 / PolyGram

FIGHTING
Ballad of a hard man / Fighting my way back / For those who love to live / Freedom song / King's vengeance / Rosalie / Silver dollar / Spirit slips away / Suicide / Wild one
CD ______ 5322962
Mercury / Mar '96 / PolyGram

JAILBREAK
Angel from the coast / Boys are back in town / Cowboy song / Emerald / Fight or fall / Jailbreak / Romeo and the lonely girl / Running back / Warriors
CD ______ 5322942
Mercury / Mar '96 / PolyGram

JOHNNY THE FOX
Boogie woogie dance / Borderline / Don't believe a word / Fool's gold / Johnny / Johnny the fox meets Jimmy the weed / Massacre / Old flame / Rocky / Sweet Marie
CD ______ 5322952
Mercury / Mar '96 / PolyGram

LIFE
Thunder and lightening / Waiting for an alibi / Jailbreak / Baby please don't go / Holy war / Renegade / Hollywood / Got to give it up / Angel of death / Are you ready / Boys are back in town / Cold sweat / Don't believe a word / Killer on the loose / Sun goes down / Emerald / Black rose / Still in love with you / Rocker
CD ______ 8128822
Vertigo / Aug '90 / PolyGram

LIVE AND DANGEROUS - IN CONCERT
Boys are back in town / Dancin' in the moonlight / Massacre / I'm still in love with you / Me and the boys / Don't believe a word / Warriors / Are you ready / Sha la la la / Baby drives me crazy
CD ______ 5322972
Mercury / Mar '96 / PolyGram

LIZZY KILLERS
Do anything you want to / Sarah / Whiskey in the jar / Jailbreak / Boys are back in town / Killer on the loose / Don't believe a word / Dancin' in the moonlight / Waiting for an alibi
CD ______ 8000602
Vertigo / '83 / PolyGram

RENEGADE
Angel of death / Renegade / Pressure will blow / Leave this town / Hollywood (down on your luck) / No one told him / Fats / Mexican blood / It's getting dangerous
CD ______ 8424352
Vertigo / Jun '90 / PolyGram

THIN LIZZY
Friendly ranger at Clontarf Castle / Honesty is no excuse / Diddy levine / Ray gun / Look what the wind blue in / Eire / Return of the farmer's son / Clifton Grange Hotel / Saga of the ageing orphan / Remembering part 1 / Dublin / Remembering part 2 / Old moon madness / Thing's ain't working out down at the farm
CD ______ 8205282
Vertigo / Jan '89 / PolyGram

THUNDER AND LIGHTNING
Thunder and lightning / This is the one / Sun goes down / Holy war / Cold sweat / Someday / She is going to hit back / Baby, please don't go / Bad habits / Heart attack / Thunder and lightening
CD ______ 8104902
Vertigo / Jun '89 / PolyGram

VAGABONDS OF THE WESTERN WORLD
Mama nature said / Hero and the madman / Slow blues / Rocker / Vagabond of the western world / Little girl in bloom / Gonna creep up on you / Song for while I'm away / Whiskey in the jar / Black boys on the corner / Randolph's tango / Broken dreams
CD ______ 8209692
Vertigo / May '91 / PolyGram

WHISKY IN THE JAR
Whiskey in the jar / Sarah / Look what the wind blew in / Return of the farmer's son / Old moon madness / Dublin / Shades of blue orphanage / Buffalo girl / Black boys on the corner / Rocker / Mama nature said / Broken dreams / Here I go again / Little darling / Vagabond of the western world / Remembering (part 2)
CD ______ 5520852
Spectrum / Mar '96 / PolyGram

WILD ONE (The Very Best Of Thin Lizzy)
Boys are back in town / Jailbreak / Don't believe a world / Waiting for an alibi / Rosalie/Cowgirl song / Cold sweat / Thunder and lightning / Out in the fields / Dancin' in the moonlight / Parisienne walkways / Sarah / Still in love with you / Emerald / Bad reputation / Killer on the loose / Chinatown / Do anything you want to / Rocker / Whiskey in the jar
CD ______ 5281132
Mercury / Jan '96 / PolyGram

Thin White Rope

EXPLORING THE AXIS/BOTTOM FEEDERS
Down in the desert / Disney girl / Soundtrack / Lithium / Dead grammas on a train / Three song / Eleven / Roger's tongue / Real West / Exploring the axis / Ain't that loving you baby / Macy's window / Waking up / Valley of the bones / Atomic imagery / Rocket USA
CD ______ DIAB 824
Diabolo / Mar '97 / Pinnacle

MOONHEAD...PLUS
Not your fault / Wire animals / Take it home / Thing / Moonhead / Wet heart / Mother / Come around / If those tears / Crawl piss freeze / Tina and Glen / Munich eunuch / God rest ye merry gentlemen / Here she comes now
CD ______ DIAB 825
Diabolo / Apr '97 / Pinnacle

WHEN WORLDS COLLIDE
CD ______ MRCD 047
Munster / May '94 / Cargo / Greyhound / Plastic Head

Things To Come

I WANT OUT
Sweetgina / Mississippi dealer / I want out / Your down / Speak of the devil / Smokestack lightnin' / Character of Caruso / Tell me why / Tomorrow / Pushin' too hard (instr.) / Show me a place / I'm a man / Home to you / Your down (instr.) / Icicles on the roof / Sweetgina (instr.) / Behold now behemoth / Darkness
CD ______ CDSC 11017
Sundazed / Jan '94 / Cargo / Greyhound / Rollercoaster

Thingy

SONGS ABOUT ANGELS, EVIL AND RUNNING AROUND ON FIRE
CD ______ HED 067
Headhunter / May '97 / Cargo

Think About Mutation

HELLRAVER
Ganglords / Overload / River / Lucky times / Rewinding seeds / Suffer / Warning / Psycho DJ / Nude / Try the way to move / View (what's this life) / Killing Zoe / 4 steps ahead
CD ______ DY 162
Dynamica / Jun '96 / Koch

HOUSE GRINDER
CD ______ DY 32
Dynamica / Oct '93 / Koch

HOUSEBASTARDS
CD ______ DY 102
Dynamica / Sep '94 / Koch

Think Twice

JOY IS FREE
CD ______ IBCD 1
Internal Bass / Feb '97 / Prime / Timewarp / Total/BMG

Thinking Fellas Union Local ...

I HOPE IT LANDS (Thinking Fellas Union Local 282)
CD ______ COMM 043CD
Communion / Dec '96 / Cargo

PORCELAIN ENTERTAINMENTS (Thinking Fellas Union Local 282)
CD ______ RTS 21
Return To Sender / Jan '96 / ADA / Direct

STRANGERS FROM THE UNIVERSE (Thinking Fellas Union Local 282)
My pal the tortoise / Socket / Bomber pilot WWII / Hundreds of years / Guillotine / Uranium / February / Pull my pants up tight / Cup of dreams / Oxenmaster / Operation / Piston and the shaft / Communication / Noble experiment
CD ______ OLE 1092
Matador / Oct '94 / Vital

WORMED BY LEONARD (Thinking Fellas Union Local 282)
CD ______ THW 0022
Thwart / Dec '96 / Cargo

Thinking Plague

IN THIS LIFE
CD ______ RERTPCD
ReR/Recommended / Apr '90 / ReR Megacorp / RTM/Disc

Third & The Mortal

NIGHTSWAN
CD ______ VOW 047CD
Voices Of Wonder / Jun '95 / Plastic Head

PAINTING ON GLASS
CD ______ VOW 051CD
Voices Of Wonder / Jan '96 / Plastic Head

TEARS LAID IN EARTH
CD ______ VOW
Voices Of Wonder / Nov '94 / Plastic Head

TEARS LAID TO REST
CD ______ VOW 041CD
Voices Of Wonder / Oct '96 / Plastic Head

THIRD & THE MORTAL
CD ______ VOW 059CD
Voices Of Wonder / Mar '97 / Plastic Head

Third Ear Band

ALCHEMY
Mosaic / Ghetto raga / Druid one / Stone circle / Egyptian book of the dead / Area three / Dragon lines / Lark rise
CD ______ DOCD 1999
Drop Out / Apr '91 / Pinnacle

LIVE GHOSTS
Hope mosaic / Druid three / Ghetto raga / Live ghosts
CD ______ MASO 90004
Materiali Sonori / '90 / Cargo / Greyhound / New Note/Pinnacle

MACBETH
Overture / Beach / Lady Macbeth / Inverness / Banquet / Dagger and death / At the well/Prince's escape/Coronation/Come sealing night / Court dance / Fleance groom's dance / Bear baiting / Ambush/ Banquo's ghost / Going to bed/Blind man's buff / Requiescant/Sere and yellow leaf / Cauldron / Prophesies / Wicca way
CD ______ BGOCD 61
Beat Goes On / Jan '89 / Pinnacle

NEW AGE MAGICAL MUSICAL
Gog and Magog / Flight of the coven / Dance of the elves / Atlantis rising / Midnight on mars
CD ______ BP 257CD
Blueprint / Apr '97 / Pinnacle

THIRD EAR BAND
Air / Earth / Fire / Water
CD ______ BGOCD 89
Beat Goes On / Dec '90 / Pinnacle

VOICEPRINT RADIO SESSION
CD ______ VPR 017CD
Voiceprint / Oct '94 / Pinnacle

Third Eye

ANCIENT FUTURE
CD ______ NZ 0242
Third Eye / Oct '94 / Total/BMG

DANCE OF CREATION
CD ______ NZ 023CD
Nova Zembla / Nov '94 / Plastic Head

Third Eye Blind

SEMI-CHARMED LIFE
Losing a whole year / Narcolepsy / Semi-charmed life / Jumper / Graduate / How's it going to be / Thanks a lot / Burning man / Good for you / London / I want you / Background / Motorcycle drive by / God of wine
CD ______ 7559620122
Elektra / Jul '97 / Warner Music

Third Eye Foundation

GHOST
What to do but cry / Corpses as bedmates / Star's gone out / Out sound from way in / I've seen the light and it's dark / Ghosts / Donald Crowhurst
CD ______ WIGCD 32
Domino / Apr '97 / Vital

IN VERSION
CD ______ LSD 04CD
Linda's Strange Day / Oct '96 / Cargo

SEMTEX
CD ______ LSD 02
Linda's Strange Day / Oct '96 / Cargo

Third Person

BENDS, THE
CD ______ KFWCD 102
Knitting Factory / Nov '94 / Cargo / Plastic Head

LUCKY WATER
Busy river / Cold call / Trick water / Bubble and crow / Bridge of a thousand tears / Globe trudgers / Old Grandad (doesn't smell too bad) / John Frum he come / Curlew's sad day / Cadillac bolero / Moro reflex / Hasten slowly
CD ______ KFWCD 156
Knitting Factory / Feb '95 / Cargo / Plastic Head

Third Sex

CARD CARRYIN'
CD ______ CHSW 15
Chainsaw / Dec '96 / Cargo

Third World

REGGAE AMBASSADORS (20th Anniversary Collection)
Satta a masagana / Brand new beggar / Freedom song / Railroad track / 1865 / Rhythm of life / Dreamland / Now that we've found love / Journey to Addis / Cool meditation / Night heat / Talk to me / Irie ites / Always around / Uptown rebel / Jah glory / African woman / Breaking up is hard to do / Roots with quality / Dancing on the floor / Try Jah love / Lagos jump / Sense of purpose / Reggae radio station / Forbidden love / Reggae ambassador / DJ ambassador / Riddim haffe rule / Committed / Mi legal / Give the people what they need
CD ______ CRNCD 3
Island / Feb '94 / PolyGram

REGGAE GREATS
Now that we've found love / Prisoner in the street / Always around / Talk to me / Cool meditation / Satta a masagana / Ninety six degrees in the shade / African woman / Rhythm of life
CD ______ 5527352
Spectrum / Jul '97 / PolyGram

ROCK THE WORLD
Rock the world / Spiritual revolution / Who gave you / Dub music / Shine like a blazing fire / Dancing on the floor / There's no need to question why / Peace and love / Standing in the rain / Hug it up
CD ______ 44879452
Columbia / Jul '97 / Sony

Third World War

THIRD WORLD WAR VOL.1
CD ______ 14504
Spalax / Jul '97 / ADA / Cargo / Direct / Discovery / Greyhound

THIRD WORLD WAR VOL.2
CD ______ 14538
Spalax / Jul '97 / ADA / Cargo / Direct / Discovery / Greyhound

Thirty Ought Six

HAG SEED
CD **CDSTUMM 86**
Mute / Apr '96 / RTM/Disc

This

LETTUCE SPRAY
Grooverang (intro) / Mind's eye / Michael / Criss cross world / Kite / Mentholated head balm / Tighter / Chicken run / Destiny / Swimming against the tide / Sandwich
CD **YM 002CD**
Yellow Moon / Oct '93 / Vital

This Ascension

LIGHT AND SHADE
CD **EFA 064812**
Tess / Mar '94 / SRD

This Heat

DECEIT
CD **HEAT 2CD**
ReR/Recommended / '91 / ReR Megacorp / RTM/Disc

MADE AVAILABLE
CD **THESE 010CD**
These / Jun '97 / SRD / These

THIS HEAT
CD **HEAT 1CD**
ReR/Recommended / '91 / ReR Megacorp / RTM/Disc

This Lush Garden

BLACK TAPE FOR A BLUE GIRL
CD **HY 39100622CD**
Hyperium / Aug '93 / Cargo / Plastic Head

This Mortal Coil

BLOOD
Lacemaker / Mr. Somewhere / Andialu / With tomorrow / Loose joints / You and your sister / Nature's way / I come and stand at every door / Bitter / Baby ray baby / Several times / Lacemaker II / Late night / Ruddy and wretched / Help me lift you up / Carolyn's song / DD and E / Till I gain control again / Dreams are like water / I am the cosmos / (Nothing but) Blood
CD **DADCD 1005**
4AD / Apr '91 / RTM/Disc

FILIGREE AND SHADOW
Velvet belly / Jeweller / Ivy and neet / Meniscus / Tears / Tarantula / My father / Come here my love / At first and then / Strength of strings / Morning glory / Inchblue / I want to live / Mama K / Filigree and shadow / Firebrothers / Thais / I must have been blind / Heart of glass / Alone / Mama K / Horizon bleeds and sucks its thumb / Drugs / Red rain / Thais
CD **DAD 609 CD**
4AD / Sep '86 / RTM/Disc

IT'LL END IN TEARS
Kangaroo / Song to the siren / Holocaust / Fyt / Fond affections / Last ray / Waves become wings / Another day / Barramundi / Dreams made flesh / Not me / Single wish
CD **CAD 411 CD**
4AD / '86 / RTM/Disc

Thistlethwaite, Anthony

AESOP WROTE A FABLE
Muddy waterboy / Let your conscience be your guide / Love that burns / Aesop wrote a fable / I just want to make love to you / Jenny / It don't make sense (You can't make peace) / Howling tom cat / Good morning Mr. Customs man / Here in my arms / Flick-knife / Blues stars
CD **ACRE 001CD**
Rolling Acres / Mar '93 / Vital

CARTWHEELS
Cartwheels / Red jeans / Farming the right / Acres / Migrating bird / Cherry dress / Tower of love / Marie Dreslerova / Somewhere across the water / Communicating / Atlas / Back to the land
CD **ACRE 002CD**
Rolling Acres / Jan '95 / Vital

Thobejane, Mabi

MADIBA
Thabo / Sidudla / Segwagwa / Thabo thando nico / Domm pass / Shapedi / Economy / Mother / Madiba / Gae way home / Madiba / Workshop
CD **BW 086**
B&W / Feb '97 / New Note/Pinnacle / SRD / Vital/SAM

Thomas, Angelika

LIEBLING DER SAISON (Thomas, Angelika & Orchestra Melange)
Overture / Jonny wenn du geburtstag hast / Ich wunsch mir zum geburtstag dich / Alles mit den beinen / Lass mich einmal deine Carmen sein / Baby / Black market / Illusions / Moonlight and shadows / Boys in the backroom / Ich bin von kopf bis fuss auf liebe eingestel / Reizend / Nimm dich in acht vor blonden Frau'n / Lola / Abschiednehmen mit musik
CD **BCD 16015**
Bear Family / Dec '96 / Direct / Rollercoaster / Swift

Thomas, B.J.

RAINDROPS KEEP FALLIN' ON MY HEAD
CD **CPCD 8228**
Charly / Aug '96 / Koch

Thomas, Bill

PREACHER'S SON
CD **422504**
Last Call / May '95 / Cargo / Direct / Discovery

Thomas, Carla

BEST OF CARLA THOMAS, THE
Where do I go / I've fallen in love / I like what you're doing (to me) / Strung out over you / Just keep on loving me: *Thomas, Carla & Johnnie Taylor* / My life: *Thomas, Carla & Johnnie Taylor* / I need you woman: *Thomas, Carla & William Bell* / I can't stop: *Thomas, Carla & William Bell* / Some other man (is beating your time) / Guide me well / Time for love / (I'm going back to) living in the City / All I have to do is dream: *Thomas, Carla & William Bell* / I loved you like I love my very life / Hi de ho (that old sweet roll) / You've got a cushion to fall on / Love means you never have to say you're sorry / Sugar / I may not be all you want (but I'm all you got) / Love among people / I have a God who loves / Gee whiz / I'll never stop loving you
CD **CDSXD 093**
Stax / Aug '93 / Pinnacle

CARLA
CD **7567823402**
Atlantic / Jul '93 / Warner Music

COMFORT ME
Comfort me / No time to lose / Yes I'm ready / Lover's concerto / I'm for you / What the world needs now / Let it be me / Woman's love / Will you love me tomorrow / Forever / Move on drifter / Another night without my man
CD **SCD 706**
Stax / Apr '96 / Pinnacle

HIDDEN GEMS
I'll never stop loving you / I wonder about love / Little boy / Loneliness / (Your love is a) lifesaver / Sweet sensation / You'll lose a good thing / I've made up my mind / My man believes in me / I like it / Runaround / Good good lovin' / That beat keeps disturbing my sleep / If it's not asking too much / It ain't no easy thing / Toe hold / Good man / I can't hide it / Thump in my heart / Goodbye my love
CD **CDSXD 039**
Stax / Oct '91 / Pinnacle

LOVE MEANS
Didn't we / Are you sure / What is love / Daughter, you're still your daddy's child / Love means you never have to say you're sorry / You've got a cushion to fall on / Il est plus doux que / Cherish / I wake up wanting you
CD **CDSXE 060**
Stax / Jul '92 / Pinnacle

QUEEN ALONE, THE
CD **8122710152**
Atlantic / Jul '93 / Warner Music

Thomas, Charlie

BIG CHARLIE THOMAS (Various Artists)
I'm gonna hoodoo you: *Martin, Sara* / Your going ain't giving me the blues: *Martin, Sara* / What more can a monkey do: *Martin, Sara* / Shake that thing: *Williams, Clarence* / Get it fixed: *Williams, Clarence* / I want plenty grease in my frying pan: *Carter, Margaret* / Come get me Papa before I faint: *Carter, Margaret* / Skunk: *Christian, Buddy's Jazz Rippers* / South Rampart Street Blues: *Christian, Buddy's Jazz Rippers* / Georgia Grind: *Morris, Thomas* / Ham gravy: *Morris, Thomas* / Look out, Mr Jazz: *Okeh Melody Stars* / Nobody but my baby is getting my love: *Brown, Bessie* / St Louis Blues: *Brown, Bessie* / Papa if you can do better (I'll let a better Papa move in): *Henderson, Rosa* / I'm saving it all for you: *Henderson, Rosa* / Dark eyes: *Dixie Washboard Band* / Gimme blues: *Dixie Washboard Band* / King of the Zulus: *Dixie Washboard Band* / Zulu blues: *Dixie Washboard Band* / What do you know about that: *Williams, Clarence & Joe Sims* / Shut your mouth: *Williams, Clarence & Joe Sims*
CD **CBC 1030**
Timeless Jazz / Aug '96 / New Note/ Pinnacle

Thomas, Chris

21ST CENTURY BLUES...FROM DA HOOD
Intro / 21 cb / Hellhounds / Kkkrossroads / Kickin' true blue / Up from da underground / Blues from da hood / Da gambler / Time bomb / Homesick blues / Phone interlude / My pain, your pleasure / Kill somebody tonight / Anotherdeadhomie
CD **01005821232**
Private Music / Jul '95 / BMG

SIMPLE
CD **HCD 8043**
Hightone / Jun '94 / ADA / Koch

Thomas, David

EREWHON (Thomas, David & Two Pale Boys)
Obsession / Planet of fools / Nowheresville / Fire / Lantern / Morbid sky / Weird Cornfields / Kathleen / Highway 61 revisited
CD **COOKCD 105**
Cooking Vinyl / Sep '96 / Vital

GIANTS DANCE (Thomas, David & Ronnie Gunn)
Great Western / I get the feeling / Somewhere upon the way / Minor epic / I knw she danced / (Give my) Love to the future / Coolly I love you / Walk to the water / Bring back the old money / Falcon rise / Hillside / Memorium / Hey lady / Go get the girl / To my surprise / Fate is a dancer / Black rat sleepy tune / Giants dance
CD **BP 223CD**
Blueprint / Oct '96 / Pinnacle

MONSTER (5CD Set)
Birds are a good / Yiki tiki / Crickets in the flats / Sound of sand / New atom mine / Big dreams / Happy to see you / Crush this horn part 2 / Confuse did / Sloop John B / Man's best friend / Pedestrian walk / Bird town / Day at the Botaical gardens / Egga and I / Whi is it / Song of the hoe / Hurry back / Rain / Semaphore / Through the magnifying glass / Enthusiastic / Whale head king / Song of bailing man / Big breezy day / Farmer's wife / About true friends / My theory of spontaneous simultude/Run tin bus / What happened to me / Monster walks the winter lake / Bicycle / Coffee train / My town / Monster magee, King of the seas / Monster thinks about the good old days / My town / Fact about trains / King knut / When love is uneven / Storm breaks / Long rain / Having time / Fields of stone / Veilovsky 2-step / Obsession / Nobody knows / Red sky / Can't help falling in love / Nowheresville / Fire / Kathleen / Surfer girl/ Around the fire / Beach boys / Weird cornfields / Busman's honeymoon
CD Set **HR 110**
Cooking Vinyl / Jun '97 / Vital

Thomas, Earl

BLUE NOT BLUES
CD **FIENDCD 740**
Demon / Aug '93 / Pinnacle

Thomas, Gary

BY ANY MEANS NECESSARY
By any means necessary / Continuum / You're under arrest / Potential hazard / To the vanishing point / Screen gem / Janala / At risk / Out of harm's way
CD **8344322**
jMT / Dec '94 / PolyGram

EXILE'S GATE
CD **5140092**
jMT / Dec '93 / PolyGram

OVERKILL: MURDER IN THE WORST DEGREE
SOL / Guaranteed flow / Have hope / Outta tha game / Terror of the streets / Barrikade'll stop ya / Doomsday booty / Fuk tha massa / Godfather waltz / Just a villain / Soulja / It's on
CD **5140242**
jMT / Mar '96 / PolyGram

TILL WE HAVE FACES
Angel eyes / Best of you / Lush life / Bye bye baby / Lament / Peace / It's you or no one / You don't know what love is
CD **5140002**
jMT / Apr '92 / PolyGram

Thomas, Guthrie

MIDNIGHT TRAIN
CD **TX 3006CD**
Taxim / Apr '96 / ADA

THROUGH THE YEARS
CD **TX 3001CD**
Taxim / Jan '94 / ADA

WRITER, THE
CD **TX 3002CD**
Taxim / Dec '93 / ADA

Thomas, Henry

COMPLETE RECORDINGS, THE
CD **YAZCD 1080**
Yazoo / Apr '91 / ADA / CM / Koch

Thomas, Hociel

HOCIEL THOMAS & LILLIE DELK CHRISTIAN 1925-1928 (Thomas, Hociel & Lillie Delk Christian)
CD **DOCD 5448**
Document / May '96 / ADA / Hot Shot / Jazz Music

Thomas, Irma

DOWN AT MUSCLE SHOALS
We got something good / Good to me / Here I am, take me / Security / Let's do it over / Somewhere crying / Woman will do wrong / Yours until tomorrow / I gave you everything / I've been loving you too long / Don't make me stop now / Cheater man / Good things don't come easy
CD **CDRED 28**
Charly / Sep '91 / Koch

LIVE - SIMPLY THE BEST
Breakaway / Time is on my side / Hip shakin' mama / That's what love is all about / Thinking of you / I need somebody / I've been loving you too long / Please please please / It's raining / I done got over/Iko iko/ Hey pocky way / Wish someone would care / You can have my husband / Oh me oh my (I'm a fool for you) / Simply the best
CD **NETCD 25**
Network / May '91 / Direct / Greensleeves / SRD

NEW RULES, THE
New rules / Gonna cry till my tears run dry / I needed somebody / Good things don't come easy / Love of my man / One more time / Thinking of you / Wind beneath my wings / I gave you everything / Yours until tomorrow
CD **ROUCD 2046**
Rounder / '86 / ADA / CM / Direct

RULER OF HEARTS
I did my part / Cry on / For goodness sake / It's raining / Look up / It's too soon to know / Somebody told you / Your love is true / (You ain't) hittin' on nothing / Gone / Two winters long / I done got over it / That's all I ask / Ruler of my heart / Girl needs boy
CD **CDCHARLY 195**
Charly / Aug '89 / Koch

SOUL QUEEN OF NEW ORLEANS
It's raining / Ruler of my heart / I did my part / Cry on / Look up / It's too soon to know / I done got over / That's all I ask / For goodness sake / Gone / Somebody told you / Two winters long / (You ain't) hittin' on nothing / Girl needs boy / In between tears / She'll never be your wife / These four walls / What's so wrong with you loving me / You're the dog (I do the barking myself) / Coming from behind / Wish someone would care / Turn my world around
CD **CPCD 8010**
Charly / Feb '94 / Koch

STORY OF MY LIFE, THE
No use talkin' / Story of my life / I count the teardrops / Cried too long / Love don't get no better than this / Hold me while I cry / I won't cry for you / We all need love / Get here / Keep the faith / Dr. Feelgood
CD **ROUCD 2149**
Rounder / Feb '97 / ADA / CM / Direct

SWEET SOUL QUEEN OF NEW ORLEANS (The Irma Thomas Collection)
CD **RAZCD 2097**
Razor & Tie / Apr '96 / Koch

TIME IS ON MY SIDE...PLUS
Take a look / Time is on my side / Baby don't look down / Times have changed / I done got over it / It's raining / Somebody told you / Wait wait wait / Break-a-way / I haven't got time to cry / Some things you never get used to / Look up (when ever) / Ruler of my heart / I need your love so bad / Wish someone would care / (I want a) True true love / I did my part / You don't miss a good thing (until it's gone) / Anyone who knows what love is (will understand) / Straight from the heart / Gone / Two winters long / Without love (there is nothing) / It's a man's-woman's world
CD **CDKEND 010**
Kent / Nov '96 / Pinnacle

WALK AROUND HEAVEN
CD **ROUCD 2128**
Rounder / Apr '94 / ADA / CM / Direct

WAY I FEEL, THE
Old records / Baby I love you / Sorry wrong number / You can think twice / Sit down and cry / All I know is the way I feel / I'm gonna hold you to your promise / I'll take care of you / Dancing in the street / You don't know nothin' about love
CD **FIENDCD 112**
Demon / Sep '91 / Pinnacle

Thomas Jefferson Slave ...

BAIT AND SWITCH (Thomas Jefferson Slave Appartments)
My mysterious death / Is she shy / Down to High Street / Quarrel with the world / Cheater's heaven / Cyclotron / Negative guestlist / Fire in the swimming girl / You can't kill stupid / Rock 'n' roll hall of fame / Contract dispute / Wrong headed
CD **74321279652**
American / Jul '95 / BMG

STRAIGHT TO VIDEO (Thomas Jefferson Slave Appartments)
CD **AW 44**
Anyway / Jun '97 / Cargo

Thomas, Jay

360 DEGREES
Cheryl / Wlatz / All too soon / Wing span / Why not / Aisha / Valse / Peacocks / Whims of chambers / My ideal / Blues for McVouty / Isfahan
CD _____ **HEPCD 2060**
Hep / Feb '95 / Cadillac / Jazz Music / New Note/Pinnacle / Wellard

BLUES FOR MCVOUTY
CD _____ **STCD 562**
Stash / May '93 / ADA / Cadillac / CM / Direct / Jazz Music

Thomas, Jesse

BLUE GOOSE BLUES
CD _____ **IMP 704**
Iris Music / Nov '95 / Discovery

LOOKIN' FOR THAT WOMAN
CD _____ **CDBT 1128**
Black Top / Mar '96 / ADA / CM / Direct

Thomas, Joe

JOE THOMAS 1945-1950
CD _____ **BMCD 1051**
Blue Moon / Apr '97 / Cadillac / Discovery / Greensleeves / Jazz Music / Jet Star / TKO Magnum

Thomas, John Charles

HOME ON THE RANGE
CD _____ **GEMMCD 9977**
Pearl / Sep '92 / Harmonia Mundi

Thomas, Kenny

VOICES
Outstanding / Best of you / Tender love / Will I ever see your face / Something special / If you believe / Thinking about your love / Voices / Girlfriend / Were we ever in love
CD _____ **CCD 1890**
Cooltempo / Sep '97 / EMI

Thomas, Nicky

DOING THE MOONWALK
CD _____ **CDTRL 288**
Trojan / Apr '91 / Direct / Jet Star

Thomas, Nigel

YOICHI (Thomas, Nigel Quintet)
CD _____ **OJIN 1**
Ojin / May '97 / Cadillac

Thomas, Pat

ST. KATHERINE
CD _____ **WSFASF 144**
Normal / May '94 / ADA / Direct

Thomas, Peter

EASY LISTENING CLASSICS
CD _____ **5294912**
Polydor / Apr '96 / PolyGram

Thomas, Peter

RAUMPATROUILLE (Thomas, Peter Soundorchester)
CD _____ **RTD 34600092**
City Slang / Nov '96 / RTM/Disc

Thomas, Ramblin'

RAMBLIN' THOMAS 1928-1932
CD _____ **DOCD 5107**
Document / Nov '92 / ADA / Hot Shot / Jazz Music

Thomas, Rene

GUITAR GENIUS
All the things you are / Body and soul / Deep purple / You go to my head / Just friends / B like Bud / 'Round midnight
CD _____ **CDSGP 009**
Prestige / Jan '94 / Else / Total/BMG

GUITAR GROOVE (Thomas, Rene Quintet)
Spontaneous effort / Ruby, my dear / Like someone in love / MTC / Milestones / How long has this been going on / Greenstreet scene
CD _____ **OJCCD 1725**
Original Jazz Classics / Jun '96 / Complete/ Pinnacle / Jazz Music / Wellard

Thomas, Ruddy

SINGS BOB MARLEY
I shot the sheriff / No woman no cry / One love / Iron lion zion / Is this love / Get up stand up / Kaya / Three little birds / Stir it up / Jammin' / Buffalo soldier / Trench town rock / Could you be loved / Exodus / Kinky reggae / Sleep on, your songs will live on
CD _____ **WB 877082**
Disky / Mar '97 / Disky / THE

WHEN I'VE GOT YOU
CD _____ **HLCD 010**
Hawkeye / Jun '94 / Jet Star

Thomas, Rufus

BEST OF RUFUS THOMAS, THE (The Singles)
Funky Mississippi / So hard to get along with / Funky way / I want to hold you / Do the funky chicken / Preacher and the bear / Sixty minute man / Do the push and pull (part 1) / Do the push and pull (part 2) / World is round / Breakdown (part 1) / Breakdown (part 2) / Do the funky penguin (part 1) / Do the funky penguin (part 2) / 6-3-8 (that's the number to play) / Itch and scratch (part 1) / Funky robot (part 1) / I know (I love you so) / I'll be your santa baby / Funky bird / Boogie ain't nuttin' (but gettin' down) / Do the double bump / Jump back '75 (part 1) / Looking for a love (part 1)
CD _____ **CDSXD 094**
Stax / Oct '93 / Pinnacle

BLUES THANG
CD _____ **NEGCD 280**
Sequel / Mar '96 / BMG

CAN'T GET AWAY FROM THIS DOG
Walking the dog / Can't get away from this dog / Forty four long / Strolling Beale no.1 / Cherry red blues / Carry me back to old Virginny / Barefootin' / Story that's never been told / Last clean shirt / Show me the way to go home / Jump back / My girl / We're gonna make it: *Thomas, Rufus & Carla* / Don't mess up a good thing: *Thomas, Rufus & Carla* / I want to hold you / Can your monkey do the dog / Stop kicking my dog around / Wang dang doodle / Reconsider baby: *Thomas, Rufus & Carla*
CD _____ **CDSXD 038**
Stax / Oct '91 / Pinnacle

CROWN PRINCE OF DANCE
Git on up and do it / I know you don't want me no more / Funkiest man alive / Tutti Frutti / Funky robot / I wanna sang / Baby it's real / Steal a little / I'm still in love with you / Funky bird
CD _____ **CDSXE 054**
Stax / Nov '92 / Pinnacle

DID YOU HEARD ME
Do the Push and pull (Parts 1 & 2) / World is round / (I love you) for sentimental reasons / Breakdown (part 1) / Breakdown (part 2) / Love trap / Do the funky penguin (part 1) / Do the funky penguin (part 2) / Ditch digging / 6-3-8 (That's the number to play)
CD _____ **CDSXE 050**
Stax / Nov '92 / Pinnacle

DO THE FUNKY CHICKEN
Do the funky chicken / Let the good times roll / Sixty minute man / Looking for a love / Bearcat / Old McDonald had a farm (parts 1 and 2) / Rufus Rastus Johnson Brown / Soul food / Turn your damper down / Preacher and the bear
CD _____ **CDSXE 036**
Stax / Mar '91 / Pinnacle

RUFUS THOMAS LIVE DOING THE PUSH AND PULL AT PJ'S
Monologue / Ooh-poo-pah-doo / Old McDonald had a farm / Walking the dog / Preacher and the bear / Night time is the right time / Push and pull / Do the funky chicken / Breakdown / Do the funky chicken / Do the funky penguin
CD _____ **CDSXE 121**
Stax / Jul '95 / Pinnacle

THAT WOMAN IS POISON
That woman is poison / Big fine hunk of woman / Somebody's got to go / Walk / I just got to know / Blues in the basement / Breaking my back / All night worker
CD _____ **ALCD 4769**
Alligator / May '93 / ADA / CM / Direct

WALKING THE DOG
Dog / Mashed potatoes / Ooh-poo-pah-doo / You said / Boom boom / It's aw'rite / Walking the dog / Ya ya / Land of 1000 dances / Can your monkey do the dog / Because I love you / I want to be loved
CD _____ **SCD 703**
Stax / Apr '96 / Pinnacle

Thompson Community Singers

THROUGH GOD'S EYES (Brunson, Rev. M. & Thompson Community Singers)
CD _____ **7019406602**
Nelson Word / Dec '93 / Nelson Word

Thompson Twins

BEST OF THE THOMPSON TWINS, THE
In the name of love / Lies / Love on your side / Lay your hands on me / Gap / Hold me now / Doctor doctor / You take me up / King for a day / Get that love
CD _____ **261220**
Arista / Mar '91 / BMG

COLLECTION, THE
Hold me now / Sister of mercy / Don't mess with Doctor Dream / Who can stop the rain / Perfect day / Day after day / Doctor doctor / You take me up / Lies / Follow your heart / Still waters / Emperor's clothes / Revolution / In the name of love
CD _____ **74321152212**
Ariola Express / Sep '93 / BMG

SINGLES COLLECTION
Perfect game / Lies / Love on your side / We are detective / Watching / Hold me now / Doctor doctor / King for a day / You take me up / Sister of mercy / Don't mess with Doctor Dream / Get that love / Revolution / Lay your hands on me / In the name of love
CD _____ **74321393352**
Arista / Jan '97 / BMG

Thompson, Barbara

BARBARA THOMPSON'S SPECIAL EDITION
Country dance / Fear of spiders / City lights / Little Annie ooh / Fields of flowers / Dusk: Nightwatch / Listen to the plants / Out to lunch / Sleepwalker / Midday riser / Times past / Voices behind locked doors
CD _____ **VBR 20172**
Vera Bra / Sep '93 / New Note/Pinnacle / Pinnacle

BREATHLESS (Thompson, Barbara Paraphernalia)
Breathless / Sax rap / Jaunty / You must be jokin' / Squiffy / Bad blues / Cheeky / Gracey / Breathless (short cuts) / Sax rap (short cuts) / Cheeky (short cuts)
CD _____ **VBR 20572**
Vera Bra / Sep '93 / New Note/Pinnacle / Pinnacle

CRY FROM THE HEART, A (Live In London) (Thompson, Barbara Paraphernalia)
CD _____ **VBRCD 20212**
Vera Bra / Sep '93 / New Note/Pinnacle / Pinnacle

EVERLASTING FLAME
Everlasting flame / Tatami / In the eye of a storm / Ode to sappho / Emerald dusky maiden / Night before culloden / Unity hymn / Ancient voices / So near, so far / Fanaid grove
CD _____ **VBR 20582**
Vera Bra / Nov '93 / New Note/Pinnacle / Pinnacle

HEAVENLY BODIES
Le grand voyage / Extreme jonction / Requiem pour deux memoire / Entre les trous de la memoire / Les barricades mysterieuses / Heavenly bodies / Love on the edge of life / Elysian fields / Flights of fancy / Tibetan sunrise / Horizons new
CD _____ **VBR 20152**
Vera Bra / Sep '93 / New Note/Pinnacle / Pinnacle

LADY SAXOPHONE
In memory / All in love is fair / Falling scars / I do it for your love / Rueben, Rueben / Out on a limb / Wastelands / Waiting for the rain / What am I here for / Lady S
CD _____ **VBR 21662**
Vera Bra / May '96 / New Note/Pinnacle / Pinnacle

LIVE IN LONDON / A CRY FROM THE HEART (Thompson, Barbara Paraphernalia)
Joyride / L'extreme jonction / Cry from the heart / Entre les trous de la memoire / Out to lunch / Close to the edge / Voices behind locked doors / Eastern Western promise Part 1 / Eastern Western promise Part 11
CD _____ **VBR 20212**
Vera Bra / Sep '93 / New Note/Pinnacle / Pinnacle

NIGHTWATCH (Thompson, Barbara Paraphernalia)
Fields of flowers / Coconut hurling game / Dusk / Nightwatch / Kafferinya / Chapter and verse / To Ceres / Listen to the plants / Pure fantasy / Firefly
CD _____ **VBR 21252**
Vera Bra / Feb '97 / New Note/Pinnacle / Pinnacle

Thompson, Bob

EV'RY TIME I FEEL THE SPIRIT
CD _____ **D 2248772**
Ichiban / Apr '96 / Direct / Koch

MAGIC IN YOUR HEART
CD _____ **ICH 1165CD**
Ichiban / Apr '94 / Direct / Koch

Thompson, Bobby

BOBBY THOMPSON COLLECTION, THE (3CD Set)
CD Set _____ **RUBCD 3238**
Rubber / Dec '96 / ADA / CM / Direct / Jazz Music / Roots

BOBBY THOMPSON LAUGH-IN, THE
CD _____ **RUBCD 038**
Rubber / Dec '96 / ADA / CM / Direct / Jazz Music / Roots

LITTLE WASTER, THE
CD _____ **RUBCD 032**
Rubber / Dec '96 / ADA / CM / Direct / Jazz Music / Roots

Thompson, Bruce

BIBLE SINGERS, THE (Thompson, Bruce & The Bible Roses)
Bible singers / Go down Moses / Sweet sweet spirit / How great thou art (O store gud) / Solid rock / I want Jesus to walk with me / When the saints go marchin' in / Sometimes I feel like a Motherless child / Oh happy day / Amazing grace
CD _____ **CD 12528**
Music Of The World / Jun '96 / ADA / Target/BMG

Thompson, Butch

BUTCH & DOC (Thompson, Butch & Doc Cheatham)
CD _____ **CD 3012**
Daring / Dec '94 / ADA / CM / Direct

BUTCH THOMPSON PLAYS JELLY ROLL MORTON
CD _____ **BCD 141**
Biograph / Apr '96 / ADA / Cadillac / Direct / Hot Shot / Jazz Music / Wellard

LINCOLN AVENUE BLUES
CD _____ **DARINGCD 3019**
Daring / Nov '95 / ADA / CM / Direct

LINCOLN AVENUE EXPRESS
Tom cat blues / Big lip blues / Basin Street blues / Weeping willow blues / New Orleans hop scop blues / Aunt Hagar's blues / Willow tree / Lincoln Avenue express / Arkansas blues / Careless love / Mr. Jelly Lord / Yellow dog blues / Atlanta blues / St. Louis blues
CD _____ **DARINGCD 3027**
Daring / Jun '97 / ADA / CM / Direct

MINNESOTA WONDER
CD _____ **DR 3004**
Daring / Mar '93 / ADA / CM / Direct

PLAYS FAVORITES (Thompson, Butch Trio)
CD _____ **SACD 113**
Solo Art / Feb '93 / Jazz Music

YULESTRIDE
CD _____ **DARING 3010CD**
Daring / Nov '94 / ADA / CM / Direct

Thompson, Carroll

OTHER SIDE OF LOVE, THE
Other side of love / I go weak / Move me / Walk away / Unity / Show some love/ Where is love / Where were you / Natural woman / Lovers and strangers / Rock me gently
CD _____ **ARICD 077**
Ariwa Sounds / Dec '92 / Jet Star / SRD

Thompson, Danny

SONGHAI (Thompson, Danny/Toumani Diabate/Ketama)
CD _____ **HNCD 1323**
Hannibal / May '89 / ADA / Vital

SONGHAI VOL.2
Sute monebo / Niani / Pozo del deseo / Monte de los suspiros / Djamana djana / De jerez a mali / Ndia / De la noche a la manana / Mail sajio
CD _____ **HNCD 1383**
Rykodisc / Aug '94 / ADA / Vital

WHATEVER
Idle Monday / Till Minne av jan / Yucateca / Lovely Joan / Swedish dance / Lament for Alex / Crusader / Minor escapade
CD _____ **HNCD 1326**
Hannibal / Jul '87 / ADA / Vital

WHATEVER NEXT
Dargai / Hopdance (invitation to dance) / Beanpole / Wildfinger / Full English basket / Sandansko oro (Bulgarian dance) / Take it off the top / Major escapade
CD _____ **IMCD 117**
Antilles/New Directions / May '91 / PolyGram

WHATEVER'S BEST
CD _____ **WHAT 001CD**
Whatdisc / Feb '95 / Vital

Thompson, Eddie

AT CHESTERS (Thompson, Eddie Trio & Spike Robinson)
'S Wonderful / Flamingo / Emily / I'm getting sentimental over you / I should care / Ow / Everything happens to me / Please don't talk about me when I'm gone
CD _____ **HEPCD 2028**
Hep / Jan '92 / Cadillac / Jazz Music / New Note/Pinnacle / Wellard

AT CHESTERS VOL.2 (Thompson, Eddie Trio & Spike Robinson)
CD _____ **HEPCD 2031**
Hep / Jun '94 / Cadillac / Jazz Music / New Note/Pinnacle / Wellard

MEMORIES OF YOU (Thompson, Eddie Trio & Spike Robinson)
Rosetta / Memories of you / C Jam blues / Misty / Paris mambo / 'Round midnight / Love will find a way / Satin doll / Memories of you (alt. take) / Round midnight / Love will find a way (alt. take)
CD _____ **HEPCD 2021**
Hep / Aug '94 / Cadillac / Jazz Music / New Note/Pinnacle / Wellard

WHEN LIGHTS ARE LOW (Thompson, Eddie Trio & Roy Williams)
Lamp is low / Keepin' out of mischief now / Never say yes / When lights are low / Don't stop the carnival / I've got the world on a string / Mister Bojangles / Fred / It never entered my mind
CD _______ HEPCD 2007
Hep / Jan '97 / Cadillac / Jazz Music / New Note/Pinnacle / Wellard

Thompson, Eric

ADAM & EVE HAD THE BLUES (Thompson, Eric & Suzy)
CD _______ ARHCD 5041
Arhoolie / Apr '95 / ADA / Cadillac / Direct

Thompson, Gail

JAZZ AFRICA
Long time in Togo / Burkina faso / Kamara river / Expedition / Stressless / Finale
CD _______ ENJ 90532
Enja / Sep '96 / New Note/Pinnacle / Vital/ SAM

Thompson, Gina

NOBODY DOES IT BETTER
Rodalude / Things that you do / Nobody does it better / Can't go another minute / Angel / Freak on / Can't help myself / He'll make a way / Put me on / Into you / Strung out / I can't wait / Things that you do
CD _______ 5320602
Mercury Black Vinyl / Sep '96 / PolyGram

Thompson, Hank

HANK THOMPSON 1946-1964 (14CD Set) (Thompson, Hank & His Brazos Valley Boys)
Swing wide your gate of love / Whoa sailor / California women / What are we gonna do about the moonlight / Lonely heart knows / Starry eyed Texas gal / Humpty dumpty heart / Today / Don't flirt with me / Rock in the ocean / My heart is a jigsaw puzzle / Yesterday's mail / I find you cheatin' on me / Second hand gal / You broke my heart / Mary had a little lamb / You remembered me / Green light / What are we gonna do about he moonlight / All that goes up must come down / Standing on the outside looking in now / Tomorrow night / My front door is open / Soft lips / Grass looks greener over yonder / She's a girl without any sweetheart / Take a look at this broken heart of mine / Give a little, take a little / Cat has nine lives / Beautiful Texas / Daddy blues / How do you feel / New rovin' gambler / Humpty Dumpty boogie / Can't feel at home in the world anymore / When God calls his children home / If I cry / Broken heart and a glass of beer / Devil in my angels eyes / Playin' possum / Where is your heart tonight / Those things money can't buy / Hangover heart / I ain't cryin' over you / You were the cause / I'll be your sweetheart for a day / Love thief / Teardrops on the tea leaves / Wild side of life / Waiting in the lobby of your heart / Don't make me cry again / Cryin' in the deep blue sea / You're walking on my heart / It's better to have loved a little / How cold hearted can you get / Rub-a-dub-dub / I'd have never found somebody new / Where my sweet baby used to walk / I'll sign my heart away / Yesterday's girl / John Henry / Letter edged in black / Mother the queen of my heart / At the rainbow's edge / When you're lovin', you're livin' / You don't have the nerve / I saw my Mothers name / No help wanted / Go cry your heart out / Wake up, Irene / Fooler / Breakin' the rules / We've gone to far / If lovin' you is wrong / Tears are only rain / Annie over / This train / Little rosewood casket / Gloria / Honky tonk girl / Jersey bounce / Sunrise serenade / Johnson rag / Dardanella / When your love burns low / New deal of love / Baby I need lovin' / I'd do it again / Dusty skies / New green light / Simple Simon / Most of all / Breakin' in another heart / Too in love / String of pearls / Big beaver / Pandhandle rag / Wildwood flower / Honey, honey bee ball / Quicksand / You can give le rag / You can give me back my heart / Don't take it all out on me / Red skin girl / Westphalia waltz / Don't be that way / It makes no difference now / Anybody's girl / Taking my chances / I'm not mad, just hurt / Blackboard of my heart / Across the alley from the Alamo / Weeping willo / Prosperity special / Under the double eagle / You'll be the one / I don't want to know / Someone can steal your love from me / Old Napoleon / I was the first one / Rockin' in the Congo / Hang your head in shame / Gypsy / Don't get around much anymore / I didn't mean to fall in love / Girl in the night / Don't look now / Bubbles in my beer / Headin' down the wrong highway / Lawdy, what a girl / After all the things I've done / Make room in your heart / I wouldn't miss it for the world / Kishamo klingo / Li'l Liza Jane / If I'm not too late / Just and old flame / How do you hold a memory / Beaumont rag / Summit ridge drive / Woodchopper's ball / Bartender's polka / Wednesday's rag / Wednesday waltz / Gold and silver waltz / Skater's waltz / Fifty year ago waltz / La zindo waltz / Anniversary waltz / Let me call you sweetheart / What will I do on Monday / You're going back to your old ways again / I've run out of tomorrows / Shenandoah waltz / Signed, sealed and delivered / In the valley of the moon / Warm red wine / Squaws along the Yukon / Two hearts deep in the blues / Gathering flowers / Little blossom / Deep elem / Rovin' gambler / Cocaine blues / May I sleep in your barn tonight mister / I'll be a bachelor till I die / Three times seven / Bumming round / I left my gal in the mountains / Teach 'em how to swim / Drunkard's blues / Dry bread / Lost John / I guess I'm getting over you / What made her change / Total strangers / Just one step away / Coconut grove / Tuxedo junction / Give the world a smile / Gypsy and the tealeaves / Fooler, a faker / Six pack to go / We will start it all over again / She's just a whole lot like you / There my future goes / Teach me how to lie / It's got to be a habit / It's my fault / I'd like to tell you / I'll be around / Just an old faded photograph / I dreamed of an old love affair / Sing me something sentimental / Paying off the interest with my tears / I keep meeting girl's like you / My old flame / Just a little while / I've convinced everybody but myself / I gotta have my baby back / Oklahoma hills / Hangover tavern / Honky tonk town / I'd look forward to tomorrow / How many teardrops will it take / Drop me gently / That's the recipe for a heartache / Blue skirt waltz / I cast a lonesome shadow / Detour / I don't hurt anymore / Pick me up on your way down / Beer barrel polka / Wabash cannon ball / Then I'll keep on loving you / Shot gun boogie / Back street affair / You nearly lose your mind / Eyes of Texas / More in love your heart is / I wasn't even in the running / Luckiest heartache in town / Whatever happend to Mary / Twice as much / Just to ease the pain / Reaching for the moon / Stirring up the ashes / Paper doll / There's no you / You always hurt the one you love / September in the rain / Til then / That's all there is to that / Don't take it out on me / Just an old flame / Life's sweetest moment / I'm gonna practice freedom / Then I'll start believing in you / In the back of your mind / Here comes Santa Claus / Gonna wrap my heart in ribbons / It's Christmas everyday in Alaska / Santa Claus is comin' to town / Blue Christams / Silver bells / It's Christmas time / I'd like to have an elephant for Christmas / White Christmas / Little Christmas angel / Mr. and Mrs. Snowman / Rudolph the red nosed reindeer / We wish you a merry Christmas / Intro / Honky-tonk girl / I'll step aside / Orange blossom special / Nine pound hammer / Have I told you lately that I love you / Steel guitar rag / Lost highway / Forgive me / Rose city chimes / That's the recipe for heartache / Darling what more can I say / Cincinnati Lou / Deep in the heart of Texas / My heart is a playground / Charmaine / News wears off too fast / Will we start all over again / River road two step / There's a little bit of everything in Texas
CD Set _______ BCD 15904
Bear Family / Jul '96 / Direct / Rollercoaster / Swift

RADIO BROADCASTS 1952 (Thompson, Hank & His Brazos Valley Boys)
CD _______ FLYCD 948
Flyright / Jul '97 / Hot Shot / Jazz Music / Wellard

Thompson, Johnny

WAKE UP NOW (Thompson, Johnny Singers)
CD _______ FA 420
Fremeaux / Apr '97 / ADA / Discovery

Thompson, Linda

DREAMS FLY AWAY
Lonely hearts / Walking on a wire / I live not where I love / Sometimes it happens / For shame of doing wrong / Talking like a man / Sisters / Shay Fan Yan Ley / One clear moment / First light / Pavanne / Many dreams must fly away / I want to see the bright lights tonight / Great Valerio / Insult to injury / Poor boy is taken away / Blackwaterside / Telling me lies / I'm a dreamer / Dimming of the day
CD _______ HNCD 1379
Hannibal / Jul '96 / ADA / Vital

Thompson, Linval

HAVE TO BE SURE
CD _______ RN 7006
Rhino / Sep '96 / Grapevine/PolyGram / Jet Star

I LOVE MARIJUANA
I love marijuana / Dread are the controller / Children of the ghetto / Don't push your brother / Begging for apology / Not follow fashion / Roots lady / Big big girl / Just another girl / Starlight / Jamaican calley
CD _______ CDTRL 151
Trojan / Feb '97 / Direct / Jet Star

LONG LONG DEADLINES
CD _______ LG 21118
Lagoon / Aug '96 / Grapevine/PolyGram

LOOK HOW ME SEXY
Are you ready / You're young / Look how me sexy / Call me / Sure of the one you love / Baby mother / I spy / Things couldn't be the same / Holding on to my girlfriend / Lick up the chalice
CD _______ GRELCD 515
Greensleeves / Aug '95 / Jet Star / SRD

SIX BABYLON
CD _______ KPTSCD 1
Thompson Sound / Mar '97 / Jet Star

STRONG LIKE SAMSON
CD _______ KPSLSCD 1
Strong Like Samson / Mar '97 / Jet Star

Thompson, Lucky

BEGINNING YEARS, THE
CD _______ IAJRCCD 1001
IAJRC / Jun '94 / Jazz Music / Wellard

LORD LORD AM I EVER GONNA KNOW
Lord Lord am I ever gonna know / Love and respect / Say that to say this / Choose your own / Beautiful Tuesday / Warm inside / Our shared blessings / Scratching the surface
CD _______ CCD 79035
Candid / Mar '97 / Cadillac / Direct / Jazz Music / Koch / Wellard

LUCKY MEETS TOMMY (Thompson, Lucky & Tommy Flanagan)
CD _______ FSRCD 199
Fresh Sound / Jan '93 / Discovery / Jazz Music

LUCKY STRIKES
In a sentimental mood / Fly with the wind / Midnite oil / Reminiscent / Mumba Neua / I forgot to remember / Prey-loot / Invitation
CD _______ OJCCD 194
Original Jazz Classics / May '93 / Complete/ Pinnacle / Jazz Music / Wellard

Thompson, Malachi

BUDDY BOLDEN'S RAG (Thompson, Malachi & Africa Brass)
Buddy Bolden's rag / World view / Chaser in Brazil / We bop / Nubian call / Chaser in America / Kojo time / Harold the great / Mouse in the house
CD _______ DE 481
Delmark / Mar '97 / ADA / Cadillac / CM / Direct / Hot Shot

JAZZ LIFE, THE
In walked John / My romance / Drown in my own tears / Mystic trumpet man / Croquet ballet / Lucky seven
CD _______ DD 453
Delmark / Mar '97 / ADA / Cadillac / CM / Direct / Hot Shot

LIFT EVERY VOICE (Thompson, Malachi & Africa Brass)
Elephantine island / Old man river / Tales of ancient Kemet / Transition / Lift ev'ry voice and sing / Nubian call / Trick of the trip / Nobody knows the trouble I've seen
CD _______ DE 463
Delmark / Mar '97 / ADA / Cadillac / CM / Direct / Hot Shot

NEW STANDARDS (Thompson, Malachi Freebop Band)
Joshua / Pinnoccio / Crescent / Resolution / If I only had a brain / We speak / Dyhia Malika / Chicago soundscapes
CD _______ DE 473
Delmark / Mar '97 / ADA / Cadillac / CM / Direct / Hot Shot

SPIRIT
Spirit of man / Back to the one / Rising daystar / Dhiya malika / I remember Clifford / Dearly beloved / No more hard times
CD _______ DD 442
Delmark / Mar '97 / ADA / Cadillac / CM / Direct / Hot Shot

Thompson, Mayo

CORKY'S DEBT TO HIS FATHER
CD _______ DC 49
Drag City / Dec '96 / Cargo / Greyhound

Thompson, Prince Lincoln

UNITE THE WORLD
CD _______ BRMCD 026
Bold Reprive / '88 / Harmonia Mundi

Thompson, Richard

ACROSS A CROWDED ROOM
When the spell is broken / You don't say / I ain't going to drag my feet no more / Love is a faithless country / Fire in the engine room / Walking through a wasted land / Little blue number / She twists the knife again / Ghosts in the wind
CD _______ BGOCD 139
Beat Goes On / Mar '92 / Pinnacle

AMNESIA
Turning of the tide / Gypsy love songs / Reckless kind / Jerusalem on the jukebox / I still dream / Don't tempt me / Yankee, go home / Can't win / Waltzing's for dreamers / Pharaoh
CD _______ CZ 399
Capitol / Mar '91 / EMI

BBC LIVE IN CONCERT
CD _______ WINCD 034
Windsong / May '93 / Pinnacle

BEAT THE RETREAT (A Tribute To Richard Thompson) (Various Artists)
Shoot the light: *X* / Wall of death: *REM* / When the spell is broken: *Raitt, Bonnie* / Turning of the tide: *Mould, Bob* / For shame of doing wrong: *Straw, Syd & Evan Dando* / Down where the drunkards roll: *Los Lobos* / Beat the retreat: *Tabor, June* / Genesis hall: *Tabor, June* / I misunderstood: *Dinosaur Jr.* / Madness of love: *Parker, Graham* / Just the motion: *Byrne, David* / Valerie: *Beausoleil* / Heart needs a home: *Colvin, Shawn & Loudon Wainwright III* / Dimming of the day: *Five Blind Boys Of Alabama* / Farewell, farewell: *Prior, Maddy* / Great Valerio: *Prior, Maddy*
CD _______ CDEST 2242
EMI / Feb '95 / EMI

DARING ADVENTURES
Bone through her nose / Valerie / Missie how you let me down / Dead man's handle / Long dead love / Lover's lane / Nearly in love / Jennie / Baby talk / Cash down never never / How will I ever be simple again / Al Bowlly's in heaven
CD _______ BGOCD 138
Beat Goes On / Mar '92 / Pinnacle

GUITAR/VOCAL
Heart needs a home / Free as a bird / Night comes in / Pitfall/Excursion / Calvary cross / Time will show the wiser / Throw away street puzzle / Mr. Lacey / Ballad of easy rider / Poor Will' and the jolly hangman / Sweet little Rock 'n' roller / Dark end of the street / It'll be me
CD _______ HNCD 4413
Hannibal / Mar '89 / ADA / Vital

HAND OF KINDNESS
Poisoned heart and a twisted memory / Tear stained letter / How I wanted to / Both ends burning / Wrong heartbeat / Hand of kindness / Devonside / Two left feet
CD _______ HNCD 1313
Hannibal / Jun '86 / ADA / Vital

HENRY THE HUMAN FLY
Roll over Vaughan Williams / Nobody's wedding / Poor ditching boy / Shaky Nancy / Angels took my racehorse away / Wheely down / New St George / Painted ladies / Cold feet / Mary and Joseph / Old changing way / Twisted
CD _______ HNCD 4405
Hannibal / May '89 / ADA / Vital

HOKEY POKEY (Thompson, Richard & Linda)
Heart needs a home / Hokey pokey / I'll regret it all in the morning / Smiffy's glass eye / Egypt / Never again / Georgie on a spree / Old man inside a young man / Sun never shines on the poor / Mole in a hole
CD _______ HNCD 4408
Hannibal / May '89 / ADA / Vital

I WANT TO SEE THE BRIGHT LIGHTS TONIGHT (Thompson, Richard & Linda)
When I get to the border / Calvary cross / Withered and died / I want to see the bright lights tonight / Down where the drunkards roll / We sing hallelujah / Has he got a friend for me / Little beggar girl / End of the rainbow / Great Valerio
CD _______ IMCD 160
Island / Mar '93 / PolyGram

INDUSTRY (Thompson, Richard & Danny Thompson)
Chorale / Sweetheart on the barricade / Children of the dark / Big chimney / Kitty "quick get up I can hear clogs going up in the street" / Drifting through the days / Lotteryland / Pitfalls / Saboteur / Mew rhythms / Last shift
CD _______ CDPCS 7383
Parlophone / May '97 / EMI

MIRROR BLUE
For the sake of Mary / I can't wake up to save my life / MGB GT / Way that it shows / Easy there, steady now / King of Bohemia / Shane and Dixie / Brando mumble, Mingus eyes / I ride in your slipstream / Beeswing / Fastfood / Mascara tears / Taking my business elsewhere
CD _______ CDEST 2207
Capitol / Jan '94 / EMI

POUR DOWN LIKE SILVER (Thompson, Richard & Linda)
Streets of paradise / For shame of doing wrong / Poor boy is taken away / Night comes in / Jet plane is a rocking chair / Beat the retreat / Hard luck stories / Dimming of the day / Dargai
CD _______ HNCD 4404
Hannibal / May '88 / ADA / Vital

RUMOR AND SIGH
Read about love / Feel so good / I misunderstood / Behind grey walls / You dream too much / Why must I plead / Vincent / Backlash love affair / Mystery wind / Jimmy Shand / Keep your distance / Mother knows best / God loves a drunk / Psycho Street
CD _______ CDEST 2142
Capitol / May '91 / EMI

SHOOT OUT THE LIGHTS (Thompson, Richard & Linda)
Man in need / Walking on a wire / Don't renage on our love / Just the motion / Shoot out the lights / Backstreet slide / Did she jump or was she pushed / Wall of death

CD _______________ HNCD 1303
Hannibal / Mar '97 / ADA / Vital

SMALL TOWN ROMANCE
Heart needs a home / Time to ring some changes / Beat the retreat / Woman or man / For shame of doing wrong / Honky tonk blues / Small town romance / I want to see the bright lights tonight / Down where the drunkards roll / Love is bad for business / Great Valerio / Don't let a thief steal into your heart / Never again
CD _______________ HNCD 1316
Hannibal / Jun '86 / ADA / Vital

STRICT TEMPO
Banish misfortune / Dundee hornpipe / Do it for my sake / Rockin' in rhythm / Random jig / Grinder / Will ye no' come back again / Cam o'er the steam Charlie / Ye banks and braes o' bonnie Doon / Rufty tufty / Nonsuch a la mode de France / Andalus / Radio Marrakesh / Knife edge
CD _______________ TSCD 460
Topic / Aug '92 / ADA / CM / Direct

SUNNYVISTA (Thompson, Richard & Linda)
Civilization / Borrowed time / Saturday rolling around / You're going to need somebody / Why do you turn your back / Sunnyvista / Lonely heart / Sisters / Justice in the streets / Traces of my love
CD _______________ HNCD 4403
Rykodisc / Oct '92 / ADA / Vital

WATCHING THE DARK (The History Of Richard Thompson 1969-1982/3CD Set)
Man in need / Can't win / Waltzing's for dreamers / Crash the party / I still dream / Bird in God's garden/Lost and found / Now be thankful / Sailor's life / Genesis hall / knife edge / Walking on a wire / Small town romance / Shepherd's march/Maggie Cameron / Wall of death / For the shame of doing wrong / Back street slide / Strange affair / Wrong heartbeat / Borrowed time / From Galway to Graceland / Tear stained letter / Keep your distance / Bogie's bonnie belle / Poor wee Jockey Clarke / Jet plane is a rocking chair / Dimming of the day / Old man inside a young man / Never again / Hokey pokey / Heart needs a home / Beat the retreat / Al Bowlly's in heaven / Walking through a wasted land / When the spell is broken / Devonside / Little blue number / I ain't going to drag my feet no more / Withered and died / Nobody's wedding / Poor ditching boy / Great valerio / Twisted / Calvary cross / Jennie / Hand of kindness / Two left feet / Shoot out the lights
CD Set _______________ HNCD 5303
Hannibal / Apr '93 / ADA / Vital

YOU ME US
Razor dance / She steers by lightning / Dark hand over my heart / Hide it away / Put it there pal / Business on you / No's not a word / Am I wasting my love on you / Bank vault in heaven / Ghost of you walks / Baby don't know what to do / She cut off her long silken hair / Burns supper / Train don't leave / Cold kisses / Sam Jones / Woods of Darney
CD _______________ CDEST 2282
Capitol / Apr '96 / EMI

Thompson, Sir Charles

TAKIN' OFF
CD _______________ DD 450
Delmark / Dec '89 / ADA / Cadillac / CM / Direct / Hot Shot

Thompson, Sonny

JAM SONNY JAM (Original Miracle & King Masters 1947-1956)
Fish / Jam Sonny jam / Long gone / Screamin' boogie / Creeping (late freight) / Walking / After sundown / I'm coming back home to stay / Harlem rug cutter / Uncle Sam blues / Smokestack blues / Clang clang clang / Flying home / Four thirty in the morning / Kenner cuts one / So-o-o-o good / Things ain't what they used to be / Cotton ball / Gum shoe
CD _______________ NEMCD 900
Sequel / Jan '97 / BMG

Thompson, Sydney

CHA CHA CHA'S AND JIVES (Thompson, Sydney & His Orchestra)
CD Set _______________ WRSTCD 5009
WRD / Aug '95 / Target/BMG

CHA CHA CHA'S AND JIVES VOL.2 (Thompson, Sydney & His Orchestra)
CD _______________ WRSTCD 5014
WRD / Oct '95 / Target/BMG

QUICKSTEPS AND FOXTROTS VOL.2 (Thompson, Sydney & His Orchestra)
CD _______________ WRSTCD 5010
WRD / Oct '95 / Target/BMG

RUMBAS & SAMBAS VOL.2 (Thompson, Sydney & His Orchestra)
CD _______________ WRSTCD 5013
WRD / Oct '95 / Target/BMG

RUMBAS AND SAMBAS (Thompson, Sydney & His Orchestra)
CD Set _______________ WRSTCD 5008
WRD / Aug '95 / Target/BMG

TANGOS AND PASO DOBLES (Thompson, Sydney & His Orchestra)
CD Set _______________ WRSTCD 5006
WRD / Aug '95 / Target/BMG

TANGOS AND PASO DOBLES VOL.2 (Thompson, Sydney & His Orchestra)
CD _______________ WRSTCD 5011
WRD / Oct '95 / Target/BMG

WALTZES & VIENNESE WALTZES VOL.2 (Thompson, Sydney & His Orchestra)
CD _______________ WRSTCD 5012
WRD / Oct '95 / Target/BMG

WALTZES AND VIENNESE WALTZES (Thompson, Sydney & His Orchestra)
CD Set _______________ WRSTCD 5007
WRD / Aug '95 / Target/BMG

Thompson, Tony

SEXSATIONAL
CD _______________ 74321276862
RCA / Jul '95 / BMG

Thompson-Clarke, Robin

PRAISE HIM ON THE CELLO
All heaven declares / I love you Lord / Emmanuel / I will sing the wondrous story / There is a redeemer / In the night / When I survey / Such love / Jesus you are changing me / My Lord, what love is this (amazing love) / Send the rain Lord / Prayer of St. Patrick
CD _______________ SOPD 2052
Spirit Of Praise / Apr '92 / Nelson Word

Thorburn, Billy

DON'T SWEETHEART ME
It's always you / Little steeple pointing to a star / What more can I say / It's foolish but it's fun / If I could paint a memory / Four buddies / I'd never fall in love again / It costs so little / I crossed the gypsy's hand with silver / Don't sweetheart me / Sometimes / My dreams are getting better all the time / I'm all alone / Echo of a serenade / Somebody else is taking my place / Journey to a star / I'll just close my eyes / There's a land of beginning again / There'll come another day / I hear bluebirds / I'll be waiting for you / Until you fall in love / Mem'ry of a rose
CD _______________ RAJCD 843
Empress / Jul '97 / Koch

Thore, Francke

ART OF RUMANIAN PAN FLUTE, THE
CD _______________ CDCH 021
Milan / Feb '91 / Conifer/BMG / Silva Screen

PIPE DREAMS
Mon amour / Greensleeves for pipes / Solvejg's song / Way he makes me feel / Entr'acte / Pipe dreams / Spain / Blue rondo a la Turk / Tretemps nippon / Thais meditation / Carillon / Thorn birds
CD _______________ CDSGP 9009
Prestige / Mar '95 / Else / Total/BMG

Thorn, Paul

HAMMER AND NAIL
Heart with 4 wheel drive / 800 pound Jesus / I bet he knows / Double wide paradise / Sure sign / Every little bit hurts / Heart like mine / Temporarily forever mine / Hammer and nail / Resurrection day
CD _______________ 5407142
A&M / Jun '97 / PolyGram

Thorn, Tracey

DISTANT SHORE, A
Smalltown girl / Simply couldn't care / Seascape / Femme fatale / Dreamy / Plain sailing / New opened eyes / Too happy
CD _______________ CDMRED 35
Cherry Red / Jul '93 / Pinnacle

Thornhill, Claude

CLAUDE THORNHILL & HIS ORCHESTRA
CD _______________ JH 1048
Jazz Hour / Jul '96 / Cadillac / Jazz Music / Target/BMG

CLAUDE THORNHILL 1947
CD _______________ HCD 108
Hindsight / Aug '94 / Jazz Music / Target/BMG

TAPESTRIES
Snowfall / Stop, you're breaking my heart / Portrait of a Guinea farm / Autumn nocturne / I'm somebody nobody loves / Smiles / Night and day / Buster's last stand / There's a small hotel / I don't know why (I just do) / Under the willow tree / Arab dance / I get the blues when it rains / Sunday kind of love / Early Autumn / La paloma / Warsaw concerto / Thriving on a riff / Sorta kinda / Robbin's nest / Lover man / Polka dots and moonbeams / Donna Lee / How am I to know / For heaven's sake / Whip-poor-will / That old feeling / Coquette / Yardbird suite / Let's call it a day
CD _______________ CDCHARLY 82
Charly / Oct '87 / Koch

TRANSCRIPTION PERFORMANCE 1984, THE
Poor little rich girl / Adios / Where or when / Spanish dance / Anthropology / Baia / Arab dance / Robbin's nest / Royal garden blues / Polka dots and moonbeams / There's a small hotel / I knew you when / Someone to watch over me / Sometimes I'm happy / I don't know why / April in Paris / Begin the beguine / Godchild / Song is you / La paloma / Lover man / To each his own / Elevation
CD _______________ HEPCD 17
Hep / Oct '94 / Cadillac / Jazz Music / New Note/Pinnacle / Wellard

Thornton, Willie Mae

BALL AND CHAIN (Thornton, Willie Mae 'Big Mama' & Lightnin' Hopkins)
CD _______________ ARHCD 305
Arhoolie / Apr '95 / ADA / Cadillac / Direct

JAIL (Thornton, Willie Mae 'Big Mama')
Little red rooster / Ball 'n' chain / Jail / Hound dog / Rock me baby / Sherriff O E and me / Oh happy day
CD _______________ VMD 79351
Vanguard / Oct '95 / ADA / Pinnacle

ORIGINAL HOUND DOG, THE
Hound dog / Walkin' blues / My man called me / Cotton pickin' blues / Willie Mae's trouble / Big change / I smell a rat / I just can't help myself / They call me Big Mama / Hard times / I ain't no fool either / You don't move me no more / Let your tears fall baby / I've searched the world over / Rock-a-bye baby / How come / Nightmare / Stop a hoppin' on me / Laugh laugh laugh / Just like a dog (barking up the wrong tree) / Fish / Mischievious boogie
CD _______________ CDCHD 940
Ace / Jun '90 / Pinnacle

RISING SUN COLLECTION
CD _______________ RSNCD 002
Just A Memory / Apr '94 / New Note/ Pinnacle

SASSY MAMA (Thornton, Willie Mae 'Big Mama')
Rolling stone / Lost city / Mr. Cool / Big Mama's new love / Private number / Sassy Mama / Everybody's happy but me
CD _______________ VMD 79354
Vanguard / Apr '96 / ADA / Pinnacle

Thorogood, George

BAD TO THE BONE (Thorogood, George & The Destroyers)
Back to Wentsville / Blue highway / Nobody but me / It's a sin / New boogie chillen / Bad to the bone / Miss Luann / As the years go passing by / No particular place to go / Wanted man
CD _______________ BGOCD 94
Beat Goes On / Nov '90 / Pinnacle

BADDEST OF GEORGE THOROGOOD AND THE DESTROYERS (Thorogood, George & The Destroyers)
Bad to the bone / Move it on over / I'm a steady rollin' man / You talk too much / Who do you love / Gear jammer / I drink alone / One bourbon, one scotch, one beer / If you don't start drinkin' (I'm gonna leave) / Treat her right / Long gone / Louis to Frisco
CD _______________ CDMTL 1070
EMI / Sep '92 / EMI

BOOGIE PEOPLE (Thorogood, George & The Destroyers)
If you don't start drinkin' (I'm gonna leave) / Long distance lover / Madman blues / Boogie people / Can't be satisfied / No place to go / Six days on the road / Born in Chicago / Oklahoma sweetheart / Hello little girl
CD _______________ BGOCD 250
Beat Goes On / Dec '94 / Pinnacle

BORN TO BE BAD
Shake your moneymaker / You talk too much / Highway 49 / Born to be bad / You can't catch me / I'm ready / Treat her right / I really like girls / Smokestack lightnin' / I'm movin' on
CD _______________ BGOCD 224
Beat Goes On / May '94 / Pinnacle

GEORGE THOROGOOD AND THE DESTROYERS (Thorogood, George & The Destroyers)
Who do you love / Bottom of the sea / Night time / I drink alone / One bourbon, one scotch, one beer / Alley oop / Madison blues / Bad to the bone / Sky is crying / Reelin' and rockin'
CD _______________ ROUCD 3013
Rounder / '88 / ADA / CM / Direct

LIVE (Thorogood, George & The Destroyers)
Who do you love / Bottom of the sea / Night time / I drink alone / One bourbon, one scotch, one beer / Alley oop / Madison blues / Bad to the bone / Sky is crying / Reelin' and rockin'
CD _______________ CDFA 3211
Fame / '93 / EMI

LIVE - LET'S WORK TOGETHER (Thorogood, George & The Destroyers)
No particular place to go / Ride on Josephine / Bad boy / Cocaine blues / If you don't start drinkin' (I'm gonna leave) / I'm ready / I'll change my style / Get a haircut / Gear jammer / Move it on over / You talk to much / Let's work together / St. Louis blues / Johnny B Goode
CD _______________ CDEMC 3718
EMI / Jul '95 / EMI

MAVERICK (Thorogood, George & The Destroyers)
Gear jammer / I drink alone / Willie and the hand jive / What a price / Long gone / Dixie fried / Crawlin' kingsnake / Memphis Marie / Woman with the blues / Go go go / Ballad of Maverick
CD _______________ BGOCD 223
Beat Goes On / Jun '94 / Pinnacle

MORE GEORGE THOROGOOD & THE DESTROYERS (Thorogood, George & The Destroyers)
I'm wanted / Kids from Philly / One way ticket / Bottom of the sea / Night time / Tip on in / Goodbye baby / House of blue lights / Just can't make it / Restless
CD _______________ FIENDCD 61
Demon / Mar '86 / Pinnacle

Those Darn Accordians

SQUEEZE THIS
CD _______________ FF 70627
Flying Fish / Nov '94 / ADA / CM / Direct / Roots

Those Unknown

THOSE UNKNOWN
CD _______________ GMM 109
GMM / Oct '96 / Cargo

Those X-Cleavers

FIRST ALBUM/THE WAITING GAME
CD _______________ OW 29313
One Way / Apr '94 / ADA / Direct / Greyhound

Thou

UNE POUPEE POUR M'AMUSER
CD _______________ BRCD 061
Brinkman / Jul '97 / Cargo

Thought Industry

MODS CARVE THE PIG ASSASSINS
CD _______________ CDZORRO 65
Metal Blade / Oct '93 / Pinnacle / Plastic Head

OUTER SPACE IS JUST A MARTINI AWAY
CD _______________ 398414101CD
Metal Blade / Jan '96 / Pinnacle / Plastic Head

SONGS FOR INSERTS
CD _______________ CDZORRO 45
Metal Blade / Jul '92 / Pinnacle / Plastic Head

Thoumire, Simon

EXHIBIT A (Thoumire, Simon & Fergus MacKenzie)
By the right / Green man / Interaction / Topless / Totally tropical / Experience the real (stop imagining) / Starjumping / Down / Overcast / Art of non-resistance
CD _______________ IRCD 031
Iona / May '95 / ADA / Direct / Duncans

MARCH, STRATHSPEY & SURREAL (Thoumire, Simon Three)
CD _______________ GLCD 1171
Green Linnet / Aug '96 / ADA / CM / Direct / Highlander / Roots

WALTZES FOR PLAYBOYS
CD _______________ ARADCD 102
Acoustic Radio / Mar '94 / CM

Thrall

CHEMICAL WEDDING
CD _______________ VIRUS 189CD
Alternative Tentacles / Oct '96 / Cargo / Greyhound / Pinnacle

Threadbare

FEELING OLDER FASTER
CD _______________ DOG 028CD
Doghouse / Jul '95 / Plastic Head

Threadgill, Henry

CARRY THE DAY
Come carry the day / Growing a big banana / Vivjanrondirkski / Between orchids, lillies, blind eyes and cricket / Hyla crucifer... silence of / Jenkins boys again / Wish somebody die / It's hot
CD _______________ 4785062
Sony Music / Apr '95 / Sony

MAKIN' A MOVE
Noisy flowers / Like it feels / Official silence / Refined poverty / Make hot and give / Mockingbird sin / Dirty in the right

CD 4811312
Sony Jazz / Oct '95 / Sony

SPIRIT OF NUFF...NUFF
CD 1201342
Black Saint / May '91 / Cadillac / Harmonia Mundi

WHERE'S YOUR CUP (Threadgill, Henry & Make A Move)
100 year old game / Laughing club / Where's your cup / And this / Feels like it / Flew / Go to far
CD 4851392
Sony Jazz / Aug '97 / Sony

Three

DARK DAYS COMING
CD DIS 33CD
Dischord / Jun '97 / SRD

Three Blue Teardrops

ONE PART FIST
Sinner's spiritual / Rough and tumble world / Cadillac Jack / Switchblade pompadour / Wanted man / Red head gal / Ricochet rhythm rockabilly / In my own time / Jenny the generator / Vaporlock / Go, She devil / Rustbelt bop / Claimjumper blues / Another doggone Saturday night
CD NERCD 075
Nervous / Mar '94 / Nervous / TKO Magnum

Three Chord Wonder

NOTHING MEANS NOTHING ANYMORE
CD LF 155CD
Lost & Found / Sep '95 / Plastic Head

Three Degrees

BEST OF THE THREE DEGREES, THE
Givin' up givin' in / My simple heart / Golden lady / Runner / Out of love again / Without you / Magic in the air / Jump the gun / Starlight / Falling in love again / Hot summer night / Woman in love / Set me free / Bodycheck / Red light / Dirty old man / I'll never love this way again / When will I see you again
CD 74321452032
Camden / Feb '97 / BMG

COLLECTION OF THEIR 20 GREATEST HITS, A
When will I see you again / Can't you see what you're doing to me / Toast of love / We're all alone / Long lost lover / Get your love back / I like being a woman / What I did for love / Standing up for love / Take good care of yourself / Dirty ol' man / Loving cup a woman needs / TSOP (The sound of Philadelphia) / Another heartache / Distant lover / Together / Here I am / Year of decision / Love train
CD 4631882
Columbia / Oct '95 / Sony

COMPLETE SWAN RECORDINGS, THE
Gee baby (I'm sorry) / Do what you're supposed to do / Let's shindig / You're gonna miss me / How did that happen / Little red riding hood (that's what they call me) / I'm gonna need you / Just right for love / I'll weep for you / Don't (leave me lover) / Someone (who will be true) / Bongo's on the beach / Close your eyes / Gotta draw the line / Mine all mine / Are you satisfied / And in return / Heartbroken memories / Signs of love / Look in my eyes / Drivin' me mad / Maybe / Yours / Tales are true / I wanna be your baby / Love of my life
CD NEMCD 631
Sequel / Nov '92 / BMG

ROULETTE YEARS, THE
Ebb tide / Trade winds / Maybe / I turn to you / Collage / I won't let you go / I do take you / Through misty eyes / You're the fool / Find my way / Grass will sing for you / Sugar on Sunday / Melting pot / Who is she (and what is she to you) / You're the one / Requiem / Stardust / Isn't it a pity / There's so much love all around me / Shades of green / Lowdown / Macarthur park
CD NEMCD 753
Sequel / Sep '95 / BMG

THREE DEGREES, THE
CD HM 022
Harmony / Jun '97 / TKO Magnum

THREE DEGREES, THE
Tie u up / Make it easy on yourself / After the night is over / Are you that kind of guy / When will I see you again / Midnight train / Dirty ol' man / Nigal Naminda / TSOP / I'm doin' fine now / I'm going to miss you / I'll be around / Do right woman do right man / Let's get it on
CD GFS 076
Going For A Song / Jul '97 / Else / TKO Magnum

WHEN WILL I SEE YOU AGAIN
CD HADCD 188
Javelin / Nov '95 / Henry Hadaway / THE

Three Deuces

KEEP ON IT (Live At The Yardbird Suite)
Keep on it / Face to face / Is that all / Mr. Ed / Down at arts / Boogie on reggae woman
CD YBR 005
Yardbird Suite / Jun '97 / Timewarp

Three Dog Night

20 GREATEST HITS
CD MPG 74015
Movieplay Gold / May '93 / Target/BMG

THAT AIN'T THE WAY TO HAVE FUN
Try a little tenderness / One / Easy to be hard / Eli's coming / Celebrate / Mama told me not to come / Out in the country / One man band / Joy to the world / Liar / Old fashioned love song / Never been to Spain / Family of man / Black and white / Pieces of April / Shamballa / Let me serenade you / Show must go on / Sure as I'm sitting / Play something sweet (brickyard blues) / Till the world ends
CD VSOPCD 211
Connoisseur Collection / Feb '95 / Pinnacle

Three Fish

THREE FISH
Solitude / Song for a dead girl / Silence at the bottom / Intelligent fish / Zagreb / All messed up / Here in the darkness / Hall of intelligent fish / Strangers in my head / Loveley meander / Elusive ones / Build / Stupid fish / Secret place / Laced / If miles were alive / Can I come along / Easy way
CD 4841182
Epic / Jun '96 / Sony

Three Johns

BEST OF THE THREE JOHNS, THE
CD DOJOCD 225
Dojo / Jul '96 / Disc

Three O'Clock

SONGS AND NAILS
CD WB 1153CD
We Bite / Sep '96 / Plastic Head

Three Peppers

CLASSICS 1937-1940
CD CLASSICS 889
Classics / Jul '96 / Discovery / Jazz Music

Three Suns

THREE SUNS VOL.1 1949-1957, THE
CD CCD 075
Circle / Oct '93 / Jazz Music / Swift / Wellard

THREE SUNS VOL.2 1949-1953, THE
CD CCD 145
Circle / Mar '95 / Jazz Music / Swift / Wellard

Threnody

AS THE HEAVENS FALL
CD MASSCD 024
Massacre / Feb '94 / Plastic Head

BEWILDERING THOUGHTS
CD MASSCD 065
Massacre / Aug '95 / Plastic Head

THRENODY
CD MASSCD 120
Massacre / Apr '97 / Plastic Head

Threshold

EXTINCT INSTINCT
Exposed / Somatography / Eat the unicorn / Forever / Virtual isolation / Whispering / Lake of despond / Clear / Life flow / Somatography
CD GEPCD 1019
Giant Electric Pea / Mar '97 / Pinnacle

LIVEDELICA
CD GEPCD 1015
Giant Electric Pea / Jun '95 / Pinnacle

PSYCHEDELICATESSEN
Sunseeker / Into the light / Under the sun / He is I am / Devoted / Tension of souls / Will to give / Babylon rising / Innocent
CD GEPCD 1014
Giant Electric Pea / Feb '95 / Pinnacle

WOUNDED LAND
Consume to live / Days of dearth / Sanity's end / Paradox / Surface of air / Mother earth / Siege of Baghdad / Keep it with mine
CD GEPCD 1005
Giant Electric Pea / Aug '93 / Pinnacle

Thrilled Skinny

SMELLS A BIT FISHY
CD LOS 3CD
Artlos / Nov '93 / SRD

Thriller U

BEST OF ME, THE
CD WRCD 006
World / Jun '97 / Jet Star / TKO Magnum

LOVE RULE
CD VPCD 1439
VP / Oct '95 / Greensleeves / Jet Star / Total/BMG

THRILLER U & SANCHEZ (Thriller U & Sanchez)
CD RFCD 005
Record Factory / Nov '96 / Jet Star

Thrillhammer

GIFTLESS
Pretty dead girl / Suffocation time / Bad trip / Laughing / Happy anniversary / Motor / Bleed / Magret / Dread / Alice's place / Jinx / Bride
CD RTD 15714012
World Service / Apr '93 / Vital

Throbbin Hoods

AMBUSH
CD BMCD 076
Raw Energy / Jun '95 / Plastic Head

Throbbing Gristle

20 JAZZ FUNK GREATS
CD TGCD 4
The Grey Area / Apr '93 / RTM/Disc

ASSUMING POWER FOCUS
CD PA 016CD
Paragoric / Jan '97 / Cargo / Plastic Head

BLOOD PRESSURE
CD DCD 9048
Dossier / Jan '97 / Cargo / SRD

DOA - THIRD AND FINAL REPORT
CD TGCD 3
The Grey Area / Apr '93 / RTM/Disc

FUNK BEYOND JAZZ
CD EFA 08450CD
Dossier / Nov '93 / Cargo / SRD

GIFTGAS
CD DCD 9058
Dossier / Jan '97 / Cargo / SRD

GRIEF
CD CDTG 24
NMC / Oct '96 / Total/Pinnacle

HEATHEN EARTH
CD TGCD 5
The Grey Area / Apr '93 / RTM/Disc

JOURNEY THROUGH A BODY
CD TGCD 8
The Grey Area / Oct '93 / RTM/Disc

LIVE VOL.1
CD TGCD 10
The Grey Area / Apr '93 / RTM/Disc

LIVE VOL.2
CD TGCD 11
The Grey Area / Apr '93 / RTM/Disc

LIVE VOL.3
CD TGCD 12
The Grey Area / Apr '93 / RTM/Disc

LIVE VOL.4
CD TGCD 13
The Grey Area / Apr '93 / RTM/Disc

MISSION OF DEAD SOULS
CD TGCD 6
The Grey Area / Apr '93 / RTM/Disc

ONCE UPON A TIME
CD OBESSCD 2
Jungle / Oct '94 / RTM/Disc / SRD

SECOND ANNUAL REPORT
CD TGCD 2
The Grey Area / Apr '93 / RTM/Disc

THROBBING GRISTLE
CD TGCD 1
Mute / '88 / RTM/Disc

VERY FRIENDLY
CD CDTG 23
NMC / Oct '96 / Total/Pinnacle

Throne Of Ahaz

NIFELHEIM
CD NFR 008
No Fashion / Oct '94 / Plastic Head

ON TWILIGHT ENTHRONED
CD NFR 016
No Fashion / Jan '97 / Plastic Head

Throneberry

TROT OUT THE ENCORES
On the strobe flume / Spellbinder / Nectarine / Hooray for everything / Unsere serenade / Cut to the chase / Widow / Drops of moxie / New year's routine / Sealboy / Truth serum / Sip of beauty
CD A 086D
Alias / Jan '96 / Vital

Thrones

ALRAUNE
CD COMM 42
Communion / Dec '96 / Cargo

Throw

INVISIBLE DAYLIGHT
CD BUZ 010
Buzz / Feb '97 / Cargo

Throwing Muses

CURSE, THE
Manic depression / Counting backwards / Fish / Hate my way / Furious / Devil's roof / Snailhead / Firepile / Finished / Take / Say goodbye / Mania / Two step / Delicate cutters / Cotton mouth / Pearl / Vic / Bea
CD TAD 2019CD
4AD / Nov '92 / RTM/Disc

HOUSE TORNADO
Colder / Mexican women / River / Juno / Marriage tree / Run letter / Saving grace / Drive / Downtown / Giant / Walking in the dark / Garoux des larmes / Pools in eyes / Feeling / Soap and water / And a she-wolf after the war / You cage
CD CAD 802CD
4AD / Mar '88 / RTM/Disc

HUNKPAPA
Devil's roof / Dizzy / Dragonhead / Fall down / Angel / Burrow / Bea / No parachutes / Say goodbye / I'm alive / Mania / Take / Santa Claus
CD CAD 901CD
4AD / Jan '89 / RTM/Disc

LIMBO
Buzz / Ruthie's knocking / Freeloader / Field / Limbo / Tar kisser / Tango / Serene / Mr. Bones / Night driving / Cowbirds / Shark
CD CAD 6014CD
4AD / Aug '96 / RTM/Disc

REAL RAMONA, THE
Counting backwards / Him dancing / Red shoes / Graffiti / Golden thing / Ellen West / Dylan / Hook in her head / Not too soon / Honeychain / Say goodbye / Two step
CD CAD 1002C
4AD / Feb '91 / RTM/Disc

RED HEAVEN
Furious / Firepile / Dio / Dirty water / Stroll / Pearl / Summer St. / Vic / Backroad / Visit / Dovey / Rosetta stone / Carnival wig
CD CAD 2013CD
4AD / Aug '92 / RTM/Disc

THROWING MUSES
Call me / Green / Hate my way / Vicky's box / Rabbits dying / America (she can't say no) / Fear / Stand up / Soul soldier / Delicate cutters
CD CAD 607CD
4AD / Nov '86 / RTM/Disc

UNIVERSITY
Bright yellow gun / Start / Hazing / Shimmer / Calm down, come down / Crabtown / No way in hell / Surf cowboy / That's all you wanted / Teller / University / Snakeface / Flood / Fever few
CD CADD 5002CD
CD CAD 5002CD
4AD / Jan '95 / RTM/Disc

Thrum

RIFFERAMA
CD FIRECD 38
Fire / Sep '94 / Pinnacle / RTM/Disc

Thulbion

TWILIGHT BOUND
King's reel/The perfect host/Boys of portaferry/Trad reel / Twilight / St. Gilbert's hornpipe/The fiddler's wife/Chromatic hornpipe / Annie / John D Burgess/Major Nickerson's fancy/Dick Gossip's reel / James F Dickie/JF Dickie's delight / Sheilis / Branden's centennial waltz / Waltz for Mary Ann / Raemona / Gravel walk / Andy Renwick's ferret / Old mountain road / Time for thought / Theodore Napier / Laird of Mackintosh / Earl of Lauderdale / Little daisy / North king street / Lady on the island / Killavil reel / Far from home / Paddy on the turnpike / Loretta / Frank and Maureen Robb / Grew's hill / Duncan Black's hornpipe / Doon hingin' tie / Eeles' dream
CD CDTRAX 088
Greentrax / Jan '95 / ADA / Direct / Duncans / Highlander

Thumbnail

RED DEAD
CD HED 064CD
Headhunter / Feb '97 / Cargo

Thunder

BACKSTREET SYMPHONY
She's so fine / Dirty love / Don't wait for me / Higher ground / Until my dying day / Backstreet symphony / Love walked in / Englishman on holiday / Girl's going out of her head / Gimme some lovin' / Distant thunder
CD CDEMC 3570
EMI / Feb '90 / EMI

BACKSTREET SYMPHONY/ BACKSTREET SYMPHONY LIVE (2CD Set)
She's so fine / Dirty love / Don't wait for me / Higher ground / Until my dying day / Backstreet symphony / Love walked in / Englishman on holiday, An / Girl's going out of her head / Gimme some lovin' / Distant thunder / Another shot of love / Girl's going out of her head (live) / Englishman on holiday / Until my dying day (live) / Fired up / Dirty love (live) / She's so fine (live) / Backstreet sym-

phony (live) / Higher ground (live) / Don't wait for me (live)
CD Set TOCP 6729
EMI / Oct '91 / EMI

BEHIND CLOSED DOORS
Moth to the flame / Fly on the wall / I'll be waiting / River of pain / Future train / Till the river runs dry / Stand up / Preaching from a chair / Castles in the sand / Too scared to live / Ball and chain / It happened in this town
CD CDEMD 1076
EMI / Jan '95 / EMI

LAUGHING ON JUDGEMENT DAY
Does it feel like love / Everybody wants her / Low life in high places / Laughing on judgement day / Empty city / Today the world stopped turning / Long way from home / Fire to ice / Feeding the flame / Better man / Moment of truth / Flawed to perfection / Like a satellite / Baby I'll be gone
CD CDEMD 1035
EMI / Feb '94 / EMI

THEIR FINEST HOUR (AND A BIT)
Dirty love / River of pain / Love walked in / Everybody wants her / In a broken dream / Higher ground / Backstreet symphony / Better man / Gimme shelter / Like a satellite / Low life in high places / Stand up / Once in a lifetime / Gimme some lovin' / Castles in the sand / She's so fine
CD CDEMD 1086
EMI / Sep '95 / EMI

THRILL OF IT ALL, THE
Pilot of my dreams / Living for today / Love worth dying for / Don't wait up for me / Something about you / Welcome to the party / Thrill of it all / Hotter than the sun / This forgotten town / Cosmetic punk / You can't live your life
CD RAWCD 115
CD RAWPD 115
Raw Power / Feb '97 / Pinnacle

Thunderballs

SUMMER HOLIDAY
CD SSHD 2
Hush / Jul '94 / Pinnacle

Thundermother

NO RED ROWAN
CD KSG 003
Kissing Spell / Jun '97 / Greyhound

Thunders, Johnny

BOOTLEGGING THE BOOTLEGGERS
You can't put your arms around a memory / Personality crisis / Sad vacation / I can tell / Little queenie / Stepping stone / As tears go by
CD FREUDCD 30
Jungle / Jan '90 / RTM/Disc / SRD

COPY CATS (Thunders, Johnny & Patti Palladin)
CD FREUDCD 20
Jungle / Jun '88 / RTM/Disc / SRD

DTK (Thunders, Johnny & The Heartbreakers)
CD FREUDCD 4
Jungle / Oct '94 / RTM/Disc / SRD

HAVE FAITH (Live In Japan 1988)
Pipeline / Blame it on mom / Personality crisis / I can tell / Who do you love / Spoonful / Joey Joey / You can't put your arms around a memory / Play with five / I only wrote this song for you / Too much junkie business / Chinese rocks / Born to lose
CD ESMCD 453
Essential / Nov '96 / BMG

HURT ME
Sad vacation / Eve of destruction / Too much too soon / Joey Joey / I'm a boy I'm a girl / Go back to go / I like to play games / Hurt me / Illagitammate song of Segovia / It ain't me babe / Diary of a lover / I'd rather be with the boys / You can't put your arms around a memory / She's so untouchable / Ask me no questions / She's so strange / Lonely planet boy / Mia / Cosa nostra
CD ESMCD 588
Essential / Aug '97 / BMG

I ONLY WROTE THIS SONG FOR YOU (A Tribute To Johnny Thunders) (Various Artists)
Leave me alone: *Palladin, Patti* / Disappointed in you: *Monroe, Michael* / In cold blood: *Kane, Arthur* / Children are people too: *Kramer, Wayne* / Some hearts: *Johansen, David* / Society makes me sad: *Sylvian Sylvian* / Just another girl: *Gordy, Alison* / Can't kick: *Filthy Lucre* / You can't put your arms around a memory: *De Ville, Willy* / Diary of a lover: *Die Toten Hosen* / I love you: *Ramones* / Let go: *Lure, Walter & The Waldoes* / So alone: *Monroe, Michael* / Help the homeless: *Screwballs* / Alone in a crowd: *Los Lobos*
CD ESMCD 401
Essential / Jan '97 / BMG

IN COLD BLOOD
In cold blood / Just another girl / Green onions / Diary of a lover / Look in my eyes / Intro/Just another girl / Too much junkie business / Sad vacation / Louie Louie / Gloria / Treat me like a nigger / Do you love me / Green onions / Commandments
CD ESMCD 589
Essential / Aug '97 / BMG

LAMF (The Lost 1977 Mixes) (Thunders, Johnny & The Heartbreakers)
CD FREUDCD 44
Jungle / Sep '96 / RTM/Disc / SRD

LIVE ALBUM
Pipeline / Countdown live / Personality crisis / Little bit of whore / MIA / Stepping stone / So alone / Endless party / Copy cats (live) / Don't mess with cupid / Born to lose / Too much junkie business (live) / Chinese rocks / Pills
CD CDGRAM 70
Anagram / Mar '96 / Cargo / Pinnacle

LIVE AT MAX'S KANSAS CITY (Thunders, Johnny & The Heartbreakers)
Milk me / Chinese rocks / Get off the phone / London / Take a chance / One track mind / All by myself / Let go / I love you / Can't keep my eyes on you / I wanna be loved / Do you love me
CD RUSCD 8219
ROIR / Feb '96 / Plastic Head / Shellshock/Disc

LIVE AT MOTHERS (Thunders, Johnny & The Heartbreakers)
CD 422168
New Rose / May '94 / ADA / Direct / Discovery
CD 422390
Last Call / Feb '97 / Cargo / Direct / Discovery

LIVE IN JAPAN
CD ESDCD 226
Essential / Nov '94 / BMG

QUE SERA SERA
CD FREUDCD 49
Jungle / Nov '94 / RTM/Disc / SRD

STATIONS OF THE CROSS
Wipeout / In cold blood / Just another girl / Too much junkie business / Sad vacation / Who needs girls / Do you love me / So alone / Seven day weekend / Chinese rocks / Re-entry interlude / Voodoo dub / Surfer jam / Just because I'm white / One track mind (dub) / Little London boys / Stepping stone / I don't mind Mr. Kowalski / Creature from ET rap / Rather be with the boys
CD RE 146CD
ROIR / Nov '94 / Plastic Head / Shellshock/Disc

STUDIO BOOTLEGS, THE
CD DOJOCD 231
Dojo / May '96 / Disc

TOO MUCH JUNKIE BUSINESS
CD RE 118CD
ROIR / Nov '94 / Plastic Head / Shellshock/Disc

Thundersteel

THUNDERSTEEL
CD BMCD 53
Black Mark / Aug '94 / Plastic Head

Thuresson, Svante

LIVE
CD SITCD 9203
Sittel / Aug '94 / Cadillac / Jazz Music

Thurman

LUX
She's a man / English tea / Cheap holiday / Famous / Clowns / It would be / Now I'm a man / Flavour explosion / Lewis Brightworth / Automatic thinker / Talk to myself / Strung out / Untitled
CD RIGHT 005CD
Righteous / Oct '95 / Vital

Thurston, Bobby

YOU GOT WHAT IT TAKES/THE MAIN ATTRACTION
You got what it takes / I wanna do it with you / Check out the groove / I want your body / Sittin' in the park / Is something wrong with you / Main attraction / Love makes it complete / Keep it going / I know you feel like I feel / Very last drop / I really didn't mean it / Life is what you make it
CD DEEPM 026
Deep Beats / Apr '97 / BMG

Thy Serpent

THY SERPENT
CD SPI 036CD
Spinefarm / Sep '96 / Plastic Head

Ti Jaz

EN CONCERT
CD Y225027
Silex / Jun '93 / ADA / Harmonia Mundi

MUSIQUE BRETONNE AUJOURD 'HUI
CD Y 225027CD
Silex / Aug '93 / ADA / Harmonia Mundi

MUSIQUES DE BASSE BRETAGNE
CD MWCD 4005
Music & Words / Jul '94 / ADA / Direct

REVES SAUVAGES
CD CD 834
Diffusion Breizh / May '93 / ADA

Tia

TIA
CD ICHI 11872
Ichiban / Jul '96 / Direct / Koch

TIA'S SIMCHA SONGS
CD GV 167CD
Global Village / May '94 / ADA / Direct

Tiajin Buddhist Music ...

BUDDHIST MUSIC OF TIANJIN (Tiajin Buddhist Music Ensemble)
CD NI 5416
Nimbus / Mar '95 / Nimbus

Tiamat

ASTRAL SLEEP, THE
CD CM 97222
Century Media / Sep '94 / Plastic Head

DEEPER KIND OF SLUMBER
CD CM 77180
Century Media / Apr '97 / Plastic Head

SLEEPING BEAUTY, THE (Remix)
CD CM 770652
Century Media / May '94 / Plastic Head

SUMERIAN CRY
CD CORE 009CD
Metalcore / Jan '92 / Plastic Head

WILDHONEY
CD CM 77080CD
Century Media / Oct '94 / Plastic Head

Tibbetts, Steve

BIG MAP IDEA
Black mountain side / Black year / Big idea / Wish / Station / Start / Mile 234 / 100 moons / Wait / Three letters
CD 8392532
ECM / Oct '89 / New Note/Pinnacle

EXPLODED VIEW
Name everything / Another year / Clear day / Your cat / Forget / Drawing down the moon / X festival / Metal summer / Assembly field
CD 8311092
ECM / Jan '87 / New Note/Pinnacle

FALL OF US ALL, THE
Dzogchen punks / Full moon dogs / Nyemma / Formless / Roam and spy / Hellbound train / All for nothing / Fade away / Drinking lesson / Burnt offering / Travel alone
CD 5211442
ECM / Apr '94 / New Note/Pinnacle

NORTHERN SONG
Form walking / Big wind / Aerial view / Nine doors, breathing space
CD 8293782
ECM / Oct '89 / New Note/Pinnacle

SAFE JOURNEY
Test / Climbing / Running / Night again / My last chance / Vision / Any minute / Mission / Burning up / Going somewhere
CD 8174382
ECM / Oct '89 / New Note/Pinnacle

YR
UR / Sphexes / Ten years / One day / Three primates / You and it / Alien lounge / Ten year dance
CD 8352452
ECM / Aug '88 / New Note/Pinnacle

Tibet, David

MUSICAL PUMPKIN COTTAGE (Tibet, David & Steven Stapleton)
CD UDORCD 1
United Durtro / Oct '96 / World Serpent

SADNESS OF THINGS, THE (Tibet, David & Steven Stapleton)
CD UD 037CD
United Dairies / Oct '96 / World Serpent

Tibetan Dixie

NOTHING TOO SERIOUS
CD LRJ 263
Larrikin / Oct '93 / ADA / CM / Direct / Roots

Tickell, Kathryn

BORDERLANDS
Mary the maid / David's hornpipe / Sidlaw Hills / Brafferton Village / Stellgreen / Loch rannoch / Gypsy's lullaby / Flowers of the forest / Alston flower show / Claudio's Polka / Tents hornpipe / Walker / Lord Gordon's reel / Robson / Roly gentle / Troy's wedding / Tartar frigate / Wark football team
CD CROCD 210
Black Crow / Feb '89 / CM / Roots

COMMON GROUND
Walsh's hornpipe / Dorrington lads / Richard Moscrop's waltzes / Another knight / Mrs. Bolowski's / Neil Gow's lament / Andrew Knight's favourite / Shining pool / Outclassed / Glen Aln / Bill Charlton's fancy / Fenham / Catch a penny fox / Bowmont water / Geoff Heslop's reel / New rigged ship / Remember me / Rafferty's reel / Wild hills o' Wannies
CD CROCD 220
Black Crow / Feb '89 / CM / Roots

GATHERING, THE
Raincheck / Lads of Alnwick / Sunderland lasses / Peacocks march / Redesdale / La bettaille dans le petit arbre acharavi waltz / Gathering / Kates house / Real blues reel / St. Kilda wedding pjotr / Green brechans O'Branton / I saw my love / Tune for Matt Robson / Kathleen / Mr Nelson's birthday waltz
CD PRKCD 39
Park / Mar '97 / Pinnacle

KATHRYN TICKELL BAND
CD CROCD 227
Black Crow / Jun '91 / CM / Roots

NORTHUMBRIAN SMALL PIPES & FIDDLE
CD CDSDL 343
Saydisc / Oct '92 / ADA / Direct / Harmonia Mundi

SIGNS
CD CROCD 230
Black Crow / Mar '94 / CM / Roots

Tickell, Mike

WARKSBURN (Tickell, Mike/Kathryn Tickell/Martin Simpson)
CD CROCD 229
Black Crow / Dec '94 / CM / Roots

Tickled Pink

TICKLED PINK
CD PINK 9301CD
Pink Kitten / Jan '94 / ADA

Tickmayer Formatio

WILHELM DANCES
CD RERTFCD
ReR/Recommended / Oct '96 / ReR Megacorp / RTM/Disc

Tielman Brothers

DIE SINGLES
Tahiti jungle / Fern am Amazonas / Java guitars / Warum wenst du, kleine Tamara / Little Hans'chen twist / Twistin' the Carioca / Hello Caterina / Say you are mine / No one but you / You are the one / Little lovely lady / Warte ab darling Rosmarie / Maria / I wonder / White Christmas / Exodus / Marabunta / Real love / Michelle / Du gehst voruber / Wanderer ohne Ziel / Viel zu spat / You've got too much going / Can't help falling in love
CD BCD 15918
Bear Family / May '96 / Direct / Rollercoaster / Swift

Tieng Hat Que Huong ...

FROM SAIGON TO HANOI (Tieng Hat Que Huong Instrumental Ensemble)
CD 74321301092
Milan / May '96 / Conifer/BMG / Silva Screen

Tiermes

TIERMES
CD SGA 011CD
Misanthropy / Nov '96 / Plastic Head

Tierra Caliente

MESTIZA
CD MWCD 3005
Music & Words / Aug '94 / ADA / Direct

Tierre Sur

AMOR AND REBELLION
CD CD 9402
Roots Collective / May '95 / Jet Star / Roots Collective / SRD

Tiger

BAM BAM
CD RASCD 3042
Ras / Sep '88 / Direct / Greensleeves / Jet Star / SRD

LOVE AFFAIR
CD RRTGCD 7787
Rohit / Jul '90 / Jet Star

ME NAME TIGER
CD RASCD 3021
Ras / '88 / Direct / Greensleeves / Jet Star / SRD

RAM DANCEHALL
CD VPCD 1052
VP / '89 / Greensleeves / Jet Star / Total/BMG

RAS PORTRAITS
No wanga gut / Bam bam / Puppy love / Don't be greedy / Decent man / Rough and cool / Me name tiger / Tiger talking / Dreadie and baldhead / Do it anyway
CD RAS 3315

Ras / Jul '97 / Direct / Greensleeves / Jet Star / SRD

TOUCH IS A MOVE
CD _____ CIDM 1056
Mango / Aug '90 / PolyGram / Vital

Tiger

WE ARE PUPPETS
My puppet pal / Shamed all over / Race / Bollinger farm / Storm injector / Depot / On the rose / Sorry monkeys / Cateader reddle / She's ok / Ray Travey / Keep in touch
CD _____ TRDCD 1002
Trade 2 / Nov '96 / PolyGram / RTM/Disc / Vital

Tiger B. Smith

TIGER B. SMITH
CD _____ SB 036
Second Battle / Jun '97 / Greyhound

Tiger Lillies

BIRTHS, DEATHS & MARRIAGES
Beatman / Hell / Normal / Heroin and cocaine / Prison house blues / Jackie / Despite / Autumn leaves / Lager lout / Open your legs / Down and out / Tears / Her room / Flowers / War / Obscene / You're world / Sense of sentiment / Wake up / Repulsion / Sodsville / Bones / Circle line / Haunting me / Lili Marlene
CD _____ TIGER 1
Gee Street / Jul '94 / PolyGram

Tiger Moth

MOTHBALLS
CD _____ OMM 2012CD
Omnium / Aug '96 / ADA

Tigerlilies USA

SPACE AGE LOVE SONGS
CD _____ ALP 307
CD _____ TRUCK 07CD
Truckstop / Jun '97 / SRD

Tigertailz

BEZERK
Sick sex / Love bomb baby / I can fight dirty too / Noise level critical / Heaven / Love overload / Action city / Twist and shake / Squeeze it dry / Call of the wild
CD _____ CDMFN 96
Music For Nations / Jan '90 / Pinnacle

TIGERTAILZ LIVE IN CONCERT
CD _____ MIN 06CD
Minority/One / Oct '96 / Pinnacle

YOUNG AND CRAZY
Star attraction / Hollywood killer / Living without you / Shameless / City kids / Shoot to kill / Turn me on / She's too hot / Young and crazy / Fall in love again
CD _____ CDMFN 78
Music For Nations / Aug '89 / Pinnacle

Tight Fit

BACK TO THE 60'S (60 Non Stop Dancing Hits)
CD _____ CDMFP 6075
Music For Pleasure / Aug '89 / EMI

BACK TO THE 60'S
Lion sleeps tonight / Dancing in the street / Satisfaction / You really got me / All day and all of the night / Do wah diddy diddy / Pretty flamingo / Back is black / Bend me, shape me / High in the sky / Mr. Tambourine man / Proud Mary / O pretty woman / Letter / Baby let me take you home / Baby come back / How do you do it / I like it / Tossing and turning / Hippy hippy shake / Mony mony / Let's hang on / Sherry / Big girls don't cry / Walk like a man / Rag doll / Dawn / Yes I will / Stay / Just one look / Here I go again / I'm alive / There's a kind of hush / No milk today / Must to avoid / Hold tight / Legend of Xanadu / Sweets for my sweet / Sugar and spice / When you walk in the room / Needles and pins / Fantasy island
CD _____ 5501172
Spectrum / Oct '93 / PolyGram

BEST OF TIGHT FIT, THE
Lion sleeps tonight / Dancing in the street/ I can't get no satisfaction/really got / Do wah diddy diddy / Black is black / Bend me shape me / When you walk in the room / Mony mony / Fantasy island / Lovers concerto / Secret heart / I'm undecided / Just a moment away / Heart of stone break hearts of glass / Love the one you're with / One two three / One thing leads to another / Magic eyes / Baby I'm lost for words / Let's hang on / Sherry / Big girls don't cry / Walk like a man / Rag doll / Dawn (go away) / Yes I will / Stay / Just one look / Here I go again / I'm alive / There's a kind of hush (all over the world) / No milk today / Must to avoid / Hold tight / Legend of xanadu / Sweets for my sweet / Sugar and spice / When you walk in the room / Needles and pins
CD _____ EMPRCD 570
Emporio / May '95 / Disc

Tikaram, Tanita

ANCIENT HEART
Good tradition / Cathedral song / Sighing innocents / I love you / World outside your window / For all these years / Twist in my sobriety / Poor cow / He likes the sun / Valentine heart / Preyed upon
CD _____ 2438772
WEA / Feb '95 / Warner Music

BEST OF TANITA TIKARAM, THE
CD _____ 0630151062
East West / Sep '96 / Warner Music

EVERYBODY'S ANGEL
Only the ones we love / Deliver me / This story in me / To wish this / Mud in any water / Sunface / Never known / This stranger / Swear by me / Hot pork sandwiches / Me in mind / Sometime with me / I love the heaven's solo / I'm going home
CD _____ 9031734982
East West / Feb '91 / Warner Music

LOVERS IN THE CITY
CD _____ 4509988042
East West / Dec '96 / Warner Music

SWEET KEEPER
Once and not speak / It all come back today / Sunset's arrived / I owe all to you / Harm in your hands / Thursday's child / We almost got it together / Little sister leaving town / Love story
CD _____ 9031708002
East West / '89 / Warner Music

Til, Sonny

SOLO FEATURING EDNA MCGRIFF
My prayer / I never knew (I could love anybody) / Fool's world / You never cared for me / For all we know / Blame it on yourself / Proud of you / No other love / Night has come / I only have eyes for you: *Til, Sonny & Edna McGriff* / Once in a while: *Til, Sonny & Edna McGriff* / Good: *Til, Sonny & Edna McGriff* / Pick-a-dilly: *Til, Sonny & Edna McGriff* / That's how I feel without you: *Til, Sonny & Edna McGriff* / Lovebirds: *Til, Sonny & Edna McGriff* / Congratulations to someone / (Danger) Soft shoulders / Have you heard / Lonely wine / Come on home / First of Summer / Panama Joe / Night and day / Shimmy time / So long
CD _____ NEMCD 737
Sequel / Mar '95 / BMG

Til Tuesday

COMING UP CLOSE: A RETROSPECTIVE
Love in a vacuum / I could get used to this / Voices carry / You know the rest / No one is watching you now / On Sunday / Coming up close / Will she just fall down / David denies / What about love / Why must I / Other end of the telescope / J for Jules / (Believed you were) Lucky / Limits to love / Long gone buddy / Do it again
CD _____ 4851132
Epic / Oct '96 / Sony

Tilbury, John

DAVE SMITH'S FIRST PIANO CONCERT
CD _____ MR 14
Matchless / '90 / Cadillac / ReR Megacorp

Tillet, Louis

CAST OF ASPERSIONS, A
CD _____ CGAS 812CD
Citadel / May '94 / ADA / Direct

EGO TRIPPING AT THE GATES OF HELL
CD _____ CGAS 802CD
Citadel / May '94 / ADA / Direct

LETTERS TO A DREAM
CD _____ CGAS 816CD
Citadel / May '94 / ADA / Direct

MIDNIGHT RAIN
CD _____ RTS 18
Return To Sender / Aug '95 / ADA / Direct

RETURN TO SENDER FESTIVAL TOUR
CD _____ NORMAL 175CD
Normal / Nov '94 / ADA / Direct

UGLY TRUTH
CD _____ RTS 5
Normal / Jul '94 / ADA / Direct

Tillis, Pam

ALL OF THIS LOVE
Deep down / Mandolin rain / Sunset red and pale moonlight / It's lonely out there / River and the highway / You can't have a good time without me / Betty's got a bass boat / Tequila mockingbird / No two ways about it / All of this love
CD _____ 07822187992
Arista / Nov '95 / BMG

GREATEST HITS
Land of the living / All the good ones are gone / Don't tell me what to do / Maybe it was Memphis / Shake the sugar tree / Let that pony run / Cleopatra, queen of denial / Spilled perfume / When you walk in the room / In between dances / Mi vida loca (my crazy life) / River and the highway
CD _____ 07822188362
Arista / May '97 / BMG

HOMEWARD LOOKING ANGEL
How gone is goodbye / Shake the sugar tree / Do you know where your man is / Cleopatra, Queen of denial / Love is only human: *Tillis, Pam & Marty Roe* / Rough and tumble heart / Let that pony run / Fine, fine, very fine love / We've tried everything else / Homeward looking angel
CD _____ 07822186492
Arista / Oct '93 / BMG

SWEETHEART'S DANCE
CD _____ 07822187582
Arista / Apr '95 / BMG

Tillotson, Johnny

ALL HIS EARLY HITS - AND MORE
Poetry in motion / It keeps right on a-hurtin' / Send me the pillow that you dream on / Without you / You can never stop me loving you / We'll I'm your man / Dreamy eyes / True true happiness / Love is blind / Why do I love you so / Never let me go / Earth angel / Pledging my love / Princess, princess / Jimmy's girl / (Little sparrow) his true love said goodbye / Cutie pie / She gave sweet love to me / What'll I do / I can't help it (if I'm still in love with you) / I'm so lonesome I could cry / Out of my mind / Empty feeling / Judy Judy Judy / Funny how time slips away / Very good year for girls / Lonely street / I got a feeling / Lonesome town / I fall to pieces
CD _____ CDCHD 946
Ace / Jul '90 / Pinnacle

FABULOUS JOHNNY TILLOTSON, THE
Poetry in motion / It keeps right on a-hurtin' / Dreamy eyes / True true happiness / Why do I love you so / Jimmy's girl / Without you / Send me the pillow that you dream on / I can't help it (if I'm still in love with you) / Out of my mind / You can never stop me loving you / Funny how time slips away
CD _____ CDFAB 003
Ace / Aug '91 / Pinnacle

HIT SINGLE COLLECTABLES
CD _____ DISK 4507
Disky / Apr '94 / Disky / THE

SHE UNDERSTANDS ME/THAT'S MY STYLE
She understands me / That's love / Busted / Willow tree / Tomorrow / Little boy / To be a child again / That's when it hurts the most / More than before / Island of dreams / Yellow bird / Take this hammer / Heartaches by the number / Without your sweet lips on mine / Countin' my teardrops / You don't want my love / Just one time / Race is on / Things / Me, myself and I / Oh, lonesome me / Then I'll count again / I've seen better days / Your mem'ry comes along
CD _____ CDCHD 345
Ace / Feb '92 / Pinnacle

TALK BACK TREMBLING LIPS/THE TILLOTSON TOUCH
Talk back trembling lips / Blue velvet / Danke schon / What am I gonna do / My little world / I can't stop loving you / Worried guy / Another you / Rhythm of the rain / All alone am I / Please don't go away / Blowin' in the wind / I rise, I fall / On the sunny side of the street / Then you can tell me goodbye / This ole house / Suff'rin from a heartache / I've got you under my skin / Worry / I'm watching my watch / When I lost you / Always / Cold cold heart / Jailer bring me water
CD _____ CDCHD 331
Ace / Aug '91 / Pinnacle

YOU'RE THE REASON
Talk back trembling lips / Another you / Worried guy / Please don't go away / I rise, I fall / Worry / Heartaches by the number / She understands me / Angel / Suff'rin from a heartache / (Wait 'till you see) My gidget / No love at all / More than before / Blue velvet / You're the reason / Dreamy eyes / Red roses for a blue lady / When I lost you / Oh, lonesome me / Danke schoen / It keeps right on hurtin' / Then you can tell me goodbye / Things / All alone am I / Cold, cold heart / Always / Without you / Race is on / I can't stop loving you / Rhythm of the rain
CD _____ CDCH 618
Ace / Jan '96 / Pinnacle

Tilston, Steve

ALL UNDER THE SUN (Tilston, Steve & Maggie Boyle)
Let your banjo ring / Maid with the bonny brown hair / Here's to Tom Paine / Fair Annie / Man gone down (Fred's song) / Linden Lea / Cage / Navvy / Dark days of war / Willie the ploughboy / Threepenny bit / Fool such as I
CD _____ CDFF 663
Flying Fish / Sep '96 / ADA / CM / Direct / Roots

AND SO IT GOES
CD _____ HR 01CD
Hubris / Jul '95 / ADA

MUSIC OF O'CAROLAN, THE (Tilston, Steve & Duck Baker/Maggie Boyle/Ali Anderson)
CD _____ SHAN 97023CD
Shanachie / Aug '93 / ADA / Greensleeves / Koch

OF MOOR AND MESA (Tilston, Steve & Maggie Boyle)
CD _____ GLCD 3087
Green Linnet / Feb '95 / ADA / CM / Direct / Highlander / Roots

Tilt

I PUT A SMELL ON YOU
CD _____ EFA 125412
Celtic Circle / Dec '95 / SRD

TILL IT KILLS
CD _____ FAT 521CD
Fatwreck Chords / Jun '95 / Plastic Head

Timber

PARTS AND LABOR
There's always 1 and 9 / At the same time / I'm 30, I'm having a heart attack / Evidence is shifting / Bad education / Belay that / Crankcase / Fatal flaw / Move / Real NY / Stupid reasons / Deer slayer / Reversile fortune / Puddle / Robins make eggs blus / Passage from Pakistan / Acid test/ Pads / Sugary peppery
CD _____ R 3142
Rift / Mar '94 / Pinnacle

Timbuk 3

LIVE
CD _____ WM 1012
Watermelon / Jun '93 / ADA / Direct

Time

TIME/SMOOTH BALL
Take me along / Make it right / Let the colours keep on / Trippin' into sunshine / Love you, cherish you / You changed it all / Make love to you / Finders keepers / What can it be / I can't find it / Label it love / Preparation G / Leavin' my home / See me as i am / I think you'd cry / I'll write a song / Lazy day blues / Do you feel it / Flowers / Morning come / Trust in men everywhere
CD _____ C5HCD 643
See For Miles/C5 / Jun '96 / Pinnacle

Time 1010

TIME 1010
CD _____ TIME 1010
Time / Apr '94 / Jet Star / Pinnacle

Time Bomb '77

PROTECT AND SERVE
CD _____ GMM 112
GMM / Jun '97 / Cargo

Time Frequency

DOMINATION
CD _____ KGBD 500
Internal Affairs / Jun '94 / Pinnacle

Time Shard

HUNAB KU
CD _____ BARKCD 018
Planet Dog / May '96 / Pinnacle

Timeless All Stars

ESSENCE
CD _____ DCD 4006
Delos / '88 / Nimbus

Times

ALTERNATIVE COMMERCIAL CROSSOVER
Obligatory grunge song / Finnegans break / How honest are Pearl Jam / Sweetest girl / Ballad of Georgie Best / Lundi bleu / Palace in the sun / Sorry, I've written a melody / Finnegans break (Corporate rock mix) / Whole world's turning scarface / All I want is you to care
CD _____ CRECD 137
Creation / Apr '93 / 3mv/Vital

BEAT TORTURE
CD _____ CRECD 038
Creation / May '94 / 3mv/Vital

E FOR EDWARD
CD _____ CRECD 053
Creation / Oct '89 / 3mv/Vital

ENJOY/UP AGAINST IT
CD _____ CREV 029CD
Rev-Ola / Nov '93 / 3mv/Vital

ET DIEU CREA LA FEMME
Septieme ciel / Chagrin d'amour / Baisers voles / Sucette / Extase / Aurore boreale / Volupte / Pour Kylie / 1990 Anee erotique
CD _____ CRECD 070
Creation / May '94 / 3mv/Vital

I HELPED PATRICK MCGOOHAN ESCAPE
Big painting / Stranger than fiction / Danger man / I helped Patrick McGoohan escape / All systems are go / Up against it

CD ________ CREV 006CD
Rev-Ola / Nov '92 / 3mv/Vital

LIVE AT THE ASTRADOME
CD ________ CRECD 123
Creation / Apr '92 / 3mv/Vital

PINK BALL, BROWN BALL, RED BALL
CD ________ CRECD 073
Creation / Jul '91 / 3mv/Vital

PURE
CD ________ CRECD 091
Creation / Mar '91 / 3mv/Vital

Timeshard

CRYSTAL OSCILLATIONS
CD ________ BARKCD 004
Planet Dog / Jun '94 / Pinnacle

Timewriter

LETTERS FROM THE JESTER
CD ________ PLACCD 006
Plastic City UK / Jun '97 / Intergroove / Prime

Timmons, Bobby

BORN TO BE BLUE (Timmons, Bobby Trio)
Born to be blue / Malice towards none / Sometimes I feel like a Motherless child / Know not one / Sit-in / Namely you / Often Annie
CD ________ OJCCD 873
Original Jazz Classics / Jun '96 / Complete/ Pinnacle / Jazz Music / Wellard

SOUL MAN, THE
Cut me loose Charlie / Tom Thumb / Ein bahn strasse / Damned I know / Tenaj / Little waltz
CD ________ PRCD 7465
Prestige / Jun '96 / Cadillac / Complete/ Pinnacle

THIS HERE IS BOBBY TIMMONS
CD ________ OJCCD 104
Original Jazz Classics / Oct '92 / Complete/Pinnacle / Jazz Music / Wellard

Timms, Sally

COWBOY SALLY
CD ________ BS 016CDEP
Bloodshot / Jun '97 / Cargo

Timmy T

TIME AFTER TIME
CD ________ TIMCD 1
Dino / Jul '91 / Pinnacle

Timoteo, Chiquinho

LA GUITARE BRESILIENNE DE CHIQUINHO TIMOTEO
CD ________ KAR 988
IMP / Nov '96 / ADA / Discovery

Tin Machine

TIN MACHINE
Heaven's in here / Tin machine / Prisoner of love / Crack city / I can't read / Under the God / Amazing / Working class hero / Bus stop / Pretty thing / Video crime / Run / Sacrifice yourself / Baby can dance / Bus stop (live country version)
CD ________ CDVUS 99
Virgin / Nov '95 / EMI

Tin Pots

DREAMS & NIGHTMARES
CD ________ TP 3
Tin Pot Productions / Apr '95 / SRD

Tinandari Male Chorus

GEORGIAN POLYPHONY VOL.3
CD ________ VICG 52252
JVC World Library / Mar '96 / ADA / CM / Direct

Tindersticks

CURTAINS
Another night in / Rented rooms / Don't look down / Dick's slow song / Fast one / Ballad of Tindersticks / Dancing / Let's pretend / Desperate man / Buried bones / Bearsuit / (Tonight) Are you trying to fall in love again / I was your man / Bathtime / Walking
CD ________ 5243442
This Way Up / Jun '97 / PolyGram / SRD

LIVE AT THE BLOOMSBURY
El diabolo en el ojo / Night in / Talk to me / She's gone / My sister / No more affairs / City slickers / Sleepy song / Jism / Drunk-tank / Mistakes / Tiny tears / Raindrops / For those
CD ________ 5285972
This Way Up / Sep '95 / PolyGram / SRD

NENETTE ET BONI (Original Soundtracks)
Ma souer / La Passerelle / Les gateaux / Camions / Nenette est la / Petites chiennes / Nosterfrau / Petites gouttes d'eau / Les Cannes a peche / La mort de Felix / Nenette s'en va / Les bebes / Les fleurs / Rumba
CD ________ 5243002
This Way Up / Oct '96 / PolyGram / SRD

SECOND ALBUM
El Diablo en El Ojo / Night in / My sister / Tiny tears / Snowy in F# minor / Seaweed / Vertrauen 2 / Talk to me / No more affairs / Singing / Travelling light / Cherry blossoms / She's gone / Mistakes / Vertrauen 3 / Sleepy song
CD ________ 5263032
This Way Up / Jun '97 / PolyGram / SRD

TINDERSTICKS, THE
Nectar / Tyed / Sweet sweet man / Whiskey and water / Blood / City sickness / Patchwork / Marbles / Walt blues / Milky teeth / Jism / Piano song / Tie dye / Raindrops / Her / Tea stain / Drunk tank / Paco de Renaldo's dream / Not knowing
CD ________ 5183062
This Way Up / Jun '97 / PolyGram / SRD

Ting, Li Xiang

SOUL OF CHINA
CD ________ CDSV 1337
Voyager / Jun '93 / Discovery

Tingstad, Eric

PASTORALE (Tingstad, Eric & Nancy Rumbel)
Elysian fields / Guinevere's lament / Jester / Savannah / Bouraree / Country dance / Roses and lace / Pastorale / Fisherman's dream / Chapel in the valley / Reverence
CD ________ ND 61061
Narada / May '97 / ADA / New Note/ Pinnacle

SENSE OF PLACE, A
Appalachia calling / Monogahela / Sense of place / Spirit of Rydal Mount / Magnolia / Sovereign of the sea / Castle by the lough / Sissinghurst / American blend / Craftsman / Moonlight blue
CD ________ ND 61048
Narada / Jul '95 / ADA / New Note/Pinnacle

STAR OF WONDER (Tingstad, Eric & Nancy Rumbel)
CD ________ ND 61043
Narada / Oct '94 / ADA / New Note/ Pinnacle

Tinkerbell's Dope Ring

BEETMAKESPITPINK
CD ________ FLOP 2
Floppy / Jul '93 / Plastic Head

Tintino

SALSA PA' ABIDJAN
CD ________ 3021672
Arcade / Jul '97 / Discovery

Tiny Monroe

LITTLE VOLCANOES
She / Cream bun / Love of the bottle / Open invitation / Snake in the grass / Vhf 855v / Brittle bones / Secret place / Skin bleach / Women in love / Bubble
CD ________ 8288042
Laurel / Jul '96 / Pinnacle / PolyGram

Tiny Monsters

LIGHTING AT THE END
CD ________ 303233
TM / May '97 / Greyhound

Tiny Tim

CHRISTMAS ALBUM
Rudolph the red nosed reindeer / All I want for Christmas is my two front teeth / That's what I want for Christmas / I saw Mommy kissing Santa Claus / White Christmas / Christmas song / O holy night / Silent night / Medley / Rainbow on the river / Mission bell / What a friend we have in Jesus
CD ________ ROUCD 9054
Rounder / Nov '96 / ADA / CM / Direct
CD ________ DURTRO 029CD
Durtro / Oct '96 / World Serpent

IMPOTENT TROUBADOUR
CD ________ DURTRO 026CD
Durtro / Oct '96 / World Serpent

LIVE IN LONDON
CD ________ DURTRO 034CD
Durtro / Apr '97 / World Serpent

PRISONER OF LOVE
CD ________ VRP 005
Vinyl Retent / Jul '97 / Greyhound

RESURRECTION - TIPTOE THROUGH THE TULIPS
Tiptoe through the tulips / Sweet Rosie O'Grady / Shine on harvest moon / Baby face / Till we meet again / It's a long way to Tipperary / Prisoner of love / Those were the days / Pennies from Heaven / When you wore a tulip / Tiny bubbles / When the saints go marching in / Just a gigolo / Happy days are here again / Bill Bailey, won't you please come home
CD ________ BCD 15409
Bear Family / Dec '87 / Direct / Rollercoaster / Swift

Tippa Irie

IS IT REALLY HAPPENING TO ME
Unlucky burglar / It's good to have the feeling you're the best / You're the best / Telephone / Heartbeat / Robotic reggae / Married life / Football hooligan / Complain neighbour / Hello darling / Is it really happening to me
CD ________ TIPCD 1
Greensleeves / Sep '86 / Jet Star / SRD

MR. VERSATILE
CD ________ DTJCD 004
Jammin' / Jun '97 / Grapevine/PolyGram / Jet Star

REBEL ON THE ROOTS CORNER
CD ________ ARICD 091
Ariwa Sounds / Dec '93 / Jet Star / SRD

Tippett, Keith

COUPLE IN SPIRIT II (Tippett, Keith & Julie)
Together / Rain-bow
CD ________ ASCCD 12
ASC / Aug '97 / Cadillac / New Note/ Pinnacle

FRAMES (Music For An Imaginary Film/ 2CD Set) (Tippett, Keith Ark)
CD Set ________ OGCD 010/011
Ogun / May '96 / Cadillac / Jazz Music / Wellard

MUJICIAN VOL.3 (August Air)
CD ________ FMPCD 12
FMP / Feb '89 / Cadillac

Tipsy

TRIP TEASE (The Seductive Sequences Of Tipsy)
CD ________ EFA 709672
Asphodel / Jan '97 / Cargo / SRD

Tipton, Glenn

BAPTIZM OF FIRE
Hard core / Paint it black / Enter the storm / Fuel me up / Extinct / Baptizm of fire / Healer / Cruise control / Kill or be killed / Voodoo brother / Left for dead
CD ________ 7567829742
Atlantic / Mar '97 / Warner Music

Tir Na Nog

STRONG IN THE SUN
Free ride / Teesside / Strong in the sun / Wind was high / In the morning / Love lost / Most magical / Fall of day
CD ________ EDCD 336
Edsel / Oct '91 / Pinnacle

TEAR AND A SMILE, THE
CD ________ EDCD 334
Edsel / Sep '91 / Pinnacle

TIR NA NOG
Time is like a promise / Mariner blues / Daisy lady / Tir na nog / Aberdeen Angus / Looking up / Boat song / Our love will not decay / Hey friend / Dance of years / Live a day / Piccadilly / Dante
CD ________ BGOCD 53
Beat Goes On / '89 / Pinnacle

Tiramakhan Ensemble

SONGS FROM GAMBIA
CD ________ SOW 90128
Sounds Of The World / Sep '94 / Target/ BMG

Tirta Sari Ensenble

GAMELAN SEMARPEGULINGAN
CD ________ VICG 50242
JVC World Library / Feb '96 / ADA / CM / Direct

Tit Wrench

8-11-96 (Live)
CD ________ VC 106
Vinyl Communication / Jan '97 / Cargo / Greyhound / Plastic Head

Titan Force

WINNER/LOSER
CD ________ SHARK 021CD
Shark / '92 / Plastic Head

Titiyo

THIS IS
This is / Back and forth / Hot gold / Deep down underground / Make my day / Way you make me feel / Spinnin' / Human climate / Defended / Never let me go / Man in the moon
CD ________ 74321188822
RCA / Jan '94 / BMG

Tittle, Jimmy

GREATEST HITS
CD ________ 473924 2
Dixie Frog / Aug '93 / Direct / TKO Magnum

IT'S IN THE ATTITUDE
CD ________ DFGCD 8438
Dixie Frog / Jun '96 / Direct / TKO Magnum

Titus Groan

TITUS GROAN...PLUS
It wasn't for you / Hall of bright carvings / Liverpool / I can't change / It's all up with us / Fuschia / Open the door homer / Woman of the world
CD ________ SEECD 260
See For Miles/C5 / Sep '89 / Pinnacle

Tjader, Cal

A FUEGO VIVO
CD ________ CCD 4176
Concord Jazz / Jul '88 / New Note/ Pinnacle

BLACK ORCHID
Mi china / Close your eyes / Mambo at the "M" / Contigo / Bonita / Lady is a tramp / Black orchid / Happiness is a thing called Joe / I've waited so long / Out of nowhere / Guajira at the blackhawk / I want to be happy / Nearness of you / Pete Kelly's blues / Minor goof / Undecided / Philadelphia mambo / Flamingo / Stompin' at the savoy / Laura / Lullaby of birdland
CD ________ FCD 24730
Fantasy / Jun '94 / Jazz Music / Pinnacle / Wellard

GOOD VIBES
Guarachi guaro / Doxy / Shoshana / Speak low / Broadway / Cuban fantasy / Good vibes
CD ________ CCD 4247
Concord Picante / Apr '90 / New Note/ Pinnacle

HERE AND THERE
Guarabe / Where is love / This masquerade / Reza / Black orchid / El muchacho / Tu crees que / Liz Anne / Morning / Here / If
CD ________ FCD 24743
Fantasy / Aug '96 / Jazz Music / Pinnacle / Wellard

JAZZ MASTERS
CD ________ 5218582
Verve / Apr '94 / PolyGram

LA ONDA VA BIEN
CD ________ CCD 4113
Concord Jazz / '88 / New Note/Pinnacle

MAMBO WITH TJADER
CD ________ OJCCD 271
Original Jazz Classics / Nov '95 / Complete/Pinnacle / Jazz Music / Wellard

MONTEREY CONCERTS
CD ________ PCD 24026
Pablo / Oct '93 / Cadillac / Complete/ Pinnacle

SENTIMENTAL MOODS
I should care / Spring is here / Time was / Star eyes / Stella by starlight / Alone together / Ode to a beat generation / Skylark / Martha / Quizas quizas quizas / Running out / Racoon Strait / Last luff / Sigmund Stern groove / Coit tower / Triple T blues / Union Square / Skyline waltz / Viva capeda / Grant Avenue suite
CD ________ FCD 24742
Fantasy / Aug '96 / Jazz Music / Pinnacle / Wellard

SOUL SAUCE
Soul sauce / Soul bird / Spring is here / Tanya / Joao / Maramoor mambo / Pantano / Somewhere is the night / Afro blue / Triste / Whiffenpoof song / Leyte / Mamblues / Curacao
CD ________ CD 62073
Saludos Amigos / Jan '96 / Target/BMG

TALKIN' VERVE (The Roots Of Acid Jazz)
CD ________ 5315622
Verve / Jun '96 / PolyGram

TKO

BELOW THE BELT
CD ________ RR 349730
Roadrunner / '89 / PolyGram

TLC

CRAZYSEXYCOOL
Intro-lude / Creep / Kick your game / Diggin' on you / Case of the fake people / Crazysexycool / Red light special / Waterfalls / Intermission-lude / Let's do it again / If I was your girlfriend / Sexy-interlude / Take our time / Can I get a witness / Switch / Sumthin' wicked this way comes
CD ________ 73008260092
Arista / May '95 / BMG

OOOOOOOH... ON THE TLC TIP
Ain't 2 proud 2 beg / Shock dat monkey / Intermission / Hat 2 da bak / Das da way we like 'em / What about your friends / His story / Intermission 2 / Bad my myself / Somethin' you wanna know / Baby-baby-baby / This is how it should be done / Depend on myself / Conclusion
CD ________ 262 878
Arista / Feb '97 / BMG

TLM

I'VE GOT THE BATTERY...WHERE'S THE SLOT
CD ____ DUKE 028CD
CD ____ DUKE 028L
Hydrogen Dukebox / Jul '96 / 3mv/Vital / Kudos / Prime

RE-CHARGED
CD ____ DUKE 030CD
Hydrogen Dukebox / Nov '96 / 3mv/Vital / Kudos / Prime

To Hell With Burgundy

3
CD ____ STIGCD 07
Stig / Aug '94 / ADA / Pinnacle

ONLY THE WORLD
CD ____ STIGCD 05
Stig / Jul '94 / ADA / Pinnacle

To Rococo Rot

TO ROCOCO ROT
CD ____ KITTY 010
Kitty-Yo International / Jul '97 / Cargo

VEICULO
Micromanaged / He loves me / Modern homes / Moto / Mit dir in der gegend / Leggiero / Geheimnis eines mantels / Extra / Fach / Lips / Merano / Allover dezent / Lift
CD ____ EFA 049902
City Slang / Feb '97 / RTM/Disc

Toad The Wet Sprocket

FEAR
Walk on the ocean / Is it for me / Butterflies / Nightingale song / Hold her down / Pray your Gods / Before you were born / Something to say / In my ear / All I want / Stories I tell / I will not take these things for granted
CD ____ 4685822
Columbia / Mar '92 / Sony

Toadies

PLEATHER
CD ____ ASS 001 2
Grass / May '93 / Pinnacle / SRD

Toast

COLLECTION, THE
CD ____ DAMGOOD 124
Damaged Goods / May '97 / Shellshock/ Disc

Toasters

FRANKENSKA
CD ____ PHZCD 60
Unicorn / Nov '93 / Plastic Head

LIVE IN LA
CD ____ EFA 046072
Pork Pie / Dec '94 / SRD

NAKED CITY
CD ____ PHZCD 55
Unicorn / Oct '89 / Plastic Head

NEW YORK FEVER
CD ____ EFA 040902
Pork Pie / Jan '93 / SRD

SKA BOOM
CD ____ EFA 046052
Pork Pie / Apr '94 / SRD

TWO TONE ARMY
CD ____ EFA 046322
Pork Pie / Sep '96 / SRD

Tobias, Nancy

BEAUTIFUL SOUNDS OF THE PANPIPE (Tobias, Nancy & Phil)
CD ____ HADCD 178
Javelin / Nov '95 / Henry Hadaway / THE

Tobin, Christine

AILILIU
CD ____ BDV 9501
Babel / Jul '95 / ADA / Cadillac / Diverse / Harmonia Mundi

YELL OF THE GAZELLE
CD ____ BDV 9613
Babel / Aug '96 / ADA / Cadillac / Diverse / Harmonia Mundi

Tobin, Penelope

WHEN
When / Love of money / Paris romancing / Leave me in peace / La vendetta / Scaredy cat / Friend into lover / Melancholy / First day of spring / Only got the moment
CD ____ DDG 001
Dodgem Discs / Jun '96 / New Note/ Pinnacle

Tobruk

PLEASURE AND PAIN
Rock 'n' roll casualty / Love is in motion / Alleyboy / No paradise in Heaven / Burning up / Two hearts on the run / Let me out of here / Cry out in the night / Set me on fire
CD ____ WKFMXD 105
FM / May '88 / Revolver / Sony

Today Is The Day

SUPERNOVA
CD ____ ARRCD 44/290
Amphetamine Reptile / Aug '93 / Plastic Head

TODAY IS THE DAY
CD ____ ARR 71014CD
Amphetamine Reptile / Apr '96 / Plastic Head

WILLPOWER
CD ____ AAR 57354CD
Amphetamine Reptile / Nov '94 / Plastic Head

Todd, Dick

CANADIAN CROSBY, THE (His Greatest Recordings 1938-1942)
All this and Heaven too / As long as we're together / Blue orchids / Blue evening / Change partner / Concerto for two / Deep purple / Gaucho serenade / Girl in the bonnet of blue / Goodnight Mother / Hi-yo silver / I can't get started (With you) / I don't want to set the world on fire / It's a hap-hap happy day / It's a hundred to one / It's the talk of the town / Lazy river / Little Sir Echo / Love doesn't grow on trees / Outside of that I love you: *Todd, Dick & Dinah Shore* / Penny serenade / Someday sweetheart / To you sweetheart aloha / When Paw was coutin' Maw / When the lights go on again / Why begin again / You can't brush me off: *Todd, Dick & Dinah Shore*
CD ____ CDAJA 5179
Living Era / Dec '95 / Select

Toe Fat

TOE FAT VOL.1 & 2
That's my love for you / Bad side of the moon / Nobody / Wherefores and the whys / But I'm wrong / Just like me / Just like all the rest / I can't believe / Working nights / You tried to take it all / Stick heat / Indian summer / Idol / There'll be changes / New way / Since you've been gone / Three time loser / Midnight sun
CD ____ BGOCD 278
Beat Goes On / Sep '95 / Pinnacle

Toe Tag

REALITY
CD ____ CHERRY 228952
Cherrydisc / Jun '94 / Plastic Head

Toe To Toe

THREATS AND FACTS
CD ____ KANG 006CD
Kangaroo / Nov '95 / Plastic Head

Toenut

INFORMATION
CD ____ CDSTUMM 89
Mute / Apr '96 / RTM/Disc

Togashi, Masahiko

COLOUR OF DREAM
CD ____ TKOJ 1502
Take One / Jan '96 / Harmonia Mundi

ISOLATION (Togashi, Masahiko & Mototeru Takagi)
CD ____ TKOJ 1503
Take One / Jan '96 / Harmonia Mundi

SONG OF SOIL
CD ____ TKOJ 1501
Take One / Jan '96 / Harmonia Mundi

Tognoni, Rob

HEADSTRONG
Times change / Got yourself to blame / Stones and colours / Roosevelt and Ira Lee / Wanna be with you / Ain't that enough / Take me away / Dark angel / Everlasting lovin' boy / Jim Beam blues / Riverside / Keep your head above water / Baby please don't go
CD ____ PRD 70982
Provogue / Mar '97 / Pinnacle

STONES AND COLOURS
CD ____ PRD 70832
Provogue / Oct '95 / Pinnacle

Toho Sara

KYOJINKAI
CD ____ FDCD 58
Fourth Dimension / Apr '97 / Cargo

Toiling Midgets

SON
Faux pony / Fabric / Slaughter of Summer St. / Mr. Foster's shoes / Process words / Clinging fire/Clams / Third chair / Listen / Chains
CD ____ HUTCD 006
Hut / Jan '93 / EMI

Token Entry

WEIGHT OF THE WORLD
CD ____ EM 93942
Roadrunner / Sep '90 / PolyGram

Token Women

OUT TO LUNCH
CD ____ NMCD 6
No Master's Voice / Feb '96 / ADA / Direct

RHYTHM METHOD, THE
CD ____ NMCD 2
No Master's Voice / Jun '97 / ADA / Direct

Tokens

WIMOWEH - THE BEST OF THE TOKENS
Lion sleeps tonight / B'wanina (pretty girl) / La bamba / Hear the bells (ringing bells) / You're nothing but a girl / Tonight I met an angel / Sincerely / When I go to sleep at night / Thousand miles away / Please write / Dream angel good night / Somewhere there's a girl / I'll do my crying tomorrow / ABC 123 / Tonight, tonight / Dry your eyes / Sweet Laurie / My candy apple vette / My fiend's car / When summer is through
CD ____ 07863664742
RCA / Nov '94 / BMG

Toker, Bayram Bilge

BAYRAM
CD ____ CDT 122
Topic / Apr '93 / ADA / CM / Direct

Tokeya Inajin

DREAM CATCHER
CD ____ CDEB 2696
Earthbeat / May '93 / ADA / Direct

Tokyo Blade

BURNING DOWN PARADISE
CD ____ SPV 08512122
SPV / Mar '96 / Koch / Plastic Head

TOKYO BLADE
CD ____ RR 349883
Roadrunner / '89 / PolyGram

Tokyo Offshore Project

AEROTEK
Children of the rainbow / Soltaire / Magic melody (remix) / Aerotek / Running thunder / Gabriella / Solitaire
CD ____ SCIENCD 001
Scien / Sep '94 / Vital

Tokyo's Coolest Combo

TOKYO'S COOLEST COMBO
CD ____ BOM 04CD
Bomba / Jul '96 / Amato Disco / Mo's Music Machine / Prime / Timewarp

Tollhouse Company

BETWEEN THE FLAT LAND AND THE SKY (A Fenman's Life In Song & Narrative) (2CD Set)
Overture / End of an era / Entire man / Good life for a young man / Between the flat land and the sky / I wished myself at home / Guns of Italy / End of everything / Forty pounds / Return home / Welcome home / Living and the dead / Silent fen / Angel of mercy / Jerusalem Drove / Stepping back into life / Cock of the walk / Shooting butterflies / Out beneath the moon / That's progress / Man from the ministry / Plastic roses / Me and Ted and Harry / Back on the old fen / Old man's happy again / Last drop from the bottle / Between the flat land and the sky (reprise)
CD Set ____ THCDCD 9701
Tollhouse / May '97 / Tollhouse

Tolliver, Charles

GRAND MAX
CD ____ BLC 760145
Black Lion / Apr '91 / Cadillac / Jazz Music / Koch / Wellard

RINGER, THE
CD ____ BLCD 760174
Black Lion / Oct '93 / Cadillac / Jazz Music / Koch / Wellard

WITH MUSIC INC. AND ORCHESTRA
Impact / Mother Wit / Grand Max / Plight / Lynnsome / Mournin' variations
CD ____ 6605 1004
Strata East / Feb '91 / New Note/Pinnacle

Tolman, Russ

ROAD MOVIE
CD ____ 422368
New Rose / May '94 / ADA / Direct / Discovery

TOTEM POLES AND GLORY HOLES
Lookin' for an angel / Talking hoover dam blues / Four winds / Everything you need and everything you want / Galveston mud / Better than before / I am not afraid / Nothin' slowing me down / Play hard to forget / Waitin' for rain
CD ____ DIAB 802
Diabolo / Oct '93 / Pinnacle

Tolonen, Jukka

HOOK/HYSTERICA
CD ____ LRCD 113/149
Love / Dec '94 / ADA / Direct / Greyhound

Tom Tom Club

TOM TOM CLUB
Wordy rappinghood / Genius of love / Tom Tom theme / L'elephant / As above so below / Lorelei / On on on on / Booming and zooming
CD ____ IMCD 103
Island / Feb '90 / PolyGram

Tomita

BEST OF TOMITA, THE
CD ____ PD 89381
RCA / '88 / BMG

FIREBIRD
Firebird suite / Prelude a l'apres midi d'un faune / Night on the bare mountain
CD ____ GD 60578
RCA Victor / Oct '91 / BMG

GREATEST HITS
CD ____ RD 85660
RCA Victor / Jul '94 / BMG

KOSMOS
Space fantasy / Unanswered question / Solvejg's song / Hora staccato / Sea named Solaris
CD ____ GD 82616
RCA Victor / Oct '91 / BMG

PICTURES AT AN EXHIBITION
Gnome / Old castle / Tuileries / Bydlo / Ballet of the chicks in their shells / Samuel Goldenberg and Schmuyle / Limoges / Catacombs / Cum mortuis in lingua mortua / Hut of Baba Yaga / Great gate of Kiev
CD ____ GD 60576
RCA Victor / Oct '91 / BMG

PLANETS, THE
CD ____ GD 60518
RCA Victor / Aug '85 / BMG

SNOWFLAKES ARE DANCING (Music Of Claude Debussy)
Snowflakes are dancing / Reverie / Gardens in the rain (estampes no 3) / Clair de Lune / Arabesque No.1 / Engulfed cathedral (preludes book no.8) / Golliwogg's cakewalk / Footprints in the snow(preludes book no.6)
CD ____ GD 60579
RCA Victor / '85 / BMG

Tommaso, Giovanni

VIA GT (Tommaso, Giovanni Quintet)
CD ____ 1231962
Red / Apr '94 / ADA / Cadillac / Harmonia Mundi

Tomokawa, Kazuki

SHIBUYA APIA
CD ____ PSFD 65
PSF / Dec '95 / Harmonia Mundi

ZEINIKU NA ASA (Fat In The Morning Light)
CD ____ PSFD 82
PSF / May '97 / Harmonia Mundi

Tomorrow

TOMORROW
My white bicycle / Colonel Brown / Real life permanent dream / Shy boy / Claremount lake / Revolution / Incredible journey of Timothy Chase / Auntie Mary's dress shop / Strawberry fields forever / Three jolly little dwarfs / Now your time has come / Hallucinations
CD ____ SEECD 314
See For Miles/C5 / Feb '97 / Pinnacle

Tomorrow's Child

ROCKY COAST
CD ____ DCD 9630
Dream Circle / Nov '96 / Cargo / Plastic Head

Tomorrow's Gift

TOMORROW'S GIFT
CD ____ SB 017
Second Battle / Jun '97 / Greyhound

Tomorrowland

STEREOSCOPIC SOUNDWAVES
CD ____ DRL 042CD
Darla / Jul '97 / Cargo

Tompkins, Ross

AKA THE PHANTOM
CD ____ PCD 7090
Progressive / Jun '93 / Jazz Music

CELEBRATES THE MUSIC OF JULIE STYNE
CD ____ PCD 7103
Progressive / Aug '95 / Jazz Music

Ton-Art

MAL VU, MAL DIT
CD _______ ARTCD 6088
Hat Art / Jan '92 / Cadillac / Harmonia Mundi

Tonar, Tidlause

TIMELESS TONES
CD _______ LMP 196CD
Laerdal Musik / May '96 / ADA

Tone Loc

COOL HAND LOC
CD _______ IMCD 247
Island / Mar '97 / PolyGram

LOC'ED AFTER DARK
On fire (remix) / Wild thing / Loc'ed after dark / I got it going on / Cutting rhythms / Funky cold medina / Cheeba cheeba / Don't get close / Loc'in on the shaw / Homies
CD _______ IMCD 125
4th & Broadway / Apr '91 / PolyGram

Tone, Yasunao

SOLO FOR THE WOUNDED
CD _______ TZA 7212
Tzadik / Jul '97 / Cargo

Toney, Kevin

LOVESCAPE
Kings / Aphrodisiac / Winds of romance / Lovescape / Sweet whispers / Intimate persuasion / Body language / Deeper shade of love / African knights / Twylight 2053 / Someone / Carnival / King's reprise
CD _______ ICH 1167CD
Ichiban / Jan '94 / Direct / Koch

Tong, Pete

DANCE NATION VOL.3 (Mixed By Pete Tong & Judge Jules/2CD Set) (Various Artists)
Remember me: *Blueboy* / You got the love: *Source & Candi Staton* / Take California: *Propeller Heads* / Get up: *Stingily, Byron* / Take me by the hand: *Submerge* / Soothe: *Furry Phreaks* / Let me tell you something: *2 Guys On Warwick* / Lost without you: *Hanna, Jayn* / Zoe: *Paganini Traxx* / Barrel of a gun: *Depeche Mode* / Closer to your heart: *JX* / Encore une fois: *Sash* / Nightmare: *Brainbug* / Breathe: *Prodigy* / Ain't talkin' 'bout dub: *Apollo 440* / She drives me crazy: *Fine Young Cannibals* / Body music intersection: *Friday Night Traffik* / I believe: *Absolute* / Gotta love for you: *Serial Diva* / Jump: *Funkatarium* / Can you feel the heat: *Carle Younge Project* / Walk with me: *Heliotropic* / Cafe Del Mar: *Energy 52* / Tempest: *Amethyst* / Offshore: *Chicane* / Take me there: *Maximum* / Sugar is sweeter: *Bolland, C.J.* / Inferno: *Souvlaki*
CD Set _______ DNCD 3
Ministry Of Sound / Mar '97 / 3mv/Sony / Mo's Music Machine / Warner Music

Tongue Man

COP THIS
CD _______ DS 005CD
Drunken Swan / Oct '96 / World Serpent

Tonic

LEMON PARADE
CD _______ 5310422
Polydor / Sep '97 / PolyGram

Tonight At Noon

DOWN TO THE DEVILS
John MacLean march / Hawks and eagles fly like doves / Travelling song / Wire the loom / People's will / Run run / Hell of a man / Down to the devils / Nae trust / Mission hall / Harry Wigwam's / Hiss of marble / Jack the tanner / Rolling seas
CD _______ LCOM 9041
Lismor / Nov '90 / ADA / Direct / Duncans / Lismor

Tonnerre, Michel

TI BEUDEFF - CHANT DE MARINS
CD _______ KMCD 39
Keltia Musique / Aug '93 / ADA / Discovery

Tonooka, Sumi

HERE COMES KAI
Giant steps / It must be real / At home / In the void / Warm valley / Upper Manhattan medical group / Mystery / Here comes Kai
CD _______ CCD 79516
Candid / Feb '97 / Cadillac / Direct / Jazz Music / Koch / Wellard

TAKING TIME
Taking time / Yours and mine / Seriously speaking / Shadow waltz / Night and day / Out of the silence / Station levitation / In the night / One for Mary Lou
CD _______ CCD 79502
Candid / Feb '97 / Cadillac / Direct / Jazz Music / Koch / Wellard

Tons Of Tones

COMPLETE CITATION SAGA, THE
CD _______ DBM 2196
Fierce / Apr '97 / SRD

Tonto Irie

JAMMY'S POSSE
CD _______ 792052
Greensleeves / Nov '92 / Jet Star / SRD

Tony D

GET YOURSELF SOME (Tony D Band)
CD _______ TRCD 9919
Tramp / Nov '93 / ADA / CM / Direct

Tony O

TOP OF THE BLUES (Tony O Blues Band)
CD _______ DELCD 3014
Deluge / Jan '96 / ADA / Direct / Koch

Tony Rebel

DANCEHALL CONFRENCE (Tony Rebel & Garnet Silk)
CD _______ CDHB 152
Heartbeat / May '94 / ADA / Direct / Greensleeves / Jet Star

MEET IN A DANCEHALL CONFERENCE (Tony Rebel & Garnet Silk)
CD _______ HBCD 152
Heartbeat / Jun '94 / ADA / Direct / Greensleeves / Jet Star

REBELLIOUS
CD _______ RASCD 3097
Ras / May '92 / Direct / Greensleeves / Jet Star / SRD

Tony Toni Tone

HOUSE OF MUSIC
Thinking of you / Top notch / Let's get down / Til last summer / Lovin' you / Still a man / Don't fall in love / Holy smoke and gee whiz / Annie May / Let me know / Tossin' 'n' turnin' / Wild child / Party don't cry / Lovin' you interlude
CD _______ 5342502
Mercury / Nov '96 / PolyGram

SONS OF SOUL
If I had no loot / What goes around comes around / My ex-girlfriend / Tell me mama / Leavin' / Slow wine (slow grind) / Lay your head on my pillow / I couldn't keep it to myself / Gangsta groove / Tonyies, In the wrong key / Dance hall / Time Square 2:30 AM (Segue) / Fun / Anniversary / Castleers
CD _______ 5149332
Polydor / Jul '93 / PolyGram

Tonyall

NEW GIRL, OLD STORY
CD _______ CRZ 016CD
Cruz / May '93 / Plastic Head

Too Slim & The Taildraggers

SWAMP OPERA
CD _______ BCD 00212
Burnside / May '96 / Koch

WANTED: LIVE
CD _______ BCD 00162
Burnside / Jun '96 / Koch

Too Strong

RABENSCHWARZE NACHT
CD _______ HAUS 1
Tribehaus Recordings / Jan '94 / Plastic Head

Tool

AENIMA
Stinkfist / Eulogy / H / Useful idiot / Forty six and 2 / Message to Harry Manback / Hooker with a penis / Intermission / Jimmy / Die Eier von Satarn / Push it
CD _______ 61422311442
Zoo Entertainment / Oct '96 / BMG

OPIATE
Sweat / Hush / Part of me / Cold and ugly / Jerk off / Opiate
CD _______ 72445110272
Zoo Entertainment / Jul '92 / BMG

UNDERTOW
Intolerance / Prison sex / Sober / Bottom / Crawl away / Swamp song / Undertow / Four degrees / Flood / Disgustipated
CD _______ 72445110522
Zoo Entertainment / Apr '93 / BMG

Toop, David

PINK NOIR
Mixed blood / Ultra-paste / Pink noir / Almost transparent blue / Sugar frosted charcoal scene / Mr. Lullaby should have rocked you / Mamba point / Slow Loris versus Poison Snail / Lime leaves / Spore divination
CD _______ AMBT 18
Virgin / Sep '96 / EMI

SCREEN CEREMONIES
Ceremonies behind screens / Darkened room / Dream fluid / Psychic / Howler monkey shits and roars / Butoh porno / Reverse world / Mica screen / I hear voices
CD _______ WIRE 9001
Wire Editions / Nov '95 / Vital

Toots & The Maytals

BLA BLA BLA
CD _______ CC 2706
Crocodisc / Jan '94 / Grapevine/PolyGram

DON'T TROUBLE
CD _______ RB 3017
Reggae Best / Jan '96 / Grapevine/ PolyGram

FUNKY KINGSTON
Sit right down / Pomp and pride / Louie Louie / I can't believe / Redemption song / Daddy's home / Funky Kingston / It was written down
CD _______ RRCD 21
Reggae Refreshers / Nov '90 / PolyGram / Vital
CD _______ CDTRL 201
Trojan / Mar '94 / Direct / Jet Star

IN THE DARK
Got to be there / In the dark / Having a party / Time tough / I see you / Take a look in the mirror / Take me home country roads / Fever / Love gonna walk out on me / Revolution / 54-46 (was my number) / Sailing on
CD _______ CDTRL 202
Trojan / Mar '94 / Direct / Jet Star

REGGAE GREATS
54-46 (was my number) / Reggae got sould / Monkey man / Just like that / Funky Kingston / Sweet and dandy / Take me home country oads / Time tough / Spititual healing / Pressure drop / Peace perfect peace / Bam bam
CD _______ 5525842
Spectrum / Jul '97 / PolyGram

ROOTS REGGAE
CD _______ RNCD 2132
Rhino / Oct '95 / Grapevine/PolyGram / Jet Star

TIME TOUGH (The Island Anthology/ 2CD Set)
Six and seven books of Moses / Broadway jungle / It's you / Never you change / John and James / 54-46 (was my number) / Do the reggay / Desmond Dekker came first / Sweet and dandy / Monkey man / Peeping Tom / One eyed enos / She's my scorcher / Pressure drop / Pomp and pride / Funky Kingston / Take me home, country roads / Time tough / In the dark / Reggae got soul / Rastaman / Living in the ghetto / Hallelujah / Get up, stand up / My love is so strong / Chatty chatty / Gee whizz / Just like that / Careless Ethiopians / Never get weary / Spend the weekend / Beautiful woman / Bam bam / Spiritual healing / B for butter / Peace, perfect peace / You know / (I've got) dreams to remember / Precious precious / Hard to handle / Freedom train
CD Set _______ 5242192
Island Jamaica / Jul '96 / Jet Star / PolyGram

TOOTS & THE MAYTALS
CD _______ EXP 033
Experience / May '97 / TKO Magnum

Top Cat

9 LIVES OF THE CAT
CD _______ NLDCD 001
9 Lives / Feb '95 / Jet Star

CAT O NINE TALES
CD _______ NLDCD 002
9 Lives / Dec '95 / Jet Star

Top, Emmanuel

ASTEROID
CD _______ NOMU 51CD
Nova Mute / Oct '96 / Prime / RTM/Disc

Topper

SOMETHING TO TELL HER
CD _______ ANKST 080CD
Ankst / Jul '97 / Shellshock/Disc

Toquinho

AMIGOS (Toquinho & Vinicius)
CD _______ 1917522
EPM / Apr '97 / ADA / Discovery

Toraia Orchestra Of Tangiers

YA BAY
CD _______ TCD 1043
Tradition / Mar '97 / ADA / Vital

Torch, Sidney

SIDNEY TORCH
CD _______ PASTCD 9747
Flapper / Jun '91 / Pinnacle

Torch Song

TOWARD THE UNKNOWN REGION
CD _______ 4509989692
Warner Bros. / Dec '96 / Warner Music

Torchure

BEYOND THE VEIL
CD _______ 1MF 3770026
1MF / Nov '92 / Plastic Head

Torero Band

EASY TIJUANA
Lonely bull / Tijuana taxi / Guantanamera / I'll never fall in love again / From me to you / Walk in the black forest / Spanish flea / Hello Dolly / All my loving / Spanish Harlem / This guy's in love with you / Casino Royale / Yesterday / A banda / America / If I were a rich man / Our day will come / Acapulco 1922 / Man and a woman / Happening
CD _______ CDMFP 6251
Music For Pleasure / Sep '96 / EMI

Torino

ROCK IT
Rock it / Nights on fire / Seven mountains / Baby blue / It takes a man to cry / Showdown / Dance all night / One in a million / Shine / Turn it up
CD _______ WKFMXD 123
FM / Mar '89 / Revolver / Sony

Torkanowsky, David

STEPPIN' OUT
CD _______ ROUCD 2090
Rounder / '88 / ADA / CM / Direct

Torme, Bernie

ARE WE THERE YET
Teenage kicks / Come the revolution / Let it rock / All around the world / Mystery train / Search and destroy / Shoorah shoorah / Wild west / Star / Turn out the lights / Lies / Chelsea girls
CD _______ HMRXD 168
Heavy Metal / Apr '91 / Revolver / Sony

BACK TO BABYLON
All around the world / Star / Eyes of the world / Burning bridges / Hardcore / Here I go / Family at war / Front line / Arabia / Mystery train / TVOD / Kerrap / Love, guns and money
CD _______ CDZEB 6
Zebra / Jul '91 / Pinnacle

DEMOLITION BALL (Torme)
Fallen angel / Black sheep / Action / Ball and chain / Slip away / Long time coming / Spinnin' your wheels / Don't understand / Industry / Draw the line / US made / Let it go / Walk it / Man o' means
CD _______ CDBLEED 2
Bleeding Hearts / Apr '93 / Pinnacle

DIE PRETTY, DIE YOUNG (Torme)
Let it rock / Real thing / Ready / Sex action / Ways of the East / Killer / Memphis / Louise / Crimes of passion / Ghost train
CD _______ HMRXD 94
Heavy Metal / Nov '89 / Revolver / Sony

OFFICIAL BOOTLEG
Front line / Turn out the lights / Hardcore / Star / Burning bridges / TVOD / My baby loves a vampire / New Orleans / Love, guns and money / All around the world / Mystery train / Front line 2
CD _______ CDTB 112
Thunderbolt / '91 / TKO Magnum

Torme, Mel

16 MOST REQUESTED SONGS
PS I love you / Second time around / Haven't we met / Nearness of you / My romance / Do I love you because you're beautiful / Isn't it a pity / I know your heart / I've got you under my skin / That's all / What is there to say / Folks who live on the hill / Everyday's a holiday / You'd better love me / Strangers in the night / Christmas song
CD _______ 4743982
Columbia / Feb '94 / Sony

A&E'S EVENING WITH MEL TORME
Just one of those things / On Green Dolphin Street / You make me feel so young / Nightingale sang in Berkeley Square / Pick yourself up / Star dust / Love for sale / Since I fell for you / Three little words/Slipped disc / Smooth one/Rachel's dream / I remember you / It's easy to remember / Lover come back to me / Stairway to the stars / Oh lady be good / Ev'ry time we say goodbye
CD _______ CCD 4736
Concord Jazz / Nov '96 / New Note/ Pinnacle

AROUND THE WORLD
Frenesi / Blue moon / You're getting to be a habit with me / Skylark / Perfidia / Autumn leaves / It's de-lovely / Recipe for romance / South of the border / Vaya con dios / I wish I were in love again / Tenderly / I've got a feeling I'm falling / Oh you beautiful doll / Sonny Boy / Bewitched, bothered & bewildered / Lullaby of the leaves / I hadn't anyone 'til you / Piccolino / Black moonlight

CD _______ CDMFP 6217
Music For Pleasure / Sep '96 / EMI

CHRISTMAS SONGS
CD _______ CD 83315
Telarc / Sep '92 / Conifer/BMG

EASY TO REMEMBER
CD _______ HCD 253
Hindsight / May '94 / Jazz Music / Target/ BMG

FUJITSU-CONCORD JAZZ FESTIVAL (Japan 1990)
Shine on your shoes / Looking at you/Look at that face / Nightingale sang in Berkeley Square / Wave / Stardust / Don't cha go 'way mad/Come to baby do / Christmas song/Autumn leaves / You're driving me crazy / Sent for you yesterday / Swingin' the blues / New York state of mind
CD _______ CCD 4481
Concord Jazz / Oct '91 / New Note/ Pinnacle

GREAT AMERICAN SONGBOOK, THE
Stardust / You make me feel so young / Riding high / All God's chillun got rhythm / I'm gonna go fishin' / Don't get around much anymore / Sophisticated lady/I diinn't know about you / Rockin' in rhythm / It don't mean a thing if it ain't got that swing / Lovely way to spend an evening / I'll remember April/I concentrate on you / Autumn in New York / You gotta try / Just one of those things/On Green Dolphin Street / Party's over / I let a song go out of my heart
CD _______ CD 83328
Telarc / Dec '93 / Conifer/BMG

IN CONCERT - TOKYO (Torme, Mel & Marty Paich Dektette)
It don't mean a thing if it ain't got that swing / Cotton tail / More than you know / Sweet Georgia Brown / Just in time / When the sun comes out / Carioca / Too close for comfort / City / Bossa nova pot pourri / On the street where you live
CD _______ CCD 4382
Concord Jazz / Jun '89 / New Note/ Pinnacle

IT'S A BLUE WORLD (Bethlehem Jazz Classics)
I got it bad and that ain't good / Till the clouds roll by / Isn't it romantic / I know why / All this and Heaven too / How long has this been going on / Polka dots and moonbeams / You leave me breathless / I found a million dollar baby / Wonderful one / It's a blue world / Stay as sweet as you are
CD _______ CDGR 135
Charly / Apr '97 / Koch

LIVE AT THE CRESCENDO
Love is just a bug / Nobody's heart / It's only a paper moon / What is this thing called love / I got plenty o' nuttin' / Taking a chance / One for my baby (and one more for the road) / Nightingale sang in Berkeley Square / Just one of those things / Autumn leaves / Girl next door / Lover come back to me / I'm beginning to see the light / Looking at you / Tender trap / Tenderly / I wish I was in love again / It's de-lovely / It's all right with me / Home by the sea / Manhattan
CD _______ CDCHARLY 60
Charly / '87 / Koch

LULU'S BACK IN TOWN
CD _______ CD 53010
Giants Of Jazz / Mar '90 / Cadillac / Jazz Music / Target/BMG

MAGIC OF MEL TORME, THE
CD _______ MCCD 198
Music Club / Mar '95 / Disc / THE

MEL AND GEORGE 'DO' WORLD WAR II (Torme, Mel & George Shearing)
Lili Marlene / I've heard that song before / I know why / Love / Aren't you glad you're you / Ellington medley / Walk medley / I could write a book / Lovely way to spend an evening / On the swing shift/Five o'clock whistle / Accentuate the positive / This is the army Mister Jones / We mustn't say goodbye
CD _______ CCD 4471
Concord Jazz / Jul '91 / New Note/Pinnacle

MEL TORME/ROB MCCONNELL AND BOSS BRASS (Torme, Mel/Rob McConnell/Boss Brass)
Just friends / September song / Don't cha go 'way mad / House is not a home / Song is you / Cow cow boogie / Handful of stars / Stars fell on Alabama / It don't mean a thing if it ain't got that swing / Do nothin' 'til you hear from me / Mood indigo / Take the 'A' train / Sophisticated lady / Satin doll
CD _______ CCD 4306
Concord Jazz / Jan '87 / New Note/ Pinnacle

NIGHT AT THE CONCORD PAVILION
Sing for your supper / Sing sing sing / Sing (sing a song) / You make me feel so young / Early Autumn / Guys and dolls medley / I could have told you / Losing my mind / Deep in a dream / Goin' out of my head / Too darn hot / Day in, day out / Down for double / You're driving me crazy / Sent for you yesterday
CD _______ CCD 4433
Concord Jazz / Nov '90 / New Note/ Pinnacle

NOTHING WITHOUT YOU (Torme, Mel & Cleo Laine)
CD _______ CCD 4515
Concord Jazz / Jul '92 / New Note/ Pinnacle

REUNION (Torme, Mel & Marty Paich Dektette)
Sweet Georgia Brown / I'm wishing / Blues / Trolley song / More than you know / For whom the bell tolls / When you wish upon a star / Walk between raindrops / Bossa nova pot porri / Get me to the church on time / Goodbye look / Spain (I can recall)
CD _______ CCD 4360
Concord Jazz / Jul '90 / New Note/Pinnacle

RIGHT NOW
Comin' home baby / Homeward bound / My little red book / Walk on by / If I had a hammer / Strangers in the night / Better use your head / Time / Secret agent man / Pretty flamingo / Red rubber ball / All that jazz / You don't have to say you love me / Dominique's discotheque / Power of love / Lover's roulette / Ciao baby / Molly Marlene / King / Lima lady / Wait until dark / Only when I'm lonely
CD _______ CK 65164
Sony Jazz / Jun '97 / Sony

SINGS FRED ASTAIRE
CD _______ CDGR 124
Charly / Mar '97 / Koch

THAT'S ALL
I've got you under my skin / That's all / What is there to say / Do I love you because you're so beautiful / Folks who live on the hill / Isn't it a pity / Ho ba la la / PS I love you / Nearness of you / My romance / Second time around / Haven't we met / I know you're heart / You'd better love me / I see it now / Once in a lifetime / Hang on to me / Seventeen / I remember Suzanne / Only the very young / Paris smiles / Ev'ry day's like a holiday / One little snowflake / Christmas song
CD _______ CK 65165
Sony Jazz / Jun '97 / Sony

TORME
All in love is fair / First time ever I saw your face / New York state of mind / Stars / Send in the clowns / Ordinary fool / When the world was young / Yesterday when I was young / Bye bye blackbird
CD _______ RHCD 3
Rhapsody / Jan '87 / Jazz Music / President / Wellard

TRIBUTE TO BING CROSBY (Paramount's Greatest Singer)
This is my night to dream / It must be true / Moonlight becomes you / I can't escape from you / With every breath I take / Man and his dream / Without a word of warning / May I / Please / Thanks / Don't let that moon get away / Soon / It's easy to remember / Love in bloom / Day you came along / Pennies from heaven / Learn to croon
CD _______ CCD 4614
Concord Jazz / Oct '94 / New Note/ Pinnacle

VELVET AND BRASS
Liza / Swing shift / I'll be around / Sweety / Love walks in / These are the things / If you could see / High & low / Have you met Miss Jones / Nobody else / Autumn serenade / I get a kick out of you / Still of the night / I'm glad
CD _______ CCD 4667
Concord Jazz / Oct '95 / New Note/ Pinnacle

Torment

HYPNOSIS
CD _______ NERDCD 057
Nervous / Jul '90 / Nervous / TKO Magnum

Tormentors

ANNO DOMINI
CD _______ ECLIPSE 004CD
Nocturnal Art / Nov '96 / Plastic Head

Torn, David

BEST LAID PLANS
Before the bitter wind / Best laid plans / Hum of its parts / Removable tongue / In the fifth direction / Two face flash / Angle of incidents
CD _______ 8236422
ECM / Mar '85 / New Note/Pinnacle

CLOUD ABOUT MERCURY
Suyafhu skin..snapping the hollow reed / Mercury grid / Three minutes of pure entertainment / Previous man / Network of sparks
CD _______ 8311082
ECM / Mar '87 / New Note/Pinnacle

POLYTOWN
Honey sweating / Palms for Lester / Open letter to the heart of Diaphora / Bandaged by dreams / Warrior horsemen... / Snail hair dune / This is the abduction scene / Red sleep / Res majuko / City of the dead
CD _______ CMPCD 1006
CMP / May '94 / Cargo / Grapevine/ PolyGram / Vital/SAM

TRIPPING OVER GOD
CD _______ CMPCD 1007
CMP / Jan '95 / Cargo / Grapevine/ PolyGram / Vital/SAM

WHAT MEANS SOLID TRAVELLER
CD _______ CMPCD 1012
CMP / Apr '96 / Cargo / Grapevine/ PolyGram / Vital/SAM

Tornados

1960'S FRENCH EPS COLLECTION, THE
CD _______ 525732
Magic / Jul '97 / Greyhound

EP COLLECTION, THE
Telstar / Popeye twist / Love and fury / Jungle fever / Ridin' the wind / Dreamin' on a cloud / Red rosesand a sky of blue / Rip it up / All the stars in the sky / Hot pot / Earthy / Chasing moonbeams / Summer place / Swinging beefeater / Breeze and I / Ready Teddy / My babe / Joy stick / Flycatcher / Costermonger / Blue moon of Kennedy / Long tall Sally / Globe trotter / Alan's tune / Night ride / Chattanooga choo-choo / Life on Venus / Robot / Locomotion with me
CD _______ SEECD 445
See For Miles/C5 / Jul '96 / Pinnacle

ORIGINAL 60'S HITS, THE
CD _______ MCCD 161
Music Club / Jul '94 / Disc / THE

Torner, Gosta

TRUMPET PLAYER
CD _______ PHONTCD 9301
Phontastic / Jun '94 / Cadillac / Jazz Music / Wellard

Toro, Yomo

CELEBREMOS NAVIDAD
CD _______ ASHECD 2003
Ashe / Nov '96 / Direct

GOLDEN HANDS
Le pepita de mango - salsa / Usted - Bolero mejicano / Curame - Salsa / Danzon criollo - Danzon instrumental / Vereda tropical / La otra - Bachara / Three minus two - Jibaro / Country / Invitacion patria - Salsa boriqua / Mi pueblo / Que es eso i jene - Guaracha jibara / Bello amanecer - Salsa / Amor sincero - Bolero romantico
CD _______ TWI 1001CD
Les Disques Du Crepuscule / Mar '96 / Discovery

Torok, Mitchell

MEXICAN JOE IN THE CARIBBEAN (4CD Set)
Nacogdoches county line / I'll get my lovin' from someone else / Clingin' heart / Piney Woods boogie / Yearnin' / Someday (when someone hurts you) / Table hoppin' blues / Sober up / Little Hoo-wee / Judalina / Caribbean / Weep away / Caribbean / Hootchy kootchy Henry / Gigolo / Edgar the eager Easter bunny / Living on love / Haunting waterfall / Dancerette / World keeps turning around / Peasant's guitar / Roulette / Havana huddle / Smooth talk / My silly old heart / Sit down you're rocking the boat / Too late now / My kind of woman / Little Hoo-wee / Marching my blues away / Country and western (that's for me) / Red light, green light / No money down / It'll be all right / Woman by your side / I wish I was a little bit younger / Memories of you haunting me night and day / When Mexico gave up the rhumba / Go ahead and be a fool / Drink up and go home / Take this heart / Pledge of love / Another love from now / What's behind the strange door / You never belonged to me / Sweet revenge / Love me like you mean it / You win again / I can't help it (if I'm still in love) / Love your touch (love you so much) / Two words (True love) / You're tempting me / You can't keep a good man down / Honolulu baby / Filipino baby / How much (Do I love you) / Be kind to me / These things I hold dear / Date with a teardrop / All over again, again / You can't get there from here / You drive Buddy / PTA rock 'n' roll / Here I come cruel world / Teenie weenie bikini / Cryin' honky tonk blues / Caribbean / New guitar / You are the one / Especially for you / Kish Leon / Johnny's gone away to college / Mexican Joe / Little Hoo-wee / Rig-a-jig-a-boom / You are the one / That's my desire / Guardian Angel / Rose covered garden / When the stars get in your eyes / I want to know everything / Guardian Angel / Pink chiffon / Seventeenth summer / What you don't know (won't hurt you) / Happy street / Little boy in love / King of Holiday Island / El Tigre / Eating my heart out / Comancheros / Rio Grande / Fool's disguise / Mighty, mighty man / For somebody who's supposed to be hurtin' / I'm not myself / Hawaiian sunset / Little secrets / I wish / Timid soul / El Tigre / Summer romance / Your love / Too bad / For your precious love / Tree / What goes on in your heart / Imagination / Hidin' the hurt / Little teenage heart / Country music I gave you the best years of my life
CD Set _______ BCD 15906
Bear Family / May '96 / Direct / Rollercoaster / Swift

Torque

TORQUE
CD _______ M 7019CD
Mascot / Apr '96 / Plastic Head

Torr, Michele

GRANDS SUCCES
CD _______ MCD 339 207
Accord / '88 / Cadillac / Discovery

Torres, Eddie Lalo

IS EVERYWHERE
Quiero / Las Lagrimas Rojas / Arriba San Antonio / Que te han Contado / Balando Cumbia / Mejor Sin Ti / Margarita / Vida de mi Vida / Munequita / Sandra / Te Seguire Queriendo / Popurri
CD _______ ROUCD 6072
Rounder / Nov '96 / ADA / CM / Direct

Torres, Jaime

CHARANGO
Chimba chica / La diablada / Naupaj tiempos jinan tatay / Mambo de machahuay / Ch'isi / Caminos en la puna / La peregrinacion / El dia que me quieras / Chacarera del tiempo / Zamba de la candeleria / Sirvinaco / Milonga de mis amores
CD _______ 1115949
Messidor / Jan '87 / ADA / Koch

Torres, Juan Pablo

TROMBONE MAN
Sweet cherry pie / From John to Johnny / Who's smoking / Fiesta for Juan Pablo / Foot tapping / Samba for Carmen / At daybreak / Four and como fue / Memories / Banana split / For Elsa
CD _______ 66058085
Bellaphon / Feb '96 / New Note/Pinnacle

Torres, Marcelo

EDAD LUZ
CD _______ F 1037CD
Sonifolk / Jun '94 / ADA / CM

Torres, Roberto

EL CASTIGADOR
CD _______ CDGR 156
Charly / May '97 / Koch

Torriani, Vico

BIEDERMANN UND COOL MAN
Waikiki / Vagliamoci Tanto Bene / Immer, immer wieder / Sieben junge madchen / Piano / Komm und tanz / Bambonella aus Turin / Hello Mary Lou / Sempre Amore / Je t'aime bien Pinocchio / Pepino O Suricillo / Bon soir, Herr Kommissar / Mister / Ave Maria no morro / De Granada a Seville / Glaub' meiner liebe / La Tua Piccola Mano / Calcutta / Lass uns mal ein Tanzchen wagen / Das ist die wahre Liebe / Chitarra Romana / Signorina Cappuccina / J'ai rendezvous avec Paris / Das hat mir keiner von dir gesagt / Come Sempre / Boa Legani / Die grossen haben grosse Sorgen / Cosi come sei / Piove
CD _______ BCD 16111
Bear Family / Nov '96 / Direct / Rollercoaster / Swift

GRANADA
Das machen nur die Beine von Dolores / Isabella (Andalusisches madchen) / Granada / Spanisches Abenteuer / Blaue nacht in Sevilla / Haya Ole / Soir Espaniol / Es war einmal ein Matador / Maria Dolores / Malaguena / Komm, wir fahren nach Venedig / Rose im Garten der Liebe / Florentinische nachte / Simonetta / Carina / Carissima / Habanera / Kleine orangenverkauferin / Barcarole / D'Amore / Wie schade, dass Venedig noch so weit ist / Buona sera, Annabell / Wenn im Tal die Glocken lauten / Oh schone Heimat / Und fuhr' ich ein Madchen / Wo meine Wiege stand / Alle kleinen Englein jetzt sur Ruh'
CD _______ BCD 16109
Bear Family / Nov '96 / Direct / Rollercoaster / Swift

Tors Of Dartmoor

HOUSE OF SOUNDS
CD _______ HY 39100642
Hyperium / Jul '93 / Cargo / Plastic Head

Tortharry

WHEN MEMORIES ARE FREE
CD _______ TAGA 001CD
MAB / Nov '94 / Plastic Head

Tortoise

DIGEST COMPENDIUM OF...
CD _______ TKCB 70932
Thrill Jockey / May '97 / Cargo / Greyhound

MILLIONS NOW LIVING
CD _____ **EFA 049722**
City Slang / Jan '96 / RTM/Disc

MILLIONS NOW LIVING (Japanese Version)
CD _____ **TKCB 70931**
Thrill Jockey / May '97 / Cargo / Greyhound

RHYTHMS, RESOLUTIONS AND CLUSTERS
CD _____ **EFA 049572**
City Slang / Jun '95 / RTM/Disc

TORTOISE
CD _____ **EFA 049502**
Sub Pop / Jan '95 / Cargo / Greyhound / Shellshock/Disc

TORTOISE REMIXED
CD _____ **TKCB 71016**
Thrill Jockey / May '97 / Cargo / Greyhound

Toscanini, Arturo

ARTURO TOSCANINI & BENNY GOODMAN PLAY GEORGE GERSHWIN (Toscanini, Arturo & Benny Goodman)
CD _____ **VJC 10342**
Vintage Jazz Classics / Oct '92 / ADA / Cadillac / CM / Direct

Toscho

SERIOUS FUN
CD _____ **INAK 9041**
In Akustik / Oct '96 / Direct / TKO Magnum

Tosh, Andrew

MAKE PLACE FOR THE YOUTH
Stop what you doin' / Things I used to do / Why did you do it / Come together / Time is longer than rope / Message from Jah / One step to happiness / Small axe / Evil ones / Make place for the youth / Stop what you doin'
CD _____ **CPCD 8186**
Charly / Oct '96 / Koch

ORIGINAL MAN, THE
Same dog bite / Too much rat / Heathen rage / My enemies / Maga dog / I'm the youngest / Poverty is a crime / Original man / My enemies (dub version) / Poverty is a crime (dub version) / Original man (dub version)
CD _____ **CDHB 140**
Heartbeat / Apr '94 / ADA / Direct / Greensleeves / Jet Star

Tosh, Peter

BUSH DOCTOR
You gotta walk don't look back / Pick myself up / I'm the toughest / Soon come / Moses the prophet / Bush doctor / Stand firm / Dem ha fe get a beatin' / Creation
CD _____ **CDTRP 100**
Trojan / Nov '90 / Direct / Jet Star

EQUAL RIGHTS
Get up stand up / Downpressor man / I am that I am / Stepping razor / Equal rights / African / Jah guide / Apartheid
CD _____ **CDV 2081**
Virgin / Nov '88 / EMI

GOLD COLLECTION, THE
Johnny B Goode / Bush doctor / (You gotta walk) don't look back / No nuclear war / Come together / Na goa jail / Coming in hot / Pick myself up / In my song / Reggaemylitis / Equal rights / Crystal ball / Vampire / Lesson in my life / Testify / Maga dog
CD _____ **CDGOLD 1007**
EMI Gold / Mar '96 / EMI

LEGALIZE IT
Legalize it / Burial / What'cha gonna do / No sympathy / Why must I cry / Igziabeher (Let Jah be praised) / Ketchy shuby / Till your well runs dry / Brand new secondhand
CD _____ **CDV 2061**
Virgin / Aug '88 / EMI

TOUGHEST, THE
Coming in hot / Don't look back / Pick myself up / Crystal ball / Mystic man / Reggaemylitis / Bush doctor / Maga dog / Johnny B Goode / Equal rights / In my song
CD _____ **CDHB 150**
Heartbeat / Mar '96 / ADA / Direct / Greensleeves / Jet Star

Toss The Feathers

AWAKENING
Fever / Sunset / Awakening / Lonely man / Heritage / Requiem for the innocent / Thorn and nail / Drifting apart / Seven / Dr. Jekyll and Mrs. Hyde / Sail away / Long forgotten line
CD _____ **FC 003CD**
Fat Cat / Feb '93 / Vital

NEXT ROUND, THE
CD _____ **MMRCD 1004**
Magnetic / Mar '96 / ADA

Total

BUFFIN' THE CELESTIAL MUFFIN
CD _____ **REP 001**
Rural Electrification Programme / Apr '97 / Cargo

KASPAR HAUSER
CD _____ **METONYMIC 003CD**
Metonymic / Jun '97 / Cargo

SKY BLUE VOID
CD _____ **FRR007**
Freek / Sep '94 / RTM/Disc / SRD

TANZMUSIC DER RENAISSANCE, THE
CD _____ **FRR 017**
Freek / Dec '95 / RTM/Disc / SRD

Total

TOTAL
CD _____ **78612730062**
Arista / Feb '96 / BMG

Total Chaos

ANTHEMS FROM THE ALLEYWAY
CD _____ **64712**
Epitaph / Jun '96 / Pinnacle / Plastic Head

PATRIOTIC SHOCK
CD _____ **864502**
Epitaph / May '95 / Pinnacle / Plastic Head

PLEDGE OF DEFIANCE
CD _____ **E 864382**
Epitaph / Apr '94 / Pinnacle / Plastic Head

Total Eclipse

DELTA AQUARIDS
CD _____ **BR 2CD**
Blue Room Released / Feb '97 / Essential/ BMG / SRD

VIOLENT RELAXATION (2CD Set)
CD Set _____ **BR 015CD**
Blue Room Released / Feb '97 / Essential/ BMG / SRD

Toto

PAST TO PRESENT 1977-1990
Love has the power / Africa / Hold the line / Out of love / Georgie Porgie / I'll be over you / Can you hear what I'm saying / Rosanna / I won't hold you back / Stop loving you / Ninety nine / Pamela / Animal
CD _____ **4659982**
CBS / Sep '90 / Sony

TAMBU
Gift of faith / I will remember / Slipped away / If you belong to me / Baby he's your man / Other end of time / Turning point / Time is the enemy / Drag him to the roof / Just can't get to you / Dave's gone skiing / Road goes on / Hold the line / Africa / Rosanna / I won't hold you back / I'll be over you
CD _____ **4812029**
Columbia / Jul '96 / Sony

TOTO IV
Rossana / Make believe / I won't hold you back / Good for you / It's a feeling / Afraid of love / Lovers in the night / We made it / Waiting for your love / Africa
CD _____ **4500882**
CBS / Mar '91 / Sony
CD _____ **CK 64423**
Mastersound / Feb '95 / Sony

Toto Bissainthe

TOTO BISSAINTHE
CD _____ **LDX 274014**
La Chant Du Monde / Oct '95 / ADA / Harmonia Mundi

Toto Coelo

I EAT CANNIBALS (& Other Tasty Tracks)
CD _____ **RE 21062**
Razor & Tie / Jul '96 / Koch

I EAT CANNIBALS
I eat cannibals / Milk from the coconut / Man o'war / (I may commit) the perfect crime / Spy versus spy / Dracula's tango / Mucho macho / Milk from the coconut / Hey rajah / I eat cannibals
CD _____ **301652**
Hallmark / Jun '97 / Carlton

Tottenham Hotspur FC

GLORY GLORY TOTTENHAM HOTSPUR (Various Artists)
Glory glory Tottenham / Ossie's dream / Hot shot Tottenham / Tottenham Tottenham / It's a grand old team to play for / When the year ends in one / We're off to Wembley / Nice one Cyril / One team in London / Tottenham win away / We are Tottenham / Tribute to Ardiles and villa / Tip top Tottenham Hotspurs / Spurs go Spurs boogie / Up the Spurs / Spurs go marching on / Cry Gazza cry / Gascoigne please / Nice one Gazza / New cockeral chorus / Ooh Gary / Gary Lineker a young girls dream / Diamond lights / It's goodbye / Fog on the Tyne / All you need is love / Happy Christmas (war is over)
CD _____ **CDGAFFER 2**
Cherry Red / Nov '95 / Pinnacle

Touch

TOUCH
CD _____ **CDMFN 107**
Music For Nations / Aug '90 / Pinnacle

Touch

TOUCH SAMPLER VOL.2
CD _____ **TZERO 2**
Touch / Dec '96 / Kudos / Pinnacle

Touchstone

JEALOUSY
Mooncoin jig/High reel/Plover's wing / Cuach mo lonndubh bui/Three sea captains / Last chance / Lonely wanderer / Primrose lass/Keel row/Green grow the rushes o / Garcon a marier/Orgies nocturnes/Dans fisel / Jealousy / King's favourite/Cook in the kitchen/Din Turrant's polka / Invisible wings/Faolean / Green gates/Pinch of snuff / White snow
CD _____ **GLCD 1050**
Green Linnet / Feb '90 / ADA / CM / Direct / Highlander / Roots

NEW LAND, THE
Kilmoulis jig/The maid at the spinning wheel / Jack Haggerty / Flowing tide/Cooley's hornpipe / Susanna Martin / Flying reel/My Maryann/Game of love / Casadh cam na Feadarnaighe / Three polkas / Farewell to Nova Scotia / Song in F / Bolen's fancy/ Dunmore lasses/Glass of beer / New land
CD _____ **GLCD 1040**
Green Linnet / Feb '88 / ADA / CM / Direct / Highlander / Roots

Toulouse

WAY THE CITY STRETCHES
CD _____ **G 005CD**
Won't Go Flat / Mar '97 / Cargo

Toups, Wayne

BACK TO THE BAYOU (Toups, Wayne & ZydeCajun)
I saw Johnny dance / Mine, mine, mine / Old fashioned two-step / Take my hand / Come on in / Oh what a night / 4.A.M Alone / Un autre biere / Ma belle / Rockin' Saturday night / Every man needs a woman / Back door
CD _____ **IRCD 036**
Iona / Jul '96 / ADA / Direct / Duncans

Toure, Ali Farke

RADIO MALI
Njarka / Yer mali gakoyoyo / Soko / Bandalabourou / Machengoidi / Samarya / hani / Gambari / Gambari (Njarka) / Biennal / Arsany / Amadinin / Seygalore / Trei kongo / Radio mali / Njarka (excerpt)
CD _____ **WCD 044**
World Circuit / Apr '96 / ADA / Cadillac / Direct / New Note/Pinnacle

SOURCE, THE
CD _____ **WCD 030**
World Circuit / Jun '92 / ADA / Cadillac / Direct / New Note/Pinnacle

TALKING TIMBUKTU (Toure, Ali Farke & Ry Cooder)
Blonde / Soukora / Gomni / Sega / Amandrai / Lasidan / Keito / Banga / Ai du / Diarabi
CD _____ **WCD 040**
World Circuit / Mar '94 / ADA / Cadillac / Direct / New Note/Pinnacle

Toure Kunda

AMADOU TILO
CD _____ **CPCD 8296**
Charly / Jul '97 / Koch

CASAMANCE AU CLAIR DE LUNE
CD _____ **CPCD 8269**
Charly / Mar '97 / Koch

LES FRERES GRIOTS
Em'ma / On verra ca / Samala / Kambe / Africa lelly / Soye / Bounane / Mango / Touty yolle
CD _____ **MPG 74041**
Movieplay Gold / Jun '97 / Target/BMG

NATALIA
Toure Kunda / Duu nya / Santhiaba silo / Natalia / M'barring / Fode / Babacady
CD _____ **CPCD 8268**
Charly / Dec '96 / Koch

TOURE KUNDA
Turu / Salaly Muhamed / Banny / Kano kano / Samba / Waar / Guedj / Hamidu / Yaya bah
CD _____ **CPCD 8295**
Charly / Apr '97 / Koch

TOURE KUNDA LIVE
CD _____ **CPCD 8226**
Charly / Aug '96 / Koch

Tournesol

KOKOTSU
Imeat / Electric church / Henka / Orange planet / Draagmad Ultramarine / Cathedral / Holy cow
CD _____ **AMB 4931CD**
Apollo / Mar '94 / Vital

MOONFUNK
Inside angel / Chords of rhythm / Junglemovie / Sunny blow / Interplanetary zonecheck / Electrowaltz / Scapeland / Break 'n' space / Voltage / Mapping your mind / Beljeane / 2095 / Clockworking clockwork clock
CD _____ **RS 95074CD**
R&S / Aug '95 / Vital

Toussaint, Allen

20 GOLDEN LOVE THEMES (Movie Themes) (Toussaint, Allen Orchestra)
CD _____ **MU 5036**
Musketeer / Oct '92 / Disc

50'S MASTERS, THE
Whirlaway / Happy times / Up the crek / Tim tam / Me and you / Bono / Java / Wham tousan / Nowhere to go / Nashua / Po' boy walk / Pelican parade / Chico / (Back home again in) Indiana / Second liner / Cow cow blues / Moo moo / Sweetie pie (twenty years later) / You didn't know, did you / Up right / Blue mood / Lazy day / Naomi / Real churchy / Real church
CD _____ **BCD 15641**
Bear Family / Mar '92 / Direct / Rollercoaster / Swift

ALLEN TOUSSAINT COLLECTION, THE
CD _____ **7599265492**
Reprise / May '95 / Warner Music

FROM A WHISPER TO A SCREAM
From a whisper to a scream / Chokin' kind / Sweet touch of love / What is success / Working in a coalmine / Everything I do gonh be funky / Either / Louie / Cast your fate to the wind / Number nine / Pickles
CD _____ **CDKENM 036**
Kent / Mar '91 / Pinnacle

MOTION
Night people / Just a kiss away / With you in mind / Lover of love / To be with you / Motion / Viva la money / Declaration of love / Happiness / Optimism blues
CD _____ **7599265972**
Reprise / Jan '96 / Warner Music

SOUND OF MOVIES, THE (Toussaint, Allen Orchestra)
CD _____ **MU 5038**
Musketeer / Oct '92 / Disc

WILD SOUND OF NEW ORLEANS PIANO, THE
Up the creek / Tim Tam / Me And You / Bono / Java / Happy Times / Nowhere to go / Nashua / Po' Boy Walk / Pelican parade / Whirlaway / Wham Tousan
CD _____ **EDCD 275**
Edsel / Apr '91 / Pinnacle

Toussaint, Jean

LIFE I WANT
Blue funk / It's for you / Island man / Life I want / Crouch End afternoon / Soho strut / Gangway / Short straw / Grooving at the hall / London / Red cross
CD _____ **NNCD 1001**
New Note / Oct '95 / Cadillac / New Note/ Pinnacle

WHAT GOES AROUND
CD _____ **WCD 029**
World Circuit / May '92 / ADA / Cadillac / Direct / New Note/Pinnacle

WHO'S BLUES
Opening gambit / Who's blues / London / Visiting / Body language / Yanar's dance / Soundtrack / Chameleon
CD _____ **JHCD 019**
Ronnie Scott's Jazz House / Jan '94 / Cadillac / Jazz Music / New Note/Pinnacle / TKO Magnum

Tovey, Frank

CIVILIAN
CD _____ **CDSTUMM 56**
Mute / Jun '88 / RTM/Disc

FAD GADGET SINGLES
Back to nature / Box / Ricky's hand / Fireside favourite / Insecticide / Lady shave / Saturday night special / King of the flies / Life on the line / 4M / For whom the bells toll / Love parasite / I discover love / Collapsing new people / One man's meat
CD _____ **CDSTUMM 37**
Mute / '86 / RTM/Disc

SNAKES AND LADDERS
CD _____ **CDSTUMM 23**
Mute / '86 / RTM/Disc

TYRANNY AND THE HIRED HAND
'31 depression blues / Hard times in the cotton mill / John Henry/Let your hammer ring / Blantyre explosion / Money cravin' folks / All I got's gone / Midwife song / Sam Hall / Dark as a dungeon / Men of good fortune / Sixteen tons / North country blues

/ Buffalo skinners / Black lung song / Pastures of plenty / Joe hill
CD ____ CDSTUMM 73
Mute / Aug '89 / RTM/Disc

Towa Tei

FUTURE LISTENING
Luv connection / I want to relax please / Technova (la em copacabana) / Meditation / Son of bambi (walk tuff) / Obrigado / Dubnova / La douce vie (amai seikatsu) / Raga musgo / Batucada
CD ____ 7559617612
Warner Bros. / Sep '95 / Warner Music

Tower City

LITTLE BIT OF FIRE, A
CD ____ 19966
MTM / Oct '96 / Cargo

Tower Of Power

BUMP CITY
You got to funkifize / What happend to the world that day / Flash in the pan / Gone / You strike my main nerve / Down to the nightclub (bump city) / You're still a young man / Skating on thin ice / Of the earth
CD ____ 7599263482
Warner Bros. / Sep '93 / Warner Music

IN THE SLOT
Just enough and too much / Treat me like your man / If I play my cards right / As surely as I stand here / Fanfare-matanuska / On the serious side / Ebony jam / You're so wonderful, so marvellous / Vuela por noche / Essence of innocence / Soul of a child / Drop it in the slot
CD ____ 7599263502
Warner Bros. / Sep '93 / Warner Music

SOULED OUT
Souled out / Taxed to the max / Keep comin' back / Soothe you / Do you wanna (make love to me) / Lovin' you forever / Gotta make a change / Diggin' on James Brown / Sexy soul / Just like you / Once you get a taste / Undercurrent
CD ____ 4809422
Epic / Sep '95 / Sony

URBAN RENEWAL
Only so much oil in the ground / Come back baby / It's not the crime / I won't leave unless you want me to / Maybe it'll rub off / (To say the least) you're the most / Willing to learn / Give me the proof / It can never be the same / I believe in myself / Walkin' up hip street
CD ____ 7599263492
Warner Bros. / Sep '93 / Warner Music

Towering Inferno

KADDISH
Rose / Prayer / Dachau / 4 By 2 / Edvard Kiraly / Memory / Not me / Reverse field / Occupation / Sto Mondo Rotondo / Organ loop / Toll / Toll (II) / Ruin / Juden / Pogrom / Partisans / Modern times / Bell / Kaddish / Weaver
CD ____ CID 8039
CD ____ CIDX 8039
Island / Aug '95 / PolyGram

Townend, Rick

MAKE THE OLD TIMES NEW (Townend, Rick & Rosie Davis)
CD ____ BOBB 001CD
British Bluegrass / Nov '95 / ADA / Direct

Towner, Ralph

ANA
Reluctant bride / Tale of saverio / Joyful departure / Green and golden / I knew it was you / Les douzilles / Veldt / Between the clouds / Child on the porch / Carib crib (1 & 2) / Slavic blood / Toru / Sage brush rider
CD ____ 5370232
ECM / Apr '97 / New Note/Pinnacle

BATIK
Waterwheel / Shades of Sutton Hoo / Trellis / Batik / Green room
CD ____ 8473252
ECM / Oct '89 / New Note/Pinnacle

BLUE SUN
CD ____ 8291622
ECM / Oct '86 / New Note/Pinnacle

CITY OF EYES
CD ____ 8377542
ECM / May '89 / New Note/Pinnacle

DIARY
Dark spirit / Entry in a diary / Images unseen / Icarus / Mon enfant / Ogden road / Erg / Silence of a candle
CD ____ 8291572
ECM / Aug '86 / New Note/Pinnacle

LOST AND FOUND
Harbringer / Trill ride / Elan vital / Summer's end / Col legno / Soft landing / Flying cows / Mon enfant / Breath away / Scrimshaw / Midnight blue...red shift / Moonless / Sco cone / Tattler / Taxi's waiting
CD ____ 5293472
ECM / Feb '96 / New Note/Pinnacle

MATCHBOOK (Towner, Ralph & Gary Burton)
CD ____ 8350142
ECM / Oct '88 / New Note/Pinnacle

OLD FRIENDS, NEW FRIENDS
CD ____ 8291962
ECM / Oct '86 / New Note/Pinnacle

OPEN LETTER
Sigh / Wistful thinking / Adrift / Infection / Alar / Short 'n' stout / Waltz for Debby / I fall in love too easily / Magic touch / Magnolia Island / Nightfall
CD ____ 5119802
ECM / Jun '92 / New Note/Pinnacle

SARGASSO SEA (Towner, Ralph & John Abercrombie)
CD ____ 8350152
ECM / Sep '88 / New Note/Pinnacle

SLIDE SHOW (Towner, Ralph & Gary Burton)
Maelstrom / Vessel / Around the bend / Blue in green / Beneath an evening sky / Donkey jamboree / Continental breakfast / Charlotte's tangle / Innocenti
CD ____ 8272572
ECM / Feb '86 / New Note/Pinnacle

SOLO CONCERT
Spirit lake / Ralph's piano waltz / Train of thought / Zoetrope / Nardis / Chelsea courtyard / Timeless
CD ____ 8276682
ECM / Dec '85 / New Note/Pinnacle

SOLSTICE
Oceanus / Visitation / Drifting petals / Numbus / Winter solstice / Piscean dance / Red and black / Sand
CD ____ 8254582
ECM / '82 / New Note/Pinnacle

SOUND AND SHADOWS
Distant hills / Balance beam / Along the way / Arion / Song of the shadows
CD ____ 8293862
ECM / Oct '89 / New Note/Pinnacle

TRIOS AND SOLOS (Towner, Ralph & Glen Moore)
CD ____ 8333282
ECM / Jul '88 / New Note/Pinnacle

WORKS: RALPH TOWNER
Oceanus / Blue sun / New moon / Beneath an evening sky / Prince and the sage / Nimbus
CD ____ 8232682
ECM / Jun '89 / New Note/Pinnacle

Townes, Billy

LIVIN' FOR YOUR LOVE
Moroccan pasta / Minutes to go / Low gear / For my friend / Snowbound / Hypnotique / And the beat goes where / Sea breeze / Sun city at night / Dawn / Livin' for your love
CD ____ 101S 71422
101 South / Nov '93 / New Note/Pinnacle

Towns, Colin

COLIN TOWNS' MASK ORCHESTRA, THE (2CD Set) (Towns, Colin Mask Orchestra)
Smack and thistle / Music to type to / Tears for a traveller / Sixpence is a long shilling / Dream of pain / Magnificent whittling stomp / Completely lost / Not waving but drowning / Truth beauty compassion dignity / Bolt from the blue / Solitude
CD Set ____ TJL 001CD
The Jazz Label / Mar '97 / New Note/Pinnacle / Vital/SAM

Townshend, Pete

ALL THE BEST COWBOYS HAVE CHINESE EYES
Stop hurting people / Sea refuses no river / Slit skirts / Somebody saved me / North country girl / Uniforms (crop d'esprit) / Stardom in Acton / Communication / Exquisitely bored / Face dances part two / Prelude
CD ____ 7567828122
Atco / Jan '96 / Warner Music

COOL WALKING SMOOTH TALKING STRAIGHT SMOKING FIRESTOKING
CD ____ 7567827122
Atco / May '96 / Warner Music

EMPTY GLASS
Rough boys / I am an animal / And I moved / Let my love open the door / Jools and Jim / Keep on working / Cats in the cupboard / Little is enough / Empty glass / Gonna getcha
CD ____ 7567828112
Atco / Nov '95 / Warner Music

PSYCHODERELICT
English boy / Meher baba M3 / Let's get pretentious / Maher baba M4 (signal box) / Early morning dreams / I want that thing / Dialogue introduction to Outlive The Dinosaur / Outlive the dinosaur / Flame (demo) / Now and then / I am afraid / Don't try to make me real / Dialogue introduction to Predictable / Predictable / Flame / Meher baba m5 / Fake it / Dialogue introduction to Now And Then (Reprise) / Now and then (reprise) / Baba O'Riley / English boy (reprise)
CD ____ 7567824942
Atco / Jun '93 / Warner Music

WHITE CITY
Second hand love / Give blood / Brilliant blues / Crashing by design / Lonely words / White City fighting / Face the face / All shall be well / Hiding out / Closing sequence
CD ____ 2523922
Atco / Apr '86 / Warner Music

WHO CAME FIRST
Pure and easy / Evolution / Forever's no time at all / Let's see action / Time is passing / There's a heartache following me / Sheraton Gibson / Content / Parvardigar / His hands / Seeker / Day of silence / Sleeping dog / Loved man / Latern cabin
CD ____ RCD 10246
Rykodisc / Mar '97 / ADA / Vital

Toxik

WORLD CIRCUS
Heart attack / Social overload / Pain and misery / Voices / Door to hell / World circus / Forty seven seconds of sanity / False prophets / Haunted earth / Victims
CD ____ RR 349572
Roadrunner / Mar '88 / PolyGram

Toy Dolls

BARE FACED CHEEK
Bare faced cheek / Yul Bryner was a skinhead / How do you deal with Neal / Howza bouta kiss babe / Fisticuffs in Frederick Street / A Diamond / Quick to quit the Quentin / Nowt can compare to Sunderland Fine-Fare / Ashbrooke launderette
CD ____ RRCD 232
Receiver / Mar '97 / Grapevine/PolyGram

ONE MORE MEGABYTE
CD ____ RRCD 236
Receiver / May '97 / Grapevine/PolyGram

RECEIVER YEARS, THE
CD Set ____ RRCDX 504
Receiver / Sep '95 / Grapevine/PolyGram

TEN YEARS OF TOYS
Florence is deaf (But there's no need to shout) / Glenda and the test tube baby / Idle gossip / Carol Dodds is pregnant / Tommy Knowey's car / Peter practise's practise place / Dierdre's a slag / Blue suede shoes / Dig that groove baby / Lambrusco kid / Doughy giro / Bless you my son / My girlfriend's Dad's a vicar / she goes to fino's / Firey Jack
CD ____ RRCD 234
Receiver / Jan '97 / Grapevine/PolyGram

Toyah

ACOUSTIC ALBUM, THE
Vow / Moonlight dancing / Revive the world / I want to be free / It's a mystery / Danced / Good morning universe / Blue meanings / Jungles of jupiter / It's a mystery (up-tempo) / Leyla / Angels and demons / I am / Thunder in the mountain / It's a mystery(string version)
CD ____ ANT 012
Tring / Nov '96 / Tring

BEST OF TOYAH, THE
It's a mystery / Good morning universe / I want to be free / Neon womb / Be proud, be loud, be heard / Bird in flight / Rebel run / Brave new world / Dawn chorus / Victims of the riddle / Vow / Tribal look / Thunder in the mountains / Angel and me / Danced / leya
CD ____ CSAPCD 115
Connoisseur Collection / Feb '94 / Pinnacle

LOOKING BACK
I wanna be free / Obsolete / It's a mystery / We are / Thunder in the mountains / Good morning universe / Angel and me / Be proud, be loud / Danced / Rebel run / leya
CD ____ QED 065
Tring / Nov '96 / Tring

PHOENIX
Now and then / Let me go / World of tension / Out of the blue / Unkind / Dreamchild / Lost and found / Over you / I don't know / Disappear / Tone poem / Now and then / Phoenix
CD ____ RRCD 235
Receiver / Apr '97 / Grapevine/PolyGram

VERY BEST OF TOYAH, THE
It's a mystery / Good morning universe / I want to be free / Be proud be loud be heard / Bird in flight / Rebel run / Brave new world / Thunder in the mountains / leya / Street creature / Elusive stranger / Martian cowboy / Love me / Broken diamonds / Castaways / She / Jungles of Jupiter / We are
CD ____ NTMCD 551
Nectar / Apr '97 / Pinnacle

Toyama, Yoshio

DUET (Toyama, Yoshio & Ralph Sutton)
CD ____ JCD 226
Jazzology / Apr '94 / Jazz Music

Toyota Pipes & Drums

AMAZING GRACE
March, strathspey and reel / Slow air, jig and hornpipe / 6/8 Marches / Amazing grace / By the rivers of Babylon / Mount Fuji / Greatest hits medley / Sands of time / Magnificent seven / Send in the clowns / Salute to America
CD ____ LCOM 5133
Lismor / Jun '93 / ADA / Direct / Duncans / Lismor

T'Pau

BRIDGE OF SPIES
Heart and soul / I will be with you / China in your hand / Friends like these / Sex talk / Bridge of spies / Monkey house / Valentine / Thank you for goodbye / You give up / China in your hand (reprise)
CD ____ CDVIP 179
Virgin VIP / Apr '97 / EMI

HEART AND SOUL (The Best Of T'Pau)
Heart and soul / Valentine / Only a heartbeat / Whenever you need me / Secret garden / Sex talk / Road to our dream / This girl / Only the lonely / Bridge of spies / I will be with you / China in your hand
CD ____ TPAUD 1
Virgin / Mar '93 / EMI

PROMISE, THE
Soul destruction / Whenever you need me / Walk on air / Made of money / Hold on to love / Strange place / One direction / Only a heartbeat / Promise / Place in my heart / Man and woman / Purity
CD ____ CDVIP 124
Virgin VIP / Mar '94 / EMI

Tracey, Clark

FULL SPEED SIDEWAYS
Revenge of Sam Tracet / They're lovely / Sherman at the Copthorne / Sphere my dear / Mark nightingale song / Arnie's barnie / Chased out
CD ____ 33JAZZ 018
33 Jazz / Apr '95 / Cadillac / New Note/ Pinnacle

WE'VE BEEN EXPECTING YOU (Tracey, Clark Quintet)
CD ____ 33JAZZ 007CD
33 Jazz / Jun '93 / Cadillac / New Note/ Pinnacle

Tracey, Stan

FOR HEAVEN'S SAKE
CD ____ SGCCD 04
Cadillac / May '96 / Cadillac / Jazz Music / Wellard

GENESIS AND MORE... (Tracey, Stan & His Orchestra)
Beginning / Light / Firmament / Gathering / Sun, moon and the stars / Feather, fin and limb / Sixth day
CD ____ SJCD 114
Steam / Nov '89 / Cadillac / Jazz Music / Wellard

LAUGHIN' AND SCRATCHIN' (Tracey, Stan Trio)
CD ____ JHAS 608
Ronnie Scott's Jazz House / Mar '97 / Cadillac / Jazz Music / New Note/Pinnacle / TKO Magnum

PLAYS DUKE ELLINGTON
I let a song go out of my heart / Prelude to a kiss / Satin doll / In a mellow tone / Daydream / Great times / Sophisticated lady / Black butterfly / Lotus blossom
CD ____ MOLECD 10
Mole Jazz / Jan '90 / Cadillac / Impetus / Jazz Music / Wellard

PORTRAITS PLUS
Newk's fluke / Rocky mount / One for Gil / Clinkscales / Spectrum No. 2 / Mainframe
CD ____ CDBLT 1006
EMI / Dec '92 / EMI

WE STILL LOVE YOU MADLY (Tribute To Duke Ellington) (Tracey, Stan & His Orchestra)
I'm beginning to see the light / Mood indigo / Blue feeling / I let a song go out of my heart / Stomp, look and listen / Festival junction / In a sentimental mood / Just squeeze me / Lay by
CD ____ MOLECD 13
Mole Jazz / Apr '89 / Cadillac / Impetus / Jazz Music / Wellard

Tractor

WORST ENEMIES
Lost on the ocean / Average man's hero / Suicidal / Argument for one / Word games / Trick of the light / Scotch boulevard / No more rock 'n' roll / Peterloo
CD ____ OZITCD 0019
Ozit / May '97 / Cargo / Direct

Tractors

HAVE YOURSELF A TRACTOR CHRISTMAS
Santa Claus is coming to town / Jingle my bells / Shelter / Rockin' this Christmas / Santa looked a lot like Daddy / Christmas

is coming / Santa Claus is comin' (in a boogie woogie choo choo train) / Baby wanna be by you / Swingin' home for Christmas / White Christmas / Santa Claus boogie / Silent night / Christmas blue
CD 07822188052
Arista / Nov '95 / BMG

TRACTORS, THE
Tulsa shuffle / Fallin' apart / Thirty days / I've had enough / Little man / Baby likes to rock it / Badly bent / Blue collar rock / Doreen / Settin' the woods on fire / Tryin' to get to New Orleans / Tulsa shuffle (Revisited)
CD 07822187282
Arista / Aug '94 / BMG

Tracy, Arthur

ALWAYS IN SONG
CD PLATCD 36
Platinum / Mar '95 / Prism

MARTA
Across the great divide / Broken hearted clown / East of the sun and west of the moon / Greatest mistake of my life / I'll see you again / I'll sing you a thousand love songs / In a little gypsy tea room / Love's last word is spoken / My curly headed baby / Marta / Music, maestro, please / Old sailor / Red maple leaves / Roses of Picardy / September in the rain / Smilin' through / South Sea island magic / Stay awhile / When I grow too old to dream / Where are you / Whistling waltz / You are my heart's delight
CD CDAJA 5095
Living Era / Sep '92 / Select

SPEAK TO ME OF LOVE
Speak to me of love / East of the Sun and West of the moon / Brokenhearted clown / September rain / Trees / Love's last word is spoken / In a little gipsy tea room / It looks like rain in Cherry Blossom Lane / Serenade / Whistling waltz / Give me a heart to sing to / Smoke gets in your eyes / Roses of Picardy / South of the border / (I'm afraid) The masquerade is over / Solitude / Where are you / Wheel of the wagon is broken / Farewell sweet senorita / It's a sin to tell a lie / Somewhere in the West / When I'm with you / Marta (rambling rose of the wild wood) / When I grow too old to dream
CD CDMOIR 517
Memoir / Aug '96 / Jazz Music / Target/ BMG

STREET SINGER, THE
There's a goldmine in the sky / Waltz for those in love / Giannina mia / Water lilies in the moonlight / When the organ played 'O promise me' / Halfway to heaven / Song of songs / Smilin' through / Faithful forever / Just a wearyin' for you / Hills of old Wyomin' / Along the Santa Fe trail / We three (my echo, my shadow and me) / Breeze and I / Shepherd's serenade / Say it (over and over again) / Shrine of St. Cecilia / When the roses bloom again / Last time I saw Paris / Somewhere in France with you / White cliffs of Dover / Marta
CD PASTCD 7006
Flapper / Mar '93 / Pinnacle

VERY BEST OF ARTHUR TRACY - THE STREET SINGER
CD SOW 906
Sound Waves / May '93 / Target/BMG

VERY BEST OF THE STREET SINGER VOL.2
CD SWNCD 002
Sound Waves / May '95 / Target/BMG

Tracy, Jeanie

IT'S MY TIME
CD PULSE 17CD
Pulse 8 / Nov '95 / BMG

Tracy, Steve

GOING TO CINCINNATI
CD BSCD 4707
Blue Shadow / '92 / Swift

Trad Gras Och Stenar

GARDET 12/6/1970
CD TILCD 01
Subliminal / Jun '97 / Greyhound

Trader Horne

MORNING WAY...PLUS
CD SEECD 308
See For Miles/C5 / '90 / Pinnacle

Tradia

TRADE WINDS
Never gonna go / Let's not turn love away / Without you / Look away / No pain, no gain / Stand your ground / Don't play your ace / Take the chance / You've got me crying again / Exiles
CD WKFMXD 108
FM / Jul '88 / Revolver / Sony

Traffic

BEST OF TRAFFIC, THE
Paper sun / Heaven is in your mind / No face, no name, no number / Coloured rain / Smiling phases / Hole in my shoe / Medicated goo / Forty thousand headmen / Feeling alright / Shanghai noodle factory / Dear Mr. Fantasy
CD IMCD 169
Island / Mar '93 / PolyGram

FAR FROM HOME
Riding high / Here comes a man / Far from home / Nowhere is their freedom / Holy ground / Some kinda woman / Every night, every day / This train won't stop / State of grace / Mozambique
CD CDV 2727
Virgin / May '94 / EMI

JOHN BARLEYCORN MUST DIE
Glad / Freedom rider / Empty page / Stranger to himself / John Barleycorn / Every mother's son
CD IMCD 40
Island / Sep '89 / PolyGram

LAST EXIT
Just for you / Shanghai noodle factory / Something's got a hold of my toe / Withering tree / Medicated goo / Feeling good / Blind man
CD IMCD 41
Island / Sep '89 / PolyGram

LOW SPARK OF HIGH-HEELED BOYS, THE
Hidden treasure / Low spark of high heeled boys / Light up or leave me alone / Rock 'n' roll stew / Many a mile to freedom / Rainmaker
CD IMCD 42
Island / Sep '89 / PolyGram

MR. FANTASY
Heaven is in your mind / Berkshire poppies / House for everyone / No face, no name, no number / Dear Mr. Fantasy / Dealer / Utterly simple / Coloured rain / Hope I never find me there / Giving to you
CD IMCD 43
Island / Sep '89 / PolyGram

ON THE ROAD
Glad/Freedom rider / Tragic magic / (Sometimes I feel so) Inspired / Shoot out at the fantasy factory / Light up or leave me alone / Low spark of high heeled boys
CD IMCD 183
Island / Mar '94 / PolyGram

SHOOT OUT AT THE FANTASY FACTORY
Shoot out at the fantasy factory / Roll right stones / Evening blue / Tragic magic / Sometimes I feel so uninspired
CD IMCD 44
Island / Sep '89 / PolyGram

TRAFFIC
You can all join in / Pearly queen / Don't be sad / Who knows what tomorrow may bring / Feeling alright / Vagabond virgin / Forty thousand headmen / Cryin' to be heard / No time to live / Means to an end
CD IMCD 45
Island / '89 / PolyGram

WELCOME TO THE CANTEEN (Recorded Live)
Medicated goo / Sad and deep / As you / Forty thousand headmen / Shouldn't have took more than you gave / Dear Mr. Fantasy / Gimme some lovin'
CD IMCD 39
Island / '89 / PolyGram

WHEN THE EAGLE FLIES
Something new / Dream Gerrard / Graveyard people / Walking in the wind / Memories of a rock and rolla / LOVE / When the eagle flies
CD IMCD 142
Island / Aug '91 / PolyGram

Traffic Sound

TRAFFIC SOUND
CD HBG 122/13
Background / Apr '94 / Background / Greyhound

TRAFFIC SOUND 1968-1969
CD HBG 122/4
Background / Mar '94 / Background / Greyhound

Tragedy Divine

VISIONS OF POWER
CD TT 00212
T&T / Mar '96 / Koch

Tragert, Walter

HEAVY JUST THE SAME
CD MRCD 1095
Club De Musique / Jun '96 / Direct

Tragic Error

KLATCH IN DIE HANDEN
CD WHOS 022CD
Who's That Beat / '90 / Vital

Tragic Mulatto

ITALIANS FALL DOWN LOOK UP
CD VIRUS 74CD
Alternative Tentacles / Jun '89 / Cargo / Greyhound / Pinnacle

Tragically Hip

LIVE BETWEEN US
CD UMD 81055
Universal / Aug '97 / BMG

UP TO HERE
Blow at high dough / I'll believe in you / New Orleans is sinking / 38 years old / She didn't know / Boots or hearts / Everytime you go / When the weight comes down / Trickle down / Another midnight / Opiated
CD MCLD 19265
MCA / Dec '94 / BMG

Trail Of Thebow

ORNAMENTATION
CD RR 69122
Relapse / Jul '96 / Pinnacle / Plastic Head

Train Journey North

FIRST TRACKS
Faca sibh mairi nighean Alisdair / Wha'll be King but Charlie/Galway Trolley/Double rise / Road to Drumlemon / Da new rigged ship/ The chanter's tune/MacArthur Road / Hebridean reel/The trip to Windsord / Skyemans jig/Skylark ascension/Alex MacDonald/Echoes of Oban / Bobs of Balmoral/Curlew / Glasgow city Police Pipe Band/Jenny Dang the weaver/Hogties / Domhnull ban nan gobhar / Melody O'Farrel / Far from home/The streaker/Rodrigo / Coille an fhabach
CD CDLDL 1207
Lochshore / Feb '97 / ADA / Direct / Duncans

Trains & Boats & Planes

ENGULFED
CD RAIN 002
Cloudland / Jan '94 / Plastic Head / SRD

HUM
CD UFO 010CD
UFO / Mar '92 / Pinnacle

Tramline

SOMEWHERE DOWN THE LINE
CD EDCD 469
Edsel / Apr '96 / Pinnacle

Trammell, Bobby Lee

YOU MOSTEST GIRL
Shirley Lee / I sure do love you baby / You mostest girl / Uh oh / Should I make amends / My Susie Jane my Susie Jane / Martha Jane / Jenny Lee / It's all your fault / Couldn't believe my eyes / You stand a chance of losing what you've got / Love don't let me down / Twenty four hours / Am I satisfying you / I tried / Just let me love you one more time / Come on and love me / If you don't wanna you don't have to / Give me that good lovin' / New dance in France / Long Tall Sally
CD BCD 15887
Bear Family / Nov '95 / Direct / Rollercoaster / Swift

Trammps

LEGENDARY ZING ALBUM, THE
Penguin at the big apple/Zing went the strings of my heart / Pray all you sinners / Sixty minute man / Scrub board / Tom's song / Rubber band / Hold back the night / Penguin at the big apple
CD CDKENM 088
Kent / Oct '88 / Pinnacle

Tramp

BRITISH BLUES GIANTS
Own up / What you gonna do when the road comes through / Somebody watching me / Baby, what you want me to do / On the scene / Hard work / Too late for that now / What you gonna do / You gotta move / Funky money / Maternity orders (keep on rolling in) / Same old thing / Too late now / Street walking blues / Month of Sundays / Another day / Now I ain't a junkie anymore / Like you used to do / Put a record on / Beggar by your side / It's over
CD SEECD 354
See For Miles/C5 / Sep '92 / Pinnacle

Trance

ROCKERS
CD 36700022
Mausoleum / Oct '91 / Grapevine/ PolyGram

Trance Groove

PARAMOUNT
Dschang thang / Stone soup / Trainspotting / Ange gardien / Morning zoo / Hotel Clapham / In a field / Paramount / Paris / Wedding / Terje rypdal

CD CIA 40002
Call It Anything / Oct '96 / New Note/ Pinnacle

SOLID GOLD EASY ACTION
Reebop / Character / Bladerunner / Waiting man / Fireball / Driving south / Swamp / Air Afrique / Mamboo moon / Water / Low tide / Bladerunner II / Reebop radio edit
CD VBR 21432
Vera Bra / Jun '94 / New Note/Pinnacle / Pinnacle

Trance Induction

ELECTRICKERY
Ambienta / Nada brahma / New edge / Heaven / New age heartcore / Spinner / Bombay / Infotask / Cyberlog / Robogroove 3 / Lit by doctor life
CD GPCD 001
Guerilla / Apr '94 / Pinnacle

Trance Mission

TRANCE MISSION
CD CDSGP 0303
Prestige / Jul '96 / Else / Total/BMG

Trance To The Sun

GHOST FOREST
CD EFA 064822
Tess / Apr '94 / SRD

Trancendental Anarchists

CLUSTER ZONE
CD SR 9462CD
Silent / Jan '95 / Cargo / Plastic Head

Tranquility Bass

LET THE FREAK FLAG FLY
Five miles high / La la la / Bird / Soldiers sweetheart / We all want to be free / Never gonna end / I'll be here / Let the freak flag fly / Lichen me to Wyomin'
CD ASW 6200CD
Astralwerks / Apr '97 / Cargo / Vital

Trans Am

SURRENDER TO THE NIGHT
Motr / Cologne / Illegalize it / Love commander / Rough justice / Zero tolerance / Tough love / Night dreaming / Night dancing / Carboforce / Surrender to the night
CD EFA 0498826
City Slang / Feb '97 / RTM/Disc

TRANSAM
CD EFA 049772
City Slang / Apr '96 / RTM/Disc

Trans-Europe Express

TRANS - EUROPE EXPRESS
CD CLEO 5878CD
Cleopatra / Jan '94 / Cargo / Greyhound / Plastic Head / RTM/Disc / SRD

Trans-Lucid

DREAM DUST
CD AQUACD 2
Aquarius / Feb '97 / Arabesque / Prime

Transambient Communications

MOONMEN
Moonmen (intro) / Radio friendly / Weightless / Bubble / V5 / Are we water / Special orgee / Armstrong / Moonbeams / Receiving transmission / Moonmen (outro)
CD STONE 025CD
3rd Stone / Apr '97 / Plastic Head / Vital

PRAZE-AN-BEEBLE
Seabeams / Ocean waves at sunset / They shoot geese don't they / Alaska pt.1 / Arcades / Mauve / Iceman / Alaska pt.2 / What is muzik / River
CD STONE 015CD
3rd Stone / Sep '95 / Plastic Head / Vital

Transcend

2001-2008 FULL LENGTH
2001 / 2002 / 2003 / 2004 / 2005 / 2006 / 2007 / 2008
CD NTONECD 007
Ntone / Sep '95 / Kudos / Vital

VERSION 8.5
CD SSR 005CD
Stormstrike / Jul '95 / Plastic Head

Transcendental Love Machine

ORGASMATRONIC
CD DUKE 032CD
Hydrogen Dukebox / Jan '97 / 3mv/Vital / Kudos / Prime

Transfinite

BUGGED
CD KINXCD 5
Kinetix / Feb '97 / Pinnacle

Transglobal Underground

DREAM OF 100 NATIONS
CD _____ NRCD 021
Nation / Oct '93 / RTM/Disc

INTERNATIONAL TIMES
CD _____ NATCD 38
Nation / Oct '94 / RTM/Disc

INTERPLANETARY MELTDOWN
CD _____ NATCD 57
Nation / Oct '95 / RTM/Disc

PSYCHIC KARAOKE
CD _____ NRCD 1067
Nation / May '96 / RTM/Disc

Transient Waves

TRANSIENT WAVES
CD _____ IRE 2042
I / Jun '97 / SRD

Transits Of Tone

SYNTHESIZED THERAPY
Audio motive / Molecular structure / Dawning / Acid bunker / Sem X 4 / Wild life / Syncrone / Dawning / Cyborg remake / Computer / Dawning / Battle zone
CD _____ INTCD 20
Intelligence / Oct '96 / Intergroove / PolyGram / RTM/Disc

Transmetal

BURIAL AT SEA
CD _____ GCI 89804
Plastic Head / Jun '92 / Plastic Head

Transmisia

DUMBSHOW
CD _____ INV 027CD
Invisible / Jun '94 / Plastic Head
CD _____ WD 010CD
Wide / Jul '97 / Plastic Head / SRD

FRIGID PROSE
CD _____ WD 024CD
Wide / Apr '97 / Plastic Head / SRD

MINCING MACHINE
CD _____ WD 019CD
Wide / Jul '97 / Plastic Head / SRD

Transmission

TRANSMISSION
CD _____ ASH 018
Audible Hiss / Mar '97 / Cargo

Transvision Vamp

POP ART
Trash city / I want your love / Sister moon / Psychosonic Cindy / Revolution baby / Tell that girl to shut up / Wild star / Hanging out with Halo Jones / Andy Warhol's dead / Sex kick
CD _____ MCLD 19224
MCA / Sep '93 / BMG

VELVETEEN
Baby I don't care / Only one / Landslide of love / Falling for a goldmine / Down on you / Song to the stars / Kiss their sons / Born to be sold / Pay the ghosts / Bad valentine / Velveteen
CD _____ MCLD 19215
MCA / Aug '93 / BMG

Transwave

PHOTOTROPIC
CD _____ SUB 48092
Distance / Dec '96 / 3mv/Sony / Prime

Traore, Boubacar

SA GOLO
Sa golo / Mouso teke soma ye / Yafa ma / Dounia / Ntaara diagnamogo fe / Ala ta deye tignaye / Je chanterai pour toi / Soundiata
CD _____ LBLC 2534
Indigo / Jul '96 / New Note/Pinnacle

Trapeze

HIGH FLYERS (The Best Of Trapeze)
CD _____ 8209572
Deram / Jan '96 / PolyGram

HOLD ON
Don't ask me how I know / Take good care / When you get to heaven / Livin' on love / Hold on / Don't break my heart / Running / You are / Time will heal
CD _____ SEECD 450
See For Miles/C5 / Aug '96 / Pinnacle

LIVE IN TEXAS (Dead Armadillos)
Black cloud / You are the music, we're just the band / Way back to the bone / Back street love / Hold on / Midnight flyer
CD _____ SEECD 462
See For Miles/C5 / Oct '96 / Pinnacle

MEDUSA
Black cloud / Jury / Your love is alright / Touch my life / Seagull / Mates you wanna cry / Medusa
CD _____ 8209552
London / Feb '94 / PolyGram

TRAPEZE
It's only a dream / Giants dead, hoorah / Over / Nancy Gray / Fairytale / Verily verily / It's my life / Am I / Suicide / Wings / Another day / Send me no more letters
CD _____ 8209542
London / Feb '94 / PolyGram

YOU ARE THE MUSIC, WE'RE THE BAND
Keepin' time / Coast to coast / What is a woman's role / Way back to the bone / Feelin' so much better now / Will our love end / Loser / We are the music
CD _____ 8209562
London / Feb '94 / PolyGram

Trapezoid

COOL OF THE DAY
CD _____ SHCD 1132
Sugar Hill / Jan '97 / ADA / CM / Direct / Koch / Roots

NOW AND THEN
CD _____ FF 239CD
Flying Fish / May '93 / ADA / CM / Direct / Roots

Trasante, Negrito

UNTIL DAWN
CD _____ 972
Kardum / Aug '93 / Discovery

Trash Can Sinatras

CAKE
CD _____ 8282012
Go Discs / Jul '90 / PolyGram

HAPPY POCKET, A
Make yourself at home / Twisted and bent / Main attraction / To Sir, with love / How can I apply / Unfortunate age / Outside / Pop place / Genius I was / Sleeping policeman / I must fly / I'll get them in / Safecracker / Therapist
CD _____ 8286962
Go Discs / Sep '96 / PolyGram

I'VE SEEN EVERYTHING
Easy road / Hayfever / Bloodrush / Worked a miracle / Perfect reminder / Killing the cabinet / Orange fell / I'm immortal / Send for Benny / Iceberg / One at a time / I've seen everything / Hairy years / Earlies
CD _____ 8284082
Go Discs / May '93 / PolyGram

Trashmen

LIVE BIRD 1965-1967
Let's go trippin' / Baja / Lovin' up a storm / Malaguena / Green onions / Surfin' bird / Henrietta / Rumble / Bird dance beat / King of the surf / The / Mashed potatoes / Ubangi stomp / Dai Winslow interview / Same lines / Keep your hands off my baby
CD _____ CDSC 11006
Sundazed / Jan '94 / Cargo / Greyhound / Rollercoaster

Traum, Artie

CAYENNE
CD _____ ROUCD 3084
Rounder / ADA / CM / Direct

LETTERS FROM JOUBEE
CD _____ SHAN 5008CD
Shanachie / Dec '93 / ADA / Greensleeves / Koch

VIEW FROM HERE, THE
CD _____ SHCD 5016
Shanachie / Mar '96 / ADA / Greensleeves / Koch

Travelin' Light

CHRISTMAS WITH TRAVELIN' LIGHT
Let it snow, let it snow, let it snow / Sleigh ride / Frosty the Snowman / Twelve days of Christmas / Carol of the bells / Have yourself a merry little Christmas / We wish you a Merry Christmas / Jingle bells / Rudolph the red nosed reindeer / Here comes Santa Claus / Winter wonderland / Christmas song / Silver bells / Silent night
CD _____ CD 83330
Telarc / Nov '93 / Conifer/BMG

COOKIN' WITH FRANK & SAM
Manior de mes beves / Monk's dream / Dark eyes / Deep purple / Say it's so / Under Paris skies / Dig / Mood indigo / Alice's fax / Nuages / FDR Jones / Smoke gets in your eyes / Song d'automne / Lover
CD _____ CCD 4647
Concord Jazz / Jun '95 / New Note/ Pinnacle

MAKIN' WHOOPEE
CD _____ CD 83324
Telarc / Feb '93 / Conifer/BMG

Traveling Wilburys

TRAVELING WILBURYS VOL.1
Handle with care / Dirty world / Rattled / Last night / Not alone anymore / Congratulations / Heading for the light / Margarita / Tweeter and the monkey man / End of the line
CD _____ 9257962
Wilbury / Oct '88 / Warner Music

TRAVELING WILBURYS VOL.3
She's my baby / Inside out / If you belonged to me / Devil's been busy / Seven deadly sins / Poor house / Where were you last night / Cool dry place / New blue moon / You took my breath away / Wilbury twist
CD _____ 7599263242
Wilbury / Nov '90 / Warner Music

Travers, Pat

BLUES TRACKS
CD _____ RR 91472
Roadrunner / Sep '96 / PolyGram

HALFWAY TO SOMEWHERE
CD _____ PRD 70842
Provogue / Oct '95 / Pinnacle

JUST A TOUCH
CD _____ RR 90452
Roadrunner / Sep '96 / PolyGram

LOOKIN' UP
CD _____ PRD 70972
Provogue / Oct '96 / Pinnacle

Travis Cut

SERIAL INCOMPETENCE
CD _____ DAMGOOD 68CD
Damaged Goods / Apr '95 / Shellshock/ Disc

Travis, Merle

COUNTRY HOEDOWN SHOWS AND FILMS OF THE 1940S/50'S
CD _____ RFDCD 14
Country Routes / Feb '95 / Hot Shot / Jazz Music

FOLKSONGS OF THE HILLS
Nine pound hammer / That's all / John Bolin / Muskrat / Dark as a dungeon / John Henry / Sixteen tons / Possum up a Simmon tree / I am a pilgrim / Over by number nine / Barbara Allen / Lost John / Black gold / Harlan County boys / Pay day comes too slow / Browder explosion / Bloody Brethitt County / Here's to the operators, Boys / Miner's wife / Courtship of second cousin Claude / Miner's strawberries / Paw walked behind us with a cabride lamp / Preacher lane / Dear old Halifax
CD _____ BCD 15636
Bear Family / May '93 / Direct / Rollercoaster / Swift

GUITAR RAGS & A TOO FAST PAST (5CD Set)
You'll be lonesome too / Steppin' out kind / When Mussolini laid his pistol down / Two time Annie / What will I do / So long, farewell, goodbye / God put a rainbow in the clouds / It may be too late / Be on your way / Rainin' on the mountains / Give me your hand / Out on the open range / Ridin' down to Santa Fe / Hominy grits / That's all / Used to work in Chicago / Boogie woogie boy / Boogie woogie boy (Alt) / Merle's buck dance / Steel guitar stomp / I used to work in Chicago / I'm all thru trusting you / Weary lonesome me / No vacancy / Cincinnati Lou / Two is a couple (And three is a crowd) / What a shame / T For Texas (Blue yodel) / Missouri / Divorce me COD / Fool at the steering wheel / Nine pound hammer / Sixteen tons / Dark as a dungeon / Over by number nine / John Henry / Muskrat / I am a pilgrim / This world is not my home / Covered wagon rolled right along / Oh why oh why did I ever leave Wyoming / Little too far / When Rosie Riccoola do the Hoola Ma Boola / Steel guitar rag (Alt) / Honey bunch (Alt) / Sweet temptation / Don't hand me that line / Steel guitar rag / Honey bunch / So round, so firm, so fully packed / Alimony bound / Follow thru / Three time's seven / I'm sick and tired of you little darlin' / Sunshine's back in town / Devil to pay / Lawdy, what a gal / Sioux City Sue / Fat gal (False start) / Fat gal / I like my chicken fryin' size / Merle's boogie woogie (Alt) / Merle's boogie woogie / Dapper Dan / When my baby double talks to me / I'm pickin up the pieces of my heart / Information please / Any old time / Kentucky means paradise / Leave my honey bee alone / I'm a natural born gamblin' man / Get along blues / Too fast past / Crazy boogie / You better try another man / Deck of cards / Wabash cannonball / Blues stay away from me / Philosophy / I got a mean old woman / Petticoat fever / Start even / Cane bottom chair / I'm knee deep in trouble / Little Miss Sherlock Holmes / Too much sugar for a dime / Spoonin' moon / Trouble, trouble / El Reno / Won't cha be my baby / Dry bread / Lost John Boogie / Deep south / Boogie in minor / Let's settle down (To runnin' around together) / Done rovin' / Faithful fool / Love must be ketchin' / Kinfolks in Carolina / Rainy day feelin' / Ain't that a cryin' shame / I'll see you in my dreams / Cannonball rag / I'll have myself a ball / Bayou baby (Cajun lullaby) / Green Cheese / Louisiana boogie / Saturday night shuffle / Waltz you saved for me / Crazy about you / Re-enlistment blues / Dance of the golden road / Gambler's guitar / Shut up and drink your beer / Seminole drag / Jolie fille / I can't afford the coffee / Blue bell / Memphis blues / Sheikh of araby / On a bicycle made for two (Daisy Belle) / Black diamond blues / Blue smoke / Walking the strings / Sleepy time gal / Tuck me to sleep in my old 'Tucky home / Rock-a-bye rock / Bugle call rag / Cuddle up a little closer / Beer barrel polka / Turn my picture upside down / If you want it, I've got it / Lazy river / Hunky dory
CD Set _____ BCD 15637
Bear Family / Jun '94 / Direct / Rollercoaster / Swift

Travis, Mike

VIEW FROM WHERE, THE (Travis, Mike EH15)
Regarding Nelson: *Travis, Mike* / Grandfather clock menace: *Travis, Mike* / Cycle time: *Travis, Mike* / Forethought: *Travis, Mike* / L'allegria: *Travis, Mike* / Moonlight over joppa: *Travis, Mike* / Shall we Mr.Witherspoon: *Travis, Mike* / Backtalk: *Travis, Mike*
CD _____ ECLCD 9105
Eclectic / Apr '96 / ADA / New Note/ Pinnacle

Travis, Randy

ALWAYS AND FOREVER
Too gone too long / My house / Good intentions / What'll you do about me / I won't need you anymore / Forever and ever, Amen / I told you so / Anything / Truth is lyin' next to you / Tonight we're gonna tear down the walls
CD _____ WX 107CD
WEA / Aug '90 / Warner Music

BEST OF RANDY TRAVIS, THE
CD _____ 9548334612
WEA / Apr '95 / Warner Music

HIGH LONESOME
Let me try / Oh what a time to be me / Heart of hearts / Point of light / Forever together / Better class of losers / I'd surrender all / High lonesome / Allergic to the blues / I'm gonna have a little talk
CD _____ 7599266612
WEA / Oct '91 / Warner Music

OLD 8 BY 10
Forever and ever, amen / Honky tonk moon / Deeper than a holler / It's out of my hands / Is it still over / Written in stone / Blues in black and white / Here in my heart / We ain't out of love yet / Promises
CD _____ WX 162CD
WEA / Jul '88 / Warner Music

Travis, Theo

2AM
CD _____ 33JAZZ 011
33 Jazz / Jun '93 / Cadillac / New Note/ Pinnacle

SECRET ISLAND
Lulworth night / Crow road / After the storm / Waterlily / Details / Out of sight, out of mind / Three people / Full moon rising / Nostalgia in Times Square
CD _____ 33JAZZ 033
33 Jazz / Sep '96 / Cadillac / New Note/ Pinnacle

VIEW FROM THE EDGE
Fort Dunlop / Love for sale / Ghosts of Witley Court / Freedom / View from the edge / Psychgroove / I'm coming home / Empathy / Purple sky
CD _____ 33JAZZ 019
33 Jazz / May '95 / Cadillac / New Note/ Pinnacle

Travis, Tom

TOM TRAVIS BLUEGRASS BAND
CD _____ BOBB 003CD
British Bluegrass / Nov '95 / ADA / Direct

Travolta, John

20 GREATEST HITS
Razzamatazz / Never gonna fall in love again / Let her in / Rainbows / I don't know what I like about you / Baby, I could be so good at loving you / It had to be you / Goodnight Mr. Moon / Slow dancin' / You set my dreams to music / Whenever I'm away from you / Settle down / Back doors crying / Moonlight / Can't let you go / What would they say / Sandy / Right time of the night / Easy evil / Greased lightnin'
CD _____ 12892
Laserlight / May '97 / Target/BMG

BEST OF JOHN TRAVOLTA, THE
Sandy / Girl like you / Whenever I'm away from you / All strung out on you / Let her in / Never gonna fall in love again / Rainbows / Razzamatazz / I don't know what I like about you baby / Big trouble / Goodnight Mr. Moon / Baby, I could be so good at lovin' you / Greased lightnin' / It had to be you / Slow dancin' / Can't let you go / Easy evil / Back doors crying / What would they say / Right time of the night / Moonlight lady / Settle down / You set my dreams to music
CD _____ 3035900072
Essential Gold / Feb '96 / Carlton

BEST OF JOHN TRAVOLTA, THE
Greased lightnin' / Sandy / I don't know what I like about you baby / What would

they say / You set my dreams to music / Goodnight Mr. Moon / Back doors crying / Let her in / Baby I could be so good at lovin' you / Easy evil / Never gonna fall in love again / Razzamatazz / Settle down / Rainbows / Big trouble / Moonlight lady / Slow dancing / Can't let you go / It had to be you / Righ time of the night
CD ______ ECD 3259
K-Tel / Jan '97 / K-Tel

GREASED LIGHTNIN'
CD ______ PLSCD 123
Pulse / Apr '96 / BMG

GREASED LIGHTNIN'
CD ______ CDPS 003
Pulsar / Feb '96 / TKO Magnum

GREASED LIGHTNIN'
Let her in / Never gonna fall in love again / Rainbows / Razzamatazz / I don't know what I like about you baby / Big trouble / Goodnight Mr. Moon / Sandy / Baby, I could be so good at lovin' you / It had to be you / Slow dancing / Can't let you go / Easy evil / Back doors crying / What would they say / Right time of the night / Moonlight lady / Greased lightnin' / Settle down / You set my dreams to music
CD ______ QED 073
Tring / Nov '96 / Tring

JOHN TRAVOLTA
Let her in / Never gonna fall in love / Rainbows / Razzamatazz / I don't know what I like / Big trouble / Goognight Mr Moon / Sandy / Baby, I could be so good at lovin' you / It had to be you / Slow dancin' / Can't let you go / Easy evil / Back doors cryin' / What would they say / Right time of the night / Moon lightnin' / Greased lightnin' / Settle down / You set my dreams to music
CD ______ EMPRCD 524
Empress / Sep '94 / Koch

SANDY
Sandy / Whenever I'm away from you / Moonlight lady / Baby, I could be so good at lovin' you / Rainbows / Girl like you / Slow dancing / Back doors crying / Let her in / Big trouble / It had to be you / Goodnight Mr. Moon / Never gonna fall in love again / You set my dreams to music / What would they say / I don't know what I like about you baby / Razzamatazz / All strung out on you / Settle down / Easy evil / Can't let you go
CD ______ 100472
CMC / May '97 / BMG

VERY BEST OF JOHN TRAVOLTA, THE
Greased lightnin' / Sandy / Let her in / Never gonna fall in love again / Rainbows / Razzamatazz / I don't know what I like about you baby / Big trouble / Goodnight Mr. Moon / Baby I could be so good lovin' you / It had to be you / Slow dancin' / Can't let you go / Easy evil / Back doors cryin' / What would they say / Right time of the night / Moonlight baby / Settle down / You set my dreams to music / Sandy
CD ______ SUMCD 4066
Summit / Nov '96 / Sound & Media

Trax Beyond Subconscious

AMBIENT CUT-OUTS VOL.1
CD ______ LABUKCD 3
Labworks / Oct '94 / RTM/Disc / SRD

Tre'

DELIVERED FOR GLORY RECLAIMING THE BLUES
One eyed man / You took the blues out of me / Midnight train for home / I'm very superstitious / Please stay / Delivered for glory / More than a woman / Hard hearted woman / Reclaiming the blues / Da blues
CD ______ JSPCD 265
JSP / Feb '96 / ADA / Cadillac / Direct / Hot Shot / Target/BMG

Tre & The Blueknights

BLUES ROCKIN' BABY
CD ______ WCD 120888
Wolf / Jun '97 / Hot Shot / Jazz Music / Swift

Tre Martelli

OMI E PAIZ
CD ______ RD 5024CD
Robi Droli / Mar '96 / ADA / Direct

Treacherous Human ...

VICE (Treacherous Human Underdogs)
CD ______ RGE 1032
Enemy / Nov '94 / Grapevine/PolyGram

Treacherous Jaywalkers

SUNRISE
CD ______ SST 126CD
SST / May '93 / Plastic Head

Treacherous Three

OLD SCHOOL FLAVA
CD ______ WRA 8128CD
Wrap / Mar '94 / Koch

Treasure Land

QUESTIONS
Gift / Misery / Why / Demons / To live again / Miracle / Spirits / Kingdom / Let the rain
CD ______ TT 00292
T&T / Mar '97 / Koch

Treatment

CIPHER CAPUT
Hidden attack / Boing song / Risky / Dissolving / Designer / Cigarettes and starling / Doubt / Better future for Britain / Big I am / Decay / Damage / Holding on
CD ______ DELECCD 026
Delerium / Nov '93 / Cargo / Pinnacle / Vital

Trebunia Family Band

POLAND
CD ______ NI 5437
Nimbus / Jul '95 / Nimbus

Tree Fort Angst

KNEE DEEP
CD ______ BUS 10072
Bus Stop / Mar '97 / Cargo / Vital

Treepeople

GUILT, REGRET AND EMBARRASSMENT
CD ______ KLP 69CD
K / Jun '97 / Cargo / Greyhound / SRD

SOMETHING VICIOUS
CD ______ CZ 040CD
C/Z / Mar '92 / Plastic Head

Trees

GARDEN OF JANE DELAWNEY
Nothing special / Great silkie / Garden of Jane Delawney / Lady Margaret / Glasgerion / She moved through the fair / Road / Epitaph / Snail's lament
CD ______ BGOCD 172
Beat Goes On / Apr '93 / Pinnacle

ON THE SHORE
Soldiers three / Murdoch / Streets of Derry / Sally free and easy / Fool / Adams toon / Geordie / While the iron is hot / Little Sadie / Polly on the shore
CD ______ BGOCD 173
Beat Goes On / Mar '93 / Pinnacle
CD ______ 4844352
Columbia / Jul '96 / Sony

Trelik

TRELIK VOL.1
CD ______ TRCD 1
Trelik / Feb '97 / Kudos / Pinnacle

Trelldom

TIL EVIGHET
CD ______ HNF 016CD
Head Not Found / Jul '96 / Plastic Head

Tremble Kids All-Stars

TREMBLE KIDS ALL-STARS
CD ______ JCD 254
Jazzology / Jul '96 / Jazz Music

Trembling Blue Stars

HER HANDWRITING
CD ______ SHINKANSEN 3CD
Shinkansen / Dec '96 / SRD

Treme Brass Band

GIMME MY MONEY BACK
CD ______ ARHCD 417
Arhoolie / Jan '96 / ADA / Cadillac / Direct

Tremeloes

GOLD
CD ______ GOLD 208
Disky / Apr '94 / Disky / THE

GOLDEN HITS
Even the bad times are good / And then I kissed her / Call me number one / Never win / St Tropez / I like it that way / Once on a Sunday Morning / Here comes my baby / Silence is golden / Me and my life / Someone / Lean on me baby / Hello world / My little lady / African lullaby / Helule helule
CD ______ 306132
Hallmark / Jan '97 / Carlton

MASTER
Wait for me / Long road / Now's the time / Try me / But then I / Before I sleep / Boola boola / I swear / Baby / By the way / Willow tree / Me and my life
CD ______ CLACD 251
Castle / '91 / BMG

SILENCE IS GOLDEN
Call me number one / Even the bad times are good / Here comes my baby / Alli-oop / Do you love me / Ain't nothing but a house party / Reach out, I'll be there / I shall be released / Yellow river / My little lady / Silence is golden / I like it that way / Cool jerk / Every day / Peggy Sue / Rag doll / Twist and shout / Every little bit hurts
CD ______ 5507422
Spectrum / Jan '95 / PolyGram

SILENCE IS GOLDEN
CD ______ MSCD 032
Music De-Luxe / Jun '96 / TKO Magnum

SINGLES, THE
Goodday sunshine / Here comes my baby / Silence is golden / Even the bad times are good / Be mine / Suddenly you love me / Helule helule / My little lady / I'm gonna try / I shall be released / Hello world / Once on a Sunday morning / (Call me) Number one / By the way / Me and my life / Right wheel, left hammer sham / Hello Buddy / Too late (to be saved) / I like it that way / Blue suede / Ride on / Make it break it / You can't touch Sue / Do I love you / Say OK / Be boppin boogie
CD ______ BX 4572
BR Music / Dec '95 / Target/BMG

STORY OF THE TREMELOES, THE
CD ______ BS 80182
BR Music / Jul '94 / Target/BMG

TREMENDOUS HITS
Silence is golden / Even the bad times are good / Here comes my baby / Me and my baby / Helule helule / (Call me) number one / My little lady / Words / Hello world / Yellow river / Blue suede tie / Be mine / Hello Buddy / Once upon a Sunday morning / I like it that way / Before I sleep / By the way / Good day sunshine / Suddenly you love me / I shall be released
CD ______ MCCD 303
Music Club / Jun '97 / Disc / THE

WORLD OF BRIAN POOLE & THE TREMELOES, THE (Poole, Brian & The Tremeloes)
Do you love me / Candy man / Someone someone / Twist and shout / What do you want with my baby / Time is on my side / I can dance / Out of my mind / Medley / Three bells / I want candy / Rag doll / We know / It's alright / Mr. Bass Man / South Street / Hey girl / Well who's that / Medley / Twelve steps to love
CD ______ 5513212
Spectrum / May '96 / PolyGram

Tremulis, Nicholas

BLOODY SHOW
CD ______ BV 170962
Black Vinyl / Nov '96 / Cargo

Trenchmouth

BROADCASTING SYSTEM, THE
CD ______ RUNT 21
Runt / Mar '97 / Cargo / Greyhound / Plastic Head

CONSTRUCTION OF NEW ACTION
CD ______ SR 89222CD
Skene / Nov '92 / SRD

Trend

BITCH
CD ______ RRS 946CD
Progress / Nov '95 / Cargo / Plastic Head

Trends Of Culture

TRENDZ
CD ______ 5302072
Polydor / Jul '93 / PolyGram

Trenet, Charles

ANTHOLOGIE
CD ______ EN 521
Fremeaux / Feb '96 / ADA / Discovery

BOUM
Fleur bleue / La polka du Roi / Y'a d'la Joie / Boum / Pigeon vole / En quittant le Ville / Le Grand Cafe / La Vielle / Miss Emily / Les Oiseaux de Paris / Beguine a Bagno / Vous Oubliez votre Cheval / Vous etes Jolie / Il Pleut dans ma Chambre / La Route Enchantee / Ah Dis, ah Dis, ah Bonjour / La Vie qui va / Annie-Anna / Tout me sourit / Hop hop / Jardin du Mois de Mai / Le Soleil et la Lune / Mam'zelle Clio
CD ______ MDF 102604
Mudisque / Nov '96 / Target/BMG

COMPLETE CHARLES TRENET VOL.1, THE (Charles & Johnny/2CD Set) (Trenet, Charles & Johnny Hess)
CD Set ______ FA 081
Fremeaux / May '96 / ADA / Discovery

COMPLETE CHARLES TRENET VOL.2, THE (2CD Set)
CD Set ______ FA 082
Fremeaux / Nov '96 / ADA / Discovery

COMPLETE CHARLES TRENET VOL.3, THE (2CD Set)
CD Set ______ FA 083
Fremeaux / Feb '97 / ADA / Discovery

DIAMOND COLLECTION, THE
CD ______ 3004452
Arcade / Jun '97 / Discovery

EXTRAORDINARY GARDEN, THE (The Very Best Of Charles Trenet)
Boum / L'ame des poetes / Moi j'aime le music hall / Vous qui passez sans me voir / La jolie sardane / En Avril a Paris / Le jardin extraordinaire / Coin de rue / Mes jeunes annes / A la porte du garage / France Dimanche / Qur reste t'il de nos amours / Y'a d'la Joie / Douce France / La polka du roi / Revoir Paris / La folle complainte / Le grand cafe / La mer / Menilmontant / Vous oubliez votre cheval / La maison du poete / La famille musicienne / Le chante
CD ______ CDP 7944642
EMI / Jul '97 / EMI

L'AIME DES POETES
CD ______ CD 314
Entertainers / Feb '95 / Target/BMG

LE FOU CHANTANT
Que reste-t-il de nos amours / Les temps des cerises / Debit de l'eau..Bonsoir Jolie Madame / Un rien me fait chanter / Swing troubadour / La romance de Paris / Verlaine / Le jardin du mais de Mai / Meinilmontant / Le soleil et la lune / Vous oubliez votre cheval / J'ai ta main / Boum..Y'a de la joie / Fleur bleue / J echante
CD ______ 995752
EPM / Apr '97 / ADA / Discovery

Treniers

COOL IT BABY
You're killing me / Day old bread / Squeeze me / Flip our wigs / Rock bottom / Give a little time / Hey you / I got the blues so bad / Straighten up baby / Cool it baby / Drinkin' wine spo-dee-o-dee / Margie / Madune / Sorrento / Lover come back to me / We want a rock and roll president / Longest walk / Ain't nothing wrong with that baby
CD ______ BCD 15418
Bear Family / Dec '88 / Direct / Rollercoaster / Swift

HEY SISTER LUCY
Hey sister Lucy / Buzz buzz buzz / But I'd rather / Hey boys better get yourself an extra / Oooh look a there ain't she pretty / Near to me / No baby no / Sometimes I'm happy / I'll follow you / It's a quiet town / Convertable cadillac / Ain't she mean / Sure had a wonderful time last night / I miss you so / Hey jacobia / Why / Lady luck / When you're finished talkin' (let's make some love)
CD ______ BCD 15419
Bear Family / Dec '88 / Direct / Rollercoaster / Swift

Trent, Jackie

BEAT SINGLES VOL.1
CD ______ RPM 161
RPM / Jun '96 / Pinnacle

TWO OF US, THE (Trent, Jackie & Tony Hatch)
Downtown / Where are you now / My love / Joanna / What would I be / Call me / Who am I / Forget him / Colour my world / Thank you for loving me / I know a place / Opposite your smile / You're everything / Other man's grass / I couldn't live without your love / Let's do it again / Look for a star / Don't sleep in the subway / Sign of the times / Two of us
CD ______ PRCD 144
President / Nov '94 / Grapevine/PolyGram / President / Target/BMG

Treorchy Male Choir

50 GOLDEN YEARS OF SONG
Cwm Rhondda / For the fallen / Men of Harlech / Soldiers' chorus from Faust / Llef / Myfanwy / Jacob's ladder / O Isi and Osiris / Gwahoddiad / Hava nagila / Softly as I leave you / Cavatina / With a voice of singing / Unwaith eto / My way
CD ______ CDMFP 6214
Music For Pleasure / Feb '96 / EMI

SHOWSTOPPERS
Another opening another show / Just one of those things / You do something to me / So in love / Who wants to be a millionaire / Love changes everything / Bring him home / Anthem / Climb every mountain / Somewhere / Do you hear the people sing / How to handle a woman / Impossible dream / Send in the clowns / On the street where you live
CD ______ CDMFP 5906
Music For Pleasure / Apr '91 / EMI

TREORCHY SING QUEEN
Overture / We are the champions / Radio ga ga / Save me / Crazy little thing called love / Flash / You're my best friend / Play the game / Good old fashioned lover boy / Don't stop me now / We will rock you / Bohemian rhapsody
CD ______ CDMFP 6365
Music For Pleasure / May '97 / EMI

Treponem Pal

EXCESS & OVERDRIVE
CD ______ CD RR 9076 2
Roadrunner / Jun '93 / PolyGram

Trettine, Caroline

BE A DEVIL
CD ______ UTIL 008 CD
Utility / Feb '90 / Grapevine/PolyGram

Trial Of The Bow

RITE OF PASSAGE
Father of the flower / Ubar / Promise / Serpent / Eyre of awakening / Ceilidh for the sallow ground / Muezin / Court of the servant / As night falls / Alizee
CD ______ RR 69502
Relapse / Jun '97 / Pinnacle / Plastic Head

Trian

TRIAN VOL.2
CD ______ GLCD 1159
Green Linnet / Dec '95 / ADA / CM / Direct / Highlander / Roots

Triarchy

BEFORE YOUR VERY EARS
CD ______ ETHEL 5
Vinyl Tap / Jan '96 / Cargo / Greyhound / Vinyl Tap

Tribal Draft

COLLECTIVE JOURNEYS
CD ______ CHILLCD 006
Chillout / Nov '95 / Kudos / Pinnacle / RTM/Disc

Tribal Drift

PRIORITY SHIFT
CD ______ ONUCD 88
On-U Sound / Nov '96 / Jet Star / SRD

Tribal Tech

FACE FIRST
Face first / Canine / After hours / Revenge stew / Salt lick / Uh...yeah Ok / Crawling horror / Boiler room / Boat gig / Precipice / Wounded
CD ______ R2 79190
Bluemoon / Apr '94 / New Note/Pinnacle

Tribe 8

SNARKISM
CD ______ VIRUS 181CD
Alternative Tentacles / May '96 / Cargo / Greyhound / Pinnacle

Tribe After Tribe

PEARLS BEFORE SWINE
Boy / Lazurus / Ballad of winnie / Uh oh / Senor / Firedancers / Bury me / Pat on the back / Heart / Murder on the lee / Hopeless the clown
CD ______ CDVEST 82
Bulletproof / Apr '97 / Pinnacle

Tribe Called Quest

BEATS, RHYMES AND LIFE
Phony rappers / Get a hold / Motivators / Jam / Crew / Pressure / 1nce again / Mind power / Hop / Keeping it moving / Baby Phife's return / Seperate/Together / What really goes on / Word play / Stressed out
CD ______ CHIP 170
Jive / Jul '96 / Pinnacle

LOW END THEORY
Excursions / Buggin' out / Rap promoter / Butter / Verses from the abstract / Show-business / Vibes and stuff / Infamous date rape / Check the rhyme / Everything is fair / Jazz (We got the) / Sky pager / What / Scenario
CD ______ CHIP 117
Jive / Mar '97 / Pinnacle

MIDNIGHT MARAUDERS
Midnight marauders tour guide / Steve Biko (Stir it up) / Award tour / 8 million stories / Sucka nigga / Midnight / We can get down / Electric relaxation / Clap your hands / Oh my God / Keep it rollin' / Chase Part II / Lyrics to go / God lives through / Hot sex
CD ______ CHIP 143
Jive / Mar '97 / Pinnacle

PEOPLE'S INSTINCTIVE TRAVELS & THE PATHS OF RHYTHM
Push it along / Luck of Lucien / After hours / Footprints / I left my wallet in El Segundo / Public enemy / Bonita Applebum / Can I kick it / Youthful expression / Rhythm (Devoted to the art of moving butts) / Mr. Muhammad / Ham 'n' eggs / Go ahead in the rain / Description of a fool
CD ______ CHIP 96
Jive / Mar '97 / Pinnacle

REVISED QUEST FOR THE SEASONED TRAVELLER
Bonita applebum / I left my wallet in El Segundo / Description of a fool / Public enemy / Check the rhyme / Luck of Lucien / Can I kick it / Scenario / If the papes came / Jazz (we've got) / Butter
CD ______ CHIP 130
Jive / Mar '97 / Pinnacle

Tribe Of Dan

SHOOK UP, SHOOK UP
CD ______ MRM 003CD
Mister M / Apr '92 / Plastic Head

Tribulation

CLOWN OF THORNS
Borka intro / Born bizarre / My world is different / Rise of prejudice / Everything's floating / Safe murder of emotions / Angst / Decide (take a stand) / angel in a winterpile / Beautiful views / Landslide of losers / Down my lungs / Pick an image (make sure it sells) / Herr Ober / Tiny little skeleton / Disgraceland / Dogmother
CD ______ 8410602
Black Mark / Feb '92 / Plastic Head

SPICY
CD ______ BHR 010CD
Burning Heart / Oct '94 / Plastic Head

Tribulation All Stars

DUB LIBERATION
CD ______ WSPCD 005
Word Sound & Power / Apr '94 / SRD

Tribute

NEW VIEWS
CD ______ EUCD 1042
ARC / '89 / ADA / ARC Music

Tribute To Nothing

STRAIGHT LINE
Straight line / Find it / Cecil / Could I / Think you should / Do something / How could things / Don't care
CD ______ LJCD 002
Lockjaw / Jun '97 / Pinnacle

Trick Babys

FOOL AND HIS MONEY, A
CD ______ GKCD 023
Go-Kart / Sep '97 / Greyhound / Pinnacle

Trickett, Katie

NEXT TIME, THE
Next time / Autumn eyes / I'll never change this lovin' feelin' / When you were here / Playin' against the best / Don't say don't / Lonley road home / She danced alone / Dancin' on the edge of a razor
CD ______ FIENDCD 768
Demon / Aug '95 / Pinnacle

Tricky

MAXINQUAYE
Overcome / Ponderosa / Black steel / Hell is round the corner / Pumpkin / Aftermath / Abbaon fat track / Brand new you're retro / Suffocated love / You don't / Strugglin' / Feed me
CD ______ BRCD 610
4th & Broadway / Feb '95 / PolyGram

NEARLY GOD (Nearly God)
CD ______ DPCD 1001
Durban Poison / Apr '96 / PolyGram

PRE-MILLENNIUM TENSION
Vent / Christiansands / Tricky kid / Bad dreams / Makes me wanna die / Ghetto youth / Sex drive / Bad things / Lyrics of fury / My evil is strong / Piano
CD ______ BRCD 623
CD ______ BRCDX 623
4th & Broadway / Nov '96 / PolyGram

Triffids

AUSTRALIAN MELODRAMA
CD ______ D 31182
Mushroom / Oct '94 / 3mv/Pinnacle

BORN SANDY DEVOTIONAL
CD ______ D 19457
Mushroom / Mar '95 / 3mv/Pinnacle

CALENTURE
Trick of the night / Bury me deep in love / Kelly's blues / Home town farewell kiss / Unmade love / open for you / Holy water / Blinder by the hour / Vagabond holes / Jerdacuttup man / Calenture / Save what you can
CD ______ D 19458
Mushroom / Feb '95 / 3mv/Pinnacle

IN THE PINES
Suntrapper / In the pines / Kathy knows / Twenty five to five / Do you want me near you / Once a day / Just might fade away / Better off this way / Only one life / Keep your eyes on the hole / One soul less on your fiery list / Born Sandy Devotional / Love and affection
CD ______ D 19480
Mushroom / Feb '95 / 3mv/Pinnacle

STOCKHOLM
CD ______ D 30231
Mushroom / Feb '95 / 3mv/Pinnacle

Trigger Happy

KILLATRON 2000
CD ______ BMCD 073
Raw Energy / Jun '95 / Plastic Head

Trigger Tha Gambler

LIFE'S A 50/50 GAMBLE
CD ______ 5334142
Talkin' Loud / Oct '96 / PolyGram

Trikha, Pandit Kanwar Sain

THREE SITAR PIECES
Bageshri in teental / Rag desh in dadra / Folk piece in kahrwa / Untitled sitar
CD ______ SEECD 481
See For Miles/C5 / Aug '97 / Pinnacle

Trimble, Gerald

CROSS CURRENTS
Bedding of the bride / Adieu my lovely Nancy / Rolling spey/Green hills of Tyrol/ Bob Walters / Blessed be (the lady's token) / Frank Gilruth/Jack Danielson's reel / Trimble's compliments to the city of Philadelphia / Breakdown / Christina Marie / Shifting paradigms
CD ______ GLCD 1065
Green Linnet / Jul '93 / ADA / CM / Direct / Highlander / Roots

FIRST FLIGHT
CD ______ GLCD 1043
Green Linnet / Nov '88 / ADA / CM / Direct / Highlander / Roots

HEARTLAND MESSENGER
Kail pot/Fisher's rant/Morayshire farmer's club/General Long / Miss Wharton Duff's jig / Coates hall/Amazon / Miss Stewart's jig/ Mrs. Rose of Kilravock/Donald MacLean / Ostinelli's reel/Miss Gunning's fancy / Heartland Messsenger trilogy
CD ______ GLCD 1054
Green Linnet / Oct '93 / ADA / CM / Direct / Highlander / Roots

Trinidad Steel Combo

STEEL DRUMS FROM THE CARIBBEAN
Pantalones de vaquero / Panguin's walk / Sexy panties / Panorama / Pan American blues / Nice pants / You look pantastic / Panatonics forever / Let's pan out the gold / Pancratic body / Black panther blues / Max loves pancakes / Happy pans / Don't panic / Panthouse in Miami
CD ______ QED 228
Tring / Nov '96 / Tring

Trinity

AFRICAN REVOLUTION
African revolution / Turn yu roll / Staff of life / Not the worst / Tan tudy / Righteous rock / Judgement day / Hard time reggae / A nuh so / Rain a fall
CD ______ CDGR 116
Charly / Jan '97 / Koch

BIG BIG MAN
CD ______ LG 21057
Lagoon / May '93 / Grapevine/PolyGram

Trio

CONFLAGRATION
CD ______ BGOCD 253
Beat Goes On / Oct '95 / Pinnacle

TRIO, THE
Oh, Dear / Dousing Rod / Silvercloud / Incantation / Caractacus / Let's stand / Foyer hall / Portes des lilas / Veritably / In between / Sixes and sevens / Green walnut / Billy the kid / Dee tune / Centering / Joachim / Drum
CD ______ BGOCD 231
Beat Goes On / Aug '94 / Pinnacle

Trio Azteca

BEST OF MEXICAN FOLK SONGS
CD ______ EUCD 1109
ARC / '91 / ADA / ARC Music

Trio Bulgarka

FOREST IS CRYING
CD ______ HNCD 1342
Hannibal / May '88 / ADA / Vital

MISSA PRIMI - MUSIC OF PALESTRINA
CD ______ 669512CD
Melodie / Apr '95 / ADA / Discovery / Grapevine/PolyGram / Greensleeves / Jet Star

Trio De Cologne

LA BELLE EXCENTRIQUE
CD ______ AS 20062
Al Segno / Jun '96 / Vital/SAM

Trio Idea

NAPOLI CONNECTION (Trio Idea & Jerry Bergonzi)
CD ______ 1232612
Red / Apr '94 / ADA / Cadillac / Harmonia Mundi

Trio Matamoros

TRIO MATAMOROS
CD ______ HQCD 69
Harlequin / Apr '97 / Hot Shot / Jazz Music / Swift / Wellard

Trio Mexico

MEXICAN LANDSCAPES VOL.1
CD ______ PS 65901
PlayaSound / Jan '92 / ADA / Harmonia Mundi

Trio Pantango

TANGO ARGENTINO
CD ______ EUCD 1334
ARC / Mar '96 / ADA / ARC Music

TANGO ARGENTINO POPULAR
CD ______ EUCD 1257
ARC / Mar '94 / ADA / ARC Music

Trio Pellen-Molard

TRYPTICH
CD ______ GWP 002CD
Gwerz / Aug '93 / ADA / Discovery

Trio Pennec

JAVADAO
CD ______ CD 847
Diffusion Breizh / Apr '94 / ADA

Trio Sautivet

PARTIR REVENIR
CD ______ 495302CD
Acousteak / Apr '96 / ADA / Discovery

Trio Trabant A Roma

STATE OF VOLGOGRAD
CD ______ FMPCD 57
FMP / Oct '94 / Cadillac

Triple X

GOOD, THE BAD & THE UGLY, THE
CD ______ UNION 057
Union / Aug '96 / Else

Tripmaster Monkey

GOODBYE RACE
Albert's twisted memory bank / Pecola / Shutter's closed / Faster than Dwight / Valium / Roman catholic haircut / Is that my bag / Dad / Gravity / Key / Night of day / Not quite sure / Depravation test
CD ______ 9362456742
Warner Bros. / Jul '94 / Warner Music

Tripping Daisy

I AM AN ELASTIC FIRECRACKER
Rocket pop / Bang / I got a girl / Piranha / Motivation / Same dress new day / Trip along / Raindrop / Step behind / Noose / Prick / High
CD ______ CIRD 1004
Island / Feb '96 / PolyGram

Tripsichord

TRIPSICHORD
CD ______ 852124
EVA / May '94 / ADA / Direct

Triptych

SLEEPLESS
CD ______ GAP 031
Gap Recordings / Nov '95 / SRD

Trisan

TRISAN
Triangle / Big trouble in old ballymore E / May yo I / Dragon / Mother and son / Wintermoon / River of life / Tri le cheile
CD ______ CDRW 32
Realworld / Nov '92 / EMI

Trisaxual Soul Champs

GO GIRL
Go girl / She said / I messed up / Coffee break / Costume party / Blue Di / Misirlou / Cool face / Blue am I / Can't keep up with you / Fatman blues / Cherry race
CD ______ FIENDCD 186
Demon / Jun '90 / Pinnacle

Trischka, Tony

ALONE & TOGETHER
CD ______ BRAM 1991242
Brambus / Nov '93 / ADA

DUST ON THE NEEDLE
CD ______ ROUCD 11508
Rounder / '88 / ADA / CM / Direct

FIRE OF GRACE (Trischka, Tony & Skyline)
CD ______ FF 479CD
Flying Fish / Jun '94 / ADA / CM / Direct / Roots

GLORY SHONE AROUND
CD ______ ROUCD 0354
Rounder / Oct '95 / ADA / CM / Direct

ROBOT PLANE FLIES OVER ARKANSAS, A
CD ______ ROUCD 0171
Rounder / May '94 / ADA / CM / Direct

SOLO BANJO WORKS (Trischka, Tony & Bela Fleck)
Ruben's wah wah: *Trischka, Tony* / Fourteen: *Trischka, Tony* / Liberec: *Trischka, Tony* / Free improvision no.2: *Trischka, Tony*

/ Assunta: *Trischka, Tony* / Old Joe Clark/ June Apple: *Trischka, Tony* / Max and Gus: *Trischka, Tony* / Beaumont rag: *Trischka, Tony* / Kingfisher's wing: *Trischka, Tony* / Earl Scrugg's medley: Nashville Skyline/ Ground speed/Shuckin: *Trischka, Tony* / Jeff Davies medley: Jeff Davies/Fort Monroe/Danville Days: *Trischka, Tony* / Yaha yaha: *Trischka, Tony* / Beatles medley: *Trischka, Tony* / Rings of saturn: *Trischka, Tony* / Green Willis/Whiskey before breakfast: *Trischka, Tony* / Killer bees of caffeine: *Trischka, Tony* / Oma and Opa: *Fleck, Bela* / Solaris: *Fleck, Bela* / Flapperette/Red pepper - Spicy rag: *Fleck, Bela* / Triplet fever: *Fleck, Bela* / Bach violin partitain D minor: *Fleck, Bela* / Did you ever meet Gary Owen, Uncle Joe: *Fleck, Bela* / Middle Eastern medley: Improv/Hilmi rit/George and Gladys ka: *Fleck, Bela* / Twisted teen: *Fleck, Bela* / Au lait: *Fleck, Bela*
CD ROUCD 0247
Rounder / Feb '93 / ADA / CM / Direct

WORLD TURNING
CD ROUCD 294
Rounder / Oct '93 / ADA / CM / Direct

Triskell

CELTIQUE HARPES
Plangstigh Ewen / Dainty Davie / Dime ramo verde / Iona / Sun and shadow / Vincenta / Enezenn du / Planxty George Barbazon / Vieux chateau sous la lune / Boulavogue / King William's march / Dafydd y garreg wen / Pardon sant fiakr / Plijadur ha displijadur
CD 3037200012
Carlton / Apr '96 / Carlton

HARPES CELTIQUES
CD KMCD 60
Keltia Musique / Jul '95 / ADA / Discovery

WAR VARC'H D'AH (Triskell & Mouez Armor)
CD KMCD 64
Keltia Musique / Jul '96 / ADA / Discovery

Trisomie 21

DISTANT VOICES
Shine ola / Touch sweet pleasure / Again and again (what a regular world) / Perfect side of doubt / Badlands / Is anybody home / Distant voices / Soft brushing speed / Jazz / Long rider
CD BIAS 212 CD
Play It Again Sam / Oct '92 / Discovery / Plastic Head / Vital

SONGS BY TRISOMIE 21 VOL.1, THE
Perfect side of doubt / Again and again (What a regular world) / New outset / Bamboo / Missing piece / Betrayed / Story so far / Sharing sensation / Sunken lives / Night flight / Last song / Waiting for / Moving by you / Is anybody home / Logical animals / Il se noie
CD BIAS 281CD
Play It Again Sam / May '94 / Discovery / Plastic Head / Vital

T21 PLAYS THE PICTURES
CD BIAS 152CD
Play It Again Sam / Apr '90 / Discovery / Plastic Head / Vital

Trisquel

AMANDI
CD 20052CD
Sonifolk / Dec '94 / ADA / CM

O CHAPEU DE MERLIN
CD J 1023CD
Sonifolk / Jun '94 / ADA / CM

Tristano, Lennie

FEATURING LEE KONITZ
CD CD 53155
Giants Of Jazz / May '95 / Cadillac / Jazz Music / Target/BMG

LENNIE TRISTANO/THE NEW TRISTANO
Line up / Requiem / Turkish mambo / East 32nd / These foolish things / You go to my head / If I had you / I don't stand a ghost of a chance with you / All the things you are / Becoming / You don't know what love is / Deliberation / Scene and variations / Love lines / G minor complex
CD 2715952
Atlantic / Jun '94 / Warner Music

TRIO, QUARTET, QUINTET & SEXTET
CD CD 53149
Giants Of Jazz / Sep '94 / Cadillac / Jazz Music / Target/BMG

Tristitia

CRUCIDICTION
CD HOLY 021CD
Holy / Dec '96 / Plastic Head

ONE WITH DARKNESS
CD HOLY 11CD
Holy / May '95 / Plastic Head

Tritt, Travis

GREATEST HITS
CD 9362460012
Warner Bros. / Oct '95 / Warner Music

RESTLESS KIND
CD 9362463042
Warner Bros. / Aug '96 / Warner Music

TEN FEET TALL & BULLETPROOF
Ten feet tall and bulletproof / Walkin' all over my heart / Foolish pride / Outlaws like us / Hard times and misery / Tell me I was dreaming / Wishful thinking / Between an old memory and me / No vacation from the blues / Southern justice
CD 9362456032
Warner Bros. / May '94 / Warner Music

Troggs

ALL THE HITS PLUS MORE
Wild thing / With a girl like you / Love is all around / Little pretty thing / Anyway that you want me / I can't control myself / I love you baby / Black bottom / Louie Louie / Save the last dance for me / I do do / Strange movies / Bass for my birthday / Last night / Hot days / I don't / Widge you / Feels like a woman
CD CDSGP 0337
Prestige / Apr '97 / Else / Total/BMG

ARCHAEOLOGY
CD 5129362
Phonogram / Jan '93 / PolyGram

ATHENS ANDOVER
Crazy Annie / Together / Tuned into love / Deja vu / Dust bowl / I'm in control / Don't you know / What's your game / Suspicious / Hot stuff
CD ESMCD 180
Essential / Aug '96 / BMG

ATHENS, GEORGIA & BEYOND
CD MCCD 242
Music Club / Jun '96 / Disc / THE

AU
CD ROSE 186 CD
New Rose / May '90 / ADA / Direct / Discovery

BEST OF THE TROGGS, THE
Wild thing / I can't control myself / Save the last dance for me / Little pretty thing / Hot days / Bass for my birthday / Last night / I don't know why / I do do / With a girl like you / Louie Louie / Black bottom / Anyway you want me / I love you baby / Widge you / Strange movie / Feels like a woman / Love is all around
CD SUMCD 4002
Summit / Nov '96 / Sound & Media

BLACK BOTTOM
CD ROSE 4CD
New Rose / Mar '85 / ADA / Direct / Discovery

CELLOPHANE/MIXED BAG
Little red donkey / Too much of a good thing / Butterflies and bees / All of the time / Seventeen / Somewhere my girl is waiting / It's showing / Her emotion / When will the rain come / My lady / Come the day / Love is all around / Surprise surprise / You can cry if you want to / Say darlin' / Marbles and some gum / Purple shades / Heads or tails / Hip hip hooray / Little girl / Maybe the madman / Off the record / We waited for someone / There's something about you
CD BGOCD 343
Beat Goes On / Mar '97 / Pinnacle

DOUBLE HITS COLLECTION (Troggs/ Dave Dee, Dozy, Beaky, Mick & Tich)
CD PLATCD 3908
Platinum / Oct '89 / Prism

EP COLLECTION, THE
Wild thing / From home / Yella in me / With a girl like you / Our love will still be there / Jingle jangle / I want you / Can't control myself / Hi hi Hazel / Gonna make you / Anyway that you want me / Cousin Jane / 66.54.321 / You can't beat it / Give it to me / You're lying / I can only give you everything / Oh no / Night of the long grass / Girl in black / Love is all around / Little girl
CD SEECD 453
See For Miles/C5 / Oct '96 / Pinnacle

FROM NOWHERE/TROGGLODYNAMITE
Wild thing / Kitty cat song / Ride your pony / Hi hi Hazel / I just sing / Evil / Our love will still be there / Louie Louie / Jingle jangle / When I'm with you / From home / Jaguar and thunderbird / I can only give you everything / Last summer / Meet Jacqueline / Oh no / It's too late / 10 Downing Street / Mona / I want you to come into my life / Let me tell you babe / Little Queenie / Cousin Jane / You can't beat it / Baby come closer / It's over
CD BGOCD 340
Beat Goes On / Feb '97 / Pinnacle

GREATEST HITS
Wild thing / Love is all around / With a girl like you / I want you / I can't control myself / Gonna make you / Good vibrations / Anyway that you want me / Give it to me / Night of the long grass / Girl in black / Hi hi Hazel / Little girl / Cousin Jane / Don't you know / Together / Nowhere Road / I'm in control / Summertime / Hot stuff / Dust bowl / I'll buy you an island / Crazy Annie / Jingle jangle / Deja vu
CD 5227392
PolyGram TV / Jul '94 / PolyGram

GREATEST HITS
CD MU 5022
Musketeer / Oct '92 / Disc

LEGENDS IN MUSIC
CD LECD 074
Wisepack / Jul '94 / Conifer/BMG / THE

LIVE AT MAX'S KANSAS CITY
Got love if you want it / Satisfaction / Love is all around / Give it to me / Feels like a woman / Strange movie / Summertime / Walking the dog / Memphis / No particular place to go / Wild thing / Gonna make you / I do I do / Call me
CD MKCD 1001
President / Oct '94 / Grapevine/PolyGram / President / Target/BMG

LOVE IS ALL AROUND
Love is all around / Wild thing / Give it to me / Hi hi Hazel / Night of the long grass / Seventeen / Kitty cat song / Little girl / I just sing / Jingle jangle / When I'm with you / Let me tell you babe / You can cry if you want to / Ride your pony / Lost girl / Hip hip hooray / I can only give you everything / Louie Louie
CD 5510452
Spectrum / Jul '95 / PolyGram

LOVE IS ALL AROUND
Love is all around / Wild thing / Black bottom / Widge you / Strange movies / Feels like a woman / Last night / Bass for my birthday / Hot days / Little pretty thing / I don't / With a girl like you / I can't control myself / Any way that you want me / I do do / Save the last dance for me / Louie Louie / Hang on Sloopy / Twist and shout / Game of love / Louie Louie (reprise)
CD QED 144
Tring / Nov '96 / Tring

LOVE IS ALL AROUND
Love is all around / Wild thing / Black bottom / Widge you / With a girl like you / Twist and shout / Louie Louie / Save the last dance for me / I do do / Last night / Feels like a woman / I can't control myself / Any way that you want me / Bass for my birthday / Hot days / Game of love / Little pretty thing
CD CD 6065
Music / Apr '97 / Target/BMG

TROGGS AU ALBUM
CD HADCD 195
Javelin / Nov '95 / Henry Hadaway / THE

WILD THING
CD 15081
Laserlight / Aug '91 / Target/BMG

WILD THING
CD MSCD 030
Music De-Luxe / May '96 / TKO Magnum

WILD THING
Wild thing / With a girl like you / I can't control myself / Any way that you want me / Give it to me / Night of the long grass / Love is all around / Little girl / Widge you / Strange movie / Feels like a woman / Last night / Bass for my birthday / Hot days / Game of love/Little pretty thing / I don't / I do do / Louie Louie/Hang on Sloopy / Twist and shout
CD PLATCD 203
Platinum / Feb '97 / Prism

WILD THING
CD CD 322699
Koch Presents / Jul '97 / Koch

WILD THINGS
I got lovin' if you want it / Good vibrations / No particular place to go / Summertime / Satisfaction / Full blooded band / Memphis, Tennessee / Peggy Sue / Wild thing / Get you tonight / Different me / Down South in Georgia / After the rain / Rock 'n' roll lady / Walking the dog / We rode through the night / Gonna make you / Supergirl / I'll buy you an island / Rollin' stone
CD SEECD 256
See For Miles/C5 / Aug '94 / Pinnacle

Troi

TROI
CD JUCCD 02
Juce / Oct '95 / Grapevine/PolyGram

Troika

GODDESS
Venus / Diana / Oya / Zorya / Kuan yin / Gwenhwyfar / Athena / Inanna
CD ND 62804
Narada / Oct '96 / ADA / New Note/ Pinnacle

Troika II

DREAM PALACE
Edge of destiny / Dream palace / Bridge to heaven / Throught the mist / Vision walk / Hall of mystery / Sea of time / Journey home
CD ND 62808
Narada / Jul '97 / ADA / New Note/Pinnacle

Troise

TROISE & HIS MANDOLIERS (Troise & His Mandoliers)
CD PASTCD 7051
Flapper / Feb '95 / Pinnacle

Trojans

CELTIC SKA
CD GAZCD 011
Gaz's Rockin' Records / Nov '94 / Shellshock/Disc

COOL RULERS
CD GAZCD 014
Gaz's Rockin' Records / Jun '96 / Shellshock/Disc

EARTH FIRST
CD GAZCD 015
Gaz's Rockin' Records / Apr '97 / Shellshock/Disc

REBEL BLUES
CD GAZCD 010
Gaz's Rockin' Records / Oct '93 / Shellshock/Disc

SKALALITUDE
CD GAZCD 007
Gaz's Rockin' Records / Sep '91 / Shellshock/Disc

STACK-A-DUB
CD GAZCD 012
Gaz's Rockin' Records / Jul '95 / Shellshock/Disc

WICKED AND WILD
CD 622382
Skydog / Mar '96 / Discovery

WILD & FREE
CD GAZCD 008
Gaz's Rockin' Records / Jun '93 / Shellshock/Disc

Troka

TROKA
CD OMCD 54
Olarin Musiiki Oy / Dec '94 / ADA / Direct

Troll

TROLLSTORM OVER NIDINGJUV
CD HNF 015CD
Head Not Found / Oct '96 / Plastic Head

Trom

EVIL
CD SR 9506CD
Shiadarshana / Sep '95 / Plastic Head

Tron

SYNDICATE
London labyrinth / It's about time / Fall angel fall / Never forever / Voices by the standing stones / Snowfall in Eden / Outside / Requiem / Kingdom of forbidden thoughts / Eternity (You are alone) / Nightfall (Chapter IV) / Syndicate / Gate number two / Death's cold glance
CD MYSCD 111
Mystic / Jul '97 / Pinnacle

Tronzo, David

NIGHT IN AMNESIA (Tronzo, David & Reeves Gabrels)
CD UPSTART 018
Upstart / Jul '95 / ADA / Direct

Tronzo Trio

ROOTS
CD KFWCD 154
Knitting Factory / Feb '95 / Cargo / Plastic Head

YO HEY
Improvisation no.1/The consequences / Bakutsi/Yo hey / Improvisation no.2/Long distance blues / Monk's dream / Church waltz/Sailing the Chicarrone
CD T&M 006
Tradition & Moderne / Nov '96 / ADA / Direct

Trooper, Greg

EVERYWHERE
CD CBM 009CD
Cross Border Media / Mar '94 / ADA / Direct / Grapevine/PolyGram

Trotsky Icepick

BABY
CD SST 197CD
SST / Sep '88 / Plastic Head

CARPETBOMB THE RIFF
CD SST 295CD
SST / Sep '93 / Plastic Head

DANNY AND THE DOORKNOBS
CD SST 254CD
SST / Sep '90 / Plastic Head

EL KABONG
CD SST 246CD
SST / Jul '89 / Plastic Head

HOT POP HELLO
CD SST 286CD
SST / May '94 / Plastic Head

POISON SUMMER
Gaslight / Nightingale drive / Just the end of the world / Clowns on fire / Ivory tour / Commissioner / Big dreams / Drawing fire / Hit parade / You look like something Goya drew
CD SST 239CD
SST / Dec '89 / Plastic Head

ULTRA-VIOLET CATASTROPHE, THE
CD SST 279CD
SST / Oct '91 / Plastic Head

Trottel

FINAL SALUTE
CD XM 028CD
X-Mist / Apr '92 / Cargo / SRD

Troubador Squat

TROUBADOR SQUAT
CD PRL 0002
Pleather / Nov '96 / Cargo

Trouble

PLASTIC GREEN HEAD
CD CDVEST 45
Bulletproof / Apr '95 / Pinnacle

PSALM 9
CD 398414068CD
Metal Blade / May '96 / Pinnacle / Plastic Head

RUN TO THE LIGHT
Misery show / Thinking of the past / Peace of mind / Born in a prison / Tuesdays child / Beginning
CD 398414051CD
Metal Blade / May '96 / Pinnacle / Plastic Head

SKULL, THE
CD 398141069CD
Metal Blade / May '96 / Pinnacle / Plastic Head

Trouble Funk

DROP THE BOMB
Hey fellas / Get on up / Let's get hot / Drop the bomb / Pump me up / Don't try to use me / My love (burning love) / Caravan to midnight / I'm out to get you / Lost in love / Fool / It's for you / Birthday boy / King of the dances / Sail on / Supergrit / Hey Fellas
CD NEBCD 663
Sequel / Oct '93 / BMG

GO-GO DANCE WITH TROUBLE FUNK (Live)
CD 74321391742
Infinite Zero / Oct '96 / BMG

Troubles

TROUBLES
CD LARRCD 316
Larrikin / Nov '94 / ADA / CM / Direct / Roots

Troup, Bobby

BOBBY TROUP 1955/59/67
CD SLCD 9009
Starline / Dec '94 / Jazz Music

IN A CLASS BEYOND COMPARE
CD ACD 98
Audiophile / Apr '93 / Jazz Music

KICKS ON 66
Route 66 / Girl talk / It happened once before / Please belong to me / For once in my life / Jack 'n' Jill / Watch what happens / Thou swell / Hungry man / Tangerine / Bright lights and you girl / (Back home again in) Indiana / Try a little tenderness / Lemon twist / Misty / Lulu's back in town
CD HCD 607
Hindsight / Nov '95 / Jazz Music / Target/BMG

Troupe, Quincy

ROOT DOCTOR
CD NAR 109CD
New Alliance / Jan '95 / Plastic Head

Trout, Jimbo

JIMBO TROUT & THE FISH PEOPLE (Trout, Jimbo & The Fishpeople)
CD EFA 800382
Twah / Sep '95 / SRD

Trout, Walter

BREAKING THE RULES (Trout, Walter Band)
CD PRD 70762
Provogue / Jun '95 / Pinnacle

LIFE IN THE JUNGLE (Trout, Walter Band)
Good enough to eat / Mountain song / Life in the jungle / Spacefosh / Red house / She's out there somewhere / Frederica (I don't need you) / In my mind / Cold cold feeling / Serve me right to suffer
CD PRD 70202
Provogue / '90 / Pinnacle

NO MORE FISH JOKES (Trout, Walter Band)
CD PRD 70512
Provogue / May '93 / Pinnacle

POSITIVELY BEALE STREET (Trout, Walter Band)
CD PRD 71042
Provogue / May '97 / Pinnacle

PRISONER OF A DREAM (Trout, Walter Band)
CD PRD 70262
Provogue / Oct '91 / Pinnacle

TRANSITION (Trout, Walter Band)
CD PRD 70442
Provogue / Nov '92 / Pinnacle

Trovesi, Gianluigi

FROM G TO G (Trovesi, Gianluigi Octet)
CD 1212312
Soul Note / Nov '92 / Cadillac / Harmonia Mundi / Wellard

LES HOMMES ARMES (Trovesi, Gianluigi Octet)
CD 1213112
Soul Note / Feb '97 / Cadillac / Harmonia Mundi / Wellard

Trower, Robin

20TH CENTURY BLUES
CD FIENDCD 753
Demon / Aug '94 / Pinnacle

ANTHOLOGY
CD VSOPCD 197
Connoisseur Collection / Apr '94 / Pinnacle

BBC LIVE IN CONCERT
CD WINCD 013
Windsong / Feb '92 / Pinnacle

CARAVAN TO MIDNIGHT/VICTIMS OF THE FURY
My love (burning love) / I'm out to get you / Lost in love / Fool / It's for you / Birthday boy / King of the dance / Sail on / Jack and Jill / Roads to freedom / Victims of the fury / Ring / Only time / Into the flame / Shout / Mad house / Ready for the taking / Fly low
CD BGOCD 352
Beat Goes On / Jun '97 / Pinnacle

COLLECTION, THE
CD CCSCD 291
Castle / Aug '91 / BMG

LIVE/FOR EARTH BELOW
Too rolling stoned / Daydream / Rock me baby / Lady love / I can't wait much longer / Alethea / Little bit of sympathy / Shame the devil / It's only money / Confessin' midnight / Fine day / Alethea / Tale untold / Gonna be more suspicious / For earth below
CD BGOCD 347
Beat Goes On / Mar '97 / Pinnacle

LONG MISTY DAYS/IN CITY DREAMS
Some rain falls / Long misty days / Hold me / Caledonia / Somebody calling / Sweet wine of love / Bluebird / Falling star / Farther on up the road / Pride / Sailing / SMO / I can't live without you / Messin' the blues
CD BGOCD 349
Beat Goes On / Apr '97 / Pinnacle

SOMEDAY BLUES
Next in line / Feel so bad / Someday blues / Crossroads / I want you to love me / Inside out / Shining through / Looking for a true love / Extermination blues / Sweet little angel
CD FIENDCD 931
Demon / Jun '97 / Pinnacle

TWICE REMOVED FROM YESTERDAY/ BRIDGE OF SIGHS
I can't wait much longer / Daydream / Hannah / Man of the world / I can't stand it / Rock me baby / Twice removed from yesterday / Sinner's song / Ballerina / Day of the eagle / Bridge of sighs / In this place / Fool and me / Too rolling stoned / About to begin / Love / Little bit of sympathy
CD BGOCD 339
Beat Goes On / Feb '97 / Pinnacle

Trowers, Robert

POINT OF VIEW
Have you met Miss Jones / Minority / Riff / Statement / Spleen bop / St. Thomas / Holiday for strings / R 'n' B / 'Deed I do / Joint is jumpin' / End of a love affair
CD CCD 4656
Concord Jazz / Jul '95 / New Note/Pinnacle

Troy, Doris

JUST ONE LOOK
CD SCL 2504
Ichiban Soul Classics / Apr '95 / Koch

Trubee, John

WORLD OF LIVING PIGS
CD EFA 113362
Musical Tragedies / Feb '94 / SRD

Truce

NOTHING BUT THE TRUCE
CD BLRCD 29
Big Life / Oct '95 / Mo's Music Machine / Pinnacle / Prime

Trudell, John

AKA GRAFFITI MAN
CD RCD 51028
Rykodisc / Sep '92 / ADA / Vital

JOHNNY DAMAS AND ME
Rant 'n' roll / See the woman / Raptor / Shadow over sisterland / Baby doll's blues / That love / Johnny Damas and me / Across my heart / Something about you / After all these years / All there is to it
CD RCD 10286
Rykodisc / Feb '94 / ADA / Vital

Trudy

TUNE-IN TO THE TRUDY LOVE-RAY
CD TDYCD 054
Planet Miron / May '90 / Pinnacle

True Believers

HARD ROAD
Tell her / Ring the bell / So blue about you / Rebel kind / Train round the bend / Lucky moon / Hard road / We're wrong / I get excited / Sleep enough to dream / Rain won't help you when it's over / She's got / All mixed up / One moment to another / Who calls my name / Outside your door / Wild eyed and wound up / Nobody's home / Only a dream / Please don't fade away
CD RCD 40287
Rykodisc / Mar '94 / ADA / Vital

True Frequencies

TRUE FREQUENCIES
Insectoid / New indegenous religion / Magick bufo / Mycellial networks / Paradize lounge / Krononcuts re-union / Firewhorshipper / Beyond the DOP / Cellular data
CD 950822CD
Source / Mar '96 / SRD / Vital

True West

HOLLYWOOD HOLIDAY/ DRIFTERS
CD ROSE 23CD
New Rose / Sep '90 / ADA / Direct / Discovery

Truffaz, Erik

OUT OF A DREAM
Down town / Of a dream / Beaute bleue / Wet in Paris / Porta camollia / Indigo saisir / Elegie / Samara / Up town / Betty
CD CDP 8558552
Blue Note / Jul '97 / EMI

Truman's Water

ACTION ORNAMENTS
CD RUNT 28
Runt / Jun '97 / Cargo / Greyhound / Plastic Head

GOD SPEED THE PUNCHLINE
CD ELM 15CD
Elemental / Feb '94 / RTM/Disc

MILKTRAIN TO PAYDIRT
CD HMS 2212
Homestead / Aug '95 / Cargo / SRD

OF THICK TUM
CD HMS 1922
Homestead / Mar '93 / Cargo / SRD

SPASM SMASH XXX OX OX OX & ASS
CD ELM 9CD
Elemental / Mar '93 / RTM/Disc

Trunk Federation

INFAMOUS HAMBURGER TRANSFER, THE
Quality burn / Original uptight / Sweet bread / Dog reject / Clyde suckfinger / Young cherry trees / Match / Alright / Over-rated / Gelatin / Pinhead / St. Francis / Beanie's soft toy factory
CD A 111D
Alias / Feb '97 / Vital

Trusty

FOURTH WISE MAN, THE
CD DIS 104CD
Dischord / Oct '96 / SRD

GOODBYE DR. FATE
CD DIS 93CD
Dischord / May '95 / SRD

Tryolia Singers

SOUND OF TYROL
CD 321680
Koch / Sep '92 / Koch

Tsatthoggua

HOSANNA BIZARRE
CD OPCD 035
Osmose / Jul '96 / Plastic Head

Tschanz, Mark

BLUE DOG
CD 0630106062
East West / Dec '96 / Warner Music

Tse Tse Fly

MUD FLAT JOEY
M 1 / Jonah / Talk to me / Pog eared / On purpose / Lido / Roo mole suit / Itchy / Some pay soon / Non-ferrous / Kitchen / Hogwash
CD CDBRED 117
Cherry Red / Oct '94 / Pinnacle

Tsiboe, Nana

ASEM NIL TROUBLE DAT
Bue bue / Kai onyame / Adum / Nana ewusi / Odumankumah boa mi / Kokofu hene mba / Ghana muntye
CD TD 8001
World Circuit / Feb '94 / ADA / Cadillac / Direct / New Note/Pinnacle

Tsinandali Choir

TABLE SONGS OF GEORGIA
Kakhuri mravaljamieri / Makruli / Shashvi, Kakabi / Orovela / Turpani skhedan / Zamtari / Diambego / Shemodzakhili / Berikatsi var / Charkrulo
CD CDRW 28
Realworld / Jan '93 / EMI

Tsitsanis, Vassilis

VASSILIS TITSANIS
CD ROUCD 1124
Rounder / Feb '97 / ADA / CM / Direct

TSOL

DANCE WITH ME
Sounds of laughter / Core blue / Triangle / Eighty times / I'm tired of life / Love storm / Silent scream / Funeral march / Die for me / Peace thru power / Dance with me
CD 64622
Epitaph / Jan '97 / Pinnacle / Plastic Head

STRANGE LOVE
CD LS 9392
Roadrunner / May '90 / PolyGram

THOUGHTS OF YESTERDAY
CD EFA 122142
Poshboy / Nov '94 / RTM/Disc

Tsunami

DEEP END
CD SMR 13D
Simple Machines / May '93 / SRD

HEART'S TREMOLO
CD SMR 25CD
Simple Machines / Jun '94 / SRD

WHO IS IT
CD DYN 101
Nova / Sep '93 / New Note/Pinnacle

WORLD TOUR AND OTHER DESTINATIONS
CD SMR 33CD
Simple Machines / Apr '95 / SRD

Tsurata, Kinshi

PLAYS SATSUMA BIWA
CD C559067
Ocora / May '91 / ADA / Harmonia Mundi

Tuatara

BREAKING THE ETHERS
Breaking the ethers/Serengeti / Dark state of mind / Saturday night church / Dreamscape / Desert sky / Goodnight La Habana / Smoke rings / Getaway / Eastern star / Burning the keys / Land of apples / Breaking the ethers/Serengeti (reprise)
CD 4875402
Epic / May '97 / Sony

Tub

WHY I DRINK
Charles Murray / Repeller / Life by beerlight / Ronald Reagan / Crash / Hardcore muscles and fitness / Teenagers from outer space / Rudy Giuliana / Two foot / Scoping / Static life
CD BLK 5001ECD
Blackout / May '96 / Plastic Head / Vital

Tubb, Ernest

IT'S COUNTRY TIME VOL.1
CD 12245
Laserlight / Jul '94 / Target/BMG

IT'S COUNTRY TIME VOL.2
CD 12246
Laserlight / Jul '94 / Target/BMG

IT'S COUNTRY TIME VOL.3
CD 12247
Laserlight / Jul '94 / Target/BMG

LEGEND AND THE LEGACY, THE (Tubb, Ernest & Friends)
Waltz across Texas: *Tubb, Ernest & Willie Nelson* / When the world has turned you

down: *Tubb, Ernest & Waylon Jennings/ Vern Gosdin* / Let's say goodbye like we said hello: *Tubb, Ernest & Marty Robbins* / Walkin' the floor over you: *Tubb, Ernest & Merle Haggard/Charlie Daniels* / Half a mind: *Tubb, Ernest & George Jones* / Jealous loving heart: *Tubb, Ernest & Johnny Cash* / Rainbow at midnight: *Tubb, Ernest & Marty Robbins* / Set up two glasses Joe: *Tubb, Ernest & Ferlin Husky/Simon Crum* / You nearly lose your mind: *Tubb, Ernest & Willie Nelson/Waylon Jennings* / You're the only good thing: *Tubb, Ernest & Charlie Rich* / Filipino baby: *Tubb, Ernest & George Jones* / Jimmie Rodger's last blue yodel: *Tubb, Ernest & Conway Twitty* / Seaman's blues: *Tubb, Ernest & Merle Haggard* / Thanks a lot: *Tubb, Ernest & Loretta Lynn* / It's been so long darling: *Tubb, Ernest & Conway Twitty* / Blue eyed Elaine: *Tubb, Ernest & Justin* / Our baby's book: *Tubb, Ernest & Cal Smith* / Soldier's last letter: *Tubb, Ernest & Johnny Cash*
CD _______________ EDCD 517
Edsel / Mar '97 / Pinnacle

LET'S SAY GOODBYE LIKE WE SAY HELLO (5CD Set)
You hit the nail right on the head / Two wrongs don't make a right / That wild and wicked look in your eye / Lonely heart knows / Don't your face look red / Answer to Rainbow At Midnight / Watching my past go by / Woman has wrecked many a good man / Headin' down the wrong highway / Let's say goodbye like we say hello / Takin' it easy here / Seaman's blues / How can I forget you / Yesterday's winner is a loser today / I'm with a crowd but so alone / Waiting for a train / Forever is ending today / Have you ever been lonely / Till the end of the world / Daddy, when is mommy coming home / Don't rob another man's castle / I'm biting my fingernails and thinking of you: *Tubb, Ernest & Andrews Sisters* / My Filipino rose / My Tennessee baby / Slippin' around / Warm red wine / Driftwood on the river / Tennessee border: *Tubb, Ernest & Red Foley* / Letters have no arms / I'll take a back seat for you / Throw your love my way / Don't be ashamed of your age: *Tubb, Ernest & Red Foley* / Stand by me / Old rugged cross / What a friend we have in Jesus / Wonderful city / When I take my vacation in heaven / Farther along / I love you because / Give me a little old-fashioned love / Unfaithful one / Hillbilly fever: *Tubb, Ernest & Red Foley* / Texas Vs Kentucky: *Tubb, Ernest & Red Foley* / G-I-R-L spells trouble / You don't have to be a baby to cry / Mother, the Queen of my heart / Goodnight Irene: *Tubb, Ernest & Red Foley* / Remember me, I'm the one who loves you / I need attention bad / I'm lonely and blue / Why did you give me your love / I'm free from the chain gang now / Why should I be lonely / Hobo's meditation / Good morning Irene: *Tubb, Ernest/Red Foley/Minnie Pearl* / Love bug itch: *Tubb, Ernest/Red Foley/ Minnie Pearl* / Don't stay too long / I'm steppin' out of the picture / May the good lord bless and keep you / When it's prayer meetin' time in the hollow / Drunkard's child / Any old time / If you want some lovin' / So long (it's been good to know yuh): *Tubb, Ernest & Red Foley* / Chicken song: *Tubb, Ernest & Red Foley* / Strange little girl / Kentucky waltz / Hey la la / Rose of the mountains / Precious little baby / So many times / My mother must have been a girl like you / Somebody's stolen my honey / Heartsick soldier on a heartbreak ridge / I'm in love with Molly: *Tubb, Ernest & Red Foley* / Too old to cut the mustard: *Tubb, Ernest & Red Foley* / Missing in action / I will miss you when you go / Fortunes in memories / Dear judge / Don't brush them on me / I love everything you do / Somebody loves you / Don't trifle on your sweetheart / Hank, it will never be the same without you / beyond the sunset / When Jimmie Rodgers said goodbye / Jimmie Rodgers' last thoughts / My wasted past / Counterfeit kisses / Honeymoon is over / No help wanted: *Tubb, Ernest & Red Foley* / You're a real good friend: *Tubb, Ernest & Red Foley* / Dear John letter: *Tubb, Ernest & Elaine 'Scooter Bill' Tubb* / Double datin': *Tubb, Ernest & Red Foley* / It's the mileage that's slowin' us down: *Tubb, Ernest & Red Foley* / Divorce granted / Honky tonk heart / I'm not looking for an angel / I met a friend / When Jesus calls / Too old to tango: *Tubb, Ernest & Red Foley* / Dr. Ketchum: *Tubb, Ernest & Red Foley* / Love lifted me / White Christmas / Blue Christmas / Christmas Island / C-H-R-I-S-T-M-A-S / We need God for Christmas / Merry Christmas you all / Blue snowflakes / I'm trimming my Christmas tree with teardrops
CD Set _______________ BCD 15498
Bear Family / Feb '91 / Direct / Rollercoaster / Swift

NASHVILLE 1946/NBC 1950 (Tubb, Ernest & T. Texas Tyler)
CD _______________ CDMR 1141
Radiola / Oct '90 / Pinnacle

STARS OVER TEXAS
You nearly lose your mind / It's been so long darlin' / Have you ever been lonely (have you ever been blue) / Sweet thang / Tomorrow never comes / (When you feel like you're in love) don't just stand there / I'm with a crowd but so alone / Soldier's last letter / Blue eyed Elaine / Thanks a lot / Half a mind / Rainbow at midnight / Jimmy Rodger's last blue yodel / Journey's end / Waltz across Texas / Filipino baby / Walkin' the floor over you / You're the only good thing / Set up two glasses, Joe / Our baby's book / Driftwood on the river / Answer the phone / Jealous loving heart / Drivin' nails in my coffin / Let's say goodbye like we said hello / I'll step aside / There's a little bit of everything in Texas
CD _______________ 3036001052
Carlton / Jun '97 / Carlton

WALKING THE FLOOR OVER YOU (8CD Set)
Passing of Jimmie Rodgers / Last thoughts of Jimmie Rodgers / Married man blues / Mean old red bug blues / My Mother is lonely / Right train to heaven / TB Is whipping me / Since that black cat crossed my path / Blue eyed Elaine / I'll never cry over you / I'll get along somehow / You broke a heart / I ain't gonna love you anymore / I'm glad I met you after all / I cared for you more than I knew / You'll love me too late / I've really learned a lot / Swell San Angelo / I know what it means to be lonely / Please remember me / My rainbow trail / Last night I dreamed / I'm missing you / My baby and my wife / Walking the floor over you / When the world has turned you down / Our baby's book / I'll always be glad to take you back / Mean Mama blues / I wonder why you said goodbye / I ain't goin' honky tonkin' anymore / I hate to see you go / Time after time / First years blues / Just rollin' on / There's nothing more to say / Wasting my life away / You may have your picture / That same old story / Try me one more time / You nearly lose your mind / That's when it's coming home to you / I don't want you after all / I'm wandering how / Tomorrow never comes / Soldier's last letter / Careless Darlin' / Yesterday's tears / I'll never cry Over's last letter / Those simple things are worth a million now / Answer to walking the floor over you / You won't ever forget me / Keep my memory in your heart / I lost my ace of hearts / Though the days were only seven / With tears in my eyes (False starts) / With tears in my eyes / Are you waiting just for me / Blue eyes Elaine / I'll never lose you though you're gone / I'm too blue to worry over you / Too late to worry, too blue to cry / I'm wondering how / This time we're really through / I ain't goin honky tonkin' anymore / Have you changed your mind / That's all she wrote / Just crying to myself / I've lived a lie / Wondering if you're wondering to / When love turns to late / There's a new moon over my shoulder / Daisy may / I hung my head and cried / There's nothin' on my mind / Too late tp worry, to blue to cry / Love gone cold / You brought sorrow to my heart / Home in San Antone / Darling what more can I do / Blue bonnet lane / I believe I'm entitled to you / You're going to be sorry / My confession / That's why I'm crying over you / Gone and left me blues / When the tumble weeds come tumbling down / I'll be true while you're gone / End of the world / It just don't matter now / You're on my mind / I'm wasting my tears on you / Ten years / Old love letters / Low and lonely / Where the deep waters flow / It's coming back to you / Over the river / You don't care / Let me smile my last smile at you / I'm tired of you / You told me a lie / Frankie and Johnny / Jealous heart / Crying myself to sleep / Fort Worth Jail / You're breaking my heart / My hillbilly baby / Farther and farther apart / I loved you once / I'll step aside / Worried mind / Year ago tonight / Time changes everything / What good will it do / My time will come someday / Grey eyed darling / I never cross your mind / I told you so / I'm beginning to forget you / I'm gonna be long gone when I go away / I walk alone / Heart of stone / You'll want me back / Our baby boy / Hang your head in shame / Last goodbye / Pins and needles (In my heart) / Love I have for you / I'll never tell you I love you / I knew the moment I lost you / I wonder you feel the way I do / I'll have to live and learn (Alt) / National lament / Tweedle O'Twill / There's a rainbow on the Rio Colorado / Action speaks louder than words / Left all alone / Two more years (And I'll be free) / Trailing home to Mother / It's been so long darling / Sould I come back home to you / There's a little bit of everything in Texas / Darling, what more can I do / There's gonna be some changes made around / You were only teasing me / I'm free at last / Filipino baby / Rainbow at midnight / I don't blame you / Get in or get out of my heart / How can I be sure / Those tears in your eyes (Were not for me) / So round, so firm, so fully pakced / Don't look now / Hundred and sixty acres / Woman has wrecked many a good man / White Christmas / It's a lonely world / Mississippi gal / Trouble with me is trouble / Heart please be still / I hope I'm wrong / Those tears in your eyes / Don't talk to me about dames / You won't ever forget me / You could have said goodbye
CD Set _______________ BCD 15853
Bear Family / Jul '96 / Direct / Rollercoaster / Swift

WALTZ ACROSS TEXAS
Waltz across Texas / When the world has turned you down / Let's say goodbye like we say hello / Answer the phone / Journey's end / Walkin' the floor over you / Half a mind / Jealous loving heart / Rainbow at midnight / Set up two glasses, Joe / You nearly lose your mind / You're the only good thing / Filipino baby / Jimmie Rodgers' last blue yodel / Seaman's blues
CD _______________ PWKS 4217
Carlton / Jul '95 / Carlton

YELLOW ROSE OF TEXAS, THE (5CD Set)
Till we two are one / Your Mother, your darling, your friend / Baby your mother (Like she babied you) / Jealous loving heart / Two glasses, Joe / Woman's touch / Journey's end / Kansas city blues / Lonely Christmas eve / I'll be walking the floor this Christmas / Have you seen my boogie woogie baby / It's a lonely world / I got the blues for Mammy / (I'm gonna make my home) A million miles from here / Yellow rose of Texas / Answer the phone / Honeymoon is over / Thirty days / Doorstep to heaven / Will you be satisfied that way / Steppin' out / If I never have anything else / So doggone lonesome / Old love letters (Bring memories of you) / Jimmie Rodgers' last blue yodel / Travellin' blues / You're the only good thing (that's happened to me) / I've got the blues for Mammy / I dreamed of an old love affair / (I know my baby loves me) in her own peculiar way / Mississippi gal / There's no fool like a young fool / I new the moment I lost you / You're breaking my heart / When a soldier knocks and finds nobody home / This troubled mind o'mine / My hillbilly baby / Daisy May / Loving you is my weakness / Treat her right / I want you know (I love you) / Don't forbid me / God's eyes / My treasure / Leave me / Mr. Love / I always went through / Go home / Hey Mr. Blubird / How do we know / House of glass / Heaven help me / Tangled mind / Home of the blues / I found my girl in the USA / Geisha girl / I wonder why I worry over you / Deep purple blues / Please keep me in mind / I'm a long gone Daddy / Your cheatin' heart / Don't trade your old fashioned sweetheart / It makes no difference now / San Antonio rose / I want you to know I love you / That, my darlin', is me / I'll get along somehow / Educated Mama / I'm waiting for the ships that never come in / Half a mind / Next time / Goodbye sunshine / Hello blues / It's the age that makes the difference / What am I living for / Next voice you hear / All of those yesterdays / Walking the floor over you / When the world has turned you down / I'll always be glad to take you back / It's been so long Darling / Careless Darlin' / Though the days were only seven / Last night I dreamed / Slippin' around / I love you because / There's nothing more to say / There's a little bit of everything in Texas / You nearly lose your mind / Blue Christmas / Don't rob another man's castle / What I don't know about her / I cried a tear / Let's say goodbye like we say hello / Driftwood on the river / I wonder why you said goodbye / Tomorrow never comes / Filipino baby / I'd rather be / Letters have no arms / Rainbow at midnight / Have you ever been lonely / I will miss you when you go / Live it up / (I've lost you) So why should I care / Accidently on purpose / Do it now / He'll have to go / Mr. Blues / Kind of love she gave to me / Pick me up on your way down / This ain't the blues (Instrumental) / You win again / I believe I'm entitled to you / Guy named Joe / Who will buy the wine / Why I'm walkin' / White silver sands / Am I that easy to forget / Everybody's somebody's fool / Let the little girl dance / Candy kisses / It happened when I really needed you / Wondering / Cold cold heart / Four walls / Bouquet of roses / Crazy arms / I love you so much it hurts / I walk the line / Little ole band of gold / Wabash cannonball / I'm movin' on / Tennessee Saturday night / Signed, sealed, delivered (I'm yours) / Thoughts of a fool / Girl from Abilene / Same thing as me / Christmas is just another day / I hate to see you go / I'm sorry now / What will you tell them / It is no secret / Don't just stand there / Big blue diamonds / I'll just have another cup of coffee
CD Set _______________ BCD 15688
Bear Family / May '93 / Direct / Rollercoaster / Swift

Tubb, Justin

ROCK ON DOWN TO MY HOUSE (2CD Set)
I'm a darn good man / Story of my life / Ooh la la / Give three cheers for my baby / Somebody ughed on you / Something called the blues / I'm looking for a date tonight / You're the prettiest thing that ever happend to me / Who will it be / Sufferin' heart / Looking back to see / Miss you so / My heart's not for little girls to play with / Little bit waltz / I'm sorry I stayed away so long / Sure fire kisses / Fickel heart / Waterloo / I gotta go get my baby / Chugachuga, chica maugal / I'm a damn good man / All alone / Within your arms / Pepper hot baby / Lucky lucky someone else / You nearly lose your mind / Oh how I miss you / Desert blues / Miss the Mississippi and you / It takes a lot of heart / I'm just fool enough / I'm a big boy now / Life I have to live / Bachelor man / Party is over (For me) / Tears of angels / If you'll be my love / Someday, you'll want me to want you / I saw your face in the moon / Try me one more time / I'd trade all of my tomorrows / Silver dew on the bluegrass / Bonaparte's retreat / There'll be no teardrops tonight / Gone and left my blues / My Mary / Into each life some rain must fall / I've gotta have my baby back / Hang your head in shame / Sugar lips / Rock it down to my house / Mine is a lonely life / Almost lonely / Giveway girl / Heart's command / Buster's gang / I wish I could love that much / I know you do
CD Set _______________ BCD 15761
Bear Family / Jun '94 / Direct / Rollercoaster / Swift

Tube, Shem

ABANA BA NASERY (Tube, Shem/Justo Osala/Enos Okola)
Atisa wangu / Khwatsia ebunangwe / Servanus andai / Nilimwacha muke risavu / Mapenzi kama karata / Noah libuko / Omukhana meri / Abasiratsi muhulire / Ndakhomela / Ebijana bie bubayi / Mushalo ebutula / Rosey wangu / Willison oluhambo
CD _______________ CDORB 052
Globestyle / Nov '89 / Pinnacle

Tubes

COMPLETION BACKWARD PRINCIPLE, THE
Talk to ya later / Let's make some noise / Matter of pride / Mr. Hate / Attack of the 50 foot woman / Think about me / Sushi girl / Don't want to wait anymore / Power tools / Amnesia / When I see you / Politics / Slave trade / Could be her...could be you / Make believe / Don't go away / Price / Animal laugh / Anything is good enough / Product of... / Perfect game / Vendredi saint
CD _______________ BGOCD 100
Beat Goes On / Mar '91 / Pinnacle

GOING DOWN...THE TUBES (2CD Set)
White punks on dope / Up from the deep / Malaguena salerosa / What do you want from life / Boy crazy / Tubes world tour / Don't touch me there / Slipped my disco / Smoke (la vie en fumer) / My head is my only house unless it rains / God-birdchange / I'm just a mess / This town / Pound of flesh / Drivin' all night / Love will keep us together / White punks on dope / Turn me on / TV is king / Prime time / I want it all now / No way out / Getoverture / No mercy / Only the strong survive / Be mine tonight / Love's a mystery (I don't understand) / Telecide / Overture / Mondo bondage / Crime medley / I was a punk before you were a punk / I saw her standing there / White punks on dope
CD Set _______________ 5405642
A&M / Oct '96 / PolyGram

LOVE BOMB
Piece by piece / Stella: *3* / Come as you are: *3* / One good reason / Bora Bora 2000 / Love bomb / Night people / Say hey / Eyes / Muscle girls / Theme from a wooly place / For a song / Say hey (part 2) / Feel it / Night people (reprise)
CD _______________ BGOCD 188
Beat Goes On / Jul '93 / Pinnacle

OUTSIDE/INSIDE
She's a beauty / No not again / Out of the business / Monkey time / Glasshouse / Wild women of Wongo / Tip of my tongue / Fantastic delusion / Drums / Theme park / Outside looking in
CD _______________ BGOCD 133
Beat Goes On / Mar '92 / Pinnacle

Tubuai Choir

POLYNESIAN ODYSSEY
CD _______________ SHAN 64049CD
Shanachie / Dec '93 / ADA / Greensleeves / Koch

Tuck & Patti

BEST OF TUCK & PATTI, THE
CD _______________ 01934111562
Windham Hill / Oct '94 / BMG

DREAM
Dream / One hand, one heart / Togetherness / Friends in high places / Voodoo music / From now on we're one / I wish / Sitting in limbo / High heel blues / All the love / As time goes by
CD _______________ 01934101302
Windham Hill / Nov '93 / BMG

LEARNING TO FLY
Live in the light / Heaven down here / Learning how to fly / Strength / Woodstock / Drum / Up from the skies / Tossin' and turnin' / Getaway / In my life / Yeah yeah / Wide awake / Still tossin' and turnin
CD _______________ 4783992
Sony Soho2 / Apr '95 / Sony

LOVE WARRIORS
Love warriors / Honey pie / They can't take that away from me / Hold out hold up and hold on / Cantador (like a lover) / On a clear day (You can see forever) / Europa / Castles made of sand / Little wing / Glory glory / If it's magic
CD _______________ 01934101162
Windham Hill / Jan '95 / BMG

TEARS OF JOY
Tears of joy / Takes my breath away / I've got just about everything / Time after time / Everything's gonna be alright / Better than anything / My romance / Up and at it / Mad mad me / Love is the key
CD ______ 01934101112
Windham Hill / Jan '95 / BMG

Tucker, Junior

DEEP INSIDE OF YOU
CD ______ DTCD 001
Don't Test / Jun '97 / Grapevine/PolyGram / Jet Star

LOVE OF A LIFETIME
CD ______ VPCD 1314
VP / Aug '93 / Greensleeves / Jet Star / Total/BMG

SECRET LOVER
CD ______ CRCD 35
Charm / Nov '94 / Jet Star

TRUE CONFESSION
CD ______ VPCD 1466
VP / May '96 / Greensleeves / Jet Star / Total/BMG

Tucker, Luther

LUTHER TUCKER & THE FORD BLUES BAND (Tucker, Luther & The Ford Blues Band)
CD ______ CCD 11040
Crosscut / Nov '95 / ADA / CM / Direct

SAD HOURS
CD ______ ANT 0026CD
Antones / Apr '94 / ADA / Hot Shot

Tucker, Marshall

FINEST SOUTH ROCK (Tucker, Marshall Band)
CD ______ 12363
Laserlight / May '94 / Target/BMG

Tucker, Mickey

GETTIN' THERE
CD ______ SCCD 31365
Steeplechase / Dec '95 / Discovery / Impetus

Tucker, Moe

DOGS UNDER STRESS
CD ______ NR 422492
New Rose / Mar '94 / ADA / Direct / Discovery

I SPENT A WEEK THERE THE OTHER NIGHT
CD ______ 422373
New Rose / May '94 / ADA / Direct / Discovery

LIFE IN EXILE AFTER ABDICATION
CD ______ CREV 011CD
Rev-Ola / Mar '93 / 3mv/Vital

OH NO, THEY'RE RECORDING THIS SHOW
CD ______ 422418
New Rose / May '94 / ADA / Direct / Discovery

Tucker, Sophie

LEGENDARY SOPHIE TUCKER, THE
I'm the last of the red hot mammas / Some of these days / Aren't women wonderful / Louisville Lou / Oh you have no idea / Life begins at forty / 'Cause I feel low-down / You can't sew a button on a heart / What good am I without you / Older they get, the younger they want them / Fifty million Frenchmen can't be wrong / After you've gone / Washing the blues from my soul / Follow a star / Who wants them tell, Dard and Handsome / My Yiddishe momme / That man of my dreams / Man I love / He hadn't up 'til yesterday / Some of these days
CD ______ PAR 2031
Parade / Sep '94 / Disc

SOME OF THESE DAYS
My Yiddishe Momme / Man I love / Fifty million Frenchmen can't be wrong / Life begins at forty / Complainin' / Some of these days / After you've gone / Oh you have no idea / He's a good man to have around / When a lady meets a gentleman down South / There'll be some changes made / Washing the blues from my soul / One I love (belongs to someone else) / You've got to see Mamma ev'ry night / Aren't women wonderful / 'Cause I feel lowdown / What'll I do / Makin' wickey wackey down in Waikiki / Moanin' low / My pet / I ain't got nobody / Man of my dreams / Foolin' with the other woman's man / (If you can't sing) you'll have to swing it
CD ______ PASTCD 7807
Flapper / Oct '96 / Pinnacle

Tucker, Tanya

COUNTRY CLASSICS
Strong enough to bend / Love me like you used to / Just another love / One love at a time / Texas (when I die) / I won't take less than your love / San Antonio stroll / Would you lay with me (in a field of stone) / What's your mama's name / Child / Blood red and going down / Highway robbery / Walkin' shoes / Jamestown ferry / If it didn't come easy / Something
CD ______ CDMFP 6323
Music For Pleasure / Apr '97 / EMI

FIRE TO FIRE
Come in out of the world / I'll take the memories / I bet she knows / Find out what's happening / Fire to fire / Between the two of them / Nobody dies from a broken heart / Love will / Love you gave to me / I'll take today
CD ______ CDEST 2254
Liberty / Apr '95 / EMI

HITS: TANYA TUCKER
San Antonio stroll / Don't believe my heart can stand another you / Jamestown ferry / Here's some love / Would you lay with me (in a field of stone) / Blood red and going down / Pecos promenade / What's your mama's name child / O Texas (when I die) / Just another love / I won't take less than your love / Daddy and home / If it don't come easy / Strong enough to bend / It won't be me / I'll come back as another woman / Love me like you used to / Down to my last teardrop / My arms stay open all night / Walking shoes / Don't go out
CD ______ CDESTU 2169
Liberty / Apr '92 / EMI

LIZZIE AND THE RAINMAN
CD ______ CDCOT 108
Cottage / Mar '94 / Koch / THE

SOON
You just watch me / I love you anyway / Soon / Black water bayou / Let the good times roll / Strong enough to bend / Hangin' in / As long as there's a heartbeat / Oh what it did to me / Sneaky moon / Come on honey / We don't have to do this / Silence is king / Blue guitar
CD ______ C2 27577
Liberty / Nov '93 / EMI

Tucker, Tommy

TOMMY TUCKER & HIS ORCHESTRA 1941-1947
CD ______ CCD 15
Circle / Mar '95 / Jazz Music / Swift / Wellard

Tud

DEUS KERNE
CD ______ CD 851
Diffusion Breizh / Jul '94 / ADA

Tuesday Weld

HERSELF
CD ______ SUPERCD 01
Supermodern / Feb '97 / Cargo

Tuff

RELIGIOUS FIX
CD ______ 9041672
Mausoleum / May '95 / Grapevine/ PolyGram

Tuff, Mikey

NAH LEF JAH JAH
CD ______ RMCD 012
Roots Man / Dec '92 / Jet Star

Tulku

TRANCENDENCE
Life force / Golden era / Agua sante / Time dances slowly / Ghost dance / Orca song / Anni rose / Trancendence / Journey of the warrior / Sacred circle / Prayer to the protector
CD ______ 72152
Triloka / Mar '96 / New Note/Pinnacle

Tulla Ceili Band

CELEBRATION OF 50 YEARS, A
Concertina reel/Coffey's reel / Imelda Roland's/Cregg's pipes / Peacock's feather / Tatter Jack Walsh/Cook in the kitchen / Four courts/Tear the calico / Battering ram/ Bill Harte's/Ward's jig / Lad O'Beirne's/ Broderick's / Battle of Aughrim / Cooley's/ The cup of tea/The wise maid / Hole in the hedge/Seamus Cooley's/Kerfunken jig / Jenny picking cockles/The Sligo maid / Castle Kelly/humours of Ballyconnell/The Duke of Leinster / Butcher's jig/The lark's march/Gander at the Pratie Hole / Joe's/ The mountain lark
CD ______ GLCD 1178
Green Linnet / Feb '97 / ADA / CM / Direct / Highlander / Roots

Tumbao

SALSA PA' GOZAR
CD ______ EUCD 1188
ARC / Apr '92 / ADA / ARC Music

Tumor Circus

TUMOR CIRCUS
CD ______ VIRUS 87CD
Alternative Tentacles / Oct '91 / Cargo / Greyhound / Pinnacle

Tungsten

183.85
CD ______ IRSCD 981202
Intercord / Jan '94 / Plastic Head

Tunic

WITHOUT LOVE, WHERE WOULD YOU BE NOW
CD ______ RYPE 303
Project Rype / May '97 / Cargo

Tunjung, Gamelan Seker

MUSIC OF K.R.T. WASITODININGRAT
CD ______ CMP CD 3007
CMP / Jul '92 / Cargo / Grapevine/ PolyGram / Vital/SAM

Tupaia, Andy

HITS SELECTION VOL.2
CD ______ S 65810
Manuiti / Sep '92 / Harmonia Mundi

Turbinton, Earl

BROTHERS FOR LIFE
CD ______ ROUCD 2064
Rounder / '88 / ADA / CM / Direct

Turbo AC's

DAMNATION OVERDRIVE
Graveyard shifter / Eat my dust / No ieNo lie / Praise the lord / Righteous ruler / BBe fast / Superbad / Puff of smoke / Twistoflex / I don't care / Last mile
CD ______ BLK 034ECD
Blackout / Jan '97 / Plastic Head / Vital

Turbonegro

ASS COBRA
CD ______ BOOMBA 0012
Boomba / Jun '96 / SRD
CD ______ SFTRI 385CD
Sympathy For The Record Industry / May '97 / Cargo / Greyhound / Plastic Head

HELTA SKELTA
CD ______ EFA 15665CD
Repulsion / Jun '93 / SRD

Turbulent Force

DISTURBING TRUTH, THE
Green sugar: *Flare* / Dreams / Media overdose / Voidcom / Metro city / Renegade / Shangri-la / Breathless / Paranoia
CD ______ SOP 010CD
Emissions / Feb '97 / Amato Disco / Vital

Turmoil

CHOKE
CD ______ CM 770752
Century Media / Sep '94 / Plastic Head

FROM BLEEDING HEARTS
CD ______ CMCD 77102
Century Media / May '96 / Plastic Head

Turn Ons

TURN ONS
CD ______ DS 45CD18
Duophonic 45's / Jul '97 / RTM/Disc

Turner, 'Big' Joe

BEST OF BIG JOE TURNER, THE
CD ______ PACD 2405404
Pablo / Jan '95 / Cadillac / Complete/ Pinnacle

BIG JOE TURNER RIDES AGAIN
CD ______ RSACD 810
Sequel / Oct '94 / BMG

BIG THREE, THE (Turner, 'Big' Joe & Joe Houston/L.C. Williams)
CD ______ CDBM 095
Blue Moon / Jul '93 / Cadillac / Discovery / Greensleeves / Jazz Music / Jet Star / TKO Magnum

BLUES BOSS, THE
Roll 'em Pete / Cherry red / Morning glories / How long blues / St. Louis blues / Piney Brown blues / Ti ri lee / In the evening / Midnight cannonball / Sweet sixteen / Low down dog / Wee baby blues / Jump for joy / Poor lover's blues / Chill is on / TV mama / Hollywood bed / Miss Brown blues / Chains of love / Don't you cry / Married woman
CD ______ CD 52008
Blues Encore / '92 / Target/BMG

BLUES SINGER 1938-1942, THE
CD ______ JZCD 347
Suisa / Jan '93 / Jazz Music / THE

BLUES TRAIN (Turner, 'Big' Joe & Roomful Of Blues)
Crawdad hole / Red sails in the sunset / Cock-a-doodle-doo / Jumpin' for Joe / I want a little girl / I know you love me / Last night / I love the way (my baby sings the blues) / Blues train
CD ______ MCD 5293
Muse / Feb '87 / New Note/Pinnacle

BOSS OF THE BLUES (That's Jazz Vol.14)
Cherry red / Roll 'em Pete / I want a little girl / Low down dog / Wee baby blues / You're driving me crazy / How long blues / Morning glories / St. Louis blues / Piney Brown blues
CD ______ 7567814592
Atlantic / Jun '93 / Warner Music

EVERY DAY I HAVE THE BLUES
Stormy Monday / Piney Brown blues / Martin Luther King southside / Everyday / Shake, rattle and roll / Lucille
CD ______ OJCCD 634
Original Jazz Classics / Jan '95 / Complete/ Pinnacle / Jazz Music / Wellard

FLIP, FLOP AND FLY (Turner, 'Big' Joe & Count Basie Orchestra)
CD ______ PACD 23109372
Pablo / Jan '92 / Cadillac / Complete/ Pinnacle

GREATEST HITS
Chill is on / After my laughter came tears / Bump Miss Suzie / Chains of love / I'll never stop loving you / Sweet sixteen / Baby I still want you / Honey hush / Crawdad hole / Oke she moke she pop / Shake, rattle and roll / Well all right / Hide and seek / Flip flop and fly / Chicken and the hawk / Boogie woogie country girl / Corrine Corrina / Midnight special train / Red sails in the sunset / Feeling happy / Blues in the night
CD ______ RSACD 809
Sequel / Oct '94 / BMG

HONEY HUSH
Shake, rattle and roll / Chains of love / Roll 'em Hawk / Piney Brown blues / Cherry red / Nothin' from nothin' / Honey hush / Corine Corina / TV Mama / Wee baby blues / Squeeze me baby
CD ______ CDMF 064
Magnum Force / Mar '95 / TKO Magnum

I DON'T DIG IT
Goin' to Chicago blues / I can't give you anything but love / Blues in the night / Rocks in my bed / Sun risin' blues / Mardi gras boogie / Cry baby blues / Rainy weather blues / I don't dig it / Boogie woogie baby / My heart belongs to you / Born to gamble / I love you, I love you / Oo-ouch-stop / Wish I had a dollar / Fuzzy wuzzy honey
CD ______ RBD 618
Mr. R&B / Oct '91 / CM / Swift / Wellard

KANSAS CITY HERE I COME
Down home blues / Call the plumber / Since I fell for you / Kansas City here I come / Big legged woman / Sweet sixteen / Time after time
CD ______ OJCCD 743
Original Jazz Classics / Jan '95 / Complete/ Pinnacle / Jazz Music / Wellard

LA SELECTION 1938-1941
CD ______ 700102
Art Vocal / Nov '92 / Discovery

LIFE AIN'T EASY
CD ______ OJCCD 809
Original Jazz Classics / Jan '95 / Complete/Pinnacle / Jazz Music / Wellard

MIDNIGHT SPECIAL
I left my heart in San Francisco / I'm gonna sit right down and write myself a letter / I can't give you anything but love / You're driving me crazy / So long / After my laughter came tears / Midnight special / Stoop down baby
CD ______ PACD 2310844
Original Jazz Classics / Jan '95 / Complete/ Pinnacle / Jazz Music / Wellard

NOBODY IN MIND (Turner, 'Big' Joe & Milt Jackson/Roy Eldridge)
CD ______ OJCCD 729
Original Jazz Classics / Jan '95 / Complete/Pinnacle / Jazz Music / Wellard

ROCK 'N' ROLL SHAKEDOWN
Shake, rattle and roll / When the sun goes down / Jump for joy / Stormy Monday / Hide and go seek / How long blues / Morning, noon and night / Everyday I have the blues / Early one morning / Chains of love / Corrina Corrina / I hear you knockin'
CD ______ CWNCD 2036
Crown / Jun '97 / Henry Hadaway

ROOTS OF ROCK 'N' ROLL VOL.6, THE (Watch That Jive)
I gotta girl (for every day of the week) / Little bittie gal's blues / Rebecca / It's the same old story / SK blues / SK blues / Johnson and Turner blues / Watch that jive / Howlin' winds / Doggin' the blues / I got my discharge papers / Miss Brown Blues / I'm still in the dark / My gal's a jockey / I got love for sale / Sunday morning blues / Mad blues / It's a low down dirty shame / I'm still in the dark / Miss Brown Blues / Sally-zu-zazz / Rock of Gibraltar / Milk and butter blues / That's when it really hurts / I'm in sharp when I hit the coast / Ooh wee baby blues
CD ______ PLCD 562
President / May '97 / Grapevine/PolyGram / President / Target/BMG

STORMY MONDAY
Long way from home / Somebody loves me / Stormy Monday / Time after time / Love is like a faucet / Things that I used to do
CD _______ CD 2310 943
Pablo / Jun '93 / Cadillac / Complete/ Pinnacle

TELL ME PRETTY BABY (Turner, 'Big' Joe & Pete Johnson Orchestra)
CD _______ ARHCD 333
Arhoolie / Apr '95 / ADA / Cadillac / Direct

TEXAS STYLE
CD _______ BLE 595472
Black & Blue / Oct '94 / Discovery / Koch / Wellard

TRUMPET KINGS MEET JOE TURNER, THE
Mornin', noon and night / I know you love me baby / TV momma / Ain't nobody's business if I do
CD _______ OJCCD 497
Original Jazz Classics / May '97 / Complete/ Pinnacle / Jazz Music / Wellard

Turner, 'Big' Joe

LIVE (Turner, 'Big' Joe Memphis Blues Caravan)
Blue monk / Thing's ain't what they used to be / Woke up this morning / Bad luck / Take home pay / Aching heart / No response / Something about you / Blood on your hands / Somebody have mercy
CD _______ MYSCD 109
Mystic / Jul '97 / Pinnacle

Turner, Bruce

THAT'S THE BLUES, DAD
CD _______ LACD 49
Lake / Nov '95 / ADA / Cadillac / Direct / Jazz Music / Target/BMG

Turner, Ike

MY BLUES COUNTRY
Get it get it / Baby baby let's get it on / Five long years / I'm blue / My babe / Fool in love / I miss you / Sexy Ida / Sweet black angel / Get it get it / Love like yours / Early one morning
CD _______ MYSCD 115
Mystic / Sep '97 / Pinnacle

RHYTHM ROCKIN' BLUES (Turner, Ike & The Kings Of Rhythm)
Rocket 88: *Brenston, Jackie* / Way you used to treat me: *Lover Boy* / I miss you so: *Binder, Dennis* / Nobody wants me: *Binder, Dennis* / Wild one: *Turner, Ike* / All the blues, all the time: *Turner, Ike* / Sitting and wondering: *Walker, J.W.* / Early times: *Binder, Dennis* / World is yours: *Wright, Johnny & Ike Turner's Orchestra* / Suffocate: *Wright, Johnny* / Talking about me: *Burton, Little Johnny* / Walk my way back home: *Burton, Little Johnny* / I ain't drunk: *Lonnie The Cat* / Road I travel: *Lonnie The Cat* / Night howler: *Gayles, Billy* / Woman won't just do: *Gayles, Billy* / I'm tired of being dogged around: *Gayles, Billy* / You got me way down here: *Binder, Dennis* / Love is scarce: *Lover Boy* / Nobody seems to want me: *Lover Boy*
CD _______ CDCHD 553
Ace / Oct '95 / Pinnacle

TRAILBLAZER (Turner, Ike & The Kings Of Rhythm)
Big question / Just one more time / Mistreater / No coming back / You found the time / She made my blood run cold / I'm tore up / Trail blazer / You've changed my love / Let's call it a day / Much later / Miserable / Do you mean it / Gonna wait for my chance / If I never had known you / Rock-a-bucket / Sad as a man can be / What can it be / Do right baby / My baby's tops / Take your fine frame home
CD _______ CDCHARLY 263
Charly / Feb '91 / Koch

Turner, Ike & Tina

18 CLASSIC TRACKS
Proud Mary / Nutbush city limits / Get back / Honky tonk women / Living for the city / I want to take you higher / Come together / Higher ground / Workin' together / Sexy Ida / I idolize you / Drift away / Sweet Rhodode Island Red / Early one morning / I'm yours / Love like yours / I heard it through the grapevine / I've been loving you too long
CD _______ CDGOLD 1049
EMI Gold / Jul '96 / EMI

BEST OF IKE & TINA TURNER, THE (18 Original Hits/3CD Set)
Acid queen: *Turner, Tina* / Nutbush city limits / Higher ground / Get back / Pick me tonight / Bootsey Whitelaw: *Turner, Tina* / Proud Mary / Under my thumb: *Turner, Tina* / I can see for miles: *Turner, Tina* / Whole lotta love: *Turner, Tina* / Sweet Rhode island red / Honky tonk woman / Let's spend the night together: *Turner, Tina* / Piece of my heart / Sexy Ida pt.1 / Rockin' and rollin': *Turner, Tina* / Baby get it on / I've been loving you too long
CD Set _______ LAD 873302
Disky / Nov '96 / Disky / THE

BOLD SOUL SISTER
Bold soul sister / Mississippi rolling stone / Living for the city / Shake a hand / It's all over / Somebody (somewhere) needs me / Too much for one woman / Rockin' and rollin' / Sugar sugar / Crazy about you baby / I've been loving you too long / Fool in love / Something's got a hold on me / It sho' ain't me / Fool for you / It's gonna work out fine / I can't stop loving you / Cussin' cryin' and carryin' on / Push / Tina's prayer
CD _______ PLATCD 211
Platinum / Feb '97 / Prism

COLLECTION, THE
Mississippi rolling stone / Living for the city / Golden empire / I'm looking for my mind / Shake a hand / Bootsie Whitelaw / Too much man for one woman / I know (you don't want me no more) / Rockin' and rollin' / Never been to spain / Sugar sugar / Push / Raise your hand / Tina's prayer / Chicken / If you want it / Let's get it on / You're up to something / You're still my baby / Jesus
CD _______ CCSCD 170
Castle / '88 / BMG

CUSSIN', CRYIN' AND CARRYIN' ON
Black angel / Getting nasty / It sho' ain't me / Fool in love / Nothing you can do boy / I better get ta steppin' / Shake a tailfeather / We need an understanding / You're so fine / Too hot to hold / I'm fed up / You got what you wanted / Betcha can't kiss me (just one time) / Cussin', cryin' and carryin' on / Ain't nobody's business if I do / Funky mule / Thinking black / Black beauty / Ghetto funk / Black's alley
CD _______ CDSB 014
Starburst / May '96 / TKO Magnum

DON'T LOOK BACK
Nutbush City limits / Come together / Oh my my (can you boogie) / Fool for you / She belongs to me / Stand by me / Shake a hand / Livin' for the city / Movin' on / I can't stop lovin' you / Stagger Lee / I wanna take you higher / I know / Something / I've never been to Spain / Feel it/Knock on wood / Twist and shout / Philadelphia freedom / Hi heel sneakers / River deep mountain high
CD _______ NTMCD 545
Nectar / Apr '97 / Pinnacle

GOOD OLD TIMES
Let's get it on / Mr. Right / Bootsie Whitelaw / Oh my my / Games people play / So fine / Something / Soul deep / You got to work it / I can't believe what you say / Stormy weather / Night time is the right time / It's gonna work out fine / Proud Mary / Endlessly
CD _______ 662171
FNAC / Dec '92 / Discovery

GREATEST HITS
Fool in love / I idolize you / It's gonna work out fine / Poor fool / Tra la la la la la / River deep, mountain high / Something / Come together / Baby get it on / Nutbush city limits / Stand by me / Philadelphia freedom / I wish it would rain / I wanna take you higher / Ooh-poo-pah-do / Twist and shout
CD _______ RM 1530
BR Music / Jul '96 / Target/BMG

IKE & TINA TURNER VOL.1
CD _______ EXP 001
Experience / May '97 / TKO Magnum

IKE & TINA TURNER VOL.2
CD _______ EXP 034
Experience / May '97 / TKO Magnum

IKE & TINA TURNER VOL.3
CD _______ EXP 035
Experience / May '97 / TKO Magnum

IKE & TINA TURNER/SLY & THE FAMILY STONE ESSENTIALS (Turner, Ike & Tina/Sly & The Family Stone)
CD _______ LECDD 636
Wisepack / Aug '95 / Conifer/BMG / THE

IT'S ALL OVER
CD _______ CDSGP 058
Prestige / Oct '93 / Else / Total/BMG

LEGENDS IN MUSIC
CD _______ LECD 102
Wisepack / Sep '94 / Conifer/BMG / THE

LET THE GOOD TIMES ROLL
Nothing you can do boy / Cussin' cryin' and carryin' on / Make em wait / You got what you wanted / I smell trouble / Rock me baby / So blue over you / Beauty is just skin deep / Funky mule / I'm fed up / I've been loving you too long / I'm a motherless child / Bold soul sister / Hunter / I know / Early in the morning / You're still my baby / You got me running / Reconsider baby / Honest I do / Good times
CD _______ MDCD 11
Music De-Luxe / Sep '95 / TKO Magnum

LIVING FOR THE CITY
Can't stop loving you / Come together / Something's on my mind / Shake a hand / Never been to Spain / Living for the city / Good good loving / Fool for you / Rockin' and rollin' / Mississippi rolling stone / Philadelphia freedom / I want to take you higher / Gotta man (not too much man for one woman) / Something / Stand by me / Don't look back / I know you don't want me / You are my sunshine / Golden empire / You'll always be my baby

CD _______ 100242
CMC / May '97 / BMG

MRS
CD _______ GRF 218
Tring / Mar '93 / Tring

OLYMPIA 1971 (The Mythical Concert)
CD _______ 472364
Flarenasch / Jul '96 / Discovery

PROUD MARY (Legendary Masters Series - The Best Of Ike & Tina Turner)
Fool in love / I idolize you / I'm jealous / It's gonna work out fine / Poor fool / Tra la la la la / You shoulda treated me right / Come together / Honky tonk women / I want to take you higher / Workin' together / Proud Mary / Funkier than a mosquita' tweeter / Ooh-poo-pah-doo / I'm yours (use me anyway you wanna) / Up in heah / River deep, mountain high / Nutbush City Limits / Sweet Rhode Island Red / Sexy Ida (part 1) / Sexy Ida (part 2) / Baby - get it on / Acid Queen
CD _______ CDP 7958462
Premier/EMI / Jul '96 / EMI

RIVER DEEP, MOUNTAIN HIGH
River deep, mountain high / I idolize you / Love like yours / Fool in love / Make 'em wait / Hold on baby / Save the last dance for me / Oh baby / Everyday I have to cry / Such a fool for you / It's gonna work out fine / I'll never need more than this
CD _______ CDMID 134
A&M / Oct '92 / PolyGram

ROCKIN' SOUL OF IKE & TINA TURNER, THE
Living for the city / Rockin' and rolin' / Sugar sugar / Chicken / Mississippi rolling stone / Golden empire / I'm looking for my mind / Shake a hand / Bootsie whitelaw / Too much man for one woman / I know (you don't want me no more) / Never been to Spain / Push / Raise your hand / Tina's prayer / If you want it / You're up to something / You're still my baby / Jesus
CD _______ QED 031
Tring / Nov '96 / Tring

SENSATIONAL IKE & TINA TURNER, THE (2CD Set)
Nutbush city limits / Golden Empire / Something / Oh my, my (can you boogie) / Stormy weather / You don't love me (yes I know) / Stand by me / Give me a chance / I idolise you / Put on your tight pants / Ain't that a shame / Rockin' and rollin' / Shake / I wish it would rain / If you can hully gully / Betcha can't kiss me (just one time) / I need a man / I wanna jump / I can't stop loving you / River deep, mountain high / Philadelphia freedom / You can't have your cake and eat it too / Baby get it on / Daily bread / Come together / He belongs to me / Ooh-poo-pah-do / I want to take you higher / We need an understanding / Never been to Spain / Country girl, city man / Ya ya / Why I sing the blues / Living for the city / Use me / Sweet Rhode Island Red / Locomotion / Stagger Lee / Sugar sugar / I'm movin' on
CD Set _______ CPCD 82572
Charly / Nov '96 / Koch

SHAKE
CD _______ MU 5068
Musketeer / Oct '92 / Disc

SPOTLIGHT ON IKE & TINA TURNER
It's gonna work out fine / Fool for you / Crazy about you baby / I can't stop loving you / Somebody somewhere needs you / Too hot to hold / Cussin', cryin' and carryin' on / I know / It sho' ain't me / You got what you wanted / Ain't nobody's business if I do / Betcha can't kiss me (Just one time) / I smell trouble / It's all over / Nothing you can do boy / All I do is cry
CD _______ HADCD 127
Javelin / Feb '94 / Henry Hadaway / THE

THOSE WERE THE DAYS
Sugar sugar / Never been to Spain / Too much for one woman / Stormy weather / Into to it / Trying to find my mind / I want to take you higher / Fool in love / I idolize you / Poor fool / Lay it down / Freedom to stay / Loving him was easier / Rescue me / Father alone / What a friend / When the saints go marching in / Near the cross / Nutbush City Limits
CD _______ 662172
FNAC / Dec '92 / Discovery

TINA
Nutbush city limits / River deep mountian high / Fool in love / Something / Come together / Baby get it on
CD _______ DS 2304
BR Music / May '96 / Target/BMG

WHAT YOU HEAR IS WHAT YOU GET (Live At Carnegie Hall)
Piece of my heart / Everyday people / Doin' the Tina Turner / Sweet soul music / Ooh-poo-pah-doo / Honky tonk women / Love like yours / Proud Mary / I smell trouble / Ike's tune / I want to take you higher / I've been loving you too long / Respect
CD _______ CTMCD 302
EMI / Feb '97 / EMI

WORKIN' TOGETHER (3CD Set)
Proud Mary / Nutbush city limits / Ooh poh pah doo / Workin' together / I'm your (use me anyway you wanna) / Living for the city / I love what you do to me / Piece of my heart (live) / Early in the morning / I wan to take you higher / What you don't see is better yet / Sexy Ida (part 1) / Way yoWay you love me / Respect (live) / Way you love me / Respect / Sweet Rhode island red / Sexy Ida (part 2) / Reconsider baby / Higher ground / Up in heah / I idolize you / I'm jealous / Dust my broom / Love like yours / Nuff said / That's my purpose / You can have it / Ike's tune / I've been loving you too long / Baby - get it on / Come together / Under my thumb / Funker than a mosquita's tweeter / Honky tonk woman / Drift away / Get back / Let it be / Let's spend the night together / She came in through the bathroom window / Baby (what you want me to do) / Doin' the Tina Turner (live) / Fool in love / I heard it through the grapevine (live)
CD Set _______ SA 872702
Disky / Sep '96 / Disky / THE

Turner, Joe

CLASSICS 1941-1946
CD _______ CLASSICS 940
Classics / Jun '97 / Discovery / Jazz Music

JOE TURNER
CD _______ SACD 106
Solo Art / Oct '93 / Jazz Music

Turner, Joe Lynn

NOTHING'S CHANGED
Promise of love / Baby's got a habit / Nothing's changed / Knock knock / I believe / Satisfy me / Liviana / Bad blood / All or nothing / Last thing / Imagination / Save a place / Let me love you
CD _______ CDMFN 189
Music For Nations / Oct '95 / Pinnacle

Turner, Ken

BEST OF THE DANSAN YEARS VOL.4, THE (Turner, Ken & His Orchestra)
CD _______ DACD 004
Dansan / Jul '92 / Jazz Music / President / Target/BMG / Wellard

BEST OF THE DANSAN YEARS VOL.5, THE (Turner, Ken & His Orchestra)
CD _______ DACD 005
Dansan / Jul '92 / Jazz Music / President / Target/BMG / Wellard

Turner, Mark

YAM YAM
CD _______ CRISS 1094
Criss Cross / Apr '95 / Cadillac / Direct / Vital/SAM

Turner, Nik

NEW ANATOMY (Turner, Nik & Inner City Unit)
Young girls / Convoy / Beyond the stars / Help sharks / Birdland / Lonesome train (on a lonesome track) / Forbidden planet / Stop the city / Dr. Strange / Wildhunt
CD _______ CDTB 096
Thunderbolt / Mar '93 / TKO Magnum

PAST OR FUTURE
CD _______ CLP 96852
Cleopatra / May '97 / Cargo / Greyhound / Plastic Head / RTM/Disc / SRD

PROPHETS OF TIME
CD _______ CLEO 69082
Cleopatra / Jun '94 / Cargo / Greyhound / Plastic Head / RTM/Disc / SRD

SPACE RITUAL
CD Set _______ CLEO 95062
Cleopatra / Feb '95 / Cargo / Greyhound / Plastic Head / RTM/Disc / SRD

SPHYNX
CD _______ CLEO 21352
Cleopatra / May '97 / Cargo / Greyhound / Plastic Head / RTM/Disc / SRD

Turner, Ruby

BEST OF RUBY TURNER, THE
I'd rather go blind / If you're ready come go with me / I'm in love / What becomes of the broken hearted / Just my imagination (running away with me) / Bye baby / In my life it's better to be in love / Signed sealed delivered I'm yours / I'm livin' a life of love / Still on my mind / Vibe is right / It's a cryin shame / It's gonna be alright / Paradise / Rumours / It's you my heart beats for
CD _______ EMPRCD 566
Emporio / May '95 / Disc

BEST OF RUBY TURNER, THE
If you're ready (come go with me): *Turner, Ruby & Jonathan Butler* / What becomes of the broken hearted: *Turner, Ruby & Jimmy Ruffin* / Merry go round / Just my imagination (running away with me): *Turner, Ruby & The Temptations* / Ooo baby baby / I'd rather go blind / Leaves in the wind / It's gonna be alright / Vibe is right / It's a cryin' shame / Rumours / I'm livin' a life of love / It's you my heart beats for / I'm in love / Paradise / Signed, sealed, delivered I'm yours / In my life (It's better to be in love) / Still on my mind

CD _____ QED 034
Tring / Nov '96 / Tring

GUILTY
You can't do that / There is something on your mind / You're pouring water on a drowning man / My oh my / Wang dang doodle / Don't mess up a good thing / Bring it on home to me / Love like blood / Ain't nobody / One time around / Guilty / Take it as it comes / That way / Over the edge / Rockin' good way / My eyes are weeping
CD _____ IGOXCD 502
Indigo / Sep '96 / ADA / Direct

RESTLESS MOODS
CD _____ MAGCD 1058
M&G / Aug '95 / 3mv/Sony

Turner, Tina

BREAK EVERY RULE
What you get is what you see / Change is gonna come / Addicted to love / In the midnight hour / 634 5789 / Land of 1000 dances / Typical male / Two people / Till the right man comes along / Afterglow / Girls / Back where you started / Break every rule / Overnight sensation / Paradise is here / I'll be thunder
CD _____ CDP 746 323 2
Capitol / Sep '86 / EMI

COLLECTED RECORDINGS, THE (Sixties To Nineties - 3CD Set)
Fool in love / It's gonna work out fine / I idolize you / Poor fool / Letter from Tina / Finger poppin' / River deep, mountain high / Crazy about you baby / I've been loving you too long / Bold soul sister / I want to take you higher / Come together / Honky tonk women / Proud Mary / Nutbush city limits / Sexy Ida / It ain't right (lovin' to be lovin') / Acid Queen / Whole lotta love / Ball of confusion / Change is gonna come / Johnny and Mary / Games / When I was young / Total control / Let's pretend we're married / It's only love: *Turner, Tina & Bryan Adams* / Don't turn around / Legs / Addicted to love / Tearing us apart: *Turner, Tina & Eric Clapton* / It takes two: *Turner, Tina & Rod Stewart* / Let's stay together / What's love got to do with it / Better be good to me / Private dancer / I can't stand the rain / Help / We don't need another hero / Typical male / What you get is what you see / Paradise is here / Back where you started / Best / Steamy windows / Foreign affair / I don't wanna fight
CD Set _____ CDEST 2240
CD Set _____ CDESTX 2240
Capitol / Nov '94 / EMI

COUNTRY CLASSICS
CD _____ HADCD 166
Javelin / May '94 / Henry Hadaway / THE

COUNTRY SIDE OF TINA TURNER
CD _____ ST 5009
Star Collection / Apr '95 / BMG

FOREIGN AFFAIR
Steamy windows / Best / You know who (is doing you know what) / Undercover agent for the blues / Look me in the heart / Be tender with me baby / You can't stop me loving you / Ask me how I feel / Falling like rain / I don't wanna lose you / Not enough romance / Foreign affair
CD _____ CDESTU 2103
Capitol / Sep '89 / EMI

IN PROFILE (Interview Disc)
CD _____ CDINPROF 002
EMI / Aug '97 / EMI

LIVE IN EUROPE (2CD Set)
What you get is what you see / Break every rule / I can't stand the rain / Two people / Typical male / Better be good to me / Addicted to love / Private dancer / We don't need another hero / What's love got to do with it / Let's stay together / Show some respect / Land of 1000 dances / In the midnight hour / 634 5789 / Change is gonna come / Tearing us apart: *Turner, Tina & Eric Clapton* / Proud Mary / Help / Tonight: *Turner, Tina & David Bowie* / It's only love: *Turner, Tina & Bryan Adams* / Nutbush City limits / Paradise is here / Let's dance: *Turner, Tina & David Bowie* / Girls / Back where you started / River deep, mountain high / Overnight sensation
CD Set _____ CDESTD 1
Capitol / Mar '88 / EMI

PRIVATE DANCER
I might have been queen / What's love got to do with it / Show some respect / I can't stand the rain / Private dancer / Let's stay together / Better be good to me / Steel claw / Help
CD _____ CDP 7460412
Capitol / Jun '84 / EMI

PRIVATE DANCER (Added Value Centenary Edition)
I might have been queen / What's love got to do with it / Show some respect / I can't stand the rain / Private dancer / Let's stay together / Better be good to me / Steel claw / Help / 1984 / I wrote a letter / Rock 'n' roll widow / Don't rush the good things / When I was young / What's love got to do with it / Better be good to me / I can't stand the rain

CD _____ CDCNTAV 1
Capitol / Feb '97 / EMI

ROUGH
Fruits of the night / Bitch is back / Woman I'm supposed to be / Viva la money / Funny how time slips away / Earthquake hurricane / Root toot undisputable rock 'n' roller / Fire down below / Sometimes when we touch / Woman in a man's world / Night time is the right time
CD _____ CDP 7952132
Capitol / Aug '95 / EMI

SIMPLY THE BEST
Best / What's love got to do with it / I don't wanna lose you / Nutbush City limits / Let's stay together / Private dancer / We don't need another hero / Better be good to me / River deep, mountain high / Steamy windows / Typical male / It takes two: *Turner, Tina & Rod Stewart* / Addicted to love / Be tender with me baby / I want you near me / Love thing
CD _____ CDESTV 1
Capitol / Oct '91 / EMI

TINA TURNER
Golden empire / Tina's prayer / You're still my baby / Sugar sugar / Loving him was easier / Gonna have fun / Don't you blame it on me / I don't need / We need an understanding / Crazy 'bout you baby / Push / Good hearted woman / Chicken shack / You're so fine / Bootsie Whitelaw / Lay it down / Shake a hand / Let's get it on
CD _____ 399561
Koch Presents / May '97 / Koch

TINA TURNER
You're up to something / I know (you don't want me no more) / Living for the city / Rock me baby / If you want it / Please love me / Freedom to stay / Stand by your man / Soul deep / Rockin' and rollin' / I'm looking for my mind / Mississippi rolling stone / Raise your hand / We had it all / If this is our last time / You ain't woman enough to take my man / If it's alright with you / Too much man for one woman
CD _____ 399547
Koch Presents / Jun '97 / Koch

TINA TURNER
CD _____ GFS 075
Going For A Song / Jul '97 / Else / TKO Magnum

WILDEST DREAMS
Do what you do / Whatever you want / Missing you / On silent wings / Thief of hearts / In your wildest dreams / Golden eye / Confidential / Something beautiful remains / All kinds of people / Unfinished sympathy / Dancing in my dreams
CD _____ CDEST 2279
Parlophone / Apr '96 / EMI

WILDEST DREAMS (2CD Special Tour Edition Set)
Do waht you do / Whatever you want / Missing you / On silent wings / Thief of hearts / In your wildest dreams / Goldeneye / Confidential / Something beautiful remains / All kinds of people / Unfinished sympathy / Dancing dreams / In your wildest dreams: *Turner, Tina & Barry White* / Something beautiful remains / Difference between us / River deep moutain high / We don't need another hero / Private dancer / Steamy windows / Best / On silent wings
CD Set _____ CDESTX 2279
Capitol / Nov '96 / EMI

Turner, Titus

JAMIE RECORDINGS, THE
CD _____ BCD 15532
Bear Family / Feb '92 / Direct / Rollercoaster / Swift

Turning Point

FEW AND THE PROUD, THE
CD _____ LF 172CD
Lost & Found / Jul '95 / Plastic Head

IT'S ALWAYS
CD _____ NA 004CD
New Age / Jul '96 / Plastic Head

Turntable Symphony

MINI LP, THE
Instructions of life (mixes) / Remix of life / Can't stop / It'll make you go ooh / Techno love
CD _____ HAPPYCD 001
Happy Music / May '93 / Vital

Turquoise

TURQUOISE TRAIL, THE
CD _____ TURQUOISE 1995
Turquoise / Aug '95 / Vital

Turre, Steve

STEVE TURRE
CD _____ 5371332
Verve / Aug '97 / PolyGram

Turrentine, Stanley

COMMON TOUCH
Buster brown / Blowin' in the wind / Lonely avenue / Boogaloo / Common touch / Living through it all / Ain't no way
CD _____ CDP 8547192
Blue Note / Feb '97 / EMI

EASY WALKER
Meat wave / They all say I'm the biggest fool / Yours is my heart alone / Easy walker / What the world needs now is love / Alone together / Foggy day / Stan's shuffle / Watch what happens / Intermission walk / Wave
CD _____ CDP 8299082
Blue Note / Jan '97 / EMI

IF I COULD
June bug / Caravan / I remember Bill / Avenue / Marvin's song / Maybe September / A luta continua / If I could
CD _____ 5184442
Limelight / Mar '93 / PolyGram

LOOK OUT
Look out / Journey into melody / Return engagement / Little Sheri / Tin tin deo / Yesterdays / Tiny capers / Minor chant
CD _____ CDP 7865432
Blue Note / May '96 / EMI

MORE THAN A MOOD
Thomasville / They can't take that away from me / In a sentimental mood / Easy walker / Triste / Pieces of a dream / Spirits up above / More than a mood
CD _____ 8442792
Limelight / Feb '92 / PolyGram

PIECES OF A DREAM
CD _____ OJCCD 831
Original Jazz Classics / Nov '95 / Complete/Pinnacle / Jazz Music / Wellard

SPOILER
Magilla / When the sun comes out / La Fiesta / Sunny / Maybe September / You're gonna hear from me / Lonesome lover
CD _____ CDP 8533592
Blue Note / Nov '96 / EMI

Turriff, Jane

SINGIN IS MA LIFE
CD _____ SPRCD 1038
Springthyme / Apr '96 / ADA / CM / Direct / Duncans / Highlander / Roots

Turtle Island String Quartet

BY THE FIRESIDE
CD _____ 01934111752
Windham Hill / Nov '95 / BMG

WHO DO YOU
CD _____ 01934101462
Windham Hill / Sep '95 / BMG

Turtlehead

BACK SLAPPING PRAISE
CD _____ BTR 012CD
Bad Taste / Nov '96 / Plastic Head

GO
CD _____ BTR 010CD
Bad Taste / Jul '96 / Plastic Head

Turtles

HAPPY TOGETHER (The Very Best Of The Turtles)
Happy together / She'd rather be with me / Too young to be one / Me about you / Think I'll run away / Can I get to know you better / Guide for the married man / Elenore / It ain't me babe / You baby / Let me be / She's my girl / You don't have to walk in the rain / You know what I mean / Lady O / You showed me / There you sit lonely / Outside chance / Buzz saw / Sound asleep
CD _____ MCCD 046
Music Club / Sep '91 / Disc / THE

TURTLE SOUP
CD _____ SC 6086
Sundazed / Feb '97 / Cargo / Greyhound / Rollercoaster

WOODEN HEAD
CD _____ SC 6087
Sundazed / Feb '97 / Cargo / Greyhound / Rollercoaster

Tuscadero

PINK ALBUM, THE
Heat lightnin' / Candy song / Game song / Latex dominatrix / Just my size / Dime a dozen / Lovesick / Mount Pleasant / Nancy Drew / Hollywood handsome / Leather idol / Crayola
CD _____ OLE 1592
Matador / Aug '95 / Vital

STEP INTO MY WIGGLE ROOM
Holidays R hell / Angel in a half shirt / Poster boy / Dreams of the tanker / Sways / Given up / Sonic yogurt / Palmer: All Star jam
CD _____ TB 1792
Teenbeat / Oct '95 / Cargo / SRD / Vital

Tusen, Till

JAZZIN' JACKS
CD _____ FLCCD 151
Four Leaf Clover / May '97 / Cadillac / Wellard

Tuskegee Institute Singers

COMPLETE RECORDING WORKS 1914-1927
CD _____ DOCD 5549
Document / Jul '97 / ADA / Hot Shot / Jazz Music

Tuu

1000 YEARS
CD _____ SDV 027CD
SDV / May '94 / Plastic Head

ALL OUR ANCESTORS
CD _____ RBADCD 9
Beyond / Oct '94 / Kudos / Pinnacle

Tuva

ECHOES FROM THE SPIRIT WORLD
CD _____ PANCD 2013
Pan / May '93 / ADA / CM / Direct

VOICES FROM THE CENTRE OF ASIA
CD _____ SFWCD 40017
Smithsonian Folkways / May '95 / ADA / Cadillac / CM / Direct / Koch

Tuxedo Moon

BEST OF TUXEDO MOON
What use / No tears / Cage / Some guys / Dark companion / In a manner of speaking / Atlantis / Waltz / L'etranger / Tritone (musica diablo) / East/jinx / Desire / You
CD _____ CBOY 1313
Crammed Discs / Jan '94 / Grapevine/PolyGram / New Note/Pinnacle / Prime / RTM/Disc

TV Personalities

AND DON'T THE KIDS JUST LOVE IT
CD _____ REF 33007
Fire / Oct '91 / Pinnacle / RTM/Disc

CHOCOLAT-ART LIVE 1984
CD _____ EFA 04320 CD
Pastell / Jun '93 / SRD

CLOSER TO GOD
You don't know how lucky you are / Hard luck story no.39 / Little works of art / Razor blades and lemonade / Coming home soon / Me and my big ideas / Honey for the bears / I see myself in you / Goodnight Mr. Spaceman / My very first nervous breakdown / We will be your gurus / You are special and you always will be / Not for the likes of us / You're younger than you know / Very dark today / I hope you have a nice day / This heart's not made of stone / Baby, you're only as good as you should be / Closer to God
CD _____ FIRECD 32
Fire / Oct '92 / Pinnacle / RTM/Disc

I WAS A MOD BEFORE YOU WAS A MOD
CD _____ OVER 41CD
Overground / Jul '95 / Shellshock/Disc / SRD

MUMMY, YOU'RE NOT WATCHING ME
CD _____ REF 33008
Fire / Oct '91 / Pinnacle / RTM/Disc

PAINTED WORD THE
CD _____ REF 33010
Fire / Oct '91 / Pinnacle / RTM/Disc

PRIVILEGE
Paradise is for the blessed / Conscience tells me no / All my dreams are dead / Man who paints the rainbows / Sad Mona Lisa / Sometimes I think you know me / Privilege / Good and faithful servant / My hedonistic tendencies / Salvador Dali's garden party / What if it's raining / Engine driver song / Better than I know myself
CD _____ FIRE 33021
Fire / Oct '91 / Pinnacle / RTM/Disc

THEY COULD HAVE BEEN BIGGER THAN THE BEATLES
Psychedelic holiday / David Hockney's diary / Boy in the paisley shirt / When Emily cries
CD _____ REF 33009
Fire / Oct '91 / Pinnacle / RTM/Disc

TOP GEAR
CD _____ OVER 48CD
Overground / Mar '96 / Shellshock/Disc / SRD

Twardzik, Richard

PACIFIC JAZZ (Twardzik, Richard Trio)
You stepped out of a dream / Bock's tops / At last / Laugh cry / Lullaby in rhythm / Joey Joey Joey / Albuquerque social swim / Yellow tango / I'll remember April / Crutch for the crab (Alt.) / Don't worry 'bout me / Yesterday's gardenias / Backfield in motion / Eye opener / Party's over / Woody's dot / Bess you is my woman now / 'Round mid-

night / Crutch for the crab / Just one of those things
CD CZ 245
Pacific Jazz / Apr '90 / EMI

Tweed, Karen

DROPS OF SPRINGWATER
CD DMP 9401CD
DMP / Jan '96 / Direct

SILVER SPIRE, THE
CD DMP 9402CD
DMP / Jan '96 / Direct

TUNES FOR THE ACCORDION VOL.1
CD PMCD 003
Punch Music / Aug '94 / ADA / Roots

TUNES FOR THE ACCORDION VOL.2
CD PMCD 004
Punch Music / Aug '94 / ADA / Roots

Twelfth Night

COLLECTORS ITEM
CD CDGRUB 18
Food For Thought / Feb '91 / Pinnacle

LIVE AND LET LIVE
Ceiling speaks / End of the endless majority / We are sane / Fact and fiction / Poet sniffs a flower / Sequences / Creepshow / East of eden / Love song
CD CYCL 050
Cyclops / Feb '97 / Pinnacle

Twenty Miles

TWENTY MILES
Intro / Junkyard blues / Place called hell / She don't know / Fred McDowell / My back door / I'm not a man / Come right in / My little baby / Mississippi bolero
CD 03022
Fat Possum / Jun '97 / Cargo / Pinnacle

Twice A Man

COLLECTION, THE
CD YELLOW 16
Yellow / Aug '88 / SRD

FROM THE NORTHERN SHORE
CD YELLOW 01CD
Yellow / '89 / SRD

Twiggy

TWIGGY AND THE GIRLFRIENDS
CD 14529
Spalax / Feb '97 / ADA / Cargo / Direct / Discovery / Greyhound

Twiggy

TWIGGY
CD PHCD 2056
Penthouse / Jan '97 / Jet Star

Twilight

EYE FOR AN EYE
CD 35641
Seagull / Nov '96 / Cargo

Twilight Circus Dub Sound ...

BIN SHAKER DUB (Twilight Circus Dub Sound System)
CD MCD 150
M / Aug '97 / SRD

OTHER WORLDS OF DUB (Twilight Circus Dub Sound System)
CD MCD 127
M / Aug '96 / SRD

Twilight Earth

INTERNATIONAL SOIREE
CD TIME 002CD
Timebase / Nov '94 / Plastic Head

Twink

MR. RAINBOW
CD TWKCD 1
Twink / Jul '90 / Pinnacle / RTM/Disc

Twinkle

GOLDEN LIGHTS
CD RPM 108
RPM / Jul '93 / Pinnacle

Twinkle Brothers

BABYLON RISE AGAIN
CD NGCD 528
Twinkle / Apr '92 / Jet Star / Kingdom / SRD

CHANT DOWN BABYLON
CD NGCD 547
Twinkle / Oct '95 / Jet Star / Kingdom / SRD

DJ SELECTION
CD NGCD 545
Twinkle / Dec '94 / Jet Star / Kingdom / SRD

DUB MASSACRE VOL.1 & 2
CD NGCD 7102
Twinkle / Dec '94 / Jet Star / Kingdom / SRD

DUB MASSACRE VOL.3 & 4
CD NGCD 505
Twinkle / Jan '96 / Jet Star / Kingdom / SRD

DUB MASSACRE VOL.6
CD NGCD 543
Twinkle / Jun '94 / Jet Star / Kingdom / SRD

DUB PLATE
CD NGCD 546
Twinkle / Dec '94 / Jet Star / Kingdom / SRD

DUB WITH STRINGS
CD NGCD 535
Twinkle / Nov '92 / Jet Star / Kingdom / SRD

ENTER ZION
CD NGCD 503
Twinkle / Jan '96 / Jet Star / Kingdom / SRD

EQUALITY AND JUSTICE
Equality and justice / Rejoice / Lamb to the slaughter / We nah go let Jah go / Blood on their hands / Wicked them a go run / Lightning and thunder / You're bound / I will praise Jah
CD NGCD 541
Twinkle / Feb '94 / Jet Star / Kingdom / SRD

FREE AFRICA
I don't want to be lonely anymore / Free Africa / Love / I love you so / Gone already / Solid as a rock / Come home / Shu be dub (you can do it too) / Patoo / Never get burn / Dread in the ghetto / Watch the hypocrites / Jahovah / Since I threw the comb away / One head / Free us
CD CDFL 9008
Frontline / Sep '90 / EMI / Jet Star

ME NO YOU
CD NGCD 632
Twinkle / Jul '94 / Jet Star / Kingdom / SRD

NEW SONGS FOR JAH
CD NGCD 518
Twinkle / Jan '96 / Jet Star / Kingdom / SRD

OTHER SIDE, THE (Twinkle Brothers & Ralston Grant)
CD RGCD 5805
Twinkle / Oct '95 / Jet Star / Kingdom / SRD

RASTA PON TOP
CD NGCD 532
Twinkle / Apr '92 / Jet Star / Kingdom / SRD

TWINKLE LOVE SONGS VOL.2
CD NGCD 536
Twinkle / Feb '93 / Jet Star / Kingdom / SRD

Twinz

CONVERSATION
Conversation / Round and round / Good times / Eyes 2 heads / Jump ta this / Eastside LB / Sorry I kept you / Conversation # 2 / Journey wit me / Hollywood / Pass it on / Don't get it twisted / 1st Round draft pick
CD 5278832
RAL / Aug '95 / PolyGram

Twisted Roots

TURN TO STONE
CD CHERRY 228932
Cherrydisc / Dec '94 / Plastic Head

Twisted Science

BLOWN
Sex, drugs and science / Bender / Beady eye / Bad head / Laptop swine / Slow blow / Magma hum / Intermission / Lube / Bad kabuki / Mr. Ray Gone / Horn / Here come the pigs / Fryed / Fin
CD LCD 04
Lo Recordings/Leaf / Jun '97 / RTM/Disc

Twisted Sister

BIG HITS AND NASTY CUTS
We're not going to take it / I wanna rock / I am (I'm me) / Price / You can't stop rock 'n' roll / Kids are back / Shoot 'em down / Under the blade / I'll never grow up now / Feel so fine / Let the good times roll / It's only rock 'n' roll / Tear it loose / What you don't know / Be chrool to your scuel
CD 7567823802
Atlantic / Mar '92 / Warner Music

LIVE AT HAMMERSMITH
What you don't know / Kids are back / Stay hungry / Destroyer / We're not gonna take it / You can't stop rock 'n' roll / Knife in the back / Shoot 'em down / Under the blade / Burn in hell / I am (I'm me) / I wanna rock / SMF / We're gonna make it / Jailhouse rock / Train kept a rollin'

CD CDMFN 170
Music For Nations / Oct '94 / Pinnacle

Twitty, Conway

BEST OF CONWAY TWITTY, THE
It's only make believe / Hello darlin' / Fifteen years ago / Danny boy / You've never been this far before / Touch of the hand / To see an angel cry / She needs someone to hold her (when she cries) / I'll try / After all the good is gone / After our last date / As soon as I hang up the phone / Baby's gone / I can't see me without you / I'm not through loving you yet / I've hurt her more than she loves me / (Lying here with) Linda on my mind / Games that Daddies play / Don't cry Joni / (I can't believe) she gives it all to me
CD CD 3558
Cameo / Mar '96 / Target/BMG

CONWAY TWITTY
Guess my eyes were bigger than my heart / Look into my teardrops / I don't want to be with me / Image of me / To see my angel cry / Hello darlin' / I can't see me without you / (Lost her love) On our last date / You've never been this far before / I'm not through loving you yet / Linda on my mind / (I can't believe) She gives it all to me / I've already loved you in my mind / Boogie grass band / Don't take it away / I'd just love to lay you down / Tight fittin' jeans / Slow hand / Rose / I don't know a thing about love / Don't call him a cowboy / Desperado love / That's my job / Goodbye time / She's got a single thing in mind
CD MCLD 19236
MCA / May '94 / BMG

CONWAY TWITTY
CD LECD 043
Dynamite / May '94 / THE

FINAL RECORDINGS OF HIS GREATEST HITS
CD PWKS 4263
Carlton / Jul '95 / Carlton

HIGH PRIEST OF COUNTRY MUSIC, THE
Image of me / Next in line / Darlin' you know I wouldn't lie / I love you more today / Hello darlin' / Fifteen years ago / How much more can she stand / I wonder what she'll think about me leaving / On our last date / I can't stop loving you / She needs someone to hold her / You've never been this far before / There's a honky tonk angel / I see the want to in your eyes / Linda on my mind / This time I've hurt her more than she loves me / That games that daddies play / Play guitar play / I've always loved you in my mind / Don't take it away / I'd love to lay you down / Rest your love on me / Tight fittin' jeans / Red neckin' love makin' night
CD EDCD 500
Edsel / May '97 / Pinnacle

ROAD THAT I WALK, THE
CD CDSGP 0170
Prestige / Sep '95 / Else / Total/BMG

ROCK 'N' ROLL WITH CONWAY TWITTY
Golly gosh oh gee / I wonder if you told her (About me) / Why can't I get through to you / This road that I walk / Crazy dreams / You made me what I am today / Born to sing the blues / Double talk baby / I need your lovin' / Maybe baby / Midnight / Shake it up baby
CD 306792
Hallmark / May '97 / Carlton

ROCK 'N' ROLL YEARS 1956-1964, THE (8CD Set)
Rock house / Crazy dreams / Give me some love / I need your lovin' kiss / Just in time / Born to sing the blues / Maybe baby / Shake it up / I need your lovin' / Golly gosh oh gee / Double talk baby / Why can't I get through to you / Crazy dreams / Give me some love / Born to sing the blues / Born to sing the blues / Born to sing the blues / Born to sing the blues / Crazy dreams / Crazy dreams / Crazy dreams / It's only make believe / I'll try / I vibrate (from my head to my feet) / Will you love me then as you love me now / Story of my love / Don't you know / When I'm not with you / Judge of hearts / Yea yea boo hoo / Heavenly / Come on home / Nobody / Sputnik / Easy to fall in love / Goin' home / Big train / Teenage heart / One and only you / When I'm not with you / Don't you know / Story of my love / My one and only you / Goin' home / Make me know you're mine / Judge of hearts / First romance / I need you so / Mona Lisa / Sentimental journey / Hallelujah I love her so / You'll never walk alone / Hey little Lucy / Halfway to Heaven / Teasin' / Heavenly / Halfway to Heaven / Just because / Cry Jane cry / Blueberry Hill / Heartbreak Hotel / You win again / Danny boy / Hey Miss Ruby / Restless / She's mine / Lonely kind of love / Beachcomber / Easy to fall in love / Because you love me / Leonora my love / Rosaleena / My adobe hacienda / Hey little Lucy / Restless / Because you love me / My adobe hacienda / Star spangled Heaven / Huggin' and a kissin' / Can't we go steady / Lonely blue boy / Sorry / Blue moon / Eternal tears / Foggy river / Platinum high school / Trouble in mind / Pretty eyed baby / Rebound / Hurt in my heart / Maybe tomorrow we'll know / Tell me one more time / What am I living for / Fallen star / I'd still play the fool / Betty Lou / Knock three times / What a dream / Is a bluebird blue / Whole lotta shakin' goin' on / My heart cries / Sweet Georgia Brown / Lonely blue boy / Betty Lou / That's where my lovin' goes / Don't you dare let me down / Send her to me / Flame / C'est si bon / Long black train / Blue suede shoes / Great balls of fire / Jailhouse rock / Treat me nice / Handy man / Girl can't help it / Shake, rattle and roll / Diana / Splish splash / Reelin' and rockin' / Million teardrops / Next kiss (is the last goodbye) / Tree in the meadow / Above and beyond / I'm in a blue blue mood: *Twitty, Conway & Roy Orbison* / Live fast, love hard, die young / Man alone / Donna's dream / Tower of tears / I can hear my heart break / Million teardrops / Prisoner of love / Unchained melody / Sweet sorrow / Little bird told me / It's driving me wild / Turn around / Walk on by / Portrait of a fool / There is something on your mind / Don't cry no more / Mr. Jones / Hang up the phone / Little piece of my heart / She knows me like a book / Comfy n' cozy / Lookin' back / Pledging my love / Prisoner of love / Unchained melody / Unchained melody / Sweet sorrow / It's driving me wild / Walk on by / Mr. Jones / Little piece of my heart / Little piece of my heart / It's too late / I almost lost my mind / I got a woman / My babe / Let the good times roll / Fever / Boss man / Don't cry no more / City lights / Faded love / Don't let the stars get in your eyes / Ages and ages ago / I hope, I think, I wish / Pickup / Hound dog / She ain't no angel / Got my mojo working / Long tall Texan / Go on and cry / She loves me / I'm sorry heart / Talkin' about you / Walk proud / Such a night / My baby left me / Where your love leadeth me / Big town / This road that I walk / Bad man / Ever since you went away / Blue is the way I feel / Turn the other cheek / Treat me mean, treat me cruel / I'm checkin' out / Heartache just walked in / I wonder if you told her about me / Girl at the bar / You made me what I am / I'll get over losing you / Have I been away too long / Let me be the judge / Sound of an angel's wings / Highland rock: *Bruno, Al* / Midnite creep: *Bruno, Al*
CD Set BCD 16112
Bear Family / May '97 / Direct / Rollercoaster / Swift

SPOTLIGHT ON CONWAY TWITTY
Fifteen years ago / To see my angel cry / I see the want to in your eyes / I'm not through loving you yet / Linda on my mind / Don't cry Joni / I've already loved you in my mind / Play guitar, play / It's only make believe / Let me be the judge / Ever since you went away / Big town / Sitting in a dim cafe
CD HADCD 121
Javelin / Feb '94 / Henry Hadaway / THE

WORLD OF CONWAY TWITTY, THE
Unchained melody / Fever / Mona Lisa / Diana / Heartbreak hotel / Splish splash / I almost lost my mind / Lonely blue boy / Blue suede shoes / Great balls of fire / Shake, rattle and roll / Blue moon / Jailhouse rock / Handy man / Let the good times roll / Blueberry Hill / Treat me nice / What am I living for / Whole lotta shakin' goin' on / It's only make believe
CD 5514322
Spectrum / May '96 / PolyGram

Two Bit Thief

ANOTHER SAD STORY IN THE BIG CITY
CD WB 070CD
We Bite / Feb '91 / Plastic Head

GANGSTER REBEL BOP
CD WB 2093CD
We Bite / Nov '92 / Plastic Head

ONE MORE FOR THE ROAD
CD WB 3103CD
We Bite / Apr '94 / Plastic Head

Two Lone Swordsmen

FIFTH MISSION (RETURN TO THE FLIGHTPATH ESTATE) (2CD Set)
Little did we know / Best of Stealth / Slow drive West / Big man original / Spark / Lino Square / Search for a car / Gang sweep shuffling / King Mob file / Enemy haze / Beacon block / Two barb quickstep / Switch it / Rico's helly / Paisley dark
CD Set SOP 009CD
Emissions / Aug '96 / Amato Disco / Vital

STOCKWELL STEPPAS
Another heady cocktail / Plunge / Spin desire / Kicking in / Kicking in / Turn the filter off / Spray can attack / We love mutronics / Because I can
CD PT 040CD
Emissions / Mar '97 / Amato Disco / Vital

SWIMMING NOT SKIMMING
Swimming not skimming / Swimming not skimming (Obo 07 mix) / Swimming not skimming (Andy Sheriff mix) / Swimming not skimming (Pod mix) / Swimming not skimming (16b & Anthony Teasdale mix) / Glide by shooting / Bim, Jack & Florence / Don't

call it jerk / Flossie wears Paco & Ralph / Swimming not skimming (ITN mix)
CD PT 035CD
Emissions / Nov '96 / Amato Disco / Vital

Two Tons

TWO TONS O'FUN/BACKATCHA
Do you wanna boogie huh / Just us / I got the feelin' / Gone away / Earth can be just like heaven / Make someone feel happy today / Taking away your space / One-sided love affair / Never like this / I depend on you / Your love is gonna see me through / It's true I do / Can't do it by myself / Cloudy with a chance of rain / I've got to make it on my own / I been down
CD CDSEWD 082
Southbound / Jul '93 / Pinnacle

Two Tunes

RAINDROPS TALKING
CD BRAM 1991272
Brambus / Nov '93 / ADA

Two Witches

AGONY OF THE UNDEAD VAMPIRE PIT VOL.2
CD CANDY 1112CD
Candy / Nov '92 / Plastic Head

VAMPIRE KISS, THE
CD CDSATE 02
Talitha / Jul '93 / Plastic Head

Ty Gwydr

292 YMLAEN AT Y FILIWN
CD ANKST 045CD
Ankst / Feb '94 / Shellshock/Disc

Tygers Of Pan Tang

CAGE, THE
Rendezvous / Lonely at the top / Letter from LA / Paris by air / Tides / Making tracks / Actor / Cage / Love potion no.9 / You always see what you want to see / Danger in paradise / Life of crime / Love's a lie / What you sayin' / Making tracks
CD EDGY 104
Neat / May '97 / Pinnacle

CRAZY NIGHTS
Slip away / Stormlands / Paradise drive / Do it good / Love don't stay / Never satisfied / Running out of time / Crazy nights / Down and out / Lonely man / Make a stand / Raised on rock
CD EDGY 103
Neat / May '97 / Pinnacle

FIRST KILL
Slave to freedom / Angel / Straight as a die / Final answer / Euthanasia / Shakespeare Road / Don't take nothing / Alright on the night / Bad times / Small town flirt
CD CLACD 258
Castle / '91 / BMG

SPELLBOUND
Gangland / Take it / Minotaur / Hellbound / Mirror / Silver and gold / Tyger Bay / Story so far / Black Jack / Don't stop by / All or nothing / Don't give a damn / Bad times / It ain't easy / Don't take nothing
CD EDGY 102
Neat / May '97 / Pinnacle

WILD CAT
Euthanasia / Slave to freedom / Don't touch me there / Money / Killers / Fireclown / Wild catz / Badger badger / Insanity / Suzie smiled / Rock and roll man / Alright on the night / Tush / Straight as a die / Don't take nothing / Bad times / Burning up / Don't touch me there
CD EDGY 101
Neat / May '97 / Pinnacle

Tyketto

SHINE
Jamie / Rawthigh / Radio Mary / Get me there / High / Ballad of Ruby / Let it go / Long cold winter / I won't cry / Shine
CD CDMFN 195
Music For Nations / Nov '95 / Pinnacle

STRENGTH IN NUMBERS
Strength in numbers / Rescue me / End of the summer days / Ain't that love / Catch my fall / Last sunset / All over me / Write your name in the sky / Meet me in the night / Why do you cry / Inherit the wind / Standing alone
CD CDMFN 157
Music For Nations / Feb '94 / Pinnacle

TAKE OUT AND SERVED UP
CD CDMFN 207
Music For Nations / Jul '96 / Pinnacle

Tyla

GOTHIC
CD REVXD 218
Revolver / Aug '97 / Revolver / Sony

LIFE AND TIMES OF A BALLAD MONGER
CD REVXD 197
Revolver / Nov '95 / Revolver / Sony

Tyla Gang

BLOW YOU OUT
CD 622392
Skydog / Apr '97 / Discovery

Tyle, Chris

SUGAR BLUES (Tyle, Chris & His Silver Leaf Jazzband)
CD SOSCD 1298
Stomp Off / Jul '96 / Jazz Music / Wellard

Tyler, Alvin 'Red'

GRACIOUSLY
CD ROUCD 2061
Rounder / '88 / ADA / CM / Direct

HERITAGE
CD ROUCD 047
Rounder / '88 / ADA / CM / Direct

Tyler, Bonnie

BEST, THE
Total eclipse of the heart / Faster than the speed of the night / Have you ever seen the rain / If you were a woman (and I was a man) / Here she comes / Loving you's a dirty job but someone's got to do it / Getting so excited / Save up all your tears / Best / Holding out for a hero / Married men / Rockin' good way / More than a lover / Don't turn around / Lovers again / Lost in France / It's a heartache / To love somebody
CD 4735222
Columbia / Oct '94 / Sony

BONNIE TYLER LOVE SONGS
CD SSLCD 206
Savanna / Jun '95 / THE

COLLECTION, THE
CD CCSCD 285
Castle / Feb '93 / BMG

FASTER THAN THE SPEED OF NIGHT
Have you ever seen the rain / Faster than the speed of night / Getting so excited / Total eclipse of the heart / It's a jungle out there / Going through the motions / Tears / Take me back / Straight from the heart
CD CD 32747
CBS / Oct '92 / Sony

FREE SPIRIT
CD 0630121082
East West / Mar '96 / Warner Music

GOODBYE TO THE ISLAND
I'm just a woman / We danced on the ceiling / Wild love / Closer you get / Sometimes when we touch / Goodbye to the island / Wild side of life / Whiter shade of pale / Sitting on the edge of the ocean / I believe in your sweet love
CD CLACD 288
Castle / Jul '92 / BMG

HEAVEN AND HELL (Tyler, Bonnie & Meatloaf)
Bat out of hell: *Meat Loaf* / Faster than the speed of night: *Tyler, Bonnie* / You took the words right out of my mouth: *Meat Loaf* / Have you ever seen the rain: *Tyler, Bonnie* / Read 'em and weep: *Meat Loaf* / Total eclipse of the heart: *Tyler, Bonnie* / Two out of three ain't bad: *Meat Loaf* / Holding out for a hero: *Tyler, Bonnie* / Dead ringer for love: *Meat Loaf* / If you were a woman (and I was a man): *Tyler, Bonnie* / If you really want to: *Meat Loaf* / Straight from the heart: *Tyler, Bonnie* / Loving you's a dirty job but somebody's got to do it: *Tyler, Bonnie* / Heaven can wait: *Meat Loaf*
CD 4736662
Columbia / May '93 / Sony

IT'S A HEARTACHE
It's a heartache / Louisiana rain / Married men / Love of a rolling stone / Blame me / My guns are loaded / Heaven / If I sing you a love song / Whiter shade of pale / Piece of my heart / If you ever need me again / Eyes of a fool / I believe in your sweet love / Living for the city / Baby I remember you / Wild side of life
CD 5507282
Spectrum / Aug '94 / PolyGram

LOST IN FRANCE
Sometimes when we touch / More than a lover / (You make me feel like) a natural woman / Goodbye to the island / Sitting on the edge of the ocean / Don't stop the music / Here I am / Get out of my head / Lost in France / Closer you get / Come on give me loving / I'm just a woman / Give me your love / Got so used to loving you / Here's Monday / Love tangle
CD 5507292
Spectrum / Mar '95 / PolyGram

LOVE COLLECTION, THE (2CD Set)
Lost in France / Baby, I remember you / Give me your love / Love of a rolling stone / World starts tonight / Piece of my heart / Love tangle / Heaven / More than a lover / Got so used to loving you / It's about time / Louisiana rain / Yesterday dreams / Baby goodnight / Living for the city / Don't stop the music / (You make me feel like) a natural woman / World is full of married men / It's a heartache / Hey love (it's a feelin') / If I sing you a love song / Too good to last / Come on, give me loving / I believe in your sweet love / What a way to treat my heart / Baby I just love you / If you ever need me again / Words can change your life / Bye bye now my sweet love / I'm just a woman / Wild love / Closer you get / Sometimes when you touch / Whiter shade of pale / We danced on the ceiling / Goodbye to the island
CD Set SMDCD 104
Snapper / May '97 / Pinnacle

NATURAL FORCE
It's a heartache / Blame me / Living for the city / If I sing you a love song / Heaven / Yesterday dreams / Hey love / (You make me feel like) a natural woman / Here I am / Baby goodnight
CD CLACD 232
Castle / Apr '91 / BMG

PIECE OF MY HEART
Lost in France / Whiter shade of pale / World starts tonight / Heaven / Here I am / More than a lover / Love tangle / Louisiana rain / My guns are loaded / Piece of my heart / Goodbye to the island / Living for the city / Love of a rolling stone / We danced on the ceiling / Bye bye now my sweet love / It's a heartache
CD 21018
Laserlight / Jul '97 / Target/BMG

STRAIGHT FROM THE HEART
CD CCSCD 801
Castle / Aug '95 / BMG

WORLD STARTS TONIGHT, THE
Got so used to loving you / Love of a rolling stone / Lost in France / Piece of my heart / More than a lover / Give me your love / World starts tonight / Here's Monday / Love tangle / Let the show begin
CD CLACD 231
Castle / Apr '91 / BMG

Tyler, Charles

EASTERN MAN ALONE
CD ESP 10592
ESP / Jan '93 / Jazz Music

Tyler, Chris

SMILER, THE
CD SOSCD 1258
Stomp Off / Dec '93 / Jazz Music / Wellard

Tyndall, Nik

AMBIENT MUSIC
CD SKYCD 3049
Sky / Feb '95 / Greyhound / Koch / Vital/ SAM

Tyner, McCoy

4 X 4 (Tyner, McCoy Quartets)
Inner glimpse / Manha de carnaval / Paradox / Backward glace / Forbidden land / Pannonica / I wanna stand over there / Seeker / Blues in the minor / Stay as sweet as you are / It's you or no one
CD MCD 55007
Milestone / Apr '94 / Cadillac / Complete/ Pinnacle / Jazz Music / Wellard

ATLANTIS
Atlantis / In a sentimental mood / Makin' out / My one and only love / Pursuit / Love samba
CD MCD 55002
Milestone / Aug '96 / Cadillac / Complete/ Pinnacle / Jazz Music / Wellard

BEST OF MCCOY TYNER, THE (The Blue Note Years)
Passion dance / Search for peace / Man from Tanganyika / Peresina / Song for my lady / Wanderer / You taught my heart to sing / Blue Monk / My one & only love
CD CDP 8370512
Blue Note / Apr '96 / EMI

BLUE BOSSA
CD CDC 9033
LRC / Jul '91 / Harmonia Mundi / New Note/Pinnacle

BLUE BOSSA
Blue bossa / Recife's blues / I'll take romance / Rotunda / We'll be together again
CD 17120
Laserlight / May '97 / Target/BMG

BON VOYAGE
Bon voyage / Don't blame me / Summertime / You stepped out of a dream / Jazz walk / How deep is the ocean / Blues for Max / Yesterdays
CD CDSJP 260
Timeless Jazz / Jul '91 / New Note/Pinnacle

EXTENSIONS
Message from the Nile / Wanderer / Survival blues / His blessings
CD CDP 8376462
Blue Note / Jun '96 / EMI

FLY WITH THE WIND
CD FCD 6019067
Fantasy / Nov '86 / Jazz Music / Pinnacle / Wellard

INCEPTION
Inception / There is no greater love / Blues for Gwen / Sunset / Effendi / Speak low
CD IMP 12202
Impulse Jazz / Apr '97 / New Note/BMG

INCEPTION/NIGHT OF BALLADS AND BLUES
Inception / Blues for Gwen / Speak / We'll be together again / For heaven's sake / Blue monk / Days of wine and roses / There is no greater love / Sunset effendi / Satin doll / 'Round midnight / Star eyes / Groove waltz
CD MCAD 42000
Impulse Jazz / Jun '89 / New Note/BMG

INFINITY (Tyner, McCoy & Michael Brecker)
Flying high / I mean you / Where is love / Changes / Happy days / Impressions / Mellow minor / Good morning heartache
CD IMP 11712
Impulse Jazz / Sep '95 / New Note/BMG

JOURNEY (Tyner, McCoy Big Band)
Samba dei ber / Juanita / Choices / You taught my heart to sing / Peresina / Blues on the corner / January in Brasil
CD 5199412
Birdology / Apr '92 / PolyGram

LIVE AT WARSAW JAZZ FESTIVAL 1991
CD CD 66050008
Bellaphon / Jul '93 / New Note/Pinnacle

MCCOY TYNER PLAYS ELLINGTON
Duke's place / Caravan / Solitude / Searchin' / Mr. Gentle and Mr. Cool / Satin doll / Gyspy without a song / It don't mean a thing... / I got it bad / Gypsy without a song
CD IMP 12162
Impulse Jazz / Apr '97 / New Note/BMG

NIGHTS OF BALLADS AND BLUES
Satin doll / We'll be together again / 'Round midnight / For heaven's sake / Star eyes / Blue monk / Groove waltz / Days of wine and roses
CD IMP 12212
Impulse Jazz / Apr '97 / New Note/BMG

PARIS BOSSA (Tyner, McCoy Quintet)
CD MCD 0342
Moon / Jan '92 / Cadillac / Harmonia Mundi

PLAYS ELLINGTON
Duke's place / Caravan / Solitude / Searchin' / Mr. Gentle and Mr. Cool / Satin doll / Gypsy without a song / It don't mean a thing if it ain't got that swing / I got it bad and that ain't good / Gypsy without a song (Alternate take)
CD MCAD 33124
Impulse Jazz / Dec '90 / New Note/BMG

PRELUDE & SONATA
CD MCD 92442
Milestone / Feb '96 / Cadillac / Complete/ Pinnacle / Jazz Music / Wellard

REAL MCCOY, THE
Passion dance / Contemplation / Four by five / Search for peace / Blues on the corner
CD CDP 7465122
Blue Note / Mar '95 / EMI

SAHARA
CD OJCCD 311
Original Jazz Classics / Apr '92 / Complete/Pinnacle / Jazz Music / Wellard

SONG FOR MY LADY
CD OJCCD 313
Original Jazz Classics / Apr '92 / Complete/Pinnacle / Jazz Music / Wellard

SUPER TRIOS
CD MCD 55003
Milestone / Oct '93 / Cadillac / Complete/ Pinnacle / Jazz Music / Wellard

TURNING POINT, THE (Tyner, McCoy Big Band)
Passion dance / Let it go / High priest / Angel eyes / Fly with the wind / Update / In a sentimental mood
CD 5131632
Birdology / Jan '93 / PolyGram

UPTOWN DOWNTOWN (Tyner, McCoy Big Band)
Love surrounds us / Three flowers / Genesis / Uptown / Lotus flower / Blues for Basie
CD MCD 9167
Milestone / Apr '94 / Cadillac / Complete/ Pinnacle / Jazz Music / Wellard

WHAT THE WORLD NEEDS NOW (The Music Of Burt Bacharach) (Tyner, McCoy Trio)
(They want to be) Close to you / What the world needs now is love / Look of love / Alfie / (There's) Always somwthing there to remind me / House is not a home / One less bell to answer / Windows of the world / You'll never get to heaven (If you break my heart)
CD IMP 11972
Impulse Jazz / May '97 / New Note/BMG

Type O Negative

OCTOBER RUST
CD RR 88742
Roadrunner / Sep '96 / PolyGram

ORIGIN OF THE FAECES
CD _______________ **RR 90062**
Roadrunner / Sep '96 / PolyGram

SLOW DEEP AND HARD
CD _______________ **RO 93132**
Roadrunner / May '91 / PolyGram

Tyrell, Sean

CRY OF A DREAMER
Mattie / Coast of Malabar / Demolition Dan / Isle of Inisfree / House of delight / November rain / Blue-green bangle / Message of peace / Cry of the dreamer / Only from day to day / No-go / Connie's song / Fortune for the finder / 12th Of July
CD _______________ **LMCD 001**
L-MCD / Jun '94 / ADA
CD _______________ **HNCD 1391**
Hannibal / Nov '95 / ADA / Vital

Tyrrall, Gordon

BRIDGE FLOWS, THE
CD _______________ **PM 001CD**
Punch Music / Jun '94 / ADA / Roots

WHERE THE RIVER FLOWS
CD _______________ **PMCD 001**
Punch Music / Aug '94 / ADA / Roots

Tyson, Ian

AND STOOD THERE AMAZED
CD _______________ **SP 1168CD**
Stony Plain / Oct '93 / ADA / CM / Direct

OLD CORRALS AND SAGEBRUSH & OTHER COWBOY CLASSIC
Gallo del cielo / Alberta's child / Old double diamond / Windy Bill / Montana waltz / Whoopie ti yi yo / Leavin' Cheyenne / Old corrals and sagebrush / Old Alberta moon / Night rider's lament / Oklahoma hills / Tom Blasingame / Colorado trial / Hot summer tears / What does she see / Rocks begin to roll / Will James / Murder steer
CD _______________ **BCD 15437**
Bear Family / Aug '88 / Direct / Rollercoaster / Swift

ONE JUMP AHEAD OF THE DEVIL
What does she see / Beverly / Turning thirty / Newtonville waltz / Lone star and coors / One too many / Texas / I miss you / Goodness of Shirley / Freddie Hall / Half a mile to hell
CD _______________ **SPCD 1177**
Stony Plain / Oct '93 / ADA / CM / Direct

Tyson, Sylvia

YOU WERE ON MY MIND
Pepere's mill / Slow moving heart / Rhythm of the road / Walking on the moon / Thrown to the wolves / Night the Chinese restaurant burned down / You were on my mind / Sleep on my mind / Trucker's cafe / River Road / Last call / Le Moulin a Pepere / Blind fiddler's waltz
CD _______________ **RTMCD 77**
Round Tower / Jun '96 / Avid/BMG

Tytot, Angelin

GIITU
CD _______________ **MIPU 204CD**
Mipu / Dec '93 / ADA / Direct

Tzuke, Judie

BEST OF JUDIE TZUKE
New friends again / Black furs / Sukarita / Sports car / For you / These are the laws / Welcome to the cruise / Come hell or waters high / Higher and higher / Chinatown / Stay with me 'til dawn / Bring the rain
CD _______________ **8113922**
Phonogram / Feb '94 / PolyGram

RITMO
Face to face / Nighthawks / How do I feel / Another country / Jeannie no / She don't live here anymore / Shoot from the heart / Walk don't walk / Push push / Chinatown / City of swimming pools
CD _______________ **BGOCD 225**
Beat Goes On / Jun '94 / Pinnacle

ROAD NOISE (The Official Bootleg)
Heaven can wait / Chinatown / I'm not a loser / Information / Flesh is weak / Sports car / For you / Come hell or waters high / Southern smiles / Kateria Island / Love on the border / Black furs / City of swimming pools / Bring the rain / Sukarita / Stay with me 'til dawn / Hunter
CD _______________ **BGOCD 212**
Beat Goes On / Dec '93 / Pinnacle

SHOOT THE MOON
Heaven can wait / Love on the border / Information / Beacon Hill / Don't let me sleep / I'm not a loser / Now there is no love at all / Late again / Liggers at your funeral / Water in motion / Shoot the moon
CD _______________ **BGOCD 226**
Beat Goes On / Oct '94 / Pinnacle

STAY WITH ME TILL DAWN
Stay with me till dawn / Bring the rain / Ladies night / Welcome to the cruise / We'll go dreaming / Let me be the pearl / Dominique / Turning stones / Choice you've made / Understanding / Living on the coast / Sports car / Higher and higher / I never know where my heart is / Come hell or waters high / Black furs
CD _______________ **5508962**
Spectrum / Aug '95 / PolyGram

WONDERLAND
Wonderland / I can read books / Man and a gun / Keep control / On a ship / Vivien / Sara's gone / She loves his hands / Fly / Swimming
CD _______________ **ESMCD 184**
Essential / Jan '97 / BMG

U

U-Men

STEP ON A BUG
Whistlin' Pete / Three year old could do that / Flea circus / Willie Dong hurts dogs / Pay the bubba / Two times four / Juice party / Too good to be food / Papa doesn't love his children anymore
CD _______________ **TUPCD 012**
Tupelo / Jun '90 / RTM/Disc

U-Roy

BABYLON KINGDOM MUST FALL
CD _______________ **ARICD 129**
Ariwa Sounds / Sep '96 / Jet Star / SRD

DREAD IN A BABYLON
Runaway girl / Chalice in the palace / I can't love another / Dreadlocks dread / Great psalms / Natty don't fear / African message / Silver bird / Listen to the teacher / Trenchtown rock
CD _______________ **CDFL 9007**
Frontline / Sep '90 / EMI / Jet Star

FLASHING MY WHIP
CD _______________ **RNCD 2130**
Rhino / Nov '95 / Grapevine/PolyGram / Jet Star

MUSIC ADDICT
I originate / Come fe warn them / King Tubby's skank / Reggae party / I feel good / Music addict / Jah Jah call you / Haul and pull / Waterboat
CD _______________ **RASCD 3024**
Ras / Aug '87 / Direct / Greensleeves / Jet Star / SRD

MUSICAL VISION
CD _______________ **LG 21080**
Lagoon / Nov '93 / Grapevine/PolyGram

NATTY REBEL
Babylon burning / Natty rebel / So Jah Jah say / Natty kung fu / If you should leave me / Do you remember / Travelling man / Have mercy / Badie boo / Go there natty / Fire in a Trench Town
CD _______________ **CDFL 9017**
Virgin / Apr '83 / EMI

ORIGINAL DJ
Babylon burning / Natty rebel / Evil doers / Jah Jah / Rule the nation / On the beach / Tide is high / Rock away / Peace and love in the ghetto / Say you / I can't love another / Trenchtown rock / Hot pop / Wear you to the ball / True confession / Everybody bawling / Words of wisdom / Great psalms / African message / Listen to the teacher / Control tower / Runaway girl / Natty don't fear / Chalice in the palace / Come home little girl
CD _______________ **CDFL 9020**
Frontline / Jun '95 / EMI / Jet Star

RASTA AMBASSADOR
Control tower / Wear you to the ball / Evil doers / Mr. Slave Driver / Small axe / Come home little girl / Say you / No more war / Tide is high / Jah Jah
CD _______________ **CDFL 9016**
Frontline / Jun '91 / EMI / Jet Star

SMILE A WHILE (U-Roy & Yabby U)
CD _______________ **ARICD 085**
Ariwa Sounds / May '93 / Jet Star / SRD

SUPER BOSS
CD _______________ **LG 21024**
Lagoon / Jul '93 / Grapevine/PolyGram

TEACHER MEETS THE STUDENT, THE (U-Roy & Josie Wales)
CD _______________ **SONCD 0028**
Sonic Sounds / Apr '92 / Jet Star

TRUE BORN AFRICAN
CD _______________ **AIRCD 071**
Ariwa Sounds / Sep '91 / Jet Star / SRD

VERSION OF WISDOM
Your ace from outer space / Rule the nation / Honey come forward / Version galore / Things you love / Wear you to the ball / On the beach / Rock away / True confession / Everybody bawling / Wake the town / Words of wisdom / Treasure isle skank / Same song / Tide is high / Hot pop / Tom drunk / Drive her home / Merry go round / What is catty
CD _______________ **CDFL 9003**
Frontline / Jul '90 / EMI / Jet Star

WAKE THE TOWN
CD _______________ **RNCD 2114**
Rhino / Jul '95 / Grapevine/PolyGram / Jet Star

WITH A FLICK OF MY MUSICAL WRIST (U-Roy & Friends)
CD _______________ **CDTRL 268**
Trojan / Sep '94 / Direct / Jet Star

YOUR ACE FROM SPACE
CD _______________ **CDTRL 359**
Trojan / Aug '95 / Direct / Jet Star

u-Ziq

BLUFF LIMBO (2CD Set)
CD Set _______________ **CAT 018CD**
Rephlex / Apr '96 / Prime / RTM/Disc

IN PINE EFFECT
Mr. Angry / Melancho / Wailing song / Iced jem / Funky pipecleaner / Phiescope / Old fun no.1 / Pine effect / Dauphine / Roy Castle / Within a sound / Rain / Tungsten carbide / Frank / Problematic / Green crumble
CD _______________ **FLATCD 20**
Hi-Rise / Oct '95 / EMI / Pinnacle

LUNATIC HARNESS
Brace yourself Jason / Hasty boom alert / Mushroom compost / Blainville / Lunatic harness / Approaching menace / My little beautiful / Secret stair / Secret stair / Wannabe / Catkin and teasel / London / Midwinter log
CD _______________ **CDPLU 005**
Planet U / Jun '97 / Prime / Vital

TANGO N'VECTIF
CD _______________ **CAT 013CD**
Rephlex / Aug '96 / Prime / RTM/Disc

URMER BILE TRAX VOL.1 & 2
Urmer bile / Let let / M5 saabtone / Fine tuning / Hydrozone / 1 Hip 007 / Hornet / Phonic socks
CD _______________ **PLUD 003**
Planet U / Feb '97 / Prime / Vital

U2

ACHTUNG BABY
Zoo station / Even better than the real thing / One / Until the end of the world / Who's gonna ride your wild horses / So cruel / Fly / Mysterious ways / Tryin' to throw your arms around the world / Ultraviolet / Acrobat / Love is blindness
CD _______________ **CIDU 28**
Island / Oct '91 / PolyGram

ALL I WANT IS (Interview Disc)
CD _______________ **3D 001**
Network / Nov '96 / Total/BMG

BOY
Twilight / An cat dubh / Out of control / Stories for boys / Ocean / Day without me / Another time another place / Electric Co / Shadows and tall trees / I will follow
CD _______________ **IMCD 211**
Island / Apr '95 / PolyGram

EVEN BETTER THAN THE REAL THING (2CD Set/Documentary and Music)
CD Set _______________ **OTR 1100043**
Metro Independent / Jun '97 / Essential/BMG

INTERVIEW DISC
CD _______________ **SAM 7003**
Sound & Media / Nov '96 / Sound & Media

JOSHUA TREE, THE
Where the streets have no name / I still haven't found what I'm looking for / With or without you / Bullet the blue sky / Running to stand still / Red hill mining town / In God's country / Trip through your wires / One tree hill / Exit / Mothers of the disappeared
CD _______________ **CIDU 26**
Island / Mar '87 / PolyGram

OCTOBER
Gloria / I fall down / I threw a brick through a window / Rejoice / Fire / Tomorrow / October / With a shout (Jerusalem) / Stranger in a strange land / Scarlet / Is that all
CD _______________ **IMCD 223**
Island / Mar '96 / PolyGram

ORIGINAL SOUNDTRACKS VOL.1 (Passengers)
United colours / Slug / Your blue room / Always forever now / Different kind of blue / Beach sequence / Miss Sarajevo / Ito okashi / One minute warning / Corpse (These chains are way too long) / Elvis ate America / Plot 180 / Theme from The Swan / Theme from Lets Go Native
CD _______________ **CID 8043**
Island / Oct '95 / PolyGram

PHILADELPHIA INTERVIEWS, THE
CD _______________ **CBAK 4006**
Baktabak / Apr '88 / Arabesque

POP
Discotheque / Do you feel loved / Mofo / If God will send his angels / Staring at the sun / Last night on Earth / Gone / Miami / Playboy mansion / If you wear that velvet dress / Please / Wake up dead man
CD _______________ **CIDU 210**
Island / Mar '97 / PolyGram

PRESS CONFERENCE MEXICO 1992
CD _______________ **MEX 1CD**
Wax / Jun '97 / RTM/Disc / Total/BMG

RATTLE AND HUM
Helter skelter / Hawkmoon 269 / Van Diemen's land / Desire / Angel of Harlem / I still haven't found what I'm looking for / When love comes to town / God pt II / Bullet the blue sky / Silver and gold / Pride (in the name of love) / Love rescue me / Heartland / Star spangled banner / All I want is you / All along the watchtower
CD _______________ **CIDU 27**
Island / Oct '88 / PolyGram

SHAPED CD INTERVIEW DISC/ADAM
CD _______________ **UFOADAM 1**
UFO / Apr '97 / Pinnacle

SHAPED CD INTERVIEW DISC/BONO
CD _______________ **UFOBONO 1**
UFO / Apr '97 / Pinnacle

SHAPED CD INTERVIEW DISC/LARRY
CD _______________ **UFOLARRY 1**
UFO / Apr '97 / Pinnacle

SHAPED CD INTERVIEW DISC/THE EDGE
CD _______________ **UFOEDGE 1**
UFO / Apr '97 / Pinnacle

TELLTALES (Interview Disc)
CD _______________ **TELL 15**
Network / Jun '97 / Total/BMG

UNDER A BLOOD RED SKY (Live)
Eleven o'clock tick tock / I will follow / Party girl / Gloria / Sunday Bloody Sunday / Electric Co / New Year's Day / 40
CD _______________ **IMCD 248**
Island / Mar '97 / PolyGram

UNFORGETTABLE FIRE, THE
Sort of homecoming / Pride (in the name of love) / 4th of July / Wire / Unforgettable fire / Promenade / Indian Summer sky / MLK / Elvis Presley and America
CD _______________ **IMCD 236**
Island / Sep '96 / PolyGram

WAR
Sunday bloody Sunday / Seconds / Like a song / New Year's Day / Two hearts beat as one / Refugee / Drowning man / Red light / 40 / Surrender
CD _______________ **IMCD 141**
Island / Aug '91 / PolyGram

WIDE AWAKE IN AMERICA
Bad / Sort of homecoming / Three sunrises / Love comes tumbling
CD _______________ **IMCD 75**
Island / Nov '89 / PolyGram

ZOOROPA
Zooropa / Babyface / Numb / Lemon / Stay (Faraway, so close) / Daddy's gonna pay for your crashed car / First time / Some days are better than others / Dirty day / Wanderer: *U2 & Johnny Cash*
CD _______________ **CIDU 29**
Island / Jun '93 / PolyGram

Uakti

TRILOBYTE
CD _______________ **4540562**
Point Music / Oct '96 / PolyGram

UB40

BAGGARIDDIM
King step / Buzz feeling / Lyric officer Mk2 / Demonstrate / Two in a one mk1 / Hold your position Mk3 / Hip hop lyrical robot / Style Mk4 / V's version / Don't break my heart / I got you babe: *UB40 & Chrissie Hynde* / Mi spliff / Fight fe come in Mk2
CD _______________ **DEPCD 10**
DEP International / Oct '85 / EMI

BEST OF UB40 VOL.1, THE
Red red wine / I got you babe / One in ten / Food for thought / Rat in mi kitchen / Don't break my heart / Cherry oh baby / Many rivers to cross / Please don't make me cry / If it happens again / Sing our own song / Maybe tomorrow / My way of thinking / King
CD _______________ **DUBTV 1**
DEP International / Oct '87 / EMI

BEST OF UB40 VOL.2, THE
Breakfast in bed / Where did I go wrong / I would do for you / Homely girl / Here I am (come and take me) / Kingston Town / Wear you to the ball / Can't help falling in love / Higher ground / Bring me your cup / C'est la vie / Reggae music / Superstition / Until my dying day
CD _______________ **DUBTV 2**
DEP International / Oct '95 / EMI

GEFFREY MORGAN
Riddle me / As always you were wrong again / If it happens again / DUB / Pillow / Nkomo a go-go / Seasons / You're not an army / I'm not fooled so easily / You're eyes were open
CD _______________ **DEPCD 6**
DEP International / Oct '84 / EMI

GROOVIN' JAMAICA PAYS TRIBUTE TO UB40 (Various Artists)
CD _______________ **RNCD 2065**
Rhino / Oct '94 / Grapevine/PolyGram / Jet Star

GUNS IN THE GHETTO
Always there / Hurry come up / I love it when you smile / I've been missing you / Oracabessa moonshine / Guns in the ghetto / Tell me is it true / Friendly fire / I really can't say / Lisa
CD _______________ **CADEP 16**
DEP International / Jun '97 / EMI

LABOUR OF LOVE VOL.1
Johnny too bad / Guilty / Sweet sensation / Many rivers to cross / Red red wine / Please don't make me cry / She caught the train / Keep on moving / Cherry oh baby / Version girl
CD _______________ **DEPCD 5**
DEP International / Jul '86 / EMI

LABOUR OF LOVE VOL.1 & 2
Cherry oh baby / Keep on moving / Please don't make me cry / Sweet sensation / Johnny too bad / Red red wine / Guilty / She caught the train / Version girl / Many rivers to cross / Here I am (come and take me) / Tears from my eyes / Groovin' / Way you do the things you do / Wear you to the ball / Singer man / Kingston town / Baby / Wedding day / Sweet cherrie / Stick by me / Just another girl / Homely girl / Impossible love
CD Set _______________ **DEPDDX 1**
DEP International / Oct '94 / EMI

LABOUR OF LOVE VOL.2
Here I am (come and take me) / Tears from my eyes / Groovin' / Way you do the things you do / Wear you to the ball / Singer man / Kingston town / Baby / Wedding day / Sweet cherrie / Stick by me / Just another girl / Homely girl / Impossible love
CD _______________ **DEPCD 14**
DEP International / Nov '89 / EMI

PRESENT ARMS
Present arms / Sardonicus / Don't let it pass you by / Wild cat / One in ten / Don't slow down / Silent witness / Lambs bread / Don't walk on the grass / Dr. X
CD _______________ **DEPCD 1**
DEP International / Apr '88 / EMI

PRESENT ARMS IN DUB
Present arms in dub / Smoke it / B line / King's row / Return of Dr. X / Walk out / One in ten / Neon haze
CD _______________ **DEPCD 2**
DEP International / '88 / EMI

PRESENT ARMS/BAGGARIDDIM/CCCP - LIVE IN MOSCOW (3CD Set)
CD Set _______________ **TPAK 20**
Virgin / Nov '91 / EMI

PROMISES AND LIES
C'est la vie / Desert sand / Promises and lies / Bring me your cup / Higher ground / Reggae music / Can't help falling in love / Now and then / Things ain't like they used to be / It's a long, long way / Sorry
CD _______________ **DEPCD 15**
DEP International / Jul '93 / EMI

RAT IN MI KITCHEN
All I want to do / You could meet somebody / Tell it like this / Elevator / Watchdogs / Rat in mi kitchen / Looking down at my reflection / Don't blame me / Sing our own song
CD _______________ **DEPCD 11**
DEP International / Apr '92 / EMI

SIGNING OFF
Tyler / King / Twelve Bar / Burden of shame / Adella / I think it's going to rain again / 25% / Food for thought / Little by little / Signing off / Madame Medusa / Strange fruit / Reefer madness
CD _______________ **CDOVD 439**
DEP International / Oct '93 / EMI

SIGNING OFF/RAT IN THE KITCHEN/ PRESENT ARMS IN DUB (3CD Set)
CD Set _______________ **TPAK 35**
Virgin / Oct '94 / EMI

UB40
Dance with the devil / Come out to play / Breakfast in bed / You're always pulling me down / I would do for you / 'Cause it isn't true / Where did I go wrong / Contaminated minds / Matter of time / Music so nice / Dance with the devil (reprise)
CD _______________ **DEPCD 13**
DEP International / Jul '88 / EMI

UB40 FILE, THE
Tyler / King / Twelve bar / Burden of shame / Adella / I think it's going to rain today / 25% / Food for thought / Little by little / Signing off / Madame Medusa / Strange fruit / Reefer madness / My way of thinking / Earth dies screaming / Dream a lie
CD _______________ **VGDCD 3511**
DEP International / Jul '86 / EMI

UB40 LIVE
Food for thought / Sardonicus / Don't slow down / Folitician / Tyler / Present arms / Piper calls the tune / Love is all is alright / Burden of shame / One in ten
CD _______________ DEPCD 4
DEP International / '88 / EMI

UB44
So here I am / I won't close my eyes (remix) / Forget the cost / Love is all is alright (re-mix) / Piper calls the tune / Key / Don't do the crime / Folitician (remix) / Prisoner
CD _______________ DEPCD 3
DEP International / Apr '86 / EMI

Ubik

JUST ADD PEOPLE
CD _______________ ZOOMCD 1
Zoom / Jul '92 / Arabesque / Mo's Music Machine / Prime / RTM/Disc

Uen, Jin Long

BUDDHIST CHANTS AND PEACE MUSIC
CD _______________ MCCD 235
Music Club / Mar '96 / Disc / THE

UFO

AIN'T MISBEHAVIN'
Between a rock and a hard place / Another Saturday night / At war with the world / Hunger in the night / Easy money / Rock boyz, rock / Lonely cities (of the heart)
CD _______________ WKFMXD 107
FM / Mar '88 / Revolver / Sony

BEST OF UFO, THE
Doctor Doctor / Only you can rock me / Let it roll / Shoot shoot / Let it rain / When it's time to rock / Rock bottom / Love to love / High flyer / Can you roll her / Pack it up (and go) / Hot & ready / This time / Long gone / Young blood / Lonely heart
CD _______________ CDGOLD 1050
EMI Gold / Jul '96 / EMI

ESSENTIAL UFO
Doctor doctor / Rock bottom / Out in the street / Mother Mary / Natural thing / I'm a loser / Only you can rock me / Lookin' out for no.1 / Cherry / Born to lose / Too hot to handle / Lights out / Love to love / This kid's / Let it roll / Shoot shoot
CD _______________ CDCHR 1888
Chrysalis / Oct '92 / EMI

HEAVEN'S GATE LIVE
Heavens' gate / Chase / This time / Mean-streets / Name of love / Only ones / Wreck-less / Night run / Only you can rock me / Doctor doctor
CD _______________ MNMCD 1
M&M / Nov '95 / Total/BMG

LIGHTS OUT
Too hot to handle / Just another suicide / Try me / Lights out / Gettin' ready / Alone again or / Electric phase / Love to love
CD _______________ ACCD 1127
Chrysalis / '87 / EMI

LIGHTS OUT IN TOKYO - LIVE
Running up the highway / Borderline / Too hot to handle / She's the one / Cherry / Back door man / One of those nights / Love to love / Only you can rock me / Lights out / Doctor doctor / Rock bottom / Shoot shoot / C'mon everybody
CD _______________ ESMCD 386
Essential / Apr '95 / BMG

MAKING CONTACT/MISDEMEANOUR
CD _______________ BGOCD 319
Beat Goes On / Jul '96 / Pinnacle

NO HEAVY PETTING/LIGHTS OUT
Natural thing / I'm a loser / Can you roll her / Belladonna / Reasons love / Highway lady / On with the action / Fool in love / Martian landscape / Too hot to handle / Just an-other suicide / Try me / Lights out / Gettin' ready / Alone again or / Electric phase / Love to love
CD _______________ BGOCD 228
Beat Goes On / Aug '94 / Pinnacle

OBSESSION/NO PLACE TO RUN
Only you can rock me / Pack it up (and go) / Arbory hill / Ain't no baby / Lookin' out for no.1 / Hot 'n' ready / Cherry / You don't fool me / Lookin' out for No.1 (Reprise) / One more for the rodeo / Born to lose / Alpha Centauri / Lettin' go / Mystery train / This fire burns tonight / Gone in the night / Young blood / No place to run / Take it or leave it / Money, money / Any day
CD _______________ BGOCD 229
Beat Goes On / May '94 / Pinnacle

PHENOMENON/FORCE IT
Too young to no / Crystal light / Doctor Doctor / Space child / Rock bottom / Oh my / Time on my hands / Built for comfort / Lipstick traces / Queen of the deep / Let it roll / Shoot shoot / High flyer / Love lost love / Out in the street / Mother Mary / Too much of nothing / Dance your life away / This kid's
CD _______________ BGOCD 227
Beat Goes On / Oct '94 / Pinnacle

TOO HOT TO HANDLE (The Best Of UFO)
Only you can rock me / Too hot to handle / Long gone / Profession of violence / We belong to the night / Let it rain / Lonely heart / This time / Lettin' go / Lights out / Natural thing / Blinded by a lie / Wreckless / When it's time to rock / Shoot shoot / Young blood / Let it roll / Doctor doctor
CD _______________ MCCD 153
Music Club / Feb '94 / Disc / THE

WILD, THE WILLING AND THE INNOCENT/MECHANIX
Chains chains / Long gone / Wild, the willing and the innocent / It's killing me / Makin' moves / Lonely heart / Couldn't get it right / Profession of violence / Writer / Something else / Back into my life / You'll get love / Doing it all for you / We belong to the night / Let it rain / Terri / Feel it / Dreaming
CD _______________ BGOCD 230
Beat Goes On / Sep '94 / Pinnacle

X-FACTOR - OUT THERE...AND BACK, THE (2CD Set)
Unidentified flying object / Boogie / C'mon everybody / Shake it about / (Come away) Melinda / Follow you home / Who do you love / Evil / Silver birdstar storm / Prince Kajaku / Loving cup / One of those nights / Ain't life sweet / Long gone / Borderline / She's the one / Running up the highway / Back door man / Let the good times roll / Cherry / Love to love / Only you can rock me / Lights out / Doctor doctor / Rock bottom / Shoot shoot
CD Set _______________ SMDCD 122
Snapper / May '97 / Pinnacle

UFO

3RD PERSPECTIVE
His name is... / Planet plan / Friends we'll be / Spy's spice(mon espionne) / Fool's paradise / Waltz (le serpent rouge) / Pica-resque eye / Nica's dream / Cosmic gypsy / Dice for a chance / Moving shadows
CD _______________ 5344872
Mercury / Jun '97 / PolyGram

Ugarte, Enrique 'Kike'

ENRIQUE UGARTE, ACCORDION CHAMPION
Bolero / Sabre dance / Czardas
CD _______________ EUCD 1151
ARC / Jun '91 / ADA / ARC Music

FOLKLORE VASCO
CD _______________ EUCD 1157
ARC / Jun '91 / ADA / ARC Music

VALSE MUSETTE
CD _______________ EUCD 1114
ARC / '91 / ADA / ARC Music

VALSE MUSETTE VOL.2
CD _______________ EUCD 1200
ARC / Sep '93 / ADA / ARC Music

Ugly Duckling

12 BARS
Ugly guys are cool / Devil's highway / Day I put the jukebox on the rails / Not that guy / Pulp fiction / What a drag / I love you for yourself / Dog eat dog / Rimbaud or Rambo / Dancing alone
CD _______________ BMCD 288
Munich / Feb '97 / ADA / CM / Direct / Greensleeves

Ugly Kid Joe

AMERICA'S LEAST WANTED
Neighbor / Goddamn devil / Come tomor-row / Panhandlin prince / Busy bee / Don't go / So damn cool / Same side / Cats in the cradle / I'll keep tryin' / Everything about you / Madman ('92 Re-mix) / Mr. Record man
CD _______________ 5125712
Mercury / Nov '92 / PolyGram

AS UGLY AS THEY WANNA BE
Madman / Whiplash / Too bad / Everything about you / Sweet leaf / Funky fresh coun-try club / Heavy metal
CD _______________ 8688232
Mercury / May '92 / PolyGram

MESSAGE TO SOBRIETY
CD _______________ 5282822
Mercury / Jun '95 / PolyGram

MOTEL CALIFORNIA (2CD Set)
It's a lie / Dialogue / Sandwich / Rage against the answering machine / Would you like to be there / Little red man / Bicycle wheels / Father / Undertow / Shine / Strange / 12 Cents / Sweeping up
CD Set _______________ RAWCD 113
Raw Power / Oct '96 / Pinnacle

Uglystick

UGLYSTICK
CD _______________ CDVEST 46
Bulletproof / Mar '95 / Pinnacle

Ui

SIDELONG
CD _______________ 185352
Southern / Apr '96 / SRD

UNLIKE
CD _______________ LUNAMOTH 05
Lunamoth / Sep '96 / SRD

Ui Cheallaigh, Aine

CUIMHNI CEOIL
CD _______________ CIC 077CD
Clo Iar-Chonnachta / Nov '93 / CM

IN TWO MINDS
CD _______________ CEFCD 158
Gael Linn / Jan '94 / ADA / CM / Direct / Grapevine/PolyGram / Roots

UK

IN THE DEAD OF THE NIGHT
Alaska / Time to kill / Only thing she needs / Carrying no cross / Thirty years / In the dead of night / Caesars Palace blues
CD _______________ BP 243CD
Blueprint / Apr '97 / Pinnacle

UK Subs

BRAND NEW AGE
You can't take it anymore / Brand new age / Public servant / Warhead / Barbie's dead / Organised crime / Rat race / Emotional blackmail / Kicks / Teenage / Dirty girls / 500 cc / Bomb factory
CD _______________ DOJOCD 228
Dojo / Jun '95 / Disc

DIMINISHED RESPONSIBILITY
You don't belong / So what / Confrontation / Fatal / Time and matter / Violent city / Too tired / Party in Paris / Gangster / Face the machine / New order / Just another jungle / Collision cult
CD _______________ DOJOCD 232
Dojo / Jun '95 / Disc

DOWN ON THE FARM
CID / I live in a car / Bic / Down on the farm / Endangered species / Countdown / Plan of action / Living dead / Ambition / Fear of girls / Lie down and die / Sensitive boys / Ice age / I Robot / Flesh wound / I don't need your love / Motivator / Combat zone / Fascist regime
CD _______________ DOJOCD 117
Dojo / Apr '93 / Disc

FLOOD OF LIES/SINGLES 1982-85
CD _______________ FALLCD 18
Fallout / '95 / RTM/Disc

GREATEST HITS LIVE
Emotional blackmail / Endangered species / Fear of girls / New York State Police / Rock 'n' roll savage / Does she suck / Organised crime / Bic / You don't belong / Confrontation street / Barbie's dead / Keep on running / Warhead / Police state / Teen-age / Telephone numbers / I couldn't be you / I live in a car / Party in Paris / Crash course / Blues / Killer / Rat race / Young criminals / Left for dead / Rockers / Be-tween the eyes / SK8 Tough / CID / To-morrow's girls / Stranglehold / New barbarians
CD _______________ DOJOCD 130
Dojo / Jun '93 / Disc

GROSS OUT USA
CD _______________ FALLCD 031
Fallout / '95 / RTM/Disc

HUNTINGTON BEACH
CD _______________ REVXD 150
FM / May '90 / Revolver / Sony

IN ACTION (10 YEARS)
CD _______________ REVXD 142
FM / Mar '90 / Revolver / Sony

JAPAN TODAY
CD _______________ FALLCD 045
Fallout / Mar '93 / RTM/Disc

KILLING TIME
CD _______________ FALLCD 047
Fallout / Mar '89 / RTM/Disc

LEFT FOR DEAD, ALIVE IN HOLLYWOOD
CD _______________ RE 412CD
ROIR / Nov '94 / Plastic Head / Shellshock/Disc

LIVE AT THE ROXY
CD _______________ RRCD 146
Receiver / Jul '93 / Grapevine/PolyGram

MAD COW FEVER
CD _______________ FALLCD 048
Fallout / Jan '91 / RTM/Disc

NORMAL SERVICE RESUMED
CD _______________ FALLCD 050
Fallout / Jun '93 / RTM/Disc

OCCUPIED
CD _______________ FALLCD 052
Fallout / Apr '96 / RTM/Disc

PEEL SESSIONS, THE (1978-1979)
CD _______________ FALLCD 53
Fallout / Mar '97 / RTM/Disc

PUNK CAN TAKE IT VOL.1
CD _______________ CLP 97032
Cleopatra / Jul '96 / Cargo / Greyhound / Plastic Head / RTM/Disc / SRD

PUNK CAN TAKE IT VOL.2 (Self Destruct 1982-1988)
CD _______________ CLP 9826
Cleopatra / Oct '96 / Cargo / Greyhound / Plastic Head / RTM/Disc / SRD

PUNK IS BACK, THE
Organised crime / Bomb factory / Dirty girls / Waiting for the man / Rat race / Teenage / Warhead / Sensitive boys / CID / Tomor-row's girls / Left for dead / She's not here / Kicks / I don't need your love / Limo life / Cocaine
CD _______________ CD 430002
Voiceprint / Apr '95 / Pinnacle

PUNK SINGLES COLLECTION, THE
CID / Stranglehold / Tomorrows girls / She's not there / Warhead / Teenage / Party in Paris / Keep on running / Countdown / Self destruct / Another typical city / Private army / Gun says / Motivator / Sabre dance / Hey Santa / Here comes Alex / Barmy London army / Freaked / New barbarians / Limo life
CD _______________ CDPUNK 66
Anagram / Aug '95 / Cargo / Pinnacle

QUINTESSENTIALS
CD _______________ FALLCD 054
Fallout / Apr '97 / RTM/Disc

RIOT
Cyberjack / Rebel radio / Power corrupts / Preacher / Riot / Chemical war / Paradise burning / House of cards / Human rights / Guilty man / Lost not found / Music for the deaf / Beggars and bums / My little red book / Flat earth society
CD _______________ CDMGRAM 113
Anagram / Jun '97 / Cargo / Pinnacle

SCUM OF THE EARTH
CD _______________ MCCD 120
Music Club / Aug '93 / Disc / THE

SINGLES 1978-1982, THE
CD _______________ GBR 001
Get Back / Apr '93 / Cargo / Pinnacle

UK SUBS BOX SET (4CD Set)
CD Set _______________ SUBBOX 1
Abstract / Nov '96 / Cargo / Pinnacle / Total/BMG

Ukamau

FOLKLORE DE BOLIVIA
CD _______________ EUCD 1023
ARC / '91 / ADA / ARC Music

MUSICA DE BOLIVIA
CD _______________ EUCD 1207
ARC / Sep '93 / ADA / ARC Music

Ukrainians

KULTURA
Polityka / Ukrain America / Kievskiy express / Smert / Horilka / Slava / Europa / Kinets / Tycha voda / Zillya zeleneke / Ya / Tsyhan-ochka / Dyakuyu i dobranich
CD _______________ COOKCD 070
Cooking Vinyl / Sep '94 / Vital

VORONY
Vorony / Chlib / Koroleva Ne Pomerla / Chi skriptsi hrayu / Sche Raz / Nadia Pishla / Doroha / Rospryahaite / Durak / Sertsem I dusheyu / Dvi Lebidky / De ye moya mila / Teper mi hovorymo / Chekannya (Venus in furs)
CD _______________ COOKCD 054
Cooking Vinyl / Feb '95 / Vital

Ulan Bator

ULAN BATOR VOL.2
CD _______________ DSA 54043
CDSA / Dec '96 / Harmonia Mundi / ReR Megacorp

Ullman, Tracey

BOBBY'S GIRL (The Very Best Of Tracey Ullman)
CD _______________ 12374
Laserlight / Sep '94 / Target/BMG

HIT SINGLE COLLECTABLES
CD _______________ DISK 4513
Disky / Apr '94 / Disky / THE

VERY BEST OF TRACY ULLMAN, THE
CD _______________ STIFFCD 19
Disky / Jan '94 / Disky / THE

YOU CAUGHT ME OUT
You caught me out / Little by little / Bad motorcycle / Loving you is easy / Sun-glasses / Helpless / If I had you / Where the boys are / I know what boys like / Give him a great big kiss / Baby I lied
CD _______________ STIFFCD 08
Disky / Jan '94 / Disky / THE

Ullmann, Gebhard

BASEMENT RESEARCH
CD _______________ 1212712
Soul Note / Apr '95 / Cadillac / Harmonia Mundi / Wellard

Ulloa, Francisco

MERENGUE
La tijera / Agua de tu fuente / La situacion / El beso robao / Tongoneate / Ramonita /

Manana por la manana / Los caballos / Linda Mujer / Lucas y radhames / La lengua / San Francisco / Homenaje a bolo
CD CDORB 020
Globestyle / Jul '90 / Pinnacle

Ullulators

FLAMING KHAOS
CD DMCD 1021
Demi-Monde / Feb '92 / RTM/Disc / TKO Magnum

Ulman Brothers

ACOUSTIC POWER
CD LZ 2122
RUM / Aug '96 / ADA

Ulmer, James 'Blood'

BLACK AND BLUES
CD DIW 845
DIW / Jul '91 / Cadillac / Harmonia Mundi

HARMOLODIC GUITAR WITH STRINGS
CD DIW 878
DIW / Feb '94 / Cadillac / Harmonia Mundi

LIVE AT THE BAYERISCHER
Burning up / Church / Crying / Let me take you home / Boss lady / Street bride / Timeless / Make it right
CD IOR 770182
In & Out / May '95 / Vital/SAM

MUSIC SPEAKS LOUDER THAN WORDS (James 'Blood' Ulmer Plays The Music Of Ornette Coleman)
CD DIW 910
DIW / Dec '96 / Cadillac / Harmonia Mundi

MUSIC SPEAKS LOUDER THAN WORDS
CD CD 378332
Koch Jazz / Jul '97 / Koch

ODYSSEY
Church / Little red house / Love dance / Are you glad to be in America / Election / Odyssey / Please tell her / Swing and things
CD 4851012
Sony Jazz / Sep '96 / Sony

Ulterior Motive Orchestra

SPY TIME
CD TCD 1033
Tradition / Nov '96 / ADA / Vital

Ultimate Concern

SHIELD BETWEEN
CD NLB 002CD
No Looking Back / Mar '96 / Plastic Head

Ultimate Kaos

ULTIMATE KAOS
Intro (Age ain't nuthin' but a number) / Hoochie booty / Some girls / This heart belongs to you / Skip to my Lou / Misdemeanour / Show a little love / Weekend girl / Cool out alley / Believe in us / Age ain't nuthin' but a number / Uptown / Falling in love / Right here
CD 5274442
Wild Card / May '95 / PolyGram

Ultimate Spinach

BEHOLD AND SEE
Behold and see / Mind flowers / Where you're at / What you're thinking of / Fragmentary march of green / Genesis of beauty suite / Fifth horseman of the apocalypse
CD CDWIKD 148
Big Beat / Oct '95 / Pinnacle

ULTIMATE SPINACH
Ego trip / Sacfifice of the moon (In four parts) / Plastic raincoats / Hung up minds / (Ballad of the) Hip death goddess / Your head is reeling / Dove in Hawk's clothing / Baarogue no.1 / Funny freak parade / Pamela
CD CDWIKD 142
Big Beat / Apr '95 / Pinnacle

ULTIMATE SPINACH VOL.3
(Just like) Romeo and Juliet / Some days you just can't win / Daisy / Reasons / Eddie's rush / Happiness, child / Strange life tragicomedy / Back door blues / World has just begun
CD CDWIKD 165
Big Beat / Jun '96 / Pinnacle

Ultranate

BLUE NOTES IN THE BASEMENT (Basement Boys)
Blue notes / Sands of time / Is it love / Deeper love (missing you) / You and me together / It's over now / Scandal / Rejoicing / Rain / Love hungover / It's my world / Funny (how things change)
CD 9031747042
WEA / Jun '91 / Warner Music

ONE WOMAN'S INSANITY
How long / You're not the only one / Show me / I'm not afraid / Incredibly you / Joy / I specialize in loneliness / One woman's insanity / Feelin' fine / Love is a many splendoured thing
CD 9362453302
WEA / Oct '93 / Warner Music

Ultravivid Scene

JOY 1967-1990
It happens every time / Three stars / Grey turns white / Guilty pleasure / Beauty No. 2 / Praise the low / Staring at the sun / Special one / Poison / Extraordinary / Kindest cut / Lightning
CD CAD CD 0005
4AD / Apr '90 / RTM/Disc

ULTRA VIVID SCENE
She screamed / Crash / You didn't say please / Lynne-Marie 2 / Nausea / Mercy seat / Dream of love / Lynne-Marie / This isn't real / Whore of God / Bloodline / How did it feel / Hail Mary
CD CAD 809CD
4AD / Oct '88 / RTM/Disc

Ultrabide

GOD IS GOD, PUKE IS PUKE
CD K 162C
Konkurrel / Nov '95 / SRD

Ultrahead

DEFINITION AGGRO
CD CDVEST 40
Bulletproof / Feb '95 / Pinnacle

Ultrahigh

VIEW OF ULTRAHIGH
CD FIM 1015
Force Inc. / Mar '95 / Amato Disco / Arabesque / SRD

Ultramarine

BEL AIR
CD 0630112062
Blanco Y Negro / Dec '96 / Warner Music

EVERY MAN AND WOMAN IS A STAR
CD R 2892
Rough Trade / Jun '92 / Pinnacle

FOLK
CD OSHCD 1
Offshore / Jan '95 / RTM/Disc

UNITED KINGDOMS
Source / Kingdom / Queen of the moon / Prince Rock / Happy land / Urf / English heritage / Instant kitten / Badger / Hooter / Dizzy fox / No time
CD 4509934252
Blanco Y Negro / Dec '96 / Warner Music

Ultramarine

DE
Djanea / U song / Dub it / Ivory coast / De / Bod kan'nal / Modakofa
CD 500052
Musidisc / Mar '90 / Discovery

E SI MALA
CD 500242
Musidisc / Nov '93 / Discovery

Ultras

COMPLETE HANDBOOK OF SONGWRITING
CD TX 92792
Roadrunner / Sep '91 / PolyGram

Ultrasonic

GLOBAL TEKNO (2CD Set)
1,2,3,4 / Out of control / Hey Mr. DJ / Make that move / 180 mph / Tic tok / Total break up / Let the muzik set you free / Dreamer of dreams / In the air tonight / There is no back-up / Do you believe in love / Joyriderz / We want one more / Star spangled tekno / Party people in the house / DJ ragga / US vs. bass baby pt. 2 / Annihilating rhythm pt. 2 / Check your head / Make that move / Tekno junkies in the mix
CD Set DCSR 007
Clubscene / Oct '95 / Clubscene / Grapevine/PolyGram / Mo's Music Machine / Prime

LIVE AT CLUB KINETIC
CD DCSR 010
Clubscene / Sep '96 / Clubscene / Grapevine/PolyGram / Mo's Music Machine / Prime

TECHNO JUNKIES 1992-94
CD DCSR 002
Clubscene / Sep '94 / Clubscene / Grapevine/PolyGram / Mo's Music Machine / Prime

Ultravibe

TRAVELS THROUGH THE ULTRAVIBE SPECTRUM
CD REVCC 008
Revco / Jul '96 / Grapevine/PolyGram / Timewarp

Ultraviolence

LIFE OF DESTRUCTOR
I am destructor / Electric chair / Joan / Hardcore motherfucker / Digital killing / Only love / We will break / Hiroshima / Destructor's fall / Death of a child
CD MOSH 103CD
Earache / Jun '94 / Vital

PSYCHODRAMA
Birth - Jessica / Reject / Disco boyfriend / Pimp / Psychodrama / Birth hitman / Stone faced / Murder academy / Hitman's heart / Contract / Lovers / Suicide pact / God's mistake / Searching hell / Heaven is oblivion
CD MOSH 142CD
Earache / Sep '97 / Vital

Ultravox

COLLECTION, THE
Dancing with tears in my eyes / Hymn / Thin wall / Voice / Vienna / Passing strangers / Sleepwalk / Reap the wild wind / All stood still / Visions in blue / We came to dance / One small day / Love's great adventure / Lament
CD CCD 1490
Chrysalis / Mar '85 / EMI

DANCING WITH TEARS IN MY EYES
Sleepwalk / Waiting / Passing strangers / Vienna / Passionate reply / Voice / Hymn / Monument / We came to dance / Dancing with tears in my eyes / Reap the wild wind / Love's great adventure / White china / All fall down / Dreams / All in one day
CD CDGOLD 1078
Music For Pleasure / Feb '97 / EMI

HA HA HA
Rock work / Frozen ones / Fear in the western world / Distant smile / Man who dies everyday / Artificial life / While I'm still alive / Hiroshima mon amour
CD IMCD 147
Island / Jul '92 / PolyGram

INGENUITY
Ingenuity / There goes a beautiful world / Give it all back / Future picture forever / Silent cries / Distance / Ideals / Who'll save you / Way out-a way through / Majestic
CD RES 109CD
Resurgence / Apr '97 / Pinnacle

MONUMENT
Monument / Reap the wild wind / Voice / Vienna / Mine for life / Hymn / Passing strangers / Visions in blue
CD CDGOLD 1025
EMI Gold / Jul '96 / EMI

RAGE IN EDEN
Voice / We stand alone / I remember death in the afternoon / Thin wall / Stranger within / Accent on youth / Ascent / Rage in Eden / Your name has slipped my mind again
CD CDGOLD 1097
EMI Gold / Jun '97 / EMI

RARE VOL.1
Waiting / Face to face / King's lead hat (live) / Passionate reply / Herr X / Alles klar / Keep talking / I never wanted to begin / Paths and angles / Private lives (live) / All stood still / Hosanna (in Excelsis deo) / Monument / Thin wall / Break your back / Reap the wild wind (live) / Overlook
CD CDCHR 6053
Chrysalis / Nov '93 / EMI

RARE VOL.2
Easterly / Building / Heart of the country / White china / Man of two worlds / Three / All in one day / Dreams / All fall down (Instrumental) / All fall down (Live) / Dream on (Live) / Prize (Live) / Stateless / One small day (Final mix)
CD CDCHR 6078
Chrysalis / Aug '94 / EMI

THREE INTO ONE
Young savage / Rock work / Dangerous rhythm / Man who dies everyday / Wild, the beautiful and the damned / Slow motion / Just for a moment / Quiet men / My sex / Hiroshima mon amour
CD IMCD 30
Island / '89 / PolyGram

ULTRAVOX
Ultravox / Saturday night in the city of the dead / Life at rainbow's end / Slip away / I want to be a machine / Wide boy / Dangerous rhythm / Lonely hunter / Wild, the beautiful and the damned / My sex
CD IMCD 146
Island / Jul '92 / PolyGram

ULTRAVOX/HA HA HA/SYSTEMS OF ROMANCE (3CD Set)
Saturday night in the city of the dead / Life at the rainbow's end / Slip away / I want to be a machine / Wide boys / Dangerous rhythm / Lonely hunter / Wild, the beautiful and the damned / My sex / Rockwrok / Frozen ones / Fear in the Western world / Distant smile / Man who dies everyday / Artificial life / While I'm still alive / Hiroshima mon amour / Slow motion / Can't stay long / Someone else's clothes / Blue light / Some of them / Quiet men / Dislocation / Maximum acceleration / When you walk through me / Just for a moment
CD Set 5241522
Island / Nov '95 / PolyGram

VIENNA
Astradyne / New Europeans / Private lives / Passing strangers / Mr. X / Sleepwalk / Western promise / Vienna / All stood still
CD CCD 1296
Chrysalis / Jul '94 / EMI

Ulver

BERGTATT
CD HNF 005CD
Head Not Found / Aug '95 / Plastic Head

KVELDSSANGER
CD HNF 014CD
Head Not Found / Feb '96 / Plastic Head

MADRIGAL OF RIGHT, THE
CD CM 77158CD
Century Media / Mar '97 / Plastic Head

Umba, Mac

DON'T HOLD YOUR BREATH
CD CDTRAX 113
Greentrax / May '96 / ADA / Direct / Duncans / Highlander

Umbra Et Imago

GEDANKEN EINES VAMPIRES
CD DW 075CD
Deathwish / Jan '96 / Plastic Head

MYSTICA SEXUALS
CD SONO 195CD
Spirit Production / Apr '97 / Plastic Head

Umbrella Heaven

DO YOU HATE ME
CD BWL 017
Boogle Wonderland / Sep '95 / SRD

Umezu, Kazutoki

ECLECTICISM
CD KFWCD 130
Knitting Factory / Feb '95 / Cargo / Plastic Head

UMO

UNIDENTICAL MUSICAL OBJECT
CD HE 013
Home Entertainment / Dec '96 / Cargo

Unaminated

GOD OF EVIL
CD NFR 009CD
No Fashion / Mar '95 / Plastic Head

IN THE FOREST OF THE DREAMING DEAD
CD NFR 004
No Fashion / Oct '94 / Plastic Head

Unbroken

LIFE LOVE REGRET
CD NA 022CD
New Age / Jul '96 / Plastic Head

RITUAL
CD NA 016CD
New Age / Jul '96 / Plastic Head

Uncanny

SPLENIUM NYKTOPHBIA
CD USR 008CD
Unisound / Nov '95 / Plastic Head

Uncle Festive

PAPER AND THE DOG, THE
Paper and the dog / Road to Kent / Jessica / Boy King / Fantastic then / Super / Green village / Sunday thoughts / All rise / Up and down (and speedin' all over) / Not for nothin'
CD R2791692
Bluemoon / Nov '91 / New Note/Pinnacle

Uncle Fish & The Cry

DUSSELDORF PHILIPSHALLE 7.12.91
CD DDICK 17CD
Dick Bros. / Sep '96 / Pinnacle

Uncle Sam

FOURTEEN WOMEN
CD CMGCD 010
Communique / Nov '93 / Plastic Head

HEAVEN OR HOLLYWOOD
Live for the day / Don't be shy / Alice D / No reason why / Candy man / Don't you ever / All alone / Peace of mind, piece of body / Under sedation / Heaven or Hollywood / Steppin stone / Train kept a rollin'
CD 3MC3
Skeller / Nov '90 / Pinnacle

Uncle Slam

WHEN GOD DIES
When God dies / My mother's son / Procreation / Smoke 'em if you got 'em / Offering to a daity / Age of agression / End of the line / Lightless sky / Summer in space / Bombs away

CD 727732
Restless / Jan '95 / Vital

Uncle Tupelo

ANODYNE
Slate / Acuff-Rose / Long cut / Give back the key to my heart / Chickamauga / New Madrid / Anodyne / We've been had / Fifteen keys / High water / No sense in lovin' / Steal the crumbs
CD 9362454242
WEA / Oct '93 / Warner Music

MARCH 16-20 1992
Grindstone / Coalminers / Wait up / Criminals / Shaky ground / Satan your kingdom must come down / Black eye / Moonshiner / I wish my baby was born / Atomic power / Lilli Schull / Warfare / Fatal wound / Sandusky / Wipe the clock
CD ROCK 6090CD
Rockville / Apr '97 / Plastic Head / SRD

NO DEPRESSION
CD ROCK 6050CD
Rockville / Apr '97 / Plastic Head / SRD

STILL FEEL GONE
Gun / Looking For A Way Out / Fall Down Easy / Nothing / Still Be Around / Watch me fall / Punch Drunk / D Boon / True To Life / Cold shoulder / Discarded / If that's alright
CD BUFF 001CD
Yellow Moon / May '93 / Vital
CD ROCK 6070CD
Rockville / May '97 / Plastic Head / SRD

Uncle Walt's Band

AMERICAN IN TEXAS REVISITED, AN
CD SHCD 1034/5
Sugar Hill / Jan '97 / ADA / CM / Direct / Koch / Roots

GIRL ON THE SUNNY SHORE, THE
CD SHCD 1032/3
Sugar Hill / Jan '97 / ADA / CM / Direct / Koch / Roots

Uncle Wiggly

JUMP BACK, BABY
Ded / Plentitude / Imbeciles / Rat's rabbits / Godfrey's cordial / Sweetheart / Francis / Purple threat / Yr hed / Arm / Head grows / Tone scrifter / Spuzzy / Mandible Jackson / Mary's crayons / Skeeny
CD TB 1852
Teenbeat / Mar '96 / Cargo / SRD / Vital

Uncurbed

MENTAL DISORDER
CD LF 094CD
Lost & Found / Jan '95 / Plastic Head

NIGHTMARE IN DAYLIGHT, A
CD FINNREC 010CD
Finn / Jun '96 / Cadillac / Plastic Head

STRIKE OF MANKIND
CD LF 061CD
Lost & Found / Aug '93 / Plastic Head

STRIKE OF MANKIND/MENTAL DISORDER
CD LF 237CD
Lost & Found / Sep '96 / Plastic Head

Under The Church

SPACE INVADERS
CD NLR 010CD
New Life / Apr '97 / Cargo

Under The Noise

OF GENERATION AND CORRUPTION
CD SPV 08434242
SPV / Apr '96 / Koch / Plastic Head

REGENERATION
CD COPCD 024
Cop International / Nov '96 / Cargo

Under The Sun

UNDER THE SUN
CD MABEL 2
Vinyl Tap / Jan '96 / Cargo / Greyhound / Vinyl Tap

Underbelly

EVERYONE LOVES YOU WHEN YOU'RE DEAD
CD SEVE 003CD
7 / Jul '95 / Pinnacle / Warner Music

MUMBLY PEG
CD OUT 1142
Brake Out / Nov '94 / Direct

Undercover

CHECK OUT THE GROOVE
CD HFCD 26
PWL / Nov '92 / Warner Music

Underdog

ATTIC TAPES (2CD Set)
Space cakes / Nose bleed / Dungeon beats / SOTA / Ugbug / Darkside / Green haze / Junk funk / Davro's wheel / Untitled / Mighty shadow / Nite moves / Break O'dawn / Doppleganger / Third kind / Angel heart / Hardcore rhymer / After hours / Vulcan gas / Strange daze / Close to the edge / Speak of the devil / Sound of the crowd / Lunatic beats / Stamp stamp / From beyond / B-boy moonstomp / Whuzzat / Live from / Brain damage
CD Set BITECD 15
Bite It / Mar '97 / RTM/Disc

Underground Lovers

LEAVES ME BLIND
CD GUCD 2
Guernica / Oct '92 / Pinnacle

Underground Resistance

X-101
CD EFA 01727CD
Tresor / Oct '96 / 3mv/BMG / Prime / SRD

Undernation

ANGER
CD OUT 1112
Brake Out / Nov '94 / Direct

SOMETHING ON THE TV
CD OUTCD 106
Brake Out / Sep '91 / Direct

Undertakers

UNEARTHED
(Do the) Mashed potatoes / Everybody loves a lover / Money (that's what I want) / What about us / Just a little bit / Stupidity / If you don't come back back / Think / Be my little girl / She said yeah / I need your lovin' / Tell me what you're gonna do / Tricky Dicky / Irresistable you / Love is a swingin' thing / Hey hey hey hey / You're so fine and sweet / Leave my kitten alone / Watch your step / Throw your love away girl / I fell in love (for the very first time)
CD CDWIKD 163
Big Beat / Feb '96 / Pinnacle

Undertones

CHER O'BOWLIES (Pick Of The Undertones)
Teenage kicks / True confessions / Get over you / Family entertainment / Jimmy Jimmy / Here comes the summer / You got my number (why don't you use it) / My perfect cousin / See that girl / Tearproof / Wednesday week / It's going to happen / Julie Ocean / You're welcome / Forever paradise / Beautiful friend / Save me / Love parade / Valentine's treatment / Love before romance
CD CDFA 3226
Fame / Oct '89 / EMI

HYPNOTISED
More songs about chocolate and girls / There goes Norman / Hypnotised / See that girl / Whizz kids / Under the boardwalk / Way girls talk / Hard luck / My perfect cousin / Boys will be boys / Tearproof / Wednesday week / Nine times out of ten / Girls that don't talk / What's with Terry / You've got my number (Why don't you use it) / Hard luck (Again) / Let's talk about girls / I told you so / I don't wanna see you again
CD ESMCD 486
Essential / Mar '97 / BMG

POSITIVE TOUCH
Fascination / Julie Ocean / Life's too easy / Crises of mine / You're welcome / His good looking girlfriend / Positive touch / When Saturday comes / It's going to happen / Sign and explode / I don't know / Hannah Doot / Boy wonder / Forever paradise
CD DOJOCD 193
Dojo / May '94 / Disc

POSITIVE TOUCH
Fascination / Julie Ocean / Life's too easy / Crisis of mine / You're welcome / Good-looking girlfriend / Fairly in the money now / Beautiful friend / Kiss in the dark / Forever paradise / Boy wonder / Hannah Doot / I don't know / Sigh and explode / It's going to happen / When Saturday comes / Positive touch
CD ESMCD 485
Essential / Mar '97 / BMG

SIN OF PRIDE, THE
Got to have you back / Untouchable / Valentine's treatment / Love before romance / Luxury / Bye bye baby blue / Love parade / Soul seven / Conscious / Chain of love / Save me / Sin of pride
CD DOJOCD 194
Dojo / May '94 / Disc

SIN OF PRIDE, THE
Got to have you back / Valentine's treatment / Luxury / Love before romance / Untouchable / Bye bye baby blue / Conscious / Chain of love / Soul seven / Love parade / Save me / Sin of pride / Bittersweet / You stand so close (But you're never there) / Turning blue / Like that / I can only dream / Window shopping for new clothes
CD ESMCD 487
Essential / Mar '97 / BMG

TEENAGE KICKS (The Best Of The Undertones)
Teenage kicks / Get over you / Male model / Jimmy Jimmy / Mars bar / My perfect cousin / Tearproof / Hypnotised / Positive touch / It's going to happen / When Saturday comes / Love parade / Casbah rock / Family entertainment / Girls don't like it / Here comes the summer / You've got my number / Let's talk about girls / Way girls talk / More songs about chocolate and girls / Wednesday week / You're welcome / Julie Ocean / Forever paradise / Soul seven
CD CCSCD 808
Renaissance Collector Series / Jan '97 / BMG

UNDERTONES
Family entertainment / Girls don't like it / Male model / I gotta getta / Teenage kicks / Wrong way / Jump boys / Here comes the summer / Get over you / Billy's third / Jimmy Jimmy / True confessions / (She's a) Runaround / I know a girl / Listening in / Casbah rock / Smarter than U / Emergency cases / Top twenty / Really really / Mars bars / She can only say no / One way love
CD ESMCD 484
Essential / Mar '97 / BMG

Undertow

EDGE OF QUARREL
CD LF 152CD
Lost & Found / May '95 / Plastic Head

Underworld

DUBNOBASSWITHMYHEADMAN
CD JBOCD 1
Junior Boys Own / May '97 / Mo's Music Machine / RTM/Disc

PEARL'S GIRL
Pearl's girl / Puppies / Oich oich / Cherry pie / Mosaic / Deep arch
CD TVT 87482
TVT / Jan '97 / Cargo / Greyhound

SECOND TOUGHEST IN THE INFANTS (2CD Set)
Juanita / Kiteless / To dream of love / Banstyle/Sappys curry / Confusion the waitress / Rowla / Pearl's girl / Air towel / Blueski / Stagger
CD Set U2 CDB
Logic / Dec '96 / Cargo
CD JBOCD 4
Junior Boys Own / May '97 / Mo's Music Machine / RTM/Disc

Undish

ACTA EST FABULA
CD MASSCD 126
Massacre / Jun '97 / Plastic Head

Undivided Roots

BEST OF UNDIVIDED ROOTS, THE
CD NTMCD 547
Nectar / Jun '97 / Pinnacle

UNDIVIDED ROOTS
Party Nite / Duke of Earl / Never get away / Mystic man / Mad about you / Stranger to my eyes / Someone to love / Rock dis ya music / To love again / Nature of love
CD CIDM 1042
Mango / Jul '90 / PolyGram / Vital

Unfolding

HOW TO BLOW YOUR MIND...
CD 3197
Head / Jun '97 / Greyhound

Ungod

CIRCLE OF THE 7 INFERNAL PACTS
CD MRCD 001
Merciless / Oct '94 / Plastic Head

Unholy

SECOND RING OF POWER, THE
CD CDAV 005
Avant / Aug '94 / Cadillac / Harmonia Mundi

Uniform Choice

STARING AT THE SUN
CD LF 176CD
Lost & Found / Jul '95 / Plastic Head

STRAIGHT AND ALERT
CD LF 175CD
Lost & Found / Jul '95 / Plastic Head

Union

UNION, THE
CD GROW 0422
Grass / Feb '95 / Pinnacle / SRD

Union 13

EAST LOS PRESENTS UNION 13
Who are you / Regrets / Fuck society / Bonded as one / Todo es una politica / Burocrata Estafador / Children's story / Falling down / Country full of lies / I can't stand it anymore / Govierno podrido / Realidad / Over the hill / Government / State of consciousness / Un muro por cruzar / Ronald's fuckhouse / Final approach
CD 64942
Scooch Pooch / Jul '97 / Cargo / Greyhound / Pinnacle

Union Avenue

UNION AVENUE
I shot the sheriff / Other side / Bad moon rising / Ace of spades / Big river
CD RAUCD 029
Raucous / May '97 / Nervous / RTM/Disc / TKO Magnum

Union Jack

THERE WILL BE NO ARMAGEDDON
CD PLAT 15CD
Platipus / Jul '95 / Prime / SRD

Uniques

BEST OF THE UNIQUES 1967-1969, THE
CD CDTRL 340
Trojan / Jun '94 / Direct / Jet Star

Unit 4+2

CONCRETE AND CLAY
CD 8442962
London / Jan '93 / PolyGram

Unit Moebius

LIFE MOOD PARTS 1-8/REMIXES
CD SIRE 001
Silver Recordings / Jul '96 / SRD

STATUS
CD KKCD 150
KK / May '96 / Plastic Head

Unit Pride

CAN I KILL A DREAM
CD LF 158CD
Lost & Found / Jun '95 / Plastic Head

United

NO IQ
CD 398414107CD
Metal Blade / Mar '96 / Pinnacle / Plastic Head

United Future Organisation

NO SOUND IT TOO TABOO
Mistress of the dance / Stolen moments / Sunday folk tale / Future light / Make it better / Magic wand of love / Bar f out / Doopsylalolic / Tears of gratitude / United future airlines
CD 5222712
Talkin' Loud / Sep '94 / PolyGram

SOUNDTRACK, THE
CD APR 003CD
April / May '95 / Plastic Head / Shellshock/Disc

United States Of Existence

COLLECTION, THE
CD 0005
US Fidelit / Jul '97 / Greyhound

Unitone Hi-Fi

BOOMSHOT
CD INCCD 3314
Incoming / Apr '97 / Pinnacle

REWOUND & RERUBBED
CD INCCD 3308
Incoming / Jun '96 / Pinnacle

Unitone Rockers

MAGIC PLANET
CD BFRCD 010
Beat Farm / Apr '93 / Total/BMG

Unity

BLOOD DAYS
CD LF 103CD
Lost & Found / Aug '94 / Plastic Head

Universal Being

ARCHIVES, THE
CD HOLCD 28
Holistic / Jun '97 / Kudos / Pinnacle / Plastic Head / Prime

HOLISTIC RHYTHMS
CD HOLCD 23
Holistic / Jan '96 / Kudos / Pinnacle / Plastic Head / Prime

JUPITER
CD HOLCD 025
Holistic / Jul '96 / Kudos / Pinnacle / Plastic Head / Prime

Universal Congress Of

ELEVENTH HOUR SHINE ON
CD EMY 1362
Enemy / Nov '92 / Grapevine/PolyGram

MECOLODICS
CD ____ **SST 204CD**
SST / May '93 / Plastic Head

SAD & TRAGIC DEMISE OF THE BIG FINE HOT SALTY BLACK WIND
CD ____ **EMY 1172**
Enemy / Nov '94 / Grapevine/PolyGram

Universal Indicator

COMPILATION VOL.1-4
CD ____ **MKS 80**
Rephlex / May '94 / Prime / RTM/Disc

Universal Order Of ...

UNIVERSAL ORDER OF ARMAGEDDON (Universal Order Of Armageddon)
CD ____ **KRS 224CD**
Kill Rock Stars / Sep '96 / Cargo / Greyhound / Plastic Head

University Of Wisconsin Band

UNIVERSITY OF WISCONSIN/EAU CLAIRE SYMPHONY BAND
CD ____ **SOSCD 1284**
Stomp Off / Dec '94 / Jazz Music / Wellard

Unknown Factor

GLOBAL FACTOR
CD ____ **DFDCD 008**
Defender / Apr '97 / Essential/BMG / Prime / SRD

Unleashed

ACROSS THE OPEN SEA
CD ____ **CM 770552**
Century Media / Nov '93 / Plastic Head

EASTERN BLOOD
CD ____ **CM 771182**
Century Media / Nov '96 / Plastic Head

LIVE IN VIENNA
CD ____ **CM 770562**
Century Media / Jan '94 / Plastic Head

VICTORY
CD ____ **CM 770902**
Century Media / May '95 / Plastic Head

WARRIOR
CD ____ **CM 77124CD**
Century Media / Jun '97 / Plastic Head

WHERE NO LIFE DWELLS
CD ____ **CM 97182**
Century Media / '92 / Plastic Head

Unleashed Power

QUINTET OF SPHERES
CD ____ **RS 101**
SORT / Nov '93 / Plastic Head

Unlimited Dream Company

VOLTAGE
Up in dub heaven / Shore gardens / As one door closes / Potion takes effect / If I should step / Feel like I'm falling / Scenic root / Sandoz by moonlight / No headaches
CD ____ **CDTOT 24**
Jumpin' & Pumpin' / Apr '95 / 3mv/Sony / Mo's Music Machine

Unlimited Sound Orchestra

CHRISTMAS IN AMERICA
CD ____ **I 3885762**
Galaxy / Dec '96 / ZYX

UNLV

NO LONGER VIRGINS
CD ____ **WRA 8119CD**
Wrap / Feb '94 / Koch

Unorthodox

ASYLUM
CD ____ **HELL 0021CD**
Hellhound / '90 / Koch

BALANCE OF POWER
CD ____ **HELL 0030CD**
Hellhound / Apr '94 / Koch

Unpure

UNPURE
CD ____ **NPR 011CD**
Napalm / Jun '95 / RTM/Disc

Unrest

BPM 1991-1994
June / Cath Carroll / When it all / So so sick / Hydrofoil / Winina XY / Winona XX / Folklore / Imperial / Cherry, Cherry / Hey London / Bavarain mods / Vibe out / Hi-tec theme / Wednesday and proud
CD ____ **TB 1752**
Teenbeat / Aug '95 / Cargo / SRD / Vital

FUCK PUSSY GALORE (AND ALL HER FRIENDS)
So you want to be a rock 'n' roll star / Scott and Zelda / Hill / Happy song / Rigor mortis / Can't sit still / Cats / Die grunen / Holiday in Berlin / 91st Century schizoid man / Hil, part 2 / Picnic at Hanging Rock / Live on a hot August night / Chastity ballad / Judy says / Tundra / Wild thang / Laughter / S Street shuffle (with a beat) / Over the life / Hope / Communist tart / She makes me free to be me / Sammy's mean mustard / Greg Hershey where are you / Egg cheer
CD ____ **OLE 0242**
Matador / Jan '94 / Vital

IMPERIAL
CD ____ **GU 1CD**
Guernica / Aug '92 / Pinnacle

PERFECT TEETH
CD ____ **CAD 3012CD**
4AD / Jun '93 / RTM/Disc

Unsane

AMREP CHRISTMAS
CD ____ **MR 069CD**
Man's Ruin / Jul '97 / Cargo / Greyhound / Plastic Head

ATTACK IN JAPAN
CD ____ **SPV 08545912**
SPV / Mar '97 / Koch / Plastic Head

SCATTERED, SMOTHERED AND COVERED
CD ____ **SPV 08445782**
SPV / Dec '95 / Koch / Plastic Head

SINGLES 1989-1992, THE
CD ____ **EFA 049132**
City Slang / Nov '92 / RTM/Disc

TOTAL DESTRUCTION
CD ____ **EFA 049262**
City Slang / Jan '94 / RTM/Disc

Unsophisticates

GUIDO
Riverbank / Maxi's dead / So long, Glasgow / Blow up / Pervert / Ain't got no life / Straitjacket / Almost normal / Ghost of tess renaudo / Israeli relations / Lie / Growth / Is it safe
CD ____ **SCANCD 23**
Passion / May '97 / 3mv/Pinnacle

Untamed Youth

PLANET MACE
CD ____ **ES 1223CD**
Estrus / Jul '97 / Cargo / Greyhound / Plastic Head

Untouchables

AGENT DOUBLE O SOUL
Agent double o soul / Stripped to the bone / World gone crazy / Cold city / Education / Let's get together / Airplay / Under the boardwalk / Sudden attack / Shama lama ding dong
CD ____ **723422**
Restless / Feb '95 / Vital

DECADE OF DANCE (Live)
CD ____ **725072**
Restless / Feb '95 / Vital

Unun

SUPER SHINY
CD ____ **BAD 001CD**
Bad Taste / Feb '96 / Plastic Head

UNV

SOMETHING'S GOIN ON
UNV thang / When will I know / Who will it be / Close tonight / Gonna give U what U want / Something's goin' on / 2 B or not 2 B / Straight from my heart / Hold on / No one compares to you
CD ____ **93624528742**
WEA / Nov '93 / Warner Music

UNIVERSAL NUBIAN VOICES
CD ____ **9362458392**
WEA / Jul '95 / Warner Music

Unwound

FUTURE OF WHAT
CD ____ **KRS 245CD**
Kill Rock Stars / Jul '95 / Cargo / Greyhound / Plastic Head

NEW PLASTIC IDEAS
Entirely different / Matters / What was wound / Envelope / Fiction friction / Abstraktions / Arboretum / Usual dosage / All souls day / Hexenszene
CD ____ **KRS 223CD**
Kill Rock Stars / Mar '94 / Cargo / Greyhound / Plastic Head

Up & Running

NOT FOR SALE
Why do you kick her while she's down / Is this the start / This one is for you / Boom / Silent but deadly / Baby, baby, babe / Thunder / No more tears / Gangland / Absolute fool / Don't set me up / Red man blues
CD ____ **PCOM 1142**
President / Oct '95 / Grapevine/PolyGram / President / Target/BMG

Up Bustle & Out

LIGHT 'EM UP, BLOW 'EM OUT
Clandestine operation / Emerald alley / Rain in Tibet / Silks, perfume and gold / Beautiful lure / Apple strudle / Compared to what / Y ahora tu / Radio Madrid / Dance of Caravan summer / Lazy daze / Hearty do-lallies / Coca conga / Coffee at Senor Rudi's / Illusion / Party with the Raj
CD ____ **ZENCD 027**
Ninja Tune / Jun '97 / Kudos / Pinnacle / Prime / Vital

ONE COLOUR JUST REFLECTS ANOTHER
Aqui no ma / Revolutionary woman of the windmill, part 1 / Running rude / Bicycles, flutes and you / 1,2,3, Alto y fuera / African friendship / Twelve penny apples / Three drunk musicians / Poncho cafe / Hand of contraband / Mr. Pavement man / Ninja's principality / Unmarked grave / Discoursing drums / Street of Huangayo, Peru
CD ____ **ZENCD 019**
Ninja Tune / Apr '96 / Kudos / Pinnacle / Prime / Vital

Up Front

PSALMS
CD ____ **RASCD 3093**
Ras / Oct '92 / Direct / Greensleeves / Jet Star / SRD

Up Organisation

(SHOW IT TO ME) FREE
(Show it to me) Free
CD ____ **EXP 3**
Essential / Jul '96 / Essential/BMG

Upchurch, Phil

ALL I WANT
Poison / When we need it bad / 12/25 / 516 / Grace / What will I do / All I want from you / U god it gowin on
CD ____ **ICH 1127CD**
Ichiban / Jan '94 / Direct / Koch

LOVE IS STRANGE (Upchurch, Phil & Chaka Khan)
CD ____ **GOJ 60142**
Go Jazz / Sep '95 / Vital/SAM

WHATEVER HAPPENED TO THE BLUES
CD ____ **GOJ 60062**
Go Jazz / Sep '95 / Vital/SAM

Upfront

SPIRIT
CD ____ **LF 087CD**
Lost & Found / Jun '94 / Plastic Head

Upper Crust

LET THEM EAT ROCK
CD ____ **UPSTART 026**
Upstart / Oct '95 / ADA / Direct

Uppsala Big Band

IN PROGRESS
CD ____ **SITCD 9206**
Sittel / Jun '94 / Cadillac / Jazz Music

RADIO UPPLAND BIG BAND 93
CD ____ **SITCD 9207**
Sittel / Jun '94 / Cadillac / Jazz Music

Upright Citizens

COLOUR YOUR LIFE
CD ____ **IRC 037**
Impact / Mar '97 / Cargo

Upsetters

UPSETTERS AND THE STUDENT
CD ____ **RN 7008**
Rhino / Sep '96 / Grapevine/PolyGram / Jet Star

Upsidedown Cross

EVILUTION
CD ____ **TAANG 70CD**
Taang / Jun '93 / Cargo

Uptighty

UPTIGHTY
CD ____ **MUDCD 003**
Mud/Parasol / Feb '97 / Cargo

Uralsky All Stars

RUSSIAN ROULETTE
Mishka, mishka / South Rampart Street parade / C'est si bon / Cabaret / Fine flowers in the spring garden / I've been dreaming of you for three years / My blue heaven / Katusha / Midnight in Moscow / Stenjka razin / Ah, Odessa / Mjasoedowskaya uliza
CD ____ **CDTTD 597**
Timeless Jazz / Sep '95 / New Note/ Pinnacle

WE'LL MEET AGAIN
Song of the Volga boatmen / Back home again in Indiana / Dream a little dream of me / Nobody's sweetheart / Just a gigolo / I ain't got nobody / Night train / Amapola / Night and day / Struttin' with some barbecue / Meet me tonight in dreamland / We'll meet again
CD ____ **CDTTD 595**
Timeless Jazz / Sep '96 / New Note/ Pinnacle

Urban Cookie Collective

HIGH ON A HAPPY VIBE
CD ____ **PULSE 13CD**
Pulse 8 / Mar '94 / BMG

Urban Dance Squad

LIFE N' PERSPECTIVES OF A GENUINE CROSSOVER
Come back / Gates of the big fruit / Life 'n' perspectives / Mr. Ezway / Thru the eyes of Jason / Routine / Son of the culture clash / Careless / Grand black citizen / Harvey quinnt / Duck ska / For the plasters / Wino the medicineman / Bureaucrat of Flaccostreet
CD ____ **261 994**
Arista / Oct '91 / BMG

PERSONA NON GRATA
Demagogue / Good grief / No honestly / Alienated / Candy strip exp / Self sufficient snake / (Some) Chit chat / Burnt up cigarette / Self styled / Mugshot / Hangout / Downer
CD ____ **CDHUT 19**
Hut / Jun '94 / EMI

PLANET ULTRA
Nonstarter / Temporarily expendable / Forgery / Planet Ultra / Dresscode / Totalled / Warzone 109 / Metaphore warfare / Ego / Carbon copy / Everyday blitzkrieg / Inside-outsider / Stark sharks & backlashes / Pass the baton right / Damn the quota / Grifter swifter / Tabloid say / Natural born communicator
CD ____ **CDVIR 53**
Virgin / Sep '96 / EMI

Urban Knights

URBAN KNIGHTS
On the radio / Wanna be with you / Chill / Hearts of longing / Friendship / Miracle / Rose / Urban samba / Forever more / Senegal
CD ____ **GRP 98152**
GRP / May '95 / New Note/BMG

URBAN KNIGHTS VOL.2
Scirroco / Get up / Come dance with me / South African jam / Brazilian rain / Interlude / Summer nights / Tell me why / Urban paradise / Drama / Step by step / Promise / Interlude / Dawn
CD ____ **GRP 98622**
GRP / Mar '97 / New Note/BMG

Urban Sax

SPIRAL
CD ____ **FCD 1125**
EPM / Jul '91 / ADA / Discovery

URBAN SAX
CD ____ **FDC 1124**
EPM / Jul '91 / ADA / Discovery

Urban Turban

URBAN TURBAN
CD ____ **SRS 4722CD**
Silence / Dec '94 / ADA / Direct

Urban Waste

URBAN WASTE
CD ____ **LF 062**
Lost & Found / Jan '94 / Plastic Head

Urbanator

URBANATOR VOL.2
Urbanate the area II / Basia / New Yorker / Magic / Urbal tea / Moody's mood for love / Anytime anywhere / Mantra / Hi ho silver / Polak
CD ____ **HIBD 8012**
Hip Bop / Oct '96 / Koch / Silva Screen

Urbani, Massimo

BLESSING, THE
CD ____ **1232572**
Red / Nov '93 / ADA / Cadillac / Harmonia Mundi

Urbaniak, Michal

FRIDAY NIGHT AT THE VILLAGE VANGUARD
CD ____ **STCD 4093**
Storyville / Feb '89 / Cadillac / Jazz Music / Wellard

TAKE GOOD CARE OF MY HEART
CD ____ **SCCD 31195**
Steeplechase / Jul '88 / Discovery / Impetus

Ure, Midge

BREATHE
Breathe / Fields of fire / Fallen angel / Free / Guns & arrows / Lay my body down / Sin-

nerman / Live forever / Trail of tears / May your good Lord / Maker
CD _____ 74321346292
Arista / May '96 / BMG

GIFT, THE
If I was / When the winds blow / Living in the past / That certain smile / Gift / Antilles / Wastelands / Edo / Chieftain / She cried / Mood music / Piano / Man who sold the world / Gift (Instrumental)
CD _____ CDGOLD 1045
EMI Gold / Jul '96 / EMI

IF I WAS (The Very Best Of Midge Ure & Ultravox)
If I was / No regrets / Love's great adventure / Dear God / Cold cold heart / Vienna / Call of the wild / Dancing with tears in my eyes / All fall down / Yellow pearl / Fade to grey / Reap the wild wind / Answers to nothing / Do they know it's Christmas
CD _____ CDCHR 1987
Chrysalis / Feb '93 / EMI

IF I WAS
If I was / That certain smile / When the winds blow / Living in the past / Wastelands / Antilles / Gift / Answers to nothing / Remembrance day / Sister and brother / Hell to heaven / Take me home / Homeland / Edo
CD _____ DC 868792
Disky / Mar '97 / Disky / THE

Urge

RECEIVED THE GIFT OF FLAVOR
Brainless / All washed up / Where do we go / Drunk asshole / Don't ask why / Open all night / Take away / Frying pan / I remember / Damn that shit is good / It's gettin' hectic / Violent opposition / Dirty rat
CD _____ 4866742
Epic / Feb '97 / Sony

Urge Overkill

10 YEARS OF WRECKING (2CD Set)
CD Set _____ 86132RAD
Edel / Jul '95 / Pinnacle

AMERICRUISER
CD _____ TGCD 52
Touch & Go / Nov '94 / SRD

EXIT THE DRAGON
Jaywalkin' / Break / Need some air / Somebody else's body / Honesty files / This is no place / Mistake / Take me / View of the rain / Last night / Tomorrow / Tin foil / Monopoly / You'll say / Digital black epilogue
CD _____ GED 24818
Geffen / Aug '95 / BMG

SATURATION
Sister Havana / Tequila sundae / Positive bleeding / Back on me / Woman 2 woman / Bottle of fur / Crackbabies / Stalker / Dropout / Erica Kane / Nite and grey / Heaven 90210
CD _____ GED 24529
Geffen / Jun '93 / BMG

STULL
CD _____ NTMCD 522
Nectar / Aug '96 / Pinnacle

SUPERSONIC STORYBOOK
CD _____ TG 70CD
Touch & Go / Nov '94 / SRD

Uriah Heep

ABOMINOG (Remastered)
Too scared to run / Chasing shadows / On the rebound / Hot night in a cold town / Ruuning all night (with the lion) / That's the way that it is / Prisoner / Hot persuasion / Sell your soul / Think it over / Tin soldier / Son of a bitch / That's the way that it is / Chasing shadows
CD _____ ESMCD 571
Essential / Aug '97 / BMG

BEST OF URIAH HEEP VOL.1, THE
Gypsy / Bird of prey / Lady in black / Salisbury / July morning / Look at yourself / Easy livin' / Wizard / Sweet Lorraine / Stealin' / Suicidal man / Return to fantasy / Misty eyes / Easy livin' / Stealin'
CD _____ ESMCD 418
Essential / Oct '96 / BMG

COLLECTION, THE
Love machine / Look at yourself / Firefly / Return to fantasy / Rainbow demon / That's the way it is / Love is blind / On the rebound / Easy livin' / July morning / Running all night (with the lion) / Been away too long / Gypsy / Wake up (set your sights) / Can't keep a good band down / All of my life
CD _____ CCSCD 226
Castle / Jul '89 / BMG

CONQUEST (Remastered)
No return / Imagination / Feelings / Fools / Carry on / Won't have to wait too long / Out on the street / It ain't easy / Been hurt / Love stealer / Think it over / My Joanna needs tuning / Lying
CD _____ ESMCD 570
Essential / Aug '97 / BMG

DEMONS AND WIZARDS
Wizard / Traveller in time / Easy livin' / Poet's justice / Circle of hands / Rainbow demon / All my life / Paradise / Spell / Why / Home again to you
CD _____ ESMCD 319
Essential / Jan '96 / BMG

DIFFERENT WORLD
Blood on stone / Which way will the wind blow / All god's children / All for one / Different world / Step by step / Seven days / First touch / One in one / Cross that line / Stand back
CD _____ CLACD 279
Castle / Feb '93 / BMG

DREAM ON (2CD Set)
CD Set _____ CDHTD 102
HTD / Oct '95 / CM / Pinnacle

FALLEN ANGEL (Remastered)
One more night / Falling in love / Woman of the night / I'm alive / Come back to me / Whad'ya say / Save it / Love or nothing / Put your lovin' on me / Fallen angel / Cheater / Gimme love / Right to live / Been hurt
CD _____ ESMCD 561
Essential / Jul '97 / BMG

FIREFLY (Remastered)
Hanging tree / Been away too long / Who needs me / Wise man / Do you know / Rollin' on / Sympathy / firefly / Crime of passion / Do you know / Far better way / Wise man
CD _____ ESMCD 559
Essential / Jul '97 / BMG

FREE ME
Wizard / Something or nothing / On the rebound / I'm so tired / Been away too long / One way or another / Return to fantasy / Free me / Woman of the world / Love or nothing / That's the way that it is / Wise man / Prima donna / Dreams
CD _____ 5507312
Spectrum / Mar '95 / PolyGram

HEAD FIRST (Remastered)
Other side of midnight / Stay on top / Lonely nights / Sweet talk / Love is blind / Roll-overture / Red lights / Rollin' the rock / Straight through the heart / Weekend warriors / Playing for time / Searching / Wizard
CD _____ ESMCD 572
Essential / Aug '97 / BMG

HIGH AND MIGHTY
One way or another / Weep in silence / Misty eyes / Midnight / Can't keep a good band down / Woman of the world / Footprints in the snow / Can't stop singing / Make a little love / Confession / Name of the game / Sundown
CD _____ ESMCD 468
Essential / Jan '97 / BMG

INNOCENT VICTIM
Keep on ridin' / Flyin' high / Roller / Free 'n' easy / Illusion / Free me / Cheat and lie / Dance / Choices / Illusion/Masquerade / River
CD _____ ESMCD 560
Essential / Jul '97 / BMG

LADY IN BLACK
Lady in black / Easy livin' / Gypsy / Spider man / Sympathy / Carry on / Think it over / Traveller in time / Shady lady / Lonely nights / Fallen angel / Come back to me / Love stealer / Stay on top
CD _____ 5507302
Spectrum / Jan '95 / PolyGram

LANSDOWNE TAPES
Born in a trunk / Simon the bullet freak / Here I am / Magic lantern / Why / Astranaz / What's within my heart / What should be done / Lucy blues / I want you babe / Celebrate / Schoolgirl / Born in a trunk (instrumental) / Look at yourself
CD _____ RMCCD 0193
Red Steel / Jun '96 / Pinnacle

LIVE AT SHEPPERTON '74 (Remastered)
Easy livin' / So tired / I won't mind / Sweet freedom / Something or nothing / Easy road / Stealin' / Love machine / Rock 'n' roll medley / Easy road/Sleazy/Easy livin'
CD _____ ESMCD 590
Essential / Aug '97 / BMG

LIVE IN EUROPE,1979
Easy livin' / Look at yourself / Lady in black / Free me / Stealin' / Wizard / July morning / Falling in love / Woman of the night / I'm alive / Who needs me / Sweet Lorraine / Free'n'easy / Gypsy
CD _____ RAWCD 030
Raw Power / Mar '87 / Pinnacle

LIVE IN MOSCOW (Cam B Mockbe)
Bird of prey / Stealin' / Too scared to run / Corinna / Mr. Majestic / Wizard / July morning / Easy livin' / That's the way that it is / Pacific highway
CD _____ CLACD 276
Castle / '92 / BMG

LOOK AT YOURSELF
Look at yourself / I wanna be free / July morning / Tears in my eyes / Shadows of grief / What should be done / Love machine / Look at yourself / What's within my heart
CD _____ ESMCD 318
Essential / Jan '96 / BMG

MAGICIAN'S BIRTHDAY, THE
Sunrise / Spider woman / Blind eye / Echoes in the dark / Rain / Sweet Lorraine / Tales / Magician's birthday / Silver white man / Crystal ball
CD _____ ESMCD 339
Essential / Jan '96 / BMG

RAGING SILENCE
Hold your head up woman / Blood red roses / Voice on my TV / Rich kids / Cry freedom / Bad bad man / More fool you / When the war is over / Lifeline
CD _____ CLACD 277
Castle / Feb '93 / BMG

RARITIES FROM THE BRONZE AGE
CD _____ NEXCD 184
Sequel / Feb '92 / BMG

RETURN TO FANTASY
Return to fantasy / Shady lady / Devil's daughter / Beautiful dream / Prima donna / Your turn to remember / Showdown / Why did you go / Year or a day
CD _____ ESMCD 381
Essential / May '96 / BMG

SALISBURY
Bird of prey / Park / Time to live / Lady in black / High priestess / Salisbury / Simon the bullet freak / High priestess (single edit)
CD _____ ESMCD 317
Essential / Jan '96 / BMG

SEA OF LIGHT
CD _____ HTCD 33
HTD / Mar '95 / CM / Pinnacle
CD _____ SPV 08576952
SPV / Dec '96 / Koch / Plastic Head

SPELLBINDER LIVE
CD _____ CD 08576992
SPV / Jul '96 / Koch / Plastic Head

STILL 'EAVY, STILL PROUD
Gypsy / Lady in black / July morning / Easy livin' / Easy road / Free me / Other side of midnight / Mr. Majestic / Rich kid / Blood red roses
CD _____ CLACD 278
Castle / '93 / BMG

SWEET FREEDOM
Dreamer / Stealin' / One day / Sweet freedom / If I had the time / Seven stars / Circus / Pilgrim / Sunshine / Stealin' / Seven stars
CD _____ ESMCD 338
Essential / Jan '96 / BMG

TIME OF REVELATION, A (2CD Set)
CD Set _____ ESFCD 298
Essential / May '96 / BMG

URIAH HEEP IN CONCERT
CD _____ 880272
King Biscuit / Jun '97 / Greyhound

URIAH HEEP LIVE 1973
Sunrise / Sweet Lorraine / Traveller in time / Easy livin' / July morning / Tears in my eyes / Gypsy / Circle of hands / Look at yourself / Magician's birthday / Love machine / Rock 'n' roll medley
CD _____ ESMCD 320
Essential / Jun '96 / BMG

URIAH HEEP STORY, THE
CD _____ ROHACD 2
EMI / Feb '90 / EMI

VERY 'EAVY, VERY 'UMBLE
Gypsy / Walking in your shadow / Come away Melinda / Lucy blues / Dreammare / Real turned on / I'll keep on trying / Wake up (set your sights) / Gypsy / Come away Melinda / Born in a trunk
CD _____ ESMCD 316
Essential / Jan '96 / BMG

WONDERWORLD
Wonderworld / Suicidal man / Shadows and the wind / So tired / Easy road / Something or nothing / I won't mind / We got we / Dreams
CD _____ ESMCD 380
Essential / May '96 / BMG

Uriel

UNDER COMPULSION
Jazz funk conspiracy / Roof top sniper / Pimp strikes back / Under compulsion / Lazy days / Precinct 25 / On the run / Flight to Sao Paulo / Planet Samba / Jeune amour
CD _____ BMCD 001
Beau Monde / Jun '97 / Kudos / Pinnacle / Vital

Urlich, Margaret

CHAMELEON DREAMS
CD _____ TIMBCD 604
Timbuktu / Aug '95 / Pinnacle

Urusei Yatsura

WE ARE URUSEI YATSURA
CD _____ CHE 54CD
Che / Apr '97 / SRD

US 3

HAND ON THE TORCH
Cantaloop (Flip fantasia) / I got it goin' on / Different rhythms, different people / It's like that / Just another brother / Cruisin' / I go to work / Tukka yoot's riddim / Knowledge of self / Lazy day / Eleven long years / Make tracks / Dark side
CD _____ CDEST 2230
Capitol / Sep '97 / EMI

US Bombs

PUT STRENGTH IN FINAL...
CD _____ DIS 1
Disaster / Jun '97 / Greyhound

US Maple

LONG HAIR IN 3 STAGES
CD _____ GR 33CD
Skingraft / Nov '95 / SRD

SANG PHAT EDITOR
CD _____ GR 44CD
Skingraft / Jun '97 / SRD

US Saucer

HELL, YES
CD _____ ACM 606
Amarillo / Jun '97 / Greyhound

UNITED STATES SAUCER
Famous dogs / Fade / Devotional Sam / Ramblin' man / Size it up / Sweet chariot / God OD / Cindy / Tres mellow / Les Mardis Gras / Run shroud run / Born free / I'll always love you
CD _____ RTS 22
Return To Sender / Oct '96 / ADA / Direct

USA All Stars

IN BERLIN FEBRUARY 1955
CD _____ EBCD 21132
Flyright / Feb '94 / Hot Shot / Jazz Music / Wellard

Used Carlotta

WASTED WORDS
CD _____ HYMN 5
Fundamental / Aug '97 / Cargo / Plastic Head / Shellshock/Disc

Usher, Raymond

USHER
I'll make it right / Can you get wit it / Think of you / Crazy / Slow love / Many ways / I'll show you love / Love was here / Whispers / You took my heart / Smile again / Final goobye / Interlude / Interlude 2 (Can't stop)
CD _____ 73008260082
Arista / Oct '94 / BMG

Usherhouse

FLUX
CD _____ CLEO 94612
Cleopatra / Apr '94 / Cargo / Greyhound / Plastic Head / RTM/Disc / SRD

MOLTING
CD _____ SATE 05
Talitha / Aug '93 / Plastic Head

Usurper

THRESHOLD OF THE USURPER
CD _____ NR 6667CD
Necropolis / May '97 / Plastic Head

Ut

IN GUT'S HOUSE
CD _____ BFFP 17CD
Blast First / RTM/Disc

Utah Saints

UTAH SAINTS
New Gold Dream / What can you do for me / Soulution / Believe in me / Too much to swallow part 1 / What can you do for me / Something good / I want you / States of mind / Trance atlantic glide / Kinetic synthetic / My mind must be free
CD _____ 8283792
FFRR / Jun '93 / PolyGram

UTE

FREE TO BE...FREE TO BREATHE
CD _____ 33JAZZ 009CD
33 Jazz / Jun '93 / Cadillac / New Note/ Pinnacle

Uthanda

GROOVE
Be my friend / Sweet soul salvation / Found out the hard way / Look away / Change in my world / Don't let me be misunderstood / To be loved / You groove / Mercy mercy / Way you are / Red September
CD _____ CD 08794
Broken / Jan '92 / Broken

Uttal, Jai

BEGGARS AND SAINTS
Lake of exploits / Hara shiva shankara / Be with you / Gopala / Rama bolo / Radhe radhe / Menoka / Beggars and saints / Lake of exploits pt.2 / Conductor / Coda
CD _____ 3202082
Triloka / Nov '94 / New Note/Pinnacle

FOOTPRINTS
Footprints / Caranan / Andobar Island / Raghupati / Madzoub / Pahari / Snowview

/ Taking the dust / Raghupati II / Bus has come
CD 3201832
Triloka / Jun '92 / New Note/Pinnacle

MONKEY
CD 3201942
Triloka / Sep '92 / New Note/Pinnacle

UVX

DOUBLE HELIX
CD EYECDLP 7
Magick Eye / Aug '94 / Cargo / SRD

RAYS
CD MEYCD 11
Magick Eye / Apr '96 / Cargo / SRD

UX

ULTIMATE EXPERIENCE
Ux part 1 / Life support technology / Chameleon / Outer reaches / Escape / Alien life activity / Pure intellect / Master of the universe / Nebula / Ux part 2
CD BFLCD 22
Dragonfly / Mar '97 / Mo's Music Machine / Pinnacle

Uys, Tessa

PIANO MUSIC
CD URCD 107
Upbeat / Nov '92 / Cadillac / Target/BMG

Uz Jsme Doma

IN THE MIDDLE OF WORDS
CD MAM 29
Indies / Jun '97 / ReR Megacorp

Uzeb

ENTRE CIEL ET TERRE
Apres les confidences / 4 P M Gate 26 / Good bye pork pie hat / Spacy country / Perrier citron / Home / Blue in green / Luna mars / Son song / Bella's lullaby / Entre ciel et terre
CD JMS 186842
Cream / Jul '96 / New Note/Pinnacle

LIVE IN EUROPE
Time Square / Mile O / 4 p.m., gate 26 / Le baiser sale / 60 Rue Des Lombards / New Funk / Slinky / La ballade bleue / Bull's nostril blues
CD JMS 186282
JMS / May '95 / New Note/BMG

Uzect Plaush

MORE BEAUTIFUL HUMAN LIFE
Violet cell edit / Wind from nowhere / Wetzone rapture / Falling dream / Auto-radia / Boiling horizon / Discrete global / Sky rolled back
CD AMB 4932CD
Apollo / Apr '94 / Vital

UZI

SLEEP ASYLUM
CD PILLMCD 4
Placebo / Feb '94 / RTM/Disc

Uzzell Edwards, Charles

OCTOPUS
CD PS 0879CD
Fax / Nov '95 / Plastic Head

V

V

SOME MOVING, SOME STOOD STILL
CD ______ **GIFTCD 1**
4AD / May '95 / RTM/Disc

V-Roys

JUST ADD ICE
Guess I know I'm right / No regrets / Pounding heart / Sooner or later / Wind down / Goodnight looser / Cry / What's she found / Lie I believe / Around you / Kick me around / Cold beer hello
CD ______ **TRACD 240**
Transatlantic / Aug '96 / Pinnacle

V2

V2 (Anthology)
CD ______ **OVER 55CD**
Overground / Aug '96 / Shellshock/Disc / SRD

V3

PHOTOGRAPH BURNS
American face / Bristol girl / Harry / Horsekick / Photograph burns / Caucasian white / Adam twelve / Torch / End of the bar / Star artist / Split dog / Hating me hating you / Super human
CD ______ **74321312642**
American / Mar '96 / BMG

Vache, Allan

ALLAN VACHE & HIS FLORIDA JAZZ ALLSTARS (Vache, Allan Florida Jazz Allstars)
CD ______ **NHCD 032**
Nagel Heyer / Mar '97 / Jazz Music

ATLANTA JAZZ PARTY
CD ______ **ACD 270**
Audiophile / Apr '93 / Jazz Music

JAZZ IN AMERIKA HAUS VOL.3 (Vache, Allan Quintet)
CD ______ **CD 013**
Nagel Heyer / May '96 / Jazz Music

ONE FOR MY BABY (Vache, Allan Quintet)
CD ______ **ACD 255**
Audiophile / '91 / Jazz Music

SWING AND OTHER THINGS (Vache, Allan Sextette)
CD ______ **ARCD 19171**
Arbors Jazz / May '97 / Cadillac

Vache, Warren Jr.

EASY GOING (Vache, Warren Sextet)
Little girl / Easy going bounce / Warm valley / You'd be so nice to come home to / Michelle / It's been so long / Was I to blame for falling in love with you / London by night / Mandy, make up your mind / Moon song (That wasn't meant for me)
CD ______ **CCD 4323**
Concord Jazz / Jul '87 / New Note/Pinnacle

FIRST TIME OUT
CD ______ **ACD 196**
Audiophile / Jan '94 / Jazz Music

LIVE AT THE VINEYARD THEATRE (Vache, Warren Trio)
CD ______ **CHR 70028**
Challenge / Sep '96 / ADA / Direct / Jazz Music / Wellard

PLAY HARRY WARREN (Vache, Warren Jr. & Brian Lemon)
CD ______ **ZECD 8**
Zephyr / May '96 / Cadillac / Jazz Music / New Note/Pinnacle

WARREN VACHE & DEREK WATKINS/ BRIAN LEMON QUARTET (Vache, Warren Jr. & Derek Watkins/Brian Lemon)
CD ______ **ZECD 9**
Zephyr / May '96 / Cadillac / Jazz Music / New Note/Pinnacle

WARREN VACHE AND THE BEAUX-ARTS STRING QUARTET (Vache, Warren & The Beaux-Arts String Quartet)
CD ______ **CCD 4392**
Concord Jazz / '89 / New Note/Pinnacle

Vache, Warren Sr.

JAZZ IN AMERIKA HAUS VOL.2 (Vache, Warren Quintet)
CD ______ **CD 012**
Nagel Heyer / May '96 / Jazz Music

WARREN VACHE & SYNCOPATIN' 7
CD ______ **CCD 57**
Circle / Apr '94 / Jazz Music / Swift / Wellard

Vada

VADA
CD ______ **MASS 64CD**
Mass Productions / Jul '95 / ADA

Vader

DE PROFUNDIS
CD ______ **IRC 067CD**
Impax / Jul '96 / Plastic Head

FUTURE OF THE PAST
Merciless death / Dethroned emperor / Death metal / Outbreak of evil / Storm of stress / Flag of hate / Deadness / IFY / We are the league / Black Sabbath / Silent scream
CD ______ **SPV 08453862**
SPV / Mar '97 / Koch / Plastic Head

SOTHIS
CD ______ **RPS 013CD**
Repulse / May '96 / Plastic Head

ULTIMATE INCANTATION
CD ______ **MOSH 059CD**
Earache / Nov '92 / Vital

Vagtazo Halottkemek

HAMMERING AT THE DOOR OF NOTHINGNESS
CD ______ **VIRUS 110CD**
Alternative Tentacles / Mar '92 / Cargo / Greyhound / Pinnacle

JUMPING OUT OF THE WORLD
CD ______ **VIRUS 92CD**
Alternative Tentacles / '92 / Cargo / Greyhound / Pinnacle

Vai, Steve

ALIEN LOVE SECRETS
Mad horsie / Juice / Die to live / Boy from Seattle / Ya yo gakk / Kill the guy with the ball / Good eaters / Tender surrender
CD ______ **4785862**
Relativity / Apr '95 / Sony

FIRE GARDEN
There's a fire in the house / Crying machine / Dyin' day / Whookam / Blowfish / Mysterious murder of Christian Tiera's lover / Hand on heart / Bangkok / Fire garden suite / Deepness / Little Alligator / All about Eve / Aching hunger / Brother / Damn you / When I was a little boy / Genocide / Warm regards
CD ______ **4850622**
Relativity / Sep '96 / Sony

FLEX-ABLE
Little green men / Viv woman / Lovers are carzy / Salamanders in the sun / Boy/girl song / Attitude song / Call it sleep / Junkie / Bill's private parts / Next stop Earth / There's something dead in here / So happy / Bledsoe Blvd / Burnin' down the mountain / Chronic insomnia
CD ______ **4878712**
Epic / Jun '97 / Sony

PASSION AND WARFARE
Liberty / Erotic nightmares / Animal / Answers / Riddle / Ballerina 12/24 / For the love of God / Audience is listening / I would love to / Blue powder / Greasy kids stuff / Alien water kiss / Sisters / Love secrets
CD ______ **4671092**
Relativity / Oct '93 / Sony

SEX AND RELIGION
Earth dweller's return / Here and now / In my dreams with you / Still my bleeding heart / Sex and religion / Dirty black hole / Touching tongues / State of grace / Survive / Pig / Road to Mt Calvary / Deep down into the pain / Rescue me or bury me
CD ______ **4739472**
Relativity / Jul '93 / Sony

Vaiana, Pierre

SHAKRA
CD ______ **CELPC 23**
CELP / Sep '93 / Cadillac / Harmonia Mundi

Vain

FADE
CD ______ **REVXD 216**
Revolver / Aug '97 / Revolver / Sony

MOVE ON IT
Breakdown / Whisper / Long time ago / Ivy's dream / Hit and run / Family / Planets turning / Get up / Crumpled glory / Resurrection / Ticket outta here
CD ______ **HMRXD 194**
Heavy Metal / Sep '94 / Revolver / Sony

Val, Joe

DIAMOND JOE
CD ______ **ROUCD 11537**
Rounder / Nov '95 / ADA / CM / Direct

LIVE IN HOLLAND (Val, Joe & New England Bluegrass Boys)
All the good times are past and gone / Lonesome river / Blue moon of Kentucky / Molly and tenbrooks / Satan's jewelled crown / Prisoner's song / Teardrops in my eyes / Ocean of diamonds / Swing low, sweet chariot / Corey is gone / Rose of old Kentucky / Sunny side of the mountain / No Mother or Dad / Don't give your heart to a rambler / Going back to old Kentucky
CD ______ **SCR 29**
Strictly Country / Feb '97 / ADA / Direct

ONE MORNING IN MAY (Val, Joe & New England Bluegrass Boys)
CD ______ **ROUCD 0003**
Rounder / Jun '96 / ADA / CM / Direct

Valance, Ricky

TELL LAURA I LOVE HER
Tell Laura I love her / Once upon a time / Movin' away / Lipstick on your lips / Jimmy's girl / Only the young / Say hello (to a new love) / Why can't we / Fisher boy / Bobby / I want to fall in love / I never had a chance / It's not true / Try to forget her / At times like these / Don't play no.9 / Til the final curtain falls / Six boys / Face in the crowd / My Summer love: *Merryweather, Jason* / Abigail: *Merryweather, Jason*
CD ______ **GEMCD 006**
Diamond / Jan '97 / Pinnacle

Valdes, Bebo

BEDO RIDES AGAIN
CD ______ **MES 158342**
Messidor / Jul '95 / ADA / Koch

DESCARGA CALIENTE (Valdes, Bebo Orchestra)
CD ______ **CCD 512**
Caney / Jul '96 / ADA / Discovery

SABOR DE CUBA (Valdes, Bebo Orchestra)
CD ______ **CCD 509**
Caney / Jul '96 / ADA / Discovery

Valdes, Carlos

MASTERPIECE
CD ______ **MES 158272**
Messidor / Dec '93 / ADA / Koch

Valdes, Chucho

GRANDES MOMENTOS
CD ______ **74321327242**
Milan / May '96 / Conifer/BMG / Silva Screen

LUCUMI
CD ______ **MES 158762**
Messidor / Apr '93 / ADA / Koch

Valdes, Merceditas

TUMI CUBA CLASSICS VOL.2 (Afro Cuban)
CD ______ **TUMICD 050**
Tumi / Aug '95 / Discovery / Stern's

Valdes, Miguelito

HAVANA 1938-1940
CD ______ **HQCD 81**
Harlequin / Apr '97 / Hot Shot / Jazz Music / Swift / Wellard

Valdespi, Armando

EN NUEVA YORK 1935
CD ______ **TCD 073**
Tumbao Cuban Classics / Jul '96 / Discovery

EN NUEVA YORK 1935 VOL.2 (Valdespi, Armando Orchestra)
CD ______ **TCD 077**
Tumbao Cuban Classics / Jan '97 / Discovery

Valens, Ritchie

BEST OF RITCHIE VALENS
Come on let's go / La bamba / Donna / Bluebirds over the mountain / Fast freight / Cry cry cry / That's my little Suzie / Stay beside me / Big baby blues / Little girl / Hurry up / Bony Moronie / We belong together / Malaguena / Framed / In a turkish town / Dooby dooby wah / Ooh my head
CD ______ **CDCHM 387**
Ace / Mar '92 / Pinnacle

LOST TAPES, THE
We belong together / Blues with drum / Ritchie's blues / Come on let's go / In a turkish town / Dooby dooby wah / Bluebirds over the mountain / That's my little Suzie / Let's rock 'n' roll / Donna / Blues instrumental / Cry cry cry / Malaguena / Blues - slow / Stay beside me / Rhythm song / Guitar instrumental / Rock lil darlin' / La bamba / Ooh my head
CD ______ **CDCHD 317**
Ace / May '92 / Pinnacle

RICHIE VALENS STORY, THE
CD ______ **DFCD 71011**
Del-Fi / Jan '97 / Cargo / Koch

RITCHIE VALENS STORY, THE
Bony Moronie / Come on let's go / That's my little Suzie / Rock little Darlin' / Bluebirds over the mountain / La bamba / Let's rock 'n' roll / Donna / Summertime blues / In a Turkish town / Paddiwack song / Big baby blues / Malaguena / Stay beside me
CD ______ **CDCHD 499**
Ace / Jan '94 / Pinnacle

RITCHIE VALENS/RITCHIE
That's my little Suzie / In a Turkish town / Come on let's go / Donna / Bony Moronie / Ooh my head / La Bamba / Bluebirds over the mountain / Hi-tone / Framed / We belong together / Dooby dooby wah / Stay beside me / Cry cry cry / Big baby blues / Paddiwack song / My darling is gone / Hurry up / Little girl / Now you're gone / Fast freight / Ritchie's blues / Rockin' all night
CD ______ **CDCHD 953**
Ace / Oct '90 / Pinnacle

Valente, Caterina

INTERNATIONAL, THE
Guardando Il cielo / Zeeman / Koini tsukarete / Adam et eve / el bardo / Hava nagila / Nessuno mai / Tintarella di luna / Es mi amor / Tra-la-la-la / Das weisse hchzeitskleid / Diz me em setemro / Mijn souvenir / Leccion de twist / Weil die sehnsucht so gross war / Don Quixote / Dindi / Hana / Morgen wird's schoner sein / Me importas tu / Caro mio / Dammi retta / Oyedo nihonbashi / Una lagrima del yuo dolore / Parlezmoi d'amour / Napule ca se sceta / Ein stern ging verloren / Scandinavian folk song
CD ______ **BCD 15604**
Bear Family / Oct '91 / Direct / Rollercoaster / Swift

ONE AND ONLY, THE
Ola, ola, ola / Un p'tit beguine / Tornera / Das kommt vom kussen / Bruxeria / Adios Panama / Habame no Utah / Amo solo te / When in Rome / Und dann kam der Mondenschein / O Erotas pou makousse / Broadway conga / La otra cara / Kumono nagareni / Twist a Napoli / Zuviel tequila / Dia de fiesta / I Melenia I yiftopoula / Amor prohibido / Kom lat ons dansen / Im Kabarett der illusionen / Una sera di Tokyo / Cua cua cua / Israeli lullaby
CD ______ **BCD 15601**
Bear Family / Oct '90 / Direct / Rollercoaster / Swift

Valentine 6

VALENTINE 6
CD ______ **EFA 043912**
Crippled Dick Hot Wax / Jul '97 / SRD

Valentine Brothers

MONEY'S TOO TIGHT TO MENTION
CD ______ **TKOCD 016**
TKO / '92 / TKO

Valentine Saloon

SUPER DUPER
CD ______ **PIPECD 001**
Pipeline / Mar '93 / Pinnacle

Valentine, 'Kid' Thomas

DANCE HALL YEARS
CD ______ **AMCD 48**
American Music / Jan '94 / Jazz Music

KID THOMAS
CD ______ **AMCD 010**
American Music / Oct '93 / Jazz Music

KID THOMAS & HIS DIXIELAND BAND 1960
CD ______ **504CD 33**
504 / Feb '95 / Cadillac / Jazz Music / Target/BMG / Wellard

KID THOMAS AT THE MOOSE HALL
CD ______ **BCD 305**
GHB / Oct '93 / Jazz Music

KID THOMAS IN CALIFORNIA
CD ______ **BCD 296**
GHB / Jan '94 / Jazz Music

KID THOMAS' DIXIELAND BAND 1957
CD ______ 504CD 37
504 / Nov '96 / Cadillac / Jazz Music / Target/BMG / Wellard

KID THOMAS/EMANUEL PAUL/BARRY MARTYN BAND
CD ______ BCD 257
GHB / Mar '95 / Jazz Music

NEW ORLEANS TRADITIONAL JAZZ LEGENDS
CD ______ MG 9004
Mardi Gras / Feb '95 / Jazz Music

SONNETS FROM ALGIERS
CD ______ AMCD 53
American Music / Jul '96 / Jazz Music

TRUMPET KING
CD ______ MG 9003
Mardi Gras / Feb '95 / Jazz Music

Valentine, Cal

TEXAS ROCKER, THE
CD ______ BMCD 9027
Black Magic / Dec '94 / ADA / Cadillac / Direct / Hot Shot

Valentine, Dickie

BEST OF DICKIE VALENTINE, THE
CD ______ SOW 704
Sound Waves / May '94 / Target/BMG

DICKIE VALENTINE & FRIENDS
CD ______ MATCD 279
Castle / Sep '93 / BMG

MR. SANDMAN
Wanted / Stay awhile / Second time around / With these hands / For all we know / Lost dreams and lonely hearts / Wait for me / No such luck / My word / In times like these / Once in each life / Build yourself a dream / Mona Lisa / It's better to have loved / Nothing but the best / Free me / Old devil moon / Come another day another love / Dreams can tell a lie / Cry my soul / Something good / Song of the trees / Kiss to build a dream on / Mr. Sandman
CD ______ C5MCD 625
See For Miles/C5 / Jul '95 / Pinnacle

MY FAVOURITE SONGS
CD ______ SSLCD 202
Savanna / Jun '95 / THE

THIS IS DICKIE VALENTINE (2CD Set)
Venus / La Rosita / Song of the trees / You touch my hand / Sometimes I'm happy / Just in time / Teenager in love / King of dixieland / Hold me in your arms / Get well soon / Homecoming waltz / Dreams can tell a lie / Long before I knew you / Blossom fell / Broken wings / Climb every mountain / Roundabout / My favourite song / Finger of suspicion / Mr. Sandman / Fool that I am / All the time and ev'rywhere / Ronettes / One more sunrise / No such luck / Where (in the old hometown) / Old pi-anna rag / Clown who cried / I'll never love again / You belong to me / Chapel of the roses / Standing on the corner / Endless / How unlucky can you be / Once, only once / Shalom
CD Set ______ CDDL 1224
Music For Pleasure / Apr '92 / EMI

VERY BEST OF DICKIE VALENTINE, THE
Finger of suspicion / Mr. Sandman / Blossom fell / Cleo and me-o / Many loves and penny loves / All the time and ev'rywhere / There'll be some changes made / Endless / Broken wings / Give me a carriage with eight white horses / Old pi-anna rag / Three sides to every story / I wonder / Runaround / Many times / Pine tree pine over me / Who's afraid (not I, not I) / Guessing / In a golden coach (there's a heart of gold) / My impossible castle
CD ______ 5520222
Spectrum / Jan '97 / PolyGram

Valentino, Vinny

VINNY VALENTINO & HERE NO EVIL
Distance between two lines / Venice / Don't blame me / Blues for a while / Secret hiding place / Full moon over the Mediterranean / Veins / Song is you / As you said / When the feeling moves you / Lu / Old folks
CD ______ PAR 2016
PAR / Aug '93 / Koch

Valera Miranda Family

VALERA MIRANDA FAMILY, THE
Llora mi nena / Bambay / Tuna, mayari, guantanamo / Juramento / Que lindo bayamo / Basta ya / Rita la caimana / Retorna / Vuela como el aguila / Dulce embeleso / Murio Valera en San Luis / El misterio de tus ojos / El calvario de un poeta / El penqquito de Coleto
CD ______ C 560107
Ocora / Jun '97 / ADA / Harmonia Mundi

Valhal

MOONSTONE
CD ______ HNF 009CD
Head Not Found / Mar '95 / Plastic Head

Vali, Justin

TRUTH, THE (Vali, Justin Trio)
Malagasy intro / Ny marina (The truth) / Sova (Malagasy rap) / Sariaka (Joy) / Rambala / Tsondrao (Benediction) / Tsingy (Sacred mountain) / Bilo (Malagasy voodoo) / Relahy / Ray sy Reny (Mum and Dad) / Manga ny Lanitr'i / Kintana (The open roof) / Vato malaza / Sova (Repeat) / Bongo lava (The broad mountain range) / Malagasy folk dance medley / Surprise tunnel track
CD ______ CDRW 51
Realworld / Jan '95 / EMI

Valitsky, Ken

SPECIES COMPATIBILITY
CD ______ KFWCD 135
Knitting Factory / Nov '94 / Cargo / Plastic Head

Valland, Asne

DEN LJOSE DAGEN
CD ______ FXCD 139
Musikk Distribujson / Jan '95 / ADA

Valle, Marcus

ESSENTIAL MARCUS VALLE VOL.1, THE
CD ______ MRBCD 003
Mr. Bongo / May '95 / New Note/Pinnacle / RTM/Disc / SRD

ESSENTIAL MARCUS VALLE VOL.2, THE
Os grilos / Tiao branco forte / Previsao do tempo / Menitira carioca / Tanta andei / Seu encanto / Gente / Com mais de 30 / Gara / Dues Brasileiro / Amor de nada / A morte de um deus de sal / Wanda vidal / Revolucao organica / Batacuda surgiu / Azimuth
CD ______ MRBCD 007
Mr. Bongo / Oct '96 / New Note/Pinnacle / RTM/Disc / SRD

Vallee, Rudy

DANCING IN THE MOONLIGHT
You're driving me crazy / My song / This is the Missus / I'll never have to dream again / Just an echo in the valley / Me minus you / I'm keepin' company / I'm playing with fire / Bed time story / My dancing lady / Earful of music / You oughta be in pictures / Dancing in the moonlight / Pretty girl is like a melody / Page Miss Glory / These foolish things / Glory of love / That's southern hospitality / Makin' whoopee / Doin' the racoon
CD ______ CD 349
Entertainers / Jun '96 / Target/BMG

HEIGH-HO EVERYBODY, THIS IS RUDY VALLEE
Heigh ho everybody, heigh ho / Betty coed / If I had a girl like you / Let's do it / I still remember / Salaaming the rajah / My heart belongs to the girl who belongs to somebody else / One in the world / I'll be reminded of you / You'll do it someday, so why not now / Kitty from Kansas City / That's when I learned to love you / Outside / Dream sweetheart / Love made a gypsy out of me / Perhaps / Little kiss each morning a little kiss each night / Verdict is life with you / Lover come back to me / Stein song
CD ______ PASTCD 7077
Flapper / Sep '95 / Pinnacle

Vallenato

PRE - LOG
CD ______ TOPYCD 074
Temple / May '94 / Pinnacle / Plastic Head

Vallhall

HEADING FOR MARS
CD ______ HNF 018CD
Voices Of Wonder / Jun '97 / Plastic Head

Valli, Frankie

20 GREATEST HITS (Valli, Frankie & Four Seasons)
Sherry / Big girls don't cry / Walk like a man / Dawn / Rag doll / Stay / Let's hang on / Working my way back to you / Opus 17 (Don't you worry about me) / I've got you under my skin / C'mon Marianne / You're ready now / Who loves you / December '63 (oh what a night) / Silver star / My eyes adored you / Swearin' to God / Fallen angel / Grease / Can't take my eyes off you
CD ______ PLATCD 4902
Platinum / Dec '88 / Prism

AIN'T THAT A SHAME/LIVE ON STAGE (Four Seasons)
Candy girl / Happy, happy birthday baby / Honey love / Soon (I'll be home again) / Stay / Dumb drum / Marlena / Long lonely nights / New Mexican rose / That's the only way / Melancholy / Ain't that a shame / Silver wings / Starmaker / Blues in the night / Just in time / Little boy (In grown up clothes) / I can dream, can't I / How do you make a hit song / By myself / Jada / We three / Day in, day out / My mother's eyes / Mack the knife / Come si bella / Brotherhood of man
CD ______ CDCHD 596
Ace / Jun '95 / Pinnacle

BIG HITS/NEW GOLD HITS (Four Seasons)
What the world needs now is love / Anyone who had a heart / There's always something there to remind me / Make it easy on yourself / Walk on by / What's new pussycat / Queen Jane approximately / Mr. Tambourine man / Like a rolling stone / Don't think twice it's alright / All I really want to do / Blowin' in the wind / C'mon Marianne / Let's ride again / Beggin' / Around and around / Goodbye girl / I'm gonna change / Tell it to the rain / Dody (I dig you) / Puppet song / Lonesome road / Opus 17 (Don't you worry 'bout me) / I've got you under my skin
CD ______ CDCHD 620
Ace / Feb '96 / Pinnacle

CHRISTMAS ALBUM/BORN TO WANDER (Four Seasons)
We wish you a merry Christmas / Angels from the realms of glory / Hark the herald angels sing / It came upon a midnight clear / What child is this / Carol of the bells / Deck the walls / Excelsis deo / O come all ye faithful (adeste fidelis) / Little drummer boy / First noel / O holy night / Silent night / Deck the halls with boughs of holly / God rest ye merry gentlemen / Away in a manger / Joy to the world / Santa Claus is coming to town / Christmas tears / I saw Mommy kissing Santa Claus / Christmas song / Jingle bells / White Christmas / Born to wander / Don't cry, Elena / Where have all the flowers gone / Cry myslef to sleep / Ballad for our time / Silence is golden / New town / Golden ribbon / Little pony get along / No surfin' today / Searching wind / Millie
CD ______ CDCHD 615
Ace / Oct '95 / Pinnacle

DAWN (GO AWAY)/RAG DOLL (Four Seasons)
Big man's world / You send me / Mountain high / Life is but a dream / Church bells may ring / Dawn / Only yesterday / Sixteen candles / Breaking up is hard to do / Earth angel / Don't let go / Do you want to dance / Save it for me / Touch of you / Danger / Marcie / No one cares / Rag doll / Angel cried / Funny face / Huggin' my pillow / Setting sun / Ronnie / On broadway tonight
CD ______ CDCHD 554
Ace / Sep '94 / Pinnacle

FOUR SEASONS ENTERTAIN YOU/ WORKING MY WAY BACK TO YOU (Four Seasons)
Show girl / Where is love / One clown cried / My prayer / Little Darlin' / Bye bye baby (baby goodbye) / Betrayed / Somewhere / Living just for you / Little angel / Big man in town / Sunday kind of love / Toy soldier / Girl come running / Let's hang on / Working my way back to you / Pity / I woke up / Beggar's parade / Can't get enough of you baby / Sundown / too many memories / Comin' up in the world / Everybody knows my name
CD ______ CDCHD 582
Ace / Feb '95 / Pinnacle

GENUINE IMITATION LIFE GAZETTE (Valli, Frankie & Four Seasons)
American crucifixion resurrection / Mrs. Stately's garden / Look up look over / Something's on her mind / Saturday's father / Wall Street village day / Genuine imitation life / Idaho / Wonder what you'll be / Soul of a woman / Watch the flowers grow / Raven / Will you love me tomorrow / Electric stories
CD ______ CDCHD 628
Ace / Oct '96 / Pinnacle

GOLD
CD ______ GOLD 212
Disky / Apr '94 / Disky / THE

HALF AND HALF (Valli, Frankie & Four Seasons)
Emily / And that reminds me (my heart reminds me) / Singles game / Circles in the sand / Sorry / Girl I'll never know (angels never fly this low) / Face without a name / She gives me light / To make my father proud / Patch of blue / Morning after loving you / Any day now / Oh how happy / Dream of Kings / You've got your troubles / Lay me down (wake me up) / Where are my dreams
CD ______ CDCHD 635
Ace / Jun '96 / Pinnacle

HARMONY (Four Seasons)
Mystic Mr. Sam / Silver star / December '63 (oh what a night) / Storybook lovers / Slip away / Harmony perfect harmony / Emily's (saille de danse) / Who loves you
CD ______ 100572
CMC / May '97 / BMG

ORIGINAL HITS 1962-1972, THE (Four Seasons)
CD ______ DCD 5367
Disky / Apr '94 / Disky / THE

SHERRY & 15 OTHERS (Four Seasons)
CD ______ DCD 5409
Disky / Oct '94 / Disky / THE

SHERRY/BIG GIRLS DON'T CRY (Four Seasons)
Sherry / I've cried before / Yes sir that's my baby / Peanuts / La dee dah / Teardrops / You're the apple of my eye / Never on a Sunday / I can't give you anything but love / Girl in my dreams / Oh Carol / Lost lullabye / Walk like a man / Silhouettes / Why do fools fall in love / Tonite, tonite / Lucky ladybug / Alone / One song / Sincerely / Since I don't have you / My sugar / Hi Lili hi lo / Big girls don't cry
CD ______ CDCHD 507
Ace / Apr '94 / Pinnacle

SOLO/TIMELESS
My funny valentine / Cry for me / (You're gonna) Hurt yourself / Ivy / Secret love / Can't take my eyes off you / My Mother's eyes / This is goodbye / Sun ain't gonna shine anymore / Trouble with me / Proud one / You're ready now / By the time I get to Phoenix / Expression of love / For all we know / Sunny / Watch where you walk / To give (the reason I live) / Eleanor Rigby / September rain (here come's the rain) / Make the music play / Stop and say hello / Donnybrook / I make a fool of myself
CD ______ CDCHD 538
Ace / Jun '94 / Pinnacle

VERY BEST OF FRANKIE VALLI & THE FOUR SEASONS, THE (Valli, Frankie & Four Seasons)
Sherry / Big girls don't cry / Walk like a man / Ain't that a shame / Rag doll / Dawn / Silence is golden / Let's hang on / Working my way back to you / Who loves you / Opus 17 (Don't you worry about me) / I've got you under my skin / Can't take my eyes off you / Night / My eyes adored you / You're ready now / Swearin' to God / December '63 (oh what a night) / Silver star / Fallen angel / We can work it out / Sun ain't gonna shine anymore / Down the hall / Grease
CD ______ 5131192
PolyGram TV / Feb '92 / PolyGram

VERY BEST OF THE FOUR SEASONS, THE (Four Seasons)
CD ______ MCCD 211
Music Club / Oct '95 / Disc / THE

Value

PULLING LEGS OFF FLIES
CD ______ BBA 10CD
Big Cat / Feb '94 / 3mv/Pinnacle

Vamp

HORISONTER
CD ______ MS 1121CD
Musikk Distribujson / Dec '94 / ADA

Van Basten

PERIMITIVE
CD ______ BRUCD 1
Brute / Oct '95 / Mo's Music Machine / RTM/Disc

Van Der Graaf Generator

1ST GENERATION
Darkness / Killer / Man erg / Theme one / Pioneers over C / Pictures/Lighthouse / Eyewitness / SHM / Presence of the night / Kosmos tours / (Custards) last stand / Clot thickens / Land's end / We go now / Refugees
CD ______ COMCD 2
Virgin / Feb '87 / EMI

AEROSOL GREY MACHINE, THE
Afterwards / Orthenthian Street / Running back / Into a game / Ferret and featherbird / Aerosol grey machine / Black smoke yen / Aquarian / Squid I / Octopus
CD ______ FIE 9116
Fie / May '97 / Vital

GODBLUFF
Undercover man / Scorched earth / Arrow / Sleepwalkers
CD ______ CASCD 1109
Charisma / Apr '88 / EMI

H TO HE, WHO AM THE ONLY ONE
Killer / With no door / Emperor in his war room / Lost / Pioneers over C
CD ______ CASCD 1027
Charisma / Nov '88 / EMI

I PROPHESY DISASTER
Afterwards / Necromancer / Refugees / Boat of millions of years / Lemmings (Including cog) / Arrow / La rossa / Ship of fools / Medley
CD ______ CDVM 9026
Virgin / Aug '93 / EMI

LEAST WE CAN DO IS WAVE TO EACH OTHER, THE
Darkness / Refugees / White hammer / Whatever would Robert have said / Out of my book / After the flood
CD ______ CASCD 1007
Charisma / '87 / EMI

NOW AND THEN
Liquidator / Gentlemen prefer blondes / Main slide / Spooks / Saigon roulette / Tropic of conversation / Tarzan the epilogue
CD ______ CDTB 042
Thunderbolt / May '88 / TKO Magnum

PAWN HEARTS
Lemmings (including Cog) / Man erg / Pictures/Lighthouse / Eyewitness / SHM / Kosmos tours / Clot thickens / Land's end / We

go now / Presence of the night / (Custards) last stand
CD CASCD 1051
Charisma / Apr '88 / EMI

QUIET ZONE PLEASURE DOME
Lizard play / Habit of the broken heart / Siren song / Last frame / Wave / Cat's eye, yellow fever (running) / Sphinx in the face / Chemical world / Sphinx returns
CD CASCD 1131
Charisma / '87 / EMI

STILL LIFE
Pilgrims / Still life / La Rossa / My room (waiting for wonderland) / Childlike faith in childhood's end
CD CASCD 1116
Charisma / Apr '87 / EMI

TIME VAULTS
Liquidator / Rift valley / Tarzan / Coil night / Time vaults / Drift / Roncevaux / It all went red / Faint and forsaken / (In the) Black room
CD CDTB 106
Thunderbolt / Dec '92 / TKO Magnum
CD 14847
Spalax / Feb '97 / ADA / Cargo / Direct / Discovery / Greyhound

VITAL
Ship of fools / Still life / Last frame / Mirror images / Medley / Plague of lighthouse keepers / Pioneers over C / Sci finance / Door / Urban / Killer / Urban (part 2) / Nadir's big chance
CD CVLCD 101
Virgin / '89 / EMI

WORLD RECORD
When she comes / Place to survive / Masks / Meurglys 111 (The songwriters guild) / Wondering
CD CASCD 1120
Charisma / Aug '88 / EMI

Van Dieren, Bernard

BERNARD VAN DIEREN COLLECTION
CD BML 001
British Music / Feb '96 / Forties Recording Company

Van Dooren, Mamie

STORY
CD MAR 062
Marginal / Jun '97 / Greyhound

Van Duser, Guy

AMERICAN FINGER STYLE GUITAR
CD ROUCD 11533
Rounder / '88 / ADA / CM / Direct

EVERY LITTLE MOMENT (Classic Jazz For Acoustic Guitar & Clarinet) (Van Duser, Guy & Billy Novick)
Let's dance / Every little moment / Wabash blues / Whose honey are you / Song is ended (but the melody lingers on) / Indian summer / Got a date with an angel / Wolverine blues / When my ship comes in / Linger awhile / I'll see you in my dreams / Moonlight serenade
CD DARINGCD 3026
Daring / Oct '96 / ADA / CM / Direct

GUY & BILLY (Van Duser, Guy & Billy Novick)
CD CD 3014
Daring / Dec '94 / ADA / CM / Direct

Van Dyke, Leroy

ORIGINAL AUCTIONEER, THE
Auctioneer / I fell in love with a pony tail / Leather jacket / I'm movin' on / My good mind (went bad on me) / Heartbreak cannonball / Chicken shack / Poor boy / What this old work needs / Every time I ask my heart / Pocketbook song / Down at the south end of town / Honky tonk song / One heart
CD BCD 15647
Bear Family / Nov '93 / Direct / Rollercoaster / Swift

WALK ON BY (Hits & Misses)
Walk on by / If a woman answers (Hang up the phone) / Black cloud / Happy to be unhappy / Night people / Big man in a big house / Faded love / Save me the moonlight / My world is caving in / Handful of friends / I got a conscience / Broken promise / Dim dark corner / I sat back and let it happen / Geh nicht vorbei / Just before dawn / Now I lay me down / Heartaches by the number / Sea of heartbreak / Love letters in the sand / Sugartime / Don't forbid me / Honeycomb / How long must you keep me a secret / Party doll / Conscience I'm guilty / Day the preacher comes / Fireball mail / If you don't, somebody else will / Put your little hand in mine
CD BCD 15779
Bear Family / Jan '94 / Direct / Rollercoaster / Swift

Van Dyke, Paul

SEVEN WAYS (2CD Set)
Home / Seven ways / I like it / Heaven / Come (and get it) / Forbidden fruit / Beautiful place / People / Greatness of Britain / I can't feel it / Words / Seven ways (beware the veil demo) / Don't imitate, innovate / Come / Sundae 6AM / Forbidden fruit / Don't imitate, innovate / I want you, I need you / Living for the night / Beautiful place
CD DVNT 014CD
CD Set DVNT 014DCD
Deviant / May '97 / Prime / Vital

Van Eps, George

KEEPIN' TIME (Van Eps, George & Howard Alden)
Blue skies / Satin doll / It had to be you / Body and soul / How high the moon / Honeysuckle rose / I cover the waterfront / Chant / Willow weep for me / Kay's fantasy / More than you know / I got rhythm
CD CCD 4713
Concord Crossover / Jul '96 / New Note/ Pinnacle

Van Halen

1984
1984 / Jump / Panama / Top Jimmy / Drop dead legs / Hot for teacher / I'll wait / Girl gone bad / House of pain
CD 9239852
WEA / Feb '95 / Warner Music

5150
Good enough / Why can't this be love / Get up / Dreams / Summer nights / Best of both worlds / Love walks in / 5150 / Inside
CD 9253942
WEA / Feb '95 / Warner Music

BALANCE
CD 9362457602
WEA / Jan '95 / Warner Music

BEST OF VAN HALEN, THE
CD 9362464742
WEA / Oct '96 / Warner Music

DIVER DOWN
Where have all the good times gone / Hang 'em high / Cathedral / Secrets / Intruder / Pretty woman / Dancing in the street / Little guitar (intro) / Little guitars / Big bad Bill is sweet William now / Bull bug / Happy trails
CD 257003
WEA / Jan '84 / Warner Music

FAIR WARNING
Mean street / Dirty movies / Sinner's swing / Hear about it later / Unchained / Push comes to shove / So this is love / Sunday afternoon in the park / One foot out of the door
CD 9235402
WEA / Jun '89 / Warner Music

FOR UNLAWFUL CARNAL KNOWLEDGE
Pound cake / Judgement day / Spanked / Runaround / Pleasure dome / In 'n' out / Man on a mission / Dream is over / Right now / 316 / Top of the world
CD 7599265942
WEA / Jun '91 / Warner Music

LIVE - RIGHT HERE, RIGHT NOW
Right now / One way to rock / Why can't this be love / Give to live / Finish what ya started / Best of both worlds / 316 / You really got me / Won't get fooled again / Jump / Top of the world / Pound cake / Judgement day / When it's love / Spanked / Ain't talkin' 'bout love / In 'n' out / Dreams / Man on a mission / Ultra bass / Pleasure dome / Panama / Love walks in / Runaround
CD 9362451982
WEA / Feb '93 / Warner Music

OU812
Mine all mine / When it's love / AFU (naturally wired) / Cabo wabo / Source of infection / Feels so good / Come back and finish what you started / Black and blue / Sucker in a 3 piece
CD 9257322
WEA / Jun '88 / Warner Music

VAN HALEN VOL.1
You really got me / Jamie's cryin' / On fire / Runnin' with the Devil / I'm the one / Ain't talkin' 'bout love / Little dreamer / Feel your love tonight / Atomic punk / Eruption / Ice cream man
CD 256470
WEA / Feb '95 / Warner Music

VAN HALEN VOL.2
You're no good / Dance the night away / Somebody get me a doctor / Bottoms up / Outta love again / Light up the sky / DOA / Women in love / Spanish fly / Beautiful girls
CD 256616
WEA / Mar '87 / Warner Music

WOMEN AND CHILDREN FIRST
Tora tora / Cradle will rock / Romeo delight / Fools / In a simply rhyme / Could this be magic / Loss of control / Take your whiskey home / Everybody wants some
CD 9234152
WEA / Jun '89 / Warner Music

Van Helden, Armand

COLLECTION, THE
CD ZYX 204302
ZYX / Feb '97 / ZYX

GREATEST HITS
Witch doktor / Zulu (change mix): *Circle Children* / Love thang: *Banji Boys* / Aw yeah: *Chupacabra* / Break night: *Mole People* / Indonesia: *Circle Children* / Rumba: *Pirates Of The Carribean* / Break da 80's / Spark da meth: *Da Mongoloids* / NY express: *Hardheads*
CD SR 329CD
Strictly Rhythm / Mar '97 / Prime / RTM/ Disc / SRD / Vital

OLD SCHOOL JUNKIES
CD HSCD 3005
Raging Bull / Mar '97 / Prime / Total/BMG

SAMPLER SLAYER ENTER THE MEAT MARKET
CD 8289402
London / Aug '97 / PolyGram

Van Helsingen, Bart

PERCUSSION DUO (Van Helsingen, Bart & Hans Hasebos)
CD HH 001
Bvhaast / Apr '92 / Cadillac

Van Hoen, Mark

FLOWERS FROM THE DARKNESS
CD TO 31
Touch / Feb '97 / Kudos / Pinnacle

Van Maasakkers, Gerard

ZONDER TITEL
CD MWCD 1002
Music & Words / Jun '92 / ADA / Direct

Van Meter, Sally

ALL IN GOOD TIME
High country / Blues for your own / Tyson's dream / Crazy creek / Anne's waltz / Weary lonesome blues / Bird that I held in my hand / Amor de mi vida / Road to Columbus / Damien Miley/The idlers of Belltown / We're not over yet
CD SHCD 3792
Sugar Hill / Jan '91 / ADA / CM / Direct / Koch / Roots

Van Peebles, Melvin

X-RATED BY AN ALL WHITE JURY (2CD Set)
Lilly done the zampoughi everytime I pulled her coat tail / Mirror mirror on the wall / Coolest place in town / You can get up before noon without being a square / Dozens / Tenth and Greenwich (women's house of detention) / Come raising your leg on me / Sera sera Jim / Catch that on the corner / Three boxes of longs please / You ain't no astronaut / Come on feet do your thing / Funky girl on Motherless Broadway / Put a curse on you / I got the blood / You gotta be holdin' out five dollars on me / Heh heh (chuckle) good morning sunshine / Salamaggi's birthday / Rufus and Ruby / Mother's prayer / Country brother and the city sister / Chippin' / Just don't make no sense / Dear Mistuh P / Love that's America / I remember / My pal Johnny
CD Set 5406942
A&M / Jun '97 / PolyGram

Van Ronk, Dave

FOLKWAYS YEARS 1959-1961
CD SFCD 40041
Smithsonian Folkways / Sep '94 / ADA / Cadillac / CM / Direct / Koch

Van Ruller, Jesse

EUROPEAN QUINTET
Debits 'n credits / Bewitched / Ruler / De poesch / I'll be seeing you / Two walk / Green's greenery / Vienna night express / You're my everything / This could be the start of something big
CD BM 1002
Blue Music / Feb '97 / New Note/Pinnacle

Van Senger, Dominik

FIRST, THE
CD VBR 20072
Vera Bra / Dec '90 / New Note/Pinnacle / Pinnacle

Van Vliet, Winanda

LUNA Y MAR
CD CHR 70037
Challenge / Sep '96 / ADA / Direct / Jazz Music / Wellard

Van Zandt, Johnny

IN CONCERT
CD 88028
King Biscuit / May '97 / Greyhound

Van Zandt, Townes

ABNORMAL
If I needed you / Pancho and Lefty / Snake mountain blues / Two girls / Kathleen / Waiting around to die / Tecumseh valley / Dead flowers / Catfish song / Flying shoes / Blazes blues / Marie / Song for lungs / Old Shep
CD RTS 24
Return To Sender / Oct '96 / ADA / Direct

AT MY WINDOW
Snowin' on Raton / Blue wind blew / At my window / For the sake of the song / Ain't leavin' your love / Buckskin stallion blues / Little sundance / Still lookin' for you / Gone gone blues / Catfish song
CD SHCD 1020
Sugar Hill / Jun '97 / ADA / CM / Direct / Koch / Roots

BEST OF TOWNES VAN ZANDT, THE
Kathleen / St John the gambler / Waiting around to die / Don't take it too bad / Colorado girl / I'll be here in the morning / Delta momma blues / Tower song / Brand new companion / Two hands / Standin' / No deal / To live is to fly / No lonesome tune / Honky tonkin' / Pancho and lefty / If I needed you / Heavenly houseboat blues / Loretta / No place to fall / Flyin' shoes
CD CPCD 8176
Charly / Jun '96 / Koch

DOCUMENTARY
Waiting around to die / Tecumseh Valley / If I needed you story / Pancho and Lefty / Blaze's blues / Marie / Hole / Cowboy junkies lament / Lightnin' Hopkins / Brand new companion / I'll be here in the morning
CD NORMAL 211CD
Normal / Jul '97 / ADA / Direct

FIRST ALBUM
For the sake of the song / Tecumseh valley / Many a fine lady / Quick silver daydreams of Maria / Waitin' around to die / I'll be there in the morning / Sad Cinderella / Velvet voices / Talkin' karate blues / All your young servants / Sixteen summers, fifteen falls
CD 598109129
Tomato / Aug '93 / Vital

FLYIN' SHOES
Loretta / No place to fall / Flyin' shoes / Who do you love / When she don't need me / Dollar bill blues / Rex's blues / Pueblo waltz / Brother flower / Snake song
CD CDCHARLY 193
Charly / Jul '89 / Koch

HIGHWAY KIND, THE
Lost highway / My proud mountains / Highway kind / Dublin blues / Blaze's blues / Wreck on the highway / Hole / (I heard that) Lonesome whistle / Rake / Banks of the Ohio / Ira Hayes / Darcey Farrow / A song for / STill lookin' for you / Joke / No deal / At my window
CD SHCD 1056
Sugar Hill / Apr '97 / ADA / CM / Direct / Koch / Roots
CD NORMAL 201CD
Normal / May '97 / ADA / Direct

LIVE AND OBSCURE (Live In Nashville 1985)
Dollar bill blues / Many a fine lady / Pueblo waltz / Talking Thunderbird blues / Loretta / Snake Mountain blues / Waitin' around to die / Tecumseh Valley / Pancho and Lefty / You are not needed now
CD SHCD 1026
Sugar Hill / Jul '97 / ADA / CM / Direct / Koch / Roots

LIVE AT THE OLD QUARTER, HOUSTON, TEXAS
Announcement / Pancho and Lefty / Mr. Mudd and Mr. Gold / Don't you take it too bad / Tow girls / Fraternity blue / If I needed you / Brand new companion / White freightliner blues / To live is to fly / She came and she touched me / Talking thunderbird blues / Rex's blues / Nine pound hammer / For the sake of the song / No place to fall / Loretta / Kathleen / Tower song / Waitin' around to die / Tecumseh valley / Lungs / Only him or me
CD CDCHARLY 183
Decal / Oct '89 / Koch

NASHVILLE SESSIONS, THE
At my window / Rex's blues / No place to fall / Buckskin stallion blues / White freightliner blues / Snake song / Loretta / Two girls / Spider song / When she don't need me / Pueblo waltz / Upon my soul
CD 598107929
Tomato / Aug '93 / Vital

NO DEEPER BLUE
CD SHCD 1046
Sugar Hill / Aug '95 / ADA / CM / Direct / Koch / Roots
CD IRS 993151
Intercord / Jun '96 / Plastic Head

PANCHO AND LEFTY (Live & Obscure)
Dollar bill blues / Many a fine lady / Nothin' / Pueblo waltz / Talking thunderbird blues / Rex's blues / White freightliner blues / Loretta / Snake Mountain blues / Waitin' round to die / Tecumseh Valley / Pancho and Lefty / You are not needed now
CD EDCD 344
Edsel / Mar '97 / Pinnacle

REAR VIEW MIRROR
CD SHCD 1054
Sugar Hill / Feb '97 / ADA / CM / Direct / Koch / Roots

ROADSONGS
Ira Hayes / Dead flowers / Automobile blues / Coo coo / Fraulein hello / Central Indian cowboy / Racing in the streets / My starter won't start this morning / Texas river song / Wabash cannonball / Short haired woman blues / Man gave names to all of the animals / Little Willie the gambler / Cocaine / You win again / High, low and in between / When he offers his hand
CD ____ SHCD 1042
Sugar Hill / Apr '94 / ADA / CM / Direct / Koch / Roots
CD ____ NORMAL 195
Normal / Feb '97 / ADA / Direct

TOWNES VAN ZANDT
For the sake of the song / Columbine / Waiting around to die / Don't take it too bad / Colorado girl / Lungs / I'll be here in the morning / Fare thee well, Miss Carousel / (Quick silver day dreams of) Maria / None but the rain
CD ____ CDCHARLY 119
Decal / Jun '88 / Koch

Van Zyl

RELIC (2CD Set)
CD Set ____ CENCD 013
Centaur / Feb '96 / Pinnacle

Vandals

FEAR OF A PUNK PLANET
CD ____ TX 51094CD
Triple X / '95 / Plastic Head

LIVE FAST DIARRHOEA
CD ____ 158022
Nitro / Oct '96 / Pinnacle / Plastic Head

OI TO THE WORLD
CD ____ KF 787622
Kung Fu / Jun '97 / Cargo

QUICKENING
CD ____ 158062
Nitro / Oct '96 / Pinnacle / Plastic Head

SWEATIN' TO THE OLDIES
CD ____ TX 51154CD
Triple X / Jul '95 / Plastic Head

Vanden Plas

ACAULT
CD ____ DCD 9629
Dream Circle / Nov '96 / Cargo / Plastic Head

Vander, Christian

65 (Vander, Christian Trio)
CD ____ A 10
Seventh / Nov '93 / Cadillac / Harmonia Mundi / ReR Megacorp

OFFERING (Parts 1 & 2)
CD ____ A 1/2
Seventh / Mar '93 / Cadillac / Harmonia Mundi / ReR Megacorp

OFFERING
CD ____ A 9
Seventh / Sep '93 / Cadillac / Harmonia Mundi / ReR Megacorp

OFFERING VOL.3 & 4
CD ____ A 5/6
Seventh / Mar '93 / Cadillac / Harmonia Mundi / ReR Megacorp

SONS - DOCUMENT 1973 - LE MANOR (Vander/Top/Blasquiz/Garber)
CD ____ AKT 2
AKT / Jan '93 / Cadillac / Harmonia Mundi

Vander, Stella

D'EPREUVES D'AMOUR
CD ____ A 8
Seventh / Mar '93 / Cadillac / Harmonia Mundi / ReR Megacorp

Vandermark, Ken

SINGLE PIECE FLOW (Vandermark Five)
Careen / Momentum / Fence / Data janitor / Mark inside / Wood-skin-metal / Billboard / Limited edition
CD ____ ALP 47CD
Atavistic / Apr '97 / Cargo / SRD

STEEL WOOD TRIO
CD ____ OD 12005
Okka Disk / Aug '95 / Cadillac / Harmonia Mundi

Vanderveen, Ad

BRAND NEW EVERYTIME
CD ____ MWCD 1008
Music & Words / Apr '96 / ADA / Direct

Vandoni, Chris

RAIN FOREST, THE
CD ____ BRAM 1991192
Brambus / Nov '93 / ADA

Vandross, Luther

BEST OF LUTHER VANDROSS, THE/ THE BEST OF LOVE (2CD Set)
Searching / Glow of love / Never too much / If this world were mine / Bad boy / Having a party / Since I lost my baby / Promise me / Till my baby comes home / In only for one night / Creepin' superstar / Until you come back to me / Stop to love / So amazing / There's nothing better than love / Give me the reason / Any love / I really didn't mean it / Love won't let me wait / Treat you right / Here and now
CD ____ 4658012
Epic / Oct '89 / Sony

BUSY BODY
I wanted your love / Busy body / I'll let you slide / Make me a believer / For the sweetness of your love / How many times can we say goodbye / Superstar (Don't you remember) / Until you come back to me
CD ____ 4879562
Epic / Jul '97 / Sony

FOREVER, FOR ALWAYS, FOR LOVE
Bad boy/Having a party / You're the sweetest one / Since I lost my baby / Forever, for always, for love / Better love / Promise me / She loves me back / Once you know how
CD ____ 4844602
Epic / Aug '96 / Sony

GIVE ME THE REASON
Stop to love / See me / I gave it up (when I fell in love) / So amazing / Give me the reason / There's nothing better than love / I really didn't mean it / Because it's really love / Anyone who had a heart
CD ____ 4501342
Epic / Jan '87 / Sony

GREATEST HITS 1981-1995
Never too much / Sugar and spice / She's a super lady / House is not a home / Give me the reason / So amazing / Stop to love / See me / I really didn't mean it / Any love / Here and now / Power of love (love power) / Best things in life are free: *Jackson, Janet & Luther Vandross* / Love the one you're with / Power of love (love power) (mix) / Thrill I'm in
CD ____ 4811002
LV / Oct '95 / Sony

LUTHER VANDROSS
Bad boy / Having a party / Since I lost my baby / She loves me back / House is not a home / Never too much / She's a super lady / Sugar and spice / Better love / You're the sweetest one
CD ____ 4606972
Epic / Feb '94 / Sony

NEVER TOO MUCH
Never too much / Sugar and spice / Don't you know that / I've been working / She's a super lady / You stopped loving me / House is not a home
CD ____ 32807 2
Epic / May '90 / Sony

NIGHT I FELL IN LOVE, THE
Till my baby comes home / Night I fell in love / If only for one night / Creepin' / It's over now / Wait for love / My sensitivity (Gets in the way) / Other side of the world
CD ____ 4624892
Epic / Mar '90 / Sony

POWER OF LOVE
She doesn't mind / Power of love/Love power / I'm gonna start today / Rush / I want the night to stay / Don't want to be a fool / I can tell you that / Sometimes it's only love / Emotional love / I who have nothing: *Vandross, Luther & Martha Wash*
CD ____ 4680122
Epic / May '91 / Sony

SONGS
Love the one you're with / Killing me softly / Endless love: *Vandross, Luther & Mariah Carey* / Evergreen / Reflections / Hello / Ain't no stoppin' us now / Always and forever / Going in circles / Since you've been gone / All the woman I need / What the world needs now / Impossible
CD ____ 4766562
Epic / Sep '94 / Sony

THIS IS CHRISTMAS
With a Christmas heart / This is Christmas / Mistletoe jam (everybody kiss somebody) / Every year, every Christmas / My favourite things / Have yourself a merry little Christmas / I listen to the bells / Please come home for Christmas / Kiss for Christmas / O come all ye faithful (adeste fidelis)
CD ____ 4813122
LV / Dec '95 / Sony

TWELVE INCH MIXES
Never too much / I gave it up (when I fell in Love) / It's over now / Never too much (mix)
CD ____ 4689862
Epic / Nov '92 / Sony

YOUR SECRET LOVE
Your secret love / Love don't love you anymore / It's hard for me to say / Crazy love / I can make it better / Too proud to beg / I can't wait no longer (let's do this) / Nobody to love / Whether or not the world gets better: *Vandross, Luther & Lisa Fischer* / This time I'm right / Knocks me off my feet / Goin' out of my head
CD ____ 4843832
CD ____ 4843839
LV / Oct '96 / Sony

Vangelis

ALBEDO 0.39
Pulstar / Freefall / Mare tranquilitatis / Main sequence / Sword of Orion / Alpha / Nucleogenesis (part 2) / Albedo 039
CD ____ ND 74208
RCA / Sep '89 / BMG

BEST OF VANGELIS, THE
Pulstar / Spiral / To the unknown man / Albedo 0.39 / Bacchanale / Aries / Beauborg / So long ago so clear
CD ____ 74321292812
RCA / Jul '95 / BMG

CHARIOTS OF FIRE (The Music Of Vangelis)
CD ____ MACCD 246
Autograph / Aug '96 / BMG

CHINA
Chung kuo (the long march) / Dragon / Himalaya / Little fete / Long march / Plum blossom / Summit / Tao of love / Yin and Yang / Chung kuo
CD ____ 8136532
Polydor / '83 / PolyGram

CITY
Dawn / Morning papers / Nerve centre / Side streets / Good to see you / Twilight / Red lights / Procession
CD ____ 9031730262
East West / Nov '90 / Warner Music

COLLECTION, THE
CD ____ 74321224152
RCA / Aug '94 / BMG

DIRECT
Motion of stars / Will of the wind / Metallic rain / Elsewhere / Glorianna (hymn a la femme) / Rotations logic / Oracle of Apollo / Message / Ave / First approach / Dial out / Intergalactic radio station
CD ____ 259149
Arista / Feb '93 / BMG

GALACTIC SOUNDS UNLIMITED PERFORM THE HITS OF VANGELIS (Galactic Sounds Unlimited)
Pulstar / Eric's theme / Italian song / Rotations logic / Will of the wind / Hymne / Elsewhere / L'apocalypse des animaux / Tao of love / To the unknown man / L'opera sauvage / I hear you now / Theme from Antarctica / I'll find my way home / Dervish D / Chariots of fire
CD ____ QED 011
Tring / Nov '96 / Tring

GIFT (The Best Of Vangelis)
Cosmos theme / Pulstar / Page of life / Alpha / 12 o'clock / Sword of Orion / Motion of stars / Way / Heaven and hell suite / Will of the wind / Glorianna / Metallic rain / Shine for me / Intergalactic radio station
CD ____ 74321393372
Camden / Jun '96 / BMG

HEAVEN AND HELL
Heaven and hell / So long long ago so'clear
CD ____ ND 71148
RCA / Sep '89 / BMG

INVISIBLE CONNECTIONS
Invisible connections / Atom blaster / Thermo vision
CD ____ 4151962
Deutsche Grammophon / Mar '85 / PolyGram

L'APOCALYPSE DES ANIMAUX
Apocalypse des animaux / Generique / Petite fille de la mer (la) / Sing bleu (le) / Mort du loup / Ours musicien / Creation du monde / Mer recommencee
CD ____ 8315032
Polydor / '88 / PolyGram

MASK
Movements 1-6
CD ____ 8252452
Polydor / Apr '85 / PolyGram

MUSIC OF VANGELIS AND JEAN MICHEL JARRE, THE (Virtual Reality)
Oxygene / Apocalypse des animaux / Eric's theme / Tao of love / Calypso / Ethnicolour / Italian song / Zoolookologie / Antartica / Souvenir de Chine / I'll find my way home / L'opera sauvage / Chariots of fire / Equinoxe / Arpegiator / China / Magnetic fields / Fourth rendezvous
CD ____ SUMCD 4018
Summit / Nov '96 / Sound & Media

OCEANIC
CD ____ 0630167612
East West / Oct '96 / Warner Music

PORTRAIT
CD ____ 5311542
Polydor / Apr '96 / PolyGram

SOIL FESTIVITIES
Movement / Movement 2 / Movement 3 / Movement 4 / Movement 5
CD ____ 8233962
Polydor / Sep '84 / PolyGram

SPIRAL
Spiral / Ballad / Dervish D / To the unknown man / Three plus three
CD ____ ND 70568
RCA / Oct '89 / BMG

VOICES
CD ____ 0630127862
East West / Feb '96 / Warner Music

Vanguard Jazz Orchestra

TO YOU (A Tribute To Mel Lewis)
CD ____ MM 5054
Music Masters / Oct '94 / Nimbus

Vanian, Dave

DAVE VANIAN & THE PHANTOM CHORDS
Voodoo doll / Screamin' kid / Big town / This house is haunted / You and I / Whiskey and me / Fever in my blood / Frenzy / Shooting Jones / Jezebel / Tonight we ride / Johnny Guitar / Chase the wild wind / Swamp thing
CD ____ CDWIKD 140
Big Beat / Mar '95 / Pinnacle

Vanilla Fudge

PSYCHEDELIC SUNDAE (The Best Of Vanilla Fudge)
You keep me hangin' on / Where is my mind / Look of love / Ticket to ride / Come by day, come by night / Take me for a little while / That's what makes a man / Season of the witch / Shotgun / Thoughts / Faceless people / Good good lovin' / Some velvet morning / I can't make it alone / Lord in the country / Need love / Street walking woman / All in your mind
CD ____ 8122711542
Atlantic / Mar '93 / Warner Music

VANILLA FUDGE
Ticket to ride / People get ready / She's not there / Bang bang (my baby shot me down) / You keep me hangin' on / Take me for a little while / Eleanor Rigby
CD ____ 7567903902
Atlantic / Mar '93 / Warner Music

Vanishing Heat

ITCH
CD ____ TEQM 93005
TEQ / Jul '97 / Cargo / Plastic Head

Vannelli, Gino

BIG DREAMERS NEVER SLEEP
CD ____ FDM 362112
Dreyfus / Oct '93 / ADA / Direct / New Note/Pinnacle

BLACK CARS
Black cars / Other man / It's over / Here she comes / Hurts to be in love / Total stranger / Just a motion away / Imagination / How much
CD ____ FDM 362102
Dreyfus / Oct '93 / ADA / Direct / New Note/ Pinnacle

Van't Hof, Jasper

AT THE CONCERTGEBOUW
CD ____ CHR 70010
Challenge / Aug '95 / ADA / Direct / Jazz Music / Wellard

BLUE CORNER
Blue balls / Blauklang / U / Before birth / Blue corner / Two brothers / Gog / L'epoque bleue / Another night in Tunesia / Icarus / Fate / Black is the colour of my true love's hair
CD ____ 92292
Act / Jun '96 / New Note/Pinnacle

EYEBALL
Bax / Viber snake / Eyeball I / Hyrax / Schwester Johanna / Laur / One leg missing / Eyeball II / Rev
CD ____ FCD 0002
Limetree / Oct '95 / New Note/Pinnacle

FREEZING SCREENS (Van't Hof, Jasper & Greetje Bijma/Pierre Favre)
Part 1 / Part 2 / Part 3 / Part 4 / Part 5
CD ____ ENJ 90632
Enja / Oct '96 / New Note/Pinnacle / Vital/ SAM

TOMORROWLAND
Whoozit / Tomorrow land / Rutherford / Wildcard / Pilansberg / Ascot / Mr. Woof / Round about / Ma belle / Ballad for a lady / Ventre a terre / Quiet American
CD ____ CHR 70040
Challenge / Mar '97 / ADA / Direct / Jazz Music / Wellard

Vanwarmer, Randy

EVERY NOW AND THEN
Stories, trophies and memories / Ain't nothin' coming / Every now and then / You were the one / Tomorrow would be better / She's the reason / Appaloosa night / Beautiful rose / Just when I needed you most / Love is a cross you bear / Safe harbour / I never got over you
CD ____ ETCD 190
Etude / Mar '96 / Grapevine/PolyGram

I WILL WHISPER YOUR NAME
I guess it never hurts to hurt sometimes / I'm in a hurry / Vital spark / Used cars / Velvet vampire / Time and money / Just when I needed you most / Silence of her

dreams / Echoes / There's a rhythm / Don't look back / I will whisper your name
CD KCD 377
Irish / Jan '96 / Target/BMG

THIRD CHILD
Follow that car / Romeo's heart / Don't want to think about it / As if my heart was not my own / Just when I needed you most / Third child / Something beautiful / Two strangers on a train / Damn this night / Whispers of emotion / Diamonds in the light
CD FIENDCD 765
Demon / May '95 / Pinnacle

VITAL SPARK, THE
CD ALCD 194
Alias / May '96 / Grapevine/PolyGram

WARMER
Losing out on love / Just when I needed you most / Your light / Gotta get out of here / Convincing lies / Call me / Forever loving you / I could sing / Deeper and deeper / One who loves you
CD 8122713982
Rhino / Jun '95 / Warner Music

Vanzyl

CELESTIAL MECHANICS
Moment of totally / Callisto / Valhalla / Celestial mechanics
CD CENCD 003
Centaur / Oct '93 / Pinnacle

Vapors

TURNING JAPANESE (The Best Of The Vapors)
Turning Japanese / News at ten / Waiting for the weekend / Spring collection / Sixty second interval / Somehow / Trains / Bunkers / Cold war / America / Letter from Hiro / Jimmie Jones / Daylight titans / Isolated case / Wasted / Billy / Talk talk / Prisoners / Spiders / Here comes the judge
CD CDGO 2071
EMI Gold / Nov '96 / EMI

Varathron

HIS MAJESTY AT THE SWAMP
CD CYBERCD 8
Cyber / Mar '94 / Amato Disco / Arabesque / Plastic Head

WALPURGISNACHI
CD USR 017CD
Unisound / Jan '96 / Plastic Head

Vardis

BEST OF VARDIS, THE
Situation negative / Let's go / 100 mph / Dirty money / If I were king / Destiny / Silver machine / Police patrol / Steamin' along / Blue rock / Jumping Jack flash / Do I stand accused / Where there's mods there's rockers / Gary glitter / Together tonight / Boogie blitz / Jeepster / Don't mess with the bet / Radio rockers / Bad company
CD CDMETAL 12
Anagram / Sep '97 / Cargo / Pinnacle

Varga

PROTOTYPE
Unconscience / Greed / Wawnan mere / Freeze don't move / Self proclaimed / Thief / Bring the hammer down / Cast into the shade / Strong / Film at eleven / Goodbye boogaloo (Instrumental) / Freeze don't move (Krash's psycho mix)
CD 74321190802
RCA / Aug '94 / BMG

Varganvinter

FROSTFOOD
CD IR 023CD
Invasion / Nov '96 / Plastic Head

Vargas, Angel

EL RUISENOR DE LAS CALLES PORTENAS
CD EBCD 79
El Bandoneon / Jul '96 / Discovery

Vargas, Pedro

BOLERO MAMBO
CD ALCD 030
Alma Latina / Jul '97 / Discovery

BOLEROS MEXICANOS VOL.1
CD ALCD 038
Alma Latina / Jul '97 / Discovery

BOLEROS MEXICANOS VOL.2
CD ALCD 040
Alma Latina / Jul '97 / Discovery

CANTA CANCIONES RANCHERAS
CD ALCD 035
Alma Latina / Jul '97 / Discovery

CANTA CON GRANDES ORQUESTAS LATINA
CD ALCD 033
Alma Latina / Jul '97 / Discovery

CANTA INOLVIDABLES BOLEROS CUBANOS
CD ALCD 027
Alma Latina / Jul '97 / Discovery

Various

MERENGUE ONLY
Sali a papa a mama / El bigote / Cerca de ti / Adivinalo / Son de la loma / La chica gomela / Punta colara / En mi pensamiento / Pan de arroz / Cebiche de camaron / La vendedora de pitos / Mete y saca / Te voy amar / Asegura tu pan / El trencito / Muneca Linda / La matica de yuca / Tu pum pum / Todo todo / Adios
CD DC 880532
Disky / May '97 / Disky / THE

Varnaline

MAN OF SIN
Hammer goes down / Gary's paranoia / Lbs / Thorns and such / Little pills / Dust / No decision, no disciple / Want you / Green again / In the year of dope
CD RCD 10368
Rykodisc / Aug '96 / ADA / Vital

Varttina

SELENIKO
CD 517466
Spirit Feel / May '93 / Koch

Varukers

BLOODSUCKERS/PREPARE FOR THE ATTACK
Protest and survive / Nowhere to go / No masters no slaves / Don't conform / Android / March of the SAS / Nodda (contraceptive machine) / Government's to blame / Tell us what we all want to hear / Don't wanna be a victim / What the hell do you know / School's out (maybe) / Killed by man's own hands / Animals / Enter a new phase / Stop the killing now / Instru-mental / Thatcher's fortress / Massacred millions / Nuclear / State enemy / Will they never learn / Bomb blast / Die for your government / Soldier boy
CD CDPUNK 56
Anagram / Oct '95 / Cargo / Pinnacle

DEADLY GAMES
CD ABBT 806CD
Abstract / Sep '94 / Cargo / Pinnacle / Total/BMG

MURDER
CD VARUCKERS 003CD
Varukers / Jul '97 / Cargo

SINGLES 1981-1985, THE
CD CDPUNK 74
Anagram / Apr '96 / Cargo / Pinnacle

STILL BOLLOX AND STILL HERE
CD WB 1136CD
We Bite / Nov '95 / Plastic Head

Vas

SUNYATA
Ningal / Saphyrro / Refuge / Sunyata / Apsara / Astrae / Iman / Rememberance / Arc of ascent / As siva's feet
CD ND 63039
Narada / May '97 / ADA / New Note/ Pinnacle

Vas Deferens Organization

TRANSCONTINENTAL
CD QU 02
Uaquaversal / May '97 / Greyhound

Vasconcelos, Monica

NOIS
CD MOVAS 001
Triple Earth / Jul '97 / Grapevine/ PolyGram / Stern's

Vasconcelos, Nana

FRAGMENTS: MODERN TRADITION
CD TZA 7506
Tzadik / Jul '97 / Cargo

STORYTELLING
Curtain (Cortina) / Fui fuio, na praca / Uma tarde no norte (An afternoon in the north) / Um dia no Amazonas (A day in the Amazon) / Clementina, no terreiro / Vento chamando vento / Tu nem quer saber (You don't want to know) / Nordeste (Northeast) / Tiroleo / Noite das estrelas (Night of stars)
CD CDEMC 3712
EMI / Sep '97 / EMI

Vaselines

ALL THE STUFF AND MORE
Son of a gun / Rory ride me raw / You think you're a man / Dying for it / Molly's lips / Teenage Jesus superstar / Jesus doesn't want me for a sunbeam / Let's get ugly / Sex sux (amen) / Dum dum / Oliver twisted / Monster pussy / Day I was a horse / Bitch / Slushy / No hope / Hairy / Dying for some blues / Lovecraft
CD ONLYCD 013
Avalanche / Sep '95 / RTM/Disc

COMPLETE HISTORY, A
CD SPCD 145
Sub Pop / Mar '94 / Cargo / Greyhound / Shellshock/Disc

Vasen

ESSENCE
CD B 6787
Auvidis/Ethnic / Oct '94 / ADA / Harmonia Mundi

LEVANDE VASEN
CD DRCD 009
Drone / Mar '96 / ADA

VARLDENS VASEN
Kapten Kapsyl / Bambodansarna / Borjar du fatta / Shapons vindaloo / Nitti pomfritti / 30 ars jiggen / Anno / Tartulingen / Sald och solde / En timme i ungern / Till farmor
CD XOUCD 118
Xource / Jul '97 / ADA / Direct

Vasmalom

VASMALOM VOL.2
CD MWCD 4012
Music & Words / Nov '95 / ADA / Direct

Vasquez, Andrew

KIOWA APACHE MUSIC
CD 14996
Spalax / Jan '97 / ADA / Cargo / Direct / Discovery / Greyhound

Vasquez, Junior

LIVE VOL.1 (2CD Set) (Various Artists)
Kimantana: *Life Force* / YDW: *S'N'S* / Excess: *X-Pact* / Burning up: *Moraes, Angel & Sally Cortes* / Mr. Fantast: *Hanson, Johnny* / Check this out: *Fisher, Cevin* / Dream drums: *Lectroluv* / Wombo lombo: *Kidjo, Angelique* / Wave speech: *Lazonby, Peter* / Come on home: *Lauper, Cyndi* / Clear: *Campbell, Sonny* / Live it cool (just do it): *Rhodes, Lydia* / Phunkee muzeek: *Shazzamm* / House of joy: *Robinson, Vickie Sue* / You got to pray: *Cardwell, Joi* / Storm in my soul: *Kamasutra* / No more I love you's: *Lennox, Annie* / If I were you: *Lang, k.d.* / Reap (what you sow): *Mitchell, Vernessa* / One by one: *Cher* / Ab fab: *Saunders, Jennifer & Joanna Lumley*
CD Set 74321477692
Logic / Apr '97 / 3mv/BMG

Vath, Sven

ACCIDENT IN PARADISE
Ritual of life / Caravan of emotions / L'esperanca / Sleeping invention / Mellow illusion / Merry go round somewhere / Accident in paradise / Drifting like whales in the darkness / Coda
CD 4509911932
Eye Q / May '93 / Vital

REMIX LP
CD 4509997022
Eye Q / Mar '95 / Vital

ROBOT, THE HARLEQUIN & THE BALLETDANCER, THE
Intro / Harlequinn plays bells / Harlequin / Beauty and the beast / Harlequin's meditation / Birth of Robby / Robot / Ballet romance / Ballet fusion / Ballet dancer
CD 4509975342
Eye Q / Sep '94 / Vital

Vatten

DIGGIN' THE ROOTS
You'll never know / Looking back / Status quo / Crossroads / Pretty woman / Stumble / First sight phenomenon / Black cat moan / Walkin' by myself / Don't try your jive on me / Prisons on the road / Little girl / Baby, baby, baby / Ervik boogie / Killing floor
CD GUTS 008CD
Gutta / Mar '93 / Plankton

Vaughan, Frankie

THERE'S ONLY ONE FRANKIE VAUGHAN
Hello Dolly / Singin' in the rain / There's no business like show business / Mame / Smoke gets in your eyes / Give my regards to Broadway / Begin the beguine / Way we were / I just called to say I love you / Can't smile without you / It's all in the game / If you were the only girl in the world / I get a kick out of you / 42nd Street / Cabaret / Lullaby of Broadway / Stella by starlight / When I fall in love
CD HADCD 215
Spotlight On / Jun '97 / Henry Hadaway

WORLD OF FRANKIE VAUGHAN, THE
Give me the moonlight, give me the girl / Tower of strength / Green door / Long time, no see / Gotta have something in the bank, Frank / Tweedle Dee / Wonderful things / Am I wasting my time on you / Hey Mama / Sometime somewhere / Hello Dolly / Man on fire / There'll be no teardrops tonight / I'm gonna clip your wings / Kewpie doll / Hercules / Judy / You're the one for me / Kookie little paradise / That's my doll
CD 5520152
Spectrum / May '96 / PolyGram

Vaughan, Jimmie

STRANGE PLEASURE
Boom-papa-boom / Don't cha know / Hey yeah / Flamenco dancer / (Everybody's got) Sweet soul vibe / Tilt a whirl / Six strings down / Just like putty / Two wings / Love the world / Strange pleasure (Modern back-port duende)
CD 4742682
Epic / Feb '97 / Sony

Vaughan, Malcolm

EMI PRESENTS THE MAGIC OF MALCOLM VAUGHAN
Chapel of the roses / Every day of my life / More than ever / My special angel / St. Therese of the roses / To be loved / Wait for me / With your love / World is mine / Hello young lovers / Heart of a child / Holy city / Lady of Spain / Love me as if there were no other / Love me as though there were no other / Wedding / You'll never walk alone / Only you (and you alone) / Oh my Papa / You were the only girl in the world / Miss you / Willingly / Bell is ringing / My foolish heart / Guardian angel / When the last rose has faded
CD CDMFP 6289
Music For Pleasure / May '97 / EMI

Vaughan, Sarah

16 MOST REQUESTED SONGS
Black coffee / That lucky old sun (Just rolls around heaven all day) / Summertime / Nearness of you / Goodnight my love / Can't get out of this mood / It might as well be spring / Come rain or come shine / Thinking of you / These things I offer you (For a lifetime) / Vanity / Pinky / Sinner or saint / My tormented heart / Linger awhile / Spring will be a little late this year
CD 4743992
Columbia / Feb '94 / Sony

20 JAZZ CLASSICS
Serenata / Baubles, bangles and beads / Star eyes / Wrap your troubles in dreams (and dream your troubles away) / My favourite things / Come spring / Taste of honey / Fly me to the moon / This can't be love / Goodnight sweetheart / On Green Dolphin Street / I'm gonna live till I die / Maria / Until I met you / Moonglow / I don't know about you / All I do is dream of you / Because
CD CDMFP 6160
Music For Pleasure / May '95 / EMI

AFTER HOURS
My favourite things / Every time we say goodbye / Wonder why / Easy to love / Sophisticated lady / Great day / Ill wind / If love is good to me / In a sentimental mood / Vanity / Through the years
CD CDP 8554682
Roulette / Mar '97 / EMI

AT MISTER KELLY'S (Vaughan, Sarah Trio)
September in the rain / Willow weep for me / Just one of those things / Be anything but darling be mine / Thou swell / Stairway to the stars / Honeysuckle rose / Just a gigolo / How high the moon / Dream / I'm gonna sit right down and write myself a letter / It's got to be love / Alone / If this isn't love / Embraceable you / Lucky in love / Dancing in the dark / Poor butterfly / Sometimes I'm happy / I cover the waterfront
CD 8327912
EmArCy / Mar '92 / PolyGram

BEST OF SARAH VAUGHAN, THE
You're blase / I've got the world on a string / Midnight sun / I gotta right to sing the blues / From this moment on / Ill wind / All too soon / Lush life / In a sentimental mood / Dindi
CD CD 2405416
Pablo / Jun '93 / Cadillac / Complete/ Pinnacle

BEST OF SARAH VAUGHAN, THE
CD DLCD 4016
Dixie Live / Mar '95 / TKO Magnum

BODY AND SOUL
CD HADCD 187
Javelin / Nov '95 / Henry Hadaway / THE

COLLECTION, THE
Whatever Lola wants / Thinking of you / Black coffee / Summertime / More I see you / My favourite things / In a sentimental mood / 'Round midnight / Hands across the table / I cried for you / Just friends / Lover man / Ooh, what-cha doin' to me / Perdido / Polka dots and moonbeams / Prelude to a kiss / Sophisticated / Star eyes / Nearness of you / You hit the spot / When sunny gets blue / When your lover has gone / You stepped out of a dream / It might as well be spring
CD COL 059
Collection / Jul '96 / Target/BMG

COPACABANA
Copacabana / Smiling hour / To say goodbye / Dreamer / Gentle rain / Tete / Dindi / Double rainbow / Bonita
CD CD 2312125
Pablo / Jan '92 / Cadillac / Complete/ Pinnacle

CRAZY AND MIXED UP
I didn't know what time it was / That's all / Autumn leaves / Love dance / Island / In love in vain / Seasons / You are too beautiful
CD _______________ CD 2312137
Pablo / Apr '94 / Cadillac / Complete/ Pinnacle

DIVINE
CD _______________ ENTCD 225
Entertainers / '88 / Target/BMG

DIVINE MISS VAUGHAN, THE (2CD Set)
CD Set _______________ JWD 102301
JWD / Nov '94 / Target/BMG

DUKE ELLINGTON SONGBOOK VOL.1, THE
In a sentimental mood / I'm just a lucky so and so / Solitude / I let a song go out of my heart / I didn't know about you / All too soon / Lush life / In a mellow tone / Sophisticated lady / Daydream
CD _______________ PACD 2312111
Pablo / Oct '93 / Cadillac / Complete/ Pinnacle

DUKE ELLINGTON SONGBOOK VOL.2, THE
I ain't got nothin' but the blues / Black butterfly / Chelsea Bridge / What am I here for / Tonight I shall sleep / Rocks in my bed / I got it bad and that ain't good / Everything but you / Mood indigo / It don't mean a thing if it ain't got that swing / Prelude to a kiss
CD _______________ CD 2312116
Pablo / Oct '93 / Cadillac / Complete/ Pinnacle

EASY LIVING (Vaughan, Sarah & Oscar Peterson)
CD _______________ JWD 102219
JWD / Jul '95 / Target/BMG

EMBRACEABLE YOU
Embraceable you / Scat blues / 'Round midnight / Sassy's blues / Misty / Just one of those things / Alfie / What now my love / I had a ball / Theme / Lover man
CD _______________ 17110
Laserlight / Mar '97 / Target/BMG

ESSENTIAL SARAH VAUGHAN, THE
CD _______________ 4671522
Columbia / Oct '93 / Sony

GEORGE GERSHWIN SONGBOOK VOL.1, THE
CD _______________ PRS 23021
Personality / Jan '95 / Target/BMG

GEORGE GERSHWIN SONGBOOK VOL.1, THE
Embraceable you / I'm kinda glad we did / They all laughed / Looking for a boy / He loves and she loves / My man's gone now / I won't say I will / Foggy day / Let's call the whole thing off / Things are looking up / Do it again / Love walked in / They can't take that away from me / 'S wonderful / Soon
CD _______________ 8468952
EmArCy / Mar '91 / PolyGram

GEORGE GERSHWIN SONGBOOK VOL.2, THE
CD _______________ PRS 23022
Personality / Jan '95 / Target/BMG

GEORGE GERSHWIN SONGBOOK VOL.2, THE
But not for me / Isn't it a pity / Of thee I sing / I'll build a stairway to paradise / Someone to watch over me / Bidin' my time / Man I love / How long has this been going on / My one and only / Lorelei / I've got a crush on you / Summertime / Fascinatin' rhythm / Maybe / Embraceable you
CD _______________ 8468962
EmArCy / Mar '91 / PolyGram

GITANES - JAZZ 'ROUND MIDNIGHT
April in Paris / Lover man / I won't say I will but I won't say I won't / I'm glad there is you / Prelude to a kiss / Jim my man / (I'm afraid) this masquerade is over / It's easy to remember / But not for me / Darn that dream / I'll never smile again / Smoke gets in your eyes / September song / Over the rainbow
CD _______________ 5100862
Verve / Apr '91 / PolyGram

HOW LONG HAS THIS BEEN GOING ON
I've got the world on a string / Midnight sun / How long has this been going on / You're blase / Easy living / More than you know / My old flame / Teach me tonight / Body and soul / When your lover has gone
CD _______________ CD 2310821
Pablo / Oct '92 / Cadillac / Complete/ Pinnacle

I'VE GOT IT GOOD
CD _______________ LDJ 274918
Radio Nights / Nov '91 / Cadillac / Harmonia Mundi

IN THE LAND OF HI-FI
Over the rainbow / Soon / Cherokee / I'll never smile again / Don't be on the outside / How high the moon / It shouldn't happen to a dream / Sometimes I'm happy / Maybe / Occasional man / Why can't I / Oh my
CD _______________ 8264542
EmArCy / Mar '94 / PolyGram

IRVING BERLIN SONGBOOK, THE (Vaughan, Sarah & Billy Eckstine)
Alexander's ragtime band / Isn't this a lovely day (to be caught in the rain) / I've got my love to keep me warm / All of my life / Cheek to cheek / You're just in love / Always / Easter parade / Girl that I marry / Now it can be told / Remember
CD _______________ 8225262
EmArCy / Feb '85 / PolyGram

IRVING BERLIN SONGBOOK, THE
CD _______________ PRS 23023
Personality / Jan '95 / Target/BMG

JAZZ MASTERS
Cherokee / September song / Shulie a bop / My funny valentine / How high the moon / It shouldn't happen to a dream / Linger awhile / Poor butterfly / Just one of those things / Lonely woman / Lullaby of birdland / Say it isn't so / Sometimes I'm happy / All the things you are / Sassy's blues / Misty
CD _______________ 5181992
Verve / May '94 / PolyGram

JAZZ MASTERS
CD _______________ CDMFP 6299
Music For Pleasure / Mar '97 / EMI

LIVE IN CHICAGO
CD _______________ JHR 73580
Jazz Hour / Jun '94 / Cadillac / Jazz Music / Target/BMG

LIVE IN JAPAN
CD _______________ 557304
Accord / Dec '89 / Cadillac / Discovery

LOVER MAN
I cried for you / But not for me / What kind of fool am I / As long as he needs me / More I see you / Stormy weather / What is this thing called love / Trouble is a man / While you are gone / Tenderly / Lover man / Love me or leave me / Penthouse serenade / What a difference a day made / Everything I have is yours
CD _______________ CDMT 031
Meteor / Jul '97 / TKO Magnum

LOVERMAN
I'll wait and pray / Signing off / Interlude / No smokes blues / East of the sun / Loverman / What more can a woman do / I'd rather have a memory than a dream / Mean to me / All too soon / Time and again / I'm scared / You go to my head / It might as well be Spring / We're through / Hundred years from today / If you could see me now / I can make you love me / My kinda love / You're blase / I'm through with love / Body and soul / Don't worry 'bout me / Time after time / September song
CD _______________ PLCD 556
President / Feb '97 / Grapevine/PolyGram / President / Target/BMG

MASTERPIECES OF SARAH VAUGHAN
Shulie a bop / Body and soul / Lullaby of Birdland / My funny valentine / Willow weep for me / Stardust / Summertime / Honeysuckle rose / Just a gigolo / Boy from Ipanema / Take the 'A' train / What is this thing called love / Everyday I have the blues / Padre / I feel pretty / Mist / Lover man
CD _______________ 8463302
EmArCy / Oct '93 / PolyGram

MEMORIAL ALBUM
CD _______________ VJC 10152
Victorious Discs / Feb '91 / Jazz Music

MY FUNNY VALENTINE AND OTHER LOVE SONGS
My funny valentine / I'm in the mood for love / Touch of your lips / All the things you are / That old black magic / Lover man / Misty / It's magic / All of me / They say it's wonderful / Prelude to a kiss / Man I love / Cheek to cheek / My romance / Love walked in / Body and soul / Just one of those things / Bewitched, bothered and bewildered / Thou swell / S'wonderful
CD _______________ PRS 23020
Personality / Nov '95 / Target/BMG

PERDIDO (Vaughan, Sarah & Dizzy Gillespie)
CD _______________ NI 4004
Natasha / Jun '93 / ADA / Cadillac / CM / Direct / Jazz Music

SARAH AND CLIFFORD (Vaughan, Sarah & Clifford Brown)
Lullaby of Birdland / April in Paris / He's my guy / Jim / You're not the kind / Embraceable you / I'm glad there is you / September song / It's crazy
CD _______________ 8146412
EmArCy / May '85 / PolyGram

SARAH AND CLIFFORD (Vaughan, Sarah & Clifford Brown)
CD _______________ JHR 73581
Jazz Hour / Jun '94 / Cadillac / Jazz Music / Target/BMG

SARAH SLIGHTLY CLASSICAL
Be my love / Intermezzo / I give to you / Because / Full moon and empty arms / My reverie / Moonlight love / Ah sweet mystery of life / Till the end of time / None but the lonely heart / Night / If you are but a dream / Only / Experience unnecessary
CD _______________ CDROU 1029
Roulette / Mar '91 / EMI

SARAH VAUGHAN
CD _______________ CD 107
Timeless Treasures / Oct '94 / THE

SARAH VAUGHAN 1944-1950
CD _______________ CD 14568
Jazz Portraits / May '95 / Jazz Music

SARAH VAUGHAN 1960-1964
CD _______________ CD 53176
Giants Of Jazz / Sep '94 / Cadillac / Jazz Music / Target/BMG

SARAH VAUGHAN COLLECTOR'S EDITION
CD _______________ DVAD 6012
Deja Vu / Apr '95 / THE

SARAH VAUGHAN IN HI-FI
East of the sun / Nice work if you can get it / Come rain or come shine / Mean to me / It might as well be spring / Can't get out of this mood / Goodnight my love / Ain't misbehavin' / Pinky / Nearness of you / Spring will be a little late this year / Ooh whatcha doin' to me / It's all in the mind
CD _______________ CK 65117
Sony Jazz / Jun '97 / Sony

SARAH VAUGHAN'S GOLDEN HITS
Misty / Broken hearted melody / Make yourself comfortable / Autumn in New York / Moonlight in Vermont / How important can it be / Smooth operator / Whatever Lola wants / Lullaby of Birdland / Eternally / Poor butterfly / Close to you / Lover man / Tenderly / Passing strangers / C'est la vie / Experience unnecessary / Banana boat song
CD _______________ 8248912
Mercury / Apr '91 / PolyGram

SARAH VAUGHAN: THE JAZZ SIDES
CD _______________ 5268172
Verve / Feb '95 / PolyGram

SASSY 1944-1950
CD _______________ CD 53162
Giants Of Jazz / Nov '95 / Cadillac / Jazz Music / Target/BMG

SASSY 1950-1954
CD _______________ CD 53165
Giants Of Jazz / Jan '94 / Cadillac / Jazz Music / Target/BMG

SASSY AT RONNIE'S
Here's that rainy day / Like someone in love / I'll remember April / Sophisticated lady / If you could see me now / Foggy day / I cried for you / But not for me/Embraceable you / Man I love / My funny valentine / Passing strangers / Blue skies / More I see you / Early Autumn / Tenderly
CD _______________ JHCD 015
Ronnie Scott's Jazz House / Jan '94 / Cadillac / Jazz Music / New Note/Pinnacle / TKO Magnum

SASSY SWINGS THE TIVOLI (Sarah Vaughan Live At The Tivoli, Copenhagen/2CD Set)
I feel pretty / Misty / What is this thing called love / Lover man / Sometimes I'm happy / Won't you come home Bill Bailey / Tenderly / Sassy's blues / Polka dots and moonbeams / I cried for you / Poor butterfly / I could write a book / Time after time / All of me / I hadn't anyone till you / I can't give you anything but love / I'll be seeing you / Maria / Day in, day out / Fly me to the moon / Baubles, bangles and beads / Lady's in love with you / Honeysuckle rose / What is this thing called love / Lover man / I cried for you / More I see you / Say it isn't so / Black coffee / Just one of those things / On Green Dolphin Street / Over the rainbow
CD Set _______________ 8327882
EmArCy / Jul '90 / PolyGram

SEND IN THE CLOWNS (Vaughan, Sarah & Count Basie)
I gotta right to sing the blues / Just friends / Ill wind / If you could see me now / I hadn't anyone till you / Send in the clowns / All the things you are / Indian summer / When your lover has gone / From this moment on
CD _______________ PACD 23121302
Pablo / Jan '94 / Cadillac / Complete/ Pinnacle

SEND IN THE CLOWNS
CD _______________ 4806822
Sony Jazz / Jan '95 / Sony

SLOW AND SASSY
No smoke blues / East of the sun / Don't blame me / All too soon / Lover man / What more can a woman do / I'd rather have a memory than a dream / Mean to me / Time and again / I'm scared / You go to my head / I can make you love me / It might as well be spring / We're through / If you could see me now / You're not the kind / My kinda love / I've got a crush on you / I'm through with love / Everything I have is yours / Body and soul / Penthouse serenade / Don't worry 'bout me / September song / Time after time
CD _______________ PASTCD 7809
Flapper / May '97 / Pinnacle

SNOWBOUND/THE LONELY HOURS
Snowbound / I hadn't anyone 'til you / What's good about goodbye / Stella by starlight / Look to your heart / Oh you crazy moon / Blah blah blah / I remember you / I fall in love too easily / Glad to be unhappy / Spring can really hang you up the most / Lonely hours / I'll never be the same / If I had you / Friendless / You're driving me crazy / Always on my mind / Look for me, I'll be around / What'll I do / Solitude / These foolish things / Man I love / So long my love
CD _______________ CTMCD 109
EMI / Jan '97 / EMI

SOFT AND SASSY
CD _______________ HCD 601
Hindsight / Apr '94 / Jazz Music / Target/ BMG

SONGS OF THE BEATLES, THE
CD _______________ 7567814832
Atlantic / Jun '93 / Warner Music

SPOTLIGHT ON SARAH VAUGHAN
That old black magic / Careless / Separate ways / Are you certain / Mary contrary / Broken hearted melody / I've got the world on a string / Friendly enemies / What's so bad about it / Sweet affection / Misty / Send in the clowns / If you could see me now
CD _______________ HADCD 108
Javelin / Feb '94 / Henry Hadaway / THE

SWINGIN' EASY
Shulie a bop / Lover man / I cried for you / Polka dots and moonbeams / All of me / Words can't describe / Prelude to a kiss / You can't take that away from me / Linger awhile
CD _______________ 5140722
EmArCy / Feb '93 / PolyGram

THAT OLD BLACK MAGIC (Vaughan, Sarah & Billy Eckstine)
That old black magic / I'm beginning to see the light / I hear a rhapsody / Misty / I apologise / Cottage for sale / More I see you / Stormy weather / As long as he needs me / My favourite things / What kind of fool am I / I'll be seeing you
CD _______________ 306492
Hallmark / May '97 / Carlton

THIS IS JAZZ
Ain't misbehavin' / Summertime / Wave / Just friends / Thinking of you / East of the sun (and west of the moon) / So many stars / It might as well be spring / Nearness of you / I cried for you / Black coffee / Nothing will be as it was / Can't get out of this mood / You're mine you / Mean to me / My man's gone now
CD _______________ CK 64974
Sony Jazz / Oct '96 / Sony

TIME AFTER TIME
I feel so smoochie / Lover man / As long as he needs me / Gentleman friend / What a difference a day made / Sometimes I feel like a Motherless child / What kind of fool am I / Trouble is a man / It's you or no one / Don't worry 'bout me / More I see you / East of the sun / September song / I'm through with love / My favourite things / Time after time
CD _______________ SUMCD 4006
Summit / Nov '96 / Sound & Media

TOUCH OF CLASS, A
Serenata / Baubles, bangles and beads / Star eyes / Wrap your troubles in dreams / My favourite things / Goodnight sweetheart / On Dolphin Street / I'm gonna live till I die / Maria / Until I met you / Invitation / Trees / Moonglow / I didn't know about you / All I do is dream of you / Come spring / Taste of honey / Fly me to the moon / This can't be love / Because
CD _______________ TC 865232
Disky / May '97 / Disky / THE

TOWN HALL CONCERT 1947 (Vaughan, Sarah & Lester Young)
Lester leaps in / Just you just me / Jumpin' with symphony Sid / Sunday / Don't blame me / My kinda lover / I cover the waterfront / I don't stand a ghost of a chance with you / Lester's bebop boogie / These foolish things / Movin' with Lester / Man I love / Time after time / Mean to me / Body and soul / I cried for you
CD _______________ CDP 8321392
Parlophone / Apr '97 / EMI

YOU'RE MINE YOU (Vaughan, Sarah & Quincy Jones)
You're mine you / Best is yet to come / Witchcraft / So long / Second time around / I could write a book / Maria / Baubles, bangles and beads / Fly me to the moon / Moonglow / Invitation / On green dolphin street / One mint julep / Mama he treats your daughter mean
CD _______________ CDP 8571572
Roulette / Jul '97 / EMI

Vaughan, Stevie Ray

COULDN'T STAND THE WEATHER (Vaughan, Stevie Ray & Double Trouble)
Scuttle buttin' / Couldn't stand the weather / Things that I used to do / Voodoo chile / Cold shot / Tin Pan Alley / Honey bee / Stang's swang
CD _______________ EK 64425
Epic / Feb '95 / Sony

COULDN'T STAND THE WEATHER/ SOUL TO SOUL/TEXAS FLOOD (3CD Set)
CD Set _______________ 4683362
Epic / Jan '94 / Sony

GREATEST HITS (Vaughan, Stevie Ray & Double Trouble)
Taxman / Texas flood / House is rockin' / Pride and joy / Tightrope / Little wing / Crossfire / Sky is crying / Cold shot / Couldn't stand the weather / Life without you
CD _____ 4810232
Epic / Nov '95 / Sony

IN STEP
House is rockin' / Tightrope / Leave my girl alone / Wall of denial / Love me darlin' / Crossfire / Let me love you baby / Travis walk / Scratch 'n' sniff / Riviera paradise
CD _____ 4633952
Epic / Jul '89 / Sony

IN THE BEGINNING (Vaughan, Stevie Ray & Double Trouble)
In the open / Slide thing / They call me guitar hurricane / All your love / I miss loving / Tin Pan alley / Love struck baby / Tell me / Shake for me / Live another day
CD _____ 4726242
Epic / Sep '94 / Sony

LIVE ALIVE
Say what / Ain't gonna give up on love / Pride and joy / Mary had a little lamb / Superstition / I'm leaving you (commit a crime) / Cold shot / Willie the wimp / Look at little sister / Texas flood / Voodoo chile / Lovestruck baby / Change it / Life without you
CD _____ 4668392
Epic / Apr '93 / Sony

LIVE FROM CARNEGIE HALL
Intro / Scuttle buttin' / Testifiyin / Love struck baby / Honey bee / Cold shot / Letter to my girl / Dirty pool / Pride and joy / Things that I used to do / COD / Iced over / Lenny / Rude mood
CD _____ 4882062
Epic / Aug '97 / Sony

SKY IS CRYING, THE (Vaughan, Stevie Ray & Double Trouble)
Boot Hill / Sky is crying / Empty arms / Little wing / Wham / May I have a talk with you / Close to you / Chitlins con carne / So excited / Life by the drop
CD _____ 4686402
Epic / Nov '91 / Sony

SOUL TO SOUL
Say what / Looking out the window / Look at little sister / Ain't gonna give up on love / Gone home / Change it / You'll be mine / Empty arms / Come on / Life without you
CD _____ 4663302
Epic / Apr '91 / Sony

TEXAS FLOOD (Vaughan, Stevie Ray & Double Trouble)
Lovestruck baby / Pride and joy / Texas flood / Tell me / Testify / Rude mood / Mary had a little lamb / Dirty pool / I'm cryin' / Lenny
CD _____ 4609512
Epic / Jul '89 / Sony

TRIBUTE TO STEVIE RAY VAUGHAN, A (Various Artists)
Pride & joy: *Raitt, Bonnie* / Texas flood: *Vaughan, Jimmie* / Telephone song: *King, B.B.* / Long way from home: *Guy, Buddy* / Ain't gone 'n give up on love: *Clapton, Eric* / Love struck baby: *Cray, Robert* / Cold shot: *Dr. John* / Six strings down-tick tock srv shuffle: *All*
CD _____ 4850672
Epic / Aug '96 / Sony

Vaughn, Ben

DRESSED IN BLACK
Big drum sound / Man who has everything / Dressed in black / Doormat / Long black hair / New wave dancing / Cashier girl / Words can't say what I want to say / Hey Romeo / Too sensitive for this world / Growin' a beard / Don't say you don't wanna / Poor Jimmy Gordon
CD _____ FIENDCD 166
Demon / Feb '90 / Pinnacle

MONO
Daddy rollin' in your arms / Cross ties / Goin' down the road / Sundown sundown / Our favourite martian / Strange desire / Jailbait / Exploration in fear / Just a little bit of you / Dark glasses / Magdalena / I waited too long too late / Out of control / Skip a rope / I'll come runnin' / That's how I got to Memphis / Sheba / We belong together
CD _____ 7882772
Sky Ranch / Sep '96 / Discovery

MOOD SWINGS
CD _____ FIENDCD 724
Demon / Nov '92 / Pinnacle

RAMBLER '65
7 Days without love / Levitation / Song for you / Heavy machinery / Boomerang / Only way to fly / Rock is dead / Beautiful self destruction / Perpetual motion machine / Soundtrack music from Rambler 65 / Main title / Piston search / Geator drive
CD _____ MRCD 066
Rubble / Jun '95 / Plastic Head
CD _____ 8122724842
Rhino / Mar '97 / Warner Music

Vaughn, Billy

22 OF HIS GREATEST HITS
CD _____ RCD 7025
Ranwood / May '89 / Jazz Music

BILLY VAUGHN
CD _____ HM 025
Harmony / Jun '97 / TKO Magnum

Vaughn, Maurice John

GENERIC BLUES ALBUM
CD _____ ALCD 4763
Alligator / Apr '93 / ADA / CM / Direct

IN THE SHADOW OF THE CITY
CD _____ ALCD 4813
Alligator / May '93 / ADA / CM / Direct

Veasley, Gerald

LOOK AHEAD
CD _____ 101S 8771312
101 South / Aug '94 / New Note/Pinnacle

SIGNS
Marvin's mood / Lasting moment / Highway home / Exit to the street / Signs / Salamanca / Imani (faith) / Soul seduction / What are you doing for the rest of your life / Walking through walls / Tranquility
CD _____ 101S 8770522
101 South / Oct '94 / New Note/Pinnacle

Ved Buens Ende

THOSE WHO CARESS THE PALE
CD _____ ALC 001
Misanthropy / Mar '97 / Plastic Head

WRITTEN IN WATERS
CD _____ AMAZON 006CD
Misanthropy / Nov '95 / Plastic Head

Vee, Bobby

BEST OF BOBBY VEE, THE
Rubber ball / Run to him / Night has a thousand eyes / More than I can say / Suzie baby / Devil or angel / Stayin' in / How many tears / Walkin' with my angel / Letter from Betty / Sharing you / Buddy's song / Charms / Take good care of my baby / Please don't ask about Barbara / Punish her / Someday / Come back when you grow up / Beautiful people / Maybe just today
CD _____ CDP 7903272
Liberty / Jul '88 / EMI

EP COLLECTION, THE
CD _____ SEECD 297
See For Miles/C5 / Mar '95 / Pinnacle

I REMEMBER BUDDY HOLLY
That'll be the day / It doesn't matter anymore / Peggy Sue / True love ways / It's so easy / Heartbeat / Oh boy / Raining in my heart / Think it over / Maybe baby / Early in the morning / Buddy's song / Wishing / Measure my love / Everyday / Love's made a fool of you / Mr. and Mrs. / Forget me not / White silver sands / Well alright
CD _____ CZ 498
EMI / May '92 / EMI

TAKE GOOD CARE OF MY BABY (22 Greatest Hits)
CD _____ RMB 75075
Remember / Sep '94 / Total/BMG

Vega, Alan

DUJANG PRANG
CD _____ 213CD 008
2.13.61 / Oct '96 / Pinnacle

JUKEBOX BABE
CD _____ 668532
Melodie / Mar '96 / ADA / Discovery / Grapevine/PolyGram / Greensleeves / Jet Star

NEW RACEION
Pleaser / Christ dice / Gamma pop / Viva the legs / Do the job / Junior's little sister dropped ta cheap / How many lifetimes / Holy skips / Keep it alive / Go trane go
CD _____ 110122
Musidisc / May '93 / Discovery

Vega, Chilton & Vaughn

CUBIST BLUES
CD _____ 7422466
Last Call / May '97 / Cargo / Direct / Discovery

Vega, Ray

RAY VEGA
Greenhouse / Tahluchahchah / Afternoon in Paris / Islands / No two people / Partido Alto / It's a New York thing / Alone together / Psalm 150
CD _____ CCD 4735
Concord Picante / Nov '96 / New Note/ Pinnacle

Vega, Suzanne

99.9 F
Rock in this pocket (Song of David) / Blood makes noise / In Liverpool / 99.9 F / Blood sings / Fat man and dancing girl / (If you were) in my movie / As a child / Bad wisdom / When heroes go down / As girls go / Song of sand / Private goes public
CD _____ 5400122
A&M / Sep '92 / PolyGram

DAYS OF THE OPEN HAND
CD _____ 3952932
A&M / Apr '95 / PolyGram

NINE OBJECTS OF DESIRE
Birth-day (Love made real) / Headshots / Caramel / Stockings / Casual match / Thin man / No cheap thrill / World before Columbus / Lolita / Honeymoon suite / Tombstone / My favourite plum
CD _____ 5405832
A&M / Feb '97 / PolyGram

SOLITUDE STANDING
Tom's diner / Luka / Ironbound / Fancy poultry / In the eye / Night vision / Solitude standing / Calypso / Language / Gypsy / Wooden horse
CD _____ SUZCD 2
A&M / May '87 / PolyGram

SUZANNE VEGA
Cracking / Freeze tag / Marlene on the wall / Small blue thing / Straight lines / Undertow / Some journey / Queen and the soldier / Night movies / Neighbourhood girls
CD _____ CDMID 177
A&M / Mar '93 / PolyGram

TOM'S ALBUM (Various Artists)
CD _____ 3953632
A&M / Oct '91 / PolyGram

Vega, Tony

APARENTEMENTE
Aparentemente / Donde estas / En resumen / Esposa / Me gusta que seas celosa / No me liames amor / Deja / Con su mejor amiga / Por fin
CD _____ 66058017
RMM / Jun '93 / New Note/Pinnacle

Vegas

VEGAS
Possessed / Walk into the wind / She's alright / Take me for what i am / Trouble with lovers / Nothing alas alack / Thought of you / Anthem / Wise guy / Day it rained forever / She
CD _____ 74321110442
RCA / Aug '96 / BMG

Vegas Beat

VEGAS BEAT
CD _____ CAR 21CD
Candy Ass / Mar '97 / Cargo

Veillon, Jean-Michel

E KOAD NIZAN
CD _____ GWP 004CD
Gwerz / Aug '93 / ADA / Discovery

JEAN-MICHEL VEILLON
CD _____ GWP 009CD
Gwerz / Aug '95 / ADA / Discovery

Vela, Rosie

ZAZU
Fool's paradise / Magic smile / Interlude / Tonto / Sunday / Taxi / Second emotion / Boxes / Zazu
CD _____ 3950162
A&M / Apr '95 / PolyGram

Velaires

SCREAMERS TO FLAIRS TO VELAIRES FROM SIOUX CITY TO PHOENIX
I dig / Roll over Beethoven / Brazil / Sticks and stones / Dream / Hey pretty baby / Scotch and soda / Ubangi stomp / Sweet little sixteen / Memories are made of this / Lotta lovin' / Mule train / Lovin' you / It's almost tomorrow / Yes it's me / Tragedy train / Don't wake me up / Locomotion / Johnny B Goode / Memory train / Summertime blues / Will I / I can never do enough for you / Sticks and stones / What did I do wrong / Ubangi stomp
CD _____ BCD 16168
Bear Family / May '97 / Direct / Rollercoaster / Swift

Velez, Glen

RAMANA
CD _____ CDH 307
Topic / Apr '93 / ADA / CM / Direct

RHYTHMCOLOUREXOTICA
CD _____ ELLICD 4140
Ellipsis Arts / May '97 / ADA / Direct

Velo Deluxe

SUPERELASTIC
Superelastic / Velo deluxe / Simple / Dirtass / Alibi / Desiree / Angels / Skin and bones / Saturday / Eleven / Said / Miracle
CD _____ DEDCD 020
Dedicated / Feb '95 / BMG / Vital

Velocette

SONORITIES
CD _____ REFCD 8
Reflective / May '96 / RTM/Disc / SRD

Velocity Girl

6 SONG CD
I don't care if you go / Always / Forgotten favorite / Why should I be nice to you / Not at all / I don't care if you go (accoustic)
CD _____ SLUM 023
Slumberland / Feb '93 / Vital

COPACETIC
CD _____ SPCD 75242
Sub Pop / Apr '93 / Cargo / Greyhound / Shellshock/Disc

GILDED STARS AND ZEALOUS HEARTS
CD _____ SPCD 340
Sub Pop / Mar '96 / Cargo / Greyhound / Shellshock/Disc

SIMPATICO
CD _____ SPCD 122/303
Sub Pop / Jul '94 / Cargo / Greyhound / Shellshock/Disc

Veloso, Caetano

CIRCULADO
Fora de orem / Circulado de fulo / Itapua / Boas vindas / Ela ela / Santa Clara padroeira da telivisiao / Baiao da penha / Neide candolina / Terciera margem do rio / O cu do mundo / Lindeza
CD _____ 5106392
Philips / Feb '94 / PolyGram

CIRCULADO VIVO
A tua presence morena / Black or white / Americanos / Um Indio circulado de fulo / Queixe / Mano a mano / Chega de saudade / Disseram que eu voltei / Americanizade / Quando eu penso na Bahia / A terceira margem do rio / Oceano / Jokerman / Voce e Linda / O leaozinho / Itapua / Debaizo dos caracois dos seus / O mais doces barbaros / A filha da chiquita bacana / Chuve suor e cerveja / Sampa
CD _____ 5180702
Philips / Oct '93 / PolyGram

FINA ESTAMPA AO VIVO
CD _____ 5289182
Verve / Mar '96 / PolyGram

Velvelettes

VELVELETTES MEET THE ROYALETTES, THE (Velvelettes & Royalettes)
CD _____ MAR 117
Marginal / Jun '97 / Greyhound

Velvet Color

LET ME HOLD YOUR HEART
CD _____ EFA 128202
Hot Wire / Feb '96 / SRD

NOW IS THE TIME
CD _____ EFA 128192
Hot Wire / Dec '95 / SRD

Velvet Crush

IN THE PRESENCE OF GREATNESS
Window to the world / Drive me down / Ash and earth / White soul / Superstar / Blind faith / Speedway baby / Stop / Asshole / Die a little every day
CD _____ CRECD 109
Creation / Oct '90 / 3mv/Vital

TEENAGE SYMPHONIES TO GOD
Hold me up / My blank pages / Why not your baby / Time wraps around you / Atmosphere / Ten / Faster days / Something's gotta give / This life is killing me / Weird summer / Star trip / Keep on lingerin'
CD _____ CRECD 130
Creation / Jun '94 / 3mv/Vital

Velvet Monkeys

RAKE
CD _____ DANCD 061
Danceteria / Feb '95 / ADA / Plastic Head / Shellshock/Disc

Velvet Sound Orchestra

INSTRUMENTAL SUMMER HITS (3CD Set)
Mes emmeredes / L'amour c'est l'affaire des gens / She / Rosa / Cafe de la paix / L'important c'est la rose / Yesterday when I was young / Mefie toi / La maladie d'amour / Little love and understanding / Ne me quitte pas / Old fashioned way / La vie devant soi / Nathalie / La France / Milonga sentimental / Lady Laura / Quiereme mucho / Y como es el / Playa / Hey / Abrazame / Que canten los Ninos / Quiero / Un canto a Galicia / Comidas / Y te vas / Por el amor de una mujer / Mi querido mi viego mi amigo / Amor de mis Amores / Stani amori / Per lei / Se bastasse una canzone / Felicita / La solitudine / Mara / Ma che bello questo amore / Liberta / Lettera martedi / Amarti e l'immenso per me / Se stiamo insieme / Stracciatella / Sincerita / Musica e

CD Set HR 880392
Disky / May '97 / Disky / THE

Velvet Underground

1969 VOL.1
Waiting for my man / Lisa says / What goes on / Sweet Jane / We're gonna have a real good time together / Femme fatale / New age / Rock 'n' roll / Beginning to see the light / Heroin
CD 8348232
Mercury / '88 / PolyGram

1969 VOL.2
Ocean / Pale blue eyes / Heroin / Some kinda love / Over you / Sweet Bonnie Brown / It's just too much / White light / White heat / I can't stand it / I'll be your mirror
CD 8348242
Mercury / '88 / PolyGram

ANOTHER VIEW
We're gonna have a real good time together / I'm gonna move right in / Hey Mr. Rain / Ride into the sun / Coney Island steeplechase / Guess I'm falling in love / Ferryboat Bill / Rock 'n' roll
CD 8294052
Polydor / Jan '94 / PolyGram

BEST OF THE VELVET UNDERGROUND, THE
I'm waiting for the man / Femme fatale / Run run run / Heroin / All tomorrow's parties / I'll be your mirror / White light, white heat / Stephanie says / What goes on / Beginning to see the light / Pale blue eyes / I can't stand it / Lisa says / Sweet Jane / Rock 'n' roll
CD 8411642
Polydor / Oct '89 / PolyGram

LIVE AT MAX'S KANSAS CITY
I'm waiting for the man / Sweet Jane / Lonesome Cowboy Bill / Beginning to see the light / I'll be your mirror / Pale blue eyes / Sunday morning / New age / Femme fatale / After hours
CD 7567903702
Atlantic / May '93 / Warner Music

LIVE MCMXCIII
We're gonna have a real good time together / Venus in furs / Guess I'm falling in love / Afterhours / All tomorrow's parties / Some kinda love / I'll be your mirror / Beginning to see the light / Gift / I heard her call my name / Femme fatale / Hey Mr. Rain / Sweet Jane / Velvet nursery rhyme / White light, white heat / I'm sticking with you / Black angel's death song / Rock 'n' roll / I can't stand it / I'm waiting for the man / Heroin / Pale blue eyes / Coyote
CD 9362454652
CD Set 9362454642
WEA / Oct '93 / Warner Music

LOADED
Who loves the sun / Sweet Jane / Rock 'n' roll / Cool it down / New age / Head held high / Lonesome Cowboy Bill / I found a reason / Train round the bend / Oh sweet nuthin' / Ride into the sun / Ocean / I'm sticking with you / I love you / Rock 'n' roll / Head held high / Satelite of love / Oh gin / Walk and talk / Sad song / Love makes you feel 10 ft tall
CD 7567903672
Atlantic / May '93 / Warner Music

LOADED (The Fully Loaded Edition/2CD Set)
Who loves the sun / Sweet Jane / Rock and roll / Cool it down / New age / Head held high / Lonesome cowboy Bill / I found a reason / Train round the bend / Oh sweet nuthin' / Ride into the sun / Ocean / I'm sticking with you / I love you / Rock & roll / Head held high / Who loves the sun / Sweet Jane / Rock and roll / Cool it down / New age / Head held high / Lonesome cowboy Bill / I found a reason / Trail round the bend / Oh sweet nuthin' / Ocean / I love you / Satellite of love / Oh gin / Walk and talk / Sad song / Love makes me feel 10 feet tall
CD Set 8122725632
Rhino / Mar '97 / Warner Music

PEEL SLOWLY AND SEE (4CD Set)
CD Set 5278872
Polydor / Sep '95 / PolyGram

VELVET DOWN UNDERGROUND, THE (Various Artists)
Sunday morning: *Painters & Dockers* / I'm waiting for the man: *Bored* / Femme fatale: *Nursery Crimes* / Venus in furs: *Glory Box* / Run run run: *Authohaze* / All tomorrow's parties: *Spleens* / Heroin: *Ripe* / There she goes again: *Cosmic Psychos* / I'll be your mirror: *Underground Lovers* / Black angel's death song: *Clowns Smiling Backwards* / European son: *Snark*
CD SUR 529CD
Survival / Jun '93 / ADA / Pinnacle

VELVET UNDERGROUND
Candy says / What goes on / Pale blue eyes / That's the story of my life / Beginning to see the light / Murder mystery / Jesus / After hours / Some kinda love / I'm set free
CD 5312522
Polydor / Apr '96 / PolyGram

VELVET UNDERGROUND AND NICO, THE (Velvet Underground & Nico)
Sunday morning / I'm waiting for the man / Femme fatale / Venus in furs / Run run run / All tomorrow's parties / Heroin / There she goes again / I'll be your mirror / Black angel's death song / European son
CD 5312502
Polydor / Apr '96 / PolyGram

WHITE LIGHT, WHITE HEAT
White light, white heat / Gift / Lady Godiva's operation / Here she comes now / I heard her call my name / Sister Ray
CD 5312512
Polydor / Apr '96 / PolyGram

Velvets

COMPLETE VELVETS, THE
Tonight (Could be the night) / Time and again / Spring fever / That lucky old sun / Laugh / Lana / Love express / Let the good times roll / Light goes on, light goes off / Crying in the chapel / Dawn / Here comes that song again / Nightmare / If / Let the fool kiss you / Baby the magic is gone / Be ever mine / You done me bad / Kiss me / Alicia / Bird dog / My love / Who has the right / I'm trusting in you / Almost but not quite / Husbands and wives / I can feel it / Poison love / That's out of my line
CD CDCHD 625
Ace / Mar '96 / Pinnacle

Velvett Fogg

VELVETT FOGG...PLUS
Yellow cave woman / New York mining disaster 1941 / Wizard of Gobsolod / Once among the trees / Lady Caroline / Come away Melinda / Owed to the dip / Within the night / Plastic man / Telstar '69
CD SEECD 259
See For Miles/C5 / Sep '89 / Pinnacle

Vendemian

BETWEEN TWO WORLDS
CD ABCD 001
Resurrection / May '94 / Plastic Head

ONE EYE OPEN
CD ABCD 014
Resurrection / Apr '97 / Plastic Head

THROUGH THE DEPTHS
CD ABCD 002
Resurrection / Jan '96 / Plastic Head

TRANSITION
CD ABCD 006
Resurrection / Mar '96 / Plastic Head

TREACHEROUS
CD ABCD 003
Resurrection / Jan '96 / Plastic Head

Vendetta

SOMEWHERE IN THE NIGHT
Somewhere in the night / So do I / 1-2-3 / I've got you in my heart / Could have done without it / Don't let the world drag you under / I've got you in my sight tonight / Living day at a time / Gotta see Jane / Somewhere in the night / So do I (AOR) / In and out of love / Stay tonight / Only you can save my life / If you want my love / One step at a time / Larsen effect / Somewhere in the night (Reprise)
CD PZA 006CD
Plaza / Mar '94 / Pinnacle

Venera

BOTH ENDS BURNING
CD GIFT 052CD
Gift Of Life / Apr '97 / Cargo

Venerea

SHAKE YOUR BOOTY
CD GIFT 048CD
Gift Of Life / Dec '96 / Cargo

Veneziano, Rondo

CONCERTO PER VIVALDI
Autumno / Inverno / Estro armonico / Il piacere / La cetra / Primavera / Cimento dell'armonico / Estate / La stravaganza
CD 262489
RCA / Jun '97 / BMG

Veni Domine

FALL BABYLON FALL
CD MASSCD 127
Massacre / Jun '97 / Plastic Head

MATERIAL SANCTUARY
CD MASSCD 074
Massacre / Oct '95 / Plastic Head

Venom

AT WAR WITH SATAN
At war with Satan / Rip ride / Genocide / Cry wolf / Stand up (and be counted) / Women, leather and hell / Aaaaarrghh
CD CLACD 256
Castle / '91 / BMG

BLACK METAL
Black metal / To hell and back / Buried alive / Raise the dead / Teacher's pet / Leave me in hell / Sacrifice / Heaven's on fire / Countess Bathory / Don't burn the witch / At war with Satan
CD CLACD 254
Castle / '91 / BMG

BLACK REIGN
CD RRCD 212
Receiver / Apr '96 / Grapevine/PolyGram

COLLECTION, THE
Welcome to hell / Dead on arrival / Snots shit / Black metal / Hounds of hell / At war with Satan / At war with Satan (Full re-edited version) / Bitch witch / Intro tapes / Possessed / Sadist (Mistress of the whip) / Manitou / Angel dust / Raise the dead / Red light fever / Venom station ids for America and Spain
CD CCSCD 367
Castle / Mar '93 / BMG

EINE KLEINE NACHTMUSIK
Too loud for the croed / Seven gates of hell / Leave me in hell / Nightmare / Countess Bathory / Die hard / Schizo / Guitar solo by Mantas / In nomine Satanus / Witching hour / Black metal / Chanting of the priest / Satanchrist / Fly trap / Warhead / Buried alive / Love amongst / Bass solo Cronos / Welcome to hell / Bloodlust
CD NEATXSO 132
Neat / Nov '87 / Pinnacle

FROM HEAVEN TO THE UNKNOWN (2CD Set)
Welcome to hell / Witching hour / Angel dust / Red light fever / Black metal / Buried alive / Teacher's pet / Countess Bathory / Don't burn the witch (at war with Satan-intro) / Rip ride / Cry wolf / Women, leather and hell / Satanachist / Possessed / Hellchild / Mystique / Too loud for the crowd / In league with Satan / Live like an angel / Bloodlust / In nomine satanas / Die hard / Acid queen / Bursting out / Warhead / Lady Lust / 7 gates of hell / Manitou / Dead of the night / Dead on arrival / Hounds of hell / Bitch bitch / Sadist / Black metal / Snots shit
CD Set SMDCD 120
Snapper / May '97 / Pinnacle

IN MEMORIUM (The Best Of Venom)
Angel dust / Raise the dead / Red light fever / Buried alive / Witching hour / At war with satan / Warhead / Manitou / Under a spell / Nothing sacred / Dead love / Welcome to hell / Black metal / Countess bathory / 1000 Days in sodom / Prime evil / If you wanna war / Surgery
CD MCCD 097
Music Club / Mar '93 / Disc / THE

LIVE OFFICIAL BOOTLEG
Leave me in hell / Countess bathory / Die hard / Seven gates of hell / Buried alive / Don't burn the witch / In nomine satanus / Welcome to hell / Warhead / Stand up and be counted / Bloodlust
CD CDTB 110
Thunderbolt / '91 / TKO Magnum

OLD, NEW, BORROWED AND BLUE
CD CDBLEED 7
Bleeding Hearts / Oct '93 / Pinnacle

POSSESSED
Powerdrive / Flytrap / Satanchist / Burn this place (to the ground) / Harmony dies / Possessed / Hellchild / Moonshine / Wing and a prayer / Suffer not the children / Voyeur / Mystique / Too loud for the croed
CD CLACD 402
Castle / Jun '94 / BMG

PRIME EVIL
CD CDFLAG 36
Under One Flag / Oct '89 / Pinnacle

SINGLES 1980-1986
In league with Satan / Live like an angel / Blood lust / In nomine satanus / Die hard / Acid queen / Bustin' out / Warhead / Lady lust / Seven gates of hell / Manitou / Dead of the nite
CD CLACD 246
Castle / '92 / BMG

TEAR YOUR SOUL APART
CD CDFLAG 50
Under One Flag / Sep '90 / Pinnacle

TEMPLES OF ICE
CD CDFLAG 56
Under One Flag / Jun '91 / Pinnacle

WASTELAND, THE
Cursed / I'm paralysed / Back legions / Riddle of steel / Need to kill / Kissing the beast / Crucified / Shadow king / Wolverine / Clarisse
CD CDFLAG 72
Under One Flag / Nov '92 / Pinnacle

WELCOME TO HELL
Sons of Satan / Welcome to hell / Schizo / Mayhem with mercy / Poison / Live like an angel / Witching hour / 1000 days in Sodom / Angel dust / In league with Satan / Red light fever
CD CLACD 255
Castle / '91 / BMG

Venom P. Stinger

TEARBUCKETER
CD SB 0512
Matador / May '96 / Vital

Vent 414

VENT
Fixer / Fits and starts / At the base of the fire / Last episode / Laying down with / Life before you / Correctional / Easy to talk / Night out with a foreign fella / Kissing the mirror / At one / 2113 / Guess my God
CD 5330482
Polydor / Oct '96 / PolyGram

Ventilators

VENTILATORS, THE
CD EFA 046222
Pork Pie / Sep '95 / SRD

Ventura, Ray

SUCCES ET RARETES 1930-1939
CD 701592
Chansophone / Sep '96 / Discovery

Ventures

ANOTHER SMASH/THE COLOURFUL VENTURES
Riders in the sky / Wheels / Lonely heart / Bulldog / Lullaby of the leaves / Beyond the reef / Rawhide / Meet Mister Callaghan / Trombone / Last date / Ginchy / Josie / Blue moon / Yellow jacket / Bluer than blue / Cherry pink and apple blossom white / Green leaves of summer / Blue skies / Green fields / Red top / White silver sands / Yellow bird / Orange fire / Silver city
CD C5HCD 619
See For Miles/C5 / Aug '94 / Pinnacle

BATMAN/TV THEMES
Batman Theme / Zocko / Cape / Get Smart theme / Man from UNCLE / Hot Line / Joker's Wild / Up, Up, And Away / Green Hornet 1966 / 00-711 / Vampcamp / Secret Agent Man / Charlie's Angels / Medical Centre / Star Trek / Streets Of San Francisco / Starsky & Hutch / Baretta's Theme / Hawaii Five-0 / SWAT / Police Story / MASH / Policewoman / Nadia's Theme (The Young And The Restless)
CD C5HCD 653
See For Miles/C5 / Jun '97 / Pinnacle

BEST OF POP SOUNDS/GO WITH THE VENTURES
Kyoto doll / Hokkaido skies / Blue chateau / Scat in the dark / Koyubino-Omoide / Sukiyake / Ginirono-Michi / Reflections in a palace lake / Ginza lights / Forbidden love / Wakareta-Hitoto / Kirino-Kanatani / Sometimes I feel longing for a motherless child / Kimito-Itsumademo / Green grass / These boots are made for walkin' / Frankie & Johnny / Ad-Venture / Monday, Monday / Good lovin' / Eight miles high / Escape / Sloop John B / Go / California dreamin'
CD C5HCD 642
See For Miles/C5 / Jun '96 / Pinnacle

DON'T WALK RUN VOL.2/KNOCK ME OUT
House of the rising sun / Diamond head / Night train / Peach fuzz / Rap city / Blue star / Walk don't run '64 / Night walk / One mint julep / Pedal pusher / Creeper / Stranger on the shore / I feel fine / Love potion no.9 / Tomorrow's love / Oh pretty woman / Mariner no.4 / When you walk in the room / Gone gone gone / Slaughter on 10th avenue / She's not there / Lonely girl / Bird rockers / Sha la la
CD C5HCD 630
See For Miles/C5 / Aug '95 / Pinnacle

EP COLLECTION VOL.2, THE
Walk don't run / Last night / Red river rock / You are my sunshine / Scratch / Action / No matter what / Wild thing / Wild cat / Walk don't run '64 / Running wild / Memphis / El cumbanchero / McCoy / Green onions / Lovesick blues / Penetration / Pipeline / Stop action / Little bit of action / Wolly and wild / Wild child / Cruel sea / Tall cool one / Tarantella / Skip to m'limbo
CD SEECD 363
See For Miles/C5 / Jan '93 / Pinnacle

EP COLLECTION, THE
No trespassing / Night train / Ram bunk shush / Lonely heart / Ups 'n' downs / Torquay / Bulldog / Meet Mr. Callaghan / Trambone / Josie / Yellow jacket / Bluer than blue / Gringo / Moon dawg / Sunny river / Guitar twist / Telstar / Percolator / Silver city / Wildwood flower / Wabash cannonball / Secret agent man / Man from UNCLE / Hot line
CD SEECD 292
See For Miles/C5 / Jan '90 / Pinnacle

FLIGHT OF FANTASY/IN SPACE
Mighty Quinn / Innermotion faze / Ballad of Bonnie and Clyde / Walking the carpet / Flights of fantasy / Soul coaxing / Green light / Cry like a baby / Fly away / Love shower / Summertime blues / Scarborough fair canticle / Out of limits / He never came back / Moon child / Fear / Exploration in terror / War of the satelites / Bat / Penetra-

Waaberi

NEW DAWN
Rogo rogosho / Cidlaan dareemaya / Heei yaa alahobalin hobalowa / Hafun / Shubahada / Ada bere chaelka / Indo ashak / Nin hun heloha modina / Ulimada / Kafiyo kaladeri
CD ____ CDRW 66
Realworld / Jul '97 / EMI

Waby Spider

SIDA
CD ____ ADC 1001
PAM / Feb '94 / ADA / Direct

Waco Brothers

COWBOY IN FLAMES
CD ____ BS 015CD
Bloodshot / Jun '97 / Cargo

Waddell, Steve

ALONG THE ROAD (Waddell, Steve & His Creole Bells)
CD ____ SOSCD 1301
Stomp Off / Jul '96 / Jazz Music / Wellard

EGYPTIAN ELLA (Waddell, Steve & His Creole Bells)
CD ____ SOSCD 1230
Stomp Off / Oct '92 / Jazz Music / Wellard

Waddle

CHEESEBURGER CHEESEBURGER CHEESEBURGER CHEESEBURGER
Jungle / Big and black / Easy / Tony / Mass pussy hunt / T&NO freightline / King Wocker / Food / Steven's new Capri / Cairo / Arsehole ride / Find / Wuss
CD ____ NBX 023
Noisebox / Aug '96 / RTM/Disc / Vital

Wade, Wayne

LADY
CD ____ RNCD 2133
Rhino / Feb '96 / Grapevine/PolyGram / Jet Star

Wades

TOUCH OF HEAVEN, A
CD ____ KMCD 822
Kingsway / Mar '95 / Complete/Pinnacle

Wagon

NO KINDER ROOM
CD ____ HCD 8072
Hightone / Jul '96 / ADA / Koch

Wagon Christ

PHAT LAB NIGHTMARE
CD ____ RSNCD 18
Rising High / Jul '94 / 3mv/Sony

THROBBING POUCH
CD ____ RSNCD 30
Rising High / Mar '95 / 3mv/Sony

Wagoner, Porter

ESSENTIAL PORTER WAGGONER & DOLLY PARTON, THE (Wagoner, Porter & Dolly Parton)
Last thing on my mind / Holding on to nothin' / We'll get ahead someday / Yours love / Always always / Just someone I used to know / Tomorrow is forever / Daddy was an old time preacher man / Better move it on home / Right combination / Burning the midnight oil / Lost forever in your kiss / Together always / We've found it / Say forever you'll be mine / If teardrops were pennies / Please don't stop loving me / Is forever longer than always / If you go I'll follow you / Making plans
CD ____ 07863668582
RCA Nashville / Aug '96 / BMG

THIN MAN FROM WEST PLAINS (4CD Set)
Settin' the woods on fire / Headin' for a weddin' / Lovin' letters / I can't live with you (I can't live without you) / Bringing home the bacon / Angel made of ice / Takin' chances / All roads lead to love / That's it / Beggar for your love / Trademark / Don't play that song (You lied) / Flame of love / Dig that crazy moon / Trinidad / Bad news travels fast / Get out of here / My bonfire / Town crier / Love at first sight / Be glad you ain't me / Our shivaree / Company's coming / Tricks of the trade / Satisfied mind / Good time was had by all / Hey maw / How quick / I like girls / Itchin' for my baby / Eat, drink and be merry / I'm stepping out tonight / Let's squiggle / Living in the past / What would you do (if Jesus came to your house) / How can you refuse him now / Tryin' to forget the blues / Uncle pen / How I've tried / I've known you from somewhere / Seeing her only reminded me of you / Midnight / I guess I'm crazy / Born to lose / Ivory tower / I should be with you / Would you be satisfied / I'm day dreamin' tonight / I'll pretend / Who will he be / Good mornin' neighbor / My brand of blues / Thinking of you / I thought I heard you call my name / Turn it over in your mind / Payday / Big wheels / Wound time can't erase / As long as I'm dreaming / Your love / Doll face / I don't want this memory / Burning bridges / Five O'clock in the morning / Heaven's just a prayer away / Tomorrow we'll retire / Just before dawn / Dear lonesome / Tell her lies and feed her candy / Haven't you heard / Don't ever leave me / Who'll buy the wine / Me and Fred and Joe and Bill / Out of sight out of mind / I thought of God / I'm gonna sing / Our song of love / Battle of little big horn / Luannie Brown / Your kind of people / Girl who didn't need love / Legend of the big steeple / Wakin' up the crowd / Old log cabin for sale / Falling again / Old Jess / Your old love letters / Heartbreak affair / Everything she touches get the blues / I cried again / My name is mud / Sugarfoot rag / I thought I heard you calling my name / One way ticket (to the blues) / Take good care of her / I went out of my way / Tennessee border / I gotta find someone (who loves like I do) / Misery loves company / Cryin' loud / I wonder where you are tonight / Frosty the snowman / Cold dark waters / Ain't it awful / Wasted years / Private little world / I've enjoyed as much of this as I can stand / Blue house painted white
CD Set ____ BCD 15499
Bear Family / May '93 / Direct / Rollercoaster / Swift

Wah

WORD TO THE WISE GUY, A (Mighty Wah)
Yuh learn I / Weekends / Lost generation / Yuh learn II / Know there was something / Yuh learn III / In the bleak (body and soul) mid winter / What's happening here / Papa crack - God's lonely man / Yuh learn IV / Come back
CD ____ BBL 54CD
Lowdown/Beggars Banquet / Jan '89 / RTM/Disc / Warner Music

Wahls, Shirley

DOWN BY THE RIVERSIDE (Wahls, Shirley Singers)
CD ____ BB 1962
Black & Blue / Feb '96 / Discovery / Koch / Wellard

Wai Fat, Chan

FOO CUP KWAN NAN
CD ____ FS 001
Fat Sound / Jun '97 / ReR Megacorp

Waikikis

HAWAIIAN FAVOURITES (Waikiki Beach Boys)
Hawaiian wedding song / Hawaiian march / Analani E / Ports of paradise / Shimmering sands / My little grass shack in Kealakekua, Hawaii / Kono knoi / Mamoola moon / Kahola march / Hawaii calls / Hawaii tattoo / Sweet Leilani / Flower of the islands / Honi kaua / Garlands for your hair / Song of the Islands / Tiny bubbles / Beautiful Moorea / Hawaiian honeymoon / March to Diamond Head
CD ____ CC 254
Music For Pleasure / May '90 / EMI

Wailer, Bunny

BLACKHEART MAN
Blackheart man / Fighting against conviction / Oppressed song / Fig tree / Dreamland / Rastaman / Reincarnated soul / Amagideon / Bide up / This train
CD ____ RRCD 6
Reggae Refreshers / Jun '90 / PolyGram / Vital

BUNNY WAILER SINGS THE WAILERS
Dancing shoes / Mellow mood / Dreamland / Keep on moving / Hypocrite / I'm the toughest / Rule this land / Burial / I stand predominate / Walk the proud land
CD ____ RRCD 8
Reggae Refreshers / Jun '90 / PolyGram / Vital

CRUCIAL ROOTS CLASSICS
CD ____ SHCD 45014
Shanachie / Apr '94 / ADA / Greensleeves / Koch

GUMPTION
CD ____ SMCD 014
Solomonic / Jul '91 / Jet Star / Pinnacle

HALL OF FAME
CD ____ RASCD 3502
Ras / Jan '96 / Direct / Greensleeves / Jet Star / SRD

JUST BE NICE
CD ____ RASCD 3121
Ras / Jul '93 / Direct / Greensleeves / Jet Star / SRD

LIBERATION
CD ____ SHANCD 43059
Shanachie / Feb '89 / ADA / Greensleeves / Koch

MARKETPLACE
CD ____ SHCD 43071
Shanachie / Jun '91 / ADA / Greensleeves / Koch

PROTEST
Moses children / Get up stand up / Scheme of things / Quit trying, follow fashion monkey / Wanted children / Who feels it / Johnny too bad
CD ____ RRCD 7
Reggae Refreshers / Jun '90 / PolyGram / Vital

RETROSPECTIVE
CD ____ SHCD 45021
Shanachie / Mar '95 / ADA / Greensleeves / Koch

ROOTS MAN SKANKING
CD ____ SHANCD 43043
Shanachie / Sep '87 / ADA / Greensleeves / Koch

ROOTS RADICS ROCKERS REGGAE
CD ____ SHANCD 43013
Shanachie / Jan '84 / ADA / Greensleeves / Koch

RULE DANCE HALL
CD ____ SHANCD 43050
Shanachie / Jun '88 / ADA / Greensleeves / Koch

Wailing Roots

FEELINGS AND DUB
CD ____ ACPCG 014
Melodie / Oct '95 / ADA / Discovery / Grapevine/PolyGram / Greensleeves / Jet Star

Wailing Souls

BEST OF THE WAILING SOULS, THE
CD ____ JJCD 167
Channel One / Apr '96 / Jet Star

FACE THE DEVIL
CD ____ CDTRL 360
Trojan / Jun '95 / Direct / Jet Star

FIRE HOUSE ROCK
Firehouse rock / Run dem down / Oh what a feeling / Kingdom rise, kingdom fall / Act of affection / Busnah / Fool will fall / Bandits taking over / Who lives it / See Baba Joe
CD ____ GRELCD 21
Greensleeves / Sep '89 / Jet Star / SRD

INCHPINCHERS
Inchpinchers / Things and time / Baby come rock / Mass charley ground / Oh what a lie / Ghetto of Kingston Town / Tom sprang / Don't get lost / Modern slavery / Infidels
CD ____ GRELCD 47
Greensleeves / Sep '92 / Jet Star / SRD

ON THE ROCKS
Down on the rocks / Sticky stay / Stop red eye / Gun / Jah is watching you / Riddim of life / What is your meaning / Ishen tree / Don't burn baby
CD ____ GRELCD 59
Greensleeves / Feb '96 / Jet Star / SRD

STRANDED
Stranded in L A / File for your machete / Thinking / Peace and love shall reign / Helmet of salvation / War deh round a John shop / Eyes of love / Divided and rule / Sunrise till sunset / Best is yet to come
CD ____ GRELCD 73
Greensleeves / Aug '95 / Jet Star / SRD

TENSION
CD ____ BSCD 8
Big Ship / Mar '97 / Jet Star

VERY BEST OF THE WAILING SOULS, THE
War / Jah give us life / Bredda / Old broom / Kingdom rise, Kingdom fall / Firehouse rock / Who no waan come / Things and time / Stop red eye / Sticky stay / They don't know Jah / War deh round a John shop
CD ____ GRELCD 99
Greensleeves / Oct '95 / Jet Star / SRD

WILD SUSPENSE
Row fisherman / Slow coach / We got to be together / Feel the spirit / Bredda Gravilicious / Wild suspense / They never knew / Black rose / Something funny / Very well / Walk but mind you don't fall / Row fisherman (dub) / Bredda Gravilicious (dub) / Slow coach (dub) / Something funny (dub) / We-'ve got to be together / Very well (dub)
CD ____ RRCD 53
Reggae Refreshers / Apr '95 / PolyGram / Vital

Wainapel, Harvey

AMBROSIA (The Music Of Kenny Barron)
Anywhere / Ambrosia / Phantoms / Lunacy / Lullabye / Sambao / Belem / Sonia braga / If and when
CD ____ AL 73060
A / Nov '96 / Cadillac / Direct

Wainwright III, Loudon

ALBUM VOL.3
Dead skunk / Red guitar / East Indian princess / Muse blues / Hometeam crown / B side / Needless to say / Smoky Joe's cafe / New paint / Trilogy (circa 1967) / Drinking song / Say that you love me
CD ____ EDCD 168
Edsel / Feb '91 / Pinnacle

ATTEMPTED MOUSTACHE
Swimming song / AM world / Bell bottom pants / Liza / I am the way / Clockwork chartreuse / Down drinking at the bar / Man who couldn't cry / Come a long way / Nocturnal stumblebutt / Dilated to meet you / Lullaby
CD ____ ED CD 269
Edsel / May '88 / Pinnacle

CAREER MOVES
Road ode / I'm alright / Five years old / Your mother and I / Westchester county / He said, she said / Christmas rap / Suddenly it's Christmas / Thanksgiving / Fine Celtic name / TSMNWA / Some balding guys / Swimming song / Absence makes the heart grow fonder / Happy birthday Elvis / Fabulous songs / Unhappy anniversary / I'd rather be lonely / Just say no / April fool's day morn / Man who couldn't cry / Acid song / Tip that waitress / Career moves
CD ____ CDV 2718
Virgin / Jul '93 / EMI

FAME AND WEALTH
Reader and advisor / Grammy song / Dump the dog / Five years old / Westchester county / Saturday morning fever / April fools day morn / Fame and wealth / Thick and thin / Revenge / Ingenue / IDTTYWLM
CD ____ ROUCD 3076
Rounder / Aug '88 / ADA / CM / Direct

GROWN MAN
Birthday present / Grown man / That hospital / Housework / Cobwebs / Year / Father/Daughter dialogue / 1994 / Iwiwal / Just a John / I suppose / Dreaming / End has begun / Human cannonball / Treasures untold
CD ____ CDV 2789
Virgin / Oct '95 / EMI

HISTORY
People in love / Men / Picture / When I'm At Your House / Doctor / Hitting You / I'd rather be lonely / Between / Talking New Bob Dylan / So many songs / Four times ten / Father And A Son / Sometimes I forget / Handful Of Dust
CD ____ CDV 2703
Virgin / Sep '92 / EMI

I'M ALRIGHT
One man guy / Lost love / I'm alright / Not John / Cardboard boxes / Screaming issue / How old are you / Animal song / Out of this world / Daddy take a nap / Ready or not / Career moves
CD ____ ROUCD 3096
Rounder / Aug '88 / ADA / CM / Direct

LIVE ONE, A
Motel blues / Hollywood hopeful / Whatever happened to us / Natural disaster / Suicide song / School days / Kings and Queens / Down drinking at the bar / B side / Nocturnal stumblebutt / Red guitar / Clockwork chartreuse / Lullaby
CD ____ ROUCD 3050
Rounder / Mar '96 / ADA / CM / Direct

MORE LOVE SONGS
Hard day on the planet / Synchronicity / Your mother and I / I eat out / No / Home stretch / Unhappy anniversary / Man's world / Vampire blues / Overseas calls / Expatriot / Back nine
CD ____ ROUCD 3106
Rounder / '88 / ADA / CM / Direct

ONE MAN GUY (The Best Of Loudon Wainwright III 1984-1989)
CD ____ MCCD 166
Music Club / Jul '94 / Disc / THE

UNREQUITED
Sweet nothin's / Lowly trust / Kings and Queens / Kick in the head / Whatever happened to us / Crime of passion / Absence makes the heart grow fonder / On the rocks / Mr. Guilty / Guru / Hardy Boys at the Y / Unrequited to the ninth degree / Rufus is a tit man
CD ______ EDCD 273
Edsel / Apr '91 / Pinnacle

Wainwright, Sloan

SLOAN WAINWRIGHT
CD ______ WBG 0023CD
Waterbug / Aug '96 / ADA

Waite, John

NO BRAKES
Saturday night / Missing you / Dark side of the sun / Restless heart / Tears / Euroshima / Dreamtime/Shake it up / For your love / Love collision
CD ______ NSPCD 514
Connoisseur Collection / Jun '95 / Pinnacle

Waiting For God

QUARTER INCH THICK
CD ______ CDREC 030
Re-Constriction / Jan '97 / Cargo

Waiting For The Sun

WAITING FOR THE SUN
CD ______ KSCD 9508
Kissing Spell / Jun '97 / Greyhound

Waits, Tom

ASYLUM YEARS
Diamonds on my windshield / Looking for the heart of Saturday night / Martha / Ghosts of Saturday night / Grapefruit moon / Small change / Burma shave / I never talk to strangers / Tom Traubert's blues / Blue valentines / Potter's field / Kentucky Avenue / Somewhere / Ruby's arms
CD ______ 9604942
Asylum / Oct '86 / Warner Music

BIG TIME
16 shells from a 30.6 / Red shoes / Underground / Cold cold ground / Straight to the top / Yesterday is here / Way down in the hole / Falling down / Strange weather / Big black Mariah / Rain dogs / Train song / Johnsburg Illinois / Ruby's arms / Telephone call from Istanbul / Clap hands / Gun street girl / Time
CD ______ IMCD 249
Island / Mar '97 / PolyGram

BLACK RIDER
CD ______ CID 8021
Island / Nov '93 / PolyGram

BLUE VALENTINE
Red shoes by the drugstore / Christmas card from a hooker in Minneapolis / Romeo is bleeding / Twenty nine dollars / Wrong side of the road / Whistlin' past the graveyard / Kentucky Avenue / Sweet little bullet from a pretty blue gun / Title track
CD ______ 7559605332
WEA / Oct '94 / Warner Music

BONE MACHINE
Earth died screaming / Dirt in the ground / Such a scream / All stripped down / Who are you this time / Ocean / Jesus gonna be here / Little rain / In the colosseum / Going out West / Murder in the red barn / Black wings / Whistle down the wind / I don't wanna grow up / Let me get up on it / That feel
CD ______ CID 9993
Island / Aug '92 / PolyGram

CLOSING TIME
Ol' 55 / Hope that I don't fall in love with you / Virginia Avenue / Old shoes / Midnight lullaby / Martha / Rosie / Ice cream man / Little trip to heaven / Grapefruit moon / Closing time
CD ______ 9608362
WEA / Feb '93 / Warner Music

EARLY YEARS VOL.1, THE
Goin' down slow / Poncho's lament / I'm your late night evening prostitute / Had me a girl / Ice cream man / Rockin' chair / Virginia avenue / Midnight lullabye / When you ain't got nobody / Little trip to heaven / Frank's song / Looks like I'm up shit creek again / SSo long I'll see ya
CD ______ EDCD 332
Edsel / Jul '91 / Pinnacle
CD ______ PT 340601
Manifesto / Feb '97 / Vital

EARLY YEARS VOL.2
Hope I don't fall in love / Ol 55 / Mockingbird / In between love / Blue skies / Nobody / I want you / Shiver me timbers / Grapefruit moon / Diamonds on my windshield / Please call me, baby / So it goes / Old shoes
CD ______ EDCD 371
Edsel / Feb '93 / Pinnacle

EARLY YEARS VOL.2, THE
Hope that I don't fall in love with you / Ol'55 / Mockin' bird / In between love / Blue skies / Nobody / I want you / Shiver me timbers / Grapefruit moon / Diamonds on my windshield / Please call me, baby / So it goes / Old shoes
CD ______ PT 340602
Manifesto / Feb '97 / Vital

FOREIGN AFFAIRS
Cinny's waltz / Muriel / I never talk to strangers / Sight for sore eyes / Potter's field / Burma shave / Barber shop / Foreign affair
CD ______ 7559606182
WEA / Feb '95 / Warner Music

FRANKS WILD YEARS
Hang on St. Christopher / Straight to the top (Rhumba) / Blow wind blow / Temptation / I'll be gone / Yesterday is here / Please wake me up / Franks theme / More than rain / Way down in the hole / Straight to the top / I'll take New York / Telephone call from Istanbul / Cold cold ground / Train song / Innocent when you dream
CD ______ IMCD 50
Island / Jun '89 / PolyGram

HEART ATTACK AND VINE
In shades / Saving all my love for you / Downtown / Jersey girl / Till the money runs out / On the nickel / Mr. Seigal / Ruby's arms / Heart attack and vine
CD ______ 7559605472
Elektra / May '93 / Warner Music

HEART OF SATURDAY NIGHT, THE
New coat of paint / San Diego serenade / Semi suite / Shiver me timbers / Diamonds on my windshield / Looking for the heart of Saturday night / Fumblin' with the blues / Please call me, baby / Depot depot / Drunk on the moon / Ghosts of Saturday night
CD ______ 7559605972
WEA / Jan '89 / Warner Music

NIGHT ON EARTH (Original Soundtrack)
CD ______ 5109292
Island / Mar '92 / PolyGram

NIGHTHAWKS AT THE DINER
Emotional weather report / On a foggy night / Eggs and sausages / Better off without a wife / Nighthawk postcards / Warm beer and cold women / Putnam county / Spare parts 1 / Nobody / Big Joe and Phantom 309
CD ______ 9606202
WEA / '89 / Warner Music

RAIN DOGS
Singapore / Clap hands / Cemetery polka / Jockey full of Bourbon / Tango till they're sore / Big black Maria / Diamonds and gold / Hang down your head / Time / Rain dogs / Midtown / Ninth and headpin / Gun Street girl / Union Square / Blind love / Walking Spanish / Downtown train / Bride of raindog / Anywhere I lay my head
CD ______ IMCD 49
Island / Aug '89 / PolyGram

RAINDOGS/SWORDFISHTROMBONES (2CD Set)
CD Set ______ ITSCD 5
Island / Nov '92 / PolyGram

SMALL CHANGE
Tom Traubert's blues / Step right up / Jitterbug boy / I wish I was in New Orleans / Piano has been drinking / Invitation to the blues / Pasties and a G string / Bad liver and a broken heart / One that got away / Small change / I can't wait to get off work
CD ______ 9606122
WEA / '89 / Warner Music

STEP RIGHT UP (The Songs Of Tom Waits) (Various Artists)
Old shoes: *Drugstore* / Mockin' bird: *Tindersticks* / Better off without a wife: *Shelley, Pete* / Red shoes by the drugstore: *Wedding Present* / Step right up: *Violent Femmes* / Downtown: *Chilton, Alex* / Big Joe & the Phantom 309: *Archers Of Loaf* / You can't unring a bell: *These Immortal Souls* / Pasties & a G-string: *Pierce, Jeffrey Lee* / Christmas card from a hooker in Minneapolis: *Magnapop* / Ol' 55: *Alvin, Dave* / Jersey girl: *Pale Saints* / Martha: *Buckley, Tim* / Ruby's arms: *Frente* / I hope that I don't fall in love with you: *10,000 Maniacs*
CD ______ CARCD 30
Caroline / Nov '95 / EMI

SWORDFISHTROMBONES
Underground / Shore leave / Dave the butcher / Johnsburg, Illinois / Sixteen shells from A 306 / Town with no cheer / In the neighbourhood / Just another sucker on the vine / Frank's wild years / Swordfishtrombones / Down down down / Soldier's things / Gin soaked boy / Trouble's braids / Rainbirds
CD ______ IMCD 48
Island / Jun '89 / PolyGram

Wake

MASKED
CD ______ CLEO 91872
Cleopatra / Mar '94 / Cargo / Greyhound / Plastic Head / RTM/Disc / SRD

TIDAL WAVE OF HYPE
Shallow end / Obnoxious Kevin / Crasher / Selfish / Provincial disco / I told you so / Britain / Back of beyond / Solo project / Down on your knees / Britain (remix) / Big nose big deal
CD ______ SARAH 618CD
Sarah / Mar '95 / Vital

Wake Ooloo

STOP THE RIDE
CD ______ K 171CD
Konkurrent / Sep '96 / SRD

Wake RSV

PRAYERS TO A BROKEN STONE
CD ______ PLASCD 025
Plastic Head / Mar '90 / Plastic Head

Wakeford, Tony

SELFISH SHELLFISH (Wakeford, Tony & Steven Stapleton)
CD ______ TURSA 004CD
Tursa / Oct '96 / World Serpent

Wakelin, Johnny

FROM ALI TO THE NAZ
CD ______ CDRPM 0003
RP Media / Nov '96 / Essential/BMG

Wakely, Graham

MANHATTAN SKYLINE
Winter games / Fascination / Solitaire / Orange coloured sky / Girl from Corsica / Devil's gallop / You make me feel brand new / Skylark / Mornings at seven / Blaze away / Missing / Love theme from St. Elmo's Fire / Manhattan skyline
CD ______ MSKY 001
Wakely Graham / Apr '94 / Wakely Graham

Wakeman, Adam

100 YEARS OVERTIME
See what you see / Too late to cry / Take my hand / 100 Years overtime / Hold on / Here with me / More to say / Too long dead / Only me missing / Someone / Sound of a broken heart / Lonely heart tonight
CD ______ RWCD 26
President / Nov '94 / Grapevine/PolyGram / President / Target/BMG

SOLILOQUY
Words of love / Don't say goodbye / There go the angels / One way down / Soliloquy / Little justice / Edge of my heart / Soliloquy part II: The act is over / No time for your love no more / Something strange / Save a tear for me
CD ______ RWCD 15
President / Nov '93 / Grapevine/PolyGram / President / Target/BMG

Wakeman, Rick

2000 AD INTO THE FUTURE
Into the future / Toward peace / 2000 AD / ADRock / Time tunnel / Robot dance / New beginning / Forward past / Seventh dimension
CD ______ RWCD 21
President / Nov '93 / Grapevine/PolyGram / President / Target/BMG

AFRICAN BACH
African Bach / Message of mine / My homeland / Liberty / Anthem / Brainstorm / Face in the crowd / Just a game / Africa east / Don't touch the merchandise
CD ______ RWCD 20
President / Nov '93 / Grapevine/PolyGram / President / Target/BMG

ASPIRANT SUNRISE
Thoughts of love / Gentle breezes / Whispering cornfields / Peaceful beginnings / Dewy morn / Musical dreams / Distant thoughts / Dove / When time stood still / Secret moments / Peaceful
CD ______ RWCD 17
President / Nov '93 / Grapevine/PolyGram / President / Target/BMG

ASPIRANT SUNSET
Floating clouds / Still waters / Dream / Sleeping village / Sea of tranquility / Peace / Sunset / Dying embers / Dusk / Evening moods
CD ______ RWCD 18
President / Nov '93 / Grapevine/PolyGram / President / Target/BMG

ASPIRANT SUNSHADOWS
Nightwind / Churchyard / Tall shadows / Shadowlove / Melancholy mood / Mount Fuji by night / Hidden reflections / Evening harp / Moonraker pond / Last lamplight / Japanese sunshadows
CD ______ RWCD 19
President / Nov '93 / Grapevine/PolyGram / President / Target/BMG

BLACK KNIGHTS AT THE COURT OF FERDINAND IV (Wakeman, Rick & Mario Fasciano)
CD ______ WCPCD 1009
West Coast / Sep '96 / Koch / Scratch/ BMG

CAN YOU HEAR ME
CD ______ HRHCD 005
Music Fusion / Mar '97 / Pinnacle

CLASSIC TRACKS, THE
Journey to the centre of the Earth / Catherine Howard / Merlin the magician
CD ______ 305632
Hallmark / Oct '96 / Carlton

CLASSIC, THE
CD ______ CDSGP 115
Prestige / Apr '94 / Else / Total/BMG

CLASSICAL CONNECTION I, THE
Gone but not forgotten / After the ball / Elgin mansions / Sea horses / Merlin the magician / Catherine of Aragon / Catherine Howard / 1984 Overture / Hymn / Finale incorporating Julia
CD ______ RWCD 13
President / Nov '93 / Grapevine/PolyGram / President / Target/BMG

CLASSICAL CONNECTION VOL.2, THE
Eleanor Rigby / Birdman of Alcatraz / Day after the fair / Opus 1 / Painter / Summertime / Dancing in heaven / A garden of music / Mackintosh / Farandol / Pont Street / Art and soul
CD ______ RWCD 14
President / May '93 / Grapevine/PolyGram / President / Target/BMG

COST OF LIVING, THE
Twij / Pandamonia / Gone but not forgotten / One for the road / Bedtime stories / Happening man / Shakespeare run / Monkey nuts / Elegy written in a country churchyard
CD ______ GCDWR 1892
Griffin / Jun '97 / Greyhound

COUNTRY AIRS
Lakeland walks / Wild moors / Harvest festival / Glade / Dandelion dreams / Ducks and drinks / Green to gold / Stepping stones / Morning haze / Waterfalls / Spring / Quiet valleys / Nature trails / Heather carpets
CD ______ NAGE 10CD
Art Of Landscape / Apr '86 / Sony

COUNTRY AIRS (1992 Version)
CD ______ RWCD 10
President / Nov '93 / Grapevine/PolyGram / President / Target/BMG

CRIMES OF PASSION
CD ______ RWCD 3
President / Nov '93 / Grapevine/PolyGram / President / Target/BMG

FAMILY ALBUM, THE
Adam (Rick's second son) / Black beauty (black rabbit) / Jemma (Rick and Nina's daughter) / Benjamin (Rick's third son) / Oscar (Rick and Nina's son) / Oliver (Rick's eldest son) / Nina (Rick's wife) / Wiggles (black and white rabbit) / Chloe / Kookie / Tilly / Mum / Dad / Day after the fair / MacKintosh
CD ______ RWCD 4
President / Nov '93 / Grapevine/PolyGram / President / Target/BMG

FIELDS OF GREEN
Election '97/Arthur / Starship trooper/wurm / Promise of love / Spanish wizard / Never ending road / Fighter / Tell me why / Rope trick / Nice man / Fields of green
CD ______ MFCD 001
Music Fusion / Aug '97 / Pinnacle

GREATEST HITS
CD Set ______ CDFRL 001
Fragile / Nov '93 / Grapevine/PolyGram

HERITAGE SUITE
Chasms / Thorwald's cross / St. Michael's isle / Spanish head / Ayres / Mona's isle / Dhoon / Bee orchid / Chapel hill / Curraghs / Painted lady / Peregrine falcon
CD ______ RWCD 16
President / Nov '93 / Grapevine/PolyGram / President / Target/BMG

JOURNEY TO THE CENTRE OF THE EARTH
Journey / Battle
CD ______ 5500614
Spectrum / May '93 / PolyGram

LIGHT AT THE END OF THE TUNNEL
CD ______ HRHCD 004
Music Fusion / Mar '97 / Pinnacle

LIVE AT HAMMERSMITH
Arthur / Three wives / Journey / Merlin
CD ______ RWCD 2
President / Nov '93 / Grapevine/PolyGram / President / Target/BMG

LIVE ON THE TEST
Recollection / Part IV, the realisation / Sir Lancelot and the black knight / Part III, the spaceman / Catherine Parr / Prisoner / Merlin the magician
CD ______ WHISCD 007
Windsong / Oct '94 / Pinnacle

MYTHS AND LEGENDS OF KING ARTHUR, THE
Arthur / Lady of the lake / Guinevere / Sir Lancelot and the black knight / Merlin the magician / Sir Galahad / Last battle
CD ______ CDMID 135
A&M / Oct '92 / PolyGram

NEW GOSPELS, THE (2CD Set)
CD Set ______ HRMCD 001
OTL Music / Nov '96 / Grapevine/ PolyGram

NIGHT AIRS
CD _______ RWCD 9
President / Nov '93 / Grapevine/PolyGram / President / Target/BMG

NO EXPENSE SPARED (Wakeman, Rick & Adam)
No expense spared / Dylic / It's your move / No one cares / Luck of the draw / Dream the world away / Is it the spring / Nothing ever changes / Number 10 / Jungle / Children of Chernobyl / Find the time
CD _______ RWCD 22
President / Nov '93 / Grapevine/PolyGram / President / Target/BMG

PHANTOM POWER
CD _______ RIOCD 1003
Rio Digital / Nov '92 / Grapevine/PolyGram

PIANO ALBUM, THE
CD _______ ESSCD 322
Essential / Nov '95 / BMG

PRIVATE COLLECTION, THE
Battle / Penny's piece / Pearl and dean piano concerto / Piece for granny / Steamhole dance (parts 1 and 2) / Mountain / Warmongers / Aberlady / Now a word from our sponsor
CD _______ RWCD 23
President / Apr '94 / Grapevine/PolyGram / President / Target/BMG

ROCK 'N' ROLL PROPHET...PLUS
Return of the prophet / I'm so straight I'm a weirdo / Dragon / Dark / Alpha sleep / Maybe '80 / March of the child soldiers / Early warning / Spy of '55 / Stalemate / Do you believe in fairies / Rock 'n' roll prophet
CD _______ RWCD 12
President / Nov '93 / Grapevine/PolyGram / President / Target/BMG

ROMANCE OF THE VICTORIAN AGE (Wakeman, Rick & Adam)
Burlington Arcade / If only / Last teardrop / Still dreaming / Memories of the Victorian age / Lost in words / Tale of love / Mysteries unfold / Forever in my heart / Days of wonder / Swans / Another mellow day / Dance of the elves
CD _______ RWCD 25
President / Nov '94 / Grapevine/PolyGram / President / Target/BMG

SEA AIRS
Harbour lights / Pirate / Storm clouds / Lost at sea / Mermaid / Waves / Fisherman / Flying fish / Marie Celeste / Time and tide / Lone sailor / Sailor's lament
CD _______ RWCD 8
President / Nov '93 / Grapevine/PolyGram / President / Target/BMG

SEVEN WONDERS OF THE WORLD, THE
Pharos of Alexandra / Colossus of Rhodes / Pyramids of Egypt / Hanging gardens of Babylon / Temple of Artemis / Statue of Zeus / Mausoleum at Halicarnassus
CD _______ RWCD 27
President / Jun '95 / Grapevine/PolyGram / President / Target/BMG

SILENT NIGHTS
Tell 'em all you know / Opening line / Opera / Man's best friend / Glory boys / Silent nights / Ghost of a rock 'n' roll star / Dancer / Elgin mansions / That's who I am
CD _______ RWCD 1
President / Nov '93 / Grapevine/PolyGram / President / Target/BMG

SIX WIVES OF HENRY VIII, THE
Catherine of Aragon / Ann of Cleves / Catherine Howard / Jane Seymour / Anne Boleyn / Catherine Parr
CD _______ CDMID 136
A&M / Oct '92 / PolyGram

SOFTSWORD
Magna charter / After prayers / Battle sonata / Siege / Rochester collage / Story of love (King John) / March of time / Don't fly away / Isabella / Softsword / Hymn of hope
CD _______ RWCD 24
President / Apr '94 / Grapevine/PolyGram / President / Target/BMG

SUITE OF GODS, A (Wakeman, Rick & Ramon Ramedios)
CD _______ RWCD 5
President / Nov '93 / Grapevine/PolyGram / President / Target/BMG

SURREAL STATE CIRCUS OF IMAGINATION
CD _______ DSHLCD 7018
D-Sharp / Jun '95 / Pinnacle

TAPESTRIES (Wakeman, Rick & Adam)
Fremiet's cat / Time will tell / Fountains of love / View from a window / Les Vendanges / Summer's end / Clair de Lune / Brighter dawn / Blue Lily / Tapestries / Garden party / Portraits in a gallery / Daydream / Storyteller
CD _______ RWCD 29
President / Jun '96 / Grapevine/PolyGram / President / Target/BMG

TIME MACHINE
Custer's last stand / Ocean city / Angel of time / Slaveman / Ice / Open up your eyes / Elizabethan rock / Make me a woman / Rock age
CD _______ RWCD 7
President / Nov '93 / Grapevine/PolyGram / President / Target/BMG

TRIBUTE
CD _______ CDRPM 0018
RP Media / May '97 / Essential/BMG

VIGNETTES (Wakeman, Rick & Adam)
Waiting alone / Wish I was you / Sun comes crying / A breath of heaven / Moment in time / Artist's dream / Change of face / Madman blues / A painting of our love / Riverside / Need you / Simply acoustic / Just another tear
CD _______ RWCD 30
President / Nov '96 / Grapevine/PolyGram / President / Target/BMG

VISIONS
Fantasy / Peace of mind / Innermost thoughts / Vision of light / Higher planes / Astral traveller / Dream on / Thought waves / Drifting patterns / Future memories / Levitation / Moondreams
CD _______ RWCD 28
President / Oct '95 / Grapevine/PolyGram / President / Target/BMG

VOYAGES (2CD Set)
Catherine of Aragon / Catherine Howard / Jane Seymour / Anne Boleyn / Arthur / Merlin the magician / Last battle / White rock / Searching for gold / After the ball / Ice run / March of the gladiators / Summertime / Temperament of mind / Journey / Recollection / Battle / Forest / Crime of passion / Judas Iscariot / Hibernation / Free song / Maker
CD Set _______ 5405672
A&M / Oct '96 / PolyGram

WAKEMAN WITH WAKEMAN (Wakeman, Rick & Adam)
Lure of the wild / Beach comber / Meglomania / Rage and rhyme / Sync or swim / Jiggajig / Caesarea / After the atom / Suicide shuffle / Past and present / Paint it black
CD _______ RWCD 11
President / Feb '93 / Grapevine/PolyGram / President / Target/BMG

ZODIAQUE (Wakeman, Rick & Tony Fernandez)
CD _______ RWCD 6
President / Nov '93 / Grapevine/PolyGram / President / Target/BMG

Wakenins, Ulf

HEART OF MINE
CD _______ DRGCD 91416
DRG / Jul '94 / Discovery / New Note/ Pinnacle

NEW YORK MEETING
Bernie's tune / Way you look tonight / Crazy he calls me / Nature of business / Spartacus / New York meeting / Jet lag / Angel eyes / Georgia on my mind
CD _______ CDLR 45082
L&R / Jul '94 / New Note/Pinnacle

Wakeooloo

HEAR NO EVIL
CD _______ EFA 262072
Pravda / Dec '94 / SRD

WHAT ABOUT IT
CD _______ EFA 061972
House In Motion / Jul '95 / SRD

Walcott, Collin

GRAZING DREAMS
Song of the morrow / Gold sun / Swarm / Mountain morning / Jewel ornament / Grazing dreams / Samba tala / Moon lake
CD _______ 8278662
ECM / Jun '86 / New Note/Pinnacle

WORKS: COLLIN WALCOTT
Scimitar / Song of the morrow / Like that of sky / Travel by night / Godumada / Hey da boom lullaby / Prancing / Cadona / Awakening / Padma / Travel by day
CD _______ 8372762
ECM / Jun '89 / New Note/Pinnacle

Walden, Myron

HYPNOSIS
My house / Telepathy / Dimensions / Hypnosis / Untitled in A flat minor / Marva / As the sun peaks / Dearted
CD _______ NYC 60252
NYC / Nov '96 / New Note/Pinnacle

Walden, Narada Michael

ECSTASY'S DANCE
White night / Delightful / First love / Rainbow sky / I cry, I smile / I don't want nobody else(to dance with you) / Awakening / I shoulda loved ya / Tonight I'm alright / Real thang / Blue side of midnight / Reach out / High above the clouds / Gimme, gimme, gimme / Divine emotions
CD _______ 8122725662
Rhino / Mar '97 / Warner Music

Waldo, Elisabeth

SACRED RITES
Serpent and the eagle / Within the temple of macuilzochitl / Papaganga lament / Ritual of the human scarifice / Festival of Texcatlipoca / Song for the mountain spirits / Penitente procession / Land of the sun kings / Song of the chasqui / Incan festival dance / Making chica / Balsa boat / Swinging the quipu / Saycuscal (weary stones) / Dance of the nustas
CD _______ GNPD 2225
GNP Crescendo / Oct '95 / ZYX

Waldo, Terry

TERRY WALDO AND THE GOTHAM CITY BAND VOL.2 (Waldo, Terry & The Gotham City Band)
CD _______ SOSCD 1201
Stomp Off / Oct '92 / Jazz Music / Wellard

Waldron, Mal

BLACK SPIRITS ARE HERE AGAIN (Waldron, Mal & Roberto Ottaviano)
CD _______ DIW 917
Ocora / Jan '97 / ADA / Harmonia Mundi

BLUES FOR LADY DAY (Personal Tribute To Billie Holiday)
Blues for Lady Day / Just friends / Don't blame me / You don't know what love is / Man I love / You're my thrill / Strange fruit / Easy living / Mean to me
CD _______ BLC 760193
Black Lion / Jun '94 / Cadillac / Jazz Music / Koch / Wellard

CROWD SCENE (Waldron, Mal Quintet)
CD _______ 1212182
Soul Note / Nov '92 / Cadillac / Harmonia Mundi / Wellard

FREE AT LAST (Waldron, Mal Trio)
Rat now / 1-3-234 / Willow weep for me / Balladina / Rock my soul / Boo
CD _______ 8313322
ECM / Aug '89 / New Note/Pinnacle

LEFT ALONE (Plays The Moods Of Billie Holiday) (Waldron, Mal Trio)
CD _______ BET 6024
Bethlehem / Jan '95 / ADA / ZYX

LIVE AT DE KAVE
CD _______ SER 01
Serene / Mar '90 / Cadillac

MUCH MORE (Waldron, Mal & Marion Brown)
CD _______ FRLCD 010
Freelance / Oct '92 / Cadillac / Koch

NO MORE TEARS (FOR LADY DAY)
Yesterdays / No more tears / Melancholy waltz / Solitude / Love me or leave me / All night through / As time goes by / Smoke gets in your eyes / Alone together
CD _______ CDSJP 328
Timeless Jazz / Aug '90 / New Note/ Pinnacle

OUR COLLINE'S A TREASURE
CD _______ 1211982
Soul Note / May '91 / Cadillac / Harmonia Mundi / Wellard

PEAK (Waldron, Mal & Steve Lacy)
CD _______ ARTCD 6186
Hat Art / Mar '97 / Cadillac / Harmonia Mundi

QUEST, THE (Waldron, Mal & Eric Dolphy)
Status seeking / Duquility / Thirteen / We did it / Warm canto / Warp and woof / Fire waltz
CD _______ OJCCD 82
Original Jazz Classics / Jun '96 / Complete/ Pinnacle / Jazz Music / Wellard

SONGS OF LOVE AND REGRET (Waldron, Mal & Marion Brown)
CD _______ FRLCD 006
Freelance / Oct '92 / Cadillac / Koch

TWO NEW (Waldron, Mal & George Haslam)
I've got the world on a string / One for Steve / Tangled lawful bells / Let's do it over / Sakura / Steps in rhythm / Datura / From charleston till now / Come Sunday / I'm old fashioned / After the carnage / Thailand dance
CD _______ SLAMCD 306
Slam / Oct '96 / Cadillac

WALDRON-HASLAM (Waldron, Mal & George Haslam)
I got it bad and that ain't good / If I were a bell / Catch as catch should / Somewhere / Variations on Brahms' Symphony no.3/ movement no.3 / Time for Duke / Vortex / Motion in order
CD _______ SLAMCD 305
Slam / Oct '94 / Cadillac

WHERE ARE YOU (Waldron, Mal Quintet)
CD _______ 1212482
Soul Note / May '94 / Cadillac / Harmonia Mundi / Wellard

Walk Away

SATURATION
Saturation / Many kochanas / For you / Bobok / Softly / Sheet / She's like a sexmachine / Joy is better / Sambula
CD _______ IOR 770242
In & Out / Sep '95 / Vital/SAM

Walkabouts

DEATH VALLEY DOLLS
CD _______ GRCD 404
Glitterhouse / Nov '96 / Avid/BMG

DEVIL'S ROAD
Light will stay on / Rebecca wild / Stopping off place / Cold eye / Christmas valley / Blue head flame / When fortune smiles / For all this / Fairground blues / Leaving kind / Forgiveness song
CD _______ CDVIR 46
Virgin / Mar '96 / EMI

JACK CANDY
CD _______ SPCD 251
Sub Pop / Jan '93 / Cargo / Greyhound / Shellshock/Disc

NEW WEST HOTEL
CD _______ GRCD 252
Glitterhouse / Nov '96 / Avid/BMG

NIGHTTOWN
Follow me an angel / These proud streets / Tremble (Goes the night) / Unwind / Lift your burdens up / Prayer for you / Immaculate / Nocturno / Heartless / Nightbirds / Forever gone / Harbour lights / Slow red dawn
CD _______ CDVIR 57
Virgin / Jun '97 / EMI

RAG AND BONE CATARACT
CD _______ GRCD 85
Glitterhouse / Nov '96 / Avid/BMG

SATISFIED MIND
CD _______ GRCD 294
Glitterhouse / Nov '96 / Avid/BMG

SCAVENGER
CD _______ GRCD 161
Glitterhouse / Nov '96 / Avid/BMG

SEE BEAUTIFUL RATTLESNAKE GARDENS
CD _______ GRCD 335
Glitterhouse / Jun '97 / Avid/BMG

SETTING THE WOODS ON FIRE
CD _______ GRCD 319
Glitterhouse / Nov '96 / Avid/BMG

Walker

STRIKE WHILE THE IRON'S HOT
Strike while the iron's hot / Mon ami / Don't look over your shoulder / It all takes time / Ships that pass in the night / Everyone was a baby / Curacao - blue sky / Tender zone / Looking for an answer / Belong / Month of Sundays / Tudor sweet
CD _______ ZYZ 077CD
Zyzzle / Jan '94 / Zyzzle

Walker Brothers

AFTER THE LIGHTS GO OUT (The Best Of The Walker Brothers 1965-1967)
Love her / Make it easy on yourself / First love never dies / My ship is coming in / Deadlier than the male / Another tear falls / Baby you don't have to tell me / After the lights go out / Mrs. Murphy / In my room / Arcangel / Sun ain't gonna shine anymore / Saddest night in the world / Young man cried / Livin' above your head / Stay with me baby / Walking in the rain / Orpheus / I can't let it happen to you / Just say goodbye / Disc and Music Interview / Japanese Interview
CD _______ 8428312
Fontana / May '90 / PolyGram

COLLECTION, THE
Lights of Cincinatti / Jackie / Joanna / If I promise / Annabella / I'll be your baby tonight / Love her / Sun ain't gonna shine anymore / (Baby) You don't have to tell me / Stay with me baby / Here comes the night / Land of 1000 dances / Living above your head / In my room / Archangel / Stand by me / Everything under the sun / People get ready
CD _______ 5502002
Spectrum / Mar '96 / PolyGram

GALA
Make it easy on yourself / Summertime / My ship is coming in / Lonely winds / There goes my baby / Livin' above your head / Here comes the night / Stay with me baby / No sad songs for me / Sun ain't gonna shine anymore / Land of 1000 dances / (Baby) You don't have to tell me / Dancing in the street / In my rain / Walking in the rain / Just say goodbye
CD _______ 8302122
Phonogram / Feb '89 / PolyGram

LINES
Lines / Taking it all in stride / Inside of you / Have you seen my baby / We're all alone / Many rivers to cross / First day / Brand new Tennessee waltz / Hard to be friends / Dreaming as one

CD 4836742
Columbia / Mar '96 / Sony

NITE FLIGHTS
Shutout / Fat Mama kick / Nite flights / Electrician / Death of romance / Den Haague / Rhythms of vision / Disciples of death / Fury and the fire / Child of flames
CD 4844382
Epic / Jul '96 / Sony

NO REGRETS
No regrets / Hold an old friend's hand / Boulder to Birmingham / Walkin' in the sun / Lover's lullaby / I've got to have you / He'll break your heart / Everything that touches you / Lovers / Burn our bridges
CD 4773542
GTO / Aug '94 / Sony

Walker, Billy

CROSS THE BRAZOS AT WACO (6CD Set)
Headin' for heartaches / I'm gonna take my heart away from you / You're gonna pay with a broken heart / You didn't try and didn't care / Too many times / Dirt 'neath your feet / I guess I'll have to die / Anything your heart desires / Last kiss is the sweetest / Alcohol love / I ain't got no roses / Beautiful brown eyes / Don't tell a soul / She's got honky tonk blood in her veins / What would you do / Always think of you / Ting a ling a school pickney sing ting / Fifteen hugs past midnight / Millie darling / Anything your heart desires / What makes me love you (like I do) / One heart's beatin', one heart's cheatin' / If I should live that long / Stolen love / Who took my ring from your finger / True love's so hard to find / You have my heart now / You know what did / One you hurt / I can tell / I didn't have the nerve it took to leave / Don't let your pride break your heart / Mexican Joe / Time will tell / Headin' for heartaches / It hurts too much to laugh (and I'm too big) / I got lost along the way / I can't keep the girls away / Thank you for calling / Candlelight / Pretend you just don't know me / I'm a fool to care / Going going gone / Kissing you / You're the only good thing (that's happened to me) / Let me hear from you / Let me hear from you / Hey / Fool that I am / Record / Which one of us is to blame / Let's make memories tonight / Whirlpool / Go ahead and make me cry / Most important thing / Can't you love me just a little / Blue mountain waltz / Why does it have to be / So far / Little baggy britches / Leavin' on my mind / I'll never stand in your way / Untamed heart / Especially for fools / If you were happy (then I'm satisfied) / Headin' down the wrong highway / On my mind again / Viva la Matador / I care no more / Image of me / I need it / Where my baby goes she goes with me / Put your hand in mine / It'll take a while / It's doggone tough on me / Ghost of a promise / Love's got a hold on me / I dreamed of an old love affair / Mr. Heartache / I thought about you / Storm within my heart / One way give and take / Woman like you / I call it heaven / Forever / Farewell party / Changed my mind / Gotta find a way / I'll be true to you / Little lover / I wish you love / Yes, I've made it / Faded lights and lonesome people / Just call me lonesome / Let's think about living / Alone with you / They'll never take love from me / I take the chance / Guess things happen that way / Remember me, I'm the one who loves you / Molly darling / Rockin' alone in an old rocking chair / Gonna find me a bluebird / There stands the glass / Jambalaya / Charlie's shoes / Funny how time slips away / Joey's back in town / Charlie's shoes / Wild colonial boy / I know I'm lying / Next voice you hear / Willie the weeper / It's me, not them / Lovely hula hands / Beggin' for trouble / Plaything / I've got a new heartache / Give me back my heart / Ancient history / Man who had everything / These arms of mine / Throw me out / Storm of love / That would sure go good / Heart be careful / Circumstances / It's lonesome / Morning paper / Coming back for more / Cross the brazos at Waco / Down to my last cigarette / If it pleases you / I'm so miserable without you / Matamoros / Samuel Colt / Blue moonlight / Come a little bit closer / Gun, the gold, the girl / Blizzard / Pancho villa / Cattle call / Amigo's guitar / Lawman / Buy Juanita some flowers / I'm nothin' to you / Smoky memories / Nobody but a fool / Pretend you don't see me / Don't change
CD Set BCD 15657
Bear Family / Oct '93 / Direct / Rollercoaster / Swift

Walker, Billy Jr.

BILLY WALKER JR.
Under the stars / 5th of July / Ballerina dance / Marotta / Hot steel / China girl / Night rider / Add two / Perfect love / Water bells
CD GEFD 24469
Geffen / Mar '92 / BMG

WALK, THE
Walk / Hourglass / Dream on / Mystery man / Street dancin' / Illusions / Free flight / Fields of stone / Crystal speak to me / Breezes
CD GEFD 24315
Geffen / May '91 / BMG

Walker, Brett

BRETT WALKER & THE RAILBIRDS (Walker, Brett & The Railbirds)
Look a little closer / Can't stay too long / Tell me why / What's still left / Drown in your ocean / Rain dance / It's a good thing / Yesterday has gone / Everything I want / I could be wrong / Take me to the river / American dreamer
CD WESTCD 9
West Coast / Nov '96 / Cargo

Walker, Clay

CLAY WALKER
Dreaming with my eyes open / What's it to you / Silence speaks for itself / How to make a man lonesome / Next step in love / White palace / Money can't buy (the love we had) / Things I should have said / Where do I fit in the picture / Live until I die / I don't know how love starts
CD 74321166762
Giant / Aug '94 / BMG

IF I COULD MAKE A LIVING
If I could make a living / Melrose Avenue cinema / My heart will never know / What do you want for nothin' / This woman and this man / Boogie till the cows come home / Heartache highway / You make it look so easy / Lose your memory / Money ain't everything / Down by the river
CD 74321250172
Giant / Apr '95 / BMG

RUMOUR HAS IT
Rumour has it / One, two, I love you / I'd say that's right / Heart over head over heels / Watch this / You'll never hear the end of it / Country boy and city girl / I need a Margarita / That's us / Then what
CD 74321454772
Giant / Apr '97 / BMG

Walker, Dee

JUMP BACK
CD TANGCD 6
Tangerine / Aug '92 / RTM/Disc

Walker, Ian

CROSSING THE BORDERLINES (Walker, Ian & Setanta)
CD FE 088CD
Fellside / Apr '93 / ADA / Direct / Target/ BMG

Walker Jazz Band

BIG BAND STORY VOL.2
CD PV 785093
Disques Pierre Verany / Feb '86 / Kingdom

Walker, Jerry Jeff

CHRISTMAS GONZO STYLE
I'll be home for Christmas / White Christmas / Santa Claus is coming to town / Christmas song / Here comes Santa Claus / Rudolph the red nosed reindeer / Jingle bells / Walking in a winter wonderland / Frosty the snowman / Jingle bell rock / Twelve days of Christmas / We wish you a Merry Christmas
CD RCD 10312
Rykodisc / Nov '94 / ADA / Vital

GYPSY SONGMAN
Gypsy songman / David and me / Mr. Bojangles / Hands on the wheel / Ramblin' hearts / Then came the children / She knows her daddy sings / Long afternoons / Borderline / Driftin' way of life / Hard livin' / Railroad lady / Jaded lover / Rain just falls / Night rider's lament / We were kind of crazy then / Cadillac cowboy / Pass it on / Charlie Dunn / Hill country rain
CD RCD 20071
Rykodisc / May '92 / ADA / Vital

HILL COUNTRY RAIN
CD RCD 10241
Rykodisc / Jun '92 / ADA / Vital

LIVE AT GRUENE HALL
Lovin' makes livin' worthwhile / Pickup truck song / Long long time / I feel like Hank Williams tonight / Man with the big hat / Quiet faith of man / Little bird / Woman in Texas / Rodeo wind / Trashy wind
CD RCD 10123
Rykodisc / May '92 / ADA / Vital

NAVAJO RUG
Navajo rug / Just to celebrate / Blue mood / Lucky man / Detour / I'm all through throwing good love after bad / Rockin' on the river / Nolan Ryan (a hero to us all) / Flowers in the snow / If I'd loved you then
CD RCD 10175
Rykodisc / Jul '91 / ADA / Vital

VIVA LUCKENBACH
Gettin' by / Viva Luckenbach / Learning to p'like and Luckenbach women's lib / Keep Texas beautiful / What I like about Texas / I'll be here in the morning / Gift / Little man / Some phone numbers / I makes money (money don't make me) / Gonzo compadres / Movin' on
CD RCD 10268
Rykodisc / Mar '94 / ADA / Vital

Walker, Jimmy

ROUGH AND READY BOOGIE WOOGIE FOR 4 HANDS (Walker, Jimmy & Erwin Helfer)
CD TCD 5011
Testament / Dec '94 / ADA / Koch

Walker, Joe

I'M IN THE DOG HOUSE
I'm in the dog house / Couche couche and ky-yay / Bullet through my heart / Give me what I want / I left my home / Watch that black cat / Tante Sarah / I screwed up / I'd like to put my hand on that / Seen it for myself / Keep on pushing / Mom and pop waltz
CD ZNCD 1006
Zane / Oct '95 / Pinnacle

ZYDECO FEVER
CD ZNCD 1004
Zane / Oct '95 / Pinnacle

Walker, Joe Louis

BLUES SURVIVOR
Help yourself / Shake for me / My dignity / Young girl's eyes / Part of me / Bad thing / You just don't know / Put you down baby / Blues survivor / Rainy nights / Workin' blues
CD 5190632
Verve / Jan '93 / PolyGram

GIFT, THE
One time around / Thin line / 747 / Gift / What about you / Shade tree mechanic / Quarter to three / Mama didn't raise no fools / Everybody's had the blues / Main goal
CD HCD 8012
Hightone / Jan '89 / ADA / Koch

GREAT GUITARS
CD 5371412
Verve / Mar '97 / PolyGram

JLW
I can't get you off my mind / I need your lovin' everyday / Rain on my mind / Inner city man / On that powerline / Hold on / 12 step lovin' / Alone / Got to find my baby / Lost the will to love me / Going to Canada
CD 5231182
Verve / Sep '93 / PolyGram

LIVE AT SLIM'S VOL.1
CD FIENDCD 212
Demon / Apr '91 / Pinnacle

LIVE AT SLIM'S VOL.2
Don't you know / Thin line / One woman / Blue guitar / Shade tree mechanic / 747 / Just a little bit / Brother go ahead and take her / Love at first sight
CD FIENDCD 716
Demon / Apr '92 / Pinnacle

Walker, John

ADVENTURE/DEVOTED TO YOU
Once upon a time in the West / I know why / To a wild rose / Breaker on the side / Memory / April in Portugal / Blue moon / Prelude no.1 / How do I love thee / Moonlight serenade / Argentine melody / Tales of the unexpected / Clair de lune / Chariots of fire / Theme from Ice Castles / Again / Hooked on classics / Adventure / Swiss piece
CD C5CD 632
See For Miles/C5 / Feb '96 / Pinnacle

MY FAVOURITE LENNON/MCCARTNEY (Walker, John & The Digital Sunset)
CD C5MCD 565
See For Miles/C5 / Jun '91 / Pinnacle

MY FAVOURITE SINATRA (Walker, John & The Digital Sunset)
New York, New York / Something stupid / Strangers in the night / It's been a long, long time / Five minutes more / Saturday night is the loneliest night of the week / Love and marriage / Three coins in the fountain / It's nice to go travellin' / I'll be seeing you / Nancy with the laughing face / I'm a fool to want you / Come fly with me / Witchcraft / Nice 'n' easy / London by night / Tender trap / Begin the beguine / I've got you under my skin / Night and day / All the way / High hopes / If you never come to me / Hey jealous lover / Lady is a tramp / My kind of town (Chicago is) / Young at heart / My way
CD C5CD530
See For Miles/C5 / May '89 / Pinnacle

PLAYS MY FAVOURITE JOHN WALKER ORIGINALS (Walker, John & The Digital Sunset)
CD C5MCD 575
See For Miles/C5 / '91 / Pinnacle

SUMMER SONG/BY SPECIAL REQUEST
Water babies / I got rhythm / S'wonderful / On the street where you live / Tritsch-tratsch polka / Island in the sun / Jamaica farewell / Mon amour / Jive alive / Forgotten dreams / Theme from "New York, New York" / Lonely shepherd / John & Julie / Chanson de matin / My favourite things / Ave Maria / Caribbean melody / In the mood / Little brown jug / American patrol / Chattanooga choo choo / Lambada / We'll be together again / Amor / If (they made me a king) / Weep they will / I left my heart in San Francisco
CD C5CD 629
See For Miles/C5 / Oct '95 / Pinnacle

TIME TO RELAX/LIVE AT TURNER'S
Atlantis / Seasons / Elizabethan serenade / Thousand and one nights / Fleur de Paris / Pastoral symphony / Jesu joy of my soul / Minuet in G / Morning / Skater's waltz / Valse des fleurs / Morgenblaetter / Wiener blut / I know not where / Stars fell on Alabama / People on the hills / Hooked in space / 2001 / Close encounters of the third kind / Star Wars / Cair paravel / Blue danube / Liebestraum / Artist's life / Cuckoo waltz / Voices of spring / Nocturne in E flat / Wine, women and song / Coppelia valse / Tales from the Vienna Woods / March of the toys / Yellow bird / Stranger in paradise / Evening clam ski Sunday / Love changes everything / Till / Jesu joy of man's desiring / Village parade / Valentino / Classical romance / Aces high / Meditation / Tico tico / Valse romantique / Sunrise / In a monastery garden / May you always
CD C5CD 626
See For Miles/C5 / Jul '95 / Pinnacle

UNCHAINED MELODIES
Unchained melody / Any dream will do / Wooden heart / Forever and ever / One day in your life / Ferry across the Mersey / Nothings gonna change my love for you / Annie's song / Clair / House of the rising sun / Puppet on a string / Take my breath away / Summer holiday / I just called to say I love you / Lady in red / Sacrifice / Those were the days / In the summertime / Hello / Dancing queen / Uptown girl / Wombling song
CD C5JCD 615
See For Miles/C5 / Apr '95 / Pinnacle

Walker, Johnny

BLUE LOVE (Walker, Johnny 'Big Moose')
Mean ol' Frisco blues / Blue shadows / Lone wolf / I'm gonna tell my Mama / Georgia on my mind / One room country shack / Blackjack / Don't cry / Who's been foolin' with you / Hallelujah I love her so / Drown in my own tears
CD ECD 260822
Evidence / Sep '96 / ADA / Cadillac / Harmonia Mundi

LIVE AT THE RISING SUN (Walker, Johnny 'Big Moose')
CD RS 0008CD
Rising Sun / Jul '95 / ADA

Walker, Junior

19 GREATEST HITS: JUNIOR WALKER
CD 5300332
Motown / Jan '93 / PolyGram

BEST OF JUNIOR WALKER & THE ALL STARS, THE (Walker, Junior & The All Stars)
CD Set 5302932
Motown / Apr '94 / PolyGram

SHAKE AND FINGERPOP
Shotgun / How sweet it is (to be loved by you) / Home cooking / Money / Pucker up buttercup / What does it take (to win your love) / Come see about me / Hip city / Cleo's mood / Shake and fingerpop / Shoot your shot
CD CDBM 072
Blue Moon / Apr '89 / Cadillac / Discovery / Greensleeves / Jazz Music / Jet Star / TKO Magnum

Walker, Philip

BIG BLUES FROM TEXAS (Walker, Philip & Otis Grand)
CD JSPCD 248
JSP / Nov '92 / ADA / Cadillac / Direct / Hot Shot / Target/BMG

BLUES
How many more years / 90 proof / What'd you hope to gain / Don't be afraid of the dark / Big rear window / Her own keys / Talk to that man / Sometime girl / I had a dream
CD FIENDCD 128
Demon / Oct '88 / Pinnacle

SOMEDAY YOU'LL HAVE THESE BLUES
CD HCD 8032
Hightone / Sep '94 / ADA / Koch

WORKING GIRL BLUES
CD CDBT 117
Rounder / Aug '95 / ADA / CM / Direct

Walker, Pipe Sergeant Gordon

PIPE BANDS OF DISTINCTION (Walker, Corporal Gordon)
CD CDMON 804
Monarch / Dec '89 / ADA / CM / Direct / Duncans

WORLD'S GREATEST PIPERS VOL.13, THE
Crags of Stirling / 71st Highlanders / Atholl Cummers / Cameronian rant / Smith of Chil-

liechassie / Mrs. Macpherson of Inveran / My love my joy / Duncan Johnstone / Doctor MacInnes' fancy / Banks of the Allan water / Colin's cattle / Carbello crossing / Highland wedding / Piper's bonnet / John Morrison of Assynthouse / High level hornpipe / Tam Bain's lum / Sweet maid of Mull / Star of Kuwait / Mo Gra's lullaby / Freedom's cry / MacPhedran's strathspey / Stumpie / Thick lies the mist on yon hill / Brolum / Scots air reel / Jimmy Blue / Duke of Hamilton's reel / Row me home / Leaving Barra / Old wife of Mill Dust / John Patterson's mare / MacKay's banner
CD ______ LCOM 5252
Lismor / Aug '96 / ADA / Direct / Duncans / Lismor

Walker, Robert 'Bilbo'

PROMISED LAND
Goin to the train station / Please love me / Just a country boy / Promised land / You took my love / Still a fool / Wild side of life / It wasn't God that made honky tonk angels / Everything gonna be alright / Baby, baby, baby / How much more / Mama talk to your daughter / Better lovin' man / Hold that train conductor / Got my mojo working / Berry pickin'
CD ______ R 2632
Rooster / Mar '97 / Direct

Walker, Sammy

IN CONCERT
CD ______ BRAM 1990162
Brambus / Nov '93 / ADA

Walker, Scott

BOY CHILD
Plague / Such a small love / Plastic palace people / Big Louis / Seventh seal / Old man's back again / Little things (that keep us together) / Girls from the streets / Copenhagen / War is over / Montague Terrace (in blue) / Amorous Humphrey Plugg / Bridge / We came through / Boy child / Prologue / Time operator / It's raining today / On your own again / Rope and the colt
CD ______ 8428322
Fontana / May '90 / PolyGram

CLIMATE OF HUNTER, THE
Rawhide / Dealer / Sleepwalkers woman / Blanket roll blues
CD ______ CDV 2303
Virgin / Nov '89 / EMI

IT'S RAINING TODAY (The Scott Walker Story 1967-1970)
CD ______ RE 21202
Razor & Tie / Dec '96 / Koch

NO REGRETS (The Best Of Scott Walker/Walker Brothers) (Walker, Scott & The Walker Brothers)
No regrets: *Walker Brothers* / Make it easy on yourself: *Walker Brothers* / Sun ain't gonna shine anymore: *Walker Brothers* / My ship is comin' in: *Walker Brothers* / Joanna: *Walker, Scott* / Lights of Cincinatti: *Walker, Scott* / Another tear falls: *Walker Brothers* / Boy child: *Walker, Scott* / Montague Terrace in blue: *Walker, Scott* / Jackie: *Walker, Scott* / Stay with me baby: *Walker Brothers* / If you go away: *Walker, Scott* / First love never dies: *Walker Brothers* / Love her: *Walker Brothers* / Walking in the rain: *Walker Brothers* / Baby you don't have to tell me: *Walker Brothers* / Deadlier than the male: *Walker Brothers* / We're all alone: *Walker Brothers*
CD ______ 5108312
Fontana / Jan '92 / PolyGram

SCOTT VOL.1
Mathilde / Montague Terrace in blue / Angelica / Lady came from Baltimore / When Joanna loved me / My death / Big hurt / Such a small love / You're gonna hear from me / Through a long and sleepless night / Always coming back to you / Amsterdam
CD ______ 5108792
Fontana / Feb '92 / PolyGram

SCOTT VOL.2
Jackie / Best of both worlds / Black sheep boy / Amourous Humphrey Plugg / Next / Girls from the streets / Plastic palace people / Wait until dark / Girls and the dogs / Windows of the world / Bridge / Come next Spring
CD ______ 5108802
Fontana / Feb '92 / PolyGram

SCOTT VOL.3
It's raining today / Copenhagen / Rosemary / Big Louise / We came through / Butterfly / Two ragged soldiers / 30 century man / Winter night / Two weeks since you've gone / Sons of / Funeral tango / If you go away
CD ______ 5108812
Fontana / Aug '92 / PolyGram

SCOTT VOL.4
Seventh seal / On your own again / World's strongest man / Angels of ashes / Boy child / Hero of the war / Old mans back again / Duchess / Get behind me / Rhymes of goodbye
CD ______ 5108822
Fontana / Aug '92 / PolyGram

SINGS JACQUES BREL
Mathilde / Amsterdam / Jackie / My death / Next / Girl and the dogs / If you go away / Funeral tango / Sons of
CD ______ 8382122
Fontana / Sep '92 / PolyGram

STRETCH/WE HAD IT ALL
CD ______ BGOCD 358
Beat Goes On / May '97 / Pinnacle

TIL THE BAND COMES IN
CD ______ BGOCD 320
Beat Goes On / Aug '96 / Pinnacle

TILT
Farmer in the city / Cockfighter / Bouncer see bouncer / Manhattan / Face on breast / Bolivia '95 / Patriot / Tilt / Rosary
CD ______ 5268592
Fontana / May '95 / PolyGram

Walker, Sylford

LAMB'S BREAD
CD ______ GRELCD 119
Greensleeves / May '90 / Jet Star / SRD

Walker, T-Bone

BEGINNING 1926-1946, THE
CD ______ 158852
Blues Collection / Feb '97 / Discovery

BLUES T-BONE STYLE (Various Artists)
Strollin' with bones: *Brown, Clarence 'Gatemouth'* / T-Bone boogie: *Earl, Ronnie* / Dedication to the late T-Bone Walker: *Guy, Buddy* / Don't leave me baby: *Walker, Philip & Otis Grand* / Blues for T-Bone: *Houston, Joe* / When the rain starts fallin': *Copeland, Johnny* / Two bones and a pick: *Roomful Of Blues* / T-Bone jumps again: *Schultz, Alex & The Mighty Flyers* / Hustle is on: *Walker, Philip* / Duke's mood: *Robillard, Duke*
CD ______ EDCD 7019
Easydisc / Jul '97 / Direct

FUNKY TOWN
Goin' to funky town / Party girl / Why my baby (keep on bothering me) / Jealous woman / Going to build me a playhouse / Long skirt baby blues / Struggling blues / I'm in an awful mood / I wish my baby (would come home at night)
CD ______ BGOCD 116
Beat Goes On / Sep '91 / Pinnacle

GOOD FEELIN'
Good feelin' / Every day I have the blues / Woman you must be crazy / Long lost lover / I wonder why / Vacation / Shake it baby / Poontang / Reconsider / Sail on little girl / When I grow up / See you next time
CD ______ 5197232
Verve / Feb '94 / PolyGram

I WANT A LITTLE GIRL
CD ______ DD 633
Delmark / Nov '92 / ADA / Cadillac / CM / Direct / Hot Shot

LOW DOWN BLUES
Don't leave me baby / I'm gonna find my baby / It's a lowdown dirty deal / I know your wig has gone / T-Bone jumps again / Stormy Monday / She's my old time used to be / Midnight blues / Long skirt baby blues / Too much trouble blues / Hypin' woman blues / Natural blues / That's better for me / Lonesome woman blues / Inspiration blues / T-Bone shuffle / That old feeling is gone / I wish you were mine / She's the no sleepin 'est woman / Plain old down home blues / Go back to the one you love / You're my best poker hand
CD ______ CPCD 8214
Charly / Feb '97 / Koch

STORMY MONDAY
Every day I have the blues / I woke up this morning / Stormy Monday blues / Why my baby (keep on bothering me) / Late blues / Sail on / T-Bone blues special / Treat me so low down / When I grow up / Long lost lover / Shake it baby
CD ______ 17103
Laserlight / Jan '97 / Target/BMG

STORMY MONDAY
Left home when I was a kid / Glamour girl / (You'll never find anyone) to be a slave like me / When we are schoolmates / Got to cross the deep blue sea / My patience keeps running out / Stormy Monday blues / Lousiana bayou drive / Don't go back to New Orleans / That evening train / All night long / T-Bone's that way
CD ______ 305992
Hallmark / Jan '97 / Carlton

T-BONE BLUES
CD ______ RSACD 811
Sequel / Oct '94 / BMG

T-BONE SHUFFLE (Charly Blues Masterworks Vol.14)
I got a break baby / No worry blues / Bobby Sox blues / I'm in an awful mood / Don't give me the runaround / Hard pain blues / Goodbye blues / I'm waiting for your call / First love blues / Born to be no good / Inspiration blues / Description blues / T-Bone shuffle / I want a little girl / I'm still in love with you / West side baby
CD ______ CDBM 14
Charly / Apr '92 / Koch

WELL DONE
Back on the scene / Good boy / No do right / Please come back to me / Natural ball / Baby / She's a hit / Treat your Daddy well / Further on / Up the road / Why don't my baby treat me right / Afraid to close my eyes / She's my old time used to be / I used to be a good boy
CD ______ CDBM 098
Blue Moon / Apr '94 / Cadillac / Discovery / Greensleeves / Jazz Music / Jet Star / TKO Magnum

Walker, Wailin'

WAILIN' WALKER
CD ______ CD 3030
Double Trouble / Oct '92 / CM / Hot Shot

Walking On Ice

NO MARGIN FOR ERROR
Jealous hearts / Set me free / Today, tomorrow / Thinking man's friend / End of an era / Walk in the rain / What you see, what you hear / Footpump / Loser's waltz / Everyman / Rock
CD ______ CYCL 009
Cyclops / Aug '97 / Pinnacle

Walking Seeds

BAD ORB...WHIRLING BALL
CD ______ PAPCD 001
Paperhouse / Apr '90 / RTM/Disc

Walking Wounded

HARD TIMES
CD ______ TX 2005CD
Taxim / Jan '94 / ADA

Wall

JAZZ IN SWEDEN 1985
CD ______ 1312
Caprice / Dec '90 / ADA / Cadillac / CM / Complete/Pinnacle

Wall Akure

AFROMORPH TEXT
CD ______ FSCD 0007
Freak Street / Sep '97 / Pinnacle

Wall, Chris

HONKY TONK HEART
CD ______ RCD 10179
Hannibal / '92 / ADA / Vital

NO SWEAT
CD ______ RCD 10219
Rykodisc / Mar '92 / ADA / Vital

Wall, Dan

OFF THE WALL
13 Steps / Black ice / I didn't know what time it was / Electric ballroom / Carol's bridge / End of a love affair / Zakatak / Waltz for John / Off the wall
CD ______ ENJ 93102
Enja / Mar '97 / New Note/Pinnacle / Vital/SAM

Wall Of Sleep

WALL OF SLEEP
CD ______ WO 24CD
Woronzow / Jun '95 / Pinnacle

Wall Of Sound

WALL OF SOUND
CD ______ EBCD 2
Eightball / Jan '95 / Vital

Wallace Brothers

LOVER'S PRAYER (Classic Southern Soul)
Lover's prayer / Love me like I love you / Faith / I'll let nothing seperate me / Who's fooling who / I'll still love you / Precious words / You're mine / One way affair / Bye bye bye / Go on girl / She loves me not / I'll step aside / Hold my hurt for awhile / No more / Darlin' I love you so / Stepping stone / Girl's alright with me / These arms of mine / Talking about my baby / Thanks a lot / Line between love and hate
CD ______ CDKEND 128
Kent / Nov '95 / Pinnacle

Wallace, Bennie

BIG JIM'S TANGO
CD ______ ENJA 40462
Enja / May '95 / New Note/Pinnacle / Vital/SAM

Wallace, Robert

BREAKOUT
Barlinnie Highlander / Great is the cause of my sorrow / Mary Horne/Lewis jig / Etain / Barra marches / Lochaber no more/Dog in the bushes / King of lies / Ane ground / Broderick's bodhran / Old woman's lullaby / Below the belt / Strathspey & reel / Leaving Lochboisdale
CD ______ LCOM 5253
Lismor / Aug '96 / ADA / Direct / Duncans / Lismor

Wallace, Sippie

WOMEN BE WISE
Women be wise / Trouble everywhere I roam / Lonesome hours blues / Special delivery blues / Murder gonna be my crime / Gambler's dream / Caldonia blues / You got to know how / Shorty George blues / I'm a mighty tight woman / Bedroom blues / Up the country blues / Suitcase blues
CD ______ ALCD 4810
Alligator / May '93 / ADA / CM / Direct
CD ______ STCD 8024
Storyville / Dec '94 / Cadillac / Jazz Music / Wellard

Wallen, Byron

EARTH ROOTS
Millenium / Mountains of the moon / Winds of change / Dream catcher / Eastern wind / Heritage / Reflections / Finery of the feast / Healing ceremony / Voices of the millennium
CD ______ BW 090
Melt 2000 / Jun '97 / Vital/SAM

SOUND ADVICE
Time and space / Rhythms of vision / Moonchild / Crazy black / Ngoba / Paradox / Let go and embrace / Sesame Street / Stay open / Sunday calling / Time and space
CD ______ BW 063
B&W / Nov '96 / New Note/Pinnacle / SRD / Vital/SAM

Waller, Fats

AIN'T MISBEHAVIN'
CD ______ CD 53078
Giants Of Jazz / Mar '92 / Cadillac / Jazz Music / Target/BMG

AIN'T MISBEHAVIN'
CD ______ 17011
Laserlight / Jan '95 / Target/BMG

AIN'T MISBEHAVIN'
Ain't misbehavin' / Flat foot floogie / A-tisket, a-tasket / All God's chillun got wings / Deep river / Go down, Moses / Water boy / Lonesome road / That old feeling: *Waller, Fats & Adelaide Hall* / Pent up in a penthouse / Music maestro please / Don't try your jive on me / I can't give you anything but love: *Waller, Fats & Adelaide Hall* / Not there, right there / Cottage in the rain / London suite / Smoke dreams of you / You can't have your cake and eat it
CD ______ QED 015
Tring / Nov '96 / Tring

AIN'T MISBEHAVIN'
Ain't misbehavin' / Sweet Sue, just you / Joint is jumpin' / Handful of keys / Your feets too big / I've got my fingers crossed / Honeysuckle rose / Crazy 'bout my baby / Hallelujah things look rosy now / Serenade for a wealthy widow / I'm gonna sit right down and write myself a letter / Thousand dreams of you / Believe it, beloved / I wish I were twins / Christopher Columbus / How can you face me
CD ______ SUMCD 4022
Summit / Nov '96 / Sound & Media

AUDIO ARCHIVE
Pent-up in a penthouse / I can't give you anything but love / Smoke dreams of you / You can't have your cake and eat it / Don't try your jive on me / All God's chillun got wings / Ain't misbehavin' / Go down Moses / Not there, right there / Flat foot floogie / Cottage in the rain / Swing low, sweet chariot / Deep river / Waterboy / Music maestro please / Lonesome road / Tisket-a-tasket / That old feeling
CD ______ CDAA 023
Tring / Jun '92 / Tring

CLASSIC JAZZ FROM RARE PIANO ROLLS
18th street strut / If I could be with you one hour tonight / I'm coming Virginia / Ain't nobody's business if I do / Clearing house blues / Squeeze me / Snake hips / Laughin' cryin' blues / You can't do what my last man did / New kind of man with a new kind of love / Nobody but my baby / Got to cool my doggies now / Ain't misbehavin'
CD ______ BCD 104
Biograph / Jul '91 / ADA / Cadillac / Direct / Hot Shot / Jazz Music / Wellard

CLASSICS 1922-1926
CD ______ CLASSICS 664
Classics / Nov '92 / Discovery / Jazz Music

CLASSICS 1926-1927
CD ______ CLASSICS 674
Classics / Nov '92 / Discovery / Jazz Music

CLASSICS 1929
CD ______ CLASSICS 702
Classics / Jul '93 / Discovery / Jazz Music

CLASSICS 1929-1934
CD ______ CLASSICS 720
Classics / Dec '93 / Discovery / Jazz Music

CLASSICS 1934-1935
CD ______ CLASSICS 732
Classics / Jan '94 / Discovery / Jazz Music

CLASSICS 1935 VOL.1
CD ______ CLASSICS 746
Classics / Aug '94 / Discovery / Jazz Music

CLASSICS 1935 VOL.2
CD ______ CLASSICS 760
Classics / Jun '94 / Discovery / Jazz Music

CLASSICS 1935-1936
CD ______ CLASSICS 776
Classics / Mar '95 / Discovery / Jazz Music

CLASSICS 1936-1937
CD ______ CLASSICS 816
Classics / May '95 / Discovery / Jazz Music

CLASSICS 1937 VOL.1
CD ______ CLASSICS 838
Classics / Sep '95 / Discovery / Jazz Music

CLASSICS 1937 VOL.2
CD ______ CLASSICS 857
Classics / Feb '96 / Discovery / Jazz Music

CLASSICS 1937-1938
CD ______ CLASSICS 875
Classics / Apr '96 / Discovery / Jazz Music

CLASSICS 1938
CD ______ CLASSICS 913
Classics / Jan '97 / Discovery / Jazz Music

CLASSICS 1938-1939
CD ______ CLASSICS 943
Classics / Jun '97 / Discovery / Jazz Music

COMPLETE EARLY BAND WORKS 1927-1929
Fats Waller stomp / Savannah blues / Won't you take me home / He's gone away / Red hot Dan / Geechee / Please take me out of jail / Minor drag / Harlem fuss / Lookin' good but feelin' bad / I need someone like you / Lookin' for another sweetie / Ridin' but walkin' / Won't you get off it / When I'm alone
CD ______ DHDL 115
Halcyon / Sep '93 / Cadillac / Harmonia Mundi / Jazz Music / Swift / Wellard

CREAM SERIES VOL.2
CD ______ PASTCD 7020
Flapper / Sep '93 / Pinnacle

DEFINITIVE FATS WALLER, THE
CD ______ STCD 528
Stash / Jan '93 / ADA / Cadillac / CM / Direct / Jazz Music

DEFINITIVE FATS WALLER, THE (2CD Set)
Baby brown / Viper's drag / How can you face me / Down home blues / Dinah / Handful of keys / Solitude / Moon is low / Moon is low / Sheik of Araby / 'E' flat blues / 'E' Flat blues / Honeysuckle rose / Honeysuckle rose / Ain't misbehavin' / Sweet Sue, just you / Nagasaki / I'm crazy 'bout my baby / I'm crazy 'bout my baby / Spider and the fly / Lonesome me / After you've gone / After you've gone / Dinah / Poor butterfly / St. Louis blues / Hallelujah / Tea for two / Handful of keys / I'm crazy about my baby / Tea for two / Sweet Sue, just you / Somebody stole my gal / Honeysuckle rose / Night wind / African ripples / Because of once upon a time / Where were you on the night of June the third / Clothesline ballet / Don't let it bother you / 'E' flat blues / Alligator crawl / Zonky / Hallelujah / Do me a favour / California, here I come / I've got a feeling I'm falling / My fate is in your hands / Ain't misbehavin' / You're the top / Blue, turning grey over you / Russian fantasy / I'm crazy about my baby / Truckin' / You can't have your cake and eat it / Not there, right there / Theme and introduction / Hallelujah / By the light of the silvery moon
CD Set ______ JZCL 5004
Jazz Classics / Nov '96 / Cadillac / Direct / Jazz Music

EARLY YEARS VOL.1, THE (Breaking The Ice 1934-1935/2CD Set)
Porter's love song / I wish I were twins / Armful o'sweetness / De me a favor / Georgia May / Then I'll be tired of you / Don't let it bother you / Have a little dream on me / Serenade for a wealthy widow / How can you face me / Sweetie pie / Mandy / Let's pretend there's a moon / You're not the only oyster in the stew / Honeysuckle rose / Belive it, beloved / Dream man (make me dream some more) / I'm growing fonder of you / If it isn't love / Breakin' the ice / I'm 100% for you / Baby brown / Night wind / Because of once upon a time / I believe in miracles / You fit into the picture / Louisiana fairy tale / I ain't got nobody (and nobody cares for me) / Who's honey are you / Rosetta / Pardon my love / What's the reason / Cinders / Oh Suzannah / Dust off that old pianna / Lulu's back in town / Sweet and slow / You've been taking lessons in love (from somebody new) / You're the cutest one
CD ______ 07863666182
RCA Victor / Aug '95 / BMG

EARLY YEARS VOL.3, THE (Fractious Fingering 1936)
Christopher Columbus (a rhythm cocktail) / Cross patch / It's no fun / Cabin in the sky / Us on a bus / Stay / More I know you / You're not the kind / Why do I lie to myself about you / Let's sing again / Big Chief de Sota / Black raspberry jam / Bach up to me / Fractious fingering / Paswonky / Lounging at the Waldorf / Latch on / I'm crazy 'bout my baby (and my baby's crazy 'bout me) / I just made up with that old girl of mine / (It will have to do) until the real thing comes along / There goes my attraction / Curse of an aching heart / Bye bye baby / S'posin' / Copper colored gal / I'm at the mercy of love / Floatin' down to Cotton Town / La-de-de la-de-da / Hallelujah / Things look rosy now / 'Tain't good (like a nickel made of wood) / Swingin' them jingle bells / Thousand dreams of you / Rhyme for love / I adore you
CD ______ 07863667472
RCA Victor / Apr '97 / BMG

ESSENTIAL COLLECTION, THE
CD Set ______ LECD 616
Wisepack / Apr '95 / Conifer/BMG / THE

FASCINATIN' FATS
CD ______ CDSG 401
Starline / Aug '89 / Jazz Music

FATS AT HIS FINEST (Waller, Fats & His Rhythm)
I'm gonna sit right down and write myself a letter / Dinah / My very good friend the milkman / Baby Brown / Whose honey are you / Blue because of you / 12th Street rag / You've been taking lessons in love (from somebody new) / Somebody stole my gal / Breakin' the ice / I ain't got nobody / Just as long as the world goes round and round / I'm on a see-saw / I got rhythm / Sweet Sue, just you / Rhythm and romance / Sweet thing / Serenade for a wealthy widow
CD ______ PAR 2003
Parade / May '90 / Disc

FATS AT THE ORGAN
Eighteenth Street strut / I'm coming Virginia / If I could be with you one hour tonight / Laughin' cryin' blues / Midnight blues / Papa better watch your step / Ain't nobody's business if I do / Your time now will be mine after a while / Nobody but my baby is getting my love / Do it Mr So-and-so / Clearing house blues / You can't do what my last man did / Don't try to take my loving man away / Squeeze me
CD ______ CDAJA 5007
Living Era / Oct '88 / Select

FATS SINGS WALLER
CD ______ JZCD 348
Suisa / Jan '93 / Jazz Music / THE

FATS WALLER
CD ______ LECD 051
Dynamite / May '94 / THE

FATS WALLER
CD ______ 887858
Milan / Jul '94 / Conifer/BMG / Silva Screen

FATS WALLER
CD ______ DVX 08102
Deja Vu / May '95 / THE

FATS WALLER
CD ______ 22712
Music / Nov '95 / Target/BMG

FATS WALLER
Laughin' cryin' blues / Midnight blues / Papa better watch yourself / Tain't nobody's bizness if I do / You can't do what my last man did / Your time now / Clearing house blues / Do it mister so and so / Don't try to take my loving man away / 18th Street strut / If I could be with you one hour tonight / Just squeeze me
CD ______ 17061
Laserlight / Aug '96 / Target/BMG

FATS WALLER
CD ______ 15711
Laserlight / Apr '94 / Target/BMG

FATS WALLER 1927-1929
CD ______ CLASSICS 689
Charly / Mar '93 / Koch

FATS WALLER 1935-1936
CD ______ CD 14569
Jazz Portraits / May '95 / Jazz Music

FATS WALLER 1936
CD ______ CLASSICS 797
Classics / Mar '95 / Discovery / Jazz Music

FATS WALLER IN LONDON
London suite / Don't try your jive on me / Ain't misbehavin' / Flat foot Floogie / Pent-up in a penthouse / Music maestro please / Tisket-a-tasket / That old feeling / I can't give you anything but love / Smoke dreams of you / You can't have your cake and eat it
CD ______ CDXP 8442
DRG / '88 / Discovery / New Note/Pinnacle

FATS WALLER VOL.13
CD ______ K 133FS
King Jazz / Nov '93 / Cadillac / Discovery / Jazz Music

FATS WALLER VOL.14
CD ______ KJ 134FS
King Jazz / Nov '93 / Cadillac / Discovery / Jazz Music

HALLELUJAH
CD ______ STCD 539
Stash / Oct '92 / ADA / Cadillac / CM / Direct / Jazz Music

HANDFUL OF KEYS 1929-1934
CD ______ CD 56049
Jazz Roots / Nov '94 / Target/BMG

HONEYSUCKLE ROSE
CD ______ JHR 73503
Jazz Hour / '91 / Cadillac / Jazz Music / Target/BMG

I'M 100% FOR YOU
My very good friend the milkman / Come down to Earth my angel / You must be losing your mind / Stop pretending / Shortnin' bread / Pantin' in the panther room / Twelfth street rag / Old grandad / I'm gonna salt away some sugar / Your socks don't match / Too tired / Your feet's too big / By the light of the silvery moon / Twenty four robbers / Bless you / Romance a la mode / Us on a bus / Pan pan / Sugar rose / I'm 100% for you / Imagine my surprise / Truckin' / Music maestro please / Ain't misbehavin'
CD ______ RAJCD 824
Empress / Mar '94 / Koch

INTRODUCTION TO FATS WALLER 1928-1942, AN
CD ______ 4006
Best Of Jazz / Mar '94 / Discovery

IT'S A SIN TO TELL A LIE (Waller, Fats & His Rhythm)
CD ______ CDSGP 0168
Prestige / Nov '95 / Else / Total/BMG

IT'S A SIN TO TELL A LIE 1935-1936 (Waller, Fats & His Rhythm)
It's a sin to tell a lie / More I know you / Let's sing again / Bye-bye, baby / I've got my fingers crossed / All my life / There'll be some changes made / Somebody stole my gal / Christopher Columbus / It's no fun / There's going to be the devil to pay / Cabin in the sky / Sweet thing / Oooh, look-a there, ain't she pretty / Sugar rose / Paswonky / Until the real thing comes along / Big chief de sota / La-de-de, la-de-da / There goes my attraction / Curse of an aching heart / Truckin' / Blue because of you
CD ______ CD 53269
Giants Of Jazz / Jul '97 / Cadillac / Jazz Music / Target/BMG

JAZZ PORTRAITS
You're not the only oyster in the stew / African ripples / Honeysuckle rose / Alligator crawl / If it isn't love / Viper's drag / I'm growing fonder of you / Do me a favour / Handful of keys / Minor drag / Numb fumblin' / Mandy / Let's pretend there's a moon / Dream man / Have a little dream on me / Smashing thirds / I wish I were twins / Armful o'sweetness
CD ______ CD 14516
Jazz Portraits / May '94 / Jazz Music

JAZZ SINGER
CD ______ JZCD 350
Suisa / Jan '93 / Jazz Music / THE

JOINT IS JUMPIN', THE
Handful of keys / Minor drag / Numb fumblin' / Ain't misbehavin' / Smashing thirds / African ripples / Alligator crawl / Viper's drag / Lulu's back in town / Crazy about my baby / S'posin' / Blues / Tea for two / I ain't got nobody / Joint is jumpin' / Sheikh of Araby / Yacht club swing / Squeeze me / Your feet's too big / Carolina shout / Honeysuckle rose
CD ______ ND 86288
Bluebird / Apr '88 / BMG

JOINT IS JUMPIN', THE (The Music Of Thomas 'Fats' Waller) (Repertory Quartet)
CD ______ MECCACD 1097
Music Mecca / May '97 / Cadillac / Jazz Music / Wellard

LOW DOWN PAPA
I'm crazy 'bout my baby / Wild cat blues / Jailhouse blues / Do it Mr So-and-So / Don't try to take my man away / Your time now / Papa better watch your step / Haitian blues / Mama's got the blues / Midnight blues / Last go round blues / Cryin' for my used to be / Low down papa
CD ______ BCD 114
Biograph / Jul '91 / ADA / Cadillac / Direct / Hot Shot / Jazz Music / Wellard

LULU'S BACK IN STORE
CD ______ HADCD 189
Javelin / Nov '95 / Henry Hadaway / THE

MASTERPIECES 1929-1941
CD ______ 158152
Masterpieces / Mar '94 / BMG

MASTERPIECES OF FATS WALLER, THE
CD ______ 393342
Music Memoria / Jul '96 / ADA / Discovery

MIDDLE YEARS VOL.1, THE (1936-1938/3CD Set) (Waller, Fats & His Rhythm)
Havin' a ball / I'm sorry I made you cry / Who's afraid of love / Please keep me in your dreams / One in a million / Nero / You're laughing at me / I can't break the habit of you / Did anyone tell you / When love is young / Meanest thing you ever did was kiss me / Cryin' mood / Where is the sun / Old plantation / To a sweet pretty thing / You've been reading my mail / Spring cleaning / You showed me the way / Boo-hoo / Love bug will bite you / San Anton, San Anton / I've got a new lease of love / I've got a new lease on love / Sweet heartache / Sweet heartache (Instrumental) / Honeysuckle rose / Smarty (you know it all) / Don't you know or don't you care / Lost love / I'm gonna put you in your place / Blue turning grey over you / You've got me under your thumb / Beat it out / Our love was meant to be / I'd rather call you baby / I'm always in the mood for you / She's tall, she's tan, she's terrific / You're my dish / More power to you / How can I (with you in my heart) / Joint is jumpin' / Hopeless love affair / What will I do in the morning / How ya baby / Jealous of me / Everyday's a holiday / Neglected / My window faces the south / I'm in another world / Why do Hawaiians sing aloha / My first impression of you / On the sunny side of the street / Georgia on my mind / Something tells me / I love to whistle / You went to my head / Florida Flo / Lost and found / Don't try to cry your way back to me / Marie / In the gloaming / You had an ev'ning to spare / Let's break the good news / Skrontch / I simply adore you / Sheikh of Araby / Hold my hand / Inside
CD Set ______ 7863660832
RCA Victor / Dec '92 / BMG

MIDDLE YEARS VOL.2, THE (A Good Man Is Hard To Find/3CD Set)
In the gloaming / I simply adore you / Sheikh of araby / Hold my hand / Inside / There's honey on the moon tonight / If I were you / Wide open spaces / On the bumpy road to love / Fair and square / We the people / Two sleepy people / Shame shame (Everybody knows your game) / I'll never forgive myself (For not forgiving you) / You look good to me / Tell me with your kisses / I wish I had you / I'll dance at your wedding / Imagine my surprise / Yacht club swing / Love / I'd give my life for you / I won't believe it (Till I hear from you) / Spider and the fly / Patty cake, patty cake / Good man is hard to find / You outsmarted yourself / Last night a miracle happened / Good for nothin' but love / Hold tight, hold tight / Kiss me with your eyes / You asked for it - you got it / Some rainy day / T'ain't what you do (it's the way that you do it) / Got no time / Step up and shake my hand / Undecided / Remember who you're promised to / Honey hush / I used to love you (But it's all over now) / Wait and see / You meet the nicest people in your dreams / Anita / What a pretty Miss / Squeeze me / Bless you / It's the tune that counts / Abdullah / Who'll take my place / Bond Street / It's you who taught me / Suitcase Susie / Your feet's too big / You're lettin' the grass grow under your feet / Darktown strutters ball / I can't give you anything but love / Swingadilla street / At twilight / Oh frenchy / Cheatin' on me / Black Maria / Mighty fine / Moon is low
CD Set ______ 7863665522
RCA Victor / Jun '95 / BMG

MISBEHAVIN'
I can't give you anything but love / Your feet's too big / Let's swing again / Viper's drag / Joint is jumpin' / Ain't misbehavin'
CD ______ BSTCD 9105
Best Compact Discs / May '92 / Complete/Pinnacle

MISBEHAVIN'
Tain't nobody's biz-ness if I do / Keepin' out of mischief now / Abercrombie had a zombie / Buckin' the dice / Ain't misbehavin' / Honeysuckle rose / (You're a) square from Delaware / Mamacita / Your feet's too big / Handful of keys / Joint is jumpin' / Cash for your trash / Alligtor crawl / Min drag / Send me Jackson / Twenty four robbers / Viper's drag / Hey, stop kissing my sister / You must be losing your mind / Pantin' in the pather room / All that meat and no potatoes / Carolina shout / Scram / You run your mouth, I'll run my business
CD ______ 74321500202
Camden / Jun '97 / BMG

OUR VERY GOOD FRIEND, FATS (Waller, Fats & His Rhythm)
12th street rag / I ain't got nobody / Dinah / My very good friend the milkman / I'm on a see-saw / I'm gonna sit right down and write myself a letter / Basin Street blues / Why do hawaiians sing aloha / Paswonky / Lost love / Don't you know or don't you care / She's tall, she's tan, she's terrific / I'm always in the mood for you / St. Louis blues / Shortnin' bread / Sugar rose / That never to be forgotten night / After you've gone / Old plantation / Honeysuckle rose

CD DBCD 16
Dance Band Days / Jul '89 / Prism

PEARL SERIES: FATS WALLER
It's a sin to tell a lie / Your feet's too big / I'm crazy 'bout my baby / Draggin' my heart around / Music, maestro, please / Flat foot floogie / You're not the only oyster in the stew / Ain't nobody's business if I do / Viper's drag / My very good friend the milkman / Write myself a letter / Truckin' / I'm on a see-saw / Handful of keys / Joint is jumpin' / I wish I were twins / Minor drag / Sweet Sue, just you / Black raspberry jam / Tisket-a-tasket / Dinah / Clothes line ballet / Nagasaki / Ain't misbehavin'
CD PASTCD 9742
Flapper / Mar '91 / Pinnacle

PHENOMENAL FATS
I'm gonna put you in your place / Patty cake, patty cake / Good for nothing (but love) / Last night a miracle happend / Twelfth street rag / Paswonky / Neglected / How ya babe / Lost love / She's tall, she's tan, she's terrific / Why do Hawaiians sing Aloha / Spider and the fly / Old plantation / I love to Whistle / That never to be forgotten night
CD PAR 2011
Parade / Jul '94 / Disc

PIANO MASTERWORKS VOL.1
CD 158922
Jazz Archives / Jun '97 / Discovery

PIANO ROLLS & ORGAN 1923-1938 (4CD Set)
Laughin' cryin' blues / Your time now / Tain't nobodies buziness if I do / Papa, better watch your step / You can't do what my last man did / Midnight blues / Don't try to take my loving man away / Clearing house blues / Do it, mister so and so / If I could be with you one hour tonight / Fats Waller stomp / Savannah blues / Won't you take me home / New kind of man with a new kind of love for me / I'm coming Virginia / Nobody but my baby / He's gone away / Red hot Dan / Gee chee / Please take me out of jail / Minor drag / Harlem fuss / Baby, oh where can you be / Lookin' good but felin' bad / I need someone like you / My fate is in your hands / Lookin' for another sweetie / Ridin' but walkin' / Won't you get off it, please / When I'm alone / I'm crazy 'bout my baby / Armful o'sweetness / Porter's love song to a chambermaid / I wish I were twins / Do me a favour / Don't let it bother you / Georgia May / Have a little dream on me / Then I'll be tired of you / Mandy / Sweetie pie / Serenade for a wealthy widow / You're not the only oyster in the stew / How can you face me / Let's pretend there's a moon / If it isn't love / Honeysuckle rose / I'm growing fonder of you / Dream man / Believe it, beloved / Breakin' the ice / African ripples / I'm a hundred percent for you / Baby brown / Baby brown / Oh Susannah / What's the reason / Who's honey are you / Lulu's back in town / Dinah / Somebody stole my gal / Take it easy / There's going to be the devil to pay / Christopher Columbus / Big chief De Sota / It's a sin to tell a lie / Curse of an aching heart / Bye bye baby / Swingin' them jingle bells / Hallelujah, things look rosy now / Thousand dreams of you / Every day's a holiday / I love to whistle / Something tells me / Hold my hand / In the gloaming / Let's break the good news
CD Set FBB 908
Ember / Nov '96 / TKO Magnum

PIANO SOLOS 1929-1941
Blue black bottom / Handful of keys / Numb fumblin' / Ain't misbehavin' / Sweet savannah Sue / I've got a feeling I'm falling in love / Love me or leave me / Gladyse / Valentine stomp / Waiting at the end of the road / Baby, oh where can you be / Goin' about / My feelin's are hurt / Smashing thirds / My fate is in your hands / Turn on the heat / St. Louis blues / After you've gone / African ripples / Clothes line ballet / Alligator crawl / Viper's drag / Down home blues / E flat blues / Zonky / Keepin' out of mischief now / Stardust / Basin Street blues / Tea for two / I ain't got nobody / Georgia on my mind / Rockin' chair / Carolina shout / Honeysuckle rose / Ring dem bells
CD Set ND 89741
Jazz Tribune / May '94 / BMG

POP SINGER
CD JZCD 349
Suisa / Jan '93 / Jazz Music / THE

PORTRAIT OF FATS WALLER, A
CD GALE 412
Gallerie / May '97 / Disc / THE

PRIVATE ACETATES & FILM SOUNDTRACKS 1939-1940
Ain't misbehavin' / Sweet Sue, just you / Nagasaki / Lonesome me / Hallelujah / Handful of keys / Then you'll remember / Sextet from Lucia Di Lammermoor / My heart at thy sweet voice / Joint is jumpin' / Your feet's too big / Honeysuckle rose / I've got my fingers crossed / I'm livin' in a great big way
CD 550222
Jazz Anthology / Feb '94 / Cadillac / Discovery / Harmonia Mundi

QUINTESSENCE, THE (1929-1943/2CD Set)
CD Set FA 207
Fremeaux / Oct '96 / ADA / Discovery

THOMAS 'FATS' WALLER (A Career Perspective 1922-1943)
Birmingham blues / Red hot Dan / Henderson stomp / I'm crazy 'bout my baby / Royal Garden blues / (I'll be glad when you're dead) you rascal you / That's what I like about you / Chances are / Mean old bed bug blues / Porters love song to a chambermaid / I wish I were twins / Let's pretend there's a moon / You're not the only oyster in the sea / Baby Brown/Viper's drag/How can you face me/Down home blues / Yacht club swing / Hold my hand / Pent up in a penthouse / Honeysuckle rose / Yacht club swing / You look good to me / Hallelujah / That ain't right / Reefer man / That's what the bird said to me
CD CDMOIR 515
Memoir / Jan '97 / Jazz Music / Target/ BMG

YOU LOOK GOOD TO ME (Waller, Fats & His Rhythm)
CD CDSGP 089
Prestige / Oct '93 / Else / Total/BMG

YOU RASCAL, YOU
Georgia May / I'm crazy 'bout my baby / Breakin' the ice / Baby, oh where can you be / If it isn't love / Won't you get up off it, please / I wish I were twins / Numb fumblin' / (I'll be glad when you're dead) you rascal you / Ain't misbehavin' / Porter's love song / Draggin' my heart around / Minor drag / My fate is in your hands / That's what I like about you / Harlem fuss / Believe it, beloved / Honeysuckle rose
CD CDAJA 5040
Living Era / Oct '88 / Select

Waller, Robert James

BALLAD OF MADISON COUNTY, THE
Madison County waltz / Wabash cannonball / Dutchman / Steamer / Blue suspenders / Tangerine / Girl from the north county / Golden apples of the sun / Idaho rain / Autumn leaves
CD 7567825112
WEA / Mar '94 / Warner Music

Wallflowers

BRINGING DOWN THE HORSE
One headlight / 6th avenue heartache / Bleeders / Three marlenas / Difference / Invisible city / Laughing out loud / Josephine / God don't make lonely girls / Angel on my bike / I wish I felt nothing
CD IND 90055
Interscope / Jun '97 / BMG

Wallgren, Jan Edvard

STANDARDS AND BLUEPRINTS
CD DRCD 246
Dragon / Oct '94 / ADA / Cadillac / CM / Roots / Wellard

Wallin, Per Henrik

DOLPHINS, DOLPHINS, DOLPHINS
CD DRCD 215
Dragon / Sep '89 / ADA / Cadillac / CM / Roots / Wellard

ONE KNIFE IS ENOUGH
CD 1273
Caprice / Feb '90 / ADA / Cadillac / CM / Complete/Pinnacle

TRIO
CD 1185
Caprice / May '89 / ADA / Cadillac / CM / Complete/Pinnacle

Wallington, George

LIVE AT CAFE BOHEMIA (Wallington, George Quintet)
Johnny one note / Sweet blanche / Monor march / Snakes / Jay Mac's crib / Bohemia after dark / Minor march (alternate)
CD OJCCD 1813
Original Jazz Classics / Apr '93 / Complete/ Pinnacle / Jazz Music / Wellard

Wallowitch, John

MY MANHATTAN
My Manhattan / Cosmic surgery / Come a little closer / Oh wow / Bruce / I live alone again / None of your business / Florida / It's come true at last / Threepenny things / Tony and I / Cheap decadent drivel / This moment / Beekman place elegy / Night train to Chicago / Oy vey / Time to come home again / Old friends
CD DRGCD 91414
DRG / Sep '93 / Discovery / New Note/ Pinnacle

Wallpaper

MAGIC STATIC THREATS
CD BBPTC 23
Black Bean & Placenta Tape Club / Oct '96 / Cargo

Walrath, Jack

HI JINX
CD STCD 576
Stash / Feb '94 / ADA / Cadillac / CM / Direct / Jazz Music

HIPGNOSIS (Walrath, Jack & The Masters Of Suspense)
Sweet hip gnosis / Hip gnosis / Trane trip / Philosopher stone / Mingus piano / Blue sinistra / Games / Baby fat / Premature optomism / Eclipse / Love enough for everybody
CD TCB 01062
TCB / Feb '96 / New Note/Pinnacle

JOURNEY, MAN (Walrath, Jack & Hard Corps)
Bouncin' with ballholzka / Ancient intrigues / When love has gone (it comes out like this) / Pete's steps / (I wanna be) out there somewhere / Butt (tails from the backside) / Sarah hurts / Song of everywhen / Orange has me down
CD ECD 221502
Evidence / Sep '96 / ADA / Cadillac / Harmonia Mundi

OUT OF THE TRADITION
Clear out this world / So long Eric / Stardust / Wake up and wash it off / Come Sunday / Brother can you spare a dime / Cabin in the sky / I'm getting sentimental over you
CD MCD 5403
Muse / Sep '92 / New Note/Pinnacle

SOLIDARITY (Walrath, Jack & Ralph Reichert)
Azathoth / Hamburg concerto / Loneliness of a child / Solidarity / Hot-dog for lunch / Political suicide / Psychotic indifference / Pegasus
CD 92412
Act / Oct '96 / New Note/Pinnacle

Walser, Don

ARCHIVES VOL.1 (Walser, Don & The Pure Texas Band)
CD WM 1041CD
Watermelon / Nov '95 / ADA / Direct

ARCHIVES VOL.2 (Walser, Don & The Pure Texas Band)
CD WM 1042CD
Watermelon / Nov '95 / ADA / Direct

ROLLING STONE FROM TEXAS
CD WMCD 1028
Watermelon / Dec '94 / ADA / Direct

Walsh, Colin

ENGLISH ORGAN MUSIC FROM LINCOLN CATHEDRAL
CD PRCD 379
Priory / Jul '92 / Priory

Walsh, Joe

BEST OF JOE WALSH, THE
CD HMNCD 007
Half Moon / Jun '97 / BMG

BUT SERIOUSLY FOLKS
Over and over / Second hand store / Indian summer / At the station / Tomorrow / Inner tube / Boat Weirdos / Life's been good
CD 7559605272
WEA / Oct '93 / Warner Music

LOOK WHAT I DID
Tuning, part 1 / Take a look around / Funk # 48 / Bomber / Tend my garden / Funk # 49 / Ashes the rain and I / Walk away / It's all the same / Midnight man / Here we go / Midnight visitor / Mother says / Turn to stone / Comin' down / Meadows / Rocky mountain way / Welcome to the club / All night laundry matt blues / Country fair / Help me thru the night / Life's been good / Over and over / All night long / Life of illusion / Theme from the island weirdos / I can play that rock and roll / ILBT'S / Space age whizz kids / Rosewood bitters / Shut up / Decades / Song for a dying planet / Ordinary average guy
CD MCD 11233
MCA / Jul '95 / BMG

SMOKER YOU DRINK, THE PLAYER YOU GET, THE
Rocky mountain way / Bookends / Wolf / Midnight moodies / Happy ways / Meadows / Dreams / Days gone by / (Daydream) prayer
CD MCLD 19020
MCA / Apr '92 / BMG

YOU BOUGHT IT YOU NAME IT
I can play that rock 'n' roll / Told you so / Here we are now / Worry song / ILBTs / Space age whizz kids / Love letters / Class of '65 / Shadows / Theme from island weirdos
CD 7559238842
WEA / Jul '96 / Warner Music

YOU CAN'T ARGUE WITH A SICK MIND/THE SMOKER YOU DRINK... (2CD Set)
Rocky mountain way / Bookends / Wolf / Midnight moodies / Happy ways / Meadows / Time out / Help me make it through the night / Turn to stone / Walk away / Dreams / Days gone by / (Daydream) prayer
CD Set MCD 33728
MCA / Jul '96 / BMG

Walsh, John

TIME TO SPARE
CD LCOM 5204
Lismor / Nov '91 / ADA / Direct / Duncans / Lismor

Walsh, Sean

HAYMAKER, THE
CD GTDCD 001
GTD / Jan '95 / ADA / Else

WILL THE CIRCLE BE UNBROKEN
CD GTD 008
GTD / Feb '95 / ADA / Else

Walshe, Seamus

CLARE ACCORDION
CD SW 003CD
SW Music / Nov '96 / ADA

Walt Mink

BAREBACK RIDE
Subway / Shine / Zero day / Disappear / Sunnymeade / Frail / Turn / Fragile / What a day / Tree in orange / Miss happiness / Chowdertown / Love you better / Showers down / Quiet time / Pink moon / Smoothing the ride / Croton-harmon (Local) / Twinkle and shine / Factory
CD QUIGD 3
Quigley / Sep '93 / EMI

COLOSSUS
CD DER 361
Deep Elm / Jul '97 / Cargo

MISS HAPPINESS
Miss Happiness / Chowdertown / Love You Better / Showers down / Quiet Time / Pink Moon / Smoothing the ride / Crowton-Harmon (Local) / Twinkle And Shine / Factory
CD QUIGD 1
Quigley / Oct '92 / EMI

Waltari

TORCHA
CD EM 91292
Roadrunner / Aug '92 / PolyGram

Walter, Dick

CAPRICORN RISING (Walter, Dick Band)
Minor march / Seventh child / Capricorn rising / Lost and found / Meeting place / East 34th Street / Cobwebs and rainbows / Tight and loose / Get moving / I'm out of here
CD MONTCD 004
Montpellier / May '96 / Jazz Music / Montpellier

Walter Elf

HOMO SAPIENS
CD XM 027 CD
X-Mist / Apr '92 / Cargo / SRD

Walter, Robert

SPIRIT OF '70 (Walter, Robert & Gary Bartz)
Corry's snail and slug death / Bidi man / Palilalia / Little miss lover / Impervious / Jan Jan / Volcanic acne
CD GBR 004CD
Greyboy / Nov '96 / Timewarp

Waltham Forest Pipe Band

TRADITIONAL SCOTTISH PIPES AND DRUMS
CD EUCD 1171
ARC / '91 / ADA / ARC Music

Walton, Bill

MEN ARE MADE IN PAINT
CD ISS 002CD
Issues / Jan '94 / Plastic Head

Walton, Brenda

MORTGAGED HEART, THE
CD HARTCD 002
Heartsongs / Apr '94 / CM

Walton, Cedar

AMONG FRIENDS (Walton, Cedar Trio)
For all we know / Without a song / Off minor / My foolish heart / Midnight waltz / Ruby my dear / My old flame / I've grown accustomed to her face
CD ECD 220232
Evidence / Aug '92 / ADA / Cadillac / Harmonia Mundi

BLUES FOR MYSELF
CD RED 1232052
Red / Aug '95 / ADA / Cadillac / Harmonia Mundi

BLUESVILLE TIME (Walton, Cedar Quartet)
Rubberman / Naima / Bluesville / I remember clifford / Ojos de rojos / 'Round midnight / Without a song
CD CRISS 1017CD

Criss Cross / Jul '97 / Cadillac / Direct / Vital/SAM

CEDAR WALTON PLAYS (Walton, Cedar, Ron Carter & Billy Higgins)
CD _______________ DCD 4008
Delos / '88 / Nimbus

CEDAR'S BLUES (Walton, Cedar Quintet)
CD _______________ 1231792
Red / Apr '95 / ADA / Cadillac / Harmonia Mundi

COMPOSER
Martha's prize / Vision / Happiness / Minor controversy / Hindsight / Underground memoirs / Theme from jobim / Groove passage / Groundwork
CD _______________ TCD 4001
Astor Place / Jul '96 / New Note/Pinnacle

EASTERN REBELLION (Walton, Cedar Quartet)
Bolivia / 5/4 thing / Mode for Joe / Naima / Bittersweet
CD _______________ CDSJP 101
Timeless Jazz / Jun '89 / New Note/ Pinnacle

FIRST SET
CD _______________ SCCD 31085
Steeplechase / Jul '88 / Discovery / Impetus

MANHATTAN AFTERNOON (Walton, Cedar Trio)
CD _______________ CRISS 1082CD
Criss Cross / May '94 / Cadillac / Direct / Vital/SAM

OFF MINOR (Walton, Cedar, David Williams, Billy Higgins)
CD _______________ 1232422
Red / Mar '92 / ADA / Cadillac / Harmonia Mundi

SOUL CYCLE
CD _______________ OJCCD 847
Original Jazz Classics / Nov '95 / Complete/Pinnacle / Jazz Music / Wellard

Walton, Frank

REALITY
Safari / Spongie / Waltz of the prophets / Shorter's vibes / Change of mode
CD _______________ DD 436
Delmark / Mar '97 / ADA / Cadillac / CM / Direct / Hot Shot

Walton, Mercy Dee

ONE ROOM COUNTRY SHACK
One room country shack / My woman knows the score / Misery blues / Great mistake / Save me some / Strugglin' with the blues / Lonesome cabin blues / Rent man blues / Fall guy / Drifter / Hear me shout / Love is a mystery / Winter blues / Pauline / Get to gettin' / Dark muddy bottom / What'cha gonna do / My woman and the devil / Big minded daddy / Perfect health / Problem child / Pull 'em and pop 'em / Eighth wonder of the world / Rock 'n' roll fever
CD _______________ CDCHD 475
Ace / Jun '93 / Pinnacle

PITY AND SHAME
CD _______________ OBCCD 552
Original Blues Classics / Jan '94 / Complete/Pinnacle / Wellard

TROUBLESOME MIND
CD _______________ ARHCD 369
Arhoolie / Apr '95 / ADA / Cadillac / Direct

Walton, Peter

DANCE GUITAR
CD _______________ DLD 1019
Dance & Listen / '92 / Savoy / Target/ BMG

Wamdue Kids

THESE BRANCHING MOMENTS
Intro / Alasque / Optimistique / These branching moments / Reflection / Time we will never share / Full metal emotion
CD _______________ PF 059CD
Peacefrog / Jan '97 / Mo's Music Machine / Prime / RTM/Disc / Vital

WAMDUE WORKS
CD _______________ K7R 006CD
Studio K7 / May '96 / Prime / RTM/Disc

Wamdue Project

RESOURCE
CD _______________ SR 328CD
Strictly Rhythm / Sep '96 / Prime / RTM/ Disc / SRD / Vital

Wamma Jamma

SIX BY FOUR
Wotcha gonna tell me / Hanging on a string / Fairer slink / Slow walk / Down the track / Six-one-two
CD _______________ WAMMA 003CD
Dr. Woolybach / Dec '94 / Dr. Woolybach

Wammack, Travis

THAT SCRATCHY GUITAR FROM MEMPHIS
Night train / Fire fly / It's karate time / Scratchy / Flip flop and bop / Your love / Louie Louie / Tech-nically speaking / Hallelujah, I love her so / Thunder road / I ain't lyin' / Upset / Super soul beat / Distortion part 2 / There's a UFO up there / Umm how sweet it is / Hideaway / Find another man / Fannie Mae / You are my sunshine / Memphis, Tennessee
CD _______________ BCD 15415
Bear Family / Nov '87 / Direct / Rollercoaster / Swift

Wampas

CHAUDS SALES ET HUMIDES
CD _______________ ROSE 161CD
New Rose / Mar '89 / ADA / Direct / Discovery

Wanamaker, Lisa

SHIRIM
CD _______________ SYNCOOP 5754CD
Syncoop / Feb '95 / ADA / Direct

Wandering Lucy

LEAP YEAR
CD _______________ KLP 53CD
K / Sep '96 / Cargo / Greyhound / SRD

Wang Chung

POINTS ON THE CURVE
Don't let go / Dance hall days / Devoted friends / Talk it out / Even if you dream / Don't be my enemy / Waves / Look at me now / Wait
CD _______________ GED 04004
Geffen / Nov '96 / BMG

TO LIVE AND DIE IN LA (Original Soundtrack)
To live and die in LA / Lullaby / Wake up stop dreaming / Wait / City of angels / Red stare / Black blue white / Every big city / Dance hall days
CD _______________ GED 24081
Geffen / Nov '96 / BMG

Wangford, Hank

COWBOYS STAY ON LONGER (Wangford, Hank Band)
Cowboys stay on longer / You turned me on / Jenny / Running backwards fast / Chico / Stranded / Whiskey on my guitar / Wild thing / She don't wanna be / All I want / Big G / DFW / Suppin' whiskey / Two time polka / Hymn / Joggin' with Jesus
CD _______________ CDSD 070
Magnum Music / '89 / TKO Magnum

HARD SHOULDER TO CRY ON (Wangford, Hank & The Lost Cowboys)
Dim lights / You're still on my mind / Jealousy / My lips want to stay (but my heart wants to go) / Birmingham hotel / Stormy horizons / My baby's gone / Gonna paint this town / Jalisco / What happens / Get rhythm / Prisoner song / Lay down my old guitar / I'm coming home / End of the road
CD _______________ HANKCD 001
Sincere Sounds / Mar '93 / Direct / Vital

WAKE UP DEAD (Wangford, Hank & The Lost Cowboys)
Wake up dead / Trail of lies / Get out / Counting the cost / Home sweet home / Wedding dress / In the palm of your hand / If you went away / Did you see me wave / Chaganuga / Johnny 55 / Mouth of the river / Simple pleasures
CD _______________ WOWCD 08
Way Out West / Jul '97 / Direct / Total/BMG

Wanna-Bees

VIOLENT VIBRATIONS
CD _______________ RA 91772
Roadrunner / Apr '92 / PolyGram

Wannabes

MOD FLOWER CAKE
CD _______________ DJD 3211
Dejadisc / Dec '94 / ADA / Direct

POPSUCKER
CD _______________ DJD 3222
Dejadisc / Nov '95 / ADA / Direct

Wannadies

AQUANAUTIC
Everything's true / Cherry man / Things that I would love to have undone / Love is dead / So happy now / Lucky you / 1.07 / December days / Something to tell / Suddenly I missed her / God knows / Never killed anyone / I love you love me love
CD _______________ SNAP 005
Soap / Jan '93 / Vital

BAGSY ME
Because / Friends / Someone somewhere / Oh yes (it's a mess) / Shorty / Damn it I said / Silent people / What you want / Hit / Bumble bee boy / Combat honey / That's all / What's the fuss

CD _______________ DIECD 008
Indolent / May '97 / 3mv/BMG / Vital

BE A GIRL
You and me song / Might be stars / Love in June / How does it feel / Sweet nymphet / New world record / Dying for more / Soon you're dead / Do it all the time / Dreamy wednesdays / Kid
CD _______________ DIECD 002
Indolent / Oct '96 / 3mv/BMG / Vital

Waorani Indians

WAORANI WAAPONI
CD _______________ TUMICD 043
Tumi / '94 / Discovery / Stern's

War

ALL DAY MUSIC
All day music / Get down / That's what love will do / There must be a reason / Nappy head / Slippin' into darkness / Baby brother
CD _______________ 74321305202
Avenue / Sep '95 / BMG

BLACK MAN'S BURDON, THE
Paint it black / Spirit / Beautiful new born child / Nights in white satin / Bird & squirrel / Nuts, seeds and life / Out of nowhere / Sun / Moon / Pretty colors / Gun / Jimbo / Bare back ride/Home cookin' / They can't take away our music
CD _______________ 74321307422
Avenue / Aug '96 / BMG

DELIVER THE WORLD
H2Overture / In your eyes / Gypsy man / Me and baby brother / Deliver the word / Southern part of Texas / Blisters
CD _______________ 74321305222
Avenue / Sep '95 / BMG

PEACE SIGN
CD _______________ 74321297662
Avenue / Jun '95 / BMG

PLATINUM JAZZ
War is coming / Slowly we walk together / Platinum jazz / I got you / LA sunshine / River Niger / H2Overture / City, country, city / Smile happy / Deliver the word / Nappy head / Four cornered room
CD _______________ 74321305242
Avenue / Sep '95 / BMG

WAR
Sun oh sun / Lonely feelin' / Back home / War drums / Vibeka / Fidel's fantasy
CD _______________ 74321307372
Avenue / Aug '96 / BMG

WAR LIVE
Introduction / Sun oh sun / Cisco kid / Slippin' into darkness / Slippin' / All day music / Ballero / Lonely feelin' / Get down
CD _______________ 74321307302
Avenue / Aug '96 / BMG

WHY CAN'T WE BE FRIENDS
Don't let no-one get you down / Lotus blossom / Heartbeat / Leroy's Latin lament / Smile happy / So / Low rider / In Mazatian / Why can't we be friends
CD _______________ 74321305232
Avenue / Sep '95 / BMG

WORLD IS A GHETTO
Cisco kid / City, country, city / Beetles in a bog / Four cornered room / Where was you at / World is a ghetto
CD _______________ 74321305212
Avenue / Sep '95 / BMG

War Collapse

ROLLED OVER BY TANKS
CD _______________ DISTCD 018
Distortion / Nov '95 / Plastic Head

War Pipes

WAR PIPES
CD _______________ BRGCD 20
Bridge / Jul '95 / Grapevine/PolyGram

Ward, Anita

ANITA WARD
CD _______________ GFS 069
Going For A Song / Jul '97 / Else / TKO Magnum

RING MY BELL
I'm ready for your love / Curtains go up / This must be love / Ring my bell / Sweet splendour / There's no doubt about it / You lied / Make believe in lovers / If I could feel that old feeling again / Spoiled by your love / I won't stop loving you
CD _______________ MSCD 17
Music De-Luxe / Apr '95 / TKO Magnum

Ward, Bill

WHEN THE BOUGH BREAKS
CD _______________ CLP 9981
Cleopatra / Jun '97 / Cargo / Greyhound / Plastic Head / RTM/Disc / SRD

Ward, Billy

21 HITS (Ward, Billy & The Dominoes)
CD _______________ KCD 5008
King / Apr '97 / Avid/BMG

SIXTY MINUTE MAN (Ward, Billy & The Dominoes)
Sixty minute man / Chicken blues / Don't leave me this way / Do something for me / That's what you're doing to me / Weeping willow blues / How long blues / I am with you / Have mercy baby / If I ever get to heaven / Pedal pushin' papa / I'd be satisfied / 'Deed I do / Bells / My baby's 3-D / Tenderly / I ain't gonna cry for you / You can't keep a good man down / I really don't want to know / I'm gonna move to the outskirts of town
CD _______________ CDCHARLY 242
Charly / Oct '90 / Koch

Ward Brothers

WAVE GOODBYE TO GRANDMA
Swing / Shadows / Take from u / Imelda / Step on it / Little boy / Shirt song / Falling / Find the groove / Footsteps / Friends
CD _______________ CDSGP 0242
Prestige / Apr '97 / Else / Total/BMG

Ward, Clifford T.

GAYE AND OTHER STORIES
Gaye / Wherewithal / Cellophane / Dubious circus company / Not waving, drowning / Time the magician / Home thoughts from abroad / Way of love / Open university / Jigsaw girl / Day to myself / Nightingale / We could be talking / Where's it going to end / Crisis / Scullery / Where would that leave me / To an air hostess / Sad affair
CD _______________ CDVM 9009
Virgin / Jun '92 / EMI

SINGER SONGWRITER PLUS
Coathanger / Leader / Anticipation / Session singer / God help me / Sympathy / You knock when you should come in / Sam / Dream / Rayne / Carrie / Cause is good / Circus girl / Sidetrack
CD _______________ SEECD 418
See For Miles/C5 / May '95 / Pinnacle

Ward, John

WATER ON THE STONE
Water on the stone / Free world market place / Paper chase / Stoney ground / Heart of the town / Status / I want to see your face / Leakin' minister / Rural vandals / Must I go bound / Way of the world / Only treasure / Binding light
CD _______________ IONGF 5
Green Fingers / Jun '92 / Green Fingers Music

Ward, Robert

BLACK BOTTOM
CD _______________ BT 1123CD
Black Top / Nov '95 / ADA / CM / Direct

FEAR NO EVIL (Ward, Robert & The Black Top All Stars)
CD _______________ ORECD 520
Silvertone / Mar '94 / Pinnacle

RHYTHM OF THE PEOPLE
CD _______________ BT 1088CD
Black Top / May '93 / ADA / CM / Direct

TWIGGS COUNTRY SOUL MAN
Your love is amazing / Newborn music / Real deal / Something for nothing / White fox / You can't stop my loving now / Silver and gold / So tired of wandering / Lonely man / I'm gonna cry a river / Black bottom
CD _______________ CDBTEL 7003
Black Top / Mar '97 / ADA / CM / Direct

Warda

WARDA
Batwanness beek (I feel safe with you) / Zarny fil dohah (He came to visit me in the morning) / Ya khsara (what a pity) / Hobak west madah (Your love reached its end) / Nar el ghera (Fire of jealousy) / Ya saeedy (Oh, my master)
CD _______________ HEMIMDCD 102
Hemisphere / Feb '97 / EMI

Wardell, Dick

STREET LIFE BLUES
Some of these days / Dream and change blues / It's too late / Birds are singing / Walking the blues / Future blues / Streeet life blues / Love will make you cry / Mean old Frisco / Midnight moon / Let's turn out the light / Katie Mae / Poor children dyin' / Play with your poodle / New day coming
CD _______________ FECD 108
Fellside / Jun '96 / ADA / Direct / Target/ BMG

Warden, Monte

HERE I AM
CD _______________ WMCD 1037
Watermelon / Aug '95 / ADA / Direct

MONTE WARDEN
CD _______________ WMCD 1015
Watermelon / May '94 / ADA / Direct

Wardog

SCORCHED EARTH
CD _______________ 398414112CD

Metal Blade / Jul '96 / Pinnacle / Plastic Head

Ware, Bill

LONG & SKINNY (Ware, Bill & The Club Bird Allstars)
CD _______ **KFWCD 131**
Knitting Factory / Feb '95 / Cargo / Plastic Head

Ware, David S.

CRYPTOLOGY (Ware, David S. Quartet)
CD _______ **HMS 2202**
Homestead / Mar '95 / Cargo / SRD

EARTHQUATION
CD _______ **DIW 892**
DIW / Jan '95 / Cadillac / Harmonia Mundi

FLIGHT OF I
CD _______ **DIW 856**
DIW / May '92 / Cadillac / Harmonia Mundi

GODSPELISED
CD _______ **DIW 916**
DIW / Dec '96 / Cadillac / Harmonia Mundi

Ware, Leon

TASTE THE LOVE
Come with me angel / Back to back / Meltdown / Love parts / Cream of love / Telepathy / Musical massage / Can't stop love / I got your recipe / I get weak / Yes / It was always you / Where do I stand / Taste the love
CD _______ **XECD 5**
Expansion / Aug '95 / 3mv/Sony

Warfare

CONFLICT OF HATRED
Waxworks / Revolution / Dancing in the flames of insanity / Evolution / Fatal vision / Death charge / Order of the dragons / Elite forces / Rejoice the feast of quarantine / Noise filth and fury
CD _______ **NEATCD 1044**
Neat / Mar '88 / Pinnacle

DECADE OF DECIBELS
CD _______ **CDBLEED 8**
Bleeding Hearts / Oct '93 / Pinnacle

HAMMER HORROR
Hammer horror / Plague of the zombies / Ballad of the dead / Phantom of the opera / Baron Frankenstein / Velvet rhapsody / Sold of shadows / Prince of Darkness / Tales of the gothic genre / Scream of the vampire
CD _______ **REVXD 147**
FM / Jun '90 / Revolver / Sony
CD _______ **FILMCD 130**
Silva Screen / Apr '93 / Koch / Silva Screen

Warfield, Derek

LEGACY
CD _______ **SHCD 52042**
Shanachie / Apr '96 / ADA / Greensleeves / Koch

Warfield, Justin

JUSTIN WARFIELD SUPERNAUT, THE
CD _______ **9362458712**
Qwest / May '95 / Warner Music

MY FIELD TRIP TO PLANET 9
Tequila flats / Introduction / Dip dip divin' / K sera sera / Fisherman's grotto / Live from the opium den / Glass tangerine / Guavafish centipede / Teenage caligula / Cool like the blues / Drug store cowboy / Pick it up y'all / B boys on acid / Stormclouds left of heaven / Thoughts in the buttermilk / Tequila flats (ghosts of Laurel Canyon)
CD _______ **9362450852**
Qwest / Jan '94 / Warner Music

Warfield, Tim

COOL BLUE, A
CD _______ **CRISS 1102**
Criss Cross / Oct '95 / Cadillac / Direct / Vital/SAM

WHISPER IN MIDNIGHT, A (Warfield, Tim Sextet)
Tin soldier / Soprano song / Speak low / I've never been blue before / Whisper in midnight / Bye bye blackbird / Prayer for Uthman
CD _______ **CRISS 1122CD**
Criss Cross / Feb '97 / Cadillac / Direct / Vital/SAM

Wargasm

FIREBALL
CD _______ **MASSCD 036**
Massacre / Jul '94 / Plastic Head

UGLY
CD _______ **MASSCD 020**
Massacre / Nov '93 / Plastic Head

Warhead

WARHEAD
CD _______ **CMGCD 011**
Communique / Nov '95 / Plastic Head

Warhorse

OUTBREAK OF HOSTILITIES
Vulture blood / No chance / Burning / St. Louis / Ritual / Solitude / Woman of the devil / Red Sea / Back in time / Confident but wrong / Feeling better / Sybilla / Mouthpiece / I who have nothing
CD _______ **CDTB 104**
Thunderbolt / May '91 / TKO Magnum

WARHORSE STORY VOL.1 & 2, THE (2CD Set)
Vulture blood / No chance / Burning / St. Louis / Ritual / Solitude / Woman of the devil / Ritual / Miss Jane / Solitude / Woman of the devil / Burning / Red Sea / Back in time / Confident but wrong / Feeling better / Sybilla / Mouthpiece / I (who have nothing) / Ritual / Bad time / She was my friend / Gypsy dancer / House of dolls / Standing right behind you
CD Set _______ **RPM 501**
RPM / Jun '97 / Pinnacle

WARHORSE STORY VOL.1, THE
Vulture blood / No chance / Burning / St. Louis / Ritual / Solitude / Woman of the devil / Ritual / Miss Jane / Solitude / Woman of the devil / Burning
CD _______ **RPM 174**
RPM / Jun '97 / Pinnacle

WARHORSE STORY VOL.2, THE
Red sea / Back in time / Confident but wrong / Feeling better / Sybilla / Mouthpiece / I (who have nothing) / Ritual / Bad time / She was my friend / Gypsy dancer / House of dolls / Standing right behind you
CD _______ **RPM 175**
RPM / Jun '97 / Pinnacle

Wariner, Steve

NO MORE MR. NICE GUY
No more Mr. Nice Guy / Big hero, little hero / Prelude/Practice your scales / Somewhere else / Theme / Forever loving you / Next March / If you can't say something good / Hap Towne breakdown / For Chester B / Brickyard boogie / Don't call me Ray / Guitar talk
CD _______ **07822188142**
Arista / Apr '96 / BMG

Waring, Fred

MEMORIAL ALBUM, THE
Farewell blues / Bolshevik / Helo Montreal / Stack O'Lee blues / What a night for spooning / Glorianna / Navy blues / Hello baby / Good for you bad for me / Red hot Chicago / How'm I doin / I heard / Old yazoo / Holding my honey's hand / Old man of the mountain / You'll get by / Fit as a fiddle / Young and healthly / Dance selections / Flying colours
CD _______ **VN 179**
Viper's Nest / Nov '96 / ADA / Cadillac / Direct / Jazz Music

Waring, Steve

GUITAR PICKING (Waring, Steve & Roger Mason)
CD _______ **LDX 274969**
La Chant Du Monde / Oct '94 / ADA / Harmonia Mundi

Warlord

MAXIMUM CARNAGE
CD _______ **NB 119CD**
Nuclear Blast / Apr '96 / Plastic Head

Warlow, Anthony

CENTRE STAGE
Music of the night / Easy to love / Luck be a lady / Somewhere / This nearly was mine / I am what I am / Anthem / Bring him home / You're nothing without me / Impossible dream / Johanna / Colours of my life / Soliloquy
CD _______ **5112232**
London / Nov '91 / PolyGram

Warm Jets

FUTURE SIGNS
CD _______ **5243542**
This Way Up / Sep '97 / PolyGram / SRD

Warm Wires

SEVERE COMFORT
CD _______ **BRCD 062**
Brinkman / Apr '97 / Cargo

Warmers

WARMERS, THE
CD _______ **DIS 102CD**
Dischord / Jun '96 / SRD

Warner, Richard

QUIET HEART, SPIRIT WIND (2CD Set)
Quiet heart / Inner flame / Dance of the birds / Riding in the carriage / Solitude / Forest spirits / Temple / Water bird / Clearing / Spirit wind / Moonlight on the mountain / Eagle dance / Gathering
CD Set _______ **ND 262805**
Narada / Dec '96 / ADA / New Note/ Pinnacle

SPIRIT OF THE TAO TE CHING
Sunrise / Water / Lake joy / Heaven / Mountains on the mist / Earth / Thunder / Wind / Tao
CD _______ **ND 61053**
Narada / Jul '96 / ADA / New Note/Pinnacle

Warner, Simon

WAITING ROOMS
Keep it down / Decorating / Wake up the street / Jamboree / Moody / Doggy / Wrong girl / Hiding / Kitchen tango / Mrs Zaniewski / Ticket collector / Proper job / Waiting rooms / Simply marvellous / Coda
CD _______ **R 4132**
Rough Trade / May '97 / Pinnacle

Warner, Tom

LONG NIGHT BIG DAY
CD _______ **804102**
New World / Jun '91 / ADA / Cadillac / Harmonia Mundi

Warnes, Jennifer

FAMOUS BLUE RAINCOAT
First we take Manhattan / Bird on the wire / Famous blue raincoat / Joan of Arc / Ain't no cure for love / Coming back to you / Song of Bernadette / Singer must die / Came so far for beauty
CD _______ **258418**
RCA / Feb '97 / BMG

HUNTER, THE
Rock you gently / Somewhere, somebody / Big noise, New York / True emotion / Pretending to care / Whole of the moon / Light of Louisanne / Way down deep / Hunter / I can't hide
CD _______ **261974**
Private Music / Feb '96 / BMG

JUST JENNIFER
Close the door / Sunny day blue / Here, there and everywhere / Chelsea morning / I want to meander in the meadow / I am waiting / Places everyone / Three hoouse of gold / It's hard to love a poet / Leaves / Park / Let the sunshine in / Easy to be hard / Saturday night the world / Time is on the run / Old folks (les vieux) / We're not gonna take it / Just like Tom Thumb's blues / Back street girl / Weather's better / Tell me again I love thee / Cajun train
CD _______ **8209892**
Deram / PolyGram

SHOT THROUGH THE HEART
Shot through the heart / I know a heartache when I see one / Don't make me over / You remember me / Sign on the window / I'm restless / Tell me just one more time / When the feeling comes around / Frankie in the rain / Hard times / Come again no more
CD _______ **74321197372**
Arista / Feb '97 / BMG

Warp Drive

GIMME GIMME
Bang the drum / I 4 U / Words / Take take me now / Stay on stay on / Moments away / Crying girl / Eyes on you / Rockin' the boat / Making time stand still
CD _______ **CDMFN 99**
Music For Nations / May '90 / Pinnacle

Warpath

KILL YOUR ENEMY
CD _______ **SPV 085182852**
SPV / Mar '96 / Koch / Plastic Head

Warrant

BELLY TO BELLY VOL.1
In the end / Feels good / Letter to a friend / AYM / Indian giver / Falling down / Interlude / Solid / All 4 U / Coffee house / Interlude / Vertigo / Room with a view / Nobody else
CD _______ **06076862002**
CMC / May '97 / BMG

BEST OF WARRANT, THE
Down boys / 32 pennies in a ragu jar / Heaven / DRFSR / Big talk / Sometimes she cries / Cherry pie / Thin disguise / Uncle Tom's cabin / I saw red / Bed of roses / Mr. Rainmaker / Sure feels good to me / Hole in my wall / Machine gun / We will rock you
CD _______ **4840122**
Columbia / Jul '96 / Sony

ULTRAPHOBIC
CD _______ **CDMFN 183**
Music For Nations / Feb '95 / Pinnacle

Warren G

REGULATE G FUNK ERA
Regulate: *Warren G & Nate Dogg* / Do you see / Gangsta sermon / Recognize / Super soul sis / '94 Ho draft / So many ways / This DJ / This is the Shack / What's next / And ya don't stop / Runnin' wit no breaks
CD _______ **5233352**
Island Red / Jul '94 / PolyGram / Vital

TAKE A LOOK OVER YOUR SHOULDER
Intro / Annie Mae / Smokin' me out / Reverend Eazy Dick / Reality / Interlude / Young fun / What we go through / We bring heat / Can you feel it / Transformers / Reel tight intro / Relax your mind / To all the DJ's / Back up / What's love got to do with it: *Warren G & Adina Howard* / I shot the sheriff
CD _______ **5334842**
Def Jam / Feb '97 / PolyGram

Warren, Nick

DJ'S IN A BOX VOL.8 (Various Artists)
CD _______ **UCCD 008**
Urban Collective / Nov '96 / Amato Disco / RTM/Disc / Total/BMG / Vital

NICK WARREN LIVE IN PRAGUE (2CD Set) (Various Artists)
Ohm sessions (coloured oxygen reprise): *Cruzeman* / Tech theme: *Cruzeman* / Nipple fish: *Coffee boys* / Schattenmund: *Mikerobenics* / Spirit: *Aquaplex System* / Noise shots: *Riot Rhythm* / Cut the midrange: *Watchman* / Boom: *LT Project* / Life on Mars: *Life On Mars* / Magic shop (fourth coded dub): *Pako, Stef & Frederik* / Credits: *Celysys, Tom* / Distant drum: *Distant Drums* / Gospel 2001: *16C+* / Pandamonia: *DJ Randy* / Ancient quest: *Dark Age* / Cafe del mar: *Energy 52* / Reach for it: *Chaser* / Seadog: *Clanger* / Submissions: *Freek & Mac Zimms* / Tempest: *Deepsky* / Sunrise: *Anjo* / Galaxia: *Moonman*
CD Set _______ **GU 003CD**
Boxed / Mar '97 / SRD

Warrior

LET BATTLE COMMENCE
Let battle commence / Long stretch Broadmoor blues / Night time girl / Memories / Yesterday's hero / Invaders / Ulster bloody Ulster / Warrior
CD _______ **ETHEL 2**
Vinyl Tap / Dec '94 / Cargo / Greyhound / Vinyl Tap

Warrior River Boys

SOUNDS LIKE HOME
CD _______ **ROUCD 310**
Rounder / Jan '94 / ADA / CM / Direct

Warrior Soul

CHILL PILL
Mars / Cargos of doom / Song in your mind / Shock um down / Let me go / Ha ha ha / Concrete frontier / I want some / Soft / High road
CD _______ **GED 24608**
Geffen / Jul '97 / BMG

DRUGS, GOD AND THE NEW REPUBLIC
CD _______ **DGCD 24389**
Geffen / May '91 / BMG

FUCKER
NYC girl / Gimme some of this / Punk rock 'n' roll / Turn on / 5 ways to the gutter / Stun fun / My sky / Makin' it / Raised on riots / American / Kiss me / This joy / Can't fix / Come to me / Last decade dead century / If you think you're dead
CD _______ **CDMFN 204**
Music For Nations / Sep '96 / Pinnacle

LAST DECADE, DEAD CENTURY
I see the ruins / We cry out / Losers / Downtown / Trippin' on ecstasy / One minute years / Super power dreamland / Charlie's out of prison / Blown away / Lullaby / In conclusion / Four more years
CD _______ **GED 24285**
Geffen / Jun '97 / BMG

SALUTATIONS FROM THE GHETTO NATION
Love destruction / Blown / Shine like it / Dimension / Punk and belligerent / Asskickin' / Party / Golden shore / Trip rider / I love you / Fallen / Ghetto nation
CD _______ **GED 24488**
Geffen / Jun '97 / BMG

SPACE AGE PLAYBOYS
CD _______ **CDMFN 172**
Music For Nations / Oct '94 / Pinnacle

Warsaw

WARSAW
CD _______ **MPG 74034**
Movieplay Gold / Feb '95 / Target/BMG

Warwick, Dee Dee

SHE DIDN'T KNOW (The Atco Sessions)
CD _______ **SCL 211112**
Ichiban Soul Classics / Mar '96 / Koch

Warwick, Dionne

AQUARELA DO BRASIL
Jobim medley / Virou areia / Oh Bahia / Piano na manquiera / Captives of the heart / Samba dobrado / Heart of Brasil / N'kosi sikelel'i - Afrika / So bashiya bahlala ekhaya / Brasil / Caravan / Flower of Bahia / 10,000 words
CD _______ 07822187772
Arista / Jan '95 / BMG

DIONNE
Who, what, when, where and why / After you / Letter / I'll never love this way again / Deja vu / Feeling old feelings / In your eyes / My everlasting love / Out of my hands / All the time
CD _______ MCCD 169
Music Club / Sep '94 / Disc / THE

DIONNE WARWICK SINGS COLE PORTER
Night and day / I love Paris / I get a kick out of you / What is this thing called love / So in love / You're the top / I've got you under my skin / Begin the beguine / It's all right with me / Anything goes / You'd be so nice to come home to / All of you / I concentrate on you / Night and day (jazz version) / Just one of those things
CD _______ 260918
Arista / Oct '90 / BMG

ESSENTIAL COLLECTION, THE (2CD Set)
Do you know the way to San Jose / Walk on by / Anyone who had a heart / Raindrops keep falling on my head / Reach out for me / I just don't know what to do with myself / Don't make me over / Always something there to remind me / This girl's in love with you / Wishin' and hopin' / House is not a home / I'll never fall in love again / I say a little prayer / Are you there with another girl / Message to Michael / Close to you / Make it easy on yourself / Promises promises / What the world needs now / Windows of the world / Alfie / Trains and boats and planes / You'll never get to heaven / Look of love / Only love can break a heart / Wives and lovers / Heartbreaker / All the love in the world / I'll never love this way again / That's what friends are for / Run to me / Love power / Yours / In your eyes / Our day will come / Night and day / So amazing / Begin the beguine / You're all I need to get by / You've lost that lovin' feelin' / Who can I turn to / (Theme from) Valley of the dolls
CD Set _______ RADCD 48
Global TV / Nov '96 / BMG

FRIENDS CAN BE LOVERS
Where my lips have been / Sunny weather lover / Age of miracles / Love will find a way: *Warwick, Dionne & Whitney Houston* / Much to much / Till the end of time / Woman that I am / Fragile / Can't break this heart / Superwoman: *Warwick, Dionne & Gladys Knight/Patti LaBelle*
CD _______ 07822186822
Arista / Mar '93 / BMG

GREAT SONGS OF THE SIXTIES
What the world needs now is love / Yesterday / Raindrops keep falling on my head / Promise, promise / You've lost that lovin' feelin' / I'm your puppet / Something / We've only just begun / Macarthur park / My way / Up, up and away / Going out of my head / People get ready / You're my world / Loving you is sweeter than ever / Put yourself in my place / Someday we'll be together / I've been loving you too long / Games people play / Windows of the world
CD _______ 3035900122
Essential Gold / May '96 / Carlton

GREATEST HITS
CD _______ 259279
Arista / Aug '95 / BMG

HEARTBREAKER
All the love in the world / I can't see anything but you / You are my love / Just one more night / Our day will come / Heartbreaker / Yours / Take the short way home / It makes no difference / Misunderstood
CD _______ 258719
Arista / Oct '87 / BMG

HERE I AM/HERE WHERE THERE IS LOVE
In between the heartaches / Here I am / If I ever make you cry / Lookin' with my eyes / Once in a lifetime / This little light / Don't go breaking my heart / Window wishing / Long day, short night / Are you there (with another girl) / How can I hurt you / I loves you Porgy / Go with love / What the world needs now is love / I just don't know what to do with myself / Here where there is love / Trains and boats and planes / Alfie / As long as he needs me / I wish you love / I never knew what you were up to / Blowin' in the wind
CD _______ NEMCD 762
Sequel / Oct '95 / BMG

JUST BEING MYSELF
CD _______ JHD 002
Tring / Jun '92 / Tring

LOVE SONGS COLLECTION
I'll never fall in love again / Let it be me / Here where there is love / I love Paris / Hurt so bad / As long as he needs me / Blowin' in the wind / One hand, one heart / You can have him / People / This girl's in love with you / You're all I need to get by / Baubles, bangles and beads / Getting ready for the heartbreak / Who can I turn to / People got to be free / It's the good life / Somewhere / Unchained melody / Valley of the dolls
CD _______ PWKS 525
Carlton / Feb '96 / Carlton

MAKE WAY FOR DIONNE WARWICK/ THE SENSITIVE SOUND OF DIONNE
House is not a home / People / (They want to be) Close to me / Last one to be loved / Land of make believe / Reach out for me / You'll never get to heaven (if you break my heart) / Walk on by / Wishin' & hopin' / I smiled yesterday / Get rid of him / Make the night a little longer / Unchained melody / Who can I turn to / How many days of sadness / Is there another way to love him / Where can I go without you / You can have him / Wives & lovers / Don't say I didn't tell you so / Only the strong, only the brave / Forever my love
CD _______ NEMCD 761
Sequel / Oct '95 / BMG

ORIGINAL HITS 1962-1972, THE
CD _______ DCD 5366
Disky / Apr '94 / Disky / THE

PRESENTING DIONNE WARWICK/ ANYONE WHO HAD A HEART
This empty place / Wishin' & hopin' / I cry alone / Zip-a-dee-doo-dah / Make the music play / If you see Bill / Don't make me over / It's love that really counts (in the long run) / Inlucky / I smiled yesterday / Make it easy on yourself / Love of a boy / Anyone who had a heart / Shall I tell her / Gettin' ready for the heartbreak / Oh Lord what are you doing to me / Any old time of day / Mr. Heartbreak / Put yourself in my place / I could make you mine / Please make him love me
CD _______ NEMCD 760
Sequel / Oct '95 / BMG

SINGS BURT BACHARACH
CD _______ ENTCD 268
Entertainers / Mar '92 / Target/BMG

SOULFUL
You've lost that lovin' feelin' / I'm your puppet / People got to be free / You're all I need to get by / We can work it out / Silent voices / Hard day's night / Do right woman, do right man / I've been loving you too long / People get ready / Hey Jude / What's good about goodbye
CD _______ DCD 5401
Disky / Oct '94 / Disky / THE

WALK ON BY AND OTHER FAVOURITES
Don't make me over / This empty place / Wishin' and hopin' / Anyone who had a heart / Make it easy on yourself / It's love that really counts / Walk on by / You'll never get to heaven (If you break my heart) / Reach out for me / I just don't know what to do with myself / I say a little prayer / Do you know the way to San Jose / I'm your puppet / Trains and boats and planes / Here where there is love / Are you there (with another girl) / Wives and lovers / Valley of the dolls / I'll never fall in love again / Make the music play
CD _______ CDCHARLY 101
Charly / Oct '87 / Koch

Warzone

OLD SCHOOL VS. NEW
CD _______ VR 015CD
Victory / Sep '96 / Plastic Head

OPEN YOUR EYES, DON'T FORGET THE STRUGGLE
Into bust / It's your choice / Crazy but not insane / Fuck your attitude / As one / We're the crew / Don't forget the struggle / In the mirror / Skinhead youth / Growing up - the next step / Judgement day / Fight for our country / Open up your eyes / Dance hard or die / Face up to it / Always - a friend for life / Racism - World history part 1 / Back to school again / American movement / Fight the oppressoh / Deceive us - no more / Striving for a better life
CD _______ LF 109CD
Lost & Found / Oct '94 / Plastic Head

SOUND OF REVOLUTION, THE
CD _______ VR 045CD
Victory / Oct '96 / Plastic Head

Was Not Was

HELLO DAD... I'M IN JAIL
Listen like thieves / Shake your head / Tell me that I'm dreaming / Papa was a rollin' stone / Are you okay / Spy in the house of love / I feel better than James Brown / Somewhere in America / There's a street named after my dad / Out come the freaks / How the heart behaves / Walk the dinosaur / Hello dad... I'm in jail
CD _______ 5124642
Fontana / Jun '92 / PolyGram

WHAT UP DOG
Somewhere in America / Spy in the house of love / Out come the freaks / Earth to Doris / Love can be bad luck / Boy's gone crazy / Eleven miles an hour / What up dog / Anything can happen / Robot girl / Wedding vows in Vegas / Anytime Lisa / Walk the dinosaur / I can't turn you loose / Shadow and Jimmy / Dad I'm in jail
CD _______ 5504042
Spectrum / May '96 / PolyGram

Washboard Rhythm Kings

WASHBOARD RHYTHM KINGS VOL.1 1931
Please don't talk about me / Minnie the moocher / One more time / Walkin' my baby back home / Porter's love song / Everyman for himself / Blues in my heart / Just one more chance / Many happy returns of the day / Shoot 'em / Wake 'em up / Georgia on my mind / Pepper steak / If you don't love me / Please tell me / (I'll be glad when you're dead) you rascal you / Crooked world blues / Call of the freaks / I'm crazy 'bout my baby / Because I'm yours sincerely / Stardust / You can't stop me from lovin' you / Boola boo / Who stole the lock
CD _______ COCD 17
Collector's Classics / Jul '96 / Cadillac / Complete/Pinnacle / Jazz Music

WASHBOARD RHYTHM KINGS VOL.2 1932
CD _______ COCD 18
Collector's Classics / Jul '96 / Cadillac / Complete/Pinnacle / Jazz Music

WASHBOARD RHYTHM KINGS VOL.3 1931-1932
CD _______ COCD 25
Collector's Classics / Jul '96 / Cadillac / Complete/Pinnacle / Jazz Music

WASHBOARD RHYTHM KINGS VOL.4 1933
CD _______ COCD 26
Collector's Classics / May '97 / Cadillac / Complete/Pinnacle / Jazz Music

Washboard Sam

WASHBOARD SAM 1935-1941
CD _______ 158662
Blues Collection / Jun '97 / Discovery

WASHBOARD SAM VOL.1 - 1935-36
CD _______ DOCD 5171
Document / Oct '93 / ADA / Hot Shot / Jazz Music

WASHBOARD SAM VOL.2 - 1937-38
CD _______ DOCD 5172
Document / Oct '93 / ADA / Hot Shot / Jazz Music

WASHBOARD SAM VOL.3 - 1938
CD _______ DOCD 5173
Document / Oct '93 / ADA / Hot Shot / Jazz Music

WASHBOARD SAM VOL.4 - 1939-40
CD _______ DOCD 5174
Document / Oct '93 / ADA / Hot Shot / Jazz Music

WASHBOARD SAM VOL.5 - 1940-41
CD _______ DOCD 5175
Document / Oct '93 / ADA / Hot Shot / Jazz Music

WASHBOARD SAM VOL.6 - 1941-42
CD _______ DOCD 5176
Document / Oct '93 / ADA / Hot Shot / Jazz Music

WASHBOARD SAM VOL.7 - 1942-49
CD _______ DOCD 5177
Document / Oct '93 / ADA / Hot Shot / Jazz Music

Washer, Bill

ASAP (Washer, Bill & Danny Gottlieb)
CD _______ ITMP 970054
ITM / Jan '91 / Koch / Tradelink

Washingmachine, George

SWEET ATMOSPHERE (Washingmachine, George & Ian Date)
CD _______ JH 2008
Jazz Hour / Oct '93 / Cadillac / Jazz Music / Target/BMG

Washington, Baby

SUE SINGLES, THE
No tears / Go on / Handful of memories / Careless hands / I've got a feeling / Hush heart / Standing on the pier / Clock / That's how heartaches are made / There he is / Leave me alone / Hey lonely / I can't wait until I see my baby's face / Who's gonna take care of me / It'll never be over for me / Move on drifter / Run my heart / Your fool / Only those in love / No time for pity / You and the night and the music / Doodlin' / Ballad of Bobby Dawn / You are what you are / Either you're with me (or either you're not) / I know / White Christmas / Silent night
CD _______ CDKEND 136
Kent / Jun '96 / Pinnacle

Washington, Dinah

50 GREATEST HITS
CD _______ DBP 102004
Double Platinum / Nov '93 / Target/BMG

BACK TO THE BLUES
Blues ain't nothing but a woman cryin' for her man / Romance in the dark / You've been a good old wagon / Let me be the first to know / How long how long blues / Don't come running back to me / It's a mean old man's world / Key to the highway / If I never get to heaven / Duck before you drown / No hard feelings / Nobody knows the way I feel this morning / Don't say nothing at all / No one man / Me and my gin
CD _______ CDP 8543342
Roulette / Mar '97 / EMI

BEST OF DINAH WASHINGTON, THE (The Roulette Years)
You're nobody 'til somebody loves you / Take you shoes off baby / Call me irresponsible / You've been a good ole wagon / He's my guy / Where are you / For all we know / Red sails in the sunset / Me and my gin / It's a mean old man's world / Is you is or is you ain't my baby / That Sunday that summer / Something's gotta give / Let me be the first to know / You're a sweetheart / Fly me to the moon / I'll close my eyes / Why was I born / Baby, won't you please come home / Drinking again / Romance in the dark / Destination moon / Nobody knows the way I feel this morning
CD _______ CDROU 1054
Roulette / Apr '92 / EMI

BEST OF DINAH WASHINGTON, THE
CD Set _______ ATJCD 8006
All That's Jazz / Aug '94 / Jazz Music / THE

CLASSIC DINAH WASHINGTON, THE (2CD Set)
Septmeber in the rain / Smoke gets in your eyes / All of me / This can't be love / I can't get started / Love is here to stay / Blue skies / Love letters / They didn't believe me / Stormy weather / Ain't misbehavin' / Ev'ry time we say goodbye / Teach me tonight / I get a kick out of you / Come rain or come shine / Love walked in / Mad about the boy / Dream / Everybody loves my baby / Manhattan / Unforgettable / It could happen to you / Stardust / This bitter Earth / I wanna be loved / Trouble in mind / You don't know what love is / What a difference a day made / Baby get lost / Since I fell for you / Love for sale / Evil gal blues / I don't hurt anymore / Feel like I wanna cry / Please send me someone to love / I won't cry anymore / Tears to burn / I could have told you / I'll never be there / Salty Papa blues / Am I blue / Cry me a river / Make the man love me / When a woman loves a man / More than you know / There is no greater love
CD Set _______ CPCD 82472
Charly / Oct '96 / Koch

COLLECTION, THE
CD _______ COL 057
Collection / Jun '95 / Target/BMG

COMPLETE DINAH WASHINGTON ON MERCURY VOL.3 1952-1954, THE (3CD Set)
CD Set _______ 8346752
Mercury / Apr '93 / PolyGram

COMPLETE DINAH WASHINGTON ON MERCURY VOL.4 1954-1956, THE (3CD Set)
CD Set _______ 8346832
Mercury / Apr '93 / PolyGram

COMPLETE DINAH WASHINGTON ON MERCURY VOL.5 1956-1958, THE (3CD Set)
CD Set _______ 8389522
Mercury / Apr '93 / PolyGram

COMPLETE DINAH WASHINGTON ON MERCURY VOL.6 1958-1960, THE (3CD Set)
CD Set _______ 8389562
Mercury / Apr '93 / PolyGram

COMPLETE DINAH WASHINGTON ON MERCURY VOL.7 1961, THE (3CD Set)
CD Set _______ 8389602
Mercury / Apr '93 / PolyGram

DINAH
Look to the rainbow / Ill wind / Cottage for sale / All of me / More than you know / There'll be some changes made / Goodbye / Willow weep for me / Make me a present of you / Smoke gets in your eyes / I could have told you / Accent on youth / What is this thing called love / Show must go on / Birth of the blues
CD _______ 8421392
EmArCy / Oct '93 / PolyGram

DINAH AND CLIFFORD
CD _______ JHR 73583
Jazz Hour / Dec '94 / Cadillac / Jazz Music / Target/BMG

DINAH JAMS
Lover come back to me / Alone together/ Summertime/Come rain or come shine / I've got you under my skin / There is no greater love / You go to my head / Darn that dream / Crazy he calls me / I'll remember April
CD _______ 8146392
EmArCy / Apr '90 / PolyGram

DINAH WASHINGTON 1954
CD _______ CD 53146
Giants Of Jazz / Nov '95 / Cadillac / Jazz Music / Target/BMG

DINAH WASHINGTON AND QUINCY JONES
CD ________ CD 53152
Giants Of Jazz / May '95 / Cadillac / Jazz Music / Target/BMG

DINAH WASHINGTON SINGS STANDARDS
CD ________ 5220552
Verve / Apr '94 / PolyGram

FATS WALLER SONGBOOK, THE
Christopher Columbus / Ain't nobody's business if I do / Jitterbug waltz / Someone's rocking my dreamboat / Ain't cha glad / Squeeze me / Ain't misbehavin' / Black and blue / Everybody loves my baby / I've got a feeling I'm falling in love / Honeysuckle rose / Keepin' out of mischief now
CD ________ 8189302
EmArCy / Apr '85 / PolyGram

FIRST ISSUE (The Dinah Washington Story/2CD Set)
CD Set ________ 5148412
Verve / Dec '93 / PolyGram

FOR THOSE IN LOVE
I get a kick out of you / Blue gardenia / Easy living / You don't know what love is / This can't be love / My old flame / I could write a book / Make the man love me / Ask a woman who knows / If I had you
CD ________ 5140732
EmArCy / Feb '93 / PolyGram

GITANES - JAZZ 'ROUND MIDNIGHT
CD ________ 5100872
Verve / Apr '91 / PolyGram

GREATEST HITS
Am I asking too much / It's too soon to know / Baby get lost / Long John blues / I only know / I wanna be loved / I'll never be free / Cold cold heart / Wheel of fortune / TV is the thing (this year) / I don't hurt anymore / Teach me tonight / What a difference a day makes / Unforgettable / Baby (you've got what it takes) / Rockin' good way / This bitter Earth / Love walked in / September in the rain / Mad about the boy
CD ________ CPCD 8008
Charly / Oct '93 / Koch

HOW TO DO IT
CD ________ PASTCD 7818
Flapper / Jun '97 / Pinnacle

IN THE LAND OF HI-FI
Our love is here to stay / Let me love you / There'll be a jubilee / My ideal / I've got a crush on you / Let's do it / Nothing ever changes my love for you / What'll I tell my heart / Sunny side of the street / Say it isn't so / Sometimes I'm happy / If I were a bell
CD ________ 8264532
EmArCy / Mar '91 / PolyGram

JAZZ MASTERS
CD ________ 5182002
Verve / May '94 / PolyGram

JAZZ PROFILE
Destination moon / Blues ain't nothin' / Lover man / Don't say nothin' at all / Coquette / Man that got away / Funny thing / Just one more chance / Miss you / To forget about you / Handful of stars / I'll never stop loving you / I wanna be around / Stranger on Earth
CD ________ CDP 8549072
Blue Note / May '97 / EMI

JAZZ SIDES OF MISS D, THE
CD Set ________ JWD 102312
JWD / Nov '94 / Target/BMG

LOW DOWN BLUES (20 Classics From Dynamic Dinah)
Mellow Mama blues / Evil gal blues / Pacific Coast blues / Embraceable you / Blow top blues / Mean and evil blues / Rich man blues / When a woman loves a man / Oowee walkie talkie / Salty Papa blues / Postman blues / Wise woman blues / How to do it / Homeward bound / Chick (on the mellow side) / I can't get started / All or nothing / That's why a woman loves a heel / Joy juice / No voot no boot
CD ________ 306502
Hallmark / Jul '97 / Carlton

MAD ABOUT THE BOY
Mad about the boy / What a difference a day makes / Unforgettable / Baby, you got what it takes / Rockin' good way / September in the rain / Love for sale / Every time we say goodbye / Makin' whoopee / All of me / Let's do it / If I were a bell / Teach me tonight / Manhattan / Everybody loves somebody / Our love is here to stay / Cry me a river
CD ________ 5122142
Mercury / Apr '92 / PolyGram

MAD ABOUT THE BOY
CD ________ MPV 5522
Movieplay / May '92 / Target/BMG

MAD ABOUT THE BOY
Mad about the boy / I wanna be loved / It's too soon to know / Unforgettable / Wheel of fortune / I only know / Am I asking too much / Soft winds / What a difference a day makes / I don't hurt anymore / Dream / Time after time / Manhattan / Trust in me / Smoke gets in your eyes / Our love is here to stay
CD ________ SUMCD 4015
Summit / Nov '96 / Sound & Media

MELLOW MAMA
CD ________ DD 451
Delmark / Dec '87 / ADA / Cadillac / CM / Direct / Hot Shot

QUEEN OF THE BLUES, THE (4CD Set)
Evil gal blues / Salty papa blues / Blow top blues / Wise woman blues / My lovin' papa / Rich man's blues / Blues for a day / Pacific coast blues / When a woman loves a man / Oo-wee walkie talkie / Slick chick (on the mellow side) / Stairway to the stars / Want to be loved / You satisfy / Since I fell for you / West side baby / You can depend on me / Walkin' and talkin' / Ain't misbehavin' / Am I asking too much / Resolution blues / I want to cry / Long John blues / It's too soon to know / Good daddy blues / Baby, get lost / I only know / Fast movin' mama / It isn't fair / Big deal / I'll never be free / I wanna be loved / Harbour lights / Time out for tears / Please send me someone to love / My heart cries for you / I apologize / I won't cry anymore / Cold cold heart / New blowtop blues / Wheel of fortune / Tell me why / Trouble in mind / When the sun goes down / Double dealing daddy / Half as much / I cried for you / Fat daddy / TV is the thing / Am I blue / I let a song go out of my heart / Blue skies / Dream / I don't hurt anymore / Soft winds / If it's the last thing I do / I've got you under my skin / Darn that dream / Teach me tonight / That's all I want from you / I concentrate on you / I could write a book / Make the man love me / Blue gardenia / Easy livin' / You might have told me / I'm lost without you tonight / Make me a present of you / Smoke gets in your eyes / Look to the rainbow / If I were a bell / Is you is or is you ain't my baby / Every time we say goodbye / I'll close my eyes / I've got a feelin' I'm fallin' / Keeping out of mischief now / It ain't nobody's business if I do / Backwater blues / What a difference a day made / Cry me a river / It could happen to you / Unforgettable / Baby (you've got what it takes): *Washington, Dinah & Brook Benton* / This bitter Earth: *Washington, Dinah & Brook Benton* / Love walked in: *Washington, Dinah & Brook Benton* / Rockin' good way (to mess around and fall in love): *Washington, Dinah & Brook Benton* / We have love: *Washington, Dinah & Brook Benton* / Early every morning (early every evening too) / Stardust / September in the rain / Our love is here to stay / Tears and laughter / Mad about the boy
CD Set ________ CDDIG 20
Charly / Nov '96 / Koch

REMEMBERING DINAH (A Tribute To Dinah Washington) (Various Artists)
Evil gal blues / Just friends / I thought about you / What a difference a day makes / All of me / If I had you / Love walked in / Willow weep for me / For all we know / Ole / Sometimes I'm happy / Teach me tonight / Centrepiece / Salty Papa blues / Makin' whoopee / Bye bye blues/Rue Chaptel
CD ________ HSR 83132
In & Out / Jun '97 / Vital/SAM

ROULETTE SESSIONS, THE
Fly me to the moon / You're a sweetheart / Our love / Love is the sweetest thing / I'll close my eyes / I didn't know about you / If it's the last thing I do / Do nothin' 'til you hear from me / My devotion / That's my desire / Was it like that / Me and the one that I love / What's new / I used to love you / Somebody else is taking my place / That old feeling / He's gone again / These foolish things
CD ________ CDROU 1038
Roulette / Aug '91 / EMI

TEACH ME TONIGHT
CD ________ JHR 73565
Jazz Hour / Oct '92 / Cadillac / Jazz Music / Target/BMG

TWO ON ONE: DINAH WASHINGTON & SARAH VAUGHAN (Washington, Dinah & Sarah Vaughan)
CD ________ CDTT 4
Charly / Apr '94 / Koch

UNFORGETTABLE
This bitter Earth / I understand / This love of mine / Alone / Somewhere along the line / Song is ended (but the melody lingers on) / Everybody loves somebody / Ask a woman who knows / Man who only does (what a woman makes him do) / Bad case of the blues / When I fall in love / Unforgettable / Lingering / Do you want it that way / Congratulations to someone / I'm in Heaven tonight / Our love is here to stay / Surprise party
CD ________ 5106022
Mercury / Apr '93 / PolyGram

WHAT A DIFFERENCE A DAY MAKES
I remember you / I thought about you / That's all there is to that / I'm through with love / Cry me a river / What a difference a day makes / Nothing in the world (could make me love you more than I do) / Manhattan / Time after time / It's magic / Sunday kind of love / I won't cry anymore
CD ________ 8188152
Mercury / Oct '84 / PolyGram

Washington, Ernestine

SISTER ERNESTINE WASHINGTON 1943-1948
CD ________ DOCD 5462
Document / Jun '96 / ADA / Hot Shot / Jazz Music

Washington, Geno

GENO
I can't turn you loose / You left the water running / In the midnight hour / Gimme a little sign/Raise your hand/I get so excited / Knock on wood / Dirty, dirty / Bring it to me baby / Alison please / I can't let you go / Michael the lover / Hold on I'm comin' / Don't fight it / Land of 1000 dances / You don't know (like I know) / Tell it like it is / Put out the fire / All I need / Water / Whatever will be will be (Que sera sera) / Hi hi Hazel
CD ________ 5507692
Spectrum / Mar '95 / PolyGram

HAND CLAPPIN' FOOT STOMPIN' FUNKY BUTT...LIVE (Hipsters, Flipsters, Finger-Poppin' Daddies) (Washington, Geno & The Ram Jam Band)
Philly dog / Up tight (everything's alright) / Hold on I'm comin' / Land of 1000 dances / Willy nilly / Michael / You don't know (like I know) / Day tripper / You left the water running / Hi-heel sneakers / Raise your hand / Things get better / She shot a hole in my soul / Ride your pony / Roadrunner / Don't fight it / Respect / Get down with it / Whatever will be will be (Que sera sera) / Herk's works / I can't turn you loose / In the midnight hour / Shotgun / Who's foolin' who / It's a wonder / Wild thing
CD ________ C5CD 581
See For Miles/C5 / Oct '96 / Pinnacle

Washington, Grover Jr.

ALL MY TOMORROWS
CD ________ 4745532
Sony Jazz / Jan '95 / Sony

ANTHOLOGY VOL.1
Best is yet to come / East River drive / Be mine tonight / Can you dig it / In the name of love / Just the two of us / Jamming / Little black samba / Jetstream / Let it flow
CD ________ 9604152
Elektra / '89 / Warner Music

BEST OF GROVER WASHINGTON, THE (2CD Set)
I loves you Porgy / Where is the love / Inner city blues (make me wanna holler) / Georgia on my mind / Trouble man / Mercy mercy me (the ecology) / Ain't no sunshine/theme from man and boy / Lean on me / Lover man / Body and soul / No tears, in the end / Until it's time for you to go / Aubrey / All the king's horses / Reed seed (trio tune) / Black frost / Mister magic / Dolphin dance / Easy loving you / Juffure / Bright moments / Snake eyes / Santa cruzin' / It feels so good
CD Set ________ 5306202
Motown / Jul '96 / PolyGram

COME MORNING
East River drive / Come morning / Be mine tonight / Reaching out / Jamming / Little black samba / Making love to you / I'm all yours
CD ________ 252337
Elektra / Apr '84 / Warner Music

INSIDE MOVES
Inside moves / Dawn song / Watching you watching me / Secret sounds / Jetstream / When I look at you / Sassy stew
CD ________ 7559603182
Elektra / Oct '94 / Warner Music

MISTER MAGIC
Earth tones / Passion flower / Mr. Magic / Black frost
CD ________ 5301032
Motown / Jan '93 / PolyGram

NEXT EXIT
Take five / Your love / Only for you (siempre para d'sers) / Greene street / Next exit / I miss home / Love like this / Summer chill / Till you return to me / Get on up / Check out Grover
CD ________ 4690882
Columbia / Jul '92 / Sony

SOULFUL STRUT
Soulful strut / Can you stop the rain / Play that groove for me / Bordertown / I can count the times / Village groove / Headman's haunt / Poacher man / Mystical force / Uptown
CD ________ 4851422
Sony Jazz / Oct '96 / Sony

THEN AND NOW
Blues for DP / Just enough / French connections / Something borrowed, something blue / Lullaby for Shana Bly / In a sentimental mood / Stella by starlight
CD ________ CK 44256
Sony Jazz / Aug '97 / Sony

WINELIGHT
Winelight / Let it flow / In the name of love / Take me there / Just the two of us / Make me a memory
CD ________ 252262
Asylum / Nov '83 / Warner Music

Washington, Keith

YOU MAKE IT EASY
Let me make love to you / Stay in my corner / Don't leave me in the dark / You always gotta go / What it takes / We need to talk/ Before I let go / trippin' / Do what you like / Believe that / No one / You make it easy
CD ________ 9362453362
Warner Bros. / Sep '93 / Warner Music

Washington, Peter

WHAT'S NEW
CD ________ DIW 605
DIW / Jun '91 / Cadillac / Harmonia Mundi

Washington, Toni Lynn

BLUES AT MIDNIGHT
CD ________ CDTC 1152
Tonecool / Apr '95 / ADA / Direct

Washington, Tuts

NEW ORLEANS PIANO (The Larry Borenstein Collection vol.3)
On the sunny side of the street / Muskrat ramble / Fast blues no.1 / Blue moon / Basin Street blues / Some of these days / Yancey special no.1 / After you've gone / Early one morning / Cow cow blues / Pinetop's boogie / Trouble trouble / Tack head blues / Yancey special no.2 / (Back home again in) Indiana / St. Louis blues
CD ________ 504CD 32
504 / Aug '94 / Cadillac / Jazz Music / Target/BMG / Wellard

NEW ORLEANS PIANO PROFESSOR
CD ________ ROUCD 11501
Rounder / '88 / ADA / CM / Direct

Washington, Walter

BEST OF NEW ORLEANS RHYTHM & BLUES VOL.2 (Washington, Walter 'Wolfman')
CD ________ MG 9008
Mardi Gras / Feb '95 / Jazz Music

BLUE MOON RISIN' (Washington, Walter 'Wolfman' & The JB Horns)
CD ________ 4TR 95112
Go Jazz / Dec '95 / Vital/SAM

GET ON UP (Charly Blues Masterworks Vol.9) (Washington, Walter 'Wolfman')
It's raining in my life / Good and juicy / Girl, don't ever leave me / Nobody's fault but mine / Honky tonk / Get on up (The Wolfman's song) / You got me worried / Sure enough it's you / Lovely day
CD ________ CD BM 9
Charly / Apr '92 / Koch

OUT OF THE DARK (Washington, Walter 'Wolfman')
CD ________ ROUCD 2068
Rounder / '88 / ADA / CM / Direct

SADA (Washington, Walter 'Wolfman')
I'll be good / Skin tight / Ain't no love in the heart of the city / Girl I wanna dance with you / Share your love / Chockin' kind / Southern comfort / I got a woman / Sada / Nothing left to be desired / What's it gonna take
CD ________ VPBCD 4
Pointblank / Jun '91 / EMI

WOLF TRACKS (Washington, Walter 'Wolfman')
CD ________ ROUCD 2048
Rounder / '88 / ADA / CM / Direct

WASP

FIRST BLOOD...LAST CUTS
Animal (fuck like a beast) / LOVE machine / I wanna be somebody / On your knees / Blind in Texas / Wild child / I don't need no doctor / Real me / Headless children / Mean man / Forever free / Chainsaw Charlie / Idol / Sunset and Babylon / Hold on to my heart / Rock 'n' roll to death
CD ________ CDESTG 2217
Capitol / Nov '93 / EMI

HEADLESS CHILDREN, THE
Heretic (the lost child) / Real me / Headless children / Thunderhead / Mean man / Neutron bomber / Mephisto waltz / Forever free / Maneater / Rebel in the FDG
CD ________ CDEST 2087
Capitol / Jul '94 / EMI

INSIDE THE ELECTRIC CIRCUS
Big welcome / I don't need no doctor / 95 nasty / Shoot from the hip / I'm alive / Easy livin' / Sweet cheetah / Mantronic / King of Sodom and Gomorrah / Rock rolls on / Restless gypsy
CD ________ CDEST 2025
Capitol / Jul '94 / EMI

KFD
Kill fuck die / Take the addiction / My tortured eyes / Killahead / Kill your pretty face / Foetus / Little death / U / Wicked death / Horror
CD ________ RAWCD 114
Raw Power / Apr '97 / Pinnacle

LIVE IN THE RAW
Inside the electric circus / I don't need no doctor / LOVE machine / Wild child / 95

nasty / Sleeping (in the fire) / Manimal / I wanna be somebody / Harder faster / Blind in Texas / Scream until you like it
CD ________ CDEST 2040
Capitol / Jul '94 / EMI

STILL NOT BLACK ENOUGH
CD ________ RAWCD 103
Raw Power / Apr '96 / Pinnacle

Wasserman, Rob

SOLO
CD ________ ROUCD 0179
Rounder / Apr '94 / ADA / CM / Direct

Wassy, Brice

SHRINE DANCE
Footprints / Shrine dance / Frenet / Ta kish / Mevum for King Nfaleu / BMF / Ku jazz / Mr. BW / All blues / Danzi
CD ________ BW 089
Melt 2000 / Jun '97 / Vital/SAM

Wasteland

DAYS OF THE APOCALYPSE
CD ________ WASTE 003CD
Nightbreed / Jun '95 / Plastic Head

Watanabe, Kazumi

KILOWATT
100 mega / Capri / No one / Jive / Papyrus / Sunspin / Pretty soon / Bernard / Dolphin dance / Goodnight machines
CD ________ 794 152
Gramavision / Mar '90 / Vital/SAM

MOBO 2
Voyage / Yatokesa / Alicia / Shang hi / All beets are coming
CD ________ GRCD 8406
Gramavision / May '85 / Vital/SAM

MOBO CLUB
CD ________ 1885062
Gaia / May '89 / New Note/Pinnacle

MOBO SPLASH
CD ________ 1886022
Gaia / May '89 / New Note/Pinnacle

PANDORA
Pandora / Peaking doll / Vega / Ashita tenki ni / Passy home / Dr. Manmbo X. / Firecracker / Kumpoo manman / Arahi no yoru kimi ni tsugu / Django 1953 / Winter swallow / Satisfaction / We got lost / Memories of Phonecia / Lady Jane / I mean you / Angie / Slippin' into the river / Continental drift
CD ________ R2 79473
Gramavision / Nov '92 / Vital/SAM

SPICE OF LIFE TOO
Andre / Fu bu ki / Small wonder / Kaimon / We planet / Rain / Concrete cows / Men and angels
CD ________ 1888102
Gramavision / Dec '88 / Vital/SAM

Watanabe, Sadao

CALIFORNIA SHOWER
California shower / Duo-creatics / Desert ride / Seventh high / Turning pages of wind / Ngoma party / My country
CD ________ JMI 20122
JVC / Apr '94 / Direct / New Note/Pinnacle / Vital/SAM

IN TEMPO
CD ________ 5272212
PolyGram Jazz / Feb '95 / PolyGram

MORNING ISLAND
Morning island / Down south / Serenade / We are the one / Home meeting / Peter Vbalse pour sadao / Samba Do Marcos / Inner embrace
CD ________ JMI 20132
JVC / Aug '96 / Direct / New Note/Pinnacle / Vital/SAM

Watchman

WATCHMAN, THE
Laundry days / Summer at the empty playground II / Captain's tune / Freddy's race / Considering the lowlands of Holland / Lowland tune / Darling angel / I wanna be with you / Wiener cowboy / After the night shift / Letter to your wedding / Farewell baby
CD ________ HNCD 1362
Hannibal / Jun '91 / ADA / Vital

Watchman

PEACEFUL ARTILLERY
CD ________ INTREPID 4202
Intrepid / Nov '95 / Direct

Water Wheel

PANCHROMA
CD ________ AS 019CD
Alley Sweeper / Mar '97 / Cargo

Waterboys

BEST OF THE WATERBOYS 1981-1990, THE (1981-1990)
Girl called Johnny / Big music / All the things she gave me / Whole of the moon / Spirit / Don't bang the drum / Fisherman's blues / Killing my heart / Strange boat / And a bang on the ear / Old England / Man is in love
CD ________ CCD 1845
Ensign / Apr '91 / EMI

DREAM HARDER
New life / Glastonbury song / Preparing to fly / Return of Pan / Corn circles / Suffer / Winter winter / Love and death / Spiritual city / Wonders of Lewis / Return of Jimi Hendrix / Good news
CD ________ GFLD 19318
Geffen / Jul '96 / BMG

FISHERMAN'S BLUES
Fisherman's blues / Strange boat / Sweet thing / Has anybody seen Hank / When ye go away / We will not be lovers / World party / And a bang on the ear / When will we be married / Stolen child
CD ________ CCD 1589
Chrysalis / Oct '88 / EMI

PAGAN PLACE, A
Church not made with hands / All the things she gave me / Thrill is gone / Rags / Somebody might wave back / Big music / Red army blues / Pagan place
CD ________ CCD 1542
Ensign / Jul '94 / EMI

ROOM TO ROAM
In search of a rose / Song from the end of the world / Man is in love / Kaliope House / Bigger picture / Natural bridge blues / Something that is gone / Star and the sea / Life of Sundays / Island man / Raggle taggle gipsies / How long will I love you / Upon the wind and waves / Spring comes to Spiddal / Trip to Broadford / Further up, further in / Room to roam
CD ________ CCD 1768
Ensign / Sep '90 / EMI

SECRET LIFE OF THE WATERBOYS 1981-1985, THE
Medicine bow / That was the river / Pagan place / Billy Sparks / Savage earth heart / Don't bang the drum / Ways of men / Rags (Second amendment) / Earth only endures / Somebody might wave back / Going to Paris / Three day man / Bury my heart / Out of control / Love that kills
CD ________ CDCHEN 35
Ensign / Sep '97 / EMI

Watercress

TRIPPED UP
Tripped up
CD ________ WCHCD 003
Creeping Herb / Jan '97 / Total/BMG

Waterlillies

ENVOLUPTUOUSITY
Sunshine like you / Hip to my way / Lie with you / Tired of you / Only one (I could stand) / Girl's affair / Nether nether / Day and age / Mermaid song
CD ________ 7599267292
Sire / Oct '92 / Warner Music

TEMPTED
Tempted / I wanna be there / Never get enough / Free / I don't want your love / Nolion doll / Take my breath away / Supersonic / She must be in love / How does it feel / Work it out / Close to you
CD ________ 9362455392
Warner Bros. / Aug '94 / Warner Music

Waterman, Steve

DESTINATION UNKNOWN
Changing places (prelude) / Mute retrieval / Long forgotten dreams / Ella's waltz / Changing places / Song for Annie / Changing places (interlude) / Reservations / Destination unkown / Changing places (epilogue)
CD ________ ASCCD 4
ASC / Oct '95 / Cadillac / New Note/ Pinnacle

Waters, Benny

(SMALL'S) TO SHANGRI-LA
CD ________ MCD 5340
Muse / Sep '92 / New Note/Pinnacle

HURRY ON DOWN
CD ________ STCD 8264
Storyville / May '97 / Cadillac / Jazz Music / Wellard

PLAYS SONGS OF LOVE
CD ________ CDJP 1039
Jazz Point / May '94 / Cadillac / Harmonia Mundi

SWINGING AGAIN (Waters, Benny Quartet)
CD ________ CDJP 1037
Jazz Point / Jan '94 / Cadillac / Harmonia Mundi

TAKE IT HOME
CD ________ BMSTRCD 001
Blues Master / Jun '94 / ADA / Direct

Waters, Crystal

CRYSTAL WATERS
CD ________ 5360142
Manifesto / Aug '97 / PolyGram

STORYTELLER
100% pure love / Ghetto day / Regardless / I believe I love you / Relax / What I need / Storyteller / Is it for me / Listen for my beep / Daddy do / Lover lay low / Piece of lonely
CD ________ 5223372
Manifesto / Nov '95 / PolyGram

Waters, Ethel

CABIN IN THE SKY
CD ________ 239772
Milan / Mar '95 / Conifer/BMG / Silva Screen

CLASSICS 1921-1923
CD ________ CLASSICS 796
Classics / Mar '95 / Discovery / Jazz Music

CLASSICS 1923-1925
CD ________ CLASSICS 775
Classics / Feb '95 / Discovery / Jazz Music

CLASSICS 1925-1926
CD ________ CLASSICS 672
Classics / Nov '92 / Discovery / Jazz Music

CLASSICS 1929-1931
CD ________ CLASSICS 721
Classics / Dec '93 / Discovery / Jazz Music

CLASSICS 1931-1934
CD ________ CLASSICS 735
Classics / Feb '94 / Discovery / Jazz Music

CLASSICS 1935-1940
CD ________ CLASSICS 755
Classics / Aug '94 / Discovery / Jazz Music

ETHEL WATERS 1926-1927
CD ________ CLASSICS 688
Charly / Mar '93 / Koch

INTRODUCTION TO ETHEL WATERS 1921-1940, AN
CD ________ 4013
Best Of Jazz / Mar '95 / Discovery

Waters, Kim

SWEET 'N' SAXY/SAX APPEAL
CD ________ FMJXD 188
FM Jazz / Dec '92 / Revolver / Sony

Waters, Muddy

AUDIO ARCHIVE
Stuff you gotta watch / She's alright / Baby, please don't go / Iodine in my coffee / So glad I'm living / Sittin' here drinkin' / One more mile / Close to you / I can't call her sugar / Trainfare blues / You gonna miss me / You can't lose what you ain't never had / I got a rich man's woman / Mean red spider / Sad letter / Mean mistreater / I can't be satisfied / Diamonds at your feet / Rollin' stone / You gonna need my help
CD ________ CDAA 034
Tring / Jun '92 / Tring

BABY PLEASE DON'T GO
CD ________ IMP 305
IMP / Apr '96 / ADA / Discovery

BEST OF MUDDY WATERS 1947-1955, THE
CD ________ MCD 09370
Chess/MCA / Jul '97 / BMG / New Note/ BMG

BLUES ANTHOLOGY
CD ________ 15719
Laserlight / Jan '95 / Target/BMG

CHICAGO BLUES BAND
CD ________ LS 2908
Landscape / Nov '92 / THE

CHICAGO BLUES MASTERS VOL.1 (Waters, Muddy/Memphis Slim)
Hoochie coochie man: *Waters, Muddy* / Walkin' thru the park: *Waters, Muddy* / Boogie woogie Memphis: *Waters, Muddy* / Rollin' and tumblin': *Waters, Muddy* / How long (live): *Waters, Muddy* / Rock me: *Waters, Muddy* / Blow wind blow: *Waters, Muddy* / John Henry: *Memphis Slim* / Stagger Lee: *Memphis Slim* / How long: *Memphis Slim* / All this piano boogie: *Memphis Slim* / Bye bye baby: *Memphis Slim* / Love my baby: *Memphis Slim* / When the sun goes down: *Memphis Slim* / Someday baby: *Memphis Slim* / Slim's slow blues: *Memphis Slim* / Gee ain't it hard to find somebody: *Memphis Slim*
CD ________ CZ 547
Capitol Jazz / Jul '95 / EMI

COLLECTION, THE
CD ________ COL 034
Collection / Feb '95 / Target/BMG

COMPLETE PLANTATION RECORDINGS, THE
Country blues / Interview 1 / I be's troubled / Interview 2 / Blur cover farm blues / Interview 3 / Ramblin' kid blues / Rosalie / Joe Turner / Pearlie May blues / Take a walk with me / Blu clover blues / Interview 4 / I be bound to write to you / You're gonna miss me when I'm gone / You got to take sick and / Why don't you live so God / Country blues / You're gonna miss me when I'm gone / 32-20
CD ________ MCD 09344
Chess/MCA / Apr '97 / BMG / New Note/ BMG

ELECTRIC MUD
I just want to make love to you / I'm your hoochie coochie man / Let's spend the night together / She's alright / Mannish boy / Herbert Harper's free press news / Tom cat / Same thing
CD ________ MCD 09364
Chess/MCA / Apr '97 / BMG / New Note/ BMG

ELECTRIC MUD AND MORE (Charly R&B Masters Vol.15)
I just want to make love to you / Hoochie coochie man / Let's spend the night together / She's alright / Herbert Harper's free press / Tom cat / Same thing / Mannish boy / Got my mojo working / I can't be satisfied / Rollin' stone
CD ________ CDRB 15
Charly / Mar '95 / Koch

EP COLLECTION, THE (Waters, Muddy & Howlin' Wolf)
Howlin' for my baby: *Howlin' Wolf* / Tell me: *Howlin' Wolf* / Back door man: *Howlin' Wolf* / My country sugar Mama: *Howlin' Wolf* / Evil: *Howlin' Wolf* / Louise: *Howlin' Wolf* / You'll be mine: *Howlin' Wolf* / You gonna wreck my life: *Howlin' Wolf* / Going down slow: *Howlin' Wolf* / 300 pounds of joy: *Howlin' Wolf* / Spoonful: *Howlin' Wolf* / Smokestack lightnin': *Howlin' Wolf* / Louisiana blues: *Waters, Muddy* / Little brown bird: *Waters, Muddy* / I'm ready: *Waters, Muddy* / I just want to make love to you: *Waters, Muddy* / Messin' with the man: *Waters, Muddy* / Got my mojo working (Live): *Waters, Muddy* / Still a fool: *Waters, Muddy* / You need love: *Waters, Muddy* / She moves on: *Waters, Muddy* / I can't be satisfied: *Waters, Muddy* / Hoochie Coochie man: *Waters, Muddy* / Wee wee baby: *Waters, Muddy*
CD ________ SEECD 379
See For Miles/C5 / Oct '93 / Pinnacle

FATHER OF CHICAGO BLUES, THE
Sugar sweet / Twenty four hours / All abroad / Hoochie coochie man / I'm ready / Long distance call / I want you to love me / Honey bee / Gone to main street / She moves me / I can't call her sugar / I can't be satisfied / Rollin' stone / You gonna miss me / Baby, please don't go / Standing around crying / Got my mojo working / Still a fool / Louisiana blues / I just want to make love to you / You can't lose what you ain't never had / Blow wind blow / Forty days and forty night / Walkin' thru the park
CD ________ CD 52001
Blues Encore / '92 / Target/BMG

FATHERS AND SONS (Waters, Muddy & Michael Bloomfield)
All aboard / Mean disposition / Blow wind blow / Can't lose what you ain't never had / Walkin' through the park / Forty days and forty nights / Standing around crying / I'm ready / Twenty four hours / Sugar sweet / Long distance call / Baby, please don't go / Honey bee / Same thing / Got my mojo working (part 1) / Got my mojo working (part 2)
CD ________ CDRED 8
Charly / Sep '88 / Koch

GOIN' HOME (Live In Paris 1970)
CD ________ 422405
WMD / Jan '97 / Discovery

GOLD
CD ________ GOLD 049
Gold / Aug '96 / Else

GOODBYE NEWPORT BLUES
I got my brand on you / Hoochie coochie man / Baby, please don't go / Soon forgotten / Tiger in your tank / I feel so good / I've got my mojo working pt.1 / I've got my mojo working pt.2 / Goodbye Newport blues / Wee wee baby / Sittin' and thinkin' / Clouds in my heart / Nineteen years old / Long distance call / Same thing
CD ________ CDBM 101
Blue Moon / May '93 / Cadillac / Discovery / Greensleeves / Jazz Music / Jet Star / TKO Magnum

GOT MY MOJO WORKING
CD ________ MACCD 193
Autograph / Aug '96 / BMG

HARD AGAIN
Mannish boy / Bus driver / I want to be loved / Jealous hearted man / I can't be satisfied / Blues had a baby and they named it rock 'n' roll / Deep down in Florida / Cross-eyed cat / Little girl
CD ________ CD 32357
Columbia / Feb '94 / Sony

HOOCHIE COOCHIE MAN
CD ________ CDC 9050
LRC / Jun '93 / Harmonia Mundi / New Note/Pinnacle

HOOCHIE COOCHIE MAN
Mannish boy / I'm ready / Champagne and reefer / I want to be loved / Baby, please don't go / Sad, sad day / I'm a king bee / Blues had a baby and they named it rock

and roll / Screamin' and cryin' / I can't be satisfied / She's nineteen years old / Hoochie coochie man
CD ____ 4611862
Epic / Aug '88 / Sony

HOOCHIE COOCHIE MAN
CD ____ 3001082
Scratch / Jul '95 / Koch / Scratch/BMG

I'M READY
I'm ready / Thirty three years / Who do you trust / Copper brown / Hoochie coochie man / Mamie / Rock me / Screamin' and cryin' / Good morning little school girl
CD ____ BGOCD 108
Beat Goes On / Aug '91 / Pinnacle

KINGS OF CHICAGO
CD Set ____ CDDIG 9
Charly / Feb '95 / Koch

LIVE AT NEWPORT
CD ____ BGOCD 314
Beat Goes On / Jun '96 / Pinnacle

LIVE IN 1958
CD ____ MW 261058
Muddy Waters / Feb '94 / Jazz Music

LIVE IN ANTIBES 1974
Honky tonk women / Blow wind blow / Off the wall / Can't get no grindin' (What's the matter with the mill) / Trouble no more / Garbage man / Hoochie coochie man / Baby, please don't go / Mannish boy / Everything gonna be alright / Got my mojo working
CD ____ FCD 116
France's Concert / Jun '88 / BMG / Jazz Music

LIVE IN PARIS 1968
CD ____ FCD 121
France's Concert / Jun '89 / BMG / Jazz Music

LIVE IN SWITZERLAND 1976 (Waters, Muddy & Chicago Blues Band)
CD ____ JH 02
Jazz Helvet / Dec '90 / TKO Magnum

LIVE IN SWITZERLAND 1976 VOL.1
CD ____ 449082
Landscape / Aug '93 / THE

LIVE IN SWITZERLAND 1976 VOL.2
CD ____ LS 2921
Landscape / Sep '93 / THE

MISSISSIPPI ROLLIN' STONE
I can't call her sugar / You can't lose what you ain't never had / Sad letter / I can't be satisfied / Baby, please don't go / Walkin' thru the park / Train fare blues / Sittin' here drinkin' / I got a rich man's woman / Mean mistreater
CD ____ CDBM 014
Blue Moon / Jul '89 / Cadillac / Discovery / Greensleeves / Jazz Music / Jet Star / TKO Magnum

MUD IN YOUR EAR
Diggin' my potatoes / Watchdog / Sting it / Why d'you do me / Natural wig / Mud in your ear / Excuse me baby / Sad day uptown / Top of the boogaloo / Long distance call / Mini dress / Remember me / Snake / Comin' home baby / Blues for hippies / Chicken shack / Love u trouble / I'm so glad / Love without jealousy / Evil
CD ____ 600630
Muse / Feb '91 / New Note/Pinnacle

MUDDY WATERS
Can't get no grindin' (What's the matter with the mill) / Trouble no more / Everything gonna be alright / Hoochie coochie man / Blues straight ahead / Rollin' and tumblin'
CD ____ BSTCD 9104
Best Compact Discs / May '92 / Complete/ Pinnacle

MUDDY WATERS
Stuff you gotta watch / Iodine in my coffee / Close to you / You gonna miss me / Mean red spider / Diamonds at your feet / You gonna need my help / She's alright / So glad I'm living / One more mile / I can't call her sugar / You can't lose what you ain't never had / Sad letter / I can't be satisfied / Baby, please don't go / Walkin' through the park / Trainfare blues / Sittin' here drinkin' / I got a rich man's woman / Mean mistreater / Forty days and forty nights / Rollin' and tumblin' / All aboard / Rock me / Rollin' stone / I'm ready
CD ____ GRF 025
Tring / '93 / Tring

MUDDY WATERS & HOWLIN' WOLF GOLD (2CD Set) (Waters, Muddy & Howlin' Wolf)
CD Set ____ D2CD 4015
Deja Vu / Jan '96 / THE

MUDDY WATERS 1941-1946
CD ____ DOCD 5146
Document / Mar '95 / ADA / Hot Shot / Jazz Music

MUDDY WATERS ANTHOLOGY (The Finest Recordings)
You shook me / I feel so good / Mannish boy / Rollin' stone / You need love / Stuff you gotta watch / Baby, please don't go / Still a fool / Evan's shuffle / Rollin' and tumblin' / Hoochie coochie man / She's into something / My home is in the Delta / I just want to make love to you / Gypsy woman / Elevate me mama / Got my mojo working / Twenty four hours / Honey Bee / Forty days and forty nights / I feel so go
CD ____ PLATCD 3911
Platinum / May '91 / Prism

MUDDY WATERS BLUE BAND, THE
CD ____ MCD 6004
Muse / Sep '92 / New Note/Pinnacle

MUDDY WATERS BLUES BAND, THE (Waters, Muddy & Dizzy Gillespie)
Nicest blues / Harmonica rockin' / Down broke down / Baby rock and roll / So long / Kansas city / Luther's blues / Got my mojo working / Portnoy's blues / Hoochie coochie man / Baby please don't go / Key Little highway
CD ____ 17102
Laserlight / Mar '97 / Target/BMG

MUDDY WATERS COLLECTOR'S EDITION
CD ____ DVBC 9042
Deja Vu / Apr '95 / THE

MUDDY WATERS IN CONCERT
Baby please don't go / Soon forgotten / Corrina, Corrina / Hoochie coochie man / Howlin' Wolf / Floyd's guitar blues / Blow wind blow / Caldonia / Screamin' and cryin' / I got my mojo working / Garbage man
CD ____ CDSGP 0150
Prestige / Mar '95 / Else / Total/BMG

MUDDY WATERS LIVE
Mannish boy / She's nineteen years old / Nine below zero / Streamline woman / Howling wolf / Baby, please don't go / Deep down in Florida
CD ____ BGOCD 109
Beat Goes On / Sep '91 / Pinnacle

MY HOME IS IN THE DELTA
CD ____ CD 52021
Blues Encore / Nov '92 / Target/BMG

ONE MORE MILE
Hard days / Muddy jumps one / Burying ground / You gonna need help / Rollin' and tumblin' part 2 / Rollin' stone / Country boy / She's so pretty / Oh yeah / I don't know why / I want to be loved / I got to find my baby / Crawlin' kingsnake / Read way back / Tiger in you tank / eMeanest woman / I got my brand on you / Lonesome room blues / Messin' with the man / Five long years / You don't have to go / Elevate me mama / Thirteen highway / Early in the morning blues / One more mile / Come back baby (let's talk it over) / My dog can't bark / Roll me over baby / Trouble in mind / Trouble trouble / My pencil won't write no more / Cold up North / Streamline woman / Rock me / Standin' round cryin' / Hoochie coochie man / Baby please don't go / You can't lose what you ain't ever had / Feel like goin' home / Where's my woman been / Rollin' and tumblin'
CD ____ MCD 09348
Chess/MCA / Apr '97 / BMG / New Note/ BMG

PARIS 1972
CD ____ PACD 5302
Pablo / Jul '97 / Cadillac / Complete/ Pinnacle

ROCK ME (Charly Blues Masterworks Vol.10)
Sugar sweet / Trouble no more / All aboard / Don't go no further / I love the life I live, I live the life I love / Rock me / Got my mojo working / She's got it / Close to you / Walking through the park / Mean mistreater / Lonesome road blues / Mopper's blues / Southbound train / Take the bitter with the sweet / She's into something
CD ____ CD BM 10
Charly / Apr '92 / Koch

ROLLIN' AND TUMBLIN'
Gypsy woman / I feel like going home / Train fare home / Down South blues / Sittin' here drinkin' / Mean red spider / Streamline woman / Little Geneva / Canary bird / Rollin' and tumblin' / You're gonna need my help / Sad letter blues / Early morning blues / Too young to know / Howling Wolf / Flood / My life is ruined / Baby, please don't go / Blow wind blow / Smokestack lightnin' / Young fashioned ways / Just to be with you / Don't go no further / I love the life I live, I live the life I love
CD ____ CDRED 17
Charly / Jun '90 / Koch

ROLLIN' STONE
Forty days and forty nights / Rollin' and tumblin' / All aboard / Rock me / Rollin' stone / I'm ready / Standing around crying / She moves me / I feel so good / Going home
CD ____ CDBM 006
Blue Moon / Jan '89 / Cadillac / Discovery / Greensleeves / Jazz Music / Jet Star / TKO Magnum

ROLLIN' STONE
I can't be satisfied / Kind hearted woman blues / Screamin and cryin / Rollin' stone / Walkin' blues / Appealing blues / Louisiana blues / Long distace call / Honey bee / She moves me / Still a fool / They call me Muddy Waters / Standing around crying / She's alright / I want you to love me / Hoochie coochie man / I just want to make love to you / I'm ready / Mannish boy / Forty days and forty nights / Crawlin' kingsnake / Just a dream / I feel good
CD ____ CDRED 1
Charly / Oct '88 / Koch

VERY BEST OF MUDDY WATERS, THE (& Roots Of the Blues Vol.2 Compilation/3CD Set)
CD ____ VBCD 302
Charly / Jul '95 / Koch

YOU'RE GONNA MISS ME WHEN I'M DEAD AND GONE (Muddy Waters Tribute Band)
Trouble no more / Clouds in my heart / I don't know why / You can't lose what you never had (you can't spend what you / Don't go no further / Going to Main Street / Going down slow / Blow wind blow / Honey bee / Sugar sweet / Messin' with the man / Muddy's shuffle / Mean mistreater / Walking through the park
CD ____ CD 83335
Telarc / Jul '96 / Conifer/BMG

Waters, Patty

COLLEGE TOUR
CD ____ ESP 10552
ESP / Jan '93 / Jazz Music

Waters, Roger

AMUSED TO DEATH
Ballad of Bill Hubbard / What God wants (pt 1) / Perfect sense / Bravery of being out of range / Late home tonight / Too much rope / What God wants (pt 2) / What God wants (pt 3) / Watching TV / Three wishes / It's a miracle / Amused to death
CD ____ 4687612
Columbia / Sep '92 / Sony

PROS AND CONS OF HITCH HIKING, THE
Apparently they were travelling abroad / Running shoes / Arabs with knives and West German skies / For the first time today (part 2) / Sexual revolution / Remains of our love / Go fishing / For the first time today (part 1) / Dunroamin' duncarin' dunlivin' / Pros and cons of hitch hiking / Every stranger's eyes / Moment of clarity
CD ____ CDP 7460292
Harvest / May '84 / EMI

RADIO KAOS
Radio waves / Who needs information / Me or him / Powers that be / Sunset strip / Home / Four minutes / Tide is turning
CD ____ CDKAOS 1
Harvest / Jun '87 / EMI

Waterson, Lal

ONCE IN A BLUE MOON (Waterson, Lal & Oliver Knight)
CD ____ TSCD 478
Topic / Feb '96 / ADA / CM / Direct

Waterson, Norma

COMMON TONGUE (Waterson, Norma & Martin/Eliza Carthy)
Rambleway/Valentine waltz / Cloudy banks / Rockabello / Lowlands of Holland / Medley / Meeting is a pleasure / Hares in the old plantation / Flash company / Maid lamenting / American stranger / French stroller / Polly's love / Stars in my crown
CD ____ TSCD 488
Topic / Mar '97 / ADA / CM / Direct

NORMA WATERSON
Black muddy river / St. Swithin's day / God loves a drunk / Birds will still be singing / There ain't no sweet man (who's worth the salt of my tears) / Rags and old iron / Pleasure and pain / Outside the wall / Anna Dixie / There is a fountain in Christ's blood / Hard times heart
CD ____ HNCD 1393
Hannibal / Sep '96 / ADA / Vital

WATERSON:CARTHY (Waterson, Norma & Martin/Eliza Carthy)
CD ____ TSCD 475
Topic / Oct '94 / ADA / CM / Direct

Watersons

EARLY DAYS
CD ____ TSCD 472
Topic / Jul '94 / ADA / CM / Direct

FOR PENCE & SPICY ALE
Country life / Swarthfell rocks / Barney / Swinton May song / Bellman / Adieu adieu / Apple tree / Wassailing song / Sheep shearing / Three day millionaire / King Pharin / T stands for Thomas / Malpas wassail song / Chickens in the garden / Good old way
CD ____ TSCD 462
Topic / May '93 / ADA / CM / Direct

Wates, Matt

RELAXIN' AT THE CAT (Wates, Matt Sextet)
Long hot / East 34th Street / Stablemates / Relaxin' at The Cat / Rio summit / Arabesque / One for JG / Never will I marry / Weaver
CD ____ ABCD 2
AB / Oct '96 / Cadillac

TWO (Wates, Matt Sextet)
Boat race / Blues from the royalty / Waltz for Frankie / Table for two / Serendipity / Jerusalem / Not forgotten / Way you look tonight
CD ____ ABCD 5
AB / Oct '96 / Cadillac

Watford, Michael

MICHAEL WATFORD
Luv 4-2 / Love me tonight / First mistake / Holdin' on / Happy man / Interlude / So into you / Love to the world / Yesterday love / Michael's prayer
CD ____ 7567923232
East West / Jan '94 / Warner Music

Watkins, Mitch

HUMHEAD
CD ____ DOS 7501
Dos / Oct '95 / ADA / CM / Direct

STRINGS WITH WINGS
Zephyr / One lost love / Oh how we danced / May your sorrows pass / Map of the dark / Suspicion / October 7 / Cry / Wildest flame / Only one moment
CD ____ TIP 8888142
Tiptoe / Nov '92 / New Note/Pinnacle

Watrous, Bill

LIVE AT THE PIZZA EXPRESS 1982
Straight no chaser / When your lover has gone / Diane / Falling in love with love / There is no greater love / Dearly beloved / I should care
CD ____ MOLECD 7
Mole Jazz / Jul '83 / Cadillac / Impetus / Jazz Music / Wellard

TIME FOR LOVE, A
Low life / Shadow of your smile / Time for love / Close enough for love / Emily / Where do you start / Shining sea / Zoot / Not really the blues
CD ____ GNPD 2222
GNP Crescendo / Jun '95 / ZYX

Watson, Bobby

BEATITUDES (Watson, Bobby & Curtis Lundy)
To see her face / Karita / Jewel / ETA / Minority / Orange blossom / Beatitudes / On the one / Karita / To see her face
CD ____ ECD 22178
Evidence / Feb '97 / ADA / Cadillac / Harmonia Mundi

GUMBO
Unit seven / Point the finger / Luqman's dream / From east to west / Gumbo / Wheel within a wheel / Premonition
CD ____ ECD 220782
Evidence / Feb '94 / ADA / Cadillac / Harmonia Mundi

INVENTOR, THE
Heckle and jeckle / Inventor / PD on Great Jones Street / Sun / For children of all ages / Dreams so real / Shaw of Newark / Homemade blues / Long way home
CD ____ CDB 191915
Blue Note / Feb '90 / EMI

JEWEL (Watson, Bobby Sextet)
To see her face / Orange blossom / Jewel / Karita / You're lucky to me / And then again
CD ____ ECD 22043
Evidence / Mar '93 / ADA / Cadillac / Harmonia Mundi

URBAN RENEWAL
Lou B / Agaya / Hi-tech trap / If / Love/hate / Beattitudes / Here's to you babe / Back in the day / P D On Great Jones Street / Reachin' and searchin' / Welcome to my world
CD ____ KOKO 1209
Kokopelli / Feb '96 / New Note/Pinnacle

Watson, Chris

STEPPING INTO THE DARK
CD ____ TO 27
Touch / Jun '96 / Kudos / Pinnacle

Watson, Dale

BLESSED OR DAMNED
CD ____ HCD 8070
Hightone / May '96 / ADA / Koch

CHEATIN' HEART ATTACK
CD ____ HCD 8061
Hightone / Jul '95 / ADA / Koch

I HATE THESE SONGS
CD ____ HCD 8082
Hightone / May '97 / ADA / Koch

Watson, Diz

TONKY HONK
CD ____ AM 91CD
Amalthea / May '96 / ADA / Direct

Watson, Doc

DOC WATSON
Nashville blues / Sitting on top of the world / Intoxicated rat / Country blues / Talk about suffering / Born about six thousand years ago / Black mountain rag / Little Omie Wise / Georgie Buck / Doc's guitar / Deep river blues / St. James' hospital / Tom Dooley
CD VMD 79152
Vanguard / Oct '95 / ADA / Pinnacle

DOC WATSON FAMILY TRADITION, THE
CD ROUCD 0129
Rounder / Aug '95 / ADA / CM / Direct

DOCABILLY
CD SHCD 3836
Sugar Hill / May '95 / ADA / CM / Direct / Koch / Roots

DOWN SOUTH (Watson, Doc & Merle)
Solid gone / Bright sunny south / Slidin' delta / Coal miner's blues / Hesitation blues / What a friend we have in Jesus / Fifteen cents / Twin sisters / Hobo / Cotton eyed Joe / Hello stranger / Down south
CD SHCD 3742
Sugar Hill / Mar '85 / ADA / CM / Direct / Koch / Roots

ELEMENTARY DOCTOR WATSON
CD SHCD 3812
Sugar Hill / Jan '94 / ADA / CM / Direct / Koch / Roots

ELEMENTARY DOCTOR WATSON/THEN AND NOW
CD CLT 5839CD
Collectables / May '97 / Greyhound

GUITAR ALBUM, THE (Watson, Doc & Merle)
Sheeps in the meadow / Stoney fork / Talking to Casey / Liza / Oh lady be good / Black pine waltz / Guitar polka / Going to Chicago blues / Black mountain rag / Cotton row / John Henry / Worried blues / Twinkle twinkle / Take me out to the ball game / Gonna lay down my old guitar
CD FF 70301
Flying Fish / Nov '96 / ADA / CM / Direct / Roots

HOME AGAIN
CD VMD 79239
Vanguard / Oct '96 / ADA / Pinnacle

MEMORIES
CD SHCD 2204
Sugar Hill / Apr '95 / ADA / CM / Direct / Koch / Roots

MY DEAR OLD SOUTHERN HOME
My dear old southern home / Ship that never returned / Your lone journey / My friend Jim / No telephone in heaven / Dream of the miner's child / Wreck of old no.9 / Grandfather's clock / Don't say goodbye if you love me / Sleep, baby, sleep / Signal light / That silver haired Daddy of mine / Life is like a river
CD SHCD 3795
Sugar Hill / Jan '91 / ADA / CM / Direct / Koch / Roots

ON PRAYING GROUND
You must come in at the door / Precious Lord / On praying ground / I'll live on / Gathering buds / Beautiful golden somewhere / We'll work 'til Jesus comes / Ninety and nine / Farther along / Christmas lullaby / Did Christ o'er sinners weep / Uncloudy day
CD SHCD 3779
Sugar Hill / Apr '90 / ADA / CM / Direct / Koch / Roots

ORIGINAL FOLKWAYS RECORDINGS 1960-1962 (Watson, Doc & Clarence Ashley)
CD SFWCD 40029
Smithsonian Folkways / Jun '94 / ADA / Cadillac / CM / Direct / Koch

PICKIN' THE BLUES (Watson, Doc & Merle Watson)
Mississipppi heavy water blues / Sittin' hear pickin' the blues / Stormy weather / Windy and warm / St. Louis blues / Jailhouse blues / Freight train blues / Hobo Bill's last ride / Carroll county blues / Blue ridge mountain blues / I'm a stranger here / Honey babe blues
CD FF 352CD
Flying Fish / Jul '92 / ADA / CM / Direct / Roots

PORTRAIT
I'm worried now / Nobody knows but me / Leaving London / Stay in the middle of the road / Risin' sun blues / George Gudger's overalls / Tucker's barn / Storms on the ocean / Prayer bell of heaven / Tough luck man / My blue eyed Jane
CD SHCD 3759
Sugar Hill / Jan '97 / ADA / CM / Direct / Koch / Roots

RED ROCKING CHAIR (Watson, Doc & Merle)
Sadie / Fisher's hornpipe / Devil's dream / Along the road / Smoke, smoke, smoke / Below freezing / California blues / John Hurt / Mole in the ground / Any old time / Red rocking chair / How long blues / Down yonder
CD FF 70252
Flying Fish / Nov '96 / ADA / CM / Direct / Roots

REMEMBERING MERLE (Watson, Doc & Merle)
Frost morn / Nine pound hammer / Omie wise / Summertime / Frankie and Johnny / New river train / Honey babe blues / Black mountain rag / St. James infirmary / Southern lady / Honey please don't go / Mama don't allow / Nancy Rowland/Salt creek / Blue suede shoes / Miss the mississippi and you / Wayfaring stranger / Thoughts of never
CD DFGCD 8427
Dixie Frog / Jun '96 / Direct / TKO Magnum
CD SHCD 3800
Sugar Hill / Jan '97 / ADA / CM / Direct / Koch / Roots

RIDIN' THE MIDNIGHT TRAIN
I'm going back to the old home / Greenville high trestle / Highway of sorrow / Fill my way with love / We'll meet again sweetheart / Ridin' that midnight train / Stone's rag / Ramshackle shack / Midnight on the stormy deep / Blue baby eyes / What does the deep sea say / Let the church roll on / Sweet heaven when I die
CD SHCD 3752
Sugar Hill / Dec '88 / ADA / CM / Direct / Koch / Roots

SONGS FOR LITTLE PICKERS
Talkin' guitar / Mole in the ground / Mama blues / Froggie went a-courtin' / Shady grove / Riddle song / Sing song kitty / John Henry / Sally Goodin / Crawdad song / Grass grew all around / Liza Jane / Tennessee stud
CD SHCD 3786
Sugar Hill / Sep '90 / ADA / CM / Direct / Koch / Roots

SONGS FROM THE SOUTHERN MOUNTAINS (Watson, Doc & Family)
CD SHCD 3829
Sugar Hill / Oct '94 / ADA / CM / Direct / Koch / Roots

SOUTHBOUND
Walk on boy / Blue railroad train / Sweet Georgia Brown / Alberta / Southbound / Windy and warm / Call of the road / Tennessee stud / That was the last thing on my mind / Little darling pal of mine / Nothing to it / Riddle song / Never no more blues / Nashville pickin'
CD VMD 79213
Vanguard / Oct '95 / ADA / Pinnacle

THEN AND NOW/TWO DAYS IN NOVEMBER (Watson, Doc & Merle)
Bonaparte's retreat / Milkcow blues / Bottle of wine / Matchbox blues / Freight train boogie / If I needed you / Frankie & Johnnie / Summertime / That's all / Corrina Corrina / Meet me somewhere in your dreams / Old camp meetin' time / Rain crow Bill / Walk on boy / Poor boy blues / I'm going fishing / Kinfolks in Carolina / Last thing on my mind / Lonesome moan / Little beggar man / Old Joe Clark / Kaw-Liga / Three times seven / Train that carried my girl from town / Snow bird / Doc's rag
CD BGOCD 297
Beat Goes On / Nov '95 / Pinnacle
CD SHCD 2205
Sugar Hill / Sep '96 / ADA / CM / Direct / Koch / Roots

TREASURES UNTOLD (Watson, Doc & Family)
Intro / Lights in the valley / Beaumont rag / I heard my mother weeping / Billy in the lowground / Omie wise / Rueben's train / Hick's farewell / Ramblin' hobo / White House blues / Jimmy Sutton / The old buck ram / I want him to love me more / Grandfather's clock / Chinese breakdown / Handsome Molly / Beaumont rag: *Watson, Doc & Clarence White* / Farewell blues: *Watson, Doc & Clarence White* / Lonesome road blues: *Watson, Doc & Clarence White* / Footprints in the snow: *Watson, Doc & Clarence White*
CD VCD 77001
Vanguard / Jan '96 / ADA / Pinnacle

VANGUARD YEARS, THE (4CD Set)
Rambling hobo / Train that carried my girl from town / Coo coo / Reuben's train / Hick's farewell / Grandfather's clock / Beaumont rag / Farewell blues / Footprints in the snow / Intoxicated rat / Talk about suffering / Omie wise / Country blues / Black mountain rag / Doc's guitar / Deep river blues / Muskrat / Dream of the miner's child / Rising sun blues / Otto Wood the bandit / Little Sadie / Windy and warm / Tennessee stud / Blue railroad train / Down in the valley to pray / Dill pickle rag / FFV / Childhood play / Streamline cannonball / Old camp meeting time / I'm thinking tonight of my blue eyes / Girl in the blue velvet band / New river train / Rank stranger / Corrina Corrina / What does the deep sea say / There's more pretty girls than one / Way downtown / Brown's ferry blues / Spike driver blues / Roll on buddy / I am a pilgrim / Wabash cannonball / Roll in my sweet baby's arms / Lawson family murder / Cuckoo / Alabama bound / Bye bye bluebells / Kinfolks in Carolina / San Antonio Rose / Blow your whistle freight train / Cannonball rag / I am a pilgrim / Arrangement blues / I got a pig at home in the pen / My rough and rowdy ways / Deep river blues / Banks of the Ohio / A-roving on a Winter's night / Southbound / Memphis blues / Salt creek/ Bill Cheatham / Brown's ferry blues / Windy and warm
CD Set VCD 4155
Vanguard / Apr '96 / ADA / Pinnacle

WATSON COUNTRY (Watson, Doc & Merle)
CD FF 651CD
Flying Fish / Aug '96 / ADA / CM / Direct / Roots

Watson, Eric

BROADWAY BY TWILIGHT
CD 500482
Musidisc / May '94 / Discovery

MEMORY OF WATER, THE (Watson, Eric & John Lindberg)
CD LBLC 6535
Label Bleu / Jun '91 / New Note/Pinnacle

Watson Family

WATSON FAMILY, THE
CD CDSF 40012
Smithsonian Folkways / Aug '94 / ADA / Cadillac / CM / Direct / Koch

Watson, Helen

NOTES ON DESIRE
CD BUILD 001CD
Building / Mar '96 / ADA / Direct

Watson, James

JAMES WATSON SOLO
Concert scherzo / Trumpet concerto (Goedicke) / Albumblat / June from The Seasons / Trumpet concerto (Arutiunian) / Vocalise / Valse sentimentale / Concert etude
CD DOYCD 036
Doyen / Oct '94 / Conifer/BMG

Watson, Johnny 'Guitar'

AIN'T THAT A BITCH
I need it / I want to ta ta you baby / Superman lover / Ain't that a bitch / Since I met you baby / We're no exception / Won't you forgive me baby
CD NEM 774
Sequel / Jan '96 / BMG

AND THE FAMILY CLONE
CD NEMCD 780
Sequel / Jun '96 / BMG

FUNK BEYOND THE CALL OF DUTY
Funk beyond the call of duty / It's all about the dollar bill / Give me my love / It's a damn shame / I'm gonna get you baby / Barn door / Love that will not die
CD NEM 776
Sequel / Jan '96 / BMG

GANGSTER OF LOVE
I got eyes / Motorhead baby / Gettin' drunk / Walkin' to my baby / Highway 60 / Space guitar / Sad fool / Half pint of whiskey / No I can't / Thinking / Broke and lonely / Cuttin' in / What you do to me / Those lonely, lonely nights / You can't take it with you / I just wants me some love / Gangster of love / Sweet lovin' mama
CD CDCHARLY 267
Charly / Feb '91 / Koch

GANGSTER OF LOVE
CD CCSCD 802
Castle / Aug '95 / BMG

GIANT
Miss Frisco (Queen of the disco) / Tu jours amour / Gangster of love / Guitar disco / Wrapped in black mink / You can stay but the noise must go / Baby face
CD NEMCD 777
Sequel / Feb '96 / BMG

HOT JUST LIKE TNT
Hot little Mama / I love to love you / Hot little Mama / Don't touch me (I'm gonna hit the highway) / Too tired / Lonely girl / Ain't gonna hush / These lonely, lonely nights / Oh baby / Someone cares for me / Ruben / Give a little / Love me baby / She moves me / Ruben / Three hours past midnight / Love bandit (gangster of love) / Telephone boogie / Dee's boogie / I got a girl (that lives over yonder) / Gangster of love / One room country shack / Deana baby / Honey / Come on baby / My baby and me / You've been gone too long / Come on baby
CD CDCHD 621
Ace / Sep '96 / Pinnacle

JOHNNY 'GUITAR' WATSON
CD EXP 045
Experience / May '97 / TKO Magnum

LISTEN
If I had the power / You've got a hard head / Loving you / It's all about you / You're the sweetest thing I've ever had / I get a feeling / Like I'm not your man / You bring love / You stole my heart / I don't want to be a lone ranger / Your new love is a player / Tripping / Lonely man's prayer / You make my heart want to sing / It's way too late / Love is sweet misery / You can stay but the noise must go / Strong vibrations
CD CDCHD 408
Ace / Sep '92 / Pinnacle

LOVE JONES
Booty ooty / Love Jones / Going up in smoke / Close encounters / Asante sana / Telephone bill / Lone Ranger / Jet plane / Children of the universe
CD NEMCD 779
Sequel / Feb '96 / BMG

REAL MOTHER FOR YA, A
Real Mother for you / Nothing left to be desired / Your love is my love / Real deal / Tarzan / I wanna thank you / Lover Jones
CD NEM 775
Sequel / Jan '96 / BMG

WHAT THE HELL IS THIS
Real mother for ya / Ain't that a bitch / Booty ooty / Mother In Law / Miss Frisco (queen of the disco) / I want to ta ta you baby / Your love is my love / It's all about the dollar bill / Lover Jones / What the hell is this / I need it / I don't want to be president / Wrapped in black mink / Strung out
CD NEMCD 778
Sequel / Feb '96 / BMG

Watson, Junior

LONG OVERDUE
CD BMCD 9021
Black Magic / Apr '93 / ADA / Cadillac / Direct / Hot Shot

Watson, Kino

TRUE 2 THE GAME
Intro....It's time / Game recognize game(whatcha want) / Got me open / I'm the man (your mama warnin' you about) / Cry no more (I'll be there for you) / It's time / Bring it on / Body language / Down 4 mine / Best things in life are free / Black beauty (interlude) / Definition of love
CD 4842342
Columbia / Aug '96 / Sony

Watt, Ben

NORTH MARINE DRIVE
On Box Hill / Some things don't matter / Lucky one / Empty bottles / North Marine Drive / Waiting like mad / Thirst for knowledge / Long time no see / You're gonna make me lonesome when you go / Walter and John / Aquamarine / Slipping slowly / Another conversation with myself / Girl in winter
CD CDBRED 40
Cherry Red / Jun '87 / Pinnacle

Watters, Lu

COMPLETE GOOD TIME JAZZ RECORDINGS, THE (4CD Set) (Watters, Lu & The Yerba Buena Jazz Band)
At a Georgia camp meeting / Irish black bottom / Original jelly roll blues / Smokey mokes / Maple leaf rag / Memphis blues / Black and white rag / Black and white rag / Muskrat ramble / High society / High society / Millenberg joys / Daddy do, Daddy do / Hot house rag / Muskrat ramble / Muskrat ramble / London cafe blues / Tiger rag / Fidgety feet / Fidgety feet / Come back sweet Papa / Sunset cafe stomp / Sunset cafe stomp / Terrible blues / Temptation rag / Riverside blues / Cake walkin' babies from home / Make me a pallet on the floor / Moose march / Jazzin' babies blues / Dippermouth blues / Fidgety feet / Kansas City stomp / Muskrat ramble / Trombone rag / Minstrels of Annie Street / Jazzin' babies blues / Easy winners / Ostrich walk / Pineapple rag / I'm goin' huntin' / Ain't gonna give nobody none o' this jelly roll / New Orleans blues / Original rag / Ory's creole trombone / Pastime rag / Canal Street blues / You can't shush Katie (the gabbiest girl in town) / Maple leaf rag / Annie Street rag / Big bear stomp / Antigua blues / Emperor Norton's hunch / Climax rage / Sage hen strut / Trombone strut / Down home rag / Harlem rag / Creole belles / Sunburst rag / That's a plenty / South / Chattanooga stomp / 1919 rag / Sunset cafe stomp / Copenhagen / Panama / Working man blues / Richard M Jones blues / Bienville blues / Triangle jazz blues / Weary blues / Friendless blues / That's a plenty / Original jelly roll blues / Muskrat ramble / Canal Street blues / Yerba buena strut / Oriental strut / Struttin' with some barbecue / Emperor Norton's hunch / Ory's creole trombone / Weary blues / Down home rag / Big bear stomp / Trombone rag / Annie Street rock / Get it right / Cake walkin' babies from home / Antigua blues / Pineapple rag / Beale Street blues / Chattanooga stomp / Jazzin' babies blues / Snake rag
CD Set 4GTJCD 4409
Good Time Jazz / Nov '96 / Complete/ Pinnacle

DAWN CLUB FAVOURITES VOL.1 (Watters, Lu & The Yerba Buena Jazz Band)
CD GTCD 12001
Good Time Jazz / Nov '95 / Complete/ Pinnacle

HAMBONE KELLY (Watters, Lu & The Yerba Buena Jazz Band)
CD _____ **MMRCD 10**
Merry Makers / Aug '95 / Jazz Music

TOGETHER AGAIN (Watters, Lu & Turk Murphy)
CD _____ **MMRCD 8**
Merry Makers / Mar '95 / Jazz Music

YERBA BUENA JAZZ BAND VOL.12
CD _____ **BCD 97**
GHB / Mar '95 / Jazz Music

Watts, Charlie

FROM ONE CHARLIE (Watts, Charlie Quintet)
CD _____ **UFO 002CD**
UFO Jazz / May '91 / Pinnacle

LONG AGO & FAR AWAY
I've got a crush on you / Long ago & far away / More than you know / I should care / Good morning heartache / Someday you'll be sorry / I get along without you very well / What's new / Stairway to the stars / In the still of the night / All or nothing at all / I'm in the mood for love / Sentimental journey / Never let me go
CD _____ **VPBCD 36**
Pointblank / Jun '96 / EMI

Watts, Ernie

ERNIE WATTS QUARTET, THE (Watts, Ernie Quartet)
Language of the heart / Continental blues / Echoes / My one and only love / On the border / Skylark / One in three / Body and soul
CD _____ **JM 120052**
JVC / Aug '96 / Direct / New Note/Pinnacle / Vital/SAM

LONG ROAD HOME
Lover man / At the end of my rope / River of light / Nostalgia in Times Square / Bird's idea / Long road home / Goodbye pork pie hat / Willow weep for me / Moonlight and shadows
CD _____ **JVC 20592**
JVC / Oct '96 / Direct / New Note/Pinnacle / Vital/SAM

REACHING UP
Reaching up / Mr. Sums / I hear a rhapsody / Transparent sea / High road / Inward glance / You leave me breathless / Juice Lucy / Angels flight / Sweet solitude
CD _____ **JVC 20312**
JVC / Feb '94 / Direct / New Note/Pinnacle / Vital/SAM

TENOR TRIO (Watts, Ernie & Pete Christlieb/Rickey Woodard)
Blues up and down / Strollin' / Groovin' high / Love for sale / St. Thomas / Fried bananas / Here's to Alvy / Holy land / Moten swing / Eternal triangle / Little pony
CD _____ **JVC 90212**
JVC / Jul '97 / Direct / New Note/Pinnacle / Vital/SAM

UNITY
You say you care / In your own sweet way / Tricotism / Unity / Silver hollow / Some kind a blue / Don't look now / Joyous reunion / Lonely hearts / Sticky kisses / Soul eyes
CD _____ **JVC 20462**
JVC / Apr '95 / Direct / New Note/Pinnacle / Vital/SAM

Watts, Jeff

MEGAWATTS (Watts, Jeff 'Tain')
CD _____ **500552**
Sunnyside / Aug '93 / Discovery

Watts, Marzette

MARZETTE WATTS
CD _____ **ESP 10442**
ESP / Jan '93 / Jazz Music

Watts, Noble

RETURN OF THE THIN MAN
CD _____ **ALCD 4785**
Alligator / May '93 / ADA / CM / Direct

Watts, Trevor

MOIRE MUSIC (Watts, Trevor Moire Music)
Egugu / Ahoom mbram / Tetegramatan / Free flow / Tetegramatan reprise / Opening gambit / Otublohu / Bomsu / Hunter's song: Ibrumankuman / Rocky road to Dublin / Brekete takai / Southern memories / We are
CD _____ **5213512**
ECM / Feb '94 / New Note/Pinnacle

WIDER EMBRACE, A
CD _____ **ECM 1449**
ECM / May '94 / New Note/Pinnacle

Waulk Elektrik

UPROOTED
West wind / Ud Nameh / Lendrick Hill / Green fingers / Uist / Breakout / Dreampad / Punch it / Stumpie/Madam Frederick's/ Hunter's purse
CD _____ **DREXCD 102**
Dangerous / Apr '94 / ADA / Direct

Wave

WAVE
CD _____ **EBCD 31**
Eightball / Jan '95 / Vital

Wax

WAX FILES, THE
CD _____ **FLYCD 10**
For Your Love / Apr '97 / 3mv/Sony

Waxworth Industries

ALIEN DISCO
CD _____ **WAX 100CD**
Abstract / Aug '94 / Cargo / Pinnacle / Total/BMG

Way, Anthony

CHOIRBOY'S CHRISTMAS, THE
CD _____ **4550502**
PolyGram TV / Nov '96 / PolyGram

Way, Darryl

CONCERTO FOR ELECTRIC VIOLIN
1st movement / Allegro moderato / 2nd movement / Slow / 3rd movement / Scherzo / 4th movement / Finale (gigue)
CD _____ **EDCD 514**
Edsel / Nov '96 / Pinnacle

Way We Live

CANDLE FOR JUDITH/TRACTOR (Way We Live/Tractor)
Kick Dick II / Squares / Siderial / Angle / Storm / Willow / Madrigal / Way ahead / All ends up / Little girl in yellow / Watcher / Reavenscroft / Bar boogie / Shubunkin' / Hope in favour / Everytime it happens / Make the journey
CD _____ **SEECD 409**
See For Miles/C5 / Sep '94 / Pinnacle

Waybill, Fee

DON'T BE SCARED BY THESE HANDS
I know you / Tall dark and harmless / Shut up and love me / Swing of things / Fools cry / Surprise yourself / I've seen this movie before / Dying of delight / What's wrong with that / Somewhere deep inside
CD _____ **WESTCD 11**
West Coast / Nov '96 / Cargo

READ MY LIPS
You're still laughing / Nobody's perfect / Who loves you baby / I don't even know your name (passion play) / Who said life would be pretty / Thrill of the kill / Saved my life / Caribbean sunsets / Star of the show / I could've been somebody
CD _____ **BGOCD 283**
Beat Goes On / Aug '95 / Pinnacle

Wayne, Jeff

WAR OF THE WORLDS (Musical Version Of The War Of The Worlds)
Coming of the Martians / Eve of the war / Horsell Common and the heat ray / Artilleryman and the fighting machine / Forever autumn / Thunder child / Earth under the Martians / Red weed / Red weed / Spirit of man / Brave new world / Dead London / Epilogue (part 1) / Epilogue (part 2)
CD Set _____ **CD 96000**
CBS / Jul '86 / Sony

WAR OF THE WORLDS (Highlights)
Eve of the war / Horsell Common and the heat ray / Forever autumn / Fighting machine / Thunderchild / Red weed / Spirit of man / Dead London / Brave new world
CD _____ **CDX 32356**
Columbia / Feb '97 / Sony

WAR OF THE WORLDS (Coming Of The Martians/Earth Under The Martians/2CD Set)
Eve of the war / Horsell Common and the heat ray / Artillery man and the fighting machine / Forever Autumn / Thunder child / Red weed / Spirit of man / Red weed / Brave new world / Dead London / Epilogue / Epilogue / Spirit of man / Dark Autumn dub / Forever Autumn / Epilogue / Eve of the war / Epilogue #2/Eve of the war
CD Set _____ **CDX 96000**
Sony Music / Jun '96 / Sony

Wayne Wonder

ALL ORIGINAL BOMBSHELL
CD _____ **PHRICD 27**
Penthouse / Jan '96 / Jet Star

DON'T HAVE TO
CD _____ **PHCD 24**
Penthouse / Oct '93 / Jet Star

WAYNE WONDER COLLECTION, THE
CD _____ **PICK 001CD**
Sprint Enterprise / Jun '97 / Jet Star

Wayra, Pukaj

BOLIVIA
CD _____ **LYRCD 7361**
Lyrichord / '91 / ADA / CM / Roots

MUSICA ANDINA
CD _____ **CD 12511**
Music Of The World / Nov '92 / ADA / Target/BMG

Waysted

GOOD, THE BAD AND THE WAYSTED, THE
Hang 'em high / Hi ho my baby / Heaven tonight / Manuel / Dead on your legs / Rolling out the pie / Land that's lost the love / Crazy about the stuff / Around and around / Won't get out alive / Price you pay / Rock steady / Hurt so good / Cinderella boys / Ball and chain
CD _____ **CDMFN 43**
Music For Nations / Dec '92 / Pinnacle

WC & The Maad Circle

CURB SERVIN'
Intro / West up / Granny nuttin' up / One / Crazy break pt.2 / Put on the set / In a twist / Homesick / Feel me / Curb servin' / Stuckie mack / Taking ova / Kill a habit / Reality check / Creator
CD _____ **8286502**
Payday / Sep '95 / PolyGram / Vital

We

AS IS
CD _____ **EFA 070972**
Asphodel / Mar '97 / Cargo / SRD

We All Together

WE ALL TOGETHER
CD _____ **HBG 122/8**
Background / Apr '94 / Background / Greyhound
CD _____ **LZ 2422**
Lazarus / Jun '97 / Greyhound

We Are Going To Eat You

EVERYWHEN
If I could / Heart in hand / This conspiracy / Each life a mystery / Glory / Ride upon the tide / Eye to eye / On a day like this / Just another one / Here always / If you believe / Her dreamworld
CD _____ **ABBCD 014**
Big Cat / Jan '90 / 3mv/Pinnacle

We The People

DECLARATION OF INDEPENDENCE
CD _____ **EVA 842144**
EVA / Nov '94 / ADA / Direct

Weak Moments

WEAK MOMENTS
CD _____ **BING 008**
Ba Da Bing / Apr '97 / Cargo

Weather Girls

DOUBLE TONS OF FUN
We're gonna party / Sweet thang / Can U feel it (dee ooh la la la) / We shall all be free / Sexy ghost / Still I'm free / Here goes my heart / Love somebody tonite / Happy, happy / I want to take you higher / Can't let you go / It's raining men
CD _____ **4509940182**
WEA / Mar '94 / Warner Music

Weather Prophets

JUDGES, JURIES AND HORSEMEN
CD _____ **CRECD 033**
Creation / May '94 / 3mv/Vital

TEMPERANCE HOTEL
CD _____ **CRECD 50**
Creation / May '94 / 3mv/Vital

WEATHER PROPHETS LIVE
CD _____ **CRECD 085**
Creation / May '94 / 3mv/Vital

Weather Report

8.30 (2CD Set)
Black market / Scarlet woman / Teen town / Remark you made / Slang / In a silent way / Birdland / Thanks for the memory / Badia / Boogie woogie waltz medley / 8.30 / Brown Street / Orphan / Sightseeing
CD Set _____ **4769082**
Sony Jazz / Jan '95 / Sony

BLACK MARKET
CD _____ **4682102**
Sony Jazz / Jan '95 / Sony

DOMINO THEORY
Can it be done / D flat waltz / Peasant / Predator / Blue sound-note / Swamp cabbage / Domino theory
CD _____ **CD 25839**
CBS / Feb '84 / Sony

HEAVY WEATHER
Birdland / Remark you made / Teen town / Harlequin / Rumba mama / Palladium / Juggler / Havona
CD _____ **4682092**
Columbia / Jan '92 / Sony

I SING THE BODY ELECTRIC
CD _____ **4682072**
Sony Jazz / Jan '95 / Sony

MR. GONE
Pursuit of the woman in the feathered hat / River people / Young and fine / Elders / Mr. Gone / Punk jazz / Pinocchio / And then
CD _____ **4682082**
Sony Jazz / Jan '95 / Sony

MYSTERIOUS TRAVELLER
CD _____ **4718602**
Sony Jazz / Jan '95 / Sony

NIGHT PASSAGE
Dream clock / Port of entry / Forlorn / Rockin' in rhythm / Fast city / Night passage / Three views of a secret / Madagascar
CD _____ **4682112**
Sony Jazz / Jan '95 / Sony

SWEETNIGHTER
Boogie woogie waltz / Manolette / Adios / 125th Street congress / Will / Non-stop home
CD _____ **4851022**
Sony Jazz / Sep '96 / Sony

TALE SPINNIN'
CD _____ **4769072**
Sony Jazz / Jan '95 / Sony

THIS IS JAZZ
Birdland / Remark you made / Black market / Man in the green shirt / Young and fine / Teen town / Moors / Mysterious traveller / Orange lady
CD _____ **CK 64627**
Sony Jazz / May '96 / Sony

THIS IS THIS
This is this / Face the fire / I'll never forget you / Jungle stuff (part 1) / Man with the copper fingers / Consequently / Update / China blues
CD _____ **CD 57052**
Sony Jazz / Jan '95 / Sony

WEATHER REPORT
Milky way / Umbrellas / Seventh arrow / Orange lady / Morning lake / Waterfall / Tears / Eurydice
CD _____ **4682122**
Columbia / Jan '95 / Sony

Weathersby, Carl

DON'T LAY YOUR BLUES ON ME
Rock your town / Things the blues will make you do / Killing floor / Your love is everything / All your affection is gone / Don't lay your blues on me / Same thing / Poverty / Somebody help me / Fannie Mae
CD _____ **ECD 260752**
Evidence / Apr '96 / ADA / Cadillac / Harmonia Mundi

Weaver, Curley

COMPLETE RECORDED WORKS 1933-35
CD _____ **DOCD 5111**
Document / Nov '92 / ADA / Hot Shot / Jazz Music

Weaver, Sylvester

COMPLETE RECORDED WORKS VOL.1
CD _____ **DOCD 5112**
Document / Nov '92 / ADA / Hot Shot / Jazz Music

COMPLETE RECORDED WORKS VOL.2
CD _____ **DOCD 5113**
Document / Nov '92 / ADA / Hot Shot / Jazz Music

Weavers

ALMANAC
When the stars begin to fall / We're all dodgin' / Brother can you spare a dime / Jackhammer John / A walkin' and a talkin' / Rally round the flag / Fight on / Bill / Get along little doggies / True religion / Which are you side on / Bye bye bye
CD _____ **VMD 79100**
Vanguard / Oct '95 / ADA / Pinnacle

TOGETHER AGAIN
CD _____ **ROUCD 1681**
Rounder / '88 / ADA / CM / Direct

WASN'T THAT A TIME
CD _____ **HMNCD 012**
Half Moon / Jun '97 / BMG

Webb, Cassell

HOUSE OF DREAMS
CD _____ **WOLCD 1025**
China / May '92 / Pinnacle

Webb, Chick

'TAIN'T WHAT YOU DO, IT'S THE WAY THAT YOU DO IT (Webb, Chick & Ella Fitzgerald)

Strictly jive / If you can't sing it, you'll have to swing it (Mr. Paganini) / Gee boy you're swell / Liza / Moonlight and magnolias / Facts and figures / T'ain't what you do (it's the way that you do it) / Love you're just a laugh / Wacky dust / Midnight in Harlem / Dipsy doodle / Congo / Rusty hinge / I've got a guy / Down home rag / Tisket-a-tasket / Take another guess / Sweet Sue, just you / Rock it for me / Go Harlem / Holiday in Harlem / Azure
CD RAJCD 836
Empress / Mar '97 / Koch

CHICK WEBB WITH GUESTS
CD CD 14548
Jazz Portraits / Jan '94 / Jazz Music

CLASSICS 1929-1934
CD CLASSICS 502
Classics / Apr '90 / Discovery / Jazz Music

CLASSICS 1935-1938
CD CLASSICS 517
Classics / Apr '90 / Discovery / Jazz Music

INTRODUCTION TO CHICK WEBB 1929-1939, AN
CD 4015
Best Of Jazz / Nov '94 / Discovery

ON THE AIR 1939
CD TAX 37062
Tax / Aug '94 / Cadillac / Jazz Music / Wellard

QUINTESSENCE, THE (1929-1939/2CD Set) (Webb, Chick & Ella Fitzgerald)
CD Set FA 214
Fremeaux / Feb '96 / ADA / Discovery

RHYTHM MAN 1931-1934 (Webb, Chick Orchestra)
Heebie jeebies / Blues in my heart / Soft and sweet / On the sunnyside of the street / At the Darktown strutter's ball / If dreams come true / Let's get together / I can't dance / Imagination / Why should I beg / Stompin' at the Savoy / Blue minor / True / Lonesome moments / If it ain't love / That rhythm man / On the sunnyside of the street / Lona / It's over because we're through / What a shuffle / Blue Lou
CD HEPCD 1023
Hep / May '92 / Cadillac / Jazz Music / New Note/Pinnacle / Wellard

Webb, Jimmy

ARCHIVE
PF Sloan / Love song / Three songs / Met her on a plane / All my love's laughter / One lady / If ships were made to sail / Galveston / Once in the morning / When can Brown begin / Piano / Highwayman / Christian no / Where the universes are / Moon is a harsh mistress / Feet in the sunshine / Lady fits her blue jeans / Just this one time / Crying in my sleep / Land's end/Asleep on the wind
CD 9548320632
WEA / Jun '93 / Warner Music

SUSPENDING DISBELIEF
Too young to die / I don't know how to love you anymore / Elvis and me / It won't bring her back / Sandy cove / Friends to burn / What does a woman see in a man / Postcard from Paris / Just like always / Adios / I will arise
CD 7559615062
WEA / Oct '93 / Warner Music

Webb, Natalie

TAKE ME TO PARADISE
CD NATCD 1
Nation / Jun '95 / RTM/Disc

Webb, Stan

40 BLUE FINGERS FRESHLY PACKED (Chicken Shack)
Letter / Lonesome whistle blues / When the train comes back / San-Ho-Zay / King of the world / See see baby / First time I met the blues / Webbed feet / You ain't no good / What you did last night
CD 4773572
Columbia / Aug '94 / Sony

CHANGES (Webb, Stan & Chicken Shack)
These foolish things / Where you pushed or did you fall / Sweetest little thing / Will you dance with me / Don't you worry about a thing / I'd rather go blind / Have you seen my heart / Burning love / Poor boy
CD INAK 9008CD
In Akustik / Jul '97 / Direct / TKO Magnum

COLLECTION, THE (Chicken Shack)
Letter / When the train comes back / Lonesome whistle blues / You ain't no good / Baby's got me crying / Right way is my way / Get like you used to be / Woman is blues / I wanna see my baby / Remmington ride / Mean ol' world / San-Ho-Zay / Way it is / Tears in the wind / Maudie / Some other time / Andalucian blues / Crazy about you baby / Close to me / I'd rather go blind
CD CCSCD 179
Castle / Jan '94 / BMG

FROM THE VAULTS (Chicken Shack)
Midnight hour / When the train comes back / Night life / It's OK with me baby / Tell me / Telling your fortune / Strange things happening / Side tracked / Lonesome whistle blues / Letter / Mean old world / Tired eyes / My mood / You've done lost your good thing now / Everyday I have the blues / Waiting for you / San ho zay / It'll be me / Hey hey hey hey
CD IGOXCD 508
Indigo / Jun '97 / ADA / Direct

IMAGINATION LADY (Chicken Shack)
Crying won't help you now / Daughter of the hillside / If I were a carpenter / Going down / Poor boy / Telling your fortune / Loser
CD IGOXCD 506
Indigo / May '97 / ADA / Direct

OK KEN (Chicken Shack)
Baby's got me crying / Right way is my way / Get like you used to be / Pony and trap / Tell me / Woman is the blues / I wanna see my baby / Remington ride / Fishing in your river / Mean ol' world / Sweet sixteen
CD BGOCD 186
Beat Goes On / Jun '93 / Pinnacle
CD 4746082
Epic / Mar '97 / Sony

PLUCKING GOOD (Webb, Stan & Chicken Shack)
Reflections / Broken hearted melody / Look out / Talk about love / I'm not sorry / Crying again / For all your love / If only / Nothing I can do / Dr. Brown / Let me love you babe / Thrill has gone
CD INAK 9019CD
In Akustik / Jul '97 / Direct / TKO Magnum

SIMPLY LIVE
CD 848824
SPV / Jan '90 / Koch / Plastic Head

STAN THE MAN LIVE
CD IGOCD 2053
Indigo / Nov '95 / ADA / Direct

WEBB'S BLUES (Webb, Stan & Chicken Shack)
CD IGOCD 2013
Indigo / Dec '94 / ADA / Direct

Webber, A.J.

RUNNING OUT OF SKY
Somewhere in the darkness / Hello old friend hello / Reservation blues / Decision / Running out of sky / Sebastapol bay / Eye of the wind / Barry's song / Chosen one / That old road back home / Seeing you again
CD AJWCD 1
Smart / Sep '93 / Sony

Webber, Dave

TOGETHER SOLO (Webber, Dave & Anni Fentiman)
CD DRGNCD 931
Dragon / Mar '94 / ADA / Cadillac / CM / Roots / Wellard

Webber, Garth

ON THE EDGE (Webber, Garth & Mark Ford)
CD CCD 11045
Crosscut / Nov '94 / ADA / CM / Direct

Weber, Eberhard

CHORUS
CD 8238442
ECM / Oct '93 / New Note/Pinnacle

COLOURS OF CHLOE, THE
CD 8333312
ECM / Jul '88 / New Note/Pinnacle

FLUID RUSTLE
CD 8293812
ECM / Oct '93 / New Note/Pinnacle

FOLLOWING MORNING, THE
T on a white horse / Moana I / Following morning / Moana II
CD 8291162
ECM / Jun '86 / New Note/Pinnacle

LATER THAT EVENING
CD 8293822
ECM / Oct '93 / New Note/Pinnacle

ORCHESTRA (Weber, Eberhard Orchestra)
CD 8373432
ECM / Feb '89 / New Note/Pinnacle

PENDULUM
Bird out of a cage / Notes after an evening / Delirium / Children's song no.1 / Street scenes / Silent for a while / Pendulum / Unfinishsed self - portrait / Closing scene
CD 5197072
ECM / Oct '93 / New Note/Pinnacle

SILENT FEET (Weber, Eberhard Colours)
CD 8350172
ECM / Sep '88 / New Note/Pinnacle

WORKS: EBERHARD WEBER
Sand / Dark spell / More colours / Touch / Eyes that can see in the dark / Moana II
CD 8254292
ECM / Jun '89 / New Note/Pinnacle

YELLOW FIELDS
Touch / Sand glass / Yellow fields / Left lane
CD 8432052
ECM / May '91 / New Note/Pinnacle

Webster, Ben

AUTUMN LEAVES
CD 152162
EPM / Mar '94 / ADA / Discovery

BEN AND 'SWEETS' (Webster, Ben & Harry 'Sweets' Edison)
Better go / How long has this been going on / Kitty / My Romance / Did you call her today / Embraceable you
CD 4606132
Sony Jazz / Jan '95 / Sony

BEN AND BUCK (Webster, Ben & Buck Clayton/Henri Chaix Quartet)
CD SKCD 2037
Sackville / Mar '97 / Cadillac / Jazz Music / Swift

BEN AND BUCK ANTWERP 1967 (Webster, Ben & Buck Clayton)
CD STCD 8245
Storyville / Jan '97 / Cadillac / Jazz Music / Wellard

BEN AND THE BOYS
Teezol / Horn / Victory stride / Body and soul / Joshua / Talk to me / Concerto for Cozy / Nice and Cozy / Sleep / Memories of you / Linger awhile / Just a riff / Blues on the delta / Honeysuckle rose / I surrender dear / Blue skies / Kat's fur / Pick-up boys / My old flame / Sheik of Araby / Conversing in blue / Limehouse blues
CD PLCD 549
President / Nov '96 / Grapevine/PolyGram / President / Target/BMG

BEN WEBSTER
Round horn / Moonglow / Satin doll / For Max / But not for me / For all we know / Sunday
CD BLCD 760141
Black Lion / Apr '90 / Cadillac / Jazz Music / Koch / Wellard

BEN WEBSTER MEETS DON BYAS (Webster, Ben & Don Byas)
Blues for Dottie Mae / Lullaby for Dottie Mae / Sundae / Perdido / When Ash meets Henry / Caravan
CD 8279202
ECM / Jun '86 / New Note/Pinnacle

BEN WEBSTER MEETS OSCAR PETERSON (Webster, Ben & Oscar Peterson)
Touch of your lips: *Webster, Ben* / When your lover has gone: *Webster, Ben* / Bye bye blackbird: *Webster, Ben* / How deep is the ocean: *Webster, Ben* / In the wee small hours of the morning: *Webster, Ben* / Sunday: *Webster, Ben* / This can't be love: *Webster, Ben*
CD 8291672
Verve / Feb '93 / PolyGram

BEN WEBSTER STORY 1937-1944
CD 158612
Jazz Archives / Oct '96 / Discovery

BIG BEN TIME (Webster, Ben Quartet)
Just a sittin' and a-rockin': *Webster, Ben* / Exactly like you: *Webster, Ben* / How deep is the ocean: *Webster, Ben* / My one and only love: *Webster, Ben* / Honeysuckle rose: *Webster, Ben* / Jeep is jumpin': *Webster, Ben* / Where or when: *Webster, Ben* / Wrap your troubles in dreams (and dream your troubles away): *Webster, Ben* / Solitude: *Webster, Ben* / You forgot to remember: *Webster, Ben*
CD 8144102
Philips / Sep '84 / PolyGram

COTTON TAIL
Cotton tail: *Ellington, Duke & His Orchestra* / All too soon: *Ellington, Duke & His Orchestra* / Toby: *Moten, Bennie Kansas City Orchestra* / Lafayette: *Moten, Bennie Kansas City Orchestra* / Voice of old man river: *Bryant, Willie & His Orchestra* / Early session hop: *Hampton, Lionel & His Orchestra* / Conga brava: *Ellington, Duke & His Orchestra* / Bojangles: *Ellington, Duke & His Orchestra* / My greatest mistake: *Ellington, Duke & His Orchestra* / Chloe: *Ellington, Duke & His Orchestra* / Mobile ray: *Stewart, Rex & His Orchestra* / Linger awhile: *Stewart, Rex & His Orchestra* / Blue serge: *Ellington, Duke & His Orchestra* / Just a sittin' and a rockin': *Ellington, Duke & His Orchestra* / Some Saturday: *Stewart, Rex & His Orchestra* / Five o'clock drag: *Ellington, Duke & His Orchestra* / Chelsea bridge: *Ellington, Duke & His Orchestra* / Rain check: *Ellington, Duke & His Orchestra* / Perdido: *Ellington, Duke & His Orchestra* / What am I here for: *Ellington, Duke & His Orchestra* / Main stem: *Ellington, Duke & His Orchestra* / Cadillac slim: *Carter, Benny & Chocolate Dandies*
CD 07863667902
RCA Victor / Sep '97 / BMG

DIFFERENT PATHS (Webster, Ben & Buck Clayton)
CD SKCD 22037
Sackville / Oct '94 / Cadillac / Jazz Music / Swift

EVOLUTION
CD TPZ 1014
Topaz Jazz / Feb '95 / Cadillac / Pinnacle

FOR THE GUV'NOR
I got it bad and that ain't good / Drop me off in Harlem / One for the guv'nor / Prelude to a kiss / In a sentimental mood / John Brown's body / Work song / Preacher / Straight no chaser / Rockin' in rhythm
CD LEJAZZCD 8
Le Jazz / Mar '93 / Cadillac / Koch

FROG 1956-62, THE
CD CD 53167
Giants Of Jazz / Jan '94 / Cadillac / Jazz Music / Target/BMG

GONE WITH THE WIND
Perdido / Yesterday / I'm gonna sit right down and write myself a letter / Set call / That's all / Gone with the wind / Over the rainbow / (Back home again in) Indiana / Misty
CD BLCD 760125
Black Lion / Apr '91 / Cadillac / Jazz Music / Koch / Wellard

HORN, THE
CD PCD 7001
Progressive / Jun '93 / Jazz Music

IN A MELLOW TONE (Archive Series - Live At Ronnie Scott's)
In a mellow tone / Over the rainbow / Gone with the wind / Someone to watch over me / C Jam blues / Perdido / Stardust / Ben's blues / My romance / Ben's theme tune
CD JHAS 601
Ronnie Scott's Jazz House / Jun '95 / Cadillac / Jazz Music / New Note/Pinnacle / TKO Magnum

JAMMIN'
Tea for two / Don't blame me / 'Nuff said / I surrender dear / Woke up clipped / Dirty deal / Teezol / Horn / Romp / Honeysuckle rose / Somebody loves me / Flying home
CD VN 1012
Viper's Nest / Aug '97 / ADA / Cadillac / Direct / Jazz Music

JAZZ MASTERS
CD 5254312
Verve / Feb '95 / PolyGram

JEEP IS JUMPING, THE
CD BLC 760147
Black Lion / Oct '90 / Cadillac / Jazz Music / Koch / Wellard

KING OF THE TENORS
Tenderly / Jive at six / Don't get around much anymore / That's all / Bounce blues / Pennies from Heaven / Cotton tail / Danny boy / Poutin' / Jive at six / That's all
CD 5198062
Verve / Oct '93 / PolyGram

LIVE AT THE HAARLEMSE JAZZCLUB
For all we know / Sunday / How long has this been going on / In a mellotone / Stardust / Perdido
CD MCD 0040
Limetree / Apr '96 / New Note/Pinnacle

LIVE AT THE JAZZHUS VOL.1
Sunday / That's all / Gone with the wind / Over the rainbow / Indiana / Misty / Our love is here to stay / My romance / Blues for Herluf / Londonderry air / Set call
CD 8747102
DA Music / Jul '96 / Conifer/BMG

LIVE AT THE JAZZHUS VOL.2
Mack the knife / I can't get started / Friskin' the fog / Stormy weather / Teach me tonight / Perdido / Yesterdays / I'm gonna sit right down and write myself a letter / Set call
CD 8747122
DA Music / Oct '96 / Conifer/BMG

LIVE AT THE KING & QUEENS, PROVIDENCE, RHODE ISLAND 1963 (Webster, Ben Quartet)
Perdido / Danny boy / On green dolphin street / Go home / Bye bye blackbird / Lover come back to me / My romance / Wee dot / Tenderly / Sometimes I'm happy / How long has this been going on / Embraceable you / Theme
CD STCD 8237
Storyville / Mar '97 / Cadillac / Jazz Music / Wellard

LIVE IN PARIS
CD LEJAZZCD 29
Le Jazz / Aug '94 / Cadillac / Koch

LIVE IN PARIS - 1972
CD FCD 131
France's Concert / '89 / BMG / Jazz Music

LIVE IN VIENNA - 1972
CD RST 91529
RST / '91 / Hot Shot / Jazz Music

MASTERS OF JAZZ VOL.5
CD STCD 4105
Storyville / Feb '89 / Cadillac / Jazz Music / Wellard

SOULVILLE
Soulville / Late date / Time on my hands / Lover come back to me / Where are you / Makin' whoopee / Ill wind / Boogie woogie / Roses of Picardy

CD 8335512
Verve / Oct '93 / PolyGram

STORMY WEATHER
CD BLCD 760108
Black Lion / Dec '88 / Cadillac / Jazz Music / Koch / Wellard

THERE IS NO GREATER LOVE
CD BLCD 760151
Black Lion / Apr '91 / Cadillac / Jazz Music / Koch / Wellard

Webster, E.T.

CHANGES
CD NGCD 527
Twinkle / Apr '92 / Jet Star / Kingdom / SRD

LAMENT OF A DREAD
Reggae symphony / Cold sweat / Loner / Same, same, same / Dem say / Lament of a dread / Experience / What about I / Deeper love / Cry cry cry
CD NGCD 539
Twinkle / Feb '94 / Jet Star / Kingdom / SRD

MANKIND
CD NGCD 551
Twinkle / Jul '96 / Jet Star / Kingdom / SRD

Webster, Gregory

MY WICKED WICKED WAYS
Forever England / Water is wide / Blue eyes crying in the rain / Last night on earth / All the greatest stories / Winter / Clock chimes / Wonderland / Foolhardy / Lonesome town
CD MASKCD 055
Vinyl Japan / Apr '96 / Plastic Head / Vinyl Japan

Webster, Joe

I'M IN THE MOOD FOR BIG BAND MUSIC (Webster, Joe & Swing Fever Band)
CD LPCD 1025
Disky / Apr '94 / Disky / THE

I'M IN THE MOOD FOR DIXIE MUSIC (Webster, Joe & His River City Jazzmen)
CD LPCD 1026
Disky / Apr '94 / Disky / THE

Webster, Katie

I KNOW THAT'S RIGHT
CD ARHCD 393
Arhoolie / Apr '95 / ADA / Cadillac / Direct

NO FOOLIN'
Little meat on the side / I'm bad / No deposit, no return / Zydeco shoes and California blues / Too much sugar for a dime / Hard lovin' mama / It's might hard / Tangled in your web / Those lonely, lonely nights / Mama cat cuttin' no slack
CD ALCD 4803
Alligator / May '93 / ADA / CM / Direct

SWAMP BOOGIE QUEEN
CD ALCD 4766
Alligator / Oct '93 / ADA / CM / Direct

TWO FISTED MAMA
CD ALCD 4777
Alligator / May '93 / ADA / CM / Direct

Webster, Roger

PIECES
Four variations on a theme of Domenico Scarlatti / Aria & Scherzo / Prelude op.8 no.11 / Allegro from Toot Suite / Sicilienne / Slavish fantasie / Nightsongs / Concerto scherzo / Reflections / Concerto (Arutiunian)
CD QPRZ 018D
Polyphonic / Nov '95 / Complete/Pinnacle

TWILIGHT DREAMS
Jubilance / I'd rather have Jesus / Russian dance / Twilight dreams / Concert study / Heavenly gales / Someone cares / Concerto for cornet and brass bands
CD QPRL 066D
Polyphonic / Jul '94 / Complete/Pinnacle

Weckl, Dave

HARD WIRED
Hard wired / Afrique / Dis' place this / In flight / Crazy horse / Just an illusion / Where's Tom / In the pocket / Tribute
CD GRP 97602
GRP / Mar '94 / New Note/BMG

HEADS UP
CD GRP 96732
GRP / '92 / New Note/BMG

MASTER PLAN
Tower of inspiration / Here and there / Festival de Ritmo / In common / Garden wall / Auratune / Softly as in a morning sunrise / Masterplan / Island magic
CD GRP 96192
GRP / Aug '90 / New Note/BMG

Wedding Anniversary

WEDDING ANNIVERSARY, THE
CD DANCD 010
Danceteria / May '89 / ADA / Plastic Head / Shellshock/Disc

Wedding Present

BIZARRO
Brassneck / Crushed / No / Thanks / Kennedy / What have I said now / Granadaland / Bewitched / Take me / Be honest
CD PD 74302
RCA / Oct '89 / BMG

EVENING SESSIONS 1986-1994, THE
Everyone thinks he looks daft / Shatner / My favourite dress / I found that essence rare / Sticky / No Christmas / Lone slave / Queen of outer space / Click click / It's a gas / Hot pants / Catwoman
CD SFRSCD 029
Strange Fruit / Jun '97 / Pinnacle

GEORGE BEST
Everyone thinks he looks daft / What did your last servant die of / Don't be so hard / Million miles / All this and more / My favourite dress / Something and nothing / It's what you want that matters / Give my love to Kevin / Anyone can make a mistake / You can't moan can you
CD LEEDS 001CD
Reception / Oct '87 / Vital

HIT PARADE VOL.1
Blue eyes / Go-go dancer / Three / Silver shorts / Come play with me / California / Cattle and cane / Don't cry no tears / Think that it might / Falling / Pleasant valley Sunday / Let's make some plans
CD 74321400732
RCA / Sep '96 / BMG

MINI
Drive / Love machine / Go, man, go / Mercury / Convertible / Sports car
CD COOKCD 094
Cooking Vinyl / Aug '97 / Vital

SATURNALIA
Snake eyes / Big boots / Spaceman / Skin diving / Real thing / Dreamworld / Kansas / Hula doll / Up / Venus / 50's / Montreal / 2,3 Go
CD COOKCD 099
Cooking Vinyl / Sep '96 / Vital

SEAMONSTERS
Dalliance / Dare / Suck / Blonde / Rotterdam / Lovenest / Corduroy / Carolyn / Heather / Octopussy
CD PD 75012
RCA / Jun '91 / BMG

TOMMY
Go out and get 'em boy / Everything's spoiled again / Once more / At the edge of the sea / Living and learning / This boy can wait / You should always keep in touch with your friends / Felicity / What becomes of the broken hearted / Never said / Every mother's son / My favourite dress
CD LEEDS 002CD
Reception / Jul '88 / Vital

UKRAINSKI VISTUPI V JOHNA PEELA
Davni chasy / Yikhav khozak za dunai / Tiutiunyk / Zadumay didochok / Svitit misyats / Katrusya / Vasya vasyl'ok / Hude dnipro hude / Verhovyno
CD PD 74104
RCA / May '89 / BMG

WATUSI
So long baby / Click click / Yeah yeah yeah yeah yeah / Let him have it / Gazebo / Shake it / Spangle / It's a gas / Swimmimg pools, movie stars / Big rat / Catwoman / Hot pants
CD CID 8014
Island / Aug '94 / PolyGram

Weddings, Parties & Anything

DIFFICULT LOVES
Father's day / Taylor Square / Difficult loves / Old Ronny / Telephone in her car / Nothin' but time / Alone amongst savages / Rambling girl / Step in, step out / Four corners of the earth / For your ears only / Do not go gently
CD COOKCD 059
Cooking Vinyl / Feb '95 / Vital

KING TIDE
Monday's experts / Live it everyday / Money cuts you out / Rain in my heart / It wasn't easy / Keep talking to me / Island of humour / Easy money / In my lifetime / Always leave something behind / If you were a cloud / Year she spent in England / Stalactites
CD 4509937732
WEA / Mar '94 / Warner Music

NO SHOW WITHOUT PUNCH
CD UTICD 4
Utility / Mar '93 / Grapevine/PolyGram

ROARING DAYS
Industrial town / Under the clocks / Gun / Brunswick / Tilting at windmills / Sergeant Small / Sisters of mercy / Roaring days / Say the word / Missing in action / Laughing boy / Big river / Summons in the morning / Morton (Song for Tex)
CD COOKCD 026
Cooking Vinyl / Nov '89 / Vital

Wedgwood, Michael

PLACES LIKE THESE
Lifeline / Places like these / Act like a dog / Loving and leaving / New man coming / Piece / Searching for a fantasy / Fundamental fool / Indigo / Cry nightly / Take me away / Looking forward to missing you / Take it as it comes / You and I combine
CD VP 143CD
Voiceprint / Nov '93 / Pinnacle

Weed, Joe

JOE WEED AND THE VULTURES (Weed, Joe & The Vultures)
CD NCD 205
Highland / Mar '96 / ADA

Weedon, Bert

KING SIZE GUITAR/HONKY TONK GUITAR
Guitar boogie shuffle / Nashville boogie / King size guitar / Apache / Teenage guitar / Querida / I wonder where my baby is tonight / Pretty baby / Elmer's tune / Charleston / Chicago / Sweet Georgia Brown / Big beat boogie / Lonely guitar / Bongo rock / Blue guitar / Bert's boogie / Summer place / Bye bye blackbird / Varsity drag / Ma, he's making eyes at me / Carolina in the morning / Jealous / (In) a shanty in old Shanty Town
CD C5HCD 617
See For Miles/C5 / Jan '97 / Pinnacle

Weekenders

THAT WAS NOW BUT THIS IS THEN
CD BLOWUP 5CD
Blow Up / Feb '96 / Arabesque / SRD

Weems, Ted

BROADCAST RECORDINGS 1940-1941 (Weems, Ted & His Orchestra)
CD JH 1032
Jazz Hour / Jul '93 / Cadillac / Jazz Music / Target/BMG

MARVELLOUS (Weems, Ted & His Orchestra)
Marvellous / Oh if I only had you / From Saturday night to Sunday morning / She'll never find a fellow like me / Chick, chick, chick, chick, chicken / Cobblestones / You're the cream in my coffee / My troubles are over / Piccolo Pete / Man from the south / Come on baby / Harmonica Harry / Mysterious Mose / Slappin' the bass / Washing dishes with my sweetie / Egyptian Ella / Jig time / Play that hot guitar / Oh Mo'nah / My favourite band
CD CDAJA 5029
Living Era / May '84 / Select

Ween

12 GOLDEN COUNTRY GREATS
CD FNCD 386
Flying Nun / Aug '96 / RTM/Disc

CHOCOLATE AND CHEESE
CD FNCD 314
Flying Nun / Jan '95 / RTM/Disc

GOD WEEN SATAN
CD TTR 891862
Twin Tone / Feb '91 / PolyGram

MOLLUSK, THE
CD MUSH 3CD
Mushroom / Aug '97 / 3mv/Pinnacle

POD, THE
CD FNCD 322
Flying Nun / Mar '95 / RTM/Disc

PURE GUAVA
Little birdy / Tender situation / Stallim / Big Jim / Push little daisey's / Goin' gets tough / Reggae junkie jew / Play it off legit / Pumpin for the man / Sarah / Sprim theme / Flies on my dick / I saw Gene crying in her sleep / Touch my tooter smoocher / Morning glory / Lovin' you through it all / Her fatboy (Asshole) / Don't get to close to my fantasy / Poor ship destroyer
CD RUST 002CD
Creation / Dec '92 / 3mv/Vital

Weezer

PINKERTON
Tired of sex / Getchoo / No other one / Why bother / Across the sea / Good life / El scorcho / Pink triangle / Falling for you / Butterfly
CD GED 25007
Geffen / Sep '96 / BMG

WEEZER
My name is Jonas / On one else / World has turned and left me here / Buddy Holly / Undone / Sweater song / Surf wax America / Say it ain't so / In the garage / Holiday / Only in dreams
CD GED 24629
Geffen / Feb '95 / BMG

Wegmuller, Walter

TAROT (CD Box Set)
CD Set 14900
Spalax / Jul '97 / ADA / Cargo / Direct / Discovery / Greyhound

Wehrmacht

BIERMACHT/SHARK ATTACK
You broke my heart / Gore fix / Beer is here / Drink beer be free / Everb / Micro E / Balance of opinion / Suck / Drink Jack / Radical dissection / Beermacht / Outro
CD SHARK 009CD
Shark / Apr '92 / Plastic Head

Weidman, James

PEOPLE MUSIC
Raw deal / Petals / Hang with the gang / Bird alone / Limehouse blues / Up on the horizon / I can tell blues / Contessa's last dance / Jeannine
CD TCB 96302
TCB / Apr '97 / New Note/Pinnacle

Wein, George

METRONOME PRESENTS JAZZ AT THE MODERN (Live In The Sculpture Garden At the Museum Of Modern Art) (Wein, George & The Storyville Sextet)
CD BET 6025
Bethlehem / Jan '95 / ADA / ZYX

Weinert, Susan

BOTTOM LINE, THE (Weinert, Susan Band)
Hombre / Triple X / Tribute T Fitzcarraldo / Don't smile to soon / Masters of the midiverse / That's for you / Kluski theory / Dakota kid / Nothing / Trabucco / Vinnie
CD VBR 21772
Vera Bra / Aug '96 / New Note/Pinnacle / Pinnacle

CRUNCH TIME (Weinert, Susan Band)
Don't try that again, MF / Hopeless case / Don't you guys know any nice songs / One for George / Member of the Syndicate / Crown / He knows / Pacific Palisades / Maybe / Guess who called
CD VBR 21442
Vera Bra / Aug '94 / New Note/Pinnacle / Pinnacle

Weir, Bob

ACE
Greatest story ever told / Walk in the sunshine / Looks like rain / One more saturday night / Black throated wind / Playing in the band / Mexicali blues / Cassidy
CD GDCD 4004
Grateful Dead / Feb '89 / Pinnacle

KINGFISH
Lazy lightnin' / Supplication / Wild northland / Asia minor / Home to Dixie / Jump for joy / Goodbye yer honer / Big iron / This time / Hypnotize / Bye and bye
CD GDCD 4012
Grateful Dead / Oct '89 / Pinnacle

Weiskopf, Walt

NIGHT LIGHTS
You go to my head / With the wind and the rain in her hair / Moonlight on the Ganges / Some other time / Baubles, bangles and beads / Night owl / Camelot / Night lights / Herbie's lament / I wish I knew
CD DTRCD 106
Double Time / Nov '96 / Express Jazz

SIMPLICITY (Weiskopf, Walt Sextet)
CD CRISS 1075CD
Criss Cross / Nov '93 / Cadillac / Direct / Vital/SAM

Weiss, Harald

OTHER PARADISE, THE
CD SM 18112
Wergo / Sep '95 / ADA / Cadillac / Harmonia Mundi

TROMMELGEFLUSTER
Trommelgefluster
CD 8492852
ECM / May '91 / New Note/Pinnacle

Weiss, Klaus

LA CALLING
Other side / LA calling / Spring passed / I've heard this before / Four four / Bad girl / I'll take it / All night through
CD CDLR 45033
L&R / Jun '91 / New Note/Pinnacle

MESSAGE FROM SANTA CLAUS, A
CD MM 801053
Minor Music / Dec '95 / Vital/SAM

Weiss, Michael

MICHAEL WEISS QUINTET FEATURING... (Tom Kirkpatrick/R. Lalama/R. Drummond)
CD CRISS 1022CD
Criss Cross / May '91 / Cadillac / Direct / Vital/SAM

Weisser, Michael

SOFTWARE VISIONS (Weisser, Michael & Peter Mergener)
CD PALM 729013
Magnum Music / Nov '89 / TKO Magnum

Weissman, Dick

NEW TRADITIONS
CD FE 1400CD
Folk Era / Dec '94 / ADA / CM

Weizmann, Danny

WET DOG SHAKES, THE
CD NAR 065CD
New Alliance / May '93 / Plastic Head

Welch, Elisabeth

ELISABETH WELCH IN CONCERT
CD OCRCD 6016
First Night / Mar '96 / Pinnacle

ELISABETH WELCH LIVE IN NEW YORK
CD CDVIR 8313
TER / Sep '91 / Koch

SOFT LIGHTS AND SWEET MUSIC
CD PASTCD 7060
Flapper / Nov '95 / Pinnacle

THIS THING CALLED LOVE
What is this thing called love / Hello my lover, goodbye / Porgy / When your lover has gone / Yesterday / Boy what love has done to me / If I ever fall in love again / Long before I knew you / I love you truly / True love / How do you do it / I'll follow my secret heart / Losing my mind / One life to live / Moon river / Give me something to remember you by
CD CDVIR 8309
TER / Sep '89 / Koch

ULTIMATE ELISABETH WELCH, THE
CD 313752
Koch / Nov '92 / Koch

WHERE HAVE YOU BEEN
It was worth it / I got it bad and that ain't good / My love is a wanderer / I always say hello (to a flower) / How little it matters, how little we know / Where have you been / Manhattan madness / He was too good to me / Little girl blue / You were there / Dancing in the dark / Mean to me / As long as I live / Come rain or come shine / Remember
CD CDSL 5202
DRG / Jun '91 / Discovery / New Note/ Pinnacle

Welch, Gillian

REVIVAL
CD ALMCD 011
Almo Sounds / May '96 / Pinnacle

Welch, Kevin

LIFE DOWN HERE ON EARTH
CD DR 003
Dead Reckoning / Aug '95 / Avid/BMG

Welch, Mike

AXE TO GRIND
Did she say / Palm of her hand / Axe to grind / Elkmont stomp / Every time you lie / Afriad of my own tears / Take your best shot / She couldn't know / Time stands still / That's my sin / My emptiness / Cruise control
CD CDTC 1159
Tonecool / Feb '97 / ADA / Direct

THESE ARE MINE
CD 8425812
Sky Ranch / Apr '97 / Discovery

THESE BLUES ARE MINE
CD CDTC 1154
Tonecool / Feb '96 / ADA / Direct

Welcome

BIEN VENUE
CD A XIX
Seventh / Feb '96 / Cadillac / Harmonia Mundi / ReR Megacorp

Welcome

LOW COST SOLUTION
CD RXR 009
RX Remedy / Nov '96 / Cargo

Weldon, Casey Bill

CASEY BILL WELDON VOL.1-3 1935-1938
CD Set DOCD 5217/8/9
Document / Jan '94 / ADA / Hot Shot / Jazz Music

HAWAIIAN GUITAR WIZARD 1935-1938, THE
CD 158292
Blues Collection / Jan '95 / Discovery

Weldon, Nick

LAVENDER'S BLUE
Mabs and tucker / Sonora / In the wee small hours of the morning / Alone together / Liffey / Never let me go / Some other time / Softly as in a morning sunrise / Lavender's blue
CD VERGE 001CD
Verge / May '96 / New Note/Pinnacle

Welk, Lawrence

22 ALL TIME BIG BAND FAVOURITES
CD RCD 7023
Ranwood / May '89 / Jazz Music

22 ALL TIME FAVOURITE WALTZES
CD RCD 7028
Ranwood / May '89 / Jazz Music

22 GREAT SONGS FOR DANCING
CD RCD 7009
Ranwood / May '89 / Jazz Music

22 OF THE GREATEST WALTZES
CD RCD 7004
Ranwood / May '89 / Jazz Music

BEST OF LAWRENCE WELK, THE
CD RCD 8226
Ranwood / May '89 / Jazz Music

DANCE TO THE BIG BAND SOUNDS
CD RCD 8228
Ranwood / May '89 / Jazz Music

Well Oiled Sisters

ALCOHOL AND TEARS
CD CYCLECD 001
Cycle / Apr '94 / CM / Direct

Weller, Don

LIVE (Weller, Don Big Band)
CD 33JAZZ 032
33 Jazz / Mar '97 / Cadillac / New Note/ Pinnacle

Weller, Paul

HEAVY SOUL
Heavy soul / Peacock suit / Up in Suzie's room / Brushed / Driving nowhere / I should have been there to inspire you / Heavy soul (part two) / Friday street / Science / Golden sands / As you lean into the light / Mermaids
CD CID 8058
Island / Jun '97 / PolyGram

INTERVIEW DISC
CD SAM 7025
Sound & Media / Jan '97 / Sound & Media

LIVE WOOD
CD 8285612
Go Discs / Sep '94 / PolyGram

PAUL WELLER
Uh huh oh yeh / Bullrush / Remember how we started / Clues / Amongst butterflies / Into tomorrow / Strange museum / Above the clouds / Bitterness rising
CD 8283432
Go Discs / Sep '92 / PolyGram

STANLEY ROAD
Changing man / Porcelein Gods / Walk on gilded splinters / You do something to me / Woodcutter's son / Time passes / Stanley Road / Broken stones / Out of the sinking / Pink on white walls / Whirlpool's end / Wings of speed
CD 8286192
CD Set 8286202
Go Discs / May '95 / PolyGram

WILD WOOD
Sunflower / Can you heal us (holy man) / Wild wood / Instrumental (pt. 1) / All the pictures on the wall / Has my fire really gone out / Country / Fifth Season / Weaver / Instrumental (pt. 2) / Foot of the mountain / Shadow of the sun / Holy man (reprise) / Moon on your pyjamas
CD 8285132
Go Discs / Sep '93 / PolyGram

Wellington, Sheena

CLEARSONG
CD DUNCD 012
Dunkeld / Jun '87 / ADA / CM / Direct

STRONG WOMEN
Strong women rule us with their tears / Dark eyed Molly / Address the haggis / Mill O'Tifty's Annie / Tryst / False bride / Glasgow councillor / Slaves lament / Seattle / Great Silkie O'Sule Skerrie / Shearin' / Waulkrife Minnie / Silver tassie / My luv's like a red red rose / Little Sunday school
CD CDTRAX 094
Greentrax / Oct '95 / ADA / Direct / Duncans / Highlander

Wellington, Valerie

LIFE IN THE BIG CITY
CD GBW 002
GBW / Feb '92 / Harmonia Mundi

MILLION DOLLAR SECRET
CD R 2619
Rooster / Apr '95 / Direct

Wellins, Bobby

MAKING LIGHT WORK
Erco makes light work / Visionaire / Bossa Oseris / Logotec logarhythm / Track sound / Downright downlight / Take the 'A' train / Just friends / I'm beginning to see the light
CD HEPCD 2070
Hep / Aug '97 / Cadillac / Jazz Music / New Note/Pinnacle / Wellard

NOMAD
CD HHCD 1008
Hot House / May '95 / Cadillac / Harmonia Mundi / Wellard

SATIN ALBUM, THE
I'm a fool to want you / For heaven's sake / You don't know what love is / I get along without you very well / For all we know / Violets for your furs / You've changed / It's easy to remember / But beautiful / Glad to be unhappy / I'll be around / End of a love affair
CD JITCD 9607
Jazzizit / Feb '97 / New Note/Pinnacle

Wells Cathedral Choir

CHRISTMAS CAROLS FROM WELLS CATHEDRAL
O come all ye faithful (adeste fidelis) / God rest ye merry gentlemen / Holly and the ivy / Unto us is born a son / Once in Royal David's City / Silent night / Away in a manger / It came upon a midnight clear / I saw three ships / O little town of Bethlehem / Ding dong merrily on high / Hark the herald angels sing / First Noel / Deck the hall / Coventry carol / While shepherds watch / Good King Wenceslas / In the bleak mid winter / Infant holy, infant lowly / We wish you a merry Christmas
CD XMAS 004
Tring / Nov '96 / Tring

Wells, Dicky

CLASSICS 1929-1946
CD CLASSICS 937
Classics / Jun '97 / Discovery / Jazz Music

DICKY'S BLUES
CD TPZ 1023
Topaz Jazz / Jul '95 / Cadillac / Pinnacle

SWINGIN' IN PARIS (Wells, Dicky & Bill Coleman)
CD LEJAZZCD 20
Le Jazz / Jun '93 / Cadillac / Koch

Wells, Jean

SOUL ON SOUL
Have a little mercy / I'll drown in my own tears / After loving you / Sit down and cry / Ease away a little bit at a time / Our sweet love turned bitter / Somebody's been loving you (but it ain't been me) / Keep your mouth shut and your eyes open / If you've ever loved someone / Broomstick horse cowboy / I couldn't love you (more than I do now) / I feel good / With my love and what you've got / Keep on doin' it / Take time to make time for me / Try me and see / Roll up your sleeves, come out lovin' (winner takes all) / What have I got to lose / Puttin' the best on the outside / He ain't doin' bad / Hello baby, goodbye too
CD CDKEND 113
Kent / Jun '94 / Pinnacle

Wells, Junior

BETTER OFF WITH THE BLUES (Wells, Junior & Buddy Guy)
CD CD 83354
Telarc / Aug '93 / Conifer/BMG

COME ON IN THIS HOUSE
What my momma told me/That's all right / Why are people like that / Trust my baby / Million years blues / Give me one reason / Ships on the ocean / She wants to sell my monkey / So glad you're mine / Mystery train / I'm gonna move to Kansas City / King fish blues / You better watch yourself / Come on in this house / Goat
CD CD 83395
Telarc Blues / Nov '96 / Conifer/BMG

COMING AT YOU
CD VMD 79262
Vanguard / Jan '96 / ADA / Pinnacle

EVERYBODY'S GETTIN' SOME
Sweet sixteen / Everybody's gettin' them some / I can't stand no signifyin' shaky ground / Trying to get over you / Use me / You're tough enough / Get down / That's what love will make you do / Don't you lie to me / Last hand of the night / Back into the fold / Keep on steppin'
CD CD 83360
Telarc / May '95 / Conifer/BMG

IT'S MY LIFE BABY
It's my life baby / Country girl / Stormy Monday blues / Checking on my baby / I got a stomach ache / Slow, slow / It's so sad to be lonely / You lied to me / Shake it baby / Early in the morning / Look how baby / Everything's gonna be alright
CD VMD 73120
Vanguard / Oct '95 / ADA / Pinnacle

LIVE AT BUDDY GUY'S LEGENDS
Broke and hungry / Messin' with the kid / Hoodoo man / Little by little / Train / Sweet sixteen / What my Momma done told me / Got my mojo working / Love her with a feeling / Help me / Today I started loving you again
CD CD 83412
Telarc Jazz / Aug '97 / Conifer/BMG

ON TOP
CD DD 635
Delmark / Oct '86 / ADA / Cadillac / CM / Direct / Hot Shot

PLEADING THE BLUES (Wells, Junior & Buddy Guy)
Pleading the blues / It hurts me too / Cut out the lights / Quit teasing my baby / I'll take care of you / Take your time baby / I smell something
CD BLE 599012
Black & Blue / Dec '90 / Discovery / Koch / Wellard
CD ECD 260352
Evidence / Sep '93 / ADA / Cadillac / Harmonia Mundi
CD IS 9012
Isabel / Mar '96 / Discovery

SOUTHSIDE BLUES JAM
CD DD 628
Delmark / Jan '93 / ADA / Cadillac / CM / Direct / Hot Shot

Wells, Kitty

GREATEST HITS VOL.1
It wasn't God who made honky tonk angels / Left to right / I don't claim to be an angel / Password / Wedding ring ago / Dust on the bible / Thank you for the roses / Whose shoulder will you cry on / Lonely street / Love makes the world go round / Loving you was all I ever needed / Amigo's guitar
CD SORCD 0046
D-Sharp / Oct '94 / Pinnacle

QUEEN OF COUNTRY MUSIC 1949-1958, THE (4CD Set)
Death at the bar / Love or hate / Gathering flowers for the master's bouquet / Don't wait til the last minute to pray / How far is heaven / My mother / Make up your mind / I'll be all smiles tonight / I'm too lonely to smile / Things I might've been / I heard the jukebox playing / Wedding ring ago / Divided by two / Crying steel guitar waltz / Paying for that back street affair / Icicles hanging from your heart / I don't claim to be an angel / Honky tonk waltz / Life they live in songs / You said you could do without me / Whose shoulder will you cry on / Hey Joe / My cold cold heart is melting now / I'll love you 'til the day I die / I've kissed you my last time / I'm a stranger in my home / I gave my wedding dress away / Cheatin's a sin / You're not easy to forget / Satisfied, so satisfied / One by one / Release me / After dark / (Don't hang around) he's married to me / Thou shalt not steal / Lonely side of town / I hope my divorce is never granted / I'm in love with you / Make believe / You and me / As long as I live / No one but you / Making believe / I'd rather stay home / I was wrong / There's poison in your heart / Goodbye Mr. Brown / Mother hold me tight / Searching / Dust on the bible / Beside you / I'm counting on you / They can't take your love / I'm tired of pretending / Oh so many years / One week later / When I'm with you / Can I find it in your heart / Repenting / I guess I'll go on dreaming / Each day / Pace that kills / Change of heart / Stubborn heart / Standing room only / Mansion on the hill / Your wild life's gonna get you down / Right or wrong / Winner of your heart / Dancing with a stranger / Three ways (to love you) / She's no angel / Broken marriage vows / What about you / Sweeter than the flowers / You can't conceal a broken heart / Just when I needed you / Lonely street / That's me without you / Cheated out of love / Waltz of the angels / May you never be alone / If teardrops were pennies / Touch and go heart / My ued to be darling / Fraulein / Love me to pieces / What I believe dear (is all up to you) / I can't stop loving you / Slowly dying / I can't help wondering / He's lost his love for me / Jealousy / Mommy for a day / Hands you're holding now / Let me help you forget / All the time / (I've got my) one way ticket to the sky / I heard my saviour call / I dreamed I searched heaven for you / Great speckled bird / Matthew 24 / I need the prayers / My loved ones are waiting for me / Lord I'm coming home / He will set your fields on fire / Lonesome valley / We buried her beneath the willows
CD Set BCD 15638
Bear Family / Jul '93 / Direct / Rollercoaster / Swift

T'WASN'T GOD THAT MADE HONKY TONK ANGELS
Don't claim to be an angel / Release me / Making believe / Whose shoulder will you cry on / One by one / Lonely side of town / Searching / Mommy for a day / From left to right / After dark / Password / I'll repossess my heart / As long as I live / Honky tonk angels / This white circle
CD PRACD 4000
Prairie / Jun '97 / Henry Hadaway

Wells, Mary

22 GREATEST HITS
My guy / Bye bye baby / I don't want to take a chance / Only one who really loves you / You beat me to the punch / Two lovers / Your old standby / Old loe (let's try again) / Oh little boy (what you did to me) / What love has joined together / You lost the

sweetness / What's easy for two is so hard for one / Two wrongs don't make a right / Everybody needs love / I'll be available / One block from heaven / When I'm gone / He's the one I love / Whisper you love me boy / Does he love me / Was it worth it
CD 5301042
Polydor / '95 / PolyGram

DEAR LOVER (The Atco Years)
CD SCL 2059
Ichiban Soul Classics / Mar '95 / Koch

MOTOWN EARLY CLASSICS
My guy / My baby just cares for me / I only have eyes for you / Shop around / When your lover comes back / Let your conscience be your guide / One who really loves you / (I guess there's) No love / You beat me to the punch / Two lovers / Together: *Wells, Mary & Marvin Gaye* / 'Deed I do: *Wells, Mary & Marvin Gaye* / Drop in the bucket / He's the one I love / After the lights go down low: *Wells, Mary & Marvin Gaye* / He holds his own / Does he love me / Whisper you love me boy
CD 5521242
Spectrum / Jul '96 / PolyGram

MY GUY (The Best Of Mary Wells)
What love has joined together / Laughing boy / What's easy for two is so hard for one / My guy / Operator / Two lovers / One who really loves you / You beat me to the punch / Your old standby / You lost the sweetest boy / Old love (let's try again)
CD CDSGP 057
Prestige / May '93 / Else / Total/BMG

NEVER, NEVER LEAVE ME (The 20th Century Sides)
CD SCL 21092
Ichiban Soul Classics / Mar '96 / Koch

SISTERS OF SOUL
CD RSACD 806
Sequel / Oct '94 / BMG

VERY BEST OF MARY WELLS, THE (The Very Best Of The Motorcity Recordings)
My guy / Hold on a little longer / Walk on the city streets / Don't burn your bridges / What's easy for two is so hard for one / Keeping my mind on love / Stop before it's too late / You're the answer to my dreams / You beat me to the punch / Once upon a time
CD 3035990122
Motor City / Feb '96 / Carlton

Wellstood, Dick

ALL STAR ORCHESTRA AND BLUE THREE (Wellstood, Dick & Kenny Davern)
CD CRD 129
Chiaroscuro / Mar '96 / Jazz Music

STRETCHING OUT (Wellstood, Dick & Kenny Davern Quartet)
CD JCD 187
Jazzology / Feb '91 / Jazz Music

THIS IS THE ONE...DIG
CD SACD 119
Solo Art / Dec '95 / Jazz Music

Welsh, Alex

CLASSIC CONCERT (Britain's Jazz Heritage)
CD BLCD 760503
Black Lion / Oct '90 / Cadillac / Jazz Music / Koch / Wellard

DOGGIN' AROUND
CD BLCD 760510
Black Lion / May '93 / Cadillac / Jazz Music / Koch / Wellard

LOUIS ARMSTRONG MEMORIAL CONCERT
Hear me talkin' to ya / Georgia on my mind / Ory's creole trombone / Rockin' chair / It's alright with me / Davenport blues / Dippermouth blues / Rose room / St. James Infirmary / Royal garden blues
CD BLCD 760515
Black Lion / Nov '95 / Cadillac / Jazz Music / Koch / Wellard

MUSIC OF THE MAUVE DECADE
Charleston / Black bottom / Lonesome and sorry / I cover the waterfront / Shimma sha wabble / Don't leave me Daddy / Nobody's sweetheart / Needle / Tell 'em bout me / I cried for you / Mammy o'mine / Down among sheltering palms / Please don't talk about me when I'm gone / Sleepy time gal / Bye bye blues
CD LACD 62
Lake / Jun '96 / ADA / Cadillac / Direct / Jazz Music / Target/BMG

Welsh Guards Band

BAND OF THE WELSH GUARDS, THE (Directed by Captain Andrew Harris)
Under the double eagle / Merry peal / Floradora / Cupid's army / Serenadeno / Voyage in a troopship / Rusticanella / London Scottish / Turkish patrol / Cavalcade of martial songs / Jungle drums / On the quarterdeck / Baby's sweetheart / Knightsbridge march / Silver stars / Children of the regiment / Bells of Somerset / Maid of the mountains
CD PASTCD 9726
Flapper / Mar '91 / Pinnacle

GILBERT AND SULLIVAN
Overture- The yeoman of the guard / Take a pair of sparkling eyes / Regular royal queen / When a wooer goes a wooing / Cheerily carols the lark / I am a courtier grave and serious / When the night wind howls / Hornpipe from Ruddigore / Man who would woo a fair maid / Refrain audacious tar / I hear the soft note / Long years ago / If you're anxious for to shine / Minerva / When the buds are blossoming / Strange adventure / Once more gondolieri
CD BNA 5022
Bandleader / Jul '88 / Conifer/BMG

HOUR OF THE GUARDS, AN (Welsh Guards & Grenadier Guards)
Nimrod: *Welsh Guards Band* / Children's patrol: *Welsh Guards Band* / Norwegian carnival: *Welsh Guards Band* / Hoch heidecksburg: *Welsh Guards Band* / I hope I get better: *Welsh Guards Band* / At the ballet: *Welsh Guards Band* / I can do that: *Welsh Guards Band* / Nothing: *Welsh Guards Band* / One: *Welsh Guards Band* / What I did for love: *Welsh Guards Band* / Entry of The Boyards: *Welsh Guards Band* / Cardiff arms: *Welsh Guards Band* / Bilitis: *Welsh Guards Band* / Abide with me: *Welsh Guards Band* / In the Dolomites: *Grenadier Guards Band* / In storm and sunshine: *Grenadier Guards Band* / Kennebec: *Grenadier Guards Band* / True comrades in arms: *Grenadier Guards Band* / Washington Grays: *Grenadier Guards Band* / Bridge too far: *Grenadier Guards Band* / Robinson's grand entree: *Grenadier Guards Band* / Birdcage walk: *Grenadier Guards Band* / Army and Marine: *Grenadier Guards Band* / Children of the regiment: *Grenadier Guards Band* / Piper in the meadow: *Grenadier Guards Band* / Man o'brass: *Grenadier Guards Band* / Always Vienna: *Welsh Guards Band* / Raiders of the Lost Ark: *Grenadier Guards Band*
CD CDB 792 188 2
Music For Pleasure / Sep '89 / EMI

LAND OF MY FATHERS (HM Welsh Guards)
Bell a' peal / Casatschok / Tsarist anthem from War & Peace / British isles medley / Liberty bell / Eye level / Sentry's song from Iolanthe / Y viva Espana / Colditz march / Amazing grace / Jerusalem / Ar hyd y nos all through the night / God bless the prince of Wales / Land of my fathers / Evening hymn and last post / Colonel Bogey / Changing of the guard / Elizabethan serenade / Radetsky march
CD EMPRCD 572
Emporio / May '95 / Disc

MUSIC FROM THE CHANGING OF THE GUARD (Band Of The Welsh Guards)
To your guard / Empire / Birdcage walk / Guardsman / Long live Elizabeth / Royal review / Oxford street / Music of the night / Waterloo march / Welsh airs and fancies / Children's patrol / Gold and silver waltz / Spirit of pageantry / Welsh rhapsody / Great and glorious / Guard's parade / Lord Rothermere's march / Guards armoured division / King's guard / Welshman
CD BNA 5045
Bandleader / '91 / Conifer/BMG

Welt

PARANOID DELUSION
CD PCD 14
Progress / May '95 / Cargo / Plastic Head

Welti, Stephen

TAKE OFF
Take off / Ocean dream / Alpine adventure / Riviera / Olympic arena / Another love / Russian vine / Stampede / Satellite / Chopper chase / Caribbean can can / Pacific paradise / Cochabamba / Return to mijas / Santa Monica freeway / Lights of Lugano / Hawaiian cocktail / Continental express
CD DLCD 107
Dulcima / Jan '90 / Savoy / THE

Wenblom, Carolyn

BEES TO THE HONEY
CD GRCD 385
Grasmere / May '97 / Highlander / Savoy / Target/BMG

Wench

TIDY SIZE CHUNK OF SOMETHING, A
CD CORECD 5
Abstract / Apr '91 / Cargo / Pinnacle / Total/BMG

Wendholt, Scott

FROM NOW ON
From now on / Magnolia tones / Solar / In a sentimental mood / At the falls / Times past / Dear old Stockholm / Promise / I remember you
CD CRISS 1123CD
Criss Cross / Feb '97 / Cadillac / Direct / Vital/SAM

SCHEME OF THINGS, THE (Wendholt, Scott Quintet)
CD CRISS 1078CD
Criss Cross / Nov '93 / Cadillac / Direct / Vital/SAM

Wendt, Joja

ART OF BOOGIE WOOGIE PIANO
Death ray boogie / Just for you / Mister Freddie's blues / Boogie woogie stomp / St. Louis blues / Boogie rocks / Bass gone crazy / Dupree blues / Bear cat crawl / Chapel blues / Honky tonk train blues / Meade's boogie / Jancey special / Sweet patootie blues / Barrelhouse boogie / Chicago in mind / Boogie woogie man / Blues on my mind / Dive bomber / Zero hour
CD QED 077
Tring / Nov '96 / Tring

Wendy & Lisa

ARE YOU MY BABY
Are you my baby / Lolly lolly / Waterfall / Satisfaction / Strung out / Rainbow lake / Tears of joy / Friut at the bottom / Skeleton key / Staring at the sun / Everyday / Why wait for heaven / Are you my baby / Waterfall
CD VI 868812
Disky / Nov '96 / Disky / THE

FRUIT AT THE BOTTOM
Lolly lolly / Satisfaction / Everyday / Tears of joy / Fruit at the bottom / Are you my baby / Always in my dreams / From now on / I think it was December / Someday
CD CDV 2580
Virgin / Apr '92 / EMI

RE-MIX-IN-A-CARNATION
Lolly Lolly / Waterfall / Are you my baby / Staring at the sun / Satisfaction / Sideshow
CD CDV 2676
Virgin / '91 / EMI

Wenguang, Wu

MUSIC OF THE QIN
CD VICG 52132
JVC World Library / Mar '96 / ADA / CM / Direct

Wentzel, Magni

ALL OR NOTHING AT ALL
CD GMCD 150
Gemini / Oct '90 / Cadillac

MY WONDERFUL ONE
CD GMCD 157
Gemini / Oct '89 / Cadillac

NEW YORK NIGHTS
CD GMCD 174
Gemini / Oct '90 / Cadillac

Werdell, Leonard

MYSTO'S HOT LIPS
CD BCD 306
GHB / Jul '93 / Jazz Music

Werefrogs

SWING
CD TOPPCD 3
Ultimate / Jul '94 / Pinnacle

Werner, Kenny

LIVE AT MAYBECK RECITAL HALL VOL.34
Roberta moon / Someday my prince will come / In your own sweet way / Naima / Autumn leaves / Try to remember / Guru / Child is born
CD CCD 4622
Concord Jazz / Nov '94 / New Note/ Pinnacle

LIVE AT VISIONES
Stella by starlight / Fall / All the things you are / Blue in green / There will never be another you / Blue train / Windows / Soul eyes / I hear a rhapsody
CD CCD 4675
Concord Jazz / Dec '95 / New Note/ Pinnacle

PRESS ENTER
CD SSC 1056D
Sunnyside / May '92 / Discovery

Wernick, Pete

I TELL YOU WHAT (Wernick, Pete Live Five)
CD SHCD 3854
Sugar Hill / Sep '96 / ADA / CM / Direct / Koch / Roots

ON A ROLL
CD SHCD 3815
Sugar Hill / Mar '94 / ADA / CM / Direct / Koch / Roots

Werth, Howard

KING BRILLIANT (Werth, Howard & The Moonbeams)
Cocktail shake / Got to unwind / Embezzler / Human note / Ugly water / Midnight flyher / Fading star / Dear Joan / Roulette / Aleph / Lucinda
CD CASCD 1104
Charisma / Jun '92 / EMI

Werup, Jacques

PROVINSENS LJUS
CD DRCD 208
Dragon / Jul '87 / ADA / Cadillac / CM / Roots / Wellard

Wesley, Fred

AMALGAMATION
CD MM 801045
Minor Music / Jan '95 / Vital/SAM

BLOW FOR ME AND A TOOT TO YOU, A (Wesley, Fred & The Horny Horns)
CD NEDCD 268
Sequel / May '94 / BMG

FINAL BLOW, THE (Wesley, Fred & The Horny Horns)
CD NEDCD 270
Sequel / May '94 / BMG

NEW FRIENDS
Rockin' in rhythm / Blue monk / Plenty plenty soul / Birk's works / Peace fugue / Eyes to beautiful / Bright Mississippi
CD ANCD 8758
Antilles/New Directions / Jun '91 / PolyGram

SAY BLOW BY BLOW BACKWARDS (Wesley, Fred & The Horny Horns)
CD NEXCD 269
Sequel / May '94 / BMG

Wess, Frank

DEAR MR. BASIE (Wess, Frank & Harry Edison Orchestra)
Jumpin' at the woodside / Very thought of you / Blue on blue / All riled up / This is all I ask / I wish I knew / Whirly bird / Li'l darlin' / Dejection blues / Battle royal / One o'clock jump
CD CCD 4420
Concord Jazz / Jul '90 / New Note/Pinnacle

TRYIN' TO MAKE MY BLUES TURN GREEN
Come back to me / Tryin' to make my blues turn green / Listen to the dawn / So it is / Short circuit / Little Esther / Stray horn / Night lights / Surprise surprise / Blues in the car / Small talk / Alfie
CD CCD 4592
Concord Jazz / Apr '94 / New Note/ Pinnacle

West Bam

BAM BAM BAM
Acid sausage from Salzburgo / Wizards of the sonic / Celebration generation / Raving society / Strictly bam / Club canossa / Escapist / Track / Bam bam bam / After hours
CD 5271122
Low Spirit/Polydor / Jun '95 / PolyGram

JOURNEYS BY DJ INTERNATIONAL VOL.4 (Various Artists)
CD JDJI 4CD
JDJ / Oct '96 / 3mv/Pinnacle / SRD

West Coast All Stars

CELEBRATION OF WEST COAST JAZZ, A
CD Set CCD 79711/12
Candid / Nov '95 / Cadillac / Direct / Jazz Music / Koch / Wellard

West Coast Pop Art ...

WEST COAST POP ART EXPERIMENTAL BAND VOL.1 (West Coast Pop Art Experimental Band)
CD SC 11047
Sundazed / Jun '97 / Cargo / Greyhound / Rollercoaster

WEST COAST POP ART EXPERIMENTAL BAND VOL.1 & 2 (West Coast Pop Art Experimental Band)
CD POP 12CD
Clear Spot / Jan '97 / Cargo / SRD
CD 3096
Head / Jun '97 / Greyhound

West, David

ARCANE
CD TX 3003CD
Taxim / Jan '94 / ADA

West Ham Utd FC

FOREVER BLOWING BUBBLES (20 Hammers Hits) (Various Artists)
I'm forever blowing bubbles: *1975 Cup Final Squad* / West ham united: *1975 Cup Final Squad* / Football mad: *Boleyn Boys* / Oh sweet England: *Boleyn Boys* / Sugar sugar: *Moore, Bobby & Friends* / West side boys: *Cockney Rejects* / Viva Bobby Moore: *Serious Drinking* / Bobby Moore was innocent: *Serious Drinking* / Leroy's boots: *Barmy Army* / Devo: *Barmy Army* / Blunted irons: *United Nations* / Billy bonds mbe: *Barmy Army* / Come on you irons (big beat centenary): *Rainbow's Quest* / Bobby Moore's

legs: *Barmy Army* / Up the hammers: *Alf's Army* / Over land and sea: *Chicken Ron* / Julian Dicks: *Flat back four* / Terminator: *Flat back four* / I'm forever blowing bubbles: *Cockney Rejects* / I'm forever blowing bubbles: *Looking for a Rainbow*
CD _______________ CDGAFFER 7
Cherry Red / Aug '96 / Pinnacle

West Indies Jazz Band

MEDLEY FOR MARIUS
CD _______________ LBLC 6542
Label Bleu / Oct '91 / New Note/Pinnacle

West, Keith

EXCERPTS FROM GROUPS AND SESSIONS
Time is on my side / Don't lie to me / That's how strong my love is / Things she says / You're on your own / I don't mind / Am I glad to see you / Blow up / Three jolly little dwarfs / Revoloution / Excerpt from a teenage opera / Sam / Shy boy / Colonel Brown / On a Staurday / Kid was a killer / Visit / She / Little understanding / Power and the glory / West country / Riding for a fall / Having someone
CD _______________ RPM 141
RPM / Jun '95 / Pinnacle

West, Leslie

BLOOD OF THE SUN 1969-1975 (West, Leslie & Mountain)
CD _______________ RVCD 49
Raven / Mar '96 / ADA / Direct

DODGIN' THE DIRT
CD _______________ RR 90262
Roadrunner / Sep '96 / PolyGram

West Lothian Schools Brass ...

CARTOON (West Lothian Schools Brass Band)
Star Wars / Trumpet tune and air / La Bamba / Concertino for trumpet and brass band / Amazing grace / Charivari / Mr. Macintyre's march / Cartoon / Pastime with God company / Li'l darlin' / Harry James' trumpet concerto / Ruby Tuesday / Highland cathedral
CD _______________ QPRL 075D
Polyphonic / Jan '96 / Complete/Pinnacle

West, Mae

I'M NO ANGEL (The Original Commercial Recordings/The Film Soundtracks)
I like a guy what takes his time / Easy rider / I'm no angel / I found a new way to go to town / I want you, I need you / They call me Sister Honky Tonk / Willie of the valley / I like a guy what takes his time / Easy rider / Frankie and Johnny / They call me Sister Honky Tonk / That Dallas man / I found a new way to go to town / I want you, I need you / I'm no angel / When a St. Louis woman comes down to New Orleans / My old flame / Memphis blues / Troubled waters / He's a bad bad man / Mon coeur s'ouvre a ta voix / I'm an Occidental in an Oriental mood for love / Mister Deep Blue Sea / Little bar butterfly / On a typical tropical night / I was saying to the moon / Fifi / Now I'm a lady
CD _______________ JASCD 102
Jasmine / Oct '96 / Conifer/BMG / Hot Shot / TKO Magnum

West, Mick

FINE FLOWERS AND FOOLISH GLANCES
CD _______________ CDLDL 1229
Lochshore / Jul '95 / ADA / Direct / Duncans

West, Mike

INTERSTATE 10
Levee song / This song / Never resist / Wedding song / Burn to drive / Buddy Holly / Don't move back / Dinosaur / Barefoot boy / 6th Street Austin / Fishin' / Blues on a C Harp / Barefoot / Not angry, tired
CD _______________ QCD 010
Quark / Sep '95 / Vital

West Section Line

MAN DOWNSTAIRS, THE
CD _______________ RXR 006CD
RX Remedy / Nov '96 / Cargo

West, Sonny

RELENTLESS
Come on everybody / Come on let's go / Guitar attack / Relentless / Think it over baby / Almost grown / Jasmine / Icehouse / Take and give / Wyle E Coyote / Blue fire / I'm a man / So long baby / Doin' the boogie / Darlene / Hot choc / Runaway girl / I'll be there
CD _______________ NERCD 067
Nervous / Apr '92 / Nervous / TKO Magnum

West, Speedy

FLAMIN' GUITARS (4CD Set) (West, Speedy & Jimmy Bryant)
Jelly beans Daddy / Just remember / Boogie barn dance / Gamblin' money / Steel strike / Bryant's boogie / Red headed polka / Railroadin' / Stainless steel / Hub cap roll / T-bone rag / Truck driver's ride / Liberty bell polka / Crackerjack / Bryant's shuffle / Roadside rag / Yodelling guitar / Georgie steel guitar / Pickin' the chicken / Midnight ramble / Comin' on / Lover / Skiddle dee boo / Serenade to a frog / Bryant's bounce / Opus I / Whistle stop / Speedin' West / Hometown polka / This ain't the blues / Jammin' with Jimmy / Two of a kind / Sunset / Steel guitar rag / Swingin' on the strings / Old Joe Clark / This is Southland / Arkansas traveller / Blue bonnet rag / Hop, skip and jump / Country capers / Low man on a totem pole / Sleepwalker's lullaby / Our paradise / Cotton pickin' / Bustin' thru / Flippin' the lid / Deep water / Stratosphere boogie / West of Samoa / Shuffleboard rag / Steelin' moonlight / Caffeine patrol / Yankee clover / Pickin' peppers / Chatter box / Frettin' fingers / Pushin' the blues / Sand canyon swing / Water baby blues / Shawnee trot / On the Alamo / Rolling sky / Night rider / Hillcrest / China boy / China boy / Hawaiian war chant / Song of the islands / On the beach of Waikiki / My tane / Drifting and dreaming / My little grass shack in Kealakekua, Hawaii / Sweet Hawaiian chimes / Blue Hawaii / Yaaka hula hickey dula / Moon of Manakoora / Ka lu a / Luna / Reflections from the moon / Spaceman in orbit / Lazy Summer evening / Double or nothing / Afternoon of a swan / Wild and woolly West / Rippling waters / Totem pole dance / Slow and easy / Speedy's special / Sunset at Waikiki / Tulsa twist / Candy kisses: *Kirk, Eddy* / Ain't nobody's business but my own: *Starr, Kay & Tennessee Ernie Ford* / I'll never be free: *Starr, Kay & Tennessee Ernie Ford* / Wild card: *Williams, Tex* / Okie boogie: *Morse, Ella Mae* / Down South: *Jones, Spike* / I've turned a gadabout: *Jones, Spike* / Stop your gamblin': *Jones, Spike* / There's a blue sky way out yonder: *Jones, Spike* / Okie boogie: *Morse, Ella Mae* / Twice the lovin' (in half the time): *Shepard, Jean* / Crying steel guitar waltz: *Shepard, Jean* / Nobody else can love you like I do: *Shepard, Jean* / Keep it a secret: *Shepard, Jean* / Y'all come: *Crosby, Bing* / Under the double eagle: *Jones, Spike* / Hot lips: *Jones, Spike* / Hotter than a pistol: *Jones, Spike* / Keystone kapers: *Jones, Spike* / Boys in the backroom: *Jones, Spike* / Whistle stop: *May, Billy* / This must be the place: *Hutton, Betty & Tennessee Ernie Ford*
CD Set _______________ BCD 15956
Bear Family / Apr '97 / Direct / Rollercoaster / Swift

Westbrook, Mike

BAR UTOPIA (Westbrook, Mike Orchestra)
Overture / Nowhere / Utopia blues / Honest love / Dialogue / Utopia ballad / Happy jazz singer / Bar Utopia
CD _______________ ASCCD 13
ASC / Nov '96 / Cadillac / New Note/ Pinnacle

BRIGHT AS FIRE (The Westbrook Blake)
CD _______________ IMPCD 18013
Impetus / Mar '92 / Cadillac / Impetus

ON DUKE'S BIRTHDAY (Westbrook, Mike Orchestra)
CD _______________ ARTCD 6021
Hat Art / Apr '94 / Cadillac / Harmonia Mundi

ROSSINI (Studio)
CD _______________ ARTCD 6002
Hat Art / Jul '88 / Cadillac / Harmonia Mundi

ROSSINI - ZURICH LIVE 1986
CD Set _______________ ARTCD 26152
Hat Art / May '94 / Cadillac / Harmonia Mundi

STAGE SET (Westbrook, Kate & Mike)
September song / Private Jenny / Clio's cosmetics / Eto nepitiaai to kpyo / Une volta C'era un re / I got it bad / Nahe des geliebten / Un avenugle chant pour sa ville / Human abstract / L'egalite des sexes / Honest love / Don't explain / You've been a good old wagon / Casablanca / As time goes by
CD _______________ ASCCD 9
ASC / Apr '96 / Cadillac / New Note/ Pinnacle

Westen, Eric

WORKING DREAMER
CD _______________ BVHAASTCD 9212
Bvhaast / Dec '89 / Cadillac

Westerberg, Paul

14 SONGS
Knockin' on mine / First glimmer / World class fad / Runaway wind / Dice behind your shades / Even here we are / Silver naked ladies / Few minutes of silence / Someone I once knew / Black eyed Susan / Things / Something is me / Mannequin shop / Down love
CD _______________ 9362452552
Sire / Jun '93 / Warner Music

EVENTUALLY
CD _______________ 9362462512
Sire / May '96 / Warner Music

Westercamp, Hildegard

TRANSFORMATIONS
CD _______________ IMED 9631
Diffunzioni Musicali / Jun '97 / ReR Megacorp

Westerman, Floyd

CUSTER DIED/THIS LAND
CD _______________ TRIK 017
Trikont / Oct '94 / ADA / Direct

Western Vacation

VIBRAUDOBLAST
CD _______________ EFA 034322
Muffin / Apr '97 / SRD

WESTERN VACATION
CD _______________ EFA 034312
Muffin / Apr '96 / SRD

Western, Johnny

GUNFIGHT AT OK CORRAL
Ghost riders in the sky / Gunfight at the OK Corral / Gunfighter / Don't take your guns to town / Ringo / Hangin' tree / Cross the Brazos at Waco / Johnny Yuma / Bonanza / Ballad of Paladin / Rawhide / Searchers / High noon / Song of the bandit / Hannah Lee / Lillies grow high / Ballad of Boot Hill / Cheyenne / Wyatt Earp / Bat Masterson
CD _______________ BCD 15429
Bear Family / Jun '89 / Direct / Rollercoaster / Swift

HEROES AND COWBOYS (3CD Set)
Ballad of Paladin / Guns of the Rio Muerto (and Richard Boone) / Gunfighter / Geronimo / Lonely man / Hannah Lee / Streets of Laredo / Cowpoke / Lillies grow high / Cotton wood tree / Rollin' dust / Searchers / Nineteen men / Long tall shadow / Last round-up / Streets of old dodge city / Mr. Rodeo cowboy / Singin' man / Big battle / Forty shades of green / Violet and a rose / Give me more, more, more (of your kisses) / Let old mother nature have her way / Little buffalo Bill / Love me love me love me / Honey, how sweet can you be / Echo of your voice / Ten years / Uh huh / Delia's gone / Time has run out on me / Willowgreen / Don't cry little girl / Darling Corey / Stranger drive away / I love you more / All by my lonesome / Just for the record / Kathy come home / Only the lonely / Light the fuse / Tender years / Turn around and look at me / Sincerely your friend / Ruby, don't take your love to town / Used to / I'll try hard to forget you if I can / Whoever finds this, I love you / Last time I saw phoenix / Hustler / You wouldn't know love / Arizona morning / Stay a little longer, stay all night (theme) / Lonely street / You weren't ashamed to kiss me last night / John Henry / Remember me / Wayward wind / Gotta travel on / Ghost riders in the sky / I still miss someone / I take a country girl for mine (Texas Bill strength) / I walk the line / Ballad of Paladin / Guns of Rio Muerto
CD Set _______________ BCD 15552
Bear Family / May '93 / Direct / Rollercoaster / Swift

Westfield, Steve

BRAINWRECK
CD _______________ BS 20232
Pandemonium / Nov '96 / RTM/Disc / Vital

REJECT ME FIRST
CD _______________ PANNCD 11
Pandemonium / Mar '96 / RTM/Disc / Vital

UNDERWHELMED (Westfield, Steve Slow Band)
Lies / Happy birthday world / Underwhelmed / Nothing left to give / Monument / Leaving town / Riding with the flood / Have no fear / Life is too long / Friend
CD _______________ PANNCD 16
Pandemonium / May '97 / RTM/Disc / Vital

Westlake, David

WESTLAKE
Word around town / Dream come true / Rings on her fingers / Everlasting / She grew and she grew / Talk like that
CD _______________ CRECD 019
Creation / Jul '93 / 3mv/Vital

Weston

GOT BEAT UP
CD _______________ GKCD 019
Go-Kart / Oct '96 / Greyhound / Pinnacle

MATINEE
CD _______________ GKCD 033
Go-Kart / Sep '97 / Greyhound / Pinnacle

Weston, Calvin

DANCE ROMANCE
Chocolate rock / I can tell / Planetarian citizen / Preview / Dance romance / House blues
CD _______________ IOR 7002
In & Out / Sep '95 / Vital/SAM

Weston, John

I'M DOIN' THE BEST I CAN
CD _______________ APCD 120
Appaloosa / Sep '96 / ADA / Direct / TKO Magnum

SO DOGGONE BLUE
CD _______________ FIENDCD 743
Demon / Nov '93 / Pinnacle

Weston, Kim

KIM, KIM, KIM
You just don't know / Love I've been looking for / What could be better / When something is wrong with my baby / Love vibrations / Buy myself a man / Got to get you off my mind / Soul on fire / Brothers and sisters (get together) / Penny blues / Choice is up to you (Walk with me Jesus)
CD _______________ CDSXE 063
Stax / Jul '92 / Pinnacle

VERY BEST OF KIM WESTON, THE
Somebody's eyes / Helpless / You hit me where it hurt me / Signal your intention / My heart's not made of stone / Doin' it for myself / Investigate / It's too late / Case of too much loves making / Talkin' loud / It should have been me / After the rain / Just one man for me / Riding on the crest of a wave / Restless feet / Oh no not my baby / Springtime in my heart / Baby I'm yours
CD _______________ 3035990012
Carlton / Oct '95 / Carlton

Weston, Paul

FLOATIN' LIKE A FEATHER/THE SWEET AND THE SWINGIN'
Breezin' along with the breeze / What can I say after I say I'm sorry / It's a lovely day today / You turned the tables on me / All of me / Just you, just me / At sundown / You took advantage of me / Keepin' out of mischief now / Cheatin' on me / Isn't it a lovely day / Floatin' like a feather / Thrill is gone / I love you / Time on my hands / I'll see you in my dreams / Lies / Dream / Blue moon / Bye bye blues / Linger awhile / All by myself / Sometimes I'm happy / Street of dreams
CD _______________ CTMCD 116
EMI / Jun '97 / EMI

Weston, Randy

BLUES TO AFRICA
African village / Bedford stuyvesant / Tangier Bay / Blues to Africa / Kasbah kids / Uhuru Kwanza / Call / Kucheza blues / Sahel
CD _______________ FCD 41014
Freedom / Sep '87 / Cadillac / Jazz Music / Koch / Wellard

CARNIVAL
Carnival / Tribute to Duke Ellington / Mystery of love
CD _______________ FCD 41004
Freedom / Sep '87 / Cadillac / Jazz Music / Koch / Wellard

EARTH BIRTH
CD _______________ 5370882
Verve / May '97 / PolyGram

HOW HIGH THE MOON
Loose wig / Run Joe / Theme for Teddy / In a Spanish town / Don't blame me / JK blues / Well you needn't / How high the moon
CD _______________ BCD 147
Biograph / Jun '97 / ADA / Cadillac / Direct / Hot Shot / Jazz Music / Wellard

MARRAKESH IN THE COOL OF THE EVENING
CD _______________ 5215882
Verve / May '94 / PolyGram

MONTEREY 1966
Call / Afro black / Little Niles / Portrait of Vivian / Berkshire blues / Blues for Strayhorn / African cookbook
CD _______________ 5196982
Verve / May '94 / PolyGram

SAGA
CD _______________ 5292372
Verve / Apr '96 / PolyGram

SELF PORTRAITS (The Last Day)
Portrait of Frank Edward Weston / Berkshire blues / African night / Night in Medina / Ganawa in Paris / Last day
CD _______________ 8413142
Verve / Sep '93 / PolyGram

SPIRITS OF OUR ANCESTORS, THE (2CD Set)
African village Bedford-Stuyvesant / Healers / African cookbook / La elaha elle Allah / Morad Allah / Call / African village Bedford-Stuyvesant / Seventh Queen / Blue Moses / African sunrise / Prayer for us all
CD Set _______________ 5118572
Verve / Feb '92 / PolyGram

UHURU AFRIKA/HIGHLIFE
Uhuru kwanza (part one) / Uhuru kwanza (part two) / African lady / Kucheza blues / Caban bamboo highlife / Niger mambo / Zulu / In memory of / Congolese children / Blues of Africa / Mystery of love
CD _____ CDP 7945102
Blue Note / Feb '97 / EMI

VOLCANO BLUES (Weston, Randy & Melba Liston)
Blue mood / Chalabati blues / Sad beauty blues / Nafs / Volcano / Harvard blues / In memory of / Blues for Strayhorn / Penny packer blues / JK blues / Mystery of love / Kucheza blues / Blues for Elma Lewis
CD _____ 5192692
Verve / Feb '93 / PolyGram

Westside Connection

BOW DOWN
World domination / Bow down / Gangsta's make the world go round / All the critics in New York / Do you like criminals / Gangstas don't dance / Gangsta, the killa & the dope dealer / Cross 'em out and out a 'K / King of the hill / 3 time felons / Westward ho / Pledge / Hoo-bangin'
CD _____ CDPTY 134
Priority/Virgin / Nov '96 / EMI

GANGSTAS MAKE THE WORLD GO ROUND
CD _____ PTYCD 119
Priority/Virgin / May '97 / EMI

Westworld

BEATBOX ROCK 'N' ROLL
Sonic boom boy / Where the action is / Beatbox rock 'n' roll / Rockulator / Psycho-tech / Silver mac / Ba-na-na-bam-boo / Mix me up / Injection / Cheap 'n' nasty / Joy rider / Painkiller / Johnny Blue / Everything good is bad / Dance on / Break your heart / Big Red Indian / Ultimate Westerner / Paper skyscraper / Whirlwind girls / Cadillac / Fly Westworld
CD _____ 74321487292
RCA / May '97 / BMG

Wet Wet Wet

10
If I never see you again / Back on my feat / Fool for your love / Only sounds / If only I could be with you / I want you / Maybe I'm in love / Beyond the sea / Lonely girl / Strange / Theme from Ten / It hurts
CD _____ 5345852
Precious / Mar '97 / PolyGram

END OF PART ONE - GREATEST HITS
Wishing I was lucky / Sweet little mystery / Temptation / Angel eyes / With a little help from my friends / Sweet surrender / Brokeaway / Stay with me heartache / Hold back the river / This time / Make it tonight / More than love / Put the light on / Goodnight girl / Lip service / Blue for you / Shed a tear / Cold cold heart
CD _____ 5184772
Precious / Nov '93 / PolyGram

HIGH ON THE HAPPY SIDE
More than love / Lip service / Put the light on / High on the happy side / Maybe tomorrow / Goodnight girl / Celebration / Make it tonight / How long / Brand new sunrise / Two days after midnite
CD _____ 5104272
Precious / Jan '92 / PolyGram

HOLDING BACK THE RIVER
Sweet surrender / Can't stand the night / Blue for you / Brokeaway / You've had it / I wish / Keys to your heart / Maggie May / Hold back the river
CD _____ 8420112
Precious / Mar '92 / PolyGram

LIVE AT THE ROYAL ALBERT HALL (Wet Wet Wet & The Wren Orchestra)
CD _____ 5147742
Precious / May '93 / PolyGram

MEMPHIS SESSIONS, THE
I don't believe / Sweet little mystery / East of the river / This time / Temptation / I remember / For you are / Heaven help us all
CD _____ 8366032
Precious / Nov '88 / PolyGram

PICTURE THIS
Julia says / After the love goes / Somewhere, somehow / Gypsy girl / Don't want to forgive me now / She might never know / Someone like you / Love is my shepherd / She's on my mind / Morning / Home tonight / Love is all around
CD _____ 5268512
Precious / Apr '95 / PolyGram

POPPED IN SOULED OUT
Wishing I was lucky / East of the river / I remember / Angel eyes / Sweet little mystery / Temptation / I can give you everything / Moment you left me
CD _____ 8327262
Precious / Sep '87 / PolyGram

Wettling, George

CLASSICS 1940-1944
CD _____ CLASSICS 909
Classics / Nov '96 / Discovery / Jazz Music

Wetton, John

AKUSTIKA LIVE IN AMERICA
CD _____ BP 226CD
Blueprint / Jul '96 / Pinnacle

BATTLE LINES
Right where I wanted to be / Battle lines / Jane / Crime of passion / Sand in my hand / Sea of mercy / Hold me now / Space and time / Walking on air / You're not the only one
CD _____ BP 240CD
Blueprint / Nov '96 / Pinnacle
CD _____ CPCD 020
Cromwell / Sep '96 / Total/BMG

CHASING THE DRAGON
Heat of the moment / Don't cry / Rendezvous / Crime of passion / Caught in the crossfire / Easy money / In the dead of the night / Thirty years / Only time will tell / Hold me now / Starless / Book of Saturday / Battle lines / Open your eyes / Smile has left your eyes
CD _____ BP 227CD
Blueprint / Nov '96 / Pinnacle

KING'S ROAD 1972-1980
Nothing to lose / In the dead of night / Baby come back / Caught in the crossfire / Night after night / Turn on the radio / Rendezvous 602 / Book of Saturday / Paper talk / As long as you want me here / Cold is the night / Eyesight to the blind / Starless
CD _____ EGCD 70
EG / Oct '87 / EMI

Whale

PAY FOR ME
Pay for me / I think no / Darling Nikki / Buzz-box babe / Trying
CD _____ DGHUTM 24
Hut / May '95 / EMI

WE CARE
Kickin' / That's where it's at / Pay for me / Eurodog / I'll do ya / Electricity / Hobo humpin' slobo babe / Tryzasnice / Happy in you / I miss me / Young, dumb and full of cum / I'm cold / Born to raise hell
CD _____ CDHUT 25
CD _____ DGHUT 25
Hut / Jul '95 / EMI

Wham

FANTASTIC
Bad boys / Ray of sunshine / Love machine / Wham rap / Club Tropicana / Nothing looks the same in the light / Come on / Young guns (go for it)
CD _____ 4500902
Epic / '91 / Sony

FINAL, THE
Wham rap / Young guns go for it / Bad boys / Club Tropicana / Wake me up before you go go / Careless whisper / Freedom / Last Christmas / Everything she wants / I'm your man / Blue (armed with love) / Different corner / Battlestations / Where did your heart go / Edge of heaven
CD _____ CD 88681
Epic / '86 / Sony

MAKE IT BIG
Wake me up before you go go / Everything she wants / Heartbeat / Like a baby / Freedom / If you were there / Credit card baby / Careless whisper
CD _____ CD 86311
Epic / Nov '84 / Sony

TWELVE INCH MIXES
Wham rap / Careless whisper / Freedom (long mix) / Everything she wants / I'm your man
CD _____ 4501252
Epic / Nov '92 / Sony

Wharton Tiers

BRIGHTER THAN LIFE
CD _____ ALP 60CD
Atavistic / Jul '97 / Cargo / SRD

Wharton, Bill

SOUTH OF THE BLUES
CD _____ KS 023
Flying Fish / Nov '94 / ADA / CM / Direct / Roots

STANDING IN THE FIRE (Wharton, Bill & The Ingredients)
CD _____ KS 036CD
Kingsnake / Oct '96 / Hot Shot

What Noise

FAT
CD _____ BND 8 CD
One Little Indian / Feb '90 / Pinnacle

Whatever

LIES AND GOLD DUST
Stepping stone / Down on the up / Tin soldiers / Good time high / Suffer immaculate / All that remains / Hero's ego / No.1 / Back from the dead / Corrosion / Brain drain
CD _____ CDMFN 220
Music For Nations / Jun '97 / Pinnacle

SUGARBUZZ
CD _____ CDMFN 193
Music For Nations / Mar '96 / Pinnacle

Whatnauts

DEFINITIVE WHATNAUTS, THE (2CD Set)
I just can't lose your love / Tweedly dum dum / She's gone to another / What life to give (after giving it all) / Fall in love all over / Just can't leave my baby / I'll erase away your pain / Please make the love go away / Souling with the Whatnauts / Dance to the music / Message from a black man / You forgot too easy / Heads up / Hurry up and wait / I'm so glad I found you / Only people can save the world / Blues fly away / Why can people be colours too / Ooh baby baby / Try me (and I'll show you) / Friends by day (lovers by night) / Alibis & lies / I dig your act / You gave me true loving / World / We will always be together / My thing / Let me be that special one / Girls (part 1): *Whatnauts & Moments* / Girls: *Whatnauts & Moments* / Help is on the way / Genuine / Give a damn / Why can't we be together / Just passing / Strolling / Gotta be a love (somewhere)
CD Set _____ DEEPD 005
Deep Beats / Nov '96 / BMG

Wheat Chiefs

REDEEMER
CD _____ BANG 10142
Bang On / Feb '97 / Cargo

Wheater, Paul

ROCK OF AGES
Lead me gently home / I'd rather have Jesus / He'll understand / When God dips his love in my heart / He walked that lonesome road / God will / What a friend we have in Jesus / I saw a man
CD _____ ALD 063
Alliance Music / Oct '96 / EMI

TWENTY GOOD YEARS
CD _____ CLCD 01
Rio Digital / Feb '91 / Grapevine/PolyGram

Wheater, Tim

HEARTLAND
CD _____ ALMOCD 006
Almo Sounds / Mar '96 / Pinnacle

Wheatstraw, Peetie

BLUES, THE (2CD Set)
CD Set _____ FA 255
Fremeaux / Nov '96 / ADA / Discovery

DEVIL'S SON-IN-LAW, THE
CD _____ SOB 035412
Story Of The Blues / Apr '93 / ADA / Koch

PEETIE WHEATSTRAW VOL.1 1930-1941
CD _____ DOCD 5241
Document / May '94 / ADA / Hot Shot / Jazz Music

PEETIE WHEATSTRAW VOL.2 1930-1941
CD _____ DOCD 5242
Document / May '94 / ADA / Hot Shot / Jazz Music

PEETIE WHEATSTRAW VOL.3 1930-1941
CD _____ DOCD 5243
Document / May '94 / ADA / Hot Shot / Jazz Music

PEETIE WHEATSTRAW VOL.4 1930-1941
CD _____ DOCD 5244
Document / May '94 / ADA / Hot Shot / Jazz Music

PEETIE WHEATSTRAW VOL.5 1930-1941
CD _____ DOCD 5245
Document / May '94 / ADA / Hot Shot / Jazz Music

PEETIE WHEATSTRAW VOL.6 1930-1941
CD _____ DOCD 5246
Document / May '94 / ADA / Hot Shot / Jazz Music

PEETIE WHEATSTRAW VOL.7 1930-1941
CD _____ DOCD 5247
Document / May '94 / ADA / Hot Shot / Jazz Music

Wheeler, Cheryl

CIRCLES AND ARROWS
I know this town / Hard line to draw / Aces / Estate sale / Don't wanna / Northern girl / Soon as I find my voice / Miss you more than I'm mad / Moonlight and roses / When you're gone / Arrow
CD _____ CDPH 1162
Philo / May '95 / ADA / CM / Direct

DRIVING HOME
CD _____ PH 1152CD
Philo / Jan '94 / ADA / CM / Direct

MRS. PINOCCI'S GUITAR
CD _____ CDPH 1192
Philo / Nov '95 / ADA / CM / Direct

Wheeler, Ian

IAN WHEELER AT FARNHAM MALTINGS
CD _____ LACD 32
Lake / Nov '94 / ADA / Cadillac / Direct / Jazz Music / Target/BMG

Wheeler, Kenny

ANGEL SONG
Nicolette / Present past / Kind folk / Unti / Angel song / Onmo / Nonetheless / Past present / Kind of gentle
CD _____ 5330982
ECM / Feb '97 / New Note/Pinnacle

AROUND 6
Mai we go round / Solo one / May ride / Follow down / Riverrun / Lost woltz
CD _____ 5291242
ECM / Feb '96 / New Note/Pinnacle

CALIFORNIA DAYDREAM (Wheeler, Kenny & Gardner/Van De Geyn/Ceccarelli)
CD _____ 500292
Musidisc / Nov '93 / Discovery

DOUBLE DOUBLE YOU
Foxy trot / Ma bel / W W / Three for D'reen / Blue for Lou / Mark time
CD _____ 8156752
ECM / Jan '90 / New Note/Pinnacle

GNU HIGH
CD _____ 8255912
ECM / Aug '85 / New Note/Pinnacle

KENNY WHEELER 1976
Hi-yo / Slofa / Quiso / Blues news / Kitts
CD _____ JAS 95062
Just A Memory / May '96 / New Note/ Pinnacle

MUSIC FOR LARGE AND SMALL ENSEMBLES
Part I (opening) / Part II (For H) / Part III (for Jan) / Part IV (for PA) / Part V (know where you are) / Part VI (consolation) / Part VII (Freddy C) / Part VIII (closing) / Sophie / Sea lady / Gentle piece / Trio / Duet I / Duet II / Duet III / By myself
CD Set _____ 8431522
ECM / Nov '90 / New Note/Pinnacle

TOUCHE (Wheeler, Kenny & Paul Bley)
Presto / Ouvre / Fausto / Doing time / Mystique / Double standard / Touche / Concours / Deja vu / Colour / Upscale / Prequel / Sortie
CD _____ JUST 972
Justin Time / Feb '97 / Cadillac / New Note/ Pinnacle

WALK SOFTLY (Wheeler, Kenny & Guildhall Jazz Band)
CD _____ WAVE CD 32
Wave / Apr '90 / Wellard

WIDOW IN THE WINDOW (Wheeler, Kenny Trio)
Aspire / Ma balle Helene / Widow in the window / Ana / Hotel le hot / Now, and now again
CD _____ 8431982
ECM / Jun '90 / New Note/Pinnacle

Wheeler, Onie

ONIE'S BOP
Jump right out of this jukebox / Tell em off / I wanna hold my baby / Onie's bop / Booger gonna getcha / Going back to the city / Long gone / Steppin' out / I'll love you for a lifetime / Beggar for your love / Walkin' shoes / That's all / Cut it out / That's what I like / She wiggled and giggled / I'm satisfied with my dreams / No, i don't guess i will / Would you like to wear a crown / I saw mother with God last night / My home is not a home at all / Little mama / Hazel / Closing time / Tried and tried, I / I'll swear you don't love me / Love me like you used to do / When we all fet there / Mother prays loud in her sleep / Million years in glory / Run 'em off / Bonaparte's retreat
CD _____ BCD 15542
Bear Family / May '91 / Direct / Rollercoaster / Swift

Wheelz

AROUND THE WORLD VOL.1 (Wheelz & Ingrid Jensen)
Wheelz newz / Balkanamera / Allah / 52nd Street / Hot wheelz / Hungarian red house / Adria / Indian summer / Naked world / Ruth / Away from home
CD _____ 92472
Act / Feb '97 / New Note/Pinnacle

Whelan, John

CELTIC CROSSROADS
Denis Dillon's square dance polka / Mabel Ruddy's the windy gap / Skimming the surface / Ceol nanolag / There were roses / Beautiful blackwater / Maggie K's / Father

Maroney's 95 south Granny Barnes / Champs Elysees / Balkans / Grosse ile / Ian's return to Ireland / Yanik's / Denis Whelan's / Flower of Magherally / Passage of time
CD ND 61060
Narada / Apr '97 / ADA / New Note/Pinnacle

CELTIC REFLECTIONS
Louise / Longing for home, longing for here / Dancing to a lot of time / Last dance / Road home / Sacred ground / From the heart / Mist-eyed morning / Breton gathering / Song for Hilary / Desaunay / Cape finisterre / Trip to Skye / My Ballingarry lady
CD ND 61052
Narada / Apr '96 / ADA / New Note/Pinnacle

FRESH TAKES (Whelan, John & Eileen Ivers)
CD GLCD 1075
Green Linnet / Feb '93 / ADA / CM / Direct / Highlander / Roots

Whellans, Mike

SWING TIME JOHNNY RED
CD COMD 2036
Temple / Feb '94 / ADA / CM / Direct / Duncans / Highlander

When

BLACK, WHITE AND GREY
CD RERWHCD
ReR/Recommended / Jan '94 / ReR Megacorp / RTM/Disc

DROWNING BUT LEARNING
CD TAT 024CD
Tatra / Aug '95 / Plastic Head

SVARTEDAVEN
CD TATCD 008
Tatra / Aug '95 / Plastic Head

When Granny Sleeps

PLANET CONSTRUCTION
CD STCD 4209
Storyville / May '97 / Cadillac / Jazz Music / Wellard

Where Eagles Fly

SCOTTISH FANTASIA
CD WEF 5
Glencoe / May '95 / Duncans

Whetstone, Dave

RESOLUTION, THE
Rocky and the gopher / Bonavista 1 & 2 / Resolution / Emilia's angels/Jolly jolly demons / Black swan / Hotfoot 2 / Henry's moat / Fish pie polka/timberline / Sherborne rose / Fingers in the jam / Sweet ginger / Candlemas moon / Cummerbund/heads up / Hare in the long grass / Rachel's delight
CD MKRCD 410
Monkey's Knib / Nov '96 / CM / Direct

Whigfield

WHIGFIELD
Think of you / Another day / Don't walk away / Big time / Out of sight / Close to you / Sexy eyes / Ain't it blue / I want to love / Saturday night
CD 8286272
Systematic / Jun '95 / PolyGram

While, Chris

IN THE BIG ROOM
CD FLED 3009
Fledg'ling / Mar '97 / ADA / CM / Direct

LOOK AT ME NOW
CD FAT 003CD
Fat Cat / Aug '94 / ADA / CM / Direct

Whiplash

CULT OF ONE
CD MASSCD 087
Massacre / Apr '96 / Plastic Head

TICKET TO MAYHEM
CD RO 95962
Roadrunner / Apr '89 / PolyGram

Whipped Cream

...& OTHER DELIGHTS
Explosion / Remember / Silver 1 / Let us try it out / Wishing / This time next time / Theodora wine / I know your mine / Whatever / Together / Come together / Explosion '93
CD RESNAP 001
Soap / Jan '94 / Vital

TUNE IN THE CENTURY
Yes / Tune in the century / Wait for a minute / Lay down beside / Give away / Sensational / Virtuosly / Observatory crest / Up the country / Come and find / Beyond the sun
CD SNAP 003
Soap / Sep '92 / Vital

Whipping Boy

HEARTWORM
Blinded / Personality / Users / Fiction / Morning rise / Twinkle / When we were young / Tripped / Honeymoon is over / We don't need nobody else
CD 4802812
Columbia / Oct '95 / Sony

Whirligig

CELTIC DAWN
CD CDLDL 1227
Lochshore / Mar '95 / ADA / Direct / Duncans

Whirling Pope Joan

SPIN
CD TAT 294CD
Panic ATC / Aug '94 / ADA / CM / Direct

Whirlpool

LIQUID GLASS
CD REV 052CD
Revelation / Dec '96 / Plastic Head

Whirlpool Productions

BRIAN DE PALMA
CD LAD 0201612
Ladomat / May '95 / Plastic Head

Whirlwind

IN THE STUDIO
Hang loose (I've gotta rock) / Boppin' high school baby / My bucket's got a hole in it / My advice / Thousand stars / One more chance / Don't be crazy / Rockin' Daddy / Slow down / Blue moon of Kentucky / Together forever / Who's that knocking / Tore apart / Do what I do / Duck tail / I only wish (That I'd been told) / Midnight blue / Teenage cutie / You got class / Honey hush / Cruisin' around / Stay cool / Running wild / Okie's in the pokie / Heaven knows / Big Sandy / Such a fool / Nightmares / If it's all the same to you / Stayin' out all night
CD CDWIKD 147
Chiswick / Jun '95 / Pinnacle

Whiskeytown

RURAL FREE DELIVERY
CD MFR 0082
Mood Food / Jun '97 / Cargo

Whisky Before Breakfast

MARY'S TEAPOT
CD WBBCD 1
Abacus / Jul '97 / Direct

Whisky Priests

BLEEDING SKETCHES
CD WPTCD 13
Whippet / Oct '95 / ADA / CM / Pinnacle

BLOODY WELL LIVE
CD WPT CD7
Whippet / May '93 / ADA / CM / Pinnacle

FIRST FEW DROPS, THE
CD WPTCD 10
Whippet / Oct '94 / ADA / CM / Pinnacle

LIFE'S TAPESTRY
CD WPTCD 14
Whippet / Sep '96 / ADA / CM / Pinnacle

NEE GUD LUCK
CD WPTCD 11
Whippet / Oct '94 / ADA / CM / Pinnacle

POWER & THE GLORY, THE
CD WPT 008CD
Whippet / Apr '94 / ADA / CM / Pinnacle

TIMELESS STREET
CD WPTCD 12
Whippet / Oct '94 / ADA / CM / Pinnacle

Whispers

30TH ANNIVERSARY ANTHOLOGY (2CD Set)
Seems like I gotta do wrong / There's a love for everyone / Can't help but love you / I only meant to wet my feet / Somebody loves you / Mother for my children / Bingo / One for the money / Living together (In sin) / Make it with you / (Let's go) All the way / Lost and turned out / Can't do without love / Song for Donny / And the beat goes on / Lady my girl / It's a love thing / I'm the one for you / I can make it better / This kind of lovin' / In the raw / Emergency / Tonight / Keep on loving me / Contagious / Some kinda lover / Rock steady / Just gets better with time / In the mood / No pain no gain / Say yes / Special F/X
CD Set NEDCD 267
Sequel / Aug '94 / BMG

AND THE BEAT GOES ON
And the beat goes on / Lady / My girl / It's a love thing / I'm the one for you / Seems like I gotta do wrong / There's a love for everyone / Headlights / All the way / One for the money / Rock steady / Emergency / Some kinda lover / Keep on loving me / This kind of lovin' / In the mood
CD 21045
Laserlight / Jul '97 / Target/BMG

BEST OF THE WHISPERS, THE
And the beat goes on / My girl / Headlights / One for the money / I can make it better / It's a love thing / In the raw / Tonight / Some kinda lover / Contagious / Rock steady / Special FX / Lady / No pain, no gain / Make it with you / Let's go all the way / Out the box / Living together
CD CCSCD 804
Renaissance Collector Series / Sep '95 / BMG

ESSENTIAL SLOW GROOVE DANCEFLOOR CLASSICS
CD DGPCD 727
Deep Beats / May '95 / BMG

IMAGINATION
It's a love thing / Say you would love for me too / Continental shuffle / I can make it better / Imagination / Girl I need you / Up on soul train / Fantasy
CD NEBCD 793
Sequel / Jul '96 / BMG

LOVE IS WHERE YOU FIND IT
In the raw / Turn me out / Cruisin' in / Emergency / Say yes / Love is where you find it / Only you / Small talkin'
CD NEBCD 840
Sequel / Jul '96 / BMG

LOVE THING
It's a love thing / And the beat goes on / My girl / Can't do without your love / Cruisin' in / Welcome into my dreams / Only you / Rock steady / Lady / Emergency / Keep on lovin' me / Tonight / Imagination / I want to make it with you
CD 5507562
Spectrum / Mar '95 / PolyGram

WHISPERS
Song for Donny / My girl / Lady can you do the boogie / and the beat goes on / I love you / Out the box / Welcome into my dream
CD NEBCD 794
Sequel / Jul '96 / BMG

Whistlebinkies

ANNIVERSARY
Farewell to Nigg / Piper, the harper, the fiddler / Fiddle Strathspey and Reel / MacBeth / Island jigs / Whistlebinkies' reel / Ane ground / Sir John Fenwick / Ailein Duinn / MacDonald of the Isles / Dominic McGowan / Fiddlers' farewell / Winter it is past / Dogs among the bushes / Rattlin' roarin' Willie / Barlinnie Highlander / Change of tune
CD CC 54CD
Claddagh / Nov '92 / ADA / CM / Direct

INNER SOUND
CD CDLOC 1063
Lochshore / Feb '95 / ADA / Direct / Duncans

WANTON FLING, A
Piper's jig / Ay waulkin o / Whistlebinkies jig / Ho ro mo chuachag / Dunkeld Bridge / Cam' ye o'er frae France / Taladh / Farewell to Muirhead's / Deireadh leave 1940 / Wee Eddie reel / Wanton fling / A'bhalsa mu dheireadh
CD CDTRAX 095
Greentrax / Feb '96 / ADA / Direct / Duncans / Highlander

Whitcomb, Ian

HAPPY DAYS ARE HERE AGAIN (Whitcomb, Ian Dance Band)
CD Set DAPCD 242
Audiophile / Apr '89 / Jazz Music

IAN WHITCOMB & HIS BUNGALOW BOYS/REGINA WHITCOMB
CD ACD 267
Audiophile / Jun '96 / Jazz Music

IAN WHITCOMB & HIS MERRY BAND 1967-1993
CD SOSCD 1276
Stomp Off / Apr '94 / Jazz Music / Wellard

LOTUS LAND
CD ACD 283
Audiophile / Jun '95 / Jazz Music

RAGTIME AMERICA
CD ACD 277
Audiophile / Aug '94 / Jazz Music

THIS SPORTING LIFE
This sporting life / Soho / Boney Maronie / Dance again / Turn a song (Test pressing version) / You turn me on (Turn a song) / Be my baby / That is rock 'n' roll / N-n-nervous / Good hard rock / Where did Robinson Crusoe go with Friday on Saturday night / Poor little bird / Your baby has gone down the plughole / Louie Louie / Lover's prayer / Naked ape / Kingfisher of the loving pack / Life has no reason / Sally sails the sky / Notable yacht club of staines / Star / When rock 'n' roll was young / Oh pretty woman / Rolling with the quake / Rocking the baby to sleep
CD CREV 032CD
Rev-Ola / Jul '94 / 3mv/Vital

White, Alan

RAMSHACKLED
CD 7567803962
Atlantic / Jan '96 / Warner Music

White, Aline

JUST A LITTLE WHILE
CD BCD 292
GHB / Oct '93 / Jazz Music

White, Andy

DESTINATION BEAUTIFUL
Street scenes from my heart / Thinking of change / John / Many's the time / Punk outside the secret police / She dosen't want to cry any more / Learning to cry / He's out there / Ciao baby / Looking into friends / I couldn't leave you / Government of love
CD COOKCD 072
Cooking Vinyl / Aug '94 / Vital

HIMSELF
In a groovy kinda way / 1,000,000 miles / Six string street / Freeze out / Just jumped out of a tree / Twenty years / Guildford four / Pale moonlight / Bird of passage / St. Patrick's good luck / Coup I / Whole love story / Six string street (30 mph) / Travelling circus
CD COOKCD 029
Cooking Vinyl / Feb '95 / Vital

OUT THERE
Palaceful of noise / Where's my home / Colour of love / Waiting for the 39 / La Rue Beaurepaire / Speechless / Berlin 6 am / James Joyce's grave / One last kiss / Na na na na / Placeful of noise
CD 9031770122
East West / Jun '92 / Warner Music

TEENAGE
Acoustic guitar / Get back home / All the things I can bring / If you don't know by now / It's gonna be like this all the time / Jacqui / Because she loves it / Don't be afraid / My gay cousin / Between the man and a woman / I couldn't do it / It's gonna be like this in the rain / Whole thing
CD COOKCD 123
Cooking Vinyl / Jan '97 / Vital

White, Artie

BEST OF ARTIE WHITE, THE
Today I started loving you again / Nothing takes the place of you / Tore up / Tired of sneaking around / Jody / Dark end of the street / That's where it's at / Nobody wants you when you're old and grey / Funny how time slips away / Hattie Mae / Thangs got to change / I need someone
CD ICH 1131CD
Ichiban / Oct '93 / Direct / Koch

THINGS GOT TO CHANGE
Things got to change / Rainy day / I ain't taking no prisoners / You upset me baby / Thank you pretty baby / Hattie Mae / I wonder why / Reconsider baby / Somebody's on my case
CD ICH 1044CD
Ichiban / Oct '93 / Direct / Koch

TIRED OF SNEAKIN' AROUND
Today I started loving you / Thinking about making a change / Jody / Peeping Tom / Tired of sneaking around / Don't pet my dog / Can't get you off my mind / I can't seem to please you / Turn about is fair play / Nose to the grindstone
CD ICH 1061CD
Ichiban / Oct '93 / Direct / Koch

WHERE IT'S AT
CD ICH 1026CD
Ichiban / Oct '93 / Direct / Koch

White, Barry

BARRY WHITE
CD EXP 046
Experience / May '97 / TKO Magnum

BARRY WHITE AND FRIENDS (2CD Set)
America / Let me in and let's begin with love / High steppin', hip dressin' fella (you got it together) / Your love, your love / We can't get go of love / Our theme / Our theme / If you want me, say it / Don't forget, remember / I'm giving you a love (every man is searchin' for) / You make my life easy livin' / It ain't love babe (until you give up) / Take a good look (and what do you see) / I'm so glad that I'm a woman / Sheet music / Never, never say goodbye / Lady, sweet lady / Love makin' music / This love / Better love is (the worse it is when it's over) / Gotta be where you are / Free / You / Hung up in your love / Jamaican girl / Didn't we make it happen baby / Relax to the max / Bayou / Life / I did it for love / In the ghetto / Your the first, the last, my everything
CD Set 24363
Laserlight / May '97 / Target/BMG

COLLECTION, THE
You're the first, the last, my everything / You see the trouble with me / Can't get enough of your love babe / I'll do for you anything you want me to / Just the way you are / Walking in the rain with the one I love / It may be Winter outside / Love's theme / Sho' you right / What am I gonna do with you / Never, never gonna give you up / Let Baby we better try and get it together / Let the music play / Don't make me wait too long / I'm gonna love you just a little more babe / Right night

CD 8347902
PolyGram TV / Feb '94 / PolyGram

HEART AND SOUL OF BARRY WHITE, THE
Come on in love / I owe it all to you / Long black veil / Out of the shadows of love / I've got the world to hold me up / Your heart and soul / Where can I turn to / Under the influence of love / All in the run of a day / Fragile handle with care
CD 305952
Hallmark / Jan '97 / Carlton

I'M GONNA LOVE YOU
CD MPG 74030
Movieplay Gold / Nov '94 / Target/BMG

ICON IS LOVE, THE
Practice what you preach / There it is / I only want to be with you / Time is right / Baby's home / Come on / Love is the icon / Sexy undercover / Don't you want to know / Whatever we had, we had
CD 5402802
A&M / Oct '94 / PolyGram

JUST FOR YOU (2CD Set)
CD Set 5141432
Phonogram / Jan '93 / PolyGram

LET THE MUSIC PLAY
CD MPG 74032
Movieplay Gold / Nov '94 / Target/BMG

LET THE MUSIC PLAY
Let the music play / I can't get enough of your love, babe / I love you more than anything (In this world girl) / Love serenade I / Hard to believe that I found you / September when I first met you / Don't make me wait too long / Look at her / I'm gonna love you just a little more, baby / Oh love, well we finally made it / Let me live my life lovin' you babe / Love serenade II
CD 5515152
Spectrum / Oct '95 / PolyGram

LOVE ALBUM, THE
I've got the whole world to hold me up / Your heart and soul / Under the influence of love / All in the run of love / Out of the shadows of love / Long black veil / Come on in love / Where can I turn to / I owe it all to you / Fragile, handle with care / My buddy / I've got the whole world to hold me up
CD PLATCD 210
Platinum / Feb '97 / Prism

LOVE ALBUM, THE
Out of the shadows of love / I owe it all to you / Where can I turn / Come on in love / Under the influence of love / I've got the whole world to hold me up / Your heart and soul / I'm fragile handle with care / All in the run of the day / Long black veil
CD 100252
CMC / May '97 / BMG

MAN IS BACK, THE
Responsible / Super lover / LA my kinda place / Follow that and see (where it leads y'all) / When will I see you again / I wanna do it good to ya / It's getting harder all the time / Don't let go / Love's interlude / Goodnight my love
CD CDA 5256
A&M / Aug '89 / PolyGram

PUT ME IN YOUR MIX
Let's get busy / Love is good for you / For real chill / Break it down with you / Volare / Put me in your mix / Who you giving your love to / Love will find us / We're gonna have it all / Dark and lovely (you over there) / Sho' you right
CD 3943772
A&M / Oct '91 / PolyGram

RIGHT NIGHT AND BARRY WHITE, THE
Sho' you right / For your love / There is a place / Love is in your eyes / Right night / I'm ready for love / Share / Who's the fool
CD CDMID 155
A&M / Oct '92 / PolyGram

SATIN AND SOUL VOL.2 (2CD Set)
Walking in the rain with the one I love / Don't make me wait too long / Don't tell me about heartaches / I won't settle for less than the best (You baby) / Didn't we make it happy baby / Let me in, let's begin with love / Let the music play / Lady sweet lady / I like you, you like me / Change / Gotta be where you are / What am I gonna do with you / You're the one I need / Life / Any fool could see / I found love / Our theme (part 2) / Baby we better try and get it together / She's everything to me / Let's make tonight an evening to remember / I can't let him down / You're the only one for me
CD Set DVSOPCD 154
Connoisseur Collection / Dec '90 / Pinnacle

SOUL SEDUCTION
Never never gonna give ya up / Standing in the shadows of love / What am I gonna do with you / Honey please can't you see / Your sweetness is my weakness / I love to sing the songs I sing / It's only love doing it's thing / Bring back my yesterday / I've got so much to give / You see the trouble with me / Playing your game baby / You're so good, you're so bad / Oh me oh my (I'm such a lucky guy)
CD 5500902
Spectrum / Oct '93 / PolyGram

SPOTLIGHT ON BARRY WHITE
My buddy / Long black veil / Where can I turn to / I've got the world to hold me up / Your heart and soul / Out of the shadows of love / Under the influence of love / Fragile hadnle with care / All in the run of love / Come on in love / I owe it all to you
CD HADCD 142
Javelin / Feb '94 / Henry Hadaway / THE

UNLIMITED LOVE COLLECTION, THE
Can't get enough of your love, babe / Just the way you are / It's ecstasy when you lay down next to me / I've got so much to give / Let the music play / Never, never gonna give you up / You see the trouble with me / You're the first, the last, my everything / I've found someone / Bring back my yesterday / Standing in the shadows of love / I'm gonna love you just a little more, baby
CD APH 102801
Audiophile Legends / Apr '96 / Total/BMG

YOU'RE THE FIRST, THE LAST, MY EVERYTHING
CD MPG 74031
Movieplay Gold / Nov '94 / Target/BMG

YOUR HEART & SOUL
CD JHD 001
Tring / Jun '92 / Tring

White, Brian

C'EST MAGNAFIQUE (White, Brian & His Magna Jazz Band)
CD JCD 248
Jazzology / Jun '95 / Jazz Music

MUGGSY REMEMBERED
CD JCD 200
Jazzology / Oct '92 / Jazz Music

PLEASURE MAD (White, Brian & His Magna Jazz Band)
CD JCD 178
Jazzology / Oct '92 / Jazz Music

RAGTIMERS VOL.1 (White, Brian & Alan Gretsy)
CD JCD 116
Jazzology / Aug '94 / Jazz Music

White, Buck

MORE PRETTY GIRLS THAN ONE
CD SHMC 3710
Sugar Hill / Mar '89 / ADA / CM / Direct / Koch / Roots

White, Bukka

1963 NOT 1962
CD EDCD 382
Edsel / Oct '94 / Pinnacle

BIG DADDY
Gibson hill / Black cat bone blues / 1936 trigger toe / Cryin' Holy unto the Lord / Shake my hand blues / Sic em dogs / Aberdeen Mississippi / Mama don low / Hot springs Arkansas / Jelly roll Morton man / Black crepe blues / Glory bound train / Hobo blues
CD BCD 145
Biograph / Jun '97 / ADA / Cadillac / Direct / Hot Shot / Jazz Music / Wellard

BIG DADDY, MISSISSIPPI BLUES
CD BG 145CD
Biograph / Dec '96 / ADA / Cadillac / Direct / Hot Shot / Jazz Music / Wellard

COMPLETE RECORDINGS, THE
Pine bluff / Arkansas / Shake'em on down / Black train blues / Strange place blues / When can I change my clothes / Sleepy man blues / Parchman farm blues / Good gin blues / High fever blues / District attorney blues / Fixin' to die blues / Aberdeen / Mississippi / Bukka's jitterbug swing / Special stream line
CD 4757042
Columbia / May '94 / Sony

COMPLETE SESSIONS 1930-1940
New Frisco train / Panama limited / I am in the heavenly way / Pine bluff Arkansas / Where can I change my clothes / Sleepy man blues / Parchman farm / Good gin blues / Special line
CD TMCD 03
Travellin' Man / Apr '90 / Hot Shot / Jazz Music / Wellard

SKY SONGS VOL.1-2
CD ARHCD 323
Arhoolie / Apr '95 / ADA / Cadillac / Direct

White Caps

BLOWN IN THE USA
CD F 003CD
Fearless / Apr '97 / Cargo / Plastic Head

White, Carla

LISTEN HERE
Devil may care / Harlem nocturne / Dreamsville / It's you or no one / Lotus blossom / It's only a paper moon / Darn that dream / I've got your number / Listen here / Feelin' good / Dream
CD ECD 221092
Evidence / Jan '95 / ADA / Cadillac / Harmonia Mundi

White Devil

REINCARNATION
CD LF 210CD
Lost & Found / Jan '96 / Plastic Head

White Eagle Jazzband

TRIBUTE TO PAUL BARBARIN, A
CD BCD 404
GHB / Mar '97 / Jazz Music

White, Georgia

GEORGIA WHITE VOL.1 1930-1936
CD DOCD 5301
Document / May '95 / ADA / Hot Shot / Jazz Music

GEORGIA WHITE VOL.2 1936-1937
CD DOCD 5302
Document / May '95 / ADA / Hot Shot / Jazz Music

GEORGIA WHITE VOL.3 1937-1939
CD DOCD 5303
Document / May '95 / ADA / Hot Shot / Jazz Music

GEORGIA WHITE VOL.4 1939-1941
CD DOCD 5304
Document / May '95 / ADA / Hot Shot / Jazz Music

TROUBLE IN MIND 1935-1941
CD 158322
Blues Collection / Apr '95 / Discovery

White Hassle

NATIONAL CHAIN
Let me drive your car / Beating of my heart / What I said / Out of control / Tom the harlequin / Don't make a sound / Oh what a feeling / Oh it's so hard / I'm so lonesome I could cry / Great ship / Adventure / I lose again / Leave my woman alone / Another day passes
CD OLE 2622
Matador / Aug '97 / Vital

White Heaven

OUT
CD PSFD 11
PSF / Sep '95 / Harmonia Mundi

White House

DEDICATED TO PETER KURTEN
CD SLCD 013
Susan Lawly / Nov '96 / Cargo

GREAT WHITE DEATH SPECIAL EDITION
CD SLCD 017
Susan Lawly / Dec '96 / Cargo

NEW BRITAIN
CD SLCD 015
Susan Lawly / Nov '96 / Cargo

QUALITY TIME
CD SLCD 012
Susan Lawly / Nov '96 / Cargo

White, Howard

NASHVILLE SIDEMAN WITH FRIENDS
Jealous heart / Blue eyes cryin' in the rain / Roly poly / Deep water / Rose of ol' Pawnee / San Antonio rose / Faded love / Midnight / Columbus Stockade blues / Before I met you / Steel guitar dowve / Ensonata / Rosette / Steel guitar swallow
CD BCD 15575
Bear Family / Apr '92 / Direct / Rollercoaster / Swift

WESTERN SWING AND STEEL INSTRUMENTALS
Jealous heart / Blue eyes cryin' in the rain / Roly poly / Deep water / Rose of ol' Pawnee / San Antonio rose / Faded love / Midnight / Columbus stockade blues / Before I met you / Steel guitar dove / Ensonata / Rosette / Steel guitar swallow
CD BCD 15575
Bear Family / Apr '93 / Direct / Rollercoaster / Swift

White, James

BUY (White, James & The Contortions)
Design to kill / My infatuation / I don't want to be happy / Anesthetic / Contort yourself / Throw me away / Roving eye / Twice removed / Bedroom athlete / Throw me away (live) / Twice removed (live) / Jailhouse rock
CD 74321327572
Infinite Zero / Mar '96 / BMG

FLAMING DEMONICS
Devil made me do it / Boulevard of broken dreams / Rantin' and ravin' / Natives are restless / Caravan/It don't mean a thing/ Melt yourself down / I danced with a Zombie
CD 74321391762
Infinite Zero / Oct '96 / BMG

OFF WHITE
CD 74321318792
Infinite Zero / Oct '95 / BMG

White, Jeff

WHITE ALBUM, THE
Cold cold heart / Right before my eyes / I never know / Old Plank Road / Cabin among the trees / All prayed up / Leavin' town / Hannah / Little lies / Little Joe / Promises you made / I'm goin' on / When the night is near
CD ROUCD 0385
Rounder / Oct '96 / ADA / CM / Direct

White, Jim

WRONG EYED JESUS
Book of angels / Burn the river dry / Still waters / When Jesus gets a brand new name / Sleepy town / Perfect day to chase tornados / Wordmule / Stabbed in the heart / Angel land / Heaven of my heart / Road that leaves to Heaven
CD 9362464722
Luaka Bop / Jun '97 / Warner Music

White, Joshua

BLUES AND...
How long blues / Careless love / Oh lula / St. Louis blues / Kansas city blues / I had to stoop to conquer you / I know how to do it / Dink's blues / One mint julep / Good morning blues
CD HILLCD 16
Wooded Hill / Apr '97 / Direct / World Serpent

JOSH WHITE VOL.1 - 1929-1933
CD DOCD 5194
Document / Oct '93 / ADA / Hot Shot / Jazz Music

JOSH WHITE VOL.2 - 1933-1935
CD DOCD 5195
Document / Oct '93 / ADA / Hot Shot / Jazz Music

JOSH WHITE VOL.3 - 1935-1940
CD DOCD 5196
Document / Oct '93 / ADA / Hot Shot / Jazz Music

LEGENDARY JOSH WHITE, THE
CD CBCD 3
Collector's Blues / Apr '96 / TKO Magnum

SOUTHERN EXPOSURE
John Henry / One meatball / Southern exposure / Did you ever love a woman / Billy boy / Beloved comrade / No more blues / Frankie and Johnny / Milkcow blues / Hard time blues / Lord Randall, my son / Jelly jelly / Watercress / Evil hearted man / Mean mistreatin' woman / Miss Otis regrets / Baby baby / Dupree / Left a good deal in mobile / Lass with the delicate air / Backwater blues / House I live in / Strange fruit / Jim Crow train / Outskirts of town
CD PASTCD 7810
Flapper / Jan '97 / Pinnacle

White Kaps

CANNONBALL
CD HR 604CD
Hopeless / Nov '95 / Plastic Head

White, Karyn

KARYN WHITE
Way you love me / Secret rendezvous / Slow down / Superwoman / Family man / Love saw it / Don't mess with me / Tell me tomorrow / One wish
CD K 9256372
WEA / Mar '94 / Warner Music

MAKE HIM DO RIGHT
Hungah / Nobody but my baby / I'm your woman / Weakness / One minute / Simple / Pleasure / I'd rather be alone / Thinkin' bout love / Make him do right / Can I stay / With you / Here comes the pain again
CD 9362454002
WEA / Sep '94 / Warner Music

RITUAL OF LOVE
Romantic / Ritual of love / Way I feel about you / Hooked on you / Walking the dog / Love that's mine / How I want you / One heart / Tears of joy / Beside you / Do unto me / Hard to say goodbye
CD 7599263202
WEA / Sep '91 / Warner Music

White Knight

WHITE KNIGHT
Twilite / Energy / Techno disco / Alarm / Gonna jack '96 / White Knight '96 / Hard drive / New world order
CD TRXUKCD 003
Trax UK / Sep '96 / Mo's Music Machine / Pinnacle / Prime

White, Lari

BEST OF LARI WHITE, THE
Amazing Grace / Itty bitty little single solitary piece of my heart / Lay around and love on you / Lead me not / What a woman wants / Wild at heart / Just thinking / That's my baby / That's how you know (when you're in love) / Now I know / Ready, willing and able / I've been waiting for your love / Helping me get over you: *White, Lari & Travis Tritt*

CD 7863669942
RCA Nashville / Jan '97 / BMG

DON'T FENCE ME IN
CD 74321339142
Camden / Jun '96 / BMG

WISHES
That's my baby / Somebody's fool / Wishes / Now I know / If I'm not already crazy / That's how you don't know / When it rains / Go on / It's love / If you only knew
CD 7863663952
RCA / Apr '95 / BMG

White, Lavelle

MISS LAVELLE
CD ANT 0031CD
Antones / Sep '94 / ADA / Hot Shot

White, Lenny

RENDERERS OF SPIRIT
CD HIBD 8014
Hip Bop / Feb '97 / Koch / Silva Screen

White Lion

BEST OF WHITE LION, THE
Wait / Radar love / Broken heart / Hungry / Little fighter / Lights and thunder / All you need is rock 'n' roll / When the children cry / Love don't come easy / Cry for freedom / Lady of the valley / Tell me / Farewell to you
CD 7567824252
Atlantic / Oct '92 / Warner Music

FIGHT TO SURVIVE
CD CDMFN 130
Music For Nations / Jul '92 / Pinnacle

MANE ATTRACTION
Lights and thunder / Leave me alone / Love don't come easy / You're all I need / Broken heart / Warsong / It's over / Till death do us part / Out with the boys / Farewell to you / She's got everything
CD 7567821932
Atlantic / Apr '91 / Warner Music

PRIDE
Hungry / Lonely nights / Don't give up / Sweet little loving / Lady of the valley / Wait / All you need is rock 'n' roll / Tell me / All join our hands / When the children cry
CD 7817682
Atlantic / Jul '87 / Warner Music

White, Lily

NO PORK LONG LINE
CD JFCD 017
Jazz Focus / May '97 / Cadillac

SOMEWHERE BETWEEN TRUTH AND FICTION
CD KFWCD 153
Knitting Factory / Feb '95 / Cargo / Plastic Head

White, Michael

EIGHTIES, THE (White, Michael & His New Orleans Music)
CD 504CDS 6
504 / Jun '96 / Cadillac / Jazz Music / Target/BMG / Wellard

MOTION PICTURES (White, Michael & Bill Frisell)
You are too beautiful / Easy living / Night has a thousand eyes / Flamingo / My shining hour / Misterioso / My one and only love
CD INT 32122
Intuition / Aug '97 / New Note/Pinnacle

White Moon

TRADITIONAL MUSIC FROM MONGOLIA
CD PANCD 2010
Pan / May '93 / ADA / CM / Direct

White Noise

ELECTRIC STORM, AN
Love without sound / My game of loving / Here comes the fleas / Firebird / Your hidden dreams / Visitation / Black mass / Electric storm in hell
CD 3DCID1001
Island / '94 / PolyGram

White Orange

WHITE ORANGE
CD 1215
Caprice / Dec '91 / ADA / Cadillac / CM / Complete/Pinnacle

White, Peter

CARAVAN OF DREAMS
Caravan of dreams: *White, Peter & Boney James* / Together again: *White, Peter & Boney James* / Venice beach / Soul embrace / Long ride home: *White, Peter & Rick Braun* / Just another day: *White, Peter & Basia* / City of lights / Cafe mystique: *White, Peter & Marc Antoine* / Bittersweet / Lullaby
CD 4851362
Sony Jazz / Aug '96 / Sony

White Plains

MY BABY LOVES LOVIN'
I've got you on my mind / When tomorrow comes tomorrow / Taffeta rose / Taffeta rose (I remember) / (I remember) Summer morning / Ecstasy / Julie Anne / Does anybody know where my baby is / Step into a dream / Dad you saved the world / I can't stop / Carolina's coming home / Gonna miss her missisippi / When you are a king / Every little move she makes / Julie do ya love me / Lovin' you baby / Honey girl / Young birds fly / Show me your hand / You've got your troubles / Today I killed a man I didn't know / My baby loves lovin' / In a moment of madness / To love you
CD 8206222
London / May '93 / PolyGram

White, Roland

TRYING TO GET TO YOU
CD SHCD 3826
Sugar Hill / May '95 / ADA / CM / Direct / Koch / Roots

White, Saylor

THAT'S JUST THE WAY IT GOES
CD 422491
New Rose / Nov '94 / ADA / Direct / Discovery

White, Sheila G.

LOVE SONG, A
CD SOW 503
Sound Waves / Jun '93 / Target/BMG

White Sister

FASHION BY PASSION
Place in the heart / Fashion by passion / Dancin' on midnight / Save me tonight / Ticket to ride / April / Until it hurts / Troubleshooters / Lonely teardrops / Place in my heart
CD WKFMXD 76
FM / Mar '87 / Revolver / Sony

White, Snowy

BEST OF SNOWY WHITE'S BLUES AGENCY, THE (White, Snowy Blues Agency)
CD SPOOKCD 004
Fantom / Sep '96 / Grapevine/PolyGram / Koch / Scratch/BMG

CHANGE MY LIFE
CD RDCD 1203
Rio Digital / Feb '91 / Grapevine/PolyGram

GOLDTOP (The Definitive Collection)
Carol / Modern times / Pigs on the wing: *Pink Floyd* / Drop in from the top: *Wright, Richard* / Renegade: *Thin Lizzy* / Memory pain / Slaybo day / In the skies: *Green, Peter* / Answer / Bird of paradise / Tailfeathers / Someone else is gonna love me / That certain thing / Out of order / Open for business / Highway to the sun / Time has come / Judgement day
CD RPM 154
RPM / Nov '95 / Pinnacle

HIGHWAY TO THE SUN
Highway to the sun / Can't find love / Burning love / Loving man / Time has come / Heartful of love / Love, pain, and sorrow / Hot Saturday night / Keep on working / I loved another woman / I can't get enough of the blues
CD 29007205
Bellaphon / Sep '95 / New Note/Pinnacle
CD CDMANU 1493
ODE / Feb '97 / CM / Discovery

NO FAITH REQUIRED (White, Snowy & The White Flames)
No faith required / Miracle I need / In the name of the Lord / Midnight blues / Slave labour / Blues like a fever / Canyon / American dream
CD CSA 107
Thunderbird / Oct '96 / Pinnacle

White Stains

WHY NOT FOREVER
CD EFA 112302
Danse Macabre / Feb '94 / SRD

White, Tam

KEEP IT UNDER YOUR HAT (White, Tam Band)
More / Dream / Coupe de Ville / Mad Sam / Good morning heartache / Street people / Stone mason's blues / Sleep-late Louie's / Woman in love / Nature of the beast / 36th Street mission blues
CD JHCD 018
Ronnie Scott's Jazz House / Jan '94 / Cadillac / Jazz Music / New Note/Pinnacle / TKO Magnum

White Town

SOCIALISM, SEXISM AND SEXUALITY
CD PARCD 004
Parasol / Nov '96 / Cargo

WOMEN IN TECHNOLOGY
Undressed / Thursday night at the Blue Note / Week next June / Your woman / White town / Shape of love / Wanted / Function of the orgasm / Going nowhere somehow / Theme for an early evening sitcom / Death of my desire / Once I flew
CD CDCHR 6120
Chrysalis / Feb '97 / EMI

White, Tony Joe

BEST OF TONY JOE WHITE, THE
Polk salad Annie / Willie and Laura Mae Jones / Soul Francisco / Don't steal my love / Roosevelt and Ira Lee / For Lee Ann / Elements and things / Rainy night in Georgia / High sheriff of Calhoun Parrish / Widow Wimberly / Stud spider / Old man Willis / Save your sugar for me / Polka salad Annie
CD 9362453052
Warner Bros. / Sep '93 / Warner Music

BEST OF TONY JOE WHITE, THE (2CD Set)
Roosevelt and Ira Lee / Stockholm blues / High sheriff of Calhoun Parrish / Old man Willis / Train I'm on / If I ever saw a good thing / As the crow flies / Even trolls love to rock and roll / Backwood preacher man / Takin' the midnight train / Did somebody make a fool out of you / Caught the Devil and put him in jail in Eudor, Arkansas / Saturday night in Oak Grove , Louisiana / I've got a thing about you baby / For ol' time sake / Ol' Mother earth
CD Set MPG 74177
Movieplay Gold / Nov '94 / Target/BMG

CLOSER TO THE TRUTH
CD 5113862
Polydor / Mar '96 / PolyGram

COLLECTION, THE
CD D 31737
Festival / Jun '97 / Greyhound

GROUPIE GIRL
CD MPG 74023
Movieplay Gold / Nov '93 / Target/BMG

LIVE
CD DFG 8407
Dixie Frog / Sep '90 / Direct / TKO Magnum

POLKA SALAD ANNIE
CD MPG 74021
Movieplay Gold / Nov '93 / Target/BMG

RAINY NIGHT IN GEORGIA
Rainy night in Georgia / Willie and Laura Mae Jones / Polk salad Annie / Groupie girl / Don't steal my love / Scratch my back / Roosevelt and Ira Lee (night of the Missacin) / I thought I knew you well / Elements and things / I want you / Save your sugar for me / Stud-spider / High Sherriff of Calhoun Parrish / Stockholm blues
CD APH 102803
Audiophile Legends / Apr '96 / Total/BMG

ROOSEVELT AND IRA LEE
CD MPG 74022
Movieplay Gold / Nov '93 / Target/BMG

White Zombie

ASTRO CREEP
Electric head pt.1 (The agony) / Supercharger heaven / Real solution # 9 / Creature of the wheel / Electric head pt.2 (The ecstasy) / Grease paint and monkey brains / I zombie / More human than human / El phantasmo and the chicken run blast-o-rama / Blur the technicolor / Blood milk and sky
CD GED 24806
Geffen / May '95 / BMG

LA SEXORCISTO DEVIL MUSIC VOL.1
Welcome to planet motherfucker/Psychoholic slag / Knuckle duster (Radio 1-A) / Thunder kiss / Black sunshine / Soul crusher / Cosmic monsters inc / Spiderbaby (yeah yeah yeah) / I am legend / Knuckle duster (Radio 2-B) / Thrust / One big crunch / Grindhouse (A go-go) / Starface / Warp asylum
CD GEFD 24460
Geffen / Mar '92 / BMG

SUPER SEXY SWINGIN'
Electric head pt.2 / More human than human / I, Zombie / Grease paint and monkey brains / Blur the technicolour / Supercharger / Heaven / El phantasmo and the chicken-run blasto-rama / Blood, milk and sky / Real solution / Electric head pt.1 / I'm your boogie man
CD GED 24976
Geffen / Aug '96 / BMG

Whitehead Brothers

SERIOUS
Forget I was a G / Your love is a 187 / Shaniqua / Change / Interlude / Late nite tip / Just a touch of love / Where ya at / Serious / Beautiful black princess / Sex on the beach / Turn U out / She needed me / Love goes on / Beautiful black princess (reprise)
CD 5303462
Motown / Jan '95 / PolyGram

Whitehead, Tim

AUTHENTIC
Falling grace / No more war / All I ever wanted / Neighbourly complaint / Aspiration / One view of Annet / Come on home / Gypsy
CD JHCD 017
Ronnie Scott's Jazz House / Jan '94 / Cadillac / Jazz Music / New Note/Pinnacle / TKO Magnum

SILENCE BETWEEN WAVES
Southend / Sky seas / Return / Third exposure / One view of Annet / Secret talks / Warners well / True to your word / 34 Cambrian road / These tears / Come on home
CD JHCD 033
Ronnie Scott's Jazz House / Nov '94 / Cadillac / Jazz Music / New Note/Pinnacle / TKO Magnum

Whitehorn, Geoff

BIG IN GRAVESEND
CD CMMR 941
Music Maker / Nov '94 / ADA / Grapevine/ PolyGram

GEOFF WHO
CD CMMR 902
Music Maker / Jun '92 / ADA / Grapevine/ PolyGram

Whiteleather, John

GO RAT GO (Whiteleather, John & The King Rats)
CD PT 601001
Part / Jul '96 / Nervous

HARD LUCK PLAN (Whiteleather, John & The King Rats)
CD PT 601003
Part / Jun '96 / Nervous

TEQUILA HANGOVER (Whiteleather, John & The King Rats)
CD PT 601002
Part / Jun '96 / Nervous

Whiteman, Paul

16 CLASSIC PERFORMANCES
Whispering / Wang wang blues / Rhapsody in blue / Washboard blues / When the day is done / Way down yonder in New Orleans / Muddy water / China boy / It's only a paper moon / Among my souvenirs / Man I love / Sugar / Mississippi mud / I'm coming, Virginia / Deep purple / Star dust
CD CWNCD 2030
Crown / Jul '96 / Henry Hadaway

BIRTH OF RHAPSODY IN BLUE, THE (Historic 1924 Aeolian Hall Concert)
CD MM 65144
Music Masters / Apr '96 / Nimbus

GREAT COMBINATION, A
This can't be love / Simple and sweet / Mexican jumpin' bean / My melancholy baby / Cuckoo in the clock / Sing for your supper / Kiss your hand Madam
CD DAWE 45
Magic / Sep '93 / Cadillac / Harmonia Mundi / Jazz Music / Swift / Wellard

JAZZ PORTRAITS
You took advantage of me / Mississippi mud / I'm coming Virginia / Whispering / Side by side / Milenberg joys / St. Louis blues / Whiteman stomp / Changes / Five step / Sensation stomp / Magnolia / Wang wang blues / Everybody step / Hot lips / Red hot Henry Brown / Charlestonette / Bell hoppin' blues
CD CD 14521
Jazz Portraits / May '94 / Jazz Music

KING OF JAZZ, THE (His Greatest Recordings 1920-1936)
Rhapsody in blue: *Whiteman, Paul & George Gershwin* / Changes / Charleston / Darktown strutters ball / Happy feet / Louisiana / Makin' whoopee / Medley / Ol' man river / Slaughter on 10th Avenue / When it's sleepy time down South / Song of India / Three o'clock in the morning / Wang wang blues / Whispering / Whiteman stomp / You took advantage of me
CD CDAJA 5170
Living Era / Mar '96 / Select

PAUL WHITEMAN AND HIS ORCHESTRA 1921-1934 (Whiteman, Paul & His Orchestra)
Southern Rose / Merry widow waltz / I'm a dreamer / Nola / Deep purple / Caprice futuristic / South Sea isles / Suite of serenades / It all depends on you / Parade of the tin soldiers / Liebestraum / Park Avenue fantasy / When you're in love / Night with Paul Whiteman at The Biltmore / Signature tune
CD PASTCD 9718
Flapper / '90 / Pinnacle

Whiteout

BITE IT
CD ORECD 536
Silvertone / Jun '95 / Pinnacle

Whiteouts

WHITEOUTS
CD _____ E 119192
Vince Lombard / Dec '93 / SRD

Whiteside, Taylor

NEW ENGLAND FAVOURITES
CD _____ FE 1406
Folk Era / Nov '94 / ADA / CM

Whitesnake

1987
Still of the night / Bad boys / Give me all your love / Looking for love / Crying in the rain / Is this love / Straight for the heart / Don't turn away / Children of the night / Here I go again / You're gonna break my heart again
CD _____ CDEMS 1531
EMI / Jul '94 / EMI

COME AN' GET IT
Come an' get it / Hot stuff / Don't break my heart again / Lonely days, lonely nights / Wine, women and song / Child of Babylon / Would I lie to you / Girl / Hit and run / Till the day I die
CD _____ CDEMS 1528
EMI / Jul '94 / EMI

FORKED TONGUE - THE INTERVIEW
CD _____ CBAK 4064
Baktabak / Feb '94 / Arabesque

GREATEST HITS
Still of the night / Here I go again / Is this love / Love ain't no stranger / Looking for love / Now you're gone / Slide it in / Slow an' easy / Judgement day / You're gonna break my heart again / Deeper the love / Crying in the rain / Fool for your loving / Sweet lady luck
CD _____ CDEMD 1065
EMI / Jun '94 / EMI

LIVE IN THE HEART OF THE CITY
Come on / Sweet talker / Walking in the shadow of the blues / Love hunter / Fool for your loving / Ain't gonna cry no more / Ready an' willing / Take me with you / Might just take your life / Lie down / Ain't no love in the heart of the city / Trouble / Mistreated
CD _____ CDEMS 1525
EMI / Jul '94 / EMI

LOVEHUNTER
Long way from home / Walking in the shadow of the blues / Help me thro' the day / Medicine man / You 'n' me / Mean business / Love hunter / Outlaw / Rock 'n' roll women / We wish you well
CD _____ CDEMS 1529
EMI / Jul '94 / EMI

READY AN' WILLING
Fool for your loving / Sweet talker / Ready an' willing / Carry your load / Blindman / Ain't gonna cry no more / Love man / Black and blue / She's a woman
CD _____ CDEMS 1526
EMI / Jul '94 / EMI

RESTLESS HEART (Coverdale, David & Whitesnake)
Don't fade away / All in the name of love / Restless heart / Too many tears / Crying / Stay with me / Can't go on / You're so fine / Your precious love / Take me back again / Woman trouble blues
CD _____ CDEMD 1104
EMI / Jun '97 / EMI

SAINTS 'N' SINNERS
Young blood / Rough and ready / Bloody luxury / Victim of love / Crying in the rain / Here I go again / Love and affection / Rock 'n' roll angels / Dancing girls / Saints and sinners
CD _____ CDEMS 1521
EMI / Jul '94 / EMI

SLIDE IT IN
Gambler / Slide it in / Standing in the shadow / Give me more time / Love ain't no stranger / Slow an' easy / Spit it out / All or nothing / Hungry for love / Guilty of love / Need your love so bad
CD _____ CZ 88
EMI / Apr '88 / EMI

SLIDE IT IN/1987/SLIP OF THE TONGUE (The Originals/3CD Set)
Gambler / Slide it in / Standing in the shadow / Give me more time / Love ain't no stranger / Slow an' easy / Spit it out / All or nothing / Hungry for love / Guilty of love / Still of the night / Bad boys / Give me all your love / Looking for love / Crying in the rain / Is this love / Straight for the heart / Don't turn away / Children of the night / Slip of the tongue / Cheap and nasty / Fool for your loving / Now you're gone / Kitten's got claws / Wings of the storm / Deeper the love / Judgement day / Slow poke music / Sailing ships
CD Set _____ CDOMB 016
EMI / Mar '97 / EMI

SLIP OF THE TONGUE
Slip of the tongue / Cheap an' nasty / Fool for your loving / Now you're gone / Kitten's got claws / Wings of the storm / Deeper the love / Judgement day / Slow poke music / Sailing ships
CD _____ CDEMS 1527
EMI / Jul '94 / EMI

TROUBLE
Take me with you / Love to keep you warm / Lie down / Day tripper / Nighthawk (vampire blues) / Time is right for love / Trouble / Belgian Tom's hat trick / Free flight / Don't mess with me
CD _____ CDFA 3234
Fame / May '90 / EMI

Whitfield, Barrence

BARRANCE WHITFIELD & THE SAVAGES (Whitfield, Barrence & The Savages)
CD _____ 422393FC058
Fan Club / Jan '95 / Direct

HILLBILLY VOO DOO
CD _____ RTMCD 55
Round Tower / Sep '93 / Avid/BMG

LET'S LOSE IT
CD _____ 422391
New Rose / May '94 / ADA / Direct / Discovery

LIVE EMULSIFIED (Whitfield, Barrence & The Savages)
CD _____ 422392
New Rose / Jan '95 / ADA / Direct / Discovery

OW OW OW (Whitfield, Barrence & The Savages)
CD _____ ROUCD 9011
Rounder / '88 / ADA / CM / Direct

RITUAL OF THE SAVAGES
CD _____ FIENDCD 760
Demon / Oct '94 / Pinnacle

SAVAGE TRACKS (Whitfield, Barrence & The Savages)
CD _____ 422402
New Rose / May '94 / ADA / Direct / Discovery

Whitfield, David

FROM DAVID WITH LOVE
CD _____ 8209482
Deram / Jan '96 / PolyGram

GREATEST HITS
Cara mia / Santo natale / Book / Mama / Everywhere / Rags to riches / When you lose the one you love / My son John / Bridge of sighs / My September love / Answer me / Beyond the stars / Adoration waltz / On the Street where you live / Willingly / I'll find you / Right to love / Cry my heart / My unfinished symphony / I believe
CD _____ 8206432
Eclipse / Nov '90 / PolyGram

WORLD OF DAVID WHITFIELD, THE
I believe / Cara mia / My September love / Answer me / If ever I would leave you / Smile / Book / Trees / Who can I turn to (when nobody needs me) / Adoration waltz / Rags to riches / Ev'rywhere / You are too beautiful / I'll never stop loving you / Rose Marie / Marta / When you lose the one you love / Stranger in paradise / Rudder and the rock / Santo natale
CD _____ 5514052
Spectrum / May '96 / PolyGram

Whitfield, Mark

FOREVER LOVE
CD _____ 5339212
Verve / Mar '97 / PolyGram

Whitfield, Norman

I HEARD IT THROUGH THE GRAPEVINE (The Motor City Stars Sing The Songs Of Norman Whitfield) (Various Artists)
Needle in a haystack: *Velvelettes* / Just my imagination: *Cameron, G.C.* / Too busy thinking about my baby: *Cameron, G.C.* / It should have been me: *Weston, Kim* / Runaway child running wild: *Cameron, G.C.* / Smiling faces sometimes: *Vee* / I can't get next to you: *Satintones* / He was really saying something: *Velvelettes* / Lonely lonely girl am I: *Velvelettes* / Ain't too proud to beg: *Wylie, Richard 'Popcorn'* / You got the love I need: *Calvin, Billie* / I heard it through the grapevine: *Gaye, Frankie* / Law of the land: *Undisputed Truth* / Too many fish in the sea: *Marvelettes*
CD _____ 305762
Hallmark / Oct '96 / Carlton

Whitfield, Weslia

LUCKY TO BE ME
Lucky to be me / Something to remember you by / Do I love you / Glad to be unhappy / Moments like this / My buddy / This funny world / He was too good to me / By myself / Be careful it's my heart / For all we know / Face like yours / Rhode Island is famous for you / Don't you know I care (or don't you care to) / Two for the road
CD _____ LCD 15242
Landmark / Aug '90 / New Note/Pinnacle

TEACH ME TONIGHT
It's a most unusual day / I've heard that song before / Almost like being in love / Teach me tonight / Pick yourself up / Don't worry about me / I fall in love too easily / I double dare you / It ain't necessarily so / When you wish upon a star / I wish I were in love again / All my tomorrows / Just in time / Until the real thing comes along / I should care
CD _____ HCD 7009
High Note / Jun '97 / New Note/Pinnacle

Whiting, Margaret

GREAT LADIES OF SONG, THE
Day in, day out / But not for me / Gypsy in my soul / Like someone in love / He's funny that way / Time after time / My heart stood still / Nobody but you / I hadn't anyone till you / I've never been in love before / But beautiful / My foolish heart / I get a kick out of you / Let's fall in love / Someone to watch over me / I could write a book / Back in your own backyard
CD _____ CDP 8303952
Capitol Jazz / Aug '95 / EMI

LADY'S IN LOVE WITH YOU, THE
CD _____ ACD 207
Audiophile / Feb '91 / Jazz Music

MARGARET WHITING
CD _____ ACD 173
Audiophile / Aug '94 / Jazz Music

THEN AND NOW
I fought every step of the way / Moonlight in Vermont / That old black magic / It might as well be Spring / Lies of handsome men / Coffee shoppe / Hell of a way to run a love affair / I got lost in his arms / Best thing for you / Our little day / Blame it on my youth / Young and foolish / Can't teach my old heart new tricks / My best friend / What is a man / Bewitched, bothered and bewildered / Old devil moon / Now that I have everything
CD _____ DRGCD 91403
DRG / Mar '92 / Discovery / New Note/ Pinnacle

TOO MARVELLOUS FOR WORDS
CD _____ ACD 152
Audiophile / Jun '95 / Jazz Music

Whitley, Keith

ESSENTIAL KEITH WHITLEY, THE
Turn me to love / Living like there's no tomorrow (finally got to me tonight) / Hard act to follow / If a broken heart could kill / If you think I'm crazy now (you should have seen me when I w / Don't our love look natural / I wonder where you are tonight / I've got the heart for you / Ten feet away / Miami my Amy / Hard livin' / Homecoming / Don't close your eyes / I'm no stranger to the rain / Would these arms be in your way / When you ssay nothing at all / It ain't nothin' / I'm over you / I wonder do you think of me / I'm losing you all over again
CD _____ 07863668532
RCA Nashville / Aug '96 / BMG

Whitman, Slim

COUNTRY CLASSICS
Rose Marie / Indian love call / Let me call you baby / Somewhere my love / My elusive dreams / When you were sweet sixteen / Love song of the waterfall / I'll take you home again Kathleen / Have I told you lately that I love you / Happy anniversary / Beautiful dreamer / When you wore a tulip and I wore a big red rose / Serenade / Roses are red (my love) / Girl of my dreams / Edelweiss / Oh my darlin'(I love you) / Twelfth of never / Can't help falling in love / You are my sunshine
CD _____ CDMFP 6319
Music For Pleasure / Apr '97 / EMI

COUNTRY STYLE
Rhinestone cowboy / Red river valley / Tumbling tumbleweeds / Kentucky waltz / Home on the range / I can't stop loving you / Cattle call / Rose Marie / Riders in the sky / From a jack to a king / Broken wings / Paper roses / It keeps right on a-hurtin' / Wayward wind / Top of the world / Cool water
CD _____ CDMFP 6035
Music For Pleasure / Nov '88 / EMI

LOVE SONGS
Rose Marie / Indian love call / Let me call you sweetheart / Somewhere my love / My elusive dreams / When you were sweet sixteen / Love song of the waterfall / I'll take you home again Kathleen / HAve I told you lately that I love you / Happy Anniversary / Beautiful dreamer / When you wore a tulip / Serenade / Roses are red / Girl of my dreams / Edelweiss / Oh my darlin' (I love you) / Twelfth of never / Can't help falling in love / You are my sunshine
CD _____ CDMFP 6113
Music For Pleasure / Mar '94 / EMI

MAGIC MOMENTS (Whitman, Slim & Byron)
I'll get by: *Whitman, Slim* / Back home again / Rose of cimarron: *Whitman, Byron* / Wabash waltz / If ever I see you again: *Whitman, Byron* / If you love me let me know / River road: *Whitman, Byron* / Before the next teardrop falls / What a fool I was: *Whitman, Slim* / Cowboy heaven / I wish I was eighteen again / Blue eyes crying in the rain
CD _____ ANT 002
Tring / Nov '96 / Tring

ROSE MARIE (1949-1959/6CD Set)
I'll do as much for you someday / I'll never pass this way again / Paint a rose on the garden wall / Tears can never drown the flame / I'm casting my lasso towards the sky / Wabash waltz / I'm crying for you / Birmingham Jail / Let's go to church / There's a rainbow in every teardrop / Love song of the waterfall / My love is growing stale / Bandera waltz / End of the world / In a hundred years or more / Why / Cold empty arms / Blue river / Indian love call / China doll / Amateur in love / Song of the old water wall / By the waters of Minnetonka / Keep it a secret / My heart is broken in three / All that I'm asking is sympathy / How can I tell / There's a rainbow in every teardrop / I'm casting my lasso towards the sky / Restless heart / There's a rainbow in every teardrop / Danny Boy / North wind / Darlin' don't cry / Stairway to heaven / Lord help me be as thou / Warm, warm lips / Ride away / Secret love / Why / We stood at the altar / There's a loveknot in my lariat / Too late now / I love the Milky Way / Rose Marie / Heart full of love / Cattle call / Beautiful dreamer / Singing hills / Haunted hungry heart / I hate to see you cry / You have my heart / When I grow too old to dream / Song of the wild / I talk to the waves / Blue eyes crying in the rain / When my blue moon turns to gold again / That silver haired Daddy of mine / Petal from a faded rose / I'll never take you back again / Lord protect my darling / Cryin' for the moon / Roll on silvery moon / Haunted hungry heart / I talk to the waves / At the end of nowhere / I'll never stop loving you / Song of the wild / Tumbling tumbleweeds / Tell me / I'll take you home again Kathleen / Serenade / First one to find the rainbow / Brahms lullaby / In the valley of the moon / Dear Mary / I'll take you home again Kathleen / Dear Mary / Cryin' for the moon / Whiffenpoof song / Curtain of tears / Smoke signals / Among my souvenirs / Tree in the meadow / At the close of a long, long day / I must have been blind / You're the only one / Riding the range for Jesus / Roundup in glory / At the end of nowhere / Careless love / Hawaiian cowboy / Warm, warm lips / I'll take you home again Kathleen / Since you've gone / Amateur in love / Lovesick blues / Many times / Forever / Unchain my heart / Once in a lifetime / Tormented / Candy kisses / Hush-a-bye / Careless hands / Very precious love / Put your trust in me / When it's springtime in the Rockies / At the end of nowhere / Mexicali rose / My best to you / Cowpoke / Wherever you are / I'll sail my ship alone / River of tears / Blues stay away from me / Fool such as I / Letter edged in black / Too tired to care / Prisoner's song / Tree in the meadow / Heartbreak hill / I'll never see Maggie alone / When I call on you / You're the only one / Blues stay away from me / I'll sail my ship alone / What kind of God (do you think you are) / Tree in the meadow / I'll walk with god / Whispering hope / I'm a pilgrim / An evening prayer / Jesus took my burden / Two loves have I / Sunrise / Walk beside me / Each step I take / Great Judgement morning / He lives on high / Today is mine / When I go to my garden / Twilia Lee / Roll river roll / Rose Marie / Indian love call / Amateur in love / Song of the old water wheel / All that I'm asking is sympathy / How can I tell / Danny Boy / Warm, warm lips / Ride away / Rose Marie / Haunted hungry heart / At the close of a long, long day / Unchain my heart / Tormented / Candy kisses / Hush-a-bye
CD Set _____ BCD 15768
Bear Family / May '96 / Direct / Rollercoaster / Swift

SLIM WHITMAN VOL.1 (2CD Set)
I'm casting my lasso towards the sky / Indian love call / Love song of the waterfall / Rose Marie / I leave the Milky Way / Tumbling tumbleweeds / Danny boy / You have my heart / I must have been blind / Lord help me be as thou / China doll / When it's springtime in the Rockies / Love knot in my lariat / Riding the range for Jesus / Poor little Angeline / Cryin' for the moon / Serenade / Many times / I'll take you home again Kathleen / First one to find the rainbow / Secret love / Stairway to heaven / I'm a fool / Heartbreak hill / Too late now / My wild Irish rose / You're the only one / Just call me lonesome / Annie Laurie / Bells that broke my heart / Sweeter than the flowers / Happy Street / Eileen / When I grow too old to dream / Tomorrow never comes / I wanna go to heaven / Blue Canadian Rockies / Yesterday's roses / I climbed the mountain / I'll see you when / Stranger on the shore / What's this world a-comin' to / Rockin' alone in an old rocking chair / Little drops of silver / Another tomorrow / Twelfth of never / It's a small world / Mr. Ting-a-Ling / It's a sin to tell a lie / As you take a walk through my mind / Happy Anniversary
CD Set _____ CDEM 1482
EMI / Mar '93 / EMI

UNDER HIS WINGS
CD _____ CDC 5383
Disky / May '94 / Disky / THE

Whitney, Dave

CREATIVE HORN OF DAVE WHITNEY, THE
CD JCD 68
Jazzology / Jun '96 / Jazz Music

Whitstein Brothers

OLD TIME DUETS
Mansion on the hill / We parted by the riverside / There's an open door waiting / Sinner you'd better get ready / We met in the saddle / I'm troubled / That silver haired daddy / Seven year blues / Weary lonesome blues / Somewhere in Tennessee / Maple on the hill / If I could hear my mother pray again / Pitfall / Beautiful lost river valley
CD ROUCD 0264
Rounder / '89 / ADA / CM / Direct

ROSE OF MY HEART
Rose of my heart / Highway headin' South / Kentucky / My curly headed baby / Weary days / Weary blues from waiting / Arkansas / Bridge over troubled water / Eighth wonder of the world / Scared of the blues / Where the old river flows / Smoky mountain memories
CD ROUCD 0206
Rounder / Oct '94 / ADA / CM / Direct

SWEET HARMONY
CD ROUCD 0344
Rounder / Mar '96 / ADA / CM / Direct

WHITSTEIN BROTHERS SING GOSPEL SONGS OF THE LOUVINS
CD ROUCD 0308
Rounder / Nov '94 / ADA / CM / Direct

Whittaker, Roger

BEST OF ROGER WHITTAKER, THE
CD MATCD 326
Castle / Feb '95 / BMG

COLLECTION, THE
CD MACCD 186
Autograph / Aug '96 / BMG

DANNY BOY...& OTHER IRISH FAVOURITES
When Irish eyes are smiling / Down by the Sally gardens / Forty shades of green / Rose of Tralee / Giant land / Star of the county down / Irish whistler / Unicorn / Minstrel boy / I'll tell me Ma / Rooney / Rising of the lark / Believe me, if all those endearing young charms / Uncle Benny / Danny boy / Kilgarry mountain
CD 09026619722
RCA / Feb '97 / BMG

EIN GLUCK, DAS ES DICH GIBT
CD INT 861 552
Interchord / '88 / CM

EVENING WITH ROGER WHITTAKER, AN
CD PLATCD 3929
Platinum / May '94 / Prism

EVENING WITH ROGER WHITTAKER, AN
Last farewell / Hello good morning happy day / If I were a rich man / Elizabethan serenade / Changelip (African whistler) / All of my life / From the people / Durham town / Mexican whistler / New world in the morning / Mammy blue / Hold on / What love is / First hello last goodbye / Hound dog / Summer in the country / Summer days / Fire and rain / Both sides now / Streets of London / River lady / Sloop John B
CD EMPRCD 522
Emporio / Sep '94 / Disc

FEELINGS
Feelings / Time in a bottle / Harbour lights / For I loved you / Love me tender / Leavin' on a jet plane / Everytime is gonna be the last time / Send in the clowns / Honey / Gentle on my mind / Unchained melody / When I need you / Miss you nights / Before she breaks my heart / Have I told you lately that I love you
CD 74321183302
RCA / Jun '94 / BMG

GREATEST HITS LIVE
Last farewell / Mexican whistler / Mammy blue / Both sides now / Streets of London / Hello good morning happy day / If I were a rich man / Elizabethan serenade / All of my life / From the people to the people / River lady / Sloop John B / New world in the morning / Hold on / What love is / First hello, last goodbye / Summer in the country / Summer days / Fire and rain
CD 100232
CMC / May '97 / BMG

HIS FINEST COLLECTION
Durham Town / Streets of London / Leaving on a jet plane / New world in the morning / Harbour lights / I don't believe in if anymore / Stranger on the shore / Feelings / Last farewell / Skye boat song: *Whittaker, Roger & Des O'Connor* / Annie's song / Gentle on my mind / Make the world go away / You were always on my mind / Twelfth of never / For the good times / Shenandoah / Amazing grace
CD 74321134632
RCA / Apr '93 / BMG

I DON'T BELIEVE IN IF ANYMORE
CD RMB 75077
Remember / Sep '94 / Total/BMG

I WILL ALWAYS LOVE YOU
A whole new world / Everything I do, I do for you / When I fall in love / Somewhere my love / Beauty and the beast / Evergreen / Wind beneath my wings / Unchained melody / Somewhere out there / High / What a wonderful world / Sunrise, sunset / You've lost that loving feeling / Born free / I will always love you
CD 09026626822
RCA / Feb '97 / BMG

IN CONCERT (2CD Set)
CD Set CPCD 82922
Charly / Jul '97 / Koch

LEGENDS IN MUSIC
CD LECD 061
Wisepack / Jul '94 / Conifer/BMG / THE

LIVE
CD MU 5062
Musketeer / Oct '94 / Disc

LIVE
CD 15089
Laserlight / Aug '91 / Target/BMG

NEW WORLD IN THE MORNING
New world in the morning / Streets of London / Early one morning / Lemon tree / Morning please don't come / Last farewell / From both sides now / Waterboy / Special kind of man / Leaving of Liverpool / Mexican whistler
CD WMCD 5697
Disky / Oct '94 / Disky / THE

NEW WORLD IN THE MORNING
Last farewell / Hello goodmorning happy day / If I were a rich man / Elizabeth serenade / Changelip (African whistler) / All of my life / From the people / Durham town / Mexican whistler / New world in the morning / Mammy blue / Hold on / What love is / First hello, last goodbye / Hound dog / Summer in the country / Summer days / Sloop John B / River lads / Streets of London / Both sides now / Fire and rain
CD 306462
Hallmark / May '97 / Carlton

PERFECT DAY
It's impossible / Smile / Hello young lovers / Raindrops keep falling on my head / There I've said it again / Anytime / Blueberry Hill / Perfect day / Whole new world / Everything I do (I do it for you) / When I fall in love / Beauty and the beast / Somewhere out there / I will always love you / Ol' man river / If ever I should leave you / Summertime / Make believe / Durham town / Last farewell / New world in the morning / I don't believe in if anymore
CD 74321371562
RCA / Apr '96 / BMG

ROGER WHITTAKER
CD HM 017
Harmony / Jun '97 / TKO Magnum

ROGER WHITTAKER
Last farewell / Hello good morning happy day / If I were a rich man / Elizabeth serenade / Changelip (African whistler) / All of my life / From the people / Durham Town / Mexican whistler / New World in the morning / Mammy blue / Hold on / What love is / First hello the last goodbye / Hound dog / Summer in the country / Summer days / Fire and rain / Both sides now / Streets of London / River lady / Sloop John B
CD GFS 066
Going For A Song / Jul '97 / Else / TKO Magnum

ROGER WHITTAKER COLLECTION
New world in the morning / Sunrise, sunset / Imagine both sides now / Love lasts forever / Send in the clowns / Wind beneath my wings / I can see clearly now / She / What a wonderful world / Evergreen / Last farewell
CD 74321339392
Camden / Jan '96 / BMG

ROGER WHITTAKER IN CONCERT (Live From The Tivoli)
New world in the morning / I love you / My land in Kenya / What a wonderful world / Mexican whistler / Wimoweh / I'll tell me ma / Skye boat song / I don't believe in if anymore / Russellin' along / Rocky top / Wilkommen / Cabaret / Oh mein papa / Send in the clowns / If I were a rich man / Thank you love / Make the world go away / Durham Town / Last farewell / Kilgarry mountain
CD PD 74854
RCA / Jan '91 / BMG

ROMANTIC SIDE OF ROGER WHITTAKER
It's your love / One another / Love will / New love / Man without love / I would if I could / See you shine / Tall dark stranger / Goodbye / My world / Don't fight / Before she breaks my heart / Time / Summer days / Pretty bird of love / Let me be your sun / Indian lady / Here we stand / Newport Belle / For I loved you
CD CDMFP 5882
Music For Pleasure / Apr '90 / EMI

SINCERELY YOURS
New world in the morning / Before she breaks my heart / Say my goodbyes to the rain / I can't help it (if I'm still in love with you) / All the way to Richmond / Summer days / Imagine / Love will / My son / Feelings / I would if I could / Man without love / It's your love / Time / Weekend in New England / Pretty bird of love / Let me be your sun / New love / Here we stand / Don't fight / One another / For I loved you / Shoe you shine / What a wonderful world
CD VSOPCD 129
Connoisseur Collection / Nov '88 / Pinnacle

STEEL MAN
Steel man / After the laughter (came tears) / You've got a friend / Impossible dream / Sinner / Charge of the light brigade / Sunrise sunset / Mud puddle / Settle down / Butterfly / Jenny's gone (and I don't care) / Handful of dreams / Acre of wheat / Santa Anna
CD 5501222
Spectrum / Oct '93 / PolyGram

TYPISCH ROGER WHITTAKER
CD INT 861 548
Interchord / '88 / CM

WORLD OF ROGER WHITTAKER, THE
Durham Town / Last farewell / Morning has broken / Mamy blue / Skye boat song / Morning, please don't come / What a wonderful world / He ain't heavy, he's my brother / New world in the morning / I don't believe in if anymore / Streets of London / Mexican whistler / Dirty old town / Taste of honey / Good morning sunshine / By the time I get to Phoenix / From both sides now / Why
CD 5517382
Spectrum / May '96 / PolyGram

Whittaker, Sebastian

ONE FOR BU
CD JR 02032
Justice / Apr '94 / Koch

SEARCHIN' FOR THE TRUTH (Whittaker, Sebastian & The Creators)
CD JR 002022
Justice / Nov '92 / Koch

Whittle, Tommy

WARM GLOW (Whittle, Tommy Quartet)
CD TEEJAY 103
Teejay / Nov '92 / Cadillac / THE

Who

30 YEARS OF MAXIMUM R'N'B (4CD Set)
I'm the face / Here 'tis / Zoot suit / Leaving here / I can't explain / Anyway anyhow anywhere / Daddy rollin' stone / My generation / Kids are alright / Ox / Legal matter / Substitute / I'm a boy / Disguises / Happy Jack / Boris the spider / So sad about us / Quick one / Pictures of Lily / Early morning cold taxi / last time / I can't reach you / Girl's eyes / Bag o' nails / Call me lightning / I can see for miles / Mary Anne with the shaky hand / Armenia city in the sky / Tattoo / Our love was / Rael 1 / Rael 2 / Sunrise / Jaguar / Melancholia / Fortune teller / Magic bus / Little Billy / Dogs / Overture / Acid queen / Underture / Pinball wizard / I'm free / See me, feel me / Heaven and hell / Young man blues / Summertime blues / Shakin' all over / Baba O'Riley / Bargain / Pure and easy / Song is over / Behind blue eyes / Won't get fooled again / Seeker / Bony Moronie / Let's see action / Join together / Replay / Real me / 5.15 / Bell boy / Love reign o'er me / Long live rock / Naked eye / Slip kid / Dreaming from the waist (Live) / Blue, red and grey / Squeeze box / My wife / Who are you / Music must change / Sister disco / Guitar and pen / You better you bet / Eminence front / Twist and shout / I'm a man / Saturday night's alright for fighting
CD Set 5217512
Polydor / Feb '94 / PolyGram

FACE DANCES (Remastered)
You better you bet / Don't let go the coat / Cache cache / Quiet one / Did you steal my money / How can you do it alone / Daily records / You / Another tricky day / I like nightmares / It's in you / Somebody save me / How can you do it alone / Quiet one
CD 5376952
Polydor / May '97 / PolyGram

IT'S HARD (Remastered)
Athena / It's your turn / Cook's country / Dangerous / Eminence front / I've known war / One life's enough / It's hard / One day at a time / Why did I fall for that / Man is a man / Cry if you want / It's hard / Eminence front / Dangerous / Cry if you want
CD 5376962
Polydor / May '97 / PolyGram

KIDS ARE ALRIGHT, THE (Original Soundtrack)
My generation / I can't explain / Happy Jack / I can see for miles / Magic bus / Long live rock / Anyway anyhow anywhere / Young man blue / Baba O'Riley / My wife / Quick one / Tommy can you hear me / Sparks / Pinball wizard / See me, feel me / Join together / Roadrunner / My generation blues / Won't get fooled again
CD 5179472
Polydor / Jun '93 / PolyGram

LIVE AT LEEDS (25th Anniversary Edition)
Heaven and hell / I can't explain / Fortune teller / Tattoo / Young man blues / Substitute / Happy Jack / I'm a boy / Quick one / Amazing journey / Summertime blues / Shakin' all over / My generation / Magic bus / Sparks
CD 5271692
Polydor / Aug '96 / PolyGram

LIVE AT THE ISLE OF WIGHT FESTIVAL 1970
Heaven and Hell / I can't explain / Young man blues / I don't even know myself / Water / Shakin' all over/Spoonful/Twist and shout / Summertime blues / My generation / Magic bus / Overture / It's a boy / Eyesight to the blind (the hawker) / Christmas / Acid queen / Pinball wizard / Do you think it's alright / Fiddle about / Go to the mirror / Miracle cure / I'm free / We're not gonna take it / Tommy can you hear me
CD EDFCD 326
Essential / Oct '96 / BMG

MY GENERATION (The Very Best Of The Who)
I can't explain / Anyway, anyhow, anywhere / My generation / Substitute / I'm a boy / Boris the spider / Happy Jack / Pictures of Lily / I can see for miles / Magic bus / Pinball wizard / Seeker / Baba O'Riley / Won't get fooled again / Let's see action / 5:15 / Join together / Squeeze box / Who are you / You better you bet
CD 5331502
Polydor / Aug '96 / PolyGram

ODDS AND SODS
Postcard / Now I'm a farmer / Put the money down / Little Billy / Too much of anything / Glow girl / Pure and easy / Faith in something bigger / I'm the face / Naked / Long live rock
CD 5179462
Polydor / Jun '93 / PolyGram

QUADROPHENIA
I am the sea / Real me / Cut my hair / Punk and the godfather / I'm one / Dirty jobs / Helpless dancer / Is it in my head / I've had enough / 5.15 / Sea and sand / Drowned / Bell boy / Dr. Jimmy / Rock / Love reign o'er me
CD 5319712
Polydor / Jun '96 / PolyGram

QUICK ONE, A (Remastered)
Run run run / Boris the spider / I need you / Whiskey man / Heatwave / Cobwebs and strange / Don't look away / See my way / Quick one / I've been away / So sad about us / Doctor doctor / Bucket T / Barbara Ann / Batman / Disguises / In the city / Man with money / Happy Jack / My generation/Land of hope and glory
CD 5277582
Polydor / Aug '96 / PolyGram

RARITIES VOL.1 & 2
CD 8476702
Polydor / Jan '91 / PolyGram

SINGLES, THE
Substitute / I'm a boy / Happy Jack / Pictures of lily / I can see for miles / Magic bus / Pinball wizard / My generation / Summertime blues / Won't get fooled again / Let's see action / Join together / Squeeze box / Who are you / You better you bet
CD 8159652
Polydor / Nov '84 / PolyGram

TALKIN' BOUT THEIR GENERATION
CD CBAK 4067
Baktabak / Feb '94 / Arabesque

TELLTALES (Interview Disc)
CD TELL 14
Network / Jun '97 / Total/BMG

TOMMY (Remastered)
Overture / It's a boy / 1921 / Amazing journey / Sparks / Eyesight to the blind (the hawker) / Christmas / Cousin Kevin / Acid Queen / Underture / Do you think it's alright / Fiddle about / Pinball wizard / There's a doctor / Go to the mirror / Tommy / Can you hear me / Smash the mirror / Sensation / Miracle cure / Sally Simpson / I'm free / Welcome / Tommy's holiday camp / We're not gonna take it
CD 5310432
Polydor / Aug '96 / PolyGram

WHO ARE YOU
New song / Had enough / 905 / Sister disco / Music must change / Trick of the light / Guitar and pen / Love is coming down / Who are you / No road romance / Empty glass / Guitan and pen / Love is coming down / Who are you
CD 5338452
Polydor / Dec '96 / PolyGram

WHO BY NUMBERS, THE
Slip kid / However much I booze / Squeeze box / Dreaming from the waist / Imagine a man / Success story / They are all in love / Blue, red and grey / How many friends / In a hand or a face / Squeeze box / Behind blue eyes / Dreaming from the waist

CD ______ 5338442
Polydor / Dec '96 / PolyGram

WHO COVERS WHO (Various Artists)
I can see for miles: *Hyperhead* / Kids are alright: *Revs* / Pictures of Lily: *McLagan, Ian & The Bump Band* / Bargain: *Buck Pets* / Good's gone: *Telescopes* / In the city: *Swervedriver* / Substitute: *Blur* / Glowgirl: *Mess* / Anyway, anyhow, anywhere: *Chilton, Alex* / Baba O'Riley: *Hinnies* / Good's gone: *Brilliant Corners*
CD ______ CM 006CD
NMC / Sep '96 / Total/Pinnacle

WHO SELL OUT, THE (Remastered)
Armenia City in the sky / Heinz baked beans / Mary Anne with the shaky hand / Odorono / Tattoo / Our love was / I can see for miles / Medac / Silas Stingy / Sunrise / I can't reach you / Relax / Rael #1/#2 / Glittering girl / Melancholia / Someone's coming / Jaguar / Early morning cold taxi / Hall of the mountain King / Girls eyes / Mary Anne with the shaky hand / Glow girl
CD ______ 5277592
Polydor / Aug '96 / PolyGram

WHO'S BETTER WHO'S BEST (Very Best Of The Who)
My generation / Anyway anyhow anywhere / Kids are alright / Substitute / I'm a boy / Happy Jack / Pictures of Lily / I can see for miles / Who are you / Won't get fooled again / Magic bus / I can't explain / Pinball wizard / I'm free / See me, feel me / Squeeze box / Join together / You better you bet / Baba O'Riley
CD ______ 8353892
Polydor / Mar '88 / PolyGram

WHO'S LAST
My generation / I can't explain / Substitute / Behind blue eyes / Baba O'Riley / Boris the spider / Who are you / Pinball wizard / See me, feel me / Love reign o'er me / Long live rock / Long live rock (reprise) / Won't get fooled again / Dr. Jimmy / Magic bus / Summertime blues / Twist and shout
CD ______ MCLD 19005
MCA / Apr '92 / BMG

WHO'S NEXT (Remastered)
Baba O'Riley / Getting in tune / Love ain't for keeping / My wife / Song is over / Bargain / Going mobile / Behind blue eyes / Won't get fooled again / Pure and easy / Baby don't you do it / Naked eye / When I was a boy / Too much of anything / I don't even know myself / Let's see action
CD ______ 5277602
Polydor / Aug '96 / PolyGram

Whodini

SIX
Brooklyn / Runnin'em / Be my lady / Here he comes / Can't get enough / Keep running back / If you want it / Turn the whole world around / Let me get some / VIP / Still want more / NBA
CD ______ 4851612
Columbia / Sep '96 / Sony

Whole Thing

WHOLE THING, THE
Another time / It's all in / Natural feeling / Missing you already / Who's got the makings / Rubberneckin' / Peer pressure / Rope walks
CD ______ JAZIDCD 088
Acid Jazz / Sep '93 / Disc

Whores Of Babylon

METROPOLIS
CD ______ CANDLE 006CD
Candlelight / Aug '94 / Plastic Head

Whyte, Ronny

ALL IN A NIGHT'S WORK
CD ______ ACD 247
Audiophile / '89 / Jazz Music

SOFT WHYTE
CD ______ ACD 204
Audiophile / Apr '94 / Jazz Music

WALK ON THE WEILL SIDE (Whyte, Ronny & Eddie Monteiro)
CD ______ ACD 289
Audiophile / Jun '96 / Jazz Music

Whyton, Wally

CHILDREN SONGS OF WOODY GUTHRIE
Put your fingers in the air / Ocean go / Little seed / Pick it up / Why oh why / Race you down the mountain / One day old / My Daddy / Goodnight little Arlo / How di do / Swimmy swim / Ridin' my car / Cleano / Dance around / Mail myself to you / Bling blang / Don't you push me down / Sleep eye
CD ______ BCD 16125
Bear Family / May '97 / Direct / Rollercoaster / Swift

Wicked Lady

AXEMAN COMETH, THE
CD ______ KSCD 9307
Kissing Spell / Jun '97 / Greyhound

PSYCHOTIC OVERKILL
CD ______ KSCD 9499
Kissing Spell / Jun '97 / Greyhound

Wicked Maraya

CYCLES
CD ______ 9040212
Mausoleum / Feb '95 / Grapevine/ PolyGram

Wicklows

OLD IRELAND (20 Traditional Irish Tunes)
Old Ireland / Old Dungannon oak / Rare old times / Mursheen Durkin / Galway shawl / Bold O'Donoghue / Fields of Athenry / Wicklow Hills / Dirty old town / Hometown on the Foyle / Do you want your old lobby washed down / Veil of white lace / Rose of Clare / Lovely Lectrim / Pretty little girls from Omagh / Cliffs of Dooneen / I'll tell me Ma / Forty shades of green / Spancil Hill / Wild Rover
CD ______ CD 6059
Music / Jan '97 / Target/BMG

Wickman, Putte

BEWITCHED (Wickman, Putte Trio)
CD ______ ABCD 051
Bluebell / Nov '96 / Cadillac / Jazz Music

IN SILHOUETTE (Wickman, Putte Quintet)
CD ______ NCD 8848
Phontastic / Aug '95 / Cadillac / Jazz Music / Wellard

IN TROMBONES
CD ______ NCD 8826
Phontastic / Aug '94 / Cadillac / Jazz Music / Wellard

SEARCHING & SWINGING 1945-1955
CD ______ PHONTCD 9304
Phontastic / Aug '94 / Cadillac / Jazz Music / Wellard

SOME OF THIS AND SOME OF THAT (Wickman/Kellaway/Mitchell)
CD ______ DRCD 187
Dragon / Jun '88 / ADA / Cadillac / CM / Roots / Wellard

VERY THOUGHT OF YOU, THE (Wickman, Putte & Red Mitchell)
CD ______ DRCD 161
Dragon / Oct '88 / ADA / Cadillac / CM / Roots / Wellard

Widespread Depression ...

DOWNTOWN UPROAR (Widespread Depression Orchestra)
CD ______ STCD 540
Stash / '91 / ADA / Cadillac / CM / Direct / Jazz Music

Widowmaker

BLOOD & BULLETS
CD ______ CDMFN 161
Music For Nations / Apr '94 / Pinnacle

STAND BY FOR PAIN
CD ______ CDMFN 175
Music For Nations / Oct '94 / Pinnacle

Wiegand, Roy

WHATEVER FLOATS YOUR BOAT HOME (Wiegand, Roy Big Band)
CD ______ SB 2081
Sea Breeze / Jan '97 / Jazz Music

Wigan's Ovation

NORTHERN SOUL DANCER
Northern soul dancer / Upon my soul / Let's get together / Be with me tonight / Stand in line / Ski-ing in the snow / Superlove / Sign on the dotted line / Personally / What's wrong with me baby / Ten miles high / My girl
CD ______ C5CD 592
See For Miles/C5 / Mar '97 / Pinnacle

Wiggins, Gary

TIME FOR SAXIN'
CD ______ BEST 1012CD
Acoustic Music / Nov '93 / ADA

Wiggins, Gerald

SOULIDARITY
Way you look tonight / You're mine you / Surprise blues / Some other spring / On Green Dolphin Street / Strip city / Child is born / What is there to say / Alexander's ragtime band / If it's the last thing I do / Lover
CD ______ CCD 4706
Concord Crossover / Jul '96 / New Note/ Pinnacle

WIG IS HERE
You are the sunshine of my life / Edith is the sweetest / Lover / Oh give me something to remember you by / Lady is a tramp / On a clear day (You can see forever) / Stolen sweets / This is the end of a beautiful friendship
CD ______ BLE 590692
Black & Blue / Dec '90 / Discovery / Koch / Wellard

Wiggs, Johnny

SOUNDS OF NEW ORLEANS VOL.2
CD ______ STCD 6009
Storyville / Jul '96 / Cadillac / Jazz Music / Wellard

Wiggs, Josephine

BON BON LIFESTYLE (Wiggs, Josephine Experience)
Make me feel like Doris Day / Head to toe / Downward facing dog / Arizona / Like a cool breeze / Trieste / Going home / Vivi's fugue / Mr. B goes surfing / Til I die / Upward facing dog / Trieste reprise
CD ______ GR 035CD
Grand Royal / Apr '97 / Cargo / Plastic Head

Wigham, Jiggs

JIGGS UP, THE
My romance / Pound cake / For someone never known / Haram / Seaflower / Milt / nightingale sang in berkeley square / Doctor is in
CD ______ CAP 740242
Capri / Oct '90 / Cadillac / Wellard

Wights, Jamie

SPREADING JOY
CD ______ JCD 232
Jazzology / Apr '94 / Jazz Music

Wigsville Spliffs

WIGSVILLE SPLIFFS, THE
CD ______ RAUCD 018
Raucous / May '96 / Nervous / RTM/Disc / TKO Magnum

Wigwam

HIGHLIGHTS
Eddie and the boys / Tramdriver / Freddie are you ready / Kite / Nuclear nightclub / Autograph / Just my situation / Cheap evening return / Frederick & Bill / Tombstone valentine / Do or die / June may be too late / Losing hold / Lost without a trace / Henry's highway code / Silver jubilee / Grass for blades / Prophet / Marvelry skimmer (friend from the fields)
CD ______ LXCD 605
Love / May '97 / ADA / Direct / Greyhound

LIGHT AGES
CD ______ WISHCD 46
Digelius / Jun '93 / Direct

LIVE MUSIC FROM THE TWILIGHT ZONE, THE
CD ______ LXCD 517
Love / Dec '95 / ADA / Direct / Greyhound

NUCLEAR NIGHTCLUB
Nuclear nightclub / Freddie are you ready / Bless your lucky stars / Kite / Do or die / Simple human kindness / Save my money and name / Pig storm / Tram driver / Wardance / Bertha come back / Better hold (and a little view) / All over too soon / Masquerade at the white palace / Goddammadog
CD ______ CDOVD 466
Virgin / Jan '96 / EMI

Wiklund/Svensson/Ekblad

SURGE
CD ______ DRCD 216
Dragon / Jun '88 / ADA / Cadillac / CM / Roots / Wellard

Wilber, Bob

BOB WILBER AND THE BECHET LEGACY
Down in Honky Tonk Town / Si tu vois ma mere / Stop shimmying sister / Lazy blues / If I let you get away with it / Roses of Picardy / Petite fleur / Rue des Champes Elysees / Chant in the night / I'm a little blackbird looking for a bluebird / Kansas City man blues / China boy
CD ______ CHR 70018
Challenge / Jun '95 / ADA / Direct / Jazz Music / Wellard

BOB WILBER AND THE SCOTT HAMILTON QUARTET (Wilber, Bob & Scott Hamilton)
CD ______ CRD 171
Chiaroscuro / Mar '96 / Jazz Music

BOB WILBER/DICK WELLSTOOD DUET (Wilber, Bob & Dick Wellstood)
CD ______ PCD 7080
Progressive / Mar '95 / Jazz Music

BUFADORA BLOW UP (Wilber, Bob Big Band)
CD ______ ARCD 19187
Arbors Jazz / May '97 / Cadillac

HAMBURG 1995 (Wilber, Bob & The Bechet Legacy)
CD ______ CD 028
Nagel Heyer / May '96 / Jazz Music

HORNS A-PLENTY
CD ______ ARCD 19135
Arbors Jazz / Nov '94 / Cadillac

IN THE MOOD FOR SWING
I'm in the mood for swing / Talk of the town / Dinah / I'm confessin' that I love you / When lights are low / Ring dem bells / Memories of you / Bei mir bist du schon / Yours and mine / Chinatown
CD ______ PHONTCD 7526
Phontastic / Apr '88 / Cadillac / Jazz Music / Wellard

JAZZ IN AMERIKA HAUS VOL.5
CD ______ CD 015
Nagel Heyer / May '96 / Jazz Music

MAN AND HIS MUSIC, A (Wilber, Bob Quintet)
World is waiting for the sunrise / Stalkin' the Bean / Do I love you / That old gang of mine / Django / I want to be happy / Chu / Freeman's way / Lazy afternoon / JJ Jump / Accent on youth / Lullaby in rhythm / Smoke rings / Bossa losada
CD ______ J&MCD 503
J&M / Aug '94 / Cadillac / Discovery / Jazz Music / Wellard

MEMORIES OF YOU/LIONEL AND BENNY (Wilber, Bob & Dany Doriz)
CD ______ BB 897
Black & Blue / Apr '97 / Discovery / Koch / Wellard

MOMENTS LIKE THIS (Wilber, Bob & Antti Sarpila)
Rent party blues / CC rider / Estrellita / Lester's bounce / Snake charmer / I want a little girl / Moments like this
CD ______ NCD 8811
Phontastic / '93 / Cadillac / Jazz Music / Wellard

ODE TO BECHET (Wilber, Bob & The Bechet Legacy)
Margie / Blues in the air / I can't believe that you're in love with me / I get the blues when it rains / Mooche / I ain't gonna give nobody none o' this jelly roll / When my dreamboat comes home / Ode to Bechet / Quincy Street stomp / Sailboat in the moonlight / High society / Bechet's fantasy / Shake it and break it
CD ______ JCD 142
Jazzology / Jul '96 / Jazz Music

RAPTUROUS REEDS
Jumpin' at the woodside / Chloe / Sherman shuffle / Sultry summer day / Stompin' at the Savoy / You are my lucky star / I've loved you all my life / I double dare you / Alone together / Linger awhile / Yours is my heart alone
CD ______ PHONTCD 7517
Phontastic / Apr '94 / Cadillac / Jazz Music / Wellard

SOPRANO SUMMIT (2CD Set) (Wilber, Bob & Kenny Davern)
Swing parade / Song of songs / Meet me tonight in dreamland / Penny rag / Mooche / Oh sister ain't that hot / Steal away / Egyptian fantasy / Fish vendor / Johnny was there / Please clarify / Where are we
CD ______ CRD 148
Chiaroscuro / Mar '96 / Jazz Music

SOPRANO SUMMIT 1977 (Wilber, Bob & Kenny Davern)
Strike up the band / Pubbles / Elsa's dream / How can you face me / Dreaming butterfly / Tracks in the snow / Lament / Panic is on / Panama rag
CD ______ CCD 4052
Concord Jazz / May '91 / New Note/ Pinnacle

SOPRANO SUMMIT CONCERTO (Wilber, Bob & Kenny Davern)
CD ______ CCD 4029
Concord Jazz / Dec '90 / New Note/ Pinnacle

SOPRANO SUMMIT LIVE (Wilber, Bob & Kenny Davern)
CD ______ J&MCD 501
J&M / May '96 / Cadillac / Discovery / Jazz Music / Wellard

SUMMIT REUNION (Wilber, Bob & Kenny Davern)
CD ______ CRD 311
Chiaroscuro / Mar '96 / Jazz Music

SUMMIT REUNION (Yellow Dog Blues) (Wilber, Bob & Kenny Davern)
CD ______ CRD 339
Chiaroscuro / Jun '96 / Jazz Music

TRIBUTE TO A LEGEND (The Bechet Legacy)
CD ______ NHCD 028
Nagel Heyer / Jul '96 / Jazz Music

Wilce, Malcolm

BEST OF FAMILY FAVOURITES (Wilce, Malcolm Duo)
CD ______ CDTS 004
Maestro / Aug '93 / Savoy

DANCE GOES ON (Wilce, Malcolm Duo)
CD ______ CDTS 039
Maestro / Nov '93 / Savoy

DANCING ALL OVER THE WORLD (Wilce, Malcolm Duo)
CD CDTS 051
Maestro / Dec '95 / Savoy

Wilco

BEING THERE (2CD Set)
Misunderstood / Forget the flowers / I got you (at the end of the century) / Red eyed and blue / (Was I) in your dreams / Dreamer in my dreams / Lonely one / Why would you wanna live / Kingpin / Someone else's song / Outta mind (outta sight) / Someday soon / Sunken treasure / Say you miss me / Hotel Arizona / What's the world got in store / Far far away / Monday
CD Set 9362462362
Warner Bros. / Feb '97 / Warner Music

Wilcox, Spiegle

JAZZ KEEPS YOU YOUNG
CD CHR 70015
Challenge / Aug '95 / ADA / Direct / Jazz Music / Wellard

Wilcoxson, Sheila

BACKWATER BLUES
CD BCD 00272
Burnside / Jul '97 / Koch

Wilczeks, Glenek

MUSIC OF THE TATRA MOUNTAINS, POLAND (Wilczeks, Glenek Bukowina Band)
CD NI 5464
Nimbus / Mar '96 / Nimbus

Wild

GOOD TO GO
CD NERCD 085
Nervous / Apr '96 / Nervous / TKO Magnum

Wild Canyon

18 GUITAR TRACKS
Enchanted canyon / Raunchy / Teen scene / Trambone / Strollin' / Mexican lady / Corn pickin' / My memories / We were born with the music of rock / Dobro / Buffalo skip / Sunny river / Skip along / Poor boy jamboree / Flamingo shuffle / Snail pace / Take me back home / Blue steel blues
CD BCD 15538
Bear Family / Nov '90 / Direct / Rollercoaster / Swift

Wild Ones

WRITING ON THE WALL
CD HMRXD 171
Heavy Metal / Apr '91 / Revolver / Sony

Wild Planet

BLUEPRINTS
CD WARPCD 11
Warp / Jun '93 / Prime / RTM/Disc

Wild Pumpkins At Midnight

SECRET OF THE SAD TREE
Entertaining Lucy / Dear Michele / Chuck it out / Vale of tears / Fruit cake recipe / Dear Jane / Stranger in the house / 7 Sisters / She wolf / Johnny Zorra / Ma
CD HOT 1061CD
Hot / Mar '97 / Hot Records

Wild Spirit

DO THAT THING
CD HMRXD 164
Heavy Metal / May '91 / Revolver / Sony

Wild Tchoupitoulas

WILD TCHOUPITOULAS, THE
Brother John / Meet de boys on de battlefront / Here dey come / Hey pocky away / Indian red / Big chief got a golden crown / Hey mama / Hey hey
CD IMCD 89
Island / Feb '90 / PolyGram

Wild Turkey

BATTLE HYMN
CD EDCD 333
Edsel / Sep '91 / Pinnacle

STEALER OF YEARS
CD HTDCD 58
HTD / Apr '96 / CM / Pinnacle

TURKEY
Good old days / Tomorrow's friend / Universal man / Eternal mother - the return / Ballad of Chuck Stallion and the Mustangs / Street / See you next Tuesday / Telephone
CD EDCD 424
Edsel / May '95 / Pinnacle

Wildchild

ATMOSPHERIC DRUM & BASS VOL.1 (Mixed By Wildchild/2CD Set) (Various Artists)
CD Set MILL 031CD
Millenium / Oct '96 / Plastic Head / Prime / SRD

BEST OF WILDTRAX, THE (Wildchild Experience)
CD LOADW 1CD
Loaded / Dec '96 / 3mv/Sony / Amato Disco / Mo's Music Machine / Pinnacle / Prime

Wilde, Eugene

I CHOOSE YOU TONIGHT
CD MCAD 42282
MCA / Jul '89 / BMG

Wilde Flowers

WILDE FLOWERS, THE
Impotence / Those words they say / Memories / Don't try to change me / Parchman farm / Almost grown / She's gone / Slow walkin' talk / He's bad for you / It's what I feel (A certain kind) / Memories (instrumental) / Never leave me
CD BP 123CD
Blueprint / Sep '96 / Pinnacle

Wilde, Kim

BEST OF KIM WILDE, THE (18 Original Hits/3CD Set)
Cambodia / Water on glass / Young heroes / Falling out / Just a feeling / You can come over / Kids in America / Everything we know / 2-6-5-8-0 / Words fell down / Chaos at the airport / Wendy said / Chequered love / View from a bridge / You'll never be so wrong / Action city / Take me tonight / Our town
CD Set LAD 873342
Disky / Nov '96 / Disky / THE

GOLD COLLECTION, THE
Kids in America / Chequered love / Water on glass / Everything we know / Young heroes / 2-6-5-8-0 / You'll never be so wrong / Falling out / Tuning in tuning on / Ego / View from a bridge / Words fell down / Action city / Just a feeling / Chaos at the airport / Take me tonight / Can you come over / Wendy said / Our town / Cambodia
CD CDGOLD 1001
EMI Gold / Mar '96 / EMI

KIM WILDE
Water on glass / Our town / Everything we know / Young heroes / Kids in America / Chequered love / 2-6-5-8-0 / You'll never be so wrong / Falling out / Tuning in, turning on
CD CDFA 3214
Fame / Nov '88 / EMI

KIM WILDE/SELECT/CATCH AS CATCH CAN (3CD Set)
Water on glass / Our town / Everything we know / Young heroes / Kids in America / Chequered love / 2-6-5-8-0 / You'll never be so wrong / Falling out / Tuning in tuning out / Ego / Words fell down / Action City / View from a bridge / Just a feeling / Chaos at the airport / Take me tonight / Can you come over / Wendy Sadd / Cambodia / House of Salome / Back street Joe / Stay awhile / Love blonde / Dream sequence / Dancing in the dark / Shoot to disable / Can you hear it / Sparks / Sing it out for love
CD Set CDOMB 012
EMI / Oct '95 / EMI

SINGLES 1981-1993, THE
Kids in America / Chequered love / Water on glass / Cambodia / View from bridge / Child come away / Love blonde / Second time / Rage to love / You keep me hangin' on / Another step (Closer to you) / You came / Four letter word / Love is holy / If I can't have you / In my life
CD MCLD 19344
MCA / Oct '96 / BMG

VERY BEST OF KIM WILDE, THE
Kids in America / Chequered love / Water on glass / 2-6-5-8-0 / Boys / Our town / Everything we know / You'll never be so wrong / Cambodia / View from a bridge / Love blonde / House of Salome / Dancing in the dark / Child come away / Take me tonight / Stay awhile
CD CDFA 3275
Fame / Oct '92 / EMI

Wilde, Marty

BEST OF MARTY WILDE, THE
Teenager in love / Donna / Sea of love / Endless sleep / Bad boy / Rubber ball / Put me down / Danny / Johnny Rocco / Ever since you said goodbye / Don't pity me / Splish splash / High school confidential / Wild cat / Blue moon of Kentucky / Teenage tears / Tomorrow's clown / Little girl / Are you sincere / Flight / Hide and seek / Jezebel / Honeycomb / Dream lover
CD 5517942
Spectrum / Nov '95 / PolyGram

SPOTLIGHT ON MARTY WILDE (Marty Wilde's Frantic Fifties)
Endless sleep / Teenager in love / Wild cat / Donna / Honeycomb / Sea of love / Bad boy / Danny / Teenage years / You've got the love / Put me down / So glad you're mine / Blue moon of Kentucky / High school confidential / Down the line / All American boy / Splish splash / Dream lover / Love of my life / Mean woman blues / I flipped / Are you sincere / Don't pity me
CD 8481682
Polydor / Jan '90 / PolyGram

TEENAGER IN LOVE
Teenager in love / Donna / Tomorrows clown / Jezebel / Sea of love / Little girl / Rubber ball / Bad boy / Johnny rocco / Fight / Hide and seek / Ever since you said goodbye / Endless sleep / Abergavenny
CD 5500852
Spectrum / Oct '93 / PolyGram

Wilden, Gert

I TOLD YOU NOT TO CRY (Swinging Themes From Thrilling Crime Films 1966-1972)
CD EFA 043802
Crippled Dick Hot Wax / Jan '97 / SRD

SCHULMADCHEN REPORT (Wilden, Gert & Orchestra)
CD EFA 043742
Crippled Dick Hot Wax / Aug '96 / SRD

Wilder, Webb

IT CAME FROM NASHVILLE (Wilder, Webb & The Beatnicks)
How long can she last / Horror hayride / I'm burning / Is this all there is / Devil's right hand / Move on down the line / One taste of the bait / I'm wise to you / It gets in your blood / Poolside / Ruff rider / Keep it on your mind
CD WM 1018CD
Watermelon / Feb '94 / ADA / Direct

TOWN & COUNTRY (Wilder, Webb & Nashvegas)
CD WMCD 1032
Watermelon / Apr '95 / ADA / Direct

Wildflowers

NEW YORK JAZZ LOFT SESSIONS VOL.1
CD WILDFLOWER 1
Douglas Music / May '97 / Cadillac / New Note/Pinnacle

NEW YORK JAZZ LOFT SESSIONS VOL.2
CD WILDFLOWER 2
Douglas Music / May '97 / Cadillac / New Note/Pinnacle

NEW YORK JAZZ LOFT SESSIONS VOL.3
CD WILDFLOWER 3
Douglas Music / May '97 / Cadillac / New Note/Pinnacle

Wildhearts

FISHING FOR LUCKIES
CD 0630148552
CD 0630148559
East West / May '96 / Warner Music

PHUQ
I wanna go where the people go / V Day / Just in lust / Baby strange / Nita nitro / Jonesing for Jones / Woah shit you got through / Cold patootie tango / Caprice / Be my drug / Naivety play / In Lilly's garden / Getting it / Don't worry 'bout me
CD 0630104042
East West / Dec '96 / Warner Music

Wilen, Barney

BARNEY WILEN
CD FSCD 48
Fresh Sound / Oct '90 / Discovery / Jazz Music

MOVIE THEMES FROM FRANCE (Wilen, Barney & Mal Waldron Trio)
Un homme et une femme / Julien dans l'ascenseur / Florence sur les Champs Elysees / Les parapluies de Cherbourg / No problem / Manha de Carnaval / Generique / Les feuilles mortes / Quiet temple
CD CDSJP 335
Timeless Jazz / Aug '90 / New Note/ Pinnacle

UN TEMOIN DANS LA VILLE/JAZZ SUR SEINE (Original Soundtrack)
Temoin danc la ville / La pendaison / Melodie pour les radio-taxis / Poursuite et metro / Ambiance pourpre / Premeditation dans l'appartement / La vie n'est qu'une lutte / Complainte du chauffer / Sur l'antenne / Blues de l'antenne / SOS radio-taxis / Final au jardin d'acclimatation / Swing 39 / Vamp / Menilmontant / John's groove / Bag's Barney blues / Swingin' Parisian rhythm / J'ai ta main / Nuages / La route enchante / Que reste t'il de nos amours / Minor's swing / Epistrophy
CD 8326582
Fontana / Mar '88 / PolyGram

Wiley, Fletch

NIGHTWATCH
Fiesta / I am what I am / People get ready / Started right / Are you ready / Nightwatch / Joy dance
CD CDPM 6000
Prestige / Mar '90 / Else / Total/BMG

Wiley, Lee

ART VOCAL 1931-1940
CD AV 015
Art Vocal / Sep '95 / Discovery

BACK HOME AGAIN
CD ACD 300
Audiophile / May '95 / Jazz Music

DUOLOGUE 1954 (Wiley, Lee & Ellis Larkins)
CD BLCD 760911
Black Lion / Jun '88 / Cadillac / Jazz Music / Koch / Wellard

HOT HOUSE ROCK
CD TPZ 1047
Topaz Jazz / Jul '96 / Cadillac / Pinnacle

LEE WILEY 1931-1937
CD VJC 1023 2
Vintage Jazz Classics / Oct '91 / ADA / Cadillac / CM / Direct

LEE WILEY AT CARNEGIE HALL 1972
CD ACD 170
Audiophile / Jul '96 / Jazz Music

LEE WILEY RARITIES
CD JASSCD 15
Jass / Oct '91 / ADA / Cadillac / CM / Direct / Jazz Music

LEE WILEY SINGS RODGERS & HART AND HAROLD ARLEN
CD ACD 10
Audiophile / Feb '91 / Jazz Music

SINGS THE SONGS OF GEORGE/IRA GERSHWIN & COLE PORTER
CD ACD 1
Audiophile / Feb '91 / Jazz Music

Wilhelm, Michael

MIKE WILHELM
CD 422394
New Rose / Feb '97 / ADA / Direct / Discovery

Wilhelm, Mick

WOOD AND FIRE
CD NR 422457
New Rose / Feb '97 / ADA / Direct / Discovery

Wilkie, David

COWBOY CELTIC
CD RHRCD 95
Red House / Sep '96 / ADA / Koch

Wilkins, Ernie

KALEIDODUKE
Johnny come lately / Mooche / Sophisticated lady / Kinda Dukish / My little brown book / Things ain't what they used to be / Good Queen Bess / Don't get around much anymore / Isfahan
CD 5193462
Birdology / Oct '94 / PolyGram

Wilkins, Jack

ALIEN ARMY (Wilkins, Jack Trio)
CD MM 5049
Music Masters / Oct '94 / Nimbus

CALL HIM RECKLESS (Wilkins, Jack Trio)
CD MM 5019
Music Masters / Oct '94 / Nimbus

KEEP IN TOUCH (Wilkins, Jack & Kenny Drew Jr.)
Short stories / Alice in wonderland / Third phase / If you could see me now / Smatter / Kiwi bird / Street of dreams / If I should lose you / Keep in touch / East coasting
CD 501295
Claves / Jun '96 / Complete/Pinnacle

MERGE
CD CRD 156
Chiaroscuro / Mar '96 / Jazz Music

Wilkins, Robert

WILKINS, DICKSON AND ALLEN 1928-35 (Wilkins, Robert, Tom Dickson & Allen Shaw)
CD DOCD 5014
Document / Dec '81 / ADA / Hot Shot / Jazz Music

Wilkinson, Jeff

BALLADS IN PLAIN TALK
CD BRAM 1990102
Brambus / Nov '93 / ADA

BRAVE & TRUE
CD BRAM 1991212
Brambus / Nov '93 / ADA

Willemark, Lena

AGRAM (Willemark, Lena & Ale Moller)
Syster Glas / Agram / Sasom Fagelem / Fastan / Bjornen / Samsingen / Per Andsu lietjin / Josef fran Arimatea / Lager och Jon

/ Blamairi / Slangpolskor / Elvedansen / Simonpolskan
CD 5330992
ECM / Oct '96 / New Note/Pinnacle

NORDAN (Willemark, Lena & Ale Moller)
CD 5231612
ECM / Sep '94 / New Note/Pinnacle

SECRETS OF LIVING (Willemark, Lena & Elise Einarsdotter)
CD 21377
Caprice / Jun '85 / ADA / Cadillac / CM / Complete/Pinnacle

Willetts, Dave

TIMELESS
CD HELPD 002
Big Help / Apr '96 / Grapevine/PolyGram

William Davis Construction ...

TOUCH MORE SPICE, A (William Davis Construction Group Band)
America/Love on the rocks / Overture from 'Phantom of the opera' / Bring him home / Invictus / Party piece / Men of Harlech / Pie Jesu / Fidgety feet / Skye boat song / Rhapsody in blue
CD QPRL 042D
Polyphonic / Jun '90 / Complete/Pinnacle

Williams, Alanda

KID DYNAMITE
Christina / You need to know / I want your love / Looking for my baby / Sailor sailor / Keep it in the groove / Out of bounds / Kid Dynamite / Big butt woman / Jacksboro highway / I wanna tell ya / One more river
CD JSPCD 292
JSP / May '97 / ADA / Cadillac / Direct / Hot Shot / Target/BMG

Williams, Alyson

RAW
Just call my name / We're gonna make it: *Williams, Alyson & Ted Mills* / I looked into your eyes / Not on the outside / Masquerade / I'm so glad: *Williams, Alyson & Chuck Stanley* / My love is so raw: *Williams, Alyson & Nikki D* / On the rocks / Still my No.1 / I need your lovin' / Sleep talk
CD 5273632
Def Jam / Jan '96 / PolyGram

Williams, Andy

16 MOST REQUESTED SONGS
Canadian sunset / Hawaiian wedding song / Can't get used to losing you / Red roses for a blue lady / Dear heart / Born free / Danny Boy / Days of wine and roses / Emily / Sweet memories / More / Maria / What now my love / Romeo and Juliet / Impossible dream
CD 4720502
Columbia / Jul '92 / Sony

ANDY WILLIAMS
CD HM 005
Harmony / Jun '97 / TKO Magnum

BEST OF ANDY WILLIAMS, THE
Moon river / Days of wine and roses / More I see you / Hawaiian wedding song / It's a most unusual day / Look of love / Music to watch the girls go by / I can't take my eyes off you / Solitaire / Happy heart / Can't get used to losing you / You lay so easy on my mind / Time for us / In the arms of love / Danny boy / May each day
CD 4810372
Columbia / Dec '95 / Sony

BUTTERFLY (His Greatest Hits 1956-1961)
Butterfly / Hawaiian wedding song / Canadian sunset / Unchained melody / I like your kind of love / Village of St. Bernadette / (In the Summertime) you don't want my love / Let it be me / Picnic / Look for the silver lining / Boom / This nearly was mine / Getting to know you / Dreamsville / Lonely Street / I'm so lonesome I could cry / In the wee small hours of the morning / Wake me when it's over / He's got the whole world in his hands / Sweet morning
CD 3036000862
Carlton / Jul '97 / Carlton

CAN'T GET USED TO LOSING YOU/ LOVE ANDY
Falling in love with love / I left my heart in San Francisco / You are my sunshine / What kind of fool am I / When you're smiling / Days of wine and roses / It's a most unusual day / My colouring book / Can't get used to losing you / I really don't want to know / Exactly like you / May each day / Somethin' stupid / Watch what happens / Look of love / What now my love / Can't take my eyes off you / Kisses sweeter than wine / Holly / When I look in your eyes / More I see you / There will never be another you / God only knows
CD 4775912
Columbia / Oct '94 / Sony

GRANDES BALADES
CD 31839
Divucsa / Oct '96 / Discovery

GREAT PERFORMANCES
CD DBP 102009
Double Platinum / Oct '95 / Target/BMG

GREATEST HITS
CD 12351
Laserlight / Aug '94 / Target/BMG

GREATEST LOVE CLASSICS (Williams, Andy & The Royal Philharmonic Orchestra)
Romeo and Juliet / Love made me a fool / Vino de amor / Different light / Another Winter's day / Vision / Journey's end / Twist of fate / Home / Brave new world / She'll never know / In my world of illusion / Words
CD CDMFP 6173
Music For Pleasure / Sep '95 / EMI

PERSONAL CHRISTMAS COLLECTION
It's the most wonderful time of the year / My favourite things / Christmas song / Bells of St. Mary's / Christmas present / Winter wonderland / First Noel / O come all ye faithful (Adeste Fidelis) / Sleigh ride / Silver bells / Hark the herald angels sing / Christmas bells / Silent night / White Christmas / Happy holiday/The holiday season
CD 4777702
Columbia / Nov '96 / Sony

REFLECTIONS
Moon river / Both sides now / Home loving man / Seasons in the sun / Days of wine and roses / Happy heart / Born free / Love story / Almost there / Can't help falling in love / Can't get used to losing you / God only knows / Solitaire / Your song / Way we were / Can't take my eyes off you / My way / May each day of the year be a good one
CD 4687812
Columbia / Jun '91 / Sony

TOUCH OF CLASS, A
Butterfly / Are you sincere / Lonely street / Canadian sunset / Village of St. Bernadette / I like your kind of love / Hawaiian love song / Lips of wine / Promise, me love / Baby doll / When your lover has gone / In the wee small hours of the morning / How wonderful to know / I'm so alone / Gone with the wind / Do you mind / You don't want my love / Walk hand in hand / Wake me when it's over / Bilbao song
CD TC 877022
Disky / May '97 / Disky / THE

WORLD OF LOVE, A
CD MCCD 218
Music Club / Oct '95 / Disc / THE

Williams, Beau

STAY WITH ME
CD MAUCD 636
Mau Mau / Apr '93 / Pinnacle

Williams, Bekki

ELYSIAN FIELDS
Megaera / Elysian fields / Charon / Moons of Artemis / Hera / Secrets of the labyrinth / Icarus / In the arms of Morpheus / Glance from Medusa / Elysian fields
CD AD 13CD
AD / Dec '96 / Disc

Williams, Big Joe

BABY PLEASE DON'T GO
CD CD 52035
Blues Encore / May '94 / Target/BMG

BIG JOE WILLIAMS & SONNY BOY WILLIAMSON VOL.1 1935-1941
CD BDCD 6003
Blues Document / '91 / ADA / Hot Shot / Jazz Music

BIG JOE WILLIAMS & SONNY BOY WILLIAMSON VOL.2 1945-1949 (Williams, 'Big Joe & Sonny Boy Williamson)
CD BDCD 6004
Blues Document / '91 / ADA / Hot Shot / Jazz Music

BIG JOE WILLIAMS AT FOLK CITY
CD OBCCD 580
Original Blues Classics / Jan '96 / Complete/Pinnacle / Wellard

BLUES ON HIGHWAY 49
CD DD 604
Delmark / Jul '93 / ADA / Cadillac / CM / Direct / Hot Shot

CLASSIC DELTA BLUES
CD OBCCD 545
Original Blues Classics / Nov '92 / Complete/Pinnacle / Wellard

DELTA BLUES 1951 (Williams, 'Big' Joe & Willie Love/Luther Huff)
CD ALCD 2702
Alligator / Oct '93 / ADA / CM / Direct

FINAL YEARS, THE
Tailormade woman / Highway / Back door / Whistling pine blues / Sunny road blues / Change gotta be made / No special rider blues / Baby please don't go / I believe I'll make a change / You're dogging me / New car blues / Black rat blues / Mama don't allow me / Down on Mr. George Mace's Farm / Meet me in the bottom / Muscle shoals blues / Big road blues
CD 5199432
Verve / Mar '93 / PolyGram

GIANT OF THE 9 STRING GUITAR 1935-1945, THE
CD 158552
Blues Collection / Mar '96 / Discovery

HAVE MERCY
CD TCD 1014
Tradition / May '96 / ADA / Vital

MISSISSIPPI'S BIG JOE WILLIAMS AND HIS NINE STRING GUITAR
CD SFWCD 40052
Smithsonian Folkways / Nov '95 / ADA / Cadillac / CM / Direct / Koch

NINE STRING GUITAR BLUES
I got the best King Biscuit / Haunted house blues / I done hollering / I got a bad mind / Long tall woman, skinny Mama too / Stack of dollars / Indiana woman blues / My baby keeps hanging around / Jiving the blues / Jump baby jump
CD DE 627
Delmark / Mar '97 / ADA / Cadillac / CM / Direct / Hot Shot

PINEY WOOD BLUES
Baby please don't go / Drop down Mama / Mellow peaches / Tailor made babe / Big Joe talking / Some day baby / Good morning little schoolgirl / Peach orchard Mama / Juanita / Shetland pony blues / Omaha blues
CD DE 602
Delmark / Jul '97 / ADA / Cadillac / CM / Direct / Hot Shot

SHAKE YOUR BOOGIE
CD ARHCD 315
Arhoolie / Apr '95 / ADA / Cadillac / Direct

STAVIN' CHAIN BLUES (Williams, 'Big' Joe & J.D. Short)
Stavin' chain blues / Roll and tumble / Mean stepfather / You got to help me some / You're gonna need King Jesus / Jumpin' in the moonlight / Rocks and gravel / Sweet old Kokomo / Nobody knows Chicago / Gonna check up on my baby / You're gonna need King Jesus / Rambled and wandered / Going back to Crawford, Miss / Stavin' chain blues / JD talks
CD DD 609
Delmark / Mar '97 / ADA / Cadillac / CM / Direct / Hot Shot

Williams, Blind Connie

PHILADELPHIA STREET SINGER
CD TCD 5024
Testament / Jul '95 / ADA / Koch

Williams, Brooks

INLAND SAILOR
CD GLCD 2114
Green Linnet / Apr '94 / ADA / CM / Direct / Highlander / Roots

KNIFE EDGE
CD GLCD 2121
Green Linnet / Aug '95 / ADA / CM / Direct / Highlander / Roots

Williams, Buster

SOMETHING MORE
Air dancing / Christina / Fortunes dance / Ballade / Deception / Sophisticated lady / I didn't know what time it was
CD IOR 70042
In & Out / Sep '95 / Vital/SAM

Williams, Carol

HAMMOND TODAY
Tico-tico / Fancy pants / Dizzy fingers / Unforgettable / What now my love / May you always / Jumpin' Jupiter / Rhapsody rag / Fools rush in / Red roses for a blue lady / We'll meet again / It's today / Kitchen rag / March: City of Chester / Bess you is my woman now / Promette / Brazil / White cliffs of Dover / Russian rag / In the news / You and the night and the music
CD MCTCD 002
Melcot / Feb '93 / Melcot Music

JUST RAGS
Leicester Square rag / Tiger rag / Black and white rag / Brittania rag / Maple leaf rag / 12th Street rag / Barrel house rag / Root beer rag / Pineapple rag / Chatterbox rag / Tin Pan Alley rag / Spaghetti rag / Ivory rag / Entertainer / Fiddlesticks rag / Coronation rag / Jingles / Kitchen rag / Zig zag rag / Temptation rag / Bugle call rag / Rhapsody rag / Peacherine rag / Russian rag (Rockies rag) / Alexander's ragtime band
CD MCTCD 007
Melcot / Aug '93 / Melcot Music

Williams, Christopher

NOT A PERFECT MAN
CD 74321254552
RCA / Jun '95 / BMG

Williams, Clarence

CLARENCE WILLIAMS COLLECTION VOL.1 1927-1928
CD COCD 19
Collector's Classics / Nov '94 / Cadillac / Complete/Pinnacle / Jazz Music

CLARENCE WILLIAMS COLLECTION VOL.2 1928
CD COCD 28
Collector's Classics / Mar '97 / Cadillac / Complete/Pinnacle / Jazz Music

CLARENCE WILLIAMS COLLECTION VOL.3 1929-1930
CD COCD 29
Collector's Classics / May '97 / Cadillac / Complete/Pinnacle / Jazz Music

CLARENCE WILLIAMS VOL.2 (1924-1930)
CD VILCD 0222
Village Jazz / Sep '92 / Jazz Music / Target/BMG

CLASSICS 1921-1924
CD CLASSICS 679
Classics / Mar '93 / Discovery / Jazz Music

CLASSICS 1924-1926
CD CLASSICS 695
Classics / Jul '93 / Discovery / Jazz Music

CLASSICS 1926-1927
CD CLASSICS 718
Classics / Jul '93 / Discovery / Jazz Music

CLASSICS 1927
CD CLASSICS 736
Classics / Feb '94 / Discovery / Jazz Music

CLASSICS 1927-1928
CD CLASSICS 752
Classics / May '94 / Discovery / Jazz Music

CLASSICS 1928-1929
CD CLASSICS 771
Classics / Aug '94 / Discovery / Jazz Music

CLASSICS 1929
CD CLASSICS 791
Classics / Jan '95 / Discovery / Jazz Music

CLASSICS 1929-1930
CD CLASSICS 810
Classics / May '95 / Discovery / Jazz Music

CLASSICS 1930-1931
CD CLASSICS 832
Classics / Sep '95 / Discovery / Jazz Music

CLASSICS 1933-1934
CD CLASSICS 871
Classics / Apr '96 / Discovery / Jazz Music

CLASSICS 1934
CD CLASSICS 891
Classics / Sep '96 / Discovery / Jazz Music

CLASSICS 1934-1937
CD CLASSICS 918
Classics / Jan '97 / Discovery / Jazz Music

Williams, Claude

LIVE AT J'S VOL.1
CD ARHCD 405
Arhoolie / Apr '95 / ADA / Cadillac / Direct

LIVE AT J'S VOL.2
CD ARHCD 406
Arhoolie / Apr '95 / ADA / Cadillac / Direct

Williams, Cootie

CLASSICS 1941-1944
CD CLASSICS 827
Classics / Sep '95 / Discovery / Jazz Music

ECHOES OF HARLEM
Stompy Jones / Diga diga doo / I can't believe that you're in love with me / Blue reverie / My honey's loving arms / Alabamy home / Stompology / Watchin' / Ring dem bells / Echoes of Harlem / Chasin' chippies / Sharpie / Boys from Harlem / Gal-avantin' / She's gone / Black beauty / Toasted pickles / Concerto for Cootie (do nothin' till you hear from me) / Royal garden blues / You talk a little trash / Sweet Lorraine / 'Round midnight / Blue garden blues
CD TPZ 1042
Topaz Jazz / Apr '96 / Cadillac / Pinnacle

INTRODUCTION TO COOTIE WILLIAMS 1930-1943, AN
CD 4018
Best Of Jazz / Apr '95 / Discovery

SEXTET AND BIG BAND 1941-1944
CD 158382
Jazz Archives / Sep '95 / Discovery

Williams, Cunnie

LOVE STARVED HEART
CD YO 4019CD
Yo Mama / Jul '96 / Cargo / Plastic Head

Williams, Danny

BEST OF DANNY WILLIAMS, THE
CD ______ CDSGP 006
Prestige / Aug '91 / Else / Total/BMG

GENTLE TOUCH, THE
Stay awhile / (With you I'm) Born again / Save the best for last / Beauty and the beast / Moon river / Where do you start / Gentle touch / Best time of my life / Maybe September / Always / Shadow of your smile / My funny valentine / Never let me go / Rainbow bridge / Someone to watch over me / Feelings / God only knows
CD ______ URCD 121
Upbeat / Jun '96 / Cadillac / Target/BMG

Williams, Dar

HONESTY ROOM
CD ______ GRACD 210
Grapevine / Nov '96 / Grapevine/PolyGram

MORTAL CITY
CD ______ GRACD 212
Grapevine / Nov '96 / Grapevine/PolyGram

MORTAL CITY/THE HONESTY ROOM (2CD Set)
CD Set ______ GRCDX 211
Grapevine / Feb '96 / Grapevine/PolyGram

Williams, David

DAVE 'FAT MAN' WILLIAMS (Williams, Dave 'Fat Man')
CD ______ BCD 355
GHB / Nov '96 / Jazz Music

Williams, Delroy

YOU SEXY THING
CD ______ CDTRL 371
Trojan / Jul '96 / Direct / Jet Star

Williams, Deniece

GONNA TAKE A MIRACLE
Free / I found love / Cause, you love me baby / That's what friends are for / God is amazing / Baby, baby, my love's all for you / When love comes calling / If you don't believe / It's gonna take a miracle / Waiting / Do what you feel / I'm so proud / Too much, too little, too late / Black butterfly / Let's hear it for the boy
CD ______ 4836752
Columbia / Jun '96 / Sony

GREATEST GOSPEL HITS
Fire inside my soul / So glad I know / My soul desire / His eye is on the sparrow / Healing / God made you special / Special love / They say / I surrender all / Every moment / God is amazing / We sing praises
CD ______ SPD 1461
Alliance Music / May '95 / EMI

Williams, Dicky

FULL GROWN MAN
CD ______ ICH 1186CD
Ichiban / Dec '95 / Direct / Koch

I WANT YOU FOR BREAKFAST
Weekend playboy / You hurt the wrong man / I've been loving you too long / Letter from a soldier / Need your love / Lost my woman to a woman / Good used man / I'm in love with two women / I want you for breakfast / Let me love you before we make love / Don't give your love to anyone but me / Little closer
CD ______ ICH 1115CD
Ichiban / Oct '93 / Direct / Koch

Williams, Don

BEST OF DON WILLIAMS LIVE, THE
Good ole boys like me / She' in love with a rodeo man / Some broken hearts never mend / Ties that bind / Louisiana Saturday night / Till the rivers all run dry / I recall a gypsy woman / It must be love / Lay down beside me Lord, I hope this day is good / (I'm juts a) Country boy / Tulsa time / Amanda / You're my best friend / Dialogue / I believe in you
CD ______ 3036300072
Country Skyline / Apr '96 / Carlton

BORROWED TALES
Fever / Crying in the rain / Lay down Sally / My rifle, my pony & me / I'll be there if you ever want me / Reason to believe / Games people play / If you could read my mind / Peace train / Long black veil / Letter / You've got a friend / Pretend
CD ______ 3036300012
Country Skyline / Apr '96 / Carlton

COUNTRY LOVE SONGS
There's never been a time / (There's) always something there to remind me / Spend some time with me / In my life / Take my hand / Where do I go from here / On her way to being a woman / Follow me back to Louisville / Apartment no.9 / Ruby Tuesday / Tears / Storybook children / Ordinary / Long walk from childhood / Coming apart / There's no angel on my shoulder
CD ______ 100502
CMC / May '97 / BMG

CURRENTS
Only water (shining in the air) / Too much love / That song about the river / Catfish bates / Back on the street again / So far, so good / Gettin' back together tonight / In the family / Standing knee deep in a river (dying of thirst) / Lone star state of mind / Old trail / It's who you love
CD ______ PD 90645
RCA / Mar '92 / BMG

DON WILLIAMS VOL.1 & 2
Come early morning / Too late to turn back now / Endless sleep / Shelter of your eyes / I recall a gypsy woman / No use running / How much time does it take / My woman's love / Don't you believe / Wish I was in Nashville / Amanda / Your sweet love / She's in love with a rodeo man / Atta way to go / We should be together / Loving you so long now / Oh misery / Miller's cave / I don't think about her no more / Down the road I go
CD ______ EDCD 499
Edsel / Mar '97 / Pinnacle

FLATLANDS
CD ______ 3036300132
Carlton / Sep '96 / Carlton

GREATEST HITS VOL.1
Amanda / Come early morning / Shelter of your eyes / Atta way to go / Don't you believe / Down the road I go / I wouldn't want to live if you don't / Love me / We should be together / Ties that bind / Ghost story / She's in love with a rodeo man / I recall a gypsy woman
CD ______ 3036300052
Country Skyline / May '97 / Carlton

IT'S GOTTA BE MAGIC
It's gotta be magic / I would like to see you again / Lay down beside me / Tears of the lonely / You've got a hold on me / Fallin' in love again / I need someone to hold me when I cry / Turn out the lights and love me tonight / Lovin' understandin' man / Fly away / Your sweet love / Tempted / No use running / Oh misery / Sweet fever / Missing you, missing me
CD ______ 3036300062
Country Skyline / Apr '96 / Carlton

LOVE SONGS
I'll never be in love again / Desparately / Heartbeat in the darkness / Jamaica farewell / Lone star state of mind / Looking back / Another place another time / Come a little closer / I've been loved by the best / Shot full of love / Come from the heart / Lovin' you's like coming home / We got love / It's who you love / Flowers won't grow (in the gardens of stone) / We've got a good fire going / Easy touch / Senorita / You love me through it all / Running out of reasons to run
CD ______ CDMFP 6109
Music For Pleasure / Dec '93 / EMI

LOVE STORIES
CD ______ 74321432562
Camden / Oct '96 / BMG

RUBY TUESDAY
CD ______ HADCD 185
Javelin / Nov '95 / Henry Hadaway / THE

SHELTER OF YOUR EYES, THE
Shelter of your eyes / Come early morning / Amanda / Atta way to go / We should be together / Down the road I go / I wouldn't want to live if you didn't love me / I recall a gypsy woman / Playing around / Miller's cafe / She's in love with a rodeo man / He's a friend of mine / Bringing it down to you / There's never been a time / Coming apart / On her way to being a woman / Follow me back to Louisville / Always something there to remind me
CD ______ CTS 55435
Country Stars / Jan '96 / Target/BMG

SOME BROKEN HEARTS
Stay young / You're my best friend / I'm just a country boy / Listen to the radio / All I'm missing is you / Some broken hearts never mend / I believe in you / Turn out the lights (love me tonight) / Tulsa time / Years from now / Say it again / Till the rivers all run dry / Amanda / I wouldn't want to live if you didn't love me / We should be together / Come early morning
CD ______ PLATCD 301
Platinum / Oct '92 / Prism

YOU'RE MY BEST FRIEND
You're my best friend / When I'm with you / It must be love / Till the rivers run dry / (Turn out the lights) And love me / Tonight / I'm just a country boy / All I'm missing is you / Don't you think it's time / Endless sleep / Some broken hearts never mend / I'm getting good at missing you / Goodbye isn't really good at all
CD ______ 3036300082
Country Skyline / Apr '96 / Carlton

YOU'RE MY BEST FRIEND
Good ole boys like me / Storybook children / Take my hand for a while / Amanda / There's never been a time / Tears / Coming apart / Follow me back to Louisville / Spend some time with me / I believe in you / Ruby Tuesday / Where do I go from here / I've been loved by the best / On her way to being a woman / Always something there to remind me / Tulsa time / Lord I hope this day is good / You're my best friend
CD ______ CD 6037
Music / Sep '96 / Target/BMG

YOU'RE MY BEST FRIEND
CD ______ CTS 55436
Country Stars / Oct '95 / Target/BMG

Williams, Freddy

BARBERSHOP FAVOURITES (Williams, Freddy Four)
Down by the riversdie / Whispering / Ragtime cowboy Joe / Carry me back to old Virginny / Heart of my heart / Drink to me only / Carolina moon / If you were the only girl in the world / Sweet Rosie O'Grady / Danny boy / Sweet sixteen / Mary Mary / Tea for two / Sixty seconds / Honeysuckle and the bee / Sleepy time girl / Genevieve / On the banks of the Wabash / If I had you / Whiffenpoof song / My evaline / When you wore a tulip / Bye bye blackbird / South Rampart Street parade / Sweet adeline / In the good old summertime
CD ______ 3036000432
Carlton / May '96 / Carlton

Williams, Geoffrey

DROP, THE
CD ______ HORCD 1001
Hands On / Apr '97 / Total/BMG

Williams, George

GEORGE WILLIAMS & BESSIE BROWN VOL.1 1923-1925 (Williams, George & Bessie Brown)
CD ______ DOCD 5527
Document / Apr '97 / ADA / Hot Shot / Jazz Music

GEORGE WILLIAMS & BESSIE BROWN VOL.2 1925-1930 (Williams, George & Bessie Brown)
CD ______ DOCD 5528
Document / Apr '97 / ADA / Hot Shot / Jazz Music

SHADES
CD ______ CDSGP 0113
Prestige / Mar '94 / Else / Total/BMG

Williams, Ginger

GREATEST HITS
In my heart / Baby we're taking a chance / As long as you love me / Mad about you / Tenderly / Strange world / Oh baby come back / He's my honey boy / I'll still love you / Here we are / Please forgive me / Holding on / I'm crying I'm crying
CD ______ WSRCD 103
World Sound / Sep '96 / Jet Star

Williams, Hank

24 GREATEST HITS VOL.1
Your cheatin' heart / Move it on over / I'm so lonesome I could cry / Ramblin' man / My heart would know / Kaw-liga / Cold cold heart / Lovesick blues / Honky tonk blues / Honky tonkin' / Mind your own business / Jambalaya / Wedding bells / Hey good lookin' / Window shopping / Settin' the woods on fire / I can't help it (if I'm still in love with you) / Half as much / Why don't you love me / You win again / May you never be alone / Baby we're really in love / Take these chains from my heart / There'll be no teardrops tonight
CD ______ 8232932
Polydor / Jul '94 / PolyGram

24 GREATEST HITS VOL.2
My bucket's got a hole in it / Crazy heart / I'll never get out of this world alive / Moanin' the blues / I could never be ashamed of you / Lost highway / You're gonna change (or I'm gonna leave) / House without love / I'd still want you / Dear John / Let's turn back the years / Howlin' at the moon / Mansion on the hill / I saw the light / (I heard that) lonesome whistle / I'm a long gone Daddy / Why should we try anymore / Long gone lonesome blues / Nobody's lonesome for me / My sweet love ain't around / I just don't like this kind of livin' / I won't be home no more / I'm sorry for you my friend
CD ______ 8232942
Polydor / Jul '94 / PolyGram

40 GREATEST HITS (2CD Set)
Move it on over / Mansion on the hill / Lovesick blues / Wedding bells / Mind your own business / You're gonna change (or I'm gonna leave) / Lost highway / My bucket's got a hole in it / I'm so lonesome I could cry / I just don't like this kind of livin' / Long gone lonesome blues / My son calls another man Daddy / Why don't you leave me / Why should we try anymore / They'll never take her love from me / Moanin' the blues / Nobody's lonesome for me / Cold cold heart / Dear John / Howlin' at the moon / I can't help it (if I'm still in love with you) / Hey good lookin' / Crazy heart / (I heard that) Lonesome whistle / I saw the light / Weary blues from waiting / I won't be home no more / Take these chains from my heart / Your cheatin' heart / Kaw-liga / I'll never get out of this world alive / You win again / Settin' the woods on fire / Window shopping / Jambalaya / Half as much / I'm sorry for you my friend / Honky tonk blues / Ramblin' man / Baby we're really in love
CD Set ______ 8212332
Polydor / Apr '89 / PolyGram

ALONE AND FORSAKEN
CD ______ 5280372
Polydor / Jan '96 / PolyGram

BEST OF HANK WILLIAMS VOL.1, THE
CD ______ 8495752
Polydor / Jul '94 / PolyGram

HANK WILLIAMS FAVOURITES (Various Artists)
CD ______ 74321378372
RCA / Jul '96 / BMG

HEALTH & HAPPINESS SHOWS (2CD Set)
CD Set ______ 5178622
Polydor / Jul '93 / PolyGram

I SAW THE LIGHT
I saw the light / Calling you / Dear brother / Wealth won't say your soul / I'm gonna sing / Message to my mother / How can you refuse him now / When God comes and gathers his jewels / Jesus remembered me / House of gold / Thank God / Angel of death
CD ______ 8119002
Polydor / Jul '94 / PolyGram

LEGEND OF COUNTRY MUSIC
Happy rovin' cowboy / Lovesick blues / Mansion on the hill / You're gonna change (or I'm gonna leave) / Tramp on the street / I'm a long gone Daddy / When God comes and gathers all his jewels / Lost highway / I'll have a new body (I'll have a new life) / I can't get you off my mind / Prodigal son / Pan American / There'll be no teardrops tonight / Mind your own business / Wedding bells / I've just told Mama goodbye / I'm so lonesome I could cry / Thy burdens are greater than mine / I saw the light / Sally Goodin
CD ______ CD 6053
Music / Jan '97 / Target/BMG

MEN WITH BROKEN HEARTS (Three Hanks)
CD ______ CURCD 029
Curb / Nov '96 / Grapevine/PolyGram

RARE DEMOS: FIRST TO LAST
Won't you sometimes think of me / Why should I cry / Calling you / You break your own heart / Pan American / Mother is gone / I watched my dreamworld crumble like clay / In my dreams you still belong to me / Wealth won't save your soul / I told a lie to my heart / Singing waterfall / I'm goin' home / Jambalaya / Heaven holds all my treasures / You better keep it on your mind / Lost on the river / Your cheatin' heart / House of gold / Honky tonk blues / Help me understand / 'Neath a cold grey tomb of stone / There's nothing as sweet as my baby / Fool about you / Log train
CD ______ CMFCD 067
Country Music Foundation / Jan '93 / ADA / Direct

Williams, Hank Jr.

WORLD OF HANK WILLIAMS JR, THE
Ring of fire / Bye bye love: *Williams, Hank Jr. & Connie Francis* / Make the world go away / I walk the line / So sad: *Williams, Hank Jr. & Lois Johnson* / Sweet dreams / North to Alaska / There goes my everything / Singin' the blues: *Williams, Hank Jr. & Connie Francis* / Folsom prison blues / I love you a thousand ways / Please help me I'm falling: *Williams, Hank Jr. & Connie Francis* / Understand your man / Long black veil / Guess things happen that way / Together again: *Williams, Hank Jr. & Lois Johnson* / Blizzard / Window up above / Your cheatin' heart
CD ______ 5520212
Spectrum / May '96 / PolyGram

Williams, Harvey

REBELLION
Song for a weekend / Gidea Park / Day the stuntman died / Song for close friends / Girl from the East tower / Don't shout at me / She sleeps around
CD ______ SARAH 406CD
Sarah / Mar '94 / Vital

Williams, Huw

NEXT EXIT, THE (Williams, Huw & Tony)
CD ______ TCS 1001CD
Tudor Crescent / Oct '94 / ADA

PARADISE CIRCUS (Williams, Huw & Tony)
CD ______ TCS 1002C
Tudor Crescent / Oct '94 / ADA

ROSEMARY'S SISTER (Williams, Huw & Tony)
CD ______ TCS 1003CD
Tudor Crescent / Jul '95 / ADA

Williams, James

LIVE AT MAYBECK RECITAL HALL VOL.42
Polka dots and moonbeams / Footprints / Dreamsville / I fall in love to easily / New

York / 'Round midnight / Inner urge / Sweet dreams / Blues etude / Holy, holy, holy / Sometimes I feel like a Motherless child / Blessed assurance / Why we sing
CD _______ CCD 4694
Concord Jazz / May '96 / New Note/ Pinnacle

MAGICAL TRIO VOL.1 (Williams, James & Ray Brown/Art Blakey)
Hammerin' / Buhaina buhaina / Night we called it a day / Old times' sake / Soulful Mr. Timmons / Love letters / Mean what you say / You're lucky to me / J's jam song
CD _______ 8328592
EmArCy / Mar '90 / PolyGram

MEET THE MAGICAL TRIO (Williams, James & Charnett Moffett/Jeff Watts)
Reebus' rendezvous / Do nothin' 'til you hear from me / Fingers / Lazy bird / By real special / Arioso / Shenanigans / Single petal of a rose / Flower is a lovesome thing
CD _______ 8386532
EmArCy / Oct '93 / PolyGram

PROGRESS REPORT (Williams, James Sextet)
Progress report / Episode from a village dance / Affaire d'amour / Mr. Day's dream / Unconscious behaviour / Renaissance lovers
CD _______ SSC 1012D
Sunnyside / Feb '86 / Discovery

TRUTH, JUSTICE & THE BLUES
Truth, justice & the blues / Self esteem / For old times sake / Yes, yes oh yes / For all intensive purposes / On his word / Take time for love / You're my alter ego / J's rhythm song / Just a feelin' / Be real special
CD _______ ECD 221422
Evidence / Mar '96 / ADA / Cadillac / Harmonia Mundi

UP TO THE MINUTE BLUES
CD _______ DIW 882CD
DIW / Apr '94 / Cadillac / Harmonia Mundi

Williams, Jerry

PARTY TONITE/CUFFED COLLARED AND TAGGED (Swamp Dogg)
CD _______ EDCD 338
Edsel / Sep '91 / Pinnacle

Williams, Jerry Lynn

PEACEMAKER
CD _______ 174512
XIII Bis / Apr '97 / Discovery

Williams, Jessica

AND THEN, THERE'S THIS
Bemsha swing / And then, there's this / All alone / Nichol's bag / Child within / Elaine / House that Rouse, built / Newk's fluke / Swanee / I mean you
CD _______ CDSJP 345
Timeless Jazz / Feb '91 / New Note/ Pinnacle

ARRIVAL
CD _______ JFCD 001
Jazz Focus / Nov '94 / Cadillac

DEDICATED TO YOU
CD _______ NWCD 100
Nightwatch / May '96 / Wellard

GRATITUDE
Sheikh / I cover the waterfront / Mr. Syms / Serenata / 'Round midnight / Nice work if you can get it / Last trane / Like Sonny / Justice
CD _______ CCD 79721
Candid / Feb '97 / Cadillac / Direct / Jazz Music / Koch / Wellard

HIGHER STANDARDS
Get out of town / When your lover has gone / Mack the knife / Night in Tunisia / Don't take your love from me / East of the sun and West of the moon / Solitude / Midnight sun / My heart belongs to Daddy
CD _______ CCD 79736
Candid / May '97 / Cadillac / Direct / Jazz Music / Koch / Wellard

IN THE POCKET
Weirdo / Gal in calico / I really love you / Driftin' / For you again / Cheek to cheek / I remember Bill / I don't stand a ghost of a chance with you / Pfrancing
CD _______ HEPCD 2055
Hep / Jun '94 / Cadillac / Jazz Music / New Note/Pinnacle / Wellard

MOMENTUM
CD _______ JFCD 003
Jazz Focus / Nov '94 / Cadillac

NEXT STEP, THE
Taking a chance on love / Stonewall blues / Easter parade / Bongo's waltz / I didn't know until you told me / Quilt / Clear blue Lou / I should care / Theme for Lester Young / Like someone in love / I'll always be in love with you / I got it bad and that ain't good / Little waltz
CD _______ HEPCD 2054
Hep / Sep '93 / Cadillac / Jazz Music / New Note/Pinnacle / Wellard

SONG THAT I HEARD, A
Make it so / Burning castle / I wish I knew / (Beautiful girl of my dreams) I love you / Geronimo / Kristen / Alone together / Blues not / Say not / Say it / Song that I heard somewhere / Blues for Mandela / I'll remember April
CD _______ HEPCD 2061
Hep / Mar '95 / Cadillac / Jazz Music / New Note/Pinnacle / Wellard

Williams, Jett

THAT REMINDS ME OF HANK
CD _______ IG 5001
Copper Creek / Feb '96 / ADA

Williams, Joe

BALLAD AND BLUES MASTER
CD _______ 5113542
Verve / Mar '92 / PolyGram

CHAINS OF LOVE
CD _______ NI 4019
Natasha / Jul '93 / ADA / Cadillac / CM / Direct / Jazz Music

COME BACK
Come back / Hold it right there / Sent for you yesterday / Yesterday / Who she do
CD _______ D/PC 2102
Delos / '88 / Nimbus

EVERY DAY (The Best Of The Verve Years/2CD Set)
CD Set _______ 5198132
Verve / Mar '94 / PolyGram

HERE'S TO LIFE
What a wonderful world / Save that time / I found a million dollar baby / When I fall in love / If I had you / Little Sir Echo / Young and foolish / I didn't know about you / Maybe September / Time for love / Here's to life
CD _______ CD 83357
Telarc / Jan '94 / Conifer/BMG

I JUST WANT TO SING (Williams, Joe & Friends)
CD _______ DCD 4004
Delos / May '94 / Nimbus

IN GOOD COMPANY
Just friends / Baby, you got what it takes / How deep is the ocean / Ain't got nothing but the blues / Love without money / Between the... / Is you is or is you ain't my baby / Too good to be true / Embraceable you / Please don't talk about me
CD _______ 8379322
Verve / Feb '90 / PolyGram

LIVE AT ORCHESTRA HALL (Williams, Joe & The Count Basie Orchestra)
CD _______ CD 83329
Telarc / Mar '93 / Conifer/BMG

NOTHIN' BUT THE BLUES
Who she do / Just a dream / Please send me someone to love / Alright, OK you win / Hold it right there / In the evening / Rocks in my bed / Sent for you yesterday / Goin' to Chicago blues / Ray Brown's in town
CD _______ DCD 4001
Delos / May '94 / Nimbus

WAR NO MORE
War no more / What a difference a day makes / After you're gone / All the things you are
CD _______ D/PC 2103
Delos / '88 / Nimbus

Williams, John

CLASSIC ROCK (Boston Pops Orchestra)
CD _______ 5501072
Spectrum / Oct '93 / PolyGram

SUMMON THE HEROES (The Official Centennial Olympic Theme) (Williams, John & The Boston Pops Orchestra)
Summon the heroes / Olympic spirit / Olympic fanfare/theme / O fortuna / Bugler's dream / Ode to Zeus / Javelin / Olympic hymn / Overture festivo / Conquest of paradise / Chariots of fire / Parade of charioteers / Toward a new life
CD _______ SK 62622
Sony Classical / Jun '96 / Sony

Williams, John

BEST OF JOHN WILLIAMS, THE
Cavatina / Horizon / Raga vilasakhani todi / Sarabande / Deer may safely graze / River God / Z, Theme from / All at sea minor / Bach changes / Dance of the emperor's clothes / Dance of the living / El tuno / Good morning freedom / JSB / Lisa Larne / Lorelei / Spanish trip
CD _______ MCCD 007
Music Club / Feb '91 / Disc / THE

PORTRAIT
CD _______ JHD 029
Tring / Jun '92 / Tring

Williams, John

JOHN WILLIAMS
CD _______ GLCD 1157
Green Linnet / Dec '95 / ADA / CM / Direct / Highlander / Roots

Williams, Juanita

INTRODUCING
CD _______ BIGMO 1024
Big Mo / Jul '94 / ADA / Direct

Williams, Larry

BEST OF LARRY WILLIAMS, THE
Short fat Fannie / Baby's crazy / Dizzy Miss Lizzy / Lawdy Miss Clawdy / Slow down / I was a fool to let you go / You bug me baby / Rockin' pneumonia and the boogie woogie flu / She said "yeah" / Hootchy-koo / Bony moronie / Little school girl / Just because / Hocus pocus / Took a trip / Jelly belly Nellie / Peaches and cream / Oh babe / Zing zing / Dummy / Bad boy
CD _______ CDCH 917
Ace / May '88 / Pinnacle

CAUSE I LOVE YOU (The Best Of Larry Williams)
CD _______ SCL 2107
Ichiban Soul Classics / Dec '95 / Koch

FABULOUS LARRY WILLIAMS
Short fat Fannie / Bony Moronie / Dizzy Miss Lizzy / Lawdy Miss Clawdy / Baby's crazy / Just because / Slow down / You dug me baby / Rockin' pneumonia and the boogie woogie flu / Little school girl / Hocus pocus / Peaches and cream
CD _______ CDFAB 012
Ace / Oct '91 / Pinnacle

LARRY WILLIAMS SHOW, THE
Slow down / Louisiana Hannah / Two hours past midnight / Baby / Out of tears / For your love / Whole lotta shakin' goin' on / Hoochie coo / Sweet little baby / Looking back / Stormsville groove / Trust in me
CD _______ EDCD 119
Edsel / Jan '92 / Pinnacle

Williams, Leona

LEONA WILLIAMS & EDNA WINSTON 1922-1927 (Williams, Leona & Edna Winston)
CD _______ DOCD 5523
Document / Apr '97 / ADA / Hot Shot / Jazz Music

Williams, Lester

I CAN'T LOSE WITH THE STUFF I USE
I can't lose with the stuff I use / My home ain't here / Crawlin' blues / Lonely heart blues / When I miss her most / Trying to forget / Let me tell you a thing or two / Lost gal / Sweet lovin' daddy / Disgusted blues / Don't leave me baby / Brand new baby / If you knew how much I loved you / Balling blues / When you're tired of running / Crazy about a woman / You're the sweetest thing / 'Bout to put you down / Going away baby / Foolin' with my heart / My time is running out / Life's no bed of roses / Waking up baby
CD _______ CDCHD 476
Ace / Jun '93 / Pinnacle

Williams, Lucinda

HAPPY WOMAN BLUES
Lafayette / I lost it / Maria / Happy woman blues / King of hearts / Rolling along / One night stand / Howlin' at midnight / Hard road / Louisiana man / Sharp cutting wings (song to a poet)
CD _______ MRCD 149
Munich / '90 / ADA / CM / Direct / Greensleeves
CD _______ SFWCD 40003
Smithsonian Folkways / Dec '94 / ADA / Cadillac / CM / Direct / Koch

RAMBLIN'
CD _______ SFWCD 40042
Smithsonian Folkways / Oct '94 / ADA / Cadillac / CM / Direct / Koch

Williams, Marion

BORN TO SING GOSPEL
CD _______ SHCD 6009
Shanachie / Mar '95 / ADA / Greensleeves / Koch

CAN'T KEEP IT TO MYSELF
CD _______ SHCD 6007
Shanachie / Dec '93 / ADA / Greensleeves / Koch

MY SOUL LOOKS BACK/THE GENIUS OF MARION WILLIAMS 1962-1992
CD _______ SHCD 6011
Shanachie / Dec '94 / ADA / Greensleeves / Koch

STRONG AGAIN
CD _______ SFCD 1013
Spirit Feel / Jun '91 / Koch

THROUGH MANY DANGERS (Classic Performances 1966-1993)
CD _______ SH 6021
Shanachie / Oct '96 / ADA / Greensleeves / Koch

Williams, Mary Lou

CLASSICS 1927-1940
CD _______ CLASSICS 630
Classics / Nov '92 / Discovery / Jazz Music

CLASSICS 1944
CD _______ CLASSICS 814
Classics / May '95 / Discovery / Jazz Music

FIRST LADY OF THE PIANO 1952-71
CD _______ CD 53180
Giants Of Jazz / Jan '94 / Cadillac / Jazz Music / Target/BMG

FREE SPIRITS
CD _______ SCCD 31043
Steeplechase / Jul '88 / Discovery / Impetus

GREATEST LADY JAZZ PIANIST 1936-1944, THE
CD _______ JZCD 357
Suisa / Feb '92 / Jazz Music / THE

KEY MOMENTS
CD _______ TPZ 1016
Topaz Jazz / Apr '95 / Cadillac / Pinnacle

LIVE AT THE COOKERY
CD _______ CRD 146
Chiaroscuro / Mar '96 / Jazz Music

ROLL 'EM
CD _______ PCD 7016
Progressive / Nov '96 / Jazz Music

TOWN HALL 1945
CD _______ VJC 10352
Vintage Jazz Classics / Oct '92 / ADA / Cadillac / CM / Direct

ZODIAC SUITE
CD _______ SFWCD 40810
Smithsonian Folkways / Nov '95 / ADA / Cadillac / CM / Direct / Koch

ZONING
CD _______ SFWCD 40811
Smithsonian Folkways / Nov '95 / ADA / Cadillac / CM / Direct / Koch

Williams, Mason

CLASSICAL GAS (Williams, Mason & Mannheim Steamroller)
CD _______ AGCD 800
American Gramophone / Oct '88 / New Note/Pinnacle

Williams, Maurice

SPOTLIGHT ON MAURICE WILLIAMS
High heeled sneakers / Bare footin' / Spanish harlem / Up on the roof / On broadway / Corine Corina / Drift away / Save the last dance for me / Raindrops keep falling on my head / Mustang Sally / Running around / Little darlin' / This feeling / Stay
CD _______ HADCD 120
Javelin / Feb '94 / Henry Hadaway / THE

Williams, Midge

CLASSICS 1937-1938
CD _______ CLASSICS 745
Classics / Aug '94 / Discovery / Jazz Music

Williams, Otis

OTIS WILLIAMS & THE CHARMS (The Original Rockin' And Chart Masters) (Williams, Otis & His Charms)
Love love stick stov / Love's our inspiration / Heart of a rose / I offer you / Fifty five seconds / My baby dearest darling / Bye bye baby / Please believe in me / When we get together / Mambo sh-mambo / Heaven only knows / Happy are we / Come to me baby / Loving baby / Let the happening happen / Quiet please / This love of mine / It's you, you, you / One fine day / What do you know about that / First time we met / Boom diddy boom boom / I'll be true / Crazy crazy love / Hearts of stone / Two hearts
CD _______ CDCHD 531
Ace / Mar '94 / Pinnacle

Williams, Pamela

SAXTRESS
CD _______ INAK 30342
In Akustik / Sep '96 / Direct / TKO Magnum

Williams, Richard

NEW HORN IN TOWN
I can dream, can't I / I remember Clifford / Ferris wheel / Raucous notes / Blues in a quandry / Over the rainbow / Renita's bounce
CD _______ CCD 79003
Candid / Feb '97 / Cadillac / Direct / Jazz Music / Koch / Wellard

Williams, Robert Pete

FREE AGAIN
CD _______ OBCCD 553
Original Blues Classics / Jan '94 / Complete/Pinnacle / Wellard

I'M AS BLUE AS A MAN CAN BE
CD _______ ARHCD 394
Arhoolie / Apr '95 / ADA / Cadillac / Direct

WHEN A MAN TAKES THE BLUES
CD ARHCD 395
Arhoolie / Apr '95 / ADA / Cadillac / Direct

Williams, Robin

ALL BROKEN HEARTS ARE THE SAME (Williams, Robin & Linda)
Rollin' and ramblin' / All broken hearts are the same / Baby rocked her dolly / Leaving this land / Annie / Riding on the Santa Fe / Pan handle wind / Pine country / Stone wall country / Across the blue mountains / After the flood
CD SHCD 1022
Sugar Hill / Jan '97 / ADA / CM / Direct / Koch / Roots

CLOSE AS WE CAN GET/9 TILL MIDNIGHT (Williams, Robin & Linda)
CD FF 359CD
Flying Fish / May '93 / ADA / CM / Direct / Roots

GOOD NEWS (Williams, Robin & Linda/ Their Fine Group)
CD SHCD 3832
Sugar Hill / Apr '95 / ADA / CM / Direct / Koch / Roots

LIVE (Williams, Robin & Linda/Their Fine Group)
CD SHCD 1043
Sugar Hill / Nov '94 / ADA / CM / Direct / Koch / Roots

RHYTHM OF LOVE, THE (Williams, Robin & Linda)
Rhythm of love / When I hear that whistle blow / House of gold / I'll remember you love in my prayers / Gone to the West / Hired gun / They all faded away / Six o'clock news / Hill county song / Devil is a mighty wind / Poor wayfaring stranger / You done me wrong
CD SHCD 1027
Sugar Hill / Jul '90 / ADA / CM / Direct / Koch / Roots

SUGAR FOR SUGAR (Williams, Robin & Linda)
CD SHCD 052
Sugar Hill / Jun '96 / ADA / CM / Direct / Koch / Roots

TURN TOWARD TOMORROW (Williams, Robin & Linda)
CD SHCD 1040
Sugar Hill / Jan '94 / ADA / CM / Direct / Koch / Roots

Williams, Rod

HANGING IN THE BALANCE
CD MCD 5380
Muse / Sep '92 / New Note/Pinnacle

Williams, Roy

GRUESOME TWOSOME (Williams, Roy & John Barnes)
CD BLCD 760507
Black Lion / Oct '93 / Cadillac / Jazz Music / Koch / Wellard

ROYAL TROMBO
CD PHONTCD 7556
Phontastic / '93 / Cadillac / Jazz Music / Wellard

SOMETHING WONDERFUL (Williams, Roy & Eddie Thompson)
Like someone in love / Is'nt it romantic / Something wonderful / I'm comin' virginia / It never entered my mind / Cheek to cheek / I'm getting sentimental over you / Folks who live on the hill / Ind's out
CD HEPCD 2015
Hep / Jul '96 / Cadillac / Jazz Music / New Note/Pinnacle / Wellard

WHEN YOU'RE SMILING (Williams, Roy & Benny Waters)
Broadway / When you're smiling / Things ain't what they used to be / Line for Lyons / Don't blame me / Just friends / Where or when / Know what I mean / Medley / Jumpin' at the woodside
CD HEPCD 2010
Hep / Aug '97 / Cadillac / Jazz Music / New Note/Pinnacle / Wellard

Williams, Rozz

DREAM HOME HEARTACHE (Williams, Rozz & Gitane Demone)
CD TX 51026CD
Triple X / Sep '95 / Plastic Head

WHORSES MOUTH
CD 600012
Hollows Hill / Jul '97 / Greyhound

Williams, Steve

FULL MOON ON BROADWAY
CD PLAN 008CD
Planet / Aug '96 / Direct

Williams, Sylvia

FROM NEW ORLEANS
CD BCD 319
GHB / Jan '94 / Jazz Music

Williams, Tom

INTRODUCING TOM WILLIAMS (Williams, Tom Quintet)
CD CRISS 1064CD
Criss Cross / Oct '92 / Cadillac / Direct / Vital/SAM

STRAIGHT STREET
CD 1091CD
Criss Cross / Jan '95 / Cadillac / Direct / Vital/SAM

Williams, Tony

BEST OF TONY WILLIAMS, THE
Sister Cheryl / Life of the party / Geo Rose / Slump / Pee Wee / Red mask / Juicy fruit / Crystal Palace / Birdland
CD CDP 8533312
Blue Note / Nov '96 / EMI

LIFETIME: THE COLLECTION
CD 4689242
Sony Jazz / Jan '95 / Sony

WILDERNESS
Wilderness rising / Chinatown / Infant wilderness / Harlem mist '55 / Night you were born / Wilderness voyager / Macchu picchu / China moon / Wilderness island / Sea of wilderness / Gambia / Cape wilderness
CD CDP 8545712
Ark/Blue Note / Nov '96 / EMI

Williams, Vanessa

IN THE COMFORT ZONE
Comfort zone / Running back to you / Work to do / You gotta go / Still in love / Save the best for last / What will I tell my heart / Stranger's eyes / Two of a kind / Freedom dance (get free) / Just for tonight / One reason / Better off now / Goodbye / Right stuff
CD 5112672
Wing / Oct '91 / PolyGram

NEXT
CD 5362602
Mercury / Aug '97 / PolyGram

RIGHT STUFF, THE
Right stuff / Be a man / Dreamin' / If you really love him / (He's got) That look / I'll be the one / Security / Darlin' I / Am I too much / Can this be real / Whatever happens
CD 8356942
Wing / Sep '88 / PolyGram

SWEETEST DAYS
Intro-lude / Way that you love / Betcha never / Sweetest days / Higher ground / You dont' have to say you're sorry / Ellamental / Sister moon / You can't run / Long way home / Constantly / Moonlight over Paris
CD 5261722
Mercury / Feb '95 / PolyGram

Williams, Victoria

LOOSE
CD 7567924302
Mammoth / Jan '95 / Vital

SWING THE STATUE
Why look at the moon / Boogieman / Clothes line / Tarbelly and featherfoot / On time / Holy spirit / Summer of drugs / I can't cry hard / Enough / Wobbling / Vieux amis / Weeds / Lift him up
CD MR 0752
Mammoth / Apr '94 / Vital

Williams, Willie

ARMAGIDEON TIME
Masterplan / See you when I get there / People / Armagideon time / All the way / Turn on the power / Easy / Burn
CD CDHB 3509
Heartbeat / '90 / ADA / Direct / Greensleeves / Jet Star

JAH WILL
CD DS 007
Drumstreet / Jun '95 / Jet Star

MESSENGER MAN (Williams, Willie & The Armagedions)
CD CRCD 42
Charm / Sep '95 / Jet Star

NATTY WITH A CAUSE
CD SHAKACD 922
Jah Shaka / Nov '92 / Jet Star / SRD

SEE ME
CD SHAKACD 949
Jah Shaka / Jul '93 / Jet Star / SRD

Williams-Fairey Engineering ...

BRASS FROM THE MASTERS VOL.1 (Williams-Fairey Band & James Gourlay/ Bryan Hurdley)
Life divine / Moor of Venice / Shining river / Energy / Variations / Severn suite op.87
CD CHAN 4547
Chandos / Aug '97 / Chandos

FREEDOM (Williams-Fairey Engineering Band)
Silkstream / Scheherazade / Laughter in the rain / Brassmens holiday / Disney fantasy / Swiss air / Lass of Richmond Hill / Thoughts of love / Freedom
CD QPRL 038D
Polyphonic / Sep '88 / Complete/Pinnacle

GOLDEN JUBILEE (Williams-Fairey Engineering Band)
Tritsch Tratsch Polka / Swing low, sweet chariot / Kim / Piper in the meadow / Pie Jesu / Marching with Sousa / Carnival for brass / Scarecrow and Mrs. King / Serenade / Bohemian rhapsody / Folk festival
CD GRACC 17
Grasmere / May '94 / Highlander / Savoy / Target/BMG

HYMNS ANCIENT AND MODERN (Williams-Fairey Engineering Band)
CD QPRL 054D
Polyphonic / Mar '93 / Complete/Pinnacle

PROCESSION TO THE MINSTER (Williams-Fairey Engineering Band)
Boys in blue / Tuesday blues / Concertino classico / Autumn leaves / Land of the mountain and the flood / Gladiator's farewell / Batman / Festival music / Caprice / Procession to the minster
CD GRCD 42
Grasmere / Nov '90 / Highlander / Savoy / Target/BMG

SPANISH IMPRESSIONS (Williams-Fairey Engineering Band)
Amparito roca / Allorada del gracioso / Maids of Cadiz / Ritual fire dance / Carmen fantasy / Andalucia / La boda de luis alonso / Bonds of friendship / Spanish march / Evocations / Four Spanish impressions
CD CHAN 4554
Chandos / Apr '97 / Chandos

TOURNAMENT FOR BRASS (Williams-Fairey Engineering Band)
President / Over the rainbow / Tournament for brass / Trouble with the tuba is... / Blenheim flourishes / Fest musik der stadt wien / Military overture / Ballycastle bay / Twin Peaks / Neapolitan scenes
CD GRCD 35
Grasmere / May '90 / Highlander / Savoy / Target/BMG

Williams-Holdings Band

DOUBLE CHAMPIONS
Land of the long white cloud / Masquerade / Devil and the deep blue sea / Rhapsody for euphonium / Capriccio / Dance sequence / Variations on a welsh theme
CD QPRL 065D
Polyphonic / Jan '94 / Complete/Pinnacle

MIDNIGHT EUPHONIUM
Midnight euphonium / Euphonism / Arioso / How soon / On my own / Concerto No. 1 / nessun dorma / Deep inside the sacred temple / Somewhere / Jeanie with the light brown hair / Your tiny hands are frozen / Carnival cocktail / Love is forever / Hail acient walls / Allegro / Ina / Pokarekareana
CD QPRL 064D
Polyphonic / Jan '94 / Complete/Pinnacle

Williamson Brothers

COMPLETE RECORDED WORKS (Williamson Brothers & Dick Justice/ Frank Hutchison)
CD DOCD 8004
Document / Jan '97 / ADA / Hot Shot / Jazz Music

Williamson, Ann

AMAZING GRACE
CD CDITV 600
Scotdisc / Mar '95 / Conifer/BMG / Duncans / Ross

FLOWER OF SCOTLAND
Water is wide / Forty shades of green / Flower of Scotland / Rose / Beyond the sunset / Crying time / Bluebells of Scotland / Wild mountain thyme / Mountains of mourne / Rowan tree / Picture of me / Star O'Rabbie Burns / Dark island / Bonnie Mary Of Argyll / Battle's o'er / Farewell my love
CD CDITV 590
Scotdisc / Aug '94 / Conifer/BMG / Duncans / Ross

VERY BEST OF ANN WILLIAMSON, THE
I can't stop loving you / I'll get over you / Tiny bubbles / Llike strangers / Cryin' time / I can't help it if I'm still in / Pal of my cradle days / She's got you / Bonaparte's retreat / Maggie / Four in the morning / Invisible tears / Is it no secret / Don't it make my brown eyes / Send me the pillow / Foresaking all the rest / Tennessee waltz / Your cheating heart / I fall to pieces / Room full of roses / Dear John
CD MCVD 30003
Emerald Gem / Nov '96 / BMG

Williamson, Claude

BLUES IN FRONT/ NEW DEPARTURE (Williamson, Claude & 7 Others)
CD STCD4163
Storyville / Feb '90 / Cadillac / Jazz Music / Wellard

MULLS THE MULLIGAN SCENE
CD FSCD 54
Fresh Sound / Oct '90 / Discovery / Jazz Music

ROUND MIDNIGHT (Bethlehem Jazz Classics) (Williamson, Claude Trio)
CD CDGR 134
Charly / Apr '97 / Koch

Williamson, Harry

TARKA (Williamson, Harry & Anthony Philips)
Movement 1 / Movement 2 / Movement 3 / Anthem
CD BP 219CD
Blueprint / Jul '96 / Pinnacle

Williamson, Robin

AMERICAN STONEHENGE (Williamson, Robin & His Merry Band)
Port London early / Pacheco / Keepsake / Zoo blues / These Islands green / Man in the van / Sands and the glass / Her scattered gold / When evening shadows / Rab's last woollen testament
CD EDCD 389
Edsel / Jun '94 / Pinnacle

CELTIC HARP AIRS AND DANCE TUNES
Lude's supper / Meggie's fou / Mwynen mon / Galway rambler / Port Atholl / Rocks of pleasure / Scholar / Glan medd dod mwyn / Old frieze britches / Blackbird / Kimiad
CD CDTRAX 134
Greentrax / Jun '97 / ADA / Direct / Duncans / Highlander

GLINT OF THE KINDLING, A (Williamson, Robin & His Merry Band)
Road to the gypsies / Me and the mad girl / Lough foyle / Woodcutter's song / By weary well / Boyhood of Henry Morgan / Poachers song / Five denials
CD TMC 9201
Music Corporation / Jan '96 / Pinnacle

ISLAND OF THE STRONG DOOR
CD TMC 9504
Music Corporation / Feb '96 / Pinnacle

JOURNEY'S EDGE
Border tango / Tune I hear so well / Red eye blues / Tomorrow / Mythic times / Lullaby for a rainy night / Rap city rhapsody / Maharajah of Mogador / Bells / Voices of the Barbary coast / Out on the water
CD EDCD 374
Edsel / Jun '93 / Pinnacle

LEGACY OF THE SCOTTISH HARPERS
Scotch cap/Scotland / Flowers of the forest/Cromlet's lilt/Chevy chase / Weel hoddled Lucky/Lochmaben harper / Gilderoy/ Cow the Gowan / MacGregor's lament/ MacGregor's search / Kilt thy coat Maggie/ Three sheepskins / Lord Dundee's lamentation/Brae's o'Killiecrankie / I'll mek ye fain to follow me / Lady Cassilis' lilt/Auld jew/ Broom o'Cowdenknowes / MacDonald of the Isles salutation / Rushes/Birk and green hollin / Soor plooms / Jockey went to the wood / Banks of Helicon/Deil tak the wars
CD CCF 12CD
Claddagh / Nov '84 / ADA / CM / Direct

MERRY BANDS FAREWELL
Wassail / Her scattered gold / By weary well / Woodcutter's song / Flower of the Briar / Legend / Five denial's on Merlin's grave / Cadgers on the cannongate
CD PWMD 5001
Pig's Whisker / Apr '97 / Pinnacle

MIRROR MAN SEQUENCES 1961-1966, THE (2CD Set)
Mirrorman's sequences / Oh Marie / Sheepish / Beat gadjies / Run run run / Kererra / Flat foot skiffle / Ironstone bit / Behold the Indian unicorn / Onion arc / To unmake demons / On the job / Hand of Fatima
CD Set PWMD 5002
Pig's Whisker / May '97 / Pinnacle

SONGS OF LOVE & PARTING/5 BARDIC MYSTERIES
CD TMC 9403
Music Corporation / Jan '96 / Pinnacle

TEN OF SONGS, THE
Ancient song / Lammas / Political lies / Scotland yet / Skull and nettlework / Barley / Here to burn / Verses at Ellesmere / Innocent love / Verses at Powis
CD FF 70448
Flying Fish / Feb '97 / ADA / CM / Direct / Roots

WINTER'S TURNING
Drive the cold winter away / Avant de s'en aller / Pastime with good company (Henry VIII)/Somerset wassail / Greensleeves morris/Green groweth the holly/Eagle's whistle / Past 1 o'clock/Great Tom's cast / Sheep under the snow/Welsh morris / Praetorius' courante clxxix/Drive the cold winter away / Blow blow thou winter wynd/Vivaldi's winter largo / Trip to the boar/Manage the miser / Carolan's quarrel with the landlady/ Christmas eve / Hunting the wren / Corelli's sonato/Scottish country dance / Polka du tapis
CD FF 70407

Flying Fish / Feb '97 / ADA / CM / Direct / Roots

Williamson, Roy

LONG JOURNEY SOUTH, THE
Long journey South / Laggan love / Skye boat song / Donald Og / Peggy Gordon / Nicky's theme / Number one / Tuscan / Long journey South (reprise)
CD _______________ MOICD 001
Moidart / Oct '91 / Conifer/BMG

Williamson, Sonny Boy

ALL TIME BLUES CLASSICS
CD _______________ 8420312
Music Memoria / Oct '96 / ADA / Discovery

ANTHOLOGY 1937-1944
CD _______________ EN 519
Encyclopaedia / Sep '95 / Discovery

BLUEBIRD RECORDINGS 1937-1938, THE
Good morning little school girl / Blue bird blues / Jackson blues / Got the bottle up and gone / Sugar mama blues / Skinny woman / Up the country blues / Worried me blues / Black gal blues / Collector man blues / Frigidaire blues / Suzanna blues / Early in the morning / Project highway / My little Cornelius / Decoration blues / You can lead me / Moonshine / Miss Louisa blues / Sunny land / I'm tired of truckin' my blues away / Down South / Beauty parlor / Until my love come down
CD _______________ 07863667232
Bluebird / Feb '97 / BMG

BLUES 1937-1945, THE
CD _______________ FA 253
Fremeaux / Jul '96 / ADA / Discovery

GOOD MORNING LITTLE SCHOOLGIRL
Good morning little school girl / Bluebird blues / Sugar Mama blues / Skinny woman / Collector man blues / Early in the morning / Black gal blues / Suzie Q / Bad luck blues / Good gravy / Honeybee blues / Decoration blues / Train fare blues / Jivin' the blues / Welfare store blues / My black name blues / Check up on my baby blues / Stop breaking down / Hoodoo hoodoo / Shake the boogie / Better cut that out
CD _______________ CD 52044
Blues Encore / Oct '96 / Target/BMG

KING OF BLUES HARMONICA 1938-1940
CD _______________ BLE 592512
Black & Blue / Dec '92 / Discovery / Koch / Wellard

NOTHING BUT THE BLUES
CD _______________ CBCD 11
Collector's Blues / Jul '96 / TKO Magnum

ORIGINAL SONNY
Bad luck blues / My baby I've been your slave / Whiskey headed blues / Susie Q / Low down ways / Insurance man blues / Good gravy / Collector man / Joe Louis and John Henry / Doggin' my love around / Until my love come down / Bad luck blues / Goodbye red / Right kind of life / Little low woman blues / Blue bird blues / Number five blues / You give an account
CD _______________ CDBM 113
Blue Moon / Feb '97 / Cadillac / Discovery / Greensleeves / Jazz Music / Jet Star / TKO Magnum

PORTRAIT OF A BLUES MAN
CD _______________ APR 3017CD
Analogue Revival / Dec '96 / ADA

SONNY BOY WILLIAMSON 1937-1939
CD _______________ 157602
Blues Collection / Feb '93 / Discovery

SONNY BOY WILLIAMSON 1940-1942
CD _______________ 158102
Blues Collection / Dec '93 / Discovery

SONNY BOY WILLIAMSON 1940-1947
CD _______________ DOCD 5521
Document / Mar '97 / ADA / Hot Shot / Jazz Music

Williamson, Sonny Boy

BLUES OF SONNY BOY WILLIAMSON, THE
CD _______________ STCD 4062
Storyville / Jun '87 / Cadillac / Jazz Music / Wellard

BOPPIN' WITH SONNY
Shuckin' woman / I'm not beggin nobody / Boppin' with Sonny / Empty bedroom / From the bottom / No nights by myself / Red hot kisses / Keep it to yourself / Going in your direction / Gettin' out of town / Sonny's rhythm / She's crazy / City of New Orleans / 309 Cat / Cat hop / Clownin' with the world
CD _______________ CDBM 088
Blue Moon / '90 / Cadillac / Discovery / Greensleeves / Jazz Music / Jet Star / TKO Magnum

BUMMER ROAD
She got next to me / Santa Claus / Little village / Your funeral and my trial (alternate) / Lonesome cabin / I can't do without you / Temperature 110 / Unseen eye / Keep your hand out of my pocket / Open road / This old life
CD _______________ MCD 09324
Chess/MCA / Apr '97 / BMG / New Note/ BMG

CLOWNIN' WITH THE WORLD
CD _______________ ALCD 2700
Alligator / Oct '93 / ADA / CM / Direct

COLLECTION, THE
CD _______________ COL 044
Collection / Feb '95 / Target/BMG

DON'T SEND ME NO FLOWERS
Don't send me no flowers / I see a man downstairs / She was so dumb / Goat / Walkin' / Little girl how old are you / It's a bloody life / Getting out of town / Slow walk / Pontiac blues / Lonesome cabin / Bye bye bird
CD _______________ CDLIK 80
Charly / Jan '93 / Koch

DOWN AND OUT BLUES
Don't start me talkin' / I don't know / All my love in vain / Key / Keep it to yourself / Dissatisfied / Fattenin' frogs for snakes / Wake up baby / Your funeral and my trail / Ninety nine / Cross my heart / Let me explain
CD _______________ CHLD 19106
Chess/MCA / Oct '92 / BMG / New Note/ BMG

EP COLLECTION PLUS, THE
Help me / Bring it on home / Checkin' up on my baby / Don't start me talkin' / Your funeral and my trial / Keep it to yourself / Cross my heart / Too old to think / One way out / Let your conscience be your guide / Temperature 110 / Tryin' to get back on my feet / You killing me / Ninety nine / I don't know / Too young to die / Dissatisfied / It's sad to be alone / Key / Trust my baby / Wake up baby / Bye bye bird / Hurts me so much / That's all I want / (I want you) close to me
CD _______________ SEECD 395
See For Miles/C5 / Feb '94 / Pinnacle

ESSENTIAL SONNY BOY WILLIAMSON, THE
Good evening everybody / Don't start me to talkin' / All my love in vain / You killing me / Let me explain / Your imagination / Don't lose your eye / Keep it to yourself / Key (to your door) / Have you ever been in love / Fattening frogs for snakes / I don't know / Like Wolf / Cross my heart / Ninety nine / Born blind / Little village / Unseen eye / Your funeral and my trial / Keep your hands out of my pocket / Unseeing eye / Let your conscience be your guide / Goat / Cool disposition / Santa Claus / Checkin' up on my baby / Temperature 110 / Lonesome cabin / Somebody help me / Down child / Trust my baby / Too close together / Too young to die / She's my baby / Stop right now / Too old to think / One way out / Nine below zero / Help me / Bye bye bird / Bring it on home / Decoration day / Trying to get back on my feet / Close to me / I can't be alone
CD _______________ CHLDD 19330
Chess/MCA / Sep '96 / BMG / New Note/ BMG

GOIN' IN YOUR DIRECTION
CD _______________ AL 2803
Alligator / Jul '94 / ADA / CM / Direct

HARP FROM DEEP SOUTH, THE
Your funeral and my trial / Wake up baby / Checkin' up on my baby / Down child / Too young to die / Fattenin' frogs for snakes / Don't start me talkin' / Sky is crying / Got to move / Help me / Bring it on home / Story of Sonny Boy Williamson / When the light went out / Keep it to yourself / Sonny's rhythm / Bye bye bird / Work with me / Movin' down the river Rhine / I wonder do I have a friend / Eyesight to the blind / Mighty long time / Nine below zero
CD _______________ CD 52018
Blues Encore / '92 / Target/BMG

HIS BEST
CD _______________ MCD 09377
Chess/MCA / Jul '97 / BMG / New Note/ BMG

KEEP IT TO OURSELVES
CD _______________ ALCD 4787
Alligator / Aug '92 / ADA / CM / Direct

KING BISCUIT TIME
CD _______________ ARHCD 310
Arhoolie / Apr '95 / ADA / Cadillac / Direct

LIVE IN ENGLAND
Bye bye bird: *Williamson, Sonny Boy & The Yardbirds* / Mr. downchild: *Williamson, Sonny Boy & The Yardbirds* / River Rhine: *Williamson, Sonny Boy & The Yardbirds* / Twenty three hours too long: *Williamson, Sonny Boy & The Yardbirds* / Lost care: *Williamson, Sonny Boy & The Yardbirds* / Take it easy: *Williamson, Sonny Boy & The Yardbirds* / Out of the water coast: *Williamson, Sonny Boy & The Yardbirds* / Western Arizona: *Williamson, Sonny Boy & The Yardbirds* / Slow walk: *Williamson, Sonny Boy & The Yardbirds* / Highway 69: *Williamson, Sonny Boy & The Yardbirds* / My little cabin: *Williamson, Sonny Boy & The Yardbirds* / Sonny's slow walk: *Williamson, Sonny Boy & The Animals* / Pontiac blues: *Williamson, Sonny Boy & The Animals* / My babe: *Williamson, Sonny Boy & The Animals* / I don't care no more: *Williamson, Sonny Boy & The Animals* / Baby don't you worry: *Williamson, Sonny Boy & The Animals* / Night time is the right time: *Williamson, Sonny Boy & The Animals* / I'm gonna put you down: *Williamson, Sonny Boy & The Animals* / Fattenin' frogs for snakes: *Williamson, Sonny Boy & The Animals* / Nobody but you: *Williamson, Sonny Boy & The Animals*
CD _______________ CDRB 21
Charly / Apr '95 / Koch

SONNY BOY WILLIAMSON & YARDBIRDS 1963 (Williamson, Sonny Boy & The Yardbirds)
CD _______________ CDLR 42020
L&R / Aug '87 / New Note/Pinnacle

SUGAR MAMA
CD _______________ IGOCD 2014
Indigo / Feb '95 / ADA / Direct

VERY BEST OF SONNY BOY WILLIAMSON, THE (& Roots Of The Blues Vol.4 Compilation/3CD Set)
Work with me / Don't start me talkin' / All my love in vein / Don't lose your eye / Keep it to yourself / Key (to your door) / Have you ever been in love / Fattening frogs for snakes / I don't know / Cross my heart / Born blind / Ninety nine / Dissatisfied / Your funeral and my trial / Wake up baby / Let your conscience be your guide / Unseeing eye / Goat / It's sad to be alone / Checkin' up on my baby / Temperature 110 / Somebody help me / Down child / Trust my baby / Too close together / Too young to die / Hunt / Nine below zero / Got to move / Bye bye bird / Help me, bring it on home / One way out / Trying to get back on my feet / Decoration / Day / Mister downchild / 23 Hours too long / Take it easy, baby / Highway 69 / My little cabin / Cool drink of water: *Johnson, Tommy* / Statesboroe blues: *McTell, 'Blind' Willie* / Candy man blues: *Hurt, 'Mississippi' John* / Nobody knows you (When you're down and out): *Smith, Bessie* / That's no way to get along: *Wilkins, Robert* / Broken hearted: *Estes, 'Sleepy' John* / Kingfisher blues: *Tampa Red* / Walking blues: *Johnson, Robert* / Sugar Mama blues: *Williamson, Sonny Boy* / Roll 'em Pete: *Turner, 'Big' Joe* / New 'shake 'em on down: *McClennan, Tommy* / Rockin' chair: *Broonzy, 'Big' Bill* / Take a little walk with me: *Lockwood, Robert Jr.* / I be's troubled: *Waters, Muddy* / Rock Island line: *Leadbelly* / Ramblin' mind blues: *Big Maceo*
CD Set _______________ VBCD 304
Charly / Jul '95 / Koch

Willie & The Poor Boys

WILLIE AND THE POOR BOYS
Baby, please don't go / Can you hear me / These arms of mine / Revenue man / You never can tell / Slippin' and slidin' / Saturday night / Let's talk it over / All night long / Chicken shack boogie / Sugar bee / Poor boy boogie
CD _______________ NEMCD 688
Sequel / Apr '94 / BMG

WILLIE AND THE POOR BOYS LIVE
High school confidential / Baby, please don't go / Mystery train / Chicken shack boogie / stagger lee / Red hot / Poor boy boogie medley / Land of 1000 dances / Tear it up / Ooh-poo-pah-doo / Rockin' pneumonia and the boogie woogie flu / What'd I say / Lovin' up a storm / Hound dog / Shake, rattle and roll / Looking for someone to love
CD _______________ NEMCD 689
Sequel / Apr '94 / BMG

Willimas, Derede

WHY NOT TONIGHT
CD _______________ FECD 11
First Edition / Apr '93 / Jet Star

Willis, Butch

REPEATS (Willis, Butch & The Rocks)
CD _______________ TB 134CD
Teenbeat / May '94 / Cargo / SRD / Vital

Willis, Chick

BACK TO THE BLUES
Don't let success (turn our love around) / Goin' to the dogs / Bow legged woman / I ain't superstitious / Tell papa / Story of my life / My adorable one / I ain't jivin' baby / Strange things happening
CD _______________ ICH 1106CD
Ichiban / Oct '93 / Direct / Koch

FOOTPRINTS ON MY BED
Love crazy / Use what you got / What's to become of the world / Roll the dice / Footprints in my bed / Big red caboose / Hello central / Jack you up / Voodoo woman / Nuts for sale
CD _______________ ICH 1054CD
Ichiban / Oct '93 / Direct / Koch

I GOT A BIG FAT WOMAN
CD _______________ ICH 1171CD
Ichiban / May '94 / Direct / Koch

NOW
I want a big fat woman / What have you got on me / I want to play with your poodle / I can't stop loving you / For your precious love / Stoop down '88 / It's all over / Garbage man
CD _______________ ICH 1029CD
Ichiban / Feb '89 / Direct / Koch

Willis, Gary

NO SWEAT
No sweat / Knothead / Everlasting night / Stagger / Liquified / Easy street / Til the cows come home / Knothead II / Ancient promise / Hymn
CD _______________ ALCD 1009
Alchemy / Apr '97 / Pinnacle

Willis, Ike

SHOULD' A GONE BEFORE I LEFT
CD _______________ EFA 034062
Muffin / Jul '94 / SRD

Willis, Larry

HEAVY BLUE (Willis, Larry Quartet)
CD _______________ SCCD 31269
Steeplechase / Oct '90 / Discovery / Impetus

SERENADE
CD _______________ SSCD 8063
Sound Hills / Jan '96 / Cadillac / Harmonia Mundi

TRIBUTE TO SOMEONE, A
King cobra / Wayman's way / Sensei / Tribute to someone / Maiden voyage / For Jean / Teasdale place
CD _______________ AQ 1022
Audioquest / Jul '95 / ADA / New Note/ Pinnacle

Willis, Ralph

RALPH WILLIS VOL.1 1944-1950
CD _______________ DOCD 5256
Document / May '94 / ADA / Hot Shot / Jazz Music

RALPH WILLIS VOL.2 1950-1953
CD _______________ DOCD 5257
Document / May '94 / ADA / Hot Shot / Jazz Music

Willis, Wesley

FABIAN ROAD WARRIOR
Shoot my jam seesion down / Ward my rock music off / Tripping daisy / Alanis Morrisette / Rock Saddam Hussein's ass / Rock the nation / Porno For Pyros / Slow cars fast cars / Quaker youth ensemble / Solid state 11 / It's against the law / Empty bottle / Firewall the throttle / Spank wagon / Reid Hyams / Rock it to Russia / Pollo / Anni Vookman / Wesley Willis / Brutal juice / Silverchair / Loud Lucy / Rock 'n' roll superhighway / Dino Paredes
CD _______________ 74321422762
American / Feb '97 / BMG

FEEL THE POWER
Fir throwing hell ride / Lonely kings / Play that rock 'n' roll / Shoot me in the ass / Thirsty whale / Rick Sims / Jello Biafra / Alice In Chains / Ice Cube / Snoop Doggy Dogg / Get me on the city bus / Rock 'n' roll power / Jason Dummeldinger / Hell me on the bus / Freak out hell bus / Shoot me down / Robin Miramontez / Greg Abramson / Mark Neiter / Scream Dracula scream / Rick Rubin / Melissa Dragich / Megan Shaw / Dust Brothers
CD _______________ 74321422752
American / Feb '97 / BMG

Willison, Christian

BOOGIE WOOGIE AND SOME BLUES
CD _______________ 10072
Blues Beacon / Apr '91 / New Note/ Pinnacle

HEART BROKEN MAN
Girl like you / Heart broken man / Congo square / Raven / New York city / Funeral / Unauthentic blues / Macho man / Drown in my own tears / On the bayou / Little voodoo baby / Man in your life
CD _______________ BLU 10262
Blues Beacon / Dec '96 / New Note/ Pinnacle

Willoughby, Mike

CRIMSON TROPHIES
CD _______________ RUCK 001CD
Rucksack / Nov '96 / ADA

Wills, Bob

AMERICAN LEGENDS
Across the alley from the Alamo / I laugh when I think how I cried over you / New San Antonio rose / Faded love / When you leave Amarillo (turn off the lights) / Elmer's tune / Bottle baby boogie / Bubbles in my beer / Big balls in cow town / Stay all night, stay a little longer / Keeper of my heart / South of the border
CD _______________ 12735
Laserlight / May '97 / Target/BMG

COUNTRY'S LEGENDARY GUITAR GENIUS
All night long / Don't cry baby / C jam blues / If he's moving in, I'm moving out / Let's get it over and done with / Right or wrong / Cotton eyed Joe / Honeysuckle rose / Linda Lou / No disappointments in heaven / Roly poly / Beaumont rag / Oh Monah / Ida Red / Faded love / I'm gonna be boss from now on / Time changes everything / Wills junction
CD ____ PRACD 4002
Prairie / Jun '97 / Henry Hadaway

LONGHORN RECORDINGS, THE
Sooner or later / Buffalo twist / All night long / You can't break a broken heart / If he's movin' in / Let's get it over and done with / Big tater in the sandy land / Mayflower waltz / Billy in the lowground / Beaumont rag / Faded love / Dian waltz / Done gone / Put your little foot / Bob's first fiddle tune / Bob's schottische / Gone indian / No disappointments in heaven / Will's junction / You'll never walk out of my heart / Betty's waltz / San Antonio rose
CD ____ BCD 15689
Bear Family / Aug '93 / Direct / Rollercoaster / Swift

ROOTS OF ROCK 'N' ROLL VOL.3, THE (The King Of Lone Star Swing) (Wills, Bob & His Texas Playboys)
Osage stomp / Cherokee maiden / Get with it / Twin guitar special / Roly poly / Take me back to Tulsa / New San Antonio Rose / Steel guitar rag / Texas Playboy Rag / Home in San Antone / Bob Wills special / Right or wrong / New Spanish two step / Time changes everything / Corrina Corrina / Big beaver / Red hot gal of mine / Whoa baby / That's what I like about the South / San Antonio Rose / Oklahoma rag / Lone star rag / Dusky skies / Bluin' the blues / No matter how she done it / Black rider / You're okay / Please don't leave me
CD ____ PLCD 553
President / Nov '96 / Grapevine/PolyGram / President / Target/BMG

SWING HI, SWING LOW (The Best Of Bob Wills & His Texas Playboys) (Wills, Bob & His Texas Playboys)
CD ____ MCCD 143
Music Club / Nov '93 / Disc / THE

Wills, Johnny Lee

BAND'S A ROCKIN', THE
CD ____ KKCD 18
Krazy Kat / Nov '96 / Hot Shot / Jazz Music

Wills, Warren

ELEVEN ASPECTS
CD ____ CDSGP 0321
Prestige / Oct '96 / Else / Total/BMG

Willson, Michelle

EVIL GAL BLUES
CD ____ BB 9550CD
Bullseye Blues / Aug '94 / Direct

SO EMOTIONAL
CD ____ CDBB 9580
Bullseye Blues / Jun '96 / Direct

Willson-Piper, Marty

ART ATTACK
CD ____ RCD 20042
Rykodisc / Jun '92 / ADA / Vital

I CAN'T CRY
CD ____ RCD 51025
Rykodisc / Jul '92 / ADA / Vital

SPIRIT LEVEL
CD ____ RCD 10197
Rykodisc / Jul '92 / ADA / Vital

Wilmot, Gary

WIND BENEATH MY WINGS
Love situation / On a way to a dream / Unchained melody / And now she's gone / Take my breath away / Star without a soul / Wind beneath my wings / Expectation road / I won't forget you / Against all odds / Danny you're a loser / There's only room for the good girls
CD ____ 306042
Hallmark / Jan '97 / Carlton

Wilson, Al

SHOW AND TELL
CD ____ CDSGP 0160
Prestige / Nov '95 / Else / Total/BMG

Wilson, Bo

MAGIC MAN (Wilson, Bo Band)
Magic man / Chevrolet / I'm tore down / Trick bag / Boogie man / Stormy Monday / Don't take advantage of me / Statsboro blues / Shake the room / If you have to know / Hard time in the land of plenty / Madhouse
CD ____ BMAC 0316
BMA / Sep '97 / Pinnacle

Wilson, Brian

AMERICAN SPRING...PLUS (American Spring)
Tennessee waltz / Thinkin' 'bout you baby / Mama said / Superstar / Awake / Sweet mountain / Everybody / This whole world / Forever / Good time / Now that everything's been said / Down home / Shyin' away / Fallin' in love / It's like Heaven / Had to phone ya
CD ____ SEECD 269
See For Miles/C5 / Dec '89 / Pinnacle

BRIAN WILSON
Love and mercy / Walkin' the line / Melt away / Baby let your hair grow long / Little children / One for the boys / There's so many / Night time / Let it shine / Rio Grande / Meet me in my dreams tonight
CD ____ 7599256692
WEA / Nov '95 / Warner Music

I JUST WASN'T MADE FOR THESE TIMES
Meant for you / This whole world / Caroline, no / Let the wind blow / Love and mercy / Do it again / Warmth of the sun / Wonderful / Still I dream of it / Melt away / Till I die
CD ____ MCD 11270
MCA / Aug '95 / BMG

ORANGE CRATE ART (Wilson, Brian & Van Dyke Parks)
CD ____ 9362454272
WEA / Nov '95 / Warner Music

Wilson, Buster

BUSTER WILSON 1947-1949
CD ____ AMCD 89
American Music / Mar '97 / Jazz Music

Wilson, Cassandra

AFTER THE BEGINNING AGAIN
There she goes / 'Round midnight / Yazoo moon / Sweet black night / My corner of the sky / Baubles, bangles and beads / Redbone / Summer wind
CD ____ 5140012
jMT / May '93 / PolyGram

BLUE LIGHT 'TIL DAWN
You don't know what love is / Come on in my kitchen / Tell me you'll wait for me / Children of the night / Hellhound on my trail / Black crow / Sankofa / Estrellas / Redbone / Tupelo honey / Blue light 'til dawn / I can't stand the rain
CD ____ CDP 7813572
Blue Note / Jan '94 / EMI

BLUE SKIES
Shall we dance / Polka dots and moonbeams / I've grown accustomed to his face / I didn't know what time it was / Gee baby ain't I good to you / I'm old fashioned / Sweet Lorraine / My one and only love / Autumn nocturne / Blue skies
CD ____ 8344192
jMT / Feb '89 / PolyGram

CASSANDRA WILSON LIVE
Don't look back / Soul melange / 'Round midnight / My corner of the sky / Desperate move / Body and soul / Rock this calling
CD ____ 8491492
jMT / Oct '91 / PolyGram

DAYS AWEIGH
Electromagnolia / Let's face the music and dance / Days aweigh / Subatomic blues / Apricots on their wings / If you only know how / You belong to you / Some other time / Black and yellow
CD ____ 8344122
jMT / Mar '94 / PolyGram

NEW MOON DAUGHTER
Strange fruit / Love is blindness / Solomon sang / Death letter / Skylark / Find him / I'm so lonesome I could cry / Last train to Clarksville / Until / Little warm death / Memphis / Harvest moon / 32.20
CD ____ CDP 8371832
Blue Note / Mar '96 / EMI

POINT OF VIEW
Square roots / Blue in green / Never desperate move / Love and hate / I am waiting / I wished on the moon / I thought you knew
CD ____ 8344042
jMT / Oct '93 / PolyGram

SHE WHO WEEPS
Iconic Memories / Chelsea bridge / Out loud (jeris' blues) / She who weeps / Angel / Body and soul / New African blues
CD ____ 8344432
jMT / Apr '91 / PolyGram

Wilson, Charles

BLUES IN THE KEY OF C
Who it's going to be / Is it over / Leaning tree / You cut off my love supply / Let's have a good time / Selfish lover / It's a crying shame / I've got a good woman
CD ____ ICH 1120CD
Ichiban / Oct '93 / Direct / Koch

Wilson, Chris

RANDOM CENTURIES
CD ____ FM 1007CD
Marilyn / Jul '92 / Pinnacle

Wilson, Delroy

22 MAGNIFICENT HITS
CD ____ BLCD 017
Graylan / Jan '96 / Grapevine/PolyGram / Jet Star

COOL OPERATOR
CD ____ MCCD 281
Music Club / Dec '96 / Disc / THE

DANCING MOOD
CD ____ SOCD 50149
Studio One / Oct '96 / Jet Star

GOLDEN MEMORIES OF DELROY WILSON, THE
CD ____ RNCD 2111
Rhino / Jul '95 / Grapevine/PolyGram / Jet Star

GOOD ALL OVER
CD ____ CSL 8014
Studio One / May '97 / Jet Star

GREATEST HITS
CD ____ JMC 200102
Jamaican Gold / Dec '92 / Grapevine/ PolyGram / Jet Star

MY SPECIAL LADY
CD ____ CDSGP 069
Prestige / Oct '94 / Else / Total/BMG

SARGE
CD ____ CD 1
Chambers / May '95 / Jet Star

SING 26 MASSIVE HITS
CD ____ RNCD 2138
Rhino / Apr '96 / Grapevine/PolyGram / Jet Star

SPECIAL
CD ____ RASCD 3119
Ras / Sep '93 / Direct / Greensleeves / Jet Star / SRD

TUNE INTO REGGAE MUSIC
CD ____ RNCD 2061
Rhino / Jun '94 / Grapevine/PolyGram / Jet Star

Wilson, Eddie

DANKESCHON, BITTESCHON, WIEDERSEHEN (2CD Set)
Wabash cannonball / Strictly nothin' / Streets of Laredo / Mid the green fields of Virginia / It's OK / I wish I could / Johnny Reb / I found my girl in the USA / Show her lots of gold / Long time to forget
CD Set ____ BCD 15615
Bear Family / Mar '93 / Direct / Rollercoaster / Swift

Wilson, Edith

EDITH & LENA WILSON 1924-1931
CD ____ DOCD 5451
Document / Jun '96 / ADA / Hot Shot / Jazz Music

HE MAY BE YOUR MAN, BUT HE COMES TO SEE ME SOMETIMES (Wilson, Edith & Little Brother Montgomery/State St. Swingers)
Mistreatin' blues / Hesitating blues / He may be your man / Easin' away from me / That same dog / Hey hey boogie / Poppa-mama blues / My handy man ain't handy anymore / Lonesome / Twiddlin' / Slow creepin' blues / Put a little love in everything you do
CD ____ DD 637
Delmark / Mar '97 / ADA / Cadillac / CM / Direct / Hot Shot

Wilson, Elder Roma

THIS TRAIN
CD ____ ARHCD 429
Arhoolie / Sep '95 / ADA / Cadillac / Direct

Wilson, Garland

CLASSICS 1931-1938
CD ____ CLASSICS 808
Classics / Apr '95 / Discovery / Jazz Music

Wilson, Glenn

BITTER SWEET (Wilson, Glenn & Stuart, Rory)
CD ____ SSC 1057D
Sunnyside / Aug '92 / Discovery

BLUE PORPOISE AVENUE
CD ____ SSC 1074
Sunnyside / Apr '97 / Discovery

Wilson, Greg

PIPER OF DISTINCTION
CD ____ CDMON 822
Monarch / Oct '94 / ADA / CM / Direct / Duncans

Wilson, Hop

HOUSTON GHETTO BLUES
CD ____ BB 9538CD
Bullseye Blues / Jan '94 / Direct

STEEL GUITAR FLASH (Wilson, Hop & His Two Buddies)
My woman has a black cat bone / I'm a stranger / I ain't got a woman / Merry christmas darling / Rockin' in the coconuts / Why do you twist / You don't move me anymore / You don't love me anymore / Feel so glad / Be careful with the blues / My woman done quit me / Dance to it / Fuss too much / Good woman is hard to find / Need your love to keep me warm / I done got over / Toot toot Tootsie goodbye / Your Daddy wants to rock / Broke and hungry / Always be in love with you / I met a strange woman / Love's got me all fenced in / Chicken stuff / Rockin' with Hop / That wouldn't satisfy
CD ____ CDCHD 240
Ace / Jun '94 / Pinnacle

Wilson, Jack

IN NEW YORK
CD ____ DIW 615
DIW / Jan '94 / Cadillac / Harmonia Mundi

RAMBLIN'
CD ____ FSRCD 152
Fresh Sound / Dec '90 / Discovery / Jazz Music

Wilson, Jackie

DYNAMIC JACKIE WILSON
Higher and higher / I get the sweetest feeling / Squeeze her, tease her (but love her) / She's alright / Think twice / I've got to get back (Country boy) / Whispers (gettin' louder) / Just be sincere / Since you showed me how to be happy / I don't want to lose you / I've lost you / Stop lying / Who am I / I believe / Even when you cry / (I can feel those vibrations) This love is real / You got me walking / No more goodbyes / Don't burn no bridges / Open the door to your heart
CD ____ CPCD 8018
Charly / Feb '94 / Koch

HIGHER AND HIGHER
Soul galore / I've lost you / I don't want to lose you / Who who song / Nothing but blue skies / I get the sweetest feeling / You brought about a change in me / I'm the one to do it / Nobody but you / Higher and higher / Uptight / Whispers (gettin' louder) / You got me walking / Let this be a letter (to my baby) / Because of you / What'cha gonna do about love / (I can feel those vibrations) This love is real / Since you showed me how to be happy
CD ____ CDKEN 901
Kent / May '86 / Pinnacle

HIGHER AND HIGHER
Reet petite / Lonely teardrops / Come back to me / Danny boy / Why can't you be mine / If I can't have you / That's why (I love you so) / I'll be satisfied / You better know it / Talk that talk / I know I'll always be in love with you / Doggin' around / Woman / Lover, a friend / Am I the man / Tear of the year / Please tell me why / I'm comin' on back to you / You don't know what it means / I just can't help it / Baby workout / Shake, shake, shake / No pity (in the naked city) / Whispers (gettin' louder) / Higher and higher / I get the sweetest feeling
CD ____ CPCD 8005
Charly / Oct '93 / Koch

HIT COLLECTION, THE
(Your love keeps lifting me) Higher and higher / Talk that talk / I'll be satisfied / That's why I love you so / I'm comin' on back to you / Am I the man / Woman, a lover, a friend / Doggin' around / Baby workout / Reet Petite / I get the sweetest feeling / Lonely teardrops / To be loved / Whispers getting louder / Shake shake shake / You better know it / All my love / Alone at last / My empty arms / Chain Gang: *Wilson, Jackie & Count Basie*
CD ____ 3036001002
Carlton / Apr '97 / Carlton

JACKIE WILSON
CD ____ HM 007
Harmony / Jun '97 / TKO Magnum

JACKIE WILSON STORY - THE CHICAGO YEARS VOL.1
Beautiful day / Pretty little angel eyes / I still love you / To change my love / I've learned about life / Just as soon as the feeling's over / Just be sincere / Tears will tell it all / That lucky old sun (just rolls around heaven all day) / Love is funny that way / Since you showed me how to be happy / My heart is calling / (Your love keeps lifting me) Higher and higher / I don't need you around / I need your loving / Let this be a letter (to my baby) / Hard to get a thing called love / Fountain / Don't you know I love you / Didn't I
CD ____ JWCD 5
Charly / Oct '95 / Koch

JACKIE WILSON STORY - THE CHICAGO YEARS VOL.2
I get lonely sometimes / Love changed her face / (I can feel those vibrations) This love is real / Because of you / Go away / Who am I / Whispers (gettin' louder) / Hum de dum de do / Somebody up there likes you / You left the fire burning / Think about the good times / Woman needs to be loved / Growin' tall / Light my fire / Try it again /

Those heartaches / With these hands / Where is love / You got me wlaking / Don't burn no bridges
CD _______________ JWCD 6
Charly / Oct '95 / Koch

JACKIE WILSON STORY - THE NEW YORK YEARS VOL.1
Etcetera / You better know it / Sazzle dazzle / Try a little tenderness / (You were made for) All my love / I'm wanderin' / I'll be satisfied / So much / Years from now / I apologize / Please tell me why / Crazy she calls me / To be loved / I'm comin' on back to you / Lonely teardrops / It's been a long time / My heart belongs to only you / Love is all / Keep smiling at trouble (trouble's a bubble) / Night
CD _______________ JWCD 1
Charly / Oct '95 / Koch

JACKIE WILSON STORY - THE NEW YORK YEARS VOL.2
CD _______________ JWCD 2
Charly / Jan '96 / Koch

JACKIE WILSON STORY - THE NEW YORK YEARS VOL.3
CD _______________ JWCD 3
Charly / Jun '96 / Koch

JACKIE WILSON STORY - THE NEW YORK YEARS VOL.4
I just can't help it / Squeeze her, please her (but love her) / kickapoo / No time out / You don't know me / To be loved / Hearts / There's nothing like this: *Wilson, Jackie & Linda Hopkins* / So you say you wanna dance / It's all my fault / Groovin' / I've got to get back (country boy) / I wanna be around / He's got the whole world in his hands: *Wilson, Jackie & Linda Hopkins* / Nobody knows the trouble I've seen: *Wilson, Jackie & Linda Hopkins* / Sing a little song / Soul time / Be my girl / Danny boy / You thing of beauty
CD _______________ JWCD 4
Charly / Sep '96 / Koch

JACKIE WILSON STORY, THE (2CD Set)
Reet petite (The finest girl you ever want to meet) / To be loved / We have love / Lonely teardrops / That's why (I love you so) / I'll be satisfied / You better know it / Talk that talk / Doggin' around / Night / Woman, a love, a friend / Am I the man / Alone at last / Passin' through / Tear of the year / My empty arms / Please tell me why / I'm coming on back on you / Lonely life / Years from now / You don't know what it means / Way I am / My heart belongs only to you / Greatest hurt / There'll be no next time / Hearts / I just can't help it / Forever and a day / Baby workout / Shake a hand / Shake shake shake / Squeeze her, tease her (But love her) / Danny Boy / Whispers (Gettin' louder) / I don't want to lose you / Just be sincere / I've lost you / (Your love keeps lifting me) Higher and higher / Since you showed me how to be happy / For your precious love / Chain gang / I get the sweetest feeling / For once in my life / Let this be a letter (To my baby) / (I can feel those vibrations) This love is real / You got me walking
CD Set _______________ DBG 53035
Double Gold / Jul '96 / Target/BMG

PORTRAIT OF JACKIE WILSON, A
CD _______________ PWKS 4238
Carlton / Feb '95 / Carlton

REET PETITE
Shake, shake, shake / Why can't you be mine / I'm wanderin' / Lonely teardrops / Yeah yeah / It's so fine / Come back to me / Shake a hand / Reet petite / If I can't have you / All my love / So much / I know I'll always be in love with you / Danny boy / Doggin' around / Do Lord: *Wilson, Jackie & Linda Hopkins*
CD _______________ CDCH 902
Ace / May '86 / Pinnacle

VERY BEST OF JACKIE WILSON, THE
Reet petite / Lonely teardrops / To be loved / That's why / I'll be satisfied / Doggin' around / Lonely life / You better know it / Talk talk talk / Am I the man / I'm comin' on back to you / Woman, a lover, a friend / Baby workout / Squeeze her, tease her (but love her) / No pity (in the naked city) / Whispers (gettin' louder) / I get the sweetest feeling / Since you showed me how to be happy / Love is funny that way / Just be sincere / Higher and higher / You got me walking / (I can feel those vibrations) this love is real
CD _______________ CDCHK 913
Ace / Nov '94 / Pinnacle

VERY BEST OF JACKIE WILSON, THE
Reet petite / Lonely teardrops / That's why I love you so / Night / You better know it / Talk that talk / To be loved / I'll be satisfied / Whispers (gettin' louder) / Higher and higher / I get the sweetest feeling / Doggin' around / Am I the man / I'm comin' on back to you / Woman, a lover, a friend / No pity (in the naked city)
CD _______________ MCCD 017
Music Club / Feb '91 / Disc / THE

VERY BEST OF JACKIE WILSON, THE
I get the sweetest feeling / In the midnight hour / Chain gang / I was made to love her / My empty arms / Please don't hurt me / Think twice / Alone at last / I'll be satisfied / For your precious love / Lonely teardrops / (You're love keeps lifting me) higher and higher / Doggin' around / Body workout / Uptight / Respect / Whispers (getting louder) / Shake a hand / Swing low, sweet chariot / He's got the whole world / Talk that talk / Reet petite
CD _______________ MOCD 3018
More Music / Nov '96 / Sound & Media

VOICE
Reet petite / I get the sweetest feeling / Lonely teardrops / Greatest hurt / Shake a hand / ALone at last / If I can't have you / Woman, a lover, a friend / I'm wandering / (You're keeps lifting me higher) Higher and higher / To be loved / All my love / Taht's why (I love you so) / You better know it / Whispers (getting louder) / I know I'll always be in love with you / You don't know what it means / Doggin' around
CD _______________ NTMCD 555
Nectar / Aug '97 / Pinnacle

Wilson, Joe Lee

ACID RAIN
CD _______________ BL 012
Bloomdido / Oct '93 / Cadillac

Wilson, Joemy

CELTIC TREASURES
CD _______________ DMCD 112
Dara / Feb '96 / ADA / CM / Direct / Else / Grapevine/PolyGram

TURLOUGH O'CAROLAN
CD _______________ DMCD 102
Dargason Music / Jun '93 / ADA

YOUNG TURLOUGH
CD _______________ DMCD 116
Dara / Feb '96 / ADA / CM / Direct / Else / Grapevine/PolyGram

Wilson, John

TELL ME SOMETHING NEW
River of love / Rainbows and you / Jump back / We all wanna be in love / Jump / Tell me something new / Is this love / Everything I need / 24 Reasons / Little Mis-treater / Daddy sang the blues
CD _______________ 3036000182
Carlton / Mar '96 / Carlton

Wilson, John

WORLD'S GREATEST PIPERS VOL.5, THE
6/8 marches / Gaelic air and 2/4 marches / Hornpipe and jigs / Strathspeys and reels / Slow air, strathspey and reel / Lowland air and two Irish reels / March, strathspey and reel / Gaelic airs and jigs / Glengarry's march / 9/8 marches / Hornpipes and jigs
CD _______________ LCOM 5170
Lismor / Oct '96 / ADA / Direct / Duncans / Lismor

Wilson, Kim

THAT'S LIFE
CD _______________ ANTCD 0034
Antones / Jul '95 / ADA / Hot Shot

TIGERMAN
CD _______________ ANTCD 0023
Antones / Nov '93 / ADA / Hot Shot

Wilson, Lena

LENA WILSON VOL.1 1922-1924
CD _______________ DOCD 5443
Document / May '96 / ADA / Hot Shot / Jazz Music

Wilson, Les

ON THE LOOSE (Wilson, Les & The Mighty Houserockers)
CD _______________ RLCD 0096
Red Lightnin' / Jun '97 / ADA / CM / Direct / Hot Shot / TKO Magnum

Wilson, Mari

RHYTHM ROMANCE, THE
CD _______________ DINCD 31
Dino / Sep '91 / Pinnacle

Wilson, Marty

RHYME
CD _______________ RCD 10114
Rykodisc / Sep '91 / ADA / Vital

Wilson, Nancy

BALLADS, BLUES & BIG BANDS (The Best Of Nancy Wilson/3CD Set)
Best is yet to come / Sophisticated lady / Close your eyes / When the world was young / Since I fell for you / Nearness of you / My one and only love / Sleepin' bee / Glad to be unhappy / If he walked into my life / Never let me go / Fly me to the moon / You'd be so nice to come home to / Don't go to strangers / Little girl blues / I'll only miss him when I think of him / Oh look at me now / Someone to watch over me / On Green Dolphin Street / Midnight sun / Our day will come / Gee baby ain't I good to you / You can have him / Angel eyes / You ain't had the blues / When he makes music / (I'm afraid) The masquerade is over / When did you leave heaven / You don't know what love is / Satin doll / This bitter Earth / Supper time / Tonight may have to last me all my life / What a little moonlight can do / I want to be with you / Very thought of you / In the dark / All night long / By myself / In a sentimental mood / Like someone in love / Days of wine and roses / You don't know me / Guess who I saw today / Song is you / Lush life / When sunny gets blue / I believe in you / Good life / Try a little tenderness / Things we did last summer / Here's that rainy day / What are you doing New Year's Eve / But beautiful / When a woman loves a man / It never entered my mind / Call me irresponsible / Willow weep for me / Sufferin' with the blues / When the sun comes out
CD _______________ PRDCD 3
Premier/EMI / Apr '96 / EMI

BEST OF NANCY WILSON, THE (Jazz & Blues Sessions)
Like someone in love / I wish I didn't love you so / Dearly beloved / Just for a thrill / I've got your number / In a sentimental mood / Getting to know you / Call it stormy monday / He's my guy / You're gonna hear from me / People / Sufferin' with the blues / Wave / Unchain my heart / Never will I marry / Green dolphin street / You don't know me / Good man is hard to find
CD _______________ CDP 8539212
Capitol Jazz / Jan '97 / EMI

IF I HAD MY WAY
Hello like before / Sweet love / If I had my way / Wish you wre here / One more try / Not a day in your life / Anything for your love / Where do I go from you / Fool in love / Loving you loving me
CD _______________ CK 67769
Sony Jazz / Aug '97 / Sony

LUSH LIFE
Free again / Midnight sun / Only the young / When the world was young / Right to love / Lush life / Over the weekend / You've changed / River shallow / Sunny / I stayed too long at the fair
CD _______________ CDP 8327452
Capitol Jazz / Aug '95 / EMI

SPOTLIGHT ON NANCY WILSON
What a little moonlight can do / Little girl blue / My one and only love / Best is yet to come / Midnight sun / Good life / You'd be so nice to come home to / Time after time / All of you / Very thought of you / Back in your own back yard / When the sun comes out / At long last love / You've changed / Someone to watch over me / I wish you love / Angel eyes / Here's that rainy day / Song is you / Miss Otis regrets
CD _______________ CDP 8285152
Capitol / Jul '95 / EMI

TODAY, TOMORROW, FOREVER/A TOUCH OF TODAY
One note Samba / Go away, little boy / Unchain my heart / (I left my heart) in San Francisco / Wives and lovers / Good life / What kind of fool am I / Can't stop loving you / On Broadway / Our day will come / Call me irresponsible / Tonight may have to last me all my life / You've got your troubles / And I love him / Uptight (everything's alright) / Have a heart / Before the rain / Shadow of your smile / Call me / Yesterday / Wasn't it wonderful / You're gonna hear from me / No one else but you / Goin' out of my head
CD _______________ CTMCD 115
EMI / Mar '97 / EMI

Wilson Phillips

SHADOWS AND LIGHT
I hear you (prelude) / It's only life / You won't see me cry / Give it up / This doesn't have to be love / Where are you / Flesh and blood / Don't take me down / All the way from New York / Fueled for Houston / Goodbye Carmen / Alone / I hear you (reprise)
CD _______________ SBKCD 18
SBK / Jun '92 / EMI

WILSON PHILLIPS
Hold on / Release me / Impulsive / Next to you (someday I'll be) / You're in love / Over and over / Reason to believe / Ooh you're gold / Eyes like twins / Dream is still alive
CD _______________ SBKCD 5
SBK / Jun '90 / EMI

Wilson, Phillip

PHILLIP WILSON PROJECT, THE (Various Artists)
CD _______________ JD 1243
Jazz Door / Oct '96 / Koch

Wilson, Reuben

BLUE MODE
Bambu / Knock on wood / Bus ride / Orange peel / Twenty five miles / Blue mode
CD _______________ CDP 8299062
Blue Note / Feb '97 / EMI

LOVE BUG
Hot rod / I'm gonna make you love me / I say a little prayer / Love bug / Stormy / Back out / Hold on I'm comin'
CD _______________ CDP 8299052
Blue Note / Jan '97 / EMI

Wilson, Rick

SUITABLE LANGUAGE
CD _______________ TFCD 001
ReR/Recommended / Feb '97 / ReR Megacorp / RTM/Disc

Wilson, Robert

VERY BEST OF ROBERT WILSON, THE
Road to the isles / Bonnie Mary of Argyle / Eriskay love lilt / Uist tramping song / My love is like a red red rose / Westering home / Maid of Kenmore / Bonnie Strathyre / Lewis bridal song / Down the glen / Bonnie Scots lassie / Gordon for me / Scotland the brave / Northern lights of Aberdeen / Tobermory Bay / Marching through the heather / Rothesay Bay / Soft lowland tongue of the borders / Song of the Clyde / Haste ye back
CD _______________ CDSL 8268
Music For Pleasure / Sep '95 / EMI

Wilson, Roger

STARK NAKED
CD _______________ WH 001CD
Whiff / Apr '94 / ADA

Wilson, Sean

50 GREAT SONGS (King & Queen Of Irish Country) (Wilson, Sean & Susan McCann)
CD _______________ PLATCD 3927
Platinum / May '94 / Prism

50 SUPER SONGS
CD _______________ SWCD 1010
TC / Apr '92 / Pinnacle / Prism

ANOTHER 50 FAVOURITE SONGS
CD _______________ SWCD 1003
TC / Aug '92 / Pinnacle / Prism

COUNTRY AND IRISH
CD _______________ SWCD 1002
TC / Jun '92 / Pinnacle / Prism

FOREVER AND EVER
CD _______________ SWCD 1004
TC / Jun '92 / Pinnacle / Prism

GREAT PARTY SINGALONG-50 SONGS
CD _______________ SWCD 1001
TC / Nov '92 / Pinnacle / Prism

SINGALONG WITH SEAN WILSON
CD _______________ SWCD 1009
TC / Jul '92 / Pinnacle / Prism

TURN BACK THE YEARS
CD _______________ PLATCD 911
Platinum / Apr '93 / Prism

WORKING MAN
CD _______________ SWCD 1007
TC / Jun '92 / Pinnacle / Prism

Wilson, Smokey

88TH STREET BLUES
CD _______________ BPCD 5026
Blind Pig / Dec '95 / ADA / CM / Direct / Hot Shot

MAN FROM MARS, THE
Thanks for making me a star / Something inside of me / Man from Mars / 44 blues / Louise / Too drunk to drive / You don't drink what I drink / Black widow / Just like a mountain / Don't want to tangle with me / Doctor blues / Easy baby
CD _______________ CDBB 9581
Bullseye Blues / Feb '97 / Direct

REAL DEAL, THE
CD _______________ CDBB 9559
Rounder / Aug '95 / ADA / CM / Direct

SMOKE 'N' FIREFIRE
CD _______________ BB 9534CD
Bullseye Blues / Jan '94 / Direct

SMOKEY WILSON WITH THE WILLIAM CLARKE BAND
CD _______________ BMCD 9013
Black Magic / Nov '93 / ADA / Cadillac / Direct / Hot Shot

Wilson, Spanky

SINGIN' AND SWINGIN'
CD _______________ BBRC 9104
Big Blue / Nov '92 / Harmonia Mundi

Wilson, Steve

BLUES FOR MARCUS (Wilson, Steve Quintet)
CD _______________ CRISS 1073CD
Criss Cross / Nov '93 / Cadillac / Direct / Vital/SAM

NEW YORK SUMMIT (Wilson, Steve Quintet)
CD _______________ CRISS 1062CD
Criss Cross / Oct '92 / Cadillac / Direct / Vital/SAM

STEP LIVELY
CD _______________ CRISS 1096
Criss Cross / Apr '95 / Cadillac / Direct / Vital/SAM

Wilson, Teddy

AIR MAIL SPECIAL
CD _______________ BLCD 760115
Black Lion / Oct '90 / Cadillac / Jazz Music / Koch / Wellard

ALONE
Tea for two / Body and soul / After you've gone / I can't get started (with you) / Moonglow / Sweet Georgia Brown / Shiny stockings / Li'l darlin' / One o'clock jump / Medley / But not for me / Sophisticated Lady / Medley / Medley
CD _______________ STCD 8211
Storyville / Mar '95 / Cadillac / Jazz Music / Wellard

BLUES FOR THOMAS WALLER
Honeysuckle rose / My fate is in your hands / Ain't cha glad / I've got a feeling I'm falling in love / Stealin' apples / Blues for Thomas Waller / Handful of keys / Striding after Fats / Squeeze me / Zonky / Blue turning grey over you / Ain't misbehavin' / Black and blue
CD _______________ BLCD 760131
Black Lion / Apr '90 / Cadillac / Jazz Music / Koch / Wellard

CLASSICS 1934-1935
CD _______________ CLASSICS 508
Classics / Apr '90 / Discovery / Jazz Music

CLASSICS 1935-1936
CD _______________ CLASSICS 511
Classics / Apr '90 / Discovery / Jazz Music

CLASSICS 1936-1937
CD _______________ CLASSICS 521
Classics / Apr '90 / Discovery / Jazz Music

CLASSICS 1937
CD _______________ CLASSICS 531
Classics / Dec '90 / Discovery / Jazz Music

CLASSICS 1938
CD _______________ CLASSICS 556
Classics / Dec '90 / Discovery / Jazz Music

CLASSICS 1939
CD _______________ CLASSICS 571
Classics / Oct '91 / Discovery / Jazz Music

CLASSICS 1942-1945
CD _______________ CLASSICS 908
Classics / Nov '96 / Discovery / Jazz Music

COLE PORTER CLASSICS
Get out of town / Just one of those things / I get a kick out of you / It's all right with me / Why shouldn't I / Love for sale
CD _______________ BLC 760166
Black Lion / '92 / Cadillac / Jazz Music / Koch / Wellard

COMPLETE ALL STAR AND V-DISCS SESSIONS
CD _______________ VJC 10132
Victorious Discs / Feb '91 / Jazz Music

EARLY YEARS, THE (Wilson, Teddy & His Piano Band)
CD _______________ CDSGP 0159
Prestige / Sep '95 / Else / Total/BMG

FINE AND DANDY (Wilson, Teddy Orchestra & Billie Holiday)
Sentimental and melancholy / This is my last affair / Carelessly / Moanin' low / Fine and dandy / There's a lull in my life / It's swell of you / How am I to know / I'm comin' Virginia / Sun flowers / Yours and mine / I'll get by / Mean to me / Foolin' myself / Easy living / I'll never be the same / I've found a new baby / You're my desire / Remember me / Hour of parting / Cocquette
CD _______________ HEPCD 1029
Hep / Oct '91 / Cadillac / Jazz Music / New Note/Pinnacle / Wellard

GENTLEMEN OF THE KEYBOARD
Somebody loves me / Sailin' / I've found a new baby / Just a mood / I got rhythm / Wham / Liza / 71 / China boy / (Back home again in) Indiana / I want to be happy / Rose room / Just like a butterfly / Fine and dandy / Under a blanket of blue / Airmail special
CD _______________ CD 53059
Giants Of Jazz / Mar '92 / Cadillac / Jazz Music / Target/BMG

GOLDEN DAYS, THE
My melancholy baby / Rosetta / Mean to me: *Wilson, Teddy & Billie Holiday* / Now it can be told: *Wilson, Teddy & Nan Wynn* / China boy: *Wilson, Teddy & Nan Wynn* / Tisket-a-tasket / Them there eyes / If I were you: *Wilson, Teddy & Nan Wynn* / Jungle love / On treasure Island / Sugar plum / I know that you know / You let me down: *Wilson, Teddy & Billie Holiday* / Mary had a little lamb: *Wilson, Teddy & Roy Eldridge* / If you were mine: *Wilson, Teddy & Billie Holiday* / All my life: *Wilson, Teddy & Ella Fitzgerald* / Sailin' / Breakin' in a pair of shoes / Hour of parting: *Wilson, Teddy & Boots Castle* / Coquette / My last affair: *Wilson, Teddy & Billie Holiday* / You brought a new kind of love: *Wilson, Teddy & Frances Hunt*
CD _______________ PASTCD 7025
Flapper / Oct '93 / Pinnacle

HOW HIGH THE MOON
CD _______________ TCD 1050
Tradition / May '97 / ADA / Vital

JAZZ PIANO (Wilson, Teddy & Mary Lou Williams/Mel Powell)
You're mine, you / I got rhythm / Someone to watch over me / Indiana / Time on my hands / Sweet Georgia Brown / I can't get started / Taking a chance on love / Melody maker / Musical express / Sometimes I'm happy / Monk's tune / Homage to Fats / Homage to Debussy / For Miss Blanc / Don't blame me
CD _______________ 303062
Hallmark / Jun '97 / Carlton

MEETS EIJI KITAMURA
CD _______________ STCD 4152
Storyville / May '96 / Cadillac / Jazz Music / Wellard

MOMENTS LIKE THIS
Alone with you / Moments like this / I can't face the music / Don't be that way / If I were you / You go to my head / I'll dream tonight / Jungle love / Now it can be told / Laugh and call it love / Tisket-a-tasket / Everybody's laughing / Here is tomorrow again / Say it with a kiss / April in my heart / I'll never fail you / They say / You're so desirable / You're gonna see a lot of me / Hello my darling / Let's dream in the moonlight / What shall I say / It's easy to blame the weather / Sugar / More than you know
CD _______________ HEPCD 1043
Hep / May '95 / Cadillac / Jazz Music / New Note/Pinnacle / Wellard

OF THEE I SWING (Wilson, Teddy & Billie Holiday)
You turned the tables on me / Sing baby sing / Easy to love / With thee I swing / Way you look tonight / Who loves you / Pennies from Heaven / That's life / Sailin' / I can't give you anything but love / I'm with you (right or wrong) / Where the lazy river goes by / Tea for two / I'll see you in my dreams / He ain't got rhythm / This year's kisses
CD _______________ HEPCD 1020
Hep / Jun '90 / Cadillac / Jazz Music / New Note/Pinnacle / Wellard

PARTNERS IN JAZZ (Classic Piano & Vocal Masterpieces) (Wilson, Teddy & Billie Holiday)
Somebody loves me / Why was I born / I've found a new baby / China boy / 711 / Wham be bop boom bam / Sailin' / Don't blame me / Way you look tonight / Blues in C sharp minor / Just a mood / More than you know / Why do I lie to myself about you / Jumpin' for joy / You can't stop me from dreaming / Jumpin' in the blacks and whites
CD _______________ 307702
Hallmark / Jul '97 / Carlton

PIANO SOLOS
Somebody loves me / Sweet and simple / Liza / Rosetta / Every now and then / It never dawned on me / I found a dream / On a treasure island / I feel like a feather in the breeze / Breakin' in a pair of shoes / Don't blame me / Between the devil and the deep blue sea / Sweat and simple
CD _______________ CDAFS 1016
Affinity / Sep '91 / Cadillac / Jazz Music / Koch

REVISITS THE GOODMAN YEARS (1980 - Copenhagen) (Wilson, Teddy Trio)
CD _______________ STCD 4046
Storyville / Feb '89 / Cadillac / Jazz Music / Wellard

RUNNIN' WILD
One o'clock jump / Mood indigo / Take the 'A' train / Satin doll / Smoke gets in your eyes / Running wild / St James infirmary blues / After you've gone
CD _______________ BLCD 760184
Black Lion / Apr '93 / Cadillac / Jazz Music / Koch / Wellard

SOLO
Get out of town / Just one of those things / I get a kick out of you / I love you / It's all right with me / Love for sale / Too damn blue / Blue turning grey over you / Ain't cha glad / I've got a feeling I'm falling / Zonky / Black and blue / Ain't misbehavin' / Honeysuckle rose
CD _______________ 8747152
DA Music / Jul '96 / Conifer/BMG

STOMPING AT THE SAVOY
I can't get started (with you) / Sometimes I'm happy / Body and soul / I'll never be the same / Easy living
CD _______________ BLCD 760152
Black Lion / Apr '91 / Cadillac / Jazz Music / Koch / Wellard

TEDDY WILSON
CD _______________ CDC 9003
LRC / Oct '90 / Harmonia Mundi / New Note/Pinnacle

TEDDY WILSON & HIS ALLSTARS (Wilson, Teddy Allstars)
CD _______________ CRD 150
Chiaroscuro / Jun '96 / Jazz Music

TEDDY WILSON & HIS ORCHESTRA VOL.5 (Wilson, Teddy & His Orchestra)
CD _______________ HEPCD 1035
Hep / May '94 / Cadillac / Jazz Music / New Note/Pinnacle / Wellard

TEDDY WILSON 1937-1938
CD _______________ CLASSICS 548
Classics / Dec '90 / Discovery / Jazz Music

TEDDY WILSON 1939-1941 (Wilson, Teddy & His Orchestra)
CD _______________ CLASSICS 620
Classics / Nov '92 / Discovery / Jazz Music

TEDDY WILSON WITH BILLIE HOLIDAY (Wilson, Teddy & Billie Holiday)
Nice work if you can get it / Where the lazy river goes by / If you were mine / My last love affair / Why do I lie to myself about you / Mood that I'm in / I'm coming Virginia / Easy living / How am I to know / Hour of parting / Coquette / You let me down / I've found a new baby / All my life / Mary had a little lamb / Miss Brown to you / What a little moonlight can do / I wished on the moon
CD _______________ CDAJA 5053
Living Era / Jun '88 / Select

THREE LITTLE WORDS
CD _______________ BB 8692
Black & Blue / Apr '96 / Discovery / Koch / Wellard

TOO HOT FOR WORDS (Wilson, Teddy Orchestra & Billie Holiday)
I wished on the moon / What a little moonlight can do / Miss Brown to you / Sun bonnet blue / It never dawned on me / Spreadin' rhythm round the world / You let me down / Sugar plum / Rosetta / Liza / Sweet Lorraine: *Wilson, Teddy & His Orchestra*
CD _______________ HEPCD 1012
Hep / Mar '90 / Cadillac / Jazz Music / New Note/Pinnacle / Wellard

WARMIN' UP
Life begins when you're in love: *Wilson, Teddy & Billie Holiday* / Rhythm in my nursery rhymes / Christopher Columbus / My melancholy baby: *Wilson, Teddy & Ella Fitzgerald* / All my life: *Wilson, Teddy & Ella Fitzgerald* / I found a dream / On treasure island / Mary had a little lamb: *Wilson, Teddy & Roy Eldridge* / Too good to be true / Warmin up / Blues in C sharp minor / It's like reaching for the moon: *Wilson, Teddy & Billie Holiday* / These foolish things: *Wilson, Teddy & Billie Holiday* / Why do I lie to myself about you / I cried for you: *Wilson, Teddy & Billie Holiday* / Guess who: *Wilson, Teddy & Billie Holiday* / I feel like a feather in the breeze / Breakin' in a pair of shoes / You came to my rescue: *Wilson, Teddy & Helen Ward* / Here's love in your eyes: *Wilson, Teddy & Helen Ward*
CD _______________ HEPCD 1014
Hep / Oct '92 / Cadillac / Jazz Music / New Note/Pinnacle / Wellard

WITH BILLIE IN MIND
CD _______________ CRD 111
Chiaroscuro / Mar '96 / Jazz Music

Wilson, Tom

TOM WILSON PRESENTS TONZ OF TEKNO (2CD Set) (Various Artists)
CD Set _______________ DBM 2026
Death Becomes Me / Aug '96 / Grapevine/ PolyGram / Pinnacle / SRD

TOM WILSON'S BOUNCIN' BEATS VOL.1 (Various Artists)
CD _______________ BNCCD 1
Rumour / Oct '94 / 3mv/Sony / Mo's Music Machine / Pinnacle

TOM WILSON'S BOUNCIN' BEATS VOL.2 (Various Artists)
CD _______________ BNCCD 2
Rumour / Jul '95 / 3mv/Sony / Mo's Music Machine / Pinnacle

TOM WILSON'S BOUNCIN' BEATS VOL.3 (Various Artists)
CD _______________ BNCCD 3
Rumour / Apr '96 / 3mv/Sony / Mo's Music Machine / Pinnacle

TOM WILSON'S TARTAN TECHNO VOL.1 (Various Artists)
CD _______________ TOONCD 101
Tempo Toons / Oct '95 / 3mv/Sony

TOM WILSON'S TARTAN TECHNO VOL.2 (2CD Set) (Various Artists)
CD Set _______________ TOONCD 102
Tempo Toons / Feb '97 / 3mv/Sony

Wilson, Tony

BEST OF TONY WILSON, THE
Give your lady what she wants / Lay next to you / Africa / New Orleans music / Love I thought I would never find love / I like your style / New York City life / Politician (A man of many words) / What does it take / Gotta make love to you / Loving you ain't the same / Better off just loving you / Legal paper / Just when I need you most / Try love / Forever young / Anything that keeps you satisfied / I can't leave it alone
CD _______________ SEECD 323
See For Miles/C5 / May '93 / Pinnacle

Wilson, U.P.

BOOGIE BOY
CD _______________ JSPCD 255
JSP / Jan '95 / ADA / Cadillac / Direct / Hot Shot / Target/BMG

THIS IS U.P. WILSON
Hold on baby / Boots and shades / Bad luck and trouble / You're one woman / Changes / Go home with me / Hold me / Peaches / Used to be mine / Fool for you
CD _______________ JSPCD 266
JSP / Jan '96 / ADA / Cadillac / Direct / Hot Shot / Target/BMG

WHIRLWIND
Roll over / Walk that walk / Your last chance / Juicin' / Going round in a daze / Who will your next fool be / Deep down inside / Bluesola / Come on baby, go home with me / If you don't know how to act (your place is at home)
CD _______________ JSPCD 277
JSP / Feb '97 / ADA / Cadillac / Direct / Hot Shot / Target/BMG

Wimbledon FC

SMELLS LIKE TEAM SPIRIT (Wimbledon FC/Supporters)
We are Wimbledon: *Wimbledon FC* / Dons song: *Wimbledon FC* / Wooly bully: *Jones, Vinnie* / Vinnie Jones is innocent: *Monty* / This is Vinnie Jones: *Monty* / When Irish eyes are smiling: *Kinnear, Joe & Friends* / Crazy games: *Jones, Vinnie* / Smells like team spirit: *Big Blue W* / Chant no.88: *Reservoir Dons & The West Bank* / All heroes (in yellow and blue): *Reservoir Dons* / Dons are coming: *Reservoir Dons* / Remember you're a Womble: *Plough Lane Boys*
CD _______________ CDGAFFER 13
Cherry Red / Apr '97 / Pinnacle

Wimme

WIMME
CD _______________ ZENCD 2043
Rockadillo / May '95 / ADA / Direct

Winans

ALL OUT
Payday / It's not heaven if you're not there / If he doesn't come tonight / That extra mile / Tradewinds / All you ever been was good / Money motive / Love will never die / Heaven belongs to you / He said go
CD _______________ 9362452132
Qwest / Aug '93 / Warner Music

Winans, Bebe & Cece

RELATIONSHIPS
Count it all joy / Love of my life / Don't let me walk down this road alone / Both day and night / Stay with me / He's always there / Right away / If anything ever happened to you / These what about's / (If I was only) Welcomed in / We can make a difference
CD _______________ CDEST 2237
Capitol / Sep '94 / EMI

Winans, Cece

ALONE IN HIS PRESENCE
Overture / Alone in his presence / I surrender all / Because of you / His strength is perfect / Every time / Great is thy faithfulness / Praise medley / Blessed assurance / Blood medley / He's always there / Alone in his presence (reprise)
CD _______________ SPD 1441
Alliance Music / Sep '96 / EMI

Winans, Vickie

VICKIE WINANS
We work it out / We shall overcome / Precious Lord / Stand up and praise him / We shall behold Him / Only one / Suddenly / I remember when / You never left me / Believing is seeing / Mary, did you know
CD _______________ CDK 9127
Alliance Music / Sep '95 / EMI

Winbush, Angela

ANGELA WINBUSH
Treat U rite / Keep turnin' me on / Too good to let you go / Baby hold on / You're my everything / Dream lover / Inner city blues / I'm the kind of woman / Sensitive heart / Hot summer love
CD _______________ 7559615912
Elektra / Apr '94 / Warner Music

Winchester Cathedral Choir

CAROLS FOR CHRISTMAS
O come all ye faithful (Adeste Fidelis) / Unto us a boy is born / Rocking / God rest ye merry gentlemen / Away in a manger / First Noel / Once in Royal David's City / Silent night / In dulci jubilo / While shepherds watched their flocks by night / Coventry

carol / O little town of Bethlehem / In the bleak midwinter / Hark the herald angels sing
CD ______ 261279
Arista / Oct '94 / BMG

Winchester, Jesse

HUMOUR ME
CD ______ SHCD 1023
Sugar Hill / Aug '96 / ADA / CM / Direct / Koch / Roots

JESSE WINCHESTER
CD ______ SPCD 1198
Stony Plain / Dec '94 / ADA / CM / Direct

LEARN TO LOVE IT
CD ______ SPCD 1205
Stony Plain / May '95 / ADA / CM / Direct

LET THE ROUGH SIDE DRAG
CD ______ SPCD 1206
Stony Plain / May '95 / ADA / CM / Direct

THIRD DOWN 10 TO GO
CD ______ SPCD 1199
Stony Plain / Dec '94 / ADA / CM / Direct

Wind In The Willows

WIND IN THE WILLOWS
Moments spent / Uptown girl / So sad (to watch good love go bad) / My uncle used to love me but she died / There is but one truth / Daddy / Friendly lion / Park Avenue blues / Djini Judy / Little people / She's fantastic and she's yours / Wheel of changes
CD ______ DOCD 1985
Drop Out / Aug '93 / Pinnacle

Wind Machine

PORTRAITS OF CHRISTMAS
CD ______ SD 606
Silver Wave / Jan '93 / Jazzizit Organisation / New Note/Pinnacle

RAIN MAIDEN
CD ______ SD 508
Silver Wave / Jan '93 / Jazzizit Organisation / New Note/Pinnacle

ROAD TO FREEDOM
CD ______ SD 602
Silver Wave / Jan '93 / Jazzizit Organisation / New Note/Pinnacle

UNPLUGGED
CD ______ SD 152
Silver Wave / Jan '93 / Jazzizit Organisation / New Note/Pinnacle

VOICES IN THE WIND
CD ______ SD 701
Silver Wave / Jan '93 / Jazzizit Organisation / New Note/Pinnacle

WIND MACHINE
CD ______ SD 151
Silver Wave / Jan '93 / Jazzizit Organisation / New Note/Pinnacle

Wind, Martin

TENDER WAVES
There's a boat that's leaving shortly for New York / Quietly / Marc's moments / You're my everything / Tender waves / Make a new start / Coracao vagabundo / You and the night and the music / Too far from you
CD ______ AL 73030
A / Nov '96 / Cadillac / Direct

Winding, Kai

BOB CITY (Small Groups 1949-1951)
CD ______ C&BCD 110
Cool & Blue / Oct '93 / Discovery / Jazz Music

CLEVELAND 1957 (Winding, Kai Septet)
CD ______ DSTS 1012
Status / '94 / Harmonia Mundi / Jazz Music / Wellard

FEATURING BILL EVANS
CD ______ CD 53150
Giants Of Jazz / May '95 / Cadillac / Jazz Music / Target/BMG

JAI AND KAI + 6 (Winding, Kai & J.J. Johnson)
Night in Tunisia / Piece for two trombonium / Rise 'n' shine / All at once you love her / No moon at all / Surrey with the fringe on top / Peanut vendor / You're my thrill / Jeanne / Four plus four / You don't know what love is / Continental (you kiss while you're dancing)
CD ______ 4809902
Sony Jazz / Dec '95 / Sony

KAI WINDING & J.J. JOHNSON (Winding, Kai & J.J. Johnson)
Out of this world / Thous sweet / Lover / Lope city / Stolen bass / It's all right with me / Mad about the boy / Yes sir that's my baby / That's how I feel about you / Gong rock
CD ______ BET 6026
Bethlehem / Jan '95 / ADA / ZYX

NUF SAID (Bethlehem Jazz Classics) (Winding, Kai & J.J. Johnson)
CD ______ CDGR 132
Charly / Apr '97 / Koch

Windows

BLUE SEPTMEBER
CD ______ 101S 70882
101 South / Nov '92 / New Note/Pinnacle

Windracht Acht

OP DE WILDE VAART
CD ______ PAN 148CD
Pan / Aug '94 / ADA / CM / Direct

Windsor For The Derby

CALM HADES FLOAT
CD ______ TR 46CD
Trance / May '96 / SRD

METROPOLITAN THEN POLAND
CD ______ TR 54CD
Trance Syndicate / Jan '97 / SRD

Winfield, Roger

WINDSONGS - THE SOUND OF THE AEOLIAN HARP
CD ______ CDSDL 394
Saydisc / Mar '94 / ADA / Direct / Harmonia Mundi

Winger, Kip

THIS CONVERSATION SEEMS LIKE A DREAM
Kiss of life / Monster / Endless circle / Angel of the underground / Steam / I'll be down / Naked son / Daniel / How far will we go / Don't let go / Here
CD ______ DOMO 710152
Domo / Feb '97 / Pinnacle

Wings

BACK TO THE EGG
Reception / Getting closer / We're open tonight / Spin it on / Again and again and again / Old Siam sir / Arrow through me / Rockestra theme / To you / After the ball / Million miles / Winter rose / Love awake / Broadcast / So glad to see you here / Baby's request / Daytime nightime suffering / Wonderful Christmas time / Rudolph the red nosed reggae
CD ______ CDPMCOL 10
Parlophone / Jun '93 / EMI

BAND ON THE RUN
Band on the run / Jet / Bluebird / Mrs. Vanderbilt / Let me roll it / Marmunia / No words / Picasso's last words / 1985
CD ______ CDPMCOL 5
Parlophone / Apr '93 / EMI

LONDON TOWN
London town / Gate on the left bank / I'm carrying / Backwards traveller / Cuff link / Chicken children / I've had enough / With a little luck / Famous groupies / Deliver your children / Name and address / Don't let it bring you down / Morse moose and the grey goose / Girlfriend / Girls school
CD ______ CDPMCOL 8
Parlophone / Apr '93 / EMI

VENUS AND MARS
Venus and Mars / Rock show / Love in song / You gave me the answer / Magneto and Titanium man / Letting go / Venus and Mars reprise / Spirits of ancient egypt / Medicine jar / Call me back again / Listen to what the man said / Treat her gently - lonely old people / Crossroads
CD ______ CDPMCOL 6
Parlophone / Apr '93 / EMI

WILD LIFE
Mumbo / Bip bop / Love is strange / Wild life / Some people never know / I am your singer / Bip bop link / Tomorrow / Dear friend / Mumbo link / Oh woman, oh why / Mary had a little lamb / Little woman love
CD ______ CDPMCOL 3
Parlophone / Apr '93 / EMI

WINGS AT THE SPEED OF SOUND
Let 'em in / Note you never wrote / She's my baby / Beware my love / Wino junko / Silly love songs / Cook of the house / Time to hide / Must do something about it / San Ferry Anne / Warm and beautiful
CD ______ CDPMCOL 7
Parlophone / Apr '93 / EMI

WINGS GREATEST
Another day / Silly love songs / Live and let die / Junior's farm / With a little luck / Band on the run / Uncle Albert / Admiral Halsey / Hi hi hi / Let 'em in / My love / Jet / Mull of Kintyre
CD ______ CDPMCOL 9
Parlophone / Jun '93 / EMI

Wink, Josh

HIGHER STATE OF WINK'S WORKS, A
Unification: *E-Culture* / I'm ready: *Size 9* / Higher state of consciousness / How's the music: *Winx* / Thoughts of a tranced love: *Winc* / Tribal confusion: *E-Culture*
CD ______ 5340572
Manifesto / Sep '96 / PolyGram

LEFT ABOVE THE CLOUDS (Winx)
CD ______ XLCD 119
XL / Sep '96 / Warner Music

Winkler, Harold

BORN WITH A KISS (Winkler, Harold & Norman Candler Orchestra)
CD ______ ISCD 156
Intersound / Jun '95 / Jazz Music

Winkler, Mark

HOTTEST NIGHT OF THE YEAR
Dancin' in the sunshine / Stain doll / Hottest night of the year / Tropical breezes / Beauty and the beast / Forward motion / Moon made me do it / Takin' chances / In a minor key
CD ______ CDLR 45015
L&R / Apr '90 / New Note/Pinnacle

Winski, Colin

HELLDORADO
CD ______ FCD 3027
Fury / Sep '93 / Nervous / TKO Magnum

Winsome

STORY OF A BLACK WOMAN
CD ______ SGCD 019
Sir George / Oct '94 / Jet Star / Pinnacle

Winston Groovy

AFRICAN GIRL
African girl / Moving on / You keep me hangin' on / From we met / Please don't go / Lay back in the arms of someone / Girl, without you / So in love with you / All because of you / Give me time / Please don't make me cry / Am I a dreamer / Oh little darling / Dear mama / Black hearted woman / Midnight train / Can't stand the morning / Anything goes with me / Old rock 'n' roller / Don't wanna hear that song again / Sea of dreams
CD ______ BRCD 3000
Blue Moon / Apr '92 / Cadillac / Discovery / Greensleeves / Jazz Music / Jet Star / TKO Magnum

COME ROCK WITH ME
CD ______ WGCD 009
Winston Groovy / Nov '95 / Jet Star

COMING ON STRONG
CD ______ WGCD 007
Winston Groovy / Oct '92 / Jet Star

Winston, George

AUTUMN
Colors/dance / Woods / Longing/love / Road / Moon / Sea / Stars
CD ______ 01934110122
Windham Hill / Jan '95 / BMG

BALLADS AND BLUES
CD ______ 08022340022
RCA / Jun '94 / BMG

DECEMBER
Thanksgiving / Jesus Jesus rest your head / Joy / Prelude / Carol of the bells / Night / Midnight (part 2) / Minstrels (part 3) / Variations on the kanon / Holly and the ivy / Some children see him / Peace / Snow
CD ______ 01934110252
Windham Hill / Jan '95 / BMG

FOREST
CD ______ 01934111572
Windham Hill / Oct '94 / BMG

LINUS AND LUCY (The Music Of Vince Guaraldi)
Cast your fate to the wind / Skating / Linus & Lucy / Great pumpkin waltz / Monterey / Charlie Brown thanksgiving / Treat Street / Eight five five / Masked marvel / Charlie brown and his All-Stars / You're in love / Charlie Brown / Peppermint Patty / Bon voyage / Young man's fancy / Remembrance / Theme to grace/Lament
CD ______ 01934111842
Windham Hill / Sep '96 / BMG

SUMMER
CD ______ 01934111072
Windham Hill / Jan '95 / BMG

WINTER INTO SPRING
January stars / February sea / Ocean waves (o mar) / Reflection / Raindance / Blossom meadow / Venice dreamer / Introduction (part 1) / Part 2
CD ______ 01934110192
Windham Hill / Jan '95 / BMG

Winstone, Eric

BY THE FIRESIDE (18 Intimate Easy Listening Classics) (Winstone, Eric & His Orchestra)
Me and my shadow / I'm in the mood for love / Rebecca / Kisses by candlelight / I'll close my eyes / That old feeling / Goodnight sweetheart / Very thought of you / You were meant for me / Unforgetaable / By the fireside / All my loving / Touch of your lips / Bye bye blues / You go to my head / Somewhere my love / Don't blame me / If I had you
CD ______ 306212
Hallmark / Jan '97 / Carlton

EASY GOING SIXTIES (18 Superb Arrangements Of 1960's Standards) (Winstone, Eric Orchestra)
Monsieur Dupont / Please please me cha cha / Last waltz / Can't take my eyes off you / Joanna / Congratulations / Can't buy me love / By the time I get to Phoenix / Strangers in the night / Sabre dance / Bonnie and Clyde / You've got your troubles / Ob-la-di ob-la-da / Something / Good vibrations / San Francisco / I wish you love / Pontinental
CD ______ 307382
Hallmark / Jul '97 / Carlton

TEACH ME TO DANCE (Winstone, Eric Orchestra)
Happy feet: *Winstone, Eric & His Band* / You've got your troubles: *Winstone, Eric & His Band* / Somewhere my love: *Winstone, Eric & His Band* / From a window: *Winstone, Eric & His Band* / Bye bye blues: *Winstone, Eric & His Band* / I'll just close my eyes: *Winstone, Eric & His Band* / Bonnie and Clyde: *Winstone, Eric & His Band* / Pepito's tune: *Winstone, Eric & His Band* / Green eyes: *Winstone, Eric & His Band* / Cuban nights: *Winstone, Eric & His Band* / Darling: *Winstone, Eric & His Band* / Last waltz: *Winstone, Eric & His Band* / Copacabana: *Winstone, Eric & His Band* / Tico tico: *Winstone, Eric & His Band* / Games that lovers play: *Winstone, Eric & His Band* / Teach me to dance: *Winstone, Eric & His Band* / International waltz: *Winstone, Eric & His Band* / Rebecca: *Winstone, Eric & His Band* / Thoughly modern Millie: *Winstone, Eric & His Band* / Goodbye blues: *Winstone, Eric & His Band* / (We're gonna) Rock around the clock: *Winstone, Eric & His Band* / Can't buy me love: *Winstone, Eric & His Band* / Congratulations: *Winstone, Eric & His Band* / Girl about town: *Winstone, Eric & His Band*
CD ______ DNSN 903
President / Apr '94 / Grapevine/PolyGram / President / Target/BMG

Winstone, Norma

WELL KEPT SECRET (Winstone, Norma & Jimmy Rowles)
Where or when / Timeless place / I dream too much / It amazes me / Prelude to a kiss / Joy spring / Remind me / Flower is a lovesome thing / Dream of you / Morning star
CD ______ 378362
Koch Jazz / Mar '97 / Koch

Winter

ETERNAL FROST
CD ______ NB 107
Nuclear Blast / Sep '94 / Plastic Head

INTO DARKNESS
CD ______ NB 064CD
Nuclear Blast / Nov '92 / Plastic Head

Winter, Cathy

NEXT SWEET TIME
CD ______ FF 598CD
Flying Fish / Feb '93 / ADA / CM / Direct / Roots

Winter, Edgar

BEST OF EDGAR WINTER, THE
CD ______ 4675072
CBS / Apr '91 / Sony

COLLECTION, THE
CD ______ 8122708952
Rhino / Jun '95 / Warner Music

HARLEM NOCTURNE
Searching / Tingo tango / Cry me a river / Save your love for me / Quiet gas / Satin doll / Jordu / Girl from Ipanema / Harlem nocturne / Come back baby / Before the sunset / Who dunnit / Please come home for Christmas
CD ______ CDTB 089
Thunderbolt / Dec '90 / TKO Magnum

I'M NOT A KID ANYMORE
Way down south / I'm not a kid anymore / Against the law / Brothers keeper / I wanta rock / Crazy / Just like you / Big city woman / Innocent lust / Frankenstein
CD ______ CDTB 152
Thunderbolt / Jan '94 / TKO Magnum

MISSION EARTH
CD ______ 8122707092
WEA / Jul '93 / Warner Music

REAL DEAL, THE
Hoochie coo / Real deal / We can't win / Good ol' rock 'n' roll / Give me the will / Nitty gritty / Eye of the storm / Sanctuary / Hot passionate love / Music is you / What do I tell my heart
CD ______ CDTB 182
Thunderbolt / May '97 / TKO Magnum

Winter, Johnny

AND
CD ______ BGOCD 105
Beat Goes On / Sep '91 / Pinnacle

BACK IN BEAUMONT (Winter, Johnny & Uncle John Turner)
Made in the shade / They call my lazy / Family rules / Ooh-poo-pah-doo / Drivin'

wheel / Allons dancez / Struggle in Houston / You're humbuggin' me / Just a little bit / Rainin' breakdown
CD CDTB 077
Thunderbolt / Apr '90 / TKO Magnum

BLUE SUEDE SHOES
Don't drink whiskey / Hook you / Blue suede shoes / Ronettes / Voodoo twist / How do you live a lie / Lost without you / Jolie blon / Bring it on home / Hello my lover / Rockin' pneumonia and the boogie woogie flu / Ice cube / Gangster of love / Parchman farm / Bad news / Roadrunner
CD CDTB 108
Thunderbolt / Feb '92 / TKO Magnum

BROKE AND LONELY
CD CDTB 165
Thunderbolt / Mar '96 / TKO Magnum

EARLY WINTER
Ease my pain / That's what love does / Crying in my heart / Guy you left behind / Shed so many tears / Creepy / Gangster of love / Roadrunner / Leave my woman alone / I can't believe you want to leave / Broke and lonely / Oh my darling / By the light of the silvery moon / Five after four AM
CD PRCD 116
President / Jan '87 / Grapevine/PolyGram / President / Target/BMG

EASE MY PAIN
CD SC 6071
Sundazed / Feb '97 / Cargo / Greyhound / Rollercoaster

ELECTRIC BLUES MAN (2CD Set)
My baby / Parchman farm / Night ride / One night of love / Thirty to twenty blues / Reelin' and rockin' / Tramp / Bad news / Bad news / Bad news / Suicide won't satisfy / Ice cube / Easy loving girl / We go back quite a ways / Hello my lover / Hook you / You'll be the death of me / Gonna miss me when I'm gone / Sloppy drunk blues / Goin' down slow / Low down gal of mine / Take my choice / Gangster of love / Eternally / Blue suede shoes / Ballad of Bertha Glutz / Living in the blues / Raindrops in my heart / Black cat bone / Talk to your daughter
CD Set CDTB 509
Thunderbolt / Jan '97 / TKO Magnum

FIVE AFTER FOUR AM
Oh my darling / Five after four AM / That's what love does / Shed so many tears / Roadrunner / Guy you left behind / Gangster of love / By the light of the silvery moon / Leave my woman alone / I can't believe you want to leave
CD CDTB 073
Thunderbolt / Nov '89 / TKO Magnum

GANGSTER OF LOVE
Gangster of love / Goin' down slow / That's what love does / Low down gal of mine / I can't believe you want to leave / Road runner / Out of sight / Five after four am / Leaving blues / Kind hearted woman / Leave my woman alone / Parchman farm
CD 305702
Hallmark / Oct '96 / Carlton

GUITAR SLINGER
It's my life baby / Iodine in my coffee / Trick bag / Mad dog / Boot Hill / I smell trouble / Lights out / Kiss tomorrow goodbye / My soul / Don't take advantage of me
CD ALCD 4735
Alligator / May '93 / ADA / CM / Direct

HEY, WHERE'S YOUR BROTHER
Johnny Guitar / She likes to boogie real low / White line blues / Please Come Home For Christmas / Hard Way / You must have a twin / You keep sayin' that you're leavin' / Treat Me Like You Wanta / Sick and tired / Blues This Bad / No More Doggin' / Check out her mama / Got my brand on you / One step forward
CD VPBCD 11
Pointblank / Sep '92 / EMI

JACK DANIELS KIND OF DAY
Sloppy drunk / Mistress / Careful with a fool / Shed so many tears / Eternally / Raining teardrops / Jack Daniels kind of a day / Going down slow / Stay by my side / We go back quite a ways / Low down gal of mine / Thirty two twenty blues / Silvery moon / I had to cry / Gonna miss me when I'm gone / Crazy baby
CD CDTB 142
Magnum Music / Dec '92 / TKO Magnum

JOHNNY B. GOODE
E Z Rider / Black cat bone / Going down slow / Five after four AM / Made in the shade / Gonna miss me when I'm gone / 32-20 Blues / Parchman farm / Don't drink whiskey / Gangster of love / Bring it on home / Hook you / Living in the blues / Hoochie coochie man / Gangster of love (Instrumental) / Messin' with the kid / Walking by myself / Johnny B Goode
CD 3036000852
Carlton / Apr '97 / Carlton

JOHNNY WINTER
I'm yours and I'm hers / Be careful with a fool / Dallas / Mean mistreater / Leland Mississippi / When you got a good friend / I'll drown my tears / Back door friend
CD 4712182
Columbia / Feb '97 / Sony

JOHNNY WINTER AND LIVE
Good morning little school girl / It's my own fault / Jumpin' Jack Flash / Great balls of fire / Long tall Sally / Whole lotta shakin' goin' on / Mean town blues / Johnny B Goode
CD BGOCD 29
Beat Goes On / Jun '92 / Pinnacle

LET ME IN
CD VPBCD 5
Pointblank / Sep '91 / EMI

LIBERTY HALL SESSIONS
CD CDTB 175
Thunderbolt / Jun '96 / TKO Magnum

LIVE IN HOUSTON, BUSTED IN AUSTIN
EZ rider / Walking by myself / Mother earth / Boney Maronie / Busted in Austin / Messin' with the kid / I can't make it by myself / Johnny B Goode / It's all over now / Jumpin' Jack flash
CD CDTB 100
Thunderbolt / Jul '91 / TKO Magnum

LIVIN' IN THE BLUES
Low down gal of mine / Going down slow / Avocado green / Parchman farm / Livin' in the blues / Leaving blues / 48-32-20 / Bad news / Kind hearted woman blues / Mojo boogie / Love, life and money / Evil on my mind / See see baby / Tin pan alley / I'm good / Third degree / Shake your moneymaker / Bad girl blues / Broke and lonely
CD SC 6070
Sundazed / Feb '97 / Cargo / Greyhound / Rollercoaster

LIVING IN THE BLUES
Goin' down slow / Kind hearted woman blues / 38-20-30 blues / Low down gal of mine / Avocado green / My world turns around her / Coming up fast / Living in the blues / Bad news / I had to cry / Kiss tomorrow goodbye / parchman farm / Tramp / Harlem nocturne
CD CDTB 083
Thunderbolt / '91 / TKO Magnum

NO TIME TO LIVE
Ain't that kindness / Stranger / Am I here / Self destructive blues / Golden days of rock and roll / Rock 'n' roll hoochie coo / Guess I'll go away / Rock 'n' roll people / Lay down your sorrows / Raised on rock / Let the music play / Prodigal son / Mind over matter / Pick up on my mojo / No time to live / On the limb
CD CDTB 136
Thunderbolt / Mar '92 / TKO Magnum

NOTHING BUT THE BLUES
Tired of tryin' / TV Mama / Sweet love and evil women / Everybody's blues / Drinkin' blues / Mad blues / It was rainin' / Bladie Mae / Walking through the park
CD BGOCD 104
Beat Goes On / Aug '91 / Pinnacle

PROGRESSIVE BLUES EXPERIMENT
Rollin' and tumblin' / Tribute to Muddy / Got love if you want it / Bad luck and trouble / Help me / Mean town blues / Broke down engine / Black cat bone / It's my own fault / Forty four
CD CDLL 57350
One Way / Jul '94 / ADA / Direct / Greyhound

RAISED ON ROCK
CD CDSGP 0306
Prestige / Aug '97 / Else / Total/BMG

RAW TO THE BONE (Winter, Johnny & Calvin Johnson)
Late on blues / They call me loudmouth / Line on your body / Once I had a woman / Take my choice / Unwelcome in your home / Gangster of love / Alone in my bedroom / hoochie coochie man / Moth balls / She's mine / Unsatisfied mind / Rock me baby
CD CDTB 126
Thunderbolt / Feb '92 / TKO Magnum
CD 8400872
Sky Ranch / May '96 / Discovery

ROCK 'N' ROLL COLLECTION (2CD Set)
Johnny B Goode / Good morning little school girl / I'll drown my tears / When you got a good friend / Be careful with a fool / Miss Ann / Hustled down in Texas / Rock 'n' roll / Hoochie koo / Rock me baby / Sitting in the jail house / Baby, watcha want me to do / Bony Moronie / It's all over now / TV Mama / Drinkin' blues / Walking thru the park / I'm not sure / Guess I'll go away / Thirty days / Come on in my kitchen / Highway 61 revisited
CD Set 4838972
Columbia / Jun '96 / Sony

SAINTS AND SINNERS
Stone County / Blinded by love / Thirty days / Stray cat blues / Bad luck situation / Rollin' cross the country / Riot in cell block 9 / Hurtin' so bad / Bony Moronie / Feedback on Highway 101 / Dirty
CD CK 66420
Columbia / Mar '96 / Sony

SEARCHIN' BLUES
Walking by myself / Diving duck / One step at a time / Bladie Mae / Mad blues / It was rainin' / Man mistreater / Mother In Law Blues / Dallas / Mean town blues
CD 4716612
Columbia / Jul '92 / Sony

SECOND WINTER
Memory pain / Good love / Miss Ann / Highway 61 revisited / Hustled down in Texas / Fast life rider / I'm not sure / Slippin' and slidin' / Johnny B Goode / I love everybody
CD EDCD 312
Edsel / Apr '89 / Pinnacle

SERIOUS BUSINESS
Master mechanic / Sound the bell / Murdering the blues / It ain't your business / Good time woman / Unseen eye / My time after awhile / Serious as a heart attack / Give it back / Route 90
CD ALCD 4742
Alligator / Oct '93 / ADA / CM / Direct

THIRD DEGREE
Mojo boogie / Love life and money / Evil on my mind / See see baby / Tin Pan Alley / I'm good / Third degree / Shake your moneymaker / Bad girl blues / Broke and lonely
CD ALCD 4748
Alligator / May '93 / ADA / CM / Direct

WHITE LIGHTNING
Mean town blues / Black cat bone / Mean mistreater / Talk to your daughter / Look up / I can love you baby
CD CDTB 149
Thunderbolt / Oct '93 / TKO Magnum

WINTER BLUES
CD CCSCD 445
Castle / May '97 / BMG

Winter, Kitty

GYPSY ALBUM, THE
CD BLDCD 539
Boulevard / Aug '97 / Grapevine/PolyGram / Total/BMG

Winter, Ophelie

SOON
Soon / Living in me / It ain't all about you / Face to face / Revolution 4 love / Best part of me / When I got the mood / Keep it on the red light / Air that I breathe / Everlasting love / Shame on U / Let the river flow / Dieu m'a donne la foi
CD 0630161122
East West / Jul '97 / Warner Music

Winter, Paul

EARTHBEAT
CD LD 0015
Living Music / Aug '88 / New Note/ Pinnacle

Winters, Ruby

RUBY WINTERS
CD RNCD 1008
Rhino / Jun '93 / Grapevine/PolyGram / Jet Star

Winther, Jens

LOOKING THROUGH (Winther, Jens Quintet)
CD STCD 4127
Storyville / Feb '90 / Cadillac / Jazz Music / Wellard

Winwood, Steve

AIYE KETA (Third World)
Happy vibes / Irin Ajo / Black beauty / Afro super / Shango
CD EDCD 513
Edsel / Feb '97 / Pinnacle

ARC OF A DIVER
While you see a chance / Second hand woman / Slowdown sundown / Spanish dancer / Night train / Dust / Arc of a diver
CD CID 9576
Island / Jan '87 / PolyGram

BACK IN THE HIGH LIFE
Higher love / Take it as it comes / Freedom overspill / Back in the high life / Finer things / Wake me up on judgement day / Split decision / My love's leavin'
CD CID 9844
Island / Jul '86 / PolyGram

CHRONICLES
Wake me up on judgement day / While you see a chance / Vacant chair / Help me angel / My love's leavin' / Valerie / Arc of a diver / Higher love / Spanish dancer / Talking back to the night
CD SSWCD 1
Island / Nov '87 / PolyGram

FINER THINGS, THE (4CD Set)
Dimples: *Davis, Spencer Group* / I Can't stand it: *Davis, Spencer Group* / Every little bit hurts: *Davis, Spencer Group* / Strong love: *Davis, Spencer Group* / Keep on running: *Davis, Spencer Group* / Somebody help me: *Davis, Spencer Group* / When I come home: *Davis, Spencer Group* / I want to know: *Clapton, Eric & The Powerhouse* / Crossroads: *Clapton, Eric & The Powerhouse* / Gimme some lovin': *Davis, Spencer Group* / I'm a man: *Davis, Spencer Group* / Paper sun: *Traffic* / Dealer: *Traffic* / Coloured rain: *Traffic* / No face, no name, no number: *Traffic* / Heaven is in your mind: *Traffic* / Smiling phases: *Traffic* / Dear Mr. Fantasy: *Traffic* / Pearly Queen: *Traffic* / Forty thousand headmen: *Traffic* / No time to live: *Traffic* / Shanghai noodle factory: *Traffic* / Medicated goo: *Traffic* / Withering tree: *Traffic* / Had to cry today: *Blind Faith* / Can't find my way home: *Blind Faith* / Sea of joy: *Blind Faith* / Sleeping in the ground: *Blind Faith* / Under my thumb: *Blind Faith* / Stranger to himself: *Traffic* / John Barleycorn: *Traffic* / Glad: *Traffic* / Freedom rider: *Traffic* / Empty pages: *Traffic* / Low spark of high heeled boys: *Traffic* / Rainmaker: *Traffic* / Shoot out at the fantasy factory: *Traffic* / (Sometimes I feel so) Uninspired: *Traffic* / Happy vibes: *Winwood, Steve & Remi Kabaka/Abdul Lasisi Amao* / Something new: *Traffic* / Dream Gerrard: *Traffic* / Walking in the wind: *Traffic* / When the eagle flies: *Traffic* / Winner/Loser: *Winwood, Steve & Stomu Yamashta* / Crossing the line (Live): *Yamashta, Stomu & Steve Winwood* / Hold on: *Winwood, Steve & Jim Capaldi* / Time is running out: *Winwood, Steve & Jim Capaldi* / Vacant chair: *Winwood, Steve & Viv Stanshall* / While you see a chance / Arc of a diver / Spanish dancer / Night train / Dust / Valerie / Talking back to the night / Your silence is your song / Higher love / Freedom overspill / Back in the high life / Finer things / Roll with it / Don't you know what the night can do / One and only man
CD Set IBXCD 2
Island / Mar '95 / PolyGram

JUNCTION 7
Spy in the house of love / Angel of mercy / Just wanna have some fun / Let your love come down / Real love / Fill me up / Gotta get back to my baby / Someone like you / Family affair / Plenty lovin' / Lord of the Street
CD CDV 2832
Virgin / Jun '97 / EMI

KEEP ON RUNNING
CD IMCD 224
Island / Mar '96 / PolyGram

REFUGEES OF THE HEART
You'll keep on searching / Every day (oh Lord) / One and only man / I will be here / Another deal goes down / Running on / Come out and dance / In the light of day
CD CDV 2650
Virgin / Nov '90 / EMI

ROLL WITH IT
Roll with it / Holding on / Morning side / Put on your dancing shoes / Don't you know what the night can do / Hearts on fire / One more morning / Shining song
CD CDV 2532
Virgin / Jun '88 / EMI

STEVE WINWOOD
Hold on / Time is running out / Let me make something in your life / Luck's in / Vacant chair / Midland maniac
CD IMCD 161
Island / Mar '93 / PolyGram

TALKING BACK TO THE NIGHT
Valerie / Big girls walk away / I go / While there's a candle burning / Still in the game / It was happening / Help me angel / Talking back to the night / There's a river
CD CID 9777
Island / Feb '87 / PolyGram

Wipers

HERD
CD TK 95CD114
Tim/Kerr / Jul '97 / Greyhound

IS THIS REAL
CD SPOD 82/253
Sub Pop / Mar '93 / Cargo / Greyhound / Shellshock/Disc

SILVER SAIL
Y I came / Back to basics / Warning / Mars / Prisoner / Standing there / Sign of the times / Line / On a roll / Never win / Silver sail
CD TK 92CD031
T/K / Jun '94 / Pinnacle

Wire

154
I should have known better / Two people in a room / 15th / Other window / Single KO / Touching display / On returning / Mutual friend / Blessed state / Once is enough / Map ref 41 degrees N 93 degrees W / Indirect enquiries / Forty versions
CD CDGO 2064
EMI / Jul '94 / EMI

BEHIND THE CURTAIN
Mary is a dyke / Too true / Just don't care / TV / New York City / After midnight / Pink flag / Love ain't polite / Oh no not so / It's the motive / Practice makes perfect / Sand in my joints / Stablemates / I feel mysterious today / Underwater experience / Dot dash / Options R / From the nursery / Finistaire / No romans / Another the letter / Forty Versions / Blessed state / Touching display / Once is enough / Stepping off too quick / Indirect inquiries / Map ref 41 degrees N 93 degrees W / Question of degree / Two people in a room / Former airline
CD CDGO 2066
EMI / May '95 / EMI

BELL IS A CUP UNTIL IT IS STRUCK, A
Silk skin paws / Finest drops / Queen's of Ur and The King of Um / Free falling divisions / It's a Bob / Boiling boy / Kidney bongos / Come back in two halves / Follow the locust / Public place
CD _____ **CDSTUMM 54**
Mute / Jun '88 / RTM/Disc

CHAIRS MISSING
Practice makes perfect / French film blurred / Another the letter / Men 2nd / Marooned / Sand in my joints / Being sucked in again / Heartbeat / Mercy / Outdoor miner / I am the fly / I feel mysterious today / From the nursery / Used to / Too late
CD _____ **CDGO 2065**
EMI / Jul '94 / EMI

EXPLODED VIEWS
CD _____ **SCONC 25**
Audioglobe / Sep '94 / Plastic Head

FIRST LETTER, THE
CD _____ **CDSTUMM 87**
Mute / Oct '91 / RTM/Disc

IDEAL COPY, THE
Point of collapse / Ahead / Madman's honey / Feed me / Ambitious / Cheeking tongues / Still shows / Over theirs / Ahead (II) / Serious of snakes / Drill / Advantage in height / Up to the sun / Ambulance chasers / Feed me (II) / Vivid riot of red
CD _____ **CDSTUMM 42**
Mute / Apr '87 / RTM/Disc

IT'S BEGINNING TO AND BACK AGAIN
Finest drops / Eardrum buzz / German shepherds / Public place / It's a boy / Illuminated / Boiling boy / Over theirs / Offer / In vivo
CD _____ **CDSTUMM 66**
Mute / Apr '89 / RTM/Disc

MANSCAPE
CD _____ **CDSTUMM 80**
Mute / Apr '90 / RTM/Disc

ON RETURNING (Wire 1977-1979)
12XU / It's so obvious / Mr. Suit / Three girl rhumba / Ex lion tamer / Lowdown / Strange / Reuters / Feeling called love / I am the fly / Practice makes perfect / French film blurred / I feel mysterious today / Marooned / Sand in my joints / Outdoor miner / Question of degree / I should have known better / Other window / Forty versions / Touching display / On returning / Another the letter / Straight line / 106 beats that / Field day for the Sundays / Dot dash / Men 2nd / Two people in room / Blessed state
CD _____ **CDP 7925352**
Harvest / Sep '96 / EMI

PINK FLAG
Reuters / Field day for the Sundays / Three girl rhumba / Ex lion tamer / Lowdown / Start to move / Brazil / It's so obvious / Surgeon's girl / Pink flag / Commercial / Straight line / 106 Beats that / Mr. Suit / Strange / Fragile / Mannequin / Different to me / Champs / Feeling called love / 12XU / Dot dash / Options R
CD _____ **CDGO 2063**
EMI / Jul '94 / EMI

TURNS AND STROKES
Safe / Lorries / Panamanian craze / Remove for improvement / Spare one / Over my head / 12XU / Inventory / Ritual view / Part of our history / Second length / Catapult 30
CD _____ **WM 004CD**
WMO / May '96 / Vital

WHORE (Various Artists Play Wire) (Various Artists)
40 Versions: *Godflesh* / Mannequin: *Lush* / It's a boy: *Resolution* / Serious of snakes: *aMiniature* / Question of degree: *Kustomized* / Ahead: *Band Of Susans* / Three girl rhumba: *Bark Psychosis* / On returning: *Ex Lion Tamers* / 12XU: *Spasm* / Lowdown: *Fudge Tunnel* / German shephers: *Laika* / Mutual friend: *Connelly, Chris* / Eastern standards: *Marks, Carl* / Our swimmer: *Petty Tyrants* / Eardrum buzz: *Scanner* / Being sucked in again: *Polar Bear* / Fragile: *Renaldo, Lee* / Map ref 41N 93W: *My Bloody Valentine* / Outdoor miner: *Transformer* / Used to: *Main* / 15th: *Watt, Mike*
CD _____ **WMO 002CD**
WMO / Feb '96 / Vital

WIRE 1985-1990
CD _____ **CDSTUMM 116**
Mute / Jun '93 / RTM/Disc

Wired To The Moon

PURE
Hold me / No way home / Pure / Same old story / Believes / Promises / This girl / World of stone / All the time / Harry's letter
CD _____ **COOKCD 104**
Cooking Vinyl / Jul '97 / Vital

Wiregrass Sacred Harp ...

COLORED SACRED HARP (Wiregrass Sacred Harp Singers)
CD _____ **804332**
New World / Feb '94 / ADA / Cadillac / Harmonia Mundi

DESIRE FOR PIETY (Wiregrass Sacred Harp Singers)
CD _____ **805192**
New World / Aug '97 / ADA / Cadillac / Harmonia Mundi

Wirtz, Mark

GO GO MUSIC OF MARK WIRTZ, THE (Wirtz, Mark Orchestra/Chorus)
Yeh yeh / If illusion met fantasy / Yellow spotted Capricorn / Come back and shake me / You didn't have to be so nice / Comin' home baby / Don't do it baby / Real Mr. Smith / Monday Monday / Touch of velvet / Sting of brass / Sunny / I can hear music / Sunday night / Riviera carnival / Chinese chequers / Watching a matchstick flight / Yesterday's laughter, today's tears / Dizzy / Ther's no business like monkey business / Thimble full of puzzles / Beyond the horizon / Dreamin' / Fantastic fair
CD _____ **RPM 172**
RPM / Dec '96 / Pinnacle

Wirtz, Rev. Billy C.

BACKSLIDER'S TRACTOR PULL
CD _____ **HCD 8024**
Hightone / Feb '96 / ADA / Koch

DEEP FRIED AND SANCTIFIED
CD _____ **HCD 8017**
Hightone / Feb '96 / ADA / Koch

PIANIST ENVY
CD _____ **HCD 8051**
Hightone / Feb '96 / ADA / Koch

SONGS OF FAITH AND INFLAMMATION
CD _____ **HCD 8069**
Hightone / Apr '96 / ADA / Koch

TURN FOR THE WIRTZ, A
CD _____ **HCD 8042**
Hightone / Feb '96 / ADA / Koch

Wisdom

SIGNS OF THE TIME
CD _____ **WBM 2002**
Wisdom Wise / Sep '93 / Jet Star

Wisdom, Norman

WISDOM OF A FOOL, THE
Don't laugh at me / Wisdom of a fool / Dream for sale / Up in the world / Narcissus: *Wisdom, Norman & Joyce Grenfell* / Beware / Me and my imagination / Skylark / Who can I turn to / Boy meets girl: *Wisdom, Norman & Ruby Murray* / You must have been a beautiful baby / Heart of a clown / I don't arf love you: *Wisdom, Norman & Joyce Grenfell* / By the fireside / Joker / Impossible / You're getting to be a habit with me / Happy ending / Make a miracle: *Wisdom, Norman & Pip Hinton* / Once in love with Amy / My darling, my darling / Leaning on a lampost / For me and my girl / Lambeth walk
CD _____ **SEECD 477**
See For Miles/C5 / Jun '97 / Pinnacle

Wisdom Tooth

MENTAL FLOSS
CD _____ **KFWCD 141**
Knitting Factory / Jun '97 / Cargo / Plastic Head

Wiseblood

PEDAL TO THE METAL
CD _____ **ABB 030CD**
Big Cat / Nov '91 / 3mv/Pinnacle

Wiseguys

EXECUTIVE SUITE
CD _____ **WALLCD 008**
Wall Of Sound / May '96 / Prime / Soul Trader / Vital

Wiseman Sextette

WISEMAN SEXTETTE/QUARTET 1923
CD _____ **DOCD 5520**
Document / Mar '97 / ADA / Hot Shot / Jazz Music

Wiseman, Bob

CITY OF WOOD
CD _____ **GRCD 324**
Glitterhouse / Sep '94 / Avid/BMG

Wiseman, Mac

TEENAGE HANGOUT
Teenage hangout / Step it up and go / Sundown / I hear you knocking / Meanest blues in the world / Hey Mr. Bluesman / One mint julep / I'm waiting for the ships that never come in / Fool / I like this kind of music / Now that you have me / Talk of the town / Glad rags / I'm eatin' high on a hog / I want someone / Camptown races / I'll still write your name in the sand / Promise of things to come / Thinkin' about you / Because we are young / Be good baby / 'Tis sweet to be remembered / Running bear / Ballad of Davy Crockett / Tom Dooley / Sixteen tons / El Paso / Old lamplighter / Three bells / I'm movin' on
CD _____ **BCD 15694**
Bear Family / Jul '93 / Direct / Rollercoaster / Swift

Wiseman, Val

LADY SINGS THE BLUES
Eeny meeny miny mo / What shall I say / One, two button your shoe / I'll never be the same / How could you / Am I blue / What a little moonlight can do / Miss Brown to you / On the sentimental side / It's easy to blame the weather / He's funny that way / If dreams come true / Lover man / Just one of those things / Easy living / You can depend on me / Don't explain / Riffin' the scotch
CD _____ **ESJCD 541**
Essential Jazz / Apr '97 / BMG

Wishbone Ash

ARGUS
Time was / Sometime world / Blowin' free / King will come / Leaf and stream / Warrior / Throw down the sword
CD _____ **MCLD 19085**
MCA / Nov '92 / BMG

ARGUS/PILGRIMAGE (2CD Set)
Time was / Sometime world / Blowin' free / King will come / Leaf and stream / Warrior / Throw down the sword / Vas dis / Pilgrim / Jailbait / Alone / Lullaby / Valediction / Where were you tomorrow
CD Set _____ **MCD 33003**
MCA / Jul '96 / BMG

BLOWIN' FREE
Blind eye / Phoenix / Persephone / Outward bound / Pilgrim / You rescue me / Time was / King will come / Blowin' free / Throw down the sword / Lady whiskey / Rock 'n' roll widow / Ballad of the beacon / Jailbait / Everybody needs a friend / Mother of pearl
CD _____ **NTRCD 014**
Nectar / Feb '94 / Pinnacle

ILLUMINATIONS
CD _____ **HTDCD 67**
HTD / Oct '96 / CM / Pinnacle

LIVE DATES
King will come / Warrior / Throw down the sword / Lady whiskey / Phoenix / Rock 'n' roll widow / Ballad of the beacon / Baby, what you want me to do / Pilgrim / Blowin' free / Jailbait
CD _____ **BGOCD 293**
Beat Goes On / Sep '95 / Pinnacle

LIVE IN GENEVA
CD _____ **HNRCD 03**
Hengest / Mar '96 / Grapevine/PolyGram

PILGRIMAGE
Vas dis / Pilgrim / Jailbait / Alone / Lullaby / Valediction / Where were you tomorrow
CD _____ **MCLD 19084**
MCA / Nov '92 / BMG

RAW TO THE BONE
Cell of fame / People in motion / Don't cry / Love is blue / Long live the night / Rocket in my pocket / It's only love / Don't you mess / Dreams (searching for an answer) / Perfect timing
CD _____ **CLACD 390**
Castle / Aug '93 / BMG

THERE'S THE RUB
Silver shoes / Don't come back / Persephone / Hometown / Lady Jay / FUBB
CD _____ **MCLD 19249**
MCA / Oct '94 / BMG

TIMELINE (Live)
CD _____ **RRCD 216**
Receiver / Jan '97 / Grapevine/PolyGram

TWIN BARRELS BURNING
Engine overheat / Can't fight love / Genevieve / Me and my guitar / Hold on / Streets of shame / No more lonely nights / Angels have mercy / Wind up
CD _____ **CLACD 389**
Castle / Aug '93 / BMG

WISHBONE ASH
Blind eye / Lady whisky / Errors of my ways / Queen of torture / Handy / Phoenix
CD _____ **BGOCD 234**
Beat Goes On / Oct '94 / Pinnacle

WISHBONE ASH IN CONCERT
CD _____ **WINCCD 4**
Windsong / Sep '91 / Pinnacle

WISHBONE FOUR
So many things to say / Ballad of the beacon / No easy road / Everybody needs a friend / Doctor / Sorrel / Sing out the song / Rock 'n' roll widow
CD _____ **MCLD 19149**
MCA / Aug '94 / BMG

Wishdokta

POST MODERN BREAKS (Wishdokta & James Hyman)
CD _____ **KICKCD 2**
Kickin' / Apr '93 / Prime / SRD

Wishing Stones

WILDWOOD
CD _____ **HVNCD 004**
Creation / Nov '91 / 3mv/Vital

Wishplants

COMA
CD _____ **WOLCD 1033**
China / Oct '93 / Pinnacle

DADDY LONGLEGS
CD _____ **WOLCD 1070**
China / Jul '96 / Pinnacle

Witch Hazel

LANDLOCKED
CD _____ **FLY 014**
Blue Rose / Dec '95 / 3mv/Pinnacle

Witchcraft

AS I HIDE
Mindfire wish / Open ways / Liquid air / X-position / Absentia / Return to me / Invocation / Iridescent / We rest / Cathedral / Love on a battleship
CD _____ **AD 24CD**
AD / Oct '96 / Disc

Witchdoktors

BRAIN MACHINE
CD _____ **LOUDEST 18**
One Louder / Mar '97 / Mo's Music Machine / Shellshock/Disc / SRD

Witchfynde

BEST OF WITCHFYNDE, THE
CD _____ **CDMETAL 1**
British Steel / Feb '97 / Cargo / Pinnacle / Plastic Head

Witchkiller

DAY OF THE SAXONS
CD _____ **047554**
Steamhammer / '89 / Pinnacle / Plastic Head

Witchman

EXPLORIMENTING BEATS
Viper flats / Amok / Stone def / Hammerhead / Chemical noir / Order of the dragon / Post trauma blues / NY 23 / No place like chrome / Palace of angels / Light at the edge
CD _____ **DVNT 019CD**
Deviant / Apr '97 / Prime / Vital

Withers, Bill

LEAN ON ME (The Best Of Bill Withers)
Ain't no sunshine / Grandma's hands / Lean on me / Use me / Kissing my love / Who is he and what is he to you / I don't want you on my mind / Same love that made me laugh / Hello like before / Lovely day / Let me be the one you need / I want to spend the night / Stepping right along / Whatever happens / Watching you watching me / Heart is your life / You try to find a love / Just the two of uus
CD _____ **4805062**
Columbia / May '95 / Sony

Witherspoon, Jimmy

AIN'T NOTHIN' NEW ABOUT THE BLUES (Witherspoon, Jimmy & Robben Ford)
CD _____ **AIM 1050**
Aim / Apr '95 / ADA / Direct / Jazz Music

BABY-BABY-BABY
CD _____ **OBCCD 527**
Original Blues Classics / Nov '92 / Complete/Pinnacle / Wellard

BIG BLUES
You got me running / Whiskey drinking woman / Once there lived a fool / Just a dream / Lotus blossom / Big boss man / Nobody knows you when you're down and out / That's the one / Let's think awhile / Swing on it / Point / Snow was falling
CD _____ **JSPCD 285**
JSP / Jul '97 / ADA / Cadillac / Direct / Hot Shot / Target/BMG

BLOWIN' IN FROM KANSAS CITY
Love my baby / There ain't nothing better / Love and frendship / TB blues / Goin' around in circles / She's evil / I'm just a country boy / Good jumping aka jump children / Blowing the blues / It's raining outside / I'm just a lady's man / I'm just wandering / Who's been jivin' you / Sweet lovin' baby / Thelma Lee blues / Slow your speed / Dr. Knows His Business aka Dr. Blues / Rain rain rain / Baby baby
CD _____ **CDCHD 279**
Ace / Feb '91 / Pinnacle

BLUES AROUND THE CLOCK
CD _____ **OBCCD 576**
Original Blues Classics / Jan '96 / Complete/Pinnacle / Wellard

BLUES FOR EASY LIVERS
Lotus blossom / Gee baby ain't I good to you / Travellin' light / PS I love you / I'll always be in love with you / Don't worry 'bout me / Easy living / Embraceable you / Blues in the night / Trouble in mind / How long will it take to be a man / I got it bad and that ain't good

CD OBCCD 585
Original Blues Classics / Oct '96 / Complete/Pinnacle / Wellard

BLUES THE WHOLE BLUES AND NOTHING BUT THE BLUES
You got a hold of my heart / It never rains but it pours / Real bad day / Sooner or later / Killing time / Blues the whole blues and nothing but the blues / Help me operator / Would man be satisfied / Two sides to every story / Wake up call / Think / You ain't foolin' me
CD IGOCD 2001
Indigo / Jul '95 / ADA / Direct

CRY THE BLUES (Witherspoon, Jimmy & Richard 'Groove' Holmes)
Tell him I was flyin' (part 1) / In blues / Loser's blues / Please send me someone to love / Life's highway / Cry the blues / Out blues / Since I fell for you / Everything / Tell him I was flyin' (part 2)
CD TKOCD 004
TKO / '92 / TKO

EVENIN' BLUES
Money's gettin' cheaper / Grab me a freight / Don't let go / I've been treated wrong / Evening / Cane River / Baby how long / Good rockin' man / Kansas city / Drinking beer
CD OBCCD 511
Original Blues Classics / Apr '94 / Complete/Pinnacle / Wellard

JAY'S BLUES
Foolish prayer / Lucille / One fine gal / Blues in trouble / Two little girls / Corn whiskey / Don't tell me now / Last mile / Day is dawning / Back door blues / Fast woman, sloe gin / Twenty four sad hours / Just for you / Sad life / Move me baby / I'm not so young / Highway to happiness / I done told you / Oh boy / Jay's blues / Back home / Miss, Miss Mistreater
CD CDCHARLY 270
Charly / Sep '91 / Koch

JIMMY WITHERSPOON
Time's gettin' tougher than tough / St. Louis blues / Trouble in mind / Goin' to Kansas city / Outskirts of town / Every day / Roll 'em Pete / CC rider / Corina Corina / How long
CD 17069
Laserlight / Aug '96 / Target/BMG

JIMMY WITHERSPOON & JAY MCSHANN (Witherspoon, Jimmy & Jay McShann)
CD BLCD 760173
Black Lion / Mar '93 / Cadillac / Jazz Music / Koch / Wellard

JIMMY WITHERSPOON SINGS THE BLUES
CD AIM 1005CD
Aim / Oct '93 / ADA / Direct / Jazz Music

LIVE AT CONDON'S, NEW YORK
Goin' to Chicago / Gee baby ain't I good to you / You got me runnin' / Big boss man / Sweet lotus blossom / I'm gonna move to the outskirts of town / If I didn't get well no more / Money's getting cheaper / In the dark / I'm knocking out your teeth tonite / Ain't nobody's business if I do / Trouble in mind / Don't you miss your baby
CD CDGATE 7023
Kingdom Jazz / Nov '90 / Kingdom

LIVE AT MONTEREY
CD M&MJ 421
Fresh Sound / Feb '88 / Discovery / Jazz Music

MIDNIGHT LADY CALLED THE BLUES
New York City blues / Barber / Blinded by love / Happy hard times / Something rotten in East St Louis / Midnight lady called the blues / Blues hall of fame
CD MCD 5327
Muse / Sep '92 / New Note/Pinnacle

ROCKIN' WITH SPOON (Charly Blues Masterworks Vol.25)
Good rockin' tonight / When I been drinkin' / Big fine girl / No rollin' blues / Ain't nobody's business if I do / Times gettin' tougher than tough / How long / Corine / CC rider / Roll 'em Pete / Everyday / Outskirts of town / Kansas city / Trouble in mind / St. Louis blues
CD CDBM 25
Charly / Apr '92 / Koch

SPOON & GROOVE (Witherspoon, Jimmy & Richard 'Groove' Holmes)
CD TCD 1015
Tradition / May '96 / ADA / Vital

SPOON SO EASY
It ain't no secret / Ain't nobody's business / Live so easy / Congratulations / I can make it without you / Goin' down slow / When the lights go out / Crying / TWA / Danger / I don't know why (why do I love you like I do) / Garfield Avenue / Mack and Jay / Just to prove my love to you
CD MCD 93003
Chess/MCA / Apr '97 / BMG / New Note/BMG

SPOON'S LIFE
Night life / Help me / Big boss man / Cold cold feeling / Worried life blues / Did you ever / Blues with a feeling / Big leg woman

CD ECD 260442
Evidence / Mar '94 / ADA / Cadillac / Harmonia Mundi

SPOONFUL
Big boss man / Nothing's changed / Sign on the building / Reds and whiskey / Moon is rising / Inflation blues / Take out some insurance / Pearly whites / Spoonful / Gloomy Sunday
CD 74321332932
RCA / Feb '97 / BMG

TOUGHER THAN TOUGH
Time's getting tougher than tough / How long / Corrina Corrina / CC rider / Roll 'em Pete / Everyday / Outskirts of town / Kansas City / Trouble in mind / St. Louis blues / In blues / Loser's blues / Please send me someone to love / Life's highway / Cry the blues / Out blues
CD CDBM 123
Blue Moon / Jun '97 / Cadillac / Discovery / Greensleeves / Jazz Music / Jet Star / TKO Magnum

Within Reach

SOMETHING'S NOT RIGHT
CD JABSC 002CD
Burning Heart / Jan '97 / Plastic Head

Within Temptation

ENTER
CD DSFA 1007CD
DSFA / May '97 / Plastic Head

Withschinsky, Hill

LATIN MOODS (2CD Set)
Girl from Ipanema / One note samba / Meditation / Volare / Spanish eyes / Quiet nights of quiet stars / Begin the beguine / How insensitive / Latin nights / Guantamera / Desafinado / Cubana / Wave / Agua de beber / Kiss of fire / Gift / Once I loved / Night and day / Lambada / Summer samba / Spanish harlem / Dindi / La cumparsita / Amor / On a clear day (You can see forever) / Evergreen / La bamba / Tango / Light my fire / Peal of bells / Killing me softly / Brasilia / Copacabana / Breeze from Rio / Tico tico / Perfidia
CD Set 3036000122
Carlton / Oct '95 / Carlton

Wizards Of Twiddly

MAN MADE SELF
CD FFPCD 2
Fracture For Pleasure / Jan '94 / SRD

Wizo

UUAARRGH
CD FAT 527CD
Fatwreck Chords / Jun '95 / Plastic Head

Wob

I CAN'T STAY LONG
Poacher / Legacy / Sometimes / Dancing for sixpence / Rapunzel / Goodbye Twyford / Mole / Kings clearing / Dusty corners / Mother Earth / London / Hardest part
CD CYCLECD 002
Cycle / Feb '96 / CM / Direct

Wobbling Woodwinds

SOLO FLIGHT (Wobbling Woodwinds & Ulf Johansson)
CD NCD 8829
Phontastic / Mar '94 / Cadillac / Jazz Music / Wellard

Wofa

GUINEA/MARTINIQUE ENCOUNTER (Wofa/Tambou Bo Kannal)
CD 926502
BUDA / Oct '96 / Discovery

Wofford, Mike

LIVE AT MAYBECK RECITAL HALL VOL.18
CD CCD 4514
Concord Jazz / Jul '92 / New Note/Pinnacle

Woggles

GET TOUGH
CD TR 023CD
Telstar / May '97 / Cargo / Greyhound

Wojtasik, Piotr

QUEST
CD PB 00147
Power Bros. / Jul '97 / Harmonia Mundi

Wolf, Kate

BACKROADS (Wolf, Kate & Wildwood Flower)
Lately / Emma Rose / Sitting on the porch / Redtail hawk / Telluride / Goodbye babe / It ain't in the wine / Tequila and me / Legend in his time / Riding in the country / Oklahoma going home / Back roads

CD R 27142
Rhino / Oct '94 / ADA

BREEZES
CD GAD 210
Gadfly / Mar '96 / ADA

CARRY IT ON
Then came the children / September song / Both sides now / We were strangers / Sweet love / Carry it on / Old and lonely sound / Boy from Oklahoma / One by one / Forsaken lover / Highway in the wind / Muddy roads
CD FR 301
Flat Rock / May '97 / ADA / Direct

CLOSE TO YOU
Across the great divide / Legget serenade / Like a river / Unfinished life / Friend of mine / Love still remains / Eyes of a painter / Here in California / Stone in the water / Close to you
CD R 271482
Rhino / Oct '94 / ADA

EVENING IN AUSTIN, AN
Eyes of a painter / Green eyes / Carolina pines / Give yourself to love / Let's get together / Friend of mine
CD R 271487
Rhino / Oct '94 / ADA

GIVE YOURSELF TO LOVE VOL.1 & 2
CD R 271483
Rhino / Oct '94 / ADA

LOOKING BACK AT YOU
CD R 71613
Rhino / Jul '94 / ADA

Wolf Spider

DRIFTEN IN THE SULLEN SEA
CD CDFLAG 63
Under One Flag / Sep '91 / Pinnacle

KINGDOM OF PARANOIA
Manifestants / Pain / Black'n'white / Foxes / Waiting for sense / Desert / Sickened nation / Nasty-ment / Survive / Weakness
CD CDFLAG 49
Under One Flag / Nov '90 / Pinnacle

Wolfe, Robert

ANY DREAM WILL DO
It's the natural thing to do / Gal in Calico / It only happens when I dance with you / Take these chains from my heart / Nobody's child / Your cheatin' heart / Crystal chandeliers / Jardin secret / Dolannes melodie / Oh lady be good / Our love is here to stay / Liza / Embraceable you / Fascinating rhythm / They can't take that away from me / Somebody loves me / Someone to watch over me / Golden wedding day (La Cinquantaine) / From a distance / Mr. Mistoffelees / Tell me on a Sunday / Close every door / Any dream will do / Chanson de Matin / I'm beginning to see the light / I've got a gal in Kalamazoo / It don't mean a thing if it ain't got that swing / Romantica / At the Cafe Continental / Serenade in the night / Florentiner march
CD GRCD 51
Grasmere / '92 / Highlander / Savoy / Target/BMG

BLACKPOOL REVISITED
High school cadets march / Wind beneath my wings / Meditation / South American Joe / Tequila / As I love you / Once in a while / Sentimental journey / She didn't say 'yes' / I'm old fashioned / Make believe / Smoke gets in your eyes / Song is you / Somewhere out there / Spanish flea / Wedding samba / Cumana / Unchained melody / True love ways / Money is the root of all evil / We're in the money / At the end of the day / Castle on a cloud / I dreamed a dream / Master of the house / Empty chairs at empty tables / On my own / Do you hear the people sing
CD CDGRS 1238
Grosvenor / '91 / Grosvenor

EVERYTHING'S IN RHYTHM
Household Brigade / If you love me / Vilia / All I do is dream of you / Hold me / Have you ever been lonely / Summer of '42 / Happy whistler / Stumbling / Nearness of you / Under the double eagle / Head over heels in love / When you've got a little springtime in your heart / Everything's in rhythm / Over my shoulder / When the midnight choo choo leaves for Alabama / Blackfoot walk / Crazy words crazy tune / Can you feel the love tonight / Oliver selection / You've got to pick a pocket or two / I'd do anything / Oom-pah-pah / As long as he needs me / Nights of gladness / Gimme dat ding / Bare necessities / Bring me sunshine / One moment in time
CD GRCD 69
Grasmere / Nov '95 / Highlander / Savoy / Target/BMG

FRIENDS FOR LIFE
Royal Air Force march past / Silver threads among the gold / When your old wedding ring was new / Till we meet again / Parade of the tin soldiers / Songs my mother taught me / My fair lady / Gymnopedie No.1 / Mona Lisa / Orange coloured sky / Those lazy-hazy-crazy days of summer / Aces high / Gold and silver waltz / I've got a pocketful of dreams / Zing went the strings of my heart / Painting the clouds with sunshine / Sanctuary of the heart / Friends for life (Amigos para siempre) / Mairzy doats and dozy doats / We're gonna hang out the washing on the siegfried line / Don't fence me in / When you tell me that you love me / Me and my girl
CD GRCD 56
Grasmere / Mar '93 / Highlander / Savoy / Target/BMG

GOLDEN WURLITZER FAVOURITES (2CD Set) (Wolfe, Robert & Nicholas Martin)
Medley / Medley / Golden wedding day / Tiger rag / Medley / Medley / Chanson de matin / Medley / Medley / Florentiner march / Medley / Medley / Medley / Medley (10) / Our director / Medley (11) / Bless this house / Medley (12) / Parade of the tin soldiers / Medley (13) / Waltz of the flowers / Kitten of the keys / Medley (14) / Leap year waltz / Aces high / Medley (15) / Songs my Mother taught me / Medley (16) / Blaze of glory
CD Set MUCD 9501
Musketeer / May '96 / Disc

HEAR MY SONG
Holyrood / Rose / Mack and Mabel / Hoagy Carmichael medley / Somewhere my love/ My own true love / Whistling waltz/Gladrag doll/My blue heaven / Hear my song, Violetta / Amapola/Guaglione / History of love/Here's that rainy day / Il silenzio / Yakety sax / Smilin' through/Always / How high the moon / It's only a paper moon / Moonlight in Vermont / Stranger on the shore/La Mer / I'm crazy 'bout my baby / On a slow boat to China / Pagan love song / That's my weakness / Don't be cross / Sons of the brave
CD GRCD 79
Grasmere / Feb '97 / Highlander / Savoy / Target/BMG

SPREAD A LITTLE HAPPINESS
CD GRCD 61
Grasmere / May '94 / Highlander / Savoy / Target/BMG

WURLITZER MAGIC
Children of the regiment / Around the world / Poeme / (Why does my heart go) Boom / 'Deed I do / Keep young and healthy / Sweet Sue, just you / Best things in life are free / Continental / Guilty / Confessin' (that I love you) / Harbour lights / Wedding of the painted doll / My heart and I / March militaire / Fascination / Under the linden tree / Mr. Sandman / Crazy people / Brown eyes, why are you blue / Rosalie / September in the rain / September song / (We're gonna) Rock around the clock / Opus one / In the mood / Pokare kareana / I still call Australia home / Now is the hour / Waltzing Matilda
CD CD 6021
Music / Apr '96 / Target/BMG

Wolfetones

25TH ANNIVERSARY: WOLFETONES
CD Set SHCD 52024/5
Shanachie / Jul '91 / ADA / Greensleeves / Koch

BELT OF THE CELTS
CD SHAN 52035CD
Shanachie / Aug '93 / ADA / Greensleeves / Koch

IRISH TO THE CORE
CD SHAN 52033CD
Shanachie / Aug '93 / ADA / Greensleeves / Koch

SING OUT FOR IRELAND
CD TRCD 1015
Triskel / '88 / CM / I&B / Roots

Wolff, Henry

TIBETAN BELLS VOL.2 (Wolff, Henry & Nancy Hennings)
CD CDCEL 005
Celestial Harmonies / Jul '88 / ADA / Select

TIBETAN BELLS VOL.3
CD CDCEL 027
Celestial Harmonies / Feb '89 / ADA / Select

Wolfgamme, Nani

20 GOLDEN HITS OF HAWAII
CD MCD 71804
Monitor / Jun '93 / CM

Wolfgang Press

BIRD WOOD CAGE
King of soul / Raintime / Bottom drawer / Kansas / Swing like a baby / See my wife / Holy man / Hang on me / Shut that door
CD CAD 810CD
4AD / Oct '88 / RTM/Disc

FUNKY LITTLE DEMONS
CD CAD 4016CD
4AD / Sep '94 / RTM/Disc

LEGENDARY WOLFGANG PRESS AND OTHER TALL STORIES
CD ___ CAD 514 CD
4AD / Feb '87 / RTM/Disc

MAMA TOLD ME NOT TO COME
CD ___ BAD 1007 CD
4AD / May '91 / RTM/Disc

QUEER
CD ___ CADCD 1011
4AD / Aug '91 / RTM/Disc

STANDING UP STRAIGHT
Dig a hole / My life / Hammer the halo / Bless my brother / Fire-fly / Rotten fodder / Forty days, thirty nights / I am the crime
CD ___ CAD 606 CD
4AD / Feb '87 / RTM/Disc

Wolfhound

HALLELUJA
CD ___ BLR 84 024
L&R / May '91 / New Note/Pinnacle

NEVER ENDING STORY, THE (Wolfhound & Anne Haigis)
CD ___ BLR 84 025
L&R / May '91 / New Note/Pinnacle

Wolfhounds

LOST BUT HAPPY (The Wolfhounds 1986-1990)
CD ___ CDMRED 126
Cherry Red / Apr '96 / Pinnacle

Wolfsbane

MASSIVE NOISE INJECTION
Protect and survive / Load me down / Black lagoon / Rope and ride / Kathy Wilson / Loco / End of the century / Steel / Temple of rock / Manhunt / Money to burn / Paint the town red / Wild thing
CD ___ ESMCD 193
Essential / Aug '96 / BMG

WOLFSBANE
Wings / Lifestyles of the broke and obscure / My face / Money talks / See how it's done / Beautiful lies / Protect and survive / Black machine / Violence / Die again
CD ___ ESMCD 396
Essential / Jan '97 / BMG

Wolfstone

CHASE, THE
Tinnie Run / Glass And The Can / Prophet / Appropriate Dipstick / Flames And Hearts / Ten pound float / Close it down / Jake's Tune / Early Mist / Cannot Lay Me Down
CD ___ IRCD 018
Iona / Aug '92 / ADA / Direct / Duncans

HALF TAIL, THE
CD ___ GLCD 1172
Green Linnet / Aug '96 / ADA / CM / Direct / Highlander / Roots

PICK OF THE LITTER (The Best Of Wolfstone)
Baffle / Tall ships / Glass and the can / Heart and soul / White gown / Glen lass / Brave foot soldiers / Dinner's set / Sleepy toon / 10 pound float / Holy ground
CD ___ IRCD 056
Lismor / Jul '97 / ADA / Direct / Duncans / Lismor

UNLEASHED
Cleveland park / Song for yesterday / Silver spear / Sleepy toon / Hector the hero / Howl / Here is where the heart is / Hard heart / Erin
CD ___ IR 014 CD
Iona / Nov '91 / ADA / Direct / Duncans

WOLFSTONE
CD ___ CMCD 072
Celtic Music / Apr '94 / CM

YEAR OF THE DOG
CD ___ GL 1145CD
Green Linnet / Jul '94 / ADA / CM / Direct / Highlander / Roots

Wolpe, Stefan

PASSACAGLIA - FIRST RECORDINGS
CD ___ ARTCD 6182
Hat Art / Oct '96 / Cadillac / Harmonia Mundi

Wolstenholme, Woolly

SONGS FROM THE BLACK BOX
Has to be a reason / Down the line / All get burned / Too much, too loud, too late / Even the night / Deceivers all / Will to fly / Sunday bells / Open / Sail away / Quiet islands / Prospect of Whitby / Lives on the line / Patriots / Gates of heaven (14/18) / American excess / Maestoso / Waveform
CD ___ BP 174CD
Blueprint / May '97 / Pinnacle

Wolz, Christian

COR
CD ___ EFA 112342
Danse Macabre / Nov '94 / SRD

INTUS MESTRA DE LA FORE
CD ___ EFA 112282
Danse Macabre / Jan '94 / SRD

Womack & Womack

CONSCIENCE
Conscious of my conscience / MPB / Friends / Slave / Teardrops / Good man monologue / Life's just a ball game / I am love / Celebrate the world
CD ___ IMCD 213
Island / Mar '96 / PolyGram

TEARDROPS
Teardrops / Celebrate the world / Slave / Conscious of my conscience / Good man monologue / MPB / Life's just a ball game / Friends (so called) / I am love / Love wars / Take me home country roads / Family / Rejoice
CD ___ 5500672
Spectrum / May '93 / PolyGram

TRANSFORMATION TO THE HOUSE OF ZEKKARIYAS
Drive (first gear) / Fiesta / Understanding / Passion and pain / Long time / Second gear / Candy world / Land of odd / Pie in the sky / Secret star / Focus
CD ___ 9362450752
Warner Bros. / May '93 / Warner Music

Womack, Bobby

COLLECTION, THE
CD ___ CCSCD 404
Castle / Apr '94 / BMG

HOME IS WHERE THE HEART IS
Home is where the heart is / Little bit salty / Standing in the safety zone / How long has this been going on / I could never be satisfied / Something for my head / Change is gonna come / We've only just begun
CD ___ EDCD 172
Edsel / Feb '91 / Pinnacle

I FEEL A GROOVE COMIN' ON
Let's get together / Broadway walk / What is this / I'm a midnight mover / Communication / I can understand it / Hang on in there / Can't stop a man in love / Let it hang out / Check it out / Daylight / I feel a groove comin' on / So many sides of you / Secrets / Stand up / Tryin' to get over you / Tell me why / Falling in love again
CD ___ CPCD 8294
Charly / Apr '97 / Koch

ONLY SURVIVOR (The MCA Years)
I wish he didn't trust me so much / Wanna make love to you / That's where it's at / Truth song / Let me kiss it where it hurts / Woman likes to hear that / So many rivers / World where no-one cries / Living in a box / I ain't got nobody else / When the weekend comes / Only survivor / Inherit the wind / (No matter how high I get)I'll still be lookin' up to you
CD ___ MCLD 19355
MCA / Apr '97 / BMG

POET TRILOGY, THE (3CD Set)
CD Set ___ CPCD 80803
Charly / Jul '94 / Koch

POET VOL.1, THE
So many sides of you / Lay your lovin' on me / Secrets / Just my imagination / Stand up / Games / If you think you're lonely now / Where do we go from here
CD ___ MUSCD 505
MCI Original Masters / Sep '94 / Disc / THE
CD ___ REC 2029
Razor & Tie / Jun '96 / Koch

POET VOL.2, THE
Love has finally come at last / It takes a lot of strength to say goodbye / Through the eyes of a child / Surprise surprise / Tryin' to get over you / Tell me why / Who's foolin' who / I wish I had someone to go home to / American dream
CD ___ MUSCD 506
MCI Original Masters / Sep '94 / Disc / THE

RESURRECTION
Good ole days / You made me love again / So high on your love / Don't break your promise (too soon) / Forever love / Please change your mind / Trying not to break down / Cousin Henry / Centerfield / Goin' home / Walking on the wildside / Cry myself to sleep / Wish / Color him father
CD ___ CDCTUM 8
Continuum / Sep '94 / Pinnacle

STOP ON BY (The Soul Of Bobby Womack)
Daylight / I can understand it / You're welcome / Stop on by / Harry hippie / Jealous love / Nobody wants you when you're down and out / Across 110th street / Across 110th street / Facts of life/He'll be there when the sun goes down / That's the way I feel about cha / Woman's gotta have it / I'm through trying to prove my love to you / Communication / (If you want my love) put something down on it / Lookin' for a love
CD ___ CTMCD 304
EMI / Feb '97 / EMI

VERY BEST OF BOBBY WOMACK, THE
I can understand it / Harry hippie / I'm a midnight mover / What is this / Somebody special / That's the way I feel about cha / Communication / California dreamin' / If you don't want my love, give it back / I wish it would rain / Nobody wants you when you're down and out / Across 110th street / If you want my love, put something down on it / Lookin' for love / I don't wanna be hurt by ya love again / Got to get you back / Woman's gotta have it / There's one thing that beats failing / You're messing up a good thing / Love ain't something you can get for free
CD ___ MCCD 018
Music Club / May '91 / Disc / THE

VERY BEST OF BOBBY WOMACK, THE (2CD Set)
What is this / Fly me to the moon / California dreamin' / I'm a midnight mover / I left my heart in San Francisco / It's gonna rain / How I miss you baby / Don't look back / I'm gonna forget about you / Preacher / More than I can stand / Communication / That's the way I feel about cha / If you don't want my love, give it back / Woman's gotta have it / I can understand it / Sweet Caroline / Nobody wants you when you're down and out / I'm through trying to prove my love to you / You're welcome / Stop on by / Harry Hippie / Across 110th Street / All along the watchtower / That's heaven to me / Lookin' for a love / I don't know what the world is coming to / I don't wanna be hurt by ya love again / If you want my love, put something down on it / Check it out / It's all over now / Where there's a will there's a way / Daylight / So many sides of you / Just my imagination / If you think you're lonely now / Love has finally come at last: *Womack, Bobby & Patti Labelle* / Tell me why / I wish I had someone to go home to
CD Set ___ CPCD 82552
Charly / Nov '96 / Koch

Womack, Lee Ann

LEE ANN WOMACK
CD ___ MCD 11585
MCA / Jul '97 / BMG

Womack/Warden

RANDOM ACTS OF SENSELESS VIOLENCE (4CD Set)
CD Set ___ 213CD 007
2.13.61 / Oct '96 / Pinnacle

Womb

BELLA
CD ___ DCD 9624
Dream Circle / Nov '96 / Cargo / Plastic Head

Wonder Stuff

CONSTRUCTION FOR THE MODERN IDIOT
Change every light bulb / I wish them all dead / Cabin fever / Hot love now / Full of life (happy now) / Storm drain / On the ropes / Your big assed Mother / Swell / Sing the absurd / Hush / Great drinker
CD ___ 5198942
Polydor / Mar '96 / PolyGram

IF THE BEATLES HAD READ HUNTER (The Singles)
Welcome to the cheap seats / Wish away / Caught in my shadow / Don't let me down gently / Size of a cow / Hot love now / Dizzy / Unbearable / Circlesquare / Who wants to be the Disco King / Golden green / Give give give me more more more / Coz I luv you / Sleep alone / Full of life (happy now) / It's yer money I'm after baby / On the ropes / It's not true
CD ___ 5213972
Polydor / Sep '96 / PolyGram

Wonder, Stevie

CONVERSATION PEACE
Rain your love down / Edge of eternity / Taboo to love / Take the time out / I'm new / My love is with you / Treat myself / Tomorrow Robins will sing / Sensuous whisper / For your love / Cold chill / Sorry / Conversation peace
CD ___ 5302382
Motown / Mar '95 / PolyGram

ESSENTIAL STEVIE WONDER, THE (2CD Set)
Yester-me, yester-you, yesterday / My cherie amour / If you really love me / We can work it out / Signed, sealed, delivered (I'm yours) / Never had a dream come true / Something out of the blue / Heaven help us all / Do yourself a favour / I was made to love her / Thank you love / Until you come back to me / I'm wondering / Shoo-be-doo-be-doo-da-day / Angie girl / More than a dream / For once in my life / You met your match / Don't know why I love you / Uptight / Music talk / Ain't that asking for trouble / Love a-go-go / Nothing's too good for my baby / Be cool be calm (and keep yourself together) / I'd cry / Travellin' man / Place in the sun / Blowin' in the wind / Fingertips / Workout Stevie,workout / Hey harmonica man / Kiss me baby / Hi-heel sneakers / Happy Street / Don't you feel it / Castles in the sand / Contract on love / I call it pretty music, but the old folks call it the blues

CD Set ___ 5300472
Motown / Jan '93 / PolyGram

FULFILLINGNESS FIRST FINALE
Smile please / Heaven is ten zillion light years away / Too shy to say / Boogie on reggae woman / Creepin' / You haven't done nothin' / It ain't no use / They won't go when I go / Bird of beauty / Please don't go
CD ___ 5301052
Motown / Jan '93 / PolyGram

HOTTER THAN JULY
Did I hear you say you love me / All I do / Rocket love / I ain't gonna stand for it / As if you read my mind / Masterblaster / Do like you / Cash in your face / Lately / Happy birthday
CD ___ 5300442
Motown / Jan '93 / PolyGram

IN SQUARE CIRCLE
Part time lover / I love you too much / Whereabouts / Stranger on the shore of love / Never in your sun / Spiritual walkers / Land of la la / Go home / Overjoyed / It's wrong (la la) / I wish he didn't trust me so much / Baby don't leave home without it / So many rivers / Got to be with you tonight / Whatever happened to those times / Let me kiss it where it hurts / Only survivor / That's where it's at / Check it out
CD ___ 5300462
Motown / Mar '96 / PolyGram

INNERVISIONS
Too high / Visions / Living for the city / Golden lady / Higher ground / Jesus children of America / All in love is fair / Don't you worry about a thing / He's misstra know it all
CD ___ 5300352
Motown / Jan '93 / PolyGram

INSTRUMENTAL MEMORIES (Various Artists)
I just called to say I love you / Superstition / My cherie amour / Signed sealed delivered I'm yours / Don't you worry about a thing / Isn't she lovely / Master blaster (jammin') / Sir Duke / Happy birthday / For once in my life / Part time lover / Lately / Ebony and ivory / You are the sunshine of my life
CD ___ 306962
Hallmark / Jun '97 / Carlton

JOURNEY THROUGH THE SECRET LIFE OF PLANTS (2CD Set)
Earth's creation / First garden / Voyage to India / Same old story / Venus flytrap and the bug / Ai no, sono / Seed's a star and treed medley / Secret life of plants / Finale / Seasons / Power flower / Send one your love (instrumental) / Race babbling / Outside my window / Black orchid / Ecclesiastes / Kesse ye lolo de ye / Come back as a flower / Send one your love
CD Set ___ 5301062
Motown / Jan '93 / PolyGram

LOVE SONGS - 20 CLASSIC HITS
Contract on love / My cherie amour / Until you come back to me / Yester-me, yester-you, yesterday / Never had a dream come true / If you really love me / Heaven help us all / Never dreamed you'd leave in Summer / Place in the sun / Alfie / Hey love / For once in my life / We can work it out / I was made to love her / Don't know why I love you / Blowin' in the wind / Shoo-be-doo-be-doo-da-day / I'm wondering / Nothing's too good for my baby / Signed, sealed, delivered (I'm yours)
CD ___ 5300372
Motown / Jan '93 / PolyGram

MUSIC OF MY MIND
Love having you around / Superwoman / I love every little thing about you / Sweet little girl / Happier than the morning sun / Girl blue / Seems so long / Keep on running / Evil
CD ___ 5300282
Motown / Jan '93 / PolyGram

NATURAL WONDER - LIVE IN CONCERT (2CD Set)
Love's in need of love today / Master blaster (Jammin') / Higher ground / Rocket love / Ribbon in the sky / Pastime paradise / If it's magic / Village ghetto land / Tomorrow Robins will sing / Overjoyed / My cherie amour / Signed, sealed, delivered I'm yours / Living for the city / Sir Duke / I wish / You are the sunshine of my life / Superstition / I just called to say I love you / For your love / Another star / Stevie Ray blues / Ms. and Mr. Little Ones / Stay gold
CD ___ 5305462
Motown / Oct '95 / PolyGram

ORIGINAL MUSIQUARIUM (2CD Set)
Isn't she lovely / You are the sunshine of my life / Higher ground / Superwoman / Send me your love / Do I do / Superstition / Living for the city / Front line / You haven't done nothin' / Sir Duke / Ribbon in the sky / Masterblaster / That girl / I wish / Boogie on reggae woman
CD Set ___ 5300292
Motown / Jan '93 / PolyGram

SONG REVIEW (The Very Best Of Stevie Wonder)
Isn't she lovely / I just called to say I love you / Superstition / Sir Duke / Master blaster (jammni') / Ebony and ivory / Happy

birthday / Living for the city / He's Misstra know it all / You are the sunshine of my life / Lately / Part-time lover / My cherie amour / Yester-me, yester-you, yesterday / Uptight (everything's alright) / I was made to love her / For once in my life / Signed, sealed, delivered, I'm yours / For your love / Kiss lonely goodbye / Redemption song
CD 5307572
Motown / Nov '96 / PolyGram

SONGS IN THE KEY OF LIFE (2CD Set)
Love's in need of love today / Have a talk with God / Village ghetto land / Confusion / I am singing / If it's magic / As / Another star / I wish / Knocks me off my feet / Pastime paradise / Summer soft / Ordinary pain / Isn't she lovely / Joy inside my tears / Black man / Sir Duke / Ngiculela es una historia
CD Set 5300342
Motown / Jan '93 / PolyGram

STEVIE WONDER SONGBOOK (Various Artists)
I was made to love you: *Khan, Chaka* / It's a shame: *Detroit Spinners* / Until you come back to me: *Franklin, Aretha* / Heaven is ten zillion light years away: *Johnson, Paul* / Try Jah love: *Third World* / Buttercup: *Anderson, Carl* / Creepin': *Vandross, Luther* / You are the sunshine of my life: *Washington, Grover Jr.* / Pastime paradise: *Barretto, Ray* / Perfect angel: *Riperton, Minnie* / Too shy to say: *Jackson, Walter* / Never said: *Reeves, Dianne* / You haven't done nothin': *Robinson, Orphy* / Do I do: *Morrissey-Mullen* / Girl blue: *Main Ingredient* / Don't you worry 'bout a thing: *Irvin, Weldon* / Tell me something good: *Rufus* / Signed, sealed, delivered I'm yours: *Gadd Gang* / Another star: *Sledge, Kathy*
CD VSOPCD 216
Connoisseur Collection / Apr '95 / Pinnacle

TALKING BOOK
You are the sunshine of my life / Maybe your baby / You and I / Tuesday heartbreak / You've got it bad, girl / Superstition / Big Brother / Blame it on the sun / Lookin' for another pure love / I believe
CD 5300362
Motown / Jan '93 / PolyGram

Wondermints

WONDERFUL WORLD OF...
CD TFCK 88799
Toys Factory / May '97 / Greyhound / Plastic Head

WONDERMINTS
CD 90332
Big Deal / Jun '97 / Greyhound

Wong, Francis

PILGRIMAGE (Wong, Francis Quartet)
CD CD 974
Music & Arts / Jul '97 / Cadillac / Harmonia Mundi

Wongraven

HELLTRONEN
CD FOG 006CD
Moonfog / Jun '95 / Plastic Head

Wonky Alice

ATOMIC RAINDANCE
Linar Adam / Radius / Sirius / Son of the sun / Sundance / Captain paranoia / Astronauts / Moon / Atomic raindance
CD ONA 001 CD
Pomona / Jan '93 / Vital

Woob

WOOB
CD EMIT 1194
Time Recordings / Aug '94 / Pinnacle

Wood Brothers

HOOKED ON COUNTRY (Wood Brothers & The Nashville Greats)
Hooked on country love / Hooked on Randy Travis / Hooked on Willie Nelson / Hooked on trains / Hooked on Merle Haggard / Hooked on George Strait / Hooked on Marty Robbins / Hooked on a waltz / Hooked on Johnny Cash / Hooked on a country party
CD ECD 3072
K-Tel / Jan '95 / K-Tel

I'M IN THE MOOD FOR COUNTRY MUSIC
CD LPCD 1027
Disky / Apr '94 / Disky / THE

Wood, Chris

LISA (Wood, Chris & Andy Cutting)
CD RUF 002CD
RUF / Sep '92 / ADA

LIVE AT SIDMOUTH (Wood, Chris & Andy Cutting)
CD RUF 003CD
RUF / Feb '95 / ADA

LUSIGNAC (Wood, Chris & Andy Cutting)
CD RUF 004CD
RUF / Nov '95 / ADA

Wood, Clynt

TEARS OF SUCCESS
CD WINK 1994
Wink / Oct '94 / Jet Star

Wood, Diana

BEST SAX EVER
Street life / Put it where you want it / Smooth operator / Inherit the wind / Your latest trick / Morning dance / This means so much to me / Lily was here / In the mood / Take five / Yakety sax / Heaven is in your heart / Girl from Ipanema / Slam / Roadblaster / Songbird / Baker street / Careless whisper / Pick up the pieces
CD QED 083
Tring / Nov '96 / Tring

Wood, Lauren

CAT TRICK
CD 7599268722
WEA / Jan '96 / Warner Music

LAUREN WOOD
CD 7599268712
WEA / Jan '96 / Warner Music

Wood, Richard

CELTIC TOUCH, THE
Jigs / Strathspeys and reels / Lament/The Celtic touch / Jigs / Clog and reels / Jigs / Lament/Memories of Dot Mackinnon / Clog reels hornpipe / Strathspeys and reels / Slow air and reels / Reels
CD IRCD 042
Iona / Feb '97 / ADA / Direct / Duncans

Wood, Ronnie

MAHONEY'S LAST STAND (Wood, Ronnie & Ronnie Lane)
Tonights number / From the late to the early / Chicken wire / Chicken wired / I'll fly away / Title one / Just for a moment / Mona the blues / Car radio / Hay tumble / Woody's thing / Rooster funeral
CD CDTB 067
Thunderbolt / '88 / TKO Magnum

Wood, Roy

BOULDERS
Songs of praise / Wake up / Rock down low / Nancy sing me a song / Dear Elaine / All the way over the hill / Irish loafer (and his hen) / Miss Clarke and the computer / When Gran'ma plays the banjo / Rockin' shoes / She's too good for me / Locomotive
CD BGOCD 219
Beat Goes On / Mar '94 / Pinnacle

DEFINITIVE ALBUM, THE
CD BRCD 50
BR Music / May '94 / Target/BMG

ROY WOOD & WIZZARD (16 Greats) (Wood, Roy & Wizzard)
Are you ready to rock / Look thru the eyes of a fool / Marathon man / You sure got it now / This is the story of my love (baby) / Indiana rainbow / I can't help my feelings / Mustard / Why does such a pretty girl sing / Such sad songs / Rattle snake roll / Any old time will do / Rain came down on everything / This is this / Get on down home / Benjal jig / Dream of unwin
CD EMPRCD 573
Emporio / Jul '95 / Disc

ROY WOOD SINGLES (Various Artists)
Night of fear: *Move* / I can hear the grass grow: *Move* / Flowers in the rain: *Move* / Fire brigade: *Move* / Blackberry way: *Move* / Curly: *Move* / Brontosaurus: *Move* / Tonight: *Move* / Chinatown: *Move* / California man: *Move* / Ball park incident: *Wizzard* / See my baby jive: *Wizzard* / Dear Elaine: *Wood, Roy* / Angel fingers: *Wizzard* / Forever: *Wood, Roy* / I wish it could be Christmas every day: *Wizzard* / Rock 'n' roll winter: *Wizzard* / Going down the road: *Wood, Roy* / This is the story of my love: *Wizzard* / Are you ready to rock: *Wizzard* / Oh what a shame: *Wood, Roy*
CD VSOPCD 189
Connoisseur Collection / Aug '93 / Pinnacle

THROUGH THE YEARS
Tonight / Chinatown / Down on the bay / California man / 10538 overture / Ball park incident / Carlsberg Special / See my baby jive / Bend over Beethoven / Angel fingers / I wish it could be Christmas very day / Dear Elaine / Forever / Music to commit suicide to / Going down the road / Premium bond theme / Green glass windows / It's not easy
CD CDGOLD 1070
EMI Gold / Oct '96 / EMI

Woodard, Rickey

CALIFORNIA COOKING
Wilbur's idea / When I fall in love / This I dig of you / Jeannine / Jet lag / Day by day / Sashay / Jake's place / My one and only love / Take your pick
CD CCD 79509
Candid / Feb '97 / Cadillac / Direct / Jazz Music / Koch / Wellard

SILVER STRUT, THE
Silver strut / Grizzly / Quick flash / Kerstin / Take your pick / Stardust / Lover man / Firm roots / Sashay
CD CCD 4716
Concord Jazz / Aug '96 / New Note/ Pinnacle

TOKYO EXPRESS, THE
Recorda-me / Very thought of you / Just friends / Sand dance / Easy living / Groovy samba / Polka dots and moonbeams / Tokyo express
CD CCD 79527
Candid / Feb '97 / Cadillac / Direct / Jazz Music / Koch / Wellard

YAZOO
Icicle / Fried bananas / Abell / Turbulence / Portrait of Jennie / Holy land / 14th and Jefferson / Tadd's delight / September in the rain / Yazoo City blues
CD CCD 4629
Concord Jazz / Jan '95 / New Note/ Pinnacle

Woodland, Nick

LIVE FIREWORKS
Rock 'n' roll man / Train (23 stops) / Worried / Freight train / Race is on / I loved another woman / Cross my heart / My babe / Got a mind to give up living / Hip shake / Double trouble
CD BLU 10272
Blues Beacon / Mar '97 / New Note/ Pinnacle

Woodruff, Bob

DESIRE ROAD
CD CURCD 37
Curb / Mar '97 / Grapevine/PolyGram

Woods

IT'S LIKE THIS
Sign of the times / Next rain / Girlfriends / Chain my heart / Some other world / I don't want her (anymore) / Battleship chains / Sand / What about me / Close as you get / Why / Come off with your lies
CD DECD 900318
Demon / '89 / Pinnacle

Woods, Chris

SOMEBODY DONE STOLE MY BLUES
CD DD 434
Delmark / Sep '87 / ADA / Cadillac / CM / Direct / Hot Shot

Wood's Famous Blind ...

WOOD'S FAMOUS BLIND JUBILEE SINGERS 1925 (Wood's Famous Blind Jubilee Singers)
CD DOCD 5039
Document / May '96 / ADA / Hot Shot / Jazz Music

Woods, Mitch

SHAKIN' THE SHACK (Woods, Mitch & His Rocket 88's)
CD BP 5008CD
Blind Pig / Mar '94 / ADA / CM / Direct / Hot Shot

STEADY DATE (Woods, Mitch & His Rocket 88's)
CD BP 1784CD
Blind Pig / Mar '94 / ADA / CM / Direct / Hot Shot

Woods, Phil

BOP STEW (Woods, Phil Quintet)
Dreamsville / Bop stew / Poor Butterfly / Yes there is a Coya
CD CCD 4345
Concord Jazz / Jul '88 / New Note/Pinnacle

CELEBRATION
Reet's neet / Nefertiti / Banja Luka / Goodbye Mr. Evans / Willow weep for me / All bird's children / My man Benny / Perils of Poda / How's your Mama
CD CCD 47702
Concord Jazz / Aug '97 / New Note/ Pinnacle

ELSA (Woods, Phil & Enrico Pieranunzi)
CD W 2062
Philology / Aug '92 / Cadillac / Harmonia Mundi

EUROPEAN TOUR
CD 1231632
Red / Apr '95 / ADA / Cadillac / Harmonia Mundi

EVOLUTION (Woods, Phil Little Big Band)
Alvin G / Black flag / Hal mallet / Miles ahead / Rain go away / Song for Sisyphus / Thaddeus / Which way is uptown
CD CCD 4361
Concord Jazz / Nov '88 / New Note/ Pinnacle

FLOWERS FOR HODGES (Woods, Phil & Jim McNeely)
CD CCD 4485
Concord Jazz / Nov '91 / New Note/ Pinnacle

FULL HOUSE
CD MCD 9196
Milestone / Oct '93 / Cadillac / Complete/ Pinnacle / Jazz Music / Wellard

HARD SOCK DANCE
CD ATJCD 5964
All That's Jazz / Jul '92 / Jazz Music / THE

HEAVEN (Woods, Phil Quintet)
I'm getting sentimental over you / Heaven / Duke / Azure / 222 / Occurrence
CD ECD 221482
Evidence / Sep '96 / ADA / Cadillac / Harmonia Mundi

INTO THE WOODS
All bird's children / Hal mallet / Bop brew / Misirlou / Tune of the unknown / Samba / I didn't know about you / Just you just me / Weaver
CD CCD 4699
Concord Jazz / Jun '96 / New Note/ Pinnacle

JAZZ 1968 (Woods, Phil & Slide Hampton)
CD 7812532
Jazztime / Aug '93 / Discovery

JAZZ LIFE, A
CD W 742
Philology / Sep '92 / Cadillac / Harmonia Mundi

LIVE AT THE CORRIDONIA JAZZ FESTIVAL (Woods, Phil & Space Jazz Trio)
CD W 2112
Philology / Aug '92 / Cadillac / Harmonia Mundi

LIVE AT THE WIGMORE HALL (The Complete Concert/2CD Set) (Woods, Phil & Gordon Beck)
Quill / Everything I love / Goodbye Mr Evans / Solar / Little D / For Keith / Isotope / Petite chanson / In your own sweet way / Harlem nocturne / Re: Person I knew / How deep is the ocean / Core of the apple / Alone together
CD Set JMS 186862
JMS / Oct '96 / New Note/BMG

MILE HIGH JAZZ (Woods, Phil Quintet)
Blues for KB / Song for Sass / Harlem nocturne / Godchild / Walkin' thing / Clairevoyance
CD CCD 4739
Concord Jazz / Nov '96 / New Note/ Pinnacle

MUSIC OF JIM NCNEELY, THE
Perfect six / If I'd only / Paper spoons / Baby faced / Hey you / New waltz / Don't even ask
CD TCB 95402
TCB / Apr '96 / New Note/Pinnacle

MUSIQUE DU BOIS
CD MCD 5037
Muse / Sep '92 / New Note/Pinnacle

ORNITHOLOGY
CD PHIL 692
Philology / Oct '94 / Cadillac / Harmonia Mundi

PHIL WOODS QUARTET LIVE 1979 VOL.1 (Woods, Phil Quartet)
Bloomdido / Everything I love / Along came Betty / Hallucinations / Phil's theme
CD CCD 702
Clean Cuts / Nov '96 / Direct / Jazz Music / Wellard

PIPER AT THE GATES OF DAWN (Woods, Phil & Chris Swansen)
CD RCD 10007
Rykodisc / Mar '92 / ADA / Vital

RIGHTS OF SWING
Prelude and part 1 / Part 2 (ballad) / Part 3 (waltz) / Part 4 (scherzo) / Part 5 (presto)
CD CCD 79016
Candid / Feb '97 / Cadillac / Direct / Jazz Music / Koch / Wellard

STOLEN MOMENTS (Woods, Phil Quartet)
CD JMY 10122
JMY / Aug '91 / Harmonia Mundi

WOODLORE (Woods, Phil Quartet)
CD OJCCD 52
Original Jazz Classics / '92 / Complete/ Pinnacle / Jazz Music / Wellard

Woods, Rosemary

WALKING TOGETHER
CD SP 1027CD
Spring / Feb '93 / ADA / Direct

Woods, Terry

GAY AND TERRY WOODS IN CONCERT (Woods, Terry & Gay)
CD WIN 071CD
Windsong / Jul '95 / Pinnacle

Woodshed

40 MILES OF ROUGH ROAD
Cropduster / Holloway to Memphis / Shootin cactus / Return of yet I / Tale from the woodshed part two / Tales from the woodshed part one / Space junk / Scuffle town shuffle / 40 Miles of rough road / No
CD _______ NLX 5008CD
Cloak & Dagger / May '96 / Vital

Wool

BUDSPAWN
CD _______ ALLCD 1
Parallel / May '93 / PolyGram / Shellshock/Disc

Wooley, Sheb

RAWHIDE/HOW THE WEST WAS WON
Rawhide / Goodnight loving trail / Shifting whispering sands / Indian maiden / Story of Billy Bardell / Enchantment of the prairie / Lonley man / Wayward wind / Bars across the widow / Cattle call / How the west was won / Gotta pull up stakes (and move on west) / High lonesome / Wagonmaster's diary / Buffalo stampede / Rosie the queen of California / Building a railroad / Plowin' in new ground / Papa's old fiddle / Silver target / I belong / Big land
CD _______ BCD 15899
Bear Family / Nov '95 / Direct / Rollercoaster / Swift

Woolpackers

EMMERDANCE
Hillbilly rock, Hillbilly roll / Chatahoochee / Line dancing / Boot scootin' boogie / Two chilli dogs / Footloose / On my radio / Horses / Baby likes to rock it / Blue rodeo / You're gonna be blue / 2 left feet / Down on the farm
CD _______ 74321444052
RCA / Dec '96 / BMG

Woosey, Dominic

STRAYLIGHT
Stay down, first light / Uncubation / Oceans of infinity / Straylightsong
CD _______ ROD 01
Recycle Or Die / Apr '96 / Kudos

Wootton, Brenda

VOICE OF CORNWALL, THE
CD _______ KM 67CD
Keltia Musique / Aug '96 / ADA / Discovery

Worcester Cathedral Choir

CHRISTMAS BY THE FIRESIDE (Best Loved Christmas Carols/2CD Set) (Worcester Cathedral & Tewkesbury Abbey Choirs)
CD Set _______ 8551036/37
Naxos / Nov '96 / Select

Wordsound & Powa

PLANET CROOKLYN
CD _______ RUSCD 8224
ROIR / Apr '97 / Plastic Head / Shellshock/Disc

Work

RUBBER CAGE
CD _______ PYO 314116
Woof / Oct '95 / Grapevine/PolyGram / ReR Megacorp

SLOW CRIMES
CD _______ MEGA 001
Woof / Oct '95 / Grapevine/PolyGram / ReR Megacorp

Work, Jimmy

MAKING BELIEVE (2CD Set)
That's the way it's gonna be / Rock Island line / Puttin' on the dog / When she said you all / Digging my own grave / Don't give me a reason to wonder why / Blind heart / You've got a heart like a merry-go-round / That cold, cold look in your eyes / Hands away from my heart / That's the way the juke box plays / There's only one you / Making believe / Blind heart / Let 'em talk / Just like downtown / My old stomping ground / Don't knock just come on in / Those Kentucky bluegrass hills / You're gone, I won't forget / Rainy rainy blues / Hear that steamboat whistle blow / Tennessee border / Your jealous heart is broken now / Bluegrass ticklin' my feet / Please don't let me love you / I would send you roses (but they cost too much) / Surrounded by water and bars / Smoky mountain moon / Who's been here since I've been gone / Mr. and Mrs. Cloud / Hospitality / Pickup truck / Do your honky tonkin' at home / Southern fried chicken / Let's live a little / If I should lose you / Don't play with my heart / I'm lonesome for someone / Puttin' on the dog (Tom cattin' around) / Crazy moon / Little popcorn man / How can I love you / Out of my mind / That's what makes the jukebox play / Don't knock, just come in / Blind heart / Let me be alone / I never thought I'd have the blues / I dreamed last night
CD _______ BCD 15651
Bear Family / Aug '93 / Direct / Rollercoaster / Swift

Working Week

PAYDAY (Collection)
Soul train / Venceremos / South Africa / King of the night / Touching heaven / Doctor / Friend / Largo / Knocking on your door / Strut / Apocalypse / I thought I'd never see you again / Storm of light / Sweet nothin's / Who's foolin' who / We will win
CD _______ CDVE 19
Venture / Jul '88 / EMI

Workman, Reggie

SYNTHESIS (Workman, Reggie Ensemble)
CD _______ CDLR 131
Leo / Feb '89 / Cadillac / Impetus / Wellard

Workshop

TALENT
CD _______ LADO 17030
Ladomat / Jan '95 / Plastic Head

Workshop

WELCOME BACK THE WORKSHOP
CD _______ CTCD 054
Captain Trip / Jul '97 / Greyhound

WORKSHOP
CD _______ CTCD 053
Captain Trip / Jul '97 / Greyhound

Workshy

COAST
Something sweeter / Never the same / Ghost train / All in the mind / Finding the feeling / Heaven sent / All is fair in love / On the inside / True to life / Breakdown / Blue murder / Too late
CD _______ CI 001CD
Pony Canyon / Mar '96 / Pinnacle

World Of Leather

JESUS CHRIST SUPERSTORE
CD _______ CAKECD 17
Soundcakes / Sep '95 / 3mv/Sony

World Of Twist

QUALITY STREET
CD _______ CIRCD 17
Circa / Nov '91 / EMI

World Party

BANG
Kingdom come / Is it like today / What is love all about / And God said.... / Give it all away / Sooner or later / Hollywood / Radio-days / Rescue me / Sunshine / All I gave / Give it all away (Reprise)
CD _______ CDCHEN 33
Ensign / Apr '93 / EMI

EGYPTOLOGY
It is time / Beautiful dream / Call me up / Vanity fair / She's the one / Curse of the mummy's tomb / Hercules / Love is best / Rolling off a log / Strange groove / Whole of the night / Piece of mind / This world / Always
CD _______ CDCHR 6124
Chrysalis / Jun '97 / EMI

GOODBYE JUMBO
Is it too late / Way down now / When the rainbow comes / Put the message in the box / Ain't gonna come til I'm ready / And I fell back alone / Take it up / God on my side / Show me to the top / Love street / Sweet soul dream / Thank you world
CD _______ CCD 1654
Ensign / Apr '90 / EMI

PRIVATE REVOLUTION
Private revolution / Making love (to the world) / Ship of fools / All come true / Dance of the happy lads / It can be beautiful (sometimes) / Ballad of the little man / Hawaiian island world / All I really want to do / World party / It's all mine
CD _______ CCD 1552
Ensign / Apr '87 / EMI

World Sax Orchestra

WORLD SAX ORCHESTRA
CD _______ BVHAASTCD 8902
Bvhaast / Oct '85 / Cadillac

World Saxophone Quartet

BREATH OF LIFE (World Saxophone Quartet & Fontella Bass)
CD _______ 7559793092
Nonesuch / Nov '94 / Warner Music

DANCES AND BALLADS
CD _______ 9791642
Nonesuch / Jun '88 / Warner Music

FOUR NOW
CD _______ JUST 832
Justin Time / May '96 / Cadillac / New Note/Pinnacle

LIVE IN ZURICH
Funny paper / Touchic / My first winter / Bordertown / Steppin' / Stick / Hattie wall
CD _______ BSR 0077
Black Saint / '86 / Cadillac / Harmonia Mundi

METAMORPHOSIS (World Saxophone Quartet & African Drums)
CD _______ 7559792582
Nonesuch / Jul '94 / Warner Music

MOVING RIGHT ALONG
CD _______ 1201272
Black Saint / May '94 / Cadillac / Harmonia Mundi

STEPPIN'
CD _______ BSR 0027
Black Saint / '86 / Cadillac / Harmonia Mundi

TAKIN' IT 2 THE NEXT LEVEL
Wiring / Soft landing / Rio / Peace before / Blues for a warrior spirit / Desegregation of our children / When the monarchs come to town / Endless flight / Ballad after us / Australopithecus
CD _______ JUST 932
Justin Time / Jan '97 / Cadillac / New Note/ Pinnacle

WORLD SAXOPHONE QUARTET PLAYS DUKE ELLINGTON, THE
CD _______ 7559791372
Nonesuch / Jul '94 / Warner Music

World Trio

WORLD TRIO
Palantir / Whirling dervish / Over there / Will o' the wisp / Dr. Do-Right / Arch mage / Billy Jean / Seven rings / Eulogy
CD _______ VBR 21522
Vera Bra / Aug '95 / New Note/Pinnacle / Pinnacle

World Without Walls

MOTHERGROOVE
Mother groove / Mama's warning / No-one's slave / Aluna / Dreams of the great mother / Big wave / Black to black / Wake up / Mama's in the mix / One human family
CD _______ WWW 001CD
X-Static / Jun '94 / Vital

Worlds Apart

TOGETHER
Could it be I'm falling in love / Papa wouldn't understand / Beggin' to be written / Everlasting love / Come back and stay / Arnold Schwarzenegger / Heaven must be missing an angel / Same old promises / Experienced / Wonderful world / September / Like it was, like it is
CD _______ 74321198122
Arista / Feb '97 / BMG

Worlds Collide

ALL HOPE ABANDON
CD _______ LF 120
Lost & Found / Mar '95 / Plastic Head

World's Greatest Jazz Band

WAY OUT WEST
CD _______ TCD 1030
Tradition / Aug '96 / ADA / Vital

Worm

AGOGO
CD _______ NZ 069CD
Nova Zembla / Oct '96 / Plastic Head

Worms, Marcel

JAZZ IN 20TH CENTURY PIANO MUSIC
CD _______ BVHCD 9403
Bvhaast / Oct '94 / Cadillac

Worrell, Bernie

BLACKTRONIC SCIENCE
CD _______ GCD 79474
Gramavision / Sep '95 / Vital/SAM

FUNK OF AGES
CD _______ GCD 79460
Gramavision / Sep '95 / Vital/SAM

Worst Case Scenario

TOTAL DISCOGRAPHY
CD _______ VMFM 26
Vermiform / Feb '97 / Cargo / Greyhound / Plastic Head

Wraith

DANGER CALLING
CD _______ WARCD 7
Warhammer / Sep '92 / Grapevine/ PolyGram

RIOT
CD _______ WARCD 9
Warhammer / May '93 / Grapevine/ PolyGram

Wrathchild

BIZ SUXX (BUT WE DON'T CARE), THE
Biz suxx / Millionaire / Hooked / (Na na) nukklear rokket / Wild wild honey / Ring my bell / Hooligunz / She'z no angel / OK UK / Noo sensation / Stikky fingerz
CD _______ HMRXD 116
Heavy Metal / Nov '88 / Revolver / Sony

DELIRIUM
Delirium / Watch me shake it / That's what U get / My girlz / Long way 2 go / Good girlz / Do what you wanna / Kid pusher / She's high on luv / Rock me over / Only 4 the fun / Drive me krazy
CD _______ WKFMXD 137
FM / Dec '89 / Revolver / Sony

STAKK ATTAKK
Stakk attakk / Too wild to tame / Trash queen / Sweet surrender / Kick down the walls / Tonight / Law abuzer / Shokker / Alrite with the boyz / Wreckless
CD _______ HMRXD 18
Heavy Metal / Apr '89 / Revolver / Sony

Wray, Link

APACHE/WILD SIDE OF THE CITY LIGHTS
Wild one / Dallas blues / Big boss man / Shawnee / Joker / Apache / Beautiful brown eyes / Stars and stripes forever / Green hornet / Dick Tracy / Private eye / Hotel Loneliness / Raunchy / Flying wedge / Don't leave me / American sunset / Little sister / Love me tender / Wild side of the city lights / Viva zapata / As long as I have you / Street beat
CD _______ CDCHD 931
Ace / Jun '90 / Pinnacle

GUITAR PREACHER (The Polygram Years/2CD Set)
La de da / Take me home Jesus / Juke box Mama / Rise and fall of Jimmy Stokes / Fallin' rain / Fire and brimstone / Ice people / Go out West / Crowbar / Black river swamp / Tail dragger / Hobo man / I'm so glad, I'm so proud / Georgia pines / Water boy / Alabama electric circus / Take my hand (precious Lord) / Walkin' in the Arizona sun / Scorpio woman / All because of a woman / On the run / Days before Custer / Be what you want to / All cried out / Tuscon, Arizona / River bend / You walked by / Walk easy, walk slow / Morning / It was a bad scene / Good time Joe / Walkin' bulldog / I got to ramble / Backwoods preacher man / She's that kind of woman / Super / Rumble
CD Set _______ 5277172
Polydor / Apr '96 / PolyGram

INDIAN CHILD
CD _______ SHED 001CD
Creation / Jun '93 / 3mv/Vital

LIVE AT THE PARADISO
Blue suede shoes / Ace of spades / Walk away from love / I saw her standing there / Run chicken run / She's no good / Rumble / Rawhide / Subway blues / Money / Shake, rattle and roll / Be bop a lula
CD _______ CDMF 008
Magnum Force / Apr '91 / TKO Magnum

LIVE IN 85/GROWLING GUITAR
Rumble / It's only words / Fire / Mystery train / I got a woman / Baby let's play house / Jack the ripper / Love me / King Creole / I'm counting on you / Rawhide / Born to be wild
CD _______ CDWIK 972
Big Beat / Apr '91 / Pinnacle

ORIGINAL RUMBLE, THE
Rumble / Swag / Batman / Ace of spades / Jack the ripper / I'm branded / Fat back / Run chicken run / Turnpike USA / Dueces wild / Mustang / Blueberry Hill / Run boy run / Sweeper / Hound dog / That'll be the day / Fuzz / Rawhide / Draggin' / Aces wild / Bull dawg / Rumble man / Copenhagen boogie
CD _______ CDCH 924
Ace / Nov '89 / Pinnacle

RUMBLE PLUS
CD _______ CDWIK 924
Big Beat / Feb '89 / Pinnacle

SHADOWMAN
Rumble on the docks / Heartbreak hotel / Geronimo / Young love / Moped baby / Run through the jungle / I can't help it (if I'm still in love with you) / Night prowler / It was so easy / Timewarp/Strider / Listen to the drums / Shadowman
CD _______ CDCHD 638
Ace / Jan '97 / Pinnacle

WALKING DOWN A STREET CALLED LOVE
Walking down a street called love / Batman / Mystery train/My babe / That's alright / I got a woman / Jailhouse rock / Mr. Guitar / Born to be wild / Rumble / Sweeper / Jack the ripper / Deuces wild / Tiger man / King Creole / Fire / I can't help it if I'm still in love with you / Run chicken run / Ace of spades / Young and beautiful

CD ______ VICD 010
Visionary/Jettisoundz / Feb '97 / Cargo / Pinnacle / RTM/Disc / THE

Wreckless Eric

AT THE SHOP
Big old world / Waiting for the shit (to hit the fan) / Bony Moronie / Our neck of the woods / If it makes you happy / Depression / Semaphore signals / You're the girl for me
CD ______ 422395
New Rose / Jun '94 / ADA / Direct / Discovery

BIG SMASH
Pop song / Tonight / Too busy / Broken doll / Can I be your hero / Back in my hometown / Whole wide world / Take the cash / Let's go to the pictures / Walking on the surface of the moon / Hit and miss Judy / I wish it would rain / It'll soon be the weekend / Strange towns / Excuse me / Break my mind / Good conversation / Out of the blue / Reconnez cherie / Veronica / Brain thieves / Semaphore signals / I need a situation / Final taxi / There isn't anything else
CD ______ STIFFCD 13
Disky / Jan '94 / Disky / THE

LE BEAT GROUP ELECTRIQUE
Tell me I'm the only one / Wishing my life away / Depression / It's a sick sick world / Just for you / Sarah / Sun is pouring down / I'm not going to cry / You sweet big thing / Fuck by fuck / Parallel beds / True happiness
CD ______ 422396
New Rose / Jun '94 / ADA / Direct / Discovery

Wreckx n' Effect

RAP'S NEW GENERATION
Intro - New generation / Tha show / Top billin / Criminal minded / Harlem (interlude) / Planet rock / Move da crowd / Funky (interlude) / Funk box / Somethin for da radio / Da vapors / Rap acting school (interlude) / Boomin system / Sucka Mc's / It's yours (play on playa) / Outro
CD ______ MCD 11174
MCA / Sep '96 / BMG

WRECKS 'N' EFFECT
Go for what you know / We be Mafia / I need money / Let's do it again / Wreckx-n-effect
CD ______ K 781 860 2
Atlantic / Jul '94 / Warner Music

Wrekking Machine

MECHANISTIC TERMINATION
CD ______ 9040182
Mausoleum / Apr '95 / Grapevine/ PolyGram

Wrench, David

BLOW WINDS BLOW
CD ______ ANKST 078CD
Ankst / Jul '97 / Shellshock/Disc

Wrens

SILVER
CD ______ GROW 0102
Grass / Apr '94 / Pinnacle / SRD

Wretched

LIFE OUT THERE
CD ______ HELL 024
Hellhound / Sep '93 / Koch

LOTTA PER VIVERE
CD ______ AD 3
Anti-Christ / Oct '96 / Cargo

PSYCHOSMATIC MEDICINE
CD ______ H 00312
Hellhound / May '94 / Koch

Wright, Andrew

PIPERS OF DISTINCTION
CD ______ CDMON 802
Monarch / Dec '89 / ADA / CM / Direct / Duncans

Wright, Betty

4U2 NJOY
4 U 2 NJOY / It's been real / Quiet storm / Keep love new / From pain to joy / Valley of lonely / Lightning / We "down" / Won't be long now
CD ______ SDCD 2
Sure Delight / Jul '89 / Jet Star

BEST OF BETTY WRIGHT, THE
Shoorah shoorah / Tonight is the night pts 1 and 2 / Where is the love / That's when I'll stop loving you / Ooh la la / Slip and do it / If I ever do you wrong / Life / Do right girl / I think I'd better think about it / Smother me / You can't see for looking / Loving is really my game / That man of mine / If you abuse my love / Sometime kind of thing / Room at the top / My love is
CD ______ NEMCD 671
Sequel / May '94 / BMG

MOTHER WIT
CD ______ MSBCD 3301
Ms. B / Oct '89 / Jet Star

Wright, Charles

EXPRESS YOURSELF (Wright, Charles & The Watts 103rd St. Rhythm Band)
Express yourself / Express yourself / 'Till you get enough / Joker (on a trip thru the jungle) / Sweet Lorene / Keep saying / Do your thing / Your love (means everything to me) / Tell me what you want to do / Spreadin' honey / Doin' what comes naturally / 90 day cycle people / One lie / 65 bars and a taste of soul / I got love / Love land / Comment
CD ______ 9362453062
Warner Bros. / Jul '96 / Warner Music

Wright, Clyde

OH WHAT A DAY
CD ______ FA 417
Fremeaux / Feb '97 / ADA / Discovery

Wright, David

BETWEEN REALITIES
Eastern innersense / Between realities / Strange liaisons / Over the edge / Taiga / Illusions
CD ______ AD 5CD
AD / Mar '97 / Disc

DISSIMILAR VIEWS
Legend of the tundra / Beijing / Rysheara / Cosmicon / Albania / Smiling shadows lie / Koroe / Room of dolphins / Borders of colour / Transformation / Benny's theme / Albania / Love remembered / Returning tides / Dissimilar views
CD ______ AD 9CD
AD / Mar '97 / Disc

LIVE AT THE LONDON PLANETARIUM
Landings / Enchantress / Rysheara / Images / London / Love theme / Running cloud / Bridge to the sun / Buffalo run / Berlin / Nomad / Legend of the Tundra
CD ______ AD 17CD
AD / Nov '96 / Disc

MARILYNMBA
Confused encounters / Marilynmba / Syntasia / Walkin' the sand / Colours of the night / Marilynmba
CD ______ AD 4CD
AD / Mar '97 / Disc

MOMENTS IN TIME
Ancient dreams / Spirit of the plains movements 1-5
CD ______ AD 7CD
AD / Mar '97 / Disc

OCEAN WATCH
Dream maker / Ocean watch / Nomad / Glass mountains / Seven seas / Desert storm / Reflections / Beyond the airwaves
CD ______ AD 6CD
AD / Mar '97 / Disc

Wright, Frank

YOUR PRAYER
CD ______ ESP 10532
ESP / Jan '94 / Jazz Music

Wright, Gary

DREAM WEAVER
CD ______ 7599272942
Warner Bros. / Nov '94 / Warner Music

Wright, John

RIDE THE ROLLING SKY
CD ______ FE 097CD
Fellside / Jan '94 / ADA / Direct / Target/ BMG

THINGS WE'VE HANDED DOWN, THE (Wright, John Band)
CD ______ FE 106CD
Fellside / May '96 / ADA / Direct / Target/ BMG

Wright, Marva

BLUESIANA MAMA
Let the good times roll / Boogie song / Little red rooster / Driving wheel / Bluesiana mama / Got my mojo working / Members only / I'd rather go blind / Go tell it on the mountain / Never make your move too soon / Mama he treats your daughter mean / CC rider / Shake, shake
CD ______ 12863
Laserlight / May '97 / Target/BMG

I STILL HAVEN'T FOUND WHAT I'M LOOKING FOR
CD ______ AIMA 2CD
Aim / Oct '95 / ADA / Direct / Jazz Music

Wright, Michelle

FOR ME IT'S YOU
Nobody's girl / Answer if yes / We've tried everything else / I'm not afraid / What love looks like / You owe me / For me it's you / Cold kisses / Crank my tractor / Love has no pride
CD ______ 74321417232
Arista / Aug '96 / BMG

Wright, O.V.

O.V. WRIGHT 45'S
CD ______ HILOCD 2
Hi / Nov '93 / Pinnacle

O.V. WRIGHT LIVE
I'd rather be blind, crippled and crazy / Eight men, four women / Love and happiness / When a man loves a woman / You're gonna make me cry / Ace of spades / Precious, precious / God blessed of our love / That's how strong my love is / Into something (can't shake loose)
CD ______ HIUKCD 426
Hi / Jul '89 / Pinnacle

THAT'S HOW STRONG MY LOVE IS
Live my life without you / God blessed our love / When a man loves a woman / That's how strong my love is / Bottom line / I don't do windows / That's the way I feel about cha / Your good thing is about to end / Let's straighten it out / I don't know why / No easy way to say goodbye / Little more time / Since you left (these arms of mine) / Long road / Rhymes / Fool can't see the light / I'm gonna be a big man
CD ______ HIUKCD 108
Hi / Dec '89 / Pinnacle

WRIGHT STUFF, THE
Into something (can't shake loose) / I feel love growin' / Precious, precious / Trying to live my life without you / Your good thing is about to end / Bottom line / I don't do windows / I don't know why / Time we have / You gotta have love / Rhymes / Without you
CD ______ HIUKCD 414
Hi / May '87 / Pinnacle

WRIGHT STUFF, THE/O.V. WRIGHT LIVE
Into something (can't shake loose) / I feel love growin' / Precious, precious / Trying to live my life without you / Your good thing is about to end / Bottom line / I don't do windows / I don't know why / Time we have / You gotta have love / Rhymes / Without you / I'd rather be blind, crippled and crazy / Ace of spades / Eight men, four women / Love and happiness / God blessed our love / When a man loves a woman / That's how strong my love is / You're gonna make me cry
CD ______ HIUKCD 103
Hi / Dec '89 / Pinnacle

Wright, Rev. Robert

REMEMBER ME
CD ______ EDCD 380
Edsel / Dec '93 / Pinnacle

Wright, Rick

BROKEN CHINA
Breaking water / Night of a thousand furry toys / Hidden fear / Runaway / Unfair ground / Satellite / Woman of custom / Interlude / Black cloud / Far from the harbour wall / Drowning / Reaching for the rail / Blue room in Venice / Sweet July / Along the shoreline / Breakthrough
CD ______ CDEMD 1098
EMI / Sep '97 / EMI

Wright, Sandra

WOUNDED WOMAN
Wounded woman / Sha-la bandit / I'm not strong enough to love you again / I come running back / Lovin' you, lovin' me / Man can't be a man (without a woman) / Midnight affair / I'll see you through / Please don't say goodbye
CD ______ VEXCD 11
Demon / Jun '92 / Pinnacle

Wright, Stephen

INTERNATIONAL CHANGE
CD ______ ROTCD 003
Reggae On Top / Nov '94 / Jet Star / SRD

Wrigley, Jennifer

WATCH STONE, THE (Wrigley, Jennifer & Hazel)
CD ______ AT 038CD
Attic / Jan '95 / ADA / CM

Wu Man

CHINESE MUSIC FOR THE PIPA
CD ______ NI 5368CD
Nimbus / Oct '93 / Nimbus

Wu Tang Clan

ENTER THE WU TANG (36 CHAMBERS)
Shaolin sword / Bring da ruckus / Shame on a nigga / Clan in da front / Wu-tang / Seventh Chamber / Can it be so simple / Wu-tang sword / Da mystery of chessboxin' / Wu-tang ain't nuthing ta taf' wit / CREAM / Method man / Protect ya neck / Tearz / Seventh Chamber
CD ______ 74321203672
Loud / Apr '94 / BMG

WU TANG FOREVER (2CD Set)
Wu revolution: *Wu Tang Clan & Poppa Wu/ Uncle Pete* / Reunited / For Heaven's sake: *Wu Tang Clan & Cappadonna* / Cash still rules/Scary hours (still don't nothing move but t / Visions / As high as Wu Tang gets / Severe punishment / Older Gods / Maria: *Wu Tang Clan & Cappadonna* / Better tomorrow / It's yours / Triumph: *Wu Tang Clan & Cappadonna* / Impossible: *Wu Tang Clan & Tekitha* / Little ghetto boys: *Wu Tang Clan & Cappadonna* / Deadly melody: *Wu Tang Clan & Cappadonna* / City / Projects / Bells of war / MGM / Dog shit / Duck season / Hells wind staff / Heaterz: *Wu Tang Clan & Cappadonna* / Black shampoo / Second coming / Sunshower
CD Set ______ 74321457682
Loud / May '97 / BMG

Wubble-U

WHERE'S WUBBLE-U
Theme from Wubble-U / Jellied eels / Petal / I like the future / Wow man / Name Czech / Europhobix / Realitea break / Down / Theme reprisal / Giantkillaz / Kazum / Ambient bingo nuns / Time / Stanley clears the throakus / Angel in Bermondsey (pt 1)
CD ______ 8286662
Go Discs / Oct '95 / PolyGram

Wumpscut

MUSIC FOR A SLAUGHTERING TRIBE
CD ______ SPV 08484782
SPV / Mar '96 / Koch / Plastic Head

Wunderlich, Klaus

GOLDEN SOUNDS OF KLAUS WUNDERLICH, THE
CD ______ GS 864362
Disky / Mar '96 / Disky / THE

KEYS FOR LOVERS
CD ______ NSPCD 507
Connoisseur Collection / Mar '95 / Pinnacle

PLAYS ABBA - THE WINNER TAKES IT ALL
CD ______ NSPCD 506
Connoisseur Collection / Jan '94 / Pinnacle

TRIBUTE TO FRANK SINATRA, A
Lady is a tramp / Strangers in the night / I only have eyes for you / Something / From here to eternity / I've got you under my skin / My way / Downtown / New York, New York / Something stupid / Someone to watch over me / What now my love / Autumn in New York / Night and day / I'm gettin' sentimental over you / Just one of those things
CD ______ NSPCD 502
Connoisseur Collection / Apr '91 / Pinnacle

WWF

WE GOTTA WRESTLE
CD ______ 0089622CTR
Concrete / Jul '97 / 3mv/Pinnacle / Prime / RTM/Disc / Total/BMG

Wyands, Richard

ARRIVAL, THE (Wyands, Richard Trio)
CD ______ DIW 611
DIW / Nov '92 / Cadillac / Harmonia Mundi

GET OUT OF TOWN
CD ______ SCCD 31401
Steeplechase / Apr '97 / Discovery / Impetus

REUNITED
CD ______ CRISS 1105
Criss Cross / Oct '95 / Cadillac / Direct / Vital/SAM

Wyatt, Robert

DONESTAN
CD ______ R 2742
Rough Trade / Sep '91 / Pinnacle

FLOTSAM AND JETSAM
CD ______ R 3112
Rough Trade / Aug '94 / Pinnacle

GOING BACK A BIT (A Little History Of Robert Wyatt)
Moon in June / Alifib / Alifie / Soup song / Calyx / Sonia / All she wanted / I'm a believer / Yesterday man
CD ______ CDVM 9031
Virgin / Jul '94 / EMI

MID EIGHTIES
CD ______ R 2952
Rough Trade / Jan '93 / Pinnacle

ROCK BOTTOM
Sea song / Last straw / Little Red Riding Hood hit the road / Alifib / Little Red Robin Hood hit the road
CD ______ CDV 2017
Virgin / Feb '89 / EMI

RUTH IS STRANGER THAN RICHARD
Soup song / Sonia / Team spirit / Song for Che / Muddy mouse / Solar flares / Muddy mouse / Five black notes and one white note / Muddy mouse / Muddy mouth
CD ______ CDV 2034
Virgin / Feb '89 / EMI

SHORT BREAK, A
Short break / Tubab / Kutcha / Ventilatir / Unmasked

CD ______ BP 108CD
Blueprint / Apr '96 / Pinnacle

Wycherley, Ellen

SCOTTISH CANTICLE, A
CD ______ EWCD 004
Auldgate / Jul '94 / CM

Wylie & The Wild West Show

WYLIE AND THE WILD WEST SHOW
CD ______ DFGCD 8436
Dixie Frog / Feb '96 / Direct / TKO Magnum

Wylie-Hubbard, Ray

LOCO GRINGO'S LAMENT
CD ______ DJD 3213
Dejadisc / Dec '94 / ADA / Direct

LOST TRAIN OF THOUGHT
CD ______ DJD 3223
Dejadisc / Nov '95 / ADA / Direct

Wyman, Bill

BILL WYMAN
Ride on baby / New fashion / Nuclear reactions / Visions / Jump up / Come back Suzanne / Rio de Janeiro / Girls / Seventeen / Si si, je suis un rock star
CD ______ NEMCD 848
Sequel / Jun '96 / BMG

MONKEY GRIP
I wanna get me a gun / Crazy woman / Pussy / Mighty fine time / Monkey grip glue / What a blow / White lightnin' / I'll pull you thro' / It's a wonder
CD ______ NEMCD 846
Sequel / Jun '96 / BMG

STONE ALONE
Quarter to three / Gimme just one chance / Soul satisfying / Apache woman / Every sixty seconds / Get it on / Feet / Peanut butter time / Wine and wimmen / If you wanna be happy / What's the point / No more foolin'
CD ______ NEMCD 847
Sequel / Jun '96 / BMG

Wyndham, Victoria

COUPLETS (Wyndham, Victoria & Charles Keating)
CD ______ SH 6023
Shanachie / Jul '97 / ADA / Greensleeves / Koch

Wyndham-Read, Martyn

BENEATH A SOUTHERN SKY (Wyndham-Read, Martyn & No Man's Band)
Shearer's lament/Orotaba waltz / Emu plains / Colonial / My eldorado / Lambs on the green hills / Heel and toe polka / Sailor home from the sea / Faithful Emma / Goorianawa / Lily/Exercise 77 / Best of Autumn / Banks of the Tees / Off to the shearing / Swaggie snake and frog/Ebb wren's schottische
CD ______ FE 115CD
Fellside / May '97 / ADA / Direct / Target/ BMG

MUSSELS ON A TREE
Bold Reynolds / Hills are clad / Irish lords / Reunion / Flash stockman / Bunch of red roses / Valley of tees / Smokestack land / Jim Jones / 'ard tack / Cockleshells / Springtime it brings on the shearing / Ginny on the moor / Van Diemen's land / Shelter
CD ______ FE 084CD
Fellside / '92 / ADA / Direct / Target/BMG

SUNLIT PLAINS
CD ______ FE 102CD
Fellside / Jan '95 / ADA / Direct / Target/ BMG

Wynette, Tammy

BEST OF TAMMY WYNETTE, THE
Stand by your man / Lonely street / DI-VORCE / Gentle on my mind / Take me to your world / Almost persuaded / Your good girl's gonna go bad / Apartment no. 9 / Hey good lookin' / I don't wanna play house / My arms stay open late / There goes my everything
CD ______ CD 32015
CBS / Jun '91 / Sony

BEST OF TAMMY WYNETTE, THE
DIVORCE / There goes my everything / Ode to Billy / No charge / Honey / Crying in the chapel / Ways to love a man / Sometimes when we touch / Stand by your man / Help me make it through the night / Hey good lookin' / I don't want to play house / Crying in the rain / Another lonely song / Funny face / Your good girl's gonna go bad / Please come to Boston / Apartment no.9
CD ______ 4840462
Epic / May '96 / Sony

COUNTRY STARS (Wynette, Tammy & George Jones)
No show jones: *Jones, George* / Race is on: *Jones, George* / Bartender blues: *Jones, George* / I always get lucky with you: *Jones, George* / She's my rock: *Jones, George* / Chicken reel: *Jones, George* / He stopped loving her today: *Jones, George* / Who's gonna fill their shoes: *Jones, George* / One I loved back then: *Jones, George* / Welcome to my world: *Wynette, Tammy* / Another chance: *Wynette, Tammy* / You good girl's gonna go bad: *Wynette, Tammy* / DI-VORCE: *Wynette, Tammy* / Singing my song: *Wynette, Tammy* / Till I can make it on my own: *Wynette, Tammy* / Womanhood: *Wynette, Tammy* / Fairy tales: *Wynette, Tammy* / When the grass grows over me: *Wynette, Tammy* / Amazing grace: *Wynette, Tammy* / I'll fly away: *Wynette, Tammy* / Will the circle be unbroken: *Wynette, Tammy* / I saw the light: *Wynette, Tammy* / Stand by your man: *Wynette, Tammy* / Crying in the rain: *Wynette, Tammy*
CD ______ PLATCD 351
Platinum / May '91 / Prism

I'LL FLY AWAY (Wynette, Tammy & George Jones)
CD ______ MU 5048
Musketeer / Oct '92 / Disc

SINGING HER SONG (In Concert)
My man (understands) / Another chance / 'Til I can make it on my own / Rocky top / Alive and well / What a difference you've made in my life / (They call it) making love / You and me / Take me to your world / Womanhood / Crying in the rain / Medley no.1 / I still believe in fairy tales / Stand by your man / Medley no.2 / Let's call it a day, today / Heart over mind
CD ______ CTS 55440
Country Stars / Feb '97 / Target/BMG

WITHOUT WALLS
It's the last thing I do / Woman's needs / Every breath you take / If you were to wake up / Glasshouses / What do they know / All I am to you / I second that emotion / This love / Girl thang
CD ______ 4748002
Epic / Apr '95 / Sony

Wynn, Steve

DAZZLING DISPLAY
CD ______ 8122028322
WEA / Mar '93 / Warner Music

FLUORESCENT
CD ______ OUT 1162
Brake Out / Nov '94 / Direct

MELTING IN THE DARK
CD ______ OUT 1242
Brake Out / Aug '96 / Direct

TAKE YOUR FLUNKY AND DANGLE
CD ______ RTS 13
Return To Sender / Dec '94 / ADA / Direct

Wynona Ryders

JD SALINGER
CD ______ LOOKOUT 104CD
Lookout / Sep '95 / Cargo / Greyhound / Shellshock/Disc

Wynter, Mark

RECOLLECTED
CD ______ NEXCD 162
Sequel / Apr '91 / BMG

X Marks The Pedwalk

AIR BACK TRAX
CD CDZOT 118
Zoth Ommog / Aug '94 / Cargo / Plastic Head

KILLING HAD BEGUN
CD CDZOT 107
Zoth Ommog / Mar '94 / Cargo / Plastic Head

PARANOID ILLUSIONS
CD CDZOT 29
Zoth Ommog / Aug '93 / Cargo / Plastic Head

X-103

ATLANTIS
CD E 01740CD
Tresor / Mar '93 / 3mv/BMG / Prime / SRD

X-ASP

TERRA FIRMA
CD CAT 028CD
Rephlex / Oct '96 / Prime / RTM/Disc

X-CNN

X-CNN 4
CD XCNN 4CD
Transglobal / May '94 / Pinnacle

X-Cops

YOU HAVE THE RIGHT TO REMAIN SILENT
CD 140802
Metal Blade / Oct '95 / Pinnacle / Plastic Head

X-Legged Sally

LAND OF THE GIANT DWARVES
CD KFWCD 182
Knitting Factory / Oct '96 / Cargo / Plastic Head

X-Mal Deutschland

FETISCH
Qual / Geheimnis / Young man / In der nacht / Orient / Hand in hand / Kaempfen / Danghem / Boomerang / Stummes kind / Qual (remix) / Sehnsucht / Zeit
CD CAD 302CD
4AD / '87 / RTM/Disc

TOCSIN
Mondicht / Eiland / Reigen / Tag fur tag (day by day) / Augen blich / Begrab / Mein herz / Nacht schatten / Christmas in Australia / Der wisch / Incubus succubus II / ViFo
CD CAD 407CD
4AD / Jun '87 / RTM/Disc

X-Rated

TIGHT PUM PUM
CD LG 21077
Lagoon / May '93 / Grapevine/PolyGram

X-Ray Spex

CONSCIOUS CONSUMER
Cigarettes / Junk food junkie / Crystal clear / India / Dog in Sweden / Hi chaperone / Good time girl / Melancholy / Sophia / Peace meal / Prayer for peace / Party
CD RRCD 205
Receiver / Oct '95 / Grapevine/PolyGram

GERM FREE ADOLESCENTS
CD CDVM 9001
Virgin / Jun '92 / EMI

X-Rays

DOUBLE GODZILLA WITH CHEESE
CD MTR 350CD
Empty / Oct '96 / Cargo / Greyhound / Plastic Head / SRD

X-Seed

DESOLATION
CD CDBLEED 19
Bleeding Hearts / Jul '96 / Pinnacle

X-Specials

COZ I LUV YOU
CD RRSCD 1010
Receiver / Feb '94 / Grapevine/PolyGram

X-Tal

BITING THE UGLY BISCUIT
Family jewels / Dear friends / White rat / Lullaby / Happy Americans / I'll believe / Cheap holiday / Encore / Kansas song / Through you (Emotional consumerism) / Your fragile mind / Dub rat / Goldfish bowl / Fatal distractions / You're not saved yet / Daddy auction / Smells like smoke / Black Russian
CD RTS 25
Return To Sender / Mar '97 / ADA / Direct

DIE MONSTER DIE
CD A 012D
Alias / Jul '92 / Vital

GOOD LUCK
Stating the obvious again / Smells like smoke / Good shepherd / Cat box / I know that / Good luck
CD A 036D
Alias / Jul '93 / Vital

Xenakis

ENSEMBLE MUSIC VOL.2
CD MODE 56
Mode / Dec '96 / Harmonia Mundi / ReR Megacorp

REBONDS/AKEA/EPICYLES
CD BVHAASTCD 9219
Bvhaast / Jun '89 / Cadillac

Xenakis, Iannis

KRAANERG (Xenakis, Iannis & DJ Spooky)
CD EFA 706752
Asphodel / Jul '97 / Cargo / SRD

Xentrix

SCOURGE
CD HMRXD 198
Heavy Metal / Nov '95 / Revolver / Sony

Xerxes

BEYOND MY IMAGINATION
CD GIT 001
General Inquisitor Torquemado's / Oct '93 / Plastic Head

Xhol-Caravan

MOTHER FUCKERS GMBH
CD 14531
Spalax / Feb '97 / ADA / Cargo / Direct / Discovery / Greyhound

Xiame

PENSA
Pensa / Tokyoto / Arastape pe / Falando / Anduva / Kleiner bar / Carioca / Nossa doce lia / Hickyoung / Dois berlinese in Rio / Goodbye, pork pie hat / Dor da floresta
CD VBR 21072
Vera Bra / Aug '92 / New Note/Pinnacle / Pinnacle

XIAME (OUR EARTH)
Xiame / Nosso destino / Minha rua / Guaratiba / Rio De Janeiro / Um brasileiro em Berlin / Mutio swer / Gone but still here / 'Round midnight / Choro de crainza / I can't stand the pain / Flor da terra
CD VRB 20362
Vera Bra / Jul '90 / New Note/Pinnacle / Pinnacle

Xid

XID
CD RTD 19519182
Our Choice / Nov '94 / Pinnacle

XIII

SALT
CD 342712
No Bull / Nov '95 / Koch

Xingu Hill

MAPS OF THE IMPOSSIBLE
CD NZ 035CD
Nova Zembla / May '95 / Plastic Head

XL

XLENT
CD OCTO 4042
Ondine / Aug '95 / ADA / Koch

XLNC

R U READY
CD DMUT 1254
Multitone / Apr '96 / BMG

Xolton, Blake

COOL ON MY SKIN
CD ROSE 166CD
New Rose / Mar '89 / ADA / Direct / Discovery

Xscape

OFF THE HOOK
Do your thang / Feels so good / Hard to say goodbye / Can't hang / Who can I run to / Hip hop barber shop request line / Do you want to / What can I do / Do like lovers do / Work me slow / Love's a funny thing / Keep it on the real
CD 4896442
Columbia / Jul '95 / Sony

XTC

BIG EXPRESS, THE
Wake up / All you pretty girls / Shake you donkey up / Seagulls screaming kiss her kiss her / This world over / Everyday story of smalltown / I bought myself a liarbird / Reign of blows / You're the wish (you are) I had / I remember the sun / Train running low on soul coal / Red brick dream / Washaway / Blue overall
CD CDV 2325
Virgin / '84 / EMI

BLACK SEA
Respectable street / Generals and majors / Living through another Cuba / Love at first sight / Rocket from a bottle / No language in our lungs / Towers of London / Paper and iron (notes and coins) / Burning with optimism's flame / Sgt. Rock (is going to help me) / Travels in nihilon / Smokeless zone / Don't lose your temper / Somnambulist
CD CDV 2173
Virgin / Jun '88 / EMI

COMPACT XTC, THE (The Singles 1978-1985)
Science friction / Making plans for Nigel / Sgt. Rock (is going to help me) / Senses working overtime / Love on a farmboy's wages / Wake up / Statue of Liberty / This is pop / Are you receiving me / Life begins at the hop / Wait till your boat goes down / Generals and majors / Towers of London / Ball and chain / Great fire / Wonderland / All you pretty girls / This world over
CD CDV 2251
Virgin / '86 / EMI

DRUMS AND WIRES
Making plans for Nigel / Helicopter / Day in, day out / When you're near me I have difficulty / Ten feet tall / Roads girdle the globe / Real by reel / Millions / That is the way / Outside world / Scissor man / Complicated game
CD CDV 2129
Virgin / Jun '88 / EMI

ENGLISH SETTLEMENT
Runaways / Ball and chain / Senses working overtime / Jason and the Argonauts / No thugs in our house / Yacht dance / All of a sudden (it's too late) / Melt the guns / Leisure / It's nearly Africa / Knuckle down / Fly on the wall / Down in the cockpit / English roundabout / Snowman
CD CDV 2223
Virgin / Dec '81 / EMI

EXPLODE TOGETHER (The Dub Experiments 1978-1980)
Part 1 (go) / Dance with me Germany / Beat the bible / Dictionary of modern marriage / Clap clap clap / We kill the beast / Part II (take away) / Commerciality / Day they pulled the North Pole down / Forgotten language of light / Steam fist futurist / Shore leave ornithology (another 1950) / Cairo / Part III (the lure of the salvage) / Rotary / Madhattan / I sit in the snow / Work away / Tokyo day / New broom
CD CDOVD 308
Virgin / Jul '93 / EMI

FOSSIL FUEL (The XTC Singles Collection 1977-1992)
Science friction / Statue of Liberty / This is pop / Are you receiving me / Life begins at the hop / Making plans for Nigel / Ten feet tall / Wait till your boat goes down / Generals & Majors / Towers of London / Sgt. Rock (is going to help me) / Love at first sight / Respectable Street / Senses working overtime / Ball and chain / No thugs in our house / Great fire / Wonderland / Love on a farmboy's wages / All you pretty girls / This world over / Wake up / Grass / Meeting place / Dear God / Mayor of Simpleton / King for a day / Loving / Disappointed / Ballad of Peter Pumpkinhead / Wrapped in grey
CD CDVDX 2811
CD CDVD 2811
Virgin / Sep '96 / EMI

GO 2
Meccanik dancing / Crowded room / Battery brides (Andy paints Brian) / Buzzcity talking / Rhythm / Beattown / Life is good in the greenhouse / I am the audience / Ted / My weapon / Jumping in Gomorrah / Super tuff / Are you receiving me
CD CDV 2108
Virgin / Jul '87 / EMI

MUMMER
Beating of hearts / Wonderland / Love on a farmboy's wages / Great fire / Deliver us from the elements / Human alchemy / Ladybird / In loving memory of a name / Me and the wind / Funk pop a roll
CD CDV 2264
Virgin / Jun '88 / EMI

NONSUCH
Ballad of Peter Pumpkinhead / My bird performs / Dear Madam Barnum / Humble daisy / Smartest monkeys / Disappointed / Holly up on poppy / Crocodile / Rook / Omnibus / That wave / She appeared / War dance / Wrapped in grey / Ugly underneath / Bungalow / Books are burning
CD CDV 2699
Virgin / Apr '92 / EMI

ORANGES AND LEMONS
Garden of earthly delights / King for a day / Loving / Across the antheap / Pink thing / Chalkhills and children / Mayor of Simpleton / Here comes President kill again / Poor skeleton steps out / Hold me daddy / Minature sun / One of the millions / Scarecrow people / Merely a man / Cynical days
CD CDV 2581
Virgin / Apr '92 / EMI

RAG 'N' BONE BUFFET (Rarities & Out-Takes)
Extrovert / Ten feet tall / Mermaid smiled / Too many cooks in the kitchen (the colonel) / Respectable street / Looking for footprints / Over rusty water / Heaven is paved with broken glass / World is full of angry young men / Punch and Judy / Thanks for Christmas (the three wise men) / Tissue tigers / I need protection (the colonel) / Another satellite / Strange tales / Officer blue / Scissor man / Cockpit dance mixture / Pulsing pulsing / Happy families / Countdown to Christmas party time / Blame the weather / Take this town / History of rock 'n' roll
CD CDOVD 311
Virgin / Jul '93 / EMI

SKYLARKING
Summer's cauldron / Grass / Meeting place / That's really super, supergirl / Ballet for a rainy day / 1000 umbrellas / Season cycle / Earn enough for us / Big day / Another satellite / Mermaid smiled / Man who sailed around his soul / Dying / Sacrificial bonfire
CD CDV 2399
Virgin / Jul '93 / EMI

TESTIMONIAL DINNER, A (A Tribute To XTC) (Various Artists)
CD NTMCD 535
Nectar / Oct '96 / Pinnacle

WHITE MUSIC
Radios in motion / Crosswires / This is pop / Do what you do / Statue of Liberty / All along the watchtower / Into the atom age / I'll set myself on fire / I'm bugged / Spinning top / Neon shuffle / New town animal in a furnished cage / Science friction / She's so square / Dance band / Hang on to the night / Heatwave / Traffic light rock / Instant tunes
CD CDV 2095
Virgin / Jun '88 / EMI

Xterminator

XTERMINATOR DUB
CD RASCD 3195
Ras / Apr '96 / Direct / Greensleeves / Jet Star / SRD

XTERMINATOR PRESENTS THE AWAKENING (Various Artists)
CD RASCD 3165
Ras / Sep '96 / Direct / Greensleeves / Jet Star / SRD

Xtraverts

SO MUCH HATE
CD RUBBISHCD 001
Bin Liner / May '97 / Detour / Greyhound

Xymox

CLAN OF XYMOX
CD CAD 503CD
4AD / '85 / RTM/Disc

HEADCLOUDS
Spiritual high / It's your life / Prophecy / Wild is the wind / Single day / Love thrills / Beginning / Reaching out / Headclouds / January
CD ZCTMT 4
Zok / May '93 / Grapevine/PolyGram / Total/BMG

MEDUSA
CD CAD 613CD
4AD / Nov '86 / RTM/Disc

METAMORPHOSIS
CD ______ ZCDXY 005
Zok / Oct '94 / Grapevine/PolyGram / Total/BMG

REMIX ALBUM
CD ______ 340372
Koch / Dec '94 / Koch

SUBSEQUENT PLEASURES
CD ______ CDP 1013DD
Pseudonym / Jun '97 / Greyhound

Xysma

DELUXE
CD ______ SP 1020
Spinefarm / Jul '94 / Plastic Head

XYZ

COMPAS-ZOUK
CD ______ STCD 1379
Stern's / Jan '91 / ADA / CM / Stern's

Xzibit

AT THE SPEED OF LIFE
Grand opening / At the speed of life / Just maintain / Eyes may shine / Positively negative / Don't hate me / Paparazzi / Foundation / Mrs. Crabtree / Bird's eye view / Hit and run (part 2) / Carry the weight / Plastic surgery / Enemies and friends / Last words
CD ______ 07863668162
Loud / Oct '96 / BMG

Y

Y&T

MUSICALLY INCORRECT
Long way down / I've got my own / 21st Century / Fly away / Nowhere land / I'm lost / Quicksand / Pretty prison / Confusion / Cold day in hell / Don't know what to do / No regrets
CD _______ CDMFN 191
Music For Nations / Sep '95 / Pinnacle

TEN
CD _______ GED 24283
Geffen / Jun '97 / BMG

YESTERDAY AND TODAY LIVE
CD _______ 398417017CD
Metal Blade / May '96 / Pinnacle / Plastic Head

Y Cyrff

MAE DDOE YN DDOE
CD _______ ANKCD 30
Ankst / Oct '92 / Shellshock/Disc

MUE DDOE VW DDOE
CD _______ ANECD 30
Ankst / Nov '92 / Shellshock/Disc

Y-Live

Y ON EARTH
Humanity takes over / Who owns your soul / I want you all / Vortex vision / Don't buy it / Killing the innocents / Earthquake at Sellafield / Death of a nation / Logo of love / Humanity (reprise)
CD _______ ICACD 001
CyberArts / Dec '93 / Electronic Synthesizer Sound Projects

Ya Ho Wha 13

PENETRATION: AQUARIAN SYMPHONY
CD _______ 001CD
Higher Key / Jul '97 / Greyhound

Yabby You

BEWARE DUB
CD _______ RE 188CD
Danceteria / Feb '95 / ADA / Plastic Head / Shellshock/Disc

DELIVER ME FROM MY ENEMIES
CD _______ YVJ 006
Vivian Jones / Apr '92 / Jet Star

KING TUBBY'S PROPHECY OF DUB
Version dub / Conquering dub / Jah love dub / Anti-Christ rock / Beware of God / Robber rock / Rock vibration / Zion is here / Hungering dub / Love and peace / Homelessness / Creations and versions
CD _______ BAFCD 5
Blood & Fire / Jan '95 / Vital

YABBY YOU & MICHAEL PROPHET MEET SCIENTIST (Yabby You & Michael Prophet)
CD _______ YVJ 008
Yabby You / May '95 / Jet Star / THE

YABBY YOU MEETS MAD PROFESSOR/ BLACK STEEL
CD _______ ARICD 083
Ariwa Sounds / Apr '93 / Jet Star / SRD

YABBY YOU MEETS TOMMY MCCOOK IN DUB
CD _______ CD 1275
Peacemaker / Apr '96 / SRD

Yacoub, Gabriel

BEL
CD _______ KMCD 15
Red Sky / '91 / ADA / CM / Direct

QUATRE
CD _______ BP 3182CD
Chantons Sous La True / Apr '95 / ADA

Yaffayo

OVERTIME
CD _______ INTER 0001
Interaction / Sep '95 / Grapevine/ PolyGram

Yage

INTEGRATION
CD _______ MRCD 068
Munster / Mar '97 / Cargo / Greyhound / Plastic Head

Yah Congo

YAH CONGO MEETS KING TUBBY/MAD PROFESSOR AT DUB TABLE (Yah Congo & King Tubby/Mad Professor)
CD _______ RUSCD 8217
ROIR / Oct '95 / Plastic Head / Shellshock/Disc

Yahel, Sam

SEARCHIN'
CD _______ 860042
Naxos Jazz / Jun '97 / Select

Yakutia

EPICS AND IMPROVISATIONS
CD _______ 925652
BUDA / Aug '93 / Discovery

Yamaha International Allstar ...

YAMAHA INTERNATIONAL ALLSTAR BAND (Yamaha International Allstar Band)
CD _______ CD 005
Nagel Heyer / May '96 / Jazz Music

Yamashita, Yosuke

ASIAN GAMES (Yamashita, Yosuke & Bill Laswell/Ryuichi Sakamoto)
Melting pot / Chasin' the air / Asian games / Ninja drive / Napping on the bamboo / Parade of rain / Moon and a bride
CD _______ 5183442
Verve / Feb '94 / PolyGram

CANVAS IN QUIET (Homage To Morio Matsui)
CD _______ 5370072
Verve / Feb '97 / PolyGram

DAZZLING DAYS
CD _______ 5213032
Verve / May '94 / PolyGram

KURDISH DANCE
Kurdish dance / Back yard / Act 3-8 / Brooklyn express / Tiny square / Subway gig / 4th street up / K's gift
CD _______ 5177082
Verve / Oct '93 / PolyGram

SAKURA
Sakura / Yurikago / Haiku / Amefuri / Ano machi / Dobarada / Sasa no ha / Sunayama / Tsuki no sabaku / Usagi no dance / Nenkorori
CD _______ 8490652
Verve / Oct '93 / PolyGram

SPIDER
CD _______ 5312712
Verve / Jun '96 / PolyGram

STONE FLOWER
Surfboard / So danco samba / Eu te amo / Chovendo na roseira / Meu amigo Radames / Stone flower / Felicidade / Homage to Jobim
CD _______ JVC 90142
JVC / Aug '97 / Direct / New Note/Pinnacle / Vital/SAM

WAYS OF TIME
CD _______ 5328412
Verve / Jun '95 / PolyGram

Yamashta, Stomu

RED BUDDHA
CD _______ SPALAX 14512
Spalax / Nov '96 / ADA / Cargo / Direct / Discovery / Greyhound

SEA AND SKY
Photon / Appeared / And / Touched / Ah / Time / To see / To know
CD _______ CDKUCK 072
Kuckuck / Jun '87 / ADA / CM

Yamato Ensemble

ART OF THE JAPANESE BAMBOOFLUTE AND KOTO
CD _______ EUCD 1248
ARC / Nov '93 / ADA / ARC Music

ART OF THE JAPANESE KOTO, SHAKUHACHI AND SHAMISEN, THE
CD _______ EUCD 1364
ARC / Nov '96 / ADA / ARC Music

Yami Sari Ensemble

GAMELAN GONG KEBYAL
Yami Sari / Ratna gurnita / Puspa raga / Giri kenaka / Legong jobog / Kapi raja
CD _______ VICG 54172
JVC / Oct '96 / Direct / New Note/Pinnacle / Vital/SAM

Yanagisawa, Rie

KUROKAMI - THE MUSIC OF JAPAN (Yanagisawa, Rie & Clive Bell)
Hari no umi (Sea in spring) / Kurokami / Disguised as a silverer of mirrors / Midare rinzetsu / Yugao (The moon-flower) / Esashi Oiwake / Aki no shirabe (Tune of Autumn)
CD _______ CDSDL 367
Saydisc / Mar '94 / ADA / Direct / Harmonia Mundi

Yancey, Jimmy

ETERNAL BLUES
CD _______ CD 52031
Blues Encore / May '94 / Target/BMG

IN THE BEGINNING
CD _______ SACD 1
Solo Art / Jul '93 / Jazz Music

JIMMY YANCEY VOL.1 1939-1940
CD _______ DOCD 5041
Document / Feb '92 / ADA / Hot Shot / Jazz Music

JIMMY YANCEY VOL.2 1940-1943
CD _______ DOCD 5042
Document / Feb '92 / ADA / Hot Shot / Jazz Music

JIMMY YANCEY VOL.3 1943-1950
CD _______ DOCD 5043
Document / Feb '92 / ADA / Hot Shot / Jazz Music

PRIVATE PARTY 1951
CD _______ DOCD 1007
Document / May '97 / ADA / Hot Shot / Jazz Music

Yancey, Mama

MAYBE I'LL CRY
Trouble in mind / Santa Fe blues / Monkey woman blues / How long, how long blues / Maybe I'll cry / Pallet on the floor / Weekly blues / Baby, won't you please come home / Four o'clock blues / Kitchen sink blues
CD _______ ECD 260782
Evidence / Apr '96 / ADA / Cadillac / Harmonia Mundi

Yankee Brass Band

YANKEE BRASS BAND, THE
Arizona quickstep / Bond's serenade / No one to love / Blondinette polka / Mabel waltz / Helene Schottisch / American hymn / Red stocking quickstep / Mockingbird quickstep / Memories of home-waltz / Schottische / Moon is above us / Brin d'amour polka / Goodnight my angel / Firemen's polka
CD _______ NW 312
New World / Aug '92 / ADA / Cadillac / Harmonia Mundi

Yankovic, Weird Al

OFF AT THE DEEP END
CD _______ 5125062
Polydor / Jan '94 / PolyGram

Yanni

CHAMELEON DAYS
Swept away / Marching season / Chasing shadows / Rain must fall / Days of summer / Reflections of passion / Walkabout / Everglade run / Word in private
CD _______ 259644
Private Music / May '89 / BMG

DARE TO DREAM
CD _______ 262667
Private Music / Aug '95 / BMG

IN CELEBRATION OF LIFE
Santorini / Song for Antarctica / Marching season / Walkabout / Keys to imagination / Looking glass / Someday / Within attraction / Standing in motion / Sand dance
CD _______ 262342
Private Music / Jan '92 / BMG

IN THE MIRROR
In the mirror / In the morning light / Love for life / One man's dream / Within attraction / Forbidden dreams / Once upon a time / Chasing shadows / Aria / Quiet man / Enchantment / Song long my friend / Before I go / End of August
CD _______ 74321471252
Private Music / May '97 / BMG

KEYS TO IMAGINATION
North shore of Matsushima / Looking glass / Nostalgia / Santorini / Port of mystery / Keys to imagination / Forgotten yesterdays / Forbidden dreams
CD _______ 259960
Private Music / Nov '89 / BMG

LIVE AT THE ACROPOLIS
Santorini / Keys to imagination / Until the last moment / Rain must fall / Acroyali/ Standing in motion / One man's dream / Within attraction / Nostalgia / Swept away / Reflections of passion / Aria
CD _______ 01005821222
Private Music / Jul '95 / BMG

NIKI NANA
Niki nana (We're one) / Dance with a stranger / Running time / Someday / Human condition / First touch / Nightbird / Quiet man
CD _______ 260208
Private Music / Oct '89 / BMG

OUT OF SILENCE
Sand dance / Standing in motion / Mermaid / With attraction / Street level / Secret vows / Point or origin / Acroyali / Paths on water
CD _______ 259965
Private Music / Nov '89 / BMG

REFLECTIONS OF PASSION
After the sunrise / Mermaid / Quiet man / Nostalgia / Almost a whisper / Acrorali / Rain must fall / Swept away / Farewell / Secret vow / Flight of fantasy / Word in private / First touch / Reflections
CD _______ 260652
Private Music / Feb '96 / BMG

Yano, Akiko

AKIKO YANO
CD _______ 7559792052
Nonesuch / Jan '95 / Warner Music

LOVE LIFE
CD _______ 7559792792
Nonesuch / Jan '95 / Warner Music

PIANO NIGHTLY
CD _______ 7559794162
Nonesuch / Jun '96 / Warner Music

Yarborough, Glenn

FAMILY PORTRAIT (Yarborough, Glenn & Holly)
CD _______ FE 1416
Folk Era / Dec '94 / ADA / CM

LIVE AT THE TROUBADOUR
CD _______ FE 1704
Folk Era / Dec '94 / ADA / CM

Yardbirds

BEST OF THE LEGENDARY YARDBIRDS, THE
CD _______ NTMCD 527
Nectar / Mar '97 / Pinnacle

BEST OF THE YARDBIRDS, THE (2CD Set)
I wish you would / Certain girl / Good morning little schoolgirl / I ain't got you / For your love / Got to hurry / Heart full of soul / Steeled blues / Evil hearted you / Still I'm sad / Shapes of things / Mister you're a better man than I / I'm a man / New York City blues / Train kept a rollin' / Paff...burn / Mr. Zero / Sweet music / Someone to love / Stroll on / Too much monkey business / Got love if you want it / Smokestack lightning / Five long years / Louise / Baby what's wrong / Boom boom / Honey in your hips / Talkin' 'bout you / Let it rock / Take it easy baby: *Yardbirds & Sonny Boy Williamson* / Highway 69: *Yardbirds & Sonny Boy Williamson* / Putty (in your hands) / I'm not talking / I ain't done wrong / My girl sloopy / Jeff's blues / Like Jimmy Reed again / What do you want / Here 'tis
CD Set _______ CPCD 82452
Charly / Dec '96 / Koch

BEST OF THE YARDBIRDS, THE
For your love / Heart full of soul / Ha ha said the clown / Goodnight sweet Josephine / Shape of things / Honey in your hips / Boom boom / Train kept a-rollin' / Ten little Indians / Certain girl / Still I'm sad / Putty / Pafff...bum / Good morning little schoolgirl / I wish you would / I'm a man
CD _______ 12900
Laserlight / Jul '97 / Target/BMG

COLLECTION, THE
I wish you would / Good morning little school girl / I ain't got you / Boom boom / Good morning little school girl / Got to hurry / For your love / Too much monkey business / Got love if you want it / Here 'tis / Pontiac blues / Twenty three hours too long / Let it rock / Smokestack lightnin' / Honey in your hips / Heart full of soul / Evil hearted you / Still I'm sad / I'm a man / Jeff's blues / You're a better man than I / Shapes of things / Stroll on
CD _______ CCSCD 141
Castle / '88 / BMG

GOOD MORNING LITTLE SCHOOLGIRL
I wish you would / Trains kept a-rollin' / New York city blues / I ain't got you / Baby what's wrong / Who do you love / I ain't done wrong / Got to hurry / I'm not talking / Good morning little schoolgirl / Smokestack lightning / 23 hours too long / Mister you're a better man than I / Jeff's blues / You can't judge a book (by looking at the cover) / I'm a man / Let it rock / Boom / Stroll on / Too much monkey business
CD _______ 3036000902
Carlton / Feb '97 / Carlton

HEART FULL OF SOUL
CD _______ 12206
Laserlight / May '94 / Target/BMG

LITTLE GAMES
Little games / Puzzles / Smile on me / White Summer / Tinker tailor / Glimpses / Ten little indians / Ha ha said the clown / Drinking muddy water / No excess baggage / Stealing stealing / Only the black rose / Little soldier boy / Think about it / I remember the night / Goodnight sweet Josephine / Together now
CD _______________ CDGOLD 1068
EMI Gold / Oct '96 / EMI

LIVE AND IN THE STUDIO
CD _______________ 472155
Flarenasch / May '96 / Discovery

ON AIR
I ain't got you / For your love / I'm not talking / I wish you would / Heart full of soul / I've been wrong / Too much monkey business / Love me like I love you / I'm a man / Evil hearted you / Still I'm sad / Hang on sloopy / Smokestack lightnin' / Mister, you're a better man than I / Train kept a rollin' / Shapes of things / Dust my blues / Scratch my back / Over under sideways down / Sun is shining / Most likely you'll go your way / Little games / Drinking muddy water / Thnik about it / Goodnight sweet Josephine / My baby
CD _______________ BOJCD 20
Band Of Joy / May '91 / Pinnacle

OVER UNDER SIDEWAYS DOWN
CD _______________ RVCD 12
Raven / May '91 / ADA / Direct

RARITIES
CD _______________ PRCDSP 501
Prestige / Aug '92 / Else / Total/BMG

ROGER THE ENGINEER
Happenings ten years time ago / Psycho daisies / Over under sideways down / Nazz are blue / Rack my mind / Lost women / I can't make your way / Farewell / Jeff's boogie / Hot house of Omagararshid / He's always there / Turn into earth / What do you want / Ever since the world began
CD _______________ EDCD 116
Edsel / Feb '83 / Pinnacle

TRAIN KEPT A ROLLIN' (The Complete Georgio Gomelsky Productions/4CD Set)
CD Set _______________ CDLIKBOX 3
Decal / Nov '95 / Koch

VERY BEST OF THE YARDBIRDS, THE
For your love / Heart full of soul / Good morning little school girl / Still I'm sad / Evil hearted you / Certain girl / Jeff's blues / I wish you would / New York City / I'm not talking / You're a better man than I / Shapes of things / I'm a man / Boom boom / Smokestack lightnin' / Let it rock / You can't judge a book by the cover / Who do you love / Too much monkey business / Pretty girl / Stroll on / Respectable
CD _______________ MCCD 023
Music Club / May '91 / Disc / THE

VERY BEST OF THE YARDBIRDS, THE
Heartful of soul / I'm a man / Baby what's wrong / New York city blues / Got to hurry / Putty in your hands / Still I'm sad / Honey in your hips / Got love if you want it / You're a better man than I / Good morning little schoolgirl / Evil hearted you / Like Jimmy Reed again / Jeff's blues / For your love
CD _______________ SUMCD 4115
Sound & Media / May '97 / Sound & Media

WHERE THE ACTION IS (Radio Sessions 1965-1968/2CD Set)
I ain't got you / For your love / I'm not talking / I wish you would / Heart full of soul / I ain't done no wrong / Too much monkey business / Love me like I love you / I'm a man / Evil hearted you / Still I'm sad / Hang on Sloopy / Smokestack lightnin' / Mister you're a better man than I / Train kept a rollin' / Shapes of things / Dust my blues / Scratch my back / Over under sideways down / Sun is shining / Shapes of things / Most likely you'll go your way / Little games / Drinking muddy water / Think about it / Goodnight sweet Josephine / My baby / Shapes of things / Heart full of soul / Mister you're a better man than I / You go your way / Over under sideways down / Little games / My baby / I'm a man
CD Set _______________ PILOT 010
Burning Airlines / Jul '97 / Total/Pinnacle

YARDBIRDS AVEC ERIC CLAPTON
CD _______________ 842148
EVA / May '94 / ADA / Direct

YARDBIRDS, THE
Heartful of soul / Still I'm sad / For your love / Shapes of things / I'm a man / Good mornng little schoolgirl / Evil hearted you / Boom boom / Big boss man / Train kept a rollin' / Stroll on / Certain girl / Honey in your hips / I wish you would / I ain't got you / Talking about you / Got to hurry / Jeff's blues
CD _______________ EXP 048
Experience / May '97 / TKO Magnum

Yared, Gabriel

MAP OF THE HUMAN HEART
CD _______________ 5149002
Polydor / Jan '94 / PolyGram

Yasar, Necdet

MUSIC OF TURKEY (Yasar, Necdet Ensemble)
CD _______________ CDT 128
Topic / Apr '93 / ADA / CM / Direct

Yasnaia

ONIRO
CD _______________ LILITH 1CD
Lilith / Oct '96 / World Serpent

Yasus Afari

MENTAL ASSASSIN
CD _______________ CDTZ 015
Tappa / Aug '93 / Jet Star

Yawp

EXCUSES FOR HATE
CD _______________ KANG 005CD
Kangaroo / Aug '95 / Plastic Head

Yazbek, David

LAUGHING MAN
CD _______________ BAH 22
Humbug / Mar '95 / Total/Pinnacle

Yazoo

UPSTAIRS AT ERIC'S
CD _______________ CDSTUMM 7
Mute / May '95 / RTM/Disc

YOU AND ME BOTH
CD _______________ CDSTUMM 12
Mute / May '95 / RTM/Disc

Yazz

ONE ON ONE
Have mercy / Calling 2 U / Child / One on one / How long / Back in love again / Baby talk / Everybody's gotta learn sometime / Look of love / Live your life / That's just the way that it is
CD _______________ 5219892
Polydor / Aug '94 / PolyGram

Ybarra, Eva

A MI SAN ANTONIO (Ybarra, Eva Y Su Conjunto)
CD _______________ ROUCD 6056
Rounder / Apr '94 / ADA / CM / Direct

ROMANCE INOLVIDABLE (Ybarra, Eva Y Su Conjunto)
CD _______________ ROUCD 6062
Rounder / Jun '96 / ADA / CM / Direct

Year Zero

CREATION
CD _______________ H 00382
Hellhound / Jul '95 / Koch

NIHIL'S FLAME
Prefall (Intro) / Planetfall / Headache station / Harsh believing / Civilisation dreaming / Wishing horse / Year zero / Evergreen / Shining violet / Invention of God / Eternal dawn
CD _______________ H 00272
Hellhound / Aug '94 / Koch

Yearwood, Trisha

EVERYBODY KNOWS
I want to live again / It's alright / Even a cowboy can dream / Believe me baby / I need you / Little hercules / Under the rainbow / Everybody knows / Hello, I'm gone / Find a river / Chance I take / Maybe it's love / Lover is forever
CD _______________ MCD 11512
MCA / Aug '96 / BMG

HEARTS IN ARMOUR
You say you will / Woman before me / When goodbye was a word / Walkaway Joe / Down on my knees / That's what I like about you / Woman walk the line / You don't have to move that mountain / Hearts in armour / Wrong side of Memphis / Like we never had a broken heart / Fools like me / Nearest distant shore / She's in love with the boy / Lonesome dove
CD _______________ MCLD 19323
MCA / Sep '96 / BMG

SONG REMEMBERS WHEN, THE
Song remembers when / Better your heart than mine / I don't fall in love so easy / Hard promises to keep / Mr. Radio / Nightingale / If I ain't got you / One in a row / Here comes temptation / Lying to the moon / Walkaway Joe / New kid in town
CD _______________ MCLD 19324
MCA / Sep '96 / BMG

THINKIN' ABOUT YOU
CD _______________ MCD 11226
MCA / Feb '95 / BMG

TRISHA YEARWOOD
She's in love with the boy / Woman before me / That's what I like about you / Like we never had a broken heart / Fools like me / Victim of the game / When goodbye was a word / Whisper of your heart / You done me wrong (and that ain't right) / Lonesome dove
CD _______________ MCLD 19322
MCA / Sep '96 / BMG

Yeats, Grainne

BELFAST HARP FESTIVAL, THE
CD _______________ CEFCD 156
Gael Linn / Jan '94 / ADA / CM / Direct / Grapevine/PolyGram / Roots

Yello

BABY
Intro / Rubber band man / Sticky jungle / Ocean club / Who's groove / Capri calling / Lazy / On the run / Blender / Sweet thunder
CD _______________ 8487912
Mercury / Jun '91 / PolyGram

CLARO QUE SI
Daily disco / No more Roger / Take it all / Evening's young / She's got a gun / Ballet mechanique / Quad el habib / Lorry / Homer hossa / Pinball cha cha
CD _______________ 8183402
Mercury / Mar '88 / PolyGram

ESSENTIAL YELLO
Oh yeah / Race / Rubberband man / Vicious games / Tied up / Lost again / I love you goodbye / Of course I'm lying / Pinball cha cha / Bostitch / Desire / Jungle Bill / Goldrush / Rhythm divine
CD _______________ 5123902
Phonogram / Sep '92 / PolyGram

FLAG
Tied up / Of course I'm lying / 3rd of June / Blazing saddles / Race / Alhambra / Tied up in gear / Otto di catania
CD _______________ 8367782
Mercury / Aug '90 / PolyGram

HANDS ON YELLO
Lost again / Excess / La habanera / L'hotel / I love you / Live at the Roxy / Oh yeah / Vicious circle / Crash dance / Dr. Van Steiner / Bostich / Ciel Ouvert / You gotta say yes to another excess / Great mission
CD _______________ 5273832
Urban / Mar '95 / PolyGram

NEW MIX IN ONE GO 1980-1985, THE
Daily disco / Swing / Evening's young / Pinball cha cha / I love you / Sometimes (Dr. Hirsch) / Base for Alec / Oh yeah / Lost again / Tub dub / Angel no / Desire / Bananas to the beat / Koladiola / Domingo / Bostich / Live at the Roxy
CD _______________ 8267732
Mercury / Jun '89 / PolyGram

ONE SECOND
Habanera / Moon on ice / Call it love / Le secret farida / Hawaiian chance / Rhythm divine / Santiago / Gold rush / Dr. Van Steiner / Si senor and the hairy grill
CD _______________ 8309562
Mercury / Jun '89 / PolyGram

POCKET UNIVERSE
CD _______________ 5343532
Mercury / May '97 / PolyGram

SOLID PLEASURE
Bimbo / Night flanger / Reverse lion / Downdown samba / Magneto / Massage / Assistant's cry / Bostich / Rock stop / Coast to polka / Blue green / Eternal legs / Stanztrigge / Bananas to the beat
CD _______________ 8183392
Mercury / Mar '88 / PolyGram

STELLA
Desire / Vicious games / Oh yeah / Desert inn / Stalakdrama / Koladiola / Domingo / Sometimes (Dr. Hirsch) / Let me cry / Ciel ouvert / Angel no
CD _______________ 8228202
Mercury / Mar '88 / PolyGram

YOU GOTTA SAY YES TO ANOTHER EXCESS
I love you / Look again / No more words / Crash dance / Great mission / You gotta say yes to another excess / Swing / Heavy whispers / Smile on you / Pumping velvet / Salut mayoumba
CD _______________ 8121662
Mercury / Mar '88 / PolyGram

ZEBRA
CD _______________ 5224962
Mercury / Nov '94 / PolyGram

Yellow Jackets

COLLECTION, THE
Wildlife / Spin / Oz / Man facing north / Revelation / Freedomland / Jacket town / Dream / Foreign correspondent / You know that / Dewey
CD _______________ GRP 98092
GRP / Mar '95 / New Note/BMG

Yellow Magic Orchestra

HI TECH-NO CRIME
CD _______________ TRUCD 1
Internal / Nov '92 / Pinnacle / PolyGram

MULTIPLIES
Technopolis / Absolute ego dance / Behind the mask / Computer game / Firecracker / Snakeman show / Nice age / Multiplies / Citizens of science / Tighten up
CD _______________ L91492
Roadrunner / Sep '92 / PolyGram

Yellow Monk

SICKS
CD _______________ 74321515792
RCA / Aug '97 / BMG

Yellowcake

INNER STATE STATIONS
CD _______________ RA 017CD
Radikal Ambience / Oct '96 / Plastic Head

Yellowman

20 SUPER HITS
CD _______________ SONCD 0006
Sonic Sounds / Oct '90 / Jet Star

BADNESS
CD _______________ LACD 005
La / May '94 / Plastic Head

BEST OF YELLOWMAN LIVE IN PARIS, THE
CD _______________ 503562
CD _______________ 503552
Blue Silver / Apr '95 / Jet Star
CD _______________ 8412162
Declic / Oct '96 / Jet Star

BEST OF YELLOWMAN, THE
CD _______________ 794502
Melodie / Dec '95 / ADA / Discovery / Grapevine/PolyGram / Greensleeves / Jet Star

BLUEBERRY HILL
Blueberry Hill / Letter to Rosey / Jean a miss follow fashion / Who say yellow don't go hotel / Nah pay no tax / Anything me say / Young girl be wise / Another Saturday night
CD _______________ GRELCD 107
Greensleeves / Sep '92 / Jet Star / SRD

DON'T BURN IT DOWN
CD _______________ GRELCD 110
Greensleeves / May '88 / Jet Star / SRD

FANTASTIC YELLOWMAN
CD _______________ LG 21091
Lagoon / Nov '93 / Grapevine/PolyGram

GALONG GALONG GALONG
Galong galong galong / Beat it / Under mi fat thing / Cus cus / Reggae get the grammy / Throw me corn / Skank quadrille / Blow saxophone / Money make friend / Bubble with mi ting
CD _______________ GRELCD 87
Greensleeves / Nov '87 / Jet Star / SRD

GOOD SEX GUIDE
CD _______________ GRELCD 217
Greensleeves / Oct '95 / Jet Star / SRD

IN BED WITH YELLOWMAN
CD _______________ GRELCD 179
Greensleeves / Feb '93 / Jet Star / SRD

KING OF THE DANCE HALL
CD _______________ RRTGCD 7717
Rohit / '88 / Jet Star

KISS ME
Kiss me / Dicky / Hot again / Jordan river / Thanks and praise / Murderer / Hek she gwan / Love is a splendid thang / Woman / Slow motion
CD _______________ 113862
Musidisc UK / Jul '95 / Grapevine/PolyGram

LIVE IN ENGLAND
CD _______________ SON 0024
Greensleeves / Apr '92 / Jet Star / SRD

MAN YOU WANT, A
CD _______________ SHCD 45011
Shanachie / Mar '94 / ADA / Greensleeves / Koch

MESSAGE TO THE WORLD
CD _______________ RASCD 3185
Ras / Jan '96 / Direct / Greensleeves / Jet Star / SRD

MISTER YELLOWMAN
Natty sat upon the rock / Lost mi love / Mr. Chin / Two to six super mix / Morning ride / How you keep a dance / Jamaica a little Miami / Yellowman get's married / Duppy or gunman / Cocky did a hurt me
CD _______________ GRELCD 35
Greensleeves / '87 / Jet Star / SRD

NEGRIL CHILL (Yellowman & Charlie Chaplin)
Arrival / Feeling sexy / Don't sell yourself / Nuff punany / Naw breed again / Undergal frock / Blueberry Hill / Reason with entertainers / Gone a South Africa / Jah mi fear / Trouble Rosie / Old lady / Listen Charlie / Same way it taste / Calypso jam / Don't drop yu pants / Rent a dread
CD _______________ RE 155CD
ROIR / Jul '97 / Plastic Head / Shellshock/Disc

NOBODY MOVE - NOBODY GET HURT
Nobody move nobody get hurt / Strictly mi belly / Bedroom mazurka / Body move / Good lovin' / Wreck a pum pum / Hill and gully rider / Yellowman a lover boy / Watch your words / Why you bad so
CD _______________ GRELCD 71
Greensleeves / Jul '89 / Jet Star / SRD

ONE YELLOWMAN AND FATMAN
CD ____ JJCD 067
Channel One / Apr '96 / Jet Star

OPERATION RADICATION
11 and 11 / Shorties / Morning ride / Eventide fire / Operation radication / Couchie / Out a hand / Mad over me / Lovers corner / Bim and Bam / Badness / My possie
CD ____ NTMCD 548
Nectar / May '97 / Pinnacle

PARTY
CD ____ RASCD 3073
Ras / Aug '96 / Direct / Greensleeves / Jet Star / SRD

RAS PORTRAITS
Reggae on the move / Party / Yellow like cheese / Prayer / God alone / AIDS / Love King Yellowman / I'm ready / Wild wild West / Gone up / Dancehall / Reggae music / Maximum / War / Got the rammer / No touch ya so
CD ____ RAS 3314
Ras / Jul '97 / Direct / Greensleeves / Jet Star / SRD

REGGAE CALYPSO ENCOUNTER
CD ____ RMJLCD 0101
Rohit / '88 / Jet Star

REGGAE ON THE MOVE
CD ____ RASCD 3094
Ras / Sep '93 / Direct / Greensleeves / Jet Star / SRD

SATURDAY NIGHT
CD ____ RB 3009
Reggae Best / Jul '94 / Grapevine/ PolyGram

THEM A MAD OVER ME
CD ____ 78249700060
Channel One / Apr '95 / Jet Star

THIS IS YELLOWMAN
CD ____ RN 7009
Rhino / Sep '96 / Grapevine/PolyGram / Jet Star

TWO GIANTS CLASH (Yellowman & Josey Wales)
Society party / Strictly bubbling / Mr. Big shot / King of the crop / Wrong girl to play with / Bobo dread / Mi have Fi get you / Cure for the fever / Jah a mi guiding star / Sorry to say
CD ____ GRELCD 63
Greensleeves / '89 / Jet Star / SRD

YELLOW LIKE CHEESE
Budget / Easy me ting / Gaze / Want a woman / To touch ya so / Yellow like cheese / No get nuthin' / Ain't no meaning / Na no lyrics / Mi mother love, my father love
CD ____ RASCD 3019
Ras / Jun '87 / Direct / Greensleeves / Jet Star / SRD

YELLOWMAN GOING TO THE CHAPEL
Look in a me eye / Rub-a-dub / Going to the chapel / Hunnu fi move / Come back to Jamaica / No lucky in gambling / Ready fe them / Amen / To the bump
CD ____ GRELCD 97
Greensleeves / '86 / Jet Star / SRD

YELLOWMAN RIDES AGAIN
CD ____ RASCD 3034
Ras / Sep '88 / Direct / Greensleeves / Jet Star / SRD

YELLOWMAN STRIKES AGAIN
CD ____ CY 78936
Nyam Up / Apr '95 / Conifer/BMG

ZUNGGUZUNGGUGUZUNGGUZENG
Zungguzungguguzungguzeng / Good, the bad and the ugly / Rub-a-dub a play / Dem sight the boss / Can't hide from Jah / Who can make the dance ram / Yellowman wise / Take me to Jamaica / Friday night jamboree / Jah Jah are we guiding star
CD ____ GRELCD 57
Greensleeves / Feb '87 / Jet Star / SRD

Yelvington, Malcolm

TENNESSEE SATURDAY NIGHT
CD ____ CLCD 4403
Collector/White Label / Oct '96 / TKO Magnum

Yelworc

COLLECTION 1988-1994, THE
CD ____ EFA 125252
Celtic Circle / Apr '95 / SRD

Yemm, Bryn

HEART 'N' SOUL (The Best Of Bryn Yemm)
Haffron / Say a little prayer / Soul of my saviour / Why me Lord / Cleanse me / Since I laid my burden down / Amazing grace / I have a dream / Old rugged cross / When a child is born / Anna Marie / Let me live / End of the day / How great thou art / Holy city / It's no secret / One day at a time / I'll fly away
CD ____ CD 101
Bay / Mar '96 / Bay Enterprises

Yes

90125
Owner of a lonely heart / Hold on / It can happen / Changes / Cinema / Leave it / Our song / City of love / Hearts
CD ____ 7901252
Atlantic / Nov '83 / Warner Music

AFFIRMATIVE (The Yes Solo Family Album) (Various Artists)
CD ____ VSOPCD 190
Connoisseur Collection / Sep '93 / Pinnacle

ANDERSON, BRUFORD, WAKEMAN, HOWE (Anderson Bruford Wakeman Howe)
Sound / Second attention / Soul warrior / Fist of fire / Brother of mine / Big dream / Nothing can come between us / Birthright / Meeting / I wanna learn / She gives me love / Who was the first / I'm alive / Teakbois / Order of the universe / Order theme / Rock gives courage / It's so hard to grow / Universe / Let's pretend
CD ____ 262155
Arista / Jan '92 / BMG

BIG GENERATOR
Rhythm of love / Big generator / Shoot high aim low / Almost like love / Love will find a way / Final eyes / I'm running / Holy lamb
CD ____ 7905222
Atlantic / Aug '87 / Warner Music

CLASSIC YES
Heart of the sunrise / Wonderous stories / Yours is no disgrace / Starship trooper / Long distance runaround / Fish / And you and I
CD ____ 7567826872
Atlantic / Sep '94 / Warner Music

CLOSE TO THE EDGE
Solid time of change / Total mass retain / I get up, I get down / Seasons of man / And you and I / Cord of life / Eclipse / Preacher / Teacher / Siberian Khatru
CD ____ 7567826662
Atlantic / Aug '94 / Warner Music

DRAMA
Machine messiah / White car / Does it really happen / Into the lens / Run through the light / Tempus fugit
CD ____ 7567826852
Atlantic / Sep '94 / Warner Music

EVENING OF YES, AN (Anderson Bruford Wakeman Howe)
CD Set ____ CDRFL 002
Fragile / Nov '93 / Grapevine/PolyGram

EVENING OF YES, AN (Anderson Bruford Wakeman Howe)
CD ____ DC 865762
Disky / Mar '96 / Disky / THE

FRAGILE
Roundabout / Cans and Brahms / We have heaven / South side of the sky / Five per cent of nothing / Long distance runaround / Fish / Mood for a day / Heart of the sunrise
CD ____ 7567826672
Atlantic / Aug '94 / Warner Music

GOING FOR THE ONE
Going for the one / Turn of the century / Parallels / Wonderous stories / Awaken
CD ____ 7567826702
Atlantic / Aug '94 / Warner Music

KEYS TO ASCENSION, THE (2CD Set)
Siberia / Revealing science / America / Onward / Awaken / Roundabout / Starship trooper / Be the one / That, that is
CD Set ____ EDFCD 417
Essential / Oct '96 / BMG

RELAYER
Gates of delirium / Sound chaser / To be over
CD ____ 7567826642
Atlantic / Sep '94 / Warner Music

SYMPHONIC MUSIC OF YES (Featuring Yes) (London Philharmonic Orchestra/ David Palmer)
CD ____ 09026619382
RCA Victor / Jan '94 / BMG

TALES FROM TOPOGRAPHIC OCEANS
Revealing science of God / Remembering / Ancient / Ritual
CD ____ 7567826832
Atlantic / Sep '94 / Warner Music

TALES FROM YESTERDAY (A Tribute To Yes) (Various Artists)
Roundabout: *Berry, Robert* / Siberian khatru: *Stanley Snail* / Mood for a day: *Morse, Steve* / Don't kill the whale: *Magellan* / Turn of the century: *Howe, Steve* / Release release: *Shadow Gallery* / Wondrous stories: *World Trade* / South of the sky: *Cairo* / Soon: *Moraz, Patrick* / Changes: *Enchant* / Astral traveller: *Banks, Peter* / Clap: *Morse, Steve* / Starship trooper: *Jeronimo Road*
CD ____ RR 89142
Roadrunner / Oct '95 / PolyGram

TIME AND A WORD
No opportunity necessary / No experience needed / Then / Everdays / Sweet dreams / Prophet / Clear days / Astral traveller / Time and a word
CD ____ 7567826812
Atlantic / Sep '94 / Warner Music

TORMATO
Future times / Rejoice / Don't kill the whale / Madrigal / Release release / Arriving UFO / Circus of heaven / Onward / On the silent wings of freedom
CD ____ 7567826712
Atlantic / Aug '94 / Warner Music

UNION
I would have waited forever / Shock to the system / Masquerade / Lift me up / Without hope you cannot start the day / Saving my heart / Miracle of life / Silent talking / More we live-let go / Angkor Wat / Dangerous / Holding on / Evensong / Take the water to the mountain / Give and take
CD ____ 261558
Arista / Apr '94 / BMG

VERY BEST OF YES, THE (Highlights)
Survival / Time and a word / Starship trooper / Life seeker / Disillusion / Wurm / I've seen all good people / Your move / All good people / Roundabout / Long distance runaround / Soon / Wonderous stories / Going for the one / Owner of a lonely heart / Leave it / Rhythm of love
CD ____ 7567825172
Atlantic / Sep '93 / Warner Music

YES
Beyond and before / I see you / Yesterday and today / Looking around / Harold land / Every little thing / Sweetness / Survival
CD ____ 7567826802
Atlantic / Aug '94 / Warner Music

YES ALBUM, THE
Yours is no disgrace / Clap / Starship trooper / Life seeker / Disillusion / Wurm / I've seen all good people / Your move / All good people / Venture / Perpetual change
CD ____ 7567826652
Atlantic / Sep '94 / Warner Music

YES YEARS, THE (4CD Set)
Something's coming / Survival / Every little thing / Then / Everydays / Sweet dreams / No opportunity necessary, no experience needed / Time and a word / Starship trooper / Yours is no disgrace / I've seen all good people / Long distance runaround / Fish (schindleria praematurus) / Roundabout / Heart of the sunrise / America / Close to the edge / Ritual / Sound chaser / Soon / Amazing grace / Vevey (part 1) / Wonderous stories / Awaken / Montreux's theme / Vevey (part 2) / Going for the one / Money / Abilene / Don't kill the whale / On the silent wings of freedom / Does it really happen / Tempus fugit / Run with the fox / I'm down / Make it easy / It can happen / Owner of a lonely heart / Hold on / Shoot high aim low / Rhythm of love / Love will find a way / Changes / And you and I / Love conquers all
CD ____ 7567916442
Atlantic / Aug '91 / Warner Music

YESSHOWS
Parallels / Time and a word / Going for the one / Gates of Delirium
CD ____ 7567826862
Atlantic / Sep '94 / Warner Music

YESSONGS (2CD Set)
Opening: Excerpt from the firebird suite / Siberian Khatru / Heart of the sunrise / Perpetual change / And you and I / Cord of life / Eclipse / Preacher and the teacher / Apocalypse / Mood for a day / Excerpts from the six wives of Henry VIII / Roundabout / Your move / I've seen all good people / Long distance runaround / Fish / Close to the edge / Solid time of change / Total mass retain / I get up, I get down / Seasons of man / Yours is no disgrace / Starship trooper / Life seeker / Disillusion / Wurm
CD Set ____ 7567826822
Atlantic / Sep '94 / Warner Music

YESSTORY (2CD Set)
Survival / No opportunity necessary, no experience needed / Time and a word / Starship trooper / I've seen all good people / Roundabout / Heart of the sunrise / Close to the edge / Ritual / Soon / Wonderous stories / Going for the one / Don't kill the whale / Does it really happen / Make it easy / Owner of a lonely heart / Rhythm of love / Changes
CD ____ 7567917472
Atlantic / Sep '91 / Warner Music

YESTERDAYS
America / Looking around / Time and a word / Sweet dreams / Then / Survival / Astral traveller / Dear father
CD ____ 7567826842
Atlantic / Sep '94 / Warner Music

Yesteryear

UNDER THE RUG
CD ____ MES 006
Magick Eye / Feb '97 / Cargo / SRD

Yetties

COME TO THE YETTIES BARN DANCE
Gay Gordons / Hello / Family waltz / Clopton bridge / Swanee river / Strip the willow / Cumberland square eight / Barn dance / Timber salvage reel / Swedish masquerade / Tom Pate / Devil's dream / Circassian circle
CD ____ GRCD 53
Grasmere / May '92 / Highlander / Savoy / Target/BMG

FIDDLER KNOWS, THE
CD ____ CDALA 3010
ASV / '89 / Select

FOLK MUSIC OF ENGLAND
John Peel / Turmit hoeing / Medley / Foggy, foggy dew / Jolly waggoner / Lincolnshire poacher / Cuckoo's nest / Sailor cut down in his prime / South Australia / Medley / Lilliburleo / Trelawney / Leaving of Liverpool / No sir no / Medley / Brigg fair / Spanish ladies / Fox / Medley / Derby ram / Home dearest home
CD ____ GRCD 82
Grasmere / Jul '97 / Highlander / Savoy / Target/BMG

MUSICAL HERITAGE OF THOMAS HARDY
CD Set ____ CDALD 4010
ASV / Feb '88 / Select

SINGALONG PARTY
CD ____ GRCD 72
Grasmere / Oct '95 / Highlander / Savoy / Target/BMG

SINGING ALL THE WAY
Over the hills and far away / Ball of yarn / Grey hawk / Polka medley / Rabbit / John Barleycorn / Winter / Poor, poor farmer / Ee weren't all bad / Man at the nore / Bread and cheese and kisses / We've got oil / Beggar's song / Beaumont rag / Back 'n' back yer you / Scarlet and the blue / Carolina moon / Beautiful dreamer / Early one evening / Linden lea / Bell ringing / Levi Jackson's rag / Wave over wave / Last rose of Summer / Praise o'Dorset
CD ____ CDALA 3009
ASV / Jul '89 / Select

TOP OF THE CROPS
CD ____ GRCD 68
Grasmere / Oct '95 / Highlander / Savoy / Target/BMG

Yiladi Trio

SONGS IN YIDDISH & LADINO VOL.3
CD ____ YILADI 9103
Yiladi / Sep '94 / Direct

Yips

BONFIRE IN A DIXIE CUP
CD ____ SB 49
Siltbreeze / Nov '96 / Cargo / Vital

YLD

FOOL'S PARADISE
CD ____ CDMFN 113
Music For Nations / Mar '91 / Pinnacle

YN-Vee

YN-VEE
Even when U sleep / All I wanna do / 4 play / I'm goin' down / Sceamin' / Sonshine's groove / Chocolate / Stra8 hustler / Tricks-n-trainin' / YN-Vee / Real G / Gangsta's prayer / We got a good thing
CD ____ 5235852
Island / Oct '94 / PolyGram

YO 3

BITTER SWEET
CD Set ____ GPRCD 5
GPR / Jun '94 / 3mv/Vital

Yo La Tengo

GENIUS + LOVE = YO LA TENGO (2CD Set)
Evanescent psychic pez drop / Demons / Fog over Frisco / Too late / Hanky panky nohow / Something to do / Ultra-powerful short wave radio picks up music from Venus / Up to you / Somebody's baby / Walking away from you / Artificial heart / Cast a shadow / I'm set free / Barnaby, hardly working / Some kinda fatigue / Speeding motorcycle / Her Grandmother's gift / From a motel 6 / Gooseneck problem / Surfin' with the Shah / Ecstasy blues / Too much, part 1 / Blitzkreig bop / One self : fish girl / Enough / Drum solo / From a motel 6 / Too much, part 2 / Sunsquashed
CD Set ____ OLE 1942
Matador / Nov '96 / Vital

I CAN HEAR THE HEART BEATING AS ONE
Return to hot chicken / Moby octopad / Sugarcube / Damage / Deeper into movies / Shadows / Stockholm syndrome / Autumn sweater / Little honda / Green arrow / One PM again / Lie and how we told it / Center of gravity / Spec bebop / We're an American band / My little corner of the world
CD ____ OLE 2222
Matador / Apr '97 / Vital

MAY I SING WITH ME
CD ____ A 021CD
Alias / Jun '92 / Vital

PAINFUL
CD ____ EFA 049272
City Slang / Sep '93 / RTM/Disc

THAT IS YOURS
CD ________ EFA 0406805
City Slang / Jan '95 / RTM/Disc

Yo Yo

YOU BETTER ASK SOMEBODY
IBWin' wit my crewin' / Can you handle it / Westside story / Mackstress / Twenty Sack / You better ask somebody / They shit don't stink / Letter to the pen / Givin' it up / Pass it on / Girl's got a gun / Bonnie and Clyde theme
CD ________ 7567922522
East West / Jun '93 / Warner Music

Yoakam, Dwight

BUENOS NOCHES FROM A LONELY ROOM
I got you / One more name / What I don't know / Home of the blues / Buenos noches from a lonely room / She wore red dresses / I hear you knocking / I sang Dixie / Streets of Bakersfield / Floyd county / Send me the pillow that you dream on / Hold onto God
CD ________ 9257492
Reprise / Jan '89 / Warner Music

DWIGHT LIVE
CD ________ 9362459072
Reprise / May '95 / Warner Music

GONE
CD ________ 9362460512
Reprise / Nov '95 / Warner Music

GUITARS CADILLACS ETC ETC
Honky tonk man / It won't hurt / I'll be gone / South of cincinnati / Bury me / Guitars and cadilacs / Twenty years / Ring of fire / Miner's prayer / Heartache by the number
CD ________ 9253722
Reprise / Feb '93 / Warner Music

HILLBILLY DELUXE
Little ways / Smoke along the track / Johnson's love / Please please baby / Readin', ritin' RT23 / Always late (with your kisses) / 1000 miles from nowhere / Throughout all times / Little sister / This drinking will kill me
CD ________ 9255672
Reprise / Jun '87 / Warner Music

IF THERE WAS A WAY
Distance between you and me / Heart that you own / Takes a lot to rock you / Nothing's changed here / Sad, sad music / Since I started drinkin' again / If there was a way / Turn it on, turn it up, turn me loose / It only hurts when I cry / Send a message to my heart / I don't need it done / You're the one
CD ________ 7599263442
Reprise / Nov '90 / Warner Music

LA CROIX D'AMOUR
Things we said today / Truckin' / If there was a way / Hey little girl / What I don't know / Here comes the night / Dangerous man / Let's work together / Doin' what I did / Takes a lot to rock you / Suspicious minds / Long white cadillac
CD ________ 9362451362
Reprise / Nov '92 / Warner Music

THIS TIME
Pocket of a clown / 1000 miles from nowhere / Home for sale / This time / Two doors down / Ain't that lonely yet / King of fools / Fast of you / Try not to look so pretty / Wild ride / Lonesome roads
CD ________ 9362452412
Reprise / Apr '93 / Warner Music

UNDER THE COVERS
Claudette / Train in vain / Tired of waiting for you / Good time Charlie's got the blues / Baby don't go / Playboy / Wichita lineman / Here comes the night / Last time / Things we said today / North to Alaska / T is for Texas
CD ________ 9362466902
Reprise / Aug '97 / Warner Music

Yodellers In Gold

BEST YODELLERS, THE
CD ________ 323010
Koch / Sep '93 / Koch

Yogeswaran, Manickam

TAMIL CLASSICS
Sapthaswaram en jeevane / Aanai muga / Ammah umah / Sri lalita - shakti
CD ________ EXIL 55342
Exil / Jun '97 / Direct

Yokota

CAT, MOUSE AND ME
Good morning / Neutral / Field / River side / Wait for a day / One way / Lemon and ginger / Ceramic flower / Cat, mouse and me / From / Middle finger / Few / In the sky / Dodo
CD ________ HHCD 22
Harthouse / Feb '97 / Mo's Music Machine / Prime / Vital

FRANKFURT/TOKYO CONNECTION
CD ________ HHCD 003
Harthouse / Apr '94 / Mo's Music Machine / Prime / Vital

Yokoyama, Katsuya

ART OF THE SHAKUHACHI (Yokoyama, Katsuya & Yoshikazu Iwamoto)
CD ________ C 560114
Ocora / Jul '97 / ADA / Harmonia Mundi

Yole

A LA SOURCE
CD ________ SCD 711
Several / Nov '95 / ADA

L'AMOUR D'ELOISE
CD ________ SCD 709
Several / Nov '95 / ADA

Yona Kit

YONA KIT
CD ________ GR 20CD
Skingraft / Sep '95 / SRD

York Minster Choir

BEST LOVED HYMNS
Royal fanfare / Let all the world in every corner sing / Praise my soul / Amazing Grace / Lord of all hopefulness / O, for a thousand tongues to sing / Love divine (Blaenern) / How sweet the name of Jesus sounds / How great thou art / Thine be the glory / Soul of my saviour / For all the saints (sine nomine) / Praise the Lord / Rejoice, the Lord is king (gospel) / Lord's my shepherd (Crimond) / O worshsip the king (Hanover) / All creatures of our God and King / Jesus shall reign / Where 'er the sun / When I survey the wondrous cross / Abide with me / Day thou gavest, Lord, is ended
CD ________ CDCFP 5023
Classics For Pleasure / Nov '96 / EMI

York, Pete

STRING TIME IN NEW YORK
CD ________ BLR 84 015
L&R / May '91 / New Note/Pinnacle

SWINGING LONDON
CD ________ 341172
Koch / Apr '94 / Koch

York Waites

1588 - MUSIC FROM THE TIME OF THE SPANISH ARMADA
Queene's visiting of the campe at Tilsburie / Spanish pavan / Galliard / Crimson velvet / La doune cella / La shy myze / La bounette / Obtaining of the great galleazzo / Browninge my dere / Browninge fantasy / Les bransles gays / Delight pavan / Galliard to delight pavan / Staines morris / Quarter brawles / Pavana / Galiarda / Coranto / Watkin's ale / Robin is to the greenwood gone / Wilson's fantasie / Spanish lady / Cushion dance / Dulcina / All you that love good fellowes / Eighty eight or Sir Francis drake / Les bransles de Champagne / Carman's whistle / Under and over / Pepper is black / Millfield / Roowe well ye marynors
CD ________ CDSDL 373
Saydisc / May '97 / ADA / Direct / Harmonia Mundi

CHRISTMAS MUSICKE (1400-1800) (York Waits & Deborah Caterall)
Personent hodie / O jesulien suss o jesulein mild / Angelus ad pastores / Von himmel hoch / Resonet in laudibus / Thys endere nyghth / As I lay on a night / Als y lay on yoolis night / Piva ferrarese / O hac quam mundam / El noi de la mare/ el desembre congelat/oi betleem/birjina g / De matin ai rescoutra lou train / Quando nascette ninno / Doux pommier/faisans rejoussance / Bergers, j'ai ouy la nouvelle / Quelle est cette odeur agreable / Bergers, par les plus doux accords / Born is the babe / Thus angels sing / Christmas cheer / Little barley corn / St Day carol / I saw three ships come sailing in / Sussex carol / Yorkshire wassail / Wexford wassail / Wexford carol / While sheperds watched / Waits(London) / Waits wassail / Ding dong merrily on high
CD ________ BHCD 9607
Brewhouse / Dec '96 / ADA / Brewhouse Music

CITY MUSICKE, THE
CD ________ BH 9409CD
Brewhouse / Jul '94 / ADA / Brewhouse Music

MUSIC FROM THE TIME OF RICHARD III
Quene note / La spanga / Mater ora filium / L'hom arme / Danse de Cleves / Le souvenir / Tuba Gallicalis / Noel nouvelet / Anxi bon youre delabonestren / Nous voici dans la ville dit le Bourguinon / Allez a la fougere / In feuers hitz / Auf rief ein huebsches freulein / Der neue bauernschwanz / Die katzen pfote / Ein vrouleen edel von naturen / Das jaegerhorn / Mercantia / Anello / Amoroso / L'amor donna ch'io te porta / Bassa con misurias danza alta / Todos los biennes del mundo dindirin dindirin
CD ________ CDSDL 364
Saydisc / May '97 / ADA / Direct / Harmonia Mundi

OLD CHRISTMAS RETURN'D
CD ________ CDSDL 398
Saydisc / Oct '92 / ADA / Direct / Harmonia Mundi

Yorkshire Building Society ...

ESSAYS FOR BRASS (Yorkshire Building Society Band)
Call of the righteous / Rhapsodic variations / My strength, my tower / Meditation / Light of the world / Lord is king / Meditation / Just as I am / Tone poem / Kingdom triumphant / Victorian snapshots / On Ratcliff Highway
CD ________ QPRL 080D
Polyphonic / Oct '96 / Complete/Pinnacle

EUROPEAN BRASS BAND CHAMPIONSHIPS 1996 (Yorkshire Building Society Band/Black Dyke Mills Band)
CD ________ DOYCD 057
Doyen / Nov '96 / Conifer/BMG

INTRODUCTION (Yorkshire Building Society Band)
Introduction / Chablis / March / Swedish hymn / Dance / Time for peace / Procession to the cathedral / Facilita / Country scene / Variations on laudate dominum / Maids of cadiz / King's herald / Cortege / Jousts
CD ________ QPRL 074D
Polyphonic / Jan '96 / Complete/Pinnacle

Yorkshire Imperial Band

FAR AND AWAY
Imperial echoes / Keel row / None shall asleep / Far and away / Somewhere over the rainbow / Thunderer / Nun's chorus / James Bond collection / Indian summer / Let's face the music and dance / With one look / Mack and Mabel / Granada / Deep inside the sacred temple / Boys of the old brigade / Crimond / William Tell
CD ________ QPRL 077D
Polyphonic / Sep '96 / Complete/Pinnacle

PAGEANTRY
Strike up the band / Chelsea bridge / Hommage march / On the way home / Can can / Girl with the flaxen hair / March: Le coq d'or / Pageantry / Arnhem / Toccata from 'Organ symphony No. 5' / Drink to me only with thine eyes / Entry of the huntresses from 'Sylvia' / Country scene / Sandpaper ballet / Norwegian wood / Downfall of lucifer
CD ________ QPRL 040D
Polyphonic / Jun '88 / Complete/Pinnacle

Yothu Yindi

FREEDOM
CD ________ TVD 93380
Mushroom / Mar '94 / 3mv/Pinnacle

You Am I

HOURLY DAILY
CD ________ 9362465202
East West / Feb '97 / Warner Music

You Fantastic

PALS
CD ________ GR 42CD
Skingraft / Jun '97 / SRD

RIDDLER
CD ________ GR 38CD
Skingraft / Oct '96 / SRD

Youmans, Vincent

VINCENT YOUMANS
CD ________ ACD 089
Audiophile / Oct '93 / Jazz Music

Young Canadians

NO ESCAPE
CD ________ ZULU 014CD
Zulu / Oct '95 / Plastic Head

Young, Claude

DJ KICKS
CD ________ K7 045CD
Studio K7 / May '96 / Prime / RTM/Disc

Young, Dave

FABLES AND DREAMS (Young, Dave & Phil Dwyer Quartet)
CD ________ JUST 532
Justin Time / Nov '93 / Cadillac / New Note/Pinnacle

PIANO-BASS DUETS VOL.1
CD ________ JUST 762
Justin Time / Sep '95 / Cadillac / New Note/Pinnacle

PIANO-BASS DUETS VOL.2
Dolphin dance / Blowin' the blues away / Make me a pallet on the floor / Moment to moment / Bass blues / Self portrait in three colors / One finger snap / Loverman / Nascimento / Pendulum at Falcon's lair / I'm all smiles / Peaceful
CD ________ JUST 812
Justin Time / May '96 / Cadillac / New Note/ Pinnacle

PIANO-BASS DUETS VOL.3
In a mellow tone / Joshua / Milestones / Is that so / Soul eyes / Juicy lucy / Lament / Count two / Think of one / Don't blame me / Marie Antoinette
CD ________ JUST 912
Justin Time / Jan '97 / Cadillac / New Note/ Pinnacle

Young Disciples

ROAD TO FREEDOM
Get yourself together / Apparently nothin' / Funky yeh funki (mek it) / Talkin' what I feel / All I have (in dub) / Move on / As we come (to be) / Step right on / Freedom / Wanting / To be free / Young Disciples theme
CD ________ 5100972
Talkin' Loud / Aug '91 / PolyGram

Young, Dougie

SONGS OF DOUGIE YOUNG, THE
CD ________ AIAS 19CD
Larrikin / Nov '94 / ADA / CM / Direct / Roots

Young, Dr. Noah

FREAKS NO FEAR OF CONTAGION
CD ________ NAR 117CD
New Alliance / Jan '95 / Plastic Head

Young, Faron

18 ORIGINAL COUNTRY CLASSICS
Four in the morning / Little green apples / City lights / Walk tall / Yellow bandana / He'll have to go / Is it really over / Welcome to my world / Four walls / I'm gonna change everything / You don't know me / Am I that easy to forget / She thinks I still care / Faded love / I can't stop loving you / San Antonio rose / Linda on my mind / Drinking champagne
CD ________ 5525542
Spectrum / Sep '96 / PolyGram

ALONE WITH YOU
Hello walls / Four in the morning / Alone with you / Heartache for keepsake / Live fast, live hard and die young / Face to the wall / Unmitigated gall / Goin' steady / Some of these memories / Three days / Cryin' time / I could never be ashamed of you / Country girl / Apartment no.9 / Memphis, Tennessee
CD ________ PRACD 4001
Prairie / Jun '97 / Henry Hadaway

CAPITOL YEARS, THE (5CD Set)
If you ain't lovin' (you ain't livin') / I've got five dollars and it's Saturday night / Place for girls like you / I can't tell my heart that / In the chapel in the moonlight / If that's the fashion / Forgive me, Dear / Just married / Baby my heart / What's the use to love you / That's what I do for you / I'm gonna tell Santa Claus on you / You're the angel on my christmas tree / I hardly knew it was you / That's what it's like to be lonesome / You're right (but I wish you were wrong) / Down Lover's Lane alone / So I'm in love with you / Goin' steady / Just out of reach / I can't wait (for the sun to go down) / Have I waited too long / Tattle tale tears / What can I do with my sorrow / Good Lord must have sent you / I knew you when / Saving my tears for tomorrow / Foolish pride / Live fast, love hard, die young / Go back, you fool / All right / For the love of a woman like you / It's a great life / Better things than these / Turn her down / You're still mine / Sweet dreams / Till I met you / I'm gonna live some before I die / Candy kisses / Have I told you lately that I love you / I'll be satisfied with love / I can't help it / Your cheatin' heart / I'll be yours / Sweethearts or strangers / Shame on you / Worried mind / I miss you already / I'm a poor boy / You call everybody darlin' / You are my sunshine / Moonlight mountain / Anything your heart desires / Vacation's over / Shrine of St. Cecilia / Love has finally come my way / Face of love / That's the way it's gotta be / We're talking it over / I made a fool of myself / I'll be all right / You old used to be / Out of my heart / Every time I'm kissing you / Alone with you / That's the way I feel / I hate myself / Last night at the party / Long time ago / Hey good lookin' / Tennessee waltz / Let old Mother Nature have her way / Making believe / Almost / Mom and Dad's waltz / Don't let the stars get in your eyes / Bouquet of roses / Slowly / Bimbo / Chattanooga shoe shine boy / I don't hurt anymore / I'll go on alone / Honey stop / Locket / Snowball / When it rains it pours / Rosalie (is gonna get married) / I can't dance / Once in a while / Riverboat / Country girl / Face to the wall / There's not any like you left / Forget the past / World so full of love / Hello walls / Is she all you thought she'd be / Congratulations / Three days / Safely in love again / Down by the river / Part where I cry / I hear you talkin' / Big shoes / Believing it yourself / Come back / Overlonely and underkissed / Things to remember / I fall to pieces / Moment isn't very long / Moments to remember / Lifetime isn't long enough / I can't find the time / Trail of tears / I let it slip away / Let's pretend we're lovers again / Backtrack / How can I forget you / I'll fly away / Mansion over the hilltop / He was there / How long has it been / Beautiful gar-

den of prayer / My home sweet home / Suppertime / May the good Lord bless and keep you / What can he do / He knows just what I need / When I've learned enough to live / Now I belong to Jesus / I won't have to cross Jordan alone / Travelling on / My wonderful Lord / I know who holds tomorrow / Where could I go but to the Lord / God bless God / Don't take your love from me / If I had you / Stay as sweet as you are / My darling, my darling / Who wouldn't love you / I can't believe that you're in love with me / Object of my affection / It all depends on you / Thank you for a lovely evening / Everything I have is yours / Nearness of you / Sweet and lovely
CD Set BCD 15493
Bear Family / Mar '92 / Direct / Rollercoaster / Swift

FOUR IN THE MORNING
If you ain't lovin' (you ain't livin') / All right / Three days / Sweet dreams / Going steady / Hello walls / Backtrack / Wine me up / Your times comin' / I miss you already / This little girl of mine / Four in the morning / Seasons come, seasons go / Alone with you / Heartache for a keepsake / Apartment no. 9 / Live fast, love hard, die young / Your cheatin' heart / Satisfied mind / As far as I'm concerned / Is it really over / Chapel in the moonlight / Some of those memories / There goes my everything / Crying time / Swingin' doors / Tiger by the tail / Here comes my baby back again / Once a day / Sweet thang / I could never be ashamed of you / Are you sincere / Memphis
CD GRF 073
Tring / Feb '93 / Tring

GREATEST HITS
CD PWKS 4221
Carlton / Nov '94 / Carlton

GREATEST HITS
Four in the morning / Sweet dreams / I miss you already / Hello walls / Riverboat / Country girl / All right / Goin' steady / Backtrack / Live fast, love hard, die young / Wine me up / Your time's comin' / This little girl of mine / If you ain't lovin' / Comeback / Alone with you / That's the way it's gotta be / I've got five dollars / Three days / Yellow bandana
CD ECD 3301
K-Tel / Mar '97 / K-Tel

HELLO WALLS
CD CDSGP 0166
Prestige / Oct '95 / Else / Total/BMG

Young Fresh Fellows

INCLUDES A HELMET
CD UTIL 010 CD
Utility / Jun '90 / Grapevine/PolyGram

SOMOS LOS MEJORES
CD MR 015CD
Munster / Apr '92 / Cargo / Greyhound / Plastic Head

Young, Gary

HOSPITAL
Plant man / First Impression / Mitchell / Foothill blud / Real crill (no video) / Warren / Hospital for the chemically insane / Birds in traffic / Where you are at / Ralph the vegetarian robot / Missing in action / Wipeout / Twentieth day / Geri / Hooks of the highway
CD ABB74CD
Big Cat / Aug '95 / 3mv/Pinnacle

Young, George

OLD TIMES
CD CRD 307
Chiaroscuro / Mar '96 / Jazz Music

SPRING FEVER
It might as well be Spring / All of me / Imagination / Bernie's tune / Mysticized / Garden of desire / Kid stuff / Little O's / Domingo en la tarde / Don't stay away / Spring fever
CD 66055009
Sweet Basil / Nov '91 / New Note/Pinnacle

Young Gods

LIVE SKY TOUR
Intro / TV sky / Jimmy / Envoye/chanson rouge / L'eau rouge / Skinflowers / She rains / Summer eyes / Pas mal / Longue route / September song / Seeräuber Jenny
CD BIAS 241CD
Play It Again Sam / Jul '93 / Discovery / Plastic Head / Vital

ONLY HEAVEN
Outside / Strangel / Speed of night / Donnez les esprits / Moon revolutions / Kissing the sun / Dreamhouse / Lointaine / Grdez les esprits / Child in the tree
CD BIAS 301CD
Play It Again Sam / Jun '95 / Discovery / Plastic Head / Vital

RED WATER, THE
CD BIAS 130CD
Play It Again Sam / Aug '89 / Discovery / Plastic Head / Vital

TV SKY
Our house / Gasoline man / TV sky / Skinflowers / Dame chance / Night dance / She rains / Summer eyes
CD BIAS 201CD
Play It Again Sam / Feb '92 / Discovery / Plastic Head / Vital

YOUNG GODS
Nous de la lune / Jusqu'au bout / Ciel ouvert / Jimmy / Fai la mouette / Percussions / Feu / Did you miss me / Si tu gardes
CD LDCD 8821
Play It Again Sam / Aug '89 / Discovery / Plastic Head / Vital

YOUNG GODS PLAY KURT WEILL, THE
CD BIAS 188CD
Play It Again Sam / Apr '91 / Discovery / Plastic Head / Vital

Young Jazz

SITTEL FROM SWEDEN
CD SITCD 9237
Sittel / May '97 / Cadillac / Jazz Music

Young, James

SONGS THEY NEVER PLAY ON THE RADIO
Mystery of love / Long wooden box / For the sunrise / Mr. Misterioso / Listen to the rain / Aphro gypsia / Curious / Tall tales / Der leiermann / Planet pussy / Silver sweet siren / Songs they never play on the radio
CD CREDCD 158
Creation / Dec '93 / 3mv/Vital

Young Jessie

I'M GONE
Mary Lou / Lonesome desert / Rabbit on a log / Don't think I will / Well baby / Nothing seems right / Down at Hayden's / I smell a rat / Why do I love you / Pretty soon / Oochie coochie / Don't happen no more / Hit, git and split / Here comes Henry / Hot dog / Do you love me / This is young Jessie / Maybelline - Fragment / I hear you knocking - Fragment
CD CDCHD 607
Ace / Nov '95 / Pinnacle

Young, Jesse Colin

HIGHWAY IS FOR HEROES, THE
CD EDCD 479
Edsel / Jun '96 / Pinnacle

LOVE ON THE WING
CD EDCD 477
Edsel / Jun '96 / Pinnacle

PERFECT STRANGER
CD EDCD 478
Edsel / Jun '96 / Pinnacle

TOGETHER
Good times / Sweet little child / Together / Sweet little sixteen / Peace song / Six days on the road / Lovely day / Creole belle / 1000 miles from nowhere / Born in Chicago / Pastures of plenty
CD EDCD 491
Edsel / Jul '96 / Pinnacle

Young, John

WATER OF LIFE, THE (Young, John & Dougie Pincock)
CD ADLCD 01
Kilmahew Music / Jun '96 / Duncans

Young, John

SERENATA
I don't wanna be kissed / Baby doll / Circus / Cubana chant / In love in vain / Bones / Serenata / When I fall in love / Circus / Baby doll / I don't wanna be kissed
CD DD 403
Delmark / Mar '97 / ADA / Cadillac / CM / Direct / Hot Shot

Young, John Paul

GREATEST HITS
Love is in the air / Lost in your love / Here we go / Hot for your baby / Yesterday's hero / St. Louis / Pasadena / Love game / Heaven sent / Standing in the rain / Day that my heart caught fire / 6 5 33 5 4 / Where the action is / I wanna do it with you / Don't sing that song / Birmingham
CD 12896
Laserlight / Feb '97 / Target/BMG

LOVE IS IN THE AIR
CD 12212
Laserlight / '93 / Target/BMG

VERY BEST OF JOHN PAUL YOUNG, THE
CD 10152
CMC / Jun '97 / BMG

Young, Johnny

CHICAGO BLUES
CD ARHCD 325
Arhoolie / Apr '95 / ADA / Cadillac / Direct

JOHNNY YOUNG AND HIS FRIENDS
CD TCD 5003
Testament / Aug '94 / ADA / Koch

Young, 'Lady' Linda

GOOD MORNING TO HEAVEN (Young, 'Lady' Linda & 'Tuba Fats' Lacen Band)
CD MECCACD 2001
Music Mecca / May '97 / Cadillac / Jazz Music / Wellard

Young, La Monte

JUST STOMPIN'
Stompin' / Young Dorian's blues in G
CD R2 71262
Gramavision / Aug '93 / Vital/SAM

SECOND DREAM OF...
CD GRV 74672
Gramavision / Oct '91 / Vital/SAM

WELL TUNED PIANO, THE
CD Set 1887012
Gramavision / Jul '90 / Vital/SAM

Young, Larry

GROOVE STREET
Groove street / I found a new baby / Sweet Lorraine / Gettin' into it / Talkin' 'bout JC
CD OJCCD 1853
Original Jazz Classics / Apr '97 / Complete/ Pinnacle / Jazz Music / Wellard

LOVE CRY WANT (Young, Larry & Nicholas/Joe Gallivan)
Peace / Tomorrow, today will be yesterday / Great medicine dance / Angel place / Ancient place / Love cry
CD NJC 001
NJC / Jun '97 / Harmonia Mundi

Young, Leo

COSMIC LAND
CD EFA 019572
KTM / Mar '97 / SRD

Young, Lester

ALTERNATIVE LESTER, THE
Way down yonder in New Orleans / Countless blues / I want a little girl / Pagin' the devil
CD TAXCDS 6
Tax / Apr '91 / Cadillac / Jazz Music / Wellard

AN INTRODUCTION TO LESTER YOUNG
CD 4042
Best Of Jazz / Apr '97 / Discovery

CLASSICS 1943-1946
CD 932
Classics / Apr '97 / Discovery / Jazz Music

COMPLETE ALADDIN RECORDINGS, THE (2CD Set)
Indiana / I can't get started (With you) / Tea for two / Body and soul / DB blues / Lester blows again / These foolish things / Jumpin' at Mesner's / It's only a paper moon / After you've gone / Lover come back to me / Jammin' with Lester / You're driving me crazy / New Lester leaps in / Lester's be bop boogie / She's funny that way / Sunday / SM blues / Jumpin' with my symphony Sid / No eyes blues / Sax-o-be-bop / On the sunny side of the street / Easy does it / Easy does it / Movin' with Lester / One o'clock jump / Jumpin' at the Woodside / I'm confessin' / Lester smooths it out / Just cooling / East of the sun and West of the moon / Sheik of Araby / Something to remember you by / Untitled / Please let me forget / He don't love me anymore / Pleasing man blues / CC rider / It's better to give than receive
CD Set CDP 8327872
Blue Note / Oct '95 / EMI

EASY DOES IT 1936-1940
Shoe shine boy / Boogie woogie / Oh lady be good / Sailboat in the moonlight / Every tub / Blue and sentimental / Jumpin' at the woodside / Way down yonder in New Orleans / Countless blues / Them there eyes / I want a little girl / Pagin' the devil / You can depend on me / Jive at five / Taxi war dance / Twelfth Street rag / Clap hands / Here comes Charlie / Dickie's dream / Lester leaps in / I left my baby / I never knew / Tickle-toe / Easy does it / Broadway
CD IGOCD 2036
Indigo / Sep '96 / ADA / Direct

IN WASHINGTON DC VOL.1
Foggy day / When you're smiling / I can't get started (with you) / Fast Bob blues / DB blues / Tea for two / Jeepers creepers
CD OJCCD 782
Original Jazz Classics / Apr '94 / Complete/ Pinnacle / Jazz Music / Wellard

JAZZ ARCHIVES 1941-1944
CD 158352
Jazz Archives / May '95 / Discovery

JAZZ MASTERS
Love me or leave me / Sometimes I'm happy / I've found a new baby / Polka dots and moonbeams / On the sunny side of the street / (Back home agin) In Indiana / Prisoner of love / In a little Spanish town / Just you, just me / Peg o' my heart / Too marvellous for words / All of me / I'm confessin' that I love you / Mean to me / I never knew

CD 5218592
Verve / Feb '94 / PolyGram

KANSAS CITY SESSIONS
Way down yonder in New Orleans / Countless blues / Them there eyes / I want a little girl / Pagin' the devil / Three little words / Jo Jo / I got rhythm / Four o'clock drag / Laughing at life / Good mornin' blues / I know you know / Love me or leave me
CD CMD 14022
Commodore Jazz / Feb '97 / New Note/ BMG

LADY BE GOOD
CD ATJCD 5968
All That's Jazz / Aug '92 / Jazz Music / THE

LESTER LEAPS AGAIN
Up 'n' at 'em / (Back home again in) Indiana / Too marvellous for words / Mean to me / Sweet Georgia Brown / I'm confessin' that I love you / Neenah / I cover the waterfront / Lester leaps in / I don't stand a ghost of a chance with you / How high the moon / Be bop boogie / DB blues / Lavender blues / These foolish things / Just you, just me / Lester leaps again
CD LEJAZZCD 4
Le Jazz / Mar '93 / Cadillac / Koch

LESTER LEAPS IN
CD JHR 73571
Jazz Hour / Nov '93 / Cadillac / Jazz Music / Target/BMG

LESTER YOUNG 1936-1944
CD CD 14551
Jazz Portraits / Jul '94 / Jazz Music

LESTER YOUNG 1943-1947
CD CD 53073
Giants Of Jazz / Mar '92 / Cadillac / Jazz Music / Target/BMG

LESTER YOUNG 1950-1958
CD CD 53193
Giants Of Jazz / Sep '94 / Cadillac / Jazz Music / Target/BMG

LESTER-AMADEUS
Moten swing / Shout and feel it / You and me that used to be / Count steps in / They can't take that away from me / I'll always be in love with you / Swing brother swing / Bugle blues / I got rhythm / Allez oop / Blues with Helen / I ain't got nobody / Don't be that way / Song of the wanderer / Mortgage stomp
CD PHONTCD 7639
Phontastic / Apr '94 / Cadillac / Jazz Music / Wellard

LIVE AT THE ROYAL ROOST 1948
Lester leaps in / I don't stand a ghost of a chance with you / Just you, just me / How high the moon / Be bop boogie / These foolish things / DB Blues / Lavender blue / Lester leaps again / Sweet Georgia Brown
CD 550092
Jazz Anthology / Jan '94 / Cadillac / Discovery / Harmonia Mundi

MASTERPIECES OF LESTER YOUNG, THE
CD 393462
Music Memoria / Aug '94 / ADA / Discovery

PRESIDENT PLAYS WITH THE OSCAR PETERSON TRIO, THE (Young, Lester & Oscar Peterson Trio)
Ad lib blues / Just you, just me / Tea for two / Indiana / These foolish things / I can't get started / Stardust / On the sunny side of the street / Almost like being in love / I can't give you anything but love / There will never be another you / I'm confessin' / It takes two to tango
CD 8316702
Verve / Feb '93 / PolyGram

PRESIDENT VOL.1, THE
CD COD 029
Jazz View / Mar '92 / Harmonia Mundi

PRESIDENT VOL.2, THE
CD COD 039
Jazz View / Jul '92 / Harmonia Mundi

PRESIDENT VOL.4, THE
CD COD 038
Jazz View / Jun '92 / Harmonia Mundi

PRESIDENT VOL.6, THE
CD COD 040
Jazz View / Aug '92 / Harmonia Mundi

PREZ AND SWEETS (Young, Lester & Harry 'Sweets' Edison)
Mean to me / Red boy blues / Pennies from Heaven / That's all / One o'clock jump / She's funny that way / It's the talk of the town / I found a new baby
CD 8493912
Verve / Mar '91 / PolyGram

PREZ AND TEDDY (Young, Lester & Teddy Wilson Quartet)
All of me / Prisoner of love / Louise / Love me or leave me / Taking a chance on love / Our love is here to stay / Prez returns
CD 8312702
Verve / Feb '87 / PolyGram

PREZ CONFERENCES
CD _______ **JASSCD 18**
Jass / Oct '91 / ADA / Cadillac / CM / Direct / Jazz Music

QUINTESSENCE, THE (1936-1943/2CD Set)
CD Set _______ **FA 210**
Fremeaux / Oct '96 / ADA / Discovery

RARITIES
CD _______ **MCD 0482**
Moon / Nov '93 / Cadillac / Harmonia Mundi

RARITIES AND JAM SESSIONS (The Golden Age of Jazz)
CD _______ **JZCD 365**
Suisa / May '92 / Jazz Music / THE

SUPER SESSIONS, THE
(Back home again in) Indiana / I can't get started (with you) / Tea for two / Body and soul / Just you / Just you, just me / I never knew / Afternoon of Basie-ite / Sometimes I'm happy / After theatre jump / Six cats and a prince / Lester leaps again / Destination KC
CD _______ **LEJAZZCD 36**
Le Jazz / May '95 / Cadillac / Koch

TENOR KING
CD _______ **CDSGP 0280**
Prestige / Jul '97 / Else / Total/BMG

THIS IS JAZZ
Shoe shine boy / Boogie woogie / He ain't got rhythm / I must have that man / Honeysuckle rose / Live and love tonight / Pound cake / Exactly like you / Clap hands / Here come Charlie / Dickie's dream / Lester leaps in / Ham 'n eggs / Man I love / Easy does it / Five o'clock whistle / All of me / I got rhythm
CD _______ **CK 65042**
Sony Jazz / May '97 / Sony

Young Marble Giants

COLOSSAL YOUTH
Searching for Mr. Right / Include me out / Taxi / Eating noddemix / Constantly changing / NITA / Colossal youth / Music for evenings / Man amplifier / Choci loni / Wurlitzer jukebox / Salad days / Credit in the straight world / Brand new life / Wind in the rigging / This way / Posed by models / Clock / Clicktalk / Zebra trucks / Sporting life / Final day / Radio silents / Cake walking / Ode to Booker T
CD _______ **TWI 9842**
Les Disques Du Crepuscule / Apr '94 / Discovery

Young MC

STONE COLD RHYMIN'
Come off / Bust a move / Name is Young / Roll with the punches / Stone cold buggin' / Principal's office / Fastest rhyme / Know how / I let 'em know / Just say no
CD _______ **IMCD 122**
4th & Broadway / Apr '91 / PolyGram

Young, 'Mighty' Joe

BLUESY JOSEPHINE
CD _______ **BLE 595212**
Black & Blue / Oct '94 / Discovery / Koch / Wellard

LIVE AT THE WISE FOOLS PUB
CD _______ **AIM 1052CD**
Aim / Oct '95 / ADA / Direct / Jazz Music

MIGHTY MAN
Starvation / Mighty man / Turning point / Got my mind on my woman / Got a hold on me / Bring it on / End of the line / Ain't goin' for that / Wishy washy woman / On the move again
CD _______ **BPCD 5040**
Blind Pig / May '97 / ADA / CM / Direct / Hot Shot

Young, Neil

AFTER THE GOLDRUSH
Tell me why / After the goldrush / Only love can break your heart / Southern man / Till the morning comes / Oh, lonesome me / Don't let it bring you down / Birds / When you dance I can really love / I believe in you / Cripple Creek ferry
CD _______ **244088**
Reprise / Mar '93 / Warner Music

AMERICAN STARS AND BARS
Old country waltz / Saddle up the palomino / Hey babe / Hold back the tears / Bite the bullet / Star of Bethlehem / Will to live / Like a hurricane / Homegrown
CD _______ **7599272342**
Reprise / Dec '96 / Warner Music

BROKEN ARROW (Young, Neil & Crazy Horse)
CD _______ **9362462912**
Reprise / Jun '96 / Warner Music

COMES A TIME
Goin' back / Comes a-time / Look out for my love / Peace of mind / Lotta love / Human highway / Already one / Field of opportunity / Motorcycle mama / Four strong winds
CD _______ **7599272352**
Reprise / Jun '93 / Warner Music

DECADE (2CD Set)
Down to the wire / Burned / Mr. Soul / Broken arrow / Expecting to fly / Sugar mountain / I am a child / Loner / Old laughing lady / Cinnamon girl / Down by the river / Cowgirl in the sand / I believe in you / After the goldrush / Southern man / Helpless / Ohio / Soldier / Old man / Man needs a maid / Heart of gold / Star of Bethlehem / Needle and the damage done / Tonight's the night / Turnstiles / Winterlong / Deep forbidden lake / Like a hurricane / Love is a rose / Cortez the killer / Campaigner / Long may you run / Harvest
CD _______ **7599272332**
Reprise / Jun '93 / Warner Music

EVERYBODY KNOWS THIS IS NOWHERE (Young, Neil & Crazy Horse)
Cinnamon girl / Everybody knows this is nowhere / Round and round / Down by the river / Losing end / Running dry (Requiem for the rockets) / Cowgirl in the sand
CD _______ **244073**
Reprise / Jun '89 / Warner Music

FREEDOM
Rockin' in the free world / Crime in the city / Don't cry / Hangin' on a limb / Eldorado / Ways of love / Someday / On Broadway / Wrecking ball / No more / Too far gone
CD _______ **9258992**
Reprise / Feb '95 / Warner Music

HARVEST
Out on the weekend / Harvest / Man needs a maid / Heart of gold / Are you ready for the country / Old man / There's a world / Alabama / Needle and the damage done / Words (between the lines of age)
CD _______ **244131**
Reprise / '92 / Warner Music

HARVEST MOON
Unknown legend / From Hank to Hendrix / You and me / Harvest moon / War of man / One of these days / Such a woman / Old king / Dreamin' man / Natural beauty
CD _______ **9362450572**
Reprise / Nov '92 / Warner Music

HAWKS AND DOVES
Little wing / Homestead / Lost in space / Captain Kennedy / Staying power / Coastline / Union man / Comin' apart at every nail / Hawks and doves
CD _______ **9362457022**
Reprise / Dec '96 / Warner Music

JOURNEY THROUGH THE PAST
For what it's worth / Mr. Soul / Rock 'n' roll woman / Find the cost of freedom / Ohio / Southern man / Alabama / Are you ready for the country / Words / Soldier
CD _______ **7599261232**
Reprise / Jun '94 / Warner Music

LANDING ON WATER
Weight of the world / Violent side / Hippie dream / Bad news beat / Touch the night / People on the street / Hard luck stories / I got a problem / Pressure / Drifter
CD _______ **GED 24109**
Geffen / Nov '96 / BMG

LIVE RUST (Young, Neil & Crazy Horse)
Sugar mountain / I am a child / Comes a-time / After the goldrush / My my, hey hey (out of the blue) / When you dance I can really love / Loner / Needle and the damage done / Lotta love / Sedan delivery / Powder finger / Cortez the killer / Cinnamon girl / Like a hurricane / Hey hey, my my (into the black) / Tonight's the night
CD _______ **7599272502**
Reprise / Jun '93 / Warner Music

LUCKY THIRTEEN
Sample and hold / Transformer man / Depression blues / Get gone / Don't take your love away from me / Once an angel / Where is the highway tonight / Hippie dream / Pressure / Around the world / Mid East vacation / Ain't it the truth / This note's for you
CD _______ **GFLD 19328**
Geffen / Sep '96 / BMG

MIRROR BALL
Song X / Act of love / I'm the ocean / Big green country / Truth be known / Downtown / What happened yesterday / Peace and love / Throw your hatred down / Scenery / Fallen angel
CD _______ **9362459342**
Reprise / Jun '95 / Warner Music

NEIL YOUNG
Emperor of Wyoming / Loner / If I could have her tonight / I've been waiting for you / Old laughing lady / String quartet from whiskey boot hill / Here we are in the years / What did you do to my life / I've loved her so long / Last trip to Tulsa
CD _______ **244059**
Reprise / Mar '93 / Warner Music

OLD WAY
CD _______ **GFLD 19356**
Geffen / Apr '97 / BMG

ON THE BEACH
Walk on / See the sky about to rain / Revolution blues / For the turnstiles / Vampire blues / On the beach / Motion pictures / Ambulance blues
CD _______ **9362456992**
Reprise / Dec '96 / Warner Music

RAGGED GLORY (Young, Neil & Crazy Horse)
Country home / White line / Fuckin' up / Over and over / Love to burn / Farmer John / Mansion on the hill / Days that used to be / Love and only love / Mother Earth (natural anthem)
CD _______ **7599263152**
Reprise / Feb '95 / Warner Music

RE-AC-TOR
Opera star / Surfer Joe and Moe the sleaze / T-Bone / Get back on it / Southern Pacific / Motor city / Rapid transit / Shots
CD _______ **7599258692**
Reprise / Jun '94 / Warner Music

RUST NEVER SLEEPS (Young, Neil & Crazy Horse)
My my, hey hey (out of the blue) / Thrasher / Ride my llama / Pocohontas / Sail away / Powder finger / Welfare mothers / Sedan delivery / Hey hey, my my (into the black)
CD _______ **7599272492**
Reprise / Jun '93 / Warner Music

SLEEPS WITH ANGELS
My heart / Prime of life / Drive-by / Sleeps with angels / Western hero / Change your mind / Blue Eden / Safeway cart / Train of love / Trans Am / Piece of crap / Dream that can last
CD _______ **9362457492**
Reprise / Aug '94 / Warner Music

THIS NOTE'S FOR YOU (Young, Neil & The Blue Notes)
Ten men workin' / This note's for you / Coupe de ville / Life in the city / Twilight / Married man / Sunny inside / Can't believe your lyin' / Hey hey / One thing
CD _______ **9257192**
Reprise / Feb '95 / Warner Music

TIME FADES AWAY
Time fades away / LA / Journey through the past / Bridge / Love in mind / Don't be denied / Last dance / Yonder stands the sinner
CD _______ **7599259342**
Reprise / Jun '94 / Warner Music

TONIGHT'S THE NIGHT
Tonight's the night / Speakin' out / World on a string / Borrowed tune / Come on baby let's go downtown / Mellow my mind / Roll another number (for the road) / Albuquerque / New mama / Look out, Joe / Tired eyes / Tonight's the night pt 2
CD _______ **7599272212**
Reprise / Jun '93 / Warner Music

TRANS
Little thing called love / Computer age / We R in control / Transformer man / Computer cowboy (aka Skycrusher) / Hold on to your love / Sample and hold / Mr. Soul / Like an Inca
CD _______ **GFLD 19357**
Geffen / Apr '97 / BMG

UNPLUGGED
Old laughing lady / Mr. Soul / World on a string / Pocahontas / Stringman / Like a hurricane / Needle and the damage done / Helpless / Harvest moon / Transformer man / Unknown legend / Look out for my love / Long may you run / From Hank to Hendrix
CD _______ **9362453102**
Reprise / Jun '93 / Warner Music

WELD (2CD Set) (Young, Neil & Crazy Horse)
Hey hey, my my (into the black) / Crime in the city / Blowin' in the wind / Welfare mothers / Love to burn / Cinnamon girl / Mansion on the hill / Fuckin' up / Cortez the killer / Powder finger / Love and only love / Rockin' in the free world / Like a hurricane / Farmer John / Tonight's the night / Roll another number (for the road) / Arc
CD Set _______ **7599266712**
Reprise / Nov '91 / Warner Music

YEAR OF THE HORSE, THE (Neil Young Live)
When you dance / Barstool blues / When your lonely heart breaks / Mr. Soul / Big time / Pocahontas / Human highway / Slip away / Scattered / Danger bird / Prisoners / Sedan delivery
CD _______ **9362466522**
Reprise / Jun '97 / Warner Music

ZUMA (Young, Neil & Crazy Horse)
Don't cry no tears / Danger bird / Pardon my heart / Looking for a love / Barstool blues / Stupid girl / Drive back / Cortez the killer / Through my sails
CD _______ **7599272262**
Reprise / Jun '93 / Warner Music

Young, Paul

FROM TIME TO TIME (The Singles Collection)
Every time you go away / Come back and stay / I'm only foolin' myself / Senza una Donna / I'm gonna tear your playhouse down / Broken man / Everything must change / Wonderland / Don't dream it's over / Love of the common people / Wherever I lay my hat (that's my home) / Both sides now / Oh Girl / Softly whispering I love you / Some people
CD _______ **4688252**
Columbia / Aug '91 / Sony

LOVE SONGS
Everytime you go away / Don't dream it's over / Broken man / Softly whispering I love you / Wonderland / It will be you / Senza una Donna (without a woman): *Young, Paul & Zucchero* / Now I know what made Otis blue / Love will tear us apart / Everything must change / Half a step away / This means anything / Won't look back / Calling you / Wherever I lay my hat (that's my home) / Follow on / Love hurts
CD _______ **4783122**
Columbia / Sep '96 / Sony

NO PARLEZ
Come back and stay / Love will tear us apart / Wherever I lay my hat (that's my home) / Ku-ku kurama / No parlez / Love of the common people / Oh women / Iron out the rough spots / Broken man / Tender trap / Sex
CD _______ **4609092**
CBS / '91 / Sony

NO PARLEZ/THE SECRET OF ASSOCIATION (2CD Set)
Come back and stay / Love will tear us apart / Wherever I lay my hat (that's my home) / Ku-ku kurama / No parlez / Love of the common people / Oh women / Iron out the rough spots / Broken man / Tender trap / Sex / Bite the hand that feeds / Everytime you go away / I'm gonna tear your playhouse down / Standing on the edge / Soldier's things / Everything must change / Tomb of memories / One step forward / Hot fun / This means anything / I was in chains / Man in the iron mask
CD Set _______ **4784812**
Columbia / Mar '95 / Sony

OTHER VOICES
Heaven can wait / Little bit of love / Softly whispering I love you / Together / Stop on by / Our time has come / Oh girl / Right about now / It's what she didn't say / Calling you
CD _______ **4844702**
Columbia / Jul '97 / Sony

PAUL YOUNG
Ball and chain / I wish you love / Tularosa / Vanish / Hard cargo / Say goodbye / In a dream gone by / You'd better run away / Across the borderline / It was a very good year / Window world
CD _______ **0630186192**
East West / May '97 / Warner Music

PAUL YOUNG AND THE Q-TIPS (Young, Paul & The Q-Tips)
CD _______ **JHD 031**
Tring / Jun '92 / Tring

SOME KIND OF WONDERFUL (Young, Paul & The Q-Tips)
SYSLJFM (the letter song) / Tracks of my tears / You are the life inside of me / Man can't lose what he don't have / Some kind of wonderful / Love hurts / I wish it would rain / Sweet talk / You're gonna love me / Empty bed
CD _______ **101172**
CMC / May '97 / BMG

TRACKS OF MY TEARS (Young, Paul & The Q-Tips)
Tracks of my tears / Love hurts / Hi-fidelity / Man can't lose (What he don't have) / Sweet have / I wish it could rain / We are the life inside of me / SYSLJFM (The letter song) / Link / Broken man / Raise your hand / Get 'em up Joe / Empty bed / You're gonna love me
CD _______ **306582**
Hallmark / May '97 / Carlton

Young Pioneers

1ST VIRGINIA VOLUNTEERS
CD _______ **VMFM 21CD**
Lookout / Jul '95 / Cargo / Greyhound / Shellshock/Disc

CRIME WAVE
CD _______ **VMFM 27CD**
Vermiform / May '97 / Cargo / Greyhound / Plastic Head

FIRST VIRGINIA VOLUNTEERS
CD _______ **VMFM 212**
Vermiform / May '95 / Cargo / Greyhound / Plastic Head

Young Rascals

ANTHOLOGY (2CD Set) (Rascals/Young Rascals)
I ain't gonna eat out my heart anymore / Good lovin' / Do you feel it / Mustang Sally / Baby let's wait / In the midnight hour / You better run / Lonely to long / Come on up / Too many fish in the sea / Love is a beautiful thing / Groovin' / Find somebody / How can I be sure / If you knew / I'm so happy now / Easy rollin' / Rainy day / It's wonderful (to be loved by you) / Silly girl / Once upon a dream / Beautiful morning / People got to be free / Island of love / Look around / Ray of hope / Heaven / See / I'd like to take you home / Temptation's bout to get me / Nubia / Real thing / Carry me back / Right on / Ready for love / I believe / Glory glory / Girl like you

CD 8122710772
Atlantic / Jul '93 / Warner Music

TIME PEACE (Greatest Hits) (Rascals/ Young Rascals)
CD 7567814412
Atlantic / Jun '95 / Warner Music

Young, Steve

ROCK, SALT & NAILS
That's how strong my love is / Rock, salt and nails / I'm a one woman man / Coyote / Gonna find me a bluebird / Love in my time / Seven Bridges Road / Kenny's song / Holler in the swamp / Hoboin' / My sweet love ain't around
CD EDCD 193
Edsel / Feb '91 / Pinnacle

SOLO/LIVE
CD WM 1004
Watermelon / Jun '93 / ADA / Direct

Young Tradition

GALLERIES/NO RELATION (Young Tradition/Royston & Heather Wood)
Intro/Ductia: *Young Tradition* / Barleystraw: *Young Tradition* / What if a day: *Young Tradition* / Loyal lover: *Young Tradition* / Entracte/Stones in my passway: *Young Tradition* / Idumea: *Young Tradition* / Husbandman and servingman: *Young Tradition* / Rolling of the stones: *Young Tradition* / Bitter withy: *Young Tradition* / Banks of the Nile: *Young Tradition* / Wondrous love: *Young Tradition* / Medieval mystery tour: *Young Tradition* / Divertissement/Upon the bough: *Young Tradition* / Ratcliff highway: *Young Tradition* / Brisk young widow: *Young Tradition* / Interlude/The Pembroke unique ensemble: *Young Tradition* / John Barleycorn: *Young Tradition* / Agincourt carol: *Young Tradition* / Chicken on a raft: *Young Tradition* / Randy-dandy-o: *Young Tradition* / Shanties: *Young Tradition* / Shepherd of the downs: *Wood, Royston & Heather* / Come ye that fear Lord: *Wood, Royston & Heather* / Foolish incredibly foolish: *Wood, Royston & Heather* / Bold Benjamin-o: *Wood, Royston & Heather* / Bold astrologer: *Wood, Royston & Heather* / St. Patrick's breastplate: *Wood, Royston & Heather* / Cutty wren: *Wood, Royston & Heather* / Will you miss me: *Wood, Royston & Heather* / Gloria laus: *Wood, Royston & Heather*
CD ESMCD 461
Essential / Jan '97 / BMG

HOLLY BEARS THE CROWN, THE
CD FLED 3006
Fledg'ling / Nov '95 / ADA / CM / Direct

YOUNG TRADITION/SO CHEERFULLY ROUND
CD ESMCD 409
Essential / Jul '96 / BMG

Young, Zora

TRAVELIN' LIGHT
Travellin' light / Queen bee / Football widow / Mama jama / Key to the highway / Daughter of a son-of-a-gun / Stumbling blocks and stepping stones / Girlfriend / Brain damage / Can't take nothin out
CD DEL 3003
Deluge / Dec '95 / ADA / Direct / Koch

Youngblood Hart, Alvin

BIG MAMA'S DOOR
Big Mama's door / Joe Friday / Them fair-weather friends / France blues / Gallows pole / Pony blues / Amazed 'n' amused / Things 'bout comin' my way / When I was a cowboy (Western Plains) / Rest your saddle / If blues was money / Hillbilly Willie's blues / Livin' in a strain / That Kate Adams jive
CD 4841092
Epic / Jun '97 / Sony

Youngblood, Sydney

FEELING FREE
Feelin' free / If only I could / I'd rather go blind / Sit and wait / Kiss and say goodbye / Ain't no sunshine / I'm your lover / Not just a lover but a friend / Congratulations / Could it me (I'm in love) / That was yesterday / Good times, bad times
CD CIRCD 9
Circa / Apr '92 / EMI

HOOKED ON YOU (The Best Of Sydney Youngblood)
If only I could / Spookey / Sit and wait / Feeling free / Hooked on you / Body and soul / Wherever you go / Feels like forever / I'm your lover / I'd rather go blind / Could it be (I'm in love) / Ain't no sunshine
CD CDVIP 129
Virgin VIP / Apr '95 / EMI

Youngbloods

EARTH MUSIC
Euphoria / All my dreams blue / Monkey Business / Dreamer's dream / Sugar Babe / Long and tall / I Can Tell / Don't Play Games / Wine song / Fool me / Reason to believe
CD EDCD 274
Edsel / Apr '91 / Pinnacle

ELEPHANT MOUNTAIN
Darkness darkness / Smug / On Sir Frances Drake / Sunlight / Double sunlight / Beautiful / Turn it over / Rainsong / Trillium / Quicksand / Black mountain breakdown / Sham / Ride the wind
CD EDCD 276
Edsel / Apr '91 / Pinnacle

YOUNGBLOODS
Grizzly bear / All over the world / Statesboro Blues / Get Together / One note man / Other side of this life / Tears Are Falling / Four In The Morning / Foolin' Around / Ain't that lovin' you / CC rider

CD EDCD 271
Edsel / Jul '91 / Pinnacle

Youngs, Richard

RED AND BLUE BEAR - THE OPERA (Book/CD Set) (Youngs, Richard & Simon Wickham Smith)
CD VHF 27
VHF / Mar '97 / Cargo

Youth Of Today

TAKE A STAND
CD LF 044CD
Lost & Found / Sep '95 / Plastic Head

Yu, Chung

CLASSICAL CHINESE PIPA
CD EUCD 1176
ARC / '91 / ADA / ARC Music

Yu, Zhou

HOMELAND
CD EUCD 1260
ARC / Mar '94 / ADA / ARC Music

Yuan, Lily

ANCIENT ART MUSIC OF CHINA
CD LYRCD 7409
Lyrichord / '91 / ADA / CM / Roots

Yugar, Zulma

TIERRA SIN MAR
CD TUMICD 059
Tumi / Sep '96 / Discovery / Stern's

Yulya

RUSSIAN ROMANTIC SONGS
CD MCD 71597
Monitor / Jun '93 / CM

Yumiko, Sato

ELFISH ECHO PRESENTS
CD KM 2002
KM20 / Oct '96 / Plastic Head

Yummy Fur

NIGHT CLUB
CD GUIDE 10CD
Guided Missile / Mar '97 / Shellshock/Disc

Yumuri Y Sus Hermanos

PROVOCATION
CD AJA 1204
JVC World Library / Jun '96 / ADA / CM / Direct

Yupanqui, Atahualpa

DON ALTA
CD 68956
Tropical / Apr '97 / Discovery

L'INTEGRALE
CD LDX 274948/52
La Chant Du Monde / Jan '93 / ADA / Harmonia Mundi

Yuro, Timi

18 HEARTBREAKING SONGS
CD RMB 75061
Remember / Oct '95 / Total/BMG

HURT
CD WMCD 5668
Disky / May '94 / Disky / THE

LEGENDS IN MUSIC
CD LECD 066
Wisepack / Jul '94 / Conifer/BMG / THE

LOST VOICE OF SOUL, THE
Hurt / Just say I love him / Trying / Smile / Let me call you sweetheart / Count everything / I know (I love you) / What's the matter baby / Only love me / That's right, walk on by / Should I ever love again / Love of a boy / I ain't gonna cry no more / Insult to injury / Make the world go away / Leavin' on your mind / She's got you / Are you sure / I'd fight the world / Gotta travel on / Down in the valley / Permanently lonely / Legend in my time / Call me / Something bad on my mind / It'll never be over for me
CD RPM 117
RPM / Oct '93 / Pinnacle

VOICE THAT GOT AWAY
Interlude / It's just a metter of time / I'll never fall in love again / When something is wrong with my baby / Nothing takes the place of my baby / Hey boy / Hallelujah I love him so / I must have been out of my mind / When he wants a woman / Loving you is all I ever had / I just got back from there / So ashamed / I apologise / All my love belongs to you / Put them aside / Wall / If you gotta make a fool of somebody / Thirteenth hour / Wrong / When you were mine / Guess who / It's too soon to know / She really loves you / I waited too long / If I never get to love you / Interlude
CD RPM 167
RPM / Aug '96 / Pinnacle

Yvert, Oller

FUNAMBULES (Yvert, Oller & Trio)
CD ARN 64235
Arion / Jun '93 / ADA / Discovery

Yves Choir

BY PRESCRIPTION ONLY
Rush hour / After the rain / Rocky Road / D B / By prescription only / Mad about town / Far side / Follow me to the edge / Bianca / Morocco junction
CD 103 254
Musidisc / Mar '90 / Discovery

Z

Z-Rock Hawaii

Z-ROCK HAWAII
CD NIPP 12142
Nipp Guitar / Jul '97 / Greyhound

Zabaleta

INFERNUKO HAUSPOA (Zabaleta & Kepa Junkera)
CD KDCD 152
Elkar / May '97 / ADA

TRIKI UP (Zabaleta & Imanol)
CD KDCD 241
Elkar / May '97 / ADA

Zabrina

Z = MC2
Take a minute / Nu sound / Sunsister / Philosophy of fiction / Tell me something good / Irresistible / Housework / Keystone groove / This gun's for hire / Killer is with me / Chosen one / Godmother / Fellas from the Southside / You can make it / Sucker for a man with a body
CD ICH 1122CD
Ichiban / Oct '93 / Direct / Koch

Zacharias, Helmut

SWING PARTY
Ich kusse ihre hand, Madame / Dark eyes / Those little white lies / Swing '48 / Kosaken patrouille / Man I love / You made me love you / Mob mob / Embraceable you / What is this thing called love / Presto / How high the moon / Tigerjagd (tiger rag) / Blue moon / C jam blues / Swing party / Schwips boogie / Ich habe rhythmus (I got rhythm) / Mr. Callahan / Carioca / Sabeltanz boogie (sabre dance) / Boogie tur Geige / Fiddler's boogie / Blue blues / China boogie / Smoky / Minne minne ha ha
CD BCD 15642
Bear Family / Jun '92 / Direct / Rollercoaster / Swift

Zachrisson, Johan

RITMO DE ESTORNINHOS
Fado da liha / No comboio descendente / Dream ourselves away / Maneno Mataamu / Chegal / Ritmo de Estorninhos / Anda Maria / Danca da Serra
CD XOUCD 102
Xource / May '97 / ADA / Direct

Zachze

HIMMEL, ARSCH & ZWIRN
CD BEST 1008CD
Acoustic Music / Nov '93 / ADA

Zadeh, Aziza Mustafa

ALWAYS
CD 4738852
Sony Jazz / Jan '95 / Sony

AZIZA MUSTAFA ZADEH
Quiet alone / Tea on the carpet / Cemetry / Inspiration / Reflection / Oriental fantasy / Blue day / Character / Aziza's dream / Chargah / My ballad / I cannot sleep / Moment / Exprompt / Two candles
CD 4682862
Columbia / Apr '94 / Sony

DANCE OF FIRE
Boomerang / Dance of fire / Sheherezadeh / Aspiration / Bana bana gel (Bad girl) / Shadow / Carnival / Passion / Spanish picture / To be continued / Father
CD 4803522
Sony Jazz / Jun '95 / Sony

SEVENTH TRUTH
Ay dilber / Lachin / Interlude 1 / Fly with me / F sharp / Desperation / Daha (again) / I am sad / Interlude 2 / Wild beauty / Seventh truth / Sea monster
CD 4842382
Sony Jazz / Jul '96 / Sony

Zaffarano, Marco

HE WAS ONCE A BEAUTIFUL WOMAN
CD SILVER 1CD
Silver Planet / Jan '97 / 3mv/Sony / Prime

Zagraj Kapela

MUSIQUES DE EUROPE
CD 829262
BUDA / Nov '96 / Discovery

Zahar

LIVE AT THE KNITTING FACTORY
CD KFWCD 112
Knitting Factory / Oct '92 / Cargo / Plastic Head

Zaiko Langa L

SANS ISSUE
CD 3018212
Arcade / Feb '97 / Discovery

Zamagni, Tony

GET DOWN WITH THE BLUES
CD CDTC 1153
Tonecool / Jul '95 / ADA / Direct

Zamfir, Gheorghe

CHRISTMAS AT NOTRE DAME
CD 5174532
Phonogram / Mar '91 / PolyGram

FOLKSONGS FROM RUMANIA (Zamfir, Gheorghe & The Ciocirlia Orchestra)
CD 15208
Laserlight / '91 / Target/BMG

GHEORGHE ZAMFIR COLLECTION, THE
Anna / Joe de doi / Breaza de la dragodana / Invirtita / Rustemul de la listeava / Coragheasca / Balada lui costea pacurarul / Sirba lui pomieru and an o mindra mititica / Miertlita cind e bolnava / Flora / Asta e poteca mea / Cintec de nunta / Bocet / Mindra mea din badulesti / Hora ca din caval / Briu oltenesc / Muntinlor cu brazi inalti si / Cintecul-lui lancu jianu / Frunzulita lemn adus / Hora din muntenia and cimpulung oras de munte / Mindrele / Sirba batrineasca / Briul de la faget / Mult ma-ntreaba inima
CD COL 075
Collection / May '97 / Target/BMG

HEART OF ROMANIA, THE (Zamfir, Gheorghe & Marcel Cellier)
Inima ci venin muit / Doina din banat / Ca din banat / Cintec muntenesc / Ciorcilia / Doina Sus pe cilmea dealului / Joc dins oas / Joc de dai din banat / In memoriam Maria Lataretu / Geampara "Lelita I Oana" / Doina Gheoghe mina boll bine / Doina Lui efta botoca / Balada sarpelui / Doina da jale
CD PV 750002
Disques Pierre Verany / Jul '94 / Kingdom

LIVE IN CONCERT FROM THEIR AMERICAN TOUR (Zamfir, Gheorghe & Marcel Cellier)
Balada sarpelui / Doina de la domasnea / Doina din jebel / Joc dins oas / Doina Sus pe culmea dealului / Doina oltului / Doina lui petru unc / Doina Rugulet cu negra mure / Doina da jale
CD PV 750001
Disques Pierre Verany / Jul '94 / Kingdom

LOVE SONGS
CD 5102122
Phonogram / Mar '91 / PolyGram

MAGIC OF THE MOMENTS
CD DCD 5358
Disky / Apr '94 / Disky / THE

MAGIC OF THE PAN PIPES, THE (27 Haunting Melodies/2CD Set)
Dormasnea / Jebel / Arad / Sarmis and trefia / Flora / Anna / Oltera / Doina de la visina / Muntilor cu brazi inalti si / Mult ma-ntreaba inima / La cules de cucuruz / Am doi frati Severin / Hora din muntenia / Suita olteneasca / Doina/Hora lautareasca / Doina de jale/Ciro cirlia / Hora din muntenia e cimpulung oras de munte / Balada lui costea Pacurarul / Coragheasca / Rustemul de la listeava / Bocet / Sirba de la gaesti / Invirita / Cintee de nunita / Breaza de la Dragodana / La marginea padurii / Asra iarna era iarna / Sirba de la comana / Joe de doi
CD Set SUDCD 4503
Summit / Nov '96 / Sound & Media

MASTER OF THE PAN PIPES
CD 11016
Laserlight / '86 / Target/BMG

MELODIES OF THE HEART
CD DCD 5327
Disky / Apr '94 / Disky / THE

MOMENTS OF MY DREAMS
CD DCD 5356
Disky / Apr '94 / Disky / THE

NAMES IN MY LIFE
CD DCD 5352
Disky / May '94 / Disky / THE

PAN FLUTES & ORGAN
CD 323123
Koch / Feb '94 / Koch

PAN PIPE DREAMS
Love changes everything / Unchained melody / Somewhere / Theme from 'Limelight' / Chariots of fire / Just the way you are / Don't cry for me Argentina / Black rose / Memory / Beautiful dream / Endless dream / Your song / Bilitis / Chanson d'amour / Rose / Run to me / Serenade / Only love
CD 5518212
Spectrum / Nov '95 / PolyGram

PAN PIPES FOR CHRISTMAS
O du frohliche / Jingle bells / O tannenbaum / Six colours / Hark the herald angels sing / Noels Roumains / White Christmas / Little drummer boy / Ave Maria / Petit Papa Noel / Pour toi Jesus / Silent night / Notre Pere / Angels we have heard on high
CD 5525812
Spectrum / Nov '96 / PolyGram

PIPE DREAMS
Chariots of fire / Aranjuez mon amour / Yesterday / Your song / Run to me / I know him so well / Andrew's theme / Annie's song / What now my love / Plasir d'amour / Rose / Lonely shepherd / Rescuerdos / Gymnopedie No.1
CD 5501202
Spectrum / Oct '93 / PolyGram

SPOTLIGHT ON GHEORGHE ZAMFIR
Stranger on the shore / Don't cry for me Argentina / Chanson d'amour / Rose / She / Yesterday / Just the way you are / Annie's song / Tema da un'estate del '42 (the summer knows) / Till / Run to me / I know him so well / If you go away / Sleepy shores / Memory / Lonely shepherd / Sleepy shores (tema da luci della rabalta) (limelight) / What now my love
CD 8483732
Phonogram / Mar '91 / PolyGram

TRANQUIL SOUND OF THE PANPIPES
CD MCCD 285
Music Club / Mar '97 / Disc / THE

WONDERFUL WORLD OF PANPIPES
CD MCCD 202
Music Club / May '95 / Disc / THE

Zanki, Edo

WACHE NACHT
CD INT 845 081
Interchord / '88 / CM

Zap Mama

7
Jogging a Timbouctou / New world / Baba hooker / Belgo Zairoise / African sunset / Damn your eyes / Poetry man / Warmth / Telephone / Nostalgie / Timidity / Ele buma / Kesia Yanga / Illiol
CD CDVIR 62
Virgin / May '97 / EMI

SABSYLMA
Fusahi / Sabsylma / Mais qu'est ce / India / De la vie a la most / Citoyen 120 / Locklat Africa / Mr. Brown / Reveil en Australie / Fi dunia / Mamadit / For no one / Mamas of the Mamas / Adjosio omonie
CD CRAW 12
Crammed Discs / Aug '95 / Grapevine/ PolyGram / New Note/Pinnacle / Prime / RTM/Disc

Zapak, Ali

MY FIRST SUICIDE
CD SMART 1CD
Fundamental / Mar '97 / 3mv/Pinnacle

Zapp

ALL THE GREATEST HITS (Zapp & Roger)
More bounce to the ounce / Be alright / I heard it through the grapevine / So ruff, so tuff / Do it Roger / Dance floor / Doo wa ditty (Blow that thing) / I can make you dance / Heartbreaker / In the mix / Midnight hour / Computer love / Night and day / I want to be your man / Curiosity / Slow and easy / Mega medley
CD 9362451432
Reprise / Dec '93 / Warner Music

NEW ZAPP IV U, THE
It doesn't really matter / Computer love / Itchin' for your twitchin' / Radio people / I only have eyes for you / Rock 'n' roll / Casta-spellome / Make me feel good / Ja ready to rock
CD 7599253272
Warner Bros. / May '94 / Warner Music

ZAPP VOL.3
CD 7599238752
Reprise / Jan '96 / Warner Music

Zappa, Dweezil

CONFESSIONS
CD CDGRUB 19
Food For Thought / Mar '91 / Pinnacle

HAVIN' A BAD DAY
CD RCD 10057
Rykodisc / May '92 / ADA / Vital

SHAMPOOHORN (Z)
CD CDGRUB 25
Food For Thought / May '93 / Pinnacle

Zappa, Frank

ABSOLUTELY FREE (Zappa, Frank & The Mothers Of Invention)
Plastic people / Uncle Bernie's farm / Brown shoes don't make it / Status back baby / America drinks and goes home / Invocation and ritual dance of the young pumpkin / Call any vegetable / Big Leg Emmas / Why don'tcha do me right / Son of Suzy Creamcheese / Duke of prunes / Amnesia vivace / Duke regains his chops / Soft sell conclusion
CD RCD 10502
Rykodisc / May '95 / ADA / Vital

AHEAD OF THEIR TIME (Zappa, Frank & The Mothers Of Invention)
CD RCD 10559
Rykodisc / May '95 / ADA / Vital

APOSTROPHE
Don't eat the yellow snow / Nanook rubs it / St. Alfonzo's pancake breakfast / Father O'Blivion / Cosmik debris / Excentrifugal forz / Apostrophe / Uncle Remus / Stinkfoot
CD RCD 10519
Rykodisc / Apr '95 / ADA / Vital

APOSTROPHE (Au20 Version)
Don't eat the yellow snow / Nanook rubs it / St. Alfonzo's pancake breakfast / Father O'Blivion / Cosmik debris / Excentrifugal forz / Apostrophe / Uncle Remus / Stink foot
CD RCD 80519
Rykodisc / Jun '96 / ADA / Vital

BABY SNAKES
CD RCD 10539
Rykodisc / May '95 / ADA / Vital

BEST BAND YOU NEVER HEARD IN YOUR LIFE, THE (2CD Set)
Heavy duty Judy / Ring of fire / Cosmik debris / Find her finer / Who needs the peace corps / I left my heart in San Francisco / Zomby woof / Zoot allures / Mr. Green Genes / Florentine pogen / Andy / Inca roads / Sofa / Purple haze / Sunshine of your love / Let's move to Cleveland / When Irish eyes are smiling / Godfather part II / Few moments with Brother AWest / Torture never stops (Part one) / Theme from Bonanza / Lonesome cowboy Burt (Swaggart version) / Torture never stops (Part two) / More trouble every day (Swaggart version) / Penguin in bondage (Swaggart version) / Eric Dolphy memorial barbeque / Stairway to heaven
CD Set RCD 10653/54
Rykodisc / Apr '96 / ADA / Vital

BONGO FURY
Debra Kadabra / Carolina hard-core ecstasy / Sam with the showing scalp flat top / Poofter's Froth Wyoming plans ahead / 200 years old / Cucamonga / Advance romance / Man with the woman head / Muffin man
CD RCD 10522
Rykodisc / Feb '96 / ADA / Vital

BROADWAY THE HARD WAY
CD RCD 10552
Rykodisc / May '95 / ADA / Vital

BURNT WEENY SANDWICH (Zappa, Frank & The Mothers Of Invention)
WPLJ / Igor's boogie, phase one / Overture to A Holiday In Berlin / Theme from Burnt Weeny Sandwich / Igor's boogie, phase two / Holiday in Berlin, full-blown / Aybe sea / Little house I used to live in / Valarie
CD RCD 10509
Rykodisc / May '95 / ADA / Vital

CHUNGA'S REVENGE
Transylvania boogie / Road ladies / Twenty small cigars / Nancy and Mary music / Tell me you love me / Would you go all the way / Chunga's revenge / Clap / Rudy wants to buy yez drink / Sharleena
CD RCD 10511
Rykodisc / May '95 / ADA / Vital

CIVILIZATION PHAZE III (2CD Set)
This is phaze III / Put a motor in yourself / Oh-umm / They made me eat it / Reagan at Bitburg / Very nice body / Navanax / How the pig's music works / Xmas values / Dark water / Amnerika / Have you heard their band / Religious superstition / Saliva can only take so much / Buffalo voice / Someplace else right now / Get a life / Kayak (on snow) / N-Lite
CD Set CDDZAP 56
Zappa / Oct '94 / Pinnacle

CRUISING WITH RUBEN & THE JETS (Zappa, Frank & The Mothers Of Invention)
CD RCD 10505
Rykodisc / May '95 / ADA / Vital

DOES HUMOR BELONG IN MUSIC
Zoot allures / Tinsel Town rebellion / Trouble every day / Penguin in bondage / Hotplate heaven at the green hotel / What's

new in Baltimore / Cocksuckers' ball / WPLJ / Let's move to Cleveland / Whipping post
CD ________ RCD 10548
Rykodisc / Feb '96 / ADA / Vital

FILLMORE EAST - JUNE 1971 (Zappa, Frank & The Mothers Of Invention)
Little house I used to live in / Mud shark / What kind of girl do you think we are / Bwana dik / Latex solar beef / Willie the pimp / Do you like my new car / Happy together / Lonesome electric turkey / Peaches en regalia / Tears begin to fall
CD ________ RCD 10512
Rykodisc / May '95 / ADA / Vital

FRANCESCO ZAPPA (Barking Pumpkin Digital Gratification Consort)
CD ________ RCD 10546
Rykodisc / May '95 / ADA / Vital

FRANK ZAPPA MEETS THE MOTHERS OF PREVENTION
We're turning again / Alien orifice / Yo cats / What's new in Baltimore / I don't even care / One man, one vote / HR 2911 / Little beige sambo / Aerobics in bondage
CD ________ RCD 10547
Rykodisc / May '95 / ADA / Vital

FRANK ZAPPA: INTERVIEW PICTURE DISC
CD ________ CBAK 4012
Baktabak / Apr '88 / Arabesque

FREAK OUT (Zappa, Frank & The Mothers Of Invention)
CD ________ RCD 10501
Rykodisc / May '95 / ADA / Vital

GRAND WAZOO, THE
For Calvin (and his next two hitch-hikers) / Grand wazoo / Gletus awreetus-awrightus / Eat that question / Blessed relief
CD ________ RCD 10517
Rykodisc / May '95 / ADA / Vital

GUITAR (2CD Set)
Sexual harassment in the workplace / Republicans / That's not really reggae / When no one was no one / Once again, without the net / Outside Now / Jim and Tammy's upper room / Were we ever really safe / That ol' G minor thing again / Move it or park it / Sunrise redeemer / But who was Fulcanelli / Winos do not match / Systems of edges / Things that look like meat / Watermelon in Easter hay
CD Set ________ RCD 10550/51
Rykodisc / May '95 / ADA / Vital

HAVE I OFFENDED SOMEONE
Bobby Brown goes down / Disco boy / Goblin girl / In France / He's so gay / Sex / Titties 'n' beer / We're turning again / Dumb all over / Catholic girls / Dinah-moe humm / Tinsel-town rebellion / Valley girl / Jewish princess / Yo cats
CD ________ RCD 10577
Rykodisc / Apr '97 / ADA / Vital

HOT RATS
Peaches en regalia / Willie the pimp / Son of Mr. Green Genes / Little umbrellas / Gumbo variations / It must be a camel
CD ________ RCD 10508
Rykodisc / May '95 / ADA / Vital

JAZZ FROM HELL
Night school / Beltway bandits / While you were out / Jazz from hell / G spot tornado / Damp ankles / St. Etienne / Massaggio galore
CD ________ RCD 10549
Rykodisc / May '95 / ADA / Vital

JOE'S GARAGE ACTS I, II & III (2CD Set)
Central scrutinizer / Joe's garage / Catholic girls / Crew slut / Wet t-shirt nite / Toad-O-Line / Why does it hurt when I pee / Lucille has messed my mind up / Token of his extreme / Stick it out / Sy Borg / Dong work for Yuda / Keep it greasy / Outside now / He used to cut the grass / Packard goose / Watermelon in Easter hay / Little green rosetta
CD Set ________ RCD 10530/31
Rykodisc / May '95 / ADA / Vital

JUST ANOTHER BAND FROM LA (Zappa, Frank & The Mothers Of Invention)
Billy the mountain / Call any vegetable / Eddie, are you kidding / Magdalena / Dog breath
CD ________ RCD 10515
Rykodisc / May '95 / ADA / Vital

LATHER (3CD Set)
Re-gyptian strut / Naval aviation in art / Little green Rosetta / Duck duck goose / Down in de dew / For the young sophisticate / Tryin' to grow a chin / Broken hearts are for assholes / Legend of the Illinois enema / Bandit / Lemme take you to the beach / Revised music for guitar and low / Budget orchestra / RDNZL / Honey, don't you want a man like me / Black page no.1 / Big leg Emma / Punky's whips / Flambe / Purple lagoon / Pedro's dowry / Lather / Spider of destiny / Duke of orchestral prunes / Filthy habits / Titties 'n' beer / Ocean is the ultimate solution / Adventures of Greggery Peccary / Re-gyptian strut / Lather goods / Revenge of the knick-knack people / Time is money

CD Set ________ RCD 10574/76
Rykodisc / Sep '96 / ADA / Vital

LONDON SYMPHONY ORCHESTRA VOL.1 & 2 (2CD Set) (London Symphony Orchestra)
CD Set ________ RCD 10540/41
Rykodisc / Apr '95 / ADA / Vital

LOST EPISODES, THE
Blackouts / Lost ina whirlpool / Ronnie sings / Kenny's booger story / Mount St. Mary's concert excerpt / Take your clothes off when you dance / Tiger roach / Run home slow theme / Fountain of love / Run home cues / Any way the wind blows / Run homes cues / Charva / Dick Kunc story / Wedding dress song / Handsome cabin boy / Cops and buns / Big Squeeze / I'm a band leader / Alley cat / Grand wazoo / Wonderful wino / Kung fu / RDNZL / Basement music / Inca roads / Lil' Clanton shuffle / I don't wanna get drafted / Sharleena
CD ________ RCD 40573
Rykodisc / Feb '96 / ADA / Vital

LUMPY GRAVY
Lumpy gravy
CD ________ RCD 10504
Rykodisc / Apr '95 / ADA / Vital

MAKE A JAZZ NOISE HERE (2CD Set)
Stinkfoot / When yuppies go to hell / Fire and chains / Let's make the water turn black / Harry, you're a beast / Orange county lumber truck / Oh no / Lumpy gravy / Eat that question / Black napkins / Big swifty / King Kong / Star Wars won't work / Black page / T'mershi duween / Dupree's paradise / City of tiny lites / Royal March (L'Histoire du Soldat)/Theme from Bartok's 3rd / Sinister footwear / Stevie's spanking / Alien orifice / Cruisin' for burgers / Advance romance / Strictly genteel
CD Set ________ RCD 10555/56
Rykodisc / May '95 / ADA / Vital

MAN FROM UTOPIA, THE
Cocaine decisions / Dangerous kitchen / Tink walks amok / Radio is broken / Moggio / Man from Utopia meets Mary Lou / Stick together / Sex / Jazz discharge party hats / We are not alone
CD ________ RCD 10538
Rykodisc / May '95 / ADA / Vital

ONE SIZE FITS ALL (Zappa, Frank & The Mothers Of Invention)
Inca roads / Can't afford no shoes / Sofa No. 1 / Po-jama people / Florentine / Pogen / Evelyn, a modified dog / San Ber'dino / Andy / Sofa No. 2
CD ________ RCD 10521
Rykodisc / May '95 / ADA / Vital

ONE SIZE FITS ALL (Au20 Version) (Zappa, Frank & The Mothers Of Invention)
Inca roads / Can't afford no shoes / Sofa No.1 / Po-jama people / Florentine Pogen / Evelyn, a modified dog / San ber'dino / Andy / Sofa No.2
CD ________ RCD 80521
Rykodisc / Jun '96 / ADA / Vital

ORCHESTRAL FAVORITES
Strictly genteel / Pedro's dowry / Naval aviation in art / Duke of prunes / Bogus pomp
CD ________ RCD 10529
Rykodisc / May '95 / ADA / Vital

OVERNITE SENSATION
Camarillo brillo / I'm the slime / Dirty love / 50/50 / Zomby woof / Dinah-Moe Humm / Montana
CD ________ RCD 10518
Rykodisc / Apr '95 / ADA / Vital

PERFECT STRANGER, THE (Boulez Conducts Zappa) (Barking Pumpkin Digital Gratification Consort)
Dupree's paradise: *Ensemble Intercontemporain* / Girl in the magnesium dress / Jonestown / Love story / Naval aviation in art: *Ensemble Intercontemporain* / Outside now, again / Perfect stranger: *Ensemble Intercontemporain*
CD ________ RCD 10542
Rykodisc / May '95 / ADA / Vital

PLAYGROUND PSYCHOTICS (2CD Set) (Zappa, Frank & The Mothers Of Invention)
CD Set ________ RCD 10557/58
Rykodisc / May '95 / ADA / Vital

ROXY AND ELSEWHERE (Zappa, Frank & The Mothers Of Invention)
Preamble / Penguin in bondage / Pygmy twylyte / Dummy up / Village of the sun / Echidna's arf (of you) / Don't you ever wash that thing / Cheepnis / Son of Orange County / More trouble every day / Be bop tango (of the old jazzmen's church)
CD ________ RCD 10520
Rykodisc / May '95 / ADA / Vital

SAARBRUCKEN 1979
Dancin' fool / Easy meat / Honey, don't you want a man like me / Keep it greasy / Village of the sun / Meek shall inherit nothing / City of tiny lights / Pound for a brown / Bobby Brown / Conehead / Flakes / Magic finger / Don't eat the yellow snow / Nanook rubs it / Sain Alphonso's pancake breakfast / Rollo / Bamboozled by love

CD ________ ESMCD 962
Essential/Page One / Aug '91 / BMG

SHEIK YERBOUTI
I have been in you / Flakes / Broken hearts are for assholes / I'm so cute / Jones crusher / Whatever happened to all the fun in the world / Rat tomago / We gotta get into something real / Bobby Brown / Rubber shirt / Sheik Yerbouti tango / Baby snakes / Tryin' to grow a chin / City of tiny lites / Dancin' fool / Jewish princess / Wild love / Yo mama
CD ________ RCD 10528
Rykodisc / May '95 / ADA / Vital

SHIP ARRIVING TOO LATE TO SAVE A DROWNING WITCH
No not now / Valley girl / I come from nowhere / Drowning witch / Envelopes / Teenage prostitute
CD ________ RCD 10537
Rykodisc / May '95 / ADA / Vital

SHUT UP 'N PLAY YER GUITAR (3CD Set)
Five, five, five / Hog Heaven / Shut up 'n' play yer guitar / While you were out / Treacherous cretins / Heavy duty Judy / Soup 'n' old clothes / Variations on the Carlos Santana / Gee I like your pants / Canarsie / Ship ahoy / Deathless horsie / Pink napkins / Beat it with your fist / Return of the son of shut up 'n play / Pinocchio's furniture / Why Johnny can't read / Stucco Homes / Canard du Jour
CD Set ________ RCD 10533/34/35
Rykodisc / May '95 / ADA / Vital

SLEEP DIRT
Filthy habits / Flambay / Spider of destiny / Regyption strut / Time is money / Sleep dirt / Ocean is the ultimate solution
CD ________ RCD 10527
Rykodisc / May '95 / ADA / Vital

STRICTLY COMMERCIAL (The Best Of Frank Zappa)
Peaches en regalia / Don't eat the yellow snow / Dancin' fool / San Ber'dino / Dirty love / My guitar wants to kill your Mother / Cosmik debris / Trouble every day / Disco boy / Fine girl / Sexual harassment in the workplace / Let's make the water turn black / I'm the slime / Joe's garage / Bobby Brown goes down / Montana / Valley girl / Be in my video / Muffin man / Tell me you love me / Planet of the baritone women
CD ________ RCD 40600
Rykodisc / Aug '95 / ADA / Vital

STRICTLY GENTEEL (A Classical Introduction To Frank Zappa)
Uncle meat (main title theme) / Regyptian strut / Pedro's dowry / Outrage at Valdez / Little umbrellas / Run home slow theme / Dwarf nebula processional march and dwarf nebula / Dupree's paradise / Opus 1, No.3, 2nd movement, presto / Duke of prunes / Aybe sea / Naval aviation in art / G spot tornado / Bob in dacron, first movement / Opus 1, no.4, 2nd movement, allegro / Dog breath variations / Uncle meat / Strictly genteel
CD ________ RCD 10578
Rykodisc / May '97 / ADA / Vital

STUDIO TAN
CD ________ RCD 10526
Rykodisc / May '95 / ADA / Vital

THEM OR US
Closer you are / In France / Ya hozna / Sharleena / Sinister footwear II / Truck driver divorce / Stevie's spanking / Baby take your teeth out / Marque - son's chicken / Planet of my dreams / Be in my video / Them or us / Frogs with dirty little lips / Whipping post
CD ________ RCD 10543
Rykodisc / May '95 / ADA / Vital

THING FISH (2CD Set)
Prologue / Mammy nuns / Harry and Rhonda / Galoot up-date / Torchum never stops / That evil prince / You are what you are / Mud club / Meek shall inherit nothing / Clowns on velvet / Harry as a boy / He's so gay / Massive improve'lence / Artificial Rhonda / Crabbgrass baby / White boy troubles / No not now / Brief case boogie / Brown Moses / Wistful wit a fist-full / Drop dead
CD Set ________ RCD 10544/45
Rykodisc / May '95 / ADA / Vital

TINSELTOWN REBELLION
Fine girl / Easy meat / For the young sophisticate / Love of my life / I ain't got no heart / Panty rap / Tell me you love me / Now you see it, now you don't / Dance contest / Blue light / Tinseltown rebellion / Pick me, I'm clean / Bamboozled by love / Brown shoes don't make it / Peaches III
CD ________ RCD 10532
Rykodisc / May '95 / ADA / Vital

TRIBUTE TO THE MUSIC OF FRANK ZAPPA (Various Artists)
CD ________ EFA 034202
Muffin / Jul '95 / SRD

UNCLE MEAT (2CD Set) (Zappa, Frank & The Mothers Of Invention)
CD Set ________ RCD 10506/7
Rykodisc / May '95 / ADA / Vital

WAKA/JAWAKA
Big Swifty / Your mouth / It might just be a one-shot deal / Waka / Jawaka
CD ________ RCD 10516
Rykodisc / May '95 / ADA / Vital

WE'RE ONLY IN IT FOR THE MONEY (Zappa, Frank & The Mothers Of Invention)
Are you hung up / Who needs the peace corps / Concentration moon / Mom and Dad / Bow tie Daddy / Harry, you're a beast / What's the ugliest part of your body / Absolutely free / Flower punk / Hot poop / Nasal retentive caliope music / Mother people
CD ________ RCD 10503
Rykodisc / Apr '95 / ADA / Vital

WEASELS RIPPED MY FLESH (Zappa, Frank & The Mothers Of Invention)
Didja get any onya / Directly from my heart to you / Prelude to the afternoon of a sexually aroused gas mask / Toads of the short forest / Get a little / Eric Dolphy memorial barbecue / Dwarf Nebula processional march / Oh no / Orange county lumber truck / Weasels ripped my flesh / Charles Ives: *Zappa, Frank*
CD ________ RCD 10510
Rykodisc / Feb '96 / ADA / Vital

YELLOW SHARK (Ensemble Modern)
CD ________ RCD 40560
Rykodisc / May '95 / ADA / Vital

YOU ARE WHAT YOU IS
Teenage wind / Harder than your husband / Doreen / Goblin girl / Third movement of sinister footwear, Theme from / Society pages / I'm a beautiful guy / Beauty knows no pain / Charlie's enormous mouth / Any downers / Conehead / You are what you is / Mudd club / Meek shall inherit nothing / Dumb all over / Heavenly bank account / Suicide chump / Jumbo go away / If only she woulda / Drafter again
CD ________ RCD 10536
Rykodisc / May '95 / ADA / Vital

YOU CAN'T DO THAT ON STAGE ANYMORE VOL.1 (2CD Set) (Zappa, Frank & The Mothers Of Invention)
CD Set ________ RCD 10561/62
Rykodisc / Jul '95 / ADA / Vital

YOU CAN'T DO THAT ON STAGE ANYMORE VOL.2 (The Helsinki Tapes/ 2CD Set)
Tush tush tush / Stinkfoot / Inca roads / RDNZL / Village of the sun / Echidna's arf (of you) / Don't you ever wash that thing / Pygmy twylyte / Room service / Idiot bastard son / Cheepnis / Approximate / Dupree's paradise / Satumaa / T'mershi duween / Dog breath variations / Uncle meat / Building a girl / Montana (whipping floss) / Big swifty
CD Set ________ RCD 10563/64
Rykodisc / Jul '95 / ADA / Vital

YOU CAN'T DO THAT ON STAGE ANYMORE VOL.3 (2CD Set)
Sharleena / Bamboozled by love / Lucille has messed my mind up / Advance romance / Bobby Brown / Keep it greasy / Honey, don't you want a man like me / In France / Drowning witch / Ride my face to Chicago / Carol you fool / Chana in the Bushwah / Joe's garage / Why does it hurt when I pee / Dicky's such an asshole / Hands with a hammer / Zoot allures / Society pages / Beautiful guy / Beauty knows no pain / Charlie's enormous mouth / Cocaine decisions / Nigger biznis / King Kong / Cosmik debris
CD Set ________ RCD 10565/66
Rykodisc / Jul '95 / ADA / Vital

YOU CAN'T DO THAT ON STAGE ANYMORE VOL.4 (2CD Set)
Little rubber girl / Stick together / My guitar / Willie the pimp / Montana / Brown Moses / Evil prince / Approximate / Love of my life / Let's move to Cleveland / You call that music / Pound for a brown on the bus / Black page 2 / Take me out to the ball game / Filthy habits / Torture never stops / Church chat / Stevie's spanking / Outside now / Disco boy / Teenage wind / Truck driver divorce / Florentine pogen / Tiny sick tears / Smell my beard / Booger man / Carolina hard-core ecstasy / Are you upset / Little girl of mine / Closer you are / Johnny darling / No no cherry / Man from Utopia meets Mary Lou
CD Set ________ RCD 10567/68
Rykodisc / Jul '95 / ADA / Vital

YOU CAN'T DO THAT ON STAGE ANYMORE VOL.5 (2CD Set)
Downtown talent scout / Charles Ives / Here lies love / Piano and drum duet / Mozart ballet / Chocolate halvah / Jimmy Carl Black and Kansas on the bus 1 / Run home slow / Little march / Right there / Where is Johnny Velvet / Return of the hunchback duke / Trouble every day / Proto-minimalism / Jimmy Carl Black and Kansas on the bus 2 / My head / Meow / Baked bean boogie / Where's our equipment / Drum duet / No waiting for the peanuts to dissolve / Game of cards / Underground freak-out music / German lunch / My guitar wants to kill your mama / East meat / Dead girls of London / Shall we take ourselves seriously / What's new in Baltimore / Moggio / Danc-

ing fool / RDNZL / Advance romance / City of tiny lites / Pound for a brown / Doreen / Black page 2 / Geneva farewell
CD Set RCD 10569/70
Rykodisc / Jul '95 / ADA / Vital

YOU CAN'T DO THAT ON STAGE ANYMORE VOL.6 (2CD Set)
Mothers Of Invention Anti-Smut Loyalty Oath / Poodle lecture / Dirty love / Magic fingers / Madison panty-sniffing festival / Honey, don't you want a man like me / Farther Oblivion / Is that guy kidding or what / I'm so cute / White person / Lonely person devices / Ms. Pinky / Shove it right in / Wind up workin' in a gas station / Make a sex noise / Tracy is a snob / I have been in you / Emperor of Ohio / Dinah-Moe Humm / He's so gay / Camarillo brillo / Muffin man / NYC Halloween audience / Illinois enema bandit / 13 / Lobster girl / Black napkins / We're turning again / Alien orifice / Catholic girls / Crew slut / Tryin' to grow a chin / Take your clothes off when you dance / Lisa's life story / Lonesome Cowboy Nando / 200 Motels finale / Strictly genteel
CD Set RCD 10571/72
Rykodisc / Jul '95 / ADA / Vital

ZAPPA IN NEW YORK
Titties and beer / Cruisin' for burgers / I promise not to come in your mouth / Punky's whips / Honey, don't you want a man like me / Illinois enema bandit / I'm the slime / Pound for a brown / Manx needs women / Black page / Big leg Emma / Sofa no.1 / Black page 2 / Torture never stops / Purple lagoon
CD RCD 10524/25
Rykodisc / May '95 / ADA / Vital

ZAPPA'S UNIVERSE (Various Artists)
CD 5135752
Verve / Apr '93 / PolyGram

ZOOT ALLURES
Wind up workin' in a gas station / Black napkins / Torture never stops / Ms. Pinky / Find her finer / Friendly little finger / Wonderful wino / Zoot allures / Disco boy
CD RCD 10523
Rykodisc / Feb '96 / ADA / Vital

Zarathustra

ZARATHUSTRA
CD SB 029
Second Battle / Jun '97 / Greyhound

Zariz, Jose

EL CONDOR PASA
CD 12411
Laserlight / Jul '95 / Target/BMG

Zawinul, Joe

BEGINNING, THE (Zawinul, Joe Trio)
CD FSRCD 142
Fresh Sound / Dec '90 / Discovery / Jazz Music

BLACK WATER (Zawinul Syndicate)
Carnavalito / Familial / In the same boat / Little rootie tootie / Black water / Medicine man / Monk's mood / They had a dream
CD 4653442
Sony Jazz / Jan '95 / Sony

JOE ZAWINUL & AUSTRIAN ALLSTARS/ SWINGING NEPHEWS 1954-1957
CD RST 91549
RST / Mar '95 / Hot Shot / Jazz Music

MY PEOPLE
Bimoya / Mi Gente / In an island way / Waraya: *Talbot, Mick & Steve White* / Many churches / Midnight rainbow / Sultan / Erdapfee blues / Otzi / Do you want to drink tea, Grandpa / Africama
CD ESC 036512
Escapade / Sep '96 / New Note/Pinnacle

RISE AND FALL OF THE THIRD STREAM/MONEY IN POCKET
Baptismal / Soul of a village (part 1) / Soul of a village (part 2) / Fifth canto / From Vienna with love / Lord, lord, lord / Concerto retitled / Money in the pocket / If / My one and only love / Midnight mood / Some more of dat / Sharon's waltz / Riverbed / Del sasser
CD 8122716752
Atlantic / Jul '94 / Warner Music

STORIES OF THE DANUBE (Czech State Philharmonic Choir/Caspar Richter)
CD 4541432
Philips / Jul '96 / PolyGram

ZAWINUL
Dr. Honoris Causa / In a silent way / His last journey / Double image / Arrival in New York
CD 7567813752
Atlantic / Apr '95 / Warner Music

Zawose, Hukwe

CHIBITE
Sisitizo la amani duniani / Chilumi / Ibarikiwe mungu yupo duniani / Munyamaye / Nyangawuya / Nghanga msakuzi / Jende chiwuyaje kukaya / Sauti za kigogo / Safari na muziki / Twendeni sote na mwanga wa amani
CD CDRW 57
Realworld / Jun '96 / EMI

Zayas, Edwin Colon

Y SU TALLER CAMPESINO BIEN JIBARO
CD ROUCD 5056
Rounder / May '94 / ADA / CM / Direct

Zazou, Hector

GEOGRAPHIES
Cine citta: Gare centrale / Denise a venise / Sidi bel abbes / Vera C / Pali kao / Motel du sud / Sous les bougainvilliers / Des cocotiers
CD MTM 5
Made To Measure / Jun '96 / New Note/ Pinnacle

GEOLOGIES
Peresphone (Nue) / Enoch arden / Livia / Tanis a tunis / Plurabelle / Al sirat / Tout l'ete (Sans Toi) / Peresphone (Suite) / In the box / Deianira (Legato) / Anna / Etudes (Strates) / Brandan
CD MTM 20
Made To Measure / Jun '96 / New Note/ Pinnacle

GUILTY (Zazou, Hector & Bony Bikaye)
Guilty / No secret / Binagwe / Ba wela / Kinshasa / My shoes / Sans musik / It's a man's man's man's world / Zuwa / Na kenda
CD CRAM 062
Crammed Discs / Nov '96 / Grapevine/ PolyGram / New Note/Pinnacle / Prime / RTM/Disc

I'LL STRANGLE YOU (Zazou, Hector & Depardieu)
CD Set CRAM 80
Crammed Discs / Oct '92 / Grapevine/ PolyGram / New Note/Pinnacle / Prime / RTM/Disc

NOIR ET BLANC (Zazou, Hector & Bony Bikaye)
M'pasi ya m'pamba / Mangungu / Dju ya feza / Munipe wa kati / Eh yaye / Mama lenvo / Lamuka / Keba / Woa / M'pasi ya m'pamba / Eh yaye
CD CRAM 2534
Crammed Discs / Nov '96 / Grapevine/ PolyGram / New Note/Pinnacle / Prime / RTM/Disc

REIVAX AU BONGO
Opening theme / In the commandant's office / Crossing the border / Chief bingo's village / Reivax in a black mood / Apparition / Bongolese song / Reivax and his horse pepito / How beautiful bongo is / Hero / Chase / Reivax's theme / By the sea / Pier / Royal bath
CD MTM 2
Made To Measure / Jun '96 / New Note/ Pinnacle

SAHARA BLUE
I'll strangle you / First evening / Ophelie / Lines / Youth / Hapolot kenym / Hunger / Sahara blues (Brussels) / Amdyaz / Black stream / Harar Et Les Gallas / Lettre au directeur des messageries maritimes
CD MTM 32
Made To Measure / Apr '96 / New Note/ Pinnacle

Ze, Tom

BRAZIL CLASSICS VOL.4
Ma / O riso e a faca / Toc / To / Um "oh" e um "ah", ui (voce inventa) / Cademar / So (solidao) / Hein / Augusta / Doi / Complexo de epico / A felicidade / Vai (menina, amanha de manha)
CD 7599263962
Sire / Dec '90 / Warner Music

BRAZIL CLASSICS VOL.5 (The Hips Of Tradition)
Ogodo, ano 2000 / Sem a letra / Fiera de santana / Sofro de juventude / Cortina 1 / Tai / Iracema / Fliperama / O amor e velho-menina / Cortina 2 / Taturamba / Jingle do disco / Lua-gira-sol / Cortina 3 / Multiplicar-se unica / Cortina 4 / O pao nosso de cada mes / Amor
CD 9362451182
Luaka Bop / Feb '93 / Warner Music

Zebra

NO TELLIN' LIES
Wait until the summer's gone / I don't like it / Bears / I don't care / Lullaby / No tellin' lies / Takin' a stance / But no more / Little things / Drive me crazy
CD 7567801592
Atlantic / Jan '96 / Warner Music

Zeigler, Diane

STING OF THE HONEYBEE
CD CDPH 1174
Philo / Apr '95 / ADA / CM / Direct

Zein Musical Party

STYLE OF MOMBASA
Mtindo wa mombasa / Maneno tisiya / Wanawake wa kiamu / Taksim bayati / Baina macho na moyo / Mwiba wa kujitoma / Binti mombasa / Nataka rafiki / Mwana hasahau mana / Taksim jirka
CD CDORBD 066
Globestyle / Nov '90 / Pinnacle

Zeitlin, Denny

CONCORD DUO SERIES VOL.8 (Zeitlin, Denny & David Friesen)
All of you / Echo of a kiss / Night has a thousand eyes / Old folks / Oleo / Turn around / Island / Signs and wonders
CD CCD 4639
Concord Jazz / Apr '95 / New Note/ Pinnacle

IN CONCERT (Zeitlin, Denny & David Friesen)
CD ITM 970068
ITM / Nov '92 / Koch / Tradelink

LIVE AT MAYBECK RECITAL HALL VOL.27
Blues on the side / Girl next door / My man's gone now / Lazy bird / 'Round midnight / Love for sale / And then I wondered if you knew / Country fair / Sophisticated lady / End of a love affair / Just passing by / What is this thing called love / Fifth house
CD CCD 4572
Concord Jazz / Sep '93 / New Note/ Pinnacle

Zeke

FLAT TRACKER
T-5000 / Eddie Hill / Chiva Knievel / Overkill / Mystery chain / Viva agnostic / Hate / Wanna fuck / Fight in the storeroom / Flat truck / Bitch / Daytona / Super six / Eliminator
CD 206162
Epitaph / Jul '97 / Pinnacle / Plastic Head

SUPER SOUND RACING
Slut / Tuned out / Relapse / Chiva / Quicksand / Runnin' shine / Wreckin' machine / Eroded / Holley 750 / Incest / West Seattle acid party / Action / Mainline / 302 cubic inch V-8 / Powered blues / Hemicuda / Maybe someday / Galaxie 500 / Highway star / Schmidt value pack / Rid
CD IFACD 001
IFA / Oct '95 / Plastic Head
CD PO 20CD
Scooch Pooch / Oct '96 / Cargo / Greyhound / Pinnacle
CD 206202
Scooch Pooch / Jul '97 / Cargo / Greyhound / Pinnacle

Zellar, Martin

BORN UNDER
Lie to me / Something's gotta happen / East side boys / Falling sky / Problem solved / Cross my heart / Lay this down gently / Summer kind of sad / Force a smile / Let's go
CD RCD 10318
Rykodisc / Mar '95 / ADA / Vital

MARTIN ZELLAR & THE HARDWAYS (Zellar, Martin & The Hardways)
Haunt my dreams / Ten year coin / Brown-eyed boy / I can't believe / Hammer's gonna fall / George and Tammy / Lullaby / Big sandals / Guilty just the same / We were young
CD RCD 10359
Rykodisc / Aug '96 / ADA / Vital

Zelmani, Sophie

SOPHIE ZELMANI
I'd be broken / Stand by / There must be a reason / So good / Always you / Thousand times / Tell me you're joking / Woman in me / You and him / Until dawn / I'll remember you / I'll see you (In another world)
CD 4809556
Columbia / Jun '96 / Sony

Zelwer

LA FIANCEE AUX YEUX DE BOIS
Foire a kamenka / J'ai vu un ange / Le reve de la fiancee / Les montreurs d'ours sont partis / Grand-pere klonimus / Le soldat tufaiev se marie / Roulette russe / Igor l'innocent mort en poche / Dikanka (le soupirant) / Le tourment de vassilissa la belle / Repose toi un moment
CD MTM 24
Made To Measure / May '96 / New Note/ Pinnacle

Zen Guerrilla

ZEN GUERILLA
CD OPS 8
Compulsive / Mar '93 / SRD

Zen Paradox

CATHARSIS
CD NZCD 051
Nova Zembla / Oct '96 / Plastic Head

FROM THE SHORE OF A DISTANT LAND
CD NZCD 014
Nova Zembla / Oct '94 / Plastic Head

INTO THE ABYSS
CD NZCD 011
Nova Zembla / Jun '94 / Plastic Head

VOYAGE, THE
CD NZCD 041
Nova Zembla / Oct '95 / Plastic Head

Zeni Geva

DESIRE FOR AGONY
CD VIRUS 135CD
Alternative Tentacles / Feb '94 / Cargo / Greyhound / Pinnacle

Zenith Brass Band

ECLIPSE ALLEY
CD AMCD 75
American Music / Aug '94 / Jazz Music

Zenith Hot Stompers

SILVER JUBILEE
CD SOSCD 1191
Stomp Off / Aug '90 / Jazz Music / Wellard

ZENITH HOT STOMPERS PLAYS JELLY ROLL MORTON
CD BCD 012
GHB / Oct '93 / Jazz Music

Zenkl, Radim

GALACTIC MANDOLIN
CD ACD 5
Acoustic Disc / May '97 / ADA / Koch

STRINGS & WINGS
CD SH 5021
Shanachie / May '96 / ADA / Greensleeves / Koch

Zeno

ZENOLOGY
CD A2Z 0023CD
A2Z / Jan '96 / Plastic Head

Zentner, Michael

PRESENT TIME
CD EFA 132472
Ozone / May '94 / Mo's Music Machine / Pinnacle / SRD

Zephaniah, Benjamin

BACK TO ROOTS
CD DUBI 01CD
Acid Jazz / Jun '95 / Disc

BELLY OF THE BEAST
CD ARICD 113
Ariwa Sounds / Jun '96 / Jet Star / SRD

Zephyr

ZEPHYR
CD BGOCD 41
Beat Goes On / '89 / Pinnacle

Zerbe-Blech, Hannez

RANDO A LA FRIED (Zerbe-Blech, Hannez Band)
CD BVHAASTCD 9207
Bvhaast / Mar '86 / Cadillac

Zeros

4-3-2-1
CD LS 92422
Roadrunner / Nov '91 / PolyGram

Zerouki, Charef

GHOZALI - MY GAZELLE
Ma andakiah tgoulili kalma / Al wa'ad arrmani / Al 'achaq / Ghozali / Al 'adra / Yamra
CD CDORB 047
Globestyle / Aug '89 / Pinnacle

Zerra One

DOMINO EFFECT
Rescue me / Domino effect / I know I feel I stand / Hands up / Forever and ever / Cry for you / All forgiven / Guardian angel / Heaven
CD 8300352
Mercury / Jan '87 / PolyGram

Z'Ev

ONE FOOT IN THE GRAVE (1968-1990/ 2CD Set)
CD Set TO 13
Touch / Mar '91 / Kudos / Pinnacle

Zevon, Warren

MUTINEER
CD 74321276852
RCA / Jun '95 / BMG

QUIET NORMAL LIFE, A (The Best Of Warren Zevon)
Werewolves of London / Play it all night long / Roland the headless Thompson gunner / Envoy / Mohammed's radio / Desperados under the eaves / I'll sleep when I'm dead / Lawyers, guns and money / Ain't that pretty at all / Poor, poor pitiful me / Accidentally like a martyr / Looking for the next best thing

CD 9605032
Asylum / Nov '86 / Warner Music

SENTIMENTAL HYGIENE
Sentimental hygiene / Boom boom Mancini / Factory / Trouble waiting to happen / Reconsider me / Detox mansion / Bad karma / Even a dog can shake hands / Heartache / Leave my monkey alone
CD CDV 2433
Virgin / Jul '93 / EMI

TRANSVERSE CITY
Transverse city / Run straight down / Long arm of the law / Turbulence / They moved the moon / Splendid isolation / Networking / Gridlock / Down in the mall / Nobody's in love this year
CD CDVUS 9
Virgin / Jan '90 / EMI

ZGA

END OF AN EPOCH
CD RERZGACD 2
ReR/Recommended / Oct '96 / ReR Megacorp / RTM/Disc

ZGAMONIUMS
CD RERZGACD
ReR/Recommended / Jan '93 / ReR Megacorp / RTM/Disc

Zhane

PRONOUNCED JAH-NAY
CD 5302832
Motown / Mar '94 / PolyGram

SATURDAY NITE
CD 5307512
CD 5305882
Motown / May '97 / PolyGram

Zhihou, Hu

MUSIC OF THE GUANZI
CD VICG 52602
JVC World Library / Mar '96 / ADA / CM / Direct

Ziegler, Anne

ANNE ZIEGLER AND WEBSTER BOOTH (Ziegler, Anne & Webster Booth)
Song of paradise / Only a rose / Paradise for two / Will you remember / Wanting you / Deep in my heart dear / Someday my heart will awake / Swing high swing low / Ah sweet mystery of life / Love steals your heart / Fruits of the Earth / Trot here trot there / I'll see you again / You just you / Fold your wings / Lift up your hearts / Dearest of all / Lover come back to me / Indian love call / Such lovely things / Gates of paradise / Throw open wide your window / Love's garden of roses / Love's last word is spoken / Hear my song, Violetta
CD CDMFP 6353
Music For Pleasure / Jun '97 / EMI

LOVE'S OLD SWEET SONG (Ziegler, Anne & Webster Booth)
CD PASTCD 7034
Flapper / Aug '94 / Pinnacle

Ziegler, Finn

ANDERSEN, NIELSEN OG DEN UKENDTE
CD MECCACD 1044
Music Mecca / Nov '94 / Cadillac / Jazz Music / Wellard

Zig Zag

ZIG ZAG'S FAMILY FUN ALBUM (Memorable Tunes For Everyone)
CD DUOCD 89025
Meridian / Dec '93 / Nimbus

Zil

ZIL
CD 8419292
Polydor / Aug '90 / PolyGram

Zimmermann, Tabea

CREAM OF VICTOR SYLVESTER, THE (Zimmermann, Tabea & Thomas Zehetmair)
You're dancing on my heart / Give a little whistle / So deep is the nght / I shall be waiting / Love bells / Fragrant flowers / It's a hap-hap-happy day / When you wish upon a star / I'm in love for the last time / Love everlasting / Blue orchids / Mist is over the moon / If I were sure of you / In the middle of a dream / Lonely sweetheart / Love never grows old / Little rain must fall / Summer sweetheart / Summer evening in Santa Cruz / Dear Madam / Where of when / Don't say goodbye
CD PASTCD 9786
Flapper / Apr '92 / Pinnacle

Zineladbidine, Mohamed

OUD
CD AAA 137
Club Du Disque Arabe / Nov '96 / ADA / Harmonia Mundi

Zinn, Rusty

SITTIN' AND WAITIN'
CD CDBT 1134
Black Top / Jul '96 / ADA / CM / Direct

Zion Harmonizers

NEVER ALONE
CD FA 411
Fremeaux / Jul '96 / ADA / Discovery

Zion Train

GREAT SPORTING MOMENTS IN DUB
CD WWCD 3
Wibbly Wobbly / Dec '93 / SRD

GROW TOGETHER
Seed / Space / La madrugada / Procession / Rise / Grow together / Babylon's burning / Stand up and fight / Harvest / Tubby's garden / Dutch flowers / Peace / Roots pt.1
CD WOLCD 1071
CD WOLCD 1071N
China / Jul '96 / Pinnacle

HOMEGROWN FANTASY
Dance of life / Free the bass / Healing of the nation / Universal communication / Venceremos / Get ready / For the revolution / Why should we have to fight / Live good (IV) / Better day / Love the earth / One world, one heart / One conscience
CD WOLCD 1060
China / Jun '95 / Pinnacle

NATURAL WONDERS OF THE WORLD IN DUB
CD WOLCD 1055
China / Jan '95 / Pinnacle

PASSAGE TO INDICA
CD WOLCD 1054
China / Jan '95 / Pinnacle

SINGLE MINDED/ALIVE (2CD Set)
Get ready/We got to be together / Power One / Zimbabwe / Power Two / Legalise it (all around the world) / Dutch flowers/Need more love / Universal communication / Dance of life / Do anything you want to do / La Madrugada / Rise/Exodus / Follow like wolves / Fuck the Nazis / Babylons burning / Dance of life / Babylons burning / Do anything you want to do / Healing of the nation / Follow like wolves / Hovercraft / Rise / Stand up and fight / Get ready / Procession
CD Set WOLCD 1073
China / Jun '97 / Pinnacle

SIREN
CD WOLCD 1056
China / Jan '95 / Pinnacle

Zion Travellers

DOOTONE MASTERS, THE
Bye and bye / Down by the river / Packing up / Every time I feel the spirit / I dreamed of a city / Jesus said / I want to go to Heaven and rest / Blood / I must tell Jesus / God I'll live / Even me / I've started / Two little fishes / Death of Jesus / Close to thee / Soldier of the cross / Since he lightened my heavy load / I won't have to cross Jordan alone / Just a little talk with Jesus / Lord hold my hand / Bless me / I'm gonna wait on Jesus / You gotta reap what you so / I got to move / Lord I'll go
CD CDCHD 637
Ace / Aug '96 / Pinnacle

Zior

ZIOR...PLUS
I really do / Za za za Zilda / Love's desire / New land / Now I'm sad / Give me love / Quabala / Oh Mariya / Your life will burn / I was fooling / Before my eyes go blind / Rolling thunder / Dudi Judy / Evolution / Cat's eyes / Strange kind of magic / Ride me baby / Entrance of the devil (the Chicago spine) / Every inch a man / Angel of the highway
CD SEECD 276
See For Miles/C5 / Oct '89 / Pinnacle

Zip

GETTIN' X-PERIMENTAL
CD 5294662
Verve / Feb '97 / PolyGram

Zipci, Ferdi

NAZOUNI
CD 087942
Fresh Sound / Nov '96 / Discovery / Jazz Music

Zipoli, Domenico

MUSICA SAGRADA DE LOS MISIONES
CD 74321476182
Jade / Jun '97 / Conifer/BMG

Zipper Spy

WATCH YOUR DAMAGE
CD VC 114
Vinyl Communication / Jun '97 / Cargo / Greyhound / Plastic Head

Ziryab Trio

MASHREQ CLASSICS
Longa riad / Sihr al-sharq / Chutwat habibi / Tawsim qanoun in homayun mode / Sama'i shat araban / Zikrayati / Sama'i nahawand / Riqq solo / Sama'i farahfaza / Suzinak sakiz kasap oyun havasi
CD CRAW 18
Cramworld / Jan '97 / New Note/Pinnacle

Zitro, James

JAMES ZITRO
CD ESP 10522
ESP / Jan '93 / Jazz Music

Zlatne Uste Blakan Brass Band

NO STRINGS ATTACHED
CD ROUCD 6054
Rounder / Aug '93 / ADA / CM / Direct

Znowhite

ACT OF GOD
Last breath / Baptised by fire / Pure blood / Thunderdome / War machine / Disease bigotry / Something wicked / Rest in peace / Soldier's greed
CD RR 95872
Roadrunner / May '88 / PolyGram

ZNR

BARRICADE 3
CD RERZNR 1
ReR/Recommended / Oct '96 / ReR Megacorp / RTM/Disc

Zodiac Mindwarp

HOODLUM THUNDER (Zodiac Mindwarp & The Love Reaction)
CD 108642
Musidisc / Jan '92 / Discovery

MY LIFE STORY
CD 109832
Musidisc / Nov '92 / Discovery

Zodiac Youth

DEVIL'S CIRCUS
CD BFLCD 25
Dragonfly / Aug '97 / Mo's Music Machine / Pinnacle

Zoe

HAMMER
CD WIRED 225
Wired / Jun '96 / 3mv/Sony / Mo's Music Machine / Prime

Zoic

TOTAL LEVEL OF DESTRUCTION
CD PLRCD 001
Powerline / Nov '96 / Plastic Head

Zoinks

PANORAMA
CD DSR 61CD
Dr. Strange / Jun '97 / Cargo / Greyhound / Plastic Head

Zoller, Attila

WHEN IT'S TIME
Joy for hoy / Lu and Shu / After the morning / Song is you / When it's time / Homage to OP / Voyage / Meant to be
CD ENJ 90312
Enja / Aug '95 / New Note/Pinnacle / Vital/SAM

Zombies

BEST OF THE ZOMBIES, THE
She's not there / Time of the season / I must move / I got my mojo working / I remember how I loved her / Summertime / What more can I do / Can't nobody love you / Can't make up my mind / Tell her no / I don't want to know / I love you / You really got a hold on me / Whenever you're ready / You make me feel good / Roadrunner
CD MCCD 002
Music Club / Feb '91 / Disc / THE

COLLECTION, THE
Goin' out of my head / Leave me be / Gotta get a hold on myself / I can't make up my mind / Kind of girl / Sticks and stones / Summertime / Woman / I got my mojo working / Roadrunner / You really got a hold on me / Nothing's changed / You make me feel good / She's not there / Don't go away / How we were before / Tell her no / Whenever you're ready / Just out of reach / Remember you / Indication / She does everything for me / Time of the season / I love you
CD CCSCD 196
Castle / Aug '88 / BMG

SINGLES A'S AND B'S
She's not there / Leave me be / Tell her no / She's coming home / I want her back / Whenever you're ready / Is this the dream / Remember you / Indication / Gotta get a hold on myself / Goin' out of my head / You make me feel good / Woman / What more can I do / I must move / I remember when I loved her / I love you / Don't go away / Just out of reach / How we were before / Way I feel inside / She does everything for me
CD SEECD 30
See For Miles/C5 / Apr '97 / Pinnacle

ZOMBIES 1964-1967, THE
She's not there / Rose for Emily / I can't make up my mind / You make me feel good / Tell her no / Kind of girl / Leave me be / Sometimes / It's all right with me / I don't want to know / I love you / Indication / Nothing's changes / Hung up on a dream / Whenever you're ready / Hold your head up: *Argent, Rod* / She's not there (live): *Argent, Rod* / Time of the season (Live): *Argent, Rod* / I'm in the mood: *Argent, Rod*
CD MOCD 3009
More Music / Feb '95 / Sound & Media

Zone

BORN OF FIRE
CD ZONECD 3
Zone / Oct '96 / World Serpent

DIVINE SIMPLICITY, THE
CD ZONECD 4
Zone / Oct '96 / World Serpent

Zoo

ZOO PRESENTS CHOCOLATE MOOSE, THE
Chocolate moose / Written on the wind / I've been waiting too long / Soul drippin's / Get some beads / Ain't nobody / Try me / Love machine / Have you been sleepin' / From a camel's hump
CD CDWIKM 123
Big Beat / Oct '93 / Pinnacle

Zoo

SHAKIN' THE CAGE
CD 9362420042
WEA / Jun '92 / Warner Music

Zoogz Rift

MURDERING HELL'S HAPPY CRETINS
CD SST 21CD
SST / Feb '89 / Plastic Head

NONENTITY WATER 3 (FAN BLACK DADA)
CD SST 184CD
SST / May '93 / Plastic Head

TORMENT
CD SST 251CD
SST / May '93 / Plastic Head

VILLAGERS
CD EFA 11372 CD
Musical Tragedies / May '93 / SRD

WATER : AT A SAFE DISTANCE
CD SST 137CD
SST / May '93 / Plastic Head

Zoom

HELIUM OCTIPEDE
Balboa's kitchen / Can fighting / Five fingers and a thumb / Ephedrine breakfast / Extrano / Letter from Allan / Bottle king / Mynr / Cycle of fifths
CD TK 93CD053
T/K / Aug '94 / Pinnacle

Zoom

BIG DADDY
CD APCD 112
Appaloosa / Sep '96 / ADA / Direct / TKO Magnum

Zorn, John

COBRA (2CD Set)
CD Set ARTCD 26040
Hat Art / '91 / Cadillac / Harmonia Mundi

DURAS: DUCHAMP
CD TZA 7023
Tzadik / Jul '97 / Cargo

FILM MUSIC VOL.7 (Cynical Hysterie Hour)
CD TZA 7315
Tzadik / Jul '97 / Cargo

FILM WORKS 1986-1990
CD 7559792702
Nonesuch / Jan '95 / Warner Music
CD TZA 7314
Tzadik / Jul '97 / Cargo

HARRAS (Zorn, John & Derek Bailey/ William Parker)
CD AVAN 056
Avant / Jan '96 / Cadillac / Harmonia Mundi

IN MEMORY OF NIKKI ARANE (Zorn, John & Eugene Chadbourne)
CD INCUSCD 23
Incus / Jan '97 / Cadillac / Cargo

JOHN ZORN'S COBRA LIVE AT THE KNITTING FACTORY
CD KFWCD 124
Knitting Factory / Feb '95 / Cargo / Plastic Head

MASADA VOL.1
CD DIW 888
DIW / Mar '95 / Cadillac / Harmonia Mundi

MASADA VOL.4
CD DIW 923
DIW / Feb '97 / Cadillac / Harmonia Mundi

MASADA VOL.5
CD DIW 899
DIW / Dec '95 / Cadillac / Harmonia Mundi

MASADA VOL.6
CD DIW 900
DIW / Feb '96 / Cadillac / Harmonia Mundi

MASADA VOL.7
CD DIW 915
DIW / Dec '96 / Cadillac / Harmonia Mundi

MORE NEWS FOR LULU (Zorn, John/ Bill Frisell/George Lewis)
CD ARTCD 6055
Hat Art / Feb '92 / Cadillac / Harmonia Mundi

NAKED CITY
CD 7559792382
Nonesuch / Jan '94 / Warner Music

NEWS FOR LULU (Zorn, John/Bill Frisell/George Lewis)
CD ARTCD 6005
Hat Art / Jul '88 / Cadillac / Harmonia Mundi

SPILLANE
CD 9791722
Nonesuch / Mar '88 / Warner Music

SPY VS. SPY (The Music Of Ornette Coleman)
CD 9608442
Nonesuch / Aug '89 / Warner Music

TOKYO OPERATIONS 1994
CD AVAN 049
Avant / Feb '96 / Cadillac / Harmonia Mundi

TORTURE GARDEN (Zorn, John & Naked City)
CD MOSH 028CD
Earache / Sep '90 / Vital

Zounds

CURSE OF ZOUNDS
Fear / Did he jump / My Mummy's gone / Little bit more / This land / New band / Dirty squatters / Loads of noise / Target / Mr. Disney / War goes on / Can't cheat karma / War / Subvert / Demystification / Great white hunter / Dancing / True love / More trouble coming every day / Knife / Not me / Biafra / Wolves
CD SEEP 006
Rugger Bugger / Jan '94 / Shellshock/Disc

Zubiria, Amaia

TASOGARE (2CD Set) (Zubiria, Amaia & Pascal Gaigne)
CD Set BELLE 96284
Belle Antique / Jun '97 / ReR Megacorp

Zubop

CYCLE CITY
CD 33JAZZ 006CD
33 Jazz / Jun '93 / Cadillac / New Note/ Pinnacle

FREEWHEELING
CD 33JAZZ 015CD
33 Jazz / Oct '94 / Cadillac / New Note/ Pinnacle

Zucchero

BEST OF ZUCCHERO, THE
CD 5338222
Polydor / Jun '97 / PolyGram

MISERERE
CD 5170972
London / Jan '93 / PolyGram

SPIRITO DI VINO
CD 5277852
London / Aug '95 / PolyGram

ZUCCHERO
Diamante / Wonderful world: *Zucchero & Eric Clapton* / Il mare / Mama / Dunes of mercy / Senza una Donna: *Zucchero & Paul Young* / You're losing me / Solo una sana / You've chosen me / Diavolo in me / Overdose (d'amore) / Nice (nietzsche) che dice
CD 8490632
London / May '91 / PolyGram

Zugasti, Olatz

KANTU BATEN BILA NABIL
CD KDCD 270
Elkar / May '97 / ADA

Zulema

BEST OF ZULEMA, THE (The RCA Years)
CD SCL 21152
Ichiban Soul Classics / Jun '96 / Koch

Zulu, Philomon

HOW LONG
CD SHCD 434048
Shanachie / Apr '92 / ADA / Greensleeves / Koch

Zulutronic

MISSION ZULU ONE
CD PHARMA 10CD
Pharma / Apr '97 / Arabesque / Plastic Head / SRD

Zumaque, Francisco

BAILA CARIBE BAILA
Chucu chucu / Cando / Salvaje amor / Sera / adios amour / Colombia caribe / Dorotea / Fantasia caribe / Macumbia
CD 68947
Tropical / Apr '97 / Discovery

RITUALES - AFROAMERINDIAN SUITE
CD 68967
Tropical / Apr '97 / Discovery

VOCES CARIBES
Cuentero / Enganadora / Cafe / Con amor / La danza / Falta tiempo / New morning / Baila caribe / Arde roma / Paginas de mujer / Balas
CD 68960
Tropical / Apr '97 / Discovery

VOICES CARIBES (Zumaque, Francisco, & Super Macumbia)
CD SH 64051
Shanachie / Dec '94 / ADA / Greensleeves / Koch

Zumi-Kai

KOTO MUSIC OF JAPAN
CD 12184
Laserlight / Aug '95 / Target/BMG

Zumpano

GOIN' THROUGH CHANGES
CD SPCD 372
Sub Pop / Sep '96 / Cargo / Greyhound / Shellshock/Disc

LOOK WHAT THE ROOKIE DID
CD SPCD 140344
Sub Pop / Jan '95 / Cargo / Greyhound / Shellshock/Disc

Zumzeaux

BLAZING FIDDLES
CD PUG 010CD
Black Pig / Mar '96 / ADA / Direct / Roots

Zunomen

PEOPLE
CD CP 03
Coop / Feb '97 / Cargo

Zuvuya

SHAMANIA (Zuvuya & Terence McKenna)
Shaman I am / FX return / Black sun yadaki / Whisper in trees / Into the future / Shamania
CD DELECCD 021
Delerium / Sep '94 / Cargo / Pinnacle / Vital

Zydeco Travelers

Z-FUNK
H-Town zydeco / We will never know / Baby let me kiss you / Bad time woman / Z-Funk / Packin' up / I don't know why / Back up and try it again / Tang the hump / Keeping me out of the storm / You got me crying / Sunday walk / Back up and try it again
CD ROUCD 2146
Rounder / Feb '97 / ADA / CM / Direct

Zydecomotion

ARE YOU READY FOR THIS
Bernadette / Dangerous man / Why you want to leave me / Joli blond / Are you ready for this / No sad songs / Rainbow / Zydecomotion theme / I done got over it / I'm a farmer / You worry me / Everybody knows / Everybody knows / Why you want to leave me
CD CDBCAT 06
Bearcat / Nov '96 / ADA / Direct

Zyklon B

ZYKLON B
CD MR 005CD
Malicious / Nov '95 / Plastic Head

Zyklus

VIRTUAL REALITIES
CD AMPCD 017
AMP / Feb '95 / Cadillac / Discovery / TKO Magnum

ZZ Top

AFTERBURNER
Sleeping bag / Stages / Woke up with wood / Rough boy / Can't stop rockin' / Planet of women / I got the message / Velcro fly / Dipping low / Delirious
CD 9253422
WEA / Mar '94 / Warner Music

ANTENNA
Pincushion / PCH / Breakaway / Lizard life / Cover your rig / Antenna head / Fuzzbox voodoo / World of swirl / T-shirt / Deal goin' down / Cherry red / Everything
CD 74321182602
RCA / Jan '94 / BMG

DEGUELLO
I thank you / She loves my automobile / I'm bad I'm nationwide / Fool for your stockings / Manic mechanic / Dust my broom / Low-down in the street / Hi-fi mama / Cheap sunglasses / Esther be the one
CD K 256701
WEA / Mar '94 / Warner Music

ELIMINATOR
Gimme all your lovin' / Got me under pressure / Sharp dressed man / I need you tonight / I got the six / Legs / Thug / TV dinners / Dirty dog / If I could only flag her down / Bad girl
CD W 37742
WEA / Mar '94 / Warner Music

FANDANGO
Thunderbird / Jailhouse rock / Backdoor medley / Backdoor love affair / Mellow down easy / Backdoor love affair no.2 / Long distance boogie / Nasty dogs and funky kings / Blue jean blues / Balinese / Mexican blackbird / Heard it on the X / Tush
CD K 256604
WEA / Mar '94 / Warner Music

GREATEST HITS
Gimme all your lovin' / Sharp dressed man / Rough boy / Tush / My head's in Mississippi / Viva Las Vegas / Legs / Doubleback / Gun love / Got me under pressure / Give it up / Sleeping bag / La grange / Tube snake boogie
CD 7599268462
WEA / Apr '92 / Warner Music

ONE FOOT IN THE BLUES
CD 9362458152
WEA / Nov '94 / Warner Music

RECYCLER
Concrete and steel / Love thing / Penthouse eyes / Tell it / My head's in Mississippi / Decision or collision / Give it up / 2000 blues / Burger man / Doubleback
CD 7599262652
WEA / Mar '94 / Warner Music

RHYTHMEEN
Rhythmeen / Bang band / Black fly / What's up with that / Vincent Price blues / Zipper job / Hairdresser / She's just killing me / My mind is gone / Loaded / Prettyhead / Hummbucking part 2
CD 74321394662
RCA / Sep '96 / BMG

RIO GRANDE MUD
Francine / Just got paid / Mushmouth shoutin' / Koko blue / Chevrolet / Apologies to pearly / Bar B Q / Sure got cold after the rain fell / Whisky 'n' mama / Down brownie
CD 7599273802
WEA / Mar '94 / Warner Music

RIO GRANDE MUD/TRES HOMBRES/ FANDANGO/TEJAS/EL LOCO/FIRST LP (ZZ Top's Sixpack/3CD Set)
(Somebody else been) shaking your tree / Brown sugar / Squank / Goin' down to Mexico / Old man / Neighbour, neighbour / Certified blues / Bedroom thang / Just got back from baby's / Backdoor love affair / Francine / Just got paid / Mushmouth shoutin' / Koko blue / Chevrolet / Apologies to Pearly / Bar B Q / Sure got cold after the rain fell / Whisky 'n' mama / Down brownie / Waitin' for the bus / Jesus just left Chicago / Beer drinkers and hell raisers / Master of sparks / Hot, blue and righteous / Move me on down the line / Precious and grace / La grange / Sheik / Have you heard / Thunderbird / Jailhouse rock / Mellow down easy / Back door love affair No.2 / Long distance boogie / Nasty dogs and funky kings / Blue jean blues / Balinese / Mexican blackbird / Heard it on the X / Tush / It's only love / Arrested for driving while blind / El diablo / Snappy kakkie / Enjoy and get it on / Ten dollar man / Pan am highway blues / Avalon hideaway / She's a heartbreaker / Asleep in the desert / Tube snake boogie / I wanna drive you home / Ten foot pole / Leila / Don't tease me / It's so hard / Pearl necklace / Groovy little hippy pad / Heaven, hell or Houston / Party on the patio
CD Set 9256612
WEA / Dec '87 / Warner Music

TEJAS
It's only love / Arrested for driving while blind / El diablo / Snappy kakkie / Enjoy and get it on / Ten dollar man / Pan Am highway blues / Avalon hideaway / She's a heartbreaker / Asleep in the desert
CD 7599273832
WEA / Mar '94 / Warner Music

TRES HOMBRES
Waitin' for the bus / Jesus just left Chicago / Beer drinkers and hell raisers / Master of sparks / Hot, blue and righteous / Move me on down the line / Precious and grace / La grange / Sheik / Have you heard
CD K 256603
WEA / Mar '94 / Warner Music

ZZ TOP'S FIRST ALBUM
(Somebody else been) shaking your tree / Brown sugar / Squank / Goin' down to Mexico / Old man / Neighbour, neighbour / Certified blues / Bedroom thang / Just got back from my baby's / Backdoor love affair
CD K 256601
WEA / Mar '94 / Warner Music

Compilations

1 IN THE JUNGLE (2CD Set)
Warning: *DJ Stretch* / Mash up yer know: *Aladdin* / Valley of the shadows: *Origin Unknown* / Feel: *Guyver* / Summer someting: *Rude Bwoy Monty* / R-Type: *Jo* / Funkula: *B-Jam* / Who runs tings: *Shy FX & David Leboom* / Living in darkness: *Top Buzz* / DNA: *DNA* / Set speed: *DJ Krust* / Music box: *Roni Size & DJ Die* / I like it: *Da Intalex* / Cold mission: *Dreamers* / London sometin': *Tek 9* / Roughest: *DJ Rap* / Chopsticks: *Special K & Roughcut* / Spiritual aura: *Engineers Without Fears* / Angel fell: *Dillinja* / Follow me: *Dillinja* / Here comes the drums: *DJ Doc Scott*
CD Set ______ **CDTAKE 1**
Take One / Jan '96 / SRD

1-800 NEW FUNK
Minneapolis: *MPLS* / Hollywood: *Clinton, George* / Love sign: *Gaye, Nona & Prince* / If I love U 2 nite: *Mayte* / Colour: *Steeles* / 2gether: *New Power Generation* / Standing at the altar: *Cox, Margie* / You will be moved: *Staples, Mavis* / Seventeen: *Madhouse* / Woman's gotta have it: *Gaye, Nona* / Minneapolis reprise: *MPLS*
CD ______ **NPG 60512**
New Power Generation / Aug '94 / EMI

3 BEAT HIGH & RISING
CD ______ **3BTTCD 1**
3 Beat / Jun '93 / PolyGram

3 MINUTE BLUNTS VOL.1 (The Sound Of Detroit Instrumental Hip Hop)
Home coming: *Parker, Terence* / Flexin': *AW* / Woodward avenue: *Kanabis The Edit Assassin* / Act a fool: *Madd Phlavor* / Crystal funk: *Kanabis The Edit Assassin* / Whodunnit: *Papa Willie* / Walk under a full moon's light: *Kanabis The Edit Assassin* / Too damn cool: *Johnson, Andre Project* / Soul searchin': *Kanabis The Edit Assassin* / Outland: *DJ Slym Fas* / Daze of native noise: *Kanabis The Edit Assassin* / Play time's over: *AW* / Unique: *Johnson, Andre Project* / Make it real: *DJ Slym Fas* / Reunion in Tennesse: *Kanabis The Edit Assassin* / Fun at the Belle Isle zoo: *DJ Slym Fas* / Romancing da drum: *Parker, Terence*
CD ______ **K7 052CD**
Studio K7 / Jan '97 / Prime / RTM/Disc

3 VOCAL GREATS OF THE 50'S (Lita Roza/Petula Clark/Marion Ryan) (3CD Set)
That's the beginning of the end: *Roza, Lita* / I've got my eyes on you: *Roza, Lita* / Oh dear what can the matter be: *Roza, Lita* / I'll never say Never Again again: *Rosa, Lita* / End of a love affair: *Rosa, Lita* / Not mine: *Rosa, Lita* / As children do: *Rosa, Lita* / There's nothing rougher than love: *Rosa, Lita* / Somewhere, somehow, someday: *Rosa, Lita* / Allentown jail: *Rosa, Lita* / Once in a while: *Rosa, Lita* / Nel blu dipinto di blu: *Rosa, Lita* / This is my town: *Rosa, Lita* / Maybe you'll be there: *Rosa, Lita* / Sorry, sorry, sorry: *Roza, Lita* / I could have danced all night: *Roza, Lita* / All alone (by a telephone): *Roza, Lita* / Other woman: *Roza, Lita* / Love can change the stars: *Roza, Lita* / I Yi Yi Yi: *Clark, Petula* / You are my lucky star: *Clark, Petula* / Afraid to dream: *Clark, Petula* / It's the natural thing to do: *Clark, Petula* / As tiem goes by: *Clark, Petula* / Slumming on Park Avenue: *Clark, Petula* / I wish I knew: *Clark, Petula* / Goodnight my love: *Clark, Petula* / Alone: *Clark, Petula* / Zing went the strings of my heart: *Clark, Petula* / Sonny boy: *Clark, Petula* / Love me forever: *Ryan, Marion* / Stairway of love: *Ryan, Marion* / Hit the road to dreamland: *Ryan, Marion* / Jeepers creepers: *Ryan, Marion* / Mr. Wonderful: *Ryan, Marion* / I'm beginning to see the light: *Ryan, Marion* / Cry me a river: *Ryan, Marion* / That's happiness: *Ryan, Marion* / There will never be another you: *Ryan, Marion* / Oh oh, I'm falling in love again: *Ryan, Marion* / I'll take romance: *Ryan, Marion* / World goes round and round: *Ryan, Marion* / If I can't take it with me: *Ryan, Marion* / My heart belongs to Daddy: *Ryan, Marion* / It might as well be spring: *Ryan, Marion* / I need you: *Ryan, Marion* / Make the man love me: *Ryan, Marion* / Always and forever: *Ryan, Marion* / High life: *Ryan, Marion* / Why do fools fall in love: *Ryan, Marion* / Wait for me: *Ryan, Marion* / Hot diggity (dog diggity boom): *Ryan, Marion* / Chantez chantez: *Ryan, Marion* / Please don't say goodnight: *Ryan, Marion* / Sailor boy: *Ryan, Marion*
CD Set ______ **MAGPIE 7**
See For Miles/C5 / Sep '95 / Pinnacle

3D COMPILATION, THE
CD ______ **TIPCD 12**
Tip / May '97 / Arabesque / Mo's Music Machine / Pinnacle / Prime

3RD CYCLOPS SAMPLER
CD ______ **CYCL 046**
Cyclops / Jan '97 / Pinnacle

3RD ST. PATRICK'S DAY FESTIVAL
CD ______ **MAG 201**
Magnetic / Mar '95 / TKO Magnum

4 BEAT (The New Happy Hardcore Phenomena)
Unity: *Jack 'n' Phil* / Seventh way: *Beatmen* / 7th Heaven: *Fast Floor* / Stomper: *Format* / Everybody can be: *Higher Level* / Emotions: *Sy Project* / Spiced up: *Frantic & Impulse* / Fantasy wonderland: *Wendy* / It's all over: *Motiv 8* / Baby baby: *Pooch & Hurse* / Peaked up: *S&A* / Higher spirits: *Higher Level*
CD ______ **CDTOT 32**
Jumpin' & Pumpin' / Sep '95 / 3mv/Sony / Mo's Music Machine

4 ON 1
CD ______ **DBMTRCD 19**
Rogue Trooper / Sep '95 / Alphamagic / SRD

4-2-4 (The El Football Scrapbook)
Nice one Cyril / I'm forever blowing bubbles / Onward Sexton soldiers / Canaries / Football football / World Cup Willie / Good old Arsenal / Back home / We are Wimbledon / Belfast boy / We are the owls / Hibernian / Going back to Derby / Boys in blue / Viva el Fulham / Sunderland
CD ______ **MONDE 15CD**
Cherry Red / Aug '93 / Pinnacle

4TH ANNUAL FLAMENCO COMPETITION OF NIMES
CD ______ **172592**
Musidisc / Jan '97 / Discovery

4TH PARIS GOSPEL FESTIVAL
CD ______ **FA 422**
Fremeaux / Jun '97 / ADA / Discovery

4TH PARIS GOSPEL FESTIVAL (2CD Set)
CD Set ______ **FA 421**
Fremeaux / Jun '97 / ADA / Discovery

5 YEARS OF NUCLEAR BLAST
CD ______ **NB 083CD**
Nuclear Blast / Dec '93 / Plastic Head

5TH ST.PATRICK'S DAY FESTIVAL
In these fields / Matt peoples / Used to / Donegal lass / Flower of Magherally / Paddy's in Japan / Newry highwayman / Terry Crehan's / Hard times / Dezi's tune / Kid on the mountain / Rocky road to dublin / B'fheidir / Four ages of man / Leslie's tune / Saratoga set / While they're all talking / Guns of the magnificent seven set / Kerry polkas / Rocks of bawn / Mountain road reels
CD ______ **MAG 601**
Magnetic / Mar '95 / TKO Magnum

7 HILLS CLASH (Deeper Signals)
What you want: *Bouncing Bomb* / Evil star: *Tocsin* / Medium: *Celsius* / 15 inches plus: *Wad* / Lethargy/Apathy: *Tonka Toi* / Chickenfoot: *Obeah* / Giant: *I Monster* / Where's the love: *Screwface* / Welfare: *Extra Breaks* / Moonstomp: *Mig* / Fashioned by convenience: *Fashioned For Convenience* / Rude: *Rude*
CD ______ **DRC 1**
Break Butt / Jun '97 / Kudos / Pinnacle

7" WONDERS OF THE WORLD
CD ______ **SST 070CD**
SST / May '93 / Plastic Head

10 GLAM STARS VOL.1
CD ______ **STACD 077**
Wisepack / Nov '93 / Conifer/BMG / THE

10 GLAM STARS VOL.2
CD ______ **STACD 078**
Wisepack / Nov '93 / Conifer/BMG / THE

10 HIT STARS VOL.1
CD ______ **STACD 071**
Wisepack / Nov '93 / Conifer/BMG / THE

10 HIT STARS VOL.2
CD ______ **STACD 072**
Wisepack / Nov '93 / Conifer/BMG / THE

10 HIT STARS VOL.3
CD ______ **STACD 073**
Wisepack / Nov '93 / Conifer/BMG / THE

10 HIT STARS VOL.4
Walking on sunshine: *Katrina & The Waves* / Sun street: *Katrina & The Waves* / Living in a box: *Living In A Box* / Room in your heart: *Living In A Box* / Too shy: *Kajagoogoo* / Big apple: *Kajagoogoo* / Cap in hand: *Proclaimers* / Letter from America: *Proclaimers* / If this is it: *Lewis, Huey & The News* / Stuck with you: *Lewis, Huey & The News* / Smile: *Pussycat* / Mississippi: *Pussycat* / Turning Japanese: *Vapors* / News at ten: *Vapors* / Fade to grey: *Visage* / Mind of a toy: *Visage* / Living on the ceiling: *Blancmange* / Day before you came: *Blancmange* / Stand up for your love rights: *Yazz* / Fine time: *Yazz*
CD ______ **STACD 074**
Wisepack / Nov '93 / Conifer/BMG / THE

10 LOVE STARS VOL.1
CD ______ **STACD 059**
Wisepack / Nov '93 / Conifer/BMG / THE

10 LOVE STARS VOL.2
CD ______ **STACD 060**
Wisepack / Nov '93 / Conifer/BMG / THE

10 LOVE STARS VOL.3
CD ______ **STACD 061**
Wisepack / Nov '93 / Conifer/BMG / THE

10 LOVE STARS VOL.4
CD ______ **STACD 062**
Wisepack / Nov '93 / Conifer/BMG / THE

10 METAL STARS VOL.1
CD ______ **STACD 075**
Wisepack / Nov '93 / Conifer/BMG / THE

10 METAL STARS VOL.2
CD ______ **STACD 076**
Wisepack / Nov '93 / Conifer/BMG / THE

10 METER OHNE KOPF
CD ______ **EFA 15179CD**
Fishcore / Sep '92 / SRD

10 ROCK STARS VOL.1
CD ______ **STACD 067**
Wisepack / Nov '93 / Conifer/BMG / THE

10 ROCK STARS VOL.2
CD ______ **STACD 068**
Wisepack / Nov '93 / Conifer/BMG / THE

10 ROCK STARS VOL.3
No particular place to go: *Berry, Chuck* / Route 66: *Berry, Chuck* / Life is for living: *Barclay James Harvest* / Just a day away: *Barclay James Harvest* / Be good to yourself: *Journey* / Who's crying now: *Journey* / San Franciscan nights: *Burdon, Eric* / Ring of fire: *Burdon, Eric* / Heat is on: *Frey, Glenn* / You belong to the city: *Frey, Glenn* / After midnight: *Cale, J.J.* / Cocaine: *Cale, J.J.* / Dust my broom: *Fleetwood Mac* / Need your love so bad: *Fleetwood Mac* / Radar love: *Golden Earring* / Back home: *Golden Earring* / Woodstock: *Matthew's Southern Comfort* / Music: *Miles, John*
CD ______ **STACD 069**
Wisepack / Nov '93 / Conifer/BMG / THE

10 ROCK STARS VOL.4
CD ______ **STACD 070**
Wisepack / Nov '93 / Conifer/BMG / THE

10 SOUL STARS VOL.1
CD ______ **STACD 063**
Wisepack / Nov '93 / Conifer/BMG / THE

10 SOUL STARS VOL.2
CD ______ **STACD 064**
Wisepack / Nov '93 / Conifer/BMG / THE

10 SOUL STARS VOL.3
CD ______ **STACD 065**
Wisepack / Nov '93 / Conifer/BMG / THE

10 SOUL STARS VOL.4
Sanctified lady: *Gaye, Marvin* / My love is waiting: *Gaye, Marvin* / Always and forever: *Heatwave* / Jitterbuggin': *Heatwave* / That lady: *Isley Brothers* / Harvest for the world: *Isley Brothers* / Cuba: *Gibson Brothers* / Ooh what a life: *Gibson Brothers* / If you asked me to: *Labelle, Patti* / Oh people: *Labelle, Patti* / Please don't go: *KC & The Sunshine Band* / That's the way I like it: *KC & The Sunshine Band* / Dominoes: *Nevil, Robbie* / C'est la vie: *Nevil, Robbie* / Slowhand: *Pointer Sisters* / Jump: *Pointer Sisters* / Heaven must be missing an angel: *Tavares* / Don't take away the music: *Tavares* / Ain't no sunshine: *Withers, Bill* / Lean on me: *Withers, Bill*
CD ______ **STACD 066**
Wisepack / Nov '93 / Conifer/BMG / THE

10 YEARS AND STILL NO HIT
CD ______ **NOHITCD 020**
No Hit / Feb '97 / Cargo / SRD

10% - FILE UNDER BURROUGHS (2CD Set)
CD Set ______ **SR 93**
Sub Rosa / Apr '96 / Direct / RTM/Disc / SRD / Vital

10TH ANNIVERSARY COLLECTION (2CD Set)
CD Set ______ **CHE 10**
Chesky / Jun '97 / Discovery / Goldring

10TH NEW ORLEANS JAZZ FESTIVAL
CD ______ **FF 099CD**
Flying Fish / May '93 / ADA / CM / Direct / Roots

12 X 12 - VOL.1 (The First Bite)
Never can say goodbye: *Communards* / Venus: *Bananamen* / Push it: *Salt n' Pepa* / Big area: *Then Jerico* / This is your life: *Banderas* / Smalltown boy: *Bronski Beat* / Living on the ceiling: *Blancmange* / I feel love: *Bronski Beat & Marc Almond* / Bass (How low can you go): *Harris, Simon* / It is time to get funky: *D-Mob* / Gun law: *Kane Gang* / I'm falling: *Bluebells*
CD ______ **5500912**
Spectrum / Oct '93 / PolyGram

12 X 12 - VOL.2 (The Second Assortment)
Night train: *Visage* / Living in America: *Brown, James* / Obsession (Dance): *Animotion* / Poison arrow: *ABC* / Talking with myself: *Electribe 101* / Say hello, wave goodbye: *Soft Cell* / Back and forth: *Cameo* / Breakout: *Swing Out Sister* / Hot water: *Level 42* / Promised land: *Style Council* / Big decision: *That Petrol Emotion* / Wipeout: *Fat Boys*
CD ______ **5500892**
Spectrum / Oct '93 / PolyGram

12 X 12 - VOL.3 (The Third Impression)
Can I kick it: *Tribe Called Quest* / Blame it on the bassline: *Cook, Norman* / Roadblock: *Stock/Aitken/Waterman* / Get busy: *Mr. Lee* / Touch me (Sexual version): *49ers* / Wee rule: *Wee Papa Girl Rappers* / I'm a wonderful thing, baby: *Kid Creole & The Coconuts* / Can I get a witness: *Brown, Sam* / Too good to be forgotten: *Amazulu* / Love's crashing waves: *Difford & Tillbrook* / Sweetest smile: *Black* / Lies: *Butler, Jonathan*
CD ______ **5501252**
Spectrum / Oct '93 / PolyGram

12 YEARS IN NOISE (Metal & Beyond/ 2CD Set)
Oernst of life: *Helloween* / Prisoner of our time: *Running Wild* / Back from the war: *Gravedigger* / Maniac forces: *Tankard* / Flag of hate: *Kreator* / Revolution command: *Vendetta* / Don't you fear the winter: *Rage* / I want you: *Helloween* / Not alone: *Scanner* / Lust for life: *Gamma Ray* / Observer from above: *Secrecy* / Spinning Jenny: *Skyclad* / My decision: *Conception* / Reaper: *Mind Odyssey* / Under permission: *Sanvoisen* / Proud nomad: *Kamelot* / Horus/Aggressor: *Hellhammer* / Into the crypts of rays: *Celtic Frost* / Innocence & wrath: *Celtic Frost* / Circle of the tyrants: *Celtic Frost* / Ravenous medicine: *Voivod* / Purple haze: *Coroner* / I want you: *Coroner* / Der Mussolini: *Coroner* / Everyday is a holiday: *Mordred* / Falling away: *Mordred* / Eldritch: *Watchtower* / Shout: *Humungous Fungus* / Identity: *Punishable Act* / Let da streetz burn: *Gunjah* / Bitter: *Shihad* / Kiss or kill: *Manhole*
CD Set ______ **N 02642**
Noise / Jun '96 / Koch

12" OF PLEASURE VOL.1
CD ______ **ALMYCD 10**
Almighty / Nov '94 / Total/BMG

12" OF PLEASURE VOL.2
CD ______ **ALMYCD 14**
Almighty / Jun '95 / Total/BMG

15 KILLERS VOL.2
CD ______ **SZ 205**
Blue Rose / Jun '95 / 3mv/Pinnacle

15 KILLERS VOL.3
CD ______ **SZ 213**
Blue Rose / Jun '95 / 3mv/Pinnacle

16 FAVOURITE LINE DANCE COUNTRY SONGS
CD ______ **I 3885832**
Galaxy / Nov '96 / ZYX

17 DUB SHOTS FROM STUDIO ONE
CD ______ **CDBH 142**
Heartbeat / Aug '95 / ADA / Direct / Greensleeves / Jet Star

18 BLUES MASTERPIECES
CD ______ **CD 52000**
Blues Encore / May '94 / Target/BMG

18 GEMS OF THE GIANTS OF JAZZ CD COLLECTION
CD ______ **CD 53000**
Giants Of Jazz / May '92 / Cadillac / Jazz Music / Target/BMG

18 SOUSA FAVOURITES
Stars and stripes / Semper fields / Diplomat march / Invincible eagle / Liberty bells / Hands across the sea / King Cotton / Bells of Chicago / Crusader / Bride elect / Gladiator march / Manhattan beach / High school cadets / Elcapitano / Washington Post / Hail to the spirit of liberty / Thunderer / US field artillery
CD ______ **GRF 157**
Tring / Apr '93 / Tring

18 STOMPIN' ROCK 'N' ROLL HITS
CD ______ **CWNCD 2022**
Javelin / Jul '96 / Henry Hadaway / THE

18 TRAILBLAZING CLASSICS
We'll rest at the end of the trail: *Wakely, Jimmy* / Have I told you lately that I love you: *Autry, Gene* / Bummin' around: *Williams, Tex* / Great speckled bird: *Acuff, Roy*

& His Crazy Tennesseans / South of the border: Autry, Gene / I'm casting my lasso towards the sky: Wakely, Jimmy / Any old time: Rodgers, Jimmie / Back in the saddle again: Autry, Gene / New San Antonio Rose: Willis, Bob & His Texas Playboys / Night train to Memphis: Acuff, Roy & His Smokey Mountain Boys / Hillbilly heaven: Acuff, Roy & His Smokey Mountain Boys / It makes no difference: Autry, Gene / Mule skinner blues: Monroe, Bill & His Bluegrass Boys / Along the Santa Fe Trail: Wakely, Jimmy / Wreck on the highway: Acuff, Roy & His Smokey Mountain Boys / Prodigal Son: Sunset Carson / Waiting for a train: Rodgers, Jimmie / You are my sunshine: Autry, Gene
CD ________________ CWNCD 2026
Javelin / Jul '96 / Henry Hadaway / THE

20 ALL STAR R&B CLASSICS
I want to hug you: Hooker, John Lee / I'll be gone: Hooker, John Lee / I wish you would: Arnold, Billy Boy / Please be cool: Magic Sam / I ain't got nobody: Sly & The Family Stone / I smell trouble: Turner, Ike & Tina / Honest I do: Reed, Jimmy / Shakin' and shoutin': Magic Sam / Shake it baby: Hopkins, Lightnin' / Dragging my tail: Clapton, Eric / Louie louie: Kingsmen / I just got some: Stewart, Rod / Watermelon man: Sly & The Family Stone / Onions: Hooker, John Lee / Just pickin': Magic Sam / Don't you lie to me: Bloomfield, Mike / Catfish: Arnold, Billy Boy / Send me your pillow: Hooker, John Lee / Bullet blues: Magic Sam / I'll put a spell on you: Hawkins, Screamin' Jay
CD ________________ CWNCD 2012
Javelin / Jul '96 / Henry Hadaway / THE

20 ALL TIME GREATS (Coasters And More)
Charlie Brown: Coasters / Little Egypt: Coasters / Why do fools fall in love: Diamonds / Poetry in motion: Tillotson, Johnny / Rubber ball: Vee, Bobby / Smoke gets in your eyes: Platters / Rock 'n' roll: Coasters / Hats off to Larry: Shannon, Del / Sealed with a kiss: Hyland, Brian / Night has a 1000 eyes: Vee, Bobby / Lion sleeps tonight: Tokens / Yakety yak: Coasters / Will you still love me tomorrow: Shirelles / Peggy Sue: Crickets / La Bamba: Tokens / Poison Ivy: Coasters / Tell Laura I love her: Peterson, Ray / Party doll: Knox, Buddy / At the hop: Original Juniors / Young blood: Coasters
CD ________________ HADCD 155
Javelin / May '94 / Henry Hadaway / THE

20 AMERICAN ROCK 'N' ROLL GREATS
Why do fools fall in love: Lymon, Frankie & The Teenagers / Barbara Ann: Regents / Honeycomb: Rodgers, Jimmie / I'm stickin' with you: Bowen, Jimmy / Tears on my pillow: Imperials / Peppermint twist: Dee, Joey & The Starliters / I'm confessin' that I love you: Chantels / I only have eyes for you: Flamingos / Forty days: Hawkins, Ronnie / Woo hoo: Rock A Teens / Walkin' miracle: Essex / Girl of my best friend: Donner, Ral / Heart and soul: Cleftones / Party doll: Knox, Buddy / Don't ask me to be lonely: Dubs / Gypsy cried: Christie, Lou / Hey lover: Dovale, Debbie / Darling how long: Heartbeats / Beep beep: Playmates / Cry like I cried: Harptones
CD ________________ CDMFP 6132
Music For Pleasure / Sep '94 / EMI

20 BEST LOVED HYMNS
CD ________________ MCCD 214
Music Club / Oct '95 / Disc / THE

20 BEST OF BLUEGRASS
CD ________________ EUCD 1333
ARC / Feb '96 / ADA / ARC Music

20 BEST OF TODAYS FOLK AND WORLD MUSIC VOL.2
CD ________________ EUCD 1141
ARC / '91 / ADA / ARC Music

20 CLASSIC IRISH LOVE BALLADS
CD ________________ CDIRISH 006
Outlet / Oct '95 / ADA / CM / Direct / Duncans / Koch / Ross

20 CLASSIC SONGS OF LOVE
True: Spandau Ballet / Room in your heart: Living In A Box / Man with the child in his eyes: Bush, Kate / Dreamin': Burnette, Johnny Rock 'N' Roll Trio / Missing you: Waite, John / Tonight I celebrate my love for you: Flack, Roberta & Peabo Bryson / More than I can say: Vee, Bobby / Why do fools fall in love: Lymon, Frankie & The Teenagers / Tears on my pillow: Imperials / God only knows: Beach Boys / Air that I breathe: Hollies / Love changes everything: Climie Fisher / Is there something I should know: Duran Duran / I apologise: Proby, P.J. / I only have eyes for you: Flamingos / I honestly love you: Newton-John, Olivia / When you're in love with a beautiful woman: Dr. Hook / Honey: Goldsboro, Bobby / Tell Laura I love her: Valance, Ricky / Crying: McLean, Don
CD ________________ CDMFP 5974
Music For Pleasure / Dec '92 / EMI

20 COUNTRY LOVE SONGS
It's only make believe: Campbell, Glen / When I dream: Gayle, Crystal / There'll be no teardrops tonight: Nelson, Willie / July you're a woman: Stewart, John / Come to me: Newton, Juice / Summer wind: Newton, Wayne / Will you still love me tomorrow: Ronstadt, Linda / You're the reason I'm living: Darin, Bobby / Misty blue: Spears, Billie Jo / For the good times: Ford, Tennessee Ernie / Sharing the night together: Dr. Hook / Let it be me: Campbell, Glen & Bobbie Gentry / I'll take you home again Kathleen: Whitman, Slim / Stand by your man: Jackson, Wanda / It doesn't matter anymore: Anka, Paul / Give me your word: Ford, Tennessee Ernie / Everything a man could ever need: Campbell, Glen / Think I'll go somewhere and cry myself to sleep: Shepard, Jean / Minute you're gone: James, Sonny / We must believe in magic: Gayle, Crystal / Don't it make my brown eyes blue: Gayle, Crystal
CD ________________ CDMFP 6036
Music For Pleasure / Oct '87 / EMI

20 EXPLOSIVE DYNAMIC SUPER SMASH HIT EXPLOSIONS
CD ________________ EFA 201152
Pravda / May '95 / SRD

20 FAVOURITE IRISH PUB SONGS VOL.1
CD ________________ DOCD 2024
Dolphin / Sep '96 / CM / Else / Grapevine/ PolyGram / Koch

20 FAVOURITE IRISH PUB SONGS VOL.2
CD ________________ DOCD 2029
Koch / Oct '93 / Koch

20 FILM AND STAGE CLASSICS JAMAICAN STYLE
People will say we're in love: Spence, Trenton Orchestra / Summertime: Clarke, Lloyd / Guns of Navarone: Skatalites / Bonanza ska: Malcolm, Carlos & Afro Caribs / Shot in the dark: Soul Brothers / From Russia with love: Alphonso, Roland / Dr. Zhivago: McCook, Tommy & The Supersonics / To sir with love: Tait, Lynn & the Jets / Ol' man river: Silvertones / Get me to the church on time: McCook, Tommy & The Supersonics / Hang 'em high: Ace, Richard / Zip a dee doo dah: Smith, Slim / Magnificent seven: Wright, Winston / Hello Dolly: Pat Satchmo / Summer place: Charmers, Lloyd / Try to remember: Pat Kelly / Shaft: Chosen Few / I'm in the mood for love: Chosen Few / Moon river: Ellis, Alton / There's no business like show business: Ellis, Alton
CD ________________ CDTRL 319
Trojan / Mar '94 / Direct / Jet Star

20 GERMAN FOLK SONGS
CD ________________ MCD 71398
Monitor / Jun '93 / CM

20 GOLDEN GREATS FROM THE BIG BAND ERA
Trumpet blues and cantabile / One o'clock jump / Yes indeed / Intermission riff / You made me love you / Four brothers / Artistry in rhythm / I've got a gal in Kalamazoo / I'll never smile again / Jeeps blues / Solitude / Don't be that way / Midnight sun / Red bank boogie / La paloma / Stardust / Skyliner / Goosey gander / Well, get it
CD ________________ HRM 7005
Hermes / Jun '87 / Nimbus

20 GOLDEN NO.1'S VOL.1
Nut rocker: B-Bumble & The Stingers / I'm alive: Hollies / Bad to me: Kramer, Billy J. & The Dakotas / Poor me: Faith, Adam / Johnny remember me: Leyton, Johnny / Do wah diddy diddy: Manfred Mann / Kon-Tiki: Shadows / January: Pilot / See my baby jive: Wizzard / Anyone who had a heart: Black, Cilla / You're my world: Black, Cilla / I'll never find another you: Seekers / Tell Laura I love her: Valence, Ricky / You'll never walk alone: Gerry & The Pacemakers / World without love: Peter & Gordon / Lily the pink: Scaffold / Only sixteen: Douglas, Craig / Little children: Kramer, Billy J. & The Dakotas / What do you want: Faith, Adam / Pretty flamingo: Manfred Mann
CD ________________ CDMFP 50491
Music For Pleasure / Oct '90 / EMI

20 GOLDEN NO.1'S VOL.2
Whiter shade of pale: Procul Harum / This is my song: Clark, Petula / Sweets for my sweet: Searchers / Have I the right: Honeycombs / Always something there to remind me: Shaw, Sandie / Sunny afternoon: Kinks / Michelle: Overlanders / Let the heartaches begin: Baldry, Long John / Blackberry Way: Move / (If paradise is) half as nice: Amen Corner / In the Summertime: Mungo Jerry / Baby, now that I've found you: Foundations / Kung fu fighting: Douglas, Carl / Matchstalk men and matchstalk cats and dogs: Brian & Michael / Sad sweet dreamer: Sweet Sensation / Out of time: Farlowe, Chris / Israelites: Dekker, Desmond / Mouldy old dough: Lieutenant Pigeon / Double barrel: Collins, Dave & Ansell / Everything I own: Boothe, Ken
CD ________________ CDMFP 5898
Music For Pleasure / Oct '90 / EMI

20 GOSPEL GREATS
Love of God: Taylor, Johnnie / Trouble in my way: Swan Silvertones / My rock: Swan Silvertones / Get away Jordan: Love Coates, Dorothy / You better run: Love Coates, Dorothy / Ninety nine and a half (won't do): Love Coates, Dorothy / Straight Street: Pilgrim Travellers / Jesus hits like the atom bomb: Pilgrim Travellers / I'm determined to run this race: Cleveland, James / Living for my Jesus: Five Blind Boys Of Alabama / Alone and motherless: Five Blind Boys Of Alabama / This may be the last time: Five Blind Boys Of Alabama / Ball game: Carr, Sister Wynona / Touch the hem of his garment: Cooke, Sam & The Soul Stirrers / Prayer for the doomed: Chosen Gospel Singers / Holy ghost: Bradford, Alex / Lifeboat: Bradford, Alex / Whosoever will: Griffin, Bessie / Wade in the water: Original Gospel Harmonettes
CD ________________ CDROP 1017
Cascade / May '90 / Pinnacle

20 GREAT BLUES RECORDINGS OF THE 50'S AND 60'S
Rolling and rolling: Hopkins, Lightnin' / Drifting: Bland, Bobby / Gone with the wind: Sykes, Roosevelt / Me and my chauffeur: Thornton, Willie Mae / No rollin' blues: Witherspoon, Jimmy / No nights by myself: Williamson, Sonny Boy / Cool little car: Hooker, John Lee / Dark and dreary: James, Elmore / Ain't drunk: Turner, Ike's Rhythm Kings / Crying at daybreak: Howlin' Wolf / Three hours past midnight: Watson, Johnny 'Guitar' / Talking woman: Fulson, Lowell / Moon is rising: Littlefield, Little Willie / Tease me baby: Hooker, John Lee / Dedicating the blues: Crayton, Pee Wee / Ten years long: King, B.B. / Beer drinking woman: McCracklin, Jimmy / Sunnyland: James, Elmore / Cow town: Dixon, Floyd / Heartache baby: Louis, Joe Hill
CD ________________ CDROP 1005
Cascade / Jan '90 / Pinnacle

20 GREAT CRUISING FAVOURITES OF THE 50'S AND 60'S VOL.1
Wake up little Susie / Nut rocker / Lonely teenager / Over and over / Church bells may ring / In the mood / Short fat Fanny / Tall Paul / Poetry in motion / Runaround Sue / I'll come back to you / I cried a tear / Tick tock / Girl of my dreams / Take a message to Mary / She say / He's so fine / Pink shoe laces / Tra la la la Suzy
CD ________________ CDROP 1014
Cascade / Jan '90 / Pinnacle

20 GREAT CRUISING FAVOURITES OF THE 50'S AND 60'S VOL.2
Wanderer: Dion / Party girl: Carroll, Bernadette / Chattanooga choo choo: Fields, Ernie Orchestra / Dizzy Miss Lizzy: Williams, Larry / Rockin' robin: Day, Bobby / Angel baby: Rosie & The Originals / Sunday kind of love: Mystics / Will you still love me tomorrow: Shirelles / Bandit of my dreams: Hodges, Eddie / Baby face: Little Richard / Denise: Randy & The Rainbows / Chantilly lace: Big Bopper / Pretty girls everywhere: Church, Eugene / No wheels: Chordettes / Problems: Everly Brothers / Way you look tonight: Jarmels / It's my party: Gore, Lesley / Heart: Chandler, Kenny / Rockin' pneumonia and the boogie woogie flu: Neville, Art / I got a feeling: Tillotson, Johnny
CD ________________ CDROP 1015
Cascade / Jan '90 / Pinnacle

20 GREAT CRUISING FAVOURITES OF THE 50'S AND 60'S VOL.3
Lovers who wander / Rock everybody / When will I be loved / She said "yeah" / Hickory dickory dock / Little star / My boyfriend's back / One fine day / I cried a tear / Lawdy Miss Clawdy / Mary Lou / Lucille / Hey doll baby / Forever / My block / Please don't tell me know / Little bitty pretty one / Buzz buzz buzz / Hey boy, hey girl / Bama lama bama loo
CD ________________ CDROP 1016
Cascade / Oct '88 / Pinnacle

20 GREAT DOOWOP RECORDINGS
Pennies from Heaven: Skyliners / Hush-a-bye: Mystics / Automobile: Stickshifts / Dearest darling: Smith, Huey 'Piano' / Penalty of love: Velvetones / Cool baby cool: Flairs / Way you look tonight: Lonely Guys / Under stars of love: Carlos Brothers / Stay where you are: Olympics / Saturday night fish fry: Blue dots / These golden rings: Strangers / Just for you and I: Supremes / Why don't you write me: Jacks / Love only you: Meadowlarks / All I do is rock: Robins / I believe: Twilighters / Please understand: Milton, Buddy & Twilighters / Please don't tell 'em: Blue dots / Cold chills: Sounds / When I fall in love: Skyliners
CD ________________ CDROP 1008
Cascade / Jan '92 / Pinnacle

20 GREAT LOVE SONGS OF THE ROCK 'N' ROLL ERA
CD ________________ CDROP 1018
Cascade / Apr '92 / Pinnacle

20 GREAT RHYTHM & BLUES OF THE 50'S
Rockin' pneumonia and the boogie woogie flu: Smith, Huey 'Piano' & The Clowns / Ain't a better story told: Littlefield, Little Willie / BB boogie: King, B.B. / Good rockin' daddy: James, Etta / Rock house boogie: Hooker, John Lee / Let the good times roll: Shirley & Lee / Bop hop: Crayton, Pee Wee / Don't you know Yockomo: Smith, Huey & The Clowns / Oop shoop: Queens / reelin' and rockin': McCracklin, Jimmy / Who's been jivin' with you: Witherspoon, Jimmy / Road I travel: Turner, Ike's Rhythm Kings / Morning at midnight: Howlin' Wolf / Is everything alright: King, Earl / Love bandit: Cadets / Goodbye baby: James, Elmore / No more doggin': Gordon, Rosco / Early times: Turner, Ike's Rhythm Kings / Gee baby: Joe & Ann / Kansas City blues: Turner, 'Big' Joe
CD ________________ CDROP 1001
Cascade / Oct '88 / Pinnacle

20 GREATEST LINE DANCE PARTY HITS
CD ________________ I 3885822
Galaxy / Nov '96 / ZYX

20 IRISH SONGS YOU KNOW
Isle of Innisfree: Dan The Street Singer / I'll take you home again Kathleen: Dan The Street Singer / Wild colonial boy: McCann, Susan / Irish rover: McCann, Susan / Boys from Killybegs: O'Neill, Stephen / Sweet sixteen: Hara, Dano / Bunch of thyme: Hara, Dano / Forty shades of green: Hara, Dano / Fields of Athenry: Kennedy, Jerome / My wild Irish rose: McGuigan, Pat / If You're Irish: Shamrock Man / Agricultural Irish girl: Shamrock Man / Hannigan's hooley: Shamrock Man / Galway shawl: Swingin' Paddy / Murphy and the bricks: Big O / Black velvet band: Duncan, Hugo / Carrickfergus: Shannon Brothers / Dan the street singer: Golden Jubilee / Three leaf shamrock: O'Neill, Stephen / Danny Boy: Kennedy, Jerome
CD ________________ RBCD 532
Sharpe / Jun '97 / Duncans / Target/BMG

20 ITALIAN SONGS OF LOVE
Come prima / Tu scienda dalle stelle (Christmas song) / Quando, quando, quando / To the door of the sun / Speak softly love / Angelina / Sicilia bedda / Instrumento italiano / Tell me that you love me tonight / Il nostro concerto / Sorriento / Eh cumpare / Mamma / Santa Lucia / Il cielo in una stanza / Viva Italia / Italian wedding song / Strings of my heart (se avessi un mandolino) / Dormi dormi / Amor, mon amor
CD ________________ 305732
Hallmark / May '97 / Carlton

20 MORE EXPLOSIVE DYNAMIC SUPER SMASH HIT EXPLOSIONS
CD ________________ EFA 201162
Pravda / May '95 / SRD

20 MORE GOSPEL GREATS
I'm climbing higher mountains: Echoes Of Zion / New walk: Swanee Quintet / Tell the angels: Angelic Gospel Singers / Let the church roll on: Barbee, Lucille / Building a home: Radio Four / Go devil, go: Littlejohn, Madame Ira Mae / Wake me, shake me: May, Brother Joe / Yea Lord: Trumpet Kings / Lord bring me down: Consolers / Earnest prayer: Radio Four / I want to see jesus: Littlejohn, Madame Ira Mae / Fadeless days: Smith Jubilee Singers / How I got over: Swanee Quintet / Bible is right: Gospel Songbirds / Dark hours of distress: Littlefield, Sister Lillie Mae / No room at the inn: Fairfield Four / On my way (part one): Chapman, Rev CC / You got to be born again: Christland singers / Mother's advice: Taylor Brothers / Father I stretch my arms to thee: Killens, Rev GW
CD ________________ CDROP 1019
Cascade / Oct '93 / Pinnacle

20 MORE REGGAE HOT SHOTS
Wonderful world, beautiful people: Cliff, Jimmy / Everything I own: Boothe, Ken / Longshot kick de bucket: Pioneers / You can get it if you really want: Dekker, Desmond / Dollar in the teeth: Upsetters / Help me make it through the night: Holt, John / Small axe: Marley, Bob & The Wailers / Black magic woman: Brown, Dennis / Hypocrite: Heptones / Band of gold: Griffiths, Marcia / My time: Isaacs, Gregory / Enter into his gates with praise: Clarke, Johnny / Singer man: Kingstonians / Hit the road Jack: Big Youth / Blame it on the sun: Inner Circle / Hurt so good: Cadogan, Susan / Kingston Town: Lord Creator / If you're ready (come go with me): Richard, Cynthia / Beat down Babylon: Byles, Junior / Barber saloon: Mikey Dread
CD ________________ 3037350012
Exodus / May '96 / Carlton

20 NO.1'S OF THE 70'S
In the summertime: Mungo Jerry / Sad sweet dreamer: Sweet Sensation / Matchstalk men and matchstalk cats and dogs: Brian & Michael / Heart of glass: Blondie / Love grows (Where my Rosemary goes): Edison Lighthouse / When you're in love with a beautiful woman: Dr. Hook / When I need you: Sayer, Leo / Kung fu fighting: Douglas, Carl / Without you: Nilsson, Harry / Oh Boy: Mud / Bye bye baby: Bay City Rollers / Blockbuster: Sweet / So you win again: Hot Chocolate / Yes sir, I can boogie: Baccara / I love you love me love: Glitter, Gary / See my baby jive: Wizzard / Make me smile (come up and see me): Harley, Steve & Cockney Rebel / Can the can: Quatro, Suzi / Seasons in the sun: Jacks, Terry / Ms. Grace: Tymes
CD ________________ CDMFP 5985
Music For Pleasure / Apr '93 / EMI

20 NO.2'S OF THE 70'S
Air that I breathe: Hollies / American pie: McLean, Don / Kissin' in the back row of the movies: Drifters / Do you wanna touch me (Oh yeah): Glitter, Gary / Don't let it die: Smith, Hurricane / Denis: Blondie / Moonlighting: Sayer, Leo / Lola: Kinks / Let's work together: Canned Heat / When I'm

dead and gone: *McGuinness Flint* / Cat crept in: *Mud* / Shang-a-lang: *Bay City Rollers* / Goodbye my love: *Glitter Band* / Hell-raiser: *Sweet* / Little bit more: *Dr. Hook* / You sexy thing: *Hot Chocolate* / Some girls: *Racey* / Loving you: *Riperton, Minnie* / Rock me gently: *Kim, Andy* / Can't get by without you: *Real Thing*
CD ______ **CDMFP 5986**
Music For Pleasure / Apr '93 / EMI

20 ONE HIT WONDERS
So much in love: *Mighty Avengers* / Birds and the bees: *Warm Sounds* / I can't let Maggie go: *Honey Bus* / She's not there: *MacArthur, Neil* / Can't you hear my heartbeat: *Goldie & The Gingerbreads* / I keep ringing my baby: *Soul Brothers* / Beggin': *Timebox* / Leaving here: *Birds* / Can't you hear my heart: *Rivers, Danny* / I was Kaiser Bill's batman: *Smith, Jack 'Whispering'* / Can can: *Jay, Peter & The Jaywalkers* / Now we're through: *Poets* / That's what I want: *Marauders* / Girl: *St. Louis Union* / Please stay: *Crying Shames* / Walk with me my angel: *Charles, Don* / Not too little not too much: *Sanford, Chris* / More I see you: *Marshall, Joy* / Goin' out of my head: *West, Dodie* / House of the rising sun: *Frijid Pink*
CD ______ **C5CD 607**
See For Miles/C5 / Oct '93 / Pinnacle

20 ORIGINAL COUNTRY GREATS
Southern nights: *Campbell, Glen* / Wichita lineman: *Campbell, Glen* / Don't it make my brown eyes blue: *Gayle, Crystal* / Talking in your sleep: *Gayle, Crystal* / When you're in love with a beautiful woman: *Dr. Hook* / Sexy eyes: *Dr. Hook* / Ode to Billy Joe: *Gentry, Bobbie* / I'll never fall in love again: *Gentry, Bobbie* / Blanket on the ground: *Spears, Billie Jo* / Sing me an old fashioned song: *Spears, Billie Jo* / Lucille: *Rogers, Kenny* / Coward of the county: *Rogers, Kenny* / Snowbird: *Murray, Anne* / You needed me: *Murray, Anne* / Games people play: *South, Joe* / Hello walls: *Nelson, Willie* / There'll be no teardrops tonight: *Nelson, Willie* / It keeps right on a-hurtin': *Shepard, Jean* / Angel of the morning: *Newton, Juice* / July you're a woman: *Stewart, John*
CD ______ **CDMFP 6084**
Music For Pleasure / Jun '90 / EMI

20 ORIGINAL DOO WOP CLASSICS
Daddy's home: *Shep & The Limelites* / Sunday kind of love: *Harptones* / Pretty little angel eyes: *Lee, Curtis* / I'm not a juvenile delinquent: *Lymon, Frankie & The Teenagers* / I only have eyes for you: *Flamingoes* / Maybe: *Chantels* / Heart and soul: *Cleftones* / Blue moon: *Marcels* / Chains: *Cookies* / Little star: *Elegants* / Thousand miles away: *Heartbeats* / Barbara Ann: *Regents* / Priscilla: *Cooley, Eddie* / Don't ask me to be lonely: *Dubs* / Tears on my pillow: *Little Anthony & The Imperials* / Why do fools fall in love: *Lymon, Frankie & The Teenagers* / Gee: *Crows* / Just to be with you: *Passion* / My melancholy baby: *Marcels* / Two people in the world: *Little Anthony & The Imperials*
CD ______ **CDMFP 6207**
Music For Pleasure / Nov '95 / EMI

20 ORIGINAL RADIO STARS
CD ______ **399236**
Koch / Feb '94 / Koch

20 R 'N' B DANCE FLOOR FILLERS
Harlem shuffle: *Traits* / Show me: *Tex, Joe* / Higher and higher: *Wilson, Jackie* / Don't mess up a good thing: *Bass, Fontella & Bobby McClure* / Gonna send you back to Georgia: *Shaw, Timmy* / Hi-heel sneakers: *Tucker, Tommy* / Shame, shame, shame: *Reed, Jimmy* / Soulful dress: *Desanto, Sugar Pie* / Put on your tight pants: *Turner, Ike & Tina* / Boom boom: *Hooker, John Lee* / Barefootin': *Parker, Robert* / We're gonna make it: *Little Milton* / Holy cow: *Dorsey, Lee* / Something's got a hold on me: *James, Etta* / You left the water running: *Maurice & Mac* / Gettin' mighty crowded: *Everett, Betty* / Everybody come clap your hands: *Moody & The Deltas* / (Down at) Papa Joe's: *Dixiebells* / Ain't love good: *Clarke, Tony* / Land of 1000 dances: *Cannibal & The Head Hunters*
CD ______ **CDRB 23**
Charly / May '95 / Koch

20 R 'N' B DIVAS
My baby just cares for me: *Simone, Nina* / It's in his kiss (The shoop shoop song): *Everett, Betty* / Hello stranger: *Lewis, Barbara* / Oh no not my baby: *Brown, Maxine* / I didn't mean to hurt you: *Shirelles* / Do right woman, do right man: *James, Etta* / Woman will do wrong: *Thomas, Irma* / You don't know: *Greenwich, Ellie* / No stranger to love: *Foxx, Inez* / Take me for a little while: *Sands, Evie* / There's gonna be trouble: *Desanto, Sugar Pie* / Selfish one: *Ross, Jackie* / Recovery: *Bass, Fontella* / I don't want to cry: *Big Maybelle* / Love of my man: *Kilgore, Theola* / Let me down easy: *Lavette, Bettye* / Sit down and cry: *Washington, Ella* / You're gonna miss me: *Sexton, Ann* / Do I make myself clear: *James, Etta & Sugar Pie DeSanto* / Shame, shame, shame: *Shirley & Company*
CD ______ **CDRB 20**
Charly / Apr '95 / Koch

20 REGGAE BLOCKBUSTERS
CD ______ **CDTRL 176**
Trojan / Mar '94 / Direct / Jet Star

20 REGGAE CLASSICS VOL.1
Red red wine: *Tribe, Tony* / Sweet sensation: *Melodians* / Love of the common people: *Thomas, Nicky* / Johnny too bad: *Slickers* / Pressure drop: *Toots & The Maytals* / Liquidator: *Harry J All Stars* / Skinhead moonstomp: *Simaryp* / Longshot kick de bucket: *Pioneers* / Please don't make me cry: *Winston Groovy* / Many rivers to cross: *Cliff, Jimmy* / 007: *Dekker, Desmond & The Aces* / Rudie, a message to you: *Livingstone, Dandy* / Version girl: *Friday, Boy* / Cherry oh baby: *Donaldson, Eric* / Fattie fattie: *Eccles, Clancy* / Keep on moving: *Marley, Bob* / Rivers of Babylon: *Melodians* / Train to Skaville: *Ethiopians*
CD ______ **CDTRL 222**
Trojan / Mar '94 / Direct / Jet Star

20 REGGAE CLASSICS VOL.2
54-46 (was my number): *Toots & The Maytals* / Phoenix city: *Alphonso, Roland* / Love I can feel: *Holt, John* / Java: *Pablo, Augustus* / Reggae in your jeggae: *Livingstone, Dandy* / Pop a top: *Andy Capp* / Double barrel: *Collins, Dave & Ansell* / Wear you to the ball: *U-Roy & John Holt* / Herbsman shuffle: *King Stitt & The Dynamites* / Small axe: *Marley, Bob* / Battle axe: *Upsetters* / Israelites: *Dekker, Desmond & The Aces* / Law: *Andy Capp* / Fat man: *Morgan, Derrick* / So easy: *Winston Groovy* / Whip: *Ethiopians* / Pomp and pride: *Toots & The Maytals* / Further you look: *Holt, John* / Return of Django: *Upsetters* / Soul shakedown party: *Marley, Bob & The Wailers* / Fire corner: *King Stitt* / Next corner: *Dynamites*
CD ______ **CDTRL 224**
Trojan / Mar '94 / Direct / Jet Star

20 REGGAE CLASSICS VOL.3
CD ______ **CDTRL 256**
Trojan / Mar '94 / Direct / Jet Star

20 REGGAE CLASSICS VOL.4
CD ______ **CDTRL 284**
Trojan / Mar '94 / Direct / Jet Star

20 REGGAE HOT SHOTS
CD ______ **PWKS 4226**
Carlton / Nov '94 / Carlton

20 ROCK 'N' ROLL GREATS
Summertime blues: *Cochran, Eddie* / Blueberry Hill: *Domino, Fats* / Rubber ball: *Vee, Bobby* / Say mama: *Vincent, Gene* / You're sixteen: *Burnette, Johnny Rock 'N' Roll Trio* / Ma, he's making eyes at me: *Otis, Johnny Show* / Why do fools fall in love: *Lymon, Frankie & The Teenagers* / Perfidia: *Ventures* / Mother In Law: *K-Doe, Ernie* / Bony Moronie: *Williams, Larry* / Stay: *Williams, Maurice & The Zodiacs* / Piltdown rides again: *Piltdown Men* / Walk don't run: *Ventures* / I'm not a juvenile delinquent: *Lymon, Frankie & The Teenagers* / Willie and the hand jive: *Otis, Johnny Show* / Dreamin': *Burnette, Johnny Rock 'N' Roll Trio* / Be bop a lula: *Vincent, Gene* / Take good care of my baby: *Vee, Bobby* / Ain't that a shame: *Domino, Fats* / C'mon everybody: *Cochran, Eddie*
CD ______ **CDMFP 6007**
Music For Pleasure / Nov '88 / EMI

20 ROCK 'N' ROLL GREATS VOL.2
Rock 'n' roll music: *Berry, Chuck* / See you later alligator: *Haley, Bill* / Rave on: *Holly, Buddy* / Hello Mary Lou: *Nelson, Rick* / Hey little girl: *Shannon, Del* / Run to him: *Vee, Bobby* / I'm in love again: *Domino, Fats* / Move it: *Richard, Cliff* / Only sixteen: *Douglas, Craig* / Shakin' all over: *Kidd, Johnny & The Pirates* / Wild cat: *Vincent, Gene* / Say man: *Diddley, Bo* / Sweetie pie: *Cochran, Eddie* / Don't ever change: *Crickets* / Night has a thousand eyes: *Vee, Bobby* / Little town flirt: *Shannon, Del* / It's late: *Nelson, Rick* / It doesn't matter anymore: *Holly, Buddy* / Shake, rattle and roll: *Haley, Bill* / No particular place to go: *Berry, Chuck*
CD ______ **CDMFP 6066**
Music For Pleasure / Oct '89 / EMI

20 SONGS OF LOVE FROM THE 70'S
All by myself: *Carmen, Eric* / Living next door to Alice: *Smokie* / Daytime friends: *Rogers, Kenny* / Emma: *Hot Chocolate* / There goes my first love: *Drifters* / Torn between two lovers: *McGregor, Mary* / Love is in the air: *Young, John Paul* / I can't stop loving you (Though I try): *Sayer, Leo* / I don't want to put a hold on you: *Flint, Bernie* / Romeo: *Mr. Big* / Give a little love: *Bay City Rollers* / Heaven must be missing an angel: *Tavares* / Where do I begin: *Bassey, Shirley* / And I love you so: *Como, Perry* / It's only make believe: *Child* / You're my everything: *Garrett, Lee* / I don't wanna lose you: *Kandidate* / If not you: *Dr. Hook* / If you go away: *Jacks, Terry* / Softly whispering I love you: *Congregation*
CD ______ **CDMFP 5987**
Music For Pleasure / Apr '93 / EMI

20 SUPERSONIC MEGA HITS
CD ______ **RUNT 04CD**
Runt / Aug '95 / Cargo / Greyhound / Plastic Head

20 WELSH FOLK DANCES
CD ______ **SCD 2094**
Sain / Mar '95 / ADA / Direct / Greyhound

20TH ANNIVERSARY COLLECTION (2CD Set)
Give me back my wig / No cuttin' loose / Black cat bone / Big chief / That's why I'm crying / Double eyed whammy / I'm free / These blues is killing me / Rain / Look but don't touch / Fannie Mae / Serves me right to suffer / Leaving / Born in Louisiana / Leaving your town / Drowning on dry land / If I hadn't been high / Trouble in mind / Brick / Pussy cat moan / You don't exist anymore / Second hand man / I've got dreams to remember / Going down to Big Mary's / 300 pounds of heavenly joy / Going back home / Strike like lightning / Middle aged blues boogie / Eyeballin' / Full moon on Main Street / Crow Jane blues / I'm the Zydeco Man / You don't know what love is / Blues after hours / Boot Hill
CD Set ______ **ALCD 1056**
Alligator / May '93 / ADA / CM / Direct

20TH ANNIVERSARY OF THE NEW YORK SALSA FESTIVAL, THE (2CD Set)
Por eso yo cnato salsa / Pedro navaja / Azucar negra / El cantante / Sonora pa'l balladore / Dejame sonar / Mi primera rumba / Mentiras / Salsa calente / Los tenis / Sonambulo / Si tu no te fueras / Experto en ti / Otra noche calente / Que manera de quererte / Salsumba / Una adventura / Torero / Sisculpeme senora / Puerto rico
CD Set ______ **6758001**
Bellaphon / Jan '96 / New Note/Pinnacle

20TH ANNIVERSARY TOUR
CD ______ **ALCD 1078**
Alligator / May '93 / ADA / CM / Direct

20TH CONCORD FESTIVAL ALL STARS
Blues for Sam Nassi / Time after time / I wish I knew / Just a closer walk with thee / Sophisticated lady / Bye bye blackbird / I got it bad and that ain't good
CD ______ **CDD 366**
Concord Jazz / Jan '89 / New Note/ Pinnacle

21 SWING BAND ALL-TIME GREATS
Cherokee: *Barnet, Charlie* / One o'clock jump: *Basie, Count* / I can't get started (with you): *Berigan, Bunny* / Honky tonk train blues: *Crosby, Bob & Bob Zurke* / Amapola: *Dorsey, Jimmy* / Besame mucho: *Dorsey, Jimmy* / Boogie woogie: *Dorsey, Tommy* / I'm gettin' sentimental over you: *Dorsey, Tommy* / Don't get around much anymore: *Ellington, Duke* / Take the 'A' train: *Ellington, Duke* / Sing sing sing: *Goodman, Benny* / Why don't you do right: *Goodman, Benny & Peggy Lee* / Flying home: *Hampton, Lionel & Illinois Jacquet* / Body and soul: *Hawkins, Coleman* / At the woodchoppers' ball: *Herman, Woody* / All or nothing at all: *James, Harry & Frank Sinatra* / Ciribiribin: *James, Harry & Frank Sinatra* / Chattanooga choo choo: *Miller, Glenn* / In the mood: *Miller, Glenn* / Back bay shuffle: *Shaw, Artie* / Begin the beguine: *Shaw, Artie*
CD ______ **CDAJA 5141**
Living Era / Sep '94 / Select

21 YEARS OF ALTERNATIVE RADIO 1
Hey Joe: *Hendrix, Jimi* / Whiter shade of pale: *Procul Harum* / Delta lady: *Cocker, Joe* / My father's gun: *John, Elton* / Fat man: *Jethro Tull* / Mandolin king: *Lindisfarne* / Keep yourself alive: *Queen* / No love for free: *Armatrading, Joan* / New rose: *Damned* / Dancin' in the moonlight: *Thin Lizzy* / Overground: *Siouxsie & The Banshees* / Read it in books: *Echo & The Bunnymen* / Can't stand losing you: *Police* / It's better this way: *Associates* / 5-8-6: *New Order* / What difference does it make: *Smiths* / Sally MacLennane: *Pogues* / Inside me: *Jesus & Mary Chain* / My favourite dress: *Wedding Present* / Ruby red lips: *Gaye Bykers On Acid* / Strong enough to change: *Unseen Terror*
CD Set ______ **SFRCD 200**
Strange Fruit / Oct '88 / Pinnacle

21ST CENTURY DUB
CD ______ **RE 147CD**
ROIR / Jul '97 / Plastic Head / Shellshock/ Disc

21ST CENTURY SOUL
Falange dos tambores: *Silva, Robertinho* / Loveless: *4 Hero* / I am the black gold of the sun: *Nu Yorican Soul* / Living on the edge: *Darnell, Jeffrey* / Digital: *Roni Size & Reprazent* / Don't xplain: *Pine, Courtney* / No government: *Nicolette* / Future unknown: *DJ Krust* / Kamikaze: *Watkiss, Cleveland* / His name is: *UFO* / Sakara: *Boland, Clarke*
CD ______ **5347422**
Talkin' Loud / Jun '97 / PolyGram

24 ALL TIME VOCAL GREATS
Zing went the strings of my heart: *Garland, Judy* / Last time I saw Paris: *Martin, Tony* / Pennsylvania 6-5000: *Andrews Sisters* / Begin the beguine: *Hutchinson, Leslie 'Hutch'* / Amapola: *Durbin, Deanna* / Wanderer: *Tracy, Arthur* / Atumn nocturne: *Carless, Dorothy* / Can't get Indiana out of my mind: *Crosby, Bing* / I yi yi yi yi (I like you very much): *Miranda, Carmen* / Autumn nocturne: *Carless, Dorothy* / Can't get Indiana off my mind: *Crosby, Bing* / You are too beautiful: *Jolson, Al* / I'll be with you in apple blossom time: *Lynn, Vera* / I'm so used to you now: *Bowlly, Al* / Boulevard of broken dreams: *Langford, Frances* / You were never lovelier: *Astaire, Fred* / Jim: *Fitzgerald, Ella* / In a moment of weakness: *Powell, Dick* / Let's do it: *Martin, Mary* / Do I worry: *Ink Spots* / Wrap yourself in cotton wool: *Shelton, Anne* / That lovely week end: *Brown, Issy* / Room 504: *Hall, Adelaide* / Nagasaki: *Mills Brothers* / I got rhythm: *Merry Macs* / Sweethearts: *Jones, Alan*
CD ______ **RAJCD 831**
Empress / Jul '94 / Koch

24 BELLES CHANSONS DE PARIS
CD ______ **995102**
EPM / Jun '93 / ADA / Discovery

24 CARAT VOL.1
CD ______ **AGCD 1**
Ore / Aug '95 / Warner Music

24 NO.1'S OF THE 60'S
I like it: *Gerry & The Pacemakers* / Bad to me: *Kramer, Billy J. & The Dakotas* / Young ones: *Richard, Cliff* / You're my world: *Black, Cilla* / Pretty flamingo: *Manfred Mann* / Apache: *Shadows* / Shakin' all over: *Kidd, Johnny & The Pirates* / Poor me: *Faith, Adam* / World without love: *Peter & Gordon* / How do you do it: *Gerry & The Pacemakers* / Bachelor boy: *Richard, Cliff* / House of the rising sun: *Animals* / Do wah diddy diddy: *Manfred Mann* / Lily the pink: *Scaffold* / I remember you: *Ifield, Frank* / Anyone who had a heart: *Black, Cilla* / I'm alive: *Hollies* / Where do you go to my lovely: *Sarstedt, Peter* / Wonderful land: *Shadows* / Little children: *Kramer, Billy J. & The Dakotas* / Summer holiday: *Richard, Cliff* / I'm into something good: *Herman's Hermits* / Walkin' back to happiness: *Shapiro, Helen* / You'll never walk alone: *Gerry & The Pacemakers*
CD ______ **CDMFP 6006**
Music For Pleasure / Oct '87 / EMI

25 ALL THE BEST IRISH PUB SONGS
CD ______ **CDIRISH 004**
Outlet / Jan '95 / ADA / CM / Direct / Duncans / Koch / Ross

25 CONTINENTAL ALL-TIME GREATS
Lili Marlene: *Andersen, Lale* / Voulez vous de la canne a sucre: *Baker, Josephine & Adrien Lamy* / Due chitarre: *Buti, Carlo* / Maria La-O: *Celis, Elyane & Lecuona Cuban Boys* / Louise: *Chevalier, Maurice* / Night and day: *Comedy Harmonists* / Ich bin vom kopf bis fuss: *Dietrich, Marlene* / Mama: *Gigli, Beniamino* / Girl like Nina: *Hendrik, John* / Darling je vous aime beaucoup: *Hildegarde* / Es lebte einst in Hamburg: *Igelhoff, Peter* / Von der puszta will ich Traumen: *Leander, Zarah* / Bir mir bist du schoen: *Marjane, Leo* / La partie de bridge: *Mireille & Jean Sablon/Pills & Tabet* / Au fond de tes yeux: *Mistinguett* / Rosa da Madrid: *Piquer, Conchita* / Nuages: *Reinhardt, Django* / Guitare d'amour: *Rossi, Tino* / J'attendrai and Je sais que vous etes jolie: *Sablon, Jean & Django Reinhardt* / Andiamo a Napoli: *Serra, Daniele* / Guter mann im mond: *Serrano, Rosita* / La canzone del domani: *Del Signore, Gino* / Lamento Borinqueno: *Supervia, Conchita* / J'ai ta main: *Trenet, Charles*
CD ______ **CDAJA 5129**
Living Era / May '94 / Select

25 FAVOURITE IRISH DRINKING SONGS
CD ______ **CDIRISH 003**
Outlet / Jan '95 / ADA / CM / Direct / Duncans / Koch / Ross

25 GREATEST HITS VOL.1
CD ______ **SPCD 355**
Disky / Nov '93 / Disky / THE

25 GREATEST HITS VOL.2
CD ______ **SPCD 356**
Disky / Nov '93 / Disky / THE

25 GREATEST HITS VOL.3
CD ______ **SPCD 357**
Disky / Nov '93 / Disky / THE

25 GREATEST HITS VOL.4
CD ______ **SPCD 358**
Disky / Nov '93 / Disky / THE

25 GREATEST HITS VOL.5
CD ______ **SPCD 359**
Disky / Nov '93 / Disky / THE

25 IRISH REBEL SONGS
CD ______ **KOL 600CD**
Outlet / Jul '95 / ADA / CM / Direct / Duncans / Koch / Ross

25 IRISH REPUBLICAN SONGS
Ireland's 32 / Gra mo chroi / Take me home to Mayo / Lonely woods of Upton / They were soldiers everyone / Four green fields / Fields of Athenry / Dying rebel / Lid of me granny's bin / IRELAND / Sean South / Ireland united / West awake / Shall my soul pass through old Ireland / Boys of the old brigade / Off to Dublin in the green / Lough Sheelin eviction / Little armalite / James Connolly / Broad black brimmer / Kevin Barry / Sniper's promise / Patriot game / Only our rivers run free / Nation once again
CD ______ **KOL 602CD**
Outlet / Jul '95 / ADA / CM / Direct / Duncans / Koch / Ross

25 USA NO.1 HITS FROM 25 YEARS
Please Mr. Postman: *Marvelettes* / My girl: *Temptations* / You can't hurry love: *Ross,*

Diana & The Supremes / I heard it through the grapevine: *Gaye, Marvin* / ABC: *Jackson Five* / Just my imagination: *Temptations* / Papa was a rollin' stone: *Temptations* / Let's get it on: *Gaye, Marvin* / Baby love: *Ross, Diana & The Supremes* / I can't help myself: *Four Tops* / Reach out, I'll be there: *Four Tops* / I want you back: *Jackson Five* / Ain't no mountain high enough: *Ross, Diana* / Tears of a clown: *Robinson, Smokey* / What's going on: *Gaye, Marvin* / You are the sunshine of my life: *Wonder, Stevie* / Keep on truckin': *Kendricks, Eddie* / Don't leave me this way: *Houston, Thelma* / Three times a lady: *Commodores* / Give it to me baby: *James, Rick* / Superstition: *Wonder, Stevie* / Got to give it up: *Gaye, Marvin* / Still: *Commodores* / Endless love: *Ross, Diana & Lionel Richie*
CD ______ **5300322**
Motown / Jan '93 / PolyGram

25 YEARS OF LOVE
CD ______ **ONECD 22**
Connoisseur Collection / Jun '97 / Pinnacle

25 YEARS OF NO.1 HITS (Country)
Hello darlin': *Twitty, Conway* / Four in the morning: *Young, Faron* / It's not love (but it's not bad): *Haggard, Merle* / (Old dogs, children and) watermelon wine: *Hall, Tom T.* / Before the next teardrop falls: *Fender, Freddy* / Rhinestone cowboy: *Campbell, Glen* / Together again: *Harris, Emmylou* / One piece at a time: *Cash, Johnny* / Don't it make your brown eyes blue: *Gayle, Crystal* / Lady lay down: *Conlee, John* / Devil went down to Georgia: *Daniels, Charlie Band* / I was country when country wasn't cool: *Mandrell, Barbara* / All my rowdy friends (have settled down): *Williams, Hank Jr.* / Don't cheat in our hometown: *Skaggs, Ricky* / On the other hand: *Travis, Randy* / I sang Dixie: *Yoakam, Dwight* / Some girls do: *Brown, Sawyer* / Achy breaky heart: *Cyrus, Billy Ray* / I still believe in you: *Gill, Vince* / She don't know she's beautiful: *Kershaw, Sammy*
CD ______ **ONECD 20**
Connoisseur Collection / Mar '97 / Pinnacle

25 YEARS OF NO.1 HITS (Soul)
Thank you (falletinme be mice elf again): *Sly & The Family Stone* / Don't play that song: *Franklin, Aretha* / I'll take you there: *Staple Singers* / Get on the good foot: *Brown, James* / LOVE (love): *Green, Al* / Fight the power: *Isley Brothers* / This will be: *Cole, Natalie* / Best of my love: *Emotions* / It's ecstasy when you lay down next to me: *White, Barry* / Too much, too little, too late: *Mathis, Johnny & Deniece Williams* / One in a million you: *Graham, Larry* / Don't stop the music: *Yarbrough & Peoples* / She's strange: *Cameo* / Rock me tonight: *Jackson, Freddie* / Do me baby: *Morgan, Meli'sa* / Nite and day: *Sure, Al B.* / I can't wait another minute: *Hi-Five* / Back and forth: *Aaliyah*
CD ______ **ONECD 21**
Connoisseur Collection / Mar '97 / Pinnacle

25 YEARS OF NO.1 HITS (Instrumentals)
TSOP: *MFSB* / Telstar: *Tornados* / Tequila: *Champs* / Popcorn: *Hot Butter* / Apache: *Shadows* / Hustle: *McCoy, Van* / Albatross: *Fleetwood Mac* / Sleepwalk: *Santo & Johnny* / Classical gas: *Williams, Mason* / Hoots mon: *Lord Rockingham's XI* / Stranger on the shore: *Bilk, Acker* / Diamonds: *Harris, Jet & Tony Meehan* / Nut rocker: *B Bumble & The Stingers* / Wonderland by night: *Kaempfert, Bert* / Cherry pink and apple blossom white: *Calvert, Eddie*
CD ______ **ONECD 23**
Connoisseur Collection / Jun '97 / Pinnacle

25 YEARS OF NO.1 HITS VOL.1
I hear you knocking: *Edmunds, Dave* / All kinds of everything: *Dana* / War: *Starr, Edwin* / Maggie may: *Stewart, Rod* / Coz I love you: *Slade* / Yellow river: *Christie* / Family affair: *Sly & The Family Stone* / Spirit in the sky: *Greenbaum, Norman* / Make it with you: *Bread* / Mama told me not to come: *Three Dog Night* / Hey girl don't bother me: *Tams* / Gypsies, tramps and thieves: *Cher* / Theme from shaft: *Hayes, Isaac* / Brand new key: *Melanie* / In the summertime: *Mungo Jerry* / Woodstock: *Matthew's Southern Comfort* / Venus: *Shocking Blue* / Hot love: *T-Rex*
CD ______ **ONECD 01**
Connoisseur Collection / Aug '96 / Pinnacle

25 YEARS OF NO.1 HITS VOL.10
Sleeping satellite: *Archer, Tasmin* / Would I lie to you: *Charles & Eddie* / Stay: *Shakespears Sister* / Young at heart: *Bluebells* / Saturday night: *Whigfield* / Here comes the hot steppa: *Kamoze, Ini* / I like the way: *Hi-Five* / Take a chance: *Erasure* / Jump: *Kriss Kross* / Inside: *Stiltskin* / Mr. Vain: *Culture Beat* / Deeply dippy: *Right Said Fred* / Unbelievable: *EMF* / Set adrift on memory bliss: *PM Dawn* / Sadness: *Enigma* / Boom, shake the room: *DJ Jazzy Jeff & The Fresh Prince* / Ebeneezer good: *Shamen*
CD ______ **ONECD 10**
Connoisseur Collection / Aug '96 / Pinnacle

25 YEARS OF NO.1 HITS VOL.2
American pie: *McLean, Don* / See my baby jive: *Wizard* / Can the can: *Quatro, Suzi* / Delta dawn: *Reddy, Helen* / Crocodile rock: *John, Elton* / Keep on truckin': *Kendricks, Eddie* / Morning after: *McGovern, Maureen* / Cum on feel the noise: *Slade* / I can see clearly now: *Nash, Johnny* / Me and Mrs Jones: *Paul, Billy* / School's out: *Cooper, Alice* / You're so vain: *Simon, Carly* / Oh girl: *Chi-Lites* / Rubber bullets: *10cc* / Lean on me: *Withers, Bill* / Midnight train to Georgia: *Knight, Gladys* / Metal guru: *T-Rex* / I'll take you there: *Staple Singers*
CD ______ **ONECD 02**
Connoisseur Collection / Aug '96 / Pinnacle

25 YEARS OF NO.1 HITS VOL.3
Angie baby: *Reddy, Helen* / Rhinestone cowboy: *Campbell, Glen* / Lovin' you: *Riperton, Minnie* / Can't get enough of your love: *White, Barry* / Can't give you anything but my love: *Stylistics* / Philadelphia freedom: *John, Elton* / Love will keep us together: *Captain & Tennille* / When will I see you again: *Three Degrees* / I can help: *Swan, Billy* / Shining star: *Earth, Wind & Fire* / Cat's in the cradle: *Chapin, Harry* / Pick up the pieces: *Average White Band* / My eyes adored you: *Valli, Frankie* / Sad sweet dreamer: *Sweet Sensation* / Make me smile: *Harley, Steve* / You're no good: *Ronstadt, Linda* / January: *Pilot* / Rock your baby: *McCrae, George*
CD ______ **ONECD 03**
Connoisseur Collection / Aug '96 / Pinnacle

25 YEARS OF NO.1 HITS VOL.4
When I need you: *Sayer, Leo* / So you win again: *Hot Chocolate* / Kiss and say goodbye: *Manhattans* / Play that funky music: *Wild Cherry* / Free: *Williams, Deniece* / Best of my love: *Emotions* / December '63: *Four Seasons* / Don't cry for me Argentina: *Covington, Julie* / Float on: *Floaters* / Car wash: *Royce, Rose* / Let your love flow: *Bellamy Brothers* / Blinded by the light: *Manfred Mann* / You to me are everything: *Real Thing* / Love rollercoaster: *Ohio Players* / Rock 'n' me: *Miller, Steve Band* / I just want to be your everything: *Gibb, Andy* / Mississippi: *Pussycat* / Southern nights: *Campbell, Glen*
CD ______ **ONECD 04**
Connoisseur Collection / Aug '96 / Pinnacle

25 YEARS OF NO.1 HITS VOL.5
Wuthering heights: *Bush, Kate* / Heart of glass: *Blondie* / When you're in love: *Dr. Hook* / We don't talk anymore: *Richard, Cliff* / My sharona: *Knack* / What a fool believes: *Doobie Brothers* / Good times: *Chic* / Brass in pocket: *Pretenders* / Geno: *Dexy's Midnight Runners* / I will survive: *Gaynor, Gloria* / I don't like mondays: *Boomtown Rats* / Video killed the radio star: *Buggles* / Going underground: *Jam* / Baby come back: *Player* / Reunited: *Peaches & Herb* / Babe: *Styx* / Funkytown: *Lipps Inc.* / Do that to me one more time: *Captain & Tennille*
CD ______ **ONECD 05**
Connoisseur Collection / Aug '96 / Pinnacle

25 YEARS OF NO.1 HITS VOL.6
Tide is high: *Blondie* / Bette Davis eyes: *Carnes, Kim* / Model: *Kraftwerk* / Centrefold: *Geils, J. Band* / Tainted love: *Soft Cell* / Celebration: *Kool & The Gang* / Fame: *Cara, Irene* / Town called malice: *Jam* / Come on Eileen: *Dexy's Midnight Runners* / Keep on loving you: *REO Speedwagon* / Down under: *Men At Work* / Total eclipse of the heart: *Tyler, Bonnie* / Wherever I lay my hat: *Young, Paul* / Give it up: *KC & The Sunshine Band* / Africa: *Toto* / Arthur's theme: *Cross, Christopher* / Baby come to me: *Austin, Patti & James Ingram* / Too shy: *Kajagoogoo*
CD ______ **ONECD 06**
Connoisseur Collection / Aug '96 / Pinnacle

25 YEARS OF NO.1 HITS VOL.7
Missing you: *Waite, John* / Power of love: *Lewis, Huey & The News* / Everybody wants to rule the world: *Tears For Fears* / I shoud've known better: *Diamond, Jim* / 99 red balloons: *Nena* / Can't fight this feeling: *REO Speedwagon* / Every time you go away: *Young, Paul* / I feel for you: *Khan, Chaka* / Owner of a lonely heart: *Yes* / I want to know what love is: *Foreigner* / Move closer: *Nelson, Phyllis* / If I was: *Ure, Midge* / Take on me: *A-Ha* / Relax: *Frankie Goes To Hollywood* / 19: *Hardcastle, Paul* / Kharma chameleon: *Culture Club*
CD ______ **ONECD 07**
Connoisseur Collection / Aug '96 / Pinnacle

25 YEARS OF NO.1 HITS VOL.8
Stuck with you: *Lewis, Huey & The News* / Don't leave me this way: *Communards* / La bamba: *Los Lobos* / Venus: *Bananarama* / Final countdown: *Europe* / Walk like an Egyptian: *Bangles* / Glory of love: *Cetera, Peter* / Always: *Atlantic Starr* / Mony mony: *Idol, Billy* / You keep me hanging on: *Wilde, Kim* / Rock me Amadeus: *Falco* / Sun always shines on TV: *A-Ha* / Caravan of love: *Housemartins* / At this moment: *Era, Billy & The Beaters* / Everything I own: *Boy George* / Died in your arms: *Cutting Crew*
CD ______ **ONECD 08**
Connoisseur Collection / Aug '96 / Pinnacle

25 YEARS OF NO.1 HITS VOL.9
Nothing's gonna change my love: *Medeiros, Glenn* / Only way is up: *Yazz* / First time: *Beck, Robin* / Eternal flame: *Bangles* / Black velvet: *Myles, Alannah* / I don't have the heart: *Ingram, James* / I think we're alone now: *Tiffany* / Wishing well: *D'Arby, Terence Trent* / Something's gotten hold of my heart: *Almond, Marc & Gene Pitney* / My perogative: *Brown, Bobby* / Killer: *Adamski* / Joker: *Miller, Steve Band* / Roll with it: *Winwood, Steve* / Right here waiting: *Marx, Richard* / Ice ice baby: *Vanilla Ice* / Tears on my pillow: *Minogue, Kylie* / Sealed with a kiss: *Donovan, Jason* / Dub be good to me: *Beats International*
CD ______ **ONECD 09**
Connoisseur Collection / Aug '96 / Pinnacle

25 YEARS OF REGGAE NUMBER ONES
Amigo: *Black Slate* / Sweat: *Shinehead* / No no no: *Penn, Dawn* / Point of view: *Matumbi* / Rumours: *Isaacs, Gregory* / Try jah love: *Third World* / Little Walter: *Paul, Frankie* / Don't look back: *Tosh, Peter* / Police officer: *Smiley Culture* / Day dreaming: *Delgado, Junior* / Cherry oh baby: *Donaldson, Eric* / 54-46 was my number: *Maytals* / Many rivers to cross: *Cliff, Jimmy* / Champion lover: *Glasgow, Deborahe* / Money in my pocket: *Brown, Dennis* / Up town top ranking: *Althia & Donna* / Good thing going: *Lewis, C.J. & Philip Leo* / Pirates anthem: *Home T & Cocoa T/Shabba Ranks* / Zungguzzung-gungguzzungguzeng: *Yellowman*
CD ______ **ONECD 24**
Connoisseur Collection / Jul '97 / Pinnacle

25 YEARS OF ROCK 'N' ROLL - 1960 VOL.2
Apache: *Shadows* / Good timin': *Jones, Jimmy* / I'm sorry: *Lee, Brenda* / You'll never know what you're missing: *Ford, Emile & The Checkmates* / Pistol packin' mama: *Vincent, Gene* / How about that: *Faith, Adam* / Misty: *Mathis, Johnny* / Mama: *Francis, Connie* / Angela Jones: *Cox, Michael* / Tell Laura I love her: *Valance, Ricky* / Red river rock: *Johnny & The Hurricanes* / So sad (to watch good love go bad): *Everly Brothers* / As long as he needs me: *Bassey, Shirley* / Stairway to heaven: *Sedaka, Neil* / Please help me, I'm falling: *Locklin, Hank* / Heart of a teenage girl: *Douglas, Craig* / What in the world's come over you: *Scott, Jack* / Be mine: *Fortune, Lance* / He'll have to go: *Reeves, Jim* / Save the last dance for me: *Drifters*
CD ______ **RRTCD 60**
Connoisseur Collection / Apr '92 / Pinnacle

25 YEARS OF ROCK 'N' ROLL - 1961 VOL.2
Runaway: *Shannon, Del* / Rubber ball: *Vee, Bobby* / Little devil: *Sedaka, Neil* / Walkin' back to happiness: *Shapiro, Helen* / Running scared: *Orbison, Roy* / Where the boys are: *Francis, Connie* / Portrait of my love: *Monro, Matt* / Big bad John: *Dean, Jimmy* / Lion sleeps tonight: *Tokens* / Stand by me: *King, Ben E.* / Walk right back: *Everly Brothers* / You always hurt the one you love: *Henry, Clarence 'Frogman'* / Take five: *Brubeck, Dave* / North to Alaska: *Horton, Johnny* / Tribute to Buddy Holly: *Berry, Mike & The Outlaws* / Michael: *Highwaymen* / Halfway to paradise: *Fury, Billy* / You don't know: *Shapiro, Helen* / Well I ask you: *Kane, Eden* / Will you still love me tomorrow: *Shirelles*
CD ______ **RRTCD 61**
Connoisseur Collection / Apr '92 / Pinnacle

25 YEARS OF ROCK 'N' ROLL - 1962 VOL.2
Wanderer: *Dion* / Crying in the rain: *Everly Brothers* / Dream baby: *Orbison, Roy* / Ain't that funny: *Justice, Jimmy* / Nut rocker: *B-Bumble & The Stingers* / Swiss maid: *Shannon, Del* / Love me warm and tender: *Anka, Paul* / Deep in the heart of Texas: *Eddy, Duane* / Take good care of my baby: *Vee, Bobby* / Happy birthday sweet sixteen: *Sedaka, Neil* / Sheila: *Roe, Tommy* / Devil woman: *Robbins, Marty* / Wimoweh: *Denver, Karl* / Walk on by: *Van Dyke, Leroy* / There comes that feeling: *Lee, Brenda* / Let there be drums: *Nelson, Sandy* / Let there be love: *Cole, Nat 'King'* / Ginny come lately: *Hyland, Brian* / Town without pity: *Pitney, Gene* / When my little girl is smiling: *Drifters*
CD ______ **RRTCD 62**
Connoisseur Collection / Apr '92 / Pinnacle

25 YEARS OF ROCK 'N' ROLL - 1964 VOL.2
All day and all of the night: *Kinks* / Don't bring me down: *Pretty Things* / Over you: *Freddie & The Dreamers* / I think of you: *Merseybeats* / Anyone who had a heart: *Black, Cilla* / Swinging on a star: *Irwin, Big Dee* / Someone, someone: *Poole, Brian & The Tremeloes* / I'm into something good: *Herman's Hermits* / Can't you hear my heartbeat: *Goldie & The Gingerbreads* / No particular place to go: *Berry, Chuck* / 5-4-3-2-1: *Manfred Mann* / Girls don't come: *Shaw, Sandie* / Everything's alright: *Mojos* / Boys cry: *Kane, Eden* / Um um um um um um: *Fontana, Wayne* / Move over darling: *Day, Doris* / Don't throw your love away: *Searchers* / She's not there: *Zombies* / Losing you: *Springfield, Dusty* / Good golly miss molly: *Swinging Blue Jeans*
CD ______ **RRTCD 64**
Connoisseur Collection / Apr '92 / Pinnacle

25 YEARS OF ROCK 'N' ROLL - 1965 VOL.2
Price of love: *Everly Brothers* / Unchained melody: *Righteous Brothers* / Mr. Tambourine Man: *Byrds* / World of our own: *Seekers* / Hang on sloopy: *McCoys* / King of the road: *Miller, Roger* / Some of your lovin': *Springfield, Dusty* / Almost there: *Williams, Andy* / Colours: *Donovan* / In the midnight hour: *Pickett, Wilson* / Leader of the pack: *Shangri-Las* / Yesterday man: *Andrews, Chris* / Funny how love can be: *Ivy League* / Looking through the eyes of love: *Pitney, Gene* / Here it comes again: *Fortunes* / I left my heart in San Francisco: *Bennett, Tony* / Trains and boats and planes: *Kramer, Billy J. & The Dakotas* / In thoughts of you: *Fury, Billy* / We gotta get out of this place: *Animals* / Go now: *Moody Blues*
CD ______ **RRTCD 65**
Connoisseur Collection / Apr '92 / Pinnacle

25 YEARS OF ROCK 'N' ROLL - 1966 VOL.2
Good vibrations: *Beach Boys* / Daydream: *Lovin' Spoonful* / Rescue me: *Bass, Fontella* / My mind's eye: *Small Faces* / Green green grass of home: *Jones, Tom* / Bus stop: *Hollies* / My girl: *Redding, Otis* / Tomorrow: *Shaw, Sandie* / With a girl like you: *Troggs* / Eight miles high: *Byrds* / Holy cow: *Dorsey, Lee* / Happy together: *Turtles* / Just one smile: *Pitney, Gene* / Little man: *Sonny & Cher* / Dead end street: *Kinks* / Get away: *Fame, Georgie & The Blue Flames* / My love: *Clark, Petula* / Hold tight: *Dave Dee, Dozy, Beaky, Mick & Tich* / Out of time: *Farlowe, Chris* / When a man loves a woman: *Sledge, Percy*
CD ______ **RRTCD 66**
Connoisseur Collection / Apr '92 / Pinnacle

25 YEARS OF ROCK 'N' ROLL - 1967 VOL.2
Respect: *Franklin, Aretha* / Knock on wood: *Floyd, Eddie* / First cut is the deepest: *Arnold, P.P.* / Flowers in the rain: *Move* / Boat that I row: *Lulu* / Itchycoo Park: *Small Faces* / Release me: *Humperdinck, Engelbert* / From the underworld: *Herd* / House that Jack built: *Price, Alan* / Groovin': *Rascals* / San Francisco: *McKenzie, Scott* / On a carousel: *Hollies* / Ode to Billy Joe: *Gentry, Bobbie* / I'll never fall in love again: *Jones, Tom* / Ballad of Bonnie and Clyde: *Fame, Georgie* / Something's gotten hold of my heart: *Pitney, Gene* / Silence is golden: *Tremeloes* / Homburg: *Procul Harum* / Sweet soul music: *Conley, Arthur* / 007: *Dekker, Desmond*
CD ______ **RRTCD 67**
Connoisseur Collection / Apr '92 / Pinnacle

25 YEARS OF ROCK 'N' ROLL - 1969 VOL.2
I can hear music: *Beach Boys* / Son of a preacher man: *Springfield, Dusty* / Hey Jude: *Pickett, Wilson* / Oh happy day: *Hawkins, Edwin Singers* / Man of the world: *Fleetwood Mac* / Natural born bugie: *Humble Pie* / Fox on the run: *Manfred Mann* / (If paradise is) Half as nice: *Amen Corner* / Time is tight: *Booker T & The MG's* / I'd rather go blind: *Chicken Shack* / Private number: *Bell, William & Judy Clay* / One road: *Love Affair* / You've made me so very happy: *Blood, Sweat & Tears* / Minute of your time: *Jones, Tom* / Sorry Suzanne: *Hollies* / In the bad bad old days: *Foundations* / First of May: *Bee Gees* / My sentimental friend: *Herman's Hermits* / Call me number one: *Tremeloes* / Boy named Sue: *Cash, Johnny*
CD ______ **RRTCD 69**
Connoisseur Collection / Jul '92 / Pinnacle

25 YEARS OF ROCK 'N' ROLL - 1970 VOL.2
Victoria: *Kinks* / Rag mama rag: *Band* / Gasoline Alley bred: *Hollies* / Spirit in the sky: *Greenbaum, Norman* / Yellow river: *Christie* / Patches: *Carter, Clarence* / Both sides now: *Collins, Judy* / Love is life: *Hot Chocolate* / My baby loves lovin': *White Plains* / In my chair: *Status Quo* / Who do you love: *Juicy Lucy* / Ruby Tuesday: *Melanie* / Make it with you: *Bread* / Cotton fields: *Beach Boys* / Venus: *Shocking Blue* / Me and my life: *Tremeloes* / Don't play that song (You lied): *Franklin, Aretha* / Can't help falling in love: *Williams, Andy* / Montego Bay: *Bloom, Bobby* / Paranoid: *Black Sabbath*
CD ______ **RRTCD 70**
Connoisseur Collection / Jul '92 / Pinnacle

25 YEARS OF ROCK 'N' ROLL - 1971 VOL.2
Strange kind of woman: *Deep Purple* / Back street luv: *Curved Air* / Malt and barley blues: *McGuinness Flint* / Reason to believe: *Stewart, Rod* / Spanish harlem: *Franklin, Aretha* / I believe (in love): *Hot Chocolate* / Tonight: *Move* / Get down and get with it: *Slade* / Witch Queen of New Orleans: *Redbone* / Baby jump: *Mungo Jerry* / When you are a king: *White Plains* / Chestnut mare: *Byrds* / Shaft: *Hayes, Isaac* / Pied piper: *Bob & Marcia* / Walkin': *CCS* / Rose garden: *Anderson, Lynn* / I will return: *Springwater* / What have they done to my song Ma: *Melanie* / Sultana: *Titanic* / Amazing grace: *Collins, Judy*
CD ______ **RRTCD 71**
Connoisseur Collection / Aug '92 / Pinnacle

25 YEARS OF ROCK 'N' ROLL - 1973 VOL.2
Paper plane: *Status Quo* / God gave rock 'n' roll to you: *Argent* / You're so vain: *Simon, Carly* / Stuck in the middle with you: *Stealer's Wheel* / If you don't know me by now: *Melvin, Harold & The Bluenotes* / Amoureuse: *Dee, Kiki* / Showdown: *ELO* /

Lamplight: *Essex, David* / Angel fingers: *Wizzard* / Dynamite: *Mud* / Cum on feel the noize: *Slade* / 48 crash: *Quatro, Suzi* / Part of the union: *Strawbs* / One and one is one: *Medicine Head* / Alright alright alright: *Mungo Jerry* / Pick up the pieces: *Hudson - Ford* / Free electric band: *Hammond, Albert* / Radar love: *Golden Earring* / Could it be I'm falling in love: *Detroit Spinners* / That lady: *Isley Brothers*
CD RRTCD 73
Connoisseur Collection / Jul '92 / Pinnacle

25 YEARS OF ROCK 'N' ROLL - 1974 VOL.2
I've got the music in me: *Dee, Kiki* / Rock your baby: *McCrae, George* / Queen of clubs: *KC & The Sunshine Band* / Love's theme: *Love Unlimited Orchestra* / Magic: *Pilot* / Touch too much: *Arrows* / Stardust: *Essex, David* / Golden age of rock 'n' roll: *Mott The Hoople* / My coo ca choo: *Stardust, Alvin* / Air that I breathe: *Hollies* / Zing went the strings of my heart: *Trammps* / Walkin' miracle: *Limmie & Family Cooking* / Never, never gonna give you up: *White, Barry* / Hang on in there baby: *Bristol, Johnny* / Most beautiful girl in the world: *Rich, Charlie* / Jukebox jive: *Rubettes* / Cat crept in: *Mud* / Na na na: *Powell, Cozy* / Slip and slide: *Medicine Head* / Pool Hall Richard: *Faces*
CD RRTCD 74
Connoisseur Collection / Aug '92 / Pinnacle

25 YEARS OF ROCK 'N' ROLL - 1975 VOL.2
That's the way I like it: *KC & The Sunshine Band* / Right back where we started from: *Nightingale, Maxine* / Best thing that ever happened to me: *Knight, Gladys & The Pips* / Mr. Raffles: *Harley, Steve* / Rock me gently: *Kim, Andy* / Motor bikin': *Spedding, Chris* / My white bicycle: *Nazareth* / Art for art's sake: *10cc* / Roll over lay down: *Status Quo* / I can do it: *Rubettes* / Good love can never die: *Stardust, Alvin* / Send in the clowns: *Collins, Judy* / Rhinestone cowboy: *Campbell, Glen* / Stand by your man: *Wynette, Tammy* / This will be: *Cole, Natalie* / Take good care of yourself: *Three Degrees* / Let me try again: *Jones, Tammy* / It's been so long: *McRae, Gordon* / Dolly my love: *Moments* / Blue guitar: *Hayward, Justin & John Lodge*
CD RRTCD 75
Connoisseur Collection / Jul '92 / Pinnacle

25 YEARS OF ROCK 'N' ROLL - 1977 VOL.2
More than a feeling: *Boston* / Show you the way to go: *Jacksons* / Whodunit: *Tavares* / Telephone line: *ELO* / Best of my love: *Emotions* / Dance, dance, dance: *Chic* / Home is where the heart is: *Knight, Gladys & The Pips* / Daddy cool: *Darts* / Girl can't help it: *Darts* / Lonely boy: *Gold, Andrew* / Lucille: *Rogers, Kenny* / Southern nights: *Campbell, Glen* / Slow down: *Miles, John* / Shuffle: *McCoy, Van* / Stop me: *Ocean, Billy* / Hurt: *Manhattans* / Ain't gonna bump no more (With no big fat woman): *Tex, Joe* / Too hot to handle: *Heatwave* / Saturday nite: *Earth, Wind & Fire* / She's a wind up: *Dr. Feelgood* / Modern world: *Jam*
CD RRTCD 77
Connoisseur Collection / Jul '92 / Pinnacle

25 YEARS OF ROCK 'N' ROLL - 1978 VOL.2
Le freak: *Chic* / September: *Earth, Wind & Fire* / Boogie shoes: *KC & The Sunshine Band* / Wishing on a star: *Rose Royce* / If I can't have you: *Elliman, Yvonne* / Just the way you are: *White, Barry* / Talking in your sleep: *Gayle, Crystal* / Boogie oogie oogie: *Taste Of Honey* / Use ta be my girl: *O'Jays* / Blame it on the boogie: *Jacksons* / Always and forever: *Heatwave* / It's raining: *Darts* / Lovely day: *Withers, Bill* / If I had words: *Fitzgerald, Scott & Yvonne Keeley* / Mr. blue sky: *ELO* / Never let her slip away: *Gold, Andrew* / Jilted John: *Jilted John* / Don't take no for an answer: *Robinson, Tom* / Ever fallen in love: *Buzzcocks* / Don't look back: *Tosh, Peter*
CD RRTCD 78
Connoisseur Collection / Jul '92 / Pinnacle

25 YEARS OF ROCK 'N' ROLL - 1979 VOL.2
I want you to want me: *Cheap Trick* / Brass in pocket: *Pretenders* / He's the greatest dancer: *Sister Sledge* / Reunited: *Peaches & Herb* / Just what I needed: *Cars* / She's in love with you: *Quatro, Suzi* / Get it right next time: *Rafferty, Gerry* / Devil went down to Georgia: *Daniels, Charlie* / Hersham Boys: *Sham 69* / Deer hunter: *Shadows* / Is it love you're after: *Rose Royce* / Get down: *Chandler, Gene* / We got the funk: *Positive Force* / I love America: *Juvet, Patrick* / Haven't stopped dancing yet: *Gonzalez* / Shake your body: *Jacksons* / Star: *Earth, Wind & Fire* / Please don't go: *KC & The Sunshine Band* / I want your love: *Chic* / Ladies night: *Kool & The Gang*
CD RRTCD 79
Connoisseur Collection / Jul '92 / Pinnacle

25 YEARS OF ROCK 'N' ROLL - 1980 VOL.2
Talk of the town: *Pretenders* / Start: *Jam* / Working my way back to you: *Detroit Spinners* / Jump to the beat: *Lattisaw, Stacy* / Nine to Five: *Easton, Sheena* / Don't stop the music: *Yarbrough & Peoples* / To be or not to be: *Robertson, B.A.* / Silver dream machine: *Essex, David* / We are glass: *Numan, Gary* / Special brew: *Bad Manners* / There there my dear: *Dexy's Midnight Runners* / Feels like I'm in love: *Marie, Kelly* / What's another year: *Logan, Johnny* / Coward of the county: *Rogers, Kenny* / Better love next time: *Dr. Hook* / Hold on to my love: *Ruffin, Jimmy* / Don't push it, don't force it: *Haywood, Leon* / Crying: *McLean, Don* / Southern freeez: *Freeze* / Dog eat dog: *Adam Ant*
CD RRTCD 80
Connoisseur Collection / Jul '92 / Pinnacle

25 YEARS OF ROCK 'N' ROLL - 1982 VOL.2
Come on Eileen: *Dexy's Midnight Runners* / Freeze frame: *Geils, J. Band* / Strange little girl: *Stranglers* / Look of love: *ABC* / Living on the ceiling: *Blancmange* / Is it a dream: *Classix Nouveaux* / I don't wanna dance: *Grant, Eddy* / Love's comin' at ya: *Moore, Melba* / Suspicious minds: *Staton, Candi* / Really saying something: *Bananarama* / Don't walk away: *Four Tops* / Night birds: *Shakatak* / Lover in you: *Sugarhill Gang* / Classic: *Gurvitz, Adrian* / Brave new world: *Toyah* / Girl crazy: *Hot Chocolate* / Ooh la la la (let's go dancin'): *Kool & The Gang* / Love makes the world go round: *Jets* / Beat surrender: *Jam* / Talk talk: *Talk Talk*
CD RRTCD 82
Connoisseur Collection / Jul '92 / Pinnacle

25 YEARS OF ROCK 'N' ROLL - 1983 VOL.2
Club Tropicana: *Wham* / Joanna: *Kool & The Gang* / What is love: *Jones, Howard* / It's raining men: *Weather Girls* / I gave you my heart (didn't I): *Hot Chocolate* / Candy girl: *New Edition* / Na na hey hey kiss him goodbye: *Bananarama* / Soul inside: *Soft Cell* / Blind vision: *Blancmange* / Cry me a river: *Wilson, Mari* / BLue world: *Moody Blues* / Oblivious: *Aztec Camera* / Speak like a child: *Style Council* / Love blonde: *Wilde, Kim* / Dark is the night: *Shakatak* / Ooh to be ah: *Kajagoogoo* / He knows you know: *Marillion* / Cutter: *Echo & The Bunnymen* / Chance: *Big Country* / Bad day: *Carmel*
CD RRTCD 83
Connoisseur Collection / Jul '92 / Pinnacle

25 YEARS OF TROJAN
CD Set CDTRD 413
Trojan / Mar '94 / Direct / Jet Star

25TH FUJITSU CONCORD JAZZ FESTIVAL
You're lucky to me: *Alden, Howard Trio* / Very thought of you: *Alden, Howard Trio* / Nobody else but me: *Alden, Howard Trio* / Crazy she calls me: *Alden, Howard Trio* / All alone/Tango el bongo: *Alden, Howard Trio* / Kung fu willie: *Harris, Gene Quartet* / Grass is greener: *Harris, Gene Quartet* / Sweet Georgia Brown: *Harris, Gene Quartet* / Just a closer walk with thee: *Harris, Gene Quartet* / Robbin's nest: *Harris, Gene Quartet* / Tenderly: *Harris, Gene Quartet* / This one's for Scott: *Harris, Gene Quartet* / There is no greater love: *McPartland, Marian Trio* / Prelude to a kiss: *McPartland, Marian Trio* / There will never be another you: *McPartland, Marian Trio* / Gone with the wind: *McPartland, Marian Trio* / My foolish heart: *McPartland, Marian Trio* / I'll remember April: *McPartland, Marian Trio*
CD CCD 7002
Concord Jazz / Mar '94 / New Note/ Pinnacle

26 HAPPY HONKY TONK MEMORIES
CD MICH 4529
Hindsight / Sep '92 / Jazz Music / Target/ BMG

26TH FUJITSU CONCORD JAZZ FESTIVAL
CD CCD 7003
Concord Jazz / Apr '95 / New Note/ Pinnacle

27TH FUJITSU-CONCORD JAZZ FESTIVAL
No more blues / You'd be so nice to come home to / Stardust / In love in vain / It might as well be spring / Blues capers / Easy living / Sweet Georgia Brown / Tenderly / Swing until the girls come home / Buhaina buhaina / Love you madly / Song is you / Owl / Just friends / Portrait of Jenny / What's new / Skylark / Donna Lee
CD CCD 7004
Concord Jazz / Apr '96 / New Note/ Pinnacle

30 SECONDS BEFORE CALICO WALL
CD AA 050
Art Art / Jul '97 / Greyhound

30 TOP TEN HITS OF THE 60'S
CD MATCD 201
Castle / Nov '93 / BMG

30 YEARS OF DUB MUSIC
CD RNCD 2046
Rhino / Mar '94 / Grapevine/PolyGram / Jet Star

30 YEARS OF DUB MUSIC ON THE GO
CD RNCD 2094
Rhino / Mar '95 / Grapevine/PolyGram / Jet Star

30 YEARS OF JAMAICAN MUSIC ON THE GO
CD Set RNCD 2034
Rhino / Jan '94 / Grapevine/PolyGram / Jet Star

30 YEARS OF JAMAICAN MUSIC VOL.2
CD RNCD 87
Rhino / Feb '95 / Grapevine/PolyGram / Jet Star

30 YEARS OF NO.1'S VOL.1 (1956-1958)
(We're gonna) Rock around the clock: *Haley, Bill & The Comets* / Memories are made of this: *Martin, Dean* / Why do fools fall in love: *Lymon, Frankie* / Singin' the blues: *Steele, Tommy* / Cumberland Gap: *Donegan, Lonnie* / All shook up: *Presley, Elvis* / That'll be the day: *Holly, Buddy* / Great balls of fire: *Belafonte, Harry* / Story of my life: *Holliday, Michael* / Whole lotta woman: *Rainwater, Marvin* / Sixteen tons: *Ford, Tennessee Ernie* / Rock 'n' roll waltz: *Starr, Kay* / Lay down your arms: *Shelton, Anne* / Garden of Eden: *Vaughan, Frankie* / Diana: *Anka, Paul* / Gamblin' man: *Donegan, Lonnie* / Mary's boy child: *Belafonte, Harry* / Jailhouse rock: *Presley, Elvis* / Magic moments: *Como, Perry*
CD TYNOCD 100
Connoisseur Collection / Nov '88 / Pinnacle

30 YEARS OF NO.1'S VOL.10 (1980-1983)
Use it up and wear it out: *Odyssey* / Start: *Jam* / Feels like I'm in love: *Marie, Kelly* / Tide is high: *Blondie* / Green door: *Stevens, Shakin'* / Japanese boy: *Aneka* / Tainted love: *Soft Cell* / Prince Charming: *Adam & The Ants* / Land of make believe: *Bucks Fizz* / Model: *Kraftwerk* / Seven tears: *Goombay Dance Band* / My camera never lies: *Bucks Fizz* / House of fun: *Madness* / Goody two shoes: *Adam & The Ants* / Happy Talk: *Captain Sensible* / Fame: *Cara, Irene* / Come on Eileen: *Dexy's Midnight Runners & Emerald Express* / Do you realy want to hurt me: *Culture Club* / I don't wanna dance: *Grant, Eddy* / Down under: *Men At Work* / Too shy: *Kajagoogoo* / Total eclipse of the heart: *Tyler, Bonnie* / Is there something I should know: *Duran Duran* / True: *Spandau Ballet*
CD TYNOCD 109
Connoisseur Collection / Apr '90 / Pinnacle

30 YEARS OF NO.1'S VOL.11 (1983-1986)
Give it up: *KC & The Sunshine Band* / Karma Chameleon: *Culture Club* / Only You: *Flying Pickets* / 99 red balloons: *Nena* / Wake me up before you go go: *Wham* / I feel for you: *Khan, Chaka* / I should have known better: *Diamond, Jim* / I want to know what love is: *Foreigner* / Nineteen: *Hardcastle, Paul* / Frankie: *Sister Sledge* / Good heart: *Sharkey, Feargal* / Sun always shines on TV: *A-Ha* / Rock me Amadeus: *Falco* / Spirit in the sky: *Dr. & The Medics* / Every loser wins: *Berry, Nick* / Final countdown: *Europe* / Reet petite: *Wilson, Jackie* / Stand by me: *King, Ben E.* / Nothing's gonna stop us now: *Starship* / Never gonna give you up: *Astley, Rick* / You win again: *Bee Gees* / I think we're alone now: *Tiffany* / Perfect: *Fairground Attraction* / Orinoco Flow: *Enya*
CD TYNOCD 110
Connoisseur Collection / Jun '90 / Pinnacle

30 YEARS OF NO.1'S VOL.2 (1958-1961)
It's all in the game: *Edwards, Tommy* / It's only make believe: *Twitty, Conway* / Smoke gets in your eyes: *Platters* / Fool such as I: *Presley, Elvis* / Only sixteen: *Douglas, Craig* / Why: *Newley, Anthony* / Running bear: *Preston, Johnny* / Three steps to heaven: *Cochran, Eddie* / Please don't tease: *Richard, Cliff* / Apache: *Shadows* / Hoots mon: *Lord Rockingham's XI* / As I love you: *Bassey, Shirley* / Side saddle: *Conway, Russ* / Living doll: *Richard, Cliff* / What do you want: *Ford, Emile* / Poor me: *Faith, Adam* / Do you mind: *Newley, Anthony* / Good timin': *Jones, Jimmy* / Shakin' all over: *Kidd, Johnny & The Pirates*
CD TYNOCD 101
Connoisseur Collection / Nov '88 / Pinnacle

30 YEARS OF NO.1'S VOL.3 (1961-1963)
Sailor: *Clark, Petula* / You're driving me: *Temperance Seven* / You don't know: *Shapiro, Helen* / Kon-Tiki: *Shadows* / Tower of strength: *Vaughan, Frankie* / Young ones: *Richard, Cliff* / Nut rocker: *B-Bumble & The Stingers* / Telstar: *Tornados* / Next time: *Richard, Cliff* / Diamonds: *Harris, Jet & Tony Meehan* / How do you do it: *Gerry & The Pacemakers* / Sweets for my sweet: *Searchers* / Blue moon: *Marcels* / Runaway: *Shannon, Del* / Johnny remember me: *Leyton, Johnny* / Walkin' back to happiness: *Shapiro, Helen* / Moon river: *Williams, Danny* / Wonderful land: *Shadows* / I remember you: *Ifield, Frank* / Lovesick blues: *Ifield, Frank* / Dance on: *Shadows* / Summer holiday: *Richard, Cliff* / I like it: *Gerry & The Pacemakers* / Do you love me: *Poole, Brian & The Tremeloes*
CD TYNOCD 102
Connoisseur Collection / May '89 / Pinnacle

30 YEARS OF NO.1'S VOL.4 (1963-1965)
You'll never walk alone: *Gerry & The Pacemakers* / Diane: *Bachelors* / Little children: *Kramer, Billy J. & The Dakotas* / Don't throw your love away: *Searchers* / House of the rising sun: *Animals* / Have I the right: *Honeycombs* / Always something there to remind me: *Shaw, Sandie* / Go now: *Moody Blues* / Tired of waiting for you: *Kinks* / It's not unusual: *Jones, Tom* / Minute you're gone: *Richard, Cliff* / I'm alive: *Hollies* / Needles and pins: *Searchers* / Anyone who had a heart: *Black, Cilla* / World without love: *Peter & Gordon* / Juliet: *Four Pennies* / Do wah diddy diddy: *Manfred Mann* / You really got me: *Kinks* / Yeh yeh: *Fame, Georgie & The Blue Flames* / You've lost that lovin' feelin': *Righteous Brothers* / I'll never find another you: *Seekers* / Concrete and clay: *Unit 4+2* / Long live love: *Shaw, Sandie*
CD TYNOCD 103
Connoisseur Collection / Jul '89 / Pinnacle

30 YEARS OF NO.1'S VOL.6 (1969-1972)
Blackberry way: *Move* / (If paradise is) half as nice: *Amen Corner* / Where do you go to my lovely: *Sarstedt, Peter* / Israelites: *Dekker, Desmond & The Aces* / Dizzy: *Roe, Tommy* / In the year 2525: *Zager & Evans* / I'll never fall in love again: *Gentry, Bobbie* / Sugar sugar: *Archies* / Love grows (Where my Rosemary grows): *Edison Lighthouse* / Wandering star: *Marvin, Lee* / In the Summertime: *Mungo Jerry* / Woodstock: *Matthew's Southern Comfort* / I hear you knocking: *Edmunds, Dave* / Baby jump: *Mungo Jerry* / Hot love: *T-Rex* / Double barrel: *Collins, Dave & Ansell* / Knock three times: *Dawn* / Chirpy chirpy cheep cheep: *Middle Of The Road* / Get it on: *T-Rex* / Hey girl don't bother me: *Tams* / Coz I luv you: *Slade* / Without you: *Nilsson, Harry* / Metal guru: *T-Rex* / Vincent: *McLean, Don*
CD TYNOCD 105
Connoisseur Collection / Jun '88 / Pinnacle

30 YEARS OF NO.1'S VOL.7 (1972-1975)
You wear it well: *Stewart, Rod* / Mouldy old dough: *Lieutenant Pigeon* / Clair: *O'Sullivan, Gilbert* / Blockbuster: *Sweet* / See my baby jive: *Wizzard* / Can the can: *Quatro, Suzi* / Rubber bullets: *10cc* / Welcome home: *Peters & Lee* / I'm the leader of the gang (I am): *Glitter, Gary* / Angel fingers: *Wizzard* / Daydreamer: *Cassidy, David* / You won't find another fool like me: *New Seekers* / Tiger feet: *Mud* / Devil gate drive: *Quatro, Suzi* / Seasons in the sun: *Jacks, Terry* / Sugar baby love: *Rubettes* / Streak: *Stevens, Ray* / Always yours: *Glitter, Gary* / Kung fu fighting: *Douglas, Carl* / Sad sweet dreamer: *Sweet Sensation* / Everything I own: *Boothe, Ken* / You're the first, the last, my everything: *White, Barry* / Down down: *Status Quo* / Ms. Grace: *Tymes*
CD TYNOCD 106
Connoisseur Collection / Dec '89 / Pinnacle

30 YEARS OF NO.1'S VOL.8 (1975-1977)
January: *Pilot* / Make me smile (come up and see me): *Harley, Steve & Cockney Rebel* / Bye bye baby: *Bay City Rollers* / Oh boy: *Mud* / Stand by your man: *Wynette, Tammy* / I'm not in love: *10cc* / Tears on my pillow: *Nash, Johnny* / Give a little love: *Bay City Rollers* / Barbados: *Typically Tropical* / Can't give you anything (but my love): *Stylistics* / Hold me close: *Essex, David* / Mamma mia: *Abba* / December '63 (oh what a night): *Four Seasons* / I love to love (but my baby loves to dance): *Charles, Tina* / Forever and ever: *Roussos, Demis* / Dancing queen: *Abba* / Mississippi: *Pussycat* / Don't give up on us: *Soul, David* / Free: *Williams, Deniece* / Lucille: *Rogers, Kenny* / Show you the way to go: *Jacksons* / So you win again: *Hot Chocolate* / Silver lady: *Soul, David* / Yes sir, I can boogie: *Baccara*
CD TYNOCD 107
Connoisseur Collection / Jan '90 / Pinnacle

30 YEARS OF NO.1'S VOL.9 (1977-1980)
Name of the game: *Abba* / Up town top ranking: *Althia & Donna* / Figaro: *Brotherhood Of Man* / Take a chance on me: *Abba* / Wuthering Heights: *Bush, Kate* / Dreadlock holiday: *10cc* / Rat trap: *Boomtown Rats* / Hit me with your rhythm stick: *Dury, Ian* / I will survive: *Gaynor, Gloria* / Ring my bell: *Ward, Anita* / Are friends electric: *Tubeway Army* / I don't like Mondays: *Boomtown Rats* / Cars: *Numan, Gary* / Video killed the radio star: *Buggles* / When you're in love with a beautiful woman: *Dr. Hook* / Too much too young: *Specials* / Coward of the county: *Rogers, Kenny* / Together we're beautiful: *Kinney, Fern* / Going underground: *Jam* / Dreams of children: *Jam* / Call me: *Blondie* / Geno: *Dexy's Midnight Runners* / Crying: *McLean, Don* / Sunday girl: *Blondie*
CD TYNOCD 108
Connoisseur Collection / Mar '90 / Pinnacle

30'S GIRLS, THE
Second hand man / Rhythm for sale / Doin' the Suzie Q / All God's chillun got rhythm / Summertime / My castles rockin'
CD CBC 1026
Timeless Jazz / Sep '95 / New Note/ Pinnacle

32 MASTERPIECES OF ROCK (2CD Set)
CD Set 24003
Delta Doubles / Jun '96 / Target/BMG

35 YEARS OF THE BEST IN BLUEGRASS 1960-1995 (Rebel Record's Anniversary Collection/4CD Set)
CD Set REB 4000CD
Rebel / Jul '97 / ADA / Direct

36 IRISH LOVE BALLADS
CD ______________ CHCD 3202
Chyme / Oct '95 / ADA / CM / Direct / Koch

36 MASTERPIECES OF JAZZ VOL.2 (2CD Set)
CD Set ______________ FA 059
Fremeaux / Apr '97 / ADA / Discovery

36 SUCCES CHANSON FRANCAISE VOL.1 (2CD Set)
CD Set ______________ FA 970
Fremeaux / May '96 / ADA / Discovery

36 SUCCES CHANSON FRANCAISE VOL.2
Vous oubliez votre cheval: *Trenet, Charles* / Coches dans le foin: *Pils Et Tabet* / La mome caoutchouc: *Gabin, Jean* / C'est vrai: *Mistinguett* / Cette petite femme la: *Simon, Michel* / Mon amant de la St Jean: *Delyle, Lucienne* / La cucaracha: *Rossi, Tino* / Sombre dimanche: *Damia* / Toulon, A: *Alibert* / Confessin': *Baker, Josephine* / Le vieux chateau: *Pills & Tabet* / Priere de la Charlotte: *Dubas, Marie* / Qui craint le grand mechant loup: *Adison, Fred* / Le fiancee du pirate: *Gauty, Lys* / Maman ne vend pas le maison: *Petit Mirscha* / Le fils de la femme poisson: *Frehel* / Ca sent si bon la France: *Chevalier, Maurice* / Tout est au duc: *Trenet, Charles* / Barnabe: *Fernandel* / Ou sont-ils tous mes copains: *Piaf, Edith* / Vous n'etes pas venue Dimanche: *Rossi, Tino* / Lily Marlene: *Solidor, Suzy* / Le marche de menilmontant: *Solidor, Suzy* / On m'suit: *Mistinguett* / On m'appelle simplet: *Fernandel* / Le chacal: *Piaf, Edith* / O corse ile d'amour: *Rossi, Tino* / Papa n'a pas voulu: *Mireille* / Vous qu'avez-vous fait de mon amour: *Ventura, Ray & Guy Berry* / La guinguette a ferme ses volets: *Damia* / Avec ma p'tit gueule: *Gabin, Jean* / Seule ce soir: *Marjane, Leo* / Folatrerie: *Fernandel* / Vous qui passez sans me voir: *Sablon, Jean* / Un seul regard: *Bauge, Andre & Sim Viva* / J'ai te main: *Trenet, Charles*
CD ______________ FA 975
Fremeaux / Apr '97 / ADA / Discovery

39 STEPS TO SEATTLE
You are my friend: *Rain Parade* / Mountain of love: *Giant Sand* / Dream is gone: *American Music Club* / It's OK: *Thin White Rope* / Ron Klaus wrecked his house: *Big Dipper* / When you smile: *Dream Syndicate* / I had a dream: *Long Ryders* / Speak the same to everyone: *Non Fiction* / Crazy girl: *Casuals* / Inside: *Sidewinder* / She's alright: *Downsiders* / Drifter: *Green On Red* / Wild dog waltz: *Band Of Blacky Ranchette* / Everything you need and everything you want: *Tolman, Russ*
CD ______________ DIAB 809
Diabolo / Apr '94 / Pinnacle

40 COMPLETE FAVOURITE IRISH BALLADS
CD ______________ CDBALLAD 002
Outlet / Jan '95 / ADA / CM / Direct / Duncans / Koch / Ross

40 COMPLETE IRISH PUB SONGS
CD ______________ CDBALLAD 001
Outlet / Jan '95 / ADA / CM / Direct / Duncans / Koch / Ross

40 DEGREES C CARNAVAL TROPICAL
CD ______________ 74321459732
Milan / Feb '97 / Conifer/BMG / Silva Screen

40 FOLK BALLADS OF IRELAND (2CD Set)
CD Set ______________ CHCD 1042
Chyme / Mar '96 / ADA / CM / Direct / Koch

40 IRISH LOVE SONGS
CD ______________ CHCD 1069
Chyme / Oct '95 / ADA / CM / Direct / Koch

40 UK TOP 10 HITS OF THE 1960'S (2CD Set)
Tobacco road: *Nashville Teens* / Midnight in Moscow: *Ball, Kenny & His Jazzmen* / Candy man: *Poole, Brian* / He's in town: *Rockin' Berries* / Roses are red: *Carroll, Ronnie* / Bobby's girl: *Maughan, Susan* / Save the last dance for me: *Drifters* / Sheila: *Roe, Tommy* / Tell him: *Davies, Billie* / Diamonds: *Harris, Jet* / Mirror mirror: *Pinkerton's Assorted Colours* / Wimoweh: *Denver, Karl* / Tell me when: *Applejacks* / Juke like Eddie: *Heinz* / You've got your troubles: *Fortunes* / I think of you: *Merseybeats* / Juliet: *Four Pennies* / Winchester Cathedral: *New Vaudeville Band* / Come back and shake me: *Rodgers, Clodagh* / I'll pick a rose for my rose: *Johnson, Marv* / Tossin' and turnin': *Ivy League* / Hello little girl: *Fourmost* / When a man loves a woman: *Sledge, Percy* / Build me up buttercup: *Foundations* / Walkin' back to happiness: *Shapiro, Helen* / But I do: *Henry, Clarence 'Frogman'* / Are you sure: *Allisons* / Game of love: *Fontana, Wayne* / Where do you go to my lovely: *Sarstedt, Peter* / You were made to love me: *Freddie & The Dreamers* / Cradle of love: *Preston, Johnny* / Wild thing: *Troggs* / Baby love: *Supremes* / Good timin': *Jones, Jimmy* / My guy: *Wells, Mary* / Ain't misbehavin': *Bruce, Tommy* / Little children: *Kramer, Billy J.* / Picture of you: *Bruvvers* / I'm into something good: *Herman's Hermits* / Love is all around: *Troggs*
CD Set ______________ 330002
Hallmark / Jul '96 / Carlton

40 UK TOP 10 HITS OF THE 1970'S (2CD Set)
Angel face: *Glitter Band* / Heaven must have sent you: *Elgins* / Billy don't be a hero: *Paper Lace* / Big seven: *Judge Dread* / Have you seen her: *Chi-Lites* / Son of my father: *Chicory Tip* / Hang on in there baby: *Bristol, Johnny* / Love grows (where my Rosemary goes): *Edison Lighthouse* / Feel the need in me: *Detroit Emeralds* / Patches: *Carter, Clarence* / Yellow river: *Christie* / Wishing on a star: *Rose Royce* / Storm in a teacup: *Fortunes* / Goodbye my love: *Glitter Band* / Love machine: *Miracles* / Oh girl: *Chi-Lites* / J'taime: *Judge Dread* / Night Chicago died: *Paper Lace* / Freedom come freedom go: *Fortunes* / Rose garden: *Anderson, Lynn* / Rock your baby: *McCrae, George* / Standing in the road: *Blackfoot Sue* / Car wash: *Rose Royce* / My ding-a-ling: *Berry, Chuck* / Don't let it die: *Smith, Hurricane* / That same old feeling: *Pickettywitch* / He's the greatest dancer: *Sister Sledge* / Pepperbox: *Peppers* / Sky high: *Jigsaw* / Stoned love: *Supremes* / We are family: *Sister Sledge* / Heaven must be missing an angel: *Tavares* / I'm a man: *Chicago* / More than a woman: *Tavares* / Honey honey: *Sweet Dreams* / Nathan Jones: *Supremes* / Band of gold: *Payne, Freda* / Oh babe what would you say: *Smith, Hurricane* / With you I'm born again: *Syreeta* / Love don't live here anymore: *Rose Royce*
CD Set ______________ 330012
Hallmark / Jul '96 / Carlton

40 VERY BEST IRISH PUB SONGS
CD ______________ CDPUB 026
Outlet / Mar '97 / ADA / CM / Direct / Duncans / Koch / Ross

48 GOLDENE INSTRUMENTALS DER VOLKSMUSIK (3CD Set)
Hoch drob'n auf dem berg: *Schultheiss, Fred* / Gamser: *Leizachter Musikanten* / Es war im Bohmerwald: *Leizachter Musikanten* / Zauberzither: *Wolf, Hubert* / Brotzeitpolka: *Hot Dogs* / Vergissmeinnicht: *Gustl's Frohliche Dorfmusik* / Der witzbold: *Kalina, Herbert* / Das kufsteinlied: *Fritz & Freddy* / Blue Hawaii: *Pokuhako, Carlos* / Marianka: *Greger, Max* / Western saloon: *Lambert, Franz* / Heizelmannchens wachtparade: *Lambert, Franz* / Greensleeves: *Schachtner, Heinz* / Dorftratsch: *Kittl, Franz* / Es schmettern die Horner: *Kittl, Franz* / Mondnacht am Konigsee: *Knabl, Rudi* / Hohe tannen: *Duo Aribert Korbel* / 'S kammerfensterlin: *Schultheiss, Fred* / Im fruhtau zu Berge: *Rheinische Waldhornquartett* / Klarinettenwilderer: *Leizachter Musikanten* / Konig-ludwig-lied: *Konig-Ludwig-Musikanten* / Du bist die Rose vom: *Alpenvorlandler* / Kirchweih in Tirol: *Knabl, Rudi* / Wo die Musikanten sind: *Fritz & Freddy* / Im Gansemarsch: *Graff, Willi* / Tolzer schutzenmarsch: *Graff, Willi* / Herbert's posaunenwalzer: *Kalina, Herbert* / Echo polka: *Gustl's Frohliche Dorfmusik* / Hawaii tatoo: *Pokuhako, Carlos* / O sole mio: *Schachtner, Heinz* / Libellentanz: *Kittl, Franz* / Der zithermuckl: *Wolf, Hubert* / Herzerl fur's Herzerl: *Leizachter Musikanten* / Santo Domingo: *Fritz & Freddy* / Annchen von Tharau: *Schultheiss, Fred* / Kaiserjager Marsch: *Knabl, Rudi* / Quecksilber: *Graff, Willi* / Ambosspolka: *Hot Dogs* / Weinberg polka: *Gustl's Frohliche Dorfmusik* / Erinnerung an Rheinbach: *Kalina, Herbert* / Mitternachtblues: *Strasser, Hugo* / Mitternachtsblues: *Strasser, Hugo* / Erinnerung au Zirkus Renz: *Lambert, Franz* / Neopolitanisches Stanchen: *Barny, Wal* / Alo ahe: *Pokuhako, Carlos* / Klarinettenklamauk: *Kittl, Franz* / Dudlsackrischer: *Wolf, Hubert* / Der mond halt seine Wacht: *Duo Aribert Korbel* / Waldandacht: *Rheinische Waldhornquartett*
CD Set ______________ HR 867772
Disky / Sep '96 / Disky / THE

50 BEST IRISH REBEL BALLADS VOL.1
CD ______________ IRB 1798CD
Outlet / Oct '95 / ADA / CM / Direct / Duncans / Koch / Ross

50 CLASSIC PUB SONGS
CD ______________ PUBCD 50
Primetime / Nov '94 / Silva Screen

50 COMPLETE IRISH REBEL SONGS VOL.2
CD ______________ IRBCD 1916
Outlet / Jun '96 / ADA / CM / Direct / Duncans / Koch / Ross

50 COUNTRY NO.1'S
CD Set ______________ DBG 53033
Double Gold / Jun '94 / Target/BMG

50 IRISH SINGALONG FAVOURITES
Come back home to Erin / Whistling Phil McHugh / Gipsy Rover / Let him go let hime tarry / Flower of sweet Strabane / Give an Irish girl to me / I never will marry / Slaney valley / Delaney's donkey Mary Mack / Maggie Pickens / Some say the devil's dead Johnny / When you die / Highland / Keel row / Have a drink of whisky Ballyhoe / Where the River Shannon flows / Erin's green shore / Cutting the corn in creeslough / Lovely Derry / If I were a blackbird / Hills of Kerry / Homes of Donegal / County Mayo / Aloysius Magee Eileen / Oge agricultural Irish girl / Take me back to Castlebar / Blue hills of Breffni / Connemara bus / Dear Doctor John / I don't mind if I do / I'll take you home again Kathleen / Bunch of thyme / Rathlin island / Westering home / Where the blarney roses grow / Abbeyshrule / Brian oge and Molly Bawn / Johnny I hardly knew ye dear / Old Donegal / Peggy O'Neil / Nora Malone / My wild Irish rose / Nellie Kelly / Kitty Kelly / Maid of Fyvie / Drunken sailor / Rattling bog / Reel / Turkey in the straw
CD ______________ EMPRCD 553
Emporio / Nov '94 / Disc

50 MILLION SELLERS (2CD Set)
CD Set ______________ CPCD 82792
Charly / Apr '97 / Koch

50 NUMBER ONE'S OF THE 60'S
Young ones: *Richard, Cliff* / Wonderful land: *Shadows* / Oh pretty woman: *Orbison, Roy* / Baby love: *Ross, Diana & The Supremes* / It's not unusual: *Jones, Tom* / Sun ain't gonna shine anymore: *Walker Brothers* / (There's) always something there to remind me: *Shaw, Sandie* / Everlasting love: *Love Affair* / Baby come back: *Equals* / Sweets for my sweet: *Searchers* / Silence is golden: *Tremeloes* / With a litte help from my friends: *Cocker, Joe* / Blue moon: *Marcels* / Three steps to heaven: *Cochran, Eddie* / You really got me: *Kinks* / I like it: *Gerry & The Pacemakers* / I'm alive: *Hollies* / Young girl: *Puckett, Gary* / Yeh yeh: *Fame, Georgie* / I'm into something good: *Herman's Hermits* / Walkin' back to happiness: *Shapiro, Helen* / Go now: *Moody Blues* / Pretty flamingo: *Manfred Mann* / Out of time: *Farlowe, Chris* / Whiter shade of pale: *Procul Harum* / You've lost that loving feeling: *Righteous Brothers* / Reach out I'll be there: *Four Tops* / You don't have to say to love me: *Springfield, Dusty* / Bad to me: *Kramer, Billy J. & The Dakotas* / World without love: *Peter & Gordon* / Do it again: *Beach Boys* / Sunny afternoon: *Kinks* / All or nothing: *Small Faces* / Blackberry way: *Move* / With a girl like you: *Troggs* / Mony mony: *James, Tommy & The Shondells* / Baby, now that I've found you: *Foundations* / Where do you go to my lovely: *Sarstedt, Peter* / Je t'aime, moi non plus: *Birkin, Jane & Serge Gainsbourg* / Fire: *Crazy World Of Arthur Brown* / Long live love: *Shaw, Sandie* / Michelle: *Overlanders* / Green green grass of home: *Jones, Tom* / I'll never find another you: *Seekers* / Don't throw your love away: *Searchers* / Mr. Tambourine Man: *Byrds* / San Francisco: *McKenzie, Scott* / Keep on running: *Davis, Spencer Group* / Make it easy on yourself: *Walker Brothers* / Albatross: *Fleetwood Mac* / Something in the air: *Thunderclap Newman*
CD ______________ RADCD 08
Global TV / Apr '95 / BMG

50 ORIGINAL DANCE GOLDEN OLDIES
CD Set ______________ 55525
Laserlight / Nov '94 / Target/BMG

50 ROMANTIC LOVE SONGS (2CD Set)
Somewhere my love / Love me tonight / What is this thing called love / Young love / Love's been good to me / Have I told you lately that I love you / Old fashioned way / You're just in love / Be my love / And I love you so / Our love affair / Secret love / Lover come back to me / Hello young lovers / When I fall in love / Love me tender / Let's fall in love / Love is blue / Love story / Love letters / Je t'aime / Why do I love you / Falling in love with love / No other love / Man and a woman / You've lost that loving feeling / Let there be love / What the world needs now / Love is here to stay / I'm in the mood for love / If I loved you / Fallin' in love / Goodbye to love / I can't stop loving you / LOVE / True love / Almost like being in love / I'll never fall in love again / I wish you love / So in love / She / Easy to love / Love grows / Love letters in the sand / Man I love / Puppy love / Can't help falling in love / Somebody loves me / People will say we're in love / This guy's in love with you
CD Set ______________ 330422
Hallmark / Mar '97 / Carlton

50'S - JUKE JOINT BLUES, THE
Three o'clock blues: *King, B.B.* / Long tall woman: *James, Elmore* / Ramblin' on my mind: *Gilmore, Boyd* / Gonna let you go: *Turner, Babyface* / Love my baby: *Bland, Bobby & Junior Parker* / Riding in the moonlight: *Howlin' Wolf* / 44 blues: *Curtis, James Peck* / Step back baby: *Blair, Sunny* / This is the end: *Reed, James* / Jake head boogie: *Hopkins, Lightnin'* / Down in New Orleans: *Smith, Little George* / Monte Carlo: *Dixie Blues Boys* / Doin' the town: *Dixon, Floyd* / Just got in from Texas: *Gordon, Rosco* / Big mouth: *Nelson, Jimmy 'T-99'* / Have you ever: *Walton, Mercy Dee* / Sputterin' blues: *Robertson, Walter* / Prowling blues: *Fuller, Johnny* / Going to New Orleans: *Tanner, Kid* / Good morning little angel: *Louis, Joe Hill* / Panic's on: *McCracklin, Jimmy* / What's the matter with you: *Horton, Big Walter*
CD ______________ CDCH 216
Ace / Jul '87 / Pinnacle

50'S - R & B VOCAL GROUPS, THE
Rock bottom: *Rams* / Hold me, thrill me, chill me: *Flairs* / My darling, my sweet: *Flairs* / I made a vow: *Robins* / Please remember my heart: *Five Bells* / My cutie pie: *Five Bells* / Girl in my dreams: *Cliques* / Even since you've been gone: *Hawks* / It's all over: *Hawks* / Please don't go: *Chanters* / Tick tock: *Marvin & Johnny* / Why did I fall in love: *Jacks* / Sweet thing: *Maye, Arthur Lee & The Crowns* / Hands across the table: *Cadets* / Hey Rube: *Rocketeers* / It won't take long/Native girl: *Native Boys* / Farewell: *Relf, Bobby & The Laurels* / At last: *Berry, Richard & the Dreamers* / Please please baby: *Five Hearts* / Love me love me love me: *Chimes* / I love you, yes I do: *Marvin, Johnny*
CD ______________ CDCH 212
Ace / Jul '87 / Pinnacle

50'S - ROCKABILLY FEVER, THE
I guess it's meant that way: *Cupp, Pat* / Long gone daddy: *Cupp, Pat* / Don't do me no wrong: *Cupp, Pat* / Everybody's movin': *Glenn, Glen* / If I had me a woman: *Glenn, Glen* / I don't know when: *Harris, Hal* / True affection: *Johnson, Byron* / Be boppin' daddy: *Cole, Les & The Echoes* / Rock little baby: *Cole, Les & The Echoes* / My big fat baby: *Hall, Sonny & The Echoes* / Rock my warriors rock: *Jackson, Joe* / Snake eyed mama: *Cole, Don* / Nuthin' but a nuthin': *Stewart, Jimmy & His Nighthawks* / Wild wild party: *Feathers, Charlie* / Pink cadillac: *Todd, Johnny* / Slippin' and slidin': *Davis, Link* / All the time: *LaBeef, Sleepy* / Go home letter: *Barber, Glen* / Boppin' wigwam Willie: *Scott, Ray* / I can't find the doorknob: *Jimmy & Johnny* / Jitterbop baby: *Harris, Hal* / Little bit more: *LaBeef, Sleepy*
CD ______________ CDCH 218
Ace / Jul '87 / Pinnacle

52 SHADES OF ORANGE (2CD Set)
CD Set ______________ CDULSTER 001
Outlet / Apr '96 / ADA / CM / Direct / Duncans / Koch / Ross

55 MILES FROM TEXACO
CD ______________ EFA 06187CD
House In Motion / Jul '93 / SRD

60 FAVOURITE HYMNS (3CD Set)
Soldiers of Christ arise: *Massed Male Voice Choirs Of Honley, Skelmanthorpe & Gledholt* / O worship the king: *Brighouse & Rastrick Band* / All creatures of our God and King: *Brighouse & Rastrick Band* / Sun of my soul: *Brighouse & Rastrick Band* / Leads us Heavenly Father lead us: *Brighouse & Rastrick Band* / O love that wilt not let me go: *Brighouse & Rastrick Band* / O God our help in ages past: *Brighouse & Rastrick Band* / Come ye thankful people come: *Brighouse & Rastrick Band* / Love divine: *Brighouse & Rastrick Band* / Crown him with many crowns: *Brighouse & Rastrick Band* / How sweet the name of Jesus sounds: *Brighouse & Rastrick Band* / Jesus keeps me near the cross: *Brighouse & Rastrick Band* / Now thank we all our God: *Brighouse & Rastrick Band* / All glory laud and honour: *Brighouse & Rastrick Band* / Were you there when they crucified my Lord: *Wallace, Ian* / How great thou art: *Wallace, Ian* / I will sing the wondrous story: *Wallace, Ian* / Behold me standing at the door: *Wallace, Ian* / He hideth my soul: *Wallace, Ian* / When I survey the wondrous cross: *Wallace, Ian* / Swing low, sweet chariot: *Wallace, Ian* / In the sweet by and by: *Wallace, Ian* / Steal away: *Wallace, Ian* / In heavenly love abiding: *Wallace, Ian* / For all the saints: *Wallace, Ian* / Deep river: *Wallace, Ian* / There is a greenhill far away: *Massed Choirs* / Rock of ages: *Massed Choirs* / Lord's my shepherd: *Massed Choirs* / Who is on the Lord's side: *Massed Choirs* / Praise to the Lord: *Massed Choirs* / All people that on earth do dwell: *Massed Choirs* / To God be the glory: *Massed Choirs* / Onward Christian soldiers: *Massed Choirs* / All hail the power of Jesus' name: *Massed Choirs* / O for a thousand tongues to sing: *Massed Choirs* / All in the April evening: *Massed Choirs* / Let all the world in every corner sing: *Massed Choirs* / He lives: *Massed Choirs* / Praise my soul: *Massed Choirs* / Jesus shall reign where're the sun: *Massed Choirs* / O Jesus I have promised: *Carousel Children* / Lord of the dance: *Carousel Children* / Jesu lover of my soul: *Monese, Valerie* / Sweet hour of prayer: *Monese, Valerie* / My Jesus I love thee: *Monese, Valerie* / Amazing grace: *Monese, Valerie* / King of love my shepherd is: *Monese, Valerie* / Lord of all hopefulness: *Monese, Valerie* / I am so glad: *Heatherbell Children*
CD Set ______________ CDTRBOX 204
Trio / Oct '95 / EMI

60 GREAT BLUES RECORDINGS (3CD Set)
Jealous woman: *Walker, T-Bone* / I'm sinking: *Fulson, Lowell* / Same old lonesome day: *Fulson, Lowell* / Rocks in my pillow: *Brown, Roy* / We can't make it: *King, B.B.* / Time to say goodbye: *King, B.B.* / Please love me: *King, B.B.* / Past day: *King, B.B.* / My own fault darlin': *King, B.B.* / TB blues: *Witherspoon, Jimmy* / I'm going around in circles: *Witherspoon, Jimmy* / Telephone blues: *Smith, George* / Women in my life: *Hooker, John Lee* / Boogie chillun: *Hooker, John Lee* / Crawlin' kingsnake: *Hooker, John Lee* / Heartache baby: *Louis, Joe Hill* / Walkin' talkin' blues: *Louis, Joe Hill* / Going down slow: *Louis, Joe Hill* / When night

falls: *Carter, Goree* / Sinful woman: *James, Elmore* / I believe: *James, Elmore* / Dust my blues: *James, Elmore* / Sho' nuff I do: *James, Elmore* / That's all I care: *Dixon, Floyd* / Houston jump: *Dixon, Floyd* / Draftin' blues: *Dixon, Floyd* / Hey Mr. Porter: *Smith, George* / Good lovin': *Bland, Bobby* / Summertime: *King, Saunders* / Everything about midnight: *King, Saunders* / I'm so worried: *King, Saunders* / I ain't in the mood: *Humes, Helen* / Central Avenue blues: *Crayton, Pee Wee* / If that's the way you feel: *Champion, Mickey* / Best friend: *Champion, Mickey* / Gene's guitar blues: *Phillips, Gene* / Gene jumps the blues: *Phillips, Gene* / Jockey blues: *Turner, 'Big' Joe* / Playful baby: *Turner, 'Big' Joe* / Johnny's lowdown blues: *Fuller, Johnny* / Riding in the moonlight: *Howlin' Wolf* / How many more times: *Wilson, Smokey* / Straighten up baby: *Wilson, Smokey* / Standing in the backdoor crying: *Thomas, Lafayette* / Tired of everybody: *Parker, Johnny* / Dr. Brown: *Reed, James* / Lonesome dog blues: *Hopkins, Lightnin'* / Jake Head boogie: *Hopkins, Lightnin'* / Mississippi blues: *Dixon, Floyd Trio* / John Henry: *Pinetop Slim* / Thrill is gone: *Hawkins, Roy* / Tennessee woman: *Robinson, Fenton* / Applejack boogie: *Pinetop Slim* / Hardhearted woman: *Horton, Big Walter* / Black gal: *Horton, Big Walter* / Big chested mama: *Cotton, Sylvester* / Love me baby: *Bland, Bobby & Junior Parker* / I may be crazy baby but (I ain't no fool): *Smith, Geechie* / Cold blooded woman: *Great Gates* / I cried: *Ace, Johnny*
CD Set ____ CBOXCD 3
Cascade / Jan '92 / Pinnacle

60'S APOCALYPSE (2CD Set)
CD Set ____ AOP 51
Age Of Panik / Apr '97 / Total/BMG

60'S ARCHIVES VOL.1 - SOUND OF THE SIXTIES
CD ____ 842039
EVA / Jun '94 / ADA / Direct

60'S ARCHIVES VOL.2 - SCARCE GARAGE RECORDS
CD ____ 842634
EVA / May '94 / ADA / Direct

60'S ARCHIVES VOL.2 - TEXAS PUNK
CD ____ 842040
EVA / Jun '94 / ADA / Direct

60'S ARCHIVES VOL.3 - LOUISIANA PUNK
CD ____ 842041
EVA / Jun '94 / ADA / Direct

60'S ARCHIVES VOL.4 - FLORIDA & NEW MEXICO PUNK
CD ____ 842042
EVA / Jun '94 / ADA / Direct

60'S ARCHIVES VOL.5 - US PUNK FROM THE 60'S
CD ____ 842043
EVA / Jun '94 / ADA / Direct

60'S ARCHIVES VOL.6
CD ____ EVA 8420448
EVA / Nov '94 / ADA / Direct

60'S ARCHIVES VOL.7 - MICHIGAN PUNK
CD ____ 842045
EVA / Jun '94 / ADA / Direct

60'S ARCHIVES VOL.8 - ACID TRIPS & HEAVY SOUNDS
CD ____ 842046
EVA / May '94 / ADA / Direct

60'S CLASSICS
CD ____ DCDCD 205
Castle / Aug '96 / BMG

60'S COLLECTION (3CD Set)
You really got me: *Kinks* / Sweets for my sweet: *Searchers* / (There's) always something there to remind me: *Shaw, Sandie* / Here comes my baby: *Tremeloes* / Catch the wind: *Donovan* / Downtown: *Clark, Petula* / 24 hours from Tulsa: *Pitney, Gene* / Go now: *Moody Blues* / Ain't nothin' but a house party: *Showstoppers* / Baby, now that I've found you: *Foundations* / Pictures of matchstick men: *Status Quo* / Summer in the city: *Lovin' Spoonful* / Even the bad times are good: *Tremeloes* / Here comes the nice: *Small Faces* / Out of time: *Farlowe, Chris* / That girl belongs to yesterday: *Pitney, Gene* / Sugar and spice: *Searchers* / Michelle: *Overlanders* / This is my song: *Clark, Petula* / First cut is the deepest: *Arnold, P.P.* / Needles and pins: *Searchers* / Silence is golden: *Tremeloes* / All day and all of the night: *Kinks* / I couldn't live without your love: *Clark, Petula* / Build me up buttercup: *Foundations* / Let the heartaches begin: *Baldry, Long John* / Colours: *Donovan* / Itchykoo park: *Small Faces* / Girl don't come: *Shaw, Sandie* / I'm gonna be strong: *Pitney, Gene* / Man of the world: *Fleetwood Mac* / Daydream: *Lovin' Spoonful* / Lazy sunday: *Small Faces* / Sunny afternoon: *Kinks* / Ice in the sun: *Status Quo* / Suddenly you left me: *Tremeloes* / When you walk in the room: *Searchers* / Don't sleep in the subway: *Clark, Petula* / Only love can break your heart: *Pitney, Gene* / America/ Second amendment: *Nice* / Waterloo sunset: *Kinks* / Susannah's still alive: *Davies, Dave* / Tomorrow: *Shaw, Sandie* / (Call me) number one: *Tremeloes* / Universal: *Small Faces* / Other man's grass (is always greener): *Clark, Petula* / Something's gotten hold of my heart: *Pitney, Gene* / I'm gonna make you mine: *Christie, Lou* / Make me an island: *Dolan, Joe* / It's too late now: *Baldry, Long John* / Judy in disguise: *Fred, John & The Playboys* / Simon says: *1910 Fruitgum Company* / Oh happy days: *Hawkins, Edwin Singers* / Just one smile: *Pitney, Gene* / Puppet on a string: *Shaw, Sandie* / In the bad, bad old days (before you loved me): *Foundations* / Green tambourine: *Lemon Pipers* / Death of a clown: *Davies, Dave* / Let's go to San Francisco: *Flowerpot Men* / Don't throw your love away: *Searchers*
CD Set ____ PBXCD 501
Pulse / Nov '96 / BMG

60'S COLLECTION VOL.1
Runaway / He's so fine / Will you love me tomorrow / 24 Hours from Tulsa / Leader of the pack / Every beat of my heart / Fools rush in / Under the boardwalk / Rubber ball / Harbour lights / Walk - don't run / Mr. Bass Man / Judy in disguise (with glasses) / I believe / Tossin' and turnin' / Don't let the sun catch you crying / Silhouettes / Tobacco road / Baby, now that I've found you / Love is all around
CD ____ QED 001
Tring / Nov '96 / Tring

60'S COLLECTION VOL.2
Remember (walkin' in the sand) / Surfin' safari / I'm gonna be strong / Chapel of love / Duke of Earl / Oh no, not my baby / Barefootin' / Soldier boy / Hats off to Larry / Save the last dance for me / Ramona / Hippy hippy shake / You'll never walk alone / There's a kind of hush / Wild thing / Here it comes again / Tell Laura I love her / Walkin' back to happiness / Hurt / Dizzy
CD ____ QED 002
Tring / Nov '96 / Tring

60'S COLLECTION, THE (3CD Set)
CD Set ____ KBOX 368
Collection / Aug '97 / Target/BMG / TKO Magnum

60'S DANCE PARTY: LET'S DANCE
CD ____ MU 5002
Musketeer / Oct '92 / Disc

60'S DECADE, THE (3CD Set)
CD Set ____ TTP 002
Tring / Nov '92 / Tring

60'S HITS COLLECTION: AT THE HOP
Leader of the pack: *Shangri-Las* / Let's twist again: *Checker, Chubby* / Then he kissed me: *Crystals* / Runaround Sue: *Dion* / Good golly Miss Molly: *Little Richard* / Blueberry Hill: *Domino, Fats*
CD ____ MU 8006
Musketeer / Nov '93 / Disc

60'S HITS COLLECTION: DA DOO RON RON
Sweet talking guy: *Chiffons* / Tell Laura I love her: *Valance, Ricky* / Rhythm of the rain: *Cascades* / Will you still love me tomorrow: *Shirelles* / Chapel of love: *Dixie Cups* / Surfin' safari: *Beach Boys*
CD ____ MU 8005
Musketeer / Dec '93 / Disc

60'S HITS COLLECTION: DOWNTOWN
Downtown: *Clark, Petula* / Ferry 'cross the Mersey: *Gerry & The Pacemakers* / Happy together: *Turtles* / Young girl: *Puckett, Gary* / Calender girl: *Sedaka, Neil* / Hold me: *Proby, P.J.*
CD ____ MU 8002
Musketeer / Nov '93 / Disc

60'S HITS COLLECTION: EVERLASTING LOVE
Wild thing: *Troggs* / Breaking up is hard to do: *Sedaka, Neil* / Everlasting love: *Love Affair* / Walkin' back to happiness: *Shapiro, Helen* / Crying game: *Berry, Dave* / California dreamin': *Mamas & The Papas*
CD ____ MU 8001
Musketeer / Nov '93 / Disc

60'S HITS COLLECTION: SILENCE IS GOLDEN
Don't take your love to town: *Rogers, Kenny* / Silence is golden: *Tremeloes* / Save the last dance for me: *Drifters* / No milk today: *Herman's Hermits* / Wishin' and hopin': *Merseybeats* / Bobby's girl: *Maughan, Susan*
CD ____ MU 8004
Musketeer / Nov '93 / Disc

60'S HITS COLLECTION: UP ON THE ROOF
I'm into something good: *Herman's Hermits* / Do you love me: *Poole, Brian* / Sugar sugar: *Archies* / Hello Mary Lou: *Nelson, Rick* / Night has a thousand eyes: *Vee, Bobby* / Moon river: *Williams, Danny*
CD ____ MU 7003
CD ____ MU 8003
Musketeer / Nov '93 / Disc

60'S LOVE SONGS: DRIFT AWAY
CD ____ MU 5001
Musketeer / Oct '92 / Disc

60'S MEGAMIXES VOL.1
CD ____ MACCD 303
Autograph / Aug '96 / BMG

60'S MEGAMIXES VOL.2
CD ____ MACCD 304
Autograph / Aug '96 / BMG

60'S MIXES
CD ____ JHD 085
Tring / Mar '93 / Tring

60'S PARTY HITS
CD ____ MATCD 222
Castle / Nov '93 / BMG

60'S POP CLASSICS
Everybody's talking: *Nilsson, Harry* / In the year 2525: *Zager & Evans* / If paradise is half as nice: *Amen Corner* / Light my fire: *Feliciano, Jose* / Go now: *Moody Blues* / Come back and shake me: *Rodgers, Clodagh* / Daydream: *Lovin' Spoonful* / Letter: *Box Tops* / Captain of your ship: *Reparata & The Delrons* / Aquarius: *Fifth Dimension* / Let the sunshine in: *Fifth Dimension* / Ain't got no...I got life: *Simone, Nina* / Breaking up is hard to do: *Sedaka, Neil* / Didn't I blow your mind this time: *Delfonics* / Working in a coalmine: *Dorsey, Lee* / Keep on: *Channel, Bruce* / Itchycoo park: *Small Faces* / Grazing in the grass: *Friends Of Distinction* / Ice in the sun: *Status Quo*
CD ____ 74321449232
Camden / Feb '97 / BMG

60'S POP CLASSICS VOL.2
Go now: *Moody Blues* / Man of the world: *Fleetwood Mac* / In the year 2525: *Zager & Evans* / Captain of your ship: *Reparata & The Delrons* / Yeah yeah: *Fame, Georgie* / Out of time: *Farlowe, Chris* / I'm a believer: *Monkees* / (If paradise is) half as nice: *Amen Corner* / Light my fire: *Feliciano, Jose* / Harlem shuffle: *Bob & Earl* / Leader of the pack: *Shangri-Las* / I'm believer: *Monkees*
CD ____ 74321339252
Camden / Jan '96 / BMG

60'S POP CLASSICS VOL.3
Good bad and the ugly: *Montenegro, Hugo* / Ain't got no - I got life: *Simone, Nina* / Eve of destruction: *McGuire, Barry* / I'm your puppet: *Purify, James & Bobby* / Simon says: *1910 Fruitgum Company* / Waterloo sunset: *Kinks* / Catch the wind: *Donovan* / Needles and pions: *Searchers* / Yummy yummy yummy: *Ohio Express* / First cut is the deepest: *Arnold, P.P.* / Let the heartache begin: *Baldry, Long John* / Aquarius/ Let the sun shine: *5th Dimension*
CD ____ 74321339262
Camden / Jan '96 / BMG

60'S SUMMER MIX (2CD Set)
CD Set ____ TCD 2908
Telstar / Jun '97 / BMG

60'S SUMMER OF LOVE
Daydream: *Lovin' Spoonful* / Sunny afternoon: *Kinks* / Whiter shade of pale: *Procul Harum* / Itchycoo park: *Small Faces* / Death of a clown: *Davies, Dave* / Blackberry way: *Move* / Lady Jane: *Garrick, David* / Man of the world: *Fleetwood Mac* / Elenore: *Turtles* / Summer in the city: *Lovin' Spoonful* / Green tambourine: *Lemon Pipers* / For your love: *Yardbirds* / Handbags and gladrags: *Farlowe, Chris* / Waterloo sunset: *Kinks* / Happy together: *Turtles* / Let's go to San Francisco: *Flowerpot Men* / Woodstock: *Matthew's Southern Comfort*
CD ____ PWKS 4182
Carlton / Feb '96 / Carlton

60'S THE HITS GO ON: LOVE IS ALL AROUND
CD ____ MU 5050
Musketeer / Oct '92 / Disc

60'S UK HITS COLLECTION: TWIST AND SHOUT
CD ____ MU 5053
Musketeer / Oct '92 / Disc

60'S USA HITS
CD ____ MACCD 116
Autograph / Aug '96 / BMG

60'S USA HITS COLLECTION: SWEET TALKIN' GUY
CD ____ MU 5052
Musketeer / Oct '92 / Disc

60'S VOL.1, THE
Speedy gonzales: *Boone, Pat* / Twist: *Checker, Chubby* / Wild one: *Rydell, Bobby* / Swingin' school: *Rydell, Bobby* / Good golly miss molly: *Swinging Blue Jeans* / Let's have a party: *Jackson, Wanda* / Pipeline: *Chantays* / Hats off to Larry: *Shannon, Del* / Let's twist again: *Checker, Chubby* / Bread and butter: *Newbeats* / Here comes my baby: *Tremeloes* / One fine day: *Chiffons* / I'm the one: *Gerry & The Pacemakers* / Pepermint Twist: *Joey Dee and the Starliters* / Mr. Bass man: *Cymbal, Johnny* / You were on my mind: *Crispin St Peters* / Up on the roof: *Drifters* / Volare: *Rydell, Bobby* / Deep Purple: *Tempo, Nino* / Sheila: *Roe, Tommy* / Corina, corina: *Peterson, Ray* / Hey baby: *Channel, Bruce* / Do you want to know a secret: *Kramer, Billy J.* / Saturday night at the movies: *Drifters* / Keep searchin'(we follow the sun): *Shannon, Del* / Save the last dance for me: *Drifters* / Runaway: *Shannon, Del* / Hippy hippy shake: *Swinging Blue Jeans* / Surf city: *Jan & Dean* / Little old lady from Pasadena: *Jan & Dean*
CD ____ ECD 3142
K-Tel / Mar '95 / K-Tel

60'S VOL.2, THE
Dizzy: *Roe, Tommy* / Silence is golden: *Tremeloes* / Don't let the sun catch you crying: *Gerry & The Pacemakers* / (Don't know why) but I do: *Henry, Clarence 'Frogman'* / Trains and boats and planes: *Kramer, Billy J.* / Sweet pea: *Roe, Tommy* / Ob-la-di, ob-la-da: *Marmalade* / Because they're young: *Eddy, Duane* / I think of you: *Merseybeats* / Under the boardwalk: *Drifters* / Good morning starshine: *Oliver* / Little town flirt: *Shannon, Del* / Pied Piper: *St. Peters, Crispian* / Chapel of love: *Dixie Cups* / Blue moon: *Marcels* / Those oldies but goodies (remind me of you): *Little Cesar and the Roma Group* / Hey Paula: *Paul & Paula* / Devil or angel: *Vee, Bobby* / So much in love: *Tymes* / Forget him: *Rydell, Bobby* / Someone someone: *Poole, Brian* / Down in the boondocks: *Royal, Billy Joe* / Games people play: *South, Joe* / Everybody: *Roe, Tommy* / Those were the days: *Hopkin, Mary* / Groovy kind of love: *Fontana, Wayne* / Goin out of my head: *Little Anthony & The Imperials* / Zip a dee-doo-dah: *Soxx, Bob B. & The Blue Jeans* / More than I can say: *Vee, Bobby* / Run to him: *Vee, Bobby*
CD ____ ECD 3143
K-Tel / Mar '95 / K-Tel

60'S YEARS VOL.1
CD ____ 519382
Magic / Jul '97 / Greyhound

60'S YEARS VOL.2
CD ____ 523302
Magic / Jul '97 / Greyhound

60'S YEARS VOL.3
CD ____ 176162
Magic / Jul '97 / Greyhound

60S COLLECTION (3CD Set)
CD Set ____ TBXCD 501
TrueTrax / Jan '96 / THE

65 RAP AND HARDCORE DANCE ORIGINALS (4CD Set)
Don't stop the music: *Carroll, Dina & Simon Harris* / Respect due: *Daddy Freddy & Heavy D/Frankie Paul* / Cooling in paradise: *Thrashpack* / These are the breaks: *DJ Hanway* / Style wars: *Hijack* / Give it a rest: *She Rockers & Betty Boo* / Powerplay megamix: *Harris, Simon* / My whole life: *Spyder D* / Whole lotta love: *Vicious Rumour Club* / Shake it up: *Duke* / Burial proceedings in the course of three nights: *3 Knights* / Go freddy go: *Daddy Freddie* / Untitled: *Hardnoise* / Boingsville: *Thrashpack* / Coronation: *Royal Rhymes* / DC Jail: *DJ Daddy* / Movement: *SL Troopers* / Back 2 tha bass: *Harris, Simon* / Ill tip: *Einstein* / Free: *MC Duke* / Lyrical culture: *Demon Boyz* / Megamix: *Sirrah, Nomis* / Ragamuffin hip hop: *Asher D & Daddy Freddy* / Who's in the house: *45 King* / Trigger happy: *Thrashpack* / Tame 1 unleashed: *Lady Tame* / Theme from disturbing the peace: *Harris, Simon* / I'm riffin': *Duke* / My beat: *Father MC* / Sparky's in the place: *Sparky D* / Hits from small arms fire: *First Frontal Assault* / Every nigga's a star: *Einstein* / Return of the dread 1: *Duke* / Dancehall clash: *Tenor Fly & Daddy Freddy* / Runaway love: *Harris, Simon & Einstein* / Summertime: *Asher D & Daddy Freddy* / Onslaught: *Standing Ovation* / Bite of love doomsday of rap: *Hijack* / Shok da house: *Harris, Simon* / This is a jam: *Demon Boyz* / Rhymes unlimited: *Einstein* / Like a bike: *Asher D* / Roughneck nuh ramp: *Daddy Freddie & Tenor Fly* / Freestyle part 1: *Duke & Merlin* / Freestyle part 2: *Duke & Merlin* / Brutality: *Asher D & Daddy Freddy* / Silk smooth: *Monte Luv & DJ Rob* / Freddy's back: *Daddy Freddie & Duke* / Ragga house: *Harris, Simon & Daddy Freddy* / Shotgun wedding: *Leslie Lyrics* / Can I get a witness: *Einstein* / My policy: *Sharkey* / Live jam: *Daddy Freddie* / Rougher than an animal: *Demon Boyz* / Never made me a man: *Big Kraze* / Friday night Saturday morning: *Einstein* / This is serious: *Harris, Simon* / Dog catcher: *Duke* / Power of evil: *Predator* / Hypnotic FX: *Infamix* / Rhymes are smokin': *Einstein* / Ragamuffin duo take charge: *Asher D & Daddy Freddy* / Final conflict: *Duke*
CD Set ____ TFP 041
Tring / Apr '95 / Tring

70'S BLOCKBUSTERS
Blockbuster: *Sweet* / Rivers of Babylon: *Boney M* / All by myself: *Carmen, Eric* / Bye bye baby: *Bay City Rollers* / Native New Yorker: *Odyssey* / Seasons in the sun: *Jacks, Terry* / Ms Grace: *Tymes* / Woman in love: *Three Degrees* / New York, New York: *Kenny, Gerard* / Ready or not here I come: *Delfonics* / Every day hurts: *Sad Cafe* / Without you: *Nilsson* / Like sister and brother: *Drifters* / If you think you know how to love me: *Smokie* / Torn between two lovers: *McGregor, Mary* / It's a heartache: *Tyler, Bonnie* / I can't stand the rain: *Eruption* / Yes sir I can boogie: *Baccara*
CD ____ 74321449242
Camden / Feb '97 / BMG

70'S COLLECTION (3CD Set)
CD Set ____ TBXCD 502
TrueTrax / Jan '96 / THE

70'S COLLECTION (3CD Set)
Down the dustpipe: *Status Quo* / Apeman: *Kinks* / After the goldrush: *Prelude* / In the summertime: *Mungo Jerry* / (It's like a) sad

old kind of movie: *Pickettywitch* / You don't mess around with Jim: *Croce, Jim* / Why did you do it: *Stretch* / This flight tonight: *Nazareth* / Swing your daddy: *Gilstrap, Jim* / Midnight train to Georgia: *Knight, Gladys & The Pips* / Natural born boogie: *Humble Pie* / Love's gotta hold on me: *Dollar* / Beach baby: *First Class* / Bad, bad Leroy Brown: *Croce, Jim* / Me and my life: *Tremeloes* / Sky high: *Jigsaw* / Man who sold the world: *Lulu* / You'll never know what your missing: *Real Thing* / Egyptian reggae: *Richman, Jonathan* / Summer of my life: *May, Simon* / It's a heartache: *Tyler, Bonnie* / Sunshine day: *Osibisa* / Operator (that's not the way it feels): *Croce, Jim* / Best thing that ever happened to me: *Knight, Gladys & The Pips* / Shooting star: *Dollar* / Making up again: *Goldie* / You to me are eveything: *Real Thing* / Girls: *Moments* / Show me you're a woman: *Mud* / Isn't she lovely: *Parton, David* / Lady rose: *Mungo Jerry* / So sad the song: *Knight, Gladys & The Pips* / Purely by coincidence: *Sweet Sensation* / In my chair: *Status Quo* / In Zaire: *Wakelin, Johnny* / Broken down angel: *Nazareth* / Now is the time: *James, Jimmy* / I'll have to say I love you with a song: *Croce, Jim* / Car 67: *Driver 67* / Can't get by without you: *Real Thing* / I wanna hold your hand: *Dollar* / Long legged woman dressed in black: *Mungo Jerry* / L-l-lucy: *Mud* / Mean girl: *Status Quo* / Love hurts: *Nazareth* / Roadrunner: *Richman, Jonathan* / Come back and finish what you started: *Knight, Gladys & The Pips* / Do you wanna dance: *Blue, Barry* / Lost in France: *Tyler, Bonnie* / This is it: *Moore, Melba* / I'm doin' fine now: *New York City* / Lean on me: *Mud* / Jack in the box: *Moments* / More, more, more: *True, Andrea Connection* / I got a name: *Croce, Jim* / Baby don't change your mind: *Knight, Gladys & The Pips* / That same old feeling: *Pickettywitch* / My white bicycle: *Nazareth* / Lola: *Kinks* / (Dancing) on a saturday night: *Blue, Barry*

CD Set ______ **PBXCD 502**
Pulse / Nov '96 / BMG

70'S COLLECTION VOL.1
Band of gold: *Payne, Freda* / I can do it: *Rubettes* / Angel face: *Glitter Band* / I only wanna be with you: *Bay City Rollers* / I love to love (but my baby just loves to dance): *Charles, Tina* / I wanna dance wit' choo: *Disco Tex & The Sexolettes* / Greased lightnin': *Travolta, John* / (Dancing) on a Saturday night: *Blue, Barry* / Hitchin' a ride: *Vanity Fare* / Baby jump: *Mungo Jerry* / Love really hurts without you: *Ocean, Billy* / Here comes that rainy day feeling again: *Fortunes* / I will survive: *Gaynor, Gloria* / Juke box jive: *Rubettes* / Goodbye my love: *Glitter Band* / Shang-a-lang: *Bay City Rollers* / Now is the time: *James, Jimmy & The Vagabonds* / Run back: *Douglas, Carl* / If you don't know me by now: *Melvin, Harold & The Bluenotes* / Woman in love: *Three Degrees*

CD ______ **QED 024**
Tring / Nov '96 / Tring

70'S COLLECTION VOL.2
Hey there lonely girl: *Holman, Eddie* / Dance little lady dance: *Charles, Tina* / Black and white: *Greyhound* / People like you and people like me: *Glitter Band* / Sandy: *Travolta, John* / In the summertime: *Mungo Jerry* / Get dancin': *Disco Tex & The Sexolettes* / Summerlove sensation: *Bay City Rollers* / Never can say goodbye: *Gaynor, Gloria* / Kung fu fighting: *Douglas, Carl* / I'm on fire: *5000 Volts* / Ring my bell: *Ward, Anita* / Hold back the night: *Trammps* / Indiana wants me: *Taylor, R. Dean* / Yellow river: *Christie* / Freedom come, freedom go: *Fortunes* / I'll go where your music takes me: *James, Jimmy & The Vagabonds* / Wake up everybody: *Melvin, Harold & The Bluenotes* / Dirty ol' man: *Three Degrees* / Me and Mrs Jones: *Paul, Billy*

CD ______ **QED 025**
Tring / Nov '96 / Tring

70'S MEGAMIXES VOL.1
CD ______ **MACCD 305**
Autograph / Aug '96 / BMG

70'S MIXES
CD ______ **JHD 086**
Tring / Mar '93 / Tring

72 TRAD JAZZ CLASSICS
CD Set ______ **MBSCD 413**
Castle / Jul '95 / BMG

80'S COLLECTION, THE (3CD Set)
CD Set ______ **KBOX 370**
Collection / Aug '97 / Target/BMG / TKO Magnum

80'S SOUL WEEKENDER VOL.1 (40 Essential Dance Classics - 2CD Set)
Never too much: *Vandross, Luther* / Outstanding: *Gap Band* / You're the one for me: *D-Train* / Shame: *King, Evelyn 'Champagne'* / Stomp: *Brothers Johnson* / Juicy fruit: *Mtume* / Now that we've found love: *Third World* / Check out the groove: *Thurston, Bobby* / All night long: *Mary Jane Girls* / Feel so bad: *Arrington, Steve* / I've found lovin': *Fatback Band* / Funkin' for Jamaica: *Browne, Tom* / Super freak: *James, Rick* / Get down saturday night: *Cheatham, Oliver* / Forget me nots: *Rushen, Patrice* / Just a touch of love: *Slave* / You're lying: *Linx* / All this love I'm givin': *Guthrie, Gwen* / Dominoes: *Byrd, Donald* / Running away: *Ayers, Roy* / Southern freeez: *Freeez* / Circles: *Atlantic Starr* / Joy and pain: *Maze* / Let the music play: *Shannon* / Take that to the bank: *Shalamar* / I want your love: *Chic* / Boogie oogie oogie: *Taste Of Honey* / Hi tension: *Hi-Tension* / Minefield: *I-Level* / Mind blowing decisions: *Heatwave* / Yah mo b there: *Ingram, James & Michael McDonald* / You know how to love me: *Hyman, Phyllis* / Sexy girl: *Thomas, Lillo* / Dancin' in the key of life: *Arrington, Steve* / Encore: *Lynn, Cheryl* / You can't hide (your love from me): *Joseph, David* / Let the music play: *Earland, Charles* / Buttercup: *Anderson, Carl* / Galaxy of love: *Crown Heights Affair* / Till you take my love: *Mason, Harvey*

CD Set ______ **DINCD 122**
Dino / Mar '96 / Pinnacle

80'S SOUL WEEKENDER VOL.2 (2CD Set)
CD Set ______ **DINCD 124**
Dino / Jul '96 / Pinnacle

80'S SOUL WEEKENDER VOL.3 (38 White Sock Soul Grooves) (2CD Set)
Sexual healing: *Gaye, Marvin* / Solid: *Ashford & Simpson* / Walking into sunshine: *Central Line* / Glow of love: *Change* / Love has come around: *Byrd, Donald* / I shoulda loved ya: *Walden, Narada Michael* / Get tough: *Kleeer* / Jump to the beat: *Lattisaw, Stacy* / Right in the socket: *Shalamar* / (Somebody) Help me out: *Beggar & Co* / Don't push it don't force it: *Haywood, Leon* / I don't wanna be a freak (but I can't help myself): *Dynasty* / Let's get serious: *Jackson, Jermaine* / Take's a little time: *Total Contrast* / Movin': *Brass Construction* / Hangin' on a string: *Loose Ends* / Come into my life: *Sims, Joyce* / Rock Creek Park: *Blackbyrds* / Secret lovers: *Atlantic Starr* / How 'bout us: *Champaign* / Don't stop the music: *Yarbrough & Peoples* / You can do it: *Hudson, Al* / Medicine song: *Mills, Stephanie* / Walkin' on sunshine: *Rockers Revenge* / Never too much: *Vandross, Luther* / Trapped: *Colonel Abrams* / It's a love thing: *Whispers* / Ai no corrida: *Jones, Quincy* / Cuba: *Gibson Brothers* / Dancing in outer space: *Atmosfear* / I love music: *O'Jays* / Ring my bell: *Ward, Anita* / Turn the music up: *Players Association* / Just be good to me: *SOS Band* / Twilight: *Maze* / Love will bring us back together: *Ayers, Roy* / Son of Slide: *Slave* / Rapper's delight: *Sugarhill Gang*

CD Set ______ **DINCD 138**
Dino / Apr '97 / Pinnacle

90'S COLLECTION, THE
CD ______ **CDTRAX 5004**
Greentrax / Oct '95 / ADA / Direct / Duncans / Highlander

94 & 10TH - A DECADE OF 4TH & BROADWAY
Somebody else's guy: *Brown, Jocelyn* / Thinking about your love: *Skipworth & Turner* / Seventh heaven: *Guthrie, Gwen* / Gotta get you home tonight: *Wilde, Eugene* / I surrender to your love: *By All Means* / Let's start over: *Jaye, Miles* / My one temptation: *Paris, Mica* / Love supreme: *Downing, Will* / Teardrops: *Womack & Womack* / Love makes the world go round: *Don-E* / Where is the love: *Paris, Mica & Will Downing* / Real love: *Driza Bone* / Try my love: *Washburn, Lalomie* / Way we are: *Affair* / Lite up your life: *Act Of Faith* / King of rock: *Run DMC* / Drop the bomb: *Trouble Funk* / Boops (here to go): *Sly & Robbie* / Chief Inspector: *Badarou, Wally* / Paid in full: *Eric B & Rakim* / Friends and countrymen: *Wild Bunch* / Straight outta Compton: *NWA* / Television, the drug of the nation: *Disposable Heroes Of Hiphoprisy* / Wash your face in my sink: *Dream Warriors* / Turn on tune in cop out: *Freakpower* / Connected: *Stereo MC's* / It was a good day: *Ice Cube* / Aftermath: *Tricky* / Braindead: *Bomb The Bass* / Best at slavery: *Silent Eclipse*

CD Set ______ **BRCDD 614**
4th & Broadway / Aug '94 / PolyGram

95 NORTH PRESENTS STIP ESSENTIAL
CD ______ **CDSTIPMX 1**
Blue Music / Apr '97 / Pinnacle

100 BLUES AND SOUL GREATS (4CD Set)
Dimples: *Hooker, John Lee* / You'll be mine: *Howlin' Wolf* / My babe: *Little Walter* / I got it bad and that ain't good: *Holiday, Billie* / Stuff you gonna watch: *Waters, Muddy* / Born blind: *Williamson, Sonny Boy* / Boogie chillun: *Williamson, Sonny Boy* / Catfish blues: *King, B.B.* / Who's been talkin': *Howlin' Wolf* / Early in the morning: *Milton, Roy* / Please don't talk about me when I'm gone: *Holiday, Billie* / Poor Howard Green corn: *Holiday, Billie* / Sad hours: *Little Walter* / Dust my broom: *James, Elmore* / Iodine in my coffee: *Waters, Muddy* / Tupelo: *Hooker, John Lee* / Nice work if you can get it: *Holiday, Billie* / Wang dang doodle: *Howlin' Wolf* / Say: *Simon, Joe* / You're so fine: *Little Walter* / Little baby: *Howlin' Wolf* / Drug store woman: *Hooker, John Lee* / BB boogie: *King, B.B.* / Work with me: *Williamson, Sonny Boy* / Close to you: *Waters, Muddy* / Little red rooster: *Howlin' Wolf* / Boom boom: *Hooker, John Lee* / God bless the child: *Holiday, Billie* / You gonna miss me: *Waters, Muddy* / Last night: *Little Walter* / You killing me: *Williamson, Sonny Boy* / Walkin' and cryin': *King, B.B.* / Boll weevil blues: *Leadbelly* / Shake for me: *Howlin' Wolf* / Frisco blues: *Howlin' Wolf* / Don't explain: *Holiday, Billie* / Look on yonder wall: *James, Elmore* / Mean red spider: *Waters, Muddy* / Blues with a feeling: *Little Walter* / Spoonful: *Howlin' Wolf* / Please love me: *King, B.B.* / No shoes: *Hooker, John Lee* / I loves you Porgy: *Holiday, Billie* / Gallis pole: *Leadbelly* / Keep it to yourself: *Leadbelly* / Diamonds at your feet: *Waters, Muddy* / Can't hold out much longer: *Little Walter* / I'm in the mood: *Hooker, John Lee* / Goin' down slow: *Howlin' Wolf* / Little rain: *Reed, Jimmy* / Baby, please don't go: *Waters, Muddy* / Hobo blues: *Hooker, John Lee* / Down in the bottom: *Howlin' Wolf* / Fine and mellow: *Holiday, Billie* / Don't lose your eye: *Williamson, Sonny Boy* / Joke: *Little Walter* / Blue tail fly: *Leadbelly* / Walkin' and talkin': *Charles, Ray* / Baby Lee: *Hooker, John Lee* / Trainfare blues: *Waters, Muddy* / Back door man: *Howlin' Wolf* / It hurts me too: *James, Elmore* / Fooling myself: *Holiday, Billie* / Everyday I have the blues: *King, B.B.* / Mean ol' world: *Little Walter* / Trouble blues: *Hooker, John Lee* / Howlin' for my baby: *Howlin' Wolf* / Where can you be: *Reed, Jimmy* / One way out: *Williamson, Sonny Boy* / Hey now: *Charles, Ray* / Easy to remember: *Holiday, Billie* / Settin' here drinkin': *Holiday, Billie* / Old time shimmy: *Hooker, John Lee* / Tell me: *Howlin' Wolf* / How long: *Leadbelly* / I got a rich man's woman: *Waters, Muddy* / When your lover has gone: *Holiday, Billie* / My baby has walked off: *Howlin' Wolf* / Little wheel: *Hooker, John Lee* / How blue can you get: *King, B.B.* / Off the wall: *Little Walter* / Cool disposition: *Williamson, Sonny Boy* / I'm wonderin' and wonderin': *Charles, Ray* / Big fat woman: *Charles, Ray* / Whiskey and wimmen: *Hooker, John Lee* / Killing floor: *Howlin' Wolf* / Easy to remember: *Holiday, Billie* / Mean mistreater: *Waters, Muddy* / Coming home: *James, Elmore* / You better watch yourself: *Little Walter* / Moanin' at midnight: *Little Walter* / Process: *Hooker, John Lee* / In New Orleans: *Leadbelly* / Commit a crime: *Howlin' Wolf* / Dusty road: *Hooker, John Lee* / Sad letter: *Waters, Muddy* / Ain't nobody's business if I do: *Holiday, Billie* / I wonder who's kissing her now: *Charles, Ray* / What do you say: *Hooker, John Lee* / Hand in hand: *James, Elmore*

CD Set ______ **TFP 006**
Tring / Nov '92 / Tring

100 COUNTRY CLASSICS (4CD Set)
Reuben James: *Rogers, Kenny* / I believe: *Laine, Frankie* / You'll always have someone: *Nelson, Willie* / Wasted days and wasted nights: *Fender, Freddy* / Burning memories: *Jennings, Waylon* / Daddy: *Fargo, Donna* / Your tender years: *Jones, George* / Come on in: *Cline, Patsy* / Take these chains from my heart: *Drusky, Roy* / Slippin' away: *Fairchild, Barbara* / Shine on Ruby Mountain: *Rogers, Kenny* / Ol' blue: *Jackson, Stonewall* / Ragged but right: *Jones, George* / Sticks and stones: *Fargo, Donna* / High noon: *Laine, Frankie* / Last letter: *Drusky, Roy* / Wild side of life: *Fender, Freddy* / Should I go home: *Jackson, Stonewall* / Dream baby: *Jennings, Waylon* / Crazy love: *Fairchild, Barbara* / Cry not for me: *Cline, Patsy* / Ruby, don't take your love to town: *Rogers, Kenny* / Luckenbach, Texas (Back to the basics of love): *Drusky, Roy* / Wishful thinking: *Fargo, Donna* / Money: *Jennings, Waylon* / Singin' the blues: *Mitchell, Guy* / Hello walls: *Drusky, Roy* / I've lost at love again: *Cline, Patsy* / Mule train: *Laine, Frankie* / Kaw-liga: *Mandrell, Barbara* / Wedding bells: *Jones, George* / Four in the morning: *Young, Faron* / Blue eyes cryin' in the rain: *Drusky, Roy* / Sally was a good old girl: *Jennings, Waylon* / It wasn't God who made honky tonk angels: *Parton, Dolly* / Touch me: *Nelson, Willie* / Release me: *Mandrell, Barbara* / Heartaches by the number: *Mitchell, Guy* / Shake 'em up roll 'em: *Jackson, Stonewall* / Sunshine: *Rogers, Kenny* / Things have gone to pieces: *Jones, George* / 9,999,999 Tears: *Bailey, Razzy* / I let my mind wander: *Nelson, Willie* / Crying: *Jennings, Waylon* / Honky tonk merry go round: *Cline, Patsy* / Ticket to nowhere: *Rogers, Kenny* / Keep off the grass: *Jackson, Stonewall* / Daddy sang bass: *Perkins, Carl* / Ghost: *Nelson, Willie* / If you ain't lovin' (you ain't livin'): *Young, Faron* / Kentucky means paradise: *Mandrell, Barbara* / Stop, look and listen: *Cline, Patsy* / I can't escape from you: *Jones, George* / Making believe: *Wells, Kitty* / Honky tonk angels: *Parton, Dolly* / Abilene: *Jennings, Waylon* / Ruby Tuesday: *Williams, Don* / Elvira: *Rogers, Kenny* / Maybellene: *Robbins, Marty* / Dream baby: *Jennings, Waylon* / Good rockin' tonight: *Lewis, Jerry Lee* / Little blossom: *Parton, Dolly* / From a Jack to a King: *Miller, Ned* / I can't find the time: *Nelson, Willie* / Love's gonna live here: *Jennings, Waylon* / Jambalaya: *Jones, George* / Where do we go from here: *Williams, Don* / Homemade lies: *Rogers, Kenny* / Turn the cards slowly: *Cline, Patsy* / Things to talk about: *Jackson, Stonewall* / Your song: *Lee, Johnny* / I didn't sleep a wink: *Nelson, Willie* / Cold cold heart: *Jones, George* / Town without pity: *Pitney, Gene* / Send me the pillow that you dream on: *Locklin, Hank* / Six days on the road: *Dudley, Dave* / Rose garden: *Anderson, Lynn* / Rawhide: *Laine, Frankie* / Walkin' after midnight: *Cline, Patsy* / Rhythm and booze: *Owens, Buck* / Wings of a dove: *Husky, Ferlin* / Always leaving, always gone: *Rogers, Kenny* / Ramblin' rose: *Lee, Johnny* / I feel sorry for him: *Nelson, Willie* / In care of the blues: *Cline, Patsy* / Have I stayed away too long: *Ritter, Tex* / I'll repossess my heart: *Wells, Kitty* / Waterloo: *Jackson, Stonewall* / Last day in the mines: *Dudley, Dave* / Moonlight gambler: *Laine, Frankie* / This ole house: *Perkins, Carl* / Candy store: *Lee, Johnny* / Don't think twice, it's alright: *Jennings, Waylon* / I can't get enough of you: *Jackson, Stonewall* / Heart you break may be your own: *Cline, Patsy* / Hey good lookin': *Cash, Johnny* / Open pit mine: *Jones, George* / If I don't understand: *Nelson, Willie* / Please don't let that woman get me: *Jones, George*

CD Set ______ **TFP 003**
Tring / '88 / Tring

100 CRUISIN' GREATS (4CD Set)
CD Set ______ **TFP 018**
Tring / Nov '92 / Tring

100 GREATEST JAZZ & SWING HITS 1917-1942 (4CD Set)
CD ______ **CDAFS 10364**
Affinity / Jun '93 / Cadillac / Jazz Music / Koch

100 HITS OF THE FIFTIES (4CD Set)
CD Set ______ **TFP 015**
Tring / Nov '92 / Tring

100 HITS OF THE SEVENTIES (4CD Set)
CD Set ______ **TFP 021**
Tring / Nov '92 / Tring

100 HITS OF THE SIXTIES VOL.1 (4CD Set)
Save the last dance for me: *Drifters* / Sweet talking guy: *Chiffons* / Let's twist again: *Checker, Chubby* / It's in his kiss (The shoop shoop song): *Everett, Betty* / Let it rock: *Berry, Chuck* / Surfin' safari: *Beach Boys* / Blueberry Hill: *Domino, Fats* / Ride the wild surf: *Jan & Dean* / Every beat of my heart: *Knight, Gladys* / Hats off to Larry: *Shannon, Del* / When a man loves a woman: *Sledge, Percy* / Venus: *Avalon, Frankie* / Limbo rock: *Checker, Chubby* / Then he kissed me: *Crystals* / Leader of the pack: *Shangri-Las* / Venus in blue jeans: *Clanton, Jimmy* / Hold on I'm comin': *Sam & Dave* / On Broadway: *Drifters* / Sixteen candles: *Crests* / Rubber ball: *Vee, Bobby* / Sugar sugar: *Archies* / My guy: *Wells, Mary* / There's a kind of hush: *Herman's Hermits* / So sad the song: *Knight, Gladys* / Runaway: *Shannon, Del* / Judy in disguise: *Fred, John & His Playboy Band* / Up on the roof: *Drifters* / Surfin': *Beach Boys* / No particular place to go: *Berry, Chuck* / Letter full of tears: *Knight, Gladys* / Soul man: *Sam & Dave* / He's so fine: *Chiffons* / Devil or angel: *Vee, Bobby* / Twist: *Checker, Chubby* / You beat me to the punch: *Wells, Mary* / Da doo ron ron: *Crystals* / Tequila: *Champs* / Drag City: *Jan & Dean* / Chapel of love: *Dixie Cups* / No milk today: *Herman's Hermits* / Duke of Earl: *Chandler, Gene* / Groovy kind of love: *Fontana, Wayne* / Under the boardwalk: *Drifters* / Behind closed doors: *Sledge, Percy* / Night has a thousand eyes: *Vee, Bobby* / Pony time: *Checker, Chubby* / Bobby sox to stockings: *Avalon, Frankie* / Ain't that a shame: *Domino, Fats* / Little old lady from Pasadena: *Jan & Dean* / Build me up buttercup: *Foundations* / There goes my baby: *Drifters* / Operator: *Knight, Gladys* / My boyfriend's back: *Angels* / Little town flirt: *Shannon, Del* / Johnny B Goode: *Berry, Chuck* / I thank you: *Sam & Dave* / Oh no not my baby: *Brown, Maxine* / Knock on wood: *Floyd, Eddie* / Run to him: *Vee, Bobby* / Surfer girl: *Beach Boys* / Give him a great big kiss: *Shangri-Las* / Rockin' Robin: *Day, Bobby* / Corine Corina: *Peterson, Ray* / Promised land: *Berry, Chuck* / GTO: *Regents* / Hucklebuck: *Checker, Chubby* / Rescue me: *Bass, Fontella* / Dead man's curve: *Jan & Dean* / He's a rebel: *Crystals* / Backfield in motion: *Mel & Tim* / Why do fools fall in love: *Diamonds* / Memphis: *Berry, Chuck* / Can't you hear my heartbeat: *Herman's Hermits* / Some kind of wonderful: *Drifters* / Soul sister brown sugar: *Sam & Dave* / Drift away: *Gray, Dobie* / Remember (walkin' in the sand): *Shangri-Las* / Rhythm of the rain: *Cascades* / Itchycoo Park: *Small Faces* / Dance with me: *Drifters* / Barefootin': *Parker, Robert* / Cry baby cry: *Angels* / It's my party: *Gore, Lesley* / Letter: *Box Tops* / Wooly bully: *Sam The Sham & The Pharaohs* / Yakety yak: *Coasters* / Little darlin': *Diamonds* / In crowd: *Gray, Dobie* / Ferry 'cross the Mersey: *Gerry & The Pacemakers* / Tell Laura I love her: *Peterson, Ray* / Barbara Ann: *Regents* / Maybellene: *Berry, Chuck* / Deep purple: *Tempo, Nino & April Stevens* / I don't know why (I just do): *Henry, Clarence 'Frogman'* / Wild thing: *Troggs* / Mrs. Brown you've got a lovely daughter: *Herman's Hermits* / Surf city: *Jan & Dean* / Don't let the sun catch you crying: *Gerry & The Pacemakers* / Nadine: *Berry, Chuck*

CD Set ______ **TFP 004**
Tring / Nov '92 / Tring

100 HITS OF THE SIXTIES VOL.2
CD Set ______________ TFP 016
Tring / Nov '92 / Tring

100 NON STOP PARTY HITS (4CD Set)
Let's have a party: *Jackson, Wanda* / Dynamite: *Mud* / Be bop a lula: *Vincent, Gene & The Bluecaps* / Some girls: *Racey* / Denis: *Blondie* / Gimme hope Jo'anna: *Grant, Eddy* / Breakaway: *Ullman, Tracey* / Can the can: *Quatro, Suzi* / My Sharona: *Knack* / Bus stop: *Hollies* / You were made for me: *Freddie & The Dreamers* / Runaway: *Shannon, Del* / Forever, forever: *Domino, Fats* / Pretend: *Stardust, Alvin* / Kids in America: *Wilde, Kim* / If this is it: *Lewis, Huey & The News* / Darlin': *Miller, Frankie* / Right back where we started from: *Nightingale, Maxine* / Showing out: *Mel & Kim* / Sex drugs and rock and roll: *Dury, Ian* / Call me: *Blondie* / Dancing in the city: *Hain, Marshall* / Don't worry be happy: *McFerrin, Bobby* / Geno: *Dexy's Midnight Runners* / Bring it on home: *Animals* / Party doll: *Knox, Buddy* / Do wah diddy diddy: *Manfred Mann* / C'mon everydogy: *Cochran, Eddie* / Hippy hippy shake: *Swinging Blue Jeans* / Barbara Ann: *Beach Boys* / Mony mony: *James, Tommy & The Shondells* / Hi ho silver lining: *Beck, Jeff* / Tiger feet: *Mud* / See my baby jive: *Wizzard* / Long tall glasses: *Sayer, Leo* / This little girl: *Bonds, Gary 'US'* / On the road again: *Canned Heat* / Roll over Beethoven: *ELO* / My girl Josephine: *Domino, Fats* / I'm into something good: *Herman's Hermits* / Surf city: *Jan & Dean* / I get around: *Beach Boys* / Rock your baby: *McCrae, George* / Don't take away the music: *Tavares* / Oh baby what would you say: *Smith, Hurricane* / Sixteen tons: *Ford, Tennessee Ernie* / Baby let me take you home: *Animals* / All around my hat: *Steeleye Span* / American pie: *McLean, Don* / You sexy thing: *Hot Chocolate* / I hear you knockin': *Edmunds, Dave* / Rubber ball: *Vee, Bobby* / Boat that I row: *Lulu* / Runaround Sue: *Dion* / Morning train: *Easton, Sheena* / Magic: *Pilot* / Cat crept in: *Mud* / Teenager in love: *Dion & The Belmonts* / I like it: *Gerry & The Pacemakers* / Buona sera: *Prima, Louis* / Mississippi: *Pussycat* / Walking back to happiness: *Shapiro, Helen* / Pretty flamingo: *Manfred Mann* / Good golly Miss Molly: *Swinging Blue Jeans* / Nutbush city limits: *Turner, Ike & Tina* / Coming on strong: *Broken English* / That's the way I like it: *KC & The Sunshine Band* / We've gotta get out of this place: *Animals* / No more heroes: *Stranglers* / Hanging on the telephone: *Blondie* / It ain't what you do: *Fun Boy Three & Bananarama* / Blue moon: *Marcels* / Kisses sweeter than wine: *Rodgers, Jimmie* / Big spender: *Bassey, Shirley* / Lily the pink: *Scaffold* / Summertime blues: *Cochran, Eddie* / Lay your love on me: *Racey* / Don't let me be misunderstood: *Animals* / World without love: *Peter & Gordon* / Baker street: *Rafferty, Gerry* / Boogie oogie oogie: *Taste Of Honey* / Heaven must be missing an angel: *Tavares* / Chequered love: *Wilde, Kim* / Oh boy: *Mud* / Tom Tom turnaround: *New World* / No milk today: *Herman's Hermits* / Devil gate drive: *Quatro, Suzi* / Stuck with you: *Lewis, Huey & The News* / Centerfold: *Geils, J. Band* / Stop stop stop: *Hollies* / Freedom come freedom go: *Fortunes* / You'll never walk alone: *Gerry & The Pacemakers* / I'm telling you now: *Freddie & The Dreamers* / Seven drunken nights: *Dubliners* / Sloop John B: *Beach Boys* / Oh Marie: *Prima, Louis* / If you can't give me love: *Quatro, Suzi* / Blueberry Hill: *Domino, Fats* / Do you want to know a secret: *Kramer, Billy J. & The Dakotas* / Thank u very much: *Scaffold*
CD Set ______________ HR 877362
Disky / May '97 / Disky / THE

100 OF THE GREATEST LOVE SONGS (4CD Set)
Then he kissed me: *Crystals* / It's in his kiss (The shoop shoop song): *Everett, Betty* / Girls: *Moments* / Remember (walkin' in the sand): *Shangri-Las* / Let there be love: *Lee, Peggy* / I'm in the mood for love: *Day, Doris* / My boyfriend's back: *Angels* / Every beat of my heart: *Knight, Gladys & The Pips* / Venus in blue jeans: *Clanton, Jimmy* / Groovy kind of love: *Fontana, Wayne* / I can't find the time: *Nelson, Willie* / Don't let the sun catch you crying: *Gerry & The Pacemakers* / Sixteen candles: *Crests* / Warm and tender love: *Sledge, Percy* / Ain't no sunshine: *Jarreau, Al* / I'm so lonesome I could cry: *Spears, Billie Jo* / Night has a thousand eyes: *Vee, Bobby* / Love walked in: *Benson, George* / Embraceable you: *Day, Doris* / Where were you on our wedding day: *Price, Lloyd* / Release me: *Mandrell, Barbara* / Shelter of my arms: *Nelson, Willie* / Ruby, don't take your love to town: *Rogers, Kenny* / Portrait of my love: *Clark, Dee* / What is this thing called love: *Lee, Peggy* / Behind closed doors: *Sledge, Percy* / Lean on me: *Jarreau, Al* / Run to him: *Vee, Bobby* / Singin' in the rain: *Day, Doris* / Oh no not my baby: *Bass, Fontella* / There goes my baby: *Drifters* / He's a rebel: *Crystals* / Letter full of tears: *Knight, Gladys* / But I do: *Henry, Clarence 'Frogman'* / My guy: *Wells, Mary* / 'S wonderful: *Day, Doris* / I've loved and lost again: *Cline, Patsy* / Save the last dance for me: *Drifters* / Home is where you're happy: *Nelson, Willie* / Kisses sweeter than wine: *Rodgers, Jimmie* / Leader of the pack: *Shangri-Las* / Just a dream: *Clanton, Jimmy* / Best thing that ever happened to me: *Knight, Gladys* / Uptown: *Crystals* / Come what may: *Crosby, Bing* / Do I love you: *Garland, Judy* / Chapel of love: *Dixie Cups* / Runaway: *Shannon, Del* / Young and in love: *Dick & Deedee* / Just one of those things: *Lee, Peggy* / Rock your baby: *McCrae, George* / When a man loves a woman: *Sledge, Percy* / Operator: *Knight, Gladys & The Pips* / Dream baby: *Shannon, Del* / Stardust: *Day, Doris* / Do it love you: *Garland, Judy* / Give him a great big kiss: *Shangri-Las* / While I dream: *Sedaka, Neil* / High noon: *Laine, Frankie* / Let your love flow: *Burke, Solomon* / So sad the song: *Knight, Gladys & The Pips* / Why do fools fall in love: *Diamonds* / Rainy night in Georgia: *Benton, Brook* / World without you: *Shannon, Del* / Rhythm of the rain: *Cascades* / I can't give you anything but love: *Garland, Judy* / Love we had: *Dells* / Make it easy on yourself: *Butler, Jerry* / Just you, just me: *Day, Doris* / So many ways: *Benton, Brook* / It coulda been me: *Spears, Billie Jo* / Sh-boom: *Crew Cuts* / Tender years: *Jones, George* / Build me up buttercup: *Foundations* / Girls: *Moments* / Stormy weather: *Horne, Lena* / If ever I should fall in love: *Knight, Gladys & The Pips* / Deep purple: *Tempo, Nino & April Stevens* / Crying my heart out for you: *Day, Doris* / When my little girl is smiling: *Drifters* / Spanish Harlem: *King, B.B.* / Lyin' eyes: *Jones, Jack* / Single girl: *Posey, Sandy* / Tell Laura I love her: *Peterson, Ray* / Under the moon of love: *Lee, Curtis* / Everything I have is yours: *Crosby, Bing* / Little darlin': *Diamonds* / You and me against the world: *Knight, Gladys & The Pips* / One who really loves you: *Wells, Mary* / Why do fools fall in love: *Diamonds* / Closer you are: *Channel* / Just the two of us: *Jones, Jack* / What a man in love won't do: *Posey, Sandy* / Because you're mine: *Day, Doris* / Young and in love: *Dick & Deedee* / Up on the roof: *Drifters* / Please love me forever: *Edwards, Tommy* / When the red roses grow: *Crosby, Bing* / Earth angel: *Penguins* / Fools rush in: *Benton, Brook*
CD Set ______________ TFP 008
Tring / Nov '92 / Tring

100 ROCK 'N' ROLL HITS (4CD Set)
Roll over Beethoven: *Berry, Chuck* / Blueberry Hill: *Domino, Fats* / Yakety yak: *Coasters* / (We're gonna) Rock around the clock: *Haley, Bill & The Comets* / Venus: *Avalon, Frankie* / Reelin' and rockin': *Berry, Chuck* / Let's twist again: *Checker, Chubby* / My boyfriend's back: *Angels* / Keep a knockin': *Little Richard* / Sweet talking guy: *Chiffons* / Personality: *Price, Lloyd* / Hats off to Larry: *Shannon, Del* / Blue Monday: *Domino, Fats* / Sweet little rock 'n' roller: *Berry, Chuck* / Tequila: *Champs* / Tutti frutti: *Little Richard* / Rock 'n' roll is here to stay: *Danny & The Juniors* / Rockin' pneumonia and the boogie woogie flu: *Smith, Huey 'Piano'* / Crossfire: *Johnny & The Hurricanes* / Then he kissed me: *Crystals* / Rubber ball: *Vee, Bobby* / Be bop a lula: *Vincent, Gene* / Runaround Sue: *Shannon, Del* / Promised land: *Berry, Chuck* / Good golly Miss Molly: *Little Richard* / Twist: *Checker, Chubby* / Duke of Earl: *Chandler, Gene* / No particular place to go: *Berry, Chuck* / Ain't that a shame: *Domino, Fats* / Da doo ron ron: *Crystals* / At the hop: *Danny & The Juniors* / Shake, rattle and roll: *Haley, Bill* / School day: *Berry, Chuck* / Long tall Sally: *Little Richard* / Stagger Lee: *Price, Lloyd* / Charlie Brown: *Coasters* / Runaway: *Shannon, Del* / Book of love: *Monotones* / Beatnik fly: *Johnny & The Hurricanes* / Night has a thousand eyes: *Vee, Bobby* / Great balls of fire: *Lewis, Jerry Lee* / Too much monkey business: *Berry, Chuck* / Little Egypt: *Coasters* / Cry baby cry: *Angels* / Rockin' Robin: *Day, Bobby* / Rip it up: *Little Richard* / I go to pieces: *Shannon, Del* / Back in the USA: *Berry, Chuck* / Cool jerk: *Capitols* / Nadine: *Berry, Chuck* / See you later alligator: *Haley, Bill & The Comets* / Red river rock: *Johnny & The Hurricanes* / Hucklebuck: *Checker, Chubby* / Johnny B Goode: *Berry, Chuck* / Ooh my soul: *Little Richard* / Whole lotta shakin' goin' on: *Lewis, Jerry Lee* / Chapel of love: *Dixie Cups* / Little town flirt: *Shannon, Del* / Sweet little sixteen: *Berry, Chuck* / Jambalaya: *Domino, Fats* / Sea cruise: *Ford, Frankie* / He's a rebel: *Crystals* / Leader of the pack: *Shangri-Las* / Poison ivy: *Coasters* / Because they're young: *Eddy, Duane* / Whole lotta shakin' goin' on: *Little Richard* / Angels listened in: *Crests* / Let it rock: *Berry, Chuck* / Matchbox: *Perkins, Carl* / Kansas City: *Harrison, Wilbert* / Brown eyed handsome man: *Lewis, Jerry Lee* / Little bitty pretty one: *Day, Bobby* / I'm walkin': *Domino, Fats* / Short fat Fanny: *Little Richard* / Almost grown: *Berry, Chuck* / Maybellene: *Berry, Chuck* / Lucille: *Little Richard* / Shout: *Dee, Joey* / Limbo rock: *Checker, Chubby* / Reveille rock: *Johnny & The Hurricanes* / Why do fools fall in love: *Diamonds* / Brown eyed handsome man: *Berry, Chuck* / Baby blue: *Vincent, Gene* / Hello Josephine: *Domino, Fats* / She's got it: *Little Richard* / Mr. Bass Man: *Cymbal, Johnny* / Say man: *Diddley, Bo* / Rock 'n' roll music: *Berry, Chuck* / Handyman: *Shannon, Del* / He's so fine: *Chiffons* / This ole house: *Perkins, Carl* / Wooly bully: *Sam The Sham & The Pharaohs* / Pony time: *Checker, Chubby* / Girl can't help it: *Little Richard* / Rebel rouser: *Eddy, Duane* / Stroll: *Diamonds* / Under the moon of love: *Lee, Curtis* / Domino twist: *Domino, Fats* / Memphis: *Berry, Chuck* / Guitar man: *Eddy, Duane*
CD Set ______________ TFP 002
Tring / Nov '92 / Tring

100 SOUL HITS (4CD Set)
Soul man: *Sam & Dave* / Papa's got a brand new bag: *Brown, James* / Knock on wood: *Floyd, Eddie* / Under the boardwalk: *Drifters* / Rescue me: *Bass, Fontella* / It's just a matter of time: *Benton, Brook* / In crowd: *Gray, Dobie* / Oh no not my baby: *Brown, Maxine* / Every beat of my heart: *Knight, Gladys* / Rock your baby: *McCrae, George* / Barefootin': *Parker, Robert* / When a man loves a woman: *Sledge, Percy* / Backfield in motion: *Mel & Tim* / You don't know what you mean to me: *Sam & Dave* / Expressway to your heart: *Soul Survivors* / Save the last dance for me: *Drifters* / When something is wrong with my baby: *Sam & Dave* / If you need me: *Pickett, Wilson* / Do the funky chicken: *Thomas, Rufus* / Please please please: *Brown, James* / Rainy night in Georgia: *Benton, Brook* / Hold on I'm comin': *Burke, Solomon* / Bring it on home to me: *Floyd, Eddie* / Stand by me: *King, Ben E.* / I got the feelin': *Brown, James* / On broadway: *Drifters* / Hold on I'm comin': *Sam & Dave* / It's a man's man's man's world: *Brown, James* / Oh what a night: *Drells* / California girl: *Floyd, Eddie* / Spanish Harlem: *King, Ben E.* / True love: *Drifters* / Soul man: *Lewis, Ramsey* / So many ways: *Benton, Brook* / Letter full of tears: *Knight, Gladys* / Walking the dog: *Thomas, Rufus* / Hi-heel sneakers: *Lewis, Ramsey* / All in my mind: *Brown, Maxine* / Best thing that ever happened to me: *Knight, Gladys* / Turn it loose: *Brown, James* / Said I wasn't gonna tell nobody: *Sam & Dave* / I who have nothing: *King, Ben E.* / My guy: *Wells, Mary* / Sweets for my sweet: *Drifters* / Georgia on my mind: *Knight, Gladys* / Boll weevil song: *Benton, Brook* / You don't know like I know: *Sam & Dave* / Get up offa that thing: *Brown, James* / Warm and tender love: *Sledge, Percy* / Challenge: *Butler, Jerry* / It's too funky here: *Brown, James* / Kiddio: *Benton, Brook* / Tighten up: *Bell, Archie & The Drells* / I thank you: *Sam & Dave* / Lovin' arms: *Gray, Dobie* / Supernatural thing: *King, Ben E.* / Dancing in the street: *Lewis, Ramsey* / There goes my baby: *Drifters* / Operator: *Knight, Gladys & The Pips* / I wanna go home: *Drells* / Try me: *Brown, James* / Uptight: *Lewis, Ramsey* / So sad the song: *Knight, Gladys & The Pips* / Fools rush in: *Benton, Brook* / Girls: *Moments* / This magic moment: *Drifters* / Behind closed doors: *Sledge, Percy* / Listen: *Impressions* / Hard day's night: *Lewis, Ramsey* / Duke of Earl: *Chandler, Gene* / You got me hummin': *Sam & Dave* / Think twice: *Benton, Brook* / Since you've been gone: *Lewis, Ramsey* / Cold sweat/I can't stand myself (medley): *Brown, James* / I who have nothing: *King, Ben E.* / Soul sister brown sugar: *Sam & Dave* / (Get up I feel like being a) sex machine: *Brown, James* / Love me again: *Knight, Gladys & The Pips* / Up on the roof: *Drifters* / Look at me (I'm in love): *Moments* / Drift away: *Gray, Dobie* / It's too late: *Pickett, Wilson* / She does it right: *King, Ben E.* / Hotel happiness: *Benton, Brook* / Louie Louie: *Kingsmen* / Get on the good foot: *Brown, James* / Soul twist: *King Curtis* / Never found a girl: *Floyd, Eddie* / Don't pull your love out on me baby: *Sam & Dave* / Dance with me: *Drifters* / If ever I should fall in love: *Knight, Gladys & The Pips* / In crowd: *Lewis, Ramsey* / Love on a two way street: *Moments* / Take time to know her: *Sledge, Percy* / I need your love: *Impressions* / Can't you find another way: *Sam & Dave* / Some kind of wonderful: *Drifters* / Thank you pretty baby: *Benton, Brook* / What shall I do: *Knight, Gladys & The Pips* / I feel good: *Brown, James*
CD Set ______________ TFP 001
Tring / Nov '92 / Tring

100 WATTS: SONGS FROM WPHK'S 'PURE HYPE'
CD ______________ HPK 01
Atavistic / Jul '97 / Cargo / SRD

100% ACID JAZZ VOL.2
CD ______________ TCD 2767
Telstar / Jun '95 / BMG

100% CHRISTMAS & NEW YEAR (2CD Set)
CD Set ______________ TCD 2878
Telstar / Nov '96 / BMG

100% DANCE HITS 1996 (2CD Set)
CD Set ______________ TCD 2868
Telstar / Sep '96 / BMG

100% DETROIT WORKOUT (4CD Set)
CD Set ______________ CDFIT 5
Music For Pleasure / Nov '95 / EMI

100% DRUM & BASS (2CD Set)
Walking wounded: *Everything But The Girl* / Inner city life: *Goldie* / Feel the sunshine: *Reece, Alex & Deborah Anderson* / F jam: *Adam F* / Valley of the shadows: *Origin Unknown* / Horizons: *LTJ Bukem* / Take me to Heaven: *Baby D* / Mutant jazz: *T-Power & MK Ultra* / Greater love: *Soundman & Don Lloydie/Elizabeth Troy* / Banstyle: *Underworld* / Rings around Saturn: *Photek* / Atmospheric funk: *Wax Doctor* / Vocal: *Peshay* / Helicopter tune: *Deep Blue* / Burial: *Leviticus* / Renegade snares: *Omni Trio* / Firestarter: *Prodigy* / Circles: *Adam F* / Sweet love: *M-Beat & Nazlyn* / Slack hands: *Galliano* / Killamanjaro: *Ed Rush* / Angels fell: *Dillinja* / It's a jazz thing: *Roni Size & DJ Die* / Dezires: *Aquasky* / Free la funk: *JMJ & Richie* / Feenin': *Jodeci* / One day I'll fly away: *Llorena, Kelly* / Links: *Chameleon* / Dark stranger: *Boogie Times Tribe* / Rays of sun: *Acetate* / Dreamland: *BLIM* / Flight of the vulture: *Nice, Peter Trio*
CD Set ______________ TCD 2847
Telstar / Sep '96 / BMG

100% HOUSE CLASSICS
CD Set ______________ TCD 2759
Telstar / Feb '95 / BMG

100% PURE DANCE
CD ______________ CDRPM 0012
RP Media / Apr '97 / Essential/BMG

100% PURE GROOVE VOL.1
CD ______________ TCD 2818
Telstar / Mar '96 / BMG

100% PURE GROOVE VOL.2
CD ______________ TCD 2840
Telstar / Jun '96 / BMG

100% PURE UNDERGROUND DANCE
CD Set ______________ XCLU 001CDC
X-Clusive / Sep '94 / Pinnacle

100% RAI
CD ______________ 952052
Pomme / Jul '97 / Discovery

100% REGGAE
CD ______________ TCD 2695
Telstar / Nov '93 / BMG

100% REGGAE ORIGINALS VOL.1
CD ______________ TCD 2775
Telstar / Jul '95 / BMG

100% REGGAE ORIGINALS VOL.2
CD ______________ TCD 2832
Telstar / May '96 / BMG

100% SUMMER JAZZ
CD ______________ TCD 2781
Telstar / Jul '95 / BMG

100% SUMMER MIX '97 (2CD Set)
Ecuador: *Sash* / Freed from desire: *Gala* / Fairground: *Simply Red* / Closer than close: *Gaines, Rosie* / Saturday night: *Whigfield* / All that she wants: *Ace Of Base* / Macarena: *Los Del Rio* / Bamboleo: *Gipsy Kings* / Fresh: *Gina G* / Sweets for my sweet: *Lewis, C.J.* / Things can only get better: *D:Ream* / Boom boom boom: *Outhere Brothers* / Bomb (These sounds fall into my mind): *Bucketheads* / Professional widow: *Amos, Tori* / Missing: *Everything But The Girl* / Lovefool: *Cardigans* / Parklife: *Blur* / Riverboat song: *Ocean Colour Scene* / Breakfast at Tiffany's: *Deep Blue Something* / Good enough: *Dodgy* / Turn on tune in cop out: *Freakpower* / Midnight at the oasis: *Brand New Heavies* / Remember me: *Blueboy* / Back to life: *Soul II Soul* / Boombastic: *Shaggy* / Mr. Loverman: *Shabba Ranks* / Cecilia: *Suggs* / Don't make me wait: *911* / I can make you feel good: *Kavana* / Horny: *Morrison, Mark* / Hey DJ (play that song): *N-Tyce* / Encore une fois: *Sash* / Keep warm: *Jinny* / I'm alive: *Stretch n' Vern* / Where love lives: *Limerick, Alison* / Ain't nobody: *Course* / Get up (everybody): *Stingily, Byron* / Let me be your fantasy: *Baby D* / I love you stop: *Red 5* / Stepping stone: *PJ & Duncan*
CD Set ______________ TTVCD 2906
Telstar TV / Jul '97 / Warner Music

100% SUMMER MIX 1996
CD Set ______________ TCD 2843
Telstar / Jun '96 / BMG

101 + 303 + 808 = NOW FORM A BAND
Metamorphic structures: *Turbulent Force* / Alpha acid: *Point Alpha* / Steel mill: *THD* / Spalding: *THD* / Mollusk: *POD* / Untitled: *Turbulent Force* / Data blast: *Point Alpha* / Street stomper: *Psyche* / Geodesic dome: *POD* / Untitled: *Lords Of Afford* / Adrenalin rush: *Psyche*
CD ______________ SBR 004CD
Sabrettes Of Paradise / Oct '95 / Vital

101% REGGAE
Sing a little song: *Dekker, Desmond* / We play record: *In Crowd* / Work all day: *Biggs, Barry* / Mad about you: *Ruffin, Bruce* / Island music: *Calendar, Phil* / Girlie girlie: *George, Sophia* / Do you really want to hurt me: *Heptones* / Sweet cherrie: *Honey Boy* / Keep on riding: *Donaldson, Eric* / Side show: *Biggs, Barry* / Take care of my heart: *Gardiner, Boris* / Blue moon: *Francis, Winston* / Come back Charlie: *Charlie Chaplin* / Rock my soul: *Pioneers* / It burn mi belly: *George, Sophia* / Happy anniversary: *Schloss, Cynthia* / Busted land: *Dekker, Desmond* / Kool and deadly: *Clint Eastwood & General Saint*
CD ______________ ECD 3074
K-Tel / Jan '95 / K-Tel

102% REGGAE
OK Fred: *Dunkley, Errol* / Three ring circus: *Biggs, Barry* / Back a yard: *In Crowd* / Love again: *George, Sophia* / Starvation: *Pioneers* / Stick by me: *Holt, John* / Night like this: *Biggs, Barry* / Baby my love: *Calendar, Fip* / Eighteen yellow roses: *Gardiner, Boris* / Maga dawg: *George, Sophia* / Everybody

join hands: *Dekker, Desmond* / Uptown Sharron: *Isaacs, Gregory* / I think I love you: *Donaldson, Eric* / You are my destiny: *Gardiner, Boris* / Please don't make me cry: *Groovy, Winston* / Everything to me: *Holt, John* / One big happy family: *Ruffin, Bruce* / Elizabethan reggae: *Gardiner, Boris*
CD ________ **ECD 3103**
K-Tel / Jan '95 / K-Tel

104.9
CD ________ **XFMCD 2**
XFM / Oct '95 / Pinnacle

200 PROOF COMPILATION
CD ________ **DESTINY 100CD**
Destiny / Oct '96 / Plastic Head

300 YEARS OF SCOTLAND'S MUSIC
CD ________ **MMSCD 951**
Scott Music / Apr '95 / Select

313 DETROIT
War of the worlds: *Dark Comedy* / Distance: *Reel By Reel* / Baby can: *KELSEY* / Unconscious world: *Subterfuge* / Electricity: *Santonio* / Warwick: *Fowlkes, Eddie* / Desire: *69* / Free Your Mind: *Piece*
CD ________ **INF 01CD**
Infonet / Nov '92 / Pinnacle / Prime / Vital

706 UNION INSTRUMENTALS
CD ________ **CPCD 8302**
Charly / May '97 / Koch

1000 VOLTS OF STAX
Hideaway: *Booker T & The MG's* / (Sittin' on the) dock of the bay: *Booker T & The MG's* / Don't you lie to me: *King, Albert* / Cupid: *Redding, Otis* / I've got dreams to remember: *Redding, Otis* / Don't worry about tomorrow: *Marchan, Bobby* / Walking the dog: *Thomas, Rufus* / Runaround: *Thomas, Carla* / Floyd's beat: *Newman, Floyd* / When my love comes down: *Johnson, Ruby* / She won't be like you: *Bell, William* / Never let me go: *Bell, William* / Sweet devil: *John, Mable* / Cloudburst: *Mad Lads* / Hippy dippy: *Mar-Keys* / Don't mess up a good thing: *Thomas, Rufus & Carla* / Just enough to hurt me: *Astors* / Knock on wood: *Floyd, Eddie*
CD ________ **CDSXD 042**
Stax / Sep '91 / Pinnacle

1327 TAGE
CD ________ **EYEUKCD 007**
Harthouse / Nov '95 / Mo's Music Machine / Prime / Vital

1943-1947
CD ________ **22026**
Caprice / Feb '89 / ADA / Cadillac / CM / Complete/Pinnacle

1991 TRIANGLE JAZZ PARTYBOYS
CD ________ **FINCD 101**
Arbors Jazz / Nov '94 / Cadillac

1993 PORTLAND WATERFRONT BLUES FESTIVAL
CD ________ **BCD 00142**
Burnside / Jul '96 / Koch

2000 VOLTS OF STAX
Kinda easy like: *Booker T & The MG's* / Ride your pony: *Thomas, Rufus* / You don't know like I know: *Taylor, Johnnie* / Pain in my heart: *Redding, Otis* / It's not that easy: *Johnson, Ruby* / How about you: *Parker, Deanie* / Hotshot: *Bar-Kays* / Come out tonight: *Astors* / Bark at the moon: *Floyd, Eddie* / I found a brand new love: *Kirk, Eddie* / Please don't go: *Tonettes* / Try me: *Thomas, Carla* / Slinky: *Mar-Keys* / Crosscut saw: *King, Albert* / She's the one: *Mad Lads* / You don't miss your water: *Bell, William* / I say a little prayer: *Booker T & The MG's* / Try a little tenderness: *Redding, Otis*
CD ________ **CDSXD 074**
Stax / Oct '92 / Pinnacle

2001: A GRASS ODYSSEY
CD ________ **GROW 0272**
Grass / May '95 / Pinnacle / SRD

3000 VOLTS OF STAX
Spoonful: *Booker T & The MG's* / Come to me: *Redding, Otis* / I'd rather fight than switch: *Johnson, Ruby* / Sixty minutes of your time: *Taylor, Johnnie* / Quittin' time: *Bell, William* / Good good lovin': *Thomas, Carla* / I got everything I need: *Floyd, Eddie* / Count your many blessings: *Stars Of Virginia* / Big bad wolf: *Jenkins, Johnny* / Rotation: *Tonettes* / Wee little bit: *Marchan, Bobby* / Juanita: *Prince Conley* / Win you over: *Porter, David* / Hunter: *King, Albert* / Per-culating: *Mar-Keys* / Patch my heart: *Mad Lads* / Remember me: *Redding, Otis* / Water: *Taylor, Johnnie* / Sock soul: *Bar-Kays* / Big bird: *Floyd, Eddie* / All I need is some sunshine in my life: *Dixie Nightingales*
CD ________ **CDSXD 102**
Stax / Mar '94 / Pinnacle

4000 VOLTS OF STAX AND SATELLITE
Home grown: *Booker T & The MG's* / Woman who needs the love of a man: *Astors* / Just to hold your hand: *Marchan, Bobby* / Ain't that good: *Prince Conley* / All that I am: *Prince Conley* / As you can see: *Chips* / Shake up: *Cobras* / I'll never give her up (My friend): *Canes* / Somewhere along the line: *Canes* / Popeye the sailor man: *Del-Rios* / Any other way: *Bell, William* / Strut this Sally: *Astors* / Uncle Willie good time: *Astors* / I wish I were that girl: *Rene, Wendy* / Hawg: *Kirk, Eddie* / I see my baby coming: *Mack, Oscar* / Please don't leave: *Drapels* / Someday: *Veltones* / All the way: *Prince Conley* / Hard times (Every dog's got his day): *Prince Conley* / About noon: *Mar-Keys* / Something is worrying me: *Redding, Otis*
CD ________ **CDSXD 107**
Stax / May '95 / Pinnacle

5000 OHM (2CD Set)
CD Set ________ **IRCD 03**
Influence / Jun '94 / Plastic Head

6000 OHM (2CD Set)
No good (Start the dance): *Prodigy* / I need your love: *Microwave Prince* / Signs of life: *Meteor Seven* / Feel the melodee: *Komakino* / Sacred cycles: *Lazonby* / Cybertrance: *Blue Alphabet* / My: *Van Dyke, Paul* / Bagdad: *Paragliders* / Perpetuum mobile: *Luxor* / Filterside: *Dimitri From Paris* / Phraser: *Bionic Boom* / Self immolation: *Hiroshima* / Torwart: *Deep Piece* / Mono 1: *Nervous Project* / Amphetamine: *Drax* / Drag: *Titan & Red Acid Jack* / Mongolian rider: *Phoenixx* / Asita: *Source T-10* / Let there by rhythm: *Mason, Steve* / Two full moons: *Union Jack*
CD Set ________ **SUCK CD6**
Suck Me Plasma / Oct '94 / Arabesque / Plastic Head

$10,000 WORTH OF DOO WOP
Pretty, pretty girl: *Timetones* / Where are you: *Bel Aires* / Why be a fool: *Nobles* / My life's desire: *Verdicts* / Ride away: *Revalons* / Tight skirt and sweater: *Versatones* / Tell me: *Mastertones* / Bang bang shoot 'em Daddy: *Emblems* / Crying for you: *Centuries* / My love: *Timetones* / Poor rock and roll: *Nobles* / Can I come over tonight: *Velours* / Tomorrow: *Decoys* / Sindy: *Squires* / Bila: *Versatones* / Oh darling: *Jaytones* / My love: *Revalons* / I love you: *4 Mosts* / Jerry: *Minors* / In my heart: *Timetones*
CD ________ **FICD 1**
Finbarr International / Dec '93 / Finbarr International

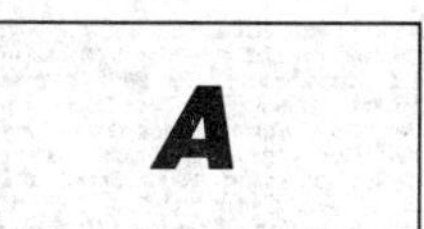

A IS FOR ACTIV
So bad: *Hagen, Nina* / American pie: *Just Luis* / Show me: *Taff, Joe* / I'll do my best: *Ritchie Family* / Always: *MK* / My sweet liar: *With It Guys* / Addicted: *Plutonic* / Hide-a-way: *Nu Soul* / Burning: *MK* / Unconditionally: *Williams, Sandra* / You shine so bright: *Dennis, Julie* / Always: *MK* / Addicted: *Plutonic* / I want it, I need it: *Williams, Sandra* / Hide-a-way: *Nu Soul* / I'll do my best: *Ritchie Family* / Burning: *MK* / Pleasure voyage: *X-Form*
CD ________ **ACTIVCD 8**
Activ / Jun '97 / Total/BMG

A NOS IDOLES
Une meche de cheveux: *Adamo* / Dominique: *Soeur Sourire* / Nous on s'aime: *Chelon, Georges* / Premier baiser, premiere larme: *Reggan, Jacky* / Come comedie: *Mars, Betty* / Les yeux d'un ange: *Fernandel, Franck* / La gendarmerie: *Topaloff, Patrick* / Mathias: *Gribouille* / C'est ma fete: *Antony, Richard* / Les ballons rouge: *Lama, Serge* / Les gens qui s'aiment: *Dumont, Charles* / Ensemble: *Sullivan, Art* / Adieu jolie Candy: *Michael, Jean Francois* / Parle mon maman: *Miras, Robert* / Souviens toi de moi: *Marie* / Comme j'ai toujours envie d'aimer: *Hamilton, Marc* / Le sud: *Ferrer, Nino* / Tout nu, tout bronze: *Carlos*
CD ________ **DC 863932**
Disky / Nov '96 / Disky / THE

A TODA CUBA LE GUSTA
CD ________ **CCD 505**
Caney / Nov '95 / ADA / Discovery

A&M RECORDS SAMPLER (2CD Set)
If it makes you happy: *Crow, Sheryl* / Everyday is a winding road: *Crow, Sheryl* / Good enough: *Dodgy* / If you're thinking of me: *Dodgy* / Marblehead Johnson: *Bluetones* / Let's make a night to remember: *Adams, Bryan* / Star: *Adams, Bryan* / I'm so happy I can't stop crying: *Sting* / Midnight in a perfect world: *DJ Shadow* / Stereo: *Spooky* / It's a sad sad planet: *Evil Superstars* / No cheap thrill: *Vega, Suzanne* / Heaven: *Washington, Sarah* / Sticky rock: *Bawl* / All gone away: *Joyrider* / 3000: *Dr. Octagon* / Berry mediatation: *UNKLE*
CD Set ________ **ARS 96**
A&M / Oct '96 / PolyGram

A-SIDES VOL.1
CD ________ **CATNO 8CD**
Crass / Nov '92 / SRD

A-SIDES VOL.2
CD ________ **CATNO 9CD**
Crass / May '93 / SRD

ABDUCTION VOL.1 (2CD Set)
Age of love: *Age Of Love* / Two moons and a trout: *Union Jack* / France: *THK* / Kinetic: *Golden Girls* / Fire of love: *Jungle High* / Le voie le soleil: *Subliminal Cuts* / Song of life: *Leftfield* / Are am eye: *Commander Tom* / Neurodancer: *Wippenberg* / Plastic dreams: *Jaydee* / Schoenberg: *Marmion* / I trance you: *Gypsy* / Domination: *Way Out West* / Vernon's wonderland: *Vernon* / Love above: *Fini Tribe* / Vicious circles: *Poltergeist*
CD Set ________ **SOLIDCD 002**
Solid State / Aug '96 / Prime / Vital

ABDUCTION VOL.2 (2CD Set)
Not forgotten: *Leftfield* / Stella: *Jam & Spoon* / De niro: *Disco Evangelists* / Chime: *Orbital* / With or without you: *Kiani, Mary* / Anything you want: *Delta Lady* / Spirits dancing: *Coyote* / Last rhythm: *Last Rhythm* / Careful: *Horse* / Shuddlefloss: *Dr. Atomic* / Intoxication: *React 2 Rhythm* / Smokebelch II: *Sabres Of Paradise* / Cafe Del Mar: *Energy 52* / Energy flash: *Beltram, Joey* / Don't be afraid: *Moonman* / Papua New Guinea: *Future Sound Of London* / Tom Tom's drum: *Eagles Prey* / Forbidden fruit: *Van Dyke, Paul* / Perfect day: *Visions Of Shiva* / Hidden sun of Venus: *LSG* / One earth beat: *Dum Dum* / Offshore: *Chicane* / Your love: *Big C* / Virginia: *Beat Foundation* / Himalayan dub: *7th Sense* / Truth: *Qattara* / Metropolis: *Evolution* / Americano slide: *Ritmo Rivals* / Yerba del diablo: *Datura* / Sonrisas: *Dos Pirates* / Collapse my love: *Dos Pirates*
CD Set ________ **SOLIDCD 010**
CD Set ________ **SOLIDSCD 010**
Solid State / Jun '97 / Prime / Vital

ABORIGINAL MUSIC OF THE WANDJINA
CD ________ **EUCD 1341**
ARC / Apr '96 / ADA / ARC Music

ABRACADABRA
CD ________ **1212012**
Soul Note / Nov '90 / Cadillac / Harmonia Mundi / Wellard

ABSOLUTE BLUES
CD ________ **JAZZFMCD 2**
Jazz FM / Feb '97 / Beechwood/BMG

ABSOLUTE COLLECTION - FEELINGS
CD ________ **LECD 425**
Wisepack / Jul '93 / Conifer/BMG / THE

ABSOLUTE COLLECTION - GOLDEN INSTRUMENTALS
CD ________ **LECD 424**
Wisepack / Jul '93 / Conifer/BMG / THE

ABSOLUTE COLLECTION - THEMES & DREAMS
CD ________ **LECD 426**
Wisepack / Jul '93 / Conifer/BMG / THE

ABSOLUTE COUNTRY VOL.1
Chattahoochee: *Jackson, Alan* / Rock my world: *Brooks & Dunn* / Desperado: *Black, Clint* / Every little thing: *Carter, Carlene* / My baby loves me: *McBride, Martina* / Fine line: *Foster, Radney* / He would be sixteen: *Wright, Michelle* / When you walk in the room: *Tillis, Pam* / Lying to the moon: *Berg, Matraca* / When she cries: *Restless Heart* / On the road: *Parnell, Lee Roy* / Dreaming with my eyes open: *Walker, Clay*
CD ________ **74321219002**
RCA / Oct '94 / BMG

ABSOLUTE COUNTRY VOL.2
CD ________ **74321279242**
RCA / Apr '95 / BMG

ABSOLUTE DANCE MIX
CD ________ **XTR 3002**
X-Treme / Feb '97 / Pinnacle / SRD

ABSOLUTE GOLD (2CD Set)
Heaven for everyone: *Queen* / Because you loved me: *Dion, Celine* / Missing: *Everything But The Girl* / Breakfast at Tiffany's: *Deep Blue Something* / Drive: *REM* / I'd lie for you (and that's the truth): *Meat Loaf* / Father and son: *Stevens, Cat* / How deep is your love: *Take That* / Where do broken hearts go: *Houston, Whitney* / Father figure: *Michael, George* / You don't understand me: *Roxette* / Always tomorrow: *Estefan, Gloria* / Missing you: *De Burgh, Chris* / Anywhere is: *Enya* / Where the wild roses grow: *Cave, Nick & Kylie Minogue* / Let it rain: *Marshall, Amanda* / Day we caught the train: *Ocean Colour Scene* / Don't look back in anger: *Oasis* / I just can't stop loving you: *Jackson, Michael* / Killing me softly: *Fugees* / Never never love: *Simply Red* / Earth, the sun, the rain: *Color Me Badd* / Open arms: *Carey, Mariah* / Anything: *3T* / I don't wanna fight: *Turner, Tina* / I'll never break your heart: *Backstreet Boys* / You're the star: *Stewart, Rod* / Secret garden: *Springsteen, Bruce* / Leningrad: *Joel, Billy* / Rocket man (I think it's going to be a long, long time): *John, Elton* / Help me: *Mike & The Mechanics* / Belfast child: *Simple Minds* / Love so beautiful: *Bolton, Michael* / All I wanna do is make love to you: *Heart* / Believer: *Glen, Marla* / You and I: *Scorpions*
CD Set ________ **SONYTV 22CD**
Sony TV / Jan '97 / Sony

ABSOLUTE PARTY PARTY
C'mon everybody: *Cochran, Eddie* / Locomotion: *Little Eva* / Shakin' all over: *Kidd, Johnny & The Pirates* / Do wah diddy diddy: *Manfred Mann* / Barbara Ann: *Beach Boys* / See my baby jive: *Wizzard* / That's the way I like it: *KC & The Sunshine Band* / Heaven must be missing an angel: *Tavares* / Devil gate drive: *Quatro, Suzi* / Kids in America: *Wilde, Kim* / Respectable: *Mel & Kim* / Whatever I do: *Dean, Hazell* / T'ain't what you do (it's the way that you do it): *Fun Boy Three & Bananarama* / Gangsters: *Specials* / Heart of glass: *Blondie* / Unbelievable: *EMF* / Geno: *Dexy's Midnight Runners* / Tiger feet: *Mud* / I'm the leader of the gang (I am): *Glitter, Gary* / Hi ho silver lining: *Beck, Jeff*
CD ________ **CDMFP 6239**
Music For Pleasure / Oct '96 / EMI

ABSOLUTE REGGAE
Everything I own: *Boothe, Ken* / Let your yeah be yeah: *Pioneers* / You make me feel: *Gardiner, Boris* / Eighteen with a bullet: *Harriott, Derrick* / Return of Django: *Upsetters* / Love of the common people: *Thomas, Nicky* / Cherry oh baby: *Donaldson, Eric* / Black and white: *Greyhound* / Reggae man: *Dekker, George* / Walk away: *Pierre, Marie* / Rain: *Ruffin, Bruce* / Young, gifted and black: *Bob & Marcia* / Lively up yourself: *Marley, Bob & The Wailers* / Then he kissed me: *Marvels* / Heart made of stone: *Hall, Audrey* / Johnny too bad: *Slickers* / Many rivers to cross: *Cliff, Jimmy* / Israelites: *Dekker, Desmond & The Aces* / Oh what a feeling: *Simon, Tito* / Hurt so good: *Cadogan, Susan* / Rivers of Babylon: *Melodians* / First time ever I saw your face: *Griffiths, Marcia* / Help me make it through the night: *Holt, John* / Suzanne beware of the devil: *Livingstone, Dandy*
CD ________ **VSOPCD 104**
Connoisseur Collection / Nov '87 / Pinnacle

ABSOLUTELY (The Very Best Of Prelude Records/2CD Set)
You're the one for me: *D-Train* / Beat the street: *Redd, Sharon* / Go with the flow: *Weeks & Co.* / Love fever: *Adams, Gayle* / Gonna get over you: *Joli, France* / You'll never know: *Hi-Gloss* / I wish you would: *Brown, Jocelyn* / Just let me do my thing: *Sine* / Come on dance, dance: *Saturday Night Band* / Keep on jumpin': *Musique* / Inch by inch: *Strikers* / I hear music in the streets: *Unlimited Touch* / Somebody else's guy: *Brown, Jocelyn* / Can you handle it: *Redd, Sharon* / Check out the groove: *Thurston, Bobby* / Feed the flame: *Johnson, Lorraine* / Music: *D-Train* / What I got is what you need: *Unique* / On a journey (I sing the Funk Electric): *Electrik Funk* / All I need is you: *Electrik Funk* / You are the one: *Pilot* / Come let me love you: *Day, Jeanette 'Lady'* / Must be the music: *Secret Weapon* / Love how you feel: *Redd, Sharon* / Ain't no mountain high enough: *Brown, Jocelyn* / I'm caught up (in a one night love affair): *Inner Life* / Come to me: *Joli, France* / In the bush: *Musique* / Body music: *Strikers* / Dyin' to be dancin': *Empress* / Give it to me (if you don't mind): *Conquest* / Searching to find the one: *Unlimited Touch* / Music got me: *Visual*
CD Set ________ **DEEPBOX 1**
Deep Beats / Feb '97 / BMG

ABSOLUTELY (The Very Best Of Disco/ 3CD Set)
Jazzy rhythm: *Wallace, Michelle* / You can't run from my love: *Singleton, Maxine* / Harder they come: *Rockers Revenge & Donnie Calvin* / We got the funk: *Positive Force* / Check out the groove: *Thurston, Bobby* / Wastin' my love: *Sticky Fingers* / Sure shot: *Weber, Tracy* / There but for the grace of God go I: *Machine* / Don't bring back memories: *Passion* / Keep giving me love: *D-Train* / Weekend: *Class Action & Chris Wiltshire* / Happiness is just round the bend: *Gooding, Cuba* / Hit 'n' run lover: *Jiani, Carol* / Ain't no mountain high enough: *Brown, Jocelyn* / I don't want to be a freak (But I can't help myself): *Dynasty* / Do you wanna funk: *Sylvester* / Night fever: *Douglas, Carol* / Ain't no need for crying: *Silk* / I'll cry for you: *Kumano* / Let's start the dance: *Bohannon, Hamilton* / Jerky rhythm: *Erotic Drum Band* / Dancin' the night away: *Voggue* / I need you: *Sylvester* / You're gonna lose my love: *Jiani, Carol* / Making love: *Todd, Pam & Love Exchange* / Your love: *Silk, Satin & Lace* / Perfect love affair: *Constellation Orchestra* / Disco stomp: *Bohannon, Hamilton* / Double dutch bus: *Smith, Frankie* / Lay it down on me: *Mallory, Gerald* / In the name of love: *Redd, Sharon* / Nice & soft: *Wish & La-Rita Gaskin* / We feel in love while dancing: *Brandon, Bill*
CD Set ________ **DEEPBOX 2**
Deep Beats / Mar '97 / BMG

ABSOLUTELY (The Very Best Of Electro/3CD Set)
White lines (Don't do it): *Grandmaster Flash & Melle Mel* / Give me tonight: *Shannon* / Uphill (Peace of mind): *COD* / Hungry for your love: *Hanson & Davis* / Crash goes love: *Holloway, Loleatta* / Boogie down bronx: *Man Parrish* / Break dancin' (Electric boogie): *West Street Mob* / Nunk: *Warp 9* / Soul makossa: *Nairobi* / Jungle rock: *Tribe* / Let the music play: *Shannon* / In the bottle: *COD* / Rock the box: *Sylvester* / And the beat goes on: *Orbit* / Mirda rock: *Griffin, Reggie & Technofunk* / Freak-a-zoid: *Midnight Star* / On journey (I sing the funk electric): *Electric Funk* / Feel the force: *G-Force* / Success: *CD III* / Rotation: *Sine* / Hip hop be bop (Don't stop): *Man Parrish* / On the upside: *Xena* / Mosquito (Aka hobo

scratch): *West Street Mob* / Jump back (Set me free): *Braxton, Dhar* / Your life: *Konk* / Message II (Survival): *Melle Mel & Duke Bootee* / Light years away: *Warp 9* / I'm the boss: *Amazing Kid & Cut Master Lee* / (I'm just a sucker) For a pretty face: *Phillips, West* / It's out of sight: *Lefturno*
CD Set — **DEEPBOX 3**
Deep Beats / Mar '97 / BMG

ABSOLUTELY (The Very Best Of Solar Records Vol.1/3CD Set)
Night to remember: *Shalamar* / It's a love thing: *Whispers* / Wet my whistle: *Midnight Star* / It's all the way live: *Lakeside* / I've just begun to love you: *Dynasty* / In the raw: *Whispers* / I gotta keep dancin' (keep smiling): *Lucas, Carrie* / Make that move: *Shalamar* / Come back lover, come back: *Sylvers* / Can-U-dance: *Deele* / Operator: *Midnight Star* / I wanna be rich: *Calloway* / Romeo where's Juliet: *Collage* / Second time around: *Shalamar* / I can make it better: *Whispers* / Headlines: *Midnight Star* / Fantastic voyage: *Lakeside* / Does that ring a bell: *Dynasty* / Friends: *Shalamar* / Show me where you're coming from: *Lucas, Carrie* / Rock steady: *Whispers* / Groove control: *Dynasty* / Get in touch with me: *Collage* / Call me: *Wolfer, Bill* / And the beat goes on: *Whispers* / Wet my whistle: *Midnight Star* / Take that to the bank: *Shalamar* / Freak-a-zoid: *Midnight Star* / There it is: *Shalamar* / Headlines: *Midnight Star* / Romeo where's Juliet: *Collage* / Night to remember: *Shalamar* / Snake in the grass: *Midnight Star* / Fantastic voyage: *Lakeside* / Scientific love: *Midnight Star* / Can-U-dance: *Deele* / Special: *Lakeside* / Restrictions: *Lakeside* / Circumstantial evidence: *Shalamar* / Hot spot: *Midnight Star* / Alien Zzz: *Collage* / Rock steady: *Whispers* / Do me right: *Dynasty* / Wet my whistle: *Midnight Star* / Midas touch: *Midnight Star* / Flavour: *Just Ice & Grandmaster Flash* / I've got it good: *Tricky Tee*
CD Set — **DEEPBOX 4**
Deep Beats / Jun '97 / BMG

ABSOLUTELY (The Very Best Of Solar Records Vol.2/3CD Set)
And the beat goes on: *Whispers* / I don't want to be a freak (but I can't help myself): *Dynasty* / Dance with you: *Lucas, Carrie* / Soul Train '75: *Soul Train Gang* / Papa was a rollin' stone: *Wolfer, Bill* / Engine no.9: *Midnight Star* / Take that to the bank: *Shalamar* / Tonight: *Whispers* / Raid: *Lakeside* / Take it to the top: *Sylvers* / Winners and losers: *Collage* / Let's get smooth: *Calloway* / There it is: *Shalamar* / Contagious: *Whispers* / Midas touch: *Midnight Star* / Do me right: *Dynasty* / I can make you feel good: *Shalamar* / Hello stranger: *Lucas, Carrie* / Shoot 'em up movies: *Deele* / I want to hold your hand: *Lakeside* / Curious: *Midnight Star* / I'm the one for you: *Whispers* / Adventures in the land of music: *Dynasty* / Groovin': *Collage* / Right in the socket: *Shalamar* / I owe you one: *Shalamar* / Take that to the bank: *Shalamar* / Second time around: *Shalamar* / Your piece of the rock: *Dynasty* / I've just begun to love you: *Dynasty* / I don't want to freak (but I can't help myself): *Dynasty* / Given in to love: *Lakeside* / It's all the way live: *Lakeside* / Two occasions: *Deele* / Lady: *Whispers* / Song for Donny: *Whispers* / And the beat goes on: *Whispers*
CD Set — **DEEPBOX 5**
Deep Beats / Aug '97 / BMG

ABSOLUTELY (The Very Best Of Old School Rap/3CD Set)
Rapper's delight: *Sugarhill Gang* / Adventures of Grandmaster Flash: *Grandmaster Flash* / Super-Wolf can do it: *Super-Wolf* / Cold gettin' dumb: *Just Ice* / Hey fellas: *Trouble Funk* / Yes we can can: *Treacherous Three* / Monster jam: *Spoonie Gee & The Sequence* / Sucker DJ: *Dimples D & Marley Marl* / Outta control: *Miracle Mike & The Ladies Of The 80's* / Ooh baby: *West Street Mob* / Message: *Grandmaster Flash & The Furious Five* / Eighth wonder: *Sugarhill Gang* / That's the joint: *Funky 4+1* / Success is the word: *12:41* / Showdown: *Furious Five & Sugarhill Gang* / Funk you up: *Sequence* / Busy Bee's groove: *Busy Bee* / Breaking bells (take me to the Mardi Gras): *Crash Crew* / Leave it to the drums (here come the drums): *Tricky Tee* / All night long (waterbed): *Kevie Kev* / Apache: *Sugarhill Gang* / It's nasty (genius of love): *Grandmaster Flash & The Furious Five* / I've got it good: *Tricky Tee* / New York New York: *Grandmaster Flash & The Furious Five* / B-boy style: *Little Jazzy Jay* / Xmas rap: *Treacherous Three* / Making cash money: *Busy Bee* / Don't rock the boat: *Midnight Star & Ecstasy* / Johnny the fox: *Tricky Tee*
CD Set — **DEEPBOX 7**
Deep Beats / Aug '97 / BMG

ABSOLUTION
Spellbound: *Siouxsie & The Banshees* / Don't let me down gently: *Wonder Stuff* / Deliverance: *Mission* / Eloise: *Damned* / Never enough: *Cure* / Ziggy Stardust: *Bauhaus* / Love like blood: *Killing Joke* / European female: *Stranglers* / Some candy talking: *Jesus & Mary Chain* / Cutter: *Echo & The Bunnymen* / Love my way: *Psychedelic Furs* / Enjoy the silence: *Depeche Mode* / Martha's harbour: *All About Eve* / Baby I love you: *Ramones* / Miss the girl: *Creatures* / No rest: *New Model Army* / Heartache: *Gene Loves Jezebel* / Moonchild (first seal): *Fields Of The Nephilim*
CD — **8457472**
Polydor / Sep '91 / PolyGram

ABSTRACT EXPRESSION VOL.1
CD — **FLAGCD 107**
Flagbearer / Jun '95 / SRD / Timewarp

ABSTRACT PHAZE
CD — **MPCD 004**
Masturi / Nov '96 / Mo's Music Machine

ABSTRACT PUNK SINGLES COLLECTION
48 Crash: *Gymslips* / Big sister: *Gymslips* / Robot man: *Gymslips* / Self destruct: *UK Subs* / Police state: *UK Subs* / War of the roses: *UK Subs* / Vengence: *New Model Army* / Nowhere to run: *Outcasts* / Denise: *Joolz* / Three Johns: *AWOL* / Great expectations: *New Model Army* / Price: *New Model Army* / Armchair: *Hagar The Womb* / Evil eye: *Gymslips* / Drink problem: *Gymslips* / Daddy's been working: *Downbeats* / Lean on me: *Redskins* / Unionise: *Redskins* / Kick out the tories: *Newtown Neurotics* / Mindless violence: *Newtown Neurotics*
CD — **CDPUNK 52**
Anagram / Apr '95 / Cargo / Pinnacle

ABSTRACT VIBES
CD — **5242522**
Quango / Jun '96 / PolyGram

ACCESS ALL AREAS (VIP)
Seven days and one week: *BBE* / Passion: *Amen UK* / Bellissima: *DJ Quicksilver* / Outragous: *Stix 'N' Stoned* / Let's groove: *Morel, George* / Party: *Fletch* / Move your body (mueve la cadera): *Reel 2 Real* / Groovebird: *Natural Born Groovers* / Techno solutions: *DJ Philip* / La batteria (the drum track): *Baby Doc* / Flash: *BBE* / Nightmare: *Brainbug* / Come with me: *Quattara* / Do that to me: *Lisa Marie Experience* / Freedom: *Black Magic* / Real vibration (want love): *Black Magic* / Stamp: *Healy, Jeremy & Amos*
CD — **CDTIVA 1015**
Positiva / Apr '97 / EMI

ACCORDEON - LA COLLECTION A SUIVRE
CD — **174522**
ARB / Jun '97 / Discovery

ACCORDEON - PARIS TANGO
CD — **175692**
ARB / Jun '97 / Discovery

ACCORDEON JAZZ 1911-1944 (2CD Set)
CD Set — **FA 038**
Fremeaux / Nov '95 / ADA / Discovery

ACCORDEON VOL.1 1913-1941 (2CD Set)
CD Set — **DH 002CD**
Fremeaux / Nov '95 / ADA / Discovery

ACCORDEON VOL.2 1942-1952 (2CD Set)
CD Set — **FA 005CD**
Fremeaux / Nov '95 / ADA / Discovery

ACCORDEON: NOSTALGIC POET OF PARIS (Poete Nostalgique De Paname)
Sous les toits de Paris: *Alexander, Maurice & His Musette Orchestra* / La mattchiche: *Vacher, Emile* / T'aimer, c'est la folie: *Vacher, Emile* / On m'suit: *Vacher, Emile* / Les momes de la cloche: *Piaf, Edith/Jean & Jacques Medinger* / Marionettes: *Marceau & His Musette Orchestra* / Napoli: *Marceau & His Musette Orchestra* / Le bonheur n'est plus un reve: *Daron, Robert & Ronaldo/Musette Orchestra* / Tel qu'il est il me plait: *Frehel & Maurice Alexander Musette Orchestra* / C'est un bureaucrate: *Alexander, Maurice & His Musette Orchestra* / Les patineurs: *Vela, Louis & Appennini* / La Java de doudoune: *Vela, Louis & Appennini* / Radieuse radiant: *Vacher, Emile* / Tant que la femme mentira: *Vacher, Emile* / Pouet poet: *Vacher, Emile* / La Java de cezigue: *Piaf, Edith/Jean & Jacques Medinger* / Souvenir de la varenne: *Marceau & His Musette Orchestra* / Athletic: *Marceau & His Musette Orchestra* / Lina: *Marceau & His Musette Orchestra* / Souvenir de Clichy: *Marceau & His Musette Orchestra* / Amusez-vous: *Gardoni, Fredo & Manuel Puig Musette Orchestra/Jean Cyrano* / Sur le plancher des vaches: *Gardoni, Fredo & Manuel Puig Musette Orchestra/ Jean Cyrano* / Musette folie: *Pesenti, Rene* / Cascadeuse: *Pesenti, Rene* / L'accordeoniste: *Lebas, Renee Orchestra*
CD — **CDAJA 5203**
Living Era / Oct '96 / Select

ACCORDEONS DIATONIQUES
CD — **CVPV 1391CD**
CVPV / Apr '96 / ADA

ACCORDION AND FIDDLES
CD — **LBP 2026CD**
Lochshore / Jun '96 / ADA / Direct / Duncans

ACCORDIONS OF THE WORLD
CD — **KAR 992**
IMP / Apr '97 / ADA / Discovery

ACCOUNTABILITY
I'm in a rush: *Joseph, Phil* / Street party: *Trampas* / Free for love: *Nelson, CJ* / No.1: *Nelson, CJ* / Precious love: *Richards, Maxine* / Gimme that love: *Ray Half Penny* / Life time: *Richards, Maxine* / Get it right: *Ray Half Penny*
CD — **FUNXD 228**
Future Underground Nation / Aug '97 / Mo's Music Machine / Pinnacle

ACCOUSTIC SAMPLER VOL.5
Secret garden: *Kostia* / Enzian: *Gratz, Wayne* / Merced: *Tingstad, Eric* / Briarcombe: *Stein, Ira* / Opal moon: *Wynberg, Simon* / Peru: *Tingstad, Eric* / La couronne: *Kolbe, Martin* / Imaginary friend: *Gratz, Wayne* / Barcelona: *White, Andrew* / Dream of the forgotten child: *Lanz, David* / Touchstone: *Ellwood, William* / Magical child: *Jones, Michael*
CD — **ND 61041**
Narada / Jul '94 / ADA / New Note/Pinnacle

ACID ATTACK VOL.3
Times fade: *Phuture The Next Generation* / Acid bites 1: *Acid Warrior* / Blanche: *Purple Plejade* / We call it acid: *Purple Plejade* / Full mane: *Laux & Olsson* / Acid code: *Beyer, Adam* / Acid marathon 1 & 2: *Acid Scout* / Hump around: *Rezzq* / Liquid: *Stoll, Steve* / Acid kraut: *Acidkraut* / Ride the rat: *Two On Acid* / Exorcisten: *Terric Krom* / Get my bearings: *Finnie, Mark* / Serial killer: *DJ Skull* / Utmosfear: *Yanni* / Hear and move: *Reich, Max* / Eazy 2 use: *Reich, Max* / Uplifting: *Proloque* / Trail: *Junk Project* / Angstman: *Metacosm* / Inside out: *Verbos, Mark* / Torn apart: *Singularity* / Dax: *Encephaloid Disturbance* / Reality: *Morant, Andrei*
CD — **MILL 042CD**
Millenium / Jul '97 / Plastic Head / Prime / SRD

ACID BOX VOL.1
CD — **ENT 3CD**
Abstract / Oct '96 / Cargo / Pinnacle / Total/BMG

ACID DREAMS TESTAMENT
CD — **2596**
Head / Jun '97 / Greyhound

ACID FLASH VOL.1 (2CD Set)
CD Set — **SPV 08938422**
SPV / Jan '96 / Koch / Plastic Head

ACID FLASH VOL.2 (2CD Set)
Heulender Wolf: *Future Breeze* / Synaesthesia: *Synaesthesiacs* / Cell: *Parts Of Console* / Southern hemisphere: *Dual Mount* / Input transformer: *Komatsu* / Upside down: *Interrupt* / Go ahead London: *Tesox* / Touch me: *Kenton Connection* / It's hot: *Brainvibe* / Evolution: *Acut Genius* / Leak: *Naomi* / Acid train: *Asys* / Inertia: *Fast Trac* / Walking: *Mo, Kevin*
CD Set — **SPV 08938672**
SPV / May '96 / Koch / Plastic Head

ACID FLASH VOL.3 (21 Acid Underground Traxx/2CD Set)
Acid NRG: *NRG Jams* / Braintool: *Junk Project* / Secret pattern: *Riot Rhythm* / Lash v 11: *Rubicon Massacre Ltd.* / Enjoy the creation: *Assym* / Reality: *Morant, Andrei* / Turn it up: *Huntemann* / Track 1 side A: *Nip Collective* / Hip: *SPAX* / Arp impression: *Driver, Jan* / Search for experience: *Noodle Project* / Strong fish taste: *Plural* / Acid house...acid: *Nostrum* / Exceed: *Junk Project* / Fusion drive: *Baj Ram* / We are not: *Jet Set* / Accent: *Acid Device* / Get out: *Terratropin* / Blame groove: *Titan & Red Acid Jack* / Countbasic: *Cellblockx* / Berlin: *Rob Acid*
CD Set — **SPV 08947082**
SPV / Sep '96 / Koch / Plastic Head

ACID FLASH VOL.4 (2CD Set)
Humanoid: *N-Son-X* / I know what U R thinking: *New Moon* / Subway: *Spick & Span* / Unicum: *DJ Tomicraft* / One and only: *Lumo* / Racha: *TB-Tuner* / Running man: *Nuclear Hyde* / Guinean folks: *Patchwork* / Sentimental circuit: *Repulsor* / Dark side of light: *Framic* / Destruction: *D-Fense & Confusion* / House muzik: *Victims Of Lobotomie* / Brain1: *Brain1* / Phuture power: *Chevalier, John* / Pattern war: *18-DB* / Girl he's fine: *Nectar* / Eject: *Acid Device* / Fear of death: *Oddball* / Streichholz: *Laux & Olsson* / Switch board: *Church Windows* / So high: *Dennmarque* / Piquant: *A Dreams A*
CD Set — **SPV 08947322**
SPV / Feb '97 / Koch / Plastic Head

ACID FLASH VOL.5
CD Set — **SPV 08947552**
SPV / Jul '97 / Koch / Plastic Head

ACID FLASHBACK
CD — **TRIPCD 1**
Rumour / Mar '95 / 3mv/Sony / Mo's Music Machine / Pinnacle

ACID JAZZ JAZZ
CD — **JAZIDCD 038**
Acid Jazz / Jul '91 / Disc

ACID JAZZ MO' JAZZ
CD — **JAZIDCD 051**
Acid Jazz / Jun '92 / Disc

ACID JAZZ VOL.1
Better half: *Funk Inc.* / Got myself a good man: *Pucho* / Houston Express: *Person, Houston* / Grits and gravy: *Kloss, Eric* / Hoochie coo chickie: *Jones, Ivan 'Boogaloo Joe'* / Lady Mama: *Ammons, Gene* / Hip shaker: *Spencer, Leon* / Psychedelic Sally
CD — **CDBGP 1015**
Beat Goes Public / Oct '91 / Pinnacle

ACID JAZZ VOL.2
Super bad: *Muhammad, Idris* / Cold sweat: *Purdie, Bernard* / Wildfire: *Bryant, Rusty* / Hot barbecue: *McDuff, Jack* / Reelin' with the feelin': *Kynard, Charles* / Spinky: *Earland, Charles* / Who's gonna take the weight: *Sparks, Melvin*
CD — **CDBGP 1017**
Beat Goes Public / Oct '91 / Pinnacle

ACID JAZZ VOL.3
I want you back: *Mabern, Harold* / Psychedelic Pucho: *Pucho* / Zebra walk: *Kynard, Charles* / Akilah: *Sparks, Melvin* / What it is: *Jones, Ivan 'Boogaloo Joe'* / Bad Montana: *Parker, Maynard* / Dig on it: *Smith, Johnny 'Hammond'* / Bowlegs: *Funk Inc.*
CD — **CDBGP 1025**
Beat Goes Public / Oct '91 / Pinnacle

ACID JAZZ VOL.3
Whole lotta love: *Goldbug* / Lovesick: *Night Trains & Marcia Johnson* / Apple green: *Mother Earth* / Exe marks the spot: *Mister Exe* / Good thing: *Taylor, James Quartet* / Rising to the top: *Blacknuss Allstars & Lisa Nilsson/Desmond Foster* / Use me: *Raw Stylus* / Up to our necks in it: *Skunkhour* / How can you forget: *Dread Flimstone & Michael Prophet* / Try me: *Isaacs, Gregory* / Unsettled life: *Emperor's New Clothes* / World peace: *African Headcharge* / Living life your own way: *Windross, Rose* / Can't get enough: *Vibraphonic* / Mambito: *Snowboy* / Hip hop beat: *Nu Perspective* / Asteroid: *Goldbug*
CD — **JAZIDCD 141**
Acid Jazz / May '96 / Disc

ACID JAZZ VOL.4
Soul dance: *Person, Houston* / Sing a simple song: *Earland, Charles* / Twang thang: *Butler, Billy* / Shaft: *Purdie, Bernard* / Sure nuff sure nuff: *Phillips, Sonny* / Mamblues: *Tjader, Cal & Bernard Purdie* / Haw right now: *Rushen, Patrice* / Life is funky: *Round Robin Monopoly*
CD — **CDBGP 1029**
Beat Goes Public / Oct '91 / Pinnacle

ACID RESISTANT VOL.1
CD — **EFA 262332**
Smile / May '95 / SRD

ACID RESISTANT VOL.2
CD — **SM 80282**
Profile / Nov '96 / Pinnacle

ACID TUNES (2CD Set)
CD Set — **560052**
Westcom / Mar '97 / Koch / Pinnacle

ACOUSTIC AID
Is this the world we created: *Mercury, Freddie* / To be with you: *Mr. Big* / Melissa: *Allman Brothers* / Blood and roses: *Allman Brothers* / Bouree: *Jethro Tull* / When I'm gone: *Schenker, Michael Group* / From the beginning: *Lake, Greg* / Prove it every night: *Money, Eddie* / Keith don't go: *Lofgren, Nils* / She talks to angels: *Black Crowes* / Tuesday afternoon: *Hayward, Justin* / Lunatic fringe: *Cochrane, Tom* / Hands of time: *Y&T* / Rad gumbo: *Little Feat* / Your love: *Outfield* / Turn turn turn: *McGuinn, Roger*
CD — **399780**
Koch Presents / Jun '97 / Koch

ACOUSTIC DISC SAMPLER VOL.1, THE (100% Handmade Music)
CD — **AC 008CDS**
Acoustic Disc / Apr '97 / ADA / Koch

ACOUSTIC DISC SAMPLER VOL.2, THE (100% Handmade Music)
CD — **ACDS 16**
Acoustic Disc / Jul '97 / ADA / Koch

ACOUSTIC DREAMS
If you leave me now / Tears in heaven / You are not alone / Back for good / Think twice / How 'bout us / Unchained melody / Just the way you are / Kiss from a rose / Sacrifice / All by myself / Always and forever / Me and Mrs Jones / One sweet day / Three times a lady / You are the sunshine of my life / And I love her / How deep is your love
CD — **CDVIP 152**
Virgin VIP / Jan '97 / EMI

ACOUSTIC FREEWAY
CD — **5257352**
PolyGram TV / Aug '95 / PolyGram

ACOUSTIC HEART (The Passion & Romance Of Acoustic Guitar Masters)
CD — **SHCD 5030**
Shanachie / Apr '97 / ADA / Greensleeves / Koch

ACOUSTIC MOODS
Lady Eleanor: *Lindisfarne* / Stuck in the middle with you: *Stealer's Wheel* / Baker Street: *Rafferty, Gerry* / Year of the cat: *Stewart, Al* / They shoot horses don't they: *Racing Cars* / Arms of Mary: *Sutherland Brothers & Quiver* / Chestnut mare: *Byrds* / Castles in the air: *McLean, Don* / Blue guitar: *Hayward, Justin & John Lodge* / Moonlight shadow: *Oldfield, Mike* / Lay down: *Strawbs* / How come: *Lane, Ronnie & Slim Chance* / Reason to believe: *Stewart, Rod* / Journey: *Browne, Duncan* / I don't mind at all: *Bourgeois Tagg* / Pinball: *Protheroe, Brian* / Streets of London: *McTell, Ralph* / Time in a bottle: *Croce, Jim* / Morning has broken: *Stevens, Cat* / After the goldrush: *Prelude*

CD ______ 5166592
PolyGram TV / Apr '94 / PolyGram

ACOUSTIC MOODS
Endless love: *In Tune* / Back for good: *In Tune* / Think twice: *In Tune* / La isla bonita: *In Tune* / Scarborough fair: *In Tune* / (Love theme from) Romeo and Juliet: *In Tune* / Get here: *In Tune* / Love is all around: *In Tune* / Save the best for last: *In Tune* / (Everything I do) I do it for you: *In Tune* / And I love her: *In Tune* / Promise me: *In Tune* / Take my breath away: *In Tune* / End of the road: *In Tune* / Gymnopedie no.1: *In Tune* / Summertime: *In Tune* / Don't let the sun go down on me: *In Tune*
CD ______ RADCD 13
Global TV / Jun '95 / BMG

ACOUSTIC MOODS (2CD Set)
Old English / Jeanne / Under ground / Ar Soudarded / First interlude / Ways / In Pappa's garden / Childhood days / King of the fairies / Romanian dance / Keel row/John Peel / Double lead through/Give us some treacle and bread / Reel of Pickering-Pick / Second interlude / Times of celebration / Mother Sea-Father Sun / Koh-I-Noor / Long Island / Slide mama / Snake river blues / Kalahari / Third interlude / Sic'e ceya ce / Fourth interlude / Calling / Sh'Dematy / Refleo del agua / Little ponies / L'isle de re / Tennessee moonlight / O ye yai quai faire / Jack hardy / Big blues / Fifth interlude / Convergence / Last stop
CD Set ______ 330112
Hallmark / Jul '96 / Carlton

ACOUSTIC MOODS (40 Timeless Instrumental Classics/2CD Set)
Yesterday / Fool on the hill / Eleanor Rigby / Wonderful tonight / Hello / Vincent / Suicide is painless / Nobody does it better / Just the two of us / No woman, no cry / Yesterday once more / Bridge over troubled water / Still crazy after all these years / Every breath you take / Just the way you are / Time after time / One more night / Raining in Ginza / Many rivers to cross / Wrapped around your finger / Smoke gets in your eyes / I only have eyes for you / Ain't misbehavin' / That ole devil called love / Strangers in the night / Blue moon / Autumn leaves / Night and day / Whispering grass / Nightingale sang in Berkeley Square / Ol' man river / Some day my prince will come / When you wish upon a star / Isn't this a lovely day / Back to the mountain / Moon river / I could / Harry Lime / Deja vu / Yatau
CD Set ______ SUDCD 4506
Summit / Nov '96 / Sound & Media

ACOUSTIC MUSIC PROJECT
Step right this way: *Prophet, Chuck & Stephanie Finch* / Trying: *Prophet, Chuck & Stephanie Finch* / On borrowed time: *Houston, Penelope* / Looking for a reason: *DeRoss, Nancie* / Say please: *Sorentino, Danny* / Such a fine line: *Shelfer, Jerry* / Hootenanny: *Muskrats* / Love's not lost: *Segal, Jonathan* / Guantanamerika: *Chilton, Alex* / Everywhere that I'm not: *Barton, Darlington & Dekker* / Words: *Movie Stars* / Penny in the sky: *Winningham, patrick* / Paint: *Hunter, Sonya* / Dreamers of the dream: *American Music Club* / Don't rewind: *Manning, Barbara* / Rude: *Haynes, Ed* / More than I will: *Champagne, Connie* / When the morning falls: *Porter, Eddie Ray*
CD ______ A 009D
Alias / Mar '93 / Vital

ACOUSTIC ROCK
Wild wood: *Weller, Paul* / Weather with you: *Crowded House* / Heal the pain: *Michael, George* / Prettiest eyes: *Beautiful South* / 74-75: *Connells* / Mmm mmm mmm mmm: *Crash Test Dummies* / Driving with the brakes on: *Del Amitri* / How men are: *Aztec Camera* / Is it like today: *World Party* / You & me song: *Wannadies* / Run baby run: *Crow, Sheryl* / Linger: *Cranberries* / Jennifer she said: *Cole, Lloyd* / Julie: *Levellers* / High and dry: *Radiohead* / Only living boy in New York: *Everything But The Girl* / It's about time: *Lemonheads* / You have place a chill in my heart: *Eurythmics* / Walk this world: *Nova, Heather* / Let it grow: *Clapton, Eric*
CD ______ 5258962
PolyGram TV / Sep '95 / PolyGram

ACOUSTIC ROUTES
CD ______ NINETY 7
Demon / Oct '93 / Pinnacle

ACOUSTICS SAMPLER, THE
Arrival of the Queen of Sheba: *Mandolin Allstars* / Musette a Teresa: *Daniels, Luke* / Laughing with the moon: *James, Hilary* / Dance of the water boatmen: *Mayor, Simon* / Plum blossoms in the snow: *Mayor, Simon & Gerald Garcia* / Sail away: *James, Hilary* / Capriol suite: *Mayor, Simon* / Green man: *Marriott, Beryl* / All hallows dance: *Mayor, Simon* / Looking after business: *Slim Panatella & The Mellow Virginians* / Apres un reve: *Mayor, Simon & Gerald Garcia* / Gipsy dance from Carmen: *Mayor, Simon Quintet* / John Watt Henry set: *Daniels, Luke* / Buttermere waltz: *Mayor, Simon* / Jump the gun/Reelin' over the rooftops: *Mayor, Simon* / Corn rigs: *James, Hilary* / Eine kleine nachtmusik: *Mandolin Allstars*
CD ______ CDACS 030
Acoustics / Jun '97 / ADA / Koch

ACROBATES ET MUSICIENS
CD ______ SHAN 21009CD
Shanachie / Nov '95 / ADA / Greensleeves / Koch

ACROSS THE GREAT DIVIDE
CD ______ DJD 3203
Dejadisc / May '94 / ADA / Direct

ACROSS THE TRACKS (Nashville R&B/ Rock'n'Roll)
She can rock: *Little Ike* / Every night in the week: *Birdsong, Larry* / Let's rock'n'roll: *'Little Shy Guy' Douglas* / Now do you hear: *Gaines, Earl* / I understand: *Allison, Gene* / Somebody somewhere: *Birdsong, Larry* / Let your will be done: *Fairfield Four* / Pipe dreams: *Beck, Jimmy* / Jump, jump hi-ho: *Gant, Clenest* / Do you love me: *Birdsong, Larry* / You gonna be sorry: *Allison, Gene* / Best of luck baby: *Gaines, Earl* / Since you left me behind: *Birdsong, Larry* / Oh baby: *Green, Rudy* / I want to be a part of you: *Chellows* / For you my love: *Lucille & The Strangers* / I know Johnny loves me: *Lucille & The Strangers* / Small town girl: *Tig, Jimmy & The Rounders* / They wanna fight: *Harrod, Chuck* / Twistin' USA: *Keaton, Johnny* / Let's twist (slow & easy): *Jarett, Ted* / Doctor Feelgood: *Hunter, Herbert* / I'm going home: *Allison, Levert* / Yesterday's mistake: *Shelton, Roscoe* / Thank God things are as well as they are: *Consolers* / Now that we're together: *Allison, Gene* / I'm just what you're looking for: *Kittrell, Christine* / Young & fancy free: *Birdsong, Larry*
CD ______ CDCHD 493
Ace / Sep '96 / Pinnacle

ACROSS THE WATERS (Irish Traditional Music From England)
CD ______ NI 5415CD
Nimbus / Oct '94 / Nimbus

ACTION
CD ______ BB 2812
Blue Beat / Oct '95 / Grapevine/PolyGram

ADAM PARFREY PRESENTS AN EVENING OF SONIC...
CD ______ MR 066
Man's Ruin / Jun '97 / Cargo / Greyhound / Plastic Head

ADDITIVE VOL.1
Journey: *Bliss 'n' Tumble* / Nightmare: *Brainbug* / Black hill: *Little Jam* / Space: *Fletch* / Disco mirror: *Plastika* / Good time: *Hipgrinders* / 104 dub: *Dub Tractor* / Acid people: *White Trash* / Techno solution: *DJ Philip* / Neuro: *X-Cabs* / Are am eye: *Commander Tom* / Space is the place: *Svenson, Johan* / Furyo: *Kayashi*
CD ______ CDADA 1002
Additive / Jun '97 / Mo's Music Machine / RTM/Disc

ADULTS ONLY VOL.1
Rub and sqeeze: *Perry, Lee 'Scratch' & The Soulettes* / Sexy Sadie: *Max Romeo* / Don't touch me tomato: *Dillon, Phyllis* / Wet dream: *Inspirations* / Adults only: *Lynch, Dermot* / Rub up push up: *Termites* / Push it in: *Versatiles* / Khaki: *Tennors* / Wreck a buddy: *Soul Sisters* / Hold the pussy: *Kid Gungo* / Birth control: *Lloydie & The Lowbites* / Barbwire: *Dean, Nora* / Open up: *Eccles, Clancy* / She want it: *Barker, Dave & The Gaylads* / Fat fat girl: *Lloydie & The Lowbites* / International pum pum: *Observers* / Punanny: *Charlie Ace & Fay* / Pussy cat: *Lloydie & The Lowbites*
CD ______ CDTRL 305
Trojan / Mar '94 / Direct / Jet Star

ADULTS ONLY VOL.2
Rub up, push up: *Hinds, Justin* / Want me cock: *Owen & Leon* / Pussy cat: *Cole, Stranger* / Dr. Dick: *Perry, Lee 'Scratch'* / Push it up: *Termites* / Adults only: *Calypso Joe* / Push push: *Itals* / Mr. Rhya: *Charmers, Lloyd* / Satan girl: *Ethiopians* / Pussy catch a fire: *Soulmates* / Big boy and teacher: *U-Roy* / Rough rider: *U-Roy* / Play with your pussy: *Max Romeo* / Papa do it sweet: *Lloyd & Patsy* / In a de pum pum: *Flowers & Alvin* / Mr. Whittaker: *Charlie Ace & Fay* / Hole under crutches: *Max Romeo* / Yum yum pussy: *Lloydie & The Lowbites*
CD ______ CDTRL 308
Trojan / Mar '94 / Direct / Jet Star

ADVENTURES IN AFROPEA VOL.3 (Afro Porto)
CD ______ 9362456692
WEA / Feb '96 / Warner Music

ADVENTURES IN TECHNO SOUL
Venus fly trap: *Too Funk* / Wake up to the source: *Hannah, Paul* / Lost point: *Naughty & Tolis* / Storm the funk: *Too Funk* / Sandcastle: *Precession* / End of the road: *Synchrojack* / Galapagos theory: *Gabriel, Russ* / Origin of species: *Gabriel, Russ*
CD ______ FERCD 001
Ferox / Jun '96 / Prime / SRD / Vital

AFRICA - NEVER STAND STILL
CD Set ______ CT 3300
Ellipsis Arts / Aug '94 / ADA / Direct

AFRICA CALLING
CD ______ RRTGCD 7734
Rohit / Mar '89 / Jet Star

AFRICA DANCE
CD ______ CDCH 366
Milan / Apr '90 / Conifer/BMG / Silva Screen

AFRICA IN AMERICA
CD Set ______ MT 115/7
Corason / Jan '94 / ADA / CM / Direct

AFRICA MOVES VOL.3
CD ______ STCD 105
Stern's / Mar '96 / ADA / CM / Stern's

AFRICA ON THE MOVE
CD ______ CDC 210
Music Of The World / Jun '93 / ADA / Target/BMG

AFRICA STAND ALONE
Sidike/Gorel megamix: *Maal, Baaba* / Zine a zine: *Khaled, Hadj Ibrahim* / Nyanama: *Keita, Salif* / Africa unite: *Bayete* / Akwaba: *Kidjo, Angelique* / Je ne sais pas: *Positive Black Soul* / Kelma: *Taha, Rachid* / Nafanta: *Lo, Ismael* / Sama duniya: *Maal, Baaba* / Return of da jelly: *Positive Black Soul*
CD ______ CDMNS 2
Mango / Aug '96 / PolyGram / Vital

AFRICA: THE MUSIC OF A CONTINENT
CD ______ PS 66006
PlayaSound / Oct '95 / ADA / Harmonia Mundi

AFRICAN ANGELS
CD ______ ARNR 0397
Amiata / Apr '97 / Harmonia Mundi

AFRICAN DUB SERIES VOL.3 & 4
CD ______ RGCD 024
Rocky One / Jan '95 / Jet Star

AFRICAN MELODICA DUB
CD ______ ROTCD 008
Reggae On Top / Jan '96 / Jet Star / SRD

AFRICAN MOVES
CD ______ ROUCD 11513
Rounder / Jan '88 / ADA / CM / Direct

AFRICAN MOVES VOL.2
Pole mama: *Somo Somo* / Amilo: *Ley, Tabu* / Boya ye: *M'Bilia Bell* / Sanza Misato: *Orchestra Africa* / Mon couer balance: *Daouda* / Gbebe mi: *Obey, Ebenezer* / Segun Adewale: *Adewale, Segun* / Yeme breoo: *African Brothers*
CD ______ STCD 1029
Stern's / Nov '89 / ADA / CM / Stern's

AFRICAN MUSEUM SELECTION
CD ______ HBCD 19
Heartbeat / May '90 / ADA / Direct / Greensleeves / Jet Star

AFRICAN RHYTHMS AND INSTRUMENTS VOL.1 (Mali, Niger, Ghana, Nigeria, Upper Volta, Senegal)
CD ______ LYRCD 7328
Lyrichord / '91 / ADA / CM / Roots

AFRICAN RUBBER DUB VOL.1
CD ______ CENCD 800
Century / Oct '96 / Shellshock/Disc

AFRICAN RUBBER DUB VOL.2
CD ______ CEND 1400
Century / Oct '96 / Shellshock/Disc

AFRICAN RUBBER DUB VOL.3
CD ______ CEND 1200
Century / Sep '94 / Shellshock/Disc

AFRICAN TRANQUILITY
CD ______ SHCD 64076
Shanachie / Nov '96 / ADA / Greensleeves / Koch

AFRICAN TRIBAL MUSIC AND DANCES
CD ______ 12179
Laserlight / Aug '95 / Target/BMG

AFRICAN TROUBADOURS (Best of African Singer/Songwriters)
CD ______ SH 6092
Shanachie / Jul '97 / ADA / Greensleeves / Koch

AFRICAN VOICES - SONGS OF LIFE
Kothbiro: *Ogada, Ayub* / Dala: *Ogada, Ayub* / Ondiek: *Ogada, Ayub* / Sutu Kun: *Diop, Vieux* / Jali: *Diop, Vieux* / Ekibobo: *Samite* / Ndere: *Samite* / Wasuze Otya: *Samite* / Ngak: *Diop, Lucky* / Igne: *Diop, Lucky* / Mamadi: *Diop, Lucky* / Woza Azania: *Nathaniel, Kevin* / Tatenda: *Nathaniel, Kevin*
CD ______ ND 63930
Narada / Nov '96 / ADA / New Note/ Pinnacle

AFRICOLOR
CD ______ 795242
Melodie / Nov '90 / ADA / Discovery / Grapevine/PolyGram / Greensleeves / Jet Star

AFRIQUE PARADE VOL.3
CD ______ 829042CD
BUDA / Jul '95 / Discovery

AFRIQUE PARADE VOL.4
CD ______ 829342CD
Melodie / Jan '97 / ADA / Discovery / Grapevine/PolyGram / Greensleeves / Jet Star

AFRIQUE PARADE-TOP DU SOUKOUS
CD ______ 828672
BUDA / Jun '93 / Discovery

AFRO BLUE
Afro blue: *Reeves, Dianne* / Capoeira: *Pullen, Don* / Home is Africa: *Parlan, Horace* / Mystery of love: *Blakey, Art* / Tin tin deo: *Moody, James* / Night in Tunisia: *Powell, Bud* / O'tinde: *Blakey, Art* / Man from Tanganyika: *Tyner, McCoy* / Appointment in Ghana: *McLean, Jackie* / Feast: *Blakey, Art* / Mr. Kenyatta: *Morgan, Lee* / Message from Kenya: *Silver, Horace* / Rhapsodia del marisillio: *Martinez, Sabu*
CD ______ BNZ 304
Blue Note / Nov '92 / EMI

AFRO CENTRICA
Mama / Okunaya / Black man's cry / Makassi again / Mona opusi / Makhombo / Explorations / Woza sihambe / Pon moun paka bouge / Ama gents
CD ______ MPG 74037
Movieplay Gold / Apr '97 / Target/BMG

AFRO CUBA: MUSICAL ANTHOLOGY
CD ______ ROUCD 1088
Rounder / Feb '94 / ADA / CM / Direct

AFRO CUBAN GROOVES
CD ______ 325042
Melodie / Apr '96 / ADA / Discovery / Grapevine/PolyGram / Greensleeves / Jet Star

AFRO LIMONESE: MUSIC FROM COSTA RICA
CD ______ LYRCD 7412
Lyrichord / '91 / ADA / CM / Roots

AFROLUSAMERICA (Africa/Brazil Pop)
CD ______ 68980
Tropical / Apr '97 / Discovery

AFROMANIA CARIBE
America latina / Hoy es viernes / El cumbanchero / Mentiras / Rumba sandunguera / La guayaba / Cafe con leche / Matilda / Eva pa've / Echao pa'lante / Dance this dance / No la dejare
CD ______ 68937
Tropical / Apr '97 / Discovery

AFROMANIA VOL.3 (Afro Dance Music)
Follow the drums: *Jambola* / Rasta: *African Vibes* / Fanfarissimo: *Ethnica* / Spirit of Africa: *SOP* / Wrassaroumba: *Mamukata* / White man, black heart: *Djibooti* / Strange: *Spacefront* / My rain: *L'Arabo, Mada & Max* / Camel song: *DJ Congano* / Cocain: *Cosmic Vibrations* / Sen culpa mare: *Papaya* / We need double light: *Mongawa*
CD ______ MNF 05252
Manifold / Apr '97 / ZYX

AFRS JUBILEE VOL.10
CD ______ JUBCD 1010
RST / Jan '97 / Hot Shot / Jazz Music

AFRS JUBILEE VOL.11
CD ______ JUBCD 1011
RST / Jan '97 / Hot Shot / Jazz Music

AFRS JUBILEE VOL.12
CD ______ JUBCD 1012
RST / Jan '97 / Hot Shot / Jazz Music

AFRS JUBILEE VOL.13
CD ______ JUBCD 1013
RST / Jan '97 / Hot Shot / Jazz Music

AFRS JUBILEE VOL.14
CD ______ JUBCD 1014
RST / Jan '97 / Hot Shot / Jazz Music

AFRS JUBILEE VOL.15
CD ______ JUBCD 1015
RST / Jan '97 / Hot Shot / Jazz Music

AFRS JUBILEE VOL.16
CD ______ JUBCD 1016
RST / Jan '97 / Hot Shot / Jazz Music

AFRS JUBILEE VOL.7
CD ______ JUBCD 1007
RST / Jul '96 / Hot Shot / Jazz Music

AFRS JUBILEE VOL.8
CD ______ JUBCD 1008
RST / Jul '96 / Hot Shot / Jazz Music

AFRS JUBILEE VOL.9
CD ______ JUBCD 1009
RST / Jul '96 / Hot Shot / Jazz Music

AFTER HOURS
Tempus fugue-it: *Powell, Bud* / Six cats and a prince: *Young, Lester* / I've never been in love before: *Peterson, Oscar* / Bemsha swing: *Evans, Bill* / Relaxing with Lee: *Parker, Charlie* / Is you is or is you ain't my baby: *Garner, Erroll* / After hours: *Brown, Patti* / Swingin' the blues: *Bryant, Ray* / Way you loook tonight: *Keynoters & Nat 'King' Cole* / Stompin' at the Savoy: *Wilson, Teddy* / Father co-operates: *Cole, Cozy* / Love for sale: *Tatum, Art* / Carioca: *Gillespie, Dizzy* / Believe it, beloved: *Jones, Hank* / Blue boy: *Tristano, Lennie* / September in the rain: *Shearing, George* / Oh, lady, be good: *Flanagan, Tommy* / Buttercorn lady: *Blakey, Art & The Jazz Messengers*
CD ______ 5526432
Spectrum / Mar '97 / PolyGram

AFTER HOURS VOL.1
CD ______ JDJAH 1CD
JDJ / Jan '96 / 3mv/Pinnacle / SRD

AFTER HOURS VOL.2 (Ultimate Deep Section)
Brooklyn heights: *Down To The Bone* / Hey hey: *Riviera Traxx Vol.1* / Dangerous jazz:

Ferry Ultra & Roy Ayers / A2 step: *Damier, Chez* / Ignorance is bliss: *Colour Climax* / Feelin' dub-e: *Miller, D. & C. Checkley* / Sun dance: *Fade 2 End* / Unification: *Doctors Of Dub* / Carreras: *MAP* / Unification II: *E-Culture* / Was I here before: *Owens, Robert* / Lonely winter: *Watergate* / Happiness: *Forthright* / Mystical journey: *Fontana, Lenny & Galaxy People* / It's music: *Century Falls & Philip Ramirez* / Gotta lotta luv: *Williams, Lenny*
CD ____ **JDJAH 2CD**
JDJ / Mar '97 / 3mv/Pinnacle / SRD

AFTER HOURS VOL.3
CD ____ **EX 3492**
Instinct / Apr '97 / Cargo

AFTER MIDNIGHT
Midnight at the Oasis: *Muldaur, Maria* / Sweet love: *Baker, Anita* / Feeling good: *Simone, Nina* / Nature boy: *Cole, Nat 'King'* / Let's face the music and dance: *Fitzgerald, Ella* / Dream a little dream of me: *Fygi, Laura* / Rockin' good way: *Washington, Dinah* / Mack the knife: *Darin, Bobby* / Cry me a river: *London, Julie* / Good morning heartache: *Holiday, Billie* / Tenderly: *Vaughan, Sarah* / Look of love: *Washington, Grover Jr.* / Like dreamers do: *Paris, Mica* / Razzamatazz: *Jones, Quincy* / Running away: *Ayers, Roy* / Cantaloop (Flip fantasia): *US 3* / Love supreme: *Downing, Will* / Time after time: *Davis, Miles* / Children of the ghetto: *Pine, Courtney* / Wrong side of town: *BBM*
CD ____ **5168712**
Polydor / Sep '94 / PolyGram

AFTER THE BREAK
Keep on movin': *Soul II Soul* / You don't love me (no no no): *Penn, Dawn* / Summer breeze: *Isley Brothers* / I can see clearly now: *Nash, Johnny* / Lean on me: *Withers, Bill* / California dreamin': *Mamas & The Papas* / Air that I breathe: *Hollies* / Spirit in the sky: *Greenbaum, Norman* / Low rider (on the boulevard): *War* / Spiritual high (State of independence): *Moodswings* / Dream a little dream of me: *Mama Cass* / Can't take my eyes off you: *Williams, Andy* / Fever: *Lee, Peggy* / Love letters: *Lester, Ketty* / Let's face the music and dance: *Cole, Nat 'King'* / Memories are made of this: *Martin, Dean* / Story of my life: *Holliday, Michael* / When you're smiling: *Armstrong, Louis* / I wanna be loved by you: *Monroe, Marilyn* / Hoots mon: *Lord Rockingham's XI*
CD ____ **SONYTV 30CD**
Sony TV / Jul '97 / Sony

AFTER THE SEPULTURE
CD ____ **RAD 003CD**
Radiation / Nov '95 / Plastic Head

AFTERBURNER (Your Gabba Nightmare)
CD ____ **CLP 9984**
Cleopatra / Jun '97 / Cargo / Greyhound / Plastic Head / RTM/Disc / SRD

AGE OF NEW WAVE, THE
25 Years: *Catch* / Doot doot: *Freur* / Stand or fall: *Fixx* / Wait a long time for you: *Thoughts* / I can't stop: *Numan, Gary* / I want to be free: *Toyah* / Bird song: *Lovich, Lena* / Louise (we get it right): *Lewie, Jona* / Ca plane pour moi: *Plastic Bertrand* / Butcher baby: *Plasmatics* / Destination Zululand: *King Kurt* / Disco in Moscow: *Vibrators* / Wonder woman: *County, Jayne* / Teenage: *UK Subs* / Nightmare continues: *Discharge* / If the kids are united: *Sham 69*
CD ____ **12841**
Laserlight / May '96 / Target/BMG

AGE OF SEARCH AND DESTRUCTION (2CD Set)
CD ____ **PLAC 0052**
Plastic City UK / Jun '97 / Intergroove / Prime

AGE OF SWING, THE (4CD Set)
In the mood / Very thought of you / Let's dance / American patrol / Artistry in rhythm / Begin the beguine / Big John special / Skyliner / What is this thing called love / Hamp's boogie woogie / I've got a gal in Kalamazoo / Cherokee / Opus in pastels / Pinetop's boogie / Snowfall / One o'clock jump / Song of India / Perdido / Sing sing sing / King Porter stomp / Little brown jug / Solitude / Eager beaver / Serenade in blue / I know why / On the Alamo / Hornet / Listen to my music / Wrappin' it up on the Lindy slide / Chatanooga choo choo / Apple honey / I'm getting sentimental over you / Harlem nocturne / Leave us leap / You made me love you / Boogie woogie Maxine / Moonlight sonata / South Rampart Street parade / St. Louis blues march / Mood indigo / Intermission riff / Jersey bounce / Hot toddy / 'S Wonderful / Oh lady be good / Chloe / Leapfrog / Pennsylvania 6-5000 / Opus / I got it bad and that ain't good / String of pearls / Sweet Georgia Brown / I'll never smile again / Stardreams / I get a kick out of you / Long John Silver / Down South camp meeting / Don't be that way / Anvil chorus / Moonlight serenade / After you've gone / Pompton turnpike / On the sunny side of the street / Do nothin' 'til you hear from me / At last / Flying home / Cotton tail / Body and soul / Painted rhythm / Tuxedo junction / Take the 'A' train / Swanee river / Don't sit under the apple tree / Sophisticated lady / Swingin' the blues / Memories of you / I can't get started (with you) / Poor butterfly / Song of the Volga boatmen / At the woodchoppers' ball
CD Set ____ **TFP 020**
Tring / Nov '92 / Tring

AGE OF SWING, THE
CD ____ **EMPRCD 507**
Emporio / Apr '94 / Disc

AGGRO AND ATTITUDE (40 Punk Classics/2CD Set)
Whips and fur: *Vibrators* / How much longer: *Alternative TV* / Kill the poor: *Dead Kennedys* / Questions: *Suburban Studs* / Solidarity: *Angelic Upstarts* / Never surrender: *Blitz* / City invasion: *Red Alert* / Killing machine: *Partisans* / Jerusalem: *One Way System* / Six guns: *Anti Pasti* / Howard Hughes: *Tights* / Animal bondage: *Art Attacks* / Ruby (don't take your love to town): *Outcasts* / Summertime now: *Erazerhead* / Bomb scare: *Dead Man's Shadow* / Nicely does it: *Instant Agony* / Violent society: *Special Duties* / Will they never learn: *Varukers* / In the future: *Riot Squad* / Do anything you wanna do: *Eddie & The Hot Rods* / Biggest prize in sport: *999* / Walk like a superstar (talk like a zombie): *Lurkers* / Where's Captain Kirk: *Spizz Energi* / Thinking of the USA: *Eater* / Just want to be myself: *Drones* / I am the bishop: *Not Sensibles* / I spy: *Rudi* / Wanna world: *Urban Dogs* / Times they are-a changin': *Vice Squad* / Little Miss Mystery: *Guitar Gangsters* / Up yer bum: *Peter & The Test Tube Babies* / Rich and hated: *Resistance 77* / Ambassador of fear: *English Dogs* / Rockers in rags: *Adicts* / What about a future: *Chaos UK* / Time is right: *Fits* / Go to hell: *Threats* / Violent world: *Disorder* / Anarchy in Woolworths: *Chaotic Dischord* / Personality crisis: *Thunders, Johnny*
CD Set ____ **SUDCD 4502**
Summit / Nov '96 / Sound & Media

AGITPROP (The Politics Of Punk/3CD Set)
CD Set ____ **DTKBOX 53**
Dressed To Kill / Sep '96 / Total/BMG

AH FEEL TO PARTY (2CD Set)
CD Set ____ **ROUCD 506667**
Rounder / Feb '96 / ADA / CM / Direct

AI CONFINI/INTERZONE
CD ____ **NT 6714**
Robi Droli / Jan '94 / ADA / Direct

AIN'T NOTHIN' BUT A HOUSE PARTY
Bless your soul: *Dreamlovers* / You gave me somebody to love: *Dreamlovers* / You ain't sayin' nothin' new: *Virgil, Henry* / You fooled me: *Virgil, Henry* / Ain't nothing but a house party: *Showstoppers* / What a man can do: *Showstoppers* / Eeeny meeny: *Showstoppers* / How easy your heart forgets me: *Showstoppers* / Suddenly: *Cherry People* / Father's angels: *Cherry People* / Bok to bak: *Cherry People* / I've been hurt: *Deal, Bill & The Rhondells* / Baby show it: *Festival* / Green grow the lilacs: *Festival* / You're gonna make it: *Devonnes* / Mob: *Devonnes* / I dig everything about you: *Devonnes* / Loan shark: *Chapter One* / Money won't do it, love will: *Chapter One* / I'll get by without you: *Gamble, Kenny & Tommy Bell* / Someday you'll be my love: *Gamble, Kenny & Tommy Bell*
CD ____ **NEMCD 678**
Sequel / Apr '94 / BMG

AIN'T NOTHIN' BUT THE BLUES (2CD Set)
Lovin' in my baby's eyes: *Taj Mahal* / Smokestack lightin': *Howlin' Wolf* / My babe: *Little Walter* / Blue collar: *Scott-Heron, Gil* / Good morning little school girl: *Winter, Johnny* / First time I met the blues: *Guy, Buddy* / Grits ain't groceries: *Blues Band* / I'm your hoochie coochie man: *Waters, Muddy* / Christo redemptor: *Musselwhite, Charley* / Little red rooster: *Howlin' Wolf* / Snake drive: *Clapton, Eric* / Need your love so bad: *Fleetwood Mac* / Every day I have the blues: *King, B.B.* / Baby please don't go: *Williams, Big Joe* / Daytime song: *Korner, Alexis* / Bleeding heart: *Hendrix, Jimi* / I'd rather go blind: *James, Etta* / Sun is shining: *James, Elmore* / I'm your witchdoctor: *Mayall, John* / Boogie chillen': *Hooker, John Lee* / Gangster of love: *Watson, Johnny 'Guitar'* / Stormy Monday: *Korner, Alexis* / Dust my broom: *James, Elmore* / Reconsider baby: *Fulson, Lowell* / Let me love you baby: *Guy, Buddy* / Worried life blues: *Big Maceo* / When the lights go out: *Witherspoon, Jimmy* / John the revelator: *House, Son* / Draggin' my tail: *Clapton, Eric & Jimmy Page* / Cruel little number: *Healey, Jeff Band* / Stealin': *Beck, Jeff* / Cold emotions, frozen hearts: *Blues Band* / Madison blues: *Thorogood, George & The Destroyers* / Bad luck blues: *Broonzy, 'Big' Bill*
CD Set ____ **RCACD 214**
RCA / Jul '97 / BMG

AIN'T NOTHIN' BUT A SHE THING
Ain't nuthin' but a she thing: *Salt n' Pepa* / Mama: *Lennox, Annie* / 69 annee erotique: *Luscious Jackson* / Weakness in me: *Etheridge, Melissa* / Woman of the ghetto: *Oliver, Andi* / Open your eyes, you can fly: *Williams, Vanessa* / Hard times: *Queen Latifah* / Cimarron: *Come* / Don't smoke in bed: *Smith, Patti* / Women of Ireland: *O'Connor, Sinead*
CD ____ **8286742**
London / Feb '96 / PolyGram

AIN'T TIMES HARD (A Modern Blues Anthology/4CD Set)
CD Set ____ **CDDIG 3**
Charly / Feb '95 / Koch

AIR BORN
Biological manipulation: *Manipulators* / Dealing with demons: *Process & Tristan* / Cyclothymic: *Process & Tristan* / Wizard: *Slinky Wizard* / Not now I've got a plane to catch: *Stripper* / Morphogenesis: *SYB Unity Nettwerk Experience* / Tranceformation: *Darshan* / Dense dawn: *Psychaos* / Beyond the internal horizon: *Process* / James Bond Theme: License To Slink: *Slinky Wizard*
CD ____ **AFRCD 3**
Flying Rhino / Jun '97 / Mo's Music Machine / Prime / SRD

AKA DUB
Dub reaction: *Black Roots* / Wipe away the tears: *Dub Judah* / Breaking barrier dub: *Jah Woosh* / We do not want them dub: *Maximillian, D.* / Blakamix country: *Mixman* / Angelic dub: *Dub Wizard* / Conscious man: *Eastwood, Kevin* / Step inside dub: *Armagideon* / Twilight circus: *Dub Frequency* / Zion: *I-Dub* / Hannibal's journey: *Dub Addxx* / Green banana: *Abeng*
CD ____ **LRCD 006**
Lush / May '97 / Prime / SRD

ALABADOS Y BAILES
CD ____ **80292**
New World / Sep '95 / ADA / Cadillac / Harmonia Mundi

ALABAMA: BLACK COUNTRY DANCE BANDS 1924-1949
CD ____ **DOCD 5166**
Document / May '93 / ADA / Hot Shot / Jazz Music

ALABAMA: SECULAR AND RELIGIOUS MUSIC
CD ____ **DOCD 5165**
Document / May '93 / ADA / Hot Shot / Jazz Music

ALADDIN RECORDS STORY, THE (2CD Set)
Flying home: *Jacquet, Illinois & His Orchestra* / Be baba leba: *Humes, Helen* / Driftin' blues: *Moore, Johnny B. & Three Blazers* / When I'm in my tea: *Davis, Maxwell* / I don't stand a ghost of a chance with you: *Harris, Wynonie* / Mother Fuyer: *Dirty Red* / He may be your man: *Humes, Helen* / Milky white way: *Trumpeteers* / Guitar in my hand: *Brown, Clarence 'Gatemouth'* / Too late: *Five Keys* / Chicken shack boogie: *Milburn, Amos* / Loch Lomond: *Rockets* / Shotgun blues: *Hopkins, Lightnin'* / 'Round midnight: *Robins* / Glory of love: *Five Keys* / Safronia B: *Boze, Calvin* / Trouble blues: *Brown, Charles* / I got loaded: *Harris, Peppermint* / Sad journey blues: *Dixon, Floyd Orchestra* / Dad gum ya hide boy: *Jordan, Louis* / Hucklebuck with jimmy: *Five Keys* / Way down boogie: *Burrage, Harold* / Blue turning grey over you: *Holiday, Billie* / Feels so good: *Shirley & Lee* / Telephone blues: *Dixon, Floyd* / Kokomo: *Gene & Eunice* / Let the good times roll: *Shirley & Lee* / How long: *Five Keys* / I need you, I want you: *Parker, Jack* / Don't let go (hold me, hold me): *Cookies* / Messy Bessy: *Jordan, Louis & His Tympany Five* / This is my story: *Gene & Eunice* / Don't leave me baby: *Fulson, Lowell* / Call operator 210: *Dixon, Floyd* / Ding dong ding: *Bip & Bop* / Remember: *Aladdins* / Rockin' with the clock: *Shirley & Lee* / Honest I do: *Foster, Cell* / Rockin' at Cosmo's: *Allen, Lee* / Be cool my heart: *Allen, Lee* / I'm so high: *Five Keys* / I'm in the mood for love: *King Pleasure* / Ray Pearl: *Jivers* / Dreamy eyes: *Squires* / Yak, yak: *Marvin & Johnny* / Darling it's wonderful: *Lovers* / Our love is here to stay: *Sharps* / King Kong: *Tyler, Big T.* / Smack, smack: *Marvin & Johnny* / Little girl in the cabin: *Sloan, Flip* / Sugar doll: *Belvin, Jesse* / Little bitty pretty one: *Harris, Thurston*
CD Set ____ **ALADDIN 1**
EMI / Jan '95 / EMI

ALAN FREED'S ROCK & ROLL DANCE PARTY
Pretzel / Rock rock rock / Maybellene / Ruby baby / Tear it up / (We're gonna) Rock around the clock / My prayer speedo / Be bop a lula / Why don't you write me / Little girl of mine / Rip it up
CD ____ **CDMF 075**
Magnum Force / '91 / TKO Magnum

ALAN LOMAX COLLECTION - SOUTHERN JOURNEY VOL.1, THE (Voices From The American South)
D Day: *Jones, Bessie* / Katy went fishing with her hook and line: *Smith, Hobart* / Walk in the parlour: *Hemphill, Sid & Lucius Smith* / Mama's gonna buy: *Hall-Ward, Vera* / Wished I was in heaven sitting down: *McDowell, Fred* / Po' lazarus: *Bright Light Quartet* / Lass of Loch Royale: *Morris, Neil* / Three nights drunk: *Mainer, J.E.* / Turkey in the straw: *Everidge, Charley & Neil Morris* / Pharaoh: *Carter, Sydney* / Cripple creek: *Higgins, Uncle Charlie & Wade Ward* / Diver boy: *Gilbert, Ollie* / Pretty Polly: *Ball, E.C.* / Sweet Roseanne: *Bright Light Quartet* / Sink 'em low: *Jones, Bessie* / Dollar Mamie: *Lewis, Ed* / I wonder will we meet again: *Crenshaw, Rev. & The Congregation* / Poor wayfaring stranger: *Riddle, Almeda* / Testimony: *Beck, I.D.* / Guide me o thou great jehovah: *Claudill, Ike* / Last words of Copernicus: *Sacred Harp Singers* / Gospel train: *Belleville A Capella Choir* / Beulah land: *Davis, John & Bessie Jones* / It just suits me: *Smith, Hobart*
CD ____ **ROUCD 1701**
Rounder / May '97 / ADA / CM / Direct

ALAN LOMAX COLLECTION - SOUTHERN JOURNEY VOL.2, THE (Ballads And Breakdowns)
Old Joe Clark: *Ward, Wade* / Poor Ellen Smith: *Ball, E.C.* / Sourwood mountain: *Smith, Hobart* / Girl I left behind: *Moore, Spencer* / John Henry: *Stoneman, Glen* / Three little babes: *Gladden, Texas* / Bonaparte's retreat: *Edmonds, Norman* / June apple: *Higgins, Charlie & Wade Ward* / Peg an'awl: *Smith, Hobart* / Sally Anne: *Stoneman, George* / Fox chase: *Ward, Wade & Bob Carpenter* / Banks of the Ohio: *Vass, Ruby* / Willow garden: *Higgins, Charlie & Wade Ward* / Graveyard blues: *Smith, Hobart* / Uncle Charlie's breakdown: *Higgins, Charlie & Wade Ward* / Burglar man: *Carpenter, Bob* / Fly around my blue eyed girl: *Smith, Hobart* / Single girl: *Vass, Ruby* / Parson Burrs: *Smith, Hobart* / Piney woods gal: *Higgins, Charlie & Wade Ward* / Hick's farewell: *Gladden, Texas* / Black Annie: *Smith, Hobart* / Little schoolboy: *Smith, Hobart* / Breaking up Christmas: *Edmonds, Norman* / Whole heap of little hors: *Gladden, Texas* / Cluck old hen: *Ward, Wade*
CD ____ **ROUCD 1702**
Rounder / May '97 / ADA / CM / Direct

ALAN LOMAX COLLECTION - SOUTHERN JOURNEY VOL.3, THE (61 Highway Mississippi)
Louisiana: *Ratcliff, Henry* / Jim and John: *Young, Ed* / 61 Highway blues: *McDowell, 'Mississippi' Fred* / Stewball: *Lewis, Ed* / Po' boy blues: *Dudley, John* / God's unchanging hand: *Burton, A. & Congregation* / Keep your lamps trimmed and burning: *McDowell, Fred* / Emmaline, take your time: *Hemphill, Sid & Lucius Smith* / I'm gonna live anyhow 'till I die: *Pratcher, Miles & Bob* / Little Sally Walker: *Gardner, Mattie* / Old devil's dream: *Hemphill, Sid & Lucius Smith* / Rolled and tumbled: *Hemphill, Rose & Fred McDowell* / Mama Lucy: *Gary, Leroy* / Soon one mornin': *McDowell, Fred* / I'm goin' home: *Webb, Ervin* / Fred McDowell's blues: *McDowell, Fred* / Tryin' to make heaven my home: *James, Viola* / Berta, Berta: *Miller, Leroy* / Germany blues: *McDowell, Fred* / Clarksdale Mill blues: *Dudley, John* / If it's all night long: *Pratcher, Miles & Bob* / Lord have mercy: *McDowell, Fred* / Didn't leave nobody but the baby: *Carter, Mrs. Sidney*
CD ____ **ROUCD 1703**
Rounder / May '97 / ADA / CM / Direct

ALAN LOMAX COLLECTION - SOUTHERN JOURNEY VOL.4, THE (Brethren, We Meet Again)
Sardinia: *Alabama Sacred Harp Singers* / Testimony on pioneer religion: *Asher, D.N.* / Amazing grace: *Adams, Howard* / Lonely tombs: *Smith, Preston & Hobart* / Guide me, o thou great Jehovah: *Spangler, George* / Old gospel ship: *Vass, Ruby* / Little family: *Gilbert, Ollie* / When the stars begin to fall: *Smith, Preston & Hobart* / Testimony: *Beck, I.D.* / When Jesus Christ was here on earth: *Beck, I.D.* / Northport: *Alabama Sacred Harp Singers* / Why must I wear this shroud: *Spangler, George* / See that my grave is kept clean: *Smith, Hobart* / My Lord keeps a record: *Mountain Ramblers* / I am a poor wayfaring stranger: *Riddle, Almeda* / Brethren, we have met again: *Spanger, George* / Jim & me: *Smith, Preston* / Joseph Looney: *Gilbert, Ollie* / Poor pilgrims of sorrow: *Beck, I.D.* / I'm on my journey home: *Alabama Sacred Harp Singers* / Closing prayer: *Alabama Sacred Harp Singers*
CD ____ **ROUCD 1704**
Rounder / May '97 / ADA / CM / Direct

ALAN LOMAX COLLECTION - SOUTHERN JOURNEY VOL.5, THE (Bad Man Ballads)
Jesse James: *Riddle, Almeda* / Po' Lazarus: *Bright Light Quartet* / Railroad Bill: *Smith, Hobart* / John Henry: *Lewis, Ed* / Willie Brennan: *Morris, Neil* / Hangman tree: *Riddle, Almeda* / Columbus stockade: *Mainer, J.E. Band* / Early in the mornin': *Moore, Johnny Lee* / Pretty Polly: *Ball, Estil C.* / Lazarus: *Morrison, Henry* / Claude Allen: *Smith, Hobart* / Cole Younger: *Gilbert, Oscar* / Lawson murder: *Moore, Spencer & Everett Blevins* / Tom Devil: *Lewis, Ed* / Hawkins County jail: *Smith, Hobart* / Dangerous blues: *Batts, Floyd* / Po' Lazarus: *Carter, James*
CD ____ **ROUCD 1705**
Rounder / May '97 / ADA / CM / Direct

ALAN LOMAX COLLECTION - SOUTHERN JOURNEY VOL.6, THE (Sheep, Don'tcha Know The Road)
Sheep, sheep, don'tcha know the road: *Jones, Bessie & The Sea Island Singers* / Juice of the forbidden fruit: *Morris, Neil* / Devil's dream: *Smith, Hobart* / You got dimples in your jaws: *Jones, Willie & Others* / Drunken hiccups: *Smith, Hobart* / You don tol' everybody: *McDowell, Fred* / House

carpenter: *Riddle, Almeda* / Straighten 'em: *Bright Light Quartet* / Corn dodgers: *Morris, Neil* / I wished I was in heaven: *Gardner, Denise & Mattie/Fred McDowell* / Tribulations: *Ball, E.C. & Lacy Richardson* / No room at the inn/Last month of the year: *Hall-Ward, Vera* / My mother died and left me: *Shorty, James & Fred McDowell* / Buttermilk: *Pratcher, Miles & Bob* / Prayer wheel: *Bright Light Quartet* / Guide me o thou great Jehovah: *Caudill, Ike & Congregation*
CD _____ ROUCD 1706
Rounder / May '97 / ADA / CM / Direct

ALAN LOMAX COLLECTION SAMPLER
Interview: *Lomax, Alan* / I'm going home: *Webb, Ervin* / Girl I left behind: *Moore, Spencer* / Titanic: *Jones, Bessie* / Sherburne: *Alabama Sacred Harp Singers* / Early in the mornin': *22 & Group* / Roll roll roll and go / Luce-o, Luce Mauvais / Sambo Caesar: *Smith, Cyprus* / War: *Growling Tiger & Lord Airey* / Religious Bhajan: *Gopaul, Ram* / Mulad tha mulad: *Nicholson, Annie* / As I roved out: *Ennis, Seamus* / Sister's lament: *McNeill, Flora* / Four loom weaver: *MacColl, Ewan* / Jovial tradesman: *Copper, Bob & Ron* / Jota manchega: *Ordonez, Jesus Orchestra* / Fandango de comares: *Munoz, Inez* / Saeta: *Radio Nacional Madrid* / Pastores de Bormujo: *Campanilleros De Bormujo* / La partenza: *Genoese Longshoreman* / O giglio e beni constrastatu: *Pingitore Family* / Stornello: *Pila, Eugenio* / Canto di carrettiere: *Lanza, Domenico* / Ballo del tamburo: *Pasquale, Aristide* / Ma uitai spre rasarit: *Lataretu, Mari* / Esashi oiwake: *Unknown Fisherman* / Gender wayang: *Ubud Gamelan* / Rain dance: *Buck, George* / John Henry: *Hemphill, Sid* / Devil's dream: *Hemphill, Sid* / Ten pound hammer: *SC Ditch Diggers* / Mailheureuse negre: *Benoit, Cleveland* / My son David: *Robertson, Jeannie* / Hawkins County jail: *Smith, Hobart* / 61 Highway: *McDowell, 'Mississippi' Fred* / Low down dirty blues: *House, Son* / Bound to lose: *Guthrie, Woody*
CD _____ ROUCD 1700
Rounder / May '97 / ADA / CM / Direct

ALANTE DI MUSICA TRADIZIONALE
CD _____ NT 6736CD
Robi Droli / Apr '95 / ADA / Direct

ALBA (New And Traditional Music From Scotland)
Alba: *British Caledonian* / Hornpipes: *British Caledonian* / Slow airs: *British Caledonian* / Cradle song: *British Caledonian* / 6/8 marches: *British Caledonian* / America - the beautiful medley: *British Caledonian* / Intercontinental gathering: *British Caledonian* / Competition medley: *British Caledonian* / Waltz and march: *British Caledonian* / 4/4 marches: *British Caledonian* / Amazing grace: *British Caledonian* / Farewell medley: *British Caledonian* / Reprise drum salute: *British Caledonian*
CD _____ LCOM 6017
Lismor / Feb '97 / ADA / Direct / Duncans / Lismor

ALBANIA: SONGS AS OLD AS THE EARTH
CD _____ T 3312
Touch / Mar '91 / Kudos / Pinnacle

ALIEN AMBIENT GALAXY
CD _____ CLEO 9683CD
Cleopatra / May '96 / Cargo / Greyhound / Plastic Head / RTM/Disc / SRD

ALIEN UNDERGROUND VOL.1
Excursions: *Floppy Sounds* / Overdrive: *Club Illusions* / Cut the midrange: *Watchman* / Rescue: *Omegaman* / Higher: *Mathumatix* / Kool kat: *Top Kat* / Soul freak: *Timewriter* / Tamburi: *Tamburi Project* / Basketball heroes: *McBride, Woody* / Alien funk: *DJ Hyperactive* / Jack in the bed: *DJ Silver*
CD _____ KICKCD 50
Kickin' / Apr '97 / Prime / SRD

ALIENS ON ACID (2CD Set)
CD Set _____ CLP 9941
X-Ray / Mar '97 / Cargo

ALIVE IN THE LIVING ROOM
CD _____ CRECD 01
Creation / May '94 / 3mv/Vital

ALL ABOUT SOUL
Divine emotions: *Narada* / Love supreme: *Downing, Will* / There's nothing like this: *Omar* / Sexual healing: *Gaye, Marvin* / How do you stop: *Brown, James* / Sha la la (make me happy): *Green, Al* / Wishing on a star: *Rose Royce* / Rainy night in Georgia: *Crawford, Randy* / Always: *Atlantic Starr* / That lady: *Isley Brothers* / Shake you down: *Abbott, Gregory* / Me and Mrs Jones: *Jackson, Freddie* / Love I lost: *Melvin, Harold* / Ain't no sunshine: *Withers, Bill* / You'll never know: *Hi-Gloss* / Cherish: *Kool & The Gang* / Softly whispering I love you: *Congregation* / I'm doing fine now: *New York City*
CD _____ RENCD 108
Renaissance Collector Series / Oct '95 / BMG

ALL AMERICAN COUNTRY
Thing called love: *Cash, Johnny* / Here comes my baby again: *Posey, Sandy* / Green green grass of home: *Miller, Roger* / Four in the morning: *Young, Faron* / Crystal chandeliers: *Drusky, Roy* / Walk on by: *Van Dyke, Leroy* / I love you because: *Jones, George* / I threw away the rose: *Williams, Hank Jr.* / Jambalaya: *Williams, Hank* / Love at the Five & Dime: *Mattea, Kathy* / Snowbird: *Glaser, Tompall & the Glaser Brothers* / Me & Bobby McGee: *Dudley, Dave* / Release me: *Lewis, Jerry Lee* / Ruby don't take your love to town: *Perkins, Carl* / Convoy: *McCall, C.W.* / I take a lot of pride in what I am: *Rodriguez, Johnny* / Make the world go away: *Arnold, Eddy* / Homecoming: *Hall, Tom T.*
CD _____ 5525572
Spectrum / Sep '96 / PolyGram

ALL AMERICAN ROCK 'N' ROLL FROM FRATERNITY RECORDS
Rock-a-bop: *Moore, Sparkle* / Flower of my heart: *Moore, Sparkle* / Killer: *Moore, Sparkle* / She's neat: *Wright, Dale* / Take hold of my hand: *Dobkins, Carl Jr.* / That's why I'm asking: *Dobkins, Carl Jr.* / Makin' love with my baby: *Turley, Richard* / That's my girl: *Turner, Jesse Lee* / Absolutely nothin': *Parsons, Bill* / Dance, dance, dance: *Parsons, Bill* / Hand me down my rockin' shoes: *Parsons, Bill* / Jungle bandstand: *Parsons, Bill* / Try it no more: *Marcum, Gene* / That's showbiz: *Wright, Dale & The Wright Guys* / You're the answer: *Wright, Dale & The Wright Guys* / Buddies with the blues: *Bare, Bobby & The All American Boys' Orchestra* / Teardrops from the eyes: *Jeffers, Jimmy & The Jokers* / Rubber dolly: *Bare, Bobby* / All American boy: *Bare, Bobby*
CD _____ CDCHD 316
Ace / Jul '91 / Pinnacle

ALL BOUNDARIES ARE ILLUSION
CD _____ TO3CD 001
21-3 Productions / Jun '97 / Arabesque / Flying UK / Prime

ALL FRUITS RIPE VOL.1
CD _____ VPCD 1242
Shocking Vibes / Jul '92 / Jet Star

ALL KINDSA GIRLS
CD _____ MRCD 108
Munster / Nov '96 / Cargo / Greyhound / Plastic Head

ALL NIGHT LONG (Dave Cash Presents The Best Of The 60's)
I can't explain: *Who* / For your love: *Yardbirds* / Daydream: *Lovin' Spoonful* / Sha la la la lee: *Small Faces* / Keep on running: *Davis, Spencer Group* / Wild thing: *Troggs* / This wheel's on fire: *Driscoll, Julie* / I'm alive: *Hollies* / Bring it on home to me: *Animals* / Concrete and clay: *Unit 4+2* / Sorrow: *Merseys* / Out of time: *Farlowe, Chris* / Let's hang on: *Four Seasons* / Days of Pearly Spencer: *McWilliams, David* / Whiter shade of pale: *Procul Harum* / Nights in white satin: *Moody Blues* / Sunny afternoon: *Kinks* / Reflections of my life: *Marmalade* / Make it easy on yourself: *Walker Brothers* / Unchained melody: *Righteous Brothers* / Groovy kind of love: *Mindbenders* / Some of your lovin': *Springfield, Dusty* / Getaway: *Fame, Georgie* / Oh not my baby: *Manfred Mann* / Hold tight: *Dave Dee, Dozy, Beaky, Mick & Tich* / Something in the air: *Thunderclap Newman*
CD _____ 5163752
PolyGram TV / Aug '93 / PolyGram

ALL NIGHT LONG THEY PLAY THE BLUES
Part time love / Country boy / I know you hear me calling / Little green house / Hey hey baby's gone / I'm serving time / Life goes on / Mama Rufus
CD _____ CDCHD 440
Ace / Jan '93 / Pinnacle

ALL OF MY APPOINTED TIME (40 Years Of Gospel)
Standing by the bedside of a neighbour: *Acapella Gospel Golden Gate Quartet* / Listen to the lambs: *Acapella Gospel Golden Gate Quartet* / Precious Lord: *Kings Of Harmony* / God shall wipe all tears away: *Kings Of Harmony* / I'm bound for Canaan land: *Blue Jay Singers* / Standing out on the highway: *Blue Jay Singers* / Well well well: *Soul Stirrers* / I'm gonna tell God: *Soul Stirrers* / Here I am, do Lord send me: *Peach, Georgia & the Harmonaires* / Where the sun will never go down: *Peach, Georgia & the Harmonaires* / Lord will make a way: *Griffin, Bessie* / Any stars in my crown: *Golden Harps* / I'll make it somehow: *Golden Harps* / They led my Lord away: *Williams, Marion* / All my appointed time: *Williams, Marion* / Groves show intro: *Golden Gate Quartet* / Polly wolly doodle: *Golden Gate Quartet* / Old Kentucky home: *Golden Gate Quartet* / On a mornin': *Golden Gate Quartet* / Take your time Miss Lucy: *Golden Gate Quartet* / Oh Noah: *Golden Gate Quartet* / Stewball: *Golden Gate Quartet* / Grove show sign off: *Golden Gate Quartet* / Hit the road to dreamland: *Charioteers* / I've got a home in that rock: *Charioteers* / Caledonia: *Charioteers* / Open the door Richard: *Delta Rhythm Boys* / Sittin' and a-rockin': *Delta Rhythm Boys*
CD _____ JCD 640
Jass / Aug '93 / ADA / Cadillac / CM / Direct / Jazz Music
CD _____ CDMOJO 308
Mojo / Nov '96 / Direct

ALL OVER THE MAP
CD _____ ROUCDAN 26
Rounder / Jun '96 / ADA / CM / Direct

ALL PLATINUM FUNK
You got it (talkin' bout my love): *Youngblood, Lonnie* / I got a suspicion: *Patterson, Bobby* / This is it: *First Class* / In the bottle: *Brother To Brother* / Funk you: *BBP* / Stay: *Moments* / Let your mind be free: *Brother To Brother* / Thump and bump: *Fisher, Eddie* / (I'm in) The prime of love: *BBP* / On top: *Youngblood, Lonnie* / I'm gonna take your love: *Brother To Brother* / Is it funky enough: *Communications & Black Experiences Band* / Cosmic blues: *Fisher, Eddie* / Chance with you: *Brother To Brother* / Walter's inspiration: *Rimshots* / Music makes me feel good: *Fisher, Eddie* / I may be right, I may be wrong: *Mill Street Depo* / Gotta get it back: *Mother Freedom Band* / Give me, lend me, loan me (let me have): *Fisher, Eddie* / 7-6-5-4-3-2-1 Blow your whistle: *Rimshots*
CD _____ CPCD 8082
Charly / Mar '95 / Koch

ALL RAVE ULTRA
CD _____ PC 002CD
Public Propaganda / Jan '95 / Plastic Head

ALL SPICE
Never like this: *Two Tons Of Fun* / I think I love you: *Shock* / Slipped away: *Allspice* / Give it up (don't make me wait): *Sylvester* / Rainy day stormy nights: *Impact* / Hungry for your love: *Allspice* / Keep it up: *Everett, Betty* / Lovin': *Hurtt, Phil* / Just us: *Two Tons Of Fun* / I ain't into that: *Rappin' Reverend* / SOS: *Side Effect* / Feel good all over: *McWilliams, Paulette* / For you: *Reason, Johnny* / I believe in you: *Muhammad, Idris* / Love's such a wonderful sound: *Reason, Johnny* / Finally found someone: *Side Effect* / Never been here before: *McWilliams, Paulette*
CD _____ CDBGPD 074
Beat Goes Public / Oct '93 / Pinnacle

ALL STAR CHA CHA CHA
New cha-cha: *Puente, Tito* / Ay, Jose: *Graciela & Machito* / Flanco's cha-cha: *Cuba, Joe Sextet* / St. Louis blues cha-cha-cha: *Gutierrez, Julio Orchestra* / El bodeguero: *O'Farrill, Chico All Star Orchestra* / No me quieras tanto: *Lupe, Tito-La* / Sabroso cha cha: *Cuba, Joe Sextet* / Improvisando cha-cha: *Morales, Obdulio Cuban Orchestra & Peruchin* / Almendra: *Candido* / Tea for two: *Puente, Tito* / Los parqueadores: *Fajardo, Jose & His Orchestra* / Holiday: *Machito*
CD _____ 12912
Laserlight / May '97 / Target/BMG

ALL STAR CHICAGO BLUES SESSION
CD _____ JSPCD 214
JSP / '88 / ADA / Cadillac / Direct / Hot Shot / Target/BMG

ALL THAT BLUES
CD _____ OBCCD 5001
Original Blues Classics / Nov '92 / Complete/Pinnacle / Wellard

ALL THAT COUNTRY
CD _____ LECD 418
Wisepack / Nov '92 / Conifer/BMG / THE

ALL THAT JAZZ (3CD Set)
CD Set _____ EMTBX 301
Emporio / Aug '97 / Disc

ALL THAT JAZZ IS BACK
Things are getting better: *Adderley, Cannonball* / How high the moon: *Baker, Chet* / Jumpin' at the Woodside: *Basie, Count* / Afro jaws: *Davis, Eddie 'Lockjaw'* / There is no greater love: *Davis, Miles New Quintet* / Latin American sunshine: *Ellington, Duke Orchestra* / Waltz for Debby: *Evans, Bill Trio* / I ain't got nothin' but the blues: *Fitzgerald, Ella & Tommy Flanagan Trio* / Foggy day: *Garland, Red* / Birk's works: *Gillespie, Dizzy* / My funny valentine: *Jackson, Milt Quartet* / Bearcat: *Jordan, Clifford Quartet* / Spring is here: *Kessel, Barney/Ray Brown/Shelly Manne*
CD _____ OJCCD 1001
Original Jazz Classics / Oct '93 / Complete/ Pinnacle / Jazz Music / Wellard

ALL THAT SAX (The Magic Of The Saxophone)
Black velvet / Lovely day / Knock on wood / One moment in time / Missing you / Piano in the dark / Don't it make my brown eyes blue / Nothing's gonna change my love for you / With a little help from my friends / Billie Jean / Groovy kind of love / Something's gotten hold of my heart / Isn't she lovely / Like dreamers do / Too much heaven / Fly robin fly / If you think you know how to love me / Way you make me feel
CD _____ ECD 3146
K-Tel / Mar '95 / K-Tel

ALL THE BEST FROM SCOTLAND VOL.1
Rowan tree / Scotland again / Dark Lochnagar / Aye ready / Ae fond kiss / Work o' the weavers / Caledonia / Skye boat song / Amazing grace / Contentment / Lord's my shepherd / Man'a man / Ye banks and braes o' bonnie Doon / Massacre of Glencoe / Auld lang syne
CD _____ LBP 2018CD
Klub / Oct '94 / ADA / CM / Direct / Duncans / Ross

ALL THE BEST FROM SCOTLAND VOL.2
Bonnie Aberdeen / Highland bridge depot / Major J McGillvary / My ain folk / Loch Lomond / Dark island / Sweet afton / Bonnie lass o'Fyvie / Jessie's hornpipe / Kirk's hornpipe / Drumlees / Island spinning song / Banjo breakdown / Fiddlers choice / Scotland your a lady / Flowers of Edinburgh / Wee dug Tim / Lucky Scaup / Rose of Allendale / Skye boat song / Morag of Dunvegan / When you and I were young Maggie / Twa racruiting sergeants
CD _____ LBP 2019CD
Klub / Oct '94 / ADA / CM / Direct / Duncans / Ross

ALL THE PRESIDENT'S MEN
CD _____ CRECD 140
Creation / Jul '92 / 3mv/Vital

ALL THE WORLD IN AN EGG
CD _____ WWCD 16
Universal Egg / Mar '96 / SRD

ALL THE WORLD NEEDS IS A LITTLE LOVE, PEACE & UNDERSTANDING
CD _____ SCL 2511
Ichiban Soul Classics / Nov '95 / Koch

ALL THROUGH THE YEAR
CD _____ HPRCD 2002
Hokey Pokey / Oct '93 / ADA / Direct

ALL TIME COUNTRY GREATS
Streets of Baltimore: *Pride, Charley* / Welcome to my world: *Reeves, Jim* / I'm movin' on: *Snow, Hank* / I'm a ramblin' man: *Jennings, Waylon* / Funny how time slips away: *Nelson, Willie* / I will always love you: *Parton, Dolly* / Send me the pillow you dream on: *Locklin, Hank* / Yakety axe: *Atkins, Chet* / Sea of heartbreak: *Gibson, Don* / End of the world: *Davis, Skeeter* / Once a day: *Smith, Connie* / She's a little bit country: *Hamilton, George IV* / Is anybody going to San Antone: *Pride, Charley*
CD _____ 74321446852
Camden / Feb '97 / BMG

ALL TIME GREATEST COUNTRY SONGS (2CD Set)
Ruby don't take your love to town: *Rogers, Kenny* / Everybody's talkin': *Nilsson* / Behind closed doors: *Rich, Charlie* / Angel of the morning: *Newton, Juice* / Lay lady lay: *Dylan, Bob* / If not for you: *Newton-John, Olivia* / Crazy: *Cline, Patsy* / He'll have to go: *Reeves, Jim* / Blue bayou: *Ronstadt, Linda* / Silver threads and golden needles: *Parton, Dolly & Loretta Lynn/Tammy Wynette* / I will survive: *Spears, Billie Jo* / Bye bye love: *Everly Brothers* / Cathy's clown: *Everly Brothers* / Language of love: *Loudermilk, John D.* / Love hurts: *Harris, Emmylou* / Me and Bobby McGee: *Kristofferson, Kris* / Take me home, country home: *Denver, John* / I don't know why: *Colvin, Shawn* / By the time I get to Phoenix: *Campbell, Glen* / Crying: *Orbison, Roy* / Don't it make my brown eyes blue: *Gayle, Crystal* / Always on my mind: *Nelson, Willie* / Islands on my mind: *Nelson, Willie* / Islands in the stream: *Rogers, Kenny & Dolly Parton* / Jolene: *Parton, Dolly* / Down to my last teardrop: *Tucker, Tanya* / Blue: *Rimes, Leann* / Let me into your heart: *Carpenter, Mary-Chapin* / Love can build a bridge: *Judds* / Good year for roses: *Costello, Elvis & The Attractions* / I'm just a country boy: *Williams, Don* / From a distance: *Griffith, Nanci* / Detroit city: *Bare, Bobby* / Ode to Billie Joe: *Gentry, Bobbie* / If I said you had a beautiful body (would you hold it agains: *Bellamy Brothers* / I will always love you: *Rogers, Kenny* / Memories: *Davies, Mac* / Kentucky woman: *Diamond, Neil* / King of the road: *Miller, Roger* / Jackson: *Cash, Johnny & June Carter* / Riders in the sky: *Cash, Johnny* / Polk salad Annie: *White, Tony Joe* / Achy breaky heart: *Cyrus, Billy Ray* / Devil went down to Georgia: *Daniels, Charlie Band* / Duelling banjos based on Feudin banjos: *Weisberg, Eric & Steve Mandell*
CD Set _____ SONYTV 24CD
Sony TV / Mar '97 / Sony

ALL TIME GREATEST LOVE SONGS, THE (2CD Set)
Julia says: *Wet Wet Wet* / Think twice: *Dion, Celine* / How deep is your love: *Bee Gees* / Always: *Atlantic Starr* / So amazing: *Vandross, Luther* / Oh baby I: *Eternal* / Soul provider: *Bolton, Michael* / On silent wings: *Turner, Tina* / Love and affection: *Armatrading, Joan* / Sexual healing: *Gaye, Marvin* / Show me heaven: *McKee, Maria* / I just want to make love to you: *James, Etta* / Wherever I lay my hat (that's my home): *Young, Paul* / (You make me feel like) A natural woman: *King, Carole* / What a wonderful world: *Armstrong, Louis* / Nothing compares 2 U: *O'Connor, Sinead* / Eternal flame: *Bangles* / Don't let the sun go down on me: *Michael, George & Elton John* / Chains: *Arena, Tina* / Back for good: *Take That* / Ocean Drive: *Lighthouse Family* / No more I love yous: *Lennox, Annie* / Your song: *John, Elton* / Love on the rocks: *Diamond, Neil* / Promise me: *Craven, Beverley* / Without you: *Nilsson, Harry* / If I could turn back time: *Cher* / Mandy: *Manilow, Barry* / Time after time: *Lauper, Cyndi* / Miss you

nights: *Richard, Cliff* / Rose: *Midler, Bette* / I say a little prayer: *Franklin, Aretha* / Stand by me: *King, Ben E.* / Don't wanna lose you: *Estefan, Gloria* / I want to know what love is: *Foreigner* / Power of love: *Rush, Jennifer* / Unchained melody: *Robson & Jerome*
CD Set ______ **SONYTV 21CD**
Sony TV / Oct '96 / Sony

ALL TIME GREATEST SAMBA SCHOOL SONGS COLLECTION, THE
CD ______ **74321467052**
Milan / May '97 / Conifer/BMG / Silva Screen

ALL TIME GREATS
Puttin' on the ritz: *Astaire, Fred* / No man is ever going to worry me: *Tucker, Sophie* / April showers: *Johnson, Al* / That's the kind of baby for me: *Cantor, Eddie* / Eadie was a lady: *Merman, Ethel* / Tisket a tasket: *Fitzgerald, Ella* / Change partners: *Astaire, Fred* / Somebody stole Gabriel's horn: *Crosby, Bing* / I come from a musical family: *Armstrong, Louis* / Man I love: *Tucker, Sophie* / Rock a bye your baby with a dixie melody: *Jolson, Al* / It never rains but it pours: *Garland, Judy* / I used to be colour blind: *Astaire, Fred* / Gotta pebble in my shoe: *Fitzgerald, Ella* / Washing the blues from my soul: *Tucker, Sophie* / Little lady make believe/Says my heart: *Cantor, Eddie* / Bob White: *Crosby, Bing & Connie Boswell* / Please: *Crosby, Bing* / I got rhythm: *Hall, Adelaide* / Solitude: *Armstrong, Louis* / Crazy feet: *Astaire, Fred* / You are too beautiful: *Jolson, Al* / Canoe song: *Robeson, Paul*
CD ______ **300462**
Hallmark / Jul '96 / Carlton

ALL TIME NUMBER ONE SONGS (2CD Set)
I believe: *Laine, Frankie* / Moulin rouge: *Mantovani & His Orchestra* / Singin' the blues: *Mitchell, Guy* / This ole house: *Clooney, Rosemary* / It's only make believe: *Twitty, Conway* / I'll be home: *Boone, Pat* / My old man's a dustman: *Donegan, Lonnie* / Smoke gets in your eyes: *Platters* / Great balls of fire: *Lewis, Jerry Lee* / Poetry in motion: *Tillotson, Johnny* / Blue moon: *Marcels* / Tell Laura I love her: *Valance, Ricky* / Runaway: *Shannon, Del* / Walkin' back to happiness: *Shapiro, Helen* / Moon river: *Williams, Danny* / Nut rocker: *B-Bumble & The Stingers* / How do you do it: *Gerry & The Pacemakers* / Sweets for my sweet: *Searchers* / Little children: *Kramer, Billy J.* / Juliet: *Four Pennies* / I'm into something good: *Herman's Hermits* / Silence is golden: *Poole, Brian & The Tremeloes* / Baby now that I've found you: *Foundations* / Everlasting love: *Ellis, Steve Love Affair* / Dizzy: *Roe, Tommy* / Sugar sugar: *Archies* / Yellow river: *Christie* / Band of gold: *Payne, Freda* / Son of my Father: *Chicory Tip* / Blockbuster: *Sweet* / Billy, don't be a hero: *Paper Lace* / January: *Pilot* / Stand by me: *King, Ben E.* / Rock your baby: *McCrae, George* / I'd like to teach the world to sing: *New Seekers* / Bye bye baby: *Bay City Rollers* / Telstar: *Tornados* / Love grows: *Edison Lighthouse* / Diane: *Bachelors* / Needles and pins: *Searchers*
CD Set ______ **MUCD 9511**
Musketeer / May '96 / Disc

ALL TIME REGGAE HITS
CD ______ **CPCD 8028**
Charly / Feb '94 / Koch

ALL WOMAN - THE BEST OF ALL WOMAN VOL.1 (2CD Set)
Show me heaven: *McKee, Maria* / From a distance: *Griffith, Nanci* / If I could turn back time: *Cher* / Sweet love: *Baker, Anita* / I say a little prayer: *Franklin, Aretha* / You're so vain: *Simon, Carly* / Stay with me baby: *Ellison, Lorraine* / Piano in the dark: *Russell, Brenda* / Stay: *Shakespears Sister* / Stop: *Brown, Sam* / Get here: *Adams, Oleta* / Mad about the boy: *Washington, Dinah* / So close: *Carroll, Dina* / Love and affection: *Armatrading, Joan* / First time: *Beck, Robin* / Remember me: *Ross, Diana* / I close my eyes and count to ten: *Springfield, Dusty* / Promise me: *Craven, Beverley* / Damn, I wish I was your lover: *Hawkins, Sophie B.* / Free: *Williams, Deniece* / Piece of my heart: *Franklin, Erma* / Eternal flame: *Bangles* / Anything for you: *Estefan, Gloria* / That ole devil called love: *Moyet, Alison* / Smooth operator: *Sade* / You gotta be: *Des'ree* / I feel the earth move: *Martika* / I'll be there: *Carey, Mariah* / See the day: *Lee, Dee C.* / True colors: *Lauper, Cyndi* / Think twice: *Dion, Celine* / Shy guy: *King, Diana* / Nothing compares 2 U: *O'Connor, Sinead* / All woman: *Stansfield, Lisa* / Why: *Lennox, Annie* / Move closer: *Nelson, Phyllis* / My one temptation: *Paris, Mica* / Another sad love song: *Braxton, Toni* / Oh baby, I: *Eternal* / Heaven is a place on earth: *Carlisle, Belinda* / Man with the child in his eyes: *Bush, Kate*
CD Set ______ **BOWOCD 001**
Dino / Sep '95 / Pinnacle

ALL WOMAN - THE BEST OF ALL WOMAN VOL.2 (2CD Set)
CD Set ______ **BOWOCD 002**
Dino / Nov '96 / Pinnacle

ALL WOMAN VOL.4
CD ______ **ALLWOCD 4**
Quality / Oct '94 / Pinnacle

ALLEY CAT
Alley cat: *Bent Fabric* / From now on: *Bent Fabric* / Norwegian sunset: *Bent Fabric* / Not a bit in love: *Bent Fabric* / Theme from 'A summer place': *Vaughn, Billy Orchestra* / Strangers in the night: *Vaughn, Billy Orchestra* / Greensleeves: *Vaughn, Billy Orchestra* / Blue: *Vaughn, Billy Orchestra* / Faded love: *Hirt, Al* / California dreaming: *Winterhalter, Hugo* / Born free: *Winterhalter, Hugo* / Killing me softly with his song: *Erling, Ole* / Yesterday: *Erling, Ole* / Sentimental journey: *Miller, Glenn & His Orchestra* / This guy's in love with you: *Ingmann, Jorgen* / La la la: *Ingmann, Jorgen*
CD ______ **101132**
CMC / May '97 / BMG

ALLIGATOR MAKES THE BLUES COME ALIVE
CD ______ **ALCD 0007**
Alligator / Jan '93 / ADA / CM / Direct

ALLIGATOR RECORDS 25TH ANNIVERSARY COLLECTION (2CD Set)
CD Set ______ **ALL 110/11CD**
Alligator / Apr '96 / ADA / CM / Direct

ALLIGATOR RECORDS CHRISTMAS COLLECTION, THE
Christmas song: *Bishop, Elvin* / Christmas on the bayou: *Brooks, Lonnie* / Let me be your Santa Claus: *Clarke, William* / Santa Claus wants some lovin': *Ellis, Tinsley* / Santa Claus Boogie: *Brown, Charles* / Christmas: *Brown, Clarence 'Gatemouth'* / I'm your santa: *Lil' Ed & The Blues Imperials* / Santa Claus: *Little Charlie & The Nightcats* / Silent night: *Musselwhite, Charley* / Christmas in the country: *Neal, Kenny* / One parent christmas: *Saffire* / Lonesome christmas: *Seals, Son* / Merry merry Christmas: *Taylor, Koko* / Deck the halls boogie: *Webster, Katie*
CD ______ **ALCDXMAS 9201**
Alligator / Oct '93 / ADA / CM / Direct

ALLIGATOR SAMPLER
CD ______ **ACDS 3657**
Alligator / Aug '90 / ADA / CM / Direct

ALLONS CAJUN ROCK 'N' ROLL
Lafayette two-step: *Roger, Aldus* / Lacassine special: *Roger, Aldus* / Mardi gras dance: *Roger, Aldus* / La valse d'ennui: *Roger, Aldus* / Diga ding ding dong: *Roger, Aldus* / Allons rock 'n' roll: *Roger, Aldus* / La valse de reno: *Roger, Aldus* / Mamou two step: *Roger, Aldus* / Hip et taiau: *Abshire, Nathan* / Cush cush: *Forester, Blackie* / Just because: *Forester, Blackie* / Hang your hat: *Forester, Blackie* / La fille de la ville: *Bruce, Vin* / Le sud de la Louisianne: *Bruce, Vin* / Lake Arthur stomp: *Thibodeaux, Rufus* / Les veuves de la coulee: *Happy Fats* / Married life: *Cormier, Louis* / Boil them cabbages down: *Guidry, Doc* / Grand mamou: *Newman, Jimmy C.* / Creole stomp: *Breaux, Jimmy* / Bosco stomp: *Breaux, Jimmy* / La valse de KLFY: *Doucet, Michael* / Ma belle Evangeline: *Doucet, Michael* / La maison a deux portes: *Doucet, Michael*
CD ______ **CDCHD 367**
Ace / Apr '91 / Pinnacle

ALMANAC
CD ______ **1238512**
IAI / May '94 / Cadillac / Harmonia Mundi

ALMIGHTY 12" VOL.1, THE
CD ______ **ALMYCD 01**
Almighty / Jan '93 / Total/BMG

ALMIGHTY 12" VOL.2, THE
CD ______ **ALMYCD 02**
Almighty / Jan '93 / Total/BMG

ALMIGHTY CLASSICS VOL.1 (Now & Then/2CD Set)
CD Set ______ **ALMYCD 17**
Almighty / May '96 / Total/BMG

ALMIGHTY CLASSICS VOL.2 (Now & Then/2CD Set)
CD Set ______ **ALMYCD 20**
Almighty / Jun '97 / Total/BMG

ALMIGHTY DEFINITIVE '95
Chains: *Rochelle* / Young hearts run free: *Respect & Hannah Jones* / Only wanna be with you: *Obsession* / Think twice: *Rochelle* / Let me feel it: *Gilles, Samantha* / Never been to me: *Rainbow Nation* / Back for good: *Lipstick* / You spin me round: *Kinky Boyz* / Until the night: *Bianca* / You are the music: *Roman Holliday* / Feels like heaven: *Jones, Hannah* / Baby don't cha leave me this way: *Royal T* / You keep me hangin' on: *Hannah & Her Sisters* / Can you feel the love tonight: *Harakuku*
CD ______ **ALMYCD 15**
Almighty / Oct '95 / Total/BMG

ALMIGHTY DEFINITIVE VOL.2
CD ______ **ALMYCD 19**
Almighty / Feb '97 / Total/BMG

ALMIGHTY DEFINITIVE VOL.3
CD ______ **ALMYCD 23**
Almighty / Aug '97 / Total/BMG

ALPINE SPIRIT (A Magical Blend Of Music And The Sounds Of Nature)
CD ______ **57782**
CMC / May '97 / BMG

ALT FREQUENCIES
CD ______ **WI 007**
Worm Interface / Oct '96 / Kudos / Pinnacle / Plastic Head

ALTER EGO
CD ______ **CDSOR 002**
Sound Of Rome / Nov '96 / SRD

ALTERED BEATS
Warning introduction: *Temporary Power Surge* / Reanimation: *DJ Rob Smith* / 3D-cut transmission: *Material & DXT/Jah Wobble/Bill Laswell* / Shin-ki-row: *DJ Krush* / Black hole universe: *DXT* / If 9 was 6: *Prince Paul & Bootsy Collins* / If 666 was 96: *DXT & Bootsy Collins* / Ancient style: *DJ Rob Smith & Liu Sola* / Invasion of the octopus people: *Invisible Scratch Pickles & DJ Q-Bert/DJ Disk* / Embryo: *DXT* / Return of the black falcon: *New Kingdom* / One-legged centipede: *Invisible Scratch Pickles & DJ Q-Bert* / Black wax: *Valis* / Dust to dust: *Spectre*
CD ______ **5242952**
Axiom / Jan '97 / PolyGram / Vital

ALTERED STATES (2CD Set)
Voodoo people: *Prodigy* / Queer: *Garbage* / Release the pressure: *Leftfield* / Everybody loves a 303: *Fatboy Slim* / People get real: *St. Etienne* / Sleeper: *Audioweb* / Hypnotisin': *Winx* / Cotton wool: *Lamb* / FEELINGCALLEDLOVE: *Pulp* / Wild wood: *Weller, Paul* / Dust up beats: *Chemical Brothers* / Echo on my mind: *Earthling* / Alien beatfreak: *Radiohead* / Born slippy: *Underworld* / 9 Acre dust: *Charlatans* / Beggin' you: *Charlatans* / 6 Underground: *Sneaker Pimps* / Statuesque: *Sleeper* / Fun for me: *Moloko* / Flowers bloom: *Mandalay* / Keep hope alive: *Crystal Method* / La Tristesse Durera: *Manic Street Preachers* / Work mi body: *Monkey Mafia* / What's in the box: *Boo Radleys* / Tiny meat: *Ruby* / Crabs: *18 Wheeler* / Loose: *Therapy* / Brand new you're retro: *Tricky* / Natural one: *Folk Implosion* / Renegade Soundwave: *Renegade Soundwave*
CD Set ______ **SOLIDCD 004**
Solid State / Oct '96 / Prime / Vital

ALTERNATIVE CURRENT VOL.1
CD ______ **CDACV 2002**
ACV / Nov '94 / Plastic Head / SRD

ALTERNATIVE CURRENT VOL.2
CD ______ **CDACV 2008**
ACV / Jan '96 / Plastic Head / SRD

ALTERNATOR
CD ______ **DINCD 125**
Dino / Sep '96 / Pinnacle

ALWAYS AND FOREVER VOL.1
Baby I'm a want you: *Bread* / When a man loves a woman: *Sledge, Percy* / Sexual healing: *Gaye, Marvin* / True: *Spandau Ballet* / Tonight I celebrate my love: *Bryson, Peabo & Roberta Flack* / Your body's callin': *Kelly, R* / Missing you: *Waite, John* / More than I can say: *Sayer, Leo* / You might need somebody: *Crawford, Randy* / There'll be sad songs (to make you cry): *Ocean, Billy* / Caravan of love: *Isley-Jasper-Isley* / Please don't go: *KC & The Sunshine Band* / Glory of love: *Cetera, Peter* / If you don't know me: *Melvin, Harold & The Bluenotes* / Zoom: *Fat Larry's Band* / After the love has gone: *Earth, Wind & Fire* / Solid: *Ashford & Simpson* / Always and forever: *Heatwave*
CD ______ **MUSCD 029**
MCI Music / Jan '97 / Disc / THE

ALWAYS AND FOREVER VOL.2
Love don't live here anymore: *Rose Royce* / Cherish: *Kool & The Gang* / So amazing: *Vandross, Luther* / I'll never fall in love again: *Deacon Blue* / For your eyes only: *Easton, Sheena* / Words: *Christians* / Darlin': *Miller, Frankie* / Hurry home: *Wavelength* / Lovin' you: *Riperton, Minnie* / Love won't let me wait: *Harris, Major* / Me and Mrs. Jones: *Paul, Billy* / Sailing: *Cross, Christopher* / I don't wanna lose you: *Kandidate* / Through the barricades: *Kandidate* / All of my heart: *ABC* / cRY FOR HELP: *Astley, Rick* / Love is the answer: *England Dan*
CD ______ **MUSCD 035**
MCI Music / May '97 / Disc / THE

AM I DREAMING
They talk about us: *Williams, Cindy* / I deserve it: *Jones, Samantha* / Town I live in: *Lee, Jackie* / You've got that hold on me: *Hillery, Jane* / I can't stop thinking about you: *Kaye, Linda* / Baby let me be your baby: *Deano* / You'd think he didn't know me: *Browne, Sandra* / Sour grapes: *Noble, Patsy Ann* / Am I dreaming: *Tiffany* / Softly in the night: *Three Bells* / Snakes and snails: *Cogan, Alma* / Wait 'til my Bobby gets home: *Jones, Beverley* / Breakaway: *Marsden, Beryl* / You don't love me no more: *Bell, Madeline* / Don't come any closer: *Jones, Samantha* / Cry to me: *Track* / Be his girl: *Sloan, Sam* / Too young to go steady: *Siver, Andee* / You kissed me boy: *Duncan, Lesley* / Biggity big: *Cope, Suzie* / Some people: *Deene, Carol* / I gotta be with you: *Rede, Emma* / Once more with feeling: *Wonder, Alison* / I didn't love him anyway: *Peanut*
CD ______ **RPM 137**
RPM / Aug '94 / Pinnacle

AM-REP SAMPLER
CD ______ **ARR 279CD**
Amphetamine Reptile / '94 / Plastic Head

AMAZING GRACE
CD ______ **MU 3012**
Musketeer / Oct '92 / Disc

AMAZING GRACE AND OTHER SCOTTISH FAVOURITES
CD ______ **CC 266**
Music For Pleasure / May '91 / EMI

AMAZONIA
CD ______ **LYRCD 7300**
Lyrichord / Feb '94 / ADA / CM / Roots

AMBASSADORS OF RHYTHM
CD ______ **CDHOT 602**
Charly / Jun '96 / Koch

AMBERDELIC SPACE (3CD Set)
CD Set ______ **DTKBOX 55**
Dressed To Kill / Sep '96 / Total/BMG

AMBIANCES DU SAHARA (Desert Blues)
CD ______ **58774CD**
World Network / Apr '96 / ADA

AMBIENT
CD ______ **EMIT 0094**
Time Recordings / Apr '94 / Pinnacle

AMBIENT AMAZON
CD ______ **TMCD 1**
Tumi Dance / Nov '95 / SRD

AMBIENT AURAS
CD ______ **CDRAID 519**
Rumour / Sep '94 / 3mv/Sony / Mo's Music Machine / Pinnacle

AMBIENT BABYLON (2CD Set)
CD Set ______ **AOP 53**
Age Of Panik / Apr '97 / Total/BMG

AMBIENT COMPILATION VOL.4
CD ______ **SR 9753**
Silent / Mar '95 / Cargo / Plastic Head

AMBIENT COOKBOOK, THE (4CD Set)
CD Set ______ **AW 007**
Ambient World / Mar '96 / Plastic Head

AMBIENT DUB VOL.4
Oracle: *Space Time Continuum* / Solar prophet: *Insanity Sect* / Callacop: *Deep Space Network* / Regina from the future: *Starseeds* / Sign: *Coldcut* / In 7: *Another Fine Day* / Warehouse 5AM: *Positive Life* / White darkness: *Sandoz* / Triangle: *Sounds From The Ground*
CD ______ **RBADCD 11**
Beyond / Jun '95 / Kudos / Pinnacle

AMBIENT FANTASY VOL.1 (L'Espirit De Ambience/2CD Set)
Morphic resonance: *Encens* / Cosmic carrot: *Timeshard* / Mystical experience: *Infinity Project* / Ether: *Neill, Ben* / Slapback: *Node* / ...From Heaven: *Manna* / Bosphoressence: *Echo System* / 3am outside here: *Elysium* / Into the void: *Mandrake* / Wobbling in space: *Optic Eye* / Sound without time: *Further* / Alien patrol: *Infinity Project* / Lady burning sky: *Neutron 9000* / Hashidity: *Optica* / 5am sunrise: *Loop Guru*
CD Set ______ **SPV 08938782**
SPV / Sep '96 / Koch / Plastic Head

AMBIENT IBIZA
Tell me what you dream: *Sergio* / Light at heart: *Bindu* / Woman is like a fruit: *Lucky People Center* / Manifest your love: *DOP* / Perimitive: *Van Basten* / Overheated living room: *Dubtractor* / Journey: *Gentle People* / Big warm glo (Planet Love): *Mind Over Rhythm* / Autumn has begun: *Fluff* / You are my desire: *Toney D & The Love Trip* / Come with me: *Affinity*
CD ______ **CDEMC 3752**
Additive / Sep '96 / Mo's Music Machine / RTM/Disc

AMBIENT MOODS
Play dead: *Bjork & David Arnold* / Protection: *Massive Attack* / Stars: *Dubstar* / Evangeline: *Cocteau Twins* / Visions of you: *Jah Wobble's Invaders Of The Heart* / Original: *Leftfield & Toni Halliday* / Missing: *Everything But The Girl* / Inner city life: *Goldie* / Little fluffy clouds: *Orb* / Sensual world: *Bush, Kate* / Sun rising: *Beloved* / Isobel: *Bjork* / Only love can break your heart: *St. Etienne* / Sadeness: *Enigma* / Raindance: *Raindance* / Moments of love: *Art Of Noise* / Ghosts: *Japan*
CD ______ **5259522**
PolyGram TV / Feb '96 / PolyGram

AMBIENT RITUALS
CD ______ **CLEO 9516CD**
Cleopatra / Jun '95 / Cargo / Greyhound / Plastic Head / RTM/Disc / SRD

AMBIENT SENSES (The Vision)
Towers of dub: *Orb* / Papua New Guinea: *Future Sound Of London* / Joyrex J9 ii: *Caustic Window* / Dreams of children: *Slater, Luke* / Earthdance: *Mandragora* / Ageispolis: *Aphex Twin* / Ready for dead: *Ready For Dead* / Minky starshine: *Seefeel* / O Locco: *Sun Electric* / Alqa: *Alien Mutation* / Galapagos: *Sunkings*
CD ______ **CDTOT 12**
Jumpin' & Pumpin' / Jun '94 / 3mv/Sony / Mo's Music Machine

AMBIENT SENSES (20 Contemporary Instrumentals)
Forbidden colours / Winter ceremony / Jesus to a child / Light of experience / Albatross / Twin Peaks theme / X-Files / Inspector Morse theme / Sadness part 1 / Crockett's theme / Play dead / Earth song / Concierto de Aranjuez / Bilitis / Parisienne walkways / Wedding song / Book of days / Love theme from the Thorn Birds / Samba Pa Ti / Chariots of fire
CD ________ **ECD 3291**
K-Tel / Jan '97 / K-Tel

AMBIENT SENSES VOL.2 (The Feeling)
Underground: Irresistable Force / My travels: Larkin, Kenny / Naiad: Ishii, Ken / Lean on me: Moby / Listening (Aural sculpture): Optic Eye / Path: El Mal / Moist mass: Locust / Stoned: Golden Claw Music / AM: Wagon Christ / Manuel versus the apaches: Deep Secret
CD ________ **CDTOT 16**
Jumpin' & Pumpin' / Oct '94 / 3mv/Sony / Mo's Music Machine

AMBIENT SENSES VOL.3
Next: Skylab / Batukau: System 7 / Potion takes effect: Unlimited Dream Company / Planet D: Sabres Of Paradise / Self perpetuating myth: Geiom / Lifewish: Optica / Polynomial-C: Aphex Twin / Hovering glows: Thaemlitz, Terre / Dust (At the crossroads): Psychik Warriors Ov Gaia / Spaced nature: Omicron / Rainforest: Trauma Club
CD ________ **CDTOT 23**
Jumpin' & Pumpin' / Mar '95 / 3mv/Sony / Mo's Music Machine

AMBIENT SYSTEMS VOL.3
CD ________ **AMB 60072**
Cleopatra / Apr '97 / Cargo / Greyhound / Plastic Head / RTM/Disc / SRD

AMBIENT WAY TO DUB
CD ________ **CLEO 9705CD**
Cleopatra / May '96 / Cargo / Greyhound / Plastic Head / RTM/Disc / SRD

AMBITION VOL.1 & 2 (The History Of Cherry Red)
CD ________ **CDBRED 140**
Cherry Red / Feb '97 / Pinnacle

AMBITION VOL.2 (A History Of Cherry Red)
Jest set junta / Night and day / From a to b / Something sends me to sleep / Plain sailing / If she doesn't smile (It'll rain) / Letter from America / Xoyo / Walter and John / Your holiness / On my mind / Mating game / Spain / Talking glamour / Foreign correspondent / Penelope tree / Taboos / Simply couldn't care / You frighten / Paraffin brain / Departure / How to die with style / English rose
CD ________ **CDBRED 96**
Cherry Red / Oct '91 / Pinnacle

AMBO: TIBETAN MONASTERY OF LABRANG
CD ________ **C 560101**
Ocora / Mar '97 / ADA / Harmonia Mundi

AMEN
Curtain: Marden Hill / I bloodbrother be: Shock Headed Peters / Vallari: King Of Luxembourg / Nice on the ice: King Of Luxembourg / You Mary you: Philippe, Louis / Nicky: Momus / O come all ye faithful (Adeste fidelis): Monochrome Set / Cecil beaton's scrapbook: Would-Be-Goods / Blue shinin' quick star: Flippers Guitar / Curry crazy: Bad Dream Fancy Dress / It's love: Hunki-Dori / Andy Warhol: Fisher-Turner, Simon / Mystery stone: Fisher-Turner, Simon / Maria Celesta: Adverse, Anthony / Whoops what a palaver: Bid / Belfast boy: Fardon, Don / Fruit paradise: Would-Be-Goods / My cherie amour: Philippe, Louis / Trial of Dr. Fancy: King Of Luxembourg / Diary of a narcissist: Momus / Temptation of the angel / Amen: Great Chefs Of Europe
CD ________ **MONDE 1CD**
Richmond / Feb '92 / Pinnacle

AMERICA IS DYING SLOWLY
CD ________ **7559619632**
East West / Dec '95 / Warner Music

AMERICAN BANJO: THREE FINGER & SCRUGGS STYLE
CD ________ **SFWCD 40037**
Smithsonian Folkways / Nov '94 / ADA / Cadillac / CM / Direct / Koch

AMERICAN BIG BANDS (2CD Set)
You're driving me crazy: May, Billy / Little brown jug: May, Billy / I guess I'll have to change my plan: May, Billy / Rose Marie: May, Billy / Tenderly: May, Billy / When I take my sugar to tea: May, Billy / Diane: May, Billy / Do you ever think of me: May, Billy / Unforgettable: May, Billy / Cocktails for two: May, Billy / Charmaine: May, Billy / Artistry in rhythm: Kenton, Stan / Printed rhythm: Kenton, Stan / I told ya I love ya, now get out: Kenton, Stan / Eager beaver: Kenton, Stan / Artistry in percussion: Kenton, Stan / Lover: Kenton, Stan / Spider and the fly: Kenton, Stan / Laura: Kenton, Stan / How high the moon: Kenton, Stan / How am I to know: Kenton, Stan / Harlem nocturne: Brown, Les & His Band Of Renown / Continental: Brown, Les & His Band Of Renown / Riding high: Brown, Les & His Band Of Renown / On a little streeet in Singapore: Brown, Les & His Band Of Renown / Hit the road to dreamland: Brown, Les & His Band Of Renown / Lover's leap: Brown, Les & His Band Of Renown / Johnson rag: Brown, Les & His Band Of Renown / Leapfrog: Brown, Les & His Band Of Renown / That certain feeling: Brown, Les & His Band Of Renown / Sentimental journey: Brown, Les & His Band Of Renown / I've got my love to keep me warm: Brown, Les & His Band Of Renown / I wonder what's become of Sally: Anthony, Ray Orchestra / Rockin' through Dixie: Anthony, Ray Orchestra / Skip to my Lou: Anthony, Ray Orchestra / Did he do right by you: Anthony, Ray Orchestra / Wanted: Anthony, Ray Orchestra / Tuxedo junction: Anthony, Ray Orchestra / It's delovely: Anthony, Ray Orchestra / Mr. Anthony's boogie: Anthony, Ray Orchestra / When the saints go marching in: Anthony, Ray Orchestra / Struggle bunny: Oliver, Joe 'King' Orchestra
CD Set ________ **CDDL 1284**
EMI / Nov '94 / EMI

AMERICAN BIG BANDS (3CD Set)
These foolish things: Carter, Benny / Drummin' man: Krupa, Gene / Nola: Hampton, Lionel / One o'clock jump: Basie, Count / Sunny side of the street: Dorsey, Tommy / Dinah: Hampton, Lionel / Mississippi mud: Beiderbecke, Bix / Jersey bounce: Nelson, Ozzie / Dippermouth blues: Dorsey, Jimmy / Christopher columbus: Goodman, Benny / Begin the beguine: Shaw, Artie / South rampart street parade: Shaw, Artie / Wrap your troubles in dreams: Gray, Glen / Honeysuckle rose: Basie, Count / In a sentmental rose: Jurgens, Dick / In the mood: Miller, Glenn / Sugerfoot stomp: Henderson, Fletcher / Perdido: Ellington, Duke / Ciribirbin: James, Harry / At the woodchoppers ball: Herman, Woody / Yes indeed: James, Harry / Drop me off at Harlem: Ellington, Duke / Unsophisticated sue: Lunceford, Jimmie / Sweet lorraine: Shaw, Artie / More than you know: Wilson, Teddy / I can't give you anything but love baby: Armstrong, Louis / nearness of you: Miller, Glenn / All of me: Dorsey, Jimmy / Stop look and listen: Dorsey, Tommy / Mean to me: Napoleon, Phil / King porter stomp: Henderson, Fletcher / California here I come: Hampton, Lionel / All or nothing at all: James, Harry / Creole love song: Ellington, Duke / May I never love again: Weems, Ted / Deep purple: Shaw, Artie / I'm coming virginia: Henderson, Fletcher / Happy feet: Whiteman, Paul / Boogie woogie man: Casa Loma Orchestra / Jitney man: Hines, Earl 'Fatha' Orchestra / American patrol: Miller, Glenn / Take the 'A' train: Ellington, Duke / Dipsy doodle: Clinton, Larry / Jazz me blues: Basie, Count / Dr. Jazz: Morton, Jelly Roll / Alligator crawl: Armstrong, Louis / Singin' the blues: Trumbauer, Frankie / Maple leaf bag: Hines, Earl 'Fatha' Orchestra / Struggle buggy: Oliver, Joe 'King' Orchestra / East st louis: Ellington, Duke / Minnie the moocher: Calloway, Cab Orchestra / Taking a chance on love: Dorsey, Tommy / Jumping at the woodside: Basie, Count / Caledonia: Herman, Woody / Skyliner: Barnet, Charlie / I'll never be the same: Krupa, Gene / My blue heaven: Lunceford, Jimmie / I wonder whose kissing her now: Lunceford, Jimmie
CD Set ________ **390182**
Hallmark / Jul '96 / Carlton

AMERICAN CLAVE - AN ANTHOLOGY
CD Set ________ **AMCL 1020/26**
American Clave / Jan '94 / ADA / Direct / New Note/Pinnacle

AMERICAN DINER (18 Rock 'n' Roll Greats)
Only you: Platters / Little darlin': Diamonds / Duke of Earl: Chandler, Gene / Tutti frutti: Little Richard / He's a rebel: Crystals / Charlie Brown: Coasters / My boyfriend's back: Angels / It's my party: Gore, Lesley / Run to him: Vee, Bobby / Sh-boom: Crew Cuts / Baby it's you: Shirelles / Poetry in motion: Tillotson, Johnny / Get a job: Silhouettes / Love potion no.9: Clovers / Maybe: Chantels / Wild one: Rydell, Bobby / Baby (you got what it takes): Benton, Brook / It's in his kiss (the shoop shoop song): Everett, Betty
CD ________ **SUMCD 4067**
Summit / Nov '96 / Sound & Media

AMERICAN DREAM
CD ________ **COA 70001CD**
North South / Feb '96 / Pinnacle

AMERICAN DREAMS 50'S VOL.1
My heart cries for you: Shore, Dinah / Be my love: Lanza, Mario / Slow poke: King, Pee Wee / C'est si bon: Kitt, Eartha / Cherry pink and apple blossom white: Prado, Perez / Cattle call: Arnold, Eddy / Rock 'n' roll waltz: Starr, Kay / Heartbreak hotel: Presley, Elvis / Banana boat song (Day O): Belafonte, Harry / Melodie d'amour: Ames Brothers / Lazy man: Monte, Lou / Oh lonesome me: Gibson, Don / Send me the pillow that you dream on: Locklin, Hank / Guess who: Belvin, Jesse / Making love: Robinson, Floyd / Three bells: Browns / Oh Carol: Sedaka, Neil / He'll have to go: Reeves, Jim
CD ________ **ND 90370**
RCA / Sep '89 / BMG

AMERICAN DREAMS 50'S VOL.2
I'm movin' on: Snow, Hank / Thing: Harris, Phil / I get ideas: Martin, Tony / Because you're mine: Lanza, Mario / Oh my papa: Fisher, Eddie / Crying in the chapel: Valli, June / Naughty lady of Shady Lane: Ames Brothers / Hot diggity (dog ziggity boom): Como, Perry / Canadian sunset: Winterhalter, Hugo / Don't be cruel: Presley, Elvis / Love is strange: Mickey & Sylvia / Mama look a boo boo: Belafonte, Harry / Four walls: Reeves, Jim / Patricia: Prado, Perez / Diary: Sedaka, Neil / Wonder of you: Peterson, Ray / Battle of Kookamonga: Homer & Jethro / Don't know you: Reese, Della / Shout: Isley Brothers
CD ________ **ND 90371**
RCA / Sep '89 / BMG

AMERICAN DREAMS 60'S VOL.1
Tell Laura I love her: Peterson, Ray / It's now or never: Presley, Elvis / Chain gang: Cooke, Sam / Last date: Cramer, Floyd / I just don't understand: Ann-Margaret / Lion sleeps tonight: Tokens / Love me warm and tender: Anka, Paul / Breaking up is hard to do: Sedaka, Neil / End of the world: Davis, Skeeter / I will follow him: March, 'Little' Peggy / Maria Elena: Los Indios Tabajaros / 500 miles away from home: Bare, Bobby / Java: Hirt, Al / Baby the rain must fall: Yarborough, Glenn / Make the world go away: Arnold, Eddy / Somebody to love: Jefferson Airplane / Light my fire: Feliciano, Jose / These eyes: Guess Who / Grazing in the grass: Friends Of Distinction / Romeo and Juliet: Mancini, Henry
CD ________ **ND 90372**
RCA / Sep '89 / BMG

AMERICAN DREAMS 60'S VOL.2
Old lamplighter: Browns / Please help me, I'm falling: Locklin, Hank / On the rebound: Cramer, Floyd / Funny how time slips away: Elledge, Jimmy / Twistin' the night away: Cooke, Sam / Steel guitar and a glass of wine: Anka, Paul / Guitar man: Eddy, Duane / Detroit city: Bare, Bobby / Abilene: Hamilton, George IV / Hello heartache, goodbye love: March, 'Little' Peggy / I can't stay mad at you: Davis, Skeeter / We'll sing in the sunshine: Garnett, Gale / Ringo: Greene, Lorne / Ballad of the Green Berets: Sadler, Sgt. Barry / My cup runneth over: Ames, Ed / Good, the bad and the ugly: Montenegro, Hugo / In the year 2525: Zager & Evans / Let's get together: Youngbloods / Everybody's talkin': Nilsson, Harry / Suspicious minds: Presley, Elvis
CD ________ **ND 90373**
RCA / Sep '89 / BMG

AMERICAN DREAMS 70'S VOL.1
Love or let me be lonely: Friends Of Distinction / American woman: Guess Who / Amos Moses: Reed, Jerry / It's impossible: Como, Perry / Without you: Nilsson, Harry / Troglodyte (caveman): Castor, Jimmy Bunch / Everybody plays the fool: Main Ingredient / Burning love: Presley, Elvis / My Maria: Stevenson, B.W. / Rock the boat: Hues Corporation / You little trustmaker: Tymes / Life is a rock (but the radio rolled me): Reunion / Lady: Styx / Miracles: Jefferson Starship / Turn the beat around: Robinson, Vickie Sue / Rich girl: Hall & Oates / Here you come again: Parton, Dolly / Shame: King, Evelyn 'Champagne'
CD ________ **ND 90374**
RCA / Sep '89 / BMG

AMERICAN FM VOL.2
CD ________ **NTRCD 029**
Nectar / Sep '94 / Pinnacle

AMERICAN FOGIES, THE
CD ________ **ROUCD 0379**
Rounder / Mar '96 / ADA / CM / Direct

AMERICAN FOLK BLUES FESTIVAL 1970
Introduction / Hard hearted woman / That ain't it / Maggie Lee / World boogie / Old lady / Going to Louisiana / Blues before sunrise / Hootin' the blues / Back water blues / Walk on / When I was drinking / Juanita / After hours / Crazy for my baby / Sittin' and cryin' the blues
CD ________ **CDLR 42021**
L&R / Jul '91 / New Note/Pinnacle

AMERICAN FOLK BLUES FESTIVAL 1972
CD ________ **CDLS 42018**
L&R / Jul '92 / New Note/Pinnacle

AMERICAN HEARTBEAT
Night train: Brown, James / What made Milwaukee famous (has made a loser out of me): Lewis, Jerry Lee / Do you know the way to San Jose: Warwick, Dionne / In a station: Band / Chattanooga choo choo: Miller, Glenn / City of New Orleans: Guthrie, Arlo / Promised land: Allan, Johnnie / California girls: Beach Boys / Woodstock: Matthew's Southern Comfort / Spanish harlem: Franklin, Aretha / Deep in the heart of Texas: Eddy, Duane / El paso: Robbins / Route 66: Troup / Twenty four hours from Tulsa: Pitney, Gene / By the time I get to Phoenix: Campbell, Glen / Walking to New Orleans: Domino, Fats / Memphis, Tennessee: Berry, Chuck / Nashville cats: Lovin' Spoonful / Meet me in St. Louis: Garland, Judy / Baltimore: Newman, Randy
CD ________ **CDV 2728**
Virgin / Apr '94 / EMI

AMERICAN INDIAN - WOUNDED KNEE
CD ________ **SM 10882CD**
Wergo / Nov '95 / ADA / Cadillac / Harmonia Mundi

AMERICAN INDIAN DANCE THEATRE
CD ________ **824312**
BUDA / Jan '90 / Discovery

AMERICAN INDIAN DANCES
CD ________ **EUCD 1317**
ARC / Jul '95 / ADA / ARC Music

AMERICAN LIVIN' BLUES FESTIVAL 1982
CD ________ **157742**
Blues Collection / Feb '93 / Discovery

AMERICAN PENSIONERS ON ECSTASY
CD ________ **CRECD 095**
Creation / Apr '91 / 3mv/Vital

AMERICAN RHYTHM 'N' BLUES
CD ________ **CDRB 27**
Charly / Aug '95 / Koch

AMERICAN ROCKABILLY
CD ________ **NERCD 048**
Nervous / Sep '95 / Nervous / TKO Magnum

AMERICAN ROOTS MUSIC
This soul is mine: Castro, Tommy / Georgia on a fast train: Shaver / Heartattack and wine: Popa Chubby / Forever: McMahan, Ken / It's in the attitude: Tittle, Jimmy / Big Bill: Ramsey, Bo / Drive to survive: Thackery, Jimmy / Every minute every hour: Principato, Tom / Midnight at a redlight: Hamilton, George V / Self sabotage: Jason & The Scorchers / Just like a fish: Garrett, Amos / Monterey: Burch, Paul / Still called the blues: Solberg, James Band / Big girl blues: Connor, Joanna / Lighting a torch: Shaver, Eddy / Everything that glitters: Seals, Dan / Honeydew: Wylie & The Wild West Show / Seven desires: Montoya, Coco
CD ________ **DFGCD 8464**
Dixie Frog / Aug '97 / Direct / TKO Magnum

AMERICAN WARRIORS
War paint/Soldier boy / In the South the birds are flying / Lakota (Sioux) Little Bighorn victory songs / Carnegie War Mothers' Chapter (Kiowa) veterans songs / World War I and II / Canadian (Lakota) flag song / American (Lakota) flag song / Four Hochunk (Winnebago) service songs / Menominee Vietnam veterans song / Indian boys from Desert Storm
CD ________ **RCD 10370**
Rykodisc / May '97 / ADA / Vital

AMERICAN WILDS
CD ________ **12148**
Laserlight / May '94 / Target/BMG

AMERICANISM
CD ________ **NTMCD 509**
Nectar / May '96 / Pinnacle

AMERICANS IN PARIS VOL.2
CD ________ **2512772**
Jazztime / Mar '90 / Discovery

AMERICANS IN PARIS VOL.7 (1946-1950)
CD ________ **8274142**
Jazztime / Jan '95 / Discovery

AMERICA'S ROCK
Burning heart: Survivor / Travellin' shoes: Bishop, Elvin / Ramblin' man: Allman Brothers / Take me home: Cher / Spooky: Atlanta Rhythm Section / Sweet dreams: Buchanan, Roy / Do you like it: Kingdom Come / Run run run: Velvet Underground / Gypsy road: Cinderella / Tom Sawyer: Rush / Midnight rider: Allman, Greg / Na na hey hey kiss him goodbye: Steam / Rock 'n' roll children: Dio / House of the rising sun: Frijid Pink
CD ________ **5506402**
Spectrum / Aug '94 / PolyGram

AMONG MY SOUVENIRS: THOSE ROMANTIC 20'S
CD ________ **8440832**
Eclipse / Mar '92 / PolyGram

AMONG MY SOUVENIRS: THOSE ROMANTIC 30'S
CD ________ **8440842**
Eclipse / Mar '92 / PolyGram

AMOUR (The Ultimate Love Collection/ 2CD Set)
Love is all around: Wet Wet Wet / Walk on by: Gabrielle / Breathe again: Braxton, Toni / Sexual healing: Gaye, Marvin / Goodbye heartbreak: Lighthouse Family / If you love me: Brownstone / Tired of being alone: Texas / Hey child: East 17 / Don't be a stanger: Carroll, Dina / Forever: Damage / Nobody knows: Rich, Tony Project / Touch me in the morning: Ross, Diana / Betcha by golly, wow: Stylistics / Don't wanna lose you: Estefan, Gloria / One day in your life: Jackson, Michael / Dreaming: MN8 / Single: Everything But The Girl / Manchild: Cherry, Neneh / What's love got to do with it: Turner, Tina / Flame: Fine Young Cannibals / Back for good: Take That / If you ever: East 17 & Gabrielle / You're gorgeous: Baby Bird / Quit playing games (with my heart): Backstreet Boys / I feel you: Andre, Peter / Words: Boyzone / Child: Owen, Mark / One more chance: One / Forever love: Barlow, Gary / Don't dream it's over: Crowded

House / Sacrifice: *John, Elton* / In too deep: *Carlisle, Belinda* / Wonderful tonight: *Clapton, Eric* / Chains: *Arena, Tina* / Woman in chains: *Tears For Fears* / Without you: *Nilsson* / So far away: *King, Carole* / Unchained melody: *Righteous Brothers* / Don't cry for me Argentina: *Covington, Julie*
CD Set _______ **5533322**
PolyGram TV / Feb '97 / PolyGram

AMP
Block rocking beats: *Chemical Brothers* / Atom bomb: *Fluke* / Pearl's girl: *Underworld* / We have explosive: *Future Sound Of London* / Ni ten ichi ryu: *Photek* / Girl boy: *Aphex Twin* / Box: *Orbital* / We all want to be free: *Tranquility Bass* / Inner city life: *Goldie* / Voodoo people: *Prodigy* / Are you there: *Wink, Josh* / Busy child: *Crystal Method* / Sick to death: *Atari Teenage Riot*
CD _______ **CAR 7550**
Astralwerks / May '97 / Cargo / Vital

AMPHETAMINE REPTILE MOTORS 1993 MODELS
CD _______ **ARRCD 42279**
Amphetamine Reptile / Jul '93 / Plastic Head

AMPHETAMINE REPTILE MOTORS 1995 MODELS
CD _______ **ARRCD 62005**
Amphetamine Reptile / May '95 / Plastic Head

AMPLIFIED VOL.1
CD _______ **AABT 807CD**
Abstract / Apr '95 / Cargo / Pinnacle / Total/BMG

AMSTERDAM SMOKERS
CD _______ **BDRCD 14**
Breakdown / May '96 / Pinnacle

AN CEOL AGAINN FHEIN
CD _______ **DUAL 3CD**
Macmeanma / Aug '95 / ADA / CM / Duncans / Highlander

AN DROICHEAD BEAG/A MIGHTY SESSION
CD _______ **DBCD 001**
Dingle Pub / Feb '96 / ADA

ANAGRAM PUNK SINGLES COLLECTION
Give us a future / Just another hero / You talk we talk / Woman in disguise / Lust for glory / Baby baby / Dragnet / Jerusalem / Pressure / Solidarity / Five flew over the cuckoo's nest / Guilty / Hang ten / Cum on feel the noize / Breakin' in / Nowhere left to run / Not just a name / This is the age / Black sheep / Children of the night / You'll never know / Legacy / Teenage rampage
CD _______ **CDPUNK 37**
Anagram / Sep '94 / Cargo / Pinnacle

ANALOGUE ELEMENTS VOL.1
CD _______ **NEUCD 1**
Neuton / May '94 / Plastic Head

ANALOGUE ELEMENTS VOL.2
CD _______ **NEUCD 2**
Neuton / Oct '94 / Plastic Head

ANCIENT CELTIC ROOTS
CD _______ **TSCD 704**
Topic / Aug '96 / ADA / CM / Direct

ANCIENT EGYPT
CD _______ **LYRCD 7347**
Lyrichord / '91 / ADA / CM / Roots

ANCIENT HEART - MANDINKA & FULANI MUSIC
CD _______ **5101482**
Axiom / Oct '92 / PolyGram / Vital

AND I LOVE YOU SO (2CD Set)
Feelings: *Albert, Morris* / And I love you so: *Bassey, Shirley* / Why can't we live together: *Thomas, Timmy* / What a difference a day makes: *Washington, Dinah* / I you don't know me by now: *Melvin, Harold & The Bluenotes* / Only love can break a heart: *Pitney, Gene* / Stand by your man: *Anderson, Lynn* / Most beautiful girl: *Rich, Charlie* / Will you love me tomorrow: *Shirelles* / Only a fool (Breaks his own heart): *Mighty Sparrow* / I'd rather go blind: *James, Etta* / Never my love: *Association* / Hurt: *Yuro, Timi* / When something is wrong with my baby: *Sam & Dave* / Ruby Tuesday: *Melanie* / Rainy night in Georgia: *White, Tony Joe* / When you wish upon a star: *Little Anthony & The Imperials* / Words of love: *Mamas & The Papas* / Three steps to heaven: *Cochran, Eddie* / Surfer girl: *Beach Boys* / It's just a matter of time: *Benton, Brook* / Daddy's home: *Shep & The Limelites* / Tonight is the night: *Wright, Betty* / If you need me: *Burke, Solomon* / Lovers concerto: *Toys* / Everybody loves somebody: *Martin, Dean* / Only you: *Platters* / Love you most of all: *Cooke, Sam* / You've lost that lovin' feelin': *Bass, Fontella* / You've got a friend: *Whittaker, Roger* / Oh girl: *Chi-Lites* / Midnight train to Georgia: *Knight, Gladys & The Pips* / Warm and tender love: *Sledge, Percy* / Remember (Walkin' in the sand): *Shangri-Las* / It's all in the game: *Edwards, Tommy* / He's so fine: *Chiffons* / Bring back my yesterday: *White, Barry* / Summer (The first time): *Goldsboro, Bobby* / Sealed with a kiss: *Hyland, Brian* / Spies and specks: *Bee Gees* / Give up your guns: *Buoys* / Raindrops keep falling on my head: *Thomas, B.J.*
CD Set _______ **DBG 53047**
Double Gold / Jul '96 / Target/BMG

AND I LOVE YOU SO
When I need you: *Sayer, Leo* / When you're in love with a beautiful woman: *Dr. Hook* / Impossible dream: *Jones, Tom* / Crazy: *Nelson, Willie* / Red sails in the sunset: *Domino, Fats* / Greatest love of all: *Bassey, Shirley* / Love me with all your heart: *Humperdinck, Engelbert* / Vaya con dios: *Orlando, Tony* / Unforgettable: *Rawls, Lou* / It started with a kiss: *Hot Chocolate* / McLean, Don: *Hot Chocolate* / My special angel: *Campbell, Glen* / That's amore: *Martin, Dean* / Spanish eyes: *Martino, Al*
CD _______ **DC 879442**
Disky / Mar '97 / Disky / THE

AND I WRITE THE SONGS (2CD Set)
I want to see the bright lights tonight: *Thompson, Richard & Linda* / Say it ain't so: *Head, Murray* / Every kinda people: *Palmer, Robert* / Lova and affection: *Armatrading, Joan* / Breakaway: *Gallagher & Lyle* / Diamonds and rust: *Baez, Joan* / Daniel: *John, Elton* / Mandolin wind: *Stewart, Rod* / Shine silently: *Lofgren, Nils* / When you see a chance: *Winwood, Steve* / Spiders and snakes: *Stafford, Jim* / Gold: *Stewart, John* / Achy breaky heart: *Cyrus, Billy Ray* / Train leaves this morning: *Dillard & Clark* / Real fine love: *Hiatt, John* / Magic smile: *Vela, Rosie* / Yellow pearl: *Lynott, Phil* / Broken English: *Faithfull, Marianne* / It's different for girls: *Jackson, Joe* / Steel claw: *Brady, Paul* / There's a guy works down the chip shop swears he's Elvis: *MacColl, Kirsty* / Don't pay the ferryman: *De Burgh, Chris* / Charlotte Street: *Cole, Lloyd & The Commotions* / If love was like guitars: *McNabb, Ian* / Lady came from Baltimore: *Hardin, Tim* / Our last song together: *Sedaka, Neil* / King of the road: *Miller, Roger* / Over the hill: *Martyn, John* / It'll take a long time: *Denny, Sandy* / Bryter later: *Drake, Nick* / Cold cold heart: *Williams, Hank* / Lake Placid blues: *White, Tony Joe* / Sunny: *Hebb, Bobby* / High flying bird: *Havens, Richie* / Let's get it on: *Gaye, Marvin* / I'll go crazy: *Brown, James*
CD Set _______ **5530622**
Debutante / Jan '97 / PolyGram

AND STILL NO HITS
CD _______ **NRCD 1100**
Nation / Aug '97 / RTM/Disc

AND STILL WE SAY NO SURRENDER
CD _______ **CDUCD 18**
Ulster Music / Apr '97 / ADA / CM / Direct / Duncans / Koch / Ross

AND THE ANGELS SING OVER THE RAINBOW - 1939
Jeepers creepers: *Armstrong, Louis* / Jive at five: *Basie, Count* / Undecided: *Webb, Chick* / Zigeuner: *Shaw, Artie* / Moonlight serenade: *Miller, Glenn* / When lights are low: *Hampton, Lionel* / Ain't she sweet: *Lunceford, Jimmie* / At the woodchoppers' ball: *Herman, Woody* / I'm checkin' out (goodbye): *Ellington, Duke* / Body and soul: *Hawkins, Coleman* / And the angels sing: *Goodman, Benny* / I wish I could shimmy like my sister Kate: *Spanier, Muggsy* / Lady's in love with you: *Miller, Glenn* / Over the rainbow: *Garland, Judy* / Sugar: *Wilson, Teddy* / Lester leaps in: *Basie, Count* / I've got my eyes on you: *Dorsey, Tommy* / Opus 5: *Kirby, John* / Flyin' home: *Goodman, Benny* / T'ain't what you do (it's the way that you do it): *Lunceford, Jimmie* / I'm coming Virginia: *Shaw, Artie*
CD _______ **PHONTCD 7667**
Phontastic / Apr '90 / Cadillac / Jazz Music / Wellard

AND THE BEAT GOES ON VOL.1 (42 Classics Of The 50's And 60's/2CD Set)
Um, um, um, um: *Fontana, Wayne & The Mindbenders* / Pamela, Pamela: *Fontana, Wayne* / Juliet: *Four Pennies* / I think of you: *Merseybeats* / Groovy kind of love: *Fontana, Wayne & The Mindbenders* / I only want to be with you: *Springfield, Dusty* / Say I won't be there: *Springfields* / Concrete and clay: *Unit 4+2* / Tell me when: *Applejacks* / Mirror, mirror: *Pinkerton's Assorted Colours* / Do you love me: *Poole, Brian & The Tremeloes* / Ain't she sweet: *Beatles* / Bobby's girl: *Maughan, Susan* / Well I ask you: *Kane, Eden* / Crying game: *Berry, Dave* / (Fool's errand) Do you really love me too: *Fury, Billy* / Leave a little love: *Lulu* / Secret love: *Kirby, Kathy* / What's new pussycat: *Jones, Tom* / Diamonds: *Harris, Jet & Tony Meehan* / Are you sure: *Allisons* / It's my party: *Gore, Lesley* / Passing strangers: *Vaughan, Sarah & Billy Eckstine* / Mack The Knife: *Fitzgerald, Ella* / My happiness: *Francis, Connie* / Good timin': *Jones, Jimmy* / As I love you: *Bassey, Shirley* / Chantilly lace: *Big Bopper* / It's all in the game: *Edwards, Tommy* / It's only make believe: *Twitty, Conway* / Stranger on the shore: *Bilk, Acker* / Wedding: *Rogers, Julie* / Rubber ball: *Wilde, Marty* / Fings ain't what they used to be: *Bygraves, Max* / Strawberry fair: *Newley, Anthony* / Sorry: *Impalas* / Smoke gets in your eyes: *Platters* / Diane: *Bachelors* / Walk on by: *Van Dyke, Leroy* / Morere I see you: *Montez, Chris* / Unchained melody: *Righteous Brothers*
CD Set _______ **5356932**
Debutante / Jul '96 / PolyGram

AND THE BEAT GOES ON VOL.2 (40 Classics Of The 60's/2CD Set)
All or nothing: *Small Faces* / Beggin': *Timebox* / Matthew and son: *Stevens, Cat* / Sitting in the park: *Fame, Georgie* / Sun ain't gonna shine anymore: *Walker Brothers* / Jesamine: *Casuals* / You've got your troubles: *Fortunes* / In thoughts of you: *Fury, Billy* / Bend me, shape me: *Amen Corner* / She's not there: *McArthur, Neil* / Bend it: *Dave Dee, Dozy, Beaky, Mick & Tich* / Lightning strikes: *Christie, Lou* / From the underworld: *Herd* / Remember: *Shangri-Las* / Rain and tears: *Aphrodite's Child* / 98.6: *Keith* / Single girl: *Posey, Sandy* / Boys cry: *Kane, Eden* / Winchester Cathedral: *New Vaudeville Band* / I was Keiser Bill's batman: *Smith, Whistling Jack* / Rainbow chaser: *Nirvana* / Hole in my shoes: *Traffic* / San Franciscan nights: *Burdon, Eric & The Animals* / Mighty Quinn: *Manfred Mann* / I can't control myself: *Troggs* / Fire: *Crazy World Of Arthur Brown* / Something in the air: *Thunderclap Newman* / This wheel's on fire: *Driscoll, Julie & Brian Auger* / Son of a preacher man: *Springfield, Dusty* / Somebody help me: *Davis, Spencer Group* / Si tu dois partir: *Fairport Convention* / Hang onto a dream: *Hardin, Tim* / I put a spell on you: *Simone, Nina* / It's a man's man's man's world: *Brown, James* / Here comes the judge: *Long, Shorty* / Long shot kick de bucket: *Pioneers* / Wonderful world, beautiful people: *Cliff, Jimmy* / Foggy mountain breakdown: *Flatt, Lester & Earl Scruggs* / River deep, mountain high: *Turner, Ike & Tina* / Ride my seesaw: *Moody Blues*
CD Set _______ **5356682**
Debutante / Jul '96 / PolyGram

AND THE BEAT GOES ON VOL.3 (2CD Set)
I can hear the grass grow: *Move* / I don't want our lovin' to die: *Herd* / My mind's eye: *Small Faces* / Get away: *Fame, Georgie & The Blue Flames* / Here it comes again: *Fortunes* / It's good news week: *Hedgehoppers Anonymous* / Everyone's gone to the moon: *King, Jonathan* / Go now: *Moody Blues* / Ha ha said the clown: *Manfred Mann* / Here we go round the mulberry bush: *Traffic* / With a girl like you: *Troggs* / Let's go to San Francisco: *Flowerpot Men* / Save me: *Dave Dee, Dozy, Beaky, Mick & Tich* / High in the sky: *Amen Corner* / Toy: *Casuals* / Creeque Alley: *Mamas & The Papas* / Game of love: *Fontana, Wayne & The Mindbenders* / Keep on running: *Davis, Spencer Group* / Pleasant Valley Sunday: *Monkees* / Rain, the park and other things: *Cowsills* / Woolly bully: *Sam The Sham & The Pharaohs* / Handy man: *Jones, Jimmy* / Let's dance: *Montez, Chris* / I'm gonna get me a gun: *Stevens, Cat* / My ship is coming in: *Walker Brothers* / You don't have to say you love me: *Springfield, Dusty* / Well I ask ya: *Kane, Eden* / It's not unusual: *Jones, Tom* / Only one woman: *Marbles* / Come and stay with me: *Faithfull, Marianne* / King of the road: *Miller, Roger* / I'm just a baby: *Cordet, Louise* / Love is blue: *Mauriat, Paul* / My boyfriend's back: *Angels* / Island of dreams: *Springfields* / Joanna: *Walker, Scott* / When will you say I love you: *Fury, Billy* / Finchley Central: *New Vaudeville Band*
CD Set _______ **5530652**
Debutante / Jan '97 / PolyGram

AND THE CRAIC WAS GOOD
I want to live: *Friday, Gavin* / Emotional time: *Hothouse Flowers* / Religious persuasion: *White, Andy* / Munster hop: *Shannon, Sharon* / Rambling Irishman: *Dannan, De* / May morning dew: *Moving Hearts* / Saturday night: *Dowdall, Leslie* / Send me a river: *Lohan, Sinead* / Adam at the window: *Black, Mary* / Island: *Brady, Paul* / Slipside: *Stockton's Wing* / From Clare to here: *Furey Brothers & Davy Arthur* / She moved through the fair: *Shades of McMurrough* / Mna na heireann: *Na Connerys* / Take my hand: *In Tua Nua* / Dark hill: *Hinterland* / November november: *Auto Da Fe* / End titles (theme from Miller's Crossing): *Burwell, Carter*
CD _______ **5533272**
Debutante / Feb '97 / PolyGram

AND THE FUN JUST NEVER ENDS
CD _______ **LF 071**
Lost & Found / Jan '94 / Plastic Head

AND THE HEAVENS CRIED (36 Progressive Rock Classics/2CD Set)
Tales of brave Ulysses: *Cream* / Mr. Fantasy: *Traffic* / Weight: *Spooky Tooth* / Meet on the ledge: *Fairport Convention* / It's only a dream: *Trapeze* / Place of my own: *Caravan* / I can take you to the sun: *Misunderstood* / Hold me back: *Patto* / Sing a song of summer: *Martyn, John* / Time has told me: *Drake, Nick* / Tiny Goddess: *Nirvana* / Strangely strange, but oddly normal: *Dr. Strangely Strange* / Breathless: *Camel* / Time goes by: *Chicken Shack* / Born to die: *Hartley, Keef Band* / Money can't save your soul: *Savoy Brown* / Jig a jig: *East Of Eden* / Those about to die: *Colosseum* / Fire: *Crazy World Of Arthur Brown* / Season of the witch: *Driscoll, Julie & Brian Auger* / House of the rising sun: *Frijid Pink* / Sky pilot: *Burdon, Eric & The Animals* / Country comfort: *Stewart, Rod* / Cry me a river: *Cocker, Joe* / Travelling man: *Dummer, John Blues Band* / Thunderback ram: *Mott The Hoople* / Room to move: *Mayall, John* / Born on the wrong side of time: *Taste* / Living in the past: *Jethro Tull* / Time seller: *Davis, Spencer* / Gungamai: *Quintessence* / Ride my seesaw: *Moody Blues* / I'm a mover: *Free* / Moon is down: *Gentle Giant* / I keep singing that same old song: *Heavy Jelly*
CD Set _______ **5356962**
Debutante / Jul '96 / PolyGram

AND THE REST IS HISTORY
Mismatch: *Disco* / Supersexy revolutionary: *Disco Pistol* / Disco dollies: *Designer* / Scooby doo: *Dweeb* / Wendyhouse: *Midget* / My nites out: *Kenickie* / In formula one: *Helen Love* / Battery power dead: *Persecution Complex* / Daddy I want a pony: *Period Pains* / Pin ups go go go: *Pin-Ups* / Hot trash: *Pink Kross* / All together now: *Bellatrix* / Disappear: *Symposium* / Blindsight: *Tampasm* / Give me a beer: *Toast* / Keep your mouth shut: *Xerox Girls*
CD _______ **ZERO 001CD**
Zerox / Jan '97 / Vital

AND THE ROAD GOES ON FOREVER VOL.1 (36 Hard Rock Classics/2CD Set)
You wear it well: *Stewart, Rod* / Benny and the Jets: *John, Elton* / You ain't seen nothin' yet: *Bachman-Turner Overdrive* / Come together in the morning: *Free* / Whiskey in the jar: *Thin Lizzy* / Down down: *Status Quo* / Love like a man: *Ten Years After* / Joy bringer: *Manfred Mann's Earthband* / Bad case of lovin' you: *Palmer, Robert* / Just a day away (forever tomorrow): *Barclay James Harvest* / I'm just a singer (in a rock and roll band): *Moody Blues* / Second chance: *.38 Special* / Wind of change: *Scorpions* / Nobody's fool: *Cinderella* / Rock'n'roll children: *Dio* / Tell Mama: *Savoy Brown* / Closer to the heart: *Rush* / St.Elmo's fire: *Parr, John* / Ramblin' man: *Allman Brothers* / Fooled around and fell in love: *Bishop, Elvin* / Show me the way: *Frampton, Peter* / Night games: *Bonnet, Graham* / Perfect strangers: *Deep Purple* / Since you been gone: *Rainbow* / 5-7-0-5: *City Boy* / Wonderland: *Big Country* / Valerie: *Winwood, Steve* / External exile: *Fish* / She's a little angel: *Little Angels* / Obsession: *Animotion*
CD Set _______ **5357172**
Debutante / Jul '96 / PolyGram

AND THE ROAD GOES ON FOREVER VOL.2 (2CD Set)
Jessica: *Allman Brothers* / Blinded by the light: *Manfred Mann's Earthband* / Look away: *Big Country* / Addicted to love: *Palmer, Robert* / Lessons in love: *Level 42* / Good thing: *Fine Young Cannibals* / Street of dreams: *Rainbow* / Show me the way: *Styx* / Eye of the tiger: *Survivor* / Caught up in you: *.38 Special* / Shelter me: *Cinderella* / Rock you like a hurricane: *Scorpions* / Roll on down the highway: *Bachman-Turner Overdrive* / Spirit of radio: *Rush* / Take me home: *Cher* / Womankind: *Little Angels* / Ballad of Jane: *LA Guns* / I'll see you in my dreams: *Giant* / One and one is one: *Medicine Head* / Stuck in the middle with you: *Stealer's Wheel* / Heart on my sleeve: *Gallagher & Lyle* / Walkin' in the Arizona sun: *Wray, Link* / Sweet dreams: *Buchanan, Roy* / Perfect skin: *Cole, Lloyd & The Commotions* / Dancin' in the moonlight: *Thin Lizzy* / All right now: *Free* / I know I'm losing you: *Stewart, Rod* / Question: *Moody Blues* / I got a line on you: *Spirit* / No mercy: *Lofgren, Nils* / Standing in the road: *Blackfoot Sue* / Webb's boogie: *Chicken Shack* / Restless: *Status Quo* / Philadelphia freedom: *John, Elton* / Walk the dinosaur: *Was Not Was* / Annie I'm not your Daddy: *Kid Creole & The Coconuts*
CD Set _______ **5530542**
Debutante / Jan '97 / PolyGram

AND THE WORLD'S ALL YOURS (An Essential Selection Of World Music/2CD Set)
No sant: *Diop, Wasis & Lena Fiagbe* / African soul: *Baroudi, Hamid* / 10th commandment: *Papa Wemba* / La ruinas en mi mente: *Soroya* / Boule fale: *Positive Black Soul & Aminata Fall* / Must must: *Khan, Nusrat Fateh Ali* / What do you want, life: *Boine, Mari* / Mansa: *Super Rail Band* / Carizzi r'amuri: *Agricantus* / Blow on my soul: *Arvanitaki, Eleftheria* / Rumba Arglina: *Radio Tarifa* / Comme un chien: *Taha, Rachid* / Sama du miya: *Maal, Baaba* / Feel ire: *Lucky Dube* / OS: *Timba Lada* / Tekere: *Keita, Salif* / Tshikunda: *Muana, Tshala* / Life: *Dreamcatcher* / LOVE: *UFO* / Mammou ayni: *Amina* / Elligibo: *Menezes, Margareth* / Aicha taadi: *Khaled, Cheb* / Lakh bi: *Africando* / No no no: *Roach, Archie* / Not an easy road: *Buju Banton* / Un aeroplane a vela: *Testa, Gianmaria* / Zan'j yo: *Boukman Experyans* / Orca's song: *Tulku* / Chimes of freedom: *N'Dour, Youssou*
CD Set _______ **5359492**
Debutante / Jan '97 / PolyGram

AND THEN SHE KISSED ME VOL.1 (38 Classic Love Songs/2CD Set)
Look of love: *ABC* / She drives me crazy: *Fine Young Cannibals* / I didn't mean to turn you on: *Palmer, Robert* / Don't go: *Hothouse Flowers* / I'm in love with a German film star: *Passions* / I got you: *Split Enz* / Will you: *O'Connor, Hazel* / No more I love you's: *Lover Speaks* / I should have known

better: *Diamond, Jim* / Sweetest smile: *Black* / Pilot of the airwaves: *Dore, Charlie* / Love hurts: *Capaldi, Jim* / Captain of her heart: *Double* / We don't cry out loud: *Brooks, Elkie* / I wanna stay with you: *Gallagher & Lyle* / Song for Guy: *John, Elton* / Cry: *Godley & Creme* / I'm not in love: *10cc* / Oh no, not my baby: *Stewart, Rod* / How can I be sure: *Springfield, Dusty* / Up where we belong: *Cocker, Joe & Jennifer Warnes* / Do that to me one more time: *Captain & Tennille* / Oh Lori: *Alessi* / Words: *Coolidge, Rita* / Me myself I: *Armatrading, Joan* / I'm your puppet: *James & Bobby Purify* / Betcha by golly wow: *Stylistics* / On the radio: *Summer, Donna* / Just the way you are: *White, Barry* / Love's theme: *Love Unlimited Orchestra* / Love town: *Newberry, Booker III* / Cherish: *Kool & The Gang* / Secret lovers: *Atlantic Starr* / Never gonna let you go: *Mendes, Sergio* / Piano in the dark: *Russell, Brenda* / Get here: *Adams, Oleta* / Love is just the great pretender: *Animal Nightlife* / You can do magic: *Limmie & Family Cooking*
CD Set _____ **5356722**
Debutante / Jul '96 / PolyGram

AND THEY DANCED THE NIGHT AWAY (39 Classic Disco Hits/2CD Set)
Word up: *Cameo* / Ladies night: *Kool & The Gang* / If I can't have you: *Elliman, Yvonne* / Hustle: *McCoy, Van & Soul City Symphony* / Let's put it all together: *Stylistics* / British hustle: *Hi-Tension* / Ain't nothin' goin' on but the rent: *Guthrie, Gwen* / Strawberry letter 23: *Brothers Johnson* / Never, never gonna give you up: *White, Barry* / Chase: *Moroder, Giorgio* / Do it again/Billy Jean: *Club House* / There's a ghost in my house: *Taylor, R. Dean* / Dr. Kiss Kiss: *5000 Volts* / I love the nightlife: *Bridges, Alicia* / Behind the groove: *Marie, Teena* / Mama used to say: *Junior* / It should have been me: *Fair, Yvonne* / Fire: *Ohio Players* / In the thick of it: *Russell, Brenda* / Never knew love like this: *Mills, Stephanie* / Night birds: *Shakatak* / Breakin'...there's no stopping us now: *Ollie & Jerry* / Get down: *Chandler, Gene* / Don't stop the music: *Yarbrough & Peoples* / Hang on in there baby: *Bristol, Johnny* / Get up I feel like being a sex machine: *Brown, James* / Funky town: *Lipps Inc.* / I feel love: *Summer, Donna* / Oops upside your head: *Gap Band* / You can't hide (your love from me): *Joseph, David* / Let the music play: *White, Barry* / I will survive: *Gaynor, Gloria* / Now that we've found love: *Third World* / Teardrops: *Womack & Womack* / Ain't nothing gonna keep me from you: *De Sario, Terri* / Burning love: *Con Funk Shun* / Dancin' the night away: *Voggue* / Shake your groove thing: *Peaches & Herb* / I was made for dancing: *Garrett, Leif* / Check this out: *LA Mix*
CD Set _____ **5356802**
Debutante / Jul '96 / PolyGram

AND THIS TIME IT'S FOR REAL (36 Classic R&B Standards/2CD Set)
Soulful dress: *Desanto, Sugar Pie* / First I look at the purse: *Contours* / He was really saying something: *Velvelettes* / Don't mess up a good thing: *Bass, Fontella & Bobby McClure* / Hey Leroy your Mama's calling you: *Castor, Jimmy* / Cleo's mood: *Walker, Junior* / Devil with the blue dress: *Long, Shorty* / Mohair Sam: *Rich, Charlie* / Thread your needle: *Dean & Jean* / Out of sight: *Brown, James* / Uptight good woman: *Lee, Laura* / Ain't nobody home: *Tate, Howard* / Got to get you off my mind: *Burke, Solomon* / Every little bit hurts: *Holloway, Brenda* / Baby I'm for real: *Originals* / Hey Western Union man: *Butler, Jerry* / Nowhere to run: *Martha & The Vandellas* / It's better to have and don't need: *Covay, Don* / Stealing in the name of the Lord: *Kelly, Paul* / Who's gonna help brother get further: *Dorsey, Lee* / I'll take you there: *Staple Singers* / Buffalo soldiers: *Flamingos* / War: *Starr, Edwin* / Bring the boys back home: *Payne, Freda* / Tell me what you want: *Ruffin, Jimmy* / Got to get enough: *Roy C* / Groovy situation: *Chandler, Gene* / Think (about it): *Collins, Lyn* / Rubberband man: *Detroit Spinners* / Deception: *Dynamic Superiors* / Sneakin' Sally through the alley: *Palmer, Robert* / Rock steady: *Franklin, Aretha* / Meet de boys on teh battlefront: *Wild Tchoupitoulas* / 18 with a bullet: *Wingfield, Pete*
CD Set _____ **5531002**
Debutante / Jan '97 / PolyGram

ANDALUSIAN FLAMENCO SONG AND DANCE
CD _____ **LYRCD 7388**
Lyrichord / '91 / ADA / CM / Roots

ANDEAN LEGACY
Tempestad: *Andina, Savia* / Encuentros: *Alturas* / Pueblo Lejano: *Viento De Los Andes* / Aranjuez: *Echoes Of Incas* / Cieldo Y Montana: *Rumillajta* / Kalasasaya: *Inkuyo* / Na Yachanichu: *Imbaya* / Tema De La Quebrada de Humahuaca: *Inti-Illimani* / Sombrero de Paja y Quina: *Andes Manta* / Ajawasi: *Inkuyo* / Akullicu: *Rumillajta* / La Samaritana: *Ancient Winds* / Concepcion: *Sukay* / El Pillan: *Caliche*
CD _____ **ND 63927**
Narada / Nov '96 / ADA / New Note/ Pinnacle

ANGEL OF THE MORNING (Rock & Pop Ballads)
CD _____ **CD 12202**
Laserlight / Aug '93 / Target/BMG

ANGELFOOD ELECTRONICS VOL.1 & 2
CD _____ **KMR 08/09CD**
Kake Mix / Mar '97 / Cargo

ANGER, FEAR, SEX AND DEATH
CD _____ **E 86402CD**
Epitaph / Nov '92 / Pinnacle / Plastic Head

ANGIE FOLK GUITAR
CD _____ **PLSCD 150**
Pulse / Jan '97 / BMG

ANGOLA PRISONERS' BLUES
Prisoner's talking blues: *Williams, Robert Pete* / Stagger Lee: *Maxey, Hogman* / Electric chair blues: *Welch, Guitar* / Some got six months: *Williams, Robert Pete* / I'm gonna leave you Mama: *Welch, Guitar* / I'm lonesome blues: *Williams, Robert Pete* / Angola bound: *Acapella Group* / Worried blues: *Maxey, Hogman* / Josephine: *Welch, Guitar* / Soldier's plea: *Young, Clara* / Moon is rising: *Mathews, Odea* / I'm still in love with you: *Joseph, Thelma Mae* / I miss you so: *Vocal Group* / Hello Sue: *Butterbeans* / Fast life woman: *Maxey, Hogman* / Careless love: *Webster, Otis* / have you ever heard the church bells tone: *Charles, Roosevelt & Otis Webster* / 61 Highway: *Welch, Guitar* / Strike at camp 1: *Charles, Roosevelt*
CD _____ **ARHCD 419**
Arhoolie / Nov '96 / ADA / Cadillac / Direct

ANNIE ON ONE
Theme: *Sabres Of Paradise* / Age of love: *Age Of Love* / Lookee here: *Transglobal Underground* / Rocks: *Primal Scream* / Vision: *Prophecy* / Da funk: *Daft Punk* / Liberation: *T-Power* / What's that sound: *Sever, Sam & The Raiders Of The Lost Art* / Clubbed to death: *Rob D* / North south east west: *Black Sheep* / Weekender: *Flowered Up*
CD _____ **HVNCD 11**
Heavenly / Feb '96 / 3mv/Pinnacle / BMG / Vital

ANOTHER ROUND OF GOLF
CD _____ **CDHOLE 009**
Golf / Jun '96 / Plastic Head

ANOTHER SATURDAY NIGHT
Before I grow too old: *McLain, Tommy* / Cajun fugitive: *Belton, Richard* / Try to find another man: *McLain, Tommy & Clint West* / Jolie blon: *Bruce, Vin* / I cried: *Cookie & The Cupcakes* / Oh Lucille: *Belton, Richard* / Who needs you so bad: *Walker, Gary* / Don't mess with my man: *White, Margo* / Another Saturday night: *White, Margo* / Un auter soir d'ennui: *Belton, Richard* / Promised land: *Allan, Johnnie* / Two steps de bayou teche: *Pitre, Austin* / Sweet dreams: *McLain, Tommy* / Breaking up is hard to do: *Cookie & The Cupcakes* / Laisser les cajun danser: *Belton, Richard* / Down home music: *Jangeaux, Rufus*
CD _____ **CDCH 288**
Ace / Feb '90 / Pinnacle

ANOTHER SENTIMENTAL JOURNEY THROUGH THE 50'S (2CD Set)
Nina never knew: *Brent, Tony* / Undecided: *Beverley Sisters* / When you lose the one you love: *Martin, Ray* / Finger of suspicion points at you: *Jupp, Eric Orchestra* / Only yesterday: *Campbell, Jean* / How wonderful to know: *Carr, Pearl* / Roulette: *Conway, Russ* / Moon is blue: *Cogan, Alma* / I'm yours: *Hughes, David* / Now and forever: *Warren, Alma* / Hold my hand: *Harris, Ronnie* / Sing little birdie: *Carr, Pearl* / Gypsy in my soul: *Boswell, Eve* / So deep my love: *Dean, Alan* / Holiday affair: *Day, Jill* / Hey there: *Hockridge, Edmund* / Donna: *Calvert, Eddie* / It's not for me to say: *Cordell, Frank* / Cinco Robles (Five oaks): *Day, Jill* / Just say I love her: *Hockridge, Edmund* / Long long ago: *Buxton, Sheila & Ronnie Harris/ Ray Martin Orchestra* / Way I feel: *Brent, Tony* / If you love me: *Brennan, Rose* / I may never pass this way again: *Lotis, Dennis* / Give her my love when you meet her: *Day, Jill* / Tammy: *Brown, Jackie* / Meet me on the corner: *Jupp, Eric Orchestra* / Charm: *Buxton, Sheila & Ronnie Harris/Ray Martin Orchestra* / Have you heard: *Brent, Tony* / No one will ever know: *Campbell, Jean* / Surprisingly: *Harris, Ronnie* / Hurry home to me: *Beverley Sisters* / Tear fell: *Day, Jill* / Royal event: *Conway, Russ* / From the time you say goodbye: *Miller, Gary* / My lucky number: *Coronets* / Lonely ballerina: *Lawrence, Lee* / How lucky you are: *Carr, Pearl* / Give me the right to be wrong: *Brent, Tony* / In-between age: *Buxton, Sheila & Ronnie Harris/Ray Martin Orchestra* / Erica: *Calvert, Eddie* / Where can I go without you: *Campbell, Jean* / No one could love you (more than I do): *Carr, Pearl* / Birds and the bees: *Lyon, Barbara* / Make me love you: *Hughes, David* / Unsuspecting heart: *Brown, Fay* / My darling, my darling: *Miller, Gary* / I'd rather take my time: *Anthony, Billie* / Waltzing the blues: *Brent, Tony* / Take me in your arms and hold me: *Carr, Pearl*
CD Set _____ **CDDL 1296**
EMI / Jun '95 / EMI

ANOTHER SHADE OF LOVERS
CD _____ **RNCD 2109**
Rhino / Jun '95 / Grapevine/PolyGram / Jet Star

ANOTHER WORLD DOMINATION SAMPLER
Soft focus am: *Lizard Music* / Carolida: *Latimer* / Life and death: *Low Pop Suicide* / Deal: *Psyclone Rangers* / Scapegoat: *Sky Cries Mary* / Supermonkey: *Stanford Prison Experiment* / Caxton Vs the fourth estate: *Elastic Purejoy* / Drug groove: *Crack Babies*
CD _____ **WDOM 018CD**
World Domination / Jul '95 / Pinnacle / RTM/Disc

ANSWER IS VOL.1, THE (The Great Answer Songs Of The 1950's)
Wild side of life: *Thompson, Hank* / It wasn't God who made honky tonk angels: *Wells, Kitty* / Back street affair: *Pierce, Webb* / Paying for that back street affair: *Wells, Kitty* / There stands the glass: *Pierce, Webb* / Please throw away the glass: *Cody, Betty* / Yesterday's girl: *Thompson, Hank* / I'm yesterday's girl: *Hill, Goldie* / I forgot more than you'll ever know: *Davis Sisters* / I found out more than you'll ever know: *Cody, Betty* / I really want you to know: *Cody, Betty* / I really don't want to know: *Arnold, Eddy* / Don't let the stars get in your eyes: *McDonald, Skeets* / I let the stars get in my eyes: *Hill, Goldie* / Long black veil: *Frizzell, Lefty* / My long black veil: *Wilkin, Marijohn* / I fall to pieces: *Cline, Patsy* / Mexican Joe: *Reeves, Jim* / Marriage of Mexican Joe: *Bradshaw, Carolyn* / Jambalaya: *Williams, Hank* / I'm Yvonne (from the bayou): *Hill, Goldie* / Dear John letter: *Husky, Ferlin* / Forgive me, John: *Husky, Ferlin* / Geisha girl: *Locklin, Hank* / Lost to a geisha girl: *Davis, Skeeter* / Fraulein: *Helms, Bobby* / I'll always be your fraulein: *Wells, Kitty*
CD _____ **BCD 15791**
Bear Family / Nov '94 / Direct / Rollercoaster / Swift

ANSWER IS VOL.2, THE (Great Answer Songs Of The 1950's)
Burning bridges: *Scott, Kjack* / You burned the bridges: *Jean, Bobbie* / Bobby's girl: *Blane, Marcie* / Stay away from Bobbie: *Sherry's Sisters* / Diana: *Anka, Paul* / Remember Diana: *Anka, Paul* / Roses are red: *Vinton, Bobby* / As long as the rose is red: *Darlin, Florraine* / Tell Laura I love her: *Peterson, Ray* / Tell Tommy I need him: *Michaels, Marilyn* / Who's sorry now: *Francis, Connie* / I'm sorry now: *Shields* / Wooden heart: *Dowell, Joe* / You know your hearts not made of wood: *Marie Ann* / Take good care of my baby: *Vee, Bobby* / I'll take good care of you: *Emery, Ralph* / Mr. Lonely: *Vinton, Bobby* / Little Miss Lonely: *Harris, Mike* / Is it true what they say about Barbara: *Regal, Mike* / Honey: *Goldsboro, Bobby* / Honey (I miss you too): *Lewis, Margaret* / Are you lonesome tonight: *Boone, Pat* / Yes I am lonesome tonight: *Carpenter, Thelma* / Fool # 1: *Lee, Brenda* / No you're the fool: *Stewart, Mark* / Who put the bomp: *Mann, Barry* / I put the bomp: *Lymon, Frankie*
CD _____ **BCD 15792**
Bear Family / Jun '95 / Direct / Rollercoaster / Swift

ANSWER IS VOL.3, THE (Great Answer Songs Of The 1960's)
Ballad of a teenage queen: *Cash, Johnny* / Return of the teenage queen: *Tucker, Tommy* / Charlie's shoes: *Walker, Billy* / Answer to Charlie's Shoes: *Mosby, Johnny & Jonie* / He'll have to go: *Reeves, Jim* / He'll have to stay: *Black, Jeanne* / She's got you: *Cline, Patsy* / She can have you: *Judy* / Almost persuaded: *Houston, David* / Almost persuaded: *Harris, Donna* / Detroit city: *Bare, Bobby* / Why don'cha come home: *Ray, Shirley* / Wolverton mountain: *King, Claude* / I'm the girl from Wolverton: *Campbell, Jo Ann* / Walk on by: *Van Dyke, Leroy* / I'll just walk on: *Singleton, Margie* / Ruby, don't take your love to town: *Rogers, Kenny* / Billy, I've got to go to town: *Stevens, Geraldine* / King of the road: *Miller, Roger* / Queen of the house: *Miller, Jody* / 5000 Miles away from home: *Bare, Bobby* / He's coming home: *Taylor, Mary* / Evil on your mind: *Howard, Jan* / Evil off my mind: *Ives, Burl* / Please help me, I'm falling: *Locklin, Hank* / (I can't help you) I'm fallin' too: *Davis, Skeeter* / Good hearted woman: *Nelson, Willie* / Good hearted man: *Cato, Connie* / Only Daddy that'll walk the line: *Shepard, Jean* / Only Mama that'll walk the line: *Shepard, Jean*
CD _____ **BCD 15793**
Bear Family / Nov '94 / Direct / Rollercoaster / Swift

ANSWERS TO THE QUESTION, THE
CD _____ **KUCD 116**
Kufe / Mar '97 / Jet Star

ANTHEMS (2CD/3CD Set)
Love is the icon: *White, Barry* / Saturday: *East 57th Street* / Harder they are: *Sounds Of Blackness* / What you want: *Future Force* / Heaven: *Washington, Sarah* / Ain't nobody's business if I do: *H2O & Billie* / Best things in life are free: *Jackson, Janet* / Voices inside my head: *Police* / Movin': *Mone* / I believe: *Absolute* / Love don't live: *Urban Blues Project* / Bring me love: *Mendez, Andrea* / I can't get no sleep: *Masters At Work* / I like it: *Moraes, Angel* / Can I get a witness: *Nesby, Ann* / We can make it: *Mone* / Ultra flava: *Heller & Farley Project* / Feel like singing: *Taktix* / Stand up: *Love Tribe* / Satisfied: *H2O & Billie* / Everything: *Washington, Sarah* / Giv me luv: *Alcatraz* / Jus' come: *Cool Jack* / I believe: *Sounds Of Blackness* / Puttin' a rush on me: *Future Force*
CD Set _____ **5406542**
CD Set _____ **5406552**
A&M / Dec '96 / PolyGram

ANTHEMS & CEREMONIALS
CD _____ **IMCD 3021**
Image / Feb '96 / Discovery

ANTHEMS VOL.1 (2CD Set)
CD Set _____ **UNCDL 003**
CD Set _____ **UNCD 003**
United Dance / Jan '97 / Alphamagic / Mo's Music Machine / Pinnacle

ANTHEMS VOL.2 1988-1992 (Mixed By Slipmatt/2CD Set)
You got the love: *Source & Candi Staton* / Baby let me love you tonite: *Kariya* / Sueno Latino: *Sueno Latino* / Break 4 love: *Raze* / Rescue me: *Malone, Debbie* / Come get my lovin': *Dionne* / I can dance: *Fast Eddie* / Acid thunder: *Fast Eddie* / Monkey say monkey do: *West Bam* / Airport 89: *Allen, Woody* / Phantom: *Renegade Soundwave* / Humanoid: *Stakker* / Bring forth the guillotine: *Silver Bullet* / 20 to get in: *Shut Up & Dance* / Total confusion: *Homeboy, A Hippy & A Funki-Dred* / Mr. Kirk's nightmare: *4 Hero* / What have you done: *One Tribe & Gem* / Papua New Guinea: *Future Sound Of London* / Dextrous: *Nightmares On Wax* / LFO: *LFO* / Give me the energy: *Pink Noise* / Pure: *GTO* / Kaos: *Dr. Baker* / Sound clash: *Kick Squad* / Go: *Moby* / Cubes: *Modular Expansion* / Just let go: *Petra & Co* / Stratosphere: *Trigger* / Quadrophonia: *Quadrophonia* / Take it easy: *Winkleburger, Cedric* / Bombscare: *2 Bad Mice* / DJ's unite: *Seduction & Fantasy* / Compounded/ Edge 1: *Edge* / Hurt you so: *Johnny L* / Hypnosis: *Psychotropic* / Panic: *Rabbit City*
CD Set _____ **UMCD 04**
United Dance / Jun '97 / Alphamagic / Mo's Music Machine / Pinnacle

ANTHOLOGIE DE LA CHANSON FRANCAISE (14CD/Book Set)
CD Set _____ **983992**
EPM / Jul '96 / ADA / Discovery

ANTHOLOGIE DE LA CHANSON FRANCAISE VOL.1 (From Troubadours To The Pleiades)
CD _____ **983152**
EPM / Jul '96 / ADA / Discovery

ANTHOLOGIE DE LA CHANSON FRANCAISE VOL.2 (French History)
CD _____ **983162**
EPM / Jul '96 / ADA / Discovery

ANTHOLOGIE DE LA CHANSON FRANCAISE VOL.3 (Ballads, Complaintes & Legends)
CD _____ **983172**
EPM / Jul '96 / ADA / Discovery

ANTHOLOGIE DE LA CHANSON FRANCAISE VOL.4 (Rites, Magic & Miracles)
CD _____ **983182**
EPM / Jul '96 / ADA / Discovery

ANTHOLOGIE DE LA CHANSON FRANCAISE VOL.5 (Soldiers, Conscripts & Deserters)
CD _____ **983192**
EPM / Jul '96 / ADA / Discovery

ANTHOLOGIE DE LA CHANSON FRANCAISE VOL.6 (The Sea, Ports & Sailors)
CD _____ **983202**
EPM / Jul '96 / ADA / Discovery

ANTHOLOGIE DE LA CHANSON FRANCAISE VOL.7 (Songs Of Labour & Toil)
CD _____ **983212**
EPM / Jul '96 / ADA / Discovery

ANTHOLOGY OF ARAB-ADALUSIAN MUSIC OF ALGERIA VOL.3
CD _____ **C 560004**
Ocora / Jan '94 / ADA / Harmonia Mundi

ANTHOLOGY OF BALI MUSIC VOL.4 (2CD Set)
CD Set _____ **926032**
BUDA / Apr '96 / Discovery

ANTHOLOGY OF BRETON TRADITIONS - ACCORDIAN
CD _____ **SCM 034CD**
Diffusion Breizh / Apr '95 / ADA

ANTHOLOGY OF BRETON TRADITIONS - BOMBARDE & BINIOU
CD _____ **SCM 032CD**
Diffusion Breizh / Apr '95 / ADA

ANTHOLOGY OF BULGARIAN FOLK MUSIC VOL.2 (Music From Rhodope/ Dobroudja)
CD _____ **LDX 274975**
La Chant Du Monde / Jun '94 / ADA / Harmonia Mundi

ANTHOLOGY OF COLUMBIANA
CD 7992342
Hispavox / Jan '95 / ADA

ANTHOLOGY OF CUBAN MUSIC
Mi son, mi son, mi son: *Miguelito Cuni Con Chappottin* / Trae rumbavana: *Conjunto Rumbavana* / Bacalao con pan: *Irakere* / Unicornio: *Rodriguez, Silvio* / Cantido Celina: *Gonzalez, Celina* / Ese sentimiento que se llama amor: *Alonso, Pacho Y Su Orquestra* / La chica mamey: *Orquesta Ritmo Oriental* / El diapason: *Orquesta Original De Manzanillo* / Que es lo que hace ud: *Gomez, Tito Con Su Conjunto* / De mis recuerdos: *Burke, Elena* / A bayomo en coche: *Son 14* / Por encima del nivel: *Los Van Van*
CD PSCCD 1010
Pure Sounds From Cuba / Feb '95 / Henry Hadaway / THE

ANTHOLOGY OF CUBAN MUSIC
Mi son, mi son, mi son: *Cuni, Miguelito & Chappottin* / Lo que te trae Rumbavana: *Conjuncto Rumbavana* / Bacalao con pan: *Grupo Irakere* / Unicornio: *Rodriguez, Silvio* / Cantido Celina: *Gonzalez, Celina* / Ese sentimiento que se llama amor: *Alonso, Pacho* / La chica mamey: *Orquesta Ritmo Oriental* / El diapason: *Orquesta Original De Manzanillo* / Que es lo que hace ud: *Gomez, Tito & Jorrin* / De mis recuerdos: *Burke, Elena* / A bayomo en coche: *Son 14* / Por encima del nivel: *Orquesta Los Van Van*
CD CD 12542
Music Of The World / May '97 / ADA / Target/BMG

ANTHOLOGY OF FLAMENCO
CD 7992362
Hispavox / Jan '95 / ADA

ANTHOLOGY OF FLAMENCO SONGS
CD Set 7914562
Hispavox / Jan '95 / ADA

ANTHOLOGY OF HOT R 'N' B FROM BATON ROUGE, AN
CD FLYCD 41
Flyright / Oct '91 / Hot Shot / Jazz Music / Wellard

ANTHOLOGY OF INDIAN CLASSICAL MUSIC, AN (A Tribute To Alain Danielou/3CD Set)
CD Set D 88270
Auvidis UNESCO / Aug '97 / Harmonia Mundi

ANTHOLOGY OF MEXICAN SONES VOL.1 (Tierra Caliente, Jalisco Y Rio Verde)
CD CO 101
Corason / Jan '94 / ADA / CM / Direct

ANTHOLOGY OF MEXICAN SONES VOL.1-3
CD Set MT 01/03
Corason / Jan '94 / ADA / CM / Direct

ANTHOLOGY OF MEXICAN SONES VOL.2 (Tixtla, Costa Chica, Istmo Y Veracruz)
CD CO 102
Corason / Jan '94 / ADA / CM / Direct

ANTHOLOGY OF MEXICAN SONES VOL.3, AN (Huasteca)
CD CO 103
Corason / Jan '94 / ADA / CM / Direct

ANTHOLOGY OF MUSIC OF BALI VOL.3 (2CD Set)
CD 926022
BUDA / Jan '97 / Discovery

ANTHOLOGY OF RUMBA
CD 7992642
Hispavox / Jan '95 / ADA

ANTHOLOGY OF SOLEA
CD 7995412
Hispavox / Feb '95 / ADA

ANTHOLOGY OF TARANTA
CD 7992662
Hispavox / Jan '95 / ADA

ANTHOLOGY OF WESTERN AUSTRALIAN TRADITIONAL JAZZ, AN
CD RQCD 1601
Request / Nov '96 / Jazz Music / Wellard

ANTOLOGIA DEL TANGO
CD BM 519
Blue Moon / Jan '97 / Cadillac / Discovery / Greensleeves / Jazz Music / Jet Star / TKO Magnum

ANTOLOGIA DEL TANGO ARGENTINO (4CD Set)
CD Set BMCD 99902
Palladium / Jul '96 / Discovery

ANTONES ANNIVERSARY ANTHOLOGY VOL.2
Chicago bound / Trouble blues / Shake for me / Everything is going to be alright / Natural ball / Sloppy drunk / Moanin' at midnight / Evan's shuffle / Black cat bone / Same thing could happen to you / High Jack
CD ANTCD 0016
Antones / Mar '92 / ADA / Hot Shot

ANTWERPEN 93
CD KK 087CD
KK / Oct '93 / Plastic Head

ANYWAY SINGLES 1992-1993
CD GH 1023CD
Get Hip / Jun '97 / Cargo / Greyhound

APHRODITE PRESENTS FULL FORCE (2CD Set)
Shadow: *Rob & Goldie* / After Dark: *A-Sides & Cool Hand Flex* / Dark coast: *DJ Creation* / Hypnosis: *Smith, Simon Bassline* / Believe: *E-Z Rollers* / Cut Throat Flow: *Optical* / Moments in space: *Nookie* / Covert: *Austin M* / Atmosphere: *DJ Phantasy* / Funk: *D'Cruze* / Acoustic vibes: *Level Vibes* / Oh gosh: *Heavyweight* / Spiral of jazz: *Ricochet* / Barter: *Sling Ting* / Punks: *A-Sides* / Bad ass: *Aphrodite & Mickey Finn* / So much trouble: *Ken, Kenny* / X-Files: *DJ Creation* / Zanzibar: *Smith, Simon Bassline* / Knowledge and wisdom: *DJ Phantasy* / Ghetto: *System 4* / Style from the dark side: *Aphrodite* / This song: *Mental Power* / Beauty and the beast: *Level Vibes* / Destroy: *Austin M* / Psycho: *Ricochet* / Bring dat beat: *Yarn & KO*
CD Set DBM 30344
Death Becomes Me / Aug '97 / Grapevine/ PolyGram / Pinnacle / SRD

APOCALYPSE NOW VOL.1 (2CD Set)
CD Set SPV 08838752
SPV / Oct '96 / Koch / Plastic Head

APOLLO VOL.1
Kinetic: *Golden Girls* / Passage: *Model 500* / Evolution: *Morley, David* / Cloudwalker: *Biosphere* / X-Tal: *Aphex Twin* / Paradise (Part 1): *Atlantis* / I love you: *Electrotete* / Calibration: *Morley, David* / Intelligent universe: *Love Craft* / Mama: *Neuro*
CD AMB 926CD
Apollo / Mar '94 / Vital

APOLLO VOL.2
Number readers: *Subsurfing* / Seal and the hydrophone: *Biosphere* / Skank: *Manna* / Too good to be strange: *Two Sandwiches Sort Of A Lunchbox* / Incidental harmony: *Global Communication* / Sick porter: *u-Ziq* / Agraphobia: *LA Synthesis* / First floor: *Morley, David* / Epique: *Felman, Thomas* / Blue orgasmic light: *Tournesol* / Like old movies: *Word Up* / Patashnik: *Biosphere* / Autophia: *Leiner, Robert* / Nine to five: *Global Communication* / Aural grey: *Meditation YS* / I feel cold inside because of the things you say: *Locust* / Stampede: *Andie* / Stardance: *Morley, David* / Traveller's dream: *Aedena Cycle*
CD Set AMB 5933CD
Apollo / May '95 / Vital

APPALOOSA ALL STARS
CD APCD 095
Appaloosa / Nov '95 / ADA / Direct / TKO Magnum

APPOINTMENT WITH FEAR
CD CYBERCD 11
Cyber / Aug '94 / Amato Disco / Arabesque / Plastic Head

APPROACHIMG INCANDESCENCE
CD CANDRCD 8010
Candor / Oct '94 / Else

AQUADELIC TRANCE FLOW
CD CLP 9972
Cleopatra / Apr '97 / Cargo / Greyhound / Plastic Head / RTM/Disc / SRD

AQUARHYTHMS (Greetings From Deepest America)
Experience remix: *Craig, Carl* / Spiritool: *Ether* / Done fukt me: *Aquarian* / Distilled: *Hydroelectric* / Ether's whisper: *Deep Dish* / Hydroelectronics: *Hydroelectric* / Who is the aquarian: *Gigi Galaxy* / Sage: *Phenom* / Deep in the feeling: *Hydronaut* / Hydr: *DJ Joost & Flux*
CD PHONOCD 2
Phono / Feb '97 / Prime / RTM/Disc

AR-TI-FAKTS
CD BONESCD 01
No Bones / Aug '97 / Kudos / Pinnacle

ARAB CLASSICAL MUSIC VOL.1
CD AAA 133
Club Du Disque Arabe / Apr '96 / ADA / Harmonia Mundi

ARAB CLASSICAL MUSIC VOL.2
CD AAA 134
Club Du Disque Arabe / Apr '96 / ADA / Harmonia Mundi

ARAB-ANDUKUSIAN ANTHOLOGY
CD C 560055
Ocora / Oct '94 / ADA / Harmonia Mundi

ARABIAN JAM
CD MHCD 0005
Madhouse / Apr '95 / Nervous

ARCANE
My mother is not the white dove: *Gifford, Alex* / Ginger: *Kennedy, Nigel* / Chinese canon: *Gifford, Alex & Simon Jeffes* / Yodel 3: *Gifford, Alex & Simon Jeffes* / Youth and age: *Gifford, Alex* / Which way out/Esmerelda Pia Fini: *Sheppard, Andy & Nana Vasconcelos* / Thoughts on the departure of a lifelong friend: *Gifford, Alex* / Cage dead (Word version): *Gifford, Alex & Simon Jeffes* / Morecambe Bay: *Gifford, Alex*
CD CDRW 40
Realworld / Oct '94 / EMI

ARCHIVES OF SPACE
CD CLP 0064
Cleopatra / Jul '97 / Cargo / Greyhound / Plastic Head / RTM/Disc / SRD

ARCHIVES OF TURKISH MUSIC VOL.1
CD C 560081
Ocora / Jul '95 / ADA / Harmonia Mundi

ARCHIVES OF TURKISH MUSIC VOL.2 (Historic Recordings 1903-1935)
CD C 560082
Ocora / Jan '96 / ADA / Harmonia Mundi

ARCTIC REFUGE
CD SP 7159CD
Soundings / Aug '96 / ADA / Else

ARE (Panpipe Ensembles From The Solomon Islands)
CD Set LDX 274961/62
La Chant Du Monde / Feb '94 / ADA / Harmonia Mundi

ARE
CD GR 4100CD
Grappa / Nov '95 / ADA

AREA CODE 212
CD CRECD 114
Creation / Nov '91 / 3mv/Vital

ARGENTINE TANGO BANDS IN SPAIN 1927-1941
CD HQCD 88
Harlequin / Nov '96 / Hot Shot / Jazz Music / Swift / Wellard

ARHOOLIE AMERICAN MASTERS VOL.1 (15 Down Home Country Blues Classics)
CD ARHCD 101
Arhoolie / Nov '96 / ADA / Cadillac / Direct

ARHOOLIE AMERICAN MASTERS VOL.2 (15 Down Home Urban Blues Classics)
Pontiac blues: *Williamson, Sonny Boy* / Big Mama's bumble bee: *Thornton, Willie Mae 'Big Mama'* / Cincinnati stomp: *Duskin, 'Big' Joe* / Anna Lee: *Hooker, Earl* / Up and down the avenue: *Musselwhite, Charley* / Been around the world: *Littlejohn, Johnny* / Wine-o-baby boogie: *Turner, 'Big' Joe & Pete Johnson* / I know that's right: *Webster, Katie* / Raven: *Shariff, Omar* / You think I'm your good thing: *Houston, Bee Bee* / Going back to the country: *Bonner, Weldon 'Juke Boy'* / Ups and downs: *Robinson, L.C. 'Good Rockin'* / Atlanta bounce: *Piano Red* / Wild wild woman: *Young, Johnny* / Gibson Creek shuffle: *Ford, Charles Band*
CD ARHCD 102
Arhoolie / Nov '96 / ADA / Cadillac / Direct

ARHOOLIE AMERICAN MASTERS VOL.3 (15 Louisiana Cajun Classics)
Le jig Francais: *Beausoleil* / Chere te mon: *Abshire, Nathan* / Port Arthur blues: *Fruge, Wade* / J'ai passe devant ta porte: *Balfa, Dewey & Marc Savoy/D.L. Menard* / Fiddle stomp: *Read, Wallis 'Cheese'* / Chicot two step: *California Cajun Orchestra* / Poor hobo: *Choates, Harry* / Jolie blonde: *Hackberry Ramblers* / Two step d'amede: *Savoy-Doucet Cajun Band* / Bernadette: *Fontenot, Canray* / Bosco stomp: *Pitre, Austin* / La robe: *Magnolia Sisters* / Basile breakdown: *Balfa, Dewey & Nathan Abshire* / Grand tasso: *Doucet, Michael* / Flames de'enfer: *Falcon, Joseph*
CD ARHCD 103
Arhoolie / Nov '96 / ADA / Cadillac / Direct

ARHOOLIE AMERICAN MASTERS VOL.4 (15 Tex Mex Conjunto Classics)
Ay te dejo en San Antonio: *Jimenez, Flaco* / Connie: *Conjunto Bernal* / Cuando se pierde le Madre: *Mendoza, Lydia* / Cada vez que cae la tarde: *Jimenez, Santiago Jr.* / Zulema: *Jimenez, Don Santiago* / Alejamiento y regreso: *Los Pavos Reales* / Atotonilco: *De La Rosa, Tony* / El canoero: *Longoria, Valerio* / Corrido de Cesar Chavez: *Los Pinguinos Del Norte* / Pasos cortos: *Lopez, Juan* / No me estorbes: *Zimmerle, Fred Rio San Antonio* / Luzita: *Martinez, Narciso* / El Mexicano-Americano: *Los Cenzontles* / Hazme caso: *Jordan, Steve* / Negra traicion: *Jimenez, Flaco*
CD ARHCD 104
Arhoolie / Nov '96 / ADA / Cadillac / Direct

ARHOOLIE AMERICAN MASTERS VOL.5 (15 Louisiana Zydeco Classics)
Zydeco sont pas sale: *Chenier, Clifton* / Lafayette special: *Sam Brothers 5* / Rag around your head: *Delafose, John* / Old time zydeco: *Sam, Ambrose* / I'm coming home: *Chenier, C.J.* / Les blues du voyager: *Ardoin, Boisec* / Tante na na: *Preston Frank's Swallow Band* / I'm on a wonder: *Chenier, Clifton* / Cofair: *Ardoin, Lawrence* / Aimez moi ce soir: *Ardoin, Amade* / Oh negresse: *Delafose, John* / Lafayette zydeco: *King, Peter & Lester Herbert* / Bee de la manche: *Fontenot, Canray* / She's my woman: *Chenier, C.J.* / Je me reveiller le matin: *Chenier, Clifton*
CD ARHCD 105
Arhoolie / May '97 / ADA / Cadillac / Direct

ARHOOLIE AMERICAN MASTERS VOL.6 (15 Regional Music Classics Of Mexico)
La chileca: *Conjunto Alma De Apatzingan* / Bala perdida: *Los Cenzontles* / La leva: *Los Caimanes* / No compro amores: *Mariachi Los Gavilanes De Oakland* / Mi texana: *Los Pinguinos Del Norte* / La guacamaya: *Conjunto alma jarocha* / El gustito: *Los Caporales De Panuco* / No es culpa mia: *Mendoza, Lydia* / La mariquita: *Mariachi De La Sierra Del Nayer* / Noes culpa mia: *Mendoza, Lydia* / Corrido de andres lopez: *Mariachi Tapatio De Jose Marmolejo* / La petenera: *Los Caimanes* / La peineta: *Los Campesinos De Michocan* / Tristeza de quertert: *Silva, Chelo* / El tilingolingo: *Conjunto alma jarocha*
CD ARHCD 106
Arhoolie / May '97 / ADA / Cadillac / Direct

ARHOOLIE AMERICAN MASTERS VOL.7 (15 World Music Classics)
Manana me voy: *Conjunto Los Amigos Del ANde* / Zmirneikos balos: *Papagika, Marika* / La tinajita: *Cuesta, Ivan* / Acuerdate bien, chaleco: *Sexteto Munamar* / El caballito: *Los Caimanes* / Di zilberne khasene: *Klezmorim* / Kozaczka szumka: *Swystum, Theodore J.* / Eldest of all: *Damessae, Seleshe* / Poor but ambitious: *Houdini, Wilmouth* / Medley of hulas: *Kalamas Quartette* / I bid you goodnight: *Spence, Joseph* / Icek w kolomej: *Orkiestra Majkuta* / Amnatine amantine: *Stellio & Son Orchestre Creole* / Irrarra hayanh gurigiya: *Chatuye* / Chareiti kaharwa: *Aziz Herawi*
CD ARHCD 107
Arhoolie / May '97 / ADA / Cadillac / Direct

ARHOOLIE AMERICAN MASTERS VOL.8 (15 Piano Blues & Boogie Classics)
Dollar Bill Boogie: *Duskin, 'Big' Joe* / Have you ever been out in the country: *Dee, Mercy* / Whistling Alex Moore's blues: *Moore, Alex* / Moaning and groaning: *Young, Johnny* / Katie's boogie woogie: *Young, Johnny* / Cruel hearted woman: *Smith, Thunder* / Ma grinder: *Shaw, Robert* / Why did you go last night: *Chenier, Clifton* / Pinetop's boogie woogie: *Robinson, L.C.* / San Francisco can be such a lonely town: *Sharriff, Imam Omar* / Rocket boogie 88: *Johnson, Pete* / Sugar hill: *White, Bukka* / You ain't got a chance: *Piano Red* / Cold chills: *Piano Red* / On the spot boogie: *Musselwhite, Charley*
CD ARHCD 108
Arhoolie / May '97 / ADA / Cadillac / Direct

ARIWA 12TH ANNIVERSARY ALBUM, THE
Together we're beautiful: *Cadogan, Susan* / Country living: *Cross, Sandra* / If I gave my heart to you: *McLean, John* / Proud of Mandela: *Macka B* / Daydreaming: *Brown, Jocelyn & Robotiks* / True born african: *U-Roy & Sister Audrey* / Show some love: *Thompson, Carroll* / Runaround girl: *Mclean, John & Dego Ranks* / Don't drink too much: *Macka B* / Creator: *Aisha* / Lonely/Love on a mountain top: *Stone, Davina & Ranking Ann* / True true loving: *Aquizim* / Stylers: *Delena* / Ganga smuggling: *Mother Nature* / Six million dub: *Mad Professor/Mafia/Fluxy*
CD ARICD 067
Ariwa Sounds / Nov '92 / Jet Star / SRD

ARIWA HITS '89
I'm in love with a dreadlock: *Kofi* / At the dance: *Simmons, Leroy* / Don't sell your body: *Macka B* / You'll never get to heaven (If you break my heart): *Annette B* / Let's make a baby: *Tajah, Paulette* / Midnight train to Georgia: *McLean, John* / Stop chat: *Lorna G.* / On my mind: *Intense* / Best friend's man: *Cross, Sandra* / Sheba's verandah: *King, Allan*
CD ARICD 050
Ariwa Sounds / Oct '89 / Jet Star / SRD

ARMENIAN FOLK MUSIC
CD SOW 90126
Sounds Of The World / Sep '94 / Target/ BMG

ARMY, THE NAVY & THE AIR FORCE, THE
Army, Navy and Airforce: *Central Band of The Royal Air Force* / Royal Air Force march past: *Central Band of The Royal Air Force* / Aces high: *Central Band of The Royal Air Force* / Battle of Britain: *Central Band of The Royal Air Force* / Evening hymn: *Central Band of The Royal Air Force* / Last post: *Central Band of The Royal Air Force* / Sunset: *Central Band of The Royal Air Force* / British Grenadiers: *Band Of The Grenadier Guards* / Old comrades: *Band Of The Grenadier Guards* / Liberty bell: *Band Of The Grenadier Guards* / Scipio march: *Band Of The Grenadier Guards* / Life on the ocean wave: *Royal Marines* / National emblem: *Royal Marines* / Sailing: *Royal Marines* / Heart of oak: *Royal Marines* / Les Huguenots: *Bandsmen From Grenadier Guards* / Radetsky march: *Bandsmen From Grenadier Guards* / Trumpet tunes: *Bandsmen From Grenadier Guards* / Amazing grace: *Regimental Band, Pipes & Drums of Royal Scots Dragoon Band* / Holyrood: *Regimental Band, Pipes & Drums of Royal Scots Dragoon Band* / Flower of Scotland: *Regimental Band, Pipes & Drums of Royal Scots Dragoon Band* / Flowers of the forest: *Regimental Band, Pipes & Drums of Royal Scots Dragoon Band*
CD CDPMFP 6131
Music For Pleasure / Sep '94 / EMI

ARNHEM (A Musical Tribute)
CD ODFRS 1002
Fragile / Sep '94 / Grapevine/PolyGram

ARNHEM LAND (Aboriginal Songs & Dances)
CD _______ CDLRH 288
Knock On Wood / Jun '97 / Discovery

AROUND THE DAY IN 80 WORLDS
CD _______ SSR 130
SSR / Feb '95 / Amato Disco / Grapevine/ PolyGram / Prime / RTM/Disc

AROUND THE WORLD (FOR A SONG)
CD _______ RCD 00217
Rykodisc / Sep '91 / ADA / Vital

ART OF FLAMENCO VOL.12, THE (El Cante En Cordoba)
CD _______ MAN 4885
Mandala / Dec '96 / ADA / Harmonia Mundi / Mandala

ART OF FLAMENCO VOL.13, THE (Nostalgia)
CD _______ MAN 4890
Mandala / Feb '97 / ADA / Harmonia Mundi / Mandala

ART OF FLAMENCO VOL.14, THE (After The War)
CD _______ MAN 4893
Mandala / Feb '97 / ADA / Harmonia Mundi / Mandala

ART OF FLAMENCO VOL.2, THE
CD _______ MAN 4878CD
Mandala / Aug '96 / ADA / Harmonia Mundi / Mandala

ART OF FLAMENCO VOL.9, THE (El Cante En Sevilla)
CD _______ MAN 4868
Mandala / Feb '96 / ADA / Harmonia Mundi / Mandala

ART OF FLAMENCO, THE
Jaleo / Solea / Tanguillo / Solo guitarra / Tangos / Nuevo flamenco / Alegrias / Buleria / Siguiriyas / Buleria rancheros / Fandango de huelva / Cantinas / Martinetes / Sevillana
CD _______ 893002
Emocion / May '94 / New Note/Pinnacle

ART OF FRANCE
CD _______ PIAS 343000212CD
Play It Again Sam / Sep '96 / Discovery / Plastic Head / Vital

ART OF HARP, THE
Wind: *Windharp* / Boy in the bush: *Hambly, Grainne* / Kid on the mountain: *Hambly, Grainne* / Kelefa: *Jobarteh, Malamini* / Coqueta / Tina Ye: *Naguru Adungu Troupe* / Berceuse: *Nogues, Kristen* / Prelude: *Mowery, Cynthia* / Kerzhadenn: *Nogues, Kristen* / Vers la source dans le bois: *Mowery, Cynthia* / Nigra sum: *Kirchner, Almut* / Blue diamonds: *Krimmel, Margot & Mark Miller* / Diatta Dinke: *Jobarteh, Malamini* / Dance with me: *Henson-Conant, Deborah* / Ambhan na leabhor/The bucks of Oranmore: *Hambly, Grainne* / Water is wide: *Krimmel, Margot* / Oro ma wangini bimu ubombo: *Naguru Adungu Troupe*
CD _______ R 272496
Earthbeat / Nov '96 / ADA / Direct

ART OF HUKWE ABI ZAWOSE
CD _______ VICG 50112
JVC World Library / Mar '96 / ADA / CM / Direct

ART OF LANDSCAPE VOL.1
CD _______ ALC 11CD
Art Of Landscape / Aug '92 / Sony

ART OF LANDSCAPE VOL.2
CD _______ ALC 12CD
Art Of Landscape / Aug '92 / Sony

ART OF THE DOTAR, THE (Music From Uzbekistan)
CD _______ C 560111
Ocora / Aug '97 / ADA / Harmonia Mundi

ART OF THE FINNISH KANTELE
CD _______ EUCD 1342
ARC / Apr '96 / ADA / ARC Music

ARTCORE VOL.1 - AMBIENT JUNGLE
Greater love: *Soundman & Don Lloydie* / Living for the future: *Omni Trio* / We enter: *Alladin* / Tranquility: *Reynolds, Austin* / Jazz note: *DJ Krust* / Jazz juice: *Jazz Juice* / Currents: *Sounds Of Life* / Sweet dreams: *DJ Crysti* / Soothe my soul: *Justice* / Dance of the saroes: *Rogue Unit* / Atmosphere: *DJ Phantasy* / Sparkling: *Little Matt* / Amenity: *Link* / Phat and phuturistic: *Little Matt* / Inhabitants of pandemonium: *Spirits From An Urban Jungle* / Deep in the jungle: *Amazon II* / Second heaven: *Atlas* / Angels in dub: *Code Blue* / Natural high: *Chaos & Julia Set*
CD _______ REACTCD 059
React / Apr '95 / Arabesque / Prime / Vital

ARTCORE VOL.2 - THE ART OF DRUM 'N' BASS
Circles: *Adam F* / I'll fly away: *Ballistic Brothers* / Total control: *Foulplay* / Sleepless: *Optical* / Drums '95: *DJ Doc Scott* / Mutante remix: *T-Power* / I wanted it more & more: *Aphrodite* / Lush life: *J-Majik* / Find me: *Skanna* / Another dream world: *Nemeton* / Three days: *Eugenix* / Can't deal with this: *Cool Breeze* / Enchanted: *Adam F* / London nights: *Dominion* / Cab Colombie: *Arteq* / Break it down: *Atomic Dog* / Fast & loose: *Bliss 'n' Tumble*
CD _______ REACTCD 075
CD _______ REACTCDX 075
React / Apr '96 / Arabesque / Prime / Vital

ARTCORE VOL.3 - EXPRESSIONS IN DRUM 'N' BASS (2CD Set - Mixed By Peshay)
Stretch: *Ishii, Ken* / F jam: *Adam F* / Journey: *Bliss 'n' Tumble* / Milk: *Garbage* / Electric soul: *Icon* / Reincarnation: *DJ Die* / Skylab: *Ed Rush* / On the nile: *Peshay* / Sea: *St. Etienne* / Expressions: *Wallace, Dave* / Motions: *Intense* / Pulse: *Zed* / Ave Maria: *A Sides & Nathan Haines* / Crossing part 2 (words): *Underwolves* / Bear: *Danny Breaks* / Solar glide: *Spirit* / Death by sax: *Tribe zero 2* / Shadow boxing: *Doc Scott* / Mysterious people: *Nookie & Larry Heard* / Homeland, xpressive journey: *Wayward Mind*
CD _______ REACTCDX 099
CD Set _______ REACTCD 099
React / Mar '97 / Arabesque / Prime / Vital

ARTE FLAMENCO
CD _______ MAN 4873CD
Mandala / Apr '96 / ADA / Harmonia Mundi / Mandala

ARTE FLAMENCO VOL.1
CD _______ MAN 4828
Mandala / May '94 / ADA / Harmonia Mundi / Mandala

ARTE FLAMENCO VOL.2
CD _______ MAN 4829
Mandala / May '94 / ADA / Harmonia Mundi / Mandala

ARTE FLAMENCO VOL.3
CD _______ MAN 4832
Mandala / May '94 / ADA / Harmonia Mundi / Mandala

ARTIFICIAL INTELLIGENCE
CD _______ WARPCD 6
Warp / Apr '96 / Prime / RTM/Disc

ARTISTRY IN JAZZ (Black Lion Jazz Sampler)
CD _______ BLCD 760100
Black Lion / '88 / Cadillac / Jazz Music / Koch / Wellard

ARTISTS FOR THE ENVIRONMENT
CD _______ 0029292
Edel / Oct '95 / Pinnacle

AS SEEN ON TV
CD _______ SPARE 001
Spare Me / May '97 / Cargo

AS TIME GOES BY (2CD Set)
Lili Marlene: *Anderson, Lale* / Moonlight serenade: *Miller, Glenn* / As time goes by: *Vallee, Rudy* / At the woodchopper's ball: *Herman, Woody* / Swinging on a star: *Crosby, Bing* / I've heard that song before: *James, Harry* / You'll never know: *Haymes, Dick* / Don't fence me in: *Andrews Sisters & Bing Crosby* / It's a lovely day tomorrow: *Lynn, Vera* / For me and my gal: *Garland, Judy & Gene Kelly* / I don't want to set the world on fire: *Geraldo* / Paper doll: *Mills Brothers* / Don't get around much anymore: *Ellington, Duke* / All or nothing at all: *Sinatra, Frank* / Tangerine: *Dorsey, Jimmy* / I don't want to walk without you: *Rhodes, Betty Jane* / Whispering grass: *Ink Spots* / Blues in the night: *Shore, Dinah* / Stardust: *Shaw, Artie* / Over the rainbow: *Garland, Judy* / You made me love you: *James, Harry* / Last time I saw Paris: *Martin, Tony* / In the mood: *Miller, Glenn* / Why don't you do right: *Lee, Peggy* / White cliffs of Dover: *Lynn, Vera* / Rum and coca cola: *Andrews Sisters* / Chattanooga choo choo: *Miller, Glenn* / I'll walk alone: *Shore, Dinah* / Waiter and the porter and the upstairs maid: *Martin, Mary & Jack Teagarden* / Yours: *Lynn, Vera* / Night and day: *Sinatra, Frank* / Begin the beguine: *Shaw, Artie* / Nightingale sang in Berkeley Square: *Shelton, Anne* / You are my sunshine: *Roy, Harry* / If I didn't care: *Ink Spots* / I know why: *Miller, Glenn* / Boogie woogie bugle boy: *Andrews Sisters* / I'll be seeing you: *Shelton, Anne* / Frenesi: *Shaw, Artie* / Moonlight becomes you: *Crosby, Bing* / Little on the lonely side: *Geraldo* / Long ago and far away: *Haymes, Dick & Helen Forrest* / Take the 'A' train: *Ellington, Duke* / You always hurt the one you love: *Mills Brothers* / Cow cow boogie: *Fitzgerald, Ella & Ink Spots* / I'll never smile again: *Sinatra, Frank* / When the lights go on again: *Monroe, Vaughan* / If I had my way: *Crosby, Bing* / I've got a gal in Kalamazoo: *Miller, Glenn* / We'll meet again: *Lynn, Vera*
CD Set _______ CPCD 8105
Charly / Jun '95 / Koch

AS TIME GOES BY
CD _______ MACCD 327
Autograph / Aug '96 / BMG

ASCENSION COLLECTION, THE
It's all we know: *OBX* / Another kind of find: *Red Red Groovy* / That's how my heart sings: *Dial 4 FX* / Freak you: *Euphoria* / Nebula: *Positive Science* / Soul feel free: *Positive Science* / Caspar ound: *House* / Eternal prayer: *OBX* / Tangled in my thoughts: *RHC & Plavka* / Maximum motion: *Plavka*
CD _______ ASCCD 1
Ascension / Apr '95 / 3mv/Sony

ASHTRAY HEART
CD _______ SRCD 1
Sorted / May '97 / Cargo

ASIA CLASSICS VOL.1 (Dance Raja Dance)
Aatavu chanda / Naane maharaja / Aase hechchagide / Prema rudaayade / Neeva nana / ellellu preethi / Ba ennalu / I love you, Yenthare / Dheem thana thana nana / Nalleya savimathe / Yerida gunginalli
CD _______ 7599268472
Luaka Bop / Jun '92 / Warner Music

ASIAN THEATRE AND DANCE (Cambodia/India/Indonesia/3CD Set)
CD Set _______ C 570303
Ocora / Mar '97 / ADA / Harmonia Mundi

ASSASSINATION
Assassination: *Dixie Nightingales* / Safety zone: *Dixie Nightingales* / There's not a friend: *Dixie Nightingales* / Hush, hush: *Dixie Nightingales* / Swing low, sweet chariot: *Revelators* / Lady called Mother: *Revelators* / In the middle of the air: *Revelators* / God is using me: *Harps Of Melody* / I'll go, send me: *Harps Of Melody* / Walk in Jerusalem: *Harps Of Melody* / Press on: *Gospel Writers* / Blind Barnabus: *Gospel Writers* / Wonderful Jesus: *Gospel Writers* / What do you know about Jesus: *Gospel Writers*
CD _______ CDZ 2019
Zu Zazz / May '96 / Rollercoaster

ASSEMBLAGE VOL.1
CD _______ XVA 001
Extreme / Feb '95 / Vital/SAM

ASSEMBLAGE VOL.2
CD _______ XVA 002
Extreme / Jun '96 / Vital/SAM

ASSORTMENT, AN
Surfer Baby: *Blind Mr. Jones* / Hey: *Blind Mr. Jones* / Brad: *Tse Tse Fly* / On purpose: *Tse Tse Fly* / PDF: *Prolapse* / Screws: *Prolapse* / Jack: *Monochrome Set* / House of God: *Monochrome Set* / Humtone 4: *Fisher, Morgan* / Humtone 4 (remix): *Fisher, Morgan*
CD _______ CDMRED 107
Cherry Red / Feb '94 / Pinnacle

ASSUMPTION OF DABRA GANNAT, THE (Ethiopian Orthodox Church of Jerusalem)
CD Set _______ C 560027/28
Ocora / Mar '92 / ADA / Harmonia Mundi

ASTURIES - CAMIN DE COMPOSTELLA
CD _______ FA 8738CD
Fono Astur / Nov '96 / ADA

ASURINI (Music From Brazil)
CD _______ C 560084
Ocora / Dec '95 / ADA / Harmonia Mundi

AT DEATH'S DOOR VOL.2
Martyr: *Fear Factory* / Stench of paradise burning: *Disincarnate* / Prelude to repulsion: *Suffocation* / Uriboric forms: *Cynic* / Hideous infirmity: *Gorguts* / Illusion of freedom: *Sorrow* / God of thunder: *Death* / Piece by piece: *Malevolent Creation* / Unspoken names: *Atrocity* / Padre nuestro: *Brujeria* / No forgiveness: *Immolation* / Sucked inside: *Skin Chamber*
CD _______ RR 91052
Roadrunner / Jan '94 / PolyGram

AT THE COURT OF CHERA KING
CD _______ WLACS 34CD
Waterlilly Acoustics / Nov '95 / ADA

AT THE DARKTOWN STRUTTER'S BALL
CD Set _______ DCD 8000
Disky / Jan '95 / Disky / THE

ATHLETICO COMPILATION VOL.1
CD _______ JAZIDCD 131
Acid Jazz / Nov '95 / Disc

ATLANTA GOSPEL 1925-1931
CD _______ DOCD 5485
Document / Nov '96 / ADA / Hot Shot / Jazz Music

ATLANTIC 252 HIT LIST
If you love me: *Brownstone* / Sweet dreams (are made of this): *Eurythmics* / Girl like you: *Collins, Edwyn* / Can't stay away from you: *Estefan, Gloria* / Dreams: *Gabrielle* / Sing hallelujah: *Dr. Alban* / Little time: *Beautiful South* / I can see clearly now: *Cliff, Jimmy* / You gotta be: *Des'ree* / Stay: *Eternal* / Sadness: *Enigma* / Open your heart: *M-People* / Why: *Lennox, Annie* / It must have been love: *Roxette* / Thinking about your love: *Thomas, Kenny* / Things can only get better: *D:Ream* / I want to know what love is: *Foreigner* / Another night: *Real McCoy* / Don't be a stranger: *Carroll, Dina* / Sweat (a la la la la long): *Inner Circle*
CD _______ SONYTV 4CD
Sony TV / Aug '95 / Sony

ATLANTIC BLUES MASTERS
Ain't nobody's business if I do: *Witherspoon, Jimmy* / T-bone blues: *Walker, T-Bone* / Laundromat blues: *King, Albert* / Rollin' and tumblin': *Leroy, Baby Face* / All your love (I miss loving): *Rush, Otis* / Little by little: *Wells, Junior* / Evening sun: *Shines, Johnny* / Short haired woman: *Hopkins, Lightnin'* / Freeze: *Collins, Albert* / Stumble: *King, Freddie* / Flood down in Texas: *Vaughan, Stevie Ray* / Sugar coated love: *Lazy Lester* / Steady: *McCain, Jerry* / Got love if you want it: *Harpo, Slim* / Shake, rattle and roll: *Turner, 'Big' Joe* / Hoy hoy: *Jones, Little Johnny* / Hello little boy: *Brown, Ruth* / I'm a woman: *Taylor, Koko* / Master charge: *Collins, Albert* / Mojo boogie: *Winter, Johnny* / Feelin' good: *Parker, Junior & The Blue Flames* / Bear cat: *Thomas, Rufus*
CD _______ 8122713862
Atlantic / Mar '94 / Warner Music

ATLANTIC BLUES: CHICAGO
Chicago blues: *Jones, Johnny* / Hoy hoy: *Jones, Johnny* / Play on little girl: *Walker, T-Bone* / T-Bone blues special: *Walker, T-Bone* / Poor man's plea: *Guy, Buddy & Junior Wells* / My baby she left me: *Guy, Buddy & Junior Wells* / Stop: *Guy, Buddy & Junior Wells* / I wonder why: *King, Freddie* / Play it cool: *King, Freddie* / Woke up this morning: *King, Freddie* / Gambler's blues: *Rush, Otis* / Feel so bad: *Rush, Otis* / Reap what you sow / Highway 49 / Honey bee: *Waters, Muddy* / Wang dang doodle: *Taylor, Koko* / Dust my broom: *Shines, Johnny* / Going down: *King, Freddie* / Please send me someone to love: *Allison, Luther* / Walking the dog: *Allison, Luther* / Feel so good: *Hutto, J.B.*
CD _______ 7567816972
Atlantic / Jan '97 / Warner Music

ATLANTIC BLUES: GUITAR
Broke down engine: *McTell, 'Blind' Willie* / Shake 'em on down: *McDowell, 'Mississippi' Fred* / My baby don't love me: *Hooker, John Lee* / Tall pretty woman: *McGhee, Stick* / Blues rock: *Brown, Texas Johnny* / There goes the blues: *Brown, Texas Johnny* / Bongo boogie: *Brown, Texas Johnny* / Two bones and a pick: *Walker, T-Bone* / Mean ol' world: *Walker, T-Bone* / Let me know: *Norris, Chuck* / It hurts to love someone: *Guitar Slim* / Down through the years: *Guitar Slim* / Okie dokie stomp: *Dupree, Cornell* / Blues nocturne: *Dupree, Cornell* / TV mama: *Turner, 'Big' Joe* / Reconsider baby: *King, Al* / Midnight midnight: *Baker, McHouston 'Mickey'* / I smell trouble: *Turner, Ike & Tina* / Why I sing the blues: *King, Albert* / Crosscut saw: *King, Albert* / Angels of mercy: *King, Albert* / Can't be satisfied: *Hammond, John* / Flood down in Texas: *Vaughan, Stevie Ray*
CD _______ 7567816952
Atlantic / Jan '97 / Warner Music

ATLANTIC BLUES: PIANO
Yancey special: *Yancey, Jimmy* / Talkin' boogie: *Montgomery, Little Brother* / Mournful blues: *Yancey, Jimmy* / Farish street jive: *Montgomery, Little Brother* / Salute to pinetop: *Yancey, Jimmy* / Vicksburg blues: *Montgomery, Little Brother* / Shave 'em dry: *Yancey, Jimmy* / Frankie and Johnny: *Walker, T-Bone* / T B blues: *Walker, T-Bone* / Strollin': *Walker, T-Bone* / Boogie woogie: *Professor Longhair* / Tipitina: *Professor Longhair* / Blue sender: *Walls, Van* / After midnight: *Walls, Van* / Roll 'em Pete: *Turner, 'Big' Joe* / 'Fore day rider: *McShann, Jay* / Cherry red: *Turner, 'Big' Joe* / My chile: *McShann, Jay* / Cow cow blues: *Atlantic* / Albert's blues: *Lewis, Meade 'Lux'* / Honky tonk train blues: *Lewis, Meade 'Lux'* / Ray's blues: *Charles, Ray* / Low society: *Charles, Ray* / Bit of soul: *Charles, Ray* / Hey bartender: *Dixon, Floyd* / Floyd's blues: *Dixon, Floyd* / After hours blues: *Brown, Texas Johnny* / Junco partner: *Jordan, Louis* / I don't know: *Mabon, Willie*
CD _______ 7567816942
Atlantic / Jan '97 / Warner Music

ATLANTIC BLUES: VOCALISTS
You got to know how: *Wallace, Sippie* / Suitcase blues: *Wallace, Sippie* / Mighty tight woman: *Wallace, Sippie* / How long blues: *Witherspoon, Jimmy* / In the evening: *Witherspoon, Jimmy* / Gimme a pigfoot and a bottle of beer / Make me a pallet on the floor: *Yancey, Mama* / St. Louis blues: *Turner, 'Big' Joe* / Oke-she-moke-she-pop: *Turner, 'Big' Joe* / I've got that feeling: *Green, Lil* / Destination love: *Harris, Wynonie* / Tell a whale of a tale: *Harris, Wynonie* / Rain is a bringdown: *Brown, Ruth* / RB blues: *Brown, Ruth* / I don't want to be president: *Mayfield, Percy* / Nothing stays the same: *Mayfield, Percy* / River's invitation: *Taylor, Ted* / Just like a fish: *Phillips, Esther* / Pouring water on a drowning man: *Clay, Otis* / Did you ever love a woman: *Thomas, Rufus* / Baby girl (parts 1 and 2): *Turner, Titus* / Ain't that lovin' you: *Bland, Bobby* / It's my own tears that's being wasted: *Copeland, Johnny* / Cheatin' woman: *Holmes, Eldridge* / I had a dream / Takin' another mans place: *Franklin, Aretha* / It's a hang up baby: *Hill, Z.Z.* / Home ain't home at suppertime: *Hill, Z.Z.*
CD _______ 7567816962
Atlantic / Jan '97 / Warner Music

ATLANTIC GROOVES - THE FUNK 'N' JAZZ EXPERIENCE VOL.1
Rock steady / Captain Buckles / Drunk man / But I was cool / Bishop school / Wild man on the loose / Little ghetto boy / Dealing with hard times / No more / Behold the day / Groovin' time / Right on / Jive Samba / Backlash / Can't git enough / Motherless child / Well I'll be white black / Funky how time can change the meaning of a word
CD _______ 9548327712
Atlantic / Aug '94 / Warner Music

ATLANTIC JAZZ - AVANT GARDE
Black mystery has been revealed / Wednesday night prayer meeting / Eventually / Lonely woman / Cherryco / Countdown / Inflated tear / Nonaah
CD _____ 7817092
Atlantic / Dec '87 / Warner Music

ATLANTIC JAZZ - BEBOP
Our love is here to stay / Evidence / Be bop / Koko / Salt peanuts / Almost like me / Allen's alley (be bop tune)
CD _____ 7817022
Atlantic / Dec '87 / Warner Music

ATLANTIC JAZZ - FUSION
Freedom jazz dance / Beaux JPooboo / Quadrant four / Beneath the earth / Homunculus / Egocentric molecules
CD _____ 7817112
Atlantic / Dec '87 / Warner Music

ATLANTIC JAZZ - INTROSPECTION
Yoruba / Tones for Joan's bones / Forest flower-sunrise / In a silent way / Standing outside / Chega de saudade / Fortune smiles
CD _____ 7817102
Atlantic / Dec '87 / Warner Music

ATLANTIC JAZZ - KANSAS CITY
You're driving me crazy / Lamp is low / Hootie blues / E flat boogie / Confessin' the blues / Jumpin' at the woodside / Until the real thing comes along / Undecided / Evening / Buster's tune / Piney brown blues
CD _____ 7817012
Atlantic / '88 / Warner Music

ATLANTIC JAZZ - MAINSTREAM
I'll be seeing you / Ain't misbehavin' / Stuffy / Django / Daphne / Perdido / Embraceable you / Four brothers / Everything happens to me / Speedy reeds
CD _____ 7817042
Atlantic / '87 / Warner Music

ATLANTIC JAZZ - NEW ORLEANS
Bourbon street parade / Burgundy St. Blues / My bucket's got a hole in it / Cielito lindo / Salty dog / Eh la bas / Maple leaf rag / Joe Avery's blues / Nobody knows the way I feel this morning / Shreveport stomp / Sing on / Shake it and break it / Tiger rag
CD _____ 7817002
Atlantic / '88 / Warner Music

ATLANTIC JAZZ - POST BOP
Lydian M-1 / I can't get started (with you) / Bag's groove / This 'n' that / Giant steps / Sister salvation / White sand / Misty (instrumental version) / Thoroughbred
CD _____ 7817052
Atlantic / Dec '87 / Warner Music

ATLANTIC JAZZ - SOUL
Think / Twist city / How long blues / Comin' home baby / Russell and Eliot / Listen here / With these hands / Compared to what / You're the one / Jive samba / Money in the pocket
CD _____ 7567817082
Atlantic / '88 / Warner Music

ATLANTIC JAZZ - WEST COAST
Sa-frantic / Not really / Paradox / Chermoya / Martians go home / You name it / Tripin' awhile / Topsy / Song is you
CD _____ 7567817032
Atlantic / Feb '94 / Warner Music

ATLANTIC JAZZ GALLERY - FLUTES
Ain't no sunshine / Laugh for Rory / Night of Nisan / Thirteenth floor / Memphis underground / Little girl of mine / Nubian lady / Stay with me / All soul / If you knew / Sombrero Sam / Journey within
CD _____ 8122716372
Atlantic / May '94 / Warner Music

ATLANTIC JAZZ GALLERY - KEYBOARDS
How long blues / Way you look tonight / Evidence / Little girl blue / C minor complex / Genius after hours / Rockin' chair / Sweet Georgia Brown / Catbird seat / Doin' that thing / My one and only love / Everything I love / Straight up and down
CD _____ 8122715962
Atlantic / Feb '94 / Warner Music

ATLANTIC JAZZ GALLERY - LEGENDS VOL.1
Hard times / Compared to what / Whispering grass / Golden striker / Inflated tear / Comin' home baby / Ramblin' / Your mind is on vacation / Sweet sixteen bars / Nubian Lady / Wednesday night prayer meeting
CD _____ 8122712572
Atlantic / Jun '93 / Warner Music

ATLANTIC JAZZ GALLERY - SAXOPHONES
If I loved you / Freedom jazz dance / Willow weep for me / Russell and Eliot / Lorelei's lament / Confirmation / Giant steps / Lonely woman / Forest flower-sunrise / Forest flower-sunset
CD _____ 8122712562
Atlantic / Jun '93 / Warner Music

ATLANTIC JAZZ GALLERY - SAXOPHONES VOL.2
Blues shout / I wish you love / Old rugged cross / Don't get around much anymore / Topsy / Love theme from the Sandpiper / Down in Atlanta / September song / Senor blues / Parker's mood / Mr. PC / Embraceable you
CD _____ 8122717262
Atlantic / Aug '94 / Warner Music

ATLANTIC JAZZ GALLERY - THE BEST OF THE 50'S
Django / All about Ronnie / Martians go home / Evidence / Backwater blues / Cousin Mary / Train and the river / Wee baby blues / Come rain or come shine / You go to my head / Fathead / Pithecanthropus erectus
CD _____ 8122712822
Atlantic / Feb '94 / Warner Music

ATLANTIC JAZZ GALLERY - THE BEST OF THE 60'S VOL.1
Comin' home baby / Equinox / Una muy bonita / Volunteered slavery / In the evening / Stop this world / Groovin' / Summertime / Yesterday / With these hands / Listen here / Ecclusiastics / Sombrero Sam
CD _____ 8122715542
Atlantic / Feb '94 / Warner Music

ATLANTIC JAZZ GALLERY - THE BEST OF THE 60'S VOL.2
Creole love call / Silver cycles / Chained no more / Soul of the village part II / Hey Jude / One note samba / You can count on me to do my part / Dervish dance / Dream weaver / Stardust / Buddy and Lou / Dick's Holler / Eat that chicken / When I fall in love / Bagpipe blues
CD _____ 8122717272
Atlantic / Aug '94 / Warner Music

ATLANTIC JAZZ GALLERY - THE BEST OF THE 70'S
Samia / Come Sunday / Freaks for the festival / Ladies man / Missy / Dedicated to you / Moonchild / In your quiet place / Blues in A minor / Birdland (Vocal) / Yoruba / Egocentric molecules / Funky thide of sings
CD _____ 8122716102
Atlantic / Feb '94 / Warner Music

ATLANTIC JAZZ VOCALS VOL.1 (Voices Cool)
CD _____ 8122717482
Atlantic / Aug '94 / Warner Music

ATLANTIC JAZZ VOCALS VOL.2 (Voices Cool)
CD _____ 8122717842
Atlantic / Oct '94 / Warner Music

ATLANTIC R & B VOL.1 (1947-1952)
Lowe groovin': *Morris, Joe* / That old black magic: *Grimes, Tiny* / Annie Laurie: *Grimes, Tiny* / Midnight special: *Grimes, Tiny* / Applejack: *Morris, Joe* / Drinkin' wine spo-dee-o-dee: *McGhee, Stick* / Coleslaw: *Culley, Frank* / So long: *Brown, Ruth* / I'll get along somehow: *Brown, Ruth* / Hey little girl: *Professor Longhair* / Mardi Gras in New Orleans: *Professor Longhair* / Tee nah nah: *Van Walls, Harry* / Anytime anyplace anywhere: *Morris, Joe* / Teardrops from my eyes: *Brown, Ruth* / One monkey don't stop no show: *McGhee, Stick* / Don't you know I love you: *Clovers* / Shouldn't I know: *Cardinals* / Chill is on: *Turner, 'Big' Joe* / Chains of love: *Turner, 'Big' Joe* / Fool, fool, fool: *Clovers* / One mint julep: *Clovers* / Wheel of fortune: *Cardinals* / Sweet sixteen: *Turner, 'Big' Joe* / 5-10-15 hours: *Brown, Ruth* / Ting a ling: *Clovers* / Gator's groove: *Jackson, Willis* / Daddy Daddy: *Brown, Ruth* / Midnight hour: *Charles, Ray*
CD _____ 7812932
Atlantic / Feb '95 / Warner Music

ATLANTIC R & B VOL.2 (1952-1955)
Beggar for your kisses: *Diamonds* / Mama he treats your daughter mean: *Brown, Ruth* / Good lovin': *Clovers* / Wild wild young men: *Brown, Ruth* / Mess around: *Charles, Ray* / Hush hush: *Turner, 'Big' Joe* / Soul on fire / Money honey: *McPhatter, Clyde & The Drifters* / Such a night: *McPhatter, Clyde & The Drifters* / Tipitina: *Professor Longhair* / White Christmas: *McPhatter, Clyde & The Drifters* / Honey love: *McPhatter, Clyde* / What'cha gonna do: *McPhatter, Clyde* / Shake, rattle and roll: *Turner, 'Big' Joe* / Sh-boom: *Chords* / Jam up: *Ridgley, Tommy* / Tomorrow night / Tweedlee dee / I got a woman: *Charles, Ray* / Door is still open: *Cardinals* / Flip flop and fly: *Turner, 'Big' Joe* / Fool for you: *Charles, Ray* / This little girl of mine: *Charles, Ray* / Play it fair / Adorable: *Drifters* / Smoky Joe's cafe: *Robins*
CD _____ 7812942
Atlantic / Feb '95 / Warner Music

ATLANTIC R & B VOL.3 (1955-1958)
Ruby baby: *Drifters* / In paradise: *Cookies* / Chicken and the hawk: *Turner, 'Big' Joe* / Devil or angel: *Clovers* / Drown in my own tears: *Charles, Ray* / Hallelujah, I love her so: *Charles, Ray* / Jim Dandy: *Baker, LaVern* / Down in Mexico: *Coasters* / Corine Corina: *Turner, 'Big' Joe* / Treasure of love: *McPhatter, Clyde* / Love love love: *Clovers* / It's too late: *Willis, Chuck* / Lonely avenue: *Charles, Ray* / Since I met you baby: *Hunter, Lloyd Serenaders* / Lucky lips: *Brown, Ruth* / Without love: *McPhatter, Clyde* / Fools fall in love: *Drifters* / Midnight special train: *Turner, 'Big' Joe* / Empty arms: *Hunter, Ivory Joe* / CC rider: *Willis, Chuck* / Betty and Dupree: *Bobbettes* / What am I living for: *Willis, Chuck* / Hang up my rock 'n' roll shoes: *Willis, Chuck* / Yakety yak: *Coasters* / Lover's question: *McPhatter, Clyde* / I cried a tear: *Charles, Ray* / Right time: *Charles, Ray* / What'd I say (parts 1 and 2): *Charles, Ray* / There goes my baby: *Drifters*
CD _____ 7812952
Atlantic / Feb '95 / Warner Music

ATLANTIC R & B VOL.4 (1958-1962)
Along came Jones: *Coasters* / Let the good times roll: *Charles, Ray* / Poison ivy: *Coasters* / Dance with me: *Drifters* / Just for a thrill: *Charles, Ray* / This magic moment: *Charles, Ray* / Save the last dance for me: *Charles, Ray* / Shopping for clothes: *Coasters* / Spanish Harlem: *King, Ben E.* / Young boy blues: *King, Ben E.* / Stand by me: *King, Ben E.* / Gee whiz: *Thomas, Carla* / Saved / Just out of reach: *Burke, Solomon* / Little Egypt: *Coasters* / Amor: *King, Ben E.* / Last night: *Mar-Keys* / I'm blue (the gong-gong song): *Ikettes* / You don't miss your water: *Bell, William* / I found a love: *Falcons* / Cry to me: *Burke, Solomon* / Don't play that song (You lied): *King, Ben E.* / Green onions: *Booker T & The MG's*
CD _____ 7812962
Atlantic / Feb '95 / Warner Music

ATLANTIC R & B VOL.5 (1962-1966)
Up on the roof: *Drifters* / CC rider / I who have nothing: *King, Ben E.* / If you need me: *Burke, Solomon* / These arms of mine: *Redding, Otis* / Hello stranger: *Lewis, Barbara* / On Broadway: *Drifters* / Just one look: *Troy, Doris* / Do the mashed potato: *Kindricks, Nat & The Swans* / Land of 1000 dances: *Kenner, Chris* / Walking the dog: *Kenner, Chris* / Release me: *Phillips, Esther* / Mercy mercy: *Covay, Don* / Under the boardwalk: *Drifters* / And I love him: *Phillips, Esther* / Hold what you've got: *Tex, Joe* / Mr. Pitiful: *Redding, Otis* / Baby, I'm yours: *Lewis, Barbara* / Teasin' you: *Tee, Willie* / I've been loving you too long: *Redding, Otis* / In the midnight hour: *Pickett, Wilson* / See saw: *Covay, Don* / Respect: *Redding, Otis* / You don't know like I know: *Sam & Dave* / When a man loves a woman: *Sledge, Percy* / Hold on I'm comin': *Sam & Dave* / Cool jerk: *Capitols* / Neighbour, neighbour: *Hughes, Jimmy*
CD _____ 7812972
Atlantic / Feb '95 / Warner Music

ATLANTIC R & B VOL.6 (1966-1969)
Land of 1000 dances: *Pickett, Wilson* / Knock on wood: *Floyd, Eddie* / Try a little tenderness: *Redding, Otis* / Mustang Sally: *Pickett, Wilson* / When something is wrong with my baby: *Sam & Dave* / Sweet soul music: *Conley, Arthur* / Soul man: *Sam & Dave* / I never loved a man (the way I love you): *Franklin, Aretha* / Do right woman, do right man: *Franklin, Aretha* / Show me: *Tex, Joe* / Tramp: *Redding, Otis & Carla Thomas* / Funky Broadway: *Pickett, Wilson* / Hip hug-her: *Booker T & The MG's* / Respect: *Franklin, Aretha* / (You make me feel like) a natural woman: *Franklin, Aretha* / Soul finger: *Bar-Kays* / Baby I love you: *Franklin, Aretha* / Skinny legs and all: *Tex, Joe* / Chain of fools: *Franklin, Aretha* / I'm in love: *Pickett, Wilson* / Memphis soul stew: *King Diamond* / (Sittin' on the) dock of the bay: *Redding, Otis* / Tighten up: *Redding, Otis* / Slip away: *Carter, Clarence* / Think: *Franklin, Aretha* / First time ever I saw your face: *Flack, Roberta* / Take a letter, Maria: *Greaves, R.B.* / Rainy night in Georgia: *Charles, Ray* / Ghetto: *Hathaway, Donny*
CD _____ 7812982
Atlantic / Feb '95 / Warner Music

ATLANTIC R & B VOL.7 (1969-1974)
Turn back the hands of time: *Davis, Walter* / Compared to what: *McCann, Les* / Don't play that song (You lied): *Franklin, Aretha* / Groove me: *Floyd, King* / Patches: *Carter, Clarence* / Funky Nassau (parts 1and2): *Beginning Of The End* / Thin line between love and hate: *Persuaders* / Rock steady: *Franklin, Aretha* / You've got a friend: *Flack, Roberta & Donny Hathaway* / Clean up woman: *Wright, Betty* / Could it be I'm falling in love: *Spinners* / Killing me softly: *Flack, Roberta* / Where is the love: *Flack, Roberta & Donny Hathaway* / I'll be around: *Spinners* / Feel like makin' love: *Flack, Roberta* / Mighty love: *Spinners* / Love won't let me wait: *Harris, Major*
CD _____ 7812992
Atlantic / Feb '95 / Warner Music

ATLANTIC SOUL BALLADS
Try a little tenderness: *Redding, Otis* / I say a little prayer: *Franklin, Aretha* / Save the last dance for me: *Drifters* / I'm in love: *Pickett, Wilson* / Warm and tender love: *Sledge, Percy* / Patches: *Carter, Clarence* / Thin line between love and hate: *Persuaders* / Spanish Harlem: *King, Ben E.* / When something is wrong with my baby: *Sam & Dave* / My girl: *Redding, Otis* / Love won't let me wait: *Harris, Major* / On Broadway: *Drifters* / Baby, I'm yours: *Lewis, Barbara* / Rainy night In Georgia: *Benton, Brook* / Hey Jude: *Pickett, Wilson*
CD _____ 2411362
Atlantic / Jun '88 / Warner Music

ATLANTIC SOUL CLASSICS
Sweet soul music: *Conley, Arthur* / In the midnight hour: *Pickett, Wilson* / Knock on wood: *Floyd, Eddie* / Soul man: *Sam & Dave* / Respect: *Franklin, Aretha* / See saw: *Covay, Don* / Everybody needs somebody to love: *Burke, Solomon* / Soul finger: *Bar-Kays* / Stand by me: *King, Ben E.* / B-A-B-Y: *Thomas, Carla* / Under the boardwalk: *Drifters* / Tramp: *Redding, Otis & Carla Thomas* / Green onions: *Booker T & The MG's* / When a man loves a woman: *Sledge, Percy* / Tribute to a king: *Bell, William* / (Sittin' on the) dock of the bay: *Redding, Otis*
CD _____ 2411382
Atlantic / May '87 / Warner Music

ATLANTIC STORY, THE (2CD Set)
Drinkin' wine spo-dee-o-dee: *McGhee, Stick* / 5-10-15 hours: *Brown, Ruth* / One mint julep: *Clovers* / Shake, rattle and roll: *Turner, 'Big' Joe* / Jim Dandy: *Baker, LaVern* / Lover's question: *McPhatter, Clyde* / What'd I say: *Charles, Ray* / Mack the knife: *Darin, Bobby* / Giant steps: *Coltrane, John* / Poison ivy: *Coasters* / Save the last dance for me: *Drifters* / Stand by me: *King, Ben E.* / Deep purple: *Tempo, Nino & April Stevens* / I got you babe: *Sonny & Cher* / Green onions: *Booker T & The MG's* / Hold on I'm comin': *Sam & Dave* / Knock on wood: *Floyd, Eddie* / When a man loves a woman: *Sledge, Percy* / Got to get you off my mind: *Burke, Solomon* / In the midnight hour: *Pickett, Wilson* / I say a little prayer: *Franklin, Aretha* / Sweet soul music: *Conley, Arthur* / (Sittin' on the) dock of the bay: *Redding, Otis* / Groovin': *Young Rascals* / You keep me hangin' on: *Vanilla Fudge* / In-A-Gadda-Da-Vida: *Iron Butterfly* / For what it's worth: *Buffalo Springfield* / Sweet Jane: *Velvet Underground* / Rock 'n' roll: *Led Zeppelin* / Can't get enough: *Bad Company* / Could it be I'm falling in love: *Detroit Spinners* / Such a night: *Dr. John* / Chanson d'amour: *Manhattan Transfer* / Soul man: *Blues Brothers* / Good times: *Chic* / We are family: *Sister Sledge* / Gloria: *Branigan, Laura* / I want to know what love is: *Foreigner* / Casanova: *Levert* / From a distance: *Levert* / Black velvet: *Myles, Alannah* / Walking in Memphis: *Cohn, Marc* / It's a shame about Ray: *Lemonheads* / Silent all these years: *Amos, Tori* / Hold on: *En Vogue*
CD Set _____ 9548324242
Atlantic / Dec '92 / Warner Music

ATMOSPHERIC DRUM 'N' BASS VOL.2
Rhode tune: *Flytronix* / Sweet mind: *Aphrodite* / Raucous grin: *Ratman* / Reaching out: *Natural Born Chillers* / Brand new heavy: *Plastic Soul* / State of grace: *Dead Calm* / Phuture subject: *Subject 13* / Abyss: *Slipstream* / We can make it happen: *Nookie* / Necessities: *Trip Wire* / Mediteranean falls: *DJ SS* / Men who fell to earth: *Marr, Leon* / Spice: *Aphrodite* / Chase: *Foulplay* / Flutes: *Alpha* / Bells of love: *DJ Special* / Something: *Sirens* / To ya: *Flytronix* / Flight: *Wallace, Dave* / Parallel life: *Starseeds* / Deep control: *Spectre* / Undefined divisions: *Nishki* / Horn section: *Rogue Unit* / True belivers: *Spectre* / Summer fresh: *Mastermind* / Biome: *Tundra* / Sly: *Shogun*
CD _____ MILL 38CD
Millenium / May '97 / Plastic Head / Prime / SRD

ATMOSPHERIC SYNTHESIZER
Theme from Antarctica / Eve of the war / Equinoxe part 5 / Tubular bells / Autobahn / Aurora / Magnetic fields part 2 / Las vegas theme from rainman / Tubbs and valerie / To the unknown man / Electrica salsa / Model / Rockit / Chariots of fire / Living on video / I'll find my way home
CD _____ QED 113
Tring / Nov '96 / Tring

ATMOSPHERIC SYNTHESIZER SPECTACULAR
CD Set _____ TFP 012
Tring / Nov '92 / Tring

ATTACK OF THE NEW KILLER SURF GUITARS
CD _____ SH 5719
Shanachie / Mar '97 / ADA / Greensleeves / Koch

ATTITUDE
CD _____ RR 87832
Roadrunner / Sep '97 / PolyGram

AUDIO ALCHEMY
CD _____ URCD 020
Ubiquity / Mar '97 / Cargo / Timewarp

AUDIOPHILE SAMPLER
CD _____ ASCD 1
Audiophile / May '95 / Jazz Music

AUDIUM CAPSULE VOL.1
CD _____ BLCCD 14
Blanc / Oct '96 / Pinnacle / Shellshock/ Disc

AURA SURROUND SOUNDBITES VOL.2 (Access All Areas)
CD _____ SUSCD 3
Aura Surround Sounds / Sep '95 / Arabesque / Grapevine/PolyGram / Mo's Music Machine / Pinnacle

AURA SURROUND SOUNDBITES VOL.3 (3CD Set)
Gotta get loose: *Must* / Scrumble: *DJ Misjah & Tim* / Dreamlab: *MLO* / Midsummer's dream: *Blokka* / Eternal: *Epik* / Axiom: *Arcana* / What is going on: *Dex* / Deltoid: *Hardline 2* / Dig deep: *Blokka* / Driver: *Epik* / Moonbase: *Sinus* / Samarkand: *MLO* / Bouncy castle: *Talisman* / Temple of acid:

Temple Of Acid / Ice station zebra: *Temple Of Acid*
CD Set ______ SUSCD 4
Aura Surround Sounds / Apr '96 / Arabesque / Grapevine/PolyGram / Mo's Music Machine / Pinnacle

AURAL GRATIFICATION VOL.1
CD ______ EFA 063522
Roundtrip / May '96 / SRD

AURAL PLEASURE
CD ______ IAAPCD 1
Inter Aspect / Oct '96 / Total/BMG

AUSTIN COUNTRY NIGHTS
CD ______ WMCD 1039
Watermelon / Dec '95 / ADA / Direct

AUSTRALIA - A MUSICAL LANDSCAPE
CD ______ IMCD 3023
Image / Mar '96 / Discovery

AUSTRALIAN STARS OF THE INTERNATIONAL MUSIC HALL VOL.1 (Boiled Beef & Cabbage)
CD ______ LARRCD 325
Larrikin / Nov '94 / ADA / CM / Direct / Roots

AUSTRALIAN STARS OF THE INTERNATIONAL MUSIC HALL VOL.2 (Is 'E An Aussie, Is 'E Lizzie)
CD ______ LARRCD 324
Larrikin / Nov '94 / ADA / CM / Direct / Roots

AUSTRIA FOLKLORE
CD ______ 399426
Koch / Jul '91 / Koch

AUSTRIAN TECHNOLOGIES VOL.1
CD ______ GELB 01CD
Gelb / Jul '94 / Plastic Head

AUSTRIAN ZITHER CLASSICS
CD ______ 995562
EPM / Mar '96 / ADA / Discovery

AUTENTICO IBIZA (4CD Set)
Spirit of the sun: *Fontana, Lenny & Harvest* / Party people: *Baltimore Soul Train & Sande* / Blackboy whiteboy: *Dockins, Charles Heritage* / Do it: *DJ Rick Lenoir & The Disco Clique* / Move your body: *Reel 2 Real* / Plastic dreams: *Jaydee* / Dancin': *Mateo & Matos* / Mans love: *Crockpot Cookers* / White powder dreams: *Fire Island* / Anytime: *Nu Birth* / Harvest for the world: *Hunter, Terry* / Sunstroke: *Chicane* / Cafe del mar: *Energy 52* / Show me love: *Fruit Loop* / Age of love: *Age Of Love* / Schoneberg: *Marmion* / Blue fear: *Armin* / Dark and long: *Underworld* / Pacific melody: *Airscape* / Arc 3: *Spacer IV* / Offshore: *Chicane* / Living in ecstasy: *Rae, Fonda* / Manic jazz day: *DJ Anthony & Georgio* / Spin spin sugar: *Sneaker Pimps* / This is the only way: *Love Beads* / Testify: *Williams, Jay* / Live your life with me: *Joseph, Corrina* / Mama: *Restless Soul* / Past silence: *DJ Restyle* / Pull me up: *Ground 96* / Boogie: *Dive* / Automatic: *Continious Cool* / Remember me: *Blueboy* / Second coming: *Livin' Large* / You better: *Mount Rushmore & The Knack* / I'm ready for a good time: *Revelation* / Falling like dominoes: *Johan S. & Jazzheads* / Midnight: *Prelude & Co.* / Make you feel: *E-N* / I luv u baby: *Original* / Harmonics track '97: *Soul Boy* / Black people have rhythm: *Leaders* / Jumping and pumping: *Son* / Erotic fantasy: *Brutal Bill & Plan B* / RIP groove: *Double 99*
CD Set ______ AUTIBCD 1
Beechwood / Jul '97 / Beechwood/BMG / Pinnacle

AUTHENTIC EXCELLO RHYTHM & BLUES
I'm evil: *Lightnin' Slim* / You're gonna ruin me baby: *Lazy Lester* / Got love if you want it: *Harpo, Slim* / Going through the park: *Anderson, Jimmy* / I'm warning you baby: *Lightnin' Slim* / Lonesome lonely blues: *Lonesome Sundown* / Wild cherry: *Washington, Leroy* / You're too late baby: *Hogan, Silas* / I'm a lover not a fighter: *Lazy Lester* / I love the life I'm livin': *Harpo, Slim* / Naggin': *Anderson, Jimmy* / I'm gonna quit you pretty baby: *Hogan, Silas* / I'm glad she's mine: *Lonesome Sundown* / I'm a king bee: *Harpo, Slim* / Mean woman blues: *Smith, Whispering* / Loving around the clock: *Lightnin' Slim* / Tell me pretty baby: *Lazy Lester* / Hoodoo party: *Thomas, Tabby* / Lonesome la la: *Hogan, Silas* / Wake up old maid: *Smith, Whispering* / I'm tired waitin' baby: *Lightnin' Slim* / Gonna stick to you baby: *Lonesome Sundown* / No naggin' no draggin': *Gunter, Arthur* / I'm doin' alright: *Shy Guy Douglas*
CD ______ CDCHD 492
Ace / Oct '93 / Pinnacle

AUTHENTIC JAMAICA SKA
CD ______ AJSCD 001
K&K / Jul '93 / Jet Star

AUTHENTIC MUSIC OF THE AMERICAN INDIAN, THE
CD ______ SPALAX 14889
Spalax / Oct '96 / ADA / Cargo / Direct / Discovery / Greyhound

AUTHENTIC NATIVE AMERICAN MUSIC
CD ______ 12551
Laserlight / Nov '95 / Target/BMG

AUTOMATIC BOP VOL.1 (31 Rockabilly Burners)
CD ______ CLCD 4433
Collector/White Label / Nov '96 / TKO Magnum

AUTUMN RECORDS STORY, THE
C'mon and swim pt.1: *Freeman, Bobby* / S-W-I-M: *Freeman, Bobby* / Scat swim: *Stewart, Sly* / Buttermilk: *Stewart, Sly* / Somebody to love: *Great Society* / Free advice: *Great Society* / She's my baby: *Mojo Men* / Jerk: *Beau Brummels & B. Freeman Band* / Sad little girl: *Beau Brummels* / No 1: *Charlatans* / Anything: *Vejtables* / Pay attention to me: *Tikis*
CD ______ EDCD 145
Edsel / May '86 / Pinnacle

AVANT GARDISM (2CD Set)
CD Set ______ LAANGE 1CD
Law & Auder/Blue Angel / Jan '97 / Prime / RTM/Disc

AVANT KNITTING TOUR
CD ______ KFWCD 142
Knitting Factory / Nov '94 / Cargo / Plastic Head

AVANTI VOL.2
CD ______ FILERCD 432
Profile / Jul '92 / Pinnacle

AVID JAZZ & VOCAL SAMPLER
CD ______ AMSC 568
Avid / May '96 / Avid/BMG / Koch / THE

AXE BRAZIL (Afro-Brazilian Music Of Brazil)
CD ______ CDP 7950572
World Pacific / Jul '91 / EMI

AZERBAIJAN - INSTRUMENTAL AND VOCAL MUSIC
CD ______ SM 1518
Wergo / May '96 / ADA / Cadillac / Harmonia Mundi

B

B IS FOR BROCCOLI
CD ______ KUDCD 007
Kudos / Jan '96 / Kudos / Pinnacle

BABY BOOMERS (4CD Set)
CD Set ______ MBSCD 418
Castle / Nov '93 / BMG

BABYLON A FALL DOWN
CD ______ CDTRL 290
Trojan / Apr '91 / Direct / Jet Star

BACHELOR'S LITTLE BLACK BOOK, THE
Patricia: *Prado, Perez* / Ruby: *Haymann, Richard Orchestra* / Jean: *Kaempfert, Bert Orchestra* / Celito linda: *Faith, Percy Orchestra* / Mr. Kelly Kelly and me: *Greenslade, Arthur & Orchestra* / Charmaine: *Mantovani & His Orchestra* / Melina: *Stanyon Strings* / Sweet Leilani: *Crosby, Bing* / Vanessa: *Winterhalter, Hugo Orchestra* / Main title from Joanna: *Greenslade, Arthur* / Anna: *Mangano, Silvana* / Gemini, summer song: *Jacobs, Dick & His Orchestra* / Hummingbird: *Paul, Les & Mary Ford* / Nola: *Paul, Les* / Virgo, blue lady: *Jacobs, Dick & His Orchestra* / Adios Marquita linda: *Esquivel, Juan Garcia*
CD ______ 12803
Laserlight / May '97 / Target/BMG

BACK FROM THE GRAVE VOL.1 (Rockin' Sixties Punkers)
CD ______ EFA 11566
Crypt / Mar '93 / Shellshock/Disc

BACK FROM THE GRAVE VOL.3 (Mid-60's Garage Punkers)
CD ______ EFA 115202
Crypt / Mar '94 / Shellshock/Disc

BACK FROM THE GRAVE VOL.4 (Mid-60's Garage Punk Screamers)
CD ______ EFA 115252
Crypt / Sep '95 / Shellshock/Disc

BACK FROM THE GRAVE VOL.8
CD ______ EFA 115922
Crypt / Feb '96 / Shellshock/Disc

BACK IN THE SADDLE AGAIN
Old Chisholm trail: *McClintock, Harry 'Haywire Mac'* / Pot wrassler: *Jackson, Harry* / Gol-durned wheel: *Holyoak, Van* / When the work's all done this fall: *Sprague, Carl T.* / Streets of Laredo: *Prude, John G.* / Sioux Indians: *Williams, Marc* / Dying cowboy: *Allen, Jules Verne* / Tyin' knots in the devil's tail: *Jack, Powder River & Kitty Lee* / Strawberry Roan: *Arizona Wranglers* / Lone star trail: *Maynard, Ken* / Ridge runnin' road: *Rice, Glen & His Beverly Hill Billies* / Whoopie ti yi yo: *White, John* / Cowhand's last ride / Little old log shack I always call my home: *Carter, Wilf* / A-ridin' old paint: *Ritter, Tex* / I want to be a cowboy's sweetheart: *Montana, Patsy* / Cattle call: *Owens, Tex* / One more ride: *Sons Of The Pioneers* / Dim narrow trail: *Ruby, Texas* / I want to be a real cowboy girl: *Girls Of The Golden West* / Back in the saddle again: *Autry, Gene* / My dear old Arizona home: *Allen, Rex* / Cowboy stomp / D-Bar-2 horse wrangler: *Critchlow, Slim* / City boarders: *Agins, Sam* / Cowboys: *Ohrlin, Glenn* / Rusty spurs: *Doux, Chris Le* / Cowboy song: *Riders In The Sky*
CD ______ NW 314/315
New World / Aug '92 / ADA / Cadillac / Harmonia Mundi

BACK ON 52ND STREET
CD ______ DIW 406
DIW / Mar '97 / Cadillac / Harmonia Mundi

BACK PORCH BLUES
CD ______ CDBM 099
Blue Moon / Apr '96 / Cadillac / Discovery / Greensleeves / Jazz Music / Jet Star / TKO Magnum

BACK PORCH BLUES
CD ______ KS 041CD
Kingsnake / Jul '97 / Hot Shot

BACK TO BASICS VOL.1
Song for Bilbao: *Brecker, Michael* / Hippest cat in Hollywood: *Silver, Horace* / Gee baby ain't I good to you: *Krall, Diana* / Hot bean strut: *Perez, Danilo* / Double indemnity: *Blacknote* / Black, as in buhaina: *Reed, Eric* / Impressions: *Tyner, McCoy*
CD ______ IMPD 207
Impulse Jazz / Oct '96 / New Note/BMG

BACK TO BASICS VOL.2
Panacea: *Three Of A Kind* / Back at the chicken shack: *Jones, Rodney* / Mime: *Bronner, Till* / Yellin' blue: *Ellis, Pee Wee* / Power of love: *Theessink, Hans* / Why did I choose you: *Lowman, Annette* / Joy to the world: *Weiss, Klaus* / Castles in Spain: *Fessler, Peter* / Serenghetti: *Cox, Bruce* / D as in David: *Denson, Karl* / Cold sweat: *Parker, Maceo*
CD ______ MM 801059
Minor Music / Oct '96 / Vital/SAM

BACK TO LOVE
CD ______ RENCD 115
Renaissance Collector Series / Mar '96 / BMG

BACK TO MONO
CD ______ WALLCD 002
Wall Of Sound / Sep '95 / Prime / Soul Trader / Vital

BACK TO THE 50'S
Love letters in the sand: *Boone, Pat* / Old cape cod: *Page, Patti* / Hernando's hideaway: *Ray, Johnnie* / Standing on the corner: *Four Lads* / Most of all: *Cornell, Don* / To each his own: *Ink Spots* / Little shoemaker: *Gaylords* / Honeycomb: *Rodgers, Jimmie* / My prayer: *Platters* / Singin' the blues: *Mitchell, Guy* / Green door: *Lowe, Jim* / 26 miles (Santa Catalina): *Four Preps* / Rose, Rose I love you: *Laine, Frankie* / Wayward wind: *Grant, Gogi* / Caribbean: *Torok, Mitchell* / Dark moon: *Guitar, Bonnie* / Marianne: *Hilltoppers* / This ole house: *Clooney, Rosemary*
CD ______ ECD 3118
K-Tel / Jan '95 / K-Tel

BACK TO THE 50'S - A BETTY PAGE TRIBUTE
CD ______ CLP 9964
Cleopatra / Jun '97 / Cargo / Greyhound / Plastic Head / RTM/Disc / SRD

BACK TO THE 60'S VOL.1
Love grows (Where my rosemary goes): *Edison Lighthouse* / With a girl like you: *Troggs* / Lightning strikes: *Christie, Lou* / Build me up buttercup: *Foundations* / How do you do it: *Gerry & The Pacemakers* / Love on a mountain top: *Knight, Robert* / Little arrows: *Lee, Leapy* / Yellow river: *Christie* / She's not there: *Zombies* / Dizzy: *Roe, Tommy* / Happy together: *Turtles* / It's my party: *Gore, Lesley* / Da doo ron ron: *Crystals* / Gimme little sign: *Wood, Brenton* / Letter: *Box Tops* / You've got your troubles (I've got mine): *Fortunes* / Groovy kind of love: *Fontana, Wayne* / Young girl: *Puckett, Gary & The Union Gap*
CD ______ ECD 3046
K-Tel / Jan '95 / K-Tel

BACK TO THE 60'S VOL.2
Ob-la-di ob-la-da: *Marmalade* / I'm gonna make you mine: *Christie, Lou* / Here it comes again: *Fortunes* / Tobacco Road: *Nashville Teens* / Any way that you want me: *Troggs* / I'm telling you now: *Freddie & The Dreamers* / I like it: *Gerry & The Pacemakers* / Elenore: *Turtles* / Baby now that I've found you: *Foundations* / Baby come back: *Equals* / Knock on wood: *Floyd, Eddie* / Soul man: *Sam & Dave* / In crowd: *Gray, Dobie* / Rescue me: *Bass, Fontella* / Tighten up: *Bell, Archie & The Drells* / Then he kissed me: *Crystals* / Sorrow: *Merseys* / Little children: *Kramer, Billy J.*
CD ______ ECD 3051
K-Tel / Jan '95 / K-Tel

BACK TO THE 60'S VOL.3
Here comes my baby: *Tremeloes* / Concrete and clay: *Unit 4+2* / Those were the days: *Hopkin, Mary* / Little things: *Berry, Dave* / Everybody: *Roe, Tommy* / Good morning sunshine: *Oliver* / Games people play: *South, Joe* / Bread and butter: *Newbeats* / Wooly bully: *Sam The Sham & The Pharaohs* / You'll never walk alone: *Gerry & The Pacemakers* / Hippy hippy shake: *Swinging Blue Jeans* / Hello little girl: *Fourmost* / Hitchin' a ride: *Vanity Fare* / Google eyes: *Nashville Teens* / You were on my mind: *St. Peters, Crispian* / Woman, woman: *Puckett, Gary & The Union Gap* / You were made for me: *Freddie & The Dreamers* / Game of love: *Fontana, Wayne*
CD ______ ECD 3123
K-Tel / Jan '95 / K-Tel

BACK TO THE 70'S
Midnight at the oasis: *Muldaur, Maria* / Love won't let me wait: *Harris, Major* / Love I lost: *Melvin, Harold & The Bluenotes* / Patches: *Carter, Clarence* / Hey girl don't bother me: *Tams* / You little trustmaker: *Tymes* / Something old something new: *Fantastics* / More more more: *True, Andrea* / Do it any way you wanna: *People's Choice* / My baby loves lovin': *White Plains* / Beg steal or borrow: *New Seekers* / Do you wanna dance: *Blue, Barry* / Let's get together again: *Glitter Band* / I can do it: *Rubettes* / In Zaire: *Wakelin, Johnny* / Baby jump: *Mungo Jerry* / Fox on the run: *Connolly, Brian* / Pepper box: *Peppers*
CD ______ ECD 3122
K-Tel / Jan '95 / K-Tel

BACK TO THE 70'S (40 Chart Busting Seventies Hits - 2CD Set)
Killer queen: *Queen* / Make me smile (come up and see me): *Harley, Steve & Cockney Rebel* / Maggie May: *Stewart, Rod* / Band on the run: *McCartney, Paul & Wings* / Lola: *Kinks* / American pie: *McLean, Don* / You're so vain: *Simon, Carly* / Never let her slip away: *Gold, Andrew* / Goodbye to love: *Carpenters* / Without you: *Nilsson, Harry* / Baker Street: *Rafferty, Gerry* / Rocket man: *John, Elton* / I don't like Mondays: *Boomtown Rats* / Hit me with your rhythm stick: *Dury, Ian & The Blockheads* / Oliver's army: *Costello, Elvis & The Attractions* / You ain't seen nothin' yet: *Bachman-Turner Overdrive* / All right now: *Free* / Wuthering Heights: *Bush, Kate* / I'm not in love: *10cc* / I want you back: *Jackson Five* / Rock your baby: *McCrae, George* / That's the way (I like it): *KC & The Sunshine Band* / Nutbush City Limits: *Turner, Ike & Tina* / You to me are everything: *Real Thing* / You're the first, the last, my everything: *White, Barry* / YMCA: *Village People* / Rivers of Babylon: *Boney M* / So you win again: *Hot Chocolate* / Let's stay together: *Green, Al* / Love don't live here anymore: *Rose Royce* / December '63 (oh what a night): *Valli, Frankie & Four Seasons* / We don't talk anymore: *Richard, Cliff* / When you're in love with a beautiful woman: *Dr. Hook* / In the summertime: *Mungo Jerry* / Ride a white swan: *T-Rex* / Coz I luv you: *Slade* / I'm the leader of the gang (I am): *Slade* / Ballroom blitz: *Sweet* / Tiger feet: *Mud* / Heart of glass: *Blondie*
CD Set ______ CDEMTV 77
EMI / Sep '93 / EMI

BACK TO THE 70'S (4CD Set)
CD Set ______ MBSCD 432
Castle / Jan '95 / BMG

BACK TO THE BLUES
CD ______ 157152
Blues Collection / Feb '93 / Discovery

BACK TO THE BLUES (2CD Set)
Easy rider: *Leadbelly* / Black train blues: *White, Bukka* / Dust my broom: *Johnson, Robert* / Mean mistreater Mama: *Carr, Leroy* / Four hands are better than two: *Johnson, Lonnie* / Georgia rag: *McTell, 'Blind' Willie* / My brownskin sugar plum: *Fuller, 'Blind' Boy* / Walkin' blues: *Johnson, Robert* / Sun risin' blues: *Turner, 'Big' Joe* / Warehouseman blues: *Dupree, 'Champion' Jack* / Got the bottle up and go: *Williamson, Sonny Boy* / Born for bad luck: *McGhee, Brownie* / Rebecca: *Turner, 'Big' Joe* / I'm calling Daisy: *McGhee, Brownie* / Sugar Mama blues: *Williamson, Sonny Boy* / Stomp down rider: *McTell, 'Blind' Willie* / Mean old bed bug blues: *Johnson, Lonnie* / Strange place blues: *White, Bukka* / Mean ol' Frisco blues: *Crudup, Arthur 'Big Boy'* / Rock Island line: *Leadbelly* / Rocks in my bed: *Turner, 'Big' Joe* / Midnight hour blues: *Carr, Leroy* / You can't get that stuff no more: *Tampa Red* / Bull cow blues: *Broonzy, 'Big' Bill* / Gamblin' man blues: *Dupree, 'Champion' Jack* / Phonograph blues: *Johnson, Robert* / Broke down engine: *McTell, 'Blind' Willie* / Bluebirds blues: *Williamson, Sonny Boy* / Baby you gotta change your mind: *Fuller, 'Blind' Boy* / Good morning blues: *Leadbelly* / Preaching blues: *Johnson, Robert* / Gonna follow my baby: *Crudup, Arthur 'Big Boy'* / Mr. Johnson's swing: *Johnson, Lonnie* / Picking my tomatoes: *McGhee, Brownie* / 15 cents a day: *Sykes, Roosevelt* / I'm a rattlesnakin' Daddy: *Fuller, 'Blind' Boy* / Worrying you off my mind: *Broonzy, 'Big' Bill* / Good woman blues: *Carr, Leroy* / You know I got a reason: *Broonzy, 'Big' Bill* / When you got a friend: *Johnson, Robert*
CD Set ______ MUCD 9508
Musketeer / May '96 / Disc

BACK TO THE STREETS
CD ______ SHACD 9006
Shanachie / Nov '93 / ADA / Greensleeves / Koch

BACKBEAT ALLSTARS COMPILATION VOL.1
Funky loisaida: *B Side* / Talk to your man: *Common Cause* / Ven a gozar: *Intergalactic Love Communication* / Funk what: *Exodus Quartet* / Slippin' and sliddin': *Exodus Quartet* / Crusader: *Fishbelly Black* / Time is on our side: *Shadow Boxers* / Catwoman: *Shadow Boxers* / Mellow mode: *DJ Hakim*
CD ____ **BBCD 721232**
Backbeat / Jul '97 / Jet Star / Timewarp

BACKDROP (The Very Essence Of Northern Soul 1974)
Where there's a will: *Thomas, Jimmy* / I got love: *Wills, Viola* / Same old thing: *Olympics* / Jumping at the go-go: *Detroit Sound* / Your personality: *Lee, Jackie* / What good am I: *Champion, Mickey* / Just like you did me: *Vernee, Yvonne* / Baby don't you weep: *Hamilton, Edward* / King for a day: *Ames, Stuart* / Look at what I almost missed: *Lewis, Pat* / Baby I'm here just to love you: *Stagemasters* / This thing called love: *Wyatt, Johnny* / Save my lovin' for you: *People's Choice* / That's why I love you: *Professionals* / Never, never: *Herbs* / You'll never make the grade: *Sunlovers* / Running wild: *Exsayvions* / Quit twistin' my arm: *Mitchell, Stanley* / Baby, baby, baby: *Tokays* / Oh yeah, yeah, yeah: *Carroll, Vivian* / Just because of you: *Rocky Roberts & The Airedales* / As long as you love me: *Ronnie & Robyn*
CD ____ **GSCD 073**
Goldmine / Feb '97 / Vital

BACKLASH
Citation collection: *Hildenbeutel, R.* / Befool: *B-Zet* / From afar: *Mir* / Moon and the sun: *Solitaire* / Under the milkyway: *Mir* / La luna de miel: *No.9 Dream* / Isn't that a funny bird: *Tollmann & Hildenbeutel* / Jazzie: *B-Zet* / Inner peace: *Hildenbeutel, R.* / Mim's french dog: *Tollmann & Hildenbeutel*
CD ____ **ROD 011**
Harthouse / May '97 / Mo's Music Machine / Prime / Vital

BACKLOG
CD ____ **VOW 050CD**
Voices Of Wonder / Jun '95 / Plastic Head

BACKTRACKIN' TO THE 70'S (4CD Set)
CD Set ____ **MBSCD 437**
Castle / Nov '95 / BMG

BACKWATER VOL.2
CD ____ **NBX 004**
Noisebox / Jun '94 / RTM/Disc / Vital

BAD, BAD WHISKEY (The Galaxy Masters)
She's looking good: *Collins, Rodger* / Rufus Jr: *Merced Blue Notes* / I got to tell somebody: *Everett, Betty* / Chicken heads: *Rush, Bobby* / Get your lie straight: *Coday, Bill* / Why do you have to lie: *Right Kind* / You better stop: *Rhodes, Sonny* / Nightingale melody: *Taylor, Little Johnny* / I pity the fool: *Saunders, Merl* / It's a shame: *Malone, J.J.* / Rainbow 71: *Holloway, Loleatta* / Foxy girls in Oakland: *Collins, Rodger* / When you find a fool bump his head: *Coday, Bill* / Mama Rufus: *Merced Blue Notes* / For your precious love: *Taylor, Little Johnny* / Abraham, Martin and John: *Brown, Charles* / Bad bad whiskey: *Merced Blue Notes* / How can I forget you: *Williams, Lenny* / Ain't nothing gonna change me: *Everett, Betty* / Woman rules the world: *Coday, Bill* / Why did our love go: *Huey, Claude 'Baby'* / Let me be your handy man: *Coday, Bill* / Fever fever fever: *Eaton, Bobby* / Lisa's gone: *Williams, Lenny* / Don't want to be a lone ranger: *Watson, Johnny 'Guitar'*
CD ____ **CDCHD 516**
Ace / Jan '94 / Pinnacle

BAD BOY
Screamin' Mimi Jeanie: *Hawks, Mickey* / Bip bop boom: *Hawks, Mickey* / Rock 'n' roll rhythm: *Hawks, Mickey* / Hidi hidi hidi: *Hawks, Mickey* / I'm lost: *Hawks, Mickey* / Cotton pickin': *Night Raiders* / Bad boy: *France, Steve* / Born to lose: *Deckelman, Sonny* / Don't hang around me anymore: *Ford, Jimmy* / You're gonna be sorry: *Ford, Jimmy* / Bad bad boy: *Lollar, Bobby* / Red hot Mama: *Williams, Wayne* / Okie's in the pokie: *Patton, Jimmy* / Yah, I'm movin': *Patton, Jimmy* / Willie was a bad boy: *Gentry, Ray* / Bad bad way: *Rodger & Tempests* / Missed the workhouse: *Watkins, Bill* / Look what I found: *Hubbar, Orangie* / Curfew: *Chuck & Gene* / Bad: *Amory, John* / Big Sandy: *Roberts, Bobby* / Hop, skip and jump: *Roberts, Bobby* / She's my woman: *Roberts, Bobby* / Go boy: *Lee, Floyd* / Take it easy, Greasy: *Lehmann, Bill* / Is there no woman for my love: *McAdams, Johnny* / All night in jail: *Bernard, Rod* / Meaner than an alligator: *Ty B & Johnny* / I've been a bad bad boy: *Kingbeats* / Teenage riot: *Portuguese Joe*
CD ____ **CDBB 55003**
Buffalo Bop / Apr '94 / Rollercoaster

BAD TASTE - THE ULTIMATE PUNK PARTY
CD ____ **BTR 013CD**
Bad Taste / Nov '96 / Plastic Head

BADAKHSHAN: MUSIC FROM THE TAJIK PAMIR MOUNTAINS
CD ____ **PAN 2024CD**
Pan / Mar '94 / ADA / CM / Direct

BAG OF GOODIES
CD ____ **LHCD 001**
Luv n' Haight / Jul '96 / Timewarp

BAGAD DU MOULIN VERT - QUIMPER
CD ____ **GRI 190842**
Griffe / Sep '96 / ADA / Discovery

BAGPIPE, THE
CD ____ **LYRCD 7327**
Lyrichord / Dec '94 / ADA / CM / Roots

BAGPIPES AND DRUMS OF SCOTLAND, THE
Inverness gathering / Australian ladies / Braig Lock Lall / Stool of repentance / Wandering hame / Inglenuek / Ye jacobites by name / Boys of blue hill / Sporting Jamie / Gallant fireman / Devil in the kitchen / Highland train / Kilt is my delight / Kate dalymple / Bluebells of Scotland / Scotland the brave / Green hills of Tyrol / Sheepwife / Brogan Lochan / Braes of Badenoch / Skye boat song / My home / Glasgow police marchpast / Black bear / Grrenwoodside / Pigeon on the gate / Cockney jocks / Bonnie lass O'Fyvie / Drum fanfare / Salute / To max rayne / Dundeach / Going to Piltlochry / Murdo's wedding / City of Hastings / Muir of Ord / Faded cabbage / Bannana fingers / Jim Tweedies sea leg
CD ____ **12713**
Laserlight / Feb '96 / Target/BMG

BAGPIPES AND HURDY GURDY
CD ____ **B 6830**
Auvidis/Ethnic / May '96 / ADA / Harmonia Mundi

BAGPIPES FROM SCOTLAND
CD ____ **HM 002**
Harmony / Jun '97 / TKO Magnum

BAGPIPES OF BRITAIN AND IRELAND
CD ____ **CDSDL 416**
Saydisc / Mar '96 / ADA / Direct / Harmonia Mundi

BAILA MI AMOR
CD ____ **DCD 5392**
Disky / Jul '94 / Disky / THE

BALAFONS OF BOBO DIOULASSO, THE
CD ____ **PS 65172**
PlayaSound / Nov '96 / ADA / Harmonia Mundi

BALI - COURT MUSIC AND BANJAR MUSIC
CD ____ **BCD 8059**
Auvidis/Ethnic / Jan '95 / ADA / Harmonia Mundi

BALI - GAMELAN & KECAK
CD ____ **7559792042**
Nonesuch / Jan '95 / Warner Music

BALI - MUSIC FROM THE MORNING OF THE WORLD
CD ____ **7559791962**
Nonesuch / Jan '95 / Warner Music

BALI - SUITE OF MUSIC AND SOUNDS
CD ____ **58397**
World Network / Mar '96 / ADA

BALI - THE CLASH OF THE GONGS
CD ____ **122119**
Long Distance / Jul '95 / ADA / Discovery

BALI - THE GREAT GONG KEBYAR
CD ____ **C 560057**
Ocora / Aug '94 / ADA / Harmonia Mundi

BALI MUSIC ANTHOLOGY VOL.2 (2CD Set)
CD ____ **926012**
BUDA / Feb '96 / Discovery

BALL TONIGHT, A
That's what I call a ball: *Donn, Larry* / Honey bun: *Donn, Larry* / Girl next door: *Donn, Larry* / Wild wild party: *Vincent, Darryl* / Ball tonight: *Campbell, Ray* / Rockin' spot: *Coldiron, Curley* / I've got love: *Deckleman, Sonny* / Forty nine women: *Irby, Jerry* / There'll be a rockin' party tonight: *Volk, Val* / I fell for your line baby: *Faire, Johnny* / Bertha Lou: *Faire, Johnny* / Hot dog: *Curtin, Lee* / Is this the place: *Queen's Royal Lancers* / Long pony tail: *Tom & Tornados* / Saturday night party: *Perkins, Reggie* / Pretty Kitty: *Perkins, Reggie* / Party time: *Noris, Bob* / Stop at the hop: *Eee, Don* / My queen and me: *Lenny & The Star Chiefs* / Rockin' bones: *Dietzel, Elroy* / Teenage ball: *Dietzel, Elroy* / Pretty baby rock: *Mayo, Danny* / Chicken walk: *Adkins, Hasil* / She's mine: *Adkins, Hasil* / Betcha I getcha: *Faire, Johnny* / Bo peep rock: *Vinyard, Eddie* / Wildwood fun: *Lefty & Leadsmen* / There's gonna be a party: *Gray, Bobby* / Dream night: *Houle Brothers* / Teen age ball: *White, Buddy*
CD ____ **CDBB 55007**
Buffalo Bop / Apr '94 / Rollercoaster

BALLADS
CD ____ **ENJ 93052**
Enja / Jul '96 / New Note/Pinnacle / Vital/ SAM

BALLADS
Seven gypsies: *Tyrrall, Gordon* / Mill O'Tifty's Annie: *McCulloch, Gordeanna* / Lord Bateman: *Knevett, Arthur* / Bonnie banks of Fordie: *Jones, Nic* / Tam Lin: *Armstrong, Frankie* / Matty Groves: *Wright, John* / Chyld Owlett: *Prior, Maddy* / Lover's ghost: *Wyndham-Read, Martyn* / Robin Hood rescuing the three Squires: *Kirkpatrick, John* / Sheath and knife: *Kydd, Christine* / Sun shines fair: *Adams, Linda* / Bonnie house of Airlie: *Eaglesham, Bobby*
CD ____ **FECD 110**
Fellside / Feb '97 / ADA / Direct / Target/ BMG

BALLADS FOR TENOR
Lover man / Lotus blossom / I can't get started / Stormy weather / Body and soul / You leave me breathless / Yesterdays / Sur les quais du vieux Paris
CD ____ **8747092**
DA Music / Oct '96 / Conifer/BMG

BALLERMANN 6
CD ____ **ZYX 550792**
ZYX / Jul '97 / ZYX

BALLERMANN 6 BALNEARIO
CD ____ **ZYX 550724**
ZYX / Dec '96 / ZYX

BALLROOM DANCING
Dr. Quick / Hallo Susi / Swingtime medley / Lambada / I concentrate on you / El toro ballade / I've seen that face / Cheim chiem cheree / Saving all my love for you / Wie ein wunder / Chattanooga cha cha / Tango noir / Severin / Only you
CD ____ **22519**
Music / Feb '96 / Target/BMG

BALLROOM DANCING FAVOURITES (3CD Set)
I don't care if I never dream: *Loss, Joe & His Orchestra* / You moved right in: *Roy, Harry & His Band* / I'll never say Never Again again: *Smith, Bryan & His Festival Orchestra* / That's a plenty: *Smith, Bryan & His Festival Orchestra* / Waltz of my heart: *Silvester, Victor* / Whisper while you waltz: *Silvester, Victor* / In the mood: *Power Pack Orchestra* / Opus 1: *Power Pack Orchestra* / Don't get around much anymore: *Power Pack Orchestra* / American patrol: *Power Pack Orchestra* / Tango Hacienda: *Smith, Bryan & His Festival Orchestra* / Tango sombrero: *Smith, Bryan & His Festival Orchestra* / I'll buy that dream: *Preager, Lou & His Orchestra* / I'm so all alone: *Fenoulhet, Paul & the Skyrockets Dance Orchestra* / Never on a Sunday: *Power Pack Orchestra* / Spanish flee: *Power Pack Orchestra* / Monday, Tuesday, Wednesday: *Dean, Syd & His Orchestra* / I should care: *Winstone, Eric & His Band* / Once in a while: *Smith, Bryan & His Festival Orchestra* / April in Paris: *Silvester, Victor* / You red head: *Dean, Syd & his Band* / Gotta be this or that: *Loss, Joe & His Orchestra* / Edwardians: *Smith, Bryan & His Festival Orchestra* / Blue Tahitian moon: *Smith, Bryan & His Festival Orchestra* / Moonlight serenade: *Power Pack Orchestra* / Mood indigo: *Silvester, Victor* / Tuxedo Junction: *Power Pack Orchestra* / It happened in Monterey: *Power Pack Orchestra* / String of pearls: *Power Pack Orchestra* / I wonder where my baby is tonight: *Silvester, Victor* / Just for a while: *Smith, Bryan & His Festival Orchestra* / Suzy: *Smith, Bryan & His Festival Orchestra* / You can't be true dear: *Rabin, Oscar & His Band with Harry Davis* / I'll be your sweetheart: *Loss, Joe & His Orchestra* / Echo told me a lie: *Adam, Paul & His Mayfair Music* / Guantanamera: *Love, Geoff & His Orchestra* / Make believe: *Smith, Bryan & His Festival Orchestra* / It looks like rain in cherry blossom: *Smith, Bryan & His Festival Orchestra* / Sobre Las Olas: *Smith, Bryan & His Festival Orchestra* / How little we know: *Winstone, Eric & His Band* / Red roses for a blue lady: *Adam, Paul & His Mayfair Music* / Rags and tatters: *Smith, Bryan & His Festival Orchestra* / Stumbling: *Smith, Bryan & His Festival Orchestra* / By candlelight: *Silvester, Victor* / Unforgettable: *Silvester, Victor* / Tango 65: *Smith, Bryan & His Festival Orchestra* / I can dream can't I: *Silvester, Victor* / Come dance with me: *Silvester, Victor* / C'est si bon: *Silvester, Victor* / Always true to you in my fashion: *Silvester, Victor* / Out of the night: *Roy, Harry & His Band* / Lipstick on your collar: *Power Pack Orchestra* / Let there be drums: *Power Pack Orchestra* / One note samba: *Love, Geoff & His Orchestra* / Sucu sucu: *Love, Geoff & His Orchestra* / Egerland march: *Smith, Bryan & His Festival Orchestra* / Bandstand march: *Smith, Bryan & His Festival Orchestra* / Turn over a new leaf: *Benson, Ivy & Her Girls Band* / Last waltz: *Power Pack Orchestra*
CD Set ____ **CDTRBOX 200**
Trio / Sep '95 / EMI

BALOUTCHISTAN: THE INSTRUMENTAL TRADITION
CD ____ **C 560105**
Ocora / Mar '97 / ADA / Harmonia Mundi

BAM BAM
CD ____ **VPCD 1237**
VP / Jul '92 / Greensleeves / Jet Star / Total/BMG

BANANAS (14 Fruity Hardcore Anthems)
Another day: *Sub State* / Gonna be alright: *DJ Vibes & Wishdokta* / Yee haa: *Forbes, Davie* / Watch me dance: *El Bruto* / I got something: *Kidz* / Everybody here tonight: *Speed, Jack* / Your love (get down): *Force & Styles* / I want your love: *Infernus* / Close your eyes: *Jimmy J & Cru-L-T* / Take me up: *Sub State* / Bassline kickin': *MC Lust* / Motorway madness: *DJ Vibes & Wishdokta* / Touch of klass: *DJ Happy Raver & The Smile-E* / Mind warp: *El Bruto*
CD ____ **DBM 2141**
Death Becomes Me / Apr '97 / Grapevine/ PolyGram / Pinnacle / SRD

BANDLEADER DIGITAL SPECTACULAR (Various Military & Brass Bands)
Berne patrol / Thunderbird / Royal salute / Regimental slow march / Motorcycle display / Chocolate dancing / Shepherd's song / Music box dancer / Canter / St. Louis blues march / Caesar's romp / Concerto for clarinet in A / Mount Longden / Drumbeatings / Rule Britannia / Jerusalem / Last post / Auld lang syne / Colonel Bogey / Artillery salvo and opening fanfare / Fanfare / God save the Queen / Bugle flute and drum calls / Precision in percussion / Tornado
CD ____ **BNA 5000**
Bandleader / Feb '85 / Conifer/BMG

BANDOLAS DE VENEZUELA
CD ____ **DIS 80114**
Dorian Discovery / Jan '94 / Conifer/BMG / Select

BANDONEON PURE - DANCES OF URUGUAY
CD ____ **SF 40431CD**
Smithsonian Folkways / Jan '94 / ADA / Cadillac / CM / Direct / Koch

BANDSTAND FAVOURITES (36 Timeless Performances/2CD Set)
Strike up the band: *Life Guards Band* / Knightsbridge march: *Blues & Royals Band* / Westminster waltz: *Blues & Royals Band* / Calling all workers: *Royal Yeomanry* / Rhapsody in blue: *Central Band Of Royal British Legion* / Army of the Nile: *Gloucestershire Regiment* / It's a long way to Tipperary: *Royal Irish Rangers* / Anything goes: *Royal Marines* / London pubs medley: *Blues & Royals Band* / Le rejouissance: *Coldstream Guards* / British grenadiers: *Cheshire Regiment* / Golden mile: *Queen's Lancashire Regiment* / Sabre dance: *Royal Marines* / Street pictures medley: *Blues & Royals Band* / Stage centre: *Coldstream Guards* / Yankee doodle dandy: *Royal British Legion Band* / Alexander's ragtime band: *Royal British Legion Band* / On Richmond hill baht 'at: *Duke Of Wellington Regiment* / Czardas: *Coldstream Guards* / Radetsky march: *Royal British Legion Band* / Glenn Miller memories: *Royal British Legion Band* / Pageantry of Gilbert & Sullivan: *Blues & Royals Band* / Colonel Bogey: *Royal British Legion Band* / Nessun Dorma: *Royal British Legion Band* / Blaze away: *Blues & Royals Band* / Tie a yellow ribbon: *Royal British Legion Band* / Greensleeves: *Blues & Royals Band* / Bells across the meadow: *Blues & Royals Band*
CD Set ____ **330492**
Hallmark / Mar '97 / Carlton

BANGING HOUSE (14 Seriously Clubbing Chuggers)
CD ____ **FIRMCD 3**
Firm / Mar '96 / Pinnacle

BANJO FESTIVAL
Banjo cantata: *McGuinn, Jim* / Banjo workout: *Maphis, Joe* / Holston valley breakdown: *Seeger, Mike* / Little boxes: *Rosmini, Dick* / There's a meeting here tonight: *Helms, Jimmy* / Cripple creek: *Cheatwood, Billy* / Goodman coonhound: *Faier, Billy* / Clinch Mountain backstop: *Lindley, David* / Johnson boys: *Lindley, David* / Red apple juice: *Rosmini, Dick* / Hundreds of miles: *Cheatwood, Billy* / Old Joe Clark: *Weissman, Dick* / Movin' down the line: *Helms, Jimmy* / Hindu stomp: *Podell, Art* / Whistle while you work: *Williams, Mason* / Mad mountain medley: *Lindley, David* / Hooka tooka: *Helms, Jimmy* / Trail ridge road: *Weissman, Dick* / Joe's breakdown: *Maphis, Joe* / Banjo tune: *Darling, Erik* / Greenback dollar: *Rosmini, Dick & Jimmy Helms* / Rumblin' on: *McGuinn, Jim* / Fast and loose: *Rosmini, Dick* / Goin' down there: *Seeger, Mike* / Earle's breakdown: *Weissberg, Eric & Marshall Brickman* / Green corn: *Faier, Billy* / Banjo hello: *Williams, Mason*
CD ____ **CD 12550**
Music Of The World / May '97 / ADA / Target/BMG

BANJO JAMBOREE
CD ____ **TCD 1019**
Tradition / May '96 / ADA / Vital

BANKLANDS
CD ____ **FE 100CB**
Fellside / Jan '95 / ADA / Direct / Target/ BMG

BAR RAM TOP 20 HITS
CD ____ **SONCD 0071**
Sonic Sounds / Sep '94 / Jet Star

BARA COUNTRY (Music From Madagascar)
CD ____ **C 560089**
Ocora / Feb '96 / ADA / Harmonia Mundi

BARBADOS SWEET FUH DAYS
CD ____ **CCD 0026**
CRS / Apr '96 / ADA / Direct / Jet Star

BARBECUE PARTY
Macarena: *Los Del Rio* / La danse de Zorba: *Trio Helenique* / Drink drink drink: *Baker,*

George Selection / Beach baby: *First Class* / Summerwine: *Roussos, Demis & Nancy Boyd* / Amor: *McKuen, Rod* / Hello summertime: *Goldsboro, Bobby* / There goes my heart again: *Domino, Fats* / Let's have a party: *Jackson, Wanda* / Poetry in motion: *Tillotson, Johnny* / Till I kissed you: *Everly Brothers* / La colegiala: *Low, Gary* / Belimbombero: *Los Reyes* / Music in the air: *US* / I'm your son South America: *Silvio* / Shame and scandal in the family: *Elliot, Shawn*
CD ______ DC 880802
Disky / May '97 / Disky / THE

BARCELONA GOLD
Barcelona: *Mercury, Freddie & Montserrat Caballe* / One song: *Campbell, Tevin* / How fast now: *Baker, Anita* / Higher baby: *DJ Jazzy Jeff & The Fresh Prince* / Keep it comin': *Sweat, Keith* / Free your mind: *En Vogue* / Don't tread on me: *Damn Yankees* / Go out dancing: *Stewart, Rod* / Texas flyer: *Tritt, Travis* / Heart to climb the mountain: *Travis, Randy* / Old soldier: *Cohn, Marc* / This used to be my playground: *Madonna* / No se tu: *Miguel, Luis* / Wonderful tonight: *Clapton, Eric* / Our love is here to stay: *Cole, Natalie* / Friends for life: *Carreras, Jose & Sarah Brightman*
CD ______ 9362450462
Warner Bros. / Aug '92 / Warner Music

BARDES FROM THE MAKRAM (Traditional Music From Baluchistan, Iran/Pakistan)
CD ______ 926332
BUDA / Feb '96 / Discovery

BARDS OF THE HIMALAYAS, THE (Epics & Trance Music)
CD ______ CNR 2741080
Le Chant Du Monde / Aug '97 / Harmonia Mundi

BARNBRACK: 22 IRISH FOLK PUB SONGS
CD ______ HRL 199CD
Outlet / Aug '94 / ADA / CM / Direct / Duncans / Koch / Ross

BARONG
CD ______ VICG 52172
JVC World Library / Mar '96 / ADA / CM / Direct

BARRELHOUSE PIANO BLUES
CD ______ DOCD 5193
Document / Oct '93 / ADA / Hot Shot / Jazz Music

BARRELHOUSE WOMEN VOL.2 (1924-1928)
CD ______ DOCD 5497
Document / Nov '96 / ADA / Hot Shot / Jazz Music

BASEMENT BOP (British Jazz In The 1950's/2CD Set)
Mike's choice: *Melody Maker New Stars* / Ten bar gait: *Whittle, Tommy Quintet* / Nemo: *Scott, Ronnie & His Orchestra* / Mango walk: *Graham, Kenny & His Afro Cubists* / For voters only: *Melody Maker All Stars* / Bremavin: *Dankworth, Johnny Quartet* / Smoke gets in your eyes: *Scott, Ronnie Quintet* / 52nd Street theme: *Scott, Ronnie Boptet* / Mop mop: *Feldman, Victor* / Flat foot: *Laurie, Cy* / It's a pity to say goodnight: *Laine, Cleo & John Dankworth* / Weaver of dreams: *Branscombe, Alan* / I can't get started: *All Star Sextet* / Not so fast: *Scott, Ronnie & Kenny Graham* / Night in Tunisia: *Dankworth, Johnny Quartet* / Close as pages in a book: *Deaucher, Jimmy* / All the things you are: *Scott, Ronnie & His Orchestra* / Fifth man: *Melody Maker New Stars* / Cotton tail: *Christie, Keith Quartet* / Scrapple from the apple: *Scott, Ronnie Boptet* / It was a lover and his lass: *Laine, Cleo & John Dankworth* / Battle royal: *Scott, Ronnie & Kenny Graham* / Pina colada: *Graham, Kenny & His Afro Cubists* / Gershwin ballad medley: *Melody Maker All Stars* / Jelly roll: *Laurie, Cy* / Stars fell on Alabama: *Whittle, Tommy Quintet* / Avalon: *Scott, Ronnie Boptet* / Oop pop a da: *All Star Sextet* / On green dolphin street: *Branscombe, Alan* / Ladybird: *Feldman, Victor*
CD Set ______ 330412
Hallmark / Mar '97 / Carlton

BASIC DANCE TRAXX
CD ______ CCC 97005
Citycat Club / Jul '97 / TKO Magnum

BASIC TECHNO
CD ______ 7700684
Omnisonus / Oct '96 / Cargo

BASIC TECHNO VOL.2
CD ______ 7702000
Omnisonus / Jun '97 / Cargo

BASS GENERATOR SINGLES COLLECTION VOL.1
CD ______ GTX 017CD
Bass Generator / Jan '96 / Alphamagic

BASS GENERATOR SINGLES COLLECTION VOL.2
CD ______ GTX 018CD
Bass Generator / Jan '96 / Alphamagic

BASS TALK VOL.4
CD ______ EFA 128222
Hot Wire / Feb '96 / SRD

BASS-IC ELEMENTS
It's a dope thang: *HED UK* / Chronicles in dub: *2 Dreds In A Dub* / Sax'n'ting: *Ruf Intelligence* / Phat and phuturistic: *Little Matt* / Future now: *Atomic Dog* / Whole world: *Endemic Void* / Deeply: *Universal Love* / T power: *Mutant Jazz* / Lid: *Eugenix* / Atmosphere: *DJ Phantasy* / Taken over: *Fallen Angels* / Phone me in the morning: *Sub Sequence*
CD ______ CDTOT 33
Jumpin' & Pumpin' / Sep '95 / 3mv/Sony / Mo's Music Machine

BASSA MUSICA
CD ______ CT 0001CD
Robi Droli / Apr '95 / ADA / Direct

BATAK OF NORTH SUMATRA
CD ______ NA 046
New Albion / Oct '92 / Cadillac / Harmonia Mundi

BATTERY POINT
Dirty mags: *Blueboy* / He gets me so hard: *Boyracer* / Autobiography: *Hit Parade* / Fran: *Aberdeen* / River: *Blueboy* / Last September's farewell kiss: *Northern Picture Library* / Wish you would: *Ivy* / Reproduction is pollution: *Shelley* / Mustard gas: *Action Painting* / Avenge: *Ivy* / Deep thinker: *Secret Shine* / Top 40 sculpture: *Sugargliders* / Paris: *Northern Picture Library* / Fireworks: *Aberdeen* / Toulouse: *Blueboy* / Hero: *Shelley*
CD ______ SARAH 359CD
Sarah / Jul '95 / Vital

BATTLE OF THE GARAGES PART 2
CD ______ VOXXCD 2068
Voxx / Oct '93 / Else / RTM/Disc

BATTLE OF THE GARAGES VOL.1, THE
CD ______ VOXXCD 2067
Voxx / Oct '93 / Else / RTM/Disc

BATTLE OF THE SAXES
CD ______ TCD 1026
Tradition / Aug '96 / ADA / Vital

BATTLE OF THE SAXES (The Great Jazz Saxophonists 1927-1946)
Battle of the saxes: *Hawkins, Coleman Sax Ensemble* / Esquire swank: *Hodges, Johnny & Duke Ellington Orchestra* / Favour of a fool: *Carter, Benny Orchestra* / Willow weep: *Jefferson, Hilton & Cab Calloway Orchestra* / Willow weep for me: *Smith, Willie Orchestra* / Ornithology: *Parker, Charlie Septet* / You need coachin': *Bostic, Earl & Don Byas/Hot Lips Page Orchestra* / Lullaby: *Hawkins, Coleman Trio* / Tea for two: *Freeman, Bud Orchestra* / I don't stand a ghost of a chance with you: *Berry, Leon 'Chu' & Cab Calloway Orchestra* / Afternoon of a Basie-ite: *Young, Lester Quartet* / Lotta sax appeal: *Wilson, Dick & Andy Kirk Orchestra* / Call me a taxi: *Miller, Eddie & The Bob Cats* / Concerto for tenor: *Auld, Georgie & His Orchestra* / Have you changed: *Webster, Ben & Harry Carney/Duke Ellington Orchestra* / Stompin' at The Savoy: *Phillips, Flip Fliptet* / Trumbology: *Trumbauer, Frankie Orchestra* / Pompton Turnpike: *Barnet, Charlie Orchestra* / Indian summer: *Bechet, Sidney New Orleans Feetwarmers* / Tired socks: *Hodges, Johnny Orchestra* / Prelude to a kiss: *Carney, Harry & Duke Ellington Orchestra* / Humouresque in swing time: *Caceras, Ernie & Emilio Trio* / Beatin' the dog: *Rollini, Adrian & Joe Venuti Blue Four*
CD ______ CDAJA 5247
Living Era / Aug '97 / Select

BATUCADA - THE SOUND OF THE FAVELAS
Ritmo no.1: *De Costa, Paulinho* / Batumata: *Fernando* / So no apito: *Padre, Miguel* / Otao e eu: *Jaritz, Nicos* / Repimar: *De Castro, Jadir & Dom Um* / Vibrando com a selecao: *Amarelo, Verde* / Ba-tu-ca-da: *Pas Ney De Castro* / Communic - Ritmo: *De Castro, Jadir & Dom Um* / Mulata Faceira: *Fernando* / Rapido: *Bateria Nota* / Pai Bene Queimou o Pe: *Fantastica Bateria* / Ozonia: *De Castro, Jadir & Dom Um* / Quando: *Fernando*
CD ______ MRBCD 005
Mr. Bongo / Mar '96 / New Note/Pinnacle / RTM/Disc / SRD

BAULE VOCAL MUSIC FROM THE IVORY COAST
CD ______ AUD 008048
Auvidis/Ethnic / Nov '93 / ADA / Harmonia Mundi

BAWDY BLUES
CD ______ OBCCD 544
Original Blues Classics / Nov '92 / Complete/Pinnacle / Wellard

BAYERN: VOLKSMUSIK 1906-1941
CD ______ US 0196
Trikont / Jul '95 / ADA / Direct

BAYOU BLUES MASTERS - GOLDBAND BLUES
I'm a country boy / Purty little dolly / Going crazy baby / Broke and hungry / Make up my mind / Need shorter hours / It ain't right / Just got to (take a) ride / Wanna do me wrong / Tin pan alley / I got fever / Life's journey / Honey bee / Sunday morning / Trouble in my home / Oh Ramona / Highway back home / I'm going / Please stand by me / Too tired / Let me hold your hand / What in the world are you gonna do / Something working baby / Pretty little red dress / C-Key blues / Catch that morning train
CD ______ CDCHD 427
Ace / Aug '93 / Pinnacle

BAYOU DANCE PARTY
CD ______ EDCD 7014
Easydisc / Aug '96 / Direct

BAZOOKA EXPLOSION, THE
CD ______ SONCD 0061
Sonic Sounds / Mar '94 / Jet Star

BBC SONGS OF PRAISE FROM OLD TRAFFORD
All people that on earth do dwell / Guide me o thou great redeemer / Amazing Grace / Thorns in the straw / Rejoice rejoice / When the saints go marching in / Mine eyes have seen the glory / Oh happy day / Shine, Jesus, shine / Alleluia / Sing to Jesus / Abide with me / You'll never walk alone
CD ______ ALD 026
Alliance Music / Jun '95 / EMI

BE BOP
What is this thing called love: *Esquire Five* / Gone with the wind: *Feldman, Victor Quartet* / Buzzy: *Jazz At The Town Hall Ensemble* / Fallonology: *All Star Sextet* / Wee dot: *Scott, Ronnie Boptet* / Too marvellous for words: *Scott, Ronnie Quartet* / Little Willie leaps: *Scott, Ronnie Boptet* / Compus mentos: *Scott, Ronnie & His Orchestra* / Loverman: *Dankworth, John* / Gone with the windmill: *Dean, Alan Beboppers* / I hear music: *Dankworth, John Seven* / Our delight: *Dankworth, John Seven* / Over the rainbow: *Graham, Kenny & His Afro Cubists* / Stars fell on Alabama: *Burns, Norman Quartet* / Johnny come lately: *Burns, Tito Sextet* / Why do I love you: *Burns, Tito Sextet*
CD ______ 305052
Hallmark / Jun '97 / Carlton

BE BOP 1945-1953
CD ______ CD 53029
Giants Of Jazz / Mar '90 / Cadillac / Jazz Music / Target/BMG

BE BOP IN PARIS VOL.1
CD ______ 2512882
Jazztime / Mar '90 / Discovery

BE BOP STORY 1944-1945, THE (3CD Set)
CD Set ______ 152362
EPM / Sep '96 / ADA / Discovery

BE BOP TO HIP HOP (A Selection Of Contemporary Scottish Jazz)
Black pyramid: *Murray, D.S. Quartet* / Guajira del sol: *Salsa Celtica* / Western ways: *Coco & The Bean* / Crazy dog theme/On the Beach Boys bus: *Hung Drawn Quartet* / Solidad: *Travis, Mike EH15* / No Romance: *Clark, Nigel Quintet* / Blue blue feeling: *White, Tam Band* / Topsy: *Severn, Eddie Quartet* / Blanks for the memory: *Conway, Dave* / Space: *Henderson, Robert Quintet*
CD ______ DEMUS 961
Demus / Aug '96 / New Note/Pinnacle

BEACH HITS - SONGS OF SUMMER
CD ______ JHD 013
Tring / Jun '92 / Tring

BEACH 'N' BOOGIE VOL.1
Shakin' dem bones: *Wilson, U.P.* / She's the one for me: *Parker, Kenny* / Here we go: *Rawls, Johnny* / Fine as wine: *Coronado, Joe* / Talkin' about love: *Butler Twins* / How much longer: *Farr, Deitra* / They killed crazy horse: *Houston, Joe & Otis Grand* / In all of my life: *Ray, Kenny 'Blue'* / Hey brother: *Morello, Jimmy* / Aunt Nancy's ball: *Griswalds* / Hoochie Mama: *Jones, Andrew 'Jr. Boy'* / Hot and saucy short and grand: *Guitar Shorty & Otis Grand* / You must be crazy: *Brown, Nappy* / Down and out: *Sayles, Charlie* / Bluesmobile: *Walker, Philip & Otis Grand* / Mo's stroll: *Buford, Mojo* / Roll over: *Wilson, U.P.* / You need to know: *Williams, Alanda*
CD ______ JSPCD 2100
JSP / Jul '97 / ADA / Cadillac / Direct / Hot Shot / Target/BMG

BEACH PARTY
Beach baby: *First Class* / Sunshine reggae: *Laidback* / Barbados: *Typically Tropical* / Red sails in the sunset: *Domino, Fats* / Mexico: *Humphries, Les Singers* / Tropicana bay: *Roussos, Demis & Nancy Boyd* / Little green bag: *Baker, George Selection* / Volare: *Martino, Al* / It never rains in Southern California: *Hammond, Albert & Albert West* / Cara mia: *Jay & The Americans* / Big bamboo: *Merry Men* / Sunglasses: *Ullman, Tracey* / Santa maria: *Tatjana* / Daydream: *Lovin' Spoonful* / Little old lady from Pasadena: *Jan & Dean* / Do wah diddy diddy: *Manfred Mann*
CD ______ DC 880772
Disky / May '97 / Disky / THE

BEACH, SUN AND SURFIN'
CD ______ 12541
Laserlight / Jul '95 / Target/BMG

BEAN STALK ALL STARS
CD ______ 793032
Melodie / Jul '97 / ADA / Discovery / Grapevine/PolyGram / Greensleeves / Jet Star

BEAT AT CINECITTA
CD ______ EFA 043822
Crippled Dick Hot Wax / Jun '97 / SRD

BEAT BOMBS VOL.1
CD ______ EFA 129602
Catch-a-Groove / Mar '97 / SRD

BEAT CLASSIC
B-Beat classic: *B+* / Something fresh to swing to: *Levi 167* / It's your rock: *Fantasy Three* / It's life: *Rock Master Scott* / Shout: *MC Craig G* / Just call us def: *Steady B* / Never satisfied: *Hi-Fidelity Three* / Throwdown: *Disco Four* / Triple threat: *Z-3 Mc's* / Funky: *Ultramagnetic MC's* / Beat bop: *Rammelzee & K-Rob*
CD ______ DC 10CDX
DC Recordings / Jun '97 / RTM/Disc

BEAT FROM THE STAR CLUB, THE (2CD Set)
CD Set ______ OTR 1100031
Metro Independent / Jun '97 / Essential/BMG

BEAT MERCHANTS
Man of the moment: *Clayson, Alan & The Argonauts* / Call of the wild: *Overlanders* / Pigtails in Paris: *MacBeth, David* / PFB: *Fabulous Flee Rekkers* / Come on baby (to the floral dance): *Eagles* / I could write a book: *Chants* / If you don't come back: *Takers* / Lies: *Sandon, Johnny & The Remo Four* / Show you mean it too: *Me & Them* / He's telling you lies: *Kingpin* / Think it over: *Hellions* / Funny how love can be: *Rockin' Berries* / Bags groove: *Sheffields* / Stage door: *Jackson, Tony* / Harry rag: *Kinks* / Lady Jane: *Garrick, David* / What a world: *Hill, Benny* / End of the season: *Uglys* / Popcorn double feature: *Searchers* / Everything's funny: *Troggs* / Born to be wild: *Nashville Teens* / Break up: *Downliners* / I'm still raving: *Sutch, Screaming Lord* / Heavy weather: *British Invasion* / Moonlight skater: *Berry, Dave*
CD ______ SEECD 430
See For Miles/C5 / Sep '95 / Pinnacle

BEAT OF NEW SOUTH AFRICA, THE
Laduma: *Ngema, Mbonegeni* / Usemncane: *Soul Brothers* / South Africa: *New South Africa* / Cry the beloved country: *Free At Last* / African solution: *Ngema, Mbonegeni* / Ndlondlo bashise: *Ngema, Mbonegeni* / Siyagiya: *Dark City Sisters* / Bazodlani: *Soul Brothers* / Daar is green: *Kerkorrel, Johannes* / Impedulo: *Elimhlophe, Ihashi* / Tumelo: *IPCC* / World: *Jambo* / Awuwa: *Kerkorrel, Johannes* / Ungakohlwa: *New South Africa* / Thwathwa: *Phale, Thomas*
CD ______ LBLV 2521
Indigo / Jul '96 / New Note/Pinnacle

BEAT OF SOWETO VOL.5
CD ______ STEW 34CD
Earthworks / Mar '96 / EMI

BEAT THE SYSTEM PUNK SINGLES COLLECTION
Stab the judge: *One Way System* / Riot torn city: *One Way System* / Youth of today: *External Menace* / Someday: *External Menace* / Die for me: *Uproar* / Better off dead: *Uproar* / Sad society: *Chaotic Youth* / No future UK: *Chaotic Youth* / I hate: *Fits* / Time is right: *Fits* / Official hooligan: *Anti Social* / No views: *External Menace* / Poor excuse: *External Menace* / Backstreet boys: *Anti Social* / Death and pure destruction: *Death Sentence* / Death sentence: *Death Sentence* / Too many people: *Anti Social* / Rebel youth: *Uproar* / Victims: *Uproar* / IRA: *Post Mortem* / Day by day: *Post Mortem* / Me and you: *One Way System* / Arms race: *Chaotic Youth* / Victims of war: *Death Sentence* / Listen to me: *Fits*
CD ______ CDPUNK 61
Anagram / Aug '95 / Cargo / Pinnacle

BEATING PUNK, PAST
CD ______ REM 20
Released Emotions / May '93 / RTM/Disc

BEATS BY DOPE DEMAND VOL.1
CD ______ KICKCD 28
Kickin' / Mar '96 / Prime / SRD

BEATS BY DOPE DEMAND VOL.2
CD ______ KICKCD 33
Kickin' / Mar '96 / Prime / SRD

BEATS BY DOPE DEMAND VOL.3 (2CD Set)
CD Set ______ KICKCD 46
Kickin' / Oct '96 / Prime / SRD

BEATS MELT DOWN
Dust bucket: *Fresh, Freddie* / Freshmess: *Hookian Mindz* / Freshmess on wax: *Riots* / Flava unit: *Playa* / aphrodite: *King Of The Beats* / Freashmess on wax: *Lyca Journey* / Interpret: *Atkins, Juan* / Citation: *Tons Of Tones* / Chiswick days: *Spectral Emotions* / Phunk=phunk: *Stalker* / Matter: *Sunrise Society* / Hayfever: *Speedy J* / System address: *ISM* / Squelch: *Fini Tribe*
CD ______ DBM 2943
Fierce / Jun '97 / SRD

BEATS RHYMES AND BASSLINES (The Best Of Rap)
Set adrift on memory bliss: *PM Dawn* / Paid in full: *Eric B & Rakim* / Say no go: *De La Soul* / Mama gave birth to the soul children: *Queen Latifah & De La Soul* / My definition of a boombastic jazz style: *Dream Warriors*

/ It's a shame (my sister): *Monie Love & True Image* / Summertime: *DJ Jazzy Jeff & The Fresh Prince* / Now that we've found love: *Heavy D & The Boyz* / Rebel without a pause: *Public Enemy* / (You gotta) Fight for your right (to party): *Beastie Boys* / Express yourself: *NWA* / U can't touch this: *MC Hammer* / Push it: *Salt n' Pepa* / Street tuff: *Rebel MC & Double Trouble* / Funky cold medina: *Tone Loc* / Got to keep on: *Cookie Crew*
CD 5153842
4th & Broadway / May '92 / PolyGram

BEATSVILLE DADDY-O
CD DADDY-OCD 001
No Hit / Feb '97 / Cargo / SRD

BEATZ BUMPS & AFROS
CD FSCD 0005
Freak Street / Oct '96 / Pinnacle

BEAUTY AN OILEAN
Seainin Mhicil O Suilleabhain / Muiris O Dalaigh / Sean O Dunnshleibhe / Sean O Cearnaigh / Padraig O Cearnaigh / Eibhlin Ni Chearna / Thomas O Dalaigh / Peaiti O Duinnshleibhe / Sean Cheaist O Cathain / Aine Ui Laoithe / Breanndan O Beaglaoich
CD CC 56 CD
Claddagh / Oct '92 / ADA / CM / Direct

BEAUTY IN DARKNESS
CD NB 166CD
Nuclear Blast / May '96 / Plastic Head

BEAUTY IN DARKNESS VOL.2
CD NB 256CD
Nuclear Blast / May '97 / Plastic Head

BEAVIS & BUTTHEAD DO AMERICA
Two cool guys: *Hayes, Isaac* / Love rollercoaster: *Red Hot Chili Peppers* / Ain't nobody: *LL Cool J* / Ratfinks, suicide tanks and cannibal girls: *White Zombie* / I wanna riot: *Rancid* / Walk on water: *Osbourne, Ozzy* / Snakes: *No Doubt* / Pimp'n ain't ez: *Madd Head* / Lord is a monkey (Rock version): *Butthole Surfers* / White trash: *Southern Culture On The Skids* / Gone shootin': *AC/DC* / Lesbian seagull: *Humperdinck, Engelbert*
CD GED 25002
Geffen / Feb '97 / BMG

BEDROOM TENORS
Don't explain: *Gordon, Dexter* / God bless the child: *Turrentine, Stanley* / Gone with the wind: *Getz, Stan* / Infant eyes: *Shorter, Wayne* / Nature boy: *Quebec, Ike* / Spring can really hang you up the most: *Sims, Zoot* / Sweet and lovely: *Jackson, Javon* / Namely you: *Rollins, Sonny* / Laura: *Henderson, Joe* / Someone to watch over me: *Hawkins, Coleman* / Love you to the letter: *Harp, Everette* / Good life: *Mobley, Hank*
CD CDP 8348732
Blue Note / Apr '96 / EMI

BEFORE THE BLUES VOL.1 (Early American Black Music Scene 1920's/1930's)
CD YAZ 2015
Yazoo / Mar '96 / ADA / CM / Koch

BEFORE THE BLUES VOL.2
CD YAZ 2016
Yazoo / Mar '96 / ADA / CM / Koch

BEFORE THE BLUES VOL.3
CD YAZ 2017
Yazoo / Mar '96 / ADA / CM / Koch

BEFORE YOU WERE PUNK
CD VR 330
Vagrant / Mar '97 / Cargo

BEGGARS BANQUET PUNK COLLECTION, THE
Shadow: *Lurkers* / Freak show: *Lurkers* / Don't tango on my heart: *Doll* / Trash: *Doll* / That's too bad: *Tubeway Army* / Ain't got a clue: *Lurkers* / Bombers: *Tubeway Army* / I don't need to tell her: *Tubeway Army* / Desire me: *Doll* / Just 13: *Lurkers* / Out in the dark: *Lurkers* / Cinderella with a husky smile: *Doll* / I don't mean it: *Carpettes* / New guitar in town: *Lurkers* / You used to be my hero: *Doll* / Johnny won't hurt me: *Carpettes* / Nothing ever changes: *Carpettes* / Last lone ranger: *Carpettes* / Laugh at me: *Stride, Pete & John Plain* / Winkers song: *Biggun, Ivor*
CD CDPUNK 73
Anagram / Mar '96 / Cargo / Pinnacle

BEGGARS OPERA
CD 8283822
London / Jan '93 / PolyGram

BEGIN THE BEGUINE - 1938
Begin the beguine: *Shaw, Artie* / Tisket-a-tasket: *Webb, Chick* / Ring dem bells: *Hampton, Lionel* / Sweet Georgia Brown: *Goodman, Benny Quartet* / I can't give you anything but love: *Armstrong, Louis* / Flat foot floogie: *Gaillard, Slim & Slam Stewart* / Music maestro please: *Dorsey, Tommy* / March of the bob cats: *Crosby, Bob* / When you're smiling: *Wilson, Teddy* / Swingin' the blues: *Basie, Count* / Louise: *Goodman, Benny* / Margie: *Lunceford, Jimmie* / Really the blues: *Ladnier, Tommy* / Little Joe from Chicago: *Kirk, Andy* / Back in your own backyard: *Holiday, Billie* / Back bay shuffle: *Shaw, Artie* / I let a song go out of my heart: *Ellington, Duke* / Jeepers creepers: *Krupa, Gene* / You must have been a beautiful baby: *Crosby, Bing* / Lullaby in rhythm: *James, Harry*
CD PHONTCD 7665
Phontastic / Apr '90 / Cadillac / Jazz Music / Wellard

BEGINNERS GUIDE TO THE GALAXY OF PSI-TRANCE (2CD Set)
CD Set ACTIVCD 9
Activ / Sep '96 / Total/BMG

BEGINNERS GUIDE TO TRADITIONAL SCOTTISH MUSIC
My fair young love/Father John MacMillan's farewell to Barra: *MacKay, Rhona* / Lude's supper: *Ossian* / Flame of wrath for squinting Patrick: *Livingstone, Pipe Major Bill* / Ewe wi'the crooked horn/Mrs. Mcpherson of Inveran: *Strathclyde Police Pipe Band* / Cradle song: *Gonnella, Ron* / Little pickle/Hare among the corn/Money in both pockets: *Glasgow Caledonian Strathspey & Reel Society* / Duke of Perth/Hunter's hill/Rakes of Mallow: *Ellis, John & His Highland Country Band* / Island of heather/Ciaro (Oran na Ciaoro): *Ellis, John & His Highland Country Band* / Puirt a beul: *MacInnes, Mairi* / Dh'theidhinn a dh'uibhist: *MacDonald Sisters* / Renfrewshire Militia/Tenpenny bit: *Stewart, Belle* / Chi mi'n geamhradh: *Runrig* / Battle of Harlaw: *Hunter, Andy* / Nicky Tams: *Stewart, Andy* / Flower o'the Quern: *Redpath, Jean* / Skye boat song: *McKellar, Kenneth* / Tartan: *Alexander Brothers* / Freedom come all ye: *Johnstone, Arthur* / Flying haggis/Peacock/MacArthur Road/Kiss the train goodbye: *Mathieson, Pipe Major Robert* / Journey to Skye: *Mathieson, Pipe Major Robert* / Ca' the yowes: *Gaelforce Orchestra* / Boys of Ballymoat: *Wolfstone*
CD LCOM 5227
Lismor / Mar '94 / ADA / Direct / Duncans / Lismor

BEGINNING, THE (Jazz At The Philharmonic)
Lester leaps in / Tea for two / Blues / Body and soul / I've found a new baby / Rosetta / Bugle call rag / How high the moon
CD LEJAZZCD 41
Le Jazz / Jun '95 / Cadillac / Koch

BEGUINE A LA CANNE A SUCRE 1946-1949
CD FA 051
Fremeaux / Oct '96 / ADA / Discovery

BEHIND THE EYE VOL.1
Cafe del mar: *Energy 52* / Magnifica: *Sonic Infusion* / Wonderer: *Vernon* / No fate: *Zyon* / See you virtual symmetry: *Odysee Of Noises* / Freebeach: *Goahead* / Airborn: *Mirage* / Sundown: *Volunteers* / Cosmos: *Java* / Synfonica: *Brainchild*
CD 4509962162
Eye Q / Feb '94 / Vital

BEHIND THE EYE VOL.2
CD 4509990922
Eye Q / Feb '95 / Vital

BELFAST BEAT - MARITIME BLUES
Don't start crying now: *Them* / Philosophy: *Them* / I can tell: *Mad Lads* / I'm leaving: *Wheels* / Road block: *Wheels* / Send me your pillow: *Wheels* / It's a cruel world: *Luvin' Kind* / Well don't that beat them all: *Just Five* / On the waterfront: *Bats* / Strangers: *Mad Lads* / Bad little woman: *Wheels* / Call my love: *Wheels* / Don't you know: *Wheels* / I'm with you: *People* / Well...alright: *People* / Little Queenie: *Mad Lads* / You got me dizzy: *Wheels* / Kicks: *Wheels* / Tell me (I'm gonna love gain): *Wheels* / I went out with my baby tonight: *Moses K & The Prophets* / Answer your phone: *Mad Lads* / I will have you: *Just Five* / Answers please: *Luvin' Kind* / Chicago calling: *Alleykatz* / Mona: *Wheels* / Gloria: *Wheels* / Bad little woman: *Wheel-a-ways*
CD CDWIKD 152
Big Beat / Apr '97 / Pinnacle

BELIEVE IN THE FREQUENCY POWER
Eternal: *Organisation* / Gotham City: *Animism* / Day of return (with dolphins): *Drawing Future Life* / Vermillion: *Suzukiski* / Colona: *Solaire* / Prussian blue smog: *Ultra AA* / Deep inside of me: *Ken Inaoka* / Halo: *Palomatic* / Dawn in the rainland: *Hazemato, Kiyoshi* / Phonetic: *Mind Design*
CD JAP 100CD
North South / May '94 / Pinnacle

BELLEVUE
CD MFCD 004
Mafia/Fluxy / Jan '94 / Jet Star / SRD

BELLISSIMO VOL.1 (The El Records Story)
La pluie fait des claquettes: *Philippe, Louis* / Ruling class: *Adverse, Anthony* / Straits of Malacca: *King Of Luxembourg* / St. Lucy: *Gol Gappas* / Nicky: *Momus* / Reach for your gun: *Bid* / It's a beautiful game: *Cavaliers* / Southern fields: *Rosemary's Children* / Our fairy tale: *Adverse, Anthony* / Valleri: *King Of Luxembourg* / Like nobody do: *Philippe, Louis* / Dreams of leaving: *Always* / Fire: *Underneath* / Curtain: *Marden Hill* / Montague terrace (In blue): *Mayfair Charm School* / Never underestimate the ignorance of the rich: *Klaxon 5* / West 14: *Gol Gappas* / Libera me: *Cagliostra* / You Mary you: *Philippe, Louis* / Picture of Dorian Gray: *King Of Luxembourg*
CD MONDE 11CD
Richmond / Apr '93 / Pinnacle

BELLISSIMO VOL.2 (The El Records Story)
Man of mine: *Florentines* / Whoops what a palaver: *Raj Quartet* / Metroland: *Always* / Fruit paradise: *Would-Be-Goods* / Imperial violets: *Adverse, Anthony* / Robe: *Marden Hill* / Anthony bay: *Philippe, Louis* / Trial of Dr. Fancy: *King Of Luxembourg* / Curry crazy: *Bad Dream Fancy Dress* / Thames Valley leather club: *Always* / Red shoes waltz: *Adverse, Anthony* / Oh Constance: *Marden Hill* / Pop up man: *Ambassador 277* / Flirt bliss love kiss: *King Of Luxembourg* / Camera loves me: *Would-Be-Goods* / Guess I'm dumb: *Philippe, Louis* / Supremes: *Bad Dream Fancy Dress* / Flair: *Bad Dream Fancy Dress* / Paradise lost: *Adverse, Anthony* / Sean Connery: *James Dean Driving Experience*
CD MONDE 12CD
Richmond / Apr '93 / Pinnacle

BELLY DANCE IN CAIRO
CD PS 65141CD
PlayaSound / Apr '95 / ADA / Harmonia Mundi

BEN & JERRY'S NEWPORT FESTIVAL
CD RHRCD 36
Red House / Jul '95 / ADA / Koch

BEND IT '91
CD PELE 001CD
Exotica / Dec '91 / SRD / Vital

BEND IT '93
It only takes a second to score a goal: *Lira* / Hotspurs boogie: *Glitterbest* / My ideal woman: *Best, George* / George (you've broken my heart): *Her* / Rah rah rah for Man Utd: *Dollies* / 1-0 for your love: *Beckenbauer, Franz* / Julie Brown loves Captain Cook: *Barrett, Les* / Le match de football: *Antoine* / Funky Manchester City: *Antoine* / Pele at Aston Villa: *Antoine* / Canoca: *Philippe, Louis* / World Cup doo wop: *Rosettes* / Don't shoot the ref: *McLeod, John X1* / Brian talk: *McLeod, John X1* / I'm football crazy: *Chinaglia, Giorgio* / Diego Armando Maradona: *Baccini, Francesco* / Fiorentina canzone viola: *Poti, Otello* / Genoa red and blue: *Baccini, Francesco & Fabrizio De Andre* / Cantona superstar: *Her* / J League freakout: *Rainbow Choir*
CD PELE 005CD
Exotica / Sep '93 / SRD / Vital

BEND IT '94 VOL.1
Goal - world cup 1966: *Sound Of Johnny Hawksworth* / Pele: *Cornelius* / Sampdoria formazione: *Cornelius* / Brazil Brazil: *Narraga O De Waldir Amaral* / World Cup football jazz: *Karie, Kahimi* / World Cup chacha: *Silvester, Victor* / Roberto Baggio - Non e un miraggio: *Il General & Ludus Pinski* / George Best - Belfast boy: *Romaine* / Georgie you've broken my heart: *Her* / George Best: *El Beatle* / World Cup chitchat: *Magnificent Andersons* / Carioca maracana: *Dreamers* / Tip top Tottenham Hotspurs: *Totnamites* / Roger Milla - My number 9 dream: *Rainbow Choir* / Ryan Giggs we love you: *Rainbow Choir* / Diego Armando Maradona: *Baggini, Francesco* / 1-0 For your love: *Bekenbaur, Franz* / Eusebio: *Philippe, Louis* / Johan Cruyff - Flying Dutchnman: *Bridge* / Pele - El Rey: *Alberto, Luis* / Manchestr United calypso: *Connor, Edric & Ken Jones* / Blackpool Blackpool: *Nolans* / World Cup doo wop: *Rosettes* / Back home - England 1970: *Stewart, Ed* / Soccer boppers: *Posh*
CD HARP 013
Exotica / Aug '94 / SRD / Vital

BEND IT '94 VOL.2
Sunshine of your smile: *Light Billy Wright* / Nice one Cyril: *Stewart, Ed Stewpot & Junior Choice* / Come on The Fish: *Fisher Athletic* / Up The Shakers: *Bury* / Sunderland are back in the First Division: *Fine Art* / We'll be with you: *Stoke City* / Oh oh oh oh oh: *West Bromwich Albion* / Georgie: *Lucy* / George Best - Belfast Boy: *Chocolate Barry* / Glory glory Man United: *Rainbow Choir* / Love only me: *Grainger, Colin* / Red red robin: *Cotton, Billy & Charlton Athletic* / We want Rodney Marsh: *Cotton, Billy & Charlton Athletic* / Good morning Mexico: *Cotton, Billy & Charlton Athletic* / My Christmas song (Cancao de natal): *Pele* / Pele: *Marsh, Peggy* / Popstyle of a Brazilian footballer: *Cezar, Paolo* / Dedicated to Giancarlo Antognoni: *Cezar, Paolo* / Roberto Mancini: *De Scalzi Brothers* / Song of the Clyde: *Rocheteau, Dominique* / Simple little things: *Charlton, Jack*
CD PELE 008CD
Exotica / Jan '95 / SRD / Vital

BENEATH THE ICY FLOW VOL.4
CD PROJEKT 14CD
Metal Blade / Apr '97 / Pinnacle / Plastic Head

BERKELEY EP'S
Bass strings: *Country Joe & The Fish* / Thing called love: *Country Joe & The Fish* / Section 43: *Country Joe & The Fish* / Hearts to cry: *Fruminous Bandersnatch* / Misty cloud: *Fruminous Bandersnatch* / Cheshire: *Fruminous Bandersnatch* / Gazelle: *Mad River* / Orange fire: *Mad River* / Windchimes: *Mad River* / Where does love go: *Notes From The Underground* / Down in the basement: *Notes From The Underground* / What am I doing here: *Notes From The Underground* / Got to get out of this dream: *Notes From The Underground* / You don't love me: *Notes From The Underground* / Let yourself fly: *Notes From The Underground* / Where I'm at today: *Notes From The Underground*
CD CDWIKD 153
Big Beat / Jun '95 / Pinnacle

BERLIN ALWAYS
Cheek to cheek: *Astaire, Fred* / This year's kisses: *Faye, Alice* / Alexander's ragtime band: *Goodman, Benny Orchestra* / Slumming on Park Avenue: *Lunceford, Jimmie & Orchestra* / I'm putting all my eggs in one basket: *Armstrong, Louis* / Waiting on the edge of the road: *Waters, Ethel* / Isn't this a lovely day (to be caught in the rain): *Ambrose & His Orchestra* / Shakin' the blues away: *Etting, Ruth* / When I lost you: *Crosby, Bing* / Always: *Goodman, Benny Orchestra* / He ain't got rhythm: *Holiday, Billie* / I've got my love to keep me warm: *Tatum, Art* / Blue skies: *Dorsey, Tommy Orchestra* / I want to be in Dixie: *American Ragtime Octette* / Let yourself go: *Astaire, Fred* / How's chances: *Hall, Henry & The BBC Dance Orchestra* / Harlem on my mind: *Waters, Ethel* / Russian lullaby: *Berigan, Bunny & His Orchestra* / How deep is the ocean: *Crosby, Bing* / When the midnight choo choo leaves for Alabam': *Dorsey, Tommy Orchestra* / Now it can be told: *Bowlly, Al*
CD AVC 517
Avid / Apr '93 / Avid/BMG / Koch / THE

BERLIN BY NIGHT
Ungarwein (gipsy wine): *Von Geczy, Barnabas & His Orchestra* / Ich tanze mit dir in den himmel hinein: *Harvey, Lilian & Willi Fritsch* / Gruss und kuss Veronika: *Die Weintraubs* / Regentropfen: *Ruth, Ludwig Orchestra & Metropol Vocalists* / Musik Musik: *Stenzel, Otto Dance Orchestra* / Arpanetta: *Gaden, Robert Orchestra* / Abends in der taverne: *Strienz, Wilhelm* / Du hast gluck bei den frau'n bel ami: *Waldmuller, Lizzi* / Wochenend und sonnenschein: *Comedy Harmonists* / Liebling mein herz lasst dich grussen: *Harvey, Lilian & Willi Fritsch* / Rosamunde: *Glahe, Will Orchestra* / Liebe is ein geheimnis: *Hildebrand, Hilde & Orchestra* / O mia bella Napoli: *Schuricke, Rudi* / Lili Marlene: *Andersen, Lale* / Schones wetter heute: *Zacharias, Helmut* / Sing: *Kunneke, Evelyn* / Liebe, kleine schaffnerin: *Carl, Rudolf* / Es geht alles voruber, es geht alles vorbei: *Andersen, Lale* / Das alte spinnrad: *Groh, Herbert Ernst & Odeon-Kunstler Orchester* / Sag' beim abschied leise "servus": *Forst, Willi*
CD CDEMS 1395
EMI / May '91 / EMI

BERSERKLEY
CD CREV 010CD
Rev-Ola / Mar '93 / 3mv/Vital

BESERK
CD DBM 2141
Happy Trax / Sep '96 / Grapevine/PolyGram / Mo's Music Machine / SRD

BEST 60'S MEGAMIX, THE
My friend Jake: *Smoke* / Take a heart: *Sorrow* / Don't stop the carnival: *Price, Alan* / Long shot kick the bucket: *Pioneers* / Red red wine: *Tribe, Tony* / Train to Skaville: *Ethiopians* / Melting pot: *Blue Mink* / I put a spell on you: *Price, Alan* / That's nice: *Christian, Neil* / Wonderful world, beautiful people: *Cliff, Jimmy* / It mek: *Dekker, Desmond* / Israelites: *Dekker, Desmond* / Shame: *Price, Alan* / More than I can say: *Vee, Bobby* / Hey baby: *Quarrymen* / Louie Louie: *Fontana, Wayne* / Love letters: *Proby, P.J.* / Tell Laura I love her: *Valance, Ricky* / Money: *Fontana, Wayne* / Groovy kinda love: *Fontana, Wayne* / Up on the roof: *Valance, Ricky* / Unchained melody: *Quarrymen* / Hold me: *Proby, P.J.* / Chains: *Four Pennies* / Johnny remember me: *Leyton, John* / Crying: *Shannon, Del* / Lonesome drums: *Nelson, Sandy* / 007: *Dekker, Desmond* / Return of Django: *Upsetters* / Liquidator: *Harry J All Stars*
CD 306812
Hallmark / May '97 / Carlton

BEST 70'S MEGAMIX, THE
If I had you: *Korgis* / Rock 'n' roll winter: *Wizzard* / Knock on wood: *Stewart, Amii* / Hellraiser: *Sweet* / Tomorrow night: *Atomic Rooster* / Clog dance: *Violinski* / Moudy old dough: *Lieutenant Pigeon* / Are you ready to rock: *Wizzard* / 7 Teen: *Regents* / Something better change: *Stranglers* / Do anything you wanna do: *Eddie & The Hot Rods* / Banana splits: *Dickies* / Silver Machine: *Hawkwind* / (Dancing) on a Saturday night: *Blue, Barry* / Chirpy, chirpy, cheep, cheep: *Kissoon, Mac & Katie* / Oh what a shame: *Wood, Roy* / Teenage depression: *Eddie & The Hot Rods* / Nice one Cyril: *Cockerel Chorus* / Snoopy & the red baron: *Hot Shots* / No honestly: *De Paul, Lynsey* / Indian reservation: *Fardon, Don* / You can get it if you really want: *Dekker, Desmond* / Young, gifted and black: *Bob & Marcia* / Everything I own: *Boothe, Ken* / Irie feelings: *Edwards, Rupie* / Double barrel: *Collins, Dave & Ansell* / Pied piper: *Bob & Mar-*

cia / Jarrow song: *Price, Alan* / Banner man: *Blue Mink* / Ballroom blitz: *Sweet* / Block buster: *Sweet* / Randy: *Blue Mink* / Help me make it through the night: *Holt, John*
CD _______________ **306352**
Hallmark / Jan '97 / Carlton

BEST 80'S ALBUM IN THE WORLD...EVER, THE (2CD Set)
Don't you want me: *Human League* / There must be an angel (playing with my heart): *Eurythmics* / Sledgehammer: *Gabriel, Peter* / Don't you forget about me: *Simple Minds* / Money for nothing: *Dire Straits* / Gimme all your lovin': *ZZ Top* / Dead ringer for love: *Meat Loaf* / Good heart: *Sharkey, Feargal* / Every breath you take: *Police* / Faith: *Michael, George* / If I could turn back time: *Cher* / Girls just wanna have fun: *Lauper, Cyndi* / Relax: *Frankie Goes To Hollywood* / House of fun: *Madness* / Going underground: *Jam* / She drives me crazy: *Fine Young Cannibals* / Golden brown: *Stranglers* / What's love got to do with it: *Turner, Tina* / I can't go for that (no can do): *Hall & Oates* / Wherever I lay my hat (that's my home): *Young, Paul* / Take on me: *A-Ha* / Freedom: *Wham* / Only way is up: *Yazz* / Ride on time: *Black Box* / Temptation: *Heaven 17* / Ain't nobody: *Rufus & Chaka Khan* / Back to life: *Soul II Soul* / All around the world: *Stansfield, Lisa* / Look of love: *ABC* / Stop: *Erasure* / Only you: *Yazoo* / Song for whoever: *Beautiful South* / You got it: *Orbison, Roy* / Heaven is a place on earth: *Carlisle, Belinda* / Alone: *Heart* / Moonlight shadow: *Oldfield, Mike* / China in your hand: *T'Pau* / Drive: *Cars* / Vienna: *Ultravox* / Enola Gay: *OMD*
CD Set _______________ **VTDCD 68**
Virgin / Oct '95 / EMI

BEST ALBUM IN THE WORLD...EVER VOL.1, THE (2CD Set)
Alright: *Supergrass* / Girls and boys: *Blur* / Waking up: *Elastica* / Girls from mars: *Ash* / Whatever: *Oasis* / Girl like you: *Collins, Edwyn* / Only one I know: *Charlatans* / Do you remember the first time: *Pulp* / Yes: *McAlmont & Butler* / Everyday is like Sunday: *Morrissey* / High and dry: *Radiohead* / Zombie: *Cranberries* / Today: *Smashing Pumpkins* / La tristesse durera (Scream to a sigh): *Manic Street Preachers* / Sit down: *James* / Wake up boo: *Boo Radleys* / Animal nitrate: *Suede* / This is music: *Verve* / I want you: *Inspiral Carpets* / Screamager: *Therapy* / This charming man: *Smiths* / April skies: *Jesus & Mary Chain* / Supersonic: *Oasis* / Fools gold: *Stone Roses* / Connected: *Stereo MC's* / Out of space: *Prodigy* / Destination eschaton: *Shamen* / True faith '94: *New Order* / Leave home: *Chemical Brothers* / Bullet: *Fluke* / Loaded: *Primal Scream* / Unbelievable: *EMF* / Real real real: *Jesus Jones* / Personal Jesus: *Depeche Mode* / Chemical world: *Blur* / Fifteen years: *Levellers* / Lenny Valentino: *Auteurs* / I can dream: *Skunk Anansie* / Captain Dread: *Dreadzone* / Lifeforms: *Future Sound Of London*
CD Set _______________ **VTDCD 58**
Virgin / Sep '95 / EMI

BEST ALBUM IN THE WORLD...EVER VOL.2, THE (2CD Set)
Wonderwall: *Oasis* / Wild wood: *Weller, Paul* / Creep: *Radiohead* / Fine time: *Cast* / Common people: *Pulp* / Life of riley: *Lightning Seeds* / Parklife: *Blur* / He's on the phone: *St. Etienne* / What do I do now: *Sleeper* / Hope street: *Levellers* / Caught by the fuzz: *Supergrass* / Hobo humpin' slobo babe: *Whale* / Angel interceptor: *Ash* / Single girl: *Lush* / Connection: *Elastica* / Queer: *Garbage* / She bangs the drum: *Stone Roses* / Blue Monday: *New Order* / How soon is now: *Smiths* / It's oh so quiet: *Bjork* / Little Britain: *Dreadzone* / Country house: *Blur* / Size of a cow: *Wonder Stuff* / Stardust: *Menswear* / Cigarettes and alcohol: *Oasis* / Kinky afro: *Happy Mondays* / Movin on up: *Primal Scream* / More you ignore me, the closer I get: *Morrissey* / History: *Verve* / Stay together: *Suede* / Just when you're thinking things over: *Charlatans* / Far gone and out: *Jesus & Mary Chain* / Great things: *Echobelly* / Might be stars: *Wannadies* / Weak: *Skunk Anansie* / Life is sweet: *Chemical Brothers* / Tosh: *Fluke* / Protection: *Massive Attack* / You do: *McAlmont & Butler*
CD Set _______________ **VTDCD 76**
Virgin / Jan '96 / EMI

BEST ALBUM IN THE WORLD...EVER VOL.3, THE (2CD Set)
Firestarter: *Prodigy* / Open up: *Leftfield* / Lust for life: *Iggy Pop* / Going out: *Supergrass* / Don't look back in anger: *Oasis* / Sandstorm: *Cast* / You've got it bad: *Ocean Colour Scene* / Stupid girl: *Garbage* / Pure: *Lightning Seeds* / What the world is waiting for: *Stone Roses* / Street spirit (fade out): *Radiohead* / Stars: *Dubstar* / Universal: *Blur* / Only love can break your heart: *St. Etienne* / Temptation: *New Order* / Garden: *Levellers* / Weirdo: *Charlatans* / Kung fu: *Ash* / Born slippy: *Underworld* / Changing man: *Weller, Paul* / Round are way: *Oasis* / Step on: *Happy Mondays* / Inbetweener: *Sleeper* / Ladykillers: *Lush* / Perseverance: *Terrorvision* / Whole lotta love: *Goldbug* / Spaceman: *Babylon Zoo* / Sleeping in: *Menswear* / Time: *Marion* / King of the kerb: *Echobelly* / My legendary girlfriend: *Pulp* / Stutter: *Elastica* / Selling Jesus: *Skunk Anansie* / Chemical beats: *Chemical Brothers* / Stay: *60ft Dolls* / Sparky's dream: *Teenage Fanclub* / For the dead: *Gene* / Life, love and unity: *Dreadzone* / Sly: *Massive Attack*
CD Set _______________ **VTDCD 84**
Virgin / Apr '96 / EMI

BEST ALBUM IN THE WORLD...EVER VOL.4, THE (2CD Set)
Some might say: *Oasis* / Alright: *Cast* / Day we caught the train: *Ocean Colour Scene* / Design for life: *Manic Street Preachers* / Trash: *Suede* / Goldfinger: *Ash* / Sale of the century: *Sleeper* / In a room: *Dodgy* / Sense: *Lightning Seeds* / Female of the species: *Space* / One to another: *Charlatans* / Loops of fury: *Chemical Brothers* / Born slippy: *Underworld* / No good (start the dance): *Prodigy* / Army of me: *Bjork* / Inner city life: *Goldie* / Walking wounded: *Everything But The Girl* / Step it up: *Stereo MC's* / Not so manic now: *Dubstar* / Sunflower: *Weller, Paul* / Orange crush: *REM* / Panic: *Smiths* / Charmless man: *Blur* / Just: *Radiohead* / Peaches: *Presidents Of The USA* / On a rope: *Rocket From The Crypt* / All I want: *Skunk Anansie* / Love spreads: *Stone Roses* / Only happy when it rains: *Garbage* / Oh yeah: *Ash* / You're gorgeous: *Baby Bird* / If you don't want me to destroy you: *Super Furry Animals* / Far: *Longpigs* / Stripper vicar: *Mansun* / Where have you been tonight: *Shed Seven* / Just the one: *Levellers* / Teenage angst: *Placebo* / Safe from harm: *Massive Attack* / 6 underground: *Sneaker Pimps* / Masterplan: *Oasis*
CD Set _______________ **VTDCD 96**
Virgin / Oct '96 / EMI

BEST ALBUM IN THE WORLD...EVER VOL.5, THE (2CD Set)
Sorted for E's and whizz: *Pulp* / Tattva: *Kula Shaker* / Live forever: *Oasis* / Everything must go: *Manic Street Preachers* / Beetlebum: *Blur* / Nancy boy: *Placebo* / Ain't talkin' 'bout dub: *Apollo 440* / Breathe: *Prodigy* / Scooby snacks: *Fun Lovin' Criminals* / Wide open space: *Mansun* / Barrel of a gun: *Depeche Mode* / Milk: *Garage* / Hedonism: *Skunk Anansie* / Beautiful ones: *Suede* / Day before yesterday's man: *Supernaturals* / Mum's gone to Iceland: *Bennet* / Nice guy Eddie: *Sleeper* / Getting better: *Shed Seven* / Lump: *Presidents Of The USA* / Into the blue: *Geneva* / Pearl's girl: *Underworld* / Out of the sinking: *Weller, Paul* / Roll with it: *Oasis* / Riverboat song: *Ocean Colour Scene* / What's the freqency Kenneth: *REM* / Hush: *Deep Purple* / Flying: *Cast* / Dark clouds: *Space* / Lucky you: *Lightning Seeds* / There she goes: *La's* / Good enough: *Dodgy* / Your woman: *White Town* / Candy girl: *Baby Bird* / Lopez: *808 State & James Dean Bradfield* / One night stand: *Aloof* / Fake plastic trees: *Radiohead* / Lost myself: *Longpigs* / Easy: *Terrorvision* / I am the resurrection: *Stone Roses*
CD Set _______________ **VTDCD 120**
Virgin / Mar '97 / EMI

BEST ALBUM IN THE WORLD...EVER VOL.6, THE (2CD Set)
CD Set _______________ **VTDCD 136**
Virgin / Jul '97 / EMI

BEST BLUES, THE
CD _______________ **CD 904**
Sound / Jun '89 / ADA

BEST CHOICE
CD _______________ **DCD 5388**
Disky / Jul '94 / Disky / THE

BEST CHRISTMAS ALBUM IN THE WORLD...EVER (2CD Set)
Happy Christmas (war is over): *Lennon, John & Yoko Ono* / Wonderful Christmastime: *McCartney, Paul* / I wish it could be Christmas every day: *Wizzard* / Merry Christmas everybody: *Slade* / Do they know it's Christmas: *Band Aid* / Fairytale of New York: *Pogues & Kirsty MacColl* / I believe in Father Christmas: *Lake, Greg* / 2000 miles: *Pretenders* / Spaceman came travelling: *De Burgh, Chris* / Power of love: *Frankie Goes To Hollywood* / Driving home for Christmas: *Rea, Chris* / Step into Christmas: *John, Elton* / Merry Christmas everyone: *Stevens, Shakin'* / Another rock and roll Christmas: *Glitter, Gary* / Little Saint Nick: *Beach Boys* / Santa Claus is coming to town: *Jackson Five* / In dulce jubilo: *Oldfield, Mike* / Stop the cavalry: *Lewie, Jona* / Christmas wrapping: *Waitresses* / Ring out, solstice bells: *Jethro Tull* / Peace on earth/Little drummer boy: *Crosby, Bing & David Bowie* / White Christmas: *Crosby, Bing* / Christmas song: *Cole, Nat 'King'* / Let it snow, let it snow, let it snow: *Martin, Dean* / Mary's boy child: *Belafonte, Harry* / When a child is born: *Mathis, Johnny* / Mistletoe and wine: *Richard, Cliff* / Walking in the air: *Jones, Aled* / I believe: *Robson & Jerome* / Winter wonderland: *Day, Doris* / Lonely pup (in a Christmas shop): *Faith, Adam* / Rockin' around the Christmas tree: *Mel & Kim* / Last Christmas: *State Of The Heart* / Happy holiday: *Williams, Andy* / Santa baby: *Kitt, Eartha* / Lonely this Christmas: *Mud* / Pretty paper: *Orbison, Roy* / Silver bells: *Reeves, Jim* / God rest ye merry gentlemen: *Como, Perry* / We wish you a merry Christmas: *Weavers* / Twelve days of Christmas: *Spinners* / Gaudette: *Steeleye Span* / In the bleak midwinter: *Jansch, Bert* / What are you doing New Year's eve: *O'Hara, Mary Margaret*
CD Set _______________ **VTDCD 103**
Virgin / Nov '96 / EMI

BEST CHRISTMAS ALBUM...EVER, THE (2CD Set)
Do they know it's Christmas: *Band Aid* / Last Christmas: *Wham* / Step into Christmas: *John, Elton* / Santa Claus is coming to town: *Jackson Five* / Merry Christmas everybody: *Slade* / In dulci jubilo: *Oldfield, Mike* / Stop the cavalry: *Lewie, Jona* / Rockin' around the Christmas tree: *Wilde, Kim* / Another rock and roll Christmas: *Glitter, Gary* / Mary had a little boy: *Snap* / Ring out, solstice bells: *Jethro Tull* / Saviour's day: *Richard, Cliff* / Mull of Kintyre: *Wings* / Spaceman came travelling: *De Burgh, Chris* / Winter's tale: *Essex, David* / Keeping the dream alive: *Freiheit* / Peace on earth - little drummer boy: *Bowie, David & Bing Crosby* / White Christmas: *Crosby, Bing* / Let it snow, let it snow, let it snow: *Martin, Dean* / Christmas song: *Fitzgerald, Ella* / Winter wonderland: *Day, Doris* / Warm December: *London, Julie* / Merry Christmas darling: *Carpenters* / Santa baby: *Kitt, Eartha* / Happy holiday: *Williams, Andy* / Lonely pup (in a Christmas shop): *Faith, Adam* / Blue Christmas: *Nelson, Willie* / Silver bells: *Reeves, Jim* / Mary's boy child: *Belafonte, Harry* / Twelve days of Christmas: *Daugherty, Jack* / Gaudete: *Steeleye Span* / Silent night: *Temptations* / Only you: *Flying Pickets* / Walking in the air: *Jones, Aled* / Christmas wrapping: *Waitresses* / Sadness part 1: *Enigma* / Merry Christmas everyone: *Stevens, Shakin'*
CD Set _______________ **VTDCD 23**
Virgin / Oct '95 / EMI

BEST CLUB ANTHEMS...EVER, THE (2CD Set)
Professional widow: *Amos, Tori* / Where love lives: *Limerick, Alison* / Don't you want me: *Felix* / I'm alive: *Stretch n' Vern* / Fairground: *Simply Red* / Klubhopping: *Klubb Heads* / Jumpin': *Lisa Marie Experience* / Scared: *Slacker* / Higher state of consciousness: *Wink, Josh* / Sugar is sweeter: *Bolland, C.J.* / Nightmare: *Brainbug* / Argentina: *Healy, Jeremy & Amos* / Bellissima: *DJ Quicksilver* / Children: *Miles, Robert* / Seven days and one week: *BBE* / Nighttrain: *Kadoc* / People of love: *Amen UK* / Give me love: *Diddy* / Born slippy: *Underworld* / I have peace: *Strike* / Remember me: *Blueboy* / You got the love: *Source & Candi Staton* / Is there anybody out there: *Bassheads* / Rhythm is a mystery: *K-Klass* / Closer than close: *Gaines, Rosie* / I'll be your friend: *Owens, Robert* / Hideaway: *De'Lacy* / Get up: *Stingily, Byron* / Ultra flava: *Heller & Farley Project* / Help me make it: *Huff & Puff* / Krupa: *Apollo 440* / Want love: *Hysteric Ego* / Offshore: *Chicane* / Rock da house: *Tall Paul* / Let me be your fantasy: *Baby D* / Walking wounded: *Everything But The Girl*
CD Set _______________ **VTDCD 124**
Virgin / Jun '97 / EMI

BEST COUNTRY ALBUM IN THE WORLD...EVER, THE (2CD Set)
Rhinestone cowboy: *Campbell, Glen* / Jolene: *Parton, Dolly* / When you're in love with a beautiful woman: *Dr. Hook* / Rose garden: *Anderson, Lynn* / Blanket on the ground: *Spears, Billie Jo* / Coward of the county: *Rogers, Kenny* / I recall a gypsy woman: *Williams, Don* / Most beautiful girl in the world: *Rich, Charlie* / Ode to Billy Joe: *Gentry, Bobbie* / Stand by your man: *Wynette, Tammy* / Crazy: *Cline, Patsy* / I love you because: *Reeves, Jim* / Don't it make my brown eyes blue: *Gayle, Crystal* / All I have to do is dream: *Gentry, Bobbie & Glen Campbell* / Wind beneath my wings: *Greenwood, Lee* / Angel of the morning: *Newton, Juice* / Banks of the Ohio: *Newton-John, Olivia* / We're all alone: *Coolidge, Rita* / Crying: *McLean, Don* / End of the world: *Davis, Skeeter* / Achy breaky heart: *Cyrus, Billy Ray* / Devil went down to Georgia: *Daniels, Charlie Band* / Promised land: *Allan, Johnnie* / I can help: *Swan, Billy* / Ring of fire: *Cash, Johnny* / I'll never fall in love again: *Gentry, Bobbie* / King of the road: *Miller, Paulette* / Games people play: *South, Joe* / Margaritaville: *Buffett, Jimmy* / Wichita lineman: *Campbell, Glen* / I will always love you: *Parton, Dolly* / From a distance: *Griffith, Nanci* / I fall to pieces: *Cline, Patsy* / Little bit more: *Dr. Hook* / Lucille: *Rogers, Kenny* / What I've got in mind: *Spears, Billie Jo* / It's over: *Orbison, Roy* / Me and Bobby McGee: *Kristofferson, Kris* / Funny how time slips away: *Nelson, Willie* / Night they drove old dixie down: *Band*
CD Set _______________ **VTDCD 146**
Virgin / Jul '97 / EMI

BEST COUNTRY DANCE ALBUM ON EARTH VOL.1, THE
Froggy went-a courtin': *Ritter, Tex* / White lightnin': *Jones, George* / Cowboys and injuns: *Savage, Big Red* / I'm a ramblin' man: *Draper, Rusty* / Games people play: *Haggard, Merle* / Wine me up: *Young, Faron* / Jambalaya: *Fender, Freddy* / Take me back to Tulsa: *Haggard, Merle* / Lonely days, lonely nights: *Loveless, Patty* / Ball and chain: *Mattea, Kathy* / Ida red: *Haggard, Merle* / Redneck girl: *Bellamy Brothers* / Johnsons of Turkey Ridge: *Paycheck, Johnny* / Teamster plan: *Thompson, Gunner* / Victory is coming: *Oak Ridge Boys* / San Antonia rose: *Haggard, Merle* / I never promised you a rose garden: *Anderson, Lynn* / Let your love flow: *Bellamy Brothers*
CD _______________ **SATRCD 0001**
Satril / Nov '96 / Henry Hadaway / THE

BEST COUNTRY DANCE ALBUM ON EARTH VOL.2, THE
Different breed of cowboy: *Thomas, Jay* / When my blue moon turns gold: *Bond, Johnny* / Bummin' around: *Williams, Tex* / Ghost riders in the sky: *Devan, Eddie* / I'm a ramblin' man: *Drusky, Roy* / Lifetime of regret: *Jones, George* / I believe she's gonna drive that rig to glory: *Davidson, Craig* / Teamster power: *Williams, Tex* / All night long: *Wills, Bob* / C-jam blues: *Wills, Bob* / Sooner or later: *Wills, Bob* / She's about a mover: *Fender, Freddy* / Love bug: *Jones, George* / I saw the light: *Monroe, Bill* / Jambalaya: *Fender, Freddy*
CD _______________ **SATRCD 0003**
Satril / Jun '97 / Henry Hadaway / THE

BEST DANCE ALBUM IN THE WORLD...EVER 1995, THE (2CD Set)
Boombastic: *Shaggy* / Stayin' alive: *N-Trance* / La la la hey hey: *Outhere Brothers* / I luv U baby: *Original* / Two can play at that game: *Brown, Bobby* / Hideaway: *De-'Lacy* / Bomb (these sounds fall into my mind): *Bucketheads* / Open your heart: *M-People* / Surrender your love: *Nightcrawlers* / Dreamer: *Livin' Joy* / 3 Is family: *Dawson, Dana* / Love enuff: *Soul II Soul* / Flavour of the old school: *Knight, Beverley* / Here comes the hotstepper: *Kamoze, Ini* / Turn on tune in cop out: *Freakpower* / Baby come back: *Pato Banton* / Right in the night (fall in love with music): *Jam & Spoon* / Run away: *Real McCoy* / Whoomp (There it is): *Clock* / Cotton eye Joe: *Rednex* / Don't you want me: *Human League* / Baby baby: *Corona* / Reach up (Papa's got a brand new pig bag): *Perfecto All Stars* / Cry India: *Umboza* / Fee fi fo fum: *Candy Girls* / Sweet harmony: *Liquid* / U sure do: *Strike* / Not over yet: *Grace* / Your loving arms: *Martin, Billie Ray* / Set you free: *N-Trance* / Axel F: *Clock* / Keep warm: *Jinny* / Shoot me with your love: *D:Ream* / I need you: *Deuce* / Freedom: *Gayle, Michelle* / Mary Jane (all night long): *Blige, Mary J.* / My prerogative: *Brown, Bobby* / La luna (to the beat of the drum): *Ethics* / I'm ready: *Size 9*
CD Set _______________ **VTDCD 67**
Virgin / Oct '95 / EMI

BEST DANCE ALBUM IN THE WORLD...EVER VOL.1
Ride on time: *Black Box* / No limit: *2 Unlimited* / What is love: *Haddaway* / It's my life: *Dr. Alban* / Power: *Snap* / Pump up the jam: *Technotronic & Felly* / All that she wants: *Ace Of Base* / Ride like the wind: *East Side Beat* / Take a chance on me: *Erasure* / Everybody's free: *Rozalla* / Pump up the volume: *MARRS* / Theme from S'Express: *S'Express* / Temptation: *Heaven 17* / Ain't no love (ain't no use): *Sub Sub & Melanie Williams* / How can I love you more: *M-People* / Phorever people: *Shamen* / 3 a.m. eternal: *KLF* / I'm gonna get you: *Bizarre Inc.* / Something good: *Utah Saints* / Run to you: *Rage* / Groove is in the heart: *Deee-Lite* / We are family: *Sister Sledge* / I'm every woman: *Khan, Chaka* / Finally: *Peniston, Ce Ce* / Big fun: *Inner City* / Got to have your love: *Mantronix* / You got the love: *Source & Candi Staton* / People everyday: *Arrested Development* / Jump: *Kriss Kross* / Gonna make you sweat: *C&C Music Factory* / Back to life: *Soul II Soul* / Dirty cash (money talks): *Adventures Of Stevie V* / Love I lost: *West End & Sybil* / Always there: *Incognito & Jocelyn Brown* / On a ragga tip: *SL2* / Oh Carolina: *Shaggy* / Mr. Loverman: *Shabba Ranks* / Thinking about your love: *Thomas, Kenny* / If only I could: *Youngblood, Sydney* / Joy: *Soul II Soul*
CD _______________ **VTDCD 17**
Virgin / Jul '93 / EMI

BEST DANCE ALBUM IN THE WORLD...EVER VOL.2
Rhythm is a dancer: *Snap* / Get up (before the night is over): *Technotronic* / Tribal dance: *2 Unlimited* / U got 2 know: *Cappella* / Boom shake the room: *DJ Jazzy Jeff & The Fresh Prince* / Boom shak-a-lak: *Apache Indian* / Jump around: *House Of Pain* / Key, the secret: *Urban Cookie Collective* / Last train to Transcentral: *KLF* / LSI: Love Sex Intelligence: *Shamen* / Out of space: *Prodigy* / It keeps rainin' (tears from my eyes): *McLean, Bitty* / Sweat (a la la la la long): *Inner Circle* / Please don't go: *KWS* / Right here: *SWV* / I love your smile: *Shanice* / Keep on movin': *Soul II Soul* / My lovin': *En Vogue* / Gypsy woman: *Waters, Crystal* / Dreams: *Gabrielle* / Set adrift on memory bliss: *PM Dawn* / Killer: *Seal* / Only way is up: *Yazz* / Peace: *Johnston, Sabrina* / When I'm good and ready: *Sybil* / I will survive: *Gaynor, Gloria* / People hold on: *Coldcut* / Slave to the vibe: *Aftershock* / Too blind to see it: *Sims, Kym* / Good life: *Inner City* / Fascinating rhythm: *Bass-O-Matic* / Open your mind: *Usura* / Don't you want me: *Felix* / Insanity: *Oceanic* / House of love: *East 17* / Shout (it out): *Louchie Lou & Michie One* / Dub be good to me: *Beats International* / Step it up: *Stereo MC's* / Magic number: *De La Soul* / Buffalo stance: *Cherry, Neneh* / Beat dis: *Bomb The Bass* / Regret: *New Order*

CD ______ VTDCD 22
Virgin / Oct '93 / EMI

BEST DANCE ALBUM IN THE WORLD...EVER VOL.3
Let the beat control your body: *2 Unlimited* / Get a life: *Soul II Soul* / Straight up: *Abdul, Paula* / Things can only get better: *D:Ream* / You got 2 let the music: *Cappella* / It's alright: *East 17* / I like to move it: *Reel 2 Real* / Sweets for my sweet: *Lewis, C.J.* / Real thing: *Di Bart, Tony* / Get-a-way: *Maxx* / Get ready for this: *2 Unlimited* / Moving on up: *M-People* / Exterminate: *Snap* / Rock my heart: *Haddaway* / Swamp thing: *Grid* / Informer: *Snow* / Long train runnin': *Doobie Brothers* / Give it up: *Goodmen* / Touch me: *49ers* / Carry me home: *Gloworm* / Let's talk about sex: *Gloworm* / Blue Monday: *New Order* / We got a love thang: *Peniston, Ce Ce* / U can't touch this: *MC Hammer* / Stay: *Eternal* / Flinstones: *BC 52s* / Come baby come: *K7* / Naked in the rain: *Blue Pearl* / Doop: *Doop* / Always: *Erasure* / Feels like heaven: *Urban Cookie Collective* / (I wanna give you) Devotion: *Nomad* / Dedicated to the one I love: *McLean, Bitty* / Light my fire: *Club House* / Ebeneezer goode: *Shamen* / Caught in the middle: *Roberts, Juliet* / Shine: *Aswad* / It's too late: *Quartz & Dina Carroll* / Show me love: *Robin S* / Real love: *Time Frequency*
CD ______ VTDCD 32
Virgin / Jul '94 / EMI

BEST DANCE ALBUM IN THE WORLD...EVER VOL.4
Confide in me: *Minogue, Kylie* / Real thing: *2 Unlimited* / Dream's a dream: *Soul II Soul* / Don't turn around: *Ace Of Base* / One night in heaven: *M-People* / Relight my fire: *Take That* / Ooops up: *Snap* / Word up: *Cameo* / Too funky: *Michael, George* / Move on baby: *Cappella* / U R the best thing: *D:Ream* / Just a step from heaven: *Eternal* / Mr. Vain: *Culture Beat* / Rhythm is a mystery: *K-Klass* / Chain reaction: *Ross, Diana* / No good (start the dance): *Prodigy* / No more (I can't stand it): *Maxx* / Total mix: *Black Box* / Tease me: *Chaka Demus & Pliers* / Searching: *China Black* / Hangin' on a string: *Loose Ends* / Let's get ready to rhumble: *PJ & Duncan* / We don't have to...: *Stewart, Jermaine* / Don't worry: *Appleby, Kim* / Relax: *Frankie Goes To Hollywood* / You don't love me (no no no): *Penn, Dawn* / Rhythm of the night: *Corona* / Incredible: *M-Beat & General Levy* / Human nature: *Clail, Gary* / Ain't nothin' goin' on but the rent: *Guthrie, Gwen* / Compliments on your kiss: *Red Dragon* / Things that make you go hmmmm: *C&C Music Factory* / Go on move: *Reel 2 Real* / Baby come back: *Pato Banton* / She's got that vibe: *R Kelly* / Unfinished sympathy: *Massive Attack* / No more tears (enough is enough): *Mazelle, Kym & Jocelyn Brown* / Turn up the power: *N-Trance* / Everything is alright (Uptight): *Lewis, C.J.* / What's going on: *Music Relief*
CD Set ______ VTDCD 40
Virgin / Nov '94 / EMI

BEST DANCE ALBUM IN THE WORLD...EVER VOL.5
Right in the night: *Jam & Spoon* / Excited: *M-People* / Dreamer: *Livin' Joy* / Don't give me your life: *Alex Party* / Scatman: *Scatman John* / Don't stop (Wiggle wiggle): *Outhere Brothers* / Bomb: *Bucketheads* / Humpin' around: *Brown, Bobby* / Push the feeling on: *Nightcrawlers* / Another night: *Real McCoy* / Zombie: *ADAM & Amy* / Whoomp (There it is): *Clock* / Cotton eye Joe: *Rednex* / Got to get it: *Culture Beat* / Baby baby: *Corona* / What's up: *DJ Miko* / Call it love: *Deuce* / Set you free: *N-Trance* / Reach up: *Perfecto All Stars*
CD ______ VIDCD 55
Virgin / Jul '95 / EMI

BEST DANCE HALL
CD ______ RNCD 2053
Rhino / Mar '94 / Grapevine/PolyGram / Jet Star

BEST DISCO ALBUM IN THE WORLD...EVER, THE (2CD Set)
I feel love: *Summer, Donna* / Funky town: *Lipps Inc.* / Shake your body (down to the ground): *Jacksons* / Boogie wonderland: *Earth, Wind & Fire & The Emotions* / Upside down: *Ross, Diana* / Le freak: *Chic* / Ladies night: *Kool & The Gang* / Young hearts run free: *Staton, Candi* / Jump to the beat: *Lattisaw, Stacy* / I'm every woman: *Khan, Chaka* / He's the greatest dancer: *Sister Sledge* / Get down tonight: *KC & The Sunshine Band* / Disco inferno: *Trammps* / Use it up, wear it out: *Odyssey* / Lady Marmalade: *Labelle* / Working my way back to you: *Detroit Spinners* / Boogie oogie oogie: *Taste Of Honey* / Shame: *King, Evelyn 'Champagne'* / Boogie nights: *Heatwave* / More than a woman: *Tavares* / Rock your baby: *McRae, George* / Never never gonna give you up: *White, Barry* / I will survive: *Gaynor, Gloria* / YMCA: *Village People* / Instant replay: *Hartman, Dan* / Best disco in town: *Ritchie Family* / Stars on 45 Abba medley: *Starsound* / Stayin' alive: *N-Trance* / Get up and boogie: *Silver Convention* / Shame shame shame: *Shirley & Company* / Feels like I'm in love: *Marie, Kelly* / Black is black: *La Belle Epoque* / DISCO: *Ottawan* / Rasputin: *Boney M* / Spacer: *Sheila B. Devotion* / Love sensation: *Holloway, Loleatta* / Let's all chant: *Zager, Michael Band* / I can make you feel good: *Shalamar* / And the beat goes on: *Whispers* / Car wash: *Rose Royce* / I shoulda loved ya: *Walden, Narada Michael* / Can you feel the force: *Real Thing* / You make me feel (Mighty real): *Sylvester* / Knock on wood: *Stewart, Amii*
CD Set ______ VTDCD 143
Virgin / Jun '97 / EMI

BEST EVER COLLECTION OF IRISH PUB SESSION, THE
CD ______ CDIRL 508
Outlet / Jul '97 / ADA / CM / Direct / Duncans / Koch / Ross

BEST EVER COLLECTION OF IRISH PUB SONGS VOL.1, THE
On Raglan road: *Kelly, Luke* / Irish Rover: *Drew, Ronnie* / Ferryman: *Dublin City Ramblers* / Sweet sixteen: *Fureys* / Lonesome boatman: *Innisfree Ceoil* / Town I love so well: *Reilly, Paddy* / Steal away: *Fureys* / Holy ground: *Dubliners* / Song for Ireland: *Kelly, Luke* / Streets of New York: *Brier Folk* / Follow me up to Carlow: *McCann, Jim* / Spanish lady: *Dubliners* / Danny Boy: *Locke, Josef* / Dicey Riley: *Drew, Ronnie* / Mary from Dungloe: *Spiceland, Emmet* / Boolavogue: *Dubliners* / Auld triangle: *Drew, Ronnie* / Fiddler's green: *Marks Men* / Fairmoyle lasses/Sportin' Paddy: *Dubliners* / God save Ireland: *Dubliners*
CD ______ CDIRL 506
Outlet / May '97 / ADA / CM / Direct / Duncans / Koch / Ross

BEST EVER COLLECTION OF IRISH PUB SONGS VOL.2, THE
Fields of Athenry: *Reilly, Paddy* / Sick-note: *Dubliners* / Dublin in the rare auld times: *Kelly, Luke* / Green fields of France: *Fureys & Davey Arthur* / Cliffs of Dooneen: *Innisfree Ceoil* / Grace: *Shamrog* / Carrickfergus: *Reilly, Paddy* / Wild rover: *Drew, Ronnie* / Spancil hill: *Reilly, Paddy* / Flight of the Earls: *Brier Folk* / John O'Dreams: *Dublin City Ramblers* / Johnston's motor car: *Drew, Ronnie* / Galway races: *Reilly, Paddy* / Crack was ninety: *Dublin City Ramblers* / Wild colonial boy: *Cane, Oliver* / Black velvet band: *Kelly, Luke* / Belfast Mill: *Dublin City Ramblers* / Rose of Allendale: *Reilly, Paddy* / Mursheen Durkin: *McEvoy, Johnny* / A nation once again: *Dubliners*
CD ______ CDIRL 507
Outlet / May '97 / ADA / CM / Direct / Duncans / Koch / Ross

BEST EVER SUMMER ALBUM, THE
Beach boys: *Beach Boys* / Let's got to San Francisco: *Flowerpot Men* / Summer breeze: *Isley Brothers* / Long hot summer: *Style Council* / Summer: *Goldsboro, Bobby* / Albatross: *Fleetwood Mac* / Bamboleo: *Gipsy Kings* / La bamba: *Los Lobos* / Diggin' your scene: *Blow Monkeys* / Sunny afternoon: *Kinks* / Sitting in the park: *Fame, Georgie* / Perfect day: *Reed, Lou* / San Francisco: *McKenzie, Scott* / Surf city: *Jan & Dean* / Surfin' USA: *Astronauts* / Walking on sunshine: *Katrina & The Waves* / In the summertime: *Mungo Jerry* / Here comes summer: *Keller, Jerry* / Summer holiday: *Richard, Cliff* / Dream a little dream of me: *Mamas & The Papas*
CD ______ 74321383162
RCA / Jun '97 / BMG

BEST FOLK, THE
CD ______ CD 902
Sound / Jun '89 / ADA

BEST FOOT FORWARD
CD ______ PUSSYCD 001
Pussy Foot / Jul '95 / RTM/Disc

BEST FOOTIE ANTHEMS IN THE WORLD...EVER (2CD Set)
We are the champions: *Queen* / World in motion: *New Order & England World Cup Squad* / Three lions: *Lightning Seeds & David Baddiel/Frank Skinner* / Back home: *England 1970 World Cup Squad* / Match of the day: *Offside* / Life of Riley: *Lightning Seeds* / Fog on the Tyne: *Gazza & Lindisfarne* / Anfield rap: *Liverpool FC* / You'll never walk alone: *Gerry & The Pacemakers* / Wonderwall: *Oasis* / Sportsnight: *Hatch, Tony* / Belfast boy: *Fardon, Don* / Come on you reds: *Manchester Utd FC* / Move move move (The Red Tribe): *Manchester Utd FC & Stryker* / Ooo aah Eric Cantona: *1300 Drums* / Grandstand: *Mansfield, Keith* / Football crazy: *Hall, Robin & Jimmy MacGregor* / Alright: *Hall, Robin & Jimmy MacGregor* / Parklife: *Blur* / Blue is the colour: *Chelsea F.C.* / Diamond lights: *Glenn & Chris* / Ossie's dream: *Tottenham Hotspur FC* / Nice one Cyril: *Cockerel Chorus* / Nessun dorma: *Pavarotti, Luciano* / Ode to joy / Always look on the bright side of life: *Monty Python*
CD Set ______ VTCD 94
Virgin / Jun '96 / EMI

BEST FUNK ALBUM IN THE WORLD...EVER VOL.1, THE
(Get up I feel like being a) Sex machine: *Brown, James* / Funky stuff: *Kool & The Gang* / Oops upside your head: *Gap Band* / She's strange: *Cameo* / My lovin': *En Vogue* / If you're ready (come go with me): *Staple Singers* / Family affair: *Sly & The Family Stone* / Inner city blues: *Gaye, Marvin* / Green onions: *Booker T & The MG's* / Papa was a rollin' stone: *Was Not Was* / Cloud 9: *Temptations* / Yum yum (gimme some): *Fatback Band* / Give up the funk: *Parliament* / Which way is up: *Starguard* / Ain't nothin' goin' on but the rent: *Guthrie, Gwen* / I gotcha: *Tex, Joe* / Got to get you into my life: *Earth, Wind & Fire* / Fire: *Ohio Players* / Use me: *Withers, Bill* / Good times: *Chic* / Strut your funky stuff: *Frantique* / Get down tonight: *KC & The Sunshine Band* / Pick up the pieces: *Average White Band* / Papa's got a brand new pigbag: *Pigbag* / Higher ground: *Red Hot Chili Peppers* / Rockit: *Hancock, Herbie* / Theme from S'Express: *S'Express* / Something got me started: *Simply Red* / Once you get started: *Rufus* / Atomic dog: *Clinton, George* / I feel sanctified: *Commodores* / Sunshine day: *Osibisa* / Hard work: *Handy, John* / Never, never gonna give you up: *White, Barry* / Mr. Big Stuff: *Knight, Jean* / Ain't gonna bump no more (with no big fat woman): *Tex, Joe* / Where is the love: *Wright, Betty* / Right place, wrong time: *Dr. John*
CD Set ______ VTDCD 44
Virgin / Feb '95 / EMI

BEST FUNK ALBUM IN THE WORLD...EVER VOL.2, THE (2CD Set)
Funky stuff: *Kool & The Gang* / Word up: *Cameo* / Atomic dog: *Clinton, George* / (Get up I feel like being a) Sex machine: *Brown, James* / Theme from Shaft: *Hayes, Isaac* / Superfly: *Mayfield, Curtis* / That lady: *Isley Brothers* / Use me: *Withers, Bill* / Funky Nassau: *Beginning Of The End* / Dance to the music: *Sly & The Family Stone* / Lady Marmalade: *Labelle* / Brick house: *Commodores* / Funkin' for Jamaica: *Browne, Tom* / Behind the groove: *Marie, Teena* / Which way is up: *Starguard* / Carwash: *Rose Royce* / Shoorah Shoorah: *Wright, Betty* / Shack up: *Banbarra* / Le freak: *Chic* / Tell me something good: *Rufus* / Oops upside your head: *Gap Band* / Give up the funk (tear the roof off the sucker): *Parliament* / Mr. Big Stuff: *Knight, Jean* / If you're ready (come go with me): *Staple Singers* / Wicky wacky: *Fatback Band* / Saturday nite: *Earth, Wind & Fire* / Fire: *Ohio Players* / Get down tonight: *KC & The Sunshine Band* / Nutbush City limits: *Turner, Ike & Tina* / Play that funky music: *Wild Cherry* / War: *Starr, Edwin* / Pick up the pieces: *Average White Band* / Move on up: *Mayfield, Curtis* / Green onions: *Booker T & The MG's* / Do what you wanna do: *T-Connection* / I gotcha: *Tex, Joe* / Rockit: *Hancock, Herbie* / Movin': *Brass Connection* / Expansions: *Smith, Lonnie Liston* / Revolution will not be televised: *Scott-Heron, Gil*
CD Set ______ VTDCD 126
Virgin / Aug '97 / EMI

BEST GIRL POWER ALBUM EVER, THE (2CD Set)
Who do you think you are: *Spice Girls* / Professional widow: *Amos, Tori* / Sisters are doing it for themselves: *Eurythmics & Aretha Franklin* / Ready to go: *Republica* / Weak: *Skunk Anansie* / Free your mind: *En Vogue* / Lady marmalade: *Labelle* / I'm every woman: *Khan, Chaka* / Give me a little more time: *Gabrielle* / Dancing in the street: *Reeves, Martha & The Vandellas* / Respect: *Franklin, Aretha* / Slowhand: *Pointer Sisters* / What's love got to do with it: *Turner, Tina* / Woman: *Cherry, Neneh* / Superwoman: *White, Karyn* / I will survive: *Savage, Chantay* / If you love me: *Brownstone* / Back and forth: *Aaliyah* / Mary Jane (All night long): *Blige, Mary J.* / Freak like me: *Howard, Adina* / Let's talk about sex: *Salt n' Pepa* / Wannabe: *Spice Girls* / (Hey now) Girls just want to have fun: *Lauper, Cyndi* / Shy guy: *King, Diana* / Buffalo stance: *Cherry, Neneh* / Ain't nothin' goin' on but the rent: *Guthrie, Gwen* / None of your business: *Salt n' Pepa* / Creep: *TLC* / Right here: *SWV* / We are family: *Sister Sledge* / Heart of glass: *Blondie* / Heaven is a place on earth: *Carlisle, Belinda* / Manic Monday: *Bangles* / Alisha rules the world: *Alisha's Attic* / You're history: *Shakespears Sister* / You lied to me: *Dennis, Cathy* / Supermodel: *Rupaul* / Short short man: *20 Fingers* / It's raining men: *Weather Girls* / Naked eye: *Luscious Jackson* / Extremis: *Hal & Gillian Anderson*
CD Set ______ VTDCD 123
Virgin / May '97 / EMI

BEST HOLIDAY ALBUM UNDER THE SUN, THE
Macarena / Saturday night / YMCA/In the navy / Locomotion / DISCO / Walking on sunshine / Lambada / Barbados / Rock the boat / Rivers of Babylon / Una paloma blanca / Hands up / Spirit in the sky / Time warp / In the summertime / Y viva Espana / Itsy bitsy teenie weenie yellow polkadot bikini / Do the conga
CD ______ ECD 3373
K-Tel / Jun '97 / K-Tel

BEST IRISH ALBUM IN THE WORLD...EVER, THE (2CD Set)
Theme from Harry's Game: *Clannad* / Riverdance: *Anderson, John Concert Orchestra* / Island: *Keane, Dolores* / Rock'n'roll kids: *Harrington, Paul & Charlie McGettigan* / Maggie: *Foster & Allen* / Summerfly: *O'Connell, Maura* / She moved through the fair: *Sharkey, Feargal* / Song for Ireland: *De Danann* / When you were sweet sixteen: *Fureys & Davey Arthur* / Hold me now: *Logan, Johnny* / Whatever happened to old fashioned love: *O'Donnell, Daniel* / All kinds of everything: *Dana* / What's another year: *Logan, Johnny* / In your eyes: *Kavanagh, Niamh* / Voice: *Quinn, Eimear* / Through the eyes of an Irishman: *Kirwan, Dominic* / Bunch of thyme: *Foster & Allen* / Danny boy: *O'Donnell, Daniel* / Galway bay: *Locke, Josef* / Hear my song Violetta: *Locke, Josef* / Whiskey in the jar: *Thin Lizzy* / Irish rover: *Pogues & The Dubliners* / Seven drunken nights: *Dubliners* / Blackbird: *Shannon, Sharon* / Brown eyed girl: *Morrison, Van* / Good heart: *Sharkey, Feargal* / Against the wind: *Brennan, Maire* / Place among the stones: *Spillane, Davy* / Homes of Donegal: *Brady, Paul* / Ride on: *Moore, Christy* / Carrickfergus: *Kennedy, Brian* / Thank you for hearing me: *O'Connor, Sinead* / Manannan/Tir Tairngiri: *Breathnach, Maire* / Dark haired lass/Biddy from Muckross/Sean Maguire's reels: *Altan* / Never mind the strangers: *Saw Doctors* / Black velvet band: *Dubliners* / Laziest gal in town: *Coughlan, Mary* / Bee in the bottle: *Lohan, Sinead*
CD Set ______ VTDCD 102
Virgin / Oct '96 / EMI

BEST IRISH REQUESTS
CD ______ DH 002
Outlet / Jul '94 / ADA / CM / Direct / Duncans / Koch / Ross

BEST JAZZ ALBUM IN THE WORLD...EVER, THE (3CD Set)
Let there be love: *Cole, Nat 'King' & George Shearing* / I get a kick out of you: *Fitzgerald, Ella* / Mad about the boy: *Washington, Dinah* / Fever: *Lee, Peggy* / Cry me a river: *London, Julie* / That ole devil called love: *Holiday, Billie* / Take the 'A' train: *Ellington, Duke* / Minnie the moocher: *Calloway, Cab* / Five guy's named Moe: *Jordan, Louis* / Hello Dolly: *Armstrong, Louis* / Ain't misbehavin': *Waller, Fats* / Relax: *Redbone, Leon* / Summertime: *Vaughan, Sarah* / Misty: *Garner, Erroll* / Foggy day: *Kessel, Barney* / Night and day: *Reinhardt, Django* / Let's get lost: *Baker, Chet* / I wish I knew: *Taylor, Billy Trio* / Kid from Red Bank: *Basie, Count* / Take five: *Brubeck, Dave* / Birdland: *Weather Report* / Running away: *Ayers, Roy* / Watermelon man: *Santamaria, Mongo* / Moondance: *Fame, Georgie & Van Morrison* / Do nothin' 'til you hear from me: *Allison, Mose* / Wade in the water: *Lewis, Ramsey Trio* / Dropping bombs on the Whitehouse: *Style Council* / Blue rondo a la Turk: *Jarreau, Al* / So what: *Jordan, Ronny* / Breezin': *Benson, George* / Morning dance: *Spyro Gyra* / Last night at danceland: *Crawford, Randy* / Girl from Ipanema: *State Of The Heart* / Travels: *Metheny, Pat* / So what: *Davis, Miles* / Cantaloupe island: *Hancock, Herbie* / 'Round midnight: *Monk, Thelonious* / Song for my father: *Andy, Horace* / Sidewinder: *Morgan, Lee* / Moanin': *Blakey, Art* / Midnight blue: *Burrell, Kenny* / Eleanor Rigby: *Jordan, Stanley* / Goodbye Pork Pie Hat: *Mingus, Charles* / Ornithology: *Parker, Charlie* / Blue train: *Coltrane, John*
CD Set ______ VTDCD 93
Virgin / Aug '96 / EMI

BEST JAZZ, THE
CD ______ CD 906
Sound / Jun '89 / ADA

BEST JOVENES FLAMENCOS, THE
El vito cante / Jaleo pa las flamencas / Vengo del mora / Mi tio el nini miguel / El reloj del carino / Lo bueno y lo malo / Vuela, vuela pajarito / Chana / Venta zoraida / Chicuelina / Nubes de colores / De perdidos al rio / Anonimo jerezano / Que no quiero dinero / Piel de habichuela / Refrito
CD ______ 93042
Emocion / Feb '95 / New Note/Pinnacle

BEST LOVED CHRISTMAS CAROLS
Hark the herald angels sing / Unto us is born a son / O little town of Bethlehem / Holly and the ivy / Away in a manger / Three Kings / O come all ye faithful (adeste fidelis) / First Noel / I saw three ships / Deck the hall / Ding dong merrily on high / Tomorrow shall be my dancing day / Of the father's heart / Cherry tree carol / I came upon a midnight clear / O come, O come Emmanuel / Once in Royal David's City / Sussex carol / As with gladness men of old / Hail blessed Virgin Mary / Jesus Christ the apple tree / Seven songs of Mary
CD ______ XMAS 010
Tring / Nov '96 / Tring

BEST MIX...EVER, THE (2CD Set)
Pump up the volume: *MARRS* / Theme from S'Express: *S'Express* / Boombastic: *Shaggy* / Groove is in the heart: *Deee-Lite* / Killer: *Adamski* / Fastlove: *Michael, George* / One night in heaven: *M-People* / Rhythm is a dancer: *Snap* / Pump up the jam: *Technotronic* / Push the feeling on: *Nightcrawlers* / Things can only get better: *D:Ream* / I like to move it: *Reel 2 Real* / Dreamer: *Livin' Joy* / Real thing: *Di Bart, Tony* / Rhythm of the night: *Corona* / Give it up: *Goodmen* / My love is for real: *Strike* / Don't you want me: *Human League* / Stamp: *Healy, Jeremy & Amos* / Born slippy (Nuxx): *Underworld* / All that she wants: *Ace Of Base* / Boom shake the room: *DJ Jazzy Jeff & The Fresh Prince* / Walk this way: *Run DMC* / Oh what a night (December '63): *Clock* / Gonna make you sweat (everybody dance now): *C&C Music Factory* / She's got that vibe: *Kelly, R* / Crazy: *Morrison, Mark* /

What is love: *Haddaway* / It's my life: *Dr. Alban* / I luv U baby: *Original* / Don't give me your life: *Alex Party* / Son of a gun: *JX* / Temptation: *Heaven 17* / Wannabe: *Spice Girls* / Mr. Vain: *Culture Beat* / Boom boom boom: *Outhere Brothers* / U got 2 let the music: *Cappella* / Right in the night (fall in love with music): *Jam & Spoon* / Reach up (Papa's got a brand new Pigbag): *Perfecto All Stars* / Seven days and one week: *BBE*
CD Set ______ **VTDCD 108**
Virgin / Nov '96 / EMI

BEST OF 2-TONE, THE
Ghost town: *Specials* / On my radio: *Selecter* / Too much too young: *Special AKA* / Do nothing: *Specials* / People do rock steady: *Bodysnatchers* / Stereotype: *Specials* / Prince: *Madness* / Rat race: *Specials* / Boiler: *Rhoda & Special A.K.A.* / I can't stand up for falling down: *Costello, Elvis* / Nelson Mandela: *Special AKA* / Missing words: *Selecter* / Message to you Rudy: *Specials* / Selecter: *Selecter*
CD ______ **CDCHRTT 5012**
Chrysalis / Nov '93 / EMI

BEST OF 90'S COUNTRY, THE
If tomorrow never comes: *Brooks, Garth* / Shotgun: *Tucker, Tanya* / Never ending song of love: *Gayle, Crystal* / On a good night: *Campbell, Glen* / I'm a survivor: *Dalton, Lacy J.* / My side of the story: *Bogguss, Suzy* / Race is on: *Brown, Sawyer* / On the bayou: *Wild Rose* / Moonshadow Road: *Brown, T. Graham* / Other side of love: *Davies, Gail* / Do you know where your man is: *Mandrell, Barbara* / Good times: *Seals, Dan* / Everything: *Chapman, Cee Cee* / What would you do about you (if you were me): *Osmond, Marie* / Country girl heart: *Gatlin, Larry & The Gatlin Brothers* / Tear it up: *Harms, Jonie*
CD ______ **CDMFP 5912**
Music For Pleasure / Apr '91 / EMI

BEST OF ACID JAZZ VOL.1, THE
CD ______ **JAZIDCD 029**
Acid Jazz / Jan '91 / Disc

BEST OF ACID JAZZ VOL.1, THE (2CD Set)
Cantaloop: *US 3 & rashaan* / Space cowboy: *Jamiroquai* / Midnight at the oasis: *Brand New Heavies* / Everyday: *Incognito* / Turn on tune in cop out: *Freakpower* / People in the middle: *Spearhead* / Feel so high: *Des'ree* / Rebirth of slick: *Digable Planets* / Feel the music: *Guru* / Been thinking about you: *Girault, Martine* / So what: *Jordan, Ronny* / Real love: *Driza Bone* / Never stop: *Brand New Heavies* / Spiritual love: *Urban Species* / Green Screen: *New Jersey Kings* / Mission impossible: *Taylor, James Quartet* / Keep steppin': *Omar* / Heavy vibes: *Vibraphonic* / Boundaris: *Conquest, Leena* / Take the L train: *Brooklyn Funk Essentials* / Whole lotta love: *Goldbug* / Apparently nothin': *Young Disciples* / Masterplan: *Sharpe, Barrie K. & Diana Brown* / Something in my eye: *Corduroy* / Venceremos: *Working Week* / Whirl keeps turning: *Jhelisa* / Dream come true: *Brand New Heavies* / Good lover: *D-Influence* / Promise me nothing: *Repercussions* / Creator has a masterplan: *Brooklyn Funk Essentials* / Now is the time: *D-Note* / Find our love: *City Lix* / 24 for betty page: *Snowboy* / Follow that arab: *Corduroy* / Turn it all around: *This I dig* / Watcha gonna do: *Xan* / Watchugot: *Groove Collective* / Funky guitar: *TC 1992* / Jesse: *Mother Earth* / Let it last: *Anderson, Carleen*
CD Set ______ **RADCD 35**
Global TV / Jun '96 / BMG

BEST OF ACID JAZZ VOL.2, THE
Don't let it go to your head: *Brand New Heavies* / Masterplan: *Brown, Diana & Barrie K Sharpe* / Peace and love: *Sewell, Janette* / Watch my garden grow: *Humble Souls* / Jazz Jupiter: *A-Zel* / Hope you're feeling better: *Mother Earth* / E-type: *Corduroy* / Lucky fellow: *Snowboy* / Ain't no use: *Pure Wildness* / Girl overboard: *Snowboy* / Living life your own way: *Windross, Rose*
CD ______ **JAZIDCD 066**
Acid Jazz / May '93 / Disc

BEST OF ACID JAZZ VOL.2, THE
CD ______ **EX 3412**
Instinct / Jan '97 / Cargo

BEST OF ACID JAZZ VOL.2, THE (2CD Set)
Virtual insanity: *Jamiroquai* / Dream on dreamer: *Brand New Heavies* / Remember me: *Blueboy* / There's nothing like this: *Omar* / Revival: *Girault, Martine* / Love the life: *Taylor, James Quartet* / High havoc: *Corduroy* / One temptation: *Paris, Mica* / Don't you worry 'bout a thing: *Incognito* / Brightest star: *Driza Bone* / Brother: *Urban Species* / Inner city blues: *Working Week* / Pushing against the flow: *Raw Stylus* / Long time gone: *Galliano* / Jackal: *Jordan, Ronny* / My definition of a bombastic style: *Definition Of Sound* / Can I kick it: *Tribe Called Quest* / Summertime: *Rebello, Jason* / Mercy mercy me: *Jazz Apostles* / Apparently nothing: *Anderson, Carleen* / Jazz in the house: *Count Basic* / You gotta be: *Des'ree* / Outside: *Omar* / Stay this way: *Brand New Heavies* / Dream warriors: *New Jersey Kings* / Friendly pressure: *Jhelisa* / Garden of earthly delight: *D-Note* / Bad as weed: *Mother Earth* / Love will keep us together: *Taylor, James Quartet* / Greenfinger: *Dr. Bong* / Beached: *Milk* / Got to be: *High Steppers* / Big city: *Outside* / Bad trip: *Night Trains* / Ain't no sunshine: *Beaujolais Band* / Corduroy orgasm club: *Corduroy* / It only gets better: *Society Of Soul* / Love supreme: *Downing, Will* / Time after time: *Tuck & Patti*
CD Set ______ **RADCD 52**
Global TV / Jan '97 / BMG

BEST OF ACID JAZZ, THE
Chicken lickin': *Funk Inc.* / Zebra walk: *Kynard, Charles* / Reelin' with the feelin': *Kynard, Charles* / Dig on it: *Smith, Johnny 'Hammond'* / Got myself a good man: *Pucho* / Super bad: *Muhammad, Idris* / Who's gonna take the weight: *Sparks, Melvin* / Sure nuff sure nuff: *Phillips, Sonny* / Cold sweet: *Purdie, Bernard* / Psychedelic Sally: *Jefferson, Eddie* / Soul dance: *Person, Houston* / Houston Express: *Person, Houston* / Smokin' at Tiffany's: *Funk Inc.*
CD ______ **CDBGP 921**
Beat Goes Public / Jun '89 / Pinnacle

BEST OF AFRICA, THE
Gerant: *Kalle, Pepe* / Loi de la nature: *4 Etoiles* / Odile: *Somo Somo* / Foolish harp: *Bhundu Boys* / Mbira jive: *Mohamed, Pops* / Bazobuya: *Soul Brothers* / Tarihinda: *Kayirebwa, Cecile* / Guy Yah: *Diabate, Sona* / Diewo: *Seck, Mansour* / Yedi Gosh: *Aweke, Aster* / Marimba song: *Amampondo*
CD ______ **RGNET 1005CD**
World Music Network / Sep '96 / ADA / New Note/Pinnacle

BEST OF AIM, THE
CD ______ **AIM 005CD**
Aim / Oct '95 / ADA / Direct / Jazz Music

BEST OF BALLROOM, THE (Strict Tempo)
Waterloo / Paperback jive / Everybody needs somebody / I'm a believer / Half a minute / All night long / One note samba / Hustle / Loco in acapulco / Boogie wonderland / Easy lover / When will I see you again / Annie's song / True love / Edelweiss / Chanson d'amour / Any dream will do / Moonlight serenade
CD ______ **QED 230**
Tring / Nov '96 / Tring

BEST OF BELLYDANCE FROM EGYPT AND LEBANON, THE
CD ______ **EUCD 1320**
ARC / Nov '95 / ADA / ARC Music

BEST OF BELLYDANCE, THE
CD ______ **EUCD 1211**
ARC / Sep '93 / ADA / ARC Music

BEST OF BGP, THE
Always there: *Side Effect* / Got myself a good man: *Pucho* / Black whip: *Jones, Ivan 'Boogaloo Joe'* / So what: *Jefferson, Eddie* / Sister Janie: *Funk Inc.* / Nuther'n like thuther'n: *Jackson, Willis* / Rock Creek Park: *Blackbyrds* / Ban montana: *Parker, Maynard* / O baby I believe I'm losing you: *Hawks, Billy* / Ping pong: *Blakey, Art & The Jazz Messengers* / Selim: *Lytle, Johnny* / Milestones: *Murphy, Mark* / Jungle strut: *Ammons, Gene* / Jazz carnival: *Azymuth*
CD ______ **CDBGP 1030**
Beat Goes Public / Oct '90 / Pinnacle

BEST OF BLUE NOTE VOL.1
Blue train: *Coltrane, John* / Maiden voyage: *Hancock, Herbie* / Christo redemptor: *Byrd, Donald* / Moanin': *Blakey, Art* / Blues walk: *Donaldson, Lou* / Song for my father: *Silver, Horace* / Back to the chicken shack: *Smith, Jimmy* / Chitlins con carne: *Burrell, Kenny* / Sidewinder: *Morgan, Lee*
CD ______ **CDP 7961102**
Blue Note / Oct '91 / EMI

BEST OF BLUE NOTE VOL.2
Senor blues: *Silver, Horace* / Decision: *Rollins, Sonny* / Three o'clock in the morning: *Gordon, Dexter* / Blues march: *Blakey, Art* / Wadin': *Parlan, Horace* / Rumproller: *Morgan, Lee* / Something else: *Adderley, Cannonball* / Blue bossa: *Henderson, Joe* / Watermelon man: *Hancock, Herbie*
CD ______ **CDP 7979602**
Blue Note / Feb '93 / EMI

BEST OF BLUE NOTE, THE (A Selection From 25 Best Albums)
Moanin': *Blakey, Art* / Midnight blue: *Burrell, Kenny* / Caravan: *Ellington, Duke* / Atomic Mr. Basie: *Basie, Count* / Un poco loco: *Powell, Bud* / Ornithology: *Parker, Charlie* / Rocker: *Davis, Miles* / I guess I'll hang my tears out to dry: *Gordon, Dexter* / Let's get lost: *Baker, Chet* / Tune up: *Rollins, Sonny* / Criss cross: *Monk, Thelonious* / Blue train: *Coltrane, John* / Maiden voyage: *Hancock, Herbie* / Song for my father: *Silver, Horace*
CD ______ **CDP 8299642**
Blue Note / Mar '95 / EMI

BEST OF BLUES, THE (2CD Set)
Boogie chillen: *Hooker, John Lee* / Roll and tumble: *Memphis Slim* / Tutti frutti: *Hawkins, Screamin' Jay* / Pinetop is just top: *Perkins, Willie 'Pinetop'* / I hate to see you go: *Walker, T-Bone* / Sweet home Chicago: *Brooks, Lonnie* / Things that I used to do: *Johnson, Luther 'Guitar Junior'* / Hands off: *McShann, Jay* / Take a lesson from your teacher: *Cousin Joe* / I can't quit my baby: *Rush, Otis* / Somebody please help me: *Clearwater, Eddy* / Every day I have the blues: *Guy, Buddy & Junior Wells* / Sloppy drunk: *Rogers, Jimmy* / So many days: *Perkins, Willie 'Pinetop'* / Highway is my home: *Magic Slim* / Impressions from France: *Johnson, Luther 'Georgia Snake Boy'* / Hey little girl: *Baker, McHouston 'Mickey'* / Railroad porter blues: *Cousin Joe* / Get back home in USA: *Hooker, John Lee* / Boogie for Meade: *Memphis Slim* / Looking back: *Rush, Otis* / Boogie woogie baby: *Clearwater, Eddy* / Country girl: *Magic Slim* / Got my mojo working: *Guy, Buddy & Junior Wells* / Slim's blues: *Memphis Slim* / Pretty baby: *Rogers, Jimmy* / Long gone blues: *Holiday, Billie* / Looking up at down: *Broonzy, 'Big' Bill* / Good morning little schoolgirl: *Williamson, Sonny Boy* / Blues on Central Avenue: *Turner, 'Big' Joe* / Mean old world: *Walker, T-Bone* / Stop breaking down: *Johnson, Robert* / That's all: *Tharpe, Rosetta* / Rich man's blues: *Washington, Dinah* / Me and my chauffeur blues: *Memphis Minnie* / Empty bed blues: *Smith, Bessie*
CD Set ______ **FA 972**
Fremeaux / Oct '96 / ADA / Discovery

BEST OF BOOGIE WOOGIE, THE
CD ______ **158482**
Jazz Archives / Feb '96 / Discovery

BEST OF BOOGIE WOOGIE, THE
Boogie woogie stomp: *Ammons, Albert* / Pine Top's boogie woogie: *Smith, Pine Top* / Yancey stomp: *Yancey, Jimmy* / Cow cow blues: *Davenport, Cow Cow* / Boogie woogie: *Basie, Count Quintet* / State street jive: *Davenport, Cow Cow* / Chicago breakdown: *Big Maceo* / Honkt tonk train blues: *Lewis, Meade 'Lux'* / Pine Top's blues: *Smith, Pine Top* / Mr. Freddie blues: *Williams, Mary Lou* / Detroit rocks: *Taylor, Montana* / Dearborn St. Breakdown: *Avery, Charles* / Yancy special: *Lewis, Meade 'Lux'* / Boogie woogie: *Basie, Count* / No.29: *Wallace, Wesley* / Head rag hop: *Nelson, Romeo* / Dirty dozen: *Speckled Red* / Shout for joy: *Ammons, Albert* / Roll 'em: *Johnson, Pete* / Right string but the wrong yo-yo: *Speckled Red*
CD ______ **304062**
Hallmark / Jun '97 / Carlton

BEST OF BOTH WORLDS, THE
CD ______ **HNCD 8304**
Hannibal / Oct '94 / ADA / Vital

BEST OF BOUZOUKI, THE
CD ______ **CD 321889**
Koch International / Jul '97 / Koch

BEST OF BRASIL, THE
CD ______ **JD 157**
Chesky / May '97 / Discovery / Goldring

BEST OF BRASS, THE (2CD Set)
CD Set ______ **CDSR 125**
Telstar / Mar '97 / BMG

BEST OF BRITISH BE-BOP, THE
Wee dot: *Scott, Ronnie* / Coquette: *Scott, Ronnie* / 52nd Street Theme: *Scott, Ronnie* / Ow: *Scott, Ronnie* / Don't blame me: *Scott, Ronnie* / Scrapple from the scrapple: *Scott, Ronnie* / Donna Lee: *Scott, Ronnie* / Too marvellous for words: *Scott, Ronnie* / Have you met Miss Jones: *Scott, Ronnie* / September song: *Scott, Ronnie* / Flamingo: *Scott, Ronnie* / Chasin' the bird: *Scott, Ronnie* / Little Willie leaps: *Scott, Ronnie* / El sino: *Scott, Ronnie* / Crazy rhythm: *Scott, Ronnie* / Lover come back to me: *Scott, Ronnie* / Compos mentos: *Scott, Ronnie* / Body beautiful: *Scott, Ronnie* / Stompin' at the Savoy: *Scott, Ronnie* / Oh lady be good: *Esquire Jazz All Stars* / Boppin' at the esquire: *Esquire Jazz All Stars* / Idapop: *Esquire Jazz All Stars* / What is this thing called love: *Esquire Jazz All Stars* / Mop mop: *Feldman, Victor* / Lady bird: *Feldman, Victor* / Quaternity: *Feldman, Victor* / Moonlight in Vermont: *Feldman, Victor* / Gone with the wind: *Feldman, Victor* / Buzy: *Jazz At The Town Hall Ensemble* / How high the moon: *Jazz At The Town Hall Ensemble* / Galaxy: *All Star Sextet* / I can't get started (With you): *All Star Sextet* / First gear: *All Star Sextet* / Confirmation: *All Star Sextet* / My baby like to bebop: *All Star Sextet* / Disc jocky jump: *All Star Sextet* / Fallonology: *All Star Sextet* / Jack Fiddles while Norman Burns: *All Star Sextet*
CD ______ **3037300037**
Carlton / Apr '96 / Carlton

BEST OF BRITISH BLUES, THE
CD ______ **CD IMB 502**
Charly / Mar '93 / Koch

BEST OF BRITISH DANCE BANDS, THE
Happy days are here again: *Ambrose & His Orchestra* / After the sun's kissed the world goodbye: *Elizalde, Fred Rhythmicians* / It's the girl: *Cotton, Billy & His Band* / By the river Sainte Marie: *Bowlly, Al* / My baby just cares for me: *Payne, Jack & The BBC Dance Orchestra* / Crazy rhythm: *Starita, Ray & His Ambassadors* / How can you say no: *Hall, Henry & The BBC Dance Orchestra* / My silent love: *Gibbons, Carroll & The Hotel Orpheans* / I'm in the market for you: *Ambrose & His Orchestra* / Too many tears: *Cotton, Billy & His Band* / Good little, bad little you: *New Mayfair Dance Orchestra* / Anytime's the time to fall in love: *New Mayfair Dance Orchestra* / Honeymoon Hotel: *Hylton, Jack & His Orchestra* / Wind's in the west: *Fox, Roy & His Band* / Baby face: *Savoy Orpheans* / Like taking candy from a baby: *Roy, Harry* / Say it: *Roy, Harry* / Play to me gypsy: *Costa, Sam* / Kiss me dear: *Jackson, Jack & His Orchestra* / For all we know: *Gibbons, Carroll & The Hotel Orpheans*
CD ______ **CDSVL 177**
Saville / Jul '86 / Conifer/BMG

BEST OF BRITISH FOLK ROCK, THE
Waiting for the wheel to turn: *Capercaillie* / Golden vanity: *Steeleye Span* / When I'm up I can't get down: *Oyster Band* / Lay down: *Strawbs* / Jewel in the crown: *Fairport Convention* / Breaking the chains: *Runrig* / Blacksmith: *Pentangle* / Lady Eleanor: *Lindisfarne* / Johnny: *New Celeste* / Pige ruadh: *Capercaillie* / One green hill: *Oyster Band* / Surfeit of lampreys: *Fairport Convention* / So early in the Spring: *Pentangle* / Tir an airm: *Runrig* / All around my hat: *Steeleye Span* / Meet me on the corner: *Lindisfarne* / Morrisons jig: *New Celeste* / Part of the union: *Strawbs*
CD ______ **PRKCD 36**
Park / Oct '96 / Pinnacle

BEST OF BRITISH FOLK, THE
Light flight: *Pentangle* / Travel away: *Humblebums* / My friend up the road: *Digance, Richard* / Byker Hill: *Swarbrick, Dave & Martin Carthy* / Spiral staircase: *McTell, Ralph* / Continental trailways bus: *Johnstons* / Streets of London: *McTell, Ralph* / Mary Skeffington: *Rafferty, Gerry* / Rosemary Lane: *Jansch, Bert* / White House blues: *Renbourn, John* / If it wasnae for your wellies: *Connolly, Billy* / Up to now: *Dransfield* / Join us in our game: *Mr. Fox* / Easy street: *James, John & Pete Berryman* / All in a dream: *Tilston, Steve* / Sir Gavin Grimbold: *Gryphon* / Ungodly: *Decameron* / Gingerbread man: *Story Teller* / Lover for all seasons: *Sallyangie* / Boxing match: *Black Country Three* / Mouse and crow: *Pegg, Carole* / Dear River Thames: *Digance, Richard* / After the dance: *Jansch, Bert & John Renbourn* / Maid that's deep in love: *Pentangle*
CD ______ **CCSCD 222**
Castle / Jun '89 / BMG

BEST OF BRITISH FOLK, THE
Streets of London: *McTell, Ralph* / Net hauling song: *Campbell, Ian Folk Group* / Drag queen blues: *Digance, Richard* / Join us in our game: *Mr. Fox* / Day at the seaside: *Renbourn, John* / Market song: *Pentangle* / Judy: *Renbourn, John* / Roisin dubh: *Dubliners* / Red's favourite: *Renbourn, John & Bert Jansch* / Light flight: *Pentangle* / Spiral staircase: *McTell, Ralph* / Travel away: *Connolly, Billy* / Pavanna (Anna Bannana): *Renbourn, John* / Off to Dublin in the green: *Dubliners* / Hermit: *Renbourn, John* / Dear river thames: *McTell, Ralph* / Young love: *Giltrap, Gordon* / No exit: *Renbourn, John & Bert Jansch* / Shoe shine boy: *Humblebums* / Willoughby's farm: *McTell, Ralph*
CD ______ **MATCD 218**
Castle / May '93 / BMG

BEST OF BRITISH FOLK, THE
CD ______ **TRTCD 156**
TrueTrax / Oct '94 / THE

BEST OF BRITISH FOLK, THE
CD ______ **DCDCD 216**
Castle / Aug '96 / BMG

BEST OF BRITISH FOLK, THE
CD ______ **PLSCD 149**
Pulse / Feb '97 / BMG

BEST OF BRITISH JAZZ FROM THE BBC JAZZ CLUB VOL.1, THE
CD ______ **URCD 118**
Upbeat / Oct '95 / Cadillac / Target/BMG

BEST OF BRITISH JAZZ FROM THE BBC JAZZ CLUB VOL.2, THE
Memphis shake / Last smile blues / Chicago buzz / Blues for an unkown gypsy / Elephant stomp blues / Under the double eagle / My gal Sal / Small hour fantasy / It's a lowdown dirty shame / March hare / Here today / PTQ Rag / Oh Dad / Sweet muscatel / Randolph Turpin / Steal away blues / Quincey Street stomp / Squatty Roo / Hard hearted Hannah / African Queen
CD Set ______ **URCD 119**
Upbeat / Feb '96 / Cadillac / Target/BMG

BEST OF BRITISH JAZZ FROM THE BBC JAZZ CLUB VOL.3, THE
Stockyard strut / If I ever cease to love / Down home rag / Chinatown, my Chinatown / Sweet Lorraine / Lil Liza Jane / Alligator hop / Beautiful dreamer / Blue blood blues / Shout 'em aunt Tillie / Pasadena / Oh, baby / Farewell blues / I've got a feeling for Orphelia / My sweetie went away / St. Louis rag / Do you know what it means to Miss New Orleans / Boodle-Am-Shake / Madeira / 20 Wang wang blues
CD ______ **URCD 120**
Upbeat / May '96 / Cadillac / Target/BMG

BEST OF BRITISH JAZZ FROM THE BBC JAZZ CLUB VOL.4, THE
'S wonderful: *Welsh, Alex Band* / Blue turning grey over you: *Welsh, Alex Band* / Chinatown, my Chinatown: *Welsh, Alex Band* / Preacher: *Welsh, Alex Band* / Sidewalk blues: *Welsh, Alex Band* / As long as I live: *Welsh, Alex Band* / On the Alamo: *Welsh, Alex Band* / Everybody loves my baby:

Welsh, Alex Band / Exactly like you: *Welsh, Alex Band* / There'll be a hot time in the old town tonight: *Welsh, Alex Band* / Between the devil and the deep blue sea: *Disley, Diz & The Soho Quintette* / Oui: *Disley, Diz & The Soho Quintette* / Shine: *Disley, Diz & The Soho Quintette* / Crying the blues: *Disley, Diz & The Soho Quintette* / Ding dong daddy from Dumas: *Mulligan, Mick Magnolia Jazz Band & George Melly* / Hesitation blues: *Mulligan, Mick Magnolia Jazz Band & George Melly* / Muddy water: *Mulligan, Mick Magnolia Jazz Band & George Melly* / Wolverine blues: *Mulligan, Mick Magnolia Jazz Band & George Melly* / It's only a shanty in Old Shanty Town: *Mulligan, Mick Magnolia Jazz Band & George Melly* / Shim-me-shawobble: *Mulligan, Mick Magnolia Jazz Band & George Melly*
CD ____ **URCD 122**
Upbeat / Sep '96 / Cadillac / Target/BMG

BEST OF BRITISH JAZZ FROM THE BBC JAZZ CLUB VOL.5, THE
Hiawatha rag: *Sunshine, Monty Jazz Band* / South: *Sunshine, Monty Jazz Band* / All the girls go crazy about the way I walk: *Sunshine, Monty Jazz Band* / Saturday night function: *Sunshine, Monty Jazz Band* / Boyfriend/Song of the Swanee: *Stewart, Graham Seven* / Tears: *Stewart, Graham Seven* / Keyhole blues: *Stewart, Graham Seven* / Down South Camp meeting: *Turner, Bruce Quartet* / Stop, look and listen: *Turner, Bruce Quartet* / One o'clock jump: *Turner, Bruce Quartet* / That's a plenty: *Ashman, Micky & His Jazzband* / London blues: *Ashman, Micky & His Jazzband* / Give me your telephone number: *Ashman, Micky & His Jazzband* / Careless love: *Barber, Chris & His Jazz Band* / As long as I live: *Barber, Chris & His Jazz Band* / Too busy: *Barber, Chris & His Jazz Band* / Tell me is fancy bred: *Barber, Chris & His Jazz Band*
CD ____ **URCD 125**
Upbeat / Mar '97 / Cadillac / Target/BMG

BEST OF BRITISH JAZZ, THE (3CD Set)
Crazy rhythm: *Daniel, Joe Jazz Group* / St. Louis blues: *Daniel, Joe Jazz Group* / Jazz me blues: *Daniel, Joe Jazz Group* / Chicago: *Daniel, Joe Jazz Group* / Little brown jug: *Daniel, Joe Jazz Group* / I wish I could shimmy like my sister Kate: *Daniel, Joe Jazz Group* / Avalon: *Daniel, Joe Jazz Group* / Marie: *Daniel, Joe Jazz Group* / Rosetta: *Daniel, Joe Jazz Group* / Susie: *Daniel, Joe Jazz Group* / Bad penny blues: *Lyttelton, Humphrey & His Band* / Heatwave: *Lyttelton, Humphrey & His Band* / Slippery horn: *Lyttelton, Humphrey & His Band* / Early call: *Lyttelton, Humphrey & His Band* / That's my home: *Lyttelton, Humphrey & His Band* / PTQ rag: *Lyttelton, Humphrey & His Band* / March hare: *Lyttelton, Humphrey & His Band* / Hoppin'mad: *Lyttelton, Humphrey & His Band* / Careless love: *Lyttelton, Humphrey & His Band* / Panama rag: *Lyttelton, Humphrey & His Band* / Maple leaf rag: *Lyttelton, Humphrey & His Band* / Alexander's ragtime band: *Phillips, Sid & His Band* / You've got to see mama ev'ry night: *Phillips, Sid & His Band* / Pasadena: *Phillips, Sid & His Band* / Disillusioned: *Phillips, Sid & His Band* / Muskrat ramble: *Phillips, Sid & His Band* / Mama don't allow it: *Phillips, Sid & His Band* / Forty cups of coffee: *Phillips, Sid & His Band* / Pete Kelly's blues: *Phillips, Sid & His Band* / Clarinet marmalade: *Phillips, Sid & His Band* / Tiger rag: *Phillips, Sid & His Band* / Sensation rag: *Randall, Freddy & His Band* / Black & blue: *Randall, Freddy & His Band* / Hotter than that: *Randall, Freddy & His Band* / Sunday: *Randall, Freddy & His Band* / Farewell blues: *Randall, Freddy & His Band* / Someday sweetheart: *Randall, Freddy & His Band* / Won't you come home Bill Bailey: *Randall, Freddy & His Band* / On Sunday I go sailing: *Richford, Doug & The London Jazzmen* / Yip-I-addy-I-ay: *Richford, Doug & The London Jazzmen* / Twelve over the eight: *Richford, Doug & The London Jazzmen* / Nagasaki: *Gonella, Nat & His Georgians* / Jubilee: *Gonella, Nat & His Georgians* / Swingin' the jinx away: *Gonella, Nat & His Georgians* / I can't dance I got ants in my pants: *Gonella, Nat & His Georgians* / Lily of the valley: *Crane River Jazz Band* / Who walks in when I walk out: *Saints Jazz Band* / Hey lawdy Papa: *Saints Jazz Band*
CD Set ____ **CDTRBOX 208**
Trio / Oct '95 / EMI

BEST OF BRITISH MELODIC TRANCE, THE
CD ____ **TLCCD 4**
Lush / Oct '97 / Prime / SRD

BEST OF BRITISH MILITARY MUSIC, THE
CD ____ **CDSR 043**
Telstar / May '94 / BMG

BEST OF BRITISH STEEL, THE (2CD Set)
Tales of destruction: *Dogs D'Amour* / Clerical conspiracy: *Sabbat* / (Na na) nukklear rokket: *Wrathchild* / Seventh church of the apocalyptic lawnmower: *Lawnmower Deth* / Low life: *Trixx Federation* / Read my lips: *Tattooed Love Boys* / Goddess: *Acid Reign* / Rock 'n' roll lady: *Dominique, Lisa* / I'm on fire: *Mantas* / Deny reality: *Re-Animator* / Surrender: *Midnight Blue* / Queen of the night: *Deathtrash* / Prey to the Lord: *Deathwish* / Living without you: *Tigertailz* / Looking for a lady: *Last Of The Teenage Idols* / Testify to me: *Virus* / Nights on fire: *Torino* / Spirit cry: *Sacrilege* / Love attack: *After Hours* / One way ride: *Lixx* / Madman: *Metal Messiah* / So alone: *Soho Roses*
CD Set ____ **WKFMXD 128**
FM / Jul '89 / Revolver / Sony

BEST OF BRITISH VOL.1, THE
Battle hymn of the republic / When you're smiling / Baker's bounce / When your lover has gone / Whispering / Groovin' high / Big noise from Winnetka / Mood indigo / Pick yourself up / Pennies from heaven / Seven come eleven / When it's sleepy time down south / Trouble with you is me / Flintstones theme / Baker's blues
CD ____ **CDSIV 6146**
Horatio Nelson / May '95 / Disc

BEST OF BRITISH, THE
CD ____ **DINCD 92**
Dino / Jun '94 / Pinnacle

BEST OF BRITISH, THE
CD ____ **TREB 5020**
Scratch / May '96 / Koch / Scratch/BMG

BEST OF BRITISH, THE
When I'm cleaning windows: *Formby, George* / It's a lovely day tomorrow: *Lynn, Vera* / Sun has got its hat on: *Ambrose* / Run rabbit run: *Flanagan & Allen* / Sally: *Fields, Gracie* / Smoke gets in your eyes: *Mantovani* / Stately homes of England: *Coward, Noel* / Parade of tin soldiers: *Dixon, Reginald* / Everything stops for tea: *Buchanan, Jack* / Man who comes around: *Cotton, Billy* / My yiddishe momma: *Shelton, Anne* / When I see an elephant fly: *Loss, Joe* / Albert and the lion: *Holloway, Stanley* / No one else will do: *Geraldo* / Laughing policeman: *Penrose, Charles* / Biggest aspidistra in the world: *Fields, Gracie* / Leaning on a lampost: *Formby, George* / Are you having any fun: *Flanagan & Allen* / Spider of the night: *Mantovani* / Nightingale sang in Berkeley Square: *Shelton, Anne* / You can't blame me for that: *Miller, Max* / Let him go, let him tarry: *Loss, Joe* / Mad dogs and Englishmen: *Coward, Noel* / We'll meet again: *Lynn, Vera*
CD ____ **CD 6034**
Music / Sep '96 / Target/BMG

BEST OF CAPITAL GOLD, THE
Something in the air: *Thunderclap Newman* / Waterloo sunset: *Kinks* / Out of time: *Farlowe, Chris* / Daydream: *Lovin' Spoonful* / Son of a preacher man: *Springfield, Dusty* / I don't want our love to die: *Herd* / I hear you knocking: *Edmunds, Dave* / Green tambourine: *Lemon Pipers* / (If paradise is) Half as nice: *Amen Corner* / This wheel's on fire: *Driscoll, Julie & The Brian Auger Trinity* / Concrete and clay: *Unit 4+2* / Jesamine: *Casuals* / Israelites: *Dekker, Desmond* / In the summertime: *Mungo Jerry* / With a little help from my friends: *Cocker, Joe* / Whiter shade of pale: *Procul Harum* / Get it on: *T-Rex* / Sweets for my sweet: *Searchers* / First cut is the deepest: *Arnold, P.P.* / Will you still love me tomorrow: *Shirelles* / Only one woman: *Marbles* / Rescue me: *Bass, Fontella* / Judy in disguise: *Fred, John & His Playboy Band* / Itchycoo Park: *Small Faces*
CD ____ **AHLCD 2**
Hit / Oct '92 / Grapevine/PolyGram

BEST OF CAPITOL CLASSICS VOL.1 & 2
Key to the world: *Reynolds, L.J.* / On the beat: *BB&Q Band* / Prance on: *Henderson, Eddie* / Love on a summer night: *McCrarys* / It's a pleasure: *Brown, Sheree* / Sound of music: *Dayton* / Doin' alright: *O'Bryan* / Music is my sanctuary: *Bartz, Gary* / Be thankful for what you've got / Hard to get around: *BB&Q Band* / Before you break my heart: *Dunlap, Gene* / Really, really love you: *Parker, Cecil* / There ain't nothin' (like your lovin'): *Laurence, Paul* / It's just the way I feel: *Dunlap, Gene & The Ridgeways*
CD ____ **CZ 208**
Capitol / Jun '89 / EMI

BEST OF CARNIVAL IN RIO VOL.1, THE
CD ____ **EUCD 1097**
ARC / '91 / ADA / ARC Music

BEST OF CARNIVAL IN RIO VOL.2, THE
CD ____ **EUCD 1136**
ARC / '91 / ADA / ARC Music

BEST OF CHARLY GROOVE, THE
Little soul party: *Ohio Players* / If she won't (find someone who will): *Dorsey, Lee* / Big legged woman: *Hobbs, Willie* / Good old funky music: *Meters* / Working in a coal mine: *Dorsey, Lee* / Give the baby anything the baby wants: *Tex, Joe* / Chokin' kind: *Toussaint, Allen* / It takes two to do wrong: *Patterson, Bobby* / Is it funky enough: *Communications & Black Experiences Band* / Thank you for letting me be myself again: *Maceo & All The King's Men* / All I do everyday: *Meters* / Full speed ahead: *Jungle Band* / Gone too far: *Toussaint, Allen* / Move on up: *Mayfield, Curtis* / Medley: *Brown, James* / It's too funky in here: *Payback* / (I got) so much trouble in my mind: *Quarterman, Sir Joe & Free Soul* / Ain't gonna bump no more (with big fat women): *Tex, Joe* / Soul music: *Mayfield, Curtis* / Tell me why: *Womack, Bobby* / Shine it on: *Sly & The Family Stone* / Cholly (funk getting ready to roll): *Funkadelic* / Mother's son: *Mayfield, Curtis* / Oh I: *Funkadelic* / Thump and bump: *Fisher, Eddie* / If it's not addin' up: *Sly & The Family Stone* / Tripping out: *Mayfield, Curtis* / One nation under a groove: *Funkadelic* / (Get up I feel like being a) sex machine: *Brown, James* / 7-6-5-4-3-2-1 Blow your whistle: *Rimshots* / Mambo mongo: *Santamaria, Mongo*
CD Set ____ **CPCD 8085**
Charly / Jun '95 / Koch

BEST OF CHESS BLUES VOL.1, THE
CD ____ **CHLD 19093**
Chess/MCA / Oct '92 / BMG / New Note/ BMG

BEST OF CHESS BLUES VOL.2, THE
CD ____ **CHLD 19094**
Chess/MCA / Oct '92 / BMG / New Note/ BMG

BEST OF CHESS R & B VOL.1
CD ____ **CHLD 19160**
Chess/MCA / Nov '91 / BMG / New Note/ BMG

BEST OF CHESS R & B VOL.2
CD ____ **CHLD 19161**
Chess/MCA / Nov '91 / BMG / New Note/ BMG

BEST OF CHESS RHYTHM, THE (2CD Set)
CD Set ____ **CHD 29376**
Chess/MCA / Mar '97 / BMG / New Note/ BMG

BEST OF CHESS VOL.1, THE
Maybellene: *Berry, Chuck* / Bo Diddley: *Diddley, Bo* / Rocket 88: *Brenston, Jackie & The Delta Cats* / See you later alligator: *Charles, Bobby* / Suzie Q: *Hawkins, Dale* / Oh oh: *Bo, Eddie* / Johnny B Goode: *Berry, Chuck* / Sincerely: *Moonglows* / Ain't got no home: *Henry, Clarence 'Frogman'* / Most of all: *Moonglows* / I'll be home: *Flamingos* / Who do you love: *Diddley, Bo*
CD ____ **CHLD 19221**
Chess/MCA / Jul '93 / BMG / New Note/ BMG

BEST OF CHESS VOL.2, THE
Happy, happy birthday baby: *Tune Weavers* / I'm so young: *Students* / Book of love: *Monotones* / Teardrops: *Andrew, Lee & The Hearts* / Ten commandments of love: *Harvey & The Moonglows* / Let me in: *Sensations* / Over the mountain across the sea: *Johnnie & Joe* / Hi-heel sneakers: *Tucker, Tommy* / Rinky dink: *Cortez, Dave 'Baby'* / Sally go round the roses: *Jaynetts* / No particular place to go: *Berry, Chuck* / Roadrunner: *Diddley, Bo*
CD ____ **CHLD 19222**
Chess/MCA / Jul '93 / BMG / New Note/ BMG

BEST OF CHOCI'S CHEWNS VOL.2 (Alternative Chunks) (2CD Set)
CD Set ____ **CCLP 001**
Choci's Chewns / Mar '97 / Arabesque / Grapevine/PolyGram / Mo's Music Machine

BEST OF CHURCH STREET STATION VOL.1, THE (Country Stars Live)
DIVORCE: *Wynette, Tammy* / Four in the morning: *Young, Faron* / Behind closed doors: *Rich, Charlie* / Mamas don't let your babies grow up to be cowboys: *Bruce, Ed* / This land is your land: *Allen, Rex Sr. & Rex Allen Jr.* / Duellin' banjos: *Devol, Skip* / Texas when I die: *Tucker, Tanya* / Before the next teardrop falls: *Fender, Freddy* / He stopped loving her today: *Jones, George* / Love in the hot afternoon: *Watson, Gene* / Detroit city: *Tillis, Mel* / He ain't heavy, he's my brother: *Osmond Brothers* / Cheating situation: *Bandy, Moe* / Wabash cannonball: *Boxcar Willie* / Big bad John: *Dean, Jimmy* / Teddy bear: *Fairchild, Barbara* / Tequila sunrise: *Bare, Bobby*
CD ____ **PLATCD 359**
Platinum / '91 / Prism

BEST OF CHURCH STREET STATION VOL.2, THE (Country Stars Live)
Delta town: *Tucker, Tanya* / Mr. Bojangles: *Nitty Gritty Dirt Band* / Heart of the country: *Mattea, Kathy* / Let your love flow: *Bellamy Brothers* / Mexico rose: *Fender, Freddy* / Secret love: *Fender, Freddy* / Who's gonna fill their shoes: *Jones, George* / Door is always open: *Dave & Sugar* / Lonely days, lonely nights: *Loveless, Patty* / Key Largo: *Higgins, Bertie* / Carmen: *Watson, Gene* / Chains of gold: *Sweethearts Of The Rodeo* / Auctioneer: *Van Dyke, Leroy* / I like beer: *Hall, Tom T.* / Love don't care: *Conley, Earl Thomas* / Please Mr. Please / God bless America: *Greenwood, Lee* / Harper Valley PTA: *Riley, Jeannie C.* / Okie from Muskogee: *Haggard, Merle*
CD ____ **PLATCD 360**
Platinum / May '91 / Prism

BEST OF COUNTRY AND IRISH, THE
CD ____ **RITZCD 0072**
Ritz / Apr '94 / Pinnacle

BEST OF COUNTRY AND WESTERN VOL.1, THE (3CD Set)
CD Set ____ **96301**
Giga / Mar '97 / ADA / Total/BMG

BEST OF COUNTRY AND WESTERN VOL.2, THE (3CD Set)
CD Set ____ **96302**
Giga / Mar '97 / ADA / Total/BMG

BEST OF COUNTRY AND WESTERN VOL.3, THE (3CD Set)
CD Set ____ **96303**
Giga / Mar '97 / ADA / Total/BMG

BEST OF COUNTRY AND WESTERN VOL.4, THE (3CD Set)
CD Set ____ **96304**
Giga / Mar '97 / ADA / Total/BMG

BEST OF COVER VERSIONS, THE
CD ____ **ZYX 810992**
ZYX / May '97 / ZYX

BEST OF DANCE '92, THE
CD ____ **TCD 2610**
Telstar / Oct '92 / BMG

BEST OF DANCE '96, THE (2CD Set)
CD Set ____ **TCD 2871**
Telstar / Oct '96 / BMG

BEST OF DANCE BAND DAYS VOL.1, THE
Moonlight serenade / Clarinade / Jumpin' at the woodside / Sweet Georgia Brown / Stars fell on Alabama / Angry / Stardust / Song of India / Caldonia / Airmail stomp / Rockin' in rhythm / Bei mir bist du schon / Little brown jug / Don't be that way / Tweet tweet / Button up your overcoat / Some people / 'S wonderful / Opus one / At the woodchoppers' ball / Blue moon / I got a girl named Netty
CD ____ **DBCD 20**
Dance Band Days / Oct '87 / Prism

BEST OF DANCE BAND DAYS VOL.2, THE
Symphony / King Porter stomp / Rockin' in rhythm / I'll be seeing you / Down the road apiece / Man with a horn / Begin the beguine / Cheek to cheek / There, I've said it again / Everybody eats when they come to my house / Newport up / Lullaby of Broadway / Seven-o-five / All the cats join in / King size blues / Fare thee well to Harlem / Bedford drive / Blue skies / Goosey gander / Cruisin' with cab / St. Louis blues / Rum and coca cola
CD ____ **DBCD 21**
Dance Band Days / Oct '87 / Prism

BEST OF DISCO ROCK, THE (2CD Set)
CD Set ____ **ZYX 811002**
ZYX / May '97 / ZYX

BEST OF DISTINCTIVE, THE
Mystic motion: *Datura* / House forever: *Billabong* / Take me away: *Westbrook* / Feel good: *B-Code* / Madness: *Nights At The Round Tables* / Get into music: *DJ's Rule* / King cone: *X-Odus* / Lellenda el espiritu: *Nights At The Round Tables* / Fall out of love: *Hybrid* / Switchead: *Marshal Stax* / Feeling: *Endive* / I could be this: *Androgeny & Michael M*
CD ____ **DISNCD 10**
Distinctive / Apr '96 / 3mv/Pinnacle / Amato Disco

BEST OF DWARF VOL.2, THE
CD ____ **DWARFCD 002**
Dwarf / Oct '96 / Mo's Music Machine

BEST OF EAST EUROPEAN SONGS AND DANCES
CD ____ **EUCD 1148**
ARC / '91 / ADA / ARC Music

BEST OF ELECTRO VOL.1, THE
Jam on it: *Newcleus* / Smurf: *Brunson, Tyrone* / Light years away: *Warp 9* / Breakin' in space: *Key-Matic* / Egypt, Egypt: *Egyptian Lover* / Party scene: *Russel Brothers* / Clear: *Cybotron* / One for the treble (fresh): *Davy DMX* / Wild style: *Timezone* / Al- naafiysh: *Hashim* / Hip hop be bop: *Man Parrish* / Break dancin' electric boogie: *Wet Street Mob*
CD ____ **SOUNDSCD 8**
Street Sounds / Oct '95 / Beechwood/BMG

BEST OF EVOLUTION, THE
CD ____ **EVGCD 1**
Evolution / Apr '96 / Alphamagic

BEST OF EYE Q CLASSICS (2CD Set)
Summerbreeze: *Summerbreeze* / 4 Monks: *Virtual Symmetry* / Vernon's wonderland: *Vernon* / No fate: *Zyon* / Magnifica: *Sonic Infusion* / Sun down: *Volunteers* / Airborn: *Mirage* / Synfonica: *Brainchild* / Troya mix '93: *Odysee Of Noises* / Cosmos: *Java* / Alienated: *Earth Nation* / Superstring: *Cygnus X* / Goahead: *Freebeach* / Symmetry: *Brainchild* / Firedance: *Odysee Of Noises* / VS: *Virtual Symmetry* / El sueno: *Aquaform* / Orange theme: *Cygnus X*
CD Set ____ **EYEUKCD 011**
Eye Q / Jul '96 / Vital

BEST OF FLAMENCO, THE
CD ____ **EUCD 1158**
ARC / Jun '91 / ADA / ARC Music

BEST OF FRANCE'S CONCERT COMPILATION, THE
CD ____ **FCD 130**
France's Concert / '89 / BMG / Jazz Music

BEST OF GOSPEL, THE (2CD Set)
CD Set 3014342
Arcade / Feb '97 / Discovery

BEST OF GOTHAM RHYTHM AND BLUES, THE
CD KKCD 04
Krazy Kat / Oct '90 / Hot Shot / Jazz Music

BEST OF GREECE VOL.2
CD EUCD 1159
ARC / Jun '91 / ADA / ARC Music

BEST OF GRENADA 1995, THE
CD JW 1017CD
JW / Jan '96 / Jet Star

BEST OF HARD HOUSE, THE (4CD Set)
CD Set DAM 002
Tring / Dec '96 / Tring

BEST OF HI-NRG, THE
Don't leave me this way: Jiani, Carol / Queen of fools: Williams, Jessica / Love fire: James, Jimmy / Satellites: Warren, Ellie / I'm living my own life: Bentley, Earlene / Whiplash: Eastbound Expressway / High energy: Thomas, Evelyn / I am what I am: La Cage / Love's gone mad: Seventh Avenue / Panic: French Kiss / Love and desire: Arpeggio / We are invincible: 501's / Fight: Lewis, Norma / I'm gonna love you forever: Ruffin, Jimmy & Jackson Moore
CD 303862
Hallmark / Jun '97 / Carlton

BEST OF HIP HOP (2CD Set)
CD Set ZYX 811102
ZYX / Jul '97 / ZYX

BEST OF HTD, THE
Down in the bottom: Terraplane / Shake for me: Terraplane / We lie: Albion Band / Thank Christ for the bomb/Soldier: Groundhogs / Land of my fathers (Hen wlad fy nhadau): Caravan / Foolish pride: McPhee, Tony / Railway station: Tylor / Children of the stones: Rose Among Thorns / Fogbound: Banks, Peter / Why: Sister Mary Elephant
CD HTDCD 20
HTD / Aug '96 / CM / Pinnacle

BEST OF INDIE METAL, THE
I survive: Terraplane / Take it all away: Girlschool / All the time: Spider / All around the world: Torme, Bernie / Motorhead: Hawkwind / Hit it: Tygers Of Pan Tang / Wind of change: Langton, Lloyd Group / We got the edge: Savage / Gimme the money: Terraplane / Too different: Persian Risk / Time for you: Scrubs / It could be better: Girlschool / Hurry on sundown: Hawkwind / Feel like a man: Spider / Star: Torme / Are you there: Tygers Of Pan Tang
CD EMPRCD 552
Emporio / Nov '94 / Disc

BEST OF INDIE, THE
CD BOTT 003CD
Beechwood / May '96 / Beechwood/BMG / Pinnacle

BEST OF IRELAND, THE (Celtic Graces)
Midnight walker: Spillane, Davy / Ballymun regatta: Whelan, Bill / Plains of Kildare: Brady, Paul / Maids of Mitchelstown: Bothy Band / Wee weaver: Keane, Dolores & John Faulkner / Aaron's key: Stockton's Wing / Arthur McBride: Brady, Paul / Eigigh suas a stoirin: Clannad / Rip the calico: Bothy Band / Mr. O'Connor: De Danann / Scar an nollaig sinn/It takes two: King, Philip & Peter Browne / Pursuit of Farmer Michael Hayes: Planxty & Christy Moore / Maid of Coolmore: Bothy Band / Declan: Lunny, Donal / Lord Franklin: Burke, Kevin & Michael O'Dohmnhaill
CD CDEMC 3693
Hemisphere / Feb '97 / EMI

BEST OF IRELAND, THE (3CD Set)
Let him go, let him tarry: Murray, Ruby / Teddy O'Neil: Murray, Ruby / Delaney's donkey: Murray, Ruby / Dear old Donegal: Murray, Ruby / McNamara's band: Murray, Ruby / When Irish eyes are smiling: Murray, Ruby / Danny boy: Murray, Ruby / Cockles and mussels: Murray, Ruby / Trottin' to the fair: Murray, Ruby / It's a great day for the Irish: Murray, Ruby / Believe me if all those endearing young charms: Murray, Ruby / Mush, mush, mush: O'Dowda, Brendan / Ballymaquilty band: O'Dowda, Brendan / Dear little shamrock: O'Dowda, Brendan / On the one road: O'Dowda, Brendan / Paddy McGinty's goat: O'Dowda, Brendan / Come back to Erin: O'Dowda, Brendan / Phil the fluter's ball: O'Dowda, Brendan / Mountains of Mourne: O'Dowda, Brendan / Come back Paddy Reilly: O'Dowda, Brendan / Are you right there Michael: O'Dowda, Brendan / Si do Mhaimeo/Peter Street: O'Duill, Brendan / Doonaree: Murray, Ruby & Brendan O'Dowda / Eileen O'Grady: Murray, Ruby & Brendan O'Dowda / Three tunes: Gallowglass Ceili Band / Reel: Gallowglass Ceili Band / I'll take you home again Kathleen: Locke, Josef / When you were sixteen: Locke, Josef / Galway Bay: Locke, Josef / Macushla: Locke, Josef / Rose of Tralee: Locke, Josef / Isle of Innisfree: Locke, Josef / Maire my girl: Locke, Josef / How can you buy Killarney: Locke, Josef / My heart's in the heart of Killarney: Cunningham, Larry / Vely Leitrim: Cunningham, Larry / Moonshiner: Murphy, Delia / Spinning wheel: Murphy, Delia / Courtin' in the kitchen: Murphy, Delia / Three drunken maidens: Planxty / Whiskey in the jar: Dubliners / Galway races: Dubliners / Kelly, the boy from Killan: Dubliners / Limerick rake: Dubliners / Bantry Bay: O'Shea, Sean / Banks of my own lovely Lee: O'Shea, Sean / Star of the County Down: McCormack, John / Jeannie with the light brown hair: McCormack, John / Down by the Sally Gardens: McCormack, John / Queen of Connemera: Ardellis Ceili Band / Jigs: Ardellis Ceili Band / Old Skibbereen: Gallagher, Bridie / Castlebar Fair: Gallagher, Bridie / Flower of sweet Strabane: Gallagher, Bridie / Where the River Shannon flows: Gallagher, Bridie / Wearin' of the green: Henry, Dermot / Ireland my home: MacEwan, Father Sydney / Mother MacHree: MacEwan, Father Sydney / Rose of Killarney: MacEwan, Father Sydney / Irish lullaby: Shannonside Ceili Band / Old bog road: Drennan, Tommy / Claddagh ring: Tulla Ceili Band / Three reels: Kilfernora Ceili Band / Kitty of Coleraine: Bunratty Singers / Coulin: O'Grady, Geraldine / My lagan love: O'Duffy, Michael / Irish salute: Band of the Irish Guards
CD Set CDTRBOX 272
Trio / May '97 / EMI

BEST OF IRELAND, THE (20 Tracks Of Traditional Irish Music)
Galway bay: Locke, Josef / Whiskey in the jar: Dubliners / Trottin' to the fair: Murray, Ruby / An Irish lullaby: Shannonside Ceili Band / When Irish eyes are smiling: Jones, Sansie / Dear old Donegal: Locke, Josef / Queen of Connemera: Ardellis ceili band & John Bennet / Danny boy: O'Se, Sean / Jigs: Ardellis Ceili Band / Mountains of Mourne: O'Dowda, Brendan / Galway races: Dubliners / When you were sweet sixteen: Locke, Josef / Reels: Gallowglass Ceili Band / A pretty Irish girl: O'Dowda, Brendan & Ruby Murray / Flower of sweet Strabane: Gallagher, Bridie / It's a great day for the Irish: Murray, Ruby / Rose of Tralee: O'Dowda, Brendan / Ireland my home: Father Sydney MacEwan / Bantry bay: O'Se, Sean / Isle of Innisfree: Locke, Josef
CD CDMFP 6231
Music For Pleasure / Jun '96 / EMI

BEST OF IRISH FOLK FEST, THE
CD CDTUT 727478
Wundertute / '89 / ADA / CM / Duncans

BEST OF IRISH FOLK, THE
Rocky road to Dublin: Dubliners / Curragh of Kildare: Furey, Finbar & Eddie / Glenside polka: Glenside Ceilidh Band / Henry joy: Grehan Sisters / Handsome cabin boy: Sweeney's Men / Frog's wedding: Johnstons / Exile's jig: Sweeney's Men / Lambs on the green hills: Johnstons / Spanish cloak: Furey, Finbar & Eddie / Golden jubilee: Glenside Ceilidh Band / Cook in the kitchen: Dubliners / Orange and the green: Grehan Sisters / St. Patrick's breastplate: Wood, Royston & Heather / Inis dhun ramha: Na Fili / Foggy dew: Imlach, Hamish / Three pieces by O'Carolan: Renbourn, John / Madame Bonaparte: Furey, Finbar / Rakish Paddy: Furey, Finbar / Roisin dubh: Dubliners / Chanters tune: Na Fili / Spanish lady: Johnstons / Killarney boys of pleasure: Swarbrick, Dave
CD CCSCD 221
Castle / Jun '89 / BMG

BEST OF IRISH FOLK, THE
CD HMCD 064
Harmac / Aug '90 / I&B

BEST OF IRISH FOLK, THE
CD PLSCD 133
Pulse / Apr '96 / BMG

BEST OF IRISH SHOWBANDS, THE
CD MATCD 231
Castle / Dec '92 / BMG

BEST OF IRISH TRADITIONAL MUSIC, THE (2CD Set)
CD Set 2CHDHX 807
Outlet / May '95 / ADA / CM / Direct / Duncans / Koch / Ross

BEST OF JAMAICA GOLD VOL.1, THE
CD JMC 200219
Jamaican Gold / May '94 / Grapevine/ PolyGram / Jet Star

BEST OF JAMAICA GOLD VOL.2, THE
CD JMC 200220
Jamaican Gold / May '94 / Grapevine/ PolyGram / Jet Star

BEST OF JAZZ FUSION VOL.2, THE
Strawberry moon: Washington, Grover Jr. / I wanna play for you: Clarke, Stanley / Give it all you've got: Mangione, Chuck / Ginseng woman: Gale, Eric / Throw down: Browne, Tom / Birdland: Weather Report / Grandma's hands: Scott-Heron, Gil / Jazz carnival: Azymuth / Liquid groove: Maria, Tania / Modern time blues: Ponty, Jean-Luc / Running away: Ayers, Roy / East river: Brecker Brothers / Sudden samba: Larsen, Neil / By all means: Mouzon, Alphonse / Spiral: Crusaders
CD NTRCD 042
Nectar / Jan '96 / Pinnacle

BEST OF JAZZ ORGANS, THE
CD CDC 9006
LRC / Oct '90 / Harmonia Mundi / New Note/Pinnacle

BEST OF JAZZ SAXOPHONES VOL.3, THE
CD CDC 9009
LRC / Oct '90 / Harmonia Mundi / New Note/Pinnacle

BEST OF JAZZ SINGERS VOL.2, THE
CD CDC 9008
LRC / Oct '90 / Harmonia Mundi / New Note/Pinnacle

BEST OF JUNGLE MASSIVE, THE (2CD Set)
CD Set SMDCD 112
Snapper / Jul '97 / Pinnacle

BEST OF JUNGLE VOL.1, THE
CD PNCCA 2
Production House / Aug '94 / Jet Star / Total/BMG

BEST OF JUNGLE VOL.3, THE
CD PNCCA 4
Production House / Jan '95 / Jet Star / Total/BMG

BEST OF JUNGLE VOL.4, THE
CD PNCCA 6
Production House / May '95 / Jet Star / Total/BMG

BEST OF LATIN AMERICA - CHANGE THE RULES, THE
La noche: Arroyo, Joe / Sobre las olas: Latin Brothers / Descarge de hoy: Alemany, Jesus / EL patillero: Fruko / Me tenian amarrado con fe: Saquito, Nico / Juana pena: Maestra, Sierra / Pregoes do rios: De Rua, Moleque / Eu quero sossego: Reiner, A / Floreaux: Os Ingenuos / Negra presuntuosa: Baka, Susana / El puente de los suspiros: Freundt, Julie / Duele: Kjarkas / Mi corazon en la ciudad: Junaro, Emma / Me gusta todo: Los Nemus Del Pacifico / La tarde: Estudiantina Invasora / Mil horas: La Sonora Dinamita / El indio sinuano: Jiminez, Maximo / Bordoneo Y 900: Mosalini, Juan Jose / Alma de loca: Varela, Adriana
CD RGNET 1013CD
World Music Network / May '97 / ADA / New Note/Pinnacle

BEST OF LATIN AMERICA - EL CONDOR PASA, THE
El condor pasa / Tres bailecitos / Mburucya nostalgia Colombiana / Frederico / Recuerdo del puno / Que nadie sepa mi sufrir / Noche del Paraquay despedida / Burrerita / Estampa Panamena / Alde viejo companario / La tropilla / Pastor de nubes Asuncion del Paraguay
CD PV 793093
Disques Pierre Verany / Oct '93 / Kingdom

BEST OF LATIN AMERICA - LA COLEGIALA, THE
La colegiala / La Peregrinacion / Palmeras / Concierto en la llanura / Sueno de angelita / Cascada la baguala / El arriero / Porque / Cruzando el dulce / Zamponas / Reservista purajhei / Villa guillermina / Paraguay pe el indio muerte / Misionera / La danza del colibri
CD PV 793094
Disques Pierre Verany / Oct '93 / Kingdom

BEST OF LATIN AMERICA - MOLIENDO CAFE, THE
Moliendo cafe / Pajaro campana / Madrecita / Indiecita Linda / Cerro cora / Che picazu mi / Kantu / Itagua poti / Guesta de pampa azui / Virginia / Sanz del destino / Estancia ava ne-e / Genoveva / Recuerdos de ipacarai / Angela Rosa / Esperanza mia
CD PV 793095
Disques Pierre Verany / Oct '93 / Kingdom

BEST OF LATIN AMERICA VOL.1, THE
CD EUCD 1115
ARC / '91 / ADA / ARC Music

BEST OF LATIN AMERICA VOL.2, THE
CD EUCD 1147
ARC / '91 / ADA / ARC Music

BEST OF LATIN JAZZ, THE
Nica's dream: Burrell, Kenny / Sambop: Adderley, Cannonball / Gunky: Lytle, Johnny / Baion baby: Stitt, Sonny / Mambo inn: Taylor, Billy / Caravan: Pucho & His Latin Soul Brothers / Montuneando: Santamaria, Mongo & La Lupe / Ping pong: Blakey, Art & The Jazz Messengers / Mau mau: Farmer, Art Septet / Manteca: Garland, Red Trio / Seafood Wally: Rodriguez, Willie / Screamin': McDuff, 'Brother' Jack / Fatman: Montego Joe / Mambo ricci: Dolphy, Eric & Latin Jazz 5
CD CDBGP 1034
Beat Goes Public / Mar '92 / Pinnacle

BEST OF LATIN JAZZ, THE
CD EMPRCD 707
Emporio / Mar '97 / Disc

BEST OF LEGGO, THE
CD 504012
Declic / Nov '95 / Jet Star

BEST OF LISTEN TO THE BAND VOL.1, THE
Mephistopheles / Carmen suite / Laura / Batman / Molly on the shore / Bolero / Overture 'Tancredi' / Over the rainbow / Rhythm and blues / Festive prelude / Pastime with good company / Music from 'Ballet Russe' / March 'Le Reve Passe' / Capriccio Espagnol / Skye boat song / Fiorentiner march / Soldiers in the park
CD DOYCD 016
Doyen / Oct '92 / Conifer/BMG

BEST OF LIVING BEAT, THE
Bass (how low can you go): Harris, Simon / Ragga house: Daddy Freddy / Grab the mike: Wildman / SuperMarioland: Ambassadors Of Funk / I'm in the mood for dancing: Nolans / Back for good: Real Emotion / Time: Leslie Lyrics / Armed and extremely dangerous: M-Brace & Angie / Who's crying now: Sims, Joyce / (I've got your)pleasure control: Harris, Simon & Lonnie Gordon / Go for the heart: Fox, Samantha / French Kiss: Big Louis / Sexy Lady: Big Dipper / Better move quick: Bassman / Don't stop the music: Harris, Simon & Dina Carroll / Boom boom boom(say what ho): Inhere sisters / Do it now: Bailey, Louise
CD ANT 004
Tring / Nov '96 / Tring

BEST OF LOADING BAY VOL.1, THE
CD LBAYCD 1
Loading Bay / Jan '93 / Loading Bay Records

BEST OF LOUISIANA MUSIC, THE
CD ROUANCD 08
Rounder / Jun '93 / ADA / CM / Direct

BEST OF LOVERS ROCK VOL.1, THE
CD RNCD 2018
Rhino / Feb '94 / Grapevine/PolyGram / Jet Star

BEST OF LOVERS ROCK VOL.2, THE
CD RNCD 2039
Rhino / Jan '94 / Grapevine/PolyGram / Jet Star

BEST OF LOVERS ROCK VOL.3, THE
CD RNCD 2062
Rhino / Jun '94 / Grapevine/PolyGram / Jet Star

BEST OF LUV 'N' HAIGHT VOL.1, THE
CD LHCD 011
Luv n' Haight / Jul '96 / Timewarp

BEST OF MEMPHIS ROOTS, THE
CD RITZRCD 537
Ritz / Dec '93 / Pinnacle

BEST OF MOUNTAIN STAGE VOL.1, THE
Such a night: Dr. John / Hell I'd go: Acoustic Warriors / Twilight: Danko, Rick / Bill of goods: Wainwright III, Loudon / O'Marie: Lanois, Daniel / Home is where the heart is: Gregson, Clive / Songbird: Winchester, Jesse / Yes, yes, yes: NRBQ / Shoot out the lights: Thompson, Richard / Bird on the wire: Groce, Larry / What you gonna do when the zydeco turn on you: Buckwheat Zydeco
CD BPM 001CD
Blue Plate / May '97 / ADA / Direct / Greyhound

BEST OF MOUNTAIN STAGE VOL.2, THE
God is a real estate developer: Shocked, Michelle / It's a big old goofy world: Prine, John / Arms of love: Hitchcock, Robyn / Red wine and promises: Tabor, June / Losing my religion: REM / Tank park salute: Bragg, Billy / Summerfly: O'Connell, Maura / You're no good: Harding, John Wesley / Where've you been: Mattea, Kathy / These blues: Gilmore, Jimmie Dale / Simply: Hickman, Sara / Standing on shaky ground: McClinton, Delbert
CD BPM 002CD
Blue Plate / May '97 / ADA / Direct / Greyhound

BEST OF MOUNTAIN STAGE VOL.3, THE
Border crossing: Timbuk 3 / Guantan America: Chilton, Alex / Superman's song: Crash Test Dummies / Never had it so good: Carpenter, Mary-Chapin / Waiting for a miracle: Cockburn, Bruce / Soy de San Louis: Texas Tornados / Misguided angel: Cowboy Junkies / Lewis: Yo La Tengo / Shelter: McLachlan, Sarah / Renegade: Zevon, Warren / Cynical girl: Crenshaw, Marshall / Romance is a slow dance: Fabulous Twister Sisters / Tear stained letter: Sonnier, Jo El
CD BPM 003CD
Blue Plate / May '97 / ADA / Direct / Greyhound

BEST OF MOUNTAIN STAGE VOL.4, THE
Big boss man: Holmes Brothers / That's enough of that stuff: Ball, Marcia / You're so fine: Hammond, John / What do you want the girl to do: Toussaint, Allen / My tears: Robillard, Duke / Crazy horse blues: Thompson, Bob / My God called me this morning: Fairfield Four / Sweet home Chicago: Edwards, Honeyboy / Move on: Nelson, Tracy / Purple haze: Bobs / It's getting warm in here: Musselwhite, Charley / Why am I treated so bad: Staples, Pops
CD BPM 004CD
Blue Plate / May '97 / ADA / Direct / Greyhound

BEST OF MOUNTAIN STAGE VOL.5, THE
Angels: *Holsapple, Peter & Chris Stamey* / Early summer rain: *Welch, Kevin* / Walkin' for your love: *Widespread Panic* / Particle man: *They Might Be Giants* / Peace: *Los Lobos* / Loves recovery: *Indigo Girls* / Responsibility: *Forbert, Steve* / Goodnite Irene: *Pere Ubu* / Any cure: *Subdudes* / Rockin' in the res: *Trudell, John*
CD ______ **BPM 005CD**
Blue Plate / May '97 / ADA / Direct / Greyhound

BEST OF MOUNTAIN STAGE VOL.6, THE
Girl from the north country: *Hornsby, Bruce* / Mister wrong: *Cracker* / World leader pretend: *REM* / Outbound plane: *Griffith, Nanci* / Black sunshine: *Me Phi Me* / Headmasters of mine: *Gaines, Jeffrey* / After you're gone: *DeMent, Iris* / Blue world: *Brady, Paul* / What a good boy: *Barenaked Ladies* / Working on a building: *Hampton, Bruce & The Aquarium Rescue Unit*
CD ______ **BPM 006CD**
Blue Plate / May '97 / ADA / Direct / Greyhound

BEST OF MOUNTAIN STAGE VOL.7, THE
Mama's got a girlfriend now: *Harper, Ben* / American music: *Violent Femmes* / Praise the lord and pass the snakes: *Hot Tuna* / You look like rain: *Morphine* / Moonshiner: *Uncle Tupelo* / Good things: *BoDeans* / Magic finger: *Fleck, Bela* / Being simple: *Judybats* / Pale sun: *Cowboy Junkies* / Mr Jones: *Counting Crows*
CD ______ **BPM 007CD**
Blue Plate / May '97 / ADA / Direct / Greyhound

BEST OF MOUNTAIN STAGE VOL.8, THE
Buildings and bridges: *Di Franco, Ani* / Dominique: *Pilgrim, Billy* / Find yourself a door: *Droge, Pete* / Happy home: *Cole, Paula* / Gypsy life: *Gorka, John* / I know better now: *Croce, A.J.* / Do not disturb: *Larkin, Patty* / Trampoline: *Lloyd, Bill* / Golden dreams: *Straw, Syd* / Howling wind: *Parker, Graham* / Mama's arms: *Kadison, Joshua* / Woman on the floor: *Band De Soleil*
CD ______ **BPM 008CD**
Blue Plate / May '97 / ADA / Direct / Greyhound

BEST OF MUSIC OF LIFE, THE
CD ______ **MOLCD 029**
Music Of Life / Apr '93 / Grapevine/ PolyGram

BEST OF NASHBORO GOSPEL, THE
Touch me Lord Jesus: *Angelic Gospel Singers* / I've fixed it with Jesus: *Boggs, Professor Harold* / Family prayer: *Bright Stars* / Milky white way: *CBS Trumpeteers* / Give me my flowers: *Consolers* / Stop gambler: *Cook, Madame Edna Gallmon* / Bible is right: *Gospel Songbirds* / Wake me, shake me: *May, Brother Joe* / Roll Jordan roll: *Famous Skylarks* / How I got over: *Swanee Quintet* / Mother's advice: *Taylor Brothers* / Step by step: *Boyer Brothers* / In my saviours care: *Sons of the south* / Jesus be my keeper: *Silvertone singers* / I'm a soldier: *Jordan River Singers* / If you miss me from praying: *Radio Four* / Sell out to the master: *Christland singers* / Since Jesus came into my heart: *Silvertone singers* / Didn't it rain children: *Sons of the south* / My life is in his hands: *Jordan River Singers* / Let the church roll on: *Barbee, Lucille* / You got to be born again: *Christland singers* / Earnest prayer: *Radio Four* / Don't drive your children away: *Fairfield Four* / I want to be just like him: *Supreme Angels* / No cross no crown: *Brooklyn Allstars* / Step by step (#2): *Swanee Quintet*
CD ______ **CDCHD 373**
Ace / Jan '93 / Pinnacle

BEST OF NEW COUNTRY LINE DANCE, THE
One step forward / There goes my heart / Wild one / Elvira / All you ever do is bring me down / Boys and me / Achy breaky heart / Bring it on down to my house / Cotton eye Joe / My baby loves me / Anyway the wind blows / Gone country
CD ______ **305932**
Hallmark / Jan '97 / Carlton

BEST OF NEW WELSH FOLK MUSIC, THE (Goreuon Canu Gwerin Newydd)
Y gog lwydlas: *James, Sian* / Hyd y frwynen/Rhuad teirw'r dyffryn: *Saith Rhyfeddod* / Os ymadael: *Bob Delyn* / Fflat huw puw: *Gwerinos* / Cefn du/Ymdeithgan gwyr dyfi/ Y derwydd: *Gwerinos* / Adar man y mynydd: *Ogam* / Jig poltague/Gyrru'r byd o'mlaen/Neidod twm bach: *Ogam* / Taflwn yr hosan: *Ogam* / Mon a Menai: *Pigyn Clust* / Hoffter menna/Ffair y borth: *Pigyn Clust* / Taith madoc: *Aberjaber* / Y march glas: *Cusan Tan* / Jigolo/Harri Morgan: *Ar-Log* / Seidir ddoe: *Plethyn* / Cariad fach tirderi: *Rodge, John* / Ysbryd y werin/Mae'r ddaer yn glasu: *Carreg Lafar* / Marwnad yr ehedydd/Ymdaith gwyr dyfnaint: *Branwen* / Suo gan/Y gelynnen/Llantony Abbey: *Calennig* / Fe drawodd yn fy meddwl: *Iwan, Dafydd*
CD ______ **SCD 2146**
Sain / Jun '97 / ADA / Direct / Greyhound

BEST OF NORTHERN SOUL, THE
Twenty four hours a day / Weak spot / Your magic put a spell on me / Breakin' down the walls of heartache / Key to my happiness / Ain't no soul left in these old shoes / Let me down easy / With this ring / Reaching for the best / Baby I'm still the same man / Our love is in the pocket / You're gonna love my baby / That's when the tears start / Doomsday / What's wrong with me baby / Goodbye cruel love / Out on the floor / There's nothing else to say / Skiing in the snow / Nothing's worse than being alone
CD ______ **QED 062**
Tring / Nov '96 / Tring

BEST OF NORTHSOUND VOL.1, THE (Harmonising Nature With Music)
CD ______ **2456**
NorthSound / Aug '96 / Gallant

BEST OF OI VOL.3, THE
CD ______ **DOJOCD 207**
Dojo / Mar '95 / Disc

BEST OF OI, THE
Suburban rebels: *Business* / Someone's gonna die: *Blitz* / George Davis is innocent: *Sham 69* / GLC: *Menace* / Police oppression: *Angelic Upstarts* / England belongs to me: *Cock Sparrer* / One law for them: *4 Skins* / King of the jungle: *Last Resort* / SPG: *Red Alert* / Summer of '81: *Violators* / Police story: *Partisans* / Smash the discos: *Business* / Runnin' riot: *Cock Sparrer* / Right to choose: *Combat 84* / Working class kids: *Last Resort* / Yesterday's heroes: *4 Skins* / Police car: *Cockney Rejects* / Razors in the night: *Blitz* / Meglomania: *Blood* / Maniac: *Peter & The Test Tube Babies* / Tuckers ruckers ain't no suckers: *Gonads* / Two pints of lager: *Splodge* / Kids of the 80's: *Infa Riot* / They don't understand: *Sham 69* / England: *Angelic Upstarts*
CD ______ **DOJOCD 94**
Dojo / Apr '93 / Disc

BEST OF OPEN, THE (2CD Set)
CD Set ______ **OPENCD 1**
Ministry Of Sound / May '96 / 3mv/Sony / Mo's Music Machine / Warner Music

BEST OF PAN PIPES, THE
Killing me softly / Lifted / Whole new world / How deep is your love / Love is all around / Everything I do (I do it for you) / Careless whisper / Drive / Mysterious girl / I will always love you / Unchained melody / Tears in heaven / I swear / Without you / First time ever I saw your face / You don't bring me flowers / Goodbye to love / Power of love / Walking in the air / Ev'ry time we say goodbye / Sacrifice / When I fall in love / Change the world / Forever love / Jesus to a child / Earth song / Think twice / El Condor Pasa / Yesterday / Back for good / Don't cry for me Argentina / Beauty & the beast / Riverdance / Orinoco flow / All by myself / Danny boy / Someday / Nothing compares 2 U / Wind beneath my wings / Memory
CD ______ **TCD 2845**
Telstar / Sep '96 / BMG

BEST OF PIANO JAZZ, THE
Sept a dire / Force tranquille / Agripaume III / Bouillie bordelaise / Adi / Valse no.2 / Sep petits jeux / Beeing sincere / Leila / E si...si...si / Voice of Zak / Trio du porto / E H F T B
CD ______ **TCB 01042**
TCB / Sep '95 / New Note/Pinnacle

BEST OF REGGAE SUNSPLASH, THE
Ital love: *Chalice* / Revival time: *Chalice* / Calling you: *Sandi & The Sunsetz* / Do you feel like dancing: *Bloodfire Posse* / Can't stop rocking tonight: *Bloodfire Posse* / It's magic: *Brown, Dennis* / Wild fire: *Brown, Dennis & John Holt* / Botha: *Cocoa T* / Medley: *Charlie Chaplin & Yellowman* / Oh what a feeling: *Isaacs, Gregory* / Let off: *Josey Wales* / Ram jam dance: *Wailer, Bunny* / Jolly session: *Wailer, Bunny* / Sabotage: *Wailer, Bunny*
CD ______ **CDCHARLY 235**
Charly / Sep '90 / Koch

BEST OF REGGAE VOL.1, THE
CD ______ **3885932**
Galaxy / Jun '97 / ZYX

BEST OF RIC RECORDS VOL.1, THE (Carnival Time)
Carnival Time: *Johnson, Al* / Cotton candy: *Capello, Lenny* / Check Mr. Popeye: *Bo, Eddie* / I don't talk too much: *Nelson, Martha* / Let's stop and talk it over: *Ridgley, Tommy* / Lena: *Johnson, Al* / Ninety pound weakling: *Capello, Lenny* / Losing battle: *Adams, Johnny* / Let's Get It: *Blanchard, Edgar* / She's got what it takes: *Ridley, Tommy* / Feeling right Sat: *Velvetiers*
CD ______ **ROUCD 2075**
Rounder / '88 / ADA / CM / Direct

BEST OF RIO CARNIVAL, THE
CD ______ **CDEB 2224**
Earthbeat / May '93 / ADA / Direct

BEST OF ROCK 'N' ROLL LOVE SONGS, THE
CD ______ **DINCD 91**
Dino / Jun '94 / Pinnacle

BEST OF ROCK 'N' ROLL VOL.2 1938-1946, THE (2CD Set)
CD Set ______ **FA 352**
Fremeaux / Feb '97 / ADA / Discovery

BEST OF ROCK ON STAGE VOL.1, THE
Come together: *MC5* / What goes on: *Velvet Underground* / Somebody to love: *Jefferson Airplane* / Shape I'm in: *Band* / Sweet Jane: *Reed, Lou* / Only women bleed: *Cooper, Alice* / It's all over now: *Faces* / Highway star: *Deep Purple* / Rosalie/Cowgirl's song: *Thin Lizzy* / I want to go to the sun: *Frampton, Peter* / All in it together: *Pirates* / All through the city: *Dr. Feelgood* / Junior's wailing: *Status Quo* / Long train runnin': *Doobie Brothers* / In trance: *Scorpions* / Messin' with the kid: *Gallagher, Rory*
CD ______ **VSOPCD 202**
Connoisseur Collection / Aug '94 / Pinnacle

BEST OF ROCK ON STAGE VOL.2, THE
Pinball wizard: *Who* / Kill the king: *Rainbow* / Stealin': *Uriah Heep* / Too old to rock 'n' roll, too young to die: *Jethro Tull* / I'm going home: *Ten Years After* / Woke up this morning and found myself dead: *Hendrix, Jimi* / Voodoo chile: *Vaughan, Stevie Ray* / Black magic woman: *Santana* / Full moon boogie: *Beck, Jeff & Jan Hammer Group* / Born to be wild: *Blue Oyster Cult* / Do the strand: *Roxy Music* / This flight tonight: *Nazareth* / Breaking the law: *Judas Priest* / Ace of spades: *Motorhead* / Parisienne walkways: *Moore, Gary*
CD ______ **VSOPCD 208**
Connoisseur Collection / Nov '94 / Pinnacle

BEST OF ROTTERDAM RECORDS, THE
CD ______ **ROF CD1**
Rotterdam / Mar '93 / SRD

BEST OF SALSA, THE
CD ______ **EUCD 1319**
ARC / Nov '95 / ADA / ARC Music

BEST OF SAN FRANCISCO LIVE, THE
White rabbit: *Jefferson Airplane* / Morning dew: *Grateful Dead* / I want to be near you: *Scaggs, Boz* / Who do you love: *Hammond, John* / Early morning rain: *Lightfoot, Gordon* / Diggy liggy lo: *Commander Cody* / White bird: *It's A Beautiful Day* / So fine: *Bishop, Elvin* / Brand new Tennessee waltz: *Winchester, Jesse* / Stagger Lee: *Taj Mahal* / Turn on your lovelight: *Grateful Dead & Janis Joplin* / Plastic fantastic lover: *Jefferson Airplane* / Time has come today: *Chambers Brothers* / Hellbound train: *Town Cryers & Marty Balin*
CD ______ **3036000702**
Carlton / Feb '97 / Carlton

BEST OF SAXON WORLD WIDE VOL.1, THE
CD ______ **SAXCD 002**
Saxon Studio / Mar '95 / Jet Star

BEST OF SAXON WORLD WIDE VOL.2, THE
CD ______ **SAXCD 0032**
Saxon Studio / Oct '95 / Jet Star

BEST OF SAXON WORLD WIDE VOL.4, THE
CD ______ **SAXCD 007**
Saxon Studio / Jun '97 / Jet Star

BEST OF SCOTLAND, THE (3CD Set)
Donald, where's yer troosers: *Stewart, Andy* / Road to the Isles: *Stewart, Andy* / Scottish soldier: *Stewart, Andy* / Campbell Town Loch: *Stewart, Andy* / Drunken piper/ Highland laddie/ Black bear: *Blackwatch 1st Battalion Pipes/Drums* / Auld Scotch sangs: *Anderson, Moira* / Rowan tree: *Anderson, Moira* / My ain house: *Anderson, Moira* / My ain folk: *Anderson, Moira* / Wild rover: *Tartan Lads* / Sky is bluer in Scotland: *Tartan Lads* / West's awake hornpipe/ Robertson hornpipe: *Johnstone, Jim & His Band* / Teviot brig jig/ Original tune/ Drummond castle/ Jennie's bl: *Johnstone, Jim & His Band* / Castles in the air: *Johnstone, Jim & His Band* / Bonnie lass o'Bon Accord: *Johnstone, Jim & His Band* / I love a lassie: *Logan, Jimmy* / Roamin' in the gloamin': *Logan, Jimmy* / My home/ Sky boat song: *Royal Scots Dragoon Guards* / Flower of Scotland: *Royal Scots Dragoon Guards* / Mull of Kintyre: *Royal Scots Dragoon Guards* / Amazing Grace: *Royal Scots Dragoon Guards* / Hiking group: *Gay Gordons* / Bonnie Dundee: *Corries* / Isle of Skye: *Corries* / Black Douglas: *Corries* / Scottish waltz selection: *Wick Scottish Dance Band* / Cock o' the North: *Scots Guards* / Garb of old cat: *Scots Guards* / Wee MacGregor: *Scots Guards* / Gathering of the clans: *Scots Guards* / Northern lights of old Aberdeen: *Shand, Jimmy* / Linton Ploughman's jig/ Muckin O'Geordies Byre: *Shand, Jimmy* / Lady Nellie Wemyss/ Braidley's house/ Major Mackie: *Shand, Jimmy* / Circle waltz/ Queen Mary Queen Mary/ If you will marry me: *Glen Lomond Scottish Dance Band* / Kate Bardier/ My wee Lauds a sojer: *Glen Lomond Scottish Dance Band* / Middleton medley/ Craighall/ Lady Carmichael: *Glen Lomond Scottish Dance Band* / Auld inn/ Fill your glasses/ Lively Tim: *Glen Lomond Scottish Dance Band* / I belong to Glasgow: *Fyffe, Will* / Para handy: *Houliston, Max & his Scottish Band* / Holy rood: *Gordon Highlanders* / National emblem: *Gordon Highlanders* / Steadfast and true: *Gordon Highlanders* / Ye banks and braes o' bonnie Doon: *MacEwan, Father Sydney* / Toronto Scottish Regiment/ Durrator Bridge/ Duntroon: *Black Watch Band* / Caledonian two step: *MacLeod, Jim* / Scotland the brave: *Wilson, Robert* / Down in the glen: *Wilson, Robert* / March selection/ O'Donnel ABU/ Dawning of the day: *Holmes, Ian* / Who fears to speak of the '98: *Holmes, Ian* / With a hundred pipers/ Finglas weeping: *2nd Battalion Scots Guards*
CD Set ______ **CDTRBOX 120**
Trio / Oct '94 / EMI

BEST OF SCOTLAND, THE (20 Tracks Of Traditional Scotish Music)
Bluebells of Scotland: *Corries* / Donald where's your troosers: *Stewart, Andy* / Scotland the brave: *Wilson, Robert* / Mairi's wedding: *Anderson, Moira* / Bluebell polka: *Shand, Jimmy* / Black Douglas: *Corries* / Rowan tree: *McKellar, Kenneth* / Road to the Isles: *Stewart, Andy* / Flower of Scotland: *Royal Scots Dragoon Guards* / Roamin' in the gloamin': *Logan, Jimmy* / Sound the pibroch: *Corries* / Westering home: *Wilson, Robert* / Mull of Kintyre: *Royal Scots Dragoon Guards* / I love a lassie: *Logan, Jimmy* / Gay Gordons medley: *Shand, Jimmy* / Dancing in Kyle: *Anderson, Moira* / Campbeltown loch: *Stewart, Andy* / I belong to Glasgow: *Fyffe, Will* / Amazing grace: *Royal Scots Dragoon Guards* / Haste ye back: *Wilson, Robert*
CD ______ **CDMFP 6230**
Music For Pleasure / Jun '96 / EMI

BEST OF SCOTTISH DANCE BANDS, THE
CD ______ **CC 264**
Music For Pleasure / May '91 / EMI

BEST OF SCOTTISH FOLK, THE
CD ______ **PLSCD 148**
Pulse / Feb '97 / BMG

BEST OF SCOTTISH PIPES AND DRUMS, THE
CD ______ **EUCD 1306**
ARC / Jul '95 / ADA / ARC Music

BEST OF SIOUX VOL.1, THE
Wave of war: *Higgs, Joe* / Pharoah's walk: *Exodus & Jam Rock* / Funny man: *King Reggie* / In the ghetto: *Dillon, Phyllis* / With these hands: *Wayne, Mark* / African people (Indian Reservation): *Brown, Funky* / Super bad: *JD* / I don't know: *Smith, Junior* / Train (Engine 54): *Lloyd The Matador* / Lay a foundation: *Higgs, Joe* / You just gotta get ready: *Jackson, Pooch* / Cool girl: *King Reggie* / Mammy blue: *Circles* / Julia sees me: *Exodus* / I'm in a dancing mood: *Smith, Junior* / World is spinning around: *Higgs, Joe* / Happy song: *Twinkle Brothers* / Young, gifted and black: *King Reggie* / Vietnam: *Smith, Sammi* / Heavy reggae: *Roosevelt Singers*
CD ______ **PRCD 602**
President / Jun '95 / Grapevine/PolyGram / President / Target/BMG

BEST OF SKA LIVE, THE
Train to skaville: *Selecter* / Gangsters: *Specials* / Tears of a clown: *Special Beat* / On my radio: *Selecter* / Nite club: *Specials* / Mirror in the bathroom: *Special Beat* / Missing words: *Selecter* / Monkey man: *Specials* / Ranking full stop: *Special Beat* / Too much pressure: *Selecter* / Longshot kick the bucket: *Specials* / Rat race: *Special Beat* / James Bond: *Selecter* / Skinhead moonstomp: *Specials* / Enjoy yourself: *Special Beat*
CD ______ **EMPRCD 579**
Emporio / Jul '95 / Disc

BEST OF SOLAR, THE
I can make you feel good: *Shalamar* / And the beat goes on: *Whispers* / Midas touch: *Midnight Star* / I don't want to be a freak (but I can't help myself): *Dynasty* / Fantastic voyage: *Lakeside* / Dance with you: *Lucas, Carrie* / Romeo where's Juliet: *Collage* / Take that to the bank: *Shalamar* / Come back lover: *Sylvers* / Body talk: *Deele* / It's a love thing: *Whispers* / Headlines: *Midnight Star* / I wanna be rich: *Calloway* / I gotta keep dancin': *Lucas, Carrie* / Make that move: *Shalamar* / Rock steady: *Whispers*
CD ______ **RENCD 106**
Renaissance Collector Series / Sep '95 / BMG

BEST OF SPLATCH, THE
CD ______ **STOAT 006**
Mother Stoat / May '97 / Shellshock/Disc

BEST OF SUGAR HILL GOSPEL VOL.1, THE (Everytime I Feel The Spirit)
CD ______ **SHCD 9102**
Sugar Hill / Jan '97 / ADA / CM / Direct / Koch / Roots

BEST OF SUGAR HILL GOSPEL VOL.2, THE (Way Down Deep In My Soul)
CD ______ **SHCD 9103**
Sugar Hill / Jan '97 / ADA / CM / Direct / Koch / Roots

BEST OF SUMMER JAM, THE
Introduction: *Sinbad* / Cisco kid: *War* / Pick up the pieces: *Average White Band* / For the love of money: *O'Jays* / Fire: *Ohio Players* / Lovegirl: *Marie, Teena* / Joy and pain: *Maze* / Midnight train to Georgia: *Knight, Gladys* / That's the way of the world: *Earth, Wind & Fire* / Celebration: *Kool & The Gang* / Shake and dance with me: *Con Funk Shun* / What is hip: *Tower Of Power* / Outstanding: *Gap Band* / Oops upside your head: *Gap Band* / I'm every woman: *Khan, Chaka*

/ Fantastic voyage: *Lakeside* / Love and happiness: *Green, Al*
CD ___ RENCD 123
Renaissance Collector Series / Jun '97 / BMG

BEST OF SUN ROCKABILLY VOL.1, THE
Ten cats down: *Cantrell & Claunch* / Jump right out of this jukebox: *Wheeler, Onie* / Gonna romp and stomp: *Rhodes, Slim* / Domino: *Phillips, Sam* / Rakin' and scrapin': *Beard, Dean* / Slow down: *Earls, Jack* / Red cadillac and a black moustache: *Thompson & May* / Break up: *Rich, Charlie* / Greenback dollar / Red headed woman: *Burgess, Sonny* / Flyin' saucer rock 'n' roll: *Scott, Ray* / Crawdad hole: *Lewis, Jerry Lee* / Love my baby: *Parker, Herman* / Red hot: *Emerson, Billy 'The Kid'* / We wanna boogie: *Burgess, Sonny* / Come on little mama: *Harris & Cogswell* / Right behind you baby: *Rich, Charlie* / Ubangi stomp: *Underwood, Charles* / Let's bop: *Earls, Jack* / Rabbit action: *Thompson, Junior* / Put your cat clothes on: *Perkins, Carl* / Rockin' with my baby: *Yelvington, Malcolm*
CD ___ CPCD 8202
Charly / Feb '97 / Koch

BEST OF SUN ROCKABILLY VOL.2, THE
Got love if you want it: *Smith, Warren* / That don't move me: *Perkins, Carl* / Itchy: *Burgess, Sonny* / Drinkin' wine: *Simmons, Gene* / How come you do me: *Thompson, Junior* / Gimme some lovin': *Jenkins, Harold* / Johnny Valentine: *Anderson, Andy* / Baby, please don't go: *Riley, Billy Lee* / Sentimental fool: *Pittman, Barbara* / Rebound: *Rich, Charlie* / Miss Froggie: *Smith, Warren* / Rock around the town: *Beard, Dean* / Wild one: *Lewis, Jerry Lee* / My baby don't rock: *McDaniel, Luke* / Find my baby for me: *Burgess, Sonny* / My gal Mary Ann: *Earls, Jack* / Me and my rhythm guitar: *Powers, Johnny* / All night rock: *Honeycutt, Glenn* / Your loving man: *Taylor, Vernon* / Madman 1: *Wages, Jimmy* / Fairlane rock: *Thompson, Hayden* / I need your loving kiss: *Jenkins, Harold* / Perkin's wiggle: *Perkins, Carl* / Ain't got a thing: *Burgess, Sonny*
CD ___ CPCD 8209
Charly / Feb '97 / Koch

BEST OF SWING '95, THE (2CD Set)
CD Set ___ TCD 2789
Telstar / Oct '95 / BMG

BEST OF SYNTHESIZER HITS, THE
CD ___ EMPRCD 506
Emporio / Apr '94 / Disc

BEST OF TANGO, THE (2CD Set)
CD ___ 3020312
Arcade / Jun '97 / Discovery

BEST OF THE '60S BRITISH BEAT VOL.2, THE
Build me up buttercup: *Foundations* / Little children: *Kramer, Billy J.* / Baby make it soon: *Marmalade* / Twist and shout: *Poole, Brian* / You were on my mind: *St. Peters, Crispian* / I understand: *Freddie & The Dreamers* / Um um um um um um: *Fontana, Wayne* / Pied piper: *St. Peters, Crispian* / Baby now that I've found you: *Foundations* / He's in town: *Rockin' Berries* / If you gotta make a fool of somebody: *Freddie & The Dreamers* / Do you love me: *Poole, Brian* / Reflections of my life: *Marmalade* / Poor man's son: *Rockin' Berries* / I'll keep you satisfied: *Kramer, Billy J.* / Game of love: *Fontana, Wayne*
CD ___ 305472
Hallmark / Oct '96 / Carlton

BEST OF THE 1960'S GOLDEN OLDIES VOL.1, THE
Monday Monday: *Mamas & The Papas* / Eve of destruction: *McGuire, Barry* / Honey: *Goldsboro, Bobby* / Tracy: *Cuff Links* / Hush, not a word to Mary: *Rowles, John* / Magic carpet ride: *Steppenwolf* / Bend me, shape me: *American Breed* / Summertime: *Stewart, Billy* / Mama told me not to come: *Three Dog Night* / Dizzy: *Roe, Tommy* / Livin' next door to Alice: *Smokie* / I'm a believer: *Monkees* / White rabbit: *Jefferson Airplane* / Letter: *Box Tops* / Deep water: *Grapefruit* / Lion sleeps tonight: *Tokens*
CD ___ MCD 30204
Ariola Express / Mar '94 / BMG

BEST OF THE BANDS, THE
Take the 'A' train: *Ellington, Duke* / Perdido: *Ellington, Duke* / Amercan patrol: *Miller, Glenn* / In the mood: *Ellington, Duke* / Little brown jug: *Miller, Glenn* / String of pearls: *Miller, Glenn* / Caldonia: *Herman, Woody* / Woodchopper's ball: *Herman, Woody* / King Porter stomp: *Goodman, Benny* / On the sunny side of the street: *Dorsey, Tommy* / Begin the beguine: *Shaw, Artie* / Stardust: *Shaw, Artie* / Texas chatter: *James, Harry* / One o'clock jump: *Basie, Count* / Jeepers creepers: *Basie, Count* / Mack the knife: *Armstrong, Louis* / High society: *Armstrong, Louis* / Stompin' at the Savoy: *Armstrong, Louis* / Royal garden blues: *Dorsey, Tommy* / After you've gone: *Hampton, Lionel*
CD ___ CD 6007
Music / Apr '96 / Target/BMG

BEST OF THE BARBER SHOP QUARTET, THE
Michelle / You'll never know (just how much I love you) / Sixteen tons / Carolina I'm coming back to you / Dear little boy of mine / You can't be a beacon (if your light don't shine) / Turn on your light / How are things in Glocca Morra / You're in style when you're wearing a smile / Sweetheart of Sigma Chi / If you can't get a girl in the summertime / Chase the rain away / Looking at the world thru' rose coloured glasses / When you wish upon a star / One rose that's left in my heart / You're some pretty doll / Tennessee waltz / I miss mother most of all / Darkness on the delta / In the good old summertime / If you were the only girl in the world / Alabama jubilee / Albamy bound
CD ___ QED 120
Tring / Nov '96 / Tring

BEST OF THE BEST VOL.2, THE
CD ___ RASCD 3133
Ras / Feb '94 / Direct / Greensleeves / Jet Star / SRD

BEST OF THE BEST VOL.3, THE
CD ___ RASCD 3149
Ras / Jun '95 / Direct / Greensleeves / Jet Star / SRD

BEST OF THE BEST VOL.4, THE
CD ___ RASCD 3153
Ras / Jun '95 / Direct / Greensleeves / Jet Star / SRD

BEST OF THE BIG BANDS, THE
CD ___ DCD 5337
Disky / Dec '93 / Disky / THE

BEST OF THE BIG BANDS, THE (36 Legendary Classics - 2CD Set)
Jumpin' at the woodside: *Basie, Count* / Do nothin' 'til you hear from me: *Herman, Woody* / Cherokee: *Barnet, Charlie* / It's the talk of the town: *Henderson, Fletcher* / Hamp's boogie woogie no.1: *Hampton, Lionel* / Tuxedo junction: *Hawkins, Erskine* / Christopher Columbus: *Kirk, Andy & His Twelve Clouds of Joy* / Jumpin' blues: *McShann, Jay* / King porter stomp: *Goodman, Benny* / One o'clock jump: *James, Harry* / Blue Lou: *Carter, Benny* / All the things you are: *Dorsey, Tommy* / Drumboogie: *Krupa, Gene* / Chattanooga choo choo: *Miller, Glenn* / There's a small hotel: *Thornhill, Claude* / Artistry in rhythm: *Kenton, Stan* / If dreams come true: *Webb, Chick* / Take the 'A' train: *Ellington, Duke* / Stompin' at the savoy: *Goodman, Benny* / Until the real thing comes along: *Kirk, Andy* / Nightmare: *Shaw, Artie* / One o'clock jump: *Basie, Count* / Snowfall: *Thornhill, Claude* / Let me off uptown: *Krupa, Gene* / I can't get started: *Berigan, Bunny* / For dancers only: *Lunceford, Jimmie* / At the woodchoppers ball: *Herman, Woody* / In the mood: *Miller, Glenn* / I'm getting sentimental over you: *Dorsey, Tommy* / Flying home: *Hampton, Lionel* / Undecided: *Webb, Chick* / Begin the beguine: *Shaw, Artie* / Rockin' in rhythm: *Ellington, Duke* / Fidgety feel: *Henderson, Fletcher* / Skyliner: *Barnet, Charlie* / Organ grinders swing: *Lunceford, Jimmie*
CD Set ___ 330052
Hallmark / Jul '96 / Carlton

BEST OF THE BIG DANCE BANDS, THE
CD ___ CDC 9010
LRC / Oct '90 / Harmonia Mundi / New Note/Pinnacle

BEST OF THE BLUES SINGERS VOL.2
CD ___ CDC 9007
LRC / Oct '90 / Harmonia Mundi / New Note/Pinnacle

BEST OF THE CEILI BANDS, THE
CD ___ EMPRCD 706
Emporio / Mar '97 / Disc

BEST OF THE DJ'S BOUT YA, THE
CD ___ SONCD 0048
Sonic Sounds / Jul '93 / Jet Star

BEST OF THE EIGHTIES VOL.1, THE
West End girls: *Pet Shop Boys* / Mickey: *Basil, Toni* / Special brew: *Bad Manners* / Feels like I'm in love: *Marie, Kelly* / Swing the mood: *Jive Bunny* / High energy: *Thomas, Evelyn* / Transfer affection: *Flock Of Seagulls* / Bass (how low can you go): *Harris, Simon* / Touch me (I want your body): *Fox, Samantha* / Can't shake the feeling: *Big Fun* / You think you're a man: *Divine* / Fantasy Island: *Tight Fit* / Hands of she's mine: *Rankin' Roger* / Jack mix IV: *Mirage* / On a crowded street: *Pennington, Barbara*
CD ___ QED 181
Tring / Nov '96 / Tring

BEST OF THE EIGHTIES VOL.2, THE
Kiss: *Jones, Tom & Art Of Noise* / Blame it on the boogie: *Big Fun* / That's what I like: *Jive Bunny* / Wishing (If I had a photograph of you): *Flock Of Seagulls* / Can can: *Bad Manners* / Lion sleeps tonight: *Tight Fit* / If you're ready (come go with me): *Turner, Ruby & Jonathan Butler* / Nothing's gonna stop me now: *Fox, Samantha* / Jack mix II: *Mirage* / Close to perfection: *Brown, Miquel* / Mirror in the bathroom: *Rankin' Roger* / Fan the flame: *Pennington, Barbara* / I eat cannibals: *Toto Coelo* / Wee rule: *Wee Papa Girl Rappers* / Walk like a man: *Divine* / Saddle up: *Christie, David* / Here comes that sound: *Harris, Simon*
CD ___ QED 182
Tring / Nov '96 / Tring

BEST OF THE EIGHTIES, THE (4CD Set)
West end girls: *Pet Shop Boys* / High energy: *Thomas, Evelyn* / More you live the more you love: *Flock Of Seagulls* / Hey there lonely girl: *Big Fun* / You think you're a man: *Divine* / Mucho macho: *Toto Coelo* / That's what I like: *Jive Bunny* / Secret heart: *Tight Fit* / Special brew: *Bad Manners* / Don't try to stop it: *Roman Holliday* / Feels like I'm in love: *Marie, Kelly* / All of me: *Sabrina* / Heaven must be missing an angel: *Tavares* / Jack mix 4: *Mirage* / Lies: *Butler, Jonathan* / Fan the flame: *Pennington, Barbara* / Here comes that sound: *Harris, Simon* / Soulmate: *Wee Papa Girl Rappers* / Swing the mood: *Jive Bunny* / Missing words: *Black, Pauline* / We are family: *Sister Sledge* / Jack mix 2: *Mirage* / I eat cannibals: *Toto Coelo* / Kiss: *Jones, Tom & Art Of Noise* / Wishing (if I had a photograph of you): *Flock Of Seagulls* / Like a yo yo: *Sabrina* / If you're ready (come go with me): *Turner, Ruby & Jonathan Butler* / Hands off she's mine: *Rankin' Roger* / Heat it up: *Wee Papa Girl Rappers* / Don't stop till you get enough: *Faye, Ash* / Lip up fatty: *Bad Manners* / Nothing's gonna stop me now: *Fox, Samantha* / Saddle up 1990: *Christie, David* / I am what I am: *Gaynor, Gloria* / Nightmares: *Flock Of Seagulls* / Nobody: *Basil, Toni* / Car wash: *Royce, Rose* / Lion sleeps tonight: *Tight Fit* / Boys: *Sabrina* / Blame it on the boogie: *Big Fun* / Walk like a man: *Divine* / Cover plus (we're all grown up): *O'Connor, Hazel* / Bass (how low can you go): *Harris, Simon* / French kiss: *Big Louie* / Sunshine: *Mills, Warren* / Can't shake the feeling: *Big Fun* / I love to love: *Charles, Tina* / He's a saint he's a sinner: *Brown, Miquel* / Frankie: *Sister Sledge* / Dracula's tango: *Toto Coelo* / Faith: *Wee Papa Girl Rappers* / Handful of promises: *Big Fun* / I'd rather be blind: *Turner, Ruby* / Magic's wand: *Whodini* / Is it love you're after: *Royce, Rose* / Back to the sixties: *Tight Fit* / Mickey: *Basil, Toni* / Space age love song: *Flock Of Seagulls* / I'm in love: *Turner, Ruby* / Fantasy island: *Tight Fit* / Move closer: *Jones, Tom* / Mirror in the bathroom: *Rankin' Roger* / Wee rule: *Wee Papa Girl Rappers* / Touch me (I want your body): *Fox, Samantha* / Twistin' the night away: *Divine* / Italo house mix: *Rococo* / Three minute hero: *Black, Pauline* / Who's that girl (she's got it): *Flock Of Seagulls* / On a crowded street: *Pennington, Barbara* / Blow the house down: *Wee Papa Girl Rappers* / Magic touch: *Royce, Rose* / I surrender to the spirit of the night: *Fox, Samantha* / Close to perfection: *Brown, Miquel* / Can can: *Bad Manners*
CD Set ___ QUAD 008
Tring / Nov '96 / Tring

BEST OF THE GUARDS, THE
Fanfare for a genial occasion: *Life Guards Band* / Knightsbridge march: *Blues & Royals Band* / Pomp and circumstance no.4: *Coldstream Guards Band* / Borough and bayonet: *Life Guards Band* / Pipe medley: *Irish Guards Band* / Royal star and garter march: *Welsh Guards Band* / Verdi airs: *Coldstream Guards Band* / Strike up the band: *Life Guards Band* / Duke of Cambridge: *Coldstream Guards Band* / Amazing grace: *Blues & Royals Band* / Old comrades: *Blues & Royals Band* / Tribute to pageantry: *Welsh Guards Band* / Pipe medley: *Irish Guards Band* / Czardas: *Coldstream Guards* / Royal salute: *Welsh Guards Band* / Radetsky: *Blues & Royals Band* / Crown imperial: *Life Guards Band*
CD ___ 306992
Hallmark / Jul '97 / Carlton

BEST OF THE MILITARY BANDS, THE (3CD Set)
Life on the ocean wave / Sailing / Anchors aweigh / Heart of oak / Hands across the sea / Stars & stripes forever / King Cotton / Semper fidelis / Washington Post / Hail to the spirit of Liberty / Thunderer / Warship / Battle of Trafalgar / Army & Marine / Fantasia on British sea songs / Light of foot / God bless the Prince of Wales / Hollyrood / Army of the Nile / Standard of St. George / Les Huguenots / Grenadiers / Scipio / Figaro / Garb of old Gaul / Let Erin remember / Men of Harlech / National emblem / Gathering of the clans / Birdcage walk / Lillibu-relo / Golden spurs / Royal Air Force March / 633 Squadron / Dam busters / Aces high / Battle of Britain / Crown Imperial / Those magnificent men in their flying machines / Evening hymn / Last post / Sunset / Old comrades / Duke of York / Blaze away / Colonel Bogey / Radetzky march / Imperial echoes / Liberty bell / Celebrated Marche Lorraine / Drum salute / Mingulay boat song / Battle of Kiltie Krankie / Money musk / Highland laddie / Campbells are coming / Battle of the Somme / Dogshai hills / Entry into the crater / Bonnie Anne / Athol Cummera / Sheepwife / Macleod of Mull / Lament / Fingal's weeping / Flower of Scotland / Mull of Kintyre / My home / Skye boat song / Scotland the Brave / Black bear / Amazing grace / Flowers of the forest
CD Set ___ CDTRBOX 216
Trio / Jul '96 / EMI

BEST OF THE REST VOL.6
CD ___ RASCD 3187
Ras / Feb '96 / Direct / Greensleeves / Jet Star / SRD

BEST OF THUNDERDOME, THE (3CD Set)
CD Set ___ 9902278
Arcade / Nov '96 / Cargo

BEST OF TODAY'S BLACK AFRICAN FOLK MUSIC, THE
CD ___ EUCD 1205
ARC / Sep '93 / ADA / ARC Music

BEST OF TOMMY QUICKLY, JOHNNY SANDON, GREGORY PHILLIPS...
Tip of my tongue: *Quickly, Tommy & The Remo Four* / Heaven only knows: *Quickly, Tommy & The Remo Four* / Lies: *Sandon, Johnny & The Remo Four* / On the horizon: *Sandon, Johnny & The Remo Four* / Yes: *Sandon, Johnny & The Remo Four* / Magic potion: *Sandon, Johnny & The Remo Four* / Kiss me now: *Quickly, Tommy & The Remo Four* / No other love: *Quickly, Tommy & The Remo Four* / Prove it: *Quickly, Tommy & The Remo Four* / Haven't you noticed: *Quickly, Tommy & The Remo Four* / I wish I could shimmy like my sister Kate: *Remo Four* / Peter Gunn: *Remo Four* / You might as well forget him: *Quickly, Tommy & The Remo Four* / It's simple as that: *Quickly, Tommy & The Remo Four* / Sally go round the roses: *Remo Four* / I know a girl: *Remo Four* / Wild side of life: *Quickly, Tommy & The Remo Four* / Forget the other guy: *Quickly, Tommy & The Remo Four* / Humpty dumpty: *Quickly, Tommy & The Remo Four* / I go crazy: *Quickly, Tommy & The Remo Four* / Everybody knows: *Phillips, Gregory & The Remo Four* / Closer to me: *Phillips, Gregory & The Remo Four* / Angie: *Phillips, Gregory* / Please believe me: *Phillips, Gregory* / Don't bother me: *Phillips, Gregory* / Make sure that you're mine: *Phillips, Gregory* / Sixteen tons: *Sandon, Johnny* / Donna means heartbreak: *Sandon, Johnny* / Some kinda wonderful: *Sandon, Johnny* / Legend in my time: *Sandon, Johnny*
CD ___ SEECD 349
See For Miles/C5 / Apr '92 / Pinnacle

BEST OF UNDERGROUND DANCE, THE
Don't stop the music: *Carroll, Dina & Simon Harris* / Theme from disturbing the peace: *Harris, Simon* / These are the breaks: *DJ Hanway* / Ragga house (all night long): *Harris, Simon & Daddy Freddy* / Freddy's back: *Daddy Freddie & Duke* / This is serious: *Harris, Simon* / I'm riffin': *MC Duke* / Back 2 tha bass: *Harris, Simon* / Summertime: *Asher D & Daddy Freddy* / Boingsville: *Thrashpack* / Shok da house: *Harris, Simon* / In the house: *Asher D* / Runaway love: *Harris, Simon & Einstein* / Vibes: *Demon Boyz* / Right here right now: *Harris, Simon* / Gotstago: *Einstein*
CD ___ QED 054
Tring / Nov '96 / Tring

BEST OF WALES, THE (3CD Set)
God bless the Prince of Wales: *Morriston Orpheus Choir* / How great thou art: *Morriston Orpheus Choir* / Hiraeth (longing): *Morriston Orpheus Choir* / Love, could I only tell thee: *Morriston Orpheus Choir* / Tros y garreg: *Morriston Orpheus Choir* / Swansea Town: *Morriston Orpheus Choir* / Land of song: *Morriston Orpheus Choir* / For King and country: *Morriston Orpheus Choir* / Steal away: *Morriston Orpheus Choir* / Old rugged cross: *Morriston Orpheus Choir* / Amazing grace: *Morriston Orpheus Choir* / David of the White Rock (Dafydd y Garreg Wen): *Morriston Orpheus Choir* / Comrades in arms: *Morriston Orpheus Choir* / Silver birch: *Morriston Orpheus Choir* / Lord's prayers: *Morriston Orpheus Choir* / Unwaith etton nghymru anwyl: *Morriston Orpheus Choir* / Cartef: *Morriston Orpheus Choir* / Morte Christe (when I survey the wondrous cross): *Treorchy Male Choir* / Easter hymn: *Treorchy Male Choir* / All through the night (Ar hyd y nos): *Treorchy Male Choir* / Llef (Deus salutis): *Treorchy Male Choir* / Tydi a roddaist (Thou gavest): *Treorchy Male Choir* / We'll keep a welcome: *Treorchy Male Choir* / Valley called the Rhondda: *Treorchy Male Choir* / Jimmy Brown song (Les trois cloches): *Treorchy Male Choir* / Diolch I'r Ior: *Treorchy Male Choir* / Speed your journey: *Treorchy Male Choir* / Counting the goats: *Treorchy Male Choir* / Gwahoddiad: *Treorchy Male Choir* / Sospan fach: *Treorchy Male Choir* / Eli Jenkins' prayer: *Dunvant Male Choir* / Llanfair: *Dunvant Male Choir* / With a voice of singing: *Dunvant Male Choir* / Dashenka (Y Sipsiwn): *Dunvant Male Choir* / Calon lan: *Treorchy Male Choir & The Cory Band* / Roman war song: *Treorchy Male Choir & The Cory Band* / Laudamus (Bryn Calfaria): *Monmouthshire Massed Choir* / Lily of the valley: *Monmouthshire Massed Choir* / Kalinka: *Orpheus Male Choir, Rhos* / Bugeilio'r Gwenith Gwyn: *Orpheus Male Choir, Rhos* / En route: *Morriston Orpheus Choir & The Band of the Welsh Guards* / March of the men of Harlech: *Morriston Orpheus Choir & The Band of the Welsh Guards* / Pilgrims' chorus: *Morriston Orpheus Choir & Gus Footwear Band* / Cavalry of the Steppes: *Morriston Orpheus Choir & Gus Footwear Band* / Goin' home: *Dowlais Male Choir* / Medley: *Second Festival Of One Thousand Welsh Male Voices*
CD Set ___ CDTRBOX 276
Trio / May '97 / EMI

BEST OF WALES, THE (20 Tracks Of Traditional Welsh Music)
We'll keep a welcome: *Morriston Orpheus & Treorchy Male Choirs* / Men of Harlech: *Morriston Orpheus & Treorchy Male Choirs/ Welsh Guards* / Myfanwy: *Cwm Rhondda Morriston Orpheus Choir* / How great thou art: *Cwm Rhondda Morriston Orpheus Choir* / Bugeilio'r Gwenith Gwyn: *Cwm Rhondda Morriston Orpheus Choir* / Gwahoddiad: *Cwm Rhondda Morriston Orpheus Choir* / Llanfair: *Cwm Rhondda Morriston Orpheus Choir* / Sospan fach: *Treorchy Male Choir & The Band Of The Welsh Guards* / Battle hymn of the republic: *Treorchy Male Choir* / Morte Christe: *Treorchy Male Choir* / Eli Jenkins Prayer: *Treorchy Male Choir* / Ar hyd y nos: *Treorchy Male Choir* / Medley: *Welsh/Scots/Irish/Coldstream/Grenadier Guards* / Lily of the valley: *Monmouthshire Massed Choir* / Jacob's ladder: *Monmouthshire Massed Choir* / Speed your journey: *Thousand Welsh Male Voices* / Chorus of the Hebrew slaves: *Thousand Welsh Male Voices* / Kumbaya: *Thousand Welsh Male Voices* / Sanctus: *Thousand Welsh Male Voices* / Hen wlad fy nhadau: *Morriston Orpheus Choir & The Band of the Welsh Guards*
CD ____ CDMFP 6232
Music For Pleasure / Jun '96 / EMI

BEST OF WOODSTOCK, THE
CD ____ 7567826182
Warner Bros. / Jun '94 / Warner Music

BEST OF ZOTH OMMOG
CD ____ CLEO 94712
Cleopatra / Jul '94 / Cargo / Greyhound / Plastic Head / RTM/Disc / SRD

BEST PARTY ALBUM IN THE WORLD...EVER, THE (2CD Set)
Wake me up before you go go: *Wham* / Good times: *Chic* / Staying alive: *N-Trance* / YMCA: *Village People* / Stars on 45 Abba medley: *Star Sounds Orchestra* / Saturday night: *Whigfield* / What is love: *Haddaway* / Rhythm of the night: *Corona* / It's my life: *Dr. Alban* / Relight my fire: *Take That* / Hey now (girls just wanna have fun): *Lauper, Cyndi* / All that she wants: *Ace Of Base* / Here comes the hotstepper: *Kamoze, Ini* / Boombastic: *Shaggy* / One step beyond: *Madness* / Baby come back: *Pato Banton* / Twist and shout: *Chaka Demus* / Give it up: *Goodmen* / Moving on up: *M-People* / Ride on time: *Black Box* / Come on Eileen: *Dexy's Midnight Runners* / Young at heart: *Bluebells* / Love shack: *B-52's* / It's in his kiss (The shoop shoop song): *Cher* / Crocodile rock: *John, Elton* / La bamba: *Los Lobos* / Reet petite: *Wilson, Jackie* / Baby love: *Supremes* / I will survive: *Gaynor, Gloria* / I'm in the mood for dancing: *Nolan Sisters* / Locomotion: *Minogue, Kylie* / Only way is up: *Yazz & The Plastic Population* / Stars on 45 disco medley: *Starsound* / Groove is in the heart: *Deee-Lite* / December '63 (oh what a night): *Four Seasons* / Let's dance: *Montez, Chris* / Shout: *Lulu & The Luvvers* / DISCO: *Ottawan* / I'm too sexy: *Right Said Fred* / Can can: *Bad Manners* / Time warp: *Damian* / Cotton eye Joe: *Rednex* / Always look on the bright side of life: *Monty Python*
CD Set ____ VTDCD 71
Virgin / Nov '95 / EMI

BEST PUNK ALBUM IN THE WORLD...EVER VOL.1, THE
Anarchy in the UK: *Sex Pistols* / Ever fallen in love: *Buzzcocks* / Teenage kicks: *Undertones* / Into the valley: *Skids* / New rose: *Damned* / Babylon's burning: *Ruts* / Sheena is a punk rocker: *Ramones* / Sound of the suburbs: *Members* / All around the world: *Jam* / Another girl another planet: *Only Ones* / Passenger: *Iggy Pop* / Making plans for Nigel: *XTC* / Peaches: *Stranglers* / Sex and drugs and rock 'n' roll: *Dury, Ian & The Blockheads* / (I don't want to go to) Chelsea: *Chelsea* / Denis: *Blondie* / 2-4-6-8 motorway: *Robinson, Tom Band* / Milk and alcohol: *Dr. Feelgood* / Looking after no.1: *Boomtown Rats* / Deutscher girls: *Adam & The Ants* / Christine: *Siouxsie & The Banshees* / Identity: *X-Ray Spex* / C30 C60 C90 Go: *Bow Wow Wow* / Public Image: *Public Image Ltd* / My way: *Vicious, Sid* / God save the queen: *Sex Pistols* / Neat neat neat: *Damned* / Gary Gilmore's eyes: *Adverts* / Top of the pops: *Rezillos* / Dancing the night away: *Motors* / What do I get: *Buzzcocks* / Jilted John: *Jilted John* / I am the fly: *Wire* / Mongoloid: *Devo* / Roadrunner: *Richman, Jonathan & Modern Lovers* / White punks on dope: *Tubes* / Blank generation: *Hell, Richard & The Voidoids* / Marquee moon: *Television* / Psycho killer: *Talking Heads* / Stop your sobbing: *Pretenders* / Is she really going out with him: *Jackson, Joe* / Ready steady go: *Generation X* / (Get a) grip (on yourself): *Stranglers* / Shot by both sides: *Magazine* / Alternative Ulster: *Stiff Little Fingers* / Eighties: *Killing Joke* / Money: *Flying Lizards* / Kung fu international: *Cooper Clarke, John*
CD Set ____ VTDCD 42
Virgin / Jan '95 / EMI

BEST PUNK ALBUM IN THE WORLD...EVER VOL.2, THE (2CD Set)
Pretty vacant: *Sex Pistols* / Lust for life: *Iggy Pop* / No more heroes: *Stranglers* / Hong Kong garden: *Siouxsie & The Banshees* / Where's Captain Kirk: *Spizz Energi 2* / Orgasm addict: *Buzzcocks* / Do anything you wanna do: *Eddie & The Hot Rods* / Eton rifles: *Jam* / My perfect cousin: *Undertones* / Hanging on the telephone: *Blondie* / This perfect day: *Saints* / Staring at the rude boys: *Ruts* / Day the world turned day-glo: *X-Ray Spex* / King rocker: *Generation X* / I want candy: *Bow Wow Wow* / Kings of the wild frontier: *Adam & The Ants* / Rock lobster: *B-52's* / Pump it up: *Costello, Elvis & The Attractions* / Sweet Gene Vincent: *Dury, Ian & The Blockheads* / So it goes: *Lowe, Nick* / Spanish stroll: *Mink Deville* / Brass in pocket: *Pretenders* / Pretty in pink: *Psychedelic Furs* / Rat trap: *Boomtown Rats* / Holiday in the sun: *Sex Pistols* / Something better change: *Stranglers* / If the kids are united: *Sham 69* / Turning Japanese: *Vapors* / I don't mind: *Buzzcocks* / Don't dictate: *Penetration* / Saints are coming: *Skids* / She does it right: *Dr. Feelgood* / Love comes in spurts: *Hell, Richard & The Voidoids* / Sonic reducer: *Dead Boys* / Rock 'n' roll nigger: *Smith, Patti Group* / Suspect device: *Stiff Little Fingers* / Smash it up: *Damned* / Don't touch me there: *Tubes* / Shake some action: *Flamin' Groovies* / Little girl: *Banned* / Whole wide world: *Wreckless Eric* / Treason (It's just a story): *Teardrop Explodes* / Outdoor miner: *Wire* / Satisfaction: *Devo* / Death disco: *Public Image Ltd* / Love will tear us apart: *Joy Division* / Beasley Street: *Cooper Clarke, John*
CD Set ____ VTDCD 79
Virgin / Mar '96 / EMI

BEST RAP ALBUM IN THE WORLD...EVER, THE (2CD Set)
I got 5 on it: *Luniz* / Gangasta's paradise: *Coolio* / Regulate (album version): *Warren G* / Mr. Wendel: *Arrested Development* / White lines (don't do it): *Grandmaster Flash & Melle Mel* / I wish (radio edit): *Skee Lo* / Boombastic: *Shaggy* / Jump around: *House Of Pain* / Boom shake the room: *DJ Jazzy Jeff & The Fresh Prince* / U can't touch this: *MC Hammer* / (You gotta) Fight for your right (to party): *Beastie Boys* / Walk this way: *Run DMC* / No fronts (clean greene edit): *Dog Eat Dog* / Come back baby: *K7* / Boom shack-a-lak (edit): *Apache Indian* / Hip hip hooray: *Naughty By Nature* / Whatta man: *Salt n' Pepa & En Vogue* / Gimme that body (radio edit): *Q-Tee* / Ain't no time to play: *Guru* / I'll be around: *Rappin' 4-Tay* / Rapper's delight: *Sugarhill Gang* / Message: *Grandmaster Flash & The Furious Five* / That's how I'm livin': *Ice-T* / Don't believe the hype: *Public Enemy* / Me, myself and I: *De La Soul* / Too hot (Clean version): *Coolio* / Getto jam: *Domino* / Round the way girl: *LL Cool J* / Love sick (upbeat mix): *Gang Starr* / Set adrift on memory bliss (Radio mix): *PM Dawn* / Karmacoma: *Massive Attack* / Brown sugar: *D'Angelo* / One shot: *Brotherhood* / Can't you see: *Total F Notorious Big* / Can I kick it: *Tribe Called Quest* / Wash your face in my sink (radio mix): *Dream Warriors* / It's a shame: *Monie Love* / Hand of the dead body: *Scarface*
CD Set ____ VTDCD 75
Virgin / Apr '96 / EMI

BEST REGGAE ALBUM IN THE WORLD...EVER VOL.1, THE (2CD Set)
Tease me: *Chaka Demus & Pliers* / Boombastic: *Shaggy* / Mr. Loverman: *Shabba Ranks* / Close to you: *Priest, Maxi* / Don't turn around: *Aswad* / Good thing going: *Minott, Sugar* / Amigo: *Black Slate* / Keep on movin': *Marley, Bob & The Wailers* / I shot the sheriff: *Inner Circle* / Now that we've found love: *Third World* / Baby come back: *Pato Banton & Ali Campbell/Robin Campbell* / I don't wanna dance: *Grant, Eddy* / You can get it if you really want: *Dekker, Desmond* / Shine: *Aswad* / Compliments on your kiss: *Red Dragon* / Searchin': *China Black* / Silly games: *Kay, Janet* / (You gotta walk) don't look back: *Tosh, Peter* / On a ragga tip: *SL2* / No no no (world a respect) / Oh Carolina: *Shaggy* / Israelites: *Dekker, Desmond* / Double barrell: *Collins, Dave & Ansell* / Return of Django: *Upsetters* / Liquidator: *Harry J All Stars* / Rudi's in love: *Locomotive* / Message to you Rudi: *Specials* / On my radio: *Selecter* / One step beyond: *Madness* / Tears of a clown: *Beat* / Uptown top ranking: *Althia & Donna* / Wonderful world beautiful people: *Cliff, Jimmy* / Love of the common people: *Thomas, Nicky* / Pressure drop: *Toots & The Maytals* / Young, gifted and black: *Bob & Marcia* / Hurt so good: *Cadogan, Susan* / Help me make it through the night: *Holt, John* / I can see clearly now: *Nash, Johnny* / Everything I own: *Boothe, Ken* / Many rivers to cross: *Cliff, Jimmy* / Every little thing she does is magic: *Chaka Demus & Pliers* / Every breath you take: *Wright, Betty*
CD Set ____ VTDCD 127
Virgin / Aug '97 / EMI

BEST REGGAE ALBUM IN THE WORLD...EVER VOL.2, THE
Baby come back: *Pato Banton* / Compliments on your kiss: *Red Dragon* / Higher ground: *UB40* / Searching: *China Black* / Wild world: *Priest, Maxi* / You don't love me (no no no): *Penn, Dawn* / Shine: *Aswad* / Everything is alright (Uptight): *Lewis, C.J.* / I like to move it: *Reel 2 Real & The Mad Stuntman* / Incredible: *M-Beat & General Levy* / Arranged marriage: *Apache Indian* / Oh Carol: *General Saint & Don Campbell* / You can get it if you really want: *Dekker, Desmond* / I shot the sheriff: *Inner Circle* / No woman no cry: *Boothe, Ken* / Pressure drop: *Toots & The Maytals* / Hurt so good: *Cadogan, Susan* / Help me make it through the night: *Holt, John* / Kingston town: *Lord Creator* / Many rivers to cross: *Cliff, Jimmy* / Silly games: *Kay, Janet* / Girlie girlie: *George, Sophia* / Living on the frontline: *Grant, Eddy* / Don't turn around: *Ace Of Base* / Yummy yummy: *Summit* / Here I stand: *McLean, Bitty* / Rudi's in love: *Locomotive* / Message to you Rudy: *Specials* / Prince: *Madness* / Tears of a clown: *Beat* / Walking on the moon: *Police* / Tide is high: *Blondie* / Games people play: *South, Joe* / Sugar sugar: *Baysee, Duke* / Pass the dutchie: *Musical Youth* / Cupid: *JC 001* / Midnight rider: *Davidson, Paul* / Walking in the sunshine: *Bad Manners* / Liquidator: *Harry J All Stars* / Everything I own: *Boy George*
CD Set ____ VIDCD 39
Virgin / Dec '94 / EMI

BEST REGGAE ALBUM IN THE WORLD...EVER, THE
Mr. Loverman: *Shabba Ranks* / Sweat (A la la la la long): *Inner Circle* / Sweets for my sweet: *Lewis, C.J.* / Dedicated to the one I love: *McLean, Bitty* / Informer: *Snow* / Close to you: *Priest, Maxi* / Oh Carolina: *Shaggy* / Riddim: *US 3* / Love you like crazy / Dance hall mood: *Aswad* / Dancing on the floor: *Third World* / Wonderful world, beautiful people: *Cliff, Jimmy* / Love of the common people: *Thomas, Nicky* / Young, gifted and black: *Bob & Marcia* / Small axe: *Marley, Bob* / Israelites: *Dekker, Desmond* / Double barrel: *Collins, Dave & Ansell* / Red red wine: *Tribe, Tony* / Return of Django: *Upsetters* / I'm in the mood for ska: *Lord Tanamo* / Money in my pocket: *Brown, Dennis* / Everything I own: *Boothe, Ken* / Rivers of Babylon: *Melodians* / It keeps rainin' (Tears from my eyes): *McLean, Bitty* / All that she wants: *Ace Of Base* / Dub be good to me: *Beats International* / On a ragga tip: *SL2* / Too much too young: *Specials* / One step beyond: *Madness* / Shout (It out): *Louchie Lou & Michie One* / Lip up fatty: *Bad Manners* / On my radio: *Selecter* / Bed's too big without you: *Hylton, Sheila* / Silly games: *Kay, Janet* / Good thing going: *Minott, Sugar* / I don't wanna dance: *Grant, Eddy* / Just don't want to be lonely: *McGregor, Freddie* / I can see clearly now: *Nash, Johnny* / Uptown top ranking: *Alfred & Donald* / Amigo: *Black Slate* / Don't look back: *Tosh, Peter* / Tomorrow people: *Marley, Ziggy* / Jamaican in New York: *Shinehead* / I want to wake up with you: *Gardiner, Boris*
CD ____ VIDCD 27
Virgin / May '94 / EMI

BEST REGGAE, THE
CD ____ CD 903
Sound / Jun '89 / ADA

BEST ROCK 'N' ROLL
CD ____ CD 901
Sound / Jun '89 / ADA

BEST ROCK 'N' ROLL ALBUM IN THE WORLD...EVER, THE
(We're gonna) Rock around the clock: *Haley, Bill & The Comets* / Ain't that a shame: *Domino, Fats* / Sweet little sixteen: *Berry, Chuck* / Bye bye love: *Everly Brothers* / La bamba: *Valens, Ritchie* / Peggy Sue: *Holly, Buddy* / That'll be the day: *Crickets* / Tutti frutti: *Little Richard* / Be bop a lula: *Vincent, Gene* / At the hop: *Danny & The Juniors* / Reet petite: *Wilson, Jackie* / Let's twist again: *Checker, Chubby* / Runaway: *Shannon, Del* / Summertime blues: *Cochran, Eddie* / Move it: *Richard, Cliff* / Locomotion: *Little Eva* / Why do fools fall in love: *Lymon, Frankie & The Teenagers* / Lipstick on your collar: *Francis, Connie* / Sealed with a kiss: *Hyland, Brian* / Teenager in love: *Wilde, Marty* / Rubber ball: *Vee, Bobby* / Wanderer: *Dion* / You're 16: *Burnette, Johnny* / Oh Carol: *Sedaka, Neil* / Chantilly lace: *Big Bopper* / Little darlin': *Diamonds* / Halfway to paradise: *Fury, Billy* / Let's dance: *Montez, Chris* / Red river rock: *Johnny & The Hurricanes* / Nutrocker: *B-Bumble & The Stingers* / Will you still love me tomorrow: *Shirelles* / Poetry in motion: *Tillotson, Johnny* / Do you love me: *Poole, Brian & The Tremeloes* / Little bitty pretty one: *Harris, Thurston* / But I do: *Henry, Clarence 'Frogman'* / Bony moronie: *Williams, Larry* / That's alright Mama: *Crudup, Arthur* / Get a job: *Silhouettes* / Twist and shout: *Isleys* / Shake, rattle and roll: *Haley, Bill & The Comets* / Wake up little Susie: *Everly Brothers* / Golly Miss Molly: *Little Richard* / C'mon everybody: *Cochran, Eddie* / Happy birthday sweet sixteen: *Sedaka, Neil* / Blueberry Hill: *Domino, Fats*
CD Set ____ VTDCD 37
Virgin / Oct '94 / EMI

BEST ROCK 'N' ROLL ALBUM IN THE WORLD...EVER, THE (2CD Set)
Tutti frutti: *Little Richard* / Chantilly lace: *Big Bopper* / At the hop: *Danny & The Juniors* / C'mon everybody: *Cochran, Eddie* / Wake up little Susie: *Everly Brothers* / That'll be the day: *Crickets* / Shakin' all over: *Kidd, Johnny & The Pirates* / Move it: *Richard, Cliff* / Lipstick on your collar: *Francis, Connie* / Bony Moronie: *Williams, Larry* / Red River rock: *Johnny & The Hurricanes* / Shake, rattle and roll: *Haley, Bill & The Comets* / Locomotion: *Little Eva* / Let's dance: *Montez, Chris* / Why do fools fall in love: *Lymon, Frankie & The Teenagers* / Little bitty pretty one: *Harris, Thurston* / Party doll: *Knox, Buddy* / Pretty little angel eyes: *Lee, Curtis* / Night has a thousand eyes: *Vee, Bobby* / Tequila: *Champs* / La bamba: *Valens, Ritchie* / Wipeout: *Surfaris* / Brand new cadillac: *Taylor, Vince & Playboys* / Promised land: *Allan, Johnnie* / Sweet little sixteen: *Berry, Chuck* / Be bop a lula: *Vincent, Gene* / Summertime blues: *Cochran, Eddie* / Rave on: *Holly, Buddy* / Rock around the clock: *Haley, Bill & The Comets* / Runaway: *Shannon, Del* / Poetry in motion: *Tillotson, Johnny* / Halfway to paradise: *Fury, Billy* / Will you still love me tomorrow: *Shirelles* / Hello Mary Lou (goodbye heart): *Nelson, Rick* / Bye bye love: *Everly Brothers* / Ain't that a shame: *Domino, Fats* / Teenager in love: *Wilde, Marty* / Twist and shout: *Isley Brothers* / Rett petite: *Wilson, Jackie* / Good golly Miss Molly: *Little Richard* / Get a job: *Silhouettes* / (I don't know why I love you) but I do: *Henry, Clarence 'Frogman'* / Personality: *Price, Lloyd* / Nutrocker: *B Bumble & The Stingers* / Oh Carol: *Sedaka, Neil* / Born too late: *Poni-Tails* / Sealed with a kiss: *Hyland, Brian* / Sea of love: *Phillips, Phil* / Blue velvet: *Vinton, Bobby* / Only the lonely: *Orbison, Roy*
CD Set ____ VTDCD 128
Virgin / Aug '97 / EMI

BEST ROCK ALBUM IN THE WORLD...EVER VOL.1, THE (2CD Set)
Are you gonna go my way: *Kravitz, Lenny* / Paradise City: *Guns n' Roses* / Walk this way: *Run DMC & Aerosmith* / Boys are back in town: *Thin Lizzy* / 20th Century Boy: *Bolan, Marc & T-Rex* / Gimme all your lovin': *ZZ Top* / Born to be wild: *Steppenwolf* / Al right now: *Free* / Simply the best: *Turner, Tina* / Girl like you: *Collins, Edwyn* / Inside: *Stiltskin* / Since you've been gone: *Rainbow* / Here I go again: *Whitesnake* / Turn it on again: *Genesis* / Do the Strand: *Roxy Music* / Passenger: *Iggy Pop* / Silver machine: *Hawkwind* / Ace of spades: *Motorhead* / Paranoid: *Black Sabbath* / Another brick in the wall: *Pink Floyd* / Owner of a lonely heart: *Yes* / Strange brew: *Cream* / Smoke on the water: *Deep Purple* / Can't get enough: *Bad Company* / In a broken dream: *Python Lee Jackson* / Mannish boy: *Waters, Muddy* / All day and all of the night: *Kinks* / Stay with me: *Faces* / You ain't seen nothing yet: *Bachman-Turner Overdrive* / Cum on feel the noize: *Slade* / No more heroes: *Stranglers* / She sells sanctuary: *Cult* / Free bird: *Lynyrd Skynyrd* / Hard rain's a-gonna fall: *Ferry, Bryan* / More than a feeling: *Boston* / (Don't fear) the reaper: *Blue Oyster Cult* / In the air tonight: *Collins, Phil* / I'd do anything for love: *Meat Loaf*
CD Set ____ VTDCD 125
Virgin / Aug '97 / EMI

BEST ROCK ALBUM IN THE WORLD...EVER VOL.2, THE (2CD Set)
Seven seas of Rhye: *Queen* / Desire: *U2* / Why can't this be love: *Van Halen* / Bad love: *Clapton, Eric* / All night long: *Rainbow* / Here I go again: *Whitesnake* / Two princes: *Spin Doctors* / Viva Las Vegas: *ZZ Top* / Stay with me: *Stewart, Rod & The Faces* / Elected: *Cooper, Alice* / Rock 'n' roll dreams come through: *Meat Loaf* / Turn it on again: *Genesis* / Waterfront: *Simple Minds* / Rocks: *Primal Scream* / Wishing well: *Free* / Crossroads: *Cream* / Join together: *Who* / Rocky Mountain way: *Walsh, Joe* / Let love rule: *Kravitz, Lenny* / Losing my religion: *REM* / Solsbury Hill: *Gabriel, Peter* / Whole of the moon: *Waterboys* / Street life: *Roxy Music* / We gotta get out of this place: *Animals* / Cum on feel the noize: *Slade* / Pretty vacant: *Sex Pistols* / Blockbuster: *Sweet* / Telegram Sam: *T-Rex* / Cigarettes and alcohol: *Oasis* / Wild thing: *Troggs* / You really got me: *Kinks* / No more heroes: *Stranglers* / Down down: *Status Quo* / Don't believe a word: *Thin Lizzy* / Out in the fields: *Moore, Gary & Phil Lynott* / Black night: *Deep Purple* / She's not there: *Santana* / Feel like makin' love: *Bad Company* / All the young dudes: *Mott The Hoople* / Walk on the wild side: *Reed, Lou*
CD ____ VTDCD 47
Virgin / Mar '95 / EMI

BEST ROCK ALBUM IN THE WORLD...EVER, THE
We willl rock you: *Queen* / Inside: *Stiltskin* / Are you gonna go my way: *Kravitz, Lenny* / I'd do anything for love (But I won't do that): *Meat Loaf* / Smoke on the water: *Deep Purple* / Pride (In the name of love): *U2* / Born to be wild: *Steppenwolf* / Free bird: *Lynyrd Skynyrd* / All right now: *Free* / (Don't fear) The reaper: *Blue Oyster Cult* / Can't get enough: *Bad Company* / School's out: *Cooper, Alice* / More than a feeling: *Boston* / Boys are back in town: *Thin Lizzy* / Since you've been gone: *Rainbow* / Walk this way: *Run DMC & Aerosmith* / Twentieth century boy: *T-Rex* / Silver machine: *Hawkwind* / Mama: *Genesis* / Sledgehammer: *Gabriel, Peter* / In the air tonight: *Collins, Phil* / Paranoid: *Black Sabbath* / Ace of spades: *Motorhead* / All day and all of the night: *Kinks* / Gimme all your lovin': *ZZ Top* / She sells sanctuary: *Cult* / Owner of a lonely heart: *Yes* / Do the strand: *Roxy Mu-*

sic / Passenger: *Iggy Pop* / Sunshine of your love: *Cream* / Mannish boy: *Waters, Muddy* / Life's been good: *Walsh, Joe* / Won't get fooled again: *Who* / Crazy crazy nights: *Kiss* / Eye of the tiger: *Survivor* / Caroline: *Status Quo* / Money for nothing: *Dire Straits* / In a broken dream: *Python Lee Jackson*
CD _______________ VTDCD 35
Virgin / Aug '94 / EMI

BEST ROCK ANTHEMS IN THE WORLD...EVER, THE (2CD Set)
We are the champions: *Queen* / Best: *Turner, Tina* / Addicted to love: *Palmer, Robert* / I found someone: *Cher* / Behind the mask: *Clapton, Eric* / Living years: *Mike & The Mechanics* / Everybody hurts: *REM* / Let's dance: *Bowie, David* / Bat out of hell: *Meat Loaf* / Are you gonna go my way: *Kravitz, Lenny* / All right now: *Free* / Inside: *Stiltskin* / Final countdown: *Europe* / Long train runnin': *Doobie Brothers* / Need you tonight: *INXS* / Don't you (forget about me): *Simple Minds* / Is this love: *Whitesnake* / In the air tonight: *Collins, Phil* / Should I stay or should I go: *Clash* / You could be mine: *Guns n' Roses* / Walk this way: *Run DMC & Aerosmith* / School's out: *Cooper, Alice* / Pinball wizard: *Who* / Changing man: *Weller, Paul* / All or nothing: *Small Faces* / 20th century boy: *T-Rex* / Cum on feel the noize: *Slade* / Slide away: *Oasis* / Life of Riley: *Lightning Seeds* / Goldfinger: *Ash* / Pretty vacant: *Sex Pistols* / Lust for life: *Iggy Pop* / Gimme all your lovin': *ZZ Top* / Paper plane: *Status Quo* / Satellite: *Hooters* / Since you've been gone: *Rainbow* / Can't get enough: *Bad Company* / Love is the drug: *Roxy Music*
CD Set _______________ VTDCD 83
Virgin / May '96 / EMI

BEST ROCK BALLADS IN THE WORLD...EVER, THE (2CD Set)
Kind of magic: *Queen* / Girl like you: *Collins, Edwyn* / Over my shoulder: *Mike & The Mechanics* / Stuck in the middle with you: *Stealer's Wheel* / Don't stop: *Fleetwood Mac* / Heaven is a place on earth: *Carlisle, Belinda* / Dignity: *Deacon Blue* / Road to hell: *Rea, Chris* / I wish it would rain down: *Collins, Phil* / Romeo and Juliet: *Dire Straits* / Don't dream it's over: *Crowded House* / Waiting for a girl like you: *Foreigner* / I'll stand by you: *Pretenders* / Show me heaven: *McKee, Maria* / Eternal flame: *Bangles* / Oh yeah (on the radio): *Roxy Music* / Drive: *Cars* / Wind of change: *Scorpions* / To be with you: *Mr. Big* / Heaven help: *Kravitz, Lenny* / I'd do anything for love (but I won't do that): *Meat Loaf* / If I could turn back time: *Cher* / Is this love: *Whitesnake* / Black velvet: *Myles, Alannah* / Days: *MacColl, Kirsty* / Pure: *Lightning Seeds* / Mary's prayer: *Danny Wilson* / Valerie: *Winwood, Steve* / Every little thing she does is magic: *Police* / Rosanna: *Toto* / Keep on loving you: *REO Speedwagon* / Hard to say I'm sorry: *Chicago* / Follow you follow me: *Genesis* / Walking in Memphis: *Cohen, Marc* / Missing you: *Waite, John* / (I just) died in your arms: *Cutting Crew* / Kayleigh: *Marillion* / Babe: *Styx* / Listen to your heart: *Roxette* / Right here waiting: *Marx, Richard*
CD Set _______________ VTDCD 60
Virgin / Aug '95 / EMI

BEST SCOTTISH ALBUM IN THE WORLD...EVER, THE (2CD Set)
Letter from America: *Proclaimers* / Every beat of my heart: *Stewart, Rod* / Sailing: *Sutherland Brothers* / Wild mountain thyme: *Silencers* / Mull of Kintyre: *McCartney, Paul & Wings* / Caledonia: *Miller, Frankie* / I should have known better: *Diamond, Jim* / Heart on my sleeve: *Gallagher & Lyle* / Perfect: *Fairground Attraction* / Stuck in the middle with you: *Stealer's Wheel* / Young at heart: *Bluebells* / Ob-la-di, ob-la-da: *Marmalade* / Shout: *Lulu* / Shang-a-lang: *Bay City Rollers* / Magic: *Pilot* / Donald where's your troosers: *Stewart, Andy* / Bluebell polka: *Shand, Jimmy* / Stop yer tickling Jock: *Lauder, Harry* / Amazing Grace: *Royal Scots Dragoon Guards* / Over the sea to Skye: *Celtic Spirit* / Rabbie Burns trilogy: *Monroes* / Auld lang syne: *Festival Singers* / Baker Street: *Rafferty, Gerry* / Mary's prayer: *Danny Wilson* / Dignity: *Deacon Blue* / Whole of the moon: *Waterboys* / Girl like you: *Collins, Edwyn* / Let's go round again: *Average White Band* / Somewhere in my heart: *Aztec Camera* / If I was: *Ure, Midge* / Shoeshine boy: *Humblebums* / I'm gonna be (500 miles): *Proclaimers* / Fields of fire (400 miles): *Big Country* / Battle: *Wolfstone* / An ubhal as airde (the highest apple): *Runrig* / Tinseltown in the rain: *Blue Nile* / Patience of angels: *Reader, Eddi* / Breislach: *Capercaillie* / Flower of Scotland: *Corries* / Knockin' on heaven's door
CD Set _______________ VTDCD 137
Virgin / Jun '97 / EMI

BEST SELLERS OF THE 1960'S AND 1970'S (4CD Set)
Let it be me: *Everly Brothers* / Walking to New Orleans: *Fats Domino* / Reflections of my life: *Marmalade* / She'd rather be with me: *Turtles* / My girl: *Temptations* / It's in his kiss (the shoop shoop song): *Everett, Betty* / Bend it: *Dave Dee, Dozy, Beaky, Mick & Tich* / It keeps right on a-hurtin': *Tillotson, Johnny* / I'm gonna knock on your door: *Hodges, Eddie* / Clementine: *Jan & Dean* / Birds and the bees: *Akens, Jewel* / Surfin' safari: *Beach Boys* / Harlem shuffle: *Bob & Earl* / Moon river: *Butler, Jerry* / Happy together: *Turtles* / Duke of Earl: *Chandler, Gene* / Moody river: *Boone, Pat* / Legend of xanadu: *Dave Dee, Dozy, Beaky, Mick & Tich* / When will I be loved: *Everly Brothers* / Hold what you got: *Tex, Joe* / Oh what a night: *Dells* / Sound of silence: *Bachelors* / Ob la di ob la da: *Marmalade* / Surfin': *Beach Boys* / Talk back tremblin' lips: *Tillotson, Johnny* / Baby talk: *Jan & Dean* / Hey Paula: *Paul & Paula* / Leader of the pack: *Shangri-Las* / Greased lightnin': *Travolta, John* / Swing your daddy: *Gilstrap, Jim* / Jeans on: *Dundas, David* / Love grows where my Rosemary goes: *Edison Lighthouse* / Something old something new: *Fantastics* / Sweet inspiration: *Johnson, Johnny & Bandwagon* / Indian reservation: *Fardon, Don* / Long tall glasses (I can dance): *Sayer, Leo* / Tie a yellow ribbon 'round the ole oak tree: *Orlando, Tony* / Sugar me: *De Paul, Lynsey* / I'm doin' fine now: *New York City* / Man who sold the world: *Lulu & David Bowie* / Don't let me be misunderstood: *Esmeralda, Santa* / Wake up and make love with me: *Dury, Ian* / Breakaway: *Ullman, Tracey* / Wunderbar: *Tenpole Tudor* / Sandy: *Johansen, Glen* / You make me feel like dancing: *Sayer, Leo* / Daughter of darkness: *Jones, Tom* / Knock three times: *Orlando, Tony* / Sugar candy kisses: *Kissoon, Mac & Katie* / Highwire: *Carr, Linda* / Show and tell: *Wilson, Al* / Only you can: *Fox* / Be thankful for what you've got: *DeVaughan, William* / Don't give up on us: *Soul, David* / Won't somebody dance with me: *De Paul, Lynsey* / Take your mama for a ride: *Lulu*
CD Set _______________ HR 871392
Disky / Jul '97 / Disky / THE

BEST SELLERS VOL.1
CD _______________ DCD 5354
Disky / Apr '94 / Disky / THE

BEST SELLERS VOL.2
CD _______________ DCD 5355
Disky / Apr '94 / Disky / THE

BEST SELLERS VOL.3
CD _______________ DCD 5379
Disky / Apr '94 / Disky / THE

BEST SIXTIES ALBUM IN THE WORLD...EVER VOL.1, THE (2CD Set)
I'm a believer: *Monkees* / I got you babe: *Sonny & Cher* / It might as well rain until September: *King, Carole* / Young ones: *Richard, Cliff & The Shadows* / Runaway: *Shannon, Del* / Let's hang on: *Four Seasons* / I only want to be with you: *Springfield, Dusty* / Price of love: *Everly Brothers* / Mony mony: *James, Tommy & The Shondells* / Hi ho silver lining: *Beck, Jeff* / Flowers in the rain: *Move* / Waterloo sunset: *Kinks* / Good vibrations: *Beach Boys* / She's not there: *Zombies* / Pretty flamingo: *Manfred Mann* / Love is all around: *Troggs* / Unchained melody: *Righteous Brothers* / Ferry cross the Mersey: *Gerry & The Pacemakers* / Whiter shade of pale: *Procul Harum* / Wichita lineman: *Campbell, Glen* / He ain't heavy, he's my brother: *Hollies* / Sun ain't gonna shine anymore: *Walker Brothers* / Downtown: *Clark, Petula* / Can't get used to losing you: *Williams, Andy* / Silence is golden: *Tremeloes* / I heard it through the grapevine: *Gaye, Marvin* / (Sittin' on the) dock of the bay: *Redding, Otis* / I say a little prayer: *Franklin, Aretha* / Do you know the way to San Jose: *Warwick, Dionne* / You can't hurry love: *Supremes* / Reach out, I'll be there: *Four Tops* / Dancing in the street: *Reeves, Martha & The Vandellas* / Uptight (everything's alright): *Wonder, Stevie* / Soul man: *Sam & Dave* / It's not unusual: *Jones, Tom* / Yeh yeh: *Fame, Georgie & The Blue Flames* / Sha la la la lee: *Small Faces* / Got to get you into my life: *Bennett, Cliff & The Rebel Rousers* / In the midnight hour: *Pickett, Wilson* / Knock on wood: *Floyd, Eddie* / I got you (I feel good): *Brown, James* / Rescue me: *Bass, Fontella* / Go now: *Moody Blues* / Brown eyed girl: *Morrison, Van* / Mr. Tambourine Man: *Byrds* / House of the rising sun: *Animals* / When a man loves a woman: *Sledge, Percy* / Crazy: *Cline, Patsy* / We have all the time in the world: *Armstrong, Louis* / Stand by me: *King, Ben E.*
CD Set _______________ VTDCD 66
Virgin / Nov '95 / EMI

BEST SIXTIES ALBUM IN THE WORLD...EVER VOL.2, THE (2CD Set)
Oh pretty woman: *Orbison, Roy* / Daydream believer: *Monkees* / How do you do it: *Gerry & The Pacemakers* / Where did our love go: *Ross, Diana* / Young girl: *Puckett, Gary & The Union Gap* / Do wah diddy diddy: *Manfred Mann* / Bend me shape me: *Amen Corner* / Baby come back: *Equals* / Let's dance: *Montez, Chris* / Heartbeat: *Holly, Buddy* / Sweets for my sweet: *Searchers* / Just one look: *Hollies* / I'm into something good: *Herman's Hermits* / Cathy's clown: *Everly Brothers* / Night has a thousand eyes: *Vee, Bobby* / Apache: *Shadows* / Concrete & clay: *Unit 4+2* / Dizzy: *Roe, Tommy* / Something's gotten hold of my heart: *Pitney, Gene* / You've lost that loving feeling: *Righteous Brothers* / Will you love me tomorrow: *Shirelles* / I can't let Maggie go: *Honeybus* / What a wonderful world: *Armstrong, Louis* / Dedicated to the one I love: *Mamas & The Papas* / Words: *Bee Gees* / I get around: *Beach Boys* / Fire brigade: *Move* / We gotta get out of this place: *Animals* / Friday on my mind: *Easybeats* / You really got me: *Kinks* / Born to be wild: *Steppenwolf* / Wild thing: *Troggs* / I fought the law: *Fuller, Bobby Four* / Itchycoo Park: *Small Faces* / Keep on running: *Davis, Spencer Group* / Dance to the music: *Sly & The Family Stone* / Respect: *Franklin, Aretha* / Mustang Sally: *Pickett, Wilson* / Green onions: *Booker T & The MG's* / My girl: *Redding, Otis* / You never can tell: *Berry, Chuck* / Three steps to heaven: *Cochran, Eddie* / Everlasting love: *Love Affair* / Elenore: *Turtles* / Make it easy on yourself: *Walker Brothers* / First cut is the deepest: *Arnold, P.P.* / Walk on by: *Warwick, Dionne* / Groovy kind of love: *Mindbenders* / Something in the air: *Thunderclap Newman* / Albatross: *Fleetwood Mac*
CD Set _______________ VTDCD 106
Virgin / Nov '96 / EMI

BEST SOUL, THE
CD _______________ CD 905
Sound / Jun '89 / ADA

BEST SUMMER ALBUM IN THE WORLD...EVER, THE (2CD Set)
I wanna be the only one: *Eternal & Bebe Winans* / Closer than close: *Gaines, Rosie* / Lovefool: *Cardigans* / Wannabe: *Spice Girls* / Se a vida e (that's the way life is): *Pet Shop Boys* / Good enough: *Dodgy* / Alright: *Supergrass* / Girls and boys: *Blur* / Day we caught the train: *Ocean Colour Scene* / Cecilia: *Suggs* / Shy guy: *King, Diana* / In the summertime: *Shaggy & Rayvon* / Tease me: *Chaka Demus & Pliers* / Shine: *Aswad* / Jump around: *House Of Pain* / Bodyshakin': *911* / Star people: *Michael, George* / I luv u baby: *Original* / Ooh ahh...just a little bit: *Gina G* / Bellissima: *DJ Quicksilver* / Seven days and one week: *BBE* / Wake up Boo: *Boo Radleys* / I believe I can fly: *R Kelly* / Summer breeze: *Isley Brothers* / Lovely day: *Withers, Bill* / Groovin': *Young Rascals* / Weather with you: *Crowded House* / Back to life: *Soul II Soul* / Pray: *Take That* / Days: *MacColl, Kirsty* / Do it again: *Beach Boys* / This summer: *Squeeze* / Echo beach: *Martha & The Muffins* / Summertime blues: *Cochran, Eddie* / Macarena: *Los Del Rio* / Guaglione: *Prado, Perez 'Prez'* / Bamboleo: *Gipsy Kings* / Now that we've found love: *Third World* / Summertime: *DJ Jazzy Jeff & The Fresh Prince* / Love shack: *B-52's* / Walking on sunshine: *Katrina & The Waves* / California girls: *Beach Boys* / Summer holiday: *Richard, Cliff & The Shadows* / Summertime: *Gerry & The Pacemakers*
CD Set _______________ VTDCD 140
Virgin / Jun '97 / EMI

BEST SUMMER...EVER, THE
In the summertime: *Shaggy* / Compliments on your kiss: *Red Dragon* / Boom boom boom: *Outhere Brothers* / Wipeout: *Fat Boys & The Beach Boys* / Hot hot hot: *Arrow* / Saturday night: *Whigfield* / Dreamer: *Livin' Joy* / Sweets for my sweet: *Lewis, C.J.* / Don't turn around: *Aswad* / You don't love me (no no no): *Penn, Dawn* / Sweat (A la la la la long): *Inner Circle* / Humpin' around: *Brown, Bobby* / Love city groove: *Love City Groove* / Grease megamix: *Travolta, John & Olivia Newton John* / Give it up: *KC & The Sunshine Band* / Wake up Boo: *Boo Radleys* / Walking on sunshine: *Katrina & The Waves* / Beach baby: *First Class* / Barbados: *Typically Tropical* / Y viva Espana: *Sylvia* / Days: *MacColl, Kirsty* / Long hot summer: *Style Council* / Summer breeze: *Isley Brothers* / Back to life: *Soul II Soul & Caron Wheeler* / Lovely day: *Withers, Bill* / Summertime: *DJ Jazzy Jeff & The Fresh Prince* / I'll be around: *Rappin' 4-Tay* / Searching: *China Black* / Now that we've found love: *Third World* / Club Tropicana: *Wham* / Do it again: *Beach Boys* / Echo beach: *Martha & The Muffins* / Somewhere in my heart: *Aztec Camera* / Summertime blues: *Cochran, Eddie* / Summer rain: *Carlisle, Belinda* / On the beach: *Rea, Chris* / Under the boardwalk: *Drifters* / Summertime: *Gerry & The Pacemakers* / Summer (The first time): *Goldsboro, Bobby* / Spanish wine: *White, Chris*
CD Set _______________ VTDCD 57
Virgin / Jul '95 / EMI

BEST SWING '96 VOL.1, THE
CD _______________ TCD 2805
Telstar / Jan '96 / BMG

BEST SWING '96 VOL.2, THE
CD _______________ TCD 2820
Telstar / Feb '96 / BMG

BEST SWING '96 VOL.3, THE
CD _______________ TCD 2837
Telstar / Jun '96 / BMG

BEST SWING ALBUM IN THE WORLD...EVER VOL.1, THE (2CD Set)
Lifted: *Lighthouse Family* / This is how we do it: *Jordan, Montell* / Return of the Mack: *Morrison, Mark* / Whoo ha got you all in check: *Busta Rhymes* / Brown sugar: *D'Angelo* / If you love me: *Brownstone* / Stay: *Eternal* / Mary Jane (All night long): *Blige, Mary J.* / Flavour of the old school: *Knight, Beverley* / She's got that vibe: *R Kelly* / I wish: *Skee Lo* / I've got a little something for you: *MN8* / I got 5 on it: *Luniz* / Boombastic: *Shaggy* / I must stand: *Ice-T* / Regulate: *Warren G* / I wanna sex you up: *Color Me Badd* / Don't walk away: *Jade* / Every little thing I do: *Soul For Real* / My prepgative: *Brown, Bobby* / Poison: *Bel Biv Devoe* / Rough with the smooth: *Nelson, Shara* / Right here: *SWV* / Freak like me: *Howard, Adina* / Real love: *Driza Bone* / Ghetto heaven: *Family Stand* / Search for the hero: *M-People* / Sensitivity: *Tresvant, Ralph* / Freek n' you: *Jodeci* / Undercover lover: *Smooth* / You love is a 187: *Whitehead Brothers* / Dance: *Whitehead Brothers* / I care: *Soul II Soul* / Hey Mr. DJ: *Zhane* / Back and forth: *Aaliyah* / Don't take it personal (Just one of dem days): *Aaliyah* / Summertime: *DJ Jazzy Jeff & The Fresh Prince* / Sweetness: *Gayle, Michelle* / Can't stop: *After 7* / 1,2,3,4 (Sumpin' new): *Coolio* / Hangin' on a string (Contemplation): *Loose Ends*
CD Set _______________ VTCD 86
Virgin / Jun '96 / EMI

BEST SWING ALBUM IN THE WORLD...EVER VOL.2, THE (2CD Set)
Crazy: *Morrison, Mark* / Bump 'n' grind: *Kelly, R* / Good thing: *Eternal* / Love II love: *Damage* / Say you'll be there: *Spice Girls* / Give me a little more time: *Gabrielle* / Ocean drive: *Lighthouse Family* / Spinning the wheel: *Michael, George* / Keep on movin': *Soul II Soul & Caron Wheeler* / Two can play that game: *Brown, Bobby* / Don't look any further: *M-People* / Down that road: *Nelson, Shara* / You gotta be: *Des'ree* / I'm goin' down: *Blige, Mary J.* / Girlfriend: *Pebbles* / Anything: *SWV* / Everyday of the week: *Jade* / Happy just to be with you: *Gayle, Michelle* / Tuff act to follow: *MN8* / Gangsta's paradise: *Coolio & LV* / Something for da honeyz: *Jordan, Montell* / Stressed out: *Tribe Called Quest & Faith Evans* / Lane: *Ice-T* / Golden brown: *Kaleef* / Feel the music: *Guru* / Age ain't nothing but a number: *Aaliyah* / I wanna be down: *Brandy* / Moving on up (on the right side): *Knight, Beverley* / Throw your hands up: *LV* / Apparently nothin': *Young Disciples* / Special kind of lover: *Nu Colours* / Who do u love: *Nu Colours* / Who do you love: *Cox, Deborah* / There's nothing like this: *Omar* / All the things (your man won't do): *Joe* / Mind blowin': *Smooth* / G Spot: *Marshall, Wayne* / Freak me: *Silk* / Feenin': *Jodeci*
CD Set _______________ VTDCD 111
Virgin / Nov '96 / EMI

BETHLEHEM SAMPLER, THE
CD _______________ CDBETH 1
Charly / Mar '97 / Koch

BETSILEO LALANGINA (Madagascar)
CD _______________ 926622
BUDA / Feb '97 / Discovery

BETWEEN FATHER SKY AND MOTHER EARTH
Ancient ground: *Nakai, R. Carlos* / Amazing grace: *Nakai, R. Carlos* / Wind spirit: *Miller, Bill* / Moonlit Stallions: *Native Flute Ensemble* / Riding with thunder: *Native Flute Ensemble* / Holy people: *Douglas Spotted Eagle* / Snow geese: *Douglas Spotted Eagle* / Ashne ate: *Silverbird, Perry* / Happy shepherd: *Silverbird, Perry* / Zuni friendship song: *Manhooty, Chester* / 500 Drums: *Adams, Mel* / Enchanted forest: *Tsa'ne Dos'e* / Kiowa hymn (III): *Pewewardy, Cornel* / Healing song: *Primeaux, Mike & Attson*
CD _______________ ND 63915
Narada / Aug '95 / ADA / New Note/ Pinnacle

BETWEEN THE GROOVES - RHYTHM 'N' BLUES
Mom's apple pie: *Davis, Tyrone* / You still love me: *King, Ben E.* / Check in the mail: *Jackson, Millie* / Strokin': *Carter, Clarence* / For your precious love: *Reed, Francine* / You're gonna come back to me: *Mitchell, Prince Phillip* / There's a change: *Chi-Lites* / Funny how time slips away: *White, Artie* / So tied up: *Clayton, Willie* / Mr. Mailman: *Graham, Jesse*
CD _______________ D 2248792
Ichiban / Sep '96 / Direct / Koch

BEVERLEY HILLS - WILD, YOUNG AND RICH VOL.1
CD _______________ DCD 5287
Disky / Feb '93 / Disky / THE

BEVERLEY HILLS - WILD, YOUNG AND RICH VOL.2
CD _______________ DCD 5288
Disky / Feb '93 / Disky / THE

BEWARE OF THE TEXAS BLUES
I'm a stepper: *Fritz, Joe 'Papoose'* / Can't sleep tonight: *Moore, Henry & Guitar Slim* / Workin' man blues: *Copeland, Johnny* / Life's highway: *Big Walter* / Empty house of so many tears: *Green, Clarence* / Drowning on dry land: *Eastwood Revue* / Rock of Gibraltar / Farther on up the road / Line your body / Freeze / That's fat / Rock me baby / It's alright / Good as old time religion
CD _______________ CDBM 064
Blue Moon / Apr '91 / Cadillac / Discovery / Greensleeves / Jazz Music / Jet Star / TKO Magnum

BEWARE OF THE TEXAS BLUES VOL.2
CD CDBM 085
Blue Moon / May '92 / Cadillac / Discovery / Greensleeves / Jazz Music / Jet Star / TKO Magnum

BEYOND BOUNDARIES
CD CDEB 2552
Earthbeat / May '93 / ADA / Direct

BEYOND MAN'S MIND (The Mystery Of Trance) (2CD Set)
Underground: *Free Inside* / Nosedive: *Boom Generation* / Best kept secrets: *Ambergriz* / Event: *Upgrade 1.2* / Key spiracy: *Zeromen* / Devil in Heaven: *Upgrade 1.2* / Bird of dawning: *Cyberheads* / Blue memories: *West & Storm* / Rich: *Paradise In Dubs* / Feel me: *Angeldust* / Fallen angel: *Cyber Prince* / Magic of light: *Ambergriz* / Mind butterflies: *Bai Oo* / Don't you like music: *Clusia Icrtal* / Nightvisions: *Dr. M* / Got to learn: *Bi Boys Action Squad* / Hostile takeover: *Foam People* / Freakin' the trance: *Upgrade 1.2* / One of the frightened: *Angeldust* / Style shifting: *Shape Shifter* / Low key scenes: *Zeromen 2*
CD Set SPV 08938802
SPV / Aug '96 / Koch / Plastic Head

BEYOND THE BEACH
CD UPSTARTCD 12
Upstart / Jan '95 / ADA / Direct

BEYOND THE CALICO WALL
CD VOXXCD 2051
Voxx / Feb '94 / Else / RTM/Disc

BEYOND THE FRONTLINE
Looks is deceiving: *Gladiators* / Message from the king: *Prince Far-I* / Right time: *Mighty Diamonds* / Wear you to the ball: *U-Roy* / If I don't have you: *Isaacs, Gregory* / Lightning flash weak heart: *Drop Big Youth* / Behold: *Culture* / Great psalms: *U-Roy* / Never get burn: *Twinkle Brothers* / Declaration of rights: *Clarke, Johnny* / Universal tribulation: *Isaacs, Gregory* / Natty rebel: *U-Roy* / Civilisation: *Hudson, Keith* / Freedom fighters: *Washington, Delroy*
CD FRONT 1
Frontline / Jul '90 / EMI / Jet Star

BEYOND THE SUN
CD DAPCD 001
Dance Arena / Sep '95 / RTM/Disc

BEYOND THE SUN VOL.2
CD DAPCD 002
Dance Arena / Mar '96 / RTM/Disc

BGP PRESENTS: BACK TO FUNK (Selection Of Killer Cuts From East/ Westbound Collective)
Back to funk: *Lowe, Robert* / Hicky burr: *Frazier, Caesar* / Monkey hips 'n' rice: *19th Whole* / Pain: *Person, Houston* / Rainy day fun: *Austin, Donald* / Stone thing: *Cash, Alvin* / Gettin' off: *Mason, Bill* / Slippin' into darkness: *19th Whole* / Whip whop: *Sparks, Melvin* / Kaleidoscope: *Chandler, Gary* / Stone thing: *Cash, Alvin*
CD CDBGPD 096
Beat Goes Public / Sep '95 / Pinnacle

BHANGRA - EAST 2 WEST
CD MCCD 121
Music Club / Aug '93 / Disc / THE

BHANGRA BEAT
Gora chitta wrang: *Ragga-Blasters* / Umbhi: *Amar* / Nukhe chakhee javana: *Achanak* / Gem song: *DJ Gem* / Tappe: *Achanak* / Ambersaria: *Eshara* / Bhangra paa: *Achanak* / Kina sona: *Achanak* / Ena akian: *Infinity* / Veh sajna: *Vocals Unlimited* / Yaada: *Amar* / Boliyan: *Anakhi* / Westworld: *East West Connection* / Mirza (Here I come junglist): *Punjabi MC*
CD SUMCD 4125
Sound & Media / Jun '97 / Sound & Media

BHANGRA NOW
Soniyae ni Soniaye: *Shoring* / Gurdh nalo ishq mitah: *Azaad* / Rail Gaddi / Jago aye: *Premi* / Ik pathli jehi mutyaar: *Sahotas* / Saun Rabdi Mauj Lag Javey: *Kapoor, Mahendra* / Paliey Punjean Waliey: *Premi* / Sanu Roki Na Kar: *Sidhu, Amarjit* / Giddh wich nachdi de: *Manak, Kuldip* / Kar Gai Jat Sharabi: *Azaad* / Giddha Penda / Bhangra rap: *Sidhu, Amarjit*
CD BHANGRA 2CD
Multitone / Apr '88 / BMG

BHANGRA POWER
Bhangra Paa Ni...: *Sidhu, Amarjit* / Bhabi gal na kari: *Kapoor, Mahendra* / Sachi Muchi: *Sachi Muchi* / Ek Sohni Jahe Mutiyear: *Paaras* / Aa Kudiye: *DCS* / Yaar pooch de yaaran nu / Nachdi di gooth khulgaye: *Premi* / Tere husan di gal: *Azaad* / Akh mar ghider vich: *Sahotas* / O mere yaaro: *Paaras* / Giddhe Wich Nach Patia: *Sachi Muchi* / Nachdi pitho da: *Premi*
CD BHANGRA 1CD
Multitone / Apr '88 / BMG

BHANGRA TOP TEN VOL.12
CD CDSR 016
Star / Aug '90 / Pinnacle / Stern's

BHANGRA WEDDING SONGS
CD BHANGRA 3CD
Multitone / Aug '88 / BMG

BIG BAD BLUES (25 Sun Blues Classics)
Before long: *Jimmy & Walter* / We all gotta go sometime: *Louis, Joe Hill* / Bear cat: *Thomas, Rufus* / Carry my business on: *Bolnes, Houston* / Baby I'm coming home: *Booker, Charlie* / Juiced: *Love, Billy* / My real gone rocket: *Brenston, Jackie* / Greyhound blues: *Hunt, D.A.* / Wolf call boogie: *Hot Shot Love* / Prison bound blues: *Nix, Willie* / Blues train: *Randolph, Tot* / Mystery train: *Parker, Junior & The Blue Flames* / Beggin' my baby: *Little Milton* / Red hot: *Emerson, Billy 'The Kid'* / Cotton crop blues: *Cotton, James* / I'm gonna murder my baby: *Hare, Pat* / Rattlesnakin' mama: *Stewart, William* / Tiger man: *Vinson, Mose* / Gonna leave you baby: *Lewis, Sammy & Willie Johnson* / Cool down mama: *Hunter, Long John* / Come back home: *Howlin' Wolf* / Come back baby: *Dr. Ross* / I feel so worried: *Lewis, Sammy & Willie Johnson* / Let's get high: *Gordon, Rosco* / Ain't that right: *Snow, Eddie*
CD CPCD 8100
Charly / Jun '95 / Koch
CD CPCD 8272
Charly / Apr '97 / Koch

BIG BAND BASH (2CD Set)
CD Set CDB 1209
Giants Of Jazz / Apr '92 / Cadillac / Jazz Music / Target/BMG

BIG BAND BLUES
Loose wig: *Hampton, Lionel Orchestra* / Things ain't what they used to be: *Ellington, Duke Orchestra* / Lonesome lover blues: *Eckstine, Billy & His Orchestra* / Uptown blues: *Lunceford, Jimmie Orchestra* / Big Jim blues: *Kirk, Andy & His Twelve Clouds of Joy* / Deep in the blues: *Krupa, Gene & His Orchestra* / Sobbin' blues: *Berigan, Bunny & His Orchestra* / Gulf coast blues: *Barnet, Charlie Orchestra* / Feet draggin' blues: *James, Harry Orchestra* / Sent for you yesterday: *Goodman, Benny & His Orchestra* / Swingin' the blues: *Basie, Count & His Orchestra* / Gin mill blues: *Crosby, Bob & His Orchestra* / My favourite blues: *Carter, Benny & His Orchestra* / Sepian bounce: *McShann, Jay & his Orchestra* / Little jazz boogie: *Eldridge, Roy Orchestra* / St. James Infirmary: *Shaw, Artie Orchestra* / Basin Street blues: *Teagarden, Jack Orchestra* / Blue garden blues: *Williams, Cootie & His Orchestra* / Down your alley blues: *Ellington, Duke* / Blowin' up a storm: *Herman, Woody & His Orchestra*
CD 304502
Hallmark / Jun '97 / Carlton

BIG BAND BOOGIE 1939-1942
CD RACD 7107
Aerospace / May '96 / Jazz Music / Montpellier

BIG BAND BOX (3CD Set)
CD Set TBXCD 512
TrueTrax / Jan '96 / THE

BIG BAND BOX (2CD Set)
CD Set PBXCD 512
Pulse / Nov '96 / BMG

BIG BAND CLASSICS
In the mood: *Miller, Glenn* / Little brown jug: *Miller, Glenn* / American patrol: *Miller, Glenn* / Moonlight serenade: *Miller, Glenn* / Tuxedo junction: *Miller, Glenn* / Pennsylvania 6-5000: *Miller, Glenn* / String of pearls: *Miller, Glenn* / Take the 'A' train: *Ellington, Duke* / Perdido: *Ellington, Duke* / Creole love call: *Ellington, Duke* / Black and tan fantasy: *Ellington, Duke* / Mood indigo: *Ellington, Duke* / Caravan: *Ellington, Duke* / Solitude: *Ellington, Duke* / Stompin' at the Savoy: *Goodman, Benny* / Avalon: *Goodman, Benny* / King Porter stomp: *Goodman, Benny* / Moonglow: *Goodman, Benny* / One o' clock jump: *Goodman, Benny* / And the angels sing: *Goodman, Benny* / Sing sing sing: *Goodman, Benny* / Pinetop's boogie: *Dorsey, Tommy* / Night and day: *Dorsey, Tommy* / After you've gone: *Dorsey, Tommy* / Song of India: *Dorsey, Tommy* / Blue skies: *Dorsey, Tommy* / I'm getting sentimental over you: *Dorsey, Tommy* / Marie: *Dorsey, Tommy*
CD KAZCD 106
Kaz / Nov '89 / BMG

BIG BAND CLASSICS
CD Set DCDCD 212
Castle / Jan '96 / BMG

BIG BAND CLASSICS VOL.2
CD KAZCD 107
Kaz / Feb '92 / BMG

BIG BAND COLLECTION (2CD Set)
CD Set DEMPCD 011
Emporio / Mar '96 / Disc

BIG BAND ERA (4CD Set)
CD Set CDDIG 15
Charly / Jun '95 / Koch

BIG BAND ERA VOL.1
CD MICH 5601 CD
Hindsight / Sep '92 / Jazz Music / Target/ BMG

BIG BAND ERA VOL.10
CD MICH 5610 CD
Hindsight / Sep '92 / Jazz Music / Target/ BMG

BIG BAND ERA VOL.2
CD MICH 5602 CD
Hindsight / Sep '92 / Jazz Music / Target/ BMG
CD CDB 103
Giants Of Jazz / Jan '96 / Cadillac / Jazz Music / Target/BMG

BIG BAND ERA VOL.3
CD MICH 5603 CD
Hindsight / Sep '92 / Jazz Music / Target/ BMG

BIG BAND ERA VOL.4
CD MICH 5604 CD
Hindsight / Sep '92 / Jazz Music / Target/ BMG

BIG BAND ERA VOL.5
CD MICH 5605 CD
Hindsight / Sep '92 / Jazz Music / Target/ BMG

BIG BAND ERA VOL.6
CD MICH 5606 CD
Hindsight / Sep '92 / Jazz Music / Target/ BMG

BIG BAND ERA VOL.7
CD MICH 5607 CD
Hindsight / Sep '92 / Jazz Music / Target/ BMG

BIG BAND ERA VOL.8
CD MICH 5608 CD
Hindsight / Sep '92 / Jazz Music / Target/ BMG

BIG BAND ERA VOL.9
CD MICH 5609 CD
Hindsight / Sep '92 / Jazz Music / Target/ BMG

BIG BAND FAVOURITES (3CD Set)
Kick off: *Parnell, Jack* / Skin deep: *Parnell, Jack* / Champ: *Parnell, Jack* / When Yuba plays the rumba: *Parnell, Jack* / Love and marriage: *Parnell, Jack* / When the saints go marching in: *Parnell, Jack* / Tender trap: *Watt, Tommy & Orchestra* / Apple for the teacher: *Watt, Tommy & Orchestra* / Crumpets for the Count: *Watt, Tommy & Orchestra* / Overdrive: *Watt, Tommy & Orchestra* / Sugar: *Watt, Tommy & Orchestra* / Won't you come home Bill Bailey: *Watt, Tommy & Orchestra* / Easy Street: *Watt, Tommy & Orchestra* / Goin' to the County Fair: *Watt, Tommy & Orchestra* / Rock bottom: *Watt, Tommy & Orchestra* / Charmaine: *May, Billy* / Mad about the boy: *May, Billy* / Always: *May, Billy* / Air express: *MacKintosh, Ken* / Crew cut: *MacKintosh, Ken* / Creep: *MacKintosh, Ken* / Creeping Tom: *MacKintosh, Ken* / Riot in Cell Block II: *MacKintosh, Ken* / Monster: *MacKintosh, Ken* / Wembley Stadium: *MacKintosh, Ken* / Hampden Park: *MacKintosh, Ken* / Misty: *MacKintosh, Ken* / Black velvet: *MacKintosh, Ken* / Woodchoppers ball: *Watt, Tommy & The Forty Two Big Band* / Tuxedo Junction: *Watt, Tommy & The Forty Two Big Band* / Cobblers song: *Ainsworth, Alyn* / Bedtime for drums: *Ainsworth, Alyn* / When the guards are on parade: *Ainsworth, Alyn* / Intermission riff: *Kenton, Stan* / Fascinating rhythm: *Kenton, Stan* / How high the moon: *Kenton, Stan* / Comin' thro' the Rye: *Geraldo* / I only have eyes for you: *Geraldo* / One o'clock jump: *Loss, Joe* / Skyliner: *Loss, Joe* / Take the 'A' train: *Loss, Joe* / I wonder what's become of Sally: *Anthony, Ray* / Columbia, the gem of the ocean: *Anthony, Ray* / Rockin' through Dixie: *Anthony, Ray* / Washington whirligig: *Rabin, Oscar & His Band with Harry Davis* / Painted rhythm: *Rabin, Oscar & His Band with Harry Davis* / Basin Street blues: *Rabin, Oscar & His Band with Harry Davis* / Crazy bear: *Squadronaires*
CD Set CDTRBOX 160
Trio / Sep '95 / EMI

BIG BAND JAZZ - TULSA TO HARLEM
CD DD 439
Delmark / Mar '89 / ADA / Cadillac / CM / Direct / Hot Shot

BIG BAND JUMP
CD VN 163
Viper's Nest / Mar '96 / ADA / Cadillac / Direct / Jazz Music

BIG BAND LATIN
Christopher Columbus: *Machito & His Afro-Cubans* / Un conga me dio la lettra: *Mendoza, Celeste* / La reina: *Morales, Noro* / Partio y pelao: *Orquesta Oriental* / Que te parece cholito: *Campo, Pupi* / Memoria a Beny More: *Orquesta Oriental* / Cha cha cha flamenco: *Valle, Joe Y Su Orquesta* / Dispierta Emilia: *Orquesta Riverside* / Gozanda la salve: *Cotto, Joe Y Su Orqesta* / Echa pa' aca: *Morales, Noro* / Mambo-scope: *Machito & His Afro-Cubans* / TNT: *Grand, Rene* / El eco y el carretero: *Cruz, Celia & Rene Hernandez* / El agua del pon pon: *Orquesta Riverside* / Pomme la mano: *Mendoza, Celeste* / Paraiso sonado: *Valle, Joe Y Su Orquesta* / Undecided: *Puente, Tito* / La culpa tiene el gallo: *Cotto, Joe Y Su Orqesta* / How high the moon: *Campo, Pupi* / Piel canela: *Cruz, Celia & Rene Hernandez*
CD CDHOT 611
Charly / Sep '96 / Koch

BIG BAND SELECTION, THE (3CD Set)
In the mood: *Miller, Glenn* / Temptation: *Shaw, Artie* / Tea for two: *Armstrong, Louis* / September song: *Brown, Les* / Blowing up a storm: *Herman, Woody* / One o'clock jump: *Goodman, Benny* / Take the 'A' train: *Ellington, Duke* / Basie boogie: *Basie, Count* / Imagination: *Dorsey, Jimmy* / Cherokee: *Barnet, Charlie* / Songs of India: *Dorsey, Tommy* / Little brown jug: *Dorsey, Tommy* / Moon glow: *Dorsey, Tommy* / Stompin' at the Savoy: *Armstrong, Louis* / Love me or leave me: *Brown, Les* / Caldonia: *Herman, Woody* / Sing sing sing: *Goodman, Benny* / Mooche: *Ellington, Duke* / April in Paris: *Ellington, Duke* / Nightmare: *Shaw, Artie* / Lover: *Armstrong, Louis* / Nutcracker suite: *Brown, Les* / Jersey bounce: *Goodman, Benny* / Caravan: *Ellington, Duke* / Lester leaps in: *Basie, Count* / Nearness of you: *Dorsey, Jimmy* / Skyliner: *Barnet, Charlie* / On the sunny side of the street: *Dorsey, Tommy* / Chattanooga choo choo: *Miller, Glenn* / Donkey serenade: *Shaw, Artie* / Jeepers creepers: *Armstrong, Louis* / How about you: *Brown, Les* / Northwest passage: *Herman, Woody* / Frankie and Johnny: *Goodman, Benny* / Pretty woman: *Ellington, Duke* / Moonlight serenade: *Miller, Glenn* / Stardust: *Shaw, Artie* / C'est si bon: *Armstrong, Louis* / It's all right with me: *Brown, Les* / Early autumn: *Herman, Woody* / There's a small hotel: *Herman, Woody* / I'll never be the same: *Krupa, Gene* / Goin' to Chicago: *Krupa, Gene* / Just you, just me: *Krupa, Gene* / Good for nothin' Joe: *Barnet, Charlie* / This love of mine: *Dorsey, Tommy* / Pennsylvania 6-5000: *Miller, Glenn* / Frenesi: *Shaw, Artie* / Tiger rag: *Armstrong, Louis* / Cabin in the sky: *Brown, Les* / After glow: *Herman, Woody* / Get happy: *Goodman, Benny* / Uptown blues: *Barnet, Charlie* / All the things you are: *Barnet, Charlie* / Blue and sentimental: *Basie, Count* / It started all over again: *Dorsey, Tommy* / Sleepy lagoon: *Dorsey, Tommy* / That old black magic: *Miller, Glenn* / Blues in the night: *Shaw, Artie* / When the saints go marching in: *Armstrong, Louis* / Sentimental journey: *Brown, Les* / Bijou: *Herman, Woody* / Stompin' at the Savoy: *Goodman, Benny* / Do nothin' 'til you hear from me: *Ellington, Duke* / Red bank boogie: *Basie, Count* / Fools rush in: *Dorsey, Jimmy* / East side, West side: *Barnet, Charlie* / Marie: *Dorsey, Tommy* / Tuxedo junction: *Miller, Glenn* / I can't get started (with you): *Miller, Glenn* / Ain't misbehavin': *Miller, Glenn* / I'm forever blowing bubbles: *Brown, Les* / At the woodchoppers' ball: *Herman, Woody* / Down south camp meeting: *Goodman, Benny* / Perdido: *Ellington, Duke* / I've got rhythm: *Dorsey, Jimmy* / Jumpin' at the woodside: *Basie, Count* / Taking a chance on love: *Dorsey, Tommy* / Trumpet blues: *James, Harry*
CD Set TFP 007
Tring / Nov '92 / Tring

BIG BAND SOUND VOL.1, THE
Jeepers creepers: *Armstrong, Louis* / Does your heart beat for me: *Morgan, Russ* / Tiger rag: *Dorsey, Jimmy* / Cherokee: *Barnet, Charlie* / Magenta haze: *Ellington, Duke* / (In) a shanty in old Shanty Town: *Long, Johnny* / Sophisticated lady: *Ellington, Duke* / Harlem nocturne: *Barnet, Charlie* / Northwest passage: *Herman, Woody* / Let's dance: *Goodman, Benny* / Begin the beguine: *Shaw, Artie* / So rare: *Dorsey, Jimmy* / Night and day: *Shaw, Artie* / Oh Johnny: *Fitzgerald, Ella & Chick Webb* / Opus one: *Dorsey, Tommy* / One o'clock jump: *Basie, Count* / C'est si bon: *Armstrong, Louis* / (Back home again in) Indiana: *Ellington, Duke* / When the saints go marching in: *Armstrong, Louis* / Woodchopper's ball: *Herman, Woody* / Summit ridge drive: *Pastor, Tony* / They can't take that...: *Basie, Count*
CD GRF 012
Tring / '93 / Tring

BIG BAND SOUND VOL.2, THE
Pompton turnpike: *Barnet, Charlie* / What is this thing called love: *Shaw, Artie* / Ain't misbehavin': *Ellington, Duke* / Take the 'A' train: *Ellington, Duke* / Frenesi: *Pastor, Tony* / My heart belongs to dad: *Shaw, Artie* / Count steps in: *Basie, Count* / Sultry sunset: *Ellington, Duke* / Dipsy doodle: *Clinton, Larry* / I want the waiter (with the water): *Webb, Chick* / Flat foot floogie: *Basie, Count* / St. Louis blues: *Dorsey, Jimmy* / Skyliner: *Barnet, Charlie* / Bijou: *Herman, Woody* / Mame: *Armstrong, Louis* / Tip toe topic: *Ellington, Duke* / Old rocking chair: *Armstrong, Louis* / Caldonia: *Herman, Woody* / Margie: *Lunceford, Jimmie* / I'm just wild about Harry: *Dorsey, Jimmy* / Just a gigolo: *Armstrong, Louis* / Body and soul: *Armstrong, Louis* / Linger awhile: *Morgan, Russ*
CD GRF 013
Tring / '93 / Tring

BIG BAND SOUND, THE
April in Paris: *Miller, Glenn* / Begin the beguine: *Shaw, Artie* / Oh Johnny, oh Johnny Oh: *Webb, Chick & Ella Fitzgerald* / Does your heart beat for me: *Morgan, Russ* / In a shanty in old Shanty Town: *Long, Johnny* / Harlem nocturne: *Barnet, Charlie* / North West passage: *Herman, Woody* / Let's dance: *Goodman, Benny* / So rare: *Dorsey, Jimmy* / Opus one: *Dorsey, Tommy* / Indi-

ana: *Ellington, Duke* / Something new: *Basie, Count* / Love me or leave me: *Day, Doris & Les Brown* / I'll never be the same: *Krupa, Gene* / Dipsy doodle: *Clinton, Larry* / Margie: *Lunceford, Jimmie* / Night and day: *Shaw, Artie* / Count steps in: *Basie, Count* / Sultry sunset: *Ellington, Duke*
CD ______ **QED 168**
Tring / Nov '96 / Tring

BIG BAND, THE
CD ______ **CD 56032**
Jazz Roots / Nov '94 / Target/BMG

BIG BANDS
Dragnet: *Anthony, Ray* / Early autumn: *Herman, Woody* / Satin doll: *Ellington, Duke* / Creep: *MacKintosh, Ken* / Brother John: *Riddle, Nelson* / September song: *Kenton, Stan* / Man with golden arm: *May, Billy* / Don't be that way: *Goodman, Benny* / All the things you are: *Barnet, Charlie* / No name jive: *Gray, Glen & The Casa Loma Orchestra* / Staccato's theme: *Bernstein, Elmer* / Sleepy lagoon: *James, Harry* / Younger than springtime: *Brown, Les* / Up a lazy river: *Zentner, Si* / Experiements with mice: *Dankworth, John* / Mama's talking soft: *Basie, Count* / Once around: *Jones, Thad & Mel Lewis* / Nightmare: *Shaw, Artie* / Midnight sleighride: *Sauter-Finegan Orchestra* / Diabolus: *Rich, Buddy*
CD ______ **CDMFP 6164**
Music For Pleasure / May '95 / EMI

BIG BANDS 1945
CD ______ **JZCD 355**
Suisa / Oct '93 / Jazz Music / THE

BIG BANDS OF THE SWINGING YEARS
CD ______ **CD 104**
Timeless Treasures / Oct '94 / THE

BIG BANDS OF THE SWINGING YEARS
CD ______ **TCD 1035**
Tradition / Nov '96 / ADA / Vital

BIG BEAT ELITE (2CD Set)
CD Set ______ **CERBAD 3**
Lacerba / Jun '97 / 3mv/Sony

BIG BEATS
Intro: *Plastic Scene* / Underground gets deep: *Unsung Heroes* / Hitman 2/Love song for a hitman: *Funky Monkey* / We're not playing God: *Mellowtrons* / Red: *Mother Nature's Cloud & Shower Show* / Bulldozer: *Moog* / Voice: *Van Cleef, Lee* / I say: *From A Dozen* / Silent partner: *Red Myers* / Get yourself organised: *Headrillaz* / Buss: *Puff* / This is the end: *Mr. Dan*
CD ______ **SPECCD 502**
Dust II Dust / May '97 / 3mv/Sony / Mo's Music Machine / Prime / SRD

BIG BLUES - BLUES MUSIC FOR KIDS
Flying lesson / Zip a dee doo dah / Skip to my blues / Candy store blues / Pancake man / Late for school blues / Pick a bale o' cotton / Funky bluesy ABC's / Rainy day blues / Waggy tailed dog / Fishin' blues / There wouldn't be a me
CD ______ **R 272534**
Music For Little People / Nov '96 / Direct

BIG BLUNTS VOL.1 (12 Smokin' Reggae Hits)
Under mi sleng teng: *Smith, Wayne* / Chalice in the palace: *U-Roy* / Herbman smuggling: *Yellowman & Fathead* / Jamaica weed: *Lone Ranger* / Legalize the herb: *Ninjaman* / One draw: *Marley, Rita* / Under mi sleng teng: *Smith, Wayne* / Herbsman hustling: *Minott, Sugar* / Under mi sensi: *Levy, Barrington* / Herb: *Tony Rebel* / Pass the tu-sheng-peng: *Paul, Frankie* / Pass the kutchie: *Mighty Diamonds*
CD ______ **TBCD 1077**
Tommy Boy / Mar '97 / RTM/Disc

BIG BLUNTS VOL.2
CD ______ **TBCD 1153**
Tommy Boy / Nov '96 / RTM/Disc

BIG BLUNTS VOL.3
CD ______ **TBCD 1167**
Tommy Boy / Nov '96 / RTM/Disc

BIG CHILL EYELID MOVIES, THE
Just close your eyes and listen: *Chameleon* / Sunchemical: *O Yuki Conjugate* / Pickyparkdickybods: *Solid Doctor* / P Phase ST: *Dun Tractor* / Aloo Astralasia: *Dun Tractor* / Harsh truth part one: *Zurich* / Respondez s'il vous plait: *Howie B* / Don: *Boymerang* / Endlessly downward: *Beat System* / Can't deal with this (kid loops mix): *Cool Breeze* / Amber: *T-Power* / Timber: *Grantby* / Long road: *Funki Porcini*
CD ______ **HEADZCD 001**
Global Headz / May '96 / Kudos / Vital

BIG CHILL PRESENTS PIPEDREAMS
CD ______ **CDRAID 537**
Rumour / Sep '97 / 3mv/Sony / Mo's Music Machine / Pinnacle

BIG CHILL VIBES COLLECTION VOL.1, THE
Mbira jam: *Another Fine Day* / Cloud: *Mr. Psyche* / Optimystic: *Morpha* / Stranger: *Earthtribe* / Sure as not: *Afro Celt Sound System* / Snow: *Sounds From The Ground* / Botswana Ben: *Diversity Of Life* / Jazz Kirk: *Knights Of The Occasional Table* / Boy from West Bronx: *Future 3* / Night time: *Mr. Scruff* / Oddments 3 & 4: *Toona* / Lite my fire: *Gentle People* / Spacefire: *Gentle People*
CD ______ **HEADZCD 002**
Global Headz / Apr '97 / Kudos / Vital

BIG CITY BLUES EAST COAST STYLE
If the blues were whiskey: *Johnson, Luther 'Guitar Junior'* / Down in Virginia: *Holmes Brothers* / Full court press: *Magic Dick & Jay Geils* / That will never do: *Roomful Of Blues* / Eddie's gospel groove: *Earl, Ronnie & The Broadcasters* / What can I do (somebody tell me): *Little Buster & The Soul Brothers* / Better left unsaid: *Willson, Michelle* / Gimme a break: *Levy, Ron* / Life is a ballgame: *Persuasions*
CD ______ **EDCD 7018**
Easydisc / Mar '97 / Direct

BIG CITY BLUES WEST COAST STYLE
Working man: *Fulson, Lowell* / Boogie on down: *McCracklin, Jimmy* / This is the thanks I get: *Lynn, Barbara* / Goin' out West: *Davis, Larry* / Don't burn down LA: *Wilson, Smokey* / Rebop jump: *Nocturne, Johnny* / My last goodbye: *Hawkins, Ted* / Can't stop these teardrops: *Strehli, Angela* / Help the bear: *McCracklin, Jimmy & Smokey Wilson/Larry Davis* / Go down sunshine: *Nelson, Tracy*
CD ______ **EDCD 7017**
Easydisc / Mar '97 / Direct

BIG CITY SOUL VOL.1
Looking for you: *Mimms, Garnet* / Love is not a game: *Soul, Sam E* / My Dear heart: *Robinson, Shawn* / Mend my broken heart: *St. John, Rose & The Wonderettes* / Hold on: *O'Jays* / Ready, willing and able: *Holiday, Jimmy & Clydie King* / Lot of love: *Banks, Homer* / Hooked by love: *Banks, Homer* / I lost a true love: *Wagner, Danny & The Kindred Soul* / Then came heart break: *Jive Five* / Strange neighbourhood: *McDaniels, Gene* / Stick close: *Brown, Estelle* / Be careful girl: *Turner, Betty* / I'll never forget you: *O'Jays* / It's what's underneath that counts: *Jackson, June* / Working on your case: *O'Jays* / My heart is in danger: *Ray, Alder* / Honest to goodness: *Diplomats* / Are you trying to get rid of me baby: *Crystals* / Breakaway (part 1): *Karman, Steve* / I only get this feeling: *Irwin, Dee* / Livin' above your head: *Jay & The Americans* / Don't: *Josie, Marva* / It's a sad thing: *Pollard, Ray* / Walk with a winner: *McDaniels, Gene* / Drifter: *Pollard, Ray* / It'll never be over for me: *Yuro, Timi*
CD ______ **GSCD 042**
Goldmine / Jul '94 / Vital

BIG CITY SOUL VOL.2
Stop and think it over: *Mimms, Garnet* / I love you baby: *Ambers* / Pretty little face: *Four Hi's* / You can split: *Youngblood Smith* / What would I do: *Superiors* / Living a lie: *High Keys* / Stop and take a look at yourself: *Shalimars* / Take a step in my direction: *Little Eva* / Real jive guy: *Ahres, Dajh* / Walkin' the duck: *Triumphs* / I can't make it without you baby: *Banks, Bessie* / Just a fool: *Gainey, Jerry* / I watched you slowly slip away: *Guyton, Howard* / Mighty good way: *Banks, Robert* / Right direction: *Ward, Clara* / My heart belongs to you: *Pickett, Wilson* / I don't want to lose your love: *Woods, Billy* / Love I give: *Murray, Louise* / (You'd better) Straighten up and fly right: *Bryant, Terry* / Born to please: *Prince Harold* / Baby I love you: *Tate, Howard* / I'm a practical guy: *Gardner, Don* / Backfield in motion: *Poindexter Brothers* / I don't need no doctor: *Ashford, Nick* / Can't deny the hurt: *Rakes, Pal & The Prophets* / Picture me gone: *Brooks, Diane* / Let's take a chance: *High Keys* / Let me be your boy: *Pickett, Wilson*
CD ______ **GSCD 044**
Goldmine / Sep '94 / Vital

BIG CITY SOUL VOL.3
I'm alive with the love feeling: *Turner, Spyder* / Street talk: *Tymes* / To the ends of the earth: *Middleton, Tony* / I'm gonna change: *Velours* / (Love) You can't just walk away: *Courtney, Dean* / I can't make it anymore: *Turner, Spyder* / Key to my happiness: *Charades* / I got what you need: *Weston, Kim* / My heart took a licking: *Jackson, Millie* / Everything you always wanted to know about love: *Roberts, Lou* / I'm gonna hold on (to your love): *Mars, Marlina* / Can't make it without you: *Superiors* / At the top of the stairs: *Formations* / Watch out girl: *Embers* / You fooled me: *Roberts, Lou & The Marks* / You're just the kind of guy: *Weston, Kim* / We got togetherness: *Jewels* / What would I do: *Tymes* / Cry your eyes out: *Cambridge, Dottie* / Wanting you: *Stevens, April* / You just don't know: *Broadways* / Weeping cup: *Charades* / Betcha can't change my mind: *Courtney, Dean* / You never know: *Nash, Johnny* / Fool that I am: *Solitaires* / You can count on me: *Hamilton, Roy* / Panic is on: *Hamilton, Roy*
CD ______ **GSCD 047**
Goldmine / Jan '95 / Vital

BIG CITY SOUL VOL.4 (2CD Set)
Fell in love with you baby: *Charts* / Wait til I give the signal: *Shirelles* / When it comes to my baby: *Mislap, Ronnie* / Not my girl: *Platters* / You can't fight love: *Shirley & Jessie* / Call on Billy: *Soul, Billy T.* / I feel better: *Bruce, Alan* / To get your love back: *Dodds, Nella* / Bricks, broken bottles and sticks: *Parish, Dean* / Never in a million years: *Honey Bees* / Glamour girls: *Hopkins, Harold* / How much pressure (do you think I can stand): *Robinson, Roscoe* / Mr. Creator: *Candy & The Kisses* / Change: *Eady, Ernestine* / Think twice before you walk away: *Porgy & The Monarchs* / Never love a robin: *Foxx, Inez & Charlie* / Tonight I'm gonna see my baby: *Hughes, Freddie* / I've got to be strong: *Jackson, Chuck* / Three rooms: *Freeman, Audrey* / Jerkin' time: *Diplomats* / Ain't that the truth: *Troy, J B* / If I'm hurt you'll feel the pain: *Barbara & Brenda* / You lie so well: *Knight, Marie* / I've got love for you: *Intruders* / First date: *Dodds, Nella* / Woman: *Esquires* / Hey girl: *Porgy & The Monarchs* / You've got my love: *Wells, Donnie* / Upset my heart (got me upset): *Clay, Judy* / Lover: *Hunt, Tommy* / Tonight's the night: *Candy & The Kisses* / Since you've been gone: *Anglos* / Magic touch: *Moore, Melba* / Try some soul: *Crossen, Ray* / You could be my remedy: *Shirelles* / No stranger to love: *Foxx, Inez & Charlie* / In the long run: *Blandon, Curtis* / Live on: *Troy, J B* / Hand it over: *Wand Orchestra* / I've got to find someone to love: *Fisher, Jerry & The Nightbeats* / Honey boy: *Dodds, Nella* / There goes a forgotten man: *Radcliffe, Jimmy* / That's no way to treat a girl: *Knight, Marie* / Fear of losing you: *Platters* / Just one more time: *Barnes, J.J.* / Silencer: *Jackson, Chuck* / There's still a tomorrow: *Diplomats* / Are you trying to get rid of me baby: *Candy & The Kisses* / Words can never tell it: *Hunt, Tommy* / Nobody made you love me: *Charts* / Keep a hold on me: *Porgy & The Monarchs* / Doesn't it ring a bell: *Platters* / Way to a woman's heart: *Soul, Billy T.* / All the way from heaven: *Chancellors* / Nobody knows: *Williams, Maurice* / Anything you do is right: *Brown, Maxine* / No doubt about it: *Shirelles* / Your kind of lovin: *Clay, Judy* / My little plaything: *Watts, Glen* / If I had you: *Big Maybelle*
CD Set ______ **GSCD 065**
Goldmine / Oct '95 / Vital

BIG COUNTRY ALBUM (40 Country Music Greats/2CD Set)
CD Set ______ **DEMPCD 015**
Emporio / Mar '96 / Disc

BIG COUNTRY LINE DANCE PARTY
CD ______ **CDTIV 620**
Scotdisc / Dec '96 / Conifer/BMG / Duncans / Ross

BIG DANCE HITS 1992
Ebeneezer Goode: *Shamen* / Rhythm is a dancer: *Snap* / Jump: *Kriss Kross* / Rock your baby: *KWS* / Don't talk just kiss: *Right Said Fred* / Are you ready to fly: *Rozalla* / I don't care: *Shakespears Sister* / Baker Street: *Undercover* / Expression: *Salt n' Pepa* / I feel love: *Messiah* / Too funky: *Michael, George* / Twilight zone: *2 Unlimited* / MASH (Suicide is painless): *Manic Street Preachers* / Blue room: *Orb* / Reality used to be a friend of mine: *PM Dawn* / I'm doing fine now: *Pasadenas* / It only takes a minute: *Take That* / Humpin' around: *Brown, Bobby* / Mutations (Chime): *Orbital* / Love makes the world go round: *Don-E* / I'm gonna get you: *Bizarre Inc.* / It's a fine day: *Opus III* / Hypnotic st8: *Altern 8* / Dream come true: *Brand New Heavies* / Make it on my own: *Limerick, Alison* / Love U more: *Sunscreem* / Everybody in the place: *Prodigy* / Crucified: *Army Of Lovers* / Kings of the ring: *Du Berry, Steve & Born 2 B* / Different strokes: *Isotonik*
CD ______ **AHLCD 4**
Hit / Nov '92 / Grapevine/PolyGram

BIG DIXIE
CD ______ **TCD 1036**
Tradition / Nov '96 / ADA / Vital

BIG FIX, THE
CD ______ **ALLIED 82CD**
Allied / May '97 / Cargo / Greyhound / Plastic Head

BIG FOLK AND PROTEST HITS OF THE 60'S
Walk right in / Puff the magic dragon / Go tell it on the mountain / If I had a hammer / Tom Dooley / Michael / House of the rising sun / Blowin' in the wind / Cotton fields / Where have all the flowers gone / San Francisco Bay blues / Little boxes / Freight train / Subterranean homesick blues / Green green / Catch the wind / Times they are a changin'
CD ______ **306032**
Hallmark / Jan '97 / Carlton

BIG HIT MIX, THE
Mysterious girl: *Andre, Peter* / Get down (You're the one for me): *Backstreet Boys* / Three lions: *Baddiel, David & Frank Skinner* / Lifted: *Lighthouse Family* / I got 5 on it: *Luniz* / Craz chance: *Kavana* / Love me for a reason: *Boyzone* / Light of life: *Louise* / Could it be forever: *Gemini* / Blue moon: *Alford, John* / Don't stop movin': *Livin' Joy* / Can't help it: *Happy Clappers* / Missing: *Everything But The Girl* / Thunder: *East 17* / What do I do now: *Sleeper* / Female of the species: *Space* / Stupid girl: *Garbage* / I wanna be a hippy: *Technohead* / Move move move (The Red Tribe): *Manchester Utd FC* / Good day: *Maguire, Sean*
CD ______ **VTCD 95**
Virgin / Jun '96 / EMI

BIG IN WIGAN - 20 NORTHERN MAMMOTHS FROM THE WHEEL TO KEELE (A Collection Of Northern Soul Oldies From 1968-1996)
It's a woman's world (you'd better believe it): *Gypsies* / Baby reconsider: *Haywood, Leon* / That's loving you: *Wiggins, Percy* / Sweet sherry: *Barnes, J.J.* / I wanna be (your everything): *Pretenders* / Happy: *Bell, William* / My man, a sweet man: *Jackson, Millie* / Little Miss Soul: *Lovettes* / I'll never fall in love again: *Freeman, Bobby* / Hey sah-lo-ney: *Lane, Mickey Lee* / Till you give: *Patterson, Bobby* / With my love and what you've got: *Wells, Jean* / Mother of shame: *Holloway, Loleatta* / Running away from love: *Mahoney, Skip & The Casuals* / You've come a long way baby: *Flower Shoppe* / Ain't that good enough: *Edwards, John* / You turned my bitter into sweet: *Love, Mary* / Baby I need you: *Lorraine & The Delights* / Can it be me: *Williams, Mel* / Our love will grow: *Showmen*
CD ______ **CDKEND 129**
Kent / Aug '96 / Pinnacle

BIG MIX '97 (2CD Set)
Who do you think you are: *Spice Girls* / Fresh: *Gina G* / Fly like an eagle: *Seal* / Ready or not: *Course* / Horny: *Morrison, Mark* / Don't you love me: *Eternal* / Professional widow: *Amos, Tori* / Dance with me: *Tin Tin Out* / Spinning the wheel: *Michael, George* / Things can only get better: *D:Ream* / Lopez: *808 State* / Nightmare: *Brainbug* / Encore une fois: *Sash* / Tha wildstyle: *DJ Supreme* / Bellissima: *DJ Quicksilver* / Theme from The Professionals: *Johnson, Laurie London Big Band* / Passion: *Amen UK* / Flash: *BBE* / Ain't talkin' 'bout dub: *Apollo 440* / I believe I can fly: *R Kelly* / You might need somebody: *Ama, Shola* / Virtual insanity: *Jamiroquai* / Remember me: *Blueboy* / MFEO: *Kavana* / Bodyshakin': *911* / You got the love: *Source & Candi Staton* / Boss: *Braxtons* / Where can I find love: *Livin' Joy* / Flame: *Crustation* / Absurd: *Fluke* / Say my name: *Zee* / Scared: *Slacker* / Just playin': *JT Playaz* / Rock da house: *Tall Paul* / Groove Bird: *Natural Born Groovers* / Extremis: *Hal & Gillian Anderson* / Come with me: *Qattara*
CD Set ______ **VTDCD 130**
Virgin / Jun '97 / EMI

BIG NOISE: A MAMBO INN COMPILATION
Dub lion (remake): *DJ Food* / Kinna sohna: *Khan, Nusrat Fateh Ali* / Did-funk club: *Khaled, Hadj Ibrahim* / Angelina: *Sweet Talks* / Zing zong: *Kanda Bongo Man* / Ussak ndja: *Tchando* / Mango mangue: *Mambomania* / El swing: *Montanez, Andy* / Elena Elena: *Libre* / Samba de flora: *Airto* / Wack wack: *Young-Holt Trio* / Do what you wanna: *Lewis, Ramsey* / You're the one: *McGriff, Jimmy* / My God can do anything: *Barnes, Luther & The Red Budd Gospel Choir*
CD ______ **HNCD 1382**
Hannibal / Nov '94 / ADA / Vital

BIG ONE, THE
CD ______ **FLIP 30CD**
Burning Heart / Sep '95 / Plastic Head

BIG PEOPLE MUSIC VOL.1
CD ______ **CRCD 56**
Jet Star / Nov '96 / Jet Star

BIG PEOPLE MUSIC VOL.2
CD ______ **CRCD 65**
Charm / Mar '97 / Jet Star

BIG SHIP OLE FUNG REGGAE SKA
CD ______ **GRELCD 242**
Greensleeves / Aug '97 / Jet Star / SRD

BIG SQUEEZE, THE
Johnny Allen's reel/Sporting Nell: *McComiskey, Billy & Sean McGlynn* / Miller of Draughin/Humours of Castlefin: *O'Brien, Paddy* / High reel/Geoghegan's reel: *Burke, Joe* / Maids of Selma/Larry Redican's/Dancing tables: *Keane, James* / Crossing the Sahannon/Lad O'Beirne's reel/Rough road: *Keane, James* / Andy Stewart's reel/Harsh February: *Cunningham, Phil* / Desaunay/Petticoat I bought in Mullingar: *Cunningham, Phil* / Sweeney's reel: *Daly, Jackie* / Bucks of Oranmore: *Burke, Joe* / Spike Island lassies/Humours of Tulla: *McComiskey, Billy* / Strathspey and reel: *O'Brien, Paddy* / La Bastringue: *Daly, Jackie* / Connaught man's rambles/Cat in the corner: *Burke, Joe* / Master Crowley's reels: *Keane, James* / Lament from Eoin Rhua/March of the Gaelic order: *O'Brien, Paddy* / Yellow tinker/Sally Gardens: *McComiskey, Billy* / Tom Fleming's reel/Kitty's wedding/Sean McGuire's reel: *Whelan, John* / Jackson's reel/Jean's reel/Moving cloud: *Cunningham, Phil*
CD ______ **GLCD 1093**
Green Linnet / Nov '90 / ADA / CM / Direct / Highlander / Roots

BIG SURF
Pipeline: *Lively Ones* / Scratch: *Lively Ones* / Misirlou: *Lively Ones* / Surfbeat: *Lively Ones* / High tide: *Lively Ones* / Baja: *Lively Ones* / Torquay: *Lively Ones* / Soul surfer: *Lively Ones* / Rik-a-tik: *Lively Ones* / Church key: *Myers, Dave & The Surftones* / Moment of truth: *Myers, Dave & The Surftones* / Bullwinkle (part 2): *Centurions* / Sano: *Centurions* / Surfin' at Mazatland: *Centurions* /

Body surfin': *Centurions* / Vesuvius: *Centurions* / Latin'ia: *Centurions* / Intoxica: *Centurions* / Steel pier: *Impacts* / Impact: *Impacts* / Blue surf: *Impacts* / Wipeout: *Impacts* / Fort Lauderdale: *Impacts* / Exotic: *Sentinals* / Pipe: *Sentinals* / Latin soul: *Sentinals* / Tor chula: *Sentinals* / Big surf: *Sentinals*
CD ____ **CDCHD 319**
Ace / Aug '91 / Pinnacle

BIG TIMES IN A SMALL TOWN
CD ____ **PH 1155CD**
Philo / Oct '93 / ADA / CM / Direct

BIG TRANCE JESUS HEAD (2CD Set)
CD Set ____ **AOP 54**
Age Of Panik / Jun '97 / Total/BMG

BIG WHEELS OF AZULI (1991-1995)
Bring me love: *Mendez, Andrea* / R U sleeping: *Indo* / Ministry of love: *Romanthony* / Anthem: *Black Shells* / Feeling: *Jasper Street Family* / Place called Heaven: *Tension* / In a fantasy: *Chocolate Fantasy* / Running: *Disco Elements* / Heaven: *KCC & Emile* / Falling from grace: *Romanthony* / Summer groove: *Sensory Elements*
CD ____ **AZNYCD 1**
Azuli / Nov '95 / Amato Disco / Azuli / Mo's Music Machine / Prime / Vital

BIGGEST BAND SPECTACULAR IN THE WORLD (1985 Military Musical Pageant Wembley Stadium/2CD Set)
General salute and opening fanfare / By beat of drum / Light of foot / Pipes and drums / Queen's guards / Massed bands / Royal military band of The Netherlands / War and peace / Finale
CD Set ____ **BNW 9002**
Bandleader / '89 / Conifer/BMG

BIGSHOT MIXES
CD ____ **DBCD 506**
Debut / May '90 / 3mv/Sony / Pinnacle

BIO BLUE (Life And Soul Of Manchester)
CD ____ **BLUCD 1**
2 Blue / Aug '96 / Grapevine/PolyGram

BIONIC DUB
CD ____ **LG 21114**
Lagoon / Aug '95 / Grapevine/PolyGram

BIORHYTHM VOL.1
Take me back (bass head mix): *Rhythmatic* / Mood (optimystic mix): *Symbols & Instruments* / Free: *Kate B* / Emanon: *Rhythm Is Rhythim* / Fall into a trance: *Critical Rhythm* / Self hypnosis: *Nexus 21* / Somebody new: *MK* / Bio rhythms: *C&M Connection* / Indulge: *Howard, Neal* / Don't lead me: *Grey, Paris*
CD ____ **BIOCD 1**
Network / Jul '90 / 3mv/Sony / Pinnacle

BIORHYTHM VOL.2
CD ____ **BIOCD 2**
Network / '92 / 3mv/Sony / Pinnacle

BIRD IN THE BUSH, THE (Traditional Songs Of Love & Lust)
Two magicians / Old man from over the sea / Wanton seed / Gathering rushes in the month of May / Bonnie black hare / Whirly whori / Pretty Polly / Old bachelor / Stonecutter boy / Mower / Bird in the bush / Pegging awl / Mortinmas time / Widow of the Westmorland's daughter
CD ____ **TSCD 479**
Topic / Jun '96 / ADA / CM / Direct

BIRTH OF BE BOP, THE (Wichita-New York 1940-1945/2CD Set)
CD ____ **FA 046**
Fremeaux / Feb '96 / ADA / Discovery

BIRTH OF BE BOP, THE (2CD Set)
Hot mallets: *Hampton, Lionel Orchestra* / Dameron stomp: *Leonard, Harlan & His Rockets* / Pitter panther patter: *Ellington, Duke & Jimmy Blanton* / I never knew: *Young, Lester & Charlie Christian* / Swing to bop: *Christian, Charlie* / Hootie blues: *McShann, Jay & his Orchestra* / Gasser: *Eldridge, Roy Orchestra* / Moose: *Barnet, Charlie Orchestra* / Sometimes I'm happy: *Young, Lester Quartet* / Honeysuckle rose: *Williams, Cootie Sextet* / Woody 'n' you: *Hawkins, Coleman Orchestra* / Disorder at the border: *Hawkins, Coleman Orchestra* / Tiny's tempo: *Grimes, Tiny Quintet* / Red cross: *Grimes, Tiny Quintet* / Flyin' Hawk: *Hawkins, Coleman Quartet* / Blowing the blues away: *Eckstine, Billy & His Orchestra* / Opus X: *Eckstine, Billy & His Orchestra* / Interlude: *Vaughan, Sarah* / East of the sun: *Vaughan, Sarah* / Sometimes for you: *Pettiford, Oscar & His 18 All Stars* / Good bait: *Gillespie, Dizzy All Stars* / Be bop: *Gillespie, Dizzy All Stars* / Night in Tunisia: *Raeburn, Boyd Orchestra* / Groovin' high: *Gillespie, Dizzy Sextet* / Blue 'n' boogie: *Gillespie, Dizzy Sextet* / All the things you are: *Gillespie, Dizzy* / Dizzy atmosphere: *Gillespie, Dizzy* / Riff tide: *Hawkins, Coleman Orchestra* / Lover man: *Vaughan, Sarah* / Salt peanuts: *Gillespie, Dizzy & His All Star Quintet* / Shaw nuff: *Gillespie, Dizzy & His All Star Quintet* / Slam slam blues: *Norvo, Red* / Congo blues: *Norvo, Red* / Good Earth: *Herman, Woody Orchestra* / Super session: *Byas, Don Quartet* / Why not: *Thompson, Lucky All Stars* / Air mail special: *Auld, Georgie & His Orchestra* / Blow Mr. Dexter: *Gordon, Dexter All Stars* / Dexter's minor mad: *Gordon, Dexter All Stars* / Now's the time: *Parker, Charlie Reboppers* / Ko ko: *Parker, Charlie Reboppers* / Slim's jam: *Gaillard, Slim*
CD Set ____ **CPCD 81942**
Charly / Sep '96 / Koch

BIRTH OF SKA, THE
Carry go bring home: *Hinds, Justin & The Dominoes* / River bank: *Brooks, Baba* / Musical communion: *Brooks, Baba* / Feeling fine: *Alphonso, Roland* / Strongarm Sampson: *Hinds, Justin & The Dominoes* / Over the river: *Hinds, Justin & The Dominoes* / Next door neighbour: *Silvera, Owen & Leon & The Skatalite Band* / When I call your name: *Brooks, Baba* / Yeah yeah baby: *Stranger & Patsy/Baba Brooks/Skatalite Band* / Hog in a cocoa: *Skatalite Band* / Musical storeroom: *Anderson, Frank & Skatalite Band* / Corner stone: *Hinds, Justin & The Dominoes*
CD ____ **CDTRL 274**
Trojan / Mar '94 / Direct / Jet Star

BIRTH OF SOUL, THE
You're not the guy for me: *Anderson, Ernestine* / Sound of my man: *Kilgore, Theola* / Hey girl don't bother me: *Tams* / Ain't nothing you can do: *Bland, Bobby* / Pain in my heart: *Redding, Otis* / Cry baby: *Mimms, Garnet & Enchanters* / How can I forget: *Holiday, Jimmy* / You don't have to be a tower of strength: *Lynne, Gloria* / He will break your heart: *Butler, Jerry* / Have fun: *Cole, Ann* / Oh my angel: *Tillman, Bertha* / Something's got a hold on me: *James, Etta* / Daddy rollin' stone: *Martin, Derek* / Mockingbird: *Foxx, Inez & Charlie* / Snap your fingers: *Henderson, Joe* / I'll come running to you: *Cooke, Sam* / Merry go round: *Johnson, Marv* / Goin' out of my head: *Little Anthony & The Imperials* / Hey girl: *Scott, Freddie* / You'll lose a good thing: *Lynn, Barbara* / Part time love: *Taylor, Little Johnny* / I'm qualified: *Hughes, Jimmy* / Any other way: *Bell, William* / She ain't ready: *Barnes, J.J.* / I do: *Marvelows* / Telephone game: *Clark, Claudine* / Mama didn't lie: *Bradley, Jan* / Gypsy woman: *Impressions*
CD ____ **CDKEND 123**
Kent / Apr '96 / Pinnacle

BIRTH OF THE THIRD STREAM
Three little feelings / Poem for brass / All about Rosie / Revelations / Suspensions / Symphony for brass and percussion / Transformation / Pharoah
CD ____ **4851032**
Sony Jazz / Sep '96 / Sony

BITING BACK
CD ____ **WOWCD 35**
Words Of Warning / Jan '94 / SRD / Total/BMG

BITTER & TWISTED (Mrs. Wood & Blu Peter) (2CD Set)
Don't stop: *Mark NRG* / Hybrid oral: *Random Generator* / Smokin' Jesus: *Summer Skool* / Tribal steps: *Kaltenbrunner* / Side on: *Space DJ's* / Phreaks: *Huntemann* / Cachka: *Bulkhead* / Ignition: *Madame Dubois* / Universal spirit: *Freak Force* / Straight forward: *Secret Cinema* / Equilibrum: *Tranquilizer* / File 003tmp: *Gravital Force II* / Trip beat: *Wave Captain* / Secret spice: *Gargano, Pablo* / Mystery: *Code 16* / Automorphism: *RND Technologies* / Darkbag: *Kool World* / Famous: *Rubicon Massacre Ltd.* / Shi du: *Khan, Reysan* / Rhythm state 2: *Prussic Acid Rhythm* / Who's gettin' it: *Naked Ape* / Be silent: *Dr. Mu* / Homecoming: *Troop* / Here is justice: *Judge S* / Magnitude 7: *Sonic Animation* / Limits: *V-Tracks* / Diadora: *Mikerobenics* / Wake up: *Mark NRG* / Starburst: *Razors Edge* / Timerunner: *16C+* / 4 times: *Racoon* / My time is yours: *LSG* / Bruised: *Spira* / Weeping waste: *Renegade Legion*
CD Set ____ **REACTCD 086**
React / Aug '96 / Arabesque / Prime / Vital

BITTER FRUITS
CD ____ **IUKCD 002**
Harthouse / Apr '95 / Mo's Music Machine / Prime / Vital

BIWA AND SHAKUHACHI
CD ____ **C 580059**
Ocora / Jan '95 / ADA / Harmonia Mundi

BLACK & WHITE BLUES
CD Set ____ **MBSCD 431**
Castle / Oct '94 / BMG

BLACK AND BLUE
CD ____ **TJ 050**
That's Jazz / Mar '94 / BMG

BLACK AND BLUES (Sweet Little Angel)
CD ____ **12207**
Laserlight / Jul '93 / Target/BMG

BLACK AND BLUES
CD ____ **VGCD 660510**
Vogue / Oct '93 / BMG

BLACK AND SOUL
CD ____ **12403**
Laserlight / Feb '95 / Target/BMG

BLACK AND TAN CLUB, THE
CD ____ **NAR 060CD**
New Alliance / May '93 / Plastic Head

BLACK AND WHITE BLUES (2CD Set)
John Lee's original boogie: *Hooker, John Lee* / Hoochie coochie man: *Waters, Muddy* / Death letter blues: *House, Son* / Mam don't like me runnin' around: *Williams, Big Joe* / Rollin' and tumblin': *Memphis Slim* / Blues jumped over the rabbit: *Turner, 'Big' Joe* / Stormy monday blues: *Lewis, Smiley* / Shotgun blues: *Hopkins, Lightnin'* / Drop down mama: *McDowell, 'Mississippi' Fred* / Key to the highway: *McGhee, Brownie & Sonny Terry* / Shrewsbury blues: *Ridgley, Tommy* / Mean old world: *Walker, T-Bone* / Drifting blues: *Moore, Johnny B. & Three Blazers* / Trouble blues: *Brown, Charles Trio* / Trian time blues: *Milburn, Amos* / Call operator 210: *Dixon, Floyd* / How many more years: *King, Freddie* / Laughnin' and clownin': *Womack, Bobby* / New boogie chillun: *Thorogood, George* / Dust my broom: *Canned Heat* / Rollin' and tumblin': *Winter, Johnny* / Groundhog blues: *Groundhogs* / Dimples: *Animals* / Shotgun blues: *Dr. Feelgood* / Egg or the hen: *Rockpile* / Got my mojo working: *Manfred Mann* / I'm tore down: *Korner, Alexis* / Mistreated: *Groundhogs* / 3 O'clock blues: *Love Sculpture* / Parchment farm: *Nashville Teens* / Eddie's blues: *Cochran, Eddie* / You shook me: *Beck, Jeff* / Come on in my kitchen: *Miller, Steve* / TV mama: *Canned Heat* / Bluest blues: *Lee, Alvin*
CD Set ____ **CDEM 1624**
EMI / Jul '97 / EMI

BLACK BOX (2CD Set)
CD Set ____ **9010552**
Immediate / Mar '97 / BMG

BLACK BOX OF JAZZ (4CD Set)
CD Set ____ **MBSCD 450**
Castle / Aug '96 / BMG

BLACK, BROWN & REGGAE
CD ____ **D 31516**
Far I / Oct '96 / Jet Star

BLACK DANCE VOL.2
CD ____ **ZYX 550632**
ZYX / Oct '96 / ZYX

BLACK GOLD
CD ____ **HRCD 8047**
Disky / Jul '94 / Disky / THE

BLACK MAGIC
Maybellene: *Berry, Chuck* / Keep a knockin': *Little Richard* / Rockin' Robin: *Day, Bobby* / Lover's question: *McPhatter, Clyde* / Dedicated to the one I love: *Shirelles* / Girl I love: *Benton, Brook* / Tears on my pillow: *Imperials* / You're just too marvellous: *Holiday, Billie* / Please love me forever: *Edwards, Tommy* / All in my mind: *Brown, Maxine* / Sixteen candles: *Crests* / Unforgettable: *Washington, Dinah* / Let the good times roll: *Shirley & Lee* / Misty: *Vaughan, Sarah* / CC rider: *Charles, Ray* / Dance with me Henry: *James, Etta* / Chains of love: *Phillips, Esther* / My way: *Simone, Nina* / Alley oop: *Hollywood Argyles* / Earth angel: *Penguins* / Baby it's you: *Labelle, Patti* / Duke of Earl: *Chandler, Gene*
CD ____ **C5LCD 586**
See For Miles/C5 / Apr '92 / Pinnacle

BLACK OUT
CD ____ **REVXD 166**
Black / Feb '91 / Revolver / Sony

BLACK ROCK/CYBERFUNK/FUTURE BLUES
CD ____ **RCD 10313**
Rykodisc / Oct '94 / ADA / Vital

BLACK ROOTS (From 1970's Funk To Hip Hop)
Payback: *Brown, James* / Sing a simple song: *Sly & The Family Stone* / Slippin' into darkness: *War* / Pusherman: *Mayfield, Curtis* / My thang: *Brown, James* / God made me funky: *Headhunters* / P-funk: *Parliament* / Revolution will not be televised: *Scott-Heron, Gil* / That's the way of the world: *Earth, Wind & Fire* / Rapper's delight: *Sugarhill Gang* / Showdown: *Furious Five & Sugarhill Gang* / Message: *Grandmaster Flash* / Sucker MC's: *Run DMC* / Keep on movin': *Soul II Soul* / Unbelievable: *Notorious BIG* / Can I kick it: *Tribe Called Quest* / Flava in ya ear: *Mack, Craig* / Cream: *Wu Tang Clan*
CD ____ **74321382942**
RCA / Jun '96 / BMG

BLACK SECULAR VOCAL GROUPS VOL.1 (1921-1929)
CD ____ **DOCD 5546**
Document / Jul '97 / ADA / Hot Shot / Jazz Music

BLACK SECULAR VOCAL GROUPS VOL.2 1931-1939
CD ____ **DOCD 5550**
Document / Jul '97 / ADA / Hot Shot / Jazz Music

BLACK TO THE FUTURE VOL.1
CD ____ **DIVCD 02**
Diverse / May '94 / Grapevine/PolyGram

BLACK TOP BAYOU STATE BOOGIE
Make a better world: *King, Earl* / Hey hey baby's gone: *Walker, Philip* / Love at first sight: *August, Lynn* / About my past: *Ridgley, Tommy* / Case of love: *Davis, James 'Thunderbird' & Earl King* / A ma maison: *Simien, Terrance* / Lookin' for that woman: *Thomas, Jesse* / Emmitt Lee: *Fran, Carol* / Second line: *Muldaur, Maria* / Buck's nouvelle jole blon: *Buckwheat Zydeco* / Mama and Papa: *Eaglin, Snooks*
CD ____ **CDBTEL 7005**
Black Top / May '97 / ADA / CM / Direct

BLACK TOP BLUES COSTUME PARTY
CD ____ **BT 1116CD**
Black Top / Jun '95 / ADA / CM / Direct

BLACK TOP BLUES VOCAL DYNAMITE
CD ____ **BT 1124CD**
Black Top / Nov '95 / ADA / CM / Direct

BLACK TOP BLUES-A-RAMA (Budget Sampler)
CD ____ **BT 002CD**
Black Top / Dec '90 / ADA / CM / Direct

BLACK TOP BLUES-A-RAMA VOL.2
CD ____ **BT 1045CD**
Black Top / '92 / ADA / CM / Direct

BLACK TOP BLUES-A-RAMA VOL.3 (Live From Tipitinas)
CD ____ **BT 1056CD**
Black Top / '92 / ADA / CM / Direct

BLACK TOP BLUES-A-RAMA VOL.4 (Down And Dirty)
CD ____ **BT 1057CD**
Black Top / '92 / ADA / CM / Direct

BLACK TOP BLUES-A-RAMA VOL.5
CD ____ **BT 1058CD**
Black Top / '92 / ADA / CM / Direct

BLACK TOP BLUES-A-RAMA VOL.6
CD ____ **BT 1073CD**
Black Top / May '92 / ADA / CM / Direct

BLACK TOP BLUES-A-RAMA VOL.7
CD ____ **BT 1089CD**
Black Top / May '93 / ADA / CM / Direct

BLACK VOCAL GROUPS 1935-44
CD ____ **RFDCD 10**
Country Routes / Feb '92 / Hot Shot / Jazz Music

BLACK VOCAL GROUPS VOL.1
CD ____ **DOCD 5340**
Document / May '95 / ADA / Hot Shot / Jazz Music

BLACK VOCAL GROUPS VOL.2
CD ____ **DOCD 5347**
Document / May '95 / ADA / Hot Shot / Jazz Music

BLACK VOCAL GROUPS VOL.3 1925-1943
CD ____ **DOCD 5551**
Document / Jul '97 / ADA / Hot Shot / Jazz Music

BLACK VOCAL GROUPS VOL.4 1927-1939
CD ____ **DOCD 5552**
Document / Jul '97 / ADA / Hot Shot / Jazz Music

BLACK VOCAL GROUPS VOL.5 1923-1941
CD ____ **DOCD 5553**
Document / Jul '97 / ADA / Hot Shot / Jazz Music

BLACK VOCAL GROUPS VOL.6 1924-1937
CD ____ **DOCD 5554**
Document / Jul '97 / ADA / Hot Shot / Jazz Music

BLACK VOCAL GROUPS VOL.7 1927-1941
CD ____ **DOCD 5555**
Document / Jul '97 / ADA / Hot Shot / Jazz Music

BLACK VOCAL GROUPS VOL.8 1926-1935
CD ____ **DOCD 5556**
Document / Jul '97 / ADA / Hot Shot / Jazz Music

BLACKEND VOL.1 (2CD Set)
CD Set ____ **BLACK 001DCD**
Blackend / Jul '96 / Plastic Head

BLACKEND VOL.2 (2CD Set)
CD Set ____ **BLACK 003DCD**
Blackend / Jul '96 / Plastic Head

BLACKPOOL MECCA STORY, THE
Love factory: *Laws, Eloise* / Seven day lover: *Fountain, James* / Bet if you ask around: *Velvet* / Get it off my conscience: *Lovelites* / I need you: *Jenkins, Dianne* / Time passes by: *Bynum, James* / Make up your mind: *Connelly, Earl* / Payback's a drag: *Smith Bros* / Destination unkown: *Delrey's Incorporated* / Ladies choice (part 1): *Franklin, Boby* / Wash and wear love: *Varnado, Lynn* / Cashing in: *Voices Of East Harlem* / Woman is hard to understand: *Mack, Jimmy* / Alone with no love: *Rock Candy* / I don't know what foot to dance on: *Tolliver, Kim* / Tow-a-way love: *Jenkins, Dianne* / Lord what's happening to your people: *Smith, Kenny* / You made me this way: *Vann, Ila* / Don't you care anymore: *Mathis, Jodi* / I can see him loving you: *Anderson Brothers* / Let our love grow higher: *Cooper, Eula* / You've been gone too long: *Sexton, Ann*
CD ____ **GSCD 068**
Goldmine / Oct '95 / Vital

BLACKPOOL TOWER CENTENARY, THE (2CD Set)
Tiger rag: *Dixon, Reginald* / Little girl: *Dixon, Reginald* / As time goes by: *Dixon, Reginald* / When I take my sugar to tea: *Dixon, Reginald* / Happy feat: *Dixon, Reginald* / Sabre dance: *Dixon, Reginald* / Symphonic poem: *Dixon, Reginald* / Samum: *Dixon, Reginald* / I love the sunshine of your smile: *Dixon, Reginald* / When I grow too old to dream: *Dixon, Reginald* / Let's have another one: *Dixon, Reginald* / Oh you beautiful doll: *Dixon, Reginald* / Have you ever been lonely: *Dixon, Reginald* / Happy wanderer: *Dixon, Reginald* / Over the waves: *Dixon, Reginald* / Ma, he's making eyes at me: *Dixon, Reginald* / We'll keep a welcome: *Dixon, Reginald* / Blaydon races: *Dixon, Reginald* / Maybe it's because I'm a Londoner: *Dixon, Reginald* / I belong to Glasgow: *Dixon, Reginald* / I do like to be beside the seaside: *Dixon, Reginald* / Quicksteps: *Kelsall, Phil* / Mr. Sandman: *Kelsall, Phil* / Avalon: *Kelsall, Phil* / Crazy rhythm: *Kelsall, Phil* / Viennese waltz: *Kelsall, Phil* / Skater's waltz: *Kelsall, Phil* / Bossa novas: *Kelsall, Phil* / Girl from Ipanema: *Kelsall, Phil* / Destination love: *Kelsall, Phil* / Barn dance: *Kelsall, Phil* / Tip toe through the tulips: *Kelsall, Phil* / I don't know why (I just do): *Kelsall, Phil* / My mammy: *Kelsall, Phil* / Cha cha cha: *Kelsall, Phil* / Cherry pink and apple blossom white: *Kelsall, Phil* / Por favor: *Kelsall, Phil* / Slow rhumbas: *Kelsall, Phil* / Here's that rainy day: *Kelsall, Phil* / La Golondrina: *Kelsall, Phil* / St. Bernard's waltz: *Kelsall, Phil* / Bless 'em all: *Kelsall, Phil* / Band played on: *Kelsall, Phil* / Ash grove: *Kelsall, Phil* / Daisy bell: *Kelsall, Phil* / Mayfair quicksteps: *Kelsall, Phil* / Little white lies: *Kelsall, Phil* / Happy feet: *Kelsall, Phil* / It's just the time for dancing: *Kelsall, Phil* / Tango: *Kelsall, Phil* / La Camparsita: *Kelsall, Phil* / Jive: *Kelsall, Phil* / Nagasaki: *Kelsall, Phil* / Sweet Georgia Brown: *Kelsall, Phil* / Gay Gordons: *Kelsall, Phil* / Scotch mist: *Kelsall, Phil* / Rosetta: *Barlow, Charles & His Orchestra* / Apple for the teacher: *Barlow, Charles & His Orchestra* / Waltzes: *Barlow, Charles & His Orchestra* / Coppelia: *Barlow, Charles & His Orchestra* / Maria Elena: *Barlow, Charles & His Orchestra* / Sambas: *Barlow, Charles & His Orchestra* / El cumbanchero: *Barlow, Charles & His Orchestra* / Hawaiian samba: *Barlow, Charles & His Orchestra* / Cha chas: *Barlow, Charles & His Orchestra* / Something stupid: *Barlow, Charles & His Orchestra* / Swingin' shepherd blues: *Barlow, Charles & His Orchestra* / Paso dobles: *Barlow, Charles & His Orchestra* / For you, Rio Rita: *Barlow, Charles & His Orchestra* / March of the matadors: *Barlow, Charles & His Orchestra* / Anniementamento: *Barlow, Charles & His Orchestra* / Foxtrots: *Barlow, Charles & His Orchestra* / Vilia: *Barlow, Charles & His Orchestra* / Red roses for a blue lady: *Barlow, Charles & His Orchestra* / Quaker girl: *Turner, Ken & His Orchestra* / Dollar princess: *Turner, Ken & His Orchestra* / Two-steps: *Turner, Ken & His Orchestra* / Semper fidelis: *Turner, Ken & His Orchestra* / Namur: *Turner, Ken & His Orchestra* / Saunters: *Turner, Ken & His Orchestra* / Oh my papa: *Turner, Ken & His Orchestra* / Trust in me: *Turner, Ken & His Orchestra* / Waltz: *Turner, Ken & His Orchestra* / Biberacher-waltzer: *Turner, Ken & His Orchestra* / Gavottes: *Turner, Ken & His Orchestra* / Country gardens: *Turner, Ken & His Orchestra* / I leave my heart in an English garden: *Turner, Ken & His Orchestra* / Way to the heart: *Turner, Ken & His Orchestra* / Tangos: *Turner, Ken & His Orchestra* / Midnight in Malaga: *Turner, Ken & His Orchestra* / Madame: *Turner, Ken & His Orchestra* / Modern waltz: *Turner, Ken & His Orchestra* / Peyton Place theme: *Turner, Ken & His Orchestra* / Manhattan: *Dixon, Reginald* / Boo hoo: *Dixon, Reginald*
CD Set ______ **CDDL 1272**
Music For Pleasure / Mar '94 / EMI

BLAME IT ON THE BOOGIE
Blame it on the boogie: *Jacksons* / Boogie nights: *Heatwave* / Dance, dance, dance: *Chic* / He's the greatest dancer: *Sister Sledge* / Get down on it: *Kool & The Gang* / Oops upside your head: *Gap Band* / Play that funky music: *Wild Cherry* / Let's groove: *Earth, Wind & Fire* / Use it up and wear it out: *Odyssey* / Never can say goodbye: *Gaynor, Gloria* / That's the way (I like it): *KC & The Sunshine Band* / Lady Marmalade: *Labelle, Patti* / Night to remember: *Shalamar* / Hot stuff: *Summer, Donna* / Rock the boat: *Hues Corporation* / Funky town: *Lipps Inc.* / Boogie oogie oogie: *Taste Of Honey* / More, more, more: *Andrea True Connection* / Disco inferno: *Trammps* / I haven't stopped dancing yet: *Gonzales*
CD ______ **5155172**
PolyGram TV / Jul '92 / PolyGram

BLANKET ON THE GROUND
CD ______ **MU 5056**
Musketeer / Oct '92 / Disc

BLAS
CD ______ **RTE 161CD**
RTE / May '93 / ADA / Koch

BLASTA (The Irish Traditional Music Special - A Gael Linn Sampler)
Cameronian wheel: *De Danann* / Doon reel: *De Danann* / Ansacht na nansact: *Ni Fhearraigh, Aoife* / Mason's apron: *Murphy, Colm* / Coinleach ghlas an fhomhair: *Clannad* / Maids of Castlebar: *McMahon, Tony & Noel Hill* / Collier's reel: *McMahon, Tony & Noel Hill* / Is fada liom uaim i: *Ni Dhomhnaill, Maighread* / Danish quadrille: *Buttons & Bows* / We venerate thy cross: *Ni Riain, Noirin & Monks Of Glenstal Abbey* / Cucanandy/The jug of brown ale: *Clannad* / Foggin reel: *Bergin, Mary* / Ivy leaf: *Bergin, Mary* / Trim the velvet: *Bergin, Mary* / Jimmy mo mhile stor: *Keane, Dolores* / John Stewart's: *Glackin, Paddy* / James Byrne's pretty peg: *Glackin, Paddy* / Miss Patterson's supper: *Glackin, Paddy* / Wee lass on the brae: *Ni Dhomhnaill, Triona* / Ballintore jig: *Keenan, Paddy*
CD ______ **CDTCD 007**
Gael Linn / May '97 / ADA / CM / Direct / Grapevine/PolyGram / Roots

BLASTING CONCEPT VOL.1
CD ______ **SST 013CD**
SST / May '93 / Plastic Head

BLAXPLOITATION VOL.1 (Soul, Funk & Jazz From The Inner City) (2CD Set)
Ghetto: *Hathaway, Donny* / Inner city blues: *Washington, Grover Jr.* / Woman of the ghetto: *Shaw, Marlena* / Pusherman: *Mayfield, Curtis* / Home is where the hatred is: *Phillips, Esther* / Stone to the bone: *Brown, James* / Expansions: *Smith, Lonnie Liston* / Also sprach zarathustra: *Deodato, Eumir* / Stratus: *Cobham, Billy* / Shaft: *Hayes, Isaac* / He's a superstar: *Ayers, Roy* / Superfly: *Mayfield, Curtis* / Summer in the city: *Jones, Quincy* / For what it's worth: *Mendes, Sergio* / Stepping stones: *Harris, Johnny* / Nubian lady: *Lateef, Yusef* / I'd rather be with you: *Collins, Bootsy* / Straussmania: *Salinas, Daniel* / Children of the ghetto: *Pine, Courtney* / Other side of town: *Joseph, Julian* / By all means: *Mouzon, Alphonse* / Look of love: *Hayes, Isaac* / If you want me to stay: *Stone, Sly* / Why can't we live together: *Thomas, Timmy*
CD Set ______ **RADCD 43**
Global TV / Sep '96 / BMG

BLAXPLOITATION VOL.2 (2CD Set)
CD Set ______ **RADCD 54**
Global TV / Feb '97 / BMG

BLECH VOL.2
CD ______ **WARPCD 44**
Warp / Sep '96 / Prime / RTM/Disc

BLESS MY BONES (Memphis Gospel Radio: The Fifties)
CD ______ **ROUCD 2063**
Rounder / '88 / ADA / CM / Direct

BLIND PIG - 20TH ANNIVERSARY COLLECTION (2CD Set)
Monkey see, monkey do: *Montoya, Coco* / Drive to survive: *Thackery, Jimmy & The Drivers* / Think: *Magic Slim & The Teardrops* / That spot right there: *Bell, Carey* / Howlin' at the moon: *Davies, Debbie* / Tricky woman: *Rogers, Jimmy* / She's as cold as ice: *Rogers, Roy* / Terraplane blues: *Hooker, John Lee* / Don't move the mountain: *Gospel Hummingbirds* / I need a real man: *Scott, E.C.* / Had enough: *Castro, Tommy* / Right place, wrong time: *Rush, Otis* / Messin' with the kid: *Guy, Buddy & Junior Wells* / Wastin' time: *Carrier, Chubby* / Big girl blues: *Connor, Joanna* / Worried life blues: *Pinetop Perkins* / Take me back: *Cotton, James* / Should I wait: *Allison, Luther* / Two time boogie: *Studebaker John & The Hawks* / My heart bleeds blue: *Coleman, Deborah* / Hey sweet baby: *Cain, Chris* / Harpin' on a riff: *Musselwhite, Charley* / Cold chills: *Gray, Henry* / La vierge: *Rapone, Al* / I won't be there: *Preacher Boy* / Blues come to Texas: *Shines, Johnny* / I got something on you baby: *Wilson, Smokey* / I been thinkin': *Campbell, Eddie C.* / That's my baby: *Clearwater, Eddy* / Bad thing: *Brown, Sarah* / If I could reach out (and help somebody): *Clay, Otis* / Old time shuffle: *Boogie Woogie Red* / Crazy 'bout my baby: *Pryor, Snooky* / I wonder: *Sykes, Roosevelt* / If I get lucky: *Horton, Walter* / Let's rock: *Commander Cody*
CD Set ______ **BPCD 2001**
Blind Pig / May '97 / ADA / CM / Direct / Hot Shot

BLIND/FRAGMENT
CD ______ **ASH 14**
Ash International / Jan '95 / Kudos / Pinnacle

BLOODSTAINS ON THE WALL
Bloodstains on the wall: *Honey Boy* / You better move on away from here: *Honey Boy* / Have you a match: *Honey Boy* / Uncle Sam blues: *Pine Blues Pete* / Woman acts funny: *Pine Blues Pete* / Going back to Mama: *Pine Blues Pete* / Got a letter this morning: *Pine Blues Pete* / Want to boogie woogie: *Pine Blues Pete* / Ride my new car with me: *Williams, Big Joe* / Rather be sloppy drunk: *Williams, Big Joe* / Dial 110 blues: *Bledsoe, Country Jim* / Hollywood boogie: *Bledsoe, Country Jim* / One thing my baby likes: *Bledsoe, Country Jim* / Stormin' and rainin': *Bledsoe, Country Jim* / I ate the wrong part: *Little Temple* / What a mistake: *Little Temple* / Mean and evil: *Little Temple* / Cold love: *Little Temple* / Black snake blues: *McKinley, Pete* / Cryin' for my baby: *McKinley, Pete* / Look-a-here boy: *McKinley, Pete* / Whistlin' blues: *McKinley, Pete* / Don't want me blues: *McKinley, Pete* / David's boogie: *McKinley, Pete* / Sail on little girl, sail on: *McKinley, Pete*
CD ______ **CDCHD 576**
Ace / Jul '94 / Pinnacle

BLOODY FUCKING HARDCORE
CD ______ **MOK 97CD**
Mokum / Mar '94 / Pinnacle

BLOW MR. HORNSMAN
Jumpin' Jack / Super Special / Death rides / Run for your life / On the moon / Undertaker's burial / Roll On / Franco Nero / Leaving Rome / Ghost capturer / Nightmare / Judgement warrant / East of the River Nile / Harvest in the East / Va Va Voom / Broken Contract / Butter sefish / If you're ready
CD ______ **CDTRL 257**
Trojan / Mar '94 / Direct / Jet Star

BLOW MY BLUES AWAY VOL.1
CD ______ **ARHCD 401**
Arhoolie / Apr '95 / ADA / Cadillac / Direct

BLOW MY BLUES AWAY VOL.2
CD ______ **ARHCD 402**
Arhoolie / Apr '95 / ADA / Cadillac / Direct

BLOW THE MAN DOWN: SEA SONGS & SHANTIES
Wild goose: *Killen, Louis* / Lovely Nancy: *Campbell, Ian* / Black ball line: *MacColl, Ewan* / Nightingale: *Tawney, Cyril* / Blow the man down: *Corbett, Harry H.* / Heave away, my Johnny: *Killen, Louis* / Lofty tall ship: *Larner, Sam* / Row bullies row: *Campbell, Ian* / Flying cloud: *Killen, Louis* / Fireship: *Tawney, Cyril* / Tom's gone to Hilo: *Tawney, Cyril* / Greenland whale fishery: *Watersons* / Ship in distress: *Killen, Louis* / Lowlands low: *Campbell, Ian* / Cod banging: *Hart, Bob* / Hilo Johnny Brown: *Killen, Louis* / Bonny ship the Diamond: *Lloyd, A.L.* / Bold Princess Royal: *Killen, Louis* / Billy boy: *Davenport, Bob* / Windy old weather: *Roberts, A.V. 'Bob'* / Bold Benjamin: *Tawney, Cyril* / Hog eye man: *Campbell, Ian* / Goodbye fare thee well: *Killen, Louis*
CD ______ **TSCD 464**
Topic / May '93 / ADA / CM / Direct

BLOW UP PRESENTS EXCLUSIVE BLEND VOL.1
CD ______ **BLOWUP 006CD**
Blow Up / Aug '96 / Arabesque / SRD

BLOWIN' UP A STORM (Jazz Sax Classics)
One for the guv'nor: *Webster, Ben* / Charity rag: *Shank, Bud* / Sunny moon for two: *Rollins, Sonny* / Like someone in love: *Rollins, Sonny* / Stan's blues: *Getz, Stan* / Ben's blues: *Webster, Ben* / Sweet Lorraine: *Webster, Ben* / Here's that rainy day: *Getz, Stan* / Tonight I sleep with a smile on my face: *Getz, Stan* / Harlem nocturne: *Bostic, Earl* / Ain't misbehavin': *Bostic, Earl* / Blowin' up a storm: *Herman, Woody* / Caldonia: *Herman, Woody* / Goodnight sweetheart: *Bostic, Earl* / Woodchopper's ball: *Herman, Woody* / Dizzy atmosphere: *Parker, Charlie*
CD ______ **SUMCD 4113**
Sound & Media / May '97 / Sound & Media

BLOWING MY HORN
Fiesta in brass: *Eldridge, Roy* / Mid-forte: *Baker, Chet* / Moon song: *Armstrong, Louis* / I'll take romance: *Dorham, Kenny* / It's a wonderful world: *Butterfield, Billy* / Where's art: *Eldridge, Roy* / La divorce de Leo Fall: *Morgan, Lee* / Si si: *Rodney, Red* / Sermonette: *Adderley, Nat* / What's new: *Brown, Clifford* / Hymn to her: *Ferguson, Maynard* / Squeaky's blues: *Terry, Clark* / I'm true to you: *Stewart, Rex* / Diner' au motel: *Davis, Miles* / Dizzy's business: *Gillespie, Dizzy* / Someone to love: *Newman, Joe* / Weather bird: *James, Harry* / Gee, baby, ain't I food to you: *Edison, Harry*
CD ______ **5526412**
Spectrum / Mar '97 / PolyGram

BLUE
CD ______ **CDSTUMM 49**
Mute / Oct '93 / RTM/Disc

BLUE
CD ______ **CDBV 001**
Blue Village / Jun '96 / SRD

BLUE BOOGIE (Boogie Woogie Stride & The Piano Blues)
Boogie woogie stomp: *Ammons, Albert* / Boogie woogie blues: *Ammons, Albert* / Chicago in mind: *Ammons, Albert* / Bass goin' crazy: *Ammons, Albert* / Blues part 1: *Lewis, Meade 'Lux'* / Honky tonk train blues: *Lewis, Meade 'Lux'* / Variations on a theme: *Lewis, Meade 'Lux'* / Nineteen ways of playing a chorus: *Lewis, Meade 'Lux'* / Bass on top: *Lewis, Meade 'Lux'* / Two's and fews: *Lewis, Meade 'Lux' & Albert Ammons/Pete Johnson* / Vine Street blues: *Johnson, Pete* / Barrelhouse breakdown: *Johnson, Pete* / Mule walk (stomp): *Johnson, James P.* / Blue note boogie: *Johnson, James P.* / Call of the blues: *Johnson, James P.* / World is waiting for the sunrise: *Benskin, Sammy* / Jug head boogie: *Hodes, Art* / Funny feathers: *Hodes, Art* / Father's gateway: *Hines, Earl 'Fatha'* / Aunt Hagar's blues: *Tatum, Art*
CD ______ **BNZ 292**
Blue Note / Apr '92 / EMI

BLUE BRAZIL (Blue Note In A Latin Groove)
Upa neguinho: *Paez, Luiz Arrunda* / Catavento: *Costa, Alaide* / Berimbau: *Som, Mandrake* / Vim de santana: *Quarteto Novo* / Deus Brasiliero: *Ribiero, Perry & Bossa 3* / Primitivo: *Milton Banana Trio* / Noa noa: *Milton Banana Trio* / Viola fora de moda: *Lobo, Edo* / Nao me diga adeus: *Bossa 3* / Batucada Sergiu: *Valle, Marcus* / Aldeia de ogum: *Joyce* / Tudo que voce podia ser: *Lo Borges* / Homenagem a mongo: *Som Tres* / Deixa isso pra la: *Soares, Elza* / Misturada: *Quarteto Novo* / Bebe: *Deodato, Eumir* / Um tema p'ro Simon: *Alf, Johnny* / Cala boca menino: *Donato, Joao* / Me deixa: *Donato, Joao* / Night and day: *Brasil, Victor Assis*
CD ______ **CDP 8291962**
Blue Note / Jun '94 / EMI

BLUE BREAK BEATS VOL.1 (You Gotta Hear Blue Note To Dig Def Jam)
Grooving with Mr G: *Holmes, Richard 'Groove'* / Sookie sookie: *Green, Grant* / Who's making love: *Donaldson, Lou* / Weasil: *Byrd, Donald* / Kudu: *Henderson, Eddie* / Harlem river drive: *Humphrey, Bobbi* / Blue juice: *McGriff, Jimmy* / Final comedown: *Green, Grant* / Turtle walk: *Donaldson, Lou* / Your love is too much: *Three Sounds* / Black Jack: *Byrd, Donald* / Olilloqui Valley: *Hancock, Herbie*
CD ______ **BNZ 288**
Blue Note / Apr '92 / EMI

BLUE BREAK BEATS VOL.2
Street lady: *Byrd, Donald* / Jasper country man: *Humphrey, Bobbi* / Kumquat kids: *Henderson, Eddie* / Higga boom: *Harris, Gene* / Orange peel: *Wilson, Reuben* / Worm: *McGriff, Jimmy* / Caterpillar: *Donaldson, Lou* / Ain't it funky now: *Green, Grant* / Ummh: *Hutcherson, Bobby* / Good humour man: *Mitchell, Blue* / Beale Street: *Byrd, Donald* / Viva Tirado: *Wilson, Gerald* / Pot belly: *Donaldson, Lou* / Spinning wheel: *Smith, Lonnie Liston* / Phantom: *Pearson, Duke*
CD ______ **BNZ 311**
Blue Note / Jul '93 / EMI

BLUE BREAK BEATS VOL.3
Walk tall: *Adderley, Cannonball* / You've made me so very happy: *Rawls, Lou* / Ode to Billy Joe: *Donaldson, Lou* / Sho' nuff nelon: *Wilson, Reuben* / Howling for Judy: *Steig, Jeremy* / Light my fire: *Bassey, Shirley* / It's your thing: *Donaldson, Lou* / Put on train: *Three Sounds* / Don't call me nigger whitey: *Harris, Gene* / Dominoes: *Byrd, Donald* / Mystic brew: *Foster, Ronnie* / Get out of my life woman: *Williams, Joe & Thad Jones/Mel Lewis Orchestra* / Ground hog: *Pearson, Duke* / Soul, soul, soul: *McLean, Jackie* / Flat backing: *Mitchell, Blue* / Down here on the ground: *Green, Grant* / Blacks and blues: *Humphrey, Bobbi* / Going down south: *Hutcherson, Bobby*
CD ______ **CDP 8543602**
Blue Note / Oct '96 / EMI

BLUE BULL (A Trip To Happy Techno)
CD ______ **SPV 08938572**
SPV / Mar '96 / Koch / Plastic Head

BLUE EYES CRYING IN THE RAIN
Blue eyes cryin' in the rain: *Drusky, Roy* / Shine on Ruby mountain: *Rogers, Kenny* / I didn't sleep a wink: *Nelson, Willie* / Daddy: *Fargo, Donna* / Your song: *Lee, Johnny* / Stop, look and listen: *Cline, Patsy* / Making believe: *Wells, Kitty* / Slippin' away: *Fairchild, Barbara* / Abilene: *Jennings, Waylon* / Ruby, don't take your love to town: *Rogers, Kenny* / I feel sorry for him: *Nelson, Willie* / Where do we go from here: *Williams, Don* / Turn the cards slowly: *Cline, Patsy* / Moonlight gondolier: *Laine, Frankie* / From a Jack to a King: *Miller, Ned* / Elvira: *Rogers, Kenny* / Have I stayed away too long: *Ritter, Tex* / Ghost: *Nelson, Willie* / 9,999,999 tears: *Baily, Razzy* / Sticks and stones: *Fargo, Donna* / Shake 'em up roll 'em: *Jackson, Stonewall* / Heartaches by the number: *Mitchell, Guy* / Homemade lies: *Rogers, Kenny* / Hello walls: *Drusky, Roy* / I let my mind wander: *Nelson, Willie*
CD ______ **GRF 121**
Tring / Feb '93 / Tring

BLUE GIRLS VOL.1 (1924-1930)
CD ______ **DOCD 5503**
Document / Nov '96 / ADA / Hot Shot / Jazz Music

BLUE GIRLS VOL.2 (1925-1930)
CD ______ **DOCD 5504**
Document / Nov '96 / ADA / Hot Shot / Jazz Music

BLUE HAWAII (A Vintage Anthology)
Little heaven of the seven seas: *Coral Islanders* / Moon of Manakoora: *Coral Islanders* / Blue Hawaii: *Crosby, Bing & Lani McIntire & Hawaiians* / Palace in paradise: *Crosby, Bing & Lani McIntire & Hawaiians* / Sweet Leilani: *Crosby, Bing & Lani McIntire & Hawaiians* / Love dreams of Lula Lu: *Ferera, Frank* / For you: *Fillis, Len* / Goodbye Hawaii: *Hall, Henry & The BBC Dance Orchestra* / Pua Kealoha: *Hoopii, Sol & Novelty Trio/Quartet* / Weave a lei: *Hoopii, Sol & Novelty Trio/Quartet* / Hawaiian paradise: *Iona, Andy & Islanders* / Night is young: *Iona, Andy & Islanders/Cliff Edwards* / St. Louis blues: *Jim & Bob, the genial Hawaiians* / Tomi, Tomi: *Kanui & Lula* / Makalapua

O Kamakeaha: *Klein, Manny & Hawaiians* / Hawaiian gems: *Mendelssohn, Felix & His Hawaiian Serenaders* / I got rhythm: *Mendelssohn, Felix & His Hawaiian Serenaders* / Sing me a song of the Islands: *Mendelssohn, Felix & His Hawaiian Serenaders* / Song of the rose: *Mendelssohn, Felix & His Hawaiian Serenaders* / Where the waters are blue: *Mendelssohn, Felix & His Hawaiian Serenaders* / Palms of paradise: *Johnny Kaonohi Pineapple & Native Islanders* / On the beach at Waikiki: *Sharpe, A.P. & Honolulu Hawaiians* / O muki, muki O: *Shaw, Al & Hawaiian Beachcombers* / Lullaby of the leaves: *Smeck, Roy & Vita Trio* / Paradise beside the sea: *Tauber, Richard*
CD ____ CDAJA 5121
Living Era / Feb '94 / Select

BLUE HIGHWAY
CD ____ BT 003CD
Black Top / Aug '94 / ADA / CM / Direct

BLUE JUICE
Streets of Calcutta: *Shankar, Anandar* / Soul mission: *Bennett, Brian* / EVA: *Perry, Jean Jacques* / For what it's worth: *Rawls, Lou* / Willie and Laura Mae Jones: *Wilson, Nancy* / Mississippi delta: *Gentry, Bobbie* / Sookie sookie: *Britt, Tina* / Tighten up: *Gordon, Benny* / Grits and gravy: *Fame Gang* / Uptight: *Preston, Billy* / Look into the flower: *Caravan, Jimmy* / Give it up or turn it loose: *Hyman, Dick* / Dancing drums: *Shankar, Anandar* / Killiano: *Lyttle, Johnny* / No problema: *Richardson, Jerome* / Samba for Maria: *Connors, Norman & Freddie Hubbard* / Mas que nada: *Soares, Elza* / Cala boca menino: *Donato, Joao* / Never come closer: *Doris* / Ode to Billie Joe: *Wilson, Nancy* / Hey girl: *Harris, Gene & Three Sounds* / MSP: *Hamilton, Chico*
CD ____ CDP 8543472
Blue Note / Oct '96 / EMI

BLUE LADIES 1934-1941
CD ____ DOCD 5327
Document / Mar '95 / ADA / Hot Shot / Jazz Music

BLUE MOODS
Chi chi: *Parker, Charlie* / You'r mine, you: *Webster, Ben* / Pick yourself up: *Carter, Benny* / Limehouse blues: *Adderley, Cannonball & John Coltrane* / Chalmeau: *Carney, Harry* / World is waiting for the sunrise: *Hawkins, Coleman* / I never has seen snow: *Woods, Phil* / That old feeling: *Mulligan, Gerry & Stan Getz* / Over the rainbow: *Byas, Don* / Just friends: *Konitz, Lee* / Baby won't you please come home: *Bechet, Sidney* / Cheek to cheek: *Phillips, Flip* / Bemoanable lady: *Dolphy, Eric* / I want to be happy: *Young, Lester* / I didn't know about you: *Hodges, Johnny* / I know that you know: *Rollins, Sonny & Sonny Stitt* / Flying home: *Jacquet, Illinois*
CD ____ 5526422
Spectrum / Mar '97 / PolyGram

BLUE MOON (20 Great Hits Of The Sixties)
What do you want to make those eyes at me for: *Ford, Emile & The Checkmates* / Venus in blue jeans: *Wynter, Mark* / There goes that song again: *Miller, Gary* / Midnight in Moscow: *Ball, Kenny & His Jazzmen* / My old man's a dustman: *Donegan, Lonnie* / Warpaint: *Brook Brothers* / Ain't that funny: *Justice, Jimmy* / Little bitty tear: *Miki & Griff* / Be mine: *Fortune, Lance* / What a crazy world we're living in: *Brown, Joe* / My friend the sea: *Clark, Petula* / Charmaine: *Bachelors* / Blue moon: *Marcels* / Them there eyes: *Ford, Emile & The Checkmates* / Go away little girl: *Wynter, Mark* / All my love: *Wilson, Jackie* / It only took a minute: *Brown, Joe* / Have a drink on me: *Donegan, Lonnie* / Romeo: *Clark, Petula* / Green leaves of summer: *Ball, Kenny*
CD ____ TRTCD 101
TrueTrax / Oct '94 / THE

BLUE 'N' GROOVY (Blue Note Connects With The Good Vibes)
Chili peppers: *Pearson, Duke* / On children: *Wilson, Jack* / Hi-heel sneakers: *Mitchell, Blue* / Senor blues: *Silver, Horace* / Meat wave: *Turrentine, Stanley* / Dem tambourines: *Wilkerson, Don* / Sidewinder: *Morgan, Lee* / Cantaloupe island: *Hancock, Herbie* / Ping pong: *Blakey, Art* / True blue: *Brooks, Tina* / Jeannine: *Byrd, Donald* / My favourite things: *Green, Grant* / 8/4 Beat: *Hutcherson, Bobby* / Tom Thumb: *Shorter, Wayne*
CD ____ BNZ 300
Blue Note / Oct '92 / EMI

BLUE NOTE BOX, THE (4CD Set)
Blue train: *Coltrane, John* / Maiden voyage: *Hancock, Herbie* / Cristo redentor: *Byrd, Donald* / Moanin': *Blakey, Art & The Jazz Messengers* / Blues walk: *Donaldson, Lou* / Song for my father: *Silver, Horace* / Back at the Chicken Shack: *Smith, Jimmy* / Chitlins con carne: *Burrell, Kenny* / Sidewinder: *Morgan, Lee* / Senor blues: *Silver, Horace* / Decision: *Rollins, Sonny* / Three o'clock in the morning: *Gordon, Dexter* / Blues march: *Blakey, Art* / Wadin': *Parlan, Horace* / Rumproller: *Morgan, Lee* / Somethin' else: *Adderley, Cannonball* / Blue bossa: *Henderson, Joe* / Watermelon man: *Hancock, Herbie* / Hold on I'm comin': *Wilson, Reuben* / It's your thing: *Green, Grant* / Scorpion: *Donaldson, Lou* / Village lee: *Patton, 'Big' John* / Spooky: *Turrentine, Stanley* / Dancin' in an easy groove: *Smith, Lonnie Liston* / You want me to stop loving you: *Turrentine, Stanley* / Do like Eddie: *Scofield, John* / Blue monk: *Tyner, McCoy & Bobby Hutcherson* / Immediate left: *Hagans, Tim* / I waited for you: *Jackson, Javon* / Take the D flat train: *Hays, Kevin* / One of another kind: *Green, Benny* / Reflections: *Fortune, Sonny* / Donna Lee: *Rubalcaba, Gonzala* / Rounders mood: *Lovano, Joe* / I love Paris: *Terrasson, Jacky*
CD Set ____ CDP 8360542
Blue Note / Nov '95 / EMI

BLUE NOTE RARE GROOVES
Bus ride: *Wilson, Reuben* / Hunk o'funk: *McDuff, Jack* / Hot rod: *Wilson, Reuben* / Bird wave: *McGriff, Jimmy* / Boogaloo: *Turrentine, Stanley* / Heaven on Earth: *Young, Larry* / Black rhythm happening: *Gale, Eddie* / String bean: *Patton, 'Big' John* / Groovin' for Mr. G: *Holmes, Richard* / Round town: *Jones, Elvin* / Soul special: *Hill, Andrew* / Blackjack: *Byrd, Donald* / Serenade to a savage: *Candido*
CD ____ CDP 8356362
Blue Note / Mar '96 / EMI

BLUE RIBBON BANJO
Adams county breakdown: *Adams, Tom* / Sleepy eyed John/Tom & Jerry: *Smith, Craig* / Clinging vine: *Keith, Bill* / Clarinet polka: *Evans, B* / Moving out: *Schatz, Mark* / Shelton special: *Shelton, Allen* / Maple leaf rag: *Whisnant, Johnnie* / Fortune: *Cockerham, Fred* / Boat's up the river: *Reed, Ola Belle* / Pea patch jig: *Hartford, John* / Jenny's wedding/Rakish Paddy: *Furtado, Tony* / Robot plane flies over Arkansas: *Trischka, Tony* / Perplexed: *Fleck, Bela* / Wired: *Vestal, Scott* / Runaround: *Crowe, J.D. & The New South*
CD ____ EDCD 7001
Easydisc / Aug '96 / Direct

BLUE RIBBON BLUEGRASS
CD ____ AN 11CD
Rounder / Jan '94 / ADA / CM / Direct

BLUE RIBBON FIDDLE
CD ____ EDCD 7004
Easydisc / Aug '96 / Direct

BLUE RIBBON GUITAR
Blackberry blossom: *O'Connor, Mark* / Tarnation: *Grier, David* / Salt Creek: *Blake, Norman & Tony Rice/Doc Watson* / Shake your hips: *McCoury Brothers* / Cooley's reel: *Barenberg, Russ* / Bury me beneath the willow: *Nygaard, Scott* / Huckleberry hornpipe: *Crary, Dan* / Back up and push: *Rice, Wyatt* / Fisher's hornpipe/Devil's dream: *Watson, Doc & Merle* / Big mon: *Rice, Tony* / Fiddler's dram/Whiskey before breakfast: *Blake, Norman* / Old, old house: *Country Cooking*
CD ____ EDCD 7006
Easydisc / Nov '96 / Direct

BLUE RIDGE OLD-TIME SAMPLER
CD ____ CUY 2701CD
County / Apr '96 / ADA / Direct

BLUE YORK, BLUE YORK
New York times: *Humphrey, Bobbi* / On Broadway: *Wilson, Reuben* / Tenderly: *Smith, Jimmy* / Stomping at the Savoy: *Hall, Jim* / Lullaby of Birdland: *Shearing, George* / Skating in Central Park: *Modern Jazz Quartet* / Blue Harlem: *Quebec, Ike* / Take the 'A' train: *Kings Sisters* / 52nd Street theme: *Powell, Bud* / Broadway: *Staton, Dakota* / City lights: *Morgan, Lee* / 116th and Lenox: *McLean, Jackie* / Jersey girl: *Cole, Holly* / Sugar hill: *Three Sounds* / Harlem river drive: *Humphrey, Bobbi*
CD ____ CDP 8543632
Blue Note / Oct '96 / EMI

BLUE-EYED RHYTHM AND BLUES
CD ____ CDRB 25
Charly / Aug '95 / Koch

BLUEBEAT, SKA & REGGAE REVOLUTION
CD ____ SEECD 319
See For Miles/C5 / May '91 / Pinnacle

BLUEBEAT, SKA & REGGAE REVOLUTION VOL.2
CD ____ SEECD 353
See For Miles/C5 / Sep '92 / Pinnacle

BLUEBELLS
CD ____ CMPCD 56
CMP / Nov '92 / Cargo / Grapevine/ PolyGram / Vital/SAM

BLUEFUNKERS VOL.1 (Pitchers, Leftfielders & Flipsiders)
CD ____ ZEN 002CD
Indochina / Jan '95 / Pinnacle

BLUEGRASS ALBUM VOL.4
Age / Cheyenne / Cora is gone / Old home town / Talk it all over with him / Head over heels / Nobody loves me / When you are lonely / I might take you back again / Lonesome wind blues
CD ____ ROUCD 0210
Rounder / Feb '95 / ADA / CM / Direct

BLUEGRASS ALBUM VOL.5 (Sweet Sunny South)
Rock hearts / Big black train / Thinking about you / Out in the cold war / On the old Kentucky shore / Preaching, praying, singing / Someone took my place with you / Foggy mountain rock / My home's across the Blue Ridge Mountains / Along about daybreak / Sweet sunny South
CD ____ ROUCD 0240
Rounder / '89 / ADA / CM / Direct

BLUEGRASS AT NEWPORT (1959/1960/1963)
Salty dog blues: *Flatt, Lester & Earl Scruggs/The Foggy Mountain Boys* / Before I met you: *Flatt, Lester & Earl Scruggs/The Foggy Mountain Boys* / Cabin on the hill: *Flatt, Lester & Earl Scruggs/The Foggy Mountain Boys* / Jimmy Brown the news boy: *Flatt, Lester & Earl Scruggs/The Foggy Mountain Boys* / Train forty-five: *New Lost City Ramblers* / Pretty little miss: *New Lost City Ramblers* / Liza Jane: *New Lost City Ramblers* / Jordan am a hard road to travel: *Logan, Tex/Eric Weissberg & The New Lost City Ramblers* / I wonder how the old folks are at home: *Wiseman, Mac & The Country Boys* / Love letters in the sand: *Wiseman, Mac & The Country Boys* / Little footsteps in the snow: *Wiseman, Mac & The Country Boys* / Way downtown: *Ahley, Clarence/Doc Watson/Clint Howard/Fred Price* / Maggie Walker blues: *Ahley, Clarence/Doc Watson/Clint Howard/Fred Price* / Girl I loved in sunny Tennessee: *Ahley, Clarence/Doc Watson/Clint Howard/Fred Price* / Lee Highway blues: *Ahley, Clarence/Doc Watson/Clint Howard/Fred Price* / Flinthill special: *Scruggs, Earl/Hylo Brown & The Timberliners* / Earl's breakdown: *Scruggs, Earl/Hylo Brown & The Timberliners* / Cumberland gap: *Scruggs, Earl/Hylo Brown & The Timberliners* / Salty dog blues: *Morris Brothers* / You give me your love and I'll give you mine: *Morris Brothers* / Border ride: *Jim & Jesse & the Virginia Boys* / Gosh I miss you all the time: *Jim & Jesse & the Virginia Boys* / Dill pickle rag: *Jim & Jesse & the Virginia Boys* / She left me standing on the mountain: *Jim & Jesse & the Virginia Boys*
CD ____ VCD 121
Vanguard / Oct '95 / ADA / Pinnacle

BLUEGRASS BREAKDOWN
New broom: *Berline, Lue & Byron* / Old Logan: *Berline, Lue & Byron* / Crazy creek: *Berline, Lue & Byron* / Dusty Miller: *Berline, Lue & Byron* / How mountain girls can love: *Stanley Brothers* / Man of constant sorrow: *Stanley Brothers* / Big Tildy: *Stanley Brothers* / Orange blossom special: *Stanley Brothers* / Leather britches: *Smith, Arthur* / Blackberry blossom: *Smith, Arthur* / Levee breakin' blues: *Greenbriar Boys* / At the end of a long lonely day: *Greenbriar Boys* / Old Joe Clark: *Dillards* / Ground hog: *Dillards* / Banjo in the hollow: *Dillards* / Polly Vaughn: *Dillards* / Duelling banjos: *Dillards* / Alabama jubilee: *McMichen, Clayton* / Sourwood mountain: *McMichen, Clayton* / You better get right little darlin': *New York City Ramblers* / I'm coming back but I don't know when: *New York City Ramblers* / Cedar hill: *New York City Ramblers* / Tell it to me: *New York City Ramblers* / Mule skinner blues: *Monroe, Bill & His Bluegrass Boys* / Blue moon of Kentucky: *Monroe, Bill & His Bluegrass Boys* / Walls of time: *Monroe, Bill & His Bluegrass Boys* / Somebody touched me: *Monroe, Bill & His Bluegrass Boys* / Bluegrass breakdown: *Monroe, Bill & His Bluegrass Boys*
CD ____ VCD 77006
Vanguard / Oct '95 / ADA / Pinnacle

BLUEGRASS COMPACT DISC
CD ____ ROUCD 11502
Rounder / '88 / ADA / CM / Direct

BLUEGRASS COMPACT DISC VOL.2
CD ____ ROUCD 11516
Rounder / '88 / ADA / CM / Direct

BLUEGRASS FROM THE GOLD COUNTRY
CD ____ ROUCD 0131
Rounder / Sep '96 / ADA / CM / Direct

BLUEGRASS GREATS
Trainwreck of emotion: *McCoury, Del* / Lost and I'll never find the way: *Skaggs, Ricky & Peter Rowan* / In my time of dying: *Stevens, Beth & April* / I never knew: *White, Jeff* / There's a brighter mansion over there: *Longview* / Mama's hand: *Morris, Lynn* / Picture in a tear: *Rice, Wyatt & Santa Cruz* / Everybody's reaching out for someone: *Cox Family* / Hard hearted: *Jim & Jesse & the Virginia Boys* / Indecision: *King, James* / I'm working on the road to gloryland: *IIIrd Tyme Out* / My better years: *Johnson Mountain Boys*
CD ____ EDCD 7007
Easydisc / Jun '97 / Direct

BLUEGRASS MUSIC
CD ____ 12181
Laserlight / May '94 / Target/BMG

BLUEGRASS REUNION
CD ____ ACD 4
Acoustic Disc / May '97 / ADA / Koch

BLUEGRASS SPECTACULAR
CD ____ CTS 55424
Country Stars / Sep '94 / Target/BMG

BLUEGRASS SPIRIT (12 Songs Of Faith)
CD ____ EDCD 7021
Easydisc / Nov '96 / Direct

BLUEGRASS TODAY - THE HITS
CD ____ EDCD 9001
Easydisc / Aug '96 / Direct

BLUES - CHICAGO STYLE (4CD Set)
What have I done: *Smith, Byther* / Going back to Louisiana: *Bell, Lurrie* / DJ play my blues: *Guy, Buddy* / If you got to love somebody: *Dawkins, Jimmy* / Where the hell were you: *Lefty Dizz* / Run don't walk: *Sumlin, Hubert* / Mean red spider: *Rogers, Jimmy* / Tina Nu: *Guy, Phil* / Ain't no sunshine: *Smith, Byther* / Addressing the nation: *Smith, Byther* / Moon is rising: *Taylor, Eddie & KC Red* / As the years go passing by: *Allen, Pete & Carey Bell/Lurrie Bell* / I need you so bad: *Bell, Lurrie* / All I can do: *Sumlin, Hubert* / Hoochie coochie: *Bell, Carey* / Minnie Sue: *Burks, JT* / Partnership woman: *Burks, JT* / Now darlin': *Wrencher, Big John* / Good morning blues: *Easy Baby* / That's alright in the dark: *Bell, Carey & Lefty Dizz* / Little Walter's blues: *Sayles, Charlie* / Watchdog: *Buford, Mojo* / Reconsider baby: *Bell, Carey & Lurrie* / Lamp post: *Sayles, Charlie* / Automobile: *Sayles, Charlie* / Rambling woman: *Harmonica Hinds & Big Moose Walker* / Burying ground: *Harmonica Hinds & Big Moose Walker* / New harp in town: *Bell, Steve* / Two old maids: *Horton, Walter* / Good lovings: *Evans, Lucky Lopez* / Tail draggin': *Evans, Lucky Lopez* / Oh baby: *Left Hand Frank* / Strange woman: *Bell, Carey* / Mighty Mars: *Mars, Johnny* / Rocket 88: *Mars, Johnny* / Same things: *Campbell, Eddie C.* / Cha cha in blues: *Campbell, Eddie C.* / I'm going upstairs: *Bell, Carey* / Extra extra: *Evans, Lucky Lopez* / Jack potato boogie: *Buford, Mojo* / Jealous of my baby: *Buford, Mojo* / Desert Island: *Mars, Johnny* / Best place: *Louisiana Red* / Valerie: *Louisiana Red* / Mama talk to your daughter: *Carter, Joe* / You're the one: *Carter, Joe* / Rock me: *Carter, Joe* / If you don't want me: *Littlejohn, Johnny* / Keep on running: *Littlejohn, Johnny* / I feel like jumping: *Lefty Dizz* / Take a walk with me: *Rogers, Jimmy* / Wee little room: *Frank JR* / Mojo: *Littlejohn, Johnny* / Looking for a woman: *Smith, Byther* / You got to help me: *Sumlin, Hubert* / It could be you: *Sumlin, Hubert* / Whisky headed woman: *Philips, Brewster* / Poison Ivy: *Philips, Brewster* / Bottleneck blues: *Smith, Big Red*
CD Set ____ PBXCD 403
Pulse / Jul '97 / BMG

BLUES - THE CHICAGO YEARS
CD ____ MACCD 195
Autograph / Aug '96 / BMG

BLUES 60'S
I have a dream: *Hancock, Herbie* / Cease the bombing: *Green, Grant* / Acid, pot & pills: *Silver, Horace* / Psychedelic: *Morgan, Lee* / Black heroes: *Hutcherson, Bobby* / There is the bomb: *Cherry, Don* / Black rhythm happening: *Gale, Eddie* / Watts happening: *Jazz Crusaders* / Blowing in the wind: *Turrentine, Stanley* / I wish I knew how it'd feel to be free: *Taylor, Billy* / Say it loud (I'm black and I'm proud): *Donaldson, Lou*
CD ____ CDP 8354722
Blue Note / Oct '95 / EMI

BLUES AFTER HOURS
Baby doll blues: *Earl, Ronnie* / They killed crazy horse: *Houston, Joe & Otis Grand* / 4811 Wadsworth (Blues for George): *Piazza, Rod & The Mighty Flyers* / Get down with the blues: *Tony Z* / Sidetrack: *Connors, Gene 'Mighty Flea'* / Down at PJ's place: *Maxwell, David* / Blues for Al and Peggy: *Morgan, Mike & The Crawl* / I'm not ashamed to play the blues: *Jones, Tutu* / Blues for Henry: *Sumlin, Hubert* / John Henry: *Rishell, Paul & Annie Raines*
CD ____ EDCD 7027
Easydisc / Jul '97 / Direct

BLUES ALBUM, THE (2CD Set)
Mannish boy: *Waters, Muddy* / Boom boom: *Hooker, John Lee* / Crossroads: *Cream* / When love comes to town: *U2 & B.B. King* / Mustang Sally: *Guy, Buddy* / Born under a bad sign: *King, Albert* / Need your love so bad: *Fleetwood Mac* / Somewhere down the crazy river: *Robertson, Robbie* / Black magic woman: *Santana* / Piece of my heart: *Franklin, Erma* / Dixie chicken: *Little Feat* / On the road again: *Canned Heat* / Smokestack lightnin': *Howlin' Wolf* / I'd rather go blind: *James, Etta* / Try a little tenderness: *Commitments* / Right next door (because of me): *Cray, Robert Band* / Fade to black: *Dire Straits* / Nineties blues: *Rea, Chris* / Bell bottom blues: *Derek & The Dominoes* / Cocaine: *Cale, J.J.* / Still got the blues: *Moore, Gary* / Hunter: *Free* / Thrill is gone: *King, B.B.* / Hoochie coochie man: *Waters, Muddy* / Muddy waters blues (acoustic version): *Rodgers, Paul* / I'm a king bee: *Harpo, Slim* / I'm in the mood: *Hooker, John Lee* / Dust my broom: *James, Elmore* / Help me: *Williamson, Sonny Boy* / Love in vain: *Johnson, Robert* / I'm a man: *Diddley, Bo* / My head's in Mississippi: *ZZ Top* / Shake your moneymaker: *Fleetwood Mac* / Shame, shame, shame: *Winter, Johnny* / I'm leaving you (commit a crime): *Vaughan, Stevie Ray* / Walkin' to my baby: *Fabulous Thunderbirds* / All your love: *Mayall, John & The Bluesbreakers* / You shook me: *Beck, Jeff* / Greeny: *Blues Breakers* / Little red rooster: *Howlin' Wolf*

CD Set ________ VTDCD 54
Virgin / Jun '95 / EMI

BLUES AND BOOGIE - EXPLOSION
CD ________ BLR 84003
L&R / May '91 / New Note/Pinnacle

BLUES AND SOUL COLLECTION
CD ________ MU 5054
Musketeer / Oct '92 / Disc

BLUES AND SOUL LEGENDS
CD ________ MACCD 185
Autograph / Aug '96 / BMG

BLUES ANYTIME VOL.1 (An Anthology Of British Blues)
I'm your witch doctor / Snake drive / Ain't gonna cry no more / I tried / Tribute to Elmore / I feel so good / Telephone blues / You don't love me / West coast idea / Ain't seen no whisky / Flapjacks / Cold blooded woman
CD ________ CDIMM 008
Immediate / Nov '93 / Koch / Target/BMG

BLUES ARCHIVE
CD ________ RMCD 204
Rialto / Sep '96 / Disc / Total/BMG

BLUES AT NEWPORT 1959-1964
Candy man: *Hurt, 'Mississippi' John* / Coffee blues: *Hurt, 'Mississippi' John* / Stagolee: *Hurt, 'Mississippi' John* / Long gone: *McGhee, Brownie & Sonny Terry* / Key to the highway: *McGhee, Brownie & Sonny Terry* / Samson and Delilah: *Davis, Rev. Gary* / I won't be back no more: *Davis, Rev. Gary* / Prodigal son: *Wilkins, Rev. Robert* / (I wish I was in) Heaven sitting down: *Wilkins, Rev. Robert* / Devil got my woman: *James, Skip* / Clean up at home: *Estes, 'Sleepy' John* / On my way from Texas: *Williams, Robert Pete* / Bulldog blues: *Williams, Robert Pete* / I double double do love you: *Fuller, Jesse* / San Francisco Bay blues: *Fuller, Jesse* / Me and the devil: *Hammond, John* / Sometimes you make me feel so bad: *Hooker, John Lee* / Hobo blues: *Hooker, John Lee* / That will never happen no more: *Ronk, Dave Van*
CD ________ VCD 115
Vanguard / Oct '95 / ADA / Pinnacle

BLUES AT XMAS VOL.3
CD ________ ICH 1173CD
Ichiban / Oct '94 / Direct / Koch

BLUES BEFORE SUNRISE: LIVE VOL.1
I'm ready: *Big Wheeler* / Down in Virginia: *Big Wheeler* / She loves another man: *Big Wheeler* / Got a feeling (I got the blues): *Big Wheeler* / I gotta go: *Big Wheeler* / Be careful: *Brim, John* / Lonesome man blues: *Brim, John* / Tough times: *Brim, John* / Ice cream man: *Brim, John* / Streetwise advisor: *Arnold, Billy Boy* / Billy Boy medley: *Arnold, Billy Boy* / You're the one: *Burns, Jimmy* / Leaving here walking: *Burns, Jimmy*
CD ________ DE 699
Delmark / Jun '97 / ADA / Cadillac / CM / Direct / Hot Shot

BLUES BEHIND THE WALL (East Berlin 1966)
Running the boogie: *Sykes, Roosevelt* / All your love: *Sykes, Roosevelt* / I keep drinking: *Little Brother Montgomery* / You shouldn't do it: *Sleepy John Estes & Yank Rachell* / Roll 'em Pete: *Turner, 'Big' Joe* / Sheckin' on my baby: *Wells, Junior* / Vietnam blues: *Wells, Junior* / Suitcase blues: *Wallace, Sippie* / Midnight boogie: *Williams, Robert Pete* / Flip flop and fly: *Turner, 'Big' Joe* / It takes time: *Turner, 'Big' Joe* / Night time is the right time: *Sykes, Roosevelt* / My own fault: *Rush, Otis* / Pinetop's boogie woogie: *Smith, Clarence 'Pinetop'* / Yelow jam blues: *Estes, 'Sleepy' John & Yank Rachell* / Over yonder walls: *Wells, Junior* / Women keep your mouth shut: *Wallace, Sippie* / Tribute to Sonny Boy Williamson: *Wallace, Sippie* / Louise: *Williams, Robert Pete* / Feeling happy: *Turner, 'Big' Joe*
CD ________ CDMOJO 309
Mojo / Nov '96 / Direct

BLUES BLUES BLUES (3CD Set)
CD Set ________ EMTBX 303
Emporio / Aug '97 / Disc

BLUES BOX
CD Set ________ 308642
Scratch / Feb '96 / Koch / Scratch/BMG

BLUES, BOOGIE & BOP (The 1940's Mercury Sessions/7CD Set)
CD Set ________ 5256092
Mercury / Feb '96 / PolyGram

BLUES BRITANNIA
CD ________ BRGCD 07CD
Music Maker / Jul '94 / ADA / Grapevine/PolyGram

BLUES BROTHER, SOUL SISTER (The Best Of Blues Brother, Soul Sister - 2CD Set)
Boom boom: *Hooker, John Lee* / Take a little piece: *Franklin, Erma* / Soul man: *Sam & Dave* / I'd rather go blind: *James, Etta* / Green onions: *Booker T & The MG's* / Think: *Franklin, Aretha* / Harlem shuffle: *Bob & Earl* / Take me to the river: *Green, Al* / Mannish boy: *Waters, Muddy* / Rescue me: *Bass, Fontella* / In the midnight hour: *Pickett, Wilson* / Knock on wood: *Floyd, Eddie* / Stormy monday: *Little Milton* / Drift away: *Gray, Dobie* / Need your love so bad: *Fleetwood Mac* / I'm in the mood: *Hooker, John Lee* / It's a man's man's man's world: *Brown, James* / Born under a bad sign: *King, Albert* / Tired of being alone: *Green, Al* / Night time is the right time: *Turner, Ike & Tina* / I'm a roadrunner: *Walker, Junior & The All Stars* / I just want to make love to you: *James, Etta* / Tell it like it is: *Neville, Aaron* / High heeled sneakers: *Tucker, Tommy* / I'll take you there: *Staple Singers* / Private number: *Bell, William* / Little red rooster: *Howlin' Wolf* / Oh no not my baby: *Brown, Maxine* / I put a spell on you: *Simone, Nina* / When a man loves a woman: *Sledge, Percy* / Respect: *Franklin, Aretha* / Thrill has gone: *King, B.B.* / Sweet soul music: *Conley, Arthur* / Smokestack lightning: *Howlin' Wolf* / What'd I say: *Charles, Ray* / Stay with me baby: *Ellison, Lorraine* / Who's that lady: *Isley Brothers* / Got my mojo working: *Waters, Muddy* / (Sittin' on the) dock of the bay: *Redding, Otis* / B-A-B-Y: *Thomas, Carla* / My guy: *Wells, Mary* / Misty blue: *Moore, Misty* / How sweet it is: *Gaye, Marvin* / Dancing in the street: *Martha & The Vandellas* / Going to a go go: *Robinson, Smokey & The Miracles* / Uptight: *Wonder, Stevie* / Midnight train to Georgia: *Knight, Gladys*
CD Set ________ DINCD 115
Dino / Nov '95 / Pinnacle

BLUES BROTHERS
Bad luck shadow: *Otis, Johnny* / Wee baby blues: *Turner, Joe* / Kidney stew: *Vinson, Eddie 'Cleanhead'* / Louie Louie: *Berry, Richard* / Beans and cornbread: *Jordan, Louis* / Pink champagne: *Liggins, Joe* / Country girl: *Otis, Johnny* / Doin' it: *Berry, Richard* / Squeeze me baby: *Turner, Joe* / Midnight creeper: *Vinson, Eddie 'Cleanhead'* / Oh baby I love you: *Berry, Richard* / Honey dipper (part one): *Liggins, Joe* / Honey dripper (part two): *Liggins, Joe* / Evening shadows coming down: *Milburn, Amos* / Cherry red: *Vinson, Eddie 'Cleanhead'* / Nothin' from nothin' blues: *Turner, Joe* / One scotch, one bourbon, one beer: *Milburn, Amos* / Boom chick a boogie: *Liggins, Joe* / Let the good times roll: *Jordan, Louis* / Person to person: *Vinson, Eddie 'Cleanhead'* / Chick shack a boogie: *Milburn, Amos* / I'm a good thing: *Jordan, Louis* / Bye bye baby: *Otis, Johnny*
CD ________ 3035900082
Essential Gold / Apr '96 / Carlton

BLUES BUSTERS VOL.2
CD ________ MSA 008CD
Munich / Apr '94 / ADA / CM / Direct / Greensleeves

BLUES BUSTERS VOL.3 (Classic Blues Rock)
CD ________ MSACD 010
Munich / Aug '96 / ADA / CM / Direct / Greensleeves

BLUES CHICAGO STYLE
CD ________ PLSCD 181
Pulse / Apr '97 / BMG

BLUES COCKTAIL PARTY
CD ________ BT 1066CD
Black Top / '92 / ADA / CM / Direct

BLUES COLLECTION (3CD Set)
CD Set ________ TBXCD 508
TrueTrax / Jan '96 / THE

BLUES COLLECTION (3CD Set)
Snake drive: *Clapton, Eric* / Dust my broom: *Waters, Muddy* / I'm in the mood: *Hooker, John Lee* / Step back baby: *King Biscuit Boy* / Telephone blues: *Mayall, John & The Bluesbreakers* / First time I met the blues: *Guy, Buddy* / Hold that train: *Smith, Byther* / LA breakdown: *All Stars & Jimmy Page* / Looking for my baby: *Johnson, Jimmy* / You upset me baby: *Allison, Luther* / I've got a mind to travel: *Collins, Albert* / Came up the hard way: *Clearwater, Eddy* / You don't love me: *McPhee, Tony* / Stormy monday blues: *Korner, Alexis* / Dimples: *Hooker, John Lee* / Howlin' wolf: *Waters, Muddy* / On top of the world: *Mayall, John & Eric Clapton* / Don't let my baby ride: *Scott, Isaac* / Good rockin' mama: *Hooker, John Lee* / Red hot mama: *Fleetwood Mac* / Red house: *Hendrix, Jimi* / How can one woman be so mean: *Guy, Buddy & Junior Wells* / Leave me alone: *Benton, Buster* / Hoochie coochie man: *Waters, Muddy* / Cold blooded woman: *Savoy Brown* / No shoes: *Hooker, John Lee* / Easy: *Horton, Big Walter* / Walking blues: *Waters, Muddy* / Somebody loan me a dime: *Robinson, Fenton* / I wish you would: *Arnold, Billy Boy & Tony McPhee* / Foxtrot: *Hooker, Earl* / Can't hold out: *Sharpville, Todd* / She's mine (keep your hands to yourself): *Hooker, John Lee* / Bad news: *Moore, Gary* / Steelin': *Clapton, Eric & Jimmy Page* / Crosstown link: *Lee, Albert* / All my money gone: *De Lay, Paul Band* / End of the blues: *Hooker, Earl* / Born with the blues: *Bell, Carey & Buster Benton* / Blue light: *Mighty Houserockers* / Blow wind blow: *Waters, Muddy* / Hobo blues: *Hooker, John Lee* / Don't stay out all night: *Arnold, Billy Boy & Tony McPhee* / I gotta new car/ Framed: *Key, Troyce & J.J. Malone* / I'm leaving: *Hooker, John Lee* / I had it so hard: *Sunnyland Slim*
CD Set ________ PBXCD 508
Pulse / Nov '96 / BMG

BLUES COLLECTION VOL.2
Step it up and go: *Fuller, 'Blind' Boy* / Diddie wa diddie: *Blind Blake* / Spoonful blues: *Patton, Charlie* / Nobody's fault but mine: *Johnson, Blind Willie* / New someday baby: *Estes, 'Sleepy' John* / Billie's blues: *Holiday, Billie* / Boogie woogie: *Young, Lester* / Down the road apiece: *Sanchez, Michael* / Cry to me: *Beaker, Norman Band* / Act like you love me: *Detonators* / Mai Lee: *Hooker, John Lee* / It's a man down there: *Bennett, Buster* / Sonny Boy Williamson: *Bruce, Jack & Paul Jones* / Married men: *McPhee, Tony & The Groundhogs* / My baby she don't look like that: *Lamb, Paul & The King Snakes* / Look out: *Webb, Stan & Chicken Shack* / Time to love: *Abrahams, Mick* / Have a little faith in me: *Farlowe, Chris* / Rockin' good way: *Turner, Ruby* / Some change: *Price, Alan & Electric Blues Company*
CD ________ IGOCD 2061
Indigo / Feb '97 / ADA / Direct

BLUES DELUXE
Clouds in my heart: *Blues Deluxe* / Hey bartender: *Taylor, Koko* / Wang dang doodle: *Dixon, Willie* / Sweet home Chicago: *Brooks, Lonnie* / Don't throw your love on me so strong: *Seals, Son* / You too might need a friend: *Young, 'Mighty' Joe*
CD ________ XRTCD 9301
Alligator / Oct '93 / ADA / CM / Direct

BLUES EXPERIENCE
When love comes to town: *U2* / Still got the blues (for you): *Moore, Gary* / Somewhere down the crazy river: *Robertson, Robbie* / Black magic woman: *Fleetwood Mac* / I'd rather go blind: *Chicken Shack* / Crossroads: *Cream* / Cocaine: *Cale, J.J.* / Please don't let me be misunderstood: *Cocker, Joe* / Ronettes: *Cray, Robert Band* / Try a little tenderness: *Commitments* / She's not there: *Santana* / On the road again: *Canned Heat* / Nineties blues: *Rea, Chris* / Fade to black: *Dire Straits* / Steamy windows: *White, Tony Joe* / Walking the dog: *Thomas, Rufus* / Who do you love: *Thorogood, George* / Red house: *Hendrix, Jimi*
CD ________ 5162282
PolyGram TV / Jun '93 / PolyGram

BLUES EXPERIENCE VOL.1
CD ________ CDRR 301
Request / May '92 / Jazz Music / Wellard

BLUES FIREWORKS
CD ________ CAD 465
Blues Collection / Apr '95 / Discovery

BLUES FOR LOVERS
CD ________ DCD 5272
Kenwest / Nov '92 / THE

BLUES FOR YOU
CD ________ ALSCD 7958
Alligator / Jul '89 / ADA / CM / Direct

BLUES FROM CHICAGO
Sweet home Chicago / Big boss man / Low down funk / I'm losing you / Lost love / Hoochie koochie man / You go me cryin' / I got to love my woman / Mess ada blues
CD ________ CDTB 174
Thunderbolt / Feb '96 / TKO Magnum

BLUES FROM DOLPHIN'S OF HOLLYWOOD
Darkest hour: *Crayton, Pee Wee* / Forgive me: *Crayton, Pee Wee* / Crying and walking: *Crayton, Pee Wee* / Pappy's blues: *Crayton, Pee Wee* / Baby, pat the floor: *Crayton, Pee Wee* / I'm your prisoner: *Crayton, Pee Wee* / Lovin' John: *Crayton, Pee Wee* / Fillmore Street blues: *Crayton, Pee Wee* / Boogie bop: *Crayton, Pee Wee* / You can't bring me down: *Little Caesar* / Cadillac baby: *Little Caesar* / WDIA station ID: *Mayfield, Percy* / Look the whole world over: *Mayfield, Percy* / Monkey song: *Mayfield, Percy* / Treat me like I treat you: *Mayfield, Percy* / My country girl: *Mayfield, Percy* / Worried life blues: *Mayfield, Percy* / Pete's boogie: *Mayfield, Percy* / Big family blues: *Witherspoon, Jimmy* / Cain River blues: *Witherspoon, Jimmy* / Teenage party: *Witherspoon, Jimmy* / SK blues: *Witherspoon, Jimmy* / Never know when a woman changes her mind: *Dixon, Floyd* / Oh baby: *Dixon, Floyd* / Cadillac funeral: *Harris, Peppermint*
CD ________ CDCHD 357
Ace / Nov '91 / Pinnacle

BLUES GIANTS
CD ________ MATCD 272
Castle / Apr '93 / BMG

BLUES GIANTS
CD ________ PLSCD 172
Pulse / Apr '97 / BMG

BLUES GIANTS IN CONCERT
Blues everywhere: *Memphis Slim* / John Henry: *Memphis Slim & Willie Dixon* / Captain captain: *Waters, Muddy* / Catfish blues: *Waters, Muddy* / In the city: *Waters, Muddy* / I feel like cryin': *Waters, Muddy* / Your love for me is true: *Williamson, Sonny Boy* / Don't misuse me: *Williamson, Sonny Boy* / I'm getting tired: *Williamson, Sonny Boy* / Getting down slow: *Spann, Otis* / Careless love: *Johnson, Lonnie* / CC rider: *Johnson, Lonnie* / TB blues: *Spivey, Victoria* / Big roll blues: *Williams, Big Joe* / Back in the bottom: *Williams, Big Joe* / Baby, please don't go: *Williams, Big Joe*

CD ________ 92052
Act / Aug '94 / New Note/Pinnacle

BLUES GOLD COLLECTION (2CD Set)
CD Set ________ D2CD 4008
Deja Vu / Jun '95 / THE

BLUES GUITAR
CD ________ PLSCD 155
Pulse / Apr '97 / BMG

BLUES GUITAR BLASTERS
After hours: *Nolan, Jimmy* / Killing floor: *King, Albert* / You threw your love on me too strong: *King, Albert* / Talkin' woman: *Fulson, Lowell* / Everytime it rains: *Fulson, Lowell* / Early in the morning: *King, B.B.* / Talkin' the blues: *King, B.B.* / Dust my blues: *James, Elmore* / Elmo's shuffle: *James, Elmore* / Hawaiian boogie: *James, Elmore* / Jumpin' in the heart of town: *Thomas, Lafayette* / Certainly all: *Guitar Slim* / Things that I used to do: *Guitar Slim* / Twistin' the strings: *Turner, Ike* / Three hours past midnight: *Watson, Johnny 'Guitar'* / Twinky: *Crayton, Pee Wee* / Mistreated so bad: *Crayton, Pee Wee* / Hey hey baby: *Walker, T-Bone* / I had a good girl: *Hooker, John Lee*
CD ________ CDCH 232
Ace / Jan '88 / Pinnacle

BLUES GUITAR GREATS
Move it on over: *Thorogood, George & The Destroyers* / Kings crosstown shuffle: *King, Little Jimmy* / Robert Nighthawk stomp: *Earl, Ronnie & The Broadcasters* / Don't stop by the creek son: *Copeland, Johnny* / Too hot to handle: *Robillard, Duke* / One way or another: *Washington, Walter 'Wolfman'* / Trouble: *Shannon, Preston Band* / Alligator boogaloo: *Brown, Clarence 'Gatemouth'* / Payback: *Lynn, Barbara* / Just for a little while: *Kubek, Smokin' Joe Band*
CD ________ EDCD 7016
Easydisc / Aug '96 / Direct

BLUES GUITAR GREATS
Down in the bottom: *Williams, Big Joe* / Government money: *Estes, 'Sleepy' John* / I don't want no woman: *Magic Sam* / Five long years: *Allison, Luther* / If you change your mind: *Hutto, J.B.* / Chitlins con carne: *Dawkins, Jimmy* / I walked all night: *Young, Joe* / Lockwood's boogie: *Lockwood, Robert Jr.* / Trouble don't last always: *Wells, Junior & Buddy Guy* / So many roads: *Rush, Otis* / Crash head on into love: *Brooks, Lonnie* / Strange how I miss you: *Johnson, Jimmy* / Why's life got to be this way: *McDaniel, Floyd & Blues Swingers* / Someday after awhile: *Barkin' Bill & Steve Freund* / West side stroll: *Specter, Dave & The Bluebirds* / West side woman: *Bell, Lurrie* / Mean mistreater: *Moore, Johnny B.*
CD ________ DE 697
Delmark / Jun '97 / ADA / Cadillac / CM / Direct / Hot Shot

BLUES GUITAR HEROES
CD ________ TRTCD 154
TrueTrax / Dec '94 / THE

BLUES GUITAR MASTERS (2CD Set)
CD Set ________ CDGR 1422
Charly / Apr '97 / Koch

BLUES GUITARISTS
CD ________ CLACD 431
Castle / Mar '97 / BMG

BLUES HARMONICA SPOTLIGHT
CD ________ BT 1083CD
Black Top / Jan '93 / ADA / CM / Direct

BLUES HARP BOOGIE
CD ________ MCCD 124
Music Club / Jan '92 / Disc / THE

BLUES HARP GREATS
Three harp boogie: *Cotton, James & Paul Butterfield/Billy Boy Arnold* / (I shoulda did) What my Mama told me: *Bell, Carey* / Come back baby: *Treat Her Right* / Oven is on: *Montgomery, James Band* / Jumpin' blues: *Magic Dick & Jay Geils* / Ol' heartbreak: *Raines, Annie & Paul Rishell* / Hey baby (Don't you know your Daddy loves you so): *Butler Twins* / Rockin' at th eRiverside: *Hummel, Mark* / Pickin' rags: *Buford, Mojo* / Lamp post: *Sayles, Charlie*
CD ________ EDCD 7023
Easydisc / Feb '97 / Direct

BLUES HOLLERIN' BOOGIE
Help: *Scott, Isaac* / Hoochie coochie man: *Waters, Muddy* / I wouldn't treat a dog (the way you treated me): *Big Twist & The Mellow Fellows* / Just a dream: *Arnold, Billy Boy & Tony McPhee* / Never let me go: *Tucker, Tommy* / Wandering blues: *Hooker, John Lee* / Lowdown and funky: *Gaines, Ropy & The Crusaders* / Sorry: *Benton, Buster & Carey Bell* / Oh what a feeling: *Ricks, Jimmy & the Ravens* / War is starting: *Hopkins, Lightnin'* / That's alright Mama: *Turner, Titus* / Cut you loose: *Smith, Byther* / Whammy: *Hawkins, Screamin' Jay* / Don't you feel my leg: *Muldaur, Maria* / Hey hey: *Turner, Ike & Jimmy Thomas* / Insane asylum: *Baldry, Long John & Kathi McDonald* / Trouble all my days: *Louisiana Red* / Touch of your love: *Sharpville, Todd* / Mayor Daley's blues: *Clearwater, Eddy* / Walk right in: *Musselwhite, Charley*
CD ________ MCCD 173
Music Club / Sep '94 / Disc / THE

BLUES IN JAZZ, THE
CD ______ CD 56002
Jazz Roots / Aug '94 / Target/BMG

BLUES IN THE MISSISSIPPI NIGHT
CD ______ RCD 10206
Rykodisc / Feb '92 / ADA / Vital

BLUES IN THE NIGHT NO.1 (Newport Jazz Festival 1958 July 3rd-6th)
CD ______ NCD 8815
Phontastic / '93 / Cadillac / Jazz Music / Wellard

BLUES IN THE NIGHT NO.2 (Newport Jazz Festival 1958 July 3rd-6th)
CD ______ NCD 8816
Phontastic / '93 / Cadillac / Jazz Music / Wellard

BLUES IS A TRAMP - LIVE PARADISO
CD Set ______ TRCD 99122
Tramp / Nov '93 / ADA / CM / Direct

BLUES JAM IN CHICAGO
Watch out / Ooh baby / South Indiana / Last night / Red hot jam / I'm worried / I held my baby last night / Madison blues / I can't hold out / I need your love / I got the blues / World's in a tangle / Talk with you / Like it this way / Someday soon baby / Hungry country girl / Black Jack blues / Rockin' boogie / Sugar mama / Homework
CD ______ 4805272
Columbia / May '95 / Sony

BLUES LADIES, THE
CC rider blues: *Rainey, Gertrude 'Ma'* / Blame it on the blues: *Rainey, Gertrude 'Ma'* / Don't advertise your man: *Smith, Clara* / Nobody knows the way I feel this mornin': *Hunter, Alberta* / How long daddy, how long: *Cox, Ida* / Black snake blues: *Spivey, Victoria* / Bedroom blues: *Wallace, Sippie* / Trouble in mind: *Hill, Chippie* / Gin house blues: *Smith, Bessie* / Nobody knows you when you're down and out: *Smith, Bessie* / I need a little sugar in my bowl: *Smith, Bessie* / My Georgia grind: *Bogan, Lucille* / Black angel blues: *Bogan, Lucille* / Ice man (come on up): *Memphis Minnie* / You done lost your good thing now: *White, Georgia* / Blues ain't nothin' but: *White, Georgia* / Hot nuts (get them from the peanut man): *Johnson, Lil* / Don't you make me high: *Johnson, Merline* / Rock me: *Tharpe, Rosetta* / I'm tired of fattein' frogs for snakes: *Crawford, Rosetta* / Romance in the dark: *Green, Lil* / Why don't you do right: *Green, Lil* / Evil gal blues: *Washington, Dinah* / Salty papa blues: *Washington, Dinah*
CD ______ IGOCD 2042
Indigo / Nov '96 / ADA / Direct

BLUES LEGENDS (4CD Set)
CD Set ______ MBSCD 416
Castle / Mar '93 / BMG

BLUES LEGENDS (4CD Set)
CD Set ______ MCBX 009
Music Club / Apr '94 / Disc / THE

BLUES LEGENDS
CD ______ MACCD 196
Autograph / Aug '96 / BMG

BLUES LEGENDS VOL.1
CD ______ 901592
FM / May '91 / Revolver / Sony

BLUES LEGENDS VOL.2
CD ______ 901602
FM / May '91 / Revolver / Sony

BLUES LEGENDS VOL.3
CD ______ 901612
FM / May '91 / Revolver / Sony

BLUES LIVE FROM THE MOUNTAIN STAGE
Leave my woman alone: *Nighthawks* / It hurts me too: *Nelson, Tracy* / Slidell blues: *Geremia, Paul* / That's the way to do it: *Pryor, Snooky* / My Daddy was a jockey: *Hammond, John* / Blues why do you worry me: *Musselwhite, Charley* / Devil's real: *Smither, Chris* / Black cat on the line: *Cephas, John 'Bowling Green' & Phil Wiggins* / Lonesome bedroom blues: *Clarke, William* / Louisiana blues: *Jackson, John* / You got love if you want it: *Legendary Blues Band* / That'll work: *Johnson, Johnnie* / Quicks and blues: *Brown, Charles* / Gee I wish: *Robillard, Duke*
CD ______ BPMCD 305
Blue Plate / May '97 / ADA / Direct / Greyhound

BLUES MASTERS
Can't get you off my mind: *Jones, Lloyd* / Kansas city monarch: *Earl, Ronnie* / Too proud: *Mighty Sam* / Bring it on home: *MacLeod, Doug* / Feel like going home: *Lucas, Robert* / Down in Mississippi: *Evans, Terry* / Feets out in the hallway: *Beard, Joe* / I'm so lonely: *Mighty Sam* / Moonshine 2: *Lucas, Robert*
CD ______ AQCD 1034
Audioquest / Feb '96 / ADA / New Note/ Pinnacle

BLUES MEN, THE
Down at the corner grocery store: *Reed, Jimmy* / Goin' mad blues: *Hooker, John Lee* / Dust my broom: *Waters, Muddy* / I wish you would: *Arnold, Billy Boy & Tony McPhee* / Your gonna need me, baby: *Louisiana Red* / Major Daley's blues: *Clearwater, Eddy* / Come on in this house: *Smith, Byther* / Still a fool: *Edwards, Clarence* / In my younger days: *Guy, Buddy & Junior Wells* / Soft and mellow Stella: *Sunnyland Slim* / Somebody loan me a dime: *Robinson, Fenton* / Mona: *Diddley, Bo* / Neighbour neighbour: *King Biscuit Boy & Ronnie Hawkins Band* / War is starting again: *Hopkins, Lightnin'* / When my first wife quit me: *Johnson, Jimmy* / Ship made of paper: *Magic Slim*
CD ______ ECD 3315
K-Tel / May '97 / K-Tel

BLUES MISTLETOE & SANTA'S LITTLE HELPER
CD ______ BT 1122CD
Black Top / Oct '95 / ADA / CM / Direct

BLUES NOTES - AND BLACK (A Blues Survey From 1920-1960)
CD ______ PHONTNCD 8827
Phontastic / '93 / Cadillac / Jazz Music / Wellard

BLUES OBSCURITIES 1923-1931
CD ______ DOCD 5481
Document / Nov '96 / ADA / Hot Shot / Jazz Music

BLUES ON FIRE
Man and the blues: *Bell, Lurrie* / Blues at my baby's house: *Guy, Buddy* / She torture me: *Walker, Philip & Otis Grand* / Small room: *Sayles, Charlie* / Down so long: *Louisiana Red* / Bad luck and trouble: *Wilson, U.P.* / Pursue your dreams: *Butler Twins* / Why don't you let me be: *Wilson, Smokey* / Desert Island: *Mars, Johnny* / I can't live happy: *Walker, Victor* / It's so easy to love you: *Bell, Carey* / Play the blues in Paris: *Smith, Byther*
CD ______ EDCD 9007
Easydisc / Feb '97 / Direct

BLUES PIANO ORGY
Blues hurt my tongue to talk: *Speckled Red* / Dresser drawers: *Sykes, Roosevelt* / Concentration blues: *Sykes, Roosevelt* / Kickin' motor scooter: *Sykes, Roosevelt* / (New Year's) resolution blues: *Sykes, Roosevelt* / My baby's coming with a marriage license: *Sunnyland Slim* / Poor boy: *Sunnyland Slim* / Every time I get to drinkin': *Sunnyland Slim* / Depression blues: *Sunnyland Slim* / Stendahl stomp: *Little Brother Montgomery* / Tremblin' blues: *Little Brother Montgomery* / No special rider: *Little Brother Montgomery* / Bass key boogie: *Little Brother Montgomery* / Five o'clock blues: *Memphis Slim* / Nat Dee special: *Memphis Slim* / Lonesome bedroom blues: *Jones, Curtis* / Takin' off: *Jones, Curtis* / Tin Pan Alley blues: *Jones, Curtis* / Three-in-one blues: *Spann, Otis*
CD ______ DE 626
Delmark / Nov '96 / ADA / Cadillac / CM / Direct / Hot Shot

BLUES ROOTS
CD ______ 2696182
Tomato / Feb '89 / Vital

BLUES ROUND MIDNIGHT
Three o'clock blues: *Davis, Larry* / Old man blues: *Copeland, Johnny* / Something about you: *Davis, Larry* / Blues around midnight: *Fulson, Lowell* / Love will lead you right: *Walker, T-Bone* / You're breaking my heart: *King, B.B.* / Down now: *King, B.B.* / Shattered dreams: *Fulson, Lowell* / T-99 Blues: *Nelson, Jimmy 'T-99'* / I'm wonderin' and wonderin': *Charles, Ray* / Second hand fool: *Nelson, Jimmy 'T-99'* / Quit hanging around: *King, Saunders* / Dragnet blues: *Ervin, Frankie* / Crazy with the blues: *Jones, Marti* / Our love is here to stay: *Holden, Lorenzo* / I need somebody: *Witherspoon, Jimmy* / Gee baby ain't I good to you: *Witherspoon, Jimmy* / Picture of you: *Green, Vivianne* / Playing the numbers: *Ervin, Frankie* / It just wasn't true: *Jones, Marl*
CD ______ CDCH 235
Ace / Apr '88 / Pinnacle

BLUES SHAKERS (20 Original Blues Grooves)
Shake your moneymaker: *James, Elmore* / Left handed woman: *Reed, Jimmy* / Fannie Mae: *Brown, Buster* / Rough dried woman: *Big Mac* / All your love: *Rush, Otis* / Look watcha done: *Magic Sam* / Big town playboy: *Taylor, Eddie* / Blues in D natural: *Hooker, Earl* / Big car blues: *Hopkins, Lightnin'* / Just a little bit: *Gordon, Rosco* / Bear cat: *Thomas, Rufus* / Roll and rhumba: *Reed, Jimmy* / Kansas City: *Harrison, Wilbert* / Good rockin' tonight: *Witherspoon, Jimmy* / This is the end: *Guy, Buddy* / Figure head: *Brooks, Lonnie* / Cut you-a loose: *Allen, Ricky* / Frisco blues: *Hooker, John Lee* / My back scratcher: *Frost, Frank* / Bowlegged woman: *Rush, Bobby*
CD ______ CDNEW 102
Charly / Dec '96 / Koch

BLUES, THE (2CD Set)
CD Set ______ R2CD 4008
Deja Vu / Jan '96 / THE

BLUES, THE
CD ______ RENCD 114
Renaissance Collector Series / Mar '96 / BMG

BLUES WITH A DIFFERENCE
CD ______ CDS 4
Rounder / '88 / ADA / CM / Direct

BLUES WITH A FEELING (2CD Set)
Introduction: *House, Son* / Preaching blues: *House, Son* / Death letter blues: *House, Son* / Empire state express: *House, Son* / Devil got my woman: *James, Skip* / Aberdeen Mississippi blues: *White, Bukka* / Levee camp blues: *Williams, Robert Pete* / Louise: *McDowell, 'Mississippi' Fred* / Don't let nobody turn you round: *Wilkins, Rev. Robert* / Keep your lamp trimmed and burning: *Brown, Rev. Pearly & Christine* / What do you think about Jesus: *McDowell, 'Mississippi' Fred & Annie Mae/Rev. Robert Wilkins* / Woman I'm loving she's taken my appetite: *Hopkins, Lightnin'* / Come on baby: *Hopkins, Lightnin'* / Baby please don't go: *Hopkins, Lightnin'* / Freddie: *Lipscomb, Mance* / So different blues: *Lipscomb, Mance* / God moves on the water (The sinking of the Titanic): *Lipscomb, Mance* / Freight train: *Cotten, Elizabeth* / Here I am Lord send me: *Hurt, 'Mississippi' John* / Pallet on your floor: *Hurt, 'Mississippi' John* / San Francisco Bay blues: *Fuller, Jesse Lone Cat* / I can't quit you baby: *Hooker, John Lee* / Stop now baby: *Hooker, John Lee* / Walkin' blues: *Waters, Muddy* / I can't be satisfied: *Waters, Muddy* / Five long years: *Boyd, Eddie & Willie Dixon* / Wrinkles: *Lafayette, Leake & Willie Dixon* / Cocaine: *Van Ronk, Dave* / Drop down mama: *Hammond, John* / Grizzly bear: *Von Schmidt, Eric* / Travelling blues: *Koerner, 'Spider' John* / CC rider: *Chambers Brothers* / Blues with a feeling: *Butterfield, Paul Blues Band* / Look over yonder wall: *Butterfield, Paul Blues Band* / Born in Chicago: *Butterfield, Paul Blues Band*
CD Set ______ VCD2 77005
Vanguard / Oct '95 / ADA / Pinnacle

BLUES WITH A FEELING
CD ______ MACCD 199
Autograph / Aug '96 / BMG

BLUES WITH THE GIRLS
CD ______ 157582
Blues Collection / Feb '93 / Discovery

BLUES WOMEN TODAY
Two bit Texas town: *Strehli, Angela* / Don't let it end: *Washington, Toni Lynn* / Girlfriend says: *Willson, Michelle* / Blue house: *Ball, Marcia* / I'll take care of you: *Thomas, Irma* / Fear no evil: *Peebles, Ann* / No I ain't gonna let you go: *Boykin, Brenda* / Come with me: *Honeycutt, Miki* / My blue mood: *Bogart, Deanna* / God's gift to women: *Block, Rory*
CD ______ EDCD 7010
Easydisc / Oct '96 / Direct

BLUES YOU HATE TO LOSE (16 Classic Blues Performances)
Country boy blues: *Span, Otis* / Have a little walk with me: *Lockwood, Robert Jr.* / El capitan: *Memphis Slim* / How long blues: *Price, Sammy* / It's your own fault: *Hopkins, Lightnin'* / New key to the highway: *Gillum, Bill 'Jazz'* / Bad luck and troubles: *Stidham, Arbee* / In the evening: *Witherspoon, Jimmy* / Mamie's blues: *Hodes, Art* / CC rider: *McGhee, Brownie & Sonny Terry* / I've been mistreated: *Fulson, Lowell* / I'm gonna move to the outskirts of town: *Jordan, Louis* / It's a low down dirty shame: *Broonzy, 'Big' Bill* / When I've been drinkin': *Smith, Carrie* / Bring it to Jerome: *Diddley, Bo* / Goin' down slow: *Waters, Muddy*
CD ______ EMPRCD 661
Emporio / Jun '96 / Disc

BLUESIANA HOT SAUCE
CD ______ SHCD 5009
Shanachie / Apr '94 / ADA / Greensleeves / Koch

BLUESIANA HURRICANE
CD ______ SHCD 5014
Shanachie / Oct '95 / ADA / Greensleeves / Koch

BLUESMEN & RHYTHM KINGS
It's so cold and mean (drug scene): *Johnson, L.V.* / Something's mighty wrong: *Davis, Tyrone* / Strange: *Haddix, Travis* / You've got all of me: *King, Ben E.* / Dark end of the street: *White, Artie* / (When I) Think of my baby: *Graham, Jesse* / Let love take care (of the rest): *Brown, Nappy* / You don't know nothing about love: *Garrett, Vernon* / Where is Leroy: *Blues Boy Willie* / I've been loving you too long to stop now: *Clayton, Willie*
CD ______ ICH 11912
Ichiban / Jun '96 / Direct / Koch

BLUESVILLE VOL.1
Judge Boushay blues: *Lewis, Walter 'Furry'* / Country girl blues: *Memphis Willie B* / Big road blues: *Douglas, K.C.* / Levee camp blues: *Williams, Big Joe* / Catfish: *Smith, Robert Curtis* / San Quentin blues: *Maiden, Sidney* / Big fat mama: *Walton, Wade* / Grievin' me: *Franklin, Pete* / Dyin' crapshooters blues: *McTell, 'Blind' Willie* / Fine booze and heavy dues: *Johnson, Lonnie* / Blues before sunrise: *Blackwell, Scrapper* / You got to move: *Davis, Rev. Gary* / Brown skin woman: *Eaglin, Snooks* / Pawn shop: *McGhee, Brownie & Sonny Terry* / T-model blues: *Hopkins, Lightnin'* / You is one black rat: *Quattlebaum, Doug* / Highway 61: *Memphis Willie B* / Shake 'em on down: *Lewis, Walter 'Furry'* / Hand me down baby: *Maiden, Sidney* / Alberta: *Eaglin, Snooks* / See what you have done: *Tate, Baby* / Goin' where the moon crosses the yellow dog: *Blackwell, Scrapper*
CD ______ CDCH 247
Ace / Jun '88 / Pinnacle

BLUESVILLE VOL.1 (Big Blues Honks & Wails)
CD ______ PRCD 9905
Prestige / Feb '96 / Cadillac / Complete/ Pinnacle

BLUESVILLE VOL.2
Train done gone: *Kirkland, Eddie* / Down on my knees: *Kirkland, Eddie* / Homesick's blues: *Homesick James* / Stones in my passway: *Homesick James* / Rack 'em back Jack: *Memphis Slim* / Happy blues for John Glenn: *Hopkins, Lightnin'* / Devil jumped the black man: *Hopkins, Lightnin'* / My baby done gone: *Terry, Sonny* / School time: *Arnold, Billy Boy* / Big legged woman: *Johnson, Lonnie* / I have to worry: *King Curtis* / Calcutta: *Sykes, Roosevelt* / Show down: *Lucas, Buddy* / How long blues: *Witherspoon, Jimmy* / You better cut that out: *Arnold, Billy Boy* / Drivin' wheel: *Sykes, Roosevelt* / It's a lonesome old world: *Witherspoon, Jimmy* / Jelly roll baker: *Johnson, Lonnie*
CD ______ CDCH 250
Ace / Oct '88 / Pinnacle

BLUESVILLE VOL.2 (Feelin' Down On The South Side)
CD ______ PRCD 9906
Prestige / Feb '96 / Cadillac / Complete/ Pinnacle

BLUESVILLE VOL.3 (Beale Street Get-Down)
CD ______ PRCD 9907
Prestige / Feb '96 / Cadillac / Complete/ Pinnacle

BLUESVILLE VOL.4 (In The Key Of Blues)
CD ______ PRCD 9908
Prestige / Feb '96 / Cadillac / Complete/ Pinnacle

BLUNT SPECIAL BLENDS
CD ______ TVT 10102
Blunt / Jan '97 / Vital

BOAT TO PROGRESS
CD ______ GRELCD 602
Greensleeves / May '90 / Jet Star / SRD

BOATS AGAINST THE CURRENT
CD ______ CAKE 012CD
Hedonist / Dec '96 / Cargo / SRD

BODY AND SOUL (2CD Set)
I say a little prayer for you: *Franklin, Aretha* / River deep, mountain high: *Turner, Ike & Tina* / Only sixteen: *Cooke, Sam* / Stand by me: *King, Ben E.* / Have you seen her: *Chi-Lites* / My guy: *Wells, Mary* / Dancing in the street: *Martha & The Vandellas* / Harlem shuffle: *Bob & Earl* / If you don't know me by now: *Melvin, Harold & The Bluenotes* / When a man loves a woman: *Sledge, Percy* / (If loving you is wrong) I don't want to be right: *Ingram, Luther* / Tell it like it is: *Neville, Aaron* / Doggin' around: *Wilson, Jackie* / If you need me: *Pickett, Wilson* / Soul man: *Sam & Dave* / Knock on wood: *Floyd, Eddie* / Be young, be foolish, be happy: *Tams* / Love don't live here anymore: *Rose Royce* / My special prayer: *Sledge, Percy* / Chain of fools: *Franklin, Aretha* / Wonderful world: *Cooke, Sam* / Spanish Harlem: *King, Ben E.* / Daddy's home: *Shep & The Limelites* / Down to my last heartbreak: *Pickett, Wilson* / Nowhere to run: *Reeves, Martha* / Release me: *Phillips, Esther* / Alone at last: *Wilson, Jackie* / Hey there lonely girl: *Holman, Eddie* / Letter full of tears: *Knight, Gladys & The Pips* / Show & tell: *Wilson, Al* / Soul sister, brown sugar: *Sam & Dave* / Love I lost: *Melvin, Harold & The Bluenotes* / Why can't we live together: *Thomas, Timmy* / Something old, something new: *Fantastics* / Hold on I'm coming: *Burke, Solomon* / It's a man's man's man's world: *Brown, James*
CD Set ______ TNC 96236
Natural Collection / Aug '96 / Target/BMG

BODY HEAT
Unbelievable: *EMF* / Your mama don't dance: *Poison* / Hot in the city: *Idol, Billy* / Hold on: *Wilson Phillips* / Coast to coast: *Shaffer, Paul* / Hot child in the city: *Gilder, Nick* / C'est la vie: *Nevil, Robbie* / We don't have to take our clothes off: *Stewart, Jermaine* / I touch myself: *Divinyls* / Right here right now: *Jesus Jones* / Land of a thousand dances: *Geils, J. Band* / Ice ice baby: *Vanilla Ice* / Some like it hot: *Power Station* / When you walk in the room: *Carrack, Paul* / I won't let the sun go down on me: *Kershaw, Nik* / So hot: *Heights* / Love blonde: *Wilde, Kim*
CD ______ DC 880752
Disky / Aug '97 / Disky / THE

BODY RAPTURES VOL.3
CD ______ CDZOT 110
Zoth Ommog / Sep '94 / Cargo / Plastic Head

BOGLE AT LARGE
CD ______ EWCD 01
Teams / Oct '92 / Jet Star

BOGLE FEVER
CD ______ WRCD 003
World / Jun '97 / Jet Star / TKO Magnum

BOGLE MANIA
CD ____ GRELCD 180
Greensleeves / Apr '93 / Jet Star / SRD

BOLERO - THE COOL COMPILATION
Popurri de boleros - si mi comprendieras: *Faz, Roberto Y Su Conjunto* / Como pienso en ti: *Alonso Y Los Bocucos* / Amor fugaz: *More, Benny Y Su Orquesta* / A mi manera (Comme d'habitude): *Alvarez, Adalberto & Su Son* / Si me pudieras querer: *Faz, Roberto Y Su Conjunto Casino* / Frenesi: *Gomez, Tito Con Su Conjunto* / Tu mi adoracion: *Faz, Roberto Y Su Conjunto Casino* / Me falabas tu: *Alonso, Pacho Y Su Orquestra* / Popurri de boleros - Irremediablemente solo: *Faz, Roberto Y Su Conjunto*
CD ____ PSCCD 1008
Pure Sounds From Cuba / Feb '95 / Henry Hadaway / THE

BOLERO MANIA (4CD Set)
CD ____ BM 99906
Blue Moon / Apr '97 / Cadillac / Discovery / Greensleeves / Jazz Music / Jet Star / TKO Magnum

BOLLOCKS TO CHRISTMAS
Christmas time again: *Bad Manners* / Christmas is really fantastic: *Sidebottom, Frank* / Step into Christmas: *Business* / Snowman: *Anti Nowhere League* / Blue Christmas: *Frantic Flintstones* / Merry Christmas everybody: *4 Skins* / O come all ye faithful (adeste fidelis): *Sidebottom, Frank* / Jingle bells: *Judge Dread* / Hey Santa: *UK Subs* / Twelve days of Christmas: *Splodge* / Stuff the turkey: *Alien Sex Fiend* / Another Christmas: *Yobs* / I wish it could be Christmas: *Sidebottom, Frank* / Jingle bells: *Macc Lads* / Christmas in Dreadland: *Judge Dread* / Turkey stomp: *Hotknives* / Santa bring my baby back: *Frantic Flintstones* / Auld Lang Syne: *UK Subs* / C-h-r-i-s-t-m-a-s: *Yobs* / White Christmas: *Gonads* / Drinking and driving: *Business* / Christmas medley: *Sidebottom, Frank* / White Christmas (live): *Stiff Little Fingers*
CD ____ DOJOCD 204
Dojo / Dec '94 / Disc

BOMBA
CD ____ MCD 71355
Monitor / Jun '93 / CM

BOMBARDES ET BINIOUS DE BRETAGNE
CD ____ ARN 64243
Arion / Aug '93 / ADA / Discovery

BONANZA SKA
CD ____ CDTRL 309
Trojan / Mar '94 / Direct / Jet Star

BONESHAKERS VOL.1 (12 Superb Funky Boneshaking Grooves)
CD ____ IBCD 2
Internal Bass / Jan '97 / Prime / Timewarp / Total/BMG

BONESHAKERS VOL.2
CD ____ IBCD 5
Internal Bass / Jan '97 / Prime / Timewarp / Total/BMG

BONNIE SCOTLAND
CD ____ PASTCD 9800
Flapper / Nov '92 / Pinnacle

BONNIE SCOTLAND
CD ____ GCMD 506
GCM / Jun '97 / Total/BMG

BOO
Mountaineering in Belgium: *Attila The Stockbroker* / Charm: *Shoulders* / Oh Marie: *Tender Trap* / Music down: *Tansads* / Carry me: *Levellers* / She drives my train: *Resque* / Shotgun: *Bleach* / Turpentine: *Newcranes* / On Sunday: *Shoulders* / Polishing your hate: *Stranglmartin* / Eye of the average: *Tansads* / Love comes through: *Tender Trap* / Trash Madonna: *Zodiac Mindwarp & The Love Reaction* / Nature's love: *Newcranes*
CD ____ 10062
Musidisc / Jan '93 / Discovery

BOOGIE WOOGIE
CD ____ CD 14552
Jazz Portraits / Jul '94 / Jazz Music

BOOGIE WOOGIE (2CD Set)
Cavalcade of boogie: *Ammons, Albert* / Boogie woogie stomp: *Ammons, Albert* / Boogie woogie blues: *Ammons, Albert* / Suitcase blues: *Ammons, Albert* / Chicago in mind: *Ammons, Albert* / Shout for joy: *Ammons, Albert* / Boogie woogie: *Ammons, Albert* / Bass goin' crazy: *Ammons, Albert* / Derborn street breakdown: *Avery, Charles* / Henry Brown blues: *Brown, Henry* / Deep Morgan blues: *Brown, Henry* / Eastern chimes blues: *Brown, Henry* / Slow drag: *Davenport, Cow Cow* / Chimes blues: *Davenport, Cow Cow* / Atlanta rag: *Davenport, Cow Cow* / Barrelhouse woman: *Ezell, Will* / Heifer dust: *Ezell, Will* / Chain em down: *Garnett, Blind Leroy* / Louisiana glide: *Garnett, Blind Leroy* / Honky tonk train blues: *Lewis, Meade 'Lux'* / Fanny Lee blues: *Wallace, Wesley* / No. 29: *Wallace, Wesley* / Jab blues: *Williams, Jabo* / Pratt city blues: *Williams, Jabo*
CD Set ____ 24321
Laserlight / Feb '96 / Target/BMG

BOOGIE WOOGIE AND BARRELHOUSE PIANO VOL.1
CD ____ DOCD 5102
Document / Nov '92 / ADA / Hot Shot / Jazz Music

BOOGIE WOOGIE AND BARRELHOUSE PIANO VOL.2
CD ____ DOCD 5103
Document / Nov '92 / ADA / Hot Shot / Jazz Music

BOOGIE WOOGIE BEAT
CD ____ CWNCD 2008
Javelin / Jun '95 / Henry Hadaway / THE

BOOGIE WOOGIE BLUES
Cow cow blues: *Davenport, Cow Cow* / 5th street blues: *Davenport, Cow Cow* / Hurry and bring it home blues: *Davenport, Cow Cow* / Harlem choc'late babies on parade: *Johnson, James P.* / Birmingham blues: *Johnson, James P.* / Sugar blues: *Williams, Clarence* / Papa de da da: *Williams, Clarence* / Gulf coast blues: *Johnson, Clarence* / You're always messin' 'round with my man: *Johnson, Clarence* / Low down papa: *Johnson, Clarence* / Chicago stomp: *Blythe, Jimmy* / Society blues: *Blythe, Jimmy* / Boogie woogie blues: *Blythe, Jimmy* / Hard luck blues: *Robbins, Everett* / Fives: *Thomas, Hersal* / Down and out blues: *Fowler, Lemuel*
CD ____ BCD 115
Biograph / Jul '91 / ADA / Cadillac / Direct / Hot Shot / Jazz Music / Wellard

BOOGIE WOOGIE GIANTS, THE
CD ____ JHR 73533
Jazz Hour / May '93 / Cadillac / Jazz Music / Target/BMG

BOOGIE WOOGIE PIANO
CD ____ CD 14525
Jazz Portraits / Jan '94 / Jazz Music

BOOGIE WOOGIE PIANO
CD ____ CD 56001
Jazz Roots / Aug '94 / Target/BMG

BOOGIE WOOGIE RIOT (Piano & Guitar Boogie Blues)
Tribute / Rocket 88 / Wine-o baby boogie / Rattler / Earl's boogie woogie / Cows / Lightnin's boogie / Atlanta bounce / Rock 'n' roll bed / Throw the boogie woogie / Down the road apiece / Fast Santa Fe / Boogie all the time / Right string baby, but the wrong yo-yo / Half tight boogie / Hammond boogie / Red light / Walter's boogie / Houston boogie / Pine top's boogie woogie / I know that's right / Fillmore street boogie / Skid row boogie
CD ____ CDCHD 526
Ace / Feb '95 / Pinnacle

BOOGIE WOOGIE SPECIAL
CD ____ TPZ 1025
Topaz Jazz / Aug '95 / Cadillac / Pinnacle

BOOGIE WOOGIE STOMP
Boogie woogie stomp: *Ammons, Albert* / Foot pedal boogie: *Ammons, Albert & Pete Johnson* / Boogie woogie prayer: *Ammons, Albert & Pete Johnson/Meade 'Lux' Lewis* / Boogie woogie: *Basie, Count* / Boogie woogie: *Brown, Cleo* / Fat fanny stomp: *Clarke, Jim* / Yancey special: *Crosby, Bob & Bob Zurke* / Rocks: *Custer, Clay* / Boogie woogie: *Dorsey, Tommy & Howard Smith* / Chain 'em down: *Garnett, Blind Leroy* / Roll 'em: *Goodman, Benny & Jess Stacy* / After hours: *Hawkins, Erskine & Avery Parrish* / Chip's boogie woogie: *Herman, Woody & Tommy Linehan* / Indian boogie woogie: *Herman, Woody & Tommy Linehan* / Boogie woogie on St. Louis blues: *Hines, Earl 'Fatha'* / Boo-woo: *James, Harry & Pete Johnson* / Bear cat crawl: *Lewis, Meade 'Lux'* / Honky tonk train blues: *Lewis, Meade 'Lux'* / Vine Street boogie: *McShann, Jay* / No special rider: *Montgomery, Little Brother* / Pinetop's boogie woogie: *Smith, Pine Top* / Wilkins Street stomp: *Speckled Red* / Roll 'em Pete: *Turner, 'Big' Joe & Pete Johnson* / Crying in my sleep: *Yancey, Jimmy* / Slow and easy blues: *Yancey, Jimmy*
CD ____ CDAJA 5101
Living Era / Feb '93 / Select

BOOGIE WOOGIE VOCALISTS
CD ____ CD 14541
Jazz Portraits / Jan '94 / Jazz Music

BOOGIE WOOGIE VOL.1 (Piano Soloists)
Pinetop's boogie woogie: *Smith, Clarence 'Pinetop'* / Jump steady blues: *Smith, Clarence 'Pinetop'* / Detroit rocks: *Taylor, Montana* / Indiana Avenue stomp: *Taylor, Montana* / Dirty dozens: *Speckled Red* / Wilkins Street stomp: *Speckled Red* / Head rag hop: *Nelson, Romeo* / Cow cow blues: *Davenport, Cow Cow* / State Street jive: *Davenport, Cow Cow* / Yancey special: *Yancey, Jimmy* / Midnight stomp: *Yancey, Jimmy* / Streamline train: *Loften, Cripple Clarence* / I don't know: *Loften, Cripple Clarence* / Shout for joy: *Ammons, Albert* / Bass goin' crazy: *Ammons, Albert* / Yancey special: *Lewis, Meade 'Lux'* / Honky tonk train blues: *Lewis, Meade 'Lux'* / Blues on the downbeat: *Johnson, Pete* / Kaycee on my mind: *Johnson, Pete* / Ross Tavern boogie: *Hodes, Art*
CD ____ JASMCD 2538
Jasmine / Feb '95 / Conifer/BMG / Hot Shot / TKO Magnum

BOOGIE WOOGIE VOL.2 (The Small Groups)
Boogie woogie stomp: *Ammons, Albert & His Rhythm Kings* / Boogie woogie: *Basie, Count* / Down the road apiece: *Bradley, Will* / Basin Street boogie: *Bradley, Will* / St. Louis blues: *Butterfield, Erskine* / Grand slam: *Goodman, Benny Sextet* / Munson Street breakdown: *Hampton, Lionel & His Orchestra* / Bouncing at the beacon: *Hampton, Lionel & His Orchestra* / We're gonna pitch a boogie woogie: *Harlem Hamfats* / Chip's boogie woogie: *Herman, Woody* / Boo woo: *James, Harry* / Boogie woogie's mother-in-law: *Johnson, Budd Orchestra* / Cherry red: *Johnson, Pete & Joe Turner* / Baby look at you: *Johnson, Pete & Joe Turner* / Far away blues: *Johnson, Pete & Joe Turner* / Bye bye baby: *Big Maceo* / Anytime for you: *Big Maceo* / Dirty dozen: *Price, Sammy* / Lead me Daddy: *Price, Sammy* / Straight to the bar: *Price, Sammy* / Rock it in rhythm: *Tampa Red* / She's love crazy: *Tampa Red*
CD ____ JASMCD 2539
Jasmine / Apr '95 / Conifer/BMG / Hot Shot / TKO Magnum

BOOGIE WOOGIE VOL.3 (The Big Bands)
Scrub me Mama with a boogie beat / Basie boogie / Beat me, Daddy, eight to the bar / Rock-a-bye boogie / Back to boogie / Yancey special / Honky tonk train blues / Boogie woogie / Roll 'em / Indian boogie woogie / Boogie woogie bugle boy / Boogie woogie on St. Louis blues / Back beat boogie / Little Joe from Chicago / Drum boogie / Teddy bear boogie / Bluebird boogie woogie / Meade lux special / Cuban boogie woogie / Rum boogie
CD ____ JASMCD 2540
Jasmine / Jun '95 / Conifer/BMG / Hot Shot / TKO Magnum

BOOGIE WOOGIE, THE
In the mood: *Miller, Glenn* / Red bank boogie: *Basie, Count* / Beulah's sister's boogie: *Hampton, Lionel* / Honky tonk train blues: *Crosby, Bob* / Yancey special: *Lewis, Meade 'Lux'* / Jammin' the boogie: *Ammons, Albert* / Hamp's boogie woogie: *Hampton, Lionel* / Pinetop's boogie woogie: *Price, Sammy* / Jimmy's boogie woogie: *Basie, Count & Jimmy Rushing* / Boogie woogie on St. Louis blues: *Hines, Earl 'Fatha'* / Hamp's walkin' boogie: *Hampton, Lionel* / Chip's boogie woogie: *Herman, Woody* / Calloway boogie: *Calloway, Cab* / Boo woo: *James, Harry & Pete Johnson* / Central Avenue breakdown: *Cole, Nat 'King' & Lionel Hampton* / Roll 'em: *Goodman, Benny* / Cow cow blues: *Zurke, Bob* / Tatum-pole boogie: *Tatum, Art* / Oscar's boogie: *Peterson, Oscar* / Just jazz boogie: *Johnson, Pete*
CD ____ CD 53003
Giants Of Jazz / Mar '92 / Cadillac / Jazz Music / Target/BMG

BOOM BOOM
CD ____ MPV 5531
Movieplay / '93 / Target/BMG

BOOM BOOM
Boom boom: *Hooker, John Lee* / Blues is my middle name: *Charles, Ray* / You step out of my dreams: *Vaughan, Sarah* / Please come back home to me: *Burke, Solomon* / Poor boy: *Howlin' Wolf* / How blue can you get: *King, B.B.* / Goodnight Irene: *Leadbelly* / Don't let the sun catch you cryin': *Big Maybelle* / They call it stormy Monday: *Turner, 'Big' Joe* / Why won't my baby treat me right: *Walker, T-Bone* / Limehouse blues: *Mills Brothers* / My man: *Holiday, Billie* / Baby, won't you please come home: *Hines, Earl 'Fatha'* / Jelly Roll blues: *Morton, Jelly Roll* / It's hard to believe you: *Rush, Otis & Little Walter* / Don't want no big fat woman: *Williams, Big Joe*
CD ____ 100932
CMC / May '97 / BMG

BOOM REGGAE HITS VOL.5
CD ____ VPCD 1449
VP / Nov '95 / Greensleeves / Jet Star / Total/BMG

BOOMING ON PLUTO (Electro For Droids - 2CD Set)
Night drive: *Model 500* / I like to watch: *Freefall 68* / Dead cities: *Future Sound Of London* / Landslide: *Cabaret Voltaire* / Planet rock: *Bambaataa, Afrika & The Soul Sonic Force* / Angry dolphin: *Plaid* / Watermelon man: *Hancock, Herbie* / Bassline: *Mantronix* / Was a dog a doughnut: *Stevens, Cat* / Organic mango barbed: *HAT* / Salsa smurf: *Special Request* / Punjabi sher: *Safri Boys* / I didn't know I loved you: *Planet Patrol* / Solina: *Jedi Knights* / Extra: *To Rococo Rot* / Apartment: *Moroder, Giorgio* / Silicon based predator: *Sidewinder* / Let's get brutal: *Nitro Deluxe* / Olivine: *Black Dog* / Ear candy: *Tales From The Hardside* / Pack jam: *Jonzun Crew* / Computer games: *Clinton, George* / Nocturnal resort: *Prime, Michael* / Digicality: *Unique 3* / Running: *Information Society* / Al-naafiysh (The soul): *Hashim* / Genki: *Bleep & Booster* / Tootak, tootak, tootiyan: *Singh, Malkit* / Automannik: *Guy Called Gerald*
CD Set ____ AMBT 20
Virgin / Apr '97 / EMI

BOOT SCOOTIN' BOOGIE (The Nashville Line Dancing Album)
Chattahoochie: *Jackson, Alan* / Mama don't get dressed up: *Brooks & Dunn* / Cherokee boogie: *BR5-49* / Big guitar: *Blackhawk* / Laid back stone cold: *Wright, Michelle* / We all get lucky sometimes: *Parnell, Lee Roy* / Betty's got a bass boat: *Tillis, Pam* / It's all in your head: *Diamond Rio* / Chain of this town: *BR5-49* / Boot scootin' boogie: *Brooks & Dunn* / Little Bitty: *Jackson, Alan* / Hammer and nails: *Foster, Radney* / House is rockin': *Parnell, Lee Roy* / Cleopatra, Queen of denial: *Tillis, Pam* / Baby likes to rock it: *Tractors* / Wake up and smell the whiskey Houdini: *Graham, Tammy* / Rock my world: *Brooks & Dunn* / You owe me: *Wright, Michelle*
CD ____ 74321461802
Arista / Feb '97 / BMG

BOP BEGINS
CD ____ TPZ 1051
Topaz Jazz / Nov '96 / Cadillac / Pinnacle

BOPPIN' THE BLUES
CD ____ CPCD 8271
Charly / Apr '97 / Koch

BOPPIN' TONIGHT
Let's go boppin' tonight: *Ferrier, Al* / Honey baby: *Ferrier, Al* / No no baby: *Ferrier, Al* / What is that thing called love: *Ferrier, Al* / My baby done gone away: *Ferrier, Al* / Couple in the car: *Earl, Little Billy* / Who's baby are you: *Earl, Little Billy* / Go dan tucker: *Earl, Little Billy* / I never had the blues: *Earl, Little Billy* / Honey baby o: *Earl, Little Billy* / Freight train: *Hart, Larry* / Oh Nellie: *Hart, Larry* / I'm just a mender: *Hart, Larry* / Coffins have no pockets: *Hart, Larry* / Come on baby: *Hart, Larry* / Flashiest classiest: *Hart, Larry* / Never run out of love: *Hart, Larry* / Hold me baby: *Bill & Carroll* / Bluff city rock: *Bill & Carroll* / Bop stop rock: *Victorian, Ray* / Oh baby: *Jano, Johnny* / Mabel's gone: *Jano, Johnny* / High voltage: *Jano, Johnny* / Castro rock: *Chevalier, Jay*
CD ____ CDCHD 442
Ace / Feb '93 / Pinnacle

BORDER MUSIC
Laissez-faire: *Daigrepont, Bruce* / Kolinda: *Beausoleil* / La Viejito: *Jimenez, Flaco* / Allons a Lafayette: *Sonnier, Jo El* / This little girl: *Menard, D.L.* / Big chief: *Richard, Zachary* / Hundred Ladrones: *Los Linces* / Corrido el aceite: *Jordan, Steve* / J'etais au bal: *Doucet, David* / Someone else is steppin' in: *Buckwheat Zydeco* / High point two step: *Riley, Steve* / La otra modesta: *Jimenez, Santiago Jr.* / Cuando me miraste: *Salvidar, Mingo* / Tennis shoes: *Newman, Jimmy C.* / Aquella noche: *Hinojosa, Tish*
CD ____ NETCD 1004
Network / Oct '92 / Direct / Greensleeves / SRD

BORDERLANDS - FROM CUNJUNTO TO CHICKEN SCRATCH
CD ____ SF 40418CD
Smithsonian Folkways / Jan '94 / ADA / Cadillac / CM / Direct / Koch

BOREDOM IS DEEP AND MYSTERIOUS VOL.1
CD ____ APR 001CD
April / Feb '95 / Plastic Head / Shellshock/ Disc

BOREDOM IS DEEP AND MYSTERIOUS VOL.2
CD ____ APR 007
April / Feb '96 / Plastic Head / Shellshock/ Disc

BOREDOM IS DEEP AND MYSTERIOUS VOL.3
CD ____ APR 023CD
April / Jul '97 / Plastic Head / Shellshock/ Disc

BORN BAD VOL.2
CD ____ BB 002CD
Born Bad / Feb '97 / Cargo

BORN BAD VOL.4
CD ____ BB 004CD
Born Bad / Feb '97 / Cargo

BORN BAD VOL.5
CD ____ BB 005CD
Born Bad / Feb '97 / Cargo

BORN BAD VOL.6
CD ____ BB 006CD
Born Bad / Feb '97 / Cargo

BORN TO BE WILD
Born to be wild: *Steppenwolf* / All right now: *Free* / Keep on running: *Davis, Spencer Group* / Green onions: *Booker T & The MG's* / That's alright Mama: *Stewart, Rod* / Need your love so bad: *Fleetwood Mac* / Got my mojo working: *Manfred Mann* / We gotta get out of this place: *Animals* / Twentieth century boy: *T-Rex* / Let's work together: *Canned Heat* / Whatever you want: *Status Quo* / Cocaine: *Cale, J.J.* / Don't mess up a good thing: *Cooder, Ry & Chaka Khan* / Smokin' gun: *Cray, Robert* / Love and marriage: *Third Man* / I'd rather go blind: *Chicken Shack* / Texas flood: *Vaughan, Stevie Ray* / Baby please don't go: *Them*

CD ___ TCD 2524
Telstar / Sep '91 / BMG

BORN TO BE WILD
Born to be wild: *Steppenwolf* / Reelin' and rockin': *Berry, Chuck* / Big road blues: *Canned Heat* / C C Ryder: *Charles, Ray* / Keep on running: *Davis, Spencer* / Hell raiser: *Sweet*
CD ___ DS 2303
BR Music / Aug '96 / Target/BMG

BORN TO BE WILD
CD ___ PLSCD 200
Pulse / Apr '97 / BMG

BORN TO BE WILD VOL.4
Since you've been gone: *Rainbow* / Killer on the loose: *Thin Lizzy* / Young blood: *Thin Lizzy* / Bomber: *Motorhead* / Down down: *Status Quo* / Never say die: *Black Sabbath* / Hush: *Deep Purple* / United: *Judas Priest* / More tha a feeling: *Boston* / Gimme all your lovin': *ZZ Top* / Feels like the first time: *Foreigner* / Run to the hills: *Iron Maiden* / God gave rock 'n' roll to you: *Argent* / You ain't seen nothing yet: *Bachman-Turner Overdrive* / These dreams: *Heart* / No more Mr. Nice Guy: *Cooper, Alice* / Owner of a lonely heart: *Yes* / Holding out for a hero: *Tyler, Bonnie*
CD ___ MUSCD 036
MCI Music / May '97 / Disc / THE

BORN TO CHOOSE
Photograph: *REM & Natalie Merchant* / She said she said: *Sweet, Matthew* / Running out of time: *Sugar* / Born to choose: *Mekons* / Rant 'n' roll: *Trudell, John* / Box spring hog: *Waits, Tom* / Pancakes: *Williams, Lucinda* / Greenlander: *Pavement* / Don't talk about my music: *NRBQ* / Lost my driving wheel: *Cowboy Junkies* / HIV Baby: *Soundgarden* / Distracted: *Helmet*
CD ___ RCD 10256
Rykodisc / Nov '93 / ADA / Vital

BORN TO SWING (4CD Set)
CD Set ___ MBSCD 444
Castle / Jul '96 / BMG

BORN UNDER A BAD SIGN
CD ___ VSOPCD 205
Connoisseur Collection / Oct '94 / Pinnacle

BORN WITH THE BLUES
Stomp boogie: *Hooker, John Lee* / I wish you would: *Arnold, Billy Boy & Tony McPhee* / Road runner: *Diddley, Bo* / Hard walking Hanna: *Reed, Jimmy* / When my first wife quit me: *Johnson, Jimmy* / Lonesome: *Memphis Slim* / Born with the blues: *Benton, Buster & Carey Bell* / Alabama train: *Louisiana Red* / I had it so hard: *Sunnyland Slim* / Don't stay out all night: *Arnold, Billy Boy & Tony McPhee* / Let the good times roll creole: *Memphis Slim* / Rent house boogie: *Hooker, John Lee* / Cry before I go: *Reed, Jimmy* / Don't know where I've been: *Diddley, Bo*
CD ___ 300932
Hallmark / Jul '96 / Carlton

BORN WITH THE BLUES VOL.1
Neighbour neighbour: *King Biscuit Boy & Ronnie Hawkins Band* / Sometimes I wonder: *Louisiana Red* / Cool drink of water: *Stackhouse, Houston* / Foxtrot: *Hooker, Earl* / She put the wammee on me: *Hawkins, Screamin' Jay* / Born with the blues: *Benton, Buster & Carey Bell* / Got me a Louisiana woman: *Hopkins, Lightnin'* / Things I used to do: *Collins, Albert* / Rode myself crazy: *Delay, Paul Band* / Honey bee: *Waters, Muddy* / Sweet Miss Bea: *Arnold, Billy Boy* / Down at the corner grocery store: *Reed, Jimmy* / Taking off: *Murphy, Matt* / Play the blues for you: *Mighty Houserockers* / Loaded: *Butterfield, Paul* / He sure could hypnotize: *Clovers* / Came up the hard way: *Clearwater, Eddy*
CD ___ EMPRCD 525
Emporio / Sep '94 / Disc

BORN WITH THE BLUES VOL.2
Can't hold out: *Sharpville, Todd* / Sinner's prayer: *Arnold, Billy Boy* / Bad news: *Sykes, Roosevelt* / St. Louis sunset twist: *Sharp, Benny* / Rocky mountains: *Edwards, Clarence* / Lightnin' bug: *Louisiana Red* / Sloppy drunk: *Williams, Big Joe* / Hey hey: *Turner, Ike* / Bye bye bird: *Williamson, Sonny Boy* / Rialto rock: *Reed, Buddy* / Leg woman: *King, Willie* / I don't know why: *Clearwater, Eddy* / In my younger days: *Guy, Buddy & Junior Wells* / You better be sure: *Gibson, Lacy* / Daddy rollin' stone: *Ricks, Jimmy & the Ravens* / Late one evening: *Lamb, Paul & The Blues Burglars* / Babe: *Orta, Paulo* / End of the blues: *Hooker, Earl*
CD ___ EMPRCD 526
Emporio / Sep '94 / Disc

BOSNIA - ECHOES FROM AN ENDANGERED WORLD
CD ___ SF 40407CD
Smithsonian Folkways / Nov '94 / ADA / Cadillac / CM / Direct / Koch

BOSSA BEACH
CD ___ DOUCE 802CD
Irma La Douce / Nov '96 / Timewarp

BOSSA BRAVA VOL.2
CD ___ EX 3452
Instinct / Mar '97 / Cargo

BOSSA NOVA
CD ___ CD 62029
Saludos Amigos / Oct '93 / Target/BMG

BOSSA NOVA & SAMBA IN CONCERTO
CD ___ CD 62011
Saludos Amigos / Oct '93 / Target/BMG

BOSSA NOVA VOL.2
CD ___ GLO 143
RGE / Aug '93 / Discovery

BOSSTOWN SOUND 1968 (The Music & The Time/2CD Set)
Ballad of the hip death goddess: *Ultimate Spinach* / Baroque no.1: *Ultimate Spinach* / Fragmentary march of green: *Ultimate Spinach* / Can't find the time to tell you: *Orpheus* / Walk away Renee: *Orpheus* / Brown arms in Houston: *Orpheus* / Tomorrow man: *Orpheus* / Maybe more than you: *Lost* / Everybody knows: *Lost* / Mystic (seven starry skies): *Lost* / Violet gown: *Lost* / Everybody knows: *Bagatelle* / Back on the farm: *Bagatelle* / Off with the old: *Chameleon Church* / In a kindly way: *Chameleon Church* / Hapiness child: *Ultimate Spinach* / Eddie's rush: *Ultimate Spinach* / Born under a bad sign: *Apple Pie Motherhood Band* / Gypsy: *Apple Pie Motherhood Band* / Goodbye girl: *Eden's Children* / Just let go: *Eden's Children* / Come in it's all for free: *Eagle* / Kickin' it back: *Eagle* / Separated: *Eagle* / Vacuum: *Puff* / Go with you: *Puff* / Looking in my window: *Puff* / Bright lit blue skies: *Rockin' Ramrods* / Can't you see: *Rockin' Ramrods* / Prophecies/Morning blue: *Front Page Review* / Silver children: *Front Page Review* / Valley of eyes: *Front Page Review* / In my dark world: *Front Page Review* / In my dark world: *Ill Wind* / High flyin' bird: *Ill Wind* / American eagle tragedy: *Earth Opera* / Red Sox are winning: *Earth Opera*
CD Set ___ CDWIK2 167
Big Beat / Oct '96 / Pinnacle

BOSTON BLUES BLAST VOL.1
CD ___ CDTC 1146
Tonecool / May '94 / ADA / Direct

BOTTLENECK BLUES
CD ___ TCD 5021
Testament / Oct '95 / ADA / Koch

BOTTOM LINE VOL.1
CD ___ NTMCD 501
Nectar / Jun '95 / Pinnacle

BOTTOM LINE VOL.2
CD ___ NTMCD 523
Nectar / Aug '96 / Pinnacle

BOUNCY TECHNO ANTHEMS VOL.1
CD ___ DBMTRCD 21
Rogue Trooper / Dec '95 / Alphamagic / SRD

BOUNCY TECHNO ANTHEMS VOL.2 (2CD Set)
CD Set ___ DBMPCHCD 2A
Punch / Jun '96 / SRD

BOUND TO PLEASE
Why U wanna play on me: *Jump Cutz* / Hooked: *Jump Cutz* / Movin' 2 da break: *Jump Cutz* / Jus' wanna be wit U: *Jump Cutz* / Deep introspection: *Jump Cutz* / Watersports: *House Of Wacks* / Runaway: *Unison* / Dancin': *Loose Baggage*
CD ___ DISCCD 01
Luxury Service / May '97 / Amato Disco / Mo's Music Machine / Prime

BOUZOUKIS & SIRTAKIS
CD ___ 995142
EPM / Jun '93 / ADA / Discovery

BOXING CLEVER
CD ___ DRGNCD 943
Dragon / May '94 / ADA / Cadillac / CM / Roots / Wellard

BOYD IN THE VOID
CD ___ D 1392
Distance / Feb '96 / 3mv/Sony / Prime

BOYS
Forever girl: *OTT* / I need you: *3T* / Flava: *Andre, Peter* / Wishes: *Human Nature* / Love me for a reason: *Boyzone* / Shout: *Ant & Dec* / Love guaranteed: *Damage* / I can make you feel good: *Kavana* / Quit playing games (with my heart): *Backstreet Boys* / Hey child: *East 17* / Day we find love: *911* / I feel you: *Andre, Peter* / Forever love: *Barlow, Gary* / Horny: *Morrison, Mark* / Let me here you say ole ole: *Outhere Brothers* / Good day: *Maguire, Sean* / Last night: *Az Yet* / Twelth of never: *Carter Twins* / I've got a little something for you: *MN8* / Pray: *Take That*
CD ___ SONYTV 27CD
Sony TV / May '97 / Sony

BOYZ OF SWING VOL.1
Return of the Mack: *Morrison, Mark* / Hey lover: *LL Cool J* / I got 5 on it: *Luniz* / Lifted: *Lighthouse Family* / Runnin': *Pharcyde* / Somethin' for the honeyz: *Jordan, Montell* / Pathway to the moon: *MN8* / Down low (nobody has to know): *R Kelly* / I'm in love: *Joe* / Candy rain: *Soul For Real* / Your love is a 187: *Whitehead Brothers* / Water runs dry: *Boyz II Men* / I'll never break your heart: *Backstreet Boys* / Freak in you: *Jodeci* / Freak me: *Silk* / Tell me what you want me to do: *Campbell, Tevin* / Feel the music: *Guru* / Do it for love: *4Mandu* / Throw your hands up: *LV* / 1,2,3,4 (Sumpin' new): *Coolio*
CD ___ 5354232
PolyGram TV / Apr '96 / PolyGram

BOYZ OF SWING VOL.2
One for the money: *Brown, Horace* / Ocean Drive: *Lighthouse Family* / Hit me off: *New Edition* / I can't sleep baby (if I): *R Kelly* / On bended knee: *Boyz II Men* / Love U 4 life: *Jodeci* / Tell me what you like: *Guy* / Housekeeper: *Men Of Vizion* / You want this party started: *Somethin' For The People* / Feel your pain: *Whitehead Brothers* / Hooked on you: *Silk* / Process of elimination: *Gable, Eric* / We've got it goin' on: *Backstreet Boys* / Let's get down: *Morrison, Mark* / Thank God it's Friday: *R Kelly* / Every little thing I do: *Soul For Real* / Happy: *MN8* / Flava: *Andre, Peter* / We got it: *Immature* / Baby don't go: *4Mandu* / This is how we do it: *Jordan, Montell* / Two can play that game: *Brown, Bobby* / Sensitivity: *Tresvant, Ralph* / So in love with you: *Duke* / Grave and the constant: *Fun Lovin' Criminals* / Doin' it: *LL Cool J* / She said: *Pharcyde* / Playa hata: *Luniz* / It's all the way live (now): *Coolio* / I must stand: *Ice-T*
CD ___ 5357552
PolyGram TV / Sep '96 / PolyGram

BOYZ WHO SOULED THE WORLD, THE
CD ___ AHLCD 18
Hit / Feb '94 / Grapevine/PolyGram

BRABANTS VOLKSORKFEST (Flemish Folk Music From Belgium)
CD ___ B 6827CD
Auvidis/Ethnic / Apr '96 / ADA / Harmonia Mundi

BRAIN TICKET - ADRENALIN TRIP
CD Set ___ SPV 08992302
Subterranean / Jul '95 / Koch / Plastic Head

BRAINDEAD VOL.3 (Hardcore Cyberspace)
CD ___ EFA 008752
Shockwave / Jan '96 / SRD

BRAINDEAD VOL.4 (2CD Set)
CD Set ___ ZYX 810872
ZYX / Nov '96 / ZYX

BRAND NEW SECONDHAND
D'yer mak'er: *Eek-A-Mouse* / Bed's too big without you: *Hylton, Sheila* / On and on: *Aswad* / Hey Joe: *Black Uhuru* / Around the world: *Krystal* / Everday people: *Brown, Rula* / Best of my love: *Aswad* / Walk on by: *I-Tones & Ram* / Just my imagination: *Murvin, Junior* / Some guys have all the luck: *Tucker, Junior* / Groovin': *Killer Bees* / Take me home country roads: *Toots & The Maytals*
CD ___ RCD 10247
Rykodisc / Feb '93 / ADA / Vital

BRASIL
Batucada 1 / Zanzibar / Amazon river / Berimbau / Capoeira / Magika / Forro / Misturada / Batucada 2
CD ___ SJRCD 022
Soul Jazz / Nov '94 / New Note/Pinnacle / Timewarp / Vital

BRASIL: A CENTURY OF SONG (Folk And Tradition/Carnaval/Bossa Nova/ Musica/4CD/Book Set)
CD Set ___ CD 50002
Blue Jackel / Mar '97 / New Note/Pinnacle

BRASILEIRO
CD ___ CD 62038
Saludos Amigos / Nov '93 / Target/BMG

BRASILIAN CHRISTMAS, A
Ave Maria / Christmas song / Air on a six string / Have yourself a merry little christmas / O little town of Bethlehem / I'll be home for Christmas / Dance Natahl / O Velhinho / Santa Claus is coming to town / White Christmas / Jingle bells / What child is this
CD ___ TCD 4006
Astor Place / Nov '96 / New Note/Pinnacle

BRASILICA
After sunrise: *Mendes, Sergio* / Barumba: *Tamba Trio* / Birimbau: *Dom Um Romao* / Vera Cruz: *Nascimento, Milton* / Roda: *Gil, Gilberto* / Solo: *Meirelles E Os Copa 5* / Crickets sing for Anamaria: *Valle, Marcus* / Blues Avolente: *Powell, Baden* / Adam Adam: *Joyce* / Tereza Sabe Sambar: *Regina, Elis* / Tamba: *Tamba Trio* / Zanzibar: *Mendes, Sergio* / Upa neguinho: *Mendes, Sergio* / Mas que nada: *Jorge, Ben* / Tudo Tom: *Donato, Joao* / Vig=digal: *Resende, Marcos*
CD ___ 5168532
Talkin' Loud / Aug '94 / PolyGram

BRASS BAND
CD ___ PDSCD 524
Pulse / Aug '96 / BMG

BRASS BAND FAVOURITES
Guns of Navarone / Magnificent seven / Over the rainbow / Trouble with the tuba is / Headless horseman / Men of Harlech / Marche militaire / Death of glass / Tea for two / Puttin' on the Ritz / Coronation Street / March of the cobblers / My way / Ein schnapps / Swan / Sailing by / Tango taquin / Can can / Semper sousa / Colonel Bogey
CD ___ CC 257
Music For Pleasure / Oct '90 / EMI

BRASS BAND SPECTACULAR
CD ___ MATCD 235
Castle / Dec '92 / BMG

BRASS BAND SPECTACULAR
CD ___ PLSCD 233
Pulse / Jul '97 / BMG

BRASS BAND WALTZES AND POLKAS
CD ___ PS 65154
PlayaSound / Sep '95 / ADA / Harmonia Mundi

BRASS FIDDLE, THE
Muilleann Na Maidi / Vincent Campbell's mazurkas / Marine / Drowsy Maggie / Doodley doodley dank / Frost is all over / Low Highland / Mary o' The Wisp / King George IV / Bagpipe March / Wild Irishman / Johnny Boyle's Jig / Biddy of Muckross / Jackson's bean a'ti ar lar / Lancers / Johnny Ward's Paddy Bartley's / La Marseillaise / Miss Drummond of Perth / Rakish Paddy / Cat that kittled in Jamie's wig / Kilcar Mazurka / On the road from glen to carrick / Old wheel of fortune / James Byrne's mazurka / Seamas O'Beirn's Highland / Ri Mhim Na Salach / Curly haired boy
CD ___ CC 44CD
Claddagh / Aug '96 / ADA / CM / Direct

BRAVE NEW WORLD VOL.6 (2CD Set)
CD Set ___ ZYX 810922
ZYX / Mar '97 / ZYX

BRAVEHARP
Loch Lomond / Dark island / Caledonia / Skye boat song / Ye banks and braes / Road and the miles to Dundee / My love is like a red, red rose / Ae fond kiss / Amazing grace / Auld lang syne/Will ye no come back again / Flower of Scotland / Wild mountain thyme / Northern lights of Old Aberdeen / Always Argyll / Island waves
CD ___ RECD 511
REL / Mar '97 / CM / Duncans / Highlander

BRAVEHEARTS (Traditional Songs From Scotland)
Campbells are coming / Annie Laurie / Bluebells of Scotland / Charlie is my darling / My heart is in the highlands / Flow gently sweet Afton / John Anderson / Wi' a hundred pipers / Comin' thro' the rye / Blythe Blythe and merry was she / Bonnie Dundee / I have heard the Mavis singing / My love she's but a lassie yet / Loch Lomond / Ye banks and braes o' bonnie doon / Rowan tree / Miss Dairymple / Weel may the Keel Row / O my love is like a red red rose / Skye boat song / Highland fling / Sword dance three and one / Sword dance four and one / March of the Cameron men / Highland fling / Robin Adair / Whistle and I'll come to you / Come o'er the stream Charlie / Scots wha' hae wi' wallace bled / Wha'll buy caller herrin / Belles o' Edinboro' / My Jo and dearie o / Moon had climbed / Years awa' / Soldier's return / Duncan Gray / Birks o' Aberfeldy / I lo'e na a laddie but Ane / Come under my plaidie / Jock o' Hazeldean / Highland lad my love was born / Man's a man for a that / Auld lang syne / Danny boy / Wee highland glen
CD ___ SUMCD 4071
Summit / Nov '96 / Sound & Media

BRAZIL
CD ___ CD 62031
Saludos Amigos / Oct '93 / Target/BMG

BRAZIL (Manha De Carnaval)
Mas que nada: *Oliveira, Valdeci* / Meia lua inteira: *Banda Brasil Corcovado* / Danca de Ana: *Da Silva, Jorginho* / Agua de beber: *Oliveira, Valdeci* / Paraiso: *Banda Brasil Corcovado* / Garot ada Ipanema: *Oliveira, Valdeci* / Bachianas Brasileiras no.5: *Braganca, Maria* / Nino de Vespa: *Da Silva, Jorginho* / Misterio do Som: *Banda Brasil Corcovado* / Noites caiocas: *Braganca, Maria* / Quebrando: *Martins, Zeduardo* / Aique saudade voce: *Banda Brasil Corcovado* / Manha de Carneval: *Braganca, Maria* / Batucada: *Banda Brasil Corcovado*
CD ___ 12548
Laserlight / Aug '96 / Target/BMG

BRAZIL
CD ___ 3003742
IMP / Jan '97 / ADA / Discovery

BRAZIL BLUE
Regra tres: *Monteiro, Doris* / Nereci (A name): *Djavan* / Cidade vazia (Empty city): *Milton Banana Trio* / Sarau para radames: *Da Viola, Paulinho* / O cantador (The street singer): *Brasil, Victor Assis* / Comecar de novo: *Lins, Ivan* / Sao Tome (St Thomas): *Venturini, Flavio* / Vento de maio: *Regina, Elis* / Bate-papo (Shoot the breeze): *Os Choroes & Radames Gnattali* / Chorando baixinho (Crying low): *Ferreira, Abel* / Copacabana: *Sete, Bola* / Samba de uma nota so: *Joyce* / Corcovado: *Gilberto, Joao* / Emotiva no.1: *Delmiro, Helio* / Ecos (Echoes): *Nascimento, Joel* / Fica mal com deus (Be bad with God): *Quarteto Novo & Hermento Pascoal* / Milage dos peixes (Miracle of the fishes): *Nascimento, Milton* / Cantareiro (Dish rack): *Mariano, Cesar Camargo* / Choro de Mae (Mother's choro): *Tiso, Wagner* / Nem uma lagrima (Not one tear): *Caymmi, Nana*

CD ______ CDEMC 3676
Hemisphere / May '94 / EMI

BRAZIL CLASSICS VOL.1 (Beleza Tropical)
Ponta de lanca Africano: *Ben, Jorge* / Sonho meu: *Bethania, Maria e Gal Costa* / So quero um xodo: *Gil, Gilberto* / Um canto de afoxe para o bloco do ile / Leaozinho: *Veloso, Caetano* / Cacada: *Buarque, Chico* / Calice: *Buarque, Chico & Milton Nascimento* / Equatorial: *Borges Lo* / San Vincente / Quilombo, O el dorado negro: *Gil, Gilberto* / Caramba...galileu de galileia: *Ben, Jorge* / Caixa de sol: *Pereira, Nazare* / Maculele: *Pereira, Nazare* / Queixa: *Veloso, Caetano* / Andar com fe: *Gil, Gilberto* / Fio maravilha: *Ben, Jorge* / Anima: *Nascimento, Milton* / Terra: *Veloso, Caetano*
CD ______ 7599258052
Sire / May '94 / Warner Music

BRAZILIAN EXPLOSION
Felix: *Faze Action* / Carlos Alberta: *Soul Generation* / Eder: *Arakatuba* / Pele: *Ballistic Brothers* / Jarzinho: *Arakatuba* / Rivelinho: *Beats & Pieces* / Junior: *Box Saga* / Josimar: *Fila Brazillia* / Dunga: *Arakatuba* / Zico: *Arakatuba* / Riva: *Lilliana*
CD ______ MRBCD 006
Mr. Bongo / Jan '97 / New Note/Pinnacle / RTM/Disc / SRD

BRAZILIAN NIGHTS
CD ______ CDCH 539
Milan / Sep '91 / Conifer/BMG / Silva Screen

BRAZILIAN NIGHTS
Samba de verao: *Valle, Marcus* / Triste: *Klugh, Earl* / Garota de impanema: *Milton Banana Trio* / Conversa de botequim: *Monteiro, Doris* / Samba do aviao: *Neco* / How insensitive: *Lagrene, Birelli* / Nereci: *Djavan* / Cidade vazia: *Milton Banana Trio* / Regra tres: *Monteiro, Doris* / Ecos: *Nascimento, Joel* / Emotiva no.1: *Delmiro, Helio* / Chorando baixinho: *Ferreira, Abel* / Bate Papo: *Os Choroes* / Quem e voce: *Razao Brasileira*
CD ______ DC 880862
Disky / May '97 / Disky / THE

BRAZILIAN THOROUGH
CD ______ LHCD 019
Luv n' Haight / Jul '96 / Timewarp

BRAZILICA VOL.2
Falange dos tambores: *Silva, Robertinho* / Taureg: *Costa, Gal* / Cravo e canela: *MPB4* / Queremos guerica: *Gil, Gilberto* / Agua de beber: *Quarteto Em Cy* / Carcara: *Nara* / Os grilles: *Soares, Claudette* / Amor no samba: *Pitman, E. & B.* / Mas que nada: *Mendes, Sergio* / Feitinho pro poeta: *Soares, Claudette* / Mano Joao: *Wanderlea* / Relance: *Costa, Gal* / Ponta de lanca Africano: *Ben, Jorge* / Consolacao: *Powell, Baden* / Imprevisto: *Bossa Tres* / Casa forte: *Regina, Elis* / Mara ton leblon: *Vaz, Celia* / Camtemplacao: *Meirelles*
CD ______ 5350272
Talkin' Loud / Jul '97 / PolyGram

BREAD AND ROSES (Festival of Acoustic Music, Greek Theatre)
CD ______ CDWIK 103
Big Beat / Mar '92 / Pinnacle

BREAK BEATS VOL.1 & 2
CD ______ WRCD 001
Warrior / '91 / Pinnacle

BREAK BEATS VOL.3 & 4
CD ______ WRCD 002
Warrior / Oct '92 / Pinnacle

BREAKING HEARTS
CD ______ DINCD 34
Dino / Feb '92 / Pinnacle

BREAKING MOULDS (Jazz Dance Live)
CD ______ JAGZCD 001
Jagz / Nov '96 / Timewarp

BREAKING THE BARRIERS WITH SOUND (Captured By The Vibes)
Captured by the vibes: *Robotiks* / Didn't I: *Kofi* / I just want to love you: *Simmons, Leroy* / Dancing time: *Aisha* / Roots and culture: *Macka B* / Let's make it work: *Cross, Sandra* / And now you're gone: *McLean, John* / Baby, baby, my love's all for you: *Tajah, Paulette* / Mellow: *Intense* / Daylight and darkness: *Sister Audrey* / Captured by the dub: *Mad Professor*
CD ______ ARICD 040
Ariwa Sounds / Sep '88 / Jet Star / SRD

BREAKING THE ICE VOL.1
CD ______ MOLECD 022
Mole / Jun '97 / Intergroove

BREAKPOINT
CD ______ LSCD 02
London Something / Aug '97 / Jet Star / SRD

BREIZH & ROLL
CD ______ 062049
Wotre Music / Jul '96 / Discovery / New Note/Pinnacle

BRESIL '90
CD ______ 824882
BUDA / Nov '90 / Discovery

BRESIL EN FETE: BRAZILIAN FOLK FESTIVITIES
CD ______ PS 65098
PlayaSound / Nov '92 / ADA / Harmonia Mundi

BRESIL ESCALE PARIS
CD ______ KAR 991
IMP / Feb '97 / ADA / Discovery

BRIEF HISTORY OF AMBIENT VOL.1, A (152 Minutes 33 Seconds/2CD Set)
Flowered knife shadows: *Budd, Harold* / Thru metamorphic rock (edit): *Tangerine Dream* / Evening star: *Fripp, Robert & Brian Eno* / Mountain goat: *Amorphous Androgynous* / Sea of vapours: *Khan, Nusrat Fateh Ali* / Forge of volcan: *Hawkwind* / Requiem: *Killing Joke* / Ending (ascent): *Eno, Brian* / Marnia's tent: *Horowitz, Richard* / Rapido de noir: *Schmidt, Irmin & Bruno Spoerri* / Kazoo: *Ashra* / Their memories: *Budd, Harold & Brian Eno* / Leave your body: *Grid* / Electric becomes eclectic: *Franke, Christopher* / Phaedra (edit): *Tangerine Dream* / Delta rain dream: *Eno, Brian & Jon Hassell* / Monkey king: *Orbit, William* / Castle in the clouds: *Gong* / Life form: *Hawkwind* / Dance: *Laraaji* / Sacred stones: *Chandra, Sheila* / Earth floor: *Earth Floor* / Gift of fire: *Hassell, Jon* / End of words: *Material* / Panorphelia: *Froese, Edgar* / Voices: *Eno, Roger* / Traum mal wieder: *Czukay, Holger* / Home: *Sylvian, David*
CD Set ______ AMBT 1
Virgin / Aug '93 / EMI

BRIEF HISTORY OF AMBIENT VOL.2, A (Imaginary Landscapes/2CD Set)
Call to prayer: *Maal, Baaba* / Tal coat: *Eno, Brian* / In mind: *Amorphous Androgynous* / Rubicon pt.2: *Tangerine Dream* / Healing place: *Sylvian, David* / Crystal clear: *Grid* / Nuages: *Sakamoto, Ryuichi* / Wind on water: *Fripp, Robert & Brian Eno* / Wildlife: *Penguin Cafe Orchestra* / When things dream: *Jansen, Steve & Richard Barbieri* / Magick mother invocation: *Gong* / Bringing down the light: *Sylvian, David & Robert Fripp* / Not another: *Jah Wobble* / One flower: *Goo Brothers* / Black Jesus: *God* / Mountain of needles: *Eno, Brian & David Byrne* / You are here: *Manzanera, Phil* / Bendel dub: *Prince Far-I* / Slow kaliuki: *Pokrovsky, Dmitri Ensemble* / Euterpe gratitude piece: *Allen, Daevid* / Water music: *Fripp, Robert* / New moon at red deer wallow: *Rain Tree Crow* / Attack of the 50 foot drum demon: *Bass-O-Matic* / Mekong: *Jam Nation* / Endless life: *Verve* / Nachtmusik schattenhaft: *Schulze, Klaus* / Arrival: *Voyager* / Specific gravity of smile: *Froese, Edgar* / Orovela: *Tsinandali Choir* / Dance no. 3: *Laraaji* / Premonition: *Sylvian, David & Holger Czukay* / Island: *Grid*
CD Set ______ AMBT 2
Virgin / Dec '93 / EMI

BRIEF HISTORY OF AMBIENT VOL.3, A (The Music Of Changes/2CD Set)
Sygyt khoomei kargyraa: *Shu-De* / When the waters came to life: *Schmidt, Irmin* / Gringatcho demento: *Orbit, William* / Red earth (As summertime ends): *Rain Tree Crow* / Last emperor (Theme variation 1): *Sakamoto, Ryuichi* / 1988: *Fripp, Robert* / Epiphany: *Sylvian, David* / Study of six guitars: *Amorphous Androgynous* / Amy yo I: *Trisan* / Kingdom come: *Laswell, Bill* / You will be all right: *Ono, Seigen* / Meditation: *Laraaji* / Pendulum man: *Bark Psychosis* / Distant village: *Brook, Michael* / Mystery R.P.S. (No.8): *Jah Wobble* / Throw away your gun (Dub): *Prince Far-I* / Wind and lonely fences: *Fripp, Robert & Brian Eno* / Nuages (That which passes, passes like clouds): *King Crimson* / Mustt mustt: *Khan, Nusrat Fateh Ali* / Concert for gender: *Shakuhachi & Zither* / Healthy colours: *Fripp, Robert & Brian Eno* / Cascade parts 2 and 3: *Future Sound Of London* / Summer storm: *Quine, Robert & Fred Maher* / Rising thermal: *Hassell, Jon & Brian Eno* / Mutability (A new begining is in the offing): *Sylvian, David*
CD Set ______ AMBT 3
Virgin / May '94 / EMI

BRIEF HISTORY OF AMBIENT VOL.4, A (Isolationism/2CD Set)
Lost: *KK Null* / Flat without a back: *O'Rourke, Jim* / Dredger: *Ice* / Strangers: *Bjorkenheim, Raoul* / Daisy gun: *Soviet France* / Air lubricated free axis trainer: *Labradford* / Self strangulation: *Techno Animal* / Hallucinations (In memory of Reinaldo Arenas): *Schutze, Paul* / Silver rain fell: *Scorn* / Lost in fog: *Disco Inferno* / Six: *Total* / Once again I cast myself into the flames of atonement: *Nijiumu* / Aphex airlines: *Aphrodisiac* / Vandoevre: *AMM* / Lief: *Seefeel* / O'rang: *Little Sister* / Hydroponic: *EAR* / Desert flower: *Sufi* / Burial rites: *Toop, David & Max Eastley* / Crater scar (Adrenchrome): *Main* / Hide: *Final* / Thoughts: *Lull* / Kamom (Part one: Brohuk): *Koner, Thomas*
CD Set ______ AMBT 4
Virgin / Aug '94 / EMI

BRILLIANCE FOR A BETTER FUTURE
CD ______ SR 9455
Silent / Nov '94 / Cargo / Plastic Head

BRING DA RUCKUS (A Loud Story)
Bring da rukus: *Wu Tang Clan* / Lump lump: *Sadat X* / When eyes may shine: *Xzibit & Mobb Deep* / Love what I feel: *April* / Protect ya neck: *Wu Tang Clan* / Everyday and everynight: *Michelle, Yvette* / Pass out: *Alkaholiks* / Paparazzi: *Xzibit* / Reality: *Evans, Adriana* / Glaciers of ice: *Raekwon The Chef* / Advance to boardwalk: *Cella Dwellas* / I don't know: *Next Level* / Drop a gem on 'em: *Mobb Deep* / Only when I'm drunk: *Alkaholiks* / Lower Eastside: *Delinquent Habits* / CREAM: *Wu Tang Clan* / Survival of the fittest: *Mobb Deep*
CD ______ 743214421628
Loud / Jan '97 / BMG

BRINGING IT ALL BACK HOME (2CD Set)
CD Set ______ HBCD 0010
Hummingbird / Feb '97 / ADA / Direct / Grapevine/PolyGram

BRINGING IT ALL BACK HOME - GUINNESS TOUR '92
CD ______ HBCD 0001
Hummingbird / Oct '93 / ADA / Direct / Grapevine/PolyGram

BRISTOL SESSIONS, THE
Skip to my Lou: *Dunford, Uncle Eck* / O Molly dear: *Shelton, B.F.* / Walking in the way of Jesus: *Shelton, B.F.* / Newmarket wreck: *Barker, J.W.* / Soldier's sweetheart: *West Virginia Coon Hunters* / Greasy string: *West Virginia Coon Hunters* / Are you washed in the blood: *Stoneman, Ernest V.* / Henry Whitter's fox chase: *Whitter, Henry* / Bury me beneath the willow: *Carter Family* / Jealous sweetheart: *Johnson Brothers* / Will they ring the golden bells: *Karnes, Alfred G.* / Sandy river belle: *Dad Blackard's Moonshiners* / Sleep: *Rodgers, Jimmie* / Johnny Goodwin: *Bull Mountain Moonshiners* / I'm redeemed: *Alcoa Quartet* / Little log cabin by the sea: *Carter Family* / Old time corn shuckin': *Blue Ridge Corn Shuckers* / I want to go where Jesus is: *Phipps, Ernest* / Midnight on the stormy deep: *Stoneman, Ernest; Irma Frost & Erk Dunford* / Wandering boy: *Carter Family* / To the work: *Karnes, Alfred G.* / Blackeyed Susie: *Nestor, J.P.* / Passing Policeman: *Johnson Brothers* / Tell mother I will meet her: *Stoneman, Ernest V.* / Single girl, married girl: *Carter Family* / Potlicker blues: *Watson, El* / Longest train I ever saw: *Tenneva Ramblers* / Resurrection: *Stoneman, Ernest V.* / Storms are on the ocean: *Carter Family* / Wreck of the Virginian: *Reed, Blind Alfred* / Billy Grimes, the Rover: *Shellor family* / Standing on promises: *Tennessee mountaineers* / Mountaineer's courtship: *Stoneman, Ernest; Irma Frost & Erk Dunford* / Poor orphan child: *Carter Family* / I am bound for the promised land: *Karnes, Alfred G.*
CD Set ______ CMFCD 011
Country Music Foundation / Jan '93 / ADA / Direct

BRIT BEAT (16 Swingin' Hits)
Hippy hippy shake: *Swinging Blue Jeans* / You were made for me: *Freddie & The Dreamers* / Concrete and clay: *Unit 4+2* / Hello little girl: *Fourmost* / Do you want to know a secret: *Kramer, Billy J.* / I think of you: *Merseybeats* / You've got your troubles: *Fortunes* / I like it: *Gerry & The Pacemakers* / Do you love me: *Poole, Brian & The Tremeloes* / Tossing and turning: *Ivy League* / Game of love: *Fontana, Wayne* / He's in town: *Rockin' Berries* / Baby now that I've found you: *Foundations* / Tell me when: *Applejacks* / Little things: *Berry, Dave* / You were on my mind: *St. Peters, Crispian*
CD ______ SUMCD 4070
Summit / Nov '96 / Sound & Media

BRIT FUNK
CD ______ AHLCD 40
Hit / Aug '96 / Grapevine/PolyGram

BRIT HOP & AMYL HOUSE
What's that sound: *Sever, Sam & The Raiders Of The Lost Art* / Real shit: *Fried Funk Food* / Dirt: *Death In Vegas* / Don't die foolish: *Lionrock* / Shaolin Buddha finger: *Depth Charge* / Voodoo people: *Prodigy* / Leave home: *Chemical Brothers* / Santa Cruz: *Fatboy Slim* / Blow the whole joint up: *Monkey Mafia* / Beat bastik: *Hard Hop Heathen* / Flow: *Model 500* / Higher state of consciousness: *Wink, Josh* / Lobotomie: *Top, Emmanuel* / Renegade Soundwave: *Renegade Soundwave* / Bug powder dust: *Bomb The Bass*
CD ______ HARD 10LPCD
Concrete / Jun '97 / 3mv/Pinnacle / Prime / RTM/Disc / Total/BMG

BRIT PACK BRAT PACK (16 Transatlantic Hits)
Itchycoo park: *Small Faces* / For your love: *Yardbirds* / Wild thing: *Troggs* / Baby come back: *Equals* / Letter: *Box Tops* / Bend me, shape me: *American Breed* / Gimme some loving: *Davis, Spencer Group* / Young girl: *Puckett, Gary & The Union Gap* / Happy together: *Turtles* / You've got your troubles: *Fortunes* / Reflections of my life: *Marmalade* / Here comes my baby: *Tremeloes* / Sugar sugar: *Archies* / 98.6: *Keith* / Judy in disguise: *Fred, John & His Playboy Band* / Woolly bully: *Sam The Sham & The Pharaohs*
CD ______ SUMCD 4065
Summit / Nov '96 / Sound & Media

BRITISH 60'S HIT COLLECTION, THE
Jesamine: *Casuals* / Just like Eddie: *Heinz* / Diamonds: *Harris, Jet* / Bobby's girl: *Maughan, Susan* / Tell him: *Davies, Billie* / Tell me when: *Applejacks* / Tossing and turning: *Ivy League* / Tobacco Road: *Nashville Teens* / Baby now that I've found you: *Foundations* / Pied piper: *St. Peters, Crispian* / You don't have to: *Caravelles* / Ain't misbehavin': *Bruce, Tommy* / Juliet: *Four Pennies* / Are you sure: *Allisons* / Walking back to happiness: *Shapiro, Helen* / Early in the morning: *Vanity Fair* / Moon river: *Williams, Danny*
CD ______ PLATCD 209
Platinum / Feb '97 / Prism

BRITISH 60'S VOL.1, THE
I'm telling you now: *Freddie & The Dreamers* / I understand: *Freddie & The Dreamers* / If you gotta make a fool of somebody: *Freddie & The Dreamers* / You were made for me: *Freddie & The Dreamers* / Sorrow: *Merseybeats* / I think of you: *Merseybeats* / Wishing and hoping: *Merseybeats* / Don't turn around: *Merseybeats* / It's love that really counts: *Merseybeats* / I love you, yes I do: *Merseybeats* / He's in town: *Rockin' Berries* / Poor man's son: *Rockin' Berries* / Little children: *Kramer, Billy J.* / I'll keep you satisfied: *Kramer, Billy J.* / Bad to me: *Kramer, Billy J.* / Do you want to know a secret: *Kramer, Billy J.*
CD ______ PLATCD 207
Platinum / Feb '97 / Prism

BRITISH 60'S VOL.2, THE
Here it comes again: *Fortunes* / You've got your troubles: *Fortunes* / Freedom come freedom go: *Fortunes* / Storm in a teacup: *Fortunes* / This gold ring: *Fortunes* / Twist and shout: *Poole, Brian* / Do you love me: *Poole, Brian* / Someone someone: *Poole, Brian* / Candy man: *Poole, Brian* / Little loving: *Fourmost* / Hello little girl: *Fourmost* / I'm in love: *Fourmost* / Game of love: *Fontana, Wayne* / Um um um um um um: *Fontana, Wayne* / Pamela Pamela: *Fontana, Wayne* / Groovy kind of love: *Fontana, Wayne*
CD ______ PLATCD 208
Platinum / Feb '97 / Prism

BRITISH BLUEGRASS VOL.1
CD ______ BBMA 1001CD
British Bluegrass / Nov '95 / ADA / Direct

BRITISH BLUES HEROES
CD ______ MCCD 194
Music Club / Mar '95 / Disc / THE

BRITISH BLUES INVASION
CD ______ MACCD 150
Autograph / Aug '96 / BMG

BRITISH DANCE BANDS
CD ______ AVC 539
Avid / May '94 / Avid/BMG / Koch / THE

BRITISH DUB FUNK VOL.1
CD ______ XEN 004CD
Funky Xen / Jul '96 / Timewarp

BRITISH DUB FUNK VOL.2
CD ______ XEN 005CD
Funky Xen / Jul '96 / Timewarp

BRITISH FOLK COLLECTION
CD ______ CDSR 048
Telstar / May '94 / BMG

BRITISH INVASION, THE
CD Set ______ TFP 025
Tring / Nov '92 / Tring

BRITISH POP HISTORY
CD ______ 16103
Laserlight / May '94 / Target/BMG

BRITISH POP HISTORY - THE 60'S
CD ______ 16081
Laserlight / Nov '93 / Target/BMG

BRITISH PUB PARTY
CD Set ______ TREB 5010
Scratch / May '96 / Koch / Scratch/BMG

BRITISH R 'N' B INVASION, THE
Stay: *Eternal* / Back to life: *Soul II Soul* / Living in the light: *Wheeler, Caron* / It's a shame (my sister): *Monie Love* / Hanging on a string (contemplating): *Loose Ends* / Let me be the one: *Five Star* / Tell me (how it feels): *52nd Street* / Say I'm your number one: *Princess* / Love zone: *Ocean, Billy* / All woman: *Stansfield, Lisa* / Never stop: *Brand New Heavies* / Tribute (right on): *Pasadenas* / Mama used to say: *Junior* / It's gonna be alright: *Turner, Ruby*
CD ______ DOMECD 8
Dome / Sep '96 / 3mv/Sony

BRITISH ROCK'N'ROLL GREATS (3CD Set)
We're gonna rock tonight: *Crombie, Tony* / Big beat: *Lang, Don* / Rockin' shoes: *King Brothers* / Cool & cosy: *Avons* / Ain't misbehavin': *Bruce, Tommy* / That rock'n'roll man: *Ellington, Ray* / Walk don't run: *Barry, John* / Rock pretty baby: *Lang, Don* / Rock'n'roll coaster: *Crombie, Tony* / You can't say I love you to a rock'n'roll tune: *Small, Joan* / Rock around the island: *Lang, Don* / Please don't touch: *Kidd, Johnny* / Don't nobody move: *Lawrence, Lee* / Stranded in the jungle: *Ellington, Ray* / Saturday night at the Duckpond: *Cougars* / London rock: *Crombie, Tony* / Queen of the hop: *Lang, Don* / Shakin' all over: *Kidd, Johnny* / Wake up little Susie: *King Brothers* / I'm a moody guy: *Fenton, Shane & The Fentones* / Teach you to rock: *Crombie, Tony* / Six Five Spe-

cial: *Lang, Don* / Five foot two eyes of blue: *Fenton, Shane & The Fentones* / Rock'n'roll opera: *Lawrence, Lee* / Skinny Lizzie: *Angelo, Bobby* / Rubber ball: *Avons* / Got the water boilin': *Bruce, Tommy* / Gypsy beat: *Packabeats* / Rock Mr. Piper: *Lang, Don* / Shortnin' bread rock: *Crombie, Tony* / This should go on forever: *Eager, Vince* / Left hand boogie: *Ellington, Ray* / Be my girl: *Dale, Jim* / Trambone: *Krew Kats* / Mexican: *Fentones* / Rock'n'roll blues: *Lang, Don* / Let's you & I rock: *Crombie, Tony* / Rock around the Cookhouse: *Lang, Don* / Giddy up a ding dong: *Ellington, Ray* / Earth angel: *Southlanders* / Red planet rock: *Lang, Don* / Don't you rock me Daddy-O: *Vipers* / That'll be the day: *Page, Larry* / Rock'n'roll boogie: *Squadronaires* / Witch doctor: *Lang, Don* / Green door: *Ellington, Ray* / Shake, rattle & roll: *Parnell, Jack* / Rock, rock, rock: *Lang, Don* / Crazy love: *Squadronaires* / Rock man rock: *MacKintosh, Ken* / Rockabilly: *Anthony, Billie* / Hush-a-bye rock: *Southlanders* / Baby sittin': *Angelo, Bobby* / Ain't that a shame: *Southlanders* / Rockin' around the world (part 1): *Kirchin Band* / Rockin' around the world (part 2): *Kirchin Band*
CD Set ______ **CDTRBOX 228**
Trio / Jul '96 / EMI

BRITISH SOUL VOL.1
This beautiful day: *Jackson, Levi* / Serving a sentence of life: *Douglas, Carl* / Beautiful night: *Thomas, Jimmy* / What love brings: *Bernard, Kenny* / I'll hold you: *Frankie & Johnny* / Don't pity me: *Lynn, Sue* / Lost summer love: *Silva, Lorraine* / Our love is getting stronger: *Night, Jason* / Love is wonderful: *Parfit, Paula* / Stop and you'll become aware: *Shapiro, Helen* / Nobody knows: *St. John, Tammy* / Everything's gonna be alright: *Arnold, P.P.* / Invitation: *Band Of Angels* / If you knew me: *Keyes, Ebony* / Number one in your heart: *Goins, Herbie* / Need your love: *Notations* / Movin' away: *Lynch, Kenny* / Baby I don't need your love: *Chants* / Stand accused: *Colton, Tony* / Never ever: *Clements, Soul Joe* / Tears of joy: *Merrell, Ray*
CD ______ **GSCD 049**
Goldmine / Feb '95 / Vital

BRITISH SOUL VOL.2
It'll never be over for me: *Yuro, Timi* / You're absolutely right: *Aldo, Steve* / It's just love: *Andrews, John* / Drifter: *Baldry, Long John* / You're ready now: *Bennett, Bobby* / He's gotta love me: *Brooks, Elkie* / What greater love: *Hammer, Jack* / Surrounded by a ray of sunshine: *Jones, Samantha* / One in a million: *Keyes, Karol* / Sweet music: *Koobas* / Can't stop talkin' 'bout my baby: *Patto, Michael* / He knows how to love me: *Shapiro, Helen* / On the brink: *Vickers, Mike* / Stay a little while: *Benson, Barry* / That's the tune: *Proby, P.J.* / Lying awake: *Chandelle, Dany* / And suddenly: *Jones, Samantha* / Too late to say you're sorry: *Soulmates* / Just like Romeo and Juliet: *West Five* / Everything I touch turns to tears: *St. John, Barry* / My own two feet: *Lynch, Kenny* / What about the music: *Spice* / When I'm gonna find her: *Loyd, Mark* / Too busy thinking about my baby: *Latter, Gene* / Marble and iron: *James, Jimmy* / Sell my soul to the devil: *Douglas, Carl*
CD ______ **GSCD 079**
Goldmine / Oct '96 / Vital

BRITISH TRADITIONAL JAZZ COLLECTIONS VOL.2
CD ______ **8307882**
Philips / Mar '93 / PolyGram

BRITJAZZ
CD ______ **MCCD 290**
Music Club / Mar '97 / Disc / THE

BRITS - THE AWARDS 1990
All around the world: *Stansfield, Lisa* / Fine time: *Yazz* / My prerogative: *Brown, Bobby* / Sowing the seeds of love: *Tears For Fears* / Best: *Turner, Tina* / My one temptation: *Paris, Mica* / Eye know: *De La Soul* / Sensual world: *Bush, Kate* / Girl I'm gonna miss you: *Milli Vanilli* / Bamboleo: *Gipsy Kings* / Best of me: *Richard, Cliff*
CD Set ______ **TCD 2386**
Telstar / Feb '90 / BMG

BRITS - THE AWARDS 1992
Innuendo: *Queen* / Calling Elvis: *Dire Straits* / Mysterious ways: *U2* / Cream: *Prince* / Rescue me: *Madonna* / Stars: *Simply Red* / Can't stop this thing we started: *Adams, Bryan* / Don't let the sun go down on me: *Michael, George & Elton John* / When a man loves a woman: *Bolton, Michael* / All woman: *Stansfield, Lisa* / Promise me: *Craven, Beverley* / Hole hearted: *Extreme* / Shiny happy people: *REM* / Love is a stranger: *Eurythmics* / Sit down: *James* / Mystify: *INXS* / Love to hate you: *Erasure* / Killer: *Seal* / Justified and ancient: *KLF* / Unbelievable: *EMF* / Just another dream: *Dennis, Cathy* / Set adrift on memory bliss: *PM Dawn* / Thinking about your love: *Thomas, Kenny* / All 4 love: *Color Me Badd* / Sunshine on a rainy day: *Zoe* / Unfinished sympathy: *Massive Attack* / Risk is half undressed: *Jellyfish* / Mustang Sally: *Commitments* / Blue hotel: *Isaak, Chris* / It had to be you: *Connick, Harry Jr.* / Caribbean blue: *Enya* / Inspector Morse: *Pheloung, Barrington*
CD Set ______ **5152072**
PolyGram TV / Feb '92 / PolyGram

BRITS - THE AWARDS 1993
Bohemian rhapsody: *Queen* / Who's gonna ride your wild horses: *U2* / Drowning in my own tears: *Simply Red* / Rhythm of my heart: *Stewart, Rod* / Drive: *REM* / Walking on broken glass: *Lennox, Annie* / Feels like forever: *Cocker, Joe* / Bad love: *Clapton, Eric* / One: *John, Elton* / Rocket man: *Bush, Kate* / End of the road: *Boyz II Men* / Stay: *Shakespears Sister* / Too funky: *Michael, George* / Sleeping satellite: *Archer, Tasmin* / Your town: *Deacon Blue* / Digging in the dirt: *Gabriel, Peter* / Sexy MF: *Prince* / People everyday: *Arrested Development* / Lay all your love on me: *Erasure* / Boss drum: *Shamen* / Blue room: *Orb* / Please don't go: *KWS* / Baker Street: *Undercover* / Ain't no man: *Carroll, Dina* / Free your mind: *En Vogue* / Friday I'm in love: *Cure* / Weather with you: *Crowded House* / Million love songs: *Take That* / Time to make you mine: *Stansfield, Lisa* / I wonder why: *Stigers, Curtis* / Crucify: *Amos, Tori* / Deeply dippy: *Right Said Fred* / Constant craving: *Lang, k.d.* / Celts: *Enya*
CD ______ **5160752**
PolyGram TV / Feb '93 / PolyGram

BRITS - THE AWARDS 1995 (2CD Set)
What's the frequency, Kenneth: *REM* / My heart: *Young, Neil & Crazy Horse* / Patience of angels: *Reader, Eddi* / Mmm mmm mmm mmm: *Crash Test Dummies* / Red shoes: *Bush, Kate* / Kiss from a rose: *Seal* / Cornflake girl: *Amos, Tori* / Sulky girl: *Costello, Elvis* / Run to you: *Adams, Bryan* / Hung up: *Weller, Paul* / You gotta be: *Des'ree* / Love town: *Gabriel, Peter* / More you ignore me, the closer I get: *Morrissey* / Thank you for hearing me: *O'Connor, Sinead* / Zombie: *Cranberries* / Motherless child: *Clapton, Eric* / I believe: *Detroit, Marcella* / Circle of life: *John, Elton* / Seven seconds: *N'Dour, Youssou* / Searching: *China Black* / Sweetness: *Gayle, Michelle* / Half the man: *Jamiroquai* / Just a step from heaven: *Eternal* / Midnight at the oasis: *Brand New Heavies* / Love the one you're with: *Vandross, Luther* / Sight for sore eyes: *M-People* / Mama said: *Anderson, Carleen* / If I only knew: *Jones, Tom* / So natural: *Stansfield, Lisa* / Sly: *Massive Attack* / Stay another day: *East 17* / Things can only get better: *D:Ream* / Girls and boys: *Blur* / Insomniac: *Echobelly* / Wild ones: *Suede* / Numb: *Portishead* / Live forever: *Oasis*
CD Set ______ **MOODCD 39**
Columbia / Feb '95 / Sony

BRITS - THE AWARDS 1996
Wonderwall: *Oasis* / Common people: *Pulp* / Universal: *Blur* / Lucky you: *Lightning Seeds* / Basket case: *Green Day* / Alright: *Supergrass* / Kelly's heroes: *Black Grape* / High and dry: *Radiohead* / Girl like you: *Collins, Edwyn* / Alright: *Cast* / Queer: *Garbage* / Afroride: *Leftfield* / Pumpkin: *Tricky* / Kung Fu: *Ash* / Down by the water: *PJ Harvey* / Stutter: *Elastica* / Isobel: *Bjork* / Roll with it: *Oasis* / Changing man: *Weller, Paul* / Perfect: *Lightning Seeds* / Hold me, thrill me, kiss me, kill me: *U2* / Hand in my pocket: *Morissette, Alanis* / Gangsta's paradise: *Coolio* / Kiss from a rose: *Seal* / Circus: *Kravitz, Lenny* / Missing: *Everything But The Girl* / Itchycoo Park: *M-People* / Rough with the smooth: *Nelson, Shara* / Protection: *Massive Attack* / Raindrops keep falling on my head: *Manic Street Preachers* / Strangers when we meet: *Bowie, David* / Sentimental fool: *Cole, Lloyd* / If I were you: *Lang, k.d.* / Shapes and sizes: *Armatrading, Joan*
CD ______ **SONYTV 10CD**
Sony TV / Feb '96 / Sony

BRITS - THE AWARDS 1997 (2CD Set)
Australia: *Manic Street Preachers* / Govinda: *Kula Shaker* / Marblehead Johnson: *Bluetones* / Sugar coated iceberg: *Lightning Seeds* / Fun lovin' criminals: *Fun Lovin' Criminals* / Oh yeah: *Ash* / You're gorgeous: *Baby Bird* / Neighbourhood: *Space* / Circle: *Ocean Colour Scene* / If it makes you happy: *Crow, Sheryl* / I am, I feel: *Alisha's Attic* / She said: *Longpigs* / Twisted (everyday hurts): *Skunk Anansie* / Good enough: *Dodgy* / Bittersweet me (Memphis soundcheck): *REM* / Mile End: *Pulp* / Stripper vicar: *Mansun* / Peaches: *Presidents Of The USA* / Lust for life: *Iggy Pop* / Don't look back in anger: *Oasis* / Breathe: *Prodigy* / Cosmic girl: *Jamiroquai* / No woman, no cry: *Fugees* / Return of the mack: *Morrison, Mark* / Angel: *Simply Red* / Say you'll be there: *Spice Girls* / Give me a little more time: *Gabrielle* / Nobody knows: *Rich, Tony Project* / You're makin' me high: *Braxton, Toni* / Ocean drive: *Lighthouse Family* / Gangsta's paradise: *Coolio* / Talk to me: *Babyface* / One and one: *Miles, Robert & Maria Naylor* / Kootchi: *Cherry, Neneh* / Born slippy: *Underworld* / Christiansands: *Tricky* / Loops of fury: *Chemical Brothers* / Final hit: *Leftfield* / Theme from mission: impossible: *Mullen, Larry & Adam Clayton*
CD Set ______ **SONYTV 23CD**
Sony TV / Feb '97 / Sony

BROKEN BEATS & DIRTY PROMISES
CD ______ **TRPHOP 2002CD**
North South / Nov '96 / Pinnacle

BROKEN HEARTED
Just walking in the rain: *Ray, Johnnie* / Love letters in the sand: *Boone, Pat* / Only you (and you alone): *Platters* / End of the world: *Davis, Skeeter* / Tell Laura I love her: *Peterson, Ray* / Hey Paula: *Paul & Paula* / Hey there lonely girl: *Holman, Eddie* / Young girl: *Puckett, Gary & The Union Gap* / Groovy kind of love: *Fontana, Wayne* / Ferry 'cross the Mersey: *Gerry & The Pacemakers* / Cryin' game: *Berry, Dave* / To know him is to love him: *Teddy Bears* / Chapel of love: *Dixie Cups* / Rhythm of the rain: *Cascades* / What becomes of the broken hearted: *Ruffin, Jimmy* / When a man loves a woman: *Sledge, Percy* / Stand by me: *King, Ben E.* / If you don't know me by now: *Melvin, Harold & The Bluenotes*
CD ______ **ECD 3049**
K-Tel / Jan '95 / K-Tel

BROKEN HEARTED (18 Bittersweet Love Songs)
Sad sweet dreamer: *Sweet Sensation* / Who were you with in the moonlight: *Dollar* / Be thankful for what you've got: *De Vaughn, William* / Way we were: *Knight, Gladys & The Pips* / I'm doin' fine now: *New York City* / Somebody else's guy: *Brown, Jocelyn* / Where did our love go: *Elbert, Donnie* / Goodbye nothing to say: *Javells* / I couldn't live without your love: *Clark, Petula* / Don't throw your love away: *Searchers* / Funny how love can be: *Ivy League* / Same old feeling: *Pickettywitch* / Let the heartaches begin: *Baldry, Long John* / Tired of waiting for you: *Kinks* / Sandy: *Travolta, John* / Making up again: *Goldie* / I'll have to go away: *Jigsaw* / Rainin' through my sunshine: *Real Thing*
CD ______ **SUMCD 4106**
Summit / Nov '96 / Sound & Media

BROTHER, CAN YOU SPARE A DIME
Were you there / Maledetto / Lungi da te / Bist du bei mir / Hear de lambs/Plenty good room / Go down Moses / Bye and bye / Steal away / Crucifixion / Roun' about de mountain / Standin' in the need of prayer / Negro spiritual medley / Heav'n heav'n / Waterboy / Go down Moses/Deep river / Couldn't hear nobody pray / Every time I feel the spirit / Swing low, sweet chariot / Goin' to shoot all over God's heaven / Ol' man river / Street cries of New Orleans / Cobbler's song / Brother can you spare a dime
CD ______ **GEMMCD 9484**
Pearl / Mar '91 / Harmonia Mundi

BROTHERHOOD
CD ______ **NLB 003CD**
No Looking Back / Mar '96 / Plastic Head

BROTHERHOOD
CD ______ **LHCD 018**
Luv n' Haight / Jul '96 / Timewarp

BROTHERS IN BLUES, SISTERS IN SOUL (18 Classic Tracks)
(Sittin' on the) Dock of the bay: *Sledge, Percy* / B-A-B-Y: *Thomas, Carla* / Harlem shuffle: *Bob & Earl* / Dancing in the street: *Reeves, Martha* / Green onions: *Cortez, Dave 'Baby'* / Ride Captain ride: *Blues Image* / It's in his kiss (the shoop shoop song): *Everett, Betty* / Knock on wood: *Floyd, Eddie* / My guy: *Wells, Mary* / Rescue me: *Bass, Fontella* / Soul man: *Sam & Dave* / I say a little prayer: *Reeves, Martha* / Tell it like it is: *Neville, Aaron* / Drift away: *Gray, Dobie* / Stand by me: *King, Ben E.* / All I could do was cry: *James, Etta* / Wake up everybody: *Melvin, Harold & The Bluenotes* / When a man loves a woman: *Sledge, Percy*
CD ______ **ECD 3066**
K-Tel / Jan '95 / K-Tel

BROWNSWOOD WORKSHOP MULTI-DIRECTION VOL.1
CD ______ **5189602**
Talkin' Loud / Mar '94 / PolyGram

BROWNSWOOD WORKSHOP MULTI-DIRECTION VOL.2
Spontaneity: *Jazz Brothers* / April in Tokyo: *Pronoia* / Hug: *Tiny Voice Production* / La lune: *Naoyuki Honzawa* / Return of the space ape: *Audio Active* / Seasons change: *Sylk 130* / Deep water: *Trio Da Lata* / Por El: *Diet Music* / Tune for us: *Kruder & Dorfmeister* / Rock 'n' roll philosophy: *Love TKO* / Is it worth it: *DJ Milo*
CD ______ **5286792**
Talkin' Loud / Mar '96 / PolyGram

BROWSER
CD ______ **SCHTUMM 001CD**
Jealous / Sep '96 / Pinnacle

BUDAL LARDIL
CD ______ **LARRCD 285**
Larrikin / Jun '94 / ADA / CM / Direct / Roots

BUDDAH DEEP SOUL
CD ______ **NEMCD 781**
Sequel / Mar '96 / BMG

BUDDHIST CHANT 1/MAHA PIRIT - THE GREAT CHANT
CD ______ **JD 6512**
Jecklin Disco / Nov '90 / Pinnacle

BUDDHIST CHANT VOL.1
CD ______ **VICG 50392**
JVC World Library / Mar '96 / ADA / CM / Direct

BUENAVENTURA DURRUTI (2CD Set)
CD Set ______ **777733**
Nato / Apr '97 / Discovery / Harmonia Mundi

BUENOS AIRES 30'S TANGOS
CD ______ **995222**
EPM / Jun '93 / ADA / Discovery

BUENOS AIRES BANONEON ORCHESTRA
CD ______ **CDCH 702**
Milan / Feb '91 / Conifer/BMG / Silva Screen

BUENOS AIRES BY NIGHT
La cumparsita: *Basso, Jose* / El firulete: *Basso, Jose* / El choclo: *Sexeto Mayor* / Adios nonino: *Sexeto Mayor* / De vuelta y media: *Varela, Hector* / Paloma blanca: *Varela, Hector* / Quejas de bandoneon: *Troilo, Anibal* / Danzarin: *Troilo, Anibal* / Verano porteno: *Garello, Paul* / Margarita de agosto: *Garello, Paul* / La Cachila: *Pugliese, Osvaldo* / La Yumba: *Pugliese, Osvaldo* / El dia que me quieras: *Gardel, Carlos* / Mi buenos aires querido: *Gardel, Carlos* / Grisel: *Mores, Mariano* / Taquito militar: *Mores, Mariano* / La punalada: *Canaro, Francisco* / La tablada: *Canaro, Francisco* / Yira yira: *Sassone, Florindo* / Adios muchachos: *Sassone, Florindo*
CD ______ **CDEMS 1487**
EMI / May '93 / EMI

BUILT
CD ______ **RI 039**
Rather Interesting / Sep '96 / Plastic Head

BULERIAS 1930-1940 (Music From Spain)
CD ______ **995792**
EPM / Sep '96 / ADA / Discovery

BULGARIA - MUSIC OF SHOPE COUNTY
CD ______ **LDX 274970**
La Chant Du Monde / Apr '94 / ADA / Harmonia Mundi

BULGARIAN BRASS
CD ______ **PAN 153CD**
Pan / Mar '95 / ADA / CM / Direct

BULGARIAN FOLK MUSIC
CD ______ **SOW 90115**
Sounds Of The World / Sep '93 / Target/BMG

BULLDOG AT NIGHT
CD ______ **USCD 3043**
Urban Sound Of Amsterdam / Jun '97 / Amato Disco / Arabesque / Intergroove / Mo's Music Machine

BULLSEYE BLUES CHRISTMAS
CD ______ **CDBB 9567**
Bullseye Blues / Oct '95 / Direct

BURIED ALIVE
CD ______ **BCD 4052**
Bomp / Feb '96 / Cargo / Greyhound / RTM/Disc / Shellshock/Disc

BURIED ALIVE VOL.2 - THE BEST OF SMOKE VOL.7
CD ______ **BCD 4058**
Bomp / Jan '97 / Cargo / Greyhound / RTM/Disc / Shellshock/Disc

BURLINGTON COFFEEHOUSE VOL.1
CD ______ **ALC 127CD**
Alcazar / Aug '96 / ADA

BURNING AMBITIONS (A History Of Punk)
Boredom: *Buzzcocks* / Bingo masters breakout: *Fall* / 12XU: *Wire* / Life: *Alternative TV* / Keys to your heart: *101'ers* / I'm alive: *999* / Gary Gilmore's eyes: *Adverts* / (Get a) grip (on yourself): *Stranglers* / Baby baby: *Vibrators* / Oh bondage up yours: *X-Ray Spex* / I'm stranded: *Saints* / Chinese rocks: *Thunders, Johnny & The Heartbreakers* / Love song: *Damned* / In a rut: *Ruts* / Stranglehold: *UK Subs* / Flares and slippers: *Cockney Rejects* / Wait: *Killing Joke* / Holiday in Cambodia: *Dead Kennedys* / Last rockers: *Vice Squad* / Someone's gonna die: *Anti Pasti* / City baby attacked by rats: *GBH* / Russians in the DHSS: *Attila The Stockbroker* / Lust for glory: *Angelic Upstarts*
CD ______ **CDBRED 3**
Anagram / Jun '96 / Cargo / Pinnacle

BURNING AMBITIONS VOL.2 (A History Of Punk)
Then he kissed me: *Hollywood Brats* / I don't care: *Boys* / Thinkin' of the USA: *Eater* / Safety pin stuck in my heart: *Fitzgerald, Patrick* / Automatic lover: *Vibrators* / Action time vision: *Alternative TV* / Murder of Liddle Towers: *Angelic Upstarts* / CID: *UK Subs* / Police car: *Cockney Rejects* / Teenage kicks: *Undertones* / Totally wired: *Fall* / Kill the Poor: *Dead Kennedys* / Exploited barmy army: *Exploited* / So what: *Anti Nowhere League* / Seventeen years of hell: *Partisans* / Stab the Judge: *One Way System* / Run like hell: *Peter & The Test Tube Babies* / Smash the discos: *Business* / Warriors: *Blitz* / Dozen girls: *Damned* / Summer of '81: *Vi-*

olators / Megalomania: *Blood* / vengeance: *New Model Army* / You'll never know: *New Model Army*
CD ______ CDPUNK 81
Anagram / Jun '96 / Cargo / Pinnacle

BURNING AMBITIONS VOL.3
If the kids are united: *Sham 69* / Warhead: *UK Subs* / Greatest cockney rip off: *Cockney Rejects* / Another dead soldier: *Anti Pasti* / Decontrol: *Discharge* / Too drunk to fuck: *Dead Kennedys* / Transvestite: *Peter & The Test Tube Babies* / Ramrton song: *Disorder* / Puppets of war: *Chron Gen* / Let's break the law: *Anti Nowhere League* / No survivors: *GBH* / Stand strong stand proud: *GBH* / Everybody jitterbug: *Toy Dolls* / Viva la revolution: *Adicts* / Burn 'em down: *Abrasive Wheels* / Jerusalem: *One Way System* / Farmyard boogie: *Chaos UK* / Die for your government: *Varukers* / Fuck religion, fuck politics, fuck the lot of you: *Chaotic Dischord* / Decapitated: *Broken Bones*
CD ______ CDPUNK 98
Anagram / Jun '97 / Cargo / Pinnacle

BURNING LOVE
CD ______ HRCD 8045
Disky / Dec '93 / Disky / THE

BURNING UP
CD ______ CDTRL 336
Trojan / Mar '94 / Direct / Jet Star

BURNING UP VOL.3
CD ______ CDBS 563
Burning Sounds / Jan '97 / Grapevine/ PolyGram / Jet Star / Total/BMG

BURNLEY BLUES FESTIVAL '89
CD ______ JSPCD 228
JSP / Jun '89 / ADA / Cadillac / Direct / Hot Shot / Target/BMG

BURRO PRESENTS BEATSPERIMENTS
CD ______ EMCD 1
Elephant Music / Oct '96 / SRD

BUSTIN' OUT
CD ______ VPRC 1046
Steely & Cleevie / May '89 / Jet Star

BUSTIN' SURFBOARDS
Surf jam: *Beach Boys* / Out of limits: *Marketts* / Fast freight: *Valens, Ritchie* / Our man Flint: *Challengers* / Curl rider: *Surf Raiders* / Our favorite Martian: *Fuller, Bobby* / Perfect wave: *Norman, Neil* / Wild weekend: *Rockin' Rebels* / Victor: *Dale, Dick & His Del-Tones* / Bustin' surfboards: *Tornadoes* / Yang bu: *Messina, Jim* / Surf rider: *Lively Ones* / Lonely surfer: *Nitzsche, Jack*
CD ______ GNPD 2152
GNP Crescendo / Jul '95 / ZYX

BUY THIS USED CD
CD ______ DE 120642
Homestead / Oct '93 / Cargo / SRD

BUYAKA (The Ultimate Dancehall Collection)
CD ______ 923722
Big Beat / Mar '94 / Pinnacle

BY ANY MEANS NECESSARY
CD ______ YRECD 001
YRE / Nov '93 / Grapevine/PolyGram

BY THE RIVERS OF BABYLON (Timeless Hymns Of Rastafari)
CD ______ SH 45031
Shanachie / Mar '97 / ADA / Greensleeves / Koch

C IS FOR CHERRIES
CD ______ KUDCD 008
Kudos / Jul '96 / Kudos / Pinnacle

CABARET CHRISTMAS, A
Winter wonderland: *Hampton Callaway, Ann & Billy Stritch* / Christmas love song: *Hampton Callaway, Ann* / I'll be home for Christmas: *Stritch, Billy* / Merry Christmas to me/Hard candy Christmas: *Sullivan, K.T.* / Let it snow, let it snow, let it snow: *Carroll, Barbara* / It must be Christmas: *Mulligan, Gerry* / After the holiday: *Marcovicci, Andrea* / Silent night: *Akers, Karen & Andrea Marcovicci* / I don't remember Christmas: *Akers, Karen* / Christmas waltz: *Whiting, Margaret* / What are you doing New Year's Eve: *Haran, Mary Cleere* / Christmas in the city: *Leonhart, Jay* / Have yourself a merry little Christmas: *Loudon, Dorothy* / White Christmas: *Cook, Barbara*
CD ______ DRGCD 91415
DRG / Nov '93 / Discovery / New Note/ Pinnacle

CABARET'S GOLDEN AGE VOL.1
Lili Marlene: *Andersen, Lale* / Suppose: *Baker, Josephine* / Just once for all time: *Garat, Henri* / La cucaracha: *Niessen, Gertrude* / Solomon: *Welch, Elisabeth* / Luxury cruise: *Andersen, Inga* / I'm one of the queens of England: *Byng, Douglas* / Il m'a vue nue: *Mistinguett* / I want yer, ma honey: *Guilbert, Yvette* / I should like to be really in love: *Ahlers, Anny* / 2-2-22 Timbuctoo: *Blaney, Norah* / Pretty little baby: *Baker, Josephine* / I'm just a poor little woman: *Leander, Zarah* / Folies musicales: *Betove* / Under the red lamps: *Andersen, Lale* / Je voudrais vous dire en Francais: *Serrano, Rosita* / Is your heart still free: *Ahlers, Anny* / Nymph errant: *Lawrence, Gertrude* / Holyhollyhollyhollyhollywood: *Hansen, Max* / Ca c'est Paris: *Mistinguett* / Symphonie: *Dietrich, Marlene* / Spring: *Byng, Douglas* / When lights are low: *Welch, Elisabeth* / La Conga: *Niessen, Gertrude* / Falling in love again: *Dietrich, Marlene*
CD ______ PASTCD 9727
Flapper / '90 / Pinnacle

CABARET'S GOLDEN AGE VOL.2
Night and day: *Hutchinson, Leslie 'Hutch'* / Darling je vous aime beaucoup: *Hildegarde* / Button up your shoes and dance: *Wall, Max* / Wistaria: *Mayerl, Billy* / Stately homes of England: *Coward, Noel* / La paloma: *Serrano, Rosita* / Drei rote rosen: *Andersen, Lale* / You've got to pay for everything you get: *Frankau, Ronald* / Hold 'em Joe: *Lili-Verona* / Je ne dis pas non: *Chevalier, Maurice* / Come and join the no-shirt party: *Long, Norman* / Am I blue: *Anona Winn* / Le chanson des rues: *Sablon, Jean* / Thank you so much, Mrs Lowsborough-Goodby: *Porter, Cole* / Where are the songs: *Coward, Noel* / Sombreros et mantillas: *Ketty, Rina* / Paddlin' Madelin' home: *Layton & Johnstone* / Room with a view: *Hildegarde* / Mon coeur: *Chevalier, Maurice* / Two little babes in the wood: *Porter, Cole* / I'm shooting high: *Marsh, Carolyn* / Her mother came too: *Buchanon, Jack* / Le potpourri d'Alain Gerbault: *Printemps, Yvonne*
CD ______ PASTCD 9737
Flapper / Mar '91 / Pinnacle

CABARETS AND CHANSONNIERS (3CD Set)
CD Set ______ 984072
EPM / Jun '97 / ADA / Discovery

CADENCE STORY, THE
Butterfly / All I have to do is dream / Poetry in motion / Lollipop / I'm gonna knock on your door / Rumble / Forty five men in a telephone booth / Dead Don / Bye bye love / Ballad of Davy Crockett / Mr. Sandman / Hernando's hideawy / I like your kind of love / Born to be with you / Lighthouse / Message from James Dean / Wake up little Susie / Baby doll / I love my girl / Swag / Cherry berry wine / Without you / (Girls, girls, girls) Made to love / Since I fell for you / IT keeps right on a-hurtin' since I left / Ain't gonna wash for a week / Ebb Tide / Eh, cumpari
CD ______ CDCHD 550
Ace / Aug '95 / Pinnacle

CAFE CLASSICS
CD ______ 74321263432
RCA / Mar '95 / BMG

CAFE DE PARIS 1930-1941 (24 Accordian Classics From The Boulevards of Paris)
Falmbee montalbanaise / L'accordeoniste / El ferrero / Enivrante / Strange harmony / Mado / Matelotte / Quand on se promene / Sporting java / Pepee / La guinguette a ferme ses volets / Swing valse / Brise napolitaine / Soir de dispute / Le charmeur de serpents / Les triolets / Gallito / Swing '39 / Pinsonnette / Rosetta / Melancolie / Jeanette
CD ______ MCCD 096
Music Club / Mar '93 / Disc / THE

CAFE DEL MAR, IBIZA VOL.1
CD ______ REACTCD 041
React / May '97 / Arabesque / Prime / Vital

CAFE DEL MAR, IBIZA VOL.2
Haunted dancehall: *Sabres Of Paradise* / Making of Jill: *Mark & Henry's* / Tarenah: *Lab* / Moment scale: *Silent Poets* / Entre dos aguas: *De Lucia, Paco* / Sunset: *TBMP* / Eugene: *Salt Tank* / Devotion: *D-Note* / Blue eyes sunrise: *Woodshed* / Easter song: *Man Called Adam* / Unity: *Antoine, Marc* / Everybody loves the sunshine: *Ramp* / La mar: *Atlas*
CD ______ REACTCD 062
React / May '97 / Arabesque / Prime / Vital

CAFE DEL MAR, IBIZA VOL.3
Blue bar: *After Life* / Dusk: *Pressure Drop* / Emotions of paradise: *Miro* / Sueno Con Mexico: *Metheny, Pat* / Nights interlude: *Nightmares On Wax* / Tones: *Nova Nova* / Asia: *Neri, Alex* / Dust of life: *Fazed Idjuts* / Walking on air: *Padilla, Jose* / My freedom: *Beat Foundation* / Redemption song: *Moodswings* / Panama bazaar: *Eighth Wave* / Last picture show: *Heavy Shift* / Spells and angels: *Minister Of Noise*
CD ______ REACTCD 084
React / May '97 / Arabesque / Prime / Vital

CAFE DEL MAR, IBIZA VOL.4
Que bonito: *Padilla, Jose* / Sun shines better: *Martyn, John* / Leo leo: *Indo Aminata* / Grillos: *Fernandez, Paco* / Return journey: *Voices Of Kwahn* / Miracle Road: *Les Jumeaux* / No sant: *Diop, Wasis & Lena Fiagbe* / Out of time: *Levitation* / Place De La Concorde: *Fila Brazillia* / Offshore: *Chicane* / Fifth and avenida: *Afterlife* / Troubled girl: *Ramirez, Karen* / Lula: *Mison, Phil* / Street tattoo: *Getz, Stan*
CD ______ 5539072
Manifesto / Aug '97 / PolyGram

CAFE LATINO
CD ______ TCD 2841
Telstar / Jun '96 / BMG

CAFE LOCAL VOL.1
CD ______ PIAS 015560120
Play It Again Sam / Sep '96 / Discovery / Plastic Head / Vital

CAFE LOCAL VOL.2
CD ______ PIAS 015561520
Play It Again Sam / Nov '96 / Discovery / Plastic Head / Vital

CAFE MAMBO (3CD Set)
CD Set ______ VTDCD 150
Virgin / Aug '97 / EMI

CAFE SOCIETY 1939
CD ______ DOCD 1003
Document / Apr '97 / ADA / Hot Shot / Jazz Music

CAINED AND ABLE
CD ______ PUSHCD 1
Push / Jul '97 / SRD

CAJUAL RELIEF
CD ______ SOMCD 3
Sound Of Ministry / Jul '95 / 3mv/Sony / Amato Disco / Prime

CAJUN AND CREOLE MASTERS
CD ______ T 138
Music Of The World / Aug '96 / ADA / Target/BMG

CAJUN CLASSICS VOL.1
Back door: *Louisiana aces* / Pine grove blues: *Abshire, Nathan* / Saturday night special: *Cormier, Lesa & The Sundown Playboys* / Jolie blon: *Bruce, Vin* / Sugar bee: *Cleveland Crochet* / Lafayette two-step: *Roger, Aldus* / Cher cherie: *Guidry, Doc* / Fumes d'enfer: *Pitre, Austin* / Step it fast: *Bonsall, Joe & the orange playboys* / Parlez vous francais: *Matte, Bill* / I'll take you home: *Bertrand, Robert* / Equand j'etais pauvre: *Balfa, Dewey* / Lemonade song: *Broussard, Leroy* / Grande bosco: *Lejeune, Iry* / Mamou two step: *Walker, Lawrence* / Hippy ti yo: *Newman, Jimmy C.* / Sha ba ba: *Brown, Sidney* / Cajun stripper: *Richard, Belton* / J'ai fait mon idee: *Bergeron, Shirley* / Choupique two step: *Greely, David* / La pointe aux pins: *Jambalaya Cajun Band & Reggie Matte* / Creole stomp: *Breaux, Jimmy* / J'ai ve le loup: *Beausoleil* / Hee haw breakdown: *Cormier, Nolan & the LA Aces*
CD ______ CDCHM 431
Ace / Mar '93 / Pinnacle

CAJUN CLASSICS VOL.2 (The Kings Of Cajun At Their Very Best)
Lacassine special / Madam boso / Sur la courtableau / La valse de reno / Les veuves de la coulee / Jolie fille / Mamou blues / Louisiana aces special / Jolie blon / Grand nuit special / I passed by your door / Cajun pogo / Starvation waltz / Mowater blues / Hippy ti yo / Les traces de mon bogue / Hold my false teeth / Hey jolie / Makes me feel like dancing / Valse de cypriere / La vie de cadjin / Le ti-mouchoir / Tu peux cogner / Going back to Louisiana
CD ______ CDCHM 519
Ace / May '94 / Pinnacle

CAJUN COUNTRY
CD ______ EDCD 7013
Easydisc / Oct '96 / Direct

CAJUN DANCE HALL
Couer des cajuns: *Daigrepont, Bruce* / Les grands bois: *Sonnier, Jo El* / La pointe aux pins: *Riley, Steve & Mamou Playboys* / J'aurais du t'aimer (I should have loved you): *Newman, Jimmy C.* / Rolling pin: *Beausoleil* / Balfa Waltz: *Doucet, David* / Grande bosco: *LeJeune, Eddie* / La danse de Mardi Gras: *Mamou* / Lafayette two step: *Menard, D.L.* / Bayou pon pon: *Doucet, Michael & Cajun Brew*
CD ______ EDCD 7011
Easydisc / Aug '96 / Direct

CAJUN DANCE HALL SPECIAL
CD ______ ROUCD 11570
Rounder / Feb '93 / ADA / CM / Direct

CAJUN EXPERIENCE
La vie Marron: *File* / Old fashioned two step: *Balfa Toujours* / Webb Pierce blues: *Fontenot, Allen* / Make my hustle: *Frank, Keith* / Cajun from Church Point: *Callier, Jackie* / La danse de Mardi Gras: *Balfa Brothers* / Back home again in Louisiana: *Cormier, Lesa & The Sundown Playboys* / Love Bridge Waltz: *Lejeune, Iry* / Games people play: *Abshire, Nathan* / Rocking Saturday night: *Toups, Wayne* / J'ai fait mon e'de: *Bergeron, Shirley* / La valse de KLFY: *Doucet, Michael* / Les flumes d'enfer: *Pitre, Austin* / Valse a Beausoleil: *Beausoleil* / Poor hobo: *Choates, Harry* / La valse de Reno: *Walker, Lawrence* / Lake Arthur Stomp: *Thibodeaux, Rufus* / Un autre soir d'ennui: *Richard, Belton* / opelousas waltz: *Pitre, Austin* / Two step de l'anse a paille: *Balfa Brothers*
CD ______ NTRCD 071
Nectar / Apr '97 / Pinnacle

CAJUN FAIS DO-DO
CD ______ ARHCD 416
Arhoolie / Jan '96 / ADA / Cadillac / Direct

CAJUN GREATS
La chere toute-toute: *Sonnier, Jo El* / La porte d'en arriere: *Newman, Jimmy C.* / Midland special: *Berard, Al & The Basin Brothers* / Jolie blon: *LeJeune, Eddie* / Chez Seychelles: *Beausoleil* / Jeune filles de la campagne: *Balfa Toujours* / J'ai passe devant ta porte: *Menard, D.L.* / Mamou two step: *Trio Cadien* / Madeleine: *LeJeune, Eddie & The Morse Playboys* / Petit mamou: *Daigrepont, Bruce* / French blues: *Doucet, David* / Jongle a moi: *Riley, Steve & Mamou Playboys*
CD ______ EDCD 7012
Easydisc / Jun '97 / Direct

CAJUN HONKY TONK
CD ______ ARHCD 427
Arhoolie / Apr '95 / ADA / Cadillac / Direct

CAJUN HOT SAUCE
Mosquito that ate up my sweetheart in New Iberia: *Beausoleil* / Kaplan waltz: *Savoy-Doucet Cajun Band* / Monsieur Leonard: *California Cajun Band* / Port Arthur blues: *Balfa, Dewey* / Two step d'amende: *Savoy-Doucet Cajun Band* / En bas du chene vert: *Menard, D.L.* / Shoo black: *Fontenot, Canray & Beausoleil* / Bosco stomp: *Clark, Octa & Hector Duhon* / Jolie blonde: *Guillory, Chuck* / Allons a lafayette: *Choates, Harry* / Bayou pom pom: *Read, Wallis 'Cheese'* / Crowley waltz: *Hackberry Ramblers* / Hey Ma: *Breaux Brothers* / Grand Texas: *Guillory, Chuck* / Valse criminelle: *Clark, Octa & Hector Duhon* / Keep a knocking: *Read, Wallis 'Cheese'* / Catch my hat: *Fruge, Wade* / Je veux me marier: *Hackberry Ramblers* / Valse du mariage: *California Cajun Orchestra* / One step d'amende: *Doucet, Michael* / Basile waltz: *Choates, Harry* / Osson two step: *Falcon, Joseph*
CD ______ CDCHD 591
Ace / Feb '96 / Pinnacle

CAJUN LOUISIANA 1928-1929 (2CD Set)
CD Set ______ FA 019CD
Fremeaux / Nov '95 / ADA / Discovery

CAJUN MOON (The Best Of The Bayou)
Tous les temps en temps (every now and then): *Reneaux, J.J. Band* / Cajun moon: *Deadweights & Memphis Roots* / Gumbo: *Milteau, J.J.* / Ye yai quoi faire: *Milteau, J.J.* / By you on the bayou tonight: *Reneaux, J.J. Band* / Crawdaddy stomp: *McCoy, Charlie & The United* / Bayou lafayette: *McCoy, Charlie & The United* / Flames d'enfer: *Reneaux, J.J. Band* / Louise (like sweet wine): *Buddy & Ghost Riders* / All you ever do is bring me down: *Deadweights & Memphis Roots* / Julie: *Ann Americana* / Down in lafayette: *Dobson, Richard & State Of The Heart* / Louisville: *Milteau, J.J.* / Julie jean bad bad girl: *Reneaux, J.J. Band* / Bootleggin': *Americana* / Leve tes fenetres haut (raise your windows high): *Reneaux, J.J. Band* / Cajun moon (reprise): *Deadweights & Memphis Roots*
CD ______ 306072
Hallmark / Jan '97 / Carlton

CAJUN MUSIC ANTHOLOGY VOL.1 (Le Gran Mamou)
Basile: *Soileau, Leo & Mayuse Lafleur* / Saut' crapaud: *Fruge, Columbus* / Quelqu' un est jaloux: *Guilory, Delin T. & Lewis Lafleur* / Les blues de voyage: *Ardoin, Amedee & Dennis McGee* / Mon vieux D'Autrefois: *Falcon Trio* / Je vais jouer celea por tois: *Guidry, Bixy & Percy Babineaux* / L'abandoner: *Montet, Bethmost & Joswell Dupois* / Trois jours apres ma most: *Soileau Couzens* / O' bebe': *Doucet, Oscar & Alius Soileau* / Ma cherie: *Doucet, Oscar & Alius Soileau* / La valse j'aime: *Falcon Trio* / Grosse mama: *Soileau, Leo & Moise Robin* / Belle of Point Claire: *Mistric, Arteleus* / One stepde Lacassine: *Abshire, Nathan & The Rayn-Bo Ramblers* / Jolie blon: *Hackberry Ramblers* / Il y a pas la Claire de Lune: *Joe's Acadians* / Lake Charles waltz: *Four Aces* / Valse de maralis bulleur: *Rayne-Bo Ramblers* / La two-step a Erby: *Thibodeaux Boys* / Le gran mamou: *Soileau, Leo & his three aces* / Alberta: *Walker, Lawrence* / Je va t'aimer quand meme: *Hackberry Ramblers* / Viens donc me rejoindre: *Fusilier, J.B. & His Merrymakers* / Barroom blues: *Dixie Ramblers* / La veuve da la coulee: *Happy Fats & His Rayne-Bo Ramblers*
CD ______ CMFCD 013
Country Music Foundation / Jan '93 / ADA / Direct

CAJUN MUSIC ANTHOLOGY VOL.2 (Raise Your Window)
Mama where are you at: *Soileau, Leo & Mayuse Lafleur* / Alone at home: *Guilory, Delin T. & Lewis Lafleur* / Je me suis en alle: *Montet, Bethmost & Joswell Dupois* / You belong to me: *Mistric, Arteleus* / When I meet you at the gate: *Doucet, Oscar & Alius Soileau* / Stop that: *Guilory, Delin T. & Lewis Lafleur* / Waltz of the bayou: *Guidry, Bixy & Percy Babineaux* / La fille que j'aime: *Creduer, Joe & Albert Babineaux* / Sur le chemin chez moi: *Couzens, Soileau* / Pauvre garcon: *Falcon Trio* / La valse de Riceville: *Abshire, Nathan & The Rayn-Bo Ram-*

blers / Raise your window: Falcon Trio / Lake Arthur stomp: Miller's Merrymakers / La vieux vals an' onc mack: Thibodeaux Boys / Si voux moi voudrais ame: Soileau, Leo & his three aces / En route chez moi: Falcon Trio / Si tu vondroit marriez avec moi: Joe's Acadians / Lonesome blues: Shreve, Floyd & the Three Aces / Crowley waltz: Hackberry Ramblers / Joilie schvr rouge: Happy Fats & His Rayne-Bo Ramblers
CD CMF 017D
Country Music Foundation / Aug '93 / ADA / Direct

CAJUN MUSIC ANTHOLOGY VOL.3 (Gran Prairie - Victor Bluebird Sessions 1935-1940)
One step de morse: Abshire, Nathan & The Rayn-Bo Ramblers / Noveau grand gueydan: Rayne-Bo Ramblers / Et la bas: Hackberry Ramblers / Les blues de bosco: Rayne-Bo Ramblers / Two step du la teil: Fusilier, J.B. & His Merrymakers / Jolie petite fille: Hackberry Ramblers / Rayne breakdown: Rayne-Bo Ramblers / Ta oblis de nernier: Happy Fats & His Rayne-Bo Ramblers / Pine island: Miller's Merrymakers / Las vas de la prison: Hackberry Ramblers / Les escrives dan plantin: Rayne-Bo Ramblers / Crap shooters hop: Werner, Joe & Ramblers / Ma chere bouclett: Fusilier, J.B. & His Merrymakers / Tickle her: Hackberry Ramblers / La response de blues de bosco: Happy Fats & His Rayne-Bo Ramblers / Hackberry hop: Soileau, Leo / La place mon coeur desire: Rayne-Bo Ramblers / La breakdown a Pete: Hackberry Ramblers
CD CMF 018D
Country Music Foundation / Aug '93 / ADA / Direct

CAJUN SOCIAL MUSIC
CD SFCD 40046
Smithsonian Folkways / Sep '94 / ADA / Cadillac / CM / Direct / Koch

CAJUN SPICE
CD ROUCD 11550
Rounder / Oct '93 / ADA / CM / Direct

CAJUN VOL.2 (Fais Do Do)
Ma blonde est partie: Breaux, Amedee / Les tracas du hobo: Breaux, Amedee / Two step de Mama: Ardoin, Amade / Two step de eunice: Ardoin, Amade / Two step de pararie soileau: Ardoin, Amade / Rasalia: Segura, Dewey / You're small and sweet: Segura, Dewey / Far away from home blues: Segura, Dewey / Fais do-do negre: Freres Breaux / Tiger rag blues: Freres Breaux / One step a Marie: Freres Breaux / Mazurka de la louisiane: Freres Breaux / Le vieux soulard et sa femme: Breaux, Cleoma / Marie buller: Breaux, Cleoma / Mon coeur t'apelle: Breaux, Cleoma / C'est si triste san lui: Breaux, Cleoma / Madam atchen: Ardoin, Amade / Taunt aline: Ardoin, Amade / Le blues du petit chien: Freres Breaux / La valse d'auguste: Freres Breaux / La valse d'utah: Freres Breaux
CD 4757032
Columbia / May '94 / Sony

CALANAIS
CD CD 001
An Lanntair / May '95 / ADA / Duncans

CALBMELAN
CD DATCD 22
Dat / Nov '95 / ADA / Direct

CALENDAR MUSIC IN THE CENTRAL VALLEYS
CD LDX 274938
La Chant Du Monde / Sep '92 / ADA / Harmonia Mundi

CALIENTE - HOT
CD NW 244
New World / Aug '92 / ADA / Cadillac / Harmonia Mundi

CALIENTE GOLD COLLECTION (2CD Set)
CD Set D2CD 4021
Deja Vu / Jun '95 / THE

CALIFORNIA COOL (Hip Sounds Of The West Coast)
This could be the start of something: Murphy, Mark / Man with the golden arm: May, Billy & His Orchestra / Black nightgown: Mulligan, Gerry & Shelly Manne / Squimp: Hamilton, Chico / But not for me: Baker, Chet Quartet / Ironic: Guiffre, Jimmy & Jack Sheldon Quartet / I hear music: Hawes, Hampton Trio / Lover man: Konitz, Lee & Gerry Mulligan Quartet / Hey Bellboy: Woods, Gloria & Peter Candoli / Diablo's dance: Pepper, Art & Shorty Rogers / Our love is here to stay: Edwards, Teddy & Les McCann Ltd / Route 66: Troup, Bobby / Two can play: Gordon, Bob & Jack Montrose Quintet / Take five: Shank, Bud / Jimmy's theme: Baker, Chet & Bud Shank Orchestra / Something cool: Christy, June / Mambo de la pinta: Pepper, Art Quartet / Do I love you: Lee, Peggy & George Shearing / Katanga: Amy, Curtis & Dupree Bolton / Handful of stars: Chaloff, Serge / West coast blues: Criss, Sonny
CD BNZ 303
Blue Note / Feb '93 / EMI

CALIFORNIA DREAMIN'
Cantamilla: Tranquility Bass / Three nudes: Hawke / Energize: Island Universe / Reality of nature: Young American Primitive / Funk you very much: Ultraviolet Catastrophe / Taste of your own medicine: Elements of Trance / Feelin' real good: Aquatherium / Transmit liberation: Single Cell Orchestra / Straight up caffeine: Up Above The World / Theme from Daisy Glow: Daisy Glow
CD TRUCD 3
Internal / Jan '94 / Pinnacle / PolyGram

CALIFORNIA DREAMIN'
California dreamin': Mamas & The Papas / Little deuce coupe: Beach Boys / Summer in the city: Lovin' Spoonful / Let's go to San Francisco: Flowerpot Men / Little old lady from Pasadena: Jan & Dean / California girls: Beach Boys / Place in the sun: Hammond, Albert / Happy together: Turtles / Hello summertime: Goldsboro, Bobby / Walking on sunshine: Katrina & The Waves / Surf city: Jan & Dean / San Franciscan nights: Burdon, Eric / Dedicated to the one I love: Mamas & The Papas / Mama told me not to come: Three Dog Night
CD DC 880482
Disky / May '97 / Disky / THE

CALIFORNIA DREAMING
CD 10512
CMC / Jun '97 / BMG

CALL DAT GEORGE
CD JWIG 002CD
JW / Jan '96 / Jet Star

CALL OF NATURE (3CD Set)
CD Set KBOX 374
Collection / Aug '97 / Target/BMG / TKO Magnum

CALL OF THE BANSHEE
CD SPV 08438932
SPV / Feb '95 / Koch / Plastic Head

CALL ON THE DARK
CD NB 233CD
Nuclear Blast / Apr '97 / Plastic Head

CALLING ALL WORKERS
FDR Jones / Bandwagon / Mrs. Bagwash / Ernie Bagwash / Bell / It's that man again / Lambeth walk / Calling all workers / I'm one of the Whitehall warriors / It's foolish but it's fun / All over the place / Chattanooga choo choo / I I-love you so / Out in Indiah / Blues in the night / Take the world exactly as you find it / Why don't you do it right / Warsaw concerto / People will say we're in love / My heart and I / This is the army / Dark music / I couldn't sleep a wink last night
CD CDCHD 302
Happy Days / Aug '94 / Conifer/BMG

CALYPSO CALALOO (Early Carnival Music From Trinidad 1914-50)
CD ROUCD 1105
Rounder / Apr '94 / ADA / CM / Direct

CALYPSO CARNIVAL
CD ROUCD 1077
Rounder / Feb '93 / ADA / CM / Direct

CALYPSO COSTA RICA
CD 926462
BUDA / Jul '96 / Discovery

CALYPSO LADIES 1926-1941
CD HTCD 06
Heritage / Feb '91 / ADA / Direct / Hot Shot / Jazz Music / Swift / Wellard

CALYPSOCA HITS VOL.1
CD JW 012
JW / Jan '96 / Jet Star

CAMBODIA - MUSIC OF THE ROYAL PALACES
CD C 5560034CD
Ocora / Jul '94 / ADA / Harmonia Mundi

CAMDEN CRAWL, THE
CD PUBE 07CD
Love Train / Nov '95 / SRD

CAMINO AL SOL
CD TUMICD 044
Tumi / Apr '95 / Discovery / Stern's

CAN YOU DIG IT
Resolution: Coltrane, John / Happy days: Tyner, McCoy / For mods only: Hamilton, Chico / Caravan: Hubbard, Freddie / Stolen moments: Nelson, Oliver / Hold 'em Joe: Rollins, Sonny / Creator has a master plan: Sanders, Pharoah / Sermonette: Jones, Quincy / Good lookin' out: Turrentine, Stanley / II BS: Mingus, Charles / Limbo jazz: Ellington, Duke & Coleman Hawkins
CD IMPD 8881
Impulse Jazz / Oct '96 / New Note/BMG

CAN YOU FEEL THE FORCE
CD PLSCD 135
Pulse / Apr '96 / BMG

CAN YOU HANDLE IT
Zoom: Fat Larry's Band / Purely by coincidence: Sweet Sensation / Jack in the box: Moments / No one can love you more: Hyman, Phyllis / Midas touch: Midnight Star / Friends: Shalamar / You to me are everything: Real Thing / Part time love: Knight, Gladys & The Pips / My girl: Whispers / Where did our love go: Elbert, Donnie / Lean on me: Moore, Melba / Can you handle it: Redd, Sharon / Best thing that ever happened to me: Knight, Gladys & The Pips / You'll never know what you're missing: Real Thing / Still in love: Lucas, Carrie / Homely girl: Chi-Lites / Casanova: Coffee / You are my starship: Connors, Norman
CD TRTCD 141
TrueTrax / Oct '94 / THE

CAN YOU SEE IT 1988-1993
CD INVCD 023
Invisible / Feb '94 / Plastic Head

CANDID JAZZ
28th and 8th: Hawkins, Coleman & Pee Wee Russell / Wrap your troubles in dreams: Eldridge, Roy / Lord, Lord am I ever gonna know: Thompson, Lucky / Hard sock dance: Bailey, Benny / Brother Terry: Terry, Clark / Deep river: Akiyoshi, Toshiko & Charlie Mariano Quartet / Sallie: Ellis, Don / Ferris Wheel: Williams, Richard / African lady: Lincoln, Abbey & Max Roach / Man of words: Little, Booker / Boo: Ervin, Booker / Criss cross: Lacy, Steve / Port of call: Taylor, Cecil / Lock 'em up: Mingus, Charles
CD CCD 79000
Candid / Feb '97 / Cadillac / Direct / Jazz Music / Koch / Wellard

CANDLELIGHT SAMPLER
CD CANDLE 011CD
Candlelight / Oct '96 / Plastic Head

CANNABIS WEEKEND
CD EFA 127022
Dope / Mar '95 / SRD

CANNED BLUES
CD HRCD 8036
Disky / Jul '94 / Disky / THE

CAN'T GET ENOUGH
CD LHCD 006
Luv n' Haight / Jul '96 / Timewarp

CAN'T KEEP FROM CRYING (Blues From The Death Of President Kennedy)
CD TCD 5007
Testament / Oct '94 / ADA / Koch

CAN'T LIVE WITHOUT IT
Can't live without it: Tucker, Luther / Voodoo man: White, Lavelle / Why'd you have to say that l'word: Kane, Candye / Bird nest on the ground: Bramhall, Doyle / Baby please don't lie to me: Wilson, Kim / Give me time: Foley, Sue / Slow down baby: Pryor, Snooky / She put the hurt on me: Sahm, Doug / It won't be long: Kane, Candye / Itchy and scratchy: Cowdrey, Lewis / Keep on drinking: Tucker, Luther / Stop these teardrops: White, Lavelle
CD ANTCD 9905
Antones / Jul '95 / ADA / Hot Shot

CANTE FLAMENCO
CD NI 5251
Nimbus / Sep '94 / Nimbus

CANTONA - THE ALBUM
Eric Cantona: Ratmond Bizarre / Have you heard about Eric: Captain Sensible / Cantona Superstar: Her / Ooh ah Cantona: Boyle, Pete & The K-Stand / Monsieur Genius: Boyle, Pete & The K-Stand / Grand old Cantona: Boyle, Pete & The K-Stand / Eric the King: Boyle, Pete & The K-Stand / 12 days of Cantona: Boyle, Pete & The K-Stand / Do the frog: Philippe, Louis / Eric (please don't go): Half Time Oranges / Eric Cantona what a bloody star: Red Deville
CD PELE 010CD
Exotica / Oct '95 / SRD / Vital

CAPE BRETON ISLAND
CD NI 5383
Nimbus / Sep '94 / Nimbus

CAPE-VERDE ISLANDS (The Roots)
CD PS 65061
PlayaSound / Nov '90 / ADA / Harmonia Mundi

CAPITOL COUNTRY MUSIC CLASSICS - 1940'S
Jingle jangle: Ritter, Tex / Texas blues: Willing, Foy / I'm wastin' my tears on you: Ritter, Tex / Oklahoma hills: Guthrie, Jack / With tears in my eyes: Tuttle, Wesley / Divorce me COD: Travis, Merle / So round, so firm: Travis, Merle / Oakie boogie: Guthrie, Jack / Silver stars, purple sage, eyes of blue: Stone, Cliffie / Smoke, smoke, smoke: Williams, Tex / Humpty dumpty heart: Thompson, Hank / Peepin' through the keyhole: Stone, Cliffie / Rye whiskey: Ritter, Tex / Cigareets, whusky and wild, wild women: Ingle, Red & The Natural Seven / Cocaine blues: Hogsed, Roy / One has my name (the other has my heart): Wakely, Jimmy / Dear Oakie: Rivers, Jack / Life gits tee-jus, don't it: Williams, Tex / Candy kisses: Kirk, Eddy & The String Band / Tennessee border: Ford, Tennessee Ernie / Gamblin' polka dot blues: Duncan, Tommy / Slippin' around: Whiting, Margaret & Jimmy Wakely / Whoa sailor: Thompson, Hank / Give me a hundred reasons: Jones, Ann / I love you because: Payne, Leon / Mule train: Ford, Tennessee Ernie
CD CDEMS 1412
Capitol / Jul '97 / EMI

CAPITOL COUNTRY MUSIC CLASSICS - 1950'S
Broken down merry-go-round: Whiting, Margaret & Jimmy Wakely / I'll never be free: Ford, Tennessee Ernie & Kay Starr / Shot gun boogie: Ford, Tennessee Ernie / Hot rod race: Dolan, Jimmy / Mockin' Bird Hill: Paul, Les & Mary Ford / Wild side of life: Thompson, Hank & His Brazos Valley Boys / High noon: Ritter, Tex / Don't let the stars get in your eyes: McDonald, Skeets / Goin' steady: Young, Faron / That's me without you: James, Sonny / Dear John letter: Shepard, Jean & Ferlin Husky / Forgive me, John: Shepard, Jean & Ferlin Husky / Wake up, Irene: Thompson, Hank / Release me: Heap, Jimmy & The Melody Mastg / You better not do that: Collins, Tommy / What'cha gonna do now: Collins, Tommy / Satisfied mind: Shepard, Jean / When I stop dreamin': Louvin Brothers / Sixteen tons: Ford, Tennessee Ernie / Waltz of the angels: Stewart, Wynn / I gotta know: Jackson, Wanda / I don't believe you've met my baby: Louvin Brothers / Young love: James, Sonny / Gone: Husky, Ferlin / Alone with you: Young, Faron / Country music is here to stay: Husky, Ferlin
CD CDEMS 1413
Capitol / Jul '97 / EMI

CAPITOL COUNTRY MUSIC CLASSICS - 1960'S
Six pack to go: Thompson, Hank / He'll have to stay: Black, Jeanne / Wings of a dove: Husky, Ferlin / Hello walls: Young, Faron / Right or wrong: Jackson, Wanda / In the middle of a heartache: Jackson, Wanda / I dreamed of a hillbilly heaven: Ritter, Tex / Sing a little song of heartache: Maddox, Rose / Must you throw dirt in my face: Louvin Brothers / Tips of my fingers: Clark, Roy / Second fiddle (to an old guitar): Shepard, Jean / I don't love you anymore: Louvin, Charlie / Just between the two of us: Owens, Bonnie & Merle Haggard / You're the only world I know: James, Sonny & the Southern Gentleman / Born to be with you: James, Sonny & the Southern Gentleman / Strangers: Haggard, Merle / Tombstone every mile: Curless, Dick / Queen of the house: Miller, Jody / Hicktown: Ford, Tennessee Ernie / Yodel, sweet Molly: Louvin, Ira / I'll take the dog: Shepard, Jean & Ray Pillow / Burning bridges: Campbell, Glen / Gentle on my mind: Campbell, Glen / It's such a pretty world today: Stewart, Wynn / Just hold my hand: Mosby, Johnny & Jonie / Mr. Walker, it's all over: Spears, Billie Jo / Okie from Muskogee: Haggard, Merle & the Strangers
CD CDEMS 1422
Capitol / Jul '97 / EMI

CAPITOL COUNTRY MUSIC CLASSICS - 1970'S
Fightin' side of me: Haggard, Merle & the Strangers / Cherokee maiden: Haggard, Merle & the Strangers / All I have to do is dream: Campbell, Glen & Bobbie Gentry / Big wheel cannonball: Curless, Dick / Snowbird: Murray, Anne / Something to brag about: Louvin, Charlie & Melba Montgomery / Empty arms: James, Sonny / I'm a truck: Simpson, Red / She's my rock: Edwards, Stoney / Comin' after Jenny: Ritter, Tex / Fiddle man: Stegall, Red / Bonparte's retreat: Campbell, Glen / Rhinestone cowboy: Campbell, Glen / Get on my love train: La Costa / I'm not Lisa: Colter, Jessi / What's happened to blue eyes: Colter, Jessi / Hurt: Connie Cato / Letter that Johnny Walker read: Asleep At The Wheel / Miles and miles of Texas: Asleep At The Wheel / Couple more years: Dr. Hook / Bluest heartache of the year: Dale, Kenny / Paper Rosie: Watson, Gene / Gambling polka dot blues: Texas Playboys / I cheated on a good woman's love: Craddock, Billy / Gambler: Schitz, Don / Ain't life hell: Cochran, Hank & Willie Nelson
CD CDEMS 1423
Capitol / Jul '97 / EMI

CAPITOL COUNTRY MUSIC CLASSICS - 1980'S
Nothing sure looked good on you: Watson, Gene / Something 'bout you baby I like: Campbell, Glen & Rita Coolidge / Could I have this dance: Murray, Anne / (You say you're) a real cowboy: Craddock, Billy / Louisiana Saturday night: McDaniel, Mel / Sweetest thing (I've ever know): Newton, Juice / Step that step: Brown, Sawyer / Meet me in Montana: Osmond, Marie & Dan Seals / I tell it like it used to be: Brown, T. Graham / Darlene: Brown, T. Graham / Heartbeat in the darkness: Williams, Don / Old coyote town: Williams, Don / Just another love: Tucker, Tanya / I don't want to set the world on fire: Bogguss, Suzy / Unconditional love: New Grass Revival / I won't take less than your love: Tucker, Tanya/Paul Davis & Paul Overstreet / I didn't (every chance I had): Rodriguez, Johnny / New never wore off my sweet baby: Dilon, Dean / Addicted: Seals, Dan / I wish I could fall in love today: Mandrell, Barbara / Much too young (to feel this damn old): Brooks, Garth / If tomorrow never comes: Brooks, Garth
CD CDEMS 1424
Capitol / Jul '97 / EMI

CAPITOL RARE VOL.1 (Funky Notes From The West Coast)
Music is my sanctuary: Bartz, Gary / Sky islands: Caldera / Annie Mae: Cole, Natalie / Sunshine: Wilson, Nancy / As: Harris, Gene / Genie: Lyle, Bobby / I love you: Taste Of Honey / While I'm alone: Maze / Peace of mind: Allen, Rance Group / Inside

you: *Henderson, Eddie* / Every generation: *Laws, Ronnie* / She's my summer breeze: *Reflections* / Losalamitos (Latinfunklove-song): *Harris, Gene* / About love: *Sidran, Ben* / Dindi: *Lawson, Janet* / Woman of the ghetto: *Shaw, Marlena* / Cheshire cat: *Foster, Ronnie*
CD **CDP 8298652**
Capitol / Jun '94 / EMI

CAPITOL RARE VOL.2
It's a pleasure: *Brown, Sheree* / Before you break my heart: *Dunlap, Gene* / La Costa: *Cole, Natalie* / Carnival de L'esprit: *Bartz, Gary* / Sunshower: *Mouzon, Alphonse* / Abdullah & Abraham: *Hamilton, Chico* / Tidal wave: *Laws, Ronnie* / Can't hide love: *McRae, Carmen* / Space spiritual: *Adderley, Nat Sextet* / Expressway to your heart: *Thunder, Margo* / Beggar for the blues: *Drew, Patti* / Windy C: *100% Pure Poison* / Theme for Relana: *Harris, Gene* / Inside my love: *Riperton, Minnie* / Nightfall: *Stratavarious*
CD **CDP 8356072**
Capitol / Oct '95 / EMI

CAPTAIN OF YOUR SHIP (New Dancehall Shots)
CD **SHCD 45006**
Shanachie / Sep '93 / ADA / Greensleeves / Koch

CARAMBOLAGE
CD **CMPCD 58**
CMP / Nov '92 / Cargo / Grapevine/ PolyGram / Vital/SAM

CARAT VOL.2
CD **PIAS 015561623**
Play It Again / Apr '97 / Silva Screen

CARIBBEAN BEAT VOL.1
La ki ni nano: *Dixie Band* / No dji m'en nouille: *Caribbean Combo* / Sally Brown: *Aitken, Laurel* / Bailando: *Orlando, Ramon* / Sans cesse di nouille: *Cabrimol, Jean Michel* / No dance: *Imagination Brass* / Argent: *Amoro, Rene Paul* / Sabor y pena: *Roque, Victor* / Pa kita' m: *Vega Band* / Lajan mwe: *Reasons Orchestra* / Gozolinn: *Rosier, Piar* / Wasmashin: *Prudencia, Macorio* / Agua: *Vargas, Wilfred*
CD **INT 31122**
Intuition / Aug '92 / New Note/Pinnacle

CARIBBEAN BEAT VOL.2
Bayoe: *Imagination Brass* / On et yo: *Toumpak* / El emneito: *La Fuerza Mayor* / Sinking ship: *Gypsy* / Bayo bayo: *Dixie Band* / Doux doux cherrie: *Heartbeat* / Enojado: *Huracan* / Which one is me home: *Exile One* / Sa ki di sa: *Dede Saint Prix* / Guns of Navarone: *Skatalites* / Party feeling: *Massive Chandelier* / Musica latina: *Fernadito Villalona* / Hot hot hot: *Arrow*
CD **INT 31262**
Intuition / Nov '93 / New Note/Pinnacle

CARIBBEAN BEAT VOL.3
El bailabien / La pachanga del futbol / Pimpele / Tafia / Mata shimaraya / Hickee / La pachanga / Pitaste / Pajaro loco / La negra quiere / No le crea / Zap zap / Laissez passer
CD **INT 31472**
Intuition / Oct '94 / New Note/Pinnacle

CARIBBEAN BEAT VOL.4
Baila / Quien ha visto por ahi mi sombrero de yarey / Moon hop / El baile del perrito / Que seria de cali / Tipico caliente / El merengue / Karayib leve / Echao pa 'lante / Para que aprendan / SOS Maya / Beberte / Losd sitio entera
CD **INT 31532**
Intuition / Oct '95 / New Note/Pinnacle

CARIBBEAN BEAT VOL.5
Pica pica: *Mendez, Kinito* / Para el llanto: *Charanga Habanera* / Soukwe: *Reasons Orchestra* / La flaca: *Coco band* / No me llores mas: *Sierra Maestra* / E alo: *Taxi Kreol* / Jugadita de engano...no: *Origina De Manzanillo* / La noche: *Arroyo, Joe* / Roots: *Palacio, Andy* / Anacaona ay: *Anacaona* / Dos mujeres: *Gitierrez, Alfredo* / Cali Aji: *Gripo Niche* / We different: *Arrow*
CD **INT 31722**
Intuition / Jul '97 / New Note/Pinnacle

CARIBBEAN COCKTAIL
Caribbean surfer / Island in the sun / Rivers of Babylon / America / Sloop John B / Montego Bay / Yellow bird / Coconut woman / Soul limbo / Underneath the mango tree / Brown girl in the ring / Jamaican coffee / Don't stop the carnival / Banana boat song / Jamaica farewell / La bamba / Guantanamera
CD **EMPRCD 580**
Emporio / Jul '95 / Disc

CARIBBEAN DREAM
CD **JWCRO 94CD**
JW / Jan '96 / Jet Star

CARIBBEAN FEELING (2CD Set)
Cumple anos: *Mandingo Y Su Familia* / Todo me gusta de ti: *America, Ima* / Salsa Caribeno: *Camino De Lobo* / Te distes cuenta: *Mandingo, Felipe* / Vals para mayra: *Teran, Sergio* / Tu y las nubes: *Alvarez, Rosario* / Sourie: *De Souza, George* / El gavilan: *Mandingo Y Su Familia* / Entre palmeras: *Vesga, Jose Luis* / Amor de mis amores: *Alvarez, Rosario* / Merengue pasion: *Camino De Lobo* / Kimbiza: *Mi Orquesta* / Juan Jose: *Mandingo Y Su Familia* / Parrandero: *Mandingo Y Su Familia* / Seis por derecho: *Mandingo Y Su Familia* / Destapa el ron: *Mandingo Y Su Familia* / Son Carebeno: *Malaquias, Aldo* / Guantanamera: *Alvarez, Rosario* / A pedir su mano: *Caribbean Orchestra* / Culo e pulla: *Mandingo Y Su Familia* / Mucho mucho: *Jerez, Mauricio* / Orgullo de ti: *Conquistador* / Teresa: *Mandingo Y Su Familia* / Olo lai lo: *Mandingo Y Su Familia* / El cumaco de San Juan: *Mandingo Y Su Familia* / Guadalajara: *Mexican Mariachi Band* / Correveula: *Maipu* / La Billirubina: *Caribbean Orchestra* / Extrano camino: *Conquistador* / Chorinho: *Teran, Sergio*
CD Set **24331**
Laserlight / Jul '96 / Target/BMG

CARIBBEAN MAGIC (A Magical Blend Of Music And The Sounds Of Nature)
CD **57862**
CMC / May '97 / BMG

CARIBBEAN MEMORIES
CD **HM 023**
Harmony / Jun '97 / TKO Magnum

CARIBBEAN PARTY
L'histoire du zouk: *Kali* / Chale lanmou: *Tabou Combo* / Serjyo: *Bago* / Pump me up: *Krosfyah* / Ice cream: *Coalishun* / Roots rock reggae: *Wailer, Bunny* / Pa fe mwen la pen: *Virgal, Eric* / Chayew ale: *Geremy, Patsy* / Dokte: *Thamar, Ralph* / Don't touch my tempo: *Arrow*
CD **PUTU 1322**
Putumayo / Aug '97 / Grapevine/PolyGram

CARIBBEAN TROPICAL DANCE PARTY - 20 HOT CARIBBEAN RHYTHMS
Marinero: *Los Latinos* / Quiero un sombrero: *Carcamo, Pablo* / Consigueme eso: *Musica Latina* / O cana sordi: *Tumbao* / Chapa'lante Catalina: *Carcamo, Pablo* / El pescador: *Carcamo, Pablo* / Un, dos, tres: *Musica Latina* / Mensaje de mi Colombia: *Carcamo, Pablo* / Villa carino: *Carcamo, Pablo* / Candela y tumbao: *Tumbao* / Fantasia caribena: *Carcamo, Pablo* / Los pirulos: *Musica Latina* / Mi alegre serenata: *Carcamo, Pablo* / Vuela paloma: *Tumbao* / Solo quedo: *Carcamo, Pablo* / Suave: *Carcamo, Pablo* / El Africano: *Musica Latina* / Ojala que llueva cafe: *Carcamo, Pablo* / Sol y arena: *Carcamo, Pablo*
CD **EUCD 1209**
ARC / Sep '93 / ADA / ARC Music

CARIBEAN STEEL DRUMS
CD **GRF 201**
Tring / Jan '93 / Tring

CARILLON - THE COMPLETE PRELUDES
CD **A 6230**
Tempo / Dec '96 / Discovery / Harmonia Mundi

CARNEGIE HALL SALUTES THE JAZZ MASTERS (Verve 50th Anniversary)
Tea for two / Tangerine / Shiny stockings / Willow weep for me / I must have that man / Desafinado / Manteca / Parisian thoroughfare / How high the moon / Turn out the stars / Eternal triangle / How insensitive / Down by the riverside / Yellowstone / It's about that time / Now's the time
CD **5231502**
Verve / Oct '94 / PolyGram

CARNIVAL
Waters of Tyne: *Sting & Jimmy Nail* / Winds from the South: *Chieftains* / Dream Angus: *Lennox, Annie* / Va pensiero: *Zucchero* / Sweet and low: *Midler, Bette* / Tu scendi dalle stelle: *Pavarotti, Luciano* / Abide with me: *John, Elton* / All through the night: *Colvin, Shawn* / Lapwony: *Oryema, Geoffrey* / Freedom: *Madonna* / No voy a dejarte arder: *Blades, Ruben* / Ufomeni uyangithanda: *Clegg, Johnny* / Ten years: *Simon, Paul* / Nkosi sikelel' i Afrika: *Katz, Sharon & The Peace Train* / I bought me a cat: *Taylor, James* / Saint Saens:Le carnaval des animaux
CD **74321447692**
RCA Victor / Sep '97 / BMG

CARNIVAL FEVER VOL.1
CD **PD 006**
Ebony / Mar '96 / Jet Star

CARNIVAL JUMP-UP
CD **DE 4014**
Delos / Feb '94 / Nimbus

CARNIVAL OF SOUL VOL.1 (Wishes)
Wishes: *Metrics* / She's so fine: *Topics* / All I need is your love: *Manhattans* / Me, myself and I: *Jenkins, Norma* / I need a guy: *Lovettes* / Forget him: *Brown, Barbara* / Nobody loves me (like my baby): *Caldwell, Harry* / I love you more: *Williams, Lee & The Cymbals* / I'll keep holding on: *Ruffin, Kenneth* / Nothing will ever change (this love of mine): *Jules, Jimmy* / My love is yours tonight: *Turner Brothers* / It's everything about you (that I love): *Williams, Lee & The Cymbals* / I wanna be (your everything): *Pretenders* / Love has passed me by: *Terrell, Phil* / I say yeah: *Pets* / I'll catch you on the rebound: *Leon & The Metronomes* / Can I come in: *Terrell, Phil* / Come home to Daddy: *Goggins, Curby* / I can tell: *Little Royal* / I'm gonna be missing you: *Bailey, Rene* / My baby's gone: *Tren-Teens* / I call it love: *Pretenders* / Until you come back to me: *Manhattans* / Go right on: *Three Reasons*
CD **CDKEND 108**
Kent / Oct '94 / Pinnacle

CARNIVAL OF SOUL VOL.2 (Feelin' Good)
I'm just a young boy: *Terrell, Phil* / So in love: *Brown, Barbara* / Hey girl (where are you going): *Topics* / There goes a fool: *Manhattans* / Please come back: *Caldwell, Harry* / Peeping through the window: *Williams, Lee & The Cymbals* / I found you: *Metrics* / That's what love will do: *Symphonies* / I'm the one love forgot: *Pretenders* / Sometimes I wonder: *Brown, Barbara* / Don't let yourself go: *Jules, Jimmy* / Boogaloo party: *Harold & Connie* / Little Miss Soul: *Lovettes* / Love is breaking out all over: *Manhattans* / Broken heart: *Pretenders* / Warm and tender love: *Bailey, Rene* / Don't you run away: *Terrell, Phil* / Need someone to love: *Jenkins, Norma* / I don't have to cry: *Topics* / I'm afraid (to say I love you): *Lovettes* / New world (is just beginning): *Caldwell, Harry* / Lost love: *Williams, Lee & The Cymbals* / Leave me if you want to: *Goggins, Curby* / Feelin' good: *Carnival Kings*
CD **CDKEND 118**
Kent / Mar '95 / Pinnacle

CARNIVAL OF SOUL VOL.3 (I Wanna Be)
I need you baby: *Williams, Lee & The Cymbals* / I'll be gone: *Williams, Lee & The Cymbals* / I'll erase you: *Terrell, Phil* / I wanna be (your everything): *Manhattans* / I call it love: *Pretenders* / If love comes knockin': *Topics* / Send him to me: *Brown, Barbara* / I'm the man for you baby: *Turner Brothers* / Just one more time: *Jules, Jimmy* / What kind of man are you: *Johnson, Dolores* / Try me one time: *Johnson, Dolores* / Oh why: *Mays, Curly* / You made me love you: *Little Royal* / Git go: *Simon, Maurice & The Pie Men* / Just be yourself: *Pretenders* / April lady: *Perry, James* / Take me back: *Three Reasons* / Lonely girl: *Lovettes* / Cry, cry, cry: *Ruffin, Kenneth* / Buy this record for me: *Leon & The Metronomes* / Your yah-yah is gone: *Trenteens* / It's too late for tears: *Bailey, Rene* / I don't wanna go: *Manhattans* / Groove in G: *Bascomb, Wilbur & The Blue Zodiact* / Love don't come easy: *New Jersey Connection*
CD **CDKEND 124**
Kent / Oct '95 / Pinnacle

CARNIVAL RHYTHMS
Mango mangue: *Parker, Charlie* / Luxo so: *Getz, Stan & Charlie Byrd* / Arinanara: *Valdes, Miguelito* / Nague: *Valdes, Miguelito* / Agueas de marco (Waters of March): *Jobim, Antonio Carlos* / Evolution of Mann: *Mann, Herbie* / Doralice: *Getz, Stan & Joao Gilberto* / Tin tin deo: *Gillespie, Dizzy* / Felicidade: *Gilberto, Astrud* / Ritmo uni: *Tjader, Cal & Eddie Palmieri* / So danco samba (I only dance samba): *Getz, Stan & Luiz Bonfa* / Manteca: *O'Farrell, Chico* / Amor em paz (Once I loved): *Jobim, Antonio Carlos* / Mambo is here to stay: *Machito* / Um abraco no bonfa (Am embrace to bonfa): *Gilberto, Joao* / Ponce: *Morales, Noro* / Boto: *Henderson, Joe* / Elation: *Bobo, Willie* / Tristeza: *Powell, Baden*
CD **5526512**
Spectrum / Mar '97 / PolyGram

CAROLINA BLUES 1926-1929
CD **DOCD 5168**
Document / May '93 / ADA / Hot Shot / Jazz Music

CAROLINA MY DARLING
CD **VPCD 1290**
VP / May '93 / Greensleeves / Jet Star / Total/BMG

CARWASH EXPERIENCE (2CD Set)
We are family: *Sister Sledge* / Let's start the dance: *Bohannon, Hamilton* / Do what you want to do: *T-Connection* / Shoot me with your love: *Thomas, Tasha* / Love sensaton: *Hartman, Dan & Loleatta Holloway* / Rappers delight: *Sugar Hill Gang* / Last night a DJ saved my life: *In Deep* / Dance across the floor: *Horne, Jimmy 'Bo'* / 7654321 blow your whistle: *Toms, Gary Empire* / You can do it: *Hudson, Al & The Partners* / Delirium: *McGhee, Fancine* / Let no man put asunder: *First Choice* / Contact Starr, Edwin: *Starr, Edwin* / Carwash: *Rose Royce* / Starsky and Hutch: *Taylor, James Quartet* / Soul power '74: *Maceo & The Macks* / Party time: *Fatback Band* / All this love that I'm giving: *McCrae, Gwen* / War: *Starr, Edwin* / Me and baby brother: *War* / Rose Royce express: *Rose Royce* / Funky man: *Brown, James* / Think: *Collins, Lyn* / Rock me again and again: *Collins, Lyn* / Blackwater gold: *Sunshine Band* / ot to be reel: *Lynn, Cheryl* / Long train bunning: *Doobie Brothers* / Give it up or turn it loose: *Brown, James* / Starting too fast: *HT's* / Machine gun: *Commodores* / Bite your granny: *Morning, Noon & Night*
CD Set **CDEM 1614**
EMI / Jul '97 / EMI

CASA DE LA TROVA: SANTIAGO DE CUBA
CD **COCD 120**
Corason / Oct '94 / ADA / CM / Direct

CASA DE SAMBA VOL.1 (10 Latin House Anthems)
What a sensation: *Kenlou III* / Sykodelik: *Restless Soul* / Fiesta de defriteus: *H-Man* / Brazil: *Master Builders* / Eu Nao: *Basement Jaxx* / Carnival: *Bah Samba* / Breaking point: *Crime* / Escucha mi funk: *High Tower Set* / Resolution: *Canto Azul* / Constant ariba: *MPQ*
CD **CDHIGH 5**
High On Rhythm / Mar '97 / 3mv/Sony

CASA DE SAMBA VOL.2
Urban haze: *Basement Jaxx* / Look who's loving me: *Smokin' Beats* / Latin seoul: *DJ Sneak* / Congo: *River Plate Samba Orchestra* / Red raw latino shakedown: *Atlanta* / Montayo: *Agora* / Spy in Rio: *Laj, Leo & Mr. Beef* / Symphony del ritmo: *Pascal's Bongo Massive* / Latin track: *Second Nature* / New York New York: *Master Builders*
CD **CDHIGH 6**
High On Rhythm / Jun '97 / 3mv/Sony

CASTLE IN THE AIR (Scottish Country Dancing)
CD **MU 3005**
Musketeer / Oct '92 / Disc

CATFISH BLUES
CD **CDBM 090**
Blue Moon / Jun '93 / Cadillac / Discovery / Greensleeves / Jazz Music / Jet Star / TKO Magnum

CATTLE CALL
CD **ROUCD 1101**
Rounder / Feb '96 / ADA / CM / Direct

CAUGHT IN THE CYCLONE
CD **CYD 102**
Cyclone / Dec '96 / Cargo / Nervous / TKO Magnum

CAVA SESSIONS
CD **TLV 003 CD**
Tennants Live Vinyl / May '90 / Pinnacle

CD 2000 (Electrecord)
2000: *Third Electric* / Drop in: *Kit Builders* / Wireless intercom: *Artificial Material* / Elastisch: *Klys-Tron* / On it: *Invisible Man* / Infanticide: *Infanticide Inc.* / Give up the funk: *Synapse* / Celestial crawlers: *Spacepawn Masters* / Foreign motel: *Artificial Material* / My melody: *Rootpowder* / EXEL: *Klys-Tron* / Defcon: *Third Electric*
CD **K7 058CD**
Studio K7 / Jun '97 / Prime / RTM/Disc

CEILI TIME IN IRELAND
CD **CDC 016**
Ceol / Feb '97 / CM

CEILIDH HOUSE SESSIONS (From The Tron Tavern Edinburgh)
Maggie Lauder / Full rigged ship / Turnpike / Trowie burn / Shady grove / Reel of tulla / Tron blues / Pottinger's reel / Mountain road / Lark in the morning
CD **CDTRAX 5002**
Greentrax / May '94 / ADA / Direct / Duncans / Highlander

CELEBRATE THIS LOVE (2CD Set)
CD Set **NSCD 006**
Newsound / Feb '95 / THE

CELEBRATION (25 Years Of The Organist Entertains)
CD **CDGRS 1273**
Grosvenor / Feb '95 / Grosvenor

CELEBRATION (Sounds Of Bournville)
Rondo / Bist du bei mir / Solveig's song / Old house / Music of the night / Tuba tune in D major / Chi mai / Salley gardens / Sunrise, sunset / All by myself / Pie jesu / Entertainer / Prelude in C minor / Salut d'amour opus 12 / How lovely are thy dwellings / Thnak you for the music / Simple a veu / Maria / Choral improvisation opus 65 / Now thank we all our God / March triomphale / Trumpet tune / As the brigegroom to his chosen
CD **CDGRS 1286**
Grosvenor / Mar '96 / Grosvenor

CELEBRATION
CD **IMCD 3013**
Image / Feb '96 / Discovery

CELEBRATION OF DUBLIN, A (24 Street Ballads From The Fair City/Dublin Millennium)
CD **DOLCD 1988**
Dolphin / Aug '96 / CM / Else / Grapevine/ PolyGram / Koch

CELEBRATION OF SCOTTISH MUSIC, A
CD **COMD 2003**
Temple / Feb '94 / ADA / CM / Direct / Duncans / Highlander

CELEBRATION OF SOUL VOL.1, A
CD **VSD 5488**
Varese Sarabande / Oct '94 / Pinnacle

CELEBRATION OF SOUL VOL.2, A
CD **VSD 5494**
Varese Sarabande / Jan '95 / Pinnacle

CELLO SOLO - ALL DIGITAL
CD **CDLR 301**
Leo / Apr '89 / Cadillac / Impetus / Wellard

CELTIC CHRISTMAS, A
Calennig / Taladh Chriosdahb / Wren hornpipe/Christmas eve/Winter apples / Oikan ayns Bethlehem / Hunting the wren / Kanomp Nouel / Dublin tune / Mari Lwyd / Da day dawns/Christmas day i da mornin/Papa Stour sword danc / Tree of life / Carval ny drogh vraane / Gower Wassail / Plygain: Wel dyma'rborau gorau i gyd / Arise and hail the glorious star / Seven rejoices of Mary / Ffarwel gyr Aberffraw / Lenabh an aigh / Highland pipe medley
CD __________ **CDSDL 417**
Saydisc / Oct '96 / ADA / Direct / Harmonia Mundi

CELTIC CIRCLE SAMPLER VOL.3
CD __________ **EFA 125322**
Celtic Circle / Oct '95 / SRD

CELTIC COLLECTION, A
CD __________ **PUTU 1252**
Putumayo / Oct '96 / Grapevine/PolyGram

CELTIC CONNECTIONS
CD __________ **LTCD 001**
Living Tradition / Jan '95 / Direct / Duncans

CELTIC DAWN
CD __________ **HCD 128**
GTD / Apr '95 / ADA / Else

CELTIC FAVOURITES
Ramblin' Irishman / Rising of the moon / Road to Sligo / Ashplant / 10 Franc piece / O'Carolan's dream / White, orange and green / High road to Linton/Mrs. McLeod's reel / Foxhunters / Fiddler's green / Rocky road to Dublin / Arthur McBride / Cherish the ladies/Paddy's Clancey's jig medley / Gravelwalk / Couragie / Bold O'Donaghue / Paddle me own canoe / Molly Malone / Doherty's reel / Ferryman / Cod-liver oil / Home boys home / Father O'Flynn / Lannigan's ball / All for me grog / Wild rover / Galway races medley / Muirsheen durkin / Paddy Fathy's reel/Dinny's fancy / Spanish lady / Maid behind the bar/Gravel walk / Holy ground / Finnegan's wake / Irish rover/ Rakes of mallow / Seven drunken nights
CD __________ **DCD 3011**
Music / Jun '97 / Target/BMG

CELTIC FOLK FESTIVAL
CD __________ **MRCD 183**
Munich / Aug '96 / ADA / CM / Direct / Greensleeves

CELTIC HARP
Tri-coloured ribbon: *Soazig* / O'Carolan's concerto: *Waxie's Dargle* / Fields of Athenrey: *Heaney, Gerry* / Marv Pontkalleg: *Soazig* / Childhood days: *Skovbye, Kim* / Currah of Kildare: *Blarney Lads* / Into the rain: *Waxie's Dargle* / Ar soundarded: *Soazig* / Tipping it up to Nancy/Swallow's tail: *Waxie's Dargle* / Come all ye young and tender maidens: *Waxie's Dargle & Berni O'Sullivan* / Sleivenamon: *Royal Irish Rangers & Anne Marie O'Farrell* / Salt hill: *Waxie's Dargle* / Dancer and the moon: *Skovbye, Kim* / Geese in the bog/Wind that shakes the barley: *Waxie's Dargle* / Skibbereen: *Heaney, Gerry* / King of the fairies: *Waxie's Dargle*
CD __________ **12857**
Laserlight / Oct '96 / Target/BMG

CELTIC HEART
Fergus sings the blues: *Deacon Blue* / Don't go: *Hothouse Flowers* / My special child: *O'Connor, Sinead* / In a lifetime: *Bono & Clannad* / Pair of brown eyes: *Pogues* / Fisherman's blues: *Waterboys* / Letter from America: *Proclaimers* / Abhainn an t-aluaigh: *Runrig* / Perfect: *Fairground Attraction* / Voyage: *Moore, Christy* / Harry's Game: *Clannad* / Island: *Brady, Paul* / N17: *Saw Doctors* / Captured: *Kennedy, Brian* / Against the wind: *Brennan, Maire* / Man is alive: *Bloom, Luka* / Coisich a ruin (walk my beloved): *Capercaillie* / Golden mile: *Black, Mary*
CD __________ **74321131662**
RCA / Feb '93 / BMG

CELTIC HEARTBEAT CHRISTMAS
Na hu o ho: *Kennedy, Fiona* / Snowy path: *Altan* / Dream in the night: *Clannad* / Snowy birch trees: *Loefke, Thomas* / Maria matrem virginem: *Anuna* / Wexford carol: *Nightnoise* / Night before christmas (the devil in the kitchen): *MacIsaac, Ashley* / No sandman, no santa: *Dunning, Brian* / Winter, fire and snow: *Hill, Benita* / Oiche nollaig: *Breatnach, Cormac* / Christmas pipes: *Celtia* / Fairy child: *Masterson, Declan* / Oiche chuain: *Minogue, Aine* / Angels are singing: *Minogue, Aine*
CD __________ **7567829292**
Warner Bros. / Oct '96 / Warner Music

CELTIC HEARTBEAT COLLECTION, THE
CD __________ **7567806102**
Atlantic / Apr '95 / Warner Music

CELTIC HEARTBEAT COLLECTION, THE
Caracena: *Whelan, Bill* / Blackbird: *Shannon, Sharon* / All the lies that you told me: *Black, Frances* / Harry's Game: *Clannad* / Hazel woods: *Masterson, Declan* / Storm: *Moving Hearts* / Road to glory: *Shanely, Elenor* / Inis sui: *Breathnach, Maire* / Chetvorno horo: *Irvine, Andy & Davy Spillane* / Down by the Sally Gardens: *Finn, Alec* / Blue bird: *Anuna* / Winter's end: *O'Flynn, Liam*
CD __________ **UND 53082**
Celtic Heartbeat / Jun '97 / BMG

CELTIC INSPIRATION VOL.1
CD __________ **NTRCD 031**
Nectar / Mar '95 / Pinnacle

CELTIC INSPIRATION VOL.2
He aint' give you none: *Morrison, Van* / Man is in love: *Waterboys* / Pair of brown eyes: *Moore, Christy* / My old friend the blues: *Proclaimers* / All or nothing: *Reader, Eddi* / Mandinka: *O'Connor, Sinead* / Flower of the west: *Runrig* / Spanish horses: *Runrig* / I need love: *Bloom, Luka* / Great song of indifference: *Geldof, Bob* / Cath: *Bluebells* / In a big country: *Big Country* / Moon over bourbon street: *Coughlan, Mary* / You will rise again: *Capercaillie* / Railway hotel: *Fureys* / Fairytale of New York: *Pogues & Kirsty MacColl*
CD __________ **NTRCD 043**
Nectar / Jan '96 / Pinnacle

CELTIC JIGS AND REELS
CD __________ **300542**
Hallmark / Feb '97 / Carlton

CELTIC LEGACY
Elnini: *Coulter, William* / Douce mousitomanie: *Orion* / Lone harper: *Barra MacNeils* / Dacw 'nghariad: *4 Yn Y Bar* / If ever you were mine: *MacMaster, Natalie* / Invernia: *Milladoiro* / Dheanainn sugradh: *Poozies* / Swans at Coole: *Breathnach, Maire* / Cailin gaelach: *Ni Dhomhnaill, Maighread* / Lorraine's waltz: *Whelan, John* / Dulaman: *Altan* / Culloden's harvest: *Deanta* / Si beag si mor: *Deiseal* / Une chanson a la mariee: *Bouchard, Dominic* / Theid mi mhachaigh: *MacKenzie, Talitha*
CD __________ **ND 63916**
Narada / Mar '95 / ADA / New Note/ Pinnacle

CELTIC MAGIC (Eleven Irish Instrumentals)
Lorraine's waltz: *Whelan, John & Eileen Ivers* / Inisheer: *Cherish The Ladies* / Bright hollow fog: *Williams, John* / I'll always remember you: *Connolly, Seamus* / If ever you were mine: *O'Sullivan, Jerry* / Farewell my gentle harp: *O'Donnell, Eugene & Rosalyn Briley* / Planxty gan ainm: *Faulkner, John* / Dobbin's flowery vale: *Altan* / Sligo lament: *McGann, John* / Whistle on the wind/Jug of punch/Dogs among the bushes: *Madden, Joanie* / Derry air (Danny boy): *O'Donnell, Eugene & James MacCafferty*
CD __________ **EDCD 9008**
Easydisc / Jun '97 / Direct

CELTIC MOODS (Musical Reflections Of Ireland)
CD __________ **DOCD 105**
Dolphin / Apr '94 / CM / Else / Grapevine/ PolyGram / Koch

CELTIC MOODS
Riverdance: *Whelan, Bill* / Only a woman's heart: *McEvoy, Eleanor* / New grange: *Clannad* / She moved through the fair: *Sharkey, Feargal* / Strange boat: *Waterboys* / Sarah: *Thin Lizzy* / abhainn an t-aluaigh: *Runrig* / Grace and pride: *Capercaillie* / Three babies: *O'Connor, Sinead* / Ride on: *Moore, Christy* / Pair of brown eyes: *Pogues* / Blackbird: *Shannon, Sharon* / Against the wind: *Brennan, Maire* / Heroine: *Edge & Sinead O'Connor* / Invisible to you: *Coughlan, Mary* / Can't help falling in love: *Bloom, Luka* / Always travelling: *Spillane, Davy* / Island: *Brady, Paul* / Woodbrook: *O'Suilleabhain, Micheal*
CD __________ **VTCD 52**
Virgin / Jun '95 / EMI

CELTIC MOODS
Swallowtail reel: *Northrop, Kate* / Kenavo cill airne: *Soazig* / Wedding gift: *Skovbye, Kim & Gabrielle Reger* / Strings in the earth and air: *Skovbye, Kim & Klaus Schonning* / Planxty brabazon: *Northrop, Kate* / Miss MacDermott: *Soazig* / Robin's tune: *Skovbye, Kim & Gabrielle Reger* / Eastbound: *Skovbye, Kim & Gabrielle Reger* / Storm clouds: *Northrop, Kate* / Pennherez keroulaz: *Soazig* / Stranger: *Skovbye, Kim & Klaus Schonning* / Portrait no.1: *Skovbye, Kim & Gabrielle Reger* / Crystal: *Skovbye, Kim & Gabrielle Reger* / Portrait no.2: *Skovbye, Kim & Gabrielle Reger* / Marche de Brian Boru: *Soazig*
CD __________ **12858**
Laserlight / May '97 / Target/BMG

CELTIC MUSIC (3CD Set)
CD Set __________ **PS 360502**
PlayaSound / Sep '96 / ADA / Harmonia Mundi

CELTIC ODYSSEY
Carolan's ramble to Chashel: *Coulter, Steve & Harris Moore* / Butterfly: *Orison* / Donal Agus Morag/the new rigged ship: *Altan* / Calliope house/the cowboy jig: *Fraser, Alasdair & Paul Machlis* / Chuaigh me 'na Rosann: *Scartaglen* / Trip to Skye: *Whelan, John & Eileen Ivers* / Are ye sleeping Maggie: *Fraser, Alasdair* / Tribute to Peadar O'Donnell: *Moving Hearts* / Siun ni dhuibhir: *Relativity* / Alasdair Mhic cholla ghasda: *Capercaillie* / Puirt a buel: *Sileas* / York reel, The/dancing feet: *Trimble, Gerald* / Morghan meaghan: *Riley, Laurie & Bob McNally* / Strathgarry: *Wynberg, Simon*
CD __________ **ND 63912**
Narada / Jul '93 / ADA / New Note/Pinnacle

CELTIC ROCK
To you I bestow: *Mundy* / Ro Ro Rosey: *Morrison, Van* / Fairytale of New York: *Pogues & Kirsty MacColl* / Dirty old town: *Pogues* / Ride on: *Moore, Christy* / Mandinka: *O'Connor, Sinead* / Fisherman's blues: *Waterboys* / Kid gloves: *Gallagher, Rory* / Mustang Sally: *Commitments* / Good heart: *Sharkey, Feargal* / Over the hills: *Moore, Gary* / What's going on: *Taste* / Dear Miss Lonely Hearts: *Lynott, Phil* / Waiting for an alibi: *Thin Lizzy* / Big decision: *That Petrol Emotion* / Wasted: *Energy Orchard* / Teenage kicks: *Undertones*
CD __________ **RENCD 117**
Renaissance Collector Series / Jun '97 / BMG

CELTIC ROOTS (2CD Set)
Fisherman's blues: *Waterboys* / Fergus sings the blues: *Deacon Blue* / Love is a stranger: *Eurythmics* / Robin (the hooded man): *Clannad* / Big yellow taxi: *Brennan, Maire* / Take the floor: *Capercaillie* / Captured: *Kennedy, Brian* / All or mothing: *Reader, Eddi* / Bring 'em all in: *Scott, Mike* / Van Diemens' land: *Dickson, Barbara* / Blues for Buddah: *Silencers* / First months of summer: *Four Men & A Dog* / Madame George: *Energy Orchard* / Caislean air: *Clannad* / When the ship come in: *Dickson, Barbara* / Newry highway men: *Johnstons* / Rocky road to Dublin: *Dubliners* / Kilarmey boys of pleasure: *Swarbrick, Dave* / Whole of the moon: *Waterboys* / Walk: *Eurythmics* / Hello in there: *Reader, Eddi* / Romeo's twin: *Kavanagh, Niamh* / Intuition: *Kennedy, Brian* / Painted moon: *Silencers* / Letter from America: *Proclaimers* / When you return: *Capercaillie* / My Johnny was a shoemaker: *Dickson, Barbara* / In your eyes: *Kavanagh, Niamh* / Handsome cabin boy: *Sweeney's Men* / Healer in your heart: *Runrig* / Perfect: *Fairground Attraction* / Modern girl: *Easton, Sheena* / Lets go round again: *Average White Band* / Can I have my money band: *Rafferty, Gerry* / Black velvet band: *Dubliners* / Hermit: *Renbourn, John*
CD Set __________ **RCACD 218**
RCA / Jul '97 / BMG

CELTIC SONGS OF LOVE (Traditional Airs & Ballads)
Boatman / Siubhan ni dhuibhir / Ploughboy lads / Bugeiliar Gwenith Gwyn / Sweet nightingale / Two magicians / Banks of the Lee / Graih my cheree / Ffarwel i Aberystwyth / Waly waly / Irree seose / Deus ganin me d'am bro / Well below the valley / How can ye gang lassie / Nee caillinyin roie / Merched / False love / Tam lin / Moorlough shore / Lloer dirion / Red top knots / Will ye go love / Bess o'bedlam
CD __________ **BEJOCD 16**
Beautiful Jo / May '97 / ADA / Direct

CELTIC SPIRIT
Ubi Caritas: *Dover, Connie* / Seacht Suailci na Maighdine Muire: *Ni Fhearraigh, Aoife* / Kyrie Eleison, An Ghloir, An Phaidir: *Minogue, Aine* / Be thou my vision: *Anjali Quartet* / Salve splendor: *Jackson, William* / Noeleen Brehed: *Groupe Vocal Jef Le Penven* / Mo ghra thu: *Ni Fhearraigh, Aoife* / Bi, a losa, im Chroi-se: *Coulter, William* / Our Father, God celestial: *Baltimore Consort* / Puer Natus: *Minogue, Aine* / Christ Child's lullaby: *Wellington, Sheena* / Rosa Mystica: *Schroeder-Sheker, Terese*
CD __________ **ND 63929**
Narada / Nov '96 / ADA / New Note/ Pinnacle

CELTIC SPIRIT
Danny boy / Wild mountain thyme / Dark island / She moved through the fair / Caledonia / Whiskey in the jar / Rowan tree / When you were sweet sixteen / Ae fond kiss / Amazing grace / Loch Lomond / My love is like a red, red rose / Bunch of thyme / Island song/Brides of Glenshiel / Will ye no come back again / Over the sea to Skye
CD __________ **RECD 513**
REL / Apr '97 / CM / Duncans / Highlander

CELTIC TAPESTRY VOL.2, A
CD __________ **SH 78006**
Shanachie / Mar '97 / ADA / Greensleeves / Koch

CELTIC TWILIGHT VOL.3
CD __________ **HS 11107CD**
Hearts Of Space / Nov '96 / ADA

CELTIC VOICES: WOMEN OF SONG
Sealwoman: *McLaughlin, Mary* / Yundah: *McLaughlin, Mary* / Bring the peace: *McLaughlin, Mary* / You saw his eyes: *McLaughlin, Mary* / Little red bird: *Christian, Emma* / Birth in Bethlehem: *Christian, Emma* / O Kirre, thou wilt leave me: *Christian, Emma* / Goodnight song: *Christian, Emma* / Cantus: *Dover, Connie* / Wishing well: *Dover, Connie* / In aimsir bhaint an fheir: *Dover, Connie* / Siuil a ruin: *Dover, Connie* / Colour me: *Sullivan, Maireid* / She moved through the fair: *Sullivan, Maireid* / Waly waly: *Sullivan, Maireid*
CD __________ **ND 63921**
Narada / Oct '95 / ADA / New Note/ Pinnacle

CELTIC WOMAN
CD __________ **CWRCD 7001**
Celtic Woman / May '96 / CM / Grapevine/PolyGram

CELTIC WORLD (2CD Set)
Swallowtail reel: *Northrop, Kate* / Church of Kildare: *Blarney Lads* / Tears in heaven: *Hamilton, C. & J. Spencer* / Everything I do (I do it for you): *Hamilton, C. & J. Spencer* / On your shore: *Hamilton, C. & J. Spencer* / Al labous marv: *Soazig* / Seoladh na ngamhna: *Campbell, D.* / Storm clouds: *Northrop, Kate* / Pennherez keroulaz: *Soazig* / Falling: *Hamilton, C. & J. Spencer* / Against all odds: *Hamilton, C. & J. Spencer* / Silkie: *Northrop, Kate* / Streets of Derry: *Campbell, D.* / O'Carolan's concerto: *Dargle, W.* / Fields of Athenrey: *Dargle, W.* / Tipping it up to Nancy/Swallow's tail: *Dargle, W.* / Ar soundarded: *Soazig* / Miss McDermott: *Soazig* / Dancer and the moon: *Skovbye, Kim Band* / Portrait no.1: *Skovbye, Kim & Gabrielle Reger* / Tri-coloured ribbon: *Soazig* / Skartinglas: *Campbell, D.* / Earth dance: *Northrop, Kate* / In the air tonight: *Hamilton, C. & J. Spencer* / I will always love you: *Hamilton, C. & J. Spencer* / Robin the hooded man: *Hamilton, C. & J. Spencer* / Stranger: *Skovbye, Kim & Klaus Schonning* / Lonely banna strand: *Soazig* / King of the fairies: *Dargle, W.* / Childhood days: *Skovbye, Kim Band* / Brezhoneg: *Soazig* / Mountain streams: *Campbell, D.* / Mo ghile near: *Campbell, D.* / Eastbound: *Skovbye, Kim & Gabrielle Reger* / Wedding gift: *Skovbye, Kim & Gabrielle Reger* / Courting is a pleasure: *Campbell, D. & M. Sands* / Danny boy: *Keaney, C.*
CD Set __________ **24343**
Laserlight / Jul '97 / Target/BMG

CELTS RISE AGAIN, THE
CD __________ **GLCD 0104**
Green Linnet / Nov '87 / ADA / CM / Direct / Highlander / Roots

CENTENARY VOL.2
CD __________ **SZCD 004**
Surr Zema Musik / Apr '96 / Jet Star

CENTRAL AFRICAN REPUBLIC: MUSIQUE GBAYA/CHANTS A PENSER
CD __________ **C 580008**
Ocora / Nov '92 / ADA / Harmonia Mundi

CENTRAL HEATING (2CD Set)
Central introduction: *Tony D* / Loop dreams: *Aim* / Spellbound: *Rae & Christian* / Its time 2: *Tony D & Chubby* / When we get: *Tony D* / Original Stuntmaster: *Aim* / How sweet it is: *Mr. Scruff & Mr. Rae* / Got to have her: *Mr. Rae & Mr. Scruff* / Like rain: *Only Child* / Pourquoi: *Only Child* / Good advice: *Rae & Chris* / Hemlocka: *Votel* / Hand of doom: *Votel* / Through these veins: *Funky Fresh Few & Afu Ra* / You mean fantastic: *Funky Fresh Few* / 2nd Street go go: *Tony D*
CD Set __________ **GCCD 101**
Grand Central / Nov '96 / Vital

CEOL TIGH NEACHTAIN (Music From Galway)
CD __________ **CEFCD 145**
Gael Linn / Jan '94 / ADA / CM / Direct / Grapevine/PolyGram / Roots

CEREMONIAL
CD __________ **IMCD 3014**
Image / Feb '96 / Discovery

CEREMONIAL AND WAR DANCES (Native American Music)
Navahoe boy / Prisoner song / Girl and many boys / Mountain by the sea / Mescalero trail / Montana grass song / Mountain spirit song / Lightning song / Song of the Black Mountain / Song of the Green Rainbow / Yei-be-chai chant / Our father's thoughts / War dance / War dance / War dance (slow/fast) / Warrior song / Honoring song / Glory song / Memorial song
CD __________ **12552**
Laserlight / Nov '95 / Target/BMG

CHA CHA CABARET
CD __________ **KLP 66CD**
K / Jun '97 / Cargo / Greyhound / SRD

CHA-CHA-CHA
CD __________ **CD 62030**
Saludos Amigos / Oct '93 / Target/BMG

CHAMAME - MUSIC OF THE PARANA
CD __________ **C 560052CD**
Ocora / Jul '94 / ADA / Harmonia Mundi

CHAMAME - RURAL MUSIC / ARGENTINA
CD __________ **KAR 989**
IMP / Apr '97 / ADA / Discovery

CHAMPION BRASS
King cotton: *Fairey Engineering Works Band* / Perpetuum mobile: *Fairey Engineering Works Band* / Send in the clowns: *Fairey Engineering Works Band* / Lohengrin intro: *Fairey Engineering Works Band* / Girl I left behind: *Fairey Engineering Works Band* / If: *Fairey Engineering Works Band* / Round the clock: *Fairey Engineering Works Band* / Queen of Sheba: *Fairey Engineering Works Band* / Can can: *Fairey Engineering Works Band* / Don't cry for me Argentina: *Fairey Engineering Works Band* / Polly wolly doodling: *Fairey Engineering Works Band* / Hustle: *Fairey Engineering Works Band* / Peace: *Fairey Engineering Works Band* / Fanfare

and soliloquy: *Fairey Engineering Works Band*
CD ____ EMPRCD 568
Emporio / May '95 / Disc

CHAMPION DJ'S FROM STUDIO ONE
CD ____ SOCD 50151
Studio One / Oct '96 / Jet Star

CHAMPIONS OF ROCK (2CD Set)
Fireball: *Deep Purple* / Cry for the nations: *Schenker, Michael Group* / Radar love: *Golden Earring* / Race with the devil: *Girlschool* / And the band played on: *Saxon* / Caledonia: *Trower, Robin* / Silver machine: *Hawkwind* / Wild child: *WASP* / Overkill: *Motorhead* / Hair of the dog: *Nazareth* / Love like a man: *Ten Years After* / (Don't fear) the reaper: *Blue Oyster Cult* / Easy livin': *Uriah Heep* / Tomorrow night: *Atomic Rooster* / Some kinda wonderful: *Grand Funk Railroad* / Face down in the gutter: *XYZ* / I'm the urban spaceman: *Bonzo Dog Band* / I like to rock: *April Wine* / These dreams: *Heart* / Paranoid: *Black Sabbath* / Gypsy: *Uriah Heep* / Doctor doctor: *UFO* / 747 (Strangers in the night): *Saxon* / Roll over Beethoven: *ELO* / On the road again: *Canned Heat* / Trouble: *Gillan* / Who do you love: *Juicy Lucy* / Heroes: *Meat Loaf* / Ace of spades: *Motorhead* / Don't do that: *Geordie* / I'm going home: *Ten Years After* / Armed and ready: *Schenker, Michael Group* / Beck's bolero: *Beck, Jeff & Rod Stewart* / Back home: *Golden Earring* / Willie and the hand jive: *Thorogood, George* / Clap for the wolfman: *Guess Who*
CD Set ____ SP 871942
Disky / Nov '96 / Disky / THE

CHAMPIONS OF ROCK VOL.1
Fireball: *Deep Purple* / Cry for the nations: *Schenker, Michael Group* / Radar love: *Golden Earring* / Race with the devil: *Girlschool* / And the band played on: *Saxon* / Caledonia: *Trower, Robin* / Silver machine: *Hawkwind* / Wild child: *WASP* / Overkill: *Motorhead* / Hair of the dog: *Nazareth* / Love like a man: *Ten Years After* / (Don't fear) the reaper: *Blue Oyster Cult* / Easy livin': *Uriah Heep* / Tomorrow night: *Atomic Rooster* / Some kinda wonderful: *Grand Funk Railroad* / Everybody wants her: *Thunder* / I like to rock: *April Wine* / Face down in the gutter: *XYZ*
CD ____ CR 871292
Disky / Mar '97 / Disky / THE

CHAMPIONS OF ROCK VOL.2
These dreams: *Heart* / Paranoid: *Black Sabbath* / Gypsy: *Uriah Heep* / Doctor doctor: *UFO* / 747 (strangers in the night): *Saxon* / Roll over Beethoven: *ELO* / On the road again: *Canned Heat* / Trouble: *Gillan* / Who do you love: *Juicy Lucy* / Heroes: *Meat Loaf* / Ace of spades: *Motorhead* / Don't do that: *Geordie* / I'm going home: *Ten Years After* / Armed and ready: *Schenker, Michael Group* / Beck's bolero: *Beck, Jeff* / Back home: *Golden Earring* / Willie and the hand jive: *Thorogood, George* / Clap for the wolfman: *Guess Who*
CD ____ CR 871302
Disky / Mar '97 / Disky / THE

CHANSONS A MENER ET A DANSER
CD ____ 983252
EPM / Oct '96 / ADA / Discovery

CHANSONS GAILLARDES ET LIBERTINES
CD ____ 983282
EPM / Oct '96 / ADA / Discovery

CHANSONS INTROUVABLES, CHANSONS RETROUVEES VOL.3
CD ____ 171272
Musidisc / Jul '95 / Discovery

CHANTS AND MUSIQUES DE PROVENCE
CD ____ PV 782 112
Disques Pierre Verany / '88 / Kingdom

CHANTS ET DANCES DE THRACE, BULGARIA
CD ____ ARN 64343
Arion / Sep '96 / ADA / Discovery

CHANTS ET DANSES
CD ____ ARN 64244
Arion / Aug '93 / ADA / Discovery

CHANTS ET TAMBOURS (Music From Venezuala)
CD ____ C 560085
Ocora / Dec '95 / ADA / Harmonia Mundi

CHANTS IN PRAISE OF KRISHNA
CD ____ VICG 50342
JVC World Library / Mar '96 / ADA / CM / Direct

CHANTS TZIGANES
CD ____ QUI 903028
Quintana / Nov '91 / Harmonia Mundi

CHARETTE
CD ____ CH 9601
Eden / May '96 / ADA

CHARLESTON CHASERS VOL.2
CD ____ SOSCD 1314
Stomp Off / Nov '96 / Jazz Music / Wellard

CHARLESTON DAYS, THE
Let's all go to Mary's house: *Whidden, Jay & His New Midnight Follies Band* / After I say I'm sorry: *Mackey, Percival & His Band* / Laugh clown laugh: *Schubert, Adrian Dance Orchestra* / Charleston: *Bell, Edison & His Dance Orchestra* / I've never seen a straight banana: *Happiness Boys* / What did I tell ya: *Savoy Orpheans* / Where's that rainbow: *Baker, Edythe Piano* / How could Red Riding Hood: *Royal Automobile Club Orchestra* / Chinese moon: *Douglas, Fred* / High up in the sky: *Maddison, Bert & Dance Orchestra* / Under the moon: *Radio Imps* / Latest dance hits of 1926: *Coliseum Dance Orchestra* / Julian: *Denza Dance Band* / Thanks for the buggy ride: *Mackey, Percival & His Band* / Breezin' along with the breeze: *Revelers* / Hitch up the horses: *Savoy Orpheans* / If I had a talking picture of you: *Alfredo & His Band* / Russian lullaby: *Bidgood, Harry & His Broadcasters* / Seven and eleven: *Corona Dance Orchestra* / Dainty Miss: *Da Costa, Raie* / Molly: *Hylton, Jack & His Orchestra* / My wife is on a diet: *Hudson, Harry Melody Men* / Barcelona: *Savoy Orpheans* / Electric flashes of 1926: *Munro, Ronnie & His Dance Orchestra*
CD ____ PASTCD 9706
Flapper / '90 / Pinnacle

CHARLESTON OF THE TWENTIES
CD ____ 995362
EPM / Dec '93 / ADA / Discovery

CHARLOTTE GOSPEL 1920-1938
CD ____ DOCD 5486
Document / Nov '96 / ADA / Hot Shot / Jazz Music

CHARLY'S SOUL TEMPO (A Soulful Experience)
CD ____ CDNEW 108
Charly / May '97 / Koch

CHARM RAGGA SAMPLER VOL.1
CD ____ MPCCD 1
Charm / Jul '94 / Jet Star

CHART '96 (2CD Set)
Wannabe: *Spice Girls* / Spaceman: *Babylon Zoo* / I am blessed: *Eternal* / Going out: *Supergrass* / Charmless man: *Blur* / Naked: *Louise* / Se a vide e: *Pet Shop Boys* / Nighttrain: *Kadoc* / Seven days and one week: *BBE* / Stamp: *Healy, Jeremy & Amos* / Jazz it up: *Reel 2 Real* / Freedom: *Williams, Robbie* / Missing: *Everything But The Girl* / Not a dry eye in the house: *Meat Loaf* / I got 5 on it: *Luniz* / Don't stop moving: *Livin' Joy* / Day we caught the train: *Ocean Colour Scene* / I just wanna make love to you: *James, Etta* / Breakfast at Tiffany's: *Deep Blue Something* / Don't look back in anger: *Oasis* / I wanna be a hippy: *Technohead* / Firestarter: *Prodigy* / Whole lotta love: *Goldbug* / It's oh so quiet: *Bjork* / Female of the species: *Space* / We've got it goin' on: *Backstreet Boys* / Thank god it's Friday: *R Kelly* / Born Slippy: *Underworld* / Gangstas Paradise: *Coolio* / Trash: *Suede* / In too deep: *Carlisle, Belinda* / Stars: *Dubstar* / Goldeneye: *Turner, Tina* / You're gorgeous: *Baby Bird* / Where love lives: *Limerick, Alison* / Insomnia: *Faithless* / No Diggity: *Blackstreet & Dr. Dre* / Creep: *TLC* / I will survive: *Savage, Chantay* / Sale of the century: *Sleeper* / Mysterious girl: *Andre, Peter*
CD Set ____ CDEMTVD 153
EMI TV / Nov '96 / EMI

CHART BUSTERS (2CD Set)
Back for good: *Take That* / Unchained melody: *Robson & Jerome* / No more I love you's: *Lennox, Annie* / Independent love song: *Scarlet* / Girl like you: *Collins, Edwyn* / Right in the night: *Jam & Spoon* / Baby baby: *Corona* / Scatman: *Scatman John* / Total eclipse of the heart: *French, Nicki* / U sure do: *Strike* / Tell me when: *Human League* / Wake up boo: *Boo Radleys* / Some might say: *Oasis* / Waking up: *Elastica* / Fool's gold '95: *Stone Roses* / In betweener: *Sleeper* / Guaglione: *Prado, Perez* / Reach up (papa's got a brnd new pig bag): *Perfecto All Stars* / Open your heart: *M-People* / Love City Groove: *Love City Groove* / I've got a little something: *MN8* / Two can play that game: *Brown, Bobby* / Dreamer: *Livin' Joy* / Don't stop (wiggle wiggle): *Outhere Brothers* / Here comes the hotstepper: *Kamoze, Ini* / It's in his kiss (the shoop shoop song): *Kikitup* / Let's get it on: *Shabba Ranks* / Run away: *Real McCoy* / Set you free: *N-Trance* / Bump 'n' grind: *Kelly, R* / Cotton eye Joe: *Rednex* / Hands up, hands up: *Zig & Zag* / Surrender your love: *Nightcrawlers* / Not over yet: *Grace* / Always something there to remind me: *Tin Tin Out* / Any time you need a friend: *New Jersey Gospel Choir* / Freedom: *Gayle, Michelle* / Your loving arms: *Martin, Billie Ray* / White cliffs of Dover: *Robson & Jerome*
CD Set ____ RADCD 15
Global TV / Jun '95 / BMG

CHART HIT HISTORY (3CD Set)
U can't touch this: *MC Hammer* / Feels like I'm in love: *Marie, Kelly* / Rock your baby: *McCrae, George* / Too shy: *Kajagoogoo* / So you win again: *Hot Chocolate* / Living in a box: *Living In A Box* / Just an illusion: *Imagination* / Solid: *Ashford & Simpson* / Loverboy: *Ocean, Billy* / Respectable: *Mel & Kim* / Some girls: *Racey* / Dancing with tears in my eyes: *Ultravox* / I don't wanna dance: *Grant, Eddy* / Dolce vita: *Paris, Ryan* / Breakaway: *Ullman, Tracey* / Denis: *Blondie* / Love changes (everything): *Fisher, Climie* / We belong: *Benatar, Pat* / China in your hand: *T'Pau* / Baker street: *Rafferty, Gerry* / Walking on sunshine: *Katrina & The Waves* / He ain't heavy he's my brother: *Hollies* / She's a lady: *Jones, Tom* / Road to nowhere: *Talking Heads* / True: *Spandau Ballet* / When I need you: *Sayer, Leo* / Kids in America: *Wilde, Kim* / Never ending story: *Limahl* / Love is a battlefield: *Benatar, Pat* / Radar love: *Golden Earring* / Heroes: *Meat Loaf* / Every rose has it's thorn: *Poison* / My sharona: *Knack* / Roll over Beethoven: *ELO* / Kayleigh: *Marillion* / Centrefold: *Geils, J. Band* / This flight tonight: *Nazareth* / Missing you: *Waite, John* / Power of love: *Lewis, Huey & The News* / Nutbush city limits: *Turner, Ike & Tina* / Ride like the wind: *Saxon* / (I just) died in your arms tonight: *Cutting Crew*
CD Set ____ HR 873902
Disky / Nov '96 / Disky / THE

CHART MACHINE
Dreamer: *Livin' Joy* / Love city groove: *Love City Groove* / Not over yet: *Grace* / Your body's calling: *R Kelly* / I'm going down: *Blige, Mary J.* / Don't stop (wiggle wiggle): *Outhere Brothers* / Two can play that game: *Brown, Bobby* / Turn on tune in cop out: *Freakpower* / One night stand: *Let Loose* / Baby baby: *Corona* / Love me for a reason: *Boyzone* / Whatever: *Oasis* / Stay another day: *East 17* / Don't give me your life: *Alex Party* / Call it love: *Deuce* / Another day: *Whigfield* / Crazy: *Morrison, Mark* / Hoochie booty: *Ultimate Kaos* / Axel F: *Ace Of Base* / Living in danger: *Ace Of Base*
CD ____ 5250392
Polydor / May '95 / PolyGram

CHART SHOW DANCE ALBUM, THE
CD ____ 5257682
PolyGram TV / Jul '95 / PolyGram

CHART SHOW ROCK ALBUM, THE
CD ____ 5354892
PolyGram TV / Jun '96 / PolyGram

CHART SHOW ULTIMATE BLUES ALBUM
CD ____ AHLCD 19
Hit / Jun '94 / Grapevine/PolyGram

CHARTBUSTERS (2CD Set)
I believe I can fly: *R Kelly* / Your woman: *White Town* / I have peace: *Strike* / Ready or not: *Course* / Encore une fois: *Sash* / Sometimes: *Brand New Heavies* / Underwater love: *Smoke City* / You're gorgeous: *Baby Bird* / Spaceman: *Babylon Zoo* / Ready to go: *Republica* / Missing: *Everything But The Girl* / Good enough: *Dodgy* / Flying: *Cast* / Alright: *Supergrass* / Tattva: *Kula Shaker* / Riverboat song: *Ocean Colour Scene* / I'm alive: *Stretch n' Vern* / You got the love: *Source & Candi Staton* / Ain't talkin' 'bout dub: *Apollo 440* / X-Files: *DJ Dado* / Remember me: *Blueboy* / Unbreak my heart: *Braxton, Toni* / If you ever: *East 17 & Gabrielle* / Quit playing games (with my heart): *Backstreet Boys* / Flava: *Andre, Peter* / Father and son: *Boyzone* / Just a little bit: *Gina G* / Back for good: *Take That* / Macarena: *Los Del Rio* / Clementine: *Owen, Mark* / Waterfalls: *TLC* / Nobody knows: *Rich, Tony* / Children: *Miles, Robert* / Forever: *Damage* / Don't make me wait: *911* / I can make you feel good: *Kavana* / Forvever love: *Barlow, Gary* / Search for the hero: *M-People* / Cecilia: *Suggs* / Female of the species: *Space* / Call around: *Livingstone* / Three lions: *Lightning Seeds & David Baddiel/Frank Skinner*
CD Set ____ RADCD 65
Global TV / May '97 / BMG

CHARTBUSTERS VOL.1 (4CD Set)
CD Set ____ MBSCD 422
Castle / Nov '93 / BMG

CHARTBUSTERS VOL.1
Tokyo blues / No room for squares / If ever I would leave you / So tired / Blues in a jiff / Una mas / Down under / Blues on the corner
CD ____ NYC 60172
NYC / Jul '95 / New Note/Pinnacle

CHARTBUSTERS VOL.2 (4CD Set)
CD Set ____ MBSCD 423
Castle / Nov '93 / BMG

CHEAP SHOTS
CD ____ BHR 022CD
Burning Heart / Mar '95 / Plastic Head

CHEAP SHOTS VOL.2
CD ____ BHR 043CD
Burning Heart / Apr '96 / Plastic Head

CHEAPO CRYPT SAMPLER VOL.2
CD ____ EFACD 12886
Crypt / Jun '97 / Shellshock/Disc

CHEATIN' FROM A MAN'S POINT OF VIEW
CD ____ SCL 2508
Ichiban Soul Classics / Mar '95 / Koch

CHEATIN' FROM A WOMAN'S POINT OF VIEW
CD ____ SCL 2507
Ichiban Soul Classics / Mar '95 / Koch

CHECK ONE (2CD Set)
CD Set ____ XTR 22CDM
X-Treme / Nov '96 / Pinnacle / SRD

CHECK OUT THE FLAVOUR
CD ____ RAPTURE 6001CD
Rapture / Sep '93 / Plastic Head

CHECK OUT THE GROOVE
CD ____ MCCD 203
Music Club / May '95 / Disc / THE

CHECK OUT THE GROOVE
CD ____ PLSCD 134
Pulse / Apr '96 / BMG

CHECK THIS OUT, BABY
CD ____ 37463405
One Foot / Apr '97 / Cargo

CHEGA DE SAUDADE (No More Blues)
CD ____ CD 53139
Giants Of Jazz / Jan '94 / Cadillac / Jazz Music / Target/BMG

CHEMICAL DUB
CD ____ RSNCD 36
Rising High / Jun '95 / 3mv/Sony

CHEN ZHONG (The Traditions Of Shanghai For Lute, Fiddle & Zither)
CD ____ C 560090
Ocora / Dec '96 / ADA / Harmonia Mundi

CHERRY RED PUNK SINGLES COLLECTION
Bad hearts / It / Cracked / Howard Hughes / China's eternal / Bored / You're gonna die / Then he kissed me / Sick on you / November 22nd 1963 / Meet the creeper / Right now / Black leather / No body knows / What do I get / Holiday in Cambodia / Police truck / Kill the poor / In sight / Too drunk to fuck / Prey
CD ____ CDPUNK 51
Anagram / Apr '95 / Cargo / Pinnacle

CHESS 50TH ANNIVERSARY COLLECTION (2CD Set)
Smokestack lightnin': *Howlin' Wolf* / Hoochie coochie man: *Waters, Muddy* / Let me love you baby: *Guy, Buddy* / Boom boom (out go the lights): *Little Walter* / Tell mama: *James, Etta* / I had a talk with my man last night: *Collier, Mitty* / Summertime: *Stewart, Billy* / I'm a man: *Diddley, Bo* / If walls could talk: *Diddley, Bo* / Entertainer: *Clark, Tony* / Flat foot Sam: *TV Slim* / ama talk to your daughter: *Lenoir, J.B.* / TWA: *Witherspoon, Jimmy* / Dirty old man: *Witherspoon, Jimmy* / Wang dang doodle: *Taylor, Koko* / So mnay roads: *Rush, Otis* / Seventh son: *Mabon, Willie* / Jock-a-mo: *Crawford, Sugar Boy* / Walk: *McCracklin, Jimmy* / Reconsider baby: *Fulson, Lowell* / One bourbon, one scotch, one beer: *Hooker, John Lee* / Roadrunner: *Diddley, Bo* / Reelin' and rockin': *Berry, Chuck* / That's all right: *Rogers, Jimmy* / My time after a while: *Guy, Buddy* / Don't know why I love you (but I do): *Henry, Clarence 'Frogman'* / Rescue me: *Bass, Fontella* / 'In' crowd: *Lewis, Ramsey Trio* / Soulful dress: *Desanto, Sugar Pie* / Stay in my corner: *Dells* / Voice your choice: *Radiants* / Talk to me baby: *James, Elmore* / Good to me: *Thomas, Irma* / Rocket 88: *Brenston, Jackie & The Delta Cats* / Selfish cone: *Ross, Jackie* / Juke: *Little Walter & His Night Cats* / Grit's ain't groceries: *Little Milton* / 29 ways: *Dixon, Willie* / Help me: *Williamson, Sonny Boy* / Rollin' stone: *Waters, Muddy*
CD Set ____ CHD 29382
Chess/MCA / Apr '97 / BMG / New Note/ BMG

CHESS BLUES (4CD Set)
CD Set ____ CHD 49340
Chess/MCA / Mar '93 / BMG / New Note/ BMG

CHESS CLUB RHYTHM AND SOUL
Mellow fellow: *James, Etta* / Messin' with the man: *Waters, Muddy* / Get out: *Collier, Mitty* / Summertime: *Stewart, Billy* / Ooh baby: *Diddley, Bo* / You left the water running: *Maurice & Mac* / Hey Mr DJ: *Moore, Bobby & The Rhythm Aces* / Can't make it without you: *Hughes, Freddie* / Ain't it: *McDuff, 'Brother' Jack* / Let's wade in the water: *Shaw, Marlena* / Fire: *Taylor, Koko* / Do I make myself clear: *James, Etta & Sugar Pie DeSanto* / Knife and a fork: *Anderson, Kip* / My babe: *Little Walter* / Help me: *Williamson, Sonny Boy* / Good morning little school girl: *Don & Bob* / Who's that guy: *Kolettes* / Here comes the judge: *Markham, Pigmeat* / Function at the junction: *Lewis, Ramsey* / Grits ain't groceries (all around the world): *Little Milton* / Must I holler: *Thomas, Jano* / Every day I have to cry: *Alaimo, Steve* / Musty rusty: *Donaldson, Lou* / I don't want a fuss: *Desanto, Sugar Pie* / High heel sneakers: *Tucker, Tommy*
CD ____ CDKEND 134
Kent / Jun '96 / Pinnacle

CHESS EP COLLECTION, THE
Long tall shorty: *Tucker, Tommy* / Suzie Q: *Hawkins, Dale* / Ain't got no home: *Henry, Clarence 'Frogman'* / Rescue: *Bass, Fontella* / You all green: *Diddley, Bo* / I got to find my baby: *Little Walter* / Good morning little school girl: *Don & Bob* / Oh baby: *Williams, Larry* / Walk: *McCracklin, Jimmy* / I don't want 'cha: *Tucker, Tommy* / When the lights go out: *Witherspoon, Jimmy* / Entertainer: *Clarke, Tony* / Summertime: *Stewart, Billy* / I had a talk with my man: *Collier, Mitty* / Sitting in the park: *Stewart, Billy* / Who's cheating who: *Little Milton* / In crowd: *Lewis, Ramsey Trio* / Leave my baby alone:

Guy, Buddy / Hi-heel sneakers: *Tucker, Tommy* / Soulful dress: *Desanto, Sugar Pie* / Crazy for my baby: *Dixon, Willie* / I can tell: *Diddley, Bo* / You gonna wreck my life: *Howlin' Wolf* / Messin' with the man: *Waters, Muddy* / Promised land: *Berry, Chuck*
CD ______ **SEECD 380**
See For Miles/C5 / Oct '93 / Pinnacle

CHESS UPTOWN SOUL
Entertainer: *Clarke, Tony* / Love ain't nothin': *Nash, Johnny* / Jerk and twine: *Ross, Jackie* / Oh what a feeling: *Phelps, James* / It ain't no big thing: *Radiants* / Sitting in the park: *Stewart, Billy* / Temptation 'bout to get me: *Knight Brothers* / Everything to me: *Elbert, Donnie* / Nothing but you: *Chessmen* / I won't need you: *Chandler, Gene* / Wear it on our face: *Dells* / Do you wanta go: *Mack, Andy* / Pushover: *James, Etta* / Believe in me baby: *Little Milton* / Searching for my love: *Moore, Bobby & The Rhythm Aces* / I had a talk with my man: *Collier, Mitty* / I believe she will: *Eddie & Ernie* / So much love: *Maurice & Mac* / Hurt so bad: *Lewis, Ramsey* / Here you come running: *De Santo, Sugar Pie* / Mama didn't lie: *Bradley, Jan* / Go away little boy: *Shaw, Marlena* / Soul of man: *Bass, Fontella* / Two in the morning: *Spooner's Crowd*
CD ______ **CDKEND 140**
Kent / Feb '97 / Pinnacle

CHIARASCURO CHRISTMAS, A
CD ______ **CRD 332**
Chiaroscuro / Nov '95 / Jazz Music

CHICAGO - THAT TOODLIN' TOWN (2CD Set)
CD Set ______ **DCD 8002**
Disky / Jan '95 / Disky / THE

CHICAGO 1935
CD ______ **CJR 1001**
Gannet / Nov '95 / Cadillac / Jazz Music

CHICAGO ALL STARS, THE (2CD Set)
Reach out: *Yesterday Dreamers* / Welcome to the storm: *Outerrealm* / Operation sneak: *DJ Sneak* / Migraine headache: *Fade 2 Tha Future* / Submarine: *Felix Da Housecat* / It's time to excel: *MD Connection* / Radikal bitch: *Armando* / Move traxx: *Professor Traxx* / Trickster: *Fiasco, Johnny* / I just need: *K-Hand* / My my my: *Alexi, Kaay* / Can u dance: *Crump, Harrison* / Metropolis: *Felix Da Housecat* / Daybreak: *Aphrohead* / Tunnel vision: *Armando* / Footsteps of rage: *Felix Da Housecat* / Spiritual drum II: *Professor Traxx* / Ruhrschellweg: *Broccoli Brothers & Righteous Men* / Wicked city: *Righteous Men* / Diafana: *Random Logic*
CD Set ______ **FEAR 025CDLTD**
Radikal Fear / Jan '96 / Vital

CHICAGO BLUES
CD ______ **CLACD 425**
Castle / Mar '97 / BMG

CHICAGO BLUES (2CD Set)
Where the hell where you when I got home: *Lefty Dizz* / Ain't it nice to be loved: *Lefty Dizz* / Keep on running: *Littlejohn, Johnny* / If you don't want me: *Littlejohn, Johnny* / You got to help me: *Sumlin, Hubert* / Tell me why: *Linkchain, Hip* / You must be shampoo baby: *Linkchain, Hip* / Good kookamaloo: *Louisiana Red* / Little boy blue: *Horton, Walter* / Cha cha in blues: *Campbell, Eddie C.* / Hello Mrs. Brown: *Smith, Byther* / Brought up the hard way: *Bell, Carey* / One eyed man: *Tre* / Young girl: *Evans, Lucky Lopez* / Good lovings: *Evans, Lucky Lopez* / Fishing in my pond: *Rogers, Jimmy* / Crazy woman blues: *Rogers, Jimmy* / Dr. Boogie: *Terry, Doc* / Things can't stay the same: *Terry, Doc* / So good to me: *Dawkins, Jimmy* / Swear to tell the truth: *Walker, Johnny 'Big Moose'* / Low down dog: *Burks, JT* / Must I holler: *Burks, JT* / From Greenwood Mississippi to Chicago: *Burks, JT* / Operator: *Burks, JT* / I'm very superstitious: *Tre* / Pickin' rags: *Buford, Mojo* / Jack potato boogie: *Buford, Mojo* / Once a gambler: *Guy, Phil* / Leaving town: *Louisiana Red* / Lonesome blues: *Granderson, John Lee* / Grease me baby: *Louisiana Red*
CD Set ______ **JSPCD 401**
JSP / Jul '97 / ADA / Cadillac / Direct / Hot Shot / Target/BMG

CHICAGO BLUES - THE GOLDEN ERA (2CD Set)
CD Set ______ **CDGR 1432**
Charly / Apr '97 / Koch

CHICAGO BLUES AT BURNLEY
CD ______ **JSPCD 247**
JSP / '91 / ADA / Cadillac / Direct / Hot Shot / Target/BMG

CHICAGO BLUES AT HOME
CD ______ **TCD 5028**
Testament / Oct '95 / ADA / Koch

CHICAGO BLUES JAM
Had it so hard: *Sunnyland Slim & Lacy Gibson* / Soft & mellow Stella: *Sunnyland Slim & Lacy Gibson* / Bessie Mae: *Sunnyland Slim & Lacy Gibson* / You went away baby: *Bell, Carey & Willie Williams* / Alcoholic man: *Bell, Carey & Willie Williams* / Showing off my car: *Bell, Carey & Willie Williams* / In the dark (that ain't right): *Magic Slim* / Cummins Prison farm: *Magic Slim* / Pretty baby: *Johnson, Jimmy* / When my first wife quit me: *Johnson, Jimmy* / Came up the hard way: *Clearwater, Eddy* / Muddy water's gonna run clear: *Clearwater, Eddy* / I don't know why: *Clearwater, Eddy* / Boogie my blues away: *Clearwater, Eddy* / Mayor Daley's blues: *Clearwater, Eddy*
CD ______ **NEBCD 852**
Sequel / Aug '96 / BMG

CHICAGO BLUES LIVE VOL.1
CD ______ **WCD 120871**
Wolf / Jul '97 / Hot Shot / Jazz Music / Swift

CHICAGO BLUES MASTERS VOL.3 (2CD Set)
Everything gonna be alright / Hold that bus, conductor / Strollin' the strip / Respect me baby / I will always love you / Three times seven / Farther on up the road / Hard road to travel / Save your money, baby / Too hot to hold / Long distance call / Don't answer the door / Love me baby / Chains of love / Sky is falling / Long distance operator / I'm a free man / Can't live without love / Kiddy boy / Mellow down easy / Can't hold on much longer / My babe / Juke / West Helena woman / Tell me Mama / Last night / You better watch yourself / Key to the highway / Everything's gonna be alright / Too late / Love with a feelin' / Goin' down slow / Just a feelin' / She moves me / Tonight I wanna love me a stranger / Nose open / Goodbye my lady / Georgia swing
CD Set ______ **CDEM 1604**
Capitol / Mar '97 / EMI

CHICAGO BLUES NIGHT
CD ______ **GBW 001**
GBW / Feb '92 / Harmonia Mundi

CHICAGO BLUES TODAY VOL.1
Help me: *Wells, Junior Chicago Blues Band* / It hurts me too (when things go wrong): *Wells, Junior Chicago Blues Band* / Messin' with the kid: *Wells, Junior Chicago Blues Band* / Vietcong blues: *Wells, Junior Chicago Blues Band* / All night long: *Wells, Junior Chicago Blues Band* / Going ahead: *Hutto, J.B. & His Hawks* / Please help: *Hutto, J.B. & His Hawks* / Too much alcohol: *Hutto, J.B. & His Hawks* / Married woman blues: *Hutto, J.B. & His Hawks* / That's the truth: *Hutto, J.B. & His Hawks* / Marie: *Spann, Otis Southside Piano* / Burning fire: *Spann, Otis Southside Piano* / SP blues: *Spann, Otis Southside Piano* / Sometime I wonder: *Spann, Otis Southside Piano* / Spann's stomp: *Spann, Otis Southside Piano*
CD ______ **VMD 79216**
Vanguard / Oct '95 / ADA / Pinnacle

CHICAGO BLUES TODAY VOL.2
Cotton crop blues: *Cotton, Jimmy Blues Quartet* / Blues keep falling: *Cotton, Jimmy Blues Quartet* / Love me or leave: *Cotton, Jimmy Blues Quartet* / Rockett: *Cotton, Jimmy Blues Quartet* / West Helena blues: *Cotton, Jimmy Blues Quartet* / Everything's going to turn out alright: *Rush, Otis Blues Band* / It's a mean old world: *Rush, Otis Blues Band* / I can't quit you baby: *Rush, Otis Blues Band* / Rock: *Rush, Otis Blues Band* / It's my own fault: *Rush, Otis Blues Band* / Dust my broom: *Homesick James & His Dusters* / Somebody been talkin': *Homesick James & His Dusters* / Set a date: *Homesick James & His Dusters* / So mean to me: *Homesick James & His Dusters*
CD ______ **VMD 79217**
Vanguard / Oct '95 / ADA / Pinnacle

CHICAGO BLUES TODAY VOL.3
One more time: *Young, Johnny South Side Blues Band* / Kid man blues: *Young, Johnny South Side Blues Band* / My black mare: *Young, Johnny South Side Blues Band* / Stealin' back: *Young, Johnny South Side Blues Band* / I got mine in time: *Young, Johnny South Side Blues Band* / Tighten up on it: *Young, Johnny South Side Blues Band* / Dynaflow blues: *Shines, Johnny Blues Band* / Black spider blues: *Shines, Johnny Blues Band* / Layin' down my shoes and clothes: *Shines, Johnny Blues Band* / If I get lucky: *Shines, Johnny Blues Band* / Rockin' my boogie: *Horton, Big Walter Blues Harp & Memphis Charlie* / Mr. Boweevil: *Horton, Big Walter Blues Harp & Memphis Charlie* / Hey hey: *Horton, Big Walter Blues Harp & Memphis Charlie*
CD ______ **VMD 79218**
Vanguard / Oct '95 / ADA / Pinnacle

CHICAGO BLUES VOL.1
CD ______ **WCD 120281**
Wolf / Dec '96 / Hot Shot / Jazz Music / Swift

CHICAGO GARAGE BAND GREATS (The Best Of Rembrandt Records 1966-1968)
Hassle: *Nite Owls* / Boots are made for talking: *Nite Owls* / Open up your mind: *Nuchez* / No reservations: *Circus* / Come on back: *Nickel Bag* / Woods: *Nickel Bag* / Games we play: *Circus* / Sands of mind: *Circus* / Long lost friend: *Monday's Child* / It's a hassle: *Nickel Bag* / I live in the springtime: *Lemon Drops* / Listen girl: *Lemon Drops* / Nobody for me: *Lemon Drops* / Flowers on the hillside: *Lemon Drops* / Trilogy: *Watermelon* / Ocean song: *Watermelon* / I can make you happy: *Buzzsaw* / Nowhere to go: *Buzzsaw* / Roll on Angeline: *Buzzsaw* / Walking through a rainbow: *Buzzsaw*
CD ______ **CDTB 164**
Thunderbolt / Mar '95 / TKO Magnum

CHICAGO GOSPEL
CD ______ **HTCD 08**
Heritage / '92 / ADA / Direct / Hot Shot / Jazz Music / Swift / Wellard

CHICAGO HOUSE 1986-1991 (3CD Set)
CD Set ______ **CHBOXCD 1**
Beechwood / Nov '96 / Beechwood/BMG / Pinnacle

CHICAGO HOUSE JAM
We can make it: *UBQ & Kathy Summers* / My underground: *Vision* / Project 3: *Two Men On A Struggle* / Feel my soul: *UBQ & Kathy Summers* / Bubbles: *Tikkle* / Seduction: *Vision* / Cosmic rhythm: *UBQ Project* / Reachin': *LNR* / Project 1: *Two Men On A Struggle* / When I fall in love: *UBQ & Kathy Summers*
CD ______ **SLIPCD 57**
Slip 'n' Slide / Mar '97 / Amato Disco / Prime / RTM/Disc / Vital

CHICAGO JUMP BANDS 1945-1953
CD ______ **RST 915772**
RST / Jun '94 / Hot Shot / Jazz Music

CHICAGO RADIO SOUL
Rescue me: *Bass, Fontella* / Don't mess up a good thing: *Bass, Fontella & Bobby McClure* / We got the winning hand: *Little Milton* / Selfish one: *Ross, Jackie* / Thousand miles away: *Garrett, Jo Ann* / Shy guy: *Radiants* / No faith, no love: *Collier, Mitty* / I can't help myself: *Gems* / Love is a five letter word: *Phelps, James* / This heart of mine: *Clarke, Tony* / Lonely girl: *Davis, Andrea* / (Don't it make you) feel kinda bad: *Radiants* / La de da, I'm a fool in love: *Phelps, James* / Only time will tell: *James, Etta* / Peak of love: *McClure, Bobby* / Bossa nova bird: *Dells* / Creeper: *Robinson, Freddie* / Heartbreak society: *Radiants* / Strange feeling: *Stewart, Billy* / Try my love again: *Moore, Bobby & The Rhythm Aces* / Sharing you: *Collier, Mitty* / Take me for a little while: *Ross, Jackie* / One day I'll show you: *Radiants* / Stay by my side: *Garrett, Jo Ann* / Love reputation: *LaSalle, Denise* / Happy new love: *Gems*
CD ______ **CDKEND 133**
Kent / Apr '96 / Pinnacle

CHICAGO SOUND VOL.1
CD ______ **CSDCD 1**
Chicago Sound / May '95 / SRD

CHICAGO SOUND VOL.2
CD ______ **CDCS 002**
Chicago Sound / Sep '96 / SRD

CHICAGO SOUNDS
CD ______ **CSCD 001**
ACV / Dec '94 / Plastic Head / SRD

CHICAGO SOUTH SIDE JAZZ 1927-1931
I'm goin' huntin' / If you want to be my sugar papa / My baby / Pleasure mad / Some do and some don't / Tack it down / Endurance stomp / Bull fiddle rag / Shake your shimmy / Shake that jelly roll / Don't cry honey / Shanghai honeymoon / Good feelin' blues / Wild man stomp / Stomp your stuff
CD ______ **NEOVOX 868**
Neovox / Mar '94 / Wellard

CHILDLINE
One: *Automatic Baby* / Feelin' alright: *Weller, Paul* / Huckleberry Grove: *Ocean Colour Scene* / Still life: *Alisha's Attic* / Punk boy: *Ash* / Ski jump nose: *Mansun* / Lazy: *Suede* / Whiskey in the jar: *Pulp* / Better man: *Cast* / Ocean Drive: *Lighthouse Family* / Can't smile without you: *Menswear* / Back street luv: *Salad* / Witchita lineman: *These Animal Men* / Dance of the bad angel: *Booth, Tim & Angelo Badalamenti* / Chaos: *Tricky* / Possibly maybe: *Bjork* / Looking for: *East 17* / Your song: *Boyzone*
CD ______ **5530302**
PolyGram TV / Nov '96 / PolyGram

CHILDREN - 100% KIDS
CD ______ **TCD 2798**
Telstar / Nov '95 / BMG

CHILDREN - 100% KIDS PARTY
Smurfsong: *Father Abraham & The Smurfs* / Toad's song: *Jones, Terry* / Help it's the hair bear bunch / Rugrats / Mr. Blobby / Ma nah ma nah / Bare necessities megamix: *UK Mixmasters* / Scooby Doo, where are you / Masked rider / Thunderbirds / We are VR: *VR Troopers* / X - Men / Clarissa explains it all / U krazy katz: *PJ & Duncan* / Hands up hands up: *Zig & Zag* / Christmas in Smurfland: *Father Abraham & The Smurfs* / Dog pound hop: *Ren & Stimpie* / Wacky races / Top cat / Tra la la song / Power Rangers / Biker mice from Mars / Captain Scarlet / Stingray / Jetsons / Remember you're a womble / Postman Pat song: *Barrie, Ken* / Rupert the bear: *Lee, Jackie* / It only takes a minute girl: *Pinky & Perky*
CD ______ **TCD 2874**
Telstar / Nov '96 / BMG

CHILDREN - A TRADITIONAL CHRISTMAS
CD ______ **CD 251**
CYP Children's Audio / Jul '94 / Total/ BMG

CHILDREN - ALL ABOARD (All Time Children's Favourites)
Laughing policeman: *Penrose, Charles* / Ugly duckling: *Kaye, Danny* / Robin Hood: *James, Dick* / Right said Fred: *Cribbins, Bernard* / Hippopotamus song: *Wallace, Ian* / Banana boat song (Day O): *Freberg, Stan* / Goodness gracious me: *Sellers, Peter & Sophia Loren* / Bee song: *Askey, Arthur* / Who's afraid of the big bad wolf: *Pinky & Perky* / I know an old lady: *Ives, Burl* / My boomerang won't come back: *Drake, Charlie* / Teddy bears' picnic: *Hall, Henry* / Nellie the elephant: *Miller, Mandy* / Sparky's magic piano: *Blair, Henry & Ray Turner* / Owl and the pussycat: *Hayes, Elton* / Ernie (the fastest milkman in the West): *Hill, Benny* / Buckingham Palace: *Stephens, Anne* / Windmill in old Amsterdam: *Hilton, Ronnie* / Grandad: *Dunn, Clive* / My brother: *Scott, Terry* / Morningtown ride: *Seekers* / Gnu song: *Flanders, Michael & Donald Swann* / Two little boys: *Harris, Rolf* / Runaway train: *Holliday, Michael*
CD ______ **CDEMS 1479**
EMI / Mar '93 / EMI

CHILDREN - CHANTEFABLES, CHANTEFLEURS (French Children's Songs, Poems & Music)
Desnos/Tardieu/Mechin
CD ______ **LDX 200314**
La Chant Du Monde / Jan '93 / ADA / Harmonia Mundi

CHILDREN - CHRISTMAS PARTY POPS
CD ______ **CD 250**
CYP Children's Audio / Oct '93 / Total/ BMG

CHILDREN - JUNIOR CHOICE VOL.1
Nellie the elephant: *Miller, Mandy* / Runaway train: *Dalhart, Vernon* / Gilly gilly ossenfeffer katzenellenbogen by the sea: *Bygraves, Max* / You're a pink toothbrush: *Bygraves, Max* / Robin Hood: *James, Dick* / I taut I taw a puddy tat: *Blanc, Mel* / Woody Woodpecker: *Blanc, Mel* / Ernie (the fastest milkman in the West): *Hill, Benny* / I've lost my mummy: *Harris, Rolf* / Jake the peg: *Harris, Rolf* / My boomerang won't come back: *Drake, Charlie* / Mr. Custer: *Drake, Charlie* / Little boy fishin': *Abicair, Shirley* / Laughing policeman: *Penrose, Charles* / Ragtime Cowboy Joe: *Chipmunks* / Buckingham Palace: *Stephens, Anne* / Hippopotamus song: *Flanders & Swann* / Ballad of Davy Crockett: *Ford, Tennessee Ernie* / Grandad: *Dunn, Clive*
CD ______ **CDMFP 5890**
Music For Pleasure / Oct '90 / EMI

CHILDREN - JUNIOR CHOICE VOL.2
Ugly ducking: *Kaye, Danny* / King's new clothes: *Kaye, Danny* / Little white duck: *Kaye, Danny* / Tubby the tuba: *Kaye, Danny* / Little red monkey: *Nicols/ Edwards/ Bentley* / Grandfather's clock: *Radio Revellers* / Kitty in the basket: *Dekker, Diana* / I know an old lady: *Ives, Burl* / Big Rock Candy Mountain: *Ives, Burl* / There's a friend for little children: *Uncle Mac* / All things bright and beautiful: *Uncle Mac* / Three billy goat gruff: *Luther, Frank* / Owl and the pussycat: *Hayes, Elton* / Puffin' Billy: *Melodi Light Orchestra* / (How much is that) doggie in the window: *Roza, Lita* / Mr. Cuckoo (sing your song): *Ross, Edmundo* / Typewriter: *Anderson, Leroy* / Little shoemaker: *Michael Twins* / Bimbo: *Miller, Suzi* / Swedish rhapsody: *Mantovani*
CD ______ **CDMFP 5891**
Music For Pleasure / Oct '90 / EMI

CHILDREN - JUNIOR PARTY POPS
CD ______ **CD 249**
CYP Children's Audio / May '93 / Total/ BMG

CHILDREN - JUNIOR PARTY POPS VOL.2
CD ______ **PT 249CD**
CYP Children's Audio / Mar '93 / Total/ BMG

CHILDREN - JUNIOR PARTY POPS VOL.2
CD ______ **PT 247CD**
CYP Children's Audio / Mar '93 / Total/ BMG

CHILDREN - MR. BOOM IS OVER THE MOON
CD ______ **MB 007CD**
Moonbeam Music / Nov '95 / Duncans

CHILDREN - MUSICAL FUN AND GAMES
Children's games / Sorcerer's apprentice / Dolly Suite: *Academy Of St. Martin in the Fields/Neville Marriner* / Musical box / Nutcracker suite: *Royal Philharmonic Orchestra* / Pied piper: *MacDonald, George & Northern Sinfonia of England* / Themes for Narnia: *Robles, Marisa Ensemble & Christopher Hyde-Smith* / Scaramouche-Braziliera: *Johnson, Emma & Gordon Back*
CD ______ **CDDCA 673**
ASV / Oct '89 / Select

CHILDREN - SONGS AND NURSERY RHYMES OF THE WORLD
Le furet / Une souris verte / Chant de deux petites filles / Los mamones / Oi cotou cotou cototchok / Barati baratin / Tutu marambaia / London Bridge / Madeira lullaby / Monday's child / Head and shoulders / Las Abejas / Grun grun grun / Assalalaa de la terre de Baffin / Simon says / Estaba el Senor Don Gato / Je te tiens par la barbichette / Alle meine entchen / Nick nack

paddy wack / Savez vous planter les choux / ABCD / Pussy cat / Water drum / Lullaby / Eenie meenie minie moe / Der wettstreit / Chicken never shows its nest / Ikh agsal / Ihumke / Bingo
CD _______________ U 310110
Auvidis Jeunesse / May '97 / Harmonia Mundi

CHILDREN - THE COMPLETE JUNIOR CHOICE
Nellie the elephant / Who's afraid of the big bad wolf / Puff the magic dragon / Old Macdonald had a farm / Runaway train / Jake the peg / Splish splash / I taut I taw a puddy-tat / I've lost my mummy / Ugly bug ball / Owl and the pussycat / Puffin' Billy / (How much) Is that doggy in the window / You're a pink toothbrush / Woody woodpecker / Whistle while you work / Winnie The Pooh / All things bright and beautiful / Teddy bears picnic / My boomerang won't come back / Laughing policeman
CD _______________ CDLFPK 2000
Listen For Pleasure / May '96 / EMI

CHILDREN - WILD WORLD OF ANIMAL SONGS
CD _______________ JJCD 477
Jumping Jack / Jul '95 / THE

CHILDREN - YOUNG AT HEART
Christopher Robin: *Lee, Mary* / Animal crackers: *BBC Dance Orchestra* / Little man you've had a busy day: *Rosing, Val & Jay Wilbur Band* / Horsey horsey: *Campbell, Big Bill & His Rocky Mountain Rhythm* / Mickey Mouse's birthday party: *Marcellion, Muzzy & Ted Fiorito Band* / Little drummer boy: *Robins, Phyllis & Jay Wilbur Band* / On the good ship Lollipop: *Geraldo & His Orchestra* / Mommy I don't want to go to bed: *Gonella, Nat & His Georgians* / Wedding of Jack and Jill: *Wilbur, Jay & his band* / Runaway train: *Dalhart, Vernon* / Trains: *Gardiner, Reginald* / Bee song: *Askey, Arthur* / Teddy bears' picnic: *Hall, Henry Orchestra* / It's my mother's birthday today: *Yates, Hal & His Orchestra* / Three little fishes: *Gonella, Nat & His Georgians* / When the circus comes to town: *Kyser, Kay Orchestra* / Hush hush hush, here comes the bogeyman: *Hall, Henry Orchestra* / Laughing policeman: *Penrose, Charles* / Lion and Albert: *Holloway, Stanley* / Buckingham Palace: *Stephens, Anne*
CD _______________ PASTCD 9769
Flapper / Oct '93 / Pinnacle

CHILDREN - YOUR FAVOURITE CHRISTMAS PARTY SONGS AND CAROLS
CD _______________ CDMFP 5955
Music For Pleasure / Dec '94 / EMI

CHILDREN'S COLLECTION, THE (3CD Set)
Grand old Duke of York / Sing a song of sixpence / Once I caught a fish alive / Hey diddle diddle / Little Jack Horner / Little Miss Muffet / Little Bo Peep / Mary Mary quite contrary / Old Macdonald had a farm / Twinkle twinkle little star / Nick-nack paddy wack / Baa baa black sheep / Bobby Shaftoe / Hush a-bye baby / Humpty Dumpty / Lavender's blue (Dilly, Dilly) / London Bridge is falling down / Oranges and lemons / Oh, dear what can the matter be / Over the hills and far away / Fox jumped up / Celementine / Three jolly rogues of Lynn / Who killed Cock Robin / Cockles and mussels / Hush little baby / What shall we do with the drunken sailor / Riddle song / Michael Finnigan / Froggy's courting / When you wish upon a star / Thomas O'Malley's cat / Give a little whistle / When I see an elephant fly / Who's afraid of the big bad wolf / Ugly bug ball / Whistle while you work / Winnie the Pooh / Heigh-ho / Siamese cat song / Supercalifragilisticexpialidocius / Bare necessities / Colonel Hathi's march / Trust in me / That's what friends are for / I wanna be like you / Never smile at a crocodile / Feed the birds / Aristocats / Hi diddle dee dee / Everybody wants to be a cat / I've got no strings / Cinderella / Goldilocks and the three bears / Little Red Riding Hood / Jack and the beanstalk / Rumplestiltskin / Sleeping Beauty
CD Set _______________ CDTRBOX 268
Trio / Oct '96 / EMI

CHILDREN'S FAVOURITES (2CD Set)
CD Set _______________ TREB 3041
Scratch / May '96 / Koch / Scratch/BMG

CHILDREN'S FAVOURITES - YOU MUST REMEMBER THIS
Puffin' Billy: *McLodi Light Orchestra/Ole Jensen* / Teddy bear's picnic: *Rosing, Val & Henry Hall/BBC Dance Orchestra* / Swinging on a star: *Crosby, Bing* / I've got no strings: *Kemp, Hal Orchestra* / Grandfather's clock: *Williams, Harold & BBC Male Chorus* / One little raindrop: *Ovaltineys & George Melachrino/Tessa Deane* / Policeman's holiday: *New Light Symphony Orchestra* / Dicky bird hop: *Fields, Gracie* / Laughing policeman: *Penrose, Charles* / One, two, button your shoe: *Swingettes & Jack Hylton Orchestra* / Buckingham Palace: *Stephens, Anne* / Rhythm in the alphabet: *Formby, George* / Little boy bubbles: *Doyle, Jack 'Trump' Aces Of Rhythm* / Animal crackers in my soup: *Robins, Phyllis & The Corona Babes* / Parade of the tin soldiers: *New Light Symphony Orchestra* / Runaway train: *Robinson, Carson & His Pioneers* / Pied piper of Hamelin: *Bowlly, Al & Ray Noble/His New Mayfair Orchestra* / Owl and the pussy cat: *Robertson, Stuart* / I'm Popeye the sailor man: *Costello, Billy* / Three little fishes: *Denham, Maurice* / Wedding of the painted doll: *Layton & Johnstone* / Ragtime cowboy Joe: *Carless, Dorothy & Johnny Green/Geraldo* / Portrait of a toy soldier: *Sandler, Albert & His Orchestra* / Balloons: *Ovaltineys & Monte Rey* / Little man, you've had a busy day: *Carlisle, Elsie* / Everything stops for tea: *Lorenzi, Mario 'Harp' & His Rhythmics* / Goodnight children eveywhere: *Lynn, Vera & Ambrose*
CD _______________ 7560552812
Happy Days / Feb '97 / Conifer/BMG

CHILDREN'S SONGS FROM SOUTH INDIA
CD _______________ ARN 6428
Arion / Oct '94 / ADA / Discovery

CHILDREN'S SONGS FROM SW CHINA
CD _______________ ARN 64365
Arion / Feb '97 / ADA / Discovery

CHILD'S CELEBRATION OF FOLK MUSIC, A
CD _______________ 9425852
Music For Little People / Aug '96 / Direct

CHILIK: SONGS AND MELODIES OF THE NAGAYBAKS (Recordings From Russian Tartar Province Of Chelyabinsk)
CD _______________ PAN 7003CD
Pan / Feb '95 / ADA / CM / Direct

CHILL FM
CD _______________ MR 14CD
Massive Respect / Apr '96 / Alphamagic / Mo's Music Machine

CHILL OUT
CD _______________ 9548345492
East West / Aug '96 / Warner Music

CHILL OUT - THE ALBUM
CD _______________ XPS 3CD
X-Treme / Feb '97 / Pinnacle / SRD

CHILL OUT CLASSICS VOL.1
CD _______________ CHILLCD 1
Chillout / May '94 / Kudos / Pinnacle / RTM/Disc

CHILL OUT FREE (2CD Set)
CD Set _______________ AVEXCD 51
Avex / Nov '96 / 3mv/Pinnacle

CHILL OUT OR DIE VOL.1
CD _______________ RSNCD 8
Rising High / Jul '93 / 3mv/Sony

CHILL OUT OR DIE VOL.2 (2CD Set)
CD Set _______________ RSNCD 17
Rising High / May '94 / 3mv/Sony

CHILL OUT OR DIE VOL.3
CD _______________ RSNCD 25
Rising High / Oct '94 / 3mv/Sony

CHILL OUT OR DIE VOL.4 (2CD Set)
CD Set _______________ RSNCD 33
Rising High / Jun '95 / 3mv/Sony

CHILLIN' (The Best Of Jazz Funk)
Sun goddess: *Lewis, Ramsey* / Expansions: *Smith, Lonnie Liston* / Keep that same old feeling: *Crusaders* / Morning dance: *Spyro Gyra* / Always and forever: *Jordan, Stanley* / School days: *Clarke, Stanley* / Mystic voyage: *Ayers, Roy* / Mr. Magic: *Washington, Grover Jr.* / Feels so good: *Mangione, Chuck* / Sneakin' up behind you: *Brecker Brothers* / Funkin' for Jamaica: *Browne, Tom* / Action speaks louder than words: *Chocolate Milk* / Jaws: *Schifrin, Lalo* / Black cow: *Connors, Norman*
CD _______________ 74321288852
Ariola / Jun '95 / BMG

CHILLOUT CLASSICS (Classical Music Mixed By Jonothan Moore)
CD _______________ 39101822
Hyperium / Jun '97 / Cargo / Plastic Head

CHILLOUT FOUREVER
CD _______________ XTR 38CDM
X-Treme / Jun '97 / Pinnacle / SRD

CHINESE BAMBOO FLUTE MUSIC
CD _______________ 12183
Laserlight / Aug '95 / Target/BMG

CHINESE HAN MUSIC
CD _______________ 117052
Musidisc / Jan '97 / Discovery

CHISWICK SAMPLER, THE (Good Clean Fun)
Beautiful Delilah: *Count Bishops* / Sweet revenge: *101'ers* / Gatecrasher: *Gorillas* / Groovy Ruby: *Moped, Johnny* / Enemies: *Radiators From Space* / Tear it up/Teenage cutie: *Whirlwind* / Train kept a rollin': *Motorhead* / I want candy: *Bishops* / Radio stars/Buy Chiswick records: *Radio Stars* / Smash it up: *Damned* / Romford girls: *Riff Raff* / Dead vandals: *Johnny & The Self Abusers* / Come on let's go: *Sharpe, Rocky & The Replays* / Driver's seat/Poison pen mail: *Sniff 'n' The Tears* / Let's talk about the weather: *Radiators* / There's a boy on our street: *Disguise* / Addicts of the first night: *Albania* / Swim the Indian ocean: *2-2* / Over the top: *Motordamn*
CD _______________ CDWIKX 162
Chiswick / Oct '95 / Pinnacle

CHISWICK STORY, THE (2CD Set)
Route 66: *Count Bishops* / Teenage letter: *Count Bishops* / Train train: *Count Bishops* / Keys to your heart: *101'ers* / She's my gal: *Gorillas* / Gorilla got me: *Gorillas* / Drip drop: *Sharpe, Rocky & The Razors* / I'm crying: *Story, Little Bob* / Dirty pictures: *Radio Stars* / No Russians in Russia: *Radio Stars* / Nervous wreck: *Radio Stars* / Real me: *Radio Stars* / Television screen: *Radiators From Space* / Motorhead: *Motorhead* / I wanna be free: *Rings* / No one: *Moped, Johnny* / Darling let's have another baby: *Moped, Johnny* / Little queenie: *Moped, Johnny* / I want you to dance with me: *Hill, Jeff* / Common truth: *Amazorblades* / Saints and sinners: *Johnny & The Self Abusers* / Hang loose (I've gotta rock): *Whirlwind* / I only wish (that I'd been told): *Whirlwind* / Heaven knows: *Whirlwind* / Million dollar hero: *Radiators* / Dancing years: *Radiators* / Cosmonaut: *Riff Raff* / I want candy: *Bishops* / Gay boys in bondage: *Drug Addix* / Rama lama ding dong: *Sharpe, Rocky & The Replays* / Imagination: *Sharpe, Rocky & The Replays* / Shout shout (knock yourself out): *Sharpe, Rocky & The Replays* / Heart: *Sharpe, Rocky & The Replays* / Driver's seat: *Sniff 'n' The Tears* / Hey baby: *Disguise* / I couldn't help but cry: *Kelleher, Dan* / Automobile: *Stickshifts* / Love song: *Damned* / Smash it up: *Damned* / Gabrielle: *Nips* / That driving beat: *Red Beans & Rice* / I can't fight it: *Textones* / Albania (are you all mine): *Albania* / Go go go: *Albania* / Tomahawk cruise: *Smith, TV's Explorers* / Tennessee stud: *Woods, Terry* / Radioactive kid: *Meteors* / Insufficient data: *2-2* / Kwagayo: *2-2* / Desire: *Radiation, Roddy & Tearjerkers* / Grab what you can (biez co mozesz): *Jakko*
CD Set _______________ CDWIK2 100
Chiswick / Mar '92 / Pinnacle

CHOIR MUSIC FROM WALES
Land of my fathers / Home / Welsh rapsody / Suo gan / God bless the Prince of Wales / Ash grove / When I survey the wonderous cross / All through the night / Arwelfa / Bells of Aberdovey / Tretswer court / Lisa Land and the ballad of Roke's drift / Welsh medley / David of the white rock / Cwm rhondda / How great thou art / Soldiers chorus / Abide with me
CD _______________ 3036100162
Pearls / May '96 / Carlton

CHOMP
CD _______________ TKCD 6
2 Kool / Apr '95 / Pinnacle / SRD

CHOROS FROM BAHAI
CD _______________ NI 5404
Nimbus / Feb '95 / Nimbus

CHRISTMAS CAROLS
God rest ye merry gentlemen / While shepherds watched their flocks by night / See amid the winter's snow / Silent night / Good King Wenceslas / O little town of Bethlehem: *Guildford Cathedral Choir* / Unto us is born a son / Away in a manger / Rocking / In dulci jubilo: *Westminster Abbey Choir* / Ding dong merrily on high / Coventry carol / I saw three ships: *St. Paul's Cathedral Choir* / Holly and the ivy / Angels from the realms of glory: *St. Paul's Cathedral Choir* / First Noel / O come all ye faithful (Adeste Fidelis) / Once in Royal David's City: *Exeter Cathedral Choir* / Hark the herald angels sing: *Exeter Cathedral Choir*
CD _______________ CC 224
Music For Pleasure / Dec '94 / EMI

CHRISTMAS COLLECTION, A
Christmas song: *Cole, Nat 'King'* / O come all ye faithful (Adeste fidelis): *Cole, Nat 'King'* / Walking in the air: *Jones, Aled* / Santa Claus is coming to town: *Lee, Peggy* / Christmas waltz: *Lee, Peggy* / Rudolph the red nosed reindeer: *Martin, Dean* / White Christmas: *Martin, Dean* / Jingle bells: *Paul, Les & Mary Ford* / Silent night: *Paul, Les & Mary Ford* / When a child is born: *Rogers, Kenny* / Christmas is my favourite time of year: *Rogers, Kenny* / Little drummer boy: *Lynn, Vera* / Mary's boy child: *Lynn, Vera* / Have yourself a merry little Christmas: *Campbell, Glen* / Christmas is for children: *Campbell, Glen* / O' holy night: *Rodgers, Jimmie* / I'll be home for Christmas: *Beach Boys* / Winter wonderland: *Mercer, Johnny* / What child is this: *Rodgers, Jimmie* / We three kings of Orient are: *Beach Boys*
CD _______________ CDMFP 5903
Music For Pleasure / Oct '96 / EMI

CHRISTMAS COUNTRY COLLECTION
CD _______________ MCCDX 004
Music Club / Nov '94 / Disc / THE

CHRISTMAS CROONERS
CD _______________ MCCDX 003
Music Club / Nov '93 / Disc / THE

CHRISTMAS FAVOURITES
CD _______________ 15463
Laserlight / Nov '95 / Target/BMG

CHRISTMAS JUBILEE
CD _______________ VJC 1016 2
Vintage Jazz Classics / Oct '91 / ADA / Cadillac / CM / Direct

CHRISTMAS MOODS
Deck the halls / First Noel / God rest ye merry gentlemen / Hark the herald angels sing / It came upon a midnight clear / Jingle bells / Joy to the world / O little town of Bethlehem / O Christmas tree / O come all ye faithful (adeste fidelis) / Silent night / We wish you a Merry Christmas / We three Kings / Angels from the realms of glory / Away in a manger
CD _______________ XMAS 011
Tring / Nov '96 / Tring

CHRISTMAS PAN PIPES
CD _______________ ROJOC 1026
Hit / Oct '96 / Grapevine/PolyGram

CHRISTMAS REFLECTIONS
CD _______________ MCCDX 005
Music Club / Nov '94 / Disc / THE

CHRISTMAS SAX
Christmas song: *Martin, Dean* / Do you hear what I hear / I believe in Father Christmas / O Christmas tree / Mary's boy child / Last Christmas / Winter wonderland / When a child is born / Mistletoe and wine / White Christmas / Silver bells / Have yourself a merry little Christmas / Let it snow, let it snow, let it snow / Silent night
CD _______________ CDMFP 6245
Music For Pleasure / Oct '96 / EMI

CHRISTMAS SOUL SPECIAL
Jingle bells / Silent night / Drummer boy / Oh holy night / Jingle bell rock / Christmas song / Santa Claus is coming to town / Noel / Winter wonderland / O come all ye faithful (Adeste Fidelis) / Frosty the snowman / Silver bells
CD _______________ CDVR 015
Varrick / '88 / ADA / CM / Direct / Roots

CHRISTMAS TIME WITH THE STARS
White Christmas / Jingle Bells / Santa Claus is coming to town / Siberian sleigh ride / Snow White and the seven dwarfs / Christmas bells at eventide / Sitting on the ice at the ice rink / Say it with carols / Kiddies go carolling / Christmas day in the cookhouse / Hansel and Gretel dance duet / Christmas dinner / Christmas swing / March of the toys / Christmas night in Harlem / It happened in sun valley / O little town of Bethlehem / Christmas song / Ghost of the turkey / Snowman / Fairy on the Christmas tree / I'm going home for Christmas / Don't wait till the night before Christmas
CD _______________ CDYULE 300
Happy Days / Oct '94 / Conifer/BMG

CHRISTMAS WITH THE STARS (3CD Set)
Christmas song: *Cole, Nat 'King'* / When a child is born: *Monro, Matt* / Let it snow, let it snow, let it snow: *Martin, Dean* / Little Saint Nick: *Beach Boys* / Blue Christmas: *Campbell, Glen* / Santo natale: *Locke, Josef* / Christmas waltz: *Lee, Peggy* / Jingle bells: *Paul, Les & Mary Ford* / Little donkey: *Lynn, Vera* / See amid the Winter's snow: *Morriston Orpheus & Treorchy Male Choirs* / Happiest Christmas of all: *Morecambe & Wise* / O' holy night: *Rogers, Jimmy* / Do you hear what I hear: *Adams, Cliff Singers* / Wassail song: *Mitchell, George Minstrels* / Christmas wish (from me to you): *Lynn, Vera* / Christmas blues: *Martin, Dean* / Mary's boy child: *Monro, Matt* / Little boy that Santa Claus forgot: *Cole, Nat 'King'* / Walking in the air: *Jones, Aled* / Frosty the snowman: *Beach Boys* / Rudolf the red nosed reindeer: *Martin, Dean* / It must be getting close to Christmas: *Campbell, Glen* / Santa Claus is coming to town: *Lee, Peggy* / Deck the halls: *Treorchy & Morriston Orpheus/Pontarddulais Choirs* / Winter wonderland: *Mercer, Johnny* / Little drummer boy: *Lynn, Vera* / Star of Bethlehem: *Locke, Josef* / Twelve days of Christmas: *Adams, Cliff Singers* / Christmas medley: *Treorchy & Morriston Orpheus/Pontarddulais Choirs* / What child is this (Greensleeves): *Rogers, Jimmy* / Shepherds lay on a lonely hill: *Mitchell, George Minstrels* / We three kings of Orient are: *Beach Boys* / White Christmas: *Martin, Dean* / O come all ye faithful (adeste fidelis): *Cole, Nat 'King'* / I'll be home for Christmas: *Beach Boys* / Silent night: *Paul, Les & Mary Ford* / Holy city: *Locke, Josef* / Christmas alphabet: *Adams, Cliff Singers* / Happy holiday: *Lee, Peggy* / Sleigh ride: *Lynn, Vera & The Mike Sammes Singers* / Firts noel: *Fitzgerald, Ella* / Ding dong merrily on high: *Treorchy & Morriston Orpheus/Pontardduiais Choirs* / Happiest Christmas tree: *Cole, Nat 'King'* / Christmas is for children: *Campbell, Glen* / Silver bells: *Whiting, Margaret & Jimmy Wakely* / Sing we now of Christmas: *Ford, Tennessee Ernie* / Christmas bells: *Mitchell, George Minstrels* / A-wassailing: *Morecambe & Wise*
CD Set _______________ CDTRBOX 240
Trio / Oct '96 / EMI

CHRISTMAS WITH THE STARS, A
CD _______________ MCCDX 008
Music Club / Nov '94 / Disc / THE

CHUNKS
CD _______________ SST 069CD
SST / May '93 / Plastic Head

CHUNKS OF THE CHOCOLATE FACTORY (Best Of Choc's Chewns Vol.1/2CD Set)
CD Set _______________ SUSCD 2
Aura Surround Sounds / Jan '95 / Arabesque / Grapevine/PolyGram / Mo's Music Machine / Pinnacle

CHURCHICAL CHANTS OF THE NYABINGI (Live Field Recordings)
Got to move / Tell them wherever I go / Weeping and moaning / I I I / Fire man / Fire burn / White boy a follower / Keep cool Babylon / Think I never know / Armagiddion
CD ____ **CDHB 20**
Heartbeat / Feb '97 / ADA / Direct / Greensleeves / Jet Star

CHUTNEY CARNIVAL
CD ____ **JMC 1124**
JMC / May '96 / Jet Star

CIAO ITALIA
Se bastasse una canzone / Il mondo / Grande grande grande / Come vorrei / Amore amore amore mio / Sara perche ti amo / Volare / L'italiano / Che sara / Guarde che luna / Gloria La mia California / Una lacrima sul viso / Sereno E' / Insieme / Vado via / Margherita / A chi
CD ____ **SP 881012**
Disky / Jul '97 / Disky / THE

CICADELIC 60'S VOL.1, THE
CD ____ **COLCD 0515**
Collectables / Jun '97 / Greyhound

CICADELIC 60'S VOL.2, THE
CD ____ **COLCD 0525**
Collectables / Jun '97 / Greyhound

CICADELIC 60'S VOL.3, THE
CD ____ **COLCD 0543**
Collectables / Jun '97 / Greyhound

CICADELIC 60'S VOL.4, THE
CD ____ **COLCD 0544**
Collectables / Jun '97 / Greyhound

CICADELIC 60'S VOL.5, THE
CD ____ **COLCD 0574**
Collectables / Jun '97 / Greyhound

CIELITO LINDO
CD ____ **CD 62021**
Saludos Amigos / Jan '93 / Target/BMG

CINCOS ANOS
CD ____ **TR 38CD**
Trance / Oct '95 / SRD

CINEMA ORGAN
Savoy hunting medley / Wedegwood blue / Mexican hat dance / Sleighride / Smoke gets in your eyes / Diane you're just in love / Royal command / Festival in Valencia / When I fall in love / Hunagry / Bluebell polka / Swingin' sleigh bells / Nola / Kitten on the keys / Always / Windows of Paris / Punch and Judy polka
CD ____ **EMPRCD 560**
Emporio / Mar '95 / Disc

CINEMA ORGAN VOL.1
CD ____ **PASTCD 9722**
Flapper / Jul '91 / Pinnacle

CINEMA ORGAN VOL.2
CD ____ **PASTCD 7052**
Flapper / Oct '94 / Pinnacle

CIRCLE DANCE (Hokey Pokey Charity Compilation)
CD ____ **CONED 1**
Hokey Pokey / Oct '90 / ADA / Direct

CITY LIMITS
CD ____ **TMPMC 016**
Temple / Oct '95 / BMG

CITY SOUL FROM PHILLY
Didn't I blow your mind: *Philly Groove Orchestra* / Have I sinned: *Labelle, Patti & The Bluebells* / La la means I love you: *Philly Groove Orchestra* / Are you ready for me: *Philly Groove Orchestra* / Love freeze: *Philly Groove Orchestra* / Armed and extremely dangerous: *First Choice* / Smarty pants: *First Choice* / Guilty: *First Choice* / This is the house (where love died): *First Choice* / When will I see you again: *Three Degrees* / I'm doing fine now: *Three Degrees* / Dirty ol' man: *Three Degrees* / I'll be around: *Three Degrees* / Seems like I gotta do wrong: *Whispers* / I walked right in: *Labelle, Patti & The Bluebells* / Decatur Street: *Labelle, Patti & The Bluebells*
CD ____ **HADCD 218**
Spotlight On / Jun '97 / Henry Hadaway

CITY SPACE VOL.2
CD ____ **E 3759CD**
Atatak / Nov '93 / SRD

CLAMCHOWDER & ICE
CD ____ **EFA 11374**
Musical Tragedies / Apr '93 / SRD

CLARE TRADITION, THE
CD ____ **GTDHCD 082**
GTD / Jul '93 / ADA / Else

CLARINET MARMALADE
Dizzy debutante: *Bailey, Buster & Rhythm Busters* / Blues in thirds: *Bechet, Sidney Trio* / Barney's concerto: *Bigard, Barney & Duke Ellington* / Dee blues: *Carter, Benny & Chocolate Dandies* / Too tight: *Dodds, Johnny* / Praying the blues: *Dorsey, Jimmy* / My inspiration: *Fazola, Irving & Bob Crosby* / Sweet Georgia Brown: *Goodman, Benny Quartet* / Sheikh of araby: *Hamilton, Jimmy & Teddy Wilson* / Woodsheddin' with Woody: *Herman, Woody* / Climax rag: *Lewis, George & New Orleans Stompers* / Reunion in Harlem: *Marsala, Joe & Delta Four* / Can't we be friends: *Matlock, Matty & Bob Crosby/Bobcats* / Everybody loves my baby: *Mezzrow, Mezz & Mezzrow-Ladnier Quartet* / High society: *Miller, Eddie & Mound City Blues Blowers* / Chinatown, my Chinatown: *Mince, Johnny & Tommy Dorsey/Clambake Seven* / Monday date: *Noone, Jimmie Apex Club Orchestra* / Stratton Street strut: *Polo, Danny & Swing Stars* / She's crying for me blues: *Roppolo, Leon & Original New Orleans Rhythm Kings* / Friars Point Shuffle: *Russell, Pee-Wee & Eddie Condon/Chicagoans* / Summit Ridge Drive: *Shaw, Artie & His Gramercy Five* / Clarinet marmalade: *Shields, Larry* / Beau Koo Jack: *Simeon, Omer* / (Back home again in) Indiana: *Teschemacher, Frank & Eddie Condon* / Pagin' the devil: *Young, Lester & The Kansas City Six*
CD ____ **CDAJA 5132**
Living Era / May '94 / Select

CLASH OF THE IRIES
CD ____ **VPCD 1235**
VP / Jul '92 / Greensleeves / Jet Star / Total/BMG

CLASH OF THE TITANS (The Reggae Giants Meet)
Holy Mount Zion: *McGregor, Freddie* / Show us the way: *Brown, Dennis* / Take my breath away: *Paul, Frankie* / Rock on: *Isaacs, Gregory* / Better days: *Heptones* / Sister Maggie Brest: *I-Roy* / Dice cup: *Don Carlos* / Brandy: *McGregor, Freddie* / He can't spell: *Brown, Dennis* / Lay your head: *Paul, Frankie* / Bad da: *Isaacs, Gregory* / Land of love: *Heptones* / Dub and come: *I-Roy* / Open up the gates: *Brown, Dennis* / On a Sunday night: *Don Carlos* / No war in the ghetto: *McGregor, Freddie* / Concentration: *Brown, Dennis* / How I care for you: *Paul, Frankie*
CD ____ **CDGR 115**
Charly / Jan '97 / Koch

CLASS & RENDEZVOUS STORY, THE
Rockin' Robin: *Day, Bobby* / Nut rocker: *B-Bumble & The Stingers* / Miami: *Church, Eugene* / In the mood: *Fields, Ernie Orchestra* / Little bitty pretty one: *Day, Bobby & The Satellites* / Hey girl, hey boy: *McLollie, Oscar & Jeanette Baker* / Bear: *Watson, Johnny 'Guitar'* / That's my desire: *Bob & Earl* / Pretty girls everywhere: *Church, Eugene & the Fellows* / Texas twister: *Fields, Ernie Orchestra* / I'm confessin' that I love you: *Belvin, Jesse* / Bluebird, the buzzard and the oriole: *Day, Bobby* / No time: *Titans* / Ez: *Rene, Googie* / You made a boo boo: *Bob & Earl* / One more kiss: *Watson, Johnny 'Guitar'* / Wow wow baby: *Searchers* / Good news: *Church, Eugene* / Alley oop: *Dynasores* / Let me know, let me know: *McLollie, Oscar & Jeanette Baker* / Mama Julie: *Terry & Gerry* / I ain't goin' for that: *Church, Eugene* / Chattanooga choo choo: *Fields, Ernie Orchestra* / Over and over: *Day, Bobby*
CD ____ **CDCHD 461**
Ace / Jun '93 / Pinnacle

CLASSIC 80'S GROOVE MASTERCUTS VOL.1
Do it to the music: *Raw Silk* / So fine: *Johnson, Howard* / After the dance is through: *Krystol* / (I'll be a) freak for you: *Royalle Delite* / Main thing: *Shot* / You used to hold me so tight: *Houston, Thelma* / Fool's paradise: *Morgan, Meli'sa* / Who do you love: *Wright, Bernard* / Hangin' on a string: *Loose Ends* / Change of heart: *Change* / Settle down: *Thomas, Lillo* / Encore: *Lynn, Cheryl*
CD ____ **CUTSCD 15**
Beechwood / Nov '93 / Beechwood/BMG / Pinnacle

CLASSIC 80'S GROOVE MASTERCUTS VOL.2
I am somebody: *Jones, Glenn* / Serious: *Serious Intention* / She's strange: *Cameo* / You aint' really down: *Status IV* / I'm in love: *Thomas, Lillo* / Twilight: *Maze* / Let's groove: *Earth, Wind & Fire* / I wonder if I take you home: *Lisa Lisa & Cult Jam/Full Force* / Thinking about your love: *Skipworth & Turner* / Stomp: *Brothers Johnson* / Breakin' down: *Julia & Co.* / Act like you know: *Fat Larry's Band*
CD ____ **CUTSCD 26**
Beechwood / Mar '95 / Beechwood/BMG / Pinnacle

CLASSIC 80'S GROOVE MASTERCUTS VOL.3
CD ____ **CUTSCD 36**
Beechwood / Feb '97 / Beechwood/BMG / Pinnacle

CLASSIC ACID MASTERCUTS VOL.1
Poke: *Endless Poker's* / Acid tracks: *Phuture* / I've lost control: *Sleazy D* / Dream girl: *Pierre's Pfantasy Club* / Acid thunder: *Fast Eddie* / Lack of love: *Charles B* / Machines: *Laurent X* / Groove that won't stop: *Saunderson, Kevin* / Acid over: *Tyree* / Fantasy girl: *Pierre's Pfantasy Club* / Land of confusion: *Armando* / Magic feet: *Dunn, Mike*
CD ____ **CUTSCD 32**
Beechwood / Feb '96 / Beechwood/BMG / Pinnacle

CLASSIC BALEARIC MASTERCUTS
Barefoot in the head: *Man Called Adam* / Snappiness: *BBG & Dina Taylor* / La passionara: *Blow Monkeys* / Josephine: *Rea, Chris* / Talking with myself: *Electribe 101* / Flotation: *Grid* / Wax the van: *Lola* / Spiritual high: *Moodswings* / Cascades: *Sheer Taft* / Sueno latino: *Sueno Latino* / Primavera: *Tullio De Piscopo* / Hoomba hoomba: *Voice Of Africa*
CD ____ **CUTSCD 34**
Beechwood / Jun '96 / Beechwood/BMG / Pinnacle

CLASSIC BANDS OF THE THIRTIES
Song of India: *Dorsey, Tommy Orchestra* / South Rampart street parade: *Crosby, Bob & His Orchestra* / Begin the beguine: *Shaw, Artie Orchestra* / I let a song go out of my heart: *Ellington, Duke Orchestra* / One o'clock jump: *Goodman, Benny Orchestra* / Sunrise serenade: *Kemp, Hal Orchestra* / At the woodchoppers' ball: *Herman, Woody & His Orchestra* / It's only a paper moon: *Whiteman, Paul & His Orchestra* / Stop, look and listen: *Dorsey Brothers Orchestra* / Minnie the moocher: *Calloway, Cab Orchestra* / My prayer: *Dorsey, Jimmy Orchestra* / Don't be that way: *Wilson, Teddy & His Orchestra* / All God's chillun got rhythm: *Berigan, Bunny & His Orchestra* / In the mood: *Miller, Glenn Orchestra* / St. Louis blues: *Lombardo, Guy & His Royal Canadians* / Jumpin' at the woodside: *Basie, Count Orchestra*
CD ____ **HADCD 160**
Javelin / May '94 / Henry Hadaway / THE

CLASSIC BIG BAND JAZZ
CD ____ **AVC 540**
Avid / May '94 / Avid/BMG / Koch / THE

CLASSIC BLUES (3CD Set)
Boom boom: *Hooker, John Lee* / Blues is my middle name: *Charles, Ray* / You step out of my dream: *Vaughan, Sarah* / Please come back to me: *Burke, Solomon* / Poor boy: *Howlin' Wolf* / How blue can you get: *King, B.B.* / Goodnight Irene: *Leadbelly* / Don't let the sun catch you cryin': *Big Maybelle* / They call it stormy Monday: *Turner, 'Big' Joe* / Why won't my baby treat me right: *Walker, T-Bone* / Limehouse blues: *Mills Brothers* / My man: *Holiday, Billie* / Baby, won't you please come home: *Hines, Earl 'Fatha'* / Jelly Roll blues: *Morton, Jelly Roll* / It's hard to believe you: *Rush, Otis & Little Walter* / Don't want no big fat woman: *Williams, Big Joe* / Good morning little schoolgirl: *Chicago Breakdown* / Every day I have the blues: *King, B.B.* / I'll never fall in love again: *Brown, Ruth* / Old piano plays the blues: *Cole, Nat 'King'* / I wonder what my baby's doing tonight: *Big Maybelle* / There's good rockin' tonight: *Hopkins, Lightnin'* / These four walls: *Thomas, Irma* / I'm going home: *Diddley, Bo* / Billie's blues: *Holiday, Billie* / Birmingham blues: *Hooker, John Lee* / Nothing can stop me: *Houston, Cissy* / It may be the last time: *Rush, Otis & Little Walter* / GI blues: *Lightnin' Slim* / Love for sale: *Brown, Roy* / How long blues: *Turner, 'Big' Joe* / Wang dang doodle: *Howlin' Wolf* / I put a spell on you: *Hawkins, Screamin' Jay* / I'm so glad I'm in love again: *Houston, Cissy* / When the saints go marching in: *Hines, Earl 'Fatha'* / Lover come back to me: *Holiday, Billie* / I guess I'm a fool: *Memphis Slim* / Hey Bo Diddley: *Diddley, Bo* / Let the four winds blow: *Brown, Roy* / When the sun goes down: *Turner, 'Big' Joe* / Crackin' up: *Diddley, Bo* / BB Boogie: *King, B.B.* / I'd rather go blind: *James, Etta* / Crazy 'bout you baby: *Lightnin' Slim* / If loving you is wrong: *Mason, Barbara* / Red rooster: *Howlin' Wolf* / I need you so bad: *Cotton, James* / Goodnight sweetheart, goodnight: *Spaniels*
CD Set ____ **100912**
CMC / May '97 / BMG

CLASSIC BLUESMEN (3CD Set)
Rocks in my bed: *Turner, 'Big' Joe* / Midnight hour blues: *Carr, Leroy* / I ain't gonna be worried no more: *Estes, 'Sleepy' John* / She's coming back some cold rainy day: *Barbeque Bob* / You can't get that stuff no more: *Tampa Red* / Bull cow blues: *Broonzy, 'Big' Bill* / Pine bluff Arkansas: *White, Bukka* / Gamblin' man blues: *Dupree, 'Champion' Jack* / It's your time now: *Broonzy, 'Big' Bill* / Phonograph blues: *Johnson, Robert* / Broke down engine: *McTell, 'Blind' Willie* / Blue disco blues: *Williamson, Sonny Boy* / I know his blood can make me whole: *Johnson, 'Blind' Willie* / Baby you gotta change your mind: *Fuller, 'Blind' Boy* / Good morning blues: *Leadbelly* / Preaching blues (up jumped the devil): *Johnson, Robert* / Gonna follow my baby: *Crudup, Arthur 'Big Boy'* / Mr.Johnson's swimg: *Johnson, Lonnie* / Picking my tomatoes: *McGhee, Brownie* / 15 cents a day: *Sykes, Roosevelt* / Jivin' the jive: *Sykes, Roosevelt* / CC rider: *Leadbelly* / Keys to the highway: *Broonzy, 'Big' Bill* / Black train blues: *White, Bukka* / I'll believe I'll dust my broom: *Broonzy, 'Big' Bill* / Mean mistreater mama: *Carr, Leroy* / Four hands are better than two: *Johnson, Lonnie* / Denver blues: *Tampa Red* / I can't be satisfied: *Broonzy, 'Big' Bill* / Motherless child blues: *Barbeque Bob* / Death valley blues: *Crudup, Arthur 'Big Boy'* / Georgia rag: *McTell, 'Blind' Willie* / Dark was the night: *McTell, 'Blind' Willie* / My brownskin sugarplum: *Fuller, 'Blind' Boy* / Walking blues: *Johnson, Robert* / Sun risin' blues: *Turner, 'Big' Joe* / Warehouse man blues: *Dupree, 'Champion' Jack* / Get the bottle up and go: *Williamson, Sonny Boy* / Born for bad luck: *McGhee, Brownie* / Little Laura blues: *Estes, 'Sleepy' John* / I'm a rattlesnakin' Daddy: *Fuller, 'Blind' Boy* / Worryin' you off your mind: *Broonzy, 'Big' Bill* / If I had my way I'd tear the building down: *Johnson, 'Blind' Willie* / Working man blues: *Estes, 'Sleepy' John* / Good woman blues: *Carr, Leroy* / You know I got a reason: *Broonzy, 'Big' Bill* / When you got a friend: *Johnson, Robert* / Rebecca: *Turner, 'Big' Joe* / I'm calling Daisy: *McGhee, Brownie* / Chain gang blues: *Dupree, 'Champion' Jack* / Sugar mama blues: *Williamson, Sonny Boy* / Western bound blues: *Tampa Red* / Stomp down rider: *McTell, 'Blind' Willie* / Keep your lamp trimmed and burning: *Johnson, 'Blind' Willie* / California blues: *Barbeque Bob* / Mean old bedbug blues: *Johnson, Lonnie* / Strange place blues: *White, Bukka* / Trouble and whiskey: *Sykes, Roosevelt* / Mean old Frisco blues: *Crudup, Arthur 'Big Boy'* / Rock Island line: *Leadbelly*
CD Set ____ **390042**
Hallmark / Jul '96 / Carlton

CLASSIC CEILI BANDS
CD ____ **MACCD 203**
Autograph / Aug '96 / BMG

CLASSIC CHRISTMAS, A
CD ____ **DCD 5311**
Disky / Dec '93 / Disky / THE

CLASSIC CLUB COLLECTIVE (A Classic Collection Of Club Anthems)
Got to have your love: *Mantronix* / Let the beat hit 'em: *Lisa Lisa & Cult Jam* / Optimistic: *Sounds Of Blackness* / Love under moonlight: *Graham, Jaki* / Twilight: *Maze & Frankie Beverly* / Secret rendezvous: *Rene & Angela* / Laughin' at you: *Dazz Band* / Come into my life: *Sims, Joyce* / Got to be real: *Lynn, Cheryl* / Sleep talk: *Williams, Alyson* / You and me tonight: *Aurra* / Good lovin': *Belle, Regina* / Heaven: *Chimes* / Can't stop: *After 7*
CD ____ **CDUBC 01**
Debut / Jan '94 / 3mv/Sony / Pinnacle

CLASSIC COUNTRY
CD ____ **9548330072**
WEA / Nov '95 / Warner Music

CLASSIC COUNTRY
CD ____ **MACCD 289**
Autograph / Aug '96 / BMG

CLASSIC COUNTRY (4 In The Morning/ Heartbreak USA/Fall To Pieces/3CD Set)
It wasn't God who made Honky Tonk Angels: *Wells, Kitty* / Ruby don't take your love to town: *Rogers, Kenny* / Baby on my mind: *Spears, Billie Jo* / Rose garden: *Anderson, Lynn* / Harper Valley: *Riley, Jeannie C.* / No tomorrow in sight: *Nelson, Willie* / Jackson: *Lewis, Jerry Lee & Linda Gail Lewis* / Big town: *Twitty, Conway* / Lonely women make good lovers: *Luman, Bob* / Music City USA: *Bare, Bobby* / Wild side of life: *Thompson, Hank* / Rhinestone cowboy: *Campbell, Glen* / Satisfied mind: *Wagoner, Porter* / Rock Island line: *Cash, Johnny* / King of the road: *Miller, Roger* / Big bad John: *Dean, Jimmy* / Take me home: *Boxcar Willie* / Four in the morning: *Young, Faron* / Heartbreak USA: *Wells, Kitty* / Please release me: *Parton, Dolly* / Let's think about living: *Luman, Bob* / Me and Bobby McGhee: *Rogers, Kenny* / Race is on: *Jones, George* / Dang me: *Miller, Roger* / Indiana wants me: *Taylor, R. Dean* / Tom Dooley: *Kingston Trio* / El paso: *Robbins, Marty* / Settin' the woods on fire: *Williams, Hank* / Sally was a good old girl: *Jennings, Waylon* / Thanks a lot: *Tubb, Ernest & Loretta Lynn* / These boots are made for walking: *Hazelwood, Lee* / Next in line: *Cash, Johnny* / Truck drivin' outlaw: *Olsen, Denis* / Rose Marie: *Whitman, Slim* / North to Alaska: *Horton, Johnny* / Oh lonesome me: *Gibson, Don* / Walkin' after midnight: *Cline, Patsy* / He'll have to go: *Reeves, Jim* / Crystal chandeliers: *Pride, Charley* / White lightning: *Jennings, Waylon* / Take this job and shove it: *Paycheck, Johnny* / Cold cold heart: *Jones, George* / Stranger in my arms: *Cline, Patsy* / Kiss an angel good morning: *Pride, Charley* / I fall to pieces: *Jackson, Wanda* / Have I told you lately that I love you: *Reeves, Jim* / Please help me I'm falling: *Locklin, Hank* / I'm the only hell Mama ever raised: *Paycheck, Johnny* / Love of the common people: *Jennings, Waylon* / Night life: *Nelson, Willie* / Church, a courtroom, then goodbye: *Cline, Patsy* / Help me make it through the night: *Pride, Charley*
CD Set ____ **55161**
Music / Oct '96 / Target/BMG

CLASSIC COUNTRY
He'll have to go / Is anybody going to San Antone / Jolene / Ruby don't take your love to town / Funny how time slips away / Delta dawn / 500 miles away from home / I can't stop loving you / Put it off until tomorrow / Mr. Bojangles / Early morning rain / Son of Hickory Holler's tramp / I know one / Green green grass of home / Honky tonk blues / Abilene / Pure love / Two doors down / I'm movin' on / Send me the pillow you dream on / Make the world go away / My last date
CD ____ **74321378352**
Camden / Apr '97 / BMG

CLASSIC COUNTRY COLLECTION, THE (2CD Set)
High powered love: *Harris, Emmylou* / Atlantic city: *Band* / Margaritaville: *Buffett, Jimmy* / Everybody's talkin': *Nilsson* / From

a distance: *Griffith, Nanci* / Southern nights: *Campbell, Glen* / Moon is over her shoulder: *Johnson, Michael* / Crescent city: *Harris, Emmylou* / I'll never fall in love again: *Gentry, Bobbie* / Okie from muskogee: *Haggard, Merle* / Is anybody going to San Antone: *Daniels, Charlie* / Honky tonk blues: *Pride, Charley* / Early morning rain: *Hamilton, George IV* / Foggy mountain breakdown: *Hall, Tom T.* / Cry me a river: *Gayle, Crystal* / It ain't me baby: *Cash, Johnny & June Carter* / Night life: *Nelson, Willie* / Ode to Billie Joe: *Gentry, Bobbie* / I got stripes: *Cash, Johnny* / I will always love you: *Parton, Dolly* / You're my best friend: *Williams, Don* / Good hearted woman: *Jennings, Waylon & Willie Nelson* / Jambalaya: *Jackson, Wanda* / By the time I get to Phoenix: *Campbell, Glen* / Mr. Bojangles: *Hall, Tom T.* / Storms never last: *Jennings, Waylon* / Delta dawn: *Tucker, Tanya* / Amanda: *Jennings, Waylon* / Coat of many colours: *Parton, Dolly* / Queen of the silver dollar: *Dave & Sugar* / Crazy: *Cline, Patsy* / My heart: *Milsap, Ronnie* / My elusive dreams: *Rich, Charlie* / I can't stop loving you: *Reeves, Jim*
CD Set ______ **RCACD 217**
RCA / Jul '97 / BMG

CLASSIC CROONERS
Anything goes: *Bennett, Tony* / Granada: *Laine, Frankie* / Love letters: *Como, Perry* / Blue skies: *Haymes, Dick* / So many ways: *Benton, Brook* / Hello Dolly: *Armstrong, Louis* / Come fly with me: *Sinatra, Frank* / My heart is taking lessons: *Crosby, Bing* / Mona Lisa: *Cole, Nat 'King'* / Cry: *Ray, Johnnie* / Life is a song: *Bennett, Tony* / Woman in love: *Laine, Frankie* / Song of songs: *Como, Perry* / Night and day: *Haymes, Dick* / Kiddio: *Benton, Brook* / Cabaret: *Armstrong, Louis* / East side of heaven: *Crosby, Bing* / Hernando's hideaway: *Ray, Johnnie* / Unforgettable: *Cole, Nat 'King'* / I've got you under my skin: *Sinatra, Frank*
CD ______ **MUCD 9012**
Musketeer / Apr '95 / Disc

CLASSIC DANCE COLLECTION VOL.1, THE (Ain't No Getting Over You)
Ain't no getting over you: *Roel, Charlotte* / Groovin': *Out Of Mind* / 24 days: *Run 4 Fun* / Love me or leave me: *Marian* / Give me your love: *Factual Beat* / Night fever: *New Suit* / On Broadway: *Dance Society* / Paradise: *Out Of Mind* / I swear: *Lulu & The Luvvers* / Every beat of my heart: *Marian* / I shot the sheriff: *Marian* / What's love got to do with it: *Buttercups* / All I wanna do: *Factual Beat* / Hands up: *Q-Generation* / Someday we'll be together: *Jackson, Latoya* / Grease: *Hairstyle 55*
CD ______ **101002**
CMC / May '97 / BMG

CLASSIC DANCE COLLECTION VOL.2, THE (You & Me Together)
If lovin' you is wrong: *Marian* / Sugar sugar: *Kissin' Cousins* / I keep gettin' higher: *Corinne* / Stop in the name of love: *Jackson, Latoya* / I believe: *Factual Beat* / Fly away: *Toolex* / Fame: *Celebrity* / Please don't talk to Jessica: *Run 4 Fun* / Kung fu fighting: *Hadiza* / locomotion: *Tax 'n' Tips* / You and me together: *Jampack & Bee* / Destination nowhere: *Out Of Mind* / Celebration: *Global Dance Party* / Groove your soul: *Factual Beat* / Surrender: *Levi Tuesday* / Stumblin' in: *Cash 'n' Carry*
CD ______ **101012**
CMC / May '97 / BMG

CLASSIC DANCE COLLECTION VOL.3, THE (Dancing With Somebody)
Dancing with somebody: *Run 4 Fun* / Summerdream: *Out Of Mind* / Born to be alive: *Street Gang* / Reminds me of you: *Marian* / Farewell my summer love: *Jampack & Bee* / Open your heart: *Toolex* / I was made to love her: *Big Lovers* / Groove your soul: *Factual Beat* / I'm 4 real: *Corinne* / Substitute: *Nouveau Sisters* / Baby love: *Jackson, Latoya* / Ma Baker: *Black On White* / Take me (beyond reality): *Simon* / Wild thing: *Hadiza* / He ain't heavy (he's my brother): *Gray & Co.* / Why: *Little C*
CD ______ **101022**
CMC / May '97 / BMG

CLASSIC DANCE COLLECTION, THE (3CD Set)
Ain't no getting over you: *Roel, Charlotte* / Groovin': *Out Of Mind* / 24 days: *Run 4 Fun* / Love me or leave me: *Marian* / Give me your love: *Factual Beat* / Night fever: *New Suit* / On Broadway: *Dance Society* / Paradise: *Out Of Mind* / I swear: *Lulu & The Luvvers* / Every beat of my heart: *Marian* / I shot the sherriff: *Hadiza* / What's love got to do with it: *Buttercups* / All I wanna do: *Factual Beat* / Hands up: *Q-Generation* / Someday we'll be together: *Jackson, Latoya* / Grease: *Hairstyle 55* / If lovin' you is wrong: *Marian* / Sugar sugar: *Kissin' Cousins* / I keep gettin' higher: *Corinne* / Stop in the name of love: *Jackson, Latoya* / I believe: *Factual Beat* / Fly away: *Toolex* / Fame: *Celebrity* / Please don't talk to Jessica: *Run 4 Fun* / Kung fu fighting: *Hadiza* / Locomotion: *Tax 'n' Tips* / You and me together: *Jampack & Bee* / Destination nowhere: *Out Of Mind* / Celebration: *Global Dance Party* / Groove your soul: *Factual Beat* / Surrender: *Tuesday, Levi* / Stumblin' in: *Cash 'n' Carry* / Dancing with somebody: *Run 4 Fun* / Summerdream: *Out Of Mind* / Born to be alive: *Street Gang* / Reminds me of you: *Marian* / Farewell my summer love: *Jampack & Bee* / Open your heart: *Toolex* / I was made to love her: *Big Lovers* / Groove your soul: *Factual Beat* / I'm 4 real: *Corinne* / Substitute: *Nouveau Sisters* / Baby love: *Jackson, Latoya* / Ma Baker: *Black On White* / Take me (beyond reality): *Simon* / Wild thing: *Hadiza* / He ain't heavy (he's my brother): *Gray & Co.* / Why: *Little C*
CD Set ______ **100992**
CMC / May '97 / BMG

CLASSIC DEEP HOUSE VOL.2
CD ______ **GR 101014**
Gravity / Dec '96 / Shellshock/Disc

CLASSIC DISCO MASTERCUTS VOL.1
Vertigo/Relight my fire: *Hartman, Dan* / Can't live without your love: *Jones, Tamiko* / I need you: *Sylvester* / This time baby: *Moore, Jackie* / Disco nights: *GQ* / Sure shot: *Weber, Tracy* / Body music: *Strikers* / Delirium: *McGee, Francine* / Casanova: *Coffee* / Shame: *King, Evelyn 'Champagne'* / Do what you wanna do: *T-Connection* / I hear music in the street: *Unlimited Touch*
CD ______ **CUTSCD 25**
Beechwood / Feb '95 / Beechwood/BMG / Pinnacle

CLASSIC DOO WOP
You promise me love: *Lewis, Earl & The Channels* / Come back to me: *Sylvia, Margo & The Tune Weavers* / Sweetest one: *Joel & The Dymensions* / At the altar: *Staton, Johnny & The Feathers* / Miracle moment of love: *West, Rudy & The Five Keys* / My angel lover: *Cox, Herb & The Cleftones* / Heaven and Cindy: *Five Boroughs & Brian Daly* / Wherever you are: *Blandon, Richard & The Dubs* / One little teardrop: *Grant, George & The Castelles* / Heaven's for real / Alice from above: *Peels, Leon & The Bluejays* / Whispering bells: *Joel & The Dymensions* / I've tried: *Sylvia, Margo & The Tune Weavers* / Play a love song: *Jaguars* / You lost the game of love: *Cox, Herb & The Cleftones* / One too many lies: *Five Boroughs & Siobhan Daly* / That's the way it goes: *Joel & The Dymensions* / Why can't you: *Wrens* / Surrender to love: *Grant, George & The Castelles* / Moonlight: *Maye, Arthur Lee* / Our love: *Julian, Don & The Meadowlarks* / Accept me for what I am: *Green, Vernon & the Medallions* / My junaita: *Joel & The Dymensions* / This time: *Blandon, Richard & The Dubs*
CD ______ **CDCHD 417**
Ace / Sep '92 / Pinnacle

CLASSIC EASY (Instrumental/The Very Best Of Easy Listening)
Strangers in the light: *Freeman, Stan* / Moon river: *Starlight Strings* / This guy's in love with you: *Goodwin, Ron & His Orchestra* / Bright eyes: *Manuel* / String of pearls: *Loss, Joe Orchestra* / Continental: *Love, Geoff & His Orchestra* / What the world needs now is love: *Goodwin, Ron & His Orchestra* / Theme from 'A Man And A Woman': *Love, Geoff & His Orchestra* / Rodrigo's guitar concerto de aranjeuz: *Manuel* / Walk in the black forest: *Love, Geoff & His Orchestra* / Say it with music: *Payne, Jack* / Unforgettable: *Starlight Strings* / Goodnight: *Loss, Joe Orchestra* / Can't take my eyes off you: *Henriques, Basil & The Wakiki Islanders* / Blarney's stoned: *Hawkshaw, Alan* / Music to drive by: *Loss, Joe Concertium* / Countdown: *Fahey, Brian* / Sucu sucu: *Jaramillo, Pepe* / Wheels: *Loss, Joe Orchestra* / At the sign of the swinging cymbal: *Fahey, Brian*
CD ______ **CDMFP 6257**
Music For Pleasure / Nov '96 / EMI

CLASSIC EASY (Vocal/The Very Best Of Easy Listening)
Unforgettable: *Cole, Nat 'King'* / True love: *Crosby, Bing & Grace Kelly* / Magic moments: *Hilton, Ronnie* / Folk who live on the hill: *Lee, Peggy* / Spanish eyes: *Martino, Al* / Memories are made of this: *Martin, Dean* / Where do I begin (love story): *Bassey, Shirley* / Why do fools fall in love: *Cogan, Alma* / It might as well rain until September: *King, Carole* / Galveston: *Campbell, Glen* / Edelweiss: *Hill, Vince* / Cry me a river: *London, Julie* / From Russia with love: *Monro, Matt* / Don't make my brown eyes blue: *Gayle, Crystal* / I don't know how to love him: *Reddy, Helen* / Very thought of you: *Wilson, Nancy* / When I fall in love: *Cole, Nat 'King'* / Nightingale sang in Beverley Square: *Darin, Bobby* / Vincent: *McLean, Don* / Carnival is over: *Seekers*
CD ______ **CDMFP 6258**
Music For Pleasure / Nov '96 / EMI

CLASSIC ELECTRO MASTERCUTS VOL.1
Walking on sunshine: *Rockers Revenge & Donnie Calvin* / Don't make me wait: *Peech Boys* / White lines (don't don't do it): *Grandmaster Flash & Melle Mel* / Hip hop be bop (Don't stop): *Man Parrish* / Rockit: *Hancock, Herbie* / Smurf: *Brunson, Tyrone* / In the bottle: *COD* / London bridge is falling down: *Newtrament* / Al-Naafiysh (The soul): *Hashim* / Magic's wand: *Whodini* / Wildstyle: *Time Zone* / Adventures of Grandmaster Flash on the wheels of steel: *Grandmaster Flash & The Furious Five*
CD ______ **CUTSCD 19**
Beechwood / May '94 / Beechwood/BMG / Pinnacle

CLASSIC EURO DANCE HITS
CD ______ **NTRCD 072**
Nectar / Feb '97 / Pinnacle

CLASSIC FUNK
CD ______ **MCCD 200**
Music Club / May '95 / Disc / THE

CLASSIC FUNK MASTERCUTS VOL.1
Who is he and what is he to you: *Creative Source* / Wicky wacky: *Fatback Band* / Gimme some more: *JB's* / For the love of money: *O'Jays* / Fire: *Ohio Players* / Pusherman: *Mayfield, Curtis* / Blow your head: *Wesley, Fred & The J.B.'s* / Fencewalk: *Mandrill* / Pick up the pieces: *Average White Band* / Rock creek park: *Blackbyrds* / NT Pts 1 and 2: *Kool & The Gang* / Stone to the bone: *Brown, James*
CD ______ **CUTSCD 6**
Beechwood / May '92 / Beechwood/BMG / Pinnacle

CLASSIC FUNK MASTERCUTS VOL.2
Movin': *Brass Construction* / Express yourself Pt.1: *Wright, Charles & The Watts 103rd St. Rhythm Band* / You can have your Watergate: *JB's* / It's alright now: *Harris, Eddie* / Funky stuff/More funky stuff: *Kool & The Gang* / Keep on steppin': *Fatback Band* / Jive turkey: *Ohio Express* / Ghetto: *Hathaway, Donny* / Baby let me take you (in my arms): *Detroit Emeralds* / Boss: *Brown, James* / Do it fluid: *Blackbyrds* / Stomp and buck dance: *Crusaders*
CD ______ **CUTSCD 14**
Beechwood / Sep '93 / Beechwood/BMG / Pinnacle

CLASSIC FUNK MASTERCUTS VOL.3
Just kissed my baby: *Meters* / Goin' to see my baby: *Fatback Band* / Turn off the light: *Young, Larry* / Hands of time: *Perfect Circle* / Let a man come in and do the popcorn: *Brown, James* / (I've got) So much trouble in my mind: *Quarterman, Sir Joe & Free Soul* / Sideway shuffle: *Lewis, Linda* / Miss Fatback: *Philips, Saundra* / This is it: *Davis, Betty* / Stop the rain: *Average White Band* / Can you get it: *Mandrill* / Who's in town: *Nature Boys*
CD ______ **CUTSCD 24**
Beechwood / Jan '95 / Beechwood/BMG / Pinnacle

CLASSIC G-FUNK MASTERCUTS VOL.1
Alwayz into somethin': *NWA* / Indo smoke: *Mista Grimm* / Keep their heads ringin': *Dr. Dre* / Regulate: *Warren G & Nate Dogg* / Dirty B side: *Da Brat & Notorious BIG* / Black superman: *Above The Law* / Gangsta's boogie: *LV* / Summer breeze: *DJ Quik* / Hand of the dead body: *Scarface & Ice Cube* / Guerilla funk: *Paris* / Ghetto jam: *Domino* / 12 pacofdoja: *Lil' Half Dead*
CD ______ **CUTSCD 39**
Beechwood / Jul '97 / Beechwood/BMG / Pinnacle

CLASSIC HIGHLIFE
CD ______ **AIM 1053**
Aim / Oct '95 / ADA / Direct / Jazz Music

CLASSIC HIP HOP MASTERCUTS VOL.1
My philosophy: *Boogie Down Productions* / It's my beat: *Sweet Tee & Jazzy Joyce* / Peter Piper: *Run DMC* / Strong island: *JVCFORCE* / Eric B for president: *Eric B & Rakim* / Have a nice day: *Shante, Roxanne* / Serious: *Steady B* / Jimbrowski: *Jungle Brothers* / Description of a fool: *Tribe Called Quest* / Talkin' all that jazz: *Stetsasonic* / King of the beats: *Mantronix*
CD ______ **CUTSCD 29**
Beechwood / Jul '95 / Beechwood/BMG / Pinnacle

CLASSIC HIP HOP MASTERCUTS VOL.2
It's yours: *TLA Rock & Jazzy Jay* / Chorus line part 1: *Ultramagnetic MC's* / It's a new style: *Beastie Boys* / Humpty dance: *Digital Underground* / Buddy: *De La Soul* / Rebel without a pause: *Public Enemy* / Paper thin: *MC Lyte* / Wrath of Kane: *Big Daddy Kane* / Peace is not the word to play: *Main Source* / Letter to the better: *Master Ace* / Uptown: *Dope On Plastic* / Choice is yours: *Black Sheep*
CD ______ **CUTSCD 35**
Beechwood / Sep '96 / Beechwood/BMG / Pinnacle

CLASSIC HOUSE MASTERCUTS VOL.1
Someday: *Rogers, Cece* / Tears: *Knuckles, Frankie* / Let the music (use you): *Night Writers* / Give it to me: *Bam Bam* / Big fun: *Inner City* / You used to hold me: *Rosario, Ralphi* / Baby wants to ride: *Principle, Jamie* / Break 4 love: *Raze* / Voodoo Ray: *Guy Called Gerald* / Devotion: *Ten City* / It's alright: *Sterling Void* / Promised land: *Smooth, Joe*
CD ______ **CUTSCD 20**
Beechwood / Jun '94 / Beechwood/BMG / Pinnacle

CLASSIC HOUSE MASTERCUTS VOL.2
Music is the key: *Silk, J.M.* / Strings of life: *Rythim Is Rythim* / Open our eyes: *Jefferson, Marshall* / I'm in love: *Sha-Lor* / Love will find a way: *Romeo, Victor* / Morning after: *Fallout* / Let's get busy: *McClaine, Curtis & On The House* / Make my body rock: *Jomanda* / Take some time out: *Jarvis, Arnold* / If you should need a friend: *Blaze* / Definition of a track: *Back Room* / Musical freedom: *Simpson, Paul*
CD ______ **CUTSCD 22**
Beechwood / Oct '94 / Beechwood/BMG / Pinnacle

CLASSIC HOUSE MASTERCUTS VOL.3
Ma foom bey: *Cultural Vibe* / Give me back the love: *On The House* / Can U dance: *Jason, Kenny 'Jammin' & Fast Eddie* / Night moves: *Rickster* / Forever together: *Raven Maize* / String free: *Phortune* / Can you party: *Royal House* / Who's gonna ease the pressure: *Thornhill, Mac* / Sound: *Reese & Santonio* / Release your party: *Bang The Party* / Can you feel it: *Mr. Fingers*
CD ______ **CUTSCD 28**
Beechwood / Jun '95 / Beechwood/BMG / Pinnacle

CLASSIC JAZZ PIANO (1927-1957)
Mr. Jelly Lord: *Morton, Jelly Roll* / Glad rag doll: *Hines, Earl 'Fatha'* / State Street special: *Yancey, Jimmy* / Honky tonk train blues: *Lewis, Meade 'Lux'* / Thou swell: *Johnson, James P.* / Rompin': *Johnson, James P.* / Smashing thirds: *Waller, Fats* / Contrary motions: *Smith, Willie 'The Lion'* / Out of nowhere: *Tatum, Art* / Where or when: *Wilson, Teddy* / Daybreak serenade: *Stacy, Jess* / Rosetta: *Hines, Earl 'Fatha'* / Honeysuckle rose: *Waller, Fats* / Solitude: *Ellington, Duke* / Tonk: *Ellington, Duke & Billy Strayhorn* / Shine on harvest moon: *Basie, Count* / All God's chillun got rhythm: *Williams, Mary Lou* / Erroll's bounce: *Garner, Erroll* / Poor butterfly: *Peterson, Oscar* / I don't stand a ghost of a chance with you: *Tristano, Lennie* / Shaw 'nuff: *Powell, Bud* / Concerto for Billy the Kid: *Evans, Bill*
CD ______ **ND 86754**
Bluebird / Apr '89 / BMG

CLASSIC JAZZ-FUNK MASTERCUTS VOL.1
Expansions: *Smith, Lonnie Liston* / Always there: *Laws, Ronnie* / Bottle: *Scott-Heron, Gil* / Change (makes you want to hustle): *Byrd, Donald* / Inherit the wind: *Felder, Wilton* / Shaker song: *Spyro Gyra* / Jazz carnival: *Azymuth* / Los conquistadores chocolates: *Smith, Johnny 'Hammond'* / Say you will: *Henderson, Eddie* / Brasilia: *Klemmer, John* / Till you take my love: *Mason, Harvey* / Unicorn: *Gillespie, Dizzy*
CD ______ **CUTSCD 2**
Beechwood / Sep '91 / Beechwood/BMG / Pinnacle

CLASSIC JAZZ-FUNK MASTERCUTS VOL.2
Could heaven ever be like this: *Muhammad, Idris* / Brazilian love affair: *Duke, George* / Easy: *Jarreau, Al* / Dominoes: *Byrd, Donald* / To prove my love: *Doheny, Ned* / Snowblower: *Baker, B.* / Poo poo la la: *Ayers, Roy* / Come with me: *Maria, Tania* / Rotation: *Alpert, Herb* / Chicago song: *Sanborn, David* / New killer Joe: *Golson, Benny* / Keep that same old feeling: *Crusaders*
CD ______ **CUTSCD 4**
Beechwood / Nov '91 / Beechwood/BMG / Pinnacle

CLASSIC JAZZ-FUNK MASTERCUTS VOL.3
Feel the real: *Bendeth, David* / Roller jubilee: *Di Meola, Al* / Saturday night: *Hancock, Herbie* / Love has come around: *Byrd, Donald* / Spring high: *Lewis, Ramsey* / Love will bring us back together: *Ayers, Roy* / Westchester lady: *James, Bob* / Summer madness: *Kool & The Gang* / Sun goddess: *Lewis, Ramsey & Earth, Wind & Fire* / Darlin' darlin' baby: *Khan, Steve* / You're a star: *Aquarian Dream* / Best of friends: *White, Lenny*
CD ______ **CUTSCD 7**
Beechwood / Jun '92 / Beechwood/BMG / Pinnacle

CLASSIC JAZZ-FUNK MASTERCUTS VOL.4
Birdland: *Weather Report* / I thought it was you: *Hancock, Herbie* / Can't you see me: *Ayers, Roy* / Dancing in outer space: *Atmosfear* / You got the floor: *Adams, Arthur* / Whistle bump: *Deodato, Eumir* / Real thing: *Mendes, Sergio* / Magic fingers: *Hamilton, Chico* / Strawberry letter 23: *Brothers Johnson* / Chief inspector: *Badarou, Wally* / Funkin' for Jamaica: *Browne, Tom* / Street life: *Crusaders*
CD ______ **CUTSCD 16**
Beechwood / Jan '94 / Beechwood/BMG / Pinnacle

CLASSIC JAZZ-FUNK MASTERCUTS VOL.5
Countdown (Captain Fingers): *Ritenour, Lee* / Grand prix: *Fuse One* / Freeze thaw: *Basia* / Sausalito: *Washington, Grover Jr.* / Intro (The River Niger): *Ayers, Roy* / Dreamin': *Heath Brothers* / Keep smiling: *Szabo, Gabor* / Watching life: *LA Boppers* / Boulevard: *White, Peter* / Let's funk tonight: *Blue Feather* / La Cuna: *Barretto, Ray* / African bird: *OPA*
CD ______ **CUTSCD 23**
Beechwood / Nov '94 / Beechwood/BMG / Pinnacle

CLASSIC JAZZ-FUNK MASTERCUTS VOL.6
Friends and strangers: *Grusin, Dave* / Deja vu: *AB's* / Mi mi Africa: *Yagi, Nobuo* / Nice shot: *Watanabe, Sadao* / Mid Manhattan: *Casiopea* / Antes de mais nada: *Pacific Jam* / Lament: *Honda, Toshiyuki* / From the lonely afternoon: *Mukai, Shigeharu* / Send me your feelings: *Hino, Terumasa* / Music inside you: *Kazu Matsui Project* / Cadillac kid: *Morizono, Katsutoshi* / Trinkets and things: *Kawaski, Ryo*
CD ____ CUTSCD 31
Beechwood / Jan '96 / Beechwood/BMG / Pinnacle

CLASSIC JAZZ-FUNK MASTERCUTS VOL.7
El bobo: *Lewis, Webster* / Valdez in the country: *Hathaway, Donny* / Family: *Laws, Hubert* / Black is the colour: *Longmire, Wilbert* / Deja vu: *Da Costa, Paulino* / Sweet power your embrace: *Mason, James* / Harlem boys: *Rollins, Sonny* / Life is like a samba: *Benoit, David* / Fifty four: *Sea Level* / Tequila mockingbird: *Lewis, Ramsey* / Straight to the bank: *Summers, Bill*
CD ____ CUTSCD 37
Beechwood / Mar '97 / Beechwood/BMG / Pinnacle

CLASSIC LOVE
CD ____ 0630150082
Warner Bros. / May '96 / Warner Music

CLASSIC LOVE DUETS
CD ____ CDMOIR 430
Memoir / Jul '95 / Jazz Music / Target/ BMG

CLASSIC LOVE SONGS PERFORMED ON PAN PIPES
If you leave me now / Killing me softly / Feelings / How deep is your love / Love is all around / When I fall in love / Hello / Endless love / Love changes everything / First man you remember / It must have been love / Eternal flame / I need to be in love / Groovy kind of love / Hopelessly devoted to you
CD ____ SUMCD 4097
Summit / Feb '97 / Sound & Media

CLASSIC MASTERCUTS (The Best Of Classic Mastercuts - 2CD Set)
Boops (here to go): *Sly & Robbie* / Ain't nothin' goin' on but the rent: *Guthrie, Gwen* / Who's zoomin' who: *Franklin, Aretha* / Love comes down: *King, Evelyn* / Big fun: *Gap Band* / Going back to my roots: *Odyssey* / Night to remember: *Shalamar* / Trapped: *Colonel Abrams* / And the beat goes on: *Whispers* / Yah mo b there: *Ingram, James* / I feel for you: *Khan, Chaka* / Never knew love like this before: *Mills, Stephanie* / Jazz carnival: *Azymuth* / Morning dance: *Spyro Gyra* / Groove: *Franklin, Rodney* / Night birds: *Shakatak* / To prove my love: *Doheny, Ned* / Sign of the times: *James, Bob* / Garden party: *Mezzoforte* / Can't you see me: *Ayers, Roy* / Pick up the pieces: *Average White Band* / Space Princess: *Smith, Lonnie Liston* / I thought it was you: *Hancock, Herbie* / Love on a summer night: *McRary's* / This feeling is killing me: *Jones Girls* / You know how to love me: *Hyman, Phyllis* / Don't look any further: *Edwards, Dennis* / Keep on movin': *Soul II Soul* / See me: *Vandross, Luther* / Unfinished sympathy: *Massive Attack* / Whole town's laughing: *Pendergrass, Teddy* / Flesh of my flesh: *Hudson, Lavine* / Between the sheets: *Isley Brothers* / (You make me feel like) A Natural woman: *Blige, Mary J.* / Love don't live here anymore: *Rose Royce* / Don't be a fool: *Loose Ends*
CD Set ____ VTDCD 101
Virgin / Sep '96 / EMI

CLASSIC MELLOW MASTERCUTS VOL.1
She's so good to me: *Vandross, Luther* / Risin' to the top (give it all you got): *Burke, Keni* / Outstanding: *Gap Band* / Joy and pain: *Maze* / Give me the sunshine: *Leo's Sunshipp* / Hold me tighter in the rain: *Griffin, Billy* / I'm out of your life: *Arnie's Love* / You'll never know: *Hi-Gloss* / What you won't do for love: *Caldwell, Bobby* / I'm back for more: *Johnson, Al & Jean Carn* / Fruit song: *Reynolds, Jeannie* / Mellow mellow right on: *Lowrell*
CD ____ CUTSCD 3
Beechwood / Sep '91 / Beechwood/BMG / Pinnacle

CLASSIC MELLOW MASTERCUTS VOL.2
Don't look any further: *Edwards, Dennis* / Baby I'm scared of you: *Womack & Womack* / Mind blowing decisions: *Heatwave* / I don't think that man should sleep alone: *Parker, Ray Jr.* / All night long: *Mary Jane Girls* / Sweet sticky thing: *Ohio Players* / It's ecstasy when you lay down next to me: *White, Barry* / Juicy fruit: *Mtume* / What'cha see is what'cha get: *Dramatics* / Yu-ma/Go away little boy: *Shaw, Marlena* / I choose you: *Paris* / So delicious: *Fatback Band*
CD ____ CUTSCD 8
Beechwood / Jul '92 / Beechwood/BMG / Pinnacle

CLASSIC MELLOW MASTERCUTS VOL.3
Never too much: *Vandross, Luther* / You're gonna get next to me: *Kirkland, Bo & Ruth Davis* / Nights over Egypt: *Jones Girls* / Now that we've found love: *O'Jays* / Don't let it go to your head: *Carne, Jean* / Do you get enough love: *Jones, Shirley* / You are my starship: *Connors, Norman* / Reasons (Live): *Earth, Wind & Fire* / Rock me tonight: *Jackson, Freddie* / Gotta get you home tonight: *Jackson, Freddie* / Wilde, Eugene: *Jackson, Freddie* / Sweet love: *Baker, Anita* / We're in this love together: *Jarreau, Al*
CD ____ CUTSCD 17
Beechwood / Feb '94 / Beechwood/BMG / Pinnacle

CLASSIC MELLOW MASTERCUTS VOL.4
Love is contagious: *Sevelle, Taja* / Headline news: *Bell, William* / Heaven sent you: *Clark, Stanley* / She's got the papers: *Fields, Richard 'Dimples'* / She's got the papers (I got the man): *Mason, Barbara* / Promise me: *Dayton* / Feel so free (won't let go): *Rushen, Patrice* / Stay: *Controllers* / Sugar free: *Juicy* / Do me baby: *Morgan, Meli'sa* / It's just the way I feel: *Dunlap, Gene & The Ridgeways* / I wish he didn't trust me so much: *Womack, Bobby*
CD ____ CUTSCD 33
Beechwood / Apr '96 / Beechwood/BMG / Pinnacle

CLASSIC MIX MASTERCUTS VOL.1
Yah mo be there: *Ingram, James* / Medicine song: *Mills, Stephanie* / You're the one for me: *D-Train* / Seventh heaven: *Guthrie, Gwen* / You don't know: *Serious Intention* / Searchin' to find the one: *Unlimited Touch* / Beat the street: *Redd, Sharon* / You can't hide (your love from me): *Joseph, David* / Ain't nothin' goin' on but the rent: *Guthrie, Gwen* / Thinking of you: *Sister Sledge* / Searching: *Change* / Running away: *Ayers, Roy*
CD ____ CUTSCD 1
Beechwood / Sep '91 / Beechwood/BMG / Pinnacle

CLASSIC NEW JACK SWING MASTERCUTS VOL.1
Rub you the right way: *Gill, Johnny* / Her: *Guy* / I got the feelin': *Today* / New Jack swing: *Wreckx n' Effect* / She's got that vibe: *R Kelly* / Do me right: *Guy* / Sensitivity: *Tresvant, Ralph* / So you like what you see: *Samuelle* / Poison: *Bel Biv Devoe* / Treat them like they want to be treated: *Father MC* / Another like my lover: *Guy, Jasmine* / Mama told me: *Jackson, Keisha*
CD ____ CUTSCD 5
Beechwood / Mar '92 / Beechwood/BMG / Pinnacle

CLASSIC NEW JACK SWING MASTERCUTS VOL.2
Is it good to you: *Lucas, Tammy & Teddy Riley* / Don't be afraid: *Hall, Aaron* / Yo that's a lot of body: *Ready For The World* / I like your style: *Bubba* / Whatever it takes: *Basic Black* / Swinging single: *Groove B Chill* / Just got paid: *Kemp, Johnny* / My fantasy: *Guy* / Why you get funky on me: *Today* / Coool aid express card: *Nation Funktasia* / Serious: *La Rue* / My prerogative: *Brown, Bobby*
CD ____ CUTSCD 9
Beechwood / Oct '92 / Beechwood/BMG / Pinnacle

CLASSIC NEW JACK SWING MASTERCUTS VOL.3
Ain't too proud to beg: *TLC* / I want her: *Sweat, Keith* / I just can't handle it: *Hi-Five* / Judy had a boyfriend: *Riff* / Somebody for me: *Heavy D & The Boyz* / I'm dreaming: *Williams, Christopher* / DOG me out: *Guy* / Rump shaker: *Wreckx n' Effect* / 69: *Father MC* / I'm so into you: *SWV* / Real love: *Blige, Mary J.* / Love thang: *Intro*
CD ____ CUTSCD 18
Beechwood / Mar '94 / Beechwood/BMG / Pinnacle

CLASSIC NEW JACK SWING MASTERCUTS VOL.4
Anything: *SWV* / Do me: *Bell biv devoe* / Do the right thing: *Redhead Kingpin & The FBI* / I found love: *Redd, Jeff* / I'm in luv: *Joe* / It's alright: *Jodeci* / Lisa baby: *Father MC* / Listen closely (bozack): *Father MC* / New jack city: *Tamrock* / She's mine: *Basic Black* / Wanna get with u: *Guy* / We've got our own thang: *Heavy D & The Boyz*
CD ____ CUTSCD 27
Beechwood / Apr '95 / Beechwood/BMG / Pinnacle

CLASSIC P-FUNK MASTERCUTS VOL.1
Disco to go: *Brides Of Funkenstein* / Dog talk: *K-9 Corporation* / Four play: *Wesley, Fred & The Horny Horns* / Funk funk: *Cameo* / Funken town: *Slave* / Get lucky: *Well Red* / Hollywood: *Red Hot Chili Peppers* / Loopzilla: *Clinton, George* / Shake: *General Caine* / Tweakin': *Clinton, George* / We came to funk ya: *Wesley, Fred & The Horny Horns* / Work that sucker to death: *Xavier*
CD ____ CUTSCD 12
Beechwood / Jan '93 / Beechwood/BMG / Pinnacle

CLASSIC PAN PIPES (Romantic Pan Pipes/For Lovers/Play Love Songs - 3CD Set)
I have a dream / Strawberry fields forever / Dark side of the sun / Scarborough fair / Sailing / Unchained melody / Amazing Grace / If you leave me now / Something / Feelings / Here comes the sun / Sara / Yesterday / MacArthur park / Bird of Paradise / House of the rising sun / Don't cry for me Argentina / Banks of the Ohio / Autumn dream / Let it be / Power of love / I've had the time of my life / We've got tonight / Eternal flame / You light up my life / Up where we belong / Everything I do (I do it for you) / Heartbreaker / For ever and ever / Do that to me one more time / When you're in love with a beautiful woman / Love changes everything / And I love her / Groovy kind of love / Have you ever really loved a woman / Light my fire / Woman in love / For your eyes only / I can't help falling in love with you / I will always love you / I don't wanna cry / Wind beneath my wings / Ebony and ivory / Fernando / I'll be there / Bridge over troubled water / Always on my mind / Can you feel the love tonight / Phantom Of The Opera / Music of the night / Orinoco flow / Flashdance...what a feeling / Top of the world / Norwegian Wood / Tears in heaven / Moonlight shadow / He ain't heavy, he's my brother / Michelle / Just when I needed you most / Begin the beguine / Take my breath away
CD Set ____ 55158
Music / Oct '96 / Target/BMG

CLASSIC PARTY HITS VOL.1
Let's have a party: *Jackson, Wanda* / Yellow river: *Christie* / Sugar baby love: *Rubettes* / Hippy hippy shake: *Swinging Blue Jeans* / Da doo ron ron: *Crystals* / I'm into something good: *Herman's Hermits* / Baby come back: *Equals* / Walkin' back to happiness: *Shapiro, Helen* / Silence is golden: *Tremeloes* / You'll never walk alone: *Gerry & The Pacemakers* / Runaway: *Shannon, Del* / Just walkin' in the rain: *Ray, Johnnie* / Something's gotten hold of my heart: *Pitney, Gene* / Speedy Gonzales: *Boone, Pat* / Coasters: *Brown, Charlie* / Papa oom mow mow: *Rivingtons* / Ob-la-di ob-la-da: *Marmalade* / Nut rocker: *B-Bumble & The Stingers*
CD ____ 11980
Music / Feb '96 / Target/BMG

CLASSIC PARTY HITS VOL.2
Words: *David, F.R.* / Under the moon of love: *Showaddywaddy* / Tonight: *Rubettes* / In the bad, bad old days (before you loved me): *Foundations* / Keep searchin': *Shannon, Del* / Walk don't run: *Ventures* / Viva Bobby Joe: *Equals* / I'm telling you now: *Freddie & The Dreamers* / Ferry cross the Mersey: *Gerry & The Pacemakers* / When a man loves a woman: *Sledge, Percy* / Someone: *Tremeloes* / Windy: *Association* / Wishin' and hopin': *Merseybeats* / Sheila: *Roe, Tommy* / Mr. Bassman: *Cymbal, Johnny* / It's my party: *Gore, Lesley*
CD ____ 11981
Music / Apr '96 / Target/BMG

CLASSIC PERFORMERS
When the saints go marching in: *Armstrong, Louis* / Shall we dance: *Astaire, Fred* / One o'clock jump: *Basie, Count* / Where the blue of the night meets the gold of the day: *Crosby, Bing* / Boogie woogie: *Dorsey, Tommy* / It don't mean a thing if it ain't got that swing: *Ellington, Duke* / Tisket-a-tasket: *Fitzgerald, Ella* / Stompin' at the savoy: *Goodman, Benny* / Easy living: *Holiday, Billie* / Moonlight serenade: *Miller, Glenn* / Begin the beguine: *Shaw, Artie* / Honeysuckle Rose: *Waller, Fats* / Boogie woogie bugle boy: *Andrews Sisters* / Two sleepy people: *Geraldo & His Orchestra* / It's a sin to tell a lie: *Ink Spots* / Woodchopper's ball: *Herman, Woody* / Over the rainbow: *Garland, Judy* / March of the bob cats: *Crosby, Bob & His Bobcats* / There's a small hotel: *Baker, Josephine* / April showers: *Jolson, Al* / Thanks for the memory: *Hope, Bob & Shirley Ross* / Swingin' with Django: *Quintette Du Hot Club De France* / Rose Marie: *Eddy, Nelson* / Time on my hands: *Bowlly, Al*
CD ____ HADCD 170
Javelin / May '94 / Henry Hadaway / THE

CLASSIC RARE GROOVE MASTERCUTS VOL.1
Turned on to you: *80's Ladies* / Riding high: *Faze-O* / Why I came to California: *Ware, Leon* / Say you love me girl: *Break Water* / Movin' in the right direction: *Parks, Steve* / Number one: *Rushen, Patrice* / Good love: *Jeffries, Rome* / So different: *Kinky Foxx* / Much too much: *Sass* / All I want is my baby: *Gilliam, Roberta* / Moonshadow: *Labelle, Patti* / It's your love: *Beatty, Ethel*
CD ____ CUTSCD 11
Beechwood / Apr '93 / Beechwood/BMG / Pinnacle

CLASSIC RARE GROOVE MASTERCUTS VOL.2
Caveman boogie: *Wilson, Lesette* / LA nights: *Agawa, Yasuko* / No.1 girl: *Light Of The World* / You need a change of mind: *Brooklyn Express* / There's a reason: *Hi-Tension* / Work it out: *Break Water* / Barely breaking even: *Universal Robot Band* / I'd like to get into you: *Kelly, Denise & Fame* / Windy city theme: *Davis, Carl* / Bump and hustle music: *Stewart, Tommy* / God made me funky: *Head Hunters* / Give me some: *LA Boppers*
CD ____ CUTSCD 21
Beechwood / Sep '94 / Beechwood/BMG / Pinnacle

CLASSIC REGGAE IN 90'S STYLE
CD ____ RASCD 3104
Ras / Jan '95 / Direct / Greensleeves / Jet Star / SRD

CLASSIC REGGAE MASTERCUTS
Very well: *Wailing Souls* / Chalice in the palace: *U-Roy* / I don't want to be left outside: *Andy, Horace* / Conscious man: *Andy, Horace* / War ina Babylon: *Romeo, Max* / Nice time (late night blues): *Carlos, Don* / Jah no dead: *Burning Spear* / Keep on knocking: *Miller, Jacob* / Hardtimes: *Gad, Pablo* / Warrior charge: *Aswad* / Prophecy: *Fabian* / Love and only love: *Fred Locks*
CD ____ CUTSCD 30
Beechwood / Oct '95 / Beechwood/BMG / Pinnacle

CLASSIC ROCK
All or nothing: *Small Faces* / Giving it all away: *Small Faces* / Daltrey, roger: *Small Faces* / Something in the air: *Thunderclap Newman* / fire: *Crazy World Of Arthur Brown* / This wheel's on fire: *Driscoll, Julie & The Brian Auger Trinity* / Cry to me: *Pretty Things* / Mighty Quinn: *Manfred Mann* / Buddy Joe: *Golden Earring* / From the underworld: *Herd* / Gin house blues: *Amen Corner* / One and one is one: *Medicine Head* / Everything's alright: *Mojos* / With a girl like you: *Troggs* / You ain't seen nothin' yet: *Bachman-Turner Overdrive*
CD ____ 5506452
Spectrum / Aug '94 / PolyGram

CLASSIC ROCK 'N' ROLL
CD ____ 66450172
In Toto / Dec '92 / Target/BMG

CLASSIC ROCKERS
Baby, I love you so: *Miller, Jacob* / King Tubby meets the rockers uptown: *Pablo, Augustus* / Isn't it time to see / Jah in the hills: *Pablo, Augustus* / Can't keep a good man down: *Immortals* / Earth, wind and fire: *Blackman, Paul* / Love won't be easy: *Sibbles, Leroy* / Changing world: *Earl 16* / Blackman's heart: *Delgado, Junior* / Jah says the time has now come: *Mundell, Hugh* / You never know: *Williams, Delroy* / You never know dub: *Rockers All Stars* / Stop the fighting: *Williams, Delroy* / Stop the fighting dub: *Rockers All Stars* / Sukiyaki: *Pablo, Augustus* / Eastern promise: *Pablo, Augustus*
CD ____ RRCD 52
Reggae Refreshers / Apr '95 / PolyGram / Vital

CLASSIC ROCKERS VOL.2
CD ____ CDRP 0121
Rockers International / Mar '97 / Greensleeves / Jet Star

CLASSIC SALSOUL MASTERCUTS VOL.1
Dreaming: *Holloway, Loleatta* / Heartbreaker: *Burgess, Leroy* / I got my mind made up: *Instant Funk* / Jingo: *Candido* / Let no man put asunder: *First Choice* / Love sensation: *Holloway, Loleatta* / Nice and nasty: *Salsoul Orchestra* / Runaway: *Salsoul Orchestra & Loleatta Holloway* / Ten percent: *Double Exposure* / Beat goes on and on: *Ripple* / Bottle: *Bataan, Joe* / You're just the right size: *Salsoul Orchestra*
CD ____ CUTSCD 10
Beechwood / Feb '93 / Beechwood/BMG / Pinnacle

CLASSIC SALSOUL MASTERCUTS VOL.2
First choice: *Dr. Love* / My love is free: *Double Exposure* / Ain't no mountain high enough: *Inner Life* / This will be a night to remember: *Holman, Eddie* / Just as long as I got you: *Love Committee* / Helplessly: *Moment Of Truth* / Spring rain: *Silvetti* / Moment of my life: *Inner Life* / Sing, sing: *Gaz* / Hit and run: *Holloway, Loleatta* / Ooh, I love it (love break): *Salsoul Orchestra* / Dancin' and prancin': *Candido*
CD ____ CUTSCD 13
Beechwood / Jun '93 / Beechwood/BMG / Pinnacle

CLASSIC SIXTIES BEAT GROUPS
Louie Louie: *Kingsmen* / You tell me why: *Beau Brummels* / How love was true: *Bee Gees* / He's in town: *Rockin' Berries* / I'm the one: *Gerry & The Pacemakers* / Jesamine: *Casuals* / Love is all around: *Troggs* / Don't want you no more: *Davis, Spencer Group* / Here it comes again: *Fortunes* / Can't you hear my heartbeat: *Herman's Hermits* / Dandy: *Herman's Hermits* / Mr. Moonlight: *Merseybeats* / When it comes to your love: *Beau Brummels* / Anyway that you want me: *Troggs* / How do you do it: *Gerry & The Pacemakers* / Walk in the room: *Searchers*
CD ____ HADCD 220
Spotlight On / Jun '97 / Henry Hadaway

CLASSIC SOUL
CD ____ PLSCD 116
Pulse / Aug '96 / BMG

CLASSIC SOUL MASTERCUTS VOL.1
Paradise: *Hutson, Leroy* / My sensitivty: *Vandross, Luther* / When love calls: *Atlantic Starr* / Love you anyway: *Cameo* / Much too much: *Miller, Marcus* / Feels like I'm falling

in love: *Bar-Kays* / Try love again: *Natural Four* / Annie May: *Cole, Natalie* / My destiny: *McClain, Alton & Destiny* / Wanna hold on to you: *Loose Change* / How can you live without love: *Terrel, Jean* / Never like this: *Weather Girls*
CD ____ CUTSCD 38
Beechwood / Jun '97 / Beechwood/BMG / Pinnacle

CLASSIC SOUL MIX
Satisfaction guaranteed: *Melvin, Harold & The Bluenotes* / Love on a mountain top: *Knight, Robert* / Jimmy Mack: *Reeves, Martha* / It's in his kiss (the shoop shoop song): *Everett, Betty* / Soul man: *Sam & Dave* / In crowd: *Gray, Dobie* / My guy: *Wells, Mary* / Saturday night at the movies: *Drifters* / Knock on wood: *Floyd, Eddie* / Stand by me: *King, Ben E.* / Hey girl don't bother me: *King, Ben E.* / BABY: *Thomas, Carla* / Duke of Earl: *Chandler, Gene* / Harlem shuffle: *Bob & Earl*
CD ____ ECD 3071
K-Tel / Jan '95 / K-Tel

CLASSIC SUBBASE
Far out: *Sonz Of A Loop Da Loop Era* / Slammer: *Krome & Time* / Tell me why: *Wallace, Rachel* / Future sound: *Phuture Assassins* / I feel this way: *M&M/Rachel Wallace* / This sound is for the underground: *Krome & Time* / Hardcore will never die: *Q-Bass* / Weird energy: *DJ Hype* / Life (hands to heaven): *D'Cruze & Rachel Wallace* / Fireball: *Timebase* / Bad boy: *Mad Ragga Jon* / Funky hardcore: *Q-Bass*
CD ____ SUBBASECD 5
Suburban Base / Apr '97 / Pinnacle / Prime

CLASSIC TO THE CORE VOL.1 (2CD Set)
Hypnosis: *Psychotropic* / Let's do it: *Cox, Carl* / Feel the rhythm (comin' on strong): *Rhythm Section* / Take no chance: *Xray Xperiments* / Some justice: *Urban Shakedown & Mickey Finn* / 40 miles: *Congress* / Narra mine: *Genaside II* / What have you done: *One Tribe & Gem* / Vamp: *Outlander* / Energy flash: *Beltram, Joey* / Feel real good: *Manix* / Take me away: *True Faith & Final Cut*
CD Set ____ BSECD 1
Bass Section / Dec '95 / Grapevine/ PolyGram

CLASSIC TO THE CORE VOL.2
CD ____ BSECD 2
Bass Section / May '96 / Grapevine/ PolyGram

CLASSICA
CD ____ 39101632
Hyperium / Jan '97 / Cargo / Plastic Head

CLASSICAL INSTRUMENT TRADITIONS
CD ____ VICG 52622
JVC World Library / Feb '96 / ADA / CM / Direct

CLASSICAL TRADITIONS (Music From Central Asia/2CD Set)
CD Set ____ C 56003536
Ocora / Nov '93 / ADA / Harmonia Mundi

CLASSICAL TURKISH MUSIC
CD ____ CMT 2741013
La Chant Du Monde / Sep '95 / ADA / Harmonia Mundi

CLASSICS OF 1975
CD ____ RNCD 2048
Rhino / Apr '94 / Grapevine/PolyGram / Jet Star

CLASSICS OF SUPERSTITION, THE (2CD Set)
CD Set ____ SUPER 2816CD
Superstition / Dec '96 / Plastic Head / SRD / Vital

CLASSICS SAMPLER
CD ____ CLASS 99
Classics / Apr '95 / Discovery / Jazz Music

CLEETHORPES STORY, THE
Can you imagine that: *Jenkins, Norma* / If I was a kid: *Kennedy, Billy* / SOS: *Today's People* / I'm your pimp: *Skull Snaps* / Your autumn of tomorrow: *Crow* / Gig: *Raw Soul* / I've got the need: *Spooky & Sue* / Spring rain: *Silvetti* / Boogie with your baby: *Willie J* / Cut your motor off: *Black Nasty* / Summer in the parks: *East Coast Connection* / Girl you better wake up: *Liberty* / Broadway sissy: *Roscoe & Friends* / Lady lady lady: *Boogie Man Orchestra* / You're the cream of the crop: *Maurice, Andre* / What took you so long: *Woodruff, Stanley* / Never gonna let you go: *Jobell Orchestra* / Hipit: *Hosanna* / If you really need a friend: *Foster, Bobby* / If I had my way: *Troy Keys* / What makes her a woman: *Reed, Danny* / What's happening to this love affair: *Hunt, Danny* / Soon everything's gonna be alright: *3rd Time Around* / What about love: *Marboo* / Long gone: *Flemming, Debbie*
CD ____ GSCD 086
Goldmine / Mar '97 / Vital

CLIMAX (Hi Energy Anthems From Start To Finish)
You think you're a man / Action / Feels like I'm in love / Male stripper / Jump, jump (a little higher) / Gimme gimme gimme (a man after midnight) / Let me feel it / Stand by your man / Rhinestone cowboy / These boots are made for walking / I feel the earth move / Relax
CD ____ ECD 3200
K-Tel / Mar '95 / K-Tel

CLOAKE AND DAGGER
CD ____ SVCD 6
Shocking Vibes / May '97 / Jet Star

CLOCKWORK ORANGE (Ibiza Experience)
CD ____ HF 48CD
PWL / Nov '95 / Warner Music

CLOSE TO THE HEART
Through Bucky's eyes: *Gettel, Michael* / Gabriel's dream: *Mann, Brian* / Portraits: *Brewer, Spencer* / Gemina: *Illenberger, Ralf* / Jonathan's lullaby: *Stein, Ira* / Summer's child: *Lanz, David* / Back home: *Lauria, Nando* / Je t'aime: *Mann, Brian* / Old house is silent: *Gettel, Michael* / Memory: *Rumbel, Nancy* / Another star in the sky: *Arkenstone, David* / Return to the heart: *Lanz, David* / Shape of her face: *Whalen, Michael*
CD ____ ND 63918
Narada / Apr '95 / ADA / New Note/Pinnacle

CLOSE TO THE HEART
CD ____ NSCD 019
Newsound / May '95 / THE

CLOSET CLASSICS VOL.2
Everything starts with an E: *Ezee Posse* / Satan's butterfly ball: *Boy George* / Deliverance: *Ezee Posse* / Let love shine: *Amos* / You can have it all: *Gallagher, Eve* / Misunderstood: *Gallagher, Eve* / Dreamtime: *Zee* / Love on love: *Ezee Posse* / Same thing in reverse: *Boy George* / Love is leaving: *Boy George* / Generations of love: *Jesus Loves You* / Broadway: *Kinky Roland* / Church of freedom: *Amos* / Come away: *Amos*
CD ____ IMPCD 002
More Protein / Apr '97 / Pinnacle / Total/ BMG

CLOSET POP FOLK
CD ____ PYCD 2
Pop Psycle / Jul '97 / Greyhound

CLOSET POP FREAK
CD ____ PYCD 1
Pop Psycle / Jul '97 / Greyhound

CLOUDS (21 Instrumental Moods)
Windmills of your mind / Just for you / Someone to watch over me / You've got a friend / This masquerade / Amanda / Cavatina / What are you doing for the rest of your life / Laura Jane / Gymnopedie / Nearness of you / Clouds / Shadow of your smile / Secret love / Air on a g-string / This guy's in love with you / Till there was you / Very thought of you / Moon river / Another suitcase in another hall
CD ____ EMPRCD 605
Emporio / Jun '96 / Disc

CLOUDWATCH VOL.1
CD ____ SCS 001
Sonic Soul / May '97 / Cargo

CLUB - JUST DANCE IT (2CD Set)
CD Set ____ 560012
Westcom / Jan '97 / Koch / Pinnacle

CLUB 2 DEF (4CD Set)
CD Set ____ BDRCD 13
Breakdown / Apr '96 / Pinnacle

CLUB 4 LIFE (2CD Set)
CD Set ____ AVEXCD 49
Avex / Aug '96 / 3mv/Pinnacle

CLUB ACID
CD ____ BB 035244CD
Broken Beat / May '96 / Plastic Head

CLUB BOMBERS VOL.2
CD ____ ZYX 811042
ZYX / May '97 / ZYX

CLUB BUZZ '95
CD ____ CUTZCD 95
CD ____ CUTZBX 95
Rumour / Nov '95 / 3mv/Sony / Mo's Music Machine / Pinnacle

CLUB BUZZ VOL.1
CD ____ CUTZCD 1
Rumour / Feb '95 / 3mv/Sony / Mo's Music Machine / Pinnacle

CLUB BUZZ VOL.2
CD ____ CUTZCD 2
Rumour / Aug '95 / 3mv/Sony / Mo's Music Machine / Pinnacle

CLUB CLASS (2CD Set)
U sure do: *Strike* / Don't give me your life: *Alex Party* / Push the feeling on: *Nightcrawlers* / Always something there to remind me: *Tin Tin Out* / Reach up (papa's got a brand new pig bag): *Perfecto All Stars* / Two can play at that game: *Brown, Bobby* / Another night: *MC Sar & The Real McCoy* / Yeke yeke: *Kante, Mory* / Axel F (short stab): *Clock* / Shelter me: *Circuit* / You bring me joy: *Rhythm Factor* / Another star: *Sledge, Kathy* / What hope have I: *Sphinx* / Respect: *Cheeks, Judy* / Message of love: *Love Happy* / Spirit inside: *Spirits* / Sight for sore eyes: *M-People* / Rockin' my body: *49ers* / Climax: *Paperclip People* / Embracing the sunshine: *BT* / Every time you touch me: *Moby* / Poison: *Prodigy*
CD Set ____ RADCD 10
Global TV / Apr '95 / BMG

CLUB CULTURE
CD ____ STRSCD 3
Stress / May '94 / Mo's Music Machine / Pinnacle / Prime

CLUB CUTS '97 VOL.2 (2CD Set)
CD Set ____ TTVCD 2916
Telstar TV / Jul '97 / Warner Music

CLUB EUROPA
CD ____ PHAZE 1
Music Factory / Jul '96 / Pinnacle / Total/ BMG

CLUB FETISH
CD ____ 953 SEQCD
Sequential / Jun '97 / Essential/BMG

CLUB FORMULA
CD ____ AB 1695292
Essential Dance / Nov '96 / RTM/Disc

CLUB GROOVES VOL.1
CD ____ DCOMPCD 2
Death Becomes Me / Apr '94 / Grapevine/ PolyGram / Pinnacle / SRD

CLUB IBIZA VOL.1 (3CD Set)
CD Set ____ QPMCD 1
QPM / Oct '95 / Beechwood/BMG

CLUB IBIZA VOL.1 (Silver Edition - 3CD Set)
CD Set ____ QPMXCD 1
QPM / Apr '96 / Beechwood/BMG

CLUB IBIZA VOL.2 (3CD Set)
CD Set ____ QPMCD 6
QPM / Sep '96 / Beechwood/BMG

CLUB JAZZ
Curro's: *Hancock, Herbie & Donald byrd* / Chantized: *Hubbard, Freddie* / Confined few: *Little, Booker* / There will never be another you: *Benson, George* / Soul power: *Hancock, Herbie* / Prophecy: *Byrd, Donald* / Out of this world: *Hancock, Herbie & Donald byrd* / Invitation: *Hancock, Herbie & Donald byrd* / Stop look and listen: *Terry, Clark & Miles Davis* / Handbags and gladrags: *Farlowe, Chris* / That's what a friend will do: *Lynn, Barbara* / Our soul brothers: *Dickens, Charles*
CD ____ CWNCD 2015
Javelin / Jul '96 / Henry Hadaway / THE

CLUB MEETS DUB VOL.1
CD ____ ZD 5CD
Zip Dog / Oct '95 / Grapevine/PolyGram / SRD / Vital

CLUB MEETS DUB VOL.2
CD ____ ZD 8CD
Zip Dog / Sep '96 / Grapevine/PolyGram / SRD / Vital

CLUB MEETS DUB VOL.3
One chill: *Dub War* / Green dub: *Xenos* / Toker smoker: *Salvo Jets* / Dis power: *Digital Science* / Dolphinalysis: *Emperor Sly* / Actions = reactions dub: *One Love Sound* / Earth a biosphere: *Salt Tank & Australasia* / Cold blooded hot head: *Ha-Lo* / Road to Basra: *Shotgun Rockers* / Smokin' weed: *Scar'd For Life* / Prophet a man: *Bloomfield, Alan* / Didgeridogs: *Emperor Sly*
CD ____ ZD 14CD
Zip Dog / Jul '97 / Grapevine/PolyGram / SRD / Vital

CLUB MIX '96 VOL.1
State of independence: *Summer, Donna* / Ultra flava: *Heller & Farley Project* / Got myself together: *Bucketheads* / Passion (Do you want it right now): *Gat Decor* / Give me luv: *Alcatraz* / Movin': *Mone* / Keep the music strong: *Bizarre Inc.* / Higher state of consciousness: *Wink, Josh* / I'm ready: *Size 9* / I wish: *Skee Lo* / Innocent: *Addis Black Widow* / Klubhopping: *Klubb Heads* / Your love: *Inner City* / America: *Full Intention* / Disco's revenge: *Gusto* / And I'm telling you I'm not going: *Giles, Donna* / Are you gonna be there: *Up Yer Ronson* / Mr. Friday night: *Moorish, Lisa* / Tell it to my heart: *Q-Club* / Disco 2000: *Pulp* / Naughty north and the sexy south: *E-Motion* / I've got the vibration: *Black Box* / I'll be there: *99th Floor Elevators* / Wham bam: *Candy Girls & Sweet Pussy Pauline* / I feel love: *Summer, Donna* / Renegade master: *Wildchild* / I believe: *Happy Clappers* / Nighttrain: *Kadoc* / To the beat of the drum (la luna): *Ethics* / Get into the music: *DJ's Rule* / Electronic pleasure: *N-Trance* / I wanna be a hippy: *Technohead*
CD ____ 5354122
PolyGram TV / Mar '96 / PolyGram

CLUB MIX '96 VOL.2
CD ____ 5357652
PolyGram TV / Jul '96 / PolyGram

CLUB MIX '97 VOL.1 (2CD Set)
Breathe: *Prodigy* / Seven days and one week: *BBE* / Real vibration (want love): *Express Of Sound* / So in love with you: *Duke* / Blue skies: *BT* / I'm alive: *Stretch n' Vern & Maddog* / Keep pushin': *Dlugosch, Boris & Booom* / Not over yet: *Grace* / Don't go: *Third Dimension & Julie McDermott* / Cuba: *El Mariachi* / Believe in me: *Mankey* / Pearl's girl: *Underworld* / Help me make it: *Huff & Puff* / Run to you: *Carroll, Dina* / It's just another groove: *Mighty Dub Katz* / Follow the rules: *Livin' Joy* / Offshore: *Chicane* / Arkham asylum: *Sasha* / Move any mountain: *Shamen* / Survive: *Brutal Bill & Saundra Marquez* / Tall 'n' handsome: *Outrage* / Yeke yeke: *Kante, Mory* / United nations of house: *United Nations Project* / Stamp: *Healy, Jeremy & Amos* / Waterfall: *Atlantic Ocean* / Access: *DJ Misjah & Tim* / Jump to my beat: *Wildchild* / Floor-essence: *Man With No Name* / Closer to you: *JX* / Groovebird: *Natural Born Groovers* / Ultimate: *Antic* / 100%: *Kiani, Mary* / Second coming: *Libido* / Floor space: *Our House* / Wizard's of the sonic: *West Bam*
CD ____ 5532012
PolyGram TV / Dec '96 / PolyGram

CLUB MIX '97 VOL.2 (2CD Set)
Discoteque: *U2* / Toxygene: *Orb* / Inferno: *Souvlaki* / Barrel of a gun: *Depeche Mode* / Rez: *Underworld* / You got the love: *Source & Candi Staton* / Take me by the hand: *Submerged* / Close to your heart: *JX* / Life's too short: *Hole In One* / Bellisima: *DJ Quicksilver* / Party people: *Pianoman* / Just playin': *JT Playaz* / Get up: *Stingily, Byron* / Sugar is sweeter: *Bolland, C.J.* / Runaway: *Nu Yorican Soul & India* / One and one: *Miles, Robert* / 7 days and one week: *BBE* / Zoe: *Paganini Traxx* / All I wanna do: *Tin Tin Out* / Love is all you need: *99 All Stars* / Girls and boys: *Hed Boys* / Up to no good: *Porn Kings* / Resonance: *Magic Alec* / Ultra Flava: *Heller & Farley Project* / Have fun: *Coma B* / Beat is over: *Basco* / Amber groove: *SAS* / Antheum: *Digital Blondes* / London x-press: *X-Press 2* / Remember me: *Blueboy* / Brooklyn beats: *Deep, Scotti* / Drive me crazy: *Partizan* / Mystery land: *Y-Traxx* / Wiggly world: *Mr. Jack* / Open up: *Leftfield & John Lydon*
CD Set ____ 5533642
PolyGram TV / Feb '97 / PolyGram

CLUB MIX '97 VOL.3 (2CD Set)
Free: *Ultranate* / Closer than close: *Gaines, Rosie* / Something's going on: *Terry, Todd* / Spin spin sugar: *Sneaker Pimps* / Naked and ashamed: *Dylan Rhymes* / Heaven on earth: *Spellbound* / My love is deep: *Parker, Sara* / Fly life: *Basement Jaxx* / Satisfied (take me higher): *H2O* / Misbehavin': *Booth, Buddy* / Invader: *Koolworld Productions* / Break it: *Mr. Spring* / Legends: *Sacred Spirit* / I love you...stop: *Red Five* / Difference: *Funny Walker* / Snow: *ORN* / Nightmare: *Brainbug* / Hondy (no access): *Hondy* / Deep (I'm falling deeper): *Ariel* / To be loved: *Drayton, Luce* / Scared: *Slacker* / Flash: *BBE* / Go with da flow: *Loop Da Loop* / Hand in hand: *Grace* / Love on and on: *Cato, Lorraine* / Rock da house: *Tall Paul* / Cafe del mar: *Energy 52* / With or without you: *Kiani, Mary* / Shine: *Space Brothers* / Never lost his hardcore: *NRG* / Can you feel the heat: *Carle Younge Project* / Someone: *Ascension* / Flowtation: *De Moor, Vincent* / Prophet: *Bolland, C.J.* / Catch: *Sunscreem*
CD ____ 5536912
PolyGram TV / Jun '97 / PolyGram

CLUB PARTY, THE (Midtown 10th Anniversary)
CD ____ MIDCD 02
Midtown / Jun '97 / SRD

CLUB SATURN
CD ____ BDRCD 17
Breakdown / Oct '96 / Pinnacle

CLUB SKA '67
Guns of Navarone: *Skatalites* / Phoenix city: *Alphonso, Roland* / Shanty town: *Dekker, Desmond* / Broadway jungle: *Flames* / Contact: *Richards, Roy* / Guns fever: *Brooks, Baba* / Rub up, push up: *Hinds, Justin* / Dancing mood: *Wilson, Delroy* / Stop making love: *Gaylads* / Pied piper: *Marley, Rita* / Lawless Street: *Soul Brothers* / Skaing West: *Sir Lord Comic* / Copasetic: *Rulers*
CD ____ IMCD 53
Mango / Jul '89 / PolyGram / Vital

CLUB TOGETHER IBIZA
CD ____ CDEMTVD 134
EMI TV / Sep '96 / EMI

CLUB TRIBUNE, THE (Compiled By DJ Moguai) (2CD Set)
Sound: *Humate* / Cum on: *DJ HMC* / Jack the beat: *Wicked Wipe* / Substance: *Incisions* / Fuck up: *Caunos* / Da phonk: *Elektrochemie UK* / Excitement: *Saturday Night Life* / Metrum reflex: *Norman* / Tryout: *Dit* / Chord memory: *Pooley, Ian* / Siren: *DJ Misjah* / Our music: *FEOS & MSO* / Shogun: *Direct Drive* / Watchman's theme: *Watchmen 2* / Torqueflight: *DJ Moguai* / Sulk: *Encephaloid Disturbance* / Toggle: *Tan Ru* / To the sky: *Pump Panel* / Take over: *Oshawa* / Forerunner: *Natural Born Groovers*
CD Set ____ SPV 08938762
SPV / Aug '96 / Koch / Plastic Head

CLUB UK (Mixed By Biko & Steve Harvey/2CD Set)
Crazy man: *Blast* / Feel so right: *Solution* / Do that to me: *Lisa Marie Experience* / Want love: *Hysteric Ego* / Let's groove: *Morel, George* / Up to no good: *Porn Kings* / Sound of Eden: *Shades Of Rhythm* / Question: *Seven Grand Housing Authority* / So in love with you: *Duke* / Into your heart: *6 By 6* / I feel so good: *Totalis* / Love resurrection: *Floor Federation* / Klubhopping: *Klubb Heads* / Tall 'n' handsome: *Outrage* / Le voie de soleil: *Subliminal Cuts* / Jus' come:

Cool Jack / Ultra flava: *Farley & Heller* / Keep pushing: *Dlugosch, Boris & Booom* / Blue skies: *BT & Tori Amos* / Huff 'n' puff: *Puff Dogs* / Curse of voodoo ray: *May, Lisa* / Dirty games: *Groove Committee* / Two fatt guitars: *Direckt* / Cangica: *Mighty Dub Katz* / Blue: *LaTour* / U can abuse my body: *Bruno, Tony* / Access: *DJ Misjah & Tim* / Gift: *Way Out West*
CD Set _______ FIRMCD 9
Firm / Dec '96 / Pinnacle

CLUB VIBE
CD _______ JAPECD 106
CD _______ JAPEPX 106
Escapade / Feb '96 / 3mv/Sony / Prime

CLUB X:PRESS
CD _______ XPS 1CDU
X-Press / May '95 / SRD

CLUB ZONE
Show me love: *Robin S* / Real vibration (I want your love): *Express Of Sound* / Celebrate the love: *Zhivago* / People hold on: *Lisa & Tori* / You're the one: *AT Project* / Jump up in the air: *London Boy* / If Madonna calls: *Vasquez, Junior* / Take me away: *Respect* / Get freaky: *Bass Symphony* / Blow job: *Shocking Rose* / Funk phenomenon: *Van Helden, Armand* / You make me feel: *Real DJ* / It must be love: *Club Freaks* / Fill me up: *Libra*
CD _______ DC 881322
Disky / Jul '97 / Disky / THE

CLUBBED OUT (2CD Set)
Flotation: *Grid* / Sweet harmony: *Beloved* / Indian vibes: *Mathar* / Another green world: *Eno, Brian* / Joy & heartbreak: *Movement .98* / Stella's cry: *Jam & Spoon* / Melt: *Leftfield* / Cherry coloured funk: *Cocteau Twins* / Stories: *Izit* / Clubbed to death: *Rob D* / Racing tracks: *Visnadi* / Huge ever growing pulsating brain that rules from the centre: *Orb* / Talking with myself: *Electribe 101* / Barefoot in the head: *Man Called Adam* / Dream beam: *Hypnotone* / Only love can break your heart: *St. Etienne* / Papua New Guinea: *Future Sound Of London* / Dredd overboard: *Nightmares On Wax* / Wilmot: *Sabres Of Paradise* / You're not alone: *Olive* / Autumn leaves: *Coldcut* / Riding to Rio: *Orbit, William* / Gift: *Way Out West* / God moving over the face of the waters: *Moby* / Zed & 2 L's: *Fila Brazillia* / Natural high: *Warp 69*
CD Set _______ SOLIDCD 005
Solid State / Oct '96 / Prime / Vital

CLUBBED TO DEATH
CD _______ RDCD 001
RDR / Feb '95 / RTM/Disc

CLUBLAND (2CD Set)
You're not alone: *Olive* / Closer than close: *Gaines, Rosie* / Ecuador: *Sash & Rodriguez* / Flylife: *Basement Jaxx* / Make the world go round: *Sandy B* / Way: *Funky Green Dogs* / I love you...stop: *Red 5* / Guidance: *Kamillion* / Oye como va: *Puente, Tito & His Latin Ensemble* / 6 underground: *Sneaker Pimps* / Help me make it: *Huff & Puff* / Scared: *Slacker* / Sound Of Eden: *Casino* / Woamnchild: *Duke* / I'll be your friend: *Owens, Robert* / What would we do: *Sol Brothers* / Morning light: *Team Deep* / I have peace: *Strike* / Shine: *Space Brothers* / Grooverbird: *Natural Born Groovers* / Flash: *BBE* / Armed and extremely dangerous: *BBE* / Encore une fois: *Sash* / Dance with me: *Tin Tin Out* / People hold on: *Stansfield, Lisa & Dirty Rotten Scoundrels* / Let's groove: *Phat & Funky* / Ready or not: *Course* / You got the love: *Source & Candi Staton* / My love is deeper: *Parker, Sara* / Out of my head 97: *Marradonna* / Harmonica track: *Soul Boy* / Flowtation: *De Moor, Vincent* / Footprint: *Disco Citizens* / Walkin' on up: *DJ Prof X Or*
CD Set _______ TCD 2912
Telstar / Jun '97 / BMG

CMCD
CD _______ RERCMCD
ReR/Recommended / Oct '96 / ReR Megacorp / RTM/Disc

COAST TO COAST
Voice of America: *Dark Star* / American fool: *Green, Jack* / Better late than never: *XS* / How far Jerusalem: *Magnum* / Call of the wild: *Sabu* / Hold back the night: *Multi-Story* / Stand me up: *Statetrooper* / Dancin' on midnight: *White Sister* / Shoot for the heart: *Lawrence, Karen* / Surrender: *Joshua*
CD _______ WKFMXD 96
FM / Jul '87 / Revolver / Sony

COASTAL BREAKS (2CD Set)
CD Set _______ AVEXCD 46
Avex / Nov '96 / 3mv/Pinnacle

COCKNEY CHRISTMAS, A
Hark the herald angels sing / O little town of Bethlehem / Once in Royal David's City / See amid the winter's snow / While shepherd's watched their flocks by night / O come all ye faithful (adeste fidelis) / Jingle bells / Good King Wenceslas / Ding dong merrily on high / God rest ye merry gentlemen / Deck the halls / White Christmas / Twelve days of Christmas / First Noel / Away in a manger / Holly & the ivy / Gloucestershire wassail / Santa Claus is coming to town / Frosty the snowman / Rudolf the red nosed reindeer / Sleigh ride / Winter wonderland / Merry Christmas everybody / All I want for Christmas is my two front teeth / Rockin' around the Christmas tree / Jingle bell rock / I wish it could be Christmas every day / Merry Christmas everybody (reprise) / Happy Christmas war is over / Mistletoe & wine / Silent night / We wish you a merry Christmas
CD _______ XMAS 005
Tring / Dec '96 / Tring

COCKNEY KINGS OF THE MUSIC HALL
CD _______ CDSDL 413
Saydisc / Oct '95 / ADA / Direct / Harmonia Mundi

COCKTAIL COMBOS (3CD Set)
Straighten up and fly right / Gee baby ain't I good to you / Sweet Lorraine / Easy listening blues / Bring another drink / I'm a shy guy / You're nobody 'til somebody loves you / Don't blame me / I'm through with love / Come to baby, do / Frim fram sauce / Loan me two till Tuesday / (Get your kicks on) Route 66 / Baby, baby all the time / Oh, but I do / But she's my buddy's chick / You can't call it madness (but I call it love) / (I love you) for sentimental reasons / You're the cream in my coffee / You don't learn that in school / I miss you so / I think you get what I mean / (Everyone has someone) but all I've got is me / What'll I do / I'll string along with you / Blazers boogie / Baby don't you cry / Drifting blues / Homesick blues / How high the moon / Get yourself another fool / In the evening when the sun goes down / Trouble blues / I don't care who knows / When your lover has gone / Tormented / Alley batting / Take me / Let's have a ball / Did you ever love a woman / Again / Gee, I've made up my mind / That old feeling / Without the one you love / Black night / Once there lived a fool / Hard times / Evening shadows / Rollin' like a pebble in the sand / Rising sun / Cryin' and driftin' blues / Goodnight my love / Cryin' mercy / PS I love you / My silent love / I want to fool around with you / Married woman / Wino blues / Empty stocking blues / Walkin' and talkin' blues / San Francisco blues / Bad neighbourhood / You played me for a fool / Telephone blues / You need me now / Broken hearted traveller / Do I love you / Long time ago / Lovin' (brought me into this world) / Tired, broke and busted / Come back baby / Call operator 210 / Wine, wine, wine / Red cherries
CD Set _______ CDEM 1605
Capitol / Mar '97 / EMI

COEUR DE FRANCE
La chavannee: *La Chavanee* / Polka du lac: *Blanchard, Jean & Eric Montbel* / Au point du jour: *Les Ecoliers De Saint Genest* / La marotte / Bourrees de Gatignol et de Leonard de la Vedrenne: *La Concorde Des Temps* / Valse a Dede: *Les Brayauds* / Le crab noir: *La Grande Bande Des Cornemuses* / Suite de bourrees: *Melusine* / Michel / Pause cafe/Grand frise: *Trio Cornemuse* / Le retour de la veillee/La polka des Coustouby: *Cafe Charbons* / Frere Nicolas: *Cafe Charbons* / Ego sum pauper/ Valse a Bouffard: *Vielleux Du Bourbonnais*
CD _______ B 6848
Auvidis/Ethnic / May '97 / ADA / Harmonia Mundi

COFFEE BAR DAYS (2CD Set)
All I have to do is dream: *Everly Brothers* / Claudette: *Everly Brothers* / Something else: *Cochran, Eddie* / Three steps to heaven: *Cochran, Eddie* / I'm not a juvenile delinquent: *Lymon, Frankie & The Teenagers* / Why do fools fall in love: *Lymon, Frankie & The Teenagers* / Pretty little angel eyes: *Lee, Curtis* / Wanderer: *Dion* / He's so fine: *Chiffons* / More than I can say: *Vee, Bobby* / Baby sittin': *Angelo, Bobby & The Tuxedos* / I'm walkin': *Domino, Fats* / Ma, he's making eyes at me: *Otis, Johnny* / Sea cruise: *Ford, Frankie* / Mother In Law: *K-Doe, Ernie* / Blue jean bop: *Vincent, Gene* / I'm a moody guy: *Fenton, Shane & The Fentones* / Ain't misbehavin': *Bruce, Tommy & The Bruisers* / Witch doctor: *Lang, Don* / Cloudburst: *Lang, Don* / Lollipop: *Mudlarks* / Don't you rock me daddy-o: *Vipers Skiffle Group* / Cumberland gap: *Vipers Skiffle Group* / It takes a worried man: *Vipers Skiffle Group* / Runaway: *Shannon, Del* / Teenager in love: *Dion & The Belmonts* / Shakin' all over: *Kidd, Johnny & The Pirates* / Cindy oh Cindy: *Brent, Tony* / Girl of my dreams: *Brent, Tony* / Someday (you'll want me to want you): *Nelson, Rick* / You're sixteen: *Burnette, Johnny Rock 'N' Roll Trio* / Tell Laura I love her: *Valance, Ricky* / Fever: *Lee, Peggy* / Send me the pillow that you dream on: *Tillotson, Johnny* / Kisses sweeter than wine: *Rodgers, Jimmie* / Volare: *Martin, Dean* / Only sixteen: *Douglas, Craig* / Be my girl: *Dale, Jim* / Big man: *Four Preps* / Love letters: *Lester, Ketty*
CD Set _______ CDDL 1254
Music For Pleasure / Jan '94 / EMI

COLDKRUSHCUTS
Groover: *Funki Porcini* / Global chaos: *KT & Hex* / Sometimes: *2 Player & The Herbaliser* / Breaks: *DJ Vadim & Mark B* / Real killer part 2: *Herbaliser* / Get your head down: *Vibert, Luke* / Goodbye cruel world: *London Funk Allstars* / Naked leaves: *Coldcut* / Spiral dub: *DJ Food* / Harmonic: *Hex* / Mod you: *Cabbageboy* / Readybrek: *DJ Toolz* / Creatures: *Amon Tobin* / Nightrous: *Peezee* / An unmarked grave: *Up Bustle & Out* / Revolutionary woman of the windmill: *Up Bustle & Out* / Mr. Chombee has the flaw: *Herbaliser* / Breaks of wrath: *DJ Food* / Alice Effekt: *DJ Food* / Glass: *Gideon* / Sunvibes: *DJ Food* / Oddly Godly: *EVA* / Going down: *Funki Porcini* / Forty winks: *Herbaliser* / B Boy: *DJ Vadim* / Headz still ain't ready: *DJ Vadim* / Aural prostitution: *DJ Vadim* / Electric lazyland: *9 Lazy 9* / Give it to me raw: *London Funk Allstars* / Broadcasting live from planet Blapps: *London Funk Allstars* / Today London, tomorrow the world: *London Funk Allstars* / Junkies bad trip: *London Funk Allstars* / Knee deep in the beats part 1: *London Funk Allstars* / Sign: *Coldcut* / Call me: *DJ Vadim* / Bass city roller: *DJ Food* / Mother: *Herbaliser* / Aural prostitution: *DJ Vadim* / Morning prayer: *DJ Vadim* / Dark lady: *DJ Food* / Lounge shiznitz: *DJ Vadim* / Love is what you need: *London Funk Allstars*
CD _______ ZENCD 026LTD
CD _______ ZENCD 026
Ninja Tune / Feb '97 / Kudos / Pinnacle / Prime / Vital

COLEURS SUD (Music From Southern France)
Nove dai corporacions: *Tesi, Riccardo & Patrick Vaillant* / Bruna de laguna: *Carlotti, Jean-Marie & Daniele Craighead/Riccardo Tesi* / Brouillard epais: *Une Anche Passe* / Tossa bonica: *Cobles* / Aquela des adrets: *Zephirin Castellon* / Maudit sia l'amour: *Jurie, Renat* / Gaztetasunak bainerabila: *Achiary, Benat* / Banbulak dantza: *Folc, Perlinpinpin* / Per non languir: *Carlotti, Jean-Marie* / Vivem totjorn en montanha: *Zephirin Castellon* / Sardana curta: *Cobles* / La mare de deu: *Achiary, Benat* / Lili purpurea: *Achiary, Benat* / La batalha d'Achos: *Folc, Perlinpinpin* / Lundi: *Jurie, Renat* / Un joen pastor quitava: *Jurie, Renat* / Ba nin adixkide bat: *Achiary, Benat* / Marche de la Saint Blaise: *Une Anche Passe*
CD _______ B 6851
Auvidis/Ethnic / Aug '97 / ADA / Harmonia Mundi

COLLABORATIONS VOL.1
CD _______ LCD 001
Lo Recordings / Nov '96 / BMG / RTM/ Disc

COLLABORATIONS VOL.2
CD _______ LCD 002
Lo Recordings / Nov '96 / BMG / RTM/ Disc

COLLECTED SOUNDS, THE
CD _______ SLIPCD 45
Slip 'n' Slide / Jun '96 / Amato Disco / Prime / RTM/Disc / Vital

COLLECTED WORKS - 15 YEARS OF MUSIC
CD _______ SP 116CD
Stony Plain / Oct '93 / ADA / CM / Direct

COLLECTION OF MODERN SOUL CLASSICS, A
Just loving you: *Andrews, Ruby* / Come back baby: *Justice Department* / I'm so glad you're mine: *Perkins, George* / Lonely girl: *Side Show* / Talkin': *Vee Gees* / Making new friends: *Tracy, Jeanie* / Girl, you're my kind of wonderful: *Relf, Bobby* / Girl I've been trying to tell you: *Ultimates* / Lightin' up: *Karim, Ty* / Teasin you again: *Tee, Willie* / Let's go fishing: *Turner Bros* / Dream: *Creations* / I need your love: *Woods, Ella* / Here stands a man who needs you: *Wilson, George* / Given up on love: *Thompson, Johnny* / If it's not love don't waste my time: *Johnson, Dorothy* / Have I really loved you: *Smoke* / Footsteps across your mind: *Shock* / Girl I love you: *Fisher, Shelley* / You're gone: *Hardin, Celest* / Better to bend than break: *Simmons, Cissie* / Colour him father: *Winstons* / Wash and wear love: *Vernado, Lynne*
CD _______ GSCD 009
Goldmine / Jan '93 / Vital

COLORES DE CUBA
CD _______ 74321283392
Milan / May '96 / Conifer/BMG / Silva Screen

COLORS OF ZOTH OMMOG, THE
CD _______ CDZOT 121
Zoth Ommog / Nov '94 / Cargo / Plastic Head

COLOURS
Understand this groove: *UFI* / Metropolis: *Metropolis* / Cry freedom: *Mombassa* / Burning: *MK* / I'm comin' hardcore: *MANIC* / Berry: *TC 1991* / Bad man: *Urban Jungle* / Funky guitar: *TC 1992* / Hyporeel: *Metropolis* / Appolonia: *BM EX* / Always: *MK* / Unity / Hold your head up high / Is this love really real: *Sure Is Pure & Aphrique*
CD _______ CDUCR1
Union City / Jan '93 / EMI

COLOURS (20 Great Hits Of The Sixties)
Needles and pins: *Searchers* / All day and all of the night: *Kinks* / I couldn't live without your love: *Clark, Petula* / Silence is golden: *Tremeloes* / Build me up buttercup: *Foundations* / Mockingbird Hill: *Migil 5* / Colours: *Donovan* / Itchycoo Park: *Small Faces* / Girl don't come: *Shaw, Sandie* / I'm gonna be strong: *Pitney, Gene* / Suddenly you love me: *Tremeloes* / First cut is the deepest: *Arnold, P.P.* / Daydream: *Lovin' Spoonful* / Funny how love can be: *Ivy League* / Ice in the sun: *Status Quo* / Something here in my heart: *Paper Dolls* / Don't sleep in the subway: *Clark, Petula* / She'd rather be with me: *Turtles* / Only love can break a heart: *Pitney, Gene* / Hello Susie: *Amen Corner*
CD _______ TRTCD 104
TrueTrax / Oct '94 / THE

COLOURS OF THE WORLD
Mama yo / Charquia walla / Simera / Fire dance / Araguaney / Roga pa Sabta Barba / Drissa barani / Fan karaibo / Vanne ca maille la / Nihon minyo kumikyoku dai ichiban / Friarhalling / Dansa / 'Lfraj rabby / Jeu de harpe / Chant of the port keats men / Jansa
CD _______ PS 66008
PlayaSound / Jun '97 / ADA / Harmonia Mundi

COLUMBIA GOSPEL 1938
CD _______ DOCD 5487
Document / Nov '96 / ADA / Hot Shot / Jazz Music

COME BACK TO ERIN AND OTHER IRISH LOVE SONGS
Come back to Erin: *O'Hara, Maureen* / Do you remember that night, love: *O'Hara, Maureen* / Next market day: *O'Hara, Maureen* / Nora Lee/I once loved a boy: *O'Hara, Maureen* / I'll take you home again Kathleen: *Parker, Frank* / Galway Bay: *Parker, Frank* / Danny Boy: *Parker, Frank* / Peggy: *Harrington, Pat* / Donnaree: *Quinn, Carmel* / Spinning wheel: *Quinn, Carmel* / If I were a blackbird: *Quinn, Carmel* / Irishmeela: *Quinn, Carmel* / Give him to me: *O'Hara, Maureen* / He moved through the fair: *O'Hara, Maureen* / Come to me, bend to me: *Parker, Frank* / Rose of Tralee: *Downey, Morton*
CD _______ CK 53630
Columbia / Mar '97 / Sony

COME DANCING QUICKSTEP
When you wish upon a star / It's a hap hap happy day / Moonlight avenue / Give a little whistle / You're dancing in my heart / In the middle of a dream / Where or when / Chicago / An apple for the teacher / Begin the beguine / In the still of the night / Walk in the black forest / L A international airport / Don't say goodbye / There will never be another you
CD _______ 306112
Hallmark / Jan '97 / Carlton

COME DANCING SALSA
Taka taka-ta / Cogo el camaron / Pare cochero / Lo que me paso en la / Mi chiquita / El coco / Eso que anda / Se muere la tia / Yo no quiero que seas celosa / El bobo de la yuca / La protesta de los chivos / Santa Barbara / Longina / Los sitios entero
CD _______ 306102
Hallmark / Jan '97 / Carlton

COME GO WITH US (25 Classic Northern Soul Tracks From The Vaults Of EMI)
Pretty little girl: *Smith, George* / I hurt on the other side: *Cook, Jerry* / With all that's in me: *Johnson, Marv* / You've got to look up: *Drapers* / You've got the love: *Little, Rosie* / What's gonna happen to me: *Hodges, Charles* / I can't help loving you: *Breedlove, Jimmy* / She blew a good thing: *Height, Donald* / Don't cry at the party: *Mad Lads* / Baby I need you: *Williams, T.J.* / No more dreams: *Patton, Alexander* / Time will change: *Inverts* / I'm not the one: *Thieves* / Can't take no more: *Turnarounds* / No explanation needed: *Themes* / River of tears: *Banks, Barbara* / You lied, I cried, love died: *Mosley, Tommy* / One day love: *Dodson, Tommy* / Watch yourself: *Nature Boys* / Sweet sweet love: *Sheen, Bobby* / Turn around baby: *Lena & The Deltanettes* / You're a puzzle: *Jive Five* / Come go with me: *Jones, Gloria* / Queen is on her knees: *Tynes, Maria* / Wrong girl: *Showmen* / Cover girl: *Spencer, Carl*
CD _______ GSCD 084
Goldmine / Sep '96 / Vital

COME ON PEEL THE NOISE
CD _______ TANGCD 11
Tangerine / Jul '95 / RTM/Disc

COMEDIENS 1930-1939 (2CD Set)
CD Set _______ 982742
EPM / Jun '93 / ADA / Discovery

COMEDIES/OPERAS FROM SRI LANKA
CD _______ CMT 2741006CD
La Chant Du Monde / Jul '95 / ADA / Harmonia Mundi

COMIN' HOME TO THE BLUES VOL.1
She's into something: *Cray, Robert* / You can't judge a book by the cover: *Buchanan, Roy* / Two fisted mama: *Webster, Katie* / Blues overtook me: *Musselwhite, Charley* / Don't you call that boogie: *Hopkins, Lightnin'* / That woman is poison: *Thomas, Rufus* / Everyday I have the blues: *Memphis Slim* / Sonny's whoopin' the doop: *Terry, Sonny* / I think I got the blues: *Dixon, Willie* / What am I living for: *Brown, Clarence 'Gatemouth'* / Don't take advantage of me: *Winter, Johnny* / Who's lovin' you tonite: *Eaglin, Snooks* / Moon is full: *Collins, Albert* / Jump for joy: *Taylor, Koko* / Whole lotta lovin':

Professor Longhair / Drinkin' wine spo-dee-o-dee: *Otis, Johnny*
CD ______ MCCD 016
Music Club / Feb '91 / Disc / THE

COMIN' HOME TO THE BLUES VOL.1-3 (3CD Set)
CD Set ______ MCBX 002
Music Club / Jan '93 / Disc / THE

COMIN' HOME TO THE BLUES VOL.2
Little red rooster: *Howlin' Wolf* / I'm a man: *Diddley, Bo* / Your funeral and my trial: *Williamson, Sonny Boy* / Wee wee hours: *Berry, Chuck* / First time I met the blues: *Guy, Buddy* / Mannish boy: *Waters, Muddy* / Dust my broom: *James, Elmore* / Juke: *Little Walter* / So many roads, so many trains: *Rush, Otis* / Tell mama: *James, Etta* / Walking the blues: *Dixon, Willie* / Sugar mama: *Hooker, John Lee* / I asked for water (she gave me gasoline): *Howlin' Wolf* / Bring it to Jerome: *Diddley, Bo* / Worried life blues: *Berry, Chuck* / Got my mojo working: *Waters, Muddy* / Don't start me talkin': *Williamson, Sonny Boy* / In the mood: *Hooker, John Lee* / Chicago bound: *Rogers, Jimmy* / Wang dang doodle: *Taylor, Koko* / I'd rather go blind: *James, Etta* / Diggin' my potatoes: *Washboard Sam* / Reconsider baby: *Fulson, Lowell* / My baby: *Little Walter*
CD ______ MCCD 026
Music Club / May '91 / Disc / THE

COMIN' HOME TO THE BLUES VOL.3
When you see the tears from my eyes: *Guy, Buddy* / Goin' mad blues: *Hooker, John Lee* / All my love in vain: *Williamson, Sonny Boy* / Standing at the burial ground: *McDowell, 'Mississippi' Fred* / Hi-heel sneakers: *Tucker, Tommy* / She's 19 years old: *Waters, Muddy* / How blue can you get: *Collins, Albert* / Hoodoo man: *Wells, Junior* / No friend around: *Hooker, John Lee* / Don't know where I've been: *Diddley, Bo* / Christo redemptor: *Musselwhite, Charley* / Blue and lonesome: *McPhee, Tony & Billy Boy Arnold* / Hoochie coochie man: *Waters, Muddy* / Baptize me in wine: *Hawkins, Screamin' Jay* / Sad hours: *Little Walter* / One room country shack: *Butterfield, Paul*
CD ______ MCCD 044
Music Club / Sep '91 / Disc / THE

COMING DOWN
CD ______ CRECD 135
Creation / Feb '95 / 3mv/Vital

COMING ON STRONG (2CD Set)
CD Set ______ NSCD 004
Newsound / Feb '95 / THE

COMMERCIAL BREAKS
Only you: *Praise* / Lovely day: *Withers, Bill* / Summer breeze: *Isley Brothers* / Love train: *O'Jays* / How 'bout us: *Champaign* / Turn turn turn: *Byrds* / It's over: *Orbison, Roy* / Move over darling: *Day, Doris* / I can see clearly now: *Nash, Johnny* / Stand by your man: *Wynette, Tammy* / Always on my mind: *Nelson, Willie* / Blue velvet: *Vinton, Bobby* / I can help: *Swan, Billy* / Take five: *Brubeck, Dave* / Summertime: *Vaughan, Sarah* / Mannish boy: *Waters, Muddy* / Should I stay or should I go: *Clash*
CD ______ 4690482
Columbia / Nov '91 / Sony

COMMITTED TO JUNGLE
CD ______ VZS 16CD
Vizion Sound / Apr '95 / Jet Star

COMMODORE STORY (2CD Set)
Love is just around the corner: *Condon, Eddie* / Strange fruit: *Holiday, Billie* / Good man is hard to find / You're some pretty doll: *Waller, Fats* / Indiana: *Byas, Don* / At a Georgia camp meeting: *Bechet, Sidney* / Way down yonder in New Orleans: *Bechet, Sidney* / Dedication: *Hawkins, Coleman* / Sugar: *Wiley, Lee* / Billie's blues: *Holiday, Billie* / My ideal: *Tatum, Art & Coleman Hawkins* / Memories of you: *Webster, Ben & Sid Catlet* / Night and day: *Wilson, Teddy & Edmond Hall* / Body and soul: *Eldridge, Roy & Berry, Leon 'Chu'* / Smack: *Carter, Benny & Coleman Hawkins* / World is waiting for the: *Goodman, Benny & Mel Powell* / Mamie's blues: *Morton, Jelly Roll* / Franklin Street blues: *Johnson, Bunk* / Willie the weeper: *Wilber, Bob* / Lazy daddy: *Original Dixieland Jazz Band* / That's a plenty: *Davison, 'Wild' Bill* / New Orleans: *Hackett, Bobby* / Memphis blues: *Spanier, Muggsy* / Sheik of Araby: *De Paris, Sidney* / You need coachin': *Hot Lips Page Trio* / Diane: *Teagarden, Jack* / Tin roof blues: *Brunies, George* / Peg o' my love: *Mole, Miff* / Keeping out of mischief now: *Russell, Pee Wee* / Man I love: *Hall, Edmond* / Blue room: *Freeman, Bud* / Sunny side of the street: *Berry, Leon 'Chu'* / Selection from the gutter: *Hodes, Art* / Summertime: *Sullivan, Joe* / Ec-Stacy: *Stacy, Jess* / Begin the beguine: *Heywood, Eddie* / Jammin' the boogie: *Ammons, Albert* / Lazy river: *Zack, George* / Finger buster: *Smith, Willie 'The Lion'* / Squeeze me: *Sutton, Ralph*
CD Set ______ CMD 24002
Commodore Jazz / Feb '97 / New Note/ BMG

COMMON GROUND - CELTIC VOICE
'O bhean a 'ti: *Brennan, Maire* / Mary of the south seas: *Finn, Tim & Neil* / Tomorrow: *Bono & Adam Clayton* / Cavan potholes: *Shannon, Sharon* / Help me to believe: *Brady, Paul* / On Raglan Road: *O'Connor, Sinead* / As I roved out: *Kennedy, Brian* / Night before Larry was stretched: *Costello, Elvis* / Mna na h'eireann: *Bush, Kate* / Whistling low/Errigal: *Spillane, Davy & Donal Lunny* / My heart's tonight in Ireland: *Irvine, Andy* / Cathain: *O'Maonlai, Liam* / Bogie's bonnie belle: *Moore, Christy*
CD ______ PRMTVCD 1
Premier/EMI / May '96 / EMI

COMMUNIQUE (2CD Set)
CD Set ______ SIXXCD 4
Six6 / Sep '96 / 3mv/Sony / Pinnacle

COMPACT D'AFRIQUE
Adjani Muana Kini: *Mabele, Aurlus* / Iyole: *Kanda Bongo Man* / Masquereau: *Les Quatre Etoiles* / Sane-mamadou: *Tchico & Les Officers Of African Music* / Lascar Pa Kapi: *Choc Stars* / Izia: *Papa Wemba Et Mavuela* / Le bon samaritain: *Sukami, Teddy*
CD ______ CDORB 907
Globestyle / Aug '86 / Pinnacle

COMPAGNU TI MANNU
CD ______ TA 012CD
Robi Droli / Apr '95 / ADA / Direct

COMPETING HIGHLAND DANCER, THE (Highland & National Dances From Beginners To Open Dancers)
CD ______ CDITV 516
Scotdisc / Jul '90 / Conifer/BMG / Duncans / Ross

COMPILATIONS
CD ______ NATCD 50
Nation / Feb '95 / RTM/Disc

COMPLETE 'D' SINGLES COLLECTION VOL.1, THE (4CD Set)
Can't play hookey: *Noack, Eddie* / My steady dream: *Noack, Eddie* / Mom and Dad I love you too: *Travis, Al* / He brough us together: *Travis, Al* / Cotton picker: *Watts, Wortham* / Lonesome: *Watts, Wortham* / Never meant for me: *Carl, Utah* / Treasured memories: *Carl, Utah* / I can't find the doorknob: *Jimmy & Johnny* / Keep telling me: *Jimmy & Johnny* / Baby, when the sun goes down: *Douglas, Tony* / World in my arms: *Douglas, Tony* / Talk to me lonesome heart: *O'Gwynn, James* / Changeable: *O'Gwynn, James* / I want to be where you're gonna be: *Singleton, Margie* / Shattered kingdom: *Singleton, Margie* / Chantilly lace: *Big Bopper* / Purple people eater meets the witch doctor: *Big Bopper* / Gonna pack up my toubles: *Hall, Sonny & The Echoes* / My big fat baby: *Hall, Sonny & The Echoes* / Walking away: *Dollar, Johnny* / No memories: *Dollar, Johnny* / Texas Alaska: *Jackson, Ray* / Alaska: *Jackson, Ray* / I played the fool: *Four B's* / Love eternal: *Four B's* / Don't hold me to a vow: *Moncrief, Bobby* / Here is my heart: *Moncrief, Bobby* / Dreaming in vain: *Sheets, Sonny* / Wheels: *Terry & The Pirates* / Blues got me: *Bond, Eddie* / Standing in your window: *Bond, Eddie* / Same old fool: *Barber, Glen* / Tomorrow: *Barber, Glen* / Hello sadness: *Barber, Glen* / Daydreaming again: *Bragg, Doug* / If I find my dreamgirl: *Bragg, Doug* / Have blues, will travel: *Noack, Eddie* / Price of love: *Noack, Eddie* / Ohh wow: *Dee & Patty* / Sweet lovin' baby: *Dee & Patty* / Understand: *Forrer, Johnnie* / Fools paradise: *Forrer, Johnnie* / Blue memories: *O'Gwynn, James* / You don't want to hold me: *O'Gwynn, James* / Draggin' the fiddle: *Choates, Harry* / Allons a lafayette: *Choates, Harry* / Jole Blon: *Choates, Harry* / Corpus Christie waltz: *Choates, Harry* / Echo mountain: *Jackson, Ray* / Tears of tomorrow: *Jackson, Ray* / Lookin: *Porter, Royce* / I still belong to you: *Porter, Royce* / Lonely night: *Mathis, James* / I've been known to cry: *Mathis, James* / Stealin' sugar: *Lindsay, Merle* / Hoy rag: *Lindsay, Merle* / I'm all wrapped up: *Doyle, Ted* / He made you mine: *Doyle, Ted* / Mean autry: *Thibodeaux, Rufus* / Cameron memorial waltz: *Thibodeaux, Rufus* / True affection: *Johnson, Byron* / You were only fooling: *Johnson, Byron* / I need someone: *Mac, Johnny* / That's all I can do: *Mac, Johnny* / Step aside old heart: *Timmons, Patsy* / I understand him: *Timmons, Patsy* / Won't you tell me: *Stanford, Doug* / Sady: *Stanford, Doug* / Men do cry: *Hall, Sonny* / Day you walked away: *Hall, Sonny* / I kept it a secret: *Edge, Dave* / I didn't think of you: *Edge, Dave* / I don't live there any more: *Noack, Eddie* / Walk' em off: *Noack, Eddie* / Reprieve of Tom Dooley: *Johnson, Rick* / Barbara Allen: *Johnson, Rick* / Maple sugar: *Allen, Ward* / Back up and push: *Allen, Ward* / Bugger burns: *Lynn, Jerry* / Queen of the moon: *Lynn, Jerry* / It'll be my first time: *Kilgore, Merle* / I take a trip to the moon: *Kilgore, Merle* / Opelousas waltz: *Choates, Harry* / Poor Hobo: *Choates, Harry* / Honky tonk boogie: *Choates, Harry* / Port arthur waltz: *Choates, Harry* / I'm all alone: *Bragg, Doug* / Calling me back: *Bragg, Doug* / Whirlwind: *Bragg, Doug* / Man I met: *Campi, Ray* / Ballad of Donna and Peggy Sue: *Campi, Ray* / Dottie: *McCoy, Doyle* / Some how I don't mind: *McCoy, Doyle* / Justice of love: *Bowman, Cecil* / Man awaitin': *Bowman, Cecil* / Penalty of love: *Velvetones* / Come back: *Velvetones* / Born to love you: *Heap, Jimmy* / Some one else is filling my shoes: *Heap, Jimmy* / I love only you: *Heap, Jimmy* / I Like it: *Heap, Jimmy* / Gold records in the snow: *Heap, Jimmy* / Happy little bluebird: *Barnes, Benny* / Chantilly lace cha cha: *Kimbrough, Bill* / Egg head: *Kimbrough, Bill* / From a kiss to the blues: *Mathis, Johnny* / Since I said goodbye to love: *Mathis, Johnny* / What makes you cry: *Jackson, Ray* / Tea leaves don't cry: *Jackson, Ray* / Trumpets and clarinets: *Kucera, Ernie* / Annie waltz: *Kucera, Ernie* / One more heartache: *Doyle, Ted* / Just for the thrill: *Doyle, Ted* / It's wrong for me to love you: *Johnson, Byron* / Our love is not worth living for: *Johnson, Byron* / Letter overdue: *Gray, Claude* / I'm not supposed: *Gray, Claude* / Don't look behind: *Noack, Eddie* / Thinking man's woman: *Noack, Eddie* / Baby don't go: *Charles, Andy & The Blues Kings* / Love come back: *Charles, Andy & The Blues Kings*
CD Set ______ BCD 15832
Bear Family / Nov '95 / Direct / Rollercoaster / Swift

COMPLETE CHRISTMAS BOX, THE (Christmas Carols/Tijuana Christmas/ Merry Christmas/3CD Set)
God rest ye merry gentlemen / While shepherd's watched / See amid the Winters snow / Silent night / Good King Wenceslas / O little town of Bethlehem / Unto us is born a son / Away in a manger / Rocking / In Dulci Jubilo / Ding dong merrily on high / Coventry carol / I saw three ships / Holly and the ivy / Angels from the realms of glory / First noel / O come all ye faithful (adeste fidelis) / Once in Royal David's city / Hark the Herald Angels sing / Jingle bells / Silent night / Hark the Herald Angels sing / Ding dong merrily on high / While shepherd's watched / Holly and the ivy / Away in a manger / We three kings of Orient are / See amid the Winter's snow / O little town of Bethlehem / Good King Wenceslas / It came upon a midnight clear / First noel / Christians awake / God rest ye merry gentlemen / O come all ye faithful (adeste fidelis) / Once in Royal David's city / White Christmas / White Christmas: *Martin, Dean* / Christmas song: *Cole, Nat 'King'* / Santa Claus is coming to town: *Lee, Peggy* / Jingle bells: *Paul, Les* / Winter wonderland: *Mercer, Johnny* / Santa Claus' party: *Baxter, Les* / Silver bells: *Whiting, Margaret & Jimmy Wakely* / Rudolph the red-nosed reindeer: *May, Billy* / Christmas waltz: *Lee, Peggy* / (All I want for Christmas is) my two front teeth: *Cole, Nat 'King'* / Christmas blues: *Martin, Dean* / Silent night: *Paul, Les & Mary Ford*
CD Set ______ CDTRBOX 244
Trio / Oct '96 / EMI

COMPLETE IRISH DANCING SET (2CD Set)
CD Set ______ CDH 1050CD
Outlet / Jul '95 / ADA / CM / Direct / Duncans / Koch / Ross

COMPLETE IRISH NATIONAL ANTHEM, THE
CD ______ IRBCD 1937
Outlet / Jul '94 / ADA / CM / Direct / Duncans / Koch / Ross

COMPLETE SONGS OF ROBERT BURNS VOL.1, THE
When rosy May comes in wi' flowers / O, that I had ne'er been married / Wee Willie Gray / O wha'll mow me now / Brose & butter / Wintry West extends his blast / Sweet Afton / Duncan Gray cam here to woo / Winter it is past / Guide 'en to you kimmer / Kellyburn braes / Slave's lament / Of a the airts the wind can blaw / What can a young lassie / Ay waulkin O / O steer her up, an huad her gaun / Cooper o' Cuddy / O rattlin roarin Willie / To the weavers gin ye go / Lady Mary Ann / Montgomerie's Peggy / Lea rig / Yestreen I had a pint o' wine
CD ______ CKD 047
Linn / Mar '96 / PolyGram

COMPLETE SONGS OF ROBERT BURNS VOL.2, THE
Soldier's return / Reel O' Stumpie / I hae a wife o'ma ain / My Nanie O / Ye Jacobites by name / Rantin, rovin Robin / O let me in this ae night / Auld man's mare's dead / How cruel are the parents / Leezie Lindsay / My wife's a wanton wee thing / To Daunton me / Hey ca' thro / De'il's awa' wi' tha exciseman / Silver tassie / Kissin my Katie / Scots wha hae / O were I on Parnassus Hill / O an ye were dead gudeman / Willie Wastle / Beware o' bonnie Ann / Willie brew'd a peck o' maut / Rosebud by my early walk / Whistle o'er the lave o't / Jumpin John / Dusty miller / My collier laddie / Weary pund o' tow / Now westlin winds
CD ______ CKD 051
Linn / May '96 / PolyGram

COMPLETE STAX/VOLT SINGLES, THE (1959-1968/9CD Set)
Fool in love: *Veltones* / Because I love you: *Carla & Rufus* / Gee whiz: *Thomas, Carla* / You make me feel so good: *Chips* / Love of my own: *Thomas, Carla* / Last night: *Mar-Keys* / I didn't believe: *Rufus & Friend* / I'm going home: *Prince Conley* / (Mama, mama) Wish me good luck: *Thomas, Carla* / Morning after: *Mar-Keys* / Life I live: *Stephens, Barbara* / About noon: *Mar-Keys* / Burnt biscuits: *Triumphs* / I kinda think he does: *Thomas, Carla* / Foxy: *Mar-Keys* / You don't miss your water/Formula of love: *Bell, William* / Goofin' off: *Skipper, Macy* / Wait a minute: *Stephens, Barbara* / Sunday jealous: *Charles, Nick* / That's the way it is with me: *Stephens, Barbara* / Pop-eye stroll: *Mar-Keys* / Three dogwoods: *Charles, Nick* / No tears: *Tonettes* / Why should I suffer: *Canes* / Whot's happenin': *Mar-Keys* / Just across the street/There's a love: *Del-Rios* / Can't ever let go: *Thomas, Rufus* / Green onions/Behave yourself: *Booker T & The MG's* / Any other way: *Bell, William* / I'll bring it home to you: *Thomas, Carla* / Sack o' woe: *Mar-Keys* / These arms of mine: *Redding, Otis* / Teardrop sea: *Tonettes* / Dog: *Thomas, Rufus* / Jelly bread: *Booker T & The MG's* / I told you so: *Bell, William* / Bo-time: *Mar-Keys* / Home grown: *Booker T & The MG's* / My imaginary guy: *Parker, Deanie* / Just as I thought: *Bell, William* / What a fool I've been: *Thomas, Carla* / Hawg: *Kirk, Eddie* / Don't be afraid of love: *Mack, Oscar* / That's my guy: *Johnson, Cheryl & Pam* / Chinese checkers: *Booker T & The MG's* / Somebody mentioned your name: *Bell, William* / What can I do: *Marchan, Bobby* / That's what my heart needs: *Redding, Otis* / What can it be: *Astors* / Bango: *Billy & The King Bees* / Them bones: *Kirk, Eddie* / Walking the dog: *Thomas, Rufus* / I'll show you: *Bell, William* / Pain in my heart: *Redding, Otis* / Gee whiz it's Christmas: *Thomas, Carla* / Mo' onions: *Booker T & The MG's* / Frog stomp: *Newman, Floyd* / Can your monkey do the dog: *Thomas, Rufus* / You won't do right: *Marchan, Bobby* / Wondering: *Drapels* / Each step I take: *Parker, Deanie* / Honeydripper: *Van-Dells* / Who will it be tomorrow: *Bell, William* / Come to me/Don't leave me this way: *Redding, Otis* / I don't want you anymore: *Jefferson, Eddie* / Restless: *Cobras* / Somebody stole my dog: *Thomas, Rufus* / Big party: *Barbara & The Browns* / That's really some good/Night time is the right time: *Rufus* / Security: *Redding, Otis* / Dream girl: *Mack, Oscar* / Closer to my baby: *Williams, Dorothy* / I've got no time to lose: *Thomas, Carla* / Young man: *Drapels* / Soul dressing: *Booker T & The MG's* / After laughter (comes tears): *Rene, Wendy* / Can't explain how it happened: *Hunter, Ivory Joe* / Bush bash: *Mar-Keys* / Please return to me: *Fleets* / Jump back: *Thomas, Rufus* / Chained and bound: *Redding, Otis* / In my heart: *Barbara & The Browns* / Spunky: *Jenkins, Johnny* / Bar B Q: *Rene, Wendy* / Sidewalk surf: *Mad Lads* / Can't be still: *Booker T & The MG's* / Woman's love: *Thomas, Carla* / Yank me (doodle): *Baracudas* / That's how strong my love is/Mr. Pitiful: *Redding, Otis* / Don't let her be your baby: *Del-Rays* / Can't see you when I want you: *Porter, David* / My lover: *Barbara & The Browns* / Got you on my mind: *Barbara & The Browns* / How do you quit (someone you love): *Thomas, Carla* / Biggest fool in town: *Gorgeous George* / Banana juice: *Mar-Keys* / Little Sally Walker: *Thomas, Rufus* / Goodnight baby: *Sam & Dave* / Bootleg/Outrage: *Booker T & The MG's* / I've been loving you too long: *Redding, Otis* / Candy: *Astors* / Give you what I got/Reap what you sow: *Rene, Wendy* / Stop look what you're doin': *Thomas, Carla* / Willy willy: *Thomas, Rufus* / Don't have to shop around: *Mad Lads* / Crying all by myself: *Bell, William* / I take what I want: *Sam & Dave* / When you move you lose: *Thomas, Rufus & Carla* / Respect: *Redding, Otis* / Make it me: *Premiers* / World is round: *Thomas, Rufus* / In the twilight zone: *Astors* / Blue groove: *Sir Isaac & The Dodads* / You don't know like I know: *Sam & Dave* / Grab this thing: *Mar-Keys* / Be my lady: *Booker T & The MG's* / Comfort me: *Thomas, Carla* / I can't turn you loose/Just one more day: *Redding, Otis* / I want someone: *Mad Lads* / Birds and the bees: *Thomas, Rufus & Carla* / Philly dog: *Mar-Keys* / I had a dream: *Taylor, Johnnie* / Satisfaction: *Redding, Otis* / Things get better: *Floyd, Eddie* / I'll run your hurt away: *Johnson, Ruby* / Hot dog: *Four Shells* / Let me be good to you: *Thomas, Carla* / Hold on I'm comin': *Sam & Dave* / Laundromat blues: *King, Albert* / Sugar sugar: *Mad Lads* / Share what you got/ Marching off to war: *Bell, William* / My lover's prayer: *Redding, Otis* / Your good thing is about to end: *John, Mable* / I got to love somebody's baby: *Taylor, Johnnie* / What will love tend to make: *Mad Lads* / Knock on wood: *Floyd, Eddie* / B-A-B-Y: *Thomas, Carla* / My sweet potato/Booker-loo: *Booker T & The MG's* / Oh pretty woman: *King, Albert* / Said I wasn't gonna tell nobody: *Sam & Dave* / Never like this before: *Bell, William* / Fa fa fa fa fa (Sad song): *Redding, Otis* / Patch my heart: *Mad Lads* / Sister's got a boyfriend: *Thomas, Rufus* / Come to me my darling/When love comes down: *Johnson, Ruby* / Try a little tenderness: *Redding, Otis* / Crosscut saw: *King, Albert* / Little bluebird/Toe hold: *Taylor, Johnnie* / Jingle bells: *Booker T & The MG's* / You got me hummin': *Sam & Dave* / You're taking up another: *John, Mable* / All I want for Christmas is you: *Thomas, Carla* / Please uncle Sam: *Charmels* / Something good: *Thomas, Carla* / Raise your head: *Floyd, Eddie* / Ain't that lovin' you: *Taylor, Johnnie* / I don't want to lose: *Mad Lads* / When something is wrong: *Sam & Dave* / Let me down slow: *Wilson, Bobby* / Hip hug-her: *Booker T & The MG's* / Everybody loves a winner: *Bell, William* / Minnie skirt Minnie:

Rice, Sir Mack / When tomorrow comes: *Thomas, Carla* / Spoiler: *Purrell, Eddie* / I love you more than words can say: *Redding, Otis* / If ever I needed love: *Johnson, Ruby* / Same time, same place: *John, Mable* / Tramp: *Redding, Otis & Carla Thomas* / Soul finger/Knucklehead: *Bar-Kays* / Shake: *Redding, Otis* / Born under a bad sign: *King, Albert* / Soothe me/I can't stand up: *Sam & Dave* / Don't rock the boat: *Floyd, Eddie* / My inspiration: *Mad Lads* / Love sickness: *Rice, Sir Mack* / How can you: *Jeanne & The Darlings* / Sophisticated Cissy: *Thomas, Rufus* / I'll always have faith in you: *Thomas, Carla* / Love is a doggone good thing: *Floyd, Eddie* / Groovin'/Slim Jenkins place: *Booker T & The MG's* / Glory of love: *Redding, Otis* / I'm a big girl now/ Wait you dog: *John, Mable* / You can't get away from it: *Taylor, Johnnie* / Eloise: *Bell, William* / Knock on wood: *Redding, Otis & Carla Thomas* / I'm glad to do it: *Blast, C.L.* / You can't run away from your heart: *Clay, Judy* / I'll gladly take you back: *Charmels* / Soul man: *Sam & Dave* / Daddy didn't tell me: *Astors* / Give everybody some: *Bar-Kays* / On a Saturday night: *Floyd, Eddie* / Don't hit me no more: *John, Mable* / Somebody's sleeping: *Taylor, Johnnie* / Winter snow: *Booker T & The MG's* / Every day: *Bell, William* / What I'll do for satisfaction: *Daye, Johnny* / Pick up the pieces: *Thomas, Carla* / Down ta my house: *Thomas, Rufus* / As long as I've got you: *Charmels* / Soul girl: *Jeanne & The Darlings* / Cold feet: *King, Albert* / I thank you/Wrap it up: *Sam & Dave* / (Sittin' on the) dock of the bay: *Redding, Otis* / Don't pass your judgement: *Memphis Nomads* / Lovey dovey: *Redding, Otis & Carla Thomas* / I got a sure thing: *Nightingales* / Big bird: *Floyd, Eddie* / Hard day's night: *Bar-Kays* / Next time: *Taylor, Johnnie* / Tribute to a king/Every man: *Bell, William* / Able mable: *John, Mable* / Memphis train/ I think I made a boo boo: *Thomas, Rufus* / What will later on be like/Hang me now: *Jeanne & The Darlings* / Soul power: *Martin, Derek* / Bring your love back to me: *Lyndell, Linda* / Dime a dozen: *Thomas, Carla* / Whatever hurts you: *Mad Lads* / Happy song: *Redding, Otis* / Lucy: *King, Albert* / I ain't particular: *Taylor, Johnnie*
CD Set ______ **7567822182**
Atlantic / May '91 / Warner Music

COMPLETE STAX/VOLT SOUL SINGLES VOL.2, THE (1968-1971/9CD Set)
I was born to love you: *Walton, Shirley* / Precious, precious: *Hayes, Isaac* / Send peace and harmony home: *Walton, Shirley* / Soul limbo: *Booker T & The MG's* / I've never found a girl: *Floyd, Eddie* / It's been a long time coming: *Delaney & Bonnie* / What a man: *Lyndell, Linda* / I like everything about you: *Hughes, Jimmy* / Stay baby stay: *Daye, Johnny* / Private number: *Clay, Judy & William Bell* / So nice: *Mad Lads* / Long walk to DC: *Staple Singers* / Give 'em love: *Soul Children* / Funky Mississippi: *Thomas, Rufus* / Lovin' feeling: *Charmels* / Where do I go: *Thomas, Carla* / Bed of roses: *Clay, Judy* / Bring it on home to me: *Floyd, Eddie* / It's unbelievable (how you control my soul): *Jeanne & The Darlings* / Who's making love: *Taylor, Johnnie* / Mighty cold Winter: *Dino & Doc* / Hang 'em high: *Booker T & The MG's* / You're leaving me: *Ollie & The Nightingales* / Copy kat: *Bar-Kays* / I forgot to be your lover: *Bell, William* / Running out: *John, Mable* / My baby specializes: *Bell, William & Judy Clay* / I'll understand: *Soul Children* / Ghetto: *Staple Singers* / Blues power: *King, Albert* / Echo: *Epsilons* / Funky way: *Thomas, Rufus* / Take care of your homework: *Taylor, Johnnie* / I like what you're doing (to me): *Thomas, Carla* / I've got to have your love: *Floyd, Eddie* / Let 'em down baby: *Hughes, Jimmy* / Love is here today and gone tomorrow: *Mad Lads* / It ain't long enough: *Clay, Judy* / Mellow way you treat your man: *Ollie & The Nightingales* / Private number: *Stitt, Sonny* / Time is tight: *Booker T & The MG's* / Double or nothing: *Mar-Keys* / (Sittin' on the) dock of the bay: *Staple Singers* / So I can love you: *Emotions* / Don't stop dancing (to the music): *Bar-Kays* / One more chance: *Joseph, Margie* / I wanna be good (to you): *Dotson, Jimmy* / Finger lickin' good: *Miller, Art Jerry* / Tighten up my thang: *Soul Children* / Whole world is falling down: *Bell, William* / Testify (I wonna): *Taylor, Johnnie* / Drowning on dry land: *King, Albert* / Do the cissy: *Stingers* / Don't tell your mama: *Floyd, Eddie* / Mrs. Robinson: *Booker T & The MG's* / Love's sweet sensation: *Bell, William & Mavis Staples* / Just because your love has gone: *Banks, Darrell* / Chains of love: *Hughes, Jimmy* / Happy: *Bell, William* / Challenge: *Staple Singers* / Soul-a-lujah: *Taylor, Johnnie/Eddie Floyd/ William Bell* / Never, never let you go: *Floyd, Eddie & Mavis Staples* / Just keep on loving me: *Taylor, Johnnie & Carla Thomas* / I need you woman: *Bell, William & Carla Thomas* / I've got a feeling: *Ollie & The Nightingales* / It's time to pay for the fun (we've had): *Jeanne & The Darlings* / I could never be president: *Taylor, Johnnie* / By the time I get to Phoenix: *Mad Lads* / Long and lonely world: *Kelly, Colette* / Midnight cowboy: *Bar-Kays* / I've fallen in love (with you): *Thomas, Carla* / Slum baby: *Booker T & The MG's* / Best part of a love affair: *Emotions* / By the time I get to Phoenix: *Hayes, Isaac* / Walk on by: *Hayes, Isaac* / Tupelo Part 1: *Staples, Pops/ Steve Cropper/ Albert King* / Water: *Staples, Pops/ Steve Cropper/ Albert King* / Sweeter he is: *Soul Children* / You're driving me (To the arms of a stranger): *Staples, Mavis* / Open up your heart: *Newcomers* / Why is the wine sweeter (on the other side): *Floyd, Eddie* / When will we be paid: *Staple Singers* / Grinder man: *Hooker, John Lee* / Born under a bad sign: *Bell, William* / What you gonna do: *Joseph, Margie* / I'm so glad: *Hughes, Jimmy* / Beautiful feelings: *Banks, Darrell* / Your love was strange: *Dramatics* / Love bones: *Taylor, Johnnie* / Hard to say goodbye: *Delaney & Bonnie* / Got to get rid of you: *Barnes, J.J.* / Habit forming love: *Milner, Reggie* / My thing is a moving thing: *TSU Tornadoes* / Stealing love: *Emotions* / Wrapped up in love again: *King, Albert* / Do the funky chicken: *Thomas, Rufus* / California girl: *Floyd, Eddie* / Tribute to a blackwoman, Part 1: *Hayes, Bernie* / Song and dance: *Bar-Kays* / Hold on I'm comin': *Soul Children* / Love's gonna tear your playhouse down Part 1: *Brooks, Chuck* / Help me put out the flame (in my heart): *Hines, Ernie* / Black boy: *Staples, Pops* / Bracing myself for a fall: *Ollie & The Nightingales* / All I have to do is dream: *Bell, William & Carla Thomas* / Singing about love: *Jeanne & The Darlings* / Goodies: *Chris & Shack* / Just the way you are today: *Lewis, Barbara* / Creeper returns: *Little Sonny* / Guide me well: *Thomas, Carla* / Give a damn: *Staple Singers* / Steal away: *Taylor, Johnnie* / Your sweet lovin': *Joseph, Margie* / I forgot to remember: *Jones & Blumenburg* / Can't see you when I want you: *Porter, David* / Never be true: *Thomas, Carla* / Can't you see what you're doing to me: *King, Albert* / Sixty minute man: *Thomas, Rufus* / Preacher and the bear: *Thomas, Rufus* / Something: *Booker T & The MG's* / Seeing is believing: *Mad Lads* / You're my only temptation: *Ryan, Roz* / What I don't know won't hurt me: *Thompson, Paul* / Right, tight and out of sight: *Branding Iron* / (What's under) The natural do: *Kasandra, John* / My girl: *Floyd, Eddie* / I have learned to do without you: *Staples, Mavis* / Play the music tornadoes: *TSU Tornadoes* / Lonely soldier: *Bell, William* / Heart association: *Emotions* / I stand accused: *Hayes, Isaac* / Brand new day: *Staple Singers* / Sweeter tomorrow: *Joseph, Margie* / Cool strut: *Hayes, Bernie* / You put the sunshine back in my world: *Newcomers* / Montego Bay: *Bar-Kays* / Got it together parts I and II: *Robinson, Rudy & The Hungry Five* / Wade in the water: *Little Sonny* / You're movin' much too fast: *Nightingales* / Best year of my life: *Floyd, Eddie* / I am somebody: *Taylor, Johnnie* / I loved you like I love my very life: *Thomas, Carla* / Soul machine: *Milner, Reggie* / (Follow her) Rules and regulations: *Temprees* / Do the Push and pull (part 1): *Thomas, Rufus* / Love changes: *Charlene & The Soul Serenaders* / Put your world in my world (Best of two worlds): *Soul Children* / Love is plentiful: *Staple Singers* / Heavy makes you happy: *Staple Singers* / Who took the merry out of christmas: *Staple Singers* / Too many lovers: *Shack* / Black christmas: *Emotions* / Mistletoe and me: *Hayes, Isaac* / Ask the lonely: *Lewis, Barbara* / Jody's got your girl and gone: *Taylor, Johnnie* / Finish me off: *Soul Children* / Oh how it rained: *Floyd, Eddie* / Look of love: *Hayes, Isaac* / Electrified love: *Hines, Ernie* / Melting pot: *Booker T & The MG's* / That's the way I like it (I like it that way): *Lewis, Barbara* / Mr. Big Stuff: *Knight, Jean* / You make me want to love you: *Emotions* / Stop, In the name of love: *Joseph, Margie* / I don't wanna lose you: *Taylor, Johnnie* / Girl I love you: *Temprees* / World is round: *Thomas, Rufus* / Penny for your thoughts: *Bell, William* / Never can say goodbye: *Hayes, Isaac* / I don't want to be like my daddy: *Nightingales* / You've got to earn it: *Staple Singers* / Hold on to it: *Limitations* / What'cha see is what'cha get: *Dramatics* / Born too late: *Branding Iron* / Just ain't as strong as I used to be: *Hughes, Jimmy* / That other woman got my man and gone: *Joseph, Margie* / If you think it (You may as well do it): *Emotions* / Shame on the family name: *Scott, Calvin* / Blood is thicker than water: *Floyd, Eddie* / Hijackin' love: *Taylor, Johnnie* / Sweetback's theme: *Van Peebles, Melvin* / Breakdown (part 1): *Thomas, Rufus* / Pin the tail on the donkey: *Newcomers* / Them hot pants: *Sain, Lee* / If that ain't a reason (for your woman to leave you): *Little Milton* / It's good to be careful (But it's better to be loved): *Shack* / Where would you be today: *Ilana* / Everybody wants to go to heaven: *King, Albert* / Got to get away from it all: *Soul Children* / Love's creepin' up on me: *United Image* / Show me how: *Emotions* / If I give it up, I want it back: *Porter, David* / Woman named trouble: *Little Sonny* / Losing boy: *Giles, Eddie* / Respect yourself: *Staple Singers* / I'll kill a brick (About my man): *Hot Sauce* / You think you're hot stuff: *Knight, Jean* / All for the love of a woman: *Bell, William* / Shaft: *Hayes, Isaac* / Jamaica this morning: *MG's* / Promises of yesterday: *Mad Lads* / Girl, come on home: *Major Lance* / (Let hurt put you in the love) Loser's seat: *Wilson, Joni* / My baby love: *Temprees* / How do you move a mountain: *Leaders* / Black nasty boogie: *Black Nasty* / Do the funky penguin (part 1): *Thomas, Rufus* / You've got a cushion to fall on: *Thomas, Carla* / Get up and get down: *Dramatics* / Son of Shaft: *Bar-Kays* / Don't you mess with my money, my honey or my woman: *Johnson, L.V.* / I can smell that funky music: *Mercury, Eric* / Sadness for things: *Scott, Calvin* / That's what love will make you do: *Little Milton* / Standing in for Jody: *Taylor, Johnnie*
CD Set ______ **9SCD 4411**
Stax / Sep '93 / Pinnacle

COMPLETE STAX/VOLT SOUL SINGLES VOL.3, THE (1972-1975/10CD Set)
Yum yum yum (I want some): *Floyd, Eddie* / Carry on: *Knight, Jean* / Do your thing: *Hayes, Isaac* / I've been lonely for so long: *Knight, Frederick* / Nothing is everlasting: *Thomas, Annette* / Hearsay: *Soul Children* / Angel of mercy: *King, Albert* / In the rain: *Dramatics* / She's my old lady too: *Sain, Lee* / Explain it to her Mama: *Temprees* / Right on: *Sons Of Slum* / Doing my own thing: *Taylor, Johnnie* / My honey and me: *Emotions* / Let's stay together: *Hayes, Isaac* / Bring it home (amd give it to me): *Hot Sauce* / Look around you: *Black Society* / Don't do it: *Nightingales* / I'm with you: *Nightingales* / I'll take you there: *Staple Singers* / Which way: *Leaders* / Living a life without you: *Brown, Veda* / What's good for you (don't have to be good to you): *Scales, Harvey* / Let me repair your heart: *Mad Lads* / What's usual seems natur'l: *Mercury, Eric* / I wanna make up (before we break up): *Major Lance* / ain't that lovin' you: *Hayes, Isaac & David Porter* / Walking the back streets and crying: *Little Milton* / Save us: *Bell, William* / 6-3-8 (that's the number to play): *Thomas, Rufus* / Starting all over again: *Mel & Tim* / Keep on loving me: *Stefan* / (I'm afraid) the masquerade is over: *Porter, David* / Going down slow (parts 1 and 2): *Little Sonny* / I could never be happy: *Emotions* / Don't take my kindness for weakness: *Soul Children* / I'll play the blues for you: *King, Albert* / I dedicate my life for you: *Hatcher, Roger* / Do the sweetback: *March Wind* / Getting funky round here: *Black Nasty* / When the chips are down: *Porter, David* / Sugar: *Thomas, Carla* / You're good enough (to be my baby): *Floyd, Eddie* / This world: *Staple Singers* / Helping man: *Knight, Jean* / Ain't I good: *Kasandra, John* / Dance, dance, dance: *Bar-Kays* / Dedicated to the one I love: *Temprees* / Toast to the fool: *Dramatics* / Stop doggin' me: *Taylor, Johnnie* / Trouble: *Knight, Frederick* / I'm gonna cry a river: *Little Milton* / Itch and scratch (part 1): *Thomas, Rufus* / What would I do: *Hines, Ernie* / I know It's not right (to be in love with a married man): *Brown, Veda* / Holy cow: *Stefan* / What goes around (must come around): *Sons Of Slum* / men: *Hayes, Isaac* / Endlessly: *Staples, Mavis* / You hurt me for the last time: *Foxx, Inez* / My sweet Lord: *Williams, John Gary* / Breaking up somebody's home: *King, Albert* / How can you mistreat the one you love: *Love, Katie* / From toys to boys: *Emotions* / Dryer: *Johnson, Roy Lee & The Villagers* / I may not be all you want (but I'm all you got): *Thomas, Carla* / Ain't no sweat: *Major Lance* / Do me: *Knight, Jean* / Rainy day: *Little Milton* / It ain't always what you do (it's who you let see you do it): *Soul Children* / I may not be what you want: *Mel & Tim* / Funky robot (part 1): *Thomas, Rufus* / Don't you fool with my soul (part 1): *Taylor, Johnnie* / Oh la de da: *Staple Singers* / What do you see in her: *Hot Sauce* / Thousand miles away: *Temprees* / Hey you get off my mountain: *Dramatics* / Rolling down a mountainside: *Hayes, Isaac* / You're still my brother: *Bar-Kays* / Stop half loving these women: *Lewis, Jimmy* / Lovin' on borrowed time: *Bell, William* / Lay your loving on me: *Floyd, Eddie* / Time: *Foxx, Inez* / Heaven knows: *Mel & Tim* / I believe in you (you believe in me): *Taylor, Johnnie* / Short stopping: *Brown, Veda* / Be what you are: *Staple Singers* / I've got to love somebody's baby: *Stefan* / Playing on me: *King, Albert* / Long as you're the one somebody in the world: *Porter, David* / This is my song of love to you: *Knight, Frederick* / Sugarcane: *MG's* / Love is a hurtin' thing: *Soul Children* / Baby, lay your head down: *Floyd, Eddie* / Check me out: *Floyd, Eddie* / Running (back and forth): *Emotions* / Crossing over the bridge: *Foxx, Inez* / Love's maze: *Temprees* / It ain't easy: *Bar-Kays* / Love among people: *Thomas, Carla* / What is it: *Little Milton* / I've got to go without you: *Bell, William* / Love is taking over: *Mercury, Eric* / Ruby Dean: *Hicks, Joe* / I'm so glad I fell in love with you: *Mad Lads* / Fell for you: *Dramatics* / Cheaper to keep her: *Taylor, Johnnie* / I know you don't want me no more: *Thomas, Rufus* / If you're ready (come go with me): *Staple Singers* / Slipped and tripped: *Sweet Inspirations* / Peace, be still: *Emotions* / I'll be the other woman: *Soul Children* / Martin hop: *Newcomers* / I had a talk with my man: *Foxx, Inez* / At last: *Temprees* / Joy: *Hayes, Isaac* / Good woman turning bad: *Hot Sauce* / Mose (part 3): *Kasandra, John* / I'll be your Santa baby: *Thomas, Rufus* / I wanna do things for you: *Floyd, Eddie* / That's what the blues is all about: *King, Albert* / One way love affair: *Hurley, Carolyn* / Tin pan alley: *Little Milton* / Funky bird: *Thomas, Rufus* / We're getting careless with our love: *Taylor, Johnnie* / What do the lonely get at Christmas: *Emotions* / Season's greetings: *Cix Bits* / Don't lose faith in me Lord: *Mercury, Eric* / Don't start lovin' me (If you're gonna stop): *Brown, Veda* / Touch a hand, make a friend: *Staple Singers* / I panicked: *Dramatics* / Change it all: *Flemming, Joy* / Gettin' what you want (losin' what you get): *Bell, William* / He's mine: *Verdell, Jackie* / My woman is good to me: *Little Sonny* / I got you and I'm glad: *Porter, David* / Put a little love away: *Emotions* / Suzy: *Knight, Frederick* / Same folks: *Mel & Tim* / You make the sunshine: *Temprees* / Whole damn world is going crazy: *Williams, John Gary* / Circuits overloaded: *Foxx, Inez* / Wonderful: *Hayes, Isaac* / Behind closed doors: *Little Milton* / Guess who: *Floyd, Eddie* / Sweet inspiration: *Dirty Tricks* / Which way did it go: *Pop Staples* / Talking to the people: *Black Nasty* / I've been born again: *Taylor, Johnnie* / Neckbone: *MG's* / Wounded woman: *Wright, Sandra* / Stop dogging me: *Hot Sauce* / Goodness gracious: *Weston, Kim* / City in the sky: *Staple Singers* / Title theme: *Hayes, Isaac* / Soul street: *Floyd, Eddie* / Flat tire: *King, Albert* / Love makes it right: *Soul Children* / Mr. Cool that ain't cool: *Temprees* / Boogie ain't nuttin' (but gettin' down): *Thomas, Rufus* / Highway to heaven: *Banks, Ron & The Dramatics* / Get it while it's hot: *Bell, William* / Passing thru: *Knight, Frederick* / Keep an eye on your close friends: *Newcomers* / My main man: *Staple Singers* / There is a God: *Staple Singers* / That's the way I want to live my life: *Mel & Tim* / Forever and a day: *Mel & Tim* / Baby, I'm through: *Emotions* / It's September: *Taylor, Johnnie* / Woman to woman: *Brown, Shirley* / Did you hear yourself: *Brown, Randy* / You need a friend like mine: *Thomas, Annette* / I love, I love: *Temprees* / Let me back in: *Little Milton* / Crosscut saw: *King, Albert* / Coldblooded: *Bar-Kays* / Bump meat: *Rice, Sir Mack* / (Too little in common to be lovers) Too much going to say go: *Newcomers* / Bump and boogie (part 1): *Wrecking Crew* / What's happening baby (part 1): *Soul Children* / Who made the man: *Staple Singers* / I keep thinking to myself: *Benton, Brook* / I got a reason to smile (cause I got you): *Floyd, Eddie* / Try to leave me if you can (i bet you can't do it): *Banks, Bessie* / Burning on both ends: *Singleton, Willie* / There are more questions than answers: *Emotions* / Santa Claus wants some lovin': *King, Albert* / I can't let you go: *Hot Sauce* / I betcha didn't know that: *Knight, Frederick* / Lovin' you, lovin' me: *Wright, Sandra* / Do the double bump: *Thomas, Rufus* / Come and get your love: *Temprees* / Dark skin woman: *Rice, Sir Mack* / It ain't no fun: *Brown, Shirley* / If you talk in your sleep: *Little Milton* / Talk to the man: *Floyd, Eddie* / You're astounding: *Barbara & Joe* / Dy-no-mite (Did you say my love): *Green Brothers* / Boom-a-rang: *Dynamic Soul Machine* / Come what may: *Williams, John Gary* / Try me tonight: *Taylor, Johnnie* / Groovin' on my baby's love: *Waters, Freddie* / I can't shake your love (can't shake you lose): *Fiestas* / I wanna play with you: *Knight, Frederick* / I'm doing fine: *King, Albert* / No way: *Davis, Theresa* / Back road into town: *Staple Singers* / I'm so glad I met you: *Floyd, Eddie* / Packed up and took my mind: *Little Milton* / Just keep on loving me: *Taylor, Johnnie* / How can I be a witness: *Hudmon, R.B.* / Jump back '75 (part 1): *Thomas, Rufus* / I got to be myself: *Staple Singers* / It's worth a whipping: *Brown, Shirley* / Holy ghost: *Bar-Kays*
CD Set ______ **10SCD 4415**
Stax / Oct '94 / Pinnacle

COMPTINES & CHANSONS - ENFANTS
CD ______ **983262**
EPM / Oct '96 / ADA / Discovery

COMPUTER MUSIC CURRENTS 12
CD ______ **WER 2032**
Wergo / Feb '96 / ADA / Cadillac / Harmonia Mundi

CONCENTRATED UNDERGROUND VOL.1
Peechi: *Reload* / Emotional experience: *Amorph* / Crying is devine: *4D* / Jacob's ladder: *A-Sides* / Deliverer: *Pergon* / Dark matter: *Subject & Jeff Mill* / Memory of God: *CYM Dimensions* / Part 5: *Hedgehog Affair* / Atmosphere: *Chaos & Julia Set* / Captain's log: *Teckno Bros* / First rebirth: *Jones & Stephenson* / Two full moons and a trout: *Union Jack* / Mad cap laughs: *Drax*
CD ______ **DCOMPCD 1**
Death Becomes Me / Mar '94 / Grapevine/ PolyGram / Pinnacle / SRD

CONCENTRATED UNDERGROUND VOL.2
CD ______ **FLAG 103CD**
Flagbearer / Nov '94 / SRD / Timewarp

CONCEPTION
CD ______ **OJCCD 172**
Original Jazz Classics / Feb '93 / Complete/Pinnacle / Jazz Music / Wellard

CONCORD JAZZ CHRISTMAS, A
Christmas time is here: *Clooney, Rosemary* / Have yourself a merry little Christmas: *Peplowski, Ken* / I'll be home for Christmas: *Harris, Gene* / Apple, an orange and a little stick doll: *Cheatham, Jeannie & Jimmy* / Angels we have heard on high: *Scaggiari Trio* / Carol of the bells: *Byrd, Charlie* / Secret of Christmas: *McCorkle, Susannah* / God rest ye merry gentlemen: *McPartland, Marian* /

Jingle bells: Vignola, Frank / Coventry carol: Allyson, Karrin / Christmas love song: Hamilton, Scott / Santa Claus is coming to town: Bruno, Jimmy / Christmas waltz: McConnell, Rob / Let it snow, let it snow, let it snow: Atwood, Eden / Little town of Bethlehem: McKenna, Dave / Winter wonderland: Alden, Howard & Ken Peplowski / What are you doing New Year's Eve: Sloane, Carol
CD ______ CCD 4613
Concord Jazz / Oct '94 / New Note/ Pinnacle

CONCORD JAZZ COLLECTOR'S SERIES SAMPLER
Sweetback / Benny's bugle / Spring is here / I'm on my way / Look for the silver lining / Summertime, bidin' my time / After you've gone / Seven come eleven / Soft shoe / Carioca hills / Embraceable you / Smooth one / I wish I were in love again / I've found a new baby
CD ______ CCD 6013
Concord Jazz / Nov '93 / New Note/ Pinnacle

CONCORD JAZZ GUITAR COLLECTION VOL.1 & 2
La petite mambo / Isn't this a lovely place / Dolphin dance / Zigeuner / Prelude to a kiss / I'm on my way / I can't get started (with you) / Side track / Georgia on my mind / You don't know what love is / Claire de Lune / Seven come eleven / When Sunny gets blue / Orange, brown and green / Don't cry for me Argentina
CD ______ CCD 4160
Concord Jazz / Mar '90 / New Note/ Pinnacle

CONCORD JAZZ GUITAR COLLECTION VOL.3
Band call / Ecaroh / Joy spring / Avalon / Count down / Ain't misbehavin' / Too marvellous for words / East to West / Beija fior / There will never be another you / Song is you / Reflections in d / Skye boat song
CD ______ CCD 4507
Concord Jazz / May '92 / New Note/ Pinnacle

CONCRETE PRESENTS STRUCTURALLY SOUND
CD ______ HARD 21LPCD
Concrete / Jun '97 / 3mv/Pinnacle / Prime / RTM/Disc / Total/BMG

CONFERENCE OF THE BIRDS - LIVE AT WILLISAU
CD ______ ITM 970070
ITM / Sep '92 / Koch / Tradelink

CONFESSIN' THE BLUES
CD ______ IGOCD 2020
Indigo / Jun '95 / ADA / Direct

CONGO DRUMS
CD ______ PS 65164
PlayaSound / May '96 / ADA / Harmonia Mundi

CONGOLESE MASS
CD ______ 087262
Melodie / Mar '96 / ADA / Discovery / Grapevine/PolyGram / Greensleeves / Jet Star

CONGRATULATIONS
CD ______ I 3896042
Galaxy / Oct '96 / ZYX

CONJUNTO VOL.1 (Tex Mex Border Music)
CD ______ ROUCD 6023
Rounder / '88 / ADA / CM / Direct

CONJUNTO VOL.2
CD ______ ROUCD 6024
Rounder / '88 / ADA / CM / Direct

CONJUNTO VOL.3
CD ______ ROUCD 6030
Rounder / ADA / CM / Direct

CONJUNTO VOL.4
CD ______ ROUCD 6034
Rounder / ADA / CM / Direct

CONJUNTO VOL.5 (Polkas De Oro)
CD ______ ROUCD 6051
Rounder / Feb '94 / ADA / CM / Direct

CONJUNTO VOL.6 (Contrabando)
CD ______ ROUCD 6052
Rounder / Apr '94 / ADA / CM / Direct

CONSCIOUS RAGGA VOL.1
CD ______ GRELCD 220
Greensleeves / Oct '95 / Jet Star / SRD

CONSCIOUS RAGGA VOL.2
CD ______ GRELCD 225
Greensleeves / Jun '96 / Jet Star / SRD

CONSPIRACAO BAIANA
CD ______ 68970
Tropical / Jul '97 / Discovery

CONTEMPORARY FLUTE
CD ______ BVHAASTCD 9211
Bvhaast / Dec '91 / Cadillac

CONTEMPORARY JAZZ MASTERS SAMPLER
Frelun brun (Brown hornet) / Moors / Two to tango / Pieces of dreams / Wings of Karma / God and the devil in the land of the sun / Chicago theme (Love loop) / Gotcha / Medieval overture / Velvet darkness / Delzura / Phenomenon / Compulsion / Skylark / Fatback / Chameleon / Such a night
CD ______ 4670862
Columbia / Jan '92 / Sony

CONTROVERSY OF PIPERS, A
CD ______ COMD 1008
Temple / Apr '95 / ADA / CM / Direct / Duncans / Highlander

COOKING VINYL SAMPLER VOL.4
Ontario, quebec and me: Bragg, Billy / Levens lament: Leven, Jackie / Jam tomorrow: Oyster Band / Memphis: Pere Ubu / Summer heat: Jansch, Bert / Cachapaya shuffle: Incantation / All our trades: Tabor, June / How can you keep on moving: McLeod, Rory / Roll on forever: Rockingbirds / Let it go: Goats Don't Shave / No dancing: Immaculate Fools / You gotta survive: TRB / Persons unkown: Poison Girls / Liberty: Barely Works / Blackberry blossom: Barely Works / Cuckoo's nest: Barely Works / Rumbidzai: Four Brothers
CD ______ GRILLCD 008
Cooking Vinyl / Aug '95 / Vital

COOKING VINYL SAMPLER VOL.5
CD ______ GRILLCD 009
Cooking Vinyl / Sep '96 / Vital

COOKING VINYL SAMPLER VOL.6 - 1997 (2CD Set)
Not like Jordan: Oyster Band / Homemade blood: Prophet, Chuck / Mari mac: Great Big Sea / Bonny besses: Rev Hammers Freeborn John / In or out: Difranco, Ani / Extremely violent man: Leven, Jackie / Sugardaddy: Bragg, Billy / Negative equity: Carter / Snake eyes: Wedding Present / Hand in my pocket: White, Andy / Hurry back: Thomas, David / Promises: Wired To The Moon / By my rambling woman: McLeod, Rory / Holding on: Difranco, Ani / Dawn: Stevenson, Savourna & Danny Thompson / Kachembere: Bhundu Boys / Codex: Pere Ubu / Makorokoto: Four Brothers / Bjorn again polka: Edward II & The Red Hot Polkas / Catchapaya shuffle: Incantation / Raining (my eyes are filled with clouds): Ancient Beatbox / Who cares: Shocked, Michelle / Back home: Jansch, Bert / Big river: Barely Works / Windy city: Tabor, June / Breaths: Sweet Honey In The Rock / Dirty old town: MacColl, Ewan / Rumours of glory: Cockburn, Bruce / Las Vegas (in the hills of Donegal): Goats Don't Shave / We had it all: Rockingbirds / Spivaye solovey: Ukrainians / Ready for me: Immaculate Fools / Loved: Robinson, Tom / Old tarts song: Poison Girls
CD Set ______ GRILLCD 010
Cooking Vinyl / Jul '97 / Vital

COOL & CRAZY
Kool kat: Sherrell, Bill / Rock on baby: Sherrell, Bill / Rock 'n' roll teenager: Sherrell, Bill / Yes, no, or maybe: Sherrell, Bill / Rock crazy baby: Adams, Art / Dancing doll: Adams, Art / Imogene: Ray, Don / Those rock 'n' roll blues: Ray, Don / Cool cat: Montgomery, Joe / Woodpecker rock: Couty, Nat / Won't you come along with me: Couty, Nat / Bon bon baby: Coulston, Jerry / Little rocker: Stuart, Scottie / Marlene: Sonics / Minus one: Sonics / Blast off: Sonics / Cool cool baby: Yarborough, Lafayette / Living doll: Yarborough, Lafayette / Rock 'n' roll fever: Graham B / Cool baby: Cole, Lee / Short fat Ben: Barclay, Phil / I love me all: Barclay, Phil / Come along with me: Parker, Malcom / Servant of love: Van Bros / Cool cats: Huften, Jim / Get hot or go home: Kerby, John / Pizza pie: Irwin, Phil / Little bitty boy: Hulin, T.K. / Cool baby cool: Hulin, T.K. / Ricky Tic: Davis, Al / She's cool: Vikings
CD ______ CDBB 55006
Buffalo Bop / Apr '94 / Rollercoaster

COOL - TALKIN' VERVE
CD ______ 5332462
Verve / May '97 / PolyGram

COOL BEAT
CD ______ RENCD 101
Castle / Jul '95 / BMG

COOL CHRISTMAS
Please come home for Christmas: Eagles / Blanche comme la neige: McGarrigle, Kate & Anna / Lights of the stable: Harris, Emmylou / Soon after Christmas: Nordenstam, Stina / White Christmas: Redding, Otis / Winter: Amos, Tori / Fairytale of New York: Pogues / Silent night: Enya / Coventry carol: Paige, Elaine / 2000 miles: Pretenders / Driving home for Christmas: Rea, Chris / Power of love: Frankie Goes To Hollywood / Walk out to winter: Aztec Camera / Winter wonderland: Booker T & The MG's / Christmas in February: Reed, Lou / Santa's beard: They Might Be Giants / Little boy that Santa Claus forgot: Associates / Christmas card from a hooker in Minneapolis: Waits, Tom
CD ______ 9548324852
WEA / Dec '93 / Warner Music

COOL RAGGA MIX
CD ______ VPCD 1477
VP / Oct '96 / Greensleeves / Jet Star / Total/BMG

COOL SOUNDS FOR WARM NIGHT
CD ______ MCCD 195
Music Club / Mar '95 / Disc / THE

COOL STRUTTIN'
CD ______ 99 2120
Ninetynine / Jul '96 / Timewarp

COOL STRUTTIN' VOL.2
CD ______ AM 00512
Amber / Aug '94 / Pinnacle

COOL TUNES
CD ______ RIPEXD 220
Ripe / Jan '97 / Pinnacle

COOL WORLD (41 Australian Rock Singles 1976-1986/2CD Set)
Deep water: Clapton, Richard / (Boys) what did the detective say: Sports / So young: Zep, Jo Jo & The Falcons / Beautiful people: Australian Crawl / Nips are getting bigger: Mental As Anything / Can't help myself: Flowers / Stay young: INXS / Unguarded moment: Church / They won't let my girlfriend talk to me: Jimmy & The Boys / Quasimodo's dream: Reels / No secrets: Angels / Happy man: Sunnyboys / Smith and Wesson blues: Radio Birdman / Know your product: Saints / Who can it be now: Men At Work / Cool world: Mondo Rock / Never gonna die: Choirboys / Breakfast at sweethearts: Cold Chisel / I hear motion: Models / Great Southern land: Icehouse / Boys in town: Divinyls / Solid rock: Goanna / Rain: Dragon / Six months in a leaky boat: Split Enz / Gimme some lovin': GANGgajang / Throw your arms around me: Hunters & Collectors / Cattle and cane: Go-Betweens / No say in it: Machinations / Big girls: Electric Pandas / Send me an angel: Real Life / We will together: Eurogliders / Girl on the wall: Clifton, Jane / No lies: Noiseworks / Great wall: Boom Crash Opera / Man overboard: Do Re Mi / Wide open road: Triffids / I want you back: Hoodoo Gurus / Weirdo libido: Lime Spiders / Sad girl: Stems / Daughters of glory: Black Sorrows / Before too long: Kelly, Paul & The Coloured Girls
CD Set ______ RVCD 55
Raven / Feb '97 / ADA / Direct

COOLIN', THE (Classic Irish Slow-Airs & Laments)
Roisin dubh: Conlan, Festy / Spailpin a ruin: Clancy, Willie / Nil se na la/The hounours of Winnington: McConnell, Cathal & Robin Morton / Paddy rambles through the park: Doherty, John / Coolin': Doran, Felix / Lark in the clear air: Pepper, Noel / Willy Reilly: Daly, Jackie / An cailin rua: McDermott, Josie / Boolavogue/The old bog road: Rowsome, Leo / Air from Thomas Moore: Solus Lillis / Se bheath mo bhfuartha: Griffin, Vincent / Molly O'Malone: Ennis, Seamus / An Eirinn no n'eosfhainn ce h'i: Droney, Chris / Red haired boy: Clifford, Julia / Lord Mayo: Mitchell, Pat / Blackbird: Kelly, John / Faithful brown cow: Walsh, Liam / Old caubeen: Kelly, Gene / Old man rocking the cradle: O'Keeffe, Padraig / Fairy child: Mac Aogain, Michael / Spalpeen's lament: Doonan, John / Bean dubh an ghleanna: McMahon, Tony / Blind Mary: McAloon, Sean / Melodious little fort of Bruff: Bailie, Brian / Lament of Aughrim: McPeake Family Trio
CD ______ CDORBD 093
Globestyle / Oct '96 / Pinnacle

COP
Sun: Under The Noise / Eclipse: Fishtank / Open your eyes: DLI / Ne plus ultra: Index / Transit: Battery / Victim (sanction of the victim): Heavy Water Factory / Orchid: Osas / Stuck: Slave Unit / Cutting thin blue lines: DLI / Christine: Battery / Halcyon ghetto: Index / Manna: Under The Noise / Angela: Razor Skyline
CD ______ COPCD 026
Cop International / Dec '96 / Cargo

COPULATIN' BLUES
CD ______ JCD 1
Jass / Oct '91 / ADA / Cadillac / CM / Direct / Jazz Music

COPULATIN' COLLECTION VOL.1
CD ______ VN 168
Viper's Nest / Aug '95 / ADA / Cadillac / Direct / Jazz Music

CORASON CALIENTE COLLECTION
Legba mia mia: Les Grandes Vissages De Cyvadier / El sombrerito (el enfermo y el doctor iii): Los Camperos De Valles / Harina de maiz: Septeto Tipico Oriental / La vieja: La Negra Graciana / Oyelos de nuevo: Los Munequitos De Matanzas / Canero no.15: Los Guanches / Laos, Cambodia y Vietnam: Grupo Changui De Guantanamo / Baile en la calle: Cachucha Y Su Conjunto / Los perros del curro: Cachucha Y Su Conjunto / Las abajenas: Mariachi Reyes Del Aserradero / La tortolita: Reynoso, Juan / Amarrao con P: Cuarteto Patria / Male amalita: Dueto De Comachuen / El canelo: Conjunto Cosamaloapan / Mayeye: Canambu / El principe de los Bongoceros: Septeto Habanero / Camino a Mayaguez: Guateque / Go mango walk: Mini-Musical Female Duet / Contigo en la distancia: Garzon, Armando & Quinteto Oriente
CD ______ CRSCD 801
CRS / Feb '97 / ADA / Direct / Jet Star

CORES DO BRASIL VOL.1 (Vozes)
Para-raio: Djavan / Ole ola: Buarque, Chico / Cavalgada: De Belem, Fafa / Mariano: Camargo, Cesar / Bodas de prata: Regina, Elis / Outubro: Nascimento, Milton / Denise rei: Ben, Jorge / Viramundo: Bethania, Maria / Maravilha: Hime, Francis & Chico Buarque / Abre alas: Lins, Ivan / Ive brussel: Ben, Jorge & Caetano Veloso / Toada: Lobo, Edo / Doce maggia: De Belem, Fafa / Ate segunda feira: Buarque, Chico / Curumin chama cunhata que eu vou contar: Ben, Jorge / Travessia: Nascimento, Milton / Preta pretinha: Baianos, Novos / Coisas cristalinas: Wando / Ventos do norte: Djavan / Faz parte do meu show: Creuza, Maria
CD ______ NSCD 001
Nascente / Jul '91 / Disc / New Note/ Pinnacle

CORES DO BRASIL VOL.2 (Samba)
Bizantina bizancia: Ben, Jorge / La vem o Brasil descendo a ladeira: Moreira, Moraes / Prata da noite: De Sa, Estacio / O bebado e o equilibrista: Bosca, Joao / Moenda: Machado, Elaine / Swing de campo grande: Balonos, Novos / Flor de lis: Djavan / Fruta mulher: Moreira, Moraes / Acorda que eu quero ver: Caymmi, Nana / O dia que o sol declarou o seu amor pela terra: Ben, Jorge / Quem te viu, quem te ve: Buarque, Chico / Brasil pandeiro: Balonos, Novos / A rita: Buarque, Chico / No reino encantado do amor: Ben, Jorge / Maria vai com as outras: Creuza, Maria / Tem que se tirar da cabeca: Do Salgeuiro, Academicos / Quilombo do dumba: De Jesus, Clementina / Roda viva: Buarque, Chico / O dia se zangou: Negra, Jovelina Perola / Era umas ves 13 pontos: Ben, Jorge / Contraste: Macale, Jards / Que maravilha: Ben, Jorge & Toquinho
CD ______ NSCD 002
Nascente / Jul '91 / Disc / New Note/ Pinnacle

CORES DO BRASIL VOL.3 (Bossa Nova)
Embola a bola: Djavan / Samba de bencao: De Moraes, Vincius / Chega de saudade: Creuza, Maria / Mais um adeus: Toquinho & Marilla Medalha / A felicidade: Dos Santos, Agostinho / Para viver um grande amor: De Moraes, Vincius / Para que digladiar: Ben, Jorge / Desencontro: Buarque, Chico & Toquinho / Samba de veloso: Zimbo Trio / Sao demals os perigos desta vida: Vinicius & Toquinho / Apelo: Bethania, Maria & Vinicius / Canto de ossanha: Creuza, Maria & Vinicius & Toquinho / Na boca de beco: Djavan / Voce abusu: Creuza, Maria / Carolina: Buarque, Chico / Girl from Ipanema: De Moraes, Vincius / Corcovado: Creuza, Maria / Morena de flor: De Moraes, Vincius / Marina: Creuza, Maria / Paiol de polvora: De Moraes, Vincius / Trocando em miudo: Hime, Francis / Katarina, Katarina: Ben, Jorge
CD ______ NSCD 003
Nascente / Jul '91 / Disc / New Note/ Pinnacle

CORES DO BRASIL VOL.4 (Samba Com Jazz)
Milagre: Quarteto Em Cy / Agua de beber: Zimbo Trio / Tres pontas: Nascimento, Milton / Samba do aviao: Jobim, Antonio Carlos & Miucha / Reza: Zimbo Trio / Mas que nada: Creuza, Maria / Samba sem voce: Passos, Rosa & Emilio Santiago / Bon tempo: Buarque, Chico / Muito obrigado: Djavan / Como diza o poeta: Vinicius & Toquinho / Noite dos mascarados: Buarque, Chico / Consolacao: Zimbo Trio / O morro nao engana: Melodia, Luiz / Cancao de busios: Sa, Sandra / Samba de verao: Valle, Marcus / Bem bem: Costa, Gal / Pra fazer o sol nascer: Gil, Gilberto / Madalena ful pro mar: Buarque, Chico / Requebra que eu dou um doce: Hime, Olivia & Dory Caymmi / Um vestido de bolero: Hime, Olivia & Dory Caymmi / Onde e que voce esteva: Buarque, Chico / Gira giro: Nascimento, Milton / Arrastao: Zimbo Trio / Espelho christalino: Valenca, Alceu
CD ______ NSCD 004
Nascente / Jul '91 / Disc / New Note/ Pinnacle

CORES DO BRASIL VOL.5 (Saudade)
No dia em que eu vim embora: Regina, Elis / Boca da noite: Toquinho / Cavaleiro: Veloso, Caetano / Primavera: Joyce / Uma vez um caso: Lobo, Edu & Joyce / Corsario: Regina, Elis / Gongaba: Hime, Olivia & Edu Lobo / Dindi: Creuza, Maria / Dreamer: Wanda / Sem fantasia: Buarque, Chico / Ultimo desejo: Bethania, Maria / Umas e outras: Buarque, Chico / Eu sei que vou te amar: Creuza, Maria & Vinicius & Toquinho / Pra nao mais voltar: De Belem, Fafa / Irmao de fe: Nascimento, Milton / How insensitive: Creuza, Maria / Sabia: Buarque, Chico / Da cor do pecado: Creuza, Maria / Acabou chorare: Baianos, Novos / Rosa flor: Vandre, Geraldo / Apelo: Toquinho & Vincius De Moraes
CD ______ NSCD 005
Nascente / Jul '91 / Disc / New Note/ Pinnacle

CORES DO BRASIL VOL.6 (Danca)
Roda: Gil, Gilberto / Besta e tu: Baianos, Novos / Fato consumado: Djavan / Te futaco: Guerreiro, Cid / Taj Mahal/Filhomaravilha/Pais Tropical: Ben, Jorge / A tongo da mironga do kabulete: Toquinho & Vinicius / Rei no bagaco coisas do vida: De Be-

lem, Fafa / Salve simpatia: *Ben, Jorge* / Tiro de misericordia: *Bosco, Joao & Chico Batera* / Adelita: *Ben, Jorge* / A banda do ze pretinho: *Ben, Jorge* / Nem ouro nem prata: *Maurity, Ruy* / Ague negra da lagoa: *Toquinho* / Africaner brother bound: *Shock, Obina & Gilberto Gil* / Gabriel Guerreiro galactico: *Ben, Jorge* / Mambembe: *De Belem, Fafa* / Perfume de cebola (Fragance of onion): *Filo* / Da cor do pecado: *Creuza, Maria* / Em matogrosso fronteira com: *Ben, Jorge*
CD **NSCD 006**
Nascente / Jul '91 / Disc / New Note/ Pinnacle

CORNEMUSE ECOSSAISE
Massed pipes and drums / Country dance / Grand march / Set dance / Pipe major march / Quick march / Piper dance / Pipes and drums in Kathmandou / Scottish dance / Royal Scots polka / Drummer's call / Hills of Glenorchy / Greenwood side / Slow march / Banks of Allan / Amazing grace / Auld Lang Syne / Military fanfare / Black bear / Fanfare Drawbridge
CD **ARN 64030**
Arion / '87 / ADA / Discovery

CORNERSTONE CONNECTION
CD **SONCD 0069**
Sonic Sounds / Oct '94 / Jet Star

CORONATION STREET (25th Anniversary Album)
Coronation street theme / Beatles medley / You needed me / This old heart of mine / Never can say goodbye / To all the men I've loved before / Unchained melody / Pop party medley / These boots are made for walkin' / Street medley / All of me / George Formby medley / You make me feel so young / Street like ours / Old time sing-a-long medley
CD **ECD 3115**
K-Tel / Jan '95 / K-Tel

CORPORATE DEATH
CD **NB 095**
Nuclear Blast / Apr '94 / Plastic Head

CORPORATE ROCK WARS
Strike it: *Dub War* / My mind still speaks: *Misery Loves Co* / Lighter form of killing: *Pitch Shifter* / Exodus: *Scorn* / Joy of irony: *Fudge Tunnel* / Freak wow: *Old* / Crush my soul: *Godflesh* / North Korea goes bang: *Violent, Johnny* / Honour code loyalty: *Misery Loves Co* / Mental: *Dub War* / NCM: *Pitch Shifter* / Sex mammoth: *Fudge Tunnel* / Glitch: *Old* / Electric chair: *Ultraviolence* / New spite: *Godflesh* / End: *Scorn*
CD **MOSH 136CD**
Earache / May '95 / Vital

CORRIB FOLK, THE
CD **CDBALLAD 006**
Outlet / Jan '95 / ADA / CM / Direct / Duncans / Koch / Ross

CORRIDINHOS
CD **PS 65093**
PlayaSound / Aug '92 / ADA / Harmonia Mundi

COSMIC CONSPIRACY
CD **IBIZAMUSIC 003**
Ibiza / Mar '97 / Mo's Music Machine

COSMIC CUBES VOL.1 (2CD Set)
CD Set **SPV 08938252**
SPV / Feb '95 / Koch / Plastic Head

COSMIC CUBES VOL.2 (2CD Set)
CD Set **SPV 08938342**
SPV / Jun '95 / Koch / Plastic Head

COSMIC CUBES VOL.3 (2CD Set)
K People: *Nailin & Kane* / Dawn goddess: *Quatermass* / Sweet gravity: *LSG* / Hovercab: *Spacebuggy* / Don't cry my love: *Love Religion* / Chemical trance: *Ethnica* / Gobi desert: *100 Monkeys & Tristan* / Bombay: *Caunos* / Intimate encounter: *New Balance Crossover* / Flow: *Model 500* / Visual imagination: *Hyber Nation* / One of the frightened: *Angeldust* / Polterguys: *Kashmir* / Positiv education: *SLAM* / Rising rissol: *Ru-Rapente* / Hopium: *Z-Plane* / Dirty life: *Illegal District* / Synasthasia: *Source Experience* / Neria fetisch: *L'Auberge* / How to bluff your way in techno music: *Max 404*
CD Set **SPV 08938662**
SPV / May '96 / Koch / Plastic Head

COSMIC CUBES VOL.4 (2CD Set)
Party spirit: *Deep Sound* / Wired: *Tenth Chapter* / All because of you: *Universal State Of Mind* / Sundae 6 am: *Van Dyke, Paul* / Train of thought: *Matipo Pyramid* / 03: *O-Lab* / Subconsiousness: *Elysium* / Afterlife: *Astralasia* / T 96: *M.A.D* / Tommy: *Terra C* / Cat and the canary: *Miherobenics* / Nautilus: *Scan Carriers* / Caunos: *Canyon* / Mission: *Watchman* / Indian flute: *Haramatix* / Cosmic wave: *DJ Warlock* / Vallhalla: *Hinetico* / Answer: *NDMA*
CD Set **SPV 08947342**
SPV / Apr '97 / Koch / Plastic Head

COSMIC ENERGY VOL.1 (2CD Set)
CD Set **IR 002CD**
Independence / Jan '96 / Plastic Head

COSMIC KURUSHI MONSTERS (Tokyo Invasion Vol.1) (2CD Set)
CD Set **TOKYO 1**
Virgin / Jul '96 / EMI

COSMIC TRANCE
CD **DI 242**
Distance / Dec '95 / 3mv/Sony / Prime

COSMIC TRANCE VOL.1 (2CD Set)
CD Set **560062**
Westcom / Mar '97 / Koch / Pinnacle

COSMIC TRANCE VOL.2
CD **SUB 48382**
Distance / Apr '97 / 3mv/Sony / Prime

COSMIC TRAVELLERS
Right stuff: *Pressurehead* / Between worlds: *Underground Zero* / We do it: *Hawkwind* / Grid cooordinate-vorp one: *Anubian Lights* / Time of: *Hawklords* / Venusian skyline: *Melting Euphoria* / Master: *Helios Creed* / Trip to G9: *Spiral Realms* / Seeing strange nights: *Dark Matter* / Pre-cambrian shuffle: *Brain* / Space does not care: *Zero Gravity*
CD **CDMGRAM 105**
Anagram / Apr '96 / Cargo / Pinnacle

COSMOSOUND (The Art Of Drum 'n' Bass & Trip Hop)
CD **CLP 9992**
Cleopatra / Jun '97 / Cargo / Greyhound / Plastic Head / RTM/Disc / SRD

COTTON CLUB
CD **15707**
Laserlight / Apr '94 / Target/BMG

COTTON CLUB - ORIGINAL MUSIC
CD **CD 53022**
Giants Of Jazz / Mar '90 / Cadillac / Jazz Music / Target/BMG

COTTON CLUB, THE
Cotton Club stomp: *Ellington, Duke Cotton Club Orchestra* / Just a crazy song: *Robinson, Bill 'Bojangles'* / Am I blue: *Waters, Ethel* / Heebie jeebies: *Webb, Chick & His Orchestra* / I must have that man: *Hall, Adelaide* / Stormy weather: *Arlen, Harold* / When you're smiling: *Armstrong, Louis Orchestra* / Lazybones: *Williams, Midge* / Old yazoo: *Calloway, Cab Orchestra* / Honey just for you: *Kirk, Andy & His Twelve Clouds of Joy* / Between the Devil and the deep blue sea: *Armstrong, Louis Orchestra* / Sweet rhythm: *Lunceford, Jimmie & his Chickasaw Syncopators* / Blues I love to sing: *Hall, Adelaide* / Kicking the gong around: *Calloway, Cab Orchestra* / Serenade to a wealthy widow: *Foresythe, Reginald* / Jubilee stomp: *Ellington, Duke Cotton Club Orchestra* / I can't give you anything but love: *Waters, Ethel* / Doin' the new low down: *Mills, Irving*
CD **CDAJA 5031**
Living Era / Oct '88 / Select

COTTON PICKIN' BLUES
Southern can is mine: *McTell, 'Blind' Willie* / Lay down St Louis blues: *Johnson, Lonnie* / Milkcow's calf blues: *Johnson, Robert* / Ain't no telling: *Hurt, 'Mississippi' John* / Pigmeat is what I crave: *Carter, Bo* / Fixing to die blues: *White, Bukka* / Lord, I just can't keep from crying: *Johnson, 'Blind' Willie* / Stormy night blues: *Carr, Leroy* / Spreadin' snakes blue: *Broonzy, 'Big' Bill* / Fort Worth and Dallas blues: *Leadbelly* / Baby won't you please come home: *Smith, Bessie* / Sweet home blues: *Wheatstraw, Peetie* / Truckin' my blues away: *Fuller, 'Blind' Boy* / Nothing in ramblin': *Memphis Minnie* / Reverence man blues: *Patton, Charlie* / Matchbox blues: *Jefferson, Blind Lemon*
CD **305682**
Hallmark / Jul '97 / Carlton

COUNTER CULTURE
Strings: *Astro Farm* / Love is what we need: *99 All Stars* / Calling: *Solar Stone* / Help me make it: *Huff & Puff* / Walk with me: *Heliotropic* / Disco screw: *Protein Boy* / Atomic life: *Atom Heart* / Snow: *ORN* / Small town boy: *Legato* / Spin spin sugar: *Sneaker Pimps* / Cafe del mar: *Energy 52* / Dark and long: *Underworld* / Galaxia: *Moonman* / May go wild: *Grooveyard*
CD **KICKCD 52**
Kickin' / Jun '97 / Prime / SRD

COUNTERFORCE
Better place: *DJ Tasmin & The Monk* / Carrie: *Inna Rhythm* / Disturbance: *Hyper On Experience* / Let it roll: *DJ Crystal* / Deep space (I see sunshine): *Lemon D* / Warpdrive: *DJ Crystal* / Lock up: *Zero B* / Deep: *Koda* / Dream of you: *DJ Flynn & Flora* / Dance of the sarooes: *Rogue Unit*
CD **TRUCD 6**
Internal / Oct '94 / Pinnacle / PolyGram

COUNTRY
Turn me loose and let me swing: *Nelson, Willie & Curtis Potter* / Brand new ways: *McCallister, Don Jr & His COwboy Jazz Revue* / Black rose: *Whitfield, Barrence & Tom Russell* / Midnight ride: *Roy, Jimmy 5 Star Hillbillies* / She makes the angels cry: *Broussard, Rick* / Undying love: *Swan, Billy & Van Duren* / Just to hear your voice: *Price, Toni* / Yeah, yeah, yeah: *Blazers* / It's over: *Flores, Rosie* / Corazon viajero: *Hinojosa, Tish* / Monterrey: *McGhee, Wes* / Border radio: *Alvin, Dave* / Prairie blues: *Bennett, Pinto & The Motel Cowboys* / Friends: *Lost Gonzo Band* / I gotta have my baby back: *Rattlesnake Annie* / Walkin' on the moon: *Moffatt, Katy* / No place to fall: *Van Zandt, Townes* / Factory town: *Donovan, Barb* / Ain't licked yet: *Hamilton, Dirk* / I don't feel that way anymore: *Robinson, Charlie* / Fool: *Picketts* / Fool such as I: *Chiavola, Kathy* / Door number one: *Fracasso, Michael & Lucinda Williams* / If you were a bluebird: *Hancock, Butch* / Pack up your lies: *Pink, Celinda*
CD **VJCD 1**
Vinyl Junkie / Jul '95 / ADA / Direct

COUNTRY 'N' IRISH ACCORDION
Country roads medley / Botany bay medley / When Irish eyes are smiling medley / These are my mountains medley / I'll take you home again Kathleen / Tom Dooley medley / All for me grog / Walkin' after midnight / Isle of Innishtree medley / When your old wedding ring was new medley / Maggie medley / Leaving of Liverpool
CD **CD 6081**
Music / Jun '97 / Target/BMG

COUNTRY 4 YOU
CD **DS 019**
Desperado / Jun '97 / TKO Magnum

COUNTRY AND WESTERN (2CD Set)
CD Set **PFCD 3001**
Scratch / Mar '97 / Koch / Scratch/BMG

COUNTRY AND WESTERN FAVOURITES (4CD Set)
CD Set **MBSCD 410**
Castle / Jan '95 / BMG

COUNTRY AND WESTERN GREATS (Sea Of Heartbreak)
I can't stop loving you: *Gibson, Don* / Almost persuaded: *Jones, George* / Ruby, don't take your love to town: *Rogers, Kenny* / Where do I go from here: *Williams, Don* / Shelter of my arms: *Nelson, Willie* / For the good times: *Husky, Ferlin* / Four in the morning: *Young, Faron* / But I do: *Fender, Freddy* / Daddy sang bass: *Perkins, Carl* / Catfish John: *Russell, Johnny* / Love's gonna live here: *Jennings, Waylon* / There goes everything: *Greene, Jack* / Things to talk about: *Jackson, Stonewall* / Send me the pillow that you dream on: *Locklin, Hank* / Son of Hickory Holler's tramp: *Darrell, Johnny* / Sea of heartbreak: *Gibson, Don* / Talk back trembling lips: *Jones, George* / Rueben James: *Rogers, Kenny* / Tears: *Williams, Don* / Broken promises: *Nelson, Willie*
CD **MUCD 9013**
Musketeer / Apr '95 / Disc

COUNTRY BALLADS (3CD Set)
Somebody loves you: *Gayle, Crystal* / Country Willie: *Nelson, Willie* / Take me in your arms and hold me: *Whitman, Slim* / All I have to do is dream: *Newton, Juice* / Better love next time: *Dr. Hook* / Love lifted me: *Rogers, Kenny* / Jambalaya: *Nitty Gritty Dirt Band* / Country girl: *Newton-John, Olivia* / Another place, another time: *Williams, Don* / Son of a preacher man: *Gentry, Bobbie* / Games people play: *South, Joe* / Rose garden: *Spears, Billie Jo* / By the time I get to Phoenix: *Campbell, Glen* / Among my souvenirs: *Whitman, Slim* / Wayward wind: *Gayle, Crystal* / If we only have love: *Newton-John, Olivia* / Funny how time slips away: *Nelson, Willie* / Misty blue: *Spears, Billie Jo* / Little bit more: *Dr. Hook* / Love me like you used to: *Tucker, Tanya* / Reason to believe: *Campbell, Glen* / Give me your word: *Ford, Tennessee Ernie* / Am I blue: *Nelson, Willie* / Dreaming my dreams with you: *Gayle, Crystal* / She believes in me: *Rogers, Kenny* / Sweet dreams: *Young, Faron* / Reuben James: *Jackson, Wanda* / My blue heaven: *Whitman, Slim* / Angel of the morning: *Newton, Juice* / Let it be me: *Gentry, Bobbie* / Country girl heart: *Gatlin, Larry & The Gatlin Brothers* / There'll be no teardrops tonight: *Nelson, Willie* / All I wanna do in life: *Gayle, Crystal* / I'm walking behind you: *Whitman, Slim* / It's only make believe: *Campbell, Glen* / You've made me so very happy: *Gentry, Bobbie* / You love me through it all: *Williams, Don* / I just had you on my mind: *Craddock, Billy* / Love song: *Newton-John, Olivia* / Sharing the night: *Dr. Hook* / What the world needs now is love: *Spears, Billie Jo* / We've got tonight: *Rogers, Kenny* / Hey Mr. Dream Maker: *West, Dottie* / Crying: *McLean, Don* / My arms stay open all night: *Tucker, Tanya*
CD Set **CDTRBOX 172**
Trio / Sep '95 / EMI

COUNTRY BALLADS
CD **DS 016**
Desperado / Jun '97 / TKO Magnum

COUNTRY BLUES COLLECTORS ITEMS 1924-1928
CD **DOCD 5169**
Document / May '93 / ADA / Hot Shot / Jazz Music

COUNTRY BLUES COLLECTORS ITEMS VOL.2
CD **SOB 035402**
Story Of The Blues / Apr '93 / ADA / Koch

COUNTRY BLUES HARD HITTERS (How You Want It Done)
How you want it done: *Broonzy, 'Big' Bill* / Walk right in: *Cannon, Gus & His Jug Stompers* / Back to the woods: *Arnold, Kokomo* / Voice throwing blues: *Hawkins, Walter 'Buddy Boy'* / Two white horses in a line: *Evans, Joe & Arthur McClain* / Dark angel: *Moore, Alice* / Statesboro blues: *McTell, 'Blind' Willie* / Believe I'll go back home: *Kelly, Jack & His South Memphis Jug Band* / Devil and my brown: *Jackson, Bo Weevil* / Rolling log blues: *Beaman, Lottie* / Don't hang my clothes on no barbed wire line: *Wheatstraw, Peetie* / Denomination blues: *Phillips, Washington* / Teasin' brown blues: *Lasky, Louie* / Diddie wah diddie: *Blind Blake* / Wild cow blues: *Williams, Big Joe* / Big chief blues: *Lewis, Furry* / Whiskey and women: *Black Ace* / Dope head blues: *Spivey, Victoria* / Girl I love she got long curly hair: *Estes, 'Sleepy' John* / See that my grave is kept clean: *Jefferson, Blind Lemon* / Chickasaw train blues: *Memphis Minnie* / Little green slippers: *Memphis Jug Band* / Right now blues: *Stokes, Frank* / I'm so glad: *James, Skip*
CD **PM 002**
Pigmeat / Sep '96 / Direct

COUNTRY BOX (3CD Set)
CD Set **TBXD 505**
TrueTrax / Jan '96 / THE

COUNTRY BOX (2CD Set)
CD Set **PBXCD 505**
Pulse / Nov '96 / BMG

COUNTRY BOYS
Country boy: *Campbell, Glen* / Amazing grace: *Campbell, Glen* / Reuben James: *Rogers, Kenny* / Son of Hickory Holler's tramp: *Rogers, Kenny* / Crazy: *Nelson, Willie* / Night life: *Nelson, Willie* / Rose Marie: *Whitman, Slim* / Red River valley: *Whitman, Slim* / Folsom Prison blues: *Haggard, Merle* / San Antonio rose: *Haggard, Merle* / Desperately: *Williams, Don* / Another place another time: *Williams, Don* / I heard you crying in your sleep: *Jones, George* / I get lonely in a hurry: *Jones, George* / Jambalaya: *Nitty Gritty Dirt Band* / Sweet dreams: *Young, Faron* / Baby's got her blue jeans on: *McDaniel, Mel* / I just had you on my mind: *Craddock, Billy* / I've got a tiger by the tail: *Owens, Buck* / Wings of a dove: *Husky, Ferlin*
CD **CDMFP 5910**
Music For Pleasure / May '91 / EMI

COUNTRY CHARTBUSTERS VOL.1
Devil went down to Georgia: *Daniels, Charlie Band* / Rose garden: *Anderson, Lynn* / Stand by your man: *Wynette, Tammy* / Always on my mind: *Nelson, Willie* / El Paso: *Robbins, Marty* / Me and Bobby McGee: *Kristofferson, Kris* / River unbroken: *Parton, Dolly* / Ring of fire: *Cash, Johnny* / Seven year ache: *Cash, Rosanne* / North to Alaska: *Horton, Johnny* / Take this job and shove it: *Paycheck, Johnny* / Banjo man: *Scruggs, Earl* / Kern river: *Haggard, Merle* / Most beautiful girl: *Rich, Charlie* / Would you lay with me: *Tucker, Tanya*
CD **4771202**
Embassy / Oct '95 / Sony

COUNTRY CHARTBUSTERS VOL.2
Kiss you all over: *Exile* / Thing called love: *Cash, Johnny* / Teddy bear song: *Fairchild, Barbara* / What a man my man is: *Anderson, Lynn* / Devil woman: *Robbins, Marty* / Help me make it through the night: *Kristofferson, Kris* / DIVORCE: *Wynette, Tammy* / Behind closed doors: *Rich, Charlie* / Sylvia's mother: *Dr. Hook* / Flowers on the wall: *Statler Brothers* / Battle of New Orleans: *Horton, Johnny* / Big bad John: *Dean, Jimmy* / Lovin' her was easier (than anything I'll ever do): *Nelson, Willie* / I can help: *Swan, Billy* / Too lonely too long: *Parton, Dolly* / Okie from Muskogee: *Haggard, Merle* / Delta dawn: *Tucker, Tanya* / High noon: *Laine, Frankie* / For the good times: *Price, Ray* / Wildfire: *Murphey, Michael*
CD **4851452**
Embassy / Aug '96 / Sony

COUNTRY CHRISTMAS
CD **DCD 5353**
Disky / Dec '93 / Disky / THE

COUNTRY CLASSICS
CD **LECD 044**
Wisepack / Jul '94 / Conifer/BMG / THE

COUNTRY CLASSICS
Rose garden: *Anderson, Lynn* / Big bad John: *Dean, Jimmy* / No charge: *Montgomery, Melba* / Harper Valley PTA: *Riley, Jeannie C.* / Four in the morning: *Young, Faron* / Abilene: *Hamilton, George IV* / Please help me, I'm falling: *Locklin, Hank* / Wolverton mountain: *King, Claude* / From a jack to a king: *Miller, Ned* / One day at a time: *Seely, Jeannie* / Mr. Walker, it's all over: *Spears, Billie Jo* / Satisfied mind: *Wagoner, Porter* / It wasn't God who made honky tonk angels: *Wells, Kitty* / Take this job and shove it: *Paycheck, Johnny* / Waterloo: *Jackson, Stonewall* / Misty blue: *Burgess, Wilma* / Ruby, don't take your love to town: *Darrell, Johnny* / End of the world: *Davis, Skeeter*
CD **ECD 3057**
K-Tel / Jan '95 / K-Tel

COUNTRY COLLECTION (3CD Set)
Rose Marie: *Whitman, Slim* / Indian love call: *Whitman, Slim* / You are my sunshine: *Whitman, Slim* / Riders in the sky: *Whitman, Slim* / Have I told you lately that I love you: *Nelson, Willie* / Crazy: *Nelson, Willie* / Country Willie: *Nelson, Willie* / Gentle on my mind: *Campbell, Glen* / Reason to believe: *Campbell, Glen* / Amazing Grace: *Campbell, Glen* / Rhinestone Cowboy: *Campbell, Glen* / Southern nights: *Campbell, Glen* / Today I started loving you again: *Spears,*

Billie Jo / What I've got in mind: Spears, Billie Jo / Blanket on the ground: Spears, Billie Jo / '57 Chevrolet: Spears, Billie Jo / Ode to Billy Joe: Spears, Billie Jo / Don't it make my brown eyes blue: Gayle, Crystal / Cry me a river: Gayle, Crystal / Wrong road again: Gayle, Crystal / Wayward wind: Gayle, Crystal / When I dream: Gayle, Crystal / You've lost that lovin' feelin': Rogers, Kenny & Dottie West / Lady: Rogers, Kenny / Lucille: Rogers, Kenny / Ruby, don't take your love to town: Rogers, Kenny / Stand by your man: Jackson, Wanda / When you're in love with a beautiful woman: Dr. Hook / Sexy eyes: Dr. Hook / I just had you on my mind: Craddock, Billy / I wish that I could fall in love today: Montgomery, Barbara / Wings of a dove: Husky, Ferlin / Oki from Muskogee: Haggard, Merle / Legend of Bonnie and Clyde: Haggard, Merle / Desperately: Williams, Don / Sweet dreams: Young, Faron / King of the road: Ford, Tennessee Ernie / Baby's got her blue jeans on: McDaniel, Mel / Raindrops keep falling on my head: Gentry, Bobbie / I'll never fall in love again: Gentry, Bobbie / All I have to do is dream: Newton, Juice / Hey Mr. Dream Maker: West, Dottie / Sing me an old fashioned song: Shepard, Jean / It keeps right on a-hurtin': Shepard, Jean / Daddy and home: Tucker, Tanya / What would you do about you (if you were me): Osmond, Marie / Still crazy after all these years: Dalton, Lacy J.
CD Set __________ **CDTRBOX 124**
Trio / Oct '94 / EMI

COUNTRY COLLECTION (Ruby Don't Take Your Love To Town)
Ruby, don't take your love to town: Rogers, Kenny / Six days on the road: Dudley, Dave / I've been everywhere: Anderson, Lynn / (There's) always something there to remind me: Williams, Don / Walk on by: Van Dyke, Leroy / 9,999,999 tears: Baily, Razzy / I gave my love to a railroad man: Mandrell, Barbara / Almost persuaded: Houston, David / It's all over: Murray, Anne / I washed my hands in muddy water: Jackson, Stonewall / I'm so lonesome I could cry: Thomas, B.J. / Release me: Parton, Dolly / Honeysuckle: Owens, Buck / Teddy Bear song: Fairchild, Barbara / Satin sheets: Pruett, Jeanne / Tender years: Jones, George
CD __________ **100962**
CMC / May '97 / BMG

COUNTRY COLLECTION (Crazy)
Denver: Milsap, Ronnie / Redneck: Perkins, Carl / Kawliga: Mandrell, Barbara / Crying: Anderson, Lynn / I want to be with you tonight: Alabama / It makes no difference now: Spears, Billie Jo / Crazy: Lynn, Loretta / Don't think twice: Jennings, Waylon / Right after the dance: Owens, Buck / Something's burning: Rogers, Kenny / Things have gone to pieces: Jones, George / Mistakes by the number: Kershaw, Doug / There's never been a time: Williams, Don / I can't help it: Shannon, Del / Because of you: Posey, Sandy / One step beyond: Nelson, Willie
CD __________ **100982**
CMC / May '97 / BMG

COUNTRY COLLECTION (Rose Garden)
Rose Garden: Anderson, Lynn / Patches: Alabama / Jambalaya: Jones, George / Green green grass of home: Ives, Burl / Abilene: Jennings, Waylon / Wayward wind: Mandrell, Barbara / For the good times: Rogers, Kenny / Look what they've done to my song: Spears, Billie Jo / Road that I walk: Twitty, Conway / Puppy love: Parton, Dolly / We did in '54: Perkins, Carl / Sunday morning coming down: Smith, Sammi / I just can't help believing: Thomas, B.J. / Boys ain't supposed to cry: Davis, Mac / Take my hand: Williams, Don / Dreamin': Gibbs, Terry
CD __________ **100972**
CMC / May '97 / BMG

COUNTRY COLLECTION (3CD Set)
Ruby, don't take your love to town: Rogers, Kenny & The First Edition / Six days on the road: Dudley, Dave / I've been everywhere: Anderson, Lynn / (There's) always something there to remind me: Williams, Don / Walk on by: Van Dyke, Leroy / 9999999 tears: Baily, Razzy / I gave my love to a railroad man: Mandrell, Barbara / Almost persuade: Houston, David / It's all over: Murray, Anne / I washed my hands in muddy water: Jackson, Stonewall / I'm so lonesome I could cry: Thomas, B.J. / Release me: Parton, Dolly / Honeysuckle: Owens, Buck / Teddy bear song: Fairchild, Barbara / Satin sheets: Pruett, Jeanne / Your tender years: Jones, George / Rose garden: Anderson, Lynn / Patches: Alabama / Jambalaya: Jones, George / Green green grass of home: Ives, Burl / Abilene: Jennings, Waylon / Wayward wind: Mandrell, Barbara / For the good times: Rogers, Kenny & The First Edition / Look what they've done to my song: Spears, Billie Jo / Road that I walk: Twitty, Conway / Puppy love: Parton, Dolly / We did in '54: Perkins, Carl / Sunday morning coming down: Smith, Sammi / I just can't help believing: Thomas, B.J. / Boys ain't suppose to cry: Davis, Mac / Take my hand: Williams, Don / Dreamin': Gibbs, Terry / Denver: Milsap, Ronnie / Redneck: Perkins, Carl / Kawliga: Mandrell, Barbara / Crying: Anderson, Lynn / I want to be with you tonight: Alabama / It makes no difference now: Spears, Billie Jo / Crazy: Lynn, Loretta / Don't think twice: Jennings, Waylon / Right after the dance: Owens, Buck / Something's burning: Rogers, Kenny & The First Edition / Things have gone to pieces: Jones, George / Mistakes by the number: Kershaw, Doug / There's never been a time: Williams, Don / I can't help it: Shannon, Del / Because of you: Posey, Sandy / One step beyond: Nelson, Willie
CD Set __________ **100952**
CMC / May '97 / BMG

COUNTRY COLORS (A Magical Blend Of Music And The Sounds Of Nature)
CD __________ **50522**
CMC / May '97 / BMG

COUNTRY COOKING (26 Bluegrass Originals)
CD __________ **ROUCD 11551**
Rounder / '88 / ADA / CM / Direct

COUNTRY CREAM VOL.1 (2CD Set)
CD Set __________ **CDSGP 0100**
Prestige / Aug '94 / Else / Total/BMG

COUNTRY DUETS
Something up my sleeve: Bogguss, Suzy & Billy Dean / We fell in love anyway: Francis, Cleve & Patti Austin / We're both to blame: Greenwood, Lee & Tanya Tucker / Bye bye love: Dalton, Lacy J. & Eddie Rabbitt / Angels love bad men: Mandrell, Barbara & Waylon Jennings / What'cha gonna do with a cowboy: LeDoux, Chris & Garth Brooks / Don't underestimate love: Nitty Gritty Dirt Band / Cowboys like a little rock 'n' roll: LeDoux, Chris & Charlie Daniels / Hopelessly yours: Greenwood, Lee & Suzy Bogguss / Don't go out: Tucker, Tanya & T. Graham Brown / You've lost that lovin' feeling: Rogers, Kenny & Dottie West / All I have to do is dream: Campbell, Glen & Bobby Gentry / Willingly: Nelson, Willie & Shirley Collie / Let your love flow: Reeves, Del & Billie Jo Spears / Something 'bout you baby I like: Campbell, Glen & Rita Coolidge
CD __________ **CDMFP 6331**
Music For Pleasure / Apr '97 / EMI

COUNTRY DUETS
Wild side of life / Slowly / Let's get together / Dear John letter / Good hearted woman / Making plans / Rings of gold / Till a tear becomes a rose / Jeanie's afriad of the dark / Under the spell again / You don't bring me flowers / Just to satisfy you / Our love / Sweet memories / I love you / Have I told you lately that I love you / Don't let me cross over / Mocking bird hill / Storms never last / Love is no excuse
CD __________ **74321378422**
Camden / Apr '97 / BMG

COUNTRY DYNASTY
Sylvia's mother: Dr. Hook / Me and Bobby McGee: Kristofferson, Kris / Crying: Orbison, Roy / Walkin' after midnight: Cline, Patsy / Golden ring: Jones, George & Tammy Wynette / Jackson: Cash, Johnny & June Carter / Thing called love: Cash, Johnny / Help me make it through the night: Kristofferson, Kris & Brenda Lee / What will baby be: Parton, Dolly / Always on my mind: Nelson, Willie / To all the girls I've loved before: Haggard, Merle / Behind closed doors: Rich, Charlie / Seven year ache: Cash, Johnny / Downtown train: Carpenter, Mary-Chapin / You're gonna love yourself in the morning: Nelson, Willie & Brenda Lee / Honey come back: Anderson, Lynn / There goes my everything: Wynette, Tammy
CD __________ **4747912**
Columbia / Nov '93 / Sony

COUNTRY FAVOURITES (4CD Set)
CD Set __________ **HADCDMS 6**
Javelin / Oct '96 / Henry Hadaway / THE

COUNTRY FAVOURITES
Where do we go from here: Williams, Don / World's worst loser: Jones, George / Love hurts: Parsons, Gram & Emmylou Harris / Hello walls: Young, Faron / Fly like an eagle: Fat Cat Band / All that's keeping me alive: Fat Cat Band / How do I hide from a memory: Pillow, Ray / It's so easy: Jennings, Waylon / By the time I get to Phoenix: Nashville West / You still want to go: Henderson, Kelvin / Release me: Parton, Dolly / Lighthouse bar: Blackwater Band / Is there something on your mind: Nelson, Willie / Way out there: Parsons, Gene / Wing of a dove: Husky, Ferlin / What she deserves: Powers, Laura / Let the sunshine on the people: Jackson, Stonewall / Silver wings: Fender, Freddy / You'll never walk alone: Twitty, Conway
CD __________ **306082**
Hallmark / Jan '97 / Carlton

COUNTRY GEMS
Honey come back: Campbell, Glen / Cry me a river: Gayle, Crystal / Daytime friends: Rogers, Kenny / Wayward wind: Ritter, Tex / Raindrops keep falling on my head: Gentry, Bobbie / Duellin' banjos: Jackson, Carl / Race is on: Jones, George / Angel of the morning: Newton, Juice / Life gits tee-jus don't it: Wiliams, Tex / Tumbling tumbleweeds: Husky, Ferlin / Lesson in leavin': West, Dottie / Sing me an old fashioned song: Spears, Billie Jo / Hello walls: Nelson, Willie / Country girl: Young, Faron / Home on the range: Whitman, Slim / Destiny: Murray, Anne / I got a new field to plough: McDonald, Skeets / Take me home country roads: Newton-John, Olivia / Loving him was easier: Carter, Anita / Jambalaya: Axton, Hoyt / Stand by your man: Jackson, Wanda / Mercy: Shepard, Jean / Mule train: Ford, Tennessee Ernie / Young love: James, Sonny
CD __________ **CC 243**
Music For Pleasure / Sep '89 / EMI

COUNTRY GENTLEMEN
Lonesome number one: Gibson, Don / I love you because: Jackson, Stonewall / Please help me, I'm falling: Locklin, Hank / There goes my everything: Greene, Jack / Convoy: Husky, Ferlin / Take this job and shove it: Paycheck, Johnny / Misery loves company: Wagoner, Porter / Jambalaya: Russell, Johnny / Alone with you: Young, Faron / Never ending song of love: Lee, Dickey / You can have her: Brown, Jim Ed / Little black book: Dean, Jimmy / Almost persuaded: Houston, David / Hitchin' a ride: Reno, Jack / Pick me up on your way down: Walker, Charlie / Juanita Jones: Phillips, Stu / Take a letter Miss Gray: Tubb, Justin / Country bumpkin: Smith, Cal
CD __________ **ECD 3068**
K-Tel / Dec '96 / K-Tel

COUNTRY GIANTS VOL.1
Reuben James: Rogers, Kenny / Honky tonk angels: Rogers, Kenny / Sweet dreams: Young, Faron / Then you'll know: Young, Faron / I'm so lonesome I could cry: Spears, Billie Jo / I can't find the time: Nelson, Willie / Ruby, don't take your love to town: Rogers, Kenny / Things to talk about: Jackson, Stonewall / Talk about me: Paycheck, Johnny / I didn't sleep a wink: Nelson, Willie / From a Jack to a King: Miller, Ned / White lightning: Jennings, Waylon / Look what they've done to my song ma: Spears, Billie Jo / Making believe: Parton, Dolly / Home is where you're happy: Nelson, Willie / Wings of a dove: Husky, Ferlin / Shine on Ruby mountain: Rogers, Kenny / Sticks and stones: Fargo, Donna / Rose garden: Anderson, Lynn / Turn the cards slowly: Cline, Patsy / Ramblin' rose: Lee, Johnny / Country girl: Young, Faron / Dear heart: Miller, Roger / Heart you break may be your own: Cline, Patsy / Little green apples: Miller, Roger
CD __________ **CDGFR 003**
Tring / Jun '92 / Tring

COUNTRY GIANTS VOL.1
Reuben James: Rogers, Kenny / Walkin' after midnight: Cline, Patsy / Country girl: Young, Faron / Face of a fighter: Nelson, Willie / Sweet evening breeze (bring my baby back to me): Reeves, Jim / Shake 'em up, roll 'em: Jackson, Stonewall / Making believe: Parton, Dolly / Six days on the road: Boxcar Willie / Wings of a dove: Husky, Ferlin / Sticks and stones: Fargo, Donna / 9,999,999 tears: Bailey, Razzy / Sally was a good old girl: Jennings, Waylon / Luckenbach Texas: Drusky, Roy / Kaw-Liga: Mandrell, Barbara / I'll repossess my heart: Wells, Kitty / That girl who waits on tables: Fender, Freddy / Fraulein: Gilley, Mickey / Jambalaya: Jones, George / Elvira: Rogers, Kenny / North to Alaska: Boxcar Willie
CD __________ **QED 003**
Tring / Nov '96 / Tring

COUNTRY GIANTS VOL.2
Is there something on your mind: Nelson, Willie / Rhythm 'n' booze: Owens, Buck / Candy store: Lee, Johnny / stop, look and listen: Cline, Patsy / Four in the morning: Young, Faron / Hello walls: Young, Faron / Wishful thinking: Fargo, Donna / Reuben James: Rogers, Kenny / Both sides now: Murray, Anne / Billy Jack Washburn: Paycheck, Johnny / Shelter of my arms: Nelson, Willie / This ole house: Perkins, Carl / Then you'll know: Cline, Patsy / Letter to heaven: Parton, Dolly / Ol' blue: Jackson, Stonewall / Sally was a good old girl: Jennings, Waylon / Honky tonk merry go round: Laine, Frankie / Moonlight gambler: Laine, Frankie / Wine me up: Young, Faron / Send me the pillow that you dream on: Locklin, Hank / Building heartaches: Nelson, Willie / Ease the want in me: Spears, Billie Jo / Sad and lonely days: Dudley, Dave / Heartaches by the number: Mitchell, Guy / Blue is the way I feel: Twitty, Conway
CD __________ **CDGFR 004**
Tring / Jun '92 / Tring

COUNTRY GIANTS VOL.2
I'm so lonesome I could cry: Spears, Billie Jo / Ruby don't take your love to town: Rogers, Kenny / Then you'll know: Cline, Patsy / Crying: Jennings, Waylon / Convoy: Boxcar Willie / Home: Reeves, Jim / Little blossom: Parton, Dolly / Ol' blue: Jackson, Stonewall / If you ain't lovin': Young, Faron / Daddy: Fargo, Donna / That heart belongs to me: Gilley, Mickey / Take this job and shove it: Paycheck, Johnny / Sweeter than candy: Perkins, Carl / What have they done to my song Ma: Spears, Billie Jo / Shine on Ruby mountain: Rogers, Kenny / Pick me up on your way down: Cline, Patsy / Roly poly: Reeves, Jim / Keep off the grass: Jackson, Stonewall / Green green grass of home: Paycheck, Johnny / Truck driving man: Boxcar Willie
CD __________ **QED 179**
Tring / Nov '96 / Tring

COUNTRY GIRL
CD __________ **11814**
Music / Feb '96 / Target/BMG

COUNTRY GIRLS
Wrong road again: Gayle, Crystal / Somebody loves you: Gayle, Crystal / What I've got in mind: Spears, Billie Jo / '57 Chevrolet: Spears, Billie Jo / Daddy and home: Tucker, Tanya / Strong enough to bend: Tucker, Tanya / All I have to do is dream: Newton, Juice / Sweetest thing (I've ever known): Newton, Juice / I wish that I could fall in love today: Mandrell, Barbara / It all came true: Mandrell, Barbara / Pinkertons flowers: Montgomery, Melba / Hey Mr. Dream Maker: West, Dottie / Still crazy after all these years: Dalton, Lacy J. / Reuben James: Jackson, Wanda / Mississippi delta: Gentry, Bobbie / Under the sun: Bogguss, Suzy / Slippin' away: Shepard, Jean / Coat of many colours: Peppers, Nancy / It's morning (and I still love you): Colter, Jessi / Simple little words: Lane, Christy
CD __________ **CDMFP 5911**
Music For Pleasure / Apr '91 / EMI

COUNTRY GIRLS
CD __________ **MACCD 114**
Autograph / Aug '96 / BMG

COUNTRY GOLD
CD __________ **LECD 42**
Wisepack / Jul '94 / Conifer/BMG / THE

COUNTRY GOLD (It's Only Make Believe)
CD __________ **MU 5055CD**
Musketeer / Oct '92 / Disc

COUNTRY GOLD (2CD Set)
Guitar man: Presley, Elvis / Rhinestone cowboy: Campbell, Glen / Crazy: Cline, Patsy / Blue bayou: Orbison, Roy / Jolene: Parton, Dolly / Ring of fire: Cash, Johnny / Stand by your man: Wynette, Tammy / Behind closed doors: Rich, Charlie / Rose garden: Anderson, Lynn / Lucille: Rogers, Kenny / I can help: Swan, Billy / Don't it make my brown eyes blue: Gayle, Crystal / I love you because: Reeves, Jim / '57 Chevrolet: Spears, Billie Jo / Funny how time slips away: Nelson, Willie / Coal miner's daughter: Lynn, Loretta / Four in the morning: Young, Faron / I'm sorry: Lee, Brenda / Sea of heartbreak: Gibson, Don / I will always love you: Parton, Dolly / Achy breaky heart: Cyrus, Billy Ray / When you're in love with a beautiful woman: Dr. Hook / Let your love flow: Bellamy Brothers / Country road: Taylor, James / Banks of the Ohio: Newton-John, Olivia / Wind beneath my wings: Greenwood, Lee / Crystal chandeliers: Pride, Charley / Sweet dreams: Cline, Patsy / All I have to do is dream: Everly Brothers / He'll have to go: Reeves, Jim / Theme from the dukes of hazard (good ol'boys): Jennings, Waylon / Honky tonk man: Yoakam, Dwight / Have mercy: Judds / Lone star state of mind: Williams, Don / Return of the grievous angel: Parsons, Gram / Together again: Harris, Emmylou / From a distance: Griffith, Nanci / Mr. Tambourine man: Byrds / End of the world: Davis, Skeeter / Love me tender: Presley, Elvis
CD Set __________ **RADCD 25**
Global TV / Mar '96 / BMG

COUNTRY GOLD
CD __________ **MACCD 112**
Autograph / Aug '96 / BMG

COUNTRY GOLD VOL.1
Sweet dreams: Cline, Patsy / You're my best friend: Williams, Don / Dream lover: Campbell, Glen & Tanya Tucker / I've cried the blue right out of my eyes: Gayle, Crystal / Coal miner's daughter: Lynn, Loretta / Ramblin' fever: Haggard, Merle / Big four poster bed: Lee, Brenda / Sail away: Oak Ridge Boys / You've never been this far before: Twitty, Conway / Hand that rocks the cradle: Campbell, Glen / Texas (When I die): Tucker, Tanya / I was country when country wasn't cool: Mandrell, Barbara / Somebody's knockin': Gibbs, Terri / There goes my everything: Greene, Jack / Satin sheets: Pruett, Jeanne / Still: Anderson, Bill / Busted: Conlee, John / Country bumpkin: Smith, Carl / My special angel: Helms, Bobby / Hello darlin': Twitty, Conway
CD __________ **MCCD 080**
Music Club / Jun '92 / Disc / THE

COUNTRY GOLD VOL.2
CD __________ **MCCD 053**
Music Club / '93 / Disc / THE

COUNTRY GOLD VOL.3
CD __________ **MCCD 132**
Music Club / Sep '93 / Disc / THE

COUNTRY GOLDEN HITS
CD __________ **DCD 5309**
Disky / Dec '93 / Disky / THE

COUNTRY GOSPEL
Hellelujah special: Perkins, Carl / Old time religion: Reeves, Jim / Pictures from life's other side: Lewis, Jerry Lee / Wreck on the highway: Pitney, Gene & George Jones / He'll do for you: Cline, Patsy / Family bible: Jones, George / When god dips his love in my heart: Reeves, Jim / Why me lord: Cash, Johnny / He means all the world to me: Oak Ridge Boys / I saw the light: Phillips, Bill / Without god: Oak Ridge Boys / Daddy sang bass: Perkins, Carl / Reuben James: Rog-

ers, Kenny / Hobo heaven: *Boxcar Willie* / Peace in the valley: *Cash, Johnny* / Old country church: *Oak Ridge Boys* / Life's railway to heaven: *Cline, Patsy* / Softly and tenderly: *Reeves, Jim* / Old brush arbors: *Jones, George* / Let me live in the light of his love: *Pride, Charley*
CD ____________ **300902**
Hallmark / Jul '96 / Carlton

COUNTRY GOSPEL 1929-1946
Motherless children: *Carter Family* / Presentjoys: *Alabama Sacred Heart Singers* / Rocky road: *Alabama Sacred Heart Singers* / There's evil in ye children: *Davis, Jimmie* / You'll never miss your mother: *Grayson & Whitter* / On the rock where Moses stood: *Carter Family* / I'll lead a Christian life: *Carter Family* / Dry bones: *Lunsford, Bascom Lamar* / We shall all be reunited: *Karnes, Alfred G.* / Old time religion: *Phipps, Ernest & Holiness Quartet* / No telephone in heaven: *Carter Family* / Mother came to get her boy from jail: *Mainer, Wade* / What would you give in exchange for your soul: *Mainer, Wade* / God holds the future in his hands: *Mainer, Wade* / Saints go marching in: *Monroe Brothers* / Shining city over the river: *Dixon Brothers* / In the vine covered chapel: *Delmore Brothers* / Heavenly light is shining on me: *Delmore Brothers* / Will the circle be unbroken: *Monroe Brothers* / Open up them pearly gates: *Robinson, Carson* / Just inside the pearly gates: *Anglin Twins* / When the golden train comes down: *Sons Of The Pioneers* / You must come in at the door: *Sons Of The Pioneers* / It won't be long: *Acuff, Roy* / Prodigal son: *Acuff, Roy* / Precious memories: *Shelton Brothers* / Address from heaven: *Armstrong Twins* / Calling you: *Williams, Hank* / Wealth won't save your soul: *Williams, Hank* / Speak to me little darling: *Blue Sky Boys* / My Lord keeps a record: *Story, Carl* / Are you afraid to die: *Story, Carl* / Echose from the burning bush: *Story, Carl* / Wicked path of sin: *Monroe, Bill* / Drunken driver: *O'Day, Molly* / Tramp on the street: *O'Day, Molly*
CD Set ____________ **FA 055**
Fremeaux / Apr '97 / ADA / Discovery

COUNTRY GOSPEL 1946-1953
CD ____________ **DOCD 5221**
Document / Apr '94 / ADA / Hot Shot / Jazz Music

COUNTRY GREATS (4CD Set)
CD Set ____________ **MBSCD 429**
Castle / Sep '94 / BMG

COUNTRY GREATS
CD ____________ **CPMV 023**
Cromwell / Sep '94 / Total/BMG

COUNTRY GREATS
CD ____________ **MACCD 115**
Autograph / Aug '96 / BMG

COUNTRY GREATS (4CD Set)
Reuben James: *Rogers, Kenny & The First Edition* / Walkin' after midnight: *Cline, Patsy* / Country girl: *Young, Faron* / Face of a fighter: *Nelson, Willie* / Sweet evening breeze bring my baby back to me: *Reeves, Jim* / Shake 'em up roll'em: *Jackson, Stonewall* / Making believe: *Parton, Dolly* / Six days on the road: *Boxcar Willie* / Wings of a dove: *Husky, Ferlin* / Luckenbach Texas: *Drusky, Roy* / Kaw-liga: *Mandrell, Barbara* / I'll reposses my heart: *Wells, Kitty* / That girl who waits on tables: *Fender, Freddy* / Fraulein: *Gilley, Mickey* / Jambalaya: *Jones, George* / Elvira: *Rogers, Kenny* / North to Alaska: *Boxcar Willie* / I'm so lonesome I could cry: *Spears, Billie Jo* / Ruby don't take your love to town: *Rogers, Kenny & The First Edition* / Then you'll know: *Cline, Patsy* / Crying: *Jennings, Waylon* / Convoy: *Boxcar Willie* / Home: *Reeves, Jim* / Little blossom: *Parton, Dolly* / Ol' blue: *Jackson, Stonewall* / If you ain't lovin': *Young, Faron* / Daddy: *Fargo, Donna* / That heart belongs to me: *Gilley, Mickey* / Take this job and shove it: *Paycheck, Johnny* / Sweeter than candy: *Perkins, Carl* / What have they done to my song ma: *Spears, Billie Jo* / Shine on ruby mountain: *Rogers, Kenny & The First Edition* / Pick me up on your way down: *Cline, Patsy* / Roly poly: *Reeves, Jim* / Keep off the grass: *Jackson, Stonewall* / Green green grass of home: *Paycheck, Johnny* / Truck driving man: *Boxcar Willie* / Sweet dreams: *Young, Faron* / I've loved and lost again: *Cline, Patsy* / Don't think twice: *Jennings, Waylon* / I can't find the time: *Nelson, Willie* / I never promised you a rose garden: *Anderson, Lynn* / Always leaving always gone: *Rogers, Kenny & The First Edition* / Hello walls: *Drusky, Roy* / Wishful thinking: *Fargo, Donna* / I can't get enough of you: *Jackson, Stonewall* / Before the next teardrop falls: *Fender, Freddy* / Release me: *Mandrell, Barbara* / Have I told you lately that I love you: *Reeves, Jim* / Lonely wine: *Gilley, Mickey* / Makin' believe: *Wells, Kitty* / Four in the morning: *Young, Faron* / Your tender years: *Jones, George* / Hungry for love: *Cline, Patsy* / She even woke me up to say goodbye: *Rogers, Kenny & The First Edition* / Last letter: *Drusky, Roy* / I don't know why I love you but I do: *Fender, Freddy* / Blue eyes cryin' in the rain: *Drusky, Roy* / Ease the want in me: *Spears, Billie Jo* / Almost persuaded: *Paycheck, Johnny* / Something's burning: *Rogers, Kenny & The First Edition* / Just out of reach: *Cline, Patsy* / He'll have to go: *Reeves, Jim* / Apartment no.9: *Young, Faron* / Dream baby: *Jennings, Waylon* / Dixie: *Boxcar Willie* / Old kentucky home: *Boxcar Willie* / Baby I want to love you: *Fender, Freddy* / Things have gone to pieces: *Jones, George* / Should I go home: *Jackson, Stonewall* / Someone to give my love to: *Paycheck, Johnny* / Shelter of your arms: *Nelson, Willie* / Night after night: *Gilley, Mickey* / Once a day: *Young, Faron* / Never no more: *Cline, Patsy* / Going out with the tide: *Fender, Freddy* / Am I losing you: *Reeves, Jim* / Sticks and stones: *Fargo, Donna* / 9,999,999 tears: *Bailey, Razzy* / Sally was a good old girl: *Jennings, Waylon*
CD Set ____________ **QUAD 003**
Tring / Nov '96 / Tring

COUNTRY GREATS (Blue Eyes Cryin' In The Rain)
Blue eyes cryin' in the rain: *Drusky, Roy* / Ease the want in me: *Spears, Billie Jo* / Almost persuaded: *Paycheck, Johnny* / Something's burning: *Rogers, Kenny & The First Edition* / Just out of reach: *Cline, Patsy* / He'll have to go: *Reeves, Jim* / Apartment 9: *Young, Faron* / Dream baby: *Jennings, Waylon* / Dixie: *Boxcar Willie* / Baby I want to love you: *Fender, Freddy* / Things have gone to pieces: *Jones, George* / Should I go home: *Jackson, Stonewall* / Someone to give my love to: *Paycheck, Johnny* / Shelter of your arms: *Nelson, Willie* / Night after night: *Gilley, Mickey* / Once a day: *Young, Faron* / Never no more: *Cline, Patsy* / Going out with the tide: *Fender, Freddy* / Am I losing you: *Reeves, Jim* / Old Kentucky home: *Boxcar Willie*
CD ____________ **QED 049**
Tring / Nov '96 / Tring

COUNTRY GREATS
She's just a girl I used to know: *Jones, George* / Will you remember mine: *Nelson, Willie* / I fall to pieces: *Young, Faron* / Treat me mean treat me cruel: *Twitty, Conway* / Daddy sang bass: *Perkins, Carl* / Livin' in the sunshine of your love: *Pillow, Ray* / Airport song: *Blackwater Band* / Georgia in a jug: *Paycheck, Johnny* / I don't need to know that right now: *Paycheck, Johnny* / Your cheatin' heart: *Young, Faron* / Can't change overnight: *Jones, George* / And so will you my love: *Nelson, Willie* / What am I living for: *Perkins, Carl* / Lighthouse bar: *Blackwater Band* / Where I stand: *Twitty, Conway* / We're together again: *Pillow, Ray*
CD ____________ **300482**
Hallmark / Jul '96 / Carlton

COUNTRY GREATS VOL.1
CD ____________ **TRTCD 174**
TrueTrax / Jun '95 / THE

COUNTRY GREATS VOL.2
CD ____________ **TRTCD 189**
TrueTrax / Feb '96 / THE

COUNTRY HALL OF FAME
CD ____________ **LECD 045**
Wisepack / Jul '94 / Conifer/BMG / THE

COUNTRY HEARTBREAKERS
Heartaches: *Cline, Patsy* / She's got you: *Cline, Patsy* / It hurts so much: *Reeves, Jim* / When two worlds collide: *Reeves, Jim* / I will always love you: *Parton, Dolly* / Daddy come and get me: *Parton, Dolly* / Don't fall in love with a dreamer: *Rogers, Kenny* / Till I can make it on my own: *Rogers, Kenny* / Cry me a river: *Gayle, Crystal* / I still miss someone: *Gayle, Crystal* / Your cheatin' heart: *Lynn, Loretta* / Paper roses: *Lynn, Loretta* / Please Mr. Please: *Newton-John, Olivia* / I honestly love you: *Newton-John, Olivia* / Honey come back: *Campbell, Glen* / Hey won't you play another somebody done somebody wrong song: *Spears, Billie Jo* / Misty blue: *Spears, Billie Jo* / I'll never fall in love again: *Gentry, Bobbie* / There'll be no teardrops tonight: *Nelson, Willie* / It keeps right on a-hurtin': *Shepard, Jean*
CD ____________ **CDMFP 6116**
Music For Pleasure / Mar '94 / EMI

COUNTRY HEROES LIVE
CD ____________ **15402**
Laserlight / Aug '91 / Target/BMG

COUNTRY HICKS VOL.1
CD ____________ **BARKLOG 1CD**
No Hit / Sep '95 / Cargo / SRD

COUNTRY JUNCTION (2CD Set)
Country junction: *Ford, Tennessee Ernie* / Goin' steady: *Young, Faron* / Satisfied mind: *Shepard, Jean* / My home town: *Husky, Ferlin* / High noon: *Ritter, Tex* / There my future goes: *Thompson, Hank* / Smoke, smoke, smoke: *Williams, Tex* / I don't hurt anymore: *Ford, Tennessee Ernie* / Cold cold heart: *Jackson, Wanda* / Ain't it funny what a fool will do: *Jones, George* / What's bad for you is good for me: *Montgomery, Melba* / I'm wasting my tears on you: *Ritter, Tex* / You're calling me sweetheart again: *Shepard, Jean* / Sixteen tons: *Ford, Tennessee Ernie* / Sioux City Sue: *Husky, Ferlin* / That's what I like about the West: *Williams, Tex* / Sweet dreams: *Young, Faron* / Streets of Laredo: *Ritter, Tex* / Tears on my pillow: *Ford, Tennessee Ernie* / Left my gal in the mountains: *Thompson, Hank* / Forget the past: *Young, Faron* / Wild side of life: *Thompson, Hank* / Funny how time slips away: *Ford, Tennessee Ernie* / My wedding ring: *Shepard, Jean* / Billy the kid: *Ritter, Tex* / My home in San Antone: *Husky, Ferlin* / Shot gun boogie: *Williams, Tex* / Silver threads and golden needles: *Jackson, Wanda* / There'll be no teardrops tonight: *Ford, Tennessee Ernie* / I can still see him in your eyes: *Mack, Billy* / You'd better go: *Shepard, Jean* / If I could keep you off my mind: *Mathis, Johnny* / We must have been out of our minds: *Jones, George & Melba Montgomery* / Alabama Jubilee: *Husky, Ferlin* / Don't let the stars get in your eyes: *McDonald, Skeets* / Mule train: *Ford, Tennessee Ernie* / I've got five dollars and it's Saturday night: *Young, Faron* / Crying steel guitar waltz: *Shepard, Jean* / Don't walk away: *Husky, Ferlin* / Rye whiskey: *Ritter, Tex*
CD Set ____________ **CDDL 1215**
Music For Pleasure / Nov '91 / EMI

COUNTRY LADIES
Gonna get along without you now: *Davis, Skeeter* / I can't stop loving you: *Wells, Kitty* / Crazy: *Jackson, Wanda* / Satin sheets: *Pruett, Jeannie* / How can I unlove you: *Anderson, Lynn* / Misty blue: *Burgess, Wilma* / Let's go all the way: *Jean, Norma* / I'll love you more: *Seely, Jeannie* / Mr. Walker it's all over: *Spears, Billie Jo* / There never was a time: *Riley, Jeannie C.* / Ain't had no lovin': *Smith, Connie* / Superman: *Fargo, Donna* / Send me the pillow you dream on: *Smith, Sammi* / Pitty pitty patter: *Raye, Susan* / It only hurts for a while: *Smith, Margo* / Shake me I rattle: *Worth, Marion* / Kid stuff: *Fairchild, Barbara* / Satisfied mind: *Shepard, Jean*
CD ____________ **ECD 3067**
K-Tel / Dec '96 / K-Tel

COUNTRY LADIES (2CD Set)
CD Set ____________ **MCD 211611**
MCA / Mar '97 / BMG

COUNTRY LADIES
CD ____________ **DS 018**
Desperado / Jun '97 / TKO Magnum

COUNTRY LADIES LIVE
CD ____________ **15404**
Laserlight / Aug '91 / Target/BMG

COUNTRY LEGENDS
Talking in your sleep: *Gayle, Crystal* / By the time I get to Phoenix: *Campbell, Glen* / Better love next time: *Dr. Hook* / Queen of the house: *Miller, Jody* / Funny how time slips away: *Nelson, Willie* / If you could read my mind: *Newton-John, Olivia* / Wichita lineman: *Campbell, Glen* / I love you because: *Spears, Billie Jo* / Gambler: *Rogers, Kenny* / Give me your word: *Ford, Tennessee Ernie* / Hey Mr. Dream maker: *West, Dottie* / All I have to do is dream: *Campbell, Glen & Bobbie Gentry* / Don't it make my brown eyes blue: *Gayle, Crystal* / Games people play: *South, Joe* / When you're in love with a beautiful woman: *Dr. Hook* / She believes in me: *Rogers, Kenny* / Ode to Billie Joe: *Gentry, Bobbie* / Crazy: *Nelson, Willie* / I honestly love you: *Newton-John, Olivia* / '57 Chevrolet: *Spears, Billie Jo*
CD ____________ **CDSL 8259**
EMI / Jul '95 / EMI

COUNTRY LEGENDS
CD ____________ **DCDCD 201**
Castle / Aug '96 / BMG

COUNTRY LEGENDS
Crazy: *Cline, Patsy* / Coward of the county: *Rogers, Kenny* / From a distance: *Griffith, Nanci* / You're my best friend: *Williams, Don* / DIVORCE: *Parton, Dolly* / Last one to know: *McEntire, Reba* / Boy named Sue: *Cash, Johnny* / Blanket on the ground: *Spears, Billie Jo* / Don't let your babies grow up to be cowboys: *Nelson, Willie* / Most beautiful girl in the world: *Rich, Charlie* / Help me make it through the night: *Kristofferson, Kris* / She's in love with the boy: *Yearwood, Trisha* / Talking in your sleep: *Gayle, Crystal* / Wind beneath my wings: *Greenwood, Lee* / El Paso: *Robbins, Marty* / Brand new heartache: *Everly Brothers* / Cola miner's daughter: *Lynn, Loretta* / It's only make believe: *Campbell, Glen*
CD ____________ **MACCD 110**
Autograph / Aug '96 / BMG

COUNTRY LEGENDS
CD ____________ **NTRCD 058**
Nectar / Feb '97 / Pinnacle

COUNTRY LINE DANCING
Boys and me / Girls with guitars / Talk dirty to me / Don't step out of line / That's what I get for losin' you / Cowboy reggae / Swamp thing / Back on the streets / Soft touch / XXX's and OOO's (An American girl) / Cotton Eye Joe / Deadwood stage / Line King / Nobody wins / Angel of the night / Any man of mine / Fast Fingers Freddie / Meet me on the corner / Wrong train, wrong line / Time won't let me slow down / When you walk in the room / Duelling banjos
CD ____________ **QED 032**
Tring / Nov '96 / Tring

COUNTRY LINE DANCING VOL.1
Achy breaky heart / Boot scootin' boogie / Down at St. Domas Walkers / Wink / Livin' on love / God bless Texas / Fast as you / Kick a little / Love bug / Ain't going down til the sun comes up / American honky tonk bar association / Holdin' heaven / I feel lucky / Down on the farm / Baby likes to rock it / Xxx's and Ooo's / Honky tonk blues
CD ____________ **CDMFP 6280**
Music For Pleasure / Nov '96 / EMI

COUNTRY LINE DANCING VOL.2
Cadillac ranch / Hillbilly rock / Chattahoochee / Rock my world (little country girl) / If bubba can dance (I can too) / Whiskey ain't workin' / Mercury blues / He thinks he'll keep her / Why haven't I heard from you lately / Neon moon / What the cowgirls do / Summertime blues / Gone country / Goin' through the big D / Little miss honky tonk / Third rate romance / Big one / Any man of mine
CD ____________ **CDMFP 6343**
Music For Pleasure / Apr '97 / EMI

COUNTRY LOVE
CD ____________ **MACCD 258**
Autograph / Aug '96 / BMG

COUNTRY LOVE (16 Country Classics)
Send me the pillow you dream on: *Locklin, Hank* / Help me make it through the night: *Bare, Bobby* / Dreams of the everyday housewife: *Campbell, Glen* / Three cigarettes in an ashtry: *Cline, Patsy* / Sweet dreams: *Jones, George* / Across the wide Missouri: *McCall, Cash* / You're my man: *Spears, Billie Jo* / Alone with you: *Young, Faron* / By the time I get to Phoenix: *Campbell, Glen* / You're eyes don't lie to me: *Anderson, Bill* / Box of memories: *Riley, Jeannie C.* / Little green apples: *Miller, Roger* / Simple thing as love: *Clark, Roy* / Love's gonna live here: *Jennings, Waylon* / Touch of my woman: *Walker, Billy* / I've loved and lost again: *Cline, Patsy*
CD ____________ **SUMCD 4050**
Summit / Nov '96 / Sound & Media

COUNTRY LOVE SONGS (3CD Set)
Hello I love you: *Gayle, Crystal* / Honey come back: *Campbell, Glen* / My elusive dreams: *Whitman, Slim* / Love letters in the sand: *Spears, Billie Jo* / Willingly: *Nelson, Willie & Shirley Collie* / Just another love: *Tucker, Tanya* / Cold cold heart: *Jackson, Wanda* / On the banks of the Ohio: *Newton-John, Olivia* / Country girl heart: *Gatlin, Larry & The Gatlin Brothers* / Someday soon: *Gayle, Crystal* / My side of the story: *Boguss, Suzy* / If not you: *Dr. Hook* / Let me call you sweetheart: *Whitman, Slim* / Lay back in the arms of someone: *Newton, Juice* / It's all right with me: *Gayle, Crystal* / Stand by your man: *Spears, Billie Jo* / Last thing on my mind: *Campbell, Glen* / I'll take you home again Kathleen: *Whitman, Slim* / Hello walls: *Nelson, Willie* / One love at a time: *Tucker, Tanya* / High noon: *Ritter, Tex* / Please Mr., please: *Newton-John, Olivia* / Ain't it funny what a fool will do: *Jones, George* / Come to me: *Newton, Juice* / Our chain of love: *Nelson, Willie & Shirley Collie* / I love you, I honestly love you: *Newton-John, Olivia* / Everything a man could ever need: *Campbell, Glen* / Still crazy after all these years: *Dalton, Lacy J.* / (We must have been) out of our minds: *Jones, George & Melba Montgomery* / All I have to do is dream: *Campbell, Glen & Bobby Gentry* / (Hey won't you play) another somebody done somebody wrong so: *Spears, Billie Jo* / Love song of the waterfall: *Whitman, Slim* / Take me as I am (or let me go): *Nelson, Willie* / Talking in your sleep: *Gayle, Crystal* / Under the gun: *Boguss, Suzy* / Oh Jessi: *Dr. Hook* / Delta dawn: *Tucker, Tanya* / Silver threads and golden needles: *Jackson, Wanda* / If: *Newton-John, Olivia* / My wedding ring: *Shepard, Jean* / I will survive: *Spears, Billie Jo* / Goin' steady: *Young, Faron* / Shotgun: *Tucker, Tanya* / I wish that I could fall in love today: *Mandrell, Barbara* / Another lonely night: *Shepard, Jean*
CD Set ____________ **CDTRBOX 236**
Trio / Oct '96 / EMI

COUNTRY MEETS SOUL
I'm so lonesome I could cry: *Green, Al* / Rainin' love: *Wood, Brenton* / No easy way to say goodbye: *Wright, O.V.* / Funny how time slips away: *Green, Al* / You win again: *Rich, Charlie* / I die a little each day: *Clay, Otis* / Say yes to love: *Clayton, Willie* / It was jealousy: *Peebles, Ann* / When something is wrong with my baby: *Rich, Charlie* / For the good times: *Green, Al* / When I'm gone: *Clayton, Willie* / Hurry up freight train: *Rich, Charlie* / You don't know me: *Johnson, Syl* / One woman: *Green, Al* / To fool a fool: *Rich, Charlie* / Time we have: *Wright, O.V.* / Since I met you baby: *Felts, Narvel* / I'll be standing by: *Green, Al* / Wedding bells: *Rich, Charlie*
CD ____________ **HILOCD 14**
Hi / Jul '95 / Pinnacle

COUNTRY MOODS
When you're in love with a beautiful woman: *Dr. Hook* / Let your love flow: *Bellamy Brothers* / Ruby, don't take your love to town: *Rogers, Kenny* / Good year for the roses: *Costello, Elvis & The Attractions* / Jolene: *Parton, Dolly* / Wichita lineman: *Campbell, Glen* / Don't it make my brown eyes blue: *Gayle, Crystal* / Thing called love: *Cash, Johnny* / ode to billy joe: *Gentry, Bobbie* / We're all alone: *Coolidge, Rita* / Blue bayou: *Ronstadt, Linda* / Horse with no name: *America* / Crazy: *Cline, Patsy* / Help me make it through the night: *Kristofferson, Kris* / Behind closed doors: *Rich, Charlie* / DIVORCE: *Wynette, Tammy* / You're my

best friend: *Williams, Don* / Four in the morning: *Young, Faron* / Here, there and everywhere: *Harris, Emmylou* / Me and Bobby McGee: *Nelson, Willie* / Angel of the morning: *Newton, Juice* / Harper Valley PTA: *Riley, Jeannie C.* / King of the road: *Miller, Roger*
CD ______ **5152992**
PolyGram TV / Apr '92 / PolyGram

COUNTRY MOODS
CD ______ **MACCD 218**
Autograph / Aug '96 / BMG

COUNTRY MUSIC INTERNATIONAL (The Best In New Country Music)
Till you love: *McEntire, Reba* / Ladder of love: *Crowell, Rodney* / Just a memory: *Mavericks* / One: *Jones, George & Tammy Wynette* / Listen to the radio: *Griffith, Nanci* / You better think twice: *Gill, Vince* / Why don't that telephone ring: *Byrd, Tracy* / I wanna go far: *Yearwood, Trisha* / Almost goodbye: *Chestnut, Mark* / Now that's country: *Stuart, Marty* / Hard lovin' woman: *Collie, Mark*
CD ______ **CMID 001**
MCA / Feb '96 / BMG

COUNTRY MUSIC VOL.1
CD ______ **3003662**
IMP / Jan '97 / ADA / Discovery

COUNTRY MUSIC VOL.2
CD ______ **3003652**
IMP / Jan '97 / ADA / Discovery

COUNTRY MUSIC: CAT'N AROUND
CD ______ **KKCD 07**
Krazy Kat / Feb '93 / Hot Shot / Jazz Music

COUNTRY NEGRO JAM SESSIONS
CD ______ **ARHCD 372**
Arhoolie / Apr '95 / ADA / Cadillac / Direct

COUNTRY NIGHTS
CD ______ **MACCD 113**
Autograph / Aug '96 / BMG

COUNTRY NUMBER ONES
Dukes Of Hazzard: *Jennings, Waylon* / Crazy: *Cline, Patsy* / I fall to pieces: *Cline, Patsy* / Lucille: *Rogers, Kenny* / Coward of the county: *Rogers, Kenny* / Nine to five: *Parton, Dolly* / Here you come again: *Parton, Dolly* / Distant drums: *Reeves, Jim* / Rhinestone cowboy: *Campbell, Glen* / Southern nights: *Campbell, Glen* / Blanket on the ground: *Spears, Billie Jo* / Love in the first degree: *Alabama* / Coal miner's daughter: *Lynn, Loretta* / Kiss an angel good morning: *Pride, Charley* / Make the world go away: *Arnold, Eddy* / Abilene: *Hamilton, George IV* / I was country when country wasn't cool: *Mandrell, Barbara* / Rose Marie: *Whitman, Slim* / Hello walls: *Nelson, Willie* / You're the best break this heart ever had: *Bruce, Ed*
CD ______ **CDMFP 6108**
EMI / Jan '94 / EMI

COUNTRY OF SONGS 1958-1995 (Music From Lithuania)
CD ______ **C 600005**
Ocora / May '97 / ADA / Harmonia Mundi

COUNTRY ORIGINALS
I will always love you: *Parton, Dolly* / Love of the common people: *Jennings, Waylon* / Guitar man: *Reed, Jerry* / I can't stop loving you: *Gibson, Don* / Tobacco road: *Loudermilk, John D.* / Gentle on my mind: *Harford, John* / Green green grass of home: *Wagoner, Porter* / In the ghetto: *Davis, Mac* / Help me make it through the night: *Kristofferson, Kris* / Singin' the blues: *Robbins, Marty* / For the good times: *Price, Ray* / Crazy: *Nelson, Willie* / Everybody's talkin': *Neil, Fred* / Rose garden: *South, Joe* / Sweet dreams: *Young, Faron* / Good year for the roses: *Jones, George* / Always on my mind: *Lee, Brenda* / From a distance: *Griffith, Nanci* / Wind beneath my wings: *Greenwood, Lee* / Misty blue: *Burgess, Wilma*
CD ______ **VSOPCD 204**
Connoisseur Collection / Nov '95 / Pinnacle

COUNTRY RADIO SHOWS VOL.1
CD ______ **OTA 101908**
On The Air / Mar '96 / Target/BMG

COUNTRY RADIO SHOWS VOL.2
Crazy: *Cline, Patsy* / Walkin' after midnight: *Cline, Patsy* / San Antonio rose: *Cline, Patsy* / I love you so much it hurts: *Cline, Patsy* / I fall to pieces: *Cline, Patsy* / Lovin' in vain: *Cline, Patsy* / Marine's hymn: *Cline, Patsy* / I love you more: *Reeves, Jim* / Home: *Reeves, Jim* / I'm beginning to forget you: *Reeves, Jim* / Have I told you lately that I love you: *Reeves, Jim* / Just call me lonesome: *Reeves, Jim* / How's the world treating you: *Reeves, Jim* / If heartaches are the fashion: *Reeves, Jim* / Till the end of the world: *Reeves, Jim* / Making believe: *Reeves, Jim* / Oklahoma Hills: *Reeves, Jim* / Highway to nowhere: *Reeves, Jim* / I've lived a lot in my time: *Reeves, Jim* / Tips of my fingers: *Young, Faron* / King of the road: *Young, Faron* / Almost persuaded: *Young, Faron* / Live fast, love hard, die young: *Young, Faron* / Apartment: *Young, Faron* / Crying time: *Young, Faron* / Together again: *Young, Faron* / Yonder comes a sucker: *Young, Faron* / Invitation to the blues: *Young, Faron*
CD ______ **OTA 101909**
On The Air / Mar '96 / Target/BMG

COUNTRY ROADS (2CD Set)
Don't it make my brown eyes blue: *Gayle, Crystal* / Mountain music: *Alabama* / Ruby don't take your love to town: *Rogers, Kenny & The First Edition* / Jolene: *Parton, Dolly* / Ladies love outlaws: *Jennings, Waylon* / Behind closed doors: *Rich, Charlie* / Blanket on the ground: *Spears, Billie Jo* / I walk the line: *Cash, Johnny* / Crystal chandeliers: *Pride, Charley* / Are you sure Hank done it this way: *Jennings, Waylon* / Crazy arms: *Nelson, Willie* / I fall to pieces: *Cline, Patsy* / Rhinestone cowboy: *Campbell, Glen* / Bargain store: *Parton, Dolly* / Mason Dixie lines: *Jennings, Waylon* / Fire and rain: *Nelson, Willie* / He'll have to go: *Reeves, Jim* / Ring of fire: *Cash, Johnny* / Orange blossom special: *Monroe, Bill & His Bluegrass Boys* / Walking after midnight: *Cline, Patsy* / Lonesome on'ry and mean: *Jennings, Waylon* / Me and Paul: *Nelson, Willie* / Harper Valley PTA: *Parton, Dolly* / Reuben James: *Rogers, Kenny* / Misty blue: *Spears, Billie Jo* / Most beautiful girl in the world: *Rich, Charlie* / I know one: *Reeves, Jim* / Me and Bobby McGee: *Pride, Charley* / Heartbreaker: *Parton, Dolly* / My home is in Alabama: *Alabama* / Whitchita lineman: *Campbell, Glen* / Gentle on my mind: *Hartford, John* / Take me home country roads: *Davis, Skeeter* / Shadows of my mind: *Everette, Leon* / Talking in your sleep: *Gayle, Crystal* / Distant drums: *Reeves, Jim* / Honky tonk blues: *Pride, Charley* / In my Tennessee mountain home: *Parton, Dolly*
CD Set ______ **RCACD 204**
RCA / Jul '97 / BMG

COUNTRY ROCKERS LIVE
CD ______ **15403**
Laserlight / Mar '95 / Target/BMG

COUNTRY SELECTION, THE (2CD Set)
Walkin' after midnight: *Cline, Patsy* / He'll have to go: *Reeves, Jim* / Crystal candeliers: *Pride, Charley* / White lightning: *Jennings, Waylon* / Take this job and shove it: *Paycheck, Johnny* / Cold cold heart: *Jones, George* / Stranger in my arms: *Cline, Patsy* / Kiss an angel good morning: *Cline, Patsy* / I fall to pieces: *Jackson, Wanda* / Have I told you lately that I love you: *Reeves, Jim* / Pease help me I'm falling: *Locklin, Hank* / I'm the only hell mama ever raised: *Paycheck, Johnny* / Love of the common people: *Jennings, Waylon* / Worlds' worst lover: *Jones, George* / Four walls: *Reeves, Jim* / Night life: *Nelson, Willie* / Church, a courtroom, then goodbye: *Cline, Patsy* / Help me make it through the night: *Cline, Patsy* / It wasn't God who made honky tonk angels: *Wells, Kitty* / Ruby don't take your love to town: *Rogers, Kenny* / Baby on my mind: *Spears, Billie Jo* / Rose garden: *Anderson, Lynn* / Harper valley PTA: *Riley, Jeannie C.* / No tomorrow in sight: *Nelson, Willie* / Jackson: *Lewis, Jerry Lee & Linda Gail Lewis* / Big town: *Twitty, Conway* / Lonely women make good lovers: *Luman, Bob* / Music city USA: *Bare, Bobby* / Wild side of life: *Thompson, Hank* / Rhinestone cowboy: *Campbell, Glen* / Satisfied mind: *Wagoner, Porter* / Rock island line: *Cash, Johnny* / King of the road: *Miller, Roger* / Big bad john: *Dean, Jimmy* / Take me home: *Boxcar Willie* / Four in the morning: *Young, Faron*
CD Set ______ **DCD 3010**
Music / Jun '97 / Target/BMG

COUNTRY SPECIAL
CD ______ **LECD 041**
Wisepack / Jul '94 / Conifer/BMG / THE

COUNTRY STAR COLLECTION (2CD Set)
Six days on the road: *Dudley, Dave* / Fraulein: *Gilley, Mickey* / Half a man: *Nelson, Willie* / Listen to a country song: *Anderson, Lynn* / Rawhide: *Laine, Frankie* / Don't think twice: *Jennings, Waylon* / It's all over: *Murray, Anne* / Home is where you're happy: *Nelson, Willie* / Wings of a dove: *Husky, Ferlin* / Devil went down to Georgia: *Anderson, Lynn* / Broken promises: *Nelson, Willie* / Paths of victory: *Murray, Anne* / Burning memories: *Jennings, Waylon* / Cheatin' kind: *Spears, Billie Jo* / Three hearts in a tangle: *Drusky, Roy* / Both sides now: *Murray, Anne* / Answer me: *Laine, Frankie* / Rose garden: *Anderson, Lynn* / Things to remember: *Nelson, Willie* / 16 tons: *Travis, Merle* / Little bitty tear: *Ives, Burl* / You can't put the city in a country girl: *Fairchild, Barbara* / Moonlight gambler: *Laine, Frankie* / Got a lot of rhythm in my soul: *Cline, Patsy* / Have I stayed away too long: *Ritter, Tex* / Making believe: *Parton, Dolly* / Dallas: *Spears, Billie Jo* / In the shelter of his arms: *Oak Ridge Boys* / Funny way of laughing: *Ives, Burl* / Lovesick blues: *Cline, Patsy* / Hillbilly heaven: *Ritter, Tex* / Gone: *Husky, Ferlin* / Cheating is: *Fairchild, Barbara* / High noon: *Laine, Frankie*
CD Set ______ **330282**
Hallmark / Mar '97 / Carlton

COUNTRY STARS OF THE 80'S - LIVE
CD ______ **15405**
Laserlight / Aug '91 / Target/BMG

COUNTRY SUPERSTARS (CD/CD Rom Set)
CD Set ______ **WWCDR 007**
Magnum Music / Apr '97 / TKO Magnum

COUNTRY WOMEN
CD ______ **NTRCD 070**
Nectar / Mar '97 / Pinnacle

COUNTRY'S MOST WANTED (20 Classic Country Hits)
No love have I: *Pierce, Webb* / Crazy: *Cline, Patsy* / Little bitty tear: *Ives, Burl* / Bridge washed out: *Mack, Warner* / Misty blue: *Burgess, Wilma* / Statue of a fool: *Greene, Jack* / Fifteen years ago: *Twitty, Conway* / One's on the way: *Lynn, Loretta* / Don't she look good: *Anderson, Bill* / Funny face: *Fargo, Donna* / Heaven is my woman's love: *Overstreet, Tommy* / This much a man: *Robbins, Marty* / Wasted days and wasted nights: *Fender, Freddy* / You rubbed it in all wrong: *Craddock, Billy* / Some broken hearts never mend: *Williams, Don* / Last cowboy song: *Bruce, Ed & Willie Nelson* / Elvira: *Oak Ridge Boys* / Ring on her finger time on her hands: *Greenwood, Lee* / Guitar town: *Earle, Steve* / Rough and rowdy days: *Jennings, Waylon*
CD ______ **MCCD 301**
Music Club / Jun '97 / Disc / THE

COVER ME (12 Klone Classics)
CD ______ **CDKOPY 106**
Klone / Mar '97 / 3mv/Sony / Pinnacle

COVER ME SOUL
CD ______ **HIUKCD 140**
Hi / May '93 / Pinnacle

COVERED IN REGGAE
CD ______ **EMPRCD 704**
Emporio / Mar '97 / Disc

COVERSATIONS WITH THE FRENCH CONNECTION
CD ______ **YP 005CD**
Yellow / Jul '96 / Timewarp

COW COW BOOGIE 1943
CD ______ **PHONTCD 7671**
Phontastic / Apr '94 / Cadillac / Jazz Music / Wellard

COWBOY COUNTRY VOL.1 (20 Country Classics)
Rawhide: *Laine, Frankie* / Wichita lineman: *Campbell, Glen* / Galveston: *Campbell, Glen* / Don't think twice it's alright: *Jennings, Waylon* / Country girl: *Young, Faron* / You're still mine: *Young, Faron* / Send me the pillow you dream on: *Locklin, Hank* / These arms you push away: *Locklin, Hank* / I wonder if God likes country music: *Anderson, Bill* / Deck of cards: *Anderson, Bill* / Poppin' Johnny: *Miller, Frankie* / Big talk of the town: *Miller, Frankie* / Tender years: *Jones, George* / My favourite lies: *Jones, George* / That's how I got to Memphis: *Bare, Bobby* / Me and Bobby McGee: *Bare, Bobby* / Twilight on the trail: *McCall, Cash* / Red river valley: *McCall, Cash* / Thousand miles of ocean: *Copas, Cowboy* / I dreamed of a hillbilly heaven: *Copas, Cowboy*
CD ______ **SUMCD 4038**
Summit / Nov '96 / Sound & Media

COWBOY COUNTRY VOL.2 (20 Country Classics)
Southern nights: *Campbell, Glen* / By the time I get to Phoenix: *Campbell, Glen* / I walk the line: *Cash, Johnny* / Folsom Prison blues: *Cash, Johnny* / Daddy don't you walk so fast: *Clark, Roy* / Most beautiful girl in the world: *Clark, Roy* / You're my man: *Spears, Billie Jo* / Dallas: *Spears, Billie Jo* / Love on borrowed time: *Steele, Jo Ann* / Beginning of goodbye: *Steele, Jo Ann* / Girl most likely: *Riley, Jeannie C.* / Cotton patch: *Riley, Jeannie C.* / Walkin' after midnight: *Cline, Patsy* / Stop, look and listen: *Cline, Patsy* / Willow tree: *Sovine, Red* / Wound time can't erase: *Sovine, Red* / San Antonio Rose: *Autry, Gene* / Dixie cannonball: *Autry, Gene* / Little green apples: *Miller, Roger* / King of the road: *Miller, Roger*
CD ______ **SUMCD 4068**
Summit / Nov '96 / Sound & Media

COWBOY RECORDS COMPILATION VOL.2
2 Damned free: *Perks Of Living Society* / I want you: *Secret Life* / Timetravellers: *Lovechild & Rolfe* / All over me: *Carr, Suzi* / Peace, love, harmony: *Re-Joice* / How sweet the sound: *Forthright* / Why why why: *Deja Vu* / Only you: *Talizman* / Trippin' on sunshine: *Pizzaman* / Rock the discotheque: *Ramp* / If this is love: *Tracey, Jeanie* / All I do: *Voodoo Blue*
CD Set ______ **RODEO 2CD**
Cowboy / Nov '94 / 3mv/Pinnacle

COWBOYS SONGS ON FOLKWAYS
CD ______ **CDSF 40043**
Smithsonian Folkways / Aug '94 / ADA / Cadillac / CM / Direct / Koch

COWPUNKS
Long time leavin': *Viceroys* / Last days of wine roses: *Blackboot Trio* / Something I said: *Condo, Ray* / Gentle: *Shivers* / He's a dick: *Golden Smog* / Feast of life: *Boneypony* / Back of my mind: *Flaming Stars* / We love you, Tipper Gore: *Furnaceface* / Jesus wrote a blank cheque: *Cake* / Playboy, the shit: *Lambchop* / Withered and died: *Freakwater* / Still be around: *Uncle Tupelo* / Questioningly: *Vidalias* / Six days on the road: *Coal Porters* / C'mon here: *Medicine Hat* / Underneath the bottle: *Go To Blazes* / Bellyfull of bullets: *Cacavas, Chris & Junkyard Love* / Something: *Price, Toni* / Country western song: *Beat Farmers* / Wild Bill Jones: *Bad Livers* / Heart of darkness: *Sparklehorse* / Hole: *Van Zandt, Townes* / No such thing as a sin: *Garing, Greg* / Let's go burn Ole Nashville Down: *Nixon, Mojo*
CD ______ **VJCD 002**
Vinyl Junkie / Jun '96 / ADA / Direct

CRACKS IN THE SIDEWALK
CD ______ **SST 092CD**
SST / May '93 / Plastic Head

CREAM - ANTHEMS
Bomb: *Bucketheads* / Let me show you how: *K-Klass* / Get your hands off my man: *Vasquez, Junior* / Caught in the middle: *Roberts, Juliet* / Love and happiness: *India* / Love: *Roberts, Joe* / Saturday night, Sunday morning: *T-Empo* / Lemon: *U2* / Girls & boys: *Hed Boys* / Hideaway: *De'Lacy* / Where love lies: *Limerick, Alison* / Musik: *X-Press 2* / Bells of NY: *Slo Moshun* / Plastic dreams: *Jaydee* / Question: *Seven Grand Housing Authority* / Is there anybody out there: *Bassheads* / Eighteen strings: *Tin Man* / Yeke yeke: *Kante, Mory* / Chemical beats: *Chemical Brothers* / My mercury mouth: *Chemical Brothers* / On ya way: *Helicopter* / Funkaterium: *Jump* / All funked up: *Mother* / Passion: *Gat Decor* / One: *Mindwarp* / Acperience: *Hardfloor* / Waterfall: *Atlantic Ocean* / Positive education: *Soma* / In the dark we live: *Aphrohead* / Into your heart: *Rozzo*
CD ______ **74321326152**
De-Construction / Oct '95 / BMG

CREAM LIVE VOL.1 (DJs Paul Oakenfold/Pete Tong/Justin Robertson/ Graeme Park)
Club lonely: *Ellis, Sam* / Keeping the jam going: *Ill Disco* / Feel it: *Bailey, Carol* / Sexual: *Rowe, Maria* / Love's got me (on a trip so high): *Clark, Loni* / Drunk on love (roger's ultimate anthem): *Basia* / True faith: *New Order* / Train of thought: *Excrima* / Sight for sore eyes: *M-People* / Always: *Tin Tin Out* / Only me: *Hyper Logic* / Sound of Eden: *Shades Of Rhythm* / Things can only get better: *D:Ream* / Witch doktor: *Van Helden, Armand* / Witch doktor (remix): *Van Helden, Armand* / Boys revenge: *Original Creators* / Wild pitch: *Music Freaks* / Yes it is: *Lady B* / Voodoo Ray: *Guy Called Gerald* / Let's get ready to rhumble: *DJ Fiovanni* / So get up: *Underground Sound Of Lisbon* / I luv you baby: *DJ Pipi* / Ajare: *Way Out West* / Your loving arms: *Martin, Billie Ray* / Save the day: *Disscuss* / Odyssey to Anyoona: *Jam & Spoon* / Let me be your fantasy: *Baby D* / Le voie: *Subliminal Cuts* / Vernon's wonderland: *Vernon* / How can I love you more: *M-People* / Kut it: *Reo Eye*
CD ______ **74321272192**
De-Construction / Apr '95 / BMG

CREAM LIVE VOL.2 (Paul Oakenfold/ Nick Warren/James Lavelle) (3CD Set)
Skin on skin: *Grace* / X'cellent: *Dubeuro* / Animal: *Lost* / My house: *BOD* / Come on: *Konya* / Coma aroma: *In Aura* / Let the hustlers play: *Pulse & Tango* / If I could fly: *Grace* / Western: *PFM* / Eugina: *Salt Tank* / Fantasya: *Miles, Robert* / Paint a picture: *Man With No Name & Hannah* / Hidden sun of Venus: *LSG* / Moon: *Virus* / New kicks: *Bley, Johann* / I like that sound: *Munsterland* / Inner energy: *Ebe Audio* / Loose caboose: *Electroliners* / Snow: *ORN* / Radiate: *Brothers Grim* / Live as one: *Sam Traxx* / Gift: *Way Out West* / Domination: *Way Out West* / Star: *Shaker* / Bjango: *Lucky Monkeys* / In my mind: *Deepsky* / Giant within: *Art Of Silence* / Tripple double: *City Wide Allstars* / Disco stomp: *Electric Fruit Orchestra* / Indoctrinate: *Castle Trancelot* / Spinners: *UNKLE* / Caught short: *Autocreation* / Drifting sounds of Wakiki: *Repeat* / Hate that hate made: *Paris* / Calm down: *Most Wanted* / Blue flowers: *Dr. Octagon* / Modular mix: *Air* / Last stop: *Groove Robbers & DJ Shadow* / Meiso: *DJ Krush* / Berry meditation: *UNKLE* / Clubbed to death II: *Clubbed To Death* / Soul food: *Tuff Crew* / Bug in the bassbin: *Inner Zone Orchestra* / Hypnotizin: *Winx* / Bee: *Scientist* / Oscillator: *Paperclip People* / Piano tune: *Peshay*
CD Set ______ **74321391252**
De-Construction / Jun '96 / BMG

CREAM OF AMBIENT VISIONS, THE
Chase the Manhattan: *Black Dog* / Dark and long: *Underworld* / My beautiful blue sky: *Moby* / Dr. Peter: *Rejuvination* / Wilmot: *Sabres Of Paradise* / Dolce vita: *Optica* / Lost continent: *Inner Circle* / Wave form: *Mono Now* / Mission impossible: *Naturists* / Dream: *Evolve Now* / Total toxic tranquillity: *Holmes & McMillan*
CD ______ **KOLDCD 008**
Arctic / Apr '95 / Pinnacle

CREAM OF IRISH FOLK
CD ______ **CHCD 1040**
Chyme / May '95 / ADA / CM / Direct / Koch

CREAM OF NEW COUNTRY, THE
Long time gone: *Starling, John & Lowell George* / Amarillo highway: *Allen, Terry* / Smokin' in the rain: *Hancock, Butch & Jimmie Dale Gilmour* / Meadow green: *Rowan, Peter & Maura O'Connell* / Road goes on forever: *Keen, Robert Earl* / Time to learn: *O'Brien, Tim & Mary Chapin Carpenter* / Lose again: *Krauss, Alison & Union Station* / I'll stay around: *Skaggs, Ricky & Emmylou*

Harris / One more ride: *Stuart, Marty & Johnny Cash/Doc Watson/Jerry Douglas* / Talk about sufferin': *Skaggs, Ricky* / Playin' fool: *Moffatt, Katy* / Whenever kindness fails: *Keen, Robert Earl* / By the Rio Grande: *Hinojosa, Tish* / New day medley: *Douglas, Jerry* / Hickory wind: *Hillman, Chris* / New Delhi freight train: *Allen, Terry*
CD _______________ MCCD 137
Music Club / Jan '94 / Disc / THE

CREAM OF TRIP HOP VOL.1, THE
Cosmic trigger happy: *Glamorous Hooligan* / Small world: *Small World* / Shaolin Buddha finger: *Depth Charge* / Electric lazyland: *9 Lazy 9* / Move ya: *Rising High Collective & Plavka* / Santa Cruz: *Fatboy Slim* / Know kname (Down): *Juryman* / Anafey: *Hip Optimist* / Showdown at Voodoo Creek: *Deep Freeze Productions* / Onamission: *Coldcut* / Shadiest breeds: *Dark Globe*
CD _______________ KOLDCD 009
Arctic / Jun '95 / Pinnacle

CREAM OF TRIP HOP VOL.2, THE
CD _______________ KOLDCD 011
Arctic / Sep '95 / Pinnacle

CREAM OF TRIP HOP VOL.3, THE
CD _______________ KOLDCD 012
Arctic / Feb '96 / Pinnacle

CREAM OF TRIP HOP VOL.4, THE
CD _______________ KOLDCD 014
Arctic / Jun '96 / Pinnacle

CREAM OF TRIP HOP VOL.5, THE
CD _______________ KOLDCD 016
Arctic / Sep '96 / Pinnacle

CREAM OF UNDERGROUND HOUSE VOL.1, THE
De Niro: *Disco Evangelists* / Ethnic Prayer: *Havanna* / Percussion obsession: *Okatu* / Devo: *Crunch* / Buruchacca: *Mukka* / Slumberland: *Solitaire Gee* / Skelph: *Harri* / Givin' you no rest: *E-Lustrious* / Le Noir: *Diceman* / Two fatt Guitars: *Direckt* / Jump to my beat: *Wildchild Experience* / Te Quiero: *La Camorra*
CD _______________ KOLDCD 001
Arctic / Mar '96 / Pinnacle

CREAM OF UNDERGROUND HOUSE VOL.2, THE
Skinnybumblebee: *Gipsy* / London x-press (the journey continues): *Xpress 2* / Tonight (dub mix): *108 Grand* / Requiem part 1: *Rejuvination* / I've got it: *Rollin' Gear* / Journey: *Rollin' Gear* / Rez: *Underworld* / Positive education: *Slam* / Babyloop: *Pizzaman* / Funk and drive: *K&M Project* / Trumpet release (no mercy mix): *Funky Punch*
CD _______________ KOLDCD 003
Arctic / Mar '96 / Pinnacle

CREAM OF UNDERGROUND HOUSE VOL.3, THE
Open up: *Leftfield & John Lydon* / Texas cowboys: *Grid* / Say what: *X-Press 2* / Good time: *Luvdup* / Saturday night party: *Alex Party* / Back stab: *Direct 2 Disc* / Theme from outrage: *Outrage* / Trancespotter: *Vinyl Blair* / Dubious kettle: *Channel* / Musik: *Technicality* / Mandala: *Monumental*
CD _______________ KOLDCD 004
Arctic / Mar '96 / Pinnacle

CREAM OF UNDERGROUND HOUSE VOL.4, THE
On ya way: *Helicopter* / Who runs the show: *Question* / In your dance: *E-Lustrious* / It's gonna be alright: *Ill Disco* / Make it funky: *Rebound* / Feeling: *Tin Tin Out* / Echo drop: *Taiko* / Choir boys and kinky girls: *Social Outrage Choir* / Psychotherapy: *Rejuvination* / Dope: *Vinyl Blair* / Blinder: *Mukkaa*
CD _______________ KOLDCD 005
Arctic / Mar '96 / Pinnacle

CREAM OF UNDERGROUND HOUSE VOL.5, THE
You and me: *Rhyme Time Productions* / Do what U like: *Goodfellos* / Partners: *Move Inc.* / No pain: *Dark Star* / 4 you: *4th Measure Men* / Beat beat: *Nostalgia Freaks* / Keep the jam going: *Ill Disco* / Cognoman: *Clubland Refugees* / So damn tuff: *Boomerang* / Retro Euro vibe piece: *Woomera* / Spirit: *Eskubar*
CD _______________ KOLDCD 006
Arctic / Mar '96 / Pinnacle

CREAM OF UNDERGROUND HOUSE VOL.6, THE
CD _______________ KOLDCD 007
Arctic / Mar '96 / Pinnacle

CREAM OF UNDERGROUND HOUSE VOL.7, THE
CD _______________ KOLDCD 010
Arctic / Mar '96 / Pinnacle

CREAM OF UNDERGROUND HOUSE, THE (La Creme De La Creme Vol.1 - 3CD Set)
CD Set _______________ KOLDCD 013
Arctic / Mar '96 / Pinnacle

CREAM OF UNDERGROUND HOUSE, THE (La Creme De La Creme Vol.2 - 3CD Set)
CD Set _______________ KOLDCD 015
Arctic / Aug '96 / Pinnacle

CREAM SEPARATES (The Collection/ 3CD Set)
Never tell you: *Rhythm & Sound/Tikiman* / Rise: *Rivera, Sandy & Kings Of Tomorrow Presents* / Flirt: *Horn* / Glide by shooting: *Two Lone Swordsmen* / Fade II black: *Kot* / Love revolution: *Mysterious People* / Fly life: *Basement Jaxx* / Untitled: *Listenin' Parlour* / Gosp: *LWS* / Summer madness: *Daemyon, Jerald* / Twenty minutes of disco glory: *DJ Garth & ETI* / Tick tock: *Chia Pet* / Don't ever stop: *Dubbing Double* / Theme from the Blue Cucaracha: *Innocent* / Samba magic: *Summer Daze* / In your soul: *Latino Circus* / Seawall: *Envoy* / Modus vivendi: *Modus Vivendi* / Paper moon: *51 Days* / Indulge: *Howard, Neal* / In a vision: *Virgo Four* / Unicorn: *Blue Maxx* / Warior: *Oniero* / Airport martini: *Curtin, Dan* / Party: *Willpower* / Sugar: *Nimbus Quartet* / Sueno latino: *Sueno Latino* / Song for Olivia: *Cliff Hanger* / Art Lukm: *Holy Ghost Inc.* / Confusion the waitress: *Underworld* / Illegal gunshot: *Ragga Twins* / Gettin' stupid: *Dirty Beatniks* / We wanna go back: *Word Up* / There's gonna be a riot: *Dub Pistols* / Trickshot: *Ceasefire* / Karaoke with Buddah: *Eboman* / King of the beats: *Mantronix* / Loose caboose: *Electroliners* / Wrecktify: *Laidback* / Scared: *Slacker* / Psychic bounty killaz: *DJ Sneak & Armand Van Helden* / Jack another day: *Innocent* / Fat cow: *Fiasco* / Body music: *Wulf n' Bear* / Theme from OP Art: *As One*
CD Set _______________ 74321463782
De-Construction / Mar '97 / BMG

CREATION REBEL
CD _______________ LG 21110
Lagoon / Jul '95 / Grapevine/PolyGram

CREATION ROCKERS VOL.1 & 2
Guns fever: *Brooks, Baba* / Message from a black man: *Harriott, Derrick* / I've got soul: *Carlton & His Shoes* / Flashing my whip: *U-Roy* / Blood and fire: *Niney The Observer* / Little way different: *Dunkley, Errol* / Reggae phenomenom: *Big Youth* / Finanacial endorsement: *Isaacs, Gregory* / Enter into his gates with praise: *Clarke, Johnny* / Big rip off: *Pablo, Augustus* / Man hungry: *Minott, Sugar* / I and I are the chosen one: *Prince Far-I* / Dance crasher: *Ellis, Alton* / My conversation: *Smith, Slim* / Caution: *Wailers* / My satisfaction: *Holt, John* / Feeling soul: *Andy, Bob* / More music: *McCook, Tommy* / Brand new second hand: *Tosh, Peter* / Glitter not gold: *Big Joe* / Pretty girl: *Wilson, Delroy* / Conquerer: *Brown, Dennis* / Step by step: *Mikey Dread* / You're no good: *Boothe, Ken*
CD _______________ CDTRL 180
Trojan / Jun '94 / Direct / Jet Star

CREATION SOUP VOL.1
CD _______________ CRECD 101
Creation / May '94 / 3mv/Vital

CREATION SOUP VOL.2
CD _______________ CRECD 102
Creation / May '94 / 3mv/Vital

CREATION SOUP VOL.3
CD _______________ CRECD 103
Creation / May '94 / 3mv/Vital

CREATION SOUP VOL.4
CD _______________ CRECD 104
Creation / May '94 / 3mv/Vital

CREATION SOUP VOL.5
CD _______________ CRECD 105
Creation / May '94 / 3mv/Vital

CREATION'S JOURNEY (Native American Music)
CD _______________ SFWCD 40410
Smithsonian Folkways / May '95 / ADA / Cadillac / CM / Direct / Koch

CREATIVE DRUM 'N' BASS (Dr. S. Gachet/DJ SS - 2CD Set)
Forbidden agenda: *Dr. S. Gachet* / Phuturistic joint: *C4* / Sea breeze: *Matrix* / Can't go wrong: *Subject To Reason* / Underwater communications: *Johnny L* / Flight: *Wallace, Dave* / Blue nights: *Zed* / 3 days: *Eugenix* / Horn section: *Rogue Unit* / Mystical people: *Nookie & Larry Heard* / Mutant jazz: *T-Power* / Helicopter '96: *Deep Blue* / Message: *Shy FX* / Twister: *Mental Power* / Sights beyond: *John B* / Future: *$ Man* / Cooper: *ICI* / Times Square: *Decoder* / Urban jazz: *Zed* / After dark: *A-Sides & DJ Flex*
CD Set _______________ ZIPCD 003
Club Masters / Mar '97 / Sound & Media

CREATIVE GARAGE (Paul 'Trouble' Anderson/Noel Watson - 2CD Set)
Cape fear: *KMA Productions* / Dreams: *Smokin' Beats* / Feel it: *Electric Circus* / French girls: *Mantronik, Curtis* / Happy days: *Hope, Alexander* / I need you now: *Sinnamon* / 10 Minute high: *Kings Of Tomorrow & Michelle Weeks* / Your heaven: *Urban Blues Project* / All the ladies: *Blackjack Collective* / Won't somebody take you home: *N V-US* / Together forever: *Raven Maize* / Times are changing: *Smokin' Beats* / Gentle touch: *Da Players* / Sunny muzik: *Roberts, Andy* / Higher and higher: *Oval Emotion* / River of love: *Splice Of Life & Shawn Benson* / Do you feel me: *Simonelli, Victor* / So in love: *Wild Pursuit & Gerideau* / Over U (big splash): *Baffled 2* / Free love: *Soul Source*
CD Set _______________ ZIPCD 002
Club Masters / Oct '96 / Sound & Media

CREATIVE HOUSE (Graham Gold/Ramp - 2CD Set)
I wanna know: *Supernature* / Up to no good: *Porn Kings* / Born workin': *Grand Larceny* / Future trance: *Sider, Jones* / Calling angels: *Ling, Andy* / First picture of you: *Beautiful Imbalance* / Rise: *Modifiers* / Systematic: *De Moor, Vincent* / Sensations: *Imperial* / Chevignon: *Shadowman 2* / Old skool: *DJ Tonka* / Use your ears: *DJ Tonka* / Never give it up: *Serena* / Lay love: *D-Crew* / Gotta keep pushin': *Z-Factor* / Bar-B-Q: *DJ Linus* / Disco fever: *Extra Lights* / New world, old ways: *Planet Heaven* / Brothers and sisters: *2 Funky 2* / Gotta get on: *Earl Grey*
CD Set _______________ ZIPCD 001
Club Masters / Oct '96 / Sound & Media

CREATIVE TECHNO
CD _______________ ZIPCD 006
Club Masters / Apr '97 / Sound & Media

CREATIVE TRANCE
CD _______________ ZIPCD 005
Club Masters / Apr '97 / Sound & Media

CREATIVE TRIP HOP (Mixed By Pressure Drop & Dave Tipper)
Weekend starts here: *Fatboy Slim* / Blood: *Juryman* / Get a grip: *Bass Kittens* / Finders Kreepers: *Run-a-ways* / Dusk: *Pressure Drop* / Mondo Scurro: *Dark Globe* / Mektob: *Les Gazons Lumieres* / Depth charge: *Depth Charge* / Train stop: *Cujo* / Revolutionary woman: *Up Bustle & Out* / 5 o'clock charlie: *DJ 10 Plate* / Bentley's gonna sort you out: *Bentley Rhythm Ace* / Jay relf: *Tokya Too* / Peter the wolf: *It Spy* / Phantom (nya binght): *Zebulon* / Hot and bothered: *Headrillaz* / Six pak: *Tipper* / Funky shit: *611* / Long time coming: *Kolonel Kurtz* / Blinky blue eyed sunrise: *Metaluna Mutant* / Anchored in acid: *Tipper, Dave* / Bassgunner: *Tipper, Dave* / Hot tuna: *Pelirocco*
CD _______________ ZIPCD 004
Club Masters / Mar '97 / Sound & Media

CREEPY CRAWL LIVE
CD _______________ AP 6007CD
Another Planet / May '97 / Pinnacle / Vital

CREOLE KINGS OF NEW ORLEANS VOL.1
Going back to New Orleans: *Liggins, Joe & His Honey Drippers* / Louisiana: *Mayfield, Percy* / River's invitation: *Mayfield, Percy* / Lawdy Miss Clawdy: *Price, Lloyd* / Where you at: *Price, Lloyd* / Frog legs: *Price, Lloyd* / Teachin' and preachin': *Royal Kings* / Things that I used to do: *Guitar Slim* / Till I say well done: *Kings* / Ay tete fee: *Chenier, Clifton* / Oh how I need your love: *Hall, Alberta* / Send me some lovin': *Price, Leontyne* / Do baby do: *Kador, Ernest* / Who's been foolin' you: *Myles, Big Boy & Sha-Weez* / Rich woman: *Millet, Lil* / Whistlin' Joe: *Lambert, Lloyd* / No buts, no maybes: *Professor Longhair* / Baby, let me hold your hand: *Professor Longhair* / Everytime I hear that mellow saxophone: *Montrell, Roy* / Bop sitin blues: *Blanchard, Edgar* / Just to hold my hand: *Myles, Big Boy* / Lights out: *Byrne, Jerry* / Cha dooky-doo: *Neville, Art* / I'm a fool to care: *Neville, Art* / Jockomo: *Williams, Larry* / Bad boy: *Williams, Larry*
CD _______________ CDCHD 393
Ace / Mar '92 / Pinnacle

CREOLE KINGS OF NEW ORLEANS VOL.2
Bouncin' the boogie: *Royal Kings* / Got a brand new baby: *Little Mr. Midnight & Paul Gayten Band* / Four o'clock blues: *Little Mr. Midnight & Paul Gayten Band* / Restless heart: *Price, Lloyd* / Ain't it a shame: *Price, Lloyd* / Say baby: *Johnson, Willie* / That night: *Johnson, Willie* / Eating and sleeping: *King, Earl* / Heavy sugar: *Lambert, Lloyd* / Think it over: *Guitar Slim* / So glad you're mine: *Kador, Ernest* / That girl I married: *Myles, Big Boy & Sha-Weez* / Squeeze box boogie: *Chenier, Clifton* / Good golly Miss Molly: *Blackwell, Bumps* / Oooh wow: *Montrell, Roy* / Stepping high: *Blanchard, Edgar* / All around the world: *Millet, Lil* / Oooh-wee baby: *Neville, Art* / Just because: *Williams, Larry* / Cry pretty baby: *Professor Longhair* / Look what you're doing to me: *Professor Longhair* / Misery: *Professor Longhair* / Look no hair: *Professor Longhair* / Rock 'n' roll fever: *Monitors* / Carry on: *Byrne, Jerry*
CD _______________ CDCHD 477
Ace / Jun '93 / Pinnacle

CREOLE MUSIC OF PERU
CD _______________ X 55520
Aspic / Sep '95 / Harmonia Mundi

CRESCENT CITY SOUL (The Sound Of New Orleans 1947-1974/4CD Set)
Mardi Gras in New Orleans: *Professor Longhair* / Fat man: *Domino, Fats* / Mighty mighty man: *Brown, Roy* / Lawdy Miss Clawdy: *Price, Lloyd* / Things that I used to do: *Guitar Slim* / I didn't want to do it: *Spiders* / Jock-a-mo: *Crawford, Sugar Boy* / I hear you knocking: *Lewis, Smiley* / Tutti frutti: *Little Richard* / Ain't that a shame: *Domino, Fats* / Let the good times roll: *Shirley & Lee* / Ain't got no home: *Henry, Clarence 'Frogman'* / Let the four winds blow: *Brown, Roy* / Monkey: *Bartholomew, Dave* / Don't you just know it: *Smith, Huey 'Piano'* / Ooh poo pah doo: *Hill, Jessie* / Walking to New Orleans: *Domino, Fats* / Mother in law: *K-Doe, Ernie* / She put the hurt on me: *Prince La La* / It will stand: *Showmen* / I know (you don't love me no more): *George, Barbara* / It's raining: *Thomas, Irma* / Working in a coal mine: *Dorsey, Lee* / Tell it like it is: *Neville, Aaron* / Cissy strut: *Meters* / Lady marmalade: *Labelle* / Boogie woogie Mama: *Ridgley, Tommy* / Detroit city blues: *Domino, Fats* / 3x7=21: *Jewel King* / That's how you got killed before: *Bartholomew, Dave* / Tee-nah-nah: *Lewis, Smiley* / Stack-a-Lee: *Archibald* / Poppa Stoppa theme song: *Bartholomew, Dave* / Jumpin' tonight: *Turner, Joe* / Ain't gonna do it: *Bartholomew, Dave* / Every night about this time: *Domino, Fats* / Shake shake baby: *Archibald* / Good jax boogie: *Bartholomew, Dave* / I'm gone: *Shirley & Lee* / Looped: *Ridgley, Tommy* / Bells are ringing: *Lewis, Smiley* / Who drank my beer while I was in the rear: *Bartholomew, Dave* / Goin' home: *Domino, Fats* / Lillie Mae: *Lewis, Smiley* / Great big eyes (those little reds): *Archibald* / Little girl sing ding a ling: *Bartholomew, Dave* / Bon Ton Roulet: *Garlow, Clarence* / You've gotta reap: *Fulson, Lowell* / Going to the river: *Domino, Fats* / Baby's gone: *Toppers* / Blue Monday: *Lewis, Smiley* / You're the one: *Spiders* / Sittin' and wonderin': *Allen, Jesse* / ABC's (part 1): *Smilin' Joe* / ABC's (part 2): *Smilin' Joe* / Toy bell: *Bees* / I'm slippin' in: *Spiders* / Single life: *Tate, Blind Billy* / Runnin' wild: *Crayton, Pee Wee* / Four winds: *Bartholomew, Dave* / Feels so good: *Shirley & Lee* / Travellin' mood: *Wayne, Wee Willie* / Would you: *Bartholomew, Dave* / Witchcraft: *Spiders* / I'm in love again: *Domino, Fats* / One night: *Lewis, Smiley* / Try rock 'n' roll: *Mitchell, Bobby* / I feel good: *Shirley & Lee* / Someday: *Lewis, Smiley* / Rockin' at Cosmo's: *Allen, Lee* / Chicken Shack boogie: *Milburn, Amos* / Please believe me: *Brown, Charles* / Shame shame shame: *Lewis, Smiley* / Sick and tired: *Kenner, Chris* / Sister Jenny: *Fuller, Johnny* / I'll be the bee: *Ruth & Al* / I'm walkin': *Domino, Fats* / Keeper of my heart: *Adams, Faye* / I'm gonna be a wheel someday: *Mitchell, Bobby* / I want to walk you home: *Domino, Fats* / Ooh poo pah doo: *Hill, Jessie* / Tiddle winks: *Allen & Allen* / Over you: *Neville, Aaron* / Whip it on me: *Hill, Jessie* / Hello my lover: *K-Doe, Ernie* / I just want you: *Charles, Bobby* / It keeps raining: *Domino, Fats* / Tain't that the truth: *K-Doe, Ernie* / Come on: *King, Earl* / Heavenly baby: *Allen & Allen* / True love never dies: *Orange, Allen* / New Orleans twist: *Blazer Boy* / Cry on: *Thomas, Irma* / It won't be me: *Diamond, Lee* / Let's live: *Neville, Aaron* / Grumblin' fussin' nag nag: *Del-Royals* / I cried my last tear: *K-Doe, Ernie* / Country fool: *Showmen* / Te ta te ta ta: *K-Doe, Ernie* / I done got over it: *Thomas, Irma* / Oogsey moo: *Hill, Jessie* / Certain girl: *K-Doe, Ernie* / Fate planned it this way: *Showmen* / I want somebody: *Taylor, Tommy* / Searching for the olive oil: *Senors* / Help yourself: *Diamond, Lee* / Blues: *Robinson, Al* / Always a first time: *King, Earl* / Fortune teller: *Spellman, Benny* / Valley of my tears: *Lee, Calvin* / Trick bag: *King, Earl* / Every now and then: *Spellman, Benny* / Never again: *Reeder, Eskew* / Lipstick traces: *Spellman, Benny* / Ruler of my heart: *Thomas, Irma* / 39-21-40: *Showmen* / Take a look: *Thomas, Irma*
CD Set _______________ CRESCENT 1
EMI / May '97 / EMI

CRIMINAL JUSTICE
Banana co: *Radiohead* / 911 is a joke: *Duran Duran* / Ground level: *Stereo MC's* / Impact: *Orbital* / Kids: *Jamiroquai* / Lay my troubles down: *Aswad* / Moment in darkness: *Shamen* / Perfect day: *EMF* / Revolution: *Dodgy* / Practice what you preach: *Corduroy* / Paranoid: *Inspiral Carpets*
CD _______________ CDCRIM 001
Ultimate / Jul '95 / Pinnacle

CRITIC'S CHOICE
Me and my baby: *Green, Benny* / Fort Worth: *Lovano, Joe* / Man talk: *Osby, Greg* / On golden beams: *De Johnette, Jack* / To know one: *Calderazzo, Joey* / Body and soul: *Margitza, Rick* / Substance of things hoped for: *Peterson, Ralph* / Capoeira: *Pullen, Don* / Twang: *Scofield, John* / Our gang: *Allen, Geri* / Airegin: *Rubalcaba, Gonzala* / Beija eu: *Monte, Marisa*
CD _______________ BNZ 293
Blue Note / Jul '92 / EMI

CROONERS
CD _______________ MCCD 104
Music Club / May '93 / Disc / THE

CROONERS (3CD Set)
CD Set _______________ MCBX 010
Music Club / Apr '94 / Disc / THE

CROONING ON VENUS
Rangers in the night: *Wyatt, Robert* / Time: *Sly & The Family Stone* / Yet so beautiful: *MacDonald, Laurel* / Cais: *Nascimento, Milton* / I still love Albert Einstein: *Earthling* / Mercury: *Royal Trux* / See through love: *Russell, Arthur* / My ideal: *Baker, Chet* / I see you again: *Nordenstam, Stina* / Take me as I am: *Hooker, John Lee* / Starsailor: *Buckley, Tim* / Rain: *Tenko* / Taity Inty: *YMA Sumac* / Dealer: *Walker, Scott* / White jam: *Captain Beefheart* / Young & supernatural:

Lilacs / Falling: Cruise, Julee / Death of Polly: Bates, Martyn / Autumn leaves: Coldcut / Prtelude/Lawns of Dawns: Mico / Protection: Massive Attack / Diabaram: Sakamoto, Ryuichi / Wind chimes: Beach Boys / Honey moon: Hosono, Haruomi / You will be loved again: O'Hara, Mary Margaret / Twilight zone: Dr. John / Higher than the sun: Primal Scream / Brilliant trees: Sylvian, David / Small hours: Martyn, John / Ever so lonely/Eyes/Ocean: Chandra, Sheila / Lifeforms: Future Sound Of London
CD AMBT 13
Virgin / May '96 / EMI

CROSS COUNTRY
Okie from Muskogee: Haggard, Merle / Rhinestone cowboy: Campbell, Glen / Blanket on the ground: Spears, Billie Jo / Coward of the county: Rogers, Kenny / Crazy: Nelson, Willie / Don't it make my brown eyes blue: Gayle, Crystal / Rose Marie: Whitman, Slim / Rawhide: Laine, Frankie / Love me like you used to do: Tucker, Tanya / Harper valley PTA: Riley, Jeannie C. / Give me your word: Ford, Tennessee Ernie / We've got tonight: Rogers, Kenny & Sheena Easton / Son of a preacher man: Gentry, Bobbie / Angel of the morning: Newton, Juice / Honey: Goldsboro, Bobby / Hello walls: Young, Faron / Country girl: Newton-John, Olivia
CD KS 875092
Disky / Jul '97 / Disky / THE

CROSSING BORDERS
CD CBM 010CD
Cross Border Media / Mar '94 / ADA / Direct / Grapevine/PolyGram

CROSSROADS - SOUTHERN ROUTES (The Music Of The American South - CD/CD-Rom Set)
Rising sun: McGhee, Brownie & Sonny Terry / Statesboro blues: Allman Brothers / Blue Monk: Dirty Dozen Brass Band / 15 ans: Les Quatre Vieux Garcons / Woke up this mornin': SNCC Freedom Singers / Brother John: Neville Brothers / Blue suede shoes: Perkins, Carl / Anque me odies: Mendoza, Lydia / Apartment: Wynette, Tammy / Too many hungry mouths: LaSalle, Denise / Southbound: Watson, Doc / There is none like him: Mississippi Mass Choir / Travellin' shoes: Hall-Ward, Vera / Mice and the bad angel: Jumper, Betty Mae / Turtle's song to the wolf: Jumper, Betty Mae / Iko iko: Neville Brothers / White House blues: Monroe, Bill / I'd rather be an old time Christian: Watson, Merle
CD Set SFWCD 40080
Smithsonian Folkways / Sep '96 / ADA / Cadillac / CM / Direct / Koch

CROSSROADS CEILI
CD CHCD 015
Chart / Oct '96 / Direct / Koch

CRUISIN'
Boom boom: Hooker, John Lee / No particular place to go: Berry, Chuck / Got my mojo working: Waters, Muddy / Working in the coalmine: Dorsey, Lee / Barefootin': Parker, Robert / Reet petite: Parker, Robert / It's in his kiss (The shoop shoop song): Everett, Betty / Wonderful world: Cooke, Sam / When a man loves a woman: Sledge, Percy / Will you still love me tomorrow: Shirelles / Twenty four hours from Tulsa: Pitney, Gene / Leader of the pack: Shangri-Las / You can't judge a book by the cover: Diddley, Bo / But I do: Henry, Clarence / Chapel of love: Dixie Cups / Oh what a night: Dells / Harlem shuffle: Bob & Earl / Smokestack lightnin': Howlin' Wolf / Walking through the park: Waters, Muddy / You can't catch me: Berry, Chuck
CD CPCD 8056
Charly / Feb '95 / Koch

CRUISIN' - CRUISIN' WITH THE BLUES
CD CPCD 8110
Charly / Apr '96 / Koch

CRUISIN' - SOUL CRUISIN'
CD CPCD 8111
Charly / Apr '96 / Koch

CRUISIN' 1955 ('Jumpin' George Oxford/KSAN San Francisco)
Rock 'n' roll: Morrow, Buddy / I got a woman: Charles, Ray / Sincerely: Moonglows / My babe: Little Walter / Earth angel: Penguins / Maybellene: Berry, Chuck / Only you: Platters / Ain't that a shame: Domino, Fats / Story untold: Nutmegs / Bo Diddley: Diddley, Bo / Pledging my love: Ace, Johnny
CD INCD 1955
Increase / Jul '96 / Discovery / EAP

CRUISIN' 1956 (Robin Seymour/WKMH Dearborn)
Robin Seymour theme: Four Lads / Roll over Beethoven: Berry, Chuck / Eddie my love: Teen Queens / Ooby dooby: Orbison, Roy / Tonite tonite: Mello Kings / Great pretender: Platters / Tutti frutti: Little Richard / Stranded in the jungle: Cadets / Oh what a night: Dells / In the still of the nite: Five Satins / Blue suede shoes: Perkins, Carl
CD INCD 1956
Increase / Jul '96 / Discovery / EAP

CRUISIN' 1957 (Joe Niagra/WIBG Philadelphia)
Suzie Q: Hawkins, Dale / Happy, happy birthday baby: Tune Weavers / School days: Berry, Chuck / Goodnight sweetheart: Spaniels / Little darlin': Diamonds / Over the mountain across the sea: Johnny & Joe / Bony Moronie: Williams, Larry / To the aisle: Five Satins / Whole lotta shakin' goin' on: Lewis, Jerry Lee / Long lonely nights: Andrews, Lee & The Hearts
CD INCD 1957
Increase / Jul '96 / Discovery / EAP

CRUISIN' 1958 (Jack Carney/WIL St. Louis)
At the hop: Danny & The Juniors / Tequila: Champs / Book of love: Monotones / Rock 'n' roll music: Berry, Chuck / Short shorts: Royal Teens / Chantilly lace: Big Bopper / Rockin' Robin: Day, Bobby / Get a job: Silhouettes / Ten commandments of love: Harvey & The Moonglows / Rebel rouser: Eddy, Duane
CD INCD 1958
Increase / Jul '96 / Discovery / EAP

CRUISIN' 1959 (Hunter Hancock/KGFJ Los Angeles)
Baby hully gully: Olympics / There is something on your mind: Big Jay McNeely / Almost grown: Berry, Chuck / What a difference a day makes: Washington, Dinah / Say man: Diddley, Bo / Sixteen candles: Crests / Personality: Price, Lloyd / It's just a matter of time: Benton, Brook / Sea of love: Phillips, Phil / Kansas City: Harrison, Wilbert
CD INCD 1959
Increase / Jul '96 / Discovery / EAP

CRUISIN' 1960 (Dick Biondi/WKBW Buffalo)
Big boy Pete: Olympics / Baby (you've got what it takes): Benton, Brook & Dinah Washington / What in the world's come over you: Scott, Jack / Angel baby: Rosie & The Originals / Alley oop: Hollywood Argyles / Stay: Williams, Maurice & The Zodiacs / Running bear: Preston, Johnny / Big hurt: Fisher, Toni / Because they're young: Eddy, Duane / Fannie Mae: Brown, Buster
CD INCD 1960
Increase / Jul '96 / Discovery / EAP

CRUISIN' 1961 (Arnie 'Woo Woo' Ginsburg/WMEX Boston)
Arnie Ginsburg theme: 3D's / My true story: Jive Five / Nadine: Berry, Chuck / But I do: Henry, Clarence 'Frogman' / Those oldies but goodies: Little Caesar & The Romans / Tossin' and Turnin': Lewis, Bobby / Daddy's home: Shep & The Limelites / Runaway: Shannon, Del / Ya ya: Dorsey, Lee / Peanut butter: Marathons / Wooden heart: Dowell, Joe
CD INCD 1961
Increase / Jul '96 / Discovery / EAP

CRUISIN' 1962 (Russ 'Weard Beard' Knight/KLIF Dallas)
Soldier boy: Shirelles / I need your lovin': Gardner, Don & Dee Dee Ford / Hey baby: Channel, Bruce / Duke of Earl: Chandler, Gene / You'll lose a good thing: Lynn, Barbara / Let me in: Sensations / What's your name: Don & Juan / Wanderer: Dion / Sealed with a kiss: Hyland, Brian / I know you don't love me no more: George, Barbara
CD INCD 1962
Increase / Jul '96 / Discovery / EAP

CRUISIN' 1963 (B. Mitchell Read/WMCA New York)
Hand clappin': Prysock, Red / Sally go round the roses: Jaynettes / He's so fine: Chiffons / Twist and shout: Isley Brothers / Baby it's you: Shirelles / It's my party: Gore, Lesley / Walk right in: Rooftop Singers / Denise: Randy & The Rainbows / Mama didn't lie: Bradley, Jan / Hey Paula: Paul & Paula / Louie Louie: Kingsmen
CD INCD 1963
Increase / Jul '96 / Discovery / EAP

CRUISIN' 1964 (Johnny Holliday/WHK Cleveland)
Harlem shuffle: Bob & Earl / Nitty gritty: Ellis, Shirley / Dang me: Miller, Roger / Chapel of love: Dixie Cups / Since I fell for you: Welch, Lenny / Girl from Ipanema: Getz, Stan & Astrud Gilberto / It's in his kiss (The shoop shoop song): Everett, Betty / Talk back tremblin' lips: Tillotson, Johnny / It's alright: Impressions / Funny: Hinton, Joe / Remember (walkin' in the sand): Shangri-Las / Suspicion: Stafford, Terry
CD INCD 1964
Increase / Jul '96 / Discovery / EAP

CRUISIN' 1965 (Robert W. Morgan/KHJ Los Angeles)
Wooly bully: Sam The Sham & The Pharaohs / You've lost that lovin' feelin': Righteous Brothers / Birds and the bees: Akens, Jewel / King of the road: Miller, Roger / Sweet little sixteen: Berry, Chuck / Name game: Ellis, Shirley / In crowd: Lewis, Ramsey / It ain't me babe: Turtles / Yes I'm ready: Mason, Barbara / Eve of destruction: McGuire, Barry
CD INCD 1965
Increase / Jul '96 / Discovery / EAP

CRUISIN' 1966 (Pat O'Day/KJR Seattle)
Sunny: Hebb, Bobby / Wipeout: Surfaris / Soul and inspiration: Righteous Brothers / Psychotic reaction: Count Five / Born a woman: Posey, Sandy / Pushin' too hard: Seeds / Walk away Renee: Left Banke / Li'l Red Riding Hood: Sam The Sham & The Pharaohs / California dreamin': Mamas & The Papas / Sweet pea: Roe, Tommy
CD INCD 1966
Increase / Jul '96 / Discovery / EAP

CRUISIN' 1967 (Dr. Don Rose/WQXI Atlanta)
Judy in disguise: John Fred & Playboy Band / Apples, peaches and pumpkin pie: Jay & The Techniques / Happy together: Turtles / Gimme little sign: Wood, Brenton / (We ain't got) nothin' yet: Blue Magoos / Snoopy Vs. the Red Baron: Royal Guardsmen / 98.6: Keith / Little bit of soul: Music Explosion / Rain the park and other things: Cowsills / Incense and peppermints: Strawberry Alarm Clock
CD INCD 1967
Increase / Jul '96 / Discovery / EAP

CRUISIN' 1968 (Johnny Dark/WCAO Baltimore)
Magic carpet ride: Steppenwolf / I wish it would rain: Temptations / Spooky: Classics IV / Cry like a baby: Box Tops / Honey: Goldsboro, Bobby / Angel of the morning: Rush, Merrilee / Girl watcher: O'Kaysions / Midnight confession: Grass Roots / Love child: Supremes / I heard it through the grapevine: Gaye, Marvin
CD INCD 1968
Increase / Jul '96 / Discovery / EAP

CRUISIN' 1969 (Harv Moore/WPGC Washington DC)
Lover please: McPhatter, Clyde / He will break your heart: Groovers / Tequila: Champs / Working on a groovy thing: 5th Dimension / Talk to me: Sunny & The Sunglows / Abraham, Martin and John: Robinson, Smokey & The Miracles / My boyfriend's back: Angels / Israelites: Dekker, Desmond / Pushin' too hard: Seeds / My cherie amour: Wonder, Stevie
CD INCD 1969
Increase / Jul '96 / Discovery / EAP

CRUISIN' 1970 (Kris Erik Stevens/WLS Chicago)
Spirit in the sky: Greenbaum, Norman / Drowning in the sea of love: Simon, Joe / Green-eyed lady: Sugar Loaf / Gypsy woman: Hyland, Brian / Commercial vehicle: Ides Of March / One less bell to answer: 5th Dimension / Don't let the green grass fool you: Pickett, Wilson / Will you love me tomorrow: Shirelles / Sunshine: Edwards, Jonathan / Celebrate: Three Dog Night / New world coming: Mama Cass
CD INCD 1970
Increase / Jul '96 / Discovery / EAP

CRUISIN' CLASSICS (2CD Set)
Knock on wood: Floyd, Eddie / Roses are red: Carroll, Ronnie / Kiddio: Benton, Brook / Charlie Brown: Coasters / Smoke gets in your eyes: Platters / Twenty five miles: Starr, Edwin / Wimoweh: Denver, Karl / Save the last dance for me: Drifters / When you're young and in love: Marvelettes / Soul man: Sam & Dave / Dizzy: Roe, Tommy / Baby love: Supremes / Good timin': Jones, Jimmy / Maybelline: Berry, Chuck / Tell me when: Applejacks / When a man loves a woman: Sledge, Percy / Personality: Price, Lloyd / Juliet: Four Pennies / Walking back to happiness: Shapiro, Helen / Patches: Carter, Clarence / California girl: Floyd, Eddie / My heart's a symphony: Lewis, Gary & The Playboys / Moon river: Williams, Danny / Nadine: Berry, Chuck / Bring it on home to me: Sledge, Percy / Boll weevil song: Benton, Brook / You were on my mind: St. Peters, Crispian / Sheila: Roe, Tommy / Going to a go go: Monitors / Yakety yak: Coasters / Don't mess with Bill: Marvelettes / Stagger Lee: Price, Lloyd / Only you: Platters / I'll pick a rose for my rose: Johnson, Marv / I believe: Laine, Frankie
CD Set 330322
Hallmark / Mar '97 / Carlton

CRUISIN' GREATS VOL.1
He's so fine: Chiffons / Runaway: Shannon, Del / Stagger Lee: Price, Lloyd / Duke of Earl: Chandler, Gene / Night has a thousand eyes: Vee, Bobby / Under the moon of love: Lee, Curtis / Under the boardwalk: Drifters / Tequila: Champs / Leader of the pack: Shangri-Las / Little darlin': Diamonds / Slippin' and slidin': Little Richard / Barefootin': Parker, Robert / Chapel of Love: Dixie Cups / 24 hours from Tulsa: Pitney, Gene / Little town flirt: Shannon, Del / Rebel rouser: Eddy, Duane / Great pretender: Platters / Save the last dance for me: Drifters / Will you love me tomorrow: Shirelles / Surfin' safari: Beach Boys
CD QED 178
Tring / Nov '96 / Tring

CRUISIN' YEARS, THE (A History Of Rock & Roll Radio)
I got a woman: Charles, Ray / Roll over Beethoven: Berry, Chuck / Suzie Q: Hawkins, Dale / At the hop: Danny & The Juniors / Hully gully: Olympics / Teen angel: Dinning, Mark / Blue moon: Marcels / My true story: Jive Five / Sally go round the roses: Jaynettes
CD INCD 1000
Increase / Jul '96 / Discovery / EAP

CRUSADE FROM THE NORTH (2CD Set)
Enslaved/Darkthrone/Storm/Satyricon/Immortal/Isengard
CD Set FOG 010CD
Moonfog / Feb '96 / Plastic Head

CRUSH (2CD Set)
Saturday night: Suede / Candy girl: Baby Bird / I am, I feel: Alisha's Attic / If you're thinking of me: Dodgy / You do something to me: Weller, Paul / Oh yeah: Ash / Find the river: REM / Chasing rainbows: Shed Seven / Something changed: Pulp / On and on: Longpigs / High and dry: Radiohead / Lovefool: Cardigans / 500 (Shake baby shake): Lush / Female of the species: Space / You and me song: Wannadies / Frog Princess: Divine Comedy / Huckleberry grove: Ocean Colour Scene / From the bench at Belvidere: Boo Radleys / Champagne supernova: Oasis / Walkaway: Cast / Being brave: Menswear / For the dead: Gene / (I'm gonna) cry myself blind: Primal Scream / Stay together: Suede / Little arithmetics: dEUS / Milk: Garbage & Tricky / Dark therapy: Echobelly / Stars: Dubstar / Missing: Everything But The Girl / Only love can break your heart: St. Etienne / Love will tear us apart '95: Joy Division / Come home: James / After all: Frank & Walters / There she goes: La's / It's about time: Lemonheads / Julie: Levellers / Mellow doubt: Teenage Fanclub / No rain: Blind Melon / To sir, with love: Trash Can Sinatras / Love song: Cure
CD Set 5532952
PolyGram TV / Feb '97 / PolyGram

CRY OF THE BLUES, THE
Don't start me talkin': Cotton, James / Georgina: Dupree, 'Champion' Jack / Kidney stew blues: Vinson, Eddie 'Cleanhead' / Sweet home Chicago: Baker, Mickey / Long John Blues: Washington, Dinah / How long blues: Memphis Slim / You got good business: Jones, Curtis / Every dog's got his day: Copeland, Johnny / Eagle rock: Memphis Slim / I'm in love: Walker, T-Bone / Saint Lewis blues: Lewis, Furry / Who she do: Williams, Joe / They call me Doctor Professor Longhair: Professor Longhair / Married man blues: Humes, Helen / Just out of Louisiana: Hopkins, Lightnin' / Backwater blues: Broonzy, 'Big' Bill / Long way home: Brown, Clarence 'Gatemouth'
CD 5526382
Spectrum / Mar '97 / PolyGram

CRYING SCENE
CD NSCD 017
Newsound / May '95 / THE

CRYPT CHEAPO SAMPLER
CD EFA 115672
Crypt / Apr '94 / Shellshock/Disc

CRYSTALIZE YOUR MIND (Nuggets From The Golden State)
Crystalize your mind: Living Children / Now it's over: Living Children / I'll be around: Poor Souls / Shadows: Vejtables / Feel the music: Vejtables / Excitation: Rear Exit / Miles beyond: Rear Exit / Train: Transatlantic Train / You're bringing me down: Transatlantic Train / She was a lady: Transatlantic Train / I'm going: Flying Circus / Midnight highway: Flying Circus / Green eyes green world: Flying Circus / Swallow the sun (dark on you now): Love Exchange / Light switch: Mourning Reign / Cut back: Mourning Reign / Kissy face: Maze / Dejected soul: Maze / Napoleon: Staff / Would you take me for a ride: Staff / Morning: Afterglow / Susie's gone: Afterglow
CD CDWIKD 131
Big Beat / Aug '94 / Pinnacle

CUBA
Mi corazon hace tic-tac: Gonzalez / El muneco: Mandingo, Felipe / Lo que me gusta de ti: America, Ima / Nuevo horizonte: Valdez, Marco / Volveras: Oliveira, Valdeci / Abomey: Mivekannin, Renaud / Guantanamera: America, Ima / Vuela: Moreno, Jorge / Pandara: Oliveira, Valdeci / Casual encuentro: Garcia, Franco / Hoy mi voz: Collantes, Posi / Si senor: Valdez, Marco / La Llegada: Garcia, Franco / Bacuranao: Collantes, Posi
CD 12603
Laserlight / Aug '96 / Target/BMG

CUBA - I AM TIME (4CD/Book Set)
El sinsonte: Quinto, Pancho & Anag 7 / Obatala: Valdes, Merceditas / La voz del congo: Clave & Guaguanco / Chacho: Los Munequitos De Matanzas / Yemaya: Conjunto Folklorico Nacional De Cuba / Pappa Aggun: Mendoza, Celeste & Los Papines / Santa Barbara: Gonzalez, Celina / Con su pin pin: Comparsa San Agustin / Bata rhythm / Osain: Valdes, Merceditas / Chivo que rompe tambo: Bola De Nieve / Soy todo: Formell, Juan Y Los Van Van / Assokere: Sintesis / Arrolla Cubano: Vera, Maria Teresa / Mamita cambia: Valdes, Miguelito / Saoco: Mendoza, Celeste / Yo si tumbo cana: Cuarteto D'Aida / Guajira Guantanamera: Fernandez, Joseito / Son de la loma: Trio Matamoros / Maria Cristina: Saquito, Nico / El derdulero: Alvarez, Paulina / El diablo tun tun: Cuni, Miguelito / Ritmo pilon: Alonso, Pacho / Y manana me caso contigo: Faz, Roberto Y Su Conjunto / Drume negrita: Valdes, Merceditas / Yayabo: Gomez, Tito / Sabanas biancas: Alfonso, Gerado / Mariposa: Ferrer, Pedro Luis /

Identidad: *Milanes, Pablo* / A Bayamo en coche: *Alvarez, Adalberto & Su Son* / Pa que te salves: *Delgado, Isaac Y Su Orquesta* / Que bueno baila usted: *More, Benny* / Rumba caliente: *Reve Y Su Charangon* / Lliana quiere chocolate: *Pello Afrokan* / Echale salista: *Pineiro, Ignacio Septeto Nacional* / Tres lindas Cubanas: *Sexteto Habanero* / Pare cochero: *Orchestra Aragon* / Sociedad Antonio Maceo: *Lopez, Israel 'Cachao'* / Mulatica revoltosa: *Arcano Y Sus Maravillas* / Adivinalo: *Rodriguez, Arsenio* / Oye el carbonero: *Cuni, Miguelito* / Que sorpresa: *Formell, Juan Y Los Van Van* / Recordando al sonero: *Alvarez, Adalberto & Su Son* / La bruja camara: *Cortes, Jose Luis Y NG La Banda* / La bola: *Mandolin El Medico De La Salsa* / Se te fue la mano: *Delgado, Isaac Y Su Orquesta* / Mambo: *Bauza, Mario* / Descarga numero dos: *O'Farrell, Chico* / Juana: *Irakere* / Nueva vision: *Salvador, Emilio* / Bemba'e cuchara: *Cachao* / Tumbao de coqueta: *Alemany, Jesus* / Sobre un canto a eleggua: *Grupo Afro-Cuba* / Parraga: *Valle, Orlando 'Maraca'* / El noticiero: *Los Terry* / Woody 'n' you: *Rubalcaba, Gonzalo* / Monturo: *Coleman, Steve Mystic Rhythm Society & Afro Cuba De Matanzas*
CD Set ____ **BJAC 50102**
Blue Jackel / Aug '97 / New Note/Pinnacle

CUBA LIBRE VOL.1 (Afro-Cuba)
Cuban lullaby: *Bauza, Mario* / Mambo: *Bauza, Mario* / Yo siempre oddara: *Bunnett, Jane* / Despojo: *D'Rivera, Paquito* / Relax: *Sandoval, Arturo* / El montuno de patatp: *Patato* / Guaguanjira: *D'Rivera, Paquito* / La comparsa: *D'Rivera, Paquito* / Come fue: *D'Rivera, Paquito* / El mansiero: *Bauza, Mario* / Comelon: *Patato* / Adios pampa mia: *Patato* / GMS: *Bunnett, Jane*
CD ____ **NSCD 007**
Nascente / Oct '95 / Disc / New Note/ Pinnacle

CUBA LIBRE VOL.2 (Latin Jazz)
Tanga: *D'Rivera, Paquito* / Snow samba: *D'Rivera, Paquito* / Lorenzo's wings: *D'Rivera, Paquito* / Bahia san juan: *Hidalgo, Giovanni* / Jazz sabor: *Seis Del Solar* / Zambia: *Bauza, Mario* / Night in Tunisia: *Bauza, Mario* / Azulito: *Bauza, Mario*
CD ____ **NSCD 008**
Nascente / Oct '95 / Disc / New Note/ Pinnacle

CUBA LIBRE VOL.3 (Made In Heaven)
CD ____ **NSCD 012**
Nascente / Nov '96 / Disc / New Note/ Pinnacle

CUBAN BOX SET (4CD Set)
CD Set ____ **320302**
Milan / Jan '96 / Conifer/BMG / Silva Screen

CUBAN CLASSICS
Taka taka-ta: *Irakere* / El coco: *Irakere* / Locas por el mambo: *More, Benny* / Mi chiquita: *More, Benny* / El bobo de la yuca: *More, Benny* / Lo que me paso en la guagua: *Alvarez, Alberto* / Longina: *Burke, Malena* / Santa Barbara: *Gonzalez, Celina* / Pare cochero: *Orquesta Aragon* / Yo no quiero que seas celosa: *Reve Y Su Charangon* / Los sitios entero: *NG La Banda* / La protesta de los chivos: *NG La Banda* / Coge el Camaron: *Origina De Manzanillo* / Se muere la tia: *Los Van Van* / Eso que anda: *Los Van Van*
CD ____ **HADCD 169**
Javelin / May '94 / Henry Hadaway / THE

CUBAN FANTASY
CD ____ **CD 62023**
Saludos Amigos / Apr '94 / Target/BMG

CUBAN RHYTHMS
CD ____ **CCD 504**
Caney / Nov '95 / ADA / Discovery

CUBAN SANTERIA
CD ____ **SFWCD 40419**
Smithsonian Folkways / Oct '95 / ADA / Cadillac / CM / Direct / Koch

CUBAN SEXTETOS/CONJUNTOS
CD ____ **HQCD 64**
Harlequin / Jun '96 / Hot Shot / Jazz Music / Swift / Wellard

CUBANS IN EUROPE VOL.1 1929-1932
Arriba guajiro: *Septeto Nacional* / Asturias partia: *Septeto Nacional* / El que siembra su maiz: *Septeto Nacional* / Bururu barara: *Septeto Nacional* / A la loma de Belen: *Septeto Nacional* / Aurora: *Septeto Nacional* / Maroxina: *Septeto Nacional* / Duo punto Cubano: *De La Cruz, Juan & Bienvenido Leon* / Bruno Zayas: *Castellanos* / Cuba en Paris: *Castellanos* / Mi tumbao: *Castellanos* / Les trois coups: *Rico* / Melody's bar: *Barreto, Don* / Negro bembon: *Grenet, Eliseo* / Merse: *Grenet, Eliseo* / Songoro cosongo: *Grenet, Eliseo* / Lamento Cubano: *Grenet, Eliseo* / Recuerdos tu: *Los Siboneyes Orquesta* / Por es yo te vanto ati: *Los Siboneyes Orquesta* / Digen que no me quieres: *Los Siboneyes Orquesta* / Caminando: *Azpiazu, Don*
CD ____ **HQCD 37**
Harlequin / Oct '96 / Hot Shot / Jazz Music / Swift / Wellard

CUBANS IN EUROPE VOL.2
Voodoo: *Azpiazu, Don* / Mulata sandunguera: *De La Cruz, Juan & Bienvenido Leon* / Mujer de fuego: *De La Cruz, Juan & Bienvenido Leon* / La negrilla: *Grenet, Eliseo* / Tanto tren: *Grenet, Eliseo* / Yo no tumbo cana: *Grenet, Eliseo* / Mueveme tu cintura: *Grenet, Eliseo* / Invitacion a la rumba: *Castellanos* / Green eyes: *Castellanos* / Chivo que rompe tambo: *Cueva, Julio* / Buscando millionarias: *Cueva, Julio* / Flan y merengue: *Cueva, Julio* / Maria la o: *Cueva, Julio* / Rico son: *Cueva, Julio* / Una cabana y una Inglesa: *Cueva, Julio* / Invitacion a la rumba: *Orchestre Cubain*
CD ____ **HQCD 56**
Harlequin / Jan '97 / Hot Shot / Jazz Music / Swift / Wellard

CUE THE MAMBO
CD ____ **CDHOT 604**
Charly / Jun '96 / Koch

CULT AGE
CD ____ **CDACV 2009**
ACV / Jun '96 / Plastic Head / SRD

CULT VOL.2 (A Miracle Summer Breeze/ The Psychedelic Trance Compilation)
Next stop oblivion: *Z To A* / Free lemonade: *Total Eclipse* / Gilis voyage: *Etnica* / Probe: *Tufaan* / Forbidden: *Disco Volante* / Mouli karaki: *Joking Sphinx* / Ushuala: *Ushuala* / Yes: *Axelerator* / Vacant vacation: *Synchro*
CD ____ **SPV 08538742**
SPV / Sep '96 / Koch / Plastic Head

CULTURE CENTRE VOL.2
CD ____ **PHCD 2050**
Penthouse / Jan '97 / Jet Star

CULTURE MIX VOL.1
CD ____ **BWD 0001**
Brickwall / May '97 / Jet Star

CUMBIA CUMBIA VOL.2
CD ____ **WCD 033**
World Circuit / Apr '93 / ADA / Cadillac / Direct / New Note/Pinnacle

CUMBIAS, BABUCOS & PASILOS
CD ____ **PS 65123**
PlayaSound / Apr '94 / ADA / Harmonia Mundi

CUP OF TEA RECORDS - A COMPILATION
Love anybody: *Barcode* / Up in the air: *Static Sound System* / Revolutionary pilot: *Static Sound System* / Secret love: *Static Sound System* / Doge of Venice: *Dedamo* / Crimes: *Spaceways* / I water my plants: *Monk & Canatella* / Rough head: *Monk & Canatella* / Squeeler: *Red* / Timber: *Grantby* / This time it's different: *Monk & Canatella* / Passion: *Purple Penguin* / Japanese flute: *Spaceways* / Float: *Oska*
CD ____ **COTCD 001**
Cup Of Tea / Jul '96 / Vital

CURRENT ARTISTS AT STUDIO ONE VOL.1
CD ____ **SOCD 50148**
Studio One / Oct '96 / Jet Star

CURRENT ARTISTS AT STUDIO ONE VOL.2
CD ____ **SOCD 50150**
Studio One / Oct '96 / Jet Star

CURTOM STORY, THE (1966-1980/2CD Set)
CD Set ____ **CDLAB 107**
Charly / Jan '96 / Koch

CURTOM SUPERPEOPLE
CD ____ **CDNEW 110**
Charly / Jul '97 / Koch

CUT THE CRAP
CD ____ **EXP 040**
Experience / May '97 / TKO Magnum

CUTTING IT TO THE X-TREME
CD ____ **XTR 11CD**
Cutting / Jun '94 / Pinnacle

CYBERNETIC BIOREAD TRANSMISSION
CD ____ **BIOCD 01**
Messerschmitt / Mar '94 / Plastic Head

CYLINDER JAZZ 1913-1927
Hungarian rag / Clarinet squawk: *Louisiana Five* / Dardanella: *Raderman, Harry's Jazz Orchestra* / Meadow lark: *Yellman, Duke & his orchestra* / Where's my sweetie hiding: *Merry Sparklers* / Blue eyed sally / Ain't she sweet / She's a cornfed Indiana gal: *Oliver, Earl's Jazz Babies* / Make that trombone laugh: *Raderman, Harry's Jazz Orchestra* / Night time in Little Italy: *Frisco Jazz Band* / I'm going to park myself in your arms: *Yellman, Duke & his orchestra* / That certain feeling: *Tennessee Happy Boys* / Do it again / Louisville Lou
CD ____ **CDSDL 334**
Saydisc / Mar '94 / ADA / Direct / Harmonia Mundi

D&D PROJECT, THE
One-two pass it: *D&D All Stars* / Look alive: *Big C* / Act up: *Ill Breed* / Da good die young: *N-Tense* / Stone to the bone: *Big Jaz* / From within out: *Fabidden Frut* / Get up: *Maniac Mob* / Just a little flava: *Il Unorthodox* / Blowin' up the spot: *Ill Will* / Rude boy: *Night Dwellers* / Nine inches hard: *Juice* / Mental illness: *2 Mental*
CD ____ **07822187802**
Arista / Jun '95 / BMG

D-DAY 50TH ANNIVERSARY: A MUSICAL TRIBUTE
CD ____ **DDAY 50**
Start / Feb '97 / Disc

D-DAY: A COMMEMORATION IN SOUND
CD Set ____ **DDCD 6644**
Conifer / May '94 / Conifer/BMG

DA MINIMAL FUNK
CD ____ **EFA 626152**
Raw Elements / Apr '97 / Plastic Head / SRD

DADDIES SING GOOD NIGHT (A Collection Of Sleepytime Songs)
CD ____ **SHCD 3821**
Sugar Hill / Mar '94 / ADA / CM / Direct / Koch / Roots

DAFFAN SINGLES (2CD Set)
These hands: *Jericho, Jerry* / Walk my way: *Jericho, Jerry* / Tangled mind: *Irby, Jerry* / Bottom of the list: *Irby, Jerry* / Heartaches for gold: *Tillman, Floyd* / Running away: *Tillman, Floyd* / Always lend a helping hand: *Jericho, Jerry* / I'm getting more than my share: *Jericho, Jerry* / Our daily bread: *McBride, Dickie* / Silent partners: *McBride, Dickie* / Call for me Darling: *Irby, Jerry* / It's time you started looking: *Irby, Jerry* / How foolish can woman be: *McBride, Laura Lee* / I want my man: *McBride, Laura Lee* / Clickety clack: *Irby, Jerry* / Man is a slave: *Irby, Jerry* / Rich and the poor: *Jericho, Jerry* / Which way are you going: *Jericho, Jerry* / Be kind to a man: *Jericho, Jerry* / So ashamed: *Jericho, Jerry* / That's too bad: *Irby, Jerry* / I'd give you anything in this world: *Irby, Jerry* / Waltz you saved for me: *Jericho, Jerry* / Floyd's song: *Tillman, Floyd* / Cold, cold beer: *Tillman, Floyd* / Hopeless: *Fidlo* / Triflin' heart: *Fidlo* / Who's getting your love: *Lee, Ted* / Blues that way: *Lee, Ted* / Dig that crazy driver: *Pennix, William* / How old do you get: *Pennix, William* / Teach 'em how to swim: *Pennix, William* / Them old blues got me: *Pennix, William* / Ride the waves of love: *Elliott, Margaret* / Last call: *Elliott, Margaret* / Strange love: *Bundrick, John 'Rabbit'* / Made in Japan: *Bundrick, John 'Rabbit'* / This wallflower's gonna bloom: *Elliott, Margaret* / What's her name: *Elliott, Margaret* / Cold grey walls of yesterday: *Pickering Bros* / Please (come back to me): *Pickering Bros* / Surviving half of a love affair: *Pickering Bros* / Lady luck my love: *Pickering Bros* / Letter from nashville: *Pickering Bros*
CD Set ____ **BCD 15878**
Bear Family / Jun '95 / Direct / Rollercoaster / Swift

DAIGAN
CD ____ **TRADD 183CD**
Fflach / May '97 / ADA

DAKAR SOUND VOL.3
CD ____ **2002853**
Dakar Sound / Jan '97 / Stern's

DAKAR SOUND VOL.4
CD ____ **2002852**
Dakar Sound / Jan '97 / Stern's

DALGAS 1928-1933
CD ____ **HTCD 34**
Heritage / Jan '97 / ADA / Direct / Hot Shot / Jazz Music / Swift / Wellard

DAN MASKS
CD ____ **C 580048**
Ocora / Nov '93 / ADA / Harmonia Mundi

DANCE '95
Cotton eye Joe: *Rednex* / Set you free: *N-Trance* / Total eclipse of the heart: *French, Nicki* / Another night: *MC Sar & The Real McCoy* / Saturday night: *Whigfield* / Let me be your fantasy: *Baby D* / Sweet love: *M-Beat & Nazlyn* / Can you feel it: *Reel 2 Real* / Baby come back: *Pato Banton* / Baby, I love your way: *Big Mountain* / Love so strong: *Secret Life* / Don't leave me this way: *Houston, Thelma* / Apparently nothin': *Anderson, Carleen* / Sweetness: *Gayle, Michelle* / Midnight at the oasis: *Brand New Heavies* / Welcome to tomorrow (are you ready): *Snap* / Texas cowboys: *Grid* / Eighteen strings: *Tinman* / What's up: *DJ Miko* / Sign: *Ace Of Base*
CD ____ **VTCD 43**
Virgin / Feb '95 / EMI

DANCE ATTACK
CD ____ **ZYX 550732**
ZYX / Feb '97 / ZYX

DANCE BAND HITS OF THE BLITZ (2CD Set)
It can't be wrong: *Geraldo & His Orchestra* / Long ago and far away: *Geraldo & His Orchestra* / Humpty Dumpty heart: *Geraldo & His Orchestra* / Every night about this time: *Geraldo & His Orchestra* / I don't want to set the world on fire: *Geraldo & His Orchestra* / Anywhere on earth is heaven: *Geraldo & His Orchestra* / I'm nobody's baby: *Gonella, Nat & His New Georgians* / Aurora: *Gonella, Nat & His New Georgians* / I can't get Indiana off my mind: *Gonella, Nat & His New Georgians* / Be careful it's my heart: *Roy, Harry & His Band* / Daddy: *Roy, Harry & His Band* / Sand in my shoes: *Roy, Harry & His Band* / Pennsylvania polka: *Roy, Harry & His Band* / That lovely weekend: *Roy, Harry & His Band* / Five o'clock whistle: *Roy, Harry & His Band* / White Christmas: *Roy, Harry & His Band* / Down Forget-Me-Not Lane: *Loss, Joe & His Orchestra* / I'll never smile again: *Loss, Joe & His Orchestra* / You made me care: *Loss, Joe & His Orchestra* / How sweet you are: *Benson, Ivy & Her Girls Band* / If I had my way: *Benson, Ivy & Her Girls Band* / I'm sending my blessing: *Benson, Ivy & Her Girls Band* / Home coming waltz: *Benson, Ivy & Her Girls Band* / Does she love me: *Leader, Harry & His Band*
CD Set ____ **CDDL 1185**
Music For Pleasure / Aug '93 / EMI

DANCE BANDS OF THE 1940'S (A Dream World Is Waiting)
Dream world is waiting: *Geraldo & His Orchestra* / Sentimental interlude: *Gonella, Nat & His New Georgians* / Night flight: *Winstone, Eric* / Let him go let him tarry: *Geraldo & His Orchestra* / Roundabout goes round: *Roy, Harry & His Band* / Hot dogs: *Gonella, Nat & His New Georgians* / Is you is or is you ain't my baby: *Barriteau, Carl & his Orchestra* / I'm looking for a melody: *Roy, Harry & His Orchestra* / Promenade: *Winstone, Eric & His Band* / And then you kissed me: *Geraldo & His Orchestra* / I'll always be with you: *Loss, Joe & His Orchestra* / Ol' Man Mose: *Barriteau, Carl & his Orchestra* / Yankee doodle came to London town: *Roy, Harry & His Band* / There I've said it again: *Geraldo & His Orchestra* / Tanks for the boogie ride: *Gonella, Nat & His New Georgians* / Blue note paper: *Gibbons, Carroll & Savoy Hotel Orpheans* / I want my Mama: *Roy, Harry & His Band* / I'll get by: *Barriteau, Carl & his Orchestra* / Ferry boat serenade: *Gibbons, Carroll & Savoy Hotel Orpheans* / Gotta be this or that: *Geraldo & His Orchestra* / No need for words: *Loss, Joe & His Orchestra* / It's always you: *Roy, Harry & His Band*
CD ____ **PLCD 543**
President / Jun '96 / Grapevine/PolyGram / President / Target/BMG

DANCE BANDS OF THE 30'S AND 40'S
You try someone else / Leave the rest to nature / Outside of you / You started me dreaming / I can't get Mississippi off my mind / She's my secret passion / Linda / My old dog / Until we meet again / Bitin' the dust / Little things that mean so much / I'm in love for the last time / It's the bluest kind of blues my baby sings / Talk to me / Ain't nobody here but us chickens / Goodnight my beautiful / Seven day's leave / We speak of you often / Don't dilly dally on the way / Bow bells / Leicester Square rag / Old music master / Shoemaker's serenade / Give me my ranch / Far away place
CD ____ **CDMFP 6362**
Music For Pleasure / Jun '97 / EMI

DANCE BUZZ
Guaglione: *Prado, Perez* / Surrender your love: *Nightcrawlers* / Your loving arms: *Martin, Billie Ray* / Scatman: *Scatman John* / Freedom: *Gayle, Michelle* / Dreamer: *Livin' Joy* / Love city groove: *Love City Groove* / Baby baby: *Corona* / Not over yet: *Grace* / Don't stop (wiggle wiggle): *Outhere Brothers* / Love and devotion: *Real McCoy* / Two can play that game: *Brown, Bobby* / Turn on tune in cop out: *Freakpower* / Open your heart: *M-People* / Max don't have sex with your ex: *Erotic* / Buring: *MK* / Call it love: *Deuce* / Steam: *East 17* / Move your body: *Eurogroove* / Sex on the streets: *Pizzaman*
CD ____ **RADCD 17**
Global TV / Jun '95 / BMG

DANCE CLASSICS
CD ____ **DSPCD 106**
Disky / Sep '93 / Disky / THE

DANCE CLASSICS FROM IBIZA (3CD Set)
CD Set ____ **ZOO 1BX**
Steppin' Out / Mar '97 / Else / Mo's Music Machine / Pinnacle / Steppin' Out / Total/ BMG / Vital

DANCE COLLECTION (3CD Set)
CD Set ____ **TBXCD 504**
TrueTrax / Jan '96 / THE

DANCE COLLECTION (3CD Set)
Get dancin': *Disco Tex & The Sexolettes* / This is it: *Moore, Melba* / (7,6,5,4,3,2,1) blow your whistle: *Rimshots* / Disco stomp pt.1: *Bohannon, Hamilton* / Sunshine day:

Osibisa / Boogie on down (get funky now): *Real Thing* / Come on dance, dance: *Saturday Night Band* / What's your name, what's your number: *True, Andrea Connection* / Take that to the bank: *Shalamar* / Shame, shame, shame: *Shirley & Company* / White lines (don't do it) pt.1: *Grandmaster Flash* / Rapper's delight: *Sugarhill Gang* / Last night a DJ saved my life: *Indeep* / Disappearing act: *Shalamar* / Get up (before the night is over): *Technotronic* / Somebody else's guy: *Brown, Jocelyn* / Can you handle it: *Redd, Sharon* / Hip hop, be bop (don't stop): *Man Parrish* / Just let me do my thing: *Sine* / Let the music play: *Shannon* / You're the one for me: *D-Train* / Foot stompin' music: *Bohannon, Hamilton* / Can you feel the force: *Real Thing* / Night to remember: *Shalamar* / Feels like I'm in love: *Marie, Kelly* / Body music: *Strikers* / Step off: *Grandmaster Flash* / Pump up the jam: *Technotronic* / What I got is what you need: *Unique* / Dancing the night away: *Voggue* / Menergy: *Cowley, Patrick* / Midas touch: *Midnight Star* / Over and over: *Shalamar* / More, more, more: *True, Andrea Connection* / Never give you up: *Redd, Sharon* / Rock steady: *Whispers* / It's not what you got (it's how you use it): *Lucas, Carrie* / When boys talk: *Indeep* / Hot love: *Marie, Kelly* / I wish you would: *Brown, Jocelyn* / Go deh yaka (go to the top): *Monyaka* / Sending out an SOS: *Young, Retta* / This beat is technotronic: *Technotronic* / Music: *D-Train* / I don't want to be a freak: *Dynasty* / Message: *Grandmaster Flash*
CD Set _______________ **PBXCD 504**
Pulse / Nov '96 / BMG

DANCE CRASHER (Ska To Rock Steady)
Big bamboo: *Lord Creator* / Latin goes ska: *Skatalites* / Garden of love: *Drummond, Don* / Rough and tough: *Cole, Stranger* / Beardman ska: *Skatalites* / Shame and scandal: *Tosh, Peter & The Wailers* / Street corner: *Skatalites* / Bonanza ska: *Malcolm, Carlos & Afro Caribs* / Dance crasher: *Ellis, Alton & The Flames* / Let George do it: *Drummond, Don* / Rudie bam bam: *Clarendonians* / Dr. Dick: *Perry, Lee 'Scratch' & The Soulettes* / Ball o' fire: *Skatalites* / Independence ska: *Brooks, Baba & Band* / Don't be a rude boy: *Rulers* / Ska jam: *McCook, Tommy & The Soulettes* / Hallelujah: *Toots & The Maytals* / Owe me no pay me: *Ethiopians*
CD _______________ **CDTRL 260**
Trojan / Mar '94 / Direct / Jet Star

DANCE CRAZY (From The Charleston To The Jive)
Charleston: *Savoy Orpheans* / Blue room: *Savoy Orpheans* / Black bottom: *Johnny Hamp's Kentucky Serenaders* / That's you, baby: *Hylton, Jack* / Walking with Susie: *Hylton, Jack* / Happy feet: *Whiteman, Paul* / Rockin' in rhythm: *Ellington, Duke* / Put on your old grey bonnet: *Casa Loma Orchestra* / Boogie woogie man: *Casa Loma Orchestra* / Man from Harlem: *Calloway, Cab* / Tiger rag: *Payne, Jack* / Tailspin: *Dorsey Brothers* / Clap hands, here comes Charlie: *Webb, Chick* / For dancers only: *Lunceford, Jimmie* / Just you, just me: *Norvo, Red* / At the swing cats' ball: *Jordan, Louis* / Deep night: *Dorsey, Tommy* / Boulder buff: *Miller, Glenn* / Jitney man: *Hines, Earl 'Fatha'* / King Porter stomp: *Crosby, Bob* / Hep hep - the jumpin' jive: *Gonella, Nat*
CD _______________ **PPCD 78104**
Past Perfect / Feb '95 / Glass Gramophone Co.

DANCE DIVAS
Express: *Carroll, Dina* / U: *Clark, Loni* / Big time sensuality: *Bjork* / Give it up, turn it loose: *En Vogue* / Don't walk away: *Jade* / So natural: *Stansfield, Lisa* / I wish: *Gabrielle* / You and me: *Lisa B* / Gotta get it right: *Fiagbe, Lena* / Everybody's free: *Rozalla* / My love is guaranteed: *Sybil* / Luv 4 luv: *Robin S* / Little bit more: *Sims, Kym* / Can't get enough of your love: *Dayne, Taylor* / Lost in music: *Sister Sledge* / Free love: *Roberts, Juliet* / I will always love you: *Washington, Sarah* / Born to BREED: *Monie Love* / Respect: *Adeva* / Alex Party: *Alex Party*
CD _______________ **5166522**
PolyGram TV / Jan '94 / PolyGram

DANCE FEVER
CD _______________ **MPV 5551**
Movieplay / May '94 / Target/BMG

DANCE FLOOR HEAVEN VOL.1
Do you wanna funk: *Sylvester* / Menergy: *Cowley, Patrick* / Somebody else's guy: *Brown, Jocelyn* / You think you're a man: *Divine* / Last night a DJ saved my life: *Indeep* / Feels like I'm in love: *Marie, Kelly* / Downtown: *Clark, Petula* / Let the music play: *Shannon* / Can you feel the force: *Real Thing* / Can you handle it: *Redd, Sharon* / Night to remember: *Shalamar* / What's your name what's your number: *Andrea True Connection* / Pump up the jam: *Technotronic* / Hip hop be bop (Don't stop): *Man Parrish* / Foot on the rock: *Cherry, Neneh & GMC*
CD _______________ **TRTCD 119**
TrueTrax / Oct '94 / THE

DANCE FLOOR HEAVEN VOL.2
Walk like a man: *Divine* / Die hard lover: *Cowley, Patrick & Linda Imperial* / I wish you would: *Brown, Jocelyn* / Band of gold: *Sylvester* / When boys talk: *Indeep* / Hot love: *Marie, Kelly* / I can make you feel good: *Shalamar* / More, more, more: *Andrea True Connection* / This is it: *Moore, Melba* / Dance with you: *Lucas, Carrie* / Get up (Before the night is over): *Technotronic* / On the dance floor: *New Guys On The Block* / Highwire: *Carr, Linda & The Love Squad* / Sending out an SOS: *Young, Retta* / Soul je t'aime: *Sylvia & Ralfi Pagan*
CD _______________ **TRTCD 143**
TrueTrax / Dec '94 / THE

DANCE GALA VOL.1
CD _______________ **CD 340052**
Koch International / Jul '97 / Koch

DANCE GALA VOL.2
CD _______________ **CD 340192**
Koch International / Jul '97 / Koch

DANCE GALA VOL.3
CD _______________ **CD 340202**
Koch International / Jul '97 / Koch

DANCE GALA VOL.4
CD _______________ **CD 340212**
Koch International / Jul '97 / Koch

DANCE HALL RAWKUS
CD _______________ **RWK 11072**
Rawkus / Mar '97 / Jet Star

DANCE HALL REGGAE
CD _______________ **MCCD 288**
Music Club / Mar '97 / Disc / THE

DANCE HEAT '95
Scatman: *Scatman John* / Dreamer: *Livin' Joy* / Your loving arms: *Martin, Billie Ray* / Don't make me wait: *Loveland* / Not over yet: *Grace* / Don't stop (wiggle wiggle): *Outhere Brothers* / Reach up: *Perfecto All Stars* / Guaglione: *Prado, Perez 'Prez'* / Bubbling hot: *Pato Banton & Ranking Roger* / Love city groove: *Love City Groove* / Crazy: *Morrison, Mark* / Two can play that game: *Brown, Bobby* / U sure do: *Strike* / Axel F: *Clock* / Max don't have sex with your ex: *E-Rotic* / Baby baby: *Corona* / Conway: *Reel 2 Real* / Always something there to remind me: *Tin Tin Out & Espiritu* / Take you there: *Simon, Ronni* / Too many fish: *Knuckles, Frankie* / I believe: *Happy Clappers* / Sex on the streets: *Pizzaman*
CD _______________ **VTCD 50**
Virgin / May '95 / EMI

DANCE HEAVEN
They say it's gonna rain: *Dean, Hazell* / On my radio: *Selecter* / Car wash: *Royce, Rose* / Close to perfection: *Brown, Miquel* / French kiss: *Big Louie* / Italio house mix: *Rococo* / Saddle up: *Christie, David* / Fan the flame: *Pennington, Barbara* / Heaven must be missing an angel: *Tavares* / Swing the mood: *Jive Bunny* / Going back to my roots: *Odyssey* / High energy: *Thomas, Evelyn* / Feels like I'm in love: *Marie, Kelly* / Jack mix 4: *Mirage* / Special brew: *Bad Manners* / Bass (how low can you go): *Harris, Simon* / Frankie: *Sister Sledge* / Hands off she's mine: *Beat*
CD _______________ **305622**
Hallmark / Oct '96 / Carlton

DANCE HITS OF THE 80'S
Let's groove: *Earth, Wind & Fire* / Ooh la la: *Marie, Teena* / Jump: *Pointer Sisters* / She wants to dance with me: *Astley, Rick* / Alice, I want you just for me: *Full Force* / Rockit: *Hancock, Herbie* / My love is so raw: *Williams, Alyson* / I'm that type of guy: *LL Cool J* / Going back to my roots: *Odyssey* / Encore: *Lynn, Cheryl* / I wonder if I take you home: *Lisa Lisa & Cult Jam/Full Force* / Roses: *Haywoode* / Love come down: *King, Evelyn* / System addict: *Five Star* / Call me: *Spagna* / My toot toot: *LaSalle, Denise*
CD _______________ **PWKS 4199**
Carlton / Aug '94 / Carlton

DANCE HITS OF THE 80'S
High energy: *Thomas, Evelyn* / Fan the flame: *Pennington, Barbara* / So many men, so little time: *Brown, Miquel* / Who knows what evil: *Man To Man* / Great minds think alike: *Wells, James* / Animal magnetism: *Pandy, Darryl* / Standing in line: *Mancha, Steve* / Take one step forward: *Wills, Viola & Noel McCalla* / Chalk it up to experience: *Thomas, Evelyn* / Close to perfection: *Brown, Miquel* / Hands off: *Pallas, Laura* / Ain't no mountain high enough: *Powell, Shezwae* / Love's gone mad: *Seventh Avenue*
CD _______________ **QED 140**
Tring / Nov '96 / Tring
CD _______________ **100092**
CMC / May '97 / BMG

DANCE INFERNO (16 Explosive Hits Of The 1990's)
Be my lover / Welcome to tomorrow / Mr. Vain / What is love / Run away / Baby baby / I luv u baby / Don't give me your life / I like to move it / Surrender your love / Hideaway / Short short man / Move on baby / Human nature / Real thing / I'm gonna get you
CD _______________ **SUMCD 4056**
Summit / Nov '96 / Sound & Media

DANCE LATINO
Tributo a Los Admirables: *Los Admirables* / La sopa en botella: *Cruz, Celia & La Sonora Matancera* / Compadre Pedro Juan: *Damiron Y Capuseaux* / Quiero Amanecer: *Lopez, Anardy* / A mayaguez: *Valle, Joe* / Que me digan feo: *Estrellas Cubanos* / Colombina: *Conjunto Tipico Cibaeno* / Maria Morena: *Beltran, Alberto & Willie Rosario Orchestra* / Mujer celosa: *Pinedo, Nelson & La Sonora Matancera* / A Puerto Rico: *Hernandez, Mario Y Sus Diablos Del Caribe* / Pa' chismoso tu: *Morel, Manolin* / Coda tierra con su ritmo: *Kalaff, Luis* / El yerbero moderno: *Cruz, Celia* / La cruz: *Damiron Y Capuseaux* / Donde vives: *Lopez, Anardy* / La lapa: *Cuba, Joe Sextet* / No hay mal que por bien no venga: *Rodriguez, Johnny* / Galletana: *America Del 55* / Potaje: *Faz, Roberto Y Su Conjunto* / Pa' despues venir llorando: *Kalaff, Luis*
CD _______________ **CDHOT 621**
Charly / Apr '97 / Koch

DANCE MIX '96 (16 Hypnotic Movers)
Feel the pulse: *Euripides* / Real beat: *Cuban Heart* / In the mix (nu disco): *Koka* / Free stylin': *Koka* / Blown away: *Beat Fantastic* / Eastern promise: *Euripides* / Hot baby: *Rap Noise* / House of scratch: *Koka* / Unstoppable: *Beat Fantastic* / Enigmatic: *Tone Poets* / Shake your move: *Euripides* / Hypnotic: *Tone Poets* / Scat new jack: *Koka* / Down on the upbeat: *Beat Fantastic* / Techno jam: *Koka* / Dance crazy: *Mister M*
CD _______________ **305612**
Hallmark / Oct '96 / Carlton

DANCE MIX UK VOL.1 (2CD Set)
Children: *Miles, Robert* / Night train: *Kadoc* / Don't you want me: *Felix* / Passion: *Gat Decor* / Missing: *Everything But The Girl* / Search for the hero: *M-People* / Just a step from heaven: *Eternal* / Whatta man: *Salt n' Pepa & En Vogue* / Gangsta's paradise: *Coolio & LV* / This is how we do it: *Jordan, Montell* / I've got a little something for you: *MN8* / I like to move it: *Reel 2 Real* / Connected: *Stereo MC's* / Here comes the hotstepper: *Kamoze, Ini* / Twist and shout: *Chaka Demus & Pliers* / Mr. Loverman: *Shabba Ranks* / Baby come back: *Pato Banton* / Baby I love your way: *Big Mountain* / Searching: *China Black* / All that she wants: *Ace Of Base* / Things can only get better: *D:Ream* / Dreamer: *Livin' Joy* / Saturday night: *Whigfield* / Sunshine after the rain: *Berri* / Swamp thing: *Grid* / Axel F: *Clock* / U sure do: *Strike* / Try me out: *Corona* / I luv you baby: *Original* / Son of a gun: *JX* / Real thing: *Di Bart, Tony* / Right in the night: *Jam & Spoon* / Move your body: *Xpansions* / Stayin' alive: *N-Trance* / Bomb: *Bucketheads* / Hideaway: *De'Lacy* / Show me love: *Robin S* / We are family: *Sister Sledge* / Gonna to make you sweat: *C&C Music Factory* / Groove is in the heart: *Deee-Lite*
CD Set _______________ **RADCD 37**
Global TV / Apr '96 / BMG

DANCE MIX UK VOL.2 (2CD Set)
Flava: *Andre, Peter* / We've got it goin' on: *Backstreet Boys* / Macarena: *Los Del Rio* / There's nothin I won't do: *JX* / Don't stop movin': *Livin' Joy* / Keep on jumpin': *Lisa Marie Experience* / Disco's revenge: *Gusto* / I need a lover tonight: *Kendoh* / Don't give me your life: *Alex Party* / Fable: *Miles, Robert* / X-Files: *DJ Dado* / Theme from s'express: *S'Express* / Where love lives: *Limerick, Alison* / Jazz it up: *Reel 2 Real* / One night in heaven: *M-People* / U r the best thing: *D:Ream* / I'm gonna get you: *Bizarre Inc.* / Everybody's free: *Rozalla* / Key the secret: *Urban Cookie Collective* / Ain't no love (ain't no use): *Sub Sub & Melanie Williams* / Run to you: *Rage* / Blue monday: *New Order* / Ooh ahh, just a little bit: *Gina G* / I need your loving (everybody's gotta learn sometimes): *Baby D* / Stay another day: *East 17* / Relight my fire: *Take That* / Finally: *Peniston, Ce Ce* / Two can play that game: *Brown, Bobby* / Luv 4 luv: *Robin S* / Now that we've found love: *Heavy D & The Boyz* / Let's talk about sex: *Salt n' Pepa* / Boom, shake the room: *DJ Jazzy Jeff & The Fresh Prince* / Boom boom boom: *Outhere Brothers* / Rhythm of the night: *Corona* / Whooph (there it is): *Corona* / Return of the mack: *Morrison, Mark* / I got 5 on it: *Luniz* / Creep: *TLC* / Dreams: *Gabrielle* / Sweetness: *Gayle, Michelle* / She's got that vibe: *R Kelly* / Sweets for my sweet: *Lewis, C.J.* / Shine: *Aswad* / Oh carolina: *Shaggy*
CD Set _______________ **RADCD 42**
Global TV / Aug '96 / BMG

DANCE MUSIC
CD _______________ **CDLBP 2024**
Lochshore / Jul '96 / ADA / Direct / Duncans

DANCE MUSIC OF IRELAND: JIGS AND REELS
Maudabawn Chapel/Wild Irishman/Moher reel: *Burke, Kevin & Michael O'Dohmnhaill* / Paddy O'Brien's/Scatter the mud/Arthur Daley's: *Trimble, Gerald* / Stone in the field/Steeplechase/Culfodda reel: *Keane, James* / Dillon's fancy/Maids in the meadow/Toss the feathers: *Crawford, Kevin* / Paddy Fahy's jig/Sean Ryan's jig: *Hayes, Martin* / Robbie Hannan's jigs: *O'Sullivan, Jerry* / Johnny Doherty's/Sean sa cheo/Lady Gordon: *Madden, Joanie* / Congress reel/Down the broom/Star of Munster: *Irish Tradition* / Humours of Ballyloughlin/Knocknagow: *Ivers, Eileen* / Green field of Woodford/Cat's rambles: *Coen, Jack* / Bucks of Oranmore/Wind that shakes the barley: *Burke, Joe & Charlie Lennon* / Cul aodh jig/Blue angel: *Buttons & Bows* / Dunmore lassies/McFadden's handsome daughter: *Moloney, Mick* / Sculley Casey's/The tidy woman: *Williams, John*
CD _______________ **CELT 9001**
Celtophile / May '97 / Direct

DANCE NATION VOL.1 (2CD Set)
CD Set _______________ **DNCD 96**
Ministry Of Sound / Apr '96 / 3mv/Sony / Mo's Music Machine / Warner Music

DANCE NATION VOL.2 (2CD Set)
CD Set _______________ **DNCD 962**
Ministry Of Sound / Jul '96 / 3mv/Sony / Mo's Music Machine / Warner Music

DANCE NRG
CD _______________ **FARECD 101**
Fanfare / Oct '92 / Total/BMG

DANCE OF HEAVEN'S GHOSTS (Music From Greece)
Les ke kratages maheria: *Vitali, Eleni* / Halali ine o erotas: *Mazaraki, Nikoletta* / I mangues then iparhoun pla: *Alexiou, Haris* / To ponemeno stithos mou: *Parios, Yannis* / To hioni: *Papadopoulou, Katerina* / Mirodia kalokeriou: *Leonardou, Sotiria* / Mia ine I oussia: *Alexiou, Haris* / O Amerikanos: *Zervoudakis, Dimitris* / Ba mazi mou: *Diamandi, Litsa* / Trikimia: *Morali, Athina* / Mia gyneka bori: *Vitali, Eleni* / Eho mia dipsa: *Patrios, Yannis* / Edo sto pezodromia: *Koumbaroulis, Andreas* / Oil me len tragoudisse: *Aidonidis, Hronis*
CD _______________ **HEMICD 24**
Hemisphere / Feb '97 / EMI

DANCE OF THE CELTS
5 Pound flute: *Old Blind Dogs* / An drochaid chluiteach: *Mhoireach, Anna* / Cregg's pipe set: *Tabache* / Inisheer: *Buttons & Bows* / Christy Barry's set: *Crawford, Kevin* / Trip to sligo set: *Dervish* / Trip to Skye: *Whelan, John* / Boy in the gap: *Kilbride, Pat* / Gavotten ar menez: *Kornog* / Andy de Jarlis: *Altan* / Gartrai na bhfeileoig: *Bergin, Mary* / Flight of the termite: *Deanta* / Finn MacCool's reel: *Kirtley, Pat* / Shetland jumper: *McGann, John* / Leis lacha: *Masterson, Declan*
CD _______________ **ND 63932**
Narada / May '97 / ADA / New Note/ Pinnacle

DANCE OPERA VOL.3
CD _______________ **PIAS 94047720CD**
Dance Opera / Apr '97 / Mo's Music Machine / Plastic Head

DANCE OPERA VOL.6 (2CD Set)
CD Set _______________ **PIAS 094045523**
Dance Opera / Jun '96 / Mo's Music Machine / Plastic Head

DANCE PARTY
CD _______________ **BLS 1015 CD**
BLS / Jul '92 / Jet Star

DANCE PARTY
Choice: *Blow Monkeys* / Never gonna give you up: *Astley, Rick* / Indestructible: *Four Tops* / Love take over: *Five Star* / I'm so excited: *Pointer Sisters* / Flashback: *Imagination* / Going back to my roots: *Odyssey* / Love come down: *King, Evelyn* / Runner: *Three Degrees* / Gonna get along without you know: *Wills, Viola* / Armed and extremely dangerous: *First Choice* / (We've got a) Good thing going: *Minott, Sugar*
CD _______________ **74321339232**
Camden / Jan '96 / BMG

DANCE PLANET - SOUNDS OF THE DETONATOR
CD _______________ **DPRCD 1**
Dance Planet / Sep '95 / SRD

DANCE PLANET - THE RETRO MIXES VOL.1 (Mixed By Jim 'Shaft' Ryan & DJ Sy/Iks - 2CD Set)
Sweet harmony: *Liquid* / Every time I see her: *Shades Of Rhythm* / Get down: *M-D Emm* / Lock up: *Zero B* / Everybody in the place: *Prodigy* / Blame: *Blame* / Dance with power: *Bass Construction* / We are ie: *Reel 2 Real* / We are hardcore: *House Crew* / This sound is for the underground: *Krome & Time* / On a ragga tip: *SL2* / Innersence: *Liquid Crystal* / Hurt you so: *Johnny L* / Fires burning: *Run Tings* / My own: *Seduction* / Far out: *Sonz Of A Loop Da Loop Era* / Rhythm for reasons: *Rhythm For Reasons* / Edge 1: *Edge 1* / Blow out: *Bass Selective* / Baptised by dub: *Criminal Minds* / Keep the fires burning: *House Crew* / Peace and loveism: *Sonz Of A Loop Da Loop Era* / Really livin': *Really Livin'* / Livin' in darkness: *Top Buzz* / EQ: *EQ* / Feel real good: *Manix* / Your love: *Prodigy* / Give it to me baby: *Love Revolution* / Can you feel it: *Elevation* / Don't go: *Awesome 3*
CD Set _______________ **IKSCD 1**
Dance Planet / Feb '97 / SRD

DANCE POWER VOL.3
CD _______________ **MNF 05272**
Manifold / Jun '97 / ZYX

DANCE SOUNDS OF DETROIT (2CD Set)
Memories & souveniers: *Payne, Freda* / I want to be loved: *Supremes* / Fear: *Starr, Edwin* / Two way street: *Jacas, Jake* / Don't wait around: *Elgins* / Sitting in the park: *Lovetones* / Right direction: *Littles, Hattie* /

Fresh out of tears: *Laurence, Lynda* / One shot at happiness: *Demps, Louvain* / Wake me up when it's over: *Ruffin, Jimmy* / Which way do I turn: *Crawford, Carolyn* / Send some love: *Barnes, Ortheia* / Lost: *Randolph, Barbara* / I'm dedicating my love: *McNeir, Ronnie* / Weak hearted: *Taylor, Sherri* / Hotter than the summer days: *Edwards, Sandra* / See this man in love: *Wylie, Richard 'Popcorn'* / Look into the future: *Leverette, Chico* / Look into the eyes of a fool: *Bristol, Johnny* / Better love next time: *Johnson, Marv* / City lights: *Lewis, Pat* / Grazing in the grass: *Monitors* / Timeless: *Crawford, Carolyn* / I've fallen and can't get up: *Fantastic Four* / Come back and start again: *Nero, Frances* / Six by six: *Van Dyke, Earl* / Sister Lee: *Ward, Sammy* / Fire alarm: *Lovetones* / One and one makes two: *Starr, Edwin* / That girl is dangerous: *Jacas, Jake* / Lovestruck: *Edwards, Sandra* / All around the motorcity: *Andantes* / Just us: *Royster, Vermettya* / Half hearted: *Gordon, Billy* / Bad case of nerves: *Marvelettes* / Breaking into my heart: *Randolph, Barbara*
CD ______ **3035990077**
Old Gold / Oct '95 / Carlton

DANCE SOUNDS OF HI
CD ______ **HILOCD 3**
Hi / Nov '93 / Pinnacle

DANCE SOUNDS OF THE 70'S
CD ______ **JHD 105**
Tring / Aug '93 / Tring

DANCE TIP 2000 (2CD Set)
Breathe: *Prodigy* / Born slippy: *Underworld* / One to one: *Miles, Robert* / Seven days and one week: *BBE* / X-files: *DJ Dado* / Wrong: *Everything But The Girl* / Offshore: *Chicane* / Higher state of consciousness: *Wink, Josh* / Klubbhopping: *Klubb Heads* / I need a lover tonight: *Kendoh* / Nighttrain: *Kadoc* / Disco's revenge: *Gusto* / Stamp: *Healy, Jeremy & Amos* / Don't you want me: *Felix* / That look: *De'Lacy* / Naughty north and the sexy south: *E-Motion* / Loving you more: *BT & Vincent Covello* / Gift: *Way Out West* / One night stand: *Aloof* / I wanna be a hippy: *Technohead* / Ooh ahh...just a little bit: *Gina G* / Flava: *Andre, Peter* / You're makin' me high: *Braxton, Toni* / Children: *Miles, Robert* / Megamix: *Corona* / Don't stop movin': *Livin' Joy* / Return of the mack: *Morrison, Mark* / Keep on jumpin': *Lisa Marie Experience* / Megamix: *Outhere Brothers* / Get down: *Backstreet Boys* / Oh what a night: *Clock* / Jazz it up: *Reel 2 Real* / I belong to you: *Gina G* / Where love lives: *Limerick, Alison* / Driving: *Everything But The Girl* / Sunshine: *Umboza* / Cuba: *El Mariachi* / Creep: *TLC* / Golden brown: *Kaleef* / Search for the hero: *M-People*
CD Set ______ **RADCD 50**
Global TV / Dec '96 / BMG

DANCE TO THE MAX VOL.1
Living on my own: *Mercury, Freddie* / Things can only get better: *D:Ream* / Relight my fire: *Take That & Lulu* / Moving on up: *M-People* / Boom shake the room: *DJ Jazzy Jeff & The Fresh Prince* / Come baby come: *K7* / Rhythm is a dancer: *Snap* / Ride on time: *Black Box* / Got to get it: *Culture Beat* / U got 2 let the music: *Cappella* / Long train runnin': *Doobie Brothers* / Give it up: *Goodmen* / No limit: *2 Unlimited* / Relax: *Frankie Goes To Hollywood* / It's my life: *Dr. Alban* / Here I stand: *McLean, Bitty* / Respect: *Sub Sub* / No matter what you do: *Flavour* / Things that make you go hmmmm: *C&C Music Factory*
CD ______ **VTCD 24**
Virgin / Mar '94 / EMI

DANCE TO THE MAX VOL.2
Real thing: *2 Unlimited* / Move on baby: *Cappella* / Light my fire: *Club House* / I like to move it: *Reel 2 Real* / Sweets for my sweet: *Lewis, C.J.* / Dedicated to the one I love: *McLean, Bitty* / Always: *Erasure* / Return to innocence: *Enigma* / Don't look any further: *M-People* / Real thing: *Di Bart, Tony* / U R the best thing: *D:Ream* / Shine on: *Degrees Of Motion* / How gee: *Black Machine* / Life: *Haddaway* / Son of a gun: *JX* / Rockin' for myself: *Motiv 8* / Real love: *Time Frequency* / Hold that sucker down: *OT Quartet* / Exterminate: *Snap* / It's alright: *East 17*
CD ______ **VTCD 29**
Virgin / May '94 / EMI

DANCE TO THE MAX VOL.3
Shine: *Aswad* / You don't love me (no no no): *Penn, Dawn* / Swamp thing: *Grid* / What goes around: *McLean, Bitty* / Just a step from heaven: *Eternal* / Key, the secret: *Urban Cookie Collective* / One night in heaven: *M-People* / Take me away: *D:Ream* / No good (Start the dance): *Prodigy* / Go on move: *Reel 2 Real* / U and me: *Cappella* / No more (I can't stand it): *Maxx* / Everybody gonfi gon: *Two Cowboys* / Think about the way: *Ice MC* / Run to the sun: *Erasure* / Let the beat control your body: *2 Unlimited* / Mr. Vain: *Culture Beat* / Power: *Snap* / Whammer slammer: *Warp 9* / Summertime: *DJ Jazzy Jeff & The Fresh Prince*
CD ______ **VTCD 33**
Virgin / Aug '94 / EMI

DANCE TRAX (18 Original Hits/3CD Set)
Love is all around: *DJ Bobo* / What is love: *Haddaway* / Shimmy shake: *740 Boyz* / Whammer slammer: *Warp 9* / Music instructor: *Hymn* / Got to move your body: *Lick & Kentucky Martha* / Jump for joy: *2 Unlimited* / Time is up: *Milton, C.B.* / Flying high: *Captain Hollywood* / I wish: *Skee Lo* / Feel my riddim: *Skibby* / Don't give me your life: *Alex Party* / Spontaneous: *Spymaster & Eric Nouhan* / Mercedes Benz: *T-Spoon & Jean Shy* / Don't stop (wiggle wiggle): *Outhere Brothers* / Try me out: *Corona* / In spirit: *Dilemma* / Total eclipse of the heart: *French, Nicki*
CD Set ______ **LAD 873822**
Disky / Nov '96 / Disky / THE

DANCE WITH ME - THE AUTUMN TEEN SOUND
Dance with me: *Mojo Men* / She goes with me: *Mojo Men* / Off the hook: *Mojo Men* / Draggin' the main: *Upsetters* / Little one: *Spearmints* / Anything: *Vejtables* / I still love you: *Vejtables* / Where did I fail: *Knight Riders* / I: *Knight Riders* / Torture and pain: *Knight Riders* / Won't you be my baby: *Knight Riders* / I should be glad: *Gear One* / Hello little girl: *Gear One* / I think it's time: *Chosen Few* / Nobody but me: *Chosen Few* / Pay attention to me: *Tikis* / I'll never forget about you: *Tikis* / Darkest night of the year: *Tikis* / Blue eyes: *Tikis* / Just me: *Us* / How can I tell her: *Us* / Mark my words: *Bundles* / Watch me girl: *Bundles* / Something bad: *Mojo Men* / My woman's head: *Mojo Men* / Can't you see that she's mine: *Mojo Men* / Why: *Mojo Men* / As I get older: *Mojo Men* / All over town: *Au Go Go's* / I still love you (version): *Vejtables*
CD ______ **CDWIKD 128**
Big Beat / Mar '94 / Pinnacle

DANCE ZONE '94 (2CD Set)
Let me be your fantasy: *Baby D* / Another night: *Real McCoy* / Saturday night: *Whigfield* / She's got that vibe: *R Kelly* / Best of my love: *Lewis, C.J.* / Confide in me: *Minogue, Kylie* / Compliments on your kiss: *Red Dragon* / Twist and shout: *Chaka Demus & Pliers* / Rhythm of the night: *Corona* / Move on baby: *Cappella* / What's up: *DJ Miko* / Incredible: *M-Beat & General Levy* / Go on move: *Reel 2 Real* / Carry me home: *Gloworm* / Swamp thing: *Grid* / Everybody gonfi gon: *Two Cowboys* / Eighteen strings: *Tinman* / No good (start the dance): *Prodigy* / 100% pure love: *Waters, Crystal* / Midnight at the oasis: *Brand New Heavies* / Whatta man: *Salt n' Pepa & En Vogue* / Doop: *Doop* / Shine on: *Degrees Of Motion* / Son of a gun: *JX* / Anything: *Culture Beat* / U and me: *Cappella* / Rock my heart: *Haddaway* / Real thing: *2 Unlimited* / Get-a-way: *Maxx* / Sweets for my sweet: *Lewis, C.J.* / Sign: *Ace Of Base* / It's alright: *East 17* / Things can only get better: *D:Ream* / Renaissance: *M-People* / Searching: *China Black* / Sweet Lullaby: *Deep Forest* / Save our love: *Eternal* / Shine: *Aswad* / You don't love me (no no no): *Penn, Dawn* / Dedicated to the one I love: *McLean, Bitty* / How gee: *Black Machine* / Light my fire: *Clubhouse & Carl* / Rockin' for myself: *Motiv 8* / Blow your whistle: *DJ Duke*
CD Set ______ **5251302**
PolyGram TV / Nov '94 / PolyGram

DANCE ZONE '95 (2CD Set)
CD Set ______ **5350452**
PolyGram TV / Oct '95 / PolyGram

DANCE ZONE MEGAMIX VOL.1
Roffo's theme V - the hitman / Termination party / I breathe you / Blue Monday / Love is a stranger / Passion / I feel love / Cocoon / Energize / Knock on wood
CD ______ **QED 074**
Tring / Nov '96 / Tring

DANCE ZONE VOL.5
I need your loving (everybody's gotta learn sometime): *Baby D* / Scatman: *Scatman John* / Boom boom boom: *Outhere Brothers* / Your loving arms: *Martin, Billie Ray* / Hold my body tight: *East 17* / Dreamer: *Livin' Joy* / Love and devotion: *Real McCoy* / Not anyone: *Black Box* / Eternity: *Snap* / I need you: *Deuce* / Two can play that game: *Brown, Bobby* / Not over yet: *Grace* / Raise your hands: *Reel 2 Real* / Respect: *Cheeks, Judy* / Open your heart: *M-People* / Love city groove: *Love City Groove* / Swing low, sweet chariot: *Ladysmith Black Mambazo & China Black* / Turn on tune in cop out: *Freakpower* / Let it rain: *East 17* / Tears don't lie: *Mark Oh* / Guaglione: *Prado, Perez 'Prez'* / Think of you: *Whigfield* / Sex on the streets: *Pizzaman* / I believe: *Happy Clappers* / JJ tribute: *ASHA* / Direct me: *Reese Project* / Take you there: *Simon, Ronni* / Work it out: *Shiva* / Everybody in the world: *Ashah* / Access: *DJ Misjah* / Move your body: *Eurogroove* / High as a kite: *One Tribe* / Love love love: *Rollo Goes Mystic* / Always something there to remind me: *Tin Tin Out & Espiritu* / Wizards of the sonic: *West Bam* / Invader: *Koolworld Productions* / Gudvibe: *Tinman* / Spirit inside: *Spirits* / Bomb (These sounds fall into my mind): *Bucketheads* / Lifting me higher: *Gems For Jem*
CD ______ **5256332**
PolyGram TV / Jul '95 / PolyGram

DANCE ZONE VOL.7
Keep on jumpin': *Lisa Marie Experience* / Nakasaki (I need a lover tonight): *Kendoh* / State of independence: *Summer, Donna* / Stars: *Dubstar* / Disco 2000: *Pulp* / Klubhopping: *Klubb Heads* / Nightrain: *Kadoc* / Over and over: *Plux & Georgia Jones* / Passion: *Gat Decor* / So pure: *Baby D* / My life is in your hands: *Meltdown* / Be as one: *Sasha & Maria* / Give me a little more time: *Gabrielle* / Do U still: *East 17* / Lifted: *Lighthouse Family* / 1,2,3,4 (sumpin' new): *Coolio* / Itychoo park: *M-People* / Everyday: *Incognito* / Are you gonna be there: *Up Yer Ronson* / I wanna be a hippy: *Technohead* / Are you out there: *Crescendo* / Give me luv: *Alcatraz* / Disco's revenge: *Gusto* / America (I love America): *Full Intention* / I got the vibration: *Black Box* / Got myself together: *Bucketheads* / Ultra flava: *Heller & Farley Project* / Skin on skin: *Grace* / Loving you more: *BT* / In spirit: *Dilemmas* / Hide-a-way: *Nu Soul & Kelli Rich* / On ya way: *Helicopter* / And I'm telling you I'm not going: *Giles, Donna* / Naughty north and the sexy south: *E-Motion* / Geve me strength: *Jon Of The Pleased Wimmin* / I'll be there: *99th Floor Elevators* / Wham bam: *Candy Girls & Sweet Pussy Pauline* / To the beat of the drum (la luna): *Ethics* / Forever young: *Interactive* / Access: *DJ Misjah & Tim*
CD ______ **5354272**
PolyGram TV / Apr '96 / PolyGram

DANCE ZONE VOL.8 (2CD Set)
I'm alive: *Stretch n' Vern & Maddog* / Let's all chant: *Gusto* / Ain't nobody's business if I do: *H2O & Billie* / We've got it goin' on: *Backstreet Boys* / Hello Honky Tonks (Rock your body): *Pizzaman* / Don't stop movin': *Livin' Joy* / There's nothing I won't do: *JX* / Ooh aah...just a little bit: *Gina G* / Everybody's free: *Rozalla* / That look: *De'Lacy* / Read my lips: *Alex Party* / Oh what a night: *Clock* / Flava: *Andre, Peter* / Groovin': *Pato Banton & The Reggae Revolution* / Return of the Mack: *Morrison, Mark* / Krupa: *Apollo 440* / Take me to heaven: *Baby D* / You're not alone: *Olive* / Sunshine: *Umboza* / Macarena: *Los Del Mar* / Keep on jumpin': *Terry, Todd & Martha Wash/Jocelyn Brown* / Tha wildstyle: *DJ Supreme* / Higher state of consciousness: *Wink, Josh* / Do that to me: *Lisa Marie Experience* / Where love lives: *Limerick, Alison* / In de ghetto: *Morales, David & The Bad Yard Club/Crystal Waters/Delta* / Move your body: *Ruffneck & Yavahn* / Wrong: *Everything But The Girl* / Stand up: *Lovetribe* / Jazz it up: *Reel 2 Real* / Klubbhopping: *Klubb Heads* / If Madonna calls: *Vasquez, Junior* / Rays of the rising sun: *Mozaic* / It's just another groove: *Mighty Dub Katz* / Jus come: *Cool Jack* / Vicious circle: *Poltergeist* / Arms of Loren: *E'voke* / One day I'll fly away: *Llorena, Kelly* / Down to earth: *Grace* / Fable: *Miles, Robert*
CD Set ______ **5359032**
PolyGram TV / Sep '96 / PolyGram

DANCE ZONE VOL.9 (2CD Set)
Shine: *Space Brothers* / Prophet: *Bolland, C.J.* / I love you...stop: *Red Five* / Reday or not: *Course* / Encore une fois: *Sash* / Lovefool: *Cardigans* / Saint: *Orbital* / Sometimes: *Brand New Heavies* / It's alright, I feel it: *Nu Yorican Soul* / Underwater love: *Smoke City* / Fired up: *Funky Green Dogs* / Sound of eden: *Casino* / People hold on: *Dirty Rotten Scoundrels & Lisa Stansfield* / My love is deep: *Parker, Sara* / Do you know: *Gayle, Michelle* / Scared: *Slacker* / Hand in hand: *Grace* / Tha wildstyle: *DJ Supreme* / Where can I find love: *Livin' Joy* / I belong to you: *Gina G* / One and one: *Miles, Robert & Maria Naylor*
CD Set ______ **5377162**
PolyGram TV / May '97 / PolyGram

DANCEFLOOR FEVER (20 Essential Grooves)
I'm doin' fine now: *New York City* / Hold back the night: *Trammps* / More more more: *True, Andrea Connection* / Shame, shame, shame: *Shirley & Company* / Swing your Daddy: *Gilstrap, Jim* / Dolly my love: *Moments* / Dial L for the love squad: *Carr, Linda* / Ride a wild horse: *Clark, Dee* / Get dancing: *Disco Tex & The Sexolettes* / This is it: *Moore, Melba* / Now is the time: *James, Jimmy & The Vagabonds* / Baby don't change your mind: *Knight, Gladys & The Pips* / Take that to the bank: *Shalamar* / Galaxy of love: *Crown Heights Affair* / I gotta keep dancin': *Lucas, Carrie* / In the bush: *Musique* / I don't want to be a freak (but I can't help myself): *Dynasty* / We got the funk: *Positive Force* / Check out the groove: *Thurston, Bobby* / Can you handle it: *Redd, Sharon*
CD ______ **SUMCD 4102**
Summit / Nov '96 / Sound & Media

DANCEHALL CONNECTION VOL.1 & 2
CD ______ **MFCD 006**
Mafia/Fluxy / Dec '92 / Jet Star / SRD

DANCEHALL DAYS
CD ______ **FILECD 458**
Profile / Jan '95 / Pinnacle

DANCEHALL HITS VOL.1
CD ______ **VPCD 1335**
Digital B / Oct '93 / Jet Star

DANCEHALL HITS VOL.1
CD ______ **PHCD 2001**
Penthouse / Aug '93 / Jet Star

DANCEHALL HITS VOL.2
CD ______ **PHCD 2003**
Penthouse / Aug '93 / Jet Star

DANCEHALL HITS VOL.2
CD ______ **VPCD 1321**
Digital B / Sep '93 / Jet Star

DANCEHALL HITS VOL.3
CD ______ **PHCD 2004**
Penthouse / Aug '93 / Jet Star

DANCEHALL HITS VOL.3
CD ______ **VPCD 1344**
VP / Dec '93 / Greensleeves / Jet Star / Total/BMG

DANCEHALL HITS VOL.4
CD ______ **PHCD 2015**
Penthouse / Aug '94 / Jet Star

DANCEHALL KILLERS
CD ______ **792092**
Jammy's / Jun '93 / Jet Star

DANCEHALL KILLERS VOL.3
CD ______ **SHCD 45018**
Shanachie / Dec '94 / ADA / Greensleeves / Koch

DANCEHALL KINGS
CD ______ **SONCD 0083**
Sonic Sounds / Apr '96 / Jet Star

DANCEHALL ROUGHNECK
CD ______ **HBCD 148**
Greensleeves / Aug '93 / Jet Star / SRD

DANCEHALL SLAM
CD ______ **SHCD 45025**
Shanachie / Mar '96 / ADA / Greensleeves / Koch

DANCEHALL STYLE
Dancehall style: *McLeod, Enos & Roots Radics* / Tears on my pillow: *Mabujah* / Sharron: *Mabujah* / Hang down your head: *Pheaney, Winston* / Children of the ghetto: *Naggo Heptones* / Gain experience: *McLeod, Enos* / Made up my mind: *McLeod, Enos* / Magic: *McLeod, Enos* / Keep away: *McLeod, Enos* / Why must I: *McLeod, Enos* / Lonely street: *McLeod, Enos* / Lonely: *McLeod, Enos* / Sparkling light: *McLeod, Enos* / Money lover: *McLeod, Enos* / Show me: *Marshall, Larry* / Channa channa: *Bobby Melody* / Answer me: *Davis, Ronnie* / Write myself a letter: *Davis, Ronnie*
CD ______ **PRCD 608**
President / May '97 / Grapevine/PolyGram / President / Target/BMG

DANCEHALL STYLEE VOL.2
Here I come (Broader than Broadway): *Levy, Barrington* / Burrup: *Nardo Ranks* / Murder dem: *Ninjaman* / Ring the alarm: *Tenor Saw* / Drum pan sound: *Reggie Stepper* / Stop loving you: *McGregor, Freddie* / Roots and culture: *Shabba Ranks* / Cabin stabbin': *Super Cat & Nico Demus/Junior Demus* / Wicked in bed: *Shabba Ranks* / DJ in my country: *Clement Irie* / Proud to be black: *Crucial Robbie* / Golden touch: *Brown, Rula & Commander Shad*
CD ______ **FILECD 291**
Profile / Feb '91 / Pinnacle

DANCEPOWER VOL.2
CD ______ **MNF 05232**
Manifold / Jan '97 / ZYX

DANCES OF THE GODS
CD ______ **C 559 051**
Ocora / Apr '89 / ADA / Harmonia Mundi

DANCES OF THE WORLD (Music From Elektra Nonesuch 'Explorer' Series)
CD ______ **7559791672**
Nonesuch / Jan '95 / Warner Music

DANCING 'TIL DAWN
Last minute miracle: *Shirelles* / Help me: *Wilson, Al* / This man / Woman lover thief: *Stemmons Express* / One in a million / Come back baby: *Dodds, Nella* / Everything is everything / Marching / Out on the street again: *Candy & The Kisses* / Love it's getting better / Get on up / Desiree / Do you believe it / I'm your yes man: *Reid, Clarence* / Work song / These chains of love (Are breaking me down): *Jackson, Chuck* / Ain't that peculiar: *Tindley, George* / Stop sign / Ain't no soul / Name it and claim it: *Stewart, Darryl* / Tightrope / You busted my mind: *Clay, Judy* / Love is a good foundation / There comes a time / I don't have a mind of my own / Lost love: *Irma & The Fascinations* / Please stay: *Ivorys* / Show me a man: *Bradshaw, Bobby* / Livin' the nightlife: *Charts* / Let me give you my lovin': *Brown, Maxine* / Black eyed girl: *Thompson, Billy*
CD ______ **CDKEND 106**
Kent / Feb '94 / Pinnacle

DANCING AT THE PALAIS (Recollections From The Palais Days)
I'm so alone: *Preager, Lou & His Orchestra* / I want my Mama: *Roy, Harry & His Band* / When the Rose Of Tralee met Danny Boy: *White, Jack & His Band* / Chatanooga choo choo: *Loss, Joe & His Orchestra* / Mean to me: *Gonella, Nat & His New Georgians* / You're breaking my heart all over again: *White, Jack & His Band* / Ashby De La Zooch: *Preager, Lou & His Orchestra* / Carolina: *Preager, Lou & His Orchestra* / Russian serenade: *Roy, Harry & His Band* / Jee bie hop: *Leader, Harry & His Orchestra* / Let him go, let him tarry: *Geraldo & His Orchestra* / Down in New Mexico: *Gonella, Nat & His New Georgians* / Sally Water: *Munn, Billy & His Orchestra* / I'm nobody's baby:

White, Jack & His Band / Woe is me: *Rabin, Oscar & His Band* / Little smile: *Leader, Harry & His Orchestra* / Good, good, good: *Preager, Lou & His Orchestra* / For all that I care: *White, Jack & His Band* / It only takes a small cloud: *White, Jack & His Band* / I'm beginning to see the light: *Geraldo & His Orchestra* / It had to be you: *Roy, Harry & His Band* / I'll always be with you: *Preager, Lou & His Orchestra*
CD ____ RAJCD 879
Empress / Apr '97 / Koch

DANCING BRAZIL
CD ____ 15343
Laserlight / May '94 / Target/BMG

DANCING IN THE STREET (2CD Set)
Standing at the crossroads: *James, Elmore* / Good Holly Miss Molly: *Little Richard* / Blueberry hill: *Domino, Fats* / That's alright Mama: *Crudup, Arthur 'Big Boy'* / Surfin' USA: *Beach Boys* / Stand by me: *King, Ben E.* / You've lost that loving feeling: *Righteous Brothers* / Mr. Tambourine man: *Byrds* / What I'd say: *Charles, Ray* / Respect: *Franklin, Aretha* / In the midnight hour: *Pickett, Wilson* / Boom boom: *Hooker, John Lee* / House of the rising sun: *Animals* / Sunshine of your love: *Cream* / Somebody to love: *Jefferson Airplane* / Ball and chain: *Big Brother & The Holding Company* / I'm waiting for the man: *Velvet Underground* / I'm eighteen: *Cooper, Alice* / Walk on the wild side: *Reed, Lou* / What do I get: *Buzzcocks* / Roadrunner: *Richman, Jonathan* / Heart of glass: *Blondie* / Please, please, please: *Brown, James* / Dance to the music: *Sly & The Family Stone* / If you don't know me by now: *Melvin, Harold* / Message: *Grandmaster Flash* / What's going on: *Gaye, Marvin* / Purple haze: *Hendrix, Jimi* / Dancing in the street: *Reeves, Martha & The Vandellas* / Rock Island line: *Donegan, Lonnie* / Da doo ron ron: *Crystals* / Holidays in the sun: *Sex Pistols* / Baby please don't go: *Them*
CD Set ____ 3036400162
Carlton / Jul '96 / Carlton

DANCING ON SUNSHINE
I got you babe: *UB40 & Chrissie Hynde* / Wild world: *Priest, Maxi* / I can see clearly now: *Nash, Johnny* / Now that we've found love: *Third World* / Don't turn around: *Aswad* / Dub be good to me: *Beats International* / Word girl: *Scritti Politti* / To love somebody: *Somerville, Jimmy* / Everything I own: *Boy George* / Love of the common people: *Thomas, Nicky* / Dreadlock holiday: *10cc* / Israelites: *Dekker, Desmond* / Double barrel: *Collins, Dave & Ansell* / Uptown top ranking: *Althia & Donna* / Tomorrow people: *Marley, Ziggy & The Melody Makers* / Silly games: *Kay, Janet* / Help me make it through the night: *Holt, John* / Just don't want to be lonely: *McGregor, Freddie* / Wonderful world, beautiful people: *Cliff, Jimmy* / I don't wanna dance: *Grant, Eddy* / Sing our own song: *UB40*
CD ____ 5155192
PolyGram TV / Jul '92 / PolyGram

DANCING STRINGS OF SCOTLAND
Reel of the 51st division / Linton ploughman / Scottish waltz / Hamilton house / Dashing white sergeant / Duke of Perth / Strip the willow / Gay Gordons / Petronella / Highland Schottische / Circassian circle
CD ____ LCOM 5175
Lismor / Nov '96 / ADA / Direct / Duncans / Lismor

DANCING TO THE BANDS AGAIN (2CD Set)
Say it everyday: *Skyrockets Orchestra* / That's my desire: *Rabin, Oscar & His Band* / I'll do it all over again: *Roy, Harry* / Another day: *Roy, Harry* / It's all over now: *Preager, Lou & His Band* / I'm always chasing rainbows: *Fenoulhet, Paul* / I walked in with my eyes open: *Fenoulhet, Paul* / Little on the lonely side: *Fenoulhet, Paul* / I wonder who's kissing her now: *Rabin, Oscar & His Band* / You can't be true dear: *Rabin, Oscar & His Band* / I'm not in love: *Rabin, Oscar & His Band* / June night: *Rabin, Oscar & His Band* / Far away place: *Rabin, Oscar & His Band* / You're still the only girl in the world: *Rabin, Oscar & His Band* / Turn over a new leaf: *Benson, Ivy* / Tree in the meadow: *Benson, Ivy* / I'm in the mood for love: *Benson, Ivy* / I cover the waterfront: *Benson, Ivy* / I'll buy that dream: *Preager, Lou & His Orchestra* / I want to learn to dance: *Preager, Lou & His Orchestra* / When the red, red robin comes bob, bob, bobbin' along: *Preager, Lou & His Orchestra* / I'm so alone: *Fenhoulet, Paul & Skyrockets Dance Orchestra* / I'll close my eyes: *Fenhoulet, Paul & Skyrockets Dance Orchestra* / In Pinetop's footsteps: *Fenhoulet, Paul & Skyrockets Dance Orchestra* / Please don't say no: *Fenhoulet, Paul & Skyrockets Dance Orchestra* / It's dreamtime: *Fenhoulet, Paul & Skyrockets Dance Orchestra* / I don't care if I never dream again: *Loss, Joe Band* / Gotta be this or that: *Loss, Joe Band* / I'll be your sweetheart: *Loss, Joe Band* / Lavender blue: *Geraldo & His Dance Orchestra* / Maria from Bahia: *Geraldo & His Dance Orchestra* / On a slow boat to China: *Geraldo & His Dance Orchestra* / After all: *Geraldo & His Dance Orchestra* / You moved right in: *Roy, Harry & His Orchestra* / Cynthia's in love: *Roy, Harry & His Orchestra* / Out of the night: *Roy, Harry & His Orchestra* / Last waltz of the evening: *Roy, Harry & His Orchestra* / You red head: *Dean, Syd & his Band* / Dreamer's holiday: *Dean, Syd & his Band* / Monday, Tuesday, Wednesday: *Dean, Syd & his Band* / Red roses: *Adam, Paul & His Mayfair Music* / Put your shoes on Lucy: *Adam, Paul & His Mayfair Music* / Echo told me a lie: *Adam, Paul & His Mayfair Music* / Two lips: *Adam, Paul & His Mayfair Music* / How little it matters, how little we know: *Winstone, Eric* / I should care: *Winstone, Eric* / There must be a way: *Foster, Teddy & The Band* / I'm in love with two sweethearts: *Foster, Teddy & The Band*
CD Set ____ CDDL 1260
Music For Pleasure / May '94 / EMI

DANCING TO THE FLUTE (Music & Dance In Indian Art)
CD ____ 131352
Celestial Harmonies / Jul '97 / ADA / Select

DANDELION SAMPLER 1969-1972, THE
Coathanger: *Ward, Clifford T.* / Nice: *St. John, Bridget* / Pictures in the sky: *Medicine Head* / Strange locomotion: *Siren* / Ruby baby: *Vincent, Gene* / Ravenscroft 13 bar boogie: *Tractor* / Missed my times: *Occasional Word* / Asmoto Running Band: *Principal Edwards Magic Theatre* / Please bring back the birch for the milkman: *Hart, Mike* / Little triple one shot: *Coxhill, Lol* / Roadrunner: *Stackwaddy*
CD ____ SFMD 96
See For Miles/C5 / Sep '96 / Pinnacle

DANGER URBAN ELECTRONIC DISORDER
Biohazard: *Dazzle T & Buzz K* / Southgates remorse: *BLIM* / Projects: *Two Plus One* / Anger: *Footloose* / Planet: *Elementz Of Noise* / Mutant revisited: *DJ Trace* / Onza: *BLIM* / Implants: *Genetix* / Jeamland '96: *DJ Trace* / Renegade fazed: *Tonic* / Vision: *Rescale* / Shadow: *Freq Nasty*
CD ____ EMFCDLP 002
Emotif / Jan '97 / SRD / Vital

DANGER ZONE
CD ____ 5538702
PolyGram TV / Aug '97 / PolyGram

DANIEL POOLE - WORLD SOUND SYSTEMS
CD ____ TLCDPCD 001
TLC / Jan '96 / SRD

DANISH TRAD JAZZ VOL.1
CD ____ MECCACD 1006
Music Mecca / Aug '90 / Cadillac / Jazz Music / Wellard

DANISH TRAD JAZZ VOL.2
CD ____ MECCACD 1031
Music Mecca / Nov '94 / Cadillac / Jazz Music / Wellard

DANISH TRAD JAZZ VOL.3
CD ____ MECCACD 1099
Music Mecca / May '97 / Cadillac / Jazz Music / Wellard

DANSE MACABRE SAMPLER
CD ____ EFA 11213
Danse Macabre / Apr '93 / SRD

DANSKE JAZZ '95
CD ____ MECCACD 1069
Music Mecca / May '97 / Cadillac / Jazz Music / Wellard

DANSKE JAZZ '96
CD ____ MECCACD 2009
Music Mecca / May '97 / Cadillac / Jazz Music / Wellard

DANZA LATINA
Todo paol no se pica: *Manaure* / El tamalito: *Hermanos Santa Cruz* / Contigo mi vida: *Selva* / Me he de guardar: *Saravia, Patricia* / Mama no deja: *Rego, Elisa* / Yo no say pilon de machacar: *Rodriguez, Lalo* / Entre rejas: *Orquesta Bamba* / Caramelos: *Los Amaya* / Contratiempos: *Navajita Platea* / Buleria del solitaire: *Arebato* / Saca los manos: *Freundt, Julie* / Ciega: *Jailene* / Tambito: *Son, Caribe Gaita Y* / Borrando fronteras: *Carabajal, Peteco* / Gitanos y morenos: *Perez, Gato* / Hablame: *Garcia, Carangano Y Jose Luis* / He vuelto para andar: *Laugart, Ziomara*
CD ____ HEMICD 25
Hemisphere / Feb '97 / EMI

DARGASON MUSIC SAMPLER
CD ____ DM 118CD
Dargason Music / Nov '96 / ADA

DARK EMPIRE STRIKES BACK
CD ____ DARK 0052
Dark Empire / Apr '94 / SRD

DARK HEARTS VOL.1
CD ____ HHSP 006CD
Harthouse / Feb '95 / Mo's Music Machine / Prime / Vital

DARK HEARTS VOL.2
CD ____ HHSP 009CD
Harthouse / Nov '95 / Mo's Music Machine / Prime / Vital

DARK PASSAGES VOL.2
CD ____ RISE 012CD
Rise Above / Jul '96 / Plastic Head / Vital

DARK PROGRESSIVE SOUND VOL.1
CD ____ EFACD 91011
Zillo / Jul '96 / SRD

DARK SIDE VOL.2
CD ____ REACTCD 032
React / Dec '93 / Arabesque / Prime / Vital

DARK SONICS
CD ____ CD 8419732
SPV / Apr '96 / Koch / Plastic Head

DARKEND GOTHIC ROCK COMPILATION
CD ____ DARK 001CD
Darkend / Feb '97 / Plastic Head

DARKEST HOUR, THE
CD ____ CLP 0029
Hypnotic / Aug '97 / Cargo / SRD

DARN IT - POEMS BY PAUL HAINES/ MUSIC BY MANY
CD ____ AMCL 1014
Normal / May '94 / ADA / Direct

DAS MACH ICH MIT MUSIK
Das mach ich mit musik: *Johns, Bibi* / Die gipsy band: *Johns, Bibi* / Bimbo: *Johns, Bibi* / Billy boy: *Sauer, Wolfgang & Angele Durand* / Das klavier uber mir: *Kuhn, Paul* / Swing hei: *Kuhn, Paul* / Federball: *Kuhn, Paul* / Chanson d'amour: *Durand, Angele* / Sailor's boogie: *Durand, Angele* / Warum strahlen heut' nacht di sterne so hell: *Sauer, Wolfgang* / Liebe im April: *Sauer, Wolfgang* / Little rock: *Durand, Angele & Bibi Johns* / Bye bye baby: *Durand, Angele & Bibi Johns* / Ich mocht auf deiner hochzeit tanzen: *Kuhn, Paul & Bibi Johns* / Lillie boogie: *Serrano, Rosita* / Mitternachts blues: *Schachtner, Heinz* / Dein herz aus stein: *De Vale, Mariette* / Willy lilly rock a billy: *Boswell, Eve* / Paris dixie: *Cordy, Annie* / Ma belle mademoiselle: *Constantine, Eddie*
CD ____ BCD 15413
Bear Family / Dec '87 / Direct / Rollercoaster / Swift

DATAFILE
CD ____ REXDF 001
Ruffex / Oct '96 / Mo's Music Machine

DAUGHTERS OF TEXAS
Young and dumb / Breaking up somebody's home / In the mood / Say the wrong thing / Rock 'n' roll fever / Horny old buzzard, dirty old man / Your magic touch (quit working on me) / Nobody knows you (when you're down and out) / Walk rightin / I can tell I'm losing you / Stepping up in class / Breaking mama's rule / Ain't nobody gonna take my man
CD ____ CDTB 080
Thunderbolt / Jan '92 / TKO Magnum

DAVE GODIN'S DEEP SOUL TREASURES (Taken From The Vaults)
I'm never gonna live it down: *Knight Brothers* / Easy as saying 1-2-3: *Willis, Timmy* / Lights out: *Hicks, Zerben R. & The Dynamics* / Anybody who knows what love is (will understand): *Thomas, Irma* / Have a little mercy: *Wells, Jean* / Try love: *Grayson, Dori* / I can't make it without him: *Davis, Brendetta* / Showdown: *Carter, Kenny* / I'm not the one: *Banks, Larry* / Turning point: *Holiday, Jimmy* / Standing here crying: *Incredibles* / She broke his heart: *Just Brothers* / You're on top: *Untouchables* / It's not that easy: *Bell, Reuben & The Casanovas* / Cry baby cry: *Van & Titus* / I still love you: *Stanback, Jean* / Try to leave me if you can (I bet you can't do it): *Banks, Bessie* / Songs to sing: *Raw Spitt* / How much longer (must I wait): *Moses, Lee* / Nothing's too much (nothing's too good): *Young, Billy* / I feel like cryin': *Sam & Bill* / I'm goin' for myself: *Eddie & Ernie* / Tried so hard to please her: *Knight Brothers* / Love of my man: *Gray, Pearlean & The Passengers* / You got me: *Jaibi*
CD ____ CDKEND 143
Kent / Apr '97 / Pinnacle

DAVID HAMILTON'S FAVOURITE MELODIES (Relaxing Moods)
Deep purple: *Temple, nino & April stevens* / Rhythm of the rain: *Cascades* / Here it comes again: *Fortunes* / You were on my mind: *St. Peters, Crispian* / It hurts to be in love: *Pitney, Gene* / Maria: *Proby, P.J.* / He's so fine: *Chiffons* / Breaking up is hard to do: *Sedaka, Neil* / Venus: *Avalon, Frankie* / Cupid: *Drifters* / Warm and tender love: *Sledge, Percy* / groovy kind of love: *Fontana, Wayne* / Here comes that rainy day feeling: *Fortunes* / Reflections of my life: *Marmalade* / Town without pity: *Pitney, Gene* / Remember(walkin' in the sand): *Shangri-Las* / Stranger on the shore: *Bilk, Acker*
CD ____ ANT 018
Tring / Nov '96 / Tring

DAVID HAMILTON'S FAVOURITE MELODIES (Sixties Hits)
Sugar sugar: *Archies* / Ruby don't take your love to town: *Rogers, Kenny* / If I had a hammer: *Lopez, Trini* / Sweet talkin guy: *Chiffons* / Sha la la la lee: *Small Faces* / Letter: *Box Tops* / Little town flirt: *Shannon, Del* / It hurts to be in love: *Pitney, Gene* / Rockin' robin: *Day, Bobby* / Barefootin: *Parker, Robert* / Duke of earl: *Chandler, Gene* / It's in his kiss (the shoop shoop song): *Everett, Betty* / I'm into something good: *Herman's Hermits* / One fine day: *Chiffons* / Backstage (I'm lonely): *Pitney, Gene* / Poetry in motion: *Tillotson, Johnny* / Louie louie: *Kingsmen* / Hit's of the 70's (David Hamilton's favourite melodies)
CD ____ ANT 019
Tring / Nov '96 / Tring

DAVID HAMILTON'S FAVOURITE MELODIES (Hits Of The 70's)
Lady rose: *Mungo Jerry* / Hitchin' a ride: *Vanity Fare* / Now is the time: *James, Jimmy & The Vagabonds* / Lets get together again: *Glitter Band* / Run back: *Douglas, Carl* / Black & white: *Greyhound* / I'm doin fine now: *New York City* / Girls: *Moments* / Freedom come freedom go: *Fortunes* / I only want to be with you: *Bay City Rollers* / Love will keep us together: *Sedaka, Neil* / Up in a puff of smoke: *Brown, Polly* / Sugar baby love: *Rubettes* / You can get it if you really want: *Decker, Desmond & the Aces* / Yellow river: *Christie* / I get a little sentimental over you: *New Seekers* / Shang a lang: *Bay City Rollers* / People like you & people like me: *Glitter Band*
CD ____ ANT 020
Tring / Nov '96 / Tring

DAVID HAMILTON'S FAVOURITE MELODIES (Disco Party Mix)
I'll go where your music takes me: *James, Jimmy & The Vagabonds* / I love to love: *Charles, Tina* / I will survive: *Gaynor, Gloria* / Hold back the night: *Trammps* / Band of Gold: *Payne, Freda* / Get dancin': *Disco Tex & The Sexolettes* / Saddle up: *Christie, David* / Twist: *Checker, Chubby* / Do the funky chicken: *Thomas, Rufus* / You little trustmaker: *Thymes* / Dance little lady dance: *Charles, Tina* / I wanna dance wit choo: *Disco Tex & The Sexolettes* / Don't take away the music: *Tavares* / High energy: *Thomas, Evelyn* / Feel like I'm in love: *Marie, Kelly*
CD ____ ANT 021
Tring / Nov '96 / Tring

DAVID HAMILTON'S FAVOURITE MELODIES (Lover's Fireside)
Night has a thousand eyes: *Vee, Bobby* / My special prayer: *Sledge, Percy* / Chapel of love: *Dixie Cups* / Something's gotten hold of my heart: *Pitney, Gene* / Everything I own: *Boothe, Ken* / Somewhere: *Proby, P.J.* / Every beat of my heart: *Knight, Gladys & The Pips* / Single Girl: *Posey, Sandy* / 24 hours from Tulsa: *Pitney, Gene* / Love is all around: *Troggs* / So many ways: *Benton, Brook* / Sixteen candles: *Crests* / Hurt: *Yuro, Timi* / Will you love me tomorrow: *Shirelles* / Like it is: *Neville, Aaron* / Letter full of tears: *Knight, Gladys & The Pips* / You'll never walk alone: *Gerry & The Pacemakers*
CD ____ ANT 022
Tring / Nov '96 / Tring

DAY MY FAVOURITE INSECT DIED, THE
CD ____ KS 14CD
Kollaps / Feb '97 / Cargo

DAY TRIPPER
Magic bus: *Swervedriver* / Mysteries: *Happy Campers* / Fun for me: *Moloko* / In a room: *Dodgy* / Simple life: *Chamberlain* / 36 degrees: *Placebo* / Tattva: *Kula Shaker* / Midnight in a perfect world: *DJ Shadow* / What now: *Pressure Drop* / Sunrise shakers: *Reef* / Straight line: *Tribute To Nothing* / Love spreads: *Stone Roses* / Worst case scenario: *Stanford Prison Experiment* / Descend: *Feeder* / Insects are all around us: *Money Mark* / Stereo: *Spooky* / Airhead: *Millencolin* / Untitled: *DJ Shadow*
CD ____ 5406772
A&M / Feb '97 / PolyGram

DAYDREAM (Summer Chart Party)
Build me up buttercup: *Foundations* / I'm gonna make you mine: *Christie, Lou* / Popcorn: *Hot Butter* / Daydream: *Lovin' Spoonful* / Waterloo sunset: *Kinks* / Yummy yummy yummy: *Ohio Express* / Mirrors: *Oldfield, Sally* / Isn't she lovely: *Parton, David* / (Dancing) on a Saturday night: *Blue, Barry* / Lady rose: *Mungo Jerry* / Ain't nothing but a house party: *Showstoppers* / Lazy Sunday: *Small Faces* / Down the dustpipe: *Status Quo* / That same old feeling: *Pickettywitch* / Roadrunner: *Richman, Jonathan & Modern Lovers* / What have they done to my song Ma: *Melanie* / Who were you with in the moonlight: *Dollar* / Surfin' safari: *Beach Boys* / Mexico: *Baldry, Long John*
CD ____ TRTCD 144
TrueTrax / Oct '94 / THE

DAYTRIPPERS (3CD Set)
CD Set ____ DTKBOX 52
Dressed To Kill / Dec '96 / Total/BMG

DE NEDERLANDSCHE UNDERGROUND
CD ____ PRIME 052CD
Prime / Oct '96 / Pinnacle / Vital

DE NOVA DA CAPO COMPILATION
CD ____ DNDC 007CD
De Nova Da Capo / Oct '96 / World Serpent

DEAR OLD ERIN'S ISLE
CD ____ NI 5350
Nimbus / Sep '94 / Nimbus

DEATH IS JUST THE BEGINNING VOL.3 (2CD+VHS Set/2CD Set)
CD Set ____ NB 1119
Nuclear Blast / Jan '95 / Plastic Head

CD Set NB 111CD
Nuclear Blast / Jun '96 / Plastic Head

DECADE OF CALLIGRAPH, A
Lady Jekyll and Mistress Hyde: *Lyttelton, Humphrey* / Black butterfly: *Lyttelton, Humphrey* / Caribana Queen: *Lyttelton, Humphrey* / Strange Mr Peter Charles: *Lyttelton, Humphrey* / My funny valentine: *Lyttelton, Humphrey* / Bad penny blues: *Lyttelton, Humphrey* / Happy go lucky local: *Lyttelton, Humphrey* / Jack the bear: *Lyttelton, Humphrey* / Madly: *Lyttelton, Humphrey* / Drop me off in Harlem: *Shapiro, Helen* / When a woman loves a man: *Shapiro, Helen* / Turner minor: *Turner, Bruce* / Buddy Tate from Texas State: *Lyttelton, Humphrey & Buddy Tate* / I got a pocket of dreams: *Daniels, Maxine & Brian Lemon* / Fascinating rhythm: *Barnes, Johnny* / Down in honky tonk town: *Lyttelton, Humphrey & Lillian Boutte* / My Mama socks me: *Davern, Kenny* / Summertime: *Lyttelton, Humphrey & Acker Bilk*
CD CLGCD 031
Calligraph / Oct '95 / Cadillac / Jazz Music / New Note/Pinnacle / Wellard

DECADE OF DECCA INSTRUMENTALS 1959-1967, THE
Entry of the gladiators: *Nero & The Gladiators* / Bongo rock: *Jetstreams* / Chariot: *Stoller, Rhet* / Taboo: *Sounds Incorporated* / Eclipse: *Greenslade, Arthur & The Geemen* / Paella: *Sunspots* / Grumbling guitar: *Other Two* / Surfside: *Revell, Digger & The Denver Men* / Saturday jump: *Midnight Shift* / Stand up and say that: *Nashville Five* / Night train: *Fifty Fingers Give Guitars* / Stand and deliver: *Snobs* / Bogey man: *Moontrekkers* / I didn't know the gun was loaded: *Cannons* / Fugitive: *Thunderbolts* / Song of Mexico / Treck to Rome: *Nero & The Gladiators* / More like Nashville: *Nashville Five* / Savage (part 2): *Sneaky Petes* / Pop the whip: *Dynamic Sounds* / Mind reader: *Howard, Johnny, Group* / Curly: *Bluesbreakers* / Feeling in the mood: *Thunderbolts* / Hall of the mountain king: *Nero & The Gladiators* / Savage: *Sneaky Petes* / Sounds like locomotion: *Sounds Incorporated*
CD SEECD 204
See For Miles/C5 / May '92 / Pinnacle

DECADE OF IBIZA, A (2CD Set)
CD Set TCD 2902
CD Set XTCD 2902
Telstar / Jun '97 / BMG

DECK THE HALLS
CD 15304
Laserlight / Nov '95 / Target/BMG

DECONSTRUCTION CLASSICS
Ride on time: *Black Box* / Rhythm is a mystery: *K-Klass* / Anthem: *N-Joi* / Dream 17: *Annette B* / Higher ground: *Sasha* / Confide in me: *Minogue, Kylie* / Sight for sore eyes: *M-People* / Don't you want me: *Felix* / Open your mind: *Usura* / Texas cowboys: *Grid* / High: *Hyper Go Go* / Carino: *T-Coy* / Movin' on up: *M-People* / Infinity: *Guru Josh* / How can I love you more: *M-People* / Packet of peace: *Lion Rock* / Love thing: *Evolution* / I'm in love: *Sha-Lor* / Everybody everybody: *Black Box* / Don't come to stay: *Hot House* / Sly one: *Van-Rooy, Marina* / Is there anybody out there: *Bassheads* / Future FJP: *Liaison D* / Ajare: *Way Out West* / Girls and boys: *Hed Boys* / Swamp thing: *Grid*
CD 74321299002
De-Construction / Aug '95 / BMG

DEDICATED TO THE ONE I LOVE
CD MCCD 087
Music Club / Dec '92 / Disc / THE

DEDICATED TO THE ONE I LOVE
Little darling: *Diamonds* / Earth angel: *Penguins* / Chapel of love: *Dixie Cups* / Fools rush in: *Benton, Brook* / Uptown: *Crystals* / Pillow you dream on: *Locklin, Hank* / Embraceable you: *Day, Doris* / Up on the roof: *Drifters* / Night has a thousand eyes: *Vee, Bobby* / So many ways: *Benton, Brook* / Runaway: *Shannon, Del* / Because you're mine: *Day, Doris* / I loved and lost again: *Cline, Patsy* / Single girl: *Posey, Sandy* / Love walked in: *Benson, George* / Just the two of us: *Jones, Jack* / Portrait of my love: *Clark, Dee* / Give him a great big kiss: *Shangri-Las* / One who really loves you: *Wells, Mary* / Why do fools fall in love: *Diamonds* / Let your love flow: *Burke, Solomon* / Singin' the blues: *Mitchell, Guy* / While I dream: *Sedaka, Neil* / Crying my heart out for you: *Day, Doris* / Tell Laura I love her: *Peterson, Ray*
CD GRF 131
Tring / Apr '93 / Tring

DEDICATED TO YOU (18 More Songs From The Heart)
Coward of the county: *Rogers, Kenny* / I will always love you: *Parton, Dolly* / Have I told you lately that I love you: *Reeves, Jim* / Roses are red: *O'Donnell, Daniel* / Who's sorry now: *Francis, Connie* / Years from now / I don't know why I love you: *Rose Marie* / Blanket on the ground: *Spears, Billie Jo* / Honey: *Goldsboro, Bobby* / Crystal chandeliers: *Pride, Charley* / Sunshine of your smile: *Berry, Mike* / You are my sunshine: *Boxcar Willie* / Love is like a butterfly: *Parton, Dolly* / I need you: *O'Donnell, Daniel* / Anniversary waltz: *Rose Marie* / Little green apples: *Miller, Roger* / Single girl: *Posey, Sandy* / Last farewell: *Whittaker, Roger*
CD PLATCD 3901
Platinum / Oct '88 / Prism

DEE JAYS RULE (2CD Set)
CD Set AVEXCD 52
Avex / Jan '97 / 3mv/Pinnacle

DEEP BLUE (Rounder 25th Anniversary Blues Anthology)
CD ROUCDAN 20
Rounder / Nov '95 / ADA / CM / Direct

DEEP BLUES
Jumper on the line: *Burnside, R.L.* / Jr Blues: *Kimbrough, Junior* / Catfish blues: *Johnson, Big Jack* / Daddy, when is Momma coming home: *Johnson, Big Jack* / Big boy now: *Johnson, Big Jack* / Midnight prowler: *Frost, Frank* / You can talk about me: *Hemphill, Jessie Mae* / Shame on you: *Hemphill, Jessie Mae* / Long haired doney: *Burnside, R.L.* / Heartbroken man: *Barnes, Roosevelt 'Booba'* / Ain't gonna worry about tomorrow: *Barnes, Roosevelt 'Booba'* / Love like I wanna: *Barnes, Roosevelt 'Booba'* / Terraplane blues: *Pitchford, Lonnie* / If I had possession over judgement day: *Pitchford, Lonnie* / Devil blues: *Owens, Jack & Bud Spires*
CD 4509919812
WEA / Mar '93 / Warner Music

DEEP CONCENTRATION (2CD Set)
CD Set OM 006CD
OM / May '97 / Cargo / SRD

DEEP DISTRAXION
Geera: *Monumental* / Not gonna do it: *S1000* / Do one more: *Spoonio* / Mandala: *Monumental* / Stoneage: *Floorjam* / Who's in the house: *S1000* / Viewfinder: *Back II Front* / Deep distraxion: *Floorjam* / I'm gonna get you: *Hook Line & Sinker* / Ibiza: *Back II Front* / By dawn's early light: *Thee Madkatt Courtship* / Lego beat: *Happy Larry*
CD SLIKCD 002
Deep Distraxion/Profile / Jul '94 / Pinnacle

DEEP DOWN IN FLORIDA (TK Deep Soul)
All because of your love: *Clay, Otis* / Honey honey: *Hudson, David* / Sometimes: *Facts Of Life* / If he hadn't slipped up and got caught: *Patterson, Bobby* / Sweet woman's love: *Clay, Otis* / God blessed our love: *Allen, Charles* / All I need is you: *Clay, Otis* / I've tried it all: *Meadows Bros.* / Baby I cried cried cried: *Johnson, Charles* / Today my whole world fell: *Clay, Otis* / It's never too late: *Willie & Anthony* / Let me in: *Clay, Otis* / Love on the phone: *Mitchell, John* / Caught in the act: *Facts Of Life* / Love you save: *Williams, Lee Shot* / When I'm loving you: *Hudson, David* / Special kind of love: *Clay, Otis*
CD NEMCD 721
Sequel / Mar '95 / BMG

DEEP DOWN SOUTH
CD CDRB 29
Charly / Nov '95 / Koch

DEEP GREEN
Save a place for me / Deep green / Carlin how / Old man of the ocean / Skinningrove bay / North country girl / Kilten castle / Abbess St. Hilda
CD FG 2803
Frog / Apr '96 / Total/BMG

DEEP HARMONICA BLUES
Courtin' in a cadillac: *McCain, Jerry* / That's what they want: *McCain, Jerry* / Calling all cows: *Blues Rockers* / Johnny Mae: *Blues Rockers* / Not welcome anymore (Sanafee): *Warren, Baby Boy & Sonny Boy Williamson* / Chuc-a-luck chicken: *Warren, Baby Boy & Sonny Boy Williamson* / Love shock: *Little Sonny* / I'll love you baby (until the day I die): *Little Sonny* / Bring me my machine gun: *Warren, Baby Boy & Sonny Boy Williamson* / Hello stranger: *Warren, Baby Boy & Sonny Boy Williamson* / You better change: *Ole Sonny Boy* / Blues & misery: *Ole Sonny Boy* / You don't love me no more: *McCain, Jerry* / Things ain't right: *McCain, Jerry* / Goin' home: *Lightnin' Slim* / I'm grown: *Lightnin' Slim* / Wonderin' & worryin': *Harpo, Slim* / They call me Lazy: *Lazy Lester* / Harmonica twist: *Smith, Whispering* / Please give me one more twist: *Smith, Whispering* / Shut your mouth: *Anderson, Jimmy* / Rats & roaches on your mind: *Anderson, Jimmy* / When I met you baby: *Jolly George* / She's got me: *Jolly George*
CD CDCHD 604
Ace / Nov '96 / Pinnacle

DEEP HOUSE VOL.1 (The Sound Of The UK Underground)
CD CDTOT 43
Jumpin' & Pumpin' / Jul '96 / 3mv/Sony / Mo's Music Machine

DEEP IN A DREAM (20 Dreamy Mood Grooves)
Dream: *Pied Pipers* / I dream of you: *Sinatra, Frank* / My dreams are getting better: *Day, Doris* / Meet me tonight in dreamland: *Mills Brothers* / Have a little dream on me: *Waller, Fats* / Dream lullaby: *Carter, Benny & His Orchestra* / Someone's rocking my dreamboat: *Ink Spots* / When or where: *Horne, Lena* / I've got a pocketful of dreams: *Ambrose & His Orchestra* / If dreams come true: *Goodman, Benny & His Orchestra* / I've got a date with my dream: *Holiday, Billie* / Dreaming a dream: *Bowlly, Al* / Laura: *Herman, Woody & His Orchestra* / I had the craziest dream: *Forrest, Helen* / Day dream: *Hodges, Johnny Orchestra* / Did you ever see a dream walking: *Crosby, Bing* / Yesterday's dreams: *Hutchinson, Leslie 'Hutch'* / Wrap your troubles in dreams: *Cole, Cozy Orchestra & Coleman Hawkins* / I'm always chasing rainbows: *Garland, Judy* / Put your dreams away: *Sinatra, Frank*
CD 305542
Hallmark / Oct '96 / Carlton

DEEP IN THE HEART OF TEXAS
Deep in the heart of Texas: *Kevin & The Blacktears* / Let somebody else drive: *Kevin & The Blacktears* / Will you love me manana: *Saldana, Sir Doug* / Whiter shade of pale: *Saldana, Sir Doug* / Black cat: *Beall, Charlie* / Take a walk in the rain: *Kosub, Kevin* / Loco vaquero: *Jimenez, Flaco* / Joint is jumpin': *Meyers, Augie* / I don't get the blues when I'm stoned: *Dogman & The Shepherds* / Mexico: *Torres, Toby* / I got it: *Mike The Leadsinger*
CD CDZ 2016
Zu Zazz / Apr '94 / Rollercoaster

DEEP IN THE HEART OF TUVA
CD ELLICD 4080
Ellipsis Arts / May '97 / ADA / Direct

DEEP IN THE PHILLY GROOVE
La la means I love you / I need your love so bad / So long, goodbye, it's over / When times are bad / Goodbye pain / Face the future / Didn't I / One and one is five / When the bottom falls out / Follow the lamb / Not goin' to let you (Talk to me that way) / Didn't we make it / Puff puff, you're gone / Ruby Lee / You are my sun sign part 1 / Handle with care / I want to be your lover / Player / Armed and extremely dangerous / Smarty pants / Delfonics theme / Can't go on living
CD CDKEND 115
Kent / May '94 / Pinnacle

DEEP LANCASHIRE (Songs & Ballads Of The Industrial North West)
Hand loom weaver's lament / Hop hop hop / Beg your leave / Ale is physic for me / Gettin' wed / Clogs / Merry little doffer / Rawtenstall annual fair / Coqlouse medley / Cob a coalin' / Seaur pies / Bury new loom / Ten per cent / Man like thee / Lancashire liar
CD TSCD 485
Topic / Jul '97 / ADA / CM / Direct

DEEP SOUTH BLUES PIANO 1935-1937
CD DOCD 5233
Document / May '94 / ADA / Hot Shot / Jazz Music

DEEPER INTO THE VAULT
CD CDMFN 124
Music For Nations / Nov '91 / Pinnacle

DEEPEST SHADE OF TECHNO VOL.1
CD REFCD 001
Reflective / Apr '94 / RTM/Disc / SRD

DEEPEST SOUL VOL.1
I'm lonely: *Sanders, Nelson* / You got me on a string: *Freeman Brothers* / You should have told me: *New Yorkers* / I'll be gone: *Turner, Tommy* / Just a little more love: *Soul Commanders* / Love as true as mine: *Rockays Band* / I've learned my lesson: *Richardson, Donald Lee* / Don't waste my time: *Sinceres* / Ain't gonna do you no good: *Willis, Betty* / These feelings: *Phil & Del* / Helpless girl: *Staten, Little Mary* / Whole lot of tears: *Stuart, Jeb* / Pick yourself up: *Taylor, E.G. & The Sound of Soul* / I'm still hurt: *Little Tom* / Human: *Ad Libs* / I worship the ground you walk on: *Ad Libs* / Teach me to love again: *Scott, Kurtis* / It won't hurt: *Bogen, Richard* / I'll be there: *Tenderonies* / Please come back: *Tate, Jimmy* / Make the best of what you've got: *Patton, Alexander* / I'm beggin' you baby: *Vibra-Tones & George Johnson* / Never let me go: *Vibra-Tones & George Johnson*
CD GSCD 016
Goldmine / Jul '93 / Vital

DEEPEST SOUL VOL.2
This beautiful day: *Jackson, Levi* / Serving a sentence of life: *Douglas, Carl* / Beautiful night: *Thomas, Jimmy* / What love brings: *Bernard, Kenny* / I'll hold you: *Frankie & Johnny* / Don't pity me: *Lynn, Sue* / Lost summer love: *Silva, Lorraine* / Our love is getting stronger: *Night, Jason* / Love is wonderful: *Parfit, Paula* / Stop and you'll become aware: *Shapiro, Helen* / Nobody knows: *St. John, Tammy* / Everything's gonna be alright: *Arnold, P.P.* / Invitation: *Band Of Angels* / If you knew me: *Keyes, Ebony* / Number one in your heart: *Goins, Herbie* / Need your love: *Notations* / Movin away: *Lynch, Kenny* / Baby I don't need your love: *Chants* / Stand accused: *Colton, Tony* / Never ever: *Clements, Soul Joe* / Tears of joy: *Merrell, Ray*
CD GSCD 041
Goldmine / Jan '95 / Vital

DEF JAM 10TH ANNIVERSARY BOX SET (4CD Set)
CD Set 5238482
Def Jam / Nov '95 / PolyGram

DEFENDERS OF THE OPPRESSED BREED (2CD Set)
CD Set VEG 001CD
Dolores / Mar '97 / Plastic Head

DEFINITION OF HARDCORE
CD RIVCD 3
Reinforced / Sep '93 / SRD

DEFINITIVE AMBIENT COLLECTION VOL.1
CD RSNCD 13
Rising High / Feb '94 / 3mv/Sony

DEFINITIVE BLUES
Boom boom: *Hooker, John Lee* / Whisky and wimmen: *Hooker, John Lee* / Time is marchin': *Hooker, John Lee* / Don't you remember me: *Hooker, John Lee* / Ain't nobody's business: *Witherspoon, Jimmy* / New Orleans woman: *Witherspoon, Jimmy* / No rolling blues: *Witherspoon, Jimmy* / Sweet lovin' baby: *Witherspoon, Jimmy* / Blowin' the fuse: *Hopkins, Lightnin'* / Don't need no job: *Hopkins, Lightnin'* / Chain gang blues: *Hopkins, Lightnin'* / Everybody's blue: *Hopkins, Lightnin'* / CC rider: *Leadbelly* / Baby don't you love me no more: *Leadbelly* / Matchbox blues: *Leadbelly* / Bourgeois blues: *Leadbelly* / Highway 49: *Howlin' Wolf* / Poor baby: *Howlin' Wolf* / Little red rooster: *Howlin' Wolf* / Wang dang doodle: *Howlin' Wolf*
CD SUMCD 4046
Summit / Nov '96 / Sound & Media

DEFINITIVE COLLECTION OF IRISH BALLADS VOL.1, A (2CD Set)
CD Set BALLAD 001CD
Outlet / Aug '94 / ADA / CM / Direct / Duncans / Koch / Ross

DEFINITIVE COLLECTION OF IRISH BALLADS VOL.2, A (2CD Set)
CD Set BALLAD 002CD
Outlet / Aug '94 / ADA / CM / Direct / Duncans / Koch / Ross

DEFINITIVE HOUSE FOR ALL
CD XTR 16CD
X-Treme / Jul '95 / Pinnacle / SRD

DEGUNG-MOJANG PRIANGAN (Sundanese Music Of West Java)
Mojang Priangan / Warung Pojok / Kedak Kesaha / Gupay Panjajab
CD SOW 90155
Sounds Of The World / Jan '97 / Target/BMG

DEL-FI AND DONNA STORY VOL.1, THE
Hippy hippy shake: *Romero, Chan* / I don't care now: *Romero, Chan* / I want some more: *Romero, Chan* / My little Ruby: *Romero, Chan* / That's my little Suzie: *Valens, Ritchie* / La Bamba: *Valens, Ritchie* / My babe: *Holden, Ron* / Love you so: *Holden, Ron* / Jungle fever: *Shadows* / Under stars of love: *Shadows* / Rumours: *Crawford, Johnny* / Proud: *Crawford, Johnny* / Little cupid: *Carlos Brothers* / Gonna see my baby: *Addrisi Brothers* / Cherrystone: *Addrisi Brothers* / Back to the old salt mine: *Addrisi Brothers* / Marie: *Dale, Dick* / Untouchables: *Hall, Rene* / Fast freight: *Valens, Ritchie* / Blabbermouth: *Fantastics* / Is it a dream: *Flamingo, Johnny* / When I do the mashed potato: *Bright, Larry* / Little more wine my dear: *Hawks* / To be loved (forever): *Pentagons* / Everything's gonna be alright: *Holden, Ron* / Please please please: *Ronnie & The Pomona Casuals* / Misirlou: *Lively Ones* / Big surf: *Sentinals* / Okie surfer: *Gates, David* / Original surferstomp: *Johnstone, Bruce* / KRLA jingle: *Surfettes*
CD CDCHD 313
Ace / Jul '91 / Pinnacle

DEL-FI AND DONNA STORY VOL.2, THE
Intro / Come on let's go: *Valens, Ritchie* / Alone and blue: *Addrisi Brothers* / Wild twist: *Roller Coasters* / For your love: *Romero, Chan* / She don't wanna dance (no more): *Little Caesar & The Romans* / Quiet as it's kept: *Nelson, Chip* / You're mine: *Flamingo, Johnny* / Fussy: *Hawks* / Big top: *Nitehawks* / Unjarro: *Addrisi Brothers* / Dancing in the sand: *Hollers, Wayne* / Watusi bongos: *Epps, Preston* / Seeing double: *Holden, Ron* / If I had my way: *Romero, Chan* / Sugar baby: *Romero, Chan* / Addrisi Brothers: *Romero, Chan* / Terror: *Grippers* / Rockin' Matilda: *Swags* / Summertime blues: *Valens, Ritchie* / Hippy hippy shake: *Romero, Chan* / Rock house party: *Romero, Chan* / Playboy: *Romero, Chan* / La Bamba: *Romero, Chan* / My little Ruby: *Romero, Chan* / Slauson sax: *Romancers* / Tell me: *Langford, Gerry* / Blowin' the blues: *Swags* / Betty Jean: *Little Caesar & The Romans* / True love can be: *Holden, Ron* / Walking alone: *Pentagons* / I want some more: *Romero, Chan*
CD CDCHD 489
Ace / Apr '94 / Pinnacle

DELETIONS VOL. 1
Surface noise: *Planetary Assault Systems* / Gruve: *Planetary Assault Systems* / Funk electric: *Planetary Assault Systems* / CVO trance: *Glenn Underground* / Seaquest: *Glenn Underground* / Cat NA thy trap: *Glenn Underground* / Summer funk: *Purveyors Of Fine Funk* / Z mood: *Purveyors Of Fine Funk* / Hot: *Purveyors Of Fine Funk* / Ashes smashing red: *Purveyors Of Fine Funk*

CD PFEC 01
Peacefrog / Jun '97 / Mo's Music Machine / Prime / RTM/Disc / Vital

DELIRIUM PRESENTS AFTER 6AM
CD DELACD 02
Delirium / Jan '94 / Arabesque / Plastic Head

DELIRIUM PRESENTS AFTER 6AM VOL.2
CD DELACD 03
Delirium / May '95 / Arabesque / Plastic Head

DELMARK 40TH ANNIVERSARY - BLUES
CD DXCD 2
Delmark / Aug '93 / ADA / Cadillac / CM / Direct / Hot Shot

DEMAGNETIZED
CD MAGNETCD 13
Magnetic North / Nov '95 / ADA / SRD

DENZ DA DENZ VOL.2
CD NL 609022
Basic Beat / Jun '97 / Arabesque / Intergroove

DER KLANG DER FAMILLE
CD NOMU 4CD
Nova Mute / Jul '92 / Prime / RTM/Disc

DESCENDENTS OF THE ITINERANT GYPSIES (Melodies Of Sorrow And Joy/ Hungary & Romania)
Khelimaski dyili / Meselaki dyili / Csardas / Funeral piece / Men's dance / Keserves / Dance piece / Wedding march / Flirtation dance for men and women
CD MCM 3010
Multicultural Media / May '97 / Direct

DESIGNER COLLECTION (2CD Set)
CD Set UMCD 001
United Dance / Oct '96 / Alphamagic / Mo's Music Machine / Pinnacle

DESPERATE DALLAS DEMOS (1950's Texas Rock & Roll)
CD NOHITCD 003
No Hit / Feb '97 / Cargo / SRD

DESPERATE ROCK 'N' ROLL VOL.1
CD FLAMECD 001
Flame / Jul '95 / Cargo / SRD

DESPERATE ROCK 'N' ROLL VOL.2
CD FLAMECD 002
Flame / Jul '95 / Cargo / SRD

DESPERATE ROCK 'N' ROLL VOL.3
CD FLAMECD 003
Flame / Jul '95 / Cargo / SRD

DESPERATE ROCK 'N' ROLL VOL.4
CD FLAMECD 004
Flame / Jul '95 / Cargo / SRD

DESPERATE ROCK 'N' ROLL VOL.5
CD FLAMECD 005
Flame / Sep '95 / Cargo / SRD

DESTINATION BOMP BOMP (2CD Set)
CD Set BCD 4048/2
Bomp/Blue Rose / Jul '96 / 3mv/Vital

DESTRUCTIVE URGES
CD BENT 009CD
Creeping Bent / May '96 / RTM/Disc

DETROIT 313
CD EFA 017922
Tresor / Apr '96 / 3mv/BMG / Prime / SRD

DETROIT SOUL FROM THE VAULTS VOL.1
Soul sloopy: *Dynamics* / Yes I love you baby: *Dynamics* / Head and shoulders: *Young, Patti* / Love keeps falling away: *Williams, Lloyd & Highlights* / It won't matter at all: *Williams, Lloyd & Highlights* / Arabia: *Royal Playboys* / What's wrong with your love (#2): *Metros* / Don't let her give you some of her love: *Metros* / It's real: *Sanders, Nelson* / Music in my soul: *Milner, Reggie* / Make a change: *Rogers, Johnny* / Soul food: *Rogers, Johnny* / Open the door to your heart: *Burdick, Doni* / I have faith in you: *Burdick, Doni* / Give my heart a break: *Turner, Sammy* / Fascinating girl: *Lemons, George* / We go to pieces: *Hairston, Forest* / Love to a guy: *Dynamics* / Keep a hold on me: *Lewis, Diane* / Kangaroo dance: *Williams, Lloyd & Highlights* / Opposites attract: *Swingers* / I'll be on my way: *Bob & Fred*
CD GSCD 019
Goldmine / Aug '93 / Vital

DETROIT SOUL FROM THE VAULTS VOL.2
Yes I love you baby: *Dynamics* / Head and shoulders: *Young, Patti* / I've got that feelin': *Garcia, Frankie* / Lovin' touch: *Satin Dolls* / First degree love: *Vaughan, Lafayette* / Arabia: *Royal Playboys* / What's wrong with your love (#1): *Metros* / We still have time: *Metros* / Candle: *Burdick, Doni* / What'cha gonna do: *Burdick, Doni* / Make a change (inst): *Rogers, Johnny* / Soul food: *Rogers, Johnny* / If you walk out of my life: *Burdick, Doni* / Bari track: *Burdick, Doni* / Merry go round: *Frontera, Tommy* / Fascinating girl: *Lemons, George* / We go to pieces: *Hairston, Forest* / Whenever I'm without you: *Dynamics* / Nobody likes me: *White, Willie* / Go down: *Highlights* / Lookin' for a woman: *Brooks Brothers* / I'll be on my way: *Bob & Fred*
CD GSCD 020
Goldmine / Aug '93 / Vital

DETROIT: BEYOND THE THIRD WAVE
Impolite to refuse: *Young, Claude* / Vortex: *Deason, Sean* / 8th wonder: *Kosmic Messenger* / Come on now baby: *K-Hand* / Sandblaster: *Shake* / Insert another data disk: *Ectomorph* / Life on tek: *Web, Will* / Solid signal: *DJ T1000* / Midnight hours: *Dixon, Terence* / Last trip: *Mode Selector*
CD ASW 6170
Astralwerks / May '96 / Cargo / Vital

DEUTSCHES JAZZ FESTIVAL 1954-1955 (8CD Set)
Jennie's ball: *2 Beat Stompers* / Flamingo: *Strasser, Hugo* / Fine and dandy: *Koller, Hans New Jazz Stars* / Just you, just me: *Edelhagen All Stars* / Is you is or is you ain't my baby: *Valente, Caterina* / I never knew: *Hipp, Jutta Combo* / Creole love call: *Bunge, Fred Star Band* / September song: *Kuhn, Rolf All Stars* / Jazz time rief: *Edelhagen, Kurt* / Paul's festival blues: *Kuhn, Paul Quartet* / Lullaby of Birdland: *Rediske, Johannes Quintet* / Klagita: *Schonberger, Heinz* / Festival jump: *Valente, Caterina* / Get out of here: *Spree City Stompers* / Just a blues: *Spree City Stompers* / Just a closer walk with thee: *Spree City Stompers* / St. James infirmary: *Spree City Stompers* / Eight bar blues: *Spree City Stompers* / That da da strain: *Spree City Stompers* / Mississippi mud: *2 Beat Stompers* / Got no blues: *2 Beat Stompers* / Panama: *2 Beat Stompers* / Black bottom blues: *2 Beat Stompers* / I'm confessin' that I love you: *2 Beat Stompers* / Music goes 'round and around: *2 Beat Stompers* / Manuskript blues: *Haensch, Delle Jump Combo* / Blue moon: *Haensch, Delle Jump Combo* / There's no one but you: *Haensch, Delle Jump Combo* / Hey good lookin': *Haensch, Delle Jump Combo* / Flamingo special: *Haensch, Delle Jump Combo* / There's no you: *Edelhagen, Kurt* / Big John special: *Edelhagen, Kurt* / You go to my head: *Edelhagen, Kurt* / Jazz 55: *Edelhagen, Kurt* / Nancy and the colonel: *Edelhagen, Kurt* / Light stuff: *Edelhagen, Kurt* / Stuff lover: *Edelhagen, Kurt* / Flying home: *Edelhagen, Kurt* / My funny valentine: *Edelhagen, Kurt* / I ain't gonna tell you: *Edelhagen, Kurt* / Don't blame me: *Edelhagen, Kurt* / T time: *Edelhagen, Kurt* / Purple hyazinth: *Edelhagen, Kurt* / All the things you are: *Francesco, Silvio Quartet* / Long journey: *Francesco, Silvio Quartet* / Ain't misbehavin': *Francesco, Silvio Quartet* / Lagwood walk: *Buschmann, Glen Quartet* / All of me: *Buschmann, Glen Quartet* / Farewell blues: *Buschmann, Glen Quartet* / St. Louis blues: *Buschmann, Glen Quartet* / Blue prelude: *Buschmann, Glen Quartet* / For you my love: *Buschmann, Glen Quartet* / Just one of those things: *Buschmann, Glen Quartet* / Shine: *Buschmann, Glen Quartet* / Embraceable you: *Buschmann, Glen Quartet* / Berlin blues: *Buschmann, Glen Quartet* / Too marvellous for words: *Kuhn, Rolf Quintet* / Frankfurt blues (now's the time): *Kuhn, Rolf Quintet* / Hipp noses: *Hipp, Jutta Quartet* / Song is you: *Hipp, Jutta Quartet* / Indian summer: *Hipp, Jutta Quartet* / Cool talk: *Hipp, Jutta Quartet* / These foolish things: *Hipp, Jutta Quartet* / Gone with the wind: *Hipp, Jutta Quartet* / Jutta: *Koller, Hans New Jazz Stars* / Iris: *Koller, Hans New Jazz Stars* / When your lover has gone: *Koller, Hans New Jazz Stars* / Porsche: *Koller, Hans New Jazz Stars* / Squeeze me: *Brandt, Helmut Combo* / Sum: *Brandt, Helmut Combo* / Breeze and I: *Brandt, Helmut Combo* / I can't believe that you're in love with me: *Brandt, Helmut Combo* / Out of nowhere: *Wenig, Erhard Quartet* / Tenor jump: *Wenig, Erhard Quartet* / September riff: *Wenig, Erhard Quartet* / Cynthia's in love: *Christmann, Freddy Quartet* / As long as there's music: *Christmann, Freddy Quartet* / First love: *Christmann, Freddy Quartet* / Passe: *Christmann, Freddy Quartet* / Theme in B: *Lauth, Wolfgang Quartet* / Tomorrow: *Lauth, Wolfgang Quartet* / Cool march: *Lauth, Wolfgang Quartet* / Cave souvenir: *Lauth, Wolfgang Quartet* / Jumpin' with Symphony Sid: *Lehn, Erwin* / Blues intermezzo: *Lehn, Erwin* / Gerry walks: *Lehn, Erwin* / Cool Street: *Lehn, Erwin* / Autumn nocturne: *Lehn, Erwin* / Conference mit mosch: *Lehn, Erwin* / What is this thing called love: *Lehn, Erwin* / Blues fur Tenorsaxophon: *Lehn, Erwin* / Lester leaps in: *Lehn, Erwin* / EVG: *Lehn, Erwin* / Indikativ: *Banter, Harald Ensemble* / Moon over Miami: *Banter, Harald Ensemble* / Autumn in New York: *Banter, Harald Ensemble* / Tabu jump: *Banter, Harald Ensemble* / Polyphona: *Banter, Harald Ensemble* / Nature boy: *Banter, Harald Ensemble* / Happy days are here again: *Banter, Harald Ensemble* / To dance or not to dance: *New Jazz Group Hannover* / I only have eyes for you: *New Jazz Group Hannover* / Lover man: *New Jazz Group Hannover* / Continuation: *New Jazz Group Hannover* / Cloe: *Rediske, Johannes Quintet* / Boptical illusion: *Rediske, Johannes Quintet* / Sweet Georgia Brown: *Rediske, Johannes Quintet* / Thou swell: *Kuhn, Paul Quintet* / Dancing in the dark: *Kuhn, Paul Quintet* / Delaunay's dilemma: *Rediske, Johannes Quintet* / Jumpin' at the rosengarten: *Rediske, Johannes Quintet* / Flip: *Rediske, Johannes Quintet* / I don't stand a ghost of a chance with you: *Rediske, Johannes Quintet* / Crazy rhythm: *Rediske, Johannes Quintet*
CD Set BCD 15430
Bear Family / Oct '90 / Direct / Rollercoaster / Swift

DEVIL'S OWN
CD TBCD 1204
Tommy Boy / Apr '97 / RTM/Disc

DEVOLUTION ALTERNATIVE ROCK CLASS
CD DEVOCD 1
Big Life / Mar '95 / Mo's Music Machine / Pinnacle / Prime

DEVOTED TO YOU (16 Songs From The Heart)
Crazy: *Cline, Patsy* / Some broken hearts never mend: *Williams, Don* / Happy anniversary: *Whitman, Slim* / Wheel of fortune: *Rose Marie* / She wears my ring: *King, Solomon* / Hurt: *Yuro, Timi* / With pen in hand: *Carr, Vikki* / Devoted to you: *Everly Brothers* / Sing me an old fashioned song: *Spears, Billie Jo* / Have I got some blues for you: *Pride, Charley* / I will love you all my life: *Foster & Allen* / Pal of my cradle days: *Breen, Ann* / When I leave the world behind: *Rose Marie* / I fall to pieces: *Cline, Patsy* / All I'm missing is you: *Williams, Don* / So sad (to watch good love go bad): *Everly Brothers* / Ebony eyes: *Everly Brothers* / Love hurts: *Everly Brothers*
CD PLATCD 21
Platinum / Apr '88 / Prism

DEWAR'S BAGPIPE FESTIVAL
CD KFWCD 133
Knitting Factory / Nov '94 / Cargo / Plastic Head

DIAL M FOR MERTHYR
CD NONG 02CD
Fierce Panda / Apr '97 / Shellshock/Disc

DIALOGUES
Frissell frazzle / Calypso Joe / Uncle Ed / Snowbound / Dream steps / Bon Ami / Stern stuff / Skylark / Simple things / Dialogue
CD CD 83369
Telarc / Nov '95 / Conifer/BMG

DIAMOND HIDDEN IN THE MOUTH OF A CORPSE, A
Won't change: *Husker Du* / Johnsonius: *Johansen, David* / Scum and slime: *Giorno, John Band* / President, Colonel Bradford, every man a god: *Burroughs, William S.* / Halloween: *Sonic Youth* / Dead man's shoes: *Cabaret Voltaire* / Eyes without blood: *Galas, Diamanda* / Neither his nor yours: *Coil* / Game: *Gira, Michael* / Out of the frying pan: *Van Tieghem, David* / Tenement lover: *Hagedorn, Jessica & The Gangster Choir*
CD VICD 011
Visionary/Jettisoundz / Apr '97 / Cargo / Pinnacle / RTM/Disc / THE

DIAMOND JUBILEE PIPE BAND CHAMPIONSHIPS
CD CDMON 809
Monarch / Sep '90 / ADA / CM / Direct / Duncans

DIE NOW VOL.1 (Engine/Blackout Sampler)
Not waving, drowning: *Sheer Terror* / Booze cabana: *Goops* / Running with scissors: *Deadguy* / Morning breath: *Sweet Diesel* / Faith healer: *Outcrowd* / Grounded ex-patriot: *New Bomb Turks* / I got your numbers: *Swinging Utters* / Wall of hate: *Killing Time* / Temple body: *Crawlpappy* / Hard way: *Outburst* / Harsh truth: *Icemen*
CD EB 024ECD
Engine / Aug '95 / Vital

DIE NOW VOL.2
Family tree: *H2O* / Empire strikes back: *Sweet Diesel* / Can't get around it: *Killing Time* / Death of a junkie: *Goops* / Beautiful wreck: *Fur* / Sell out: *Plow United* / Hardcore muscle and fitness: *Tub* / Righteous ruler: *Turbo AC's* / American soul spiders: *New Bomb Turks* / Evil: *Awkward thought* / Sitting around at home: *Gorilla Biscuits* / Ashes: *Sheer Terror* / Coming down: *Skin Candy*
CD BLK 5003ECD
Blackout / Jun '96 / Plastic Head / Vital

DIEHARD SAMPLER
CD PCD 24
Die Hard/Progress / Nov '96 / Plastic Head

DIFFERENT COLOURS OF DRUM AND BASS (2CD Set)
Razorback: *Deason, Sean* / Future reality part 1: *Deason, Sean* / Mood swing: *Dead Calm* / Sphing: *Dead Calm* / Nine miles deep: *Ronnie & Clyde* / Soul of darkness: *Omni Trio* / Mr. Bond: *Nicky Blackmarket & D-Lux* / Turn it up: *S-Man* / Wave: *Wallace, Dave* / Port Rhombus: *Squarepusher* / Tian Craxx: *Plastik & Feedback* / Rhode tune: *Flytronix* / DJ DManifest: *D-Lux* / King of the beats: *Amazon II* / Mash up yer know: *Aladdin* / Dred BWhat the time dred: *Dred Bass* / Dub plate circles: *Undercover Agent* / Jungle makes me: *Green Piece* / U down: *DJ Pulse & The Jazz Cartel* / Drop top: *Aphrodite & Mickey Finn*
CD Set 560142
Nova Tekk / Aug '97 / Pinnacle

DIG THE NU BREED
Contraflow: *Synchromesh* / Rattlesnake: *Scare-Electric* / Drifter: *Fruit Loop* / Who da fuck: *Semi-Detached Production* / Touching bass: *Tiny Stars* / Vanishin' point: *Tipper* / Sub zero: *Red Myers* / Daylight robbery: *Wide Receiver* / Big rock: *Barillo, Sloop John* / Dalai beats: *Mr. Natural*
CD WALLCD 012
Wall Of Sound / Mar '97 / Prime / Soul Trader / Vital

DIGGIN' DEEPER (2CD Set)
Pastime paradise: *Barretto, Ray* / Am I black enough for you: *Paul, Billy* / Cloud nine: *Santamaria, Mongo* / Also sprach zarathustra: *Deodato, Eumir* / Kissing my love: *Withers, Bill* / Home is where the hatred is: *Phillips, Esther* / So what: *Benson, George* / Right down here: *Puthli, Asha* / Love for a day: *Lewis, Ramsey* / Latin America: *Walton, Cedar* / In the park: *Smith, Lonnie Liston* / Consolacao: *Os Ipanemas* / Brazil: *Jobim, Antonio Carlos* / On the path: *Franklin, Rodney*
CD Set 4838992
Sony Jazz / Jul '96 / Sony

DIGGIN' DEEPER VOL.2
Superstrut: *Deodato, Eumir* / Sideman: *Smith, Lonnie* / Use me: *Phillips, Esther* / Living for the city: *Lewis, Ramsey* / I remember Wes: *Benson, George* / Lookin' good: *Gale, Eric* / Midnight at the oasis: *Hubbard, Freddie* / Ricky tick: *Santamaria, Mongo* / Berimbau: *Os Ipanemas* / Old castle: *Barretto, Ray* / Nunya: *Scott, Tom* / Sugar Loaf Mountain: *Duke, George* / Just around the corner: *Hancock, Herbie*
CD 4874782
Sony Jazz / Jun '97 / Sony

DIGGIN' IN THE CRATES (Profile Rap Classics Vol.1)
Sucker MC's (Krush-groove 1): *Run DMC* / King Kut: *Word Of Mouth & DJ Cheese* / Genius rap: *Dr. Jekyll & Mr. Hyde* / Drag rap: *Showboys* / Fly guy: *Pebblee-Poo* / I can't wait (To rock the mike): *Spyder D & DJ Doc* / Beat bop: *Rammelzee & K-Rob* / Here comes that beat: *Pumpkin & The Profile All Stars* / Rock box: *Run DMC* / Lifestyles Of The Fresh And Fly: *MC Dollar Bill* / Fresh: *Fresh 3 MC's* / Nightmares: *Dane, Dana*
CD FILERCD 449
Profile / Jun '94 / Pinnacle

DIGNITY OF HUMAN BEING IS VULNERABLE
CD AWA 1993CD
Konkurrel / May '93 / SRD

DIMENSION VOL.2
CD EFA 200872
Trip Trap / Jul '95 / SRD

DIMENSIONE JAZZ
CD RTCL 810CD
Right Tempo / Jul '96 / New Note/ Pinnacle / Timewarp

DINNER AT EIGHT (The Great London Dance Bands)
Dancing in the dark / Without rhythm / This'll make you whistle / Honey coloured moon / Star fell out of heaven / You turned the tables on me / You / I won't dance / It's easy to remember / Dinner at eight / My romance / Zing, went the strings of my heart / One, two, button your shoe / Toy trumpet / Soft lights and sweet music / Alone / Nice work if you can get it / When you've got a little springtime in your heart / Tinkle, tinkle, tinkle / Over my shoulder / Not bad / Here's to the next time / Auf wiedersehen, my dear / Smoke gets in your eyes / Keep a twinkle in your eye
CD PLCD 539
President / Oct '95 / Grapevine/PolyGram / President / Target/BMG

DINNER JAZZ
CD MUSCD 024
MCI Music / Nov '94 / Disc / THE

DINNER JAZZ AMERICAN CLASSICS
CD JAZZFMCD 1
Jazz FM / Oct '96 / Beechwood/BMG

DIRE TEMPO
CD RTCL 803CD
Right Tempo / Jul '96 / New Note/ Pinnacle / Timewarp

DIRECT HITS FROM BULLSEYE
CD BB 9001CD
Bullseye Blues / May '93 / Direct

DIRECTION
CD POLYVINYL 5CD
Polyvinyl / Nov '96 / Cargo

DIRECTION AFRICA (A Collection Of African Grooves From Celluloid)
CD CDNEW 106
Charly / Apr '97 / Koch

DIRTY HOUSE VOL.1
Indoctrinate: *Castle Trancelot* / Don't stop my beat: *Trigger* / Disco's revenge: *Gusto Love* / Danger zone: *Dangerous Society* / Rhythm graffitt: *Crime* / Things I like: *Aaliyah* / Driftwood: *Foot Club* / Shake your booty: *Ill Disco* / Rollerskate disco: *Pooley, Ian* / I just can't go: *Space Warlock* / Turn me on:

Brown, Kathy / Never be the same: *Northbound* / I think about you: *King, Evelyn 'Champagne'*
CD ____ CDHIGH 2
High On Rhythm / Nov '95 / 3mv/Sony

DIRTY HOUSE VOL.2 (14 Tough Euro/ US/UK House Anthems - Mixed By DJ Bambach)
All of me: *Brunson, Tyrone & Chanelle* / On my knees: *Skiffle* / Satisfied: *H2O & Billie* / America: *Full Intention* / Work it out: *RIP Productions* / Screamer: *Yosh & Lovedeejay Akemi* / Feel good: *B-Code* / Jump for joy: *2 Unlimited* / Drop: *Mr. Whippy* / Wanna drop a house (on that bitch): *Urban Discharge & She* / I get high: *Upstate* / Remember me: *Jubb, Phil* / VII: *XVX* / Up and down: *D&T*
CD ____ CDHIGH 3
High On Rhythm / Jun '96 / 3mv/Sony

DIRTY ROCK VOL.1
CD ____ KNEWCD 736
Kenwest / Apr '94 / THE

DIRTY ROCK VOL.2
CD ____ KNEWCD 737
Kenwest / Apr '94 / THE

DISAGREEMENT OF THE PEOPLE, THE
Ain't but just one way: *Cope, Julian* / Justice/Injustice: *Chumbawamba* / Guildford Four: *White, Andy* / Won't get fooled away: *McNabb, Ian* / Birmingham six: *Pogues* / All our trades: *Tabor, June* / How can you keep moving on: *McLeod, Rory* / Electro Ray's: *Back To The Planet* / Hobo: *Reservoir Frogs* / Men of England: *New Model Army & Joolz* / One green hill: *Oyster Band* / Babylon: *Det-Ri-Mental* / Clay jugg: *Leven, Jackie & Mike Scott* / Stonehenge: *Poison Girls* / Pastor Niemoler's lament (Never Again): *Kitchens Of Distinction* / Come dancing: *Credit To The Nation* / This land: *Bragg, Billy*
CD ____ COOKCD 088
Cooking Vinyl / Jun '95 / Vital

DISAPPEARING WORLD, THE
CD ____ CDSDL 376
Saydisc / Mar '94 / ADA / Direct / Harmonia Mundi

DISCLOSURE - VOICES OF WOMEN
CD ____ NAR 067CD
New Alliance / May '93 / Plastic Head

DISCO BISCUITS
CD ____ HF 52CD
PWL / Mar '97 / Warner Music

DISCO CLASSICS (2CD Set)
Going back to my roots: *Odyssey* / Shake your body: *Jacksons* / Funkytown: *Lipps Inc.* / Family affair: *Sly & The Family Stone* / September: *Earth, Wind & Fire* / Boogie nights: *Heatwave* / Never can say goodbye: *Gaynor, Gloria* / Lady Marmalade: *Labelle* / Jump to it: *Franklin, Aretha* / Night to remember: *Shalamar* / Love come down: *King, Evelyn 'Champagne'* / You make me feel (mighty real): *Sylvester* / I can't stand the rain: *Eruption* / Can you feel the force: *Real Thing* / System addict: *Five Star* / Automatic: *Pointer Sisters* / Shame: *King, Evelyn 'Champagne'* / Theme from Shaft: *Hayes, Isaac* / You're the first, my last, my everything: *White, Barry* / Disco nights: *GQ* / Low rider: *War* / I can make you feel good: *Shalamar* / Sing a simple song: *Sly & The Family Stone* / Dare me: *Pointer Sisters* / And the beat goes on: *Whispers* / Use it up, wear it up: *Odyssey* / Love really hurts without you: *Ocean, Billy* / Contact: *Starr, Edwin* / Ms. grace: *Tymes* / Giving up, giving in: *Three Degrees* / Is this a love thing: *Raydio* / Morning dance: *Spyro Gyra* / Rivers of Babylon: *Boney M* / You're more than a number in my little red book: *Drifters* / Rock the boat: *Hues Corporation* / Yes sir I can boogie: *Baccara*
CD Set ____ RCACD 206
RCA / Jul '97 / BMG

DISCO COLLECTION (3CD Set)
I will survive: *Gaynor, Gloria* / I wanna get next to you: *Rose Royce* / Beat goes on: *Dells* / Who loves you: *Four Seasons* / Saddle up: *Christie, David* / Fly Robin fly: *Silver Convention* / Doctor's orders: *Douglas, Carol* / Get ready: *Temptations* / Feels like I'm in love: *Marie, Kelly* / On the run (the battle is over): *Ocean, Billy* / Dancing in the street: *Reeves, Martha & The Vandellas* / Shake it, shake it: *Whispers* / Singing in the rain: *Taco* / Show and tell: *Wilson, Al* / I'm in the mood for dancing: *Nolans* / Come on in love: *White, Barry* / Dance little lady dance: *Charles, Tina* / Harmony, perfect harmony: *Four Seasons* / Dancing Queen: *Douglas, Carol* / I wish it would rain: *Temptations* / Wishing on a star: *Rose Royce* / Jimmy Mack: *Reeves, Martha & The Vandellas* / Needle in a haystack: *Whispers* / Living it up: *Christie, David* / Disco kid: *First Class* / Puttin' on the ritz: *Taco* / Clapping song: *Humphries, Les Singers* / Out of the shadows of love: *White, Barry* / You can get it if you really want: *Dekker, Desmond* / Don't take away the music: *Tavares* / Boogie oogie oogie: *Dells* / Thank you Mr. DJ: *Silver Convention* / Get up and boogie: *Silver Convention* / Ain't no stopping us now: *Dells* / Attention to me: *Nolans* / December '63 (oh what a night): *Four Seasons* / More, more, more: *True, Andrea Connection* / Dance dance dance: *Humphries, Les Singers* / For once in my life: *Dekker, Desmond* / Rock your baby: *McCrae, George* / I love to love: *Charles, Tina* / Night fever: *Douglas, Carol* / Car wash: *Rose Royce* / Heatwave: *Reeves, Martha & The Vandellas* / It only takes a minute: *Tavares* / Be my baby: *Svenne & Lotta* / Dr. Love: *Whispers* / I owe it all to you: *White, Barry*
CD Set ____ 101032
CMC / May '97 / BMG

DISCO COLLECTION VOL.1 (I Will Survive)
I will survive: *Gaynor, Gloria* / I wanna get next to you: *Rose Royce* / Beat goes on: *Dells* / Who loves you: *Four Seasons* / Saddle up: *Christie, David* / Fly Robin fly: *Silver Convention* / Doctor's orders: *Douglas, Carol* / Get ready: *Temptations* / Feels like I'm in love: *Marie, Kelly* / On the run (the battle is over): *Ocean, Billy* / Dancing in the street: *Reeves, Martha & The Vandellas* / Shake it shake it: *Whispers* / Singing in the rain: *Taco* / Show and tell: *Wilson, Al* / I'm in the mood for dancing: *Nolans* / Come on in love: *White, Barry*
CD ____ 101042
CMC / May '97 / BMG

DISCO COLLECTION VOL.2 (Dance Little Lady Dance)
Dance little lady dance: *Charles, Tina* / Harmony perfect harmony: *Four Seasons* / Dancing Queen: *Douglas, Carol* / I wish it would rain: *Temptations* / Wishing on a star: *Rose Royce* / Jimmy Mack: *Reeves, Martha & The Vandellas* / Needle in a haystack: *Whispers* / Living it up: *Christie, David* / Disco kid: *First Class* / Puttin' on the ritz: *Taco* / Clapping song: *Humphries, Les Singers* / Out of the shadows of love: *White, Barry* / You can get it if you really want: *Dekker, Desmond* / Don't take away the music: *Tavares* / Boogie oogie oogie: *Dells* / Thank you Mr. DJ: *Silver Convention*
CD ____ 101052
CMC / May '97 / BMG

DISCO COLLECTION VOL.3 (Get Up & Boogie)
Get up and boogie: *Silver Convention* / Ain't no stopping us now: *Dells* / Attention to me: *Nolans* / December '63 (oh what a night): *Four Seasons* / More more more: *True, Andrea Connection* / Dance dance dance: *Humphries, Les Singers* / For once in my life: *Dekker, Desmond* / Rock your baby: *McCrae, George* / I love to love: *Charles, Tina* / Night fever: *Douglas, Carol* / Car wash: *Rose Royce* / Heatwave: *Reeves, Martha & The Vandellas* / It only takes a minute: *Tavares* / Be my baby: *Svenne & Lotta* / Dr. Love: *Whispers* / I owe it all to you: *White, Barry*
CD ____ 101062
CMC / May '97 / BMG

DISCO DANCE CATS
CD ____ 12547
Laserlight / Jul '95 / Target/BMG

DISCO DAZE
CD ____ MATCD 261
Castle / May '93 / BMG

DISCO DEATH RACE 2000
CD ____ MM 800452
Moonshine / Apr '96 / Mo's Music Machine / Prime / RTM/Disc

DISCO EXPLOSION
CD ____ GRF 211
Tring / Apr '93 / Tring

DISCO FEVER (4CD Set)
Feels like I'm in love: *Marie, Kelly* / Dance little lady dance: *Charles, Tina* / Rock your baby: *McCrae, George* / Kung fu fighting: *Douglas, Carl* / Cuba: *Gibson Brothers* / I wanna dance wit choo: *Disco Tex & The Sexolettes* / Boys: *Sabrina* / Summer of '42: *Biddu Orchestra* / High energy: *Thomas, Evelyn* / Love I lost, The: *Melvin, Harold & The Bluenotes* / More more more: *True, Andrea* / Hey there, lonely girl: *Holman, Eddie* / Reach out I'll be there: *Gaynor, Gloria* / Now is the time: *James, Jimmy & The Vagabonds* / Hands up: *Ottawan* / You little trustmaker: *Tymes* / So many men, so little time: *Brown, Miquel* / Runner, The: *Three Degrees* / My hearts beating wild (tic tac tic tac): *Gibson Brothers* / Hold back the night: *Trammps* / DISCO: *Ottawan* / I'm on fire: *5000 Volts* / Boogie nights: *Heatwave* / On a crowded street: *Pennington, Barbara* / I will survive: *Gaynor, Gloria* / It's been so long: *McCrae, George* / Ooh what a life: *Gibson Brothers* / All of me: *Sabrina* / Rain forest: *Biddu Orchestra* / He's a saint, he's a sinner: *Brown, Miquel* / Hey girl don't bother me: *Tams* / Disco fever: *James, Jimmy & The Vagabonds* / Look back over your shoulder: *Bell, Archie & The Drells* / Love's gone mad: *Seventh Avenue* / Wake up everybody: *Melvin, Harold & The Bluenotes* / My simple heart: *Three Degrees* / If you want it (do it yourself): *Gaynor, Gloria* / Fairytales: *Charles, Tina* / Latin america: *Gibson Brothers* / Dance the kung fu: *Douglas, Carl* / I love to love: *Charles, Tina* / Better do it salsa: *Gibson Brothers* / Saddle up: *Christie, David* / I am what I am: *Gaynor, Gloria* / Get dancin': *Disco Tex & The Sexolettes* / Fan the flame: *Pennington, Barbara* / Always and forever: *Heatwave* / You're ok: *Ottawan* / Run back: *Douglas, Carl* / Close to perfection: *Brown, Miquel* / I can't leave you alone: *McCrae, George* / Love really hurts without you: *Ocean, Billy* / Satisfaction guaranteed: *Melvin, Harold & The Bluenotes* / Don't stop till you get enough: *Ashaye* / You to me are everything: *Real Thing* / My claim to fame: *Wells, James* / Treat her like a lady: *Cornelius Brothers* / Masquerade: *Thomas, Evelyn* / Trippin' on a soul cloud: *Biddu Orchestra* / Dancin' on a Saturday night: *Blue, Barry* / Ring my bell: *Ward, Anita* / Que sera mi vida: *Gibson Brothers* / Love train: *Three Degrees & Harold Melvin* / Stress: *Christie, David* / Can't take my eyes off you: *Gaynor, Gloria* / Do it any way you wanna: *People's Choice* / Metropolis: *Gibson Brothers* / Heartless: *Thomas, Evelyn* / If you don't know me by now: *Melvin, Harold & The Bluenotes* / Help me get some help: *Ottawan* / Hey girl: *James, Jimmy & The Vagabonds* / Reaching for the best: *Exciters* / Twenty four hours a day: *Pennington, Barbara* / Mariana: *Gibson Brothers* / Reflections: *Thomas, Evelyn* / Doctor's orders: *Sabrina* / Love I lost: *Seventh Avenue* / When will I see you again: *Three Degrees* / I'll go where the music takes me: *James, Jimmy & The Vagabonds* / Never can say goodbye: *Gaynor, Gloria*
CD Set ____ TFP 031
Tring / Jan '95 / Tring

DISCO FEVER (18 All-Time Dancefloor Favourites)
Feels like I'm in love: *Marie, Kelly* / Hang on in there baby: *Bristol, Johnny* / I will survive: *Gaynor, Gloria* / Feel the need in me: *Detroit Emeralds* / Band of gold: *Payne, Freda* / Rock your baby: *McCrae, George* / You little trustmaker: *Tymes* / Heaven must have sent you: *Elgins* / Harlem shuffle: *Bob & Earl* / High energy: *Thomas, Evelyn* / Nathan Jones: *Supremes* / Going back to my roots: *Odyssey* / More, more, more: *True, Andrea* / Hey girl don't bother me: *Tams* / Knock on wood: *Floyd, Eddie* / Ring my bell: *Ward, Anita* / Heaven must be missing an angel: *Tavares* / Frankie: *Sister Sledge*
CD ____ ECD 3257
K-Tel / Feb '97 / K-Tel

DISCO FOX VOL.4
CD ____ ZYX 810912
ZYX / Feb '97 / ZYX

DISCO GENERATION (2CD Set)
Don't let me be misunderstood: *Santa Esmerelda* / Move your feet: *Hithouse* / Motorcity mix: *Beatsamatic* / Living on video: *Trans X* / Let's all chant: *Zager, Michael* / Walk in the park: *Straker, Nick* / Let your love flow: *Bellamy Brothers* / Love is in the air: *Young, John Paul* / Knock on wood: *Stewart, Amii* / I'm on fire: *5000 Volts* / Dreams are ten a penny: *Kincaid* / Under the moon of love: *Showaddywaddy* / I'm the leader of the gang: *Glitter, Gary* / Kung fu fighting: *Douglas, Carl* / Typically tropical: *Barbados* / Two man sound: *Brown, Charlie* / Paloma blanca: *Baker, George Selection* / Bino: *Mama Leone* / Live is life: *Opus* / Rain in May: *Werner, Max* / Jeans on: *Dundas, David* / Get down: *O'Sullivan, Gilbert* / Substitute: *Clout* / Standing in the rain: *Young, John Paul* / Love me like a lover: *Charles, Tina* / Disco stomp: *Bohannon* / Miss Broadway: *Belle Epoque* / Fire in the night: *Hotshots* / Dance all night: *Block* / Yes sir I can boogie: *Baccara* / Ooh, yes I do: *Luv* / Sun of Jamaica: *Goombay Dance Band* / It's a heartache: *Tyler, Bonnie* / More than I can say: *Sayer, Leo* / Train to yesterday: *Christie, Tony* / Tried so hard: *Outsiders*
CD Set ____ 24345
Laserlight / Feb '97 / Target/BMG

DISCO INFERNO
I wanna dance wit' choo: *Disco Tex & The Sexolettes* / Ring my bell: *Ward, Anita* / I will survive: *Gaynor, Gloria* / Kung fu fighting: *Douglas, Carl* / Dance little lady dance: *Charles, Tina* / Rain forest: *Biddu Orchestra* / I'll go where your music takes me: *James, Jimmy & The Vagabonds* / Hold back the night: *Trammps* / Reaching for the best: *Exciters* / (Dancing) on a Saturday night: *Blue, Barry* / Saddle up: *Christie, David* / Band of gold: *Payne, Freda* / Run back: *Douglas, Carl* / I love to love (but my baby just loves to dance): *Charles, Tina* / Love really hurts without you: *Ocean, Billy* / Boogie nights: *Heatwave*
CD ____ QED 048
Tring / Nov '96 / Tring

DISCO INFERNO VOL.1
Lost in music: *Sister Sledge* / Le Freak: *Chic* / You make me feel (Mighty real): *Sylvester* / I'm every woman: *Khan, Chaka* / Young hearts run free: *Staton, Candi* / Is it love you're after: *Rose Royce* / Jump to the beat: *Lattisaw, Stacy* / Working my way back to you: *Detroit Spinners* / Here I go again: *Bell, Archie* / Supernature: *Cerrone* / Disco Inferno: *Trammps* / dance, dance, dance: *Chic* / Nights on Broadway: *Staton, Candi* / Lover's holiday: *Change* / I shoulda loved ya: *Walden, Narada Michael* / Then came you: *Warwick, Dionne & The Detroit Spinners* / Spacer: *Sheila B. Devotion* / Searching: *Change* / We are family: *Sister Sledge* / Shaft: *Hayes, Isaac*
CD ____ 9548319632
East West / Jul '95 / Warner Music

DISCO INFERNO VOL.2
Shame: *King, Evelyn 'Champagne'* / Funkin' for Jamaica: *Browne, Tom* / Thinking of you: *Sister Sledge* / Native New Yorker: *Odyssey* / I'll be around: *Detroit Spinners* / Keep the fire burning: *McCrae, Gwen* / Love has come around: *Byrd, Donald* / You're a star: *Aquarian Dream* / Southern Freeez: *Freeez* / He's the greatest dancer: *Sister Sledge* / Everybody dance: *Chic* / It makes you feel like dancin': *Rose Royce* / Just a touch of love: *Slave* / Glow of love: *Change* / Ghetto child: *Detroit Spinners* / Funky nassau: *Beginning Of The End* / Get up and boogie: *Silver Convention* / Funky sensation: *McCrae, Gwen* / Forget me nots: *Rushen, Patrice*
CD ____ 9548324232
East West / Dec '93 / Warner Music

DISCO MIX '96 (2CD Set)
CD Set ____ 9548348072
Warner Bros. / Oct '96 / Warner Music

DISCO MIXES
CD ____ JHD 087
Tring / Mar '93 / Tring

DISCO NIGHTS
Disco nights: *GQ* / Car wash: *Rose Royce* / Boogie wonderland: *Earth, Wind & Fire* / Rock the boat: *Hues Corporation* / Use it up wear it out: *Odyssey* / Turn the beat around: *Robinson, Vickie Sue* / Ms. Grace: *Tymes* / Which way is up: *Starguard* / Shame: *King, Evelyn* / Instant replay: *Hartman, Dan* / Hi fidelity: *Kids from Fame* / Daddy cool: *Boney M* / One way ticket: *Eruption* / Givin' up givin' in: *Three Degrees* / You're more than a number in my little red book: *Drifters* / Disco lady: *Taylor, Johnny* / Everybody up: *Ohio Players* / YMCA: *Village People*
CD ____ 74321290382
Ariola / Feb '97 / BMG

DISCO PARTY
That's the way I like it: *KC & The Sunshine Band* / Dance across the floor: *Horne, Jimmy 'Bo'* / One for you one for me: *La Bionda* / Heaven must be missing an angel: *Tavares* / This is my life: *Bassey, Shirley* / Get off: *Foxy* / Hot shot: *Young, Karen* / Ring my bell: *Ward, Anita* / Follow me: *Lear, Amanda* / Saddle up: *Christie, David* / Gonna get along without you now: *Wills, Viola* / Can you feel the force: *Real Thing* / Let's all chant: *Zager, Michael Band* / Feels like I'm in love: *Marie, Kelly* / Do it: *BT Express* / Swing your daddy: *Gilstrap, Jim*
CD ____ DC 880272
Disky / Jul '97 / Disky / THE

DISCO SEXY (2CD Set)
I can make you feel good: *Shalamar* / Shame, shame, shame: *Shirley & Company* / Red light spells danger: *Ocean, Billy* / Think I'm gonna fall in love with you: *Dooleys* / Smarty pants: *First Choice* / Contact: *Starr, Edwin* / Hold on to my love: *Ruffin, Jimmy* / Mr. Tamborine man: *Johnson, Johnny & Bandwagon* / Love I lost: *Melvin, Harold & The Bluenotes* / Yes sir I can boogie: *Baccara* / I'm gonna run away from you: *Lynn, Tammi* / Everybody plays the fool: *Main Ingredient* / Spacer: *Sheila B. Devotion* / Sound of Philadelphia: *MFSB* / More, more, more: *True, Andrea Connection* / Everything's Tuesday: *Chairmen Of The Board* / New York, New York: *Kenny, Gerard* / Jump to the beat: *Lattisaw, Stacy* / Let's go round again: *Average White Band* / Hallelujah freedom: *Campbell, Junior* / Funkytown: *Lipps Inc.* / Hustle: *McCoy, Van* / Nights on Broadway: *Staton, Candi* / Queen of the rapping scene: *Modern Romance* / Pillow talk: *Sylvia* / Lincoln county: *Love Affair* / La la means I love you: *Delfonics* / You're more than a number in my little red book: *Drifters* / Baby blue: *Springfield, Dusty* / Jack and Jill: *Raydio* / I love to love (but my baby just loves to dance): *Charles, Tina* / All I have to do is dream: *Matthews, Al* / It's up to you Petula: *Edison Lighthouse* / Feel the need in me: *Detroit Emeralds* / Candida: *Dawn* / Come back and shake me: *Rodgers, Clodagh* / Galaxy of love: *Crown Heights Affair* / Mind blowing decisions: *Heatwave* / Intuition: *Linx* / Jack in the box: *Moments*
CD Set ____ 3036400292
Carlton / Mar '97 / Carlton

DISCO SUBVERSION (2CD Set)
CD Set ____ FIM 1020
Force Inc. / May '96 / Amato Disco / Arabesque / SRD

DISCO SUCKS
CD ____ CHE 60CD
Che / Jul '96 / SRD

DISCO TECH
Papillon: *Vandross, Luther & Cissy Houston* / More, more, more (parts 1 & 2): *Andrea True Connection & Samantha Fox* / Paradise diamond: *Vandross, Luther & Cissy Houston* / Chain diamonds: *Vandross, Luther & Cissy Houston* / Cream always rises to the top diamond: *Vandross, Luther & Cissy Houston* / More, more ,more (part 3): *Bananarama* / Hot butterfly: *Khan, Chaka* / Risky changes diamond: *Bionic Boogie* / Starcruiser diamond: *Starcruiser Band* / Fancy dancer diamond: *Starcruiser Band* / Tiger, tiger: *Vandross, Luther & Cissy Houston* / Crazy luck diamond: *Vandross, Luther* / Most of all diamond: *Gaynor, Gloria*
CD ____ CDPS 001
Pulsar / Sep '95 / TKO Magnum

DISCO-VERED
CD ______ **ALMYCD 21**
Almighty / Aug '97 / Total/BMG

DISCOVER NARADA
From the forge to the field: *Arkenstone, David & Kostia/David Lanz* / Day by day by day: *Mann, Brian* / Americana: *Rubaja, Bernardo* / Behind the waterfall/Desert rain: *Lanz, David* / Rug merchant: *Arkenstone, David* / Millennium theme: *Zimmer, Hans* / Seven days: *Kolbe, Martin* / Parterre: *Tingstad, Eric & Nancy Rumbel* / Simple joys: *Souther, Richard* / Overture: *Mirowitz, Sheldon* / Lament for Hetch Hetchy: *Fraser, Alasdair* / New Amazon: *Junior Homrich* / Stand and water: *Kostia* / Nebraska: *Buffett, Peter* / Hawk: *Trapezoid* / Endings: *Jones, Michael*
CD ______ **CD 9002**
Narada / Jun '92 / ADA / New Note/ Pinnacle

DISCOVER NARADA VOL.2
CD ______ **ND 69008**
Narada / Nov '93 / ADA / New Note/ Pinnacle

DISCOVER SCOTLAND VOL.1
Original: *Carmichael, John & His Band* / Kathleen's reel: *Carmichael, John & His Band* / Bauaria: *Carmichael, John & His Band* / Dixie: *Carmichael, John & His Band* / Do you think you could love me again: *MacLeod, Jim & His Band* / Skye boat song: *Scott, Tommy Strings of Scot* / Richmora: *Oakbank Sound* / Pomander jig: *Oakbank Sound* / Wee sergeant: *Oakbank Sound* / Rab Smillies JG: *Oakbank Sound* / Maggie: *Gillies, Alasdair* / Silver darlin': *Marlettes* / Marie's wedding: *Garden, Bill & His Highland Fiddle Orchestra* / Vist tramping songs: *Garden, Bill & His Highland Fiddle Orchestra* / Marquis of Huntly: *Garden, Bill & His Highland Fiddle Orchestra* / Roxburgh Castle: *Garden, Bill & His Highland Fiddle Orchestra* / Scotland the brave: *Garden, Bill & His Highland Fiddle Orchestra* / From Scotland with love: *Scott, Tommy Strings of Scot* / Wild mountain thyme: *Marlettes* / Marching through the heather: *Frazer, Grant* / Johnny lad: *Frazer, Grant* / Flower of Scotland: *Frazer, Grant* / Jig time: *Garden, Bill & His Highland Fiddle Orchestra* / McFlannels: *Garden, Bill & His Highland Fiddle Orchestra* / Para Handy: *Garden, Bill & His Highland Fiddle Orchestra* / Man's a man for a' that: *Harper, Addie & The Wick Trio* / Scots wha hae: *Harper, Addie & The Wick Trio* / Auld lang syne: *Harper, Addie & The Wick Trio* / I love a lassie: *Anderson, Stuart* / Roamin' in the gloamin': *Anderson, Stuart* / Wee Deoch an' Doris: *Anderson, Stuart* / Stop your ticklin' Jock: *Anderson, Stuart* / Keep right on to the end of the road: *Anderson, Stuart* / Denny and Dunipace Pipe Band: *Denny & Dunipace Pipe Band* / Major Bobby: *Denny & Dunipace Pipe Band* / Muckin' o' Geordie's byre: *Denny & Dunipace Pipe Band* / Glendaurel highlanders: *Denny & Dunipace Pipe Band* / Bonnie Dundee: *Denny & Dunipace Pipe Band*
CD ______ **CDITV 428**
Scotdisc / Aug '88 / Conifer/BMG / Duncans / Ross

DISCOVERED '97
CD ______ **SUGA 14CD**
Sugar / May '97 / RTM/Disc

DISTANCE TO ACID TRANCE VOL.1
CD ______ **DI 192**
Distance / Dec '95 / 3mv/Sony / Prime

DISTANCE TO ACID TRANCE VOL.2
CD ______ **SUB 48102**
Distance / Jul '96 / 3mv/Sony / Prime

DISTANCE TO GOA VOL.1
CD ______ **DI 152**
Distance / Dec '95 / 3mv/Sony / Prime

DISTANCE TO GOA VOL.2
CD ______ **DI 172**
Distance / Dec '95 / 3mv/Sony / Prime

DISTANCE TO GOA VOL.3 (2CD Set)
CD Set ______ **SUB 48022**
Distance / Mar '96 / 3mv/Sony / Prime

DISTANCE TO GOA VOL.4
CD ______ **SUB 48169**
Distance / Jul '96 / 3mv/Sony / Prime

DISTANCE TO GOA VOL.5 (2CD Set)
Deranger: *Hallucinogen* / Stardiver: *Electric Universe* / Phenomena: *Miranda* / Wizard: *Deedrah* / Lepton Head: *Shakta* / Land of freedom: *Transwave* / Dreampod: *Psychopod* / Hybrid: *Eat Static* / Walk on the moon: *Antidote* / Spiral spit trick: *Katayama* / Chitty bang: *Ololluqut* / Liquid: *Orion* / Free return: *Alienated* / Simplicity: *Project System* / I wanna expand: *Cwithe* / Radio SPACE: *Electric Universe* / Malaka dance: *Transwave* / Alien pets: *Prana* / SPQR: *Shiva Chandra* / Reefer madness: *Lunar Asylum*
CD Set ______ **SUB 48352**
Distance / Apr '97 / 3mv/Sony / Prime

DISTANCE TO HAPPY TRANCE - THE ENERGISER
CD ______ **DI 232**
Distance / Dec '95 / 3mv/Sony / Prime

DISTANCE TO TECHNOLAND (2CD Set)
CD Set ______ **SUB 48179**
Distance / Nov '96 / 3mv/Sony / Prime

DISTORTION TO HELL
CD ______ **DISTCD 5**
Distortion / Oct '94 / Plastic Head

DISTORTION TO HELL AGAIN
CD ______ **DISTCD 16**
Distortion / Feb '96 / Plastic Head

DISTURB MY SOUL (Gospel From Stax Records' Chalice Label)
Assassination: *Dixie Nightingales* / Nail print: *Dixie Nightingales* / Hush hush: *Dixie Nightingales* / He's a friend of mine: *Jubilee Hummingbirds* / Our freedom song: *Jubilee Hummingbirds* / All I need is some sunshine in my life: *Dixie Nightingales* / I don't know: *Dixie Nightingales* / All these things to me: *Stars Of Virginia* / Wade in the water: *Stars Of Virginia* / God's promise: *Pattersonaires* / I learned to pray: *Pattersonaires* / Stop laughing at your fellow man: *Jubilee Hummingbirds* / Jesus will fix it: *Jubilee Hummingbirds* / This is our prayer: *Dixie Nightingales* / It comes at the end of the race: *Dixie Nightingales* / He's worthy: *Pattersonaires* / Child of God: *Pattersonaires* / Till Jesus comes: *Pattersonaires* / Give me one more chance: *Jubilee Hummingbirds* / Press my dying pillow: *Jubilee Hummingbirds* / There's not a friend: *Dixie Nightingales* / Forgive these fools: *Dixie Nightingales* / Son of God: *Stars Of Virginia* / Even me: *Stars Of Virginia*
CD ______ **CDSXD 086**
Stax / Feb '94 / Pinnacle

DIVA X MACHINA
CD ______ **COPCD 027**
Cop International / May '97 / Cargo

DIVANA (Music Of Rajasthan Vol.2)
CD ______ **3018632**
Long Distance / Feb '97 / ADA / Discovery

DIVAS
CD ______ **MOTCCD 67**
Motor City / Oct '92 / Total/BMG

DIVAS EN ROOTS
CD ______ **ARICD 089**
Ariwa Sounds / Jul '96 / Jet Star / SRD

DIVAS OF JAZZ SING (20 Classics)
CD ______ **CWNCD 2027**
Javelin / Jul '96 / Henry Hadaway / THE

DIVAS OF MALI (Great Vocal Performances From A Fabled Land)
Sekou semega: *Damba, Fanta* / Banga diabate: *Kouyate, Tata Bambo* / Kotuba: *Koita, Ami* / Djina Moussou: *Doumbia, Nahawa* / Youcoba sylla: *Sidibe, Sali* / Jakha: *Kouyate, Kandia* / Karamoko: *Kouyate, Sanougoue*
CD ______ **SH 64078**
Shanachie / Dec '96 / ADA / Greensleeves / Koch

DIVINE DIVAS (3CD Set)
Tierradentro: *Gomez, Claudia* / La sombra negra: *La Mompasina, Toto* / Rain song: *Burch, Sharon* / Femmes d'Afrique: *Bell, Nayanka & Tshala Muana/Djanka Diabate* / Comment te dire adieu: *Hardy, Francoise* / Dejame llorar: *Hinojosa, Tish* / Canto di Hecate: *Belloni, Alessandra* / Your scarf will not hold your hair: *Leskaj, Zana & Luljeta Hia* / Mai kai no kauai: *Moe, Rose* / Emo neuvoi: *MeNaiset* / Amazing grace: *Di Franco, Ani* / Foggy dew: *O'Sullivan, Cathie* / Dejate amar: *India* / Laban Ko: *Doumbia, Nahawa* / Receita de samba: *Joyce* / Jheel mai chand: *Najma* / Maria Lando: *Baca, Susana* / Ya habibi: *Maideh, Malouma Mint* / Wayala: *Fadela & Sahrawi* / Baby, now that I've found you: *Krauss, Alison* / Thugamar fein an samradh linn: *Ni Riain, Noirin* / Sorban palid: *Kurnia, Detty* / Lamara: *Bel, M'Bilia* / Stepping out of babylon: *Griffiths, Marcia* / Illoqarfik: *Marina* / Durme hermoza donzella: *Frankel, Judy* / Come on in my kitchen: *Wilson, Cassandra* / Sekusile: *Dark City Sisters* / La Guyanaise: *Cedia, Sylviane* / Mango mangue: *Valdes, Merceditas* / Mal' de amor: *Saozinha* / Prisoner's song: *Molnar, Eva & Vasmalom* / Moritat: *Krause, Dagmar* / Sudden waves: *Tabor, June* / Viento Pasajero: *Junaro, Emma* / Navai: *Deyhim, Sussan* / Souffle van: *Bissainthe, Toto*
CD Set ______ **ROUCD 507123**
Rounder / Mar '97 / ADA / CM / Direct

DIWAN OF BISKRA, THE (Music From Algeria)
CD ______ **C 5560088**
Ocora / Jan '97 / ADA / Harmonia Mundi

DIX IMPROVISATIONS - VICTORIAVILLE 1989
CD ______ **VICTOCD 09**
Victo / Nov '94 / Harmonia Mundi / ReR Megacorp

DIXIELAND
CD ______ **CD 53041**
Giants Of Jazz / Mar '90 / Cadillac / Jazz Music / Target/BMG

DIXIELAND
CD ______ **490311**
RCA / Jul '95 / BMG

DIXIELAND FAVOURITES
Muskrat ramble / Canal street blues / When you're smiling / Doctor Jazz / Tishomingo blues / Black and blues / I want a big butter and egg man / Memphis blues / At the jazz band ball / Do you know what it means to miss New Orleans / Just a closer walk with thee / High society / Maple leaf rag / When you wore a tulip (and I wore a big red rose)
CD ______ **EMPRCD 521**
Emporio / Oct '94 / Disc

DIXIELAND FAVOURITES
Make up my mind: *Teagarden, Jack* / Prelude in C minor: *Teagarden, Jack* / Original Dixieland one step: *Teagarden, Jack* / High society: *Teagarden, Jack* / Shine: *Teagarden, Jack* / Down by the riverside: *Jones, Jonah* / Beale street blues: *Jones, Jonah* / Sheik of Araby: *Jones, Jonah* / California here I come: *Russell, Pee Wee* / Love is here to stay: *Russell, Pee Wee* / Coquette: *Russell, Pee Wee* / Royal garden blues: *Hunt, Pee Wee* / After you've gone: *Hunt, Pee Wee* / Basin street blues: *Hunt, Pee Wee* / Creole love call: *Kid Ory* / Muskrat rumble: *Kid Ory* / That's a plenty: *Kid Ory* / At the Jazz Band Ball: *Spanier, Muggsy* / Sugar foot stomp: *Spanier, Muggsy* / Dinah: *Spanier, Muggsy*
CD ______ **SUMCD 4107**
Sound & Media / Mar '97 / Sound & Media

DIXIELAND JAZZ - THE COLLECTION
Tiger rag: *Original Dixieland Jazz Band* / Look at 'em doing it now: *Original Dixieland Jazz Band* / Copenhagen: *Wolverine Orchestra* / Careless love: *Original Tuxedo Jazz Orchestra* / She's crying for me: *Original New Orleans Rhythm Kings* / That's no bargain: *Nichols, Red & His Five Pennies* / Way down yonder in New Orleans: *Trumbauer, Frank & His Orchestra* / I'm more than satisfied: *Chicago Loopers* / Royal goden blues: *Beiderbecke, Bix & His Gang* / Nobody's sweetheart: *McKenzie & Condon's Chicagoans* / Coquette: *Whiteman, Paul & His Orchestra* / I found a new baby: *Chicago Rhythm Kings* / There'll be some changes made: *Chicago Rhythm Kings* / Shake your can: *Dodds, Johnny* / Moanin' low: *Mole, Miff Molers* / Strut Miss Lizzie: *Mills, Irving & His Hotsy Totsy Gang* / Georgia on my mind: *Carmichael, Hoagy Orchestra* / After you've gone: *Venuti-Lang All Stars* / Spider crawl: *Banks, Billy & His Orchestra* / Eel: *Condon, Eddie & His Orchestra* / When the saints go marching in: *Armstrong, Louis* / At the jazz band ball: *Rhythm Cats* / Relaxin' at the touro: *Spanier, Muggsy* / Muskrat ramble: *Armstrong, Louis*
CD ______ **QED 101**
Tring / Nov '96 / Tring

DIXIELAND JUBILEE (2CD Set)
CD Set ______ **DBG 53030**
Double Gold / Jan '94 / Target/BMG

DIXIELAND TO SWING GOLD (2CD Set)
CD Set ______ **D2CD 4009**
Deja Vu / Jun '95 / THE

DIXIELAND VOL.1
Joshua fit de battle of Jericho: *Original Dixieland Stompers* / When the saints: *Original Dixieland Stompers* / Buddy Bolden blues: *Original Dixieland Stompers* / Sweet Georgia Brown: *Brixie Dixie Jazz Band* / When you're smiling: *Brixie Dixie Jazz Band* / Honeysuckle rose: *Brixie Dixie Jazz Band* / Down by the riverside: *Original Dixieland Stompers* / Go tell it to the mountains: *Original Dixieland Stompers* / Lizzy's rag: *Original Dixieland Stompers* / I want a little girl: *Brixie Dixie Jazz Band* / When my sugar walks down the street: *Brixie Dixie Jazz Band* / Georgia: *Dutch Swing College Band* / Bad, bad Leroy Brown: *Dutch Swing College Band* / Play it to me: *Original Dixieland Stompers* / Champs Elysses: *Dutch Swing College Band* / Ice cream: *Brixie Dixie Jazz Band*
CD ______ **12460**
Laserlight / Nov '95 / Target/BMG

DIXIELAND VOL.2
Midnight in Moscow: *Ball, Kenny* / Riverboat shuffle: *Dukes Of Dixieland* / Winin' boy blues: *Dukes Of Dixieland & Danny Barker* / Eh, la bas: *Original Dixieland Stompers* / My bonnie is over the ocean: *Original Dixieland Stompers* / Black roses blues: *Original Dixieland Stompers* / It's a plenty: *Brixie Dixie Jazz Band* / Somebody loves me: *Brixie Dixie Jazz Band* / March of the Siamese children: *Ball, Kenny* / Alexander's ragtime band: *Dukes Of Dixieland* / Bugle call blues: *Original Dixieland Stompers* / CC rider: *Original Dixieland Stompers* / Basin Street blues: *Brixie Dixie Jazz Band* / Raggie time: *Original Dixieland Stompers* / Casey Jones: *Station Hall Jazz Band* / Over in the Gloryland: *Original Dixieland Stompers*
CD ______ **12461**
Laserlight / Nov '95 / Target/BMG

DJ BOX VOL.1, THE (40 Drum & Bass Anthems/3CD Set)
CD Set ______ **BDRCD 12**
Breakdown / Apr '96 / Pinnacle

DJ BOX VOL.2, THE (40 Drum 'n' Bass Anthems/3CD Set)
CD Set ______ **BDRCD 18**
Breakdown / Nov '96 / Pinnacle

DJ CULTURE VOL.1 (Vintage Mixes 1992-1994/Sasha/Seaman/Digweed/2CD Set))
CD Set ______ **STRMIX 1CD**
Stress / Sep '96 / Mo's Music Machine / Pinnacle / Prime

DJ CULTURE VOL.2 (Mixed By Seaman/ Whitehead/Warren - 3CD/MC Set)
CD Set ______ **STRMIX 2CD**
Stress / Sep '96 / Mo's Music Machine / Pinnacle / Prime

DJ CULTURE VOL.3 (Mixed By Kaye/ Bouthier/Pappa - 3CD/MC Set)
Orange sunshine: *Superstars Of Rock* / Coming home: *Visions & Dianne Lynne* / When you love someone: *Daphne* / Don't fail: *Johnny Fiasco* / LA nights: *Prince Of Bel Air* / Journey: *Spastik Plastik* / Planet funk: *Neri, Alex* / Final: *Hustlers Convention* / Watcha gonna do: *Joy For Life* / I found it: *Daphne* / Last rhythm: *Last Rhythm* / Everything is gonna change: *Rusty* / Warm it up: *Joy For Life* / Watcha gonna do (master mix): *Joy For Life* / Release the tension: *Greed* / Get down: *Hustlers Convention* / Uptown downtown: *Full Intention* / Return to the rare groove republic: *Route 66* / Spirits dancing: *Coyote* / Last rhythm (Way Out West mix): *Last Rhythm* / Tune in: *Chris & James* / Decadence: *Reefa* / America (I love America): *Full Intention* / Everything is gonna change (Sasha's dub): *Rusty* / Love me tonight: *White, Anthony* / Dub up the volume: *Greed* / Planet funk (Moonchild mix): *Neri, Alex* / Wildstyle groove: *Paninaro* / Gimme your love: *Sharon S* / Coming home (Freefall remix): *Visions & Dianne Lynne* / For what you dream of: *Bedrock & KYO* / Spirits dancing (mix): *Coyote* / Last rhythm (Way Out West remix): *Last Rhythm* / Send your drummage: *Reefa* / Send your spirit: *Reefa* / On my way: *Reefa* / Healing dream: *Sunday Club* / Coming home (Sunday Club remix): *Visions & Dianne Lynne* / Way it is: *Chameleon*
CD Set ______ **STRMIX 3CD**
Stress / Sep '96 / Mo's Music Machine / Pinnacle / Prime

DJ JUNGLE FEVER UK
CD ______ **RSNCD 35**
Rising High / Jun '95 / 3mv/Sony

DJ MORPHEUS PRESENTS LYSERGI
Jeune amour: *Uriel* / Butterfly: *Craig, Carl* / No 100 flow: *Cambio* / Whispers special: *Sluta Leta* / Breakers special 93: *Zeb-Roc-Ski & Stieber Twins* / Yoshi: *Dunderhead* / Chart flow: *Eight Miles High* / Norton midgate: *Eight Miles High* / Rather be here: *Random House* / Why things change: *Spank Da Monkey* / Sykodelic: *Spank Da Monkey*
CD ______ **SSR 178**
SSR / Mar '97 / Amato Disco / Grapevine/ PolyGram / Prime / RTM/Disc

DJ POWER VOL.1
CD ______ **POWCD 1**
Escapade / Aug '94 / 3mv/Sony / Prime

DJ POWER VOL.2
CD ______ **POWCD 2**
Escapade / Nov '94 / 3mv/Sony / Prime

DJ REMIX CULTURE
CD ______ **STRSCD 5**
CD ______ **STRSCDDJ 5**
Stress / Nov '94 / Mo's Music Machine / Pinnacle / Prime

DJ SELECTIONS VOL.1
CD ______ **ZZCD 022**
Zola & Zola / Sep '96 / Jet Star

DJ SY
CD Set ______ **SDIMCD 2**
Sound Dimension / Jun '95 / Total/BMG

DJ'S DEELITE
CD ______ **504582**
Declic / Nov '95 / Jet Star

DJ'S DELITE - THE GOLD COLLECTION (3CD Set)
Vol.4: *SMD* / Feel free: *Dougal & Vibes* / Vol.1: *Norty Norty* / Vol.1: *Ravers Choice* / Six days: *Jay, Jimmy & Cru-L-T* / Da vibes: *Remarc* / Zurich: *Dougal* / Perfect dreams: *DJ Force & Evolution* / Crowd control: *Ramos & Supreme* / Vol.2: *DJ Anthems* / You are the one: *DJ Red Alert & Mike Slammer* / Vol.3: *SMD* / Vol.2: *Crowd Pleasers* / Sky high: *Dougal* / Sweetest love: *Vibes & Wishdokta* / Take me away: *Jay, Jimmy & Cru-L-T* / We got it: *Substate* / Feel good: *Vibes & Wishdokta* / 95 Rampage: *In Between The Lines* / Hello lover: *Hello Lover* / Rollige: *DJ SS* / We enter: *Alladin* / Really love: *Ascend & Ultravibe* / Lighter: *Sound Of The Future* / Dubwars: *Badman* / Mood of music: *Tekniq* / Hearing is believing: *MA2* / DJ SS: *Tarzan* / Easy men: *Easy Men* / Half step: *International Rude* / Black: *Black* / Hot flames: *Dextrous & H Pee* / Reality: *Phaze 3 & Klass A* / White: *White* / Jungle: *Smith, Simon Bassline* / Badman tings: *Terrible Tings* / Lazy bones: *Smith, Simon Bassline* / Systematic: *Brown, Scott* / Faze 1: *Forbes & Cyclone* / Do what you like: *Brown, Scott* / Higher: *Kinetic Pleasure* / Rock this place: *DJ Chewy* / Around the world: *Sense Of Summer* / Let yourself go: *DJ Ham* / Samplemania: *DJ Seduction* / No more tears: *Vibes & Wishdokta* / Take me up: *Substate* / Bust the new jam: *Seduction & Eruption* / Ultimate seduction: *DJ Hixxy* / Come together: *Storm Syndicut* / Party pumper: *DJ Brisk & Rebel Alliance* / Groovy dimensions: *WE-3* / Give yourself to me: *Icon* / Home: *Alk E-D* / Misunderstanding: *DJ Slam* / Another day: *Substate*

CD Set DBM 2204
Death Becomes Me / Jan '97 / Grapevine/ PolyGram / Pinnacle / SRD

DJ'S DELITE VOL.1
CD TROOPCD 6
Rogue Trooper / Jan '95 / Alphamagic / SRD

DJ'S DELITE VOL.2
CD DBMTROOPCD 9
Rogue Trooper / Jun '95 / Alphamagic / SRD

DJ'S DELITE VOL.3
CD DBMTRCD 22
Rogue Trooper / Nov '95 / Alphamagic / SRD

DJ'S DELITE VOL.4 (Mixed By Marc Smith)
CD DBM 2011
DJ's Delite / Sep '96 / SRD

DJ'S IN A BOX VOL.4 (Mixed By Phil Jubb)
CD UCCD 004
Urban Collective / Jun '96 / Amato Disco / RTM/Disc / Total/BMG / Vital

DJ'S IN A BOX VOL.6 (Mixed By Anthony Papa)
CD UCCD 006
Urban Collective / Aug '96 / Amato Disco / RTM/Disc / Total/BMG / Vital

DJ'S IN A BOX VOL.7
CD UCCD 007
Urban Collective / Sep '96 / Amato Disco / RTM/Disc / Total/BMG / Vital

DJ'S IN THE HOUSE
CD MACCD 160
Autograph / Aug '96 / BMG

DJ'S MEET THE SINGERS VOL.2
CD SONCD 0049
Sonic Sounds / Jul '93 / Jet Star

DJ'S TAKE CONTROL (All Mixed Up - Mixed by Sanchez/Deep Dish/Colon/ 3CD Set)
CD Set ORCD 032
One / Aug '97 / Total/BMG

DJ'S TAKE CONTROL - THE COLLECTION (3CD Set)
CD Set ORCD 030
One / Apr '97 / Total/BMG

DJ'S UNITE - THE COMPLETE SERIES (3CD Set)
Hypnosis: *Smith, Simon Bassline* / Twisted girl: *Ruff With The Smooth & Donovan Bad Boy Smith* / Engineers without fears: *DJ Rap* / Life began changing: *Van Cleef* / Natural high: *Chaos & Julia Set* / I feel free: *DJ Phantasy & Gemini* / You take me up: *DJ Aphrodite* / Dream on: *Phantasy & Smooth* / Ruffer: *DJ Force & Evolution* / Hear me: *Slipmatt* / Summer Breeze: *Bonnie The Highlander* / Above the clouds: *Sunshine Productions* / Cops: *DJ Hype* / Take your soul: *NC & Asend* / Big boo yaa: *Aphrodite & Tony B* / Rollin' voodoo: *DJ Spatts* / Hitman: *Marvellous Caine* / You as one: *Ryder, Ned* / Atmosphere: *DJ Phantasy* / Long time coming: *Danny Breaks* / Dubwars: *Badman* / Rollers convention part 3: *DJ SS* / Out in the streets: *Rude Bwoy Monty* / Use of weapons: *Chaos & Julia Set* / Tuneful: *Nut-E-1 & Technarchy* / Passion: *DJ Vibes & Wishdokta* / Party pumper: *DJ Brisk & Rebel Alliance* / Kick some ass: *DJ Druid & Rebel Alliance* / Rhythm: *Just Another Artist* / Cheddar 3: *DJ Sy* / Carousel: *Dougal & Micky Skeedale* / World war part 1: *DJ Hixxy* / Influence: *DJ Slam* / Perfect dreams: *DJ Force & Evolution* / Let yourself go: *DJ Ham* / Disco hardcore: *DJ Seduction* / I need you: *Sub-State & DJ Jack B*
CD Set DBM 2516
Death Becomes Me / Jan '97 / Grapevine/ PolyGram / Pinnacle / SRD

DJ'S UNITE VOL.1
CD TROOPCD 2
Rogue Trooper / Oct '94 / Alphamagic / SRD

DJ'S UNITE VOL.2
CD TROOPCD 10
Rogue Trooper / May '95 / Alphamagic / SRD

DJ'S UNITE VOL.3
CD DBMTRCD 20
Rogue Trooper / Oct '95 / Alphamagic / SRD

DJ'S UNITE VOL.4 (2CD Set)
Let yourself go: *El Bruto* / Your love (get down): *Force & Styles/Jenna* / I got something: *DJ Reno & Eatsum & The Kidz* / Rock dis place: *DJ Elevation* / Touch of klass: *DJ Happy Raver & The Smile-E* / Giving all my love: *Forbes, Davie* / Givin' all I got: *DJ Vibes & Wishdokta* / Everybody here tonight: *Jack Speed* / It's gonna be: *DJ Poosie* / Raw: *Alk E-D* / Let's go: *Jimmy J & Cru-L-T* / It would be: *DJ Ham* / You're gonna love me: *DJ Pleasure* / Smile, fuck up: *DJ Psycangle*
CD Set DBM 2521
Death Becomes Me / Jan '97 / Grapevine/ PolyGram / Pinnacle / SRD

DO IT FLUID/B&G PARTY (14 Rare Grooves)
Fantasy: *Smith, Johnny 'Hammond'* / Shifting gears: *Smith, Johnny 'Hammond'* / Joyous: *Pleasure* / Hump: *Rushen, Patrice* / Always there: *Side Effect* / Keep that same old feeling: *Side Effect* / Do it fluid: *Blackbyrds* / Rock creek park: *Blackbyrds* / Concrete jungle: *Three Pieces* / Glide: *Pleasure* / Ghettos of the mind: *Pleasure* / Straight to the bank: *Summers, Bill* / I've learned from my burns: *Spyder's Webb* / Sister Jane: *Funk Inc.*
CD CDBGPD 035
Beat Goes Public / Apr '92 / Pinnacle

DO NOT ADJUST YOUR SET
Burnin' down: *Strange Brew* / Angel: *Friday, Gavin* / Watch me now: *Grooveyard* / Freak of the week: *Freakpower* / Too far gone: *13th Sign* / Release one: *Leftfield* / Dubilicious demo groove: *Crystal Method* / Rematerialized: *Death In Vegas* / Yimpop: *Hardfloor* / Fuck dub: *Tosca* / Weekend starts here: *Fatboy Slim* / Keep on: *Wiseguys* / Six underground: *Sneaker Pimps* / Ticket: *11-59* / Heidi: *Ruby*
CD IMPCD 003
More Protein / Feb '97 / Pinnacle / Total/ BMG

DO THE CROSSOVER BABY
I'll never stop loving you: *Thomas, Carla* / I got the vibes: *Armstead, Jo* / Stars: *Lewis, Barbara* / I'm the one who loves you: *Banks, Darrell* / I may not be what you want: *Mel & Tim* / Whole damned world gone crazy: *Williams, John Gary* / Be my lady: *Astors* / Since I lost my baby's love: *Major Lance* / Bark at the moon: *Floyd, Eddie* / Catch that man: *John, Mable* / Little by little and bit by bit: *Weston, Kim* / You're my only temptation: *Ryan, Roz* / Whole world's a picture show: *Newcomers* / Special kind of woman: *Thompson, Paul* / I play for keeps: *Thomas, Carla* / Sweet sherry: *Barnes, J.J.* / Sacrifice: *Bell, William* / Loving by the pound: *Redding, Otis* / Just keep on loving me: *Mancha, Steve* / Man in the street: *Bell, William* / Trippin' on your love: *Staple Singers* / Did my baby call: *Mad Lads* / Where would you be today: *Ilana* / One more chance: *Joseph, Margie*
CD CDKEND 105
Kent / Aug '93 / Pinnacle

DO THE NUCLEAR TESTS IN PARIS AND BEIJING
Queenie: *Pimlico* / 911 KGGI: *Citrus* / Face on the bar room floor: *Flaming Stars* / Spineless little shit: *Thee Headcoatees* / GLC: *Armitage Shanks* / I'm afraid they're all talking about me: *Mickey & Ludella* / Shit parade: *Tokyo Skunx* / Jet tone boogie: *Rockings* / I wanna go to Coney Island: *Jet Boys* / Hello there: *Gigantor* / Scuba scuba: *Revillos* / Little terrors: *Revolta* / Hangover head: *Diaboliks* / He used to paint in colours: *TV Personalities* / Mud: *Grape* / My boy and his motorbike: *Carousel* / Nostalgia: *Weekend* / New crush: *Bugbear* / Winona, I'll be up my Nan's: *Parker, Pop* / Clearly: *McTells* / Open to persuasion: *Chesterfields* / I wanna bang on the drum: *Dee, Johnny* / Cars in the grass: *Moxham, Stuart & The Original Artists* / Good enough: *Holly Golightly* / Cheat: *Earls Of Suave*
CD MASKCD 058
Vinyl Japan / Feb '96 / Plastic Head / Vinyl Japan

DO THE OOBY DOOBY
Good rockin' tonight: *Wray, Link* / Cat all nite: *Flynn, Lee* / Rockin' Robin: *Henchmen* / Big bounce: *Caddell, Shirley* / Shake: *Fleming, George* / Paul Jones rock: *Ginger & Johnny* / Rock a square dance: *Reilly, Tommy & The QC Boys* / Ooby dooby: *Teen Kings* / Wild wild party: *Dickie Doo & The Don'ts* / Wash machine boogie: *Echo Valley Boys* / Buck dancin': *Kennedy, Ace* / Birmingham bounce: *Gunter, Hardrock* / Georgia slop: *Downing, Big Al* / Rock rock: *Powers, Johnny*
CD 305242
Hallmark / Jun '97 / Carlton

DO YOU BELIEVE IN LOVE
CD CRECD 063
Creation / May '94 / 3mv/Vital

DO YOU BELIEVE IN LOVE (2CD Set)
CD Set NSCD 007
Newsound / Feb '95 / THE

DO YOU WANNA DANCE (Hits Of The 70's)
Flight tonight: *Nazareth* / Brand new key: *Melanie* / Baby jump: *Mungo Jerry* / That same old feeling: *Pickettywitch* / In my chair: *Status Quo* / Part time love: *Knight, Gladys & The Pips* / Do you wanna dance: *Blue, Barry* / After the goldrush: *Prelude* / Bad, Bad Leroy Brown: *Croce, Jim* / Lola: *Kinks* / Kung fu fighting: *Douglas, Carl* / Sad sweet dreamer: *Sweet Sensation* / What have they done to my song Ma: *Melanie* / Medley: *Knight, Gladys & The Pips* / Alright alright alright: *Mungo Jerry* / Black superman (Muhammed Ali): *Wakelin, Johnny* / Time in a bottle: *Croce, Jim* / Shame, shame, shame: *Shirley & Company* / Swing your daddy: *Gilstrap, Jim* / Have you seen her: *Chi-Lites*
CD TRTCD 108
TrueTrax / Dec '94 / THE

DO YOUR DUTY
CD IMP 940
Iris Music / Jul '95 / Discovery

DO Y'SELF A FAVOUR (The Countdown Years 1975-1979)
CD RVCD 35
Raven / Jan '94 / ADA / Direct

DOCTOR JAZZ SAMPLER
CD STCD 6040
Storyville / Aug '94 / Cadillac / Jazz Music / Wellard

DOCUMENT 01
CD DOROB 001CD
Dorobo / Sep '95 / Plastic Head

DOES THE WORD 'DUH' MEAN ANYTHING TO YOU
CD CHE 40CD
Che / Sep '95 / SRD

DOGS 4 LIFE
CD GOGZ 4CD1
Rude & Deadly / May '97 / Shellshock/ Disc

DOIN' IT
Zaius: *Russ, Eddie* / Groove: *Franklin, Rodney* / Always there: *Bobo, Willie* / That's the way of the world: *Lewis, Ramsey* / Reach out: *Duke, George* / Doin' it: *Hancock, Herbie* / Sneaking up behind you: *Brecker Brothers* / Funkin' for Jamaica: *Browne, Tom* / Get down everybody (it's time for world peace): *Smith, Lonnie Liston* / Johannesburg: *Scott-Heron, Gil* / Hooked on young stuff: *Tempo, Nino & 5th Avenue Sax* / Street wave: *Brothers Johnson*
CD RNBCD 104
Connoisseur Collection / Aug '93 / Pinnacle

DOING GOD'S WORK (A Creation Compilation)
Ten miles: *Wilson, Phil* / In a mourning town: *Biff Bang Pow* / Murderers, the hope of women: *Momus* / Shine on: *House Of Love* / Cut me deep: *Jasmine Minks* / Word around town: *Westlake* / Kiss at dawn: *Sudden, Nikki* / Catch me: *Blow Up*
CD CRECD 024
Creation / May '94 / 3mv/Vital

DOING IT FOR THE KIDS
Cut me deep: *Jasmine Minks* / Ballad of the band: *Felt* / Christine: *House Of Love* / Well done sonny: *Weather Prophets* / All fall down: *Primal Scream* / She paints: *Biff Bang Pow* / Loft 49: *Jazz Butcher* / North shore train: *Berry, Heidi* / Death is hanging over me: *Sudden, Nikki* / Cigarette in my bed: *My Bloody Valentine* / Jetstream: *Pacific* / Godevil: *Times* / Complete history of sexual jealousy Parts 17 - 24: *Momus* / Reflects of rye: *Emily* / Brighter now: *Razorcuts*
CD CRECD 037
Creation / Aug '88 / 3mv/Vital

DONE STILL GOT THE BLUES
CD MACCD 200
Autograph / Aug '96 / BMG

DONEGAL FIDDLE, THE
CD RTE 196CD
RTE / Nov '96 / ADA / Koch

DON'T ASK FOR THE MOON, WE HAVE THE STARS
Way you look tonight: *Astaire, Fred* / Let there be love: *Hutchinson, Leslie 'Hutch'* / Boy next door: *Garland, Judy* / September song: *Huston, Walter* / She's funny that way: *Sinatra, Frank* / You're a sweetheart: *Bowlly, Al* / I'm making believe: *Ink Spots & Ella Fitzgerald* / Amor amor: *Rey, Monte* / I'm knee deep in daisies: *Smith, Whispering* / How do I know it's real: *Sullivan, Maxine* / That old feeling: *Lee, Peggy & Capitol Jazzmen* / Too marvellous for words: *Stafford, Jo* / That old black magic: *Whiting, Margaret & Freddie Slack* / Sweet Lorraine: *Cole, Nat 'King' Trio* / It can't be wrong: *Carless, Dorothy* / Let's do it: *Martin, Mary* / Never took a lesson in my life: *Carlisle, Elsie* / Let's get away from it all: *Lane, Muriel & Woody Herman* / Long ago and far away: *Forrest, Helen & Dick Haymes* / Only forever: *Crosby, Bing* / Dinah: *Cantor, Eddie* / I've got a heart filled with love: *Desmond, Johnny & Glenn Miller* / Very thought of you: *Holiday, Billie* / Boy what love has done to me: *Froman, Jane* / I remember you: *Forrest, Helen & Harry James* / Now voyager: *Davis, Bette & Paul Henried*
CD UCD 400
Happy Days / Feb '97 / Conifer/BMG

DON'T CALL ME SKA FACE (3CD Set)
CD Set DTKBOX 56
Dressed To Kill / Sep '96 / Total/BMG

DON'T CRY FOR ME ARGENTINA
CD MACCD 307
Autograph / Aug '96 / BMG

DON'T FENCE ME IN (Western Music)
CD ROUCD 1102
Rounder / Mar '96 / ADA / CM / Direct

DON'T FORGET TO BREATHE
CD E 802042
Crank / Mar '97 / Cargo

DON'T MESS WITH THE BLUES
CD MACCD 197
Autograph / Aug '96 / BMG

DON'T SHOOT
Bend in the road: *Danny & Dusty* / Hello walls: *Jimmy & The Rhythm Pigs* / I'll get out somehow: *McCarthy, Steve* / Wreckin' ball: *Doe, John* / Almost persuaded: *Christensen, Julie* / Tears fall away: *Divine Horsemen* / Tear it down: *Gilkyson, Terry* / Never get out of this world alive: *Waterson, Jack* / Blind justice: *Band Of Blacky Ranchette* / Freight train: *Allison, Clay* / Tear it all to pieces: *Romans*
CD MAUCD 606
Mau Mau / Jul '91 / Pinnacle

DON'T STOP THE MUSIC (Dance Favourites From The 1970's-1990's/2CD Set)
Rock your baby: *McCrae, George* / Feels like I'm in love: *Marie, Kelly* / Fan the flame: *Pennington, Barbara* / So many men so little time: *Brown, Miquel* / High energy: *Thomas, Evelyn* / After dark: *Brookes, Patti* / He's number one: *Fantasy* / Something old, something new: *Fantastics* / Feel the need in me: *Detroit Emeralds* / Love and desire: *Arpeggio* / Frankie: *Sister Sledge* / Queen of fools: *Williams, Jessica* / I'm in the mood for dancing: *Nolans* / Saddle up: *Nolans* / Love machine: *Miracles* / Satellites: *Warren, Ellie* / Heaven must be missing an angel: *Tavares* / Going back to my roots: *Odyssey* / Love in the night: *VHF* / It's too late: *Core & Louise* / That's when we'll be free: *State Of Grace* / Heart of glass: *Desiderata* / Car wash: *Rose Royce* / Medley: *Gaynor, Gloria* / Footsteps following me: *Nero, Frances* / Haven't stopped dancing yet: *Faces* / Ain't nothing but a house party: *Contours* / Get dancin': *Bombers* / Don't stop the music: *Carroll, Dina* / Love I lost: *Seventh Avenue* / Another man: *Mason, Barbara*
CD Set 330302
Hallmark / Mar '97 / Carlton

DON'T TALK JUST KISS
CD UPCD 05
Nitro / Sep '95 / Pinnacle / Plastic Head

DON'T TOUCH THAT DIAL VOL.1 (Johnnie Walker On Radio Caroline 1968)
Because they're young: *Eddy, Duane* / Judy in disguise: *Fred, John & His Playboy Band* / Rescue me: *Bass, Fontella* / She'd rather be with me: *Turtles* / Spooky: *Classics IV* / Days of Pearly Spencer: *McWilliams, David* / Harlem shuffle: *Bob & Earl* / B-A-B-Y: *Thomas, Carla* / Soul man: *Sam & Dave* / Knock on wood: *Floyd, Eddie* / Stand by me: *King, Ben E.* / All my loving: *Martin, George* / Warm and tender love: *Sledge, Percy* / For your love: *Yardbirds* / Livin' above your head: *Jay & The Americans*
CD TJLCD 1968A
Jumbo / Jul '96 / Discovery / EAP

DON'T TOUCH THAT DIAL VOL.2 (Bob Stewart On Radio Caroline 1966)
Shapes of things: *Yardbirds* / What'd I say: *Lewis, Jerry Lee* / Sha la la la lee: *Small Faces* / You send me: *Cooke, Sam* / Oh no not my baby: *Brown, Maxine* / My babe: *Little Walter* / Backstage: *Pitney, Gene* / Hard day's night: *Lewis, Ramsey Trio* / Love letters: *Lester, Ketty* / It's in his kiss (the shoop shoop song): *Everett, Betty*
CD TJLCD 1966
Jumbo / Jul '96 / Discovery / EAP

DON'T YOU FEEL MY LEG
Buy me some juice: *Barker, 'Blue' Lu* / Where's Joe: *Barker, 'Blue' Lu* / Lyin' in jail: *Barker, 'Blue' Lu* / Easy riding blues: *Booze, Wee Bea* / I just ain't feelin' right: *Booze, Wee Bea* / Feel it: *Dee, Baby* / I want to see my Daddy: *Dee, Baby* / Don't you feel my leg: *Barker, 'Blue' Lu* / That made him mad: *Barker, 'Blue' Lu* / I feel like laying in another woman's husband's arms: *Barker, 'Blue' Lu* / Don't tell me nothin' 'bout my man: *Booze, Wee Bea* / I'm gonna put you down: *Booze, Wee Bea* / I just ain't feelin' right: *Booze, Wee Bea* / Look what baby's got for you: *Dee, Baby* / Baby Dee blues: *Dee, Baby* / Buy me some juice: *Barker, 'Blue' Lu* / You gotta show it to me baby: *Barker, 'Blue' Lu* / There was a l'il mouse: *Barker, 'Blue' Lu*
CD DE 684
Delmark / Nov '96 / ADA / Cadillac / CM / Direct / Hot Shot

DOO WOP - UNDER THE COVERS
Why do fools fall in love: *Essex* / Out of sight, out of mind: *Essex* / Gee whizz (look at his eyes): *Essex* / We belong together: *Essex* / Creation of love: *Essex* / Thousand miles away: *Anthony, Wayne* / Silhouettes: *Lymon, Frankie* / Buzz buzz buzz: *Lymon, Frankie* / I cover the waterfront: *Little Anthony & The Imperials* / Please say you want me: *Little Anthony & The Imperials* / Over the rainbow: *Little Anthony & The Imperials* / When you wish upon a star: *Little Anthony & The Imperials* / Earth angel: *Cleftones* / Glory of love: *Cleftones* / Hundred pounds of clay: *Cleftones* / Red sails in the sunset: *Cleftones* / Heavenly father: *Span, Patricia & The Cleftones* / Tonight's the night: *Teenagers* / Diamonds and pearls: *Turbans* / I'm confessin': *Uniques* / Beside you: *Flamingos* / Gee: *Harmony Grits* / Come softly to me: *Barrett, Richard & The Sevilles* / Blue velvet: *Page, Joey* / Glory of love: *Angels* / (I love you) for sentimental reasons: *Devotions*

CD NEMCD 917
Sequel / Jul '97 / BMG

DOO WOP ALBUM, THE
For your precious love: *Impressions* / Red sails in the sunset: *Spaniels* / I only have eyes for you: *Flamingos* / Zoom zoom zoom: *Collegians* / In the still of the night: *Five Satins* / Could this be magic: *Dubs* / Maybe: *Chantels* / Bim bam bam: *El Dorados* / I just got lucky: *Orioles* / I understand: *G-Clefs* / Speedo: *Cadillacs* / Don't do that: *Five Tinos* / Real gone Mama: *Moonglows* / Lover's prayer: *Delltones* / Heart and soul: *Cleftones*
CD SUMCD 4118
Sound & Media / May '97 / Sound & Media

DOO WOP CLASSICS
Book of love: *Monotones* / Over and over again: *Harvey & The Moonglows* / Please come back come: *Flamingos* / Heart and soul: *Cleftones* / Baby, please don't go: *Orioles* / Tell it to the judge: *Monotones* / Real gone Mama: *Harvey & The Moonglows* / Chica boom (that's my baby): *Flamingos* / Little girl of mine: *Cleftones* / Crying in the chapel: *Orioles* / Look in my eyes: *Chantels* / Secret love: *Harvey & The Moonglows* / I found a new baby: *Flamingos* / Maybe: *Chantels* / Sixteen candles: *Crests* / Blue moon: *Marcels* / Just for a trick: *Flamingos* / Blue velvet: *Harvey & The Moonglows* / Legend of sleepy hollow: *Monotones*
CD GRF 196
Tring / Jan '93 / Tring

DOO WOP FROM DOLPHIN'S OF HOLLYWOOD VOL.1
Goose is gone aka the nest is warm: *Turbans* / Tick tock a woo: *Turbans* / No no cherry: *Turbans* / When I return: *Turbans* / Two things I love: *Voices* / Why: *Voices* / Crazy: *Voices* / Takes two to make a home: *Voices* / Hunter Hancock radio ad: *Voices* / My aching feet: *Gassers* / Why did you leave me: *Gassers* / Tell me: *Gassers* / Beloved: *Gassers* / Hum-de-hum: *Gassers* / Untitled blues: *Relf, Bobby & The Laurels* / Our love: *Relf, Bobby & The Laurels* / Honey bun: *Turks* / It can't be true: *Turks* / How to be a lover: *Hodge, Gaynell & The Blue Aires* / Love you right: *Hodge, Gaynell & The Blue Aires* / One time is enough: *Byrd, Bobby* / Hold me baby: *Byrd, Bobby* / Girl named Joe: *Miracles* / My angel: *Miracles* / Nine Boogie: *Miracles* / Let us be as one (aka Sweet thing): *Miracles*
CD CDCHD 364
Ace / Jan '92 / Pinnacle

DOO WOP GROUPS & CROONERS
CD CWNCD 2019
Javelin / Jul '96 / Henry Hadaway / THE

DOOTONE STORY VOL.1, THE
Ding a ling: *Crescendos* / Baby doll: *Crescendos* / I can't go on: *Milton, Roy & his Orchestra* / You got me reelin' and rockin': *Milton, Roy & his Orchestra* / My girl: *McCullough, Charles & the Silks* / I got tore up: *Julian, Don & The Meadowlarks* / This must be paradise: *Julian, Don & The Meadowlarks* / Please Mr. Jordan: *Duncan, Cleve & the Penguins* / Flee oo wee: *Calvanes* / Wet back hop: *Higgins, Chuck* / Don't you know I love you: *Higgins, Chuck* / Boogie woogie teenage: *Meadowlarks* / Be fair: *Pipes* / Buick '59: *Green, Vernon & the Medallions* / Magic mountain: *Green, Vernon & the Medallions* / Jump and hop: *Romancers*
CD CDCHD 579
Ace / Jan '96 / Pinnacle

DOOTONE STORY VOL.2, THE
Crazy over you: *Calvanes* / Heaven and paradise: *Julian, Don & The Meadowlarks* / I wonder why: *Fascinators* / I still remember: *Romancers* / Honey gee: *Saigons* / Lawful wedding: *Cuff Links* / Ay si si (mambo): *Dootones* / Baby come on come: *Calvanes* / Jump and hop: *Romancers* / I ain't gonna cry no more: *Penguins* / Did I do wrong: *Cuff Links* / Tell me baby: *Collins, Lee* / Sailor boy: *Dootones* / Speedin': *Medallions* / You're heavenly: *Saigons* / My heart: *Cuff Links* / I'm betting my heart (on you): *Duncan, Cleve & The Radiants* / You're an angel: *Pipes* / House cat: *Romancers* / If you were my darling: *Dootones* / One more kiss: *Calvanes* / That'll make it nice: *Eli & The Manhattans* / I'll never love again: *Johnny Twovoice & The Medallions* / Two crazy scientists: *Collins, Lee* / May we be on better terms: *Debonaires* / So long Daddy: *Souvenirs* / Ding a ling: *Maye, Arthur Lee* / This is goodbye: *Romancers*
CD CDCHD 588
Ace / Feb '97 / Pinnacle

DOPE CLASSICS (2CD Set)
Mother fuckin' remix: *East Side Hoods* / DJ talk: *Kicks Like A Mule* / Depth charge: *Depth Charge* / Wede man: *Selectah* / Zulu war chant: *Afrika Bambaataa Presents Time Zone* / Theme from funky killer: *S'Express* / Knife and a fork: *Think Tank* / Ride the pressure: *Coldcut* / Alarm clock: *Westbam* / Untitled: *Hardnoise* / Ozone breakdown: *Renegade Soundwave* / Intoxication: *React 2 Rhythm* / Who's the bad man: *Patten, Dee* / Poor man's glory: *LS Diezel & Launch Dat* / Not forgotten: *Leftfield* / Dance: *Rhythim Is Rhythim* / Rush: *Rhythm Masters* / You won't get away: *Pirates Of The Carribean* / Walk on: *Smith & Mighty* / DJ premier in deep concentration: *Gang Starr* / 20 seconds to comply: *Silver Bullet* / Keep it up: *YBU* / Hey hey can u relate: *DJ Mink* / Sleng teng: *Smith, Wayne*
CD Set REACTCD 104
React / Sep '97 / Arabesque / Prime / Vital

DOPE GUNS 'N' FUCKING IN THE STREETS VOL.8-11
CD ARRCD 80023
Amphetamine Reptile / Apr '97 / Plastic Head

DOPE ON PLASTIC VOL.1
Ode to a blunt: *Men With Sticks* / Dubble agent (Spying On-u): *Strange Brew* / Is it a wizard or a blizzard: *Mighty Truth* / Reefer man cometh: *Woodshed* / Conversations with Julian Dexter: *Grassy Knoll* / Snapper: *Red Snapper* / Cities: *APE* / Steppin': *Box Saga* / Inner spaces: *Digi Alliance* / Black jesus: *9 Lazy 9* / Tempest dub: *Edge Test 2* / Seashell: *Skylab*
CD REACTCD 055
React / Jan '95 / Arabesque / Prime / Vital

DOPE ON PLASTIC VOL.2
Radio Woodshed: *Woodshed* / Jailbird: *Primal Scream* / Spirit: *Kitachi* / To the hip: *Bootman* / Striplight: *APE* / Tribhuwan: *Purple Penguin* / Sinsemilia: *Dillingers Massive Dub Beats* / Wildfire: *Disciples* / Now or never: *Crustation* / Acoustic blues: *Cool Breeze* / It's not a man's world: *Strata 3*
CD REACTCD 065
React / Jul '95 / Arabesque / Prime / Vital

DOPE ON PLASTIC VOL.3
Worlds: *Midfield General* / Go off (cut le roc goes off): *Midfield General* / Mountain: *Purple Penguin* / DD Luxe: *Clutch Deluxe* / Livin free: *Small World* / GBH Dub: *Death In Vegas* / Scratch: *Kitachi* / Wallop: *DJ Food* / Just a lil dope: *Masters At Work* / 29: *Turntable TEchnova* / Bobimore dub: *Henry & Louis* / We wanna go back: *Word Up* / Images: *Aquasky* / 89: *Funky Fresh News* / Shine the light: *Wood, Matt* / Bean to the world: *Cabbage Boy*
CD REACTCD 073
CD REACTCDX 073
React / Feb '96 / Arabesque / Prime / Vital

DOPE ON PLASTIC VOL.4 (2CD Set)
Indian summer: *Saber, Danny* / Insomniac: *Killer Moses* / Herb: *Hidden Chipsters* / Angel dust: *Dragonfly* / Let me clear my throat: *DJ Kool* / Ride on: *Little Axe* / Work mi' body: *Monkey Mafia* / Time out: *Kitachi* / Confusion: *Dubdog* / Mo' bounce: *Love Lee* / For those who like to groove: *Scope* / Third eye: *Finger* / Return of the rebel: *Raw Deal* / Remember me: *Blueboy* / Phat 'n' fresh: *Gee, Tommy* / Apache rock: *Roxy Breaks* / Watch me rollin': *Cut & Paste* / Ahooga: *Awesome 2* / Dedication: *DJ Eclipse* / Shoplifter: *Red Myers* / Bouncy lady: *Danny Hibrid* / Tee meenie: *Tee Noize* / My mate Paul: *Holmes, David* / Goodbye cruel world: *London Funk Allstars*
CD REACTCDX 097
CD Set REACTCD 097
React / Jan '97 / Arabesque / Prime / Vital

DORADO - FINE GOLD
CD DOR 48CD
Dorado / Feb '96 / Pinnacle

DORADO COMPILATION VOL.1
Scheme of things: *D-Note* / Impressions: *Giant Steps NYC* / Sally's knocking: *Jhelisa* / Thirteenth key: *Sunship* / Rain: *D-Note* / Ain't no fun: *Monkey Business* / Circle of cruelty: *Circle in the sand*
CD DOR 8
Dorado / Sep '92 / Pinnacle

DORADO COMPILATION VOL.2
CD DOR 16CD
Dorado / Oct '93 / Pinnacle

DORADO COMPILATION VOL.3
CD DOR 20CD
Dorado / May '94 / Pinnacle

DORKCRUSHER
CD TUPEPCD 031
Tupelo / Jul '91 / RTM/Disc

DOT ROCK 'N' ROLL
Fool: *Clark, Sanford* / Chicken shack: *Van Dyke, Leroy* / Set it up and go: *Wiseman, Mac* / You're late Miss Kate: *Dee, Jimmy & The Offbeats* / Transfusion: *Nervous Norvous* / It ain't me: *Campi, Ray* / Playboy: *Denton, Bob* / Ballroom baby: *Lory, Dick* / I like this kind of music: *Ringo, Jimmy* / Pucker paint: *Wolfe, Danny* / Big door: *Brown, Gene* / Trapped love: *Courvale, Keith* / Johnny Johnny Johnny: *Jones, Kay Cee* / It's all over: *Sullivan, Niki* / Oh my baby's gone: *Sharpe, Ray* / Let's flat git it: *Wolfe, Danny* / Stop let me off the bus: *Lanson, Snooky* / Oh yeah: *Danton, Tommy* / Baby you've had it: *Paul, Joyce* / Skinnie Minnie: *Denton, Bob* / Call me Shorty: *Gilley, Mickey* / That's the way I feel: *Sharpe, Ray* / Carry on: *Newman, Jimmy C.* / Jitterbuggin': *Five Bops* / Modern romance: *Clark, Sanford* / You heard me knocking: *Adams, Billy* / Henrietta: *Dee, Jimmy & The Offbeats*
CD CDCHD 592
Ace / Oct '96 / Pinnacle

DOT'S COVER TO COVER (Hit Upon Hit)
Hearts of stone: *Fontane Sisters* / Two hearts: *Boone, Pat* / Maybellene: *Lowe, Jim* / Why don't you write me: *Lanson, Snooky* / Ain't that a shame: *Boone, Pat* / Only you (and you alone): *Hilltoppers* / Rollin' stone: *Fontane Sisters* / At my front door: *Boone, Pat* / Blue suede shoes: *Lowe, Jim* / Eddie my love: *Fontane Sisters* / Ka-ding-dong: *Hilltoppers* / I hear you knocking: *Storm, Gale* / Seventeen: *Fontane Sisters* / I'll be home: *Boone, Pat* / Why do fools fall in love: *Storm, Gale* / Seven days: *Lanson, Snooky* / Long tall Sally: *Boone, Pat* / Ivory tower: *Storm, Gale* / I'm in love again: *Fontane Sisters* / I almost lost my mind: *Boone, Pat* / Please don't leave me: *Fontane Sisters* / Chains of love: *Boone, Pat* / Lucky lips: *Storm, Gale* / Young love: *Hunter, Tab* / Marianne: *Hilltoppers* / Plaything: *Todd, Nick* / Raunchy: *Vaughn, Billy* / Get a job: *Mills Brothers* / Joker: *Hilltoppers* / At the hop: *Todd, Nick*
CD CDCHD 609
Ace / May '95 / Pinnacle

DOUBLE AGENT 1980
CD AGENT 1980
Double Agent / Feb '97 / Cargo

DOUBLE ARTICULATION (Folds And Rhizomes Remixed)
CD SR 110
Sub Rosa / Feb '97 / Direct / RTM/Disc / SRD / Vital

DOUBLE D'OR - ITALIE (2CD Set)
CD Set 3030822
Arcade / Jun '97 / Discovery

DOUBLE ECLIPSE - TRIBUTE TO NEDLY ELSTAK
CD BVHAASTCD 9210
Bvhaast / Dec '89 / Cadillac

DOWN AND OUT BLUES (4CD Set)
CD Set MBSCD 434
Castle / Nov '95 / BMG

DOWN MEMORY LANE
Fine romance: *Dieval, Jack* / Cheek to cheek: *Osborne, Tony* / By the light of the silvery moon/On Moonlight Bay: *John, Michael Singers* / I'm beginning to see the light: *Moorhouse, Alan* / Yours: *Ternent, Billy* / I won't dance: *Dieval, Jack* / Quando, quando: *Tait, Basil* / I've got my love to keep me warm: *Osborne, Tony* / Way you look tonight: *Dieval, Jack* / Five foot two, eyes of blue: *Ternent, Billy* / Three o'clock in the morning: *Moorhouse, Alan* / Broken doll: *John, Michael Singers* / Anything goes: *Britannia Band* / You were meant for me: *Ternent, Billy* / I only have eyes for you: *Evans, Tony* / Fascination: *Sherwood Foresters* / Stars fell on Alabama: *Ternent, Billy* / Is it true what they say about Dixie: *John, Michael Singers* / Goodnight sweetheart/I'll see you in my dreams: *John, Michael Singers*
CD 305182
Hallmark / Jul '97 / Carlton

DOWN TO THE ROACH (New Trip Hop - The Ultimate In Tripped Out Beats)
Theme from Lounge: *Lounge* / Freshmess: *Hookian Mindz* / Talking drum: *APE* / Desire: *69* / Tow truck: *Sabres Of Paradise* / Essential philosophy: *Fire & Theft* / Sisterettes and Brotherettes: *8 Up* / Temple trax 003: *4E* / Freedom: *DJ Food* / Fourth way: *Daddy Longlegs* / Natural high: *Warp 69*
CD CDTEP 9
Step 2 / Sep '95 / 3mv/Sony

DOWNLOW HIP HOP (The Hip Hop Underground)
Die young: *Intro* / I was forgotten: *Godfather Don* / Frankenstein's pain: *Frankenstein* / Do yo' thing: *Tariq, Al* / Next type of motion: *Roots Manuva* / Let me know something: *Chill Rob G* / Mysteries of life: *Parker, Lewis* / Tried by 12: *East Flatbush Project* / Real estate: *Blak Twang* / Braggin writes: *J-Live* / You made me: *Prince Paul* / TCB: *Outro*
CD SOUNDSCD 10
Street Sounds / Oct '96 / Beechwood/BMG

DOWNTOWN (20 Great Hits Of The Sixties)
You really got me: *Kinks* / Sweets for my sweet: *Searchers* / Always something there to remind me: *Shaw, Sandie* / Here comes my baby: *Tremeloes* / Catch the wind: *Donovan* / Downtown: *Clark, Petula* / Twenty four hours from Tulsa: *Pitney, Gene* / Go now: *Moody Blues* / Baby, now that I've found you: *Foundations* / Sugar and spice: *Searchers* / Cast your fate to the wind: *Sounds Orchestral* / Elenore: *Turtles* / Tossin' and turnin': *Ivy League* / Here comes the nice: *Small Faces* / Out of time: *Farlowe, Chris* / Louie Louie: *Kingsmen* / That girl belongs to yesterday: *Pitney, Gene* / Michelle: *Overlanders* / This is my song: *Clark, Petula* / Don't throw your love away: *Searchers*
CD TRTCD 103
TrueTrax / Oct '94 / THE

DR. BOB JONES PRESENTS THE FUNK CONNECTION
CD PAZ 802CD
La Plaza / Sep '97 / Essential/BMG

DRAG ADDICT
Work to do: *Roach Motel* / Diva (Diva's talk): *Club 69* / Sugar pie guy (the absolute high): *Club 69* / Ku koo for cocoanuts: *One Groovy Cocoanut* / Oh Daddy shit (big Daddy remix): *That Kid Chris* / Men adore (12 inches just the right size): *Fierce Child* / Give it to Mama: *Yvette* / Accident: *Ride Committee* / Officer where's your brother (get her): *Morel's Grooves* / Wham bam (Sharon's supa-sonic mix): *Candy Girls* / Down to the waistline (honey): *Morel's Grooves* / Radikal bitch (London fierce pussy mix): *Armando* / Get your hands off my man (a dub 4 junior): *Junior* / X-Xuses (Acapella): *Blacktivity* / Filthy hetro (nu industrial mix): *Tracy & Sharon* / Love to do it: *Ride* / Boyfriend (sweet machine mix): *Love & Sex* / Get to know me: *Tracy & Sharon*
CD CDHUT 34
Hut / Feb '96 / EMI

DRAG CITY HOUR
CD SN 2
Sea Note / Dec '96 / Cargo

DRAUMKVEDET
CD HCD 7098CD
Musikk Distribujson / Apr '95 / ADA

DREAD BEAT & RIDDIMS VOL.2
CD CRSCD 902
CRS / Aug '96 / ADA / Direct / Jet Star

DREAD POETS SOCIETY
CD EFA 11665CD
T'Bwana / Apr '93 / SRD

DREAM IN COLOUR
CD NTHEN 9
Now & Then / Sep '95 / Plastic Head

DREAM INJECTION VOL.2 (2CD Set)
Bass cadet: *Autechre* / Oil zone: *Speedy J* / Welcome home: *Kosmik Kommando* / Malmo: *Capslock* / First mechanical: *Red Sector A* / Chemical: *Tapeworm* / Dark: *Fini Tribe* / Windscreen wiper: *Shaolin Wooden Men* / Herbstwald: *Time Modem* / Ereximus: *Xyphax* / Start as you mean to go on: *Aphex Twin* / Ballad of Nicky McGuire: *Sabres Of Paradise* / Java: *Larkin, Kenny* / Envelope: *Immersion* / Credo: *Pentatonik* / Manifestation: *Haujobb* / Open mind: *Orbital* / Luxor: *Code* / Sudafelm: *Beaumont Hannant* / Nutrient: *Brain Pilot* / Attalal: *Download* / Swan Vesta: *u-Ziq*
CD Set 08938692
Westcom / Apr '96 / Koch / Pinnacle

DREAM INJECTION VOL.3 (Trance & Ambience/2CD Set)
Deep blue sea: *Scuba* / Halcyon and on and on: *Orbital* / Blueprints: *Price, Darren* / Affective: *Lobe* / Con spirito: *C.J. Bolland* / Casablanca: *Ambush* / Stardancer: *Morley, David* / Psi-onyx (mmm): *Beaumont Hannant* / Low-key sonics: *Zero Men* / TN-forces: *Xyphax* / Union of ilk: *Nuw Idol* / Atlantis: *Red Sector A* / Traume: *Cosmic Baby* / Surrender: *Interloper* / Dynamic solution: *Plastic System* / Dark side: *Resistance D* / No future: *Klange* / Corporate anthem pt.1: *Soma* / Muta 3: *Anibaldi, Leo* / On: *Aphex Twin* / Love song: *Influx* / Dream injection: *It*
CD Set SPV 08947432
Westcom / Feb '97 / Koch / Pinnacle

DREAM INJECTION VOL.4 (2CD Set)
CD Set DCD 08947522
Westcom / May '97 / Koch / Pinnacle

DREAM TEAM IN THE MIX (The London Dream Team In Session)
Closer than close: *Gaines, Rosie* / Love can't turn around: *Farley Jackmaster Funk* / Keep on moving: *DJ Disciple* / Find the path: *New Horizon* / Special: *Colour Girl* / Freaky: *Timmi Magic* / Wanna spend the night: *Lewis, Danny J.* / Things are never: *Operator & Baffled* / Deliver me: *Urban Blues Project* / Dreams: *Smokin' Beats* / Bad boys: *Baffled Republic* / Release the pressure: *Foster, Danny* / Lift me up: *Vasquez, Junior* / One more time: *King, Evelyn 'Champagne'*
CD LIBTCD 002
4 Liberty / Jun '97 / BMG / Mo's Music Machine / Pinnacle / SRD

DREAM TOPPING
Hangover square: *Always* / Ulysses and the siren: *Adverse, Anthony* / Tidal wave: *Apples* / Discotheque: *Bad Dream Fancy Dress* / Pele: *Cornelius* / 6 A.M.: *Daily Planet* / Trouble in ten town: *Darlene Fanclub* / Mike alway's diary: *Karie, Kahimi* / Zoom up: *Karie, Kahimi* / Where have all the schoolboys gone: *King Of Luxembourg* / Martine: *Philippe, Louis* / Hot cherry love bombs: *Magnificent Andersons* / Toffee spot: *Magnificent Andersons* / Grant me the day: *Marbles* / Our man in: *Marden Hill* / You're an angel: *Mr. Martini* / Sadness of things: *Momus* / Jackie Onassis: *Milky* / Noise: *Monochrome Set* / Big beat Jesus cheat: *Pink Kross* / Pure: *Pulling Jessica's Hair* / Take three girls: *Romaine* / Sit down I think I love you: *Fisher-Turner, Simon* / Ecuador days: *Would-Be-Goods* / Camera loves me: *Would-Be-Goods*
CD MONDE 21CD
Richmond / Sep '95 / Pinnacle

DREAMHOUSE VOL.1 (Le Voyage)
Fly: *D'Agostino Planet* / Jack of the green: *Land Of Oz* / Bakerloo symphony: *Picotto, Mauro* / Giallone remix: *D'Agostino, Gigi* / Happily: *D'Agostino, Gigi* / Hit the bang: *Groove Park* / Children: *Miles, Robert* / Noise maker theme: *D'Agostino, Gigi* / My house: *Picotto, Mauro* / Harmonic: *D'Agostino, Gigi* / Marimba: *D'Agostino Planet* / Melody voyager:

D'Agostino Planet / Android: *2 Culture In A Room* / For love: *D'Agostino Planet* / Groovebird: *Natural Born Groovers*
CD ___ MCD 60015
MCA / Jul '96 / BMG

DREAMS AND THEMES (20 Synth Classics)
Chase / Magic fly / Axel F / Moments in love / I hear you now / Second time / Equinoxe / Chariots of fire / Eve of the war / Dune / Oxygene / Theme from Rainman / Take my breath away / Falling / Tao of love / Crockett's theme / Lily was here / Another day in paradise / Eternal flame
CD ___ SUMCD 4011
Summit / Nov '96 / Sound & Media

DREAMS IN THE WITCHOUSE
CD ___ FETISH 666CD
Grave News / May '96 / Plastic Head

DREAMS OF ANGELS (A Magical Blend Of Music And The Sounds Of Nature)
CD ___ 57672
CMC / May '97 / BMG

DREAMS OF FLYING - ASTRAL JAZZ
CD ___ WCL 11014
White Cloud / Feb '96 / Select

DRINK ME SAMPLER '96
CD ___ DRINK 1
Echo / Jan '96 / EMI / Vital

DRINKING AND LOVE SONGS OF SOUTH WEST CHINA
CD ___ ARN 64363
Arion / Sep '96 / ADA / Discovery

DRIVE TIME - THE VERY BEST OF DRIVE TIME (2CD Set)
CD Set ___ DINCD 137
Dino / Apr '97 / Pinnacle

DRIVE TIME VOL.1 (2CD Set)
CD Set ___ DINCD 96
Dino / Mar '95 / Pinnacle

DRIVE TIME VOL.2 (2CD Set)
Weather with you: *Crowded House* / Valerie: *Winwood, Steve* / Addicted to love: *Palmer, Robert* / Everybody's talkin': *Beautiful South* / Brown eyed girl: *Morrison, Van* / American pie: *McLean, Don* / Heat is on: *Frey, Glenn* / Walking in Memphis: *Cohn, Marc* / How soon is now: *Smiths* / Black velvet: *Myles, Alannah* / Right beside you: *Hawkins, Sophie B.* / Walking on sunshine: *Katrina & The Waves* / Calling all the heroes: *It Bites* / Living in America: *Brown, James* / Imagination: *Belouis Some* / Mr. Blue Sky: *ELO* / Broken land: *Adventures* / Is it like today: *World Party* / Brass in pocket: *Pretenders* / Show me heaven: *McKee, Maria* / Wake up Boo: *Boo Radleys* / Love shack: *B-52's* / Sit down: *James* / Independent love song: *Scarlet* / Crazy for you: *Let Loose* / Suspicious minds: *Fine Young Cannibals* / Thorn in my side: *Eurythmics* / Road to hell: *Rea, Chris* / Bridge to your heart: *Wax* / Summer in the city: *Lovin' Spoonful* / Come undone: *Duran Duran* / Stay: *Shakespears Sister* / Waiting for a star to fall: *Boy Meets Girl* / Kyrie: *Mr. Mister* / Glory of love: *Cetera, Peter* / Driver's seat: *Sniff 'n' The Tears* / Everybody's gotta learn sometime: *Korgis* / (Feels like) Heaven: *Fiction Factory* / Sailing on the seven seas: *OMD* / Race: *Yello*
CD Set ___ DINCD 99
Dino / Jul '95 / Pinnacle

DRIVE TIME VOL.3 (40 Of The Greatest Radio Anthems Of All Time - 2CD Set)
74-75: *Connells* / It's in his kiss (The shoop shoop song): *Cher* / Here I stand: *Milltown Brothers* / There she goes: *La's* / Flashdance what a feeling: *Cara, Irene* / She drives me crazy: *Fine Young Cannibals* / Can you dig it: *Mock Turtles* / Different for girls: *Jackson, Joe* / Lost weekend: *Cole, Lloyd* / Stir it up: *Labelle, Patti* / Maniac: *Sembello, Michael* / Olivers army: *Costello, Elvis* / Moon light shadow: *Oldfield, Mike* / Girl like you: *Collins, Edwyn* / Sleeping satellite: *Archer, Tasmin* / Will you: *O'Connor, Hazel* / Walk of life: *Dire Straits* / I could be so good to you: *Waterman, Dennis* / Lessons in love: *Level 42* / Once in a lifetime: *Talking Heads* / Baker Street: *Rafferty, Gerry* / Betty Davis eyes: *Carnes, Kim* / Fall at your feet: *Crowded House* / Airport: *Motors* / Everybody wants to rule: *Tears For Fears* / I don't want a lover: *Texas* / Letter from America: *Proclaimers* / Missing you: *Waite, John* / Blinded by the light: *Manfred Mann* / Mustang Sally: *Commitments* / Eloise: *Damned* / I want your love: *Transvision Vamp* / Good tradition: *Tikaram, Tanita* / Your so vain: *Simon, Carly* / Owner of a lonely heart: *Yes* / Constant craving: *Lang, k.d.* / Somewhere in my heart: *Aztec Camera* / Life in a northern town: *Dream Academy* / Kiss from a rose: *Seal* / I got my mind set on you: *Harrison, George*
CD Set ___ DINCD 119
Dino / Dec '95 / Pinnacle

DRIVE TIME VOL.4 (2CD Set)
Lucky you: *Lightning Seeds* / Run baby run: *Crow, Sheryl* / Harvest for the world: *Christians* / Kiss this thing goodbye: *Del Amitri* / Goodbye Yellow Brick Road: *John, Elton* / How long: *Ace* / Love and affection: *Armatrading, Joan* / Never let her slip away: *Gold, Andrew* / Running up that hill: *Bush, Kate* / Getting away with it: *Electronic* / Jessie: *Kadison, Joshua* / Golden brown: *Stranglers* / Rush hour: *Wiedlin, Jane* / I got you: *Split Enz* / One by one: *Cher* / Would I lie to you: *Charles & Eddie* / Yah mo B there: *Ingram, James & Michael McDonald* / Pick up the pieces: *Average White Band* / Don't stop: *Fleetwood Mac* / Stuck in the middle with you: *Stealer's Wheel* / Love of the common people: *Young, Paul* / War baby: *Robinson, Tom* / Horse with no name: *America* / Let your love flow: *Bellamy Brothers* / Real gone kid: *Deacon Blue* / Sweet sixteen: *Idol, Billy* / Shout: *Tears For Fears* / All right now: *Free* / Power of love: *Lewis, Huey & The News* / Two Princes: *Spin Doctors* / Sweet talkin' woman: *ELO* / Walk like an Egyptian: *Bangles* / Make me smile (come up and see me): *Harley, Steve & Cockney Rebel* / Come on Eileen: *Dexy's Midnight Runners & Emerald Express* / Young at heart: *Bluebells* / If you let me stay: *D'Arby, Terence Trent*
CD Set ___ DINCD 128
Dino / Aug '96 / Pinnacle

DRIVIN' COUNTRY
Rhinestone cowboy: *Campbell, Glen* / Talking in your sleep: *Gayle, Crystal* / Blanket on the ground: *Spears, Billie Jo* / Rose Marie: *Whitman, Slim* / Have I told you lately that I love you: *Nelson, Willie* / Another place another time: *Williams, Don* / Sweet dreams: *Young, Faron* / I'll never fall in love again: *Gentry, Bobbie* / Stand by your man: *Jackson, Wanda* / All I have to do is dream: *Newton, Juice* / Wings of a dove: *Husky, Ferlin* / King of the road: *Ford, Tennessee Ernie* / When you're in love with a beautiful woman: *Dr. Hook* / I honestly love you: *Newton-John, Olivia* / Games people play: *South, Joe* / I just had you on my mind: *Caddock, Billy 'Crash'* / Crazy: *Nelson, Willie* / Still crazy after all these years: *Dalton, Lacy J.*
CD ___ CDMFP 6228
Music For Pleasure / Aug '96 / EMI

DRIVIN' EASY
Fever: *Lee, Peggy* / Memories are made of this: *Martin, Dean* / Let there be love: *Cole, Nat 'King'* / Cry me a river: *London, Julie* / Angie baby: *Reddy, Helen* / Portrait of my love: *Monro, Matt* / Volare: *Martino, Al* / And I love you so: *Bassey, Shirley* / Don't it make my brown eyes blue: *Gayle, Crystal* / Galveston: *Campbell, Glen* / If not you: *Dr. Hook* / Crying: *McLean, Don* / Wind beneath my wings: *Keel, Howard* / On the street where you live: *Damone, Vic* / Moon river: *Williams, Danny* / You belong to me: *Stafford, Jo* / I'll never find another you: *Seekers* / He ain't heavy, he's my brother: *Hollies*
CD ___ CDMFP 6238
Music For Pleasure / Aug '96 / EMI

DRIVIN' HITS
Simply irresistable: *Palmer, Robert* / Nutbush City limits: *Turner, Ike & Tina* / My Sharona: *Knack* / Call me: *Blondie* / Bang bang (my baby shot me down): *Cher* / Missing you: *Waite, John* / Bette Davies eyes: *Carnes, Kim* / Vienna: *Ultravox* / True: *Spandau Ballet* / Golden brown: *Stranglers* / Running up that hill: *Bush, Kate* / Here comes the sun: *Harley, Steve & Cockney Rebel* / Walking on sunshine: *Katrina & The Waves* / Geno: *Dexy's Midnight Runners* / Call me: *Go West* / Baker St.: *Rafferty, Gerry* / Roll over Beethoven: *ELO* / Hi ho silver lining: *Beck, Jeff*
CD ___ CDMFP 6227
Music For Pleasure / Aug '96 / EMI

DRIVIN' ROCK 'N' ROLL
Blueberry Hill: *Domino, Fats* / Take good care of my baby: *Vee, Bobby* / Walk don't run: *Ventures* / Be bop a lula: *Vincent, Gene* / Somethin' else: *Cochran, Eddie* / I'm walkin': *Domino, Fats* / Why do fools fall in love: *Lymon, Frankie & The Teenagers* / Rubber ball: *Vee, Bobby* / Summertime blues: *Cochran, Eddie* / Willie and the hand jive: *Otis, Johnny Show* / Dreaming: *Burnette, Johnny* / Blue Jean bop: *Vincent, Gene* / I'm not a juvenile delinquent: *Lymon, Frankie & The Teenagers* / Shakin' all over: *Kidd, Johnny & The Pirates* / Only sixteen: *Douglas, Craig* / Blue moon: *Marcels* / Love potion no.9: *Clovers* / Tell Laura I love her: *Valence, Ricky* / You've got what it takes: *Johnson, Mary* / Party doll: *Knox, Buddy* / You're sixteen: *Burnette, Johnny* / Saturday night at the Duck Pond: *Cougars*
CD ___ CDMFP 6229
Music For Pleasure / Aug '96 / EMI

DRIVIN' ROCK VOL.1
CD ___ KNEWCD 729
Kenwest / Feb '94 / THE

DRIVIN' ROCK VOL.2
CD ___ KNEWCD 730
Kenwest / Feb '94 / THE

DRIVIN' ROCK VOL.3
CD ___ KNEWCD 731
Kenwest / Feb '94 / THE

DRIVIN' ROCK VOL.4
CD ___ KNEWCD 732
Kenwest / Feb '94 / THE

DRIVING ROCK (2CD Set)
Radio ga ga: *Queen* / Here I go again: *Whitesnake* / Legs: *ZZ Top* / Rhiannon: *Fleetwood Mac* / Long train runnin': *Doobie Brothers* / Rock 'n' me: *Miller, Steve Band* / Two princes: *Spin Doctors* / Mm mm mm mm: *Crash Test Dummies* / Inside: *Stiltskin* / Lil' devil: *Cult* / Can't get enough: *Bad Company* / Black velvet: *Myles, Alannah* / You can go your own way: *Rea, Chris* / Rocky mountain way: *Walsh, Joe* / Well all right: *Santana* / Dead ringer for love: *Meat Loaf* / If I could turn back time: *Cher* / Voodoo chile: *Hendrix, Jimi* / Drive: *Cars* / Hazard: *Marx, Richard* / To be with you: *Mr. Big* / Show me heaven: *McKee, Maria* / Abracadabra: *Miller, Steve Band* / Stop draggin my heart around: *Nicks, Stevie* / Because the night: *Smith, Patti* / Sweet home Alabama: *Lynyrd Skynyrd* / There goes another love song: *Outlaws* / More than a feeling: *Boston* / Hold the line: *Toto* / Love is the drug: *Roxy Music* / China in your hand: *T'Pau* / Life's been good: *Walsh, Joe* / I can't go for that (no can do): *Hall & Oates* / Nothing's gonna stop us now: *Starship* / Broken wings: *Mr. Mister* / Time after time: *Lauper, Cyndi* / Black betty: *Ram Jam* / I want to know what love is: *Foreigner*
CD Set ___ GLOCD 3
Global TV / Jul '97 / BMG

DRONES AND THE CHANTERS, THE
CD ___ CC 61CD
Claddagh / Mar '95 / ADA / CM / Direct

DROP IN THE OCEAN, A
CD ___ ETCD 10
Semantic / Feb '94 / Plastic Head

DROP OF THE IRISH, A
CD ___ PASTCD 9799
Flapper / Sep '92 / Pinnacle

DROP THE BOX
CD ___ CDLDL 1234
Lochshore / Oct '95 / ADA / Direct / Duncans

DROS BIANT Y BYD
CD ___ SCD 2113
Sain / Aug '95 / ADA / Direct / Greyhound

DRUG TEST VOL.1
CD ___ INV 081CD
Invisible / May '97 / Plastic Head

DRUM, CHANT & INSTRUMENTAL MUSIC OF NIGER, MALI & UPPER VOLT
CD ___ 7559720732
Nonesuch / Jan '95 / Warner Music

DRUM CRAZY VOL.1
CD ___ DCCD 001
Drum Crazy / Jul '96 / Timewarp

DRUM CRAZY VOL.2
CD ___ DCCD 002
Drum Crazy / Jul '96 / Timewarp

DRUM CRAZY VOL.3
CD ___ DCCD 003
Drum Crazy / Jul '96 / Timewarp

DRUM CRAZY VOL.4
CD ___ DCCD 004
Drum Crazy / Jul '96 / Timewarp

DRUM CRAZY VOL.5
CD ___ DCCD 005
Drum Crazy / Jul '96 / Timewarp

DRUM 'N' BASS COLLECTION VOL.1 (Drum 'n' Bass Selection Vol.1 & 2/4CD Set)
CD ___ BDRBOX 1
Breakdown / Nov '95 / Pinnacle

DRUM 'N' BASS COLLECTION VOL.2 (Drum 'n' Bass Selection Vol.3 & 4/ Telepathy/5CD Set)
CD Set ___ BDRBOX 2
Breakdown / Nov '95 / Pinnacle

DRUM 'N' BASS FEVER
CD ___ TOYCD 1002
Intrinsic / Nov '96 / Pinnacle

DRUM 'N' BASS MANIA
CD ___ EMPRCD 702
Emporio / Mar '97 / Disc

DRUM 'N' BASS MIX 1997 (2CD Set)
Ain't talkin' 'bout dub: *Apollo 440* / Sweet love: *M-Beat & Nazlyn* / Inner city life: *Goldie* / Feel the sunshine: *Reece, Alex* / Sea: *St. Etienne* / One day I'll fly away: *Llorena, Kelly* / Far away: *Doc Scott* / Wetern tune: *PFM* / To give but not forget: *Outside* / It's a jazz thing: *Roni Size* / Impact: *City Connection* / Psychosis: *Peshay* / Horn section: *Rogue Unit* / Mindz: *Mind 21* / Rhode tune: *Flytronix* / Take me to heaven: *Baby D* / Do U know: *M-Beat & Jamiroquai* / Greater love: *Soundman & Don Lloydie/Elizabeth Troy* / Morning will come: *M-Beat & Junior Giscombe* / Smooth note: *Mouse, Jason* / Piano tune: *Peshay* / Rays of sun: *Acetate* / Bubblegum: *One True Parker* / Wishing on a star: *88.3 & Lisa May* / Renegade snares: *Omni Trio* / So many dreams: *Guy Called Gerald* / Moments in space: *Nookie* / Urban blues: *Gurley, S.* / Spectrum: *Wax Doctor* / Play the game: *Freestyles* / Feenin': *Jodeci* / F-Jam: *Adam F* / Walking wounded: *Everything But The Girl* / Can't knock the hustle: *Jay-Z & Mary J. Blige* / Cotton wool: *Lamb*
CD Set ___ 5533952
PolyGram TV / Mar '97 / PolyGram

DRUM 'N' BASS SELECTION VOL.2 (2CD Set)
Rrroll da bbeats: *DJ Hype* / Maximum style: *Tom & Jerry* / Hello lover: *Fallen Angel* / Sweet vibrations: *DMS & Boneman X* / Maniac music: *Lick Back Organisation* / Johnny 94: *Johnny Jungle* / It's a jazz thing: *Roni Size* / Mo musik: *DJ Ron* / Stand easy: *JB* / Callin' all the people: *A-Zone* / Terrorist: *Renegade* / You must think first: *Dope Style* / Predator: *Shimon* / Ruff revival: *Run Tings* / Droppin' science vol.1: *Droppin' Science* / Screw face: *Brain Killers* / Time to move: *DJ Dextrous* / Kall da kops: *Sacred* / What kind of world: *Send* / Burial: *Leviticus*
CD Set ___ BDRCD 3
Breakdown / Sep '94 / Pinnacle

DRUM 'N' BASS SELECTION VOL.3 (2CD Set)
Cool down: *Andy C* / Lionheart: *Bert & Dillinger* / King of the jungle: *King Of The Jungle* / Feel the magic: *Sophisticated Bad Boyz* / War in '94: *Badman* / Dead bass: *Dead Dred* / Air freshener: *Tom & Jerry Vol 9* / Booyaaa: *Amazon II* / Rude boy: *Flex* / Hitman: *Marvellous Caine* / Ganja man: *Krome & Time* / Little roller Vol 1: *L-Double* / Sound murderer: *Remarc* / Heavenly body: *DJ Dextrous* / Firing line: *Droppin' Science* / Mash up da place: *Ganga Vol 4* / Ali Baba: *Hopa & Bones* / Yeah man: *Dream Team* / Alive and kicking (origin unknown mix): *Red One* / Selectors roll: *Rus De Tox & Teebone*
CD Set ___ BDRCD 5
Breakdown / Nov '94 / Pinnacle

DRUM 'N' BASS SELECTION VOL.4 (2CD Set)
CD Set ___ BDRCD 6
Breakdown / Apr '95 / Pinnacle

DRUM 'N' BASS SELECTION VOL.5 (2CD Set)
CD ___ BDRCD 9
Breakdown / Sep '95 / Pinnacle

DRUM SONG (Mighty Mike's Continuous Mix)
CD ___ RN 0047
Rhino / Feb '97 / Grapevine/PolyGram / Jet Star

DRUMMERS FANFARE
Drum fanfare: *Shotts & Dykehead Caledonia Pipe Band* / Selection: *Cook, Arthur* / March, strathspey and reel: *Kilpatrick, Jim* / Selection: *Ward, Eric*
CD ___ LCOM 5174
Lismor / Feb '97 / ADA / Direct / Duncans / Lismor

DRUMS OF SOUTH AMERICA (Guadeloupe/Venezuela/Cuba/3CD Set)
CD Set ___ C 570302
Ocora / Mar '97 / ADA / Harmonia Mundi

DRUMS OF THE EARTH VOL.1
CD ___ AUB 6773
Auvidis/Ethnic / Mar '93 / ADA / Harmonia Mundi

DRUMS OF THE EARTH VOL.2 (Asia)
CD ___ AUB 6774
Auvidis/Ethnic / Apr '93 / ADA / Harmonia Mundi

DRUMS PARADE 1937-1945
CD ___ 158692
Jazz Archives / Jan '97 / Discovery

DRY LUNGS (2CD Set)
CD Set ___ DVLR 1DCD
Dark Vinyl / Aug '93 / Plastic Head / World Serpent

DUB EXPLOSION
CD ___ CDTRL 366
Trojan / Jan '96 / Direct / Jet Star

DUB FROM JAMAICA ROOTS
CD ___ OMCD 034
Original Music / Sep '96 / Jet Star / SRD

DUB HOUSE DISCO VOL.1
CD ___ GRCD 004
Guerilla / Aug '92 / Pinnacle

DUB HOUSE DISCO VOL.2 (2000)
Land of Oz: *Spooky* / I still want ya: *Outer Mind* / Feel: *Chameleon Project* / Schudelfloss: *Dr. Atomic* / Product: *10th Chapter* / Alchemy: *Drum Club* / Oh yeah: *DOP* / Dub house disco: *2 Shiny Heads* / Feeling warm: *Eagles Prey* / Supereal: *One Nation* / Intoxication: *React 2 Rhythm* / Schmoo: *Spooky*
CD ___ GRCD 007
Guerilla / Jul '94 / Pinnacle

DUB HOUSE DISCO VOL.3 (The Third)
Little bullet: *Spooky* / Here I go: *DOP* / Underground: *Matter* / Aquamarine: *Lemon Sol* / Blue beyond: *Supereal* / Persuasion: *Martin, Billie Ray & Spooky* / Come into my life: *Abfahrt* / Higher: *Code MD* / Columbia: *Chameleon Project* / Prologue: *10th Chapter* / Solar: *Shape Navigator* / Persuasion (mix): *Martin, Billie Ray & Spooky*
CD ___ GRCD 012
Guerilla / Jul '94 / Pinnacle

DUB OR DIE VOL.1
CD ___ RE 099CD
ROIR / Jul '97 / Plastic Head / Shellshock/ Disc

DUB OR DIE VOL.2
CD ________ RE 098CD
ROIR / Jul '97 / Plastic Head / Shellshock/ Disc

DUB OUT WEST VOL.1 (Roots Cultivatas)
Bongo dub: *Jackson, Dan* / Jah pure and clean: *Peter D* / Beulah unforsaken land: *Henry & Louis* / Addis dub: *Armagideon* / Freedom part III: *Dub Crusaders* / Fanfare: *Ratman* / Promised land: *Alpha & Omega* / Glory dub: *Stryka Dread* / Agent dub: *Dub Plate Vibes Crew* / Tribute to the gentle giant: *Blue & Red* / Take heed: *Black Roots* / Dub robery: *High Tech Roots Dynamics* / Mother Africa: *I-Phonic* / Ark of the covenant: *Inner State*
CD ________ NRCD 014
Nubian / Mar '96 / Jet Star / Vital

DUB OUT WEST VOL.2 (Roots: Forward Ever)
Fishtown dub: *Shotgun Rockers* / Kalahari dub: *Inner State* / Selassie I feeling: *Skelly Roots* / Tribulation dub: *Culture D* / Kick down vatican: *Stryka Dread* / In captivity: *Black Roots* / Ras is head dub: *Reading Music Collective* / Chemical reaction dub: *Dub Chasm* / Dub symphony: *Daddy Roots* / Jah love dub: *Armagideon* / Scorcher dub: *Imperial Force* / Only Jah: *Dub Ghecko* / Rightful ruler: *Alpha & Omega* / Storm, steal and fire: *Rhythm-Ites* / Salvation dub: *Yagga Dan & Daddy Skrew* / King David symphony: *Dub Plate Vibes Crew*
CD ________ NRCD 015
Nubian / Nov '96 / Jet Star / Vital

DUB OUT WEST VOL.3 (Change Of Step)
Black woman dub: *Stryka Dread* / Looking for Eden: *Dub Chandra* / Conflicts with the police: *Alpha & Omega* / Everytime: *Dub Ghecko* / Good, the dub and the free: *Black Roots* / Hydro dub: *Armagideon* / Judas: *Ratman* / Hiroshima part 2: *Dub Nation* / Stop fighting: *Rose, Peter D. & Felix* / Unite against war and famine: *Blue & Red* / Grip: *Equinox* / Nosferatu: *Shotgun Rockers*
CD ________ NRCD 016
Nubian / May '97 / Jet Star / Vital

DUB OVER DUB
CD ________ CDHB 202203
Heartbeat / Feb '96 / ADA / Direct / Greensleeves / Jet Star

DUB PLATE SELECTION
CD ________ STHCCD 15
Strictly Hardcore / Sep '95 / SRD

DUB REVOLUTION
CD ________ RUSCD 8207
ROIR / Jul '95 / Plastic Head / Shellshock/ Disc

DUB, TRIP AND HOP
CD ________ FRCD 5
Flex / Jun '95 / Jet Star / Plastic Head / SRD

DUBBED OUT IN DC
CD ________ ESL 006
18th Street Lounge / Jun '97 / Cargo

DUBBLE ATTACK (Dee-Jay Collection 1972-1974)
No. 1 in the world: *U-Roy* / Opportunity rock: *Big Youth* / Meaning of one: *Prince Jazzbo* / Rasta on a Sunday: *I-Roy* / Father's call: *Beckford, Dean* / This is a year for rebels: *Godsons* / Spider to the fly: *Big Youth* / Brother Toby is a movie from London: *I-Roy* / Mr. Harry Skank: *Prince Jazzbo* / Dubble attack: *Big Youth* / Whole lot of sugar: *Prince Hammer* / Festive season: *I-Roy* / Mr. Want All: *Prince Jazzbo* / Butter bread: *Young, Lloyd*
CD ________ GRELCD 601
Greensleeves / May '90 / Jet Star / SRD

DUBHEAD - THE 90'S DUB SAMPLER VOL.1
CD ________ IVECD 2
Shiver / Oct '95 / SRD

DUBHEAD - THE 90'S DUB SAMPLER VOL.2
CD ________ IVECD 4
Shiver / Mar '96 / SRD

DUBHEAD - THE 90'S DUB SAMPLER VOL.3
CD ________ IVE 005CD
Shiver / Jul '97 / SRD

DUBITAMIN
Repetitive beats: *Retribution* / No dog bark: *Dub Syndicate* / Earth rocker: *Bush Chemists* / I wah 4000: *Mixman* / Zion ring: *Zion Train* / Splash say the fishes in the sea: *Wimbish, Doug* / Tabla school: *Suns Of Arqa* / High speed dubbing: *Bush Chemists & Culture Freeman* / Rightway: *Power Steppers* / Mastermonk: *Electric Source* / Outer space: *Tassilli Players* / Circle line: *Blue / Sunshine* dub: *Vibe Tribe Soundsystem & Don Abi*
CD ________ EFA 063512
Roundtrip / Jan '97 / SRD

DUBLIN ONE RECORDINGS VOL.1
CD ________ DONECD 1
Dublin One / Apr '97 / Prime / SRD

DUBLIN SONGS
Molly Malone: *Band Of Dubs* / Rocky road to Dublin: *Dubliners* / Spanish lady: *Reilly, Paddy* / Biddy Mulligan: *Grace, Brendan* / Rare ould times: *Dubliners* / St. Laurence O'Toole: *Fureys & Davey Arthur* / Dublin, my Dublin: *Reilly, Paddy* / Ringsend rose: *Grace, Brendan* / Raglan Road: *McCann, Jim* / Dublin saunter: *Reilly, Paddy* / Night ferry: *Fureys & Davey Arthur* / Dublin town: *Grace, Brendan* / Foggy dew: *McCann, Jim* / Auld triangle: *Dubliners* / Summer in Dublin: *McCann, Jim* / Anna Liffey: *Dubliners* / Dublin in my tears: *Fureys & Davey Arthur* / Jem: *Drew, Ronnie* / Dublin - take me: *Fureys & Davey Arthur*
CD ________ MCCD 042
Music Club / Sep '91 / Disc / THE

DUBMISSION VOL.1
Destination unknown: *Sly & Robbie* / Demolition city: *Sly & Robbie* / Ion storm: *Black Uhuru* / Boof n' baff n' biff: *Black Uhuru* / Flikaflame: *Aswad* / Tuffist: *Aswad* / I and I survive: *Burning Spear* / Reality: *Johnson, Linton Kwesi* / Shocking: *Johnson, Linton Kwesi* / Night nurse: *Isaacs, Gregory*
CD ________ 5242942
Quango / Aug '97 / PolyGram

DUBMISSION VOL.2 (The Remixes)
Night nurse: *Isaacs, Gregory* / Boof n' baff n' biff: *Black Uhuru* / Destination unknown: *Sly & Robbie* / I and I survive: *Burning Spear* / Boof n' baff n' biff: *Black Uhuru* / Demolition city: *Sly & Robbie* / Demolition city: *Sly & Robbie* / Ion storm: *Black Uhuru* / Boof n' baff n' biff: *Black Uhuru* / Night nurse: *Isaacs, Gregory*
CD ________ 5244212
Quango / Aug '97 / PolyGram

DUBNOLOGY VOL.1
CD ________ MIDDL 4CD
Middle Earth / Nov '95 / RTM/Disc

DUBNOLOGY VOL.2 (Lost In Bass/2CD Set)
CD Set ________ MIDDLE 7CD
Middle Earth / Oct '96 / RTM/Disc

DUBS FOR DAZE VOL.1 (Jim Fox Dubs Up The Ras Tapes/2CD Set)
Knock knock dub: *Don Carlos* / Rastafari dub: *Broggs, Peter* / Got to be dub: *Broggs, Peter* / Dub rider: *Don Carlos* / Leaving dub: *Don Carlos* / Jah a de dub: *McGregor, Freddie* / Cool dub: *Don Carlos* / Dub sheriff: *Broggs, Peter* / Sunshine dub: *Don Carlos* / Nice to be dub: *Roots Radics* / General dub: *Charlie Chaplin* / Always dub: *Brown, Foxy* / Dub farmer: *Broggs, Peter* / Hungry dub: *McGregor, Freddie* / Coming home dub: *Broggs, Peter* / Live as dub: *Brown, Foxy* / Lyrics of dub: *Brigadier Jerry* / Dub divorce: *Sanchez* / Mandela dub: *Brigadier Jerry* / Dub we land: *Roots Radics* / Crucial dub: *Lazo* / Don't you dub: *Lazo* / Game called dub: *Isaacs, Gregory* / Whole world dub: *Ras Pidow* / Dub overdue: *Ras Pidow* / Afrika dub: *Ras Pidow* / Real dub: *Lazo* / Give a little dub: *Isaacs, Gregory* / Dub and go: *Isaacs, Gregory* / Broken dub: *Pardon Me* / Roots dub: *Ras Pidow* / Peace and dub: *Lazo* / Dreamer dub: *Lazo* / Shabada dub: *Lazo* / House of rising dub: *Isaacs, Gregory*
CD ________ RAS 3504
Ras / May '97 / Direct / Greensleeves / Jet Star / SRD

DUBS FOR DAZE VOL.2 (Scientist Dubs Up The Ras Tapes/2CD Set)
Goon a dub: *Eek-A-Mouse* / Ready for dub: *Yellow Man* / Praising dub: *Broggs, Peter* / Dub belly: *McGregor, Freddie* / Wild wild dub: *Yellow Man* / Aids man: *Yellow Man* / Bossman dub: *Smith, Wayne* / Mess with dub: *Broggs, Peter* / Me oh my oh dub: *Eek-A-Mouse* / Mama mama dub: *McGregor, Freddie* / Lying dub: *Eek-A-Mouse* / Dub gone dub: *Broggs, Peter* / Virgin dub: *Yellow Man* / Merry dub / Jingle bells / Do dub: *Eek-A-Mouse* / Pass the dub: *Michigan & Smiley* / International dub: *Broggs, Peter* / Damn dub: *Smith, Wayne* / Ease up dub: *Yellow Man* / Ethiopia dub: *Broggs, Peter* / Dubbing home: *McGregor, Freddie* / Golden dub: *Broggs, Peter* / Girlish dub: *Eek-A-Mouse* / Too hot dub: *Yellow Man* / Party dub: *Yellow Man* / Boys want dub: *Yellow Man* / Here we dub: *Michigan & Smiley* / Loving dub: *Yellow Man* / Freaky dub: *Eek-A-Mouse*
CD Set ________ RAS 3505
Ras / May '97 / Direct / Greensleeves / Jet Star / SRD

DUBWISE VOL.1 & 2
CD ________ PRFCD 45
Phase One / Aug '97 / Pinnacle / SRD

DUCK AND COVER
CD ________ SST 263CD
SST / Aug '90 / Plastic Head

DUENDE
CD ________ ELLICD 3350
Ellipsis Arts / Oct '94 / ADA / Direct

DUETS
CD ________ CWNCD 2004
Javelin / Jun '95 / Henry Hadaway / THE

DUETS - DITHYRAMBISCH
CD ________ FMPCD 1920
FMP / Nov '87 / Cadillac

DULCE & FORTISSIMAE
CD ________ NT 6733CD
Robi Droli / Apr '95 / ADA / Direct

DUM TRAX
CD ________ DUM 100
Dum / Mar '95 / Plastic Head

DUNGEON OF DELIGHT (2CD Set)
CD Set ________ NZ 010CD
Nova Zembla / Jun '94 / Plastic Head

DUSTY AND FORGOTTEN (1950's Vocal Groups)
CD ________ FLYCD 54
Flyright / Feb '94 / Hot Shot / Jazz Music / Wellard

DUTCH HARBOR
CD ________ ALP 85CD
Atavistic / Apr '97 / Cargo / SRD

DYNAMO OPEN AIR 10TH ANNIVERSARY
Self-bias resistor: *Fear Factory* / Once solemn: *Paradise Lost* / Blood and fire: *Type O Negative* / Ball of destruction: *Madball* / Gorrit: *Dub War* / No fronts: *Dog Eat Dog* / Paint it black: *Grip Inc.* / Old: *Machine Head* / Till the end of time: *Trouble* / Proof: *Eleven Pictures* / Still pounds: *Mental Hippie Blood* / Systems failing: *Nevermore* / On the toad again: *Motorpsycho* / Pump it up: *Warrior Soul* / Liefe: *Waving Corn* / Whatever that hurts: *Tiamat* / Body cry: *Downset* / Falling: *Biohazard*
CD ________ RR 89272
Roadrunner / Sep '96 / PolyGram

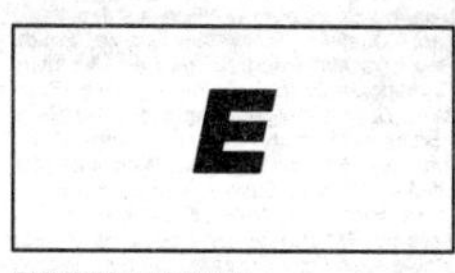

EAR PIERCING PUNK
CD ________ AIPCD 1056
Archive / Jan '97 / RTM/Disc / Shellshock/ Disc

EARLY AMERICAN RURAL MUSIC VOL.1 (Times Ain't Like They Used To Be - 1920's/1930's)
CD ________ YAZ2030
Yazoo / May '97 / ADA / CM / Koch

EARLY AMERICAN RURAL MUSIC VOL.2 (Times Ain't Like They Used To Be - 1920's/1930's)
CD ________ YAZ 2031
Yazoo / May '97 / ADA / CM / Koch

EARLY CANADIAN ROCKERS VOL.3
CD ________ CLCD 4432
Collector/White Label / Sep '96 / TKO Magnum

EARLY CANTE FLAMENCO VOL.1 (The Early 1930's)
CD ________ ARHCD 326
Arhoolie / Apr '95 / ADA / Cadillac / Direct

EARLY GIRLS VOL.1 (Popsicles & Icicles)
Doo wah diddy: *Exciters* / You're no good: *Everett, Betty* / Name game: *Ellis, Shirley* / Chains: *Cookies* / It might as well rain until September: *King, Carole* / I'm into something good: *Earl Jean* / I can't stay mad at you: *Davis, Skeeter* / I wish I were a princess: *March, 'Little' Peggy* / I told every little star: *Scott, Linda* / Triangle: *Grant, Janie* / West of the wall: *Fisher, Toni* / Pink shoelaces: *Stevens, Dodie* / Music music music: *Sensations* / Dear Abby: *Hearts* / Whenever a teenager cries: *Reparata & The Delrons* / Popsicles and icicles: *Murmaids* / Wonderful summer: *Ward, Robin & The Rainbows* / I love how you love me: *Paris Sisters* / Dark moon: *Guitar, Bonnie* / You: *Aquatones* / Till: *Angels* / Great pretender: *Young, Kathy* / Angel baby: *Rosie & The Originals* / Eddie my love: *Teen Queens* / He's gone: *Chantels* / Dedicated to the one I love: *Shirelles* / Son in law: *Blossoms* / Easier said than done: *Essex*
CD ________ CDCHD 608
Ace / Sep '95 / Pinnacle

EARLY GIRLS VOL.2
My boy lollipop: *Gaye, Barbie* / Tell him: *Exciters* / Our day will come: *Ruby & The Romantics* / Boy next door: *Secrets* / Every beat of my heart: *Knight, Gladys* / Cry baby: *Bonnie Sisters* / You don't own me: *Gore, Lesley* / Street: *Terry & The Tunisians* / Bobby's girl: *Blane, Marcie* / Sugartime: *McGuire Sisters* / Tonight you belong to me: *Patience & Prudence* / Kind of boy you can't forget: *Raindrops* / Fever: *Lee, Peggy* / September in the rain: *Washington, Dinah* / I'll save the last dance for you: *Jo, Damita* / Teach me tiger: *Stevens, April* / I just don't understand: *Ann-Margaret* / I met him on a Sunday: *Shirelles* / Lonely blue nights: *Rosie & The Originals* / Forgive me (for giving you such a bad time): *Tino, Babs* / Thousand stars: *Young, Kathy* / Let me in: *Sensations* / Well, I told you: *Chantels* / Lonely nights: *Hearts* / Duchess of earl: *Pearlettes* / Move on: *Blossoms* / Letter full of tears: *Knight, Gladys & The Pips* / What's a matter baby (is it hurting you): *Yuro, Timi*

CD ________ CDCHD 657
Ace / Jun '97 / Pinnacle

EARLY KLEZMER 1903-1926
CD ________ ARHCD 7034
Arhoolie / Nov '96 / ADA / Cadillac / Direct

EARLY MUSIC OF THE NORTH CARIBBEAN 1916-1920
CD ________ HQCD 67
Harlequin / May '96 / Hot Shot / Jazz Music / Swift / Wellard

EARLY NEGRO VOCAL GROUPS VOL.2 1893-1923
CD ________ DOCD 5288
Document / Dec '94 / ADA / Hot Shot / Jazz Music

EARLY NEGRO VOCAL GROUPS VOL.3 1921-1924
CD ________ DOCD 5355
Document / Jun '95 / ADA / Hot Shot / Jazz Music

EARLY NEGRO VOCAL GROUPS VOL.4 1921-1924
CD ________ DOCD 5531
Document / Apr '97 / ADA / Hot Shot / Jazz Music

EARLY RHYTHM 'N' BLUES 1943-1953
Five guys named moe: *Jordan, Louis* / Marry a woman uglier than you: *Duke Of Iron* / Whitman platter: *Whitman, Ernest 'Bubbles'* / Honky tonk train blues: *Lewis, Meade 'Lux'* / I'm gonna move to the outskirts of town: *Jordan, Louis* / Infantry blues: *Jordan, Louis* / In the mood: *Morris, Ernie* / Comedy routine: *McQueen, Butterfly & Ernest 'Bubbles' Whitman* / This train: *Tharpe, Sister Rosetta* / Knock me a kiss: *Jordan, Louis* / Pink champagne: *Liggins, Joe 'Honeydripper'* / Harlem nocturne: *Otis, Johnny Band* / Goof: *McNeely, 'Big' Jay Band* / Serenade in blue: *McNeely, 'Big' Jay Band* / Deacon's parade: *McNeely, 'Big' Jay Band* / Boogie in the front: *McNeely, 'Big' Jay Band* / Body and soul: *McNeely, 'Big' Jay Band* / Deacon's hop: *McNeely, 'Big' Jay Band* / I'm just a fool in love: *Milburn, Amos* / Charmaine: *Vinson, Eddie 'Cleanhead'* / Didn't it rain children: *Tharpe, Sister Rosetta* / Time alone will tell: *Jackson, Bull Moose* / Let's ball tonight
CD ________ CDMOJO 307
Mojo / Nov '96 / Direct

EARLY SHAKER SPIRITUALS
CD ________ ROUCD 0078
Rounder / Aug '96 / ADA / CM / Direct

EARLY WAR YEARS, THE
We're gonna hang out the washing: *Flanagan & Allen* / Yours: *Lynn, Vera* / Nearness of you: *Hutch* / I'm stepping out with a memory: *Mesene, Jimmy & Al Bowlly* / Wings over the navy: *Stone, Lew & Sam Browne* / I haven't time to be a millionaire: *Mesene, Jimmy & Al Bowlly* / Our sergeant major: *Formby, George* / American patrol: *Miller, Glenn* / It's a hap-hap-happy day: *Roy, Harry & Ray Ellington* / Run rabbit run: *Flanagan & Allen* / It's a pair of wings for me: *Gonella, Nat & His New Georgians* / Bless 'em all: *Cotton, Billy & Allan Breeze* / Turn the money in your pocket: *Mesene, Jimmy & Al Bowlly* / I'll never smile again: *Mesene, Jimmy & Al Bowlly* / We'll go smiling along: *Mesene, Jimmy & Al Bowlly* / We must all stick together: *Geraldo & Cyril Grantham* / White cliffs of Dover: *Lynn, Vera* / My prayer: *Henderson, Chick & Joe Loss Orchestra* / Oh buddy I'm in love: *Gonella, Nat* / Oh Johnny oh: *Roy, Harry & His Tiger Ragamuffins* / Kiss me goodnight sergeant major: *Cotton, Billy & Allan Breeze* / Juke box saturday night: *Miller, Glenn* / All over the place: *Thorburn, Billy & His Dance Band* / Moonlight serenade: *Miller, Glenn* / Wish me luck as you wave me goodbye: *Fields, Gracie*
CD ________ PASTCD 7017
Flapper / Mar '97 / Pinnacle

EARLY YEARS VOL.2
CD ________ WBRCD 802
Business / Nov '92 / Jet Star

EARLY YEARS VOL.3
CD ________ WBRCD 803
Business / Mar '94 / Jet Star

EARPLUGGED
CD ________ MOSH 115CD
Earache / Sep '94 / Vital

EARPLUGGED 2
Breed to breathe: *Napalm Death* / Stained glass horizon: *Cathedral* / Keep on rotting in the free world: *Carcass* / Blinded by fear: *At The Gates* / Circle of shit: *Godflesh* / Strike it: *Dub War* / Hippy fascist: *Pulkas* / Million lies: *Misery Loves Co* / Strangled: *Ultraviolence* / Undead: *Haunted* / Big loader: *Iron Monkey* / Underachiever: *Pitch Shifter* / Stranger aeons: *Entombed* / Technology's Gay: *AC* / Damage 381: *Extreme Noise Terror*
CD ________ MOSH 187CD
Earache / Sep '97 / Vital

EARTH BEAT
Mental cube-Q: *Mental Cube* / Quazi: *Yage* / You took my love: *Candese* / Papua New Guinea: *Future Sound Of London* / So this is love: *Mental Cube* / Child of the bass generation: *Mental Cube* / Tingler: *Smart*

Systems / Coda coma: *Yage* / Owl: *Indo Tribe* / People livin' for today: *Semi Real* / Theme from Hot Burst: *Yage* / Shrink: *Indo Tribe* / Stakker humanoid: *Humanoid* / In the mind of a child: *Indo Tribe* / Creator: *Smart Systems* / Bite the bullet baby: *Indo Tribe*
CD **CDTOT 7**
Jumpin' & Pumpin' / Nov '91 / 3mv/Sony / Mo's Music Machine

EARTH SONGS (12 Original Songs Honouring The Earth)
My heart soars: *Friedmann* / Out of the earth: *Wynberg, Simon* / Desert song: *Stein, Ira* / Thousand small gold bells: *Arkenstone, David* / Earth cry mercy: *Gettel, Michael* / In return: *Tingstad, Eric & Nancy Rumbel* / Calling: *Jones, Michael* / Universal garden: *Kostia* / Remember remember: *Mirowitz, Sheldon* / Forgotten places: *Illenberger, Ralf* / Which is yes: *Brewer, Spencer* / Earth tribe: *Lauria, Nando*
CD **ND 63913**
Narada / Oct '93 / ADA / New Note/ Pinnacle

EARTHQUAKE ALBUM, THE
Smoke on the water: *Rock Aid Armenia* / All right now: *Free* / Since you've been gone: *Rainbow* / Headless cross: *Black Sabbath* / Turn it on again: *Genesis* / Fool for your loving: *Whitesnake* / Heat of the moment: *Asia* / We built this city: *Starship* / Run to the hills: *Iron Maiden* / Silent running: *Mike & The Mechanics* / Amanda: *Boston*
CD **ANT 010**
Tring / Nov '96 / Tring

EARTHRISE (The Rainforest Album)
I still haven't found what I'm looking for: *U2* / Here comes the rain again: *Eurythmics* / Don't give up: *Gabriel, Peter & Kate Bush* / Saltwater: *Lennon, Julian* / How many people: *McCartney, Paul* / Is this the world we created: *Queen* / Walk of life: *Dire Straits* / Brazilian: *Genesis* / Yes we can: *Artists United For Nature* / Spirit of the forest: *Spirit Of The Forest* / Fragile: *Sting* / Crazy: *Seal* / Under African skies: *Simon, Paul* / Learning to fly: *Pink Floyd* / Wake me up on judgement day: *Winwood, Steve* / It's the end of the world as we know it (and I feel fine): *REM* / I'm still standing: *John, Elton*
CD **5154192**
Polystar / Jun '92 / PolyGram

EARTHRISE SHADOW VOL.3
Azulee: *Shantel* / Maxwell's demon: *Taran* / Lo: *Megashira* / Blind television: *Jammin' Unit* / Mosaik: *Kosma* / Splendid: *Marschmellows* / Sighting: *Cujo* / Charlie X: *Spaceways* / On the loose: *Slowly* / Le funkster: *Le Gooster* / Blow jam: *Mr. Electric Triangle* / Free radicals: *Futique* / Blind man's bluff: *Spectral Assignment*
CD **SDW 0262**
Shadow / Jun '97 / Cargo / Plastic Head

EARTH'S ANSWER
CD **CDCEL 016**
Celestial Harmonies / Aug '88 / ADA / Select

EARTHTRANCE
Invocation: *Medicine Drum* / G Spot: *Speedy J* / Kincajou: *Banco De Gaia* / Osmosis: *Man With No Name* / Chlorophyte: *Eat Static* / Point of no return: *Kox Box* / Orphic resonance: *Hallucinogen* / Guajibo: *Indigo* / Environmental breakdown: *Source Experience* / Rainforest is calling: *Vath, Sven* / On the 7th night: *System 7*
CD **CDTIVA 1011**
Positiva / Sep '97 / EMI

EASIN' IN (Essential Texas Blues)
Cottonfield blues: *Thomas, Henry* / Bulldoze blues: *Thomas, Henry* / Fishing blues: *Thomas, Henry* / Dallas rag: *Dallas String Band* / Got the blues: *Jefferson, Blind Lemon* / Long lonesome blues: *Jefferson, Blind Lemon* / Bad luck blues: *Jefferson, Blind Lemon* / Match box blues: *Jefferson, Blind Lemon* / See that my grave's kept clean: *Jefferson, Blind Lemon* / Doggone my good luck soul: *Hudson, Hattie* / Double crossing blues: *Alexander, Texas* / Hungry wolf blues: *Smith, J.T. 'Funny Paper'* / Ground hog blues: *Ramblin' Thomas* / Easin' in: *Cadillac, Bobbie* / Elm Street blues: *Day, Texas Bill* / Thieving blues: *Ranger, Jack* / Hurry blues: *Jones, Little Hat* / Blue goose blues: *Thomas, Jesse* / Black gal what makes your head so hard: *Pullum, Joe* / Ninth Street stomp: *Edwards, Bernice* / Bull cow blues: *Moore, Alex* / Trifling woman: *Black Ace* / You gonna need my help some day: *Black Ace* / Got a break baby: *Walker, T-Bone*
CD **IGOCD 2043**
Indigo / Nov '96 / ADA / Direct

EAST COAST ASSAULT VOL.1
CD **TOODAMNHY 22**
Too Damn Hype / May '97 / Cargo / SRD

EAST COAST ASSAULT VOL.2 (2CD Set)
CD Set **TDH 020**
Too Damn Hype / Feb '97 / Cargo / SRD

EAST COAST BLUES
CD **FLYCD 45**
Flyright / Nov '92 / Hot Shot / Jazz Music / Wellard

EAST COAST BLUES
Crow Jane blues: *Daniels, Julius* / You gonna quit me blues: *Blind Blake* / Church bells blues: *Jordan, Louis* / Pick poor Robin clean: *Jordan, Louis* / Cocaine blues: *Jordan, Louis* / Barbershop rag: *Moore, William* / Old country rock: *Moore, William* / Raggin' the blues: *Moore, William* / Every day in the week blues: *Anderson, Pink & Simmie Dooley* / Brownie blues: *Tarter & Gay* / Unknown blues: *Tarter & Gay* / Dupree blues: *Walker, Willie* / South Carolina rag: *Walker, Willie* / Good gal: *White, Joshua* / Low cotton: *White, Joshua* / Blood red river: *White, Joshua* / I'm throwin' up my hands: *Davis, 'Blind' Gary* / Cross and evil woman blues: *Davis, 'Blind' Gary* / Farewell to you baby: *Martin, Carl* / Badly mistreated man: *Martin, Carl* / Crow Jane: *Martin, Carl* / Old time blues: *Martin, Carl* / Picking my tomatoes: *McGhee, Brownie* / Dealing with the devil: *McGhee, Brownie*
CD **IGOCD 2044**
Indigo / Mar '97 / ADA / Direct

EAST COAST BLUES IN THE THIRTIES
CD **SOB 035282**
Story Of The Blues / Feb '93 / ADA / Koch

EAST COAST JIVE (Apollo Theatre Recordings)
Everything's cool: *Gonzales, Babs* / 1280 special: *Gonzales, Babs* / Phipps' deep: *Gonzales, Babs* / It takes a long, tall, brown skin gal: *Four Blues* / Re bop de boom: *Four Blues* / It ain't what you had: *Four Blues* / Call the police: *Simms, Artie* / Take it easy baby: *Simms, Artie* / Darktown strutters ball: *Morgan, Loumell* / Bow tie Jim: *Morgan, Loumell* / Blackstick boogie: *Smith, Ben* / Travelin' Papa: *Smith, Ben* / No lovin' woman: *Smith, Ben* / Roy's groove: *Gonzales, Babs* / Phipps' deep: *Gonzales, Babs* / Blues in the night: *Morgan, Loumell* / Old man river: *Morgan, Loumell* / Whistlin' at the chicks: *Wallace, Babe* / Ain't gonna worry 'bout nothin': *Wallace, Babe* / I'd rather have you fat and happy: *Four Blues* / Vegetable song: *Four Blues*
CD **DE 669**
Delmark / Mar '97 / ADA / Cadillac / CM / Direct / Hot Shot

EAST COAST VOL.1
CD **ECCD 0001**
East Coast / May '96 / Jet Star

EAST COAST VOL.2
CD **ECCD 00022**
East Coast / Jul '97 / Jet Star

EAST-WESTERCISM (2CD Set)
CD Set **LAANGE 2CD**
Law & Auder/Blue Angel / May '97 / Prime / RTM/Disc

EASTERN UPRISING (2CD Set)
Goddess: *Joi* / Core: *Cocoon* / Sitar funk: *Earthtribe* / Harmon dub: *Black Star Liner* / Dum maro dum: *Safri Goes To Bollywood* / Return of the shankar: *Krome Assassins* / Temple of doom: *Tango Padre* / Ruffistahn: *Bedouin Ascent* / RAFI: *Asian Dub Foundation* / Loaded mantra: *Masters Of Sound* / Earthtribe: *Earthtribe* / Om: *Patrina*
CD **4872162**
Higherground / Apr '97 / Sony

EASTSIDE SOUND, THE
CD **BA 08CD**
Bacchus Archives / Apr '96 / Cargo / Plastic Head

EASY AND SLOW
CD **HCD 127**
GTD / Apr '95 / ADA / Else

EASY LISTENING (2CD Set)
Il senzio: *Rosso, Nini* / Wonderland by night: *Strings Of Paris* / Brazil: *Papetti, Fausto* / Stranger on the shore: *Bilk, Acker* / Red roses for a blue lady: *Dana, Vic* / Guitar tango: *Vandyke, Lex* / Tequila: *Prado, Perez* / Midnight cowboy: *Strings Of Paris* / You're nobody till somebody loves you: *Martin, Dean* / Girl from Ipanema: *Ipanema Beach Orchestra* / More I see you: *Humperdinck, Engelbert* / Besame mucho: *Vandyke, Lex* / Fool on the hill: *Ipanema Beach Orchestra* / MacArthur Park: *Ipanema Beach Orchestra* / One note samba: *Ipanema Beach Orchestra* / Somethin stupid: *Ipanema Beach Orchestra* / Aqua de beber: *Ipanema Beach Orchestra* / Malaguena: *Trio Trakitan* / Quizas quizas quizas: *Trio Trakitan* / Shadow of your smile: *Papetti, Fausto* / My way: *Papetti, Fausto* / Raindrops keep falling on my head: *Thomas, B.J.* / Hooked on a feeling: *Thomas, B.J.* / Hawaiian wedding song: *Waikiki Minstrels* / Moon river: *Valentino, Serge* / I say a little prayer: *Warwick, Dionne* / Do you know the way to San Jose: *Warwick, Dionne* / El condor pasa: *Bomha, Dinu* / La montanara: *Rosso, Nini* / Petite fleur: *Kaper, Bob* / Amor, amor, amor: *Vandyke, Lex* / La comparsa: *Vandyke, Lex* / Et maintenant: *Strings Of Paris* / Man and a woman: *Strings Of Paris* / Send in the flowers: *Gorme, Eydie* / You'll always be the one I love: *Martin, Dean* / Patricia: *Prado, Perez* / Once upon a time in the west: *Soho Strings* / Sleepwalk: *Santo & Johnny* / Deep purple: *Tempo, Nino & April Stevens* / Georgia on my mind: *Kaper, Bob* / In crowd: *Lewis, Ramsey Trio*
CD Set **DBG 53053**
Double Gold / Jul '96 / Target/BMG

EASY LISTENING
I just called to say I love you: *Strasser, Hugo & Sein Tanzorchester* / They can't take that away from me/C'est si bon: *Wunderlich, Klaus* / Moonlight serenade: *Manuel & The Music Of The Mountains* / Vaya con dios: *Love, Geoff & His Orchestra* / Cherry pink and apple blossom white: *Calvert, Eddie* / Breeze and I/More/I could have danced all night: *Wunderlich, Klaus* / Rivers of Babylon: *Loss, Joe* / Mr. Sandman: *Silvester, Victor & His Ballroom Orchestra* / Ella: *Moss, Andre* / Du schwarzer Zigeuner: *Orchestre Grand Cafe* / Sleepy shores: *Pearson, Johnny*
CD Set **KS 875102**
Disky / Jul '97 / Disky / THE

EASY LISTENING COLLECTION, THE (3CD Set)
Moonlight serenade: *Miller, Glenn Orchestra UK* / Solitaire: *Vaughn, Billy Orchestra* / Raindrops keep falling on my head: *Winterhalter, Hugo* / Sandy roads: *Bent Fabric* / Glutrote rosen: *Ingmann, Jorgen* / Love story: *Vaughn, Billy Orchestra* / How deep is your love: *Erling, Ole* / Never my love: *Winterhalter, Hugo* / Red roses for a blue lady: *Vaughn, Billy Orchestra* / Stranger, where are you now: *Bent Fabric* / Blue eyes crying in the rain: *Hirt, Al* / Fernando: *Erling, Ole* / Rose from Santa Monica: *Ingmann, Jorgen* / Spanish eyes: *Vaughn, Billy Orchestra* / Taste of honey: *Winterhalter, Hugo* / Wonderland by night: *Hirt, Al* / Alley cat: *Bent Fabric* / Theme from 'A Summer Place': *Vaughn, Billy Orchestra* / Faded love: *Hirt, Al* / California dreaming: *Winterhalter, Hugo* / From now on: *Bent Fabric* / Killing me softly with his song: *Erling, Ole* / Sentimental journey: *Miller, Glenn Orchestra UK* / Strangers in the night: *Vaughn, Billy Orchestra* / This guy's in love with you: *Ingmann, Jorgen* / Born free: *Winterhalter, Hugo* / Yesterday: *Erling, Ole* / Norwegian sunset: *Bent Fabric* / Greensleeves: *Vaughn, Billy Orchestra* / La la la: *Ingmann, Jorgen* / Not a bit in love: *Bent Fabric* / Is blue: *Vaughn, Billy Orchestra* / Sail along silvery moon: *Vaughn, Billy Orchestra* / Theme from 'Love Story': *Winterhalter, Hugo* / Oh my papa (Oh mein papa): *Hirt, Al* / Matador: *Bent Fabric* / Long and winding road: *Winterhalter, Hugo* / Wishing and hoping: *Ingmann, Jorgen* / Matrimony: *Erling, Ole* / Java: *Hirt, Al* / Stranger on the shore: *Vaughn, Billy Orchestra* / When shadows fall: *Bent Fabric* / Rhapsody in blue: *Hirt, Al* / La mer: *Ingmann, Jorgen* / Love is a riddle: *Bent Fabric* / Love theme from 'Romeo & Juliet': *Winterhalter, Hugo* / Tie a yellow ribbon round the old oak tree: *Erling, Ole* / Only yesterday: *Vaughn, Billy Orchestra*
CD Set **101112**
CMC / May '97 / BMG

EASY LISTENING MOODS
CD **5404142**
A&M / Sep '95 / PolyGram

EASY LISTENING VOL.3
CD **NORMAL 192CD**
Normal / Aug '95 / ADA / Direct

EASY PROJECT VOL.1, THE (20 Lounge Favourites)
Shake: *Johnston, Laurie Orchestra* / Kinda kinky: *McVay, Ray Orchestra* / Mas que nada: *Sounds Orchestral* / Lunar walk: *Hawksworth, Johnny Orchestra* / Walk on the wild side: *Tew, Alan Orchestra* / It's murder: *Hawksworth, Johnny Orchestra* / Theme from San Benedict: *Keating, Johnny Orchestra* / House of the rising sun: *Synthesonic Sound* / Blue 'n' groovy: *Paraffin Jack Flash Ltd* / Clown: *Keating, Johnny Orchestra* / Echo four two: *Johnson, Laurie Orchestra* / Mucho Mexico Seven-O: *Shakespeare, John Orchestra* / High society: *Reed, Les Piano* / Staccato: *Eliminators* / Ironside: *Tew, Alan Orchestra* / Getaway: *Keating, Johnny & The Z Men* / Superfly: *Synthesonic Sound* / Revenge: *McVay, Ray Orchestra* / But she ran the other way: *Schroeder, John Orchestra* / Spiral: *Roache, Harry Constellation*
CD **NEMCD 772**
Sequel / Oct '95 / BMG

EASY PROJECT VOL.2, THE (Welcome To The House Of Lounge)
Fear is the key: *Budd, Roy Orchestra* / Out of this world: *Hatch, Tony* / Funko: *Saint Orchestra* / West End: *Saint Orchestra* / Mr. Rose: *Budd, Roy* / Sportsnight: *Hatch, Tony Orchestra* / Pinball wizard: *Roche, Harry Constellation* / Wana nana wana nana: *Schroeder, John Orchestra* / Turnpike Lane: *Moore, Pete Orchestra/Chorus* / Love today, cry tomorrow: *Stapleton, Cyril* / Man alive: *Hatch, Tony Sound* / Blue streak: *Allen, Jerry Trio* / Sleep walk: *Killer Watts* / Virgin soldiers march: *Schroeder, John Orchestra* / Le blon: *City Of Westminster String Band* / Colditz march: *Ainsworth, Alyn Orchestra* / Peter Popgunn: *Schroeder, John Orchestra* / Limehouse: *Johnson, Laurie Orchestra* / London life: *Harris, Anita* / Bird has flown: *Schroeder, John Orchestra* / Car chase: *Budd, Roy Orchestra* / We can work it out/Hey Jude: *Killer Watts*
CD **NEMCD 842**
Sequel / Jun '96 / BMG

EASY TEMPO VOL.1
CD **RTCL 813CD**
Right Tempo / Jul '96 / New Note/ Pinnacle / Timewarp

EASY TEMPO VOL.3 (A Further Cinematic Easy Listening Experience)
Saudade / Nago / I cavalli / Bob E Hellen / North Pole penguin / Frenesia / La bikinia / Il Libanese / Lady Magnolia / Diamond bossa nova / Amanda's train / Beryl's tune / La seduzione / Easy lovers / Flute sequence / Beryl's tune / Soul samba / Casa di moda / Honey, rhythm and butter / Danza citar free / Esquetando os tambourinos e cuica
CD **ET 904CD**
Easy Tempo / Jun '97 / New Note/Pinnacle

EBB STORY VOL.1, THE
I've got a feeling / What is life without a home / If you please / Time brings about a change / Look what you're doing to me / True lips / Buzz buzz buzz / Way you carry on / Love like a fool / Look no hair / I wanna know / Darkness / Keep walkin' on / Good mornin' baby / Sure nuff / You fascinate me / Mine all mine / Voodoo love / Never let me go / Wrapped up in a dream / She's my witch / Oh Linda / Lucky Johnny / Need your lovin' / Much too much / Come on / My silent prayer / Run run run / Kiss me squeeze me / Hali-lou
CD **CDCHD 524**
Ace / Feb '95 / Pinnacle

EBB STORY VOL.2, THE
Everywhere I go: *Taylor, Ted* / Live like a king: *Twilighters* / Days are dark: *Taylor, Ted* / Very truly yours: *Taylor, Ted* / If I don't see you again: *Taylor, Ted* / Hold on (I've got the chills): *Taylor, Ted* / Picadilly: *Jaguars* / Hold me tight: *Jaguars* / Trinidad woman: *Ebb Tones* / Beautiful city: *Zion Travellers* / Believe in me: *Zion Travellers* / When I get you back: *Harris, Tony* / Give me back my heart: *Hollywood Flames* / Two little bees: *Hollywood Flames* / There is something on your mind: *Hollywood Flames* / Just for you: *Hollywood Flames* / Close to you: *Fabulous Tones* / Burning desire: *Tempo-Mentals* / Weathers stormy: *Lampkin, Tony* / True confession: *Ruffin, Riff* / Look up: *Erkard, Tommy* / Bump de bump: *Souvenirs* / When the deal goes down: *Agee, Ray* / Why in the world: *Allen, Tony* / Heavenly escort: *5 Orleans* / Baby let me hold your hand: *Professor Longhair* / Misery: *Professor Longhair* / Harlem nocturne: *Jones, JJ*
CD **CDCHD 603**
Ace / Jun '97 / Pinnacle

EBONY ELEMENTS VOL.1
CD **NL 703024**
Essential Dance Music / Jun '97 / Intergroove / RTM/Disc

EC PUNK ROCK MOUNTAIN
CD **FRIGHT 056**
Fierce / Jun '97 / Cargo

ECHOES OF MADISON COUNTY
CD **2148**
NorthSound / Aug '96 / Gallant

ECHOES OF THE ANDES (A Magical Blend Of Music And The Sounds Of Nature)
CD **50532**
CMC / May '97 / BMG

ECHOES OF THE NILE (Aspects Of Egyptian Music)
Bell announcing Sunday morning mass / Paean from mass for day of fasting / Sample performances of small cymbals / Church bell/Coptic bible recitation / Coptic wedding reception/Song and dance / Qu'ran recitation and azan / Muhammad festival / Ud improvisation / Bashraf / Ruins / Rhythm patterns / Rhythmic improvisation / Sounds of the Mizmar / Farewell beloved / Get our old stuff / Nubian girl
CD **MCM 3005**
Multicultural Media / May '97 / Direct

ECHOES OF THE OZARKS VOL.1
CD **COCD 3506**
County / May '96 / ADA / Direct

ECHOES OF THE OZARKS VOL.2
CD **COCD 3507**
County / May '96 / ADA / Direct

ECLECTRO (2CD Set)
Return of the rebel: *Raw Deal* / Duden: *Atlas, Natacha* / Somatime: *Click & Cycle* / Moody pan pipes: *Zone 12* / Kush: *Zone 12* / Deep blue "C": *Alien 3* / Raw uncut: *Roots Manuva* / Positive polarity: *T-Power* / Hell bent: *BLIM* / Machines: *Doc Scott* / Mutant revisited: *DJ Trace* / One man dead: *Native Bass* / Dawn breaker: *Jazzed Up* / Blown it: *Infinite Wheel* / Global game: *Interference*
CD Set **ANTICDLP 001**
Anti-Static / Oct '96 / Pinnacle / Vital

ECLIPSE PRESENTS (NORTH)
Go: *Moby* / Activ 8: *Altern 8* / Hardcore heaven: *DJ Seduction* / Hardcore uproar: *Together* / Lock up: *Zero B* / Peace and harmony: *Brothers In Rhythm* / Total confusion: *Homeboy, A Hippy & A Funki-Dred* / Way in my brain: *SL2* / Feel so real: *Dream Frequency & Debbie Sharp* / Injected with a poison: *Khan, Praga* / Some justice '96: *Urban Shakedown* / Dominator: *Human Re-*

source / Playing with knives: Bizarre Inc. / I want you (forever): Cox, Carl / Is anybody out there: Bassheads / Rhythm is a mystery: K-Klass / Not forgotten: Leftfield / Gonna make you sweat (Everybody dance now): C&C Music Factory / Theme (unique radio edit): Unique 3 / Is there anybody out there: Bassheads / Free (c'mon): Catch / Let me see ya move: Visa / Hurt you so: Johnny L / On a ragga tip: SL2 / Far out: Sonz Of A Loop Da Loop Era
CD ______ VTDCDN 73
Virgin / Mar '96 / EMI

ECLIPSE PRESENTS (SOUTH)
Go (woodtick mix): Moby / Activ 8: Altern 8 / Hardcore heaven: DJ Seduction / Hardcore uproar: Together / Lock up: Zero B / Peace and harmony: Brothers In Rhythm / Total confusion: Homeboy, A Hippy & A Funki-Dred / Way in my brain: SL2 / Feel so real (edit): Dream Frequency & Debbie Sharp / Injected with a poison: Khan, Praga / Some justice '95: Urban Shakedown / Dominator: Human Resource / Playing with knives: Bizarre Inc. / I want you (forever): Cox, Carl / Is there anybody out there: Bassheads / Rhythm is a mystery: K-Klass / Not forgotten: Leftfield / Gonna make you sweat (everybody dance now): C&C Music Factory / Theme (unique radio edit): Unique 3 / Go: Moby / DJ'S take control: SL2 / Insomniak: DJ PC / Anathasia: T-99 / Feel so real: Dream Frequency & Debbie Sharp / Night in motion: Cubic 22 / Nightbird: Convert / It's just a feeling: Terrorize / Far out: Sonz Of A Loop Da Loop Era / Some jsutice '95: Urban Shakedown / Feel real good: Manix / Don't go: Awesome 3 / On a ragga tip: SL2
CD ______ VTDCDS 73
Virgin / Mar '96 / EMI

ECSTATIC VOL.1 (2CD Set)
CD Set ______ PACT 1CD
Impact / Sep '96 / Mo's Music Machine / SRD

ECSTATIC VOL.2 (2CD Set)
Hallelujah: DJ Seduction / Hop on the dancefloor: Bunter & Seduction / Let the bass kick: Sy & Unknown / Higher now: DJ Seduction / Sensation: Vibes & Wishdokta / Come down: Rise & Shine / Show me your love: Euphoria / Touch the magic: Stripey J / DJ's mixing: Edit V / Bust the new jam: Seduction & Eruption / Imagination: DJ Seduction / Got to believe: DJ DNA / Go with the flow: DJ Unknown / Live for the future: DJ Pooch / Down to Love: Force & Styles / It's not over: Dougal & Seduction / Want to be free: Sedders
CD Set ______ PACT 2CD
Impact / Feb '97 / Mo's Music Machine / SRD

EDINBURGH MILITARY TATTOO 1996
CD ______ EMTCD 113
Tattoo / Jul '96 / Duncans

EDINBURGH MILITARY TATTOO 1997
CD ______ EMTCD 114
Tattoo / Aug '97 / Duncans

EDISON DIAMOND DISC HOT DANCE BANDS 1927-1929
CD ______ NEOVOX 969
Neovox / Oct '93 / Wellard

EIGHT BALL - THE SOUND OF NEW YORK
CD ______ XTR 13CD
X-Treme / Sep '94 / Pinnacle / SRD

EIGHT OVER THE EIGHT BALL
CD ______ EBALL 2CD
Produce / Feb '95 / 3mv/Sony

EIGHTBALL RECORDS COMPILATION VOL.1
CD ______ EBCD 1
Eightball / Jan '95 / Vital

EIGHTBALL RECORDS COMPILATION VOL.2
CD ______ EBCD 3
Eightball / Jan '96 / Vital

EIGHTBALL RECORDS COMPILATION VOL.3 (Mixed By Bill Coleman/Live From The Peace Bisquit Lounge)
Intoxication: Aaron, Robert & Edwige / Boom: Peace Bureau / Tell me what's on your mind: La Desirade / Struck by luv: Lectroluv & Alvaughn Jackson / Thoughts of you: Wave / Hands of a raindrop: Tiny Bubbles / Hallelujah: Funky Fusion Band / Rejoice: 250lbs Of Blue & Elizabeth Mordaunt / On the sand: Groove Thing / Try my lovin': Bluejean / Black thoughts: African Dream / I can't let you go: Mack Vibe & Jacqueline / Risin' to the top: 250lbs Of Blue & Storm / Trouble: Cardwell, Joi / Real thing: Screamin' Rachel
CD ______ EBCD 52
Eightball / Jan '95 / Vital

EIN SCHIFFWIRD KOMMEN
Komm wi machen eine kleine reise: Lind, Gitta & Christa Williams / Vaya con dios: Lind, Gitta & Christa Williams / Kein auto: Lind, Gitta & Christa Williams / Denn sic fahren hinaus auf das meer: Brown, Peggy / Musik von zuckerhut: Club Jamaika / Augen has du wie kakao: Club Jamaika / Adieu lebewohl goodbye (Tonight is so right for love): Bottcher, Gerd / Ich komme wieder: Bottcher, Gerd / Abends in Athen: Andersen, Lale / Ein schiff wird kommen: Andersen, Lale / Ein fremder mann: Andersen, Lale / Bahama melodie: Bertelmann, Fred / Das blaue meer und du: Bertelmann, Fred / Einen ring it zwei blutroten steinen: Valente, Caterina / Wos ist das land: Valente, Caterina / Schick mir einen gruss: Valente, Caterina / Weisse mowe flieg in die ferm: Valente, Caterina / Wenn die sonne scheint in Portugal: Assia, Lys / Zeig mir bei nacht die sterne: Engel, Detlef / Mr. Blue: Engel, Detlef / Komm zu mir wenn du einsam bist: Torriani, Vico / Sweet Hawaii: Gitte & Rex Gildo / Fern von de Heimat: Lind, Gitta / Wo die sonne in das meer versinkt: Durand, Angele / Heim, heim mocht ich zienn: Bottcher, Gerd & Detlef Engel
CD ______ BCD 15414
Bear Family / Dec '87 / Direct / Rollercoaster / Swift

EITHER SIDE OF MIDNIGHT (30 Cool Jazz Classics/2CD Set)
I'm a fool to want you: Morgan, Lee / All blues: Bridgewater, Dee Dee / But not for me: Jamal, Ahmad / I don't know what time it was: Shorter, Wayne / Willow weep for me: Edison, Harry / Here's the rainy day: Bridgewater, Dee Dee / Make the man love me: Kelly, Wynton / I got it bad and that ain't good: Webster, Ben / Lover man: McRae, Carmen / 'Round midnight: Ellington, Duke / Little girl blue: Simone, Nina / Tenderly: Byas, Don / I loves you porgy: Simone, Nina / My one and only love: Grappelli, Stephane / Mellow mood: Marmarosa, Dodo / Star eyes: Kral, Irene / Pleasingly plump: Basie, Count / Turn out the stars: Evans, Bill / Blue gardenia: Washington, Dinah / Come rain or come shine: Kelly, Wynton / Why try to change me now: Foster, Frank / What are you doing the rest of your life: Evans, Bill / Indian summer: Hawkins, Coleman / Darn that dream: Washington, Dinah / Mr. Lucky: Byrd, Donald / Moonlight in Vermont: McRae, Carmen / Waltz Latino: Feldman, Victor / In a sentimental mood: Stitt, Sonny
CD Set ______ CPCD 82302
Charly / Oct '96 / Koch

EITHER SIDE OF MIDNIGHT VOL.2 (2CD Set)
Blue room: Sims, Zoot / More I see you: Vaughan, Sarah / Detour ahead: Evans, Bill / Just in time: Morgan, Lee / Girl talk: Burrell, Kenny / Misty: Bridgewater, Dee Dee / All or nothing at all: Shorter, Wayne / Everything happens to me: Marmarosa, Dodo / Crazy he calls me: Washington, Dinah / In a mellow tone: Ellington, Duke / Lonely melody: Ashby, Dorothy / My funny Valentine: Farmer, Art / Lullaby of Birdland: Torme, Mel / You've changed: Weller, Don / Theodora: Taylor, Billy / Playtime: Rich, Buddy / I could write a book: McRae, Carmen / In a sentimental mood: Webster, Ben / 'S wonderful: Braff, Ruby / All the things you are: Jamal, Ahmad / Lulu's back in town: Torme, Mel / Here's that rainy day: Montgomery, Wes / Prelude to a kiss: Stitt, Sonny / Autumn leaves: Kelly, Wynton / How long has this been going on: Connor, Chris / Confessin': Norvo, Red / Hey there: Gray, Wardell / When the world was young: Bryant, Ray / Love me or leave me: Simone, Nina
CD Set ______ CDPCD 81402
Charly / Oct '95 / Koch

EL CAIMAN
CD ______ CORA 129
Corason / Aug '96 / ADA / CM / Direct

EL CHA CHA CHA DE CU
CD ______ 283382
Total / Jan '96 / Total/BMG

EL CHE VIVE
CD ______ 3018342
Arcade / Feb '97 / Discovery

EL CONDOR PASA (South American Indian Harp & Flute Music)
CD ______ 15163
Laserlight / May '94 / Target/BMG

EL CONDOR PASA
CD ______ CD 62042
Saludos Amigos / Nov '93 / Target/BMG

EL CONDOR PASA (Traditional Pan Pipes - 2CD Set)
Mon amour: Thore, Francke / Pipe dreams: Thore, Francke / Greensleeves: Thore, Francke / Blue rondo a la turk: Thore, Francke / Meditation: Thore, Francke / Carillon: Thore, Francke / Spain: Thore, Francke / Solvejg's song: Thore, Francke / Entre des aguas: Barreros, Paco / Manha de carnaval: Barreros, Paco / New Year: Barreros, Paco / Papel de plata: Barreros, Paco / Lotus feet: Barreros, Paco / Alturas: Barreros, Paco / Dentro de tu alma: Barreros, Paco / Toki Doki: Barreros, Paco / Rio Ancho: Barreros, Paco / Moyobamaba: Los Indios De Cuzco / El indio del Altiplano: Los Indios De Cuzco / Pa'ti cholita: Patoruzu Y Su Conjunto / El pajaron: Patoruzu Y Su Conjunto / El zaino: Patoruzu Y Su Conjunto / Pajaritos: Patoruzu Y Su Conjunto / Diecenueve de enero: Patoruzu Y Su Conjunto / Kena misky: Patoruzu Y Su Conjunto / Francisca Teresa Luisa: Patoruzu Y Su Conjunto / Huayno di Juanico: Patoruzu Y Su Conjunto / Naco del carnaval: Patoruzu Y Su Conjunto / La piojosa: Patoruzu Y Su Conjunto / Chasquinanes: Patoruzu Y Su Conjunto / Sentimientos: Patoruzu Y Su Conjunto / Yaravi de San Lorenzo: Patoruzu Y Su Conjunto / La feria de los flores: Santiago Conjunto Viracocha / Vicunitas: Santiago Conjunto Viracocha / Misteru: Los Indios De Cuzco
CD Set ______ RCACD 209
RCA / Jul '97 / BMG

EL CONDOR PASA
CD ______ MACCD 306
Autograph / Aug '96 / BMG

EL PRIMITIVO (American Rock 'n' Roll & Rockabilly)
Save it: Robbins, Mel / Oh yeah: Jeffrey, Wally / I wanna dance all night: Wiley, Chuck / It's love: Wiley, Chuck / Bandstand: Nash, Cliff / Times is tough: Wiley, Chuck / Are you with me: Robbins, Mel / I wanna shake it: Hobock, Curtis / I love you dearly: Hurt, Jimmy & the Del Rio's / Thump: Embers / Baby moon: Smith, Herbie / Best dressed beggar in town: Turner, Buck / Door to door: Wiley, Chuck / Uh oh: Imps / I walked all night: Embers / Explosion: Nash, Cliff / Out of gas: Howard, Chuck / Tell me baby: Nash, Cliff / Why worry about me: Wiley, Chuck / That'll get it: Imps / No time for sister: Nash, Cliff / I love you so much: Wiley, Chuck / Jenny Lou: Nash, Cliff
CD ______ CDCHD 473
Ace / Aug '93 / Pinnacle

EL RITMO LATINO VOL.1 (18 Classic Latin Grooves)
Hit the bongo: Puente, Tito / Muneca: Palmieri, Eddie / El escencia del guaguanco: Pacheco, Johnny / Senor Serano: Miranda, Ismael / Jive samba: Constanzo, Jack & Gerry Woo / La verdad: Palmieri, Eddie / El malecon: Orchestra Harlow / Manteca: Alegre All Stars / Aguzate: Ray, Ricardo / Mambo tipico: Puente, Tito & His Orchestra / Fever: La Lupe / Wipeout: Barretto, Ray / La jicota: Ruiz, Rosendo Jr. / Work song: Puente, Tito / Mambo Manila: Rodriguez, Tito & His Orchestra / Carmelina: Valdes, Alfredito / Song for my father: Valentin, Bobby / Arsenio: Harlow, Larry
CD ______ MCCD 025
Music Club / May '91 / Disc / THE

EL RITMO LATINO VOL.2
CD ______ MCCD 232
Music Club / Mar '96 / Disc / THE

EL SALAO
CD ______ TUMICD 023
Tumi / '92 / Discovery / Stern's

EL SON DE CUBA
CD ______ 283432
Total / Jan '96 / Total/BMG

ELECTRIC BALLROOM (Synthetic Pop from the 1980's/1990's/2CD Set)
True faith: New Order / Temptation: Heaven 17 / My soul unwraps tonight: Savage Progress / Waves: Blancmange / Golden brown: Stranglers / Hymn: Ultravox / Bird song: Lovich, Lena / It's my party: Stewart, Dave & Barbara Gaskin / Hey little girl: Icehouse / Are friends electric: Numan, Gary & Tubeway Army / (I want to live) In harmony: Boytronic / This city: Foxx, John / Kitchen at parties: Lewie, Jona / Thank God it's friday: Automatic / In a manner of speaking: Tuxedo Moon / Fall: Endzeit / Africa: Twice A Man / Blue moon: De/Vision / Moonlight lovesong: Second Decay / Good bye horses: Psyche / Boat on the river: Blind Passengers / Stranged: SPOCK / Save me: Elegant Machinery / Lost little robot: Beborn Beton / Imagination: Daily Planet / Over my home: Northern Territories / Morning light: Silent Gift / Just in case: Philtron / Midnight: Chateau De Joie / Space's embrace: Rame / Holegrain: Statemachine / Pictures: X-Act / In your heart: Infame / Rosen: Spell Inside
CD Set ______ SPV 08847242
SPV / Apr '97 / Koch / Plastic Head

ELECTRIC DREAMS
CD ______ NTRCD 033
Nectar / Mar '95 / Pinnacle

ELECTRIC DREAMS
Blue Monday: New Order / Love is a stranger: Eurythmics / Mirror man: Human League / Tainted love: Soft Cell / Victim of love: Erasure / If I was: Ure, Midge / Heart of glass: Blondie / Mad world: Tears For Fears / Come live with me: Heaven 17 / Wood beez (pray like Aretha Franklin): Scritti Politti / Living on the ceiling: Blancmange / Situation: Yazoo / Careless memories: Duran Duran / Quiet life: Japan / All stood still: Ultravox / Chant no.1 (I don't need this pressure on): Spandau Ballet / Talk Talk: Talk Talk / We close our eyes: Go West / Politics of dancing: Re-Flex / Together in electric dreams: Moroder, Giorgio & Philip Oakey / Enola Gay: OMD / Change: Tears For Fears / Fade to grey: Visage / Never never: Assembly / Are friends electric: Tubeway Army / Wishing (If I had a photograph of you): Flock Of Seagulls / Wishful thinking: China Crisis / I'm in love with a German film star: Passions / Don't go: Yazoo / Torch: Soft Cell / Is it a dream: Classix Nouveaux / Treason: Teardrop Explodes / Love on your side: Thompson Twins / Change your mind: Sharpe & Numan / Sgt. Rock (Is going to help me): XTC / Wouldn't it be good: Kershaw, Nik / Love shadow: Fashion / Vienna: Ultravox
CD Set ______ 5254352
PolyGram TV / Feb '95 / PolyGram

ELECTRIC ENIGMA, THE (2CD Set)
CD Set ______ 62 IRDTCP2
Irdial / Apr '96 / RTM/Disc

ELECTRIC GUITAR STORY 1935-1945, THE
CD ______ 158522
Jazz Archives / Jul '96 / Discovery

ELECTRIC LADYLAND VOL.1
CD ______ EFA 006692
Mille Plateau / Nov '95 / SRD

ELECTRIC LADYLAND VOL.2
CD ______ EFA 006742
Mille Plateau / Apr '96 / SRD

ELECTRIC LADYLAND VOL.3
CD ______ EFA 006792
Mille Plateau / Oct '96 / SRD

ELECTRIC LADYLAND VOL.4
CD ______ EFA 006892
Mille Plateau / May '97 / SRD

ELECTRIC RADIO SAMPLER MUSIC TEST
CD ______ TEST 001CD
Haven / Sep '93 / Pinnacle / Shellshock/ Disc

ELECTRIC SUGAR CUBE FLASHBACKS
CD ______ AIPCD 1054
Archive / Mar '93 / RTM/Disc / Shellshock/ Disc

ELECTRICITY (18 Synth Pop Hits)
CD ______ MUSCD 008
MCI Music / Sep '93 / Disc / THE

ELECTRO BEATS
Cuts it up: Grandmixer DST / Home of hip hop: Grandmixer DST / Megamix: Grandmixer DST / Mean machine: Grandmixer DST & Jalal / Change the beat: Fab Five Freddy / Escapades of Futura 2000: Futura 2000 & The Clash / Wild style: Time Zone / World destruction: Time Zone
CD ______ CDNEW 103
Charly / Jan '97 / Koch

ELECTRO JUICE
CD ______ SABO 12CD
Sabotage / Nov '96 / Plastic Head

ELECTROCITY VOL.4
CD ______ EFA 063212
Ausfahrt / Dec '93 / SRD

ELECTROCITY VOL.5
CD ______ EFA 053232
Ausfahrt / Aug '94 / SRD

ELECTROCITY VOL.6
CD ______ EFA 063262
Ausfahrt / Apr '95 / SRD

ELECTROCITY VOL.7
CD ______ EFA 063292
Ausfahrt / Feb '96 / SRD

ELECTROCITY VOL.8
CD ______ EFA 063322
Dossier / Apr '97 / Cargo / SRD

ELECTRONIC FRANKFURT (2CD Set)
CD Set ______ PODDCD 023
Pod / Sep '94 / Total/BMG

ELECTRONIC SPECIES
CD ______ EFA 120952
Estontrager / May '96 / SRD

ELECTRONIC TOYS
CD ______ QDKCD 013
QDK Media / Aug '96 / Direct

ELECTRONIC WARFARE (Mixed By Mr. C)
Versuvius: Stranger / Two: Morohas, Hiroshi / Fog of the unknown: God Of The Machine / Plutobeat: Pluto / Limbo of the vanished poss: Tone Theory / Sea 2 sea: Kosmic Messenger / Nude machinery: God Of The Machine / Rize: Mantrac / Scenic route: Urban Groove / Darkness: Megalon / MASP: Insync & Invisible Force / Incoming: Urban Groove / Niteflight: Somnambulist / Idax: Megalon / Waterwurld: Underground Science / Fax wars: Innersound / Motion: Megalon / Found object: Else / Reflex: Underground Science
CD ______ PLKMCD 7
Plink Plonk / Jun '97 / Prime / SRD

ELECTRONIC YOUTH
CD ______ MRSP 001
Music Research / Feb '94 / Plastic Head

ELECTRONICA (Full-On Big Beats) (2CD Set)
Block rockin' beats: Chemical Brothers / Nightmare: Brainbug / Take California: Propeller Heads / It's no good: Depeche Mode / Open up: Leftfield & John Lydon / Absurd: Fluke / We have explosive: Future Sound Of London / Naked and ashamed: Dylan Rhymes / Encore une fois: Sash / Groovebird: Natural Born Groovers / Satan: Orbital / Going out of my head: Fatboy Slim / Rollercoaster: Grid / For what you dream of: Bedrock & KYO / Bullet (bitten): Fluke / Scared: Slacker / Ain't talkin' about dub: Apollo 440 / Children: Miles, Robert / Seven days and one week: BBE / Born slippy: Un-

derworld / Breathe: *Prodigy* / Life is sweet: *Chemical Brothers & Tim Burgess* / Come with me: *Qattara* / Extremis: *Hal & Gillian Anderson* / Earth angel: *Dreadzone* / Valley of the shadows: *Origin Unknown* / Spin spin sugar: *Sneaker Pimps* / Wilmot: *Sabres Of Paradise* / Zoe: *Paganini Traxx* / You're not alone: *Olive* / Inner City Life: *Goldie* / Walking wounded: *Everything But The Girl* / Protection: *Massive Attack*
CD Set VTDCD 131
Virgin / Jun '97 / EMI

ELEMENTAL FORCE OF PHUNKEE NOIZE VOL.1
CD RSNCD 35
Rising High / May '95 / 3mv/Sony

ELEMENTAL FORCE OF PHUNKEE NOIZE VOL.2
CD RSNCD 44
Rising High / Jul '96 / 3mv/Sony

ELEMENTS
Stratus: *Cobham, Billy* / Back together again: *Mouzon, Alphonse & Larry Coryell* / Oceanliner: *Passport* / Black market: *Weather Report* / Birds of fire: *Mahavishnu Orchestra* / Hello Jeff: *Clarke, Stanley* / Dinner music of the gods: *Di Meola, Al* / Romantic warrior: *Corea, Chick & Return To Forever* / Nuclear burn: *Brand-X* / War dance: *Colosseum II*
CD VSOPCD 218
Connoisseur Collection / Aug '95 / Pinnacle

ELEMENTS OF JAZZ
CD KICKCD 41
Kickin' / Sep '96 / Prime / SRD

ELEMENTS OF JAZZ VOL.2
Mercy no mercy: *Caron, David* / Morning session: *Martin, Alex Ensemble* / Transparent: *Reflection* / Silicon jazz: *Wavescape* / Piano: *Read, Jaime* / Soul searcher dub: *Underground Evolution* / Destination other: *As One* / Dayride: *O'Brian, Ian* / Snooky's spirit: *Black Jazz Chronicles* / Scuba: *Scuba* / Astralwerks: *Model 500*
CD KICKCD 54
Kickin' / Aug '97 / Prime / SRD

ELEPHANT TABLE ALBUM
CD XXCD 001
Xtract / Oct '89 / RTM/Disc

ELEVEN YEARS FROM YESTERDAY
CD FMRCD 02
Future / Feb '88 / ADA / Harmonia Mundi

EMERALD FAVOURITES (24 Best Irish Songs)
An Irish harvest day / Danny Boy / Galway shawl / Dirty old town / Castle of Dromore / Golden jubilee / Holy ground / Courtin' in the kitchen / Let him go let him tarry / Good ole mountain dew / Donegal shore / Red rose cafe / Town I love so well / Boys from Killybegs / Mountains of Mourne / Green Glens of Antrim / Mary from Dungloe / Forty shades of green / McAlpines fusiliers / Black velvet band / Fields of Athenry / Three leaf Shamrock / Sweet sixteen
CD RBCD 521
Sharpe / Jun '97 / Duncans / Target/BMG

EMERALD ISLE DREAMS
CD 57572
CMC / May '97 / BMG

EMERALD MOODS (Pan Pipes Collection/25 Timeless Irish Evergreens)
When Irish eyes are smiling/Mountains of Mourne / Bunch of thyme/Fields of Athenry / How can you buy Killarney/Mother MacRee/Tooraloora loora / Danny boy / Will you go lassie go/The spinning wheel / Carrickfergus / Forty shades of green/Sweet sixteen / Galway Bay/Isle of Innisfree / Mary from Dungloe/Magpie / Cockles and mussles/Black velvet band/The wild rover / I'll take you home again Kathleen / Cliffs of Doonreen/Rose of Tralee / On the banks of my own lovely Lee / I'll tell my Ma/Courtin' in the kitchen
CD COMCD 08
Sharpe / Oct '96 / Duncans / Target/BMG

EMERALD ROCK
Where the streets have no name: *U2* / Linger: *Cranberries* / Whole of the moon: *Waterboys* / Small bit of love: *Saw Doctors* / Real real gone: *Morrison, Van* / I don't like Mondays: *Boomtown Rats* / Dancin' in the moonlight: *Thin Lizzy* / Nowhere: *Therapy* / Teenage kicks: *Undertones* / Somebody to love: *In Tua Nua* / Don't go: *Hothouse Flowers* / Mandinka: *O'Connor, Sinead* / Nobody knows: *Brady, Paul* / Parisienne walkways: *Moore, Gary & Phil Lynott* / Good heart: *Sharkey, Feargal* / After all: *Frank & Walters* / In the midnight hour: *Commitments* / She's the one that I adore: *Energy Orchard* / Big decision: *That Petrol Emotion* / In the name of the Father: *Bono & Gavin Friday*
CD 5149442
Polydor / Mar '95 / PolyGram

EMIT 1197
Vox 25: *Bone, Richard* / What's in the box: *Bad Data* / Unc: *8M2 Stereo* / Giant stroke: *Woob* / Oxygen: *Gas* / Imagination satellite: *International People's Gang* / Waterpump: *Simpson, Dallas* / Dead eye: *Miasma* / Apus apus: *Davies, Hywel*
CD EMIT 1197
Emit / Jun '97 / Pinnacle

EMIT 2296
CD EMIT 2296
Time Recordings / Dec '96 / Pinnacle

EMOTIONS FOR THE WEISHUI RIVER
CD PAN 149CD
Pan / Aug '94 / ADA / CM / Direct

EMPIRE STATE RECORDS DJ MASTERMIX
CD EBCD 9
Eightball / Jan '95 / Vital

EMPORIUM OF DANCE (2CD Set)
CD Set CATCD 001
Scratch / Nov '95 / Koch / Scratch/BMG

EMPTY BED BLUES
CD PLSCD 115
Pulse / Apr '96 / BMG

EMPTY SAMPLER VOL.1
CD MTR 273CD
Empty / Jun '94 / Cargo / Greyhound / Plastic Head / SRD

EMPTY SAMPLER VOL.2
CD MTR 353CD
Empty / May '97 / Cargo / Greyhound / Plastic Head / SRD

EN ATTENDANT LE TOUR
CD DEM 015
IMP / Feb '96 / ADA / Discovery

EN VISITANT L'EXPO
CD DEM 014
IMP / Feb '96 / ADA / Discovery

ENCHANTED CAROLS
Church bells: *Townsend, Dave & Nick Hooper* / Hark the herald angels sing / Virgin most pure: *Dartington Handbell Choir* / Jingle bells: *Penny piano* / Star of Bethlehem / Angels from the realms of glory: *Grosmont Handbell Ringers* / Away in a manger: *Grosmont Handbell Ringers* / O little town of Bethlehem: *Grosmont Handbell Ringers* / First Noel: *Grosmont Handbell Ringers* / As, with gladness, men of old: *Sun Life Stanshawe Band* / Glory to God in the highest: *Sun Life Stanshawe Band* / See amid the winter's snow: *Sun Life Stanshawe Band* / O come all ye faithful (Adeste Fidelis) / Silent night / Down in yon forest: *Dartington Handbell Choir* / Good King Wenceslas / Little Jesus sweetly sleep: *Launton Handbell Ringers* / Little drummer boy: *Launton Handbell Ringers* / Deck the halls with boughs of holly: *Launton Handbell Ringers* / Little donkey: *Launton Handbell Ringers* / While shepherds watched their flocks by night: *Barrel Organ* / Auld lang syne
CD CDSDL 327
Saydisc / '85 / ADA / Direct / Harmonia Mundi

ENCHANTED MOODS (3CD Set)
CD Set EMTBX 310
Emporio / Aug '97 / Disc

ENCHANTING MONGOLIA
CD EFA 119492
Nebelhorn / Feb '94 / SRD

ENCHANTMENTS
CD CLEO 95202
Cleopatra / Aug '95 / Cargo / Greyhound / Plastic Head / RTM/Disc / SRD

ENCOUNTER
CD EFA 11606CD
EFA / Apr '93 / SRD

END OF MUSIC
CD DANCD 078
Danceteria / Nov '94 / ADA / Plastic Head / Shellshock/Disc

ENDLESS JOURNEY VOL.2
CD FARCD 405
Family Affair / Jul '96 / Timewarp

ENDLESS LOVE (2CD Set)
One last love song: *Beautiful South* / Bump 'n' grind: *R Kelly* / Crazy for you: *Let Loose* / Around the world: *East 17* / I'll stand by you: *Pretenders* / Crash boom bang: *Roxette* / Kiss from a rose: *Seal* / Stay: *Eternal Basement* / Stars: *China Black* / Don't be a stranger: *Carroll, Dina* / Can't stay away from you: *Estefan, Gloria* / Love ain't here anymore: *Take That* / Now and forever: *Marx, Richard* / I'll never fall in love again: *Deacon Blue* / When love breaks down: *Prefab Sprout* / Ordinary world: *Duran Duran* / La la (means I love you): *Swing Out Sister* / Nothing compares 2 U: *O'Connor, Sinead* / Love me for a reason: *As We Speak* / Endless love: *Ross, Diana & Lionel Richie* / Love don't live here anymore: *Nail, Jimmy* / Jealous guy: *Roxy Music* / Every breath you take: *Police* / I don't want to talk about it: *Everything But The Girl* / Don't let the sun go down on me: *John, Elton* / Unchained melody: *Righteous Brothers* / Without you: *Nilsson, Harry* / If you leave me now: *Chicago* / My love: *McCartney, Paul* / Man with the child in his eyes: *Bush, Kate* / On the wings of love: *Osborne, Jeffrey* / Secret lovers: *Atlantic Starr* / Love and affection: *Armatrading, Joan* / Babe: *Styx* / I wanna stay with you: *Gallagher & Lyle* / Love is all around: *Troggs* / Nights in white satin: *Moody Blues* / I'm not in love: *10cc*
CD Set 5253412
Polydor / Jan '95 / PolyGram

ENDLESS LOVE (18 Instrumental Love Songs)
Still / Hello / Lady / Endless love / Touch me in the morning / I don't wanna lose you / When you tell me that you love me / One more night / Against all odds / Sorry seems to be the hardest word / Where do broken hearts go / Didn't we almost have it all / I'm still waiting / One day in your life / Blue eyes / Lately / My cherie amor / You are the sunshine of my life
CD SUMCD 4063
Summit / Nov '96 / Sound & Media

ENERGY 1994 & STREET PARADE
Milky way: *Borealis, Aurora* / Bagdad: *Paragliders* / Spoken word is weak: *Mike Ink & Burger Industries* / House of house: *DJ Yves De Ruyther & DJ Franky* / Orient: *Luke Slaters 7th Pain* / Ambulance two: *Armani, Robert* / Primitive passion: *Dee, Alici & Ralphie* / Boo ya: *Jens* / Symphony: *Gangsta* / We don't care: *T-Bass & O. Kunze* / Aural 721: *Hood, Robert* / Helix: *Synetics* / M 3 of canes venatici: *Direct Force* / Kneels before me: *Agent Loft*
CD SUPER 2022CD
Superstition / Aug '94 / Plastic Head / SRD / Vital

ENERGY 1996
CD CDACV 2010
ACV / Feb '97 / Plastic Head / SRD

ENERGY RAVE VOL.5 (2CD Set)
CD Set 9010722
Immediate / Mar '97 / BMG

ENERGY RAVE VOL.6 (2CD Set)
CD Set 9010762
Immediate / Mar '97 / BMG

ENERGY RUSH XTERMINS
CD DINCD 84
Dino / May '94 / Pinnacle

ENERGY TRANCE (The Ultimate Trance Collection)
CD 341642
Koch / Dec '94 / Koch

ENEZ EUSA OUESSANT
CD 861CD
Escalibur / Nov '96 / ADA / Discovery / Roots

ENFORCERS - ABOVE THE LAW (2CD Set)
CD Set RIVETCD 7
Reinforced / Oct '96 / SRD

ENFORCERS VOL.4
CD RIV 490
Reinforced / Sep '93 / SRD

ENFORCERS VOL.5
CD RIVET 52CD
Reinforced / Oct '93 / SRD

ENGLAND'S GLORY 1966 (From 1966 To Euro '96)
CD CDGAFFER 6
Cherry Red / May '96 / Pinnacle

ENGLISH & SCOTTISH FOLK BALLADS
Henry Martin: *Lloyd, A.L.* / Baron of Brackley: *MacColl, Ewan* / Reynardine: *Briggs, Anne* / Bramble briar: *Killen, Louis* / Jack Orion: *Lloyd, A.L.* / Cruel ships carpenter: *Waterson, Mike* / Cruel mother: *Lloyd, A.L.* / Lord Randal: *MacColl, Ewan* / Bitter withy: *Lloyd, A.L.* / Forester: *Kennedy, Norman* / Willie O'Winsbury: *Briggs, Anne* / Sweet Kumadie: *MacColl, Ewan* / Demon lover: *Lloyd, A.L.* / Young Edwin in the Lowlands: *Lloyd, A.L.* / Hughie The Graeme: *MacColl, Ewan* / Drumdelgie: *Kennedy, Norman* / Prickly bush: *Lloyd, A.L.* / Beggar man: *MacColl, Ewan*
CD TSCD 480
Topic / Jun '96 / ADA / CM / Direct

ENGLISH FOLK SONGS (A Selection From The Penguin Book Of English Folk Songs)
When I was young / Gaol song / Whale catchers / Young and single sailor / False bride / Ratcliffe highway / Grey cock / Basket of eggs / One night as I lay on my bed / Banks of Green Willow / All things are quite silent / Banks of Newfoundland
CD FE 047CD
Fellside / Nov '95 / ADA / Direct / Target/BMG

ENGLISH FREAKBEAT VOL.1
CD AIPCD 1039
Archive / May '95 / RTM/Disc / Shellshock/Disc

ENGLISH FREAKBEAT VOL.2
CD AIPCD 1047
Archive / Feb '96 / RTM/Disc / Shellshock/Disc

ENGLISH FREAKBEAT VOL.6
CD AIPCD 1055
Archive / Oct '96 / RTM/Disc / Shellshock/Disc

ENJA - 20TH ANNIVERSARY
Dance Benita dance: *Blythe, Arthur* / Maybe September: *Flanagan, Tommy* / Sossity; you're a woman: *Krantz, Wayne* / Wow: *Dennerlein, Barbara* / Green chimneys: *Reedus, Tony* / Time until: *Degen, Bob* / Storyteller: *Abou-Khalil, Rabih* / Giant steps: *Tyner, McCoy* / Phantoms: *Barron, Kenny* / You and I: *Lincoln, Abbey* / Lakutshon ilanga: *Ibrahim, Abdullah* / Straight no chaser: *Wallace, Bennie* / Yawn: *Scofield, John* / Ballad to Mahalia: *Tsilis, Gust William* / Edge to edge: *Formanek, Michael* / My funny valentine: *Baker, Chet*
CD ENJACD 80602
Enja / Jun '94 / New Note/Pinnacle / Vital/SAM

ENTER THE CYBER LOUNGE (The Best In Trip Hop & Psychedelic Rhythms)
Can't deal with this: *Cool Breeze* / Atlas Earth: *Spacer* / Aqualibra: *Cold Blue* / Cap Colombie: *Arteq* / Fast and loose: *Bliss 'n' Tumble* / Who are you: *Larceny* / At Least the American Indian people know exactly how...: *Fire This Time* / Spirit: *Kitachi* / Definition: *Dom & Roland* / No inference: *Fire & Theft* / Satellite: *Ryder, Mark* / Dust bucket: *Freddie Fresh*
CD CDTOT 42
Jumpin' & Pumpin' / Jul '96 / 3mv/Sony / Mo's Music Machine

ENTER THE HARDBAG
Fee fi fo fum: *Candy Girls & Sweet Pussy Pauline* / Something about you: *Mr. Roy* / Move your body: *Xpansions* / Son of a gun: *JX* / It's what's upfront that counts: *Yosh* / Diablo: *Grid* / Conway: *Reel 2 Real* / I'm rushin': *Bump* / Bullet: *Fluke* / Deeper: *Funky See Funky Do* / Happiness (is just around the bend): *Brooklyn's Poor & Needy* / Joanna: *Mrs. Wood* / Sweet harmony: *Liquid* / Don't you want me: *Felix* / Blue Monday: *New Order* / Club America: *Club America* / All night: *Tocayo* / Housework: *Rizzo* / Burning up: *De Vit, Tony* / Magic: *Blu Peter* / Hooked: *99th Floor Elevators* / Only me: *Hyperlogic* / I need a man: *Li Kwan* / Stomp: *Ramp* / Let the rhythm flow: *Diva Rhythms* / Want me love me: *Justine*
CD 5404572
A&M / Dec '95 / PolyGram

EP COLLECTION SAMPLER, THE
I'll keep you satisfied: *Kramer, Billy J.* / I go to pieces: *Peter & Gordon* / Jennifer Juniper: *Donovan* / Perfidia: *Shadows* / Rocky road blues: *Vincent, Gene* / Look through any window: *Hollies* / Do wah diddy: *Manfred Mann* / I'm into something good: *Herman's Hermits* / Pipeline: *Ventures* / I like it: *Gerry & The Pacemakers* / Little devil: *Shapiro, Helen* / I'm telling you now: *Freddie & The Dreamers* / Take good care of my baby: *Vee, Bobby* / Summertime blues: *Cochran, Eddie* / Ain't that a shame: *Domino, Fats* / Good things are coming my way: *Proby, P.J.*
CD SFMEP 101
See For Miles/C5 / Oct '96 / Pinnacle

EPIC HOUSE EXPERIENCE
CD TRIPCD 5
Rumour / Jun '96 / 3mv/Sony / Mo's Music Machine / Pinnacle

EPIDEMIC
CD SABOTAGE 01CD
Sabotage / May '95 / Plastic Head

EPITONE
CD BTR 002CD
Bad Taste / Nov '95 / Plastic Head

ESCAPE FROM SAMSARA
CD SETCD 1
Secret / Apr '97 / SRD

ESCAPE TO TRANSCYBERIA
CD K7 036CD
Studio K7 / Oct '96 / Prime / RTM/Disc

ESQUIRE ALL AMERICAN JAZZ CONCERT 1944
CD 158262
Jazz Archives / Jan '95 / Discovery

ESQUIRE JAZZ CONCERT, METROPOLITAN OPERA HOUSE
CD CD 53035
Giants Of Jazz / Jan '89 / Cadillac / Jazz Music / Target/BMG

ESSENCE OF FUNK
Cornbread / Loose change / Slow drag / Eternal flame / Freedom jazz dance / Jive samba / Comin' home baby
CD HIBD 8007
Hip Bop / Oct '95 / Koch / Silva Screen

ESSENCE OF JUNGLE
CD NURCD 1
Nur Ents / Jun '96 / Jet Star

ESSENCE OF THE BLUES, THE (3CD Set)
CD Set MCBX 015
Music Club / Dec '94 / Disc / THE

ESSENTIAL 60'S NORTHERN SOUL DANCEFLOOR CLASSICS VOL.1
Purple haze: *Jones, Johnny & The King Casuals* / Baby boy: *Hughes, Freddie* / Tryin to find my woman: *Courtney, Lou* / There was a time: *Chandler, Gene* / Who who song: *Wilson, Jackie* / Marble and iron: *Douglas, Carl* / Our love is getting stonger: *Knight, Jason* / What about the music: *Harner, Billy* / Boc to bach: *Father's Angels* / What love brings: *Bernard, Kenny* / Everything's gonna be alright: *Arnold, P.P.* / Scrub board: *Trammps* / Ton of dynamite: *Crocker, Frankie 'Loveman'* / Soul improvisations: *McCoy, Van* / Goodbye nothing to say: *Javells* / Bring him back: *Starr, Stella* / Stop what you're doing to me: *Playthings* /

I get the sweetest feeling: Wilson, Jackie / Love makes a woman: Acklin, Barbara / I'm gonna miss you: Artistics / Stay close to me: Five Stairsteps / Hold back the night: Trammps
CD _______________ DGPCD 704
Deep Beats / Sep '94 / BMG

ESSENTIAL 60'S NORTHERN SOUL DANCEFLOOR CLASSICS VOL.2
This is the house where love died: First Choice / Turning my heartbeat up: MVP's / Help me: Wilson, Al / Glad all over: Young, Leon Strings / Sally saying something: Harner, Billy / Don't just look at me: Farlowe, Chris / Good things come to those who wait: Jackson, Chuck / Don't take it out of this world: Adam's Apples / Under my thumb: Gibson, Wayne / Livin' the nightlife: Charts / I'm so glad I found you: Jones, Linda & The Whatnauts / I don't want to lose you: Wilson, Jackie / Last minute miracle: Shirelles / One in a million: Brown, Maxine / Black eyed girl: Thompson, Billy / I'm gonna pick up my toys: Devonnes / You're puttin' me on: Taylor, Carmen / Have more time: Smith, Marvin / In the long run: Blandon, Curtis / Just in the nick of time: Lamarr, Tony / California montage: Young-Holt Unlimited
CD _______________ DGPCD 728
Deep Beats / Jun '95 / BMG

ESSENTIAL BIG BANDS
CD _______________ 4671502
Sony Jazz / Jan '95 / Sony

ESSENTIAL BLUES
Cry before I go: Reed, Jimmy / Hard walking Hanna: Reed, Jimmy / Hi heel sneakers: Tucker, Tommy / Drunk: Tucker, Tommy / House rent boogie: Hooker, John Lee / Stomp boogie: Hooker, John Lee / Dust my broom: James, Elmore / Coming home: James, Elmore / Little red rooster: Howlin' Wolf / I ain't superstitious: Howlin' Wolf / Lonesome: Memphis Slim / Let the good times roll creole: Memphis Slim / 40 days and 40 nights: Waters, Muddy / Rollin' and tumblin': Waters, Muddy / Don't stay out all night: Arnold, Billy Boy & Tony McPhee / I wish you would: Arnold, Billy Boy & Tony McPhee
CD _______________ ECD 3106
K-Tel / Jan '95 / K-Tel

ESSENTIAL CLUBSCENE VOL.3
CD _______________ CSR 011
Clubscene / Jan '97 / Clubscene / Grapevine/PolyGram / Mo's Music Machine / Prime

ESSENTIAL COLLECTION FROM SCOTLAND, THE
CD _______________ RECD 496
REL / May '95 / CM / Duncans / Highlander

ESSENTIAL COUNTRY COLLECTION, THE (3CD Set)
CD Set _______________ EMTBX 304
Emporio / Aug '97 / Disc

ESSENTIAL DANCE TRAXX
CD _______________ CCC 97001
Citycat Club / Jul '97 / TKO Magnum

ESSENTIAL DANCEFLOOR LABELS CLASSICS VOL.2 (The Best Of Sutra)
So different: Kinky Foxx / Don'tcha go nowhere: Dee, Donald / Last night a DJ saved my life: Indeep / Keep on tryin': Sizzle / Bad times (I can't stand it): Captain Rapp / Thanks to you: Sinnamon / In motion: Payne, Freda / Every way but loose: Plunky & The Oneness Of Ju Ju / Ain't no stoppin' (ain't no way): McFadden & Whitehead / Rock the beat: Jamaica Girls / Happy feeling: Morgan, Denroy / Treat yourself to my love: Gonzales, Terri
CD _______________ DGPCD 797
Deep Beats / Jul '96 / BMG

ESSENTIAL DETROIT SOUL COLLECTION, THE
CD _______________ GSCD 003
Goldmine / Mar '92 / Vital

ESSENTIAL DRUM 'N' BASS
CD _______________ DBMEM 1
Essential Dance / Dec '95 / RTM/Disc

ESSENTIAL DRUM 'N' BASS
Bonus hop: Half Breed / Booya: Insolent Bo / Dark justice: Evil-Ed / Every posse: Shaper / Good old days: Fader / Chainsaw: Scan / Sizeable respect: Scan / Criminal: Half Breed / Need you: Redneck / Selecta: Rockers / Lazy Sunday: Roots / Icecold: Ken, Kenny & Cool Breeze / Live and direct: Facs / Beware: Facs / Stand bold: Universal Flava / Work dat sucker: Smokey Joe / Dogs on the set: Grimm, Ben / Crazy juice: Headman / Jazz creation: Universal Flava / Mistical journey: Elusive
CD _______________ ESSECD 1
Beechwood / Jun '97 / Beechwood/BMG / Pinnacle

ESSENTIAL ELEMENTS VOL.6
CD _______________ 703011
CD _______________ 703011X
Essential Dance / Feb '96 / RTM/Disc

ESSENTIAL ELEMENTS VOL.7
CD _______________ NR 0192
Essential Dance / Jun '97 / RTM/Disc

ESSENTIAL ELLA, BILLIE, SARAH, ARETHA, MAHALIA
CD _______________ 4737332
Sony Jazz / Jan '95 / Sony

ESSENTIAL FOLK VOL.1
CD _______________ NTRCD 030
Nectar / Mar '95 / Pinnacle

ESSENTIAL FOLK VOL.2
CD _______________ NTRCD 047
Nectar / May '96 / Pinnacle

ESSENTIAL GARAGE DANCEFLOOR CLASSICS VOL.1
In and out of my life: Adeva / You don't know: Serious Intention / Ma foom bey: Cultural Vibe / Jazzy rhythm: Wallace, Michelle / Tee's happy: Northend / You're all played out: Life / Touch me: Rae, Fonda / Standing right there: Moore, Melba / I'm caught up (in a one night love affair): Inner Life / What I got is what you need: Unique
CD _______________ DGPCD 686
Deep Beats / Jun '94 / BMG

ESSENTIAL GARAGE DANCEFLOOR CLASSICS VOL.2
Music is the answer: Abrams, Colonel / You can't run from my love: Singleton, Maxine / Who's gonna ease the pressure: Thornhill, Mac / Touch me (love me tonight): Keith, Brian / I can't wait too long: Church, Joe / Music's got me: Visual / One hot night: Pure Energy & Lisa Stevens / Love itch: Flemming, Rochelle / You are the one: Pilot / I'd like to: Feel / I need you now: Sinnamon
CD _______________ DGPCD 739
Deep Beats / Nov '95 / BMG

ESSENTIAL GROOVE
This DJ: Warren G / Bump 'n' grind: R Kelly / Cry for you: Jodeci / Your love is a 187: Whitehead Brothers / Midnight at the oasis: Brand New Heavies / Everything's gonna be alright: Sounds Of Blackness / Blow your mind: Jamiroquai / Ease my mind: Arrested Development / Anything: SWV / True spirit: Anderson, Carleen / Looking through patient eyes: PM Dawn / Sly: Massive Attack / All about Eve: Marxman / Spiritual love: Urban Species / Twyford Down: Galliano / You know how we do it: Ice Cube / Outside: Omar / Love makes the world go round: Don-E / Get in touch: Freakpower / Don't you worry about a thing: Incognito
CD _______________ 5254382
Polydor / Mar '95 / PolyGram

ESSENTIAL HARDCORE
Understand your destiny: Suzy Shoes / Ard corr: Well Ard / Parsley: DJ Splix / Blue skies: Because I Am / Dance with power: Bass Construction / Tingler: Smart Systems / Q: Mental Cube / Wonderful day: Flag / Quazi: Yage / Fire when ready: G Double / Can you feel me: Circa 91 / Heavy ride: China Boy / Owl: Indo Tribe / 550 state: Blood Brothers / 54321 carry on: AWOL / Braineater (I need my hardcore): Danse City
CD _______________ 305102
Hallmark / Jun '97 / Carlton

ESSENTIAL HOLLYWOOD JAZZ
CD _______________ 4743732
Sony Jazz / Jan '95 / Sony

ESSENTIAL IRISH COLLECTION, THE
Miss Mcleod's reel / Whiskey in the jar / I'll tell me Ma / Muirsheen Durkin / Lord of the dance / Gypsy rover / Boys of County Armagh / Black velvet band / Wild rover / Danny boy / Higgins hornpipe / Lanigans ball / Drowsy Maggie's / Leaving of Liverpool / Roddy McCauley / Irish rover / Patsy McCann / Far away in Australia / Spancil Hill / Molly Malone / Maggie / Red is the rose / After all these years / Irish washerwoman / Captain Pugwash / Fields of Athenry / Hills of Donegal / Holy ground / Mason's apron / Keel row / Scotland the brave / Minstrel boy / MacNamara's band / Peter Street
CD _______________ QED 136
Tring / Nov '96 / Tring

ESSENTIAL IRISH FOLK COLLECTION, THE (2CD Set)
CD Set _______________ DOL2CD 100
Dolphin / Oct '96 / CM / Else / Grapevine/PolyGram / Koch

ESSENTIAL ITALIAN HOUSE
CD _______________ DBMEM 3
Death Becomes Me / Sep '96 / Grapevine/PolyGram / Pinnacle / SRD

ESSENTIAL JAZZ
Ain't misbehavin': Armstrong, Louis / I can't get started: Parker, Charlie / God bless the child: Holiday, Billie / Last night a miracle happened: Waller, Fats / Stormy weather: Garner, Erroll / High society: Morton, Jelly Roll / I got rhythm: Reinhardt, Django / Yardbird suite: Davis, Miles / C'est si bon: Armstrong, Louis / Honey hush: Waller, Fats / Stardust: Garner, Erroll / Lover man: Holiday, Billie / Ballin' the jack: Morton, Jelly Roll / Sweet Georgia Brown: Reinhardt, Django / I get a kick out of you: Parker, Charlie / Ornithology: Davis, Miles
CD _______________ ECD 3105
K-Tel / Jan '95 / K-Tel

ESSENTIAL JAZZ (18 Classic Jazz Tracks)
I wish I knew (how it would feel to be free): Taylor, Billy / Night in Tunisia: Parker, Charlie & Miles Davis / I got it bad and that ain't good: Ellington, Duke / Alfie's theme: Rollins, Sonny / It's only a paper moon: Fitzgerald, Ella / Nuages: Reinhardt, Django / 'Round midnight: Gordon, Dexter / Double-O: Basie, Count / Love for sale: Adderley, Cannonball & Miles Davis / My man: Holiday, Billie / My funny valentine: Baker, Chet & Gerry Mulligan Quartet / Midnight blue: Burrell, Kenny / So relax: Redbone, Leon / So it may secretly begin: Metheny, Pat Group / Morning dance: Spyro Gyra
CD _______________ MUSCD 30
MCI Music / Jan '97 / Disc / THE

ESSENTIAL JAZZ CONCERTS
CD _______________ 4685742
Sony Jazz / Jan '95 / Sony

ESSENTIAL JAZZ DRUMMERS
Sing sing sing: Woody, Sam / Hi fi fo fum: Bellson, Louie & Duke Ellington / Skin Deep: Roach, Max / Drum suite (pts 1-5): Rich, Buddy / Sugarfoot stomp: Morello, Joe / Flash: Morello, Joe / C jam blues: Blakey, Art / Sacrifict: Woodyard, Sam / Duel fuel (pts 1-3): Woodyard, Sam
CD _______________ 4685732
Columbia / Jul '93 / Sony

ESSENTIAL JAZZ LEGENDS
CD _______________ 4716842
Sony Jazz / Jan '95 / Sony

ESSENTIAL JAZZ PIANO
CD _______________ 4685722
Sony Jazz / Jan '95 / Sony

ESSENTIAL JAZZ SAX
CD _______________ 4741862
Sony Jazz / Jan '95 / Sony

ESSENTIAL JAZZ VOL.1
Take five: Brubeck, Dave / Girl from Ipanema: Getz, Stan & Astrud Gilberto / One note samba: Gillespie, Dizzy / I've got you under my skin: Washington, Dinah / Summertime: Vaughan, Sarah / Foggy day: Marsalis, Wynton / Take the 'A' train: Marsalis, Wynton / Love for sale: Davis, Miles / God bless the child: Holiday, Billie / Laird baird: Parker, Charlie / Polka dots and moonbeams: Peterson, Oscar / Autumn leaves: Evans, Bill / Goodbye Pork Pie Hat: Mingus, Charles / Soul eyes: Coltrane, John / Ain't misbehavin': Armstrong, Louis / I can't get started: Parker, Charlie
CD _______________ MUSCD 005
MCI Music / Nov '92 / Disc / THE

ESSENTIAL JAZZ VOL.2 (15 Classic Jazz Tracks)
Take the 'A' train: Ellington, Duke / Straighten up and fly right: Cole, Nat 'King' / Sidewinder: Morgan, Lee / I guess I'll hang my tears out to dry: Gordon, Dexter / Laura: Parker, Charlie / Folks who live on the hill: Grappelli, Stephane & George Shearing / They can't that away from me: Gillespie, Dizzy / Lullaby of birdland: Jones, Quincy / April in Paris: Basie, Count / Fever: Lee, Peggy / Misty: Garner, Erroll / On green dolphin street: Peterson, Oscar / Nuit sur Les Champs Elysees: Davis, Miles / Watermelon man: Hancock, Herbie / More I see you: Mobley, Hank
CD _______________ MUSCD 031
MCI Music / Jan '97 / Disc / THE

ESSENTIAL MELLOW GROOVE, THE
CD _______________ GSCD 005
Goldmine / Sep '92 / Vital

ESSENTIAL MERENGUE - STRIPPING THE PARROTS
CD _______________ CORACD 122
Corason / Feb '95 / ADA / CM / Direct

ESSENTIAL MIX VOL.1 (Tong/Cox/Sasha/Oakenfold/2CD Set)
Hide-a-way: Rich, Kelli / Over and over: Plux & Georgia Jones / Nakasaki: Kendoh / Tempo fiesta: Itty Bitty Boozy Woozy / Dancing daffodils: Beat Syndicate / Are you out there: Crescendo / I need you: Pendulum / Access: DJ Misjah & Tim / Are you ready to fly: Dune / Neurodancer: Wippenberg / Harmonio groove: Garnier, Laurent / Outrage: DJ Powerout / Dance 2 the music: Men With Rhythm / Education: Pox And Cowell / Mantra to the Buddha: Hyperspace / Cut for life: Leftfield / Static: Markey / Step back: Slam / Thunder: Clarke, Dave / Lets turn it on: Doof / Paradise regime: Blue Amazon / Save me: Beat Foundation / Wired: Tenth Chapter / Rays of the rising sun: Mozalo / Runaway: Evoke / Coma aroma: Inaura / Survive: Brothers Grimm / Skylined: Prodigy / Floor essence: Man With No Name / Down to earth: Grace / Star: Utah Saints / Sun: Virus
CD Set _______________ 8287012
FFRR / Nov '95 / PolyGram

ESSENTIAL MIX VOL.2
Call on me: Johnny X / Lover that you are: Pulse / Heaven knows: Moraes, Angel / Keep on jumpin': Lisa Marie Experience / Cut the midrange: Watchman / Read my lips: Future Breeze / There's nothing I won't do: JX / Eugina: Salt Tank / Stand up: Love Tribe / What you want: Future Force / Day in the life: Terry, Todd / Edge of time: FK / What a sensation: Kenlou III / Everybody be somebody: Ruffneck / Pearl's girl: Underworld / Straight forward: Secret Cinema / Circuit maximus: Unknown Force / Side on: Space DJ's / Cantina tango: Dirty House Crew / Spacewreck: Manmade / Flash: Cosmic Messenger / Bite and scratch: Vogel, Christian
CD _______________ 5354312
CD _______________ 5354242
FFRR / Apr '96 / PolyGram

ESSENTIAL MIX VOL.3 (Tong/Seaman/Judge Jules/Carter) (Ltd Edition 2CD/Rom Set)
To be real: Fuzz / La tropicana: La Tropicana / It's just another groove: Mighty Dub Katz / Windows: SIL / Blue room: T-Empo / Mystery land: Y-Traxx / Born slippy: Underworld / Quattara: Quattara / Last rhythm: Last Rhythm / I am: Chakra / Coming home: Visions / Horn: Digidance / Ain't no way: Nemen / Always on my mind: Pink Noise / Outrageous: Stix 'N' Stoned / Kiss of life: Fanny Flow / Difference: Funny Walker / U (I got the feeling): Scot Project / Imagination: Time Zone / I'm alive: Stretch n' Vern / Jumpin': Terry, Todd / Life: Blair / Disco cubism: I-Cube / Carry on: Washington, Martha / Future: Armando / One for MAW: Jedi Knights / I think of you: Rednail Kidz / This is the house: Freaks / Shout & out: Lood / Feeling mm-pa-paa-paa: Dee
CD _______________ 5358262
CD Set _______________ 5358292
FFRR / Sep '96 / PolyGram

ESSENTIAL MIX VOL.4 (Pete Tong/Paul Oakenfold/Dave Carter - 2CD Set)
Pushing against the flow: Raw Stylus / Fired up: Funky Green Dogs / Fly life: Basement Jaxx / Flame: Fine Young Cannibals / She drives me crazy: Fine Young Cannibals / Ride a rocket: Li / Warning: Fah / Ice rain: Whitcombe, Alex & Big C / Offshore: Chicane / Run to you: Carroll, Dina / Closer to you: JX / Life's too short: Hole In One / Trommelaschine: Der Dritte Raum / Arkham asylum: Sasha / Places: Tilt / Mammal: Virtual Symmetry / Inner city life: Goldie / Say my name: Zee / Voices of KA: Van Leeuwen, Sjef / Blue skies: BT & Tori Amos / Off shore: Chicane / Eternally: Quadran / Anomaly: Libra / Words: Van Dyke, Paul / Pan fried: Light / Sensemilla: Dillingers Massive Dub Beats / Phantom: Trippatrazz / Zig it up: Ninjaman & Flourgan / Let me clear my throat: DJ Kool / Enter/Other: Q-Burns Abstract Message / Mad them: General Levy / Silence go boom: Sons Of Silence / Filthy: St. Etienne & Q-Tee / Trickshot: Ceasefire / Blow the whole joint up: Monkey Mafia / Just feel it (Live '92): Kix / Inspire me: Frontier Man / Killa: Smith & Mighty / Who da fuck: Semi-Detached Production / There's gonna be a riot: Dub Pistols / In da jungle: Playboy / Wickedest sound: Rebel MC / Breaking into a sweat: Interspin / Narramine: Genaside II / Killin': Ghostrider & Special K / Super sharp shooter: Ganja Kru / Neptune: Blame / Buddy bye bye: Osbourne, Johnny
CD Set _______________ 5531532
CD Set _______________ 5531672
FFRR / Nov '96 / PolyGram

ESSENTIAL MODERN SOUL COLLECTION VOL.1, THE
CD _______________ GSCD 002
Goldmine / Mar '93 / Vital

ESSENTIAL MODERN SOUL COLLECTION VOL.3, THE
For real: Flowers / Alone again: Baker, Ernest / Da da da da da (I love you): Naturals / I think I've got a good chance: Barnes, J.J. / Can this be real: Perfections / He's a better liar than me: Lampkin, Tony / I just want to do my own thing: Reachers / That's the way the world should be: Up From The Bottom / All work and no play: Jordan, Vivalore / Put your lovin' on me: Fisher, Willie / Since you said you'd be mine: Ragland, Lou / Can't nobody love me like you do: Storm / I gotta make you believe in me: BJB / I'll do anything for you: McDonald, Lee / Doin' it cause it feels good: Strong, Chuck / All of a sudden: Moore, Melvin / Ain't nothing like the love: Simmons, John / Hungry: Sandy's Gang / What does the future hold: 24 Karat Gold
CD _______________ GSCD 040
Goldmine / Jun '94 / Vital

ESSENTIAL NASHVILLE
CD _______________ 74321367022
RCA / Apr '96 / BMG

ESSENTIAL NORTHERN SOUL COLLECTION, THE
CD _______________ GSCD 001
Goldmine / Sep '91 / Vital

ESSENTIAL OLD SCHOOL HARMONY DANCEFLOOR CLASSICS VOL.2
That's the way it's got to be (body and soul): Soul Generation / Friends just friends: Courtship / My ebony princess: Briscoe, Jimmy & The Little Beavers / It's gotta be love: Trumains / In your way: Soul Generation / Super love: Futures / Love ain't love (til you give it to somebody): Briscoe, Jimmy & The Little Beavers / I choose you: Chicago Gangsters / Caught in the act (of loving you): Courtship / Million dollars: Soul Generation / Girl don't let me down: Trumains / Forever: Briscoe, Jimmy & The Little Beavers / (Love lives on a) windy hill: Futures / Wait so long: Soul Generation / Oops it just slipped out: Courtship / Love foundation: Electrified Action / I only feel this way when I'm with you: Briscoe, Jimmy & The Little Beavers / (I'll know) when true

love really passes by: *Ebonys* / Gotta let some sunshine: *Exceptionals* / For the chance of loving you: *Courtship*
CD ________ **DGPCD 784**
Deep Beats / Jul '96 / BMG

ESSENTIAL OLD SCHOOL RAP DANCEFLOOR CLASSICS VOL.1
Funky sound (Tear the roof off): *Sequence* / Do you want to rock (before I let go): *Funky Four* / King Heroin: *Funky Four* / Showdown: *Furious Five & Sugarhill Gang* / Pump me up: *Trouble Funk* / Birthday party: *Grandmaster Flash & The Furious Five* / Apache: *Sugarhill Gang* / Feel it (The Mexican): *Funky Four* / Eighth wonder: *Sugarhill Gang* / Ice cream dreams: *Lady L* / Mosquito: *West Street Mob* / Message: *Grandmaster Flash & The Furious Five*
CD ________ **DGPCD 708**
Deep Beats / Mar '95 / BMG

ESSENTIAL OLD SCHOOL RAP DANCEFLOOR CLASSICS VOL.2
Adventures of Grand Master Flash on the wheels of steel: *Grandmaster Flash & The Furious Five* / Hey fellas: *Trouble Funk* / Sucker DJ: *Dimples D & Marley Marl* / Got it good: *Tricky Tee* / Success is the word: *12:41* / Fat boys: *Disco 3* / Ya mama: *Wuf Ticket* / Our picture of a man: *Playgirls* / It's good to be the queen: *Sylvia* / Monster jam: *Spoonie Gee & The Sequence*
CD ________ **DGPCD 741**
Deep Beats / Nov '95 / BMG

ESSENTIAL REGGAE (16 Reggae Hits)
Uptown top ranking: *Althia & Donna* / Hurt so good: *Cadogan, Susan* / Irie feelings: *Edwards, Rupie* / Red red wine: *Tribe, Tony* / Double barrel: *Collins, Dave & Ansell* / Wonderful world, beautiful people: *Cliff, Jimmy* / Liquidator: *Harry J All Stars* / Black pearl: *Faith, Horace* / Some guys have all the luck: *Harriott, Derrick* / Money in my pocket: *Brown, Dennis* / You can get it if you really want it: *Dekker, Desmond* / Love of the common people: *Thomas, Nicky* / Help me make it through the night: *Holt, John* / Let your yeah be yeah: *Pioneers* / Black and white: *Greyhound* / Young, gifted and black: *Bob & Marcia*
CD ________ **CDGOLD 1056**
EMI Gold / Oct '96 / EMI

ESSENTIAL ROCK
Dirty love: *Thunder* / All the young dudes: *Dickinson, Bruce* / Fireball: *Deep Purple* / Mean man: *WASP* / I've done everything for you: *Hagar, Sammy* / Your mamma don't dance: *Poison* / 747 (strangers in the night): *Saxon* / Silver machine: *Hawkwind* / Something better change: *Stranglers* / Ships in the night: *Be-Bop Deluxe* / Down at the doctors: *Dr. Feelgood* / Centrefold: *Geils, J. Band* / Let's work together: *Canned Heat* / Garden party: *Marillion* / Roll over Beethoven: *ELO* / Whole lotta love: *CCS*
CD ________ **CDGOLD 1037**
EMI Gold / May '96 / EMI

ESSENTIAL SELECTION SUMMER '97, THE
CD ________ **5538862**
PolyGram TV / Aug '97 / PolyGram

ESSENTIAL SLOW GROOVE DANCEFLOOR CLASSICS VOL.2
I'm the one for you: *Whispers* / Over and over: *Shalamar* / Show me where you're coming from: *Lucas, Carrie* / Window on a dream: *Wolfer, Bill* / Curious: *Midnight Star* / Winners and losers: *Collage* / Two occasions: *Deele* / Don't keep me waiting: *Whispers* / Hello stranger: *Lucas, Carrie* / Feels so good: *Midnight Star* / One girl: *Dynasty* / No pain, no gain: *Whispers* / This is for the lover in you: *Shalamar*
CD ________ **DGPCD 711**
Deep Beats / Feb '95 / BMG

ESSENTIAL SOUL
Tainted love: *Jones, Gloria* / Right back where we started from: *Nightingale, Maxine* / Good time tonight: *Soul Sisters* / Looking for you: *Mimms, Garnet* / Lot of love: *Banks, Homer* / Everybody needs help: *Holiday, Jimmy* / Ready, willing and able: *Holiday, Jimmy & Clydie King* / Better use your head: *Little Anthony & The Imperials* / Dance, dance, dance: *Casualeers* / No.1 in your heart: *Goins, Herbie* / In the midnight hour: *Preston, Billy* / Who's that lady: *Isley Brothers* / Lipstick traces: *O'Jays* / You got what it takes: *Johnson, Marv* / Do wah diddy diddy: *Exciters* / Love potion no.9: *Clovers* / What's wrong with me baby: *Invitations* / Seven days too long: *Woods, Chuck* / I'm on my way: *Parrish, Dean* / Drifter: *Pollard, Ray*
CD ________ **CDGOLD 1031**
EMI Gold / May '96 / EMI

ESSENTIAL SUN ROCKABILLIES VOL.1
Put your cat clothes on: *Perkins, Carl* / Red hot: *Riley, Billy Lee* / We wanna boogie: *Burgess, Sonny* / Tennessee zip: *Parchman, Kenny* / Rabbit action: *Haggett, Jimmy* / Come on little mama: *Harris, Ray* / Madman: *Wages, Jimmy* / Red cadillac and a black moustache: *Smith, Warren* / Mama mama mama: *Thompson, Hayden* / Flat foot Sam: *Blake, Tommy* / Crowdad hole: *Earls, Jack* / Goin' crazy: *Self, Mack* / Crazy woman: *Simmons, Gene* / Tough tough tough: *Anderson, Andy* / Huh babe: *McDanie, Luke* / Ten cats down: *Miller Sisters* / Rakin' and scrapin': *Beard, Dean* / Rockin' with my baby: *Yelvington, Malcolm* / Bottle to the baby: *Feathers, Charlie* / This ole heart of mine: *Bond, Eddie* / Milkshake mademoiselle: *Lewis, Jerry Lee* / Your lovin' man: *Taylor, Vernon* / Me and my rhythm guitar: *Powers, Johnny* / Just in time: *Jenkins, Harold* / Ooby dooby: *Orbison, Roy*
CD ________ **CPCD 8099**
Charly / Jun '95 / Koch

ESSENTIAL SUN ROCKABILLIES VOL.2
CD ________ **CPCD 8118**
Charly / Aug '95 / Koch

ESSENTIAL SUN ROCKABILLIES VOL.3
CD ________ **CPCD 8161**
Charly / Mar '96 / Koch

ESSENTIAL SUN ROCKABILLIES VOL.4
Red headed woman: *Burgess, Sonny* / High high high: *McDaniel, Luke* / Lonely woman: *Harris, Ray* / I feel like rockin': *Parchman, Kenny* / You better believe it: *Blake, Tommy* / Don't lie to me: *Beard, Dean* / Pop and Mama: *Simmons, Gene* / Fairlane rock: *Thompson, Hayden* / Miss Pearl: *Wages, Jimmy* / Lovin' memories: *Self, Mack* / Blue day tomorrow: *Taylor, Vernon* / Drive in: *Vickery, Mack* / Oh yeah: *McVoy, Carl* / I need your lovin': *Jenkins, Howard* / My bonnie: *Hoback, Curtis* / Love is my business: *Greaves, Cliff* / Whole lotta shakin' goin' on: *Gilley, Mickey* / Cindy Lou: *Penner, Dick* / Donna Lee: *Rich, Charlie* / To be with you: *Dorman, Harold* / Thousand guitars: *Pendarvis, Tracy* / Honey bee: *Hinton, Don* / Heart throb: *Frost, Jack* / Watch that stuff: *Skipper, Macy* / My girl and his girl: *Hall, Roy* / Frankie and Johnny: *Feathers, Charlie* / Linda: *Chaffin, Ernie* / My babe: *Felts, Narvel*
CD ________ **CPCD 8236**
Charly / Nov '96 / Koch

ESSENTIAL SWEET SOUL SELECTION, THE
We're gonna be together: *Dynamics* / Hey foxy lady: *Natural Resources* / Why should I forgive you: *Clock* / Tricky dick: *Train Robbers* / Vibrations: *5 Farenheit* / What a lovely way to meet: *True Movement* / Don't ask me: *Norfolk* / Turned around over you: *Imperial Wonders* / I stand alone: *Malibus, Calif* / How do you say goodbye: *Heartbreakers* / Let me take care of your heart: *Smith Brothers* / I do love my lady: *Haze* / Stop to think it over: *God's Gift To Women* / Young hearts get lonely too: *New Young Hearts* / No one in this world: *Enchanting Enchanters* / Now I know: *Final Chapter* / Bet you didn't know: *Mind Readers* / Don't let go: *Sweet Berry* / You mean everything to me: *Four Tracks* / Never turn your back on the one you love: *Stone Luv* / I love you, baby: *Moovers*
CD ________ **GSCD 120**
Goldmine / Apr '97 / Vital

ESSENTIAL TECHNO (3CD Set)
CD Set ________ **DBMEM 2**
Death Becomes Me / Jun '96 / Grapevine/ PolyGram / Pinnacle / SRD

ETERNAL FLAME (Baltimore Jam)
CD ________ **STBCD 2504**
Stash / Sep '95 / ADA / Cadillac / CM / Direct / Jazz Music

ETERNAL FREQUENCY, THE
Kraton 3: *Manmademan* / Solar nomads: *Shakta* / Carnival On Mars: *Mindfield* / Venusian illusion: *Nervasystem* / OO7 in heaven: *Orion* / My world (doesn't follow any other): *Subclouds* / Zarkon principle: *Dimension 5* / Moondog: *Lunar Asylum* / Journey Inside: *Moonweed* / Rezorector: *Metronome*
CD ________ **PTM 135CD**
Phantasm / Mar '97 / Arabesque / Plastic Head / Prime / Vital/SAM

ETERNAL LOVE
CD ________ **WBRCD 1001**
Business / Aug '94 / Jet Star

ETERNAL VOICES (2CD Set)
CD Set ________ **NAR 053**
New Alliance / May '94 / Plastic Head

ETERNALLY
CD ________ **STACD 052**
Wisepack / Sep '93 / Conifer/BMG / THE

ETERNALLY ALIVE VOL.2
CD ________ **MILL 017CD**
Millenium / Nov '95 / Plastic Head / Prime / SRD

ETERNALLY ALIVE VOL.3
CD ________ **MILL 027CD**
Millenium / Sep '96 / Plastic Head / Prime / SRD

E'THING YOU ALWAYS WANT...
CD ________ **AA 041**
Arf Arf / Jul '97 / Greyhound

ETHNO PUNK - AROUND THE WORLD WITH ATTITUDE
Children come and go: *Poliker, Yehuda* / Mireme miss: *Jardin, Ciudad* / Lena gia mena: *Pyx-Lax* / More and more: *Salt & Nails* / Det ar jag: *Den Fule* / Sid h'bidi: *Mano Negra* / Katami-bushi: *Parsha Club* / I tak warto zyc: *Raz Daw Trzy* / Make mana: *Mau Mau* / Rockin' the Bronx: *Black 47* / Nao me estrague o dia: *Os Paralamas Do Sucesso* / Wild on the snow: *Ciu Jian* / Waiting for Conrad: *Shooglenifty* / Aivoton: *Hadningarna* / Mamo feber: *Wilmer X*
CD ________ **CDEMC 3750**
Premier/EMI / May '96 / EMI

EUPHORIA
CD ________ **CDRAID 516**
Rumour / Mar '94 / 3mv/Sony / Mo's Music Machine / Pinnacle

EUPHORIA
CD Set ________ **SPV 08538892**
SPV / Jul '94 / Koch / Plastic Head

EUROBEAT 2000
CD ________ **KICKCD 32**
Slip 'n' Slide / Jan '96 / Amato Disco / Prime / RTM/Disc / Vital

EUROBEAT 2000 - CLUB CLASSICS VOL.1
CD ________ **KICKCD 13**
Kickin' / Oct '94 / Prime / SRD

EUROBEAT 2000 - CLUB CLASSICS VOL.2
CD ________ **KICKCD 19**
Kickin' / Mar '95 / Prime / SRD

EUROBEAT 2000 - CLUB CLASSICS VOL.4
Prepare to jam: *Lindsay, Patrick* / Pain in my brain: *Outsider* / Circuit sex: *Blunted Boy Wonder* / Paroles: *Mike Ink* / Thunder: *Clarke, Dave* / Game form: *Beltram, Joey* / Bite and scratch: *Vogel, Christian* / Rabbits name was: *A&E Dept* / Der klang der familie: *3 Phase* / Strange funk: *Aura-Z* / Acid memory: *Dearborn, Mike* / Robot rebellion: *Sunrise Society*
CD ________ **KICKCD 48**
Kickin' / Jan '97 / Prime / SRD

EUROCLUB VOL.1
Get up: *Technotronic* / Jack to the sound of the underground: *Hithouse* / Don't let me be misunderstood: *Santa Esmerelda* / James Brown in still alive: *Holy Noise* / Quadraphonia: *Quadrophonia* / Sonar system: *Meng Syndicate* / To piano: *Clarke, Rozline* / Dancing is like making love: *Mainx* / Can this be love: *Eden* / Make my day: *Grace Under Pressure* / Move: *Guaranteed Raw* / Fell the groove: *Cartouche* / I won't let you down: *Two Boys* / Nightlife: *TPFF* / Feel good: *Chique* / Keep the fire burning: *Bass X* / Let your love flow: *Melissa* / Down on the street: *Glow* / This beat is technotronic: *Technotronic*
CD ________ **EUROCD 1**
Charly / Jul '95 / Koch

EUROCLUB VOL.2
Pump up the jam: *Technotronic* / Voices: *KC Flightt* / Good love: *Xaviera Gold* / Alice (who the fuck is Alice): *Steppers* / Wave of the future: *Quadrophonia* / Go with love: *Black Diamond* / I can handle it: *MSD* / 99 Luftballons: *Donn-Ah* / Fue amor: *Jazzy Mel* / Glow of love: *Grace Under Pressure* / Hot (wonderful world): *Reggie* / Touch the sky: *Cartouche* / Just the two of us: *2 Boy's* / Just a little pain: *Laurenz* / Rage: *Twins* / Night is mine (x-tra compact mix): *MC-X* / Give me your love: *Bobbylone* / Gonna move your body: *Voice Over*
CD ________ **EUROCD 2**
Charly / Jul '95 / Koch

EUROPEAN CLUB SHOES
Search: *Trancesetters* / Work it: *Liquid Groove* / Perception: *R-Factor* / Shine on: *Sirius 5* / You make me happy: *Danceorder 2* / Sides of iron: *Chaser* / First word: *Soundsurf* / Jack the beat: *Wicked Wipe* / Extra: *Ishii, Ken* / Needle damage: *Autorepeat* / Amazing space funk: *Silent Breed*
CD ________ **SPV 08768262**
SPV / Apr '96 / Koch / Plastic Head

EUROPEAN POLKA HITS
Trumpet echo / Cross polka / Polka from Tegernsee / Fast polka
CD ________ **15282**
Laserlight / '91 / Target/BMG

EUROPEAN TRUMPET SUMMIT
CD ________ **EFA 064282**
Konnex / Apr '95 / SRD

EVE COMPILATION
CD ________ **EVRCD 19**
Eve / Mar '93 / Grapevine/PolyGram

EVE OF THE WAR (Synthesizer Hits)
CD ________ **MACCD 314**
Autograph / Aug '96 / BMG

EVEN SANTA GETS THE BLUES
Christmas celebration: *King, B.B.* / I'll be coming home for Christmas: *Brooks, Hadda* / Merry Christmas baby: *Brown, Charles* / I want you with me at Christmas: *Belvin, Jesse* / White Christmas: *Brooks, Hadda* / La Christmas blue: *Brooks, Hadda* / Please come home for Christmas: *Winter, Johnny* / I wanna spend Christmas with you: *Fulson, Lowell* / Only if you were here: *Hayes, Isaac* / So glad you were born: *Hayes, Isaac*
CD ________ **VPBCD 28**
Virgin / Nov '95 / EMI

EVENING CONCERTS - NEWPORT FOLK FESTIVAL 1963
CD ________ **VCD 77002**
Vanguard / Jan '96 / ADA / Pinnacle

EVENING SESSION - PRIORITY TUNES (2CD Set)
Babies: *Pulp* / Changing man: *Weller, Paul* / Day we caught the train: *Ocean Colour Scene* / Something 4 the weekend: *Super Furry Animals* / Lump: *Presidents Of The USA* / Does your mother know: *Ash* / Fine time: *Cast* / Born slippy: *Underworld* / Firestarter: *Prodigy* / Valley of the shadows: *Origin Unknown* / Box: *Orbital* / Eurochild: *Massive Attack* / Street spirit: *Radiohead* / I believe: *Booth, Tim & Angelo Badalamenti* / Wrong: *Everything But The Girl* / Stars: *Dubstar* / What do I do now: *Sleeper* / Vow: *Garbage* / Drowners: *Suede* / Female of the species: *Space* / Champagne supernova: *Oasis* / Far: *Longpigs* / Connection: *Elastica* / Speakeasy: *Shed Seven* / Lose it: *Supergrass* / Weak: *Skunk Anansie* / Pig valentine: *60ft Dolls* / Rollercoaster: *Northern Uproar* / Ladykillers: *Lush* / Kandy pop: *Bis* / Take it easy chicken: *Mansun* / Just: *Radiohead* / Bank holiday: *Blur* / Penny royalty: *Manic Street Preachers* / Caught in session: *Snuff* / Born in '69: *Rocket From The Crypt* / Wuthering heights: *China Drum* / Come home: *Placebo* / Shining in the wood: *Tiger* / Chart rider space invader: *Dweeb* / Come out 2nite: *Kenickie*
CD Set ________ **VTDCD 88**
Virgin / Aug '96 / EMI

EVERY BEAT YOU EAT
CD ________ **DQCD 01**
Don Q / Aug '97 / Shellshock/Disc / SRD

EVERY DAY I HAVE THE BLUES
Crawling Kingsnake: *Hooker, John Lee* / Blues after hours: *Crayton, Pee Wee* / Straighten up baby: *Wilson, Smokey* / Lonesome dog blues: *Hopkins, Lightnin'* / TV Mama: *Turner, Joe* / Me and my chauffer: *Thornton, Willie Mae 'Big Mama'* / Shattered dreams: *Fulson, Lowell* / Every day I have the blues: *King, B.B.* / Sneakin' around: *King, B.B.* / House rockin' boogie: *Howlin' Wolf* / Too many drivers: *Fulson, Lowell* / Have mercy someone: *Hill, Z.Z.* / Chains of love: *Turner, Joe* / Good morning little school: *Hogg, Smokey* / Telephone blues: *Smith, Little George* / Gone with the wind: *Roosevelt Skyes* / Jealous woman: *Walker, T-Bone* / Happy home: *James, Elmore*
CD ________ **306652**
Hallmark / May '97 / Carlton

EVERY SONG TELLS A STORY
Boxer: *Simon & Garfunkel* / Candle in the wind: *John, Elton* / Praying for time: *Michael, George* / Little time: *Beautiful South* / Alison: *Costello, Elvis* / Hazard: *Marx, Richard* / Romeo and Juliet: *Dire Straits* / Living years: *Mike & The Mechanics* / Dignity: *Deacon Blue* / Up the junction: *Squeeze* / You're so vain: *Simon, Carly* / WOLD: *Chapin, Harry* / Ode to Billy Joe: *Gentry, Bobbie* / Ruby, don't take your love to town: *Rogers, Kenny* / Babooshka: *Bush, Kate* / Vincent: *McLean, Don* / Uptown, uptempo woman: *Edelman, Randy* / Waterloo sunset: *Kinks* / Classic: *Gurvitz, Adrian*
CD ________ **5251702**
PolyGram TV / Apr '95 / PolyGram

EVERYBODY DANCE
CD ________ **RENCD 110**
Renaissance Collector Series / Mar '96 / BMG

EVERYBODY IS LINE DANCIN' (2CD Set)
CD Set ________ **KEG 101**
Southbound / Jul '97 / Grapevine/ PolyGram

EVERYBODY'S GOTTA LEARN SOMETIME (International Hostage Release album)
Give blood: *Townshend, Pete* / Architectural number: *Holland, Jools* / Almost seems (too late to turn): *Clannad* / Answers to nothing: *Ure, Midge* / If you really love me: *Woore, Colin* / Desert island: *Harper, Roy* / Nothing too serious: *Icehouse* / It's my life: *Talk Talk* / Candles: *Rea, Chris* / My nation underground: *Cope, Julian* / War baby: *Robinson, Tom* / Everybody's gotta learn sometime: *Korgis* / Driftwood: *Moody Blues* / Happy ending: *Dorsey, Gail Ann* / Hostage: *Oldfield, Mike* / Morning side: *Winwood, Steve* / Belfast child: *Simple Minds* / We don't need another hero: *Turner, Tina* / Never promise anyone forever: *All About Eve* / Man's too strong: *Dire Straits* / Don't give up: *Gabriel, Peter & Kate Bush*
CD ________ **WKFMXD 155**
FM / Jan '91 / Revolver / Sony

EVERYTIME I FEEL THE SPIRIT
CD ________ **CPCD 8164**
Charly / Mar '96 / Koch

EVIDENCE BLUES SAMPLER VOL.1
CD ________ **ECD 260002**
Evidence / Jan '92 / ADA / Cadillac / Harmonia Mundi

EVIDENCE BLUES SAMPLER VOL.2
Johnnie's boogie: *Johnson, Johnnie* / Ramblin' on my mind: *Lockwood, Robert Jr.* / Worried about the blues: *Fulson, Lowell* / You say that you love me honey: *Odom, Andrew* / Giving up on love: *Davis, Larry* / Choo choo ch' boogie: *Brown, Clarence 'Gatemouth'* / Trouble in mind: *Smith, Carrie*

/ Blues is alright: *Little Milton* / Orange driver: *Burns, Eddie Band* / My baby and me: *Shaw, Eddie* / Talking to anna mae, part 1: *Taylor, Melvin* / Takes money: *Young, Joe* / Special road: *Robinson, Fenton* / Young man young woman blues: *Robinson, Fenton* / That's your thing: *Benton, Buster* / All for business: *Dawkins, Jimmy*
CD ______ **ECD 260402**
Evidence / Sep '93 / ADA / Cadillac / Harmonia Mundi

EVIDENCE BLUES SAMPLER VOL.3
House cat blues: *Linkchain, Hip* / Don't throw your love on me so strong: *Campbell, Eddie C.* / Boxcar shorty: *Cousin Joe* / Giving up on love: *Davis, Larry* / Little red rooster: *Peterson, Lucky* / Night life: *Witherspoon, Jimmy* / That's alright: *Rogers, Jimmy* / Cold cold feeling: *Taylor, Melvin* / You've got me running: *Johnson, Luther 'Georgia Snake Boy'* / Don't you lie to me: *Edwards, Honeyboy* / It hurts me too: *Wells, Junior* / You just a baby child: *Dawkins, Jimmy* / Broke and hungry: *Sumlin, Hubert* / I can't quit you baby: *Rush, Otis*
CD ______ **ECD 260482**
Evidence / Mar '94 / ADA / Cadillac / Harmonia Mundi

EVITA'S TANGO (The Golden Age Of The Tango 1945-1952)
CD ______ **74321447932**
Milan Sur / Feb '97 / Conifer/BMG

EVOLUTION
CD ______ **LHCD 009**
Luv n' Haight / Jul '96 / Timewarp

EVOLUTION'S CHRISTMAS
CD ______ **EVCD 3**
Evolution / Dec '95 / Alphamagic

EVOLVING TRADITION
Trip to Fowey/Indian Queen: *Kings Of Calicut* / Tom Clarke's trip to Russia: *Henderson, Ingrid & Allan* / Johnny 'Watt' Henry's/Aly Bain's: *Daniels, Luke Trio* / Flower of Magherallyo: *Oige* / Flatulent Friar of Frome/Lizzie Watling's jig: *Plews, Dan & Cath James* / Tamlin's reel/Bucks of Oranmore/Bunker Hill: *Sherburn, Chris & Denny Bartley* / Bonny Light Horseman/Michael Turner's waltz: *Carthy, Eliza & Nancy Kerr* / PJ Cunningham's old dance: *Cythara* / Doon hingin tie/Tammy Anderson: *Shetland's Young Heritage* / Recruited collier: *Rusby, Kate & Kathryn Roberts* / Raag kirvani/Tintaal: *Sood, Rajan & Rakhi* / Faroe rum/Andowin ida bow/Sleep soond ida moarnin/Lasses tru: *MacDonald, Catriona & Ian Lowthian* / Robin Hood/The tolling bell: *Hedgerows* / Left side jigs: *Thoumire, Simon & Ian Carr* / Jolie Bassette: *Lewery, Gavin & Jock Tyldesley* / Tralee gaol/The chanter: *Van Eyken, Tim & Kerensa Wragg* / Road to recovery/Humours of Galway/Farewell to the Shetland: *Anglim, Carlene & Simon Howarth* / Lord Gresham: *Bohinta* / Tom and Jerry: *Wrigley, Jennifer & Hazel* / Fairfield march/Pit stop/The rushing reel: *Lakeman Brothers* / Bransle du chien/Bar room brawl: *Chipolata 5*
CD ______ **MCRCD 5991**
Mrs. Casey / Apr '95 / ADA / Direct

EXCELLO HITS
Little darlin': *Gladiolas* / Raining in my heart: *Harpo, Slim* / Oh Julie: *Crescendos* / Prisoner's song: *Storm, Warren* / Rollin' stone: *Marigolds* / Pleadin' for love: *Birdsong, Larry* / Congo mombo: *Guitar Gable* / Hey baby: *Ferrier, Al* / Emmitt Lee: *Fran, Carol* / Shoop shoop: *Gladiolas* / I'm a mojo man: *Lonesome Sundown* / This should go on forever: *King Karl* / I'm a lover not a fighter: *Lazy Lester* / Now that she's gone: *King Crooners* / Doin' the horse: *Brooks, Skippy* / Rooster blues: *Lightnin' Slim* / Please think it over: *Shelton, Roscoe* / School daze: *Little Rico & The King Crooners* / Hello Mary Lee: *Lightnin' Slim* / You know baby: *Meloaires* / Baby scratch my back: *Harpo, Slim* / Snake out of the grass: *Anderson, Rosheil*
CD ______ **CDCHD 400**
Ace / Jan '94 / Pinnacle

EXCLUSIVE ALTERNATIVES
CD ______ **CLP 9948**
Cleopatra / Jun '97 / Cargo / Greyhound / Plastic Head / RTM/Disc / SRD

EXCURSIONS (2CD Set)
Fantasy on a fantasy: *Caron, David* / Claire: *10* / Firescratch: *Midnight Funk Association* / Warrior: *Stasis* / Summer madness: *DJ Solo & DJ Aura* / Harry's law: *Twig Bud* / Twice the lips: *Midnight Funk Association* / Altares: *Stasis* / Night-side: *Prunes* / Libre: *10* / Take heed: *DJ Solo & DJ Aura* / Davoff: *Twig Bud* / Plot: *Prunes* / Mr. Jolly lives next door: *Prunes* / Hardcore hip hop: *DJ Shadow* / Night shade: *Prunes* / Last stop: *DJ Shadow* / Libro: *10* / Time in advance: *Stasis* / In from the cold: *Stasis* / Pressure: *DJ Solo*
CD Set ______ **MW 056CD**
Mo Wax / Dec '96 / PolyGram / Vital

EXIT DANCE
CD ______ **HHCD 011**
Harthouse / Mar '97 / Mo's Music Machine / Prime / Vital

EXOTIC VOICES & RHYTHMS OF BLACK AFRICA
CD ______ **EUCD 1204**
ARC / Sep '93 / ADA / ARC Music

EXOTIC VOICES & RHYTHMS OF THE SOUTH SEAS
CD ______ **EUCD 1254**
ARC / Mar '94 / ADA / ARC Music

EXPANSION PHAT JAMS VOL.1
Just let me be close to you: *Valentine Brothers* / No more tears: *Jeter, Genobia* / Beverly: *Jamariah* / You know what it's like: *Brooks, Calvin* / Callin' up (Old memories): *Haynes, Victor* / Shoulda been you: *Ware, Leon* / Didn't mean to hurt you: *Valentine, Billy* / Starlite: *Ballin, Chris* / Victory: *Baylor, Helen* / Kissing in the dark: *Rodni* / Miss you: *Fresh Air* / Love hurts: *Glaze* / Show your love: *Hutson, Leroy* / I can't stand the pain: *Lorenzo* / If you don't want my love: *Williams, Lewis*
CD ______ **EXCDP 3**
Expansion / Jun '94 / 3mv/Sony

EXPANSION PHAT JAMS VOL.2
Morning glow: *James, Josie* / Any time, any place: *Gary* / I'll treat U rite: *Perry, Trina* / No one move me like you do: *Gaines, Billy & Sarah* / Whenever I'm lonely: *Dawkins & Dawkins* / I need your help: *Austin, Dennis* / Memory: *King, James* / This love: *Baylor, Helen* / We got something: *Valentine, Billy* / Share your love: *Hutson, Leroy* / Talk to me: *Brooks, Calvin* / I'll always love you: *Robbins, Rockie* / Another lonely night: *Jous* / You are my one and only love: *Webb, Rick* / Let's turn the lights down low: *Jamariah*
CD ______ **EXCDP 4**
Expansion / Jul '95 / 3mv/Sony

EXPANSION SOUL SAUCE VOL.1
My favourite thing: *Brooks, Calvin & Hari Paris* / Share your love: *Hutson, Leroy* / Oasis: *Baylor, Helen* / I found someone: *Gaines, Billy & Sarah* / Shine: *Aja* / Heartbeat: *Ware, Leon* / Win your love: *James, Josie* / Everybody's in a hurry: *McNeir, Ronnie* / Main squeeze: *Crook, General* / Hang on: *Robbins, Rockie* / Love is the magic: *Blu, Peggi* / We got one: *Covington, Matt* / Power to the people: *Linsey* / Friends or lovers: *Burke, Keni* / Promises: *Glaze*
CD ______ **CDEXP 1**
Expansion / Jul '93 / 3mv/Sony

EXPANSION SOUL SAUCE VOL.2
Late night hour: *Waters, Kim* / Surrender (my soul): *Skinner, Belinda A.* / Paradise: *Tankard, Ben* / Give me all your love: *Ballin, Chris* / You are my star: *Reeves, Paulette* / Forever: *Felder, Wilton* / I can only think of you: *McCrae, Gwen* / Fool for love: *Warren, Tony* / It's up to me: *James, Josie* / One step back for love: *El Coco* / Stay with me: *Clear, Crystal* / Shame on you: *Lovesmith, Michael* / Goodbye song: *Vanesse & Carolyn* / Look of love: *Hutson, Leroy* / After affect: *Taylor, Gary*
CD ______ **CDEXP 3**
Expansion / May '93 / 3mv/Sony

EXPANSION SOUL SAUCE VOL.3
Think about it: *Webb, Rick* / Ja miss me: *Valentine, Billy* / I don't know why: *White, Lynn* / One and only: *Rodni* / Take a little time: *James, Josie* / Days and nights: *Haynes, Victor* / Blind to it all: *Taylor, Gary* / Love's gonna bring you home: *Rockmelons* / All my love: *Carmichael, James* / This kind of love (so special): *Valentine Brothers* / I'd like to into you: *Kelly, Denise & Fame* / Get into your life: *Beloyd* / Losers weepers: *Blackfoot, J.* / If you don't want my love: *Williams, Lewis*
CD ______ **CDEXP 6**
Expansion / Nov '93 / 3mv/Sony

EXPANSION SOUL SAUCE VOL.4
Down low: *Redd, Jeff* / When ever you're ready: *Purnell, Tiffany* / Keep holdin' on: *Tyronza* / Deeper and deeper: *Wilson, Pauline* / Fly away: *Wall, Jeremy* / Rockin' you tonite: *Gary* / Any kind of love: *Tankard, Ben* / Miracle: *Dawkins & Dawkins* / Come share your love: *Kymiztre* / Heart is a house for love: *Valentine, Billy* / You got what I want: *Jous* / Love at first sight: *Epps, James* / If it was me: *Sunday Tucker* / I get high on your memory: *Jacobs, Sheila*
CD ______ **CDEXP 9**
Expansion / Feb '95 / 3mv/Sony

EXPANSION SOUL SAUCE VOL.5
So good: *Bristol, Johnny* / I need: *Coleman, Margi* / U should be with me: *Bleu, Mikki* / Can't miss: *Jackson, Nicole* / Don't keep me waiting: *Wilde, Dee Dee* / Solitaire: *Davis, Michael* / My joy (is you): *Wanda* / No one (can give the love you give): *Simpson, Nate* / All out of love: *Morgan, Cozette* / You're so good: *Martinez, Nigel* / Jive: *Jive* / Soap opera love affair: *Clayton, Willie* / Night like this in Georgia: *Cameron, G.C.* / I think I'm falling in love with you: *Natural High*
CD ______ **CDEXP 11**
Expansion / Apr '96 / 3mv/Sony

EXPERIENCE IN KOOL VOL.1
CD ______ **TKCD 14**
2 Kool / Oct '95 / Pinnacle / SRD

EXPERIENCE IN KOOL VOL.2
Skyline: *Pure Instinct* / Let sleeping dogs lie: *Deep Freeze Productions* / Original bedroom rockers: *Kruder & Dorfmeister* / Falling: *Mr. Electric Triangle* / Inhale: *Digi Alliance* / Strange noises: *Redeye Knights* / Ombre: *Fresh Lab* / Psycho: *Marden Hill* / Scaramanga's revenge: *Freakniks* / Flamingo down: *Jung Collective* / Revolutionary pilot: *Statik Sound System* / Lament: *Resonators* / Instrumental themes: *Experimental Pop Band*
CD ______ **TKCD 25**
2 Kool / Jun '96 / Pinnacle / SRD

EXPERIENCE IN KOOL VOL.3
CD ______ **TKCD 43**
2 Kool / Mar '97 / Pinnacle / SRD

EXPLICIT BASS (2CD Set)
CD Set ______ **B2BCD 1**
Back 2 Basics / Nov '96 / RTM/Disc / SRD

EXPLORATIONS VOL.1
CD ______ **URCD 006**
Ubiquity / Jul '96 / Cargo / Timewarp

EXPLORATIONS VOL.2
CD ______ **URCD 008**
Ubiquity / Jul '96 / Cargo / Timewarp

EXPLORATIONS VOL.3
CD ______ **URCD 013**
Ubiquity / Jul '96 / Cargo / Timewarp

EXPLORE NARADA
Dreamer's waltz: *Lanz, David* / Path with heart: *Lanz, David* / Planxty Burke/Planxty Drew: *Phillips, Shelley* / Si bheag, si mhor: *Coulter, William* / South by winterwest: *McLaughlin, Billy* / Daisy goes a dancing: *Kirtley, Pat* / Doce moreana: *Lauria, Nando* / Thinking of Recife: *Lauria, Nando* / Louise: *Whelan, John* / Dancing to a lot of time: *Whelan, John* / Gift of the sea: *Gratz, Wayne* / At sunrise: *Gratz, Wayne* / Mori sonando: *De La Bastide, Miguel* / Into the dark: *Cook, Jessse* / Invitation: *Kostia* / For you: *Kostia* / Water: *Warner, Richard*
CD ______ **ND 69007**
Narada / Oct '96 / ADA / New Note/ Pinnacle

EXPLOSAO DO BRASIL
CD ______ **1918202**
EPM / Jul '97 / ADA / Discovery

EXPLOSIVE ROCKSTEADY/JACKPOT OF HITS
I'm moving on: *Pioneers* / Miss Tourist: *Pioneers* / Just like a river: *Cole, Stranger & Gladstone Anderson* / Uncle Sam's country: *Walks, Dennis* / Long shot: *Pioneers* / Train to soulsville: *Cool Sticky* / Love love everyday: *Pioneers* / Hold them: *Shirley, Roy* / Come brothers: *Malcolm, Hugh* / Give me a little loving: *Pioneers* / Push it in: *Versatiles* / Love brother love: *Dunkley, Errol* / Jackpot: *Pioneers* / Feel good: *Mellotones* / No dope me pony: *Pioneers* / Secret weapon: *Collins, Ansell* / El Casino Royale: *Tait, Lynn & the Jets* / What Moma no want she gets: *Cole, Stranger* / Catch the beat: *Pioneers* / Good time rock: *Malcolm, Hugh* / Hurry come up: *Crashers* / Just can't win: *Versatiles* / Seeing is knowing: *Cole, Stranger & Gladstone Anderson* / Holding out: *Creations*
CD ______ **CDTRL 377**
Trojan / Mar '97 / Direct / Jet Star

EXPOSED
CD ______ **IYF 01CD**
In Yer Face / Sep '96 / Else

EXPRESSIONS (The Violin - Its Many Moods And Styles)
Partita / Autumn from 'The Four Seasons' / King of the fairies / Kalinka / Honeysuckle rose / Bobby's blues / Pie Jesu / Caprice Viennoise / Danny air / Bahr bela ma / Raving / Jigs and reels medley / Mrs. Hamilton of Pencaitland / Eriskay love lilt / Double violin concerto in A major / Age of glass
CD ______ **303732**
Hallmark / Jun '97 / Carlton

EXPRESSIONS (The Electric Guitar - It's Many Moods And Styles)
Maverick / Driving seat / Echo sixties / Country pickin' / Rollin' / Julie / Time and again / RADIO / Gambler / Interlude / Nevada / Holiday blues / Guy in a hole / Cat Billy / Woman in love / Groove / Cacoethes/ Flip flap / Highway driver / Heading home
CD ______ **304542**
Hallmark / Jun '97 / Carlton

EXTRA HOT VOL.10
CD ______ **DMUT 1306**
Multitone / Mar '96 / BMG

EXTREME MUSIC FROM AFRICA
CD ______ **SLCD 016**
Susan Lawly / Feb '97 / Cargo

EXTREME ROCK - A NEW AGE
CD ______ **M 7021CD**
Mascot / Sep '96 / Plastic Head

EYE ON THE PRIZE
Together forever: *Exodus* / Keep in touch: *Shades Of Love* / Heavy vibes: *Montana, Vince Jr.* / Get down: *Aleem & Leroy Burgess* / Long enough: *Last Poets* / Barely breaking even: *Universal Robot Band* / Weekend: *Class Action* / What happend to the music: *Trammps*
CD ______ **SURCD 02**
Grapevine / Jun '94 / Grapevine/PolyGram

FAB HITS OF THE 60'S
Ob-la-di-ob-la-da: *Marmalade* / Girl don't come: *Shaw, Sandie* / Venus in blue jeans: *Wynter, Mark* / Poor man's son: *Rockin' Berries* / Picture of you: *Brown, Joe & The Bruvvers* / Don't sleep in the subway: *Clark, Petula* / Theme from Z cars: *Keating, Johnny & The Z Men* / Warpaint: *Brook Brothers* / Ice in the sun: *Status Quo* / (Call me) number one: *Tremeloes* / Tin soldier: *Small Faces* / Sugar and spice: *Searchers* / Twist and shout: *Isley Brothers* / Barefootin': *Parker, Robert* / In the bad old days before you loved me: *Foundations* / Make me an island: *Dolan, Joe* / Cast your fate to the wind: *Sounds Orchestral* / Colour of my love: *Jefferson* / Ain't nothing but a house party: *Showstoppers* / Natural born bugie: *Humble Pie*
CD ______ **MCCD 296**
Music Club / May '97 / Disc / THE

FABULOUS 30'S, THE
CD ______ **DCD 5335**
Disky / Dec '93 / Disky / THE

FABULOUS FIFTIES ROCK 'N' ROLL
Great balls of fire: *Lewis, Jerry Lee* / Shake, rattle and roll: *Haley, Bill & The Comets* / Bony moronie: *Williams, Larry* / Raunchy: *Justis, Bill* / Lucille: *Little Richard* / Tiger: *Fabian* / Claudette: *Everly Brothers* / Leroy: *Scott, Jack* / Rave on: *Holly, Buddy & The Crickets* / Johnny B Goode: *Berry, Chuck* / (We're gonna) Rock around the clock: *Haley, Bill & The Comets* / Blue suede shoes: *Perkins, Bill* / When: *Kalin Twins* / Tallahassie lassie: *Cannon, Freddy* / Good golly Miss Miss: *Little Richard* / Wake up little Susie: *Everly Brothers* / Lawdy Miss Clawdy: *Price, Lloyd* / Whole lotta shakin' goin' on: *Lewis, Jerry Lee*
CD ______ **PWKS 4180**
Carlton / Oct '94 / Carlton

FABULOUS FLIPS VOL.1
Slow down: *Williams, Larry* / Give me love: *Rosie & The Originals* / Leroy: *Scott, Jack* / I wonder if I care as much: *Everly Brothers* / Sweetheart please don't go: *Gladiolas* / Miss Ann: *Little Richard* / Crazy: *Hollywood Flames* / Train to nowhere: *Champs* / My little girl: *Crescendos* / What'cha gonna do: *Kuf Linx* / Did you cry: *Dicky Doo & Don'ts* / Can it be: *Titans* / Swag: *Wray, Link & His Raymen* / She's the one for me: *Aquatones* / Flippin': *Hall, Rene* / Gotta getta date: *Jan & Arnie* / Over and over: *Day, Bobby* / One night, one night: *Skyliners* / Beside you: *Crests* / Crazy baby: *Rockin' R's* / Rock 'n' roll cha cha: *Eternals* / Love me as I love you: *Cortez, Dave 'Baby'* / Taking care of business: *Turner, Titus* / Last night I dreamed: *Fiestas* / Sweet thing: *Bland, Billy* / My babe: *Holden, Ron*
CD ______ **CDCHD 444**
Ace / Oct '93 / Pinnacle

FABULOUS FLIPS VOL.2
Little Billy boy / Lonesome for a letter / Trouble, trouble / It's really you / Why / Well / Little Queenie / Ch-kow-ski / I can't hold out any longer / Don't start cryin' now / Cast iron arm / Bad boy / Gee how I wish you were here / Sail along sil'vry moon / Red sails in the sunset / Rubber dolly / Living's loving you / Sweet was the wine / Tight capris / Girl of my dreams / Love is a swingin' thing / Gunshot / Chicken necks / Havin' so much fun / Back shack track / Monster
CD ______ **CDCHD 560**
Ace / Apr '95 / Pinnacle

FABULOUS FLIPS VOL.3
I can't go on (Rosalie): *Dion & The Belmonts* / Wail: *Royaltones* / Dirty robber: *Wailers* / Fortune teller: *Spellman, Benny* / Am I asking to much: *String-A-Longs* / I am lonely: *Silhouettes* / That's the way it's gonna be: *Shields* / Red sails in the sunset: *Sharpe, Ray* / Smoke from your cigarette: *Belmonts* / Getting dizzy: *Elegants* / Stay awhile: *Clovers* / Mr. Dillon: *Delacardos* / Before I grow too old: *Domino, Fats* / Rockin' shoes: *Ames Brothers* / Come my little baby: *Chantels* / Goddess of angels: *Falcons* / Cincinnati fireball: *Falcons* / Big fat woman: *Freeman, Bobby* / Ooh la la: *Avalon, Frankie* / Waddle: *Slades* / High school dance: *Williams, Larry* / I ain't goin' for that: *Church, Eugene* / Country fool: *Showmen* / Beverly Jean: *Lee, Curtis* / Saccharin Sally: *Tu-Tones* / Down at the beach: *Pentagons*
CD ______ **CDCHD 645**
Ace / Feb '97 / Pinnacle

FACE OF THE FUTURE
CD ______ **BDRCD 4**
Breakdown / Nov '94 / Pinnacle

FACE THE CHALLENGE IN MUSIC VOL.1
CD ______ **CHR 70020**
Challenge / Sep '95 / ADA / Direct / Jazz Music / Wellard

FACE THE CHALLENGE IN MUSIC VOL.3 (Today's Jazz Classics)
Three for two: *Alter, Myriam* / Toda a gente que passa: *Bacan & Lilian Vieira* / 13 bar blues: *Margitza, Rick* / Kidney stew: *Davis, Spanky & Roy Eldridge* / Wheeling: *Baseline* / Ascot: *Van't Hof, Jasper* / Speak low: *Citroen, Soesja* / Take the 'A' train: *Houdinis* / Blue again: *McHugh, Jimmy & Dorothy Fields* / Elephant walk: *Vloeimans, Eric* / Los aretes de la luna: *Winanda Del Sur* / You took advantage of me: *Kellaway, Roger* / Grand slam: *De Graaf, Dick & Tony Lakatos Trio*
CD _______________ CHR 719970
Challenge / Jul '97 / ADA / Direct / Jazz Music / Wellard

FACE THE MUSIC - TORVILL & DEAN
Mack and Mabel / Summertime / Barnum / Bolero / Capriccio / Song of India / Venus / Love duet from Fire and Ice / Snow maiden - the Procession of the Tsar Berendey / Incantation / Oscar tango / Iceworks / Skaters' waltz / Let's face the music and dance / History of love / Medley
CD _______________ 8450652
PolyGram TV / Feb '94 / PolyGram

FACES OF THE HARP
Austin's planxty: *Doyle, Dennis* / Tipsy elk: *Loefke, Thomas* / Dance of the lambs: *Robertson, Kim* / Saguaro: *Riley, L & M. MacBean* / Castlebay scrap/Stuart's rant: *Sileas* / Dialogue with a brook: *Woods, Sylvia* / Bennachie sunrise/Willie trip to Toronto: *Sedrenn* / Waterdance/Gay feather: *Waldren, K.L. & C. Kreitlow* / Memories of that isle: *Bell, Derek* / Eclipse: *Williams, Ani* / Blessing way: *Haines, Julia* / Mushrooms of Fagernes: *Northern Lights* / Bas alastruim/McAlistrum's march: *Heymann, Ann & Alison Kinnaird* / Wedding of pysche and eros: *Pinter, Judith* / Spring: *Lee, R.*
CD _______________ ND 63934
Narada / Jun '97 / ADA / New Note/ Pinnacle

FACING THE WRONG WAY
CD _______________ FTWW 1
4AD / Sep '95 / RTM/Disc

FACTOR 20
Karma chameleon: *Culture Club* / Tide is high: *Blondie* / Turn to gold: *Austin, David* / Love in our hearts: *Brown, Peter* / Night in New York: *Elbow Bones & Racketeers* / Everything I own: *Boy George* / Kiss me: *Duffy, Stephen* / On my way to LA: *Carmen, Phil* / Baby I need your lovin': *Turner, Ruby & The Four Tops* / Calyso crazy: *Ocean, Billy* / Place in the sun: *Winjama* / Don't go lose it baby: *Masekela, Hugh* / One cup of coffee: *Shaffer, Paul* / You can leave your hat on: *Chippendales* / Lion sleeps tonight: *Tight Fit* / Queen of clubs: *KC & The Sunshine Band* / Wonderful world beautiful people: *Amazulu* / Tena's song: *Foxy*
CD _______________ DC 880812
Disky / May '97 / Disky / THE

FADO DE LISBOA
CD _______________ HTCD 14
Heritage / Jan '93 / ADA / Direct / Hot Shot / Jazz Music / Swift / Wellard

FAIKAVA: THE TONGAN KAVA CIRCLE
CD _______________ PAN 2022CD
Pan / Oct '93 / ADA / CM / Direct

FAITH, A MESSAGE FROM THE SPIRITS
Introduction, faith / Chango / Damaru drum/ Chant for deity dharmaraja / Evangelist sheila / Djouba / Gaj jatra / Tsok choe / I specialize / Mravaldzanier / Torah recital/ Yaashe shalom / Koran recital / Eleggua / Tsmindao upalo / Bells / Let god turn it around for you / Tsok choe
CD _______________ SJRCD 034
Soul Jazz / Mar '97 / New Note/Pinnacle / Timewarp / Vital

FAKE FRUIT AND HORRIBLE SHOES (A Pure Plastic Compilation No.1)
Funked up / Halcyon / Spring / Endless filters / 20ft scarf / Nine open / Slingshot / Room and air / Tropica
CD _______________ PPCDCOMP 1
Pure Plastic / Jun '97 / Kudos / Pinnacle / Vital

FALLOUT PUNK SINGLES COLLECTION, THE
Fallen hero: *Enemy* / Viva la revolution: *Adicts* / Suicide bag: *Action Pact* / Punks alive: *Enemy* / Jubilee: *Rabid* / New barbarians: *Urban Dogs* / People: *Action Pact* / Limo life: *Urban Dogs* / Last rites: *Enemy* / London bouncers: *Action Pact* / Another typical city: *UK Subs* / Question of choice: *Action Pact* / Decapitated: *Broken Bones* / Amphetamine blues: *Fallen Angels* / Private army: *UK Subs* / Cruxifix: *Broken Bones* / Yet another dole queue song: *Action Pact* / Inner planet love: *Fallen Angels* / Cocktail credibility: *Action Pact* / Seeing through my eyes: *Broken Bones* / This gun says: *UK Subs* / Champs Elysees: *Adicts* / Never say die: *Broken Bones* / Hey Santa: *UK Subs* / Jodie Foster: *UK Subs*
CD _______________ CDPUNK 30
Anagram / Mar '94 / Cargo / Pinnacle

FAMILY CIRCLE FAMILY TREE
Off with the old: *Chameleon Church* / Ina kindly way: *Chameleon Church* / Here's a song: *Chameleon Church* / Ready Eddie: *Chameleon Church* / Camellia is changing: *Chameleon Church* / Your golden love: *Chameleon Church* / Remembering's all I can do: *Chameleon Church* / Blueberry pie: *Chameleon Church* / Tompkins square park: *Chameleon Church* / Spring this year: *Chameleon Church* / Maybe more than you: *Lost* / Back door blues: *Lost* / I want to know: *Lost* / Here she comes: *Lost* / Everybody knows: *Lost* / Violet gown: *Lost* / Mystic: *Lost* / Kaleidoscope: *Lost* / Ultimate spinach III: *Lost* / Happiness child: *Lost*
CD _______________ CDWIKD 146
Chiswick / Jan '96 / Pinnacle

FAMILY TREE INTERNATIONAL
CD _______________ 99 2146
Ninetynine / Jul '96 / Timewarp

FAMOUS CHARISMA BOX, THE (4CD Set)
Hoopoe's tales: *Stanshall, Vivian* / Sympathy: *Rare Bird* / Refugees: *Van Der Graaf Generator* / Lady Eleanor: *Lindisfarne* / Knife: *Genesis* / Indian summer: *Audience* / Witchi-tai-to: *Topo D Bil* / Terry keeps his clips on: *Stanshall, Vivian* / Hungarian peasant girl: *Billmuss, Trevor* / Regent stereet incident: *String Driven Thing* / Gaye: *Ward, Clifford T.* / Imperial zeppelin: *Hammill, Peter* / Painted ladies: *Moore, G T* / Money game: *Hull, Alan* / Ooh mother: *Unicorn* / Liar: *Brown, Capability* / Intermezzo from Karelia suite: *Nice* / Quark, strangeness and charm: *Hawkwind* / Solsbury Hill: *Gabriel, Peter* / Lucinda: *Werth, Howard* / Why can't I be satisfied: *Jack The Lad* / Doubting Thomas: *Heights, Jackson* / Fog on the Tyne: *Lindisfarne* / I get a kick out of you: *Shearston, Gary* / Ritt Mickley: *Refugee* / Disco suicide: *Brand-X* / Working in line: *Rutherford, Mike* / Go placidly: *Every Which Way* / Robot man: *Wakeman, Rick* / And the wheels keep turning: *Banks, Tony* / Out in the sun: *Moraz, Patrick* / How can I: *Hackett, Steve* / Too many people: *Bell, Graham* / Happy the man: *Genesis* / She belongs to me: *Bell & Arc* / Window city: *Stanshall, Vivian* / Travel agent sketch (Live at Drury Lane): *Monty Python* / Cultural attache: *Humphries, Barry* / Talks turf: *O'Sullevan, Peter* / Three fold attunement: *Turner, Gordon* / Talks cricket: *Arlott, John* / One and tow: *Lang, R D* / Sir Henry at Rawlinson End: *Stanshall, Vivian* / Finland: *Monty Python* / Varsity students rag: *Betjeman, John* / I bet you they won't play this song on the radio: *Monty Python* / Theme one: *Van Der Graaf Generator* / Window city (Fade): *Stanshall, Vivian* / Chasing sheep is best left to shepherds: *Nyman, Michael* / Front door: *Isaacs, Gregory* / Cloudy day: *Congo Ashanti Roy* / Put it out: *Prince Far-I* / Don't leave me this way: *Desperadoes* / Move it on up: *Moore, G T* / (Hey you) the Rocksteady crew: *Rocksteady Crew* / Hey DJ: *World's Famous Supreme Team* / Paperheart: *King, Robert* / Anticipation: *Delta 5* / All about you: *Scars* / Ten don't for honeymooners: *Monochrome Set* / Making time: *Creation* / Freedom dance jazz: *Emerson, Keith* / It's all over now baby blue: *Wray, Link* / Embezzler: *Werth, Howard & The Moonbeams* / Kittiwake: *Jansch, Bert* / Too late for goodbyes: *Lennon, Julian* / God rock: *Turner, Nik*
CD Set _______________ CASBOX 1
Charisma / Nov '93 / EMI

FAMOUS SPIRITUAL & GOSPEL FESTIVAL 1965
Jesus said if you go / Lord send the rain / Travelling shoes / Preaching/Exodus, 3rd / Tell me how long the train been gone / It's a needed time / It's in my heart / What love / Good somewhere / John saw the number / O why / Lord you have been good to me
CD _______________ CDLR 44005
L&R / Feb '92 / New Note/Pinnacle

FANFARE (20 Brass Band Classics)
Fanfare: *GUS Footwear Band Quartet* / Elegy from a 'Downland suite': *Cory Band* / Snowy polka: *Royal Doulton Band* / Austria: *Wingates Temperance Band* / Pixies parade: *Foden Motor Works Band* / Eye level: *Hendon Brass Band* / Prelude for an occasion: *Black Dyke Mills Band* / El matador: *Cambridge Band* / Slavonic dance no.8: *Carlton Main Colliery Band* / Waltz from memories of Schubert: *Cambridge Band* / Top o' the morning: *Wingates Temperance Band* / Comedians gallop: *Hammonds Sauce Works Band* / Pineapple poll: *Black Dyke Mills Band* / Zorba's dance: *Hammonds Sauce Works Band* / Promenade: *Cory Band* / Contestor: *Black Dyke Mills Band* / Entertainer: *Royal Doulton Band* / Shepherd's song: *GUS Footwear Band Quartet* / Streets of Paris: *CWS Band* / Entry of the gladiators: *Cambridge Band*
CD _______________ TRTCD 127
TrueTrax / Oct '94 / THE

FANITULLEN VOL.1 & 2
CD _______________ GR 4098CD
Grappa / Jun '96 / ADA

FANTASTIC 40'S, THE
CD _______________ DCD 5336
Disky / Dec '93 / Disky / THE

FANTASTIC FIFTIES, THE (2CD Set)
Great pretender: *Platters* / Bernadine: *Boone, Pat* / Rock around the clock: *Haley, Bill & The Comets* / Personality: *Price, Lloyd* / Suzie Q: *Hawkins, Dale* / Yakety yak: *Coasters* / Lover's question: *McPhatter, Clyde* / Kansas City: *Harrison, Wilbert* / Donna: *Valens, Ritchie* / Stardust: *Cole, Nat 'King'* / Glow worm: *Mills Brothers* / Tom Dooley: *Kingston Trio* / Sleep walk: *Santo & Johnny* / One summer night: *Danleers* / Sea of love: *Phillips, Phil & The Twilights* / Answer me: *Laine, Frankie* / Somebody stole my gal: *Ray, Johnnie* / Do you wanna dance: *Freeman, Bobby* / Blue suede shoes: *Perkins, Carl* / Send me the pillow: *Locklin, Hank* / To be loved: *Wilson, Jackie* / Stagger Lee: *Price, Lloyd* / Tequila: *Champs* / Charlie Brown: *Coasters* / Smoke gets in your eyes: *Platters* / Tears on my pillow: *Little Anthony & The Imperials* / It's all in the game: *Edwards, Tommy* / Great balls of fire: *Lewis, Jerry Lee* / Come go with me: *Del-Vikings* / Reveille rock: *Johnny & The Hurricanes* / I believe: *Laine, Frankie* / Alone: *Shepherd Sisters* / Walkin' my baby back home: *Ray, Johnnie & Frankie Laine* / Be bop a lula: *Vincent, Gene* / Rockin' Robin: *Day, Bobby* / Alley oop: *Hollywood Argyles*
CD Set _______________ TNC 96227
Natural Collection / Aug '96 / Target/BMG

FANTASTIC ROCK 'N' ROLL
CD _______________ CLCD 4402
Collector/White Label / Nov '96 / TKO Magnum

FANTAZIA HOUSE COLLECTION CLUB CLASSICS VOL.1 (3CD Set)
CD _______________ FHCCC 1CDSL
CD Set _______________ FHCCC 1CD
Fantazia / Feb '96 / 3mv/Sony / Prime

FANTAZIA HOUSE COLLECTION CLUB CLASSICS VOL.2 (2CD Set)
CD Set _______________ FHCCC 2CD
CD Set _______________ FHCCC 2CDL
Fantazia / Sep '96 / 3mv/Sony / Prime

FANTAZIA HOUSE COLLECTION CLUB CLASSICS VOL.3 (3CD Set)
Think about: *DJ H & Steffy* / Let your body be free: *Volcano* / Where love lives (come on in): *Limerick, Alison* / 40 Miles: *Congress* / Perfect motion: *Sunscreem* / It's gonna be a lovely day: *SOUL System* / Plastic dreams: *Jaydee* / Out there: *Friends Of Matthew* / Everybody's free: *Rozalla* / Berry: *TC 1991* / Kenetic: *Golden Girls* / Degrees of passion: *Gat Decor* / Belfast: *Orbital* / Keep on jumpin': *Terry, Todd* / London X-Press: *X-Press 2* / Girls and boys: *Hed Boys* / Trippin' on sunshine: *Pizzaman* / Reach: *Lil' Mo' Yin Yang* / Everybody be somebody: *Ruffneck* / Give me luv: *Alcatraz* / And I'm telling you I'm not going: *Giles, Donna* / Been a long time: *Fog* / Who keeps changing your mind: *South Street Players* / Direct me: *Reece Project* / Caught in the middle: *Roberts, Juliet* / Saturday night Sunday morning: *T-Empo* / Let no man put asunder: *First Choice* / Runaway: *Nu Yorican Soul* / I get high: *Upstate* / So in love with you: *Duke* / Scared: *Slacker* / Life's too short: *Hole In One* / Flowtation: *De Moor, Vincent* / Cafe del mar: *Energy 52* / Walk with me: *Heliotropic* / Small town boy: *Legato* / Just come back to me: *Hypertrophy* / Come with me: *Qattara* / Offshore: *Chicane*
CD Set _______________ FHCCC 3CD
Fantazia / May '97 / 3mv/Sony / Prime

FANTAZIA HOUSE COLLECTION VOL.1 (2CD Set)
Lifting me higher: *Gems For Jem* / Sexy movemaker: *Fifth Circuit* / Anthem: *Black Shells* / Choose me: *Cookie* / Angel: *Sub Sub* / I'm in love: *Summers, Kathy* / Make my love: *Christopher, Shawn* / All over me: *Carr, Suzi* / Get down to love: *Music Choir* / You can't turn around: *Bottom Dollar* / Trouble: *Cardwell, Joi* / Time to stop: *Sanchez, Roger* / House luck: *Jump Cutz* / 2 Fatt guitars: *Direckt* / Le voie le soleil: *Subliminal Cuts* / Action: *Alfredo* / I've got the freedom: *Tin Tin Out* / Retro Euro vibe peace: *Woomera* / Callin': *Callin* / Foreplay EP: *UK Movin* / Ibiza go wild: *Pedro & Raoul* / Into your heart: *Rozzo* / Calm down: *Chris & James* / Voices inside my handbag: *Patterson & Price* / So damn tuff: *Boomerand* / Hot dog: *Key Aura* / Better with Gee: *Thermo Statik* / Time travellers: *Love Child & Rolfe* / Never gonna give you up: *Turner, Ruby* / Ay ninos: *Amnesia* / 2 Fatt guitars (mix): *Direckt* / Tripping on sunshine: *Pizzaman* / Echo drop: *Taiko* / You and me: *Rhyme Time Productions* / Testiment one: *Chubby Chunks* / Beatniks: *Delorme* / Shake your body: *LWS* / Better vibes: *Funky Monkey* / Acid folk: *Perplexer*
CD Set _______________ FHC 1CD
Fantazia / Nov '94 / 3mv/Sony / Prime

FANTAZIA HOUSE COLLECTION VOL.2 (2CD Set)
Useless man: *Minty* / House fever: *Burger* / G marks the spot: *Sensoria* / Throw: *Paperclip People* / Sweet attitude: *Sophie's Boys* / Easy does it: *Sound Crowd* / Throw reprise: *Paperclip People* / Liberation: *Lippy You* / Love Vs. Hate: *League Of Sinners* / Nu energy: *Hard 2 Dance* / Why are your feet stompin': *Hard 2 Dance* / Cod n' chips EP: *Hard 2 Dance* / Pitch 'n' drop: *Cakebread, Lee* / Where's the party: *DJ Saab* / It's alright: *Sain II* / Manhattan attement: *East Village Loft Society* / Feel it: *Creation* / Submarine: *Submarine* / In T house: *Johan S* / You took my lovin': *Total Control* / Basement in sound: *More & Groove* / Feel the music: *BBR Street Gang* / Stomp: *Shimmon* / Funky thing: *Indigo* / Everybody is somebody: *Flipped Out* / Tall and handsome: *Outrage* / Hey man: *Artyma* / Son of Eilmot: *Mighty Dub Katz* / Strong: *Phorce* / Cry boy: *Cosmo, olitan* / Krazy noise: *Numerical Value* / Driftwood: *Tom Tom* / Mooncat: *Shaker* / Good times: *Funkydory* / Hooked: *99th Floor Elevators* / Bits and pieces: *Artomesia* / Burning up: *De Vit, Tony* / Gotta get: *Must* / Keep ya head on: *Rizzo* / Organgrinder: *Deeper Cut* / Rock express: *Wizzard*
CD Set _______________ FHC 2CD
Fantazia / Apr '95 / 3mv/Sony / Prime

FANTAZIA HOUSE COLLECTION VOL.3 (2CD Set)
CD Set _______________ FHC 3CD
Fantazia / Sep '95 / 3mv/Sony / Prime

FANTAZIA HOUSE COLLECTION VOL.4 (2CD Set)
CD Set _______________ FHC 4CD
Fantazia / Jun '96 / 3mv/Sony / Prime

FANTAZIA HOUSE COLLECTION VOL.5 (2CD Set)
Whitehead, Alistair & Tall Paul
Isn't it time: *Kuva* / Keep hope alive: *Serial Diva* / Fired up: *Funky Green Dogs* / I'm still waiting: *Angel Heart* / Watcha gonna do: *Joy For Life* / I get high: *Upstate* / Jus' come: *Cool Jack* / Jumangi's house: *RM Project* / Keep pushin': *Z-Factor* / Feels so right: *Solution* / Don't lose the love: *Hit The Boom* / Do you feel me: *NY's Finest* / White love: *One Dove* / Sugar is sweeter: *Bolland, C.J.* / Bifter: *Low Pressure* / Phunkee muzeek: *Shazzamm* / Living in danger: *Ace Of Base* / Curse of Voodoo Ray: *May, Lisa* / Let the music hypnotize you: *Blue Lagoon* / 100%: *Kiani, Mary* / Forerunner: *Natural Born Groovers* / Love resurrection: *Floor Federation* / Antheum: *Digital Blondes* / This love: *Red Sun* / Feel the beat: *Sunglasses Ron* / Global fazes: *Jon The Dentist*
CD Set _______________ FHC 5CD
Fantazia / Mar '97 / 3mv/Sony / Prime

FANTAZIA PRESENT THE DJ COLLECTION VOL.1
Deep in Milan: *Hyper Space Europa* / Sun dreams: *Wax* / Infanta-ci: *Baby Doc & The Dentist* / Midi function: *System* / In the dark we live: *Aphrohead Aka Felix Da Housecat* / Mania: *Rainforest* / Shivaratri: *Fsom* / Mr. Peacock goes to Boscaland: *White Label* / Moonflux: *Black & Brown* / Nervous distortion: *Judge Dread* / Second rebirth: *Jones & Stephenson* / Killer: *Buzz & Ace* / Odyhand trance: *Osysee* / Ride: *English Muffin* / Do you wanna party: *DJ Scott* / Inflitrator: *Technosis* / Mad one: *Smith, Marc* / Varispeed: *DJ Edge* / On the groove: *Interstate* / Point break: *Sulfurex* / Storm: *Jack Speed*
CD _______________ FANTA 7CD
Fantazia / Oct '94 / 3mv/Sony / Prime

FANTAZIA TAKES YOU INTO THE JUNGLE VOL.2 (3CD Set)
Awareness: *Interrogator* / London something: *Tek 9* / Unkown: *Mental Power* / Touch my toes: *Dr. S. Gachet* / Lipsing jam ring: *T-Power* / Sovereign melody: *Dillinja* / Half step: *Photek* / Sound murderer: *Remark* / Driftin' thru the galaxy: *White Label* / Tiger style: *DJ Hype* / Flavour of a sound: *Photek* / Lionheart: *Berty B & Dillinja* / Alive and kickin: *Red 1* / Can U feel it: *School Of Hard Knocks* / Hitman: *Marvellous Caine* / Relics of pressure: *Studio Pressure* / Still lets me down: *Tom & Jerry* / World of confusion: *DJ Rap* / Wheel and deal: *DJ Gunshot* / Calling the people: *A-Zone* / Spiritual aura: *DJ Rap* / Safety zone: *A-Zone* / Big band: *Flatliner* / Just play music: *4th Dimension* / Switch: *DJ Rap* / Digable bass: *DJ Rap* / Gimp: *DJ Rap* / Intelligent w'man: *DJ Rap* / License: *Krome & Time* / World of music: *Peshay* / Yeah man: *Dream Team* / Tibetan jungle: *DJ Rap* / Shadow: *Dream Team* / Universal: *4 Hero* / Release the bells: *Sounds Of Life* / Dope: *Good Looking* / All around the world: *Grooverider* / Plasmic life volume 1: *Water BaBy* / Voyager 2: *Lucky Spin* / Force 10: *White Label* / Journies: *FBD Project* / Intense: *Genesis Project* / Cold fresh air: *Higher Sense* / Photek 2: *Photek* / Only you: *Nookie* / Sound control: *Andy C* / Champion sound: *Q-Project* / Thunder: *Rood Project*
CD Set _______________ FADJ 002CD
Fantazia / Nov '94 / 3mv/Sony / Prime

FANTAZIA VOL.1 (The First Taste)
I got the real feel: *Sunset Regime* / Operation acid: *New Age* / Rock to the max: *Ellis Dee* / Worldwide regime: *Top Buzz* / CFU play DAT: *Cybertronic* / Sonar: *Orca* / Looking out my window: *Ratpack* / EBE 1: *PSI* / Good for me: *4 Real* / Feel my love: *Mac, Nikky* / PSI: *Fantazia* / Aquabatics: *Orca* / Give me a rush: *New Age*
CD _______________ FANTA 1CD
Fantazia / Nov '92 / 3mv/Sony / Prime

FANTAZIA VOL.1 & 2 (The First Taste/ Twice As Nice/3CD Set)
Lords of the dance: *Ratpack* / Live 4 the feeling: *DJ Vibes* / Desire: *Ellis Dee* / Psikop: *PSI* / Don't hold back: *Mac, Nikky* / Forever (free your mind): *PSI* / Pulse: *St. Ives* / You gotta believe: *Sunset Regime* / Your love is taking me: *St. Ives* / Free: *Shake Ya Bones* / Baby: *Transhuman* / Innerunderstanding:

PSI / Indonesia: *Transhuman* / Astral: *Orca* / Raja: *Orca* / What is art: *Orca* / Substance: *Orca* / Love makes it easy: *Orca* / I got the real feel: *Sunset Regime* / Operation Acid: *New Age* / Rock to the max: *Ellis Dee* / Worldwide regime: *Top Buzz* / CFU play DAT: *Cybertronic* / Sonar: *Orca* / Looking out my window: *PSI* / EBE 1: *Ratpack* / Good for me: *4 Real* / Feel my love: *Mac, Nikky* / Fantazia: *PSI* / Aquabatics: *Orca* / Give me a rush: *New Age*
CD Set ______ **FANTA 001/2CD**
Fantazia / Dec '94 / 3mv/Sony / Prime

FANTAZIA VOL.3 (Made In Heaven)
Montana: *Way Out West* / Natural high: *Q-Tex* / Majorca: *Nevins, Jason* / Move on: *Secret Society* / Space: *Omer & Crooks* / Musika: *Lost Tribe* / We gonna funk: *DJ Pierre* / Megwana: *Moon* / Big bang: *Luxor* / You got me: *NRG* / Free the feeling: *Ellis Dee* / Looking into the light: *DJ Slam* / What a dream: *True Life* / No way: *PSI* / Power of love: *Q-Tex* / How can I love: *Akki* / Shake ya bones: *Shake Ya Bones* / Bring it down: *Wildchild Experience* / Time to let go: *KOTT*
CD ______ **FANTA 5CD**
Fantazia / Apr '94 / 3mv/Sony / Prime

FANTAZIA VOL.4 (The Fourth Dimension)
Let's groove: *Morel's Grooves* / Feels good: *Osibisa* / Everybody get up: *Two Amigos* / Rock to the beat: *RM Project* / Short dick man: *20 Fingers* / Take over: *Reznor, Bridget* / Plastic dreams: *Jaydee* / Sensastion of the mind: *Elysian* / Treaty: *Yothu Yindi* / Tribal love: *Ramone'll Ropiak* / Makes me feel like: *Capital Underground* / Cosmic love: *V-Tracks* / Dosh: *Netherland Power* / My dreams: *Transfiguartion* / Mistral: *Gad* / Laika: *H-Foundation* / Black dragon: *Van Basten* / Mesquite: *Hyperspectres* / June project: *Berra* / Move your tetas: *Outdance* / Ohm: *Shafty*
CD ______ **FANTA 8CD**
Fantazia / Jun '95 / 3mv/Sony / Prime

FAR OUT
CD ______ **ASSCD 003**
Funky Ass / Jul '96 / Else / Timewarp

FAREWELL TO LISSY CASEY
CD ______ **OSS 79CD**
Ossian / Aug '95 / ADA / CM / Direct / Highlander

FARMER'S WEDDING IN JOURE
CD ______ **PAN 2004CD**
Pan / Aug '94 / ADA / CM / Direct

FASCINATION (2CD Set)
CD Set ______ **24021**
Delta Doubles / Mar '95 / Target/BMG

FASHION STATEMENT, A
CD ______ **RASCD 3172**
Ras / Apr '96 / Direct / Greensleeves / Jet Star / SRD

FAST FALLS THE RAIN (A Compilation Of Moravian Folk Music)
CD ______ **LT 0014**
Lotos / Nov '95 / Czech Music Enterprises

FAST FORWARD (Mixed By DJ Jesse)
CD ______ **IDT 000557**
ID&T / Nov '96 / Plastic Head

FAT FAT FAT (Now Even Fatter)
CD ______ **BLUBBACD 484848**
No Hit / Feb '97 / Cargo / SRD

FATHER'S FAVOURITES
CD ______ **CDC 5388**
Disky / May '94 / Disky / THE

FAULT IN THE NOTHING, A (2CD Set)
CD Set ______ **ASH 26CD2**
Ash International / Mar '96 / Kudos / Pinnacle

FAVOURITE CAROLS
CD Set ______ **XMASCD 992**
Castle / Nov '96 / BMG

FAVOURITE HYMNS
CD ______ **300562**
Carlton / May '97 / Carlton

FAVOURITE IRISH DRINKING SONGS
If you're Irish / Bold O'Donaghue / I'll tell me ma / Courtin' in the kitchen / Wild Rover / Molly Malone / I belong to Glasgow / Loch Lomond / When Irish eyes are smiling / Irish rover / Brennan on the moor / Wild colonnial boy / Mursheen Durkin / Rose of Aranmore / Where the three counties meet / Danny boy / Galway bay rose of Tralee / Goodbye oh Johnny dear / Old bog road / Farewell to Galway / Whiskey in the jar / Waxies dargle / Dicey Riley / Whiskey you're the devil / Holy ground / It's a long way to Tipperary / Hello Patsy Fagan / Come down the mountain Katie Daly / When I was single / Love is teasing / Never wed an old man / Boys of Killybegs / Tim Kinnegan's wake / Old maid in a garret / Goodbye Mick / Dublin O'Shea / Moonshiner / Juice of the barley / Rosin' the bow / Maggie / Silver threads among the gold / Fiddlers green / Fiddler's green / Black velvet band / Boul'thady quill / Boys from the CoArmagh / Garden where the praties grow / Dan O'Hara / Home, boys, home / Tongs by the fire / Hannigan's hooley / Mcnamara's band / Humour is on me now / Westmead bachelor / Blackthorn stick
CD ______ **EMPRCD 520**
Emporio / Jul '94 / Disc

FAVOURITE IRISH SONGS
Mountains of Mourne: *McCann, Jim* / Green fields 'round Ferbane: *Far Tulla* / Isle of Innisfree: *Kerr, John* / Fields of Athenry: *Reilly, Paddy* / Dingle Bay: *Margo* / Spancil Hill: *Far Tulla* / Green hills of Sligo: *Murrihy, P.J.* / Grace: *Kenny, Tony* / Rose of Mooncoin: *McEvoy, Johnny* / Rare oul times: *Erin's Isle Singers* / Shanagolden: *Margo* / Cliffs of Doneen: *Margo* / Flight of earls: *Kerr, John* / Banks of the Lee/Come back Paddy Reilly: *Erin's Isle Singers*
CD ______ **CHCD 033**
Chart / Oct '96 / Direct / Koch

FAX IT, CHARGE IT, DON'T ASK ME WHAT'S FOR DINNER
CD ______ **SHCD 8018**
Shanachie / Oct '95 / ADA / Greensleeves / Koch

FEAR OF A RUFF PLANET
CD ______ **RUF 026**
Ruff Neck / Oct '96 / Mo's Music Machine

FEARLESS FLUSH SAMPLER, THE
CD ______ **F 0272**
Fearless / Jun '97 / Cargo / Plastic Head

FEASTS MUSIC FROM MEDITERRANEAN COUNTRIES
CD ______ **926542**
BUDA / Sep '96 / Discovery

FEASTS OF THE SAVANNA (A Musical Journey Through East & West Africa)
Sock selue / Yentchable / Initiation dance / Kbunse / Nje / Ceremonial drums / Traditional doctor's cure / Drum session / Sansa / Dingidi song / Jopadhola malinda / Enanga / Werga / Children's song / Dogon children's flute / Dogon harp / Narrative/ Kora accompaniment
CD ______ **MCM 3006**
Multicultural Media / May '97 / Direct

FEDERATION OF TECHNO HOUSE VOL.1 (2CD Set)
CD Set ______ **LD 9455CD**
LD / Feb '95 / Vital

FEED YOUR HEAD
CD ______ **BARKCD 022**
Planet Dog / Nov '96 / Pinnacle

FEEL LIKE MAKING LOVE
CD ______ **AHLCD 25**
Hit / Feb '95 / Grapevine/PolyGram

FEEL THE FIRE DUETS
CD ______ **12544**
Laserlight / May '95 / Target/BMG

FEEL THE FORCE (20 Smash Hits Of The Seventies)
I wanna hold your hand: *Dollar* / Long legged woman dressed in black: *Mungo Jerry* / L-L-Lucy: *Mud* / Man who sold the world: *Lulu* / Love hurts: *Nazareth* / Roadrunner twice: *Richman, Jonathan & Modern Lovers* / Come back and finish what you started: *Knight, Gladys & The Pips* / Burlesque: *Family* / Lost in France: *Tyler, Bonnie* / You don't have to go: *Chi-Lites* / Dance the body music: *Osibisa* / Lean on me: *Mud* / Jack in the box: *Moments* / More, more, more: *Andrea True Connection* / I got a name: *Croce, Jim* / Baby don't change your mind: *Knight, Gladys & The Pips* / Mirrors: *Oldfield, Sally* / My white bicycle: *Nazareth* / Love's gotta hold on me: *Dollar* / Can you feel the force: *Real Thing*
CD ______ **TRTCD 110**
TrueTrax / Oct '94 / THE

FEELIN' GOOD
CD ______ **LHCD 024**
Luv n' Haight / Jul '96 / Timewarp

FEELIN' GOOD - AMERICAN R&B HITS VOL.1
CD ______ **CDRB 11**
Charly / Nov '94 / Koch

FEELING THE BLUES
Poor boy blues: *Atkins, Chet & Mark Knopfler* / I'd rather go blind: *Chicken Shack* / Hoochie coochie man: *Waters, Muddy* / Ain't gone 'n' give up on love: *Vaughan, Stevie Ray & Double Trouble* / Cheap tequila: *Winter, Johnny* / Tabacco road: *Winter, Edgar* / Gamblers roll: *Allman Brothers* / Need your love tonight: *Fleetwood Mac* / Tuff enuff: *Fabulous Thunderbirds* / Season of the witch: *Bloomfield, Mike & Al Kooper* / Skyscraper blues: *Derringer, Rick* / Down in Mississippi: *Omar & The Howlers* / Boogie my way back home: *Moore, Gary* / Brothers: *Vaughan Brothers* / Schoolgirl: *Argent* / Killing floor: *Electric Flag*
CD ______ **4758282**
Columbia / Oct '95 / Sony

FEELINGS (Romantic Guitar)
CD ______ **MACCD 326**
Autograph / Aug '96 / BMG

FEELINGS
Love story (where do I begin) / Strangers in the night / Something / Bright eyes / Woman / You are the sunshine of my life / Michelle / Lara's theme / To all the girls I loved before / Spanish eyes / Don't it make my brown eyes blue / Tara's theme / Feelings / Annie's song / Love is blue / If you leave me now / Unchained melody / Memory / Nights in white satin / Song sung blue / Guantanamera / Don't cry for me Argentina / Oh happy day / Fool on the hill / September wind / Bilitis / Last farewell / Sailing / Greensleeves / Eleanor Rigby / House of the rising sun / Banks of the Ohio / Cast your fate to the wind / Whiter shade of pale / My way
CD Set ______ **DCD 3008**
Music / Jun '97 / Target/BMG

FEELINGS NOT FREQUENCIES
CD ______ **ABCD 001**
Holistic / Feb '95 / Kudos / Pinnacle / Plastic Head / Prime

FEELINGS... (Beautiful Songs & Wonderful Performances/2CD Set)
Something to remember you by: *Dale, Syd & His Orchestra* / Misty: *Sentimental Sax* / I wish you love: *Emblow, Jack* / Love walked in: *Osborne, Tony Orchestra* / Sentimental journey: *Dale, Syd & His Orchestra* / No other love: *Osborne, Tony Orchestra* / Sounds of romance: *Master Strings* / Stay as sweet as you are: *Dale, Syd & His Orchestra* / Summertime: *Sentimental Sax* / Man and a woman: *Dale, Syd & His Orchestra* / It could happen to you: *London Theatre Orchestra* / Because of you: *Master Strings* / Body and soul: *Sentimental Sax* / Moonglow: *London Theatre Orchestra* / In a sentimental mood: *Sentimental Sax* / Woman in love: *Aprile, J.C. & His Orchestra* / Days of wine and roses: *London Theatre Orchestra* / Foggy day in London town: *Swift, Roger* / Nuances: *Master Strings* / Lady: *Dale, Syd & His Orchestra* / Gigi: *John, Michael Singers* / Party's over: *Dale, Syd & His Orchestra* / Feelings: *Aprile, J.C. & His Orchestra* / Once in a while: *London Theatre Orchestra* / Shadow of your smile: *Angelo, Michael & his Orchestra* / Wisteria: *Master Strings* / Almost there: *Dale, Syd & His Orchestra* / My ideal: *John, Michael Singers* / Yesterday: *London Theatre Orchestra* / Second time around: *Dale, Syd & His Orchestra* / Way we were: *Aprile, J.C. & His Orchestra* / All the love in the world: *Aprile, J.C. & His Orchestra* / How insensitive: *London Theatre Orchestra*
CD Set ______ **330452**
Hallmark / Mar '97 / Carlton

FELIDAE (A Benefit For Cedarhill Animal Sanctuary)
CD ______ **EXIT 1CD**
Last Exit / May '97 / Cargo

FEMALE BLUES 1922-1927
CD ______ **JPCD 1526**
Jazz Perspectives / Jan '97 / Hot Shot / Jazz Music

FEMALE BLUES SINGERS 1921-1928 (The Remaining Titles)
CD ______ **DOCD 1005**
Document / Apr '97 / ADA / Hot Shot / Jazz Music

FEMALE BLUES SINGERS VOL.1 1924-1932
CD ______ **DOCD 5505**
Document / Jan '97 / ADA / Hot Shot / Jazz Music

FEMALE BLUES SINGERS VOL.10 1923-1929
CD ______ **DOCD 5514**
Document / Jan '97 / ADA / Hot Shot / Jazz Music

FEMALE BLUES SINGERS VOL.11 1921-1931
CD ______ **DOCD 5515**
Document / Jan '97 / ADA / Hot Shot / Jazz Music

FEMALE BLUES SINGERS VOL.12 1922-1935
CD ______ **DOCD 5516**
Document / Jan '97 / ADA / Hot Shot / Jazz Music

FEMALE BLUES SINGERS VOL.13 1921-1931
CD ______ **DOCD 5517**
Document / Mar '97 / ADA / Hot Shot / Jazz Music

FEMALE BLUES SINGERS VOL.14 1923-1932
CD ______ **DOCD 5518**
Document / Mar '97 / ADA / Hot Shot / Jazz Music

FEMALE BLUES SINGERS VOL.2 1922-1928
CD ______ **DOCD 5506**
Document / Jan '97 / ADA / Hot Shot / Jazz Music

FEMALE BLUES SINGERS VOL.3 1923-1928
CD ______ **DOCD 5507**
Document / Jan '97 / ADA / Hot Shot / Jazz Music

FEMALE BLUES SINGERS VOL.4 1921-1940
CD ______ **DOCD 5508**
Document / Jan '97 / ADA / Hot Shot / Jazz Music

FEMALE BLUES SINGERS VOL.5 1921-1929
CD ______ **DOCD 5509**
Document / Jan '97 / ADA / Hot Shot / Jazz Music

FEMALE BLUES SINGERS VOL.6 1922-1928
CD ______ **DOCD 5510**
Document / Jan '97 / ADA / Hot Shot / Jazz Music

FEMALE BLUES SINGERS VOL.7 1922-1929
CD ______ **DOCD 5511**
Document / Mar '97 / ADA / Hot Shot / Jazz Music

FEMALE BLUES SINGERS VOL.8 1923-1928
CD ______ **DOCD 5512**
Document / Jan '97 / ADA / Hot Shot / Jazz Music

FEMALE BLUES SINGERS VOL.9 1923-1930
CD ______ **DOCD 5513**
Document / Jan '97 / ADA / Hot Shot / Jazz Music

FEMALE COUNTRY BLUES VOL.1 (The Twenties)
CD ______ **SOB 035292**
Story Of The Blues / Dec '92 / ADA / Koch

FEMME FATALE (3CD Set)
CD Set ______ **DTKBOX 64**
Dressed To Kill / Jun '97 / Total/BMG

FEMO JAZZ FESTIVAL - 25TH ANNIVERSARY
CD ______ **MECCACD 1038**
Music Mecca / Nov '94 / Cadillac / Jazz Music / Wellard

FERIA - THE BEST SEVILLANAS
Rociadora / Y las arenas / Desde el alma / Voy pal rocio / Mi medalla rociera / Acurela del rocio / Cuardo paso triana / Coria del rio / Cebolla, pimiento y colifior / La marisma se alborota / Mi devocion / Por las arenas / Y todos los afios / Antes de nacer / Po "Poeso" / Tengo que volver / Stones rocleros / Noches del camino / Bambolero / Cantinero de cuba / Djobi, djoba / Se pasavan los pias / Me, va, me va / Mi guitarra / Color moreno / Ay peregrinal / Que sabre la gente / Salve rociera del ole, ole
CD ______ **EMO 93072**
Emocion / Jun '96 / New Note/Pinnacle

FERRY ACROSS THE MERSEY
Ferry Across the Mersey: *Gerry & The Pacemakers* / Sweets for my sweet: *Searchers* / Lily the pink: *Scaffold* / You're my world (il mio mondo): *Black, Cilla* / Hippy hippy shake: *Swinging Blue Jeans* / Hello little girl: *Fourmost* / Do you want to know a secret: *Kramer, Billy J. & The Dakotas* / Breakaway: *Marsden, Beryl* / I like it: *Gerry & The Pacemakers* / America: *Storm, Rory & The Hurricanes* / Little loving: *Fourmost* / Needles and pins: *Searchers* / Bad to me: *Kramer, Billy J. & The Dakotas* / You're no good: *Swinging Blue Jeans* / You'll never walk alone: *Gerry & The Pacemakers* / Thank u very much: *Scaffold*
CD ______ **DC 878872**
Disky / Jul '97 / Disky / THE

FEST NOZ DE KLEG
CD ______ **GLEG 001CD**
Diffusion Breizh / Aug '95 / ADA

FEST NOZ LIVE
CD ______ **KMCD 76**
Keltia Musique / Jun '97 / ADA / Discovery

FEST-DEIZ ACCORDEONS
CD ______ **CD 427**
Diffusion Breizh / Jul '94 / ADA

FESTIVAL DE MUSIQUES IRLANDAISES VOL.3
CD ______ **GRI 190812**
Griffe / Sep '96 / ADA / Discovery

FESTIVAL FLAMENCO
CD ______ **EUCD 1210**
ARC / Sep '93 / ADA / ARC Music

FESTIVAL FLAMENCO GITANO VOL.3
CD ______ **CDLR 44015**
L&R / New Note/Pinnacle

FESTIVAL INTERCELTIQUE DE L'ORIENT/CONCERT BINIOU BOMBARDE
CD ______ **ERO 057**
Eromi / Nov '96 / ADA

FESTIVAL ITALIANO 1994
CD ______ **472072**
Flarenasch / May '96 / Discovery

FESTIVAL LATINO (20 Seeco Latin Hits)
Cachondea: *Feliciano, Jose 'Cheo'* / Besito de coco: *Rivera, Ismael* / Cuca la loca: *Bienvenido Granda* / Un mondo raro: *Flores, Lola* / Luna de miel en Puerto Rico: *Capo, Bobby* / Ave Maria Lola: *Argentino, Carlos* / Besame morenita: *Pinedo, Nelson* / Fina estampa: *Alfaro, Xiomara* / Desolacion: *Jaramillo, Julio* / Borracho no vale: *Santos, Daniel* / Ya no tengo amigos: *Feliciano, Jose 'Cheo'* / El chivo de la campana: *Rivera, Ismael* / Rico guaguanco: *Bienvenido*

Granda / Tu rica boca: *Flores, Lola* / La coca leca: *Capo, Bobby* / Ay que rico amor: *Argentino, Carlos* / El vaquero: *Pinedo, Nelson* / Cuando ya no me quieras: *Alfaro, Xiomara* / Amor sin esperanza: *Jaramillo, Julio* / El cornetta: *Santos, Daniel*
CD CDHOT 614
Charly / Dec '96 / Koch

FESTIVAL MUSIC OF KERALA
CD VICG 53502
JVC World Library / Mar '96 / ADA / CM / Direct

FESTIVAL OF BRASS
CD DOYCD 008
Doyen / Oct '92 / Conifer/BMG

FESTIVAL OF CAROLS
Once in Royal David's City: *Guildford Cathedral Choir* / While shepherds watched their flocks by night: *Sunbury Junior Singers Of The Salvation Army* / Holly and the ivy: *St. Paul's Cathedral Choir* / God rest ye merry gentlemen: *Guildford Cathedral Choir* / Unto us is born a son: *Westminster Abbey Choir* / As with gladness men of old: *Guildford Cathedral Choir* / O little town of Bethlehem: *St. Paul's Cathedral Choir* / Hark the herald angels sing: *Guildford Cathedral Choir* / I saw three ships: *St. Paul's Cathedral Choir* / Silent night: *Sunbury Junior Singers Of The Salvation Army* / In dulci jubilo: *Westminster Abbey Choir* / First Noel: *Guildford Cathedral Choir* / In the bleak midwinter: *St. Paul's Cathedral Choir* / Good King Wenceslas: *Guildford Cathedral Choir* / Rocking: *Sunbury Junior Singers Of The Salvation Army* / Coventry carol: *St. Paul's Cathedral Choir* / It came upon a midnight clear: *Guildford Cathedral Choir* / Away in a manger: *Westminster Abbey Choir* / Ding dong merrily on high: *Sunbury Junior Singers Of The Salvation Army* / O come all ye faithful (Adeste Fidelis): *Guildford Cathedral Choir*
CD CDMFP 6080
Music For Pleasure / Dec '94 / EMI

FESTIVAL OF FOLK, A (2CD Set)
CD Set DEMPCD 002
Emporio / Mar '96 / Disc

FESTIVAL OF GOSPEL AND NEGRO SPIRITUAL (2CD Set)
CD Set FA 403
Fremeaux / Nov '95 / ADA / Discovery

FESTIVAL OF GROUPS (New York Doo Wop 1958-1966)
Love bound: *Universals* / Dreaming: *Universals* / Kisses in my dreams: *Universals* / Ol' man river: *Ricks, Jimmy & the Ravens* / Daddy rollin' stone: *Ricks, Jimmy & the Ravens* / You've got just what I need: *Ricks, Jimmy & the Ravens* / Deep river: *Ricks, Jimmy & the Ravens* / Homesick: *Ricks, Jimmy & the Ravens* / Oh what a feeling: *Ricks, Jimmy & the Ravens* / Cecilia: *Ricks, Jimmy & the Ravens* / Umgowa twist: *Ricks, Jimmy & the Ravens* / Night and day: *Orioles* / So long: *Orioles* / Sincerely: *Orioles* / Some of this, some of that: *Orioles* / Poor baby: *Clovers* / He sure could hypnotise: *Clovers* / Do the zombie: *Symbols* / Snatchin' peaches: *Chanteclairs* / Invasion: *Dovers* / Sha-he-be: *Essentials* / Daddy can I go to the hop: *Cashmeres & Eddie Jones* / Sardines: *Magnetics* / (Down at) Ling Ting laundry: *Chanteclairs* / Earth cousins: *Middleton, Tony & Jack Hammer*
CD NEMCD 939
Sequel / Jul '97 / BMG

FESTIVAL OF IRISH FOLK MUSIC VOL.1 (2CD Set)
Cliffs of Dooneen: *Dublin City Ramblers* / Slievenamon: *Dublin City Ramblers* / Finnegan's wake: *Dublin City Ramblers* / Town I loved so well: *Dublin City Ramblers* / Sea around us: *Dublin City Ramblers* / Four green fields: *Dublin City Ramblers* / My lovely rose of Clare: *Reilly, Paddy* / Snowy breasted pearl: *Reilly, Paddy* / Rose of Allendale: *Reilly, Paddy* / Come back Paddy Reilly: *Reilly, Paddy* / Down by the Sally gardens: *Reilly, Paddy* / Black velvet band: *Dubliners* / McAlpine's fusiliers: *Dubliners* / Fairmoye lasses/Sporting Paddy: *Dubliners* / Seven drunken nights: *Dubliners* / Home boys home: *Dubliners* / Blue mountain rag: *Dubliners* / Raglan road: *Reilly, Paddy* / Steal away: *Furey Brothers & Davy Arthur* / Now is the hour: *Furey Brothers & Davy Arthur* / Silver threads among the gold: *Furey Brothers & Davy Arthur* / When you were sweet sixteen: *Furey Brothers & Davy Arthur* / My love is like a red red rose: *Furey Brothers & Davy Arthur* / Song for Ireland: *Furey Brothers & Davy Arthur* / Dirty old town: *Dubliners* / Farewell to Carlingford: *Dubliners* / Foggy dew: *Dubliners* / Parcel o' rogues: *Dubliners* / Bunclody: *Dubliners* / Rare ould times: *Dubliners* / Man you don't meet every day: *Barleycorn* / Donegal Danny: *Barleycorn* / Only our river run free: *Barleycorn* / Lakes of Coolfin: *Barleycorn* / This land is your land: *Barleycorn* / Buachaill an Eirne: *Barleycorn*
CD Set CHCD 1013
Chyme / Oct '90 / ADA / CM / Direct / Koch

FESTIVAL OF IRISH FOLK MUSIC VOL.2 (2CD Set)
Butterfly: *Bothy Band* / Kesh jig: *Bothy Band* / Sixteen come next Sunday: *Bothy Band* / Rip the calico: *Bothy Band* / Strayaway child: *Bothy Band* / Death of Queen Jane: *Bothy Band* / Dheanainn sugradh: *Clannad* / By chance it was: *Clannad* / Rince Briotanach: *Clannad* / Dulaman: *Clannad* / Mo mhaire: *Clannad* / Cumha eoghain rue ui neill: *Clannad* / Teddy bears head: *Wolfetones* / Ode to Biddy Magee: *Wolfetones* / Foggy dew: *Wolfetones* / Tricoloured ribbon: *Wolfetones* / Banks of the Ohio: *Wolfetones* / Black Ribbon Band: *Wolfetones* / Whiskey in the jar: *Dubliners* / Town I loved so well: *Dubliners* / Free the people: *Dubliners* / Lord of the dance: *Dubliners* / Musical priest/Blackthorn stick: *Dubliners* / Finnegan's wake: *Dubliners* / Green fields of France: *Furey Brothers & Davy Arthur* / Garrett Barry's jig: *Furey Brothers & Davy Arthur* / Reason I left Mullingar: *Furey Brothers & Davy Arthur* / Morning lies heavy: *Furey Brothers & Davy Arthur* / Ted Furey's selection: *Furey Brothers & Davy Arthur* / Lament: *Furey Brothers & Davy Arthur* / Ril gan ainm/Cinnte le dia/The union reel: *Bergin, Mary* / Garrai na bhfeileoig/Miss Galvin: *Bergin, Mary* / Step it out Mary: *Doyle, Danny* / Irish soldier laddie: *Doyle, Danny* / Red haired Mary: *Doyle, Danny* / Whiskey on a Sunday: *Doyle, Danny*
CD Set CHCD 1035
Outlet / Sep '93 / ADA / CM / Direct / Duncans / Koch / Ross

FESTIVAL OF IRISH FOLK VOL.1 (2CD Set)
Seven drunken nights: *Dubliners* / Auld triangle: *Dubliners* / Finnegan's wake: *Dubliners* / Holy ground: *Dubliners* / Joe Hill: *Kelly, Luke* / Song for Ireland: *Kelly, Luke* / Tomorrow morning: *McGuire, Sean & Joe Burke* / Friendly visit: *McGuire, Sean & Joe Burke* / Farl O'Gara: *McGuire, Sean & Joe Burke* / Trim the velvet: *McGuire, Sean & Joe Burke* / Copperplate 1: *McGuire, Sean & Joe Burke* / Copperplate 2: *McGuire, Sean & Joe Burke* / Port padraig na cara: *Burke, Joe* / Frost is all over: *Burke, Joe* / Spike island lassies: *Burke, Joe* / Farewell to Leitrim: *Burke, Joe* / Return from Camden Town: *Burke, Joe* / Tom Moyland's frolic: *Burke, Joe* / Green fields of France: *Fureys & Davey Arthur* / Steal away: *Fureys & Davey Arthur* / Gallipoli: *Fureys & Davey Arthur* / Old bush: *Bealfeirste* / Bucks of Oranmore: *Bealfeirste* / Toss the feathers: *Bealfeirste* / Toss the feathers: *Bealfeirste* / Out in the ocean: *Bealfeirste* / Hag with the money: *Bealfeirste* / Galway races: *McCann, Jim* / Easy and slow: *McCann, Jim* / Irish ways and Irish laws: *Close, John* / Back home in Derby: *Close, John* / Botany bay: *McEvoy, Johnny* / Murshesen Durkin: *McEvoy, Johnny* / Coulin: *Innisfree Ceoil* / Roisin dubh: *Innisfree Ceoil* / Lonesome boatman: *Innisfree Ceoil* / King of the fairies: *Innisfree Ceoil* / Carrickfergus: *Innisfree Ceoil* / Dawning of the day: *Innisfree Ceoil* / Sam Hall: *Reilly, Paddy* / Spancil hill: *Reilly, Paddy* / Rocky road to Dublin: *Reilly, Paddy* / Sullivans: *Reilly, Paddy* / Rose of Allandale: *Reilly, Paddy*
CD Set PTICD 2001
Pure Traditional Irish / Mar '97 / ADA / CM / Direct / Ross

FESTIVAL OF IRISH FOLK VOL.2 (2CD Set)
On Raglan Road: *Kelly, Luke* / Foggy dew: *Kelly, Luke* / Wild rover: *Dubliners* / Dublin in the rare oul times: *Dubliners* / Molly Maguires: *Dubliners* / Musical priest: *Dubliners* / Blackthorn stick: *Dubliners* / Last night's fun: *Dubliners* / Congress reel: *Dubliners* / Four green fields: *Dubliners* / Black velvet band: *Dubliners* / Miss McNamara: *Na Fili* / Follow me down to Limerick: *Na Fili* / Boulavouge: *McHaile, Tom* / Gooseberry bush: *McHaile, Tom* / Maid behind the bar: *McHaile, Tom* / Coolies No.3: *McHaile, Tom* / Miss Monaghan's: *McKillop, Jim* / Spey in spate: *McKillop, Jim* / Mist in the glenn: *McKillop, Jim* / Knights of St. Patrick: *McKillop, Jim* / Nancy Spain: *Dublin City Ramblers* / John O'Dreams: *Dublin City Ramblers* / Ferryman: *Dublin City Ramblers* / Fields of Athenry: *Reilly, Paddy* / Carrickfergus: *Reilly, Paddy* / Town I loved so well: *Reilly, Paddy* / Fairy: *Tansey, Seamus* / Clougher: *Tansey, Seamus* / Round Kilavelle: *Tansey, Seamus* / Mail coach road to Silgo: *Tansey, Seamus* / Richards Dwyer's reel: *Burke, Joe* / Paddy Kelly's reel: *Burke, Joe* / Jackson's jig: *Burke, Joe* / Monaghan's jig: *Kelly, John & James* / Ceathru cavan: *Kelly, John & James* / Wild Irishman: *Kelly, John & James* / Irish rover: *Drew, Ronnie* / Song for Ireland: *Kelly, Luke* / Lord Inchquinn: *Dubliners* / Down the broom: *Ceannt, Eamonn Ceili Band* / Saint Ruth's brush: *Ceannt, Eamonn Ceili Band* / Preston's: *Ceannt, Eamonn Ceili Band* / Woeful widow: *Ceannt, Eamonn Ceili Band* / New York jig: *Ceannt, Eamonn Ceili Band* / Tie the bonnet: *Shaskeen* / Innisfree: *Innisfree Ceoil* / Give me your hand: *Innisfree Ceoil* / Women of Ireland: *Innisfree Ceoil*
CD Set PTICD 2002
Pure Traditional Irish / Mar '97 / ADA / CM / Direct / Ross

FESTIVAL OF IRISH MUSIC
CD EUCD 1156
ARC / Jun '91 / ADA / ARC Music

FESTIVAL OF IRISH MUSIC VOL.1
CD EUCD 1323
ARC / Nov '95 / ADA / ARC Music

FESTIVAL OF IRISH MUSIC VOL.2
CD EUCD 1160
ARC / '91 / ADA / ARC Music

FESTIVAL OF IRISH MUSIC VOL.3
Summer in Ireland: *Oisin* / Mungo Kelly's: *Oisin* / Winds of change: *Oisin* / Blantyre explosion: *Dubliners* / Botany Bay: *McLoughlin, Noel* / Baloo baleerie: *Butler, Margie* / Kid on the mountain: *Pied Pipers* / Leithrim fancy: *Pied Pipers* / Cold blow and the rainy night: *McLoughlin, Noel* / Star of the county down: *Golden Bough* / Hare's paw and Jackie Coleman's No 2: *Golden Bough* / Carrickfergus: *McLoughlin, Noel* / Samhradh samradh: *Tara* / Chief O'Neill's favourite: *Pied Pipers* / Nine points of rougery: *Pied Pipers* / Faral O'Gara: *Pied Pipers* / Spancil hill: *McLoughlin, Noel* / Wake of the barrel: *Golden Bough* / Lea Rig: *Butler, Margie* / Kind Robin: *Butler, Margie* / Foggy dew: *Dubliners* / Jeannie C: *Oisin*
CD EUCD 1212
ARC / Sep '93 / ADA / ARC Music

FESTIVAL OF SAN MIGUEL TZINACAPAN, MEXICO
CD C 560099
Ocora / Nov '96 / ADA / Harmonia Mundi

FESTIVAL OF TRADITIONAL IRISH MUSIC (2CD Set)
CD Set CHCD 1037
Chyme / Aug '94 / ADA / CM / Direct / Koch

FESTIVAL OF YORKSHIRE VOICES, A
March of the peers / Let there be peace on earth / Song of the jolly Roger / Valse / Funiculi, funicula / Softly as I leave you / Finlandia / On Ilkley moor baht'at / Lost chord / When the saints go marching in / Sound an alarm / Morte Criste / Gwahoddiad / Ouverture solenelle (1812) / Pomp and circumstance No.1
CD QPRZ 008D
Polyphonic / Mar '92 / Complete/Pinnacle

FESTIVAL TROPICAL
CD EUCD 1250
ARC / Mar '94 / ADA / ARC Music

FEVER IN THE JUNGLE VOL.1
CD F2FCD 1
Fist 2 Fist / Oct '94 / Jet Star

FEVER IN THE JUNGLE VOL.2
CD F2FCD 2
Fist 2 Fist / Apr '95 / Jet Star

FEVER PITCH
CD FADCD 028
Fashion / Aug '93 / Jet Star / SRD

FFIDIL (Traditional Welsh Fiddle Music)
CD TRADD 182CD
Fflach / May '97 / ADA

FIAFIA (Dances From The South Pacific)
CD PAN 150CD
Pan / Dec '94 / ADA / CM / Direct

FIDDLE MUSIC OF DONEGAL, THE
CD CNF 001CD
CNF / Nov '96 / ADA

FIDDLE STICKS
CD NI 5320
Nimbus / Sep '94 / Nimbus

FIDJERI - SONGS OF THE PEARL DIVERS (Music from Bahrain)
CD AUD 08046
Auvidis/Ethnic / Feb '93 / ADA / Harmonia Mundi

FIFTY YEARS OF SUNSHINE
CD PS 9333
Pulse Sonic / Jul '93 / Plastic Head

FILL YOUR HEAD WITH PHANTASM VOL.1
CD PTM 131
Phantasm / May '95 / Arabesque / Plastic Head / Prime / Vital/SAM

FILL YOUR HEAD WITH PHANTASM VOL.2
CD PTM 133
Phantasm / Feb '96 / Arabesque / Plastic Head / Prime / Vital/SAM

FILL YOUR HEAD WITH PHANTASM VOL.3 (Future Psychedelic Techno)
Pile: *Semsis* / Liquid lifeform: *Nervasystem* / Alfalfa: *Amanite FX* / 20,000 worlds in a perspex box: *Mindfield* / Virus: *Virus* / Martians on motorcycles: *Moonweed & Squid* / Foxglove: *Shakta* / Night spacer: *Quatermass* / Touch the sun: *Sundog* / Kundalini: *OOOD*
CD PTM 134
Phantasm / Oct '96 / Arabesque / Plastic Head / Prime / Vital/SAM

FILTERLESS COLLECTIVE VOL.1 & 2
CD 12FKFCDLP
Filterless / Jul '97 / Arabesque / Kudos / Pinnacle / Prime

FILTERLESS COLLECTIVE VOL.1, THE
CD 5FKFCD
Filterless / Jul '95 / Arabesque / Kudos / Pinnacle / Prime

FINE AS WINE
CD FLYCD 30
Flyright / Apr '91 / Hot Shot / Jazz Music / Wellard

FINEST VINTAGE JAZZ (Greatest Jazz 1918-1940)
Savoy blues: *Armstrong, Louis* / When it's sleepy time down South: *Armstrong, Louis* / Jumpin' at the woodside: *Basie, Count* / Blues in thirds: *Bechet, Sidney & Earl Hines* / Singin' the blues: *Beiderbecke, Bix* / Symphony in riffs: *Carter, Benny* / Big noise from Winnetka: *Crosby, Bob Orchestra* / Marie: *Dorsey, Tommy* / East St. Louis toodle-oo: *Ellington, Duke* / Sing me a swing song: *Fitzgerald, Ella* / Roll 'em: *Goodman, Benny* / Creole love call: *Hall, Adelaide* / Running wild: *Hampton, Lionel* / Crazy rhythm: *Hawkins, Coleman* / Easy living: *Wilson, Teddy & Billie Holiday* / Walkin' and swingin': *Kirk, Andy & His Twelve Clouds of Joy* / Handful of riffs: *Lang, Eddie & Lonnie Johnson* / Honky tonk train blues: *Lewis, Meade 'Lux'* / Feelin' no pain: *Nichols, Red & His Five Pennies* / Livery stable blues: *Original Dixieland Jazz Band* / I got rhythm: *Reinhardt, Django & Stephane Grappelli* / St. Louis blues: *Smith, Bessie & Louis Armstrong* / Relaxin' at the Touro: *Spanier, Muggsy* / I gotta right to sing the blues: *Teagarden, Jack & Benny Goodman* / Honeysuckle rose: *Waller, Fats*
CD CDAJA 5117
Living Era / Oct '93 / Select

FINGERPRINTS
CD 02602
Glitterhouse / May '95 / Avid/BMG

FINNISH TECHNO COMPILATION
CD FU 502CD
Function / Nov '96 / Plastic Head

FIRE DOWN BELOW
Fire down below: *Burning Spear* / African skank: *Prince Francis* / Love and peace: *Marshall, Larry* / No happiness: *Webber, Marlene* / What does it take: *Francis, Winston & Alton Ellis* / Nite ride: *'Im & Dave* / Up park camp: *Jarrett, Winston* / Reggae children: *Richards, Roy* / What is love: *Brown, Errol* / Midnight soul: *'Im & The Invaders* / Sweet talking: *Heptones* / Love again: *Jackie & The Invaders* / Rainy night in Georgia: *Parker, Ken* / Mission impossible: *Mittoo, Jackie*
CD CDHB 81
Heartbeat / Sep '90 / ADA / Direct / Greensleeves / Jet Star

FIRE/FURY STORY (2CD Set)
CD Set CDLAB 102
Charly / Mar '96 / Koch

FIRED
CD FI 001
Fire Island / Oct '96 / SRD

FIREPOINT
See me running: *Cooper, Mike* / I wouldn't mind: *Moore, Gerald* / No whiskey: *Robinson, Tom* / Here's to the future kid: *Cooper, Mike* / No more doggin': *Kelly, Dave* / City woman: *Power, Duffy* / Oh really: *Cooper, Mike* / Leaf without a tree: *Mitchell, Sam* / Big boss man: *Robinson, Tom* / Sunflower: *Robinson, Tom* / Halfway: *Power, Duffy*
CD C5CD 593
See For Miles/C5 / Aug '96 / Pinnacle

FIRST CIRCLE SAMPLER, THE
CD CSCD 1
Circle / Jan '97 / Jazz Music / Swift / Wellard

FIRST FLIGHT
CD ARFCD 1
Flying Rhino / Jun '96 / Mo's Music Machine / Prime / SRD

FIRST LIGHT - PIANO SOLOS
Private thoughts: *Paul, Glenn* / Rainforest: *Paul, Glenn* / Eleanora's falcon: *Paul, Glenn* / Poetic justice: *Larkin, Sheila* / Cape clear: *Larkin, Sheila* / Provincetown set: *Larkin, Sheila* / Loving the unknown: *Jang, Mia* / Silent song: *Jang, Mia* / Waiting: *Jang, Mia* / Bridge: *Dehaas, John B* / San blas: *Dehaas, John B* / Healing: *Dehaas, John B* / Colour of love: *Carr, Adrian* / Rachel: *Carr, Adrian* / You don't know me: *Carr, Adrian*
CD ND 61059
Narada / Dec '96 / ADA / New Note/ Pinnacle

FIRST XI, THE
CD WALLCD 004
Wall Of Sound / Jun '96 / Prime / Soul Trader / Vital

FISH SMELL LIKE CAT
Moon shaker: *Water Melon* / Albatross: *Water Melon* / Urin: *Chari Chari* / Sea breeze: *Chari Chari* / Round and round: *Typhoon Tosh* / She was beautiful: *Ahh Foll Yet* / Snakes and ladders: *Typhoon Tosh* / Bugis folktales: *Chari Chari* / Mr. Sales man: *Fantastic Plastic Machine* / Mahalo hotel: *Arrow Tour* / Sound is: *Mad Vibes & Kensuke Shina* / Ring of fire: *Shina, Kensuke* / Bamboo love shack: *Water Melon* / Utaki: *Chari Chari*
CD PUSSYCD 005
Pussy Foot / Apr '97 / RTM/Disc

FISTFUL OF PUSSIES/FOR A FEW PUSSIES MORE, A
Repo man: *Meteors* / Mystery street: *Batmobile* / Alley cat king: *Frantic Flintstones* / Spy catcher: *Guana Batz* / Brand new Cadillac: *Milkshakes* / No dog: *Turnpike Cruisers* / Hangman's Caesars: *Quakes* / Cyclonic: *Quakes* / I knew sky: *Golden Horde* / My brain is in the cupboard: *Alien Sex Fiend* / Surf city: *Meteors* / I get so exited: *Dexter, Levi & The Ripchords* / Rumble in the jungle: *Rochee & The Sarnos* / Holy hack Jack: *Demented Are Go* / Thirteen lines: *Wigs* / Boneshaker baby: *Alien Sex Fiend* / She's gone: *Riverside Trio* / Thee holy jukebox: *Raymen*
CD ______ CDMGRAM 36
Anagram / May '93 / Cargo / Pinnacle

FLAMENCO HIGHLIGHTS FROM SPAIN
CD ______ 15162
Laserlight / '91 / Target/BMG

FLAMENCO RUMBA GITANA
CD ______ EUCD 1208
ARC / Sep '93 / ADA / ARC Music

FLAMENCO VIVO COLLECTION (Gypsies & Flamenco/2CD Set)
CD Set ______ B 6824
Auvidis/Ethnic / Feb '97 / ADA / Harmonia Mundi

FLAMENCO, FIRE AND GRACE
Mori sonando: *De La Bastide, Miguel* / Callejon De Las Canteras: *Tomatito* / Crisol: *Morente, Enrique* / Bulleriando: *Moraito* / Aguita clara: *Riqueni, Rafael* / Mi hijo jonato: *El Viejin* / Viajero: *De La Bastide, Miguel* / Chicuelina: *Riqueni, Rafael* / Voz de referencia: *Carrasco, Diego* / Caminillo viejo: *Tomatito* / Tangos de la plaza: *Morente, Enrique* / Into the dark: *Cook, Jesse*
CD ______ ND 63924
Narada / May '96 / ADA / New Note/ Pinnacle

FLAMES OF HELL (Swamp Music Vol.1)
CD ______ TRIKONT 0156
Trikont / Jan '95 / ADA / Direct

FLAMIN'
CD ______ TX 51218CD
Triple X / Mar '96 / Plastic Head

FLAPPER BOX, THE (5CD Set)
Begin the beguine: *Shaw, Artie* / Drum stomp: *Hampton, Lionel* / Bugle call rag: *Roy, Harry* / Georgia on my mind: *Gonella, Nat* / Stompin' at the Savoy: *Goodman, Benny* / Love is the sweetest thing: *Bowlly, Al* / Save it pretty Mama: *Armstrong, Louis* / World is waiting for the sunrise: *Geraldo & His Orchestra* / Continental: *Stone, Lew* / One o'clock jump: *Basie, Count* / On the air: *Gibbons, Carroll* / Say it with music: *Payne, Jack* / Whispering: *Fox, Roy* / Take the 'A' train: *Ellington, Duke* / Sweetest music this side of Heaven: *Winnick, Maurice* / Somebody stole my gal: *Cotton, Billy* / In the mood: *Loss, Joe* / Here's to the next time: *Hall, Henry* / At the woodchoppers' ball: *Herman, Woody* / I used to be colour blind: *Hylton, Jack* / Trumpet blues and cantabile: *James, Harry* / Hors d'oeuvres: *Ambrose & His Orchestra* / Donkey serenade: *Jones, Allan* / You've done something to my heart: *Laye, Evelyn* / Night and day: *Astaire, Fred* / Indian love call: *Eddy, Nelson & Jeanette MacDonald* / My heart belongs to Daddy: *Martin, Mary* / Louise: *Chevalier, Maurice* / Amapola: *Durbin, Deanna* / Goodnight Vienna: *Buchanan, Jack* / Let yourself go: *Rogers, Ginger* / One night of love: *Moore, Grace* / Little white room: *Day, Frances & John Mills* / Inka dinka doo: *Durante, Jimmy* / Lovely to look at: *Dunn, Irene* / I'll see you again: *Coward, Noel* / Falling in love again: *Dietrich, Marlene* / I'll get by: *Haymes, Dick* / I can give you the starlight: *Ellis, Mary* / Experiment: *Lawrence, Gertrude* / Thanks for the memory: *Hope, Bob & Shirley Ross* / Dancing on the ceiling: *Matthews, Jessie* / I get a kick out of you: *Merman, Ethel* / We're gonna hang out the washing on the Siegfried line: *Flanagan & Allen* / Yours: *Lynn, Vera* / Nearness of you: *Hutchinson, Leslie 'Hutch'* / I'm stepping out with a memory tonight: *Bowlly, Al & Jim Mesene* / I haven't time to be a millionaire: *Bowlly, Al & Jim Mesene* / Wings over the Navy: *Stone, Lew* / Our Sergeant Major: *Formby, George* / American patrol: *Miller, Glenn* / It's a hap-hap-happy day: *Roy, Harry* / Run rabbit run: *Flanagan & Allen* / It's a pair of wings for me: *Gonella, Nat* / Bless 'em all: *Cotton, Billy* / Turn the money in your pocket: *Bowlly, Al & Jim Mesene* / I'll never smile again: *Bowlly, Al & Jim Mesene* / We'll go smiling along: *Bowlly, Al & Jim Mesene* / We must all stick together: *Geraldo & Cyril Grantham* / White cliffs of Dover: *Lynn, Vera* / My prayer: *Henderson, Chick* / Oh buddy I'm in love: *Gonella, Nat* / Oh Johnny oh: *Roy, Harry & His Tiger Ragamuffins* / Kiss me goodnight, Sergeant Major: *Cotton, Billy* / Jukebox Saturday night: *Cotton, Billy* / All over the place: *Thorburn, Billy* / Moonlight serenade: *Miller, Glenn* / Wish me luck as you wave me goodbye: *Fields, Gracie* / If you were the only girl in the world: *Ziegler, Anne & Webster Booth* / Be careful it's my heart: *Sinatra, Frank* / Bless you: *Ink Spots* / Little white gardenia: *Brisson, Carl* / Very thought of you: *Bowlly, Al* / J'Attendrai: *Rossi, Tino* / Stop beatin' around the mulberry bush: *Merry Macs* / What do you know Jo: *Stafford, Jo & The Pied Pipers* / Great mistake of my life: *Henderson, Chick* / Body and soul: *Boswell, Connee* / Sonny boy: *Jolson, Al* / Tisket-a-tasket: *Fitzgerald, Ella* / Without a song: *Dennis, Denny* / How about you: *Carless, Dorothy* / Where the blue of the night meets the gold of the day: *Crosby, Bing* / Trans-Atlantic lullaby: *Hall, Adelaide* / Last time I saw Paris: *Martin, Tony* / Fools rush in: *Shelton, Anne* / My very good friend the milkman: *Waller, Fats* / Pennsylvania 6-5000: *Andrews Sisters* / These foolish things: *Layton, Turner* / Someone to watch over me: *Langford, Frances* / Ma, I miss your apple pie: *Ambrose & His Orchestra* / There's a land of Begin Again: *Loss, Joe* / Don't sit under the apple tree: *Andrews Sisters* / I'll never smile again: *Sinatra, Frank* / You are my sunshine: *Roy, Harry* / I don't want to walk without you: *Lipton, Celia* / String of pearls: *Miller, Glenn* / When I see an elephant fly: *Lea, Jimmy* / That lovely weekend: *Carless, Dorothy & Geraldo* / Moonlight becomes you: *Crosby, Bing* / Someone's rocking my dreamboat: *Crosby, Bing* / Drummin' man: *Squadronaires* / Who wouldn't love you: *Ink Spots* / Elmer's tune: *Miller, Glenn* / Kiss the boys goodbye: *Martin, Mary* / My devotion: *Winstone, Eric & His Band* / Rancho pillow: *Martin, Freddy* / Beat me Daddy, eight to the bar: *Shearing, George* / Daybreak: *Sinatra, Frank* / I've got a gal in Kalamazoo: *Andrews Sisters* / Nightingale sang in Berkeley Square: *Shelton, Anne* / White Christmas: *Crosby, Bing*
CD Set ______ PASTCDS 7010
Flapper / Jun '93 / Pinnacle

FLASH OF '29 (Portrait Of Music In 1929)
Some of these days / If I had a talking picture of you / Mess-a-stomp / Louise / Dinah / Button up your overcoat / Honey / Won't you get up off it, please / Muskrat ramble / After you've gone / Black and blue / When you're smiling / Wang wang blues / I'm a dreamer (aren't we all) / Everybody loves my baby / Bashful baby
CD ______ PHONTCD 7608
Phontastic / '93 / Cadillac / Jazz Music / Wellard

FLASHBACK
Flashback: *Imagination* / Let's groove: *Earth, Wind & Fire* / Celebration: *Kool & The Gang* / Contact: *Starr, Edwin* / Love come down: *King, Evelyn 'Champagne'* / Gangsters of the groove: *Heatwave* / Cuba: *Gibson Brothers* / Going back to my roots: *Odyssey* / Don't stop the music: *Yarbrough & Peoples* / Oops upside your head: *Gap Band* / Funky town: *Lipps Inc.* / I will survive: *Gaynor, Gloria* / DISCO: *Ottawan* / YMCA: *Village People* / Car wash: *Rose Royce* / Hustle: *McCoy, Van* / I love to love (but my baby loves to dance): *Charles, Tina* / You're the first, the last, my everything: *Charles, Tina*
CD ______ MUSCD 004
MCI Music / Nov '92 / Disc / THE

FLASHBACK TO THE 50'S (2CD Set)
Wanted: *Martino, Al* / Comes a-long-a-love: *Starr, Kay* / That's how a love song was born: *Burns, Ray* / Fever: *Lee, Peggy* / Story of my life: *Holliday, Michael* / Undecided: *Radio Revellers & Geraldo/Orchestra* / I'll be around: *Boswell, Eve & Chorus/Orchestra* / True love: *Crosby, Bing & Grace Kelly/ Johnny Green* / Volare: *Martin, Dean* / Pretend: *Dawn, Julie & Norrie Paramor/Orchestra* / Bewitched, bothered and bewildered: *Torme, Mel* / Cry me a river: *London, Julie* / Young and foolish: *Lawrence, Lee & Ray Martin Orchestra* / Happy days and lonely nights: *Murray, Ruby* / When I fall in love: *Cole, Nat 'King'* / No other love: *Hilton, Ronnie* / I'll be hanging around: *MacKintosh, Ken* / It breaks my heart: *Carr, Carole & Frank Cordell Orchestra* / Eternally: *Campbell, Jean & Philip Green Orchestra* / Keep me in mind: *Buxton, Sheila & Ronnie Harris/Ray Martin Orchestra* / Holiday affair: *Day, Jill & Frank Cordell Orchestra* / Blacksmith blues: *Rabin, Oscar & His Band* / Story of Tina: *Bereton, Gerry & Philip Green Orchestra* / Ciao ciao Bambina: *Cardinali, Roberto & the Rita Williams singers* / Stealin': *Warren, Alma & Ron Goodwin Chorus/Orchestra* / Ferryboat Inn: *Cogan, Alma & Frank Cordell Chorus/Orchestra* / Lucky lips: *Cogan, Alma & Frank Cordell Chorus/Orchestra* / Me and my imagination: *Peers, Donald & Sydney Torch/Orchestra* / Poor little fool: *Nelson, Rick* / My love and devotion: *Johnson, Teddy* / Met me on the corner: *Coronets* / Every day of my life: *Vaughan, Malcolm* / Oh oh I'm falling in love again: *Rodgers, Jimmie & Hugo Peretti Orchestra* / Jezebel: *Loss, Joe & His Orchestra* / He's got the whole world in his hands: *London, Laurie & Geoff Love Orchestra* / Oh my papa (O mein Papa): *Klooger, Annette & Teddy Foster Orchestra* / I will never change: *James, Dick & Ron Goodwin Orchestra* / Small talk: *Small, Joan & Peter Knight Orchestra* / My heart belongs to only you: *Morton, Peter & Ray Martub Orchestra* / Buona Sera: *Prima, Louis & Sam Butera/ Witnesses* / Band of gold: *Lyon, Barbara & Ray Martin Orchestra* / Strange: *Vaughan, Frankie & Ken MacKintosh Orchestra* / With these hands: *Hughes, David & Frank Cordell Orchestra* / Get with it: *Kentones & Ron Goodwin Orchestra* / Zambezi: *Bousch, Lou & His Orchestra* / Dance with me Henry: *Kirchin Band* / If you go: *Dean, Alan* / Things go wrong: *Anthony, Billie* / Seven little girls sitting in the back seat: *Avons* / Chances are: *Desmond, Michael & Bill Shepherd Orchestra*
CD Set ______ CDDL 1236
Music For Pleasure / Nov '92 / EMI

FLASHBACK TO THE 60'S (2CD Set)
I like it: *Gerry & The Pacemakers* / World without love: *Peter & Gordon* / Walkin' back to happiness: *Shapiro, Helen* / One way love: *Bennett, Cliff & The Rebel Rousers* / Kites: *Dupree, Simon & The Big Sound* / Anyone who had a heart: *Black, Cilla* / Bad to me: *Kramer, Billy J. & The Dakotas* / Look through my window: *Hollies* / I'm telling you now: *Freddie & The Dreamers* / Kon-Tiki: *Shadows* / You're driving me crazy: *Temperance Seven* / Pretty flamingo: *Manfred Mann* / little lovin': *Fourmost* / I'm the urban spaceman: *Bonzo Dog Band* / What do you want: *Faith, Adam* / Surfin' USA: *Beach Boys* / I remember you: *Ifield, Frank* / House of the rising sun: *Animals* / I'm into something good: *Herman's Hermits* / Up on the roof: *Lynch, Kenny* / Lily the pink: *Scaffold* / I'm a tiger: *Lulu* / I'll never fall in love again: *Gentry, Bobbie* / I've been a bad bad boy: *Jones, Paul*
CD Set ______ CDDL 1112
Music For Pleasure / Jun '91 / EMI

FLASHBACK TO THE 70'S (2CD Set)
I hear you knocking: *Edmunds, Dave* / When I'm dead and gone: *McGuinness Flint* / Strange kind of woman: *Deep Purple* / Don't let it die: *Smith, Hurricane* / California man: *Move* / Crash: *Quatro, Suzi* / See my baby jive: *Wizzard* / Cat crept in: *Mud* / Bump: *Kenny* / Rock your baby: *McCrae, George* / You sexy thing: *Hot Chocolate* / That's the way I like it: *KC & The Sunshine Band* / Motor bikin': *Spedding, Chris* / Moonlighting: *Sayer, Leo* / Little bit more: *Dr. Hook* / They shoot horses don't they: *Racing Cars* / Spanish stroll: *Mink Deville* / Peaches: *Stranglers* / Dancing in the dark: *Marshall Hain* / More than a woman: *Tavares* / Wuthering Heights: *Bush, Kate* / Ever fallen in love: *Buzzcocks* / Hanging on the telephone: *Blondie* / Darlin': *Miller, Frankie* / My Sharona: *Knack* / Tears of a clown: *Beat* / Message to rudy: *Specials* / On my radio: *Selecter* / American pie: *McLean, Don* / Roll over Beethoven: *ELO* / Nutbush City Limits: *Turner, Ike & Tina* / Dance with the devil: *Powell, Cozy* / Right back where we started from: *Nightingale, Maxine* / Make me smile (come up and see me): *Harley, Steve & Cockney Rebel* / Loving you: *Reddy, Helen* / Angie baby: *Robinson, Tom* / 2-4-6-8 Motorway: *Robinson, Tom* / Baker Street: *Rafferty, Gerry* / Rich kids: *Rich Kids* / Milk and alcohol: *Dr. Feelgood*
CD Set ______ CDDL 1233
Music For Pleasure / Nov '92 / EMI

FLATLINE
CD ______ MGOUTCD 7
Granite / Sep '96 / Pinnacle

FLAVAS
Tha crossroads / Gangsta's paradise / Diggin' on you / Waterfalls / I got 5 on it / Loungin' / Get money / Fu-gee-la / California love / Get on up / You're the one / Return of the mack / I wish / Too hot / Flava/1,2,3,4 sumpin' new
CD ______ SUMCD 4108
Summit / Feb '97 / Sound & Media

FLAVOURS OF JAZZ FUN
CD ______ RENCD 112
Renaissance Collector Series / Mar '96 / BMG

FLEADH CEILI
CD ______ CDC 007
Ceol / Feb '97 / CM

FLESH EATERS (The Return Of The Undead/3CD Set)
CD Set ______ DTKBOX 57
Dressed To Kill / Oct '96 / Total/BMG

FLESH, FANGS AND FILIGREE (3CD Set)
CD Set ______ DTKBOX 60
Dressed To Kill / Dec '96 / Total/BMG

FLICKNIFE PUNK SINGLES COLLECTION
Shake some action / Total control / Shell shock / Waiting for the man / Teenage in love / Do the geek / Thatcher / Follow the leader / Fight to win / Let's get crazy / Werewolf / We don't care / Wanna world / No romance / No sign of life / Leaders of tomorrow / Respectable / Playing cards with dead men / Summertime now / Nicely does it
CD ______ CDPUNK 42
Anagram / Feb '95 / Cargo / Pinnacle

FLIGHT OF THE CONDOR
CD ______ CDSR 065
Telstar / May '95 / BMG

FLIGHT OF THE CONDOR (2CD Set)
CD Set ______ DCDCD 211
Castle / Aug '96 / BMG

FLIGHT OF THE GREEN LINNET
CD ______ RCD 20075
Rykodisc / May '96 / ADA / Vital

FLIGHTS OF FANCY (Beautiful Sound Of The Panpipes)
Light of experience / El condor pasa / Picnic at hanging rock / Cacharpaya / First time ever I saw your face / Godfather / Endless love / True / Bluebird / Do you know where you're going to / And I love her / Tara's theme / Once upon a time in the west / Flame Trees of Thika / Feelings / True love ways / Why can't it wait till morning
CD ______ CDMFP 5896
Music For Pleasure / Sep '90 / EMI

FLOORPACKIN'
You should of held on: *7th Avenue Aviators* / Tears: *Roye, Lee* / I'm where it's at: *Jades* / If that's what you wanted: *Beverly, Frankie* / Soul self satisfaction: *Jackson, Earl* / Little togetherness: *Young Hearts* / You didn't have to leave: *Ellusions* / Nothing can compare to you: *Velvet Satins* / I'm not strong enough: *Four Perfections* / Stick by me baby: *Salvadors* / That beatin' rhythm: *Temple, Richard* / Sliced tomatoes: *Just Brothers* / Double cookin': *Checkerboard Squares* / Try a little harder: *Fi Dels* / Countdown: *Tempos* / Per-so-nally: *Paris, Bobby* / Lend a hand: *Hutton, Bobby* / She'll come running back: *Britt, Mel* / Hung up on your love: *Montclairs* / You've been gone too long: *Sexton, Ann* / Dearly beloved: *Montgomery, Jack* / I'm comin' home: *Pride, Lou* / I'm not built that way: *Hesitations* / My sugar baby: *Clarke, Connie* / Put your arms around me: *Sherrys* / It's all over: *Mann, Charles*
CD ______ SSCD 004
Goldmine / Mar '97 / Vital

FLOW: AN EXPERIENCE IN DRUM 'N' BASS
Alltitude: *Architex* / Airtight: *Funki Technicians* / Drifting: *KMC* / Coming on strong: *Cold Mission* / Inertia: *Mouly & Lucinda* / Sorrow: *Future Bound* / Liquid velvet: *J-Majik* / Sound ceased: *Xedos* / Can't you see: *Technical Itch* / Oceans: *Subject 13* / Generations: *Intensity*
CD ______ KUB 932
Kubin / Jun '97 / Arabesque / Timewarp

FLOWER POWER
CD ______ HRCD 8041
Disky / May '94 / Disky / THE

FLOWER POWER
CD ______ TIN 861212
Disky / Aug '96 / Disky / THE

FLOWER POWER DAZE VOL.1
CD ______ DCD 5297
Disky / Sep '93 / Disky / THE

FLOWER POWER DAZE VOL.2
CD ______ DCD 5359
Disky / Apr '94 / Disky / THE

FLOYD'S CAJUN FAIS DO DO
Wafus two step: *Sundown Playboys* / Valse de soleil coucher: *Cormier, Lesa & The Sundown Playboys* / Back home again in Louisiana: *Cormier, Lesa & The Sundown Playboys* / La valse san espoir: *Cormier, Lesa & The Sundown Playboys* / Step it fast: *Bonsall, Joe* / La pointe au pain: *Hebert, Adam* / I can't sleep at night: *Hebert, Adam* / Rosalie: *Hebert, Adam* / Valse de toute le monde: *Prejean, Leeman* / Teardrop special: *Barro & The Teardrops* / 73 special: *Lejeune, Rodney* / Flumes d'enfer: *Pitre, Austin* / Fee Fee can't dance: *Cajun Trio + 1* / One step de duson: *Cormier, Louis* / Ville platte widow: *Fontenot, Allen* / Bachelor's life: *Badeaux & The Louisiana Aces* / Valse de meche: *Barzas, Maurice & The Mamau Playboys* / Rodare special: *Thibodeaux, Eugene* / Webb Pierce blues: *Fontenot, Allen* / Si tu m'aimes: *Bruce, Vin* / Bo Sparkle waltz: *Broussard, August* / Calcasieu rambler's special: *Broussard, August*
CD ______ CDCH 304
Ace / Oct '90 / Pinnacle

FLUTE & SITAR MUSIC OF INDIA
CD ______ 12178
Laserlight / Aug '95 / Target/BMG

FLUTE AND GAMELAN MUSIC OF WEST JAVA
CD ______ TSCD 913
Topic / Apr '95 / ADA / CM / Direct

FLUTES OF THE MANDARA MOUNTAINS, THE (Music From Cameroon)
CD ______ C 560110
Ocora / Jan '97 / ADA / Harmonia Mundi

FLUTES OF THE WORLD
CD ______ PS 660077
PlayaSound / Oct '96 / ADA / Harmonia Mundi

FLUXTRAX VOL.1 (2CD Set)
CD Set ______ EXPCD 001
EXP / Jul '96 / 3mv/Pinnacle / RTM/Disc

FLUXTRAX VOL.2 (2CD Set)
CD Set ______ EXPCD 003
EXP / Jun '96 / 3mv/Pinnacle / RTM/Disc

FLY AFRICAN EAGLE (The Best Of African Reggae)
CD ______ SH 45033
Shanachie / Jul '97 / ADA / Greensleeves / Koch

FLY DE GATE
CD VPCD 1285
VP / May '93 / Greensleeves / Jet Star / Total/BMG

FLYIN' HIGH
CD RNBCD 107
Connoisseur Collection / Jan '94 / Pinnacle

FLYING HIGH
Mooncat: *Shaker* / Euro friendly: *Bootleg Boys* / Toccata: *Childs, Sky* / Gotta get (Loose): *Must* / Keep your luv: *Partisans* / Krazy noise: *Numerical Value* / On ya way: *Helicopter* / Flagship: *Blue Peter* / Driver: *Epik* / Tree frog: *Hope Experience* / Check it out: *Kinky Riba* / Organ grinder: *Deeper Cut* .
CD CDTOT 25
Jumpin' & Pumpin' / Apr '95 / 3mv/Sony / Mo's Music Machine

FLYING NUN SAMPLER
CD FNCD 377
Flying Nun / Sep '96 / RTM/Disc

FLYING TRANCE CLASSICS (2CD Set)
CD Set ZYX 811122
ZYX / Aug '97 / ZYX

FOLDS AND RHIZOMES
CD SR 99
Sub Rosa / Feb '96 / Direct / RTM/Disc / SRD / Vital

FOLK & CEREMONIAL MUSIC FROM CAMBODIA
CD D 8068
Unesco / Feb '96 / ADA / Harmonia Mundi

FOLK AND SACRED SONGS FROM ITALY
CD 926522
BUDA / Sep '96 / Discovery

FOLK BOX (2CD Set)
CD Set TBXCD 513
TrueTrax / Jan '96 / THE

FOLK BOX (2CD Set)
CD Set PBXCD 513
Pulse / Nov '96 / BMG

FOLK COLLECTION VOL.1, THE
Another Irish rover: *Four Men & A Dog* / Carthy's reel/The return to Camden Town: *Carthy, Martin & Dave Swarbrick* / Almost every circumstance: *Prior, Maddy & June Tabor* / Oh I swear: *Thompson, Richard* / Company policy: *Carthy, Martin* / I specialise: *Gregson & Collister* / Party's over: *Albion Band* / Brighton camp/March past: *Kirkpatrick, John* / Good old way: *Watersons* / Johnny Cope: *MacColl, Ewan* / Battle of Falkirk Muir: *Battlefield Band* / Reaper: *Tabor, June* / Farewll to the gold: *Jones, Nic* / Reconciliation: *Alias Ron Kavana* / Walsh's polkas: *Patrick Street* / Lakes of ponchartrain: *Simpson, Martin* / Mariano: *Keen, Robert Earl* / Through moorfields: *Cronshaw, Andrew* / Now westlin' winds: *Gaughan, Dick*
CD TSCD 470
Topic / Oct '93 / ADA / CM / Direct

FOLK COLLECTION VOL.2, THE
CD TSCD 481
Topic / Oct '95 / ADA / CM / Direct

FOLK GUITAR
CD TRTCD 216
TrueTrax / Jul '96 / THE

FOLK HEARTBEAT
Can't help falling in love: *Lick The Tins* / Bride 1945: *Matthews, Iain* / Choo choo ch'boogie: *Chilli Willi & Red Hot Peppers* / False knight on the road: *Hart, Tim & Maddy Prior* / Hal-an-tow: *Collins, Shirley & The Albion Country Band* / Belle of Belfast city: *Lick The Tins* / Female drummer: *Steeleye Span* / This train: *Denny, Sandy* / Ramblin' boy: *Denny, Sandy* / Blacksmith: *Steeleye Span* / Rave on: *Steeleye Span* / Dalesman litany: *Hart, Tim & Maddy Prior* / Midnight bus: *Chilli Willi & Red Hot Peppers* / Famous flower of serving men: *Carthy, Martin* / Marrowbones: *Steeleye Span* / Claudy banks: *Collins, Shirley & The Albion Country Band*
CD EMPRCD 595
Emporio / Jun '96 / Disc

FOLK HERITAGE VOL.1
Fiddle diddle: *Chilli Willi & Red Hot Peppers* / Dalesman's litany: *Hart, Tim & Maddy Prior* / Calling on song: *Steeleye Span* / Handsome Polly-O: *Carthy, Martin* / Copshawholme Fair: *Steeleye Span* / Sing me back home: *Matthews, Iain* / My ramblin' boy: *Denny, Sandy* / Fool like you: *Moore, Tim* / Famous flower of serving men: *Carthy, Martin* / Adieu sweet lovely Nancy: *Hart, Tim & Maddy Prior* / Blacksmith: *Steeleye Span* / Just as the tide was flowing: *Collins, Shirley* / Rock 'n' roll love letter: *Moore, Tim* / Last thing on my mind: *Denny, Sandy* / Lark in the morning: *Steeleye Span* / Wager a wager: *Hart, Tim & Maddy Prior*
CD MCCD 043
Music Club / Sep '91 / Disc / THE

FOLK HERITAGE VOL.1-3 (3CD Set)
CD Set MCBX 004
Music Club / Jan '93 / Disc / THE

FOLK HERITAGE VOL.2
Time to ring some changes: *Thompson, Richard* / Not a day passes: *Gregson & Collister* / Ramble away: *Albion Band* / Music for a found harmonium: *Patrick Street* / Song of the iron road: *MacColl, Ewan* / Band played waltzing Matilda: *Tabor, June* / Handsome Molly: *Simpson, Martin* / World turned upside down: *Gaughan, Dick* / Sovay: *Carthy, Martin & Dave Swarbrick* / All things are quite silent: *Collins, Shirley* / Spaghetti panic: *Blowzabella* / Hidden love/ Sheila Coyles: *Four Men & A Dog* / Fine horsemen: *Silly Sisters* / Lovely cottage/ Gold ochra at Killarney point to points: *Alias Ron Kavana* / Canadee-I-O: *Jones, Nic* / Country life: *Watersons*
CD MCCD 049
Music Club / Mar '92 / Disc / THE

FOLK HERITAGE VOL.3
Granite years: *Oyster Band* / Who cares: *Shocked, Michelle* / First time ever I saw your face: *MacColl, Ewan* / Mississippi summer: *Tabor, June & The Oyster Band* / Hush little baby: *Horseflies* / Breaths: *Sweet Honey In The Rock* / Hopak: *Ukrainians* / Silver wheels: *Cockburn, Bruce* / Byker hill: *Barely Works* / Angry love: *McLeod, Rory* / Six string street: *White, Andy* / Sea never dry: *God's Little Monkeys* / Turn things upside down: *Happy End* / That's entertainment: *Colorblind James Experience* / Free Mexican airforce: *Jimenez, Flaco* / Raining: *Ancient Beatbox*
CD MCCD 076
Music Club / Jun '92 / Disc / THE

FOLK LIVE FROM THE MOUNTAIN STAGE
It sure was better back then: *Forbert, Steve* / Fishin' in the dark: *Nitty Gritty Dirt Band* / Sweet is the melody: *DeMent, Iris* / Gentle on my mind: *Hartford, John* / Beat the retreat: *Thompson, Richard* / Driving home: *Wheeler, Cheryl* / Time passage: *Stewart, Al* / Take this hammer: *Taj Mahal* / Letter from heaven: *Morrissey, Bill* / Lives in the balance: *Havens, Richie* / John Wayne lives in Hoboken: *Delevantes* / Sun won't stop: *Near Holly*
CD BPM 310CD
Blue Plate / May '97 / ADA / Direct / Greyhound

FOLK MASTERS
CD SF 40047CD
Smithsonian Folkways / Dec '94 / ADA / Cadillac / CM / Direct / Koch

FOLK MASTERS
CD CDAR 1017
Action Replay / Oct '94 / Tring

FOLK MUSIC FROM BELGIUM (2CD Set)
CD Set B 6844
Auvidis/Ethnic / Feb '97 / ADA / Harmonia Mundi

FOLK MUSIC FROM NORTHEN IRELAND
CD CDN 1101
Outlet / Apr '97 / ADA / CM / Direct / Duncans / Koch / Ross

FOLK MUSIC FROM NORTHERN SPAIN
CD CMT 2741003CD
La Chant Du Monde / Jul '95 / ADA / Harmonia Mundi

FOLK MUSIC FROM SCOTLAND
CD 12250
Laserlight / Apr '94 / Target/BMG

FOLK MUSIC IN SWEDEN VOL.11 (Fiddlers From Five Provinces)
CD CAP 21487CD
Caprice / Aug '96 / ADA / Cadillac / CM / Complete/Pinnacle

FOLK MUSIC IN SWEDEN VOL.12 (The Songs Of The Tornedalen)
CD CAP 21485CD
Caprice / Nov '96 / ADA / Cadillac / CM / Complete/Pinnacle

FOLK MUSIC IN SWEDEN VOL.13 (Nordic Folk Instruments)
CD CAP 21484CD
Caprice / Aug '96 / ADA / Cadillac / CM / Complete/Pinnacle

FOLK MUSIC IN SWEDEN VOL.14 (Folk Tunes From Jamtland)
CD CAP 21489CD
Caprice / Nov '96 / ADA / Cadillac / CM / Complete/Pinnacle

FOLK MUSIC IN SWEDEN VOL.15 (Songs Of Sailors & Navies)
CD CAP 21540CD
Caprice / May '97 / ADA / Cadillac / CM / Complete/Pinnacle

FOLK MUSIC IN SWEDEN VOL.16 & 17 (Tunes From Rattvik, Boda & Binsjo/ 2CD Set)
CD Set CAP 22044CD
Caprice / May '97 / ADA / Cadillac / CM / Complete/Pinnacle

FOLK MUSIC IN SWEDEN VOL.18 (Tunes From Dala Floda, Enviken & Ore)
CD CAP 21541CD
Caprice / May '97 / ADA / Cadillac / CM / Complete/Pinnacle

FOLK MUSIC IN SWEDEN VOL.5
CD CAP 21476CD
Caprice / Nov '95 / ADA / Cadillac / CM / Complete/Pinnacle

FOLK MUSIC IN SWEDEN VOL.9 & 10
CD CAP 22043
Caprice / May '96 / ADA / Cadillac / CM / Complete/Pinnacle

FOLK MUSIC OF ALBANIA
CD TSCD 904
Topic / Oct '94 / ADA / CM / Direct

FOLK MUSIC OF BULGARIA
CD TSCD 905
Topic / Sep '94 / ADA / CM / Direct

FOLK MUSIC OF CUBA
CD D 8064
Unesco / Oct '95 / ADA / Harmonia Mundi

FOLK MUSIC OF GREECE
CD TSCD 907
Topic / Sep '94 / ADA / CM / Direct

FOLK MUSIC OF NORTHERN SPAIN
CD CMT 2741003
La Chant Du Monde / Apr '95 / ADA / Harmonia Mundi

FOLK MUSIC OF TURKEY
CD TSCD 908
Topic / Sep '94 / ADA / CM / Direct

FOLK MUSIC OF YUGOSLAVIA
CD TSCD 906
Topic / Sep '94 / ADA / CM / Direct

FOLK MUSIC VOL.1
CD D8005
Auvidis/Ethnic / Jun '89 / ADA / Harmonia Mundi

FOLK MUSIC VOL.2
CD D8003
Auvidis/Ethnic / Jun '89 / ADA / Harmonia Mundi

FOLK 'N' HELL
Flick it up and catch it: *Sutherland, Jim* / Half way round/walking the line: *Burach* / If and when: *Bongshang* / Pipe tunes: *Shooglenifty* / Passing away: *Mounsey, Paul* / Sun fire majestic: *Colour Of Memory* / Jolly beggar/man in black: *Coelbeg* / Superwasp/ Along the coast of Norway/Neckbuster: *Seelyhoo* / All together: *MacLean, Dougie* / By the right: *MacKenzie, Fergus & Simon Thoumire* / Beaujolais nouveau: *Humpff Family* / Grandmother's eyes: *Rock, Salt & Nails* / Hoagies/Porshe: *Poozies* / Burning of Auchindoun/Turn again: *Iron Horse* / O ho na Ribeannan/Sean triubhas/Faca tu saor an T-Sabhaidh: *Tannas* / Bitter honey: *Khartoum Heroes* / Willie's aul' trews/Auld reel 1/Auld reel 2: *Old Blind Dogs*
CD PRMDCD 16
Hemisphere / Oct '96 / EMI

FOLK ROUTES
Siege of Yaddlethorpe: *Amazing Blondel* / Matty Groves: *Fairport Convention* / John Barleycorn: *Traffic* / Seven black roses: *Martyn, John* / It suits me well: *Denny, Sandy* / Road: *Drake, Nick* / When I get to the border: *Thompson, Richard & Linda* / Strangely strange but oddly normal: *Dr. Strangely Strange* / Black Jack David: *Incredible String Band* / Nutting girl: *Hutchings, Ashley* / She moved through the fair: *Fairport Convention* / I was a young man: *Albion Country Band* / Peace in the end: *Fotheringay* / Long odds/Mr. Cosgill's delight: *Hutchings, Ashley & John Kirkpatrick* / Audrey: *Heron, Mike* / Man of iron: *Denny, Sandy* / Girl in the month of May: *Bunch* / Hornpipe: *Locke, John*
CD IMCD 197
Island / Jul '94 / PolyGram

FOLK SONGS OF NORTH EAST SCOTLAND
CD CDTRAX 5003
Greentrax / Nov '95 / ADA / Direct / Duncans / Highlander

FOLK SONGS VOL.1
CD VICG 50222
JVC World Library / Feb '96 / ADA / CM / Direct

FOLK SONGS VOL.2
CD VICG 50232
JVC World Library / Feb '96 / ADA / CM / Direct

FOLK THEATRE OF NORTH VIETNAM
CD ARN 64368
Arion / Nov '96 / ADA / Discovery

FOLKLORE FROM VENEZUELA
CD EUCD 1237
ARC / Nov '93 / ADA / ARC Music

FOLKLORIC INSTRUMENTAL TRADITIONS OF KOREA VOL.1
CD VICG 50202
JVC World Library / Mar '96 / ADA / CM / Direct

FOLKLORIC INSTRUMENTAL TRADITIONS OF KOREA VOL.2
CD VICG 50212
JVC World Library / Mar '96 / ADA / CM / Direct

FOLKS LIVE
CD BPCD 1003
Blue Planet / Mar '96 / ADA

FOLKSONGS (Old Time Country Music 1926-1944/2CD Set)
CD FA 047
Fremeaux / Apr '96 / ADA / Discovery

FOLKSONGS OF THE LOUISIANA ARCADIANS VOL.1
CD ARHCD 359
Arhoolie / Apr '95 / ADA / Cadillac / Direct

FOLLOW THAT ROAD (2nd Annual Vineyard Retreat/2CD Set)
CD Set PH 1165/66CD
Philo / Sep '94 / ADA / CM / Direct

FONG NAAM (Ancient Contemporary Music From Thailand)
CD 140982
Celestial Harmonies / Oct '95 / ADA / Select

FOOM FOOM
CD BFCD 05
Bruce's Fingers / Oct '93 / Cadillac / Discovery

FOOTBALL CRAZY
Blue is the colour: *Chelsea F.C.* / Can we kick it (no we can't): *World Of Orange* / Wooly bully: *Jones, Vinnie* / You reds: *Resistance 77* / Andy Cole song: *Palmer, Harry* / Soccer fan: *Real Sounds Of Africa* / Roger Milla is my no.9 dream: *Rainbow Choir* / Do it cos you like it: *Rainbow Choir* / Arsenal rap: *A-Team* / Nice one Gazza: *New Cockney Chorus* / Cry Gazza cry: *Spittin' Image* / Ohh Gary Gary: *Her* / Milan Milan: *West, Keith* / Super Marco Van Basten: *Rainbow Choir* / Ryan Giggs we love you: *Rainbow Choir* / Glory glory Man Utd: *Stretford End Boys* / Canaries: *Norwich City* / Alouette: *Webb, David* / We will follow united: *Palmer, Harry* / You'll never walk alone: *Liverpool FC*
CD EMPRCD 626
Emporio / Jun '96 / Disc

FOOTBALL HEAVEN
Match of the day / Grandstand / Aztec Gold / Tutti al mondo / You are the number one / We are the champions / To be the number one / Gloryland / World in motion / When the saints go maching in / Whatever will be will be (Que sera sera) / That's amore / Life of riley / Guantanamera / John Brown's Body / Champions league / You'll never walk alone / March of triumph / Ode to joy / Nessun dorma
CD ANT 011
Tring / Nov '96 / Tring

FOR A LOVELY MOTHER
CD DCD 5382LM
Disky / May '94 / Disky / THE

FOR A LOVELY MOTHER (Instrumental)
CD CNCD 5994LM
Disky / May '94 / Disky / THE

FOR COLLECTORS ONLY (Kent/ Modern's Serious Shades Of Soul)
You brought it all on yourself: *Hammond, Clay* / Burning out: *Garrett, Vernon* / Long as I've got my baby: *Day, Jackie* / I've been done wrong: *Holiday, Jimmy* / Nobody but me: *Other Brothers* / I'm coming home: *John, Bobby* / Remove my doubts: *Johnson, Stacey* / You make me feel like someone: *Gilliam, Johnny* / You are my sunshine: *Shane, Jackie* / Baby I'm sorry: *Hill, Z.Z.* / Them love blues: *Wright, Earl* / Beauty is just skin deep: *Sweethearts* / You are my first love: *Hunt, Pat* / I'm lonely for you: *Adams, Arthur* / All that shines isn't gold: *Windjammers* / One more chance: *Four Tees* / My love, she's gone: *Intentions* / I'm in love: *Sanders, Larry* / Would you like to love me: *Holiday, Jimmy* / Like it stands: *Ramsey, Robert* / You make me cry: *Adams, Arthur* / I was born to love you: *Copeland, Johnny* / I need money: *Davis, Ruth* / It's been a long time baby: *Other Brothers* / Think it over baby: *Love, Mary*
CD CDKEND 119
Kent / Sep '95 / Pinnacle

FOR DANCERS FOREVER (25 Storming 60's Soul Sounds)
You turned my bitter into sweet: *Love, Mary* / Baby, without you: *Monday, Danny* / Before it's too late: *Day, Jackie* / Your love has made me a man: *Hutch, Willie* / You just cheat and lie: *Hill, Z.Z.* / This man wants you: *Cox, Wally* / Three lonely guys: *Brilliant Corners* / My baby needs me: *Baker, Yvonne* / I don't need: *Turner, Ike & Tina* / You better be good: *Woods, Peggy* / Lay this burden down: *Love, Mary* / If I could turn back the hands of time: *Garrett, Vernon* / Can it be me: *Williams, Mel* / Dancing fast, dancing slow: *Intentions* / My jealous girl: *Hammond, Clay* / My aching back: *Fulson, Lowell* / I can't believe what you say: *Turner, Ike & Tina* / This couldn't be me: *Sweethearts* / Love is gonna get you: *Woods, Peggy* / I can feel your love: *Taylor, Felice* / Oh what heartaches: *Day, Jackie* / No puppy love: *Copeland, Johnny* / What more: *Hill, Z.Z.* / I'm so thankful: *Ikettes* / I'm in your hands: *Love, Mary*
CD CDKEND 100
Kent / Sep '92 / Pinnacle

FOR MILLIONAIRES ONLY
Say something nice to me: *Kline, Bobby* / Heartaches I can't take: *Gaylettes* / I'll be back: *Wallace, Jimmy* / Girls are against me: *Utopias* / Go for yourself: *Antiques* / That's the kind of man I am: *Adams, Bobby* / Heart you're made of stone: *Magnetics* / My love gets stronger: *Ridgley, Tommy* / Bring your fine self home: *Soulettes* / I'm still young: *Summers, Johnny* / Soul step: *Dogs* / One way or the other: *Roberts, Tina* / Female ingenuity: *Ruby* / Lady lady: *Colt 45's* / Heartaches, Souvenirs: *Powell, Will* / Lonely girl: *Mercury, Eric* / I got the power: *Coarcy, Joanne* / What more do you want: *Toones, Gene* / I'm going over: *Honeycutt, Johnny* / I couldn't care less: *Fredreick, Carol*
CD ____ **GSCD 099**
Goldmine / Nov '96 / Vital

FOR MY VALENTINE
CD ____ **WMCD 5677VT**
Disky / Feb '94 / Disky / THE

FOR ONE AND ALL
CD ____ **9425742**
Music For Little People / Jan '96 / Direct

FOR SENTIMENTAL REASONS
Mountain greenery: *Torme, Mel* / Blueberry Hill: *Armstrong, Louis* / Tammy: *Reynolds, Debbie* / Too close for comfort: *Gorme, Eydie* / (I love you) for sentimental reasons: *Fitzgerald, Ella* / Standing on a corner: *Mills Brothers* / True love ways: *Holly, Buddy* / Dream a little dream of me: *Mama Cass* / Friendly persuasion: *Boone, Pat* / Pretty blue eyes: *Lawrence, Steve* / Love me or leave me: *Davis, Sammy Jr.* / Unchained melody: *Hibbler, Al* / Lollipops and roses: *Jones, Jack* / Sweet old fashioned girl: *Brewer, Teresa* / Around the world: *Crosby, Bing* / Mr. Wonderful: *Lee, Peggy* / Love is a many splendoured thing: *Four Aces* / Moonglow and theme from picnic: *Stoloff, Morris*
CD ____ **3035900032**
Carlton / Oct '95 / Carlton

FOR YOU WITH LOVE
CD ____ **I 3896022**
Galaxy / Oct '96 / ZYX

FOR YOUR PRECIOUS LOVE (2CD Set)
CD Set ____ **DBG 53040**
Double Gold / Jun '95 / Target/BMG

FORCE 1 - THE CLUB IS HERE
CD ____ **343322**
Koch Dance Force / Nov '95 / Koch

FOREGANGARE
CD ____ **MNW 240/2**
MNW / Jan '94 / ADA / Vital

FOREVER AND ALWAYS
Father and son / Why / Someday / Love me for a reason / Because you loved me / I love you always forever / Killing me softly / Forever love / Spinning the wheel / Always be my baby / One sweet day / How deep is your love / You are not alone / Words / Count on me / Give me a little more time / I am blessed / Unbreak my heart
CD ____ **305962**
Hallmark / Jan '97 / Carlton

FOREVER AND EVER (18 Songs From The Heart)
Gambler: *Rogers, Kenny* / True love ways: *Holly, Buddy* / You're breaking my heart: *Rose Marie* / What a wonderful world: *Armstrong, Louis* / When your old wedding ring was new: *Longthorne, Joe* / Love letters: *Lester, Ketty* / Something's gotten hold of my heart: *Pitney, Gene* / It's only make believe: *Twitty, Conway* / Wind beneath my wings: *Greenwood, Lee* / Long arm of the law: *Rogers, Kenny* / Sweet dreams: *Cline, Patsy* / You're my best friend: *Williams, Don* / If I were you: *Judds* / Someone loves you honey: *Pride, Charley* / Jackson: *Sinatra, Nancy & Lee Hazelwood* / Just beyond the moon: *Ritter, Tex* / Dedicated to the one I love: *Mamas & The Papas* / Moonlight and roses: *Reeves, Jim*
CD ____ **PLATCD 3906**
Platinum / Jun '89 / Prism

FOREVER CELTIC
Still in love with you: *Thin Lizzy* / Deep in your heart: *Brady, Paul* / Borderline: *De Burgh, Chris* / Ancient rain: *Coughlan, Mary* / Gone to Pablo: *Bloom, Luka* / Gort na sailean: *Tamalin* / Against the wind: *Brennan, Maire* / New grange: *Clannad* / You're in my love: *Lohan, Sinead* / Wonderful thing: *Dowdall, Leslie* / Song for Ireland: *Black, Mary* / Forever frozen: *Spillane, Davy* / Place among the stones: *Spillane, Davy* / Three babies: *O'Connor, Sinead* / Ansacht na nansacht: *Aoife* / Parisienne walkways: *Moore, Gary* / Lonesome boatman: *Fureys* / Wall of tears: *Black, Frances* / Weakness in me: *Goss, Kieran*
CD ____ **RENCD 116**
Renaissance Collector Series / Jun '97 / BMG

FOREVER DOO WOP VOL.1 (2CD Set)
CD Set ____ **KNEWCD 738**
Kenwest / Apr '94 / THE

FOREVER DOO WOP VOL.2 (2CD Set)
CD Set ____ **KNEWCD 739**
Kenwest / Apr '94 / THE

FORMULE TECHNO VOL.1 (2CD Set)
CD Set ____ **7142615**
Fairway / Dec '96 / Cargo

FORMULE TECHNO VOL.2 (2CD Set)
CD Set ____ **7142628**
Fairway / Apr '97 / Cargo

FORTIES DANCE BAND HITS
There's a harbour of dreamboats / I'm gonna get lit up (when the lights go on in London) / Baby please stop and think about me / As time goes by / Coming in on a wing and a prayer / Why don't you fall in love with me / Ragtime cowboy Joe / I left my heart at the stage door canteen / Lady who didn't believe in love / Lover lullaby / Don't get around much anymore / It can't be wrong / Pistol packin' Mama / Sunday, Monday or always / Walkin' by the river / Mr. Five by five / If I had my way / In the blue of evening / Johnny Zero / What's the good word Mr Bluebird / Tell me the truth / Where's my love / So long Sarah Jane
CD ____ **RAJCD 818**
Empress / Jul '94 / Koch

FORTY SHADES OF GREEN
CD ____ **DCDCD 219**
Castle / Apr '96 / BMG

FORTY YEARS OF WOMEN IN JAZZ
CD Set ____ **JCD 09/10**
Jass / Oct '91 / ADA / Cadillac / CM / Direct / Jazz Music

FORWARD (Selection Of Top Greensleeves Singles 1977-1982)
Another one bites the dust: *Clint Eastwood & General Saint* / Wa-do-dem: *Eek-A-Mouse* / Diseases: *Michigan & Smiley* / Gun man: *Prophet, Michael* / Fattie boom boom: *Ranking Dread* / Born for a purpose: *Dr. Alimantado* / Bathroom sex: *General Echo* / War: *Wailing Souls* / Yellowman get's married: *Yellowman* / Fat she fat: *Holt, John*
CD ____ **GRELCD 60**
Greensleeves / Mar '94 / Jet Star / SRD

FOUND IN THE FLURRY
CD ____ **BEST 1073CD**
Acoustic Music / Nov '95 / ADA

FOUNDATIONS (The Big Issue LP - Coming Up From The Streets)
Talk show host: *Radiohead* / Tranquiliser busy tranquilising: *Orbital* / Mellow madness: *Guy Called Gerald, A & GK* / Spikee: *Underworld* / Mondays: *808 State* / Stunt bubble: *Fluke* / Hanging in midair: *Bomb The Bass* / Russian roulette: *Ultramarine* / Mother India: *Fun-Da-Mental* / Four friends and a microphone: *Black Dog* / Jat Scheelan: *Scanner* / Escape from Tokyo: *DJ Evolution & MC Teebag* / Bil let: *Bandulu* / Big sky city: *System 7* / Space shanty: *Leftfield* / Distant lands: *Menni* / Strange fever: *Future Loop Foundation* / Bambient: *Ege Bam Yasi* / Suck me up dub: *Massive Attack* / Only love (will lift us up): *Healing Arts & Jane Walker* / Let it roll: *DJ Crystal* / Saynaha: *Atlas* / March 19th: *Moody Boyz* / Bitter sweet: *Aloof*
CD ____ **FCL 002CD**
Feedback / Jan '97 / RTM/Disc

FOUR BITCHIN' BABES
CD ____ **SH 8018CD**
Shanachie / Nov '95 / ADA / Greensleeves / Koch

FOUR DECADES OF POP (2CD Set)
CD Set ____ **MBSCD 433**
Castle / Feb '95 / BMG

FOUR IN THE MORNING
It wasn't God that made honky tonk angels: *Wells, Kitty* / Ruby, don't take your love to town: *Rogers, Kenny* / Rose garden: *Anderson, Lynn* / Harper Valley PTA: *Riley, Jeannie C.* / No tomorrow in sight: *Nelson, Willie* / Jackson: *Lewis, Jerry Lee* / Big town: *Twitty, Conway* / Lonely woman make good lovers: *Luman, Bob* / Music city USA: *Bare, Bobby* / Wild side of life: *Thompson, Hank* / Rhinestone cowboy: *Campbell, Glen* / Satisfied mind: *Wagoner, Porter* / Rock Island line: *Cash, Johnny* / King of the road: *Miller, Roger* / Big bad John: *Dean, Jimmy* / Take me home: *Boxcar Willie* / Four in the morning: *Young, Faron*
CD ____ **11977**
Music / Feb '96 / Target/BMG

FOUR TRUMPET STARS: LOUIS, DIZZY, MILES & CHET
CD ____ **4749242**
Sony Jazz / Jan '95 / Sony

FOUR WOMEN BLUES (The Victor/ Bluebird Recordings)
I'm goin' back home: *Memphis Minnie* / Bumble bee blues: *Memphis Minnie* / I never told a lie: *Memphis Minnie* / Don't want no woman: *Memphis Minnie* / Georgia skin: *Memphis Minnie* / You wrecked my happy home: *Memphis Minnie* / I'm waiting on you: *Memphis Minnie* / Keep on goin': *Memphis Minnie* / When the sun goes down: *Memphis Minnie* / Hustlin' woman blues: *Memphis Minnie* / Selling my pork chops: *Memphis Minnie* / Doctor, doctor blues: *Memphis Minnie* / Hardworking woman blues: *Mississippi Matilda* / Happy home blues: *Mississippi Matilda* / Christmas mornin' blues: *Kansas City Kitty* / Double trouble blues: *Kansas City Kitty* / Leave my man alone: *Kansas City Kitty* / Mistreatin' easy rider: *Kansas City Kitty* / Staggering blues: *Moore, Miss Rosie Mae* / Ha ha blues: *Moore, Miss Rosie Mae* / School girl blues: *Moore, Miss Rosie Mae* / Stranger blues: *Moore, Miss Rosie Mae*
CD ____ **7863667192**
RCA / Feb '97 / BMG

FRANCOPHONIX
CD ____ **CPCD 8132**
Charly / Oct '95 / Koch

FRANKFURT HARD TRANCE HISTORY (3CD Set)
CD Set ____ **PIAS 556200825**
DJ's Present / Dec '96 / Plastic Head

FRANKLINTON MUSCATEL SOCIETY
CD ____ **CDBM 091**
Blue Moon / Apr '93 / Cadillac / Discovery / Greensleeves / Jazz Music / Jet Star / TKO Magnum

FREAKTOWN
CD ____ **EFA 12739CD**
Subterfuge / Mar '97 / SRD

FREAKY DANCE TRAXX
CD ____ **CCC 97002**
Citycat Club / Jul '97 / TKO Magnum

FREDDIE MCGREGOR PRESENTS THE BEST OF BIG SHIP
CD ____ **RASCD 3162**
Ras / Dec '95 / Direct / Greensleeves / Jet Star / SRD

FREE AT LAST (South Africa Outernational Meltdown Series)
Hungry on arrival / Giya kasiamore / Sanibonani / Ningakhali / Don't cry / Long walk to freedom / Bongani's theme
CD ____ **BW 076**
B&W / Nov '96 / New Note/Pinnacle / SRD / Vital/SAM

FREE SPIRIT
I want it all: *Queen* / If I could turn back time: *Cher* / Poison: *Cooper, Alice* / Talking to myself: *Terraplane* / It must have been love: *Roxette* / Need you tonight: *INXS* / Touch: *Noiseworks* / Best: *Tyler, Bonnie* / You took the words right out of my mouth: *Meat Loaf* / You give love a bad name: *Bon Jovi* / How can we be lovers: *Bolton, Michael* / I don't love you anymore: *Quireboys* / Carrie: *Europe* / Black velvet: *Myles, Alannah* / (I just) died in your arms: *Cutting Crew* / Flame: *Cheap Trick* / Living years: *Mike & The Mechanics*
CD ____ **MOODCD 16**
Columbia / Apr '91 / Sony

FREE THE FUNK VOL.1
Philip Marlow: *Word Up* / Where I'm going: *Fried Funk Food* / Punks not dead: *Dadamo* / Sundown: *Koh Tao* / Step into Eden: *Ballistic Brothers* / Dark jazz: *Daphreephunkateerz* / Drakes equation: *Spacer* / On da rocks: *Bangalter, Thomas* / Sportif: *Heights Of Abraham* / Hot flush: *Red Snapper* / Flow: *Model 500* / What I'm feelin' (good): *Nightmares On Wax*
CD ____ **RS 95085CD**
R&S / Jan '96 / Vital

FREE THE FUNK VOL.2
CD ____ **RS 96102CD**
R&S / Jul '96 / Vital

FREESTYLE CANDIES
CD ____ **KLNAGCD 2**
Klang / Dec '96 / Plastic Head

FREESTYLE VOL.4
Play your own risk: *Planet Patrol* / Promise me: *Lil Suzy* / I wanna be the one: *Stevie B* / Now I found you: *Garcia, Tony* / Don't go away: *Johnny O* / Bad of the heart: *Lamond, George* / Can I stop the love: *Naif* / I need you: *GT* / Someone to hold: *April* / If you were mine: *D'Lan, Lorenzo* / I believe: *April* / I can't live without you: *Garcia, Tony* / Up and down: *Chicco* / You are the only one: *Giant* / I'll be loving you: *Collage* / Holding on: *Torrez, Judy* / Shake your body: *Beat Production* / Limelight: *Dee, Gina*
CD ____ **ZYX 550772**
ZYX / Apr '97 / ZYX

FREEWAY
CD ____ **5259192**
PolyGram TV / Feb '96 / PolyGram

FREEZONE VOL.1 (The Phenomenology Of Ambient - 2CD Set)
CD Set ____ **SSR 129**
SSR / May '94 / Amato Disco / Grapevine/ PolyGram / Prime / RTM/Disc

FREEZONE VOL.3 (2CD Set)
CD Set ____ **SSR 167CD**
SSR / May '96 / Amato Disco / Grapevine/ PolyGram / Prime / RTM/Disc

FREEZONE VOL.4 (Dangerous Lullaby/ 2CD Set)
Space pin: *Basement Jaxx* / One: *Thievery Corporation* / Offset acoustics: *Flytronix* / Never tell you: *Rhythm & Sound* / Columbus: *Four Ears* / Key: *Tosca* / Lust in space: *Dimitri From Paris* / Trip to nowhere: *Funki Porcini* / Enlightment: *Endemic Void* / Supersex: *Morphine* / Once around the moon: *Stasis* / Blowin' it: *Only Child* / I wnt to...: *Geist, Morgan* / Night of the living blenders: *Fields, Jordan* / It could be g: *Craig, Carl* / Through the surface: *Jimpster* / Turn and waist: *Treva Whateva* / Young at heart: *Herbert & Love From San Francisco* / Boneskin: *Crewmunity* / Starting block: *Stade* / RSI: *Juryman & Spacer* / 10: *Juryman & Spacer* / Zoned: *Niew*
CD Set ____ **SSR 187CD**
SSR / Jun '97 / Amato Disco / Grapevine/ PolyGram / Prime / RTM/Disc

FRENCH COLLECTION
CD ____ **CDWNCD 2009**
Javelin / Jun '95 / Henry Hadaway / THE

FRENCH COLLECTION VOL.1
CD ____ **LECD 121**
Wisepack / Nov '94 / Conifer/BMG / THE

FRENCH COLLECTION VOL.1, THE
CD ____ **CD 352070**
Duchesse / May '93 / Pinnacle

FRENCH COLLECTION VOL.2
CD ____ **LECDD 635**
Wisepack / Aug '95 / Conifer/BMG / THE

FRENCH COLLECTION VOL.2, THE
CD ____ **CD 352133**
Duchesse / Jul '93 / Pinnacle

FRENCH COLLECTION VOL.3, THE
CD ____ **CD 352134**
Duchesse / Jul '93 / Pinnacle

FRENCH COLLECTION, THE (3CD Set)
CD Set ____ **CD 333503**
Duchesse / Nov '93 / Pinnacle

FRENCH FRIED FUNK (2CD Set)
CD Set ____ **SLIPCD 63**
Slip 'n' Slide / Aug '97 / Amato Disco / Prime / RTM/Disc / Vital

FRENCH-BELGIAN INDUSTRIES
CD ____ **MA 432**
Machinery / Apr '94 / Koch

FRENCHY SCISSORHANDS (The True Story Of Flicknife Records)
CD ____ **CDMGRAM 59**
Anagram / Jul '88 / Cargo / Pinnacle

FRENESI - 1940
Frenesi: *Shaw, Artie* / Koko: *Ellington, Duke* / Sweet Lorraine: *Cole, Nat 'King'* / Gilly: *Goodman, Benny* / Laughin': *Holiday, Billie* / Boo wah, boo wah: *Calloway, Cab* / Fats Waller's original E-flat blues: *Waller, Fats* / Swingtime up in Harlem: *Dorsey, Tommy* / When day is done: *Hawkins, Coleman* / Just like taking candy from a baby: *Astaire, Fred* / Boogie woogie on St. Louis blues: *Hines, Earl 'Fatha'* / Jack hits the road: *Freeman, Bud* / Louisiana: *Basie, Count* / I'll never smile again: *Dorsey, Tommy* / Boog it: *Miller, Glenn* / Singin' the blues: *Hackett, Bobby* / Okay for baby: *Lunceford, Jimmie* / 2.19 blues: *Armstrong, Louis* / Jazz me blues: *Bobcats* / King Porter stomp: *Metronome All Star Band*
CD ____ **PHONTCD 7668**
Phontastic / Apr '90 / Cadillac / Jazz Music / Wellard

FRESH BLUES
I've got the blues: *Blues Company* / Texas: *Connor, Joanna Band* / Broken hearted melody: *Webb, Stan & Chicken Shack* / Good morning love: *Allison, Luther* / Remembering love: *Cadillac Blues Band* / Red blood: *Blues Company* / Going down: *Allison, Bernard* / Roberta: *Electric Blues Duo* / It hurts me too: *Kelly, Dave Band* / Sky is crying: *Connor, Joanna Band* / Thrill is gone: *Farlowe, Chris & Peter York* / Don't you worry about a thing: *Webb, Stan & Chicken Shack* / Silent nite: *Blues Company*
CD ____ **INAK 19001CD**
In Akustik / Jul '97 / Direct / TKO Magnum

FRESH EMISSIONS (2CD Set)
Frust: *Being* / Try: *Being* / Anackrohn: *Vermin* / Afflicted: *Vermin* / Pedal bin liner boy melts the bag: *Bishop* / Charic roots: *Herb* / Splinter group: *Conemelt* / Hats off to tracksuit: *Conemelt* / Funny five minutes: *Panash* / Lemmy parts 1 and 2: *Panash* / Space is forever: *Uriel* / Andromeda session: *Uriel* / Through mist at one hundred: *Two Lone Swordsman* / Midnight automatic: *Day, Deanne* / No-fi: *Corridor* / 1: *Bios* / 2: *Bios*
CD Set ____ **SOP 005CD**
Emissions / Nov '95 / Amato Disco / Vital

FRESH HITS 1996
Killing me softly: *Fugees* / Macarena: *Los Del Rio* / Crazy: *Morrison, Mark* / Mysterious girl: *Andre, Peter* / Better watch out: *Ant & Dec* / Nobody knows: *Rich, Tony Project* / You're making me high: *Braxton, Toni* / Because you loved me: *Dion, Celine* / We're in this together: *Simply Red* / Three lions: *Baddiel & Skinner & Lightning Seeds* / We've got it goin' on: *Backstreet Boys* / Naked: *Louise* / Freedom 90: *Michael, George* / Walking wounded: *Everything But The Girl* / Don't stop movin': *Livin' Joy* / Good thing: *Eternal* / Fable: *Miles, Robert* / X files: *DJ Dado* / That look: *De'Lacy* / Where love lives: *Limerick, Alison* / Krupa: *Apollo 440* / Born Slippy: *Underworld* / Design for life: *Manic Street Preachers* / Oh yeah: *Ash* / Tattva: *Kula Shaker* / Trash: *Suede* / Day we caught the train: *Ocean Colour Scene* / Sale of the century: *Sleeper* / Champagne supernova: *Oasis* / Peaches: *Presidents Of The USA* / 500 (Shake baby shake): *Lush* /

Female of the species: *Space* / 24/7: *3T* / Lifted: *Lighthouse Family* / Do you know where you're coming from: *M-Beat & Jamiroquai* / Woo hah got you all in check: *Busta Rhymes* / Tha crossroads: *Bone Thugs n' Harmony* / You're the one: *SMV* / I can't sleep baby (If I): *R Kelly* / Something for the weekend: *Divine Comedy* / Daydream believer: *Robson & Jerome*
CD ____ **MOODCD 46**
Sony Music / Aug '96 / Sony

FRESH HITS 1997 (2CD Set)
CD Set ____ **RADCD 70**
Global TV / Aug '97 / BMG

FRESH RECORDS PUNK SINGLES COLLECTION
My friends: *Dark* / John Wayne: *Dark* / Einstein's brain: *Dark* / On the wires: *Dark* / Masque: *Dark* / Punk rock stars: *Art Attacks* / Rat city: *Art Attacks* / Madman: *Cuddly Toys* / Astral Joe: *Cuddly Toys* / Someone's crying: *Cuddly Toys* / It's a shame: *Cuddly Toys* / Hawaii Five-O: *Dark* / Young one's: *Menace* / Debbie Harry: *Family Fodder* / I've had the time of my life: *Manufactured Romance* / Hobby for a day: *Wall* / Earbending: *JC's Mainmen* / Poison takes hold: *Play Dead* / Rebecca's room: *Wasted Youth* / Puppets of war: *Chron Gen* / TV eye: *Play Dead*
CD ____ **CDPUNK 32**
Anagram / May '94 / Cargo / Pinnacle

FRESH, SHARP AND SWEET
CD ____ **NTRCD 056**
Nectar / Jun '97 / Pinnacle

FRESHEN UP VOL.1
U sure do: *Strike* / Love come rescue me: *Lovestation* / Saved: *Mr. Roy* / Feel the spirit: *Giant City* / Do U feel 4 me: *Eden* / Open sesame: *Jinx* / Love (A wonderful thing): *Karess* / Shine on me: *Lovestation* / Formula 1: *Strike* / Something about U: *Mr. Roy* / Best of my love: *Lovestation* / Control: *Time Of The Mumph*
CD ____ **FRSHCD 1**
Fresh / May '95 / 3mv/Sony / Mo's Music Machine / Prime

FRESHNESS ON WAX - PHUNK NOT PUNK (Further Adventures In Quality Dope Beats)
CD ____ **DBMFLAGCD 113**
Flagbearer / Jun '96 / SRD / Timewarp

FRESKA VOL.2
Dreamer: *Livin' Joy* / Don't wait for me: *Loveland* / I believe: *Happy Clappers* / Taking me higher: *Gems For Jem* / Invader: *Kool World* / Horny as funk: *Soapy* / Love and sex: *Boyfriend* / Ooh baby: *Raw Tunes* / Hot: *Majick Village* / It's alright: *SAIN* / Dance MF: *Nelson, Grant* / Latinos on parade: *Franco, Chinco* / Let the rhythm flow: *Diva Rhythms* / You can have it: *Casanova, Charlie* / Fe fi fo fum: *Raw* / Do you wanna party: *Wand & Storm HQ* / Sex on the streets: *Pizzaman* / Krazy noise: *Numerical Value*
CD ____ **REACTCDX 061**
CD ____ **REACTCD 061**
React / Jun '95 / Arabesque / Prime / Vital

FRIED TO PERFECTION BY EXPERTS
Mary Queen of Scots: *Eugenius* / Pillow fight: *18 Wheeler* / Wet dream: *18 Wheeler* / Butterfly boy: *Shonen Knife* / Get the wow: *Shonen Knife* / Apple: *Boyfriend* / Summer thing: *Boyfriend* / Don't get 2 close 2 my fantasy: *Ween* / Sarah: *Ween* / She must be Spanish: *Autohaze* / Here tonight: *Autohaze* / Plant me: *Suddenly Tammy*
CD ____ **RUST 011CD**
August / Sep '93 / 3mv/Vital

FRIENDS IN HIGH PLACES VOL.1 (14 Urban Contemporary Gospel & Inspired Soul Performances)
More than a friend: *Baylor, Helen* / Out front: *Angel* / You changed my life: *Marquis Ubu* / Thank you Jesus: *Jasper, Chris* / Call me: *Smith, Kenny* / Step by step: *Hammond, Fred* / One love one people: *Taylor, Gary* / I'll shine for you: *Austin, Dennis* / Empty promises: *Futrel* / God in you: *Dawkins & Dawkins* / Will you be ready: *Redeemed* / It's only natural: *Thomas, Keith* / Be for real: *Mitchell, Vernessa* / Love's the key: *Gaines, Billy & Sarah*
CD ____ **CDEXP 5**
Expansion / Dec '93 / 3mv/Sony

FRIENDS IN HIGH PLACES VOL.2 (14 Urban Contemporary Gospel & Inspired Soul Performances)
Any way: *Garmon, Terry* / Every time: *Winans, Cece* / My treasure: *Baker, Sam* / If I ever fall: *Winans* / Don't be afraid: *Kingdom* / Turn to Jesus: *Moss, J.* / Heaven is mine: *Futch Brothers* / Thank you Lord: *Disciples Of Christ* / Miracle: *Clarke Sisters* / Never alone: *Williams, Kelli* / Call on me: *Staten, Keith* / Over and over again: *Sapp, Marvin* / Whatever it takes: *Sign Of The Times* / Call his name: *Hewett, Howard*
CD ____ **CDEXP 10**
Expansion / Jun '96 / 3mv/Sony

FRIFOT
CD ____ **CAP 2138CD**
Caprice / Nov '95 / ADA / Cadillac / CM / Complete/Pinnacle

FROM ACOUSTIC TO ELECTRIC BLUES
CD ____ **D2CD 08**
Deja Vu / Dec '92 / THE

FROM BAM BAM TO CHERRY OH BABY
Bam bam: *Toots & The Maytals* / Ba ba boom: *Jamaicans* / Intensified: *Dekker, Desmond* / Sweet and dandy: *Toots & The Maytals* / Boom shacka lacka: *Lewis, Hopeton* / Unity is love: *Dice, Billy* / Da da: *Byles, Junior* / Pomp and pride: *Toots & The Maytals* / Festival 10: *Morgan, Derrick* / Cherry oh baby: *Donaldson, Eric*
CD ____ **JMC 200101**
Jamaican Gold / Nov '92 / Grapevine/ PolyGram / Jet Star

FROM BRUSSELS WITH LOVE
CD ____ **TWI 0072**
Les Disques Du Crepuscule / Mar '96 / Discovery

FROM DIXIELAND TO SWING
CD ____ **D2CD 09**
Deja Vu / Dec '92 / THE

FROM GALWAY TO DUBLIN
CD ____ **ROUCD 1087**
Rounder / Feb '93 / ADA / CM / Direct

FROM HERE TO TRANQUILITY VOL.1
CD ____ **PS 9336**
Silent / Nov '93 / Cargo / Plastic Head

FROM HERE TO TRANQUILITY VOL.2
CD ____ **SR 9343**
Silent / May '94 / Cargo / Plastic Head

FROM HERE TO TRANQUILITY VOL.3
CD ____ **SR 9460**
Silent / Feb '95 / Cargo / Plastic Head

FROM HORSE TO TANK
Boots and saddles: *Queen's Royal Hussars* / Royal Tank Regiment: *Royal Tank Regiment Bands* / Light Cavalry Overture: *9/12 Royal Lancers* / Fear naught: *Royal Tank Regiment Bands* / With sword and lance: *16th/5th Queen's Royal Lancers* / Vimy ridge: *Royal Tank Regiment Bands* / Old grey mare: *16th/5th Queen's Royal Lancers* / Blue flash: *Royal Tank Regiment Bands* / Final charge: *Queen's Dragoon Guards* / Scarlet and green: *16th/5th Queen's Royal Lancers* / Fifth Royal Tank Regiment: *Royal Tank Regiment Bands* / St. Cecilia: *9th/12th Royal Lancers* / Evening hymm and cavalry last post: *9th/12th Royal Lancers* / Tank town: *Royal Tank Regiment Bands* / Thin red line: *16th/5th Queen's Royal Lancers* / March past: *Royal Tank Regiment Bands*
CD ____ **305192**
Hallmark / Jun '97 / Carlton

FROM MOUNTAIN AND VALLEY
CD ____ **QPRZ 006D**
Polyphonic / Jun '91 / Complete/Pinnacle

FROM NASHVILLE WITH LOVE
CD ____ **CURCD 035**
Curb / Apr '97 / Grapevine/PolyGram

FROM OUT OF NOWHERE VOL.1
Shove: *Cosmic Psychos* / Modern girl: *Dubrovniks* / Heading right back to you: *Dubrovniks* / Build it up: *Nursery Crimes* / Eleanor Rigby: *Nursery Crimes* / Fatal fascination: *Screaming Tribesmen* / Bugging: *Screemfeeder* / End of this day: *Screemfeeder* / Dreaming: *Chevelles* / Run and hide: *Chevelles* / Degenerate boy: *Bored* / Rain: *Bored* / Shame: *You Am I* / Snake tide: *You Am I* / Cheers: *Front & Loader* / Me to know: *Front & Loader* / Chrysalidz: *Mass Appeal*
CD ____ **SUR 525CD**
Survival / Jun '93 / ADA / Pinnacle

FROM REELS TO RAGA (A Musical Journey Around The World/2CD Set)
Lodge road/From night till morn / Scotland the brave / Road to Sligo/Tripping up the stairs / All through the night / Le village Francais / La vino chianti / Refleo del agua / Cantares do emigrante / Eine kleine biermusik / Alpenzauber / Szomoru vasarnap / Danse Roumaine / Svietit Miessiatz / Nasza muzyka / Enzeli / A night in Plaka / Loukoum / Sh' dematy / Bedouin music & dance / Ras el hanout / Banani / Ewondo / Benguela / Upendo wa bwana / Tugela kwela / Raga bhairava / Tarian Asyek / Tchang fou / Tchango-tchoum / Summer / Umeke ohana / Milongueo del ayer / Rin del angelito / Huayno de la roca / Las calenas / Samba carnaval / Antigua / Mambo y cha cha cha / La cucaracha / Tender hearted cowboys
CD Set ____ **330172**
Hallmark / Jul '96 / Carlton

FROM SWEDEN TO AMERICA
CD ____ **CAP 21552CD**
Caprice / Aug '96 / ADA / Cadillac / CM / Complete/Pinnacle

FROM THE CORNERS OF THE WORLD
CD ____ **CAP 21468CD**
Caprice / May '97 / ADA / Cadillac / CM / Complete/Pinnacle

FROM THE DANUBE TO THE BALKAN (Music From Bulgaria)
CD ____ **CMT 274981**
La Chant Du Monde / Dec '95 / ADA / Harmonia Mundi

FROM THE DERWENT TO THE GARONNE
CD ____ **ALIENCD 6**
Alienor / May '97 / Cargo

FROM THE HEART
CD ____ **STACD 051**
Wisepack / Sep '94 / Conifer/BMG / THE

FROM THE HEART (Corason Sampler)
CD ____ **CORACD 701**
Corason / Feb '95 / ADA / CM / Direct

FROM THE IRISH TRADITION VOL.3
CD ____ **CDTCD 003**
Gael Linn / Dec '94 / ADA / CM / Direct / Grapevine/PolyGram / Roots

FROM THE MOUNTAINS TO THE SEA (The Music Of Peru/The 1960's)
El contrapunto: *Los Mensajeros De La Libertad* / El inmenso altiplano: *Los Kcollas* / El penado: *Barssy, Jorge Y Su Conjunto* / Separacion: *Los Tupas* / Soy trujillanita: *Banda Sinfonica Sunicancha* / Manana me voy: *Solitaria Andajina* / Ayhuala: *Banda Filarmonica Andajina* / Te quiero porque me queres: *Boachet, Beto* / Mi china Lola: *Conjunto Cachicadan* / El pelicano: *Coronado, Blackie* / El serranito: *Los Ases Del Ande* / El Alcatraz: *Coronado, Blackie* / Que viva el Santo: *Conjunto Los Chiroques* / Cachirpunta: *Conjunto Virgen De Natividad De Cajamarquilla* / Ingrata huancay bambina: *Los Canarios Del Peru* / El proletario: *Conjunto Los Condores De Parinacocha* / Pretenciosa huancaynita: *Trio Los Andes* / Gorrioncito: *Picaflor De Los Andes* / Vicunita de ancahuasi: *Conjunto Costumbrista* / Ardorosa pasion: *Juajina, Alam Conjunto* / Ayacuchana: *Conjunto Lira Folklorica Del Peru* / Vicunitas de atlas punas: *Conjunto San Cristobel De Bishongo* / La ultima copa: *Jara, Alberto* / 039: *Avila, Tito Y Sus Costenos* / El consuelo de llorar: *Los Yungas* / Los pampa y la puna: *Los Dandys Y Su Conjunto* / Soy criollo: *Los Monarcos*
CD ____ **ARHCD 400**
Arhoolie / Nov '96 / ADA / Cadillac / Direct

FROM YOURS TO YOU...A VALENTINE BOUQUET (20 Sweet & Sentimental Love Songs)
My melancholy baby: *Crosby, Bing* / Begin the beguine: *Andrews Sisters* / I should care: *Winstone, Eric & His Orchestra* / In a shady nook by a babbling brook: *Peers, Donald* / Very thought of you: *Holiday, Billie* / All I do is dream of you: *Miller, Glenn Orchestra* / That's my home: *Gonella, Nat & His New Georgians* / Laura: *Shelton, Anne* / Kiss me again: *Sinatra, Frank* / I remember you: *Dorsey, Jimmy & His Orchestra* / I'll close my eyes: *Squires, Dorothy* / I had the craziest dream: *Lynn, Vera* / No one else will do: *Preager, Lou & His Orchestra* / It can't be wrong: *Carless, Dorothy* / Way you look tonight: *Astaire, Fred* / Masquerade is over: *Daniels, Bebe* / Nearness of you: *Lombardo, Guy & His Royal Canadians* / Night and day: *Bowlly, Al* / At last: *Geraldo & His Orchestra* / Embraceable you: *Garland, Judy*
CD ____ **EMPUCD 1**
Empress / Jan '97 / Koch

FRONTLINE REGGAE
CD ____ **CONQ 998CD**
Conqueror / May '95 / Grapevine/ PolyGram / Jet Star

FROZEN BRASS: AFRICA & LATIN AMERICA
CD ____ **PAN 2026CD**
Pan / Oct '93 / ADA / CM / Direct

FRUIT OF THE ORIGINAL SIN
CD ____ **TWI 0352**
Les Disques Du Crepuscule / Mar '96 / Discovery

FRYING THE FAT
Jazz hypnosis: *First Priority* / Concentrate: *Aim* / In Rhodes: *Rae & Christian* / Dirty dog: *Tony D* / Diggin' Dizzy: *Aim* / Free rolling: *Rae* / I thought I'd find you here: *Howie, Alex* / Still blowin' free: *Funky Fresh Few* / Ways of the underground: *Funky Fresh Few* / Pure arithmetic: *First Priority* / Let the funk ride: *Aim* / Bang bang: *Howie, Alex* / Fat slug: *Mr. Scruff* / First cut is the deepest: *First Priority* / Central J Parlay: *Tony D*
CD ____ **GCCD 100**
Grand Central / Jun '96 / Vital

FUBAR CLUB, THE (2CD Set)
CD Set ____ **FARCD 1**
Inner Rhythm / Jul '96 / Alphamagic

FUCKING HARDCORE VOL.1
CD ____ **MOK 99CD**
Mokum / Sep '93 / Pinnacle

FUCKING HARDCORE VOL.3
Fucking hardcore: *Chosen Few* / I wanna be a hippy: *Technohead* / Freak tonight: *Speedfreak* / Edge of panic: *Cyanide* / Realm of darkness: *Annihilator* / Abba gabba: *Riot Nation* / Toxic waste 396: *High Energy* / Headsex: *Technohead* / Don't fuck with me: *Original Gabber* / To da rhythm: *Dee, Lenny* / Voodoo vibe: *Tellurian* / Happ-e-people: *Search & Destroy* / We keep going on: *Riot Nation* / This is not the end: *One, Walter* / Energy boost: *DJ Dano & Liza N. Eliaz*
CD ____ **DB 47932**
Deep Blue / Jul '95 / PolyGram

FUCKING HARDCORE VOL.4
CD ____ **DB 47882**
Deep Blue / Apr '96 / PolyGram

FUCKING HARDCORE VOL.5
CD ____ **DB 47842**
Deep Blue / Nov '96 / PolyGram

FUCKING HARDCORE VOL.6
Fucking hardcore no.6: *Chosen Few* / Sound of the underground: *Tellurian* / Hardcore headz: *Outside Agency* / T-1000: *Fear Factory* / Thermal fuse: *Demolition Team* / Big time noise: *DJ Dano* / Stormfront: *Painkiller* / Live in hell: *Walter One* / Zlam (here it comez): *Chosen Few* / Speaker blow: *Ceasefire* / Name of the DJ: *Chosen Few* / I won't stop rocking: *Tellurian* / Narcoterror: *Elvis Jackson* / Touch the darkness: *Outside Agency* / Trip 2 pussyland: *Search & Destroy* / Speedjack: *Walter One* / Starcore: *Aggroman*
CD ____ **DB 47822**
Mokum / Jul '97 / Pinnacle

FUCKING HARDFLOOR VOL.1 & 2 (2CD Set)
CD Set ____ **ATOM 005DCD**
Atomic Fate Inc / Oct '95 / Plastic Head

FULL ENERGY VOL.1
CD ____ **ZEN 007CD**
Indochina / Feb '96 / Pinnacle

FULL VELOCITY (Progressive Drum 'n' Bass)
CD ____ **RZ 012CD**
Runningz / May '97 / SRD

FULL-E RECORDS VOL.1
CD ____ **FUE C1**
Full-E / Nov '95 / Plastic Head

FULSOM PRISON BLUES
CD ____ **MACCD 215**
Autograph / Aug '96 / BMG

FUN OF THE FAIR
Cabaret / Me and my shadow / Ciribiribin / Stripper / Can can / My blue heaven / Viva Espana / Twelfth street rag / I do like to be beside the seaside / At the Darktown strutter's ball / King cotton / Waiting for the Robert E Lee / Carolina in the morning / Pretty baby / Toot toot tootsie goodbye / I'm sitting on top of the world / I'm looking over a four leaf clover / Chinatown, my Chinatown / Baby face / California here I come / Avalon / Little boogie / Skokiaan / Annen polka / Day trip to Bangor / Roses from the South / Eleanor waltz / Dinah / Alexander's ragtime band
CD ____ **SOV 007CD**
Sovereign / Jun '92 / Target/BMG

FUN WHILE IT LASTED
Safety net: *Shop Assistants* / Cuticles: *Househunters* / E 102: *BMX Bandits* / Steaming train: *Talulah Gosh* / Assumption as an elevator: *Boy Hairdressers* / Son of a gun: *Vaselines* / You make my head explode: *Groovy Little Numbers* / Talulah Gosh: *Talulah Gosh* / Johnny Alucard: *BMX Bandits* / Surf's up: *Beat Poets* / Molly's lips: *Vaselines* / Strawberry girl: *Talulah Gosh*
CD ____ **ONLYCD 006**
Avalanche / May '97 / RTM/Disc

FUN WITH MUSHROOMS
Toadstool soup (slight send slight return): *Boris & His Bolshie Balalaika* / Night descent: *Bazaar, Saddar* / Electric sensation: *Praise Space Electric* / Yuppi deadhead party: *14th Wray* / Government surplus 3am: *Carter, Dean & The High Commission* / Awakened: *Omnia Opera* / Who's my name: *Inn* / Uncle Sam: *Juana, Harold* / Chocolate staircase: *Dead Flowers* / Half moon flower: *Tangle Edge* / Did you feed the fish: *Watch children* / Thoughts of the sky: *Wobble jaggle jiggle* / Thought dial: *Mooseheart Faith* / Ritual people: *Cosmic kangaroos* / Mr. and Mrs. Creature: *Reefus moons* / Thirteen ghosts: *Marshmallow Overcoat* / Freakbeat: *Dr. Brown* / River: *Jasmine Love Bomb*
CD ____ **DELECCD 009**
Delerium / Jun '93 / Cargo / Pinnacle / Vital

FUNKIEST LINE DANCE ALBUM IN THE WORLD, THE
Why'da pick on me: *Swamp Honkys* / Fool and his money: *Hawks, Chip* / What a man's gotta do: *Shot To Pieces* / Thinkin' 'bout you: *Capricorn* / I don't do sad anymore: *Richmond, Simon* / No money: *Payne, Les* / Honky tonk ballroom: *Richmond, Simon* / Freeze: *Caffrey, Phil* / Arlene: *Capricorn* / Outta my head: *Swamp Honkys* / Bullet proof vest: *Shot To Pieces* / Picture frame: *Capricorn* / R 'n' R time capsule: *Weller, Freddy* / I must be stupid: *Swamp Honkys* / Don't let go: *Shot To Pieces* / Whatever it takes: *Richmond, Simon* / Born in Britain: *Corridor 38* / Goodbye love (hello heartache): *Richmond, Simon* / Hand clappin', foot tappin', good lookin' girl: *Capricorn* / Caroline: *Richmond, Simon*
CD ____ **ECD 3374**
K-Tel / Jun '97 / K-Tel

FUNKMASTER MIX (2CD Set)
Word up: *Cameo* / Oops up side your head: *Gap Band* / Movin': *Brass Construction* / Funky Nassau: *Beginning Of The End* / Brick house: *Commodores* / (Are you ready) Do the bus stop: *Fatback Band* / Papa's got

a brand new pigbag: *Pigbag* / Get up offa that thing: *Brown, James* / Funkin' for Jamaica: *Browne, Tom* / Stomp: *Brothers Johnson* / Tell me something good: *Rufus* / War: *Starr, Edwin* / Shaft: *Hayes, Isaac* / Cuba: *Gibson Brothers* / Shoorah shoorah: *Wright, Betty* / Funky weekend: *Stylistics* / That lady: *Isley Brothers* / Sound that funky horn: *KC & The Sunshine Band* / Play that funky music: *Wild Cherry* / Hang on in there baby: *Bristol, Johnny* / Le freak: *Chic* / Lady Marmalade: *Labelle* / Get down on it: *Kool & The Gang* / Let's groove: *Earth, Wind & Fire* / Shake your body: *Jacksons* / Rock the boat: *Hues Corporation* / Move on up: *Mayfield, Curtis* / Strut your funky stuff: *Frantique* / Car wash: *Rose Royce* / Shame: *King, Evelyn 'Champagne'* / Ain't no stoppin' us: *McFadden & Whitehead* / Family affair: *Sly & The Family Stone* / If you're ready (come go with me): *Staple Singers* / Behind the groove: *Marie, Teena* / Forget me nots: *Rushen, Patrice* / Use it up and wear it out: *Odyssey* / Boogie nights: *Heatwave* / Pick up the pieces: *Average White Band* / Rock it: *Hancock, Herbie* / Green onions: *Booker T & The MG's*
CD Set ______ **5355762**
PolyGram TV / May '96 / PolyGram

FUNKY ALTERNATIVES (The Best Of Funky Alternatives)
CD ______ **INDIGO 41412**
Echo Beach / May '97 / Cargo / Shellshock/Disc

FUNKY ALTERNATIVES VOL.7
CD ______ **CPRODCD 021**
Concrete Productions / Feb '94 / Cargo / Plastic Head

FUNKY ALTERNATIVES VOL.8
Menofearthe reaper: *Pop Will Eat Itself* / Pure spite: *Godflesh* / Crackin' up: *Revolting Cocks* / You coma: *Optimum Wound Profile* / Bombs in my head: *Ultraviolence* / Momentous lamentous: *Pig* / Mind razor: *Gunshot* / Untitled: *Surfers for Satan* / Obsession: *Shining* / We know who you are: *Judda* / Compassion: *Mussolini Headkick*
CD ______ **CPRODCD 026**
Concrete Productions / Mar '95 / Cargo / Plastic Head

FUNKY CHICKEN
CD ______ **CDTBL 137**
Trojan / Aug '96 / Direct / Jet Star

FUNKY GUITAR BEATS
Fire eater: *Bryant, Rusty* / Odds on: *Kynard, Charles* / Dirty apple: *Smith, Johnny 'Hammond'* / Thank you: *Sparks, Melvin* / Sweet Georgia Brown: *Butler, Billy* / We'll be together: *Jones, Ivan 'Boogaloo Joe'* / Shadow dancers: *Benson, George* / Swivel hips: *Jackson, Willis* / Thrill is gone: *Funk Inc.* / Billie Jean: *Ponder, Jimmy*
CD ______ **PRCD 24162**
Prestige / Jun '96 / Cadillac / Complete/ Pinnacle

FUNKY JAMS VOL.1
Space funk: *Manzel* / Did you mean it: *Bell, Arlene* / Family tree: *Family Tree* / Give the drummer some more: *Little Hooks & Ray Nato/The Kings* / Searching for the soul pt.1 and 2: *Wade, Jake & The Soul Searchers* / Watermelon man: *Smith, Miss Elsie* / Sorry 'bout that: *Poole, Benny* / For your love: *1619 Bab* / Lunar funk: *Fabulous Counts* / Superpeople: *Notations* / Cold bear: *Gaturs* / Skin it back pt.1 and 2: *Bush, Tommy*
CD ______ **HUBCD 1**
Hubbub / Aug '95 / Beechwood/BMG / SRD / Timewarp

FUNKY JAMS VOL.2
Whatcha want us to do pt.1: *Dynamic Concepts* / Sweet Peter pt.1 and 2: *Nichols, Frieda & Homer Brown Group* / Chocolate sugar: *Berry Street Station* / D minor vamp: *Yesterday, Today & Tomorrow* / Honey trippin': *Mystic Moods* / Let's keep on jukin': *King Tutt & The Untouchables* / Wastin' no time: *New Editions* / Nabbit juice pt.1: *Eastwind* / Do what you want to do: *Chapter II* / Whole thing: *Big Barney* / Impeach the president: *Honey Drippers*
CD ______ **HUBCD 2**
Hubbub / Sep '95 / Beechwood/BMG / SRD / Timewarp

FUNKY JAMS VOL.3
Cornbread and beans: *Brodie, Hugh* / Can you feel it: *SOUL* / Stand up and be counted: *Getto Kitty* / Machine shop pt.2: *Untouchable Machine Shop* / My friend: *Marrero, Ricardo & The Group* / Freakin' time: *Asphalt Jungle* / Ain't it good enough: *Nu Sound Express Ltd* / Funky key: *Dynamics* / Funky four corners: *Marks, Richard* / She's a love maker: *Fields, Lee* / Time to love: *Candy Coated People* / Boot's groove: *Soul Tornadoes*
CD ______ **HUBCD 4**
Hubbub / Nov '95 / Beechwood/BMG / SRD / Timewarp

FUNKY JAMS VOL.4
Swivel your hips: *Gaturs* / Fatbackin': *Fatback Band* / Reborn: *Barbarin, Marilyn* / Crackerjack: *Mickey & His Mice* / Hey Ruby (shut your mouth): *Ruby & The Party Gang* / Stories: *Chakchas* / Cookies: *Brother Soul* / Earthquake pt.1 & 2: *Brand New* / World: *1619 Bab* / Don't push your luck: *Peacemakers* / Soul Makossa: *Kenyatta, Simon Troup* / Catch a groove: *Juice*
CD ______ **HUBCD 6**
Hubbub / Mar '96 / Beechwood/BMG / SRD / Timewarp

FUNKY JAMS VOL.5
CD ______ **HUBCD 7**
Hubbub / May '96 / Beechwood/BMG / SRD / Timewarp

FUNKY JAMS VOL.6
CD ______ **HUBCD 10**
Hubbub / Sep '96 / Beechwood/BMG / SRD / Timewarp

FUNKY JAMS VOL.7
CD ______ **HUBCD 15**
Hubbub / Feb '97 / Beechwood/BMG / SRD / Timewarp

FUNKY JAMS VOL.8
I'm a carpenter: *Robinson, David* / Down the line: *Chocolate Fudge Express* / I've got reasons: *Hooper, Mary Jane* / Live it up: *James K Nine* / In one piece: *In One Piece* / Funk time: *Funk Proof* / Can I be your squeeze: *Garbo, Chuck* / Spread the news: *Perfect Circle* / Beaver shot: *Atlantics* / Inside America: *Murray, Juggy* / Kickin' the habit: *Johnson, Jesse* / Kiss by kiss: *Johnson, Syl*
CD ______ **HUBCD 18**
Hubbub / Mar '97 / Beechwood/BMG / SRD / Timewarp

FUNKY NIGHTS (2CD Set)
Heaven must be missing an angel: *Tavares* / Car wash: *Rose Royce* / We are family: *Sister Sledge* / More than woman: *Tavares* / He's the greatest dancer: *Sister Sledge* / Wishing on a star: *Rose Royce* / Medley 1: *Tavares* / I wanna get next to you: *Rose Royce* / True love: *Sister Sledge* / Motown Philly: *Tavares* / Brother brother stop: *Sister Sledge* / Frankie: *Sister Sledge* / Bad times: *Tavares* / Is it love you're after: *Rose Royce* / Never had love like this before: *Tavares* / Medley 2: *Sister Sledge* / Do your dance: *Rose Royce* / Turn your love around: *Tavares* / I'm in love (and I love the feeling): *Rose Royce* / Everybody dance: *Sister Sledge* / Can't take the blame for losing you: *Tavares* / Love of the Lord: *Sister Sledge* / You are the words: *Tavares*
CD Set ______ **TNC 96212**
Natural Collection / Aug '96 / Target/BMG

FUNKY TALES (Southern Fried Funk From Excello, A-Bet & Mankind Records)
Little Royal freeze: *Little Royal* / Daddy don't know about Sugar Bear: *Whitney, Marva* / Baby don't do it to me: *Washington, Jerry* / Funky tale to tell: *Maceo & All The King's Men* / I ain't gonna tell (nobody): *Brown, Shirley* / Maybe your baby: *Nazty* / I got my finger on your trigger: *Harpo, Slim* / Chain of fools: *Brown, Jimmy* / Boogaloo investigator: *Exotics* / Music for the brothers: *Solicitors* / Bus stop: *Sain, Oliver* / Shaky pudding: *Morrison, Jesse* / Precious woman: *Dynamic Corvettes* / Keep on loving: *Little Royal* / Love to hate: *North, Freddie* / Your good good loving: *Powell, Bobby* / Ain't nothing in the streets: *Stanback, Jean* / I'd do it all over you: *Duke, Doris* / Do your thing: *Whitney, Marva* / I got to move: *Nazty* / Let our music make love to you: *Ureaus* / Party hearty: *Sain, Oliver* / Born to wander: *Maceo & All The King's Men* / We need more (but somebody gotta sacrifice): *Marva & Ellis*
CD ______ **CDSEWD 111**
Southbound / Jun '96 / Pinnacle

FUNKYDESERTBREAKS
CD ______ **MM 800542**
Moonshine / Sep '96 / Mo's Music Machine / Prime / RTM/Disc

FURRY LOGIC VOL.1
Microgravity: *Heard, Larry* / Obrigado: *Fila Brazillia* / Donau experience: *Count Basic* / Orbit 1: *Playing For The City* / Sugarplums: *Marden Hill* / Wild strawberry: *Dub Alchemist* / Frozen hands: *Neotropic* / I see: *Ozman* / Post-sunset misunderstanding: *Fauna Flash* / Finley's rainbow: *Guy Called Gerald* / Bengali song: *Sawhney, Nitin* / One day in paradise: *Padilla, Jose*
CD ______ **FLCD 001**
Furry Logic / Jul '97 / Pinnacle

FURTHER EAST
CD ______ **SPCD 07**
Superpower / Mar '97 / Jet Star

FURTHER SELF EVIDENT TRUTHS VOL.1
CD ______ **RSNCD 31**
Rising High / Apr '95 / 3mv/Sony

FURTHER SELF EVIDENT TRUTHS VOL.2
CD ______ **RSNCD 39**
Rising High / Aug '95 / 3mv/Sony

FURTHER SELF EVIDENT TRUTHS VOL.3
CD ______ **RSNCD 43**
Rising High / Apr '96 / 3mv/Sony

FURTHUR MORE
CD ______ **HY 20003**
Hybrid / Jul '97 / Greyhound

FURY, THE
CD ______ **DBM 2053**
Death Becomes Me / Jul '97 / Grapevine/ PolyGram / Pinnacle / SRD

FURY-MENTAL
Surfin' gorilla: *Surfin' Gorillas* / Friction: *Arousers* / Rhythm riot: *Potter, Jeff* / Mooncrest: *Muskrats* / Fury: *Razorbacks* / Warpath: *Rough Diamonds* / Bronco loco: *Condo, Ray* / Strollin' guitar: *Higham, Darrel* / Mohawk twist: *Jackals* / Green Jeans: *Rapiers* / Stampede: *Bopshack Stompers* / Stiletto: *Blue Devils* / Dinosaur: *Hot Boogie Chillun* / Lockjaw: *Roadrunners* / Rattlesnake: *Haywire* / Roswell crash: *Atomic Spuds* / Gypsy beat: *Flames* / Invitation to death: *Playboys* / Haunted highway: *Terry, Iain* / Run chicken run: *School House Rock*
CD ______ **FCD 3051**
Fury / May '97 / Nervous / TKO Magnum

FUSE VOL.1 & 2
CD ______ **NATCD 35**
Nation / Jul '94 / RTM/Disc

FUSE VOL.3 (Global Chaos)
CD ______ **NRCD 1063**
Nation / May '96 / RTM/Disc

FUSED (35 New Directions In Indie-Dance/2CD Set)
Saint: *Orbital* / It's no good: *Depeche Mode* / Scared: *Slacker* / Prophet: *Bolland, C.J.* / Firestarter: *Prodigy* / Ain't talkin' 'bout dub: *Apollo 440* / 9 acre dust: *Charlatans* / Open up: *Leftfield & John Lydon* / Ready to go: *Republica* / Lopez: *808 State* / Diablo: *Grid* / World: *New Order* / Skin on skin: *Grace* / Children: *Miles, Robert* / Ride a rocket: *Lithium & Sonya Madan* / Naked and ashamed: *Dylan Rhymes* / Higher state of consciousness: *Wink, Josh* / Asylum: *Orb* / Underwater love: *Smoke City* / Sour times: *Portishead* / Goreki: *Lamb* / Dark and long: *Underworld* / Box: *Orbital* / Trigger hippie: *Morcheeba* / Spin spin sugar: *Sneaker Pimps* / Hyperballad: *Bjork* / Wild wood: *Weller, Paul* / Wish you were here: *Aloof* / Original: *Leftfield & Toni Halliday* / Stay: *18 Wheeler* / Papau New Guinea: *Future Sound Of London* / So many dreams: *Guy Called Gerald* / Angel: *Goldie* / Feel the sunshine: *Reece, Alex & Deborah Anderson* / Darkheart: *Bomb The Bass*
CD Set ______ **5534822**
PolyGram TV / May '97 / PolyGram

FUSION OF CLASSICAL AND POP STYLES VOL.2, A
CD ______ **SPOTS 14**
Intersound / Oct '91 / Jazz Music

FUSION OF CLASSICAL AND POP STYLES, A
CD ______ **SPOTS 13**
Intersound / Oct '91 / Jazz Music

FUSION PHEW VOL.1
Sudden samba: *Larson, Neil* / Latin America: *Walton, Cedar* / Hip skip: *Williams, Tony* / El bobo: *Lewis, Webster* / Hump: *Rushen, Patrice* / Rio: *Glenn, Roger* / Caveman boogie: *Wilson, Lesette* / Harlem boys: *Rollins, Sonny* / Walk tall: *Soskin, Mark* / Do it to it: *Owens, Jimmy* / Little sunflower: *Hubbard, Freddie* / On the path: *Franklin, Rodney*
CD ______ **CDELV 10**
Elevate / Dec '93 / 3mv/Sony

FUSION PHEW VOL.2
Ju ju: *McDuff, Jack* / He loves you: *Seawind* / Goldenwings: *OPA* / Bittersweet: *Escovedo, Pete* / Sugar loaf mountain: *Duke, George* / Happy song: *Foster, Ronnie* / Baby don't you know: *Humphrey, Bobbi* / I'm staying forever: *Henderson, Wayne* / Life is like a samba: *Benoit, David* / There are many stops along the way: *Sample, Joe* / Scapegoat: *Johnson, Al* / Slick Eddie: *Stitt, Sonny*
CD ______ **CDELV 15**
Elevate / Jun '94 / 3mv/Sony

FUTILITY OF A WELL-ORDERED LIFE
CD ______ **VIRUS 147CD**
Alternative Tentacles / May '95 / Cargo / Greyhound / Pinnacle

FUTURE (A Journey Through The Electronic Underground)
Extremis: *Hal & Gillian Anderson* / Atom bomb: *Fluke* / KJZ: *Photek* / Smokin' Japanese babe: *Future Sound Of London* / Karmacoma: *Massive Attack* / Winter ceremony: *Sacred Spirit* / Loops of fury: *Chemical Brothers* / Snake hips: *Future Sound Of London* / Extremis: *Hal & Gillian Anderson* / Absurd: *Fluke* / Salsa with mesquite: *u-Ziq* / Ostiak: *Hal* / Water from a vine leaf: *Orbit, William* / Smokebelch II: *Sabres Of Paradise* / Crystal clear: *Grid* / Space diary 1: *Jah Wobble & Brian Eno* / Sleep 2: *Schutze, Paul* / Spiritual invocation: *Air* / Lizard point: *Eno, Brian* / Mr. lullaby should have rocked you: *Toop, David* / Their memories: *Budd, Harold & Brian Eno* / Home: *Sylvian, David*
CD ______ **VTDCD 118**
Virgin / Jun '97 / EMI

FUTURE COOL (Drum 'n' Bass Jazz Space)
CD ______ **CKR 002CD**
Cooker / Jun '97 / 3mv/Pinnacle / Prime / Timewarp

FUTURE FORCES
What you want: *Future Force* / Heaven: *Washington, Sarah* / Pleasure principle: *Jackson, Janet* / Klubbhopping: *Klubb Heads* / Stand up: *Love Tribe* / Bring me love: *Mendez, Andrea* / Girls and boys: *Morel's Grooves*
CD ______ **FFCD 2**
AM:PM / May '96 / PolyGram

FUTURE FUNK VOL.1 (2CD Set)
Inner city life: *Goldie & The Metalheadz* / Inspection: *Leftfield* / Leave home: *Chemical Brothers* / Clank: *Spooky* / Salt water fish: *Ruby* / Born slippy: *Underworld* / Cool kids of death: *St. Etienne* / Bump: *Angel, Dave* / Mutant jazz: *T-Power* / I'll fly away: *Ballistic Brothers* / Peace: *DJ Food* / Barbola work: *Black Dog* / Space junk: *Burning Bush* / Karmacoma: *Massive Attack* / One to one religion: *Bomb The Bass* / Journeyman part 2: *Outside* / Isobel: *Bjork* / Killing: *Olive* / Friendly pressure: *Jhelisa* / Only the strong survive: *DJ Krush* / Fallen: *APE* / Tosh: *Fluke* / Drum head: *Stoppa* / Clubbed to death: *Rob D* / Nights introlude: *Nightmares On Wax* / Garden of earthly delights: *D-Note*
CD Set ______ **5404952**
A&M / Feb '96 / PolyGram

FUTURE FUNK VOL.2 (2CD/2CD Ltd Set)
Take California: *Propeller Heads* / We are one: *DJQ* / Eva: *Perry, Jean Jacques* / When you feel good, things can turn: *Peanutbutter Wolf* / Chicken in a box: *Mr. Scruff* / Chupacasbbra: *Fresh, Freddie* / Life is sweet: *Chemical Brothers* / Brut force: *Roni Size* / Lick: *Earl Grey* / One night stand: *Aloof* / Lopez: *808 State* / ETA: *Casual Sub* / Box: *Orbital* / Bug in the bassbin: *Inner Zone Orchestra* / Midnight in a perfect world: *DJ Shadow* / Casanova 70: *Air* / Toxygene: *Orb* / Remember me: *Blueboy* / Drumming up business: *Stoppa* / Atomic moog 2000: *Coldcut* / Rock the funky beat: *Natural Born Chillers* / Spin spin sugar: *Sneaker Pimps* / Rekkit: *Death In Vegas* / Believe: *Gus Gus* / Scared: *Slacker* / Naked and ashamed: *Dylan Rhymes* / Outta space: *Tenor, Jimi*
CD Set ______ **SOLIDCD 008**
CD Set ______ **SOLIDSCD 008**
Solid State / Apr '97 / Prime / Vital

FUTURE PERFECT
Domus in nebulae: *Eno, Roger* / Saint columbas walk: *Eno, Roger* / Western island of apples: *Partridge, Andy* / Bruegel: *Partridge, Andy* / Stravinsky: *Eno, Brian* / Distant hill: *Eno, Brian* / Radiothesia III: *Eno, Brian* / Testify: *Channel Light Vessel* / Faint aroma of snow: *Channel Light Vessel* / For the love of you: *St. John, Kate* / Your promised land: *St. John, Kate* / Big noise in Twangtown: *Nelson, Bill* / Her presence in flowers: *Nelson, Bill*
CD ______ **ASCD 024**
All Saints / Mar '95 / Discovery / Vital

FUTURE SHOCK
CD ______ **CDTB 012**
Magnum Music / Oct '94 / TKO Magnum

FUTURE SOUL
CD ______ **5243332**
Quango / Jan '97 / PolyGram

FUTURE SOUND OF CHICAGO
CD ______ **SOMCD 5**
Ministry Of Sound / Jun '96 / 3mv/Sony / Mo's Music Machine / Warner Music

FUTURE SOUND OF HARDCORE, THE
CD ______ **KFCD 002**
Knite Force / Jan '96 / Grapevine/ PolyGram / Jumpstart / Mo's Music Machine

FUTURE SOUND OF JAZZ VOL.1
CD ______ **COMP 010**
Compost / Jan '97 / Plastic Head / SRD / Timewarp

FUTURE SOUND OF JAZZ VOL.2
CD ______ **COMP 017CD**
Compost / Jan '97 / Plastic Head / SRD / Timewarp

FUTURE SOUND OF JAZZ VOL.3 (2CD Set)
CD Set ______ **COMP 030CD**
Compost / Jan '97 / Plastic Head / SRD / Timewarp

FUTURE SOUND OF PARIS
Away: *Nature* / Bad vibes: *Motorbass* / Psycho phunk reaction: *Daphreephunkateerz* / Bill collector: *Trankilou* / Just about right: *Dimitri From Paris* / Free Jah: *Zend Avesta* / Rock it tonight: *Seven Dub* / Earth whispers: *Aphrodisiac* / Solar sequences experience: *Solar Side's Experience* / Make it freaky: *Malca, Stephane* / Disco 2000 selector: *Space Funk Project* / She's a model: *Magenta* / Feet Food's theme: *Dirty Jesus* / Soul experience: *Dax Riders*
CD ______ **5337382**
London / Feb '97 / PolyGram

FUTURSONICS (2CD Set)
CD Set ______ **PIAS 26000223**
Elypsia / Jun '96 / Arabesque / Plastic Head / Vital

FX FILES (5CD Set)
CD Set ______ **DTKBOX 67**
Doppelganger / Aug '97 / Total/BMG

G-SPOT VOL.1 (Club Classics)
CD ______ GSPOTCD 1
Beechwood / Mar '97 / Beechwood/BMG / Pinnacle

G-SPOT VOL.2 (Swing)
You might need somebody: *Ama, Shola* / Can we: *SWV* / Can I get you home: *Brown, Foxy* / Everytime I close my eyes: *Babyface* / I shot the sheriff: *Warren G* / Can't knock the hustle: *Jay Z & Mary J. Blige* / For you I will: *Monica* / Sometime: *Brand New Heavies* / Don't you love me: *Eternal* / Moan and groan: *Morrison, Mark* / Hold on: *En Vogue* / Doin' it: *LL Cool J* / I believe I can fly: *R Kelly* / Tha crossroads: *Bone Thugs n' Harmony* / Cold rock the party: *MC Lyte* / Sumthin' sumthin': *Maxwell* / Love guarenteed: *Damage* / One in a million: *Aaliyah* / Give me the night: *Crawford, Randy* / Crush on you: *Lil' Kim* / 5 miles to empty: *Brownstone* / Request line: *Zhane*
CD ______ GSPOTCD 2
Beechwood / Jun '97 / Beechwood/BMG / Pinnacle

GAGAKU
CD ______ LYRCD 7126
Lyrichord / Aug '94 / ADA / CM / Roots

GAGAKU
CD ______ VICG 53542
JVC World Library / Mar '96 / ADA / CM / Direct

GAL YU GOOD
CD ______ VPCD 1123
VP / Oct '90 / Greensleeves / Jet Star / Total/BMG

GALAXY TRIBE (A Drum 'n' Bass Odyssey)
CD ______ MEYCD 20
Magick Eye / Aug '97 / Cargo / SRD

GAMELAN ENSEMBLE OF BATUR
CD ______ C559 002
Ocora / '88 / ADA / Harmonia Mundi

GAMELAN GONG GEDE
CD ______ VICG 52162
JVC World Library / Mar '96 / ADA / CM / Direct

GAMELAN GONG KEBYAR VOL.1
CD ______ VICG 52152
JVC World Library / Mar '96 / ADA / CM / Direct

GAMELAN GONG KEBYAR VOL.2
CD ______ VICG 52652
JVC World Library / Mar '96 / ADA / CM / Direct

GAMELAN OF SURAKARTA
CD ______ VICG 52632
JVC World Library / Mar '96 / ADA / CM / Direct

GAMELAN SEMAR PAGULINGAN FROM BESANG ABABI (Music From Bali)
CD ______ SM 1609
Wergo / Oct '96 / ADA / Cadillac / Harmonia Mundi

GAMES AND RITES OF THE LOBI PEOPLE (Music From Burkina Faso/ Ivory Coast/Ghana)
CD ______ ARN 64341
Arion / Apr '96 / ADA / Discovery

GARAGE MIX VOL.1 (Roger Sanchez)
CD ______ GMCD 001
Dance Mix / Jul '94 / Vital

GARAGE MIX VOL.2 (David Morales)
CD ______ GMCD 002
Dance Mix / Jul '94 / Vital

GARAGE PRESSURE (2CD Set)
Alright: *Urban Soul* / Love and happiness: *River Ocean* / Beautiful people: *Tucker, Barbara* / Caught in the middle: *Roberts, Juliet* / Pennies from heaven: *Inner City* / Can I get a witness: *Nesby, Ann* / Do you want it right now: *Degrees Of Motion* / Colour of my skin: *Swing 52* / Push the feeling on: *Nightcrawlers* / Nitelife: *English, Kim* / What would we do: *DSK* / Hideaway: *DeLacy* / Where love lives: *Limerick, Alison* / I'll be your friend: *Owens, Robert* / Pride (a deeper love): *C&C Music Factory* / Been a long time: *Fog* / Lift every voice: *Mass Order* / Walkin' on: *Sheer Bronze* / Always: *MK & Alana* / Who keeps changing your mind: *South Street Player* / God made me funky: *MD X-Press* / Question: *Seven Grand Housing Authority* / Closer: *Gaines, Rosie* / Reach for me: *Funky Green Dogs* / Luv dancin': *Underground Solution* / House of love: *Smooth Touch* / Blues for you: *Logic* / Fired up: *Funky Green Dogs* / Turn me on: *Brown, Kathy* / Dreams: *Smokin' Beats*
CD Set ______ SOLIDCD 009
CD Set ______ SOLIDSCD 009
Solid State / Jun '97 / Prime / Vital

GARAGE PUNK UNKNOWNS VOL.2
CD ______ EFA 115802
Crypt / Jun '95 / Shellshock/Disc

GARAGE SOUNDS VOL.4
CD ______ CDRAID 531
Rumour / Jul '96 / 3mv/Sony / Mo's Music Machine / Pinnacle

GARGULA MECANICA
CD ______ BIOCD 03
Messerschmitt / Mar '94 / Plastic Head

GARNI: ARMENIAN DANCES
CD ______ VANGEEL 9404
Van Geel / Aug '95 / ADA / Direct

GARO OF THE MUDHUPAR FOREST, THE
CD ______ C 580054
Ocora / May '94 / ADA / Harmonia Mundi

GATHERING OF THE ELDERS, THE
CD ______ WLAAS 25CD
Waterlilly Acoustics / Nov '95 / ADA

GATHERING, THE
Lay dee at de / Spence's reel / Faery reel / Mrs. Hamilton of Pitcaithland / Untitled / Lord MacDonald's reel / Horseshoe harbour / Christy Barry's / Mrs. Heidi Hendy / Sandymount / Untitled / Lucy Campbell's / Fermoy lasses / Last chance / Venus jig / Reel du pendu (hangman's reel) / Kildare fancy / Golden eagle / Sweep's hornpipe / Lafferty's / Grogans / Star of Munster / L'air du menuisier / Kola stala vlajna / Valse clog / Green brechans of Branton / Peacock's march / I saw my love come passing me by / Rathlin island / Braes of Mar / Jenny Dang the weaver / Miss Girdle / Tail toddle / Canto de afiador / Huriondo / Jig jazz
CD ______ CDRW 62
Realworld / Apr '97 / EMI

GAY 90'S, THE (Musical Boxes/ Pianolas)
Runaway girl / Robin Hood / Florodora / Belle of New York / Geisha / Greek slave and San toy / Dozen discs / Canary and nightingale warble / Evergreens / Stephen Foster favourites / Gay 90's favourites / Miscellany
CD ______ CDSDL 312
Saydisc / Jun '92 / ADA / Direct / Harmonia Mundi

GAY ANTHEMS
CD ______ ALMYCD 11
Almighty / Feb '95 / Total/BMG

GAY ANTHEMS VOL.2
CD ______ ALMYCD 16
Almighty / Nov '95 / Total/BMG

GAY ANTHEMS VOL.3
CD ______ BLSTCD 06
Blast / Aug '97 / Total/BMG

GAY CLASSICS VOL.1 (Over The Rainbow)
CD ______ BLSTCD 01
Blast / Aug '95 / Total/BMG

GAY CLASSICS VOL.2 (Over The Rainbow)
CD ______ BLSTCD 02
Blast / Mar '96 / Total/BMG

GAY CLASSICS VOL.3 (Over The Rainbow)
CD ______ BLSTCD 04
Almighty / Sep '96 / Total/BMG

GAY DANCING (2CD Set)
CD Set ______ ZYX 811112
ZYX / Aug '97 / ZYX

GAY, FREE & HAPPY
This wheels on fire: *Suns Of Shiva* / Give it to me good: *Freaky Baby* / Pardon me: *Kon Kan* / Fantasia 2: *Suns Of Shiva* / Here and now: *Kater* / In fron wan'it: *New York Connection* / Entangled: *Numan, Wayne* / Back again: *General Base* / I will stand by you: *Petroleum Jell* / Who's gonna cry: *Taylor, Ann Marie* / You could have been with me last night: *Primitive Fire* / Strong to survive: *Shaker* / Poison: *General Base* / Breathless: *Gold, Angie*
CD ______ ST 9601
Stonewall / Jun '96 / Koch

GBG HARDCORE 1981-1985
CD ______ DOLCD 9
Distortion / Sep '93 / Plastic Head

GEE WIZZ - THE BEST IN THE HOUSE (2CD Set)
CD Set ______ WIZZD 23
Wizz / Oct '95 / Grapevine/PolyGram

GEMS OF THE MUSIC HALL
I love a lassie: *Lauder, Harry* / Every little movement: *Lloyd, Marie* / Lily of Laguna: *Stratton, Eugene* / Gas inspector: *Little Tich* / 'E can't take a roise out of oi: *Chevalier, Albert* / Put on your slippers: *Lloyd, Marie* / Burlington Bertie from Bow: *Shields, Ella* / Little idea of my own: *Robey, George* / Little Dolly daydream: *Elliott, G.H.* / When I took my morning parade: *Lloyd, Marie* / Has anyone here seen Kelly: *Forde, Florrie* / Whistling bowery boy: *Whelan, Albert* / Same as his father did before him: *Lauder, Harry* / Archibald certainly not: *Robey, George* / Going to the races: *Leno, Dan* / When father papered the parlour: *Williams, Billy* / Old bull and bush: *Forde, Florrie* / Preacher and the bear: *Whelan, Albert* / Hold your hand out, naughty boy: *Forde, Florrie* / Fill 'Em Up: *King, Hetty* / 'E dunno where 'E are: *Elen, Gus* / Three trees: *Whelan, Albert*
CD ______ PASTCD 7005
Flapper / Mar '93 / Pinnacle

GENERAL MEETS THREE BLIND MICE
CD ______ 790092
King Dragon / Jun '93 / Jet Star

GENERATION MEDIA TROPICAL
CD ______ 3013512
Flarenasch / Jan '97 / Discovery

GENERATION X - THE DEFINITIVE SOUND OF 90'S INDIE (3CD Set)
CD Set ______ GENXBXCD 1
Generation X / Jun '96 / Total/Pinnacle

GENERATIONS 1 (A Punk Look At Human Rights)
Generations: *Electric Dog House* / Alien song: *Red Aunts & Exene Cervernkova* / Legend of Pat Brown: *Assorted Jellybeans* / Nervous breakdown: *Pennywise* / 21 GUNS: *Good Riddance* / Coming to America: *Me First & The Gimme Gimmes* / Do da da: *Green Day* / Criminal: *John Doe Thing* / Synthetic world: *Swamp Dogg Does Moon Dogg* / Jilted John: *Vandals* / Don't bother me: *Bad Brains* / BUGS: *Bugs* / That last: *Fetish* / Ya ya ya ya: *Mr.T Experience* / Can't make love: *Pansy Divison & Tre Cool* / Push shove: *X-Members* / Health care for all Americans: *DFL*
CD ______ CTMARK 1000
EMI / Apr '97 / EMI

GENERICS
Cakewalk of crime: *Jonathan Fire Eater* / Something for nothing: *Spoiler* / Black eyed girl: *Speedball Baby* / Sun to sun: *Spitters* / Milky white entropy: *Poem Rocket* / Aurora F: *Slug* / Welcome to my head: *Noisext* / Boppin high school baby: *'68 Comeback* / Drag house: *Chrome Cranks* / Brad Mayor PhD: *Slowworm* / Pro choice: *Fuse* / Ordinary nights: *Railroad Jerk*
CD ______ PCP 0222
PCP / Nov '95 / Vital

GENETIC DRIFT (2CD Set)
CD Set ______ PKPWPS 5
Fax / Oct '96 / Plastic Head

GENIOS DE LA GUITARRA FLAMENCA VOL.1
Alegrias: *Sabicas* / Sevillanas: *Sabicas* / Bulerias: *Martinez, Pepe* / Fandangos: *Martinez, Pepe* / Malaguena: *De Lucia, Paco* / Tangos de la Vieja Rica: *De Lucia, Paco* / Campanilleros: *Martinez, Pepe* / Zapateado: *Martinez, Pepe* / Granadinas: *Sabicas* / Bulerias: *Sabicas* / Zapateado: *De Sanlucar, Esteban* / Farruca: *De Sanlucar, Esteban* / Molienda Cafe: *De Lucia, Paco* / Maria de la O: *De Lucia, Paco*
CD ______ CD 62095
Saludos Amigos / Mar '97 / Target/BMG

GENIOS DE LA GUITTARA FLAMENCA VOL.2
Fantasia Salinera: *Ricardo, Nino* / Nostalgia Granadina: *Ricardo, Nino* / Soleares: *Simon, Paquito* / Aires de Cadiz: *Simon, Paquito* / Zapateado: *Albaicin, Antonio* / Tientos: *Albaicin, Antonio* / Granadinas Hidalgas: *Serrano, Juanito* / Soleares: *Serrano, Juanito* / Jaleos Cale: *Serrano, Juanito* / Temas farrucos: *Ricardo, Nino* / Soleares #2: *Ricardo, Nino* / Fiesta en la Muralla: *Serrano, Juanito* / Seguiriyas: *Serrano, Juanito* / Verdiales: *Simon, Paquito* / Danza Mora: *Simon, Paquito* / Por lo Mudable: *De Lucia, Paco* / De Puerta a Puerta: *De Lucia, Paco*
CD ______ CD 62099
Saludos Amigos / Mar '97 / Target/BMG

GENIUS OF BOOGIE-WOOGIE
CD ______ CD 53053
Giants Of Jazz / Mar '90 / Cadillac / Jazz Music / Target/BMG

GENTLE MOODS
Chi mai / Bilitis / Holding back the years / Feelings / Sadness / Evergreen / Mahogany / Here comes the sun / Tubular bells / Long and winding road / Stranger on the shore / Sailing / Talking in your sleep / People / If you leave me now / I made it through the rain / Something / Chariots of fire / Yesterday / Last farewell
CD ______ GRF 313
Tring / Apr '93 / Tring

GENTLE MOODS (4CD Set)
Holding back the years: *Intimate Orchestra* / Sailing: *Intimate Orchestra* / Stranger on the shore: *Intimate Orchestra* / Twin Peaks theme: *Intimate Orchestra* / Just the way you are: *Intimate Orchestra* / Do you know where you're going to: *Intimate Orchestra* / Unchained melody: *Intimate Orchestra* / Love's theme: *Intimate Orchestra* / Rose: *Intimate Orchestra* / Chariots of fire: *Intimate Orchestra* / Tubular bells theme: *Intimate Orchestra* / What a wonderful world: *Intimate Orchestra* / Nights in white satin: *Intimate Orchestra* / I write the songs: *Intimate Orchestra* / What I did for love: *Intimate Orchestra* / Evergreen: *Intimate Orchestra* / Careless whisper: *Intimate Orchestra* / Nikita: *Intimate Orchestra* / Everything I do (I do it for you): *Intimate Orchestra* / Endless love: *Intimate Orchestra* / Sadness (part one): *Intimate Orchestra* / Third man theme: *Intimate Orchestra* / Bright eyes: *Intimate Orchestra* / Feelings: *Intimate Orchestra* / Way we were: *Intimate Orchestra* / Theme from the Godfather: *Intimate Orchestra* / One day in your life: *Intimate Orchestra* / Sacrifice: *Intimate Orchestra* / Oxygene: *Intimate Orchestra* / Ebony and ivory: *Intimate Orchestra* / That's what friends are for: *Intimate Orchestra* / Hopelessly devoted to you: *Intimate Orchestra* / Send in the clowns: *Intimate Orchestra* / Let it be: *Intimate Orchestra* / To all the girls I've loved before: *Intimate Orchestra* / Chi mai: *Intimate Orchestra* / Do that to me one more time: *Intimate Orchestra* / Strangers in the night: *Intimate Orchestra* / Saltwater: *Intimate Orchestra* / Last farewell: *Intimate Orchestra* / Aria: *Intimate Orchestra* / Love theme from Romeo and Juliet: *Intimate Orchestra* / Albatross: *Intimate Orchestra* / Hymne: *Intimate Orchestra* / Whiter shade of pale: *Intimate Orchestra* / When I fall in love: *Intimate Orchestra* / There'll be sad songs: *Intimate Orchestra* / Lady: *Intimate Orchestra* / Lost without your love: *Intimate Orchestra* / Aranjuez: *Intimate Orchestra* / Mon amour: *Intimate Orchestra* / Sealed with a kiss: *Intimate Orchestra* / Toccata: *Intimate Orchestra* / Heartbreaker: *Intimate Orchestra* / Something: *Intimate Orchestra* / You don't bring me flowers: *Intimate Orchestra* / (Sittin' on the) dock of the bay: *Intimate Orchestra* / Never on Sunday: *Intimate Orchestra* / Misty: *Intimate Orchestra* / If you leave me now: *Intimate Orchestra* / Cavatina: *Intimate Orchestra* / Bilitis: *Intimate Orchestra* / Almaz: *Intimate Orchestra* / La vie en rose: *Intimate Orchestra* / Woman in love: *Intimate Orchestra* / Up where we belong: *Intimate Orchestra* / Maid of New Orleans: *Intimate Orchestra* / I guess that's why they call it the blues: *Intimate Orchestra* / Out of Africa: *Intimate Orchestra* / Man and a woman: *Intimate Orchestra* / Moon river: *Intimate Orchestra* / Bridge over troubled water: *Intimate Orchestra* / Song sung blue: *Intimate Orchestra* / Amazing Grace: *Intimate Orchestra* / Your song: *Intimate Orchestra* / Don't cry for me Argentina: *Intimate Orchestra* / Help me make it through the night: *Intimate Orchestra* / Magnetic fields part 2: *Intimate Orchestra* / Do that to me one more time: *Intimate Orchestra* / Midnight: *Intimate Orchestra* / Song for Guy: *Intimate Orchestra*
CD Set ______ TFP 047
Tring / Apr '95 / Tring

GENTLE RAIN (A Magical Blend Of Music And The Sounds Of Nature)
CD ______ 57722
CMC / May '97 / BMG

GENTLEMEN OF SONG (2CD Set)
All the way: *Sinatra, Frank* / Blue skies: *Como, Perry* / You're a sweet little headache: *Crosby, Bing* / Lazy: *Haymes, Dick* / Darling, Je vous aime beaucoup: *Cole, Nat 'King'* / My Mammy: *Jolson, Al* / My heart cries for you: *Mitchell, Guy* / I guess I'll have to change my plans: *Bennett, Tony* / Answer me: *Laine, Frankie* / Same one: *Benton, Brook* / On the sunny side of the street: *Sinatra, Frank* / I love you: *Como, Perry* / Apple for the teacher: *Crosby, Bing* / Thinking of you: *Haymes, Dick* / It's crazy but I'm in love: *Cole, Nat 'King'* / There's a rainbow round my shoulder: *Jolson, Al* / Side by side: *Mitchell, Guy* / Jeepers creepers: *Bennett, Tony* / I believe: *Laine, Frankie* / Think twice: *Benton, Brook* / On the road to Mandalay: *Sinatra, Frank* / Goodbye Sue: *Como, Perry* / April played the fiddle: *Crosby, Bing* / Nevertheless: *Haymes, Dick* / Thou swell: *Cole, Nat 'King'* / Sonny boy: *Jolson, Al* / Call Rosie on the phone: *Mitchell, Guy* / With plenty of money and you: *Bennett, Tony* / There must be a reason: *Laine, Frankie* / Lie to me: *Benton, Brook* / I've got my love to keep me warm: *Sinatra, Frank* / All through the day: *Como, Perry* / I have eyes: *Crosby, Bing* / That lucky old sun: *Haymes, Dick* / You stepped out of a dream: *Cole, Nat 'King'* / Let me sing and I'm happy: *Jolson, Al* / Music, music, music: *Mitchell, Guy* / Chicago: *Bennett, Tony* / Wheel of fortune: *Laine, Frankie* / Revenge: *Benton, Brook*
CD Set ______ MUCD 9512
Musketeer / May '96 / Disc

GENTLEMEN OF THE COUNTRY
CD ______ HADCD 177
Javelin / Nov '95 / Henry Hadaway / THE

GENTLEMEN PIPERS, THE (Classic Recordings Of Irish Traditional Piping)
Banks of the Suir: *Walsh, Liam* / Portlaw reel: *Walsh, Liam* / Ask my father/The mountain lark: *Andrews, William* / May day/The Cuckoo's nest: *Andrews, William* / Top of the Cork road/The Irish washerwoman: *Rowsome, Leo* / Kiss the maid behind the barrel/Touch me if you dare: *Rowsome, Leo* / Snowy breasted pearl: *Rowsome, Leo* / Langstern pony: *Clancy, Willie* / Dear Irish boy: *Clancy, Willie* / Flogging reel: *Clancy, Willie* / Boys of Bluehill/Dunphy's hornpipe: *Ennis, Seamus* / Flags of Dublin/Wind that shakes the barley: *Ennis, Seamus* / Wandering minstrel/Jackson's morning brush: *Ennis, Seamus* / Blackbird: *Ennis, Seamus* / First house in Connaught/The copperplate: *McAloon, Sean & John Rea* / An buachaill caol dubh/Drops of brandy: *McAloon, Sean* / Ash plant: *Doran, Felix* / Lark in the morning: *Doran, Felix* / Mary of Murroe/The

green gates: *Doran, Felix* / Boys of the lough: *Doran, Felix* / Frieze breeches: *Mitchell, Pat* / Mairseail alasdruim: *Mitchell, Pat* / Garrett Barry's/The Virginia reel: *Mitchell, Pat* / Ballyoran: *O'Brien, Michael* / Rakish Paddy/Castle Kelly: *O'Brien, Michael*
CD _______ CDORBD 084
Globestyle / Mar '94 / Pinnacle

GENUINE HOUSEROCKIN' VOL.1
CD _______ ALCD 101
Alligator / Oct '93 / ADA / CM / Direct

GENUINE HOUSEROCKIN' VOL.2
CD _______ ALCD 102
Alligator / Oct '93 / ADA / CM / Direct

GENUINE HOUSEROCKIN' VOL.3
CD _______ ALCD 103
Alligator / Oct '93 / ADA / CM / Direct

GENUINE HOUSEROCKIN' VOL.4
CD _______ ALCD 104
Alligator / Oct '93 / ADA / CM / Direct

GENUINE HOUSEROCKIN' VOL.5
CD _______ ALCD 109
Alligator / Nov '93 / ADA / CM / Direct

GEORGE PHANG PRESENTS POWERHOUSE VOL.1
CD _______ SONCD 0007
Sonic Sounds / Feb '91 / Jet Star

GEORGIA BLUES
CD _______ IGOCD 2045
Indigo / Jun '96 / ADA / Direct

GEORGIA BLUES & GOSPEL 1927-1931
CD _______ DOCD 5160
Document / May '93 / ADA / Hot Shot / Jazz Music

GEORGIA SEA ISLAND SONGS
Moses: *Davis, John* / Kneebone: *Armstrong, Joe* / Sheep, sheep, don't you know the road: *Jones, Bessie* / Live humble: *Davis, John* / Daniel: *Proctor, Willis* / O Death: *Jones, Bessie* / Read 'em John: *Davis, John* / Beulah land: *Davis, John* / Buzzard lope: *Jones, Bessie* / Raggy Levi: *Davis, John* / Ain't I right: *Morrison, Henry* / See Aunt Dinah: *Jones, Bessie* / Walk, Billy Abbot: *Proctor, Willis* / Reg'lar reg'lar rollin' under: *Jones, Bessie* / Pay me: *Armstrong, Joe* / Carrie Belle: *Davis, John* / Laz'rus: *Morrison, Henry* / Titanic: *Jones, Bessie*
CD _______ 802782
New World / Mar '96 / ADA / Cadillac / Harmonia Mundi

GEORGIA STRING BANDS 1928-1930
CD _______ SOB 035162
Story Of The Blues / Feb '93 / ADA / Koch

GEORGIAN POLYPHONY
CD _______ VICG 50032
JVC World Library / Mar '96 / ADA / CM / Direct

GEORGIE - THE BEST ALBUM
CD _______ PELE 13CD
Exotica / Mar '97 / SRD / Vital

GERMAN BIERFEST FAVOURITES
O du lieber Augustin: *Bavarian Oompah Band* / Du kannst nicht treu sein: *Bavarian Oompah Band* / Bierwalzer: *Bavarian Oompah Band* / Oompah polka: *Bavarian Oompah Band* / Auf lustiger fahrt: *Big Bavarian Band* / Mariandi: *Bavarian Oompah Band* / Hans und Liesel: *Bavarian Oompah Band* / In den wald: *Bavarian Oompah Band* / Hoch die tassen: *Big Bavarian Band* / Trudies tanz: *Bavarian Oompah Band* / Phyllis und die mutter: *Bavarian Oompah Band* / Urbummelied: *Bavarian Oompah Band* / Die lorelei: *Bavarian Oompah Band* / In Munchen steht ein hofbrauhaus: *Bavarian Oompah Band* / Muss I denn, muss I denn zum stadtele 'naus: *Bavarian Oompah Band* / Der mai ist gekommen: *Bavarian Oompah Band* / Auf wiedersehn: *Bavarian Oompah Band* / Lieb heimatland ade: *Bavarian Oompah Band* / Rose: *Bavarian Oompah Band* / Es zogen drei buschen wohl uber den Rhein: *Bavarian Oompah Band* / Im schwarzen walfisch: *Bavarian Oompah Band* / Das war der herr von Rodenstein: *Bavarian Oompah Band* / Trumpeten echo: *Big Bavarian Band*
CD _______ 300572
Hallmark / Jul '96 / Carlton

GERMAN DRINKING SONGS
CD _______ MCD 71419
Monitor / Jun '93 / CM

GERMAN MYSTIC SOUND SAMPLER
CD _______ EFA 910102
Zillo / Dec '95 / SRD

GET DANCIN' (16 Original Soul Hits)
CD _______ 12214
Laserlight / Jan '94 / Target/BMG

GET DANCING (Disco Classics)
Get dancing: *Disco Tex & The Sexolettes* / 7-6-5-4-3-2-1 Blow your whistle: *Rimshots* / Shame, shame, shame: *Shirley & Company* / Disco stomp: *Bohannon, Hamilton* / Swing your daddy: *Gilstrap, Jim* / I get the sweetest feeling: *Wilson, Jackie* / Take that to the bank: *Shalamar* / This is it: *Moore, Melba* / Rapper's delight: *Sugarhill Gang* / Sunshine day: *Osibisa* / Now is the time: *James, Jimmy & The Vagabonds* / Boogie down (Get funky now): *Real Thing* / What's your name what's your number: *Andrea True Connection* / White lines (don't don't do it): *Grandmaster Flash & Melle Mel* / Disappearing act: *Shalamar* / You don't have to go: *Chi-Lites*
CD _______ TRTCD 118
TrueTrax / Dec '94 / THE

GET DANCING
CD _______ MU 5044
Musketeer / Oct '92 / Disc

GET DANCING (2CD Set)
CD Set _______ DCDCD 213
Castle / Jan '96 / BMG

GET DOWN TONIGHT
CD _______ PLSCD 143
Pulse / Apr '96 / BMG

GET HOT OR GO HOME (Vintage RCA Rockabillies 1956-1959 - 2CD Set)
Duck tail: *Clay, Joe* / Sixteen chicks: *Clay, Joe* / Doggone it: *Clay, Joe* / Goodbye goodbye: *Clay, Joe* / Slipping out and sneaking in: *Clay, Joe* / Get on the right track baby: *Clay, Joe* / You look that good to me: *Clay, Joe* / Crackerjack: *Clay, Joe* / Did you mean jelly bean (what you said cabbage head): *Clay, Joe* / Ooh-eee: *Cartey, Ric* / Heart throb: *Cartey, Ric* / I wancha to know: *Cartey, Ric* / Mellow down easy: *Cartey, Ric* / My babe: *Cartey, Ric* / Two tone shoes: *Homer & Jethro* / Catty Town: *King, Pee Wee* / Sugar sweet: *Houston, David* / Honky tonk mind: *Blake, Tommy & the rhythm rebels* / All night long: *Blake, Tommy & the rhythm rebels* / Now stop: *Carson, Martha* / Love me to pieces: *Martin, Janis* / Two long years: *Martin, Janis* / All right baby: *Martin, Janis* / Chicken house: *Rich, Dave* / Teen Billy Baby: *Sprouts* / Don't bug me baby: *Allen, Milt* / Rainbow Doll: *Dell, Jimmy* / It ain't right: *Terry, Gordon* / Let's get goin': *Morgan Twins* / Almost eighteen: *Orbison, Roy* / Little boy blue: *Johnson, Hoyt*
CD _______ CMFCD 014
Country Music Foundation / Jan '93 / ADA / Direct

GET INLINE
Funk phenomenon: *Van Helden, Armand* / Got myself together: *Bucketheads* / Spontaneous: *Spymaster & Eric Nouhan* / Let yourself go: *DJ Jean & Peran* / Da beat goes on: *Red 5* / Up to no good: *Porn Kings* / Jump up in the air: *London Boy* / Mental atmosphere: *Klubber's Revenge* / Fever: *Jaimin & Djaybee* / Real vibration (I want love): *Express Of Sound* / You're the one: *AT Project* / Take me away: *Respect* / People hold on: *Lisa & Tori* / Get freaky: *Bass Symphony*
CD _______ DC 881394
Disky / Jul '97 / Disky / THE

GET INTO JAZZ
CD _______ 5250302
Polydor / Nov '94 / PolyGram

GET INTO THE GROOVE
Keep that same old feeling: *Side Effect* / Jazz carnival: *Azymuth* / Rock Creek Park: *Blackbyrds* / Do it fluid: *Blackbyrds* / Walking in rhythm: *Blackbyrds* / Joyous: *Pleasure* / Beale Street: *Adams, Arthur* / Dancin': *McWilliams, Paulette* / Midnight and you: *Turrentine, Stanley* / Giving it back: *Hurtt, Phil* / I don't know what's on your mind: *Spider's Webb* / Will they miss me: *Simmons, David* / Ghettos of the mind: *Pleasure* / Space bass: *Slick* / I don't want to be alone ranger: *Watson, Johnny 'Guitar'* / Sweet Dan: *Everett, Betty* / Let your heart be free: *Rushen, Patrice*
CD _______ CDSEWD 034
Southbound / Jan '91 / Pinnacle

GET LOST (2CD Set)
CD Set _______ MPCD 02
Multiplex / Nov '96 / Plastic Head

GET ME JESUS ON THE LINE
Good news: *Staple Singers* / He has a way: *Greatest Harvest Choir* / See how he kept me: *Argo Singers* / It's Jesus in me: *Caravans* / This may be the last time: *Staple Singers* / Will the circle be unbroken: *Staple Singers* / Working on the building: *Highway QC's* / I'm going through: *Caravans* / Please hear my call: *Bells Of Joy* / One talk with Jesus: *Five Blind Boys Of Mississippi* / Where there's a will: *Five Blind Boys Of Mississippi* / Father I stretch my hand to thee: *Harmonizing Four* / I can see everybody's Mother: *Five Blind Boys Of Alabama* / He saved my soul: *Swan Silvertones* / Oh Mary don't you weep: *Swan Silvertones* / Get your soul right: *Swan Silvertones* / What about you: *Swan Silvertones* / God is standing by: *Soul Stirrers* / Wade in the water: *Harmonizing Four*
CD _______ NTMCD 519
Nectar / Oct '95 / Pinnacle

GET ON BOARD LITTLE CHILDREN
Get on board little children / Climbing Jacob's ladder / Go devil / Satisfied / Steal away to Jesus / Brother Noah / Charge to keep I have / Just a little talk with Jesus / Why should I worry / Jesus said if you go / In my saviour's care / Heavenly highway / Those chiming bells / Sun will never go down / Dig a little deeper / I took my master's hand / God rode into the windstorm / Take your burdens to the Lord / I John Saw / King Jesus is listening / I wanna see Jesus / Daniel / I'll rest after a while / Lord remember me / On the battlefield for the Lord / Father I Stretch my arms to thee / On my way (got my travellin' shoes)
CD _______ CDCHD 537
Ace / Feb '95 / Pinnacle

GET RIGHT WITH GOD VOL.1 (Hot Gospel 1947-1953)
Tree of life: *Powers, Prophet* / Blood done signed my name: *Radio Four* / I got good religion: *National Independent Gospel Singers* / Tell me why you like Roosevelt: *Jackson, Otis*
CD _______ HTCD 01
Heritage / Jan '89 / ADA / Direct / Hot Shot / Jazz Music / Swift / Wellard

GET THE PARTY MOVIN'
CD _______ ASTCD 4003
Telstar / Nov '96 / BMG

GET THE RHYTHM (2CD Set)
CD Set _______ 24302
Delta Doubles / May '94 / Target/BMG

GET WEAVING VOL.1
CD _______ GWCD 001
Weaving / Jun '92 / ADA / Direct / Koch

GET WEAVING VOL.2 (The Cajun/ Zydeco Collection)
CD _______ GWD 02CD
Weaving / Aug '93 / ADA / Direct / Koch

GET WEAVING VOL.3 (Country & Americana)
CD _______ GWCD 006
Weaving / Mar '96 / ADA / Direct / Koch

GET WITH THE BEAT - THE MAR-VEL MASTERS (A Lost Decade of American Rock & Roll)
Get with the beat: *Nix, Billy* / Honky tonkin' rhythm: *Sisco, Bobby* / Come on let's go: *Dallis, Chuck* / Jump baby jump: *Carter, Harry* / My friend: *Dallis, Chuck* / Seven lonely days: *Carter, Ginny* / Out of the picture: *Bradshaw, Jack* / I'm settin' you free: *Allen, Harold & J T Watts* / I need some lovin': *Allen, Harold* / Heartsick and blue: *Wall, Rem* / Count down: *Smith, Lorenzo* / Hot lips baby: *Duncan, Herbie* / Ha ha hey hey: *Kimbrough, Mel* / Would it matter at all: *Gatlin, Jim* / Boogie woogie baby of mine: *Burton, Bob* / I don't want you: *Carter, Harry* / Basil Smith stomp: *Smith, Basil* / Way you're treating me: *Gatlin, Jim* / Forty acres of my heart: *Burton, Bob* / Panhandle rag: *Durbin, Ronnie* / A-sleepin' at the foot: *Ashford, Shorty* / Let me love you: *Hall, Billy* / Ronnie's boogie: *Durbin, Ronnie* / Tired of rocking: *Burton, Bob* / Itchy feet: *Jennings, Rex* / Sweet Lucy: *Ashford, Shorty*
CD _______ RCD 20126
Rykodisc / Feb '93 / ADA / Vital

GETTIN' IT OFF - WESTBOUND FUNK
Gettin' it off (Instrumental): *Haskins, Fuzzy* / Just us: *Crowd Pleasers* / Thinking single: *Counts* / Funk it down: *Frazier, Ceasar* / Super funk: *Erasmus Hall* / In the pocket: *Boots & His Buddies* / Walt's first trip: *Ohio Players* / Funky world part 1 and 2: *Silky Vincent* / Get down with the get down: *Sparks, Melvin* / Super J: *Morrison, Junie* / Which way do I disco: *Haskins, Fuzzy* / Be what you is: *US Music & Funkadelic* / Funky Beethoven: *Anderson, Gene* / Crazy legs: *Austin, Donald* / What's up front that counts: *Counts* / Loose booty: *Funkadelic* / Satan's boogie: *Ohio Players* / Sweet thing: *Houston Outlaws* / Hit it and quit it: *Bobby Franklin's insanity* / Hicky Burr: *Frazier, Ceasar*
CD _______ CDSEWD 061
Westbound / Apr '93 / Pinnacle

GHAFRAN
CD _______ MFTEQ 931
NMC / Jun '93 / Total/Pinnacle

GHANA - ANCIENT CEREMONIES/ DANCE MUSIC & SONGS
CD _______ 7559720822
Nonesuch / Jan '95 / Warner Music

GHANA - THE NORTHERN TRIBES
CD _______ LYRCD 7321
Lyrichord / '91 / ADA / CM / Roots

GHETTO BLASTER
CD _______ KTR 100022
K-Town / Dec '96 / ZYX

GHETTO CELEBRITY
CD _______ BB 2811
Blue Beat / Apr '95 / Grapevine/PolyGram

GHETTO FEEL
Part time lover: *Yinka* / Bustin' outta play pen: *Da Bigg Kidz* / Get with you tonight: *Montage* / Friend not a lover: *Serenade* / You make me feel: *Rhythm Within* / Don't lead me on: *Serenade* / Blast from the past: *Da Bigg Kidz* / Come correct: *Yinka* / Tell me: *Da Fellas* / You're the one for me: *Montage*
CD _______ CDMISH 1
Mission / Dec '93 / 3mv/Sony

GHOSTS OF CHRISTMAS PAST
CD _______ TWI 0582
Les Disques Du Crepuscule / Jan '91 / Discovery

GI JIVE
GI jive: *Miller, Glenn* / At last: *Miller, Glenn* / My blue heaven: *Miller, Glenn* / Money is the root of all evil: *Andrews Sisters* / Rumours are flying: *Andrews Sisters* / Coax me a little: *Andrews Sisters* / Shoo shoo baby: *Andrews Sisters* / One meat ball: *Andrews Sisters* / Who's sorry now: *Miller, Glenn* / Put the blame on Mame: *Herth, Milt Trio* / Who told you that lie: *Boswell, Connee & The Paulette Sisters* / Come to baby do: *Dorsey, Jimmy Orchestra* / You always hurt the one you love: *Barnet, Charlie Orchestra* / Little John Ordinary: *Barnet, Charlie Orchestra* / Serenade in blue: *Langford, Frances* / Jumpin' jive: *Hampton, Lionel & His Orchestra* / Into each life some rain must fall: *Barnet, Charlie Orchestra* / Yes indeed: *Dorsey, Tommy & His Orchestra* / I'm gonna see my baby: *Moore, Phil Four* / Together: *Moore, Phil Four* / I'm beginning to see the light: *Fitzgerald, Ella & The Ink Spots*
CD _______ RAJCD 888
Empress / Jul '97 / Koch

GI JUKEBOX (100 Original Hits From The Swing Era 1936-46 - 5CD Set)
CD Set _______ H5CD 3345
Hindsight / Sep '93 / Jazz Music / Target/ BMG

GI JUKEBOX VOL.2
CD _______ HCD 2002
Hindsight / Sep '93 / Jazz Music / Target/ BMG

GI JUKEBOX VOL.4
CD _______ HCD 2004
Hindsight / Sep '93 / Jazz Music / Target/ BMG

GI JUKEBOX VOL.5
CD _______ HCD 2005
Hindsight / Sep '93 / Jazz Music / Target/ BMG

GIANT JINGLES - 60 OF THE BEST FROM THE 70'S
CD _______ GJ 001CD
Giant Jingles / Nov '93 / THE

GIANT JINGLES - 99 ORIGINAL CUTS
CD _______ GJ 003CD
Giant Jingles / Nov '93 / THE

GIANTS IN ROCK 'N' ROLL
CD _______ LECD 053
Wisepack / Jul '94 / Conifer/BMG / THE

GIANTS OF BOOGIE WOOGIE, THE
CD _______ CD 53083
Giants Of Jazz / Mar '92 / Cadillac / Jazz Music / Target/BMG

GIANTS OF COUNTRY (4CD Set)
CD Set _______ HADCDMS 4
Javelin / Oct '96 / Henry Hadaway / THE

GIANTS OF JAZZ COLLECTION, THE (2CD Set)
CD Set _______ CDB 912
Giants Of Jazz / Jan '93 / Cadillac / Jazz Music / Target/BMG

GIANTS OF ROCK
CD _______ MACCD 119
Autograph / Aug '96 / BMG

GIANTS OF ROCK 'N' ROLL ESSENTIALS
CD _______ LECDD 627
Wisepack / Aug '95 / Conifer/BMG / THE

GIANTS OF ROCK 'N' ROLL VOL.1
CD _______ 11819
Music / Feb '96 / Target/BMG

GIANTS OF ROCK 'N' ROLL VOL.2
CD _______ 11820
Music / Feb '96 / Target/BMG

GIANTS OF ROCK 'N' ROLL VOL.3
CD _______ 11821
Music / Feb '96 / Target/BMG

GIFT OF SONG, THE
Breaking hearts (ain't what it used to be): *John, Elton* / I found someone: *Cher* / Goodnight girl: *Wet Wet Wet* / Throwing it all away: *Genesis* / One more night: *Collins, Phil* / Bad love: *Clapton, Eric* / Time to make you mine: *Stansfield, Lisa* / Precious: *Lennox, Annie* / Some people: *Richard, Cliff* / Heaven: *Adams, Bryan* / I can't stand the rain: *Turner, Tina* / This woman's work: *Bush, Kate* / Little time: *Beautiful South* / Living years: *Mike & The Mechanics* / Violet: *Seal* / Missing you: *De Burgh, Chris* / Yesterday's men: *Madness* / Winter in July: *Bomb The Bass*
CD _______ 5160582
Polystar / Jun '93 / PolyGram

GIN HOUSE BLUES
What have you done to make me feel this way: *Smith, Mamie* / Graysom Street blues: *Johnson, Margaret* / Gin house blues: *Smith, Bessie* / Sweet Virginia blues: *Smith, Mamie* / Low down dirty: *McGraw, Lether* / When a 'gator hollers, folk say its a sign of rain: *Johnson, Margaret* / After you've gone: *Smith, Bessie* / Way after one and my daddy ain't come home yet: *Winston, Edna* / Rent man blues: *Winston, Edna* / Goin' crazy with the blues: *Smith, Mamie* / Hard driving papa: *Smith, Bessie* / If you're a viper: *Howard, Rosetta* / Do your duty: *McGraw, Lether* / My daddy rocks me (Parts 1 and 2): *Smith, Trixie* / I've lost my head over

you: *Hines, Babe* / I'm tired of fattenin' frogs for snakes: *Crawford, Rosetta* / Young woman's blues: *Smith, Bessie* / Double crossin' papa: *Crawford, Rosetta* / This is the end: *Hines, Babe* / What's the matter now: *Smith, Bessie*
CD PASTCD 9788
Flapper / Jun '92 / Pinnacle

GIRL FROM IPANEMA, THE
CD CD 53124
Giants Of Jazz / Nov '92 / Cadillac / Jazz Music / Target/BMG

GIRL FROM IPANEMA, THE (Samba & Bossa Nova)
CD CD 56046
Jazz Roots / Nov '94 / Target/BMG

GIRL FROM IPANEMA, THE
CD CD 62022
Saludos Amigos / Jan '93 / Target/BMG

GIRL POWER (2CD Set)
CD Set RADCD 56
Global TV / Feb '97 / BMG

GIRLS AND GUITARS VOL.1
Stay I missed you: *Loeb, Lisa* / Show me heaven: *McKee, Maria* / Constant craving: *Lang, k.d.* / Rooms on fire: *Nicks, Stevie* / Hazy shade of winter: *Bangles* / Love and affection: *Armatrading, Joan* / I believe: *Detroit, Marcella* / Hold on: *Wilson Phillips* / Chuck e's in love: *Jones, Rickie Lee* / Blue: *Mitchell, Joni* / You've placed a chill in my heart: *Eurythmics* / You're so vain: *Simon, Carly* / Luka: *Vega, Suzanne* / At 17: *Ian, Janis* / Good tradition: *Tikaram, Tanita* / Good times: *Brickell, Edie* / Anchorage: *Shocked, Michelle* / From a distance: *Griffith, Nanci* / Passionate kisses: *Carpenter, Mary-Chapin* / Girls and guitars: *Judd, Wynonna*
CD RADCD 06
Global TV / Feb '95 / BMG

GIRLS FROM IPANEMA, THE (The Best Of Bossa Nova/2CD Set)
CD Set 8413962
Verve / Jan '90 / PolyGram

GIRLS GIRLS GIRLS
CD TMPCD 009
Temple / Jan '95 / BMG

GIRLS GIRLS GIRLS
CD 12522
Laserlight / May '95 / Target/BMG

GIRLS GIRLS GIRLS
CD RNCD 2112
Rhino / Jul '95 / Grapevine/PolyGram / Jet Star

GIRLS GIRLS GIRLS
I heard it through the grapevine: *Reeves, Martha* / Rescue me: *Bass, Fontella* / My guy: *Wells, Mary* / Gee whiz: *Thomas, Carla* / Baby it's you: *Shirelles* / Love makes a woman: *Acklin, Barbara* / He's a rebel: *Crystals* / Midnight at the oasis: *Muldaur, Maria* / I will: *Winters, Ruby* / just one look: *Troy, Doris* / It's in his kiss (the shoop shoop song): *Everett, Betty* / Heatwave: *Reeves, Martha* / BABY: *Thomas, Carla* / I'm a woman: *Muldaur, Maria* / There's no other: *Crystals* / I know (you don't love me no more): *George, Barbara* / Two lovers: *Wells, Mary* / Will you still love me tomorrow: *Shirelles*
CD ECD 3125
K-Tel / Jan '95 / K-Tel

GIRLS GIRLS GIRLS
CD 10532
CMC / Jun '97 / BMG

GIRLS IN GARAGE VOL.2
CD UFOX 122
Romulan / Jul '97 / Greyhound

GIRLS OF REGGAE
Girlie girlie: *George, Sophia* / First cut is the deepest: *Penn, Dawn* / Rock my soul: *Griffiths, Marcia* / Angel of the morning: *Jones, Barbara* / Own true love: *Davis, Maureen* / Love me for a reason: *Miller, Maxine* / O mama: *Dean, Nora* / Cry me a river: *Davis, Carlene* / Dynamic: *Paula* / Baby lay down: *Schaffer, Doreen* / All the way in or all the way out: *Schloss, Cynthia* / Just for a night: *Sterling, Yvonne* / Ba bo ba: *Griffiths, Marcia* / Love again: *George, Sophia* / Come to me softly: *Davis, Carlene* / Heroes: *Ford, Charmaine* / Happy anniversary: *Schloss, Cynthia* / Could I have this dance: *Schaffer, Doreen*
CD ECD 3317
K-Tel / Jun '97 / K-Tel

GIRLS' SOUND 1957-1966, THE (2CD Set)
CD Set DBG 53032
Double Gold / Jun '94 / Target/BMG

GIVE 'EM ENOUGH BEATS
CD WALLCD 4
Wall Of Sound / May '95 / Prime / Soul Trader / Vital

GIVE 'EM ENOUGH DOPE VOL.1
CD WALLCD 001
Wall Of Sound / Feb '95 / Prime / Soul Trader / Vital

GIVE 'EM ENOUGH DOPE VOL.3
CD WALLCD 010
Wall Of Sound / Sep '96 / Prime / Soul Trader / Vital

GIVE 'EM HELL
Don't take mothing: *Tygers Of Pan Tang* / Backs to the grind: *White Spirit* / Don't need your money: *Raven* / Name rank and serial number: *Fist* / To hell and back: *Venom* / Buried alive: *Quartz* / Backstreet woman: *Jaguar* / Music: *Witchfinder General* / I survive: *Terraplane* / Take it all away: *Girlschool* / All the time: *Spider* / All around the world: *Torme, Bernie* / Give 'em hell: *Witchfynde* / One of these days: *Trespass* / Straight from hell: *Angel Witch* / Am I evil: *Diamond Head*
CD NTMCD 513
Nectar / Sep '95 / Pinnacle

GIVE 'EM THE BOOT
Brothels: *Rancid* / Watch this: *Slacker* / Can't wait: *Hepcat* / New breed: *Pietasters* / Spirit of the streets: *Business* / Los hombres no lloran: *Voodoo Glowskulls* / Barroom hereos: *Dropkick Murphys* / SkDoes he love you: *Skinner Box* / 17 at 17: *Upbeat* / OPen season: *Upbeat* / Beautiful girl: *Gadjits* / Roots radical: *Union 13* / Jaks: *US Bombs* / Fifteenth & T: *Swinging Utters* / Latin goes ska: *Skatalites* / Policeman: *Silencers* / Heart like a lion: *Pressure Point* / Infested: *Choking Victim* / No time: *F-Minus* / Playtime: *Hillyard, Dave Rocksteady 7*
CD 04022
Epitaph / Jul '97 / Pinnacle / Plastic Head

GIVE ME A HOME AMONG THE GUM TREES
CD LARRCD 232
Larrikin / Nov '94 / ADA / CM / Direct / Roots

GIVING PEOPLE CHOICES
CD AA 1001CD
Actionaid / Nov '93 / ADA

GLAD I'M A GIRL
CD EFA 061942
House In Motion / Aug '95 / SRD

GLAD TO BE GAY VOL.1
Don't leave me this way: *Communards* / You make me feel: *Sylvester* / Smalltown boy: *Bronski Beat* / Tainted love: *Soft Cell* / Shoot your shot: *Divine* / High energy: *Thomas, Evelyn* / I am what I am: *Gaynor, Gloria* / Crucified: *Army Of Lovers* / Do you really want to hurt me: *Culture Club* / I love men: *Kitt, Eartha* / Heaven in pain: *Our Heaven & Darrian Huss* / Where is my man: *Kitt, Eartha* / I'm too sexy: *Right Said Fred* / You think you're a man: *Divine* / Boogie woogie dancing shoes: *Barry, Claudja* / Persuasion: *Martin, Billie Ray & Spooky*
CD SPV 08493982
SPV / Dec '96 / Koch / Plastic Head

GLAD TO BE GAY VOL.2
Why: *Bronski Beat* / Can't take my eyes off you: *Boystown Gang* / West End Girls: *Pet Shop Boys* / I'm on fire: *Salico* / Power of love: *Texture* / Somebody else's guy: *Brown, Jocelyn* / Wind beneath my wings: *New York City Gay Men's Chorus* / Angel lies sleeping: *Psyche* / Fly to me: *Aleph* / Knock on wood: *Hot Stuff*
CD SPV 08496232
SPV / Dec '96 / Koch / Plastic Head

GLAD TO BE GAY VOL.3
Heartbeat: *Somerville, Jimmy* / I believe: *Roland, Calvin* / Hand up lovers: *Right Said Fred* / It's raining men: *Weather Girls* / Blame it on the boogie: *Big Fun* / Let me be your underwear: *Club 69* / Sex Dwarf: *Soft Cell* / I'm so beautiful: *Divine* / In the navy: *Village People* / Legendary children (all of them queer): *Johnson, Holly* / Free gay and happy (coming out anthem): *Coming Out Krew* / Lover come back to me: *Dead Or Alive* / She drives me crazy: *Fine Young Cannibals* / Walk on the wide side: *No Soul* / Rumpelstilzchen: *Golden Shower*
CD CD 08589912
SPV / Dec '96 / Koch / Plastic Head

GLAM PARTY SUPERMIX (The Glam Rock All-Stars)
Hello hello I'm back again / I'm the leader of the gang I am / Glisten yeah / Rock 'n' roll part 1 / I didn't know I loved you (till I saw you rock'n'roll) / Do you wanna touch me (Oh yeah) / I love you love me love / Blockbuster / Teenage rampage / Wig-wam bam / Ballroom blitz / Hell raiser / Fox on the run / Daytona demon / Can the can / Devilgate Drive / 48 Crash / You you you / Red dress / My coo ca choo / Jealous mind / Hot love / Metal guru / Get it on / 20th century boy / Shang-a-lang / All of me loves all of you / Remember (sha-la-la) / Bye bye baby / Skweeze me pleeze me / Cum on feel the noize / Mama we're all crazee now / Gudbuy t'Jane / Tears I cried / Let's get together again / Angelface / Goodbye my love / Waterloo / Mamma Mia / SOS / Dynamite / Crazy / L-L-Lucy / Tiger feet / Rebel rebel / Diamond dogs / Jean Genie / John I'm only dancing / Bump / Fancy pants / Sugar baby love / I can do it / Tell him / New York groove / Glass of champagne / (Dancing) On a Saturday night
CD 3036000762
Carlton / Feb '97 / Carlton

GLAM ROCK SPECIAL
CD 12539
Laserlight / May '95 / Target/BMG

GLASS OF CHAMPAGNE
CD 10452
CMC / Jun '97 / BMG

GLEN OF TRANQUILLITY
Rosebud / Annie Laurie / Glen of tranquillity / Morning has broken / My heart is in the highlands / Rowan tree / Flow gently sweet Afton / Mother nature's son / Rest thy weary head / Come oe'r the stream Charlie / Wee highland glen / Land o' the Leel / Ye banks and braes
CD RECD 512
REL / Apr '97 / CM / Duncans / Highlander

GLENFIDDICH PIPING CHAMPIONSHIP (Ceol Mor Piobaireachd)
CD CDMON 811
Monarch / Jul '94 / ADA / CM / Direct / Duncans

GLENFIDDICH PIPING CHAMPIONSHIP (Ceol Beag - March, Strathspey & Reel)
CD CDMON 812
Monarch / Jul '94 / ADA / CM / Direct / Duncans

GLITTERS IS GOLD
Tyger tyger: *Jah Wobble* / Songs of innocence: *Jah Wobble* / Whole wide world: *Eno, Roger* / In water: *Eno, Roger* / Sidelong glance from my round Nefertiti: *Budd, Harold* / Feral: *Budd, Harold* / Swanky: *Eno, Brian* / Blissed: *Eno, Brian* / Coventry carol: *St. John, Kate* / Notti senza amore: *St. John, Kate* / Sphere of no form: *Biosphere* / Kobresia: *Biosphere*
CD ASCD 031
All Saints / May '97 / Discovery / Vital

GLOBAL BRAZILIANS
CD EFA 064622
Metalimbo / Aug '95 / SRD

GLOBAL CELEBRATION (4CD Set)
CD Set ELLICD 3230
Ellipsis Arts / Apr '94 / ADA / Direct

GLOBAL CUTS VOL.1
Piano power: *Remy & Sven* / 20 Hz: *Capricorn* / Hectic boogie: *X-Tatic* / Hammond groove: *Mr. Marvin* / Monkey forest: *X-Tatic* / Cool lemon: *Cool Lemon* / Tsjika boem tsjak: *Remy & Sven* / Ride the wave: *Manpower* / Warwick: *Fowlkes, Eddie 'Flashin'* / LFOhhhh: *Remy & Sven* / Tribal zone: *OHM* / Crystal clear: *Soul Searchers*
CD RSGC 012CD
Global Cuts / Jul '93 / Vital

GLOBAL CUTS VOL.2
In thee garden: *Aphrohead* / Soul glow: *Soap Factory* / Planet jupiter 6: *Van Hees, Sven* / Saints go marching on: *K-Hand* / Smoke: *Dynetic* / Inside your mind: *God* / One dance: *Fowlkes, Eddie 'Flashin'* / Psychedelic bellydance: *Van Hees, Sven* / Harder: *FRS* / Drop (take off): *Symmetrics* / Lush: *Orbital* / Dynetic: *Smoke*
CD RSGC 026CD
Global Cuts / Nov '95 / Vital

GLOBAL DIVAS (3CD Set)
CD Set ROUCD 5062/3/4
Rounder / Dec '95 / ADA / CM / Direct

GLOBAL HOUSE GROOVES VOL.1
CD BDRCD 2
Breakdown / Jul '94 / Pinnacle

GLOBAL HOUSE GROOVES VOL.2
CD BDRCD 7
Breakdown / Apr '95 / Pinnacle

GLOBAL HOUSE VOL.1
CD SUN 49892
Mokum / Nov '95 / Pinnacle

GLOBAL HOUSE VOL.2
CD SUN 49882
Mokum / May '96 / Pinnacle

GLOBAL MEDITATION (4CD Set)
CD Set ELL 3210
Ellipsis Arts / Oct '93 / ADA / Direct

GLOBAL NITE LIFE VOL.1 (4CD Set)
Disco love: *Uncut Grooves* / Will there be: *Anorak Trax* / Surrender: *Love De Luxe* / Work: *Dynamic Kutz* / Funky groove: *Windross, Norris* / What is going on: *Dex* / Cookie crumbs: *Bash Street Kids* / Falling like dominoes: *Jazzheads* / Don't go away: *Mauritio* / Native love: *Wild Women Of Wonga* / So addicted: *XXX & Eliza* / Can't fight this feeling: *Hyper Rhythm* / Chant: *Gangster Hood Corp* / Nature: *Nature* / Luv it up: *Jump* / Trance dance: *Njoko* / Thank you: *Wild Women Of Wonga* / Gotta get loose: *Must* / No rich fat Daddy: *Jump* / Samarkand: *MLO* / Way down inside: *Fat Tulips* / Perfect chaos: *Justice* / Place called acid: *Thursday Club* / Ooh boy: *Ellis D* / My generation: *Peter Piper* / Space traveller: *New London Jazz Connection* / Squelch: *Fini Tribe* / On T go: *RAW* / Give me a wink: *Fingers Project* / Ska kore: *Mass Energy* / Beyond motion: *Incisions* / London's on acid: *Cabbage Patch* / Calling the people: *A-Zone* / In the heart of the night: *Overhead Noise* / Ibiza: *Denia* / To amora: *Mamba*
CD Set GLNCD 001
Global Nite Life / Jul '97 / Pinnacle

GLOBAL PARTNERSHIP VOL.1
CD GP 001CD
Labarynth / Nov '94 / Pinnacle

GLOBAL PARTNERSHIP VOL.2
CD RGNET 1003CD
World Music Network / Oct '95 / ADA / New Note/Pinnacle

GLOBAL PSYCHEDELIC TRANCE COMPILATION VOL.1
Zoa: *Kuro* / Solar energy: *Electric Universe* / Telepathy: *Infinity Project* / Seventh L: *Crossbreed* / Harddome 140: *Adrenalin Drum* / Neutron dance: *Electric Universe* / Binary neuronaut: *Infinity Project* / Hypnotiser: *Adrenalin Drum* / Brix: *Crossbreed*
CD SPIRIT 4006
Spiritzone / May '95 / Vital

GLOBESTYLE WORLDWIDE - YOUR GUIDE
Saludando / Yachilvi veyachail / Kesetse Mahiomolenu / Chorepste / Raha manina / Sirvientas / El anillo / Le Brijano / Iyole / El Beso / Ah laa jarah / Knowale / Chedh Hime Dh'Loumayere / Fuego Lento / Les Dorlanes / Feam Baliha
CD CDORB 018
Globestyle / Mar '88 / Pinnacle

GLORIOUS SUNRISE (A Magical Blend Of Music And The Sounds Of Nature)
CD 57612
CMC / May '97 / BMG

GLORY OF CHRISTMAS, THE (4CD Set)
O come all ye faithful (adeste fidelis) / God rest ye merry gentlemen / Holly and the ivy / Unto us is born a son / Once in Royal David's city / Silent night / Away in a manger / It came upon a midnight clear / I saw three ships / O little town of Bethlehem / Ding dong merrily on high / Hark the herald angels sing / First Noel / Deck the halls / Coventry carol / While shepherd's watch / Good King Wenceslas / In the bleak mid winter / Infant holy, infant lowly / We wish you a merry Christmas / O little town of Bethlehem / O come all ye faithful (adeste fidelis) / God rest ye merry gentlemen / Silent night / Hark the herald angels sing / While shepherds watched their flocks / Good King Wenceslas / We wish you a merry Christmas / Twelve days of Christmas / Torches / Christmas is coming / Of the father's heart begotten / Personent hodie / O come, O coem Emmanuel / Holly and the ivy / As with gladness men of old / We three Kings / Personent hodie / Infant King / Quiem pastores laudavere / In dulci jubilo / Sussex carol / Adam lay y bounden / Whence is that goodly fragrance / Of the Father's heart begotten / In the bleak mid winter / Cherry tree carol / Tomorrow shall be my dancing day / Virgin most pure / O come, O come Emmanuel / Joys seven / Twelve days of Christmas / See amid the winter's snow / Past three o'clock / Jingle bells / King Jesus hath a garden / Shepherd's pipe carol / Christmas is coming / Sans day carol / Torches / Great and mighty wonder / Angels from the realms of glory / Jesus Christ the apple tree / O little town of Bethlehem / Infant holy, infant lowly / Candlelight carol / Once in Royal David's City / Star carol / In the winter darkness / Carol of the children / Here comes Christmas / Silver sleigh / Christmas cheer / Away in a manger / Nativity carol / I saw three ships / In the bleak mid winter / Mary had a baby / Sussex carol / Little Jesus sweetly slept / While shepherds watched their flocks / Child in the manger / Unto us is born a son / Cowboy carol
CD Set QUAD 019
Tring / Nov '96 / Tring

GLORY OF GOSPEL (2CD Set)
CD Set DEMPCD 003
Emporio / Mar '96 / Disc

GLORY OF LOVE
CD 12204
Laserlight / Dec '94 / Target/BMG

GLORY OF SPAIN
CD CDMOIR 416
Memoir / Oct '92 / Jazz Music / Target/ BMG

GLORY OF THE MUSIC HALL VOL.1, THE
Let's have a song upon the gramophone: *Williams, Billy* / Seaside holiday at home: *Campbell, Herbert* / Man who broke the bank at Monte Carlo: *Coborn, Charles* / Two lovely black eyes: *Coborn, Charles* / Topsy turvy: *Roberts, Arthur* / Fishing club: *Anderson, Harry* / I wouldn't leave my little wooden hut for you: *Shepard, Burt* / Something tickled her fancy: *Randall, Harry* / Our little nipper: *Chevalier, Albert* / Adam missed it: *Knowles, R.G.* / Girl, the woman and the widow: *Knowles, R.G.* / Little Dolly Daydream: *Stratton, Eugene* / Wait 'til I'm his father: *Leno, Dan* / Wait 'til the work comes round: *Elen, Gus* / Never introduce yer Donah to a pal: *Elen, Gus* / There's another fellow looks like me: *Lashwood, George* / Piccaninny: *Hurley, Alec* / What a nut: *Tilley, Vesta* / There's a good time coming for the ladies: *Tilley, Vesta* / You can't help laughing can yer: *Champion, Harry* / Wotcher, my old brown son: *Champion, Harry* / Paperbag cookery: *Fragson, Harry* / Goodbye Dolly Gray: *Stormont, Leo* / Bel-

gium put the kibosh on the Kaiser: *Sheridan, Mark* / Here we are again: *Sheridan, Mark*
CD GEMMCD 9475
Pearl / Feb '91 / Harmonia Mundi

GLORY OF THE MUSIC HALL VOL.2, THE
Poor, proud and particular: *Ford, Harry* / Tally ho: *Little Tich* / Best man: *Little Tich* / Editress: *Robey, George* / Servants' registry office: *Robey, George* / Something on his mind: *Lloyd, Marie* / Wee Jean McGregor: *Lauder, Harry* / Rob Roy-Tam-O-Chanter O'Brian: *Lauder, Harry* / Cuckoo: *Wallace, Nellie* / Mother's pie crust: *Wallace, Nellie* / Honeysuckle and the bee: *Davies, Belle* / While you wait: *Albert, Ben* / I'll be your sweetheart: *Hawthorne, Lil* / Fishing: *Tate, Harry* / I was having my breakfast in bed: *Mayo, Sam* / Put that gramophone record on again: *Mayo, Sam* / I shall sulk: *Pleasants, Jack* / I'm shy, Mary Ellen, I'm shy: *Pleasants, Jack* / Give it a smile: *Whelan, Albert* / Everybody loves me: *Terriss, Ellaline* / I can say 'truly rural': *Bard, Wilkie* / It's nice to have a friend: *Forde, Florrie* / Old Bull and Bush: *Forde, Florrie* / Come into the garden John: *Williams, Billy* / Here we go again: *Williams, Billy*
CD GEMMCD 9476
Pearl / Feb '91 / Harmonia Mundi

GLORY OF THE MUSIC HALL VOL.3, THE
If you knew Susie like I know Susie: *Shields, Ella* / Ours is a nice 'ouse, ours is: *Lester, Alfred* / Germs: *Lester, Alfred* / Odds and ends, or Sunday mornings: *Formby, George* / I kept on waving my flag: *Formby, George* / If the wind had only blown the other way: *Scott, Maidie* / Spaniard who blighted my life: *Merson, Billy* / I've had my future told: *Elliott, G.H.* / I can't do my bally bottom button up: *Mayne, Ernie* / Moonlight bay: *Connolly, Dolly* / Agatha Green: *Cooper, Margaret* / So long Sally: *Weldon, Harry* / What do you want to make (parody): *Weldon, Harry* / Gretchen: *Moore Duprez, May* / And it was: *Laurier, Jay* / Anna Gray: *Gitana, Gertie* / Never mind: *Gitana, Gertie* / Rickety stairs: *Latona, Jen* / Come over the garden wall: *Mayne, Clarice & That* / Mr. and Mrs. Smith: *Mayne, Clarice & That* / Don't have any more, Mrs. Moore: *Morris, Lily* / I want a girl - just like the girl that married dear old Dad: *Ward, Dorothy* / Oh Mr. Porter: *Blaney, Norah* / 'E can't take a roise out of oi: *Chevalier, Albert*
CD GEMMCD 9477
Pearl / Feb '91 / Harmonia Mundi

GLUCKLICH VOL.2
CD COMP 021CD
Compost / Jun '96 / Plastic Head / SRD / Timewarp

GNAWA FROM MARRAKECH (Songs For Sidi Mimoun)
CD RDC 5035CD
Robi Droli / May '97 / ADA / Direct

GO AHEAD PUNK MAKE MY DAY
CD 158092
Nitro / Nov '96 / Pinnacle / Plastic Head

GO AHEAD VOL.3 (2CD Set)
CD Set H&GCD 004
H&G / Jun '97 / Intergroove

GO BANG 2.5
CD TNO 5101CD
Techno 404 / May '94 / Koch

GO GO POWER
Go go power: *Desanto, Sugar Pie* / Let's wade in the water: *Shaw, Marlena* / Jerk and twine: *Ross, Jackie* / Love ain't nothin': *Nash, Johnny* / Secret love: *Stewart, Billy* / In the basement: *Desanto, Sugar Pie & Etta James* / Mellow fellow: *James, Etta* / Grits ain't groceries: *Little Milton* / Ain't love good, ain't love proud: *Clarke, Tony* / Look at me now: *Callier, Terry* / Peak of love: *McClure, Bobby* / Do I make myself clear: *Desanto, Sugar Pie & Etta James* / Seven day fool: *James, Etta* / That'll get it: *Knight Brothers* / I don't wanna fuss: *Desanto, Sugar Pie* / Strange feeling: *Nash, Johnny* / Take me for a little while: *Ross, Jackie* / Love is a five letter word: *Phelps, James* / Ain't no big deal: *Little Milton*
CD CDARC 512
Charly / Jan '93 / Koch

GO SKA GO
CD CDHB 199
Heartbeat / Nov '95 / ADA / Direct / Greensleeves / Jet Star

GO WITH THE FLOW
Dream on dreamer: *Brand New Heavies* / Always there: *Incognito & Jocelyn Brown* / Space cowboy: *Jamiroquai* / Apparently nothin': *Young Disciples* / Long time gone: *Galliano* / Dream's a dream: *Soul II Soul* / Everthing is going to be alright: *Sounds Of Blackness* / Real love: *Driza Bone* / Mama said: *Anderson, Carleen* / Pushing against the flow: *Raw Stylus* / Turn in turn on cop out: *Raw Stylus* / Everyday: *Incognito* / Midnight at the oasis: *Brand New Heavies* / Moving on up: *M-People* / Masterplan: *Brown, Diana & Barrie K Sharpe* / Love the life: *Taylor, James Quartet* / Won't talk about it: *Beats International* / People in the middle: *Spearhead* / Everybody's got summer: *Atlantic Starr* / Cantaloop: *US 3*
CD 5352412
PolyGram TV / Feb '96 / PolyGram

GO-KART VS. THE CORPORATE GIANT
CD GKCD 021
Go-Kart / Mar '97 / Greyhound / Pinnacle

GOA HEAD VOL.1
CD 560002
Westcom / Oct '96 / Koch / Pinnacle

GOA HEAD VOL.2 (2CD Set)
CD Set 560072
Westcom / Mar '97 / Koch / Pinnacle

GOA HEAD VOL.3 (2CD Set)
Ionised: *Astral Projection* / Astral voyage: *Electric Universe* / UX: *Dominion* / Taiyo: *Prana* / SecrPagan dance: *Secret* / Audio engine: *Multiplex* / Neuromancer: *Shakta* / Million miles an hour: *Beach Buddha* / MiGreen man: *Miranda* / Jungle storm: *Talamasca* / Ancient forest: *Sundog* / Sunset skyline: *Electric Universe* / Zero: *Astral Projection & Dedrah* / Overwind: *Infinity Project* / Two vindaloos and an onion bhagee: *Green Nuns Of The Revolution* / Tribalistic: *Ominus* / Deep space 5d: *Dimension 5* / To eternity: *MFG* / Answer: *NDMA* / AlphaNew shoes: *Alphanaut*
CD Set 560172
Nova Tekk / Aug '97 / Pinnacle

GOA RAUME VOL.1 (A Journey Into Psychedelic Trance/2CD Set)
Trommelmaschine: *Der Dritte Raum* / Braindance: *Kaaya* / Stratosfearless: *Kox Box* / UX: *Disco Volante* / Padomania: *Charm* / Zeta reticuli: *Pleindians* / Viral spiral: *Deviant Electronics* / Enter the 2nd earth: *Schuldt, Tim* / Great sin: *Spacetribe* / Psycho activity: *X-Dream* / Liquid troll: *Chakra & Edi Mis* / Satellite: *Moon & The Sun* / Step to the star: *Miranda* / Close zen counters: *Tristan* / Online information: *Electric Universe* / Pile: *Semsis* / Smell's electronic: *Metal Spark*
CD Set SPV 08992562
SPV / Mar '97 / Koch / Plastic Head

GOA TRANCE VOL.1
CD TRIPCD 2
Rumour / Oct '95 / 3mv/Sony / Mo's Music Machine / Pinnacle

GOA TRANCE VOL.2
CD TRIPCD 3
Rumour / Jan '96 / 3mv/Sony / Mo's Music Machine / Pinnacle

GOA TRANCE VOL.3
CD TRIPCD 4
Rumour / May '96 / 3mv/Sony / Mo's Music Machine / Pinnacle

GOA TRANCE VOL.4
CD TRIPCD 6
Rumour / Aug '96 / 3mv/Sony / Mo's Music Machine / Pinnacle

GOA TRANCE VOL.5
CD TRIPCD 09
Rumour / Jan '97 / 3mv/Sony / Mo's Music Machine / Pinnacle

GOA TRANCE VOL.6
Project Oblivion: *Conspiracy Theory* / Spirit: *Sourmash* / Drama: *Manmademan* / Alien hitmen: *Slide* / Starkissed: *Secret* / Crowd nine: *Eco* / Abraxis: *Shining Path* / Omnifarious Splifferous: *Shamanic Tribes On Acid* / Planet Bliss: *Super Skunk* / Spectre: *Blue Book*
CD TRIPCD 11
Rumour / Jun '97 / 3mv/Sony / Mo's Music Machine / Pinnacle

GOA TRANCENDENTAL VOL.1
CD TRIPCD 8
Rumour / Nov '96 / 3mv/Sony / Mo's Music Machine / Pinnacle

GOA TRANCENDENTAL VOL.2
CD TRIPCD 10
Rumour / Mar '97 / 3mv/Sony / Mo's Music Machine / Pinnacle

GOD IS THE OWNER OF THEE WORLD
CD ALCHECD 001
Spinefarm / Feb '94 / Plastic Head

GOD LESS AMERICA
CD EFA 115952
Crypt / Nov '95 / Shellshock/Disc

GOD SAVE THE QUEEN (20 Years Of Punk - 3CD Set)
CD Set KITOFF 50
Dressed To Kill / Apr '97 / Total/BMG

GODFATHERS OF BRITPOP, THE
CD 5352572
PolyGram TV / Jan '96 / PolyGram

GODFATHERS OF GERMAN GOTH VOL.2
CD SPV 08438372
SPV / Jul '95 / Koch / Plastic Head

GODS OF GRIND
Stranger aeons: *Entombed* / Incarnated solvent abuse: *Carcass* / Soul sacrafice: *Cathedral* / Condemned: *Confessor* / Tools of the trade: *Carcass* / Dusk: *Entombed* / Golden blood (flooding): *Cathedral* / Pyosisified (Still rotten to the gore): *Carcass* / Shreds of flesh: *Entombed* / Autumn twilight: *Cathedral* / Last judgement: *Confessor* / Hepatic tissue fermentation: *Carcass* / Frozen rapture: *Cathedral* / Endtime: *Confessor*
CD MOSH 063CD
Earache / Mar '92 / Vital

GOIN' COUNTRY (The Definitive Line Dancing Album)
Goin' country: *Watermelon Henry* / There you go: *White, Martin* / EJ's bar: *Richmond, Simon* / Country married rock 'n' roll: *Anton & The Buzz Band* / Line dancin' days: *Capricorn* / Country music hall of fame: *McCall, T.J.* / This don't feel like dancin': *Lee, Bobby* / No honky tonks in Heaven: *Hollywood Hillbillies* / Too easy: *Shot To Pieces* / Good times come around: *Richmond, Simon* / Love my car: *Watermelon Henry* / Love kept it's hold on my heart: *Sayer, Chris* / I learnt a thing or two: *Horton, Quinton* / Ain't life wonderful: *Shot To Pieces* / Saddle up country style: *Christ[illegible]avid* / Louisiana: *Watermelon Henry* / Daddy's got his blue jeans on: *Richmond, Simon* / Oregon trail: *Cheap Seats* / Three time loser: *Hollywood Hillbillies* / Here, there and everywhere: *Cheap Seats* / Situation vacant: *Northern Lights* / Burnin' fire: *Watermelon Henry* / Let's hear it for the ladies: *Richmond, Simon*
CD 5526492
Spectrum / Jan '97 / PolyGram

GOING BACK IN TIME
CD KWCD 807
Kenwest / Jul '94 / THE

GOLD HEART LOVE SONGS
CD FEBCD 14
Connoisseur Collection / Jan '94 / Pinnacle

GOLDEN AGE OF AMERICAN ROCK 'N' ROLL VOL.1, THE (Hard-To-Get Hot 100 Hits From 1954-1963)
Denise: *Randy & The Rainbows* / Sally go round the roses: *Jaynetts* / Mule skinner blues: *Fendermen* / Sixteen candles: *Crests* / Pretty little angel eyes: *Lee, Curtis* / Love how you love me: *Paris Sisters* / Big hurt: *Fisher, Miss Toni* / Thousand stars: *Young, Kathy* / Rockin' robin: *Day, Bobby* / Earth angel: *Penguins* / Bongo rock: *Epps, Preston* / Tossin' and turnin': *Lewis, Bobby* / My true story: *Jive Five* / Stranded in the jungle: *Cadets* / Angel baby: *Rosie & The Originals* / Party lights: *Clark, Claudine* / When we get married: *Dreamlovers* / Cindy's birthday: *Crawford, Johnny* / Let's dance: *Montez, Chris* / Who's that knocking: *Genies* / Love you so: *Holden, Ron* / Cherry pie: *Skip & Fly* / Since I don't have you: *Skyliners* / Louie Louie: *Kingsmen* / Since I fell for you: *Welch, Lenny* / Image of a girl: *Safaris* / Smoky places: *Corsairs* / Gee whiz: *Innocents* / Little bit of soap: *Jarmels* / Eddie my love: *Teen Queens*
CD CDCHD 289
Ace / Oct '91 / Pinnacle

GOLDEN AGE OF AMERICAN ROCK 'N' ROLL VOL.2, THE (Hot 100 Hits From 1954-1963)
Memphis: *Mack, Lonnie* / I sold my heart to the junkman: *Blue Belles* / You belong to me: *Duprees* / Your Ma said you cried in your sleep last night: *Dino, Kenny* / Million to one: *Charles, Jimmy* / Rockin' in the jungle: *Eternals* / Wild weekend: *Rockin' Rebels* / Stay: *Williams, Maurice & The Zodiacs* / Down the aisle of love: *Quintones* / Mountain of love: *Dorman, Harold* / Nag: *Halos* / Let the little girl dance: *Bland, Billy* / There's a moon out tonight: *Capris* / Get a job: *Silhouettes* / You: *Aquatones* / Buzz buzz buzz: *Hollywood Flames* / I've had it: *Bell Notes* / I know (you don't love me no more): *George, Barbara* / Mr. Lonely: *Videls* / In the still of the nite: *Five Satins* / Church bells may ring: *Willows* / That's life (that's tough): *Gabriel & the angels* / Rumble: *Wray, Link* / Let's stomp: *Comstock, Bobby* / Oh Julie: *Crescendos* / Little darlin': *Gladiolas* / Teen beat: *Nelson, Sandy* / Diamonds and pearls: *Paradons* / Alley oop: *Hollywood Argyles* / California sun: *Rivieras*
CD CDCHD 445
Ace / May '93 / Pinnacle

GOLDEN AGE OF AMERICAN ROCK 'N' ROLL VOL.3, THE (Hot 100 Hits From 1954-1963)
All American boy: *Parsons, Bill* / Kansas city: *Harrison, Wilbert* / My true love: *Scott, Jack* / Jennie Lee: *Jan & Arnie* / Joker: *Myles, Billy* / Beat: *Rockin R's* / To know him is to love him: *Teddy Bears* / When you dance: *Turbans* / Love letters: *Lester, Ketty* / So tough: *Kuf Linx* / To the aisle: *Five Satins* / La dee dah: *Billie & Lillie* / Endless sleep: *Reynolds, Jody* / Chicken baby chicken: *Harris, Tony* / Lover's island: *Blue Jays* / No chemise please: *Granahan, Gerry* / It was I: *Skip & Flip* / Tonight I fell in love: *Tokens* / Happy birthday blues: *Young, Karen & The Innocents* / Rockin' little angel: *Smith, Ray* / Tonite tonite: *Mello Kings* / Cha hua hua: *Pets* / Western movies: *Olympics* / Girl in my dreams: *Cliques* / Sugar shack: *Fireballs* / There is something on your mind: *McNeely, 'Big' Jay* / Womans a mans best friend: *Teddy & The Twilights* / Sacred: *Castells* / Freeze: *Tony & Joe* / Click clack: *Dicky Doo & Don'ts*
CD CDCHD 497
Ace / Jan '94 / Pinnacle

GOLDEN AGE OF AMERICAN ROCK 'N' ROLL VOL.4, THE (Hot 100 Hits From 1954-1963)
Linda Lou: *Sharpe, Ray* / Little by little: *Brown, Nappy* / Rama lama ding dong: *Edsels* / Flamingo express: *Royaltones* / New Orleans: *Bonds* / Maybe: *Chantels* / Drip drop: *Dion* / Start movin' (in my direction): *Mined, Sal* / Lonely Saturday night: *French, Don* / Don't let go: *Hamilton, Roy* / Pop pop pop-pie: *Sherrys* / Life's too short: *Harris, Lafayette Jr.* / High school USA: *Facenda, Tommy* / Glory of love: *Roomates* / Peanuts: *Little Joe & The Thrillers* / Need you: *Owens, Donnie* / Party doll: *Knox, Buddy* / Could this be magic: *Dubs* / Killer Joe: *Rocky Fellers* / Barbara: *Temptations* / Peek-a-boo: *Cadillacs* / You'll lose a good thing: *Lynn, Barbara* / Lucky ladybug: *Billie & Lillie* / Tears on my pillow: *Imperials* / Baby talk: *Jan & Dean* / Here I stand: *Rip Chords* / Do the mashed potato: *Kendrick, Nat* / Why don't you write me: *Jacks* / Barbara Ann: *Regents* / Those oldies but goodies (remind me of you): *Little Caesar & The Romans*
CD CDCHD 500
Ace / Oct '94 / Pinnacle

GOLDEN AGE OF AMERICAN ROCK 'N' ROLL VOL.5, THE (Hot 100 Hits From 1954-1963)
Wiggle wiggle: *Accents* / Love potion no. 9: *Clovers* / I'm leaving it up to you: *Dale & Grace* / You cheated: *Shields* / It will stand: *Showmen* / Sleepwalk: *Santo & Johnny* / Nothin' shakin': *Fontaine, Eddie* / Happy, happy birthday baby: *Tune Weavers* / Heart and soul: *Jan & Dean* / What's your name: *Don & Juan* / Little bitty pretty one: *Harris, Thurston & The Sharps* / Darling Lorraine: *Knockouts* / Tallahassee lassie: *Cannon, Freddy* / Tell me why: *Belmonts* / Over the mountain, across the sea: *Johnnie & Joe* / Ka-ding dong: *G-Clefs* / Underwater: *Frogmen* / She cried: *Jay & The Americans* / Just a little bit: *Gordon, Rosco* / Sometime: *Thomas, Gene* / Ain't gonna kiss ya: *Ribbons* / Midnight stroll: *Revels* / Walk: *McCracklin, Jimmy* / Hey little girl: *Clark, Dee* / This is the nite: *Valiants* / Tell him no: *Travis & Bob* / Bad boy: *Jive Bombers* / Stranded in the jungle: *Jayhawks* / Duke of Earl: *Chandler, Gene* / Goodnight sweetheart goodnight: *Spaniels*
CD CDCHD 600
Ace / Sep '95 / Pinnacle

GOLDEN AGE OF AMERICAN ROCK 'N' ROLL VOL.6, THE (Hot 100 Hits From 1954-1963)
Shirley: *Fred, John* / Come go with me: *Del-Vikings* / Black slacks: *Bennett, Joe & The Sparkletones* / Lollipop: *Ronald & Ruby* / Ten commandments of love: *Harvey & The Moonglows* / Love bug crawl: *Edwards, Jimmy* / Do you want to dance: *Freeman, Bobby* / Hard times (the slop): *Watts, Noble 'Thin Man'* / Imagination: *Quotations* / I wonder (if your love will ever belong to me): *Pentagons* / At my front door: *El Dorados* / You're so fine: *Falcons* / Tall cool one: *Wailers* / Shape I'm in: *Restivo, Johnny* / Little star: *Elegants* / Lover please: *McPhatter, Clyde* / Charlena: *Sevilles* / Pledging my love: *Ace, Johnny* / Itchy twitchy feeling: *Hendricks, Bobby* / Priscilla: *Cooley, Eddie & The Dimples* / Hold back the tears: *Delacardos* / You can make it if you try: *Allison, Gene* / Real wild child: *Ivan* / Quarter to four stomp: *Stompers* / Don't you just know it: *Smith, Huey 'Piano' & The Clowns* / I'm walkin': *Nelson, Rick* / I love an angel: *Little Bill & The Bluenotes* / Short shorts: *Royal Teens* / Hide and go seek: *Hill, Bunker* / Papa-oom-mow-mow: *Rivingtons*
CD CDCHD 650
Ace / Jan '97 / Pinnacle

GOLDEN AGE OF BEGUINE, THE
CD 995672
EPM / Jul '96 / ADA / Discovery

GOLDEN AGE OF BLACK MUSIC VOL.1, THE
Don't play that song: *Franklin, Aretha* / Day dreaming: *Franklin, Aretha* / Until you come bakc to me (That's what I'm gonna do): *Franklin, Aretha* / Groove me: *Floyd, King* / Precious, precious: *Moore, Jackie* / Don't let the green grass fool you: *Pickett, Wilson* / Don't knock my love (part 1): *Pickett, Wilson* / First time I ever saw your face: *Flack, Roberta* / Killing me softly: *Flack, Roberta* / Feel like makin' love: *Flack, Roberta* / Could it be I'm falling in love: *Spinners* / Then came you: *Warwick, Dionne & The Detroit Spinners* / Sideshow: *Blue Magic* / They just can't stop it (games people play: *Blue Magic*
CD 7567819122
Atlantic / Jan '97 / Warner Music

GOLDEN AGE OF BLACK MUSIC VOL.2, THE
Dance dance dance: *Chic* / Le freak: *Chic* / Closer I get to you: *Flack, Roberta & Donny Hathaway* / We are family: *Sister Sledge* / Good times: *Chic* / You are in the system: *System* / Don't disturb this groove: *System* / (Pop, pop, pop) Goes my mind: *Levert* / Casanova: *Levert* / Miki Howard come share my love: *Levert* / So amazing: *Albright, Gerald*

CD 7567819132
Atlantic / Jan '97 / Warner Music

GOLDEN AGE OF BOLERO, THE
CD 995662
EPM / May '96 / ADA / Discovery

GOLDEN AGE OF SWING VOL.1 1929-1939, THE (Big Band Legends)
CD 158452
Jazz Archives / Nov '95 / Discovery

GOLDEN AGE OF SWING VOL.1, THE (20 Greatest Hits)
Eager beaver: Kenton, Stan / Yes indeed: Dorsey, Tommy & Jo Stafford/Sy Oliver / Perdido: Ellington, Duke / Let me off uptown: Krupa, Gene & Anita O'Day/Roy Eldridge / Don't be that way: Lunceford, Jimmie & Dan Grissom / Blues in the night: Goodman, Benny / Woodchoppers ball: Herman, Woody / Chatanooga choo choo: Miller, Glenn & Tex Beneke/Dorothy Dandridge / Concerto for clarinet: Shaw, Artie / Tangerine: Dorsey, Jimmy & Bob Eberly/Helen O'Connell / South Rampart Street parade: Crosby, Bob / Any old time: Shaw, Artie & Billie Holiday / And the angels sing: Elman, Ziggy / Why don't you do right: Goodman, Benny & Peggy Lee / Cherokee: Barnet, Charlie / Mr. Paganini: Webb, Chick & Ella Fitzgerald / One o'clock jump: Basie, Count / Two o'clock jump: James, Harry / Sing sing sing: Henderson, Fletcher & Georgia Boy Simpkins / Flying home: Hampton, Lionel
CD DBMCD 3001
Horatio Nelson / Nov '96 / Disc

GOLDEN AGE OF SWING VOL.2, THE (Big Band Legends)
CD 158462
Jazz Archives / Jul '96 / Discovery

GOLDEN AGE OF SWING VOL.3 (1929-1945)
CD 158882
Jazz Archives / Jun '97 / Discovery

GOLDEN COLLECTION OF IRISH MUSIC (2CD Set)
CD Set DCDP 3
Dolphin / Sep '96 / CM / Else / Grapevine/ PolyGram / Koch

GOLDEN COUNTRY VOL.1 (Let Your Love Flow)
CD MU 5029
Musketeer / Oct '92 / Disc

GOLDEN COUNTRY VOL.2 (From A Jack To A King)
CD MU 5030
Musketeer / Oct '92 / Disc

GOLDEN COUNTRY VOL.3 (Love Hurts)
CD MU 5031
Musketeer / Oct '92 / Disc

GOLDEN COUNTRY VOL.4 (Love Me Tender)
CD MU 5032
Musketeer / Oct '92 / Disc

GOLDEN COUNTRY VOL.5 (Games People Play)
CD MU 5033
Musketeer / Oct '92 / Disc

GOLDEN DAYS, THE
Route 66: Cole, Nat 'King' / You're the cream in my coffee: Cole, Nat 'King' / Too marvellous for words: Cole, Nat 'King' / When you're smiling (The whole world smiles with you): Cole, Nat 'King' / Into each life some rain must fall: Fitzgerald, Ella & Ink Spots / In the mood: Miller, Glenn / Friendship: Garland, Judy & Johnny Mercer / Opus No.1: Dorsey, Tommy / Shine: Crosby, Bing & The Mills Brothers / MacPherson is rehearsin' (To swing): Fitzgerald, Ella / Take the "A" train: Ellington, Duke / In a moment of weakness: Powell, Dick / Sunshine of your smile: Sinatra, Frank / Zing a little zong: Crosby, Bing & Jane Wyman / Taking a chance on love: Fitzgerald, Ella / Chattanooga choo choo: Miller, Glenn / Ida sweet as apple cider: Mills Brothers / How about you: Sinatra, Frank / Civilization (bongo, bongo, bongo): Andrews Sisters & Danny Kaye / Little Miss Broadway: Temple, Shirley & George Murphy / Darktown strutter's ball: Fitzgerald, Ella / You were never lovelier: Astaire, Fred / Connecticut: Garland, Judy & Bing Crosby / I'll be seeing you: Sinatra, Frank
CD ECD 3328
K-Tel / Mar '97 / K-Tel

GOLDEN FLUTE
CD GRF 238
Tring / Aug '93 / Tring

GOLDEN GIRLS OF THE 60'S
CD PLATCD 344
Platinum / Oct '90 / Prism

GOLDEN GROUPS
Tears on my pillow: Chimes / I'll find her: Dukes / Don't you know (I love you so): Maye, Arthur Lee & The Crowns / Nite owl: Allen, Tony & The Champs / Love you so: Crystals / Chimes ring out: Chimes / Foolish fool: Zeppa, Ben Joe & The Zephyrs / So long love: Dukes / Cool loving: Maye, Arthur Lee & The Crowns / She's gone: Metronomes / Sweet sixteen: Tropicals / My little girl: Pharaohs / It's true: Twilighters / Chop chop: Chimes / Gloria: Maye, Arthur Lee & The Crowns / I want cha baby: Gipson, Byron 'Slick' & The Sliders / Our romance: King, Clydie / Over the rainbow: Echoes / It's spring again: Pentagons / Silly dilly: Pentagons / Arlene: Titans / What have I done: Titans / Our school days: Monitors / Closer to heaven: Monitors / Miracle: Five Knights
CD CDCHD 515
Ace / Jan '94 / Pinnacle

GOLDEN HYMNS
CD CDSR 040
Telstar / May '94 / BMG

GOLDEN IRISH FAVOURITES
CD MACCD 311
Autograph / Aug '96 / BMG

GOLDEN MILES
CD RVCD 39
Raven / Dec '94 / ADA / Direct

GOLDEN ORGAN FAVOURITES
So what's new/Tie a yellow ribbon/Try a little kindness / Frenesi/Girl from Ipanema/In a little Spanish town/Elizabeth / We've only just begun/Strangers in the night/If / Anna/ Amorada/Tico tico / Waterloo/Ring ring/ Money money money / Swingin' shepherd blues / For the good times/Don't it make my brown eyes blue/After th / Beautiful Sunday/Knock three times/Yellow river / Breeze and I/The shadow of your smile/Perfidia/In the mood / Hi lili hi lo/Falling in love again/ The last waltz / Rivers of Babylon/Love is in the air/Feelings / Trumpet voluntary
CD QED 142
Tring / Nov '96 / Tring

GOLDEN PAN FLUTES
CD TREB 3001
Scratch / Mar '95 / Koch / Scratch/BMG

GOLDEN PIANO FAVOURITES
Almaz / When I fall in love / One more night / Song for Guy / Lara's theme / My way / Just the way you are / Cavatina / Endless love / Over the rainbow / Love story / Softly as I leave you / Way we were / Don't it make my brown eyes blue / Everything I do (I do it for you)
CD QED 069
Tring / Nov '96 / Tring

GOLDEN SAXOPHONE
CD GRF 239
Tring / Aug '93 / Tring

GOLDEN SHOWER OF 73 HITS
CD LF 200DCD
Lost & Found / Aug '95 / Plastic Head

GOLDEN SOUNDS OF HOME
CD 321062
Koch / Sep '92 / Koch

GOLDEN SWING BANDS OF THE FORTIES
Blue Lou / Blues / Livery stable blues / At the jazz band Ball / Big butter and egg man / Dippermouth blues / Bach goes to town / Farewell blues / One o'clock jump / Bugle call rag / I wish I could shimmy like my sister Kate / Eccentric / Uptown blues / Liza (all the clouds roll away) / Cheatin' on me / 'Taint what you do (it's the way that you do it) / Four or five times / I've found a new baby / Honeysuckle rose
CD QED 141
Tring / Nov '96 / Tring

GOLDEN TORCH STORY VOL.1, THE
Just like the weather: Chance, Nolan / I've got something: Sam & Kitty / Sliced tomatoes: Just Brothers / Sweet darlin': Clarke, Jimmy 'Soul' / Our love: Barnes, J.J. / Honey bee: Johnson, Johnny / I can't get away: Garrett, Bobby / I still love you: Superlatives / Crackin' up over you: Hamilton, Roy / Love you baby: Parker, Eddie / Personally: Paris, Bobby / One in a million: Brown, Maxine / Thumb a ride: Wright, Earl / I'm standing: Lumley, Rufus / I feel an urge: Armstead, Jo / I don't want to cry: Gray, Pearlean & The Passengers / Exus trek: Ingram, Luther / Keep on keeping on: Porter, N.F. / I'm so glad: Johnson, Herb / Quick change artist: Soul Twins / One wonderful moment: Shakers / Hit and run: Shakers / Soul self satisfaction: Jackson, Earl / That's alright: Crook, Ed / Compared to what: Mr. Floods Party / Blowing up my mind: Exciters / Please let me in: Barnes, J.J. / I love you baby: Scott, Cindy / Queen of the Go-Go: Garvin, Rex / Angel baby: Banks, Darrell
CD GSCD 061
Goldmine / May '95 / Vital

GOLDEN TORCH STORY VOL.2, THE (Revisited)
Just ask me: Guess, Lenis / Surprise party: Vibratin' Vibrations / What kind of lady: Sharp, Dee Dee / Free for all: Mitchell, Phillip / It ain't necessary: Galore, Mamie / I got the fever: Prophets / Breakaway: Valentines / Suzy's serenade: Wilson, Bob / Inky dinky wang dang doo: Dramatics / What would I do: Superiors / Unsatisfied: Johnson, Lou / Running for my life: Shelton, Roscoe / What would I do: Tymes / Case of love: Sequins / Love game A-Z: Royal Jokers / Too much: Conwell, Jimmy / They say: Ovations / If it's all the same to you babe: Ingram, Luther / Music: White, Jeanette / Bingo: Dynamics / Frantic escape: Innocent Bystanders / Don't be sore at me: Parliaments / Prove yourself a lady: Bounty, James / Number one: Exciters / I love the life I live: Michaels, Tony
CD GSCD 092
Goldmine / May '97 / Vital

GOLDEN TREASURY OF ELIZABETHAN MUSIC
Sellengers round: Broadside Band / This is the record of John: Red Byrd & The Rose Consort Of Viols / Bergamasqa: Broadside Band / In nomine a 5: Fretwork Consort Of Viols / Coventry carol: Sneak's Noyse / Passamezzo pavan: Weigand, George / Sing unto God: Red Byrd & The Rose Consort Of Viols / Spanish pavan/Galliard la gamba: York Waites / Go cristall tears: Trevor, Caroline & The Rose Consort Of Viols / A toye: Burnett, Richard / La doune cella: York Waites / Pavan - Lachrimae coactae: Rose Consort Of Viols / Greensleeves: Potter, John & The Broadside Band / Crimson velvet: York Waites / There dwelt a man in Babylon: Roberts, Deborah & The Broadside Band / Almain - The Night watch: York Waites / Come live with me: Potter, John & The Broadside Band / Bonny sweet Robin: Weigand, George / Pavan - Heigh ho Holyday: York Waites / Sweet was the song the virgin sung: Red Byrd & The Rose Consort Of Viols / Staines Morris: York Waites / Libera nos - salva nos a 5: Fretwork Consort Of Viols / Fortune my foe: Roberts, Deborah & The Broadside Band / Dulcina/ All you that love good fellowes: York Waites / Poor soul sat sighing: Roberts, Deborah & The Broadside Band / Fantasy a 5: Browning: Rose Consort Of Viols / Pavan - The cradle: York Waites / Farewell dear love: Potter, John & The Broadside Band / La bounette: York Waites
CD CDSAR 62
Amon Ra / Feb '96 / Harmonia Mundi

GOLDEN TRUMPET GREATS
Somewhere / Groovy kind of love / I don't know how to love him / If / What a wonderful world / All I ask of you / From a distance / Wind beneath my wings / It had to be you / Somewhere out there / Unchained melody / Everything I do (I do it for you) / Saltwater / Music of the night / That's what friends are for / Unforgettable
CD QED 119
Tring / Nov '96 / Tring

GOLDEN YEARS OF JAZZ VOL.1, THE
Muskrat ramble: Armstrong, Louis / St. Louis blues: Tatum, Art / Saving myself for you: Fitzgerald, Ella / Beale Street blues: Teagarden, Jack / Lady is a tramp: Horne, Lena / I got rhythm: Reinhardt, Django / Swing low, sweet clarinet: Herman, Woody & His Thundering Herd / Relaxin' at the Touro: Spanier, Muggsy / Original Jelly Roll blues: Morton, Jelly Roll & His Red Hot Peppers / Tenor king: Young, Lester / Stompin' at the Savoy: Wilson, Teddy / Body and soul: Goodman, Benny Quartet / Doggin' that thing: Allen, Henry 'Red' / Sophisticated lady: Ellington, Duke Orchestra / Harlem lament: Hines, Earl 'Fatha' / Loverman: Holiday, Billie
CD CDSGPBJZ 31
Prestige / Mar '97 / Cadillac / Complete/ Pinnacle

GOLDEN YEARS OF JAZZ VOL.10, THE
Do nothin' 'til you hear from me: Ellington, Duke Orchestra / Avalon: Hawkins, Coleman / First time I saw you: Lunceford, Jimmie / Tiger rag: Armstrong, Louis / Sheik of Araby: Tatum, Art / Nobody knows the trouble I've seen: Horne, Lena / Just wild about Harry: Bechet, Sidney / In the mood: Miller, Glenn / Easy money: Henderson, Fletcher / China boy: Wilson, Teddy / Livery stable blues: Spanier, Muggsy / Lullaby of Birdland: Fitzgerald, Ella / Take your tomorrow: Beiderbecke, Bix / Boogie woogie: Dorsey, Tommy Orchestra / Someday sweetheart: Morton, Jelly Roll & His Red Hot Peppers / Sax a plenty: Young, Lester
CD CDSGPBJZ 40
Prestige / Mar '97 / Cadillac / Complete/ Pinnacle

GOLDEN YEARS OF JAZZ VOL.2, THE
Someday sweetheart: Spanier, Muggsy / Diminuendo and crescendo in blue: Ellington, Duke Orchestra / Strange fruit: Holiday, Billie / Honky tonk train blues: Lewis, Meade 'Lux' / Stardust: Hawkins, Coleman / It's a sin to tell a lie: Waller, Fats & His Rhythm / Stardust: Morton, Jelly Roll & His Red Hot Peppers / Doctor Jazz stomp: Fitzgerald, Ella / We can't go on this way: Fitzgerald, Ella / Flat hat blues: Young, Lester / Blue and sentimental: Basie, Count Orchestra / Bugle call rag: Goodman, Benny Orchestra / Coquette: Wilson, Teddy & His Piano Orchestra / St. James Infirmary: Armstrong, Louis / Sweet Lorraine: Tatum, Art / Masquerade is over: McRae, Carmen
CD CDSGPBJZ 32
Prestige / Mar '97 / Cadillac / Complete/ Pinnacle

GOLDEN YEARS OF JAZZ VOL.3, THE
Time on my hands: Goodman, Benny Quartet / Honeysuckle rose: Waller, Fats & His Rhythm / Moonglow: Garner, Erroll / Chicago flyer: Lewis, Meade 'Lux' / Moonlight serenade: Miller, Glenn Orchestra / My melancholy baby: Teagarden, Jack / It's only a paper moon: Young, Lester / Fine romance: Horne, Lena / Henderson stomp: Henderson, Fletcher / Freight train blues: Bechet, Sidney / My melancholy baby: Lunceford, Jimmie / Jeepers creepers: Reinhardt, Django / Oh lady be good: Hawkins, Coleman / Chicago rhythm: Hines, Earl 'Fatha' / All of me: Holiday, Billie / Deep purple: Tatum, Art
CD CDSGPBJZ 33
Prestige / Mar '97 / Cadillac / Complete/ Pinnacle

GOLDEN YEARS OF JAZZ VOL.4, THE
You look good to me: Waller, Fats & His Rhythm / Basin Street blues: Fitzgerald, Ella / Begin the beguine: Shaw, Artie Orchestra / Chimes blues: Armstrong, Louis / Black bottom stomp: Morton, Jelly Roll & His Red Hot Peppers / Lullaby of the leaves: Tatum, Art / One o'clock jump: Basie, Count Orchestra / Best years of my life: Christy, June / Got a penny: Cole, Nat 'King' Trio / Characteristic blues: Bechet, Sidney / Sweet Georgia Brown: Reinhardt, Django / Take the 'A' train: Ellington, Duke Orchestra / Love me or leave me: Horne, Lena / Chimes in blues: Hines, Earl 'Fatha' / Mad house: Goodman, Benny Orchestra / That sugar baby o' mine: Holiday, Billie
CD CDSGPBJZ 34
Prestige / Mar '97 / Cadillac / Complete/ Pinnacle

GOLDEN YEARS OF JAZZ VOL.5, THE
Dippermouth blues: Spanier, Muggsy / April in Paris: Parker, Charlie / So many times: Teagarden, Jack / Carnival of Venice: James, Harry Orchestra / Moonlight in Vermont: Fitzgerald, Ella / Prisoner of love: Wilson, Teddy / Closing hour blues: Lewis, Meade 'Lux' / Solitude: Ellington, Duke Orchestra / Rhythm club stomp: Oliver, Joe 'King' / St. Louis shuffle: Henderson, Fletcher / Doggin' around: Basie, Count Orchestra / Out of nowhere: Hawkins, Coleman / Sad eyes: Young, Lester / Whose honey are you: Waller, Fats & His Rhythm / Indian summer: Bechet, Sidney / Stormy weather: Tatum, Art
CD CDSGPBJZ 35
Prestige / Mar '97 / Cadillac / Complete/ Pinnacle

GOLDEN YEARS OF JAZZ VOL.6, THE
Stompology: Hampton, Lionel Orchestra / Alligator crawl: Waller, Fats & His Rhythm / Nice work if you can get it: Goodman, Benny Quartet / Jelly roll blues: Armstrong, Louis / I'll remember: Teagarden, Jack / Now will you be good: Basie, Count Orchestra / Georgia on my mind: Holiday, Billie / Piano man: Hines, Earl 'Fatha' / Skyliner: Barnet, Charlie Orchestra / Wild man blues: Morton, Jelly Roll & His Red Hot Peppers / Honey keep your mind on me: Lunceford, Jimmie / Don't you think I love you: Oliver, Joe 'King' / Black and tan fantasy: Ellington, Duke Orchestra / Loverman: Horne, Lena / Polka dot rag: Bechet, Sidney Orchestra / April in Paris: Fitzgerald, Ella
CD CDSGPBJZ 36
Prestige / Mar '97 / Cadillac / Complete/ Pinnacle

GOLDEN YEARS OF JAZZ VOL.7, THE
I only have eyes for you: Holiday, Billie / Dippermouth blues: Armstrong, Louis / Dinah: Waller, Fats & His Rhythm / Down home jump: Hampton, Lionel Orchestra / Flying home: Fitzgerald, Ella / Vom vim veedle: Cole, Nat 'King' Trio / I'll keep remembering: Basie, Count Orchestra / Muddy river blues: Teagarden, Jack / All or nothing at all: James, Harry Orchestra / One o'clock jump: Ellington, Duke Orchestra / Hyena stomp: Morton, Jelly Roll & His Red Hot Peppers / Crazy rhythm: Reinhardt, Django / Pennsylvania 6-5000: Miller, Glenn Orchestra / Bugle call rag: Wilson, Teddy / My honey's lovin' arms: Goodman, Benny Orchestra / Takin' a chance on love: Young, Lester
CD CDSGPBJZ 37
Prestige / Mar '97 / Cadillac / Complete/ Pinnacle

GOLDEN YEARS OF JAZZ VOL.8, THE
Memories of you: Wilson, Teddy / King Porter stomp: Henderson, Fletcher / My man: Holiday, Billie / Crying all day: Beiderbecke, Bix / Fly me to the moon: Elgart, Les & His Orchestra / Chinatown, my chinatown: Dorsey, Tommy Orchestra / Serenade in blue: Miller, Glenn Orchestra / Love me or leave me: Young, Lester / My old flame: Clayton, Buck Orchestra & Frankie Laine / Jamaica shout: Hawkins, Coleman / Loverman: Parker, Charlie / C jam blues: Ellington, Duke Orchestra / Smoke house blues: Morton, Jelly Roll & His Red Hot Peppers / Flight of the bumble bee: James, Harry Orchestra / Royal Garden blues: Armstrong, Louis / Roseland shuffle: Basie, Count Orchestra
CD CDSGPBJZ 38
Prestige / Mar '97 / Cadillac / Complete/ Pinnacle

GOLDEN YEARS OF JAZZ VOL.9, THE
Don't you miss your baby: Basie, Count Orchestra / Wolverine blues: Morton, Jelly Roll & His Red Hot Peppers / Oh lady be good: Fitzgerald, Ella / Black snake blues: Oliver, Joe 'King' / I'm crazy 'bout my baby: Spanier, Muggsy / Summertime: Bechet, Sidney / Table in a corner: Teagarden, Jack / Creole rhapsody: Ellington, Duke Orchestra / Stormy weather: Holiday, Billie / Patrol

wagon blues: *Allen, Henry 'Red'* / Somebody loves me: *Hawkins, Coleman* / I surrender dear: *Wilson, Teddy* / Stardust: *Garner, Erroll* / Moonglow: *Goodman, Benny Quartet* / Honeysuckle rose: *Reinhardt, Django* / Ain't misbehavin': *Armstrong, Louis*
CD ______________ **CDSGPBJZ 39**
Prestige / Mar '97 / Cadillac / Complete/ Pinnacle

GOLDEN YEARS OF MUSIC HALL, THE
CD ______________ **CDSDL 380**
Saydisc / Mar '94 / ADA / Direct / Harmonia Mundi

GONE SURFIN'
CD ______________ **74321500272**
RCA / Jun '97 / BMG

GOOD BLUES TONIGHT
Church bell blues: *Jordan, Luke* / Mr. McTell got the blues: *McTell, 'Blind' Willie* / She stays out all night long: *Memphis Jug Band* / Suzie Q: *Williamson, Sonny Boy* / Good morning blues: *Leadbelly* / Roberta: *Leadbelly* / 32-20 blues: *Johnson, Robert* / Terraplane blues: *Johnson, Robert* / Stompin' 'em along slow: *Johnson, Lonnie* / Southern Casey Jones blues: *James, Jesse* / Lonesome day blues: *James, Jesse* / State Street blues: *Theard, Sam* / Macon blues: *Everetts, Dorothy* / Fat mouth blues: *Everetts, Dorothy* / Tight in Chicago: *Anderson, Mozelle* / Sadie's servant room blues: *Burleson, Hattie* / Superstitious blues: *Burleson, Hattie* / Heavenly sunshine: *Henton, Laura* / Dirty TB blues: *Spivey, Victoria* / Chicago stomp: *Blythe, Jimmy* / Armour Avenue struggle: *Blythe, Jimmy* / Big Bill blues: *Broonzy, 'Big' Bill* / Truckin' little woman: *Broonzy, 'Big' Bill* / Southern flood blues: *Broonzy, 'Big' Bill* / Good old cabbage greens: *Washboard Sam*
CD ______________ **CDMOIR 503**
Memoir / Aug '93 / Jazz Music / Target/ BMG

GOOD GROOVIN'
Last night a DJ saved my life / Never knew love like this before / Rock the boat / Ooh what a life / Gloria / Car Wash / Walking on sunshine / Don't take away the music / Black is black / Rescue me / Strut your funky stuff / Feels like I'm in love
CD ______________ **ECD 3202**
K-Tel / Mar '95 / K-Tel

GOOD MORNIN' BLUES
Went out on the mountain: *Leadbelly* / Whoa back: *Leadbelly* / Worried blues: *Leadbelly* / Good morning blues: *Leadbelly* / You can't lose me Charlie: *Leadbelly* / Boll weevil song: *Leadbelly* / Babylon is falling down: *Smith, Dan* / Where shall I be: *Smith, Dan* / Lining the track: *Smith, Dan* / Cotton needs pickin': *Smith, Dan* / Candy man: *Davis, Rev. Gary* / Hesitation blues: *Davis, Rev. Gary* / Whistlin' blues: *Davis, Rev. Gary* / How happy I am: *Davis, Rev. Gary* / Soon my work will all be done: *Davis, Rev. Gary*
CD ______________ **BCD 113**
Biograph / Jul '91 / ADA / Cadillac / Direct / Hot Shot / Jazz Music / Wellard

GOOD MORNING BLUES (4CD Set)
CD Set ______________ **CDDIG 18**
Charly / Jun '95 / Koch

GOOD MORNING LITTLE SCHOOLGIRL
Good morning little schoolgirl: *Chicago Breakdown* / Everyday I have the blues: *Chicago Breakdown* / I'll never fall in love again: *Brown, Ruth* / Old piano plays the blues: *Cole, Nat 'King'* / I wonder what my baby's doing tonight: *Big Maybelle* / There's good rockin' tonight: *Hopkins, Lightnin'* / These four walls: *Thomas, Irma* / I'm going home: *Diddley, Bo* / Billie's blues: *Holiday, Billie* / Birmingham blues: *Hooker, John Lee* / Nothing can stop me: *Houston, Cissy* / It may be the last time: *Rush, Otis & Little Walter* / GI blues: *Lightnin' Slim* / Love for sale: *Brown, Roy* / How long blues: *Turner, 'Big' Joe* / Wang dang doodle: *Howlin' Wolf*
CD ______________ **100922**
CMC / May '97 / BMG

GOOD MORNING VIETNAM (3CD Set)
Somebody to love: *Jefferson Airplane* / California dreamin': *Mamas & The Papas* / On the road again: *Canned Heat* / Magic carpet ride: *Steppenwolf* / Games people play: *South, Joe* / Time of the season: *Zombies* / Mellow yellow: *Donovan* / Aquarius: *5th Dimension* / Let the sunshine in: *5th Dimension* / Happy together: *Turtles* / He ain't heavy, he's my brother: *Hollies* / Letter: *Box Tops* / River deep, mountain high: *Turner, Ike & Tina* / In the year 2525: *Zager & Evans* / Tell it like it is: *Neville, Aaron* / Drift away: *Gray, Dobie* / Time in a bottle: *Croce, Jim* / Five o'clock world: *Vogues* / Bring it on home to me: *Animals* / God only knows: *Beach Boys* / Give up your guns: *Buoys* / White rabbit: *Jefferson Airplane* / Monday Monday: *Mamas & The Papas* / Friday on my mind: *Easybeats* / Born to be wild: *Steppenwolf* / Let's go to San Francisco: *Flowerpot Men* / She's not there: *Eve Of Destruction* / Weight: *Band* / Judy in disguise: *Fred, John & The Playboys* / Spirit in the sky: *Greenbaum, Norman* / Universal soldier: *Donovan* / Without you: *Nilsson* / Bad bad Leroy Brown: *Croce, Jim* / Hereos and villains: *Beach Boys* / Tossin' and turnin': *Ivy League* / I fought the law: *Bobby Fuller Four* / Incense and peppermints: *Strawberry Alarm Clock* / Sunny afternoon: *Kinks* / Sympathy: *Rowland, Steve & Family Dog* / I'm the urban spaceman: *Bonzo Dog Band* / Ball of confusion (that's what the world is today): *Temptations* / Going up the country: *Canned Heat* / (Don't fear) the reaper: *Blue Oyster Cult* / I get around: *Beach Boys* / Spooky: *Classics IV* / Brother Louie: *Stories* / Honky tonk woman: *Turner, Ike & Tina* / Fireball: *Deep Purple* / Up on cripple creek: *Band* / Elenore: *Turtles* / Soldier boy: *Shirelles* / San Franciscan nights: *Burdon, Eric* / Jenny take a ride: *Ryder, Mitch & The Detroit Wheels* / It's a long way there: *Little River Band* / Paranoid: *Black Sabbath* / Hooked on a feeling: *Thomas, B.J.* / Long tall glasses (I can dance): *Sayer, Leo* / Showdown: *ELO* / Who do you love: *Quicksilver Messenger Service* / Louie Louie: *Kingsmen*
CD Set ______________ **HR 863812**
Disky / Sep '96 / Disky / THE

GOOD MORNING VIETNAM VOL.1
Somebody to love: *Jefferson Airplane* / California dreamin': *Mamas & The Papas* / On the road again: *Canned Heat* / Magic carpet ride: *Steppenwolf* / Games people play: *South, Joe* / Time of the season: *Zombies* / Mellow yellow: *Donovan* / Aquarius: *5th Dimension* / Let the sunshine in: *5th Dimension* / Happy together: *Turtles* / He ain't heavy, he's my brother: *Hollies* / Letter: *Box Tops* / River deep mountain high: *Turner, Ike & Tina* / In the year 2525: *Zager & Evans* / Tell it like it is: *Neville, Aaron* / Drift away: *Gray, Dobie* / Time in a bottle: *Croce, Jim* / Five o'clock world: *Vogues* / Bring it on home to me: *Animals* / God only knows: *Beach Boys* / Give up your guns: *Buoys*
CD ______________ **LB 8049**
Disky / Nov '96 / Disky / THE

GOOD MORNING VIETNAM VOL.2
White rabbit: *Jefferson Airplane* / Monday monday: *Mamas & The Papas* / Friday on my mind: *Easybeats* / Born to be wild: *Steppenwolf* / Lets go to San Francisco: *Flowerpot Men* / She's not there: *Zombies* / Eve of destruction: *MacGuire, Barry* / Weight: *Band* / Judy in disguise: *Fred, John & The Playboys* / Spirit in the sky: *Greenbaum, Norman* / Universal soldier: *Donovan* / Without you: *Nilsson* / Bad bad Leroy Brown: *Croce, Jim* / Heroes and villains: *Beach Boys* / Tossin' and turnin': *Ivy League* / I fought the law: *Bobby Fuller Four* / Incense and peppermints: *Strawberry Alarm Clock* / Sunny afternoon: *Kinks* / Sympathy: *Rowland, Steve & Family Dog* / I'm the urban spaceman: *Bonzo Dog Band*
CD ______________ **DCA 863832**
Disky / Nov '96 / Disky / THE

GOOD MORNING VIETNAM VOL.3
Ball of confusion: *Temptations* / Going up the country: *Canned Heat* / (Don't fear) the reaper: *Blue Oyster Cult* / I get around: *Beach Boys* / Spooky: *Classics IV* / Brother Louie: *Stories* / Honky tonk woman: *Turner, Ike & Tina* / Fireball: *Deep Purple* / Up on cripple creek: *Band* / Elenore: *Turtles* / Soldier boy: *Shirelles* / San Franciscan nights: *Burdon, Eric* / Jenny take a ride: *Ryder, Mitch & The Detroit Wheels* / It's a long way there: *Little River Band* / Paranoid: *Black Sabbath* / Hooked on a feeling: *Thomas, B.J.* / Long tall glasses: *Sayer, Leo* / Showdown: *ELO* / Who do you love: *Quicksilver Messenger Service* / Louie louie: *Kingsmen*
CD ______________ **DCA 863842**
Disky / Nov '96 / Disky / THE

GOOD NEWS (22 Gospel Greats)
I'm going through: *Caravan* / It's Jesus in me: *Caravan* / I'm a rollin': *Five Blind Boys Of Mississippi* / Where there's a will: *Five Blind Boys Of Mississippi* / Wade in the water: *Harmonizing Four* / Father I stretch my arms to thee: *Harmonizing Four* / Nobody knows: *Highway QC's* / Working on the building: *Highway QC's* / Uncloudy day: *Staple Singers* / This may be the last time: *Staple Singers* / Going away: *Staple Singers* / Good news: *Staple Singers* / Don't drive me away: *Staple Singers* / Will the circle be unbroken: *Staple Singers* / Too close: *Staple Singers* / Great day in December: *Swan Silvertones* / Oh Mary don't you weep: *Swan Silvertones* / How I got over: *Swan Silvertones* / What about you: *Swan Silvertones* / Brighter day ahead: *Swan Silvertones* / Seek, seek: *Swan Silvertones* / I'll search heaven: *Swan Silvertones*
CD ______________ **CPCD 8215**
Charly / Feb '97 / Koch

GOOD RECORDS
Diskoking: *Hacienda* / Ycool: *Ceiver, Jiri & Jinks* / Drums in a grip: *De Wulf, Frank* / 10" of funk: *Bill & Ben* / Monster: *Planet Jazz* / Chupacabbra: *Freddie Fresh* / Phat jive: *Lindsey, Patrick* / Wait for a day: *Yokota* / Evil needle: *Alter Ego & David Holmes* / Beavis at bat: *Hardfloor* / One way: *Yokota* / Peterson session: *Braincell*
CD ______________ **HHUKCD 003**
Harthouse / Jun '97 / Mo's Music Machine / Prime / Vital

GOOD THINGS ARE HAPPENING (Nuggets From The Golden State)
Hide yourself: *Vejtables* / Better rearrange: *Vejtables* / Good things are happening: *Vejtables* / Good times: *Vejtables* / Time and place: *Vejtables* / I can't do it: *E-Type* / Long before: *E-Type* / I'm over you: *Shillings* / Part time man: *Shillings* / Going home: *Engle, Butch & The Styx* / Hey I'm lost: *Engle, Butch & The Styx* / If you believe: *Engle, Butch & The Styx* / I call her name: *Engle, Butch & The Styx* / I can't hide: *Soul Owners* / I'll cry: *Soul Owners* / In my way: *Dutch Masters* / Revenge: *Others* / I'm in need: *Others* / Satisfaction guaranteed: *Mourning Reign* / Our fate: *Mourning Reign* / I'm a lover not a fighter: *Pullice* / Little girl: *Pullice* / Tomorrow is another day: *Navarros* / Sad man: *Navarros* / My chance will come: *Origianl Wild Oats* / I'll get my way: *Chimney Sweeps* / Knock knock: *Innocents*
CD ______________ **CDWIKD 133**
Big Beat / Oct '94 / Pinnacle

GOOD TIME JAZZ STORY, THE (4CD Set)
Honky tonk music: *Morton, Jelly Roll* / Winin' boy blues: *Morton, Jelly Roll* / Finger buster: *Morton, Jelly Roll* / Creepy feeling: *Morton, Jelly Roll* / Temptation rag: *Bales, Burt* / New Orleans joys: *Bales, Burt* / Black bottom stomp: *Lingle, Paul* / Yellow dog blues: *Lingle, Paul* / Nothin': *Roberts, Luckey* / Railroad blues: *Roberts, Luckey* / Relaxin': *Smith, Willie 'The Lion'* / Between the devil and the deep blue sea: *Smith, Willie 'The Lion'* / Black and white rag: *Rose, Wally* / Pearls: *Rose, Wally* / Harlem rag: *Rose, Wally* / I wonder who's kissing her now: *Banjo Kings* / By the light of the silvery moon: *Banjo Kings* / Bill Bailey: *Banjo Kings* / Take this hammer: *Fuller, Jesse* / Leavin' Memphis: *Fuller, Jesse* / Frisco bound: *Fuller, Jesse* / San Francisco bay blues: *Fuller, Jesse* / John Henry: *Fuller, Jesse* / Storyville blues: *Johnson, Bunk* / Moose march: *Johnson, Bunk* / Careless love: *Johnson, Bunk* / Down by the riverside: *Johnson, Bunk* / Blues for Jimmie Noone: *Ory, Kid Creole Jazz Band* / Do what Ory say: *Ory, Kid Creole Jazz Band* / 1919 rag: *Ory, Kid Creole Jazz Band* / Burgundy Street blues: *Lewis, George* / Mama don't allow: *Lewis, George* / Walk through the streets of the city: *Lewis, George* / Gallatin Street grind: *Wiggs, Johnny* / Everybody loves my baby: *Wiggs, Johnny* / Gettsyburg march: *Pierson, Eddie Band* / Alabamy bound: *Pecora, Santo & The Tailgators* / My old time sweetheart: *Hug, Armand Trio* / Look what you've missed: *Bonano, Sharkey* / Too late: *Barbarin, Paul* / Maryland, my Maryland: *Matthews, Bill* / Doctor Jazz: *Girard, George* / Congo Square: *Silver Leaf Jazz Band* / Jelly roll blues: *Silver Leaf Jazz Band* / Snake rag: *Hot Horns* / Muskrat ramble: *Watters, Lu & The Yerba Buena Jazz Band* / Riverside blues: *Watters, Lu & The Yerba Buena Jazz Band* / Friendless blues: *Watters, Lu & The Yerba Buena Jazz Band* / Annie Street rock: *Watters, Lu & The Yerba Buena Jazz Band* / That's a plenty: *Watters, Lu & The Yerba Buena Jazz Band* / Kansas City stomp: *Strickler, Benny* / Brother lowdown: *Murphy, Turk Jazz Band* / Chimes blues: *Murphy, Turk Jazz Band* / Trombone rag: *Murphy, Turk Jazz Band* / St. James infirmary: *Murphy, Turk Jazz Band* / Minstrel of Annie Street: *Murphy, Turk Jazz Band* / Bay city: *Murphy, Turk Jazz Band* / Oh Daddy: *Murphy, Turk Jazz Band & Claire Austin* / Dippermouth blues: *Scobey, Bob Frisco Band* / Wolverine blues: *Scobey, Bob Frisco Band* / Ace in the hole: *Scobey, Bob Frisco Band* / Silver dollar: *Scobey, Bob Frisco Band* / Angry: *Scobey, Bob Frisco Band* / Battle hymn of the republic: *Scobey, Bob Frisco Band* / Indiana: *Scobey, Bob Frisco Band* / Arab strut: *Bay City Jazz Band* / New Orleans stomp: *Bay City Jazz Band* / Monday date: *Ewell, Don* / Blues my naughty sweetie gives to me: *Ewell, Don* / Honeysuckle rose: *Hayes, Clancy* / Ain't she sweet: *Hayes, Clancy* / Clarinet marmalade: *Daily, Pete Rhythm Kings* / Jazz man strut: *Daily, Pete Rhythm Kings* / St. Louis blues: *Ory, Kid Creole Jazz Band* / South Rampart Street parade: *Ory, Kid Creole Jazz Band* / Down hearted blues: *Ory, Kid Creole Jazz Band & Claire Austin* / Indiana: *Ory, Kid Creole Jazz Band* / Oh didn't he ramble: *Ory, Kid Creole Jazz Band* / Creole song: *Ory, Kid Creole Jazz Band* / Torch: *Castle Jazz Band* / Careless love: *Castle Jazz Band* / Five pennies: *Castle Jazz Band* / When the saints go marching in: *Castle Jazz Band* / Firehouse stomp: *Firehouse Five Plus Two* / Mississippi rag: *Firehouse Five Plus Two* / At a Georgia camp meeting: *Firehouse Five Plus Two* / Tishomingo blues: *Firehouse Five Plus Two* / Hindustan: *Firehouse Five Plus Two* / Isle of Capri: *Firehouse Five Plus Two* / Storyville blues: *Firehouse Five Plus Two* / Smokey mokes: *Firehouse Five Plus Two* / High society: *Firehouse Five Plus Two*
CD Set ______________ **4GTJCD 4416**
Good Time Jazz / Nov '96 / Complete/ Pinnacle

GOOD VIBRATIONS PUNK
Big time / Strange things by night / Love is for sops / Emergency cases / Dance away love / Don't ring me up / Listening in / Parents / Dancing in the street / Cops are comin' / Overcome by fumes / Cross the line / Love affair / Ya don't do ya / I spy / Airline disaster / Self concious over you / Love you for never / On my mind / Decisions / Original terminal / Belfast telegraph / I don't want you / Bondage in Belfast / Laugh at me
CD ______________ **CDPUNK 36**
Anagram / Sep '94 / Cargo / Pinnacle

GOOD VIBRATIONS STORY, THE
Big time: *Rudi* / Eye spy: *Rudi* / Overcome by fumes: *Rudi* / Strange things by night: *Victims* / Teenage kicks: *Undertones* / True confessions: *Undertones* / Right way home: *X-Dreamysts* / Don't ring me up: *Protex* / Cops are coming: *Outcasts* / Self conscious over you: *Outcasts* / One by one: *Ruefrex* / Love affair: *Tearjerkers* / She's 19: *Moondogs* / Doctor head love: *Teevees* / Airline disaster: *Shapes* / Big day: *PBR Street Gang* / Artificial joy: *Kameras* / On my mind: *Bank Robbers* / Dancing on the street: *Spider* / Laugh at me: *Hooley, Terry*
CD ______________ **DOJOCD 180**
Dojo / Jun '94 / Disc

GOOD WHISKEY BLUES VOL.1 (Collection Of Contemporary Blues Songs From Tennessee)
CD ______________ **TX 1004CD**
Taxim / Jan '94 / ADA

GOOD WHISKEY BLUES VOL.2 (Collection Of Contemporary Blues Songs From Tennessee)
CD ______________ **TX 1010CD**
Taxim / Jan '94 / ADA

GOODNIGHT SAIGON (3CD Set)
Nutbush city limits: *Turner, Ike & Tina* / Vietnam: *Cliff, Jimmy* / War drags on: *Donovan* / Brother Louie: *Hot Chocolate* / Proud Mary: *Turner, Ike & Tina* / Melting pot: *Blue Mink* / Why can't we live together: *Thomas, Timmy* / Baby I need your loving: *Rivers, Johnny* / Rubber bullets: *10cc* / We've gotta get out of this place: *Animals* / Love potion no.9: *Searchers* / House of the rising sun: *Animals* / Air that I breathe: *Hollies* / Ain't got no home: *Band* / I put a spell: *Price, Alan* / Black night: *Deep Purple* / You're the one: *Vogues* / Let's work together: *Canned Heat* / Roll over Beethoven: *ELO* / 10538 overture: *ELO* / Baby Jane (Mo-Mo Jane): *Ryder, Mitch & The Detroit Wheels* / Some kind of wonderful: *Grand Funk Railroad* / Silver machine: *Hawkwind* / Who do you love: *Juicy Lucy* / Gimme shelter: *Grand Funk Railroad* / Green tambourine: *Lemon Pipers* / Don't let me be misunderstood: *Animals* / I'm coming on: *Ten Years After* / American dream: *Dirt Band* / Summer in the city: *Lovin' Spoonful* / When I'm dead and gone: *McGuinness Flint* / Little green bag: *Ten Years After* / Sister golden hair: *America* / You don't mess around with Jim: *Croce, Jim* / She'd rather be with me: *Turtles* / Darlin' be home soon: *Lovin' Spoonful* / Lay down candles in the rain: *Melanie* / Mr. Bojangles: *Nitty Gritty Dirt Band* / Timothy: *Buoys* / Where peaceful waters flow: *Knight, Gladys & The Pips* / Soldier: *Groundhogs* / I'd love to change the world: *Ten Years After* / Do wah diddy diddy: *Manfred Mann* / Cotton fields: *Beach Boys* / Lucky man: *Emerson, Lake & Palmer* / Where's the playground, Susie: *Campbell, Glen* / Hi-ho silver lining: *Beck, Jeff & Rod Stewart* / American pie: *McLean, Don* / Horse with no name: *America* / I can hear music: *Beach Boys* / Light my fire: *Thomas, B.J.* / Feeling alright: *Grand Funk Railroad* / Good vibrations: *Beach Boys* / Stagger Lee and Billy: *Turner, Ike & Tina* / Clap for the wolfman: *Guess Who* / Midnight train to Georgia: *Knight, Gladys & The Pips* / Blowin' in the wind: *James, Etta* / Good morning freedom: *Blue Mink* / Peace will come: *Melanie* / Smoke on the water: *Deep Purple*
CD Set ______________ **HR 864252**
Disky / Oct '96 / Disky / THE

GORAU GWERIN CYFROL (The Best of Welsh Folk Music)
Torth of fara / Y gwr a'i farch / Mi gysgi di' maban / Cerrig yr afon / Mor o gariad / Mae 'ngHariad i'n fenws / Llancesau trefaldwyn / Bachgen bach o dincer / Y g'lomen / Ymryson canu / Ar gyfer heddiw'r bore / Clychau Aberdyfi / Ymdaith milwr mwnc / Cyfri'r geifr / Machynlleth / Cwm rhymni / Ffidl ffadl / Ffarwel i ddociau lerpwl / Wyres Megan / Gwrachod Llanddona / Mil harddach wyt / Yma o hyd
CD ______________ **SCD 2006**
Sain / Oct '88 / ADA / Direct / Greyhound

GORGEOUS (37 Irresistible Songs)
You're gorgeous: *Baby Bird* / 2 Become 1: *Spice Girls* / Nobody knows: *Rich, Tony Project* / Kiss from a rose: *Seal* / If you ever: *Gabrielle & East 17* / Goodbye heartbreak: *Lighthouse Family* / Thrill me: *Simply Red* / Cosmic girl: *Jamiroquai* / I can make you feel good: *Kavana* / Quit playing games (with my heart): *Backstreet Boys* / Day we find love: *911* / If you love me: *Brownstone* / My lovin': *En Vogue* / Trippin': *Morrison, Mark* / I feel you: *Andre, Peter* / Forever: *Damage* / Searching: *China Black* / Bill: *Scott-Adams, Peggy* / Natural: *Andre, Peter* / Undivided love: *Louise* / Don't make me wait: *911* / When I fall in love: *Ant & Dec* / Crazy for you: *Let Loose* / Love me for a reason: *Boyzone* / I just wanna make love to you: *James, Etta* / Girl like you: *Collins, Edwyn* / Best: *Turner, Tina* / Heaven is a place on earth: *Carlisle, Belinda* / Cecilia: *Suggs* / Dark clouds: *Space* / Oh yeah: *Ash* / Saturday night: *Suede* / Missing: *Everything But The Girl* / Don't dream it's over: *Crowded House* / Chains: *Arena, Tina* /

Child: *Owen, Mark* / Sometimes when we touch: *Newton*
CD ____ VTDCD 121
Virgin / Apr '97 / EMI

GOSPEL (3CD Set)
CD Set ____ EMTBX 308
Emporio / Aug '97 / Disc

GOSPEL & NEGRO SPIRITUAL FESTIVAL (2CD Set)
CD Set ____ FA 412
Fremeaux / Oct '96 / ADA / Discovery

GOSPEL AT NEWPORT 1959 & 1963-1966
CD ____ VCD 77014
Vanguard / Jan '96 / ADA / Pinnacle

GOSPEL CHRISTMAS
Hark the herald angels sing: *Hutchins, Norman* / O holy night: *Smallwood, Richard* / Away in a manger/Silent night: *West Angeles COGIC Angelic & Mass Choir* / Angels we have heard on high: *Crouch, Sandra* / Joy to the world: *West Angeles COGIC Angelic & Mass Choir* / First Noel: *Grundy, Rickey Chorale* / Go tell it on the mountain: *Winans, Mom & Pop* / O come, o come: *Coley, Daryl* / Hallelujah chorus: *Alford, Pastor Donald & The Progressive Radio Chorus*
CD ____ CDMFP 6196
Music For Pleasure / Oct '96 / EMI

GOSPEL CLASSICS
CD ____ DOCD 5190
Document / Mar '95 / ADA / Hot Shot / Jazz Music

GOSPEL CLASSICS 1950-1958
CD ____ DOCD 5464
Document / Jun '96 / ADA / Hot Shot / Jazz Music

GOSPEL CLASSICS VOL.2 1927-1935
CD ____ DOCD 5313
Document / Dec '94 / ADA / Hot Shot / Jazz Music

GOSPEL CLASSICS VOL.3
CD ____ DOCD 5350
Document / May '95 / ADA / Hot Shot / Jazz Music

GOSPEL COLLECTION, THE
CD ____ DCD 5271
Disky / Aug '92 / Disky / THE

GOSPEL COUNTRY
CD ____ DCD 5314
Disky / Nov '93 / Disky / THE

GOSPEL EVANGELISTS
CD ____ HTCD 09
Heritage / '92 / ADA / Direct / Hot Shot / Jazz Music / Swift / Wellard

GOSPEL LIVE FROM MOUNTAIN STAGE
This little light of mine: *Bass, Fontella* / Brother Moses: *Five Blind Boys Of Alabama* / Dig a little deeper: *Fairfield Four* / I want Jesus to walk with me: *Holmes Brothers* / Ring them golden bells: *Gospel Christian Singers* / Up above my head: *Austin, Ethel Caffie* / Beatitudes/Peace: *Sweet Honey In The Rock* / Fix it Jesus: *Sounds Of Heaven* / Why am I treated so bad: *Staples, Pops* / Standing in the safety zone: *Fairfield Four* / Leaning on the everlasting arms: *Bass, Fontella*
CD ____ BPM 309CD
Blue Plate / May '97 / ADA / Direct / Greyhound

GOSPEL SHIP, THE
CD ____ 802942
New World / Oct '94 / ADA / Cadillac / Harmonia Mundi

GOSPEL SINGERS AND CHOIRS
CD ____ TPZ 1011
Topaz Jazz / Jun '95 / Cadillac / Pinnacle

GOSPEL SOUND OF CHICAGO
CD ____ SHAN 6008CD
Shanachie / Dec '93 / ADA / Greensleeves / Koch

GOSPEL TRAIN
Lift up your hands / Constant love / Potter's house / Somebody somewhere / It's mighty nice to be on the Lord's side / He's got up / What shall I do / Give me Jesus / Want to get to know you / Holy is your name / Lord's prayer / Joyful, joyful
CD ____ ALD 027
Alliance Music / Jan '96 / EMI

GOSPEL VOL.3 1927-1944 (2CD Set)
CD Set ____ FA 044
Fremeaux / Nov '95 / ADA / Discovery

GOSPELS AND SPIRITUALS (2CD Set)
CD Set ____ R2CD 4026
Deja Vu / Jan '96 / THE

GOSPELS AND SPIRITUALS GOLD (2CD Set)
CD Set ____ D2CD 4026
Deja Vu / Jun '95 / THE

GOT A GOOD THING GOING (25 R&B Radio Hits Of The 1960's)
You're no good: *Warwick, Dee Dee* / Cry to me: *Harris, Betty* / Hey girl: *Scott, Freddie* / I'll find you: *Valerie & Nick* / You better go: *Martin, Derek* / Bitter with the sweet: *Gardner, Don* / But it's all right: *Jackson, J.J.* / It's all in the game: *Ricks, Jimmy* / Say you'll never (never leave me): *Clark, Alice* / Forget it: *Sandpebbles* / Lookin' for a home: *Little Buster* / Baby, you're my everything: *Williams, Jerry* / I'm gonna change my life for you: *Love, Jimmy* / Something I want to tell you: *Johnny & The Expressions* / Brand new world: *Scott, Freddie* / Doctor: *Wells, Mary* / Tired of being nobody: *Valentinos* / Don't let me down: *Height, Donald* / People sure act funny (when they've got a little money): *Turner, Titus* / Hymn no.5: *Mighty Hannibal* / Snap your fingers: *Ricks, Jimmy* / Little blue girl: *Gardner, Don* / I've got a good thing going: *Little Buster* / You got a deal: *Clark, Alice* / Your Daddy wants his baby back: *Martin, Derek*
CD ____ NEMCD 785
Sequel / Apr '96 / BMG

GOT HARP IF YOU WANT IT
CD ____ CCD 11030
Crosscut / '92 / ADA / CM / Direct

GOT TO GET YOUR OWN (Some Rare Grooves, Vol 1)
Got to get your own: *Wilson, Reuben* / Black water gold: *African Music Machine* / Goo bah: *Continental Showstoppers* / Funky song: *Ripple* / Moon walk: *Ellis, Pee Wee* / Tropical: *African Music Machine* / You're losing me: *Sexton, Ann* / I don't know what it is but it sure is funky: *Ripple* / (I've got) so much trouble in my mind: *Quatermain, Joe* / That thang: *Ellis, Pee Wee* / Dapp: *African Music Machine* / I don't dig no phony, part 2: *Scott, Moody* / Brother man, sister Ann: *Smith, Clemon*
CD ____ CDINS 5050
Charly / Sep '91 / Koch

GOTH BOX, THE (4CD Set)
CD Set ____ CLP 9798
Cleopatra / Oct '96 / Cargo / Greyhound / Plastic Head / RTM/Disc / SRD

GOTHAM BEAT
CD ____ HCD 258
Hindsight / Aug '95 / Jazz Music / Target/BMG

GOTHIC ROCK VOL.1
CD ____ FREUDCD 38
Jungle / Nov '91 / RTM/Disc / SRD

GOTHIC ROCK VOL.2 (2CD Set)
CD Set ____ FREUDCD 051
Jungle / Jul '95 / RTM/Disc / SRD

GOTHIC SOUND OF NIGHTBREED, THE
CD ____ NIGHTCD 010
Nightbreed / Jul '96 / Plastic Head

GOTHIC SPIRIT VOL.1
CD ____ SPV 07625242
SPV / Oct '94 / Koch / Plastic Head

GOTH'S UNDEAD (3CD Set)
CD ____ CLP 0038
Cleopatra / Aug '97 / Cargo / Greyhound / Plastic Head / RTM/Disc / SRD

GRAMAVISION'S 10TH ANNIVERSARY
CD ____ GV 794612
Gramavision / Dec '90 / Vital/SAM

GRAMMY LYRICS VOL.2
CD ____ VPRL 1170
VP / May '97 / Greensleeves / Jet Star / Total/BMG

GRAMMY NOMINEE ALBUM, THE
CD ____ 5332922
Polydor / Feb '97 / PolyGram

GRAMMY'S GREATEST MOMENTS (2CD Set)
What's love got to do with it: *Turner, Tina* / Sweet dreams: *Eurythmics* / She works hard for the money: *Summer, Donna* / Thing called love: *Raitt, Bonnie* / Don't wanna lose you: *Estefan, Gloria* / Another day in paradise: *Collins, Phil* / Unforgettable: *Cole, Natalie & Nat 'King' Cole* / Cradle of love: *Idol, Billy* / Sexual healing: *Gaye, Marvin* / Russians: *Sting* / You don't bring me flowers: *Streisand, Barbra & Neil Diamond* / We didn't start the fire: *Joel, Billy* / Heart of rock 'n' roll: *Lewis, Huey & The News* / Come together: *Aerosmith* / Vision of love: *Carey, Mariah* / What a fool believes: *Doobie Brothers* / Save the best for last: *Williams, Vanessa* / Respect: *Franklin, Aretha* / How am I supposed to live without you: *Bolton, Michael & Kenny G* / If you let me stay: *D'Arby, Terence Trent* / Constant craving: *Lang, k.d.* / One moment in time: *Houston, Whitney* / Tears in heaven: *Clapton, Eric*
CD Set ____ 7567805822
Atlantic / Apr '94 / Warner Music

GRAND AIRS OF CONNEMARA (Various Traditional Irish Songs)
Mainistir na buille: *MacDonnchadha, Sean* / An Caisdeach ban: *O'Cathain, Padraic* / Piopa Andy mhoir: *O'Neachtain, Tomas* / Una bhan: *O'Connluain, Feichin* / Bean on fhir rua: *O'Cathain, Padraic* / Stor mo chroi: *MacDonnchadha, Sean* / Noirin mo mhian: *MacDonnchadha, Sean* / Cailin schoth na luachra: *O'Cathain, Padraic* / Peigi Misteal: *O'Neachtain, Tomas* / An goirtin eornan: *O'Connluain, Feichin* / Cuaichin Ghleann Neifin: *O'Cathain, Padraic* / An spailpin fanach: *MacDonnchadha, Sean*
CD ____ OSS 28CD
Ossian / Dec '93 / ADA / CM / Direct / Highlander

GRAND CONCERT OF SCOTS PIPING
CD ____ TRAXCD 110
Greentrax / May '96 / ADA / Direct / Duncans / Highlander

GRAND HIT PACK, THE
CD ____ HRCD 8044
Disky / Jul '94 / Disky / THE

GRAND PIANO (2CD Set)
CD Set ____ ND 261062
Narada / Aug '97 / ADA / New Note/ Pinnacle

GRAND ROYAL MIX
Hurra: *Hurricane* / Skills to pay the bills: *Beastie Boys* / I wish I was him: *Noise Addict* / State of the world: *Luscious Jackson* / DFL: *DFL* / Carjack: *Moistboyz* / Boomin' granny: *Beastie Boys* / Can we all get along: *Hurricane* / Find your mind: *Luscious Jackson* / Pizza man: *DFL* / Transit cop demo: *Beastie Boys* / Stick 'em up: *Hurricane* / She be wantin' it more: *Luscious Jackson* / America's most hardcore: *DFL*
CD ____ TOCP 8915
Mushroom / Nov '96 / Cargo

GRANDES ORCHESTRES MUSIC HALL VOL.1
CD ____ 984042
EPM / Jun '97 / ADA / Discovery

GRANDES ORCHESTRES MUSIC HALL VOL.2
CD ____ 984052
EPM / Jun '97 / ADA / Discovery

GRANDES ORQUESTAS LATINAS
CD ____ CCD 903
Caney / Jul '97 / ADA / Discovery

GRANDES VALSES POPULAIRES 1900-1920
CD ____ 983962
EPM / Apr '97 / ADA / Discovery

GRANDS AUTEURS DU XIX SIECLE
CD ____ 983272
EPM / Oct '96 / ADA / Discovery

GRASS ROOTS VOL.9
CD ____ LACD 9
La / Sep '94 / Plastic Head

GREAT 1955 SHRINE CONCERT, THE
Spoken introduction: *Pilgrim Travellers* / All the way: *Pilgrim Travellers* / Straight Street: *Pilgrim Travellers* / Since I met Jesus: *Caravans* / What kind of man is this: *Caravans* / It's a long, long way: *May, Brother Joe* / I'm happy working for the Lord: *May, Brother Joe* / Consider me: *May, Annette* / I have a friend above all others: *Soul Stirrers* / Be with me, Jesus: *Soul Stirrers* / Nearer to thee: *Soul Stirrers* / My troubles are so hard to bear: *Davenport, Ethel* / Medley: *Love Coates, Dorothy*
CD ____ CDCHD 483
Ace / Jul '93 / Pinnacle

GREAT ACOUSTICS
CD ____ CIC 067CD
Clo Iar-Chonnachta / Nov '93 / CM

GREAT AMERICAN BIG BANDS
Sent for you yesterday: *Basie, Count* / Chicks is wonderful: *Teagarden, Jack* / These foolish things: *Carter, Benny* / When I get low I get high: *Webb, Chick* / Christopher Columbus: *Goodman, Benny* / I never knew: *Armstrong, Louis* / Flop: *Venuti, Joe* / Take the 'A' train: *Ellington, Duke* / Strictly instrumental: *James, Harry* / All of me: *Dorsey, Jimmy* / Prisoner's song: *Berigan, Bunny* / Barrelhouse Bessie from Basin Street: *Crosby, Bob* / My blue heaven: *Lunceford, Jimmie* / String of pearls: *Miller, Glenn* / Run little rabbit: *Calloway, Cab* / Twin City blues: *Herman, Woody* / I wonder who's kissing her now: *Weems, Ted* / Stop, look and listen: *Dorsey, Tommy* / I hope Gabriel likes my music: *Trumbauer, Frankie* / Study in brown: *Casa Loma Orchestra* / Deep purple: *Shaw, Artie* / Drummin' man: *Krupa, Gene* / Nola: *Hampton, Lionel*
CD ____ PPCD 78101
Past Perfect / Feb '95 / Glass Gramophone Co.

GREAT AMERICAN COMPOSERS
CD ____ CD 112
New Note / Jul '94 / Cadillac / New Note/ Pinnacle

GREAT AMERICAN SONGWRITERS, THE (5CD Set)
CD Set ____ 15991
Laserlight / Oct '95 / Target/BMG

GREAT BANDS OF TANGO'S GOLDEN AGE 1936-1947
CD ____ HQCD 89
Harlequin / Apr '97 / Hot Shot / Jazz Music / Swift / Wellard

GREAT BANDS, THE
Begin the beguin: *Shaw, Artie & His Orchestra* / Drum stomp: *Hampton, Lionel & His Orchestra* / Bugle call rag: *Roy, Harry & His Orchestra* / Gonna go on my mind: *Gonella, Nat & His Georgians* / Stompin' at the Savoy: *Goodman, Benny & His Orchestra* / Love is the sweetest thing: *Bowlly, Al & Ray Noble* / Save it pretty mama: *Armstrong, Louis Orchestra* / World is waiting for the sunrise: *Geraldo & His Orchestra* / Continental: *Stone, Lew & His Band* / One o'clock jump: *Basie, Count & His Orchestra* / On the air: *Gibbons, Carroll & The Savoy Hotel Orpheans* / Say it with music: *Payne, Jack & His Band* / Whispering: *Fox, Roy & His Band* / Take the 'A' train: *Ellington, Duke & His Orchestra* / Sweetest music this side of heaven: *Winnick, Maurice & his Orchestra* / Somebody stole my gal: *Cotton, Billy & His Band* / In the mood: *Loss, Joe & His Orchestra* / Here's to the next time: *Hall, Henry & His Orchestra* / At the woodchopper's ball: *Herman, Woody & His Orchestra* / I used to be colour blind: *Hilton, Jack & His Orchestra* / Trumpet blues and cantabile: *James, Harry & His Band* / Hors d'Oeuvres: *Ambrose & His Orchestra*
CD ____ PASTCD 7015
Flapper / Mar '97 / Pinnacle

GREAT BERLIN BAND SHOW, THE
National anthems / Fanfare - Union Jack / Jupiter / Posthorn galop / Crown of state / Per mare per terram / Globe and lauret / Rule Britannia / Pipes and drums / Glendaurel highlanders / Skye boat song / Caledonian canal / Lexy border / Bugler's delight / Light infantry / Londonderry air / St. Patrick's Day / Caubeen trimmed with blue / Irish washerwoman / Flight of the bumble bee / Brandenburg concerto / David of the White Rock / Men of Harlech / All through the night / God bless the Prince of Wales / Radetzky march / Prussia's glory / Drum display / British Grenadiers / Yorkshire march / Muss I dehn / Royal standard / Zadok the priest / Water music / Music from the Royal fireworks / Lament / Salute to Berlin / Berliner luft / Auld lang syne
CD ____ BNA 5047
Bandleader / '91 / Conifer/BMG

GREAT BIG BAND SINGERS
CD ____ HCD 326
Hindsight / Jun '95 / Jazz Music / Target/ BMG

GREAT BIG BAND THEMES
CD ____ HCD 321
Hindsight / Mar '95 / Jazz Music / Target/ BMG

GREAT BIG BANDS OF THE '50S
Fanfare boogie: *Winstone, Eric* / Drum crazy: *Johnson, Laurie* / Rhythm and blues: *Winstone, Eric* / Anticipation: *Winstone, Eric* / Nexy train out of town: *Miller, Betty* / Cobbler's song: *Winstone, Eric* / Heatwave: *Johnson, Laurie* / In a Persian market: *Johnson, Laurie* / Fascinating rhythm: *Clark, Petula* / Hallelujah: *Johnson, Laurie* / Frustration: *Winstone, Eric* / Treasure of love: *Shepherd, Pauline* / Jamboree: *Johnson, Laurie* / Slow train blues: *Winstone, Eric* / Cat walk: *Winstone, Eric* / Georgia's got a moon: *Miller, Betty* / Opus one mambo: *Winstone, Eric* / Heartbreak: *Winstone, Eric* / It might as well be spring: *Johnson, Laurie* / Robber's march: *Winstone, Eric* / Majorca: *Clark, Petula* / Stick or twist: *Johnson, Laurie* / Things we did last summer: *Johnson, Laurie*
CD ____ C5LCD 601
See For Miles/C5 / May '94 / Pinnacle

GREAT BLUES GUITAR LEGENDS, THE (4CD Set)
CD Set ____ HRCD 8030
Disky / May '93 / Disky / THE

GREAT BLUES GUITARISTS - STRING DAZZLERS
Hot fingers: *Johnson, Lonnie & Eddie Lang* / Handful of riffs: *Johnson, Lonnie & Eddie Lang* / Work ox blues: *Johnson, Lonnie & Eddie Lang* / I'm busy and you can't come in: *Weaver, Sylvester* / Georgia rag: *McTell, 'Blind' Willie* / Warm it up for me: *McTell, 'Blind' Willie* / Untitled: *Weaver, Sylvester* / When the war was on: *Johnson, 'Blind' Willie* / It's nobody's fault but mine: *Johnson, 'Blind' Willie* / How you want it done: *Broonzy, 'Big' Bill* / Getting older every day: *Broonzy, 'Big' Bill* / Guitar swing: *Weldon, Casey Bill* / Bullfrog moan: *Johnson, Lonnie & Eddie Lang* / Black snake moan: *Jefferson, Blind Lemon* / Little brother blues: *White, Joshua* / Prodigal son: *White, Joshua* / Denver blues: *Tampa Red* / Away down in the alley blues: *Johnson, Lonnie* / I love you Mary Lou: *Johnson, Lonnie*
CD ____ 4678942
Columbia / May '91 / Sony

GREAT BLUES SESSIONS
CD ____ CWNCD 2035
Crown / Jun '97 / Henry Hadaway

GREAT BLUESMEN (Newport 1959, 1960 & 1963)
Midnight boogie: *Williams, Robert Pete* / Levee camp blues: *Williams, Robert Pete* / My baby done changed the lock on the door: *Terry, Sonny & Brownie McGhee* / Tupelo: *Hooker, John Lee* / Bus station blues: *Hooker, John Lee* / Son's blues: *House, Son* / Death letter: *House, Son* / Pony blues: *House, Son* / Mailman blues: *Estes, 'Sleepy' John* / Clean up at home: *Estes, 'Sleepy' John* / Hey rattler: *Reese, Dock* / Oh my Lord: *Reese, Dock* / Sliding Delta: *Hurt, 'Mississippi' John* / Trouble, I've had it all my days: *Hurt, 'Mississippi' John* / Hard times: *James, Skip* / Killing floor blues: *James, Skip* / Cherry ball blues: *James, Skip* / Illinois blues: *James, Skip* / Death don't have no mercy: *Davis, Rev. Gary* / Catfish blues: *Doss, Willie* / I had a woman: *Doss, Willie* / I'm going down south: *Mc-*

Dowell, 'Mississippi' Fred / If the river was whisky: McDowell, 'Mississippi' Fred / Cotton field blues: Hopkins, Lightnin' / Shake that thing: Hopkins, Lightnin'
CD ____ VCD 77
Vanguard / Oct '95 / ADA / Pinnacle

GREAT BRASS BANDS
633 squadron: Grand Massed Bands / Tricky trombones (Trombone trio): Grand Massed Bands / Colditz march: Grand Massed Bands / Three trumpeters: Grand Massed Bands / HMS Pinafore (overture): Grand Massed Bands / Thunderbirds march: Grand Massed Bands / Can can: Grand Massed Bands / Rover's return: Grand Massed Bands / New world fantasy: Grand Massed Bands / Beau ideal: Grand Massed Bands / Fireman's gallop: Grand Massed Bands / Out of the blue: GUS Footwear Band / Samum: GUS Footwear Band / Espana: GUS Footwear Band / Royal Air Force march past: GUS Footwear Band / Spanish gypsy dance: GUS Footwear Band / New Colonial dance: GUS Footwear Band / Estudiantina: GUS Footwear Band / Sons of the brave: GUS Footwear Band / Bells across the meadow: GUS Footwear Band / Seventy six trombones: GUS Footwear Band / Tango taquin: GUS Footwear Band / Lisbon carnival: GUS Footwear Band / London Bridge march: GUS Footwear Band
CD ____ CDEMS 1394
EMI / Mar '91 / EMI

GREAT BRITISH BANDS (4CD Set)
CD Set ____ HRCD 8026
Disky / May '93 / Disky / THE

GREAT BRITISH DANCE BANDS, THE
Did you mean it: Hylton, Jack / I guess I'll have to change my plan: Ambrose / Got to dance my way to heaven: Hall, Henry / You go to my head: Loss, Joe / One in a million: Lawrence, Brian / I've got beginner's luck: Fox, Roy / From the top of your head: Gibbons, Carroll / Eyes of the world are on you: Levy, Louis / My heart belongs to Daddy: Cotton, Billy / Just as long as the world goes round and around: Wilbur, Jay / Mr. Rhythm Man: Gonella, Nat / You turned your head: Jackson, Jack / Let's fall in love for the last time: Mantovani / Temptation rag: Roy, Harry / Walkin' by the river: Geraldo / Crazy rhythm: Silvester, Victor / Organ grinder swing: Payne, Jack / Plain Mary Jane: Hylton, Mrs Jack / Stars fell on Alabama: Stone, Lew / My pet: Firman, Bert / Palais de Danse: Phillips, Sid / Shout for happiness: Noble, Ray
CD ____ PPCD 78112
Past Perfect / Feb '95 / Glass Gramophone Co.

GREAT BRITISH JAZZ BANDS
Jazz ma blues / Someday sweetheart / Imagination / Petite fleur / Original dixieland one step / Prelude to a kiss / Idaho / Very thought of you / K.C. BLUES / Nightingale sang in Berkeley Square / Gypsy / Limehouse blues
CD ____ EMPRCD 709
Emporio / Apr '97 / Disc

GREAT BRITISH PSYCHEDELIC TRIP VOL.1 1966-1969
Tales of Flossie Fillett: Turquoise / Baked jam roll in your eye: Timebox / In your tower: Poets / Leave me here: 23rd Turnoff / Muffin man: World Of Oz / anniversary of love: Ice / Shades of orange: End / Ice man: Ice / Come on back: Paul & Ritchie & The Cryin' Shames / Vacuum cleaner: Tintern Abbey / Love: Virgin Sleep / Saynia: Turquoise / Romeo and Juliet: Toby Twirl / Magician: Amazingly Friendly Apple / Beeside: Tintern Abbey / Stepping stone: Flies / Red sky at night: Accent / Renaissance fair: Human Instinct / Miss Pinkerton: Cuppa T / Toffee apple Sunday: Toby Twirl / Green plant: Cherry Smash / Follow me: Californians / Just one more chance: Outer Limits / Heavenly club: Sauterelles / Deep inside your mind: Shields, Keith / Elf: Stewart, Al
CD ____ SEECD 225
See For Miles/C5 / May '88 / Pinnacle

GREAT BRITISH PSYCHEDELIC TRIP VOL.2 1965-1970
That's the way it's got to be: Poets / I lied to Auntie May: Neat Change / Movin' in: Toby Twirl / Glasshouse green, splinter red: Kinsmen / Lazy day: Tinkerbell's Fairydust / Water woman: Pacific Drift / Paper chase: Love Children / Whisper her name (Maria Laine): Ice / Peacefully asleep: Life 'n' Soul / Turn into earth: Stewart, Al / Baby get your head screwed on: Double Feature / Eighty hours of paradise: Elastic Band / Fade away Maureen: Cherry Smash / Gotta wait: Game / 8.35 on the dot: Stirling, Peter Lee / All our Christmases: Majority / Requiem: Chocolate Watch Band / I'll be home (in a day or so): Dream Police / Walking through the streets of my mind: Timebox / Happy castle: Crocheted Doughnut Ring / Death at the seaside: Human Instinct / Secret: Virgin Sleep / In my magic garden: Tinkerbell's Fairydust / Woodstock: Turquoise
CD ____ SEECD 226
See For Miles/C5 / May '88 / Pinnacle

GREAT BRITISH PSYCHEDELIC TRIP VOL.3
My white bicycle: Tomorrow / Skeleton and the roundabout: Idle Race / In the land of the few: Idle Race / Kites: Dupree, Simon & The Big Sound / Mr. Armageddon: Locomotive / You've got a habit of leaving: Jones, Davy & The Lower Third / Excerpt from a teenage opera: West, Keith / Rumours: Kippington Lodge / It's so nice to come home: Lemon Trees / Real love guaranteed: Gods / We are the moles (part one): Moles / Friendly man: July / SF Sorrow is born: Pretty Things / I see: July / Lady on a bicycle: Kippington Lodge / On a saturday: West, Keith / Worn red carpet: Idle Race / Strawberry fields forever: Tomorrow / She says good morning: Pretty Things / Hey bulldog: Gods / William Chalker's time machine: Lemon Trees / Little games: Yardbirds / Puzzles: Yardbirds / First cut is the deepest: Koobas / Sabre dance: Love Sculpture
CD ____ SEECD 76
See For Miles/C5 / Jan '90 / Pinnacle

GREAT BRITISH PUNK ROCK EXPLOSION VOL.1
Anarchy in the UK: Sex Pistols / No time to be 21: Adverts / First time: Boys / New rose: Damned / I hate people: Anti Nowhere League / Homicide: 999 / I live in a car: UK Subs / Blind ambition: Partisans / Dogs of war: Exploited / Flares and slippers: Cockney Rejects / Murder of liddle towers: Angelic Upstarts / Harry May: Business / I wanna be me: Sex Pistols / Let's break the law: Anti Nowhere League / Disco man: Damned / One chord wonders: Adverts / Ain't got a clue (Live): Lurkers / Tin soldier: Stiff Little Fingers / Borstal breakout: Sham 69 / CID: UK Subs / Baby baby: Vibrators
CD ____ DOJOCD 122
Dojo / Feb '94 / Disc

GREAT BRITISH PUNK ROCK EXPLOSION VOL.2, THE
Safety in numbers: Adverts / Woman in disguise: Angelic Upstarts / Pretty vacant: Sex Pistols / Brickfield nights: Sex Pistols / Everybody's happy nowadays: Buzzcocks / BIC: UK Subs / Nobody's heroes: Stiff Little Fingers / Feelin' alright with the crew: 999 / Ignite: Damned / Streets of London: Anti Nowhere League / Bored teenagers: Adverts / I don't need to tell her: Lurkers / National insurance blacklist: Business / Viv la revolution: Adicts / Punk's not dead: Exploited / You'll never know: Vice Squad / Judy says: Vibrators / Warriors: Blitz / Something that I said: Ruts / I think I'm wonderful: Damned / For you: Anti Nowhere League / Jinx: Peter & The Test Tube Babies / Alternative: Exploited / Angels with dirty faces: Sham 69
CD ____ DOJOCD 131
Dojo / May '93 / Disc

GREAT CLASSIC BLUES SINGERS
CD ____ 158092
Blues Collection / Oct '93 / Discovery

GREAT COUNTRY LEGENDS
Walkin' after midnight: Cline, Patsy / Walk on by: Van Dyke, Leroy / Rose garden: Anderson, Lynn / What a way to live: Nelson, Willie / If I needed you: Van Zandt, Townes / Alligator man: Newman, Jimmy C. / Girl most likely: Riley, Jeannie C. / There you go: Cash, Johnny / In the jailhouse now: Pierce, Webb / You win again: Lewis, Jerry Lee / King of the road: Miller, Roger / Tennessee waltz: Page, Patti / Abilene: Jennings, Waylon / Stand by your man: Spears, Billie Jo / From a jack to a king: Miller, Ned / CB savage: Hart, Rod / I can't help you (I'm fallin' too): Davis, Skeeter / Me and my old CB: Dudley, Dave / Walk through this world with me: Jones, George / Send me the pillow you dream on: Locklin, Hank
CD ____ 306842
Hallmark / Jun '97 / Carlton

GREAT DANCE FAVOURITES
CD ____ HCD 328
Hindsight / Jun '95 / Jazz Music / Target/BMG

GREAT DAYS OF MUSIC HALL
Jolly good luck to the girl who loves a soldier: Tilley, Vesta / When father papered the parlour: Williams, Billy / Gas inspector: Little Tich / I may be crazy: Stratton, Eugene / Has anybody here seen Kelly: Forde, Florrie / Archibald certainly not: Robey, George / Burlington Bertie from Bow: Shields, Ella / Lily of Laguna: Stratton, Eugene / Every little movement: Lloyd, Marie / My old Dutch: Chevalier, Albert / Naughty Victorian days: Byng, Douglas / Mocking bird: Leno, Dan / It's a big shame: Elen, Gus / 'Arf a pint of ale: Elen, Gus / Three trees: Whelan, Albert / Preacher and the bear: Whelan, Albert / Don't send my boy to prison: Williams, Billy / Music Hall medley: Retford, Ella / PC 49: Fay, Harry / Two lovely black eyes: Coburn, Charles / Three times a day: Wallace, Nellie
CD ____ RAJCD 834
Empress / Oct '94 / Koch

GREAT DAYS OF THE ACCORDION BANDS
Old timer: Geraldo & His Orchestra / Sleepy time in sleepy hollow: Geraldo & His Orchestra / Marching along together: Geraldo & His Orchestra / At eventide: Geraldo & His Orchestra / Song of the bells: Geraldo & His Orchestra / Silver hair and heart of gold: Geraldo & His Orchestra / Sing a new song: Geraldo & His Orchestra / Clouds will soon roll by: Geraldo & His Orchestra / Marta: Geraldo & His Orchestra / Sweetest song in the world: Reid, Billy & His Orchestra / First time I saw you: Reid, Billy & His Orchestra / Blossoms on broadway: Reid, Billy & His Orchestra / Remember me: Reid, Billy & His Orchestra / Little drummer boy: Reid, Billy & His Orchestra / Moonlight on the waterfall: Reid, Billy & His Orchestra / So many memories: Reid, Billy & His Orchestra / Sweetest sweetheart: Reid, Billy & His Orchestra / My heaven in the pines: Reid, Billy & His Orchestra / Are you sincere: Reid, Billy & His Orchestra / Rose covered shack: Reid, Billy & His Orchestra / Chocolate soldier's daughter: Reid, Billy & His Orchestra / Apple blossom time: London Piano Accordion Band / South of the border (Down Mexico way): London Piano Accordion Band / All alone with my shadow: London Piano Accordion Band / Whose little what's it are you: London Piano Accordion Band / For all that I care: Scala, Primo Accordion Band / Down forget-me-not lane: Scala, Primo Accordion Band / I yi yi yi yi (I like you very much): Scala, Primo Accordion Band / There goes that song again: Scala, Primo Accordion Band / Hey little hen: Scala, Primo Accordion Band
CD ____ RAJCD 828
Empress / Jul '97 / Koch

GREAT DOBRO SESSIONS, THE
CD ____ SHCD 2206
Sugar Hill / Oct '94 / ADA / CM / Direct / Koch / Roots

GREAT FEMALE JAZZ SINGERS
CD ____ VN 164
Viper's Nest / Mar '96 / ADA / Cadillac / Direct / Jazz Music

GREAT FIGURES OF FLAMENCO VOL.1-4 (4CD Set)
CD Set ____ CMX 2741057-60
Le Chant Du Monde / May '97 / Harmonia Mundi

GREAT FIGURES OF FLAMENCO VOL.13-16 (4CD Set)
CD Set ____ CMX 2741069-72
Le Chant Du Monde / May '97 / Harmonia Mundi

GREAT FIGURES OF FLAMENCO VOL.17-20 (4CD Set)
CD Set ____ CMX 2741073-76
Le Chant Du Monde / May '97 / Harmonia Mundi

GREAT FIGURES OF FLAMENCO VOL.5-8 (4CD Set)
CD Set ____ CMX 2741061-64
Le Chant Du Monde / May '97 / Harmonia Mundi

GREAT FIGURES OF FLAMENCO VOL.9-12 (4CD Set)
CD Set ____ CMX 2741065-68
Le Chant Du Monde / May '97 / Harmonia Mundi

GREAT GENTLEMEN OF SONG VOL.1 (Hooray For Love)
In the wee small hours of the morning: Sinatra, Frank / Imagination: Martin, Dean / My buddy: Torme, Mel / There, I've said it again: Damone, Vic / PS I love you: Manning, Bob / Cuddle up a little closer: MacRae, Gordon / I'm beginning to see the light: Monro, Matt / I get along without you very well: Monro, Matt / Too marvellous for words: Russell, Andy / I guess I'll have to change my plan: Bennett, Tony / When I fall in love: Haymes, Dick / That's all: Haymes, Dick / My funny valentine: Baker, Chet / Just squeeze me: Armstrong, Louis / Affair to remember: Martino, Al / Hooray for love: Mercer, Johnny / Stardust: Ifield, Frank / Stormy weather: Rawls, Lou / Impossible: Jones, Jack / You are my lucky star: Davis, Sammy Jr.
CD ____ CDP 8317742
Capitol / Apr '95 / EMI

GREAT GIRL SINGERS
It's been so long: Forrest, Helen / If that's the way you want it baby: Forrest, Helen / I couldn't sleep a wink last night: Forrest, Helen / At least you could say hello: O'Connell, Helen / I'm steppin' out with a memory tonight: O'Connell, Helen / Just for a thrill: O'Connell, Helen / Them there eyes: Starr, Kay / It's a good day: Starr, Kay / I only have eyes for you: Starr, Kay / I'll never forget you: Clooney, Rosemary / You make me feel so young: Clooney, Rosemary / Don't worry 'bout me: Clooney, Rosemary
CD ____ HCD 320
Hindsight / Apr '95 / Jazz Music / Target/BMG

GREAT GIRL SINGERS
CD ____ HCD 414
Hindsight / Sep '92 / Jazz Music / Target/BMG

GREAT GOOGA MOOGA VOL.1 (Rhythm 'n' Bluesin' With King/Federal/Deluxe Vocal Groups)
Bo peep: Lamplighters / No other one: Tenderfoots / I wasn't thinkin', I was drinkin': Checkers / Baby let's play house: Thunderbirds / Good googa mooga: Magic Tones / Midnight hours: Drivers / So fine: Sheiks / That's your mistake: Williams, Otis New Group / All night long: Orchids / One moment with you: Ward, Billy & The Dominoes / Chicken backs: Carpets / Hug a little, kiss a little: Lamplighters / Oh Miss Nellie: Drivers / Cool cool baby: Magic Tones / Only you: Platters / La verne: Tenderfoots / Mama's daughter: Checkers / And I need you: Pyramids / Goodbye baby: Four Jacks / Be bop wino: Lamplighters
CD ____ NEMCD 907
Sequel / Jan '97 / BMG

GREAT GOSPEL CHOIRS
CD ____ HRCD 8054
Disky / Apr '94 / Disky / THE

GREAT GOSPEL MEN
CD ____ SHAN 06005CD
Shanachie / Aug '93 / ADA / Greensleeves / Koch

GREAT GOSPEL SONGS (2CD Set)
Oh happy day: Hawkins, Edwin Singers / Amen: Impressions / Hallelujah: Gayle, Crystal / Lord's prayer: Adams, Johnny / I don't know how to love him: Phillips, Ann / Farewell: Belafonte, Harry / Lay down (candles in the rain): Melanie & The Edwin Hawkin Singers / Swing down chariot: Staple Singers / God bless the child: Cooke, Sam / Down by the riverside: Jericho Group / Just a closer walk with thee: Abend, Joe Singers / Army of the Lord: King, B.B. / Joy to the world: Wilson, Jackie / It's me oh Lord: Jericho Group / Sundays are the sun days for my Lord: Perkins, Carl / Jesus loves me (this I know): Abend, Joe Singers / I know I've got religion: Staple Singers / Read your bible: Jericho Group / He's got the whole world in his hands: Simone, Nina / Amazing Grace: Phillips, Ann / When the saints go marchin' in: Lewis, Jerry Lee / Ave Maria: Stuarti, Enzo / Michael row the boat ashore: Lopez, Trini / My true confession: Benton, Brook / Joshua fit de battle of Jericho: Jericho Group / God's wonderful love: Staple Singers / Save a seat for me: King, B.B. / Hallelujah special: Perkins, Carl / Ol' man river: Cooke, Sam / Old time religion: Jericho Group / What child is this: Jackson, Mahalia / All God's lonely children: Rogers, Kenny / Something's got a hold on me: James, Etta / Go tell it on the mountain: Abend, Joe Singers / Go down Moses: Jericho Group / I got a jump: Belafonte, Harry
CD Set ____ TNC 96238
Natural Collection / Aug '96 / Target/BMG

GREAT GOSPEL WOMEN
CD ____ SHAN 06004CD
Shanachie / Aug '93 / ADA / Greensleeves / Koch

GREAT GOSPEL WOMEN VOL.2
CD ____ SHCD 6017
Shanachie / Mar '96 / ADA / Greensleeves / Koch

GREAT GUITARS
CD ____ CCD 6004
Concord Jazz / Jul '88 / New Note/ Pinnacle

GREAT HARP PLAYERS
CD ____ DOCD 5100
Document / Nov '92 / ADA / Hot Shot / Jazz Music

GREAT HYMNS OF WALES, THE
CD ____ SCD 2116
Sain / Feb '96 / ADA / Direct / Greyhound

GREAT INSTRUMENTAL FAVOURITES
CD ____ HCD 325
Hindsight / May '95 / Jazz Music / Target/BMG

GREAT JAZZ BANDS
Rock-a-bye Basie: Basie, Count / Baby, won't you please come home: Basie, Count / Jumpin' at the woodside: Basie, Count / Someone: Ellington, Duke / Suddenly it jumped: Ellington, Duke / Perdido: Ellington, Duke / Jeep is jumpin': Ellington, Duke / Together: Kirk, Andy / 9.20 Special: Kirk, Andy / For dancers only: Lunceford, Jimmie / Holiday for strings: Lunceford, Jimmie / Wham: Lunceford, Jimmie
CD ____ HCD 413
Hindsight / Sep '92 / Jazz Music / Target/BMG

GREAT JAZZ BANDS
CD ____ HCD 323
Hindsight / Apr '95 / Jazz Music / Target/BMG

GREAT JAZZ PIANISTS, THE
Carolina shout: Waller, Fats / Ain't misbehavin': Waller, Fats / Fifty seven varieties: Hines, Earl 'Fatha' / My melancholy baby: Hines, Earl 'Fatha' / Snowy morning blues: Johnson, James P. / You've got to be modernistic: Johnson, James P. / King Porter stomp: Morton, Jelly Roll / Original rags: Morton, Jelly Roll / Swampy river: Ellington, Duke / Passionette: Smith, Willie 'The Lion' / Morning air: Smith, Willie 'The Lion' / Humoresque: Tatum, Art / Begin the beguine: Tatum, Art / Tiger rag: Wilson, Teddy / When you and I were young: Wilson, Teddy / Maggie: Wilson, Teddy / Finishing up a date: Kyle, Billy / My blue heaven: Weatherford, Teddy / Pilgrim's chorus: Lambert, Donald / Rockin' chair: Wilson, Garland / Swingin' for joy: Williams, Mary Lou / Ladder: Turner, 'Big' Joe / Little Rock getaway: Sullivan, Joe
CD ____ PPCD 78107

Past Perfect / Feb '95 / Glass Gramophone Co.

GREAT JAZZ VOCALISTS, THE
Now you has jazz: *Crosby, Bing & Louis Armstrong* / Late late show: *Staton, Dakota* / Pete Kelly's blues: *Fitzgerald, Ella* / I know that you know: *Cole, Nat 'King'* / Midnight sun: *Christy, June* / Satin doll: *Wilson, Nancy* / Dinah: *Williams, Joe* / Call me irresponsible: *Washington, Dinah* / Honeysuckle rose: *Dankworth, John Seven & Cleo Laine* / Lulu's back in town: *Hi-Lo's* / I got rhythm: *Vaughan, Sarah* / Star eyes: *McCrae, Carmen & Dave Brubeck* / Got the gate on the golden gate: *Torme, Mel* / Things are swinging: *Lee, Peggy* / Her tears flowed like wine: *O'Day, Anita* / Love is just around the corner: *Four Freshmen* / Walk in the Black Forest: *Jones, Salena* / Lil' darlin: *Lambert, Hendricks & Ross* / Jon Hendricks: *Four Brothers* / God bless the child: *Holiday, Billie*
CD __________ CDMFP 6162
Music For Pleasure / May '95 / EMI

GREAT LADIES OF SONG (2CD Set)
Lover man: *Horne, Lena* / Too young: *Lee, Peggy* / Taking a chance on love: *Fitzgerald, Ella* / Them there eyes: *Starr, Kay* / Moon river: *Garland, Judy* / My blue Heaven: *Day, Doris* / St. Louis blues: *Holiday, Billie* / More I see you: *Vaughan, Sarah* / Manhattan serenade: *Shore, Dinah* / South American way: *Andrews Sisters* / I've got my love to keep me warm: *Starr, Kay* / September in the rain: *Day, Doris* / Yes my darling daughter: *Shore, Dinah* / I've got the world on a string: *Vaughan, Sarah* / Honeysuckle rose: *Horne, Lena* / As long as he needs me: *Garland, Judy* / Just one more chance: *Lee, Peggy* / All of me: *Holiday, Billie* / Imagination: *Fitzgerald, Ella* / Boogie woogie bugle boy: *Andrews Sisters* / Lady is a tramp: *Lee, Peggy* / I'm nobody's baby: *Garland, Judy* / Blue skies: *Day, Doris* / Pretty baby: *Starr, Kay* / Oh Johnny, oh Johnny oh: *Andrews Sisters* / I hear a rhapsody: *Shore, Dinah* / Love can change the stars: *Horne, Lena* / Three little words: *Fitzgerald, Ella* / I'll be seeing you: *Vaughan, Sarah* / God bless the child: *Holiday, Billie* / These foolish things: *Lee, Peggy* / I got it bad and that ain't good: *Fitzgerald, Ella* / Am I blue: *Holiday, Billie* / Are you certain: *Vaughan, Sarah* / You and I: *Shore, Dinah* / Fly me to the moon: *Garland, Judy* / 'S wonderful: *Day, Doris* / My man: *Fitzgerald, Ella* / You've got to see Mama every night: *Starr, Kay* / Bei mir bist du schon: *Andrews Sisters*
CD Set __________ MUCD 9514
Musketeer / May '96 / Disc

GREAT MALE JAZZ SINGERS
CD __________ VN 166
Viper's Nest / Mar '96 / ADA / Cadillac / Direct / Jazz Music

GREAT MARCHES VOL.1, THE
Colonel Bogey / Blaze away / On the quarterdeck / Liberty bell / Washington greys / Army of the Nile / Berliner luft / Great little army / Radetzky march / With sword and lance / National emblem / Holyrood / Semper fidelis / Boots and saddles / La reve passe / Scarlet and gold / Thunderer / Fehrbelliner reitermarsch / Thin red line / Anchors aweigh / Old comrades / Standard of St. George
CD __________ BNA 5006
Bandleader / Apr '87 / Conifer/BMG

GREAT MARCHES VOL.3, THE
Voice of the guns / Golden spurs / Wings / Royal Air Force march past / Black horse troop / Gunners / Barvada / Officer of the day / Mad major / Red cloak / Down the Mall / Iron regiment / Trombone king / Cavalry of the clouds / Imperial Life Guards / Trumpet major / Grid iron club / My congratulations / Royal standard / Purple pageant / Marche des parachutistes belges / Chief of staff / Inkerman / Pentland hills / Imperial march
CD __________ BNA 5029
Bandleader / Aug '89 / Conifer/BMG

GREAT MARCHES VOL.5, THE
Contemptibles / On the square / Aces high / King's guard / Hoch und deutschmeister / Vedette / Cavalry walk / Carmen march / H M Jollies / Alma / Sounding brass / BB and CF / March of the Royal British Legion / British Eighth / Barnum and Bailey's favourite / Guard's parade / Old gray mare / Grandioso / Flying eagle / Cavalry of the steppes / Through night to light / Blue devils / Marche Americaine / My regiment
CD __________ BNA 5060
Bandleader / Apr '92 / Conifer/BMG

GREAT MARCHES VOL.7, THE
Stars and stripes forever / Imperial echoes / Army and marine / Father Rhine / Wait for the wagon / Sarie Marais / Grenadier Mars / Gladiator's farewell / Thundering guns / Quality plus / Under freedom's banner / Royal buglers
CD __________ BNA 5112
Bandleader / Nov '94 / Conifer/BMG

GREAT MARCHES VOL.8, THE
Bond of friendship / 3 DG's / Washington Post / Fortune favours the bold / Chimes of liberty / Salamanca / Queen's division / Rifle Regiment / Quickest and best / Battleaxe company / El Capitan / Cockney cockney / Viscount Nelson U / Red Square review / Regimentsgruss / Swift and sure / Under the Allied banner / Blow away the morning's dew / Marche vanier / Ship to shore / All American soldier / Agrippa / First post / Pride of lions / St. Louis blues march
CD __________ BNA 5128
Bandleader / Dec '96 / Conifer/BMG

GREAT MUSICAL MEMORIES
CD __________ HCD 322
Hindsight / Jul '95 / Jazz Music / Target/BMG

GREAT NEW YORK SINGLES
CD __________ RE 116CD
ROIR / Nov '94 / Plastic Head / Shellshock/Disc

GREAT RADIO STARS OF THE 30'S VOL.1
It's that man again: *Handley, Tommy* / Mermaid: *Fletcher, Cyril* / Down upon the farm: *Sarony, Leslie & Leslie Holmes* / On the telephone: *Mrs. Feather* / Goes naughty: *Oliver, Vic* / Gert, Daisy and a piano: *Waters, Elsie & Doris* / Play the game, you cads: *Western Brothers* / Police station: *Wilton, Robb* / Kiss me goodnight, Sergeant Major: *Carlisle, Elsie* / Last year's calendar: *Stainless Stephen* / Bugginses at the seaside: *Constandurous, Mabel/Michael Hogan & Company* / We must all stick together: *Murgatroyd & Winterbottom* / Tomsky, the great counter-spy: *Handley, Tommy* / It's an overrated pastime: *Frankau, Ronald* / I taught her to play br-oop, br-oop: *Fields, Gracie* / Joe Ramsbottom at the dentist: *Evans, Norman* / Woodland romance: *Gourley, Ronald* / Play up and pay the dame: *Wakefield, Oliver* / Why should the dustman get it all: *Miller, Max* / Good old General Guiness: *Handley, Tommy*
CD __________ PASTCD 9721
Flapper / '90 / Pinnacle

GREAT RADIO STARS VOL.2
Bee song / I didn't orter a'ett it: *Warner, Jack* / Laughing bachelor: *Penrose, Charles* / Trains: *Gardiner, Reginald* / Rachmaninov's prelude: *Henson, Leslie* / Annual dinner of the slate club secretaries: *Johnson, Cecil* / Chin chin cheerio: *Frankau, Ronald* / Stanelli and his hornchestra: *Stanelli* / Much ado about little or nothing: *Wakefield, Oliver* / More chestnut corner: *Askey/Murdoch* / Pussy cat news: *Flotsam & Jetsam* / Splitting up: *Flanagan & Allen* / Teasing tongue twisters: *Comber, Bobbie* / Fiddling and fooling: *Ray, Ted* / I must have one of those: *Henry, Leonard* / Lion and ALbert: *Holloway, Stanley* / Jolly old ma, jolly old Pa: *Sarony, Leslie* / Truth about society: *Potter, Gillie*
CD __________ PASTCD 9728
Flapper / '90 / Pinnacle

GREAT SEX
Bump 'n' grind: *Kelly, R* / Sexual healing: *Gaye, Marvin* / Move closer: *Nelson, Phyllis* / Between the sheets: *Isley Brothers* / Slow hand: *Pointer Sisters* / Get up, I feel like being a sex machine: *Brown, James* / I want to sex you up: *Color Me Badd* / Body talk: *Imagination* / All night long: *Mary Jane Girls* / If only for one night: *Vandross, Luther* / Touch me in the morning: *Ross, Diana* / I'm gonna love you just a little more babe: *White, Barry* / Your body's calling: *Kelly, R* / Let's get it on: *Jade* / Stroke you up: *Changing Faces* / I'm goin' down: *Blige, Mary J.* / G-spot: *Marshall, Wayne* / Slow tongue: *Jackson, Millie* / Love won't let me wait: *Harris, Major* / Je t'aime, moi non plus: *Sweet Sex Symphony*
CD __________ RADCD 16
Global TV / Jun '95 / BMG

GREAT SOUND OF COUNTRY VOL.1, THE
CD __________ EMPRCD 541
Emporio / Sep '94 / Disc

GREAT SOUND OF COUNTRY VOL.2, THE
Five minutes of the latest blues: *Tubb, Justin* / Down the street to 301: *Cash, Johnny* / He made a women out of me: *Riley, Jeannie C.* / Down on the corner of love: *Owens, Buck* / I think I'll just stay here and drink: *Haggard, Merle* / Single girl: *Posey, Sandy* / Up against the wall, redneck cowboy: *Hubbard, Ray Wylie* / How the time flies: *Wallace, Jerry* / Yellow rose: *Lee, Johnny* / Comin' on strong: *Lee, Brenda* / Whispering pines: *Anderson, Bill* / Yesterday when I was young: *Clarke, Roy* / Most beautiful girl in the world: *Stampley, Joe* / Best years of my life: *Red Sovine* / Midnight driver: *Weller, Freddy* / I wished a thousand times: *Husky, Ferlin* / That's the way I feel: *Jones, George*
CD __________ EMPRCD 542
Emporio / Sep '94 / Disc

GREAT SOUND OF COUNTRY VOL.3, THE
I saw your face in the moon: *Pierce, Webb* / One is a lonely number: *Jones, George* / I heard the jukebox playing: *Young, Faron* / There you go: *Cash, Johnny* / Seasons of my heart: *Jones, George* / Help me make it through the night: *Pride, Charley* / Hello walls: *Young, Faron* / Hooked on a feeling: *Thomas, B.J.* / I've loved and lost again: *Cline, Patsy* / What am I doing in your world: *Sealey, Jeannie*
CD __________ EMPRCD 543
Emporio / Nov '94 / Disc

GREAT SOUND OF COUNTRY VOL.4, THE
Sweethearts in heaven: *Owens, Buck* / Ruebens train: *Dillards* / Just out of reach: *Cline, Patsy* / Coalminer's daughter: *Lynn, Loretta* / Garden party: *Nelson, Rick* / Lovesick blues: *Cline, Patsy* / Sticks and stones: *Fargo, Donna* / Mama tried: *Haggard, Merle* / Kiss an angel good morning: *Pride, Charley* / She's a lady: *Stampley, Joe* / Wait a little longer baby: *Thompson, Hank* / Freight train blues: *Dean, Jimmy* / Too much: *Red Sovine* / Boll weevil: *Glazer, Jim* / King of the road: *Miller, Roger* / I love you because: *Jones, George* / Done rovin': *Harton, Johnny*
CD __________ EMPRCD 544
Emporio / Nov '94 / Disc

GREAT SOUND OF COUNTRY, THE (4CD Set)
CD Set __________ EMPRBX 006
Emporio / Sep '94 / Disc

GREAT SWEET BANDS
CD __________ HCD 324
Hindsight / Jul '95 / Jazz Music / Target/BMG

GREAT SWING JAM SESSIONS 1938-1939
Keep smilin' at trouble / Just the blues / China boy / Someday sweetheart / Sugar / St. Louis blues / You took advantage of me / Someday sweetheart / Basin Street blues / Honeysuckle rose / (I would do) anything for you / Boogie woogie blues / I'm coming Virginia
CD __________ JUCD 2029
Storyville / Mar '95 / Cadillac / Jazz Music / Wellard

GREAT TENORS OF WALES, THE
CD __________ SCD 2129
Sain / Nov '96 / ADA / Direct / Greyhound

GREAT VOCALISTS, THE
If you were the only girl in the world: *Ziegler, Anne & Webster Booth* / Be careful, it's my heart: *Sinatra, Frank & Tommy Dorsey Orchestra* / Bless you: *Ink Spots* / Little white gardenia: *Brisson, Carl* / Very thought of you: *Bowlly, Al* / J'attendrai: *Rossi, Tino* / Stop beating around the mulberry bush: *Merry Macs* / What do you know Jo: *Stafford, Jo & The Pied Pipers* / Great mistake of my life: *Henderson, Chick* / Body and soul: *Boswell, Connee* / Sonny boy: *Jolson, Al* / Tisket a tasket: *Fitzgerald, Ella* / Without a song: *Dennis, Denny* / How about you: *Carless, Dorothy* / Where the blue of the night: *Crosby, Bing* / Transatlantic lullaby: *Hall, Adelaide* / Last time I saw Paris: *Martin, Tony* / Fools rush in: *Shelton, Anne* / My good friend the milkman: *Waller, Fats* / Pennsylvania 6-5000: *Andrews Sisters* / These foolish things: *Layton, Turner* / Someone to watch over me: *Langford, Frances*
CD __________ PASTCD 7018
Flapper / Mar '97 / Pinnacle

GREAT XPECTATIONS - LIVE (X-rated vol.1)
Colour me grey: *Family Cat* / Armchair anarchist: *Kingmaker* / Queen Jane: *Kingmaker* / Chrome: *Catherine Wheel* / I want to touch you: *Catherine Wheel* / Keepsake: *Senseless Things* / Walter's trip: *Frank & Walters* / Full moon: *Belly* / Empty heart: *Belly* / Dusted: *Belly* / Cheer up, it might never happen: *Carter USM* / Bloodsports for all: *Carter USM* / Just like heaven: *Cure* / Disintegration: *Cure* / For tomorrow: *Blur*
CD __________ XFMCD 1
XFM / Jul '93 / Pinnacle

GREATEST ALL-TIME NEW COUNTRY LINE DANCE
CD __________ MCCD 284
Music Club / Dec '96 / Disc / THE

GREATEST BALLADS
Would I lie to you: *Charles & Eddie* / Release me: *Wilson Phillips* / Cambodia: *Wilde, Kim* / Orchard road: *Sayer, Leo* / Mated: *Grant, David & Jaki Graham* / Suddenly last summer: *Motels* / Whenever you need me: *T'Pau* / I've been in love before: *Cutting Crew* / Harder I try: *Brother Beyond* / Sweet sixteen: *Idol, Billy* / Missing you: *Waite, John* / For your blue eyes only: *Hadley, Tony* / Home on Monday: *Little River Band* / What other reason: *Johnny Hates Jazz* / Something's gotten hold of my heart: *Almond, Marc & Gene Pitney* / Caravan of love: *Housemartins*
CD __________ BXB 877442
Disky / Jul '97 / Disky / THE

GREATEST COUNTRY SHOW, THE
CD __________ HRCD 8020
Disky / Jul '93 / Disky / THE

GREATEST DANCE ALBUM EVER MADE, THE (3CD Set)
Encore une fois: *Sash* / Freed from desire: *Gala* / I love u baby: *Original* / Offshore: *Chicane* / Sandman: *Blueboy* / Passion: *Gat Decor* / Don't stop movin': *Livin' Joy* / I believe: *Happy Clappers* / U sure do: *Strike* / Two can play that game: *Bobby Brown* / Everybody's free (to feel good): *Rozalla* / No limit: *2 Unlimited* / Stayin' alive: *N-Trance* / Whoomph (there it is): *Clock* / LSI: *Shamen* / Born slippy: *Underworld* / Open up: *Leftfield & John Lydon* / Closer than close: *Gaines, Rosie* / You got the love: *Source* / Ecuador: *Sash* / Ready or not: *Course* / Show me love: *Robin S* / Key the secret: *Urban Cookie Collective* / He's on the phone: *St. Etienne* / Keep warm: *Jinny* / I wanna give you devotion: *Nomad* / Killer: *Adamski* / Age of love: *Age Of Love* / I love you...stop: *Red 5* / Flylife: *Basement Jaxx* / So in love with you: *Duke* / Just gets better: *TJR & Xavier* / Just playin': *JT Playaz* / Short short man: *20 Fingers* / Jump around: *House Of Pain* / Boom shake the room: *DJ Jazzy Jeff & The Fresh Prince* / Come baby come: *K7* / All about us: *Peter Andre* / Remember me: *Blueboy* / Can I kick it: *Tribe Called Quest* / Magic number: *De La Soul* / She's got that vibe: *R Kelly* / Everybody (backstreets back): *Backstreet Boys* / Oh Carolina: *Shaggy* / Too hot: *Coolio* / We come to party: *N-Tyce* / Love to love: *Damage* / Something about you: *New Edition* / My father's son: *Conner Reeves* / Underwater love: *Smoke City*
CD Set __________ TTVCD 2918
Telstar / Aug '97 / BMG

GREATEST DANCE ALBUM IN THE WORLD, THE
CD __________ VTCD 13
Virgin / Jul '92 / EMI

GREATEST DANCE ALBUM OF ALL TIME, THE
Rhythm of the night: *Corona* / Back to life: *Soul II Soul* / Opps up side your head: *Gap Band* / You're the one for me: *D-Train* / No limit: *2 Unlimited* / I feel for you: *Khan, Chaka* / Pump up the volume: *MARRS* / Connected: *Stereo MC's* / Play that funky music: *Wild Cherry* / Le freak: *Chic* / Out of space: *Prodigy* / Push it: *Salt n' Pepa* / I will survive: *Gaynor, Gloria* / Blame it on the boogie: *Jacksons* / Things can only get better: *D:Ream* / We are family: *Sister Sledge* / You make me feel: *Sylvester* / Young hearts run free: *Staton, Candi* / Dance to the music: *Sly & The Family Stone* / One nation under a groove: *Funkadelic* / Grooves is in the heart: *Deee-Lite* / Let the music play: *Shannon* / I found lovin: *Fatback Band* / I like to move it: *Reel 2 Real & The Mad Stuntman* / Ebenezer good: *Shamen* / Contact: *Starr, Edwin* / Jump to the beat: *Lattisaw, Stacy* / Message: *Grandmaster Flash* / Word up: *Cameo* / Move on up: *Mayfield, Curtis* / Y M C A: *Village People* / Come in to my life: *Sims, Joyce* / Don't stop (Wiggle wiggle): *Outhere Brothers* / Night to remember: *Shalamar* / Power: *Snap* / Just be good to me: *SOS Band* / Ride on time: *Black Box* / Celebration: *Kool & The Gang* / Car wash: *Rose Royce*
CD __________ DINCD 108
Dino / Oct '95 / Pinnacle

GREATEST EVER CHRISTMAS PARTY MEGAMIX, THE
Merry Christmas everybody / I wish it could be Christmas every day / Winter wonderland / All I want for Christmas is my two front teeth / Rockin' around the Christmas tree / Jingle bell rock / Santa Claus is coming to town / Silver bells / Gloucestershire wassail / Mistletoe & wine / Silent night / We wish you a Merry Christmas / Happy Christmas war is over / When a child is born / Christmas song / Winter wonderland / Here comes Santa Claus / Santa Claus is coming to town / Frosty the snowman / Rudolph the red nosed reindeer / Sleigh ride / Blue Christmas / Mary's boy child / Good King Wenceslas / Ding dong merrily on high / God rest ye merry gentlemen / Deck the halls / I believe in Father Christmas / Do they know it's Christmas / Auld lang syne
CD __________ XMAS 006
Tring / Nov '96 / Tring

GREATEST EVER JUNIOR PARTY MIX, THE
Ghostbusters / Doin' the doo / Holiday / You got it (the right stuff) / Chicken song / Lambada / Got to get it / Birdie song / Hound dog / Look / Oops upside your head / Turtle power / Brown girl in the ring / Angel face / Ain't nothin' but a house party / Locomotion / Hand on your heart / Happenin' all over again / All shook up / Great balls of fire / Don't be cruel / See you later alligator / Let's twist again / Rock around the clock / Hound dog (reprise) / When the going gets tough / Agadoo / Too many broken hearts / Simple Simon / Itsy bitsy teeny weeny / Bat dance / Baggy trousers / Star treckin' / Ghostbusters (reprise)
CD __________ XMAS 008
Tring / Nov '96 / Tring

GREATEST FOLK SINGERS OF THE SIXTIES
You were on my mind: *Ian & Sylvia* / Now that the buffalo's gone: *Sainte-Marie, Buffy* / Walk right in: *Rooftop Singers* / East Virginia: *Baez, Joan* / Old Blue: *Houston, Cisco* / I feel like I'm fixin' to die rag: *Country Joe & The Fish* / John Henry: *Odetta* / Pack up your sorrows: *Farina, Richard* / Greenland whale fisheries: *Collins, Judy & Theodore Bikel* / Well, well, well: *Gibson, Bob & Hamilton Camp* / Ramblin' boy: *Paxton, Tom* / La Bamba: *Feliciano, Jose* / Virgin Mary had one son: *Baez, Joan & Bob Gibson* / Salty dog blues: *Flatt, Lester & Earl Scruggs* / Blowin' in the wind: *Dylan, Bob* / There but

for: *Ochs, Phil* / Violets of the dawn: *Anderson, Eric* / Sittin' on top of the world: *Watson, Doc* / Travelling riverside: *Hammond, John* / Crazy words crazy tune: *Kweskin, Jim & The Jug Band* / Candy man: *Hurt, 'Mississippi' John* / Erie canal: *Weavers* / Wish I had answered: *Staple Singers* / Ballad of Springhill: *Seeger, Peggy & Ewan MacColl* / Mellow down easy: *Butterfield, Paul* / I got it: *Chambers Brothers* / Whistling gypsy: *Makem, Tommy* / Paper of pins: *Brand, Oscar & Jean Ritchie* / East Virginia blues: *Seeger, Pete*
CD ____________ **VCD 17**
Vanguard / Oct '95 / ADA / Pinnacle

GREATEST GOSPEL GEMS VOL.1 & 2
Last mile of the way: *Cooke, Sam & The Soul Stirrers* / Touch the hem of his garment: *Cooke, Sam & The Soul Stirrers* / Search me, Lord: *May, Brother Joe* / Do you know him: *May, Brother Joe* / Mother bowed: *Pilgrim Travellers* / Straight street: *Pilgrim Travellers* / Jesus met the woman at the well: *Pilgrim Travellers* / Oh Lord, stand by me: *Five Blind Boys Of Alabama* / I'll fly away: *Five Blind Boys Of Alabama* / Too close to heaven: *Bradford, Alex* / Lord, Lord, Lord: *Bradford, Alex* / Get away Jordan: *Love Coates, Dorothy* / He's calling me: *Love Coates, Dorothy* / I'm sealed: *Love Coates, Dorothy* / My rock: *Swan Silvertones* / Jesus is a friend: *Swan Silvertones* / Let god abide: *Anderson, Robert* / Prayer for the doomed: *Chosen Gospel Singers* / Ball game: *Carr, Sister Wynona* / By and by: *Soul Stirrers* / Love of God: *Taylor, Johnnie* / I'm determined to run this race: *Meditation Singers* / Lead me, guide me: *May, Brother Joe* / Now the day is over: *Cleveland, James*
CD ____________ **CDCHD 344**
Ace / May '91 / Pinnacle

GREATEST HITS OF 1970, THE
In the summertime: *Mungo Jerry* / Rag mama rag: *Band* / Lola: *Kinks* / Down the dustpipe: *Status Quo* / Brontosaurus: *Move* / Whole lotta love: *CCS* / Black night: *Deep Purple* / Let's work together: *Canned Heat* / Voodoo chile: *Hendrix, Jimi* / Question: *Moody Blues* / Ride a white swan: *T-Rex* / I hear you knocking: *Edmunds, Dave* / When I'm dead and gone: *McGuinness Flint* / Neanderthal man: *Hotlegs* / I can't tell the bottom from the top: *Hollies* / Blame it on the Pony Express: *Johnson, Johnny & Bandwagon* / Love grows (where my Rosemary goes): *Edison Lighthouse* / Ruby Tuesday: *Melanie*
CD ____________ **CDGH 1970**
Premier/MFP / Jul '91 / EMI

GREATEST HITS OF 1971, THE
Maggie May: *Stewart, Rod* / Get it on: *T-Rex* / Malt and barley blues: *McGuinness Flint* / Strange kind of woman: *Deep Purple* / Tonight: *Move* / Tap turns on the water: *CCS* / Coz I luv you: *Slade* / Witch Queen of New Orleans: *Redbone* / Your song: *John, Elton* / Hot love: *T-Rex* / Double barrel: *Collins, Dave & Ansell* / Banner man: *Blue Mink* / Pushbike song: *Mixtures* / Something old, something new: *Fantastics* / I believe (in love): *Hot Chocolate* / If not for you: *Newton-John, Olivia* / Rose garden: *Anderson, Lynn* / Chestnut mare: *Byrds*
CD ____________ **CDGH 1971**
Premier/MFP / Jul '91 / EMI

GREATEST HITS OF 1972, THE
Rocket man: *John, Elton* / You wear it well: *Stewart, Rod* / Rock 'n' roll (part 2): *Glitter, Gary* / Metal guru: *T-Rex* / Ball park incident: *Wizzard* / Gudbuy t' Jane: *Slade* / Hold your head up: *Argent* / Family affair: *Sly & The Family Stone* / All the young dudes: *Mott The Hoople* / American pie: *McLean, Don* / 10538 overture: *ELO* / Telegram Sam: *T-Rex* / Mama weer all crazee now: *Slade* / California man: *Move* / I didn't know I loved you (till I saw you rock 'n' roll): *Glitter, Gary* / Brand new key: *Melanie* / Say you don't mind: *Blunstone, Colin* / Sylvia's mother: *Dr. Hook*
CD ____________ **CDGH 1972**
Premier/MFP / Jul '91 / EMI

GREATEST HITS OF 1973, THE
Caroline: *Status Quo* / Roll over Beethoven: *ELO* / Whiskey in the jar: *Thin Lizzy* / Do you wanna touch me (oh yeah): *Glitter, Gary* / Dance with the devil: *Powell, Cozy* / Can the can: *Quatro, Suzi* / Cum on feel the noize: *Slade* / All the way from Memphis: *Mott The Hoople* / Twentieth century boy: *T-Rex* / I'm the leader of the gang (I am): *Glitter, Gary* / Nutbush City Limits: *Turner, Ike & Tina* / See my baby jive: *Wizzard* / Rubber bullets: *10cc* / One and one is one: *Medicine Head* / Rock on: *Essex, David* / If you don't know me by now: *Melvin, Harold & The Bluenotes* / Me and Mrs. Jones: *Paul, Billy* / Daniel: *John, Elton*
CD ____________ **CDGH 1973**
Premier/MFP / Jul '91 / EMI

GREATEST HITS OF 1974, THE
You ain't seen nothin' yet: *Bachman-Turner Overdrive* / Down down: *Status Quo* / Always yours: *Glitter, Gary* / Tiger feet: *Mud* / Sugar baby love: *Rubettes* / Wall Street shuffle: *10cc* / Waterloo: *Abba* / Far far away: *Slade* / Gonna make you a star: *Essex, David* / You're the first, the last, my everything: *White, Barry* / Never can say goodbye: *Gaynor, Gloria* / Summer breeze: *Isley Brothers* / Most beautiful girl: *Rich, Charlie* / Candle in the wind: *John, Elton* / You make me feel brand new: *Stylistics* / Rock your baby: *McCrae, George* / Judy Teen: *Harley, Steve & Cockney Rebel* / I can help: *Swan, Billy*
CD ____________ **CDGH 1974**
Premier/MFP / Jul '91 / EMI

GREATEST HITS OF 1975, THE
Jive talkin': *Bee Gees* / Lady Marmalade: *Labelle, Patti* / Hold back the night: *Trammps* / Can't give you anything (but my love): *Stylistics* / Take good care of yourself: *Three Degrees* / You sexy thing: *Hot Chocolate* / I can do it: *Rubettes* / Best thing that ever happened to me: *Knight, Gladys & The Pips* / Loving you: *Riperton, Minnie* / I'm not in love: *10cc* / Tears on my pillow: *Nash, Johnny* / Hold me close: *Essex, David* / I'm stone in love with you: *Mathis, Johnny* / Make me smile (come up and see me): *Harley, Steve & Cockney Rebel* / Mamma mia: *Abba* / Doing alright with the boys: *Glitter, Gary* / Thanks for the memory (wham bam thank you mam): *Slade* / Oh boy: *Mud* / Goodbye my love: *Glitter Band* / Moonlighting: *Sayer, Leo*
CD ____________ **CDGH 1975**
Premier/MFP / Nov '91 / EMI

GREATEST HITS OF 1976, THE
Pinball wizard: *John, Elton* / Boys are back in town: *Thin Lizzy* / Here comes the sun: *Harley, Steve & Cockney Rebel* / Devil woman: *Richard, Cliff* / Boston tea party: *Harvey, Alex Band* / You make me feel like dancing: *Sayer, Leo* / Little bit more: *Dr. Hook* / Things we do for love: *10cc* / Harvest for the world: *Isley Brothers* / You should be dancing: *Bee Gees* / Don't go breaking my heart: *John, Elton & Kiki Dee* / Dr. Kiss Kiss: *5000 Volts* / Dancing queen: *Abba* / I love to love (but my baby loves to dance): *Charles, Tina* / I love music: *O'Jays* / More, more, more: *Andrea True Connection* / Love really hurts without you: *Ocean, Billy* / Music: *Miles, John* / You to me are everything: *Real Thing* / Miss you nights: *Richard, Cliff*
CD ____________ **CDGH 1976**
Premier/MFP / Nov '91 / EMI

GREATEST HITS OF 1977, THE
Rockin' all over the world: *Status Quo* / Dancin' in the moonlight: *Thin Lizzy* / She's not there: *Santana* / Spanish stroll: *Mink De-ville* / Peaches: *Stranglers* / All around the world: *Jam* / Lido shuffle: *Scaggs, Boz* / Whodunit: *Tavares* / Ain't gonna bump no more (with no big fat woman): *Tex, Joe* / Don't leave me this way: *Melvin, Harold & The Bluenotes* / Jack in the box: *Moments* / shuffle: *McCoy, Van* / How deep is your love: *Bee Gees* / When I need you: *Sayer, Leo* / They shoot horses don't they: *Racing Cars* / It's a heartache: *Tyler, Bonnie* / Knowing me, knowing you: *Abba* / So you win again: *Hot Chocolate* / 2-4-6-8 motorway: *Robinson, Tom* / No more heroes: *Stranglers*
CD ____________ **CDGH 1977**
Premier/MFP / Nov '91 / EMI

GREATEST HITS OF 1978, THE
Night fever: *Bee Gees* / September: *Earth, Wind & Fire* / If I can't have you: *Elliman, Yvonne* / Dancing in the city: *Marshall Hain* / Every 1's a winner: *Hot Chocolate* / Stayin' alive: *Bee Gees* / Take a chance on me: *Abba* / Dreadlock holiday: *10cc* / Lovely day: *Withers, Bill* / Song for Guy: *John, Elton* / Wuthering Heights: *Bush, Kate* / Darlin': *Miller, Frankie* / You took the words right out of my mouth: *Meat Loaf* / (Don't fear) the reaper: *Blue Oyster Cult* / Denis: *Blondie* / If the kids are united: *Sham 69* / Down in the tube station at midnight: *Jam* / Rat trap: *Boomtown Rats* / Hanging on the telephone: *Blondie* / Baker Street: *Rafferty, Gerry*
CD ____________ **CDGH 1978**
Premier/MFP / Nov '91 / EMI

GREATEST HITS OF 1979, THE
Eton rifles / I don't like Mondays: *Boomtown Rats* / Hersham boys: *Sham 69* / Duchess: *Stranglers* / Heart of glass: *Blondie* / Gangster: *Special AKA* / Tears of a clown: *Beat* / On my radio: *Selecter* / Milk and alcohol: *Dr. Feelgood* / Waiting for an alibi: *Thin Lizzy* / Whatever you want: *Knack* / When you fall in love with a beautiful woman: *Dr. Hook* / I have a dream: *Abba* / I will survive: *Gaynor, Gloria* / Tragedy: *Bee Gees* / Ring my bell: *Ward, Anita* / Sunday girl: *Blondie*
CD ____________ **CDGH 1979**
Premier/MFP / Nov '91 / EMI

GREATEST HITS OF THE 60'S/70'S
CD ____________ **HRCD 8046**
Disky / Dec '93 / Disky / THE

GREATEST HITS OF THE 70'S
CD ____________ **MACCD 122**
Autograph / Aug '96 / BMG

GREATEST HITS OF THE 70'S
CD ____________ **101802**
CMC / Jun '97 / BMG

GREATEST HITS OF THE SEVENTIES (3CD Set)
In the summertime: *Mungo Jerry* / I'll go where the music takes me: *Charles, Tina* / Don't make waves: *Nolans* / Mama Loo: *Humphries, Les Singers* / Beach baby: *First Class* / You can get it if you really want: *Dekker, Desmond* / Love really hurts without you: *Ocean, Billy* / Popcorn: *Hot Butter* / Sandy: *Travolta, John* / Speak to the sky: *Springfield, Rick* / Do you wanna dance: *Svenne & Lotta* / Achy breaky heart: *Black Lace* / I just can't help believin': *Thomas, B.J.* / I only wanna be with you: *Bay City Rollers* / Laughter in the rain: *Sedaka, Neil* / Even the bad times are good: *Tremeloes* / Garden party: *Nelson, Rick* / Something's burning: *Rogers, Kenny* / Lean on me: *Jarreau, Al* / Timothy: *Buoys* / Operator: *Knight, Gladys & The Pips* / Jealous guy: *Feliciano, Jose* / Precious and few: *Climax Blues Band* / Sooner or later: *Grass Roots* / Rainy night in Georgia: *Benton, Brook* / Rainbow: *Marmalade* / Three times a lady: *Drifters* / Silver star: *Four Seasons* / Street called hope: *Pitney, Gene* / Whenever I'm away from you: *Travolta, John* / Rock 'n' roll lullaby: *Thomas, B.J.* / Last farewell: *Whittaker, Roger* / Bye bye baby: *Bay City Rollers* / December '63 (oh what a night): *Four Seasons* / This diamond ring: *Lewis, Gary & The Playboys* / Heaven must be missing an angel: *Tavares* / Israelites: *Dekker, Desmond* / Mexico: *Humphries, Les Singers* / Angel face: *Glitter Band* / I love to love: *Charles, Tina* / Car wash: *Rose Royce* / Freedom come, freedom go: *Fortunes* / Feels like I'm in love: *Marie, Kelly* / Julie, do ya love me: *Sherman, Bobby* / Bang-a-boomerang: *Svenne & Lotta* / Radancer: *Marmalade* / Dragonfly: *Nolans* / Get up and boogie: *Silver Convention*
CD Set ____________ **100832**
CMC / May '97 / BMG

GREATEST HITS OF THE SEVENTIES VOL.1 (In The Summertime)
In the summertime: *Mungo Jerry* / I'll go where the music takes me: *Charles, Tina* / Don't make waves: *Nolans* / Mama Loo: *Humphries, Les Singers* / Beach baby: *First Class* / You can get it if you really want: *Dekker, Desmond* / Love really hurts without you: *Ocean, Billy* / Popcorn: *Hot Butter* / Sandy: *Travolta, John* / Speak to the sky: *Springfield, Rick* / Do you wanna dance: *Svenne & Lotta* / Achy breaky heart: *Black Lace* / I just can't help believin': *Thomas, B.J.* / I only wanna be with you: *Bay City Rollers* / Laughter in the rain: *Sedaka, Neil* / Even the bad times are good: *Tremeloes*
CD ____________ **100842**
CMC / May '97 / BMG

GREATEST HITS OF THE SEVENTIES VOL.2 (Garden Party)
Garden party: *Nelson, Rick* / Something's burning: *Rogers, Kenny & The First Edition* / Lean on me: *Jarreau, Al* / Timothy: *Buoys* / Operator: *Knight, Gladys & The Pips* / Jealous guy: *Feliciano, Jose* / Precious and few: *Climax Blues Band* / Sooner or later: *Grass Roots* / Rainy night in Georgia: *Benton, Brook* / Rainbow: *Marmalade* / Three times a lady: *Drifters* / Silver star: *Four Seasons* / Street called hope: *Pitney, Gene* / Whenever I'm away from you: *Travolta, John* / Rock 'n' roll lullaby: *Thomas, B.J.* / Last farewell: *Whittaker, Roger*
CD ____________ **100852**
CMC / May '97 / BMG

GREATEST HITS OF THE SEVENTIES VOL.3 (Bye Bye Baby)
Bye bye baby: *Bay City Rollers* / December '63 (oh what a night): *Four Seasons* / This diamond ring: *Lewis, Gary & The Playboys* / Heaven must be missing an angel: *Tavares* / Israelites: *Dekker, Desmond* / Mexico: *Humphries, Les Singers* / Angel face: *Glitter Band* / I love to love: *Charles, Tina* / Car wash: *Rose Royce* / Freedom come, freedom go: *Fortunes* / Feels like I'm in love: *Marie, Kelly* / Julie do ya love me: *Sherman, Bobby* / Bang-a-boomerang: *Svenne & Lotta* / Radancer: *Marmalade* / Dragonfly: *Nolans* / Get up and boogie: *Silver Convention*
CD ____________ **100862**
CMC / May '97 / BMG

GREATEST IN COUNTRY BLUES VOL.1, THE
CD ____________ **SOB 35212**
Story Of The Blues / Dec '92 / ADA / Koch

GREATEST IN COUNTRY BLUES VOL.2, THE
CD ____________ **SOB 35222**
Story Of The Blues / Dec '92 / ADA / Koch

GREATEST IN COUNTRY BLUES VOL.3, THE
CD ____________ **SOB 35232**
Story Of The Blues / Dec '92 / ADA / Koch

GREATEST JAZZ, BLUES AND RAGTIME OF THE CENTURY
Squeeze me: *Waller, Fats* / I'm crazy 'bout my baby: *Waller, Fats* / Ivy: *Johnson, James P. & J. Russell Robinson* / Charleston: *Johnson, James P.* / Daddy blues: *Jones, Clarence* / Doggone blues: *Jones, Clarence* / Fast stuff blues: *Blythe, Jimmy* / Alley rat blues: *Blythe, Jimmy* / Charleston blues: *Blake, Eubie* / Maple leaf rag: *Joplin, Scott* / Gin mill blues: *Fowler, Lemuel* / Fowler's hot strut: *Fowler, Lemuel* / King Porter stomp: *Morton, Jelly Roll* / Bucksnort stomp: *Tichenor, Trebor*
CD ____________ **BCD 116**
Biograph / Jul '91 / ADA / Cadillac / Direct / Hot Shot / Jazz Music / Wellard

GREATEST JUKE BOX COLLECTION EVER
CD ____________ **HADCD 209**
Javelin / Jul '96 / Henry Hadaway / THE

GREATEST LOVE
CD ____________ **DCDCD 202**
Castle / Aug '96 / BMG

GREATEST LOVE SONGS
Honey: *Goldsboro, Bobby* / Seasons in the sun: *Jacks, Terry* / Without you: *Nilsson, Harry* / Torn between two lovers: *McGregor, Mary* / Dedicated to the one I love: *Mamas & The Papas* / Sealed with a kiss: *Hyland, Brian* / Drift away: *Gray, Dobie* / I am sorry: *Lee, Brenda* / Parisienne walkways: *Moore, Gary* / I got you babe: *Sonny & Cher* / If I only had time: *Rowles, John* / Somebody to love: *Jefferson Airplane* / Escape (Pina colada song): *Holmes, Rupert* / Fire: *Pointer Sisters* / Lady: *Styx* / Love story: *Lai, Francis* / Thrill is gone: *King, B.B.*
CD ____________ **MCD 30201**
Ariola Express / Mar '94 / BMG

GREATEST LOVE SONGS, THE (3CD Set)
Just one look: *Hollies* / Bus stop: *Hollies* / I can't let go: *Hollies* / I'm in the mood for love: *Cogan, Alma* / You're nobody 'til somebody loves you: *Martin, Dean* / That's amore (That's love): *Martin, Dean* / True love (all over the world): *Martin, Dean* / Zing went the strings of my heart: *Garland, Judy* / Let's do it: *Hutchinson, Leslie 'Hutch'* / What now my love: *Bassey, Shirley* / Something: *Bassey, Shirley* / Love story: *Bassey, Shirley* / My funny valentine: *MacRae, Gordon* / Begin the beguine: *MacRae, Gordon* / What I've got in mind: *Spears, Billie Jo* / Blanket on the ground: *Spears, Billie Jo* / Stand by your man: *Spears, Billie Jo* / All my loving: *Monro, Matt* / With these hands: *Monro, Matt* / Speak softly love: *Monro, Matt* / There's a kind of hush (all over the world): *Herman's Hermits* / Moon river: *Williams, Danny* / You're so good to me: *Beach Boys* / Wouldn't it be nice: *Beach Boys* / Then I kissed her: *Beach Boys* / You are so beautiful: *Rogers, Kenny* / Lady: *Rogers, Kenny* / Love changes everything: *Keel, Howard* / Wind beneath my wings: *Keel, Howard* / I love you because: *Martino, Al* / Can't help falling in love: *Martino, Al* / Don't it make my brown eyes blue: *Gayle, Crystal* / Cry me a river: *London, Julie* / Fly me to the moon: *London, Julie* / Rose Marie: *Whitman, Slim* / For all we know: *Cole, Nat 'King'* / Let's fall in love: *Cole, Nat 'King'* / To know you is to love you: *Peter & Gordon* / And I love you so: *Reddy, Helen* / I didn't mean to love you: *Reddy, Helen* / Spanish eyes: *Martino, Al* / I'll be with you in apple blossom time: *Stafford, Jo & Nat 'King' Cole* / Honey: *Goldsboro, Bobby* / By the time I get to Phoenix: *Campbell, Glen* / I love you bit: *Cogan, Alma & Lionel Bart* / All I have to do is dream: *Campbell, Glen & Bobbie Gentry* / I am in love: *Damone, Vic* / You belong to me: *Stafford, Jo*
CD Set ____________ **CDTRBOX 112**
Trio / Oct '94 / EMI

GREATEST LOVE VOL.1
CD ____________ **TMPCD 004**
Temple / Jan '95 / BMG

GREATEST LOVE VOL.2
CD ____________ **TMPCD 005**
Temple / Jan '95 / BMG

GREATEST LOVE VOL.3
CD ____________ **TMPCD 006**
Temple / Jan '95 / BMG

GREATEST LOVE, THE
CD ____________ **MACCD 102**
Autograph / Aug '96 / BMG

GREATEST NON-STOP PARTY UNDER THE SUN, THE (2CD Set)
Ohh ahh..just a little bit: *Gina G* / Baby baby: *Corona* / I like to move it: *Reel 2 Real & The Mad Stuntman* / Two can play that game: *Brown, Bobby* / We are family: *Sister Sledge* / She's got that vibe: *Kelly, R* / Macarena: *Los Del Mar* / Guaglione: *Prado, Perez 'Prez'* / Dizzy: *Reeves, Vic & Wonder Stuff* / Love shack: *B-52's* / Hey now (girls just want to have fun): *Lauper, Cyndi* / Compliments on your kiss: *Red Dragon & Brian & Tony Gold* / Don't stop: *Outhere Brothers* / Cotton eye joe: *Rednex* / Mr. Vain: *Culture Beat* / No limit: *2 Unlimited* / Don't give me your life: *Alex Party* / U sure do: *Strike* / One night in heaven: *M-People* / Rhythm is a dancer: *Snap* / Sunshine after the rain: *Berri* / Everybody's free to feel good: *Rozalla* / Your loving arms: *Martin, Billie Ray* / Another night: *MC Sar & The Real McCoy* / Rock my heart: *Haddaway* / Now that we've found love: *Heavy D & The Boyz* / Naked: *Louise* / Sweets for my sweet: *Lewis, C.J.* / Deeply dippy: *Right Said Fred* / Sweetness: *Gayle, Michelle* / Oh what a night: *Clock* / Its alright: *East 17* / Boom shake the room: *DJ Jazzy Jeff & The Fresh Prince* / Killer: *Adamski* / Always there: *Brown, Jocelyn* / I luv u baby: *Original* / Rhythm is a mystery: *K-Klass* / Swamp

thing: *Grid* / Reach up (papa's got a brand new pig bag): *Perfecto All Stars* / All that she wants: *Ace Of Base*
CD Set ______ **CDEMTVD 149**
EMI TV / Nov '96 / EMI

GREATEST PARTY BOX, THE (4CD Set)
Happy birthday to you / 21 today / Celebration / Congratulations / Happy birthday / Birthday medley / Wedding march / Wedding march / Conga / Knees up Mother Brown / Hokey cokey / Charleston / Glenn Miller / Essential wally party medley / Anniversary waltz / Last waltz / Agadoo / Can can / Birdie song / Simple Simon says / Big Ben strikes / Auld lang syne / National Anthem / Merry Christmas everybody / I wish it could be Christmas everyday / Winter wonderland / All I want for Christmas is my two front teeth / Rockin' around the Christmas tree / Jungle bell rock / Santa Claus is coming to town / Silver bells / Gloucestershire Wassail / Mistletoe and wine / Silent night / We wish you a Merry Christmas / Happy Christmas (war is over) / When a child is born / Christmas song / Here comes Santa Claus / Frosty the snowman / Santa Claus is coming to town / Rudolph the red nosed reindeer / Sleigh ride / Blue Christmas / Mary's boy child / Good King Wenceslas / Ding dong merrily on high / God rest ye merry gentlemen / Deck the halls / I believe in Father Christmas / Do they know it's Christmas / Auld lang syne / Ghostbusters / Doin' the doo / Holiday / You got it (the right stuff) / Chicken song / Lambada / Got to get it / Hound dog / Look / Oops upside your head / Turtle power / Brown girl in the ring / Angel face / Ain't nothin' but a house party / Locomotion / Hand on your heart / Happenin' all over again / All shook up / Great balls of fire / Don't be cruel / See you later alligator / Let's twist again / Rock around the clock / Hound dog (reprise) / When the going gets tough / Agadoo / Too many broken hearts / Simmple Simon says / Itsy bitsy teeny weeny yellow polka dot bikini / Bat dance / Baggy trousers / Star treckin' / Ghostbusters (reprise) / Rudolph the red nosed reindeer: *Dixie Cups* / White Christmas: *Ford, Frankie* / Frosty the snowman: *Coasters* / Christmas song: *Drifters* / Deck the halls: *Crickets* / Sleigh ride: *Diamonds* / If I could spend Christmas with you: *Roe, Tommy* / Little drummer boy: *Tokens* / Silent night: *Shirelles* / New baby for Christmas: *Preston, Johnny* / Winter wonderland: *Rockin' Robin* / Rockin' around the Christmas tree: *Jones, Davy*
CD Set ______ **QUAD 020**
Tring / Nov '96 / Tring

GREATEST POP BALLADS (3CD Set)
Rush rush: *Abdul, Paula* / Eyes without a face: *Idol, Billy* / Dum dum girl: *Talk Talk* / I touch myself: *Divinyls* / Love is love: *Culture Club* / Kayleigh: *Marillion* / Move closer: *Nelson, Phyllis* / True: *Spandau Ballet* / Room in your heart: *Living In A Box* / Looking for Linda: *Hue & Cry* / Stay: *Thomas, Kenny* / Turn back the clock: *Johnny Hates Jazz* / Mary's prayer: *Danny Wilson* / Tracks of my tears: *Go West* / Love don't live here anymore: *Nail, Jimmy* / Closest thing to heaven: *Kane Gang* / Save a prayer: *Duran Duran* / Picture postcards from LA: *Kadison, Joshua* / So long: *Fischer Z* / Everything I own: *Boy George* / Walking on ice: *River City People* / This must be the night: *Mink Deville* / Good heart: *Sharkey, Feargal* / She makes my day: *Palmer, Robert* / I'll never fall in love: *Harry, Deborah* / True love: *Benatar, Pat* / You could have been with me: *Easton, Sheena* / Love disappears: *Gaines, Jeffrey* / Don't turn away: *Go For It* / Lover spurned: *Almond, Marc* / Heaven is a secret: *Spandau Ballet* / When you walk in the room: *Carrack, Paul* / Would I lie to you: *Charles & Eddie* / Release me: *Wilson Phillips* / Cambodia: *Wilde, Kim* / Orchard Road: *Sayer, Leo* / Mated: *Grant, David & Jaki Graham* / Suddenly last summer: *Motels* / Whenever you need me: *T'Pau* / I've been in love before: *Cutting Crew* / Harder I try: *Brother Beyond* / Sweet sixteen: *Idol, Billy* / Missing you: *Waite, John* / For your blue eyes only: *Hadley, Tony* / Home on Monday: *Little River Band* / What other reason: *Johnny Hates Jazz* / Something's gotten hold of my heart: *Almond, Marc & Gene Pitney* / Caravan of love: *Housemartins*
CD Set ______ **HR 877412**
Disky / Mar '97 / Disky / THE

GREATEST POP BALLADS VOL.1
Rush rush: *Abdul, Paula* / Eyes without a face: *Idol, Billy* / Dum dum girl: *Talk Talk* / I touch myself: *Divinyls* / Love is love: *Culture Club* / Kayleigh: *Marillion* / Move closer: *Nelson, Phyllis* / True: *Spandau Ballet* / Room in your heart: *Living In A Box* / Looking for Linda: *Hue & Cry* / Stay: *Thomas, Kenny* / Turn back the clock: *Johnny Hates Jazz* / Mary's prayer: *Danny Wilson* / Tracks of my tears: *Go West* / Love don't live here anymore: *Nail, Jimmy* / Closest thing to heaven: *Kane Gang*
CD ______ **BXA 877422**
Disky / May '97 / Disky / THE

GREATEST POP BALLADS VOL.2
Save a prayer: *Duran Duran* / Picture postcards from LA: *Kadison, Joshua* / So long: *Fischer Z* / Everything I own: *Boy George* / Walking on ice: *River City People* / This must be the night: *Mink Deville* / Good heart: *Sharkey, Feargal* / She makes my day: *Palmer, Robert* / I'll never fall in love: *Harry, Deborah* / True love: *Benatar, Pat* / You could have been with me: *Easton, Sheena* / Love dissapears: *Gaines, Jeffrey* / Don't turn away: *Go For It* / Lover spurned: *Almond, Marc* / Heaven is a secret: *Spandau Ballet* / When you walk in the room: *Carrack, Paul*
CD ______ **BXA 877432**
Disky / May '97 / Disky / THE

GREATEST POP BALLADS VOL.3
Would I lie to you: *Charles & Eddie* / Release me: *Wilson Phillips* / Cambodia: *Wilde, Kim* / Orchard road: *Sayer, Leo* / Mated: *Grant, David & Jaki Graham* / Suddenly last summer: *Motels* / Whenever you need me: *T'Pau* / I've been in love before: *Cutting Crew* / Harder I try: *Brother Beyond* / Sweet sixteen: *Idol, Billy* / Missing you: *Waite, John* / For your blue eyes only: *Hadley, Tony* / Home on Monday: *Little River Band* / What other reason: *Johnny Hates Jazz* / Something's gotten hold of my heart: *Almond, Marc & Gene Pitney* / Caravan of love: *Housemartins*
CD ______ **BXA 877442**
Disky / May '97 / Disky / THE

GREATEST RAGTIME OF THE CENTURY
Shreveport stomp: *Morton, Jelly Roll* / Sweet man: *Morton, Jelly Roll* / Tom cat blues: *Morton, Jelly Roll* / New kind of man: *Waller, Fats* / Nobody but my baby: *Waller, Fats* / Got to cool my doggies now: *Waller, Fats* / Maple leaf rag: *Joplin, Scott* / Weeping willow rag: *Joplin, Scott* / Something doing: *Joplin, Scott* / Steeplechase rag: *Johnson, James P.* / Twilight rag: *Johnson, James P.* / Charleston rag: *Blake, Eubie* / It's right here for you: *Blake, Eubie* / Fare thee honey blues: *Blake, Eubie* / Mr. Freddie blues: *Blythe, Jimmy* / Regal stomp: *Blythe, Jimmy*
CD ______ **BCD 103**
Biograph / Jul '91 / ADA / Cadillac / Direct / Hot Shot / Jazz Music / Wellard

GREATEST ROCK 'N' ROLL PARTY EVER
Blue suede shoes: *Perkins, Carl* / Be bop a lula: *Vincent, Gene* / Peggy sue: *Holly, Buddy* / Three steps to heaven: *Cochran, Eddie* / Razzle dazzle: *Haley, Bill & The Comets* / Good golly Miss Molly: *Little Richard* / Roll over Beethoven: *Berry, Chuck* / Rockin' Robin: *Day, Bobby* / Tiger: *Fabian* / Runaround Sue: *Dion* / Why do fools fall in love: *Lymon, Frankie & The Teenagers* / Hello Mary Lou: *Nelson, Ricky* / Bye bye love: *Everly Brothers* / There goes my heart again: *Fats Domino* / Not fade away: *Crickets* / Party doll: *Knox, Buddy* / Great balls of fire: *Lewis, Jerry Lee* / Red hot: *Riley, Billy Lee*
CD ______ **DC 880212**
Disky / Jul '97 / Disky / THE

GREATEST ROCK 'N' ROLL SHOW
CD ______ **HRCD 8021**
Disky / Jul '93 / Disky / THE

GREATEST SINGERS, GREATEST SONGS (3CD Set)
Over the rainbow: *Garland, Judy* / Zing went the strings of my heart: *Garland, Judy* / Little children: *Kramer, Billy J. & The Dakotas* / Dance, ballerina, dance: *Cole, Nat 'King'* / Smile: *Cole, Nat 'King'* / Let there be love: *Cole, Nat 'King'* / It must be him: *Carr, Vikki* / When you're in love with a beautiful woman: *Dr. Hook* / Climb every mountain: *Bassey, Shirley* / On the street where you live: *Damone, Vic* / Dreamboat: *Cogan, Alma* / Lady: *Rogers, Kenny* / Lucille: *Rogers, Kenny* / Shrimp boats: *Stafford, Jo* / Portrait of my love: *Monro, Matt* / Softly as I leave you: *Monro, Matt* / Walk away: *Monro, Matt* / Folks who live on the hill: *Lee, Peggy* / Story of my life: *Holliday, Michael* / Starry eyed: *Holliday, Michael* / Talking in your sleep: *Gayle, Crystal* / Don't it make my brown eyes blue: *Gayle, Crystal* / Volare: *Martin, Dean* / Memories are made of this: *Martin, Dean* / That's amore (That's love): *Martin, Dean* / Come along a love: *Starr, Kay* / Still: *Dodd, Ken & Geoff Love Orchestra* / He was beautiful: *Williams, Iris* / Honey: *Goldsboro, Bobby* / Air that I breathe: *Hollies* / Cry me a river: *London, Julie* / Dreams of an everyday housewife: *Campbell, Glen* / To sir with love: *Lulu* / Sing me an old fashioned song: *Spears, Billie Jo* / What I've got in mind: *Spears, Billie Jo* / O what a beautiful morning: *Keel, Howard* / Walkin' back to happiness: *Shapiro, Helen* / And I love you so: *Reddy, Helen* / And I love you so: *McLean, Don* / Loving you: *Riperton, Minnie* / Spanish eyes: *Martino, Al* / Carnival is over: *Seekers* / Call me irresponsible: *Washington, Dinah* / Edelweiss: *Hill, Vince* / Good vibrations: *Beach Boys*
CD Set ______ **CDTRBOX 136**
Trio / Oct '94 / EMI

GREATEST SOUL ALBUM OF ALL TIME, THE (2CD Set)
You are everything: *Ross, Diana & Marvin Gaye* / Rock me tonight: *Jackson, Freddie* / Ain't no sunshine: *Withers, Bill* / How 'bout us: *Champaign* / Me & Mrs. Jones: *Paul, Billy* / Cherish: *Kool & The Gang* / Gotta get you home: *Wilde, Eugene* / Juicy fruit: *Mtume* / You body's callin': *R Kelly* / Body talk: *Imagination* / Always: *Atlantic Starr* / Shake you down: *Abbott, Gregory* / Streetlife: *Crusaders* / Rock wit'cha: *Brown, Bobby* / I wanna get next to you: *Royce, Rose* / Do you wanna make love: *Jackson, Michael & Isaac Hayes* / Let's stay together: *Green, Al* / Midnight train to Georgia: *Knight, Gladys & The Pips* / Be thankful for what you: *De Vaughn, William* / It's a man's man's man's world: *Brown, James* / Don't leave me this way: *Melvin, Harold* / Do what you do: *Jackson, Jermaine* / Sexual healing: *Gaye, Marvin* / There's nothing like this: *Omar* / Love supreme: *Downing, Will* / Joy and pain: *Maze* / Strawberry letter 23: *Johnson, Bros* / I found lovin': *Fatback Band* / If loving you is wrong: *Jackson, Millie* / Hold back the night: *Trammps* / It's a love thang: *Whispers* / Love come down: *King, Evelyn 'Champagne'* / Stay with me tonight: *Osborne, Jeffrey* / Misty blue: *Moore, Dorothy* / You're the first the last my everything: *White, Barry* / Lovin' you: *Riperton, Minnie* / Dolly my love: *Moments* / This is it: *Moore, Melba* / Now is the time: *James, Jimmy* / Rescue me: *Bass, Fontella*
CD Set ______ **DINCD 113**
Dino / Nov '95 / Pinnacle

GREATEST TRANCE TRACKS
CD ______ **IG 0042**
Intergroove / Jun '97 / Intergroove

GREATEST TROUSERS
CD ______ **EYEUKCD 003**
Harthouse / Jun '95 / Mo's Music Machine / Prime / Vital

GREATEST VOICES OF OUR TIME VOL.1
CD ______ **GCMD 504**
GCM / Jun '97 / Total/BMG

GREECE - BYZANTINE MUSIC
CD ______ **LDX 274971**
La Chant Du Monde / Apr '94 / ADA / Harmonia Mundi

GREEN LINNET 20TH ANNIVERSARY COLLECTION (2CD Set)
CD Set ______ **GLCD 106**
Green Linnet / Aug '96 / ADA / CM / Direct / Highlander / Roots

GREEN VELVET (4CD Set)
CD Set ______ **MBSCD 436**
Castle / Nov '95 / BMG

GREEN VELVET - THE IRISH FOLK COLLECTION
She moved through the fair: *Shades of McMurrough* / From Clare to here: *Fureys & Davey Arthur* / Shane boy: *Bards* / Cliffs of Dooneen: *Dublin City Ramblers* / Emigrant: *Fureys & Davey Arthur* / Shores of Loch Bran: *De Danann* / Follow me up to Carlo: *Shades of McMurrough* / Lonesome boatman: *Fureys & Davey Arthur* / Sligo Fair: *Fergia* / Ramblin' Irishman: *De Danann* / Wind in the willows: *Spud* / Slipside: *Stockton's Wing* / Tabhair dom do lamh: *Shades of McMurrough* / Silver in the stubble: *Dublin City Ramblers*
CD ______ **5501842**
Spectrum / Mar '94 / PolyGram

GREENBELT FRINGE '95
Defiled: *Fresh Claim* / Magnum mysterium: *Eve & The Garden* / Paper chain: *3rd Day* / Who you really are: *Before & Beyond* / Take me: *Rumours Are True* / Wake me when the madness ends: *Full Circle* / Isn't he: *Catley, Marc* / Thank God for car stockers: *Catley, Marc* / Set the moose loose: *Moose Machine* / Bold love: *Red Delivery Animal* / It's like everything else: *Worner-Phillips, Nigel* / Never mind: *Bernards's Dog* / Calling: *Skellig* / Watching the war: *Ryder, Pete* / Children: *Mudhead's Monkey* / Really me: *Obviously 5 Believers* / Flawed: *Days, Jonathan Earthhouse* / Just one minute: *Bickley, Jon & Angel Train* / Rain people: *Hunt* / Art of the artsong song: *Paley's Watch* / Dreamscape: *Asylum*
CD ______ **PCDN 147**
Plankton / Nov '95 / Plankton

GREENLAND CALLING VOL.1
CD ______ **ULO 75**
Ulo / May '96 / ADA

GREENLAND CALLING VOL.2
CD ______ **ULO 76**
Ulo / May '96 / ADA

GREENSLEEVES SAMPLER VOL.1
Crazy list: *Brown, Dennis* / Feel the rydim: *Minott, Sugar* / Zungguzungguguzungguzeng: *Yellowman* / Pass the Tu-Sheng-Peng: *Paul, Frankie* / Let off supm: *Isaacs, Gregory* / Africa must be free by 1983: *Mundell, Hugh* / I love King Selassie: *Black Uhuru* / They don't know Jah: *Wailing Souls* / Dematerialise: *Scientist* / Ganja smuggling: *Eek-A-Mouse* / Stop that train: *Eastwood & Saint* / We are going: *Burning Spear* / Winnie Mandela: *Davis, Carlene* / Real enemy: *Mighty Diamonds*
CD ______ **GREZCD 1**
Greensleeves / Jun '87 / Jet Star / SRD

GREENSLEEVES SAMPLER VOL.10
Under mi sensi: *Levy, Barrington & Beenie Man* / Gangster: *Lieutenant Stitchie* / No no no (World a respect mix): *Penn, Dawn* / Can't stop the dance: *Yardcore Collective* / Down in the ghetto: *Bounty Killer* / Bumptious girl: *Sanchez & Stingerman* / Press button (Remix): *Beenie Man* / Fowl affair: *Silver Cat* / All over you: *Roach, Colin* / Shoo-be-doo: *Papa San* / Reminiscing: *Redrose & Spragga Benz* / One love: *Cocoa T & Shaka Shamba* / Bad publicity: *Ninjaman* / One good turn: *Isaacs, Gregory & Beres Hammond* / Runaround girl: *Bounty Killer & Chuck Turner* / You don't love me (no no no): *Penn, Dawn*
CD ______ **GREZCD 10**
Greensleeves / Sep '94 / Jet Star / SRD

GREENSLEEVES SAMPLER VOL.13
CD ______ **GREZCD 13**
Greensleeves / Mar '96 / Jet Star / SRD

GREENSLEEVES SAMPLER VOL.14
CD ______ **GREZCD 14**
Greensleeves / Aug '96 / Jet Star / SRD

GREENSLEEVES SAMPLER VOL.15
Man tief sonata: *Buccaneer* / Rumours: *McGregor, Freddie* / Shelly Ann: *Red Rat* / This is the time: *Luciano* / Healing: *Lady Saw & Beenie Man* / Living dangerously: *Levy, Barrington* / Slop dem: *Stephens, Richie* / Rude boy life: *Bushman* / Bounce along: *Wayne Wonder & Spragga Benz* / Time is slipping away: *Redd, Jeff* / Mr. Hardcore: *Mad Cobra* / Girls galore: *Stephens, Richie & General Degree* / Nuff gal: *Beenie Man* / So many girls: *Merciless* / Rub a dubit: *Reid, Junior & Outlaw Candy* / Tears: *Papa San*
CD ______ **GREZCD 15**
Greensleeves / May '97 / Jet Star / SRD

GREENSLEEVES SAMPLER VOL.2
Telephone love: *Lodge, J.C.* / She loves me now: *Hammond, Beres* / Rock me: *Mowatt, Judy* / Man is a man: *Boothe, Ken* / Knight in shining armour: *Glasgow, Deborahe* / Fly me to the moon: *Burning Spear* / Rumours: *Isaacs, Gregory* / Tonight I'm going to take it easy: *Mighty Diamonds* / Girl E: *Kamoze, Ini* / Magnet and steel: *Fraser, Dean* / Miserable woman: *McGregor, Freddie* / Blueberry Hill: *Yellowman* / More them chat: *Cocoa T & Krystal* / Golden touch: *Shabba Ranks*
CD ______ **GREZCD 2**
Greensleeves / Sep '88 / Jet Star / SRD

GREENSLEEVES SAMPLER VOL.3
CD ______ **GREZCD 3**
Greensleeves / Oct '89 / Jet Star / SRD

GREENSLEEVES SAMPLER VOL.4
Twice my age: *Shabba Ranks & Krystal* / Report to me: *Isaacs, Gregory* / Love me baby: *Tiger* / Pirate's anthem: *Home T & Cocoa T/Shabba Ranks* / No more walls: *Brown, Dennis* / Wicked and wild: *Little Lenny* / Mr. Loverman: *Glasgow, Deborahe & Shabba Ranks* / Blinking something: *Pinchers* / Round table talk: *Papa San* / Why turn down the sound: *Cocoa T* / Make up your mind: *Brown, Dennis & Tiger* / Tell me which one: *Admiral Tibet*
CD ______ **GREZCD 4**
Greensleeves / Apr '90 / Jet Star / SRD

GREENSLEEVES SAMPLER VOL.5
Your body's here with me: *Home T & Cocoa T/Shabba Ranks* / It's not enough: *Papa San & Fabian* / Ruling cowboy: *Cocoa T* / Home boy: *Brown, Dennis* / Gun talk: *Redrose & Tony Rebel* / Roughneck sound: *Robinson, Ed 'Roughneck'* / Going is rough: *Home T & Cocoa T/Shabba Ranks* / Monday morning blues: *Mikey Melody* / Shepherd be careful: *Cocoa T & Dennis Brown* / Guilty: *Mowatt, Judy* / More them chat: *Cocoa T & Krystal* / Golden touch: *Shabba Ranks*
CD ______ **GREZCD 5**
Greensleeves / Nov '90 / Jet Star / SRD

GREENSLEEVES SAMPLER VOL.6
Fanciness: *Shabba Ranks & Lady G* / One way woman: *Cocoa T* / John Law: *Isaacs, Gregory & Freddie McGregor/Ninjaman* / Mr. Bodyguard: *Mighty Diamonds* / Something in my heart: *Levy, Barrington & Reggie Stepper* / Mixed feelings: *Brown, Dennis & Fabiana* / Another one for the road: *Home T & Cocoa T/Shabba Ranks* / Midnight Lover: *McGregor, Freddie* / Looking for love: *Cutty Ranks & Barrington Levy* / Fancy girl: *Fabiana & Shabba Ranks* / I'm your man: *Brown, Dennis & Reggie Stepper* / Stallion: *Chaka Demus*
CD ______ **GREZCD 6**
Greensleeves / Apr '92 / Jet Star / SRD

GREENSLEEVES SAMPLER VOL.7
Oh Carolina: *Shaggy* / Bed work sensation: *Bajja Jedd* / I Spy: *General TK* / Getting closer: *Cocoa T* / Yardie: *Buju Banton* / Don man girl: *Isaacs, Gregory* / Ting a ling a ling a school pickney sing ting: *Ninjaman* / Tender loving: *Cocoa T & Shaka Shamba* / Wealth: *Cutty Ranks* / Playing hard to get: *McGregor, Freddie* / After dark: *Capleton* / I need a roof: *Mighty Diamonds* / Screwface: *General TK* / Bedroom eyes: *Yellowman* / Certain friends: *Lady G* / Dance hall queen: *Lloyd, Peter*
CD ______ **GREZCD 7**
Greensleeves / May '93 / Jet Star / SRD

GREENSLEEVES SAMPLER VOL.8
CD ______ **GREZCD 8**
Greensleeves / Nov '93 / Jet Star / SRD

GREENSLEEVES SAMPLER VOL.9
Two sounds: *Levy, Barrington & Beenie Man* / Gimme little sign: *Harvey, Maxine* / Tune in: *Cocoa T* / Statement: *Bounty Killer* / One way ticket: *Luciano* / I will forever love you: *Sanchez* / More than loving: *Capleton & Nadine Sutherland* / Love and devotion: *Hammond, Beres* / One jamaican: *Osbourne, Johnny* / Nice and lovely: *Shaggy & Rayvon* / Not because I smile: *Isaacs, Gregory* / He will see you through: *Griffiths, Marcia* / Inna de dance: *Reid, Junior* / More love: *French, Robert & Heavy D* / Rude boys ride again: *Cutty Ranks* / There's nothing like this: *Brown, Dennis*
CD **GREZCD 9**
Greensleeves / Apr '94 / Jet Star / SRD

GREETINGS FROM GOA (2CD Set)
CD Set **560102**
Nova Tekk / Apr '97 / Pinnacle

GREETINGS FROM HAWAII
CD **15184**
Laserlight / '91 / Target/BMG

GREETINGS FROM LUGANO
Amapola / Marina / Amore a Rivabella / Limon Limonero
CD **15447**
Laserlight / Jun '92 / Target/BMG

GRETSCH DRUM NIGHT AT BIRDLAND
Wee dot / Now's the time / Tune up / El Sino / Night in Tunisia
CD **CDROU 1057**
Roulette / Feb '94 / EMI

GRINDCORE
CD **NB 084CD**
Nuclear Blast / Dec '93 / Plastic Head

GROOVE IS IN THE HEART (Sample Of Dance Classics)
Every little thing I do: *Soul For Real* / Love supreme: *Downing, Will* / Say no go: *De La Soul* / Set adrift on memory bliss: *PM Dawn* / Downtown: *SWV* / Thinking of you: *Usher* / My definition of a boombastic: *Dream Warriors* / Believe in me: *Utah Saints* / Shout: *Louchie Lou & Michie One* / Can you handle it: *DNA & Sharon Redd* / Ice ice baby: *Vanilla Ice* / People everyday: *Arrested Development* / Can I kick it: *Tribe Called Quest* / Down for whateva: *Nuttin' Nyce* / Summertime: *DJ Jazzy Jeff & The Fresh Prince* / Boom shake the room: *DJ Jazzy Jeff & The Fresh Prince* / Rappers delight: *Sugarhill Gang*
CD **RENCD 120**
Renaissance Collector Series / Mar '97 / BMG

GROOVEADELIC (2CD Set)
Psychic bounty killaz: *DJ Sneak & Armand Van Helden* / Happy days: *Happy Days* / Maw War (Gotta get that groove thang): *Kenlou* / I like it: *Tyree* / Heart but house: *De Borah, Nathalie* / Emancipation of my soul: *Parker, Terence* / Lift me up: *MK & Claire Rivers* / Hear the music: *Johnson, Paul* / Alabama blues: *St. Germain* / Don't stop the feelin': *Gu & Terence FM* / In de ghetto: *Morales, David & The Bad Yard Club* / Dancer: *Moodyman* / Handbag: *Eric KJ Project* / We are one: *DJ Q* / Da lost trip: *Clubheroes* / It's so hard: *Moraes, Angel* / Morel s sax groove: *Morel Inc* / Only 4 U: *Cajmere* / I need you know: *Sinnamon* / Make the world go round: *Sandy B*
CD Set **SPVDCD 08947312**
SPV / Mar '97 / Koch / Plastic Head

GROOVES - 80'S DANCE
CD **PDSCD 539**
Pulse / Aug '96 / BMG

GROOVIN' (20 Soulful Summer Grooves)
Regulate: *Warren G & Nate Dogg* / Summertime: *DJ Jazzy Jeff & The Fresh Prince* / Breakadawn: *De La Soul* / Set adrift on memory bliss: *PM Dawn* / Back and forth: *Aaliyah* / Lover: *Roberts, Joe* / Your body's calling: *R Kelly* / I'm in luv: *Joe* / Long time gone: *Galliano* / Joy: *Soul II Soul* / Connected: *Stereo MC's* / People everyday: *Arrested Development* / It was a good day: *Ice Cube* / Brother: *Urban Species* / Turn on tune in cop out: *Freakpower* / Be thankful for what you've got: *Massive Attack* / Apparently nothin': *Young Disciples* / Still a friend of mine: *Incognito* / There's nothing like this: *Omar* / Groovin': *Tyson*
CD **5169682**
Polydor / Aug '94 / PolyGram

GROOVIN'
Peaceful easy feeling: *Alexander, Rob* / Money runner: *Jones, Quincy* / Funky sensation: *McCrae, Gwen* / World is a ghetto: *War* / Viva tirado: *El Chicano* / Mama said: *Anderson, Carleen* / Mr. Magic: *Washington, Grover Jr.* / All for you: *Van Dyke, Earl* / When the world turns blue: *Clayton, Merry* / Holy ghost: *Bar-Kays* / Billy's bag: *Preston, Billy* / You've got it bad girl: *Jones, Ivan 'Boogaloo Joe'*
CD **JAZZFMCD 3**
Jazz FM / Mar '97 / Beechwood/BMG

GROOVIN' AT THE GO-GO
Not only the girl knows: *Victors* / Hurt: *Victors* / Stay mine for heaven's sake: *Holman, Eddie* / Eddie's my name: *Holman, Eddie* / I'll cry 1000 tears: *Holman, Eddie* / I can't break the habit: *Garrett, Lee* / One more year: *United 4* / It's gonna be a false alarm: *Volcanos* / Deeper than that: *Preludes* / Shiggy diggy: *Preludes* / Groovin' at the Go-Go: *Four Larks* / She's puttin' you on: *United 4* / I still love you: *Four Larks* / Another chance: *Four Larks* / Without you baby: *Larks* / For the love of money: *Larks* / I surrender: *Holman, Eddie* / Where I'm not wanted: *Holman, Eddie* / Hurt: *Holman, Eddie* / She's wanted: *Clinton, Larry* / Focused on you: *Williams, B.* / It's needless to say: *Williams, B.*
CD **GSCD 026**
Goldmine / Nov '93 / Vital

GROOVIN' HIGH (The Age Of Modern Jazz Begins)
Groovin' high: *Gillespie, Dizzy & Charlie Parker* / All the things you are: *Gillespie, Dizzy & Charlie Parker* / Salt peanuts: *Gillespie, Dizzy & Charlie Parker* / Hallelujah: *Norvo, Red & Dizzy Gillespie/Charlie Parker* / Lonesome lover blues: *Eckstine, Billy* / Disorder at the border: *Hawkins, Coleman* / Bu-dedah: *Hawkins, Coleman* / Jumpin' blues: *McShann, Jay* / Co pilot: *Auld, Georgie* / I'll wait and pray: *Vaughan, Sarah* / Street beat: *Vaughan, Sarah* / Night in Tunisia: *Raeburn, Boyd & Dizzy Gillespie* / I can't get started: *Gillespie, Dizzy* / Apple honey: *Herman, Woody* / Buster's last stand: *Thornhill, Claude* / Blue 'n' boogie: *Gillespie, Dizzy & Dexter Gordon* / Now's the time: *Parker, Charlie* / Red cross: *Grimes, Tiny* / Koko: *Parker, Charlie*
CD **306322**
Hallmark / Jan '97 / Carlton

GROOVSVILLE REVIEW, THE
Has it happened to you yet: *Starr, Edwin* / Let's party: *Mancha, Steve* / Happiness is here: *Mercer, Barbara* / Heart trouble: *Parliaments* / I miss my baby / That's why I love you: *Professionals* / Searching: *Hatcher, Willie* / I need my baby: *Davis, Melvin & Steve Mancha* / Trying to forget you: *Turner, Spyder* / Good understanding: *Mancha, Steve* / You're gonna be sorry / Solid as a rock: *Vincent, Joyce* / You're my mellow: *Starr, Edwin* / Chains of love: *Davis, Melvin* / He stole the love that was mine: *Davis, Melvin* / Time fades away: *Henry, Andrea* / Need to be needed: *Mancha, Steve* / Pigfeet (deeper in love): *Ward, Robert* / I'm the one who loves you: *Banks, Darrell* / Goings on: *Barnes, J.J.* / Unyielding: *Mancha, Steve* / Everloving / You're still in my heart: *Ruffin, David*
CD **GSCD 121**
Goldmine / Apr '97 / Vital

GROOVY KIND OF SAX, A
We've only just begun / All the things you are / If / Saving all my love for you / Just the way you are / Moon river / I love you because / Just for you / Love me tender / Always / Sometimes when we touch / Rose / Very thought of you / Beautiful friendship / Chanson d'amour / Killing me softly / Groovy kind of love / Arthur's theme / Misty / My cherie amour
CD **EMPRCD 601**
Emporio / Jun '96 / Disc

GROOVY REGGAE STARS (2CD Set)
CD Set **24314**
Delta Doubles / Oct '95 / Target/BMG

GROOVY SHUFFLE
CD **CHILLCD 005**
Chillout / Nov '95 / Kudos / Pinnacle / RTM/Disc

GROUPS OF WRATH, THE (Songs of the Naked City)
CD **DANCD 080**
Danceteria / Feb '95 / ADA / Plastic Head / Shellshock/Disc

GROWIN' UP TOO FAST (The Girl Groups Anthology)
My boyfriend's back: *Angels* / Remember (walkin' in the sand): *Shangri-Las* / My best friend Barbara: *Francis, Connie* / Navy blue: *Renay, Diane* / She don't deserve you: *Honey Bees* / Please don't talk to the lifeguard: *Ray, Diane* / It comes and goes: *Sadina* / Maybe I know: *Gore, Lesley* / It's gonna take a miracle: *Royalettes* / Boy next door: *Secrets* / I wish I knew what dress to wear: *Arnell, Ginny* / 442 Glenwood Avenue: *Pixies Three* / Johnny's back in town: *D'Andrea, Ann* / Stay awhile: *Springfield, Dusty* / So soft, so warm: *Nu Luvs* / Look of love: *Gore, Lesley* / Beatles, please come back: *Parker, Gigi & The Lonelies* / Summertime USA: *Pixies Three* / Can't he take a hint: *Woods, Kenni* / Wow wow wee (he's the boy for me): *Angels* / Always waitin': *Paris Sisters* / Watch out Sally: *Renay, Diane* / Wonder boy: *Gore, Lesley* / Hey big boy: *Secrets* / Sweet sounds of summer: *Shangri-Las*
CD **5281712**
Mercury / Nov '96 / PolyGram

GRP SOUNDS OF 1996
Playtime: *Spyro Gyra* / Thinking about you: *Daemyon, Jerald* / I apologize: *Howard, George* / Virtual reality: *Rippingtons* / Cold and windy: *Lewis, Ramsey* / Yesterday: *Kishino, Yoshiko* / Columbia: *Acoustic Alchemy* / Duck's 'n' cookies: *Gessinger, Nils* / Moment's notice: *Sandoval, Arturo* / Love walked in: *Schurr, Diane* / Wave: *Eubanks, Kevin* / Gee baby ain't I good to you: *Krall, Diana* / She's so heavy: *Groove Collective*
CD **GRP 88902**
GRP / Oct '96 / New Note/BMG

GS I LOVE YOU (Japanese Garage Bands Of The 1960's)
You gat a call me: *Out Cast* / Everything's alright: *Out Cast* / Dynamite: *Spiders* / Monkey dance: *Spiders* / One more please: *Blue Jeans* / Stop dance: *Terrys* / Shevidevi de Yuko: *Playboy* / Kaette okure: *Playboy* / Kokoro no tokimeki (ajoen ajoen): *Swing West* / Let's go Rangers: *Rangers* / Koi O Kesunda: *Napoleon* / Aphrodite: *Cougars* / Suki Nanda: *Cougars* / Wipeout: *Spiders* / Furi furi: *Spiders* / I saw her standing there: *Burns* / Bara O Anokoni: *Days & Nights* / Let's go on the beach: *Out Cast* / Bokuno Sobakara: *Out Cast* / Hold on I'm comin': *Voltage* / J & A: *Cougars* / Seishun a go go: *Spiders* / Hey girl: *Van Dogs* / Omiyasan: *Toys* / Long tall Sally: *Out Cast* / Kimamana Shelly: *Out Cast* / Jane Jane: *Out Cast* / Fire: *Swing West*
CD **CDWIKD 159**
Big Beat / Jun '96 / Pinnacle

GUADELOUPE VOL.1
CD **C 560030**
Ocora / Jan '93 / ADA / Harmonia Mundi

GUADELOUPE VOL.2
CD **C 560031**
Ocora / Jan '93 / ADA / Harmonia Mundi

GUANTANAMERA - SON DE CUBA
CD **3015992**
Flarenasch / Feb '97 / Discovery

GUERILLA IN DUB
Rhythm is life: *Lemon Sol* / Schmooo/ aqualung: *Spooky* / Alchemy: *Drum Club* / Oh no: *DOP* / Dub house disco: *2 Shiny Heads* / Intoxication: *React 2 Rhythm* / Schudelfloss: *Dr. Atomic* / Higher: *Code MD* / Dub house disco (reprise): *2 Shiny Heads*
CD **GRCD 011**
Guerilla / Jul '94 / Pinnacle
CD **PWD 7450**
Pow Wow / May '94 / Jet Star

GUINEA: RECITS ET EPOPEES
CD **C 560009**
Ocora / Nov '92 / ADA / Harmonia Mundi

GUITAR BLUES
CD **12336**
Laserlight / May '94 / Target/BMG

GUITAR EVANGELIST
CD **DOCD 5101**
Document / Nov '92 / ADA / Hot Shot / Jazz Music

GUITAR EXPLORATION
CD **WKFMXXD 169**
FM / Apr '91 / Revolver / Sony

GUITAR FINGERSTYLE
Little Martha: *Farrell, Tim* / Crow: *Gerbard, Edward* / South by winterwest: *McLaughlin, Billy* / Daisy goes a dancing: *Kirtley, Pat* / That'll be the phone: *Ross, Don* / Soul discovery: *Woolman, Benjamin* / Lunar eclipse: *Juber, Laurence* / To B or not To B: *Anderson, Muriel* / Peristroika: *Bennett, Stephen* / If I only had wings: *Auten, D.R.* / First ride: *Ross, Don* / It never gets easier: *Anderson, Muriel* / Helms place: *McLaughlin, Billy* / Only my heart: *Jones, Tommy* / Angela: *Auten, D.R.* / Grandpa's lullaby: *Kirtley, Pat*
CD **ND 61056**
Narada / Aug '96 / ADA / New Note/ Pinnacle

GUITAR HEROES
CD Set **KBOX 350**
Collection / Oct '95 / Target/BMG / TKO Magnum

GUITAR HEROES
Apache: *Shadows* / Hawaii Five-O: *Ventures* / Guitar boogie shuffle: *Weedon, Bert* / Telstar: *Tornados* / Raunchy: *Justis, Bill* / Cruel sea: *Dakotas* / Pipeline: *Chantays* / Rumble: *Wray, Link* / Sleepwalk: *Santo & Johnny* / Mexican, The: *Fentones* / Wipe out: *Surfaris* / Memphis: *Mack, Lonnie* / Tico tico: *Paul, Les* / Walk don't run: *Ventures* / FBI: *Shadow Talk* / Fireball XL5: *Flee Rekkers*
CD **DC 880192**
Disky / Jul '97 / Disky / THE

GUITAR KINGS VOL.1
CD **EXP 039**
Experience / May '97 / TKO Magnum

GUITAR KINGS VOL.2
CD **EXP 040**
Experience / May '97 / TKO Magnum

GUITAR MAN
CD **NSCD 022**
Newsound / May '95 / THE

GUITAR MOODS
CD **MACCD 325**
Autograph / Aug '96 / BMG

GUITAR PARADISE OF EAST AFRICA
Sukuma songa: *Sukuma Bin Ongaro* / Achi Maria / Mumbi ni wakwa: *Kamau, Daniel* / Odesia: *Les Mangelpa* / Wana wanyika: *Wanyika, Simba* / Mama kamale: *Sukuma Bin Ongaro* / Shauri yako: *Orchestra Super Mazembe* / Ndia: *Mwambi, Peter* / Harare: *Les Mangelpa* / Ndiretikia ni nii: *Famous Nyahururu Boys* / Mwendwa Jane: *Kilimambogo Brothers*
CD **CDEWV 21**
Earthworks / Oct '90 / EMI

GUITAR ROCK
CD **STACD 045**
Wisepack / Sep '94 / Conifer/BMG / THE

GUITAR WORKS
Monogahela: *Tingstad, Eric* / Barcelona: *White, Andy* / Hexagram of the heavens: *Kolbe, Martin* / Light a candle: *Ellwood, William* / Inner movement: *Illenberger, Ralf* / Leaving home: *Mirowitz, Sheldon* / Nocturne: *Wynberg, Simon* / Maria's watermill: *Wynberg, Simon* / Sonho (Dream): *Lauria, Nando* / Since you asked: *Mirowitz, Sheldon* / Amber: *Montfort, Matthew* / Remembering greensleeves: *Doan, John* / By bye lullaby: *Kolbe, Martin*
CD **ND 31032**
Narada / Nov '92 / ADA / New Note/ Pinnacle

GUITAR WORKSHOP IN LA
Take it all / Bawls / Donna / Bull funk / Blues for Ronnie / Skunk blues / Hyper stork / Vicky's song / Beverly Hill / Roppongi
CD **JD 3314**
JVC / May '89 / Direct / New Note/Pinnacle / Vital/SAM

GUITAR WORKSHOP VOL.1
Trout joins the cavalry: *Boswell, Simon* / Nefarious doings: *Hardy, Chris* / Black scrag: *Lee, Philip John* / One blue guitar: *Berryman, Peter* / Loneliness of the long distance acoustic guitarist: *Barrett, Willy* / Ferdinand the spider: *Murrell, Davey* / Rock salmon suite: *Tilston, Steve* / South Devon atmospheric: *Rogers, Mike* / Mica: *Hardy, Chris* / Trout sundae: *Boswell, Simon* / Stalks and seeds: *Lee, Philip John* / Entertainer: *Rogers, John* / Kenneth's riverbank song: *Murrell, Davey* / Hair accross the frets: *Barrett, Willy* / Brother nature: *Rogers, John & Mike*
CD **ESMCD 495**
Essential / Apr '97 / BMG

GUITAR WORKSHOP VOL.2
Fingerlude: *Guillory, Isaac* / Quasimodo: *Guillory, Isaac* / Northside 33: *Foster, Bob* / Annie Lou: *Foster, Bob* / Modulations: *Legg, Adrian* / Hackney picker: *Legg, Adrian* / Valse: *Holland, Bernie* / Autumn song: *Holland, Bernie* / Minda: *Willsher, Pete* / Stealin' and dealin': *Willsher, Pete* / Dancing angel: *Banks, Peter* / Warning: Rumble strips: *Banks, Peter* / Lucifer's cage: *Giltrap, Gordon* / Confusion: *Giltrap, Gordon* / Marigold chrome: *Rogers, Mike* / And the dog was sleeping in the corner: *James, John* / Two fifteen string guitars for nice people: *Geesin, Ron*
CD **ESMCD 496**
Essential / Jul '97 / BMG

GUITARES CELTIQUES
CD **GR 1190602**
Griffe / Nov '95 / ADA / Discovery

GUITARES DE PARIS
CD **995612**
EPM / Mar '96 / ADA / Discovery

GUITARIST COLLECTION VOL.1, THE
CD **BRGCD 011**
Music Maker / Aug '94 / ADA / Grapevine/ PolyGram

GUITARIST OF THE YEAR '94
CD **CMMR 951**
Music Maker / Apr '95 / ADA / Grapevine/ PolyGram

GUITARS UNLIMITED (2CD Set)
CD Set **BB 895**
Black & Blue / Jun '97 / Discovery / Koch / Wellard

GULF COAST BLUES
Everyday is not the same / Emmitt Lee / Miss too fine / Apron strings / Lonesome saxophone part I / Lonesome saxophone part II / Young girl's got a lot of patience / I work five days a week / I don't want your money / Texas son
CD **BT 1055CD**
Black Top / Sep '94 / ADA / CM / Direct

GULF COAST GREASE: THE SANDY STORY VOL.1
Rockin' in the graveyard: *Morningstar, Jackie* / No date tonight: *Morningstar, Jackie* / Sugar baby: *Bozeman, Helen* / Because I love you: *Vincent, Darryl* / Wild wild party: *Vincent, Darryl* / I saw a dream walking: *Clark, Billy* / I know why: *Clark, Billy* / Juke box rock: *Wainwright, Happy* / Brand new baby: *Whitehurst, Floyd* / Juke box Queen: *Keenan, Ronny* / Stpo sign on your heart: *Keenan, Ronny* / Stop sign on your heart: *Keenan, Ronny* / Rockin' satellite: *Sawyer, Roy* / Walking and talking: *Wainwright, Happy* / Shenandoah waltz: *Simmons, Morris* / Trackdown: *Bozeman, Ken* / Close to you: *Richardson, George* / I'm gonna leave: *Sawyer, Roy* / Daddy's goin' batty: *Vincent, Darryl* / Woke up this morning: *Spivey, Kenny* / My baby don't love me no more: *Wainwright, Happy* / Jungle rock: *Bo & Jo* / Knocking at your door: *Bunyard, Curtis* / Mercy me: *Vincent, Darryl*
CD **CDCHD 595**
Ace / Nov '96 / Pinnacle

GUMBO STEW VOL.1 (New Orleans R&B)
Olde wine: *Afo executives* / I know (You don't love me no more): *George, Barbara* / Mojo hanna: *Lynn, Tammi* / Things have

changed: *Prince La La* / Tee na na na na: *Bo, Eddie* / My key don't fit: *Dr. John & Ronnie Barron* / Mary: *Tick tocks* / All for one: *Tee, Willie* / Private eye: *Johnson, Wallace* / Pot: *Dr. John* / Keep on lovin' you: *Pistol* / Time has expired: *Carson, Charles* / I'll make a bet: *Nookie boy* / True love: *Lee, Robbie* / I found out (You are my cousin): *Tee, Willie* / Is it too late: *Tick tocks* / Tell me the truth: *Turquinettes* / Tuned in, turned on: *Robinson, Alvin* / Give her up: *Robinson, Alvin* / Ignat: *Lastie, Melvin & Harold Battiste/Cornell Dupree* / Empty talk: *Robinson, Alvin* / I shall not be moved: *Pastor*
CD CDCHD 450
Ace / Apr '93 / Pinnacle

GUMBO STEW VOL.2
Ya yá: *Dorsey, Lee* / Clap your hands: *Johnson, Wallace* / Always accused: *Tee, Willie* / Need you: *Prince La La* / You better check: *Bo, Eddie* / Talk that talk: *Dr. John & Ronnie Barron* / World of dreams: *Lynn, Tammi* / Gonna get you yet: *Tick tocks* / Peace of mind: *Johnson, Wallace* / Two weeks three days: *Duvall, Joan* / Fix (One naughty flat): *Dr. John* / Try me: *George, Barbara* / Make her you wife: *Pistol* / It was you: *Tee, Willie* / Wyld: *Afo executives* / Let me know: *Lee, Robbie* / Better be cool: *Robinson, Alvin* / I've never been in love: *Robinson, Alvin* / Light my fire: *Lynn, Tammi* / Johnny A's blues: *Adams, Johnny*
CD CDCHD 462
Ace / Sep '93 / Pinnacle

GUN COURT DUB VOL.1
CD SBCD 002
Soul Beat / Aug '94 / Jet Star / SRD

GUN COURT DUB VOL.2
CD SBCD 008
Soul Beat / May '95 / Jet Star / SRD

GUN COURT DUB VOL.3
CD SBCD 010
Soul Beat / Aug '96 / Jet Star / SRD

GUN SHOT LICKS
CD RNCD 2069
Rhino / Jul '94 / Grapevine/PolyGram / Jet Star

GUNS OF NAVARONE/RIDE YOUR DONKEY
Guns of Navarone: *Skatalites* / River bank: *Brooks, Baba* / Illya Kuryakin: *Bennett, Ike & The Crystalites* / Saboo: *McCook, Tommy & The Supersonics* / Bonanza ska: *Malcolm, Carlos & His Jamaican Rhythms* / Vitamin A: *Brooks, Baba* / Something stupid: *Tait, Lynn & the Jets* / Copy me donkey: *Tennors* / El pussy cat ska: *Alphonso, Roland* / Penny reel: *Morris, Eric* / Sound pressure: *Soul Brothers* / Napoleon solo: *Tait, Lynn & the Jets* / Guns fever: *Brooks, Baba* / Ride your donkey: *Tennors* / Save a bread: *Hinds, Justin & The Dominoes* / Rude boy gone jail: *Clarendonians* / Combination: *Beckford, Kelynne* / One Scotch one bourbon one beer: *Brown, Alfred* / Rub and squeeze: *Perry, Lee 'Scratch' & The Soulettes* / Hold your jack: *Morgan, Derrick* / Dr. Dick: *Perry, Lee 'Scratch'* / Silent river runs deep: *Gaylettes* / Congo war: *Lord Brynner* / Dance all night: *Tartans* / I'm in a dancing mood: *Wilson, Delroy* / I like your world: *Gaylettes* / Penny for your song: *Federals*
CD CDTRL 384
Trojan / Jul '97 / Direct / Jet Star

GWLAD I MI VOL.2 (The Best Of Welsh Country Music)
Disgwyl: *John Ac Alun* / Clywed swn: *Iwcs a Doyle* / Weithiau bydd y fflam: *Iwan, Dafydd* / Eiddo i arall: *Parry, Dylan & Neil* / Yr uffern hon: *Cajuns Denbo* / Milltiroedd: *Iona Ac Andy* / Rho i mi dy galon: *Broc Mor* / Beth yw lliw y Gwynt: *Iona Ac Andy* / Hen wlad llyn: *Parry, Dylan & Neil* / Os na ddaw yfory: *John Ac Alun* / Elen: *Cajuns Denbo* / Celwydd yn dy lygaid: *Broc Mor* / Ffydd y crydd: *Iwcs a Doyle* / I'r gad: *Iwan, Dafydd*
CD SCD 2166
Sain / May '97 / ADA / Direct / Greyhound

GYPSY JAZZ
CD JHR 73588
Jazz Hour / Oct '95 / Cadillac / Jazz Music / Target/BMG

GYPSY MUSIC
CD HM 009
Harmony / Jun '97 / TKO Magnum

GYPSY MUSIC FROM MACEDONIA
CD TSCD 514
Topic / Aug '96 / ADA / CM / Direct

GYPSY PASSION
Lucia: *Lopez, Oscar* / Gipsy: *Cook, Jesse* / Gypsy flame: *Armik* / Dulce libertad: *Lara & Reyes* / 2 In the night: *Liebert, Ottmar* / Bola: *Strunz & Farah* / Danza Mora: *Tingstad, Eric* / Rumba rumba gitanita: *Romero, Ruben & Lydia Torea* / Torero: *Govi* / Istanbul: *BecVar, Bruce* / Torrecillo del leal: *De La Bastide, Miguel* / Rockin' gypsies: *Willie & Lobo*
CD ND 63931
Narada / Apr '97 / ADA / New Note/Pinnacle

GYPSY PASSIONS: THE FLAMENCO GUITAR
CD LYRCD 7399
Lyrichord / '91 / ADA / CM / Roots

GYPSY SONGS AND MUSIC
CD CDCH 295
Milan / Feb '91 / Conifer/BMG / Silva Screen

HADRA OF THE GNAWA OF ESSAOUIRA
CD C 560006
Ocora / Mar '93 / ADA / Harmonia Mundi

HAIL ROCK 'N' ROLL (3CD Set)
CD Set KBOX 375
Collection / Aug '97 / Target/BMG / TKO Magnum

HAIL VARIETY
At the Holborn Empire: *Miller, Max* / Come into the garden Maud: *Nash, Heddle* / Boiled beef and carrots: *Champion, Harry* / Burlington Bertie from Bow: *Shields, Ella* / When father papered the parlour: *Williams, Billy* / Little of what you fancy: *Lloyd, Marie* / Tower of London: *Leno, Dan* / To suffer for the likes of him: *Elen, Gus* / Don't have any more Mrs. Moore: *Morris, Lily* / My old Dutch: *Chevalier, Albert* / Goodbye Johnny I must leave you / Sons of the sea: *Reece, Arthur* / If you were the only girl in the world: *Robey, George & Violet Loraine* / I'm one of the boys of the Old Brigade: *Little Tich* / Nellie Dean: *Gitana, Gertie* / Roamin' in the gloamin': *Lauder, Harry* / PC Parker: *Austin, Charles* / In his new motor car: *Tait, Harry* / Magna Carta: *Hay, Will & his Scholars* / Lily of Laguna: *Stratton, Eugene* / Down at the old Bull & Bush: *Forde, Florrie* / Jolly brothers: *Whelan, Albert* / Man who broke the bank at Monte Carlo: *Coburn, Charles* / Love will find a way: *Collins, Jose* / And her mother comes too: *Buchanan, Jack* / He never said he loved me: *Lawrence, Gertrude* / I'll see you again: *Laye, Evelyn* / She's my lovely: *Howes, Bobby* / Mad dogs and Englishmen: *Coward, Noel* / When day's done: *Ambrose & His Orchestra* / Say it with music: *Payne, Jack & His Orchestra* / Here's to the next time: *Hall, Henry* / Coal black Mammy: *Hylton, Jack* / Sally: *Fields, Gracie* / Underneath the arches: *Flanagan & Allen* / Navy sketch: *Handley, Tommy* / Bee: *Askey, Arthur* / Auf wiederseh'n sweetheart: *Lynn, Vera* / Tulips from Amsterdam: *Bygraves, Max* / Don't laugh at me: *Wisdom, Norman* / Charmaine: *Mantovani* / Garden of Eden: *Vaughan, Frankie* / With all my heart: *Clark, Petula* / Cumberland gap: *Donegan, Lonnie* / Lay down your arms: *Shelton, Anne* / We will make love: *Hamilton, Russ* / Cara Mia: *Whitfield, David* / Rock with the caveman: *Steele, Tommy*
CD LCOM 5249
Lismor / Feb '96 / ADA / Direct / Duncans / Lismor

HAILE SELASSIE CENTENARY VOL.2
CD SZCD 4
Surr Zema Musik / May '96 / Jet Star

HAILE SELLASSIE CENTENARY DUB VOL.2
CD S 200002
Surr Zema Musik / Apr '94 / Jet Star

HAITI RAP & RAGGA
CD 3192
Declic / Apr '95 / Jet Star

HAKKEUH (HARDCORE) (2CD Set)
CD Set IDT 001505
ID&T / Mar '97 / Plastic Head

HALLELUJAH
CD AVC 528
Avid / Nov '93 / Avid/BMG / Koch / THE

HALLELUJAH (18 Uplifting Gospel Songs Of Faith & Inspiration)
In the hands of the Lord: *Five Blind Boys Of Mississippi* / Canaan: *Ward, Clara & The Ward Sisters* / Ways of the Lord: *Ward, Clara & The Ward Sisters* / Bedside of a neighbour: *Ward, Clara & The Ward Sisters* / Motherless children: *Gospelaires* / You're gonna need somebody: *Andrews, Inez* / If it's alright: *Jackson Southernaires* / Friend in Jesus: *Mighty Clouds Of Joy* / Old ship of Zion: *Pilgrim Jubilee Singers* / Burying ground: *Sensational Nightingales* / Spirit of Memphis: *Spirit Of Memphis Quartet* / Oh Jesus programme: *Sunset Travellers* / He's my saviour: *Williams Bros. & Ida Lee Brown*
CD MCCD 298
Music Club / May '97 / Disc / THE

HAMBURG STRIKES BACK
CD HY 21034CD
Hypertension / Nov '92 / ADA / CM / Direct / Total/BMG

HAMMER DOWN (20 Driving Classics)
Workin' at the car wash blues: *Croce, Jim* / Long legged woman dressed in black: *Mungo Jerry* / Roadrunner: *Diddley, Bo* / All day and all of the night: *Kinks* / Kentucky sundown: *Tennessee* / Why do you love: *Juicy Lucy* / Mean girl: *Status Quo* / You don't mess around with Jim: *Croce, Jim* / Freightloader: *Clapton, Eric & Jimmy Page* / Bad, Bad Leroy Brown: *Croce, Jim* / This flight tonight: *Nazareth* / It's a heartache: *Tyler, Bonnie* / Car 67: *Driver 67* / Race with the devil: *Girlschool* / Born to be wild: *Blue Oyster Cult* / Roadrunner twice: *Richman, Jonathan* / Spinning wheel blues: *Status Quo* / Snake drive: *Clapton, Eric & The Immediate All-Stars* / Eye of the tiger: *Nighthawks* / Blues for dancers: *Hooker, Earl*
CD TRTCD 123
TrueTrax / Oct '94 / THE

HAMMOND STYLE SINGALONG
CD SWBCD 206
Sound Waves / Oct '95 / Target/BMG

HAND PICKED (25 Years Of Rounder Bluegrass)
CD ROUCDAN 22
Rounder / Nov '95 / ADA / CM / Direct

HAND THAT HOLDS THE BREAD, THE (Songs Of Progress & Protest In The Gilded Age)
CD 802672
New World / Aug '97 / ADA / Cadillac / Harmonia Mundi

HANDFUL OF KEYS (13 Great Jazz Pianists)
Monday date: *Hines, Earl 'Fatha'* / I ain't got nobody: *Hines, Earl 'Fatha'* / Black beauty: *Ellington, Duke* / Swampy river: *Ellington, Duke* / Don't blame me: *Wilson, Teddy* / Every now and then: *Wilson, Teddy* / Honky tonk train blues: *Lewis, Meade 'Lux'* / Shout for joy: *Ammons, Albert* / How long blues: *Basie, Count* / Dirty dozens: *Basie, Count* / Between sets: *Kyle, Billy* / Finishing up a date: *Kyle, Billy* / Handful of keys: *Waller, Fats* / Numb fumblin': *Waller, Fats* / Overland: *Williams, Mary Lou* / Pearls: *Williams, Mary Lou* / Gin mill blues: *Sullivan, Joe* / Onyx bringdown: *Sullivan, Joe* / In a mist: *Beiderbecke, Bix* / In the dark: *Stacy, Jess* / Flashes barrelhouse: *Stacy, Jess* / World is waiting for the sunrise: *Stacy, Jess* / Gone with the wind: *Tatum, Art* / Stormy weather: *Tatum, Art*
CD CDAJA 5073
Living Era / Sep '90 / Select

HANDLE WITH CARE
CD SAB 05CD
Sabotage / Mar '96 / Plastic Head

HANG ELEVEN (MUTANT SURF PUNKS)
I want my woody back: *Barracudas* / Who stole the summer: *Surfin' Lungs* / 308: *Malibooz* / Herman's new woody: *Palominos* / Fun at the beach: *B-Girls* / Gas money: *Lloyd, Bobby & The Windfall Prophets* / Pipeline: *Agent Orange* / Tuff little surfer boy: *Truth & Beauty* / Girls cars girls sun girls surf girls fun girls: *Corvettes* / Automobile: *Stickshifts* / Day they raised the Thames barrier: *Beach Bums* / Shotgun: *Beach Coma* / Surfin' CIA: *Buzz & The B-Days* / Mighty morris ten: *Episode Six* / Depth charge: *Jon & The Nightriders*
CD CDGRAM 23
Cherry Red / May '95 / Pinnacle

HANG IT OUT TO DRY
CD 1008
Satan / May '97 / Greyhound

HANG ON (Vintage Jazz At The Hayes Country Club 1996)
CD PKCD 066
PEK / Mar '97 / Cadillac / Jazz Music / Wellard

HAPPY ALBUM VOL.2
Stomp it up: *JDS* / Kaos: *Q-Tex* / Looking for love: *New Motion* / Paradise lost: *Citadel Of Kaos* / Dancing thru the knite: *DJ Brisk* / Horny raver: *D-Zyne Fury* / Metamorphisis: *Ramos & Supreme/Sunset Regime* / Deep in the underground: *Lock Jaw* / Now is the time: *Brown, Scott* / Going crazy: *Rave Nation* / As cold as ice: *Stingray* / Raging desire: *Happy Tunes*
CD CDTOT 34
Jumpin' & Pumpin' / Oct '95 / 3mv/Sony / Mo's Music Machine

HAPPY ANTHEMS VOL.1
CD CDRAID 520
Rumour / Oct '94 / 3mv/Sony / Mo's Music Machine / Pinnacle

HAPPY ANTHEMS VOL.2
CD CDRAID 522
Rumour / Mar '95 / 3mv/Sony / Mo's Music Machine / Pinnacle

HAPPY ANTHEMS VOL.3
CD CDRAID 526
Rumour / Oct '95 / 3mv/Sony / Mo's Music Machine / Pinnacle

HAPPY ANTHEMS VOL.4
CD CDRAID 528
Rumour / Feb '96 / 3mv/Sony / Mo's Music Machine / Pinnacle

HAPPY BIRTHDAY BABY JESUS (2CD Set)
CD Set SFTRI 1396CD
Sympathy For The Record Industry / Nov '95 / Cargo / Greyhound / Plastic Head

HAPPY BIRTHDAY/AULD LANG SYNE/ FOR HE'S A JOLLY GOOD FELLOW..
CD PARCD 001
Image / Mar '96 / Discovery

HAPPY DAYS
CD DSPCD 112
Disky / Sep '94 / Disky / THE

HAPPY DAZE
Died in your arms tonight: *Go Mental* / Your my life: *DJ Synergy* / My love: *DJ Codeine* / Raise your hands: *H-Men* / Rushing: *DJ Mixmatt & Rebel Alliance* / Life force generator: *Ramos & Supreme/Sunset Regime* / Party pumper: *DJ Brisk* / Flashdance (What a feeling): *Magika* / Check dis out: *Serious* / Let the music: *Eruption* / Harmony: *Force & Styles* / Positive energy: *Happy Tunes*
CD CDELIC 1
Passion / Jun '96 / 3mv/Pinnacle

HAPPY DAZE VOL.2
There she goes: *La's* / Box set go: *High* / All on you (perfume): *Paris Angels* / Wonderment / Wagon: *Dinosaur Jr.* / Godlike / Falling on a bruise: *Carter USM* / Sweetness and light: *Lush* / Something's got to give: *Spooky* / She's got all the world: *Top* / Window pane: *Real People* / Pearl / Close to me: *Cure*
CD CIDTV 3
Island / Apr '91 / PolyGram

HAPPY HARDCORE ANTHEMS (4CD Set)
CD Set DAM 004
Tring / Dec '96 / Tring

HAPPY HARDCORE FEVER VOL.1
CD TROOPHTCD 16
Happy Trax / Jul '95 / Grapevine/ PolyGram / Mo's Music Machine / SRD

HAPPY HARDCORE FEVER VOL.2 (Mixed By D.J. Vibes)
CD DBMPCHCD 1A
CD DBMPCHCD 1
Punch / May '96 / SRD

HAPPY HARDCORE FEVER VOL.4 (Includes Bonus Megamix CD/2CD Set)
Runaway: *Jimmy J & Cru-L-T* / Higher: *DJ Ham* / Survival: *Tailbone* / Yee-haaa: *Forbes, Davie* / Flava: *DJ Happy Raver* / Motorway madness: *DJ Vibes & Wishdokta* / Heaven: *El Bruto* / Piano obsession: *Luna-C* / Gimme the world: *T3* / Gimme the world: *DJ Pleasure* / Love is: *DJ Brian* / Airhead: *DJ Brisk* / Inner access: *DJ Demo* / Simply electric: *DJ Force & Evolution* / Lift me up: *Future Primitive*
CD Set DBM 2738
Death Becomes Me / Feb '97 / Grapevine/ PolyGram / Pinnacle / SRD

HAPPY HARDCORE VOL.1
Breakin' free: *Slipmatt* / Visions of light: *Higher Level* / Don't beg 4 love: *Jack 'n' Phil* / Ronnie's revenge (remix): *Citadel Of Kaos* / Kounter attack: *Druid & Vinyl Groover* / Rhythm: *Just Another Artist* / Drop the bass: *DJ Seduction* / Positive: *Love Nation* / Piano progression (mix): *Luna-C* / In complete darkness: *Fat Controller* / Take me away: *Jimmy J & Cru-L-T* / Let's do it: *DJ Red Alert & Mike Slammer*
CD CDTOT 18
Jumpin' & Pumpin' / Oct '94 / 3mv/Sony / Mo's Music Machine

HAPPY HARDCORE VOL.2
Make it ruff: *DJ Brisk* / Play the theme: *Sy & Unknown* / Feel so real: *DJ Red Alert & Mike Slammer* / Better day: *DJ Seduction & Dougal* / Hold me in your arms: *Storm Syndicut* / Feels good: *Vibes & Wishdokta* / Movin': *Justin Time* / Burn baby burn: *Sensitize* / Summer vibe: *DEA* / Lust: *Just Another Artist* / Slave to the rave: *Love Nation* / Lift me up: *Future Primitive*
CD CDTOT 22
Jumpin' & Pumpin' / Jan '95 / 3mv/Sony / Mo's Music Machine

HAPPY HARDCORE VOL.3
Hardcore business: *Vibes & Wishdokta* / Take me to the top: *Sunshine Productions* / I just can't stop: *Brisk* / Ultimate seduction: *DJ Hixxy* / Drop the bass: *DJ Seduction* / Teknomancer: *Sunset Regime* / I need somebody: *Eruption* / JT Goes north: *Justin Time* / Looking into the night: *DJ Slam* / Groove control: *Midas* / Detrimental: *DJ Demand* / Warped: *Citadel Of Kaos*
CD CDTOT 30
Jumpin' & Pumpin' / Jun '95 / 3mv/Sony / Mo's Music Machine

HAPPY HARDCORE VOL.4
Ride like the wind: *Bunter, Billy & D'Zyne/ JDS* / Luv you more: *Elstak, Paul* / Higher love: *JDS* / Just like that: *Terrible twins* / Let the music: *Eruption* / Help me: *Justin Time* / It's gonna be: *DJ Poosie* / Shout now: *Time Span & Bertie* / Looking for love: *New Motion* / Woo woo wanting you: *Icon* / Take me up: *Sub State* / Red alert: *Red Alert*
CD CDTOT 37
Jumpin' & Pumpin' / Mar '96 / 3mv/Sony / Mo's Music Machine

HAPPY HARDCORE VOL.5
Better day: *GBT Inc. & Joanne Robertson* / Freedom: *DJ Unity* / Died in your arms: *Go Mental* / Giving it all I've got: *Vibes & Wishdokta* / Simply electric: *Force & Evolution* /

Is there anybody out there: *DJ Ham* / Lift me up: *DJ Demo* / Go insane: *DJ DNA* / Get down: *M-D Emm* / Life force generator: *Ramos & Supreme* / Burning love: *Critical Mass* / Keep on loving: *Grassie, Donna*
CD CDTOT 44
Jumpin' & Pumpin' / Aug '96 / 3mv/Sony / Mo's Music Machine

HAPPY MAIO FAMILY, A (Dance & Song From SW China)
CD PANCD 2023
Pan / Aug '94 / ADA / CM / Direct

HAPPY MEALS
CD MYRECORDS 001CD
My Records / Mar '96 / Plastic Head

HAPPY TO MEET (Classic Recordings Of Traditional Irish Dance Music)
Bridie Morley/Duigan's favourite: *Duigan, Packie* / Knights of St. Patrick: *Doherty, John & Tommy McMahon* / I have a bonnet trimmed with blue/The rakes of Mallow: *O'Sullivan, Bernard & Tommy McMahon* / Peg McGrath/Ganley's reel: *McDermott, Josie* / Pipe on the hob: *Clancy, Willie* / Boil the breakfast early: *Tansey, Seamus & Eddie Corcoran* / Mountain hornpipe/Kingston hornpipe: *Rea, John* / Tommy Glenny's reel: *Russell, Micko & Packie* / Gillian's apples: *Doonan, John & John Wright* / St. Anne's reel: *Pepper, Noel* / Kerry Mills: *Teahan, Terry* / Two Woodford flings: *Coen, Jack & Charlie* / Night in Ennis/The maid behind the bar: *Griffin, Vincent* / Port Liadroma/Sean Tiobraidd Arann: *Mitchell, Pat* / Duke of Leinster: *Duigan, Packie & Seamus Horan* / Cuckoo hornpipe: *Droney, Chris* / Bonny Kate/Jenny's chickens: *Tansey, Seamus & Eddie Corcoran* / Untitled mazurka: *Doherty, John* / Tatter Jack Walsh: *Russell, Micko & Gussie* / Teetotaller/Bunch of keys: *Murphy, Rose* / Ashplant/Maid of Mont Cisco: *O'Sullivan, Bernard* / Boys of the town/Dwyer's jig: *McDermott, Josie* / George White's favourite/Ivy leaf: *Doran, Felix* / We were drinking & kissing the ladies/Old Tipperary: *Kelly, John* / Barn dance: *O'Dwyer, Ellen* / Kitty's fancy/Lady Anne Hope: *Rea, John* / Sean Hayes/If there weren't any women in the world: *Kelly, Gene* / Irish washerwoman/Father O'Flynn/Lilting fisherman: *Doonan, John* / Happy to meet, sorry to part: *Ennis, Seamus* / Foxhunter's jig: *Neylan, Paddy*
CD CDORBD 092
Globestyle / Oct '96 / Pinnacle

HAPPY TOGETHER
CD TRTCD 158
TrueTrax / Feb '96 / THE

HARD AS HELL VOL.3
CD MODEF 3CD
Music Of Life / May '88 / Grapevine/ PolyGram

HARD AS HELL VOL.4
CD MODEF 4CD
Music Of Life / Dec '90 / Grapevine/ PolyGram

HARD CELL
CD MAUCD 622
Mau Mau / Aug '92 / Pinnacle

HARD EDUCATION
Untitled 1: *Surgeon* / Untitled 2: *Surgeon* / Untitled 1: *Regis* / Untitled 2: *Regis* / Untitled 1: *Female* / Untitled 2: *Female* / Untitled 1: *Portion Reform* / Untitled 2: *Portion Reform*
CD DNCD 003
Downwards / Jun '97 / Plastic Head

HARD HOP AND TRYPNO VOL.1
CD MM 800442
Moonshine / Feb '96 / Mo's Music Machine / Prime / RTM/Disc

HARD HOP AND TRYPNO VOL.2
Fire like dis: *Hard Knox* / Chemical meltdown: *Tales From The Hardside* / Monster: *Planet Jazz* / Yass waddah: *Darkglobe* / Moondusted: *Uberzone* / Botanical blipz: *Supersoul* / You better work it out: *Control X* / Too: *Immigrant* / Punk to funk: *Fatboy Slim* / Life in mono: *Mono* / Nipple fish: *Coffee boys* / This is the bass: *Mental box*
CD MM 800582
Moonshine / Feb '97 / Mo's Music Machine / Prime / RTM/Disc

HARD LEADERS (The History Of Drum & Bass/4CD Set)
CD Set KICKCD 35
Kickin' / Feb '96 / Prime / SRD

HARD LEADERS VOL.3
CD KICKCD 7
Kickin' / Oct '93 / Prime / SRD

HARD LEADERS VOL.4
CD KICKCD 8
Kickin' / Apr '94 / Prime / SRD

HARD LEADERS VOL.7
CD Set KICKCD 23
Kickin' / May '95 / Prime / SRD

HARD ROCK
Spirit of radio: *Rush* / You ain't seen nothin' yet: *Bachman-Turner Overdrive* / Come on Eileen: *Dexy's Midnight Runners & Emerald Express* / Final countdown: *Europe* / Living after midnight: *Judas Priest* / Pretty in pink: *Psychedelic Furs* / Paranoid: *Black Sabbath* / Bat out of hell: *Meat Loaf* / Down down: *Status Quo* / Bark at the moon: *Osbourne, Ozzy* / Cum on feel the noize: *Quiet Riot* / Skin deep: *Stranglers* / Ace of spades: *Motorhead* / Gypsy: *Uriah Heep* / Start talking love: *Magnum* / St. Elmo's fire: *Parr, John* / Rock 'n' roll children: *Dio* / Silver machine: *Hawkwind*
CD STACD 003
Wisepack / Oct '91 / Conifer/BMG / THE

HARD ROCK
Tower of strength: *Mission* / St. Elmo's fire: *Parr, John* / Eye of the tiger: *Survivor* / Stone cold: *Rainbow* / Losing my grip: *Samson* / I didn't know I loved you (till I saw you rock 'n' roll): *Rock Goddess* / Whatever you want: *Status Quo* / Epic: *Faith No More* / Bastille day: *Rush* / Mystery: *Dio* / It's all over now baby blue: *Bonnet, Graham* / Perfect strangers: *Deep Purple* / Central park arrest: *Thunderthighs* / Get it on: *Kingdom Come*
CD 5506492
Spectrum / Aug '94 / PolyGram

HARD STEP DRUM AND BASS VOL.1
Regulators remix: *Marvellous Caine* / International: *Eskubar* / Boogie down: *Marvellous Caine* / Heroes welcome: *Dextrous & T-Bone* / Bump 'n' bounce: *T-Bones* / Da bass 11 dark: *Asylum* / This is LA: *Lemon D* / Sample and hold: *Psykus* / Get on the mike: *Eskubar* / Beyond all reasonable doubt: *Keith, Ray* / Jazz and all dat: *Eskubar* / Lighter: *Keith, Ray* / Babylon remix 2: *DJ Trace* / Selectors roll VIP: *Tom & Jerry* / Step pon dub: *Faze 1 FM* / She's so revisited: *Neal Trix & DJ Apollo* / Jungle blanca: *Faze 1 FM* / So this is love: *Essence Of Aura*
CD STORM 1 CD
Desert Storm / Jan '96 / Sony

HARD TECHNO
CD 7142616
Fairway / Dec '96 / Cargo

HARD TECHNO CLASSICS (The Complete Series)
CD DBM 2460
Death Becomes Me / May '97 / Grapevine/PolyGram / Pinnacle / SRD

HARD TECHNO CLASSICS FROM DEEPEST GERMANY VOL.1
Phasematic: *Colone* / Distursancing: *X-Ray* / Nervous acid: *Nervous Project* / Hidden: *4D* / Crush: *Colone* / Jumping golliwogs: *Integrated Circuits* / Moby tits: *Cellblockx* / Art mechanique: *Sectral Emotions* / Yip: *Integrated Circuits* / Foible: *4D* / Caffeine rush: *SDL* / God assists: *Integrated Circuits*
CD LABUKCD 1
Labworks / Mar '94 / RTM/Disc / SRD

HARD TECHNO CLASSICS FROM DEEPEST GERMANY VOL.2
CD UNDLAB 24CD
Labworks / May '95 / RTM/Disc / SRD

HARD TECHNO CLASSICS FROM DEEPEST GERMANY VOL.3
CD DBLABCD 13
Labworks / Apr '96 / RTM/Disc / SRD

HARD TIMES AND HEARTACHES
Preachin' blues: *Johnson, Robert* / Long tall Mama: *Broonzy, 'Big' Bill* / Ain't it a cryin' shame: *Fuller, 'Blind' Boy* / Packin' trunk: *Leadbelly* / Dark was the night: *Johnson, 'Blind' Willie* / Denver blues: *Tampa Red* / Bukka's jitterbug swing: *White, Bukka* / Southern can is mine: *McTell, 'Blind' Willie* / Steppin' on the blues: *Johnson, Lonnie* / Goodbye now: *McGhee, Brownie* / St. Louis blues: *Smith, Bessie* / Hurry down sunshine: *Dupree, 'Champion' Jack* / Death letter: *House, Son* / I can't be satisfied: *Waters, Muddy* / Dust my broom: *Taj Mahal* / Stateboro blues: *Rising Sons*
CD 4766832
Columbia / May '94 / Sony

HARD TRANCE AND PSYCHEDELIC TECHNO VOL.1
CD PTM 129
Phantasm / Feb '95 / Arabesque / Plastic Head / Prime / Vital/SAM

HARD TRANCE AND PSYCHEDELIC TECHNO VOL.2
CD PTM 130CD
Phantasm / Feb '95 / Arabesque / Plastic Head / Prime / Vital/SAM

HARD TRANCE CLASSICS - THE COMPLETE SERIES (3CD Set)
D-9-5: *Colone* / This ain't no 303: *SDL* / Kayht: *Sabotage* / Science: *Spectral Emotions* / Feel: *Icons* / Elevator regained: *Colone* / Time mode: *Intergrated Circuits* / Ascend from the mind: *SDL* / Chiswick days: *Spectral Emotions* / Mission: *SDL* / Beets: *4D* / Milchglas: *Josef & His Cousin* / Accelerator: *Syntax Morph* / Centrifugal force: *SDL* / Patience: *Intergrated Circuits* / Dro-gen: *Elin* / Trip to Africa: *MG-3* / Plastic sex: *Nervous Project* / Drop: *Church Windows* / Oceanic: *Trax Beyond Subconscious* / Alfa test: *Pagan Acid* / Mirror of J: *Integrated Circuits* / Atom V20: *Syntax Morph* / Sauna: *Pleasure* / Nightrocker: *Just, Christopher* / Attractor V20: *Syntax Morph* / Head is not longer than the body: *4D* / Before the day: *Hemisphear* / Audition Colouree: *Pagan Acid* / Rattlesnake: *Integrated Circuits* / Transabotage: *Sabotage* / Alex the sugar daddy: *4D* / Danger: *Radiation* / Lock 2: *Doorkeeper* / Darkside: *Colone* / Incline: *Integrated Circuits* / Screw loose: *Doorkeeper* / hard trance: *Doorkeeper*
CD Set DBM 2459
Death Becomes Me / Jan '97 / Grapevine/ PolyGram / Pinnacle / SRD

HARD TRANCE CLASSICS FROM DEEPEST GERMANY VOL.1
CD LABUKCD 2
Labworks / Apr '94 / RTM/Disc / SRD

HARD TRANCE CLASSICS FROM DEEPEST GERMANY VOL.2
CD UNDLABCD 025
Labworks / Feb '95 / RTM/Disc / SRD

HARD TRANCE CLASSICS FROM DEEPEST GERMANY VOL.3
CD DBMLABCD 12
Labworks / Dec '95 / RTM/Disc / SRD

HARDBEATS AND SOFT DRINKS
CD OZONCD 25
Ozone / Apr '92 / SRD

HARDCLUBBING VOL.3
CD SUB 48522
Dunkla / Jul '97 / Prime

HARDCORE
CD AUM 004116
80 AUM / Nov '96 / ZYX

HARDCORE - LEADERS OF THE NEW SCHOOL VOL.1
CD KICKCD 3
Kickin' / Nov '92 / Prime / SRD

HARDCORE - LEADERS OF THE NEW SCHOOL VOL.2
CD KICKCD 5
Kickin' / Mar '93 / Prime / SRD

HARDCORE - LEADERS OF THE NEW SCHOOL VOL.5 (Jungle Dub)
CD KICKCD 12
Kickin' / Aug '94 / Prime / SRD

HARDCORE ALLIANCE
CD STAGE 1CD
Stage One / Nov '95 / Pinnacle

HARDCORE BLAST
Name of the DJ: *Chosen Few* / Cocaine: *Technohead* / Hardcore motherfuckers: *Tellurian* / Mad creator: *Santana, Omar* / Out of focus: *Brown, Scott* / Der computer ist tot: *Narcanosis* / Brainwaves: *Outside Agency* / Slapback: *Titanium Steel* / Fukem all: *DJ Dano* / Chosen paradize: *Chosen Few* / Ye shall die: *Brown, Scott* / Misadventures of the spiegel man pt 1: *Party Animals* / Abba gabba: *Riot Nation* / Hardcore suckers: *One, Walter* / Come with me (into the stars): *Narcanosis* / Put it on the table: *DJ Dano*
CD DB 47832
Mokum / Apr '97 / Pinnacle

HARDCORE CHEDDAR VOL.1 (Dutch Masters)
CD CDRAID 527
Rumour / Oct '95 / 3mv/Sony / Mo's Music Machine / Pinnacle

HARDCORE CHEDDAR VOL.2 (Dutch Masters)
CD CDRAID 530
Rumour / Jun '96 / 3mv/Sony / Mo's Music Machine / Pinnacle

HARDCORE CHEDDAR VOL.4
CD CDRAID 533
Rumour / Nov '96 / 3mv/Sony / Mo's Music Machine / Pinnacle

HARDCORE DOO-WOP (In The Hallway - Under The Street Lamp)
Wheel of fortune: *Four Flames* / Dream girl: *Jesse & Marvin* / Nite owl: *Allen, Tony & The Champs* / Oooh-Rooba-Lee: *Maye, Arthur Lee & The Crowns* / Where's my girl: *Belvin, Jesse* / I: *Allen, Tony & The Champs* / Sweet breeze: *Green, Vernon & The Phantoms* / Check yourself baby: *Allen, Tony & The Chimes* / Foot loose and fancy free: *Gipson, Byron 'Slick' & The Sliders* / Gloria: *Maye, Arthur Lee & The Crowns* / Especially: *Allen, Tony & The Chimes* / Baby need (ting-a-ling): *Zeppa, Ben Joe & The Zephyrs* / Old willow tree: *Green, Vernon & The Phantoms* / Cool loving: *Maye, Arthur Lee & The Crowns* / Pretty little girl: *Chimes* / How long: *Church, Eugene* / Malinda: *Mandolph, Bobby* / Hold me tight: *Jaguars* / Don't you know: *Maye, Arthur Lee & The Crowns* / Never let you go: *Ambers & Ralph Mathis* / Open up your heart: *Church, Eugene* / Mine all mine: *Jaguars* / Guardian angel: *Selections* / Soft and sweet: *Selections*
CD CDCHD 514
Ace / Jan '94 / Pinnacle

HARDCORE ECSTASY
CD DINCD 29
Dino / Nov '91 / Pinnacle

HARDCORE FOR THE MASSES VOL.2
CD BHR 101CD
Burning Heart / Oct '94 / Plastic Head

HARDCORE FUTURE VOL.5
Listen carefully: *Wagner, Robert* / Hardcore power: *Brown, Scott* / Centre of the earth: *Zelator* / We'll tear your soul apart: *Leviathan* / CryRise and shine: *Crypt 1* / At war: *Syphax* / Whiteline: *Trickster* / Don't fuck with me: *Dark Destination* / Stab ya brain: *Too Hostile* / Suffer: *DJ Fuckface & DJ Crizz*
CD CDRAID 536
Rumour / Aug '97 / 3mv/Sony / Mo's Music Machine / Pinnacle

HARDCORE HAPPINESS VOL.1
CD J4U 001CD
Just 4 U / Mar '95 / SRD

HARDCORE HAPPINESS VOL.3 (2CD Set)
CD Set J4U 003CD
Just 4 U / Apr '96 / SRD

HARDCORE HEAVEN VOL.2 (2CD Set)
CD Set HMLCD 102
Heaven / Jul '97 / Grapevine/PolyGram

HARDCORE HOLIDAY
CD 420172
Frantic / Nov '96 / Cargo

HARDCORE HURRICANE
Second coming: *DJ Rob* / Original: *SPC Hardcore* / Cool please brother: *Brown, Scott* / Sarin: *DJ Jordens* / Jaxx eargasm: *DJ Fuckface* / Tell me what your find: *Wasting Program* / Destronation: *Dark Destination* / Slow as fuck: *DJ Attik & DJ Stylzz* / Enjoy the pain: *DJ Epitaph* / Rob's 20 seconds: *DJ Rob* / Don't ever stop: *Brown, Scott* / We like da music: *DJ Perpetrator* / Mother fuckin' motherfucker: *Stunned Guys* / Outro: *Rave Creators* / Drifting: *DNM*
CD DC 878852
Disky / May '97 / Disky / THE

HARDCORE JUNGLIST FEVER VOL.1
CD STHCCD 6
Strictly Underground / Aug '94 / SRD

HARDCORE JUNGLIST FEVER VOL.2
CD STHCCD 7
Strictly Underground / '94 / SRD

HARDCORE MASSIVE VOL.1
CD TROOPCD 14
Rogue Trooper / Jul '95 / Alphamagic / SRD

HARDCORE RAGGAMUFFIN
CD GRELCD 151
Greensleeves / Nov '90 / Jet Star / SRD

HARDCORE SLAM (32 Happy Gabba Monsters/2CD Set)
CD Set 560032
Nova Tekk / Apr '97 / Pinnacle

HARDCORE SLAM VOL.2 (2CD Set)
Good to go: *MC Remsey* / One to two: *Forze DJ Team* / Your local DJ: *DJ Delirium* / Feel the rhythm: *Prezioso* / Like a dream: *Bass D and King Matthew feat XD* / Slaves to the raves: *Inferno Brothers* / With u: *Fuzz* / Ouzo: *Goliath* / Beast time: *DJ Waxweazle* / On a posse: *Old School Terrorists* / Used & abused: *Party Animals* / Fatal morgana: *Fuzz* / I am the future: *Angel* / Da bat device: *Dr. Z-Vago* / Get this motherfucker: *Guys* / You're dealin' with...: *Corps* / Hardcore to da bone: *Masters Of Ceremony* / 909 Trauma: *Forze DJ Team* / Jungle sickness: *Miss Groovey* / Unfucking believable: *DJ Waxweazle* / Out of order: *Physical Force* / Work that body: *Guys* / Superior: *Dr. Z-Vago* / Da east: *Bruyaa & Ozonic* / No happy shit: *Corps* / Message from hell: *Euromasters*
CD Set 560152
Nova Tekk / Aug '97 / Pinnacle

HARDCORE UPROAR
CD DINCD 20
Dino / Mar '91 / Pinnacle

HARDCORE WARRIORS
CD AUM 004079
80 AUM / Nov '96 / ZYX

HARDCORE XPERIENCE VOL.1
CD I 2884362
Galaxy / Jul '97 / ZYX

HARDCORE XPERIENCE VOL.2
CD I 3884372
Galaxy / Jul '97 / ZYX

HARDCORE XPERIENCE VOL.3
CD I 3884382
Galaxy / Jul '97 / ZYX

HARDER THAN THE REST
Signe says: *Killout Trash* / Deutschland: *ATR* / We need a chance: *EC8OR* / Suicide: *Empire, Alec* / Sweat shizuo: *Shizuo* / Turntable terrorist: *Sonic Subjunkies* / Nizza: *Hanin* / Deaf dumb and blind: *DJ Bleed* / Into the death: *Atari Teenage Riot* / Straight outa Berlin: *Killout Trash* / Discriminate: *ES8TOR* / Central industrial: *Sonic Subjunkies* / Smash him to ground: *EC8TOR & Moonraker* / Anarchy: *Shizuo* / Destroyer pt.2: *Empire, Alec*
CD DHRCD 002
Digital Hardcore / Oct '95 / Vital

HARDVIBE '96 (4CD Set)
CD Set CDB 140
Michelle / Aug '96 / Total/BMG

HARDWARE VOL.2
CD HARD 2
PSY Harmonics / Sep '95 / Plastic Head

HARJEDALSPIPAN
CD DR 08CD
Drone / Aug '96 / ADA

HARK THE HERALD ANGELS SING
CD ________ **XMASCD 991**
Castle / Nov '96 / BMG

HARLEM BIG BANDS 1925-1931
Don't forget you'll regret day by day: *Johnson, Charlie & His Paradise Orchestra* / Meddlin' with the blues: *Johnson, Charlie & His Paradise Orchestra* / Paradise wobble: *Johnson, Charlie Paradise Ten* / Birmingham black bottom: *Johnson, Charlie Paradise Ten* / Don't leave me here: *Johnson, Charlie Paradise Ten* / You ain't the one: *Johnson, Charlie Paradise Ten* / Charleston is the best dance of all: *Johnson, Charlie Paradise Ten* / Hot tempered blues: *Johnson, Charlie Paradise Ten* / Boy in the boat: *Johnson, Charlie Paradise Ten* / Walk that thing: *Johnson, Charlie Paradise Ten* / Harlem drag: *Johnson, Charlie & His Paradise Orchestra* / Hot bones and rice: *Johnson, Charlie & His Paradise Orchestra* / Harlem shuffle: *Scott, Lloyd & his orchestra* / Symphonic scronch: *Scott, Lloyd & his orchestra* / Happy hour blues: *Scott, Lloyd & his orchestra* / Lawd, lawd: *Scott, Cecil & his Bright Boys* / In a corner: *Scott, Cecil & his Bright Boys* / Bright boy blues: *Scott, Cecil & his Bright Boys* / Springfield stomp: *Scott, Cecil & his Bright Boys* / (I'll be glad when you're dead) you rascal you: *Russell, Luis & His Orchestra* / Goin' to town: *Russell, Luis & His Orchestra* / Say the word: *Russell, Luis & His Orchestra* / Freakish blues: *Russell, Luis & His Orchestra* / I've found a new baby: *Preer, Andy & The Cotton Club Orchestra*
CD ________ **CBC 1010**
Timeless Historical / Aug '94 / New Note/ Pinnacle

HARLEM COMES TO LONDON
Silver rose: *Plantation Orchestra* / Arabella's wedding day: *Plantation Orchestra* / Smilin' Joe: *Plantation Orchestra* / For baby and me: *Plantation Orchestra* / Camp meeting day: *Sissle, Noble Orchestra* / Sophisticated lady: *Ellington, Duke Orchestra* / Ike: *Ellington, Duke Orchestra* / Dinah: *Hatch & his Harlem Stompers* / Some of these days: *Hatch & his Harlem Stompers* / I can't dance / I must have that man: *Valaida* / Keep a twinkle in your eye: *Nicholas Brothers* / Your heart and mine: *Nicholas Brothers* / Dixie isn't Dixie any more: *Carter, Lavaida* / Jo Jo the cannibal kid: *Carter, Lavaida* / Breakfast in Harlem: *Buck & Bubbles* / I ain't got nobody: *Buck & Bubbles* / Sweet Georgia Brown: *Buck & Bubbles* / Harlem in my heart: *Welch, Elisabeth* / Ain't misbehavin': *Waller, Fats & His Continental Rhythm* / I can't give you anything but love
CD ________ **DRGCD 8444**
DRG / Sep '93 / Discovery / New Note/ Pinnacle

HARLEM JOYS
Riffs: *Johnson, James P.* / Handful of keys: *Waller, Fats* / Ain't misbehavin': *Armstrong, Louis* / New call of the freaks: *Russell, Luis* / Horse feathers: *Jackson, Cliff* / Jungle nights in Harlem: *Ellington, Duke* / Stop crying: *Oliver, Joe 'King'* / Sugarfoot stomp: *Henderson, Fletcher* / Trickeration: *Calloway, Cab* / Hot and anxious: *Redman, Don* / Strange as it seems: *Hall, Adelaide* / Swing it: *Carter, Benny* / Harlem joys: *Smith, Willie 'The Lion'* / I cried for you: *Holiday, Billie* / Brittwood stomp: *Newton, Frankie* / Church street sobbin' blues: *Hopkins, Claude* / King Porter stomp: *Hill, Teddy* / Jammin' for the jackpot: *Milinder, Lucky & Mills Blue Rhythm Band* / Time out: *Basie, Count* / Harlem congo: *Webb, Chick* / In the mood: *Hayes, Edgar* / Miss Annabella Brown: *Hawkins, Erskine* / Honey in the bee ball: *Jordan, Louis* / Tea for two: *Profit, Clarence* / Uptown blues: *Lunceford, Jimmie*
CD ________ **CDMOIR 507**
Memoir / Apr '94 / Jazz Music / Target/BMG

HARLEM SHUFFLE (Charly R&B Masters Vol. 18)
Gimme little sign: *Wood, Brenton* / Dancin' holiday: *Olympics* / Love makes the world go round: *Jackson, Deon* / Spring: *Birdlegs & Pauline* / Expressway to your heart: *Soul Survivors* / Ooh wee baby: *Hughes, Freddie* / Baby, I'm yours: *Lewis, Barbara* / Cool jerk: *Capitols* / Get on up: *Esquires* / And get away: *Esquires* / Duck: *Lee, Jackie* / I know: *George, Barbara* / Snake: *Wilson, Al* / Harlem shuffle: *Bob & Earl* / Hello stranger: *Lewis, Barbara* / Oh how happy: *Shades Of Blue* / Oogum boogum song: *Wood, Brenton* / Bounce: *Olympics* / Backfield in motion: *Mel & Tim* / Make me your baby / You can make it if you try
CD ________ **CDRB 18**
Charly / Mar '95 / Koch

HARLEM SHUFFLE (The Sound Of Blaxploitation)
CD ________ **PLRCD 002**
Plastic / Jun '97 / Cargo / Essential/BMG

HARMONICA BLUES 1927-1941 (2CD Set)
CD Set ________ **FA 040**
Fremeaux / Nov '95 / ADA / Discovery

HARMONICA BLUES 1929-1940
CD ________ **WSECD 106**
Wolf / Jul '96 / Hot Shot / Jazz Music / Swift

HARMONICA BLUES OF THE 1920S AND 1930S
CD ________ **YAZCD 1053**
Yazoo / Apr '91 / ADA / CM / Koch

HARMONICA MASTERS
CD ________ **YAZCD 2019**
Yazoo / May '96 / ADA / CM / Koch

HARMONY AND INTERPLAY
CD ________ **ELL 3210B**
Ellipsis Arts / Oct '93 / ADA / Direct

HARP BLOWERS 1926-1929
CD ________ **DOCD 5164**
Document / May '93 / ADA / Hot Shot / Jazz Music

HARP OF APOLLO, THE
CD ________ **VICG 50132**
JVC World Library / Mar '96 / ADA / CM / Direct

HARPBEAT OF THE SWAMP (Kingsnake Harp Classics)
CD ________ **KS 033CD**
Kingsnake / Jul '97 / Hot Shot

HARPS OF THE WORLD
CD ________ **PS 66004CD**
PlayaSound / Jul '95 / ADA / Harmonia Mundi

HARTHOUSE 100
CD ________ **HH 100CD**
Harthouse / Jul '96 / Mo's Music Machine / Prime / Vital

HARTHOUSE VOL.2 (Dedicated To The Omen)
Clapconfusion: *Zaffarano, Marco* / Spirit of fear: *Spicelab* / Astralis: *Frankfurt/Tokyo Connection* / Adventure of dama: *Cybordelics* / Mikado: *Pulse* / X-plain the un-x-plained: *Arpeggiators* / Human: *Resistance D* / Mecon: *Aurin* / Multiplex: *Aurin* / Secrets of love: *Progressive Attack* / Schneller pfeil: *Curare*
CD ________ **4509942612**
Harthouse / Dec '96 / Mo's Music Machine / Prime / Vital

HARTHOUSE VOL.8 (2CD Set)
CD Set ________ **HHSP 12CD**
Harthouse / Nov '96 / Mo's Music Machine / Prime / Vital

HARVEST STORM
CD ________ **TUT 727493**
Wundertute / Jan '94 / ADA / CM / Duncans

HAUNTED HOUSE PARTY
CD ________ **JCD 623**
Jass / Dec '87 / ADA / Cadillac / CM / Direct / Jazz Music

HAUSFLOOR VOL.4
CD ________ **UCACD 009**
UCA / Jun '97 / Intergroove / Prime

HAUSMUSIK: FESTPLATTE
CD ________ **HM 21CD**
Hausmusik / Dec '96 / Cargo

HAVANA CLUB
CD ________ **74321378102**
Milan / Jul '96 / Conifer/BMG / Silva Screen

HAVANA CUBA BOYS VOL.1
CD ________ **HQCD 48**
Harlequin / Jan '95 / Hot Shot / Jazz Music / Swift / Wellard

HAVANA FLUTE SUMMIT
CD ________ **860052**
Naxos Jazz / Jun '97 / Select

HAVE A WONDERFUL CHRISTMAS
CD ________ **CNCD 5955**
Disky / Dec '93 / Disky / THE

HAVE I TOLD YOU LATELY THAT I LOVE YOU
CD ________ **295732**
Ariola Express / May '92 / BMG

HAVE YOURSELF A SOULFUL CHRISTMAS
CD ________ **CPCD 8145**
Charly / Nov '95 / Koch

HAVE YOURSELF AN EASY LISTENING CHRISTMAS
Christmas is here to stay: *Crosby, Bing* / Baby's first Christmas: *Francis, Connie* / White Christmas: *Platters* / Little drummer boy: *Simeone, Harry Chorale* / Winter's tale: *Essex, David* / Sleigh ride: *Simeone, Harry Chorale* / Little shepherd: *Whittaker, Roger* / I believe in Father Christmas: *Swingles* / Christmas song: *St. Clair, Isla* / Holly and the ivy: *Gregory, John Strings & Voices* / Mary's boy child: *Peters & Lee* / And Kings came a calling: *Beverley Sisters* / Must be Santa: *Steele, Tommy* / First Noel: *Kerr, Anita Singers* / Bambino: *Springfields* / Christmas Eve: *Statler Brothers* / Musical Christmas card: *Sweet Substitute* / Christmas Day is coming: *Blue Diamonds* / Greensleeves: *Martin, Sari* / Rudolph the red nosed reindeer: *New Jordal Singers*
CD ________ **5521102**
Spectrum / Nov '96 / PolyGram

HAVIN' IT IN THE UK VOL.2
Havin' it anthem: *Stonedrive & Dee & Wee* / 2 For joy: *Bliss* / Flight high: *Classwork* / Voices inside my head: *Police* / Reach me: *Anita K* / Take you there: *Simon, Ronni* / Deliver me: *Hawkshaw, Geoffrey* / Music takes you: *Carpe Diem 7* / Get your hands off my man: *Vasquez, Junior* / Love it: *Gorgeous Darling* / Yeow: *Buckle & Fogey* / Prayer to the music: *Polo, Marco* / Direct me: *Reese Project* / Invader: *Kool World*
CD ________ **HAVINCD 005**
21st Century Opera / Sep '95 / Total/BMG

HAVIN' IT STATESIDE VOL.1
Forever: *Key To Life* / Love is what we need: *Dream Team* / Satisfied: *H2O & Billie* / Gotta new love: *Blakely, Donna* / Body to body: *Shades Of Love* / Keep on luvin': *Myles, Maydie* / Feel it: *Workin' Happily* / Murder track: *Delgado, Mike* / Sex with him: *Rosario, Ralphi* / I know a place: *Sound Of One* / Premonition of lost love: *Heard, Larry* / I've got something for you: *Federal Hill* / Souffles H: *Mondo Grosso* / Huh I gotta: *Shoot Tha' Juice*
CD ________ **HAVINCD 004**
21st Century Opera / Jun '95 / Total/BMG

HAWAIIAN CHRISTMAS, A
White Christmas / Silent night / Rudolph the red nosed reindeer / I'll be home for Christmas / I saw Mommy kissing Santa Claus / Peace Carol / It came upon a midnight clear / Snowy white snow and jingle bells / Jingle bells / Silver bells / Have yourself a merry little Christmas / Winter wonderland / Sleigh ride / We wish you a merry christmas / We three kings / Away in a manger / Holly and the ivy / We wish you a merry Christmas (reprise)
CD ________ **CDVIP 140**
Virgin VIP / Nov '96 / EMI

HAWAIIAN DREAMS (2CD Set)
CD Set ________ **24025**
Delta Doubles / Jun '96 / Target/BMG

HAWAIIAN DRUM DANCE CHANTS (Sounds Of Power In Time)
CD ________ **SFWCD 40015**
Smithsonian Folkways / May '95 / ADA / Cadillac / CM / Direct / Koch

HAWAIIAN SLACK KEY GUITAR
CD ________ **DCT 38032CD**
Dancing Cat / Mar '96 / ADA

HAWZI (Music From Algeria)
CD ________ **AAA 149**
Club Du Disque Arabe / Mar '97 / ADA / Harmonia Mundi

HEADING BACK TO HOUSTON (Texas Country & Western 1950-1951)
CD ________ **KKCD 12**
Krazy Kat / Apr '97 / Hot Shot / Jazz Music

HEADING IN THE RIGHT DIRECTION
CD ________ **LHCD 023**
Luv n' Haight / Jul '96 / Timewarp

HEADPHONE HOUSE
CD ________ **SLIPCD 46**
Slip 'n' Slide / Jul '96 / Amato Disco / Prime / RTM/Disc / Vital

HEADZ VOL.1 (2CD Set)
Freedom now: *Patterson* / Contemplating jazz: *Attica Blues* / Symmetrical jazz: *Awunsound* / Stars: *Nightmares On Wax* / Ravers suck our sound: *La Funk Mob* / Miles out of time: *MF Outa National* / Inside: *RPM* / Lowride: *Autechre* / Wildstyle - The krush handshake: *Oldie Scottish* / Lost and found (SFL): *DJ Shadow* / Destroy all monsters: *Skull* / Don't fake it: *Sallahr, Deflon* / 2000: *RPM* / Slipper suite: *Palm Skin Productions* / Time has come: *UNKLE & The Major Force Orchestra* / Head west - gun fight at the OK Corrall: *Howie B* / They came in peace: *Tranquility Bass* / In flux: *DJ Shadow*
CD Set ________ **MW 026CD**
Mo Wax / May '96 / PolyGram / Vital

HEADZ VOL.2A (2CD Set)
Nights interlude: *Nightmares On Wax* / Cantona style: *Prunes* / Real thing: *Peshay* / Modulor: *Air* / Searchin': *Dust Brothers* / Flow: *RPM* / My bloody valentine: *DJ Wally* / Garage piano: *UNKLE* / Kemuri: *DJ Krush* / Do you understand: *Sever, Sam & The Raiders Of The Lost Art* / What is soul: *Stereo MC's* / Covet action: *Urban Tribe* / Cabin fever: *Lo-fi Sensibilities* / Code: *Midnight Funk Association* / Concentric circle: *DJ Food* / 27 years of solitude: *Cool Breeze* / Discotron: *Stasis* / Mango maracuta: *Scott Free & Cybil Ant* / Source of uncertainity: *Tortoise* / Karmacoma: *Massive Attack* / Bodhisattva Vow: *Beastie Boys* / Simean groove: *Folk Implosion* / Martian economics: *Oldie Scottish* / Eastward: *Urban Tribe* / Spacewalk: *Lunar Funk* / New element: *Forme* / Pressure II: *Solo* / Organized crimes: *Innervisions* / KRB parts 1-8: *DJ Krush*
CD Set ________ **MW 061CD**
Mo Wax / Oct '96 / PolyGram / Vital

HEADZ VOL.2B (2CD Set)
Spectral arc: *Luminis* / Sharp AZ: *Vibert, Luke* / World lesson II: *Money Mark* / Swiss air: *Twig Bud* / Time has come: *UNKLE* / It's coming: *Grantby* / Wirecutter: *Donut Productions* / Intermission part 3: *Prunes* / Groomsman: *Dust Brothers* / Crash: *Skull* / Flute loop: *Beastie Boys* / Maze: *DJ Krush* / Sketch: *Attica Blues* / Ultimatum: *Jungle Brothers* / Science Fu beats: *Danny Breaks* / Future tense: *Force* / Beast: *Palmskin Productions* / Real thing: *Peshay* / In the mood: *Dillinja* / Tribetoon: *Roni Size & DJ Krush* / Silent witness: *Source Direct* / Counterpoint: *As One* / Bug in the bassbin: *Inner Zone Orchestra* / Object Orient: *Black Dog* / Trilogy: *Special Forces* / Quiddity: *Max 404* / Shadow's legitimate mix: *Zimbabwe Legit* / Intermission parts 1&2: *Prunes* / Intermission parts 4-8: *Prunes*
CD Set ________ **MW 062CD**
Mo Wax / Oct '96 / PolyGram / Vital

HEALER'S BREW (South Africa Outernational Meltdown Series)
Blessing ceremony / Marimba song / Mamgobhozi - a woman's name / Healers brew / Amen / Bazophumula abangkwele / Mangibe nawe baba / Djembe amam / Togetherness
CD ________ **BW 077**
B&W / Nov '96 / New Note/Pinnacle / SRD / Vital/SAM

HEART AND SOUL (2CD Set)
Midnight train to Georgia: *Knight, Gladys* / Summer breeze: *Isley Brothers* / Love train: *O'Jays* / That's what friends are for: *Williams, Deniece* / Sexual healing: *Gaye, Marvin* / Show me the way: *Belle, Regina* / Heaven must be missing an angel: *Tavares* / Night to remember: *Shalamar* / Tonight I celebrate my love to you: *Flack, Roberta & Peabo Bryson* / Mighty love: *Stansfield, Lisa* / Lean on me: *Withers, Bill* / It's a love thing: *Whispers* / I'll take you there: *Staple Singers* / When something is wrong with my baby: *Purify, James & Bobby* / Private number: *Clay, Judy & William Bell* / Angel of the morning: *Rush, Merilee* / To love somebody: *Simone, Nina* / Didn't I (blow your mind this time): *Delfonics* / I have learned to respect the power of love: *Mills, Stephanie* / That lady: *Isley Brothers* / Just don't want to be lonely: *Main Ingredient* / Love I lost: *Melvin, Harold & The Bluenotes* / Best thing that ever happened to me: *Knight, Gladys* / First cut is the deepest: *Arnold, P.P.* / Rescue me: *Bass, Fontella* / Mockingbird: *Foxx, Inez & Charlie* / Rock your baby: *McCrae, George* / I'm your puppet: *Purify, James & Bobby* / Kissin' in the back row of the movies: *Drifters* / Spooky: *Classics IV* / Ride your pony: *Dorsey, Lee* / Shoorah shoorah: *Wright, Betty* / Nothin' but a house party: *Showstoppers* / Walkin' in rhythm: *Blackbyrds* / Respect yourself: *Staple Singers* / Didn't it rain: *Jackson, Mahalia* / Ain't got no...I got life: *Simone, Nina*
CD Set ________ **RCACD 207**
RCA / Jul '97 / BMG

HEART AND SOUL
Three steps from true love: *Reflections* / Love is the key: *Maze* / Everything is cool: *T-Connection* / Bad times: *Tavares* / I'd give it to you: *Tee, Willie* / Before you break my heart: *Dunlap, Gene & The Ridgeways* / LOVE: *Green, Al* / Falling: *Moore, Melba* / Memory lane: *Riperton, Minnie* / Help (somebody please): *O'Jays* / Round and around: *Graham, Jaki* / LOVE U: *Brass Construction* / Heaven in your arms: *RJ's Latest Arrival* / Medley: *Womack, Bobby*
CD ________ **CDTMCD 317**
EMI / May '97 / EMI

HEART AND SOUL OF ROCK & ROLL, THE
CD ________ **TCD 2351**
Telstar / Oct '88 / BMG

HEART AND SOUL OF..., THE (Gladys Knight/The Supremes/The Marvelettes/ Martha Reeves)
Every beat of my heart: *Knight, Gladys* / Letter full of tears: *Knight, Gladys* / Operator: *Knight, Gladys* / Come see about me: *Knight, Gladys* / Baby love: *Supremes* / Stop in the name of love: *Supremes* / Stoned love: *Supremes* / Love child: *Supremes* / When you're young and in love: *Marvelettes* / Don't mess with Bill: *Marvelettes* / Secret love affir: *Marvelettes* / Too many fish in the sea: *Marvelettes* / Dancing in the street: *Martha & The Vandellas* / Heatwave: *Martha & The Vandellas* / Jimmy Mack: *Martha & The Vandellas* / Nowhere to run: *Martha & The Vandellas*
CD ________ **PLATCD 212**
Platinum / Feb '97 / Prism

HEART AND SOUL OF..., THE (Gloria Gaynor/Kool & The Gang/Rose Royce/ Tavares)
Celebration: *Kool & The Gang* / Ladies night: *Kool & The Gang* / Get down on it: *Kool & The Gang* / Cherish: *Kool & The Gang* / I will survive: *Gaynor, Gloria* / Every time you go away: *Gaynor, Gloria* / What a wonderful world: *Gaynor, Gloria* / Every breath you take: *Gaynor, Gloria* / Car wash: *Rose Royce* / Wishing on a star: *Rose Royce* / Love don't live here anymore: *Rose Royce* / Is it love you're after: *Rose Royce* / Heaven must be missing an angel: *Tavares* / More than a woman: *Tavares* / Don't take away the music: *Tavares* / She's gone: *Tavares* / Whodunnit: *Tavares* / Check it out: *Tavares* / It only takes a minute girl: *Tavares* / Remember what I told you to forget: *Tavares*
CD ________ **PLATCD 213**
Platinum / Feb '97 / Prism

HEART AND SOUL OF..., THE (Edwin Starr/Percy Sledge/Chi-Lites/Brook Benton)
25 miles: *Starr, Edwin* / Stop her on sight (SOS): *Starr, Edwin* / Where is the sound: *Starr, Edwin* / Just another fool in love: *Starr, Edwin* / Warm and tender love: *Sledge, Percy* / When a man loves a woman: *Sledge, Percy* / Tell it like it is: *Sledge, Percy* / Take time to know her: *Sledge, Percy* / Have you seen her: *Chi-Lites* / You and I: *Chi-Lites* / I want to pay you back: *Chi-Lites* / Toby: *Chi-Lites* / Rainy night in Georgia: *Benton, Brook* / Endlessly: *Benton, Brook* / It's just a matter of time: *Benton, Brook* / Kiddio: *Benton, Brook*
CD ______ **PLATCD 214**
Platinum / Feb '97 / Prism

HEART AND SOUL OF..., THE (Sister Sledge/Eddie Floyd/Detroit Emeralds/ Sam & Dave)
Soul man: *Sam & Dave* / Soul sister, brown sugar: *Sam & Dave* / Hold on I'm comin': *Sam & Dave* / Soothe me: *Sam & Dave* / We are family: *Sister Sledge* / Frankie: *Sister Sledge* / Thinking of you: *Sister Sledge* / Lost in music: *Sister Sledge* / Knock on wood: *Floyd, Eddie* / Bring it on home to me: *Floyd, Eddie* / Things get better: *Floyd, Eddie* / Raise your hand: *Floyd, Eddie* / Feel the need in me: *Detroit Emeralds* / You want it you got it: *Detroit Emeralds* / Dance school: *Detroit Emeralds* / Cutting the groove: *Detroit Emeralds*
CD ______ **PLATCD 215**
Platinum / Feb '97 / Prism

HEART OF AMERICA
CD ______ **RENCD 105**
Castle / Jul '95 / BMG

HEART OF ARGENTINIAN TANGO, THE
Taquito militar / Romance de barrio / Los mareados / El dia que me quieras / Corralera / Caseron de tejas / Niebla de reachuelo / Fuimos / Elegie / El portenito / La cumparsita
CD ______ **PV 795052**
Disques Pierre Verany / Jul '95 / Kingdom

HEART OF DARKNESS
CD ______ **MEZCD 2**
China / Aug '96 / Pinnacle

HEART OF IRELAND
Whiskey in the jar / Four country roads / Green fields of France / Irish rover / When you were sweet sixteen / Boys from Killybegs / You seldom come to see me anymore / Boston burglar / After all these years / Isle of Innisfree / Black velvet band / Our house is not a home / Old bog road / Town I love so well / I'll take you home again Kathleen / Any Tipperary town / Hills of Kerry / Mountains of Mourne / Maggie / Rose of Tralee
CD ______ **CD 6020**
Music / Apr '96 / Target/BMG

HEART OF SOUL
CD ______ **EXP 041**
Experience / May '97 / TKO Magnum

HEART OF SOUTHERN SOUL VOL.1
Falling in love again: *Kelly Brothers* / You're that great big feelin': *Kelly Brothers* / That's all I can do: *Anderson, Kip* / Snake out of the grass (part 1): *Anderson, Roshell* / Snake out of the grass (part 2): *Anderson, Roshell* / Soldier's sad story: *Watkins, Tiny* / Pretty little thing: *Interpreters* / Your love is worth the pain: *Truitt, Johnny* / Talk to me: *Avons* / Your love's so good: *Webber, Lee* / Somewhere out there: *Matthis, Lucille* / Mr. Fortune teller: *Dee & Don* / Midnight tears: *Watkins, Tiny* / Woman in me: *Mariann* / Steppin' stone: *Wallace Brothers* / Gonna need somebody: *Lane, Stacy* / I went off and cried: *Anderson, Kip* / You'll never know: *Brown, Shirley* / CC rider: *Powell, Bobby* / Price is too high: *Harpo, Slim* / There goes a girl: *Truitt, Johnny* / Do your thing: *Whitney, Marva* / Power is gone: *Kemp, Eugene*
CD ______ **CDCHD 568**
Ace / Sep '94 / Pinnacle

HEART OF SOUTHERN SOUL VOL.2 (No Brags - Just Facts)
Letter from my darling: *Anderson, Kip* / My love grows stronger: *Kelly Brothers* / I can't stand it: *Dee & Don* / (Those) Precious words: *Wallace Brothers* / You'll lose a good thing: *Anderson, Kip* / Way cross town: *Watkins, Tiny* / Here I am: *Whitney, Marva* / Don't let me be a cryin' man: *Truitt, Johnny* / I will: *Brown, Lattimore* / Seventh son: *Webber, Lee* / Look what I've done: *Wiggins, Percy* / Let me be a part of you: *Exotics* / Am I asking too much: *Mathis, Lucille* / Lifetime of a man: *Lane, Stacy* / Watch you work it out: *Anderson, Kip* / Forbidden fruit: *Watkins, Tiny* / Right here is where you belong: *Washington, Jerry* / Let's try to build a love affair: *Exotics* / Funky little train: *Lane, Stacy* / Let's walk down the street together: *Chuck & Mariann* / I don't want to go through life (being a fool): *Mathis, Lucille* / I'm through with you: *Truitt, Johnny* / No pity in the city: *Kemp, Eugene* / No brags just facts: *Lane, Stacy*
CD ______ **CDCHD 601**
Ace / Jun '96 / Pinnacle

HEART OF THE GAELS
CD ______ **GLCD 0105**
Green Linnet / Jun '88 / ADA / CM / Direct / Highlander / Roots

HEART OF THE LION
CD ______ **IR 022CD**
Iona / Mar '94 / ADA / Direct / Duncans

HEARTACHES (20 Songs Of Love)
No more the fool: *Brooks, Elkie* / Let the heartaches begin: *Baldry, Long John* / I don't believe in miracles: *Blunstone, Colin* / Angel of the morning: *Arnold, P.P.* / Red red wine: *James, Jimmy* / It's a heartache: *Tyler, Bonnie* / You to me are everything: *Real Thing* / I'll have to say I love you in a song: *Croce, Jim* / Mirrors: *Oldfield, Sally* / Just one smile: *Pitney, Gene* / Sorry doesn't always make it right: *Knight, Gladys & The Pips* / Handbags and gladrags: *Farlowe, Chris* / Ruby Tuesday: *Melanie* / Darling be home soon: *Lovin' Spoonful* / Man of the world: *Fleetwood Mac* / Kiss me for the last time: *Brooks, Elkie* / Love's gotta hold on me: *Dollar* / Oh girl: *Chi-Lites* / Days: *Kinks* / One less set of footsteps: *Croce, Jim*
CD ______ **TRTCD 113**
TrueTrax / Feb '96 / THE

HEARTBEAT OF SOWETO
Nwana wamina: *Chauke, Thomas* / Thathezakho: *Mlokothwa* / Jabula mfana: *Emvelo, Amaswazi* / Nsati wa wina: *Shirinda, M.D. & Family* / Siyoklishaya kusasa: *Elimnyama, Kati* / Waqala Ngowendlala: *Usuthu* / Mashama: *ChiJumane, Arando Bila* / Xumaxilovile: *Chauke, Thomas & Shinyori* / Yithinamhlaje: *Mlokothwa* / Bumnandi utshwala bakho: *Elimnyama, Kati* / Kamakhalawana: *ChiJumane, Arando Bila* / Ndzi Hkensa: *Shirinda, M.D. & Family*
CD ______ **SHANCD 43051**
Shanachie / Mar '89 / ADA / Greensleeves / Koch

HEARTBEAT REGGAE NOW
CD ______ **HBCDAN 9**
Greensleeves / Jun '93 / Jet Star / SRD

HEARTBREAK USA
Hertbreak USA: *Wells, Kitty* / Please release me: *Parton, Dolly* / Let's think about living: *Luman, Bob* / Me and Bobby McGee: *Rogers, Kenny* / Race is on: *Jones, George* / Dang me: *Miller, Roger* / Indiana wants me: *Taylor, R. Dean* / Tom Dooley: *Kingston Trio* / El paso: *Robbins, Marty* / Settin' the woods on fire: *Williams, Hank* / Sally was a good old girl: *Jennings, Waylon* / Thanks a lot: *Tubb, Ernest* / These boots are made for walking: *Hazelwood, Lee* / Next in line: *Cash, Johnny* / Truck drivin' outlaw: *Olsen, Denis* / Rose Marie: *Whitman, Slim* / North to Alaska: *Horton, Johnny* / Oh, lonesome me: *Gibson, Don*
CD ______ **11978**
Music / Feb '96 / Target/BMG

HEARTBREAKERS
CD ______ **STACD 053**
Wisepack / Sep '93 / Conifer/BMG / THE

HEARTBREAKERS
Power of love: *Rush, Jennifer* / Afer the love has gone: *Earth, Wind & Fire* / I love you too much: *Santana* / Do I love you too much: *Lake* / Do I love you: *Blunstone, Colin* / Me and Mrs Jones: *Paul, Billy* / Kiss and say goodbye: *Manhattans* / In my dreams: *REO Speedwagon* / Most beautiful girl in the world: *Rich, Charlie* / You made me so very happy: *Blood, Sweat & Tears* / When your heart is weak: *Cock Robin* / Longer: *Fogelberg, Dan* / Something's gotten hold of my heart: *Window Speaks* / Long distance love: *Bailey, Philip* / Only one woman: *Belcanto* / How 'bout us: *Champaign*
CD ______ **4804442**
Columbia / Oct '95 / Sony

HEARTBREAKERS
CD ______ **MACCD 147**
Autograph / Aug '96 / BMG

HEARTBREAKERS (18 Classic Tear Jerkers)
Don't play that song (you lied): *King, Ben E.* / Goin' out of my head: *Little Anthony & The Imperials* / I will: *Fury, Billy* / What's a matter baby (is it hurting you): *Yuro, Timi* / It's just a matter of time: *Benton, Brook* / Since I don't have you: *Skyliners* / Behind closed doors: *Sledge, Percy* / Never my love: *Association* / Harbor lights: *Platters* / If loving you is wrong (I don't want to be right): *Drifters* / For the good times: *Price, Ray* / You'll lose a good thing: *Lynn, Barbara* / What in the world's come over you: *Scott, Jack* / Teen angel: *Dinning, Mark* / Then you can tell me goodbye: *Casinos* / Born a woman: *Posey, Sandy* / I can't help it (if I'm still in love with you): *Thomas, B.J.* / Going, going, gone: *Greenwood, Lee*
CD ______ **ECD 3213**
K-Tel / Mar '95 / K-Tel

HEARTCORE DEMOS, THE
CD ______ **PACEMAKER 001CD**
Burning Heart / Sep '95 / Plastic Head

HEARTLANDS
Desire: *U2* / Real gone kid: *Deacon Blue* / Whole of the moon: *Waterboys* / Wonderland: *Big Country* / Don't go: *Hothouse Flowers* / Somewhere in my heart: *Aztec Camera* / Broken land: *Adventures* / Mary's prayer: *Danny Wilson* / I don't like Mondays: *Boomtown Rats* / Move any mountain: *Shamen* / Movin' on up: *Primal Scream* / Labour of love: *Hue & Cry* / Strange kind of love: *Love & Money* / Rip it up: *Orange Juice* / Irish rover: *Pogues & The Dubliners* / Las Vegas (in the hills of Donegal): *Goats Don't Shave* / Flower in the West: *Runrig* / My special child: *O'Connor, Sinead*
CD ______ **NTRCD 069**
Nectar / Mar '97 / Pinnacle

HEARTS DESIRE
CD ______ **RENCD 103**
Castle / Jul '95 / BMG

HEAT
CD ______ **FADCD 026**
Fashion / Nov '92 / Jet Star / SRD

HEAT IS ON, THE (2CD Set)
CD Set ______ **NSCD 002**
Newsound / Feb '95 / THE

HEATHEN CHANT, THE
CD ______ **RN 004**
Runn / Jun '96 / Grapevine/PolyGram / Jet Star / SRD

HEAVEN
Stop: *Brown, Sam* / Come into my life: *Sims, Joyce* / Poison arrow: *ABC* / Message is love: *Baker, Arthur & The Backbeat Disciples* / Have you ever had it blue: *Style Council* / Cry: *Godley & Creme* / I'll find my way home: *Jon & Vangelis* / Suspicious minds: *Fine Young Cannibals* / Your history: *Shakespears Sister* / Running in the family: *Level 42* / Closest thing to Heaven: *Kane Gang* / If I can't have you: *Elliman, Yvonne* / You make me feel brand new: *Stylistics* / Oh what a circus: *Essex, David*
CD ______ **5501492**
Spectrum / Jan '94 / PolyGram

HEAVENLY GROOVES
CD ______ **39101612**
Hyperium / Jan '97 / Cargo / Plastic Head

HEAVENLY HARDCORE
CD ______ **DINCD 35**
Dino / Mar '92 / Pinnacle

HEAVENLY VOICES
CD Set ______ **HY 39100852**
Hyperium / Feb '94 / Cargo / Plastic Head

HEAVENLY VOICES VOL.4
CD ______ **39101792**
Hyperium / Jan '97 / Cargo / Plastic Head

HEAVY GUITAR (2CD Set)
CD Set ______ **24079**
Delta Doubles / Mar '95 / Target/BMG

HEAVY METAL HEROES VOL.1 & 2
I won't surrender: *Twisted Ace* / Reaper: *Grim Reaper* / Stormchild: *Jaguar* / Storm of steel: *Soldier* / Strangers on the shore: *Bitches Sin* / Hard life: *Metal Mirror* / Cold as night: *Buffalo* / Rock Japan: *Expozer* / Running wild: *Split Beaver* / Do it: *Dragster* / Rabies: *Witchfinder General* / Lionheart: *Lionheart* / What the hells going on: *Mendes Prey* / Ice cold diamond: *Mantle Swallow Palmer* / Out of my head: *Overkill* / Devil's triangle: *Cox, Jess* / This fire inside: *Twisted Ace* / Free country: *Witchfinder General* / Oh well: *No Faith* / Calling for you: *Persian Risk* / Power and the key: *No Quater*
CD ______ **CDMETAL 9**
Anagram / Feb '97 / Cargo / Pinnacle

HEAVY METAL HEROES VOL.3
CD ______ **HMRXD 153**
Heavy Metal / Aug '90 / Revolver / Sony

HEAVY METAL RECORDS COMPILATION
CD ______ **HMRXD 143**
Heavy Metal / Jul '90 / Revolver / Sony

HEAVY METAL SINGLES COLLECTION
CD ______ **CDMETAL 003**
British Steel / Feb '97 / Cargo / Pinnacle / Plastic Head

HEAVY OVERDOSE OF LYTE PSYCH
CD ______ **AA 062**
Arf Arf / Jul '97 / Greyhound

HEAVYWEIGHT SOUND VOL.1 (A Blood & Fire Sampler)
Real gone crazy dub: *King Tubby & The Aggrovators* / Jah is I guiding star: *Tappa Zukie & The Aggrovators* / Falling dub: *Prince Philip & The Musical Intimidators* / Marcus children suffer: *Burning Spear & The Black Disciples* / Black heart: *Hudson, Keith & The Soul Syndicate* / Problems: *Andy, Horace* / Problems dub: *Andy, Horace & Prince Jammy* / Rock vibration: *Yabby You & King Tubby* / War and friction: *I-Roy & The Aggrovators* / Living style: *Yabby You & King Tubby* / Black right: *Hudson, Keith & The Soul Syndicate* / Judgement dub: *Prince Philip & The Musical Intimidators* / Marcus say Jah no dead: *Burning Spear & The Black Disciples* / Dub fi gwan: *King Tubby & The Aggrovators*
CD ______ **BAFCD 7**
Blood & Fire / Mar '96 / Vital

HEAVYWEIGHT SOUND VOL.2 (Another Blood & Fire Sampler)
Late hour: *I-Roy* / World dub - away with the bad: *Brown, Glen & King Tubby* / Ragga muffin style: *Jah Stitch* / La la bam bam: *Congos* / Shooter dub: *King Tubby & Santic Allstars* / You're no good: *Fraser, Philip* / Wrong time: *Congos* / Only love can conquer: *Prince Alla* / Jah help the dread: *Jah Stitch* / Dub bible: *Scientist & The Soul Syndicate* / Higher ranking: *King Tubby & The Aggrovators* / Black rose: *Prince Alla & Philip Fraser* / Great stone: *King Tubby & The Soul Syndicate* / Version 78 style: *Brown, Glen & King Tubby* / Superfly: *I-Roy* / Drums of Africa: *Prince Jammy & The Aggrovators*
CD ______ **BAFCD 17**
Blood & Fire / Feb '97 / Vital

HECTIC - CHAPTER ONE
CD ______ **HECTCD 001**
Hectic / Oct '95 / Grapevine/PolyGram / Jumpstart / Mo's Music Machine / RTM/ Disc

HEIDI SEZ LOOKOUT
CD ______ **LOOKOUT 169CD**
Lookout / Oct '96 / Cargo / Greyhound / Shellshock/Disc

HEIVA I TAHITI - FESTIVAL OF LIFE
CD ______ **EUCD 1238**
ARC / Nov '93 / ADA / ARC Music

HELENA BLUES LEGACY, THE
CD ______ **BLUESUN 2000**
Blue Sun / May '97 / Hot Shot

HELLS BENT ON ROCKIN'
CD ______ **NERCD 017**
Nervous / Nov '91 / Nervous / TKO Magnum

HELL'S KITCHEN
CD ______ **DIW 405**
DIW / Mar '97 / Cadillac / Harmonia Mundi

HELLSOUND VOL.5 (Blessed Are The Sick)
CD ______ **HSCOMP 005**
ID&T / Apr '97 / Plastic Head

HELP
Fade away: *Oasis* / Oh brother: *Boo Radleys* / Love spreads: *Stone Roses* / Lucky: *Radiohead* / Adnan: *Orbital* / Mourning air (war child): *Portishead* / Fake the aroma: *Massive Attack* / Shipbuilding: *Suede* / Time for loving: *Charlatans & The Chemical Brothers* / Sweetest truth: *Stereo MC's* / Ode to Billy Joe: *O'Connor, Sinead* / Search light: *Levellers* / Raindrops keep falling on my head: *Manic Street Preachers* / Tom Petty loves Veruca Salt: *Terrorvision* / Magnificent: *One World Orchestra* / Message to crommie: *Planet 4 Folk Quartet* / Dream a little dream: *Hall, Terry & Salad* / 1,2,3,4,5: *Cherry, Neneh & Trout* / Eine kleine lift muzik: *Blur* / Come together: *Smokin' Mojo Filters*
CD ______ **8286822**
Go Discs / Sep '95 / PolyGram

HELPING YOU BACK TO WORK
CD ______ **LJCD 03**
Lockjaw / Jul '97 / Pinnacle

HELTER SHELTER BOX (Elastica/Gene/ Supergrass/S*M*A*S*H)
CD Set ______ **SP 1776**
Sub Pop / Jul '95 / Cargo / Greyhound / Shellshock/Disc

HELTER SKELTER (3CD Set)
CD Set ______ **CDHSR 004**
Helter Skelter / Jun '97 / Pinnacle / Plastic Head / SRD

HELTER SKELTER - THE DRUM'N'BASS ANNUAL (2CD Set)
CD Set ______ **CDHSR 097**
Helter Skelter / Nov '96 / Pinnacle / Plastic Head / SRD

HELTER SKELTER - THE TECHNO ANNUAL (2CD Set)
CD Set ______ **CDHSR 098**
Helter Skelter / Nov '96 / Pinnacle / Plastic Head / SRD

HEMISPHERE NO MORE (A Listener Friendly Guide To Music Of The World)
Sango ya mawa: *Dabany, Patience* / La Cosecha De Mujeres: *Tribu Band* / Nereci (A name): *Djavan* / Konifale: *Tangara, Kadja* / Cortina: *Vasconcelos, Nana* / Midnight walker: *Spillane, Davy* / Khafet dhamon: *Fouad, Mohamed* / Sweet reggae: *Harley & The Rasta Family* / Yele congo: *Ketu, Ara* / Africa: *Depeu, Dave* / Madambadamba: *Tshola, Tsepo* / Koufenko: *Manfila, Kante* / E dai (A queda): *Nascimento, Milton* / Hujara: *Inti-Illimani* / Rag Pahadi: *Sharma, Shivkumar*
CD ______ **CDHEMI 2**
Hemisphere / Jun '95 / EMI

HEMPILATION
CD ______ **5325512**
Mercury / Sep '96 / PolyGram

HENT SANT JAKEZ
CD ______ **SHAM 1018CD**
Shamrock / Aug '93 / ADA / Wellard

HEP CATS FROM BIG SPRING
Move mama: *Hall, Ben* / Be bop ball: *Hall, Ben* / Blue days black nights: *Hall, Ben* / Honey you talk too much: *Fox, Orville & The Harmony Masters* / Silly Sally: *Lara, Sammy* / Tell me: *Regals* / Waitin' (on the steps at school): *Regals* / Lover's regret: *Classics* / Hep cat: *Teen Kings* / Some day sweet day: *Box, David & The Ravens* / That's all I want from you: *Box, David & The Ravens* / I do

the best I can: *Box, David & The Ravens* / Waitin' (don't wait too long): *Box, David & The Ravens* / Guitar hop: *Welborn, Larry* / It's gonna happpen: *Osburn, Bob* / Heart theif: *Osburn, Bob* / Goin' back to Louisiana: *Osburn, Bob* / Too young to love to old to cry: *Nicholas, Don & The Four Teens* / Bark like a dog: *Allison, Bobby*
CD ________ RCCD 3003
Rollercoaster / Oct '91 / Rollercoaster / Swift

HER SONG (Exotic Voices of Women From Around the World)
Great Grampah's banjo: *Pura Fe* / Yola: *Irena* / Apne Hathon: *Najma* / Kirya: *Haza, Ofra* / Jiva mukti: *Shakti, Nada* / 'S Muldach mi's air: *MacKenzie, Talitha* / Return home: *Solas & Karan Casey* / Compassion: *Flesh & Bone* / Messenger: *Shanandoa, Joanne* / In your dark eyes: *Ankri, Etti*
CD ________ SH 64077
Shanachie / Dec '96 / ADA / Greensleeves / Koch

HERE COME THE BOYS VOL.1
Make up or break up: *Leslie, Michael* / Save your love: *Rich, Tony* / Stage door: *Jackson, Tony* / Can I get to know you better: *Wynter, Mark* / I could write a book: *Chants* / Bubop-a-lu-bop-a-lie: *Storme, Robb & Whispers* / Just as long as (you belong to me): *Hill, Vince* / Ecstasy: *Reed, Oliver* / Please don't cry: *Newman, Brad* / I don't care: *Chants* / That's the way love goes: *Dickens, Charles* / Don't fool yourself: *Sumers, John* / Lookin' for love: *Watson, John L* / Big black smoke: *Mick & Malcolm* / Seven lonely days: *Migil 5* / Everything: *Darrell, Guy* / Leave a little love: *Anton, Terry* / Comes the dawn: *Galt, James* / That man's got no luck: *Benson, Gary* / My world fell down: *Ivy League* / Looking back: *West Coast Consortium* / One day: *Sands Of Time* / Only heartbreaks for me: *Justice, Jimmy* / Leave it to me: *Band Of Angels*
CD ________ NEMCD 844
Sequel / Jul '97 / BMG

HERE COME THE GIRLS VOL.1 (British Girl Singers Of The Sixties)
That's how it goes: *Breakaways* / We were lovers (when the party began): *Barry, Sandra* / There he goes (the boy I love): *Antoinette* / He knows I love him too much: *Macari, Glo* / As long as you're happy baby: *Shaw, Sandie* / Song without end: *Ruskin, Barbara* / Tell me what to do: *Jackson, Simone* / Put yourself in my place: *Panter, Jan* / It's hard to believe it: *Collins, Glenda* / So much in love: *Brown, Polly* / Very first day I met you: *Cannon, Judy* / How can I hide from my heart: *Darren, Maxine* / No other baby: *Davis, Billie* / Listen people: *Lane, Sarah* / Come to me: *Grant, Julie* / Dark shadows and empty hallways: *St. John, Tammy* / Happy faces: *Silver, Lorraine* / Something must be done: *Harris, Anita* / You'd better come home: *Clark, Petula* / When my baby cries: *Prenosilova, Yvonne* / Something I've got to tell you: *Honeycombs* / I want you: *Jeannie & The Big Guys* / I can't believe what you say: *McKenna, Val* / If you love me (really love me): *Trent, Jackie*
CD ________ NEXCD 111
Sequel / Mar '90 / BMG

HERE COME THE GIRLS VOL.3 (Run Mascara)
Easier said than done: *Essex* / Walkin' miracle: *Essex* / She's got everything: *Essex* / Run mascara: *Exciters* / I want you to be my boy: *Exciters* / There they go: *Exciters* / Kind of boy you can't forget: *Raindrops* / What a guy: *Raindrops* / That boy is messing up my mind: *Raindrops* / My one and only Jimmy boy: *Girlfriends* / For my sake: *Girlfriends* / Lover's concerto: *Toys* / What's wrong with me baby: *Toys* / Can't stop lovin' the boy: *Carolines* / Evening time: *Elena* / Girl is not a girl: *Wine, Toni* / Johnny Angel: *Fabares, Shelly* / He don't love me: *Fabares, Shelly* / I'm into something good: *Earl Jean*
CD ________ NEXCD 193
Sequel / Mar '92 / BMG

HERE COME THE GIRLS VOL.4 (You Can Be Wrong About Boys)
He doesn't love me: *Breakaways* / I've found love: *Tandy, Sharon* / Pay you back with interest: *Gillespie, Dana* / Thank goodness for the rain: *Peanut* / It's so fine: *King, Dee* / Where am I going: *Clark, Petula* / You can be wrong about boys: *Page, Mally* / He's the one for me: *St. John, Tammy* / Don't you know: *Darren, Maxine* / Thinking of you: *West, Dodie* / Well how does it feel: *Ruskin, Barbara* / You can't take it away: *Reed, Tawney* / When love slips away: *Margo & The Marvettes* / There he goes: *Pickettywitch* / London life: *Harris, Anita* / As I watch you walk away: *Smith, Martha* / Lonely without you: *Grant, Julie* / You really have started something: *Britt* / Someone has to cry (Why must I): *Kay, Barbara* / My life (is in your hands): *Paper Dolls* / Untrue unfaithful (That was you): *Rossi, Nita* / Scratch my back: *Panter, Jan* / Love ya Ilya: *Angela & The Fans*
CD ________ NEXCD 238
Sequel / Jun '93 / BMG

HERE COME THE GIRLS VOL.5 (Sisters From The City)
CD ________ NEMCD 675
Sequel / Sep '94 / BMG

HERE COME THE GIRLS VOL.6
Question: *Barry, Sandra* / I'm tired just lookin' at you: *St. John, Tammy* / Life and soul of the party: *St. John, Tammy* / Take me away: *Trent, Jackie* / Reach out, I'll be there: *Clark, Petula* / Thank you for loving me: *Antoinette* / Here she comes: *Breakaways* / Donna Star: *Douglas, Donna* / Love is a many splendoured thing: *Saxone, Linda* / Please don't talk about me when I'm gone: *Stern, Nina* / Halfway to paradise: *Ruskin, Barbara* / Come on baby: *Kim D* / He don't want your love anymore: *Doll, Linda & the Sundowners* / Something I've got to tell you: *Collins, Glenda* / Da-di-da-da: *Satin Bells* / So goes love: *Abicair, Shirley* / Thank you boy: *Gillespie, Dana* / I know you'll be there: *Silver, Lorraine* / I know you: *Angela & The Fans* / He's no good: *Baker Twins* / Heaven is being with you: *Brook, Patti* / Long after tonight is all over: *Rogers, Julie* / In the deep of the night: *West, Dodie* / You make my head spin: *Lee, Jackie*
CD ________ NEMCD 718
Sequel / Feb '95 / BMG

HERE COME THE GIRLS VOL.7 (The Trouble With Boys)
Baby baby (I still love you): *Cinderellas* / Please don't wake me: *Cinderellas* / Baby toys: *Toys* / See how they run: *Toys* / May my heart be cast in stone: *Toys* / Curfew lover: *Essex* / What did I do: *Essex* / Are you going my way: *Essex* / Moon of love: *Bobbettes* / Will you love me in heaven: *Del-Vetts* / Send him to me: *Uniques* / Breaking up is hard to do: *Fabares, Shelly* / Toom Toom (is a little boy): *Applebee, Marie* / Down by the sea (end of summer): *Applebee, Marie* / Hey lover: *Dovale, Debbie* / Opportunity: *Jewels* / I never wonder where my baby goes: *Elaine* / There's danger ahead: *Elaine* / It should'a been me (instead of company): *Elaine* / Get him: *Little Eva* / Trouble with boys: *Little Eva*
CD ________ NEMCD 752
Sequel / Aug '95 / BMG

HERE COME THE GIRLS VOL.8
Fancy dancin' man: *Clark, Petula* / Love is a gamble: *Lee, Jackie* / Other side of love: *Caravelles* / Mixed up, shook up girl: *McKenna, Val* / Lost summer love: *Silver, Lorraine* / You can't blame a girl for trying: *Ruskin, Barbara* / All the time in the world: *Paper Dolls* / Dream world: *Pickettywitch* / My heart didn't lie: *Collins, Glenda* / That boy of mine: *Breakaways* / Can you keep a secret: *Sparling, Candy* / Just wait till spring is here: *Moray, Moya* / I love you, I need you: *Brook, Patti* / Home of the brave: *Peanut* / We'll start the party again: *Young, Karen* / (Walk tall) like a man: *New Faces* / Burning in the background of my mind: *Tott, Tina* / Here before the sun: *Balmer, Lori* / I've got to get a grip of myself: *Dulittle, Liza* / That's what angels are for: *Kay, Barbara* / Trains and boats and planes: *Harris, Anita* / Take it from me (little girl): *Stern, Nina* / I'm for you: *Antoinette* / Either way I lose: *Trent, Jackie*
CD ________ NEMCD 845
Sequel / Jul '97 / BMG

HERE COMES MY BABY (Hits Of The Swinging Sixties)
CD ________ PLSCD 189
Pulse / Apr '97 / BMG

HERE COMES THE SUMMER
Hooray hooray it's a holi-holiday: *Boney M* / Summer love sensation: *Bay City Rollers* / Down on the beach tonight: *Drifters* / Farewell my summer love: *Kaos* / Everybody's got summer: *Atlantic Starr* / Gimme the sunshine: *Curiosity* / Loco in Acapulco: *Four Tops* / Fantastic day: *Haircut 100* / Surfin' USA: *Astronauts* / Surfin' in the summertime: *Ronnie & The Daytonas* / Summer (the first time): *Goldsboro, Bobby* / Aquarius (let the sunshine in): *5th Dimension* / Seasons in the sun: *Jacks, Terry* / Good thing going: *Minott, Sugar* / Montego bay: *Sugar Cane* / Sunshine reggae: *Laidback* / Sun will shine: *Feliciano, Jose* / Island in the sun: *Belafonte, Harry* / Santa Monica sunshine: *Sweet* / Current of love: *Hasselhoff, David*
CD ________ 74321286102
Ariola / May '95 / BMG

HERITAGE 14-HIP HOP
We got our own thing: *Heavy D & The Boyz* / Hip hop junkies: *Nice 'n Smoothe* / Mama said knock you out: *LL Cool J* / I come off: *Young MC* / It takes two: *Rob Base & DJ E-Z Rock* / Make it happen: *Ultramagnetic MC's* / Flavor of the month: *Black Sheep* / OPP: *Naughty By Nature* / Jump: *Kriss Kross* / Express yourself: *NWA* / Fuck Compton: *Dog, Tim* / I'm ready: *Caveman*
CD ________ CDELV 08
Elevate / Jul '93 / 3mv/Sony

HERITAGE OF SCOTLAND
CD ________ 302692
Hallmark / Jan '97 / Carlton

HERITAGE OF THE CELTS
CD ________ 302732
Hallmark / Jan '97 / Carlton

HERITAGE-COLOSSUS STORY, THE
When we get married: *Dreamlovers* / Ain't nothing but a house party: *Showstoppers* / May I: *Deal, Bill & The Rhondells* / And suddenly: *Cherry People* / Ma belle Amie: *Tee Set* / Venus: *Shocking Blue* / Check yourself: *Italian Asphalt & Paving Co* / Little green bag: *Baker, George Selection* / Sooner I get to you: *Biddu* / Carolina on my mind: *Crystal Mansion* / Don't hang me up girl: *Cherry People* / I've been hurt: *Deal, Bill & The Rhondells* / Everything is beautiful: *Ross, Jerry* / You're gonna make it: *Festivals* / Give it to me: *Mob* / Venus: *Ross, Jerry* / Pick up my toys: *Devonnes* / What kind of fool do you think I am: *Deal, Bill & The Rhondells* / I dig everything about you: *Mob* / Goodnight my love: *Duprees*
CD ________ NEMCD 677
Sequel / Nov '94 / BMG

HEROES OF POP MUSIC, THE (2CD Set)
CD Set ________ 24004
Delta Doubles / Jun '96 / Target/BMG

HEROES OF ROCK 'N' ROLL (4CD Set)
Heartbreak hotel: *Presley, Elvis* / Long tall Sally: *Presley, Elvis* / I was the one: *Presley, Elvis* / Money Honey: *Presley, Elvis* / I got a woman: *Presley, Elvis* / Blue suede shoes: *Presley, Elvis* / Hound dog: *Presley, Elvis* / Baby let's play house: *Presley, Elvis* / Maybelline: *Presley, Elvis* / That's alright Mama: *Presley, Elvis* / Blue moon of Kentucky: *Presley, Elvis* / Good rockin' tonight: *Presley, Elvis* / Great balls of fire: *Lewis, Jerry Lee* / What'd I say: *Lewis, Jerry Lee* / Lucille: *Lewis, Jerry Lee* / Brown eyed handsome man: *Lewis, Jerry Lee* / Hey good lookin': *Lewis, Jerry Lee* / Roll over Beethoven: *Lewis, Jerry Lee* / Chantilly lace: *Lewis, Jerry Lee* / Little queenie: *Lewis, Jerry Lee* / Johnny B Goode: *Lewis, Jerry Lee* / No headstone on my grave: *Lewis, Jerry Lee* / Mexicali rose: *Lewis, Jerry Lee* / I'll find it where I can: *Lewis, Jerry Lee* / High school confidential: *Lewis, Jerry Lee* / Boogie woogie country man: *Lewis, Jerry Lee* / You are my sunshine: *Lewis, Jerry Lee* / Meat man: *Lewis, Jerry Lee* / Big legged woman: *Lewis, Jerry Lee* / Rockin' my life away: *Lewis, Jerry Lee* / Who's gonna play this old piano: *Lewis, Jerry Lee* / Whole lotta shakin' goin' on: *Lewis, Jerry Lee* / Blueberry hill: *Domino, Fats* / I'm ready: *Domino, Fats* / Ain't that a shame: *Domino, Fats* / My girl Josephine (hello Josephine): *Domino, Fats* / Blue monday: *Domino, Fats* / Jambalaya: *Domino, Fats* / What a price: *Domino, Fats* / I'm in the mood for love: *Domino, Fats* / Let the four winds blow: *Domino, Fats* / I want to walk you home: *Domino, Fats* / I'm gonna be a wheel someday: *Domino, Fats* / Whole lotta lovin': *Domino, Fats* / Dance with me Mr.Domino (Domino twist): *Domino, Fats* / Fat man: *Domino, Fats* / Please don't leave me: *Domino, Fats* / I'm in love again: *Domino, Fats* / Be my guest: *Domino, Fats* / Red sails in the sunset: *Domino, Fats* / Goin' home: *Domino, Fats* / Lucille: *Little Richard* / Long tall Sally: *Little Richard* / Whole lotta shakin' goin' on: *Little Richard* / Good golly miss molly: *Little Richard* / Tutti frutti: *Little Richard* / Rip it up: *Little Richard* / Keep a knockin': *Little Richard* / Jenny jenny: *Little Richard* / Girl can't help it: *Little Richard* / Slippin' and slidin': *Little Richard* / She's got it: *Little Richard* / Money honey: *Little Richard* / Groovy little Suzy: *Little Richard* / Talking 'bout soul: *Little Richard* / Baby face: *Little Richard* / Blueberry hill: *Little Richard* / Hound dog: *Little Richard* / Send me some lovin': *Little Richard*
CD Set ________ QUAD 016
Tring / Nov '96 / Tring

HET DAGHET INDEN OOSTEN (Bagpipes Of The Low Countries)
CD ________ PANCD 2025
Pan / May '97 / ADA / CM / Direct

HEX FILES VOL.1 (The Goth Bible - Compiled By Mick Mercer/2CD Set)
CD Set ________ 9040124
Nova Tekk / Apr '97 / Pinnacle

HEX FILES VOL.2 (2CD Set)
Pantomime Clown: *Damien Youth* / Souvenirs: *Life in Sodom* / Descend: *Falling Janus* / This is the only name: *Evidence* / Autumn song: *Darkside cowboys* / Suenos: *Nubis* / This empty ocean: *Love Like Blood* / Swollen head: *Gotterdammerung* / Glitter: *Suspiria* / Velvet fuck: *Trance To The Sun* / Lost inside: *Machine In The Garden* / New dress: *Cat fud* / Yesterday's gone: *Vendemian* / Aglon: *Rosa crux* / New Christ: *Gothic sex* / I'd like to feel: *Gothic sex* / return: *Engelsstaud* / Breath of de Sade: *Cruciform* / Magnet and the power: *Black Tape For A Blue Girl* / Nothing is real: *Veil of thorns* / Blind: *Messiah of pain* / Let me hold on: *Shroud* / Eyelid backspace poem: *Catastrophe ballet* / Final day: *Meridian* / Lucrezia: *Artica* / Your soul is not enough: *Lux solemnis* / Eden: *Sofia run* / Zennor: *Mothburner* / Oduarpa: *Ataraixa* / Wedding day: *Damien Youth*
CD Set ________ 9040324
Nova Tekk / Aug '97 / Pinnacle

HEXENTEXT
CD ________ CODE 1
Overground / Oct '94 / Shellshock/Disc / SRD

HEY BABY (The Rockin' South/30 Rockabilly Gems From Excello/Nasco)
Hey baby: *Ferrier, Al* / I'm the man: *Ferrier, Al* / Kiss a me quick: *Toombs, Jackson* / Big hearted Joe: *Lindsey Brothers* / Let's get down to business: *Lindsey Brothers* / Stealin' sugar: *Batts, Ray* / Somebody clipped your wings: *Haggard, Don & The Sunset Drifters* / Havin' a whole lot of fun: *Jano, Johnny* / I'd make a good man for you: *Jano, Johnny* / Trapped: *Fortune, Billy* / Bobby sox baby: *Harpo, Slim* / My baby's gone: *Jenkins, Bobby* / I'm out: *Surf Riders* / Little Andy: *Trent, Jackie* / Spellbound: *McGuire, Lowell* / Leave my girlie alone: *McGuire, Lowell* / Mama Mama Mama (look what your little boy's done): *Storm, Warren* / Swamp gal: *Bell, Tommy* / Little baby: *Facenda, Tommy* / It's love baby: *Monorays* / Werewolf: *Warren, Gary* / Shorty shorty: *Bob & Ray* / Troubles troubles: *Storm, Warren* / So long so long (goodbye goodbye): *Storm, Warren* / Honey bee (I love you): *Angel, Tommy* / Mama doll: *Teo, Roy* / Tell me: *Trends* / I'm a little boy (looking for love): *Storm, Warren*
CD ________ CDCHD 641
Ace / Apr '97 / Pinnacle

HEY DRAG CITY
CD ________ WIGCD 16
Domino / Oct '94 / Vital

HEY MARDI GRAS
CD ________ EDCD 7015
Easydisc / Feb '97 / Direct

HEY MOM, THE GARAGE IS ON MY FOOT
CD ________ DAMGOOD 102CD
Damaged Goods / Nov '96 / Shellshock/ Disc

HI AND EASY
Windy: *Mitchell, Willie* / Take five: *Mitchell, Willie* / Louie louie: *Mitchell, Willie* / I say a little prayer: *Mitchell, Willie* / Sunshine of your love: *Mitchell, Willie* / Singing the blues: *Cannon, Ace* / It's all in the game: *Cannon, Ace* / Never on sunday: *Cannon, Ace* / Somewhere my love: *Cannon, Ace* / Blowing in the wind: *Cannon, Ace* / Yesterday: *Cannon, Ace* / Michelle: *Cannon, Ace* / Hard day's night: *Black, Bill Combo* / Tea for two cha cha: *Black, Bill Combo* / Nadine: *Black, Bill Combo* / Johnny B Goode: *Black, Bill Combo* / Java: *Black, Bill Combo* / Deep in the heart of Texas: *Black, Bill Combo*
CD ________ HILOCD 20
Hi / Sep '96 / Pinnacle

HI GIRLS
You gotta take the bitter with the sweet: *Starks, Veniece* / What more do you want from me: *Starks, Veniece* / Step child: *Starks, Veniece* / Eighteen days: *Starks, Veniece* / Every now and then: *Starks, Veniece* / Trying to live my life without you: *Starks, Veniece* / I still love you: *Starks, Veniece* / Without a reason: *Janet & The Jays* / Hurting over you boy: *Janet & The Jays* / Love what you're doing to me: *Janet & The Jays* / Pleading for your love: *Janet & The Jays* / When the battle is over: *Joint Venture* / I'd rather hurt you now: *Joint Venture* / Quiet elegence: *Joint Venture* / Mama said: *Joint Venture* / I need love: *Joint Venture* / Love will make you feel better: *Joint Venture* / Your love is strange: *Joint Venture* / Roots of love: *Joint Venture* / Look at the boy: *Plum, Jean* / Here I go again: *Plum, Jean* / Pour on the lovin': *Plum, Jean* / You ask me: *Plum, Jean* / It's you that I need (Part 1): *Duncan Sisters* / Anyway the wind blows: *Coffee, Erma* / You made me what I am: *Coffee, Erma* / He's got it: *Known Facts* / How can I believe you: *Known Facts*
CD ________ HILOCD 7
Hi / Mar '94 / Pinnacle

HI RECORDS STORY, THE
CD ________ HIUKCD 101
Hi / Jul '89 / Pinnacle

HI RECORDS: THE EARLY YEARS VOL.1
Tootsie: *McVoy, Carl* / You are my sunshine / Little John's gone / Daydreaming / Skating in the blue light: *Charmettes* / You made a hit: *Fuller, Joe* / Please please: *Coburn, Kimball* / Teenage love / I'm so lonely: *Loyd, Jay B* / Going back to Memphis: *Simmons, Gene* / Lovin' Lil: *Tucker, Tommy* / Man in love: *Tucker, Tommy* / Millers cave: *Tucker, Tommy* / Stranger: *Tucker, Tommy* / Pipliner: *Reddell, Teddy* / Want to hold you: *Reddell, Teddy* / There was a time: *Reeder, Bill* / Till I Waltz again with you: *Reeder, Bill* / Judy: *Reeder, Bill* / Secret love: *Reeder, Bill* / Twenty six miles to Joliet: *Wallace, Darlen* / Smokie: *Black, Bill Combo*
CD ________ HIUKCD 127
Hi / Apr '92 / Pinnacle

HI RECORDS: THE EARLY YEARS VOL.2
My girl Josephine: *Jayes, Jerry* / Five miles from home: *Jayes, Jerry* / Middle of nowhere: *Jayes, Jerry* / Long black veil: *Jayes, Jerry* / Sugar bee: *Jayes, Jerry* / I'm in love again: *Jayes, Jerry* / I washed my hands in muddy water: *Jayes, Jerry* / Shackles and chains: *Tucker, Tommy* / I'm in love with a shadow: *Tucker, Tommy* / Wild side of life: *Tucker, Tommy* / Since I met you baby: *Felts, Narvel* / Dee Dee: *Felts, Narvel* / Eighty six miles: *Felts, Narvel* / Little bit of soap: *Felts, Narvel* / Dark shaded glasses: *Eldred, Charles* / Long tall texan: *Kellum, Murray & Rhythm Four* / I gotta leave this town: *Sutton, Glenn* / Shame, shame, shame: *Tucker, Tommy* / Listen to me lie: *Simmons, Gene* / Wedding bells: *Simmons,*

Gene / Invitation to the blues: *Simmons, Gene* / Time is right: *Lloyd, Jay B.* / Honey babe: *Arnold, Jerry* / Son of Smokie: *Black, Bill Combo* / Crank case: *Black, Bill Combo* / TD's boogie woogie: *Black, Bill Combo* / Deep elem blues: *Cannon, Ace & Bill Black's combo* / Sittin' tight: *Cannon, Ace*
CD ________ HIUKCD 128
Hi / Apr '92 / Pinnacle

HI-BIAS EXPERIENCE, THE
CD ________ CTR 20CDM
X-Treme / Mar '96 / Pinnacle / SRD

HI-BOP SKA
CD ________ 45019
Shanachie / Dec '94 / ADA / Greensleeves / Koch

HI-FI ROCK 'N' ROLL PARTY
Lights out: *Byrne, Jerry* / Roll hot rod roll: *McLollie, Oscar* / Runaround sue: *Dion* / Sea cruise: *Ford, Frankie* / Little bit of soap: *Jarmels* / Thinking of you: *Beasley, Jimmy* / Maybellene: *Walton, Mercy Dee* / Poetry in motion: *Tillotson, Johnny* / Tutti frutti: *Little Richard* / Wake up little Susie: *Everly Brothers* / Peanut butter: *Marathons* / Promised land: *Allan, Johnnie* / Wanderer: *Dion* / Deuces wild: *Wray, Link* / Hush-a-bye: *Mystics* / Teenager in love: *Dion & The Belmonts* / Lollipop: *Chordettes* / My true story: *Jive Five* / Goodnight my love: *Belvin, Jesse* / He's so fine: *Chiffons* / Way I like it: *Gunter, Shirley* / Reet petite: *Wilson, Jackie*
CD ________ CDCH 904
Ace / May '86 / Pinnacle

HI-FIDELITY HOUSE VOL.1
Theme from guidance: *Heard, Larry* / Wind on water: *Fresh & Low* / Opinion rated: *Wamdue Kids* / Echoes and instruments: *Wamdue Kids* / Karma: *Carlos, Don* / When the voices come: *Projekt PM.* / My planet rocks: *Abacus* / Groove: *Calysto* / Dope eyes: *I-Level* / Natural high: *Yost, Kevin*
CD ________ GDRC 501
Guidance / Mar '97 / RTM/Disc

HI-NRG HEAVEN (The Cream Of Hi-NRG)
Hi-energy: *Thomas, Evelyn* / So many men so little time: *Brown, Miquel* / Love I lost: *Seventh Avenue* / Sky high: *Jigsaw* / Emergency: *Pallas, Laura* / Catch me I'm falling in love: *Raven, Marsha* / I'm living my own life: *Raven, Marsha* / Visitors: *Moonstone* / Hit and run lover: *Jiani, Carol* / Frantic love: *Eastbound Expressway* / He's a saint, he's a sinner: *Brown, Miquel* / Action: *Pearly Gates* / Who knows what evil: *Man To Man* / Earthquake: *Benson, Vicki* / On a crowded street: *Pennington, Barbara* / Do you know the way to San Jose: *Croisette* / Masquerade: *Thomas, Evelyn* / Wanted for murder boys: *Boystown Gang* / This old heart of mine: *Morris, Gee* / Satisfy my desire: *Havana*
CD ________ SUMCD 4112
Sound & Media / Mar '97 / Sound & Media

HIDDEN BEAUTY
Sunshower: *Friedemann* / Baghdad: *Cook, Jesse* / Tree of life: *Rumbel, Nancy* / Magic forest: *Arkenstone, David* / Ancient legend: *Arkenstone, David* / Shape of her face: *Whalen, Michael* / Through the parched land: *Whalen, Michael* / Ancestor: *Roos, Randy* / Heartsounds: *Lanz, David* / Leaving home: *Mirowitz, Sheldon* / L'Accordion: *Mann, Brian* / Mil amores: *Cameron, Doug* / Long riders: *Souther, Richard*
CD ________ ND 63922
Narada / Mar '96 / ADA / New Note/ Pinnacle

HIDDEN ENGLISH
CD ________ TSCD 600
Topic / Oct '94 / ADA / CM / Direct

HIDDEN ROOMS
Jump MkII: *Studio Pressure* / Relics: *Studio Pressure* / Workout: *Klute* / Hidden rooms: *Sounds Of Life* / Currents: *Sounds Of Life* / Spice of jazz: *Sounds Of Life* / Wise movements: *Motive One* / FPOP: *Klute* / Right or wrong: *Klute* / Relics: *Studio Pressure* / Release the bells: *Sounds Of Life* / Presha III: *Sounds Of Life* / Funk 78 remix: *Motive One* / Technical wizardry: *Motive One*
CD ________ CERT18CD 001
Certificate 18 / Mar '97 / Prime / SRD / Vital

HIGH ATMOSPHERE
CD ________ ROUCD 0028
Rounder / Apr '95 / ADA / CM / Direct

HIGH ENERGY
CD ________ JHD 042
Tring / Jun '92 / Tring

HIGH GEAR
CD ________ VPCD 2059
Steely & Cleevie / May '97 / Jet Star

HIGH IN A BASEMENT
Full length: *Idjut Boys & LAJ* / Original disco motion: *Faze Action* / Downtime: *Paper music issue one* / Que tal America: *Man Called Adam* / Feel the warmth: *Reel Howze* / Chrystal wave: *Century Falls* / Rump funk: *DIY* / My sisters daughter: *House Of Wacks* / Zombie dawn: *Tranquil Elephantizer* / Jazz the sea turtle: *4AM* / Jihad: *Man Called Adam* / Big C: *Dawn* / Jazz fuk: *Idjut Boys & LAJ* / In the trees: *Faze Action*
CD ________ HVNLP 14CD
Heavenly / Aug '96 / 3mv/Pinnacle / BMG / Vital

HIGH ON DANCE
Baby, I love your way: *Big Mountain* / Twist and shout: *Chaka Demus & Pliers* / Sweets for my sweet: *Lewis, C.J.* / Sign: *Ace Of Base* / What is love: *Haddaway* / Moving on up: *M-People* / Mr. Vain: *Culture Beat* / It's my life: *Dr. Alban* / Real thing: *Di Bart, Tony* / Move on baby: *Cappella* / Here we go: *Stakka Bo* / Connected: *Stereo MC's* / Anything: *SWV* / Dreams: *Gabrielle* / Return to innocence: *Enigma* / Incredible: *M-Beat & General Levy* / Set the world on fire: *E-Type* / Penso positivo (Molella remix): *Jovanotti* / Got to give it up: *Masterboy* / Somewhere over the rainbow: *Marusha*
CD ________ 5251432
PolyGram TV / Oct '94 / PolyGram

HIGH PERFORMANCE
CD ________ MB 60082
Instinct Electronica / May '97 / Cargo

HIGH PLATEAUX SONGS (Music From Madagascar)
CD ________ PS 65096
PlayaSound / Oct '92 / ADA / Harmonia Mundi

HIGH STREET
Different world: *DJ Stix* / Forbidden territories: *Avenue A* / Adelphi's ladder: *Adelphi* / Jah weybridge: *Adelphi* / Imprint: *Blindside* / Mellow bug thunk: *Plastic Digger* / Greed: *Avenue A* / Boned: *Meat Katie* / Infix: *P-Method* / Silent partner: *Red Myers* / Weightless: *P-Method* / Palnet circus: *DJ Stix*
CD ________ KSRCD 1
Kingsize / Jun '97 / Mo's Music Machine / SRD

HIGH VOLTAGE BLUES
Nervous: *Dixon, Willie* / Tramp: *Fulson, Lowell* / Things that I used to do: *Guitar Slim* / Baby let's play house: *Gunter, Arthur* / Baby scratch my back: *Harpo, Slim* / I'm a King Bee: *Harpo, Slim* / I'm gonna quit you pretty baby: *Hogan, Silas* / Boogie chillen: *Hooker, John Lee* / I'm in the mood: *Hooker, John Lee* / Little boy blue: *Horton, Walter* / Riding in the moonlight: *Howlin' Wolf* / House rockin' boogie: *Howlin' Wolf* / Dust my blues: *James, Elmore* / Homesick James: *Homesick James* / Crosscut saw: *King, Albert* / Sweet little angel: *King, B.B.* / Rock me baby: *King, B.B.* / I'm a lover not a fighter: *Lazy Lester* / Rooster blues: *Lightnin' Slim* / I'm a mojo man: *Lonesome Sundown* / Little Johnny Taylor: *Taylor, Little Johnny* / Those lonely, lonely nights: *Watson, Johnny 'Guitar'*
CD ________ 3035900182
Essential Gold / Jul '96 / Carlton

HIGH VOLTAGE VOL.1
CD ________ RNCD 2091
Rhino / Mar '95 / Grapevine/PolyGram / Jet Star

HIGHLIFE (2CD Set)
CD Set ________ NDCD 025
Night & Day / Jan '97 / ADA / Direct / Discovery

HIGHLIGHTS FROM EDINBURGH TATTOO 1965-1979 (2CD Set)
Fanfare: *Royal Marines School Of Music* / My love she's but a lassie yet: *Massed Pipes & Drums* / Haughs o' Cromdale: *Massed Pipes & Drums* / Mrs. MacDougall: *Massed Pipes & Drums* / Angus McKinnon: *Massed Pipes & Drums* / Thunderbirds: *Massed Military Bands* / 633 squadron: *Massed Military Bands* / Burns on the march: *Massed Military Bands* / Scotland the brave: *Massed Military Bands* / Athol Highlanders: *Brigade Of Gurkhas* / Dear old donegal: *Brigade Of Gurkhas* / Lutzow's wild hunt: *Brigade Of Gurkhas* / Sirmoor rifles: *Brigade Of Gurkhas* / Barren rocks Aden: *Brigade Of Gurkhas* / Dundee city: *Brigade Of Gurkhas* / Get me to the church on time: *Corps Of Drums* / Wonderful Copenhagen: *Corps Of Drums* / Cock o' the North: *Massed Military Bands* / British Grenadiers: *Massed Military Bands* / Soldiers in the park: *Massed Military Bands* / Dovecote park: *Scots College Sydney* / Road to the Isles: *Scots College Sydney* / Meetings of the waters: *Scots College Sydney* / Old rustic bridge: *Scots College Sydney* / Highland cradle song: *Scots College Sydney* / Whistle o'er the lave o't: *Scots College Sydney* / Earl of Mansfield: *Scots College Sydney* / HM Jollies: *Massed Bands Of The Royal Marines* / Blaze of brass: *Massed Bands Of The Royal Marines* / Edinburgh castle: *Massed Bands Of The Royal Marines* / Life on the ocean wave: *Massed Bands Of The Royal Marines* / Prinz Carlmarsch: *Massed Pipes, Drums & Military Bands* / Caubeen trimmed with blue: *Massed Pipes, Drums & Military Bands* / Heart of oak: *Massed Pipes, Drums & Military Bands* / Royal artilary slow march: *Massed Pipes, Drums & Military Bands* / Abide with me: *Massed Pipes, Drums & Military Bands* / Royal artillery slow match: *Massed Pipes, Drums & Military Bands* / Royal artillery last post: *Massed Pipes, Drums & Military Bands* / Lament for Red Hector of the Battles lone piper: *Massed Pipes, Drums & Military Bands* / Zum staedtli hinavs: *Massed Pipes, Drums & Military Bands* / We're no awa' tae bide awa': *Massed Pipes, Drums & Military Bands* / Loch Lomond: *Massed Pipes, Drums & Military Bands*
CD Set ________ CDMFP 5993
Music For Pleasure / Jun '93 / EMI

HIGHLY RECOMMENDED
CD ________ FORMCD 3
Formation / Nov '95 / SRD

HIGHTONE RECORDS FIRST TEN YEARS SAMPLER, THE
CD ________ HCD 2002
Hightone / Jul '94 / ADA / Koch

HIGHWAY AND LANDSCAPE (Chill Out Classics & Ethereal Anthems/2CD Set)
Qualia: *Sun Electric* / Curiosity (what is it): *Molasses* / Ultraviolet: *International People's Gang* / Joy to the world: *T-Tauri* / Out of body experience: *Rabbit In The Moon* / Eric: *Amalgamation Of Soundz* / Teleport to origin: *Valleyman* / Emotive: *SLAM* / Funkyar: *Spacetime Continuum* / Fallen destiny: *Angel, Dave* / Sueno Plutino: *Pluto & Manuel Gottsching* / Earthshake: *Gas* / Pickyparkdickbods: *Solid Doctor* / On a rowing trip: *Valleyman* / V-chip: *Sie* / Transmit liberation: *Single Cell Orchestra* / Amazing discoveries: *Move D* / Collage of dreams: *Beltran, John* / Toast: *Q-Burns Abstract Message*
CD Set ________ SUB 48342
Distance / Jun '97 / 3mv/Sony / Prime

HILLBILLY FILLIES AND ROCKIN' CHICKS
Ten cats down: *Miller Sisters* / Welcome to the club: *Chapel, Jean* / I need a man: *Pittman, Barbara* / I wanna rock: *Holcolm, Patsy* / I won't be rockin' tonight: *Chapel, Jean* / You can't break the chains of love: *Miller Sisters* / Sentimental fool: *Pittman, Barbara* / Ain't got a worry: *Ballman, Wanda* / Heartbreak girl: *Ballman, Wanda* / Ooh that's good: *Holcolm, Patsy* / I can't show how I feel: *Wood, Anita* / Red velvet: *Kirby Sisters* / (I get the) Craziest feeling: *Kirby Sisters* / Two young fools in love: *Pittman, Barbara* / Memories of you: *Priesman, Magel* / Rock 'n' roll cinnamon tree: *Wimberly, Maggie Sue* / Jumpin' Jack: *Thomas, Cliff & Barbara* / Everlasting love: *Pittman, Barbara* / Voice of a fool: *Pittman, Barbara* / Just one day: *Pittman, Barbara* / No matter who's to blame: *Pittman, Barbara* / Call me anything but call me: *Wimberly, Maggie Sue* / Someday you will pay: *Miller Sisters* / There's no right way to do me wrong: *Miller Sisters* / Love is a stranger: *Sunrays* / Got you on my mind: *Miller Sisters* / I know I can't forget you but I'll try: *Miller Sisters* / You can tell me: *Miller Sisters* / How long can it be: *Wimberly, Maggie Sue*
CD ________ CPCD 8182
Charly / Jun '96 / Koch

HILLBILLY ROCK
Watchdog / Everybody's rockin' but me / Oh yeah / Roughneck blues / Red hen boogie / Too many / Get me on your mind / Hey, honey / Started out a walkin' hey Mae / Good deal Lucille / Looking for love / What's the use (I still love you) / I ain't gonna waste my time / Billy goat boogie / I've got a brand new baby / Start all over / Lonesome journey / Hey you there / No help wanted
CD ________ CDMF 034
Magnum Force / '91 / TKO Magnum

HILLS OF HOME: 25 YEARS OF FOLK MUSIC ON ROUNDER (2CD Set)
CD ________ ROUCDAN 16/17
Rounder / Jul '95 / ADA / CM / Direct

HIM DUB VOL.1
CD ________ SZCD 002
Surr Zema Musik / Mar '94 / Jet Star

HINDU CEREMONY AT MINAKSI-SUNDARESVARA TEMPLE, A
CD ________ VICG 53482
JVC World Library / Mar '96 / ADA / CM / Direct

HIP CITY
CD ________ LHCD 016
Luv n' Haight / Jul '96 / Timewarp

HIP HOP AND MORE
CD ________ 12610
Laserlight / Oct '95 / Target/BMG

HIP HOP DON'T STOP (27 Classic Hip Hop Super Jams/2CD Set)
I'm ready: *Caveman* / It takes two: *Rob Base & DJ E-Z Rock* / Peter piper: *Run DMC* / For those who like to groove: *Twin Hype* / Treat 'em right: *Chubb Rock* / Last night: *Kid 'n' Play* / Let it roll: *Lazy, Doug* / Mistadobilina: *Del Tha Funky Homosapien* / Dowatchulike: *Digital Underground* / OPP: *Naughty By Nature* / Eye know: *De La Soul* / Talkin' all that jazz: *Stetsasonic* / Who is it: *Mantronix* / Just to get a rep: *Gangstarr* / Message: *Grandmaster Flash* / Rappers delight: *Sugarhill Gang* / Jump around: *House Of Pain* / 900 number: *45 King* / I know you got soul: *Eric B & Rakim* / Have a nice day: *Shante, Roxanne* / Hold it now hit it: *Beastie Boys* / Paid in full: *Eric B & Rakim* / Know how: *Young MC* / Can I kick it: *Tribe Called Quest* / My philosophy: *BDP* / Back by dope demand: *King Bee* / Strong island: *JVC Force*
CD Set ________ SOLIDCD 006
CD Set ________ SOLIDSCD 006
Solid State / Jan '97 / Prime / Vital

HIP HOP DON'T STOP VOL.2 (2CD Set)
Bring the noize: *Public Enemy* / My definition: *Dream Warriors* / Breaks: *Blow, Kurtis* / I come off: *Young MC* / Follow the leader: *Eric B & Rakim* / Straight outta tha jungle: *Jungle Brothers* / Children's story: *Slick Rick* / Sucker MC's: *Run DMC* / It's my beat: *Sweet Tee & Jazzy Joyce* / Lovesick: *Gangstarr* / King of the beats: *Mantronix* / Express yourself: *NWA* / Strictly business: *EPMD* / Sound of the police: *KRS 1* / Left my wallet: *Tribe Called Quest* / Saturday night: *Schoolly D* / Just buggin': *Whistle* / Godfather: *Spoonie Gee* / 3 is the magic number: *De La Soul* / Hip hop hooray: *Naughty By Nature* / Humpty dance: *Digital Underground* / Planet rock: *Bambaataa, Afrika* / Mighty hard rocker: *Cash Money & Marvellous* / Don't scandalise mine: *Sugar Bear* / Travelling at the speed of thought: *Ultramagnetic MC's* / Hip hop bebop: *Man Parrish* / Adventures on the wheels of steel: *Grandmaster Flash*
CD Set ________ SOLIDCD 011
Solid State / Jul '97 / Prime / Vital

HIP HOP HURRAY
People every day: *Arrested Development* / Got to have your love: *Mantronix* / Mass appeal: *Gang Starr* / Moira Jane's Cafe: *Definition Of Sound* / Sugar hill: *AZ* / Back for more: *Cash Crew* / Georgia: *Klio* / Oregano flow: *Digital Underground* / Bonita applebum: *Tribe Called Quest* / Turn this mutha out: *MC Hammer* / PYT (playin young thugs): *Smooth featuring 2Pac* / I wish: *Skee Lo* / Nice and slow: *Redhead Kingpin* / '93 'til infinity: *Souls Of Mischief* / Monie in the middle: *Monie Love* / In my nature: *Nuttin' Nyce*
CD ________ DC 881362
Disky / Jul '97 / Disky / THE

HIP HOP PARADISE
CD ________ XPS 4CD
X-Treme / Feb '97 / Pinnacle / SRD

HIP HOP UNLIMITED
CD ________ ZYX 550712
ZYX / Jan '97 / ZYX

HIP IS HERE (A Hemisphere Sampler)
Yo no soy pilon de Machucar: *Rodriguez, Lalo* / De noite na cama: *Monteiro, Doris* / Verano porte am: *Garello, Raul* / Mirodia Kalokeriou: *Leonardou, Sotiria & Babis Stokis* / Orchestra replies: *Yosefa* / En el estribo: *Moreno, Gabriel* / Serevende: *Mapfumo, Thomas* / Rosa enjeitada: *De Noronha, Marie Teresa* / Ijex: *Nunes, Clara & Gilberto Gil* / Children come and go: *Poliker, Yehuda* / L'ombra della luce: *Battiato, Franco*
CD ________ HEMISCD 3
Hemisphere / Jun '97 / EMI

HIPPY HOUSE AND HAPPY HOP VOL.2
To the rhythm: *Dayglo, Johnny* / Manifesto: *Extasis* / Mainstream: *Sons of be-bop* / Aftertouch: *Prophet Five* / Let the good times roll: *Quiet Boys & Galliano* / Drop it: *MC Sleaze & Solid Gone* / Jack to this: *A Silent Way*
CD ________ JAZIDCD 054
Acid Jazz / Oct '92 / Disc

HIPPYDIP (2CD Set)
Gimme dat harp boy: *Captain Beefheart* / My dark hour: *Miller, Steve* / It takes a lot to laugh it takes a train to cry: *Russell, Leon* / Rag mamma rag: *Band* / Down in Texas: *Hourglass* / I got love if you want it: *Winter, Johnny* / Little games: *Yardbirds* / Shape of things: *Beck, Jeff Group* / Happy birthday: *Idle Race* / Walking down their outlook: *High Tide* / 10538: *ELO* / Speed king: *Deep Purple* / Machines: *Lothar & The Hand People* / Out demons out: *Broughton, Edgar Band* / Songs from the bottom of a well: *Ayers, Kevin* / Octupus: *Barrett, Syd* / Mona: *Quicksilver Messenger Service* / I'm going home: *Ten Years After* / Shake some action: *Flamin' Groovies* / Clifton in the rain: *Stewart, Al* / Superlungs my supergirl: *Reid, Terry* / Trip: *Donovan* / Mockingbird: *Harvest, James* / Leaving my home: *TIME* / Cherry red: *Groundhogs* / Evil woman: *Canned Heat* / Can blue men sing the whites: *Bonzo Dog Band* / Country girl: *Schwarz, Brinsley* / Mythical kings and iguanas: *Previn, Dory* / Wall: *Haphash & The Coloured Coat* / Hang on to a dream: *Gandalf* / Living in the past: *Jethro Tull* / Daughter of the fireplace: *Man* / Seven by seven: *Hawkwind* / Do ya: *Move* / Sylvia: *Focus*
CD Set ________ CDEM 1623
EMI / Jul '97 / EMI

HISTORICAL CD OF DIGITAL SOUND SYNTHESIS 1957-1966
CD ________ WER 2033
Wergo / Feb '96 / ADA / Cadillac / Harmonia Mundi

HISTORY OF BRITISH POP, THE (2CD Set)
Do wah diddy diddy: *Manfred Mann* / I like it: *Gerry & The Pacemakers* / I'm telling you now: *Freddie & The Dreamers* / Bad to me: *Kramer, Billy J. & The Dakotas* / I'm the urban spaceman: *Bonzo Dog Band* / Got to get you into my life: *Bennett, Cliff & The Rebel Rousers* / Don't let me be misunderstood: *Animals* / Tobacco Road: *Nashville*

Teens / Shakin' all over: *Kidd, Johnny & The Pirates* / Hippy hippy shake: *Swinging Blue Jeans* / Dandy: *Herman's Hermits* / Stop stop stop: *Hollies* / Bus stop: *Hollies* / Pretty flamingo: *Manfred Mann* / World without love: *Peter & Gordon* / Boat that I row: *Lulu* / Do you want to know a secret: *Kramer, Billy J. & The Dakotas* / Good golly Miss Molly: *Swinging Blue Jeans* / Super girl: *Bonney, Graham* / You were made for me: *Freddie & The Dreamers* / I'm into something good: *Herman's Hermits* / Walkin' back to happiness: *Shapiro, Helen* / You'll never walk alone: *Gerry & The Pacemakers* / Bring it on home to me: *Animals*
CD Set ______________ 24349
Laserlight / Mar '97 / Target/BMG

HISTORY OF CANADIAN 80'S GARAGE PUNK AND SURF
CD ______________ STOMP 008
Stomp / Jan '97 / Pinnacle

HISTORY OF CARNIVAL 1929-1939
CD ______________ MBCD 3012
Matchbox / Feb '93 / Cadillac / CM / Jazz Music / Roots

HISTORY OF CHESS JAZZ, THE (2CD Set)
Poinciana: *Jamal, Ahmad* / My main man: *Stitt, Sonny & Benny Green* / Shaw' nuff: *Rodney, Red* / Killer Joe: *Jazztet* / Man I love: *Sims, Zoot* / Soul station: *Kirk, Rahsaan Roland* / Parker's mood: *Moody, James* / Keep on keepin' on: *Herman, Woody* / Gotta travel on: *Bryant, Ray* / Benny rides again: *Goodman, Benny* / My love has butterfly wings: *Klemmer, John* / At last: *James, Etta* / In crowd: *Lewis, Ramsey* / Ornithology: *Harris, Barry* / Last train from Overbrook: *Moody, James* / My foolish heart: *Ammons, Gene* / Baltimore oriole: *Alexandria, Lorez* / Bientot: *Nelson, Oliver* / Morning (excerpt): *Lateef, Yusef* / Mellow yello: *Brown, Odell & The Organizers* / Tonk: *Farmer, Art* / You're my thrill: *Jacquet, Illinois* / House warmin': *McGhee, Howard* / Tiny's blues: *Jackson, Chubby* / Candy: *Terry, Clark* / Touch: *Golson, Benny* / Silent night: *Burrell, Kenny*
CD Set ______________ GRP 2812
GRP / Feb '96 / New Note/BMG

HISTORY OF COUNTRY MUSIC - THE 1940S VOL.1 (2CD Set)
Bouquet of roses: *Arnold, Eddy* / When it's lamplighting time in the valley: *Ritter, Tex* / Guitar polka: *Dexter, Al* / Smoke on the water: *Foley, Red* / I'm biting my fingernails and thinking of you: *Tubb, Ernest & Andrews Sisters* / At mail call today: *Autry, Gene* / Detour: *Willing, Foy* / Prodigal son: *Acuff, Roy* / Lovesick blues: *Williams, Hank* / No letter today: *Daffan, Ted & The Texans* / Each night at nine: *Tillman, Floyd* / I'll hold you in my heart: *Arnold, Eddy* / I want to be a cowboy's sweetheart: *Allen, Rosalie* / Soldier's last letter: *Tubb, Ernest* / Shame on you: *Cooley, Spade* / Pistol packin' mama: *Dexter, Al* / New Spanish two-step: *Wills, Bob & His Texas Playboys* / Riders in the sky: *Monroe, Vaughan* / New San Antonio rose: *Wills, Bob & His Texas Playboys* / It's been so long Darling: *Tubb, Ernest* / Waltz of the wind: *Acuff, Roy* / It's a sin: *Arnold, Eddy* / Cool water: *Sons Of The Pioneers* / They took the stars out of heaven: *Tillman, Floyd* / New Jole blonde: *Foley, Red* / There's a new moon over my shoulder: *Javis, Jimmie* / Someday you'll want me to want you: *Britt, Elton* / Candy kisses: *Morgan, George* / I'll forgive you, but I can't forget: *Acuff, Roy* / Sugar moon: *Wills, Bob & His Texas Playboys* / Rainbow at midnight: *Tubb, Ernest* / Deep in the heart of Texas: *Autry, Gene* / Wedding bells: *Williams, Hank* / Tennessee saturday night: *Foley, Red* / Don't rob another man's castle: *Arnold, Eddy* / Pistol packin' mama: *Crosby, Bing & Andrews Sisters*
CD Set ______________ KNEWCD 715
Kenwest / Mar '93 / THE

HISTORY OF COUNTRY MUSIC - THE 1940S VOL.2 (2CD Set)
CD Set ______________ KNEWCD 716
Kenwest / Jan '93 / THE

HISTORY OF COUNTRY MUSIC - THE 1950S VOL.1 (2CD Set)
Crazy arms: *Price, Ray* / Rumba boogie: *Snow, Hank* / Let old mother nature have her way: *Smith, Carl* / Jambalaya: *Williams, Hank* / Always late (With your kisses): *Frizzell, Lefty* / Gambler's guitar: *Draper, Rusty* / Chattanooga shoe shine boy: *Foley, Red* / I take the chance: *Browns* / In the jailhouse now: *Pierce, Webb* / Cattle call: *Arnold, Eddy* / White lightning: *Jones, George* / It wasn't God who made honky tonk angels: *Wells, Kitty* / Slow poke: *King, Pee Wee* / Mexican Joe: *Reeves, Jim* / So many times: *Acuff, Roy* / Singin' the blues: *Robbins, Marty* / Golden rocket: *Snow, Hank* / Blue suede shoes: *Perkins, Carl* / Story of my life: *Robbins, Marty* / I let the stars get in my eyes: *Hill, Goldie* / Let me go, lover: *Snow, Hank* / Four walls: *Reeves, Jim* / I wanna play house with you: *Arnold, Eddy* / Don't just stand there: *Smith, Carl* / I want to be with you always: *Frizzell, Lefty* / Birmingham bounce: *Foley, Red* / I forgot more than you'll ever know: *Davis Sisters* / There you go: *Cash, Johnny* / Hey Sheriff: *Rusty & Doug* / Your cheatin' heart: *Williams, Hank* / When it's springtime in Alaska: *Horton, Johnny* / City light: *Price, Ray* / Why baby why: *Pierce, Webb & Red Sovine* / Blue blue day: *Gibson, Don* / I walk the line: *Cash, Johnny* / One by one: *Wells, Kitty & Red Foley*
CD Set ______________ KNEWCD 717
Kenwest / Mar '93 / THE

HISTORY OF COUNTRY MUSIC - THE 1950S VOL.2 (2CD Set)
CD Set ______________ KNEWCD 718
Kenwest / Jan '93 / THE

HISTORY OF COUNTRY MUSIC - THE 1960S VOL.1 (2CD Set)
CD Set ______________ KNEWCD 719
Kenwest / Mar '93 / THE

HISTORY OF COUNTRY MUSIC - THE 1960S VOL.2 (2CD Set)
CD Set ______________ KNEWCD 720
Kenwest / Jan '93 / THE

HISTORY OF COUNTRY MUSIC - THE 1970S VOL.1 (2CD Set)
Kiss an angel good morning: *Pride, Charley* / Hello darlin': *Twitty, Conway* / I ain't never: *Tillis, Mel* / Happiest girl in the whole USA: *Fargo, Donna* / All for the love of sunshine: *Williams, Hank Jr.* / Chantilly lace: *Lewis, Jerry Lee* / Country bumpkin: *Smith, Carl* / Wasted days and wasted nights: *Fender, Freddy* / Riding my thumb to Mexico: *Rodriguez, Johnny* / Year that Clayton Delaney died: *Hall, Tom T.* / Only one love in my life: *Milsap, Ronnie* / On my knees: *Rich, Charlie & Janie Frickie* / Luckenbach, Texas (Back to the basics of love): *Jennings, Waylon* / Lizzie and the rainman: *Tucker, Tanya* / She never knew me: *Williams, Don* / Hey won't you play another somebody done somebody wrong song: *Thomas, B.J.* / Georgia on my mind: *Nelson, Willie* / Here you come again: *Parton, Dolly* / Rose garden: *Anderson, Lynn* / watermelon wine: *Hall, Tom T.* / Linda on my mind: *Twitty, Conway* / There must be more to love than this: *Lewis, Jerry Lee* / Most beautiful girls: *Rich, Charlie* / Coca cola cowboy: *Tillis, Mel* / Teddy bear song: *Fairchild, Barbara* / I'm a ramblin' man: *Jennings, Waylon* / Eleven roses: *Williams, Hank Jr.* / Rub it in: *Craddock, Billy* / Golden tears: *Dave & Sugar* / You're my best friend: *Williams, Don* / Sunday morning coming down: *Cash, Johnny* / El paso city: *Robbins, Marty* / Coal miner's daughter: *Lynn, Loretta* / Blue eyes cryin' in the rain: *Nelson, Willie* / You can't be a beacon (If your lights don't shine): *Fargo, Donna* / Secret love: *Fender, Freddy*
CD Set ______________ KNEWCD 721
Kenwest / Mar '93 / THE

HISTORY OF COUNTRY MUSIC - THE 1970S VOL.2 (2CD Set)
Tulsa time: *Williams, Don* / I can help: *Swan, Billy* / You've never been this far before: *Twitty, Conway* / Satin sheets: *Pruett, Jeanne* / Jolene: *Parton, Dolly* / Soul song: *Stampley, Joe* / Grand tour: *Jones, George* / Funny face: *Fargo, Donna* / Why me: *Kristofferson, Kris* / Are you sure Hank done it this way: *Jennings, Waylon* / Would you lay with me: *Tucker, Tanya* / Before the next teardrop falls: *Fender, Freddy* / Blue skies: *Nelson, Willie* / How can I unlove you: *Anderson, Lynn* / Good woman blues: *Tillis, Mel* / It was almost like a song: *Milsap, Ronnie* / Behind closed doors: *Rich, Charlie* / Take this job and shove it: *Paycheck, Johnny* / PS I love you: *Hall, Tom T.* / It's gonna take a little bit longer: *Pride, Charley* / I will always love you: *Parton, Dolly* / Paper roses: *Osmond, Marie* / Fifteen years ago: *Twitty, Conway* / Some broken hearts never mend: *Williams, Don* / I won't mention it again: *Price, Ray* / Bedtime story: *Wynette, Tammy* / Amanda: *Jennings, Waylon* / One piece at a time: *Cash, Johnny* / Ruby baby: *Craddock, Billy* / When the snow is on the roses: *James, Sonny* / I'm just me: *Pride, Charley* / You'll lose a good thing: *Fender, Freddy* / When you're hot, you're hot: *Reed, Jerry* / Door is always open: *Dave & Sugar* / Do you know you are my sunshine: *Statler Brothers* / You always come back: *Rodriguez, Johnny*
CD Set ______________ KNEWCD 722
Kenwest / Jan '93 / THE

HISTORY OF COUNTRY MUSIC - THE 1980S VOL.1 (2CD Set)
Nine to Five: *Parton, Dolly* / City of New Orleans: *Nelson, Willie* / Love in the first degree: *Alabama* / Dukes of Hazzard: *Jennings, Waylon* / Thank god for the radio: *Kendalls* / My heart: *Milsap, Ronnie* / She got the goldmine (I got the shaft): *Reed, Jerry* / True love ways: *Gilley, Mickey* / Seven year ache: *Cash, Rosanne* / I believe in you: *Williams, Don* / Give me wings: *Johnson, Michael* / You look so good in love: *Strait, George* / He's back and I'm blue: *Desert Rose Band* / Goin' gone: *Mattea, Kathy* / Whatever happened to old fashioned love: *Thomas, B.J.* / Fire I can't put out: *Strait, George* / I wouldn't change you if I could: *Skaggs, Ricky* / Can't stop my heart from loving you: *O'Kanes* / Have mercy: *Judds* / Lost in the fifties tonight: *Milsap, Ronnie* / My heroes have always been cowboys: *Nelson, Willie* / Somebody lied: *Shelton, Ricky Van* / Cajun moon: *Skaggs, Ricky* / He stopped loving her today: *Jones, George* / Bobbie Sue: *Oak Ridge Boys* / Fourteen carat mind: *Watson, Gene* / Never been so loved (In all my life): *Pride, Charley* / Older women: *McDowell, Ronnie* / Drifter: *Sylvia* / Wanderer: *Rabbitt, Eddie* / I'll still be loving you: *Restless Heart* / I think I'll just stay here and drink: *Haggard, Merle* / Radio heart: *McClain, Charly* / Common man: *Conlee, John* / Take me down: *Alabama* / Elizabeth: *Statler Brothers*
CD Set ______________ KNEWCD 723
Kenwest / Mar '93 / THE

HISTORY OF COUNTRY MUSIC - THE 1980S VOL.2 (2CD Set)
CD Set ______________ KNEWCD 724
Kenwest / Jan '93 / THE

HISTORY OF DANCE VOL.1, A (1978)
Keep on jumpin': *Musique* / Boogie oogie oogie: *Taste Of Honey* / Galaxy: *War* / British hustle: *Hi-Tension* / You make me feel (mighty real): *Sylvester* / Now that we've found love: *Third World* / Galaxy of love: *Crown Heights Affair* / Eve of the war: *Wayne, Jeff* / Disco nights (rock freak): *GQ* / Instant replay: *Hartman, Dan* / Hit me with yor rhythm stick: *Dury, Ian & The Blockheads* / I thought it was you: *Hancock, Herbie*
CD ______________ CDOVD 474
Virgin / Jun '97 / EMI

HISTORY OF DANCE VOL.1, THE (1959-1979 - 5CD Set)
Shout: *Isley Brothers* / Green onions: *Booker T & The MG's* / Walking the dog: *Thomas, Rufus* / Knock on wood: *Floyd, Eddie* / Soul finger: *Bar-Kays* / Sweet soul music: *Conley, Arthur* / Chain of fools: *Franklin, Aretha* / Do the funky chicken: *Thomas, Rufus* / Family affair: *Sly & The Family Stone* / Could it be I'm falling in love: *Detroit Spinners* / Sound your funky horn: *KC & The Sunshine Band* / Satisfaction guaranteed: *Melvin, Harold & The Bluenotes* / Walking in rhythm: *Blackbyrds* / Get up offa that thing: *Brown, James* / Funky weekend: *Stylistics* / Movin': *Brass Construction* / Can't get by without you: *Real Thing* / Car wash: *Royce, Rose* / Do what you wanna do: *T-Connection* / Darlin' darlin' baby: *O'Jays* / Free: *Williams, Deniece* / If I can't have you: *Elliman, Yvonne* / I love the nightlife: *Bridges, Alicia* / Take that to the bank: *Shalamar* / September: *Earth, Wind & Fire* / Groove line: *Heatwave* / I want your love: *Chic* / Backstrokin': *Fatback Band* / Locomotion: *Little Eva* / Tell him: *Exciters* / Time is on my side: *Thomas, Irma* / Um um um um um um: *Major Lance* / In the midnight hour: *Pickett, Wilson* / Rescue me: *Bass, Fontella* / See saw: *Covay, Don* / Papa's got a brand new bag: *Brown, James* / Recovery: *Bass, Fontella* / Mustang Sally: *Pickett, Wilson* / B-A-B-Y: *Thomas, Carla* / I got you (I feel good): *Brown, James* / Satisfaction: *Redding, Otis* / Soul man: *Sam & Dave* / Hard to handle: *Redding, Otis* / Who's making love: *Taylor, Johnny* / Soul serenade: *Mitchell, Willie* / Time is tight: *Booker T & The MG's* / Move on up: *Mayfield, Curtis* / Hey girl don't bother me: *Tams* / Walking in the rain with the one I love: *Love Unlimited Orchestra* / Where did our love go: *Elbert, Donnie* / Little bit of leather: *Elbert, Donnie* / Nutbush City limits: *Turner, Ike & Tina* / Why can't we live together: *Thomas, Timmy* / Respect yourself: *Staple Singers* / Love on a mountain top: *Knight, Robert* / Rock your baby: *McCrae, George* / Love's theme: *Love Unlimited Orchestra* / TSOP (The sound of Philadelphia): *MFSB & Three Degrees* / Ms. Grace: *Tymes* / Zing went the strings of my heart: *Trammps* / Can't get enough of your love babe: *White, Barry* / Thanks for saving my life: *Paul, Billy* / Kissing in the back row of the movies: *Drifters* / Foot stompin' music: *Bohannon, Hamilton* / Once you get started: *Rufus & Chaka Khan* / Expansions: *Smith, Lonnie Liston* / I'll go where your music takes me: *James, Jimmy & The Vagabonds* / Dr. Love: *Charles, Tina* / Don't take away the music: *Tavares* / Who'd she coo: *Ohio Players* / Midnight train to Georgia: *Knight, Gladys & The Pips* / Dance little lady: *Charles, Tina* / Party time: *Fatback Band* / Change (makes you want to hustle): *Byrd, Donald* / Love me: *Elliman, Yvonne* / Bottle: *Scott-Heron, Gil* / Saturday night: *Earth, Wind & Fire* / Whodunnit: *Tavares* / Shake your rump to the funk: *Bar-Kays* / Once I've been there: *Connors, Norman* / Shake your groove thing: *Peaches & Herb* / Let's start the dance: *Bohannon, Hamilton* / Jack and Jill: *Raydio* / Love don't live here anymore: *Rose Royce* / You make me feel (mighty real): *Sylvester* / Let the music play: *Earland, Charles* / Do you want to get funky with me: *Brown, Peter* / Sugar pie guy: *Joneses* / Street life: *Crusaders* / Too hot: *Kool & The Gang* / Second time around: *Shalamar* / Boogie town: *Fat Larry's Band* / Please don't go: *KC & The Sunshine Band* / Runner: *Three Degrees* / Fire: *Pointer Sisters* / Contact: *Starr, Edwin* / I haven't stopped dancing yet: *Gonzales* / Reunited: *Peaches & Herb* / We got the funk: *Positive Force* / Stomp: *Brothers Johnson*
CD Set ______________ DBOX 001
Connoisseur Collection / Dec '96 / Pinnacle

HISTORY OF DANCE VOL.2, A (1979)
Ladies night: *Kool & The Gang* / Looking for love tonight: *Fat Larry's Band* / Contact: *Starr, Edwin* / Get down: *Chandler, Gene* / Heart of glass: *Blondie* / I will survive: *Gaynor, Gloria* / All this love I'm giving: *McCrae, Gwen* / Stomp: *Brothers Johnson* / Rapper's delight: *Sugarhill Gang* / Boogie wonderland: *Earth, Wind & Fire* / This time baby: *Moore, Jackie* / It's a disco night: *Isley Brothers*
CD ______________ CDOVD 475
Virgin / Jun '97 / EMI

HISTORY OF DANCE VOL.2, THE (1980-1992 - 5CD Set)
Check out the groove: *Thurston, Bobby* / Brazilian love affair: *Duke, George* / Can you handle it: *Redd, Sharon* / Risin' to the top (give it all you got): *Burke, Keni* / You're the one for me: *D-Train* / Zoom: *Fat Larry's Band* / Last night a DJ saved my life: *Indeep* / Hold me tighter in the rain: *Griffin, Billy* / Sweet somebody: *Shannon* / Trapped: *Abrams, Colonel* / Solid: *Ashford & Simpson* / Tossing and turning: *Windjammer* / Finest: *SOS Band* / Love supreme: *Downing, Will* / My perogative: *Brown, Bobby* / Going back to my roots: *FPI Project & Rich In Paradise/ Sharon Dee Clark* / Heaven: *Chimes* / Wash your face in my sink: *Dream Warriors* / Got to have your love: *Mantronix & Wondress* / Power: *Snap* / Finally: *Peniston, Ce Ce* / How can I love you more: *M-People* / Love power: *Vandross, Luther* / Sensitivity: *Tresvant, Ralph* / Key, the secret: *Urban Cookie Collective* / In the thick of it: *Russell, Brenda* / Thighs high (grip your hips and move): *Browne, Tom* / I don't want to be a freak (but I can't help myself): *Dynasty* / Use it up and wear it out: *Odyssey* / Casanova: *Coffee* / Stop to love: *Vandross, Luther* / Gangsters of the groove: *Heatwave* / Intuition: *Linx* / It's a love thing: *Whispers* / Jitterbuggin': *Heatwave* / Body talk: *Imagination* / Love come down: *King, Evelyn 'Champagne'* / Love's comin' at ya: *Moore, Melba* / I can make you feel good: *Shalamar* / Suspicious minds: *Staton, Candi* / Dead giveaway: *Shalamar* / I'm so excited: *Pointer Sisters* / Give it up: *KC & The Sunshine Band* / Dancing tight: *Fearon, Phil & Galaxy* / I just gotta have you (lover turn me on): *Kashif* / Watching you watching me: *Grant, David* / I am somebody: *Jones, Glenn* / You can't hide (your love from me): *Joseph, David* / Do it again/Billie Jean: *Club House* / Just be good to me: *SOS Band* / Prime time: *Mtume* / Let's hear it for the boy: *Williams, Deniece* / You get the best from me: *Myers, Alicia* / Backfield in motion: *JB's Allstars* / Somebody else's guy: *Brown, Jocelyn* / Round and round: *Graham, Jaki* / Axel F: *Faltermeyer, Harold* / Body and soul: *Mai Tai* / Let's talk: *One Way* / Romeo where's Juliet: *Collage* / Who's zoomin' who: *Franklin, Aretha* / Mr. DJ: *Concept* / Oh Sheila: *Ready For The World* / History: *Mai Tai* / We don't have to take our clothes off: *Stewart, Jermaine* / Rain: *Jones, Oran 'Juice'* / Don't waste my time: *Hardcastle, Paul* / You can't blame love: *Thomas & Taylor* / Headlines: *Midnight Star* / Looking for a new love: *Watley, Jody* / Rock steady: *Whispers* / Jingo: *Jellybean* / FLM: *Mel & Kim* / Sho' you right: *White, Barry* / Wet my whistle: *Midnight Star* / Girlfriend: *Pebbles* / Dreaming: *Goldsmith, Glen* / Roses are red: *Mac Band* / Don't be cruel: *Brown, Bobby* / Indestructible: *Four Tops* / Tell it to my heart: *Dayne, Taylor* / Good life: *Inner City* / Touch me: *49ers* / Respect: *Adeva* / I need your lovin': *Williams, Alyson* / 1-2-3: *Chimes* / Venus: *Don Pablo's Animals* / Lover in me: *Easton, Sheena* / Poison: *Bel Biv Devoe* / Don't go messin' with my heart: *Mantronix* / Killer: *Adamski* / Fantasy: *Black Box* / Natural thing: *Innocence* / Everybody's free (to feel good): *Rozalla* / Where love lives: *Limerick, Alison* / Another sleepless night: *Christopher, Shawn* / (I wanna give you) devotion: *Nomad & MC Mikee Freedom* / Such a good feeling: *Brothers In Rhythm* / Are you ready to fly: *Rozalla* / Feel so high: *Des'ree*
CD Set ______________ DBOX 002
Connoisseur Collection / Dec '96 / Pinnacle

HISTORY OF DANCE VOL.3, A (1980)
Just a touch of love: *Slave* / Let's go round again: *Average White Band* / And the beat goes on: *Whispers* / I shoulda loved ya: *Walden, Myron* / Celebration: *Kool & The Gang* / I owe you one: *Shalamar* / Don't stop the music: *Yarbrough & Peoples* / OOps upside your head: *Gap Band* / Taste of bitter love: *Knight, Gladys* / Walk in the park: *Straker, Nick Band* / Breaks: *Blow, Kurtis*
CD ______________ CDOVD 476
Virgin / Jun '97 / EMI

HISTORY OF DANCE VOL.4, A (1981)
I'm in love: *King, Evelyn 'Champagne'* / Girls om film: *Duran Duran* / Rapture: *Blondie* / Chant no.1 (I don't need this pressure on): *Spandau Ballet* / Tears are not enough: *ABC* / Favourite shirts (boys meets girl): *Spandau Ballet* / Love action (I believe in love): *Human League* / Going back to my roots: *Odyssey* / Pull up to the bumper: *Jones, Grace* / Body talk: *Imagination* / Let's groove: *Earth, Wind & Fire* / Never too much: *Vandross, Luther*
CD ______________ CDOVD 477
Virgin / Jun '97 / EMI

HISTORY OF DUB: THE GOLDEN AGE
CD ______________ MRMCD 10
Munich / Jul '96 / ADA / CM / Direct / Greensleeves

HISTORY OF HARDCORE, A
CD ______ JOINT 3CD
Suburban Base/Moving Shadow / Nov '95 / SRD

HISTORY OF JAMAICAN VOCAL HARMONY, A
CD ______ MRMCD 11
Munich / Jul '96 / ADA / CM / Direct / Greensleeves

HISTORY OF POP 1958-1965 (2CD Set)
CD Set ______ MBSCD 424
Castle / Nov '93 / BMG

HISTORY OF POP 1966-1973 (2CD Set)
CD Set ______ MBSCD 425
Castle / Nov '93 / BMG

HISTORY OF POP 1974-1982 (2CD Set)
CD Set ______ MBSCD 426
Castle / Nov '93 / BMG

HISTORY OF POP MUSIC
CD ______ HRCD 8019
Disky / Mar '93 / Disky / THE

HISTORY OF PUNK VOL.1, A
God save the Queen: *Sex Pistols* / Sex and drugs and rock 'n' roll: *Dury, Ian* / King Rocker: *Generation X* / Shot by both sides: *Magazine* / Day the world turned day glo: *X-Ray Spex* / Rich Kids: *Rich Kids* / Love song: *Damned* / Don't dictate: *Penetration* / Into the valley: *Skids* / Automatic lover: *Vibrators* / Peaches: *Stranglers* / Babylon's burning: *Ruts* / Satisfaction (I can't get me no): *Devo* / Typical girls: *Slits* / Ever fallen in love: *Buzzcocks* / Kill the poor: *Dead Kennedys* / Jilted John: *Jilted John* / Hersham boys: *Sham 69* / Do anything you wanna do: *Eddie & The Hot Rods* / Eton rifles: *Jam*
CD ______ CDOVD 486
Virgin / Jun '97 / EMI

HISTORY OF PUNK VOL.2, A
Deutscher girls: *Adam & The Ants* / Sound of the suburbs: *Members* / Take me I'm yours: *Squeeze* / Public Image: *Public Image Ltd* / At the edge: *Stiff Little Fingers* / All around the world: *Jam* / I just can't be happy today: *Damned* / I'm in love with a German film star: *Passions* / Life in a day: *Simple Minds* / Controversial subject: *The The* / Mannequin: *Wire* / Baby let's play house: *Sweet, Rachel* / Nellie the elephant: *Sweet, Rachel* / Banana splits: *Dickies* / Lucky number: *Lovich, Lena* / Dead cities: *Exploited* / Cruisers creek: *Fall* / Money: *Flying Lizards* / Airport: *Motors* / Science friction: *XTC*
CD ______ CDOVD 487
Virgin / Jun '97 / EMI

HISTORY OF SKA (3CD Set)
CD Set ______ CLP 9986
Cleopatra / Jun '97 / Cargo / Greyhound / Plastic Head / RTM/Disc / SRD

HISTORY OF SKA VOL.1, THE
CD ______ LG 21060
Lagoon / Mar '93 / Grapevine/PolyGram

HISTORY OF SKA VOL.2, THE
CD ______ LG 21097
Lagoon / May '94 / Grapevine/PolyGram

HISTORY OF TECHNO, THE (4CD Set)
CD Set ______ ZYX 740042
ZYX / Nov '96 / ZYX

HISTORY OF THE BLUES (2CD Set)
Boogie chillun: *Hooker, John Lee* / Dimples: *Hooker, John Lee* / Little rain: *Reed, Jimmy* / Where can you be: *Reed, Jimmy* / Diggin' my potatoes: *Memphis Slim* / Boll weevil blues: *Leadbelly* / In New Orleans: *Leadbelly* / Sometimes she will: *Hopkins, Lightnin'* / It's my own fault baby: *King, B.B.* / How many more times you gonna dog me around: *Brookes, Robert C. & The Dan Band* / Hey now: *Charles, Ray* / I'm wonderin' I'm wonderin': *Charles, Ray* / On the road again: *Brookes, Robert C. & The Dan Band* / Send me to the 'lectric chair: *Smith, Bessie* / Careless love: *Smith, Bessie* / Fine and mellow: *Holiday, Billie* / Georgia on my mind: *Holiday, Billie* / Ain't nobody's business if I do: *Brookes, Robert C. & The Dan Band* / Terraplane blues: *Brookes, Robert C. & The Dan Band* / Dust my broom: *James, Elmore* / I believe: *James, Elmore* / Glory be: *Hopkins, Lightnin'* / Iodine in my coffee: *Waters, Muddy* / I'm glad I'm living: *Waters, Muddy* / I can't call her sugar: *Waters, Muddy* / Commit a crime: *Howlin' Wolf* / My mind is ramblin': *Howlin' Wolf* / Hold onto your money: *Howlin' Wolf* / Rollin' and tumblin': *Waters, Muddy* / I can't be satisfied: *Waters, Muddy* / Sadie: *Brookes, Robert C. & The Dan Band* / Letter: *King, B.B.* / Evil child: *King, B.B.* / Everybody has their turn: *Moore, Arnold 'Gatemouth'* / Boogie woogie Papa: *Moore, Arnold 'Gatemouth'* / Boom boom: *Hooker, John Lee* / Whisky and women: *Hooker, John Lee* / Shake that thing: *Hopkins, Lightnin'* / Rock me: *Waters, Muddy* / Union Hall jump: *Brookes, Robert C. & The Dan Band*
CD Set ______ SAV 002
Tring / Apr '96 / Tring

HISTORY OF THE TANGO
CD ______ 10498
Laserlight / May '95 / Target/BMG

HISTORY OF TRANCE VOL.1 1991-1996, THE (2CD Set)
Wake up: *Garnier, Laurent* / Skyline: *Resistance D* / Fragile: *LSG* / Love stimulation: *Humate* / Trancescript: *Hardfloor* / Una musica senza ritmo: *Degeneration* / Unknown track: *Unknown* / Tranceslyvania x-press: *X-Dream* / Little fluffy clouds: *Orb* / Two full moons and a troat: *Union Jack* / Mantra: *Bolland, C.J.* / Spectrum: *Metal Master* / How much can you take: *Visions Of Shiva* / Eternal spirit: *4 Voice 4* / Paraglide: *Paragliders* / With a medium into trance: *Hearts Of Space* / Contrex ville: *Redeye* / Beat just goes on and on: *Perry & Rhodan* / Acid Eiffel: *Choice* / Alcatraz: *Peyote*
CD Set ______ SPV 08947062
SPV / Sep '96 / Koch / Plastic Head

HISTORY OF TRANCE VOL.2, THE (2CD Set)
Hymn: *Moby* / Stars: *Microglobe* / X-Plain: *Arpeggiators* / Transformation: *Transform* / Samurai: *Juno Reactor* / Gloria: *Art Of Trance* / Papua New Guinea: *Future Sound Of London* / Dark and long: *Underworld* / Alice in wonderland: *Cybordelics* / Planet sex: *Garnier, Laurent* / Trancition: *Choci & Freedom Of Sound* / Sundown: *Overlords* / Cosmic evolution: *Microbots* / Lubiantia: *Blue Planet Co-operation* / Catching the scent of mystery: *4 Voices* / Moments in noise: *Sequencer* / We came in peace: *Dance 2 Trance* / Lollipop man: *Union Jack* / Love letter: *Van Dyke, Paul* / Into my dream: *Krid Snero* / Be yourself: *Rotortype* / Meltdown: *Lunatic Asylum*
CD Set ______ SPV 08947412
SPV / Apr '97 / Koch / Plastic Head

HISTORY OF TROJAN RECORDS VOL.1 (1968-1971 - 2CD Set)
Jezebel: *Gray, Owen* / Miss Jamaica: *Cliff, Jimmy* / Silver dollar: *McCook, Tommy & The Skatalites* / New boss: *Smith, Slim* / Train to Skaville: *Ethiopians* / Tide is high: *Paragons* / ABC rock steady: *Gaylads* / Israelites: *Dekker, Desmond & The Aces* / Say I'm back: *Morris, Eric* / It mek: *Dekker, Desmond & The Aces* / If you can't beat them join them: *Conquerors* / Red red wine: *Tribe, Tony* / Fire corner: *King Stitt* / Long shot kick de bucket: *Pioneers* / Burial of Long Shot: *Prince Of Darkness* / Reggae in your jeggae: *Dandy* / Build my whole world around you: *Barker, Dave & Upsetters* / Weep: *Andy, Bob* / Sun is shining: *Marley, Bob & The Wailers* / Return of Django: *Upsetters* / Wonderful world beautiful people: *Cliff, Jimmy* / Each day: *Isaacs, Gregory* / Rain: *Ruffin, Bruce* / Black and white: *Greyhound* / Shocks of mighty: *Barker, Dave & Upsetters* / Montego Bay: *Notes, Freddie & The Rudies* / Monkey spanner: *Collins, Dave & Ansell* / Let your yeah be yeah: *Pioneers* / Foolish plan: *Osbourne, Johnny & The Sensations* / Rivers of Babylon: *Melodians* / Liquidator: *Harry J All Stars* / Everybody loves a winner: *Dandy* / Pickney girl: *Dekker, Desmond* / Barbwire: *Dean, Nora* / Kaya: *Marley, Bob & The Wailers* / I can't hide: *Parker, Ken* / Skinhead girl: *Symarip* / You can get it if you really want: *Dekker, Desmond* / Little love: *London, Jimmy* / Young gifted and black: *Bob & Marcia* / Birth control: *Lloydie & The Lowbites* / African Herbsman: *Marley, Bob & The Wailers* / Ride your donkey: *Tennors* / Copy me donkey: *Tennors* / Double barrel: *Collins, Dave & Ansell* / Pop a top: *Andy Capp* / Musical fever: *Enforcers* / Black pearl: *Faith, Horace* / My sweet Lord: *Rudies* / Crying every night: *Cole, Stranger* / Tom Drunk: *U-Roy* / Singer man: *Kingstonians* / My woman's love: *Uniques* / Love of the common people: *Thomas, Nicky* / Boom shacka lacka: *Lewis, Hopeton* / Niyah man: *Rico* / Pied piper: *Bob & Marcia* / Warrior: *Osbourne, Johnny & The Sensations* / Give and take: *Pioneers* / Moon river: *Greyhound*
CD Set ______ CDTAL 700
Trojan / Feb '95 / Direct / Jet Star

HISTORY OF TROJAN RECORDS VOL.2 (1972-1995 - 2CD Set)
Them a fe get a beatin': *Tosh, Peter* / This beautiful land: *Melodians* / Addisababa: *Wilson, Delroy* / Festival da da: *Byles, Junior* / Merry up: *Godsons* / Keep on moving: *Marley, Bob & The Wailers* / All that we need is love: *Ellis, Alton* / S90 skank: *Big Youth* / Time has come: *Smith, Slim* / Yim mas gan: *Abyssinians* / Lorna banana: *Alcapone, Dennis & Prince Jazzbo* / Money in my pocket: *Brown, Dennis* / Salvation train: *Scotty* / Loving pauper: *Isaacs, Gregory* / Pauper and the King: *I-Roy* / African Queen: *Pablo, Augustus* / Words of my mouth: *Gatherers* / Purify your heart: *Osbourne, Johnny* / Higher the mountain: *U-Roy* / Stranger on the shore: *Isaacs, David* / John devour: *Dillinger* / Have I sinned: *Charmers, Lloyd* / Hail rasta brother hail: *Ethiopians* / Everything I own: *Boothe, Ken* / Help me make it through the night: *Holt, John* / Fire burning: *Andy, Bob* / Sweet bitter love: *Griffiths, Marcia* / Stalag 17: *Collins, Ansell* / Here I am baby: *Brown, Al* / None shall escape the judgement: *Clarke, Johnny* / Ire feelings: *Edwards, Rupie* / Play de music: *Stewart, Tinga* / Forward jah jah children: *Inner Circle* / Jah Jah bless the Dreadlocks: *Mighty Diamonds* / Hurt so good: *Cadogan, Susan* / Duke Of Earl: *Campbell, Cornell* / Duke Of Earl dub: *McCook, Tommy & The Aggrovators* / Soldering: *Starlights* / Keep cool Babylon: *Ras Michael & The Sons Of Negus* / Baby hang up the phone: *Parks, Lloyd* / Dreadlocks: *Heptones* / Ram goat liver: *Shervington, Pluto* / Heavy manners: *Prince Far-I* / Key of keys: *Rose, Michael* / People got to know: *Minott, Sugar* / Love the dread: *Mikey Dread* / I am a madman: *Perry, Lee 'Scratch'* / You are the sun: *Paul, Frankie*
CD Set ______ CDTAL 900
Trojan / Feb '96 / Direct / Jet Star

HIT BOUND (The Revolutionary Sound Of Studio 1)
CD ______ CDHB 43
Heartbeat / Jan '91 / ADA / Direct / Greensleeves / Jet Star

HIT LOVE SONGS (CD/CD Rom Set)
CD Set ______ WWCDR 009
Magnum Music / Apr '97 / TKO Magnum

HIT ME WITH A FLOWER (The New Sounds Of San Francisco)
CD ______ SPEXCD 5901
Normal / Mar '94 / ADA / Direct

HIT MIX '97 (2CD Set)
CD Set ______ ZYX 810892
ZYX / Jan '97 / ZYX

HIT SOUND OF NEW ORLEANS
CD ______ CDRB 24
Charly / Aug '95 / Koch

HIT THE DECKS VOL.2
CD ______ QTVCD 008
Quality / Jul '92 / Pinnacle

HIT THE DECKS VOL.3
Ultimation: *Megabass* / Learn to love: *Marveline* / Sesame's treet: *Smart E's* / Rumblism: *Serotonin* / Protein: *Sonic Experience 3* / Come on: *DJ Seduction* / Manic stampede: *Krome & Time* / Voice of Buddha: *Aurora* / On a ragga tip: *SL2* / Sound is for the underground: *Krome & Time* / Trip II the moon: *Acen* / Bad boy: *Bad Boy* / Hypnosis: *Psychotropic* / DJ's unite: *DJ's Unite* / Does it feel good to you: *Cox, Carl* / Temple of dreams: *Messiah* / Feel the rhythm: *Terrorize* / Peace and loveism: *Sonz Of A Loop Da Loop Era* / Keep you movin': *Nu Matic* / Bass shake: *Urban Shakedown* / Eliminator: *Radioactive* / Mother Dawn: *Blue Pearl* / Moog eruption: *Digital Orgasm* / 2 B Reel: *Zone Ranger* / Mind on the beat: *Groove Technology* / Jimi Hendrix was deaf: *Two Little Boys* / Revelations: *HHFD* / Million colours: *Channel X* / Sunshine: *Aurora* / Spectral bass: *Aurora* / Obumbratta: *Apotheosis* / Rave alert: *Khan, Praga* / Can we do it: *General Max*
CD ______ QTVCD 017
Quality / Oct '92 / Pinnacle

HIT THE FLOOR VOL.1
CD ______ CDMUT 1123
Multitone / Apr '90 / BMG

HIT THE FLOOR VOL.2
CD ______ CDMUT 1124
Multitone / Apr '90 / BMG

HIT ZONE SUMMER '97
CD ______ 5538262
PolyGram TV / Aug '97 / PolyGram

HITALIA VOL.4
CD ______ 472362
Flarenasch / Jul '96 / Discovery

HITS '96
I believe: *Robson & Jerome* / Anywhere is: *Enya* / Missing: *Everything But The Girl* / Fairground: *Simply Red* / Waterfalls: *TLC* / I don't wanna be a star: *Corona* / Stayin' alive: *N-Trance* / Sunshine after the rain: *Berri* / I luv u baby: *Original* / What's that tune: *Dorothy* / Never forget: *Take That* / Eye of the tiger: *Bruno, Frank* / Hideaway: *DeLacy* / Happy just to be with you: *Gayle, Michelle* / Something about u (can't be beat): *Mr. Roy* / If you wanna party: *Molella & The Outhere Brothers* / Searching for the golden eye: *Motiv 8 & Kym Mazelle* / Guaglione: *Prado, Perez* / Living next door to Alice (who the fuck is Alice): *Smokie & Roy Chubby Brown* / Wonderwall: *Oasis* / Common people: *Pulp* / Alright: *Supergrass* / It's so quiet: *Bjork* / Queer: *Garbage* / King of the kerb: *Echobelly* / Girl like you: *Collins, Edwyn* / Fingers and thumbs: *Erasure* / He's on the phone: *St. Etienne* / What do I do know: *Sleeper* / Walkin' in memphis: *Cher* / Waiting in vain: *Lennox, Annie* / Prayer for the dying: *Seal* / I'm only sleeping: *Suggs* / Love rendezvous: *M-People* / (You make me feel like a) natural woman: *Blige, Mary J.* / Yah mo be there: *Seville, Louise* / You remind me of something: *R Kelly* / Boom, shake the room: *DJ Jazzy Jeff & The Fresh Prince*
CD Set ______ RADCD 30
Global TV / Dec '95 / BMG

HITS '97
CD ______ MOODCD 49
Sony Music / Dec '96 / Sony

HITS FROM THE 40'S (3CD Set)
That lovely weekend: *Roy, Harry & His Band* / Madelaine: *Roy, Harry & His Band* / Put your arms around me honey: *Loss, Joe & His Orchestra* / I've got the sun in the morning: *Loss, Joe & His Orchestra* / Jenny: *Loss, Joe & His Orchestra* / Gal in Calico: *Loss, Joe & His Orchestra* / I'll string along with you: *Peers, Donald* / When you wish upon a star: *Bowlly, Al* / Who's taking you home tonight: *Bowlly, Al* / Blow, blow thou winter wind: *Bowlly, Al* / It was a lover and his lass: *Bowlly, Al* / Oh Buddy I'm in love: *Gonella, Nat* / What'll I do: *Lewis, Archie* / I dream of you: *Lewis, Archie* / In the land of beginning again: *Lewis, Archie* / Promenade: *Winstone, Eric & His Band* / Dreams of yesterday: *Winstone, Eric & His Band* / I'll buy that dream: *Preager, Lou & His Orchestra* / Was it love: *Roy, Harry & His Band* / Gettin' nowhere: *Geraldo & His Dance Orchestra* / Hey little hen: *Gonella, Nat & His Georgians* / That's my home: *Gonella, Nat & His Georgians* / I haven't time to be a millionaire: *Gonella, Nat & His Georgians* / I'd rather be me: *Roy, Harry & His Band* / Safari: *Winstone, Eric & His Band* / Bitin' the dust: *Winstone, Eric & His Band* / My sister and I: *Loss, Joe & His Orchestra* / They say it's wonderful: *Hutchinson, Leslie 'Hutch'* / Five o'clock whistle: *Roy, Harry & His Orchestra* / Sentimental interlude: *Roy, Harry & His Orchestra* / Whispering grass: *Winstone, Eric & His Band* / I know why: *Winstone, Eric & His Band* / Dreamer's holiday: *Winstone, Eric & His Band* / When that man is dead and gone: *Bowlly, Al* / Can't get Indiana off my mind: *Gonella, Nat & His Georgians* / Aurora: *Gonella, Nat & His Georgians* / Vox: *Gonella, Nat & His Georgians* / Tiggerty boo: *Warner, Jack* / Long ago and far away: *Geraldo & His Orchestra* / I'm not in love: *Rabin, Oscar & His Band* / You made me care: *Loss, Joe & His Orchestra* / I'm gonna love that guy (like he's never been loved before): *Green, Paula & Her Orchestra* / Candy: *Roy, Harry & His Band* / I fell in love with an airman: *Roy, Harry & His Band* / I understand: *Gonella, Nat & His Georgians* / No orchids for my lady: *Gonella, Nat & His Georgians* / Takin' the trains out (chasin' after you): *Foster, Teddy & The Band*
CD Set ______ CDTRBOX 176
Trio / Oct '95 / EMI

HITS FROM THE 50'S (3CD Set)
Twenty tiny fingers: *Cogan, Alma* / Love and marriage: *Cogan, Alma* / You belong to me: *Cogan, Alma* / Ricochet: *Cogan, Alma* / Wake up little Susie: *King Brothers* / In the middle of the island: *King Brothers* / Stairway of love: *Holliday, Michael* / I saw Esau: *Holliday, Michael* / My house is your house: *Holliday, Michael* / Treasure of love: *Anthony, Billie* / This ole house: *Anthony, Billie* / Tammy: *Lotis, Dennis* / Idle gossip: *Campbell, Jean* / Answer me: *Campbell, Jean* / Istanbul: *Vaughan, Frankie* / Look at that girl: *Vaughan, Frankie* / Don't let the stars get in your eyes: *MacKenzie, Giselle* / Slow coach: *Radio Revellers* / Wake the town and tell the people: *Brennan, Rose* / Heartbeat: *Murray, Ruby* / Softly, softly: *Murray, Ruby* / Mule train: *Ford, Tennessee Ernie* / At last at last: *Hughes, David* / Mangoes: *Day, Jill* / Happiness Street: *Day, Jill* / Sincerely: *Day, Jill* / Day that the rains came: *Jones Boys* / Somewhere along the way: *Cole, Nat 'King'* / Mona Lisa: *Cole, Nat 'King'* / Orange coloured sky: *Cole, Nat 'King'* / If I give my heart to you: *Shelton, Anne* / Story of Tina: *Harris, Ronnie* / Man from Laramie: *Hockridge, Edmund* / Hey there: *Hockridge, Edmund* / Have I told you lately that I love you: *Tanners Sisters* / Bewitched, bothered and bewildered: *Boswell, Eve* / I'd love to fall asleep: *Nichols, Penny* / My foolish heart: *Conway, Steve* / Mr. Wonderful: *Yana* / Suddenly there's a valley: *Lawrence, Lee* / I talk to the trees: *Nicholls, Joy* / Green door: *Ellington, Ray* / (We're gonna) Rock around the clock: *Deep River Boys* / Wanted: *Brent, Tony* / Wheel of fortune: *Starr, Kay*
CD Set ______ CDTRBOX 144
Trio / Oct '94 / EMI

HITS FROM THE 60'S (3CD Set)
Surfin' USA: *Beach Boys* / Without you: *Monro, Matt* / Let true love begin: *Cole, Nat 'King'* / Pasadena: *Temperance Seven* / Just one look: *Hollies* / From a window: *Kramer, Billy J.* / Who could be bluer: *Lordan, Jerry* / Rubber ball: *Avons* / Pistol packin' mama: *Vincent, Gene* / She wears my ring: *King, Solomon* / Little lovin': *Fourmost* / Thank U very much: *Scaffold* / Lucky five: *Conway, Russ* / As you like it: *Faith, Adam* / Games people play: *South, Joe* / Goldfinger: *Bassey, Shirley* / Don't let me be misunderstood: *Animals* / I'm a tiger: *Lulu* / Happiness: *Dodd, Ken* / It's all in the game: *Richard, Cliff* / Don't let the sun catch you crying: *Gerry & The Pacemakers* / Hanky panky: *James, Tommy & The Shondells* / Got to get you into my life: *Bennett, Cliff* / Wild cat: *Vincent, Gene* / Fever: *Shapiro, Helen* / Lucky devil: *Ifield, Frank* / Hippy hippy shake: *Swinging Blue Jeans* / One fine day: *Chiffons* / Moon river: *Williams, Danny* / Way you look tonight: *Lettermen* / Poison ivy: *Paramounts* / 5-4-3-2-1: *Manfred Mann* / Bang bang (my baby shot me down): *Cher* / Oh no not my baby: *Manfred Mann* / James Bond: *Barry, John* / Apache: *Shadows* / Seventy six trombones: *King Brothers* / Tell Laura I love her: *Valance, Ricky* / Royal event: *Conway, Russ* / There's a kind of hush: *Herman's Hermits* / Do you want to know a secret: *Kramer, Billy J. & The Dakotas* / I'm crying: *Animals* / It must be him: *Carr, Vikki* / Morningtown ride: *Seekers* / Poor me: *Faith, Adam* / I'm telling you now: *Freddie & The Dreamers* / Sabre dance: *Love Sculpture* / Bus stop: *Hollies*

CD Set _______________ CDTRBOX 104
Trio / Oct '94 / EMI

HITS FROM THE 70'S (3CD Set)
48 crash: *Quatro, Suzi* / If you can't give me love: *Quatro, Suzi* / It's the same old song: *KC & The Sunshine Band* / How much love: *Sayer, Leo* / Let's work together: *Canned Heat* / Dynamite: *Mud* / I don't wanna lose you: *Kandidate* / Magic: *Pilot* / Down at the doctors: *Dr. Feelgood* / Spanish stroll: *Mink Deville* / Heart of stone: *Kenny* / Fancy pants: *Kenny* / Touch too much: *Arrows* / Judy Teen: *Harley, Steve & Cockney Rebel* / Here comes the sun: *Harley, Steve & Cockney Rebel* / Ships in the night: *Be-Bop Deluxe* / Ranking full stop: *Beat* / Heaven is in the back seat of my cadillac: *Hot Chocolate* / Every 1's a winner: *Hot Chocolate* / On my radio: *Selecter* / Cotton fields: *Beach Boys* / Gertcha: *Chas & Dave* / Freedom come freedom go: *Fortunes* / Better use your head: *Imperials* / 10538 overture: *ELO* / My Sharona: *Knack* / Malt and barley blues: *McGuinness Flint* / Journey: *Browne, Duncan* / Rich kids: *Rich Kids* / Right back where we started from: *Nightingale, Maxine* / Rag mama rag: *Band* / Tonight: *Move* / You're my everything: *Garrett, Lee* / Peaches: *Stranglers* / Darlin': *Miller, Frankie* / Ball park incident: *Wizzard* / Movin': *Brass Construction* / This will be: *Cole, Natalie* / Softly whispering I love you: *Congregation* / Oh you pretty thing: *Noone, Peter* / Whole lot of love: *CCS* / Dancing in the city: *Marshall Hain* / Na na na: *Powell, Cozy* / Motor bikin': *Spedding, Chris* / Boogie oogie oogie: *Taste Of Honey* / Crazy: *Mud* / More like the movies: *Dr. Hook* / Prince: *Madness*
CD Set _______________ CDTRBOX 108
Trio / Oct '94 / EMI

HITS FROM THE 80'S (3CD Set)
Freeze: *Spandau Ballet* / Wizard: *Hardcastle, Paul* / Classic: *Gurvitz, Adrian* / What's wrong with dreaming: *River City People* / Mony mony: *Amazulu* / Lawn chairs: *Our Daughters Wedding* / People do rock steady: *Bodysnatchers* / Modern girl: *Easton, Sheena* / Missing you: *Waite, John* / It started with a kiss: *Hot Chocolate* / You're lying: *Linx* / Plan B: *Dexy's Midnight Runners* / This little girl: *Bonds, Gary 'US'* / View from a bridge: *Wilde, Kim* / Respect: *Adeva* / Girl crazy: *Hot Chocolate* / Talk talk: *Talk Talk* / Bette Davis eyes: *Carnes, Kim* / Tarzan boy: *Baltimore* / Crying: *McLean, Don* / Searchin' (I gotta find a man): *Dean, Hazell* / Missing words: *Selecter* / Sleep walk: *Ultravox* / Politics of dancing: *Re-Flex* / C30 C60 C90 Go: *Bow Wow Wow* / Summertime: *Fun Boy Three* / Oh well: *Oh Well* / I could be so good for you: *Waterman, Dennis* / Goodbye girl: *Go West* / Can you keep a secret: *Brother Beyond* / Rise to the occasion: *Climie Fisher* / Strange little girl: *Stranglers* / There there my dear: *Dexy's Midnight Runners* / Comin' on strong: *Broken English* / C'est la vie: *Nevil, Robbie* / I'm forever blowing bubbles: *Cockney Rejects* / Somebody let me out: *Beggar & Co* / Freeze frame: *Geils, J. Band* / That certain smile: *Ure, Midge* / Summer fun: *Barracudas* / Dancing with myself: *Generation X* / Round and round: *Graham, Jaki* / Turning Japanese: *Vapors* / I shot the sheriff: *Light Of The World* / Love missile F1-11: *Sigue Sigue Sputnik* / Big apple: *Kajagoogoo* / Is it a dream: *Classix Nouveaux*
CD Set _______________ CDTRBOX 152
Trio / Oct '94 / EMI

HITS, HITS AND MORE DANCE HITS (2CD Set)
Another night: *Real McCoy* / Let me be your fantasy: *Baby D* / Welcome to tomorrow: *Snap* / Sweetness: *Gayle, Michelle* / She's got that vibe: *R Kelly* / Rhythm of the night: *Corona* / Special kind of love: *Carroll, Dina* / Movin' on up: *M-People* / Get away: *Maxx* / Swamp thing: *Grid* / Boom shake the room: *DJ Jazzy Jeff & The Fresh Prince* / Things can only get better: *D:Ream* / Ain't no love, ain't no use: *Sub Sub* / Show me love: *Robin S* / We are family: *Sister Sledge* / Now that we've found love: *Heavy D & The Boyz* / Mr. Vain: *Culture Beat* / It's my life: *Dr. Alban* / What is love: *Haddaway* / Let the beat control your body: *2 Unlimited* / Baby I love your way: *Big Mountain* / Searching: *China Black* / Compliments on your kiss: *Red Dragon* / Mr. Loverman: *Shabba Ranks* / Best of my love: *Lewis, C.J.* / Things that make you go hmmm: *C&C Music Factory* / Love I lost: *West End* / Don't you want me: *Felix* / Open your mind: *Usura* / Long train running: *Doobie Brothers* / Right here: *SWV* / My lovin': *En Vogue* / Push it: *Salt n' Pepa* / Finally: *Peniston, Ce Ce* / Key the secret: *Urban Cookie Collective* / Fantasy: *Black Box* / Run to you: *Rage* / Deep: *East 17* / Confide in me: *Minogue, Kylie* / Re-light my fire: *Take That & Lulu*
CD Set _______________ RADCD 02
Global TV / Nov '94 / BMG

HITS IN THE FIRST DEGREE (2CD Set)
CD Set _______________ NSCD 013
Newsound / Feb '95 / THE

HITS OF 1930
Happy days are here again: *Hylton, Jack & His Orchestra* / With a song in my heart: *Hutch* / Puttin' on the rinse: *Astaire, Fred & Debroy Somers Band* / Little white lies: *Hanshaw, Annette & Her Sizzling Syncopators* / Falling in love again: *Dietrich, Marlene & Friedrich Hollander Orchestra* / Happy feet: *Whiteman, Paul & His Orchestra* / Georgia on my mind: *Carmichael, Hoagy & Orchestra* / When you're smiling: *Armstrong, Louis Orchestra* / Dancing with tears in my eyes: *Layton & Johnstone* / You brought a new kind of love to me: *Chevalier, Maurice* / Exactly like you: *Carlisle, Elsie* / It happened in Monterey: *Boles, John* / Ten cents a dance: *Etting, Ruth* / Let me sing and I'm happy: *Jolson, Al & Brunswick Studio Orchestra* / Three little words: *Rhythm boys & Duke Ellington Orchestra* / Beyond the blue horizon: *MacDonald, Jeanette* / I'm confessin' that I love you: *Lombardo, Guy & His Royal Canadians* / My baby just cares for me: *Payne, Jack & His Band* / If I had a talking picture of you: *Hylton, Jack & His Orchestra* / Oh, Donna Clara: *Metaxa, George & The New Mayfair Orchestra* / You're driving me crazy: *Vallee, Rudy & His Connecticut Yankees* / Without a song: *Tibbett, Lawrence & Nat Shilkret Orchestra* / Body and soul: *Hanshaw, Annette*
CD _______________ CDAJA 5195
Living Era / Jun '97 / Select

HITS OF 1931
Stardust: *Crosby, Bing & Victor Young Orchestra* / Please don't talk about me when I'm gone: *Austin, Gene & trio* / Between the devil and the deep blue sea: *Calloway, Cab Orchestra* / Rockin' chair: *Robeson, Paul & Ray Noble New Mayfair Orchestra* / Peanut vendor: *Ambrose & His Orchestra* / Nevertheless: *Etting, ruth & orchestra* / Life is just a bowl of cherries: *Hutchinson, Leslie 'Hutch'* / When I take my sugar to tea: *Boswell Sisters & Dorsey Brothers Orchestra* / Cuban love song: *Tibbett, Lawrence & Stewart Wille* / Just one more chance: *Crosby, Bing & Victor Young Orchestra* / Lady of Spain: *Folgar, Tino* / Marta: *Tracy, Arthur* / Walkin' my baby back home: *Chevalier, Maurice* / Would you like to take a walk: *Hanshaw, Annette* / I don't know why, I just do: *Layton & Johnstone* / Prisoner of love: *Columbo, Russ & Nat Shilkret orchestra* / Dancing in the dark: *Revellers* / Sweet and lovely: *Bowlly, Al & Savoy Orpheans* / Lazy river: *Armstrong, Louis* / River stay 'way from my door: *Robeson, Paul & Ray Noble orchestra* / Sally: *Fields, Gracie & Jay Wilbur orchestra* / Dream a little dream of me: *Nelson, Ozzie* / Wrap your troubles in dreams: *Crosby, Bing & Gus Arnheim orchestra* / Goodnight, sweetheart: *Metaxa, George & Ray Noble & the New Mayfair Dance orchestra*
CD _______________ CDAJA 5190
Living Era / Dec '96 / Select

HITS OF 1932
As time goes by: *Hale, Binnie* / Sun has got his hat on: *Ambrose & His Orchestra* / Clouds will soon roll by: *Ambrose & His Orchestra* / Please: *Crosby, Bing* / It don't mean a thing if it ain't got that swing: *Ellington, Duke* / Love is the sweetest thing: *Bowlly, Al* / Goodbye blues: *Mills Brothers* / I'll never be the same: *Malneck, Matty & His Orchestra* / Mad dogs & Englishmen: *Coward, Noel* / Mad about the boy: *Lawrence, Gertrude* / I don't stand a ghost of a chance with you: *Austin, Gene* / Happy-go-lucky you and broken-heart me: *Lipton, Sydney & His Grosvenor House Orchestra* / Underneath the arches: *Flanagan & Allen* / By the fireside: *Noble, Ray* / Gipsy moon: *Crooks, Richard* / Isn't it romantic: *MacDonald, Jeanette* / Song is you: *Tibbett, Lawrence* / I've told ev'ry little star: *Ellis, Mary* / When we're alone: *Fox, Roy* / Say it isn't so: *Keller, Greta* / Paradise: *Crosby, Bing* / Sleepy-time down South: *Robeson, Paul* / Auf wiederseh'n, my dear: *Robeson, Paul* / Let's put out the lights and go to sleep: *Vallee, Rudy & His Connecticut Yankees*
CD _______________ CDAJA 5182
Living Era / Oct '96 / Select

HITS OF 1933
Did you ever see a dream walking: *Crosby, Bing & Lennie Hayton Orchestra* / Butterflies in the rain: *Browne, Sam & Ambrose & His Orchestra* / Lover: *Fulton, Jack & Paul Whiteman Orchestra* / My song goes round the world: *Schmidt, Joseph & George Walter Orchestra* / It's the talk of the town: *Boswell, Connee & Victor Young Orchestra* / I'm getting sentimental over you: *Layton & Johnstone* / There's a cabin in the pines: *Armstrong, Louis Orchestra* / Try a little tenderness: *Crosby, Bing & Lennie Hayton Orchestra* / Lazybones: *Mills Brothers* / Dinner at eight: *Rowland, Helen & Ben Selvin Orchestra* / Night and day: *Astaire, Fred* / Sophisticated lady: *Ellington, Duke Orchestra* / Stormy weather: *Arlen, Harold & Leo Reisman Orchestra* / Blue prelude: *Robeson, Paul & Ray Noble New Mayfair Orchestra* / I cover the waterfront: *Fox, Roy Band* / Brother can you spare a dime: *Crosby, Bing & Lennie Hayton Orchestra* / Close your eyes: *Bowlly, Al & Ray Noble Orchestra* / By a waterfall: *Powell, Dick & Victor Young Orchestra* / Don't blame me: *Hutchinson, Leslie 'Hutch'* / Shadow waltz: *Burke, Marie & Albert Sandler Orchestra* / I gotta right to sing the blues: *Teagarden, Jack & Benny Goodman Orchestra* / How deep is the ocean: *Browne, Sam & Ambrose* / Temptation: *Crosby, Bing & Lennie Hayton Orchestra* / Last round-up: *Autry, Gene*
CD _______________ CDAJA 5183
Living Era / Aug '96 / Select

HITS OF 1934
Love in bloom: *Crosby, Bing* / April in Paris: *Hall, Henry* / My old flame: *Anderson, Ivie* / Smoke gets in your eyes: *Dunne, Irene* / Miss Otis regrets: *Byng, Douglas* / Everything I have is yours: *Austin, Gene* / Very thought of you: *Bowlly, Al* / All I do is dream of you: *Ferdinando, Angelo* / Stay as sweet as you are: *Browne, Sam* / Carioca: *Boswell, Connee* / Let's fall in love: *Tracy, Arthur* / Isle of Capri: *Fields, Gracie* / Continental: *Browne, Sam* / Dancing on the ceiling: *Matthews, Jessie* / I'll string along with you: *Powell, Dick* / For all we know: *Hutchinson, Leslie 'Hutch'* / One night of love: *Moore, Grace* / It's only a paper moon: *Edwards, Cliff* / Moonglow: *Waters, Ethel* / What a difference a day made: *Roy, Harry & His Orchestra* / Two cigarettes in the dark: *Crosby, Bing* / Honeysuckle rose: *Waller, Fats* / Tiger rag: *Mills Brothers* / Stars fell on Alabama: *Teagarden, Jack* / Little man you've had a busy day: *Robeson, Paul*
CD _______________ CDAJA 5184
Living Era / Jun '96 / Select

HITS OF 1935
Top hat, white tie & tails: *Astaire, Fred* / Cheek to cheek: *Astaire, Fred* / La Cucaracha: *Roy, Harry* / Anything goes: *Aubert, Jeanne* / I get a kick out of you: *Merman, Ethel* / Easter Parade: *Hall, Henry* / Everything stops for tea: *Buchanan, Jack* / Lovely to look at: *Dunne, Irene* / What a difference a day made: *Dennis, Denny & Roy Fox* / I'm gonna sit right down and write myself a letter: *Waller, Fats* / Alone: *Dorsey, Tommy* / Top of your head: *Crosby, Bing & the Dorsey Brothers Orchestra* / Your feet's too big: *Ink Spots* / I'm in the mood for love: *Langford, Frances* / Canoe song: *Robeson, Paul* / Bess you is my woman now: *Tibbett, Lawrence & Helen Jepson* / My very good friend, the milkman: *Waller, Fats* / Darling, je vous aime beaucoup: *Hildegarde* / East of the Sun and West of the moon: *Tracy, Arthur* / Red sails in the sunset: *Fields, Gracie* / Blue moon: *Trumbauer, Frankie* / I wished on the moon: *Holiday, Billie & Teddy Wilson* / Lullaby of Broadway: *Powell, Dick*
CD _______________ CDAJA 5185
Living Era / Apr '96 / Select

HITS OF 1937
Bei mir bist du schon: *Andrews Sisters* / On the sunny side of the street: *Armstrong, Louis* / Rockin' chair: *Bailey, Mildred* / That old feeling: *Boswell, Connee* / Will you remember: *Costa, Sam* / Bob White: *Crosby, Bing & Connie Boswell* / Moon got in my eyes: *Crosby, Bing* / Sweet Leilani: *Crosby, Bing* / I've got you under my skin: *Day, Frances* / Marie: *Dorsey, Tommy* / Moon at sea: *Fields, Shep* / Leaning on a lamp-post: *Formby, George* / All God's chillun got rhythm: *Garland, Judy* / To Mary with love: *Geraldo* / Oh they're tough, mighty tough in the West: *Gonella, Nat* / Pennies from heaven: *Gonella, Nat* / Nice work if you can get it: *Holiday, Billie* / Slap that bass: *Ink Spots* / Was it rain: *Langford, Frances* / Greatest mistake of my life: *Mesene, Jimmy* / I've got my love to keep me warm: *Powell, Dick* / Broken hearted clown: *Roy, Harry* / Can I forget you: *Sablon, Jean* / September in the rain: *Tracy, Arthur* / Where is the sun: *Valaida*
CD _______________ CDAJA 5116
Living Era / Nov '93 / Select

HITS OF 1938
Oh ma-ma: *Andrews Sisters* / Ti-pi-tin: *Andrews Sisters* / Change partners: *Astaire, Fred* / I used to be colour blind: *Astaire, Fred* / Nice work if you can get it: *Astaire, Fred* / Bei mir bist du schon: *Bowlly, Al* / You couldn't be cuter: *Bowlly, Al* / Somebody's thinking of you tonight: *Browne, Sam* / Me and my girl: *Cooper, Jack* / Big noise from Winnetka: *Crosby, Bob* / My heart is taking lessons in love: *Crosby, Bing* / On the sentimental side: *Crosby, Bing* / Boogie woogie: *Dorsey, Tommy* / Donkey serenade: *Fields, Gracie* / Whistle while you work: *Fields, Shep* / Tisket-a-tasket: *Fitzgerald, Ella* / Just let me look at you: *Geraldo* / Dipsy doodle: *Gonella, Nat* / Flat foot floogie: *Gonella, Nat* / Two sleepy people: *Lynn, Vera & Denny Dennis* / I hadn't anyone till you: *Martin, Tony* / Down and out blues: *Mesene, Jimmy* / Begin the beguine: *Shaw, Artie* / Music maestro please: *Waller, Fats*
CD _______________ CDAJA 5104
Living Era / May '93 / Select

HITS OF 1939
Small town: *Bowlly, Al* / What do you know about love: *Bowlly, Al* / Oh you crazy moon: *Clare, Wendy* / I cried for you: *Crosby, Bing* / My melancholy baby: *Crosby, Bing* / I'm falling in love with someone: *Crosby, Bing & Frances Langford* / On the outside looking in: *Currie, Bill* / (I'm afraid) the masquerade is over: *Dennis, Denny* / FDR Jones: *Fitzgerald, Ella* / Over the rainbow: *Garland, Judy* / Blue orchids: *Grantham, Cyril* / Wish me luck as you wave me goodbye: *Grantham, Cyril* / I get along without you very well: *Hall, Adelaide* / Transatlantic lullaby: *Hall, Adelaide* / At the woodchoppers' ball: *Herman, Woody* / My prayer: *Ink Spots* / Deep purple: *Layton, Turner* / And the angels sing: *Lenner, Anne* / We'll meet again: *Lynn, Vera* / Wishing: *Lynn, Vera* / They say: *Melachrino, George* / In the mood: *Miller, Glenn* / Goodnight children everywhere: *Roy, Harry* / Indian summer: *Simms, Ginny*
CD _______________ CDAJA 5086
Living Era / Mar '92 / Select

HITS OF 1940
Beat me Daddy, eight to the bar: *Andrews Sisters* / Woodpecker song: *Andrews Sisters* / If I had my way: *Crosby, Bing* / I haven't time to be a millionaire: *Crosby, Bing* / Only forever: *Crosby, Bing* / I can't love you anymore: *Daniels, Bebe* / Amapola: *Durbin, Deanna* / Love is all: *Durbin, Deanna* / Shake down the stars: *Hall, Adelaide* / Begin the beguine: *Henderson, Chick & Joe Loss* / Maybe: *Ink Spots* / Whispering grass: *Ink Spots* / It's a hap-hap-happy day: *Lipton, Celia* / Faithful forever: *Carmen & Guy Lombardo* / I'm in love for the last time: *Lynn, Vera* / It's a lovely day tomorrow: *Lynn, Vera* / Nearness of you: *Miller, Glenn* / Pennsylvania 6-5000: *Miller, Glenn* / Tuxedo junction: *Miller, Glenn* / Comes love: *O'Connell, Helen & Jimmy Dorsey* / Vagabond song: *O'Connor, Cavan* / I'm stepping out with a memory tonight: *Shelton, Anne & Ambrose* / Fools rush in: *Sinatra, Frank & Tommy Dorsey* / I'll never smile again: *Sinatra, Frank & Tommy Dorsey*
CD _______________ CDAJA 5087
Living Era / Oct '92 / Select

HITS OF 1941
When that man is dead and gone: *Bowlly, Al* / I'd know you anywhere: *Crosby, Bing* / San Antonio rose: *Crosby, Bing* / You are my sunshine: *Crosby, Bing* / Six lessons from Madame La Zonga: *Dorsey, Jimmy* / Beneath the lights of home: *Durbin, Deanna* / It's foolish but it's fun: *Durbin, Deanna* / Down Forget-Me-Not Lane: *Flanagan & Allen* / Daddy: *Geraldo* / Hey little hen: *Gonella, Nat* / Oh buddy I'm in love: *Gonella, Nat* / Five o'clock whistle: *Herman, Woody* / Yesterday's dreams: *Hutchinson, Leslie 'Hutch'* / Ring, telephone, ring: *Ink Spots* / We three: *Ink Spots* / Amapola: *Loss, Joe* / Yours: *Lynn, Vera* / Last time I saw Paris: *Martin, Tony* / Johnson rag: *Miller, Glenn* / Yes my darling daughter: *Miller, Glenn* / Frenesi: *Shaw, Artie* / There goes that song again: *Shelton, Anne*
CD _______________ CDAJA 5100
Living Era / Feb '93 / Select

HITS OF 1942
Don't sit under the apple tree: *Andrews Sisters* / Pennsylvania polka: *Andrews Sisters* / Green eyes: *Barreto, Don* / Deep in the heart of Texas: *Crosby, Bing & Woody Herman* / Moonlight becomes you: *Crosby, Bing* / White Christmas: *Crosby, Bing* / Zoot suit: *Crosby, Bob* / Skylark: *Eckstine, Billy & Earl Hines* / Always in my heart: *Geraldo* / Lamplighter's serenade: *Geraldo* / Jingle jangle jingle: *Gonella, Nat* / That lovely weekend: *Henderson, Chick & Joe Loss* / Anywhere on Earth is heaven: *Hutchinson, Leslie 'Hutch'* / Who wouldn't love you: *Ink Spots* / You made me love you: *James, Harry* / Where in the world: *Martin, Tony* / Chattanooga choo choo: *Miller, Glenn* / I know why: *Miller, Glenn* / Miss you: *Roy, Harry* / Sailor with the navy blue eyes: *Roy, Harry* / Three little sisters: *Shore, Dinah* / How about you: *Sinatra, Frank & Tommy Dorsey* / Without a song: *Sinatra, Frank & Tommy Dorsey* / Someone's rocking my dreamboat: *Winstone, Eric*
CD _______________ CDAJA 5103
Living Era / Mar '93 / Select

HITS OF 1943
He's my guy: *Fitzgerald, Ella* / I'm thinking tonight of my blue eyes: *Crosby, Bing* / I left my heart at the stage door canteen: *Winstone, Eric* / Johnny Zero: *Song Spinners* / Murder he says: *Dorsey, Jimmy* / What's the good word Mr. Bluebird: *Roy, Harry* / Mr. Five by five: *Andrews Sisters* / Dearly beloved: *Astaire, Fred* / Every night about this time: *Geraldo* / G'bye now: *Tilton, Martha* / Let's get lost: *Winstone, Eric* / Coming in on a wing and a prayer: *Song Spinners* / That old black magic: *Barnet, Charlie* / Ain't got a dime to my name: *Crosby, Bing* / In the blue of evening: *Geraldo* / I'm gonna get lit up (when the lights go on in London): *Loss, Joe* / When Johnny comes marching home: *Miller, Glenn* / Don't get around much anymore: *Ink Spots* / Hit the road to dreamland: *Roy, Harry* / I had the craziest dream: *Lynn, Vera* / Better not roll those blye blue eyes: *Ambrose* / Be honest with me: *Heist, Horace* / Really and truly: *Lynn, Vera*
CD _______________ RAJCD 829
Empress / Jan '97 / Koch

HITS OF 1945
One meat ball: *Andrews Sisters* / More I see you: *Cavallaro, Carmen* / Tampico: *Christy, June & Stan Kenton* / Temptation: *Como, Perry* / Till the end of time: *Como, Perry* / Nina: *Coward, Noel* / Accentuate the positive: *Crosby, Bing* / Baia: *Crosby, Bing* / I can't begin to tell you: *Crosby, Bing* / Sentimental journey: *Day, Doris & Les Brown* / Opus No.1: *Dorsey, Tommy* / There's no you: *Dorsey, Tommy* / I'm beginning to see the light: *Fitzgerald, Ella & Ink Spots* / Together: *Haymes, Dick & Helen Forrest* / Laura: *Herman, Woody* / Estrellita: *James,*

Harry / Cocktails for two: *Jones, Spike* / Caldonia: *Jordan, Louis* / Little on the lonely side: *Lombardo, Guy* / Juke box Saturday night: *Miller, Glenn* / Cool water: *Monroe, Vaughan* / Cow cow boogie: *Morse, Ella Mae* / Conversation while dancing: *Stafford, Jo & Johny Mercer* / We'll gather lilacs: *Tauber, Richard* / Moonlight in Vermont: *Whiting, Margaret*
CD ______ CDAJA 5186
Living Era / Jan '96 / Select

HITS OF 1946
On the Atchison, Topeka and the Santa Fe: *Garland, Judy* / It might as well be Spring: *Haymes, Dick* / McNamara's band: *Crosby, Bing* / Prisoner of love: *Como, Perry* / To each his own: *Ink Spots* / Green cockatoo: *Inglez, Roberto Orchestra* / I fall in love too easily: *Sinatra, Frank* / All through the day: *Haymes, Dick & Helen Forrest* / Route 66: *Cole, Nat 'King'* / Laughing on the outside: *Shore, Dinah* / South America, take it away: *Crosby, Bing & Andrews Sisters* / Humoresque: *Lombardo, Guy* / You make me feel so young: *Haymes, Dick* / Ole buttermilk sky: *Carmichael, Hoagy* / You keep coming back like a song: *Hutch* / They say it's wonderful: *Como, Perry* / Choo choo ch'boogie: *Jordan, Louis* / Gypsy: *Ink Spots* / Aren't you glad you're you: *Crosby, Bing* / Nancy with the laughing face: *Sinatra, Frank* / Rockabye your baby with a dixie melody: *Jolson, Al* / I'll buy that dream: *Haymes, Dick & Helen Forrest* / Come closer to me: *Ros, Edmundo* / September song: *Huston, Walter* / It's a pity to say goodnight: *Fitzgerald, Ella*
CD ______ CDAJA 5246
Living Era / Feb '97 / Select

HITS OF 1960-1964
How do you do it: *Gerry & The Pacemakers* / Love of the loved: *Black, Cilla* / Nobody I know: *Peter & Gordon* / Somewhere: *Proby, P.J.* / How about that: *Faith, Adam* / Tell me what he said: *Shapiro, Helen* / Time: *Douglas, Craig* / Sun arise: *Harris, Rolf* / Little children: *Kramer, Billy J. & The Dakotas* / Little loving: *Fourmost* / Hungry for love: *Kidd, Johnny & The Pirates* / Wonderful world of the young: *Williams, Danny* / Legion's Last Patrol: *Thorne, Ken* / You can never stop me loving you: *Lynch, Kenny* / Sharing you: *Vee, Bobby* / You're no good: *Swinging Blue Jeans* / I understand: *Freddie & The Dreamers* / From a Jack to a King: *Miller, Ned* / Beatnik fly: *Johnny & The Hurricanes* / Unchained melody: *Young, Jimmy*
CD ______ CDSL 8270
Music For Pleasure / Sep '95 / EMI

HITS OF 1965-1969
Sloop John B: *Beach Boys* / Jennifer Juniper: *Donovan* / Supergirl: *Bonney, Graham* / I've been wrong before: *Black, Cilla* / Elusive butterfly: *Doonican, Val* / Lover's concerto: *Toys* / Trains and boats and planes: *Kramer, Billy J.* / Ode to Billy Joe: *Gentry, Bobbie* / Come tomorrow: *Manfred Mann* / Got to get you into my life: *Bennett, Cliff* / On the road again: *Canned Heat* / Sunny: *Hebb, Bobby* / Kites: *Dupree, Simon & The Big Sound* / Wichita lineman: *Campbell, Glen* / Me the peaceful heart: *Lulu* / Mockingbird: *Foxx, Inez & Charlie* / Georgy girl: *Seekers* / Rudi's in love: *Locomotive* / We gotta get out of this place: *Animals* / He ain't heavy, he's my brother: *Hollies*
CD ______ CDSL 8271
Music For Pleasure / Sep '95 / EMI

HITS OF 1993
CD ______ PHCD 001
Penthouse / Apr '94 / Jet Star

HITS OF INVICTUS & HOT WAX, THE
You've got me: *Chairmen Of The Board* / Crumbs off the table: *Glass House* / Give me just a little more time: *Chairmen Of The Board* / Somebody's been sleeping in my bed: *100 Proof (Aged In Soul)* / Band of gold: *Payne, Freda* / She's not just another: *Eighth Wonder* / Finders keepers: *Chairmen Of The Board* / While you're out: *Honey Cone* / Westbound no.9: *Flaming Ember* / Chairman of the board: *Chairmen Of The Board* / One monkey: *Chairmen Of The Board* / Want ads: *Honey Cone* / Stick up: *Honey Cone* / Girls it ain't easy: *Honey Cone* / Everything's Tuesday: *Chairmen Of The Board* / Women's love rights: *Lee, Laura* / If you can beat me rockin': *Lee, Laura* / Mind, body and soul: *Flaming Ember* / Bring the boys home: *Payne, Freda* / Deeper and deeper: *Payne, Freda* / I'm on my way: *Chairmen Of The Board*
CD ______ HDH CD 501
HDH / Jul '89 / Pinnacle

HITS OF THE 50'S
CD ______ MATCD 208
Castle / Dec '92 / BMG

HITS OF THE 50'S
CD ______ 101532
CMC / Jun '97 / BMG

HITS OF THE 50'S VOL.1
Singin' the blues: *Mitchell, Guy* / Smoke gets in your eyes: *Platters* / All my love: *Page, Patti* / At the top: *Danny & The Juniors* / Love letters in the sand: *Boone, Pat* / Cry: *Ray, Johnnie* / Mr. Blue: *Fleetwoods* / Three coins in the fountain: *Four Aces* / This ole house: *Clooney, Rosemary* / Ain't that a shame: *Boone, Pat* / Tom Dooley: *Kingston Trio* / Answer me: *Lane, Frankie* / Great balls of fire: *Lewis, Jerry Lee* / Tequila: *Champs* / Heartache by the number: *Mitchell, Guy* / My prayer: *Platters* / (How much is that) doggie in the window: *Page, Patti*
CD ______ MUCD 9005
Musketeer / Apr '95 / Disc

HITS OF THE 50'S VOL.1, THE (Rock Around The Clock)
Rock around the clock: *Haley, Bill & The Comets* / It's late: *Nelson, Rick* / Great pretender: *Platters* / Blue suede shoes: *Perkins, Carl* / Long tall Sally: *Little Richard* / That'll be the day: *Holly, Buddy* / Dance with me: *Drifters* / Red River rock: *Johnny & The Hurricanes* / Singing the blues: *Mitchell, Guy* / Rock 'n' roll music: *Berry, Chuck* / Remember when: *Platters* / Charlie Brown: *Coasters* / Such a night: *McPhatter, Clyde* / Stagger Lee: *Price, Lloyd* / Shakin' all over: *Valance, Ricky* / Be bop a Lula: *Vincent, Gene*
CD ______ 100762
CMC / May '97 / BMG

HITS OF THE 50'S VOL.2
(We're gonna) Rock around the clock: *Haley, Bill & The Comets* / April love: *Boone, Pat* / Great pretender: *Platters* / Sleep walk: *Santo & Johnny* / Rockabilly: *Mitchell, Guy* / Half as much: *Clooney, Rosemary* / Sh-boom: *Crew Cuts* / I believe: *Laine, Frankie* / It's only make believe: *Twitty, Conway* / Stagger Lee: *Price, Lloyd* / Tennese waltz: *Page, Patti* / Party doll: *Knox, Buddy* / Love is a many splendoured thing: *Four Aces* / Just walking in the rain: *Ray, Johnnie* / Twilight time: *Platters* / Come softly to me: *Fleetwoods* / I'll be home: *Boone, Pat* / I went to your wedding: *Page, Patti*
CD ______ MUCD 9006
Musketeer / Apr '95 / Disc

HITS OF THE 50'S VOL.2, THE (Only You)
Only you: *Platters* / Lonesome Town: *Nelson, Rick* / Tell Laura I love her: *Valance, Ricky* / Answer me: *Laine, Frankie* / Blueberry Hill: *Domino, Fats* / Just a dream: *Clayton, Jimmy* / This is goodbye, goodbye: *Haley, Bill & The Comets* / Why do fools fall in love: *Diamonds* / Dear John letter: *Husky, Ferlin* / Love is a many splendoured thing: *Four Aces* / For your precious love: *Butler, Jerry* / Heartaches by the number: *Mitchell, Guy* / What am I living for: *Perkins, Carl* / Kissin' time: *Rydell, Bobby* / Kisses sweeter than wine: *Rogers, Jimmy* / There goes my baby: *Drifters*
CD ______ 100772
CMC / May '97 / BMG

HITS OF THE 50'S VOL.3, THE (Good Golly Miss Molly)
Whole lotta shakin' goin' on: *Lewis, Jerry Lee* / Yakety yak: *Coasters* / Waterloo: *Jackson, Stonewall* / Shake, rattle and roll: *Haley, Bill & The Comets* / Ain't that a shame: *Domino, Fats* / Oh boy: *Holly, Buddy* / At the hop: *Danny & The Juniors* / Good golly Miss Molly: *Little Richard* / Rocking Robin: *McPhatter, Clyde* / Lawdy Miss Clawdy: *Price, Lloyd* / I'm walkin': *Nelson, Rick* / Go Jimmy go: *Clayton, Jimmy* / Sweet little sixteen: *Berry, Chuck* / Reveille rock: *Johnny & The Hurricanes* / (You've got) that magic touch: *Platters* / Born to boogie: *Perkins, Carl*
CD ______ 100782
CMC / May '97 / BMG

HITS OF THE 50'S, THE (3CD Set)
Rock around the clock: *Haley, Bill & The Comets* / It's late: *Nelson, Rick* / Great pretender: *Platters* / Blue suede shoes: *Perkins, Carl* / Long tall Sally: *Little Richard* / That'll be the day: *Holly, Buddy* / Dance with me: *Drifters* / Red river rock: *Johnny & The Hurricanes* / Singing the blues: *Mitchell, Guy* / Rock 'n' roll music: *Berry, Chuck* / Oh Carol: *Sedaka, Neil* / Charlie Brown: *Coasters* / Such a night: *McPhatter, Clyde* / Stagger Lee: *Price, Lloyd* / Shakin' all over: *Valance, Ricky* / Be bop a Lula: *Vincent, Gene* / Only you: *Platters* / Lonesome town: *Nelson, Rick* / Tell Laura I love her: *Valance, Ricky* / Answer me: *Laine, Frankie* / Blueberry Hill: *Domino, Fats* / Just a dream: *Clanton, Jimmy* / All alone am I: *Lee, Brenda* / Why do fools fall in love: *Diamonds* / Dear John letter: *Husky, Ferlin* / Love is a many splendoured thing: *Four Aces* / For your precious love: *Butler, Jerry* / Heartaches by the number: *Mitchell, Guy* / What am I living for: *Perkins, Carl* / Kissin' time: *Rydell, Bobby* / Kisses sweeter than wine: *Rogers, Jimmy* / There goes my baby: *Drifters* / Whole lotta shakin' goin' on: *Lewis, Jerry Lee* / Yakety yak: *Coasters* / Waterloo: *Jackson, Stonewall* / Shake, rattle and roll: *Haley, Bill & The Comets* / Ain't that a shame: *Domino, Fats* / Oh boy: *Holly, Buddy* / At the hop: *Danny & The Juniors* / Good golly Miss Molly: *Little Richard* / Rockin' Robin: *McPhatter, Clyde* / Lawdy Miss Clawdy: *Price, Lloyd* / I'm walkin': *Nelson, Rick* / Go Jimmy go: *Clanton, Jimmy* / Sweet little sixteen: *Berry, Chuck* / Reveille rock: *Johnny & The Hurricanes* / Sweet nothings: *Lee, Brenda* / Born to boogie: *Perkins, Carl*
CD Set ______ 100752
CMC / May '97 / BMG

HITS OF THE 60'S
Needles and pins / Always something there to remind me / Have I the right / Downtown / Catch the wind / Tossing and turning / Hang on Sloopy / Michelle / Out of time / Sunny afternoon / Summer in the city / Itchycoo Park / Let the heartaches begin / Silence is golden / First cut is the deepest / Build me up buttercup / Pictures of matchstick men / (If paradise is) Half as nice
CD ______ MCCD 028
Music Club / Sep '91 / Disc / THE

HITS OF THE 60'S (2CD Set)
Sunny afternoon: *Kinks* / Do wah diddy diddy: *Manfred Mann* / Daydream: *Lovin' Spoonful* / Lazy Sunday: *Small Faces* / Pictures of matchstick men: *Status Quo* / Flowers in the rain: *Move* / Man of the world: *Fleetwood Mac* / Out of time: *Farlowe, Chris* / Everlasting love: *Love Affair* / Go now: *Moody Blues* / Waterloo sunset: *Kinks* / Natural born boogie: *Humble Pie* / Light my fire: *Feliciano, Jose* / Death of a clown: *Davies, Ray* / Pretty flamingo: *Manfred Mann* / First cut is the deepest: *Arnold, P.P.* / Stop stop stop: *Hollies* / Hurdy gurdy man: *Donovan* / Albatross: *Fleetwood Mac* / Itchycoo park: *Small Faces* / Dedicated follower of fashion: *Kinks* / Sabre dance: *Love Sculpture* / Let's go to San Francisco: *Flowerpot Men* / In the year 2525: *Zager & Evans* / (If you're going to): *McKenzie, Scott* / Mr. Tambourine man: *Byrds* / Something's gotten hold of my heart: *Pitney, Gene* / Carrie Anne: *Hollies* / House of the rising sun: *Animals* / Bang bang: *Cher* / Get out my life woman: *Dorsey, Lee* / Ain't got no I got life: *Simone, Nina* / Ob-la-di ob-la-da: *Marmalade* / Tired of waiting for you: *Kinks* / Silence is golden: *Tremeloes* / Working in a coalmine: *Dorsey, Lee* / Aquarius/Let the sun shine in: *Fifth Dimension* / Colours: *Donovan* / Oh happy day: *Hawkins, Edwin Singers*
CD Set ______ RCACD 201
RCA / Jul '97 / BMG

HITS OF THE 60'S
Let's have a party: *Jackson, Wanda* / My boyfriend's back: *Angels* / Tobacco road: *Nashville Teens* / With a girl like you: *Troggs* / Hats off to Larry: *Shannon, Del* / Ferry cross the Mersey: *Gerry & The Pacemakers* / Coming on strong: *Lee, Brenda* / Ob-la-di ob-la-da: *Marmalade* / Viva Bobby Joe: *Equals* / Then he kissed me: *Crystals* / He's so fine: *Chiffons* / Hippy hippy shake: *Swinging Blue Jeans* / Swiss maid: *Shannon, Del* / If I were a carpenter: *Darin, Bobby* / (Dance with) the guitar man: *Eddy, Duane* / Sea of heartbreak: *Gibson, Don* / Love is all around: *Troggs* / Only sixteen: *Cooke, Sam* / I heard it through the grapevine: *Gaye, Marvin* / Leader of the pack: *Shangri-Las*
CD ______ CD 6078
Music / Jun '97 / Target/BMG

HITS OF THE 60'S
CD ______ 101742
CMC / Jun '97 / BMG

HITS OF THE 60'S VOL.1 (4CD Set)
CD Set ______ MBSCD 401
Castle / Nov '95 / BMG

HITS OF THE 60'S VOL.1
Chapel of love: *Dixie Cups* / Will you still love me tomorrow: *Shirelles* / I'm into something good: *Herman's Hermits* / I'm telling you now: *Freddie & The Dreamers* / Nut rocker: *B-Bumble & The Stingers* / Young girl: *Puckett, Gary* / King of the road: *Miller, Roger* / Sheila: *Roe, Tommy* / Hey Paula: *Paul & Paula* / Save the last dance for me: *Drifters* / I'm sorry: *Lee, Brenda* / My old man's a dustman: *Donegan, Lonnie* / Little children: *Kramer, Billy J.* / Harper Valley PTA: *Riley, Jeannie C.* / Everlasting love: *Love Affair* / Baby come back: *Equals* / Sugar sugar: *Archies* / You'll never walk alone: *Gerry & The Pacemakers*
CD ______ MUCD 9007
Musketeer / Apr '95 / Disc

HITS OF THE 60'S VOL.1
CD ______ PLSCD 137
Pulse / Apr '96 / BMG

HITS OF THE 60'S VOL.1, THE (It's In His Kiss)
It's in his kiss (the shoop shoop song): *Everett, Betty* / Duke of Earl: *Chandler, Gene* / Surf city: *Jan & Dean* / Ruby, don't take your love to town: *Rogers, Kenny & The First Edition* / How do you do it: *Gerry & The Pacemakers* / You're the one: *Vogues* / Stay: *Williams, Maurice* / Downtown: *Clark, Petula* / Mrs. Brown you've got a lovely daughter: *Herman's Hermits* / Fools rush in: *Nelson, Rick* / Lovin' things: *Marmalade* / Diamond ring: *Lewis, Gary & The Playboys* / Walk on by: *Van Dyke, Leroy* / Under the boardwalk: *Drifters* / Let's go to San Francisco: *Flowerpot Men* / Get ready: *Temptations*
CD ______ 100802
CMC / May '97 / BMG

HITS OF THE 60'S VOL.2 (4CD Set)
CD Set ______ MBSCD 427
Castle / Nov '93 / BMG

HITS OF THE 60'S VOL.2
CD ______ MCCD 193
Music Club / Mar '95 / Disc / THE

HITS OF THE 60'S VOL.2
Runaway: *Shannon, Del* / Bachelors: *Diane* / Bad to me: *Kramer, Billy J.* / Ob-la-di ob-la-da: *Marmalade* / It's my party: *Gore, Lesley* / Do you love me: *Poole, Brian* / I like it: *Gerry & The Pacemakers* / Leader of the pack: *Shangri-Las* / Telstar: *Tornados* / When a man loves a woman: *Sledge, Percy* / Baby, now that I've found you: *Foundations* / Moody river: *Boone, Pat* / Alley oop: *Hollywood Argyles* / Big bad John: *Dean, Jimmy* / Deep purple: *Tempo, Nino & April Stevens* / Stranger on the shore: *Bilk, Acker* / Blue moon: *Marcels* / Those were the days: *Hopkin, Mary*
CD ______ MUCD 9008
Musketeer / Apr '95 / Disc

HITS OF THE 60'S VOL.2
CD ______ PLSCD 138
Pulse / Apr '96 / BMG

HITS OF THE 60'S VOL.2, THE (Sweets For My Sweet)
Sweets for my sweet: *Drifters* / Sugar sugar: *Archies* / Telstar: *Tornados* / Hello Mary Lou: *Nelson, Rick* / Light my fire: *Feliciano, Jose* / Dancing in the street: *Reeves, Martha & The Vandellas* / Winchester Cathedral: *New Vaudeville Band* / You're the one: *Clark, Petula* / Bad to me: *Kramer, Billy J.* / Raindrops keep falling on my head: *Thomas, B.J.* / Love grows (where my Rosemary goes0: *Edison Lighthouse* / I got rhythm: *Happenings* / Do you love me: *Poole, Brian* / There's a kind of hush: *Herman's Hermits* / Wait for me Marianne: *Marmalade* / Wild thing: *Troggs*
CD ______ 100812
CMC / May '97 / BMG

HITS OF THE 60'S VOL.3
CD ______ PLSCD 139
Pulse / Apr '96 / BMG

HITS OF THE 60'S VOL.3, THE (You'll Never Walk Alone)
You'll never walk alone: *Gerry & The Pacemakers* / When a man loves a woman: *Sledge, Percy* / My girl: *Temptations* / Stand by me: *King, Ben E.* / Teenage idol: *Nelson, Rick* / Strangers in the night: *Martino, Al* / Venus in blue jeans: *Clanton, Jimmy* / My love: *Clark, Petula* / Where have all the flowers gone: *Kingston Trio* / Love is all around: *Troggs* / Do you want to know a secret: *Kramer, Billy J.* / Silence is golden: *Tremeloes* / To know him is to love him: *Shirelles* / Que sera: *Feliciano, Jose* / With this ring: *Platters* / Someone, someone: *Poole, Brian*
CD ______ 100822
CMC / May '97 / BMG

HITS OF THE 60'S VOL.4
CD ______ PLSCD 140
Pulse / Apr '96 / BMG

HITS OF THE 60'S, THE
Longshot kick de bucket: *Pioneers* / That's nice: *Christian, Neil* / Tribute to Buddy Holly: *Berry, Mike* / 007: *Dekker, Desmond* / Wonderful world, beautiful people: *Cliff, Jimmy* / Lonely city: *Leyton, Johnny* / Red red wine: *Tribe, Tony* / Train to skaville: *Ethiopians* / My friend Jack: *Smoke* / Return of Django: *Upsetters* / Take a heart: *Sorrows* / Melting pot: *Blue Mink* / I put a spell on you: *Price, Alan* / Liquidator: *Harry J All Stars* / Shame: *Price, Alan* / Lone rider: *Leyton, Johnny*
CD ______ EMPRCD 574
Emporio / Jul '95 / Disc

HITS OF THE 60'S, THE
CD ______ PDSCD 540
Pulse / Aug '96 / BMG

HITS OF THE 60'S, THE (3CD Set)
It's in his kiss (the shoop shoop song): *Everett, Betty* / Duke of Earl: *Chandler, Gene* / Surf city: *Jan & Dean* / Ruby, don't take your love to town: *Rogers, Kenny* / How do you do it: *Gerry & The Pacemakers* / You're the one: *Vogues* / Stay: *Williams, Maurice* / Downtown: *Clark, Petula* / Mrs. Brown you've got a lovely daughter: *Herman's Hermits* / Fools rush in: *Nelson, Rick* / Lovin' things: *Marmalade* / This diamond ring: *Lewis, Gary & The Playboys* / Walk on by: *Van Dyke, Leroy* / Under the boardwalk: *Drifters* / Let's go to San Francisco: *Flowerpot Men* / Get ready: *Temptations* / Sweets for my sweet: *Drifters* / Sugar sugar: *Archies* / Telstar: *Tornados* / Hello Mary Lou: *Nelson, Rick* / Light my fire: *Feliciano, Jose* / Dancing in the street: *Reeves, Martha & The Vandellas* / Winchester cathedral: *New Vaudeville Band* / You're the one: *Clark, Petula* / Bad to me: *Kramer, Billy J.* / Raindrops keep falling on my head: *Thomas, B.J.* / Love grows (where my Rosemary goes): *Edison Lighthouse* / I got rhythm: *Happenings* / Do you love me: *Poole, Brian* / There's a kind of hush: *Herman's Hermits* / Wait for me Marianne: *Marmalade* / Wild thing: *Troggs* / You'll never walk alone: *Gerry & The Pacemakers* / When a man loves a woman: *Sledge, Percy* / My girl: *Temptations* / Stand by me: *King, Ben E.* / Teenage idol: *Nelson, Rick* / Strangers in the night: *Martino, Al* / Venus in blue jeans: *Clanton, Jimmy* / My love: *Clark, Petula* / Where have all the flowers gone: *Kingston Trio* / Love is all around: *Troggs* / Do you want to know a secret: *Kramer, Billy J.* / Silence is golden: *Tremeloes* / To know him is to love him: *Shirelles* / Que sera: *Felici-*

ano, Jose / With this ring: *Platters* / Someone, someone: *Poole, Brian*
CD Set 100792
CMC / May '97 / BMG

HITS OF THE 70'S (2CD Set)
Denis: *Blondie* / Peaches: *Stranglers* / Mr. Blue sky: *ELO* / Daniel: *John, Elton* / Roadrunner: *Richman, Jonathan & Modern Lovers* / Apeman: *Kinks* / Cars: *Numan, Gary* / Baker Street: *Rafferty, Gerry* / Walk on the wildside: *Reed, Lou* / All the young dudes: *Mott The Hoople* / Love train: *O'Jays* / Heart of glass: *Blondie* / Show you the way to go: *Jacksons* / Vincent: *McLean, Don* / Native New Yorker: *Odyssey* / Make me smile: *Harley, Steve & Cockney Rebel* / Without you: *Nilsson* / Sylvia's mother: *Dr. Hook & The Medicine Show* / September: *Earth, Wind & Fire* / Lean on me: *Withers, Bill* / Egyptian reggae: *Richman, Jonathan & Modern Lovers* / All right now: *Free* / In the summertime: *Mungo Jerry* / Down down: *Status Quo* / Rasputin: *Boney M* / That lady: *Isley Brothers* / Rock your baby: *McRae, George* / Love grows where my Rosemary goes: *Edison Lighthouse* / See my baby jive: *Wizzard* / Blockbuster: *Sweet* / I'm the leader of the gang: *Glitter, Gary* / Who do you love: *Juicy Lucy* / Seasons in the sun: *Jacks, Terry* / Knock three times: *Dawn* / Best of my love: *Emotions* / Like sister and brother: *Drifters* / Lost in France: *Tyler, Bonnie*
CD Set RCACD 202
RCA / Jul '97 / BMG

HITS OF THE 70'S (18 Original Hits By The Original Stars)
Banner man: *Blue Mink* / (To be) young gifted and black: *Bob & Marcia* / If I had you: *Korgis* / Clog dance: *Violinski* / Oohh I do: *De Paul, Lynsey* / Nice one Cyril: *Cockerel Chorus* / Tomorrow night: *Atomic Rooster* / Love of the common people: *Thomas, Nicky* / Moon river: *Greyhound* / Suzanne beware of the devil: *Livingstone, Dandy* / Desperate Dan: *Lieutenant Pigeon* / Brandy scott: *English, Scott* / Snoopy vs the red dragon: *Hotshots* / 7 Teen: *Regents* / Chirpy chirpy cheep cheep: *Kissoon, Mac & Katie* / Hotshot: *Blue, Barry*
CD EMPRCD 583
Emporio / Oct '95 / Disc

HITS OF THE 70'S, THE
CD PDSCD 525
Pulse / Aug '96 / BMG

HITS OF THE 80'S
Love action (I believe in love): *Human League* / Church of the poison mind: *Culture Club* / Temptation: *Heaven 17* / Echo beach: *Martha & The Muffins* / Black Man Ray: *China Crisis* / Love don't live here anymore: *Nail, Jimmy* / You little thief: *Sharkey, Feargal* / Driving away from home: *It's Immaterial* / We don't have to take our clothes off: *Stewart, Jermaine* / (I just) died in your arms: *Cutting Crew* / Shattered dreams: *Johnny Hates Jazz* / China in your hand: *T'Pau* / Sinful: *Wylie, Pete* / Dream kitchen: *Frazier Chorus* / Straight up: *Abdul, Paula* / Mary's prayer: *Danny Wilson* / If only I could: *Youngblood, Sydney*
CD CDVIP 126
Virgin / Jul '94 / EMI

HITS OF THE 80'S
Centrefold: *Geils, J. Band* / Road to nowhere: *Talking Heads* / French kissin' in the USA: *Harry, Deborah* / Nineteen: *Hardcastle, Paul* / Wishful thinking: *China Crisis* / Running up that hill: *Bush, Kate* / If I was: *Ure, Midge* / She makes my day: *Palmer, Robert* / Heart and soul: *T'Pau* / True: *Spandau Ballet* / Cushed by the wheels of industry: *Heaven 17* / Dancing with tears in my eyes: *Ultravox* / Don't worry, be happy: *McFerrin, Bobby* / We close our eyes: *Go West* / Letter from America: *Proclaimers* / More than I can say: *Sayer, Leo*
CD CDMFP 6136
Music For Pleasure / Feb '95 / EMI

HITS OF THE 80'S (2CD Set)
This is the right time: *Stansfield, Lisa* / True: *Spandau Ballet* / Don't stop the dance: *Ferry, Bryan* / Harry's Game theme: *Clannad* / Simply irresistable: *Palmer, Robert* / Call me: *Blondie* / I scare myself: *Dolby, Thomas* / Would I lie to you: *Eurythmics* / Chain reaction: *Ross, Diana* / Sometimes: *Erasure* / Walk like an Egyptian: *Bangles* / Only you: *Yazoo* / It doesn't have to be this way: *Blow Monkeys* / Do you really want to hurt me: *Culture Club* / Power of love: *Rush, Jennifer* / Ghostbusters: *Parker, Ray Jr.* / It ain't what you do: *Fun Boy Three & Bananarama* / Wherever I lay my hat: *Young, Paul* / White wedding: *Idol, Billy* / Walking on sunshine: *Katrina & The Waves* / Band of gold: *Sylvester* / Atmospherics: *Robinson, Tom* / I can't go for that (no can do): *Hall & Oates* / Love is a battlefield: *Benatar, Pat* / No more the fool: *Brooks, Elkie* / We built this city: *Starship* / Favourite shirts (Boy meets girl): *Haircut 100* / Modern girl: *Meat Loaf* / System addict: *Five Star* / Loco in Acapulco: *Four Tops* / Who's zoomin' who: *Franklin, Aretha* / 19: *Hardcastle, Paul* / I'm so excited: *Pointer Sisters* / Ghost town: *Specials* / Perfect: *Fairground Attraction* / Friends: *Stewart, Amii*
CD Set RCACD 212
RCA / Jul '97 / BMG

HITS OF THE 80'S VOL.1
Love is a stranger: *Eurythmics* / Who's zoomin' who: *Franklin, Aretha* / Never gonna give you up: *Astley, Rick* / Perfect: *Fairground Attraction* / Slow hand: *Pointer Sisters* / Funkin' for Jamaica: *Browne, Sandra* / Ride on time: *Black Box* / I can't go for that (no can do): *Hall & Oates* / Runaway boys: *Stray Cats* / Broken wings: *Mr. Mister* / Every day hurts: *Sad Cafe* / Love plus one: *Haircut 100*
CD 74321446882
Camden / Feb '97 / BMG

HITS OF THE 80'S VOL.1, THE
West End girls: *Pet Shop Boys* / Mickey: *Basil, Toni* / Special brew: *Bad Manners* / Feels like I'm in love: *Marie, Kelly* / Swing the mood: *Jive Bunny* / High energy: *Thomas, Evelyn* / Move closer: *Jones, Tom* / Transfer affection: *Flock Of Seagulls* / Bass (how low can you go): *Harris, Simon* / Touch me (I want your body): *Fox, Samantha* / Can't shake that feeling: *Big Fun* / You think you're a man: *Divine* / Fantasy Island: *Tight Fit* / Hands off she's mine: *Beat* / Jack mix IV: *Mirage* / On a crowded street: *Pennington, Barbara*
CD 100102
CMC / May '97 / BMG

HITS OF THE 80'S VOL.2
Days: *MacColl, Kirsty* / Do you really want to hurt me: *Culture Club* / Christian: *China Crisis* / Life's what you make it: *Talk Talk* / Looking for Linda: *Hue & Cry* / Turning Japanese: *Vapors* / This is not a love song: *Public Image Ltd* / Sit and wait: *Youngblood, Sydney* / Come live with me: *Heaven 17* / Calling all the heroes: *It Bites* / Big fun: *Inner City* / Wild world: *Priest, Maxi* / Night boat to Cairo: *Madness* / Moonlight shadow: *Oldfield, Mike* / Too late for goodbyes: *Lennon, Julian* / Turn back the clock: *Johnny Hates Jazz* / Heart and soul: *T'Pau* / Bette Davis eyes: *Carnes, Kim* / Enola Gay: *OMD*
CD CDVIP 136
Virgin / Sep '95 / EMI

HITS OF THE 80'S VOL.2
Who's that girl: *Eurythmics* / Japanese boy: *Aneka* / Kyrie: *Mr. Mister* / Man eater: *Hall & Oates* / You're the voice: *Farnham, John* / Radio Africa: *Latin Quarter* / No memory: *Scarlet Fantastic* / Star: *Dee, Kiki* / Funkin' for Jamaica: *Browne, Tom* / Loco in Acapulco: *Browne, Tom* / Favourite shirts: *Haircut 100* / Einstein a go go: *Landscape* / First picture of you: *Lotus Eaters* / Automatic: *Pointer Sisters* / Doctor doctor: *Thompson Twins* / Crash: *Primitives* / Nothing's gonna stop us now: *Starship* / All out of love: *Air Supply*
CD 743215002628
Camden / Jun '97 / BMG

HITS OF THE 80'S VOL.2, THE
Kiss: *Jones, Tom & Art Of Noise* / Blame it on the boogie: *Big Fun* / That's what I like: *Jive Bunny* / Wishing (if I had a photograph of you): *Flock Of Seagulls* / Can can: *Bad Manners* / Lion sleeps tonight: *Tight Fit* / If you're ready (come go with me): *Turner, Ruby & Jonathan Butler* / Nothing's gonna stop me now: *Fox, Samantha* / Jack mix II: *Mirage* / Close to perfection: *Brown, Miquel* / Mirror in the bathroom: *Beat* / Fan the flame: *Pennington, Barbara* / I eat cannibal: *Toto Coelo* / Wee rule: *Wee Papa Girl Rappers* / Walk like a man: *Divine* / Saddle up: *Christie, David* / Here comes that sound: *Harris, Simon*
CD 100112
CMC / May '97 / BMG

HITS OF THE 80'S, THE (3CD Set)
High energy: *Thomas, Evelyn* / Fan the flame: *Pennington, Barbara* / So many men, so little time: *Brown, Miquel* / Who knows the devil: *Man To Man* / Great minds think alike: *Wells, James* / Animal magnetism: *Pandy, Darryl* / Standing in line: *Mancha, Steve* / Take one step forward: *Wills, Viola & Noel McCalla* / Chalk it up to experience: *Thomas, Evelyn* / Close to perfection: *Brown, Miquel* / Hands off: *Pallas, Laura* / Ain't no mountain high enough: *Powell, Shezwae* / Love's gone mad: *Seventh Avenue* / West End girls: *Pet Shop Boys* / Mickey: *Basil, Toni* / Special brew: *Bad Manners* / Feels like I'm in love: *Marie, Kelly* / Swing the mood: *Jive Bunny* / High energy: *Thomas, Evelyn* / Move closer: *Jones, Tom* / Transfer affection: *Flock Of Seagulls* / Bass (how low can you go): *Harris, Simon* / Touch me (I want your body): *Fox, Samantha* / Can't shake that feeling: *Big Fun* / You think you're a man: *Divine* / Fantasy Island: *Tight Fit* / Hands off she's mine: *Beat* / Jack mix IV: *Mirage* / On a crowded street: *Pennington, Barbara* / Kiss: *Jones, Tom & Art Of Noise* / Blame it on the boogie: *Big Fun* / That's what I like: *Jive Bunny* / Wishing (if I had a photograph of you): *Flock Of Seagulls* / Can can: *Bad Manners* / Lion sleeps tonight: *Tight Fit* / If you're ready (come go with me): *Butler, Jonathan* / Nothing's gonna stop me now: *Fox, Samantha* / Jack mix II: *Mirage* / Close to perfection: *Brown, Miquel* / Mirror in the bathroom: *Beat* / Fan the flame: *Pennington, Barbara* / I eat cannibal: *Toto Coelo* / Wee rule: *Wee Papa Girl Rappers* / Walk like a man: *Divine* / Saddle up: *Christie, David* / Here comes that sound: *Harris, Simon*
CD Set 101212
CMC / May '97 / BMG

HITS OF THE 90'S
Whole of the moon: *Waterboys* / Thinking about your love: *Thomas, Kenny* / King of the road: *Proclaimers* / Ring my bell: *Adeva & Monie Love* / Is it like today: *World Party* / Got to have your love: *Mantronix* / Love and anger: *Bush, Kate* / Hold on: *Wilson Phillips* / I believe: *EMF* / Faithful: *Go West* / One and only: *Hawkes, Chesney* / Don't worry: *Appleby, Kim* / U can't touch this: *MC Hammer* / Ice ice baby: *Vanilla Ice* / Turtle power: *Partners In Kryme* / Counting every minute: *Sonia*
CD CDMFP 6139
Music For Pleasure / Feb '95 / EMI

HITS OF THE BLITZ
If a grey-haired lady says How's yer father: *Wilbur, Jay & his band* / We'll meet again: *Petersen, Joe* / It's a hap-hap-happy day: *Roy, Harry & His Orchestra* / We must all stick together: *Geraldo & His Orchestra* / Mem'ry of a rose: *Loss, Joe Band* / Man who comes around: *Connelly, Campbell & Co. Ltd* / Oh Johnny oh Johnny: *Young, Arthur* / Run rabbit run: *Ambrose & His Orchestra* / Careless: *White, Jack & His Collegians* / Memories live longer than dreams: *Dash, Irwin & Monte Ray* / I haven't time to be a millionaire: *Gonella, Nat & His New Georgians* / It's a lovely day tomorrow: *Hutchinson, Leslie 'Hutch'* / nightingale sang in berkeley square: *Layton, Turner* / I hear bluebirds: *Organ Dance Band & Me* / Tiggerty boo: *Geraldo & His Orchestra* / (We're gonna hang out the) washing on the Siegfried Line: *Ambrose & His Orchestra* / Make believe island: *Bowlly, Al & Jim Mesene* / I shall be waiting: *Lipton, Sydney & His Grosvenor House Orchestra* / Arm in arm: *Lipton, Sydney & His Grosvenor House Orchestra* / FDR Jones: *Askey, Arthur & Jack Hylton* / Crash bang I want to go home: *Robins, Phyllis* / In the mood: *Philips, Sid Trio*
CD PASTCD 9754
Flapper / Mar '92 / Pinnacle

HITS OF THE PAST VOL.2
CD ANGCD 017
Angela / Jul '96 / Jet Star

HITS OF THE WAR YEARS
CD CWNCD 2003
Javelin / Jun '95 / Henry Hadaway / THE

HITS REVIVAL
It's in his kiss (the shoop shoop song): *Everett, Betty* / Love on a mountain top: *Knight, Robert* / Dancing in the street: *Reeves, Martha* / Dizzy: *Roe, Tommy* / Happy together: *Turtles* / She's not there: *Zombies* / Harlem shuffle: *Bob & Earl* / Under the boardwalk: *Drifters* / Rock your baby: *McCrae, George* / In crowd: *Gray, Dobie* / It's my party: *Gore, Lesley* / What becomes of the broken hearted: *Ruffin, Jimmy* / If you don't know me by now: *Melvin, Harold & The Bluenotes* / Great pretender: *Platters* / Groovy kind of love: *Fontana, Wayne* / When a man loves a woman: *Sledge, Percy* / End of the world: *Davis, Skeeter* / Sorrow: *Merseys*
CD ECD 3050
K-Tel / Jan '95 / K-Tel

HITS THAT LIVE FOREVER - 1950'S (2CD Set)
When I fall in love: *Cole, Nat 'King'* / Blueberry Hill: *Domino, Fats* / Seven little girls sitting on the back seat: *Avons* / Why do fools fall in love: *Lymon, Frankie & The Teenagers* / Sixteen tons: *Ford, Tennessee Ernie* / This ole house: *Anthony, Billie* / Oh mein Papa: *Calvert, Eddie* / Dreamboat: *Cogan, Alma* / C'mon everybody: *Cochran, Eddie* / Side saddle: *Conway, Russ* / Cry me a river: *London, Julie* / No other love: *Hilton, Ronnie* / True love: *Crosby, Bing & Grace Kelly* / Comes-a-long-alove: *Starr, Kay* / That's amore: *Martin, Dean* / Lollipop: *Mudlarks* / Softly softly: *Murray, Ruby* / Stairway of love: *Holiday, Michael* / Kisses sweeter than wine: *Rodgers, Jimmie* / He's got the whole world in his hands: *London, Laurie* / Witch Doctor: *Lang, Don* / Be my girl: *Dale, Jim* / Come softly to me: *Fleetwoods* / Great pretender: *Parkinson, Jimmy* / Indian love call: *Whitman, Slim* / Fever: *Lee, Peggy* / Only sixteen: *Douglas, Craig* / Story of my life: *Holiday, Michael* / Pickin' a chicken: *Boswell, Eve* / Unchained melody: *Baxter, Les* / Memories are made of this: *Martin, Dean* / White sports coat: *King Brothers* / Ain't that a shame: *Domino, Fats* / Dragnet: *Anthony, Ray* / Zambesi: *Busch, Lou* / Ma he's making eyes at me: *Otis, Johnny* / Ragtime Cowboy Joe: *Chipmunks* / Here in my heart: *Martino, Al* / Tom Dooley: *Kingston Trio* / Be bop a lula: *Vincent, Gene* / St. Therese of the roses: *Vaughan, Malcolm* / Ballad of Davy Crocket: *Ford, Tennessee Ernie* / Don't laugh at me: *Wisdom, Norman* / Mad passionate love: *Bresslaw, Bernard* / Rose Marie: *Whitman, Slim* / Pretend: *Cole, Nat 'King'* / Cherry pink & apple blossom white: *Calvert, Eddie* / Big man: *Four Preps* / Teenager in love: *Douglas, Craig* / Bell bottom blues: *Cogan, Alma*
CD Set CDDL 1308
Music For Pleasure / Jun '96 / EMI

HITS THAT LIVE FOREVER - 1960'S (2CD Set)
House of the rising sun: *Animals* / God only knows: *Beach Boys* / Here I go again: *Hollies* / I'm telling you now: *Freddie & The Dreamers* / Hi Ho silver lining: *Beck, Jeff* / Do wha diddy diddy: *Manfred Mann* / Carnival is over: *Seekers* / Yesterday: *Monro, Matt* / Three steps to heaven: *Cochran, Eddie* / Walkin' back to happiness: *Shapiro, Helen* / How do you do it: *Gerry & The Pacemakers* / Poor me: *Faith, Adam* / What now my love: *Bassey, Shirley* / Shakin' all over: *Kidd, Johnny & The Pirates* / She wears my ring: *King, Solomon* / Little children: *Kramer, Billy J. & The Dakotas* / True love ways: *Peter & Gordon* / Wonderful land: *Shadows* / Standing on the corner: *King Brothers* / High time: *Jones, Paul* / A little loving: *Fourmost* / He ain't heavy, he's my brother: *Hollies* / There's a kind of hush: *Herman's Hermits* / You're sixteen: *Burnette, Johnny* / Boom bang-a-bang: *Lulu* / Good vibrations: *Beach Boys* / Anyone who had a heart: *Black, Cilla* / Pasadena: *Temperance Seven* / Where do you go to my lovely: *Sarstedt, Peter* / Mony Mony: *James, Tommy & The Shondells* / Michael: *Highwaymen* / A world of our own: *Seekers* / I remember you: *Ifield, Frank* / Somewhere: *Proby, P.J.* / Lily the pink: *Scaffold* / Prety flamingo: *Manfred Mann* / Hippy hippy shake: *Swinging Blue Jeans* / Rubber ball: *Vee, Bobby* / I'm the urban spaceman: *Bonzo Dog Band* / Up on the roof: *Lynch, Kenny* / Blue moon: *Marcels* / All I have to do is dream: *Campbell, Glen & Bobbie Gentry*
CD Set CDDL 1311
Music For Pleasure / Jun '96 / EMI

HITS THAT LIVE FOREVER - 1970'S (2CD Set)
Heart of glass: *Blondie* / Air that I breathe: *Hollies* / Make me smile (Come up and see me sometime): *Harley, Steve & Cockney Rebel* / Wow: *Bush, Kate* / Tap turns on the water: *CCS* / Baker Street: *Rafferty, Gerry* / Let's work together: *Canned Heat* / See my baby jive: *Wizzard* / American Pie: *McLean, Don* / I hear you knocking: *Edmunds, Dave* / So you win again: *Hot Chocolate* / Oh boy: *Mud* / Motor Bikin': *Spedding, Chris* / Summer(The First Time): *Goldsboro, Bobby* / Can the Can: *Quatro, Suzi* / Roll over Beethoven: *ELO* / Some girls: *Racey* / Don't let it die: *Smith, Hurricane* / January: *Pilot* / Tears of a Clown: *Beat* / You sexy thing: *Hot Chocolate* / Nutbush City Limits: *Turner, Tina* / Tiger Feet: *Mud* / Judy Teen: *Harley, Steve & Cockney Rebel* / Denis: *Blondie* / A little bit more: *Dr. Hook* / Devil Gate Drive: *Quatro, Suzi* / Queen of Clubs: *KC & The Sunshine Band* / Vincent: *McLean, Don* / 2-4-6-8 Motorway: *Robinson, Tom* / Sylvia: *Focus* / If I only had words: *Fitzgerald, Scott & Yvonne Keeley* / Living on the Frontline: *Grant, Eddy* / Where is the love: *Wright, Betty* / Dancing easy: *Williams, Danny* / Fancy pants: *Kenny* / Dance with the Devil: *Powell, Cozy* / Rock your baby: *McCrae, George* / Right back where we started from: *Nightingale, Maxine* / Dancing in the City: *Hain, Marshall*
CD Set CDDL 1314
Music For Pleasure / Jun '96 / EMI

HITSMANIA '96 VOL.1
CD TCD 2822
Telstar / Feb '96 / BMG

HITSVILLE USA (The Tamla Motown Singles Collection 1959-1971/4CD Set)
Money (That's what I want): *Strong, Barrett* / Shop around: *Miracles* / Please Mr. Postman: *Marvelettes* / Jamie: *Holland, Eddie* / One who really loves you: *Wells, Mary* / Do you love me: *Contours* / Beechwood 4-5789: *Marvelettes* / You beat me to the punch: *Wells, Mary* / Stubborn kind of fellow: *Gaye, Marvin* / Two lovers: *Wells, Mary* / You really got a hold on me: *Miracles* / Come and get these memories: *Reeves, Martha & The Vandellas* / Pride and joy: *Gaye, Marvin* / Fingertips-Part 2: *Wonder, Stevie* / Heatwave: *Reeves, Martha & The Vandellas* / Mickey's monkey: *Miracles* / Leaving here: *Holland, Eddie* / Way you do the things you do: *Temptations* / My guy: *Wells, Mary* / Devil with the blue dress: *Shorty Long* / Every little bit hurts: *Holloway, Brenda* / Baby I need your loving: *Four Tops* / Dancing in the street: *Reeves, Martha & The Vandellas* / My smile is just a frown (turned upside down): *Crawford, Carolyn* / Needle in a haystack: *Velvelettes* / Baby love: *Supremes* / Come see about me: *Supremes* / How sweet it is (to be loved by you): *Gaye, Marvin* / My Girl: *Temptations* / My girl: *Temptations* / Really saying something: *Velvelettes* / Ask the lonely: *Four Tops* / Shotgun: *Walker, Junior & The All Stars* / Nowhere to run: *Reeves, Martha & The Vandellas* / When I'm gone: *Holloway, Brenda* / Ooo baby baby: *Miracles* / I can't help myself: *Four Tops* / First I look at the purse: *Contours* / Tracks of my tears: *Miracles* / It's the same old song: *Four Tops* / Love (makes me do foolish things): *Reeves, Martha & The Vandellas* / Take me in your arms: *Weston, Kim* / Uptight: *Wonder, Stevie* / Don't mess with Bill: *Marvelettes* / Darling baby: *Elgins* / This old heart of mine (is weak for you): *Isley Brothers* / Greetings (this is Uncle Sam): *Monitors* / Function at the junction: *Shorty Long* / Roadrunner:

Walker, Junior & The All Stars / Ain't too proud to beg: *Temptations* / What becomes of the broken hearted: *Ruffin, Jimmy* / How sweet it is (to be loved by you): *Walker, Junior & The All Stars* / Love's gone bad: *Clark, Chris* / You can't hurry love: *Supremes* / Beauty is only skin deep: *Temptations* / Heaven must have sent you: *Elgins* / Reach out, I'll be there: *Four Tops* / I'm losing you: *Temptations* / Standing in the shadows of love: *Four Tops* / It takes two: *Gaye, Marvin & Kim Weston* / Hunter gets captured by the game: *Marvelettes* / Jimmy Mack: *Reeves, Martha & The Vandellas* / Bernadette: *Four Tops* / Ain't no mountain high enough: *Gaye, Marvin & Tammi Terrell* / More love: *Robinson, Smokey & The Miracles* / I heard it through the grapevine: *Knight, Gladys & The Pips* / I second that emotion: *Robinson, Smokey & The Miracles* / I wish it would rain: *Temptations* / I can't give back the love I feel for you: *Wright, Rita* / Does your mama know about me: *Taylor, Bobby & The Vancouvers* / Ain't nothing like the real thing: *Gaye, Marvin & Tammi Terrell* / Love child: *Ross, Diana & The Supremes* / For once in my life: *Wonder, Stevie* / Cloud 9: *Temptations* / I heard it through the grapevine: *Gaye, Marvin* / Baby, baby, don't cry: *Robinson, Smokey & The Miracles* / Twenty five miles: *Starr, Edwin* / My whole world ended (the moment you left me): *Starr, Edwin* / What does it take (to win your love): *Walker, Junior & The All Stars* / I can't get next to you: *Temptations* / Baby I'm for real: *Originals* / Up the ladder to the roof: *Supremes* / I want you back: *Jackson Five* / Bells: *Originals* / Get ready: *Rare Earth* / ABC: *Jackson Five* / Ball of confusion: *Temptations* / Love you save: *Jackson Five* / Signed, sealed, delivered (I'm yours): *Wonder, Stevie* / War: *Starr, Edwin* / It's a shame: *Spinners* / Ain't no mountain high enough: *Temptations* / Still water (love): *Four Tops* / I'll be there: *Jackson Five* / Stoned love: *Supremes* / If I were your woman: *Knight, Gladys & The Pips* / Just my imagination: *Temptations* / What's going on: *Gaye, Marvin* / Never can say goodbye: *Jackson Five* / Nathan Jones: *Supremes* / I don't want to do wrong: *Knight, Gladys & The Pips* / Smiling faces sometimes: *Undisputed Truth* / Mercy mercy me: *Gaye, Marvin* / I just want to celebrate: *Rare Earth*
CD Set ______ 5301292
Motown / Jan '93 / PolyGram

HITZ BLITZ
Never forget: *Take That* / Search for a hero: *M-People* / Girl like you: *Collins, Edwyn* / Whiter shade of pale: *Lennox, Annie* / Boom boom boom: *Outhere Brothers* / Love rules: *West End* / Stuck on you: *PJ & Duncan* / Where is the feeling: *Minogue, Kylie* / Bomb: *Bucketheads* / Try me out: *Corona* / Surrender your love: *Nightcrawlers* / Shoot me with your love: *D:Ream* / Keep warm: *Jinny* / Right in the night (fall in love with the music): *Jam & Spoon* / Sing it: *Mozaic* / Humpin' around: *Brown, Bobby* / Freek n' you: *Jodeci* / Your loving arms: *Martin, Billie Ray* / Whoomph (there it is): *Clock* / Freedom: *Gayle, Michelle* / Hands up, hands up: *Zig & Zag* / Unchained melody: *Robson & Jerome*
CD ______ RADCD 23
Global TV / Aug '95 / BMG

HITZ BLITZ
Ooh ah, just a little bit / We've got it going on / Macarena / Wannabe / Keep on jumpin' / X-files / Children / So pure / I don't wanna be a star / Missing / Born slippy / Mysterious girl / How bizarre / Return of the mack / 1,2,3,4,(sumpin' new) / Spaceman / How deep is your love / Breakfast at Tiffany's
CD ______ SUMCD 4085
Summit / Nov '96 / Sound & Media

HITZONE '97 (2CD Set)
If you ever: *East 17 & Gabrielle* / I'll never break your heart: *Backstreet Boys* / Father and son: *Boyzone* / Lifted: *Lighthouse Family* / Flame: *Fine Young Cannibals* / Make it with you: *Let Loose* / How bizarre: *OMC* / Flava: *Andre, Peter* / Do you still: *East 17* / When I fall in love: *Ant & Dec* / Breathe: *Prodigy* / Born slippy: *Underworld* / Wrong: *Everything But The Girl* / Hyperballad: *Bjork* / Sugar is sweeter: *C.J. Bolland* / So pure: *Baby D* / I'm alive: *Stretch n' Vern & Maddog* / There's nothing I won't do: *JX* / Follow the rules: *Livin' Joy* / Blurred: *Pianoman* / Peacock suit: *Weller, Paul* / One to another: *Charlatans* / Twisted: *Skunk Anansie* / Getting better: *Shed Seven* / Sandstorm: *Cast* / Good enough: *Dodgy* / Goldfinger: *Ash* / Trash: *Suede* / You're gorgeous: *Baby Bird* / Day we caught the train: *Ocean Colour Scene* / Breakfast at Tiffany's: *Deep Blue Something* / She said: *Longpigs* / You and me versus the world: *Space* / One of us: *Osbourne, Joan* / So in love with you: *Duke* / Stressed out: *Tribe Called Quest & Faith Evans* / Golden brown: *Kaleef* / California love: *2Pac & Dr Dre* / Whole lotta love: *Goldbug* / Theme from Mission: Impossible: *Mullen, Larry & Adam Clayton*
CD Set ______ 5331872
PolyGram TV / Dec '96 / PolyGram

HMV SAMPLER
Sleepy lagoon: *Coates, Eric* / Springtime suite fresh morning: *Coates, Eric* / Springtime suite noonday song: *Coates, Eric* / London suite (part 2): *Coates, Eric* / Saxo-rhapsody: *Coates, Eric* / Calling all workers: *Coates, Eric* / Coronation Scot: *Torch, Sidney* / Jumping bean: *Torch, Sidney* / Dambusters march: *Torch, Sidney* / Horse guards, Whitehall: *Torch, Sidney* / Barwick Green: *Torch, Sidney* / Smilin' through: *Booth, Webster* / Roses of Picardy: *Oldham, Derek* / I'll walk beside you: *McCormack, John* / Perfect day: *Robeson, Paul* / Bless this house: *Midgley, Walter* / Kashmiri love song: *Dawson, Peter* / Over the gate: *Miles, Bernard* / Me an' old Charlie: *Miles, Bernard* / Mind your heads please: *Miles, Bernard* / Danny Deever: *Miles, Bernard*
CD ______ CDHRS 1
HMV / May '92 / EMI

HOBO BOP
Hobo bop: *Nelson, Tommy* / That long black train: *Franklin, Stewart* / Hey Mr. Porter: *Pruitt, Ralph* / I'm so lonely: *Flagg, Bill* / Goodbye train: *Foley, Jim* / Mystery train: *Taylor, Vernon* / Ho bo: *Money, Curley* / Midnight line: *Riley, Bob* / Long gone night train: *Norman, Gene* / One way track: *Davis, Hank* / Boxcar blues: *Spurling, Hank* / I'm a hobo: *Reevers, Danny* / Loco choo choo: *Miller Bros.* / Ride that train: *James, Leon* / Midnite express: *Tremaines* / Going back to Dixie: *Busbice, Wayne* / Big black train: *Johnston, Stan* / Midnight train: *Newman, Wayne* / Train wistle boogie: *Dean, Charles* / Big train: *Law, Art* / Lonely lonely train: *Anderson, Sonny* / Folsom prison blues: *Tidwell, Billy* / Train: *Runabouts* / Haunted train: *Millionaires* / Woman train: *Davis, Hank* / Miami road: *Phillipson, Larry Lee* / Kansas city train: *Lowery, Frankie* / Long black train: *Farmer, Larry* / Train rock: *Boni, Johnny*
CD ______ CDBB 55012
Buffalo Bop / Apr '94 / Rollercoaster

HOKUM BLUES 1924-1929
CD ______ DOCD 5370
Document / Jul '95 / ADA / Hot Shot / Jazz Music

HOLD THAT DREAM
CD ______ NTHEN 026CD
Now & Then / Mar '96 / Plastic Head

HOLD TIGHT - IT'S THE 60'S (2CD Set)
CD Set ______ PBXCD 401
Pulse / Nov '96 / BMG

HOLD YOUR GROUND
CD ______ LF 131CD
Lost & Found / Jan '95 / Plastic Head

HOLDING ON
CD ______ SHCD 6015
Shanachie / Oct '95 / ADA / Greensleeves / Koch

HOLDING UP HALF THE SKY (Roots Daughters - Women In Reggae)
CD ______ SH 45027
Shanachie / Oct '96 / ADA / Greensleeves / Koch

HOLDING UP HALF THE SKY (Voices Of African Women)
CD ______ SHCD 64073
Shanachie / Apr '97 / ADA / Greensleeves / Koch

HOLDING UP HALF THE SKY (Voices of Celtic Women)
CD ______ SH 78011
Shanachie / Jul '97 / ADA / Greensleeves / Koch

HOLIDAY GREETINGS
CD ______ SOW 90142
Sounds Of The World / Oct '95 / Target/ BMG

HOLIDAY IN GREECE (2CD Set)
Zorba the Greek / Thekos din karthoula sou / Doxa te theo / Lemaishani / Meray / To bouzouki echi kefia / Fantasia / Adzenta / State of angels / Medelinyia / Poune ta kronia / To yelasto pedi / Horos tou sakena / Aprillis / I kambanes / Oli nichta / Siko horepse sirtaki / Kai mis e dris ston kafenai / Lefteris / Sinchoriste to apopse to pedi / to ena ftero mou ekopses / mikhalis / Epifania / Psilli sta ftiamo / Traditional bouzouki solo / Srata te strata / Kaymos / Palanta tou antrikou / Vraho vraho / Ekeine / O delefdaos mou stathmos / Thello varya thiblo benya
CD Set ______ 330192
Hallmark / Jul '96 / Carlton

HOLIDAY TRAILS FROM ROUMANIA
CD ______ CNCD 5983
Disky / Apr '94 / Disky / THE

HOLIDAYS IN THE SUN VOL.1
CD ______ HITS 01
Visionary/Jettisoundz / Jun '97 / Cargo / Pinnacle / RTM/Disc / THE

HOLIDAYS IN THE SUN VOL.2
CD ______ HITS 02
Visionary/Jettisoundz / Jun '97 / Cargo / Pinnacle / RTM/Disc / THE

HOLLERIN'
CD ______ ROUCD 0071
Rounder / Jul '95 / ADA / CM / Direct

HOLLYWOOD ROCK 'N' ROLL VOL.1 (12 Rare Rockabilly Tracks)
Blue jeans: *Glenn, Glen* / Everybody's movin': *Glenn, Glen* / Would you: *Rock 'n' Roll* / Goofin' around: *Glenn, Glen* / I'm glad my baby's gone away: *Glenn, Glen* / One cup of coffee: *Glenn, Glen* / Don't push: *Deal, Don* / Topsy turvy: *Zeppa, Ben Joe* / Great shakin' fever: *Burnette, Dorsey* / Ezactly: *Busch, Dick* / Hollywood party: *Busch, Dick* / He will come back to me: *Leslie, Alis*
CD ______ CDCHM 1
Ace / Oct '89 / Pinnacle

HOLLYWOOD ROCK 'N' ROLL VOL.2
She just tears me up: *Stewart, Wynn* / Down on the farm: *Downing, Big Al* / So tough: *Kuf Linx* / Three months to kill: *Duvall, Huelyn* / Kee-ro-ryin': *Johnny & Jonie* / Jungle hop: *Tyler, Kip* / Gotta lot of rhythm in my soul: *Cline, Patsy* / Shiver: *Burgess, Dave* / Uncle Tom got caught: *Stewart, Wynn* / Oh babe: *Downing, Big Al* / Come on: *Stewart, Wynn* / Go little go cat: *Four Teens* / Spark plug: *Four Teens* / Didn't it rock: *Jim 'n' Rod* / Bad Dad: *Davis, Gene* / Great day in the morning: *Four Teens* / Life begins at four o'clock: *Milano, Bobby* / Shiverin' and shakin': *Beard, Dean* / Egad, Charlie Brown: *Beard, Dean* / Eyeballin': *Kuf Linx* / You can say that again: *Four Teens* / Double talkin' baby: *Milano, Bobby* / Machine gun: *Rip Tides* / Hey little car hop: *Weston, George* / Sneakin': *Weston, George* / Boo-be-ah-bee: *Coburn, Kimball* / Annie's not an orphan anymore: *Rochell & The Candles* / Rock roma rock it: *Crothers, Scat Man*
CD ______ CDCHD 494
Ace / Mar '94 / Pinnacle

HOLLYWOOD SINGS - THE GIRLS
It's foolish but it's fun: *Durbin, Deanna* / Body and soul: *Langford, Frances* / Lovely to look at: *Dunne, Irene* / Waltzing in the clouds: *Durbin, Deanna* / Jitterbug: *Garland, Judy* / Mister Five By Five: *Andrews Sisters* / Kiss the boys goodbye: *Martin, Mary* / When the roses bloom again: *Durbin, Deanna* / Man with the lollipop song: *Miranda, Carmen* / Someone to watch over me: *Langford, Frances* / One I love: *Fitzgerald, Ella* / Ferryboat serenade: *Andrews Sisters* / Falling in love again: *Dietrich, Marlene* / Over the rainbow: *Garland, Judy* / Say 'si si': *Andrews Sisters* / It never rains but it pours: *Garland, Judy* / Moon song: *Smith, Kate* / Cock eyed Major of Kaunakakai: *Andrews Sisters* / Katie went to Haiti: *Martin, Mary* / I've got you under my skin: *Langford, Frances*
CD ______ 304112
Hallmark / Jun '97 / Carlton

HOLLYWOOD SINGS - THE GUYS
Moonlight becomes you: *Crosby, Bing* / Always in my heart: *Baker, Kenny* / Farming: *Kaye, Danny* / I'm thinking tonight of my blue eyes: *Crosby, Bing* / Rock-a-bye your baby with a Dixie melody: *Jolson, Al* / Fairy pipers: *Kaye, Danny* / Tchaikovsky (and other Russians): *Kaye, Danny* / There are two rivers to cross: *Baker, Kenny* / Stein song: *Powell, Dick* / 'Tis autumn: *Martin, Tony* / April showers: *Jolson, Al* / I have eyes: *Crosby, Bing* / Love walked in: *Baker, Kenny* / Blue Tahitian moon: *Baker, Kenny* / Moon and the willow tree: *Crosby, Bing* / I haven't time to be a millionaire: *Crosby, Bing* / Cancel the flowers: *Martin, Tony* / Indian summer: *Martin, Tony* / In a moment of weakness: *Powell, Dick* / Anatole of Paris: *Kaye, Danny*
CD ______ 304102
Hallmark / Jun '97 / Carlton

HOLY BIBLE, THE
CD ______ HOLY 019CD
Holy / Jul '96 / Plastic Head

HOMAGE TO NEW ORLEANS
CD ______ CD 53087
Giants Of Jazz / Mar '92 / Cadillac / Jazz Music / Target/BMG

HOME COOKIN'
CD ______ URCD 001
Ubiquity / Jul '96 / Cargo / Timewarp

HOME ON THE RANGE
No one to call me darling: *Autry, Gene* / When the moon hangs high: *Hillbillies* / Any old time: *Rodgers, Jimmie* / Old trail: *Autry, Gene* / Why there's a tear in my eye: *Rodgers, Jimmie & Sara Carter* / Sunset trail: *Hillbillies* / Dusk: *Autry, Gene* / I've only loved three women: *Rodgers, Jimmie* / Home on the range: *Hillbillies* / Wonderful city: *Rodgers, Jimmie & Sara Carter* / Yodelling hobo: *Hillbillies* / Dying cowboy: *Hillbillies* / Round up time out west: *Rodgers, Jimmie* / Blue yodel No. 5: *Autry, Gene* / Colorado sunset: *Rogers, Roy* / There's a bridle hangin' on the wall: *Robison, Carson & His Pioneers* / I've got the jailhouse blues: *Autry, Gene* / Whisper your mother's name: *Autry, Gene* / There's a ranch in the rockies: *Rogers, Roy* / Pistol packin' papa: *Autry, Gene* / Blue river train: *Robison, Carson & His Pioneers* / I'll always be a rambler: *Autry, Gene*
CD ______ PASTCD 7028
Flapper / Jan '94 / Pinnacle

HOME TO IRELAND
Ramblin' Irishman / Rising of the moon / Road to Sligo/Tripping up the stairs / Ashplant / 10 franc pieces/St. Anne's reel/The scolair / O'Carolan's dream / White, orange and green / High road to Linton/Mrs. McLeod's reel / Foxhunters / Fiddler's green / Rocky road to Dublin / Arthur McBride / Cherish the ladies/Paddy Clancey's jig/Gillan's apples/Fathe / Gravelwalk / Couragie
CD ______ CD 6044
Music / Sep '96 / Target/BMG

HOMELAND (Collection of Black South African Music)
Ngayishela / Ea nyoloha khanyapa / Maraba start 500 / Ntlela a tingangeni / Nginbonile ubaba / Sayishayinduku / Khutsana / Umuntu / Mti wa ngwenda / Ntate bereng / Yashimizi / Nayintombi ibaleka
CD ______ GRELCD 2002
Greensleeves / Jun '88 / Jet Star / SRD

HOMMAGE A ALFRED MONTMARQUETTE
CD ______ TR 9501CD
Transit / Apr '96 / ADA

HONEYSUCKLE ROSE
CD ______ CECD 5
Collector's Edition / Apr '96 / TKO Magnum

HONEYWIND (Sounds From A Santal Village, India)
CD ______ SM 16122
Wergo / Jul '97 / ADA / Cadillac / Harmonia Mundi

HONKERS AND BAR WALKERS VOL.2
Pee wee (call of the Gators): *Jackson, Willis* / Return of BO plenty: *Lane, Morris & His Orchestra* / Gitchie gitchie-goomba: *Lane, Morris & His Orchestra* / Joe's beat: *Lane, Morris & His Orchestra* / Blue jeans: *Lane, Morris & His Orchestra* / Benson bounce: *Francis, Panama* / Darkness of the Delta: *Francis, Panama* / Bess's blues: *Francis, Panama* / 12:00 jump: *Francis, Panama* / I love her: *Harvey, Bill & His Orchestra* / Walk right in: *Harvey, Bill & His Orchestra* / Doll baby: *Ferguson, Charlie & His Orchestra* / Bean head: *Ferguson, Charlie & His Orchestra* / Hard times: *Ferguson, Charlie & His Orchestra* / Big G: *Ferguson, Charlie & His Orchestra* / That's for sure: *Smith, Bobby* / That's it: *Ferguson, Charlie & His Orchestra* / Low lights: *Ferguson, Charlie & His Orchestra* / Hi beam: *Ferguson, Charlie & His Orchestra* / I got it bad: *Ferguson, Charlie & His Orchestra* / Rush hour: *King Curtis* / Dynamite at midnite: *King Curtis*
CD ______ DD 452
Delmark / Mar '97 / ADA / Cadillac / CM / Direct / Hot Shot

HONKY TONK FAVOURITES
CD ______ SWBCD 205
Sound Waves / Sep '94 / Target/BMG

HONKY TONK JUMP PARTY
Honky tonk / Jump children (vooit vooit) / House party / Strato cruiser / Breaking up the house / Good morning judge / Special delivery stomp / Club Savoy / Hucklebuck with Jimmy / Flying home / Joe Joe jump / Mighty mighty man / Deacon moves in / I want you to be my baby / Joops jump / Train kept a rollin' / Have mercy baby / Harlem nocturne / Kidney stew / Bloodshot eyes / Love don't love nobody
CD ______ CDCHARLY 22
Charly / Aug '86 / Koch

HOOKED ON BIG BANDS
Don't sit under the apple tree / Mack the knife / Boogie woogie bugle boy / Lady is a tramp / Chattanooga choo choo / Take the 'A' train / Boogie blues / Night train / Tommy's boogie woogie / Pennsylvania 6-5000 / Le vie en rose / I got you under my skin / St. Louis blues / C'est magnifique / Begin the beguine / It had to be you / You're nobody / I just called to say I love you / Sunny side of the street / C'est si bon / American patrol / C Jam blues / Little brown jug / Goody goody / Woodchoppers ball / Tie a yellow ribbon round the old oak tree / Song of India / It happened in Monterey / Perido / Lullaby of birdland / Frankie and Johnny / In the mood / How high the moon
CD ______ EMPRCD 540
Emporio / Sep '94 / Disc

HOOKED ON COUNTRY (3CD Set)
CD Set ______ TREB 3011
Scratch / Mar '95 / Koch / Scratch/BMG

HOOKED ON DISCO (45 Non-Stop Disco Classics)
Fifth of Beethoven / Disco inferno / Salsation / Manhattan skyline / Calypso breakdown / K-Lee / More than a woman / Boogie shoes / Open sesame / Turn the beat around / Hustle / Dance, dance, dance (yowsah, yowsah, yowsah) / TSOP (The sound of Philadelphia) / Dance with me / Don't leave me this way / Shame / He's the greatest dancer / Rock the boat / I love music / Can't get enough of your love babe / Disco lady / Ring my bell / Rock your baby / I want your love / Reunited / You'll never find another love like mine / When will I see you again / Don't let me be misunderstood / Shake your groove thing / Heart of glass / Good times / Boogie fever / Never can say goodbye / Funkytown / Boogie oogie oogie / We are family / Disco nights (rock freak) / Le freak / In the navy / Get off / I will survive

/ That's the way (I like it) / That's where the happy people go / Love I lost
CD ECD 3343
K-Tel / May '97 / K-Tel

HOOKED ON DIXIE
Bugle call rag medley / Ja-da medley / Struttin' with some barbecue medley / Sweet gypsy rose medley / Piano roll blues medley / Sleepytime down south medley / Royal garden blues medley
CD EMPRCD 517
Emporio / Jul '94 / Disc

HOOKED ON MELODIES AND MEMORIES (Hooked On 40's/Dixie/Big Bands/Switched On Swing - 4CD Set)
CD Set EMPRBX 001
Emporio / Sep '94 / Disc

HOOKED ON NUMBER ONES
CD 74321101122
RCA / Aug '92 / BMG

HOOMII AND URTIN DUU
CD VICG 52112
JVC World Library / Feb '96 / ADA / CM / Direct

HOOTENANNY
Raining: *Ancient Beatbox* / Just as the ...: *Edward II & The Red Hot Polkas* / Valentine's: *Tabor, June & The Oyster Band* / Wind and the ...: *Weddings, Parties & Anything* / Vimbayi: *Four Brothers* / Frontera del ensueno: *Rey De Copas* / See how I miss you: *Cockburn, Bruce* / Liberty: *Barely Works* / Polka girl: *Colorblind James Experience* / Gastown: *God's Little Monkeys* / Travelling circus: *White, Andy* / Pigeon on the gate: *Spillane, Davy* / Tape decks all over hell: *Boiled In Lead* / Rumba for Nicaragua: *Happy End* / Collectorman: *McLeod, Rory* / Back to back: *Jolly Boys*
CD GRILLCD 003
Cooking Vinyl / May '90 / Vital

HOPELESSLY DEVOTED TO YOU
CD HR 6142
Hopeless / Jan '97 / Plastic Head

HORIZONS
Children: *Miles, Robert* / Eugina: *Salt Tank* / X files: *DJ Dado* / Superstring: *Cygnus X* / Floating: *Terra Ferma* / Are you out there: *Crescendo* / Age of love: *Age Of Love* / Vernon's wonderland: *Vernon's Wonderland* / Magic fly: *Space Blaster* / Odyssey to Anyoona: *Jam & Spoon* / Alegrya: *Extasia* / Smokebelch II: *Sabres Of Paradise*
CD 8287932
PolyGram TV / Jun '96 / PolyGram

HORN, THE (The Tenor Sax In Jazz)
Bird of Prey blues: *Hawkins, Coleman* / Newport news: *Freeman, Bud* / Prelude to a kiss: *Webster, Ben* / Neenah / No dues: *Cobb, Arnett* / You are too beautiful: *Davis, Eddie 'Lockjaw'* / Hey there: *Gray, Wardell* / Darn that dream: *Gordon, Dexter* / Going South: *Ammons, Gene* / Jive at five / Chase is on: *Rouse/Quinchette* / Way you look tonight: *Stitt/Holloway* / A la carte / I didn't know what time it was: *Shorter, Wayne* / I want to talk about you: *Coltrane, John* / Big George: *Coleman, George*
CD CDCHARLY 114
Charly / Apr '88 / Koch

HOSPITAL
Ultrasound: *London Electricity* / Fight the vulture: *Nice, Peter Trio* / Brother ignoramus: *London Electricity* / Sister stalking: *London Electricity* / Flight of the vulture: *Nice, Peter Trio* / Harp of gold: *Nice, Peter Trio* / Last supper: *Nice, Peter Trio* / Fear and loathing: *Dwarf Electro* / Agent orange: *Dwarf Electro* / Scrutiny: *E.S.T.* / Zed between the eyes: *Izit*
CD NHS 4CD
NHS / Apr '97 / Prime

HOT AND SWEATY
Feel my riddim: *Skibby* / Oh Carolina: *Shaggy* / Dedicated to the one I love: *McLean, Bitty* / Everything I own: *Boy George* / You sexy thing: *Stanfield & Brown* / La bamba: *Jungle Twins* / Tracks of my tears: *Anbessa* / Lay down: *Invaders and George Hughes* / Buk-in-ham palace: *Tosh, Peter* / I want to break free: *Los Angels* / Summertime: *La Danz & Van B King* / Somebody loves you honey: *T-Spoon* / It keeps rainin' (tears from my eyes): *McLean, Bitty* / Get up: *Inner Soul Expression* / I started a joke: *Skibby* / Fat bottomed girls: *Marga Dredd* / Sweets for my sweet: *Lewis, C.J.*
CD DC 880852
Disky / May '97 / Disky / THE

HOT AIRE (American Hot Bands Of The Twenties)
Hot aire: *Olsen, George & His Music* / If I had a girl like you: *Seattle Harmony Kings* / Darktown shuffle: *Seattle Harmony Kings* / I'm goin' out if Lizzie comes in: *Romano, Phil & His Orchestra* / Keep on croonin' a tune: *Romano, Phil & His Orchestra* / Melancholy Lou: *Lanin, Howard & His Ben Franklin Dance Orchestra* / Don't wake me up, let me dream: *Lanin, Howard & His Ben Franklin Dance Orchestra* / Paddlin' Madelin' home: *White Kaufman & His Orchestra* / Breezin' along with the breeze: *Seattle Harmony Kings* / How many times: *Seattle Harmony Kings* / Tiger rag: *Dornberger, Charles & His Orchestra* / Does she love me - positively, absolutely: *Garber, Jan & His Orchestra* / What do I care what somebody said: *Garber, Jan & His Orchestra* / You don't like it, not much: *Garber, Jan & His Orchestra* / Swanee shore: *Crawford, Jack & His Ochestra* / Sugar babe I'm leavin': *Blue Steele & His Orchestra* / When the Morning Glories wake up in the morning: *Renard, Jacques & His Cocoanut Grove Orchestra* / Baltimore: *Crawford, Jack & His Ochestra*
CD DHAL 16
Halcyon / Sep '93 / Cadillac / Harmonia Mundi / Jazz Music / Swift / Wellard

HOT BISCUITS (House Of Blues Sampler)
Cold comfort: *Rip, Jimmy* / Hand me down: *Gales Brothers* / I'm somebody: *Houston, Cissy* / Sacred ground: *Mooney, John* / Satisfy me: *Barksdale, Becky* / Moo goo: *Black, Paul* / Didn't it rain: *Five Blind Boys Of Alabama* / Mojo hand: *Hopkins, Lightnin'*
CD HBSCD 87008
House Of Blues / Apr '96 / ADA / BMG
CD 70010870082
House Of Blues / Jun '96 / ADA / BMG

HOT BRITISH DANCE BANDS 1925-1937
Riverboat shuffle: *Kit Kat Band* / Sugarfoot stomp: *Devonshire Restaurant Dance Band* / Stomp your feet: *Elizalde, Fred* / Buffalo rhythm: *Piccadilly Revels Band* / That's a plenty: *Rhythm Maniacs* / Tiger rag: *Hylton, Jack* / 11.30 Saturday night: *Arcadian Dance Orchestra* / Kalua: *Hughes, Spike* / Choo choo: *Payne, Jack* / Bessie couldn't help it: *Cotton, Billy* / Stomping: *Wornell, Jimmy Hot Blue-Bottles* / Nobody's sweetheart: *Fox, Roy* / White jazz: *Stone, Lew* / Sentimental gentleman from Georgia: *Loss, Joe* / Rockin' in rhythm: *Madame Tussaud's Dance Orchestra* / Your mother's son-in-law: *Six Swingers* / Shine: *Lawrence, Brian* / China boy: *Bond Street Swingers* / Milenberg joys: *Roy, Harry* / Cotton pickers' congregation: *Ambrose* / What a perfect combination: *Noble, Ray*
CD CBC 1005
Timeless Historical / Jan '92 / New Note/ Pinnacle

HOT CURLY WEENIE
CD RECESS 39
Roo Art / Feb '97 / PolyGram

HOT DANCE TRACKS
Captain Jack: *Captain Jack* / Allright: *Double Vision* / Got myself together: *Bucketheads* / Read my lips: *Alex Party* / Turn it up and down: *Capella* / I'm a raver: *Lipstick* / Smiling: *T-Spoon* / Hymn: *Music Instructor* / Spread your love: *2 Unlimited* / Deep in you: *Louise, Tania* / Spontaneous: *Spymaster & Eric Nouhan* / Let me be free: *Fox, Samantha* / Because you loved me: *Lost & Hally* / Higher state of consciousness: *Wink, Josh*
CD DC 879182
Disky / Aug '97 / Disky / THE

HOT GYPSY SUMMER
CD HRCD 8058
Disky / Jul '94 / Disky / THE

HOT HATS INCLUDING FATS
CD NCD 8812
Phontastic / Dec '94 / Cadillac / Jazz Music / Wellard

HOT HOT REGGAE VOL.1 & 2
CD 840602
FM / '91 / Revolver / Sony

HOT HOT SOCA
CD RRTGCD 7706
Rohit / '88 / Jet Star

HOT JAZZ 1928-1930
CD HRM 6004
Hermes / Jan '89 / Nimbus

HOT JAZZ BISCUITS
Who do you love: *White, Lenny* / Hot jazz biscuits: *Urbanator* / Bluesanova: *Browne, Tom* / Luny tune: *Essence All-Stars* / Funk in a deep freeze: *Bop City* / Jam for real: *Browne, Tom* / Up jumped Spring: *Essence All-Stars* / Late one night: *Meeting* / Dr. Jackle: *Essence All-Stars* / Cubano chant: *Essence All-Stars* / Magic: *Urbanator* / Savant: *White, Lenny* / Bass blues: *Essence All-Stars* / Freedom jazz dance: *Essence All-Stars*
CD HIBD 8801
Hip Bop / Apr '97 / Koch / Silva Screen

HOT JAZZ FROM NEW ORLEANS (20 Dixieland Stompers)
Tiger rag: *Original Dixieland Jazz Band* / Stockyard strut: *Keppard, Freddie* / Squeeze me: *Miller, Punch* / Ory's creole trombone: *Ory, Kid* / Careless love: *Original Tuxedo Jazz Orchestra* / Tar paper stomp: *Manone, Wingy* / Sobbin' blues: *New Orleans Rhythm Kings* / Someday sweetheart: *Condon, Eddie Orchestra* / 6th Street: *Armstrong, Lil Dixielanders* / Dinah: *Russell, Pee Wee Rhythmakers* / Dippermouth blues: *Oliver, Joe 'King' & His Creole Jazz Band* / Black bottom stomp: *Red Miff's Stompers* / Really the blues: *Ladnier, Tommy* / Eel: *Freeman, Bud Summa Cum Laude Orchestra* / Sweet and lowdown: *Smith, Jabbo & His Rhythm Aces* / Down by the riverside: *Johnson, Bunk* / All the jazz band ball: *Beiderbecke, Bix & His Gang* / Roof blues: *Crosby, Bob & His Bobcats* / Harlem joys: *Smith, Willie 'The Lion' & His Cubs*
CD 306702
Hallmark / Jul '97 / Carlton

HOT JAZZ ON BLUE NOTE (4CD Set)
Blues whistle: *Lewis, Meade 'Lux'* / Careless love: *White, Josh Trio* / Profoundly blue no.2: *Hall, Edmond Quartet* / Gettysburg march: *Lewis, George & His New Orleans Stompers* / Burgundy street blues: *Lewis, George & His New Orleans Stompers* / Over the waves: *Lewis, George & His New Orleans Stompers* / When you wore a tulip: *Lewis, George & His New Orleans Stompers* / Days beyond recall: *Jones, Bunk & Sidney Bechet* / High society: *Bechet, Sidney & His Blue Note Jazzmen* / Mr. Jelly lord: *Hode's, art hot seven* / Wolverine blues: *Hode's, art hot seven* / Winin' boy blues: *Dodds, Baby Jazz Four* / Doctor jazz: *Hodes, Art & His Chicagoans* / Shoe shiners dinner: *Hodes, Art & His Chicagoans* / Blame it on the blues: *Bechet-Nicholas Blue Five* / Weary way blues: *Bechet-Nicholas Blue Five* / Moose march: *De Paris, Sidney & His Blue Note Stompers* / Careless lover: *Dodds, Baby Jazz Four* / Memphis blues: *Hodes, Art Hot Five* / St.Louis blues: *Bechet, Sidney & His Blue Note Stompers* / Yellow dog blues: *Hodes, Art & His Chicagoans* / Weary blues: *Bechet, Sidney & His Blue Note Stompers* / Tiger rag: *Bechet, Sidney & His Blue Note Stompers* / Original dixieland one step: *Bechet, Sidney & His Hot Six* / Dark strutters ball: *Hodes, Art Hot Five* / Fidgety feet: *Bechet, Sidney & His Blue Note Jazzmen* / At the jazz band ball: *Bechet, Sidney & His Blue Note Jazzmen* / That eccentric rag: *Hodes, Art Trio* / Royal garden blues: *Hall, Edmond & His Blue Note Jazzmen* / Sugar foot stomp: *Hodes, Art Blue Note Jazzmen* / Bugle call rag: *Bechet, Sidney & His Blue Note Jazzmen* / Roof blues: *Bechet, Sidney & His Blue Note Jazzmen* / Tishomingo blues: *Bechet, Sidney & His Blue Note Jazzmen* / That's a plenty: *Bechet, Sidney & His Hot Six* / Low down blues: *Hodes, Art Back Room Boys* / Cake walking babies from home: *Bechet, Sidney & His Blue Note Jazzmen* / Everybody loves my baby: *De Paris, Sidney & His Blue Note Stompers* / Mandy make up your mind: *Bechet, Sidney & His Blue Note Jazzmen* / Squeeze me: *Hodes, Art Blue Note Jazzmen* / Runnin' wild: *Bechet, Sidney & His Blue Note Jazzmen* / Clark & Randolph: *Hodes, Art & His Chicagoans* / Muskat ramble: *Bechet, Sidney & His Blue Note Jazzmen* / Apex blues: *Hodes, Art Blue Five* / Blues my naughty sweetie gives to me: *Bechet, Sidney & His Hot Six* / Nobody's sweetheart: *Hodes, Art Blue Five* / Please don't talk about me when I am gone: *De Paris, Sidney & His Blue Note Stompers* / Save it pretty mama: *Hodes, Art Hot Five* / There'll be some changes made: *Bechet, Sidney & His Hot Six* / Jug head boogie: *Hodes, Art Back Room Boys* / Jazz me blues: *Bechet, Sidney & His Blue Note Jazzmen* / Night shift blues: *Hall, Edmond & His Blue Note Jazzmen* / China boy: *Bechet, Sidney & His Blue Note Jazzmen* / Nobody knows when you are down and out: *Bechet, Sidney & His Blue Note Jazzmen* / Walkin' the dog: *Johnson, James P. Blue Note Jazzmen* / Blues at the blue note: *Hall, Edmond & His Blue Note Jazzmen* / Ballin' the jack: *Paris, Sidney de Blue Note Jazzmen* / Shine: *Hodes, Art Hot Five* / KMH Drag: *Hodes, Art Hot Five* / At the ball: *Johnson, James P. Blue Note Jazzmen* / Slow em down blues: *Hodes, Art & His Chicagoans* / Shim me sha wobble: *Hodes, Art & His Chicagoans* / Easy rider: *Johnson, James P. Blue Note Jazzmen* / Jammin' in four: *Hall, Edmond Celeste Quartet* / Avalon: *Bechet, Sidney & His Hot Six* / Feelin' at ease: *Dodds, Baby Jazz Four* / Who's sorry now: *Paris, Sidney de Blue Note Jazzmen* / Call of the blues: *Paris, Sidney de Blue Note Jazzmen* / SCH Blues: *Hodes, Art Back Room Boys* / Sweet georgia brown: *Hodes, Art Blue Note Jazzmen* / Blue Horizon: *Bechet, Sidney & His Blue Note Jazzmen*
CD Set CDP 8358112
Blue Note / Dec '96 / EMI

HOT MUSIC FROM CUBA 1907-1936
CD HQCD 23
Harlequin / Oct '93 / Hot Shot / Jazz Music / Swift / Wellard

HOT NIGHTS IN THE CITY
CD WKFMXD 134
FM / Nov '89 / Revolver / Sony

HOT NOTES
CD DGF 8
Frog / Jul '96 / Cadillac / Jazz Music / Wellard

HOT REGGAE FEVER
CD 12232
Laserlight / Sep '93 / Target/BMG

HOT RHYTHM AND COOL BLUES - TEXAS STYLE
CD IMP 702
Iris Music / Jul '95 / Discovery

HOT ROCKIN' INSTRUMENTALS
CD CLCD 4430
Collector/White Label / Sep '96 / TKO Magnum

HOT ROCKIN' INSTRUMENTALS
CD CLCD 4436
Collector's Edition / Mar '97 / TKO Magnum

HOT ROD GANG
Big wheel: *Benton, Walt* / This old bomb of mine: *Stange, Howie* / Hot rod: *Berry Brothers* / Spinning my wheels: *Brooks, Chuck* / Spinner hub caps: *Davis, Pat* / Full racing cam: *Ringo, Eddie* / Girl and a hot rod: *Deram, Richie* / Big green car: *Carroll, Jimmy* / Gas money: *Carroll, Jimmy* / Hot rod baby: *Davis, Rocky* / Long John's flagpole rock: *Roller, Long John* / Hot rod boogie: *Brady, Howard W* / Robin Hood and his '56 Ford: *Ball, Woody* / Shot rod: *Conny & Bellhops* / Ford and shaker: *Gallagher, James* / Hot-rodders dream: *Burden, Ray* / Hot rod race: *Williams, Rob* / Daddy Joe: *Ciolino, Pete* / Sidewalk rock 'n' roll: *Warden, J.W.* / I'll be leavin' you: *Moore, Turner* / Brake Jake: *Fern, Mike* / Cruisin': *Bucky & Premiers* / Red hot car: *Verne, Bobby* / Lorene: *Lemons, Bill* / Speedway rock: *Woodard, Jerry* / Stop jivin' start drivin': *Keyes, Burt* / Dig that crazy driver: *Penix, William* / Car hop: *Export* / High way robbery: *Fry, Bobby* / Cop car: *West, Rick*
CD CBBB 55005
Buffalo Bop / Apr '94 / Rollercoaster

HOT ROD HITS
Double a fueler: *Deuce Coupes* / Nite prowler: *Deuce Coupes* / Road rattler: *Deuce Coupes* / Tijuana gasser: *Deuce Coupes* / Gear masher: *Deuce Coupes* / Candy apple blues: *Deuce Coupes* / Satan's chariot: *Deuce Coupes* / Monkey see: *Deuce Coupes* / Nite surfer: *Deuce Coupes* / Dawn patrol: *Deuce Coupes* / Smooth stick: *Deuce Coupes* / Top eliminator: *Darts* / Street machine: *Darts* / Corn pone: *Darts* / Hollywood drag: *Darts* / Alky burner: *Darts* / Slauson and soto: *Darts* / Detroit iron: *Darts* / Cruisin': *Darts* / Four banger: *De-Fenders* / Deuces wild: *De-Fenders* / Taco wagon: *De-Fenders* / Movin' and groovin': *De-Fenders* / Skin diver: *De-Fenders* / Loose nuts: *De-Fenders* / Little Deuce Coupe: *De-Fenders* / Drag beat: *De-Fenders* / Wheelin' home: *De-Fenders* / Tequila Joe: *De-Fenders* / Rum runner: *De-Fenders* / Roadrunner: *De-Fenders*
CD CDCHD 303
Ace / Feb '91 / Pinnacle

HOT RODS FROM HELL
CD BREPD 5001
Blood Red Discs / Aug '96 / Greyhound / Nervous

HOT TRUMPETS (25 Great Jazz Trumpeters)
West End blues: *Armstrong, Louis Hot Five* / Swing out: *Allen, Red* / Singin' the blues: *Beiderbecke, Bix* / I can't get started: *Berigan, Bunny* / I'm free: *Butterfield, Billy* / Fiesta in blue: *Clayton, Buck* / What's the reason: *Coleman, Bill* / Heckler' shop: *Eldridge, Roy* / Swing high: *Elman, Ziggy* / Just a mood: *James, Harry* / If you see me comin': *Ladnier, Tommy* / Five point blues: *Lawson, Yank* / Swingin' at the Hickory House: *Manone, Wingy* / Black and tan fantasy: *Miley, Bubber* / Parkway stomp: *Miller, Punch* / Take the 'A' train: *Nance, Ray* / Panic is on: *Newton, Frankie* / That's no bargain: *Nichols, Red* / Dippermouth blues: *Oliver, Joe 'King'* / At the fat man's: *Shavers, Charlie* / Jazz battle: *Smith, Jabbo* / Baby doll: *Smith, Joe* / Relaxin' at the Touro: *Spanier, Muggsy* / Menelik - The Lion of Judah: *Stewart, Rex* / Cootie's concerto (Echoes of Harlem): *Williams, Cootie*
CD CDAJA 5208
Living Era / Jun '96 / Select

HOT WAX EXCURSION
CD VPCD 2041
VP / Apr '96 / Greensleeves / Jet Star / Total/BMG

HOT WIRED '97
CD EFA 128352
Hotwire / Jul '97 / SRD

HOT WIRED MONSTERTRUX
Intro / Wish: *Nine Inch Nails* / Finger on the trigger: *Excessive Force* / Tool and die: *Consolidated* / Godlike: *KMFDM* / Jesus built my hotrod: *Ministry* / Kooler than Jesus: *My Life With The Thrill Kill Kult* / Provision: *Frontline Assembly* / Looking forward: *CNN* / Murder Inc: *Murder Inc.* / Edge of no control: *Meat Beat Manifesto* / Skinflower: *Young Gods* / Motorbike: *Sheep On Drugs* / Headhunter: *Front 242* / Family man: *Nitzer Ebb*
CD 9548318112
East West / Feb '93 / Warner Music

HOTDOGS, HITS & HAPPY DAYS VOL.1
CD LPCD 1011
Disky / May '94 / Disky / THE

HOTDOGS, HITS & HAPPY DAYS VOL.10
CD LPCD 1020
Disky / May '94 / Disky / THE

HOTDOGS, HITS & HAPPY DAYS VOL.2
CD LPCD 1012
Disky / May '94 / Disky / THE

HOTDOGS, HITS & HAPPY DAYS VOL.3
CD _______________ LPCD 1013
Disky / May '94 / Disky / THE

HOTDOGS, HITS & HAPPY DAYS VOL.4
CD _______________ LPCD 1014
Disky / May '94 / Disky / THE

HOTDOGS, HITS & HAPPY DAYS VOL.5
CD _______________ LPCD 1015
Disky / May '94 / Disky / THE

HOTDOGS, HITS & HAPPY DAYS VOL.6
CD _______________ LPCD 1016
Disky / May '94 / Disky / THE

HOTDOGS, HITS & HAPPY DAYS VOL.7
CD _______________ LPCD 1017
Disky / May '94 / Disky / THE

HOTDOGS, HITS & HAPPY DAYS VOL.8
CD _______________ LPCD 1018
Disky / May '94 / Disky / THE

HOTDOGS, HITS & HAPPY DAYS VOL.9
CD _______________ LPCD 1019
Disky / May '94 / Disky / THE

HOTEL EASY VOL.1 (Golden Cavalcade Casino)
Grandstand / Competitors / Thrills and spills / Where the action is (aka Mono ski) / Guitar gambler / Tycoon / Jackpot / Top chrono / Dangerous assignment / Go getter / Action line / Risk business / Syndicate / City in the sun / Hot property / Sporting highlights / Ill winds / Hollywood scene / Hot module / Organ blower / Trombones in the night / Calender girl / French kick
CD _______________ CDOVD 490
Virgin / Jun '97 / EMI

HOTEL EASY VOL.2 (La Scandale Discotheque)
Boogie juice / Hot pants / Espresso bongo / Young generation / Jet setters / Pulsator / Cutting the funk / Friday feeling / Trend setters / Pop package / Freak out / Thunderbird / Crime squad / World Cup / On the South Side / 49th Street shakedown / Soul city / Making it / Soul organ impromptu / Thunder thighs / Night fever / Disco disco / Mission just possible
CD _______________ CDOVD 491
Virgin / Jun '97 / EMI

HOTEL EASY VOL.3 (Playmates Penthouse)
Penthouse suite / Secret service / Butterfly / Florida playboy / Good thing going / Club 69 / Teen lovers / Call me / Beat me till I'm blue / Time for romance / Gingerbread / Theme for a dream / Satin sounds / Je reviens / Solitaire / Summer love / Young emotions / First affair / Girl with the beautiful hair / Half forgotten daydreams / Kiss in the moonlight / Pussycat / Bed of roses
CD _______________ CDOVD 489
Virgin / Jun '97 / EMI

HOTEL EASY VOL.4 (Paco's Poolside Bar)
Girl in a sportscar / Eurotrash / Fun in the sun / Riviera affair / Lazy day / Sandals in the sand / Clear waters / International playground / Millionaires / Never a dull moment / Beauty Parade / New image / Going places / Holiday commercial / Travelling free / Pacific playground / Caribbean cruise / Montego Bay / Brazil Brazil / Free life / Sunny speed / Summer convertible / Scooter girl
CD _______________ CDOVD 488
Virgin / Jun '97 / EMI

HOTLINES 6
CD _______________ HOT 006
Hot Hands / Dec '96 / Total/BMG

HOTTER THAN HELL
CD _______________ BMCD 50
Black Mark / Mar '94 / Plastic Head

HOTTEST BBQ ALBUM THIS SUMMER, THE
Sweat (a la la la la song) / Baby come back / Sweets for my sweet / I can see clearly now / Bambeleo / Brasil / Soca dance / Dancando lambada / Rivers of Babylon / Kingston Town / Island in the sun / Girl from Ipanema / Calypso medley / One note samba / Samba de Soho / Saudade / O tucano / Best years of our lives / Cuba / Hot hot hot / Spanish Harlem / Lambada
CD _______________ SUMCD 4069
Summit / Sep '96 / Sound & Media

HOTTEST HITS VOL.2
CD _______________ SOCD 1267
Studio One / Oct '96 / Jet Star

HOUSE 2 HOUSE MEGA RAVE VOL.1
CD _______________ DCD 5317
Disky / Nov '93 / Disky / THE

HOUSE BOMBS
CD _______________ ZYX 550642
ZYX / Nov '96 / ZYX

HOUSE FUNKIN' VOL.1
CD _______________ JAPECD 102
Escapade / Sep '94 / 3mv/Sony / Prime

HOUSE FUNKIN' VOL.2
CD _______________ JAPECD 103
Escapade / Feb '95 / 3mv/Sony / Prime

HOUSE FUNKIN' VOL.3
CD _______________ JAPECD 104
Escapade / Jun '95 / 3mv/Sony / Prime

HOUSE KISSES (2CD Set)
Feel what you want: *Kristine W* / No love lost: *Rogers, Cece* / Set U free: *Planet Soul* / I like it: *Jomanda* / We can make it: *Mone* / Break night: *Mole People* / Beautiful people: *Tucker, Barbara* / Can we live: *Jesto Funk* / Universal love: *Natural Born Groovers* / Forever and a day: *Brothers In Rhythm* / Sing a song: *Harding, Carolyn & Damon Horton* / You deserve the best: *Wag Ya Tail* / (You're my one and only) True love: *Smith, Ann-Marie* / Don't give up (love will come around): *Morel, George* / I get lifted: *Tucker, Barbara* / Love thang: *Banji Boys* / If Madonna calls: *Vasquez, Junior* / Anything U want: *McCrae, Gwen* / Be sexy: *Justine* / Weekend: *Shock* / (Who) Keeps changing your mind: *South Street Player* / Make the world go round: *Sandy B* / Change: *Daphne* / Freedom (make it funky): *Black Magic* / I'm so grateful: *Kings Of Tomorrow*
CD Set _______________ ZYX 810962
ZYX / Apr '97 / ZYX

HOUSE LOOP
CD _______________ SM 80262
Profile / Aug '96 / Pinnacle

HOUSE MARKE VOL.2 (25 Brand New & Hot House Trax/2CD Set)
In the morning: *Key* / I want you: *Shandrew* / Baby Baby: *DJ E.B.O.* / My house: *Nap, J. Project* / Party groove: *DJ Kalpa* / Deep side: *Bass Symphony* / Bass: *DJ Micky* / Future: *Big Sound Association* / Ooh yeah: *Syntone* / Wobile: *Boedha* / You got it: *Prophase* / Neuro: *X-Cabs* / Morninglight: *Team Deep* / Ultimate seduction: *Ultimate Seduction* / Summer: *Central Bass* / Magnet: *Klubb Heads* / Rabahouse: *Pro Doctors* / Work: *Fudge* / Guido the killer wimp: *Allium* / House project: *DJ Trax* / Hoover: *Daddy Cool* / Get to this: *Tecmania Rebel* / Solar cycle: *Third Man* / Sirius: *Moon & The Sun* / House show: *Fact Of Life*
CD Set _______________ DCD 08947272
SPV / Mar '97 / Koch / Plastic Head

HOUSE NATION VOL.1
CD _______________ REACTCD 047
React / Sep '94 / Arabesque / Prime / Vital

HOUSE NOT JAZZ VOL.1
Struck by luv: *Lectroluv & Alvaughn Jackson* / Sax in the ozone: *Aaron, Robert* / Fired up: *Girl* / Soweto stomp: *Funky Fusion Band* / All the same family: *African Dream* / Critical: *Wall Of Sound* / Rejoice: *250lbs Of Blue* / Thoughts of you: *Wave* / Loving you in Heaven: *Aaron, Robert & Michou* / African dreams: *African Dream*
CD _______________ EBCD 54
Eightball / Jan '95 / Vital

HOUSE OF BAMBOO PRESENTS DANCE AND MOOD MUSIC
No man's land / Ahmedabab theme / Man from nowhere / Strange galaxy / Jungle soul / Land of Marlene / Soft winds / Pictures of oceania / Following you / Magazine / Planification / Psycedelic portrait / Pictures of Saint Tropez / Psychedelic portrait / Ambiance heure zero / Strange valley / Rhythm's dealer / Picture of spring / Picture of summer / Picture of winter / De Paris a Liverpool
CD _______________ CDV 2831
Virgin / May '97 / EMI

HOUSE OF DREAMS (2CD Set)
CD Set _______________ 560042
Westcom / Apr '97 / Koch / Pinnacle

HOUSE OF DREAMS VOL.1
CD _______________ ASCCD 2
Ascension / Jun '96 / 3mv/Sony

HOUSE OF HANDBAG - AUTUMN/ WINTER COLLECTION, THE (2CD Set)
CD Set _______________ USCD 4
Ultrasound / Oct '95 / Grapevine/ PolyGram

HOUSE OF HANDBAG - SPRING/ SUMMER COLLECTION, THE (2CD Set)
CD Set _______________ USCD 3
Ultrasound / Jul '95 / Grapevine/PolyGram

HOUSE OF HANDBAG, THE (Nuovo Disco Collection/Mixed By Mark Moore/ 2CD Set)
K-Jee: *Shell Shock* / Jumpin': *Terry, Todd* / Just another groove: *Mighty Dub Katz* / Disco's revenge: *Gusto* / Jumpin': *Lisa Marie Experience* / Get on up: *Stingily, Byron* / Odysee at hysteria: *Last Disco Superstars* / Two fatt guitars: *Direktt* / Funkatarium: *Jump* / Ain't talkin' 'bout dub: *Apollo 440* / Hey Mr. DJ: *Screen II* / Theme from S'Express: *S'Express* / Techdisco EP: *DJ Duke* / Forget about the world: *Gabrielle* / Remember me: *Blueboy* / You got the love: *Staton, Candi* / I'm alive: *Stretch n' Vern* / Ultra flava: *Farley & Heller* / Positive vibration: *Black Box* / Cuba: *El Mariachi* / Kick up the volume: *Tissera, Rob* / You should be dancing: *E Sensual* / All funked up: *Mother* / Manhattan: *Stars & Stripes* / Find the groove: *Aquarius* / Can you feel the force: *Real Thing* / Little closer: *Rio Rhythm Band* / Diskfunktional: *Doc Martin* / Footstompin': *Klatsch* / Disco kicks: *BTG* / Different shapes and sizes: *DJ Sneak* / Just playin': *JT Playaz* / There will come a day: *Absolute* / Brazen hussies: *Brazen Hussies*
CD Set _______________ SOLIDCD 007
CD Set _______________ SOLIDSCD 007
Solid State / Mar '97 / Prime / Vital

HOUSE OF LIMBO
CD _______________ LIMB 18CD
Limbo / Jul '93 / Amato Disco / Pinnacle / Prime

HOUSE OF LIMBO - TRILOGY
Cry India: *Umboza* / So good: *DJ Fade* / Live in peace: *Tocayo* / It's what's upfront that counts: *Yosh* / Let the love: *Q-Tex* / Funk of tha' month: *Dark Sessions* / Sunshine: *Umboza* / Talk to me: *Planet 95* / Kiss my acid: *Mukkaa* / Screamer: *Yosh* / I trance you: *Gypsy* / Spirit is justified: *Ritmo De Vida* / Thoughts of a tranced love: *Winc* / Gotta get next to you: *Yosh* / Slip: *Soul Surfers* / Best served chilled: *Havana*
CD _______________ LIMB 61CD
Limbo / Oct '96 / Amato Disco / Pinnacle / Prime

HOUSE OF LIMBO - TRILOGY (Remixed/2CD Set)
Cry India: *Umboza* / I trance you: *Gypsy* / Best served chilled: *Havana* / Live in peace: *Tocayo* / So good: *DJ Fade* / Funk of tha month: *Dark Sessions* / It's what's upfront that counts: *Yosh* / Sunshine: *Umboza* / Let the love: *Q-Tex* / Spirit is justified: *Ritmo De Vida* / Gotta get next to you: *Yosh* / Screamer: *Yosh* / Talk to me: *Planet 95* / Thoughts of a tranced love: *Winc* / Thoughts of a tranced love: *Winc* / Kiss my acid: *Mukkaa* / Slip: *Soul Surfers*
CD _______________ LIMB 61CDX
CD Set _______________ LIMB 61LE
Limbo / Oct '96 / Amato Disco / Pinnacle / Prime

HOUSE OF LONDON VOL.1
CD _______________ OCEANCD 001
Ocean / Apr '95 / Else

HOUSE OF LONDON VOL.2
CD _______________ OCEANCD 002
Ocean / Sep '95 / Else

HOUSE OF LOVERS VOL.1
CD _______________ RECD 01
Rupie Edwards / Apr '93 / Jet Star

HOUSE OF OLDSCHOOL
CD _______________ IDTCD 1420
ID&T / Mar '97 / Plastic Head

HOUSE ON FIRE
CD _______________ RHRCD 58
Red House / Oct '95 / ADA / Koch

HOUSE PARTY (20 Great Hits Of The Sixties)
Ain't nothing but a house party: *Showstoppers* / When you walk in the room: *Searchers* / Summer in the city: *Lovin' Spoonful* / Colour my world: *Clark, Petula* / Even the bad times are good: *Tremeloes* / Sunny afternoon: *Kinks* / Nobody needs your love: *Pitney, Gene* / Message understood: *Shaw, Sandie* / Lazy Sunday: *Small Faces* / Universal soldier: *Donovan* / Pictures of matchstick men: *Status Quo* / Angel of the morning: *Arnold, P.P.* / Judy in disguise: *Fred, John & His Playboy Band* / Let the heartaches begin: *Baldry, Long John* / Long live love: *Shaw, Sandie* / My love: *Clark, Petula* / Love potion no.9: *Searchers* / Death of a clown: *Davies, Dave* / Looking through the eyes of love: *Pitney, Gene* / Happy together: *Turtles*
CD _______________ TRTCD 105
TrueTrax / Dec '94 / THE

HOUSE RARITIES
CD _______________ XTR 17CDM
CD _______________ XTR 17CDU
X-Treme / Oct '95 / Pinnacle / SRD

HOUSE ROCKIN' BLUES
I got to go: *Little Walter* / Mama talk to your daughter: *Lenoir, J.B.* / Young fashioned ways: *Waters, Muddy* / I have a little girl: *Howlin' Wolf* / You don't love me (you don't care): *Diddley, Bo* / Tired of crying: *Pejoe, Morris* / I'm leaving you: *Spann, Otis* / Rattlesnake: *Brim, John* / Poison Ivy: *Mabon, Willie* / You got to love me: *Arnold, Billy Boy* / Mellow down easy: *Little Walter* / Little girl: *Diddley, Bo* / Date bait: *Blue Smitty* / I would hate to see you go (Be careful): *Brim, John* / If it ain't me: *Rogers, Jimmy* / Who will be next: *Howlin' Wolf* / Close to you: *Waters, Muddy* / Sweet on you baby: *Arnold, Billy Boy* / Goat: *Williamson, Sonny Boy* / He knows the rules: *McCracklin, Jimmy* / I'm satisfied: *Rush, Otis* / Let me love you baby: *Guy, Buddy* / Madison blues: *James, Elmore* / Look out Mabel: *Crockett, G.L.* / Twirl: *Little Luther* / Someday: *Nighthawk, Robert* / Let's go out tonight: *Hooker, John Lee*
CD _______________ CDCHD 610
Ace / Mar '95 / Pinnacle

HOUSE THAT TRAX BUILT VOL.1, THE
Your love: *Knuckles, Frankie* / No way back: *Adonis* / Love can't turn around: *Farley Jackmaster Funk* / I've lost control: *Sleazy D* / Washing machine: *Fingers Inc.* / Move your body: *Jefferson, Marshall* / Rock me: *Screaming Rachel* / House Nation: *House Master Boyz* / U used to hold me: *Rosario, Ralphi*
CD _______________ TRXUKCD 001
Trax UK / May '96 / Mo's Music Machine / Pinnacle / Prime

HOUSE THAT TRAX BUILT VOL.2, THE
R U hot enough: *Virgo* / Liquid love: *Hardy, Ron* / You got the love: *Knuckles, Frankie* / This is acid: *Maurice* / Sensuous woman goes disco: *Jackmaster D* / 7 ways to jack: *Hercules* / Your only friend: *Phuture* / Can U feel it: *Fingers* / Bringing down the walls: *Owens, Robert* / Waiting on my angel: *Knuckles, Frankie* / Real thing: *Screamin' Rachael* / We're rocking down the house: *Adonis*
CD _______________ TRXUKCD 004
Trax UK / Aug '97 / Mo's Music Machine / Pinnacle / Prime

HOW BIG IS YOUR WOOFER
Baia: *Puente, Tito Orchestra & Buddy Morrow Orchestra* / Saturday night in Knightsbridge: *McKuen, Rod* / Breeze and I: *Esquivel, Juan Garcia* / High and the mighty: *Young, Victor & His Orchestra* / Taurus, island meeting: *Jacobs, Dick & His Orchestra* / Delicado: *Faith, Percy & His Orchestra* / Theme from Star Wars: *Cinema Sound Stage Orchestra* / Cas is a gas: *Greenslade, Arthur Trio* / So long San Francisco: *Stanyon Strings* / Listen to the warm: *Greenslade, Arthur & Orchestra* / Woman in love: *Laine, Frankie* / Up a lazy river: *Zentner, Si & His Orchestra* / In someone's shadow: *Greenslade, Arthur & Orchestra* / La marche de Sacco et Vanzetti: *Cinema Sound Stage Orchestra* / Fourth of July in Sioux falls: *San Sebastian Strings* / Bon chance, Jack: *Cinema Sound Stage Orchestra*
CD _______________ 12802
Laserlight / May '97 / Target/BMG

HOW CAN I KEEP FROM SINGING VOL.1 (Early American Rural Religious Music & Song)
CD _______________ YAZ 2020
Yazoo / Jun '96 / ADA / CM / Koch

HOW CAN I KEEP FROM SINGING VOL.2 (Early American Rural Religious Music & Song)
CD _______________ YAZ 2021
Yazoo / Jun '96 / ADA / CM / Koch

HOW DO YOU LIKE YOUR BLUES
Life is a ballgame: *Persuasions* / Can't see for lookin': *Kubek, Smokin' Joe* / You don't drink what I drink: *Wilson, Smokey* / Trombone Porky: *Cohen, Porky & Michelle Willson* / Hot leftover no.1: *Magic Dick & Jay Geils/Bluestime* / Running out of time: *Roomful Of Blues* / Promised land: *Holmes Brothers* / No use talkin': *Thomas, Irma* / Talkin' is over (the walkin' has begun): *Sansone, Jumpin' Johnny* / Longwallin': *Boyack, Pat & The Prowlers* / Check out yourself: *Jones, Tutu* / Let me play with your poodle: *Ball, Marcia* / Hot leftover no.3: *Magic Dick & Jay Geils/Bluestime* / I need time: *Jones, Andrew 'Jr. Boy'* / One foot in the blues: *Adams, Johnny* / Soldier for the blues: *King, Jimmy* / I don't know: *Brown, Ruth & Johnny Adams* / Mean case of the blues: *Clearwater, Eddy*
CD _______________ CDBBAN 27
Bullseye Blues / Jul '97 / Direct

HOW DOES IT FEEL
CD _______________ 8283832
London / Jan '93 / PolyGram

HOW I LEARNED TO STOP WORRYING AND LOVE THE BOMB
CD _______________ DIAB 820
Diabolo / Jun '96 / Pinnacle

HOW LONG HAS THIS BEEN GOING ON
CD _______________ CD 20044
Pablo / May '86 / Cadillac / Complete/ Pinnacle

HOW TO START A FIGHT
CD _______________ SD 1202
Side One / Oct '96 / Cargo

HOW TO USE MACHINERY
CD _______________ MA332
Machinery / Nov '93 / Koch

HOW YOU FE SEY DAT PRESENTS "HOT"
CD _______________ SONCD 0052
Sonic Sounds / Jul '93 / Jet Star

HOWDY (25 Hillbilly All Time Greats)
Goin' to the barn-dance tonight: *Robinson, Carson & His Pioneers* / It ain't gonna rain no mo': *Hall, Wendell* / Wreck of the old '97: *Dalhart, Vernon* / Runaway train: *Dalhart, Vernon* / Red wing: *Puckett, Riley* / Blue yodel: *Rodgers, Jimmie* / Brakeman's blues: *Rodgers, Jimmie* / My clinch mountain home: *Carter Family* / Foggy mountain top: *Carter Family* / Little Bessie: *Alabama Barnstormers* / She's too good for me: *Cole, Rex Mountaineers* / In the Cumberland mountains: *Robinson, Carson* / When the curtains of the night are pinned back by the stars: *Layman, Zora & The Hometowners* / Atlanta bound: *Autry, Gene* / She came rollin' down the mountain: *Aarons Sisters* / Little old sod shanty on my claim: *Williams, Marc* / Ragtime Cowboy Joe: *Hillbillies* / I want to be a cowboy's sweetheart: *Montana, Patsy & The Prairie Ramblers* / Meet me by the icehouse, Lizzie: *Original Hoosier Hotshots* / Wabash cannonball: *Acuff, Roy & His Crazy Tennesseans* / Golden lariat: *Montana Slim* / New San Antonio Rose: *Wills, Bob & His Texas Playboys* / Walkin' the floor over you: *Tubb, Ernest* / Born to lose: *Daffan, Ted &*

The Texans / West ain't what it used to be: *Robinson, Carson & His Pioneers*
CD _______ CDAJA 5140
Living Era / Apr '96 / Select

HOWL - A FAREWELL COMPILATION OF UNRELEASED SONGS
CD _______ GRCD 352
Glitterhouse / Dec '94 / Avid/BMG

HUAYNO MUSIC OF PERU VOL.1 1949-89
CD _______ ARHCD 320
Arhoolie / Apr '95 / ADA / Cadillac / Direct

HUAYNO MUSIC OF PERU VOL.2 1960-70
CD _______ ARHCD 338
Arhoolie / Apr '95 / ADA / Cadillac / Direct

HUBERT GREGG SAYS THANKS FOR THE MEMORY
China stomp: *Hampton, Lionel & His Orchestra* / Transatlantic lullaby: *Layton, Turner* / There's a small hotel: *Daniels, Bebe* / Scatterbrain: *Brisson, Carl* / Thanks for the memory: *Hope, Bob & Shirley Ross* / Baby face: *Jolson, Al* / Too romantic: *Dorsey, Tommy Orchestra* / Wind in the willows: *Hutchinson, Leslie 'Hutch'* / Physician: *Lawrence, Gertrude* / You're driving me crazy: *Reinhardt, Django & Stephane Grappelli* / After you've gone: *Venuti, Joe & Eddie Lang* / Sugarfoot stomp: *Goodman, Benny Orchestra* / Super special picture of the year: *Yacht Club Jazz Band* / Let's put out the lights and go to sleep: *Howes, Bobby* / Dinah: *Crosby, Bing* / Tea for two: *Tatum, Art* / One I'm looking for: *Buchanan, Jack* / I'm gonna get it up (when the lights go on in London): *Gregg, Hubert* / Si tu m'aimes: *Sablon, Jean* / At the Darktown strutter's ball: *Dorsey, Jimmy Orchestra* / Jealous of me: *Waller, Fats* / Begin the beguine: *Shaw, Artie* / Princess is awakening: *Laye, Evelyn* / Maybe it's because I'm a Londoner: *Gregg, Hubert*
CD _______ PASTCD 7024
Flapper / Sep '93 / Pinnacle

HUGE COMPILATION
CD _______ ORBITCD 4
Orbital / Aug '92 / BMG

HUGE HITS '96 (2CD Set)
Virtual insanity: *Jamiroquai* / Breakfast at Tiffany's: *Deep Blue Something* / You're gorgeous: *Baby Bird* / Ooh ahh...just a little bit: *Gina G* / Macerena: *Los Del Rio* / Mysterious girl: *Andre, Peter* / How deep is your love: *Take That* / Fairground: *Simply Red* / Cecilia: *Suggs* / We've got it goin' on: *Backstreet Boys* / Oh what a night: *Clock* / Return of the Mack: *Morrison, Mark* / Creep: *TLC* / Gangsta's paradise: *Coolio* / Children: *Miles, Robert* / X-Files: *DJ Dado* / Gift: *Way Out West* / Don't stop movin': *Livin' Joy* / Firestarter: *Prodigy* / Born slippy: *Underworld* / I wanna be a hippy: *Technohead* / Don't look back in anger: *Oasis* / Tattva: *Kula Shaker* / Design for life: *Manic Street Preachers* / Stupid girl: *Garbage* / One to another: *Charlatans* / Trash: *Suede* / Day we caught the train: *Ocean Colour Scene* / Sale of the century: *Sleeper* / Oh yeah: *Ash* / Wonderwall: *Oasis* / Missing: *Everything But The Girl* / One by one: *Cher* / Falling in to you: *Dion, Celine* / 24/7: *3T* / I will survive: *Savage, Chantay* / Like a woman: *Rich, Tony Project* / I just wanna make love to you: *James, Etta* / Search for the hero: *M-People* / Neighbourhood: *Space* / Three lions: *Baddiel & Skinner & Lightning Seeds*
CD Set _______ MOODCD 50
Sony Music / Oct '96 / Sony

HUMAN MUSIC
CD _______ HMS 100CD
Homestead / Sep '88 / Cargo / SRD

HUMBUGGARY
CD _______ BAH 13
Humbug / May '95 / Total/Pinnacle

HUNGARIAN TRADITIONAL MUSIC
CD _______ PS 65117
PlayaSound / Nov '93 / ADA / Harmonia Mundi

HUNGARY - THE LAST PASSAGE
CD _______ C 580031
Ocora / Oct '94 / ADA / Harmonia Mundi

HUNTINGDON FOLK
CD _______ SVL 04
Speaking Volumes / Aug '97 / PolyGram / Reed

HURDY GURDY IN FRANCE, THE
CD _______ Y 225109CD
Silex / Feb '95 / ADA / Harmonia Mundi

HURRA SCHOOL IS OUT (2CD Set)
Action: *Sweet* / Sky high: *Jigsaw* / Glad all over: *Quatro, Suzi* / Get down: *O'Sullivan, Gilbert* / Over & over: *James Boys* / Hitchin' a ride: *Vanity Fare* / Beach baby: *First Class* / Happy together: *Turtles* / Jeans on: *Dundas, David* / Wild thing: *Fancy* / I feel free: *Amboy Dukes* / Good times: *Easybeats* / I get so excited: *Equals* / Good morning freedom: *Blue Mink* / Hi-Lili Hi-Lo: *Price, Alan* / Sunglasses: *Ullman, Tracey* / Da doo ron ron: *Cassidy, Shaun* / Surfin' safari: *Beach Boys* / LA International Airport: *Raye, Susan* / Barbados: *Typically Tropical* / Another day in paradise: *Brown, Dennis* / Castles in the air: *McLean, Don* / Stop, girls go crazy: *Moti Special* / L'amour a la Francaise: *Sullivan, Art & Kiki* / Agadoo: *Black Lace* / Africa: *Laurens, Rose* / Kingston Kingston: *Lou & The Hollywood Bananas* / Disco samba: *Two Man Sound* / Let's all chant: *Zager, Michael Band* / Seasons of gold: *Gidea Park* / Red skies: *Fixx* / California sunshine: *Climax Blues Band*
CD Set _______ 24334
Laserlight / Jul '96 / Target/BMG

HURRY THE JUG (Classic Songs/Lilting/Storytelling In The Irish Tradition)
Talk about Garret Barry and Hurry the jug: *Lenihan, Tom* / Humours of whiskey (Paddy's panacea): *Lenihan, Tom* / Talk about music at Lenihans: *Lenihan, Tom* / John and the farmer: *Byrne, Packie Manus* / Lament to the moon: *Byrne, Packie Manus* / Bold Doherty: *Carolan, Mary-Ann* / Tinker's old budget: *Carolan, Mary-Ann* / Bonny green tree: *Reilly, John* / Raggle taggle gypsy: *Reilly, John* / Waterford boys: *Tunney, Paddy* / Sean O'Dwyer a Gleanna: *Tunney, Paddy* / Peigin is Peader: *Heaney, Joe* / Rocks of Baun: *Heaney, Joe* / Jolly thresher: *Makem, Sarah* / Banks of red roses: *Makem, Sarah* / Drowsy Maggie: *Cinnamond, Robert* / On yonder hill there sits a hare: *Hanna, George* / Erin's lovely home: *Hanna, George* / A stor mo chroi: *MacDonnchadha, Sean* / An buinnean bui: *MacDonnchadha, Sean* / Two strings on a bow: *Mitchell, Kevin* / Boys of Mullaghbawn: *Mitchell, Kevin* / Moorlough Mary: *McDermott, Josie* / Collier's reel/The Bank Of Ireland: *McDermott, Josie*
CD _______ CDORBD 090
Globestyle / Jul '96 / Pinnacle

HUSH RECORDS STORY, THE
Little girl: *Syndicate Of Sound* / Get outta my life: *Syndicate Of Sound* / Someday: *Brogues* / But now I find: *Brogues* / Believe me: *Penn, William & The Quakers* / Hey hey hey: *Penn, William & The Quakers* / I ain't no miracle worker: *Penn, William & The Quakers* / Don't shoot me down: *Brogues* / Looking for the good times (the robot): *Syndicate Of Sound* / That kind of man: *Syndicate Of Sound* / Rumours: *Syndicate Of Sound* / Say I love you: *Syndicate Of Sound* / I like that girl: *Gerry & Leslie* / Ghost of the monks: *Penn, William & The Quakers* / Care free: *Penn, William & The Quakers* / Coming up my way: *Penn, William & The Quakers* / Mary: *Syndicate Of Sound* / Games: *Syndicate Of Sound* / Nothing matters now: *Stop Sign* / Little girl: *Penn, William & The Quakers* / Doctor dear: *Diminished Fifth* / Do you hear: *Diminished Fifth* / Saturday night: *Syndicate Of Sound* / Someday: *Brogues*
CD _______ CDWIKD 154
Big Beat / Jan '97 / Pinnacle

HYMNE AN DIE POSIE
CD _______ EFA 127142
Weisser Herbst / Apr '95 / SRD

HYMNODY OF THE GREEK ORTHODOX CHURCH
CD _______ VICG 53462
JVC World Library / Mar '96 / ADA / CM / Direct

HYMNS FROM NORWICH CATHEDRAL
Praise my soul the king of heaven / Just as I am / We plough the fields and scatter / Holy, holy, holy / Through all the changing scenes of life / Onward Christian soldiers / Abide with me / Christ triuimphant ever reigning / God of Abraham / Lift high the cross / We sing the praise / Crimond / Alleluia sing to Jesus / Angel voices / Be thou my vision / Praise to the holiest / Eternal father / Jesus christ is risen today / O worship the king / For all the saints / Head that once was crowned / Lift up your hearts / All my hope on god is founded
CD _______ ANT 015
Tring / Nov '96 / Tring

HYMNS FROM TRURO CATHEDRAL
O praise ye the lord / Come thou long expected Jesus / O come o come emmanuel / All things bright and beautiful / All creatures of the God and King / Dear Lord and father / My song is love unknown / Forth in thy name o Lord I go / City of god / There is a green hill / When I survey the wondrous cross / Jesus lives / Come down oh loove divine / God be in my head / Oh Jesus I have promised / Fight the good fight / Glorious things / Day thou gavest, the / Before the ending of the day / Jerusalem
CD _______ ANT 014
Tring / Nov '96 / Tring

HYMNS OF OUR FATHERS
Holy Virgin by God's decree: *Galway Singers* / Be thou my vision: *Galway Singers* / Watch the sunrise: *Galway Singers* / Morning has broken: *Hamilton, Claire* / Lady full of God's own grace: *Galway Singers* / Soul of my saviour: *Galway Singers* / Pie Jesu: *Edwards-Jones, Gill* / Seoladh na Ngamhna: *Galway Singers* / Viderunt Omnes: *Cantus Novus* / Sweet heart of Jesus: *Galway Singers* / Faith of our fathers: *Coppin, Johnny* / Hail Queen of heaven: *Galway Singers* / Daily daily sing to Mary: *Galway Singers* / Ireland, I'll not tell her name: *Sands, Mick* / Ave Maria: *Edwards-Jones, Gill* / Hail glorious St. Patrick: *Galway Singers* / This is my body, broken for you: *Galway Singers* / I heard the voices of Jesus say: *Hamilton, Claire* / Domino fidelium: *Cantus Novus* / Immaculate Mary: *Galway Singers* / Blessed are the pure in heart: *Galway Singers* / Lord's prayer: *Galway Singers*
CD _______ 3036000932
Carlton / Mar '97 / Carlton

HYPE (Life Inside The North West)
CD _______ SPCD 371
Sub Pop / Oct '96 / Cargo / Greyhound / Shellshock/Disc

HYPER COOL VOL.1
CD _______ ZYX 550682
ZYX / Nov '96 / ZYX

HYPER COOL VOL.2
CD _______ ZYX 550782
ZYX / Feb '97 / ZYX

HYPERTENSION SAMPLER
CD _______ HY 153CD
Hypertension / Apr '95 / ADA / CM / Direct / Total/BMG

HYPNOTIZING (2CD Set)
CD Set _______ CLP 9971
Cleopatra / Apr '97 / Cargo / Greyhound / Plastic Head / RTM/Disc / SRD

HYPOCRITE INNA DANCE HALL STYLE
CD _______ JJCD 192
Channel One / Apr '96 / Jet Star

HYRDESTUND (Early Norwegian Flutes & Whistles)
CD _______ HCD 7116
Helio / Aug '96 / ADA

HYSTERICAL YEARS 1986-1990, THE
CD _______ ACHECD 020
Manic Ears / Jun '90 / Target/BMG

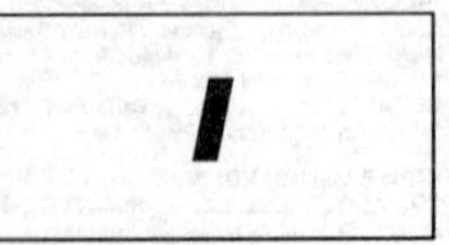

I ASKED FOR WHISKEY
CD _______ IGOCD 2028
Indigo / Aug '95 / ADA / Direct

I BELIEVE
CD _______ TCD 2811
Telstar / Dec '95 / BMG

I CAN EAGLE ROCK (1940-1941)
CD _______ TMCD 09
Travellin' Man / May '96 / Hot Shot / Jazz Music / Wellard

I CAN HEAR MUSIC
I can hear music: *Beach Boys* / Hippy hippy shake: *Swinging Blue Jeans* / Do wah diddy diddy: *Manfred Mann* / Proud Mary: *Turner, Ike & Tina* / C'mon everybody: *Cochran, Eddie* / Rubber ball: *Vee, Bobby* / Hello Mary Lou: *Nelson, Ricky* / Till I kissed you: *Everly Brothers* / Summer in the city: *Lovin' Spoonful* / Wanderer: *Dion* / Games people play: *South, Joe* / Keep searching: *Shannon, Del* / Sloop John B: *Beach Boys* / We've gotta get out of this place: *Animals* / Jenny take a ride: *Ryder, Mitch & The Detroit Wheels* / Some kinda wonderful: *Grand Funk Railroad*
CD _______ DC 880792
Disky / May '97 / Disky / THE

I CAN'T BE SATISFIED VOL.1 (Early American Women Blues Singers Town & Country)
CD _______ YAZ 2026
Yazoo / Apr '97 / ADA / CM / Koch

I CAN'T BE SATISFIED VOL.2 (Early American Women Blues Singers Town & Country)
CD _______ YAZZ 2027
Yazoo / Apr '97 / ADA / CM / Koch

I CAN'T BELIEVE IT'S NOT TRIP HOP
CD _______ NOR 001CD
North South / Mar '96 / Pinnacle

I FALL TO PIECES (Classic Country)
Walkin' after midnight: *Cline, Patsy* / He'll have to go: *Reeves, Jim* / Crystal chandeliers: *Pride, Charley* / White lightning: *Jennings, Waylon* / Take this job and shove it: *Paycheck, Johnny* / Cold cold heart: *Jones, George* / Stranger in my arms: *Cline, Patsy* / Kiss an angel good morning: *Pride, Charley* / I fall to pieces: *Jackson, Wanda* / Have I told you lately that I love you: *Reeves, Jim* / Please help me I'm falling: *Locklin, Hank* / I'm the only hell mama ever raised: *Paycheck, Johnny* / Love of the common people: *Jennings, Waylon* / World's worst lover: *Jones, George* / Four walls: *Reeves, Jim* / Night life: *Nelson, Willie* / Church, a courtroom, then goodbye: *Cline, Patsy* / Help me make it through the night: *Pride, Charley*
CD _______ CD 6045
Music / Sep '96 / Target/BMG

I GOT IT BAD AND THAT AIN'T GOOD
I got it bad and that ain't good: *Holiday, Billie* / Sad letter: *Waters, Muddy* / Dusty road: *Hooker, John Lee* / Commit a crime: *Howlin' Wolf* / Cool disposition: *Williamson, Sonny Boy* / Little rain: *Reed, Jimmy* / Blues with a feeling: *Little Walter* / Please don't talk about me when I'm gone: *Holiday, Billie* / Mean mistreater: *Waters, Muddy* / Process: *Hooker, John Lee* / Moanin' at midnight: *Howlin' Wolf* / Blue tail fly: *Leadbelly* / Dust my broom: *James, Elmore* / Nice work if you can get it: *Holiday, Billie* / Whiskey and wimmen: *Hooker, John Lee* / Diamonds at your feet: *Waters, Muddy* / I'm in the mood: *Hooker, John Lee* / In New Orleans: *Leadbelly* / Killing floor: *Howlin' Wolf* / Fine and mellow: *Holiday, Billie* / How blue can you get: *King, B.B.* / Off the wall: *Little Walter* / Mean red spider: *Waters, Muddy* / Goin' down slow: *Howlin' Wolf* / Frisco blues: *Hooker, John Lee*
CD _______ GRF 127
Tring / '93 / Tring

(I GOT NO KICK AGAINST) MODERN JAZZ
Long and winding road: *Benson, George* / She's leaving home: *Tyner, McCoy* / She's so heavy: *Groove Collective* / And I love her: *Krall, Diana* / Fool on the hill: *Scott, Tom* / Michelle: *Lewis, Ramsey* / Day in the life: *Ritenour, Lee* / Let it be: *Rangell, Nelson* / Eleanor Rigby: *Corea, Chick* / While my guitar gently weeps: *Freeman, Russ & The Rippingtons* / In my life: *Spyro Gyra* / Here there and everywhere: *Benoit, David* / Blackbird: *Sandoval, Arturo* / Yesterday: *Grusin, Dave* / Imagine: *Kishino, Yoshiko*
CD _______ GRP 98322
GRP / Oct '95 / New Note/BMG

I HAVE TO PAINT MY FACE
CD _______ ARHCD 432
Arhoolie / Jan '96 / ADA / Cadillac / Direct

I KNOW WHAT BOYS LIKE (Great Girl Pop Hits Of 1980/1990's)
CD _______ SH 5713
Shanachie / Oct '96 / ADA / Greensleeves / Koch

I LIKE IT (BGP Presents The Vanguard Experience)
EVA: *Perrey, Jean Jacques* / Take yo' praise: *Yarborough, Camille* / I like it: *Players Association* / Rigor mortez: *Burns, Dave* / Work song: *Pazant Brothers* / Funk ain't a word: *Green, Bunky* / Lavendar Thursday: *Natal, Nannette* / Cat in the night: *Perrey, Jean Jacques* / Funky monkey: *Hills, Chris* / Loose and juicy: *Pazant Brothers* / Richie's dream: *Burns, Dave* / Mas que nada: *Perrey, Jean Jacques*
CD _______ CDBGPD 106
Beat Goes Public / Jun '96 / Pinnacle

I LOVE FUSE
CD _______ FUSE 001CD
Fuse / Jan '96 / Plastic Head

I LOVE NY JUNGLE
CD _______ JSK 011
Jungle Sky / Dec '96 / Cargo

I LOVE TECHNO
CD _______ ILT 01CD
News / Sep '96 / Plastic Head

I LOVE YOU (18 Classic Country Love Songs)
Sharing the night together: *Dr. Hook* / Never ending song of love: *Gayle, Crystal* / Take me in your arms and hold me: *Whitman, Slim* / Love me like you used to: *Tucker, Tanya* / What the world needs now is love: *Spears, Billie Jo* / Honey come back: *Campbell, Glen* / Loving him was easier: *Carter, Anita* / Stand by your man: *Jackson, Wanda* / All I have to do is dream: *Newton, Juice* / Crazy: *Nelson, Willie* / Young love: *James, Sonny* / Sweet dreams: *Young, Faron* / Somebody loves you: *Gayle, Crystal* / My blue heaven: *Whitman, Slim* / You love me through it all: *Williams, Don* / When you're in love with a beautiful woman: *Dr. Hook* / Everything a man could ever need: *Campbell, Glen* / Love song: *Newton-John, Olivia*
CD _______ CDMFP 6281
Music For Pleasure / Jan '97 / EMI

I PUT A SPELL ON YOU
I put a spell on you: *Hawkins, Screamin' Jay* / I'm so glad I'm in love again: *Houston, Cissy* / When the saints go marching in: *Hines, Earl 'Fatha'* / Lover come back to me: *Holiday, Billie* / I guess I'm a fool: *Memphis Slim* / Hey Bo Diddley: *Diddley, Bo* / Let the four winds blow: *Brown, Roy* / When the sun goes down: *Turner, 'Big' Joe* / Crackin' up: *Diddley, Bo* / BB boogie: *King, B.B.* / I'd rather go blind: *James, Etta* / Crazy 'bout you baby: *Lightnin' Slim* / If loving you is wrong: *Mason, Barbara* / Red rooster: *Howlin' Wolf* / I need you so bad: *Cotton, James* / Goodnight sweetheart, goodnight: *Spaniels*
CD _______ 100942
CMC / May '97 / BMG

I SHALL SING VOL.1
CD _______ CDTRL 289
Trojan / Mar '94 / Direct / Jet Star

I SHALL SING VOL.2
Best thing for me: *Powell, June* / I see you my love: *Griffiths, Marcia* / Silly wasn't it: *Forrester, Sharon* / Love that a woman should give a man: *Dillon, Phyllis* / She kept on talking: *Mowatt, Judy* / Please Mr. Please: *Powell, June* / Mother nature: *Sweet, Roslyn* / Heart made of stone (Vocal): *Hall, Audrey* / Heart made of stone (Version): *Hit Squad* / You can wake up with me: *Powell, June* / Love the one you're

with: *Dillon, Phyllis* / Promises: *Richard, Cynthia* / You're not my kind: *Naomi* / I can't help it darling: *Jones, Barbara* / Put a little love away: *Forrester, Sharon* / Something about you: *Jordon, Sidonie* / I'll be everything to you (Vocal): *Powell, June* / I'll be everything to you (Version): *Hit Squad*
CD ______ CDTRL 316
Trojan / Mar '94 / Direct / Jet Star

I TURNED INTO A HELIUM BALLOON
Mirror of your mind: *We The People* / Color of love: *We The People* / You burn me up and down: *We The People* / St. John's shop: *We The People* / In the past: *We The People* / Half of wednesday: *We The People* / My brother, the man: *We The People* / Free information: *We The People* / Too much noise: *We The People* / By the rule: *We The People* / Alfred, what kind of man are you: *We The People* / Beginning of the end: *We The People* / I ain't no miracle worker: *Brogues* / Don't shoot me down: *Brogues* / Let it be: *Blaskey, Lindy & The Lavelles* / You ain't tuff: *Blaskey, Lindy & The Lavelles* / Spinach: *Boston Tea Party* / Words: *Boston Tea Party* / I'm spinning: *Fenwyck* / Mindrocker: *Fenwyck* / State of mind: *Fenwyck* / Away: *Fenwyck* / I wanna die: *Fenwyck* / Iye: *Fenwyck* / Show me the way: *Free For All* / Psychedelic siren: *Daybreakers* / Somebody's son: *Tikis* / Thoughts: *Front Page News* / Lies: *Knickerbockers* / My feet are off the ground: *Knickerbockers*
CD ______ CDWIKD 130
Big Beat / Jun '94 / Pinnacle

I WALK THE LINE
CD ______ MACCD 214
Autograph / Aug '96 / BMG

I WILL ALWAYS LOVE YOU (Romantic Panpipes)
I honestly love you / What are you doing / What is this thing called love / With you I'm born again / Softly as I leave you / When you're in love / Someone to watch over me / Miss you nights / Where is the love / Nearness of you / Up where we belong / Speak softly love / Tonight I celebrate my love / I will always love you
CD ______ CDMFP 6270
Music For Pleasure / Sep '96 / EMI

I-5 KILLERS VOL.3
What used to be: *Gift* / Blondes: *Everclear* / Crash: *Kpants* / Punch: *Thirty Ought Six* / Lines: *Kaia* / Simeon flick: *Skiploader* / Edward Hopper song: *Whirlees* / Jake's dream: *Time Killing Isabel* / Never win: *Wipers* / It's a lie: *Gravel Pit* / Ugly stick: *Ice Cream Headache* / Get outta my way: *Starlite Trio* / Rock your baby: *Oblivion Seekers* / Evil style: *Anal Solvent* / Josh has a crush: *New Bad Things* / Metropolis 2664: *Caveman Shoestore* / Aloha Steve and Dan-O: *Oswald 5-O* / Your Mom rules: *Supersuckers*
CD ______ SZ 0213
T/K / Jun '94 / Pinnacle

IAI FESTIVAL
CD ______ 1238592
IAI / Nov '93 / Cadillac / Harmonia Mundi

IBIZA - FOLKLORE Y CANCIONES
CD ______ 31374
Divucsa / Oct '96 / Discovery

IBIZA '95
Closer: *Mood II Swing* / Ultra flava: *Heller & Farley Project* / One love: *Coccoluto, Claudio* / Do U wanna funk: *Space 2000* / Come with me: *Zero The Hero* / Weekend: *Terry, Todd* / You gotta get up: *Perfectly Ordinary People* / Do you feel: *Effective* / Stick together: *Miss Stuck Up* / Where's my man: *EL Fredo* / Red hot in Ibiza: *DJ Pants* / Born to synthesize: *Mona Lisa Overdrive* / Honk: *Hullabaloo* / Come on y'all: *Rhythm Masters* / Mambo white: *Nox Alba* / Spiritualize: *We Shape Space* / Magic in you: *Sugar Babies*
CD ______ 21 CCCD 001
21st Century Opera / Oct '95 / Total/BMG

IBIZA HITS (2CD Set)
CD Set ______ ZYX 811142
ZYX / Aug '97 / ZYX

ICED GROOVES
No control: *Control Z* / Soul survivor: *Lenii B* / Your love: *Inner City* / Right and exact: *Ward, Chrissy* / Got myself together: *Bucketheads* / Sweetest day of may: *Vannelli, Joe T. Project* / Weekend: *Terry, Todd Project* / Break of dawn: *Rhythm On The Loose* / Passion: *Gat Decor* / Naughty North and the sexy South: *E-Motion* / Hideaway: *De-'Lacy* / Love has changed my mind: *Skinnee* / I believe: *Happy Clappers* / Eternity: *Happy Clappers*
CD ______ FI 408
Telstar / Nov '95 / BMG

ICH BIN (Mixed by Dr. Motte)
CD ______ EFA 004202
Space Teddy / Aug '97 / SRD

ICHIBAN BLUES AT CHRISTMAS
(All I want for Christmas is to) lay around: *Willis, Chuck* / Absent minded Santa: *McCain, Jerry* / Lonesome Christmas: *Blues Boy Willie* / Santa Claus is back in town: *Brown, Nappy* / Christmas is here again: *Taylor, Johnny* / Christmas time (comes but once a year): *Lynn, Trudy* / I didn't get nothin' for Christmas: *Garrett, Vernon* / Christmas tears: *Dee, David* / Christmas, don't forget about me: *Drink Small* / Please come home for Christmas: *Willis, Chuck*
CD ______ ICH 1126CD
Ichiban / Nov '91 / Direct / Koch

ICHIBAN SAMPLER
CD ______ ICH 7802CD
Ichiban / Jan '94 / Direct / Koch

IF A TREE FALLS
Song of the trees: *Trudell, John* / Devil and the trees: *Zero* / Trees: *Hoyt, Robert* / Never alone: *Cockburn, Bruce* / Kiss Mother Nature goodbye: *Williams, Hank Jr.* / Priests of the golden bull: *Sainte-Marie, Buffy* / Cry in the forest: *Fogelberg, Dan* / Where are we gonna work when the trees are gone: *Biafra, Jello & Mojo Nixon* / Trees like to rot in the forest: *Tinklers* / You can't clearcut your way to Heaven: *Cherney, Darryl* / Defend the Earth: *Di Micele, Alicia* / Farewell to Clayoquot sound: *Wyrd Sisters* / Heart of destruction: *Ferron* / Only green world: *Rumors Of The Big Wave*
CD ______ R 272495
Earthbeat / Nov '96 / ADA / Direct

IF IT AIN'T A HIT I'LL EAT MY....BABY
Think twice: *Wilson, Jackie & Laverne Baker* / Two time Slim/Hey, shine: *Snatch & The Poontangs* / Somebody else was suckin' my dick last night: *Wolff, Fred Combo* / Meat man: *Vickery, Mack* / Stoop down baby: *Willis, Chuck* / Deacon Jones/LA women love Uncle Bud: *Chavis, Boozoo* / Don't fuck around with love: *Blenders* / Long John/Short John: *Washington, Dinah* / Rotten cocksuckers' ball: *Clovers* / Hard driving blues: *Milburn, Amos* / Butcher Pete: *Brown, Roy* / Joe's joint: *Ferre, Cliff* / Fuck off (You dirty rooster): *Gaillard, Slim*
CD ______ CDZ 2009
Zu Zazz / Apr '94 / Rollercoaster

IF YOU JUST TUNED IN (Live From The Mean Fiddler's Acoustic Room)
Dollar tree: *Hawkins, Ted* / When we were young: *Orchard, Pat* / Love your shoes: *Cunningham, Andrew* / Rover: *Sons Of The Desert* / Down the wine garden: *Little Big Band* / It's not that bad anymore: *Barely Works* / White cloud: *To Hell With Burgundy* / Spitting: *And All Because The Lady Loves* / Three legged men: *Harding, John Wesley* / Tree to breathe: *Dinner Ladies* / Partisan: *Keineg, Katell* / I ain't got nothin' yet: *Hawkins, Ted*
CD ______ AWCD 1017
Awareness / Apr '90 / ADA

IF YOU WANT REGGAE VOL.1
CD ______ TMPCD 028
Temple / Jun '96 / BMG

IF YOU WANT REGGAE VOL.2
CD ______ TMPCD 029
Temple / Jun '96 / BMG

IF YOU WANT REGGAE VOL.3
CD ______ TMPCD 030
Temple / Jun '96 / BMG

IFI PALASA - TONGAN BRASS
CD ______ PANCD 2044
Pan / May '94 / ADA / CM / Direct

IGL ROCK STORY VOL.1
CD ______ AA 046
Arf Arf / Jul '97 / Greyhound

IL BALLO DEI PAZZI
CD ______ ACB 07CD
ACB / Mar '96 / ADA

IL SUONO DI ROMA
CD ______ ACVCD 2001
ACV / Oct '94 / Plastic Head / SRD

I'LL BE SEEING YOU
CD ______ CECD 2
Collector's Edition / Jan '96 / TKO Magnum

I'LL BE SEEING YOU: THOSE ROMANTIC 40'S (Nice 'n' Easy Series)
CD ______ 8440852
Eclipse / Mar '92 / PolyGram

I'LL DANCE TILL DE SUN BREAKS THROUGH (Ragtime, Cakewalks & Stomps 1898-1923)
That moaning saxophones rag: *Six Brown Brothers* / Florida rag: *Van Eps Trio* / Bacchanal rag: *Peerless Orchestra* / Alabama skedaddle: *Mitcham, William* / Castle walk: *Europe's Society Orchestra* / From soup to nuts: *Arndt, Felix* / Smoky mokes: *Metropolitan Orchestra* / Eli Green's cake walk: *Cullen & Collins* / Cake walk: *Victor Minstrels* / I'll dance till de sun breaks through: *Joyce, Archibald & His Orchestra* / Ain't nobody's business if I do: *Matson, Charles Creole Serenaders* / Whistling Rufus: *Oakley, Olly* / Wild cherries rag: *Victor Orchestra* / Won't you come home, Bill Bailey: *Collins, Arthur* / Stomp dance: *Victor Military Band* / Calico rag: *Banta, Frank & Howard Kopp* / Smiles and chuckles - A jazz rag: *Six Brown Brothers* / On the Levee: *Victor Minstrels* / Trombone sneeze - a humoresque cakewalk: *Sousa's Band* / Two key rag: *Conway's Band*
CD ______ CDSDL 336
Saydisc / Mar '94 / ADA / Direct / Harmonia Mundi

ILL ST. PRESENTS SUBTERRANEAN HITZ VOL.1
CD ______ WSCD 014
Word Sound Recordings / Jan '97 / Cargo / SRD

ILLEGAL JUNGLE VOL.2
Lovin' you: *Suburban Soul* / Worries 'n' trouble: *Stache & Michael X* / Little star: *Elegant Posse* / Keep risin': *Stache & Roger Payne* / Coming from behind: *Dubologist & MCG* / Runnin': *Mix Factory* / Nex'd Ardsteppa: *DJ Nexus Scott Potential* / Hi-ya: *Twilight Dawn* / Smells like lithium: *Cartell & D-Tone* / Something's gotta hold: *Scott Potential* / Lighter: *Co-Accused* / Shadow: *Dubscientist* / Jack's back: *Hyper X* / Prophecy: *Ridley E* / Just walk: *Rosencrantz, Phillistine & Jake* / Wake: *Killer M*
CD ______ JARCD 17
Cookie Jar / Jun '95 / SRD

ILLEGAL PIRATE RADIO VOL.1
CD ______ STHCCD 3
Strictly Underground / Aug '93 / SRD

ILLEGAL PIRATE RADIO VOL.2
CD ______ STHCCD 4
Strictly Underground / Apr '94 / SRD

ILLEGAL PIRATE RADIO VOL.3
CD ______ STHCCD 9
Strictly Hardcore / May '95 / SRD

ILLEGAL RAVE VOL.2
CD ______ STHCCD 2
Strictly Underground / Jun '93 / SRD

ILLEGAL RAVE VOL.3
CD ______ STHCCD 5
Strictly Underground / Jun '94 / SRD

I'M BEGINNING TO SEE THE LIGHT
Opus one: *Dorsey, Tommy* / Saturday night: *Sinatra, Frank* / I only have eyes for you: *Hawkins, Coleman* / As time goes by: *Holiday, Billie* / Lady Day: *Shaw, Artie* / Somebody loves me: *Condon, Eddie* / Blue Lester: *Young, Lester* / GI jive: *Jordan, Louis* / Red cross: *Parker, Charlie* / I'm beginning to see the light: *Ellington, Duke* / Night and day: *Hall, Edmond* / Down by the riverside: *Johnson, Bunk* / I'm confessin' that I love you: *James, Harry* / Exercise in swing: *Guarnieri, Johnny & Lester Young* / Someone to watch over me: *Wiley, Lee* / All the cats join in: *Goodman, Benny* / Jack Armstrong blues: *Teagarden, Jack & Louis Armstrong* / Sentimental journey: *Day, Doris & Les Brown* / Skyliner: *Barnet, Charlie* / Don't fence me in: *Bailey, Mildred* / Woody 'n' you: *Hawkins, Coleman & Dizzy Gillespie* / There'll be a hot time in the town of Berlin: *Miller, Glenn*
CD ______ PHONTCD 7672
Phontastic / Jun '94 / Cadillac / Jazz Music / Wellard

I'M IN THE MOOD FOR BLUES
CD ______ DCD 5322
Disky / Dec '93 / Disky / THE

I'M IN THE MOOD FOR SAX
I'm in the mood for love / True love / You belong to me / Jane / Secret love / Unforgettable / Dreaming / Send in the clowns / Summer the first time / Nightingale sang in Berkeley Square / Once in a while / Nearness of you / Someone to watch over me / When I fall in love / Certain smile / Evergreen / Scarborough fair / Try to remember / Feelings / Wind beneath my wings / This masquerade
CD ______ EMPRCD 602
Emporio / Jun '96 / Disc

I'M LEAVING TIPPERARY - CLASSIC IRISH TRADITIONAL MUSIC (Recorded In America In The 1920's & 1930's)
Lord Gordon's reel: *Hanafin, Michael* / I'm leaving Tipperary: *Sullivan, Dan & Shamrock Band* / My darling asleep/Maids on the green: *McGettigan, John* / Martha, the flower of sweet Strabane: *McGettigan, John* / Curlew hills/Peach Blossoms: *Morrison, James* / Frieze breeches: *Ennis, Tom* / Auld blackthorn: *Flanagan Brothers* / My Irish Molly-O: *Flanagan Brothers* / Irish mazurka: *Gillespie, Hugh* / Jenny's welcome to Charlie: *Gillespie, Hugh* / Stone outside Dan Murphy's door: *McGettigan, John* / Tailor's twist/Flower of Spring: *Morrison, James* / Billy Hanafin's reel: *Hanafin, Michael* / Green grow the rushes-o: *Sullivan, Dan & Shamrock Band* / Beggarman song: *Flanagan Brothers* / Tickling Mary Jane: *Rabbet, Murty & Gaelic Band* / Miller's reel/Duffy the dancer: *Nolan, Neil* / Moneymusk/Johnny will you marry me/Keel row: *Morrison, James* / Kildare fancy/Stack of wheat: *Ennis, Tom* / New steamboat/Bucks of Oranmore/Gardeners daughter: *Morrison, James & Tom Ennis* / Erin's lovely lea: *McGettigan, John* / Dowd's No. 9/Jackson's: *Gillespie, Hugh* / Versevanna: *Gillespie, Hugh* / Irish delight: *Flanagan Brothers*
CD ______ CDORBD 082
Globestyle / Jan '94 / Pinnacle

I'M ROMANTIC
CD ______ BB 2809
Blue Beat / Aug '96 / Grapevine/PolyGram

I'M SO LONESOME I COULD CRY
CD ______ MU 5057
Musketeer / Oct '92 / Disc

I'M SURE WE'RE GONNA MAKE IT
CD ______ 64862
Epitaph / Jan '97 / Pinnacle / Plastic Head

IMAGINE (2CD Set)
CD Set ______ DEMPCD 008
Emporio / Mar '96 / Disc

IMAGINE ANOTHER IRELAND VOL.1
Summer in Siam: *Pogues* / Strathspey: *Altan* / Harry's game: *Clannad* / All the lies: *Black, Frances* / Idir eatarthu: *O'Suilleabhain, Micheal* / Seo leo'thoil: *Casey, Nollaig & Arty McGlynn* / Lucy's tune: *Spillane, Davy* / Dul dti's raiseanna: *Begley, Seamus & Stephen Cooney* / Gardiner Street blues: *Drew, Ronnie* / Blackbird: *Shannon, Sharon* / Rights of man: *De Danann* / O'Rourke's: *O'Flynn, Liam* / Geantrai: *Anuna* / Pachelbel's frolics: *Ivers, Eileen* / Nocturne: *Irish Chamber Orchestra*
CD ______ KMCD 63
Keltia Musique / Jul '96 / ADA / Discovery

IMAGINE ANOTHER IRELAND VOL.2 (Encore)
CD ______ KMCD 75
Keltia Musique / May '97 / ADA / Discovery

IMMEDIATE BLUES ANTHOLOGY, THE (3CD Set)
I'm your witchdoctor: *Mayall, John & The Bluesbreakers* / Snake drive: *Clapton, Eric* / Ain't gonna cry no more: *McPhee, Tony* / I tried: *Savoy Brown Blues Band* / Tribute to Elmore: *Clapton, Eric* / I feel so good: *Kelly, Jo Ann* / Telephone blues: *Mayall, John & The Bluesbreakers* / You don't love me: *McPhee, Tony* / West coast idea: *Clapton, Eric* / Ain't seen no whisky: *Kelly, Jo Ann* / Flapjacks: *Stone's Masonry* / Cold blooded woman: *Savoy Brown Blues Band* / On top of the world: *Mayall, John & The Bluesbreakers* / Someone to love me: *McPhee, Tony* / Can't quit you baby: *Savoy Brown Blues Band* / Draggin' my tail: *Clapton, Eric & Jimmy Page* / Dealing with the devil: *Dharma Blues Band* / Look down at my woman: *Spencer, Jeremy* / Roll em pete: *Dharma Blues Band* / Choker: *Clapton, Eric & Jimmy Page* / True Blue: *Savoy Brown Blues Band* / When you got a good friend: *McPhee, Tony* / Someday baby: *Davies, Cyril & the Rhythm & Blues All Stars* / Steelin': *All Stars & Jeff Beck* / LA Breakdown: *All Stars & Jimmy Page* / Chuckles: *All Stars & Jeff Beck* / Down in the boots: *All Stars & Jimmy Page* / Piano shuffle: *All Stars & Nicky Hopkins* / Miles road: *Clapton, Eric & Jimmy Page* / Porcupine juice: *Santa Barbara Machine Head* / Howlin for my darling: *Stuff Smith* / Next milestone: *Lee, Albert & Tony Colton* / Someone's gonna get their head kicked in tonight: *Vince, Earl & The Valients* / New death master: *Kelly, Dave* / Back water blues: *Kelly, Jo Ann* / So much to say: *Stewart, Rod* / Married woman blues: *Kelly, Dave* / Water on my fire: *Lee, albert & paul williams* / Kepp your hands out of my pockets: *Kelly, Jo Ann* / Alabama woman: *Kelly, Dave* / Crosstown link: *Lee, Albert* / All night long: *Kelly, Dave* / Down and dirty: *Simon & Steve* / Not fade away: *Davies, Cyril & the Rhythm & Blues All Stars* / Come home baby: *Stewart, Rod & P.P.Arnold* / Life is but nothing: *Arnold, P.P.* / Little miss understood: *Stewart, Rod*
CD Set ______ CDIMMBOX 4
Charly / Jun '96 / Koch

IMMEDIATE COLLECTION, THE (16 Legendary Recordings From The Era That Inspired Britpop)
Hello Suzie: *Amen Corner* / Natural born bugie: *Humble Pie* / Out of time: *Farlowe, Chris* / Hang on to a dream: *Nice* / All or nothing: *Small Faces* / Hang on sloopy: *McCoys* / Man of the world: *Fleetwood Mac* / Angel of the morning: *Arnold, P.P.* / First cut is the deepest: *Arnold, P.P.* / Sittin' on a fence: *Twice As Much* / Lazy Sunday: *Small Faces* / Little Miss Understood: *Stewart, Rod* / Handbags and gladrags: *Farlowe, Chris* / (If paradise is) half as nice: *Amen Corner* / Itchycoo park: *Small Faces* / America: *Nice*
CD ______ SUMCD 4036
Summit / Nov '96 / Sound & Media

IMMEDIATE RECORD COMPANY ANTHOLOGY, THE (3CD Set)
CD Set ______ DOBOX 1
Dojo / Aug '92 / Disc

IMMORTAL INSTRUMENTALS
CD ______ KLMCD 051
BAM / Jan '95 / Koch / Scratch/BMG

IMMORTAL US NO.1 HITS
CD ______ KLMCD 044
BAM / Jan '95 / Koch / Scratch/BMG

IN A COCKTAIL MOOD
CD ______ TCD 1037
Tradition / Nov '96 / ADA / Vital

IN BED WITH MARINA
CD ______ MA 21
Marina / Feb '97 / SRD

IN CASE YOU MISSED IT - JAZZ FESTIVAL VOL.1
Schalfe mein prinzchen: *Bue, Papa Viking Jazz Band* / Muskrat ramble: *Collie, Max Rhythm Aces* / Mood indigo: *Ball, Kenny* / Bourbon street parade: *Dutch Swing College Band* / Flyin' house: *Dr. Dixie Jazz*

Band / That's a plenty: *Prowizorka Dzezz Bed* / Stranger on the shore: *Bilk, Acker* / Struttin' with some barbecue: *Down Town Jazzband* / Ice cream: *Sunshine, Monty Jazz Band* / Basin Street blues: *Sunshine, Monty Jazz Band* / Jumpin' at the woodside: *Huub Janssen's Amazing Jazz Band* / World is waiting for the sunrise: *Huub Janssen's Amazing Jazz Band* / Bye and bye: *Boutte, Lillian* / Petite fleur: *Lightfoot, Terry* / West End blues: *Mason, Rod Hot Five* / At the jazz band ball: *World's Greatest Jazz Band* / Jambalaya: *Barber, Chris & His Jazz Band* / As I go to the quick river: *Uralsky All Stars*
CD ____ **CDTTD 522**
Timeless Jazz / Feb '95 / New Note/ Pinnacle

IN CASE YOU MISSED IT - JAZZ FESTIVAL VOL.2
Midnight in Moscow: *Ball, Kenny* / Aria: *Bilk, Acker* / It's a sin to tell a lie: *Deep Creek Jazzuits* / Mishka, mishka: *Uralsky All Stars* / What a friend: *Boutte, Lillian* / You are woman: *Jazz Band Ball Orchestra* / Song was born: *Papa Blue's Viking Jazzband* / Royal flush: *Berkhout, Bernard '5'* / Storyville: *Houlind, Doc & His Copenhagen Ragtime Band* / Old rugged cross: *Monty's Sunshine Jazz Band* / Limehouse blues: *Dixie-O-Naires* / Washboard wiggle: *Prowizorka Jazzband* / Kansas City blues: *Collie, Max Rhythm Aces* / Hundred years from today: *Willcox, Spiegle* / Drop that sack: *Mason, Rod Hot Five* / I wish'd I could shimmy like my sister Kate: *Barber, Chris* / Dr. Jazz: *Davison, Bill* / I would do'most anything for you love: *Paramount Jazzband Of Boston* / When we danced at the Mardi Gras: *Lightfoot, Terry & His Jazzmen* / Manana: *Dutch Swing College Band* / All the girls go crazy: *Stable Roof Jazzband* / Nagasaki: *Funny House Jazzband* / When I take my sugar to tea: *Revival Jazzband* / Someday you'll be sorry / 'Deed I do
CD ____ **TTD 531532**
Timeless Jazz / Aug '96 / New Note/ Pinnacle

IN CROWD, THE (20 Mod Classics 1964-1997)
I can't explain: *Who* / Whatcha gonna do about it: *Who* / In crowd: *Gray, Dobie* / Good morning little schoolgirl: *Stewart, Rod* / Night train: *Brown, James* / I'm the face: *High Numbers* / (I'm a) roadrunner: *Walker, Junior & The All Stars* / Leaving here: *Birds* / There's a ghost in my house: *Taylor, Dean* / I'M A MA: *Taylor, Dean* / Town called malice: *Jam* / Maybe tomorrow: *Chords* / POison ivy: *Lambrettas* / There she goes: *La's* / Snake: *Dodgy* / Getting better: *Shed Seven* / Fightting fit: *Gene* / Sleeping in: *Menswear* / Alright: *Cast* / Into tomorrow: *Weller, Paul*
CD ____ **5359182**
Deram / Jun '97 / PolyGram

IN CRUST WE TRUST
CD ____ **LF 050CD**
Lost & Found / Aug '93 / Plastic Head

IN DEFENCE OF ANIMALS VOL.1
Porch: *Pearl Jam* / Arms of love: *Stipe, Michael* / Too many puppies: *Primus* / Ode to groovy: *Skinny Puppy* / Crystal blue persuasion: *Concrete Blonde* / Velvet dog: *Sister Psychic* / Untold stories: *Meat Beat Manifesto* / For love: *Lush* / Praxis 'Bold as love': *Consolidated* / Beef: *Boogie Down Productions* / Shelter: *McLachlan, Sarah* / Hyperreal selector: *Shamen* / Language of violence: *Disposable Heroes Of Hiphoprisy* / You borrowed: *Helmet* / Clean: *Grotus* / Desert Star: *Material* / Hey hey high class butcher: *Cope, Julian*
CD ____ **727472**
Restless / Nov '93 / Vital

IN DEFENCE OF ANIMALS VOL.2
Brighton rock: *Elastica* / Electric head pt.2: *White Zombie* / Enjoy: *Bjork* / We done it again: *Meat Beat Manifesto* / Chemical beats: *Chemical Brothers* / Son of neckbone: *Beastie Boys* / Tiny meat: *Ruby* / Spaceman: *Belly* / Let's go free: *Moby* / Me-Jane: *PJ Harvey* / Truth: *KRS 1* / Cosmic dub: *Massive Attack & The Mad Professor* / Amnesty report: *Watt, Mike* / Moon pie: *Alice Donut* / Note to a friend: *Aleka's Attic* / Slug dub: *Orb* / Sundayafternoonweightlessness: *Morphine*
CD ____ **BIAS 300CD**
Play It Again Sam / Oct '96 / Discovery / Plastic Head / Vital

IN FLIGHT ENTERTAINMENT VOL.1
Mambo mania: *Kaempfert, Bert* / Light my fire: *Ros, Edmundo* / Il fait beau, il fait bon (freedom come, freedom go): *Mauriat, Paul* / Discotheque: *Alguero, Augusto* / Big train: *Greger, Max* / Catwalk: *Moore, Pete* / Blues-a-go-go: *Schifrin, Lalo* / Come Ray come Charles: *Legrand, Michel* / Look of love: *Shaw, Roland* / Paramiribo: *Schroeder, John* / St Tropez: *Bardot, Brigitte* / Tu veut, tu veut pas: *Bardot, Brigitte* / They call me Mr Tibbs: *Chaquito* / Tequila: *Button Down Brass* / Cerveza: *Kaempfert, Bert* / Great expectations: *Alguero, Augusto* / Digue-ding-ding: *Legrand, Michel* / I like London in the rain: *Dearie, Blossom* / Let the love come through: *Shaw, Roland*
CD ____ **5353002**
Deram / Mar '96 / PolyGram

IN FLIGHT ENTERTAINMENT VOL.2 (Further In Flight Entertainment)
CD ____ **5531262**
Deram / Mar '97 / PolyGram

IN FLIGHT PROGRAM (Revelation Compilation)
CD ____ **REV 050CD**
Revelation / Dec '96 / Plastic Head

IN GOTH DAZE
Hex: *Specimen* / Vegas: *Nico* / I walk the line: *Alien Sex Fiend* / Psychotic Louie Louie: *Alien Sex Fiend* / Kicking up the sawdust: *Bone Orchard* / Can't stop smoking: *Alien Sex Fiend* / Sharp teeth pretty teeth: *Specimen* / Last year's wife: *Zero Lacreche* / Carnivale of the gullible: *In Excelsis* / Tenant: *Play Dead* / Beating my head: *Red Lorry Yellow Lorry* / Mind disease: *Ritual* / Creatures of the night: *Screaming Dead* / Hole: *Specimen* / Alone she cries: *Skeletal Family* / Legacy: *Furyo* / Boys 18: *Bauhaus* / Caged 19: *1919* / Hollow eyes: *Red Lorry Yellow Lorry* / So sure: *Skeletal Family*
CD ____ **CDMGRAM 89**
Anagram / Oct '94 / Cargo / Pinnacle

IN LOVE WITH JAZZ
CD ____ **ASTCD 4007**
Telstar / Nov '96 / BMG

IN LOVE WITH SOUL VOL.1
CD ____ **261471**
Ariola / Jun '91 / BMG

IN LOVE WITH THESE TIMES
CD ____ **FNE 28CD**
Normal / Mar '94 / ADA / Direct

IN MEMORIUM - GILLES DELEUZE (2CD Set)
CD Set ____ **EFA 006722**
Mille Plateau / Mar '96 / SRD

IN ORDER TO DANCE VOL.1
Electrowave: *Space Opera* / Get busy time: *Ceejay* / Here we go: *Project* / Theme of St. Baafs: *Mental Overdrive* / Brasil: *Spectrum* / Acid pandemonium: *Mundo Muzique* / Music: *Sonic Solution* / Poison: *Angel*
CD ____ **RSCD 1**
R&S / Nov '91 / Vital

IN ORDER TO DANCE VOL.4
Andromeda: *Mundo Muzique* / Nightbreed: *Bolland, C.J.* / Rise from your grave: *Phuture* / Bounce back: *Angel, Dave* / Neuromancer: *Source* / Mama: *Neuro* / My definition of house music: *DJ Hell* / Flying dreams: *Afrotrance* / Analogue bubblebath: *Aphex Twin* / Shades: *House Of Usher* / Dream: *Music Of Life Orchestra* / Plastic dreams: *Music Of Life Orchestra*
CD ____ **RS 932CD**
R&S / Jun '93 / Vital

IN ORDER TO DANCE VOL.5 (2CD Set)
CD Set ____ **RS 94036CDXX**
CD Set ____ **RS 94036CD**
R&S / Sep '94 / Vital

IN ORDER TO DANCE VOL.6 (2CD Set)
Loop 2: *Larkin, Kenny* / Glide: *Expansions* / Punk jazz: *Justice, Tony* / Rare tear part 1: *Flytronix* / Destiny: *DJ Pulse* / Stretch: *Ishii, Ken* / Aquisse: *Justice, Tony* / Manhattan melody: *Lemon D* / 5 Miles high: *TMF* / Noone in the world: *Locust* / Detroit: *Reece, Alex* / Eclosed spaces: *Skindivers* / Wind dancer: *Shogun* / Music is the basis of all life (pt.3): *Mystic Moods* / Kid caprice: *Wax Doctor* / Cool summer breeze: *Original Playboy* / I wanna be there: *Model 500* / Flow: *Model 500* / Solar feelings: *Jacob's Optical Stairway* / Feversih: *Justice, Tony* / Solar system: *Lemon D*
CD Set ____ **RS 96090CD**
R&S / May '96 / Vital

IN PRAISE OF GOD
CD ____ **CDDCA 573**
ASV / Dec '88 / Select

IN SEARCH OF THE FREEDOM
CD ____ **CDMF 090**
Magnum Force / Nov '93 / TKO Magnum

IN THE AIR TONIGHT (Synthesizer Hits)
CD ____ **MACCD 310**
Autograph / Aug '96 / BMG

IN THE AIR TONIGHT (Virgin's Greatest Hits/2CD Set)
I'd do anything for love (but I won't do that): *Meat Loaf* / I can't help falling in love: *UB40* / That's the way love goes: *Jackson, Janet* / Are you gonna go my way: *Kravitz, Lenny* / Boom boom: *Hooker, John Lee* / Unfinished sympathy: *Massive Attack* / Sailing on the sevens seas: *OMD* / It ain't over 'til it's over: *Kravitz, Lenny* / Stil got the blues: *Moore, Gary* / Sadness: *Enigma* / Close to you: *Priest, Maxi* / You got it: *Orbison, Roy* / Another day in paradise: *Collins, Phil* / Back to life: *Soul II Soul* / Belfast child: *Simple Minds* / Straight up: *Abdul, Paula* / Buffalo stance: *Cherry, Neneh* / Let's stick together: *Ferry, Bryan* / Heaven is a place on Earth: *Carlisle, Belinda* / China in your hand: *T'Pau* / Everything I own: *Boy George* / Sledgehammer: *Gabriel, Peter* / Rise: *Public Image Ltd* / Separate lives: *Collins, Phil & Marilyn Martin* / Waterfront: *Simple Minds* / Karma chameleon: *Culture Club* / Mama: *Genesis* / Temptation: *Heaven 17* / Ghosts: *Japan* / It must be love: *Madness* / In the air tonight: *Collins, Phil* / Love action: *Human League* / Pretty vacant: *Sex Pistols* / Love is the drug: *Roxy Music* / Tubular bells: *Oldfield, Mike* / Virgin 21: *Wainwright III, Loudon*
CD Set ____ **VTDCD 26**
Virgin / Aug '95 / EMI

IN THE BELLY OF THE WHALE
CD ____ **HCD 7005**
Hightone / Aug '94 / ADA / Koch

IN THE CEILIDH AND DANCE TRADITION
CD ____ **LC 5246CD**
Lismor / Nov '95 / ADA / Direct / Duncans / Lismor

IN THE CELTIC TRADITION
CD ____ **LC 5245CD**
Lismor / Nov '95 / ADA / Direct / Duncans / Lismor

IN THE GROOVES
Dixie fried / Pain killer / Voice in the wind / Burn up / Shakin' all over / Good times / Everyday / Don't you lie to me / Got to hurry / Boll Weevil song / You might have Jesus / Too much monkey business
CD ____ **CDTB 053**
Thunderbolt / '91 / TKO Magnum

IN THE LAND OF BEGINNING AGAIN - NOW THE WAR IS OVER (2CD Set)
In the land of beginning again: *Layton, Turner* / How lucky you are: *Layton, Turner* / Primrose Hill: *Layton, Turner* / I'll always love you: *Clark, Petula* / Put your shoes on Lucy: *Clark, Petula* / House in the sky: *Clark, Petula* / On the 545: *Peers, Donald* / Strawberry moon (in a blueberry sky): *Peers, Donald* / Oh my darling: *Shelton, Anne* / You've changed: *Shelton, Anne* / I keep forgetting to remember: *Shelton, Anne* / If you ever fall in love again: *Shelton, Anne* / You're my thrill: *Campbell, Bruce & his band* / I never lived until I met you: *Campbell, Bruce & his band* / Once upon a wintertime: *Lynn, Vera* / You're the one I care for: *Lynn, Vera* / Again: *Lynn, Vera* / You keep coming back like a song: *Hutchinson, Leslie 'Hutch'* / Till then: *Hutchinson, Leslie 'Hutch'* / Dream: *Green, Paula & Her Orchestra* / Let's keep it that way: *Green, Paula & Her Orchestra* / Be true: *Goff, Reggie* / Crystal gazer: *Goff, Reggie* / I love you so much it hurts: *Goff, Reggie* / Olwen: *Goff, Reggie* / My bolero: *Goff, Reggie* / Am I wasting my time on you: *Goff, Reggie* / I'm gonna let you cry for a change: *Goff, Reggie* / Time may change: *Williams, Rita* / My happiness: *Williams, Rita* / Take me to your heart again: *Williams, Rita* / My lovely world and you: *Lewis, Archie* / Bless you: *Lewis, Archie* / Maybe you'll be there: *Conway, Steve* / In all the world: *Conway, Steve* / Sweetheart we'll never grow old: *Harris, Doreen* / When you're in love: *Harris, Doreen*
CD Set ____ **CDDL 1263**
Music For Pleasure / May '94 / EMI

IN THE LAND OF MANTRA
CD ____ **3012132**
Mantra / Oct '96 / Cargo / Direct / Discovery

IN THE MIX (2CD Set)
CD Set ____ **IDT 000591**
ID&T / Dec '96 / Plastic Head

IN THE MIX '96 VOL.1 (2CD Set)
Every little step: *Brown, Bobby* / Boombastic: *Shaggy* / Hideaway: *De'Lacy* / Renegade master: *Wildchild* / Got myself together: *Bucketheads* / I know the Lord: *Tabernacle* / I believe: *Happy Clappers* / Your love: *Inner City* / Naughty North and the sexy South: *E-Motion* / And I'm telling you: *Giles, Donna* / La luna: *Ethics* / Sunshine after the rain: *Berri* / Little Britain: *Dreadzone* / Common people: *Pulp* / Fee fi fo fum: *Candy Girls* / Runaway: *E'voke* / Mr. Friday night: *Moorish, Lisa* / Sex on the streets: *Pizzaman* / I imagine: *Kiani, Mary* / Gangsta's paradise: *Coolio* / Why you treat me so bad: *Shaggy* / Too hot: *Coolio* / I'm ready: *Size 9* / Mr. Wendal: *Arrested Development* / Chemical beats: *Chemical Brothers* / Passion: *Gat Decor* / Everybody be somebody: *Ruffnecks* / Fairground: *Simply Red* / I love you baby: *Original* / Reach: *Cheeks, Judy* / Boom boom boom: *Outhere Brothers* / He's on the phone: *St. Etienne* / Baby baby: *Corona* / Wham bam: *Candy Girls* / I wanna be a hippy: *Technohead*
CD ____ **VTDCD 77**
Virgin / Feb '96 / EMI

IN THE MIX '96 VOL.2 (2CD Set)
Children: *Miles, Robert* / Nightrain: *Kadoc* / Firestarter: *Prodigy* / Keep on jumpin': *Lisa Marie Experience* / Trippin' on sunshine: *Pizzaman* / Not over yet: *Grace* / Klubhoppin: *Klubb Heads* / I need a lover: *Kendoh* / Are you out there: *Crescendo* / Missing: *Everything But The Girl* / Good thing: *Eternal* / State of independence: *Summer, Donna* / Way it is: *Chameleon* / For what you dream of: *Bedrock* / Don't you want me: *Felix* / Satellite: *Beloved* / America (I love America): *Full Intention* / Love is the drug: *Roxy Music* / I got five on it: *Luniz* / Give me a little more time: *Gabrielle* / Lifted: *Lighthouse Family* / Spaceman: *Babylon Zoo* / 1234: *Coolio* / Return of the Mack: *Morrison, Mark* / Giv me luv: *Alcatrazz* / I got the vibration: *Black Box* / Stars: *Dubstar* / Stay another day: *East 17* / Over and over: *Plux* / Eugina: *Salt Tank* / Landslide: *Harmonix* / Be as one: *Sacha & Maria* / Lovelight: *Hanna, Jayn* / Reach up: *Perfecto All Stars* / Theme from S'Express: *S'Express* / Walking wounded: *Everything But The Girl* / So pure: *Baby D*
CD Set ____ **VTDCD 85**
Virgin / May '96 / EMI

IN THE MIX '96 VOL.3 (2CD Set)
I'm alive: *Stretch n' Vern & Maddog* / Krupa: *Apollo 440* / Fastlove: *Michael, George* / Ain't nobody's business if I do: *H2O & Billie* / Where love lives: *Limerick, Alison* / Keep on jumpin': *Terry, Todd* / Disco's revenge: *Gusto* / Don't go: *Third Dimension* / Are you ready for some more: *Reel 2 Real* / Don't stop movin': *Livin' Joy* / My love is for real: *Strike* / Help me make it: *Huff & Puff* / All I wanna do: *Tin Tin Out* / Ooh aah...just a little bit: *Gina G* / There's nothing I won't do: *JX* / Just another groove: *Mighty Dub Katz* / Come on: *Konya* / Higher state of consciousness: *Wink, Josh* / Arms of Loren: *Evoke* / Flava: *Andre, Peter* / That look: *De-'Lacy* / Wrong: *Everything But The Girl* / Throb: *Jackson, Janet* / Cuba: *El Mariachi* / That girl: *Priest, Maxi & Shaggy* / Naked: *Louise* / Sunshine: *Umboza* / Want love: *Hysteric Ego* / Love me the right way: *Rapination* / Stamp: *Healy, Jeremy & Amos* / Gift: *Way Out West* / Wannabe: *Spice Girls* / Creep: *TLC* / Bom digi bom (think about the way): *TLC* / Seven days & one week: *BBE* / Macarena: *Los Del Rio* / Born slippy: *Underworld* / You give me love: *Clock*
CD Set ____ **VTDCD 97**
Virgin / Oct '96 / EMI

IN THE MIX '97 (2CD Set)
One and one: *Miles, Robert* / Stupid girl: *Garbage* / Moving on up: *M-People* / Nite life: *English, Kim* / Spinning the wheel: *Michael, George* / Hold that sucker down: *QT Quartet* / Insomnia: *Faithless* / Up to no good: *Porn Kings* / Say my name: *Zee* / Waterfall: *Atlantic Ocean* / Kick up the volume: *Tissera, Rob* / Breathe: *Prodigy* / Jump up to my beat: *Wildchild* / U girls: *Nush* / All I wanna do: *Tin Tin Out* / I am: *Chakra* / Tall 'n handsome: *Outrage* / Sugar is sweeter: *Bolland, C.J.* / Remember me: *Blueboy* / Girls and boys: *Blur* / Space cowboy: *Jamiroquai* / You got the love: *Source & Candi Staton* / Take California: *Propeller Heads* / She drives me crazy: *Fine Young Cannibals* / Arkham asylum: *Sasha* / Dreamer: *Livin' Joy* / Atom bomb: *Fluke* / Offshore: *Chicane* / Lost without you: *Hanna, Jayn* / On a ragga tip '97: *SL2* / Bjango: *Lucky Monkeys* / Zoe: *Traxx* / Wiggly world: *Mr. Jack* / Seven days and one week: *BBE* / Passion: *Amendi*
CD Set ____ **VTDCD 116**
Virgin / Jan '97 / EMI

IN THE MIX '97 VOL.2 (2CD Set)
CD Set ____ **VTDCD 132**
Virgin / Apr '97 / EMI

IN THE MIX '97 VOL.3 (2CD Set)
CD Set ____ **VTDCD 135**
Virgin / Jul '97 / EMI

IN THE MIX - '90S HITS (2CD Set)
Wrong: *Everything But The Girl* / Two can play that game: *Brown, Bobby* / Show me luv: *Robin S* / Higher state of consciousness: *Wink, Josh* / Is there anybody out there: *Bassheads* / Bomb: *Bucketheads* / Renaissance: *M-People* / Let me show you: *K-Klass* / Chant: *Gusto* / Such a good feeling: *Brothers In Rhythm* / Go: *Moby* / Jazz it up: *Reel 2 Real* / Ain't no love ain't no use: *Sub Sub & Melanie Williams* / Give it up: *Goodmen* / Latin Thing: *Latin Touch* / U sure do: *Strike* / Don't stop movin': *Livin' Joy* / Cry india: *Umboza* / Everybody's free: *Rozalla* / Blurred: *Pianoman* / Girls and boys: *Hed Boys* / Let the music lift you up: *Loveland* / Even better than the real thing: *U2* / Playing with knives: *Bizarre Inc.* / Always something there to remind me: *Tin Tin Out & Espiritu* / Son of a gun: *JX* / Your loving arms: *Martin, Billie Ray* / Key, the secret: *Urban Cookie Collective* / I believe: *Happy Clappers* / Sweet harmony: *Liquid* / Rockin' for myself: *Motiv 8* / Waterfall: *Atlantic Ocean* / Disco 2000: *Pulp* / Let me be your fantasy: *Baby D* / Swamp thing: *Grid* / Born slippy: *Underworld* / Children: *Miles, Robert*
CD Set ____ **VTDCD 89**
Virgin / Jul '96 / EMI

IN THE MIX BY DJ PAVO
CD ____ **IDTMIX 96002**
ID&T / Mar '97 / Plastic Head

IN THE PIPING TRADITION
CD ____ **LC 5243CD**
Lismor / Nov '95 / ADA / Direct / Duncans / Lismor

IN THE POPULAR SONG TRADITION
CD ____ **LC 5244CD**
Lismor / Nov '95 / ADA / Direct / Duncans / Lismor

IN THE SMOKE (Classic Traditional London Irish Music 1950-1970's)
Bank of Ireland/Woman of the house/Morning dew: *Casey, Bobby* / Blue riband/Up and away: *Clifford, John & Julia* / Boys of the lough/Trip to Durrow: *Pepper, Noel & Paddy Moran* / Rich man's daughter: *Byrne, Packie* / Jackie Coleman's/The castle: *Power, Jimmy* / Kesh jig/Morrison's/Old

Joe's: *Doonan, John* / Bucks of Oranmore/ The wind that shakes the barley: *O'Halloran Brothers* / Rights of man/Honeysuckle hornpipe: *Healy, Tommy & Johnny Duffy* / Galway shawl: *Barry, Margaret* / Callaghan's reel: *Curtin, Con & Denis McMahon* / Ballydesmond/Knocknabowl: *Clifford, Julia* / Maid behind the bar: *Wright Brothers & Paddy Neylan* / Coolin': *Pepper, Noel* / Granuaile: *O'Halloran, Des* / Follow me down to Limerick/Hardiman the fiddler: *Power, Jimmy* / Shannon breeze/Heathery breeze/Green fields of America: *Doonan, John* / Cavan lasses/Rose of the heather: *Healy, Tommy & Johnny Duffy* / Creel: *Byrne, Packie* / Moher reel: *Farr, Lucy & Bobby Casey* / Cherish the ladies: *Doonan, John* / Dublin porter/Mountain lark: *Star Of Munster Trio* / Paddy Ryan's dream: *Meehan, Danny* / Flower of sweet Strabane: *Barry, Margaret* / Maguire's favourite/Tralee gaol/Maggie in the wood: *Barry, Margaret* / Coleman's favourite/Promenade: *Power, Jimmy* / Lucy Campbell/Toss the feathers: *McMahon, Tony/Andy Boyce/Mairtin Byrnes* / Blackbird: *Doonan, John*
CD CDORBD 088
Globestyle / Mar '95 / Pinnacle

IN THE SPIRIT
CD AL 2801
Alligator / Jul '94 / ADA / CM / Direct

IN THE SUMMERTIME
CD PLSCD 142
Pulse / Apr '96 / BMG

IN THE SWISS MOUNTAINS
CD 399408
Koch / Jul '91 / Koch

IN THE WEE SMALL HOURS
Passion flower: *Hodges, Johnny* / It's the talk of the town: *Jacquet, Illinois* / I'll never smile again: *Garner, Erroll* / Laura: *Thielemans, 'Toots'* / Chelsea bridge: *Gillespie, Dizzy* / Tangerine: *Hawkins, Coleman & Ben Webster* / Street scene: *Carter, Benny* / It was a very good year: *Montgomery, Wes* / I can't get started: *Young, Lester & Oscar Peterson* / All across the city: *Evans, Bill & Jim Hall* / Willow weep for me: *Eldridge, Roy* / High and the mighty: *Hampton, Lionel* / In the wee small hours of the morning: *Mulligan, Gerry & His New Sextet* / Child is born: *Peterson, Oscar* / I wrote my song: *Smith, Stuff & Dizzy Gillespie/Oscar Peterson* / I remember Clifford: *Getz, Stan* / Were you there: *Burrell, Kenny*
CD 5526742
Spectrum / Mar '97 / PolyGram

IN THERE - MUTANT POP HYBRIDS
CD TBPICD 004
T&B / Jun '96 / Plastic Head

IN TO THE MIX (2CD Set)
Voodoo people: *Prodigy* / Mindstream: *Meat Beat Manifesto* / Instruments of darkness: *Art Of Noise* / Eternal zerne: *Talla 2XLC* / Netherworld: *LSG* / Alpha wave: *System 7* / Re-united mix 4: *Psychic TV* / Renegade soundwave: *Renegade Soundwave* / Clown: *Switchblade Symphony* / Feel the universe: *Juno Reactor* / Trance in time: *Kraftwerk* / Aqualite megga mix: *LCD* / Out of reality: *Sunbeam* / Outface: *Komaidno* / Helium: *Bypass Unit* / Pink button: *Kinder Atom* / Stab: *Din* / Sack says air: *Glez* / In a gentle mood: *Nature* / Concentration: *Surface 10* / Now is forever: *Brain* / Ba and the ka: *Anubian Lights* / Into the abyss: *R-Escape-R* / Funky alienation: *Xylon* / Hymlock: *Cathexis* / Oblivion: *Dilate*
CD CLP 9991
Cleopatra / Jul '97 / Cargo / Greyhound / Plastic Head / RTM/Disc / SRD

INCANDESCENCE
CD CDREP 8013
Elusive / Sep '94 / RTM/Disc

INCREDIBLE MUSIC ALL STARS
CD IMCD 0015
Incredible Music / Apr '97 / Jet Star / SRD

INCREDIBLY STRANGE - ONLY IN AMERICA
CD AA 049
Arf Arf / Jul '97 / Greyhound

INCURSIONS IN ILLBIENT
CD ASP 0968D
Asphodel / Nov '96 / Cargo / SRD

INDEPENDENCE BREAKS
Bass gunner: *Tipper* / Chemical meltdown: *Santana, Omar* / Miami breaks: *PSS* / Loisiana hayride: *Silicon Valley Def Stars* / Blazer beats: *Roxy Breaks* / Air guitar: *Frog Junkies* / Humaniser: *Humanizer* / Six pak: *Tipper* / Nine ways: *JDS* / QUick release: *Quick Release* / Pulse: *Reel* / Scared: *Altered States*
CD CDTOT 49
Jumpin' & Pumpin' / Jun '97 / 3mv/Sony / Mo's Music Machine

INDEPENDENT SOUL VOL.1 (14 Hard To Find Tracks From The 80's)
All night love affair: *Roosevelt Carter* / Right track: *Roosevelt Carter* / You must go on: *Junei* / Weak man: *Morris, Lee* / This time it's real: *Nevilles, Larry* / Gotta give your own love story: *Wilkerson, James JD* / I think I'm gonna be blue: *Buford, Larry* / Don't snatch it back: *Daniel, Harold* / Too many irons in the fire: *Hightower, Willie* / Tell me what you want: *Hightower, Willie* / It's no wonder (you drove me crazy): *Dee, Larry* / I could paint a picture: *Hudmon, R.B.* / Caught in the middle: *Cobbin, James & Prime Cut* / Girl you should have known: *Hudson, Johnny*
CD GSCD 080
Goldmine / Feb '97 / Vital

INDIA O FAST DHRUPAD
CD SM 1517CD
Wergo / Oct '94 / ADA / Cadillac / Harmonia Mundi

INDIAN FLUTES OF SOUTH AMERICA VOL.1
CD PS 65060
PlayaSound / Nov '90 / ADA / Harmonia Mundi

INDIAN FLUTES OF SOUTH AMERICA VOL.2
CD PS 65090
PlayaSound / Jul '92 / ADA / Harmonia Mundi

INDIAN MEDITATION
CD CD 6063
Music / Apr '97 / Target/BMG

INDIGENOUS TRIBES
Alba: *Mounsey, Paul* / Forced to return/ Spootisferry: *Rock, Salt & Nails* / Reconciliation set: *Runt O' The Litter* / Reprobate's lament: *Imlach, Hamish* / 7 down: *Thoumire, Simon & Fergus MacKenzie* / Irish reels set: *Morrison, Fred* / Scarboro' settler's lament: *Bruce, Ian* / Hooleyganz jig: *Hooleyganz Band* / Henryetta: *Humpff Family* / 70 years/ Caber: *New Celeste* / Floggin' set: *Bongshang* / St Francis songs: *Pearlfishers* / Tinne run: *Wolfstone* / Ae fond kiss: *Dalriada* / New pipe order: *Tartan Amoebas*
CD IRCD 054
Lismor / Jul '97 / ADA / Direct / Duncans / Lismor

INDIGO BLUES COLLECTION VOL.1 (Budget Sampler)
CD IGOCD 2033
Indigo / Sep '95 / ADA / Direct

INDUSTRIAL ARMAGEDDON (2CD Set)
CD Set AOP 56
Age Of Panik / Jun '97 / Total/BMG

INDUSTRIAL CHRISTMAS CAROL
CD INV 053CD
Invisible / Jan '96 / Plastic Head

INDUSTRIAL FUCKING STRENGTH (2CD Set)
Mescalinium united: *Mescalium United* / Locked on target: *Disintegrator* / Blood of an English muffin: *English Muffin* / Fuckin' hostile '96: *DJ Skinhead* / Raw: *OTT* / Utopia project: *Strychnine* / Mad as hell: *Dee, Ralphie* / Never stop: *Delta 9* / Gabber up your ass: *Gee, Rob* / Wanna be a gangsta: *DOA* / Ya mutha: *DOA* / Cunt face: *Bloody Fist* / Cock sucker: *Bloody Fist* / Extreme terror: *DJ Skinhead* / Anthem: *Temper Tantrum* / Romper stomper: *Liza N Eliaz* / Paris hardcore: *Le Malin, Manu*
CD Set MOSH 150CD
CD Set MOSH 150CDSL
Earache / Apr '96 / Vital

INDUSTRIAL MIX MACHINE (2CD Set)
CD Set CLP 9969
Cleopatra / Jun '97 / Cargo / Greyhound / Plastic Head / RTM/Disc / SRD

INDUSTRIAL REVOLUTION 2ND EDITION
CD CLEO 77712
Cleopatra / May '94 / Cargo / Greyhound / Plastic Head / RTM/Disc / SRD

INDUSTRIAL VIRUS (3CD Set)
CD Set DTKBOX 61
Dressed To Kill / Feb '97 / Total/BMG

INDUSTRIAL WAR (The Agony & The Ecstasy Of Industrial Music)
CD SHCD 5722
Shanachie / Apr '97 / ADA / Greensleeves / Koch

INESS MEZEL
Wedfel / Ado / Taiga / Aya hedat / Agour / Ifassen / Slassen kan / Laaven yissnay / Our yi nouy / Awah / Lahvev
CD Y 225066
Auvidis/Ethnic / May '97 / ADA / Harmonia Mundi

INFINITE SUMMER OF LOVE
CD TX 2016CD
Taxim / Jul '94 / ADA

INFINITY HERZ (2CD Set)
CD Set MPTCD 12
Matsuri / Jul '97 / Amato Disco / SRD

INFLUENCE: HARD TRANCE
CD CLEO 94762
Cleopatra / Jun '94 / Cargo / Greyhound / Plastic Head / RTM/Disc / SRD

INNINGS AND QUARTERS
CD NAR 069CD
New Alliance / May '93 / Plastic Head

INNOVATIVE/INTELLIGENT DRUM AND BASS VOL.1
Horizons: *LTJ Bukem* / Rain: *Photek* / High flyers: *Area 39* / Heavy vibes: *Origination* / Jazzmin: *Cloud 9* / Western: *PFM* / Into the 90's: *Photek* / Sunshine: *Eugenix & Corelle* / Universal horn: *JMJ & Richie* / Maracas beach: *Origination* / Projection: *Timeline* / Jazz and all dat: *Eskubar* / Rhys project: *James, Mikey* / Come to me: *Street Science* / Wired: *Fokus* / Part of life: *Timeline* / Are we in: *D'Cruze* / Searchin': *Dead Calm*
CD STORM 2 CD
Desert Storm / Jan '96 / Sony

INNOVATOR
CD NWKCD 21
Network / '92 / 3mv/Sony / Pinnacle

INNOVATORS FUTURE TECHNO
CD BDRCD 10
Breakdown / Feb '96 / Pinnacle

INNSBRUCK, THE BEAUTIFUL ALPINE CITY
CD 399425
Koch / Jul '91 / Koch

INOLVIDABLES DUOS LATINOS
CD CCD 902
Caney / Jul '96 / ADA / Discovery

INSIDE OUT
Inside out / California soul / Liberation song / Eternal journey / Chocolate candy / Blue monsoon / Long goodie / I am the blackgold of the sun / Dancing girl / Prayer for peace
CD CDARC 513
Charly / Jan '93 / Koch

INSIDE VOL.1 (Celebrating The Best In British Soul)
When we're making love: *Opaz* / Be still: *French, Michelle* / Me O my: *Mid 8 Production* / Been fooled: *Caitaine, Ria* / Fight: *McKoy* / Whole thing: *Act Of Faith* / Even when you're gone: *Gems For Jem* / Mystery girl: *Green, Tee* / If I knew: *D-Swing* / Hold me closer: *Circle Of Life* / Love away: *Pearce, Mary* / Coming closer: *Feel* / Simple solution: *Dee, Jay* / Running to my baby's arms: *Ipso Facto* / Slow down: *Metropolis* / Through all times: *Perfect Taste*
CD CDTEP 1
Debut / Nov '92 / 3mv/Sony / Pinnacle

INSIDE VOL.2
Greater love: *Nu Colours* / Reach out: *Perception* / Take me: *D-Swing* / Just don't care: *Funhill* / Visions: *Julianne* / I'll be good to you: *Green, Tee* / Time for love: *Gems For Jem* / Doing it for love: *Act Of Faith* / Get it on: *Solid State Sound* / Sunday morning blue: *Mapp, Chantel* / I know how: *Stevens, Kenni* / Calling her name: *Ipso Facto* / 2 be a friend: *Pearce, Mary* / Love when it's like this: *Antony, Joseph* / Your love my love: *Nazlyn* / Give it (this love song): *Caitaine, Ria*
CD CDTEP 2
Debut / Jun '93 / 3mv/Sony / Pinnacle

INSIDE VOL.3
Movin' in the right direction: *FM Inc* / Fever (rider): *D-Swing* / So much feeling: *Closer Than Close* / Gotta get it: *Index* / Deeper: *Uschi* / Fallin': *Tyson* / Heaven: *Menzies, Steve* / I Luv U: *Sovereign* / I like the way: *Everis* / Hurt so bad (till U like it): *Marshall, Wayne* / Learned my lesson: *Smith, Charlene* / There ain't enough love: *Zushii* / You belong to me: *Fyza* / Searching: *Robyn*
CD CDTEP 3
Debut / Mar '94 / 3mv/Sony / Pinnacle

INSIDE VOL.4
Feel the good times: *Smith, Charlene* / If it's to be: *Max* / Feel the heat: *Sugartrain* / We've got here: *Edwards, Kim* / It takes two: *What's Happening* / I can't hide: *Prime, Nathan* / My pain: *LIFE* / You shouldn't lie: *Brown, Dana* / Slow motion: *Groove Nation* / September rain: *Riviera* / I love the summertime: *Silver* / Obsession: *Duverney, Ondrea* / Do without you: *Zaeus* / Where's the sunshine: *Way 2 Go*
CD CDTEP 5
Debut / Oct '94 / 3mv/Sony / Pinnacle

INSPIRATION - BRAZIL (Forest Of The Amazon)
CD CDM 5658802
EMI Classics / Mar '96 / EMI

INSPIRATION - INDIA (Duets For Sitar)
CD CDM 5658812
EMI Classics / Mar '96 / EMI

INSPIRATION - JAPAN (Gagaku - Ancient Japanese Koto Melodies)
CD CDM 5659102
EMI Classics / Mar '96 / EMI

INSPIRATIONAL SAX
Will you still love me tomorrow / I can't stop loving you / Holding back the years / To all the girls I've loved before / Against all odds / Moonlight shadow / I guess why they call it the blues / How deep is your love
CD GRF 193
Tring / Jun '92 / Tring

INSPIRE TO PERSPIRE (Best Of Sweat & Underground Vibe/3CD Set)
CD Set SWHCD 1
Sweat/Underground Vibe / Jul '96 / Grapevine/PolyGram / Mo's Music Machine

INSPIRED
Petrol: *Ash* / Dragging me down: *Inspiral Carpets* / Low place like home: *Sneaker Pimps* / I Messiah, am jailer: *AC Acoustics* / Sucrose: *Delgados* / Fingerpops: *Garageland* / Exclusive: *Velvet Jones* / Two clear eyes: *Gallon Drunk* / Sex sells: *Deadstar* / Wailing words: *Scarfo* / Ten feet tall: *Flaming Stars* / I'm doing fine: *TC Hug* / Mrs. Hoover: *Candyskins* / I wanna be adored: *Stone Roses* / Can't be sure: *Sundays* / Montreal: *Wedding Present* / It's not what you know: *New FADS* / Everything flows: *Teenage Fanclub* / Little girl (with blue eyes): *Pulp* / Underground: *Folds, Ben Five*
CD NTRCD 080
Nectar / Apr '97 / Pinnacle

INSTRUMENTAL BLUES
CD CLACD 432
Castle / Mar '97 / BMG

INSTRUMENTAL BLUES DYNAMITE
CD CDBT 1135
Black Top / Jun '96 / ADA / CM / Direct

INSTRUMENTAL CLASSICS VOL.1
CD MODUB 2CD
Music Of Life / Aug '92 / Grapevine/ PolyGram

INSTRUMENTAL DIAMONDS VOL.2 - HIGHLY STRUNG (British 60's Instrumentals)
Music train: *Honeycombs* / Cleopatra's needle: *Ahab & The Wailers* / Red dragon: *Black Jacks* / Ghoul friend: *Ravens* / Jump Jeremiah: *Ford, Mike & The Consuls* / Ten swinging bottles: *Chester, Peter & The Consulate* / Pompeii: *Checkmates* / Husky: *Nicol, Jimmy* / Packabeat: *Packabeats* / First love: *Clark, Dave Five* / Man in space: *Vigilantes* / Organiser: *Organisers & Harold Smart* / Mad goose: *Sons Of The Piltdown Men* / Eliminator: *Eliminators* / Switch: *Brown, Joe* / Neb's tune: *Ahab & The Wailers* / Traitors: *Packabeats* / Caroline: *Jay, Peter & The Jaywalkers* / Husky team: *Saints* / Dream lover: *Packabeats* / Highly strung: *Rustlers* / Pigtails: *Saints* / Evening in Paris: *Packabeats* / Thunderbirds theme: *Eliminators* / Hurricane: *Honeycombs*
CD NEXCD 150
Sequel / Feb '91 / BMG

INSTRUMENTAL FIRE
CD SICK 01
Musick / Apr '97 / Cargo

INSTRUMENTAL FOLK MUSIC FROM GREECE
CD TSCD 915
Topic / Aug '96 / ADA / CM / Direct

INSTRUMENTAL GEMS VOL.1
Last night: *Ede, David* / Man in space: *Vigilantes* / John Peel: *Rowena, Jeff Group* / Weekend: *Red Price* / Cleopatra's needle: *Ahab & The Wailers* / Forest fire: *Chester, Pete Group* / Pop corn: *Brown, Joe* / Sunburst: *Fabulous Flee Rekkers* / Raunchy: *McVay, Ray Sound* / Peter Gunn: *Remo Four* / La cucaracha: *Rowena, Jeff Group* / Green man: *Ford, Mike & The Consuls* / Night train: *Nicol, Jimmy & The Shubdubs* / Rockin' minstrel: *Checkmates* / Dream lover: *Packabeats* / Hot toddy: *Original Checkmates* / Exodus: *Eagles* / Tequila: *Shepherd, Bill Orchestra* / Red cabbage: *Jay, Peter & The Jaywalkers* / Matter of who: *Rustlers* / No hats on Ilkley: *Ede, David* / Cerveza: *Wainer, Cherry* / Eliminator: *Eliminators* / Sneeze: *Red Price* / Sleep walk: *Willsher, Pete*
CD GEMCD 008
Diamond / Feb '97 / Pinnacle

INSTRUMENTAL GOLD (3CD Set)
CD Set TREB 5023
Scratch / May '96 / Koch / Scratch/BMG

INSTRUMENTAL LOVE
I will always love you / Everything I do (I do it for you) / Unchained melody / Power of love / I'm not in love / Annie's song / If you leave me now / Saving all my love for you / Wind beneath my wings / Careless whisper / Fool if you think it's over / He ain't heavy, he's my brother / Have I told you lately / Hero / If you don't know me by now / Jealous guy
CD QED 219
Tring / Nov '96 / Tring

INSTRUMENTAL MAGIC (2CD Set)
CD Set CDSR 121
Telstar / Mar '97 / BMG

INSTRUMENTAL MOODS
Riverdance: *Anderson, John Concert Orchestra* / Cacharpaya: *Incantation* / Return to innocence: *Enigma* / Yeha noha: *Sacred Spirit* / Celts: *Enya* / Sentinel: *Oldfield, Mike* / Samba pa ti: *Santana* / Albatross: *Fleetwood Mac* / Love's theme (from Midnight Express): *Moroder, Giorgio* / Adiemus: *Adiemus* / Songbird: *Kenny G* / Cavatina: *Williams, John* / Don't cry for me Argentina: *Shadows* / Inspector Morse theme: *Pheloung, Barrington* / Brideshead revisited: *Burgon, Geoffrey* / Theme from Soldier Soldier: *Parker, Jim* / Chi mai: *Morricone, Ennio* / Stranger on the shore: *Bilk, Acker* / People's Century: *People's Century Orchestra* / Panis Angelicus: *Way, Anthony*
CD VTCD 65
Virgin / Nov '95 / EMI

INSTRUMENTAL TANGOS OF THE GOLDEN AGE
El monito: *De Carlo, Julio* / Colombina: *De Carlo, Julio* / Derecho viejo: *De Carlo, Julio*

/ Boedo: *De Carlo, Julio* / La cumparista: *Laurenz, Pedro* / Mala junto: *Laurenz, Pedro* / Orgullo criollo: *Laurenz, Pedro* / Re-fa-si: *De Dois Filiberto, Juan* / El 16: *De Dois Filiberto, Juan* / Fuegos artificiales: *Firpo, Roberto* / El once: *Firpo, Roberto* / La payanca: *Firpo, Roberto* / Don Enrique: *Firpo, Roberto* / Belen: *Di Sarli, Carlos* / La guitarrita: *Di Sarli, Carlos* / Organito de la tarde: *Di Sarli, Carlos* / 9 puntos: *Di Sarli, Carlos* / El amanecer: *Di Sarli, Carlos* / El portentito: *Quinteto Pirincho* / Don Juan: *Quinteto Pirincho* / Rodriguez Pena: *Quinteto Pirincho* / La vuelta da rocha: *Canaro, Francisco* / El gavilan: *Canaro, Francisco* / Punto bravo: *Canaro, Francisco* / Guapeando: *Troilo, Anibal* / La tablada: *Troilo, Anibal*
CD _______ **HQCD 45**
Harlequin / Jun '96 / Hot Shot / Jazz Music / Swift / Wellard

INSTRUMENTAL TANGOS OF THE OLD GUARD
CD _______ **HQCD 70**
Harlequin / May '96 / Hot Shot / Jazz Music / Swift / Wellard

INSTRUMENTALLY YOURS
Blue roofs of Ispahan: *Philippe, Louis* / March of the eligible bachelors: *Monochrome Set* / Constance from Cadaquez: *Marden Hill* / Another conversation with myself: *Watt, Ben* / 1000 guitars of St. Dominiques: *Fantastic Something* / Hasta pronto: *King Of Luxembourg* / All day and all of the night: *Page, Larry Orchestra* / Maestoso con anima: *Deebank, Maurice* / You're the queer one, Les Mun: *Hepburns* / Aperitivo: *Philippe, Louis* / Star trek for jazz guitar: *Posh* / West End: *Leer, Thomas* / Through Eastfields: *Eyeless In Gaza* / Zophia: *Underneath* / Falling: *Beech, Isadora* / Ballet of the red shoes: *Adverse, Anthony* / Execution of Emperor Maximillian: *Marden Hill* / Fantasia, childhood memories: *Fisher-Turner, Simon* / Twangy twangy: *Philippe, Louis* / Park row: *Always* / Flying with lux: *Blind Mr. Jones* / Tender bruises and scars: *Hewick, Kevin* / Geneve: *Fisher, Morgan* / Yo ho ho (and three bottles of wine): *Monochrome Set* / Cavaliere servente: *Philippe, Louis*
CD _______ **MONDE 18CD**
Cherry Red / Oct '93 / Pinnacle

INSTRUMENTOS MUSICAIS POPULARES GALEGOS
CD _______ **H 026CD**
Sonifolk / Jun '94 / ADA / CM

INSTRUMENTS (Hannibal Sampler)
CD _______ **HNCD 8302**
Hannibal / May '93 / ADA / Vital

INTELLIGENT COMPILATION, AN
CD _______ **K7 035CD**
Studio K7 / Oct '96 / Prime / RTM/Disc

INTELLIGENT DRUM & BASS VOL.1
CD _______ **STHCCD 12**
Strictly Hardcore / Jun '95 / SRD

INTELLIGENT DRUM & BASS VOL.2
CD _______ **STHCCD 13**
Strictly Hardcore / Jul '95 / SRD

INTELLIGENT SELECTA
CD _______ **PNCCA 5**
Production House / Apr '95 / Jet Star / Total/BMG

INTENT - NATTY MUSIC (Mixed By Simon 'Bassline' Smith)
CD _______ **DBM 2035**
Rogue Trooper / Oct '96 / Alphamagic / SRD

INTERFERENCE LIVE AT LOVE PARADE 94
CD _______ **EFA 001452**
Interference / Aug '95 / SRD

INTERNAL JOURNAL VOL.2
CD _______ **NAR 115CD**
New Alliance / Nov '94 / Plastic Head

INTERNATIONAL CEILIDH BAND CHAMPIONSHIP, THE
Strip the willow / Songs and reels / Songs (Keltie Clippie) / Reels / Highland Schottische / Song / Dashing white sergeant / Boston two step / Song (Sound of Pibroch) / Selection / Dance 13, Jig
CD _______ **LCOM 5218**
Lismor / Jan '93 / ADA / Direct / Duncans / Lismor

INTERNATIONAL DJ SYNDICATE MIX VOL.1-TAKKYU ISHINO
DDTV u-ziq invade: *Dum Dum T.V.* / Gamer's night: *Mijk's Magic Marble Box* / Voyager: *Beltram, Joey* / Knock knock: *DJ Funk* / Take it to the floor: *K-Hand & Parris Love* / Da mindfuck: *Thee Madkatt Courtship* / Trak 11: *Phylyps* / Acsperience 5: *Hardfloor* / M 04: *Maurizio* / In the bush: *Purpose Maker* / Nagelbrett: *Sensorama* / Don't stop: *Whirlpool Productions* / Das telefon sagt acid: *Ink, Mike & Andreas Dorau* / Fuckin' suckin': *Traxmen* / Mickiee House 2: *Mickiee* / Micro 2: *Tanaka, Fumiya* / Up and down: *Up & Down* / Who da funk: *Dogtrax* / Forerunner: *Natural Born Groovers* / I thought 3, but were 4 in fact: *Ishino, Takkyu*
CD _______ **REACTCD 085**
React / Sep '96 / Arabesque / Prime / Vital

INTERNATIONAL DJ SYNDICATE MIX VOL.2-DJ CHER
Struggle: *Aquatherium* / Future shock: *Seraphim Odyssey* / Listen carefully: *HOW* / Nu energy: *Cosmic Duo* / Canis loopus: *Yekuana* / Passion devotion: *Free Spirit* / Loos caboos: *Electroliners* / Last prayer: *Chapel Of Rest* / Vertigo: *Transcendental Experience* / Ancient forest: *Sun God* / Warning: *Shay, Dan* / Amplexus: *Entropic* / One: *Aria* / Kaleidoscope: *Art Of Trance* / Rain or shine: *Beat Foundation*
CD _______ **REACTCD 103**
React / Jul '97 / Arabesque / Prime / Vital

INTERNATIONAL FESTIVAL OF COUNTRY MUSIC, FRUTIGEN (Live May 1987)
I'm goin', I'm leaving: *Hollow, Traver* / Lonesome, on'ry and mean: *Young, Steven & Tom Russell Band* / Mezcal: *Russell, Tom* / Alkali: *Russell, Tom* / Walkin' after midnight: *Moffatt, Katy & Tom Russell Band* / First taste of Texas: *Bruce, Ed* / Man who turned my mama on: *Bruce, Ed* / Summer wages: *Tyson, Ian & Andrew Hardin* / Someday soon: *Tyson, Ian & Andrew Hardin* / Navajo rug: *Russell, Tom* / Edge of a heartbreak: *Moeller, Dee* / Where is the magic: *Moeller, Dee* / Mamas don't let your babies grow up to be cowboys: *Bruce, Ed*
CD _______ **BCD 15466**
Bear Family / Jun '89 / Direct / Rollercoaster / Swift

INTERNATIONAL GUITAR FESTIVAL
CD _______ **BEST 1051CD**
Acoustic Music / Jul '94 / ADA

INTIMATE LOVERS VOL.1
CD _______ **VGCD 015**
Virgo / Dec '94 / Jet Star

INTIMATE SOUND VOL.1 1989-1993, THE
Please come back: *Edwards, Dean* / Way we are: *Affair* / There is no way: *Sound Principle* / Bring me back: *Davis, Richard Anthony* / Welcome to yesterday: *Sound Principle* / Keep it comin': *Julianne* / I'm back for more: *Lulu & Bobby Womack* / Getting on with my own life: *Jones Girls* / Lovers for life: *Davis, Richard Anthony* / Is it true: *Drakes, Anthony*
CD _______ **EMHCD 1**
Intimate / Mar '94 / Jet Star / Total/BMG

INTO THE EIGHTIES (2CD Set)
Two tribes: *Frankie Goes To Hollywood* / Every breath you take: *Police* / Who's that girl: *Eurythmics* / Sometimes: *Erasure* / Girls on film: *Duran Duran* / Shout: *Tears For Fears* / Call me: *Blondie* / Don't go: *Yazoo* / I go to sleep: *Pretenders* / How soon is now: *Smiths* / Geno: *Dexy's Midnight Runners* / Ghost town: *Specials* / Our lips are sealed: *Fun Boy Three* / House of fun: *Madness* / Do you really want to hurt me: *Culture Club* / Golden Brown: *Stranglers* / It's my life: *Talk Talk* / Look of love: *ABC* / Gold: *Spandau Ballet* / Love plus one: *Haircut 100* / No more I love you's: *Lover Speaks* / Blue Monday: *New Order* / Model: *Kraftwerk* / Temptation: *Heaven 17* / I second that emotion: *Japan* / Enola Gay: *OMD* / Echo Beach: *Martha & The Muffins* / Sound of the crowd: *Human League* / Pop musik: *M* / Somewhere in my heart: *Aztec Camera* / I don't want to talk about it: *Everything But The Girl* / You're the best thing: *Style Council* / Is Vic there: *Department S* / Go wild in the country: *Bow Wow Wow* / Crash: *Primitives* / Killing moon: *Echo & The Bunnymen* / Down in the tube station at midnight: *Jam* / I can't stand up: *Costello, Elvis & The Attractions* / Einstein a go-go: *Landscape* / Vienna: *Ultravox*
CD Set _______ **RADCD 09**
Global TV / Apr '95 / BMG

INTO THE FORTIES
Ma I miss your apple pie: *Ambrose & His Orchestra* / There's a land of begin again: *Loss, Joe Band & Chick Henderson* / Don't sit under the apple tree: *Andrews Sisters* / I'll never smile again: *Sinatra, Frank & Tommy Dorsey Orchestra* / You are my sunshine: *Roy, Harry & His Band* / I don't want to walk without you: *Lipton, Celia* / String of pearls: *Miller, Glenn* / When I see an elephant fly: *Leach, Jimmy & His New Organolians* / That lovely weekend: *Carless, Dorothy & Geraldo/Ted Heath* / Moonlight becomes you: *Crosby, Bing* / Someone's rocking my dream boat: *Hutch* / Drummin' man: *Squadronaires* / Who wouldn't love you: *Ink Spots* / Elmer's tune: *Miller, Glenn Orchestra* / Kiss the boys goodbye: *Martin, Mary* / My devotion: *Winstone, Eric Band & Julie Dawn* / Rancho pillow: *Martin, Freddy & His Orchestra* / Beat me daddy eight to the bar: *Shearing, George* / Daybreak: *Sinatra, Frank & Tommy Dorsey Orchestra* / I've got a gal in Kalamazoo: *Andrews Sisters* / Nightingale sang in Berkeley square: *Shelton, Anne & Ambrose* / White christmas: *Crosby, Bing*
CD _______ **PASTCD 7019**
Flapper / Mar '97 / Pinnacle

INTRODUCING
CD _______ **101S 77772**
101 South / Jun '93 / New Note/Pinnacle

INTRODUCTION TO AMIATA'S SECRET WORLD, AN
CD _______ **ARNR 0296**
Amiata / Apr '97 / Harmonia Mundi

INTROSPECTIVE OF HOUSE VOL.1 (3CD Set)
Do me right: *Inner City* / To be real: *Lady Cop* / Don't leave me this way: *Houston, Thelma* / Love can't turn around: *Heavy Weather* / English 101: *Afrowax* / Real vibration: *Express Of Sound* / Believe in me: *Raw Stylus* / Give me back: *Sensoria* / Looking glass: *I Spy* / Rok the disco: *Big Echo* / Loveboy: *Foot Club* / Galaxia: *Moonman* / Believer: *DJ Energy* / Gift: *Way Out West* / Never gonna give you up: *Turner, Ruby* / 100%: *Kiani, Mary* / Star: *Shaker* / Don't be afraid: *Moonman* / Voyager: *Mr. Spring* / Horn: *Digi Dance* / Brain bug: *Nightmare* / United nations of house: *United Nations Project* / Diesirae: *Andy & The Lamboy* / Love and respect: *Supa T* / You're surrounded: *Skins/Jules* / So in love with you: *Duke* / Groovebird: *Natural Born Groovers* / French kiss: *Lil' Louis* / Feel the beat: *Sunglasses Ron* / Hi Q: *Stereogen* / Footprint: *Disco Citizens* / All I wanna do: *Tin Tin Out* / Antheum: *Digital Blondes* / Turkish bizzare: *Blade Racer* / U...: *Scott Project* / Petal: *Wubble-U* / Bellissima: *DJ Quicksilver*
CD Set _______ **SDIMCD 7**
Sound Dimension / Nov '96 / Total/BMG

INTROSPECTIVE OF HOUSE VOL.2 (3CD Set)
CD Set _______ **SDIMCD 8**
Sound Dimension / Jun '97 / Total/BMG

INTUITION...
At 17: *Ian, Janis* / No frontiers: *Black, Mary* / When I was a boy: *Williams, Dar* / Welcome me: *Baez, Joan* / Jerusalem tomorrow: *Harris, Emmylou* / Words: *Tamalin* / Wonderful thing: *Dowdall, Leslie* / You're in my love: *Lohan, Sinead* / Tenderness: *Ian, Janis* / Bee in the bottle: *Lohan, Sinead* / As cool as I am: *Williams, Dar* / Going back to Harlan: *Harris, Emmylou* / Libertango: *McCall, Kirsty and Sharon Shannon* / Kilkelly: *Shanley, Eleanor* / There's a train that leaves tonight: *Black, Mary* / Down by the sally gardens: *Tamalin* / Rise again: *Rankin Family*
CD _______ **GRACD 224**
Grapevine / Aug '97 / Grapevine/PolyGram

INUIT GAMES AND SONGS
CD _______ **AUD 8032**
Auvidis/Ethnic / Mar '93 / ADA / Harmonia Mundi

INVICTUS UNCONQUERED (The Best Of Invictus Records Vol.1)
Give me just a little more time: *Chairmen Of The Board* / You've got extra added power in your love: *Chairmen Of The Board* / I shall not be moved: *Barrino Brothers* / Trapped in a love: *Barrino Brothers* / You made me over: *Davis, Melvin* / Can't get enough of you: *Edwards, Tyrone* / She's not just another woman: *8th Day* / You've got to crawl (before you walk): *8th Day* / I need it just as bad as you: *Lee, Laura* / Don't leave me starving for your love: *Lee, Laura* / Don't leave me: *Holland & Dozier* / Why can't we be lovers: *Holland & Dozier* / Giving up the ring: *Glass House* / Crumbs off the table: *Glass House* / Bring the boys home: *Payne, Freda* / Band of gold: *Payne, Freda* / Only time will tell: *General Johnson* / Breakdown: *Parliament* / VIP: *Payne, Sherrie* / Unhooked generation: *Payne, Freda* / I'm so glad: *Holland, Brian* / Roller coaster: *Woods, Danny*
CD _______ **DEEPM 028**
Deep Beats / Jul '97 / BMG

INVISIBLE ROUTE 666
CD _______ **INV 666**
Invisible / Nov '95 / Plastic Head

INVISIBLE SOUNDTRACKS (Macro 1)
Menage a trois: *Thomas, Richard* / Harsh truth: *Zurich* / Crater rim cafe: *Sons Of Silence* / Beachside FX: *Nonplace Urban Field* / Here I am: *Thomas, Richard* / Cue: *Being* / If mountains could sing: *Bedouin Ascent* / Vistic: *Disjecta* / Intrusion reported by witness: *Thomas, Richard* / Sloop B: *Twisted Science* / Muffin Spencer-Devlin/Hawaii II: *Thomas, Richard* / Dirt vs Earth: *Thomas, Richard* / Nevada 2007: *Air Miami* / Bronchusix: *Gescom* / Tema: *Seymour & Van Hoen* / Pendulum: *Vendor Refill*
CD _______ **REEL 12CD**
Leaf / May '97 / RTM/Disc

IOWA STATE FARE - MUSIC FROM THE HEARTLAND (Celebrating 150 Years Of Iowa Statehood)
CD _______ **SFWCD 40083**
Smithsonian Folkways / Sep '96 / ADA / Cadillac / CM / Direct / Koch

IRAN: MASTERS OF TRADITIONAL MUSIC VOL.1
CD _______ **C 560024**
Ocora / Aug '91 / ADA / Harmonia Mundi

IRAN: MASTERS OF TRADITIONAL MUSIC VOL.2
CD _______ **C 560025**
Ocora / Aug '91 / ADA / Harmonia Mundi

IRAN: MASTERS OF TRADITIONAL MUSIC VOL.3
CD _______ **C 560026**
Ocora / Nov '92 / ADA / Harmonia Mundi

IRELAND - A SONG FOR EVERY COUNTY (2CD Set)
CD Set _______ **CHCD 3201**
Chyme / Mar '96 / ADA / CM / Direct / Koch

IRELAND TODAY
CD _______ **B 6838**
Auvidis/Ethnic / Nov '96 / ADA / Harmonia Mundi

IRELAND'S GREATEST LOVE SONGS
CD _______ **TCD 2753**
Telstar / Nov '94 / BMG

IRELAND'S GREATEST LOVE SONGS (A Collection Of 20 Romantic Ballads From The Emerald Isle)
On Raglan road: *Kelly, Luke* / Will ye go lassie go: *Barnbrack* / Fields of Athenry: *Reilly, Paddy* / Ringsend Rose: *Tara* / Song for Ireland: *Kelly, Luke* / Grace: *Brier* / Carrickfergus: *McCann, Jim* / Danny Boy: *Locke, Josef* / John O'dreams: *Dublin City Ramblers* / First of May: *Close, John* / Spanish lady: *Dubliners* / Sweet sixteen: *Fureys & Davey Arthur* / Rose of Allendale: *Reilly, Paddy* / She moved thro' the fair: *Locke, Josef* / Last farewell: *Brier* / Town I loved so well: *McEvoy, Johnny* / Old man: *Fureys & Davey Arthur* / Mountains of Mourne: *Locke, Josef* / Lagan love: *Shannon Singers* / Star of County Down: *Barnbrack*
CD _______ **CHCD 1099**
Chyme / Mar '97 / ADA / CM / Direct / Koch

IRIE IRIE (A Ragamuffin Showcase)
CD _______ **MSACD 003**
Munich / Nov '94 / ADA / CM / Direct / Greensleeves

IRIE IRIE (The Ras Sampler)
CD _______ **MSACD 002**
Munich / May '97 / ADA / CM / Direct / Greensleeves

IRISH CEILI (Reels & Jigs)
Piper's Chair/Bill Hart's jig/Nights of St. Patrick: *Dubliners* / Sheebans/Merry blacksmith/Music in the Glen: *Kilfernora Ceili Band* / Paddy on the railroad: *Gallowglass Ceili Band* / Liffey barges: *Owens, Jesse* / Galway races: *Dubliners* / Irish soldier: *Owens, Jesse* / Eavesdropper/Donnybrook boys/A visit to Ireland: *Ardellis Ceili Band* / Haste to the wedding/Leslie's hornpipe/German Beau: *Gallowglass Ceili Band* / Queen of Connemara: *Ardellis Ceili Band* / Claddagh ring: *Tulla Ceili Band* / Finnegan's wake: *Irish National Orchestra & Choir* / Donnybrook Fair/Tate's tantrums/Rake of Kildare: *Irish National Orchestra & Choir* / Johnny I hardly knew ye: *Murphy, Mary* / Paddy's gone to France/Skylark: *Dubliners* / Barn/My own backyard: *Dun Carmel Band* / Bucks of Oranmore: *Gor Jus Wrex*
CD _______ **CDMFP 6348**
Music For Pleasure / May '97 / EMI

IRISH CELEBRATION, AN (3CD Set)
CD Set _______ **EMTBX 307**
Emporio / Aug '97 / Disc

IRISH COLLECTION
CD _______ **RITZRCD 553**
Ritz / Oct '95 / Pinnacle

IRISH COUNTRY
Forty shades of green: *McBride, Frankie* / Gentle mother: *Big Tom & The Mainliners* / My wild Irish rose: *Quinn, Brendan* / Two little orphans: *Quinn, Philomena* / I'll take you home again Kathleen: *Coll, Brian* / Rose is a rose: *McGeegan, Pat* / I'll get over you: *McCaffery, Helen* / Wonderin' what to do: *Duffy, Teresa* / Mother's love's a blessing: *Quinn, Brendan* / How are things in Gloccamorra: *McBride, Frankie* / Rose of Tralee: *Coll, Brian* / She's got you: *Quinn, Philomena* / That silver haired daddy of mine: *McCaffery, Helen* / Sunset years of life: *Big Tom & The Mainliners* / Nobody's child: *Morelli, Tony* / Irish way to love: *McGoldrick, Anna*
CD _______ **EMPRCD 665**
Emporio / Oct '96 / Disc

IRISH DANCE MUSIC
CD _______ **TSCD 602**
Topic / Oct '95 / ADA / CM / Direct

IRISH FAVOURITES
CD _______ **MATCD 216**
Castle / Dec '92 / BMG

IRISH FAVOURITES
CD _______ **CPMV 028**
Cromwell / Sep '94 / Total/BMG

IRISH FAVOURITES
CD _______ **PLSCD 166**
Pulse / Apr '97 / BMG

IRISH FAVOURITES VOL.1
CD _______ **DMC 4370**
Disky / May '94 / Disky / THE

IRISH FAVOURITES VOL.2
CD _______ **DMC 4371**
Disky / May '94 / Disky / THE

IRISH FOLK BALLADS
CD _______ **MACCD 317**
Autograph / Aug '96 / BMG

IRISH FOLK COLLECTION (3CD Set)
CD Set _______________ TBXCD 509
TrueTrax / Jan '96 / THE

IRISH FOLK COLLECTION (2CD Set)
CD Set _______________ PBXCD 509
Pulse / Nov '96 / BMG

IRISH FOLK COLLECTION VOL.2
CD _______________ CCSCD 312
Castle / Feb '93 / BMG

IRISH FOLK FAVOURITES (4CD Set)
CD Set _______________ MBSCD 404
Castle / Nov '94 / BMG

IRISH FOLK FEST - BACK TO THE FUTURE
CD _______________ CDTUT 727490
Wundertute / '89 / ADA / CM / Duncans

IRISH FOLK FEST - JUBILEE
CD _______________ CDTUT 727491
Wundertute / '89 / ADA / CM / Duncans

IRISH FOLK LEGENDS
CD _______________ CDC 013
Ceol / Feb '97 / CM

IRISH HEARTBEAT (2CD Set)
Old Ireland / Old Dungannon Oak / Rare Old Times / Muirsheen Durkin / Galway shawl / Bold O'Donoghue / Fields of Athenry / Wicklow Hills / Dirty Old Town / Hometown on the Foyle / Do you want your old lobby washed down / Veil of white lace / Rose of Clare / Lovely lectrim / Pretty little girls from Omagh / Cliffs of Donneen / I'll tell me ma / Forty shades of green / Spancil hill / Wild rover / Whiskey in the jar / Four country roads / Green fields of France / Irish rover / When you were sweet sixteen / Boys from Killybegs / You seldom come to see me anymore / Boston burglar / Ilse of Innisfree / After all these years / Black velvet band / Our house is not a home / Old bog road / Town I love so well / I'll take you home again Kathleen / Any Tipperary town / Hills of Kerry / Mountains of Mourne / Maggie / Rose of Tralee
CD Set _______________ DCD 3001
Music / Jun '97 / Target/BMG

IRISH LOVE SONGS YOU KNOW BY HEART VOL.1
CD _______________ HBCD 116
Outlet / Dec '96 / ADA / CM / Direct / Duncans / Koch / Ross

IRISH LOVE SONGS YOU KNOW BY HEART VOL.2
CD _______________ HBCD 117
Outlet / Dec '96 / ADA / CM / Direct / Duncans / Koch / Ross

IRISH MELODIES
Darlin' girl from Clare: *O'Dowda, Brendan* / Molly Brannigan: *O'Dowda, Brendan* / Trottin' to the fair: *O'Dowda, Brendan* / La galondrina (The Swallow): *O'Dowda, Brendan* / Believe me, if all those endearing young charms: *Murray, Ruby* / Meeting of the waters: *Murray, Ruby* / Little bit of heaven: *Murray, Ruby* / Marie my girl: *Locke, Josef* / Macushla: *Locke, Josef* / When it's moonlight in Mayo: *Locke, Josef* / Rose of Tralee: *Locke, Josef* / Star of County Down: *MacEwan, Father Sydney* / Killarney in the spring: *MacEwan, Father Sydney* / Connemara: *O'Dowda, Brendan & Ruby Murray* / Pretty Irish girl: *O'Dowda, Brendan & Ruby Murray* / Dan O'Hara: *Gallagher, Bridie* / Old Skibbereen: *Gallagher, Bridie* / Jaunting car: *Nelson, Havelock & Orchestra* / Minstrel boy: *Nelson, Havelock & Orchestra* / Old turf fire: *Hinds, Eric* / Bonny wee lass: *Hinds, Eric* / My singing bird: *Dunne, Veronica* / I have a bonnet trimmed with blue: *Dunne, Veronica* / Wearing of the green: *Henry, Dermot* / My lagan love: *O'Duffy, Michael* / Scorn not his simplicity: *Carroll, Alma*
CD _______________ CC 291
Music For Pleasure / Dec '92 / EMI

IRISH MEMORIES (40 Gems From The Emerald Isle/2CD Set)
Dermot Hegarty: *Black Velvet Band* / Sean O'Se: *Beautiful City* / Barley corn: *Sing Irishman Sing* / Shaskeen: *Shaskeen* / Roads and the miles to Dundee: *Margo* / Pretty little girl from Omagh: *Cunningham, Larry* / Music in the glen: *Owenmore Ceili Band* / Far from Erne's shore: *Stuart, Gene* / Red is the rose: *Margo* / Paddy McGinty's goat: *Dunphy, Sean* / Old Claddagh ring: *O'Brien, Dermot* / Asthoreen Bawn: *Coll, Brian* / Town I loved so well: *Hegarty, Dermot* / Green hills of Kerry: *Doyle, Danny* / West of the old river Shannon: *Margo* / Golden jubilee: *Dunphy, Sean* / Give an Irish girl to me: *Coll, Brian* / Home boys home: *O'Brien, Dermot* / Rose of Tralee: *Curtin, D.J.* / When my blue moon turns to gold again: *Coll, Brian* / You and me, her and him: *Lynham, Ray & Philomena Begley* / Hold me just one more time: *Hurley, Red* / Forty shades of green: *Cunningham, Larry* / Tears on my pillow: *Rock, Dickie* / Anything's better than nothing: *Lynham, Ray & Philomena Begley* / I love you because: *Cunningham, Larry* / If teardrops were pennies: *Two's Company* / Jimmy Brown the newsboy: *Hegarty, Dermot* / We go together: *Lynham, Ray & Philomena Begley* / Fool's castle: *Coll, Brian* / Poor man's roses: *Hurley, Red* / Sweet dreams: *Two's Company* / Daddy was an old time preacher man: *Lynham, Ray & Philomena Begley* / I've been everywhere: *Hegarty, Dermot* / Arkansas: *Hurley, Red* / Petal from a faded rose: *Coll, Brian* / Made for each other: *Two's Company* / Sing me back home: *Coll, Brian* / I'll take you home again Kathleen: *McCaffrey, Frank* / From a jack to a king: *Rock, Dickie*
CD Set _______________ 330392
Hallmark / Mar '97 / Carlton

IRISH MUSIC TO SET YOU DANCING
CD _______________ CHCD 2003
Chyme / Dec '96 / ADA / CM / Direct / Koch

IRISH PUB BALLADS COLLECTION
CD _______________ DOCDK 110
Dolphin / Aug '96 / CM / Else / Grapevine/ PolyGram / Koch

IRISH SHOW BAND YEARS
CD _______________ CHCD 1060
Chyme / Oct '95 / ADA / CM / Direct / Koch

IRISH SHOW BANDS (The Best Of Irish Show Bands)
CD _______________ PLSCD 176
Pulse / Apr '97 / BMG

IRISH SONGBOOK, THE
Killarney: *McCormack, John* / Last rose of summer: *Austrel, Florence* / Father O'Flynn: *Santley, Charles* / Kathleen Mavoureen: *Butt, Clara* / Trottin' to the fair: *Greene, Harry Plunket* / Garden where the praties grow: *Greene, Harry Plunket* / Minstrel boy: *Burke, Tom* / I know where I'm going: *Sheridan, Margaret* / Kerry dance: *Dawson, Peter* / Next market day: *McCormack, John* / Boat song: *Kirkby-Lunn, Louise* / Believe me, if all those endearing young charms: *Tibbett, Lawrence* / Kitty of Coleraine: *O'Doherty, Seamus* / Danny Boy: *Labette, Dora* / Kitty my love will you marry me: *McCafferty, James* / Open the door softly: *McCafferty, James* / Love at my heart: *Robeson, Paul* / Lover's curse: *Hill, Carmen* / Mother Machree: *Crooks, Richard* / She moved through the fair: *MacEwan, Sydney* / Come back to Erin: *Sheridan, Margaret* / Phil the fluter's ball: *Dawson, Peter*
CD _______________ MIDCD 006
Moidart / Apr '95 / Conifer/BMG

IRISH SONGS YOU KNOW AND LOVE VOL.1
CD _______________ HBCD 114
Outlet / Dec '96 / ADA / CM / Direct / Duncans / Koch / Ross

IRISH SONGS YOU KNOW AND LOVE VOL.2
CD _______________ HBCD 115
Outlet / Dec '96 / ADA / CM / Direct / Duncans / Koch / Ross

IRISH TIMES
CD _______________ TUT 494
Wundertute / Oct '94 / ADA / CM / Duncans

IRISH TIN WHISTLES
CD _______________ TRADHCD 007
GTD / Jul '93 / ADA / Else

IRISH TOWN
CD _______________ HBCD 0006
Hummingbird / May '97 / ADA / Direct / Grapevine/PolyGram

IRISH VOICES
Humours of the King of Ballyhooley: *Patrick Street* / Stor mo chroi: *MacDonnchadha, Sean* / Blackwaterside: *Kavana, Ron* / Traveller all over the world: *Harte, Frank* / Raggle taggle gypsy: *Reilly, John* / P for Paddy: *Irish Country Four* / Rollicking boys of Tandaragee: *Tunney, Paddy* / Bucket of the mountain dew: *McPeake Family Trio* / Bean an Leanna: *Heaney, Joe* / Wind that shakes the barley: *Makem, Sarah* / Song of the riddles: *Clancy, Willie* / An sgeilpin droighneach: *O'Neachtain, Tomas* / Maid on the shore: *Lyons, John* / Lake of coolfin: *Lenihan, Tom* / John Reilly: *O'Neill, Sarah Ann* / Green fields of America: *Graham, Len* / High on a mountain: *Four Men & A Dog*
CD _______________ TSCD 702
Topic / Feb '97 / ADA / CM / Direct

IRISH WHISTLES
CD _______________ HCD 007
GTD / Apr '95 / ADA / Else

IRON MUSE, THE (A Panorama Of Industrial Folk Music)
Sangate girl's lament/Elsie Marley: *High Level Ranters* / Doon the waggonway: *High Level Ranters* / Miner's life: *Gilfellon, Tom* / Coal-owner and the pitman's wife: *MacColl, Ewan & Peggy Seeger* / Trimdon Grange explosion: *Killen, Louis* / Blackleg miner: *Killen, Louis* / Auchengeich disaster: *Gaughan, Dick & Alistair Anderson* / Ee aye, aa cud hew: *Pickford, Ed* / Durham lockout: *Craik, Maureen* / Aa'm glad the strike's done: *High Level Ranters* / Weaver's march: *Celebrated working man's band* / Spinner's song: *Fisher, Ray* / Oh, dear me: *MacColl, Ewan & Peggy Seeger* / Doffin mistress: *Briggs, Anne* / Little piecer: *Brooks, Dave* / Hand loom weaver's lament: *Boardman, Harry* / Dundee lassie: *Fisher, Ray* / Success to the weavers: *Oldham Tinkers* / Fourpence a day: *MacColl, Ewan & Peggy Seeger* / Up the raw: *Killen, Louis* / Row between the cages: *Davenport, Bob* / Aw wish pay Friday would come: *Killen, Louis & Colin Ross* / Keep your feet still Geordie Hinny: *Killen, Louis & Colin Ross* / Farewell to the Monty: *Killen, Louis*
CD _______________ TSCD 465
Topic / May '93 / ADA / CM / Direct

IS IT COOL
Linda who: *Crothers, Scott* / Blitz: *Three Blue Teardrops* / Red hot and ready: *Memphis Mafia* / Rockabilly baby: *Erik & The Dragtones* / Tear it up: *High Noon* / Pushrod: *Potter, Jeff* / Bad cat: *Scoffed* / Hillibilly hell: *Wreckin' Ball* / Chicken walk: *Mustang Lightning* / What'd I do now: *Whole Lotsa Papa* / Naked cowboy: *Rotgut* / Rockabilly not fade away: *LeVey, Larry* / Long hard night: *Three Blue Teardrops* / Hey baby: *Wreckin' Ball* / Itchen fer lovin': *Scoffed* / Blackjack county chains: *Whole Lotsa Papa* / Wild wild women: *Mustang Lightning* / Sun # 209: *Thompson, Danny* / Lonesome road: *Rockabilly 88* / Buzz and the flyers: *Is It Cool*
CD _______________ NERCD 081
Nervous / Jun '95 / Nervous / TKO Magnum

IS IT LOVE (Music From The Lovers' Guide)
Theme for lovers / Tender invitation / Touch me / Secret whispers / Echoes of love / I need your love / Toledo / Making love in the rain / Love ocean / Now that you're a part of me / Hold me close
CD _______________ PWKS 4133
Carlton / Feb '96 / Carlton

IS THAT JAZZ
CD _______________ URCD 007
Ubiquity / Jul '96 / Cargo / Timewarp

IS THIS LOVE (2CD Set)
CD Set _______________ NSCD 008
Newsound / Feb '95 / THE

ISLAND 40TH ANNIVERSARY VOL.1
CD _______________ 5243932
Island / Sep '97 / PolyGram

ISLAND 40TH ANNIVERSARY VOL.2
CD _______________ 5243942
Island / Sep '97 / PolyGram

ISLAND MUSIC
CD _______________ RNCD 2077
Rhino / Oct '94 / Grapevine/PolyGram / Jet Star

ISLAND OF ST. HYLARION, THE
CD _______________ NA 038
New Albion / Apr '91 / Cadillac / Harmonia Mundi

ISLAND OF THE GODS, THE (Balinese Gamelan Gong)
Puspa Wresti / Topeng Keras / Legong / Kepyar Duduk dance - Turuna Jaya / Kupu Kupu Taram / Oleg Tamulilingan / Jauk / Closing instrumental music
CD _______________ SOW 90154
Sounds Of The World / Jan '97 / Target/ BMG

ISLANDS
CD _______________ PUTU 1292
Putumayo / Jun '97 / Grapevine/PolyGram

ISLE OF WIGHT FESTIVAL 1970, THE
CD _______________ EDFCD 327
Essential / Dec '95 / BMG

ISN'T IT ROMANTIC (Songwriters In Jazz)
CD _______________ 5297012
Verve / Mar '96 / PolyGram

ISTANBUL 1925
CD _______________ CD 4266
Traditional Crossroads / Dec '94 / CM / Direct

IT 1 ELECTRO
CD _______________ ITCD 1
Psychic / May '96 / 3mv/Pinnacle

IT AIN'T WHERE YOU'RE FROM...IT'S WHERE YOU'RE AT
CD _______________ LF 281CD
Lost & Found / Jun '97 / Plastic Head

IT CAME FROM BENEATH LA
CD _______________ TX 51213CD
Triple X / Jan '96 / Plastic Head

IT CAME FROM MEMPHIS
CD _______________ UPSTART 022
Upstart / Nov '95 / ADA / Direct

IT CAME FROM OUTER SPACE VOL.1
CD _______________ OUTERSPACE 11
Neuton / Jan '95 / Plastic Head

IT CAME FROM OUTER SPACE VOL.2
CD _______________ OUTERSPACE 23
Neuton / Jun '94 / Plastic Head

IT CAME FROM OUTER SPACE VOL.3
CD _______________ OUTERSPACE 25
Neuton / Sep '95 / Plastic Head

IT DON'T MEAN A THING IF IT AIN'T GOT THAT SWING
My heart belongs to Daddy: *Shaw, Artie* / I got rhythm: *Dorsey, Tommy* / Frankie and Johnny: *Goodman, Benny* / Basin Street blues: *Fitzgerald, Ella & Chick Webb* / Moonlight serenade: *Miller, Glenn* / Taking a chance on love: *Dorsey, Tommy* / Jumpin' at the Woodside: *Basie, Count* / Take the 'A' train: *Ellington, Duke* / September song: *Day, Doris & Les Brown* / Blowin' up a storm: *Herman, Woody* / Skyliner: *Barnet, Charlie* / Linger awhile: *Morgan, Russ* / Fools rush in: *Dorsey, Jimmy* / On the sunny side of the street: *Dorsey, Tommy* / Perdido: *Ellington, Duke* / My heart stood still: *Shaw, Artie* / Jersey bounce: *Goodman, Benny* / Blue and sentimental: *Basie, Count* / Caldonia: *Herman, Woody* / I'm forever blowing bubbles: *Brown, Les*
CD _______________ QED 124
Tring / Nov '96 / Tring

IT STARTED WITH A KISS
(You're) having my baby: *Anka, Paul* / Tonight I celebrate my love: *Bryson, Peabo & Roberta Flack* / Rock me tonight (for old times sake): *Jackson, Freddie* / I thought I'd ring you: *Bassey, Shirley & Alain Delon* / For a moment of your time: *Hammond, Albert* / Could it be I'm falling in love: *Grant, David & Jaki Graham* / Loving you: *Riperton, Minnie* / When I need you: *Sayer, Leo* / I'll fly for you: *Spandau Ballet* / Everytime I think of you: *Babys* / Dedicated to the one I love: *McLean, Bitty* / Move closer: *Nelson, Phyllis* / It started with a kiss: *Hot Chocolate* / When you're in love with a beautiful woman: *Dr. Hook*
CD _______________ WLT 874602
Disky / Oct '96 / Disky / THE

IT TAKES TWO
Don't let the sun go down on me: *Michael, George & Elton John* / You are everything: *Ross, Diana & Marvin Gaye* / Easy lover: *Collins, Phil & Phillip Bailey* / With you I'm born again: *Preston, Billy & Syreeta* / It takes two: *Gaye, Marvin & Kim Weston* / Up where we belong: *Cocker, Joe & Jennifer Warnes* / I've had the time of my life: *Medley, Bill & Jennifer Warnes* / I'm gonna make you love me: *Temptations & Diana Ross/Supremes* / You've lost that loving feeling: *Righteous Brothers* / If you don't know me by now: *Melvin, Harold & The Bluenotes* / Tonight I celebrate my love: *Bryson, Peabo & Roberta Flack* / Midnight train to Georgia: *Knight, Gladys & The Pips* / I got you babe: *Sonny & Cher* / Relight my fire: *Take That & Lulu* / Baby come back: *Pato Banton & Ali Campbell/Robin Campbell* / Missing: *Everything But The Girl* / Would I lie to you: *Charles & Eddie* / Senza una donna: *Young, Paul & Zucchero* / Every time you go away: *Hall & Oates* / Sisters are doing it for themselves: *Eurythmics & Aretha Franklin* / It's too late: *Quartz & Dina Carroll* / Somethin's gotten hold of my heart: *Pitney, Gene & Marc Almond* / Stop draggin' my heart around: *Nicks, Stevie & Tom Petty & The Heartbreakers* / Say goodbye to Hollywood: *Spector, Ronnie & the E Street Band* / Whole new world: *Bryson, Peabo & Regina Belle* / From now on: *Bolton, Michael & Suzie Benson* / Delicate: *D'Arby, Terence Trent & Des'ree* / Kiss: *Jones, Tom & Art Of Noise* / Up on the roof: *Robson & Jerome*
CD _______________ MOODCD 43
Sony Music / Apr '96 / Sony

IT TAKES TWO
CD _______________ PDSCD 544
Pulse / Aug '96 / BMG

IT WILL TAKE US A NATION OF MILLIONS TO HOLD US BACK
CD _______________ BBECD 006
Barely Breaking Even / Jun '97 / Beechwood/BMG

ITALIA - 20 GRANDS SUCCES
CD _______________ 3003752
IMP / Jan '97 / ADA / Discovery

ITALIAN DANCE CLASSICS - DOWN BEAT AND SOUL
CD _______________ 4784512
Irma / Jun '97 / Essential/BMG

ITALIAN DANCE CLASSICS - FUNKY AND DISCO
CD _______________ 4784492
Irma / Jun '97 / Essential/BMG

ITALIAN DANCE CLASSICS - HOUSE
CD _______________ 4784482
Irma / Jun '97 / Essential/BMG

ITALIAN DANCE CLASSICS - TECHNO
CD _______________ 4784522
Irma / Jun '97 / Essential/BMG

ITALIAN DANCE CLASSICS - UNDERGROUND AND GARAGE
CD _______________ 4784502
Irma / Jun '97 / Essential/BMG

ITALIAN HOUSE COLLECTION
CD _______________ FIRMCD 5
Firm / Jun '96 / Pinnacle

ITALIAN MANDOLINE
CD _______________ 15441
Laserlight / Nov '91 / Target/BMG

ITALIAN STRING VIRTUOSI
CD _______________ ROUCD 1095
Rounder / Mar '95 / ADA / CM / Direct

ITALY AFTER DARK - ITALIA NOSTALGICA
Vivere: *Buti, Carlo* / Amami se vuoi: *Fiordaliso, Marisa* / Venezia la luna e tu: *Virgili, Luciano* / Volare: *Arigliano, Nicola* / Bella ragazza dalle trecce bionde: *Buti, Carlo* / Capriccio mazurka: *Gargano, Guiseppe* / Santa Lucia: *De Muro Lomanto, Enzo* / Come prima: *Eigs, Franco* / Sul Lungarno: *Buti, Carlo* / Papavari e papere: *Barimar e*

La Sua Orchestra / Reginella: *Buti, Carlo* / Whatever will be will be (Que sera sera): *Power, Romina* / Luna rossa: *Ricci, Franco* / Guaglione: *Carosone, Renato* / Mama: *Gigli, Beniamino* / Anema e core: *De Palma, Jula* / Violino tzigano: *Virgili, Luciano* / Piano fortissimo: *Carosone, Renato* / Stornellando alla toscana: *Villa, Claudio* / Arrivederci Roma: *Gilardini, Renzo*
CD ____ **CDEMS 1458**
EMI / Sep '92 / EMI

ITP SELECTED WORKS 1993-1996
CD ____ **ITPAL 03CD**
ITP / Jul '96 / Jumpstart / Kudos / Pinnacle

IT'S A HEARTACHE
CD ____ **PLSCD 141**
Pulse / Apr '96 / BMG

IT'S A LOVE THING VOL.1
CD ____ **DTCD 18**
Discotex / Nov '93 / Jet Star

IT'S A LOVE THING VOL.2
CD ____ **DTCD 22**
Discotex / Apr '95 / Jet Star

IT'S A MAN'S MAN'S MAN'S WORLD
Walking the dog: *Thomas, Rufus* / Change is gonna come: *Redding, Otis* / You don't know like I know: *Sam & Dave* / I'll take good care of you: *Mimms, Garnet* / It's a man's man's man's world: *Brown, James* / Summertime: *Stewart, Billy* / Everybody needs somebody: *Pickett, Wilson* / Gimme a little sign: *Wood, Brenton* / I've never found a girl: *Floyd, Eddie* / I forgot to be your lover: *Bell, William* / Walk on by: *Hayes, Isaac* / Only the strong survive: *Butler, Jerry* / Your good thing is about to end: *Rawls, Lou* / Drowning in a sea of love: *Simon, Joe* / I've been lonely for so long: *Knight, Frederick* / Why can't we live together: *Thomas, Timmy* / Take me to the river: *Green, Al* / You and your baby blues: *Burke, Solomon* / It's ecstasy when you're next to me: *White, Barry* / Hang on in there baby: *Bristol, Johnny*
CD ____ **RNBCD 103**
Connoisseur Collection / Jul '93 / Pinnacle

IT'S A TRIPLE EARTH
CD ____ **TRECD 114**
Triple Earth / Oct '95 / Grapevine/ PolyGram / Stern's

IT'S ALL BECOMING CLEAR
CD ____ **CLR 400CD**
Clear / Mar '96 / Prime / RTM/Disc

IT'S DOUBLE JAZZ TIME (2CD Set)
CD Set ____ **ATJCD 5974**
Disky / May '93 / Disky / THE

IT'S DOUBLE SWING TIME (2CD Set)
CD Set ____ **ATJCD 5973**
Disky / May '93 / Disky / THE

IT'S FOR LIFE
CD ____ **VD 01CD**
Victory / Apr '97 / Plastic Head

IT'S GOT TO BE LOVE
It's got to be love: *Fox, Roy & His Orchestra/Mary Lee* / Embraceable you: *Sinatra, Frank* / Cheek to cheek: *Astaire, Fred* / Life begins when you're in love: *Hildegarde* / Love is the sweetest thing: *Noble, Ray & His Orchestra & Al Bowlly* / I've got my love to keep me warm: *Powell, Dick* / With all my heart: *Boswell, Connee* / There isn't any limit to my love: *Ambrose & His Orchestra/Jack Cooper* / Dearest love: *Coward, Noel* / That sentimental sandwich: *Lamour, Dorothy* / Until today: *Weems, Ted & His Orchestra/Perry Como* / Goodnight my love: *Hylton, Jack & His Orchestra/Bert Yarlett* / Trusting my love: *Matthews, Jessie* / When did you leave Heaven: *Martin, Tony* / You made me love you: *Crosby, Bing & The Merry Macs* / It had to be you: *Gibbons, Carroll & Savoy Hotel Orpheans/Julie Dawn* / You are my love song: *Hutchinson, Leslie 'Hutch'* / Sweet someone: *Fox, Roy & His Orchestra/Denny Dennis* / Nearness of you: *Shore, Dinah* / PS I love you: *Geraldo & His Sweet Music/Cyril Graham* / Man I love: *Langford, Frances* / Long ago and far away: *Haymes, Dick & Helen Forrest*
CD ____ **PPCD 78119**
Past Perfect / Mar '95 / Glass Gramophone Co.

IT'S HARD BUT IT'S FAIR (The Blues Today)
CD ____ **MCCD 147**
Music Club / Nov '93 / Disc / THE

IT'S JAZZ (Sampler)
CD ____ **22700**
Music / Feb '96 / Target/BMG

IT'S JESUS Y'ALL
Jesus you've been good to me: *Gospel Keynotes* / Hungry child: *Salem travellers* / Thankyou Lord: *Salem travellers* / I can't stop holding on: *Ramey, Troy* / I know a man from Galilee: *Ramey, Troy* / It's Jesus y'all: *Ramey, Troy* / Borrowed time: *Swanee Quintet* / Oh yes he did: *Swanee Quintet* / I've got that feeling: *Swanee Quintet* / I want to be loved: *Ellison, Tommy* / Grandma's hands: *Robinson, Cleophus* / Gamblin' man: *Angelic Gospel Stars* / I'm going to serve Jesus: *Supreme Angels* / Crown of life: *Supreme Angels* / I stood on the banks of Jordan: *Brooklyn Allstars* / People get ready: *Brooklyn Allstars* / That's my son: *Gospel Keynotes* / Won't it be grand: *Consolers* / Lord give me strength: *Boggs, Harold*
CD ____ **CDCHM 381**
Ace / Apr '94 / Pinnacle

IT'S MY PARTY
CD ____ **12168**
Laserlight / Jul '93 / Target/BMG

IT'S OKEH UP NORTH
I don't want to discuss it: *Little Richard* / I'm coming to your rescue: *Triumphs* / Don't fight it: *Major Lance* / Right track: *Butler, Billy* / This heart of mine: *Artistics* / Investigate: *Major Lance* / Quitter never wins: *Williams, Larry & Johnny Watson* / He who picks a rose: *Carstairs* / You don't want me no more: *Major Lance* / You're gonna make me love you: *Sheldon, Sandi* / This old heart (is so lonely): *Williams, Larry* / Finding out the hard way: *Vibrations* / I'm taking on pain: *Tate, Tommy* / Get my hat, nothing can stop me: *Major Lance* / Too late: *Williams, Larry & Johnny Watson* / Where have all the flowers gone: *Jackson, Walter* / Gonna get along without you now: *Vibrations* / I still love you: *Seven Souls* / Everybody loves a good time: *Major Lance* / I can't do it: *Autographs* / Call me tomorrow: *Harris, Major* / Beat: *Major Lance* / It's an uphill climb to the bottom: *Jackson, Walter* / Ain't no soul left in these old shoes: *Major Lance*
CD ____ **SSCD 1**
Goldmine / Nov '96 / Vital

IT'S ONLY LEISURE TIME
CD ____ **OER 004CD**
Orange Egg / May '97 / Alphamagic / Pinnacle / Vital

IT'S ONLY ROCK & ROLL (Album Tracks & New Music From Virgin 1215 - 2CD Set)
CD Set ____ **CDFRL 1004**
Fragile / Oct '94 / Grapevine/PolyGram

IT'S PARTY TIME
Monster mash: *Pickett, Bobby 'Boris'* / Seven little girls: *Evans, Paul* / Speedy gonzales: *Boone, Pat* / Rubber ball: *Vee, Bobby* / Does your chewing gum lose its flavour: *Donegan, Lonnie* / Purple people eater: *Wooley, Sheb* / Charlie Brown: *Coasters* / How much is that doggy in the window: *Page, Patti* / I taut I taw a puddy tat: *SJ Group* / Mr. Bass Man: *Cymbal, Johnny* / I'd like to teach the world to sing: *New Seekers* / In the summertime: *Mungo Jerry* / Birds and the bees: *Akins, Jewel* / Freight train: *McDevitt, Chas* / Zip a dee doo dah: *Soxx, Bob B. & The Blue Jeans* / I'm Henry the eighth I am: *Brown, Joe* / My old man's a dustman: *Donegan, Lonnie* / Little arrows: *Lee, Leapy*
CD ____ **ECD 3079**
K-Tel / Jan '95 / K-Tel

IT'S REGGAE TIME
CD ____ **EXP 036**
Experience / May '97 / TKO Magnum

IT'S SWING TIME (3CD Set)
CD Set ____ **55144**
Laserlight / Oct '95 / Target/BMG

IT'S THE 70'S (20 Sensational Hits)
Band of gold: *Payne, Freda* / Give me just a little more time: *Chairmen Of The Board* / That same old feeling: *Pickettywitch* / Popcorn: *Hot Butter* / Burlesque: *Family* / Mean girl: *Status Quo* / Alright alright alright: *Mungo Jerry* / Dancing on a Saturday night: *Blue, Barry* / Man who sold the world: *Lulu* / Who do you think you are: *Candlewick Green* / Get dancin': *Disco Tex & The Sex-olettes* / Shame shame shame: *Shirley & Company* / Dolly my love: *Moments* / El bimbo: *Bimbo Jet* / Ride a wild horse: *Clark, Dee* / Sky high: *Jigsaw* / Why did you do it: *Stretch* / Lost in France: *Tyler, Bonnie* / Isn't she lovely: *Parton, David* / Fanfare for the common man: *Emerson, Lake & Palmer*
CD ____ **MCCD 300**
Music Club / Jun '97 / Disc / THE

IT'S THE SENSATIONAL 70'S
Sugar baby love: *Rubettes* / I'm the leader of the gang (I am): *Glitter, Gary* / Save your kisses for me: *Brotherhood Of Man* / Beach baby: *First Class* / Sugar candy kisses: *Kissoon, Mac & Katie* / You won't find another fool like me: *New Seekers* / Doctor's orders: *Sunny* / Boogie on up: *Rokotto* / Where is the love: *Delegation* / Don't throw it all away: *Benson, Gary* / I love you love me love: *Glitter, Gary* / Jukebox jive: *Rubettes* / Love grows (where my Rosemary goes): *Edison Lighthouse* / Falling apart at the seams: *Marmalade* / Figaro: *Brotherhood Of Man* / Don't do it baby: *Kissoon, Mac & Katie* / You've been doing me wrong: *Delegation* / Something old, something new: *Fantastics* / Daddy don't you walk so fast: *Boone, Daniel* / Sweet inspiration: *Johnson, Johnny & Bandwagon*
CD ____ **MCCD 051**
Music Club / Mar '92 / Disc / THE

IT'S THE TALK OF THE TOWN
Marie: *Dorsey, Tommy* / It's the talk of the town: *Henderson, Fletcher* / Lonesome nights: *Carter, Benny* / My fine feathered friend: *Miller, Glenn* / Song of India: *Dorsey, Tommy* / Devil's holiday: *Carter, Benny* / Silhoutted in the moonlight: *Miller, Glenn* / Down a Carolina Lane: *Ellington, Duke* / Queer notions: *Henderson, Fletcher* / Stardust: *Dorsey, Tommy* / Blue Lou: *Carter, Benny* / Everyday's a holiday: *Miller, Glenn* / Nagasaki: *Henderson, Fletcher* / Six bells stampede: *Carter, Benny* / Music maestro please: *Dorsey, Tommy* / Don't wake up my heart: *Miller, Glenn* / Night life: *Henderson, Fletcher* / Who: *Dorsey, Tommy* / Sophisticated lady: *Ellington, Duke*
CD ____ **MUCD 9027**
Musketeer / Apr '95 / Disc

IT'S WHAT WE DO VOL.1
CD ____ **DRCD 3020**
Daring / Feb '96 / ADA / CM / Direct

I'VE GOT MY FRIENDS
CD ____ **FR 6869**
Flat / Mar '97 / Cargo

I'VE LOVED AND LOST AGAIN
CD ____ **MU 5059**
Musketeer / Oct '92 / Disc

IVOR NOVELLO - CENTENARY CELEBRATION
CD ____ **GEMMCD 9062**
Pearl / Nov '93 / Harmonia Mundi

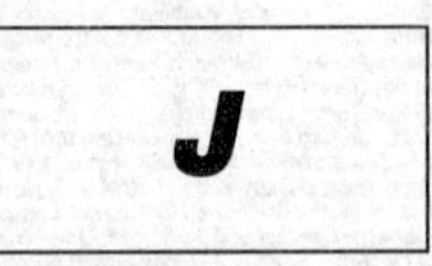

J-GROOVE (The Soul Of Japan/16 Cool Jams)
Embarrassing touch: *Yonekura, Toshinori* / Everytime we walk: *Katsumi* / I've been loving you so long: *Kobayashi, Tomiko* / I want you to say: *Yonekura, Toshinori* / Crimes of love: *Kojima, Michiru* / Early Spring: *Nakanishi, Keizo* / All of this love: *Katoh, Reiko* / 2am: *Nakanishi, Keizo* / Starting over: *Nakanishi, Keizo* / Give me your loneliness: *Katoh, Reiko* / Miracle of love: *Kobayashi, Tomiko* / Dance around: *E-Zee Band* / Dreamin': *Katsumi* / Delicate rain: *Yonekura, Toshinori* / Can't stop my love: *Kobayashi, Tomiko* / Pieces of mind: *Lam, Sandy*
CD ____ **MOCD 3017**
More Music / Nov '96 / Sound & Media

JA JA OOMPAH PAH (24 Traditional German Drinking Songs)
Schuplatter / Tiroler holzhackerbaum / O du lieber Augustin / Der frohliche wandersmann / Phyllis und die Mutter / Es war einmal ein treur husar / Oompah polka / Klarinetten polka / Schneewalzer / Zum volksfest / Im schwarzen walfisch / Die dorfmusikanten / Rixdorfer polka / Das war der Herr Von Rodenstein / Bauren polka / Muss I den, muss I den zum / Stadtele 'naus / Bierwalzer / Die lorelei / Anneliese / In Munchen steht ein / Hofbrauhaus / Hans und Liesel / Urbummelied / Lieb heimatland, ade / Alte kameraden
CD ____ **SUMCD 4037**
Summit / Nov '96 / Sound & Media

JABBERJAW GOOD TO THE LAST DROP
Mogattraction: *Girls Against Boys* / Broken E strings: *Unwound* / Rock star (Alternate version): *Hole* / Cleaning woman: *Hammerhead* / In a cold ass fashion: *Beck* / Total weirdness: *Teenage Fanclub* / Borax: *Slug* / Narrow: *Chokebore* / Charger: *Mule* / Turned out (Live): *Helmet* / Jabberjammin': *Southern Culture On The Skids* / Rocky mountain rescue: *Karp* / Chump II: *Jawbox* / Little girl: *Surgery* / Blew: *Unsane* / My letters: *Seaweed* / Buzzers and bells: *Inch* / Explain: *That Dog* / Rich kids: *Further*
CD ____ **MR 0812**
Mammoth / Jul '94 / Vital

JABBERJAW: PURE SWEET HELL
Burn it down: *Fitz Of Depression* / Skybolt X-66: *Hi-Fives* / Go: *Brainiac* / Birthday boy: *Lord, Mary Lou* / How soon is now: *Everclear* / Earth station radio: *Man Or Astro Man* / Sister: *Jawbreaker* / Charm: *Steel Pole Bath Tub* / Librarian: *Clikatat Ikatowi* / Star lust: *Red Kross* / Fibreglass jungle: *Bomboras* / Heaven isn't Hollywood: *Godheadsilo* / I started a joke: *Low* / Shine: *Laughing Hyenas* / Gripper bite: *Cocktails*
CD ____ **MR 1332**
Mammoth / Sep '96 / Vital

JACKPOT - THE WINNING TICKETS
CD ____ **CDWON 1**
Jackpot / Mar '97 / 3mv/Sony / Amato Disco / Prime

JACKSON BLUES 1928-1938
CD ____ **YAZCD 1007**
Yazoo / Jul '91 / ADA / CM / Koch

JAH JAH DREADER THAN DREAD
You can hold the handle: *Wailing Souls* / Jah jah dreader than dread: *Thompson, Linval* / Lonely man: *McKay, Freddie* / Jah help the people: *McGregor, Freddie* / Come we just a come: *Irie, Welton* / Come closer: *Viceroys* / Humble man: *Wade, Wayne* / Rubadub session: *Palmer, Tristan* / Rock to the riddim: *U-Brown* / Follow fashion: *Sammy Dread* / Follow the dub / Message: *McKay, Freddie* / Round the world: *Wade, Wayne* / Round the dub / Six babylon: *Thompson, Linval* / Six dub / Jah help people dub
CD ____ **MRCD 1005**
Majestic Reggae / May '97 / Direct

JAH LOVE INA WI
CD ____ **SKYHIGHCD 2002**
Sky High / Oct '95 / Direct / Jet Star

JAH PEOPLE (3CD Set)
CD Set ____ **DTKBOX 63**
Dressed To Kill / Jun '97 / Total/BMG

JAH REGGAE
CD ____ **EXP 037**
Experience / May '97 / TKO Magnum

JAH WISDOM
CD ____ **86102**
Greensleeves / Jun '93 / Jet Star / SRD

JAHMENTO RECS
CD ____ **HCD 7006**
Hightone / Aug '94 / ADA / Koch

J'AI ETE AU BAL VOL.1 (Cajun & Zydeco Music Of Louisiana Vol.1)
CD ____ **ARHCD 331**
Arhoolie / Apr '95 / ADA / Cadillac / Direct

J'AI ETE AU BAL VOL.2 (Cajun & Zydeco Music of Louisiana)
CD ____ **ARHCD 332**
Arhoolie / Apr '95 / ADA / Cadillac / Direct

JAKE LEG BLUES
CD ____ **JCD 642**
Jass / Jun '94 / ADA / Cadillac / CM / Direct / Jazz Music

JAKIE JAZZ 'EM 'UP (Old Time Klezmer Music 1912-1926)
CD ____ **GV 101CD**
Global Village / Nov '93 / ADA / Direct

JAM DOWN VIBRATIONS
CD ____ **RR 88812**
Roadrunner / Jul '96 / PolyGram

JAM JAM JAM (Original Full Length Sugarhill 12" Mixes)
Rapper's delight: *Sugarhill Gang* / That's the joint: *Funky 4+1* / Adventures of Grandmaster Flash on the wheels of steel: *Grandmaster Flash* / Rapper's reprise: *Sugarhill Gang & Sequence* / Message: *Grandmaster Flash & The Furious Five* / Making cash money: *Busy Bee* / Mirda rock: *Griffin, Reggie & Technofunk* / White lines (Don't don't do it): *Grandmaster Flash & Melle Mel* / Pump me up: *Trouble Funk*
CD ____ **MUSCD 016**
MCI Music / May '94 / Disc / THE

JAM SESSION
CD ____ **CD 53098**
Giants Of Jazz / May '93 / Cadillac / Jazz Music / Target/BMG

JAM SESSIONS MONTREUX '77
CD ____ **OJCCD 385**
Original Jazz Classics / Feb '92 / Complete/Pinnacle / Jazz Music / Wellard

JAMIE/GUYDEN DOO WOP COLLECTION VOL.1 (Echoes Of The Vocal Group Era)
Dry your eyes: *Inspirations* / Summertime angel: *Intentions* / I want her to love me: *Larks* / Play those oldies Mr. Bassman: *Anthony & The Sophomores* / My love will follow you: *Continental Gems* / Sweet sweetheart: *Sharps* / Bells: *Creations* / Until then: *Pentagons* / Where is he: *Clickettes* / Girl from across the sea: *Ernie & The Halos* / God gave me you: *Allen, Tony & The Wonders* / For me and my girl: *Four J'S* / No one but you: *Fantasys* / When I get older: *Butlers* / One million years: *Heartbeats* / Maybe you'll be there: *Billy & The Essentials* / I wish on a star: *Pentagons* / Love is like music: *Five Chords* / Foolish one: *Stompers* / One more time: *Four Evers* / Tonight and forever: *Clickettes* / Steamboat: *Webs* / One summer night: *Anthony & The Sophomores* / I see a star: *Little Stevie* / Loveable girl: *Butlers* / I wonder: *Pentagons* / Love: *No Names* / Crazy rock: *Five Chords* / Chapel of love: *Sundials* / Nasty breaks: *Dandevilles* / Loving you: *Allen, Tony & The Wonders* / Come on: *Sharps* / Goodbye: *Inspirations*
CD ____ **BCD 15885**
Bear Family / Jan '97 / Direct / Rollercoaster / Swift

JAMIE/GUYDEN STORY, THE (2CD Set)
Rebel rouser: *Eddy, Duane* / You'll lose a good thing: *Lynn, Barbara* / Quarter to four stomp: *Stompers* / Pink chiffon: *Torok, Mitchell* / One million years: *Heartbeats* / Maybe you'll be there: *Billy & The Essentials* / Pop pop pop pie: *Sherrys* / Unchained melody: *Blackwells* / Mother nature: *Robinson, Floyd* / Girl from across the sea: *Ernie & The Halos* / Sound off: *Turner, Titus* / Sweet dreams: *McLain, Tommy* / Yes I'm ready: *Mason, Barbara* / Going back to Louisiana: *Channel, Bruce* / I wonder: *Pentagons* / Sea of love: *Kit Kat's* / Dry your eyes: *Brenda & Tabulations* / I really love you: *Ambassadors* / Won't find better than me: *New Hope Singers* / Horse: *Nobles, Cliff* / Let me be your man: *Ashley, Tyrone* / Ain't nothin' but a house party: *Show Stoppers* /

Storm warning: *Volcanoes* / Tell me: *Ethics* / Here am I broken hearted: *Four J'S* / Oh la la limbo: *Danny & The Juniors* / Hole in the ground: *Rivers, Johnny* / I'm a poor loser: *Davis, Mac* / Time out for tears: *Churchill, Savannah* / Linda Lu: *Sharpe, Ray* / Because they're young: *Eddy, Duane* / Dancing the strand: *Gray, Maureen* / Ring a rockin': *Sedaka, Neil* / Dry your eyes: *Inspirations* / Words mean nothing: *Hazelwood, Lee* / Jam: *Gregg, Bobby* / Need you: *Owens, Donnie* / Have love, will travel: *Sharps* / Dance is over: *Billy & The Essentials* / Never never: *Jordan Brothers* / Darling I want to get married: *Heartbeats* / Come on in: *Alden, Craig* / Forty miles of bad road: *Eddy, Duane* / Son of a gun: *Clark, Sanford* / I'm in love: *Pentagons* / (I cried at) Laura's wedding: *Lynn, Barbara* / Caribbean: *Torok, Mitchell* / Strollin' after school: *Fields, Ernie* / Get out: *Melvin, Harold & The Bluenotes* / Slop time: *Sherrys* / Love (can make you happy): *Merci* / Living doll: *Bond, Bobby* / Oh how it hurts: *Mason, Barbara* / For your prescious love: *Davis, Geater* / Boogaloo down broadway: *Fantastic Johnny C* / Don't make the good girls go bad: *Humphries, Della* / Love addict: *Honey & The Bees* / Right on the tip of my tongue: *Brenda & Tabulations* / Goodbye: *Temptones*
CD Set ________ **BCD 15874**
Bear Family / Oct '95 / Direct / Rollercoaster / Swift

JAMMIN' THE BOOGIE WOOGIE
CD ________ **CD 56025**
Jazz Roots / Nov '94 / Target/BMG

JAPAN - KABUKI MUSIC
CD ________ **BCD 6809**
Auvidis/Ethnic / Jan '95 / ADA / Harmonia Mundi

JAPAN - THE NEW PSYCHEDLIC UNDERGROUND
CD ________ **BOB 107**
Bob's Airport / Nov '96 / Cargo

JAPAN CONNECTION (East Meets West) (2CD Set)
Set me free: *Hall, Latonia & Satoshi Tomie* / To another galaxy: *Tokyo Ghetto Pussy* / Flashback: *DJ Tonka* / Kotoba: *Oka, Kenichi* / Garden on the palm: *Ishii, Ken* / Quazar gamer's night: *Mijk's Magic Marble Box* / Extra: *Ishii, Ken* / Telecomposer: *Wasaki, Norihiko* / Rendezvous de telepathie: *Biomehanika, Yoji* / Merry Christmas Mr. Lawrence: *Sakamoto, Ryuichi* / Candy girls: *Wham Bam* / Let's get closer baby: *F-Action* / On and on: *Direct Drive* / Did my time: *Timewriter* / Need you: *28 East Boyz* / Find a way: *Yoki Boys* / Shine on: *Sirius 5* / Ain't got no time: *Big Light* / I like house: *Ed's Experience* / SLO: *Spice*
CD Set ________ **SPV 08968312**
SPV / Aug '96 / Koch / Plastic Head

JAPANESE HARDCORE VOL.3
CD ________ **DISCCD 013**
Voices Of Wonder / Jun '95 / Plastic Head

JAPANESE KOTO ORCHESTRA
CD ________ **LYRCD 7167**
Lyrichord / '91 / ADA / CM / Roots

JAPANESE MASTERPIECES FOR THE SHAKUHACHI
CD ________ **LYRCD 7176**
Lyrichord / '91 / ADA / CM / Roots

JAPPIN' PSYCHO BOMB VOL.1
Jungle boy: *Scamp* / My babe: *Scamp* / Bamboo bomb: *Scamp* / Somebody's gonna get their head kicked in tonight: *Hornets* / Mechagodzilla: *Hornets* / Rebel: *Pharaoh* / Wild cat blues: *Pharaohs* / Ten dollars Bucato: *Tokyo Skunx* / Brand new wagon: *Tokyo Skunx* / Tokyo nuclear nitek-lub: *Tokyo Skunx* / Bad dream: *Crackpot* / Spray with machine gun: *Crackpot* / Batman: *Biscuits* / Long separation: *Floozy Drippy's* / Tiny cowboy: *Floozy Drippy's* / She's the bad girl: *Jap Kat* / Angry hungry eyes: *Jap Kat*
CD ________ **JRCD 32**
Jappin' & Rockin' / Jun '97 / Swift / TKO Magnum

JAPPIN' PSYCHO BOMB VOL.2
Hallucination: *Mad Mongols* / Indian slap shot: *Mad Mongols* / Chicken choke: *Wood Chuck '91* / Facts of war: *Wood Chuck '91* / No stopping: *Wood Chuck '91* / Here we are nowhere: *Wood Chuck '91* / Tokyo lonesome train: *Jap Kat* / Into the mirror: *Jap Kat* / I'll just stay with rock 'n' roll: *Crazy Billy Rats* / Winter sky: *Crazy Billy Rats* / Love me: *Spikes* / Over heat: *Spikes* / Touch of God's hand: *Dog Eat Dog* / Bounty killer: *Dog Eat Dog* / I'm down: *Wankers* / Rock around the jukebox: *Wankers* / Getting me down: *Dark Ages* / Dark ages: *Dark Ages* / Vanity girl is pretty girl: *Floozy Drippy's* / Phi Phi Island: *Floozy Drippy's*
CD ________ **JRCD 33**
Jappin' & Rockin' / Jun '97 / Swift / TKO Magnum

JARGALANT ALTAI
CD ________ **PAN 2050CD**
Pan / Apr '96 / ADA / CM / Direct

JAVA - ART OF THE GAMELAN DEGUNG
CD ________ **C 560097**
Ocora / Aug '96 / ADA / Harmonia Mundi

JAVANESE COURT GAMELAN
CD ________ **7559720442**
Nonesuch / Jan '95 / Warner Music

JAZZ - FEMININE
CD Set ________ **308662**
Scratch / Feb '96 / Koch / Scratch/BMG

JAZZ - MASCULINE
CD Set ________ **308652**
Scratch / Feb '96 / Koch / Scratch/BMG

JAZZ - SACRED AND SECULAR
CD ________ **DM 25CD**
Dormouse / Jun '92 / Jazz Music / Target/BMG

JAZZ AFTER HOURS
'Round midnight: *Gales, Larry* / Over the rainbow: *Webster, Ben* / I don't stand a ghost of a chance with you: *Jacquet, Illinois* / Autumn leaves: *Scott, Shirley* / Willow weep for me: *Edison, Harry* / I can't get started: *Gillespie, Dizzy* / Passion flower: *Ellington, Duke* / Tenderly: *Byas, Don* / Body and soul: *Hawkins, Coleman* / Embraceable you: *Eldridge, Roy* / Deep forest: *Hines, Earl 'Fatha'* / You've changed: *Thompson, Lucky* / Mighty low: *Buckner, Milt*
CD ________ **EMPRCD 571**
Emporio / May '95 / Disc

JAZZ ALBUM, THE
Leroy Brown: *Kidd, Carol* / Eye witness: *Newton, David* / Moon ray: *Martin, Claire* / Ally: *Smith, Tommy* / Partners in crime: *Martin, Claire* / Gentle rain: *Taylor, Martin* / Don't take your love: *Kidd, Carol* / It's only a paper moon: *Grappelli, Stephane & Martin Taylor* / Lean baby: *Kidd, Carol* / Home from home: *Newton, David* / Old boyfriends: *Martin, Claire* / Angel's camp: *Taylor, Martin* / Please don't talk about me: *Kidd, Carol*
CD ________ **AKD 032**
Linn / Sep '94 / PolyGram

JAZZ AND BIG BAND (4CD Set)
On the sunny side of the street: *Armstrong, Louis* / Everything goes: *Ellington, Duke* / Bird of paradise: *Davis, Miles & Charlie Parker* / Ain't misbehavin': *Waller, Fats* / When my dreamboat comes home: *Rushing, Jimmy* / St. Louis blues: *Witherspoon, Jimmy* / Me and the blues: *Bailey, Mildred* / Moose the mooche: *Davis, Miles* / Sweet Georgie Brown: *Cole, Nat 'King' Trio* / When the saints go marching in: *Armstrong, Louis* / Darktown strutters ball: *Lewis, Meade 'Lux'* / Jazz me blues: *Bechet, Sidney* / My man: *Holiday, Billie* / Street beat: *Parker, Charlie* / Tip toe topic: *Ellington, Duke* / St. Louis blues: *Dorsey, Jimmy* / Smooth sailing: *Fitzgerald, Ella* / Georgia on my mind: *Carmichael, Hoagy Orchestra* / Slow boat to China: *Parker, Charlie* / Honey honey: *Charles, Ray* / C'est si bon: *Armstrong, Louis* / Don't blame me: *Davis, Miles & Charlie Parker* / Harlem speaks: *Ellington, Duke* / Tiger rag: *Henderson, Fletcher* / Mame: *Armstrong, Louis* / Four hands: *Mingus, Charles* / Sonny moon for two: *Rollins, Sonny* / Meet me where they play the blues: *Teagarden, Jack* / South rampart street parade: *Fountain, Pete* / Jelly roll blues: *Morton, Jelly Roll* / Tune of the hickory stick: *Adderley, Cannonball* / Lover man: *Holiday, Billie* / How high the moon: *Wilson, Teddy* / 'Round midnight: *Parker, Charlie* / Crosstown: *Ellington, Duke* / Scrapple from the apple: *Davis, Miles* / Crazeology: *Parker, Charlie & Dizzy Gillespie* / Panama rag: *Ory, Kid & Jimmy Noone* / Tea for two: *Armstrong, Louis* / Yes sir that's my baby: *Cole, Nat 'King' Trio* / April in Paris: *Miller, Glenn* / Begin the beguine: *Shaw, Artie* / Oh Johnny oh johnny oh: *Webb, Chick & Ella Fitzgerald* / Does your heart beat for me: *Morgan, Russ* / Cherokee: *Barnet, Charlie* / In a shanty in old shanty town: *Long, Johnny* / Harlem nocturne: *Barnet, Charlie* / Northwest passage: *Herman, Woody* / Let's dance: *Goodman, Benny* / So rare: *Dorsey, Jimmy* / Opus one: *Dorsey, Tommy* / Indiana: *Ellington, Duke* / Something new: *Basie, Count* / Love me or leave me: *Brown, Les & Doris Day* / I'll never be the same: *Krupa, Gene* / Dipsy doodle: *Clinton, Larry* / Margie: *Lunceford, Jimmie* / Night and day: *Shaw, Artie* / Count steps in: *Basie, Count* / Sultry sunset: *Ellington, Duke* / My heart belongs to daddy: *Shaw, Artie* / I got rhythm: *Dorsey, Jimmy* / Frankie and Johnny: *Goodman, Benny* / Basin street blues: *Webb, Chick & Ella Fitzgerald* / Moonlight serenade: *Miller, Glenn* / Taking a chance on love: *Dorsey, Tommy* / Jumpin' at the woodside: *Basie, Count* / Take the 'a' train: *Ellington, Duke* / September song: *Brown, Les & Doris Day* / Blowin' up a storm: *Herman, Woody* / Skyliner: *Barnet, Charlie* / Linger awhile: *Morgan, Russ* / Fools rush in: *Dorsey, Jimmy* / On the sunny side of the street: *Dorsey, Tommy* / Perdido: *Ellington, Duke* / My heart stood still: *Shaw, Artie* / Jersey bounce: *Goodman, Benny* / Blue and sentimental: *Basie, Count* / Caldonia: *Herman, Woody* / I'm forever blowing bubbles: *Brown, Les*
CD Set ________ **QUAD 005**
Tring / Nov '96 / Tring

JAZZ ANTHOLOGY 1942 (2CD Set)
CD Set ________ **152052**
EPM / Mar '94 / ADA / Discovery

JAZZ ANTHOLOGY 1943-1944 (2CD Set)
CD ________ **152302**
EPM / Apr '95 / ADA / Discovery

JAZZ ANTHOLOGY 1945 (2CD Set)
CD ________ **152342**
EPM / Jul '96 / ADA / Discovery

JAZZ AT THE FLAMINGO (2CD Set)
All star special: *Flamingo All Stars* / Hucklebuck: *Dankworth, John Quintet* / Let's call the whole thing off: *Klein, Harry & Derek Smith Trio* / Yesterday: *Rendell, Don Quartet* / Early one morning: *Crombie, Tony Orchestra* / Basie talks: *Scott, Ronnie & His Orchestra* / Mama, he treats your baby mean: *Ross, Annie & Tony Crombie Orchestra* / C'est si bon: *Ross, Annie & Tony Crombie* / IPA special: *Scott, Ronnie Sextet* / Royal Ascot: *Jazz Couriers* / Plebus: *Jazz Couriers* / Serpent: *Jazz Couriers* / Stompin': *Scott, Ronnie Quintet* / Lucky bean: *Scott, Ronnie Quintet* / 12x5: *Whittle, Tommy Quintet* / Jamba: *Crombie, Tony & Jazz Inc* / Just play: *Thompson, Eddie Trio* / Moveable: *Thompson, Eddie Trio* / Wait and see: *London Jazz Quartet* / Fishin' the blues: *London Jazz Quartet* / Gut bucket: *McNair, Harold Quintet* / Girl in blue: *Kinsey, Tony Quintet* / I only have eyes for you: *Holiday, Billie* / Foggy day in London town: *McRae, Carmen* / Robbin's nest: *Fitzgerald, Ella* / I've got the world on a string: *Torme, Mel* / Misty: *Eckstine, Billy* / Autumn in Cuba: *Le Sage, Bill & Ronnie Ross Quartet* / Gentlemen friend: *Vaughan, Sarah* / Zsa Zsa Gabor: *Moule, Ken & The London Jazz Chamber Group*
CD Set ________ **FBB 911**
Ember / Nov '96 / TKO Magnum

JAZZ AT THE PHILHARMONIC (The First Concert 1944)
Lester leaps in / Tea for two / Blues / Body and soul / I've found a new baby / Rosetta / Bugle call rag
CD ________ **5216462**
Verve / Jan '94 / PolyGram

JAZZ AT THE PHILHARMONIC - LONDON 1969 (2CD Set)
Ow / Stardust / Yesterdays / You go to my head / Tin tin deo / Champ / Woman you must be crazy / Goin' to Chicago / Stormy Monday / Shiny stockings / Undecided / I've got the world on a string / LOVE / Blue Lou / I can't get started (with you) / September song / Body and soul / Bean stalkin' / What is this thing called love
CD Set ________ **2PACD 26201192**
Pablo / Apr '94 / Cadillac / Complete/ Pinnacle

JAZZ AT THE PHILHARMONIC - STOCKHOLM '55 (The Exciting Battle)
Little David / Ow / Sticks / Man I love / I'll never be the same / Skylark / My old flame
CD ________ **PACD 23107132**
Pablo / Apr '94 / Cadillac / Complete/ Pinnacle

JAZZ AT THE PHILHARMONIC: HARTFORD 1953
Cotton tail / Airmail special / Swinging on a star / Man I love / Seven come eleven / DB blues / I cover the waterfront / Up-'n'-Adam
CD ________ **CD 2308240**
Pablo / Apr '94 / Cadillac / Complete/ Pinnacle

JAZZ, BLUE & SENTIMENTAL
CD ________ **DCD 5310**
Disky / Dec '93 / Disky / THE

JAZZ CAFE VOL.1
So what: *Johnson, J.J.* / Lullaby: *Johnson, J.J.* / Watermelon man: *Hendricks/Lambert* / On Green Dolphin Street: *Burton, Gary* / 'Round midnight: *Rollins, Sonny* / King Porter stomp: *Evans, Gil* / Night in Tunisia: *Gillespie, Dizzy* / Milestones: *Hargrove, Roy* / Every time we say goodbye: *Hollyday, Christopher* / Superwoman: *Woods, Phil* / Expansions: *Woods, L.L.* / Autumn leaves: *Moody, James* / Somewhere over the rainbow: *Baker, Chet* / My funny valentine: *Desmond, Phil* / Just a lucky so and so: *Ellington, Duke* / Take the 'A' train: *Ellington, Duke* / Love me or leave me: *Horne, Lena* / Creole love call: *Nelson, Oliver* / April in Paris: *Davison, 'Wild' Bill* / Naima: *Ruiz, Hilton* / lady day and john coltrane: *Scott-Heron, Gil*
CD ________ **74321131382**
Novus / Feb '93 / BMG

JAZZ CAFE: AFTERHOURS
Somewhere over the rainbow: *Baker, Chet* / April in Paris: *Hawkins, Coleman* / Yesterday: *Feliciano, Jose* / I'll never be the same: *Reinhardt, Django*
CD ________ **74321214472**
Jazz Cafe / Aug '94 / BMG

JAZZ CAFE: AT THE MOVIES
What a wonderful world: *Armstrong, Louis* / Every time we say goodbye: *Baker, Chet* / My man: *Hawkins, Coleman* / Oh green Dolphin Street: *Hodges, Johnny*
CD ________ **74321263672**
Jazz Cafe / Mar '95 / BMG

JAZZ CAFE: FOR LOVERS
Petite fleur: *Bechet, Sidney* / My funny valentine: *Desmond, Paul* / Nearness of you: *Mulligan, Gerry* / Lover man: *Gillespie, Dizzy*
CD ________ **74321214492**
Jazz Cafe / Aug '94 / BMG

JAZZ CAFE: GUITAR
Blue Lou: *Norvo, Red & Tal Farlow* / Beautiful moons ago: *Pizzarelli, John* / Spoons: *Scofield, John* / For BB King: *Walker, T-Bone*
CD ________ **74321263692**
Jazz Cafe / Mar '95 / BMG

JAZZ CAFE: LATIN
Manteca: *Gillespie, Dizzy* / Cherry pink: *Prado, Perez* / Mambo Inn: *Ruiz, Hilton* / Manna de carnaval: *Thielemans, Jean 'Toots'*
CD ________ **74321263702**
Jazz Cafe / Mar '95 / BMG

JAZZ CAFE: STANDARDS
After you've gone: *Basie, Count* / Mood indigo: *Bechet, Sidney* / Georgia on my mind: *Beiderbecke, Bix* / Blue skies: *Goodman, Benny*
CD ________ **74321263722**
Jazz Cafe / Mar '95 / BMG

JAZZ CAFE: SUMMERTIME
Norwegian wood: *Burton, Gary* / Birdland after dark: *Puente, Tito* / Sidewinder: *Ruiz, Hilton* / Expansions: *Smith, Lonnie Liston*
CD ________ **74321214442**
Jazz Cafe / Aug '94 / BMG

JAZZ CAFE: SWINGTIME
Take the 'A' train: *Ellington, Duke* / Flying home: *Hampton, Lionel* / Song of the Volga boatmen: *Miller, Glenn* / Creole love call: *Nelson, Oliver*
CD ________ **74321214482**
Jazz Cafe / Aug '94 / BMG

JAZZ CAFE: THE BLUES
Back o' town blues: *Armstrong, Louis* / Stormy Monday blues: *Eckstine, Billy* / Ain't nobody's business if I do: *Waller, Fats* / Everyday I have the blues: *Williams, Joe*
CD ________ **74321214452**
Jazz Cafe / Aug '94 / BMG

JAZZ CAFE: THE PIANO
'Round midnight: *Monk, Thelonious* / Pitter panther patter: *Ellington, Duke* / My blue heaven: *Peterson, Oscar* / Freakish: *Morton, Jelly Roll*
CD ________ **74321131382**
Jazz Cafe / Jun '94 / BMG

JAZZ CAFE: THE SINGERS
I'm just a lucky so and so: *Ellington, Duke* / How long has this been going on: *Horne, Lena* / Any old time: *Holiday, Billie* / lady day and john coltrane: *Scott-Heron, Gil*
CD ________ **74321214462**
Jazz Cafe / Aug '94 / BMG

JAZZ CAFE: TRUMPET & SAXOPHONE
Wee: *Hargrove, Roy* / Blue Getz blues: *Herman, Woody & Stan Getz* / Angel: *Evans, Gil* / Two of a mind: *Mulligan, Gerry & Paul Desmond*
CD ________ **74321263682**
Jazz Cafe / Mar '95 / BMG

JAZZ CELEBRATION (A Tribute To Carl Jefferson/4CD Set)
CD Set ________ **CCD 7005**
Concord Jazz / Nov '96 / New Note/ Pinnacle

JAZZ CITIES (4CD Set)
CD Set ________ **211761**
Radio France Jazz / Feb '97 / Harmonia Mundi

JAZZ CLASSICS
It's a sin to tell a lie / Potato head blues / Ostrich walk / Riverboat shuffle / Georgia on my mind / Struttin' with some barbecue / Creole jazz / I'm gonna sit right down and write myself a letter / Bourbon Street parade / Snag it / Sweet Georgia Brown / Sophisticated lady / This can't be love / I can't get started (with you) / After you've gone / Old grey bonnet / Old rugged cross / There will never be another you / Ain't misbehavin' / At the woodchoppers' ball
CD ________ **KAZCD 11**
Kaz / Feb '90 / BMG

JAZZ CLUB - TENOR SAX
CD ________ **8400312**
Verve / Jun '89 / PolyGram

JAZZ CLUB MAINSTREAM - TENOR AND BARITONE SAX
CD ________ **8451462**
Verve / Apr '91 / PolyGram

JAZZ COLLECTION (3CD Set)
CD Set ________ **TBXCD 507**
TrueTrax / Jan '96 / THE

JAZZ COLLECTION (2CD Set)
CD Set ________ **PBXCD 507**
Pulse / Nov '96 / BMG

JAZZ COLLECTION VOL.1, THE (When The Saints Go Marching In)
When the saints go marching in: *Armstrong, Louis* / Cotton tail: *Ellington, Duke* / Bugle call rag: *Goodman, Benny* / They can't take that away from me: *Holiday, Billie* / Jumpin' at the Woodside: *Basie, Count* / How high the moon: *Fitzgerald, Ella* / That old black

magic: *Calloway, Cab* / I can't give you anything but love: *Armstrong, Louis* / I can't believe that you're in love with me: *Garner, Erroll* / Morning after: *Lunceford, Jimmie* / Ain't misbehavin': *Waller, Fats* / Night and day: *Horne, Lena* / East of the sun: *Vaughan, Sarah* / High society: *Teagarden, Jack* / Take the 'A' train: *Ellington, Duke* / Love is a many splendoured thing: *Lynne, Gloria*
CD **100882**
CMC / May '97 / BMG

JAZZ COLLECTION VOL.2, THE (Sweet Georgia Brown)
Sweet Georgia Brown: *Cole, Nat 'King'* / Royal Garden blues: *Armstrong, Louis* / Lover come back to me: *Holiday, Billie* / I'm gonna sit right down and write myself a letter: *Waller, Fats* / What a difference a day makes: *Washington, Dinah* / Do nothin' 'til you hear from me: *Ellington, Duke* / Moonglow: *Garner, Erroll* / Mad about the boy: *Horne, Lena* / Swing low, sweet chariot: *Herman, Woody* / Jeepers creepers: *Armstrong, Louis* / If you can't sing it, you'll have to swing it (Mr. Paganini): *Fitzgerald, Ella* / In a mellow tone: *Basie, Count* / My romance: *Blakey, Art & The Jazz Messengers* / One o'clock jump: *Adderley, Cannonball* / Shine on harvest moon: *Dorsey, Jimmy* / I guess I'll have to change my plans: *Bennett, Tony & Count Basie Orchestra*
CD **100892**
CMC / May '97 / BMG

JAZZ COLLECTION VOL.3, THE (I Got Rhythm)
I got rhythm: *Dorsey, Jimmy* / Sophisticated lady: *Ellington, Duke* / Lady is a tramp: *Horne, Lena* / Nobody knows the trouble I've seen: *Armstrong, Louis* / Northwest passage: *Herman, Woody* / This could be the start of something else: *Lynne, Gloria* / I've got you under my skin: *Calloway, Cab* / Maple leaf rag: *Joplin, Scott* / Caravan: *Ellington, Duke* / Limehouse blues: *Mills Brothers* / Lemon drop: *Fitzgerald, Ella* / Stompin' at the Savoy: *Garner, Erroll* / Beau night in Hotchkiss Corners: *Day, Doris & Les Brown* / Yes sir that's my baby: *Cole, Nat 'King'* / Lulu's back in town: *Waller, Fats* / Swing brother swing: *Holiday, Billie*
CD **100902**
CMC / May '97 / BMG

JAZZ COLLECTION, THE (3CD Set)
When the saints go marching in: *Armstrong, Louis* / Cotton tail: *Ellington, Duke* / Bugle call rag: *Goodman, Benny* / They can't take that away from me: *Holiday, Billie* / Jumpin' at the Woodside: *Basie, Count* / How high the moon: *Fitzgerald, Ella* / That old black magic: *Calloway, Cab* / I can't give you anything but love: *Armstrong, Louis* / I can't believe that you're in love with me: *Garner, Erroll* / Morning after: *Lunceford, Jimmie* / Ain't misbehavin': *Waller, Fats* / Night and day: *Horne, Lena* / East of the sun and west of the moon: *Vaughan, Sarah* / High society: *Teagarden, Jack* / Take the 'A' train: *Ellington, Duke* / Love is a many splendoured thing: *Lynne, Gloria* / Sweet Georgia Brown: *Cole, Nat 'King'* / Royal Garden blues: *Armstrong, Louis* / Lover come back to me: *Holiday, Billie* / I'm gonna sit right down and write myself a letter: *Waller, Fats* / What a difference a day makes: *Washington, Dinah* / Do nothin' 'til you hear from me: *Ellington, Duke* / Moonglow: *Garner, Erroll* / Mad about the boy: *Horne, Lena* / Swing low, sweet chariot: *Herman, Woody* / Jeepers creepers: *Armstrong, Louis* / If you can't sing it, you'll have to swing it (Mr. Paganini): *Fitzgerald, Ella* / In a mellow tone: *Basie, Count* / My romance: *Blakey, Art & The Jazz Messengers* / One o'clock jump: *Adderley, Cannonball* / Shine on harvest moon: *Dorsey, Jimmy* / I guess I'll have to change my plans: *Bennett, Tony & Count Basie Orchestra* / I got rhythm: *Dorsey, Jimmy* / Sophisticated lady: *Ellington, Duke* / Lady is a tramp: *Horne, Lena* / Nobody knows the trouble I've seen: *Armstrong, Louis* / Northwest passage: *Herman, Woody* / This could be the start of something else: *Lynne, Gloria* / I've got you under my skin: *Calloway, Cab* / Maple leaf rag: *Joplin, Scott* / Caravan: *Ellington, Duke* / Limehouse blues: *Mills Brothers* / Lemon drop: *Fitzgerald, Ella* / Stompin' at the Savoy: *Garner, Erroll* / Beau night at Hotchkiss Corners: *Day, Doris & Les Brown* / Yes sir that's my baby: *Cole, Nat 'King'* / Lulu's back in town: *Waller, Fats* / Swing brother swing: *Holiday, Billie*
CD Set **100872**
CMC / May '97 / BMG

JAZZ COLLECTIVE
Blackbyrds' theme / EBFS / Golden wings / Mambo Inn / African bird / Casa forte / Cornbread / Reggins / Scarborough street fair / Lady smooth / You're gonna lose me / Backed up against the wall / Lifestyles / Quiet storm / Open your eyes you can fly / Ina's song
CD **CDBGPD 076**
Beat Goes Public / Feb '94 / Pinnacle

JAZZ COM BOSSA
CD **99 1602**
Ninetynine / Jul '96 / Timewarp

JAZZ COMEDY CLASSICS
CD **JCD 20**
Jass / Jan '87 / ADA / Cadillac / CM / Direct / Jazz Music

JAZZ CUTS VOL.1
CD **TMPCD 010**
Temple / Jun '95 / BMG

JAZZ CUTS VOL.2
CD **TMPCD 011**
Temple / Jun '95 / BMG

JAZZ CUTS VOL.3
CD **TMPCD 012**
Temple / Jun '95 / BMG

JAZZ DANCE CLASSICS VOL.1
CD **LHCD 010**
Luv n' Haight / Jul '96 / Timewarp

JAZZ DANCE CLASSICS VOL.2
CD **LHCD 013**
Luv n' Haight / Jul '96 / Timewarp

JAZZ DANCE CLASSICS VOL.3
CD **LHCD 015**
Luv n' Haight / Jul '96 / Timewarp

JAZZ DANCE CLASSICS VOL.4
CD **LHCD 021**
Luv n' Haight / Jul '96 / Timewarp

JAZZ DE SCENE VOL.1
CD **251 278 2**
Jazztime / Mar '90 / Discovery

JAZZ DE SCENE VOL.3 1938-1950
CD **8270962**
Jazztime / Dec '93 / Discovery

JAZZ ECHOES (A Magical Blend Of Music And The Sounds Of Nature)
CD **57772**
CMC / May '97 / BMG

JAZZ EVENT
CD **MECCACD 1034**
Music Mecca / Nov '94 / Cadillac / Jazz Music / Wellard

JAZZ FAVOURITES (3CD Set)
CD Set **KBOX 367**
Collection / Aug '97 / Target/BMG / TKO Magnum

JAZZ FOR JOY
CD **5319602**
Verve / Nov '96 / PolyGram

JAZZ FOR LOVERS
CD **DCD 5275**
Kenwest / Nov '92 / THE

JAZZ FOR LOVERS
CD **TRTCD 170**
TrueTrax / Feb '96 / THE

JAZZ FOR LOVERS
CD **CD 3538**
Cameo / Aug '95 / Target/BMG

JAZZ FOR LOVERS
I've got a crush on you: *Braff, Ruby* / When I fall in love: *Woodard, Rickey* / C'est si bon: *Armstrong, Louis* / Time after time: *Baker, Chet* / Love me: *Sims, Zoot* / More I see you: *Vaughan, Sarah* / Prelude to a kiss: *Vaughan, Sarah* / Blue and sentimental: *Powell, Seldon* / Gee baby ain't I good to you: *Greco, Buddy* / Love story: *Philips, Flip* / I like you you're nice: *Kral, Irene* / Can't we be friends: *Harrow, Nancy* / Teach me tonight: *Newton, David* / When a man loves a woman: *Scott, Shirley*
CD **EMPRCD 635**
Emporio / Jun '96 / Disc

JAZZ FOR SENSUAL LOVERS
CD **STB 2510**
Stash / Sep '95 / ADA / Cadillac / CM / Direct / Jazz Music

JAZZ FOR SENSUAL LOVERS: ROMANTIC GUITARS
CD **STB 2515**
Stash / Sep '95 / ADA / Cadillac / CM / Direct / Jazz Music

JAZZ FOR SENSUAL LOVERS: ROMANTIC SAXOPHONES
CD **STB 2512**
Stash / Sep '95 / ADA / Cadillac / CM / Direct / Jazz Music

JAZZ FOR YOU
CD **NNCD 901**
GRP / May '90 / New Note/BMG

JAZZ FROM ATLANTA 1923-1929
Eskimo song / Black cat blues / Georgia stomp / Home sweet home blues / My pretty girl / After that / Daylight's breaking blues / Hey hey / Atlanta gal / Lonesome lovesick got to have my daddy blues / Mean eyes / Bessie couldn't help it / When my sugar walks down the street / Blues have got me / Cheatin' on me / Go get 'em Caroline / Breakin' the leg / Tweedle dee tweedle doo / Hangin' around / Who'd be blue / Don't take that black bottom away / That's my girl / When Jenny does her low down dance
CD **CBC 1038**
Timeless Historical / Sep '97 / New Note/ Pinnacle

JAZZ FROM THE WINDY CITY 1927-1930
Sugar: *McKenzie & Condon's Chicagoans* / China boy: *McKenzie & Condon's Chicagoans* / Nobody's sweetheart: *McKenzie & Condon's Chicagoans* / Liza: *McKenzie & Condon's Chicagoans* / Bullfrog: *Pierce, Charles & his Orchestra* / Jazz me blues: *Pierce, Charles & his Orchestra* / I wish I could shimmy like my sister Kate: *Pierce, Charles & his Orchestra* / There'll be some changes made: *Chicago Rhythm Kings* / I've found a new baby: *Chicago Rhythm Kings* / Friars Point Shuffle: *Jungle Kings* / Darktown strutters ball: *Jungle Kings* / Jazz me blues (II): *Teschemacher, Frank* / Baby, won't you please come home: *Louisiana Rhythm Kings* / Copenhagen: *Schoebel, Elmer* / Prince of wails: *Schoebel, Elmer* / Wailing blues (I and II): *Cellar Boys* / Barrel House stomp (I, II and III): *Cellar Boys*
CD **CBC 1021**
Timeless Historical / Aug '94 / New Note/ Pinnacle

JAZZ FUNK AND FUSION
To prove my love: *Doheny, Ned* / Lion dance: *Hiroshima* / Hunt up wind: *Fukumura, Hiroshi* / Thighs high (grip your hips and move): *Browne, Tom* / By all means: *Mouzon, Alphonse & Herbie Hancock* / No problem: *Watanabe, Sadao* / Fly by night: *Ritenour, Lee* / Rag bag: *Grusin, Dave* / Central park: *Corea, Chick* / Disco dancing: *Turrentine, Stanley*
CD **VSOPCD 219**
Connoisseur Collection / Aug '95 / Pinnacle

JAZZ FUNK REVIVAL
Chameleon: *Jefferson, Eddie* / In the meantime: *Barron, Kenny* / Thank you falletinme be mice elf agin: *Jefferson, Eddie* / Walk that funky dog: *Bronstein, Stan* / Philadelphia bright: *Bishop, Walter Jr.* / In the middle of it all: *Creque, Neal* / Mean street nobridges: *Ponder, Jimmy* / Black love: *Garnett, Carlos* / Mystery of ages: *Garnett, Carlos* / Let us go (to higher hights): *Garnett, Carlos*
CD **PHOCD 8003**
Muse / Sep '95 / New Note/Pinnacle

JAZZ FUSION
Appetizer / Pulse / Blue love / Slow down / Safari / Elemental force / Razzia 1 / Miles gloriosus / Temesvar / Zick-o-mat / Mys chindli, chum weidli / Mediterranean / Square times on Times Square
CD **303242**
Hallmark / Jun '97 / Carlton

JAZZ FUSION VOL.1
Saxman: *Koz, Dave* / After the dance: *Fourplay* / Anniversary: *Albright, Gerald* / Thinkin' about tomorrow: *Incognito* / My summer vacation: *Patitucci, John* / Sade: *Kenny G* / Tourist in paradise: *Rippingtons* / Heart station: *Laws, Ronnie* / Come with me: *Jordan, Ronny* / Love will make it right: *Watanabe, Sadao* / Up town east: *Special EFX* / Show me the way: *Grant, Tom* / Reed my lips: *Scott, Tom*
CD **FUSIONCD 1**
Jazz Fusions / Jul '94 / Total/BMG

JAZZ FUSION VOL.2
After the love has gone: *Benoit/Freeman Project* / I don't know: *Wright, Betty* / Back to Memphis: *Sanborn, David* / Wind cries Mary: *Harrison, Donald* / Strutt everette: *Harp, Everette* / Restless: *James, Bob* / Walking in rhythm: *McBride, Joe* / Waiting in vain: *Ritenour, Lee* / Juju: *Miller, Marcus* / Save the best for last: *Meadows, Marion* / That's enough for me: *Austin, Patti* / Rainforest: *Hardcastle, Paul* / Love will find a way: *Lewis, Ramsey* / Justice's groove: *Clarke, Stanley*
CD **FUSIONCD 2**
Jazz Fusions / Oct '94 / Total/BMG

JAZZ FUSION VOL.3
Undercover: *Porter, Art* / Happy home: *James, Boney* / Doin' it: *Klugh, Earl* / Love is like a river: *Fattburger* / Between the sheets: *Fourplay* / 500 miles to go: *Duke, George* / Daydream: *Johnson, Mark* / For the love of you: *Brown, Norman* / Here to stay: *Metheny, Pat* / Goodbye Manhattan: *Pieces Of A Dream* / Mercy mercy me: *Special EFX* / Fine time to explain: *Spyro Gyra* / Don't get any better: *Scott, Tom* / Laid back: *Breaux, Zachary*
CD **FUSIONCD 3**
Jazz Fusions / Jul '95 / Total/BMG

JAZZ FUSION VOL.4
Fantasy: *Chinn, Daryle* / Whisk away: *Gable, Tony & 206* / Sunday mornin': *Powell, Doc* / Better days ahead: *Brown, Norman* / Secret garden: *Jones, Quincy* / Take me home to you: *Culbertson, Brian* / Wishful thinking: *Porter, Art* / Going all the way: *Rangell, Nelson* / We belong together: *Ravel, Freddie* / Back in the day: *White, Michael* / Summer nights: *Impromp2* / In the rhythm of my heart: *Mariano, Torcuato* / Play lady play: *Fourplay* / I just wanna stop: *Taylor, Joe*
CD **FUSIONCD 4**
Jazz Fusions / Nov '96 / Total/BMG

JAZZ FUTURES (Live In Concert)
Mode for John / Sterling Sylvia / Blue moon / Piccadilly square / Bewitched, bothered and bewildered / Stardust / Medgar Evers blues / You don't know what love is / Public eye
CD **02141631582**
Novus / Sep '93 / BMG

JAZZ GOES TO THE MOVIES
Puttin' on the Ritz / Crazy feet / Alone with my dreams / How I'm doin'/Dinah / One little kiss from you / I like a guy what takes his time / You're hi-de-hi-ing me / Gold diggers song / Pettin' in the park / Wo ist der mann / Nasty man / My future star / Oh I didn't know (you'd get that way) / Lulu's back in town / You are my lucky star / I've got a feeling you're fooling / Got a bran' new suit / Stompin' at the Savoy / Swing Mister Charlie / Smarty (you know it all) / I go for that / Who cares (as long as you care for me) / Just like taking candy from a baby / My my
CD **CBC 1020**
Timeless Historical / Aug '94 / New Note/ Pinnacle

JAZZ GREATS (2CD Set)
CD Set **DEMPCD 013**
Emporio / Mar '96 / Disc

JAZZ GUITAR CLASSICS
CD **OJCCD 6012**
Original Jazz Classics / Apr '92 / Complete/Pinnacle / Jazz Music / Wellard

JAZZ GUITAR VOL.1, THE
CD **CD 14528**
Jazz Portraits / Jan '94 / Jazz Music

JAZZ GUITAR VOL.1, THE
CD **CD 56007**
Jazz Roots / Aug '94 / Target/BMG

JAZZ GUITAR VOL.2, THE
CD **CD 14535**
Jazz Portraits / Jan '94 / Jazz Music

JAZZ GUITAR VOL.3, THE
CD **CD 14538**
Jazz Portraits / Jan '94 / Jazz Music

JAZZ GUITAR VOL.3, THE
CD **CD 56034**
Jazz Roots / Jul '95 / Target/BMG

JAZZ GUITAR VOL.4, THE
CD **CD 14542**
Jazz Portraits / Jan '94 / Jazz Music

JAZZ HOUSE GROOVES VOL.1
House jazz: *Don Carlos* / Ponteio: *JD's Jam* / Call me: *Everyday People* / Happy to love: *Bradshaw, Ricky* / Sax in the ozone: *Aaron, Robert* / Fuze: *Natarel Elamant* / People think I'm crazy: *Davis, Roy Jr. & Peven Everett* / Need: *4th Measure Men* / Gabrielle: *Davis, Roy Jr.* / Capital swing: *Jazz Doubt*
CD **CDHIGH 4**
High On Rhythm / Jan '97 / 3mv/Sony

JAZZ IN CALIFORNIA 1923-1930
CD **CBC 1034**
Timeless Historical / Jun '97 / New Note/ Pinnacle

JAZZ IN JAMAICA
CD **LG 21093**
Lagoon / Apr '94 / Grapevine/PolyGram

JAZZ IN ST. LOUIS 1924-1927
CD **CBC 1036**
Timeless Historical / Jun '97 / New Note/ Pinnacle

JAZZ IN TEXAS 1924-1930
CD **CBC 1033**
Timeless Historical / Jun '97 / New Note/ Pinnacle

JAZZ IN THE HOUSE VOL.1
Our mute horn: *Masters At Work* / Gummed: *Zig Zag* / I got jazz in my soul: *Just 4 Groovers* / Into the kick with Tito: *Deep Audio Penetration* / Way I feel: *Musical Expression* / Sublime: *Tickle* / Bassline: *DC Track Team* / Secret code: *Jazz Documents* / Supreme law: *Harmonious Thump* / Warehouse Vs the Ritz: *Battle Of The D.J's* / Sax track: *M&J Project* / Souffle: *Mondo Grosso*
CD **SLIPCD 025**
Slip 'n' Slide / Mar '95 / Amato Disco / Prime / RTM/Disc / Vital

JAZZ IN THE HOUSE VOL.2
Theme from change: *Daphne* / Buff dance: *Masters At Work* / My Mama said: *St. Germain* / Foot therapy: *Damier, Chez* / I'm leaving you: *Ulysses* / Innocence and inspiration: *Elements Of Live* / New Jersey deep: *Black Science Orchestra* / Tank: *Global Logic* / Moonshine: *Kenlou* / Equinox: *Code 718* / Acid ensemble: *Drivetrain* / Wet dreams: *Mada*
CD **SLIPCD 030**
Slip 'n' Slide / Sep '95 / Amato Disco / Prime / RTM/Disc / Vital

JAZZ IN THE HOUSE VOL.3 (2CD Set)
CD Set **SLIPCD 47**
Slip 'n' Slide / Sep '96 / Amato Disco / Prime / RTM/Disc / Vital

JAZZ IN THE HOUSE VOL.4
CD **SLIPCD 60**
Slip 'n' Slide / Jul '97 / Amato Disco / Prime / RTM/Disc / Vital

JAZZ IN THE THIRTIES (2CD Set)
CD Set **CDSW 8457/8**
DRG / '88 / Discovery / New Note/ Pinnacle

JAZZ JAMAICA
CD **SOCD 1140**
Studio One / Aug '94 / Jet Star

JAZZ JAZZ JAZZ
CD REVCC 003
Revco / Aug '94 / Grapevine/PolyGram / Timewarp

JAZZ JUICE VOL.1
Miles: *Davis, Miles* / Jeannine: *Jefferson, Eddie* / Boss tres bien: *Quartette Tres Bien* / Cubano chant: *Blakey, Art* / Rhoda: *Mendes, Sergio* / Mas que nada: *Mendes, Sergio* / I'll bet you thought I'd never find you: *Hendricks, Jon* / It don't mean a thing if it ain't got that swing: *Schurr, Diane* / I believe in love: *Longo, Pat* / Crickets sing for anamaria: *Valle, Marcus* / Do it fluid: *Dirty Dozen Brass Band* / Take five: *McCrae, Carmen & Dave Brubeck* / Dat dere: *Brown, Oscar Jr.* / Sidewinder: *Herman, Woody & His Herd* / Wack wack: *Young-Holt Trio* / It's a trip: *Last Poets*
CD SOUNDSCD 2
Street Sounds / Oct '94 / Beechwood/BMG

JAZZ JUICE VOL.2
Pigmy part 1: *Larkin, Billy & The Delegates* / Cerveza: *Brown, Boots & His Blockbusters* / Do it the hard way: *Baker, Chet* / Who's afraid of Virginia Woolf: *Brown, James* / Got my mojo working: *Smith, Jimmy* / Listen love: *Lucien, Jon* / Jazz jump: *King Pleasure* / Mardi gras: *Smith, Lonnie Liston* / Minor chant: *Smith, Lonnie* / Girl from Ipanema: *Rawls, Lou* / Ain't nobody here but us chickens: *Murphy, Mark* / Call me: *Wilson, Nancy* / Work song: *Brown, Oscar Jr.* / Fever: *Lee, Peggy* / Samba: *Mullins, Rob* / Hit the road Jack: *Davison, 'Wild' Bill*
CD SOUNDSCD 4
Street Sounds / Mar '95 / Beechwood/BMG

JAZZ JUICE VOL.3
Hey Leroy, your Mama's callin' you: *Castor, Jimmy* / Shoshana: *Tjader, Cal* / Tema da alma Latina: *Matos, Bobby* / Take five: *Puente, Tito* / Yumbamabe: *Sanchez, Poncho* / Don't be blue: *Jackie & Roy* / So high: *Lawson, Janet* / You've got to have freedom: *Sanders, Pharoah* / Soul bossa nova: *Jones, Quincy* / Triste: *Shepherd, Cybill* / Bossa nova ova: *Mitchell, Billy* / Boogaloo in room 802: *Bobo, Willie* / Never was love: *Roberts, Judy* / Who will buy: *Lucien, Jon* / Ordinary guy: *Bataan, Joe*
CD SOUNDSCD 6
Street Sounds / Jul '95 / Beechwood/BMG

JAZZ JUNGLE
CD JAZIDCD 142
Acid Jazz / Jun '96 / Disc

JAZZ KANSAS CITY STYLEZ
CD TPZ 1036
Topaz Jazz / Jan '96 / Cadillac / Pinnacle

JAZZ LADIES VOL.4
Burst in with the dawn / Everything must change / I'm coming home / St. Louis blues / Sorrowful blues / Baby doll / My foolish heart / As time goes by / I only have eyes for you / Where or when / It's a blue world / Saving myself for you / You can't be mine / Sugar blues
CD CDSGPBJZ 29
Prestige / May '96 / Cadillac / Complete/ Pinnacle

JAZZ LADIES VOL.5
Empty bed blues / Chicago bound blues / Alexander's ragtime band / Back water blues / Georgia on my mind / I cried for you / Love me or leave me / Man I love / Strictly for Dixie / Undecided / Angel eyes / My one and only love / Masquerade is over / Mr. Magic
CD CDSGPBJZ 30
Prestige / May '96 / Cadillac / Complete/ Pinnacle

JAZZ LIMITED VOL.1
CD DE 226
Delmark / Jun '95 / ADA / Cadillac / CM / Direct / Hot Shot

JAZZ LINKS
Be bop - what's the matter: *Murata, Yoichi & Solid Brass* / Impressions: *Kankawa* / Hopscotch: *Smith, Roger* / Real deal: *Special EFX* / Whisper not: *Nakamoto, Mari* / Cavendo na rosiera: *Yamashita, Yosuke* / Willow weep for me: *Watts, Ernie* / Danae: *Malta* / Leilani: *Minucci, Chieli* / Deep focus: *Johnson, Mark* / Back in love again: *Sea, David* / Straight no chaser: *Holman, Bill Band* / I didn't know what time it was: *Lundy, Carmen*
CD JVC 90202
JVC / Aug '97 / Direct / New Note/Pinnacle / Vital/SAM

JAZZ LOFT SESSIONS
CD ADC 3
Douglas Music / May '97 / Cadillac / New Note/Pinnacle

JAZZ MASTERPIECES VOL.1
CD PLSCD 151
Pulse / Feb '97 / BMG

JAZZ MASTERPIECES VOL.2
CD PLSCD 152
Pulse / Feb '97 / BMG

JAZZ MASTERS
BK's broiler: *Katz, Bruce* / Aurora: *Calderazzo, Joey* / Sensei: *Willis, Larry* / Blues on the corner: *Palmer, Jeff* / Tuda muda: *Lewis, Vic* / Angels at play: *Fambrough, Charles* / Mirror puzzle: *Akagi, Kei* / Suite for Frida Kahlo: *Newton, James* / Gloria's step: *Mokave* / Mermaid: *Arbuckle, Les* / My one and only love: *Wallace, Bennie* / Free to dream: *Binney, David*
CD AQCD 1035
Audioquest / Mar '96 / ADA / New Note/ Pinnacle

JAZZ MASTERS (The Best Of Jazz Masters)
Sweet Georgia Brown: *Reinhardt, Django & Stephane Grappelli* / Jam blues: *Hampton, Lionel & Oscar Peterson* / I've got my love to keep me warm: *Fitzgerald, Ella & Louis Armstrong* / Last night when we were young: *Burrell, Kenny & Gil Evans* / Polka dots and moonbeams: *Young, Lester* / Ricardo's dilemma: *Nelson, Oliver* / Organ grinder's swing: *Smith, Jimmy* / Stormy weather: *Holiday, Billie* / Ballad: *Mulligan, Gerry* / Soul sauce: *Tjader, Cal* / March on, swan lake: *Kirk, Rahsaan Roland* / Words can't describe: *Vaughan, Sarah* / Cocktails for two: *Hawkins, Coleman & Ben Webster* / Summertime: *Baker, Chet* / Cherokee: *Brown, Clifford & Max Roach* / Peanut vendor: *Mann, Herbie*
CD 5298662
Verve / Oct '96 / PolyGram

JAZZ MASTERS (Big Band Jazz)
CD CDMFP 6294
Music For Pleasure / Mar '97 / EMI

JAZZ MASTERS (Jazz Vocalisers)
CD CDMFP 6295
Music For Pleasure / Mar '97 / EMI

JAZZ MASTERS VOL.1
CD MATCD 333
Castle / Apr '95 / BMG

JAZZ MASTERS VOL.2
CD MATCD 334
Castle / Apr '95 / BMG

JAZZ MEETS AFRICA
CD 5317202
MPS Jazz / Feb '97 / PolyGram

JAZZ MEETS BRAZIL
CD 5331332
MPS Jazz / Mar '97 / PolyGram

JAZZ MESSENGERS VOL.1, THE
CD CD 53128
Giants Of Jazz / Nov '92 / Cadillac / Jazz Music / Target/BMG

JAZZ MESSENGERS VOL.2, THE
CD CD 53129
Giants Of Jazz / Nov '92 / Cadillac / Jazz Music / Target/BMG

JAZZ MOODS
CD TRTCD 126
TrueTrax / Dec '94 / THE

JAZZ MOODS
CD MACCD 133
Autograph / Aug '96 / BMG

JAZZ MOODS VOL.1
CD JWD 102206
JWD / Sep '93 / Target/BMG

JAZZ 'N' STEEL
CD DE 4013
Delos / Feb '94 / Nimbus

JAZZ NEW ORLEANS STYLE
CD TPZ 1049
Topaz Jazz / Jun '96 / Cadillac / Pinnacle

JAZZ NEWBEATS VOL.1 (Good Feelings)
Goodfeelin': *DJ First Klas* / Rebel: *Delaney's Rhythm Section* / High hopes: *Forest Mighty Black* / Moodswing: *Outside* / Searching: *Takemura, Nobukazu & D.C. Lee* / Underwater love: *Smoke City* / Revolutionary woman of the windmill: *Up Bustle & Out* / Son of mook: *Red Snapper* / Mella: *DJ Food* / Strange life: *Count Basic* / Zitti zitti: *Aeroplanitaliani* / Psycodelico: *Reminiscence Quartet*
CD CDNBT 1
New Beats / Jun '96 / 3mv/Sony

JAZZ NEWBEATS VOL.2 (Mind Fluid)
Scat attack: *Michiru, Monday* / Ghittoni: *Derek Jarman Blues* / At home in space: *Fila Brazillia* / Pleasure and pain: *Project 23* / Creator has a matter plan: *Routine* / Blowin' it: *Herbaliser & Chris Bowden* / Jazz hypnosis: *First Priority* / Cosmic jam: *DJ Food* / Tutta la notte: *Zona 45* / Mind fluid: *Nu Yorican Soul* / Let the hustlers play: *Pulse & Tango* / Latin joint: *Baby Buddah Heads*
CD CDNBT 2
New Beats / Apr '97 / 3mv/Sony

JAZZ NOT HOUSE VOL.1
Satsuki: *Giant Step* / Vibe Providin': *Peace Bureau* / Black thoughts: *African Dream* / Set me free: *Watts, Alvin 'Bobby'* / Try my lovin': *Bluejean* / On the sand: *Groove Thing* / Jazz impressions: *African Dream* / Hands of a raindrop: *Tiny Bubbles*
CD EBCD 53
Eightball / Jan '95 / Vital

JAZZ NOT JAZZ VOL.2 (The New Breed)
New jazz swing: *Now School* / Yeah: *Jazzy Grooves* / Love's fantasy: *Now School* / Ain't really down: *Shaft, Jon* / Lost: *Headshock* / Work: *Bedroom Boys* / Rize: *Fuzion* / Keep on: *Jazz not Jazz*
CD WORLD 003CD
World Series / Aug '93 / Vital

JAZZ ON A SUMMER'S DAY
Take five: *Brubeck, Dave* / Summertime: *Vaughan, Sarah* / Moanin': *Blakey, Art & The Jazz Messengers* / Man I love: *Lee, Peggy* / Girl from Ipanema: *Getz, Stan & Astrud Gilberto* / So what: *Davis, Miles* / Mack the knife: *Armstrong, Louis* / Got my mojo working: *Smith, Jimmy* / Birdland: *Weather Report* / Hymn to freedom: *Peterson, Oscar*
CD CTVCD 108
Castle / Jan '95 / BMG

JAZZ PARADE 1940-1960'S
CD CD 53025
Giants Of Jazz / Mar '92 / Cadillac / Jazz Music / Target/BMG

JAZZ PIANO VOL.1 (1935-1942)
CD 251 282 2
Jazztime / Mar '90 / Discovery

JAZZ PIONEERS VOL.2 (The Sound Of London)
CD EX 3392
Instinct / Nov '96 / Timewarp

JAZZ ROMANCE, A
Speak low: *Schurr, Diane* / One heart calling: *Rangell, Nelson* / Cross your mind: *Howard, George* / Hurricane country: *Grusin, Dave* / First time love: *Austin, Patti* / Malibu: *Ritenour, Lee* / Pieces of a heart: *Anderson, Carl* / Sarah Jane: *Lewis, Ramsey* / Kei's song: *Benoit, David*
CD GRP 97902
Golden Encore / Sep '94 / BMG

JAZZ 'ROUND MIDNIGHT - PIANO
CD 8409372
Verve / Feb '91 / PolyGram

JAZZ 'ROUND MIDNIGHT - SAXOPHONE
CD 8409512
Verve / Feb '91 / PolyGram

JAZZ 'ROUND MIDNIGHT - TRUMPET
CD 5110372
Verve / Apr '91 / PolyGram

JAZZ 'ROUND MIDNIGHT - VOICES
CD 8409462
Verve / Feb '91 / PolyGram

JAZZ SAMPLER
CD GMCD 6239
Gemini / Dec '89 / Cadillac

JAZZ SATELLITES VOL.1 (Electrification/2CD Set)
I am an epigram for life: *Styler, Divine* / Mars in Libra: *Henderson, Eddie* / Karin's mode: *Garbarek, Jan* / Universal conciousness: *Coltrane, Alice* / Gospel comes to New Guinea: *23 Skidoo* / Andromeda strain: *Melle, Gil* / Internal bleeding: *Bedouin Ascent* / Twilight zone: *Connors, Norman* / Satelittes are spinning: *Sun Ra* / 3.38: *Pop Group* / Man without a country: *Martin, Stu & John Surman* / Bullroarer: *Krakatu* / Milk rock: *Organization* / Rated X: *Davis, Miles* / Equals: *Macero, Teo* / Black mystery has been revealed: *Roland* / Beyond games: *Williams, Tony* / Bride of sloth: *Slab* / Goose and lucky: *Cooder, Ry* / Water: *Henderson, Joe* / Rima: *Headhunters* / Brown rice: *Cherry, Don* / Drive towards the smoke: *UI* / New power: *Fat* / Science fiction: *Coleman, Ornette* / Attack impulse: *16-17* / Nobu: *Hancock, Herbie*
CD Set AMBT 12
Virgin / Jul '96 / EMI

JAZZ SAXOPHONE, THE
Five four train: *Fortune, Sonny* / Sometimes I feel like a Motherless child: *Freeman, Chico* / Celebration: *Giuffre, Jimmy* / If I could be with you one hour tonight: *Hawkins, Coleman* / Passion flower: *Hodges, Johnny* / Thanks for the memory: *Konitz, Lee* / Out of nowhere: *Liebmann, David* / Spanish eyes: *Philips, Flip* / Nuestro bolero: *Paquito D'Rivera* / Let me tell you why: *Shanky, Bud* / Fred: *Sims, Zoot* / Ballad: *Woods, Phil*
CD EMPRCD 609
Emporio / Jun '96 / Disc

JAZZ SCENE, THE
CD 5216612
Verve / Feb '95 / PolyGram

JAZZ SELECTION VOL.1, THE
On the sunny side of the street: *Armstrong, Louis* / Everything goes: *Ellington, Duke* / Bird of paradise: *Davis, Miles & Charlie Parker* / Ain't misbehavin': *Waller, Fats* / When my dreamboat comes home: *Rushing, Jimmy* / St. Louis blues: *Witherspoon, Jimmy* / ME and the blues: *Bailey, Mildred* / Moose the mooche: *Davis, Miles* / Sweet Georgia brown: *Cole, Nat 'King' Trio* / When the Saints go marching in: *Armstrong, Louis* / Darktown strutters ball: *Lewis, Meade 'Lux'* / Jazz me blues: *Bechet, Sidney* / My man: *Holiday, Billie* / Street beat: *Parker, Charlie* / Tip toe topic: *Ellington, Duke* / St. Louis blues: *Dorsey, Jimmy* / Flying home: *Fitzgerald, Ella* / Georgia on my mind: *Carmichael, Hoagy Orchestra* / Slow boat to China: *Parker, Charlie* / Honey honey: *Charles, Ray*
CD QED 022
Tring / Nov '96 / Tring

JAZZ SELECTION VOL.2, THE
C'est si bon / Don't blame me / Harlem speaks / Tiger rag / Mame / Four hands / Sonny moon for two / Meet me where they play the blues / South Rampart street parade / Jelly roll blues / Tune of the hickory stick / Lover man / How high the moon / 'Round midnight / Crosstown / Scrapple from the apple / Crazeology / Panama rag / Tea for two / Yes sir, that's my baby
CD QED 023
Tring / Nov '96 / Tring

JAZZ SELECTION, THE (4CD Set)
One O'clock jump: *Basie, Count* / 'Round midnight: *Parker, Charlie* / At long last love: *Horne, Lena* / Something new: *Basie, Count* / Out of nowhere: *Davis, Miles* / King Porter stomp: *Goodman, Benny* / Lover come back to me: *Fitzgerald, Ella* / How high the moon: *Parker, Charlie* / Sweet Georgia Brown: *Cole, Nat 'King'* / Mooche: *Ellington, Duke* / More than you know: *Horne, Lena* / Mission to Moscow: *Horne, Lena* / Night in Tunisia: *Davis, Miles* / Basin Street blues: *Fitzgerald, Ella* / Crosstown: *Ellington, Duke* / My blue heaven: *Shaw, Artie* / Street beat: *Parker, Charlie* / All of me: *Basie, Count* / Black and tan fantasy: *Ellington, Duke* / Basin Street blues: *Armstrong, Louis* / Yardbird suite: *Davis, Miles* / I struck a match in the dark: *Basie, Count* / Rumbop concerto: *Gillespie, Dizzy* / Nobody knows the trouble I've seen: *Horne, Lena* / Starlit hour: *Fitzgerald, Ella* / On the sunny side of the street: *Cole, Nat 'King'* / Caravan: *Ellington, Duke* / Fascinating rhythm: *Goodman, Benny* / My heart stood still: *Shaw, Artie* / Ornithology: *Davis, Miles* / Tiger rag: *Armstrong, Louis* / Blue juice: *Barnet, Charlie* / Platterbrains: *Basie, Count* / Blue prelude: *Horne, Lena* / Stompin' at the Savoy: *Horne, Lena* / Yes sir that's my baby: *Cole, Nat 'King'* / Move: *Parker, Charlie* / Bugle call rag: *Goodman, Benny* / Sophisticated lady: *Ellington, Duke* / Moose the mooche: *Davis, Miles* / Cannon's blues: *Adderley, Cannonball* / When the saints go marching in: *Armstrong, Louis* / Embraceable you: *Davis, Miles* / It's only a paper moon: *Cole, Nat 'King'* / Down for double: *Basie, Count* / Little girl blue: *Basie, Count* / Bird of paradise: *Parker, Charlie* / Study in soulphony: *Gillespie, Dizzy* / Stairway to the stars: *Fitzgerald, Ella* / Ring dem bells: *Ellington, Duke* / Sugarfoot stomp: *Ellington, Duke* / Scuttlebutt: *Shaw, Artie* / Northwest passage: *Herman, Woody* / It's a rainy day: *Horne, Lena* / (Back home again in) Indiana: *Armstrong, Louis* / Feather merchant: *Basie, Count* / Riff raff: *Parker, Charlie* / Trouble with me is you: *Cole, Nat 'King'* / Somebody stole my gal: *Goodman, Benny* / There is no greater love: *Adderley, Cannonball* / That old magic: *Fitzgerald, Ella* / Honeysuckle rose: *Ellington, Duke* / Yes sir that's my baby: *Cole, Nat 'King'* / My old flame: *Basie, Count* / Love me or leave me: *Horne, Lena* / On the sunny side of the street: *Armstrong, Louis* / Parker's mood: *Parker, Charlie* / Three hearts in a tangle: *Gillespie, Dizzy* / Bijou: *Herman, Woody* / Don't be that way: *Goodman, Benny* / I can't get started (with you): *Shaw, Artie* / I can't remember to forget: *Barnet, Charlie* / Flying home: *Fitzgerald, Ella* / Ease it: *Adderley, Cannonball* / How high the moon: *Ellington, Duke* / Slow boat to China: *Parker, Charlie* / Don't blame me: *Parker, Charlie* / (Back home again in) Indiana: *Armstrong, Louis* / Fiesta in blue: *Basie, Count* / Bird of paradise: *Davis, Miles* / Get happy: *Goodman, Benny*
CD Set TFP 005
Tring / Nov '92 / Tring

JAZZ SHOWCASE
Basie: *Basie, Count Orchestra* / Reunion blues: *Peterson, Oscar* / So wistfully sad: *Brubeck, Dave* / Gone with the wind: *Short, Bobby* / Jo-Wes: *Pass, Joe* / Paraiso: *Mulligan, Gerry & Jane Duboc* / Little suede shoes: *Ruiz, Hilton* / Tour de force: *Hampton, Slide & The Jazz Masters* / Here's to life: *Williams, Joe & George Shearing* / Bird feathers: *Shearing, George* / I'm gonna go fishin': *Torme, Mel* / In the wee small hours of the morning: *Brown, Ray Trio* / Bittersweet: *Bryson, Jeanie* / Lullaby of Birdland: *Jamal, Ahmad*
CD CD 83342
Telarc / Apr '94 / Conifer/BMG

JAZZ THAT THE WORLD FORGOT VOL.1 (Jazz Classics Of The 1920's)
CD YAZ 2024
Yazoo / Nov '96 / ADA / CM / Koch

JAZZ THAT THE WORLD FORGOT VOL.2 (Jazz Classics Of The 1920's)
CD YAZ 2025
Yazoo / Nov '96 / ADA / CM / Koch

JAZZ TO THE WORLD
Winter wonderland: *Alpert, Herb* / Baby it's cold outside: *Reeves, Dianne* / It came upon a midnight clear: *Fourplay* / Have yourself a merry little Christmas: *Krall, Diana* / O Tannenbaum: *Duke, George* / Let it snow, let it snow, let it snow: *Franks, Michael* / Christmas waltz: *Brecker Brothers* / Little drummer boy: *Wilson, Cassandra* / I'll be home for Christmas: *Hancock, Herbie* / O come o come Emmanuel: *Hancock, Herbie* / Christmas blues: *Cole, Holly* / Angels we have heard on high: *Steps Ahead* / Christmas song: *Baker, Anita* / What child is this: *Co-*

rea, Chick / Il est ne, le divin enfant: Dr. John
CD CDP 8321272
Blue Note / Dec '95 / EMI

JAZZ TODAY VOL.1
Sunday in New York: *Cole, Richie* / OTVOG: *Rollins, Sonny* / Scrapple from the apple: *Morgan, Frank Quartet* / If dreams come true: *White, Carla* / Movin' on: *McGriff, Jimmy* / Vicki: *Crawford, Hank* / Underground express: *Campbell, Kerry* / Samba for Isabelle: *Habian, Cliff* / Toc de bola: *Azymuth* / Jacaranda: *Roditi, Claudio*
CD CDBGP 1026
Beat Goes Public / Oct '93 / Pinnacle

JAZZ TREATS FOR THE HOLIDAYS
CD ARCD 19122
Arbors Jazz / Nov '94 / Cadillac

JAZZ TRIBE, THE
CD 1232542
Red / Nov '92 / ADA / Cadillac / Harmonia Mundi

JAZZ TRUMPET
Hard sock dance: *Bailey, Benny* / Isn't it romantic: *Baker, Chet* / Open the door: *Curson, Ted* / Red bank shuffle: *Edison, Harry* / Wrap your troubles in dreams: *Eldridge, Roy* / Sallie: *Ellis, Don* / Strength and sanity: *Little, Booker* / What am I here for: *Nance, Ray* / Rua dona Margarida: *Roditi, Claudio* / Casa de luz: *Rogers, Shorty* / No problem: *Terry, Clark* / Ferris wheel: *Williams, Richard*
CD EMPRCD 610
Emporio / Jun '96 / Disc

JAZZ ULTIMATE
CD PDSCD 536
Pulse / Aug '96 / BMG

JAZZ VALENTINE
CD MM 65091
Music Masters / Oct '94 / Nimbus

JAZZ VOCAL GROUPS 1927-1944 (2CD Set)
CD Set FA 041
Fremeaux / Sep '95 / ADA / Discovery

JAZZ VOCALISTS
On the sunny side of the street: *Hampton, Lionel* / Ain't misbehavin': *Waller, Fats* / That ain't right: *Bailey, Mildred* / St. Louis blues: *Teagarden, Jack* / Stars fell on Alabama: *Wiley, Lee* / One o'clock jump: *Lambert, Dave* / Every day I have the blues: *Williams, Joe* / My man's gone now: *Simone, Nina* / Careless love: *Turner, 'Big' Joe* / What a wonderful world: *Armstrong, Louis* / Fine and mellow: *Rushing, Jimmy*
CD 07863660722
Bluebird / Oct '92 / BMG

JAZZ YEAR 1935, THE
Bubbling over / Stardust / Solo hop / In a sentimental mood / New Orleans twist / Sleepy time gal / Bouncin' in rhythm / King Porter stomp / Harlem heat / Miss brown to you / Baby won't you please come home / Truckin' / Swingin' em down / Djangology / Every now and then / Facts and figures / In the dark/flashes / Jazz me blues / Rosetta / Buzzard / Willow tree / Muskrat ramble / Chicken and waffles
CD TPZ 1045
Topaz Jazz / May '96 / Cadillac / Pinnacle

JAZZ YEAR 1946, THE
SNAFU / Mellow mood / I can't escape from you / Confirmation / Allen's alley / Cool breeze / Ten lessons with Timothy / Ornithology / Tippin' out / 52nd Street theme / Five o'clock shadow / Sam beeps and bops / Everything's cool / Under the willow tree / Things to come / Opus in pastels / Opus de bop / Living my life / Cadillac slum / Be bop boogie / She's funny that way / Back talk / Mahogany Hall stomp / Saint
CD TPZ 1063
Topaz Jazz / Feb '97 / Cadillac / Pinnacle

JAZZ YEAR BOOK 1936, THE (2CD Set)
CD Set 74321345462
Milan / Feb '97 / Conifer/BMG / Silva Screen

JAZZ YEAR BOOK 1945, THE (2CD Set)
CD Set 74321313312
Milan / Feb '97 / Conifer/BMG / Silva Screen

JAZZIER RHYTHMS VOL.1
CD HUBCD 9
Hubbub / Jun '96 / Beechwood/BMG / SRD / Timewarp

JAZZIER RHYTHMS VOL.2
Panamanian aire: *Morris, Byron* / Sun shower: *Morris, Byron* / Music in my heart: *Moses, Kathryn* / Brazil: *Gibbs, John* / Known unknown: *Jamal, Khan* / Poquito soul: *One G plus three* / Ron con-con: *El Chicano* / Feelings: *Cheyenne* / Universe: *Semper, George* / Gwee: *Fudoli, Richard* / Moondance: *Feather, Lorraine* / Love for sale: *Anderson, Ernestine*
CD HUBCD 17
Hubbub / Mar '97 / Beechwood/BMG / SRD / Timewarp

JAZZIN' AT RONNIE'S
CD MCCD 212
Music Club / Oct '95 / Disc / THE

JAZZIN' BABY BLUES
Poor papa: *Jones, Clarence* / Look what a fool I've been: *Johnson, James P.* / Jazzin' baby blues: *Jones, Clarence* / Mama's got the blues: *Waller, Fats* / Mama's gone goodbye: *Montgomery, Mike* / Goodbye: *Montgomery, Mike* / Baby, won't you please come home: *Jones, Clarence* / Play 'em for mama and sing 'em for me: *Baker, Edythe* / He's my man: *Johnson, James P.* / When you're good you're lonesome: *Baker, Edythe* / Cryin' Blues: *Randolph, Mandy* / Blooie blooie: *Baker, Edythe* / Changes: *Lawnhurst, Vee* / Yearning (just for you): *Lawnhurst, Vee* / I'm gonna jazz my way: *Randolph, Mandy*
CD BCD 117
Biograph / Jul '91 / ADA / Cadillac / Direct / Hot Shot / Jazz Music / Wellard

JAZZIN' THE BLUES
CD MCCD 186
Music Club / Nov '94 / Disc / THE

JAZZIN' THE BLUES
Jelly bean blues: *Rainey, Gertrude 'Ma'* / Cold in hand blues: *Smith, Bessie* / Sugar foot stomp: *Oliver, Joe 'King'* / Creole love call: *Ellington, Duke* / West End blues: *Armstrong, Louis* / Good morning blues: *Basie, Count* / I thought I heard Buddy Bolden say: *Morton, Jelly Roll* / Winin' boy blues: *Morton, Jelly Roll* / 2.19 blues: *Armstrong, Louis* / Geechy Joe: *Calloway, Cab* / Rusty dusty blues: *Jordan, Louis* / Across the track blues: *Ellington, Duke* / Trouble in mind: *Millinder, Lucky* / Blue serge: *Ellington, Duke* / What's the use of getting sober: *Jordan, Louis* / Harvard blues: *Basie, Count* / Good Jelly blues: *Eckstine, Billy* / Lady in bed: *Page, Hot Lips* / Hurry hurry: *Millinder, Lucky* / Take me back baby: *Basie, Count*
CD 19133
Forlane / Jan '97 / Target/BMG

JAZZIN' THE BLUES 1936-1946
CD JPCD 1515
Jazz Perspectives / May '95 / Hot Shot / Jazz Music

JAZZIN' THE BLUES VOL.2 (1939-1946)
CD DOCD 5468
Document / Jul '96 / ADA / Hot Shot / Jazz Music

JAZZIN' THE BLUES VOL.3 1937-1941
CD DOCD 5536
Document / Jun '97 / ADA / Hot Shot / Jazz Music

JAZZIN' UNIVERSALLY (South Africa Outernational Meltdown Series)
Migrant worker / Phambili / Hug courtney pine / Bo molelekwa / Dance to Africa / Nikiwe / Nobohle
CD BW 078
B&W / Nov '96 / New Note/Pinnacle / SRD / Vital/SAM

JAZZSPEAK
CD NAR 054CD
New Alliance / May '93 / Plastic Head

JAZZY LITTLE CHRISTMAS
CD 8405012
Verve / Apr '90 / PolyGram

JDJ ALIVE AT PRIDE 1996
CD JDJP 1CD
JDJ / Aug '96 / 3mv/Pinnacle / SRD

JDJ MARATHON (2CD Set)
CD Set ADMCD 1
JDJ / Oct '96 / 3mv/Pinnacle / SRD

JE T'AIME
Cherish: *Kool & The Gang* / Everlasting love: *Gibb, Andy* / Breaking up is hard to do: *Sedaka, Neil* / Son of a preacher man: *Springfield, Dusty* / Stuck in the middle with you: *Stealer's Wheel* / All kinds of everything: *Dana* / Je t'aime... moi non plus: *Birkin, Jane & Serge Gainsbourg* / You see the trouble with me: *White, Barry* / Love town: *Newbury, Booker* / Do that to me one more time: *Captain & Tennille* / Can't give you anything (but my love): *Stylistics* / Baby come back: *Player* / Captain of her heart: *Double* / Marguerita time: *Status Quo*
CD 5501462
Spectrum / Jan '94 / PolyGram

JEKURA - THE DEEP ETERNAL FOREST CD
CD EFA 015582
Apocalyptic Vision / May '95 / Cargo / Plastic Head / SRD

JESSE'S JUBILEE ALBUM
CD CD 2030S
Jesse's Jazz / Jul '96 / Jazz Music

JEUNES SONNEURS DU CENTRE BRETAGNE
CD 437
Arfolk / Mar '96 / ADA / Discovery / Roots

JEWELS OF CAJUN MUSIC
CD TRIK 0157
Trikont / Oct '94 / ADA / Direct

JIMMY JAY PRESENTS : LES COOL SESSIONS
CD CDVIR 18
Virgin / Aug '93 / EMI

JINGLE BELLS IN THE SNOW
CD CNCD 5931
Disky / Nov '92 / Disky / THE

JITTERBUG JIVE (Texas Swing 1940-1941)
CD KKCD 19
Krazy Kat / Apr '97 / Hot Shot / Jazz Music

JIVING JAMBOREE
Saturday night fish fry / Ain't got no home / Something's goin' on in my room / They call me big Mama / Honeydripper / Love love of my life / I want you / Buzz buzz buzz / Wet back hop / Ding dong daddy / Music goes 'round and around / Don't stop loving me / Nite life boogie / Opus one / Hit, git and split / Rockin' Robin / My baby's rockin / That's all / You got me reelin' and rockin' / O sole mio boogie / Free and easy / Hey girl, hey boy / Rock that boogie / Flat foot Sam / My man
CD CDCHD 561
Ace / Apr '95 / Pinnacle

JJ COMPILATION
CD JJCD 1
JJ / Jun '95 / Alphamagic / Plastic Head

JOCKOMO NEW ORLEANS RHYTHM AND BLUES
CD MCCD 206
Music Club / Jul '95 / Disc / THE

JODLER DU TYROL AU TEXAS
CD AT 8001
ARB / Jun '97 / Discovery

JOE FRASIER PRESENTS
CD JFCD 4649
VP / Aug '95 / Greensleeves / Jet Star / Total/BMG

JOE KING PRESENTS (More Bounce To The Ounce/2CD Set)
CD Set LK 154CD
Lookout / Aug '97 / Cargo / Greyhound / Shellshock/Disc

JOINT VENTURES
CD NOZACD 006
Ninebar / Jul '97 / Kudos / Prime / RTM/ Disc

JOURNEY DOWN THE RHINE (Popular Music About The Rhine Area)
CD 15371
Laserlight / '91 / Target/BMG

JOURNEY INTO AMBIENT GROOVE VOL.1, A
CD 5243302
Quango / Jan '97 / PolyGram

JOURNEY INTO AMBIENT GROOVE VOL.2, A
CD 5242242
Axiom / Jun '96 / PolyGram / Vital

JOURNEY THROUGH THE UNDERGROUND
CD PLUGCD 1
Produce / Nov '94 / 3mv/Sony

JOURNEY TO BRAZIL, A
CD PS 66508
PlayaSound / Apr '95 / ADA / Harmonia Mundi

JOURNEY TO INDIA, A
CD PS 66512
PlayaSound / Feb '96 / ADA / Harmonia Mundi

JOURNEY TO LOUISIANA, A
CD PS 66511
PlayaSound / Dec '95 / ADA / Harmonia Mundi

JOURNEY TO PORTUGAL, A
CD PS 66507
PlayaSound / Apr '95 / ADA / Harmonia Mundi

JOURNEY TO SENEGAL, A
CD PS 66513
PlayaSound / Oct '96 / ADA / Harmonia Mundi

JOURNEY TO THE EDGE (Progressive Rock Classics)
Living in the past: *Jethro Tull* / Joybringer: *Manfred Mann's Earthband* / America: *Nice* / Cirkus: *King Crimson* / In-a-gadda-da-vida: *Iron Butterfly* / Forty thousand headmen: *Traffic* / You keep me hangin' on: *Vanilla Fudge* / Child of the universe: *Barclay James Harvest* / Wishing well: *Free* / Tomorrow night: *Atomic Rooster* / Jerusalem: *Emerson, Lake & Palmer* / Freefall: *Camel* / Back street luv: *Curved Air* / Surprise surprise: *Caravan* / Natural born bugie: *Humble Pie* / Love like a man: *Ten Years After* / Burlesque: *Family* / My room (Waiting for wonderland): *Van Der Graaf Generator*
CD MUSCD 018
MCI Music / May '94 / Disc / THE

JOURNEY TO VIETNAM, A
CD PS 66509
PlayaSound / Apr '95 / ADA / Harmonia Mundi

JOURNEYS BY DJ PRESENTS TRIPTONITE (3CD Set)
Turn off the light: *Shades Of Rhythm* / Private funk: *Private Funk* / Summer bummer: *Crazy Penis* / Klarky Cat: *Gumbo* / Nu odyssey: *Departure Lounge* / Wayward mind: *Homeland* / Lick: *Earl Grey* / Reverberations: *Webster, Charles* / Delirious: *OHMSS* / Terry's house: *Brown Junior, Terry Lee* / Drop: *Hot Lizard* / Calypso theme: *Pooley, Ian* / Sunseeker: *Solar Perplexed* / You gonna make me love somebody else: *Colourblind* / My love turns to liquid: *Dream 2 Science* / That Elvis track: *Sol Brothers* / Drop the boom: *Freestylers* / Manic jazz day: *DJ Anthony & Georgio* / Renegade: *Hip Hop Renegade* / C and P electric bonus beats: *Cut & Paste* / Chicky disco: *Stout The Dodge* / Auburn: *Skylab 2000* / Shock the beat: *Electric Choc* / What would we do: *Sol Brothers* / Laydown: *2B Continued* / Timeless: *Quake-X* / Energy 52: *Cafe Del Mar* / Encore une fois: *Sash* / Guidance: *Kamillion* / Calm down: *Kamillion* / Fantasy: *Alter Egos* / Thoughts: *Altered States* / Flute lore: *Infinite Wheel* / Luv is all you need: *99 All Stars* / Floorburn: *Chapp'd Out* / Destination eschaton: *Shamen* / Dialogue: *3 Dubs In A Sleeve* / Mickey and Mallory: *Natural Born Groovers* / Scotti deep: *Brooklyn Beats* / Pandomia: *DJ Randy* / Bad man: *Sister Bliss* / Flowtation: *De Moor, Vincent* / Groove seekers allowance: *Swag* / Auburn: *Skylab 2000* / Party: *Fletch* / Acid energy: *DJ Misjah & Groovehend* / State of play: *SNJ Works* / Flamenco trip: *TUSOM*
CD Set JDJCD 14
JDJ / May '97 / 3mv/Pinnacle / SRD

JOURNEYS BY DJ VOL.5
CD JDJCD 5
JDJ / Jun '94 / 3mv/Pinnacle / SRD

JOURNEYS BY DJ VOL.6 (The Ultimate House Party Mix)
CD JDJCD 6
JDJ / Oct '94 / 3mv/Pinnacle / SRD

JOURNEYS BY DJ VOL.7 (Rocky & Diesel)
CD JDJCD 7
JDJ / Jun '95 / 3mv/Pinnacle / SRD

JOURNEYS BY DJ VOL.9 (The Ultimate Beach Party)
CD JDJCD 9
JDJ / Dec '95 / 3mv/Pinnacle / SRD

JOURNEYS INTO JUNGLE
CD JIJCD 001
JDJ / Jun '95 / 3mv/Pinnacle / SRD

JOURNEYS THROUGH CYBERSEX (Mixed By DJ Alan TG)
CD TGCD 0012
Torture Garden / Jun '97 / Intergroove

JOY OF CHRISTMAS, THE (Christmas Crooners/Christmas With Bing Crosby/ Angel Voices)
CD Set MCBX 012
Music Club / Apr '94 / Disc / THE

JOY OF CHRISTMAS, THE (2CD Set)
Once in Royal David's city / Ave Maria / Ding dong merrily on high / Silent night / Panis angelicus / Holly and the ivy / Jingle bells/Deck the hall / Good King Wenceslas / O Holy night / O little town of Bethlehem / In dulci jubilo / First Noel / Pastoral sinfonia / O thou that tellest good tidings to Zion / For unto us a child is born / God rest ye merry gentlemen / Away in a manger / What child is this / O come all ye faithful (adeste fidelis) / Twelve days of Christmas / Sussex carol / Star carol / Mary's boy child / King Jesus hath a garden / Up good Christian folk and listen / Child in a manger / Mille cherubini in coro / Lullaby / In the bleak mid Winter / Gesu bambino / Trio for two flutes and a harp / Slumber aria / See amid the Winter's snow / Shepherd's in the field abiding / While shepherds watched / Ave Maria / Hark the herald angels sing
CD Set 4524502
Decca / Nov '96 / PolyGram

JOY RIDE VOL.2
CD DCCD 4001
Joe Frazier / Apr '97 / Jet Star

JOYEUX NOEL
CD DCD 5338
Disky / Dec '93 / Disky / THE

JUBILEE JEZEBELS VOL.1
Drive Daddy drive: *Little Sylvia* / I went to your wedding: *Little Sylvia* / Ain't gonna do it: *Little Sylvia* / Blue heaven: *Little Sylvia* / Everything I need but you: *Little Sylvia* / It must be love: *Watkins, Viola* / Really real: *Watkins, Viola* / There goes my heart: *Watkins, Viola* / I've lost: *Enchanters* / Housewife blues: *Enchanters* / How could you: *Enchanters* / Boogie woogie Daddy: *Enchanters* / Heavenly father: *McGriff, Edna* / It's raining: *McGriff, Edna* / I love you: *McGriff, Edna* / Edna's blues: *McGriff, Edna* / Why oh why: *McGriff, Edna* / I'll surrender anytime: *McGriff, Edna* / It's my turn now: *Fran, Carol* / You can't stop me: *Fran, Carol* / I know: *Fran, Carol* / Any day love walks in: *Fran, Carol* / Just a letter: *Fran, Carol* / World without you: *Fran, Carol*
CD NEMCD 750
Sequel / Aug '95 / BMG

JUBILEE JEZEBELS VOL.2
Ooh little daddy: *McGriff, Edna* / I'll be around: *McGriff, Edna* / These things shall be: *McGriff, Edna* / I found somebody to love: *Little Sylvia* / Kiss for my baby: *Little Sylvia* / I miss you: *Little Sylvia* / Ring: *Little Sylvia* / Million tears: *Little Sylvia* / Don't blame my heart: *Little Sylvia* / Paint a sky for me: *Watkins, Viola* / Goodnight sweetheart, goodnight: *Mann, Gloria* / Love me

boy: *Mann, Gloria* / Today is your birthday: *Enchanters* / When I say my prayer: *Lynne, Gloria* / Uncloudy day: *Lynne, Gloria* / After the lights go down low: *Jerome, Patti* / Johnny has gone: *Jerome, Patti* / I cried for you: *Reese, Della* / Runaround: *Marie Ann* / I can see through you: *Simmons, Fay* / Hangin' around: *Simmons, Fay* / Crying in the chapel: *Fran, Carol* / I'm gonna try: *Fran, Carol* / Let me go: *Big Maybelle* / No better for you: *Big Maybelle*
CD NEMCD 916
Sequel / Jun '97 / BMG

JUBILEE/JOSIE VOCAL GROUPS VOL.3
CD NEMCD 756
Sequel / Mar '96 / BMG

JUBILEE/JOSIE VOCAL GROUPS VOL.4
CD NEMCD 757
Sequel / Mar '96 / BMG

JUBILEE/JOSIE VOCAL GROUPS VOL.5
Cruise to the moon: *Chaperones* / Shining star: *Chaperones* / Man from the moon: *Chaperones* / Teenage paradise: *Volumes* / Sandra: *Volumes* / Night and day: *Til, Sonny* / Shimmy time: *Til, Sonny* / So long: *Til, Sonny* / Crazy love: *Knight, Bob Four* / Memories: *Knight, Bob Four* / Dancing alone: *Emeralds* / Did you ever love a guy: *Emeralds* / This I swear: *Dubs* / Wisdom of a fool: *Dubs* / Our wedding day: *Shells* / Deep in my heart: *Shells* / Lonely road: *Passions* / School bells to chapel bells: *Styles* / I love you for sentimental reasons: *Styles* / Shangri-la: *Parakeets* / Elaine: *Glenwoods* / That's the way it'll be: *Glenwoods* / If you love me, really love me: *Jordan & The Fascinations* / Who needs love: *Ovations* / Remembering: *Ovations* / Two friends: *Knight, Bob Four* / Far from your love: *Appreciations* / Our song: *Volumes*
CD NEMCD 758
Sequel / Jun '96 / BMG

JUG & WASHBOARD BANDS 1928-1930
CD SOBCD 35142
Story Of The Blues / Mar '92 / ADA / Koch

JUJU ROOTS 1930S-50S
CD ROUCD 5017
Rounder / Feb '93 / ADA / CM / Direct

JUKE BOX GIANTS (4CD Set)
CD Set MBSCD 414
Castle / Nov '93 / BMG

JUKE BOX JIVE (The Birth Of Rock 'n' Roll/2CD Set)
CD Set CPCD 82702
Charly / Apr '97 / Koch

JUKE BOX R & B
I got loaded: *Cadets* / Wiggie waggie woo: *Cadets* / Sixty minute man: *Cadets* / Dance the thing: *Dixon, Floyd Orchestra* / Baby, baby every night: *James, Etta* / How big a fool: *James, Etta* / One whole year baby: *Curry, Earl* / This is the night for love: *Flairs* / She wants to rock: *Flairs* / Hit, git and split: *Young Jessie* / Everyday I have the blues: *King, B.B.* / Don't you want a man like me: *King, B.B.* / She moves me: *Watson, Johnny 'Guitar'* / Standing at the crossroads: *James, Elmore* / Rumba rock: *Beasley, Jimmy* / I'm so blue: *Beasley, Jimmy* / Chicken shack: *Turner, Ike & Tina* / Shattered dreams: *Fulson, Lowell* / Let's make with some love: *Berry, Richard & The Flairs* / Double crossin' baby: *Robins* / My darling: *Jacks* / Rock everybody: *Teen Queens*
CD CDCHD 335
Ace / Sep '91 / Pinnacle

JUKE JOINT BLUES
Statesboro blues: *McTell, 'Blind' Willie* / Good morning schoolgirl: *Williamson, Sonny Boy* / Summertime: *Holiday, Billie* / It hurts me too: *Tampa Red* / Cross road blues: *Johnson, Robert* / Nobody knows when you're down and out: *Smith, Bessie* / You just as well let her go: *Weldon, Casey Bill* / Key to the highway: *Broonzy, 'Big' Bill* / Catfish blues: *Petway, Robert* / Stones in my passway: *Johnson, Robert* / What's the matter with the mill: *Memphis Minnie* / I be troubled: *Waters, Muddy* / Midnight special: *Leadbelly* / I feel so good: *Broonzy, 'Big' Bill* / Midnight hour blues: *Carr, Leroy* / I been dealing with the devil: *Williamson, Sonny Boy* / Baby please don't go: *Williams, Big Joe* / Nobody's fault but mine: *Johnson, Blind Willie* / Roll and tumble blues: *Newbern, Hambone Willie* / Strange fruit: *Holiday, Billie* / Winnie the wailer: *Johnson, Lonnie* / Bull frog blues: *Harris, William* / Lone wolf blues: *Woods, Oscar 'Buddy'* / Ramblin' on my mind: *Johnson, Robert* / Don't you lie to me: *Tampa Red*
CD EMPRCD 669
Emporio / Oct '96 / Disc

JUKE JOINT'S 5TH ANNIVERSARY COLLECTION, THE
Jumpin' at Deke's: *Abdabs* / Ain't gonna put me down: *Taylor, Matt* / Blues is king: *Grand, Otis* / Can you dig it: *Clayton, Steve 'Big Man' & The 44's* / Long way to go: *Al Morocco 5* / Ain't holding my breath: *Out Of The Blue* / Hedgehog: *Booze & Blues* / Parchment farm: *Receeders* / Let it go: *Rockin' Armadillos* / Shake it and break it: *Marques Brothers* / Brokenhearted blues: *Elmores* / You got me: *Motel Kings* / Fun with the blues: *Packham, Kit One Jump Ahead* / Down in the bottom: *Slim Tim & Lightnin' Phil* / Good morning little schoolgirl: *Bullet Blues Band*
CD 01702002
Lunch / Jun '97 / Direct

JUKEBOX COWBOY
One foot in the honky tonk: *Henderson, Mike* / Fool on a stool: *Preston, Leroy* / Tearjoint: *Penn, Dan* / Careless coin: *Burdett, Phil* / Ain't it funny: *McCallister, Don Jr.* / Sworn to pride: *Cutrufello, Mary* / Cryin' over you: *Intveld, James* / Listen to your heart: *Heinrich, Roy* / Western life: *Cowboys & Indians* / 7 Cups of coffee 14 cigarettes: *Hurd, Cornell Band* / Indians: *Gordon, Roxy* / Luther played guitar: *Ridgway, Stan* / Take me back in your arms: *Coyne, Kevin* / Let me mend your broken heart: *Moll, Erik* / I'll never be free: *Robertson, Kathy & Chris Gaffney* / Hillbilly hula gal: *Haoles* / Two long years: *Liberty Ranch* / 5 Dollars and a heartache: *Peters, Debra & Wayne Hancock* / Cowboy nation: *Cowboy Nation* / 300 Miles: *Holcombe, Malcolm* / I'll be here in the morning: *Van Zandt, Townes & Barb Donovan* / Til we meet again: *Power, Duffy* / Good the bad and the ugly: *Chardiet, Simon*
CD VJCD 003
Vinyl Junkie / Mar '97 / ADA / Direct

JUKEBOX GIANTS
CD MACCD 107
Autograph / Aug '96 / BMG

JUKEBOX JIVES 1936-1946
CD MICH 7126
Hindsight / Nov '94 / Jazz Music / Target/ BMG

JUMP AND SWING WITH BLACK TOP
Trane diggin': *Copley, Al & Hal Singer* / Hit it: *Holmstrom, Rick* / That's it: *Big Joe & The Dynaflows* / Ain't you trouble: *Primich, Gary* / I'll take you back home: *King, Earl* / Mushmouth: *Piccolo, Greg* / Stand by me: *Zimm, Rusty* / I never thought: *Guitar Shorty* / Jumbo: *Gaines, Grady* / Low down dirty dog: *Piazza, Rod & The Mighty Flyers* / Go girl: *Tri-Saxual Soul Champs*
CD CDBTEL 7007
Black Top / May '97 / ADA / CM / Direct

JUMP AROUND - RAP'S HALL OF FAME
CD XPS 4CD
X-Press / Jun '96 / SRD

JUMP BLUE (Rockin' The Joints)
Jump children: *Bartholomew, Dave* / King kong: *Tyler, Big T.* / Hucklebuck with Jimmy: *Five Keys* / Flying home part 1: *Jacquet, Illinois* / Deacon rides again: *McNeely, 'Big' Jay* / Safronia B: *Boze, Calvin & His All Stars* / Messy Bessy: *Jordan, Louis* / I ain't drunk: *Liggins, Joe & Jimmy* / Fine brown frame: *Lutcher, Nellie* / CC rider: *Markham, Pigmeat* / He may be your man: *Humes, Helen* / Yes it's you: *Clovers* / Daybreak: *Crayton, Pee Wee* / When I'm in my tea: *Adams, Jo Jo* / I got loaded: *Harris, Peppermint* / Fool in love: *Turner, Ike & Tina* / Sax shack boogie: *Milburn, Amos* / Cleo's boogie: *Brown, Cleo* / Great big eyes: *Archibald* / Let the four winds blow: *Brown, Roy* / Teenage baby: *Walker, T-Bone* / Don't leave me baby: *Fulson, Lowell* / Wine wine wine: *Dixon, Floyd* / Let the good times roll: *Shirley & Lee* / I need you, I want you: *Parker, Jack* / Jumpin' tonight: *Turner, 'Big' Joe & His Band*
CD CDP 8543642
Blue Note / Oct '96 / EMI

JUMPIN'
Keep on jumpin': *Musique* / Runaway: *Salsoul Orchestra & Loleatta Holloway* / Disco juice: *Cloud One* / There but for the grace of God go I: *Machine* / Thousand finger man: *Candido* / Touch and go: *Ecstasy, Passion & Pain* / It's all over my face: *Loose Joints* / Love money: *T.W. Funkmasters* / Got the feeling: *Two Tons Of Fun* / Funkanova: *Wood, Brass & Steel* / Tee's happy: *Northend* / Go bang: *Dinosaur L*
CD HURTCD 002
CD HURTCDL 002
Harmless / Apr '97 / RTM/Disc

JUMPIN' AND JIVIN'
Something's goin' on in my room: *Daddy Cleanhead* / Tell it like it is: *Milton, Roy* / Lucy Brown: *Henderson, Duke* / Mad lad returns: *Parker, Leo* / Drink up light up: *Alexander, Nelson Trio* / Baby don't do that to me: *Milton, Roy* / Sometimes: *Easton, Amos* / When the rooster crows: *Turner, Joe* / Hep cat boogie: *Liggins, Jimmy* / Baby you don't know: *Milton, Roy* / Red top: *King Pleasure* / Ida Red: *Easton, Amos* / Cool goofin': *Ferguson, Rudy* / Wine woogie: *Phillips, Marvin* / Twisted: *Ross, Annie* / Tiny's boogie: *Easton, Amos* / If you don't know: *Milton, Roy* / I must have been an ugly baby: *Perry, King* / Stop talkin' start walkin': *Jefferson, Eddie* / Gonna leave you baby: *Milton, Roy* / Squattin': *Davis, Eddie 'Lockjaw'* / Hole in the wall: *Dixon, Floyd* / Got a penny Benny: *Carroll, Joe* / Make me know it: *Milton, Roy* / Moody's mood for love: *King Pleasure*
CD CDCHD 654
Ace / May '97 / Pinnacle

JUMPIN' AND PUMPIN' VS. ELICIT
Papua new guinea: *Future Sound Of London* / Fire when ready: *G Double E* / Visitor: *DJ Space* / Stakker humanoid: *Humanoid* / Dominate: *Flag* / Alchemist: *Geneside 11* / Tainted love: *Impedence* / Zum zum: *Love Men* / Check how we jam: *Bass Construction* / We can ride the boogie rock with you: *Bubbles* / Get on the move: *Psychopaths*
CD CDTOT 6
Jumpin' & Pumpin' / Jul '93 / 3mv/Sony / Mo's Music Machine

JUMPIN' IN CHICAGO
CD CDGR 175
Charly / Jul '97 / Koch

JUMPIN' JAZZ
Iron city: *Green, Grant* / Speak low: *Sparks, Melvin* / Harold's house of jazz: *Cole, Richie* / Mambo Inn: *Donaldson, Lou* / Possum grease: *Lytle, Johnny* / As time goes by: *Murphy, Mark* / Prodigal son: *Ousley, Harold* / Street song: *Hutcherson, Bobby* / Heavy juice: *Person, Houston* / Things are getting better: *Jefferson, Eddie* / So what: *Lytle, Johnny*
CD PHOCD 8005
PHQ / Jun '96 / New Note/Pinnacle

JUMPIN' JIVE (2CD Set)
Jumpin' jive: *Calloway, Cab* / Five guys named Moe: *Jordan, Louis & His Tympany Five* / Hurry hurry: *Harris, Wynonie* / All that meat & no potatoes: *Waller, Fats* / Is you is or is you ain't my baby: *Vinson, Eddie 'Cleanhead'* / Why don't you do right: *Treen, Lil with Broonzy, 'Big' Bill* / Watch that jive: *Turner, 'Big' Joe & His Band* / Caldonia: *Herman, Woody & His Orchestra* / B-flat blues: *King, Saunders & His Blues Band* / Pagin' Mr Page: *Page, Hot Lips & His Orchestra* / Share-croppin' blues: *Starr, Kay* / 'Taint what you do (it's the way that cha do it): *Waller, Fats* / Evil gal blues: *Washington, Dinah* / Shout, sister, shout: *Bradshaw, Tiny & His Orchestra* / At the swing cat's ball: *Jordan, Louis & His Tympany Five* / Hey lawdy mama: *Kirk, Andy & His Twelve Clouds of Joy* / You'se a viper: *Smith, Stuff & His Onyx Club Boys* / Knock me a kiss: *Krupa, Gene & His Orchestra* / Ram session: *Buck Ram Allstars* / Boogie woogie dance: *Calloway, Cab Orchestra* / What's the use of getting sober (when you're gonna get drunk: *Jordan, Louis & His Tympany Five* / Your feet's too big: *Waller, Fats* / Boog it: *Armstrong, Louis & Mills Brothers* / After hours: *Hawkins, Erskine & His Orchestra* / Jive (page one of the hepsters dictionary): *Calloway, Cab Orchestra* / Hamps boogie woogie: *Hampton, Lionel & His Orchestra* / Here comes the man with the jive: *Smith, Stuff & His Onyx Club Boys* / Ride Red ride: *Millinder, Lucky & His Orchestra* / Rosetta: *Newton, Frankie & His Orchestra* / Sweet Lorraine: *Cole, Nat 'King' Trio* / You meet the nicest people in your dreams: *Waller, Fats* / Do you wanna jump children: *Rushing, Jimmy/Count Basie & His Orchestra* / Harlem joys: *Smith, Willie 'The Lion' & His Cubs* / Reefer man: *Calloway, Cab Orchestra* / Swing with me rhythm: *Prima, Louis & His New Orleans Gang* / Jumpin' the blues: *Cooper, Al & His Savoy Sultans* / Roll 'em: *Goodman, Benny & His Orchestra* / Squeeze me: *Waller, Fats* / I got rhythm: *Spirits Of Rhythm* / Doug the jitterbug: *Jordan, Louis & His Tympany Five*
CD Set 330182
Hallmark / Jul '96 / Carlton

JUMPIN' LIKE MAD COOL CATS AND HIP CHICKS (2CD Set)
Jumpin' tonight (midnight rockin') / Safronia B / Cow cow boogie / Jumpin' with Symphony Sid / Jump it with a shuffle / Oh babe / Stingy blues / Oo-pa-pa-da / Hypin' women blues / Fine brown frame / Baby, let's be friends / Be baba leba / Frim fram sauce / Solid potato salad / Pork chops and mustard greens / Jack's town / This joint's too hip for me / Marihuana boogie / Pachuko hop / Juice head baby / Cheap old wine and whiskey / Looped / I ain't drunk / All that wine is gone / I seen what'cha done / No more alcohol / Insect ball / Gee / House of blue lights / Hustle is on / Blowin' Red's top / He should'a flip'd when he flop'd / He's a real gone guy / My baby done left me / Chicas patas boogie (oh babe) / Chittlin' ball / Wrong neighbourhood / Jumpin' Jack / Fat and forty / No name boogie / Concentration / Two cats / Yeah yeah yeah / I'll die happy / I may be easy, but I'm no fool / Travellin' baby / Blow man blow / Boogie woogie king / Keep your nose out of my business / Talking that talk / 5 Months, 2 weeks, 2 days
CD Set CDEM 1608
Capitol / Mar '97 / EMI

JUMPIN' THE BLUES
Damp rag / New kind of feelin' / Big Bob's boogie / Elephant rock / Riff / Fat man blues / There ain't enough room here to boogie / Dr. Jives / Cadillac boogie / Tra-la-la / Race horse / Pelican jump / Hi-Yo Silver / We're gonna rock this morning
CD CDCHD 941
Ace / Jun '90 / Pinnacle

JUMPING AT JUBILEE
Hole in the ground: *Kohlman, Freddie Orchestra* / You'll never get nothing without trying: *Cousin Joe* / Ramblin' woman: *Cousin Joe* / Can't help myself (pts 1 and 2): *Powell, Jesse* / I'm all alone: *Powell, Jesse* / Don't pass me by: *Brown, Piney* / Battle with the bottle: *Brown, Piney* / 3-D Loving: *Brown, Piney* / You bring out the wolf in me: *Brown, Piney* / Ay la bah: *Cobb, Danny* / Everyday I weep and moan: *Willis, Ralph* / Somebody's got to go: *Willis, Ralph* / Blue blues blues: *Willis, Ralph* / I got a letter: *Willis, Ralph* / Too late to scream and shout: *Willis, Ralph* / Hoodoo man: *Willis, Ralph* / Income tax: *Willis, Ralph* / Bed tick: *Willis, Ralph* / Yes he did: *La Verne, Ray* / Rock on the bop: *La Verne, Ray* / Drunk, that's all: *La Verne, Ray* / Rock 'n' roll: *La Verne, Ray*
CD NEMCD 749
Sequel / Aug '95 / BMG

JUNGLE - THE EXTREME COLLECTION VOL.1
Kills some sound / Screwface / Move on up / Morning star / Fantasy / Sensation / Didi ji / Thunder / Dance a come / Pass me a dub plate / Darkside of the moon / What a feeling / Snare time / Kaos
CD CDB 9005
B9 / Oct '94 / Pinnacle / Plastic Head

JUNGLE - THE EXTREME COLLECTION VOL.1 & 2 (2CD Set)
CD Set CDB 9008
B9 / Jun '96 / Pinnacle / Plastic Head

JUNGLE - THE EXTREME COLLECTION VOL.2
Junglist raver: *Alexander, Dean* / Zulu riddim: *Major Popular* / Authority: *Darkus* / I believe in love: *New Age & C J Nelson* / Rass clart money: *Darkus* / Ruler: *Major Popular* / Emotions: *New Age & C J Nelson* / Blessed relief: *Darkus* / Cafe le jungle: *Dubtronix* / Special girl: *New Age & Phil Joseph* / Time is right: *Darkus* / Vision: *Frixion*
CD CDB 9006
B9 / Sep '95 / Pinnacle / Plastic Head

JUNGLE - THE EXTREME COLLECTION VOL.3
Kick 'em higher: *Dubtronix* / Man from jungle: *Frixion* / Crime: *New Age* / Tropical storm: *Three The Hardway* / Joy: *Darkus* / Alien: *Frixion* / Swerve 3: *Three The Hardway* / Touched me: *Darkus* / Pyramids: *Frixion* / Hear my voice: *Dubtronix*
CD CDB 9007
B9 / Jun '97 / Pinnacle / Plastic Head

JUNGLE BIZZNIZZ VOL.1
CD SCRCD 007
Scratch / Sep '96 / Koch / Scratch/BMG

JUNGLE BOOK
CD RIVETCD 6
Reinforced / Aug '95 / SRD

JUNGLE CHICH 5
CD 31062
Kakchich / Dec '95 / Jet Star

JUNGLE COLLECTION, THE
Sucker: *Vibe Posse* / Do it: *Wee Papa Girl Rappers* / Rude boy: *Wee Papa Girl Rappers* / Ethereal: *Motive 9* / No pressure: *Motive 9* / Aqua marine: *Taskmasters* / Shimmering light: *Tayce* / Heaven and earth: *Wicked Wayne* / Hiding in the tall grass: *Hiding In The Tall Grass* / Big shot: *Wee Papa Girl Rappers* / Ethereal: *Motive 9* / Sucker: *Vibe Posse*
CD QED 170
Tring / Nov '96 / Tring

JUNGLE DUB (14 Jungle Tracks For The Serious Jungalist)
Run 4 da sound clash: *Formula 7* / Dance hall massive: *DJ Massive* / I spy: *DJ Monk* / Phizical: *Roni Size* / Feel it: *Lemon D* / You don't know: *Dillinga* / Twisted brain: *Area 39* / Religion: *Formula 7* / Jazz note: *DJ Krust* / Deep love: *Dillinga* / Maximum style dubplate: *Tom & Jerry & D J Stretch* / Bionic: *G-Kelly* / R 'n' B Collection: *Noodles & Wonder* / Money in your pocket: *Crown Jewels & MC Dett*
CD KICKCD 17
Kickin' / Dec '94 / Prime / SRD

JUNGLE DUB EXPERIENCE VOL.1 (Mazaruni)
CD ARICD 09
Ariwa Sounds / Mar '95 / Jet Star / SRD

JUNGLE DUB EXPERIENCE VOL.2 (Rapununi Safari)
Perry in the dub jungle / Kunte kinte jungle / Organic pressure / Ecologically speaking / Desolate lagoon / Steamy jungle / Natural ras / Beat of the wild beast / Rapununi savannah / Juffre view / Banjui belly
CD ARICD 111
Ariwa Sounds / Jun '95 / Jet Star / SRD

JUNGLE EXOTICA VOL.1
CD E 11565CD
Crypt / Mar '93 / Shellshock/Disc

JUNGLE EXOTICA VOL.2
CD EFACD 12888
Crypt / Apr '97 / Shellshock/Disc

JUNGLE FEVER
CD 12606
Laserlight / Oct '95 / Target/BMG

JUNGLE HEAT '95
Melody madness: *Coolhand Flex & Michelle Thompson* / Gangsta: *Trinity* / Shadow: *Dynamic Duo* / Living for the night: *Stakka & K-Tee* / Bastard: *Blackman* / Bring you down: *Tek 9* / Reality: *DJ Swift* / It's a jazz thing: *Roni Size* / Wheel up: *Lion Man* / Set

speed: *DJ Krust* / Jazzmin: *Cloud 9* / I'll always be around: *Dub Hustlers* / Essences so sweet: *Jon-E-Z-Bad* / Silver haze: *Area 39 & Corelle*
CD ________ **VTCD 51**
Virgin / Jun '95 / EMI

JUNGLE HITS VOL.1
CD ________ **STRCD 1**
Street Tuff / Sep '94 / Jet Star

JUNGLE HITS VOL.2
CD ________ **STRCD 2**
Street Tuff / Dec '94 / Jet Star

JUNGLE HITS VOL.3
CD ________ **STRCD 3**
Street Tuff / Jul '95 / Jet Star

JUNGLE MASSIVE VOL.1
CD ________ **HFCD 42**
PWL / Sep '94 / Warner Music

JUNGLE MASSIVE VOL.2
CD ________ **HFCD 43**
PWL / Nov '94 / Warner Music

JUNGLE MASSIVE VOL.3
CD ________ **HFCD 44**
PWL / Mar '95 / Warner Music

JUNGLE MASSIVE VOL.4
CD ________ **HF 46CD**
PWL / Jul '95 / Warner Music

JUNGLE ON THE STREETS
CD ________ **GTOL 93**
Land Of The Giants / Apr '95 / Jet Star

JUNGLE RENEGADES VOL.1
CD ________ **ANIMATE 3CD**
Re-Animate / Mar '95 / SRD

JUNGLE RHYTHMS VOL.1
CD ________ **SCRCD 004**
Scratch / Nov '94 / Koch / Scratch/BMG

JUNGLE ROCK - 1ST EDITION
CD ________ **SUMACD 001**
Jungle Rock / Nov '92 / Jet Star

JUNGLE SKY VOL.4 (Nirvana)
Ali rocks: *DJ Soulslinger* / Eastern influence: *DJ Ani* / Bac: *Inna-most & Origin* / We are not alone: *1.8.7.* / Mundo civilizado: *Lindsay, Arto* / Cloze u'r eyez: *Kingsize* / All natural: *Tube* / I wish: *Marshall H.* / Dirty call: *Scissor Hands* / Flotation device: *Neill, Ben*
CD ________ **JS 116CD**
Liquid Sky / Mar '97 / Cargo / SRD

JUNGLE SOUNDCLASH VOL.1
CD ________ **STHCCD 8**
Strictly Underground / '94 / SRD

JUNGLE SOUNDCLASH VOL.2
CD ________ **STHCCD 10**
Strictly Underground / May '95 / SRD

JUNGLE SPLASH PRESENTS JUNGLISM VOL.1 (No Retreat No Surrender)
CD ________ **UKBLKCD 1**
UK Black / Feb '95 / SRD

JUNGLE TEKNO - IN THE MIX
Drowning: *Four Horsemen Of The Apocalypse* / Champion sound: *Q-Project* / We enter: *Aphrodite* / Phat and phuturistic: *Matt* / MArvelous cain: *Hit Man* / See no, hear no: *Motherland* / War in '94: *Badman* / State of mind: *Sub-Sequence* / Tibetan jungel: *DJ Rap* / Peace in our time: *Van Kleef* / What kind of world: *Ascend & Ultravibe* / Scottie: *Sub Nation* / RAzor's edge: *Steve C & Monita* / Calling all people: *Azone* / gangster lean: *NW 1* / Tonight: *A-Sides & Nut E-1* / Breakin free: *Slipmatt* / Who's that: *Coolhand Flex* / Wiplash: *Coolhand Flex* / Hold back: *Coolhand Flex*
CD ________ **CDTOT 28**
Jumpin' & Pumpin' / Jun '95 / 3mv/Sony / Mo's Music Machine

JUNGLE TEKNO VOL.1
Music takes you: *Blame* / Ten BandH: *Freshtrax & Ace* / We can ride the boogie: *Bubbles* / Drop the bass: *Out-Phaze* / We have it: *CMC* / Bomb scare: *2 Bad Mice* / Run come quick: *Audio* / Dance with the speaker: *Noise Factory* / Extreme: *Tripper* / Jungle mayhem: *Primatives* / Mind games: *Power Zone* / Sonata No.6: *D-Major* / Logical progression: *LTJ Bukem* / Control: *DJ MCM & DJ Smiley* / Junglest: *Rudeboy* / Please your soul: *Tomczak*
CD ________ **CDTOT 5**
Jumpin' & Pumpin' / Jun '92 / 3mv/Sony / Mo's Music Machine

JUNGLE TEKNO VOL.2 (Happiness & Darkness)
Don't need your love: *DJ Red Alert & Mike Slammer* / Valley of the shadows: *Origin Unknown* / Euphoria (Nino's dream): *Origin Unknown* / House Crew: *Origin Unknown* / Can you feel the rush: *Noise Factory* / Shining in da darkness: *Nookie* / Full logic control: *Higher Octave* / Axis: *DJ Solo & DJ Devine* / Who's that: *Coolhand Flex* / Touch: *Origin Unknown* / Storm trooper: *DJ Mayhem* / Terminator: *Metal Heads* / Whiplash: *Coolhand Flex* / Desire: *Weekend Rush* / Just a little: *M-Beat* / Girl it ever: *Kenetic*
CD ________ **CDTOT 10**
Jumpin' & Pumpin' / Nov '93 / 3mv/Sony / Mo's Music Machine

JUNGLE TEKNO VOL.3 (Drum 'n' Bass A Way Of Life)
19.5 HZT: *LTJ Bukem & Peshay* / Tibetan jungle: *DJ Rap* / One 2 one: *Johnson, Roger* / Skyliner: *Invisible Man* / Let the drummer go: *Invisible Man* / Gangster lean: *NW 1* / Skanka: *Hardware* / Scottie: *Sub Nation* / Stay calm: *Pulse* / Ominous clouds: *Interception* / Fallen angels: *Wax Doctor* / Champion sound: *Alliance* / Breakin' free: *Slipmatt* / Inesse: *DJ Mayhem*
CD ________ **CDTOT 14**
Jumpin' & Pumpin' / Jun '94 / 3mv/Sony / Mo's Music Machine

JUNGLE TEKNO VOL.4 (Intelligence & Technology)
Sound control: *Randall & Andy C* / Attitude: *Area 39* / What kind of world: *Ascend & Ultravibe* / Hit man: *Marvellous Caine* / Jungle warrior: *N-ZO & DJ Invincible* / What the... remix: *Sonz Of A Loop Da Loop Era* / Listen up: *Higher Sense* / Calling all people (remix): *Azone* / Basher: *M6 Crew* / Stand easy: *JB* / Tonight: *A-Sides & Nut E-1* / Natural high: *Chaos & Julia Set*
CD ________ **CDTOT 15**
Jumpin' & Pumpin' / Sep '94 / 3mv/Sony / Mo's Music Machine

JUNGLE TEKNO VOL.5 (The Deep Side)
Resolution: *Photek* / Music is so special: *Brothers With Soul* / Twisted girl: *Ruff With Smooth* / Close encounter: *Jeep Head* / Peace in our time: *Van Kleef* / Rollin' intelligence: *Urban Wax* / Dub plate '94 lick: *Keith, Ray* / License: *Krome & Time* / Flying remix: *Basement Phil* / Razor's edge: *Steve C & Monita* / Fall down on me: *Original Substitute* / Change: *Fast Floor*
CD ________ **CDTOT 20**
Jumpin' & Pumpin' / Nov '94 / 3mv/Sony / Mo's Music Machine

JUNGLE TEKNO VOL.6 (Phat & Phuturistic)
Phat and phuturistic: *Matt* / Champion sound: *Q-Project* / War in '94: *Badman* / I bring you the future: *Noise Factory* / Hit man: *Marvellous Caine* / Dibi DJ: *DJ Invincible & Matticus* / Presha III: *Studio Pressure* / Drowning: *Four Horsemen Of The Apocalypse* / We enter: *Aphrodite* / See no, hear no: *Motherland* / State of mind: *Sub Sequence* / All you wanted: *Graham, John*
CD ________ **CDTOT 21**
Jumpin' & Pumpin' / Jan '95 / 3mv/Sony / Mo's Music Machine

JUNGLE TEKNO VOL.7
Pulse of life: *Sentinal* / Virtual heaven: *Alliance* / Switch: *DJ Rap* / Melody of life: *Noise Factory* / Respected no accepted: *Touch Of Jazz* / Fall down on me: *Original Substitute* / I like it: *Jack 'n' Phil* / New vision: *Big Bud* / Deep love: *Dillinja* / Studio one: *Krome & Time* / Gangster love: *EP Man* / Walter jelly: *New Jack Pimps*
CD ________ **CDTOT 27**
Jumpin' & Pumpin' / Mar '95 / 3mv/Sony / Mo's Music Machine

JUNGLE TEKNO VOL.8
Ecstatic: *Intense* / Oh gosh: *Undercover Agent* / Twisted brain: *Area 39* / 100 Tons of bass: *J&J* / Rollidge: *DJ SS* / Free me: *Bliss 'n' Tumble* / Play the music: *Just Intelligence* / Hypnosis: *Smith, Simon* / Unplugged: *Appaloosa* / Mindscape: *Dub Technicians* / Peace 'n' luv: *Unity* / I don't owe you shit: *Smak*
CD ________ **CDTOT 31**
Jumpin' & Pumpin' / Jul '95 / 3mv/Sony / Mo's Music Machine

JUNGLE USA (The New Sound Of The East Coast)
CD ________ **VTX 1CD**
Vortex / Jun '95 / SRD

JUNGLE VIBES VOL.1
CD ________ **SPVCD 8455362**
Red Arrow / Apr '95 / Jet Star / Koch / SRD

JUNGLE VOCAL
Vocal: *Peshay* / Heavy vibes: *Origination* / Yearnin': *Annette B & Chuckleberry* / Hit after hit: *Baby Wayne & Michael Rose* / Silver haze: *Area 39 & Corelle* / World is our future: *Origination* / Murder: *Beenie Man & Chuckleberry* / Tell me baby: *Faze 1 FM & R. Rankin* / Junglist lover: *Ron Tom & Julie* / Money money: *Andy, Horace & Ron Tom* / Talk: *Garnet Silk & Chuckleberry* / Good love: *Ron Tom & Marsha Red* / Flip flop: *Tenor Senior & Garnet Silk* / Sunshine: *Eugenix & Corelle* / Gal tune (ooh boy): *Medoza* / Blood sweat and tears: *Roger Robin & Chuckleberry*
CD ________ **STORM 3 CD**
Desert Storm / Jan '96 / Sony

JUNGLE WARFARE (2CD Set)
CD Set ________ **MMBK 272**
Moonshine / Apr '95 / Mo's Music Machine / Prime / RTM/Disc

JUNGLISM
CD ________ **SOURCDLP 2**
SOUR / Jul '95 / SRD

JUNGLIZED
CD ________ **SEL 14**
Crammed Discs / Jul '96 / Grapevine/ PolyGram / New Note/Pinnacle / Prime / RTM/Disc

JUNIOR BOYS OWN COLLECTION VOL.1
CD ________ **JBOCD 2**
Junior Boys Own / May '97 / Mo's Music Machine / RTM/Disc

JUNIOR BOYS OWN COLLECTION VOL.2
Ultra flava: *Heller & Farley Project* / Naked and ashamed: *Dylan Rhymes* / Shame: *PLC* / Pearl's girl: *Underworld* / Peckings: *Ballistic Brothers* / Downtown Science: *Black Science Orchestra* / Chemical beats: *Chemical Brothers* / Wild luv: *Roach Motel* / Rock 2 house: *X-Press 2* / Traditional height: *Sycamore* / Tranz euro xpress: *X-Press 2* / Born slippy: *Underworld*
CD ________ **JBOCD 6**
Junior Boys Own / Mar '97 / Mo's Music Machine / RTM/Disc

JURABEG NABIEV (Music From Tadjikstan)
CD ________ **C 560102**
Ocora / Aug '97 / ADA / Harmonia Mundi

JUS' HOUSE (14 Essential House Grooves)
Slam me baby: *4 To The Bar* / Get huh: *Ride Committee* / Let the music set you free: *House Culture* / Sax in the ozone: *Aaron, Robert* / TT Lover: *Jus Us* / Way I feel: *Tears Of Velva* / I wanna be your lover: *Nuphonic* / My prayer: *Carroll, Ronnie* / Time for change: *Ulysses* / Come on baby: *Faces* / Get down: *Mixx Vibes* / Everything I got: *Faces* / Must be the music: *Serious Rope* / Friend not lover: *Serenade*
CD ________ **CDELV 12**
Elevate / Jul '93 / 3mv/Sony

JUS' JEEPIN' VOL.1
Deep cover: *Dr. Dre* / I made love (4 da very 1st time): *Little Shawn* / Live at the barbeque: *Main Source* / How I could just kill a man: *Cypress Hill* / You can't see what I can see: *Heavy D & The Boyz* / Fudge pudge: *Organized Konfusion* / True fuschnick: *Fu-Schnickens* / Blue cheese: *UMC's* / Lisa baby: *Father MC* / Scenario: *Tribe Called Quest* / Half time: *Nas* / Horny lil devil: *Ice Cube* / Dwyck: *Gang Starr* / Daddy: *ADL*
CD ________ **CDELV 09**
Debut / Jun '94 / 3mv/Sony / Pinnacle

JUS' JEEPIN' VOL.2 (Jus' Jeepin' Again)
Electric relaxation: *Tribe Called Quest* / Wreckx shop: *Wreckx n' Effect* / Ghetto red hot: *Supercat* / CREAM: *Wu Tang Clan* / Chief rocka rumblin': *Lords Of The Underground* / Down with the king: *Run DMC* / Make room: *Alkaholiks* / Zulu war chant: *Bambaataa, Afrika* / Remains: *Gang Starr* / Danger: *Murray, Keith* / 93 Til infinity: *Souls Of Mischief* / Best kept secret 45: *Diamond D & The Psychotic Neurotics* / Murdered ova nuttin': *Hoodratz* / Shit's real: *Geronimo, Mic*
CD ________ **CDELV 19**
Elevate / Jun '95 / 3mv/Sony

JUS' TRAX
Wair a pear: *Carter, Derrick & Chris Nazuka* / Living in Brooklyn: *Product Of Da Neighbourhood* / Stella Sunday: *Glasgow Underground* / B-Boy black: *Heller & Farley Project* / Version 1: *Swag* / Odyssey: *7th Movement* / I'm back: *Sessomatto* / Version 9: *Swag* / Living in Brooklyn (Roach Motel dub): *Product Of Da Neighbourhood* / Duro: *Ospina, Davidson* / Pain in my brain: *Outsider*
CD ________ **JSTCD 1**
Jus' Trax / Feb '97 / Amato Disco / Mo's Music Machine / Prime / RTM/Disc

JUST A LITTLE OVERCOME (The Stax Vocal Groups)
No strings attached: *Mad Lads* / These old memories: *Mad Lads* / I'm so glad I fell in love with you: *Mad Lads* / Highway to Heaven: *Dramatics* / Since I've been in love: *Dramatics* / Mannish boy: *Newcomers* / Girl this boy loves you: *Newcomers* / Just a little overcome: *Nightingales* / Baby, don't do it: *Nightingales* / I'm with you: *Nightingales* / Whole bit of love: *Temprees* / Your love (is all I need): *Temprees* / I refuse to be lonely: *Stingers* / Showered with love: *Ollie & The Nightingales* / Mellow way you treat your man: *Ollie & The Nightingales* / All because of you: *Limitations* / Echo: *Epsilons* / Make this young lady mine: *Mad Lads* / Your love was strange: *Dramatics* / Open up your heart (let me come in): *Newcomers* / Anyone can: *Leaders* / Love's creepin' up on me: *United Image*
CD ________ **CDSXD 019**
Stax / Feb '89 / Pinnacle

JUST ANOTHER ASSHOLE
CD ________ **ALP 39CD**
Atavistic / Jan '97 / Cargo / SRD

JUST COUNTRY (40 Golden Greats - 2CD Set)
Hello darlin': *Twitty, Conway* / Streets of Baltimore: *Bare, Bobby* / She even woke me up to say goodbye: *Rogers, Kenny* / On her way to being a woman: *Williams, Don* / Swinging doors: *Jones, George* / Your cheatin' heart: *Shannon, Del* / Burning memories: *Jennings, Waylon* / She thinks I still care: *Pitney, Gene* / Wild side of life: *Thompson, Hank* / Honky tonkitis: *Walker, Billy* / Take these chains from my heart: *Gibson, Don* / End of understanding: *Nelson, Willie* / I fall to pieces: *Houston, David* / King of the road: *Miller, Roger* / Here comes my baby back again: *Young, Faron* / Jukebox Charlie: *Paycheck, Johnny* / Just because: *Fender, Freddy* / Why baby why: *Jones, George & Gene Pitney* / Beautiful lady: *Greene, Jack* / Jambalaya: *Russell, Johnny* / Me and Bobby McGee: *Rogers, Kenny* / Good year for the roses: *Jones, George* / Sweet dreams: *Gibson, Don* / There's never been a time: *Williams, Don* / Detroit City: *Bare, Bobby* / Moment isn't very long: *Nelson, Willie* / Wine me up: *Young, Faron* / I recall a gypsy woman: *Thompson, Hank* / Release me: *Paycheck, Johnny* / I can't help it: *Shannon, Del* / Sally was a good old girl: *Jennings, Waylon* / Almost persuaded: *Houston, David* / Funny how time slips away: *Walker, Billy* / Most beautiful girl in the world: *Clark, Roy* / Heartaches by the number: *Miller, Roger* / Bridge washed out: *Mack, Warner* / Luckenbach Texas: *Russell, Johnny* / It's only make believe: *Twitty, Conway* / Don't rob another man's castle: *Jones, George & Gene Pitney* / Green green grass of home: *Wagoner, Porter*
CD Set ________ **MUCD 9502**
Musketeer / May '96 / Disc

JUST IN TIME TOO LATE
CD ________ **SOHO 16CD**
Suburbs Of Hell / Nov '94 / Kudos / Pinnacle / Plastic Head

JUST KEEP ON DANCING (Chess Northern Soul)
Look at me now: *Callier, Terry* / Baby hang on: *McAllister, Maurice & The Radiants* / After the laughter (here comes the tears): *Chandler, Gene* / Strange change: *Ward, Herb* / I just kept on dancing: *Banks, Doug* / Fat boy can cry: *Stewart, Billy* / More love that's what we need: *Gospel Classics* / Tired of being lonely: *Jacobs, Eddy* / Sweeter than the day before: *Valentinos* / Landslide: *Clarke, Tony* / In orbit: *Lovejoy, Joy* / We go together: *Barnum, Eve* / Ain't no more room: *Kittens* / Hold on: *Radiants* / What can I do: *Kirby, George* / Love control: *Perry, Greg* / Do the pearl girl: *Matta Baby* / Devil made me do it: *Natural Four* / Why can't I be your man: *Chessmen* / Seven day fool: *James, Etta* / Lend me your hand: *Kindly Shepherds* / I'm so glad: *Cato, Joe* / Thinkin' about you: *Dells* / Ol' man river: *Stewart, Billy*
CD ________ **CDKEND 138**
Kent / Oct '96 / Pinnacle

JUST MY IMAGINATION VOL.1
CD ________ **CDTRL 286**
Trojan / Mar '94 / Direct / Jet Star

JUST MY IMAGINATION VOL.2
CD ________ **CDTRL 298**
Trojan / Mar '94 / Direct / Jet Star

JUST MY IMAGINATION VOL.3
(Sittin' on the) dock of the bay: *Brown, Dennis* / Private number: *Honey Boy* / Forgot to be your lover: *Dennis, Denzil* / Yesterday once more: *Woung, Beverley* / Stop the war: *Parks, Lloyd* / Na na hey hey kiss him goodbye: *Pioneers* / Band of gold: *Griffiths, Marcia* / It's too late: *Now Generation* / Look what you've done for me: *Boothe, Ken* / Everybody plays the fool: *Chosen Few* / Summertime: *Johnson, Domino* / If you don't know me by now: *Zap Pow* / (If loving you is wrong) I don't want to be right: *Maytones* / One bad people: *Briggs, Barry* / Boogie on reggae woman: *Briggs, Barry* / In my life: *Robinson, Jackie* / Blood brothers: *Boothe, Ken* / United we stand: *Wally Brothers* / Man who sold the world: *Wally Brothers*
CD ________ **CDTRL 311**
Trojan / Mar '94 / Direct / Jet Star

JUST MY IMAGINATION VOL.4
I love the way you love me: *Chosen Few* / Speak softly: *Spence, Barrington* / It's all in the game: *Gaylads* / Only you: *Gaylads* / What'cha gonna do about it: *Simpson, Jeanette* / What does it take (to win your love): *Ellis, Alton* / Don't let me be lonely tonight: *Forrester, Sharon* / Crazy: *Dobson, Dobby* / California dreamin': *Francis, Winston* / What's going on: *Pat Satchmo* / Only the strong survive: *Mighty Diamonds* / Queen majesty: *Chosen Few* / Midnight train to Georgia: *Brown, Teddy* / Can't get used to losing you: *Ray, Danny* / Endlessly: *Dobson, Dobby* / Dark end of the street: *Pat Kelly* / I second that emotion: *Chosen Few* / Lonely for your love: *Uniques* / There's no me without you: *Parks, Lloyd* / I love the way you love me (part 2): *Parks, Lloyd*
CD ________ **CDTRL 328**
Trojan / Mar '94 / Direct / Jet Star

JUST RAGGA
CD ________ **CRCD 14**
Charm / Jul '92 / Jet Star

JUST RAGGA VOL.10
CD ________ **CRCD 50**
Charm / Jun '96 / Jet Star

JUST RAGGA VOL.11
CD _______________ **CRCD 62**
Charm / Mar '97 / Jet Star

JUST RAGGA VOL.2
CD _______________ **CRCD 15**
Charm / Oct '92 / Jet Star

JUST RAGGA VOL.3
Action: *Nadine & Terror Fabulous* / Hands on lover: *Brown, Dennis & Lovindeer* / Step aside: *Ninja Ford* / Protein, vitamin and mineral: *Galaxy* / Clap dance: *Red Dragon* / Dead and bury: *Powerman* / Boom bye bye: *Ninja Kid* / Tickie: *Daddy Mite* / Butterfly: *Bailey, Admiral* / Broke wine butterfly: *Terror Fabulous & Daddy Screw* / Don't touch the coke: *Cobra* / No retreat: *Terror Fabulous* / Diseases: *Major Mackerel* / Racist: *Sweetie Irie*
CD _______________ **CRCD 16**
Charm / Mar '93 / Jet Star

JUST RAGGA VOL.4
CD _______________ **CRCD 18**
Charm / Jun '93 / Jet Star

JUST RAGGA VOL.5
CD _______________ **CRCD 25**
Charm / Nov '93 / Jet Star

JUST RAGGA VOL.6
CD _______________ **CRCD 28**
Charm / Apr '94 / Jet Star

JUST RAGGA VOL.7
CD _______________ **CRCD 34**
Charm / Oct '94 / Jet Star

JUST RAGGA VOL.8
CD _______________ **CRCD 39**
Charm / Jun '95 / Jet Star

JUST RAGGA VOL.9
CD _______________ **CRCD 47**
Charm / Dec '95 / Jet Star

JUST THE TWO OF US
I've had the time of my life: *Medley, Bill & Jennifer Warnes* / Don't wanna lose you: *Estefan, Gloria* / Up where you belong: *Cocker, Joe & Jennifer Warnes* / Too much, too little, too late: *Mathis, Johnny & Deniece Williams* / On the wings of love: *Osborne, Jeffrey* / Through the storm: *Franklin, Aretha & Elton John* / With you I'm born again: *Preston, Billy & Syreeta* / Endless love: *Ross, Diana & Lionel Richie* / Eternal flame: *Bangles* / I know you by heart: *Parton, Dolly & Smokey Robinson* / All the love in the world: *Warwick, Dionne* / Sometimes when we touch: *Wynette, Tammy & Mark Gray* / All I want is forever: *Taylor, James 'JT' & Regina Belle* / I knew you were waiting (for me): *Franklin, Aretha & George Michael* / Wind beneath my wings: *Knight, Gladys*
CD _______________ **MOODCD 11**
Epic / Mar '90 / Sony

JUST THE TWO OF US
CD _______________ **JHD 023**
Tring / Jun '92 / Tring

JUSTICE SAMPLER VOL.2
CD _______________ **JR 00052**
Justice / Mar '94 / Koch

JUSTIN TIME FOR CHRISTMAS
CD _______________ **JUST 752**
Justin Time / Dec '95 / Cadillac / New Note/Pinnacle

JVC WORLD CLASS MUSIC
CD _______________ **JD 3307**
JVC / Jul '88 / Direct / New Note/Pinnacle / Vital/SAM

JVC WORLD CLASS MUSIC VOL.2
Maracuja: *Castro-Neves, Oscar* / Donna: *Guitar Workshop In LA* / Face to face: *Okoshi, Tiger* / Cool shadow: *Okoshi, Tiger* / Front runner: *Holman, Bill Band* / Beverly Hills: *Guitar Workshop In LA* / Over the rainbow: *Okoshi, Tiger* / Yamato dawn: *Neptune, John Kaizan* / New face: *Watts, Ernie Quartet*
CD _______________ **JD 3319**
JVC / Aug '89 / Direct / New Note/Pinnacle / Vital/SAM

JW CALYPSOCA 1997 HITS VOL.1
CD _______________ **JW 127CD**
JW / Jun '97 / Jet Star

KALON AR C'HAB
CD _______________ **CDCA 001**
Diffusion Breizh / Apr '94 / ADA

KANSAS CITY
CD _______________ **5295542**
Verve / Aug '96 / PolyGram

KANSAS CITY
Blues in the dark: *Basie, Count* / Sittin' in: *Berry, Leon 'Chu'* / Moten swing: *Basie, Count* / How long, how long blues: *Varsity Seven* / Hootie blues: *McShann, Jay* / I surrender dear: *Chocolate Dandies* / Queer notions: *Hawkins, Coleman & Fletcher Henderson* / 627 Stomp: *Johnson, Pete* / Mary's idea: *Kirk, Andy & His Twelve Clouds of Joy* / I left my baby: *Basie, Count Orchestra* / Yeah man: *Basie, Count Orchestra* / Goon drag (gone wid de goon): *Price, Sammy & His Bluesicians* / Froggy bottom: *Kirk, Andy & His Twelve Clouds of Joy* / Blue room: *Moten, Bennie Kansas City Orchestra* / Kansas city stride: *Basie, Count Orchestra* / Pagin' the Devil: *Kansas City Six* / La Fayette: *Page, Hot Lips & His Orchestra* / Solitude: *Ellington, Duke Orchestra* / One o'clock jump: *Basie, Count Orchestra* / Blue Lester: *Young, Lester Quintet*
CD _______________ **CD 53300**
Giants Of Jazz / Feb '97 / Cadillac / Jazz Music / Target/BMG

KANSAS CITY AND SOUTH WEST
CD _______________ **DCD 8004**
Disky / Jan '95 / Disky / THE

KANSAS CITY BLUES (3CD Set)
Moten swing / Come on over to my house / Trouble in mind / On the sunny side of the street / Confessin' the blues / Walkin' blues (aka Walking) / Hard working man blues / When I've been drinking / Merry-go-round blues / Bad tale boogie / McShann's boogie blues / Everything will be all right / Pic's boogie / Scotty's / Cover up / (Scotty can blow) kicks / Tonight's the night / My man stands out / Do you want it / It comes in like a lion / When you want chili / It's hard to laugh or smile / You'll wind up on top / On the gravy train / Don't come too soon / Ugly Papa / Don't save it too long (The money song) / After hours waltz / I ain't gonna give nobody none of my jelly roll / Sugar daddy blues / Gone / Gotta good reason for being bad / Play the blues / What evil have I done / Gonna play with your woman / Work don't bother me / Goosed / Jackson County romp / Mizzou / Hot sauce / Inform me baby / Lyin' woman blues / Suppressin' the blues / Hello and goodbye / You ain't got it no more / When your lover has gone / Oh chuck it (in a bucket) / Decent woman blues / Dragging my heart around / Kickapoo / Tea for Tommy / If you don't why don't ya / I want you to be my guy / Douglas boogie / Killion / Leaving town blues / Lights out / Turn it over / That did it / Best friend blues / Baby you messed up / You better leave my gal alone / Lou, Cindy Lou / Squabblin' woman / I'm gonna get married / New style baby / Let's love awhile / Nasty attitude / Slow down baby / Lady with the black dress on / Sister flattop / It ain't no use / Jumpin' little woman
CD Set _______________ **CDEM 1607**
Capitol / Mar '97 / EMI

KANSAS CITY LEGENDS 1929-1942
CD _______________ **158432**
Jazz Archives / Nov '95 / Discovery

KARAOKE - 50'S & 60'S FAVOURITES
Teddy bear / Peggy Sue / Lipstick on your collar / Blue suede shoes / living doll / shake, rattle and roll / Vaya con dios / Rave on / Be bop a lula / That'll be theday / Love me tender / (We're gonna) Rock around the clock / Hey Jude / Da doo ron ron / Ferry 'cross the Mersey / I want to hold your hand / Bachelor boy / House of the Rising Sun / Congratulations / Delilah / Wooden heart / Return to sender / You'll never walk alone / It's now or never
CD _______________ **CC 279**
Music For Pleasure / Nov '91 / EMI

KARAOKE - 70'S
Mull of Kintyre / Don't go breaking my heart / Hi ho silver lining / Wonder of you / Dancing queen / I love you love me love / Hold me close / Love grows (where my Rosemary goes) / Waterloo / In the summertime / Knock three times / You're the one that I want / I can't tell the bottom from the top / American pie / Summer nights / Sailing
CD _______________ **CC 287**
Music For Pleasure / Nov '92 / EMI

KARAOKE - 80'S
Uptown girl / I should be so lucky / Ebony and ivory / Karma Chameleon / Never gonna give you up / Eye of the tiger / I just called to say I love you / I want to break free / Hello / Winner takes it all / Thank you for the music / Super trouper / Chain reaction / Come on Eileen
CD _______________ **CC 288**
Music For Pleasure / Nov '92 / EMI

KARAOKE - 90'S
Achy breaky heart / All right now / Would I lie to you / Should I stay or should I go / It only takes a minute / Get here / Heartbeat / Baker Street / Heal the world / Tears on my pillow / Too much love will kill you / It must have been love / Everything I do (I do it for you) / Itsy bitsy teeny weeny yellow polka dot bikini
CD _______________ **CC 8231**
Music For Pleasure / Nov '93 / EMI

KARAOKE - CHART HITS
Back for good / Wonderwall / Crazy for you / Stay another day / Re-light my fire / Love me for a reason / Eternal love / If you only let me in / Unchained melody
CD _______________ **AVC 581**
Avid / Dec '96 / Avid/BMG / Koch / THE

KARAOKE - CHILDREN'S KARAOKE FAVOURITES
There's no one quite like Grandma / Grandad / (How much is that) doggie in the window / Ugly duckling / Lily the pink / Teddy bears' picnic / Hippopotamus song / Runaway train / Ten green bottles / Matchstalk men and matchstalk cats and dogs / London Bridge is falling down / Birdie song / My grandfather's clock / Windmill in old Amsterdam / Three little fishes / Handful of songs / Animals went in two by two / Simon says / Boomps a daisy / Christopher Robin at Buckingham Palace / If you're happy / Hokey Cokey dance
CD _______________ **CC 8243**
Music For Pleasure / Oct '94 / EMI

KARAOKE - CHRISTMAS KARAOKE PARTY VOL.1
Merry Christmas everybody / Mistletoe and wine / When a child is born / Jingle bells / Santa Claus is coming to town / Mary's boy child / I wish it could be Christmas every day / Silent night / We three Kings / Last Christmas / Good King Wenceslas / Frosty the snowman / Stop the cavalry / God rest ye merry gentlemen / Saviour's day / Have yourself a merry little Christmas / We wish you a Merry Christmas / Auld lang syne
CD _______________ **CC 278**
Music For Pleasure / Dec '94 / EMI

KARAOKE - CHRISTMAS KARAOKE VOL.2
Sleigh ride / Let it snow, let it snow, let it snow / Happy holiday / When Santa got stuck up the chimney / Rudolph the red nosed reindeer / O little town of Bethlehem / I saw mommy kissing Santa Claus / It came upon a midnight clear / Little donkey / Rockin' around the Christmas tree / Winter wonderland / Jolly old St. Nicholas / All I want for Christmas (is my two front teeth) / I saw three ships / Silver bells / Fairy on the Christmas tree / Christmas alphabet / Good Christian men rejoice / Little drummer boy / Ding dong merrily on high / Deck the halls with boughs of holly / Away in a manger / White Christmas
CD _______________ **CC 8230**
Music For Pleasure / Dec '94 / EMI

KARAOKE - CLASSICS
Back for good / YMCA / (The shoop shoop song) it's in his kiss / Summer nights / Unchained melody / Rock around the clock / Summer holiday / New York, New York / Knowing me, knowing you / You can't hurry love / Re-light my fire / Suspicious minds / Don't go breaking my heart / You'll never walk alone / Greatest love of all / (They long to be) close to you
CD _______________ **AVC 580**
Avid / Dec '96 / Avid/BMG / Koch / THE

KARAOKE - GREATEST KARAOKE ALBUM IN THE WORLD (14 Sing-A-Long Party Favourites)
YMCA / Summer nights / Wake me up before you go go / Fame / Holiday / Saturday night / I will survive / La bamba / Let's twist again / It's not unusual / Cokey cokey / Tiger feet / All shook up / New York, New York
CD _______________ **SUMCD 4058**
Summit / Nov '96 / Sound & Media

KARAOKE - HIT FACTORY
Hand on your heart / Another night / Better the devil you know / Never too late / Got to be certain / Especially for you / When you come back to me / I should be so lucky / Too many broken hearts / You'll never stop me loving you / Together forever / Never gonna give you up / Toy boy / Wouldn't change a thing / This time I know it's for real / Nothing can divide us / Take me to your heart / Nothing's gonna stop me now
CD _______________ **CDMFP 5968**
Music For Pleasure / Oct '92 / EMI

KARAOKE - IRISH KARAOKE
With a shillelagh under my arm / If you're Irish come into the parlour / Galway bay / Mountains of Mourne / Minstrel boy / Cockles and mussels / How are things in Glocca Morra / Delaney's donkey / I dream of Jeannie with the light brown hair / When Irish eyes are smiling / It's a long way to Tipperary / Little bit of heaven / Black velvet band / I'll take you home again Kathleen / Believe me, if all those endearing young charms / Rose of Tralee / How can you buy Killarney / Mother Machree / It's a great day for the Irish / Danny boy
CD _______________ **CC 8227**
Music For Pleasure / Nov '93 / EMI

KARAOKE - IRISH KARAOKE CLASSICS
CD _______________ **AVC 596**
Avid / Mar '97 / Avid/BMG / Koch / THE

KARAOKE - MORE CHRISTMAS KARAOKE
I believe in Father Christmas / Jingle bell rock / Here we come a-wassailing / Christmas alphabet / Twelve days of Christmas / Hark the Herald Angels sing / Wonderful Christmas time / First noel / Do you hear what I hear / Baby it's cold outside / While sheperds watched their flocks by night / Rocking carol
CD _______________ **CDSL 8281**
EMI Solo / Oct '96 / EMI

KARAOKE - PARTY CLASSICS
When a man loves a woman / Dancing queen / When will I see you again / My girl / Sailing / Delilah / Wooden heart / Peggy Sue / Crocodile rock / Love is all around / Can't smile without you / Summer of '69 / Like a virgin / I will survive / Black is black / It only takes a minute
CD _______________ **AVC 579**
Avid / Dec '96 / Avid/BMG / Koch / THE

KARAOKE - PIONEER KARAOKE VOL.1
Addicted to love / Summer nights / Killing me softly / Candle in the wind / Crazy little thing called love / Great balls of fire / Girls just wanna have fun / All right now / House of the rising sun / I will survive / I heard it through the grapevine / Billie Jean / Locomotion / It's my party / Hey Jude / You'll never walk alone
CD _______________ **CDMFP 6124**
Music For Pleasure / Jul '94 / EMI

KARAOKE - PIONEER KARAOKE VOL.2
It's not unusual / Love shack / Night fever / Stand by your man / He ain't heavy, he's my brother / Let's dance / Hi ho silver lining / Venus / Daydream believer / If you don't know me by now / Crazy / I wanna dance with somebody (who loves me) / Boys are back in town / Summer of '69 / New York, New York / King of the road
CD _______________ **CDMFP 6125**
Music For Pleasure / Jul '94 / EMI

KARAOKE - PIONEER KARAOKE VOL.3
You can't hurry love / Fame / Mony mony / Stop in the name of love / Super trouper / Tainted love / Greatest love of all / Close to you / Blues suede shoes / If I could turn back time / Livin' on a prayer / Up where we belong / Don't it make my brown eyes blue / Bye bye love / Wild thing / Big spender
CD _______________ **CDMFP 6126**
Music For Pleasure / Jul '94 / EMI

KARAOKE - PIONEER KARAOKE VOL.4
American pie / Like a virgin / In the summertime / Hello Dolly / Oh pretty woman / Annie's song / (Sittin' on the) dock of the bay / Daniel / Bachelor boy / Endless love / Help me Rhonda / Hopelessly devoted to you / Geno / Unchain my heart / Bang a gong (get it on) / (We're gonna) Rock around the clock
CD _______________ **CDMFP 6140**
Music For Pleasure / Oct '94 / EMI

KARAOKE - PIONEER KARAOKE VOL.5
Delilah / Hello Mary Lou / Nine to Five / California dreamin' / Crocodile rock / I can see clearly now / Eye of the tiger / Band on the run / Every time we say goodbye / Don't go breaking my heart / Blue moon / We are family / Itchycoo Park / Bobby's girl / All day and all of the night / Ferry across the Mersey
CD _______________ **CDMFP 6141**
Music For Pleasure / Oct '94 / EMI

KARAOKE - PIONEER KARAOKE VOL.6
Are you lonesome tonight / Grease / I left my heart in San Francisco / Best / I will always love you / Dizzy / Groovy kind of love / You're so vain / 2-4-6-8 Motorway / Power of love / I got you babe / Tiger feet / Everybody wants to rule the world / When you're in love with a beautiful woman / Breaking up is hard to do / La bamba
CD _______________ **CDMFP 6142**
Music For Pleasure / Nov '94 / EMI

KARAOKE - PIONEER KARAOKE VOL.7
Love is all around / Centrefold / Unchained melody / Crocodile shoes / All I have to do is dream / Miss you nights / Angie baby / Purple rain / Cry me a river / Knowing me, knowing you / Nothing compares 2 U / With or without you / Lady is a tramp / I'm still standing / I swear / Something gotten hold of my heart
CD _______________ **CDMFP 6167**
Music For Pleasure / Jun '95 / EMI

KARAOKE - PIONEER KARAOKE VOL.8
It's now or never / I'd do anything for love (but I won't do that) / YMCA / Careless whisper / Take a chance on me / Sweet dreams (are made of this) / Dizzy / Baby, I love your way / We are family / Unbelieveable / Singin' in the rain / These dreams / Shine / Moving on up / Mmm mmm mmm mmm / Most beautiful girl in the world
CD _______________ **CDMFP 6168**
Music For Pleasure / Jun '95 / EMI

KARAOKE - SCOTTISH KARAOKE
Donald, where's yer troosers / Loch Lomond / Roamin' in the gloamin' / Bluebells of Scotland / Scotland the brave / Dancing in Kyle / Skye boat song / Northern lights of old Aberdeen / My ain folk / Gordon for me / My love is like a red red rose / I love a lassie / Amazing grace / Ye banks and braes o' bonnie Doon / Annie Laurie / I belong to Glasgow / Charlie is my darling / Mull of Kintyre / Westering home / Just a wee deoch an' Doris / Comin' thro' the rye / Auld lang syne
CD _______________ **CC 8228**
Music For Pleasure / Nov '93 / EMI

KARAOKE - THE GREATEST KARAOKE
Killing me softly / Big spender / You'll never walk alone / It's not unusual / Three lions / Yesterday / How deep is your love / (Can't help) falling in love / Always on my mind /

Alright / Stand by your man / Crazy / I will survive / Back for good / Hi-ho silver lining / Hey Jude
CD ________ **AVC 578**
Avid / Dec '96 / Avid/BMG / Koch / THE

KARAOKE BALLADS
CD ________ **CDSL 8282**
EMI Solo / Oct '96 / EMI

KARAOKE CELEBRATION
Bells / Wedding (La novia) / She wears my ring / Get me to the church on time / You are my sunshine / Band of gold / If you were the only girl in the world / Happy birthday to you / I'm twenty-one today / When I'm sixty four / Nobody loves a fairy when she's forty / Anniversary waltz / My ole dutch / Twenty tiny fingers / You must have been a beautiful baby / When a child is born / Congratulations / It's my party / Welcome home (Vivre) / Green green grass of home / For he's a jolly good fellow / Bachelor boy / From me to you / Especially for you / Auld land syne
CD ________ **CC 8237**
Music For Pleasure / May '94 / EMI

KARAOKE COUNTRY
Rhinestone cowboy / Coalminer's daughter / Green green grass of home / Here you come again / Honey come back / Nobody's child / I walk the line / Blanket on the ground / Last thing on my mind / Crazy / Wayward wind / Your cheatin' heart / Welcome to my world / Distant drums / Stand by your man / Try a little kindness / Help me make it through the night / Take me home country roads / Jambalaya / Harper Valley PTA / Sixteen tons
CD ________ **CC 280**
Music For Pleasure / Jul '92 / EMI

KARAOKE CROONERS
Born free / Spanish eyes / Close to you / New York, New York / I left my heart in San Francisco / Magic moments / Strangers in the night / Are you lonesome tonight / Smoke gets in your eyes / Release me / Love is a many splendoured thing / Unforgettable / What a wonderful world / I can't stop lovin' you / Moon river / When I fall in love / Answer me / Unchained melody / More / That's amore / Somewhere
CD ________ **CC 281**
Music For Pleasure / Jul '92 / EMI

KARAOKE DUETS
Somethin' stupid / Two sleepy people / I got you babe / Don't go breaking my heart / Endless love / It takes two / Cinderella Rockefella / Tonight I celebrate my love for you / Ebony and ivory / Something's gotten hold of my heart / Especially for you / I'd do anything / Who wants to be a millionaire
CD ________ **CDSL 8263**
EMI / Oct '95 / EMI

KARAOKE GLAM ROCK
I'm the leader of the gang (I am) / Hell raiser / Do you wanna touch me (Oh yeah) / Cat crept in / Can the can / Doing alright with the boys / Blockbuster / Get it on / Hello hello I'm back again / 48 crash / Tiger feet / Devil gate drive / Oh boy / I love you love me love
CD ________ **CC 8242**
Music For Pleasure / Oct '94 / EMI

KARAOKE GREASE/SATURDAY NIGHT FEVER
How deep is your love / Jive talking / Night fever / Stayin' alive / If I can't have you / You should be dancing / Rock'n'roll is here to stay / Grease / Hopelessly devoted to you / It's raining on Prom night / Summer nights / You're the one that I want / Tears on my pillow
CD ________ **CDSL 8266**
Virgin / Oct '95 / EMI

KARAOKE LEGENDS - ELVIS PRESLEY
Heartbreak Hotel / Blue suede shoes / Hound dog / Love me tender / All shook up / Teddy bear / Jailhouse rock / King Creole / One night / Girl of my best friend / It's now or never / Are you lonesome tonight / Wooden heart / Can't help falling in love / Return to sender / Crying in the chapel / If I can dream / Wonder of you / Always on my mind / Moody blue / My way
CD ________ **CC 297**
Music For Pleasure / May '93 / EMI

KARAOKE LEGENDS - LENNON & MCCARTNEY VOL.1
She loves you / Sergeant Pepper's lonely hearts club band / With a little help from my friends / Help / Penny Lane / All you need is love / Can't buy me love / Love me do / Eleanor Rigby / I want to hold your hand / Back in the USSR / When I'm sixty four / Please please me / Michelle / From me to you / Let it be / Ticket to ride / Yellow submarine / Hard day's night / Yesterday / Hey Jude
CD ________ **CC 8229**
Music For Pleasure / Nov '93 / EMI

KARAOKE LEGENDS - LENNON & MCCARTNEY VOL.2
Magical mystery tour / Nowhere man / Lady Madonna / I should have known / Fool on the hill / Paperback writer / Things we said today / I feel fine / I wanna be your man / Ob-la-di ob-la-da / Long and winding road / Drive my car / Eight days a week / And I love her / Get back / We can work it out / All my loving / Hello goodbye / I saw her standing there / Day tripper / Strawberry fields
CD ________ **CC 8241**
Music For Pleasure / Feb '95 / EMI

KARAOKE LOVE SONGS
We've only just begun / Suddenly / True love ways / Fever / Silly love songs / Endless love / Power of love / Move closer / When the girl in your arms (is the girl in your heart) / It must have been love / Love letter / And I love you so / Always on my mind / On the wings of love / Fool (if you think it's over) / Three times a lady
CD ________ **CC 286**
Music For Pleasure / Nov '92 / EMI

KARAOKE MILLION SELLING HITS
Roll over Beethoven / Mona Lisa / Sealed with a kiss / Monday, Monday / Ain't that a shame / Tears / Bright eyes / It's all in the game / Things we do for love / Under the moon of love / Rivers of Babylon / Wichita lineman / He ain't heavy, he's my brother / Anyone who had a heart / World of our own / There's a kind of hush (all over the world) / Diana / He's got the whole world in his hands
CD ________ **CC 8245**
Music For Pleasure / Oct '94 / EMI

KARAOKE NO. 1'S
Bohemian rhapsody / Everything I do (I do it for you) / Groovy kind of love / You'll never stop me from loving you / Singin' the blues / Long haired lover from Liverpool / Don't go breaking my heart / I remember you / Power of love / Imagine / Whatever will be will be (Que sera sera) / House of the rising sun / Something's gotten hold of my heart / Especially for you / I just called to say I love you
CD ________ **CC 8232**
Music For Pleasure / Nov '93 / EMI

KARAOKE ROCK 'N' ROLL
Chantilly lace / It's my party / Bird dog / Locomotion / Shake, rattle and roll / Great balls of fire / Giddy up a ding dong / Lipstick on your collar / That'll be the day / Bye bye love / Rubber ball / Blue suede shoes / Born too late / Peggy Sue / Long tall Sally / Be bop a lula / Teenager in love / Whole lotta shakin' goin' on / Rave on / Good golly Miss Molly / (We're gonna) Rock around the clock / Halfway to paradise / Blueberry Hill / C'mon everybody
CD ________ **CC 296**
Music For Pleasure / Jun '93 / EMI

KARAOKE SOUL
Save the last dance for me / (Sittin' on the) dock of the bay / When a man loves a woman / In the midnight hour / It takes two / Reach out, I'll be there / What becomes of the broken hearted / How sweet it is (to be loved by you) / Give me just a little more time / Saturday night at the movies / Band of gold / Try a little tenderness / This old heart of mine / My guy / Stand be me / At the club / Rescue me / My girl / Private number
CD ________ **CC 285**
Music For Pleasure / Nov '92 / EMI

KARAOKE TOP 10 HITS OF THE 60'S
Summer holiday / Tears / Speedy Gonzales / Anyone who had a heart / Private number / Whiter shade of pale / Seven little girls sitting in the back seat / Do wah diddy diddy / Yeh yeh / What do you want / Puppet on a string / You're sixteen / Pretty flamingo / Boom bang a bang / Lily the pink / Where do you go to my lovely / Tell Laura I love her / What do you want to make those eyes at me for / Blue moon / Three steps to heaven
CD ________ **CC 8246**
Music For Pleasure / Oct '94 / EMI

KARAOKE TOP 10 HITS OF THE 80'S
Call me / Freedom / True / House of fun / Is there something I should know / When the going gets tough / Wherever I lay my hat (that's my home) / Good heart / With a little help from my friends / Careless whisper / Only way is up / Two hearts
CD ________ **CDSL 8264**
EMI / Oct '95 / EMI

KARAOKE TOP 10 HITS OF THE 90'S
I'm too sexy / Dizzy / Million love songs / We have all the time in the world / Pray / Rhythm of my heart / Sleeping satellite / Love is all around / Crocodile shoes / Could it be magic
CD ________ **CDSL 8265**
EMI / Oct '95 / EMI

KARAOKE WARTIME FAVOURITES
There'll always be an England / Kiss me goodnight / Lili Marlene / (We're gonna hang out) The washing on the Siefried line / White cliffs of Dover / Nightingale sang in Berkeley Square / Run rabbit run / Now is the hour / Roll out the barrel / I've got sixpence / It's a long way to Tipperary / Bless 'em all / Yours / Quartermaster's stores / Coming in on a wing and a prayer / I don't want to set the world on fire / Goodnight sweetheart / I'm gonna get lit up (when the lights go on in London) / You are my sunshine / I'll be seeing you / We'll meet again / Reprise - There'll always be an England
CD ________ **CC 8236**
Music For Pleasure / May '94 / EMI

KARENNI
CD ________ **PAN 2040**
Pan / Oct '94 / ADA / CM / Direct

KASIO GEMS
CD ________ **CD 025C**
Carotte / May '97 / Jet Star

KATZ KEEP ROCKIN' VOL.1
CD ________ **LOMACD 39**
Loma / Nov '94 / BMG

KAUSTINEN FOLK MUSIC FESTIVAL 1990
CD ________ **BHCD 9130**
Brewhouse / Jul '91 / ADA / Brewhouse Music

KAZAAM
I am Kazaam: *O'Neal, Shaq* / I'll make your dreams come true: *Subway* / I swear I'm in love: *Usher* / Wishes: *Morris, Nathan* / All out on my own: *Shyheim* / No tighter wish: *Tangi & Lisa 'Left Eye' Lopes* / Lay light (one for the money): *Almighty Arrogant* / Show me your love: *Immature* / We genie: *O'Neal, Shaq & Wade Robson* / Dance wit' me: *Weaver, Jason* / If you believe: *Spinderella* / Key to my heart: *Choice* / I get lifted: *Barrio Boyzz* / Get down: *YBTO* / Boys will be boys: *Backstreet Boys* / Best of me: *Jamecia* / Mr. Material: *O'Neal, Shaq*
CD ________ **5490272**
A&M / Aug '96 / PolyGram

KAZAKH SONGS AND EPIC TRADITION OF THE WEST
CD ________ **C 580051**
Ocora / Nov '93 / ADA / Harmonia Mundi

KCRW: VOL.3 (Rare On Air)
State trooper: *Cowboy Junkies* / Dancing barefoot: *Smith, Patti* / Twister: *Zero, Remy* / Never is a promise: *Apple, Fiona* / Fall in love with me: *Booth & The Bad Angel* / Alice childress: *Folds, Ben Five* / Official ironmen rally song: *Guided By Voices* / Spinal column: *Stereolab* / She's gone: *Tindersticks* / 23 Minutes in brussels: *Luna* / Ecclesiastes: Free my heart: *Ndegeocello, Me'shell* / Angel on my bike: *Wallflowers* / Imagine: *Rubalcaba, Gonzala* / Secret o' life: *Taylor, James & Don Grolnick*
CD ________ **MR 1622**
Mammoth / Apr '97 / Vital

KEB DARGE'S LEGENDARY DEEP FUNK
Fun company: *Zambezi* / Dap walk: *Ernie & The Top Notes* / I who have nothing: *Frazier, Ray & The Shades Of Madness* / Gimme some skin: *Penn, Frank* / Kick the habit: *Prophet Soul* / Too hot to hold: *UFO's* / Sagittarus black: *McNealy, Timothy* / Quit jive'in: *Pearly Queen* / Put your own words to it: *Billy* / Cross Bronx expressway: *Cross Bronx Expressway* / Grease wheels: *Smoki' Shades Of Dub* / (Rockin') courtroom: *Judge Suds & The Soul Detergents* / How about it: *Big Bo Thomas & The Arrows* / Who dun it: *Originals Orchestra* / Soul power: *Lil' Ray & The Fantastic Four* / Ouwee man: *Serrano, Dave* / Going down for the last time: *Keaton, David* / First thing I do in the morning: *Williams, Joyce* / Can't fight the feeling: *Norwich Street Extension* / I wanna be loved by you: *Family of Eve* / Please be truthful: *Family of Eve*
CD ________ **BBECD 004**
Barely Breaking Even / Jun '97 / Beechwood/BMG

KECAK VOL.1
CD ________ **VICG 50272**
JVC World Library / Mar '96 / ADA / CM / Direct

KECAK VOL.2
CD ________ **VICG 53512**
JVC World Library / Mar '96 / ADA / CM / Direct

KEEP A ROCKIN' (2CD Set)
CD Set ________ **PFCD 3003**
Scratch / Mar '97 / Koch / Scratch/BMG

KEEP MOVIN' ON
Swingin': *Light Of The World* / Somebody help me out: *Beggar & Co* / North London boy: *Incognito* / You're lying: *Linx* / Walking into sunshine: *Central Line* / Southern Freeez: *Freeez* / Mama used to say: *Giscombe, Junior* / Easier said than done: *Shakatak* / Wings of love: *Level 42* / Dancing in outer space: *Atmosfear* / Time machine: *Direct Drive* / Give me: *I-Level*
CD ________ **RNBCD 102**
Connoisseur Collection / Jul '92 / Pinnacle

KEEP ON COMING THROUGH THE DOOR
Dance beat / Jack of my trade / Sounds of Babylon / Fire corner / Heart don't leap / To the fields / Mosquito one / Mr. Harry Skank / Alpha and omega
CD ________ **CDTRL 255**
Trojan / Mar '94 / Direct / Jet Star

KEEP ON RUNNING
CD ________ **CDTRL 334**
Trojan / Feb '94 / Direct / Jet Star

KEEP THE BEAT
CD ________ **HB8 001**
Hairball 8 / Oct '96 / Cargo

KEEP THE DREAM ALIVE (Now And Then Singles)
CD ________ **NTHEN 19**
Now & Then / May '95 / Plastic Head

KEEP THE FAITH
Change my darkness into light: *Flirtations* / Time marches on: *Hill, Lainie* / Good little you: *Dee, Joey* / Real thing: *Britt, Tina* / I'd rather die: *Superiors* / Think about the good times: *Washington, Baby* / Heartbreaker: *Barnum, H.B.* / Ecstasy: *Holloway, Patrice* / Hotline: *Garner, Reggie* / You should know: *Notations* / Love is dangerous: *Polk, Frank* / Girl's got it: *Preston, Billy* / What can go wrong: *Thrills* / Love man from Carolina: *Rollins, Bird* / I know the inside story: *Chubby & The Turnpikes* / Take your time and love kill: *Mitchell, Grover* / So Anna just love me: *Johnson, Roy Lee* / La de da I love you: *Foxx, Inez & Charlie* / Livin' in love: *Anthony, Sheila* / Time can change a love: *Scott, Cindy* / Too many people: *Goldsboro, Bobby* / Put your heart in it: *Dee, Joey* / It's too late: *Goldsboro, Bobby* / Love in my heart: *Entertainers* / I can't do it: *Eddie & Ernie*
CD ________ **GSCD 098**
Goldmine / Jun '96 / Vital

KEEP THE HOME FIRES BURNING (Songs & Music From The First World War)
Here we are, here we are: *Wheeler, F. & Chorus* / Goodbye-ee: *Various Narrators* / Just before the battle mother: *Oakland, Will & Chorus* / Your King and country want you: *Clarke, Helen & Chorus* / Trumpeter: *Newell, Raymond & Ian Swinley* / Deathless army: *Kinniburgh, T.F.* / medley: *NMB Flying Squadron* / Tramp, tramp, tramp: *Harlan & Stanley/chorus* / Keep the home fires burning: *Various Narrators* / Boys of the old brigade: *NMB Flying Squadron* / Boys in khaki, boys in blue: *Wheeler, F. & Chorus* / Colonel Bogey: *Coldstream Guards Band* / Pack up your troubles in your old kit bag: *Coldstream Guards Band* / It's a long way to Tipperary: *Coldstream Guards Band* / Roses of Picardy: *Murray, Templeton* / Passing Review Patrol: *Not Advised* / What has become of hinkey-dinky-parlay-voo: *Bernard, Al & Chorus*
CD ________ **CDSDL 358**
Saydisc / Mar '94 / ADA / Direct / Harmonia Mundi

KEEP YOUR ARMS AROUND ME
CD ________ **IMP 941**
IMP / Sep '96 / ADA / Discovery

KEEP YOUR SUNNY SIDE UP
CD ________ **SOW 512**
Sound Waves / Jul '94 / Target/BMG

KEEPING THE FAITH 1990
CD ________ **CRECD 081**
Creation / Jan '91 / 3mv/Vital

KEF TIME
CD ________ **CD 4269**
Traditional Crossroads / Feb '95 / CM / Direct

KENT'S MAGIC TOUCH
Magic touch: *Moore, Melba* / Things are getting a little tough: *Carlton, Eddie* / You fixed my heartache: *Foxx, Inez & Charlie* / Quit twistin' my arm: *Mitchell, Stanley* / This diamond ring: *Ambrose, Sammy* / Biggest man: *Hunt, Tommy* / Crying like a baby: *Jive Five* / You lie so well: *Knight, Marie* / I got my heart set on you: *Toys* / On top of the world: *SOUL* / Funny how we've changed places: *Anderson, Debra* / You shouldn't have set my soul on fire: *Foxx, Inez* / Tomorrow keeps shining: *Bartley, Chris* / I'm so glad I found you: *Diplomats* / Maybe maybe baby (baby baby baby): *Turner, Dee Dee* / This time round: *SOUL* / I wouldn't come back: *Bethea The Masked Man & The Agents* / Hole in the wall: *Stone, George* / Bricks, broken bottles and sticks: *Parrish, Dean* / You'll fall in love: *Jive Five* / Sweet sweet lovin': *Platters* / Never love a robin: *Hunt, Tommy* / My heart cries for you: *Porgy & The Monarchs* / Don't cry sing along with the music: *Moore, Melba* / That's enough: *Barbara & Brenda* / There comes a time: *Kitt, Eartha* / Long after tonight is all over: *Radcliffe, Jimmy*
CD ________ **CDKEND 146**
Kent / May '97 / Pinnacle

KENYA/TANZANIA - WITCHCRAFT & RITUAL MUSIC
CD ________ **7559720662**
Nonesuch / Jan '95 / Warner Music

KERALA: THE THAYAMBAKA (Music Of South India)
CD ________ **C 560047**
Ocora / Mar '97 / ADA / Harmonia Mundi

KERRANG VOL.1
Jesus Christ pose: *Soundgarden* / Another wordly device: *Prong* / Punishment: *Biohazard* / Autosurgery: *Therapy* / Territory: *Sepultura* / Sweating bullets: *Megadeth* / Shedding skin: *Pantera* / Caffeine bomb: *Wildhearts* / My house: *Terrorvision* / Give it away: *Red Hot Chili Peppers* / Warfair: *Clawfinger* / Believe in me: *McKagan, Duff* / Ten miles high: *Little Angels* / Over the edge: *Almighty* / Down in a hole: *Alice In Chains* / Ace of spades (Live): *Motorhead* / Paranoid: *Black Sabbath* / Smoke on the

water: Deep Purple / Victim of change (Live): Judas Priest / Stargazer: Rainbow / Bat out of hell: Meat Loaf / Cats in the cradle: Ugly Kid Joe / In my darkest hour: Megadeth / Doctor doctor: UFO / Spirit of radio: Rush / Epic: Faith No More / Angel of death: Slayer / Youth gone wild: Skid Row / Born to be wild: Steppenwolf / Freebird: Lynyrd Skynyrd
CD AHLCD 21
Hit / Jun '94 / Grapevine/PolyGram

KERRANG VOL.2 (The Kutting Edge)
CD STVCD 27
Hit / Mar '95 / Grapevine/PolyGram

KERRANG VOL.3 (2CD Set)
CD Set RR 88572
Roadrunner / Aug '96 / PolyGram

KERRY FIDDLES
CD OSS 10CD
Ossian / Mar '94 / ADA / CM / Direct / Highlander

KETTLE DRUM
CD DBCD 2039
Digital B / Feb '96 / Jet Star

KEYS OF LIFE
CD CDCEL 017
Celestial Harmonies / Jun '87 / ADA / Select

KHARTOUM HEROES
Cat gut: Khartoum Heroes / St. Swithin: Khartoum Heroes / Mother Hubbard: Khartoum Heroes / Space hopper: Khartoum Heroes / Charles and die laughing: Khartoum Heroes / Interference: Khartoum Heroes / Heaven: Khartoum Heroes / Bitter honey: Khartoum Heroes / Colossal angel: Khartoum Heroes / Song for a flower: Khartoum Heroes / Leaves: Khartoum Heroes / Out of bounds: Khartoum Heroes / Saints within: Khartoum Heroes / Moon barking: Khartoum Heroes
CD CDLDL 1222
Lochshore / Feb '97 / ADA / Direct / Duncans

KICK UP THE 80'S VOL.9
Never stop: Echo & The Bunnymen / I wanna be a flintstone: Screaming Blue Messiahs / Life in a northern town: Dream Academy / She bangs the drum: Stone Roses / More you live, the more you love: Flock Of Seagulls / I'm falling: Bluebells / Disenchanted: Communards / All of my heart: ABC / Steppin' out: Jackson, Joe / Never take me alive: Spear Of Destiny / Whistle down the wind: Heyward, Nick / Radio Africa: Latin Quarter / Crash: Primitives / No memory: Scarlet Fantastic / Obsession: Animotion / Honey thief: Hipsway / Big area: Then Jerico / Let my people go go: Rainmakers
CD OG 3528
Old Gold / Nov '92 / Carlton

KICKIN' HOUSE TUNES (2CD Set)
Promised land: FUSE / In the morning: Key / Ooo-la-la-la: Earp, Justine / Keep on jumpin': Zoe S / It's movin': DJ Linus / Check your feelings: Deeper Love / Music is my life: Creative House Boys / Do it now: Luvly Housebee / Take me to the top: MNA Project / Brooklyn beats: Deep, Scotti / Legacy: Natural Forces / Secret love: Magnetic Pulstar / All night: BOP Gun / It's so good: L&G Project / U: DJ Scott Project / Let the rhythm pump: Pigalle / Are you ready: Moves / I want you: Shandrew / Morning light: Team Deep / Candy girls: Wham Bam / Magic melody: Groove Solution / Tones in my mind: Cyborg / Jaba noba: CYB / My house: Nap, J. Project
CD Set DCD 08947292
SPV / Mar '97 / Koch / Plastic Head

KICKIN' HOUSE TUNES VOL.5 (2CD Set)
CD Set DCD 08947542
SPV / Jul '97 / Koch / Plastic Head

KICKIN' THE 3 (The Best Of Organ Trio Jazz)
Kiko: McGriff, Jimmy / Kickin' the 3: Earland, Charles / Evidence: DeFrancesco, Joey / Blues for J: Smith, Jimmy / Slouchin': Smith, Lonnie / Little green men: Goldings, Larry / Misty: Holmes, Richard 'Groove' / Lid flippin': Smith, Johnny 'Hammond' / After hours: McDuff, 'Brother' Jack / Bedeah: Medeski, John & Billy Martin/Chris Wood / Monk's dream: Young, Larry
CD SH 5034
Shanachie / Jun '97 / ADA / Greensleeves / Koch

KID'S RHYTHM 'N' BLUES KAFFEE SUMMER '97
CD STINGCD 041
Blue Sting / Jul '97 / CM / Hot Shot / Jazz Music / Swift

KILLER VOICES
What do you want from me: White, Dougie / She goes down: Di'Anno, Paul / Body rock: Stratton, Dennis / Stranger to your heart: Bodimead, Jackie / Miles away: Stratton, Dennis / No repair: Di'Anno, Paul / All shook up: White, Dougie / Show some emotion: Sloman, John / Cut loose: White, Dougie / Forever: Overland, Steve & Jackie Bodimead / So far away: Hart, Lea
CD CDTB 177
Thunderbolt / Aug '97 / TKO Magnum

KILLING MUSIC
Blackfly: Box Saga / Initiation: Sunship / Alien resident: Kid Loops / We are one: DJ Q / Porknow fish: Violet / At least American Indian people know exactly how they've bee: Fire This Time / 13th key: Sunship / Waiting hopefully: D-Note / Bury the hatchet: Local Zero / Urban hustle: DJ Q / Nine lives: Underwolves / Offshore: Chicane
CD FILT 010CD
Filter / Sep '96 / Pinnacle / Prime / RTM/ Disc

KINDA COUNTRY
CD PLSCD 170
Pulse / Apr '97 / BMG

KINDA COUNTRY VOL.1
CD MATCD 221
Castle / Dec '92 / BMG

KINDA COUNTRY VOL.2
CD MATCD 265
Castle / Apr '93 / BMG

KING KONK VOL.1
CD K 152C
Konkurrel / Mar '94 / SRD

KING KONK VOL.2
CD K 168
Konkurrel / Aug '96 / SRD

KING OF SKA VOL.1
CD KECD 01/02
King Edwards / Feb '93 / Jet Star

KING OF SKA VOL.2
CD KECD 03/04
King Edwards / Feb '93 / Jet Star

KING OF SWING, THE
CD MACCD 253
Autograph / Aug '96 / BMG

KING OF THE ROAD
CD MU 5058
Musketeer / Oct '92 / Disc

KING R 'N' B BOX SET, THE (4CD Set)
CD Set KBCD 7002
King / Apr '97 / Avid/BMG

KING SIZE DUB VOL.1 (2CD Set)
CD Set EB 001
Echo Beach / Jun '97 / Cargo / Shellshock/Disc

KING SIZE DUB VOL.2 (2CD Set)
CD Set EB 006
Echo Beach / Jun '97 / Cargo / Shellshock/Disc

KING SIZE DUB VOL.3 (2CD Set)
CD Set EB 009
Echo Beach / Jun '97 / Cargo / Shellshock/Disc

KINGDOM OF METAL (18 Killer Tracks)
Iron fist: Motorhead / (Don't fear) the reaper: Blue Oyster Cult / Kingdom of madness: Magnum / Urban guerilla: Hawkwind / Broken down angel: Nazareth / Stay on top: Uriah Heep / Angel witch: Angel Witch / Race with the devil: Girlschool / Sudden life: Man / Who do you love: Juicy Lucy / Heartline: George, Robin / Me and my guitar: Wishbone Ash / Nuclear attack: Moore, Gary / In league with satan: Venom / Come to the sabbat: Black Widow / Too hot to handle: UFO / Nobody's hero: Raven / Bomber: Headgirl
CD SUMCD 4105
Summit / Nov '96 / Sound & Media

KINGDOM OF THE SUN - FIESTAS OF PERU
CD 7559791972
Nonesuch / Jan '95 / Warner Music

KINGS & QUEENS OF COUNTRY
CD CPMV 027
Cromwell / Sep '94 / Total/BMG

KINGS AND QUEEN OF QAWWALI, THE (Love & Devotion)
CD SHCD 64083
Shanachie / Apr '97 / ADA / Greensleeves / Koch

KINGS OF AFRICAN MUSIC
CD NSCD 009
Nascente / Nov '96 / Disc / New Note/ Pinnacle

KINGS OF BLACK MUSIC, THE
CD 15169
Laserlight / Aug '91 / Target/BMG

KINGS OF CAJUN
Les filles du Canada: Abshire, Nathan / Acadian two step: Balfa Brothers / Triangle special: Pitre, Austin / French fiddle boogie: Bonsall, Joe / Midnight special: Balfa Brothers / Oson two step: Roger, Aldus / La queue de torture: Abshire, Nathan / Love bridge waltz: Duhon, Bessyl / One is a lonely number: Menard, Phil / Fee fee ponchot: Montoucet, Don / Old fashioned two step: Balfa Brothers / Zydeco hee haw: Chavis, Boozoo / That's what makes the cajun dance: Bearb, Ricky / Hick wagon wheel special: Montoucet, Don / Me and my counsin: Doucet, Camey / Mamou hot step: Ardoin Brothers / L'anne tu partit: Fruge, Ronnie / Jolie catin: Chavis, Boozoo / Lacassine special: Balfa Brothers / Johnny can't dance: Ardoin Family Orchestra / Sheryl's special: Cormier, Sheryl
CD MCCD 066
Music Club / '92 / Disc / THE

KINGS OF CAJUN (3CD Set)
CD Set MCBX 013
Music Club / Dec '94 / Disc / THE

KINGS OF CAJUN
CD TRIK 0158
Trikont / Oct '94 / ADA / Direct

KINGS OF CAJUN VOL.2
CD MCCD 116
Music Club / Jun '93 / Disc / THE

KINGS OF CAJUN VOL.3
CD MCCD 171
Music Club / Sep '94 / Disc / THE

KINGS OF CALYPSO
CD MATCD 244
Castle / Dec '92 / BMG

KINGS OF CALYPSO
CD PLSCD 229
Pulse / Jul '97 / BMG

KINGS OF COUNTRY
I can't stop lovin' you: Gibson, Don / Talk back trembling lips: Jones, George / Reuben james: Rogers, Kenny / Shelter of your arms: Nelson, Willie / Loves gonna live here: Jennings, Waylon / There goes my everything: Greene, Jack / Send me the pillow that you dream on: Locklin, Hank / Heartaches by the number: Paycheck, Johnny / For the good times: Husky, Ferlin / Where do I go from here: Williams, Don / Sea of heartbreak: Gibson, Don / Almost persuaded: Jones, George / Ruby don't take your love to town: Rogers, Kenny / Broken promises: Nelson, Willie / Son of Hickory Holler's tramp: Darrell, Johnny / Catfish john: Russel, Johnny / Four in the morning: Young, Faron / Things to think about: Jackson, Stonewall / Tears: Williams, Don / Daddy sang bass: Perkins, Carl
CD 300722
Hallmark / Jul '96 / Carlton

KINGS OF COUNTRY LIVE
CD JHD 009
Tring / Jun '92 / Tring

KINGS OF DUB
CD RB 3019
Reggae Best / Jan '96 / Grapevine/ PolyGram

KINGS OF DUB ROCK VOL.1 & 2 (Sir Coxsone Sound)
CD TMCD 3
Tribesman / Feb '95 / Jet Star / SRD

KINGS OF GYPSY MUSIC
Son son sera mix / Dale dale al bordon / Gitana / Morena / Venga valiente / Esa amor que me enganaba / Rumba para ti / Amor impoible / Vive a tu manera gitanita nos queremoos / Vete mujer / Juntos los dos / Los lachos te cantan / A-chi-li-pu / No chute / Siego tu vueli / Mejor separanos / Amores pasajeros / Perdido / Amor / Larga espre / Maria dell mar / No vuelvas a sonar
CD GRF 084
Tring / Apr '93 / Tring

KINGS OF HIP HOP, THE (4CD Set)
CD Set DAM 003
Tring / Dec '96 / Tring

KINGS OF RHYTHM AND BLUES
Willie and the hand jive: Otis, Johnny / Brown angel: Liggins, Joe / Bad bad whisky: Milburn, Amos / Outskirts of town: Jordan, Louis / Juice head baby: Vinson, Eddie 'Cleanhead' / Baby baby all the time: Milburn, Amos / Baby I've got news for you: Otis, Johnny / Tanya: Liggins, Joe / Helping hand: Jordan, Louis / Going back to LA: Liggins, Joe / Cleanhead's blues: Vinson, Eddie 'Cleanhead' / Have love will travel: Berry, Richard / Barrelhouse blues: Otis, Johnny / Yama yama pretty mama: Berry, Richard / Corine corine: Turner, Joe / I got the walkin' blues: Jordan, Louis / Trackin machine: Berry, Richard / TV mama: Turner, Joe / Old maids boogie: Vinson, Eddie 'Cleanhead' / Honey hush: Turner, Joe
CD 306002
Hallmark / Jan '97 / Carlton

KINGS OF THE BLUES
Sweet little angel: King, B.B. / She moves me: Watson, Johnny 'Guitar' / I'll get along somehow: Sims, Frankie Lee / Blues serenade: Turner, Babyface / On my way back home: Flash Terry / Odds against me: Hooker, John Lee / Sittin' here thinkin': Walker, T-Bone / Problem child: Walton, Mercy Dee / Lonesome old feeling: Bumble Bee Slim / I tried: Young Wolf / Cotton picker: Higgins, Chuck & The Melotones / Wild hop: Crayton, Pee Wee / Worried about my baby: Howlin' Wolf / Tavern lounge boogie: Burns, Eddie 'Guitar' / Believe I'll change towns: Hogg, Smokey / Too many rivers: Fulson, Lowell / Yesterday: Chenier, Clifton / Lonesome dog blues: Hopkins, Lightnin' / Hard times: Fuller, Johnny / Riding mighty high: Dixon, Floyd / Please find my baby: James, Elmore
CD CDCH 276
Ace / Jul '89 / Pinnacle

KINGS OF THE ROAD
CD DS 017
Desperado / Jun '97 / TKO Magnum

KINGSTON TOWN
CD HBCD 82
Heartbeat / May '93 / ADA / Direct / Greensleeves / Jet Star

KINKY TRAX VOL.3
CD REACTCD 030
React / Nov '93 / Arabesque / Prime / Vital

KINKY TRAX VOL.4 (The Big Apple: Divas And Dubs)
CD REACTCD 045
React / Aug '94 / Arabesque / Prime / Vital

KISS CLUB ANTHEMS (2CD Set)
Encore une fois: Sash / Scared: Slacker / Born slippy: Underworld / Not forgotten: Leftfield / You got the love: Source & Candi Staton / My love is deep: Parker, Sara / Funk phenomena: Van Helden, Armand / Give me luv: Alcatraz / Higher state of consciousness: Wink, Josh / Keep on jumpin': Terry, Todd & Martha Wash/Jocelyn Brown / Chime: Orbital / Playing with knives: Bizarre Inc. / Sound of Eden: Shades Of Rhythm / Go: Moby / La luna '95: Ethics / Groovebird: Natural Born Groovers / Don't you want me: Felix / Le voie le soleil: Subliminal Cuts / Difference: Funny Walker / Push the feeling on: Nightcrawlers / Tears: Knuckles, Frankie / Beautiful people: Tucker, Barbara / Reach: Lil Mo Yin Yang / Who keeps changing your mind: South Street Players / Missing: Everything But The Girl / Show me love: Robin S / Hideaway: De'Lacy / Get up (everybody): Stingily, Byron / Space cowboy: Jamiroquai / Deeper love: C&C Music Factory / 40 miles: Congress / Testament 1: Chubby Chunks / I'm alive: Stretch n' Vern & Maddog / Not over yet: Grace / Drive me crazy: Partizan / Children: Miles, Robert
CD Set 5534792
PolyGram TV / Apr '97 / PolyGram

KISS IN IBIZA
CD 5259112
PolyGram TV / Sep '95 / PolyGram

KISS IN IBIZA '96 (2CD Set)
I'm alive: Stretch n' Vern / Keep on jumpin': Terry, Todd / Let's all chant: Gusto / Ain't nobody's business if I do: H2O & Billie / Help me make it: Huff & Puff / Want love: Hysteric Ego / Feel my body: O'Moiraghi, Frank / Professional widow: Amos, Tori / Tall and handsome: Outrage / Do that to me: Lisa Marie Experience / That look: De'Lacy / Don't go: 3rd Dimension / High: Hyper Go Go / If I could fly: Grace / Hi energy: Maltese Massive / Tha wildstyle: DJ Supreme / Trans Euro Express: X-Press 2 / 7 days and one week: BBE / Groovebird: Natural Born Groovers / Gift: Way Out West / Bombscare: 2 Bad Mice / Stamp: Healy, Jeremy & Amos / Jus come: Cool Jack / Sugar is sweeter: Bolland, C.J. / It's gonna be alright: Technocat / Up to no good: Porn Kings / Higher state of consciousness: Wink, Josh / All I want to do: Tin Tin Out / Krupa: Apollo 440 / Horny as funk: Soapy / Nocturnal: Q-Dos / Antheum: Digital Blondes / Believe in me: Mankey / 2nd coming: Libido
CD Set 5359672
PolyGram TV / Oct '96 / PolyGram

KISS ME I'M IRISH
If it weren't for the Irish: Parker, Frank / Miss O'Leary's Irish fruitcake: Harrington, Pat / Murphy bed: Harrington, Pat / Which of them will I marry: O'Hara, Maureen / I'm going to be married on Sunday: O'Hara, Maureen / Johnny I hardly knew ye: O'Hara, Maureen / It's a great day for the Irish: Porter, Frank / When Irish eyes are smiling: Porter, Frank / Molly Malone: Porter, Frank / Macushla: Porter, Frank / MacNamara's band: Porter, Frank / Mick McGalligan's ball: Quinn, Carmel & Arthur Godfrey / Humour is on me now: Quinn, Carmel & Arthur Godfrey / Bally McQuilty band: Quinn, Carmel / With my shillelagh under my arm: Quinn, Carmel / There was an old woman: O'Hara, Maureen / Danny boy: O'Hara, Maureen / Macushla: Smith, Kate / Little bit of heaven (sure, they call it Ireland): Smith, Kate
CD CK 53631
Columbia / Mar '97 / Sony

KISS MIX '96 (2CD Set)
Blurred: Pianoman / Female of the species: Space / Disco frenzy (got to be there): Divine Intervention / It's gonna be alright: Technocat / Latin thing: Latin Thing / Klubhopping: Klubb Heads / On ya way: Helicopter / Le voie le soliel: Subliminal Cuts / Outrageous: Stix 'N' Stoned / Beginning: Dex & Jonesy / Into your heart: 6 By 6 / Theme from S'Express: S'Express / There's nothing I won't do: JX / Deep: Ariel / Schoneberg: Marmion / Baby talk: Future Files / Born slippy: Underworld / Hot and wet (believe it): Tzant / Solution (feels so right): Simonelli, Victor / Keep on jumpin': Lisa Marie Experience / Madagascar: Madagascar / Find your way: Crosby, B.J. / Stand up: Love Tribe / Lover that you are: Pulse / Can't help it: Happy Clappers / Saved my life: Edwards, Todd / Are you gonna be there: Up Yer Ronson / What you want: Future Force / Do me right: Inner City / Pushing against the flow: Ray Stylus

CD Set ______ 5357012
PolyGram TV / Jul '96 / PolyGram

KISS MIX '97 (2CD Set)
You are the universe: *Brand New Heavies* / Free: *Ultranate* / RIP groove: *Double 99* / Magic carpet ride: *Mighty Dub Katz* / Invader: *Koolworld* / Something's goin' on: *Terry, Todd* / Sunstroke: *Chicane* / Pacific melody: *Airscape* / Ecuador: *Sash* / Catch: *Sunscreem* / AsceSomeone: *Ascension* / QuatTruth: *Quattara* / Blaming June: *BT* / Frontiers: *Spirito* / Deep (I'm falling deeper): *Ariel* / Down to earth: *Grace* / Sharp tools volume three: *Sharp Boys* / Freed from desire: *Gala* / Still a thrill: *Sybil* / Show me love: *Fruit Loop* / Get up stand up: *Phunky Phantom* / Get down to the beat: *Brain Bashers* / Go with the flow: *Loop Da Loop* / Bring the beat back: *De Vit, Tony* / Don't be afraid: *Moonman* / Epidemic: *Exit EEE* / Rock the turntables: *Floorshow* / Discohopping: *Klubb Heads* / Sweet lips: *Monaco* / Flowtation: *De Moor, Vincent*
CD Set ______ 5538402
PolyGram TV / Jul '97 / PolyGram

KISS 'N' TELL
Celebrate your victory: *Shirelles* / Remember me: *Shirelles* / You're under arrest: *Shirelles* / Devil in his heart: *Donays* / Bad boy: *Donays* / Party lights: *Donays* / Silly little girl: *Dean & Jean* / Casanova: *Earline & her girlfriends* / Because of you: *Earline & her girlfriends* / Little girl lost: *Brown, Maxine* / Peaches 'n' cream: *Ikettes* / (He's gonna be) fine fine fine: *Ikettes* / Are you trying to get rid of me: *Candy & The Kisses* / You did the best you could: *Candy & The Kisses* / You got it baby: *Toys* / Try to get you out of my heart: *Toys* / I just couldn't say: *Lorraine & The Delights* / stop, look and listen: *Les girls* / Kiss and tell: *Julie & The Desires* / Better be ready: *Annette B* / Leave us alone: *Del-rons* / Don't hurt me: *Carroll, Bernadette* / Nicky: *Carroll, Bernadette* / Only seventeen: *Martin sisters* / Stay at home, Sue: *Linda Laurie* / Hey there, hey there: *Gypsies* / You don't love me anymore: *Dodds, Nella* / I wonder why: *Chiffons* / Foolish little girl: *Chiffons* / Three dips of ice cream: *Chiffons*
CD ______ CDCHD 330
Ace / Feb '93 / Pinnacle

KISS SMOOTH GROOVES
Cosmic girl: *Jamiroquai* / Sometimes: *Brand New Heavies* / Love is all we need: *Blige, Mary J.* / Doin' it: *LL Cool J* / I believe I can fly: *R Kelly* / Wonderful tonight: *Damage* / Sugar honey ice tea: *Goodfellaz* / Request line: *Zhane* / Ain't no playa: *Jay-Z & Foxxy Brown* / Spirit: *Sounds Of Blackness* / Let's get down: *Tony Toni Tone* / Tell me do U wanna: *Ginuwine* / Don't wanna be a player: *Joe* / Me and those dreamin' eyes: *D'Angelo* / Steelo: *702* / Heavenly daughter: *Kwesi* / Shake it: *D-Influence* / It's alright: *Hines, Deni* / I'm not feeling you: *Michelle, Yvette* / Only you: *112* / Lougin': *LL Cool J* / Anggel: *Simply Red* / Touch me tease me: *Case & Foxy Brown* / Trippin': *Morrison, Mark* / Nobody knows: *Rich, Tony* / If you love me: *Brownstone* / One for the money: *Brown, Horace* / Creep: *TLC* / Stressed out: *Tribe Called Quest & Faith Evans* / 1st of the month: *Bone Thugs n' Harmony* / Step into a world: *KRS 1* / This DJ: *Warren G* / Sentimental: *Cox, Deborah* / Ocean drivw: *Lighthouse Family* / Like this and like that: *Monica* / Down with the ckique: *Aaliyah* / Do you know: *Gayle, Michelle* / Fell so high: *Des'ree* / Remember me: *Blueboy*
CD ______ 5333412
PolyGram TV / Jun '97 / PolyGram

KITTEN ON THE KEYS (Pianorola Favourites)
Bye bye blackbird / Thora / Miss Annabelle Lee / For me and my gal / Stars and stripes forever / Sweet Genevieve / J'en ai marre / Alexander's ragtime band / I want to be happy / Doll dance / Moon river / Lovable and sweet / Me and Jane in a plane / Kitten on the keys / Stealing / Tippy canoe / Among my souvenirs / More we are together / Three o'clock in the morning
CD ______ CDJ 115
Australian Jazz / Nov '96 / Jazz Music

KK COMPILATION
Fire: *2nd Communication* / Second episode: *Sloppy Wrenchbody* / Chasin' the flame: *Minister Of Noise* / Warp: *DRP* / BPM: *Sterotaxic Device* / Curse: *Numb* / Disobey: *Kode IV* / What a life: *Exquisite Corpse* / Burning bodies: *Blue Eyed Christ* / Point of no return: *Cat Rapes Dog* / Zoeloe noizz: *Insekt* / Surely get's me: *Swains* / Patience: *Psychik Warriors Ov Gaia*
CD ______ KK 088CD
KK / Dec '92 / Plastic Head

KLEZMANIA (Tradition & Beyond)
CD ______ SH 67007
Shanachie / Mar '97 / ADA / Greensleeves / Koch

KLEZMER 1993 - TRADITION CONTINUES ON THE LOWER EAST SIDE
CD ______ KFWCD 123
Knitting Factory / Feb '95 / Cargo / Plastic Head

KLEZMER PIONEERS
CD ______ ROUCD 1089
Rounder / Jun '93 / ADA / CM / Direct

KLEZMOKUM
CD ______ BVHAASTCD 9209
Bvhaast / May '89 / Cadillac

KLONED VOL.2
CD ______ CDKOPY 102
Klone / Dec '93 / 3mv/Sony / Pinnacle

KLONED VOL.3
CD Set ______ CDKOPY 103
Klone / Nov '94 / 3mv/Sony / Pinnacle

KLONED VOL.4
CD ______ CDKOPY 104
Klone / Jan '96 / 3mv/Sony / Pinnacle

KLUBBTRAX VOL.3 (Mixed By The Klubbheads)
CD ______ BLUECD 03
Dutch Blue / Jun '97 / Mo's Music Machine

KLUBHOPPIN' (2CD Set)
Underwater love: *Smoke City* / Fired up: *Funky Green Dogs From Outer Space* / Ready Or Not: *Course* / People hold on: *Stansfield, Lisa & Dirty Rotten Scoundrels* / Where can I find lovev: *Livin' Joy* / Keep on jumpin': *Terry, Todd & Martha Wash/Jocelyn Brown* / Funk phenomena: *Van Helden, Armand* / Giv me luv: *Alcatraz* / Can't knock the hustle: *Jay Z & Mary J. Blige* / Release yo'self: *Transatlantic Soul* / Ultra flava: *Heller & Farley Project* / One and one: *Miles, Robert & Maria Naylor* / Hypnotizin': *Winx* / Landslide: *Harmonix* / Show me love: *Robin S* / I'll be your friend: *Owens, Robert* / You got the love: *Source & Candi Staton* / Remember me: *Blueboy* / Ain't talkin' about dub: *Apollo 440* / Breathe: *Prodigy* / Stamp: *Healy, Jeremy & Amos* / Don't you want me: *Felix* / Gift: *Way Out West* / Inferno: *Souvlaki* / Klubhopping: *Klubb Heads* / I'm alive: *Stretch n' Vern & Maddog* / Rollin' on: *Lazy, Doug* / Seven days and one week: *BBE* / Offshore: *Chicane* / Be as one: *Sasha & Maria*
CD Set ______ RADCD 60
Global TV / Apr '97 / BMG

KNEELIN' DOWN INSIDE THE GATE
CD ______ ROUCD 5035
Rounder / Jul '95 / ADA / CM / Direct

KNIGHTS OF THE TURNTABLE VOL.1
CD ______ BMRCD 01
Boomerang / Nov '94 / Jet Star

KNITE FORCE - VINYL IS BETTER
CD ______ GUMH 010
Gumh / Nov '94 / SRD

KNITTING FACTORY BOX SET (5CD Set)
CD Set ______ KFWCD 12345
Knitting Factory / Nov '92 / Cargo / Plastic Head

KNITTING FACTORY GOES TO THE NORTH WEST
CD ______ KFWCD 101
Knitting Factory / Nov '94 / Cargo / Plastic Head

KNITTING FACTORY TOURS EUROPE
CD ______ KFWCD 105
Knitting Factory / Nov '94 / Cargo / Plastic Head

KNOCK OUT BLUES
CD ______ RST 915782
RST / Jun '94 / Hot Shot / Jazz Music

KNOCK OUT IN THE FIRST ROUND
CD ______ KOCD 038
Knock Out / Oct '96 / Cargo

KNOCKOUT, IN THE SECOND ROUND
CD ______ KOCD 062
Knock Out / Jun '97 / Cargo

KNOW YOUR ENEMY
CD ______ EMY 1392
Enemy / Nov '94 / Grapevine/PolyGram

KODEX VOL.4
CD ______ EFA 119152
Kodex / Nov '94 / SRD

KONGPILATION
CD ______ BJ 999
Bananajuice / Jan '96 / Nervous

KOOL FM PRESENTS THE FEVER (2CD Set)
CD Set ______ BDRCD 20
Breakdown / Jun '97 / Pinnacle

KOOL REVOLUTION, A
CD ______ TKCD 8
2 Kool / Aug '95 / Pinnacle / SRD

KORA AND THE XYLOPHONE, THE
CD ______ LYRCD 7308
Lyrichord / '91 / ADA / CM / Roots

KOREAN COURT MUSIC
CD ______ LYRCD 7206
Lyrichord / '91 / ADA / CM / Roots

KRALINGEN POP FESTIVAL
CD ______ KRCD 1
Headlite / Mar '97 / Cargo

KRANKENHOUSE (2CD Set)
Transaxual: *Armando* / Alabama blues: *St. Germain* / Old skool: *DJ Tonka* / Organic technology: *Johnson, Paul* / Non stop: *Herbert* / House of God: *D.H.S.* / Rex attitude: *Garnier, Laurent* / Strikeout: *Hardfloor* / Times fade: *Phuture* / Quo vadis: *G-Man* / Pure madness: *Wax, Tom* / DJ kicks: *Young, Claude* / Chord memory: *Pooley, Ian* / Praline horse: *Landstrumm, Neal* / Cowgirl: *Underworld* / Kraak: *PWOG* / Terminator: *West Bam* / Who's got the flave: *Kirlian* / Loop 2: *Larkin, Kenny* / Bruce Lee MC: *MC Quincy* / Precipice: *Turntable Terranova* / Circus bells: *Armani, Robert*
CD Set ______ SPV 08947162
SPV / Feb '97 / Koch / Plastic Head

KRAUTROCK ARCHIVE VOL.1 (The Cologne Tapes)
Orion wakes: *Golem* / Leaves are falling: *Temple* / Black light: *Temple* / Dark path: *Cozmic Corriders* / Niemand versteht: *Cozmic Corriders* / Interstellar shortwave: *Astral Army* / Lunarscape: *Galactic Explorers* / Ganz wie du willst: *Feuerrote*
CD ______ CDOVD 468
Virgin / Jul '96 / EMI

KRAUTROCK ARCHIVE VOL.2 (Unknown Deutschland)
Message: *Spirulina* / Innerst: *Ten To Ten* / Heathen temple: *Temple* / Age of ages: *Temple* / Tower of Barad-Dur: *Nazgul* / Godhead dance: *Golem* / Moutainside: *Cozmic Corriders* / Summit: *Cozmic Corriders*
CD ______ CDOVD 472
Virgin / Jun '97 / EMI

KRAUTROCK ARCHIVE VOL.3 (Unknown Deutschland)
Feuerwerk: *Anderson, Neil* / Ethereal jazz: *Galactic Explorers* / Stellar launch: *Golem* / Dead marshes: *Nazgul* / No God/Astaroth: *Baal* / Schaudernacht: *Chronos* / Ship on fire: *Temple*
CD ______ CDOVD 473
Virgin / Jun '97 / EMI

KRAZY KATS CAJUN
CD ______ TRIK 0167
Trikont / Oct '94 / ADA / Direct

KRIS NEEDS MUST
Jailbird: *Primal Scream* / Mr Vinegar: *Mr. Parkers Band* / Let the fun begin: *Secret Knowledge* / Lair: *Wulf n' Bear* / Cold house yellow curtains: *Absolute State* / Dreamer: *Longman* / Sonic stiffy: *Kris N' Dave* / Speedway: *Prodigy* / Frontier: *Digital Destroyer* / Rabbits name was: *A&E Dept* / Lazarus: *Boo Radleys*
CD ______ CDRAID 534
Rumour / Mar '97 / 3mv/Sony / Mo's Music Machine / Pinnacle

KUDIYATTAM DANCE DRAMA, THE
CD ______ VICG 50372
JVC World Library / Mar '96 / ADA / CM / Direct

KUDOS DIGEST - ISSUE A (IS FOR APPLE), THE
Electric arc: *Nuron* / Jupiter: *Pluto* / End of an era: *Balony, B.J.* / Chevy rainbow: *Perbec* / Midst of tumult: *Roxy* / Griptape: *Spira* / Check it out: *PVP* / Solitude: *Stasis* / Different emotions: *Insync & Mysteron* / Honda Suzuki's last motorcycle ride: *Le Panel De Pants* / Rustless: *Beautyon*
CD ______ KUDCD 006
Kudos / Jun '95 / Kudos / Pinnacle

KULT DANCE KLASSIX VOL.2
CD ______ SPV 79908692
SPV / Aug '93 / Koch / Plastic Head

KUULAS HETKI
CD ______ OMCD 46
Digelius / Jun '93 / Direct

KWANZAA PARTY
Roaring lion: *Mary Ann* / Ng la banda: *La Expresiva* / I'll take you there: *Staple Singers* / Kanda bongo man: *Liza* / Toinho de Alagoas: *Balanco da Canao* / Sekusile: *Dark City Sisters* / Fidelina: *Duran, Alejo* / Rhythme commercial: *Ensemble Nemours Jean Baptiste* / Gouye gui: *Africando* / Flotation merengue: *Blinky & The Roadmasters* / Shaure Yako: *Orchestre Super Mazembe* / Caliventura: *Afrosound* / Same thing: *Copeland, Johnny* / Ede M chante: *Boukan Ginen*
CD ______ ROUCD 2153
Rounder / Oct '96 / ADA / CM / Direct

KYOTO JAZZ MASSIVE
CD ______ 99 2137
Ninetynine / Jul '96 / Timewarp

L

LA CHANRANGA
CD ______ 283402
Total / Jan '96 / Total/BMG

LA COLLECTION VOL.1 (2CD Set)
Lost illusions: *Shazz* / Prelusion: *Deepside* / Aurora Borealis: *Aurora Borealis* / French: *Deepside* / Alabama blues: *St Germain* / How do you plead: *Soofle* / Modus Vivendi: *Modus Vivendi* / Quarter 2: *Orange* / Lost in Alaska: *Alaska* / Yantra: *Scan X* / Acid Eiffel: *Choice* / First time: *Alaska* / Disco inferno: *LN's* / Wake up: *Garnier, Laurent* / Sexual behaviour: *Deep Contest* / Breathless: *Garnier, Laurent* / Weeping waste: *Renegade Legion* / Planet sex: *Garnier, Laurent* / Art of stalking: *Suburban Knight* / Meltdown: *Lunatic Asylum* / Shazz: *Shazz*
CD Set ______ 3018912
FNAC Dance / Dec '96 / Cargo

LA COLLECTION VOL.2 (2CD Set)
Deep in it: *St. Germain* / DJGG: *Nova Nova* / Move: *Nuages* / Leave me: *Shazz* / Alabama blues: *St. Germain* / Too late: *Iberian* / Cold fresh air: *Mono, Toni* / Le marias: *Shazz* / Baddest bitch: *Bell, Norma Jean* / Wanna dance: *Aqua Bassino* / Rainforest: *Alaska* / Aleph: *Nova Nova* / Dub experience: *St. Germain* / Astral dreams: *Garnier, Laurent* / Rainfall: *Feedback* / Groove is going: *Lady B* / Obtuse corner: *Square* / Jack on the groove: *DS* / Bleu-process cyan: *Scan X* / Crusher: *Iberian* / Louis's cry: *Juantrip* / Milky way: *Borealis, Aurora* / Eternal deep: *Scan X* / 2019: *Taho* / Dance to the music: *Garnier, Laurent* / Orgasm: *Garnier, Laurent* / It's not enough: *Madame B.* / Theisme: *St. Germain* / Cafe bassino: *Aqua Bassino* / Louis' cry: *Juantrip* / Shake it up: *Nova Nova* / percussion: *St. Germain*
CD Set ______ F 045DCD
F-Communications / Jul '96 / Prime / Vital

LA CONDITION FEMININE
CD ______ 983242
EPM / Oct '96 / ADA / Discovery

LA FLEUR DE MON SECRET
Ay amor: *Bola De Nieve* / Tonada de luna llena: *Diaz, Simon* / En el ultimo trago: *Sandoval, Jose Alfredo Jimenez* / Titulos: *Iglesias, Alberto* / Casa con ventanas y libros: *Iglesias, Alberto* / Brevemente: *Iglesias, Alberto* / Retrato de Amanda Gris: *Iglesias, Alberto* / Tango de parla: *Iglesias, Alberto* / En Madrid nunca es tarde: *Iglesias, Alberto* / Facinacion: *Iglesias, Alberto* / Existe alguna posibilidad por pequena que sea de salvar lo n: *Iglesias, Alberto* / Interior: *Iglesias, Alberto* / Escribe compulsivamente: *Iglesias, Alberto* / Duo: *Iglesias, Alberto* / Ingenua: *Iglesias, Alberto* / Mi aldea: *Iglesias, Alberto* / Que Leo: *Iglesias, Alberto* / Vertigo: *Iglesias, Alberto* / Sola: *Iglesias, Alberto* / La flor de mi secreto: *Iglesias, Alberto* / Solea: *Iglesias, Alberto* / Poesia recitada: *Iglesias, Alberto*
CD ______ 4814442
Columbia / Jan '96 / Sony

LA FREEWAY
CD ______ DINCD 25
Dino / Aug '91 / Pinnacle

LA GALOUBET TAMBOURIN
CD ______ C 560073
Ocora / Nov '95 / ADA / Harmonia Mundi

LA GRANDE PARADE DES CHANSONS D'AMOUR (2CD Set)
CD Set ______ 983832
EPM / Jul '96 / ADA / Discovery

LA HAPPENING (The Mid-60s Soul Sides Of Vault, Fat Fish & Autumn Records)
Nobody but you: *Wooden Nickels* / I'll never fall in love again: *Freeman, Bobby* / Baby reconsider: *Haywood, Leon* / Wishing and hoping: *Keen, Billy* / My heart's beating stronger: *Fisher, Andy* / That little old heartbreaker me: *Freeman, Bobby* / Tell me tomorrow: *Mandolph, Bobby* / Little girl: *Washington, Lee* / Tender tears: *Montgomery, Bobby* / Ain't no use: *Haywood, Leon* / Head over heels: *Bridges, Chuck & The LA Happening* / Going to a happening: *Neal, Tommy* / Got to get you back: *Mandolph, Bobby* / Fine, fine, fine: *Hughes, Judy* / More than a friend: *Wooden Nickels* / I've been crying: *Jones, Jesse* / Cross my heart: *Keen, Billy* / Mean ol' world: *Casualairs* / I have seniority over your love: *Kimball, Bobby* / I'm your stepping stone: *Montgomery, Bobby* / Wee bit longer: *Fisher, Andy* / Out of sight: *Sly* / Honey: *Averhart, Booker T. & The Mustangs* / You're flying high now baby: *Kimble, Neal* / LA happening: *Bridges, Chuck & The LA Happening* / Soul cargo: *Haywood, Leon*
CD ______ CDKEND 122
Kent / May '95 / Pinnacle

LA IGUANA - SONS JAROCHOS FROM MEXICO
CD ______ CO 127
Corason / May '96 / ADA / CM / Direct

LA KORA DES GRIOTS
CD ______ PS 65079
PlayaSound / Nov '91 / ADA / Harmonia Mundi

LA LEGENDE DES CORNOUAILLES
CD ______ 3015902
Arcade / Feb '97 / Discovery

LA LEGENDE DU MUSETTE
CD Set ______ 982732
EPM / Jun '93 / ADA / Discovery

LA RESISTANCE (Songs/Poetry Of The French Resistance)
CD LDX 274734
La Chant Du Monde / Jul '94 / ADA / Harmonia Mundi

LA RUMBA
CD 283422
Total / Jan '96 / Total/BMG

LA SEGUNDA INTERNACIONAL
CD MRCD 109
Munster / Nov '96 / Cargo / Greyhound / Plastic Head

LA TRADITION AMOUREUSE
CD 983232
EPM / Oct '96 / ADA / Discovery

LA YAYA
CD HCD 8022
Hightone / Jul '94 / ADA / Koch

LA YELLOW COLLECTION (2CD Set)
Trailer: *La Yellow 357* / Souvenir de Paris: *Dimitri From Paris* / Peau d'ane: *Vertigo, Louise* / Nangadef maafric: *Galliano, Frederick* / Wrong number: *Kid Loco* / Fort alamo: *Murat, Jean-Louis* / Astral waves: *Papp, Julius* / Quelle sensation bizarre: *La Yellow 357* / Jazzhead: *Ex-Press* / Jazz thing: *Reminiscence Quartet* / Sentiments: *Fresh Lab* / DJ Cam theme: *DJ Cam* / Freestyle linguistique: *Mighty Pop* / Onde anda meu amor: *Reminiscence Quartet* / Return of the forgotten groove: *Bronco* / Rock solid: *Sinclair, Bob* / Ride away: *Mighty Bop* / L'element manquant: *Menelik* / Experience: *Cutee B.* / Psychodelico: *Reminiscence Quartet* / La blues: *De Lambre, Ingrid*
CD Set 0630183912
East West / Jul '97 / Warner Music

LABELLED WITH LOVE
Magic smile: *Vela, Rosie* / On the wings of love: *Osborne, Jeffrey* / Every breath you take: *Police* / Love and affection: *Armatrading, Joan* / Stuck in the middle with you: *Stealer's Wheel* / Pearl's a singer: *Brooks, Elkie* / Steppin' out: *Jackson, Joe* / Love will keep us together: *Captain & Tennille* / Lady in red: *De Burgh, Chris* / I should have known better: *Diamond, Jim* / Heart on my sleeve: *Gallagher & Lyle* / Wonderful life: *Black* / We're all alone: *Coolidge, Rita* / Babe: *Styx* / Pick up the pieces: *Hudson - Ford* / Labelled with love: *Squeeze* / Will you: *O'Connor, Hazel* / Goodbye to love: *Carpenters* / Oh, Lori: *Alessi*
CD 5518342
Spectrum / Nov '95 / PolyGram

LABELLO BLANCO - A DIFFERENT CLASS
CD GUMH 9
Labello Blanco / Jul '94 / SRD

LACH'S ANTIHOOT (Live From The Fort At Sidewalk Cafe)
CD SH 5707
Shanachie / Jun '96 / ADA / Greensleeves / Koch

LADIES OF GASCONY - THE BAGPIPES
CD C 560051
Ocora / Aug '96 / ADA / Harmonia Mundi

LADIES OF JAZZ
Starlit hour: *Fitzgerald, Ella* / Tisket-a-tasket: *Fitzgerald, Ella* / Basin street blues: *Fitzgerald, Ella* / Freight train blues: *Smith, Trixie* / Can't make another day: *Johnson, Edith North* / Trouble in mind: *Hill, Bertha* / Chain gang blues: *Rainy, Ma* / Billie's blues: *Holiday, Billie* / I'm tired of fattening frogs for snakes: *Crawford, Rosetta & James P. Johnson's Hep Cats* / I love you Porgy: *Holiday, Billie* / Stormy weathr: *Horne, Lena* / September song: *Vaughan, Sarah* / What a difference a day makes: *Vaughan, Sarah* / Alone with the blues: *Wiley, Lee* / September in the rain: *Lee, Peggy* / All of me: *Irvin, Frances* / That old gang of mine: *Lee, Peggy* / Moon faced and starry eyed: *Forrest, Helen* / Straighten up and fly right: *McRae, Carmen* / Inside a silent tear: *McRae, Carmen* / Imagination: *McRae, Carmen* / Fine and mellow: *Holiday, Billie*
CD 22727
Music / Jun '96 / Target/BMG

LADIES OF LATIN
CD CDHOT 623
Charly / Jul '97 / Koch

LADIES OF PENTHOUSE
CD PHCD 2047
Penthouse / Oct '96 / Jet Star

LADIES OF SWING, THE
Tisket-a-tasket: *Fitzgerald, Ella* / My blue heaven: *Horne, Lena* / What a difference a day made: *Vaughan, Sarah* / On the sunny side of the street: *Lee, Peggy & Woody Herman* / St. Louis blues: *Holiday, Billie* / Body and soul: *McRae, Carmen* / C'est si bon: *Ross, Annie* / Honeysuckle rose: *Horne, Lena* / Little white lies: *Fitzgerald, Ella* / Up a lazy river: *Lee, Peggy & Woody Herman* / Fly me to the moon: *Smith, Keely* / Georgia on my mind: *Holiday, Billie* / September song: *Vaughan, Sarah* / Baby won't you please come home: *Fitzgerald, Ella* / I hear music: *Holiday, Billie* / Somebody loves me: *Lee, Peggy* / Lover man: *Vaughan, Sarah* / Lady is a tramp: *Horne, Lena*
CD ECD 3290
K-Tel / Jan '97 / K-Tel

LADIES SING JAZZ VOL.3 (1928-1945)
CD 158642
Jazz Archives / Jun '97 / Discovery

LADIES SING THE BLUES
Downhearted blues: *Bailey, Mildred* / Break o'day blues: *Brown, Ada* / Evil mama blues: *Brown, Ada* / Hangover blues: *Carlisle, Una Mae* / Hard time blues: *Cox, Ida* / Take him off my mind: *Cox, Ida* / Cravin' a man blues: *Glinn, Lillian* / Blues I love to sing: *Hall, Adelaide* / Billie's blues: *Holiday, Billie* / Long gone blues: *Holiday, Billie* / Let your linen hang low: *Howard, Rosetta* / Rosetta blues: *Howard, Rosetta* / Electrician blues: *Miles, Lizzie* / My man o'war: *Miles, Lizzie* / Booze and blues: *Rainey, Gertrude 'Ma'* / Toad frog blues: *Rainey, Gertrude 'Ma'* / Empty bed blues: *Smith, Bessie* / St. Louis blues: *Smith, Bessie* / Jelly jelly look what you done done: *Smith, Clara* / Don't you leave me here: *Smith, Laura* / Goin' crazy with the blues: *Smith, Mamie* / Freight train blues: *Smith, Trixie* / Moaning the blues: *Spivey, Victoria* / I'm a mighty tight woman: *Wallace, Sippie*
CD CDAJA 5092
Living Era / Jun '92 / Select

LADY LOVE
CD DCD 5293
Disky / Feb '94 / Disky / THE

LADY LOVE
CD DC 860552
Disky / Mar '96 / Disky / THE

LADY LOVE - SWEET LOVE GROOVES
CD 12217
Laserlight / Jul '93 / Target/BMG

LADYKILLERS VOL.1 (23 Tracks To Die For)
Stupid girl: *Garbage* / What do I do now: *Sleeper* / Great things: *Echobelly* / Ladykillers: *Lush* / Weak: *Skunk Anansie* / Zombie: *Cranberries* / Drink the elixir: *Salad* / Feed the tree: *Belly* / Lost cat: *Catatonia* / She: *Tiny Monroe* / Rise and shine: *Cardigans* / Crash: *Primitives* / Night in my veins: *Pretenders* / Love your money: *Daisy Chainsaw* / Husband: *Fluffy* / Bright yellow gun: *Throwing Muses* / Fader: *Drugstore* / Ping pong: *Stereolab* / Night: *Intastella* / He's on the phone: *St. Etienne* / Missing: *Everything But The Girl* / Tishbite: *Cocteau Twins* / Fun for me: *Moloko*
CD 5355362
PolyGram TV / May '96 / PolyGram

LADYKILLERS VOL.2 (2CD Set)
CD Set 5533812
PolyGram TV / May '97 / PolyGram

LAFAYETTE SATURDAY NIGHT
One scotch, one bourbon, one beer: *Roger, Aldus* / Mean woman: *Roger, Aldus* / Zydeco et pas sale: *Roger, Aldus* / Recorded in England: *Bernard, Rod* / 2 fee: *Bernard, Rod* / Kidnapper: *Jewel & The Rubies* / Allons a Lafayette: *Newman, Jimmy C.* / Hippy ti yo: *Newman, Jimmy C.* / Lena Mae: *Walker, Lawrence* / Memphis: *Shondells* / Slow down: *Shondells* / Alligator Bayou: *Raven, Eddy* / I got loaded: *Lil' Bob & The Lollipops* / Come on over: *Gee Gee Shinn* / Colinda: *Guidry, Doc* / What's her name: *Forester, Blackie* / Domino: *Miller, Rodney* / Before I grow too old: *Miller, Rodney* / Just because: *King Karl* / Everybody's feeling good: *King Karl* / I'm cajun cool: *Cajun Born* / Getting late in the evening: *Neal, Raful* / Candy Ann: *Jewel & The Rubies* / That's what's wrong with the church today: *Consoling Clouds Of Joy*
CD CDCHD 371
Ace / Apr '92 / Pinnacle

LALABELLA
CD FLCD 2057
Flames / Jan '97 / Jet Star

LAMBADA
CD DINCD 6
Dino / Jan '90 / Pinnacle

LAMBADA
Lambada / Mar de emocoes / Lambada do galo / Lambada de salvador / Maris Mariazinha / Louca Magia / Mule fubanga / Dancando lambada / Merequeza / Blanco do merengue (el organito) / Isso e bom / Forregae / Brilho Jamaica / Lambada (instrumental)
CD 4660552
CBS / Nov '89 / Sony

LAMBADA BRAZIL
Lambada do remelxo: *Banda Cheiro De Amor* / Zorra: *Caldas, Luiz* / Algeria da cidade: *Menezes, Margareth* / Meia lua inteira: *Veloso, Caetano* / Ve estrelas: *Ramalho, Elba* / Roda baiana: *Banda Cheiro De Amor* / Dancando merengue: *Banda Tomalira* / Tenda do amor (magia): *Menezes, Margareth* / La vem o trio: *Banda Tomalira* / Lambada: *Carioca* / Doida: *Ramalho, Elba* / Ode e adao: *Caldas, Luiz* / Vou te pegar: *Nonato Do Cavaquinho* / Grande Gandhi: *Caldas, Luiz* / Careou: *Caldas, Luiz*
CD 8415802
Polydor / Nov '89 / PolyGram

LAMBADAS OF BRAZIL
CD EMPRCD 512
Emporio / Apr '94 / Disc

LAMBARENA - BACK TO AFRICA (Gabonese Music Inspired By Bach)
CD SK 64542
Sony Classical / Jun '96 / Sony

LAMBS ON THE GREEN HILLS
CD OSS 9CD
Ossian / Oct '89 / ADA / CM / Direct / Highlander

L'AME CORSE
Pricantula: *Nous Deux* / Manetta: *Chants Corses* / La violetta: *Le Choeur D'Hommes De Sartene* / Padre: *Donnisulana* / U pino tunisianu: *Chants Corses* / Agnes dei: *Micaelli, Jacky* / Bernardinu: *Tavagna* / Lamentu di ghjesu: *Micaelli, Jacky* / Paghjella per agata: *Donnisulana* / U viaghju: *Cesari, Mighela* / Morte de fillicone: *Chants Corses* / Cantu di a tribbiera: *Le Choeur D'Hommes De Sartene* / Lamentu di una minnana: *Tavagna* / Sanctus: *Chants Religieux De Tradition* / Quantu soli: *Nous Deux*
CD B6849
Auvidis/Ethnic / May '97 / ADA / Harmonia Mundi

LAMENT
Lament for the dead of the north: *Spillane, Davy* / Bright lady: *Masterson, Declan* / Sean O Duibhir a Ghleanna: *Ni Dhomhnaill, Maighread* / An droighnean donn: *Glackin, Paddy* / Plunkett: *O'Suilleabhain, Micheal* / One breath: *O'Kelly, Alanna* / Port na bpucai: *MacMahon, Tony* / Danny boy: *Moore, Christy* / Taimse I'm chodladh: *Og Potts, Sean* / Sliabh geal gcua: *Conneff, Kevin* / Carolan's devotion: *Sheahan, John* / An bonnan bui: *Potts, Sean* / John O'Dwyer of the glen: *Martin, Neil* / O'Carolan's farewell: *Bell, Derek*
CD CDRW 27
Realworld / Mar '93 / EMI

LAND OF 1000 DUNCES
CD CR 007
Candy / Jun '97 / Greyhound

LAND OF BABOON
CD SR 9607
Silent / Feb '97 / Cargo / Plastic Head

LAND OF DRUMMERS, A
CD VPU 1007CD
Village Pulse / May '97 / ADA

LAND OF HOPE AND GLORY
Rule Britannia / Strike up the band / British Grenadiers / Here's a health unto her Majesty / Royal ceremony / Marchalong / Cavalry of the clouds / Navy day / Normandy veterans march / Battle of Britain march / Drum and bugle display / Soldiers of the sea / Lionheart / Aces high / Sir John Moore concert march / Abide with me / Land of hope and glory / Life on an ocean wave / Heart of oak / Dam busters march / Bridge too far / On the march
CD MUCD 9004
Musketeer / Apr '95 / Disc

LAND OF MY FATHERS (Welsh Choral Classics)
CD MATCD 227
Castle / Dec '92 / BMG

LAND OF MY MOTHERS
CD CRAICD 048
Crai / Aug '95 / ADA / Direct

LAND OF SONG (Welsh Choral Classics)
CD PLSCD 173
Pulse / Apr '97 / BMG

LANOR RECORDS STORY 1960-1992, THE
J'ai fait mon idee: *Bergeron, Shirley* / Parlez vous francais: *Matte, Bill* / I love my baby: *Eltradors* / Life problem: *Anderson, Elton* / Can't stop loving you: *Little Victor* / Drifting cloud: *Drifting Charles* / Keep your arms around me: *Mann, Charles* / Your no longer mine: *Mann, Charles* / I'll be your Jim: *Mallory, Willie* / Runnin' out of fools: *Boynton, Hugh* / Love don't love nobody: *Brown, Ella* / Red red wine: *Mann, Charles* / Crazy face: *Randall, Jay & The Dialtones* / Hot hot lips: *Prescott, Ralph* / I found my woman: *Carrier, Roy* / Chewing gum: *Jacob, Donald* / Walk of life: *Mann, Charles* / Accordion player waltz: *Broussard, Tim* / Drop that ego: *Generation Band* / Zydeco all night: *Walker, Joe* / My name is Beau Jocque: *Jocque, Beau*
CD ZNCD 1009
Zane / Jul '95 / Pinnacle

L'APPEL DE LA MUSE VOL.2
CD AJE 04CD
Vinyl Solution / Nov '92 / RTM/Disc

LARGIN' IT (3CD Set)
Give me luv: *Alcatraz* / Livin' in danger: *Ace Of Base* / Access: *DJ Tim & DJ Misjah* / Let's rock: *E-Trax* / Tempo fiesta: *Boozy Woozy* / Nakasaki: *Kendoh* / Hideaway: *DeLacy* / Trippin' on sunshine: *Pizzaman* / Groovebird: *Natural Born Groovers* / Indica: *Movin' Melodies* / I'm alive: *Stretch n' Vern* / Jumpin': *Terry, Todd* / Jus come: *Cool Jack* / Remember me: *Jubb, Phil* / DAncin': *Casa Royale* / Shout: *Staxx* / Make the world go round: *Sandy B* / Wrong: *Everything But The Girl* / Tart: *Divine Intervention* / Loe don't live: *Proctor, Michael* / Feel like movin': *Anorak Trax Vol.5* / I can't help it: *Happy Clappers* / Sax in the ozone: *Aaron, Robert* / Open your mind: *Thompson, Keith* / You can't turn around: *Bottom $* / So in love: *Wild Pursuit* / Cut for life: *Leftfield* / We're going on down: *Deadly Sins* / Funkatarium: *Jump* / Reach: *Lil Mo Yin Yang* / Subliminal cuts: *Le Voie De Soleil* / Search: *Trancesetters* / Yeke yeke: *Kante, Mory* / No other love: *Blue Amazon* / Stormy weather: *Ultrahigh* / Stand up: *Lovetribe* / Feel love: *Hysteric Ego* / Feel my body: *O'Moiraghi, Frank & Amnesia*
CD Set SOLIDCD 001
CD Set SOLIDSCD 001
Solid State / Jul '96 / Prime / Vital

LARK IN THE CLEAR AIR
CD OSS 13CD
Ossian / Dec '94 / ADA / CM / Direct / Highlander

L'ART DU KHEN (Vietnamese Mouth Organ)
CD ARN 60367
Arion / Feb '97 / ADA / Discovery

LAS VEGAS GRIND VOL.2
CD EFA 11512CD
Crypt / Mar '93 / Shellshock/Disc

LAS VEGAS GRIND VOL.3
CD 12887
Strip / Jul '97 / Greyhound

LAS VEGAS GRIND VOL.5
CD EFACD 12887
Crypt / Apr '97 / Shellshock/Disc

LAST GREAT ROCKABILLY SATURDAY NIGHT, THE
CD STCD 3
Stomper Time / Sep '93 / TKO Magnum

LATE NIGHT COOL
CD NTRCD 054
Nectar / Jun '97 / Pinnacle

LATE NIGHT JAZZ
What's new: *Paich, Marty* / Summer wishes, winter dreams: *Raney, Sue* / Bewitched: *Chamber Jazz Sextet* / Emily: *Daniels, Eddie* / In a sentimental mood: *Brookmeyer, Bob* / I remember clifford: *Getz, Stan* / Lotus bud: *Shank, Bud* / Please send me someone to love: *De Franco, Buddy* / I waited for you: *Baker, Chet* / Handful of stars: *Konitz, Lee* / On green dolphin street: *Liebmann, David* / I never told you: *Thielemans, 'Toots'* / You go to my head: *Holiday, Billie* / La vie en rose: *Holiday, Billie*
CD EMPRCD 664
Emporio / Oct '96 / Disc

LATE NIGHT LATIN
To be with you: *Cuba, Joe Sextet* / Si te di un beso sin importancia: *Mendoza, Celeste* / Mi pobre corazon: *Duo Los Compadres* / Noro in rumbaland: *Morales, Noro* / Lentamente: *Concepcion, Cesar* / Quien sera: *Lopez, Virginia* / Dandole a la rumba: *Rodriguez, Johnny* / El yoyo: *Puente, Tito* / Mula ta Linda: *Argentino, Carlos* / La noche morena: *Valdes, Vicentico* / De mi no se burla: *Ross, Julita* / Caravan: *Puente, Tito* / No etamos cansao: *Concepcion, Cesar* / Asi son los quereres: *Capo, Bobby* / El rumor de las olas: *Duo Los Compadres* / Eras diferente: *Mendoza, Celeste* / Tu regresso: *Morales, Noro* / Siempre nos pasa lo mismo: *Rodriguez, Johnny* / Y que: *Argentino, Carlos* / Bendicion: *Valdes, Vicentico*
CD CDHOT 609
Charly / Sep '96 / Koch

LATE NIGHT REGGAE
Some guys have all the luck: *Harriott, Derrick* / There's a place called Africa: *Byles, Junior* / Give me your love: *McGregor, Freddie* / Long long winter: *Marley, Bob & The Wailers* / You're gonna lose: *Paragons* / Meet me tonight: *Miller, Jacob* / Strange but true: *McKay, Freddie* / Make a move: *U-Roy* / Perfida: *Dillon, Phyllis* / I've got a feeling: *Byles, Junior* / Ride the donkey: *Tenors* / Boom shacka lacka: *Lewis, Hopeton* / I don't know: *Brown, Dennis* / Barbwire: *Dean, Nora* / Hey fat man: *Morgan, Derrick* / Future is here: *Melodians* / Stop loving you: *McGregor, Freddie* / Poor chubby: *Byles, Junior* / Take me back to Africa: *Dekker, Desmond*
CD CDGR 117
Charly / Jan '97 / Koch

LATER VOL.1 (Brit Beat)
Changing man: *Weller, Paul* / Just lookin': *Charlatans* / Alright: *Supergrass* / Car song: *Elastica* / Girl like you: *Collins, Edwyn* / Day we caught the train: *Ocean Colour Scene* / Goldfinger: *Ash* / Heroine: *Suede* / Yes: *McAlmont & Butler* / Wonderwall: *Oasis* / Bends: *Radiohead* / If you don't want me to destroy you: *Super Furry Animals* / Sleeper: *Audioweb* / Lenny Valentino: *Auteurs* / Fine time: *Cast* / Slight return: *Bluetones* / Universal: *Blur* / Small black flowers that grow in the sky: *Manic Street Preachers* / I spy: *Pulp*
CD CID 8053
Island / Sep '96 / PolyGram

LATER VOL.2 (Slow Beats)
Karmakoma: *Massive Attack* / Tape loop: *Morcheeba* / Brown sugar: *D'Angelo* / Watusi: *Cherry, Neneh* / Glory box: *Portishead* / I must stand: *Ice-T* / Whipping boy: *Harper, Ben* / Single: *Everything But The Girl* / Suffocated love: *Tricky* / Possibly maybe: *Bjork* / She's a lover: *Martyn, John* / Don't you dream: *Soul II Soul* / Paraffin: *Ruby* /

Blues music: *G-Love & Special Sauce* / Feel the music: *Guru* / Inside out: *Nelson, Shara* / People in tha middle: *Spearhead*
CD ______ CID 8054
Island / Dec '96 / PolyGram

LATEX TV OBLIVION
CD ______ MHCD 008
Minus Habens / Nov '93 / Plastic Head

LATIN AMERICAN HOLIDAYS
CD ______ CD 62019
Saludos Amigos / Jan '93 / Target/BMG

LATIN AMERICAN MUSIC
CD ______ 301062
Musidisc / Aug '90 / Discovery

LATIN AMERICAN PERCUSSION (3CD Set)
CD Set ______ PS 360501
PlayaSound / Sep '96 / ADA / Harmonia Mundi

LATIN CARNIVAL
CD ______ CDHOT 608
Charly / Aug '96 / Koch

LATIN CARNIVAL (A Musical Celebration Of The Magic Of Latin America)
Estar Enamorado / Todo se derrumbo / Atrevette / La Ladrona / O me quieres O me dejas / Don diablo / Has nacido libre / Amor ne me ignores / Simple magica / Ella se llambada / Dueno de nada / Preso / Terciopelo y piedra / Si el llama a tu puerta
CD ______ ECD 3256
K-Tel / Jan '97 / K-Tel

LATIN FOR LOVERS
CD ______ CDHOT 618
Charly / Mar '97 / Koch

LATIN JAZZ
Cappuccino: *La Sonora Poncena* / Diecisiete punto uno: *Palmieri, Eddie* / Blues a la Machito: *Machito & His Afro-Cuban Salseros* / Noble cruise: *Palmieri, Eddie* / Ran kan kan: *Puente, Tito* / Manteca: *Santamaria, Mongo* / Night love: *La Sonora Poncena* / Introvisate: *Impacto Crea* / Mambo jazz: *Ray, Ricardo & Bobby Cruz* / Night in Tunisia: *Barretto, Ray* / Mambo a la tito: *Puente, Tito* / New one: *Santamaria, Mongo*
CD ______ CDHOT 520
Charly / Apr '95 / Koch

LATIN JAZZ
Power struggle / Fiesta a la king / Druma / Sal sangre / Manteca 77 / Camino a casa / Start the world, I want to get on / Zimbabwe
CD ______ JWD 102220
JWD / Apr '96 / Target/BMG

LATIN JAZZ DANCE CLASSICS VOL.1
CD ______ CBCD 004
Cubop / Nov '96 / Timewarp

LATIN JAZZ VOL.1
Nica's dream: *Burrell, Kenny* / Gunky: *Lytle, Johnny* / Mambo inn: *Taylor, Billy Trio* / Caravan: *Pucho & His Latin Soul Brothers* / Sambop: *Adderley, Cannonball* / Baion baby: *Stitt, Sonny* / Tin tin deo: *Forrest, Jimmy* / Montuneando: *Santamaria, Mongo*
CD ______ CDBGP 1023
Beat Goes Public / Mar '93 / Pinnacle

LATIN JAZZ VOL.2
Ping pong: *Blakey, Art & The Jazz Messengers* / Mau mau: *Farmer, Art Septet* / Manteca: *Garland, Red Trio* / Sea food wally: *Rodriguez, Willie* / Screamin': *McDuff, 'Brother' Jack* / Fat man: *Montego Joe* / Mambo ricci: *Dolphy, Eric & Latin Jazz* / Chop sticks: *Braith, George*
CD ______ CDBGP 1027
Beat Goes Public / Aug '89 / Pinnacle

LATIN ONLY
El Africano / A mi dios todo le debo / Se me perdio la cadenita / Ligia / El merecumbe / La cocaleca / El beso / La casa de Fernando / El ciclon / Ella es mi Gloria / La conga / Ni cuerpo ni corazon / La brujita / Corazol y sincelejo / La pachango del futbol / El tizon / La gorra / La mucura / Ella ma vacila / La muchacha del conejo
CD ______ DC 880552
Disky / May '97 / Disky / THE

LATIN SOUL BOOGALOO
Bang: *Cuba, Joe Sextet* / Aye que Rico: *Palmieri, Eddie* / Para ti mi boogaloo: *Cruz, Celia* / Aqui: *Puente, Tito* / Ismael y Monchito: *Rivera, Ismael* / You're looking fine: *Orquesta Broadway* / Palo de mango: *Palmieri, Eddie* / Bambo cure: *Cortijo, Ralph & Ismael Rivera* / El Pito (I'll never go back to Georgia): *Cuba, Joe Sextet* / Steak-o-lean: *Puente, Tito* / El watusi: *Barretto, Ray*
CD ______ 12913
Laserlight / Aug '96 / Target/BMG

LATIN SUMMER (3CD Set)
CD Set ______ KBOX 373
Collection / Aug '97 / Target/BMG / TKO Magnum

LATINAS
CD ______ N 17028CD
Nimbus / Aug '95 / Nimbus

LATINO CLUB
Coro miyare: *Pacheco, Johnny* / Acid: *Barretto, Ray* / Ajiaco caliente: *DR* / Fania: *Bolanos, Reinaldo* / Ay mi cuba: *More, Benny* / Elpito (I'll never go back to Georgia): *Sabater, Cuba* / Vente conmigo: *Fania Allstars* / Taste of latin: *Merraro, R.* / Nadie se salya de la rumba: *Rodriguez, Siro* / Que sabroso
CD ______ CDCHARLY 227
Charly / Jul '90 / Koch

LATINO LATINO
Chacha la vie: *Kaoma* / Yiri yiri bon: *Lemvo, Ricardo* / Arranca: *Manzanita* / Volver a verte: *D'Leon, Oscar* / Los pasillos de tia conga: *Cespedes, Conjunto* / Besame mama: *Sanchez, Poncho* / Son flamenco: *Del Caney, Los* / Asia: *Colon, Willie* / Chi chi mani: *La Momposina, Toto* / No me llores: *Maestra, Sierra*
CD ______ PUTU 1312
Putumayo / Aug '97 / Grapevine/PolyGram

LAUGHTER ON THE HOME FRONT (Songs/Comedy That Kept A Nation Going During The Great War)
CD ______ PASTCD 7047
Flapper / Sep '94 / Pinnacle

LAURIE VOCAL GROUPS - THE 60'S SOUND
Denise: *Randy & The Rainbows* / Little star: *Randy & The Rainbows* / Why do kids grow up: *Randy & The Rainbows* / Don't worry I'm gonna make it: *Randy & The Rainbows* / Happy teenager: *Randy & The Rainbows* / Sharin': *Randy & The Rainbows* / Bye bye: *Bon-Aires* / Jeannie baby: *Bon-Aires* / Lovely way to spend an evening: *Four Graduates* / Candy queen: *Four Graduates* / Please write: *Tokens* / Cry and be on my way: *Demilles* / In the beginning: *Illusions* / I love you Diane: *Four Epics* / Dance Joanne: *Four Epics* / Judy: *Rayvons* / I'll always love you: *Tokens* / Away: *Concords* / Four seasons: *Coleman, Lenny & The Ebbtides* / Let's dance close: *Curtiss, Jimmy & The Regents* / Starlit night: *Emotions* / My heart cries: *Vera, Billy* / Donna Lee: *Demilles* / Tomorrow we'll be married: *Knight, Bob Four* / My dream: *Dino & the diplomats* / Does my love stand a chance: *Del-Satins* / Love boat: *Karillions* / This whole wide world: *Ovations* / Nicky: *Bernadette* / You just you: *Criterions* / Rock 'n' roll revival: *Five Discs* / Champaign lady: *Teardrops* / Walk down the aisle: *Monte, Vinnie* / Marie: *Harps*
CD ______ CDCHD 346
Ace / Feb '92 / Pinnacle

LAURIE VOCAL GROUPS - THE DOO WOP SOUND
Queen of the angels: *Orients* / I shouldn't: *Orients* / Zoom, zoom, zoom: *Enchords* / I need you baby: *Enchords* / Gloria: *Passion* / Oh melancholy me: *Passion* / Just to be with you: *Passion* / This is my love: *Passion* / I only want you: *Passion* / I remember: *Five Discs* / World is a beautiful place: *Five Discs* / Angel in my eyes: *Premiere, Ronnie* / Hello Dolly: *Vito & The Salutations* / Daddy's going away again: *Harps* / Shrine of St. Cecilia: *Bon-Aires* / Hush-a-bye my love: *Dino & the diplomats* / I can't believe: *Dino & the diplomats* / You, you my love: *Jo-vals* / Remain truly yours: *Criterions* / Wake up: *Elegants* / Mr. Night: *Motions* / Falling star: *Premiers* / Karen: *Lane, Rusty & The Mystics* / Who knows, who cares: *Holidays* / Stars will remember: *Holidays* / My lullabye: *Ovations* / She's my angel: *Randy & The Rainbows* / Again: *Four Epics* / Picture an angel: *Four Graduates* / I'll never know: *Del-Satins*
CD ______ CDCHD 309
Ace / Feb '91 / Pinnacle

LE CHANT DES ENFANTS DU MONDE
CD ______ ARN 64320
Arion / Jul '95 / ADA / Discovery

LE FRONT POPULAIRE (Songs From Paris 1934-1939/2CD Set)
CD Set ______ FA 049
Fremeaux / Jul '96 / ADA / Discovery

LE MEJOR DE LA SALSA
CD ______ BM 516
Blue Moon / Feb '97 / Cadillac / Discovery / Greensleeves / Jazz Music / Jet Star / TKO Magnum

LE MIROIR D'ARGENT
CD ______ CVPV 1390CD
CVPV / Apr '96 / ADA

LE MONDE DE L'ACCORDEON
CD ______ 3015712
Arcade / Apr '97 / Discovery

LE MOULIN ROUGE 1889-1940
CD ______ 983802
EPM / Jul '96 / ADA / Discovery

LE MUSETTE A PARIS
CD ______ B 6817CD
Auvidis/Ethnic / Nov '95 / ADA / Harmonia Mundi

LE PLUS BELLES FRANCAIS
CD ______ DCD 5321
Disky / Dec '93 / Disky / THE

LE PLUS GRAND ZOUK
CD ______ 4742112
AB/Sonodisc / Jan '97 / Stern's

LE SON DE PARIS
CD ______ 325012
Melodie / Sep '96 / ADA / Discovery / Grapevine/PolyGram / Greensleeves / Jet Star

LE TANGO A PARIS 1907-1941 (2CD Set)
CD Set ______ FA 012CD
Fremeaux / Nov '95 / ADA / Discovery

LE TEMPS D'UN SLOW (2CD Set)
Comme j'ai toujours envie d'aimer / Un amour de vacances: *Rippert, Christophe* / Et toute la ville en parle: *Torr, Michele* / Elle: *Barbelivien, Didier* / Dinons ce soir en amoureux: *Valery, Francois* / Je n'aime que toi: *Manson, Jean* / Si ca va pas ce soir: *Barzotti, Claude* / Et j'ai le mal de toi: *Sweet People* / Angelique: *Vidal, Christian* / Si: *Cheryl, Karen* / Dis cette melodie: *Dumont, Charles* / Butterfly: *Gerard, Daniel* / Fleur du mal: *Stephanie* / Affaire etrangere: *Dave* / Tous les je vous aime: *Roussos, Demis* / Envie de t'aimer: *Roussos, Demis* / Mise au point: *Quartz, Jakie* / Pour le plaisir: *Leonard, Herbert* / Un homme et une femme: *Croisille, Nicole & Francis Lai* / Les maries de vendee: *Barbelivien, Didier & Anais* / Amoureux fous: *Leonard, Herbert & Julie* / Maitre pierre: *Darel, Sophie & Pierre Perret* / Lindberg: *Charlebois, Robert & Louise Forestier* / Besoin de rien, envie de toi: *Peter & Sloane* / Comme une histoire d'amour: *Fugain, Michel & Veronique Genest* / Dream in blue: *Valery, Francois & Sophie Marceau* / L'enfant de l'univers: *Fernandel, Franck & Vincent* / Prends une rose: *Mardel, Guy & Chantal Goya* / Amoureux sans baggages: *Soul, David & Claire Severac* / Et si tu pars: *Sullivan, Art & Kiki* / Aime moi: *Barzotti, Claude & Estelle Esse* / L'aventura: *Charden, Stone & Eric* / Cet enfant que je t'avais fait: *Higelin, Jacques & Brigitte Fontaine* / Quoi ca sert l'amour: *Piaf, Edith & Theo Sarapo* / Si ca fait mal: *Hardy, Francoise & Alain Lubrano* / Il faut laisser le temps au temps: *Gray & Barbelivien*
CD ______ SP 876722
Disky / Nov '96 / Disky / THE

LE TEMPS DES 60'S (2CD Set)
Twist a Saint Tropez: *Les Chats Sauvages & Dick Rivers* / Tu marches et tu pleures: *Les Dauphins* / Les garcons: *Dona, Alice* / C'est pas serieux: *Les Chats Sauvages & Dick Rivers* / Baby John: *Rivers, Dick* / Aux jeunes loups: *Annoux, Jean Claude* / En avant l'amour: *Les Chats Sauvages & Dick Rivers* / La terre promise: *Anthony, Richard* / Tu n'es plus la: *Rivers, Dick & The Gladiators* / La playa: *Ciari, Claude* / Lecon de twist: *Anthony, Richard* / Hey pony: *Les Chats Sauvages & Dick Rivers* / Ya ya twist: *Anthony, Richard* / Mon train de banlieue: *Dona, Alice* / Sa grande passion: *Les Chats Sauvages & Dick Rivers* / Et quelque chose me dit: *Bartock, Ria* / Alligator: *Hector* / Les cavaliers du ciel: *Les Bourgeois De Calais* / Hong kong: *Hector* / Chante alleluia: *Les Guitares Seches* / Couleurs: *Rivers, Dick* / Anthony, Richard: *Rivers, Dick* / Jette-la: *Greco, Larry* / L'argent de poche: *Winter, Pat Et Les Saunders* / Mister pitiful: *Winter, Pat Et Les Saunders* / Sur notre plage: *Anthony, Richard* / Peut etre demain: *Triangle* / Fou roi pantin: *Komintern* / Down the road: *Les Variations*
CD Set ______ SP 876732
Disky / Nov '96 / Disky / THE

LEAD WITH THE BASS VOL.1
CD ______ WWCD 8
Wibbly Wobbly / Jul '97 / SRD

LEAD WITH THE BASS VOL.2
CD ______ WWCD 17
Universal Egg / Mar '96 / SRD

LEADER OF THE PACK (Girl Group Greats From The Rock 'n' Roll Era)
Leader of the pack: *Shangri-Las* / Soldier boy: *Shirelles* / One fine day: *Chiffons* / Chapel of love: *Dixie Cups* / Da doo ron ron: *Crystals* / Lover's concerto: *Toys* / My boyfriend's back: *Angels* / Remember (walkin' in the sand): *Shangri-Las* / Will you love me tomorrow: *Shirelles* / He's so fine: *Chiffons* / Iko iko: *Dixie Cups* / Then he kissed me: *Crystals* / Sally go round the roses: *Jaynettes* / To know him is to love him: *Teddy Bears* / He's a rebel: *Crystals* / Mr. Lee: *Bobbettes*
CD ______ SUMCD 4025
Summit / Nov '96 / Sound & Media

LEADERS OF THE PACK (The Very Best Of 60's Girl Groups)
Dancing in the street: *Reeves, Martha & The Vandellas* / Baby love: *Supremes* / It's in his kiss (The shoop shoop song): *Everett, Betty* / Leader of the pack: *Shangri-Las* / Locomotion: *Little Eva* / Shout: *Lulu & The Luvvers* / Sweet talking guy: *Chiffons* / It's my party: *Gore, Lesley* / Will you still love me tomorrow: *Shirelles* / My guy: *Wells, Mary* / Needle in a haystack: *Velvelettes* / Da doo ron ron: *Crystals* / He's so fine: *Chiffons* / Where did our love go: *Supremes* / Remember (walkin' in the sand): *Shangri-Las* / Jimmy Mack: *Reeves, Martha & The Vandellas* / Chapel of love: *Dixie Cups* / When you're young and in love: *Marvelettes* / Really saying something: *Velvelettes* / One fine day: *Chiffons* / Then he kissed me: *Crystals* / My boyfriend's back: *Angels* / Past, present and future: *Shangri-Las*
CD ______ 5163762
PolyGram TV / Aug '93 / PolyGram

LEAF
CD ______ LEAFCD 1
Psychic / May '96 / Total/BMG

LEAPIN' GUITARS (Rockin' Roulette Instrumentals)
Ramrod: *Rogers, Johnny* / Sassy: *Rogers, Johnny* / Chase: *Wild Bill & The Blue Denims* / Mona my love: *Wild Bill & The Blue Denims* / Woo hoo: *Rock-a-Teens* / Pagan: *Rock-a-Teens* / Offbeat: *Rock-a-Teens* / Oh, my nerves: *Rock-a-Teens* / Twangy: *Rock-a-Teens* / War paint: *Haley, Bill & The Comets* / Riviera: *Haley, Bill & The Comets* / El Rancho Grande: *Eddy, Duane* / Poppa's movin' on: *Eddy, Duane* / Poor boy: *Royaltones* / Wail: *Royaltones* / See saw: *Royaltones* / Little Bo: *Royaltones* / Cha hua hua: *Platt, Eddie* / Salty: *Castle, Tony & The Raiders* / Hi Lili, hi lo: *Castle, Tony & The Raiders* / Sincerely: *Castle, Tony & The Raiders* / Tara's theme: *Castle, Tony & The Raiders* / Leapin' guitar: *Chapparals* / Beer barrel rock: *Chapparals* / Bikini: *Bikinis* / Boogie rock 'n' roll: *Bikinis* / Down yonder rock: *Gone All Stars*
CD ______ NEMCD 923
Sequel / Jul '97 / BMG

LEATHER AND LACE VOL.1 (The Men & Women Of Rock)
CD ______ DINCD 9
Dino / Jun '90 / Pinnacle

LEATHER AND LACE VOL.2 (The Second Chapter)
Radio ga ga: *Queen* / Black velvet: *Myles, Alannah* / Road to hell: *Rea, Chris* / Rooms on fire: *Nicks, Stevie* / Hurting kind (I've got my eyes on you): *Palmer, Robert* / Edge of a broken heart: *Vixen* / Better days: *Gun* / I don't want a lover: *Texas* / Run to you: *Adams, Bryan* / Big love: *Fleetwood Mac* / Radar love: *Golden Earring* / Get your love: *Black Velvette* / From out of nowhere: *Faith No More* / Martha's harbour: *All About Eve* / I'm a believer: *Giant* / First time: *Beck, Robin* / Centrefold: *Geils, J. Band*
CD ______ DINCD 12
Dino / Nov '90 / Pinnacle

LEGACY (A Tribute To The First Generation Of Bluegrass)
CD ______ SHCD 9202
Sugar Hill / Jun '97 / ADA / CM / Direct / Koch / Roots

LEGACY OF GENE 'BOWLEGS' MILLER
Call of distress: *Bryant, Don* / Doin' the mustang: *Bryant, Don* / Sho is good: *Miller, Gene 'Bowlegs'* / Goodest man: *Miller, Gene 'Bowlegs'* / I was wrong: *Miller, Gene 'Bowlegs'* / What do you mean: *Miller, Gene 'Bowlegs'* / Frankenstein walk: *Miller, Gene 'Bowlegs'* / Everybody got soul: *Miller, Gene 'Bowlegs'* / Love what you're doing to me: *Janet & The Jays* / Pleading for your love: *Janet & The Jays* / Walk away: *Peebles, Ann* / I can't let you go: *Peebles, Ann* / My man: *Peebles, Ann* / Chain of fools: *Peebles, Ann* / Rescue me: *Peebles, Ann* / Won't you try me: *Peebles, Ann* / Respect: *Peebles, Ann*
CD ______ HILOCD 15
Hi / Jul '95 / Pinnacle

LEGACY OF TURLOUGH O'CAROLAN, THE
Planxty Burke: *Phillips, Shelley* / Planxty Drew: *Phillips, Shelley* / Squire Parsdons: *Orion* / Eleanor Plunkett: *Deanta* / Lord Inchiquin: *Deiseal* / Hawk of Ballyshannon: *Heymann, Ann* / Loftus Jones: *Dordan* / Si Bheag, Si Mhor: *Coulter, William* / Captain O'Kane: *McGuire, Seamus* / Colonel John Irwin: *Newman, Chris* / Mrs. Judge: *Long, Donna* / Bridget Cruise: *Bouchard, Dominic & Cyrille Colas* / John O'Connor: *Bouchard, Dominic & Cyrille Colas* / George Bravazon: *Bouchard, Dominic & Cyrille Colas* / Fanny Power: *McMeen, El* / Coralan's concerto: *Whelan, John* / Coralan's farewell to music: *O'Sullivan, Jerry*
CD ______ ND 63925
Narada / Jun '96 / ADA / New Note/ Pinnacle

LEGACY'S RHYTHM 'N' SOUL REVUE SAMPLER
Wake up everyone: *Melvin, Harold & The Bluenotes* / Caravan of love: *Isley-Jasper-Isley* / Me and Mrs. Jones: *Paul, Billy* / Kiss and say goodbye: *Manhattans* / Ain't no sunshine: *Withers, Bill* / Piece of my heart: *Franklin, Erma* / I feel so bad: *Willis, Chuck* / Backstabbers: *O'Jays* / Everyone eats when they come to my house: *Calloway, Cab* / Who loves you better: *Isley Brothers* / Hey little girl: *Major Lance* / One girl too late: *Brenda & Tabulations* / Cowboys and girls: *Intruders* / My ship is coming in: *Jackson, Walter* / Love is the message: *MFSB* / You are my friend: *Labelle, Patti* / It rocks, it swings: *Treniers* / Lady Marmalade: *Labelle, Patti*
CD ______ 4805122
Columbia / May '95 / Sony

LEGAL TENDER
CD ______ VPRL 1111
VP / May '97 / Greensleeves / Jet Star / Total/BMG

LEGALIZE DE HERB VOL.1
Kaya: *Marley, Bob* / One draw: *Marley, Rita* / Herbsman shuffle: *King Stitt* / Under me sleng teng: *Smith, Wayne* / Smoking my ganja: *Capital Letters* / Judge Natty: *Jah Lloyd* / Better collie: *Andy, Horace* / Real thing: *Levy, Barrington* / Legalize it: *Clarke,*

Johnny / Love mi sess: *Top Cat* / Spliff tail: *Palmer, Tristan* / Weedfields: *Desi Roots*
CD ______ KICKCD 50
Kickin' / Mar '97 / Prime / SRD

LEGEND OF NEW ORLEANS, THE
Dr. Jazz / Sweetie dear / Alligator crawl / Too tight / That's a plenty / Pleasin' Paul / High society / Astoria strut / Weatherbird / Turtle twist / Maple leaf rag / Perdido Street blues / Clarinet marmalade / Apex blues / Ory's Creole trombone / New Orleans stomp / Sweet lovin' man / Tiger rag / Duet stomp / Cannonball blues / Beau Koo Jack / I know that you know / Franklin Street blues / As you like it / Panama
CD ______ CD 53016
Giants Of Jazz / Jul '88 / Cadillac / Jazz Music / Target/BMG

LEGENDARY DIG MASTERS VOL.2 (Dig These Blues)
Old folk's boogie: *Simmons, Al* / You ain't too old: *Simmons, Al* / Country home: *Sailor Boy* / What have I done wrong (parts 1 and 2): *Sailor Boy* / Hand me down baby: *Maiden, Sidney* / Going back to the plow: *Hozay* / I've got an expensive woman: *Hozay* / Wrong doin' woman: *John, Moose* / Talkin' 'bout me: *John, Moose* / Springtime blues: *Sams, TW* / Come on home: *Nolen, Jimmy* / If you ever get lonesome: *Easter, Roy 'Happy'* / My woman done quit me: *Green, Slim* / Moore boogie: *Moore, Abe* / S and J: *Moore, Abe* / Singin' the blues: *Robbins, Little Bill* / Full grown woman: *Waters, Larry* / Don't tell me that you love me: *Waters, Larry* / Bring her back to me: *Robbins, Billy* / Elim stole my baby (boo hoo): *Cane, Sugar* / They say you never can miss: *Cane, Sugar*
CD ______ CDCHD 334
Ace / Jan '92 / Pinnacle

LEGENDARY DIG MASTERS VOL.3 (Dapper Cats, Groovy Tunes & Hot Guitars)
Telephone boogie: *Watson, Johnny & Jeannie* / I got a girl (that lives over yonder): *Watson, Johnny 'Guitar'* / My aching feet: *Strogin, Henry* / I've been blind, blind, blind: *Strogin, Henry* / Jimmy's jive: *Nolen, Jimmy* / Hey little girl: *Lewis, Richard* / Bingo: *Moore, Abe* / Talk to me baby: *Easter, Roy 'Happy'* / Sad stories: *Waters, Larry* / Check yourself: *Allen, Tony & Barbara* / Someday: *Sams, TW* / Country boogie: *Love, Preston & Orchestra* / Get away from here: *Lewis, Pete 'Guitar'* / Ain't gonna tell: *Ray, Dessa* / Wiggle walk: *Otis, Johnny* / Things won't be right without you: *Williams, Devonia 'Lady Dee'* / Much more: *Jessie & Joyce* / Itty bitty bee: *Johnson, Ray* / Baby please come home: *Robbins, Little Billy* / Gotta have lovin': *Robbins, Little Billy* / Blooper: *Otis, Johnny & The Jayos* / Bad Bad Bulldog: *Matthews, Little Arthur* / Hot diggity (dog ziggity boom): *Matthews, Little Arthur* / Dead man's shop: *Otis, Johnny & His Orchestra*
CD ______ CDCHD 351
Ace / Oct '92 / Pinnacle

LEGENDARY DIG MASTERS VOL.4 (Shoo-Be-Doo-Be-Ooh)
Shoobie dooby Mama: *Phantoms* / My baby doll: *Gladiators* / Girl of my heart: *Gladiators* / Another chance: *Foster, Cell* / Millie's chilli: *Foster, Cell* / Fools prayer: *Maye, Arthur Lee* / Honey honey: *Maye, Arthur Lee* / This is the night for love: *Maye, Arthur Lee* / Whispering wind: *Maye, Arthur Lee* / Crazy bells: *Stevens, Julie* / Blue mood: *Stevens, Julie* / Have a heart: *Premiers* / My darling: *Premiers* / Can it be real: *Premiers* / Take my heart: *Stevens, Julie* / You think I'm just your fool: *Stevens, Julie* / Ding a ling a ling: *Jayos* / Dying love: *Jayos* / I plead guilty: *Jayos* / Wedding ring: *Jayos* / What am I gonna do: *Jayos* / In exhange for your love: *Jayos* / Sweet thing: *Ding Dongs*
CD ______ CDCHD 569
Ace / Sep '94 / Pinnacle

LEGENDARY VOICES
CD ______ CWNCD 2002
Javelin / Jun '95 / Henry Hadaway / THE

LEGENDS OF BRITISH TRADITION (Bulls Head Barns)
Sweet Georgia Brown / Of all the wrongs / Weary blues / Baby, won't you please come home / When your lover has gone
CD ______ CMJCD 014
CMJ / Oct '91 / Jazz Music / Wellard

LEGENDS OF LATIN MUSIC
Relax & mambo: *Machito* / Dile que por mi no tema: *Cruz, Celia* / Que problema: *Cuba, Joe Sextet* / Camina y ven: *La Lupe* / Guantanamera: *Machito* / Kon-kun mambo: *Valdes, Minuelito & Machito Orchestra* / La plena bomba me llaman: *Cruz, Celia* / Lindo yambu: *Palmieri, Eddie* / Guajira: *Bobo, Willie* / Cha cha chick: *Herman, Woody & Tito Puente* / Odiame: *La Lupe*
CD ______ 12916
Laserlight / Aug '96 / Target/BMG

LEGENDS OF MUSIC
CD ______ CD 322701
Koch Presents / Jul '97 / Koch

LEGENDS OF ROCK 'N' ROLL, THE
Reelin' and rockin': *Berry, Chuck* / Johnny B Goode: *Berry, Chuck* / Memphis Tennessee: *Berry, Chuck* / Nadine: *Berry, Chuck* / Sweet little sixteen: *Berry, Chuck* / Rock around the clock: *Haley, Bill & The Comets* / Shake, rattle and roll: *Haley, Bill & The Comets* / See you later alligator: *Haley, Bill & The Comets* / Razzle dazzle: *Haley, Bill & The Comets* / Saints rock 'n' roll: *Haley, Bill & The Comets* / This ol' house: *Perkins, Carl* / Dixie fried: *Perkins, Carl* / That's right: *Perkins, Carl* / All Mama's children: *Perkins, Carl* / Blue suede shoes: *Perkins, Carl* / Good golly Miss Molly: *Little Richard* / Lucille: *Little Richard* / She's got it: *Little Richard* / Girl can't help it: *Little Richard* / Tutti frutti: *Little Richard*
CD ______ SUMCD 4048
Summit / Nov '96 / Sound & Media

LEIF 'SMOKE RINGS' ANDERSON PRESENTS...
CD ______ ANC 9096
Ancha / Aug '94 / Cadillac / Jazz Music / Wellard

LES ANTILLES
Ernestine attention / Ce les Antilles / Ba moin un tibo, doudou / Mr. Leonard / bande Zaoua / La ronde des cuisinieres / Serpent maigre / L'ete en pyjama / Maladie d'amour / Guitare des Antilles / Le rocher / Oh pere / Ninon, merengue, merengue / Danse de gros ca / Guyane, o Guyana / Sans chemise, sans pantalon / Maman, maman / Biguine a Henri / Aye Tumbaye / Roro / Madiana / Papillon vole / Adieu foulard / Adieu madras
CD ______ ARN 64034
Arion / May '88 / ADA / Discovery

LES BALALAIKAS DES TZIGANES RUSSES
Les yeux verts / Boublitchki / Ne sois pas jaloux, ne sois pas Fache / Mon bohemien / Ne pars pas / Plaine, ma plaine / Le sarafan rouge / Kalinka / Tzigane et samovar / L'amour s'est enfui / Le vieux Tzigane / Vradanka / Pourquoi m'astu aime
CD ______ ARN 64019
Arion / May '88 / ADA / Discovery

LES CHANSONS A VOIX 1900-1920
CD ______ 983952
EPM / Apr '97 / ADA / Discovery

LES CHANSONS DE 1935
CD ______ UCD 19094
Forlane / Apr '95 / Target/BMG

LES CHANSONS DE 1936
CD ______ UCD 19095
Forlane / Apr '95 / Target/BMG

LES CHANSONS DE 1937
CD ______ UCD 19096
Forlane / Apr '95 / Target/BMG

LES CHANSONS DE 1938
CD ______ UCD 19097
Forlane / Apr '95 / Target/BMG

LES CHANSONS DE 1939
CD ______ UCD 19098
Forlane / Apr '95 / Target/BMG

LES CINGLES DU MUSIC HALL 1932
Complainte de mackie: *Florelle* / C'est Parisien: *Milton, Georges* / Un seul regard: *Bauge, Andre & Sim Viva* / Il est charmant: *Lemonnier, Meg* / En parlant un peu de Paris: *Garat, Henri* / Confessin': *Baker, Josephine* / One hour with you: *Chevalier, Maurice & Jeanette Macdonald* / Couches dans le foin: *Pills & Tabet* / La fiancee du pirate: *Gauty, Lys* / Beguin-beguine: *Sablon, Jean* / Zou un peu d'aiou: *Alibert, Georges* / Quand on est au volant: *Mireille & Jean Sablon* / Papa n'a pas voulu: *Mireille* / Si petite: *Boyer, Lucienne* / Adieu, adieu: *Milton, Georges* / Mimi: *Chevalier, Maurice* / Au joyeux tyrol: *Milton, Georges* / Le doux caboulot: *Dubas, Marie* / Le doux cabulot: *Mirielle* / Un soir a la havane: *Caire, Reda* / Vous ne savez pas: *Germaine & Jean Sablon* / Je t'ai donne mon coeur: *Thunis, Willy* / J'ai reve d'une fleur: *Alibert, Henri & Jenny Helia* / Fleur de Paris: *Gilles & Julien*
CD ______ CMH 32
Fremeaux / Oct '96 / ADA / Discovery

LES CINGLES DU MUSIC HALL 1933
CD ______ CMH 33
Fremeaux / Jul '96 / ADA / Discovery

LES CINGLES DU MUSIC HALL 1934
CD ______ CMH 34
Fremeaux / May '96 / ADA / Discovery

LES COMEDIAN HARMONISTS (2CD Set)
CD Set ______ 983782
EPM / Oct '96 / ADA / Discovery

LES COMIQUES TROUPIERS 1900-1920
CD ______ 984022
EPM / Jun '97 / ADA / Discovery

LES CONGES PAYES
CD ______ DEM 019
IMP / Sep '96 / ADA / Discovery

LES GRANDS MESSIEURS DU MUSIC HALL 1931-1943
CD ______ 983472
EPM / Jul '95 / ADA / Discovery

LES PLUS BELLES VALSES MUSETTE
CD ______ FA 014CD
Fremeaux / Nov '95 / ADA / Discovery

LES PLUS GRANDS SUCCES DU PUNK
CD ______ SKYD 622282
Skydog / May '97 / Discovery

LES TOPS DU TANGO (2CD Set)
CD Set ______ 887997
Milan Sur / Feb '97 / Conifer/BMG

LESS ROCK MORE TALK
CD ______ ALLIED 87CD
Allied / Jul '97 / Cargo / Greyhound / Plastic Head

LESSON ONE
Tell me why: *Freakniks* / Miss Thang: *Unsung Heroes* / Original oddstep: *Vert* / River: *Freakniks* / Minkey part 1: *Soniq* / Action tape 1: *Search* / One we made earlier: *Unsung Heroes* / Slide up: *Next Men* / Cougar: *Search* / Change of plan: *DC 3* / Uncivilized: *Freakniks* / Lost: *Freakniks* / Easy alibi: *Freakniks* / Slow roll '77: *Freakniks*
CD ______ SCCD 002
Scenario / Jul '97 / Essential/BMG

LESSONS FROM THE UNDERGROUND VOL.1
CD ______ TILTCD 1
Tilt / Jun '97 / Total/BMG

LESSONS IN LOVE
Comment te dire adieu: *Somerville, Jimmy* / Obsession: *Animotion* / I hear you now: *Jon & Vangelis* / Sing baby sing: *Stylistics* / I know there's something going on: *Frida* / Giving it all away: *Daltrey, Roger* / Never again: *Faltskog, Agnetha* / Lessons in love: *Level 42* / I should have known better: *Diamond, Jim* / I'm Mandy fly me: *10cc* / On the wings of a nightingale: *Everly Brothers* / When Smokey sings: *ABC* / Just a day away (forever tomorrow): *Barclay James Harvest* / Lilac wine: *Brooks, Elkie*
CD ______ 5501472
Spectrum / Jan '94 / PolyGram

LET 'EM IN
CD ______ 12219
Laserlight / Nov '93 / Target/BMG

LET IT POUR (A Deluge Records Sampler)
CD ______ DELD 3016
Deluge / Oct '96 / ADA / Direct / Koch

LET IT SNOW
Sleigh ride: *Williams, Andy* / Have yourself a merry little Christmas: *Mathis, Johnny* / Let it snow, let it snow, let it snow: *Day, Doris* / White world of winter: *Crosby, Bing* / Secret of Christmas: *Andrews, Julie* / Snowfall: *Bennett, Tony* / Christmas song: *Torme, Mel* / Joy to the world: *Faith, Percy* / When a child is born: *Mathis, Johnny* / Silver bells: *Day, Doris* / Do you hear what I hear: *Williams, Andy* / Winter wonderland: *Clooney, Rosemary* / Pretty paper: *Orbison, Roy* / Christmas eve in my hometown: *Vinton, Bobby* / Christmas time again: *Humperdinck, Engelbert* / Twelve days of Christmas: *Conniff, Ray*
CD ______ 4746372
Columbia / Nov '96 / Sony

LET THERE BE SINGLES
CD ______ VIRUS 182CD
Alternative Tentacles / Sep '96 / Cargo / Greyhound / Pinnacle

LET'S DANCE
Night fever: *UK Mixmasters* / Going back to my roots: *Odyssey* / Everybody plays the fool: *Main Ingredient* / Hot hot hot: *Poindexter, Buster* / Knock three times: *Dawn* / Hooked on swing: *Kings Of Swing Orchestra* / Let's twist again: *Checker, Chubby* / He's a rebel: *Crystals* / Shout: *Isley Brothers* / Diana: *Anka, Paul* / Wooly bully: *Sam The Ram & The Fairisles* / Ballroom blitz: *Sweet*
CD ______ 74321339272
Camden / Jan '96 / BMG

LET'S DANCE FOR LOVE '95
CD ______ FTICD 1
Freetown / Jul '95 / 3mv/Sony

LET'S DO IT
CD ______ PHONTCD 7669
Phontastic / '93 / Cadillac / Jazz Music / Wellard

LET'S GET IT ON
CD ______ NSCD 021
Newsound / May '95 / THE

LET'S GO DISCO
YMCA: *Village People* / That's the way I like it: *KC & The Sunshine Band* / Play that funky music: *Wild Cherry* / Lady marmalade: *Labelle, Patti* / Boogie nights: *Heatwave* / Shake your body: *Jacksons* / Love machine (part 1): *Miracles* / Boogie wonderland: *Earth, Wind & Fire* / Heaven must be missing an angel: *Tavares* / Let's all chant: *Zager, Michael Band* / Use it up and wear it out: *Odyssey* / Funky town: *Lipps Inc.* / And the beat goes on: *Whispers* / Oops upside your head: *Gap Band* / Celebration: *Kool & The Gang* / It's a disco night (rock don't stop): *Isley Brothers* / Car wash: *Rose Royce* / I will survive: *Gaynor, Gloria* / Shame: *King, Evelyn 'Champagne'* / Turn the music up: *Players Association* / Shame, shame, shame: *Shirley & Company* / More, more, more: *Andrea True Connection* / Best of my love: *Emotions* / Hold back the night: *Trammps* / Love I lost: *Melvin, Harold & The Bluenotes* / Hustle: *McCoy, Van* / Rock your baby: *McCrae, George* / Rock the boat: *Hues Corporation* / I love music: *O'Jays* / This is it: *Moore, Melba* / Knock on wood: *Stewart, Amii* / Red light spells danger: *Ocean, Billy* / Ain't gonna bump no more (with no big fat woman): *Tex, Joe* / In the bush: *Musique* / Boogie oogie oogie: *Taste Of Honey* / September: *Earth, Wind & Fire* / If I can't have you: *Elliman, Yvonne* / Do what you wanna do: *T-Connection* / Disco stomp: *Bohannon, Hamilton* / Girls: *Moments & Whatnauts*
CD ______ CDEMTV 78
EMI / Oct '93 / EMI

LET'S GO JIVIN' TO ROCK & ROLL
Say yeah: *Salvo, Sammy* / I've got a dollar: *Dell, Jimmy* / Love makes the world go round: *Como, Perry* / Rock-a-bye boogie: *Davis Sisters* / Plantation boogie: *King, Pee Wee* / Tennessee rock 'n' roll: *Sons Of The Pioneers* / Hubba hubba hubba: *Como, Perry* / Jackpot: *Pedicin, Mike Quintet* / TV hop: *Morgan Twins* / Shape I'm in: *Restivo, Johnny* / You gotta learn your rhythm and blues: *Sedaka, Neil* / Kewpie doll: *Como, Perry* / Blue suede shoes: *King, Pee Wee* / Fiddle diddle boogie: *Davis Sisters* / You gotta go: *Pedicin, Mike Quintet* / Jukebox baby: *Como, Perry* / Boom de de boom: *Baker, Jane* / Rock and stroll room: *Mickey & Sylvia* / When the cats come marching in: *Pedicin, Mike Quintet* / Idaho red: *Ray, Wade*
CD ______ BCD 15533
Bear Family / Oct '90 / Direct / Rollercoaster / Swift

LET'S GO TRIPPIN'
Let's go trippin': *Rogers, Milt* / Surfer Joe: *Surfaris* / Wipeout: *Surfaris* / Three surfer boys: *Usher, Gary & The Usherettes* / Boss: *Rumblers* / Move it: *Chantays* / Pipeline: *Chantays* / Little stick nomad: *Competitors* / Samoa: *Beachcomas* / Beach girl: *Boone, Pat* / Boss strikes back: *Rumblers* / Ballad of Bonneville: *Brandon, Don* / Monsoon: *Chantays* / Power shift: *Competitors* / 409: *Competitors* / You can't sit down: *Surfaris* / Little Honda: *Boone, Pat* / It's a gas: *Rumblers* / Linda's tune: *Rancheros* / Green onions: *Surfaris* / Space probe: *Chantays* / Little deuce coupe: *Competitors* / Bugged: *Rumblers* / Angry sea: *Rumblers* / Milky way: *Usher, Gary & The Usherettes* / Surfer's stomp: *Monroe, Vaughan* / Maybe baby: *Chantays* / Chicago green: *Surfaris* / Showbiz: *Surfaris*
CD ______ CDCHD 630
Ace / Apr '96 / Pinnacle

LET'S GO ZYDECO
Cher catin / Petite et la grosse / Used and abused / Walking down the interstate / Zydeco two step / Crying in the streets / Midland two step / Shake what you got / Lafayette special / Lonesome road / I'm coming home / I've been there / Mardi gras song / Je suis en recolteur / Check out the zydeco / Zolo go / Green's zydeco / King's zydeco / Allons a Lafayette / Moman couche / Two step de grand mallet / Home sweet home
CD ______ CDCHD 543
Ace / Feb '95 / Pinnacle

LET'S GO, LET'S GO, LET'S GO
CD ______ 12105
Laserlight / Dec '94 / Target/BMG

LET'S HAVE A BALL TONIGHT: THE PIONEERS OF R & B
CD ______ NI 4025
Natasha / Feb '94 / ADA / Cadillac / CM / Direct / Jazz Music

LET'S HAVE A BLUES BALL
I'm having a ball: *Young, Johnny* / Dream: *Littlejohn, Johnny* / Swing it on home: *Thornton, Willie Mae 'Big Mama'* / Anna Lee: *Hooker, Earl* / Going back to the country: *Bonner, Juke Boy* / It's hard: *Chenier, Clifton* / Come on baby: *Hopkins, Lightnin'* / Nine below zero: *Williamson, Sonny Boy* / Gambling blues: *Jackson, Lil' Son* / Pontiac blues: *Williamson, Sonny Boy* / I'm in the big city: *Bonner, Juke Boy* / Meet you at the chicken shack: *Hopkins, Lightnin'* / Rag around your head: *Delafose, John* / Blues (Won't let me take my rest): *Gray, Henry* / Shake your money maker: *Littlejohn, Johnny* / If trouble was money: *Musselwhite, Charley* / Wild wild woman: *Young, Johnny* / Gimme a penny: *Thornton, Willie Mae 'Big Mama'* / On the road again: *Young, Johnny* / Mojo in my hand: *Robinson, L.C.*
CD ______ CDCHD 590
Ace / Mar '96 / Pinnacle

LET'S HEAR IT FOR THE GIRLS
All I wanna do: *Crow, Sheryl* / Girls just wanna have fun: *Lauper, Cyndi* / Ain't no man: *Carroll, Dina* / Every day of the week: *Jade* / Just a step from heaven: *Eternal* / Whatta man: *Salt n' Pepa & En Vogue* / Free your mind: *En Vogue* / Same thing: *Carlisle, Belinda* / Right beside you: *Hawkins, Sophie B.* / All I want: *Those Two* / Little bird: *Lennox, Annie* / Trouble: *Shampoo* / Go away: *Estefan, Gloria* / Jump: *Pointer Sisters* / It's raining men: *Weather Girls* / Only way is up: *Yazz* / I love your smile: *Shanice* / Gotta get it right: *Fiagbe, Lena* / Walk like an Egyptian: *Bangles* / Patience of angels: *Reader, Eddi*
CD ______ 5165522
Polydor / Apr '95 / PolyGram

LET'S PARTY (21 Favourites)
Zorba's dance / For he's a jolly good fellow / Congratulations / Hokey cokey / Conga / Superman / Birdie song / Oops upside your head / Celebration / Loco-motion / Saturday night / YMCA / Time warp / Hot hot hot / Anniversary waltz / Lambada / Swing low, sweet chariot / You'll never walk alone / Happy birthday to you / Auld lang syne / Gay Gordons
CD ______ AVC 562
Avid / May '96 / Avid/BMG / Koch / THE

LET'S ROCK TOGETHER (2CD Set)
CD Set ______ NSCD 001
Newsound / Feb '95 / THE

LET'S TALK ABOUT LOVE
CD ______ DINCD 39
Dino / May '92 / Pinnacle

LET'S TALK ABOUT SEX
CD ______ 15491
Laserlight / Aug '92 / Target/BMG

LIBRARY OF CONGRESS ARCHIVE OF FOLK CULTURE (Negro Blues & Hollers)
Camp hollers: *House, Son & Willie Brown/ Fiddlin' Joe Martin* / Cornfield hollers: *Berry, Charley* / I'm a soldier in the army of the Lord: *Silent Grove Baptist Church Congregation* / I'm gonna lift up a standard for my King: *Church Of God In Christ Congregation* / Worried life blues: *Edwards, David* / Ragged and dirty: *Brown, William* / Special rider blues: *House, Son* / Depot blues: *House, Son* / Mississippi blues: *Brown, William* / Four o'clock flower blues: *Blackwell, William & William Brown* / East St. Louis blues: *Brown, William* / Low down dirty dog blues: *House, Son*
CD ______ ROUCD 1501
Rounder / May '97 / ADA / CM / Direct

LIBRARY OF CONGRESS ARCHIVE OF FOLK CULTURE (Songs & Ballads Of The Anthracite Miners)
Down down down: *Keating, William E.* / Avondale mine disaster: *Quinn, John J.* / Me Johnny Mitchell man: *Byrne, Jerry* / Boys on the hill: *Muldowney, James* / On Johnny Mitchell's train: *Byrne, Jerry* / Rolling on the rye grass: *Muldowney, James* / Old miner's refrain: *Walsh, Daniel* / John J Curtis: *Rada, Andrew* / Celebrated workingman: *Walsh, Daniel* / When the breaker starts up full time: *Byrne, Jerry* / Union man: *Morgan, Albert* / Miner's doom: *Walsh, Daniel* / Down in a coalmine: *Jones, Morgan* / Shoofly: *Walsh, Daniel*
CD ______ ROUCD 1502
Rounder / May '97 / ADA / CM / Direct

LIFE AFTER BLOOM
CD ______ GRCD 015
Guerilla / Jun '94 / Pinnacle

LIFE IN BLUES
CD ______ 157362
Blues Collection / Feb '93 / Discovery

LIFE IN THE FOLK LANE VOL.2
Iron masters: *Men They Couldn't Hang* / Faithful departed: *Chevron, Philip* / Do you hear me now: *Jansch, Bert* / Devil's real: *Smither, Chris* / Changes: *Clark, Gene* / Voices of the Barbary Coast: *Williamson, Robin & His Merry Band* / Limit: *Rainer & Das Combo* / Pick up your coat: *Hitchcock, Nicola* / Runaway train: *Gutter Brothers* / Caribbean wind: *Revelators* / Hard day on the planet: *Wainwright III, Loudon* / Upon a veil of midnight blue: *Coughlan, Mary* / My sweet potatoe: *Renbourn, John* / Dance to your Daddy: *Sweeney's Men* / That'll do baby: *McTell, Ralph* / Sally go round the roses: *Pentangle* / They watered my whiskey down: *Burdett, Phil & The New World Troubadours*
CD ______ DIAB 808
Diabolo / Jun '94 / Pinnacle

LIFE IS CHANGE VOL.3
CD ______ EFA 11654 D
Beri-Beri / Jul '93 / SRD

LIFE MADE ME BEAUTIFUL AT FORTY
CD ______ ITM 1498
ITM / Nov '95 / Koch / Tradelink

LIFE ON THE OCEAN WAVE
Sailor's hornpipe / Sailing / Fantasy on British sea songs / Leaving of Liverpool / Cockleshell heroes / A-roving / Blow the man down / Hearts of oak / Skye boat song / Pump shanty / Dartmouth mariner / Shenandoah / Soldiers of the sea / Rollin' home / What shall we do with the drunken sailor / Life on the ocean wave
CD ______ 303772
Hallmark / Jun '97 / Carlton

LIFE SUCKS GET A CRASH HELMET
CD ______ RRCD 001
Retch / Oct '93 / Cargo / Plastic Head

LIFTING THE SPIRIT
CD ______ SCL 2510
Ichiban Soul Classics / Nov '95 / Koch

LIGHT FLIGHT (Instrumental Favourites)
Midnight in Moscow: *Ball, Kenny & His Jazzmen* / Aria: *Bilk, Acker, His Clarinet & Strings* / Floral dance: *Brighouse & Rastrick Band* / Walk in the Black Forest: *Conway, Russ* / Cast your fate to the wind: *Sounds Orchestral* / Popcorn: *Hot Butter* / Sweet Georgia Brown: *Grappelli, Stephane* / Somewhere my love: *String Chorale* / Zorba's dance: *Tacticos, Manos & His Bouzoukis* / Girl from Ipanema: *Patrick, Johnny* / Moon river: *String Chorale* / Guantanamera: *Strings Go Latin* / Petite fleur: *Barber, Chris Jazz Band & Monty Sunshine* / Light flight: *Pentangle* / Hello Dolly: *Ball, Kenny & His Jazzmen* / Amazing grace: *Royal Scots Dragoon Guards* / Moonglow: *Sounds Orchestral* / Forsyte saga (Elizabeth Tudor): *Stapleton, Cyril* / Nuages: *Reinhardt, Django* / Sleepy shores: *Sounds Orchestral*
CD ______ TRTCD 121
TrueTrax / Oct '94 / THE

LIGHTING A MATCH UNDERWATER
CD ______ DE 1
Detroit Electric / Apr '97 / Cargo

LIGHTNING RECORDS PUNK COLLECTION
CD ______ CDPUNK 79
Anagram / Jun '96 / Cargo / Pinnacle

LIGHTS CAN GO ON AGAIN - NOW THE WAR IS OVER, THE (2CD Set)
I'll string along with you: *Peers, Donald* / Nice to know you care: *Hutchinson, Leslie 'Hutch'* / People will say we're in love: *Hutchinson, Leslie 'Hutch'* / Either it's love or it isn't: *Hutchinson, Leslie 'Hutch'* / I never loved anyone: *Hutchinson, Leslie 'Hutch'* / Peg O' my heart: *Hutchinson, Leslie 'Hutch'* / Far away places: *Radio Revellers* / Shoemaker's serenade: *Radio Revellers* / You're breaking my heart: *Goff, Reggie* / How lucky you are: *Lynn, Vera* / Time after time: *Conway, Steve* / Let bygones be bygones: *Harris, Doreen* / There's no one but you: *Harris, Doreen* / I only have eyes for you: *Stapleton, Cyril* / In my dreams: *Goff, Reggie* / All's well that ends well: *Goff, Reggie* / My silent love: *Shelton, Anne* / Love of my life: *Shelton, Anne* / Say something sweet to your sweetheart: *Simpson, Jack* / I'd give the world (To you sweetheart): *Simpson, Jack* / I'll make up for everything: *Conway, Steve* / Moment I saw you: *Conway, Steve* / There, I've said it again: *Green, Paula & Her Orchestra* / Who do you love I hope: *Stapleton, Cyril* / Say that you're mine: *Carr, Pearl* / PS I love you: *Carr, Pearl* / Be mine beloved: *Davis, Beryl* / You, you, you are the one: *James, Dick* / When you're in love: *Goff, Reggie* / Blue ribbon gal: *Chester, Charlie & His Gang* / Clancy lowered the boom: *Clark, Petula* / I'll keep you in my heart: *Lynn, Vera* / I wonder who's kissing her now: *Layton, Turner* / I'd break my heart again: *Conway, Steve* / My love is only for you: *Williams, Rita* / Say it every day: *Goff, Reggie* / Stars will remember (So will I): *Rey, Monte*
CD Set ______ CDDL 1269
Music For Pleasure / May '94 / EMI

LIKE A GIRL I WANT TO KEEP YOU COMING
Invocation to Papa Legba: *Harry, Deborah* / Sister Ray: *New Order* / Just say no to drugs hysteria: *Burroughs, William S.* / Dead soul: *Burroughs, William S.* / Song for the trees (or) I know sometimes the world is wrong: *Byrne, David* / Tri-power: *Live Skull* / Living on the outside (fucked up world): *Pre-Metal Syndrome* / Party animal: *Finley, Karen* / It's a mistake to think you're special: *Giorno, John* / Hard: *Rollins Band*
CD ______ VICD 009
Visionary/Jettisoundz / Oct '96 / Cargo / Pinnacle / RTM/Disc / THE

LINE DANCE
Riverdance / Heart's cry / Lift the wings / Cotton eye Joe / Any man of mine / Deadwood stage / Wrong train, wrong line / Fast fingers Freddie / Soft touch / Boys and me
CD ______ QED 135
Tring / Nov '96 / Tring

LINE DANCE ALBUM, THE
Line dancing / Redneck girl / Brown eyed girl / Hey good lookin' / Walking after midnight / Let me dance with you / Start with the talking / I tried at first not to (fall in love with you) / If you don't think I'm leaving / Zydeco ball / When daddy played the fiddle / Cotton eyed Joe / Guitar boogie / You left the water running / Abilene / Gentle on my mind / Orange blossom guitars / Midnight flyer and showboat gambler
CD ______ SUMCD 4100
Summit / Feb '97 / Sound & Media

LINE DANCE FEVER VOL.1
CD ______ CURCD 027
Curb / Jul '96 / Grapevine/PolyGram

LINE DANCE FEVER VOL.2
CD ______ CURCD 033
Curb / Jan '97 / Grapevine/PolyGram

LINE DANCE FEVER VOL.3
CD ______ CURCD 043
Curb / Jun '97 / Grapevine/PolyGram

LINE DANCE FEVER VOL.4
Jose Cuervo: *Clayton,Kimber* / Mull River Shuffle: *Rankin Family* / Road Runner: *Microwave Dave* / Line Dance Crazy: *Kenny, Sean* / Down on the farm: *McGraw, Tim* / Cowboy boots: *Backsliders* / Dancing shoes: *McDowell, Ronnie* / Crash boom bang: *Cane Honey, T.* / You're not in Kansas: *Messina, JoDee* / Everyday I have to cry: *Woodruff, Bob* / Two more to drive away: *Brannon, Kippi* / Nice work if you can get it: *Burnin' daylight* / Do it again: *Carson, Jeff* / I saw the light: *Wyonna* / Another perfect day: *Blake and Brian* / Race is on: *Brown, Sawyer* / My hat's off to him: *Auston, Jim* / Under the hood: *Anderson, Al*
CD ______ CURCD 045
Curb / Aug '97 / Grapevine/PolyGram

LINE DANCE SPECTACULAR
CD ______ PLSCD 220
Pulse / Jul '97 / BMG

LINE UP AND DANCE (The Best Of New Country Line Dance)
Achy breaky heart: *Blueberry Hill* / There goes my heart: *Memphis Roots* / One step away: *Bayou Boys* / Elvira: *Memphis Roots* / One more last chance: *Blueberry Hill* / Six days on the road: *Moody, George & The Country Squires* / Passionate kisses: *Blueberry Hill* / Watermelon crawl: *Memphis Roots* / He thinks he'll keep her: *Blueberry Hill* / Tempted: *Memphis Roots* / Hard way: *Blueberry Hill* / I couldn't leave if I tried: *Bayou Boys* / Smokey places: *Memphis Roots* / Cotton eye Joe: *Blueberry Hill* / Fly like a bird: *Memphis Roots* / Crying shame: *Blueberry Hill* / Good noise: *Memphis Roots* / Old flames (can't hold a candle to you): *Moody, George & The Country Squires* / Lovin' all night: *Bayou Boys* / Honky tonk blues: *Blueberry Hill* / Folsom Prison blues: *Moody, George & The Country Squires* / Love's got a hold on you: *Blueberry Hill* / Cannibals: *Memphis Roots* / Big river: *Blueberry Hill* / Crazy Mama: *Memphis Roots* / One step forward: *Blueberry Hill* / Summertime blues: *Bayou Boys* / Gulf of Mexico: *Moody, George & The Country Squires* / Hillbilly rock, hillbilly roll: *Blueberry Hill* / Fool for you: *Memphis Roots* / Mercury blues: *Blueberry Hill* / Living on love: *Moody, George & The Country Squires* / Black coffee: *Memphis Roots* / Cherokee boogie: *Memphis Roots* / Don't close your eyes: *Moody, George & The Country Squires* / Bootscootin' boogie: *Blueberry Hill* / Good hearted woman: *Moody, George & The Country Squires* / Chattahoochee: *Blueberry Hill* / All you ever do is bring me down: *Memphis Roots* / Down at the twist and shout: *Bayou Boys* / Bug: *Blueberry Hill* / Me and Bobby McGee: *Moody, George & The Country Squires* / Fast as you: *Blueberry Hill* / I should have asked her faster: *Memphis Roots* / You got it: *Blueberry Hill* / (They call me) the breeze: *Moody, George & The Country Squires* / You can feel bad: *Blueberry Hill* / South of the border: *Memphis Roots*
CD ______ 3036300175
Country Skyline / Jul '97 / Carlton

LINN COLLECTION 1994, THE
CD ______ AKD 027
Linn / Oct '94 / PolyGram

LIPSTICK TRACES
Boring life / It's too soon to know: *Orioles* / L'amiral cherche une maison a louer: *Tzara, Tristan* / Roadrunner: *Richman, Jonathan* / Excerpt from "Hurlements en faveur de Sade": *Debord, Guy* / Instrumentation verbale: *Brau, Jean-Louis* / Boredom: *Buzzcocks* / One chord wonders: *Buzzcocks* / Phoneme bbbb: *Hausmann, Raoul* / At home he's a tourist: *Gang Of Four* / Gary Gilmore's eyes: *Adverts* / U: *Kleenex* / Excerpt from "Critique de la separation": *Debord, Guy* / Stage talk: *Clash* / Never been in a riot: *Mekons* / Split: *Liliput* / Rohrenhose...: *Blegvad, Peter* / Wake up: *Essential Logic* / You: *Kleenex* / Megapneumanies: *Wolman, Gil* / In love: *Raincoats* / Karawane: *Osmond, Marie* / I wish I was a mole in the ground: *Lunsford, Bascom Lamar* / Building: *Mekons* / Lipstick traces: *Spellman, Benny*
CD ______ R 2902
Rough Trade / Jul '93 / Pinnacle

LIQUID CALIFORNIA (The Sound Of The West Coast/2CD Set)
CD Set ______ SUB 11D
Subversive / Mar '96 / 3mv/Sony / Amato Disco / Mo's Music Machine / Prime / Vital

LIQUID SKY ADVENTURE SERIES VOL.1, THE
CD ______ EBCCD 1
Electro Bunker Cologne / Apr '97 / SRD

LIQUID SKY ADVENTURE SERIES VOL.2, THE
CD ______ EBCCD 2
Electro Bunker Cologne / Apr '97 / SRD

LISMOR 21ST ANNIVERSARY ALBUM
Rolling in the high grass/Scalloway lasses/ Haint dykes o'Voe: *Bain, Aly & Phil Cunningham* / Waulking song: *MacInnes, Mairi* / MacEwan's barn/Islay teenager/Lewis Road dance/'Horse on' So: *McDonald, Fergie* / Sonny's dream: *Imlach, Hamish* / Links of Forth/Atholl Cummers/MacAllister's dirk: *Strathclyde Police Pipe Band* / Wee china pig: *Alexander Brothers* / Camptown races/ Steamboat Bill/Oh Susanna: *Box & Banjo Band* / Dumbarton's drums: *Gaelforce Orchestra* / Muckin' O' Geordie's byre: *Stewart, Andy* / Gates of Edinburgh reel: *Ellis, John & His Highland Country Band* / Wiggly jig: *New Celeste* / My ain folk: *Anderson, Moira* / Spin and glow/McDowall's breakdown: *Cowie, Charlie* / Sonny's mazurka/ Foxhunters: *Mathieson, Pipe Major Robert* / Bonnie lass o'Ballochmyle: *Morrison, Peter* / Bonnie lass o'Bon Accord: *Gordon, Rob & His Band* / Lewis sailing song: *Solley, David* / West Highland way: *McKellar, Kenneth* / Lord Lovat's lament: *78th Fraser Highlander's Pipe Band* / Barren rocks of Aden/ Duke of Atholl's Highlanders: *Dancing Strings* / De niand puirt - A Beul: *Runrig*
CD ______ LCOM 5228
Lismor / Apr '94 / ADA / Direct / Duncans / Lismor

LISTEN TO THE BANNED (20 Risque Songs 1927-1933)
I've gone and lost my little yo-yo: *Cotton, Billy* / With my little ukelele in my hand: *Formby, George* / Guy what takes his time: *West, Mae* / She was only a postman's daughter: *Durium Dance Band* / Nellie the nudist queen: *Ross & Sargent* / My private affair: *Davies, Dawn* / What's it: *Rodgers, Jimmie* / He hadn't up 'til yesterday: *Tucker, Sophie* / Winnie the worm: *Frankau, Ronald* / I'm a bear in a lady's boudoir: *Edwards, Cliff* / Everyone's got sex appeal for someone: *Frankau, Ronald & Monte Crick* / All poshed up with my daisies in my hand: *Higgins, Charlie* / Pu-leeze Mr. Hemingway: *Carlisle, Elsie* / Let's all be fairies: *Durium Dance Band* / I'm going to give it to Mary with love: *Edwards, Cliff* / Physician: *Lawrence, Gertrude* / No wonder she's a blushing bride: *Fowler, Art* / Flora McDonald: *Byng, Douglas* / Or anything else I've got: *Sutton, Randolph* / And so does he: *Davies, Dawn*
CD ______ CDAJA 5030
Living Era / Oct '88 / Select

LISTEN TO THE PLANET (A Musical Journey Around The World)
CD ______ 74321372432
Milan / Oct '96 / Conifer/BMG / Silva Screen

LITTLE BIT OF HEAVEN, A (A Vintage Anthology Of 25 Irish Songs)
A little bit of heaven: *McCormack, John* / Kerry dance: *Dawson, Peter* / Lark in the clear air: *MacEwan, Sydney* / Off to Philadelphia: *McCafferty, James* / Meeting of the waters: *Sheridan, Margaret* / That's how I spell IRELAND: *O'Connor, Cavan* / Kathleen Mavourneen: *McCormack, John* / Tumbledown shack in Athlone: *Munn, Frank* / Garden where the praties grow: *Plunket-Greene, Harry* / Macushla: *Crooks, Richard* / When they sing 'The wearing o'the green' in syncopated blues: *Downey, Morton* / Last rose of summer: *Austral, Florence* / Rose of Tralee: *McCormack, John* / Rory O'Moore: *Lawrence, Brian* / Dawning of the day: *MacEwan, Sydney* / Mountains of Mourne: *Daly, Jackie* / Oft in the stilly night: *Teyte, Maggie* / Mother Machree: *White, Joseph* / Star of County Down: *McCormack, John* / Spinning wheel: *Murphy, Delia* / Green hills of Ireland: *Crooks, Richard* / She moved thro' the fair: *McEwan, Sydney* / Pride of Tipperary: *Davison, Peter* / Danny boy: *Sheridan, Margaret* / Ireland, mother Ireland: *McCormack, John*
CD ______ CDAJA 5202
Living Era / Sep '96 / Select

LITTLE DARLA HAS A TREAT FOR YOU VOL.6
CD ______ DRL 030
Darla / Mar '97 / Cargo

LITTLE DARLA HAS A TREAT FOR YOU VOL.7
CD ______ DRL 040
Darla / Jun '97 / Cargo

LITTLE RAMBLERS 1924-1927, THE
Deep blue sea blues / I'm satisfied behind that sweetie of mine / Those pananma mamas / Prince of wails / Cross words between that sweetie and me / Don't bring Lulu / Look who's here / Gotnot ti me / Melancholy Lou / Deep elm / Fallin' down / I love my baby / Tomorrow mornin' / In your green hat / In your green hat / Could I I certainly could / Here comes Malinda / I wonder whats become of Joe / Hot Henry / And then I forget / My cutey's due at two to two today / Play it / Swamp blues
CD ______ CBC 1037
Timeless Historical / Sep '97 / New Note/ Pinnacle

LITTLE RED ROOSTER - ORIGINAL R & B
Tell it like it is / Have you changed your mind / Can't hold out much longer / Through the alley / We're gonna make it / Love you like a woman / Don't you just know it / Tell mama / But I do / Cops and robbers / No money down / Born blind / Get closer together / Say boss man / You never can tell / Ya ya / Cool disposition / Juke / Little red rooster
CD ______ CDAA 043
Tring / Jun '92 / Tring

LITTLE SOUND BOY
CD ______ VPCD 1441
VP / Apr '96 / Greensleeves / Jet Star / Total/BMG

LIVE
CD ______ TUT 781
Wundertute / Oct '94 / ADA / CM / Duncans

LIVE 1955
CD ____ **JCD 17**
Jass / Nov '86 / ADA / Cadillac / CM / Direct / Jazz Music

LIVE AND WIRED - ROCK ANTHEMS
Number of the beast: *Iron Maiden* / Black night: *Deep Purple* / Only you can rock me: *UFO* / Trees: *Rush* / Fool for your loving: *Whitesnake* / Rock you like a hurricane: *Scorpions* / Shapes of things: *Moore, Gary* / Freebird: *Lynyrd Skynyrd* / Boys are back in town: *Thin Lizzy* / Show me the way: *Frampton, Peter* / Wheels of steel: *Saxon* / Voodoo chile: *Hendrix, Jimi* / Long live rock 'n' roll: *Rainbow*
CD ____ **CDEMS 1610**
EMI / May '97 / EMI

LIVE AND WIRED - ROCK BALLADS
November rain: *Guns n' Roses* / Empty rooms: *Moore, Gary* / Sugar mice: *Marillion* / Can't fight this feeling: *REO Speedwagon* / Every rose has it's thorn: *Poison* / I want you to want me: *Cheap Trick* / Still in love with you: *Thin Lizzy* / Ain't no love in the heart of the city: *Whitesnake* / Love walked in: *Thunder* / Two out of three ain't bad: *Meat Loaf* / Smile has left your eyes: *Asia* / Baby I love your way: *Frampton, Peter* / Wind of change: *Scorpions*
CD ____ **CDEMS 1609**
EMI / May '97 / EMI

LIVE AND WIRED - ROCK CLASSICS
Ace of spades: *Motorhead* / Are you ready: *Thin Lizzy* / 747 strangers in the night: *Saxon* / Neon knights: *Black Sabbath* / Attack of the mad axeman: *Schenker, Michael Group* / Ready and willing: *Whitesnake* / Victims of the future: *Moore, Gary* / All right now: *Free* / Doctor Doctor: *UFO* / Green Manalishi (with the two pronged crown): *Fleetwood Mac* / Bat out of hell: *Meat Loaf* / Run to the hills: *Iron Maiden* / Bastille day: *Rush* / School's out: *Cooper, Alice* / Smoke on the water: *Deep Purple*
CD ____ **CDEMS 1611**
EMI / May '97 / EMI

LIVE AT ANTONE'S ANNIVERSARY ANTHOLOGY VOL.2
CD ____ **ANT 00016**
Antones / Sep '95 / ADA / Hot Shot

LIVE AT MIDEM, 1979
CD ____ **500402**
Musidisc / May '94 / Discovery

LIVE AT RAUL'S
CD ____ **DJD 3216**
Dejadisc / Sep '95 / ADA / Direct

LIVE AT RONNIE SCOTT'S
CD ____ **MATCD 256**
Castle / Apr '93 / BMG

LIVE AT RONNIE SCOTT'S
This love of mine: *Scott, Ronnie Quintet* / High on you: *Cohn, Al & The Jazz Seven* / Spring can really hang you up the most: *Hayes, Tubby* / Evensong: *Taylor, John Trio* / Never let me go: *Coleman, George Quintet* / J 'n' B: *Sharpe, Jack Big Band* / Over the rainbow: *Webster, Ben Quartet* / La Pastora: *Irakere* / Man I love: *Vaughan, Sarah* / Donna Lee: *Sandoval, Arturo* / This can't be love: *Shaw, Ian* / All the things you are: *Scott, Ronnie Quintet*
CD ____ **3036001132**
Carlton / Jun '97 / Carlton

LIVE AT RONNIE SCOTT'S
CD ____ **PLSCD 236**
Pulse / Jul '97 / BMG

LIVE AT ROSKILDE '94
CD ____ **STOKES 001**
Roskilde / Jun '95 / SRD

LIVE AT THE BIG RUMBLE
CD ____ **NERCD 066**
Nervous / Nov '91 / Nervous / TKO Magnum

LIVE AT THE CAVERN
Dr. Feelgood / Keep on rolling / She's sure the girl I love / You've really got a hold on me / Everybody loves a lover / Devoted to you / You better move on / Somebody to love / I got a woman / Little queenie / Diddley daddy / Bring it on home to me / Skinny Minnie / Jezebel / I'm talking about you / Little Egypt / What'd I say / Don't start running away / Zip a dee doo dah / Reelin' and rockin'
CD ____ **SEECD 385**
See For Miles/C5 / Dec '93 / Pinnacle

LIVE AT THE EEL PUNK ROCK MOUNTAIN
CD ____ **FRIGHT 065CD**
Fierce / Feb '92 / RTM/Disc

LIVE AT THE GALWAY SHAWL
CD ____ **CIC 065CD**
Clo Iar-Chonnachta / Nov '93 / CM

LIVE AT THE KNITTING FACTORY VOL.1
CD ____ **KFWCD 097**
Knitting Factory / Nov '94 / Cargo / Plastic Head

LIVE AT THE KNITTING FACTORY VOL.2
CD ____ **KFWCD 098**
Knitting Factory / Nov '94 / Cargo / Plastic Head

LIVE AT THE KNITTING FACTORY VOL.3
CD ____ **KFWCD 099**
Knitting Factory / Nov '94 / Cargo / Plastic Head

LIVE AT THE KNITTING FACTORY VOL.4
CD ____ **KFWCD 100**
Knitting Factory / Nov '94 / Cargo / Plastic Head

LIVE AT THE KNITTING FACTORY VOL.5
CD ____ **KFWCD 108**
Knitting Factory / Nov '94 / Cargo / Plastic Head

LIVE AT THE KNITTING FACTORY VOL.6
CD ____ **KFWCD 161**
Knitting Factory / Feb '95 / Cargo / Plastic Head

LIVE AT THE ROXY
Strange boy / Smile and wave goodbye / Relics from the past / I live in a car / Telephone numbers / Get yourself killed / Never wanna leave / Here comes the knife / TV drink / Sniper / Tough on you / Fun, fun, fun / Vertigo / Lullabies lie
CD ____ **CDTB 011**
Thunderbolt / Mar '95 / TKO Magnum

LIVE AT THE SOCIAL VOL.1
Cut man: *Meat Beat Manifesto* / DMX will rock: *Davy DMX* / Mighty hard rocker: *Cash Money & Marvellous* / Yes we can: *Crooklyn Clan* / Doing it after dark: *Berrios, Carlos* / Can't: *Tainted Glass* / Juice: *Eric B & Rakim* / Wesley don't surf: *Red Snapper* / Packet of peace: *Lionrock* / P b4 U go 2 bed: *DJ Who* / To a nation rocking: *Metro* / Get up on it like this: *Chemical Brothers* / Again son: *Love Lee* / Nine acre dust: *Charlatans* / Jack me off: *Funk D'Void* / Mirrorshades: *Webb, Will* / Wede man: *Selectah* / We're doing it (Thang): *Bo, Eddie*
CD ____ **HVNLP 13CD**
Heavenly / May '96 / 3mv/Pinnacle / BMG / Vital

LIVE AT THE VORTEX
Can't wait till '78: *Wasps* / Waiting for my man: *Wasps* / Bunch of stiffs: *Mean Street* / Small lives: *Neo* / Tell me the truth: *Neo* / Living for kicks: *Torme, Bernie* / Streetfighter: *Torme, Bernie* / Animal bondage: *Art Attacks* / Frankenstein's heartbeat: *Art Attacks* / Nothing to declare: *Suspects* / You don't break my heart: *Maniacs* / I ain't gonna be history: *Maniacs*
CD ____ **CDPUNK 68**
Anagram / Nov '95 / Cargo / Pinnacle

LIVE AT YORK MINSTER
Trumpet prelude / Festive overture / Irish tune from County Derry / Pipe set / Cortege from Mlada / Nimrod / Suite in E flat / Ode to joy / Epilogue from things to come
CD ____ **3036100082**
Pearls / Apr '96 / Carlton

LIVE FROM THE CHARLOTTE
CD ____ **RAUCD 010**
Raucous / Feb '94 / Nervous / RTM/Disc / TKO Magnum

LIVE PARTY MIX
CD ____ **DO 476CD**
Dance Opera / Nov '96 / Mo's Music Machine / Plastic Head

LIVE ROCK
Life is for living: *Barclay James Harvest* / Statesboro blues: *Allman Brothers* / Show me the way: *Frampton, Peter* / From out of nowhere: *Faith No More* / Wild and wonderful: *Almighty* / Delilah: *Harvey, Alex Sensational Band* / Good morning judge: *10cc* / Delta Lady: *Cocker, Joe* / Stay with me: *Faces* / Spirit of radio: *Rush* / Roll over lay down: *Status Quo* / Mama weer all crazee now: *Slade*
CD ____ **5506462**
Spectrum / Aug '94 / PolyGram

LIVE ROCK VOL.5
CD ____ **XSRCD 3005**
XS / Mar '95 / Grapevine/PolyGram

LIVE ROCK VOL.6
CD ____ **XSRCD 3006**
XS / Mar '95 / Grapevine/PolyGram

LIVE STIFFS
I knew the bride: *Lowe, Nick* / Let's eat / Semaphore signals / Reconnez cherie / Police car: *Wallis, Larry* / I just don't know what to do with myself: *Costello, Elvis* / Miracle man: *Costello, Elvis* / Wake up and make love with me: *Dury, Ian* / Billericay Dickie: *Dury, Ian* / Sex and drugs and rock 'n' roll / Chaos
CD ____ **MAUCD 621**
Mau Mau / Aug '92 / Pinnacle

LIVERPOOL 1963-1968
Ferry 'cross the Mersey: *Gerry & The Pacemakers* / Skinny Lizzie: *Gerry & The Pacemakers* / Abyssinian secret: *Black, Cilla* / For no one: *Black, Cilla* / Sandy: *Swinging Blue Jeans* / It's too late now: *Swinging Blue Jeans* / Everything in the garden: *Fourmost* / Breakaway: *Marsden, Beryl* / Whatever will be will be (Que sera sera): *Royce, Earl & The Olympics* / I really do: *Royce, Earl & The Olympics* / America: *Storm, Rory & The Hurricanes* / I got a woman: *Black Knights* / Angel of love: *Black Knights* / I love her: *Kubas* / Magic potion: *Kubas* / First cut is the deepest: *Kubas* / Why don't you love me: *Blackwells* / One way ticket / Don't you do it no more: *Kramer, Billy J. & The Dakotas* / How I won the war: *Musketeer Gripweed & The Third Troup*
CD ____ **SEECD 370**
See For Miles/C5 / Aug '94 / Pinnacle

LIVING BEAT HOUSE CLASSICS
CD ____ **LBLCD 7**
Living Beat / May '97 / Grapevine/ PolyGram

LIVING CHICAGO BLUES VOL.1
Your turn to cry / Serves me right to suffer / Ain't that just like a woman / Feel like breaking up somebody's home / It's alright / Out of bad luck / Stoop down baby / Sittin' on top of the world / My baby's so ugly / Come home darling / Blues won't let me be / One room country shack / Linda Lou / Too late / Laundromat blues / One day / Woman in trouble
CD ____ **ALCD 7701**
Alligator / May '93 / ADA / CM / Direct

LIVING CHICAGO BLUES VOL.2
Don't answer the door / Two headed man / Cold lonely nights / Move over, little dog / Would you, baby / Worry worry / Sunnyland blues / Cry cry darlin' / Stranded on the highway / Dirty mother for you / Spider in my stew / Don't say that no more / Take it easy, baby / Blues after hours / Little angel child / How much more longer
CD ____ **ALCD 7702**
Alligator / May '93 / ADA / CM / Direct

LIVING CHICAGO BLUES VOL.3
Hard times / She's fine / Moving out of the ghetto / Going to New York / Big leg woman / Careless with our love / Roadblock / Poison ivy / I dare you / Nobody knows my troubles / Sweet little girl / Naptown / Drown in my own tears / Crying for my baby / Feel so bad / Wish me well / Have you ever loved a woman / Berlin Wall / Prisoner of the blues
CD ____ **ALCD 7703**
Alligator / May '93 / ADA / CM / Direct

LIVING CHICAGO BLUES VOL.4
Hard times: *Reed, A.C. & The Spark Plugs* / She's fine: *Reed, A.C. & The Spark Plugs* / Moving out of the ghetto: *Reed, A.C. & The Spark Plugs* / Going to New York: *Reed, A.C. & The Spark Plugs* / Big legged woman: *Scotty & The Rib Tips* / Careless without love: *Scotty & The Rib Tips* / Roadblock: *Scotty & The Rib Tips* / Poison ivy: *Scotty & The Rib Tips* / I dare you: *Lee, Lovie & Carey Bell* / Nobody knows my troubles: *Lee, Lovie & Carey Bell* / Sweet little girl: *Lee, Lovie & Carey Bell* / Nap town: *Lee, Lovie & Carey Bell*
CD ____ **ALCD 7704**
Alligator / May '93 / ADA / CM / Direct

LIVING MUSIC OF THE STEPPES (Instrumental Music & Song Of Mongolia)
Blue silk overcoat / Leafy tree / River of Uliastay / Snow crowned Altai Mountain / Hallowed road / Sunder mountain / Altai Mountain paean / Jonon Qara's run / Shiilen boor / Full moon / To run like flowing camel's water / Copper and steel / Flow of the Eveen river / Ayi nan ayi/Two hearts / Bishur appeal / Beloved otter coloured horse / Dungshang googoo / Dugureng zaan / Tale of janggar / Oyrad un daguu / Holbolog a
CD ____ **MCM 3001**
Multicultural Media / May '97 / Direct

LIVING ON THE FRONT LINE
CD ____ **CDTB 154**
Thunderbolt / Jul '94 / TKO Magnum

LIVING THE NIGHTLIFE
Carlena: *Just Brothers* / Dearly beloved: *Montgomery, Jack* / Black eyed girl: *Thompson, Billy* / Livin' the nightlife: *Charts* / Groovy guy: *Shirelles* / It's torture: *Brown, Maxine* / Gonna give her all the love I've got: *Gordon, Benny* / I refuse to give up: *Reid, Clarence* / Send my baby back: *Hughes, Freddie* / Good things come to those who wait: *Jackson, Chuck* / Do you love me baby: *Masqueraders* / Please stay: *Ivorys* / Pretty part of you: *Hunt, Tommy* / My sweet baby: *Esquires* / Love ain't what it used to be: *Diplomats* / Yesterday's kisses: *Big Maybelle* / (Happiness will cost you) One thin dime: *Lavette, Bettye* / I want you: *Clay, Judy* / Since I found a love: *Hadley, Sandy* / Love keeps me crying: *Johnson, Walter* / You can't keep a good man down: *Gentlemen Four* / I don't want to lose you: *Wynn, Mel* / Look my way: *Williams, Maurice* / You must be losing your mind: *Raye, Jimmy*
CD ____ **CDKEND 104**
Kent / Jun '93 / Pinnacle

LIVING THING, A
CD ____ **CDORBD 094**
Globestyle / Jun '97 / Pinnacle

LKJ PRESENTS
CD ____ **LKJCD 014**
LKJ / Apr '96 / Grapevine/PolyGram / Jet Star

LO MEJOR DE LA SALSA
CD ____ **DMA 5011**
Blue Moon / Jan '97 / Cadillac / Discovery / Greensleeves / Jazz Music / Jet Star / TKO Magnum

LO RECORDINGS VOL.4
Feelin' brown: *Twisted Science* / Pooo: *Kraut, Peter* / Spiegels: *Vibert, Luke* / Blasted wook: *Vibert, Luke* / See sawing sea: *Kristian, David* / Clockwork: *Cujo* / Time T-bone: *Sycophants* / We can't play from shit E: *Wormhole* / DMN 97: *Burzootie* / Wooden league: *Voafose* / Feelin' brown: *Twisted Science* / Lo-band-width: *Hood* / My name is sugar cane: *Barbed* / Space notes: *Mellowtrons* / Cry from the city: *Fish Out Of Water* / Cloaking device: *Underdog* / Scratch: *Ganger* / An itch you can't fucking scratch: *Thomas, Richard* / Epicycle: *Chasm* / Eternal boy: *Bedouin Ascent* / I'm going to hit the ground running: *Thomas, Richard* / Careful with that rake Eugene: *Moore, Thurston & Eugene Chadbourne* / 2player: *2 Player & DJ Vadim* / Demo: *Freezer*
CD ____ **LCD 05**
Lo / Jul '97 / RTM/Disc

LOADED LOCK IN
CD ____ **VVR 1000222**
V2 / May '97 / 3mv/Pinnacle

LOCA MIA
CD ____ **TUMICD 025**
Tumi / '92 / Discovery / Stern's

LOCKED INTO SURF VOL.1
CD ____ **WIGCD 002**
Alopecia / Jul '96 / Plastic Head

LOCKED ON
Joy: *Rushmore, Janet* / Space cowboy: *Jamiroquai* / Freak in you: *Jodeci* / Inside your mind: *God* / Saved my life: *Edwards, Todd* / Diamond rings: *X-Presidents* / Misled: *Dion, Celine* / Runnin' away: *Nicole* / Closer: *Mood II Swing* / Let's groove: *Morel's Grooves* / Alabama blues: *St. Germain* / Are u sleeping: *Indo* / Nite life: *English, Kim* / Satisfied: *H2O & Billie* / Spend the night: *Lewis, Danny J.* / Never gonna let you go: *Moore, Tina*
CD ____ **8287512**
CD ____ **8287732**
London / May '96 / PolyGram

LOGIC TRANCE VOL.2
Stella: *Jam & Spoon* / Transformation: *Transform* / Trans-o-phobia: *Dance Trance* / Schoneberg: *Marmion* / Midsummernight: *Glass Ceiling* / Fragile: *LSG* / Brainticket 2: *Ramin* / Rez: *Underworld* / Eternal spirit: *4 Voices* / Wake up: *Garnier, Laurent* / Fires of Ork II: *Fires Of Ork* / What is sound: *Blyz* / Little fluffy clouds: *Orb* / Paradise II: *Atlantis* / Papua New Guinea: *Future Sound Of London* / Silence of the water: *Emojonal* / I love you: *Electrotete* / How much can you take: *Visions Of Shiva* / Evolution: *Experience* / Spacetrack: *Cosmic Baby* / Love stimulation: *Humate* / Orbital: *Lush 3.1* / Logic trance: *Microbots*
CD ____ **74321212342**
Logic / Jun '94 / 3mv/BMG

LOLO SY NY TARINY (Music From Madagascar)
CD ____ **PS 65121**
PlayaSound / Feb '94 / ADA / Harmonia Mundi

LONDON BLUES FESTIVAL (2CD Set)
CD Set ____ **ITM 960017**
ITM / Feb '94 / Koch / Tradelink

LONDON JAZZ CLASSICS VOL.1
Skindo le'le: *Alive* / Jump: *Airto* / Welcome new warmth: *Sardaby, Michel* / Salsa Mama: *Richardson, Doug* / Te' Caliente: *Gallant, Patsy* / Searching: *McClerkin, Corky* / Atlas: *Jones, Robin Seven* / I feel the earth move: *First Gear & Larnelle Harris*
CD ____ **SJRCD 008**
Soul Jazz / Jul '94 / New Note/Pinnacle / Timewarp / Vital

LONDON JAZZ CLASSICS VOL.2
Samba de flora: *Moreira, Airto* / Get with it: *Parker, Billy* / Ain't no sunshine: *Sivuca* / Cocoa funk: *Franzetti, Carlos* / Forty days: *Brooks, Billy* / Sophie's gift: *Synthesis* / Feel like makin' love: *Marrero, Ricardo* / Fenway funk: *Paunetto, Bobby*
CD ____ **SJRCD 017**
Soul Jazz / Jun '94 / New Note/Pinnacle / Timewarp / Vital

LONDON JAZZ CLASSICS VOL.3
L'eroe di plastica: *Esposito, Tony* / Mr. Blindman: *McGhee, Donna* / Manha: *Azymuth* / Taz: *Paunetto, Bobby* / A assim que eu sou: *Papete* / Bananas: *Irvine, Weldon* / Bananeira: *Santiago, Emilio* / Mother's land: *Hannibal* / Cascavel: *Adolfo, Antonio*
CD ____ **SJCD 026**
Soul Jazz / May '95 / New Note/Pinnacle / Timewarp / Vital

LONDON PAVILION VOL.3
CD ____ **ACME 21CD**
El / May '89 / Pinnacle

LONDON UPDATE OF DRUM 'N' BASS (DJ Wildchild Presents)
CD ____ **MILL 39CD**
Millenium / May '97 / Plastic Head / Prime / SRD

LONELY IS AN EYESORE
Hot doggie: *Colourbox* / Acid bitter and sad: *This Mortal Coil* / Cut the tree: *Wolfgang Press* / Fish: *Throwing Muses* / Frontier: *Dead Can Dance* / Crushed: *Cocteau Twins* / No motion: *Dif Juz* / Muscoviet musquito: *Clan Of Xymox* / Protagonist: *Dead Can Dance*
CD ____________ CAD 703CD
4AD / '88 / RTM/Disc

LONG LIVE LOVE
CD ____________ PLSCD 234
Pulse / Jul '97 / BMG

LONG LIVE TIBET
Jesus Christ revisited: *Longpigs* / Govinda Hari and Saint George: *Kula Shaker* / Lining your pockets: *Ocean Colour Scene & Paul Weller* / Planet of dreams: *Bowie, David & Gail Ann Dorsey* / She's so high: *Blur* / Live bedshow: *Pulp* / Four walls: *Cast* / Too handsome to be homeless: *Baby Bird* / Possibly maybe: *Bjork* / Egoiste: *James* / Dark therapy: *Echobelly* / Polo mint city: *Texas* / Sunrise shakers: *Reef* / Bends: *Radiohead* / Moonage daydream: *Terrorvision* / Wait for the sun: *Supergrass*
CD ____________ CDEMC 3768
EMI / Jun '97 / EMI

LONG TALL SALLY (Original Rock 'n' Roll)
(We're gonna) Rock around the clock / Keep a knockin' / Personality / Be bop a lula / Johnny B Goode / At the hop / Great balls of fire / Tutti frutti / Duke of Earl / Shake, rattle and roll / Sea cruise / Stagger Lee / Whole lotta shakin' goin' on / Long tall Sally / Runaway / This ole house / Sweet little sixteen / Yakety yak / Book of love / Roll over Beethoven
CD ____________ CDAA 041
Tring / Oct '92 / Tring

LONG WALK, THE (The Sky Ranch Sampler)
CD ____________ 841422
Sky Ranch / Sep '96 / Discovery

LOOK OF LOVE, THE
Can't get by without you: *Real Thing* / Best thing that ever happened to me: *Knight, Gladys & The Pips* / Don't throw your love away: *Searchers* / (If paradise is) half as nice: *Amen Corner* / Always something there to remind me: *Shaw, Sandie* / First cut is the deepest: *Arnold, P.P.* / Just when I needed you most: *Vanwarmer, Randy* / Love hurts: *Nazareth* / Isn't she lovely: *Parton, David* / Way we were: *Knight, Gladys & The Pips* / Baby, now that I've found you: *Foundations* / Funny how love can be: *Ivy League* / Angel of the morning: *Arnold, P.P.* / Colour of my love: *Jefferson* / That same old feeling: *Pickettywitch* / You to me are everything: *Real Thing* / Sad sweet dreamer: *Sweet Sensation* / When you walk in the room: *Searchers*
CD ____________ MCCD 039
Music Club / Sep '91 / Disc / THE

LOOK OF LOVE, THE
Don't leave me this way: *Communards* / Heartache: *Pepsi & Shirlie* / She ain't worth it: *Medeiros, Glenn & Bobby Brown* / Look of love: *ABC* / You're the best thing: *Style Council* / Robert De Niro's waiting: *Bananarama* / Pale shelter: *Tears For Fears* / Wonderful life: *Black* / Senza una Donna: *Zucchero & Paul Young* / Never knew love like this before: *Mills, Stephanie* / Look away: *Big Country* / Watching you: *Shakatak* / Don't walk away: *Four Tops* / Leaving me now: *Level 42*
CD ____________ 5501452
Spectrum / Jan '94 / PolyGram

LOOK OF LOVE, THE
CD ____________ 5351902
PolyGram TV / Jan '96 / PolyGram

LOOKEY DOOKEY
CD ____________ EFA 11569CD
Crypt / Jun '93 / Shellshock/Disc

LORD OF THE DANCE
CD ____________ 5337572
PolyGram TV / Oct '96 / PolyGram

LOS TIEMPOS CAMBIAN
CD ____________ X 55519
Aspic / Sep '95 / Harmonia Mundi

LOST BLUES TAPES VOL.1
Della Mae: *Hooker, John Lee* / Hound dog: *Thornton, Willie Mae* / Captain Captain: *Waters, Muddy* / I got to cut out: *Williamson, Sonny Boy* / Blues harp shuffle: *Horton, Big Walter* / Strong brain - broad mind: *Dixon, Willie* / Big leg woman: *Dixon, Willie* / You got me runnin': *Desanto, Sugar Pie* / South side jump: *Guy, Buddy* / If I get lucky: *Lenoir, J.B.* / Got a letter this morning: *McDowell, 'Mississippi' Fred* / Sail on: *Sykes, Roosevelt* / Memphis boogie: *Memphis Slim* / Your best friend's gone: *Estes, John & Hammie Nixon* / Farewell baby: *Ross, Dr. Isiah* / Della Mae: *Hooker, John Lee*
CD ____________ 92042
Act / Apr '94 / New Note/Pinnacle

LOST GROOVES, THE
Hold on I'm comin': *Wilson, Reuben* / It's your thing: *Green, Grant* / Scorpion: *Donaldson, Lou* / Hey western union man: *Green, Grant* / Brother soul: *Donaldson, Lou* / Village lee: *Patton, 'Big' John* / Spooky: *Turrentine, Stanley* / Dancin' in a easy groove: *Smith, Lonnie Liston* / You want me to stop loving you: *Turrentine, Stanley*
CD ____________ CDP 8318832
Blue Note / Apr '95 / EMI

LOST HITS
CD ____________ SKYDOG 622312
Skydog / May '97 / Discovery

LOST HITS AND GOLDEN MEMORIES VOL.1
Let's face the music and dance: *Cole, Nat 'King'* / Hit 'n' miss: *Barry, John Seven* / Surfin' USA: *Beach Boys* / Mockinbird: *Foxx, Inez* / Locomotion: *Little Eva* / Lovers' concerto: *Toys* / My heart's symphony: *Lewis, Gary & The Playboys* / Snoopy VS the Red Baron: *Royal Guardsmen* / Footsee: *Wigan's Chosen Few* / But it's alright: *Jackson, J.J.* / Hi ho silver lining: *Beck, Jeff* / Whole lotta love: *CCS* / Here comes that rainy day feeling again: *Fortunes* / Too much foolin' around: *Tams* / Too late to turn back now: *Cornelius Brothers & Sister Rose* / This will be: *Cole, Natalie* / (Take me for) A night in New York: *Bones, Elbow & Racketeers* / Right back from where we started from: *Nightingale, Maxine* / You sexy thing: *Hot Chocolate* / It only takes a minute: *Tavares* / Taste of honey: *Boogie Oogie Oogie* / On the beat: *BB & Q Band* / Loverboy: *Chairmen Of The Board* / Point of view: *Matumbi* / Rock me tonight (for old time's sake): *Jackson, Freddie*
CD ____________ KRLCD 002
KRL / May '96 / Vital

LOST IN LOVE
Walk on by: *Warwick, Dionne* / Missing you: *Waite, John* / I've got you on my mind: *Cole, Natalie* / Air that I breathe: *Cole, Natalie* / No doubt about it: *Hot Chocolate* / No regrets: *Walker Brothers* / Crying in the rain: *A-Ha* / jJust when I need you most: *Vanwarmer, Randy* / Especially for you: *Minogue, Kylie & Jason Donovan* / Tonight I celebrate my love for you: *Bryson, Peabo & Roberta Flack* / Something's gotten hold of my heart: *Almond, Marc & Gene Pitney* / WOuld I lie to you: *Charles & Eddie* / Love is in the air: *Young, John Paul* / I'll never fall in love again: *Deacon Blue* / You might need somebody: *Crawford, Randy* / Cry me a river: *Wilson, Mari* / Love of the common people: *Young, Paul* / Mon ami m'a quittee: *Dion, Celine*
CD ____________ NTRCD 087
Nectar / Aug '97 / Pinnacle

LOST IN SPACE DRUM 'N' BASS VOL.1 (A Smarter Than Average Jungle Collection)
CD ____________ CERBAD 1
Lacerba / Jul '96 / 3mv/Sony

LOST IN SPACE DRUM 'N' BASS VOL.2 (2CD Set)
CD Set ____________ CERBAD 2
Lacerba / Jan '97 / 3mv/Sony

LOST IN SPACE DRUM 'N' BASS VOL.3 (2CD Set)
CD Set ____________ CERBAD 4
Lacerba / Jun '97 / 3mv/Sony

LOST MUSIC OF CELTARABIA, THE
CD ____________ GRIN 942CD
Grinnigogs / Jul '95 / ADA

LOST PROPERTY (2CD Set)
Love will tear us apart: *Joy Division* / Blue Monday: *New Order* / This charming man: *Smiths* / Sit down: *James* / Getting away with it: *Electronic* / Step on: *Happy Mondays* / Cutter: *Echo & The Bunnymen* / Reward: *Teardrop Explodes* / I will follow: *U2* / I travel: *Simple Minds* / Happy house: *Siouxsie & The Banshees* / Lovecats: *Cure* / Temple of love: *Sisters Of Mercy* / Ziggy Stardust: *Bauhaus* / Lust for life: *Iggy Pop* / Whole of the moon: *Waterboys* / Psycho killer: *Talking Heads* / Magnificent 7: *Clash* / Mandinka: *O'Connor, Sinead* / Song from under the floorboards: *Magazine* / Story of the blues: *Wah* / Loaded: *Primal Scream* / Going underground: *Jam* / It's the end of the world as we know it: *REM* / Route 66: *Depeche Mode* / Size of a cow: *Wonder Stuff* / Uncertain smile: *The The* / Drug train: *Cramps* / Release the bats: *Birthday Party* / Teenage kicks: *Undertones* / Altogether now: *Farm* / Geno: *Dexy's Midnight Runners* / Rock lobster: *B-52's* / Can't be sure: *Sundays* / Rip it up: *Orange Juice* / I am the fly: *Wire* / Ghost town: *Specials* / Mirror in the bathroom: *Beat* / Fiery Jack: *Fall* / Happy hour: *Housemartins* / Song to the siren: *This Mortal Coil* / Everyday is like Sunday: *Morrissey* / She sells sanctuary: *Cult*
CD Set ____________ CDEMTVD 122
EMI TV / May '96 / EMI

LOST SOUL OF DETROIT, THE VOL.1
She's not everybody's girl: *Metros* / That's bad: *Harris, Lafayette Jr.* / I hold the key: *Sanders, Nelson* / I'm leaving baby: *White, Willie* / Leave me alone: *White, Willie* / I gotta know: *Hutcher, Willie* / Standing on the sideline: *Williams, Lloyd* / Can't live without you: *Milner, Reggie* / In the middle: *Reynolds, L.J.* / Stop lost over your past: *Reynolds, L.J.* / I don't mess around: *Reynolds, Jeannie* / People make the world: *Reynolds, Jeannie* / I found the right girl: *Swingers* / Alone in the chapel: *Doe & Joe* / Do you want a love: *Milner, Reggie* / She's alright: *Milner, Reggie* / Somebody help me: *Milner, Reggie* / Uphill climb to the bottom: *Lemons, George* / Nothing can seperate our love: *Turner, Sammy*
CD ____________ GSCD 021
Goldmine / Aug '93 / Vital

LOST TREASURES CONCERTO FOR SONIC CIRCLES (Mixed By DJ Tiesto)
CD ____________ NLGUARD 052
Guardian Angel / Jun '97 / Intergroove

LOUD, PROUD & PUNK
CD ____________ PLSCD 105
Pulse / May '96 / BMG

LOUDEST VOL.1
CD ____________ LOUDEST 001
Outland / Jun '94 / Plastic Head / Vital

LOUISIANA CAJUN MUSIC SPECIAL VOL.1 (Swallow Records)
Hee haw breakdown: *Cormier, Nolan & the LA Aces* / Pine grove blues: *Abshire, Nathan* / Triangle club special: *Prejean, Leeman* / Louisiana aces special: *Badeaux* / Lacassine special: *Balfa Brothers* / Cypress inn special: *Cormier, Nolan & the LA Aces* / Zydeci Cha Cha: *Mouton* / Cankton two step: *Prejan* / Cajun ramblers special: *Derouen, Wallace* / Eunice two step: *Barzas, Maurice* / Hippy ti yo: *Bonsall, Joe* / I am so lonely: *Herbert, Adam* / Choupique two step: *Abshire, Nathan* / Waltz of regret: *Mate, Doris* / Two steps de vieux temps: *Rambling Aces*
CD ____________ CDCH 914
Ace / Jan '92 / Pinnacle

LOUISIANA CAJUN MUSIC SPECIAL VOL.2 (Swallow Records)
Choupique two step: *Abshire, Nathan* / Cypress inn special: *Cormier, Lionel* / Chinaball blues: *Pitre, Austin* / Cameron two step: *Barro* / Calcasieu rambler's special: *Broussard, August* / Waltz of regret: *Matte, Doris* / Little cajun boy: *Leger, Bobby* / Zydeco cha cha: *Mouzas & Lignos* / Mamou hot step: *Mamou Playboys* / Every night when it's dark: *Hebert, Adam* / La valse de grand bois: *Balfa Brothers* / Cankton two step: *Prejean, Leeman* / She didn't know I was married: *Menard, D.L.* / Family waltz: *Menard, Phil & Don Guillory* / Two steps de vieux temps: *Rambling Aces* / One step de duson: *Cormier, Louis*
CD ____________ CDCH 368
Ace / Mar '92 / Pinnacle

LOUISIANA CHANKY-CHANK
CD ____________ ZNCD 1002
Zane / Oct '95 / Pinnacle

LOUISIANA LIVE FROM MOUNTAIN STAGE
La danse de la vie: *Beausoleil* / Ayiti: *Neville Brothers* / Louisiana two step: *Chenier, Clifton & His Red Hot Louisiana Band* / Long hard journey home: *Radiators* / Such a night: *Dr. John* / Evegeline special: *Sonnier, Jo El* / Mother in law: *Toussaint, Allen* / Lipstick traces: *Toussaint, Allen* / Chere Duloone: *Rapone, Al* / La toussaint: *Riley, Steve & Mamou Playboys* / Choupik two step: *Queen Ida & The Bon Temps Zydeco Band* / Johnny can't dance: *Toups, Wayne & ZydeCajun* / Jeleron: *Buck Wheat Zydeco* / Don't wanna cry no more: *Simien, Terrance*
CD ____________ BPM 306CD
Blue Plate / May '97 / ADA / Direct / Greyhound

LOUISIANA PIANO RHYTHMS
Deep creek blues: *Morton, Jelly Roll* / Rum and coca cola: *Professor Longhair* / So long: *Domino, Fats* / You always hurt the one you love: *Henry, Clarence 'Frogman'* / Ain't misbehavin': *Toussaint, Allen* / Rockin' chair blues: *Charles, Ray* / Who will play this old piano: *Lewis, Jerry Lee* / Lucille: *Little Richard* / Rockin' pneumonia and the boogie woogie flu: *Smith, Huey 'Piano'* / Sea cruise: *Ford, Frankie* / Happiness is in your bed: *Dr. John* / Send me some lovin': *Little Richard* / Can't you see darling: *Charles, Ray* / On the sunny side of the street: *Toussaint, Allen* / Big chief: *Professor Longhair* / What made Milwaukee famous (has made a loser out of me): *Lewis, Jerry Lee* / I'm walkin': *Domino, Fats*
CD ____________ 598109420
Tomato / Nov '93 / Vital

LOUISIANA ROCKERS
Cindy Lou: *Terry, Gene* / Come along with me: *Perrywell, Charles* / Yankee danky doodle: *Wilson, Jimmy* / Baby you been to school: *Page, Charles* / Bye bye baby: *Gerdsen, Ray & the Yellow Jackets* / Catch that train: *Anderson, Elton* / Chickee town rock: *Yellow Jackets* / Clemae: *Morris, Jerry* / I keep cryin': *Cookie* / Why did you leave me: *Lowery, Frankie* / Wiggle rock: *Richards, Jay* / I love you: *Anderson, Elton* / Orelia: *Jackson, Ivory Lee* / Flim flam: *Prevost, Lionel* / No mail today: *Terry, Gene* / Emmagene: *Stevens, Duke* / Slop and stroll jolie blonde: *Dean, Gabe* / Fattie Hattie: *Gerdsen, Ray & the Yellow Jackets* / Do you take me for a fool: *Hillier, Chuck* / Silly dilly: *Nelson, Jay* / Sweet potato mash (Part 1): *Parker, Bill Showboat Band* / Linda Lou: *Little Eddie* / Devil made me say that: *James, Danny* / Muscadine mule: *Ferrier, Al*
CD ____________ CDCHD 491
Ace / Mar '94 / Pinnacle

LOUISIANA SATURDAY NIGHT
Louisiana man: *Kershaw, Rusty & Doug* / I cried: *Allan, Johnnie* / Mathilda: *Cookie & The Cupcakes* / My jolie blonde: *Bernard, Rod & Clifton Chenier* / She wears my ring: *Bo, Phil* / Feed the flame: *Broussard, Van* / Little cajun girl: *King, Gene* / Big boys cry: *Charles, Bobby* / Sugar bee: *Cleveland Crochet* / Jailbird: *Shurley, Bob & The Vel-Tones* / Legend in my time: *McLain, Tommy* / Diggy liggy lo: *Kershaw, Rusty & Doug* / You had your chance: *White, Margo* / You ain't nothing but fine: *Rockin' Sidney* / Big blue diamonds: *West, Clint* / Rubber dolly: *Allan, Johnnie* / There goes that train: *Martin, Lee* / Let's do the cajun twist: *Randy & The Rockets* / Crazy baby: *Rogers, Buck* / Can't stand to see you go: *Allen, Dave* / Whole lotta shakin' goin' on: *Thomas, Prentice* / I'm not a fool anymore: *Broussard, Van* / Back door: *Rufus* / Whiskey heaven: *Ford, Frankie* / Seven letters: *Storm, Warren* / I love my Saturday night: *Stutes, Herbie*
CD ____________ CDCHD 490
Ace / Oct '93 / Pinnacle

LOUISIANA SCRAPBOOK
Mardi gras in New Orleans: *Dirty Dozen Brass Band* / New rules: *Thomas, Irma* / She said the same things to me: *Adams, Johnny* / We don't see eye to eye: *Adams, Johnny* / Wondering: *Walker, Philip* / Song for Renee: *Brown, Clarence 'Gatemouth'* / It's you I love: *Beausoleil* / Louisiana blues: *Sonnier, Jo El* / Bachelor's life: *Menard, D.L. & Louisiana Aces* / Don't you know I love you: *Ball, Marcia* / Think it over one more time: *Buckwheat Zydeco* / Steppin' up in class: *Lonesome Sundown & Phillip Walker* / No relations: *Tyler, Alvin 'Red'* / One for the highway: *Booker, James* / You got me worried: *Washington, Walter 'Wolfman'* / Gonna cry till my tears run dry: *Thomas, Irma* / Flintstones meets the president: *Dirty Dozen Brass Band* / When the saints go marching in: *Washington, Tuts*
CD ____________ RCD 20058
Rykodisc / Dec '92 / ADA / Vital

LOUISIANA SPICE (25 Years Of Louisiana Music)
CD ____________ ROUCDAN 1819
Rounder / Jun '95 / ADA / CM / Direct

LOUISIANA SWAMP BLUES
Cryin' in the morning / Bad luck is on me (aka Woman troubles) / New arrival / Standin' at the station / New bon ton roulay (aka bon ton #2) / Hey, Mr. Bon Ton / You got me crying / Dreaming / I'm hurt / Flip flop / Jumping at the Zadacoe / I can't fly (aka Date with an angel) / My love (she's gone) / Low and lonesome / Country woman / Louisiana stomp / Cliston blues / Tell me (aka I'll be on my way aka Just a lonely boy) / Rockin' hop / Country bred / Rockin' the bop / Boo zoo stomp / Paper in my shoe
CD ____________ CDEMS 1606
Capitol / Mar '97 / EMI

LOVE ALBUM VOL.1, THE (2CD Set)
Don't be a stranger: *Carroll, Dina* / If you don't know me by now: *Simply Red* / Can't help falling in love: *UB40* / Searching: *China Black* / Move closer: *Nelson, Phyllis* / Again: *Jackson, Janet* / Against all odds: *Collins, Phil* / Don't let the sun go down on me: *Michael, George & Elton John* / It must have been love: *Roxette* / Don't wanna lose you: *Estefan, Gloria* / One day I'll fly away: *Crawford, Randy* / Sweet love: *Baker, Anita* / Never too much: *Vandross, Luther* / Piece of my heart: *Franklin, Erma* / Come in out of the rain: *Moten, Wendy* / When you tell me that you love me: *Ross, Diana* / Save the best for last: *Williams, Vanessa* / Zoom: *Fat Larry's Band* / Heartbreaker: *Warwick, Dionne* / Million love songs: *Take That* / If you leave me now: *Chicago* / I want to know what love is: *Foreigner* / I'll stand by you: *Pretenders* / Why: *Lennox, Annie* / Crazy: *Cline, Patsy* / Up where we belong: *Cocker, Joe & Jennifer Warnes* / Slave to love: *Ferry, Bryan* / Circle in the sand: *Carlisle, Belinda* / Rush rush: *Abdul, Paula* / I'd do anything for love (but I won't do that): *Meat Loaf* / Good heart: *Sharkey, Feargal* / (I just) died in your arms: *Cutting Crew* / Who's that girl: *Eurythmics* / You're all that matters to me: *Stigers, Curtis* / Someday (I'm coming back): *Stansfield, Lisa* / Just another day: *Secada, Jon* / Don't turn around: *Aswad* / All that she wants: *Ace Of Base* / Compliments on your kiss: *Red Dragon*
CD Set ____________ VTDCD 38
Virgin / Nov '94 / EMI

LOVE ALBUM VOL.2, THE (2CD Set)
Goodnight girl: *Wet Wet Wet* / One more night: *Collins, Phil* / I found someone: *Cher* / Let's stay together: *Turner, Tina* / All around the world: *Stansfield, Lisa* / Ain't no man: *Carroll, Dina* / I knew you were waiting (for me): *Franklin, Aretha & George Michael* / Sexual healing: *Gaye, Marvin* / Endless love: *Ross, Diana & Lionel Richie* / Unchained melody: *Righteous Brothers* / When a man loves a woman: *Sledge, Percy* / My girl: *Temptations* / Little time: *Beautiful South* / I don't want to talk about it: *Everything But The Girl* / Hazard: *Marx, Richard* / Show me heaven: *McKee, Maria* / Eternal flame: *Bangles* / Without you: *Nilsson* / Walk on by: *Warwick, Dionne* / Get here: *Adams, Oleta* / Power of love: *Rush, Jennifer* / You don't have to say you love me: *Springfield,*

Dusty / Cry me a river: *Welch, Denise* / Stand by me: *King, Ben E.* / When I fall in love: *Cole, Nat 'King'* / China girl: *Bowie, David* / It must be love: *Madness* / Every time you go away: *Young, Paul* / Damn I wish I was your lover: *Hawkins, Sophie B.* / Independant love song: *Scarlet* / China in your hand: *T'Pau* / I wonder why: *Stigers, Curtis* / Pray: *Take That* / Love me for a reason: *Boyzone* / Crazy for you: *Let Loose* / Love don't live here anymore: *Nail, Jimmy* / Jealous guy: *Roxy Music* / True: *Spandau Ballet*
CD Set _______ VTDCD 69
Virgin / Nov '95 / EMI

LOVE ALBUM VOL.2, THE
CD _______ PDSCD 533
Pulse / Aug '96 / BMG

LOVE ALBUM VOL.3, THE (2CD Set)
Greatest love of all: *Benson, George* / You've lost that lovin' feelin': *Righteous Brothers* / What's love got to do with it: *Righteous Brothers* / If I could turn back time: *Cher* / Breakfast at Tiffany's: *Deep Blue Something* / Hard to say I'm sorry: *Chicago* / Groovy kind of love: *Collins, Phil* / Waiting for a girl like you: *Foreigner* / Living years: *Mike & The Mechanics* / Missing you: *Waite, John* / Nothing compares 2 U: *O'Connor, Sinead* / Angel: *Franklin, Aretha* / Help me make it through the night: *Knight, Gladys & The Pips* / Still: *Commodores* / Tonight I celebrate my love: *Flack, Roberta & Peabo Bryson* / All the love in the world: *Warwick, Dionne* / Your song: *John, Elton* / Make it with you: *Bread* / It's all coming back to me now: *Pandora's Box* / Say you'll be there: *Spice Girls* / Coming home now: *Boyzone* / I am blessed: *Eternal* / Babe: *Take That* / Dreams: *Gabrielle* / Ocean Drive: *Lighthouse Family* / Kiss from a rose: *Seal* / That look in your eye: *Campbell, Ali* / No more I love you's: *Lennox, Annie* / Oh pretty woman: *Orbison, Roy* / Heaven is a place on Earth: *Carlisle, Belinda* / Easy lover: *Collins, Phil & Phillip Bailey* / I just want to make love to you: *James, Etta* / Try a little tenderness: *Commitments* / Mysterious girl: *Andre, Peter* / What becomes of the brokenhearted: *Ruffin, Jimmy* / Unchained melody: *Robson & Jerome* / Can't stay away from you: *Estefan, Gloria* / Dance away: *Roxy Music* / I'd lie for you (and that's the truth): *Meat Loaf*
CD Set _______ VTDCD 104
Virgin / Nov '96 / EMI

LOVE ALBUM, THE
CD _______ DSPCD 114
Disky / Feb '94 / Disky / THE

LOVE ALBUM, THE
Everytime you go away: *Gaynor, Gloria* / Cupid: *Drifters* / For your precious love: *Impressions* / I who have nothing: *King, Ben E.* / You'll lose a good thing: *Lynn, Barbara* / Tell it like it is: *Neville, Aaron* / Lovin' arms: *Gray, Dobie* / You keep me hangin' on: *Simon, Joe* / Bring it on home to me: *Floyd, Eddie* / I've been loving you too long: *Sledge, Percy* / I've passed this way before: *Ruffin, Jimmy* / You've lost that lovin' feeling: *Yuro, Timi* / Only the strong survive: *Butler, Jerry* / Hold me, thrill me, kiss me: *Carter, Mel* / So many ways: *Benton, Brook* / Too weak to fight: *Carter, Clarence* / Take good care of her: *Wade, Adam* / You always hurt the one you love: *Henry, Clarence 'Frogman'*
CD _______ ECD 3126
K-Tel / Jan '95 / K-Tel

LOVE AND DEVOTION
How deep is your love: *Take That* / Ocean drive: *Lighthouse Family* / No more I love you's: *Lennox, Annie* / Love is in my soul: *M-People* / I believe: *Robson & Jerome* / Forever love: *Barlow, Gary* / Nobody knows: *Rich, Tony Project* / Nothing compares 2 U: *O'Connor, Sinead* / She makes my day: *Palmer, Robert* / Love and understanding: *Cher* / I just want to make love to you: *James, Etta* / Mysterious girl: *Andre, Peter & Bubbler Ranx* / Light of my life: *Louise* / So natural: *Stansfield, Lisa* / You're all that matters to me: *Stigers, Curtis* / I will survive: *Savage, Chantay* / Show me heaven: *McKee, Maria* / Breathe again: *Braxton, Toni* / Don't look back in anger: *Oasis*
CD _______ 74321427282
RCA / Nov '96 / BMG

LOVE AND NAPALM
CD _______ TR 15CD
Trance / Apr '93 / SRD

LOVE BALLADS (5CD Set)
Me and Mrs. Jones: *Paul, Billy* / Love won't let me wait: *Harris, Major* / Get as much love as you can: *Jones Girls* / Forever falling in love: *Johnson, Howard* / Joy: *Pendergrass, Teddy* / Serious: *Griffin, Billy* / Used to be my girl: *O'Jays* / Hurt: *Manhattans* / You're gonna make me love somebody else: *Jones Girls* / Love I lost: *Melvin, Harold & The Bluenotes* / Does she have a friend: *Chandler, Gene* / House is not a home: *Vandross, Luther* / Love train: *O'Jays* / We ought to be doin' it: *Brown, Randy* / Special lady: *Ray, Goodman & Brown* / Ooh boy: *Rose Royce* / Do that to me one more time: *Captain & Tennille* / Before you go: *Skool Boyz* / Ooh child: *Williams, Lenny* / Don't leave me this way: *Melvin, Harold & The Bluenotes* / Brandy: *O'Jays* / Flowers: *Emotions* / Mother for my children: *Whispers* / Ain't no sunshine: *Withers, Bill* / Love ballad: *LTD* / Reasons: *Earth, Wind & Fire* / Float on: *Floaters* / Dreamer: *Jacksons* / Nights over Egypt: *Jones Girls* / Letter to my friends: *O'Jays* / At peace with woman: *Jones Girls* / You'll never find: *Rawls, Lou* / Hey there lonely girl: *Holman, Eddie* / Kiss and say goodbye: *Manhattans* / Love TKO: *Pendergrass, Teddy* / I'm in love (and I love the feeling): *Rose Royce* / After the love has gone: *Earth, Wind & Fire* / Who has the time: *Con Funk Shun* / Don't let it go to your head: *Carne, Jean* / So good, so right: *Russell, Brenda* / Caravan of love: *Isley-Jasper-Isley* / Come into my life: *Sims, Joyce* / Glow of love: *Change* / (We have come into) our time for love: *Detroit Spinners* / Sweet sensation: *Mills, Stephanie* / Sparkle: *Cameo* / Yearning for your love: *Gap Band* / It's our time: *Bailey, Philip* / Jones vs. Jones: *Kool & The Gang* / How long: *Lipps Inc.* / Never let her slip away: *Walters, Trevor* / Love has found its way: *Brown, Dennis* / Touch a four leaf clover: *Atlantic Starr* / Take my heart (you can have it if you want it): *Kool & The Gang* / Every time you go away: *Young, Paul* / Lover's holiday: *Change* / Someday: *Gap Band* / Each and every one: *Everything But The Girl* / Wherever I lay my hat (that's my home): *Young, Paul* / I can't imagine: *Bryson, Peabo & Regina Belle* / Stand by me: *King, Ben E.* / When a man loves a woman: *Sledge, Percy* / Then came you: *Detroit Spinners* / It's a man's man's man's world: *Brown, James* / Wonderful world: *Armstrong, Louis* / Lovely day: *Withers, Bill* / I've been loving you too long: *Redding, Otis* / I never loved a man (the way I love you): *Franklin, Aretha* / Warm and tender love: *Sledge, Percy* / Let the music play: *White, Barry* / Stay with me baby: *Ellison, Lorraine* / I'm your puppet: *Purify, James & Bobby* / Please please please: *Brown, James* / Lady love: *Rawls, Lou* / I say a little prayer: *Franklin, Aretha* / Turn off the lights: *Pendergrass, Teddy* / Free: *Williams, Deniece* / Let's make a baby: *Paul, Billy* / Can't get enough of your love babe: *White, Barry* / Honest I do love you: *Staton, Candi* / Loving you: *Byrd, Donald* / Shining star: *Manhattans* / Natural high: *Bloodstone* / Warm weather: *Pieces Of A Dream* / Mysteries of the world: *MFSB* / You're a star: *Aquarian Dream* / Sneaking out the back door: *Matt Bianco* / Day by day: *Shakatak & Al Jarreau* / Valdez in the country: *Hathaway, Donny* / You send me: *Ayers, Roy* / That's the way of the world: *Lewis, Ramsey* / Since I lost my baby: *Vandross, Luther* / Juicy fruit: *Mtume* / Between the sheets: *Isley Brothers* / Sexual healing: *Gaye, Marvin* / And don't you say no: *Ayers, Roy* / Weekend girl: *SOS Band* / Love don't love nobody: *Carne, Jean* / Leaving me now: *Level 42* / TSOP (The sound of Philadelphia): *MFSB*
CD Set _______ LOVECD 2
Connoisseur Collection / Dec '96 / Pinnacle

LOVE BITES
CD _______ QTVCD 022
Quality / Apr '93 / Pinnacle

LOVE COLLECTION (3CD Set)
CD Set _______ TBXCD 510
TrueTrax / Jan '96 / THE

LOVE COLLECTION (2CD Set)
CD Set _______ PBXCD 510
Pulse / Nov '96 / BMG

LOVE COLLECTION VOL.1, THE
Let there be love: *Cole, Nat 'King'* / Folks who live on the hill: *Lee, Peggy* / With these hands: *Monro, Matt* / True love ways: *Peter & Gordon* / Tonight: *Damone, Vic* / Where do you go to my lovely: *Sarstedt, Peter* / Rose Marie: *Whitman, Slim* / I've got my love to keep me warm: *Martin, Dean* / What now my love: *Bassey, Shirley* / Honey: *Goldsboro, Bobby* / Tears: *Dodd, Ken* / Let me go, lover: *Murray, Ruby* / Here in my heart: *Martino, Al* / Somewhere my love: *Sammes, Mike Singers* / She wears my ring: *King, Solomon* / Hymn a l'amour: *Piaf, Edith* / I pretend: *O'Connor, Des* / My special angel: *Vaughan, Malcolm* / He was beautiful: *Williams, Iris* / Wonder of you: *Hilton, Ronnie*
CD _______ CDMFP 5878
Music For Pleasure / Mar '92 / EMI

LOVE COLLECTION VOL.2, THE
Let's fall in love: *Cole, Nat 'King'* / Autumn leaves: *Cole, Nat 'King'* / True love: *Crosby, Bing & Grace Kelly* / Softly as I leave you: *Monro, Matt* / And we were lovers: *Monro, Matt* / Something: *Bassey, Shirley* / Where do I begin: *Bassey, Shirley* / Lady: *Rogers, Kenny* / Don't fall in love with a dreamer: *Rogers, Kenny* / Cry me a river: *London, Julie* / Spanish eyes: *Martino, Al* / By the time I get to Phoenix: *Campbell, Glen* / Don't it make my brown eyes blue: *Gayle, Crystal* / Somebody loves you: *Gayle, Crystal* / That's amore (That's love): *Martin, Dean* / I've got my love to keep me warm: *Martin, Dean* / Till there was you: *Lee, Peggy* / La vie en rose: *Piaf, Edith* / On the street where you live: *Damone, Vic* / How deep is the ocean: *Haymes, Dick*
CD _______ CDMFP 5960
Music For Pleasure / Dec '92 / EMI

LOVE COLLECTION, THE
CD _______ MACCD 159
Autograph / Aug '96 / BMG

LOVE CONNEXION
CD _______ DMUT 1363
Multitone / Jul '96 / BMG

LOVE CRAZY MEETS TALAWA
CD _______ 790152
Melodie / Nov '93 / ADA / Discovery / Grapevine/PolyGram / Greensleeves / Jet Star

LOVE HURTS
CD _______ MATCD 275
Castle / Apr '93 / BMG

LOVE HURTS (Timeless Rock Classics)
CD _______ PLSCD 199
Pulse / Apr '97 / BMG

LOVE II SWING
CD _______ TCD 2817
Telstar / Apr '96 / BMG

LOVE IS
Unchained melody: *Drifters* / Rainy night in Georgia: *Benton, Brook* / What kind of fool (do you think I am): *Tams* / Will you love me tomorrow: *Shirelles* / Love letters: *Lester, Ketty* / Since I don't have you: *Skyliners* / All I could do was cry: *James, Etta* / To know him is to love him: *Teddy Bears* / Only you (and you alone): *Platters* / Sea of love: *Phillips, Phil* / I will: *Winters, Ruby* / You send me: *Drifters* / If loving you is wrong (I don't want to be right): *Sledge, Percy* / Don't play that song (you lied): *King, Ben E.* / Smoke gets in your eyes: *Platters* / Rhythm of the rain: *Cascades* / He will break your heart: *Butler, Jerry* / Dedicated to the one I love: *Shirelles*
CD _______ ECD 3076
K-Tel / Jan '95 / K-Tel

LOVE IS IN THE AIR VOL.1
Somewhere in my heart: *Aztec Camera* / Missing you: *Waite, John* / I don't want to talk about it: *Everything But The Girl* / Crazy: *Cline, Patsy* / Do what you do: *Jackson, Jermaine* / Misty blue: *Moore, Dorothy* / Raincoat and a rose: *Rea, Chris* / He ain't heavy he's my brother: *Hollies* / I can't stop loving you: *Turner, Ike & Tina* / Torn between two lovers: *MacGregor, Mary* / Dedicated to the one I love: *Mamas & The Papas* / Together we are beautiful: *Kinney, Fern* / On and on: *Bishop, Stephen* / When I fall in love: *Astley, Rick* / Broken wings: *Mr. Mister* / Love changes everything: *Climie Fisher* / Move closer: *Jones, Tom* / Love is in the air: *Young, John Paul*
CD _______ NTRCD 034
Nectar / Feb '97 / Pinnacle

LOVE IS IN THE AIR VOL.2
From a distance: *Griffith, Nanci* / Without you: *Nilsson* / When a man loves a woman: *Sledge, Percy* / All out of love: *Air Supply* / Way we were: *Knight, Gladys & The Pips* / (If loving you is wrong) I don't want to be right: *Jackson, Millie* / You to me are everything: *Real Thing* / She's in love with the boy: *Yearwood, Trisha* / Bette Davis eyes: *Carnes, Kim* / Wind beneath my wings: *Greenwood, Lee* / Fantasy: *Kenny, Gerard* / Lost in France: *Tyler, Bonnie* / All the love in the world: *Warwick, Dionne* / If you don't know me by now: *Melvin, Harold & The Bluenotes* / Loving you: *Riperton, Minnie* / I'll have to say I love you in a song: *Croce, Jim* / (If paradise) Is half as nice: *Amen Corner* / House of the rising sun: *Animals*
CD _______ NTRCD 037
Nectar / Feb '97 / Pinnacle

LOVE IS IN THE AIR VOL.3
With a little help from my friends: *Cocker, Joe* / Love hurts: *Nazareth* / Best thing that ever happened to me: *Knight, Gladys & The Pips* / Something: *Turner, Ike & Tina* / Talking in your sleep: *Gayle, Crystal* / Seasons in the sun: *Jacks, Terry* / Man of the world: *Fleetwood Mac* / Every day hurts: *Sad Cafe* / Don't let the sun catch you crying: *Gerry & The Pacemakers* / Just when I needed you most: *Vanwarmer, Randy* / How long: *Ace* / I will: *Winters, Ruby* / My simple heart: *Three Degrees* / Sad sweet dreamer: *Sweet Sensation* / Have you seen her: *Chi-Lites* / I get the sweetest feeling: *Wilson, Jackie* / First cut is the deepest: *Arnold, P.P.* / Pretty flamingo: *Manfred Mann*
CD _______ NTRCD 038
Nectar / Feb '97 / Pinnacle

LOVE IS IN THE AIR VOL.4
True: *Spandau Ballet* / You are so beautiful: *Cocker, Joe* / I want to wake up with you: *Gardiner, Boris* / Tell it like it is: *Neville, Aaron* / My baby just cares for me: *Simone, Nina* / Cry me a river: *Wilson, Mari* / No regrets: *Ure, Midge* / Slow hand: *Pointer Sisters* / Heartbreaker: *Warwick, Dionne* / Love is a battlefield: *Benatar, Pat* / Tide is high: *Blondie* / Let your love flow: *Bellamy Brothers* / Will you still love me tomorrow: *Bellamy Brothers* / To be loved: *Wilson, Jackie* / Didn't I (blow your mind this time): *Delfonics* / Body talk: *Imagination* / Just my imagination (running away with me): *Turner, Ruby & The Temptations* / Night and day: *Everything But The Girl*
CD _______ NTRCD 039
Nectar / Feb '97 / Pinnacle

LOVE IS IN THE AIR VOL.5
Oh girl: *Young, Paul* / If she knew what she wants: *Bangles* / Blue hat for a blue day: *Heyward, Nick* / No more the fool: *Brooks, Elkie* / Midnight train to Georgia: *Knight, Gladys & The Pips* / Love all the hurt away: *Franklin, Aretha & George Benson* / Drift away: *Gray, Dobie* / Words of love: *Holly, Buddy* / Catch the wind: *Donovan* / Valentine: *Nelson, Willie* / I will always love you: *Parton, Dolly* / As time goes by: *Nilsson* / One more try: *Timmy T* / Lucky stars: *Friedman, Dean* / There'll be sad songs to make you cry: *Ocean, Billy* / Can't get by without you: *Real Thing* / Feel the need in me: *Detroit Emeralds* / It's a love thing: *Whispers*
CD _______ NTRCD 040
Nectar / Feb '97 / Pinnacle

LOVE IS IN THE AIR VOL.6
Lady: *Rogers, Kenny* / Summer breeze: *Isley Brothers* / Friends: *Stewart, Amii* / Hands to heaven: *Breathe* / See the day: *Lee, Dee C.* / I still haven't found what I'm looking for: *Chimes* / I gave you my heart (didn't I): *Hot Chocolate* / How can you mend a broken heart: *Green, Al* / Every time you say goodbye: *McCrae, George* / I'll never love this way again: *Three Degrees* / All by myself: *Carmen, Eric* / Gaye: *Ward, Clifford T.* / Sometimes when we touch: *Hill, Dan & Rique Franks* / (Something inside) So strong: *Siffre, Labi* / Sad eyes: *John, Robert* / Tears on my pillow: *Minogue, Kylie* / Find my love: *Fairground Attraction* / Spend a little time: *Armatrading, Joan*
CD _______ NTRCD 041
Nectar / Feb '97 / Pinnacle

LOVE OVER GOLD
CD _______ TCD 2684
Telstar / Feb '94 / BMG

LOVE PARADE 1994 (2CD Set)
CD Set _______ D 945013
Bunker/D'Vision / Dec '94 / Plastic Head

LOVE, PEACE AND HAPPINESS (2CD Set)
CD Set _______ DBG 53037
Double Gold / Jun '95 / Target/BMG

LOVE POWER (Hard To Find US Hot 100 Hits Of The 60's)
I got rhythm: *Happenings* / I'm gonna love you too: *Hullabaloo* / Music to watch girls by: *Crewe, Bob Generation* / Walkin' my cat named dog: *Tanega, Norma* / Attack: *Toys* / Her lover: *Dovale, Debbie* / Her Royal Majesty: *Darren, James* / Big wide world: *Randazzo, Teddy* / When she needs good lovin': *Chicago Loopers* / Leader of the laundromat: *Detergents* / But it's alright: *Jackson, J.J.* / That boy John: *Raindrops* / Soul heaven: *Dixie Drifter* / Opportunity: *Jewels* / Love power: *Sandpebbles* / Happy: *Blades of Grass* / You better go: *Martin, Derek* / Countdown: *Cortez, Dave 'Baby'* / Double O seven: *Detergents*
CD _______ NEMCD 669
Sequel / Jun '94 / BMG

LOVE PROGE (Love Records 1968-1979/ 2CD Set)
Semi-circle solitude: *Blues Section* / Somebody keeps calling my name: *Baby Grandmothers* / Luulosairas: *Wigwam* / Sisaltani portin loysin: *Pekka Streng* / Deep thinker: *Tasavallan Presidentti* / Ajatukset: *Willberg, Pepe* / Like the purpose told me: *Charlies* / Elavien hauta: *Magyar* / Black Friday: *Ferris* / Lounge: *Tasavallan Presidentti* / Virtojen kiharat: *Pekka Pohjola* / Crisader: *Wigwam* / Ode to eagle: *Nimbus* / Don't wake me now: *Mandala* / Persialaisella torilla: *Session* / No new games: *Pembroke, Jim* / Tie: *Manifest* / Do or die: *Wigwam* / Enema syringe: *Hauru, Jukka* / Vuorellaistuja: *Tabula Rasa* / Epilogi: *Donna* / Atlantis: *Nova* / Huono juttu: *Janus* / Summer '72: *Hurmerinta, Sami* / Passenger to Paramaribou: *Tolonen, Jukka* / Oh Marlene: *Wigwam* / Yksin yhdessa (osa): *Gustavson, Jukka* / Just my situation: *Royals* / Pablo: *Finnforest* / Savitaipaleen polkka: *Sukellusvene* / No why, nobody there: *Limousine*
CD Set _______ LXCD 613
Love / May '97 / ADA / Direct / Greyhound

LOVE SONGS (4CD Set)
Will you love me tomorrow: *Shirelles* / Only you: *Platters* / Something's gotten hold of my heart: *Pitney, Gene* / Remember (Walkin' in the sand): *Shangri-Las* / Fools rush in: *Benton, Brook* / Save the last dance for me: *Drifters* / Letter full of tears: *Knight, Gladys & The Pips* / Ain't no sunshine: *Jarreau, Al* / Let it be me: *Butler, Jerry & Betty Everett* / Groovy kind of love: *Fontana, Wayne* / Build me up buttercup: *Foundations* / With a girl like you: *Troggs* / Earth angel: *Penguins* / I've loved and lost again: *Cline, Patsy* / Portrait of my love: *Clark, Dee* / He's so fine: *Chiffons* / Harbour lights: *Platters* / Cupid: *Drifters* / Feelings: *Gaynor, Gloria* / Hurt: *Yuro, Timi* / Love is all around: *Troggs* / One fine day: *Chiffons* / Everalsting love: *Love Affair* / Love grows (where my Rosemary goes): *Edison Lighthouse* / You always hurt the one you love: *Yuro, Timi* / Smoke gets in your eyes: *Platters* / Every beat of my heart: *Knight, Gladys & The Pips* / Chapel of love: *Dixie Cups* / Run to him: *Vee, Bobby* / Looking through the eyes of love: *Pitney, Gene* / Funny how love can be: *Ivy League* / Baby, now that I've found you: *Foundations* / Dedicated to the one I love:

Shirelles / Under the boardwalk: *Drifters* / Twilight time: *Platters* / Can't take my eyes off you: *Gaynor, Gloria* / There's a kind of hush: *Herman's Hermits* / You were on my mind: *St. Peters, Crispian* / Here it comes again: *Fortunes* / Little things: *Berry, Dave* / When a man loves a woman: *Sledge, Percy* / For your precious love: *Butler, Jerry* / Band of gold: *Payne, Freda* / It hurts to be in love: *Pitney, Gene* / Love will keep us together: *Sedaka, Neil* / Broken promises: *Shannon, Del* / More I see you: *Platters* / Gentle on my mind: *Campbell, Glen* / Rose garden: *Anderson, Lynn* / This magic moment: *Drifters* / Guess who: *Knight, Gladys & The Pips* / It's just a matter of time: *Benton, Brook* / Feel the need in me: *Detroit Emeralds* / She even woke me up to say goodbye: *Rogers, Kenny* / Walkin' after midnight: *Cline, Patsy* / My heart cries out for you: *Mitchell, Guy* / Moonlight in Vermont: *Fitzgerald, Ella* / Night and day: *Holiday, Billie* / How high the moon: *Gaynor, Gloria* / Love for sale: *Benson, George* / Make it easy on yourself: *Butler, Jerry* / So many ways: *Benton, Brook* / Warm and tender love: *Sledge, Percy* / Breaking up is hard to do: *Sedaka, Neil* / Crying: *Campbell, Glen* / For the good times: *Rogers, Kenny* / Godnight my love: *Knight, Gladys & The Pips* / Stand by me: *Drifters* / Just out of reach: *Cline, Patsy* / If you ever should leave me: *Fitzgerald, Ella* / More than you know: *Holiday, Billie* / I love how you love me: *Yuro, Timi* / There will never be another you: *Benson, George* / Give him a great big kiss: *Shangri-Las* / To know him is to love him: *Shirelles* / Let's pretend: *Nelson, Willie* / Just one smile: *Pitney, Gene* / Sweet dreams: *Young, Faron* / It had to be you: *Travolta, John*
CD Set ______ QUAD 018
Tring / Nov '96 / Tring

LOVE SONGS COLLECTION VOL.1
Will you love me tomorrow / Only you / Something's gotten hold of my heart / Remember (walkin' in the sand) / Fools rush in / Save the last dance for me / Letter full of tears / Ain't no sunshine / Let it be me / Groovy kind of love / Build me up buttercup / With a girl like you / Earth angel / I've loved and lost again / Portrait of my love / He's so fine / Harbour lights / Cupid / Feelings / Hurt
CD ______ QED 004
Tring / Nov '96 / Tring

LOVE SONGS COLLECTION VOL.2
Love is all around / One fine day / Everlasting love / Love grows (where my Rosemary goes) / You always hurt the one you love / Smoke gets in your eyes / Every beat of my heart / Chapel of love / Run to him / Looking through the eyes of love / Funny how love can be / Baby, now that I've found you / Dedicated to the one I love / Under the boardwalk / Twilight time / Can't take my eyes off you / There's a kind of hush / You were on my mind / Here it comes again / Little things
CD ______ QED 042
Tring / Nov '96 / Tring

LOVE SONGS OF DETROIT (3CD Set)
Ain't no mountain high enough: *Payne, Sherrie* / Baby I'm for real: *Originals* / Yes I'm ready: *Weston, Kim* / If this world were mine: *Lawrence, Lynda* / Reach for the sky: *Jacas, Jake* / My heart won't say no: *Demps, Louvain* / Baby baby: *Lewis Sisters* / London bridge is falling down: *Cameron, G.C.* / Slow motion: *Barnes, J.J.* / Does your Mama know about me: *Taylor, Bobby & The Vancouvers* / If I were your woman: *Royster, Vermettya* / It's impossible: *Eckstine, Billy* / Easy to love: *Griner, Linda* / Two out of three: *Stubbs, Joe* / You're love is wonderful: *Littles, Hattie* / Take me in your arms and love me: *Nero, Frances* / Give me your love: *Royster, Vermettya* / Heaven knows: *Miracles* / You'll be sorry: *Fantastic Four* / Come back to me: *Cameron, G.C.* / Special day: *Gaye, Frankie* / Soul searching: *Randolph, Barbara* / Cloudy day: *Taylor, Bobby & The Vancouvers* / Reluctant lover: *Griffin, Billy* / Hold out my hand: *Jacas, Jake* / Ain't understanding mellow: *Harris, Joey* / Sell me soul: *Littles, Hattie* / Wholeheartedly: *McNeir, Ronnie* / Smiling faces sometimes: *Vee* / Teardrops: *Starr, Edwin* / Keeping my mind on love: *Wells, Mary* / Ask the lonely: *Eckstine, Billy* / Watching the hands of time: *Preston, Billy & Syreeta* / Tracks of my tears: *Contours* / Every little bit hurts: *Holloway, Brenda* / Time is on my side: *Littles, Hattie* / Gentle lady: *Eckstine, Billy* / Free: *Greene, Susaye* / Cry to me: *Crawford, Carolyn* / Love still lives in my heart: *Originals* / Keep this thought in mind: *Bristol, Johnny* / You haven't seen my love: *Taylor, Bobby & The Vancouvers* / With you I'm born again: *Syreeta* / For old times sake: *Jacas, Jake* / Too great a price to pay: *Lavette, Bettye* / Just my imagination: *Cameron, G.C.* / Let's get it on: *McNeir, Ronnie* / OOO Baby baby: *Robinson, Claudette* / Wishing on a star: *Calvin, Billie* / Save me I'm all alone: *Dixon, Hank* / Your precious love: *Parks, Fino & Frances Nero* / We're incredible: *McNeir, Ronnie* / Written in stone: *Gaye, Frankie* / No more heartaches: *Bristol, Johnny*
CD Set ______ 3035990065
Motor City / Jan '96 / Carlton

LOVE SONGS OF THE 50'S (3CD Set)
My special agent: *Vaughan, Malcolm* / Tammy tell me true: *Murray, Ruby* / Stairway of love: *Holliday, Michael* / It's late: *Nelson, Rick* / May you always: *Regan, Joan* / I still believe: *Hilton, Ronnie* / Somebody loves me: *Shore, Dinah* / True love: *Crosby, Bing & Grace Kelly* / Only sixteen: *Douglas, Craig* / Holiday affair: *Day, Jill* / What do you want: *Faith, Adam* / Give a fool a chance: *Cogan, Alma* / Volare: *Martin, Dean* / If I give my heart to you: *Shelton, Anne* / Forgotten dreams: *Conway, Russ* / Now and forever: *Warren, Alma* / I may never pass this way again: *Lotis, Dennis* / Bewitched, bothered and bewildered: *Squires, Dorothy* / Skye boat song: *Holliday, Michael* / St Therese of the roses: *Vaughan, Malcolm* / No other love: *Hilton, Ronnie* / Do do do do it again: *Vaughan, Frankie* / Secret that's never been told: *Squires, Dorothy* / Folks who live on the hill: *Holliday, Michael* / Sugar bush: *Boswell, Eve* / More than ever: *Vaughan, Malcolm* / Garden of Eden: *James, Dick* / That's happiness: *Cogan, Alma* / Happy days and lonely nights: *Murray, Ruby* / When I fall in love: *Cole, Nat 'King'* / Song of the valley: *Squires, Dorothy* / I'm in love again: *Domino, Fats* / Arrivederci darling: *Shelton, Anne* / Sugartime: *Dale, Jim* / If you love me: *Boswell, Eve* / Lonely ballerina: *Lawrence, Lee* / To be worthy of you: *Squires, Dorothy* / Young and foolish: *Hilton, Ronnie* / From the time you say goodbye: *Miller, Gary* / How wonderful to know: *Carr, Pearl* / Never be anyone else but you: *Nelson, Rick* / Little things mean a lot: *Cogan, Alma* / Pickin' a chicken: *Boswell, Eve* / Did you ever see a dream walking: *Holliday, Michael* / Fever: *Lee, Peggy* / Be my girl: *Dale, Jim* / Wheel of fortune: *Starr, Kay* / For all we know: *Cole, Nat 'King'* / Around the world: *Fields, Gracie* / Heartbeat: *Murray, Ruby* / Our song: *Squires, Dorothy* / Blueberry hill: *Domino, Fats* / Till there was you: *Lee, Peggy* / Too young: *Cole, Nat 'King'* / Nevertheless (I'm in love with you): *Murray, Ruby* / Very thought of you: *Cole, Nat 'King'* / Gypsy in my soul: *Boswell, Eve* / My darling, my darling: *Miller, Gary* / Blue tango: *Cogan, Alma* / Wonder of you: *Hilton, Ronnie*
CD Set ______ CDTRBOX 180
Trio / Oct '95 / EMI

LOVE SONGS OF THE 60'S
God only knows: *Beach Boys* / Moon river: *Williams, Danny* / I'll never fall in love again: *Gentry, Bobbie* / I remember you: *Ifield, Frank* / To know you is to love you: *Peter & Gordon* / If you gotta go, go now: *Manfred Mann* / She wears my ring: *King, Solomon* / I could easily fall: *Richard, Cliff* / Step inside love: *Black, Cilla* / Softly as I leave you: *Monro, Matt* / When the girl in your arms (is the girl in your heart): *Richard, Cliff* / Here I go again: *Hollies* / Starry eyed: *Holiday, Michael* / Portrait of my love: *Monro, Matt* / Love's just a broken heart: *Black, Cilla* / All I have to do is dream: *Campbell, Glen & Bobbie Gentry* / Michelle: *David & Jonathan* / Up on the roof: *Lynch, Kenny* / As long as he needs me / There's a kind of hush: *Herman's Hermits*
CD ______ CDMFP 6041
Music For Pleasure / Jan '97 / EMI

LOVE SONGS OF THE 60'S (3CD Set)
I can't give you anything but love: *Cogan, Alma* / Now that I've found you: *Cogan, Alma* / Eight days a week: *Cogan, Alma* / Up on the roof: *Lynch, Kenny* / Ramblin' rose: *Cole, Nat 'King'* / Look through any window: *Hollies* / We're through: *Hollies* / Yes I will: *Hollies* / I'm alive: *Hollies* / Love letters: *Black, Cilla* / I've been wrong before: *Black, Cilla* / Lover's concerto: *Black, Cilla* / One little voice: *Black, Cilla* / Poor boy: *Black, Cilla* / Don't answer me: *Black, Cilla* / Got to get you into my life: *Bennett, Cliff & The Rebel Rousers* / Something wonderful: *Shapiro, Helen* / I wish I'd never loved you: *Shapiro, Helen* / Tell me what he said: *Shapiro, Helen* / Walk on by: *Shapiro, Helen* / Boy without a girl: *Hilton, Ronnie* / It's yourself: *Bassey, Shirley* / Don't take the lovers from the world: *Bassey, Shirley* / I (who have nothing): *Bassey, Shirley* / Message to Martha: *Faith, Adam* / Cheryl's goin' home: *Faith, Adam* / We're gonna change the world: *Monro, Matt* / Yesterday: *Monro, Matt* / Portrait of my love: *Monro, Matt* / Hello young lovers: *Monro, Matt* / True love ways: *Peter & Gordon* / Woman: *Peter & Gordon* / If we only have love: *Lynn, Vera* / Somewhere: *Proby, P.J.* / I'm coming home: *Proby, P.J.* / You've come back: *Proby, P.J.* / To make a big man cry: *Proby, P.J.* / Some enchanted evening: *Proby, P.J.* / You don't know: *Shapiro, Helen* / Let's pretend: *Lulu* / Without him: *Lulu* / Best of both worlds: *Lulu* / There must be a way: *Vaughan, Frankie* / There I go: *Carr, Vikki* / Michelle: *David & Jonathan* / Someone other than me: *Squires, Dorothy* / Say it with flowers: *Squires, Dorothy* / How deep is the ocean: *Squires, Dorothy* / Do you want to know a secret: *Kramer, Billy J. & The Dakotas* / Trains and boats and planes: *Kramer, Billy J. & The Dakotas* / Edelweiss: *Hill, Vince* / Look around: *Hill, Vince* / Moon river: *Williams, Danny* / Wonderful world of the young: *Williams, Danny* / More: *Williams, Danny* / Girl on a swing: *Gerry & The Pacemakers* / Fly me to the moon: *Cogan, Alma* / Here there and everywhere: *Kirby, Kathy* / Love is all: *Roberts, Malcolm*
CD Set ______ CDTRBOX 184
Trio / Oct '95 / EMI

LOVE SONGS OF THE 70'S
If I had words: *Fitzgerald, Scott & Yvonne Keeley* / Loving you: *Riperton, Minnie* / When you're in love with a beautiful woman: *Dr. Hook* / And I love you so: *McLean, Don* / I don't wanna lose you: *Kandidate* / Love hit me: *Nightingale, Maxine* / More than a woman: *Tavares* / Storm in a teacup: *Fortunes* / I can't tell the bottom from the top: *Hollies* / Talking in your sleep: *Gayle, Crystal* / You'll always be a friend: *Hot Chocolate* / Softly whispering I love you: *Congregation* / Honey come back: *Campbell, Glen* / Lay your love on me: *Racey* / What I've got in mind: *Spears, Billie Jo* / Let me be the one: *Shadows* / I honestly love you: *Newton-John, Olivia* / Summer (the first time): *Goldsboro, Bobby* / Oh babe what would you say: *Smith, Hurricane* / Lucille: *Rogers, Kenny*
CD ______ CDMFP 5894
Music For Pleasure / Jan '97 / EMI

LOVE SONGS OF THE 70'S (3CD Set)
Air that I breathe: *Hollies* / When you're in love with a beautiful woman: *Dr. Hook* / Journey: *Browne, Duncan* / Storm in a teacup: *Fortunes* / Both sides now: *Laine, Cleo* / Softly whispering I love you: *Congregation* / Talking in your sleep: *Gayle, Crystal* / Put your love in me: *Hot Chocolate* / Living nest door to Alice: *Smokie* / I will survive: *Spears, Billie Jo* / Dream baby: *Campbell, Glen* / Dancing in the city: *Marshall Hain* / Right back where we started from: *Nightingale, Maxine* / Everyday: *McLean, Don* / January: *Pilot* / Where do I begin: *Bassey, Shirley* / And you smiled: *Monro, Matt* / She believes in me: *Rogers, Kenny* / This will be: *Cole, Natalie* / I don't want to put a hold on you: *Flint, Bernie* / If you can't give me love: *Quatro, Suzi* / If we only have love: *Newton-John, Olivia* / You take my heart away: *Bassey, Shirley* / Little bit more: *Dr. Hook* / He was beautiful: *Williams, Iris* / Just a smile: *Pilot* / Honey come back: *Campbell, Glen* / Somebody loves you: *Gayle, Crystal* / Darlin': *Miller, Frankie* / Love you more: *Buzzcocks* / I don't know how to love him: *Trent, Jackie* / Amoureuse: *Newton-John, Olivia* / If you think you know how to love me: *Smokie* / And I love you so: *McLean, Don* / Don't it make my brown eyes blue: *Gayle, Crystal* / Winterwood: *McLean, Don* / Make the world a little younger: *Bassey, Shirley* / She's in love with you: *Quatro, Suzi* / My last night with you: *Arrows* / Hi ho silver lining: *Beck, Jeff* / Freedom come, freedom go: *Fortunes* / What am I supposed to do: *Williams, Iris* / I'll put you together again: *Hot Chocolate* / Sam: *Newton-John, Olivia* / Lovin' you: *Riperton, Minnie*
CD Set ______ CDTRBOX 188
Trio / Oct '95 / EMI

LOVE SONGS OF THE 80'S
Missing you: *Waite, John* / Crying: *McLean, Don* / Better love next time: *Dr. Hook* / Unchain my heart: *Cocker, Joe* / Round and round: *Graham, Jaki* / It started with a kiss: *Hot Chocolate* / Classic: *Gurvitz, Adrian* / Lady: *Rogers, Kenny* / Chequered love: *Wilde, Kim* / Love changes everything: *Climie Fisher* / Tonight I celebrate my love: *Bryson, Peabo & Roberta Flack* / Rock me tonight: *Jackson, Freddie* / Let's go all the way: *Sly Fox* / Save a prayer: *Duran Duran*
CD ______ CDMFP 5927
Music For Pleasure / Jan '97 / EMI

LOVE SONGS OF THE 80'S (3CD Set)
We close our eyes: *Go West* / Sharing the night together: *Dr. Hook* / Maybe (we should call it a day): *Dean, Hazell* / Too shy: *Kajagoogoo* / One man woman: *Easton, Sheena* / Love don't live here anymore: *Nail, Jimmy* / Respect: *Adeva* / I'll fly for you: *Spandau Ballet* / Lady: *Rogers, Kenny* / Passing strangers: *Ultravox* / Tears on the telephone: *Hot Chocolate* / Chequered love: *Wilde, Kim* / Let's go all the way: *Sly Fox* / Could it be I'm falling in love: *Grant, David & Jaki Graham* / Turn back the clock: *Johnny Hates Jazz* / California dreamin': *River City People* / love action: *Human League* / Searchin': *Dean, Hazell* / Years from now: *Dr. Hook* / Walking on sunshine: *Katrina & The Waves* / It started with a kiss: *Hot Chocolate* / Just another broken heart: *Easton, Sheena* / When he shines: *Easton, Sheena* / Castles in the air: *McLean, Don* / Have you ever been in love: *Sayer, Leo* / If I only could: *Youngblood, Sydney* / Set me free: *Graham, Jaki* / Goodbye girl: *Go West* / When will I see you again: *Brother Beyond* / Rise to the occasion: *Climie Fisher* / Love changes everything: *Climie Fisher* / View from a bridge: *Wilde, Kim* / That certain smile: *Ultravox* / We've got tonight: *Rogers, Kenny* / Harder I try: *Brother Beyond* / Who's leaving who: *Dean, Hazell* / Kayleigh: *Marillion* / Summertime: *Fun Boy Three* / Love will find a way: *Grant, David* / Crying: *McLean, Don* / Until you come back to me: *Sayer, Leo* / Shattered dreams: *Johnny Hates Jazz* / Missing you: *Waite, John* / Round and round: *Graham, Jaki* / Unchain my heart: *Cocker, Joe*
CD Set ______ CDTRBOX 192
Trio / Oct '95 / EMI

LOVE SONGS OF VIDYAPATI (Traditional Indian Songs)
CD ______ C 580063CD
Ocora / Apr '95 / ADA / Harmonia Mundi

LOVE SONGS WITH SOUL
You bring out the best in me: *Armstrong, Vanessa* / Tide is turning: *Jackson, Millie* / Woman: *Jones, Glenn* / At this moment: *Jones, Glenn* / More than friends: *Butler, Jonathan* / Stay with me tonight: *Smith, Richard Jon* / Penny lover: *Kissoon, Katie* / When only a friend will do: *Davis, Mike* / An imitation of love: *Jackson, Millie* / Move closer: *Jones, Tom* / Living in the limelight: *Jones, Glenn* / In the night: *Smith, Richard Jon*
CD ______ EMPRCD 551
Emporio / Nov '94 / Disc

LOVE SUPREME, A
CD ______ DINCD 19
Dino / Jun '91 / Pinnacle

LOVE THEMES OF THE PAN PIPES (18 Greatest Hits)
Tears in Heaven / Another day in paradise / Lady in red / Three times a lady / With you I'm born again / Careless whisper / Just the way you are / I don't know much / Fool (If you think it's over) / Wind beneath my wings / Tonight I celebrate my love / Power of love / Everything I do (I do it for you) / If you don't know me by now / Wonderful tonight / I'm not in love / Didn't we almost have it all / Against all odds
CD ______ PLATCD 156
Platinum / Mar '96 / Prism

LOVE TO LOVE YOU
Daniel: *John, Elton* / Baby makes her blue jeans talk: *Dr. Hook* / Day by day: *Shakatak* / Fresh: *Kool & The Gang* / Nothing's gonna change my love for you: *Medeiros, Glenn* / Forever and ever: *Roussos, Demis* / Love me: *Elliman, Yvonne* / Reason to believe: *Stewart, Rod* / Soul and inspiration: *Walker Brothers* / I'm not in love: *10cc* / Sun ain't gonna shine anymore: *Walker Brothers* / Let's put it all together: *Stylistics* / Don't stop the music: *Yarbrough & Peoples* / Tahiti: *Essex, David*
CD ______ 5501442
Spectrum / Jan '94 / PolyGram

LOVER'S DELIGHT
Don't let me be lonely: *Kofi* / I'll never fall in love: *Klearview Harmonix* / Children of the night: *Cross, Sandra* / Give you love: *Jones, Vivian* / I'm the one who loves you: *Hartley, Trevor* / Can't hold on: *McLean, John* / Even though you're gone: *Kemi* / Hottest shot: *Kingpin* / Last night: *Tajah, Paulette* / Love in your heart: *Shaloma*
CD ______ ARICD 090
Ariwa Sounds / Oct '93 / Jet Star / SRD

LOVERS FASHION VOL.1
CD ______ FADCD 033
Fashion / Mar '96 / Jet Star / SRD

LOVERS FASHION VOL.2
CD ______ FADCD 034
Fashion / Oct '96 / Jet Star / SRD

LOVERS FOR LOVERS VOL.1
CD ______ WBRCD 901
Business / Jan '91 / Jet Star

LOVERS FOR LOVERS VOL.10
I miss you: *Heptones* / Just my imagination: *Mighty Diamonds* / Blackbirds singing: *Paragons* / Chuck E's in love: *Walker, Paulette* / Make up to break up: *Heptones* / Dance the reggae: *Harriott, Derrick* / Paradise: *Gayle, Erica* / Last chance: *Pat Kelly* / Don't draw the line: *Gayle, Erica* / Golden touch / All that glitters
CD ______ WBRCD 910
Business / Dec '95 / Jet Star

LOVERS FOR LOVERS VOL.2
CD ______ WBRCD 902
Business / Jan '91 / Jet Star

LOVERS FOR LOVERS VOL.3
CD ______ WBRCD 903
Business / Jan '91 / Jet Star

LOVERS FOR LOVERS VOL.4
CD ______ WBRCD 904
Business / Jan '92 / Jet Star

LOVERS FOR LOVERS VOL.5
CD ______ WBRCD 905
Business / Jan '92 / Jet Star

LOVERS FOR LOVERS VOL.5 & 6
CD ______ WBRCD 905/6
Business / Oct '95 / Jet Star

LOVERS FOR LOVERS VOL.6
CD ______ WBRCD 906
Business / Aug '92 / Jet Star

LOVERS FOR LOVERS VOL.7
CD ______ WBRCD 907
Business / Jan '93 / Jet Star

LOVERS FOR LOVERS VOL.8
CD ______ WBRCD 908
Business / Dec '93 / Jet Star

LOVERS FOR LOVERS VOL.9
CD ______ WBRCD 909
Business / Dec '94 / Jet Star

LOVERS FOREVER
CD ______ VPCD 2051
VP / Jul '96 / Greensleeves / Jet Star / Total/BMG

LOVERS FOREVER VOL.3
CD ______ JFCD 0004
Joe Frazier / Jun '94 / Jet Star

LOVERS LEAP
CD _______ ARICD 119
Ariwa Sounds / Oct '96 / Jet Star / SRD

LOVERS MOODS VOL.2
CD _______ VPCD 1447
VP / Nov '95 / Greensleeves / Jet Star / Total/BMG

LOVERS MOODS VOL.3
CD _______ VPCD 1458
VP / Mar '96 / Greensleeves / Jet Star / Total/BMG

LOVERS ROCK SERIOUS SELECTIONS VOL.1
Key to the world: *Thomas, Ruddy* / Baby my love: *Callender, Fil* / After tonight: *Matumbi* / Natty dread a weh she want: *Andy, Horace & Tapper* / Wide awake in dreams: *Biggs, Barry* / Let me be your angel: *Morgan, Portia* / Ting a ling: *Tamlins* / Betcha by Golly Wow: *Dunkley, Errol* / Paradise: *Adebambo, Jean* / Lady of magic: *Maloney, Bunny* / Walk on by: *Motion* / Caught you in a lie: *Marks, Louisa*
CD _______ CDREG 1
Rewind Selecta / Feb '95 / Grapevine/ PolyGram

LOVERS ROCK SERIOUS SELECTIONS VOL.2
CD _______ CDREG 4
Rewind Selecta / Jan '96 / Grapevine/ PolyGram

LOVERS ROCK SERIOUS SELECTIONS VOL.3
CD _______ CDREG 7
Rewind Selecta / Mar '97 / Grapevine/ PolyGram

LOVE'S OLD SWEET SONG
Myself when young: *Allin, Norman* / Homing: *D'Alvarez, Marguerite* / Deep river: *Anderson, Marian* / Fairytales of Ireland: *Austral, Florence* / Ciribiribin: *Bori, Lucrezia* / She wandered down the mountainside: *Buckman, Rosina* / Fairy went a-marketing: *Butt, Clara* / For you alone: *Caruso, Enrico* / Blind ploughman: *Chaliapin, Feodor* / Ich liebe dich, my dear: *Crabbe, Armand* / Song of songs: *Crooks, Richard* / Green hills o' Somerset: *Dawson, Peter* / Love's old sweet song: *Galli-Curci, Amelita* / I love you truly: *Giannini, Dusolina* / World is waiting for the sunrise: *Hackett, Charles* / Danny boy: *Labette, Dora* / Bird songs at Eventide: *McCormack, John* / By the waters of Minnetonka: *Melba, Nellie* / By the bend of the river: *Moore, Grace* / Last rose of Summer: *Patti, Adelina* / Love sends a little gift of roses: *Piccaver, Alfred* / Perfect day: *Ponsella, Rosa* / Kashmiri song: *Tauber, Richard* / I know of two bright eyes: *Widdop, Walter* / Leanin': *Williams, Harold*
CD _______ CDAJA 5130
Living Era / May '94 / Select

LOVIN' YOU
CD _______ MACCD 129
Autograph / Aug '96 / BMG

LOVING TIME, THE
Land of love: *Brazil, Noel* / Farewell to the bad times: *Brazil, Noel* / To Ramona: *Lohan, Sinead* / You're in my love: *Lohan, Sinead* / Deep in your heart: *Brady, Paul* / Helpless heart: *Brady, Paul* / All the lies that you told me: *Black, Frances* / Send him a letter: *Black, Frances* / Captured: *Kennedy, Brian* / Forgiveness: *Kennedy, Brian* / Summer sent you: *Black, Mary* / Loving time: *Black, Mary* / Reach out (I'll be there): *Goss, Kieran* / Wonderful thing: *Dowdall, Leslie*
CD _______ TORCD 085
Dara / Jun '97 / ADA / CM / Direct / Else / Grapevine/PolyGram
CD _______ BLX 10034CD
Blix Street / May '97 / ADA

LOVING YOU (4CD Set)
CD Set _______ MBSCD 428
Castle / Nov '93 / BMG

LOVING YOU
Do you really want to hurt me: *Culture Club* / Home on Monday: *Little River Band* / Baker street: *Rafferty, Gerry* / When I need you: *Sayer, Leo* / Spanish stroll: *Mink Deville* / On the border: *Stewart, Al* / True: *Spandau Ballet* / Air that I breathe: *Hollies* / Winter in America: *Ashdown, Doug* / Where do you go to my lovely: *Sarstedt, Peter* / Love hurts: *Nazareth* / Kids in America: *Wilde, Kim* / Love is forever: *Ocean, Billy* / Unforgettable: *Rawls, Lou*
CD _______ DC 878542
Disky / Aug '97 / Disky / THE

LOW BLOWS (An Anthology Of Chicago Harmonica Blues)
CD _______ R 2610
Rooster / Feb '97 / Direct

LUCKY HOUSE (2CD Set)
CD Set _______ SFT 200232
Shift / Oct '96 / ZYX

LUO ROOTS
Jadiyana: *Kapere Jazz Band* / Nath oindo: *Kapere Jazz Band* / Amagy lando: *Kapere Jazz Band* / Tuni nyamwalo: *Kapere Jazz Band* / Samwel adinda: *Kapere Jazz Band* / Jacob Omolo: *Okoth, Ogwang Lelo* / Lando nyajomere: *Kapere Jazz Band* / Amisijamoko: *Kapere Jazz Band* / John Wangu: *Okoth, Ogwang Lelo* / Lynette: *Onono, Paddy J*
CD _______ CDORBD 061
Globestyle / Jun '90 / Pinnacle

LUTZ R MASTERHAYER
CD _______ SPCD 111287
Sub Pop / Aug '93 / Cargo / Greyhound / Shellshock/Disc

LYRICS PUISSANCE VOL.4
CD _______ 503822
Declic / Apr '95 / Jet Star

LYTIC COCKTAIL
CD _______ COMP 025CD
Compost / Jan '97 / Plastic Head / SRD / Timewarp

M8 - THE ANTHEMS
CD _______ MR 021CD
Massive Respect / May '96 / Alphamagic / Mo's Music Machine

M8 DJ TECHNOTRANCE
Natural born killers: *DJ Technotrance* / Now is the time: *Brown, Scott* / Pump that body: *Scientists* / There goes the boom: *Eruption* / Disco hardcore: *DJ Seduction* / Chromedome: *Active Force* / Forbidden territory: *Active Force* / Gazometer: *Brown, Scott* / Oh yeah: *Ultimate Elation* / Shaftman: *Shaftman* / 123: *Digital Nation* / On ya knees: *Eytronix* / Can can party: *Sandman* / Hardcore science: *Q-Tex* / Rave dog: *Technoterrier* / Hardcore euphoria: *Sub Source* / Fuck the DEA: *DJ Technotrance* / Don't you want my lovin': *DJ Demand* / Strobelight: *Chill FM* / Kiss my ass seduction: *DJ Technotrance* / Splosh: *Water Pistol* / Do what you like: *Brown, Scott*
CD _______ CDTOT 35
Jumpin' & Pumpin' / Jan '96 / 3mv/Sony / Mo's Music Machine

M8 EUROPEAN TECHNO HEAVEN
Only if I had one more: *Dyewitness* / Ultimate sextrack: *Dyewitness* / Check your head: *Ultrasonic* / Power people II: *Rhythmic State Crew* / Set you free: *N-Trance* / Feel free: *Dougal & Vibes* / Sweet in pocket: *Justin Time* / Anthem: *N-Joi* / I'm the fuck you man: *Wedlock* / Sound of Rotterdam: *Human Resource* / Don't fuck with a redneck: *Juggernaut* / Cocaine: *Neuro-Tek* / Strobelight: *Chill FM* / Believe: *Q-Tex*
CD _______ CDTOT 29
Jumpin' & Pumpin' / May '95 / 3mv/Sony / Mo's Music Machine

M8 EUROPEAN TECHNO HEAVEN
Luv U more: *Elstak, Paul* / Back in the UK: *Scooter* / I wanna be a hippy: *Technohead* / Now is the time: *Brown, Scott* / Future: *Dyewitness* / Fight for your rights: *Phonki* / On and beyond: *Chill FM* / Party time: *Dougal & Eruption* / XTC love: *Feranzano, Berto* / Go get busy: *DJ Weirdo & DJ Sim* / Strict stomp: *Strictly Verbal*
CD _______ CDTOT 39
Jumpin' & Pumpin' / Apr '96 / 3mv/Sony / Mo's Music Machine

MACARENA (Swingin' Summer Instrumentals)
Macarena / Lambada / Una paloma blanca / Mexico / La bamba / Tijuana taxi / Sun of Jamaica / Girl from Ipanema / Ole guapa / Guantanamera / El condor pasa / Ciclito lindo / Un canto a galicia / Jamaica farewell / Volare / Spanish flea / Ticket to the tropics
CD _______ DGR 1112
DGR / Sep '96 / Target/BMG

MACEDONIAN DANCES
CD _______ PS 65076
PlayaSound / Jul '91 / ADA / Harmonia Mundi

MACHINE CODES COMPILATION 1993-1997
CD _______ CODEFCD
Machine Codes / Sep '97 / 3mv/Pinnacle / Kudos / SRD

MACHINE HEADS
CD _______ HEAD 6
Machinehead / Apr '97 / Cargo

MACHINO WEIRDER
CD _______ DUKE 017CD
Hydrogen Dukebox / Jun '95 / 3mv/Vital / Kudos / Prime

MACRO DUB INFECTION VOL.1 (2CD Set)
Struggle of life: *Disciples* / Double edge: *Spring Heel Jack* / Sergio Mendez part 1: *2 Bad Card* / Astral altar dub: *Automaton* / Broadway boogie woogie: *Bedouin Ascent* / Wadada: *Rootsman* / Hills are alive: *Coil* / Half cut: *Omni Trio* / If you miss: *Laika* / Crush your enemies: *New Kingdom* / Gorirr: *Tortoise* / Operation mind control: *Skull Vs Ice* / Morocco: *Alzir, Bud* / Beta, seekers of smooth things: *Plutobeat* / Paranormal in four forms: *4 Hero* / This is how it feels: *Golden Palominos* / Ragga doll: *Mad Professor* / Phora ride: *Wagon Christ* / End: *Scorn* / Ambient pumpkin: *Tricky* / Iration Steppas vs Dennis Rootical: *Iration Steppas* / Come forward: *Bandulu* / Nothingness: *Earthling*
CD Set _______ AMBT 7
Virgin / May '95 / EMI

MACRO DUB INFECTION VOL.2 (2CD Set)
M6: *Maurizio* / Sacred system: *Laswell, Bill* / Beware soul snatchers: *Rome* / Altesse: *Chatham, Rhys & Martin Wheeler* / Libel: *Pin* / Liquid boy: *Him* / A presente: *Zulutronic* / Miles to go: *Magnet* / Keen as mustard: *Plug* / Sehn sud: *Mouse On Mars* / Esoteric red: *Tao* / When you reach your peak: *Empire, Alec* / Flump: *Skull* / Shades of nature: *Ear Drum* / Nautical dub: *Porter Ricks* / Strong heart: *Disciples & Rootsman* / El Qadim: *Gedulah & Terminal Cheesecake* / Revelation of wrath: *Andre Gurov Units* / Brother no blood: *Prince Paul* / Handbag dub: *Jammin' Unit* / Rat day: *Bio Muse* / Shot in the head: *Third Eye Foundation* / Sub version: *Spectre* / Inbred version: *Ice & Palace*
CD Set _______ AMBT 14
Virgin / Oct '96 / EMI

MAD ABOUT THE BOY (Songs From The Best Known TV Commercials)
CD _______ MPV 5521
Movieplay / Jun '92 / Target/BMG

MAD ABOUT THE BOY
CD _______ CDKOPY 105
Klone / Oct '96 / 3mv/Sony / Pinnacle

MAD ABOUT THE GIRLS
Mad about the boy: *Washington, Dinah* / All through the night: *Lauper, Cyndi* / Dreams: *Gabrielle* / I ain't movin': *Des'ree* / Our love is here to stay: *Fitzgerald, Ella* / Shadow of your smile: *Gilberto, Astrud* / Bewitched, bothered and bewildered: *Fygi, Laura* / Fever: *Lee, Peggy* / Don't let me be misunderstood: *Simone, Nina* / Gone with the wind: *Page, Patti* / Make yourself comfortable: *Vaughan, Sarah* / Some of your lovin': *Springfield, Dusty* / Use me: *Goodman, Gabrielle* / Bad day: *Carmel* / Lover man: *Holiday, Billie* / 'Round midnight: *Wilson, Cassandra* / I should care: *London, Julie* / Move over darling: *Day, Doris* / Crazy: *Cline, Patsy* / Perfect year: *Carroll, Dina*
CD _______ 5255552
PolyGram TV / Jun '95 / PolyGram

MAD DOG
CD _______ NWSCD 5
New Sound / Apr '93 / Jet Star

MAD LOVE
Slowly slowly: *Magnapop* / Scratch: *7 Year Bitch* / Here come my girl: *Throneberry* / Mokingbirds: *Grant Lee Buffalo* / Glazed: *Rocket From The Crypt* / Fallout: *Florescien* / Mona Lisa fallout: *Head Candy* / Ultra anxiety: *Madder Rose* / Icy blue: *7 Year Bitch* / As long as you hold me: *MacColl, Kirsty*
CD _______ DEDCD 022
Dedicated / Dec '95 / BMG / Vital

MADAGASIKARA VOL.1
Afindrafindraq: *Rakotoarimanana, Rakotofra & Martin* / Feam baliha: *Tombo, Daniel & Marceline Vaviroa* / Dia mahaory: *Tombo, Daniel & Marceline Vaviroa* / Bonne annee amin ny tanana: *Norbert, Georges & L. Honore Rosa* / Mamakivaky alankiminina: *Norbert, Georges & L. Honore Rosa* / Fambelo eto madagasikara: *Rabenalvo Group* / Nilentika: *Andriamamonjy, David* / Tazana kely: *Andriamamonjy, David* / Mahatsiarotsiaro fanina aeo zeho: *Volambita, Tsimialona* / Nametaa imainto: *Volambita, Tsimialona* / King's song: *Rakotoarimanana, Martin* / Viavy rosy: *Randriamainty, Emmanuel* / Kilalao: *Ze Ze et groupe son*
CD _______ CDORBD 012
Globestyle / Oct '90 / Pinnacle

MADAGASIKARA VOL.2
Raha mania any / Ento rora / Madirovalo / Tsapika 2000 / Totoy tsara / Sarotra / Voromby / Ny any / Malaza avaratna / Aza mba manary toky
CD _______ CDORBD 013
Globestyle / Nov '90 / Pinnacle

MADCHESTER
CD _______ MADCCD 1
Beechwood / Oct '95 / Beechwood/BMG / Pinnacle

MADE ON EARTH (2CD Set)
CD Set _______ BR 026CD
Blue Room Released / Mar '97 / Essential/ BMG / SRD

MADE TO MEASURE RESUME...
CD _______ MTM 16
Made To Measure / Mar '88 / New Note/ Pinnacle

MADE TO MEASURE VOL.1
Pieces for nothing / A la recherche: *Lew, Benjamin* / Un chien: *Maboul, Aksak* / Scratch holiday: *Maboul, Aksak* / Verdun: *Tuxedo Moon*
CD _______ MTM 1CD
Made To Measure / '88 / New Note/ Pinnacle

MADHOUSE ACTION PACK
CD _______ MHCD 001
Penthouse / Jun '96 / Jet Star

MADHOUSE CREW LIVE
CD _______ 793012
Jammy's / Jan '94 / Jet Star

MADNESS INVASION VOL.1
CD _______ 842624
EVA / Jun '94 / ADA / Direct

MAESTROS DE LA GUITARRA FLAMENCA VOL.1
CD _______ BM 517
Blue Moon / Jan '97 / Cadillac / Discovery / Greensleeves / Jazz Music / Jet Star / TKO Magnum

MAESTROS DE LA GUITARRA FLAMENCA VOL.2
CD _______ BM 518
Blue Moon / Jan '97 / Cadillac / Discovery / Greensleeves / Jazz Music / Jet Star / TKO Magnum

MAESTROS DEL TANGO ARGENTINO (2CD Set)
CD Set _______ BMT 001
Blue Moon / Jan '97 / Cadillac / Discovery / Greensleeves / Jazz Music / Jet Star / TKO Magnum

MAFIA & FLUXY PRESENT...
Money first (Mystery mix): *Mega Banton* / World a girls: *Chaka Demus & Pliers* / Looking girl: *Ricky General* / Nah let go: *Junior Demus* / Take a gal man: *Johnny P* / Armed and dangerous (Remix): *Cutty Ranks* / Where did you get your looks from: *Sweetie Irie & Debbie G* / Gun legalize: *Dirtsman* / Hugging and kissing: *Judas* / Feelings: *Jack Radics* / Money first: *Mega Banton* / Armed and dangerous: *Cutty Ranks*
CD _______ 74321209972
RCA / Oct '94 / BMG

MAGIC AND MYSTERY (Music From Scotland & Ireland)
Frideray: *Pincock, Dougie & Alan Reid* / Fornethy house: *Heritage* / Lady Iveagh: *Heymann, Ann* / Togail curs air Leodhas: *Battlefield Band* / Air for Jakes: *McCusker, John* / An cailin rua: *McDermott, Josie* / Taimse in', chodladh: *Dykehead Caledonia Pipe Band* / Braidwood waits: *Kinnaird, Alison* / Peace and plenty: *Battlefield Band* / Miss Hamilton: *McNeill, Brian* / She's late but she's timely: *Battlefield Band* / Hollin green hollin/Thomas the rhymer/Young Benjie/ Tam Lin: *Battlefield Band* / Planxty sudley: *Maire Ni Chathasaigh* / Mrs. Jamieson's favourite: *Mac-Talla* / Craigs of Ailsa/Staffa's shore: *Kinnaird, Alison* / A stor mo chroi: *Rigler, Eric* / Brigid's waltz: *McCusker, John*
CD _______ COMD 2062
Temple / Feb '97 / ADA / CM / Direct / Duncans / Highlander

MAGIC CHRISTMAS
CD _______ 15148
Laserlight / Nov '95 / Target/BMG

MAGIC FLY (Synthesizer Hits)
Star Wars suite / Magic fly / Moonraker / St. Elmo's Fire / Rambo / First Blood part II / Oxygene / Aurora / Old and wise / Merry Christmas Mr. Lawrence / Live and let die / Ode to Amadeus / Funky Town / Don't you want me / Don't go / Too shy / Model / Friends of Mr. Cairo / Man with the golden gun / Godfather theme / Going home
CD _______ MU 5005
Musketeer / Oct '92 / Disc

MAGIC GROOVE RIDERS VOL.1 (21 House Club Traxx Inside/2CD Set)
Psychic bounty killers: *Van Helden, Armand & DJ Sneak* / Funky mustique: *Sunday Afternoon* / JW's unreleased tracks: *JW* / Sweet music: *Trancelate* / Don't take your love: *Diesal Disco Jointz* / Ruhr cowboy: *Criss Source* / Leaving: *Digital Disco* / Take control: *Fix To Fax* / You got me: *DJ Eclipse* / Disco town: *Stressman* / Dialogue: *3 Dubs In A Sleeve* / Discodamned nation: *Frank Popp* / U got me: *Belmonthe* / Symphonic days: *Powerplant Revisited* / Nite trax vol.1: *Ultrasonix* / Love hurts: *Paris Red* / Phunky Pheelings: *La Foule* / Dancin: *Mateo & Matos* / Old skool: *DJ Tonka* / Feel that groove: *Farley & Muscle*
CD Set _______ 560182
Nova Tekk / Aug '97 / Pinnacle

MAGIC MOMENTS
CD _______ CWNCD 2005
Javelin / Jun '95 / Henry Hadaway / THE

MAGIC OF ANDREW LLOYD WEBBER, THE
Journey of a lifetime: *Willetts, Dave* / Last man in my life: *Hendley, Fiona* / Rolling stock: *Jones, Paul* / Another suitcase in another hall: *Lawrence, Stephanie* / Close every door: *Willetts, Dave* / Everything's alright: *Hendley, Fiona* / Gethsemane: *Willetts, Dave* / Introduction, theme and variations 1 - 4: *Price, Jonathan* / Old deuteronmoy: *Jones, Paul* / High flying adored: *Willetts, Dave* / Don't cry for me Argentina: *Hendley, Fiona* / First man you remember: *Lawrence, Stephanie & Dave Willetts*
CD _______ PWKS 4110
Carlton / Jul '92 / Carlton

MAGIC OF BRASS, THE
Macarthur park / Always on my mind / Don't leave me this way / Bohemian rhapsody / Tritsch tratsch polka / You can call me Al / Carnival for brass / You've lost that lovin' feelin' / Get back / All I ask of you / Shepherd's song / Hello / Pie jesu / Puttin' on the ritz
CD ______ **MUCD 9003**
Musketeer / Apr '95 / Disc

MAGIC OF DETROIT VOL.1, THE
Find a quiet place and be lonely: *Davis, Melvin* / Dont't do nothing I wouldn't do: *Van Dyke, Connie* / Jack the playboy: *Rogers, Lee* / My love looks good on you: *Fabulous Peps* / You got the lovin' touch: *Lamp, Buddy* / His majesty my love: *Edwards, Dee* / They loved to be loved: *Heart, Don* / I wanna tell my baby: *Precisions* / Walk on by: *Rogers, Lee* / Hide & seek: *Dupree, Lillian* / I will give you love: *Dupree, Lillian* / Me & my baby: *Magic Tones* / Detroit, michigan: *Love, Ronnie* / Same thing that makes you laugh: *Rogers, Lee* / Hurt by love: *Hargreaves, Silky* / I'm gonna try to get over: *Hentley, Chuck* / Next best thing: *Lamp, Buddy* / Love and war: *Rogers, Lee* / Too careless with love: *Edwards, Dee* / Too many irons in the fire: *Black, Cody* / With these eyes: *Fabulous Peps* / You're the cream of the crop: *Rogers, Lee* / Together we shall overcome: *Magic Tones* / Cracked up over you: *Rogers, Lee* / Quittin' time': *International Kansas City Playboys*
CD ______ **GSCD 093**
Goldmine / Nov '96 / Vital

MAGIC OF IRELAND
Riverdance / White, orange and green / Scarce O'Tatties / Feilims little boat Phelims / Ballinasloe / Fiddler's green / Three young ladies drinking whisky before breakfast / Port Laige / If you're Irish / Arthur McBride / Morrison merrily kissed the quaker / Ramblin' Irishman / Ministrel boy / Rising of the moon / Little fairy big fairy / Beggarman / Roscabury / Nightingale / Sport of the chase / Whiskey in the jar
CD ______ **CD 6077**
Music / Jun '97 / Target/BMG

MAGIC OF IRELAND, THE (4CD Set)
CD Set ______ **EMPRBX 007**
Emporio / Oct '95 / Disc

MAGIC OF PANPIPES
Here comes the sun / Maybe / Light my fire / Forse / When you're in love with a beautiful woman / Dim all the lights / On the radio / Feelings / Sailing / Let it be / Dolanne's melody / Don't cry for me Argentina / Un jour d'ete / Autumn dream / Klavier konzert No.1 / Schusscher / Sinfonie / Barcarolle / Largo from the new world symphony / Sleepwalk / Lonely shepherd
CD ______ **QED 020**
Tring / Nov '96 / Tring

MAGIC OF THE INDIAN FLUTE VOL.1
CD ______ **EUCD 1090**
ARC / '89 / ADA / ARC Music

MAGIC OF THE INDIAN FLUTE VOL.2, THE
CD ______ **EUCD 1129**
ARC / '91 / ADA / ARC Music

MAGIC SOUND OF THE PAN PIPES VOL.1, THE
El condor pasa / Do that to me one more time / Long and winding road / For your eyes only / Ebony and ivory / If you leave me now / Lady / Unchained melody / Endless love / You light up my life / We've got tonight / Something / Arthur's theme / Feelings
CD ______ **EMPRCD 537**
Emporio / Nov '96 / Disc

MAGIC SOUND OF THE PAN PIPES VOL.2, THE
Dolanne's melodie / Fernando / Heartbreaker / Strawberry fields forever / Sara / Moonlight shadow / Up where we belong / All time high / Don't cry for me Argentina / Woman in love / Sailing / Yesterday / I have a dream / Bridge over troubled water
CD ______ **EMPRCD 538**
Emporio / Nov '96 / Disc

MAGIC SOUND OF THE PAN PIPES, THE
CD ______ **EMPRCD 511**
Emporio / Apr '94 / Disc

MAGIC SOUND OF THE PAN PIPES, THE (4CD Set)
CD Set ______ **EMPRBX 005**
Emporio / Sep '94 / Disc

MAGIC SOUNDS OF THE PIPES, THE
CD ______ **CDMFP 5615**
EMI Gold / Feb '97 / EMI

MAGIC WONDERLAND VOL.1
CD ______ **PLUMPCD 100**
Plumphouse / Feb '97 / Prime

MAGIC WURLITZER VOL.1, THE
CD ______ **PLATCD 31**
Platinum / Apr '92 / Prism

MAGIC WURLITZER VOL.2, THE
CD ______ **PLATCD 34**
Platinum / Jul '92 / Prism

MAGICAL 50'S, THE (3CD Set)
Fanfar boogie: *Winstone, Eric & His Orchestra* / Rhythm and blues: *Winstone, Eric & His Orchestra* / Anticipation: *Winstone, Eric & His Orchestra* / Cobblers song: *Winstone, Eric & His Orchestra* / Deep sleep: *Winstone, Eric & His Orchestra* / Frustration: *Winstone, Eric & His Orchestra* / Slow train blues: *Winstone, Eric & His Orchestra* / Cat walk: *Winstone, Eric & His Orchestra* / Opus one: *Winstone, Eric & His Orchestra* / Heartbreak: *Winstone, Eric & His Orchestra* / Robber's march: *Winstone, Eric & His Orchestra* / I don't care: *Winstone, Eric & His Orchestra* / Angelina: *Winstone, Eric & His Orchestra* / At the woodchoppers: *Winstone, Eric & His Orchestra* / Drum crazy: *Johnson, Laurie Orchestra* / Heatwave: *Johnson, Laurie Orchestra* / In a persian market: *Johnson, Laurie Orchestra* / Fascinating rhythm: *Johnson, Laurie Orchestra* / Hallelujah: *Johnson, Laurie Orchestra* / Jamboree: *Johnson, Laurie Orchestra* / It might as well be spring: *Johnson, Laurie Orchestra* / Majorca: *Johnson, Laurie Orchestra* / Stick and twist: *Johnson, Laurie Orchestra* / Things we did last summer: *Johnson, Laurie Orchestra* / Next train out of town: *Osbourne, Tony* / Treasure of love: *Osbourne, Tony* / Wait for me: *Ryan, Marion* / Bell bottom blues: *Radio Revellers* / No not much: *Shepherd, Pauline* / Answer me: *Goff, Reggie* / Allen town jail: *Roza, Lita* / Maybe you'll be there: *Roza, Lita* / Once in a while: *Roza, Lita* / Sixteen tons: *Hockridge, Edmund* / Tomorrow: *Brandon, Johnny* / Bidge of sighs: *Goff, Reggie* / So many times I cried over you: *Goff, Reggie* / Arrivederci darling: *Radio Revellers* / That's how a love song is born: *Clark, Petula* / Moon above Malaya: *Goff, Reggie* / Mariandl: *Young, Jimmy & Petula Clark* / Hot diggity: *Ryan, Marion* / Rags to riches: *Goff, Reggie* / Who are we: *Miller, Betty* / Memories are made of this: *Clark, Petula* / Young and foolish: *Hockridge, Edmund* / Too young: *Young, Jimmy* / Undecided: *Roy, Harry* / I'll follow you: *Preager, Lou & His Orchestra* / Oranges and lemons: *Delaney, Eric & His Band* / Three bears: *Ellington, Ray Quartet* / Baker's boogie: *Baker, Kenny Orchestra* / Mountain greenery: *Roy, Harry & His Orchestra* / Stranger than fiction: *Geraldo & His Orchestra* / Over wyoming: *Gibbons, Carroll* / Please Mr. Sun: *Roy, Harry* / Rocking the tymps: *Delaney, Eric & His Band* / Francesca: *Gibbons, Carroll* / Egon: *Preager, Lou & His Band* / That's my girl: *Ellington, Ray* / Do do do do it again: *Lipton, Sydney* / Our love is here to stay: *Baker, Kenny Orchestra* / Cross hands boogie: *Roy, Harry* / Pianno rag: *Preager, Lou & His Orchestra* / Teddy bears picnic: *Ellington, Ray Quartet* / I'm beginning to see the light: *Delaney, Eric & His Band* / Flirtation waltz: *Roy, Harry & His Band*
CD Set ______ **MAGPIE 5**
See For Miles/C5 / Sep '95 / Pinnacle

MAGICAL SOUND OF THE PAN PIPES VOL.4
Un-break my heart / In the air tonight / Man I love / Kiss from a rose / Unforgettable / Careless whisper / Take a look at me now / Your song / Lady in red / Words / Everything I do / Theme from Harry's game / True / Shadow of your smile / On your shore / Tears in heaven / Love changes everything / All by myself
CD ______ **306452**
Hallmark / May '97 / Carlton

MAGICAL SOUND OF THE PANPIPES VOL.3, THE
Flight of the condor / Do you know where you're going to / Flame trees of Thika / Ballerina girl / No more the fool / Bluebird / Morning has broken / Paradise bird / Sunny / If you leave me now / Autumn breeze / Don't cry for me Argentina / Orinoco flow / Ma baker / Daniel / Mull of kintyre / Once upon a time in the west / El condor pasa
CD ______ **305462**
Hallmark / Oct '96 / Carlton

MAGICAL SOUND OF THE WURLITZER ORGAN, THE
Beyond the blue horizon: *Ogden, Nigel* / Sweet and lovely: *Ogden, Nigel* / It's a raggy waltz: *Ogden, Nigel* / In a clock store: *Ogden, Nigel* / Whistler and his dog: *Ogden, Nigel* / Quickstep medley: *Martin, Nicholas* / Tango medley: *Martin, Nicholas* / Rhumba medley: *Martin, Nicholas* / El relicario: *Gledhill, Simon* / These foolish things: *Gledhill, Simon* / My silent love: *Gledhill, Simon* / Veradero: *Gledhill, Simon* / Autumn crocus: *Gledhill, Simon* / Calling all workers: *Sharp, Brian* / Roses of Picardy: *Sharp, Brian* / Coronation Scot: *Sharp, Brian* / In the news: *Sharp, Brian* / I'd give you the world: *Sharp, Brian* / Wurlitzer march: *Loxam, Arnold* / Grasshoppers dance: *Loxam, Arnold* / Narcissus: *Loxam, Arnold* / Windermere march: *Loxam, Arnold* / Dickie bird hop: *Loxam, Arnold*
CD ______ **MCCD 207**
Music Club / Jul '95 / Disc / THE

MAGICAL SOUNDS OF HAWAII
Honolula dance / Aloha de / Sarina / Hilo march / Beautiful Isle / Terang bular / Aloen ajoen / Hukilau song / Mama / Pau ika lani / Mauna kea / Blue wahini / Imiau ea auwey / Sophisticated Hula / Little cani Joe / Sari nande / Footprints in the sun / Nina bobo / Goro gone no / Mine ha ha / Lime lime / Sejang kene / Honolula / Moon over Maui / Mauri chimes / Kaneuche kiss
CD ______ **GRF 202**
Tring / Apr '93 / Tring

MAGIE DES ANDES
CD ______ **GRI 190522**
Griffe / Feb '96 / ADA / Discovery

MAGNETIC SUBMISSION
CD ______ **EFA 200792**
Submission / Dec '95 / SRD

MAGNIFICENT 14, THE
CD ______ **CDTRL 283**
Trojan / Mar '94 / Direct / Jet Star

MAGNIFICENT THUNDERSTORM
CD ______ **57702**
CMC / May '97 / BMG

MAGNUM MYSTERIUM
CD ______ **CDCEL 1635188**
Celestial Harmonies / Jun '87 / ADA / Select

MAGYARPALATKA
CD ______ **SYNCD 152**
Syncoop / Jun '93 / ADA / Direct

MAH NA MAH NA (The Complete Remix Project)
Karmexperience mix: *Karminski Experience* / King of Favelas mix: *Scotti, Paolo* / L'amour mix: *Sebbag, Raphael* / Space go go mix: *Gak Sato & DJ Massive* / Tiki mix: *Sato, Gak* / Mah na mammato mix: *Coccoluto, Claudio & Savino Martinez* / Football club mix: *Sweet Dick Willy & Zbouby/Zebla* / Smash on the beatbox mix: *DJ Smash* / Dub mix: *Coccoluto, Claudio & Savino Martinez*
CD ______ **MET 201204**
Right Tempo / Sep '97 / New Note/Pinnacle / Timewarp

MAIN COURSE
CD ______ **REDEURO 2**
Red Eye / Nov '94 / Direct

MAINSTREAM MASTERS, THE
CD ______ **JHR 73529**
Jazz Hour / May '93 / Cadillac / Jazz Music / Target/BMG

MAKE IT EASY
Make it easy on yourself: *Walker Brothers* / Unchained melody: *Righteous Brothers* / Green grass of home: *Jones, Tom* / Blue velvet: *Vinton, Bobby* / Most beautiful girl in the world: *Rich, Charlie* / Always on my mind: *Nelson, Willie* / Lovely day: *Withers, Bill* / January February: *Dickson, Barbara* / I can see clearly now: *Nash, Johnny* / Sylvia's mother: *Dr. Hook* / Release me: *Humperdinck, Engelbert* / Nights in white satin: *Moody Blues* / I just don't know what to do with myself: *Springfield, Dusty* / Forever autumn: *Hayward, Justin* / King of the road: *Miller, Roger* / You're a lady: *Skellern, Peter* / Stand by your man: *Wynette, Tammy* / Last farewell: *Whittaker, Roger*
CD ______ **MUSCD 003**
MCI Music / Nov '92 / Disc / THE

MAKE IT FUNKY
Movin': *Brass Construction* / Shack up: *Banbarra* / Hustle on up: *Hidden Strength* / Funky stuff: *Kool & The Gang* / Who'd she coo: *Ohio Players* / Put your body in it: *Mills, Stephanie* / Make it funky: *Brown, James* / Rigor mortis: *Cameo* / Givin' up food for funk: *JB's* / Zone: *Rhythm Makers* / We got the funk: *Positive Force* / Hypertension: *Calender* / Changin': *Brass Construction*
CD ______ **RNBCD 105**
Connoisseur Collection / Oct '93 / Pinnacle

MAKE MINE MAMBO
CD ______ **NSCD 011**
Nascente / Nov '96 / Disc / New Note/ Pinnacle

MAKE THE WORLD GO AWAY (20 Classic Love Songs)
Ain't no pleasing you: *Chas & Dave* / Whispering: *Bachelors* / This is my song: *Clark, Petula* / Make me an island: *Dolan, Joe* / Make the world go away: *Rose Marie* / When my little girl is smiling: *Justice, Jimmy* / Medley: *Knight, Gladys & The Pips* / One day at a time: *Martell, Lena* / Little bitty tear: *Miki & Griff* / Story of my life: *Miller, Gary* / Vaya con dios: *Millican & Nesbitt* / Michelle: *Overlanders* / Isn't she lovely: *Parton, David* / (It's like a) Sad old kinda movie: *Pickettywitch* / Something's gotten hold of my heart: *Pitney, Gene* / Always something there to remind me: *Shaw, Sandie* / Too young: *Young, Jimmy* / Party's over: *Donegan, Lonnie* / Moon river: *Butler, Jerry* / Cry me a river: *Knight, Marie*
CD ______ **TRTCD 112**
TrueTrax / Oct '94 / THE

MAKE YOU SWEAT
CD ______ **TCD 2542**
Telstar / Sep '91 / BMG

MAKING UP AGAIN
We've got tonight: *Brooks, Elkie* / It's too late now: *Baldry, Long John* / First cut is the deepest: *Arnold, P.P.* / Out of time: *Farlowe, Chris* / Time in a bottle: *Croce, Jim* / After the goldrush: *Prelude* / Part time love: *Knight, Gladys* / Lost in France: *Tyler, Bonnie* / Can't get by without you: *Real Thing* / Love hurts: *Nazareth* / Second time around: *Shalamar* / Go now: *Moody Blues* / Summer of my life: *May, Simon* / Say you don't mind: *Blunstone, Colin* / Shooting star: *Dollar* / Love is love: *Brooks, Elkie* / Making up again: *Goldie* / Walk on by: *D-Train* / Tired of waiting for you: *Kinks* / It doesn't have to be that way: *Croce, Jim*
CD ______ **TRTCD 140**
TrueTrax / Feb '96 / THE

MALAWI - A KWELA CONCERT
CD ______ **LDX 274972**
La Chant Du Monde / Apr '94 / ADA / Harmonia Mundi

MALE BLUES OF THE TWENTIES VOL.1 1922
CD ______ **DOCD 5482**
Document / Nov '96 / ADA / Hot Shot / Jazz Music

MALE BLUES OF THE TWENTIES VOL.2 1923-1928
CD ______ **DOCD 5532**
Document / Apr '97 / ADA / Hot Shot / Jazz Music

MAMADOU - THE DRUMS OF MALI
CD ______ **PS 65132CD**
PlayaSound / Jul '94 / ADA / Harmonia Mundi

MAMBA PERCUSSIONS VOL.1
CD ______ **PV 782 91**
Disques Pierre Verany / '88 / Kingdom

MAMBO
CD ______ **CD 62020**
Saludos Amigos / Oct '93 / Target/BMG

MAMBO EN LA HABANA
CD ______ **CD 018**
Egrem / Mar '96 / Discovery

MAMBO EXPLOSION
Anabacoa: *Prado, Perez & Benny More* / Mambo mucho mambo: *Machito* / Mambo diablo: *Puente, Tito* / Mambo no.5: *Puente, Tito* / Alex Mambo: *Machito* / Maria Cristina: *Prado, Perez & Benny More* / Mamborama: *Puente, Tito* / Clave mambo: *Cuba, Joe Sextet* / Scharneco's mambo: *Morales, Noro* / Baile de san vito: *Valdes, Minuelito*
CD ______ **12911**
Laserlight / Feb '97 / Target/BMG

MAMBO KINGS, THE
CD ______ **MPV 5524**
Movieplay / Aug '92 / Target/BMG

MAMBO MANIA
Siempre en orbita: *Toro, Yomo* / Mambo para que goche: *Gonzalez, Celio* / Mambo con cha cha cha: *Faz, Roberto* / Donkey serenade: *Puente, Tito* / Guajiriando: *Bienvenido Granda* / Kandela: *Prado, Perez* / El pescador: *Figueroa, Wilfredo* / Otro coco: *Yayo El Indio* / Mambo pide le gente: *Santos, Daniel* / Eslava 22: *Damiron* / Ricci Ricci: *Puente, Tito* / Cachondea: *Feliciano, Jose 'Cheo'* / El cucu: *Capo, Bobby* / Sambrosito: *Santos, Daniel* / Me miraste y te mire: *Machito Y Sus Afro Cubanos* / Oy este mambo: *La Sonora Matancera* / Aguantando: *Paunetto, Bobby* / Go go mambo: *Grand, Rene* / Lleque: *Cuba, Joe Sextet* / Adivinanza: *Machito Y Sus Afro Cubanos*
CD ______ **CDHOT 619**
Charly / Apr '97 / Koch

MAN I LOVE, THE
I got rhythm: *Ballew, Smith & Fred Rich Orchestra* / My Marguerita: *Viennese Seven Singing Sisters* / Why do I love you: *Elwin, Maurice & The Rhythmic Eight* / You do something to me: *Dietrich, Marlene* / Uncle Bill has much improved: *Frankau, Ronald* / Copper coloured gal: *Dawn, Dolly & Her Dawn Patrol* / Man I love: *Layton & Johnstone* / Miss Annabelle Lee: *Kent, Betty & Jack Simpson's Sextet* / There's something about a soldier: *Baker, George & Jack Hylton Orchestra* / Have you met Miss Jones: *Hall, Adelaide* / King's a queen at heart: *Rees, Judd* / Pretty girl is like a melody: *Hildegarde* / I must have that man: *Browne, Sam & Jack Hylton Orchestra* / For me and my gal: *Garland, Judy & Gene Kelly* / Ten cents a dance: *Hutchinson, Leslie 'Hutch'* / If you knew Susie (like I know Susie): *Shields, Ella* / Far away in a shanty town: *Grantham, Cyril & Geraldo Orchestra* / Masculine women feminine men: *Mayall, Billy & Gwen Farrar* / Mother's walking round in father's trousers: *Higgins, Charlie* / Sally: *Fields, Gracie* / Cabaret boys: *Bing, Douglas & Lance Lister* / Ida, sweet as apple cider: *Kent, Betty & Jack Simpson's Sextet* / Can't help lovin' dat man: *Layton & Johnstone* / I'm no angel: *West, Mae* / There ain't no sweet man that's worth the salt of my tears: *Rhythm Boys & Paul Whiteman Orchestra*
CD ______ **75605522802**
Happy Days / Aug '96 / Conifer/BMG

MANCHESTER VOL.1
CD ______ **SWDCD 001**
Swamp Donkey / Nov '94 / Else

MANCHESTER VOL.2 (Streetscene)
CD ______ **BOPCD 002**
Boptop / Dec '95 / Else

MANHATTAN SERENADES (Classic Songs Of New York)
CD JCD 641
Jass / Nov '93 / ADA / Cadillac / CM / Direct / Jazz Music

MANIFESTO
CD MASO 33045CD
Materiali Sonori / Nov '88 / Cargo / Greyhound / New Note/Pinnacle

MANIFESTO MONSTERS (2CD Set)
I got the vibration: *Black Box* / Let's all chant: *Gusto* / I'm free: *Robinson, Janice* / Tell it to my heart: *Q-Club* / In de ghetto: *Waters, Crystal* / Vicious circles: *Poltergeist* / I feel love: *Summer, Donna* / Arms of Loren: *E'voke* / Hondy (no access): *Hondy* / Relax: *Waters, Crystal* / Feel tha vibe: *That Kid Chris* / Keep pushin': *D'Lugosch, Boris* / State of independence: *Summer, Donna* / Keep on jumpin': *Wash, Martha & Jocelyn Brown* / Disco's revenge: *Gusto* / Stand the test of time: *Wiseass* / Higher state of consciousness: *Wink, Josh* / Say what: *Groove Park* / Voyager: *Mr. Spring* / Can U feel it: *Squad* / La Campana: *DJ Dero*
CD Set 5341152
Manifesto / Nov '96 / PolyGram

MANY FACES OF BOOGIE WOOGIE, THE
CD AMSC 553
Avid / Jun '96 / Avid/BMG / Koch / THE

MANY MOODS OF LOVE
CD RN 0036
Runn / May '97 / Grapevine/PolyGram / Jet Star / SRD

MARCHING AROUND THE WORLD
Friedlander march: *Band of the Royal Tank Regiment* / Radetzsky march: *Band of H.M. Royal Marines* / Gibraltar: *Band of H.M. Royal Marines* / Marche des parachutistes belges: *Band Of The Parachute Regiment* / Army of the nile: *Band of the Glosters* / Marche lorraine: *Band of the Cheshire Regiment* / Bridge too far: *Band Of The Parachute Regiment* / Golden mile: *Band of the Cheshire Regiment* / Cairo road: *Band of the Cheshire Regiment* / Die soldaten von celle: *Band of the Royal Tank Regiment* / Hands across the sea: *Band of the Royal British Legion* / Hyde park: *Band of the H.M. Royal Marines* / India, Arabia: *Band of the Cheshire Regiment* / Arromanches: *Band of the Royal British Legion* / Valdres march: *Band of the Royal Tank Regiment* / Road to Vitez: *Band of the Cheshire Regiment*
CD 300622
Hallmark / Jul '96 / Carlton

MARDI GRAS - PARADE MUSIC FROM NEW ORLEANS
CD BCD 107
GHB / Jul '93 / Jazz Music

MARIJUANA'S GREATEST HITS REVISITED
CD SKYCD 5024
Sky / Sep '94 / Greyhound / Koch / Vital/ SAM

MARIMAC ANTHOLOGY, THE
CD ROUCD 0364
Rounder / Aug '96 / ADA / CM / Direct

MARINES
CD DEM 018
IMP / May '96 / ADA / Discovery

MARK GOODIER SESSIONS
CD MARK 1
Night Tracks / Mar '92 / Grapevine/ PolyGram / Pinnacle

MARK OF THE CELTS
CD Y 225057
Silex / Feb '96 / ADA / Harmonia Mundi

MARQUEE 30 LEGENDARY YEARS (32 Classic Rockr Tracks)
Pride (in the name of love): *U2* / Solid rock: *Dire Straits* / Turn it on again: *Genesis* / Run to you: *Adams, Bryan* / White wedding: *Idol, Billy* / Love song: *Simple Minds* / Don't stand so close to me: *Police* / Going underground: *Jam* / No more heroes: *Stranglers* / Rat trap: *Boomtown Rats* / Matthew and son: *Stevens, Cat* / Living in the past: *Jethro Tull* / Dreamer: *Supertramp* / Another brick in the wall pt 2: *Pink Floyd* / Kayleigh: *Marillion* / Killer queen: *Queen* / Saturday night's alright for fighting: *John, Elton* / Get it on: *T-Rex* / All the young dudes: *Mott The Hoople* / You wear it well: *Stewart, Rod* / Boys are back in town: *Thin Lizzy* / Caroline: *Status Quo* / Layla: *Derek & The Dominoes* / Substitute: *Who* / All right now: *Free* / Badge: *Cream* / Gimme some lovin': *Davis, Spencer Group* / Need your love so bad: *Fleetwood Mac* / For your love: *Yardbirds* / Sha la la la lee: *Small Faces* / Purple haze: *Hendrix, Jimi* / Space oddity (original version): *Bowie, David*
CD 8400102
Polydor / Jan '89 / PolyGram

MARQUEE METAL
We will rock you: *Queen* / Smoke on the water: *Deep Purple* / Wishing well: *Free* / Voodoo chile: *Hendrix, Jimi* / Down down: *Status Quo* / Epic: *Faith No More* / She's a little angel: *Little Angels* / Killer on the loose: *Thin Lizzy* / School's out: *Cooper, Alice* / Crazy crazy nights: *Kiss* / Can't get enough: *Bad Company* / Ace of spades: *Motorhead* / Paranoid: *Black Sabbath* / Walk this way: *Run DMC & Aerosmith* / Is there anybody there: *Scorpions* / Wizard: *Uriah Heep* / Days of no trust: *Magnum* / Living after midnight: *Judas Priest* / Free 'n' easy: *Almighty*
CD 8454172
Polydor / Apr '91 / PolyGram

MARSEILLE, MES AMOURS
CD 878302
Music Memoria / Jun '93 / ADA / Discovery

MAS - A CARIBBEAN CHRISTMAS PARTY
Party for Santa Claus: *Lord Nelson* / Nwel la rive: *Benjamin, Lionel* / Santa Claus (do you ever come to the ghetto): *Davis, Carlene* / Soca santa: *Machel* / Noel pou yo: *Claudette Et Ti Pierre* / Asalto navideno: *El Gran Combo* / Deck the halls with boughs of holly: *Miller, Jacob* / Santa Claus is coming to town: *Spence, Joseph* / Quand j'entends chante Noel: *Gustave, Eddy*
CD RCD 10150
Rykodisc / Nov '93 / ADA / Vital

MAS' HYSTERIA
CD NSCD 010
Nascente / Nov '96 / Disc / New Note/ Pinnacle

MASCULINE WOMAN AND FEMININE MEN
CD PASTCD 7072
Flapper / May '95 / Pinnacle

MASHING UP CREATION
CD CCDUBM 001
Dubmission / Feb '97 / SRD

MASSEY HALL TORONTO MAY 15TH 1953
CD CD 53036
Giants Of Jazz / Mar '90 / Cadillac / Jazz Music / Target/BMG

MASSIVE REGGAE PARTY 1996
Baby I love your way: *Doctor* / I swear: *Rockets* / Shine: *RR Band* / Games people play: *RR Band* / You don't love me (no no no): *Just A Minute* / Don't turn around: *Just A Minute* / Sweets for my sweet: *George X* / Away from home: *Doctor* / Bayangena Baya Phuma: *Dr. Victor* / Iron lion Zion: *Dr. Victor* / Mr. Loverman: *D&V* / Oh Carolina: *Gringo* / Informer: *Show 2* / Higher ground: *100% Dance* / Can't help falling in love: *100% Dance* / Sweat (la la long): *Easy Groove*
CD 343112
Koch International / Jun '96 / Koch

MASSIVE SOUND OF RAP, THE (4CD Set)
CD Set MSCD 4
Mo's Music Machine / Jun '97 / Mo's Music Machine / Pinnacle

MASSIVE SOUNDS OF AURA SURROUND SOUNDS (4CD Set)
NEW generation: *MLO* / One million faces: *Incisions* / Understood: *Must* / Thunderdome: *Thursday Club* / London's on acid: *Cabbage Patch* / Give me a wink: *Fingers Project* / In the heat of the night: *Overhead Noise* / Shofou: *Tyoussi* / Scrumble: *DJ Misjah & Tim* / Temple of acid: *Temple Of Acid* / Deltoid: *Hardline 2* / Overload: *DJ Misjah & Tim* / Dreamlab: *MLO* / Chafs: *Sinus* / Eternal: *Epik* / Dig deep: *Blokka* / Place called acid: *Thursday Club* / Squelch: *Fini Tribe* / Play D musik: *OCP* / Want you now: *Must* / Breakdown: *Incisions* / Exploration: *Blokka* / Feel it: *Renegade* / What is going on: *Dex* / Man woman love: *DJ Misjah & Groovehend* / Blob: *Epik* / Ice Station Zebra: *Temple Of Acid* / Axiom: *Arcana* / Trancition: *Choci & Freedom Of Sound* / Samarkand: *MLO* / Driver: *Epik* / Midsummers dream: *Blokka*
CD Set MSCD 1
Aura Surround Sounds / Mar '97 / Arabesque / Grapevine/PolyGram / Mo's Music Machine / Pinnacle

MASSIVE SOUNDS OF UNDERGROUND VIBE, THE (4CD Set)
CD Set MSCD 1
Mo's Music Machine / Mar '97 / Mo's Music Machine / Pinnacle

MASSIVE VOL.4
Twice my age: *Krystal & Shabba Ranks* / Worried over you: *Davis, Janet-Lee & C.J. Lewis* / Poco man jam: *Peck, Gregory* / Shaka on the move: *Chaka Demus* / Holy water: *Bailey, Admiral* / New talk: *Sweet Irie & Joe 90* / I know love: *Priest, Maxi & Tiger* / Mr. Loverman: *Glasgow, Deborahe & Shabba Ranks* / Good thing going: *Leo, Phillip & C.J. Lewis* / One blood: *Reid, Junior* / Proud of Mandela: *Macka B & Kofi* / Guidance: *Nerious Joseph* / Dub be good to me: *Beats International & Lindy Layton* / I wanna rock: *Paul, Frankie* / First date: *Cocoa T* / Tears: *Sanchez* / Glide gently: *Anthony, Mike* / If you want it: *Hunningale, Peter* / Hurry over: *Boom, Barry* / Dancing with my baby: *Foster, Royden* / Let's start over: *Winsome & Frankie Paul* / Are you going my way: *Home T* / Baby don't go too far: *Hartley, Trevor* / Paradise: *Smith, Karen* / You are the one: *Intense*
CD Set 8282102
FFRR / Jun '90 / PolyGram

MASTER AND DISCIPLES
CD CDBM 092
Blue Moon / May '93 / Cadillac / Discovery / Greensleeves / Jazz Music / Jet Star / TKO Magnum

MASTER BRASS VOL.1 (All England Masters Championship 1990)
French military march / Light Cavalry Overture / Miss blue bonnet / Elegy from a 'Downland Suite' / Coriolanus / Marching through Georgia / Blitz / Someone to watch over me / Sun has got his hat on / Thre negro spirituals / Neapolitan scenes / Blenheim flourishes / Nightfall in camp
CD QPRL 046D
Polyphonic / Aug '91 / Complete/Pinnacle

MASTER BRASS VOL.2 (All England Masters Championship 1991)
Morning, Noon and night / Overture: Candide / Allerseelen / Marche slave / Harmony music / American fanfare / Jaguar / Ballet music / Robert le diable / Cornet carillon / Bandology / Great gate of Kiev / Witches sabbath / Evening hymn and sunset
CD QPRL 048D
Polyphonic / Sep '91 / Complete/Pinnacle

MASTER BRASS VOL.3 (All England Masters Championship 1992)
Midwest / Overture: Zampa / Summertime / Music from the XVI century / Cambridge variations / Introduction act 3 / Lohengrin / Pineapple Poll / Pantomime / Wedding procession 'Le coq d'or' / Pastime with good company / Procession to the minster / Finlandia
CD QPRL 052D
Polyphonic / Aug '93 / Complete/Pinnacle

MASTER BRASS VOL.4 (All England Masters Championship 1993)
Overture: The marriage of Figaro / Sorcerer's apprentice / Pandora / Spider and the fly / Grand march from Aida / English heritage / Blue rondo a la Turk / Lost chord / Festival overture
CD QPRL 060D
Polyphonic / Sep '93 / Complete/Pinnacle

MASTER BRASS VOL.5 (All England Masters Championship 1994)
Jubilee prelude / Someone to watch over me / Hailstorm / Eighteenth Variation (On a theme of) / Montage / Folk festival / Pavanne / Take your picc / Russian and Ludmilla / Georgia on my mind / Jerusalem / Entry of the Gods into Valhalla
CD QPRL 067D
Polyphonic / Aug '94 / Complete/Pinnacle

MASTER BRASS VOL.6 (All England Masters Championship 1995)
Victors' return / Dancing in the park / Deep inside the sacred temple / Paganini variations / La danza / Oberon / Hoe down / Zimba zamba / Dance of the comedians / Bolero
CD QPRL 073D
Polyphonic / Aug '95 / Complete/Pinnacle

MASTER BRASS VOL.7 (All England Masters Championship 1996)
Washington Grays: *Yorkshire Building Society Band* / Aye waukin' o: *Yorkshire Building Society Band* / Alloway tales: *Yorkshire Building Society Band* / Only love: *Yorkshire Building Society Band* / Savonic rhapsody no.2: *Yorkshire Building Society Band* / Hymns at sunrise: *Williams-Fairey Engineering Band* / Malaguena: *Grimethorpe Colliery Band* / Scottish dances: *Grimethorpe Colliery Band* / Satchmo: *Grimethorpe Colliery Band* / Sugar blues: *Grimethorpe Colliery Band* / In perfect peace: *Grimethorpe Colliery Band* / McArthur Park: *Grimethorpe Colliery Band*
CD QPRL 083D
Polyphonic / Sep '96 / Complete/Pinnacle

MASTERPIECE VOL.3
CD LDRCD 019
Londisc / Aug '95 / Jet Star

MASTERS OF FRENCH JAZZ 1937-1944
CD 2512802
Jazztime / Feb '91 / Discovery

MASTERS OF HARDCORE VOL.2 (2CD Set)
CD Set IDT 000768
ID&T / Dec '96 / Plastic Head

MASTERS OF HOUSE, THE (2CD Set)
CD Set BB 35243DCD
Broken Beat / May '96 / Plastic Head

MASTERS OF PERCUSSION, THE
CD MRCD 1012
Moment / Jan '95 / ADA / Koch

MASTERS OF ROCK, THE (3CD Set)
CD Set DTKBOX 54
Dressed To Kill / Sep '96 / Total/BMG

MASTERS OF SWING, THE
It's only a paper moon: *Cole, Nat 'King'* / Jeepers creepers: *Bennett, Tony* / I can't give you anything but love: *Torme, Mel* / Trolley song: *Sinatra, Frank* / Say it isn't so: *Crosby, Bing* / Cottage for sale: *Eckstine, Billy* / Blue skies: *Crosby, Bing* / Surrey with the fringe on top: *Sinatra, Frank* / I've got the world on a string: *Torme, Mel* / That old black magic: *Eckstine, Billy* / Embraceable you: *Cole, Nat 'King'* / Chicago (that toddlin' town): *Bennett, Tony* / I'm getting sentimental over you: *Torme, Mel* / Misty: *Eckstine, Billy* / Cheek to cheek/All by myself: *Crosby, Bing* / Life is a song: *Bennett, Tony* / How deep is the ocean: *Cole, Nat 'King'* / Lullaby of Broadway: *Sinatra, Frank*
CD ECD 3284
K-Tel / Jan '97 / K-Tel

MASTERS OF THE FOLK VIOLIN, THE
CD ARHCD 434
Arhoolie / Apr '95 / ADA / Cadillac / Direct

MASTERS OF THE PANPIPES, THE
CD EUCD 1318
ARC / Nov '95 / ADA / ARC Music

MASTERS OF TURKISH MUSIC VOL.2 1906-1949, THE
CD ROUCD 1111
Rounder / Sep '96 / ADA / CM / Direct

MASTERS OF ZEN, THE
CD PS 65153
PlayaSound / Sep '95 / ADA / Harmonia Mundi

MASTERS SOLO DRUMMING CHAMPIONSHIP 1997 (2CD Set)
CD Set COMD 2066
Temple / Jul '97 / ADA / CM / Direct / Duncans / Highlander

MATADOR'S ARENA VOL.1 (1968-1969)
CD JMC 200222
Jamaican Gold / Jun '95 / Grapevine/ PolyGram / Jet Star

MATADOR'S ARENA VOL.2
CD JMC 200223
Jamaican Gold / Aug '95 / Grapevine/ PolyGram / Jet Star

MATADOR'S ARENA VOL.3
CD JMC 200224
Jamaican Gold / Aug '95 / Grapevine/ PolyGram / Jet Star

MATCHBOX DAYS (Really The English Country Blues)
Bulldog blues: *Cooper, Mike* / Few short lines: *Kelly, Dave* / Say no to the Devil: *Prager, Simon & Steve Rye* / Nothin' in ramblin': *Kelly, Jo Ann* / Cottonfield blues: *Anderson, Ian A.* / Whitewash station: *Panama Ltd. Jug Band* / Searchin' the desert: *Jones, Al* / Dark road blues: *Missouri Compromise* / Spoonful: *Jones, Wizz* / Meeting house rag: *Cooper, Mike* / Blues walking like a man: *Kelly, Dave* / Stop breaking down: *Prager, Rye & Hall* / Rowdy blues: *Anderson, Ian A.* / Wildcat: *Panama Ltd. Jug Band* / Travellin' blues: *Kelly, Dave* / Bread of heaven: *Rye, Steve* / Black snake moan: *Cooper, Mike* / Cocaine habit: *Panama Ltd. Jug Band* / Friday evening blues: *Anderson, Ian A.* / If I had possession over Judgement Day: *Missouri Compromise* / Black Mary: *Kelly, Jo Ann* / Inverted world: *Anderson, Ian A. & Mike Cooper*
CD CDWIKD 168
Big Beat / Feb '97 / Pinnacle

MATRIX DUB
CD CEND 1300
Century / Jan '97 / Shellshock/Disc

MAU MAU JUNGLE
CD CD 007
Sky High / Jan '93 / Direct / Jet Star

MAURITIUS - SEGAS
CD C 580060
Ocora / Oct '94 / ADA / Harmonia Mundi

MAX POWER - MAX BASS VOL.1
CD BDRCD 15
Breakdown / Oct '96 / Pinnacle

MAX POWER - MAX BASS VOL.2
Switch: *Dream Team* / Symetrix: *Future Force* / Wolf: *Shy FX* / Twisted: *Swift* / Style: *Ill Figure* / Stick 'em up: *Remarc* / Mode one: *IQ Collective* / Nightflight: *Andy C & Shimon* / Twister: *Decoder* / International: *MTS* / Who is it: *Firefox* / Reply: *Mask* / Rucus: *Gang Related* / Throat: *Dream Team*
CD BDRCD 19
Breakdown / Apr '97 / Pinnacle

MAX THE DOG SAYS... DO THE SKA
CD DOJOCD 92
Dojo / Dec '92 / Disc

MAXI DANCE (2CD Set)
And the beat goes on: *Whispers* / Just an illusion: *Imagination* / Jump on the rhythm and ride: *Imagination* / From East to West: *Voyage* / Papa was a rolling stone: *Third World* / High energy: *Thomas, Evelyn* / Shoot your shot: *Divine* / Passion: *Flirts* / Can you feel the force: *Real Thing* / Jeopardy: *Kihn, Greg* / Pop muzik: *M* / Rapper's delight: *Sugarhill Gang* / Freedom: *Grandmaster Flash & The Furious Five* / Uptown festival: *Shalamar* / Baby now that I've found you: *Foundations* / Boogie on up: *Rokotto* / Music and lights: *Imagination* / Never can say goodbye: *Gaynor, Gloria* / Feels like I'm in love: *Marie, Kelly* / Ring my bell: *Ward, Anita* / West End girls: *Pet Shop Boys*
CD Set 24360
Laserlight / Feb '97 / Target/BMG

MAXI-MUM TENAGLIA
CD XTR 18CDM
X-Treme / Nov '95 / Pinnacle / SRD

MBUKI MVUKI
CD _______ OMCD 017
Original Music / May '93 / Jet Star / SRD

MBUTI PYGMIES OF THE ITURI RAINFOREST
CD _______ SFCD 40401
Smithsonian Folkways / Sep '94 / ADA / Cadillac / CM / Direct / Koch

ME GONE BUCK WILD (Reggae Dancehall Killers)
CD _______ 322664
Shanachie / Apr '97 / ADA / Greensleeves / Koch

ME NAISET
CD _______ KICD 37
Kansanmusiikki Instituutti / Nov '95 / ADA / Direct

MEATMEN
CD _______ VPCD 2055
VP / Oct '96 / Greensleeves / Jet Star / Total/BMG

MECHANICAL MUSIC HALL
Burlington Bertie from Bow / After the ball / Nellie Dean / Where did you get that hat / K-K-K-Katy / Flanagan / Down at the old Bull and Bush / Lily of Laguna / If it wasn't for the 'ouses in between / Bill Bailey, won't you please come home / Beside the seaside / Ask a policeman / Don't have any more, Mrs. Moore / Any old iron / My old dutch / Boiled beef and carrots / Ta-ra-ra-boom-de-ay
CD _______ CDSDL 232
Saydisc / Jan '92 / ADA / Direct / Harmonia Mundi

MECHANICAL PARADISE
CD _______ NBX 007
Haven / Oct '94 / Pinnacle / Shellshock/ Disc

MEDITATION
CD _______ 22515
Music / Feb '96 / Target/BMG

MEDITATION - REFLECTIONS (2CD Set)
CD Set _______ 24059
Delta Doubles / Sep '92 / Target/BMG

MEDITATIONS AND RELAXATION
CD _______ ACH 035 CD
Milan / Feb '89 / Conifer/BMG / Silva Screen

MEDLEY TRAIN
CD _______ CDTRL 350
Trojan / Mar '95 / Direct / Jet Star

MEET ME TONIGHT
CD _______ BB 2810
Blue Beat / Apr '95 / Grapevine/PolyGram

MEGA BODY BEATS
Seven days and one week: *BBE* / Soldier soldier: *Captain Jack* / Sing: *Nakatomi* / Freed from desire: *Gala* / Black Betty: *Flashback* / Don't stop movin': *Livin' Joy* / You make me feel: *Real DJ* / Big beat: *Capella* / Believe in the future: *Critical Mass* / My little fantasy: *4 Tune* / Street life: *Peroni Project & Jessica* / Up to no good: *Porn Kings* / Too beautiful: *Blue Zone* / Take my love: *Alitha* / El tiburon: *Project Uno* / U gotta get down: *Pryme*
CD _______ DC 881652
Disky / Jul '97 / Disky / THE

MEGA BODY VIBES
Captain Jack: *Captain Jack* / Jump for joy: *2 Unlimited* / We've got it goin' on: *Backstreet Boys* / I got 5 on it: *Luniz* / Time is up: *Milton, C.B.* / I need your love: *Cappella* / Babies are crazy: *Chakra* / Ultra flava: *Heller & Farley Project* / Children: *Miles, Robert* / Theme from S'Express: *S'Express* / Night train: *Kadoc* / In spirit: *Dilemma* / Give me luv: *Alcatraz* / Party over here: *740 Boyz* / Spank: *D-Xpress & Farida Melville* / Black is black: *Belle Epoque*
CD _______ WLT 874592
Disky / Oct '96 / Disky / THE

MEGA ITALIA (4CD Set)
CD Set _______ 3008002
Arcade / Feb '97 / Discovery

MEGA REGGAE DANCE (4CD Set)
CD _______ 3008392
Arcade / Feb '97 / Discovery

MEGA SALSA (4CD Set)
CD Set _______ 3011972
Arcade / Feb '97 / Discovery

MEGA ZOUK (2CD Set)
CD Set _______ 3005012
Arcade / Feb '97 / Discovery

MEGA-LO-MANIA
Ain't no love (ain't no use): *Sub Sub & Melanie Williams* / Beneath the sheets: *Vertigo* / Meglomania: *Duberry* / I believe in you: *Our Tribe* / Music is my life: *Chase* / U to 2 know: *Cappella* / Do u feel 4 me: *Eden* / Corporation your eyes: *Groove* / Let freedom reign: *Nu Colours* / Shine on me: *Lovestation* / Sanctuary of love: *Source* / So deep: *Reese Project* / Appolonia: *BM EX* / Devo: *Crunch* / Feels so good: *Watchman* / Love thing: *Evolution* / (You give me) All your love: *Pro-gressive* / Thankyou: *Tuff Productions* / Soul survivors: *Prohibition*
CD _______ 5158132
PolyGram TV / Apr '93 / PolyGram

MEGASOFT OFFICE '97
Way form one (so hard): *Elegia* / Saulbass theme: *Ready Made* / Seasons: *Feedback* / Bewildered: *Nova Nova* / No way out: *Chaotik Ramses* / Na Na's waltz: *Aqua Bassino* / Footprints: *Reminiscent Drive* / Downward rush of the stream: *Juantrip* / NYC dharma: *Reminiscent Drive* / Ibiza: *Aqua Bassino*
CD _______ F 066CD
F-Communications / Jun '97 / Prime / Vital

MEGATRIPOLIS (3CD Set)
CD Set _______ FUNKYPCD 1
Funky Peace / Jul '96 / Total/BMG

MEINE TEXTE, MEINE LIEDER (3CD Set)
CD Set _______ BCD 15603
Bear Family / Jul '91 / Direct / Rollercoaster / Swift

MELLOW AND WARM
CD _______ NTRCD 055
Nectar / Jun '97 / Pinnacle

MELLOW TUNES (2CD Set)
CD Set _______ 560092
Nova Tekk / Apr '97 / Pinnacle

MELLOW'S PLACE
CD _______ IDT 000331
ID&T / Nov '96 / Plastic Head

MELODEON GREATS
CD _______ TSCD 601
Topic / Aug '95 / ADA / CM / Direct

MELODICA
Children: *Miles, Robert* / Sky plus: *Nylon Moon* / Anomaly: *Libra & Taylor* / Stella: *Jam & Spoon* / De Niro: *Disco Evangelists* / Sueno Latino: *Sueno Latino* / Magic fly: *Spaceblaster* / White horses: *Lenny D* / Smokebelch: *Sabres Of Paradise* / Moons waterfalls: *Brant, Roland* / Floating: *Terra Firma* / Pyramid: *Remark, Alex* / Psalms: *Skintrade*
CD _______ CDTIVA 1013
Positiva / Sep '97 / EMI

MELODIES FROM MADAGASCAR
CD _______ PS 65124
PlayaSound / Apr '94 / ADA / Harmonia Mundi

MELODIES OF LOVE (2CD Set)
Always on my mind: *Presley, Elvis* / When I fall in love: *Cole, Nat 'King'* / We have all the time in the world: *Armstrong, Louis* / Mad about the boy: *Washington, Dinah* / Unchained melody: *Righteous Brothers* / Fever: *Lee, Peggy* / (I left my heart) in San Francisco: *Bennett, Tony* / Cry me a river: *London, Julie* / That ole devil called love: *Holiday, Billie* / I wanna be loved by you: *Monroe, Marilyn* / Memories are made of this: *Martin, Dean* / Passing strangers: *Vaughan, Sarah & Billy Eckstine* / Summertime: *Fitzgerald, Ella* / As time goes by: *Nilsson* / I put a spell on you: *Simone, Nina* / Call me irresponsible: *Washington, Dinah* / Nature boy: *Cole, Nat 'King'* / Lover man (oh, where can you be): *Holiday, Billie* / Moonlight serenade: *Miller, Glenn Orchestra* / White christmas: *Crosby, Bing* / Only the lonely: *Orbison, Roy* / Blue velvet: *Vinton, Bobby* / Will you still love me tomorrow: *Shirelles* / Breaking up is hard to do: *Sedaka, Neil* / Love letters: *Lester, Ketty* / Crazy: *Cline, Patsy* / And I love you so: *Como, Perry* / Stranger in paradise: *Bennett, Tony* / Moon river: *Williams, Andy* / Something's gotten hold of my heart: *Pitney, Gene* / It's now or never: *Presley, Elvis* / Stand by your man: *Wynette, Tammy* / All I have to do is dream: *Everly Brothers* / Oh, Carol: *Sedaka, Neil* / Born free: *Monro, Matt* / Goldfinger: *Bassey, Shirley* / Magic moments: *Como, Perry* / Diamonds are a girl's best friend: *Monroe, Marilyn* / Ain't misbehavin': *Vaughan, Sarah* / What a wonderful world: *Armstrong, Louis*
CD Set _______ GLOCD 29
Global TV / Jul '97 / BMG

MELODY TIME VOL.1 (2CD Set)
Feeling fine: *Drummond, Don* / If I could rule the world: *Ellis, Alton* / Sinners: *Hinds, Justin & The Dominoes* / Ethiopians: *Mother's Tender Care* / Do it right: *Three Tops* / On the beach: *Paragons* / You don't care: *Techniques* / Don't stay away: *Dillon, Phyllis* / I'll be lonely: *Holt, John* / Moonlight Lover: *Landis, Joya* / Jimmy Brown: *Parker, Ken* / To the other man: *Lewis, Hopeton* / Stampede: *McCook, Tommy & The Supersonics* / Weather report: *Tennors* / Where must I go: *Dunkley, Errol* / Sincerely: *Russell, Dorothy and Ken Parker* / I fell in love: *Conquerors* / Loving wine: *Cole, Stranger and Hortense Ellis* / Dearest: *Dotty and Bonny featuring Don Drummond* / Musical communion: *Brooks, Baba* / Corner stone: *Hinds, Justin & The Dominoes* / Rock steady: *Ellis, Alton* / Ba ba boom: *Jamaicans* / Ride mi donkey: *Tennors* / Don't touch me tomato: *Dillon, Phyllis* / Angel of the morning: *Landis, Joya* / You don't need me: *Melodians* / Everyday is like a holiday: *Sensations* / DJ's choice: *Alcapone, Dennis* / Wear you to the ball: *U.Roy* / Ball a fire: *McCook, Tommy & The Supersonics* / True true true: *Parker, Ken* / Loving pauper: *Dobson, Dobby* / Raindrops: *Silvertones* / You were to be: *Gladiators* / Love up kiss up: *Termites* / Rukumbiine: *Duffus, Shenley* / Next door neighbour: *Grey, Owen and Leon Silvera* / Musical storeroom: *Skatalites*
CD Set _______ RN 7025
Rhino / Aug '97 / Grapevine/PolyGram / Jet Star

MELTING PLOT
CD _______ SST 249CD
SST / Jan '89 / Plastic Head

MEMORIES (18 Love Songs From The 1960's)
Groovy kind of love: *Fontana, Wayne* / Crying game: *Berry, Dave* / You've got your troubles (I've got mine): *Fortunes* / Bad to me: *Kramer, Billy J.* / You're no good: *Swinging Blue Jeans* / With a girl like you: *Troggs* / Someone, someone: *Poole, Brian* / I think of you: *Merseybeats* / She's not there: *Zombies* / Sweets for my sweet: *Drifters* / Somewhere: *Proby, P.J.* / Rhythm of the rain: *Cascades* / Goin' out of my head: *Little Anthony & The Imperials* / Then you can tell me goodbye: *Casinos* / Woman, woman: *Puckett, Gary & The Union Gap* / Silence is golden: *Tremeloes* / You were on my mind: *Crispin St Peters* / Happy together: *Turtles*
CD _______ ECD 3078
K-Tel / Dec '96 / K-Tel

MEMORIES ARE STILL MADE OF HITS VOL.1
Under the moon of love: *Lee, Curtis* / Baby oh baby: *Shells* / If you gotta make a fool of somebody: *Ray, James* / Million to one: *Charles, Jimmy* / My true story: *Jive Five* / Once in a while: *Chimes* / One track mind: *Lewis, Bobby* / Tell me why: *Belmonts* / It's unbelievable: *Larks* / Pretty little angel eyes: *Lee, Curtis* / All in my mind: *Brown, Maxine* / Itty bitty pieces: *Ray, James* / What time is it: *Jive Five* / Soul twist: *King Curtis* / Tossin' and turnin': *Lewis, Bobby* / I'm in the mood for love: *Chimes* / Come on little angel: *Belmonts* / Til then: *Classics* / I knew it all the time: *Clark, Dave Five* / 81: *Candy & The Kisses* / Barefottin': *Parker, Robert* / Then you can tell me goodbye: *Casinos* / You've gotta be loved: *Montanas* / American boys: *Clark, Petula* / Precious and few: *Climax* / Show and tell: *Wilson, Al*
CD _______ NEMCD 924
Sequel / Mar '97 / BMG

MEMORIES DU SEGA
CD _______ PS 65139CD
PlayaSound / Apr '95 / ADA / Harmonia Mundi

MEMORIES OF IRELAND
CD _______ ECD 3113
K-Tel / Jun '95 / K-Tel

MEMORIES OF SCOTLAND
CD _______ ACD 101
Koch / Oct '93 / Koch

MEMORY LINGERS ON, THE (40 Easy Listening Classics/2CD Set)
Everybody loves somebody: *Martin, Dean* / I'm in the mood for love: *Day, Doris* / Nancy (with the laughing face): *Sinatra, Frank* / Mona Lisa: *Cole, Nat 'King'* / I hear music: *Connor, Chris* / 'Till the end of time: *Como, Perry* / Stormy weather: *Vaughan, Sarah* / I apologise: *Eckstine, Billy* / Old devil moon: *Horne, Lena* / I can't begin to tell you: *Crosby, Bing* / Thou swell: *McRae, Carmen* / Let's face the music and dance: *Astaire, Fred* / One I love (belongs to someone else): *Fitzgerald, Ella* / Love walked in: *Armstrong, Louis* / How about you: *Garland, Judy* / You'll never know: *Haymes, Dick* / Since I fell for you: *Gorme, Eydie* / Our love is here to stay: *Washington, Dinah* / Prelude to a kiss: *Torme, Mel* / Georgia on my mind: *Holiday, Billie* / Saturday night (is the loneliest night in the week): *Sinatra, Frank* / It's only a paper moon: *Fitzgerald, Ella* / I can't believe that your in love with me: *Torme, Mel* / I got it bad and that ain't good: *Day, Doris* / Autumn leaves: *Cole, Nat 'King'* / Send in the clowns: *Gorme, Eydie* / You belong to my heart: *Crosby, Bing* / Let's do it, lets fall in love: *Holiday, Billie* / Foggy day: *Astaire, Fred* / They can't take that away from me: *McRae, Carmen* / Walkin' my baby back home: *Armstrong, Louis* / Love me or leave me: *Horne, Lena* / If I loved you: *Como, Perry* / As long as he needs me: *Vaughan, Sarah* / Misty: *Eckstine, Billy* / It's all right with me: *Connor, Chris* / It can't be wrong: *Haymes, Dick* / Love for sale: *Washington, Dinah* / Boy next door: *Garland, Judy* / You're nobody 'till somebody loves you: *Martin, Dean*
CD _______ CPCD 81442
Charly / Jun '96 / Koch

MEMPHIS BLUES 1927-1938
CD _______ DOCD 5159
Document / May '93 / ADA / Hot Shot / Jazz Music

MEMPHIS JAZZ MEETING
CD _______ DIW 613
DIW / Sep '93 / Cadillac / Harmonia Mundi

MEMPHIS JAZZ MEETING : MEMPHIS CONVENTION
CD _______ DIW 874
DIW / Sep '93 / Cadillac / Harmonia Mundi

MEMPHIS MASTERS: EARLY AMERICAN BLUES CLASSICS 1927-1934
CD _______ YAZCD 2008
Yazoo / Nov '94 / ADA / CM / Koch

MEMPHIS SOUL GREATS
Hey little girl: *West, Norm* / Baby please: *West, Norm* / So good to me: *Jackson, George* / I'm gonna wait: *Jackson, George* / Aretha, sing one for me: *Jackson, George* / Patricia: *Jackson, George* / Let them know you care: *Jackson, George* / Tumbling down: *Fry, James* / Still around: *Fry, James* / Mama's boy: *Fry, James* / I've got enough: *Fry, James* / Without you: *Wright, O.V.* / Rhymes: *Wright, O.V.* / I love my baby: *Hill, Lindell* / Love map: *Hill, Lindell* / Very first time: *Hill, Lindell* / Be good to the one (That's good to you): *Mack, Jimmy* / I love her: *Walker, Willie* / Sweet thing: *Walker, Willie* / Fried chicken: *Thomas, Rufus* / I ain't got time: *Thomas, Rufus*
CD _______ HILOCD 17
Hi / Jul '95 / Pinnacle

MEN IN COUNTRY
Storm in the heartland: *Cyrus, Billy Ray* / Third rate romance: *Kershaw, Sammy* / Little more love: *Gill, Vince* / Here comes the rain: *Mavericks* / Maybe we should just sleep on it: *McGraw, Tim* / That's right you're not from Texas: *Lovett, Lyle* / On the verge: *Raye, Collin* / Dirt road: *Brown, Sawyer* / I know where love lives: *Ketchum, Hal* / Ten feet tall and bullet proof: *Tritt, Travis* / Pocket of a clown: *Yoakam, Dwight* / They're playing our song: *McCoy, Neal* / Almost Saturday night: *Woodruff, Bob* / Just like you: *Keb Mo'* / Running out of reasons to run: *Trevino, Rick* / Like the rain: *Black, Clint* / Nobody wins: *Foster, Radney* / Life down on Earth: *Welch, Kevin*
CD _______ AHLCD 46
Hit / Jul '97 / Grapevine/PolyGram

MEN OF HARLECH (Welsh Choral Classics)
We'll keep a welcome: *Canoldir Male Voice Choir* / How great thou art: *Canoldir Male Voice Choir* / Lord's prayer: *Canoldir Male Voice Choir* / Land of my fathers (Hen wlad fy nhadau): *Moriston Orpheus Choir & The Bedwas, Trethomas & Machin Band* / Where shall I be: *Moriston Orpheus Choir & The Bedwas, Trethomas & Machin Band* / Calon lan: *Moriston Orpheus Choir & The Bedwas, Trethomas & Machin Band* / Rise up shepherd and follow: *Moriston Orpheus Choir* / Anvil chorus: *Moriston Orpheus Choir* / Deep harmony: *Moriston Orpheus Choir* / Goin' home: *Moriston Orpheus Choir* / Mil harddach wyt na'r rhosyn gwyn: *Pontarddulais Male Voice Choir* / Christus redemptor (hyfrydol): *Pontarddulais Male Voice Choir* / Jesu lover of my soul: *Treorchy Male Choir* / Unwaith eto'n nghymru annwyl: *Treorchy Male Choir* / Dove: *Emanuel, Ivor & The Rhos Male Voice Choir* / Ash grove: *Emanuel, Ivor & The Rhos Male Voice Choir* / Deus salutis: *Dunvant Male Choir* / Sarah: *Dunvant Male Choir* / Ar hyd y nos: *Dunvant Male Choir* / My little Welsh home: *Emanuel, Ivor & The Rhos Male Voice Choir* / God bless the Prince Of Wales: *Rhos Male Voice Choir* / Men of Harlech: *Emanuel, Ivor & The Rhos Male Voice Choir*
CD _______ TRTCD 133
TrueTrax / Oct '94 / THE

MERCURY BLUES 'N' RHYTHM STORY 1945-1955 (8CD Set)
CD Set _______ 5282922
Mercury / Nov '96 / PolyGram

MERCURY BLUES 'N' RHYTHM STORY 1945-1955 (Highlights)
It's just the blues: *Four Jumps Of Jive* / Bar fly blues: *Witherspoon, Jimmy* / If it's good: *Lee, Julia* / Gonna send you where I got you from: *Vinson, Eddie 'Cleanhead' & Orchestra* / Record ban blues: *Washington, Dinah* / Been fooling around: *Byrd, Roy & His Blues Jumpers* / Streetwalkin' daddy: *Mondy, Alma* / Papa said yes, mama said no, no, no: *Graves, Lee* / West coast lover: *Sims, Robert 'Snake'* / (All alone) I sit and cry: *Hall, Violet* / Let me fly your kite: *Hopkins, Lightnin'* / Get back (black, brown and white): *Broonzy, 'Big' Bill* / No mail blues: *Memphis Slim* / Baby baby blues: *Otis, Johnny* / Hittin' on me: *Johnson, Ella* / Boogie the blues: *Johnson, Ray* / Talk about me: *Hawkins, Jay* / All around the world: *Turner, Titus* / Rhythm rockin' blues: *McGill, Rollee* / Woke up this moring: *Prysock, Arthur*
CD _______ 5329702
Mercury / Jan '97 / PolyGram

MERENGUE (Dominican Music & Identity)
Merengue Cibaeno: *Lora, Nico* / En la batea: *Lora, Nico* / Santiago: *Menendez, Nilo Orquesta* / Juangomero: *Morel, Antonio* / Compadre Pedro Juan: *Vasquez, Nini* / jardinera: *Mateo, Joseito* / Volvimos de nuevo: *Guandulito* / El virony: *Viloria, Angel & Conjunto Tipico Cibaeno* / Me dejaste sola: *Belkis Concepcion* / Consejo a la mujeres: *Duran, Blas* / El diente de oro: *El Ciego de Nagua* / Merengue Palo Echao: *Mercedes Moreno, Juan A.* / Merengue de Tables: *Mojita, Francisco* / Merengue redondo: *Azolo, Domingo & Pascual Salmon*

CD ROUCD 1130
Rounder / Mar '97 / ADA / CM / Direct

MERINGUE
CD CO 107
Corason / Jan '94 / ADA / CM / Direct

MERRY CHRISTMAS
CD ENTCD 200
Entertainers / '88 / Target/BMG

MERRY CHRISTMAS
CD CNCD 5932
Disky / Nov '92 / Disky / THE

MERRY CHRISTMAS
CD CNCD 5969
Disky / Dec '93 / Disky / THE

MERRY CHRISTMAS
CD I 3896012
Galaxy / Oct '96 / ZYX

MERRY CHRISTMAS FROM MOTOWN
Little Christmas tree: *Jackson, Michael* / Christmas lullaby: *Robinson, Smokey & The Miracles* / This Christmas: *Ross, Diana* / Christmas song: *Gaye, Marvin* / Wish you a merry Christmas: *Weston, Kim* / Silent night: *Ross, Diana & The Supremes* / Christmas in the city: *Gaye, Marvin* / Everyone's a kid at Christmas time: *Wonder, Stevie* / Winter wonderland: *Funk Brothers* / I want to come home for Christmas: *Gaye, Marvin* / Just a lonely Christmas: *Ross, Diana & The Supremes* / Won't be long before Christmas: *Ross, Diana & The Supremes* / Miracles of Christmas: *Wonder, Stevie* / Purple snowflake: *Gaye, Marvin*
CD 5507192
Spectrum / Nov '96 / PolyGram

MERSEYMANIA (20 Fab Sounds Of The Sixties)
I saw her standing there / Charmless man / Won't you come out tonight / I'll have to get another girl / She loves you / What shall I do / There I go / Please please me / Tell me now / Your me now / Your kind of love / You don't tell me you don't know / Tell me I'm the one / This is what I mean / This what I mean / In a little while / I want to hold your hand / I don't need you / Joshua / Maybe I will / Seems to me / Baby you can do no wrong / Night without end
CD 306022
Hallmark / Jan '97 / Carlton

MESMER VARIATIONS (Works Inspired By Mesmer/2CD Set)
CD Set ASH 18CD
Ash International / Oct '95 / Kudos / Pinnacle

MESSAGE - THE HISTORY OF RAP VOL.1
CD NTRCD 024
Nectar / Sep '94 / Pinnacle

MESSAGE - THE HISTORY OF RAP VOL.2, THE
CD NTRCD 046
Nectar / May '96 / Pinnacle

MESSAGE - THE HISTORY OF RAP VOL.3
CD NTRCD 075
Nectar / Mar '97 / Pinnacle

MESSAGE IN THE MUSIC
CD ABYSSCD 1
Abyss / May '90 / Total/BMG

METAL BOX (3CD Set)
CD Set TBXCD 506
TrueTrax / Jan '96 / THE

METAL BOX (2CD Set)
CD Set PBXCD 506
Pulse / Nov '96 / BMG

METAL COMPILATION, THE
I'd rather go wild: *Witchfynde* / Take it all away: *Girlschool* / Fighting chance: *Heritage* / Love, guns and money: *Torme, Bernie* / Angels of death: *Hawkwind* / I will survive: *Terraplane* / See you in heaven: *Ace Lane* / First (the only one): *Tygers Of Pan Tang* / Runnin' scared: *Savage* / Sweet dream maker: *Gaskin* / In the stars: *Witchfynde* / Battlezone: *Mournblade* / All the time: *Tiger* / Hardcore: *Torme, Bernie* / Hideaway: *Tygers Of Pan Tang* / Sky's falling down: *Persian Risk* / Eye for an eye: *Savage* / Motorhead: *Hawkwind*
CD SUMCD 4093
Summit / Jan '97 / Sound & Media

METAL ERUPTION
CD 398414212CD
Metal Blade / Jun '96 / Pinnacle / Plastic Head

METAL KILLERS
White line fever: *Motorhead* / Blood guts and beer: *Tank* / Nothing to lose: *Girlschool* / Urban guerilla: *Hawkwind* / Now comes the storm: *Thor* / Not for sale: *Girlschool* / Run like hell: *Tank* / Beer drinkers and hell raisers: *Motorhead* / Start raisin' hell: *Thor* / Last flight: *Jaguar* / Bump and grind: *Williams, Wendy O.*
CD MATCD 264
Castle / May '93 / BMG

METAL MANIA (2CD Set)
CD Set DCDCD 206
Castle / Jun '95 / BMG

METAL MANIA
CD MACCD 158
Autograph / Aug '96 / BMG

METAL MASSACRE
CD 398414082CD
Metal Blade / Nov '95 / Pinnacle / Plastic Head

METAL MASSACRE 10
CD CDZORRO 4
Metal Blade / May '94 / Pinnacle / Plastic Head

METAL MONOLITHS (2CD Set)
CD Set 24076
Delta Doubles / Jun '96 / Target/BMG

METAL MONSTERS
CD CDTB 507
Thunderbolt / May '96 / TKO Magnum

METAL PRAISE
Rock of ages / Jehovah Jireh / Holy holy holy / What a friend we have in Jesus / O come, o come Emmanuel / We exalt thee / Spirit song / I love you Lord / Life begun / He's the Lord
CD 7016944611
Myrrh / Apr '92 / Nelson Word

METARD NTAMAGANYA (Rwandan Court And Folk Songs)
CD W 260075
Inedit / Apr '97 / ADA / Discovery / Harmonia Mundi

METEOR ROCKABILLIES
Mama's little baby: *Thompson, Junior* / Raw deal: *Thompson, Junior* / Tongue tied Jill: *Feathers, Charlie* / Get with it: *Feathers, Charlie* / Rock, roll and rhythm: *McGinnis, Wayne* / Lonesome rhythm blues: *McGinnis, Wayne* / Don't shoot me baby (I'm not ready to die): *Bowen, Bill* / Have myself a ball: *Bowen, Bill* / All messed up: *Hooper, Jess* / Sleepy time blues: *Hooper, Jess* / Latch on to your baby: *Lamberth, Jimmy* / Bop baby bop: *Suggs, Brad* / Charcoal suit: *Suggs, Brad* / Can't steal my way around: *Burcham, Barney* / Much too young for love: *Burcham, Barney* / Curfew: *Carl, Steve & The Jags* / Eighteen year old blues: *Carl, Steve & The Jags* / Gonna shut you off baby: *Haggett, Jimmy* / Women: *Smith, Lendon & The Jesters* / Brother that's all: *Hadley, Red* / Real gone baby: *Velvetones* / Gal named Joe: *Sales, Mac* / Yakety yak: *Mac & Jake* / Don't worry 'bout nothin': *Dixon, Mason*
CD CDCHM 484
Ace / Jul '93 / Pinnacle

MEXICAN INDIAN TRADITIONS : CELEBRATIONS
CD AUD 08304
Auvidis/Ethnic / Feb '93 / ADA / Harmonia Mundi

MEXICAN LANDSCAPES VOL.3
CD PS 65903
PlayaSound / Mar '92 / ADA / Harmonia Mundi

MEXICAN LANDSCAPES VOL.4
CD PS 65904
PlayaSound / Apr '92 / ADA / Harmonia Mundi

MEXICAN LANDSCAPES VOL.5
CD PS 65905
PlayaSound / Sep '92 / ADA / Harmonia Mundi

MEXICAN LANDSCAPES VOL.7
CD PS 65907
PlayaSound / Nov '93 / ADA / Harmonia Mundi

MEXICAN REVOLUTION, THE (4CD/ Book Set)
Ignacio Parra: *Los Alegres De Teran* / Valentin Mancera: *Trio Los Aguilillas* / Corrido de Macario Romero: *Abrego Y Picazo* / Potro Lobo Gateada: *Mariachi Mexico Del Norte* / Jesus Leal: *Robinson, Rafael Herrera* / Jesus Leal: *Rocha, Pedro & Lupe Martinez* / Heraclio Bernal: *Trio Nava* / Benito Canales: *Hernandez Y Sifuentes* / Nuevo corrido de madero: *Comacho, Manuel & Regino Perez* / El cuartelazo: *Los Hermanos Chavarria* / El cuartelazo: *Hermanas Mendoza* / Fusilamiento de General Argumendo: *Hernandez Y Sifuentes* / Benjamin Argumendo: *Berlanga, Andres & Francisco Montalvo* / Fusilamiento de Felipe Angeles: *San Roman Y Vera* / Corrido de durango: *Los Darados De Durango* / Gral Francisco Villa: *Los Cuatezones* / La toma de torreon: *Los Alegres De Teran* / Toma de Guadalajara: *Las Jilguerillas* / La toma de zacatecas: *Los Errantes* / Pancho Villa: *Los Hermanos Chavarria* / La punitiva: *Hernandez Y Sifuentes* / La toma de celaya: *Hermanos Banuelos* / Derrota de villa en celaya: *Rocha, Pedro & Jose Angel Colunga* / Rendecion de pancho villa: *Rocha, Pedro & Lupe Martinez* / Corrido historia y muerte del Gral Francisco Villa: *Rubi Y Vivo* / Adelita: *Trio Gonzalez* / Valentina: *Mendoza, Lydia & Family* / Corrido de Juan Vasquez: *Mendoza, Juanita & Maria* / Corrido de Juan Carrasco: *Meza, Luis Perez* / Corrido de palomon: *Los Montaneses Del Alamo* / Corrido de Juan Villarreal: *Los Hermanos Garza* / La toma de matamoros: *Lara, Augustin & A. Novelo* / Corrido de almazan: *Mendez & Gonzalez* / Amadour maldonado: *Conjunto Tamaulipas* / Corrido de margarito: *Dueto America* / Refugio solano: *Dueto Sandoval* / Julian Del Real: *Hermanos Yanez* / Corrido de Inez Chavez Garcia: *Hermanos Banuelos* / Quirino Navarro: *Trio Los Aguilillas* / Tragedia de Maximiliano Vigueras: *Medellin, Emilio & Lupe Posada* / Corrido de cedillo: *Los Morenos* / Corrido de Yurecuaro y Tanhuato: *Hermanos Banuelos* / Marijuana la soldadera: *Hermanos Banuelos* / Revolucion de Adolfo De La Huerta: *Briceno, Alcides & Jorge Anez* / La pura pelada: *Trio Luna* / El arreglo religioso: *Duo Coahuila* / La nueva revolucion: *San Roman Y Vera* / Ortiz rubio: *La Bella Netty & Jesus Rodriguez* / El corrido del agrarista: *Trovadores Tamaulipecos* / General Obregon: *Trio Luna* / El radiograma: *Guzman & Rosales* / Corrido de toral: *Trovadores Tapatinos* / General Emiliano Zapata: *Trio Luna* / Corrido del General Cardenas: *Del Valle Y Rivas* / El corrido del petroleo: *Ray Y Laurita* / La rielera: *Mendoza, Lydia & Family* / Gral Porfirio Diaz: *Dueto Acosta* / Tiempos amargos: *Dueto America*
CD Set ARHCD 7041/44
Arhoolie / Nov '96 / ADA / Cadillac / Direct

MEXICAN-AMERICAN BORDER MUSIC VOL.1 (The Pioneer Recordings Artists 1928-1959)
CD ARHCD 7001
Arhoolie / Apr '95 / ADA / Cadillac / Direct

MEXICAN-AMERICAN BORDER MUSIC VOL.3 (Norteno & Tejano Accordion Pioneers)
CD ARHCD 7016
Arhoolie / Jan '96 / ADA / Cadillac / Direct

MEXICAN-AMERICAN BORDER MUSIC VOL.4 (Orquestas Tipicas/Pioneer Dance Orchestras 1926-1938)
Ofelia: *Enriquez, Jose Perches Orquesta* / Coquetona y juguetona: *Quinteto Tipico Mexicano* / Por vida de dios: *Orquesta Acosta-Rosette* / Alicia: *Enriquez, Jose Perches Orquesta* / Alma mia de mi grandota: *Orquesta Del Norte* / Monterrey alegre: *Orquesta Mexicana Calvillo* / Sonador: *Los Desvelados* / Mondragon: *Orquesta De La Familia* / Aborrecido: *Tipica Martinez* / El manoso: *Orquesta Tipica Fronteriza* / Pensado en ti: *Garza, Alfredo M. Orquesta* / La negra: *Banda Chihuahua* / La prieta, la guera y la chata: *Los Desvelados* / Los canedistas: *Orquesta De Guadalupe Acosta* / Adios mi chaparrita: *Caceres, Emilio Y Su Orquesta Del Club Aguila* / El sueno de califas: *Orquesta Tipica Fronteriza* / La reina de las flores: *Orquesta Tipica Fronteriza* / Adios amor mio: *Orquesta Tipica Fronteriza* / Siempre alegre: *Orquesta Tipica Fronteriza* / Es imposible: *Nunez, Tomas Orquesta* / Las gaviotas: *Nunez, Tomas Orquesta* / Penumbra: *Arredondo, Jose Maria Trio* / Besos y cerezas: *Los Cuatezones* / Celosa: *Garza, Eva Con Orquesta* / Jig in G: *Caceres, Emilio Y Su Orquesta Del Club Aguila* / Alma Angelina: *Las Hermanas Padilla & Orquesta De Manuel S. Acuna*
CD ARHCD 7017
Arhoolie / Nov '96 / ADA / Cadillac / Direct

MEXICAN-AMERICAN BORDER MUSIC VOL.5 (Orquestas De Cuerdas/The End Of A Tradition 1926-1938)
El gato negro: *El Ciego Melquiades* / Sobre las olas: *Quinteto Tipico Mexicano* / No te ruborices: *Orquesta De La Familia Ramos* / La paloma: *Sanchez, Eulalio Y Su Quinteto Mexicao* / A mi juana: *Cuarteto Carta Blanca* / El charrio: *Los Desvelados* / Tamaulipeco: *Trovadores Tamaulipecos* / Ay te va de canto: *El Trio Crudo* / A la orilla de un palomar: *Trio Alegre* / Anhelando: *Trio Alegre* / La maestrita: *Cuarteto De Cuerdo De F. Facio* / Carino: *Cuarteto De Cuerdo De F. Facio* / De aquella crena: *Trio Alegre* / El poder del amor: *Trio Alegre* / La bola: *Cuarteto Monterrey* / Panchita: *Familia Mendoza* / Jesusita en chihuahua: *Los Desvelados* / Marosovia: *Los Alegres* / La respingona: *Morales, Santiago* / Porque eres ansina: *Trio Alamo* / Andale vamos platicando: *Medina River Boys* / Maria Christina: *El Ciego Melquiades* / Jallisco nunca pierde: *El Ciego Melquiades* / Se murio la cucaracha: *Mendoza, Lydia* / Montana: *Marmolejo, Juan Mariachi Tapatio* / New Spanish two step: *Boyd, Bill Cowboy Ramblers*
CD ARHCD 7018
Arhoolie / Nov '96 / ADA / Cadillac / Direct

MEXICO
CD CD 62025
Saludos Amigos / Oct '93 / Target/BMG

MEXICO
CD Y 225712
Silex / Dec '96 / ADA / Harmonia Mundi

MEXICO - FIESTAS OF CHIAPAS & OAXACA
CD 7559720702
Nonesuch / Jan '95 / Warner Music

MICRODELIA
Happenings ten years time ago: *Yardbirds* / Moonshine heather: *Parliament* / Candy Cane madness: *George, Lowell* / Faded picture: *Seeds* / Life is just beginning: *Creation* / Flowers never cry: *Mystic Astrological Crystal Band* / Driftin': *Buckley, Tim* / Country boy: *HP Lovecraft* / Bleeker Street: *HP Lovecraft* / Levity Ball: *Cooper, Alice* / Spinning wheel: *Flaming Ember* / Somebody to love: *Great Society* / Christopher Lucifer: *Nirvana* / Don't talk to strangers: *Beau Brummels* / Trip: *Fire Escape* / Revelation in slow motion: *Count Five* / Down on me: *Big Brother & The Holding Company* / Charlie: *Deviants* / Aton 1: *Ceyleib People*
CD DIAB 811
Diabolo / Jun '94 / Pinnacle

MID ATLANTIC SESSIONS
CD MMB 92
Moonshine / Sep '94 / Mo's Music Machine / Prime / RTM/Disc

MIDNIGHT BLUE
Ill wind: *Quebec, Ike* / Please send me someone to love: *Smith, Jimmy* / Lover man: *Marable, Lawrence Quartet & James Clay* / Nearness of you: *Hartman, Johnny* / Smoke gets in your eyes: *Shank, Bud & The Lee Mercer Strings* / Autumn leaves: *Hawkins, Coleman* / Fly me to the moon: *Cole, Nat 'King' & George Shearing* / After the rain: *Pearson, Duke* / Sweet and lovely: *Perkins, Bill & Richie Kamuca* / You don't know what love is: *Wilson, Cassandra* / Nancy (with the smiling face): *Green, Grant* / (It will have to do) until the real thing comes along: *Gordon, Dexter* / Willow weep for me: *Turrentine, Stanley & Three Sounds* / I can't get started: *Young, Lester & Nat Cole*
CD CDP 8543652
Blue Note / Oct '96 / EMI

MIDNIGHT CRUISING
You: *Ten Sharp* / Time after time: *Lauper, Cyndi* / Daniel: *John, Elton* / Hold on: *Wilson Phillips* / Higher love: *Winwood, Steve* / Woman in chains: *Tears For Fears* / It's my life: *Talk Talk* / Mercy mercy me/I want you: *Palmer, Robert* / Feel so high: *Des'ree* / Tunnel of love: *Dire Straits* / Jade idol: *Stray Cats* / Driver's seat: *Sniff 'n' The Tears* / How long: *Ace* / Missing you: *Waite, John* / Africa: *Toto* / Sweet freedom: *McDonald, Michael* / Drive: *Cars*
CD DINCD 40
Dino / Jul '92 / Pinnacle

MIDNIGHT FLUTE
If you leave me now / Air that I breathe / Wind of change / Tears in heaven / Everything I do (I do it for you) / All I have to do is dream / Massachussetts / California dreamin' / I will always love you / When a man loves a woman / Fly away / One moment in time / I just called to say I love you / San Francisco / All that she wants / Half a minute / Tenderness / Air on a G string
CD CD 6043
Music / Sep '96 / Target/BMG

MIDNIGHT GUITAR
CD GRF 194
Tring / Jun '92 / Tring

MIDNIGHT GUITAR
Just the way you are / Yesterday / All my love / At seventeen / It's all clear to me now / Something / Moonlight serenade / Mama, I'll be home someday / This can't be love / I write the songs / You needed me / Hey Jude / Feels so good / What are you doing for the rest of your life / At the Copa / Late last night
CD CD 6027
Music / Jun '96 / Target/BMG

MIDNIGHT GUITAR MOODS
What I did for love / Take that look off your face / Evergreen / Close to you / As time goes by / Where is love / On this night of a thousand stars / Do you know where you're going to / He ain't heavy, he's my brother / Crazy / Vaya con dios / Smoke gets in your eyes
CD CDMFP 6222
Music For Pleasure / May '96 / EMI

MIDNIGHT HOUR
CD RNCD 2090
Rhino / Feb '95 / Grapevine/PolyGram / Jet Star

MIDNIGHT IN JAMAICA (2CD Set)
CD Set SMDCD 111
Snapper / Jul '97 / Pinnacle

MIDNIGHT JAZZ MOODS VOL.1
CD TMPCD 019
Temple / Mar '96 / BMG

MIDNIGHT JAZZ MOODS VOL.2
CD TMPCD 020
Temple / Jul '96 / BMG

MIDNIGHT JAZZ MOODS VOL.3
CD TMPCD 021
Temple / Jul '96 / BMG

MIDNIGHT MOODS (The Lighter Side Of Jazz)
Unforgettable: *Cole, Nat 'King'* / Fever: *Lee, Peggy* / Mad about the boy: *Washington, Dinah* / Girl from Ipanema: *Gilberto, Astrud* / Smooth operator: *Sade* / Lily was here: *Stewart, David A. & Candy Dulfer* / It had to be you: *Connick, Harry Jr.* / Take five: *Brubeck, Dave* / Fine romance: *Holiday, Billie* / Every time we say goodbye: *Fitzgerald, Ella* / Misty: *Garner, Erroll* / Cry me a river: *Wilson, Mari* / Goin' out of my head: *Montgomery, Wes* / Take the 'A' train: *O'Day, Anita* / Walk on the wild side: *Smith, Jimmy* / Shadow of your smile: *Peterson, Oscar* / Summertime: *Vaughan, Sarah* / Relax: *Redbone, Leon* / Passing strangers: *Vaughan,*

Sarah & Billy Eckstine / What a wonderful world: *Armstrong, Louis*
CD 5158162
PolyGram TV / Apr '93 / PolyGram

MIDNIGHT MOODS (3CD Set)
As long as he needs me / I dreamed a dream / Born free / I know him so well / With one look / Bright eyes / It's all in the game / Sailing / Memory / Endless love / Moon river / My way / Sometimes when we touch / Groovy kind of love / Without you / You needed me / I've never been to me / Three times a lady / Love changes everything / I will always love you / Yesterday / Summertime / Imagine / True love ways / Last night of the world / Love letters / Get here / When I fall in love / Nobody does it better / Tell me on a Sunday / Body and soul / We have all the time in the world / Embraceable you / Help me make it through the night / How deep is the ocean / Wherever I lay my hat (that's my home)
CD Set CDTRBOX 260
Trio / Oct '96 / EMI

MIDNIGHT MOODS (Midnight Guitar/ Midnight Sax/Midnight Flute - 3CD Set)
Just the way you are / Yesterday / All my love / At seventeen / It's all clear to me now / Something / Moonlight serenade / Mama, I'll be home someday / This can't be love / I write the songs / You needed me / Hey Jude / Feels so good / What are you doing the rest of your life / At the Copa / Late last night / Love is all around / Whiter shade of pale / Long and winding road / Woman / Lean on me / How deep is your love / Just the way you are / When I fall in love / Said I loved you...but I lied / Candle in the wind / Will you be there / You've lost that loving feeling / Blue eyes / Dreamlover / We've only just begun / One sweet day / I can love you like that / Can I touch you...there / If you leave me now / Air that I breathe / Wind of change / Tears in heaven / Everything I do (I do it for you) / All I have to do is dream / Massachusetts / California dreamin' / I will always love you / When a man loves a woman / Fly away / One moment in time / I just called to say I love you / San Francisco / All that she wants / Half a minute / Tenderness / Air on a G string
CD Set 55160
Music / Oct '96 / Target/BMG

MIDNIGHT PIANO MOODS
Heal the world / Goodbye yellow brick road / Next time you fall in love / Lady in red / Day by day / Fool on the hill / Make up my heart / Blue moon / On the street where you live / Can't help falling in love / How to handle a woman / Somethin' stupid
CD CDMFP 6223
Music For Pleasure / May '96 / EMI

MIDNIGHT ROCK PRESENTS...
CD MR 001CD96
Midnight Rock / Jul '96 / Grapevine/ PolyGram / Jet Star

MIDNIGHT SAX
Love is all around / Whiter shade of pale / Long and winding road / Woman / Lean on me / How deep is your love / Just the way you are / When I fall in love / Said I loved you...but I lied / Candle in the wind / Will you be there / You've lost that loving feeling / Blue eyes / Dreamlover / We've only just begun / One sweet day / I can love you like that / Can I touch you...there
CD CD 6028
Music / Jun '96 / Target/BMG

MIDNIGHT SAX (2CD Set)
On Broadway: *Zorn, Pete* / Moon ray: *Zorn, Pete* / Songbird: *Zorn, Pete* / Holding back the years: *Zorn, Pete* / Wonderful world: *Zorn, Pete* / Shadow of your smile: *Zorn, Pete* / Baker Street: *Zorn, Pete* / Misty blue: *Zorn, Pete* / Georgia on my mind: *Zorn, Pete* / Crazy: *Zorn, Pete* / Wild horses: *Zorn, Pete* / Girl from Ipanema: *Zorn, Pete* / Nature boy: *Zorn, Pete* / It ain't necessarily so: *Hastings, Jimmy* / My funny Valentine: *Hastings, Jimmy* / Moon river: *Hastings, Jimmy* / Unforgettable: *Abrams, Frank* / Man I love: *Abrams, Frank* / Lily was here: *Sodout, Chris* / Cry me a river: *Sodout, Chris* / Feelings: *Sodout, Chris* / Manha de carnaval: *Sodout, Chris* / Sax for love: *Sodout, Chris* / Warm and blue: *Gaucher, Michael* / Midnight magic: *Gaucher, Michael* / After hours: *Gaucher, Michael* / Belvedere Hotel: *Gaucher, Michael* / Golden gate: *Gaucher, Michael* / Summertime: *Arnopp, Tony* / Misty: *Arnopp, Tony* / Body and soul: *Arnopp, Tony* / Soul view: *Aspery, Ronnie* / Alright tonight: *Aspery, Ronnie* / Midnight song: *Aspery, Ronnie*
CD Set RCACD 210
RCA / Jul '97 / BMG

MIDNIGHT SAX (38 Safe Sax Sounds For Lovers/2CD Set)
How deep is your love / Just the way you are / Wonderful tonight / True / Feelings / Unforgettable / Another day in paradise / Lily was here / It ain't necessarily so / Summertime / My funny valentine / Moon ray / Cry me a river / Wonderful world / Georgia on my mind / Moon river / Shadow of your smile / Misty / Everytime you go away / Holding back the years / Baker Street / Air that I breathe / Candle in the wind / Every time we say goodbye / Yesterday / Don't let the sun go down on me / Nature boy / Girl from Ipanema / Save a prayer / You're so vain / My way / I just called to say I love you / Up on the roof / Misty blue / Crazy / On Broadway / Careless whisper / Songbird
CD Set SUDCD 4504
Summit / Nov '96 / Sound & Media

MIDNIGHT SAX MOODS
Can you feel the love tonight / Mind if I make love to you / Dancing in the dark / Long and winding road / Too much love will kill you / Mona Lisa / I left my heart in San Francisco / It's now or never / Unfogettable / Help me make it through the night / How deep is the ocean / Wherever I lay my hat (that's my home)
CD CDMFP 6221
Music For Pleasure / May '96 / EMI

MIDNIGHT SLOWS VOL.1 (2CD Set)
CD BB 896
Black & Blue / Apr '97 / Discovery / Koch / Wellard

MIDNIGHT SLOWS VOL.6
CD BLE 190932
Black & Blue / Apr '91 / Discovery / Koch / Wellard

MIDNIGHT SLOWS VOL.8
CD BLE 193582
Black & Blue / Apr '91 / Discovery / Koch / Wellard

MIDNIGHT SOUL
Never too much: *Vandross, Luther* / Harvest for the world: *Isley Brothers* / Street life: *Crusaders* / Higher and higher: *Wilson, Jackie* / Never knew love like this before: *Mills, Stephanie* / I'm your puppet: *Purify, James & Bobby* / Have you seen her: *Chi-Lites* / Dance to the music: *Sly & The Family Stone* / Lean on me: *Withers, Bill* / Come into my life: *Sims, Joyce* / Move on up: *Mayfield, Curtis* / I love music: *O'Jays* / It's man's world: *Brown, James* / Love I lost: *Melvin, Harold* / Reunited: *Peaches & Herb* / rescue me: *Bass, Fontella* / Way we were: *Knight, Gladys & The Pips* / Soul city walk: *Bell, Archie & The Drells*
CD MUSCD 006
MCI Music / Nov '92 / Disc / THE

MIDSUMMER NIGHT DREAMS
I feel free: *Cream* / Making time: *Creation* / Children of the sun: *Misunderstood* / Season of the witch: *Donovan* / I can hear the grass grow: *Move* / Night of the long grass: *Troggs* / Days of Pearly Spencer: *McWilliams, David* / Paper sun: *Traffic* / Flight from Ashiya: *Kaleidoscope* / Tiny goddess: *Nirvana* / My white bicycle: *Tomorrow* / From the underworld: *Herd* / King Midas in reverse: *Hollies* / I can see for miles: *Who* / Skeleton and the round about: *Idle Race* / Me my friend: *Family* / It's alright, It's only witchcraft: *Family* / Can't find my way home: *Blind Faith*
CD 5535992
Debutante / Jun '97 / PolyGram

MIGHTY BOX PLAYING
CD GTDCD 007
GTD / Jan '95 / ADA / Else

MIGHTY MOON, THE
CD MRSP 003
Music Research / Aug '94 / Plastic Head

MIGHTY WURLITZER VOL.1, THE (50 All Time Favourites)
CD SWBCD 201
Sound Waves / Sep '94 / Target/BMG

MIGHTY WURLITZER VOL.1, THE
Let's twist again/Let's dance/Oh boy / Sweet Caroline/Hi ho silver lining/My boy lollipop / Locomotion/That's livin' alright/ Atmosphere / Is this the way to Amarillo/I only want to be with you/Will / Fame/Happy heart/Young ones / What'll I do/At the end of the day/'Till we meet again / Bless 'em all/After the ball/I'm forever blowing bubbles / My bonnie lies over the ocean/Down at the old bull and bush / It's a sin to tell a lie/ Who's taking you home tonight/Alway / Walkin' my baby back home/Maybe it's because I'm a Londoner// For me and my gal/ Show me the way to go home / Can't help falling in love/Wonder of you / Birdie song
CD QED 084
Tring / Nov '96 / Tring

MIGHTY WURLITZER VOL.2, THE (50 All Time Favourites)
CD SWBCD 202
Sound Waves / Sep '94 / Target/BMG

MIGHTY WURLITZER VOL.2, THE
Around the world/Pal of my cradle days/ Edelweiss / Are you lonesome tonight/ When I grow too old to dream / California here I come/Five foot two, eyes of blue/ When you' / Don't dilly dally on the way/ Happy wanderer/Pack up your tro / Who were you with last night/A long way to Tipperary / American patrol/Little brown jug/ Don't sit under the apple t / Raining in my heart/Downtown/Do wah diddy diddy / Teenager in love/YMCA/Diana / I should be so lucky/Rockin' all over the world/Knock three / Ob-la-di ob-la-da/Beautiful Sunday/ Rhinestone cowboy / Can't take my eyes off you/Sugar sugar / Rock around the clock/Teddy bear/When the saints go marching / Over the rainbow/Unchained melody/You'll never walk alone / In the news
CD QED 085
Tring / Nov '96 / Tring

MIGHTY WURLITZER, THE
Chattanooga choo choo / You'll never know / September in the rain / Jeepers creepers / Pasadena / Happy days are here again / I wonder where my baby is tonight / Saturday rag / Let's face the music and dance / Top hat, white tie and tails / You were never lovelier / Cheek to cheek / I'm beginning to see the light / I've got a gal in Kalamazoo / It don't mean a thing if it ain't got that swing / Fascinating rhythm / They can't take that away from me / Somebody loves me / Someone to watch over me / Wonderful guy / My favourite things / Wonderful day / Mona Lisa / Orange coloured sky / Those lazy crazy days of Summer / I've got a pocketful of dreams / Zing went the strings of my heart / Painting the clouds with sunshine / Me and my girl / Maizy doats and doazy doats / Don't fence me in / We're gonna hang out the washing on the Siegfried line / Oh lady be good / Our love is here to stay / Liza / Embraceable / My fair lady
CD SUMCD 4030
Summit / Nov '96 / Sound & Media

MILESTONE AT THE GARDEN
CD ROU 1123
Rounder / May '96 / ADA / CM / Direct

MILESTONES (20 Rock Operas)
Bohemian rhapsody: *Queen* / I don't like Mondays: *Boomtown Rats* / Bat out of hell: *Meat Loaf* / Don't let the sun go down on me: *John, Elton* / Samba pa ti: *Santana* / Hotel California: *Eagles* / I'm not in love: *10cc* / 10538 overture: *ELO* / Wuthering Heights: *Bush, Kate* / Oxygene IV: *Jarre, Jean Michel* / Vienna: *Ultravox* / Nights in white satin: *Moody Blues* / Let's work together: *Canned Heat* / Layla: *Derek & The Dominoes* / Tubular bells: *Oldfield, Mike* / Smoke on the water: *Deep Purple* / Whiter shade of pale: *Procul Harum* / Music: *Miles, John* / Albatross: *Fleetwood Mac* / Drive: *Cars*
CD TCD 2379
Telstar / Dec '89 / BMG

MILITANT SCIENCE
Imaginary world: *Raw Deal* / Ladder: *Purple Kola* / Headless horseman: *Raw Deal* / Renegade: *Tonic* / Mindset: *Native Bass* / Pornagraphica: *Glowball* / Smash & Grab The Flowers: *Asian Dub Foundation & Native Bass* / Tabstramental: *Native Bass* / PKNB: *ADF* / Dalek tune: *Hempolics* / Militant scientist: *ADF & Ramjack Corporation & Master D* / Death is coming: *Todd, Jamie* / Mellow to freedom: *BLIM & MP*
CD BOSCD 001
Botchit & Scarper / Feb '97 / SRD / Vital

MILITARY BAND SPECTACULAR
CD 8441742
Deram / Jan '96 / PolyGram

MILITARY CLASSICS (2CD Set)
Blaze away / High on a hill / It's a long way to Tipperary / Colonel Bogey / Soldiers in the park / There's something about a soldier / Beer barrel polka / Quartermaster's store / Lili Marlene / Soldier's chorus / A Scottish soldier / Changing of the guard / Amazing grace / Where have all the flowers gone / Sodiers of the Queen / Royal ceremony / Victory display / Royal salute / Spitfire prelude / Spitfire fugue / La Rejouissance / Army, the navy & the air force / Calling all workers / Guns of Navarone / Lonely bugler / Fanfare for the common man / Aces high / Greensleeves / On Richmond hill baht'at / Boots & saddles / Homeward / Soldiers on parade / Yankee doodle dandy / Soldier alone / Northern echoes suite / Mist covered mountains / Navy day / V for victory / Marchalong / Day thou gavest
CD Set 330122
Hallmark / Jul '96 / Carlton

MILK FOR PUSSY
CD MQCD 9301
Mad Queen / Jan '94 / SRD

MILLENNIUM GROOVES
CD SPECCD 501
Dust II Dust / Mar '97 / 3mv/Sony / Mo's Music Machine / Prime / SRD

MILLENNIUM: ETERNALLY ALIVE
CD MILL 009CD
Millenium / Nov '94 / Plastic Head / Prime / SRD

MILLION SELLERS - THE BEST OF THE MILLION SELLERS
CD MSCD 1950
Disky / Apr '94 / Disky / THE

MILLION SELLERS - THE EIGHTIES VOL.1
CD MSCD 1971
Disky / Apr '94 / Disky / THE

MILLION SELLERS - THE EIGHTIES VOL.2
CD MSCD 1973
Disky / Oct '94 / Disky / THE

MILLION SELLERS - THE EIGHTIES VOL.3
CD MSCD 1974
Disky / Oct '94 / Disky / THE

MILLION SELLERS - THE EIGHTIES VOL.4
CD MSCD 1975
Disky / Oct '94 / Disky / THE

MILLION SELLERS - THE EIGHTIES VOL.5
CD MSCD 1976
Disky / Oct '94 / Disky / THE

MILLION SELLERS - THE FIFTIES VOL.1
CD MSCD 1951
Disky / Apr '94 / Disky / THE

MILLION SELLERS - THE FIFTIES VOL.2
CD MSCD 1952
Disky / Apr '94 / Disky / THE

MILLION SELLERS - THE FIFTIES VOL.3
CD MSCD 1953
Disky / Apr '94 / Disky / THE

MILLION SELLERS - THE FIFTIES VOL.4
CD MSCD 1954
Disky / Apr '94 / Disky / THE

MILLION SELLERS - THE SEVENTIES VOL.1
CD MSCD 1963
Disky / Apr '94 / Disky / THE

MILLION SELLERS - THE SEVENTIES VOL.2
CD MSCD 1964
Disky / Apr '94 / Disky / THE

MILLION SELLERS - THE SEVENTIES VOL.3
CD MSCD 1965
Disky / Apr '94 / Disky / THE

MILLION SELLERS - THE SEVENTIES VOL.4
CD MSCD 1966
Disky / Apr '94 / Disky / THE

MILLION SELLERS - THE SEVENTIES VOL.5
CD MSCD 1967
Disky / Apr '94 / Disky / THE

MILLION SELLERS - THE SEVENTIES VOL.6
CD MSCD 1968
Disky / Apr '94 / Disky / THE

MILLION SELLERS - THE SEVENTIES VOL.7
CD MSCD 1969
Disky / Apr '94 / Disky / THE

MILLION SELLERS - THE SEVENTIES VOL.8
CD MSCD 1970
Disky / Apr '94 / Disky / THE

MILLION SELLERS - THE SIXTIES VOL.1
CD MSCD 1955
Disky / Apr '94 / Disky / THE

MILLION SELLERS - THE SIXTIES VOL.2
CD MSCD 1956
Disky / Apr '94 / Disky / THE

MILLION SELLERS - THE SIXTIES VOL.3
CD MSCD 1957
Disky / Apr '94 / Disky / THE

MILLION SELLERS - THE SIXTIES VOL.4
CD MSCD 1958
Disky / Apr '94 / Disky / THE

MILLION SELLERS - THE SIXTIES VOL.5
CD MSCD 1959
Disky / Apr '94 / Disky / THE

MILLION SELLERS - THE SIXTIES VOL.6
CD MSCD 1960
Disky / Apr '94 / Disky / THE

MILLION SELLERS - THE SIXTIES VOL.7
CD MSCD 1961
Disky / Apr '94 / Disky / THE

MILLION SELLERS - THE SIXTIES VOL.8
CD MSCD 1962
Disky / Apr '94 / Disky / THE

MILLION SELLING HITS OF THE 50'S
Mona Lisa: *Cole, Nat 'King'* / That's amore: *Martin, Dean* / Blueberry Hill: *Domino, Fats* / Rock 'n' roll waltz: *Starr, Kay* / Shotgun boogie: *Ford, Tennessee Ernie* / Mockin' Bird Hill: *Paul, Les & Mary Ford* / Unchained melody: *Baxter, Les* / Come softly to me: *Fleetwoods* / Shrimp boats: *Stafford, Jo* / You send me: *Cooke, Sam* / Fever: *Lee, Peggy* / Here in my heart: *Martino, Al* / On the street where you live: *Damone, Vic* / Oh mein papa: *Calvert, Eddie* / Vaya con dios: *Paul, Les & Mary Ford* / Sixteen tons: *Ford, Tennessee Ernie* / Wheel of fortune: *Starr, Kay* / Ain't that a shame: *Domino, Fats* / Return to me: *Martin, Dean* / Blossom fell: *Cole, Nat 'King'*
CD CDMFP 6047
Music For Pleasure / Jan '89 / EMI

MILLION SELLING HITS OF THE 60'S
Next time: *Richard, Cliff* / I'm telling you now: *Freddie & The Dreamers* / Sloop John B: *Beach Boys* / Sealed with a kiss: *Hyland, Brian* / He ain't heavy, he's my brother: *Hollies* / World of our own: *Seekers* / Tracy: *Cuff Links* / Michael, row the boat ashore: *Highwaymen* / Wichita lineman: *Campbell, Glen* / Carrie Anne: *Hollies* / There's a kind of hush: *Herman's Hermits* / Don't let the sun catch you crying: *Gerry & The Pacemakers* / Little arrows: *Lee, Leapy* / Lucky lips: *Richard, Cliff* / You were made for me:

Freddie & The Dreamers / Tears: *Dodd, Ken* / Monday, Monday: *Mamas & The Papas* / Carnival is over: *Seekers* / Little children: *Kramer, Billy J. & The Dakotas* / Anyone who had a heart: *Black, Cilla*
CD ________ **CDMFP 6063**
Music For Pleasure / Aug '89 / EMI

MIND OF GOA VOL.1
Keeper of the dream: *Angeles* / No other love: *Blue Amazon* / Goaway: *Power Source* / Tantilus: *Shamanic Tribes On Acid* / Balck rain: *Prana* / Wicked mille: *Orichalcum* / Over drive: *Switchblade* / Riding high: *Evolution* / Bubble: *Bubble* / Anjuna: *V* / Miles and smile: *Sit On The Lungi* / Pulsar glitch: *Total Eclipse* / Acid friction: *Shay, Danny & Danny Clapham* / Awakening: *Fahrenheit* / Endorphin: *Spirit Level* / Ni nuclear mushrooms: *Amanite FX*
CD ________ **CDTOT 41**
Jumpin' & Pumpin' / May '96 / 3mv/Sony / Mo's Music Machine

MIND OF GOA VOL.2 (2CD Set)
CD Set ________ **CDTOT 46**
Jumpin' & Pumpin' / Nov '96 / 3mv/Sony / Mo's Music Machine

MIND POLLUTION VOL.1
CD ________ **WOWCD 11**
Words Of Warning / May '93 / SRD / Total/BMG

MIND POLLUTION VOL.2
CD ________ **WOWCD 29**
Words Of Warning / Sep '93 / SRD / Total/BMG

MIND THE GAP VOL.2 (Ultimate Breaks & Beats)
Night time: *Mr. Scruff* / Days gone: *Doppelganger* / Astrologikal: *Droppin' Science* / Fuck dub pt.1: *Droppin' Science* / Stoned groove: *DJ Die* / Dave Yang & Steve Yin dewish t'swish: *Fila Brazillia* / O ze (move d's joint): *Shantel* / Homeboy: *Eskubar* / That was no martian: *Airgoose* / Liquid velvet: *J-Majik* / Mad different methods: *Rush, Ed & Trace & Nico* / Jos dis: *DJ DSL*
CD ________ **GAP 00252**
Groove Attack / Feb '97 / SRD

MINDCONTROL BY JENS (3CD Set)
CD Set ________ **PIAS 556450525**
Plastic Head / Jun '97 / Plastic Head

MINIATURES (A Sequence Of 51 Tiny Masterpieces)
CD ________ **RSG 159**
Resurgence / Mar '97 / Pinnacle

MINIMAL EXPRESSIONS
Blowout expressions: *Blowout Express* / Harmonica track: *Soulboy* / Love in return: *Brown, Diana* / It's the time: *Criminal Element Orchestra* / Ultimate: *Pavonia Ave* / You're mine: *Blowout Express* / Let the fun begin: *Secret Knowledge*
CD ________ **MINX 11CD**
Dorado / Jul '97 / Pinnacle

MINISTRY OF SOUND - CLASSICS (2MC Set)
After the love: *Jesus Loves You* / Always: *MK* / Blow your whistle: *DJ Duke* / Blue: *LaTour* / Energy flash: *Beltram, Joey* / Finaaly: *Peniston, Ce Ce* / For you: *4th Measure Men* / Slve to the vibe: *Aftershock* / Stella: *Jam & Spoon* / Witch doctor: *Van Helden, Armand* / Phantom: *Renegade Soundwave* / Nervous track: *Nu Yorican Soul* / Inside your mind: *Nelson, Grant* / God made me funky: *MD X-Press* / Voices in my mind: *Voices* / (Who) keeps changing: *South Street Players* / Throw: *Paperclip People* / Voodoo ray: *Guy Called Gerald* / Pride: *Clivilles & Cole* / Do you want it right now: *Degrees Of Motion* / Teas: *Knuckles, Frankie* / Passion: *Gat Decor* / French Kiss: *Lil' Louis* / Burning: *MK* / Get busy: *Mr. Lee* / Push the feeling on: *Nightcrawlers* / Progen - move any...: *Shamen* / Alright: *Shamen* / O: *28th Street Crew*
CD Set ________ **CLACD 1**
Ministry Of Sound / Jun '97 / 3mv/Sony / Mo's Music Machine / Warner Music

MINISTRY OF SOUND - LATE NIGHT SESSIONS (Mixed By DJ Harvey)
Bone: *Persuasion* / Garden of Earthly delights: *D-Note* / New Jersey deep: *Black Science Orchestra* / Hiroshi's dub: *TPO* / No excuses dub: *Hunter, Terry* / Jazz y motion: *Batamania* / Souffles H: *Mondo Grosso* / Thank u Mum: *St. Germain* / New day: *Round Two* / Not reggae: *Idjut Boys & LAJ* / Still holdin' on: *Elements Of Life* / Peace: *DJ Food*
CD ________ **SOMCD 4**
Sound Of Ministry / Jul '97 / 3mv/Sony / Amato Disco / Prime

MINISTRY OF SOUND - THE ANNUAL VOL.1 (2CD Set)
CD Set ________ **ANNCD 95**
Ministry Of Sound / Nov '95 / 3mv/Sony / Mo's Music Machine / Warner Music

MINISTRY OF SOUND - THE ANNUAL VOL.2 (2CD Set)
CD Set ________ **ANNCD 96**
Ministry Of Sound / Nov '96 / 3mv/Sony / Mo's Music Machine / Warner Music

MINISTRY OF SOUND - THE SESSIONS VOL.1 (Mixed By Tony Humphries)
All funked up: *Mother* / Mings incredible disco machine: *Brothers Love Dubs* / Let's dance: *Mr. Peach* / Movin' on: *Roach Motel* / Take a ride: *Club 69* / Dreams: *Gabrielle* / Take it to the top: *New Dance Republic* / London x-press: *Xpress 2* / Black sky: *Shakespears Sister* / Question: *Seven Grand Housing Authority* / Slide on the rhythm: *Arizona & Zietia* / Testament one: *Chubby Chunks Vol.1*
CD ________ **MINCD 1**
Ministry Of Sound / Jul '97 / 3mv/Sony / Mo's Music Machine / Warner Music

MINISTRY OF SOUND - THE SESSIONS VOL.2 (Mixed By Paul Oakenfold)
CD ________ **MINCD 2**
Ministry Of Sound / Jul '97 / 3mv/Sony / Mo's Music Machine / Warner Music

MINISTRY OF SOUND - THE SESSIONS VOL.3 (Mixed By Clivilles & Cole)
CD ________ **MINCD 3**
Ministry Of Sound / Jul '97 / 3mv/Sony / Mo's Music Machine / Warner Music

MINISTRY OF SOUND - THE SESSIONS VOL.4 (Mixed By CJ MacKintosh)
CD Set ________ **MINCDB 4**
Ministry Of Sound / Apr '95 / 3mv/Sony / Mo's Music Machine / Warner Music
CD ________ **MINCD 4**
Ministry Of Sound / Jul '97 / 3mv/Sony / Mo's Music Machine / Warner Music

MINISTRY OF SOUND - THE SESSIONS VOL.5 (Mixed By Masters Of Work - 2CD Set)
CD ________ **MINCD 5**
Ministry Of Sound / Jul '97 / 3mv/Sony / Mo's Music Machine / Warner Music

MINISTRY OF SOUND - THE SESSIONS VOL.6 (Mixed By Frankie Knuckles - 2CD Set)
Good love: *Incognito* / Joy you bring: *Swing 52* / So special: *Spice Of Life & Gina Foster* / I appreciate: *Brown, Kathy* / Race of survival: *Sonz Of Soul & Steven Ville* / Another day: *Sledge, Kathy* / Skyhigh: *Voices & Individual* / I remember dance: *Chuggles* / Freedom (Make it funky): *Black Magic* / Live in unity: *Dangerous Minds* / Day in the life: *Terry, Todd* / Keep movin': *Mone* / Love rendezvous: *M-People* / In the trees: *Faze Action* / Hypnodelic: *FK* / Heavy gospel meeting: *Black Science Orchestra* / I'm so grateful: *Kings Of Tomorrow & Densaid* / Alabama blues: *St. Germain* / Bounce: *Kenlou* / Sound: *X-Press 2* / Limbo of vanished: *Tone Theory* / Theme: *Hot Lizard* / Reach: *Lil' Mo' Yin Yang* / Baby can you reach: *Limelife*
CD Set ________ **MINCD 6**
Ministry Of Sound / Jul '97 / 3mv/Sony / Mo's Music Machine / Warner Music

MINISTRY OF SOUND - THE SESSIONS VOL.7 (Mixed By David Morales - 2CD Set)
CD Set ________ **MINCD 7**
Ministry Of Sound / Jul '97 / 3mv/Sony / Mo's Music Machine / Warner Music

MINISTRY OF SOUND PRESENTS AWOL - LIVE
CD ________ **AWOLCD 1**
Ministry Of Sound / Jul '95 / 3mv/Sony / Mo's Music Machine / Warner Music

MINISTRY OF SOUND PRESENTS THE FUTURE SOUND OF NEW YORK
CD ________ **SOMCD 1**
Ministry Of Sound / Mar '95 / 3mv/Sony / Mo's Music Machine / Warner Music

MINIT/INSTANT STORY, THE (2CD Set)
CD Set ________ **CDLAB 101**
Charly / Jan '96 / Koch

MINSTREL BANJO STYLE
CD ________ **ROUCD 0321**
Rounder / Dec '94 / ADA / CM / Direct

MINSTREL BOY, THE (Irish Singers Of Great Renoun)
CD ________ **GEMMCD 9989**
Pearl / Nov '92 / Harmonia Mundi

MIRKKOCALBMI
CD ________ **DATCD 21**
Dat / Nov '95 / ADA / Direct

MISAS Y FIESTAS MEXICANAS
Misa panamericana (messe des mariachis) / Misa tepozteca / La charreada / Sones de michoacan / El taconaso / Hymne au soleil / Danza de los negritos / Danza de los voladores / Danza de los viejitos
CD ________ **ARN 64017**
Arion / '88 / ADA / Discovery

MISCELLANEOUS VOL.1
Under pressure: *Bluefoot* / Unix: *Biomuse* / Lowdown: *Tranquil Elephantizer* / Lunar tunes: *ARC* / Subether: *Endemic Void* / AEA: *Circadian Rhythms* / Moonrise: *Pooley, Ian* / Jinn: *Tao* / Pentax: *Launchdat* / Shapeshifter: *Fantomas* / Living dust: *Toop, David* / Sub evening lullaby: *Takshaka*
CD ________ **WORDD 1**
Language / Jul '95 / Grapevine/PolyGram / Prime / Vital

MISCELLANEOUS VOL.2
Infinitesimal: *Nad* / Miracle tonic: *Mr. Foster* / Ghost submarine: *Bermuda Triangle* / Sniper: *Occupiers* / Waiting wall: *Steve C* / We R walkin': *Phume* / Alpha Beta Gamma: *Buckfunk 3000* / Why we feel so uncomfortable about the future: *Skrew & Wrap* / Earth hum: *No Sleep* / March of Osiris: *Elixir* / 80's funky: *Decal* / Ouagga: *Phluide* / Zeitgeist: *Isis* / Uncitizen: *Deform*
CD ________ **WORDD 003**
Language / Sep '96 / Grapevine/PolyGram / Prime / Vital

MISFITS OF SKA VOL.1
CD ________ **AM 002**
Asian Man / Feb '97 / Cargo / Greyhound / Plastic Head

MISFITS OF SKA VOL.2
CD ________ **AM 006**
Asian Man / Feb '97 / Cargo / Greyhound / Plastic Head

MISS MONEYPENNY'S GLAMOROUS ONE (Mixed By Tony De Vit/Mark Moore/Jim Ryan - 3CD Set)
You got me: *DJ Eclipse* / Show me love: *Fruit Loop* / Motor: *Experts* / Pump up the jam '96: *Technotronic* / Trippy: *De Vit, Tony* / Bette Davis eyes: *Carnes, Kim* / Don't ever stop: *De Vit, Tony* / Amber groove: *SAS* / Give me love: *Diddy* / Hey child: *East 17* / Fever: *SJ* / Take me away: *Brainbashers* / Boopaloopa: *Bi Boys Action Squad* / Killa beat: *NY Alliance* / Funk me: *Clank* / Slip: *Soul Surfers* / Female of the species: *Space* / Vis r' vis: *R-Factor* / Theme from s'express: *S'Express* / Discotecs: *Playmate Puzzle* / Tall n' handsome: *Outrage* / Europhoria: *Last Disco Superstars* / Child: *Baby Blue* / It's about rhythm: *Baby Blue* / Remember me: *Blueboy* / Higher: *Richardson, Kim* / Deep in you: *Louise, Tania* / Do without: *Retrakt* / Messin' with my mind: *Dominatrix* / Good times: *Twangling, Mike* / Sexy thing: *JP Presents* / Eastern promise: *Travis Bickle* / TGV: *Sublime* / Atom bomb: *Fluke* / Victor Imbres presents fire: *Imbres, Victor* / Los puerbos: *Two Amigos* / Dodo bassburger dub: *UCC* / Alright: *BOP & Earl Bennett*
CD Set ________ **MPENNYCD 1**
Miss Moneypenny's / Mar '97 / Total/BMG

MISSED BEATS
CD ________ **BBJCD 002**
Black On Black / Jul '96 / Pinnacle / Prime / Vital

MISSING CHORD, THE
CD ________ **GASH 1**
Snatch / Feb '97 / Nervous

MISSING YOU (Sentimental Songs Of World War II)
CD ________ **VJCD 1049**
Vintage Jazz Classics / Feb '94 / ADA / Cadillac / CM / Direct

MISSING YOU - THE BEST OF MISSING YOU
Missing you: *De Burgh, Chris* / It must have been love: *Roxette* / Just another day: *Secada, Jon* / I don't wanna lose you: *Turner, Tina* / Power of love: *Rush, Jennifer* / Come in out of the rain: *Moten, Wendy* / Get here: *Adams, Oleta* / Wishing on a star: *Rose Royce* / Everytime you go away: *Young, Paul* / Missing you: *Waite, John* / Fool (if you think it's over): *Rea, Chris* / She's gone: *Hall & Oates* / Different corner: *Michael, George* / After the love has gone: *Earth, Wind & Fire* / This time: *Carroll, Dina* / Move closer: *Nelson, Phyllis* / Please don't go: *KC & The Sunshine Band* / Unchained melody: *Righteous Brothers* / I miss you: *Haddaway* / Someday (I'm coming back): *Stansfield, Lisa* / Stay: *Eternal* / Teardrops: *Womack & Womack* / Don't turn around: *Ace Of Base* / Dedicated to the one I love: *McLean, Bitty* / Can't stay away from you: *Estefan, Gloria* / When you tell me that you love me: *Ross, Diana* / Up where we belong: *Cocker, Joe & Jennifer Warnes* / Nothing compares 2 U: *O'Connor, Sinead* / Crazy: *Cline, Patsy* / Without you: *Nilsson, Harry* / Your song: *John, Elton* / God only knows: *Beach Boys* / Now and forever: *Marx, Richard* / Promise me: *Craven, Beverley* / Don't know much: *Ronstadt, Linda & Aaron Neville* / All by myself: *Carmen, Eric* / Loving you: *Riperton, Minnie*
CD Set ________ **CDEMTVD 86**
EMI TV / Oct '94 / EMI

MISSION
CD ________ **TYCD 001**
Tan Yah / Jun '92 / Jet Star

MISSION IMPOSSIBLE TO FINAL MISSION
CD ________ **SONCD 0058**
Sonic Sounds / Mar '94 / Jet Star

MISSISSIPPI BLUES
CD ________ **TMCD 07**
Travellin' Man / Oct '91 / Hot Shot / Jazz Music / Wellard

MISSISSIPPI BLUES (2CD Set)
CD Set ________ **PBXCD 402**
Pulse / Dec '96 / BMG

MISSISSIPPI BLUES
Down the dirt road blues: *Patton, Charlie* / Maggie Campbell blues: *Johnson, Tommy* / Canned heat blues: *Johnson, Tommy* / Big fat Mama: *Johnson, Tommy* / Mississippi jail house groan: *Lacy, Rube* / Dough roller blues: *Akers, Garfield* / M & O blues: *Brown, Willie* / Dry spell blues: *House, Son* / I'm so glad: *James, Skip* / Special rider blues: *James, Skip* / Hard time killin' floor blues: *James, Skip* / 22-20 blues: *James, Skip* / 49 Highway blues: *Williams, Big Joe* / Lead pencil blues: *Temple, Johnny* / Fixin' to die blues: *White, Bukka* / Parchman farm blues: *White, Bukka* / Ride 'em on down: *Petway, Robert* / Black spider blues: *Lockwood, Robert Jr.* / Little boy blues: *Lockwood, Robert Jr.* / Crosscut saw blues: *McClennan, Tommy* / Machine gun blues: *Blackwell, Willie '61'* / If I get lucky: *Crudup, Arthur 'Big Boy'* / Mean old 'Frisco blues: *Crudup, Arthur 'Big Boy'*
CD ________ **IGOCD 2039**
Indigo / Mar '97 / ADA / Direct

MISSISSIPPI BLUES & GOSPEL (Field Recordings 1934-1942)
CD ________ **DOCD 5320**
Document / Mar '95 / ADA / Hot Shot / Jazz Music

MISSISSIPPI BLUES VOL.1
CD ________ **DOCD 5157**
Document / May '93 / ADA / Hot Shot / Jazz Music

MISSISSIPPI BLUES VOL.2
CD ________ **DOCD 5158**
Document / May '93 / ADA / Hot Shot / Jazz Music

MISSISSIPPI CIVIL RIGHTS MOVEMENT
CD ________ **FE 1419**
Folk Era / Dec '94 / ADA / CM

MISSISSIPPI DELTA BLUES
CD ________ **IGOCD 2025**
Indigo / Jul '95 / ADA / Direct

MISSISSIPPI DELTA BLUES JAM IN MEMPHIS VOL.1
CD ________ **ARHCD 385**
Arhoolie / Apr '95 / ADA / Cadillac / Direct

MISSISSIPPI DELTA BLUES JAM IN MEMPHIS VOL.2
CD ________ **ARHCD 386**
Arhoolie / Apr '95 / ADA / Cadillac / Direct

MISSISSIPPI GIRLS 1928-1931
CD ________ **SOBCD 3515**
Story Of The Blues / Mar '92 / ADA / Koch

MISSISSIPPI MASTERS: EARLY AMERICAN BLUES CLASSICS
CD ________ **YAZ 2008CD**
Yazoo / Nov '94 / ADA / CM / Koch

MISSISSIPPI: FROM CANADA TO LOUISIANA
CD ________ **PS 65099**
PlayaSound / Nov '92 / ADA / Harmonia Mundi

MISSOURI 1950'S ROCKERS
CD ________ **CLCD 4434**
Collector/White Label / Nov '96 / TKO Magnum

MIST MASTERS - FLEDGLING
Lap of God: *Couch* / Freud's feild day: *Delgados* / Absence: *Supernaturals* / Didn't laugh at all: *Saidflorence* / Spooky: *Love Joy & Happiness* / Eurostar: *Margins* / Bring down the sky: *August* / Fashion victim: *Colour Wheel* / Fugue: *Philo* / Divine in water: *Fuel* / Mary Jane: *Limit Club* / Thank funk it's Friday: *Captain Shifty* / Only one: *Jellyhead* / G 12: *Microwave Babe* / Make it happen: *Skunk Tree* / Awkward: *Geiger Babies* / No reason: *Laughing club* / Coral: *Homecoming* / Banging the drum: *Bond*
CD ________ **IGCD 209**
Iona / Jan '95 / ADA / Direct / Duncans

MISTURADA VOL.2
Tempos atraz: *Flytronix* / Preficiao: *4 Hero* / Jazz carnival: *Global Communication* / Ausgang: *Ze's Trip* / Calma: *Lumen* / Faca de conta: *Roni Size* / Tudo que voce podia ser: *Flytronix* / A quem e roupa: *DJ First Klas* / Tempos atraz: *APE* / Orange sour ouica: *Azymuth*
CD ________ **FARO 15CD**
Far Out / Jun '97 / Amato Disco / New Note/ Pinnacle

MIX ZONE, THE (2CD Set)
There's nothing I won't do: *JX* / Blurred: *Pianoman* / On ya way: *Helicopter* / Read my lips: *Alex Party* / Push the feeling on: *Nightcrawlers* / Heaven knows: *Moraes, Angel* / Keep on jumpin': *Lisa Marie Experience* / Nakasaki (I need a lover tonight): *Kendoh* / Klubhopping: *Klubb Heads* / Giv me luv: *Alcatrazz* / Dreamer: *Livin' Joy* / Higher state of consciousness: *Wink, Josh* / Over and over: *Plux & Georgia Jones* / Lover that you are: *Pulse* / Disco's revenge: *Gusto* / I feel love: *Summer, Donna* / Trippin' on sunshine: *Pizzaman* / Trance piano: *Y-Traxx* / Call on me: *Johnny X* / Are you out there: *Crescendo* / Way it is: *Chameleon* / Yeke yeke: *Kante, Mory* / Have fun: *Coma B* / Children: *Miles, Robert* / Be as one: *Sasha & Maria* / Let me be your fantasy: *Baby D* / Theme from S'Express: *S'Express* / Tempo fiesta: *Itty Bitty Boozy Woozy* / Resonance: *Resonance* / Sunshine after the rain: *Berri* / I need you: *Pendulum* / For what you dream

of: *Bedrock & KYO* / Access: *DJ Misjah & Tim* / X files: *DJ Dado*
CD 5355822
PolyGram TV / Jun '96 / PolyGram

MIXED CD, A
Dr Wheeler: *Statik Sound System* / Way it is: *Dextrous* / Mrs Jones: *Red* / Mountain: *Purple Penguin* / Raw elementz: *State Of Mind* / Sole sentiment: *Ratman* / Timber: *Grantby* / Big duck: *Egg* / In our own time: *Statik Sound System* / Skafter: *Tundra* / Street reality: *Southern Comfort* / Double culture: *Henry & Louis* / Path: *Ratman* / Instruments like this: *Statik Sound System* / Razor: *Purple Penguin* / Shopping: *Egg* / Japanese flute: *Spaceways* / Ghetto blaster: *Pendulum* / Timbuktu: *Disciples*
CD COTCD 007
Cup Of Tea / Mar '97 / Vital

MIXED EMOTIONS (Jazz In The Eighth Dimension)
I'm on: *DJ BMF* / To trap a spy: *Pimp Daddy Nash* / Dub systems go: *Dubmarine* / Uncertain T: *Q-Burns Abstract Message* / Funk is free: *DJ BMF* / Vibe checkin': *Q-Burns Abstract Message* / Wendy lost in velvet: *Pimp Daddy Nash* / Feel the sauce: *Dubmarine* / Wendy lost in jungle: *Pimp Daddy Nash* / Dubmission: *Dubmarine*
CD KOBICD 002
On Delancey Street / Jul '96 / Vital

MIXED EMOTIONS (2CD Set)
If I never see you again: *Wet Wet Wet* / Alone: *Bee Gees* / What becomes of the broken hearted: *Robson & Jerome* / I heard it through the grapevine: *Gaye, Marvin* / After the love has gone: *Earth, Wind & Fire* / Love don't live here anymore: *Rose Royce* / Ain't no sunshine: *Withers, Bill* / Tired of being alone: *Green, Al* / You might need somebody: *Crawford, Randy* / Please don't go: *KC & The Sunshine Band* / eVERYTime you: *KC & The Sunshine Band* / Love on the rocks: *Diamond, Neil* / Sorry seems to be the hardest word: *John, Elton* / Miss you nights: *Richard, Cliff* / Without you: *Nilsson* / All by myself: *Carmen, Eric* / Missing you: *Waite, John* / You've lost that lovin' feelin': *Righteous Brothers* / Sun ain't gonna shine anymore: *Walker Brothers* / Power of love: *Dion, Celine* / Million love songs: *Take That* / When a man loves a woman: *Sledge, Percy* / Endless love: *Ross, Diana & Lionel Richie* / Tonight I celebrate my love: *Bryson, Peabo & Roberta Flack* / Move closer: *Nelson, Phyllis* / get here: *Adams, Oleta* / On the wings of love: *Osborne, Jeffrey* / Always and forever: *Heatwave* / Escaping: *Carroll, Dina* / Eternal flame: *Bangles* / When I need you: *Sayer, Leo* / My love: *McCartney, Paul & Wings* / Here there and everywhere: *Harris, Emmylou* / Love and affection: *Armatrading, Joan* / Lady in red: *De Burgh, Chris* / She makes my day: *Palmer, Robert* / Up where we belong: *Cocker, Joe & Jennifer Warnes* / Glory of love: *Cetera, Peter*
CD Set 5536842
PolyGram TV / Jun '97 / PolyGram

MIXIN'
CD REVCC 005
Revco / May '95 / Grapevine/PolyGram / Timewarp

MIXING IT
CD CHILLCD 004
Chillout / Nov '94 / Kudos / Pinnacle / RTM/Disc

MIXMAG LIVE VOL.1 (Carl Cox/Dave Seaman)
CD MMLCD 001
Mixmag Live / Jul '96 / Pinnacle

MIXMAG LIVE VOL.10 (Dave Seaman/ Masters At Work)
CD MMLCD 010
Mixmag Live / Jul '96 / Pinnacle

MIXMAG LIVE VOL.11 (Big Guns Techno - Sven Vath/Mr. C)
CD MMLCD 011
Mixmag Live / Jul '96 / Pinnacle

MIXMAG LIVE VOL.12 (Jon Pleased Wimmin/LuvDup)
CD MMLCD 012
Mixmag Live / Jul '96 / Pinnacle

MIXMAG LIVE VOL.13 (Techno - Darren Emerson/Dave Angel)
CD MMLCD 013
Mixmag Live / Jul '96 / Pinnacle

MIXMAG LIVE VOL.14 (Mad Hatter's Tea Party - Jeremy Healy/Brandon Block)
CD MMLCD 014
Mixmag Live / Jul '96 / Pinnacle

MIXMAG LIVE VOL.15 (Jumping Jack Frost/Randall)
CD MMLCD 015
Mixmag Live / Jul '96 / Pinnacle

MIXMAG LIVE VOL.16 (Americana - Roger Sanchez/DJ Pierre)
CD MMLCD 016
Mixmag Live / Jul '96 / Pinnacle

MIXMAG LIVE VOL.17 (Future Sound Of Europe - Nick Warren/Dimitri)
CD MMLCD 017
Mixmag Live / Jul '96 / Pinnacle

MIXMAG LIVE VOL.18 (Hardcore Happiness - Stu Allen/Slipmatt)
CD MMLCD 018
Mixmag Live / Jul '96 / Pinnacle

MIXMAG LIVE VOL.19 (Laurent Garnier)
CD MMLCD 019
Mixmag Live / Jul '96 / Pinnacle

MIXMAG LIVE VOL.2 (Grooverider/Justin Robertson)
CD MMLCD 002
Mixmag Live / Jul '96 / Pinnacle

MIXMAG LIVE VOL.20 (Richie Hawtin)
Dry ray: *Lausen* / Quo vadis: *G-Man* / Empower: *Octave One* / Jump: *Broom, Mark* / Wipe: *Teste* / 5 Mouths: *Fred Fresh* / Basic needs: *Goio* / Substance abuse: *FUSE* / Spaz: *Plastikman* / helicopter: *Plastikman* / Percussion electrique: *Dwarf* / Spastik: *Plastikman* / Eye trip: *Bryant, Akilah* / Boiling point: *Xtrak* / Electricity: *Naughty & Tolls* / Dollar: *Schmidt, Tobias* / Live wire: *DBX* / Venus fly trap: *Too Funk* / Cash machines: *Synchrojack* / Key follow: *Hannah, Paul* / Harz: *Sensorama* / Altes testametn: *Roman IV*
CD MMLCD 020
Mixmag Live / Jul '96 / Pinnacle

MIXMAG LIVE VOL.21 (LTJ Bukem)
On link: *Fokus* / Source direct: *Exit 9* / Sorrow and liquid groove: *Future Bound* / Airtight: *Funky Technicians* / No mysery: *Funky Technicians* / One and only: *PFM* / Music: *LTJ Bukem* / We can change the future: *Code Of Practice* / Breathless: *Intense* / Just visiting Mars: *FBD Project* / Free la funk: *JMJ & Richie*
CD MMLCD 021
Mixmag Live / Jul '96 / Pinnacle

MIXMAG LIVE VOL.22 (Doc Scott)
Trichonic cycle: *Jonny L* / Last day: *DJ Krust* / Eye of a needle: *Art Of Noise* / Retransistions: *Deep Blue & Blame* / Life: *Decoder* / Threshold: *Dillinja* / Metropolis: *Adam F* / Shadow boxing: *Nasty Habits* / Brief encounter: *DJ Krust* / Trippin' on broken beats: *Omni Trio* / Circuit breaker: *Decoder* / Red lights: *Hokusai* / Symbiosis: *Jonny L*
CD MMLCD 022
Mixmag Live / Nov '96 / Pinnacle

MIXMAG LIVE VOL.3 (Sasha/CJ Mackintosh)
CD MMLCD 003
Mixmag Live / Jul '96 / Pinnacle

MIXMAG LIVE VOL.4 (Danny Rampling/ Graeme Park)
CD MMLCD 004
Mixmag Live / Jul '96 / Pinnacle

MIXMAG LIVE VOL.5 (Kevin Saunderson/Slipmatt & Lime)
CD MMLCD 005
Mixmag Live / Jul '96 / Pinnacle

MIXMAG LIVE VOL.6 (Joey Beltram/E-Lustrious))
CD MMLCD 006
Mixmag Live / Jul '96 / Pinnacle

MIXMAG LIVE VOL.7 (Moby/Slam)
CD MMLCD 007
Mixmag Live / Jul '96 / Pinnacle

MIXMAG LIVE VOL.8 (Gordon Kaye/ John Digweed)
CD MMLCD 008
Mixmag Live / Jul '96 / Pinnacle

MIXMAG LIVE VOL.9 (Dr. Alex Patterson/Mixmater Morris)
CD MMLCD 009
Mixmag Live / Jul '96 / Pinnacle

MIXOLOGY PRESENTS...TOTALLY KLUBBED UP (2CD Set)
CD Set TKUCD 1
Mixology / Mar '97 / Total/Pinnacle

MLLE. SWING ET M. ZAZOU
CD DEM 017
Chansons Actualites / Nov '95 / Discovery

MO' COOKIN'
CD URCD 004
Ubiquity / Jul '96 / Cargo / Timewarp

MO' HOUSE YO MAMA
CD MM 800242
Moonshine / Mar '96 / Mo's Music Machine / Prime / RTM/Disc

MO' STEPPERS
Grazing in the grass: *Wonder, Stevie* / Use it or lose it: *Gotham* / Open your door: *Guinn* / Brickhouse: *Commodores* / Bad weather: *Supremes* / Too high: *Brown, Norman* / I can't help it: *Washington, Grover Jr.* / Break the ice: *Lovesmith, Michael* / Jones': *Temptations* / Can I get a witness: *Randolph, Barbara* / All night long: *Mary Jane Girls* / Tell me tomorrow (12" mix): *Robinson, Smokey* / T plays it cool: *Gaye, Marvin* / Love just wouldn't be right: *Marie, Teena* / World of ours: *Alston, Gerald* / It's a shame: *Detroit Spinners*
CD 5302332
Motown / Mar '94 / PolyGram

MOD JAZZ (60's Discotheque Dancers For The Cool School)
Soul shoutin': *Scott, Shirley* / Collard greens: *McCoy, Freddie* / Tengo tango: *Adderley, Cannonball* / Why don't you do right: *Murphy, Mark* / Money's gettin' cheaper: *Witherspoon, Jimmy* / Step out & git it: *Nomos* / Theme from The Carpetbaggers: *McDuff, 'Brother' Jack* / Theme from NYPD: *Smith, Johnny 'Hammond'* / Whip it on me: *Hawks, Billy* / Evil ways: *Tjader, Cal* / Yeh yeh: *Santamaria, Mongo* / Watermelon man: *Santamaria, Mongo* / Seventh son: *Allison, Mose* / I'm ready: *Spann, Otis* / Pool shark: *Jackson, Willis* / Soul shack: *Stitt, Sonny* / Filthy McNasty: *Jefferson, Eddie* / Love me right: *Witherspoon, Jimmy* / I've got your number: *Bowie, Pat* / Black talk: *Earland, Charles* / Mama Rufus: *Merced Blue Notes* / Soul liberation: *Bryant, Rusty* / Games: *Jones, 'Boogaloo' Joe* / Kenny's theme: *Burrell, Kenny* / Pink Panther: *McDuff, 'Brother' Jack*
CD CDKEND 139
Kent / Sep '96 / Pinnacle

MODERN ARCHITECTURE OF HOUSE
CD D 945002
Bunker/D'Vision / Jan '95 / Plastic Head

MODERN ART OF JAZZ, THE
CD BCD 120
Biograph / '92 / ADA / Cadillac / Direct / Hot Shot / Jazz Music / Wellard

MODERN CAJUN LOVERS
CD TRIK 0166
Trikont / Oct '94 / ADA / Direct

MODERN CHICAGO BLUES
CD TCD 5008
Testament / Oct '94 / ADA / Koch

MODERN ELECTRONICS VOL.1
CD SUB 2D
Subversive / Sep '95 / 3mv/Sony / Amato Disco / Mo's Music Machine / Prime / Vital

MODERN ELECTRONICS VOL.2
CD SUB 8D
Subversive / Feb '96 / 3mv/Sony / Amato Disco / Mo's Music Machine / Prime / Vital

MODERN ELECTRONICS VOL.3
CD SUB 19D
Subversive / Jul '96 / 3mv/Sony / Amato Disco / Mo's Music Machine / Prime / Vital

MODERN LOVE (17 Of Today's Classic Love Songs)
Don't let the sun go down on me: *Michael, George & Elton John* / Save the best for last: *Williams, Vanessa* / Stay: *Shakespears Sister* / Goodnight girl: *Wet Wet Wet* / You: *Ten Sharp* / Fall at your feet: *Crowded House* / I wonder why: *Stigers, Curtis* / Time to make you mine: *Stansfield, Lisa* / Everytime you go away: *Young, Paul* / Promise me: *Craven, Beverley* / Get here: *Adams, Oleta* / When you tell me that you love me: *Ross, Diana* / My girl: *Temptations* / Every kinda people: *Palmer, Robert* / Coming out of the dark: *Estefan, Gloria* / Unchained melody: *Righteous Brothers* / Valerie: *Winwood, Steve*
CD 5155182
PolyGram TV / Jun '92 / PolyGram

MODERN NEW ORLEANS MASTERS
CD ROUCD 11514
Rounder / '88 / ADA / CM / Direct

MODERN SOUL VOL.2 (Boss Grooves)
Show me the way: *Seville* / I can't get over losing you: *Butler, Sam* / Take another look: *Saunders, Frankie* / Try love again: *Pro-fascination* / Let me give love: *Empire, Freddie* / Give me love: *EKG* / You keep holding back on love: *Sue, Carletta* / This time it's real: *Nevilles, Larry* / Something inside: *Raj* / What's the use: *Troutman, Tony* / I'll cry over you: *Sheeler, Cynthia* / You're gonna wreck my life: *Guitar Ray* / Where is the love: *Calton, Richard* / Very special girl: *White, Earl* / Man in love: *Wright, Bill* / Sexy lady: *Sideshow* / I've got to have your love: *Robertson, Chuck*
CD GSCD 015
Goldmine / May '93 / Vital

MODERN SOUL VOL.4
Your love's got me: *Satin* / Time is right for love: *Reed, Bobby* / My heart just can't take it: *Essex IV* / Beggin' for a broken heart: *Jackson, Otis* / Now you're gone: *Smoke* / I get groove from you: *Shannon, Bobby* / One shirt: *Marshall, Gene & The Ghetto Sons* / This I've gotta see: *Shaw, Cecil* / Love in my heart: *Gunter, Cornell* / I know you're leaving me: *Hightower, Sy* / Here we go: *Spread Love* / Decisions: *Lowe, Freddie* / Sexy lady: *Giles, Eddie & The Numbers* / Breaking training: *Brown, Larry* / Don't it: *Dawson, Roy* / I wish our love would last forever: *Swiss Movement* / You beat me at my game like a lady: *Strong, Chuck*
CD GSCD 057
Goldmine / Jul '95 / Vital

MODERN SOUL VOL.5
It takes heart: *Perry, Greg* / Hardest part: *Anderson, Curtis* / You're the best thing: *Baker, Larom* / You got me hung up: *King Tutt* / What it takes to live: *Chosen Few* / Paradise: *Jewel* / I'll make it on my own: *Lyde, Cecil* / They don't make 'em like you: *Horizon* / Space lady: *Bill* / Help is on the way: *Whatnauts* / Loveland: *SPG* / My lovely lady: *Scott, Moody* / What you do to me: *Best, William* / I'm gonna see you through: *Pictures* / What am I going to do without your love: *Johnson, Willie* / Check your direction: *Cloud, Michael* / Slowly turning to love: *Taylor, Alex*
CD GSCD 078
Goldmine / Mar '96 / Vital

MODERN SOUL VOL.6
I can't stop loving you: *Love Affair* / All alone by the telephone: *Bingham, J.B.* / Thousand years: *Brand New* / Ain't nothing for a man in love: *Bell, Archie & The Drells* / If you want my love: *Horne, Jimmy 'Bo'* / Can't get along without you: *Robinson, Dutch* / Don't take your sweet lovin': *Ghetto children* / Man up in the sky: *Strong, Barrett* / Key to the world: *Reynolds, L.J.* / Trying to find a new love: *Percy & Them* / If you and I had never met: *Magic Night* / He's comin' in the morning: *York, Patti* / Gift wrap my love: *Reflections* / Tryin' to love two women: *Persuaders* / Tell me you love me: *Hill, Bobby* / Just to be with you: *Dukes, Bobby* / Look in the mirror of my eyes: *Percy & Them* / It's not easy to say goodbye: *Ghetto children* / Something special: *Kirton, Lou* / I can't control this feelin': *Dean, Snoopy* / Tears of the world: *Moore, Robert* / Lady be mine: *King, Willard* / Make believe everything's alright: *Jones, Jimmy* / How can I go on without you: *Blake, Cory*
CD GSCD 082
Goldmine / Sep '96 / Vital

MODROPHENIA (2CD Set)
Sha la la la lee: *Small Faces* / Green onions: *Booker T & The MG's* / Papa's got a brand new bag: *Brown, James* / Double barrell: *Collins, Dave & Ansell* / Israelites: *Dekker, Desmond* / Baby come back: *Equals* / Poison ivy: *Paramounts* / Sunny afternoon: *Kinks* / Dancing in the street: *Reeves, Martha & The Vandellas* / Needle in a haystack: *Velvelettes* / You can't hurry love: *Ross, Diana & The Supremes* / Out of time: *Farlowe, Chris* / We've got to get out of this place: *Animals* / Liquidator: *Harry J All Stars* / Let your yeah be yeah: *Pioneers* / You can get it if you really want it: *Dekker, Desmond* / Band of gold: *Payne, Freda* / Itchycoo park: *Small Faces* / With a girl like you: *Troggs* / Tobacco road: *Nashville Teens* / Everlasting love: *Love Affair* / Red red wine: *Tribe, Tony* / Going to a go go: *Robinson, Smokey* / Shout: *Isley Brothers* / Think: *Franklin, Aretha* / In the midnight hour: *Pickett, Wilson* / Knock on wood: *Floyd, Eddie* / Rescue me: *Bass, Fontella* / (I'm a) roadrunner: *Walker, Junior & The All Stars* / Wade in the water: *Lewis, Ramsey* / In crowd: *Gray, Dobie* / Got my mojo workin': *Smith, Jimmy* / Letter: *Box Tops* / Give me just a little more time: *Chairmen Of The Board* / Young, gifted and black: *Bob & Marcia* / Wonderful world, beautiful people: *Cliff, Jimmy* / 007 (shanty town): *Dekker, Desmond* / Monkey spanner: *Collins, Dave & Ansell* / Lazy sunday: *Small Faces* / If paradise is as half as nice: *Amen Corner* / Mony mony: *James, Tommy & The Shondells* / Waterloo sunset: *Kinks* / Pictures of matchstick men: *Status Quo* / Groovy kind of love: *Fontana, Wayne & The Mindbenders*
CD Set RADCD 62
Global TV / May '97 / BMG

MODS MAYDAY VOL.1
CD RRCD 225
Receiver / May '97 / Grapevine/PolyGram

MODS MAYDAY VOL.2
CD RRCD 228
Receiver / Jul '96 / Grapevine/PolyGram

MODULATION & TRANSFORMATION
CD EFA 006652
Mille Plateau / Jun '95 / SRD

MOJO ROCKSTEADY
CD HBCD 134
Heartbeat / Jun '94 / ADA / Direct / Greensleeves / Jet Star

MOJO WORKIN'
CD ASTCD 4006
Astrion Audio / Nov '96 / BMG

MOJO WORKING (The Best Of Ace Blues)
Dust my blues: *James, Elmore* / Boogie chillun: *Hooker, John Lee* / Little school girl: *Hogg, Smokey* / Happy payday: *Littlefield, Little Willie* / Blues after hours: *Crayton, Pee Wee* / Please love me: *King, B.B.* / Lonesome dog blues: *Hopkins, Lightnin'* / Riding in the moonlight: *Howlin' Wolf* / Things that I used to do: *Guitar Slim* / I miss you so: *Turner, Ike* / Three hours past midnight: *Watson, Johnny 'Guitar'* / Baby let's play house: *Gunter, Arthur* / I'm a mojo man: *Lonesome Sundown* / I'm a King Bee: *Harpo, Slim* / Hoodoo blues: *Lightnin' Slim* / I'm a lover not a fighter: *Lazy Lester* / Rock me baby: *King, B.B.* / Part time love: *Taylor, Little Johnny* / Black nights: *Fulson, Lowell* / Born under a bad sign: *King, Albert*
CD CDCHK 964
Ace / Jan '95 / Pinnacle

MOLTEN GOLD (The Best Of Hot Wax Records)
While you're out looking for sugar: *Honey Cone* / Day I found myself: *Honey Cone* / Girls it ain't easy: *Honey Cone* / Truth will come out: *Honey Cone* / Want ads: *Honey Cone* / One monkey don't stop no show: *Honey Cone* / Women's love rights: *Lee, Laura* / Wedlock is a padlock: *Lee, Laura* / Crumbs off the table: *Lee, Laura* / Rip off:

Lee, Laura / Somebody's been sleeping (in my bed): 100 Proof (Aged In Soul) / 90 day freeze: 100 Proof (Aged In Soul) / If I could see the light in the window: 100 Proof (Aged In Soul) / If I could see the light in the window: 100 Proof (Aged In Soul) / I'm mad as hell (and I ain't gonna take no more): 100 Proof (Aged In Soul) & New York Port Authority / Frightened girl: Silent Majority / Colors of my love: Silent Majority / Love machine: Jackson, McKinley & The Politicians / I just want to be loved: Charles, Lee / Free your mind (it's instrumental to be free): Politicians / Westbound no.9: Flaming Ember / Mind, body and soul: Flaming Ember
CD ______ DEEPM 029
Deep Beats / Jul '97 / BMG

MOMENT RECORDS COLLECTION VOL.1
CD ______ MR 1008CD
Moment / Apr '95 / ADA / Koch

MOMENTS IN LOVE VOL.1
You've lost that lovin' feelin': Righteous Brothers / Without you: Nilsson, Harry / Cherish: Kool & The Gang / Keep on loving you: REO Speedwagon / I'm not in love: 10cc / Total eclipse of the heart: Tyler, Bonnie / Broken wings: Mr. Mister / Suddenly: Ocean, Billy / Stay with me 'til dawn: Tzuke, Judie / There's nothing better than love: Vandross, Luther / All the love in the world: Warwick, Dionne / You're the best thing: Style Council / Do what you do: Jackson, Jermaine / Just the way you are: White, Barry / Best thing that ever happened to me: Knight, Gladys & The Pips / Oh girl: Chi-Lites / All out of love: Air Supply / Every day hurts: Sad Cafe
CD ______ MUSCD 002
MCI Music / Nov '92 / Disc / THE

MOMENTS IN LOVE VOL.3
It started with a kiss: Hot Chocolate / Just the way you are: White, Barry / Almaz: Crawford, Randy / Every time you go away: Young, Paul / Lost without your love: Brad / Fool if you think it's over: Brooks, Elkie / Rock me tonight: Jackson, Freddie / I don't know how to love him: Elliman, Yvonne / I'm stone in love with you: Mathis, Johnny / He was beautiful: Williams, Iris / Superwoman: White, Karyn / You're the best thing: Style Council / Sign your name: D'Arby, Terence Trent / Mind blowing decisions: Heatwave / Love and affection: Armatrading, Joan / Room in your heart: Living In A Box / Always: Atlantic Starr / Wind beneath my wings: Greenwood, Lee
CD ______ MUSCD 034
MCI Music / May '97 / Disc / THE

MOMENTS OF LOVE
CD ______ DCD 5307
Disky / Dec '93 / Disky / THE

MONDO DRIVE IN
CD ______ BRCD 5003
Blood Red Discs / Mar '97 / Greyhound / Nervous

MONKEY BUSINESS
Tighten up: Untouchables / Fatty fatty: Eccles, Clancy / 54-46 (was my number): Toots & The Maytals / 007: Dekker, Desmond / Liquidator: Harry J All Stars / Fire corner: Eccles, Clancy / Double barrel: Collins, Dave & Ansell / Birth control: Lee, Byron / Herbsman: King Stitt & The Dynamites / Elizabethan reggae: Gardiner, Boris / Return of django: Upsetters / Monkey spanner: Collins, Dave & Ansell / Longshot kick de bucket: Pioneers / Young, gifted and black: Bob & Marcia / Monkey man: Toots & The Maytals / Dollar in the teeth: Upsetters / Barbwire: Dean, Nora / Shocks of mighty: Collins, Dave & Ansell / Them laugh and kiki: Soulmates / Cherry oh baby: Donaldson, Eric
CD ______ CDTRL 188
Trojan / Jan '95 / Direct / Jet Star

MONKEY SKA
Monkey ska: Harriott, Derrick / Really now: Dreamletts / Vat seven: Drummond, Don / I don't need your love: Chuck & Dobby / Don't throw it away: Itals / Out of space: McCook, Tommy & The Supersonics / Sammy no dead: Eccles, Clancy / I'm so in love with you: Techniques / Make yourself comfortable: Los Caballeros Orchestra / Cling to me: Dawkins, Horrell / Open the door: Clive & Naomi / Live wire: Soul Brothers / Seed you sow: Bonny / True confession: Silvertones / Girl next door: Blues Blenders / Jam session: Brooks, Baba / What a good woodman: Perry, Lee 'Scratch' / Tender loving care: Tait, Lynn / Paradise: Shirley, Roy / Third man theme: Williams, Granville Orchestra
CD ______ CDTRL 323
Trojan / Mar '94 / Direct / Jet Star

MONOLOGUE (2CD Set)
CD Set ______ GEN 005CD
Generations / Jul '96 / Vital

MONSTER BOP
Rockin' in the graveyard: Morningstar, Jackie / Werewolf: Bonafede, Carl / Story that's true: Bonafede, Carl / Caveman hop: Coulston, Jerry / Cat: Willis, Rod / Midnight monsters: Jack & Jim / Nightmare: Stuart, Scottie / Graveyard: Bowman, Leroy / Skeleton fight: Smith, Allen / Monster hop: Dee, Jimmy / Gorilla: Convy, Bert / Leopard man: Wallace, Joe / Nightmare hop: Patterson, Earl / Monster: Please, Bobby / Caveman: Roe, Tommy / Mad house jump: Daylighters / Jekyll and Hyde: Burgett, Jim / Haunted house: Kevin, Cris / Head hunter: Fern, Mike / I'm the wolfman: Round Robin Monopoly / Frankenstein's den: Hollywood Flames / Don't meet Mr. Frankenstein: Casal, Carlos Jr. / I was a teenage monster: Keytones / You can get him Frankenstein: Castle Kings / Gila monster: Johnson, Joe / Frankenstein rock: Thomas, Eddie / I was a teenage cave man: Luck, Randy / Frank Frankenstein: Ivan
CD ______ CDBB 55013
Buffalo Bop / Apr '94 / Rollercoaster

MONSTER HITS - DRAG CITY
Shut down: Beach Boys / Drag city: Jan & Dean / Wheel stands: Super Stocks / Night rumble: Cole, Jerry & His Spacemen / Stick shift: Duals / 409: Beach Boys / Road runner: Gants / Dead Man's Curve: Jan & Dean / Four on the floor: Super Stocks / Chicken: Convy, Bert & The Cheers / Hot rod race: Dolan, Jimmy / Black denim trousers and motorcycle boots: Cheers / Little deuce coupe: Beach Boys / Boss dance: Cole, Jerry & His Spacemen / Little old lady (from Pasadena): Jan & Dean / Fun fun fun: Beach Boys / Wide track: Super Stocks / Car trouble: Eligibles / Little Honda: Beach Boys / Brontosaurus stomp: Piltdown Men / Mr. Grasser: Mr. Grasser & The Weirdos / Street machine: Super Stocks / Ballad of Thunder Road: Mitchum, Robert / Cheater slicks: Super Stocks / Driving little deuce: Cole, Jerry & His Spacemen / Shutdown part II: Beach Boys
CD ______ CTMCD 318
EMI / Jun '97 / EMI

MONSTER HITS - WILD SURF
Surfin': Beach Boys / Surf city: Jan & Dean / Surfer's stomp: Marketts / Theme from 'Endless Summer': Sandals / Hawaii Five-O: Ventures / Surfin' safari: Beach Boys / Finksville USA: Mr. Grasser & The Weirdos / Shoot the curl: Honeys / Tell 'em I'm surfin': Fantastic Baggys / Ride the wild surf: Jan & Dean / Surfin' bird: Trashmen / Surf age: Cole, Jerry & His Spacemen / I live for the sun: Sunrays / Surfin' USA: Beach Boys / Papa-oom-mow-mow: Rivingtons / Wipe out: Ventures / Pipeline: Cole, Jerry & His Spacemen / Summer means fun: Fantastic Baggys / Pray for the surf: Honeys / Surfer girl: Beach Boys / Goofy-foot Glen: Severson, John / Sidewalk surfin': Jan & Dean / Surf route 101: Super Stocks / Doin' the surfink: Mr. Grasser & The Weirdos / Muscle beach party: Super Stocks / Come September: Severson, John
CD ______ CTMCD 319
EMI / Jun '97 / EMI

MONSTERS OF GOTH (3CD Set)
CD Set ______ CLP 0006
Cleopatra / Jul '97 / Cargo / Greyhound / Plastic Head / RTM/Disc / SRD

MONSTERS OF ROCK
CD ______ SMR 29
Simple Machines / Jun '94 / SRD

MONSTERS OF ROCK (4CD Set)
CD Set ______ MBSCD 435
Castle / Mar '95 / BMG

MONSTERS, ROBOTS & BUG MEN
Tantric porno: Bardo Pond / (A) Man Ray: Long Fin Killie / Gold teeth: God / Sleep: Third Eye Foundation / Star: Hair & Skin Trading Company / Photon: Fuxa / Pretty note: Run On / Grand piano: Ul / Slow thrills: Bowery Electric / Neither yield nor reap: Brise Glace / Sea swells & distant squalls: Pram / Chance was: Magic Hour / SEDR 77: Labradford / Everlasting arm: Mercury Rev / Feedback song: Flying Saucer Attack / Ordinary sleep: Jessamine / Dancing sumo wrestlers: Yona Kit / Preparation: Windy & Carl / Crush my soul: Godflesh / Lonesome death of Elijah P Woods: Sabalon Glitz / Les Yper-Yper sound: Stereolab / Doldrums: Cul De Sac / Departing the body: Montgomery, Roy / Aplomado: US Maple / Before I lose my style: Space Needle / Good night: Stars Of The Lid
CD ______ AMBT 11
Virgin / May '96 / EMI

MONTEREY INTERNATIONAL POP FESTIVAL (Definitive Document Of The First Great Rock Festival)
CD Set ______ ROCCD 2
Essential / Feb '94 / BMG

MONTREUX FESTIVAL
In view: Hamilton, Chico / Let me down easy: Little Milton / We're gonna make it: Little Milton / Don't make no sense: Little Milton / Stormy Monday: Little Milton / For the love of a woman: King, Albert
CD ______ CDSXE 070
Stax / Nov '92 / Pinnacle

MOODS (A Collection Of Mellow Masterpieces)
Ese amigo de alma: Vitale, Lito Cuarteto / El vuelo: Montes, Osvaldo / La mer: Edison / Un amour dans l'apres-midi: Edison / Island: Argol, Sebastian / Winds of the stars in their eyes: Popol Vuh / Sayoko se souvient: Edison / Horseman in the wind: Argol, Sebastian / Suitor's visit: Auckland Philharmonia Orchestra / A viajem: Gismonti, Egberto / Homenaje a Anibal: Maiz, Sampayo / So sad: Faltermeyer, Harold / Dixie: Edelman, Randy / Exuadi-nos: Musy, Jean / Genesis: Shankar, Ravi
CD ______ EMPRCD 907
Emporio / Jan '97 / Disc

MOODS FOR LOVER
Chi mai / Concerto de aranjuez / Bilitis / Holding back the years / That old devil called love again / Morning has broken / Crying / Chariots of fire / Aria / Sadness pt.1 / Cavatina / Piano in the dark / Tara's theme / Imagine / Lily was there / Yesterday / Eternal flame / True
CD ______ 301172
Hallmark / Jul '96 / Carlton

MOODS FOR LOVERS (3CD Set)
Power of love / Heartbreaker / Woman in love / September in the rain / Tonight she comes / Cherish / Song for Guy / Imagine / Stranger on the shore / Lady / Glory of love / Somewhere out there / Bright eyes / Just like paradise / Chi mai / El condor pasa / Adagio / Big my secret / As if we never said goodbye / Holding back the years / Eternal flame / I miss you / Nocturne / That ole devil called love / Soleado / Dream on / Edelweiss / Lost in emotion / I'm not in love / Feelings / Love changes everything / Nikita / Spanish eyes / Albatross / Last farewell / Blue moon / Careless whisper / Sadness part 1 / I swear / Aria / We've got tonite / Cavatina / Nights in white satin / Long and winding road / Stand by me / My way / Save a prayer / On my own / Rose / Lara's theme / Time after time / Dreamin'
CD Set ______ 390222
Hallmark / Jul '96 / Carlton

MOODS ORCHESTRAL (4CD Set)
CD Set ______ MBSCD 445
Castle / Nov '95 / BMG

MOON OF ROSES
CD ______ ITM 1487
ITM / Apr '94 / Koch / Tradelink

MOONGLOW
Wavy gravy: Burrell, Kenny & Stanley Turrentine / Days of wine and roses: Lawson, Hugh / Made in France: Lagrene, Birelli / Summertime: Jones, Hank / My old flame: Sims, Zoot & John Eardley / Hot sauce: Hope, Elmo Trio / Moonglow: Goodman, Benny Quintet / Take the 'A' train: Newborn, Phineas Trio / Breeze and I: Pepper, Art & Carl Perkins / Lady is a tramp: Lee, Peggy / Swingin' the blues: Basie, Count Orchestra / Moonlight in Vermont: Smith, Johnny Quintet / Angelina: Klugh, Earl / Almost like being in love: Hipp, Jutta & Zoot Sims/Jerry Lloyd / Opus de funk: Silver, Horace / In a sentimental mood: Ellington, Duke
CD ______ CDJA 4
Premier/MFP / Oct '91 / EMI

MOONLIGHT MEMORIES
Night is young and you're so beautiful: Sinatra, Frank & Dinah Shore / Indian love call: McDonald, Jeanette / Moonlight serenade: Miller, Glenn / Moon came up with a grand idea: Crosby, Bing & Peggy Lee / My man (Mon homme): Fitzgerald, Ella / Stardust: Sinatra, Frank / There will never be another you: Cole, Nat 'King' / On a slow boat to China: Haymes, Dick / Elmer's tune: Fields, Shep / Moonlight bay: Crosby, Bing & Gary Crosby / Without a song: Sinatra, Frank / Mona Lisa: Cole, Nat 'King' / Serenade in blue: Miller, Glenn / If I didn't care: Ink Spots / I'm confessin' (that I love you): Fitzgerald, Ella / My funny valentine: Cole, Nat 'King' / Just you just me: Cole, Nat 'King' / Unforgettable: Cole, Nat 'King' / I've heard that song before: James, Harry / Polka dots and moonbeams: Sinatra, Frank / You made me love you: Garland, Judy / String of pearls: Miller, Glenn / Cheek to cheek: Haymes, Dick / Best things in life are free: Allyson, June & Peter Lawford / Thanks for the memory: Hope, Bob & Shirley Ross / Zing went the strings of my heart: Garland, Judy
CD ______ ECD 3329
K-Tel / Mar '97 / K-Tel

MOONLIGHT SERENADE
Moonlight serenade: Miller, Glenn & His Orchestra / Solitaire: Vaughn, Billy Orchestra / Raindrops keep falling on my head: Winterhalter, Hugo / Sandy roads: Bent Fabric / Glutrote rosen: Ingmann, Jorgen / Rose from Santa Monica: Ingmann, Jorgen / Love story: Vaughn, Billy Orchestra / Red roses for a blue lady: Vaughn, Billy Orchestra / Spanish eyes: Vaughn, Billy Orchestra / How deep is your love: Erling, Ole / Fernando: Erling, Ole / Never my love: Winterhalter, Hugo / Taste of honey: Winterhalter, Hugo / Stranger where are you now: Bent Fabric / Blue eyes crying in the rain: Hirt, Al / Wonderland by night: Hirt, Al
CD ______ 101122
CMC / May '97 / BMG

MOONRAKER
CD ______ SPV 08538942
SPV / Sep '94 / Koch / Plastic Head

MOONRAKER VOL.3 (2CD Set)
Rain: Steril / Cowgirl: Underworld / Tabula rasa: Covenant / Dizzy divination: Evil's Toy / Waterdome: Signal Aout 42 / City sleeps: Trauma / Tied up tied up: LFO / Like a flow: Cyan / Exile on mainline: Chemlab / Kruppel: Oomph / Al-Giabr: Esplendor Geometrico / Ich bin der Bennende Komet: Lacrimosa / Catherine: Inkubus Sukkubus / Xodus: Nefilim / Democracy: Killing Joke / Sick to death: Atari Teenage Riot / Wilde kinder: Sabotage QCQC / Nezzwerk: Haujobb / Let your body die: Cyber-Tec / Narcotic influence: Empirion / Facer: X Marks The Pedwalk / Other world: Noise Unit / Red: Click Click / Friction friction: Velvet Acid Christ / Burn baby burn: Suicide Commando / Become an angel: In Strict Confidence / You are: Cobalt 60 / Kerosene: Think About Mutation / Circuitry: Frontline Assembly / Goodbye horses: Psyche
CD Set ______ SPV 8747212
SPV / Jun '97 / Koch / Plastic Head

MOONSHINE MIXER VOL.1
Lunatix: Blakdoktor / Celebrate: Ellimac / Free: Doc Martin & Discfunktional / Celebrate: Ellimac / De la casa: EKO / Gonna make it: Stateside / De la casa: EKO / Gonna make it: Stateside
CD ______ MM 800622
Moonshine / Mar '97 / Mo's Music Machine / Prime / RTM/Disc

MORE CAJUN MUSIC AND ZYDECO
CD ______ ROUCD 11573
Rounder / Aug '95 / ADA / CM / Direct

MORE HOTTEST HITS FROM TREASURE ISLE
CD ______ HB 109CD
Heartbeat / Jul '94 / ADA / Direct / Greensleeves / Jet Star

MORE, MORE, MORE (More Classic Soul)
I wanna dance wit' choo: Disco Tex & The Sexolettes / I'm doing fine now: New York City / Dolly my love: Moments / Higher and higher: Wilson, Jackie / In Zaire: Wakelin, Johnny / More, more, more: Andrea True Connection / Hold back the night: Trammps / Dance the body music: Osibisa / Can you feel the force: Real Thing / I owe you one: Shalamar / And the beat goes on: Whispers / Check out the groove: Thurston, Bobby / Foot stompin' music: Bohannon, Hamilton / I'll go where your music takes me: James, Jimmy / Too good to be forgotten: Chi-Lites / We got the funk: Positive Force
CD ______ TRTCD 142
TrueTrax / Dec '94 / THE

MORE THAN A FEELING
You're the voice: Farnham, John / Nothing's gonna stop us now: Starship / More than a feeling: Boston / You took the words right out of my mouth: Meat Loaf / Can't fight this feeling: REO Speedwagon / Don't stop believin': Journey / Rosanna: Toto / Satellite: Hooters / Final countdown: Europe / Broken wings: Mr. Mister / When I see you smile: Bad English / (Don't fear) The reaper: Blue Oyster Cult / Flame: Cheap Trick / So tired: Osbourne, Ozzy / Rock 'n' roll dreams come through: Steinman, Jim / Stairway to heaven: Far Corporation
CD ______ 4730452
Columbia / Feb '93 / Sony

MORE THAN UNPLUGGED
Mandolin wind: Stewart, Rod / You have placed a chill in my heart: Eurythmics / Your song: John, Elton / Lean on me: Withers, Bill / Down to zero: Armatrading, Joan / Water of love: Dire Straits / Carry on: Cale, J.J. / Anchorage: Shocked, Michelle / Brown eyed girl: Morrison, Van / Suzanne: Cohen, Leonard / Luka: Vega, Suzanne / Mr. Tambourine man: Byrds / Ruby Tuesday: Melanie / Catch the wind: Donovan / Stuck in the middle with you: Stealer's Wheel / After the goldrush: Prelude / I'll have to say I love you in a song: Croce, Jim / Perfect: Fairground Attraction / Nobody does it better: Simon, Carly
CD ______ NTRCD 068
Nectar / Mar '97 / Pinnacle

MORLEY, PARLSEY, INGLOTT
CD ______ PRCD 396
Priory / Jul '92 / Priory

MORNING AFTER
Out of body: Innersphere / Repro house: Justice & Blame / As fast as I could look away she was still there: Budd & Zazou / Indigo: T-Power / Flying again: Spring Heel Jack / Angry dolphin: Plaid / MHT: Subtropic / Nautilus: Appaloosa & Oribit / T'raenon: Photek / Ride: Soft Ballad / Night moves: Foulplay / Scary HH loop: Dub Tractor / Flowers for the moonlight: Reflections / String of pearls: Spacetime Continuum / Sarcacid part 1: Alroy Road Tracks & Duke Of Haringay / F-jam: Adam F / Overheated livingroom: Dub Tractor / Diosa de la luna: Baby Doc / Come with me: Quattara / Acid people: White Trash
CD ______ CDTIVAX 1014
Positiva / Feb '97 / EMI

MOROCCAN TRANCE MUSIC VOL.2 (Sufi)
CD ______ SR 97
Sub Rosa / Jul '97 / Direct / RTM/Disc / SRD / Vital

MOROCCO
Mimoun sadie / Bar'ka ti ati a houssa / Gnawi / Hessaoui / Ian minna zin n souss /

Moulay' brahim (touichya) / Al ghazzel / Kalali sahib mina nas / Raila / Slam habibi jani / Hadra / Tahdira / Beggar's song / Anta laziz ya Mohamed
CD ____ YA 225713
Silex / Jul '97 / ADA / Harmonia Mundi

MOROCCO/MAROC (Berber Music From High/Anti Atlas Region)
CD ____ LDX 274991
La Chant Du Monde / Jun '94 / ADA / Harmonia Mundi

MORTAR
CD ____ PPP 104NP
PDCD / Jan '94 / Plastic Head

MORTUARY VOL.1
CD ____ SKELETON 93
Skeleton / Sep '94 / Plastic Head

MOSCOW NIGHTS
CD ____ MCD 71590
Monitor / Jun '93 / CM

MOST BEAUTIFUL SONGS OF AFRICA
CD ____ EUCD 1239
ARC / Nov '93 / ADA / ARC Music

MOST BEAUTIFUL YODELLING FROM THE ALPS VOL.1, THE
CD ____ 321122
Koch / Sep '92 / Koch

MOST BEAUTIFUL YODELLING FROM THE ALPS VOL.2, THE
CD ____ 330023
Koch / Sep '92 / Koch

MOST BEAUTIFUL YODELLING FROM THE ALPS VOL.3, THE
CD ____ 330039
Koch / Sep '92 / Koch

MOST POPULAR 34 IRISH AND SCOTTISH SONGS
Scotland the brave / Let's have a ceili / Johnny lad / Donald where's your trousers / Fyfe o / If you're Irish / Agricultural Irish girl / Hannigan's hooley / Northern lights of Old Aberdeen / River Clyde / I belong to Glasgow / Rambles of spring / Finnegan's wake / Town of Ballybay / McNamara's band / Dear old Donegal / Home boys home / Bonnie Charlie / I love a lassie / Loch Lomond / Roamin' in the gloamin' / Keep right on to the end of the road / Ring your mother wore / Gentle mother / Medals for mother / Mother for mine / Cambletown loch / Bonnie wee Jenny McCaul / Fair Isles / I used to love her / Rambling banjo man / Hills of Donegal / Irish rover
CD ____ PLMCD 30
Sharpe / Jun '97 / Duncans / Target/BMG

MOST UPLIFTING VOCAL ANTHEMS
CD ____ CDSAS 1
Stage One / Aug '96 / Mo's Music Machine / SRD

MOTHER OF ALL MIX ALBUMS, THE (2CD Set)
CD Set ____ TCD 2890
Telstar / Feb '97 / BMG

MOTHER OF ALL SWING ALBUMS, THE (2CD Set)
No diggity: *Blackstreet & Dr. Dre* / Return of the mack: *Morrison, Mark* / Love to love: *Damage* / Ocean Drive: *Lighthouse Family* / Gangsta's paradise: *Coolio* / We've got it goin' on: *Backstreet Boys* / Thank God it's Friday: *R Kelly* / Hit me off: *New Edition* / Woo hah got you all in check: *Busta Rhymes* / Flava: *Andre, Peter* / Forget the world: *Gabrielle* / I'm going down: *Blige, Mary J.* / All the things (your man won't do): *Joe* / Get on up: *Jodeci* / Stressed: *Tribe Called Quest & Faith Evans* / Get money: *Junior MAFIA* / Every little thing I do: *Soul For Real* / Tell me what you like: *Guy* / We got it: *Immature* / Believe in me: *Raw Stylus* / Every little step: *Brown, Bobby* / Rump steak: *Wreckx n' Effect* / Poison: *Bell biv devoe* / Boom boom shake the room: *DJ Jazzy Jeff & The Fresh Prince* / Forget I was a G: *Whitehead Brothers* / Super woman: *White, Karyn* / Freek 'n' you: *Jodeci* / It's too late: *Quartz & Dina Carroll*
CD Set ____ TCD 2877
Telstar / Oct '96 / BMG

MOTHER OF ALL SWING VOL.2, THE (2CD Set)
CD Set ____ TTVCD 2896
Telstar TV / Jul '97 / Warner Music

MOTHER VOLGA (Recordings From The Banks Of The Volga River)
CD ____ PANCD 2008
Pan / May '93 / ADA / CM / Direct

MOTOR CITY (The Music Of Detroit)
CD Set ____ TFP 014
Tring / Nov '92 / Tring

MOTOR CITY BLUES
CD ____ NEXCD 274
Sequel / Feb '96 / BMG

MOTOWN CHARTBUSTERS VOL.2
Ain't nothing like the real thing: *Gaye, Marvin & Tammi Terrell* / If I could build my whole world around you: *Gaye, Marvin & Tammi Terrell* / Reflections: *Ross, Diana & The Supremes* / Some things you never get used to: *Ross, Diana & The Supremes* / If you can want / I second that emotion / You keep running away: *Four Tops* / If I were a carpenter: *Four Tops* / I could never love another (after loving you): *Temptations* / You're my everything: *Temptations* / I heard it through the grapevine: *Knight, Gladys & The Pips* / I'm wondering: *Wonder, Stevie* / Shoo-be-doo-be-doo-da-day: *Wonder, Stevie* / I've passed this way before: *Ruffin, Jimmy* / Gotta see Jane: *Taylor, R. Dean* / Honey chile: *Reeves, Martha*
CD ____ 5300672
Motown / Jan '93 / PolyGram

MOTOWN CHARTBUSTERS VOL.4
I want you back: *Jackson Five* / ABC: *Jackson Five* / Onion song: *Gaye, Marvin & Tammi Terrell* / Too busy thinking about my baby: *Gaye, Marvin* / I can't help myself: *Four Tops* / Do what you gotta do: *Four Tops* / Up the ladder to the roof: *Supremes* / Someday we'll be together: *Ross, Diana & The Supremes* / Cloud 9: *Temptations* / I can't get next to you: *Temptations* / I second that emotion: *Temptations & Diana Ross/Supremes* / Yester-me, yester-you, yesterday: *Wonder, Stevie* / Farewell is a lonely sound: *Ruffin, Jimmy* / What does it take (to win your love): *Walker, Junior & The All Stars*
CD ____ 5300592
Motown / Jan '93 / PolyGram

MOTOWN CHARTBUSTERS VOL.5
Tears of a clown: *Robinson, Smokey* / War: *Starr, Edwin* / Love you save: *Jackson Five* / I'll be there: *Jackson Five* / Ball of confusion: *Temptations* / It's all in the game: *Four Tops* / Still water (love): *Four Tops* / Heaven help us all: *Wonder, Stevie* / Signed, sealed, delivered (I'm yours): *Wonder, Stevie* / I'll say forever my love: *Wonder, Stevie* / Ain't no mountain high enough: *Ross, Diana* / Stoned love: *Supremes* / Abraham, Martin and John: *Gaye, Marvin* / Forget me not: *Reeves, Martha* / It's a shame: *Motown Spinners* / Never had a dream come true: *Wonder, Stevie* / It's wonderful (To be loved by you): *Four Tops*
CD ____ 5300602
Motown / Jan '93 / PolyGram

MOTOWN CHARTBUSTERS VOL.7
Automatically sunshine: *Supremes* / Floy Joy: *Supremes* / You gotta have love in your heart: *Supremes & Four Tops* / Surrender: *Ross, Diana* / Doobedood'ndoobe, doobedood'ndoobe: *Ross, Diana* / Just walk in my shoes: *Knight, Gladys & The Pips* / Rockin' robin: *Jackson, Michael* / Ain't no sunshine: *Jackson, Michael* / Got to be there: *Jackson, Michael* / Take a look around: *Temptations* / Superstar (Remember how you got where you are): *Temptations* / If you really love me: *Wonder, Stevie* / Bless you: *Reeves, Martha* / Walk in the night: *Walker, Junior & The All Stars* / Festival time: *San Remo Strings* / My guy: *Wells, Mary*
CD ____ 5300622
Motown / Jan '93 / PolyGram

MOTOWN EARLY CLASSICS SAMPLER
Come see about me: *Ross, Diana & The Supremes* / Baby I need your loving: *Four Tops* / Way over there: *Robinson, Smokey & The Miracles* / Wait till my Bobby gets home: *Reeves, Martha & The Vandellas* / He's the one I love: *Wells, Mary* / Headline news: *Starr, Edwin* / Behind a painted smile: *Isley Brothers* / Ain't too proud to beg: *Temptations* / Goin' back to Indiana: *Jackson Five* / Can I get a witness: *Gaye, Marvin* / I'll say forever my love: *Ruffin, Jimmy* / People make the world go round: *Jackson, Michael*
CD ____ 5524342
Spectrum / Jul '96 / PolyGram

MOTOWN HEARTBREAKERS
CD ____ TCD 2343
Telstar / Sep '89 / BMG

MOTOWN SONGBOOK
CD ____ VSOPCD 180
Connoisseur Collection / Jan '93 / Pinnacle

MOUNTAIN MUSIC
CD ____ SFWCD 40038
Smithsonian Folkways / Dec '94 / ADA / Cadillac / CM / Direct / Koch

MOUNTAIN MUSIC OF KENTUCKY VOL.2 (2CD Set)
CD Set ____ SFWCD 40077
Smithsonian Folkways / May '96 / ADA / Cadillac / CM / Direct / Koch

MOUNTAIN MUSIC OF PERU VOL.1
CD ____ CDS 40020
Smithsonian Folkways / Aug '94 / ADA / Cadillac / CM / Direct / Koch

MOUNTAIN MUSIC OF PERU VOL.2
CD ____ SFWCD 40406
Smithsonian Folkways / Aug '95 / ADA / Cadillac / CM / Direct / Koch

MOUNTAIN MYSTIQUE (The Authentic Sounds Of The Pan Pipes)
Cuando el sole sal / La vierge sola / Carnavalito / Primavera / El Indio del Antiplano / Zagoria / El poncho rojo / Sikuereada / Los barriadas / El chuianco / Llamada de los buitres / Rin del angelito / Servania / La marcha / El pobrecito / Las flores de mi pais / Sol inca / Canto del cuculi / Vicunitas / Las chullpas / Lagrima India / Indiecito soy / La bruja / Rosita / El condor pasa
CD ____ SUMCD 4031
Summit / Nov '96 / Sound & Media

MOUNTAIN SERENITY (A Magical Blend Of Music And The Sounds Of Nature)
CD ____ 57582
CMC / May '97 / BMG

MOUVANCES TZIGANES - NOMAD'S LAND
CD ____ PS 65134CD
PlayaSound / Jul '94 / ADA / Harmonia Mundi

MOVE CLOSER (19 Romantic Melodies)
Move closer / Ti amo / Right here waiting / Saving all my love for you / Unchained melody / With you I'm born again / It must have been love / Too much Heaven / How deep is your love / Can't stay away from you / Greatest love of all / Don't wanna lose you now / Anything for you / How am I supposed to live without you / I just can't stop loving you / When a man loves a woman / I'll be there / Eternal flame / Save the best for last
CD ____ SUMCD 4010
Summit / Nov '96 / Sound & Media

MOVEMENTS IN BULGARIAN FOLK MUSIC
CD ____ VGR 9405CD
Van Geel / Jul '95 / ADA / Direct

MOVIE MONDO
Newsreader / Thrill Killers trailer / Rat Pfink theme / Rat emerges / You is a Rat Pfink / Running Wild / Big boss a go-go party: *Haydock, Ron & The Boppers* / ISC trailer / Shook out of shape: *Kay, Carol & The Stone Tones* / Wild Guitar trailer / Twist fever: *Hall, Arch & The Archers* / Brain Eaters trailer / Lemon Grove kids: *Snyder, Don/Peewee Flyn/Linda & Tickles Steckler* / Plan 9 From Outer Space / Night Of The Ghouls / Maniacs Are Loose trailer / Jayne speaks / Bird's the word: *Roberts, Rocky & The Airedales* / Jayne is dead / Girl From SIN trailer / Another day, another man / Mr. Mari's girls trailer / Get off the road / She Devils instrumental: *Lewis, R Band* / She speech / Strange Rampage trailer / Spoken intro / Hypnovista trailer / Hell's Angels / Warning
CD ____ CDWIK 90
Big Beat / Nov '90 / Pinnacle

MOVIN' ON VOL.1
Introduce me to love: *Absolute* / Overjoy: *S'Mone, Guy* / It's over: *Perfect Taste* / Searching: *China Black* / Falling by dominoes: *Music & Mystery* / Keep it comin': *Jullianne* / Never gonna give you up: *Watergates* / Takes time: *Funhill* / Bring me back: *Drakes, Anthony* / Pushin' against the flow: *Raw Stylus* / Mr. Magic: *Dreaming A Dream* / Reconsider: *Bell, Melissa*
CD ____ RUCD 300
Rumour / May '92 / 3mv/Sony / Mo's Music Machine / Pinnacle

MOVIN' ON VOL.2
Revival: *Girault, Martine* / Love guaranteed: *Ferrier, Robert* / Something inside: *Deep Joy* / I want you back: *Sinclair* / Got to be you: *Koo Koo* / You turn me on: *Everis* / Call me anytime: *FM Inc* / One girl too late: *Pure Silk* / 2.B.A.S.1: *Ballin, Chris* / Warm love: *Law, Joanna* / Intimate connection: *Delano, Rohan* / Yes, yes, yes: *Applemountain* / Higher love: *Naked Funk*
CD ____ RUCD 301
Rumour / Oct '92 / 3mv/Sony / Mo's Music Machine / Pinnacle

MOVIN' ON VOL.3
Don't go walking (out that door): *Watergates* / Keep on giving: *BCA* / Turn me on: *A Certain Ratio* / What you won't do for love: *Nu Visions* / Girl overboard: *Snowboy* / It's not alright: *Stirling McLean* / No man the vibe: *Vibe & Delroy Pinnock* / Poetical love: *Fyza* / Slow and easy: *Moving In The Right Direction* / Coming on to me: *Mo & Beev* / No time for change: *Outside* / Joy is free: *Think 2wice* / Revelation: *Simon, Vannessa* / Oh happy day: *Beat System*
CD ____ RUCD 302
Rumour / Jun '91 / 3mv/Sony / Mo's Music Machine / Pinnacle

MOVIN' RECORDS - THE REAL SOUND OF NEW JERSEY
CD ____ WORLD 004CD
World Series / Oct '93 / Vital

MOVING HOUSE
CD ____ SSR 169CD
SSR / Sep '96 / Amato Disco / Grapevine/ PolyGram / Prime / RTM/Disc

MOZAMBIQUE VOL.1
Magalango / Mutcico/Munguenisso / Enhipiti esquissirua / Mama na wamina anga monanga / Unabadera uhema / N'kissa / Ndiribe nyumba / Tira hikhubula mondlane / Utemdene / Ntabuya mundzuku / Essifa zonhipiti / Chihire / Komvarava kovela / Saudamos o grupo ladysmith black mambazo / Nisalili aussiwanini
CD ____ CDORBD 086
Globestyle / May '94 / Pinnacle

MOZAMBIQUE VOL.2
Muticitco / Simbiane / Enhipiti kahi yankhani / Amiravo amutane / Amigos, somos un enxame / Chinhambalala / Ukapata lya, ukapela bai / Mocambicano / Maria, kwadoca / Allahi ka salauto wahi wa-salaam / Frelimo quire echemi / Arminda / Mubedo wamina ysati wana wamina / Ndjemu / Onhipiti / Amigos, somos um enxame
CD ____ CDORBD 087
Globestyle / Nov '94 / Pinnacle

MPS PIANO HIGHLIGHTS
CD ____ 5195022
MPS Jazz / Mar '93 / PolyGram

MR. ROCK GUITAR
Sunshine of your love / Relax / Layla / Samba pa ti / Honky tonk woman / Hey Joe / Wonderful tonight / Crying / Blue time / I shot the sherriff / Every breath you take / How many more time / WHole lotta love / Roccata / All along the watch tower / Stairway to heaven
CD ____ ANT 017
Tring / Nov '96 / Tring

MRG 100
CD ____ MRG 100CD
Merge / Apr '97 / Cargo / Greyhound / SRD

MTM MUSIC VOL.1
Holding on to the night: *Axe* / When only love can ease the pain: *Ten* / We'll find a way: *Hugo* / Fighting the good fight: *Stone Soup* / Heat of emotion: *CITA* / After the love has gone: *Ten* / 98 in the shade: *Harlan Cage* / No rest for the wounded heart: *Tepper, Robert* / Love is the ritual: *Burtnick, Glenn* / Life in paradise: *Storming Heaven* / Talking to Sarah: *Tower City* / Don't Cry: *Ten* / Two hearts: *CITA* / Outlaw: *Captive Heart* / Best of my heart: *Kyle, Jaime* / Wanted man: *Burtnick, Glenn*
CD ____ MTM 199618
MTM / Feb '97 / Cargo

MULL OF KINTYRE (2CD Set)
CD Set ____ DCDCD 220
Castle / Nov '95 / BMG

MUMTAZ MAHAL
CD ____ WLACS 46CD
Xenophile / Jun '95 / ADA / Direct

MUNCHEN - VOLKSANGER 1902-1948
CD ____ US 0199
Trikont / Jul '95 / ADA / Direct

MUNDO AFRIKA
African dream: *Diop, Wasis & Lena Fiagbe* / Sunshine day: *Osibisa* / Scatterlings of Africa: *Juluka Radio Africa & Latin Quarter* / Biko: *Gabriel, Peter* / Nelson Mandela: *Special AKA* / Jit jive: *Bhundu Boys* / Diamonds on the soles of her shoes: *Simon, Paul* / Rain, rain, beautiful rain: *Ladysmith Black Mambazo* / Shakin' the tree: *Gabriel, Peter & Youssou N'Dour* / Happy ever after: *Fordham, Julia* / Sweet lullaby: *Deep Forest* / Temple head: *Transglobal Underground* / Father of our nation: *Masekela, Hugh* / Reckless: *Bambaataa, Afrika & UB40* / Yeke yeke: *Kante, Mory* / Yela: *Maal, Baaba* / Wombo lombo: *Kidjo, Angelique* / Africa: *Keita, Salif* / Shosholoza: *Ladysmith Black Mambazo*
CD ____ MOODCD 44
Sony Music / Jul '96 / Sony

MUNDO LATINO
Guaglione: *Prado, Perez* / La cumparsita: *Cugat, Xavier* / Oye mi canto: *Estefan, Gloria* / Soul limbo: *Mr. Bongo* / Something in my eye: *Corduroy* / La bamba: *Los Lobos* / Oye como va: *Santana* / Libertango: *Piazzolla, Astor* / Soul sauce: *Tjader, Cal* / Soul bossa nova: *Jones, Quincy* / Mas que nada: *Mendes, Sergio* / Watermelon man: *Santamaria, Mongo* / Eso beso: *Ames, Nancy* / More, more, more: *Carmel* / Hot hot hot: *Arrow* / Cuba: *Gibson Brothers* / Got myself a good man: *Pucho* / Curveza: *Brown, Boots & His Blockbusters* / Tequila: *Champs*
CD ____ SONYTV 2CD
Sony TV / Jul '96 / Sony

MURDER ONE (Mixed By Lenny Dee - 2CD Set)
CD Set ____ CSCPC
Crap Shoot / Nov '96 / Mo's Music Machine

MURRAY THE K'S HOLIDAY REVUE (Live At The Brooklyn Fox - December 1964)
He's so fine: *Chiffons* / Denise: *Randy & The Rainbows* / My boyfriend's back: *Randy & The Rainbows* / Linda: *Jan & Dean* / Surf City: *Jan & Dean* / So much in love: *Tymes* / Be my baby: *Ronettes* / She cried: *Jay & The Americans* / Town without pity: *Pitney, Gene* / Shop around: *Robinson, Smokey & The Miracles* / You can't sit down: *Dovells* / Walk on by: *Warwick, Dionne* / Hang on sloopy: *Vibrations* / Thou shalt not steal: *Dick & Deedee* / Leader of the pack: *Shangri-Las* / Since I don't have you: *Jackson, Chuck* / Any day now: *Jackson, Chuck* / Stand by me: *King, Ben E.* / Under the boardwalk: *Drifters* / Saturday night at the movies: *Drifters* / Baby it's you: *Shirelles* / Boys: *Shirelles* / Mama said: *Shirelles* / Tonight's the night: *Shirelles*
CD ____ CDMF 094
Magnum Force / Mar '95 / TKO Magnum

MUSCLE BUSTLE
Rendezvous stomp: *Rhythm Rockers* / Slide: *Rhythm Rockers* / Barefoot adventure: *Four Speeds* / RPM: *Four Speeds* / My stingray: *Four Speeds* / Four on theefloor:

Four Speeds / Cheater slicks: *Four Speeds* / Bite barracuda: *Knickerbockers* / Mighty barracuda: *Knickerbockers* / Midsummer night's dream: *Jan & Dean* / Heart and soul: *Jan & Dean* / Those words: *Jan & Dean* / Playmate of the year: *Sunsets* / Chug-a-lug: *Sunsets* / CC Cinder: *Sunsets* / Lonely surfer boy: *Sunsets* / Burnin' rubber: *Moles, Gene & The Softwinds* / Twin pipes: *Moles, Gene & The Softwinds* / Mag wheels: *Usher, Gary* / Power shift: *Usher, Gary* / Muscle bustle: *Loren, Donna* / Loophole: *Royal Coachmen* / Repeating: *Royal Coachmen* / Ski storm: *Snowmen* / 20,000 leagues: *Champs*
CD ____ **CDCHD 533**
Ace / Apr '94 / Pinnacle

MUSCLE PACK VOL.1
CD ____ **LOOPCD 102**
Loop / Feb '97 / Prime

MUSETTE DANCE, THE (Music From Italy)
CD ____ **YA 225056**
Silex / Dec '95 / ADA / Harmonia Mundi

MUSETTE FROM PARIS
Moulin Rouge / Milord / Souvenir de Montmartre / Marianne
CD ____ **15207**
Laserlight / '91 / Target/BMG

MUSHROOM JAZZ (CD/CDR Set)
CD Set ____ **OM 005**
OM / Mar '97 / Cargo / SRD

MUSIC AND DANCE OF ITALY VOL.12
CD ____ **TAO 12CD**
Taranta / Mar '96 / ADA

MUSIC AND DANCES OF OLD IRELAND
CD ____ **KAR 987**
IMP / Jan '97 / ADA / Discovery

MUSIC AND DANCES OF ROMANIA
CD ____ **KAR 990**
IMP / Feb '97 / ADA / Discovery

MUSIC AND SONG OF EDINBURGH, THE
Links of Forth / Rattlin' roarin' Willie / Capernaum / Holyrood House / Lion Wallace saw / Johnny Cope / Loose noose / Deacon Brodie / Sandy Bell's man / Festival lights / Duchess of Edinburgh / Caller oysters / Fisherrow / Mallie Lee / Black swan / Roslin castle / Edinburgh town / Flowers of Edinburgh / Waly waly / Willie's gane tae Melville castle / Union canal / Burning bing / Auld lang syne
CD ____ **CDTRAX 090**
Greentrax / Apr '95 / ADA / Direct / Duncans / Highlander

MUSIC AND SONG OF GREENTRAX
Nodding song / Tunes / Terror time / Venus in tweeds / Eilean m'araich / Set of tunes / Rosie Anderson / Liathach / Sands of the shore / Somewhere in America / Up the Noran water / Dream Angus / Niel Gow's apprentice / Strong woman / No Gods / Nuair bha mi og / '45 Revolution / Summer of '46 / Jamie come try me / Silence of tears / Yellow on the broom / Roy's wife / Chaidh mi' na ghleannan as t-fhoghar / Song of the fishgutters / Cullden's harvest / Moon and St. Christopher
CD ____ **CDTRAX 8696**
Greentrax / Jul '96 / ADA / Direct / Duncans / Highlander

MUSIC AND SONG OF SCOTLAND (A Greentrax Showcase)
Scotland the brave: *Lothian & Borders Police Band* / Bonnie Galloway: *Lothian & Borders Police Band* / Rowan tree: *Lothian & Borders Police Band* / Highland laddie: *Lothian & Borders Police Band* / Dumbarton's drums: *Redpath, Jean* / Rolling hills of the borders: *McCalmans* / Burke and Hare: *Laing, Robin* / Bonnie moorhen: *Heywood, Heather* / Old bean waltz: *Hardie, Ian* / Hospital wood: *Hardie, Ian* / Auchope cairn: *Hardie, Ian* / Glasgow that I used to know: *McNaughtan, Adam* / Bleacher lass o' Kelvinhaugh: *Paterson, Rod* / If wishes were fishes: *Bogle, Eric* / Yonder banks: *Fisher, Archie* / Shipyard apprentice: *Fisher, Archie* / Carls o'Dysart: *Russell, Janet & Christine Kydd* / De'il's awa' wi' tha exciseman: *Russell, Janet & Christine Kydd* / Farm auction: *MacKintosh, Iain* / Donald MacLean's farewell to Oban: *Bain, Aly & Phil Cunningham* / Sands of Burness: *Bain, Aly & Phil Cunningham* / Miller's reel: *Bain, Aly & Phil Cunningham* / Maid of Islay: *MacDonald, Iain* / Canan nan gaidheal: *MacPhee, Catherine-Anne* / Birnie bouzie: *Beck, Jack* / Fife and a' the lands about it: *Heritage* / Freedom come all ye: *Porteous, Lindsay & Friends*
CD ____ **CDTRAX 030**
Greentrax / Dec '89 / ADA / Direct / Duncans / Highlander

MUSIC AND SONGS FROM THE DOGON, MALI
CD ____ **926672**
BUDA / Jul '97 / Discovery

MUSIC AND SONGS OF MINORITIES, VIETNAM
CD ____ **926692**
BUDA / Jul '97 / Discovery

MUSIC AT MATT MOLLOY'S
CD ____ **CDRW 26**
Realworld / Aug '92 / EMI

MUSIC AT THE EDGE
CD ____ **74321268552**
RCA / Jul '95 / BMG

MUSIC BOX
CD ____ **FCYCD 01**
Full Cycle / Jun '97 / SRD

MUSIC FOR A CHANGING WORLD
CD ____ **XENO 401CD**
Xenophile / Jun '95 / ADA / Direct

MUSIC FOR A COUNTRY COTTAGE
Merry maker's overture / Starlings / Vanity fair / Little serenade / Woodland revel / Walk to the paradise garden / Galloping major / Watermill / Shepherd fennel's dance / A la Claire Fontaine / Waltz for string orchestra / Jenny pluck pears / Dick's maggot / Nonesuch / Woodicock / Demande et response / Patorale / Elizabethan masque / Sailing by / Dusk
CD ____ **CDGO 2039**
EMI / Jun '92 / EMI

MUSIC FOR COFFEESHOPS (2CD Set)
CD Set ____ **CDKTB 20**
Dreamtime / Mar '96 / Kudos / Pinnacle

MUSIC FOR DREAMS (2CD Set)
CD Set ____ **FRCD 6**
Flex / Jun '95 / Jet Star / Plastic Head / SRD

MUSIC FOR INTELLIGENT RAVERS
CD ____ **IRCD 03**
Influence / Jun '94 / Plastic Head

MUSIC FOR LIFE
Sweet savour / As the deer / After the flood / O perfect love / His love endures for ever / Sixth day / Somebody / Give thanks / Give you the glory / That great day / Second coming (cloudburst, rapture, eternal rest)
CD ____ **GHOUSE CD1**
Gloryhouse / Dec '96 / Gloryhouse

MUSIC FOR LOVERS
CD ____ **EMPRBX 002**
Empress / Sep '94 / Koch

MUSIC FOR MAIDS AND TAXI DRIVERS (Brazil Forro)
Balenco da canoa: *Toinho De Alagaos* / De pernambulco aomaranhao: *Duda Da Passira* / Eu tambem quero beijar: *Orlando, Jose* / Bicho da cara preta: *Toinho De Alagaos* / Comeco de verao: *Heleno Dos Oito Baixos* / Peca licenca pra falar de alagoas: *Toinho De Alagaos* / Recorda cao da passira: *Duda Da Passira* / Agricultor p'ra frente: *Orlando, Jose* / Entra e sai: *Heleno Dos Oito Baixos* / Linda menina: *Orlando, Jose* / Casa de tauba: *Duda Da Passira* / Morena da palmeira: *Orlando, Jose* / Carater duro: *Toinho De Alagaos* / Minha zeze: *Orlando, Jose* / Sonho de amor: *Toinho De Alagaos* / Namoro no escuro: *Toinho De Alagaos* / Forro da minha terra: *Duda Da Passira*
CD ____ **CDORB 048**
Globestyle / Aug '89 / Pinnacle

MUSIC FOR MY LOVE
CD ____ **WMCD 5689VT**
Disky / Feb '94 / Disky / THE

MUSIC FOR RELAXATION
CD ____ **CDCH 606**
Milan / Feb '91 / Conifer/BMG / Silva Screen

MUSIC FOR STRINGS FROM TRANSYLVANIA (Romanian Instrumental Dances)
CD ____ **LDX 274937**
La Chant Du Monde / Jul '92 / ADA / Harmonia Mundi

MUSIC FOR THE ARABIAN DULCIMER AND LUTE
Badru zahur / Nida insan / Zubida / Altaf / Taqsim / Moulana / Salaam / Taqsim raad / Munawaat ablam
CD ____ **CDSDL 415**
Saydisc / Mar '96 / ADA / Direct / Harmonia Mundi

MUSIC FOR THE GOD'S
CD ____ **RYKO 10315CD**
Rykodisc / Apr '95 / ADA / Vital

MUSIC FOR THE JET SET
CD ____ **TCD 1038**
Tradition / Nov '96 / ADA / Vital

MUSIC FOR THE QIN, ZHENG AND PIPA
CD ____ **D 8071**
Unesco / Feb '97 / ADA / Harmonia Mundi

MUSIC FORM THE SHRINES OF AJMER AND MUNDRA
CD ____ **TSCD 911**
Topic / Apr '95 / ADA / CM / Direct

MUSIC FROM BRAZIL
CD ____ **15497**
Laserlight / Feb '94 / Target/BMG

MUSIC FROM CAPE VERDE
CD ____ **CAP 21451CD**
Caprice / Nov '95 / ADA / Cadillac / CM / Complete/Pinnacle

MUSIC FROM ECUADOR
CD ____ **CAP 22031CD**
Caprice / Nov '95 / ADA / Cadillac / CM / Complete/Pinnacle

MUSIC FROM ETHIOPIA
CD ____ **TSCD 910**
Topic / Sep '94 / ADA / CM / Direct

MUSIC FROM ETHIOPIA
CD ____ **CAP 21432CD**
Caprice / Nov '95 / ADA / Cadillac / CM / Complete/Pinnacle

MUSIC FROM KARPATHOS, THE
CD ____ **926442**
BUDA / Jul '96 / Discovery

MUSIC FROM PARAGUAY
CD ____ **15467**
Laserlight / Aug '92 / Target/BMG

MUSIC FROM PORTUGAL
CD ____ **15495**
Laserlight / Jun '94 / Target/BMG

MUSIC FROM RUSSIA
CD ____ **15186**
Laserlight / '91 / Target/BMG

MUSIC FROM SOUTH AMERICA - VENEZUELA
CD ____ **15442**
Laserlight / Nov '91 / Target/BMG

MUSIC FROM TAJIKSTAN/UZBEKISTAN
CD ____ **926392**
BUDA / Jul '96 / Discovery

MUSIC FROM THE ANDES & ARGENTINA
CD ____ **CDT 112**
Topic / Apr '93 / ADA / CM / Direct

MUSIC FROM THE BASQUE COUNTRY (2CD Set)
CD Set ____ **KD 416/417CD**
Elkar / Nov '96 / ADA

MUSIC FROM THE HEART
CD ____ **ELL 3212D**
Ellipsis Arts / Oct '93 / ADA / Direct

MUSIC FROM THE IVORY COAST & FODONON
CD ____ **LDX 274838**
La Chant Du Monde / Oct '94 / ADA / Harmonia Mundi

MUSIC FROM THE NIGER REGION
CD ____ **D 8006**
Auvidis/Ethnic / Jun '89 / ADA / Harmonia Mundi

MUSIC FROM THE PUNJAB
CD ____ **ARN 64278**
Arion / Oct '94 / ADA / Discovery

MUSIC FROM THE ROYAL PAGEANT OF THE HORSE
Opening fanfare / Young horse / Rise, rise thou merry lark/Horsey, horsey don't you stop / Queen of Sheba / English country garden / Songs of the country medley / Post horn gallop / John Peel/Old Towler / Devil's gallop / Lilliburlero / Men at arms / Let battle commence / Charge March from Battle of Vittoria / Solitary traveller / Pack up your troubles / Mahler's 5th symphony / Elgar's 1st symphony / O Fortuna / Oranges and lemons / Cockney cavalcade / Pomp and circumstance no.4 / Boys and girls come out to play / Musical joke / Entry of the Gladiators / They're changing the guards at Buckingham Palace / Galloping Major/Charlie is my darlin'/Comin' thro' the rye / We'll keep a welcome/St. Patrick's day / She's a lassie from Lancashire/The Lincolnshire poacher / Blaydon races/Round the Marble Arch / Procession of the knights / Praise my soul / Coronation march from Le Prophete / Zadok the priest / Ode to the horse / National anthem / We said we wouldn't look back / Closing fanfare
CD ____ **3036001032**
Carlton / Jun '97 / Carlton

MUSIC FROM THE SILK ROADS (Music From China, Mongolia & The C.I.S.)
CD ____ **AUB 6776**
Auvidis/Ethnic / Feb '93 / ADA / Harmonia Mundi

MUSIC FROM THE TROOPNG OF THE COLOUR, THE
CD ____ **CDPR 106**
Premier/MFP / May '93 / EMI

MUSIC FROM UGANDA VOL.1 (Traditional)
CD ____ **CAP 21495CD**
Caprice / Nov '96 / ADA / Cadillac / CM / Complete/Pinnacle

MUSIC FROM UGANDA VOL.2 (Modern Traditional)
CD ____ **CAP 21553CD**
Caprice / Nov '96 / ADA / Cadillac / CM / Complete/Pinnacle

MUSIC FROM VIETNAM
CD ____ **CAP 21406CD**
Caprice / Nov '95 / ADA / Cadillac / CM / Complete/Pinnacle

MUSIC HALL MEMORIES (24 Great Singalong Favourites)
I belong to Glasgow: *Fyffe, Will* / When I'm cleaning windows (The window cleaner): *Formby, George* / 'Arf a pint of ale: *Elen, Gus* / Laughing policeman: *Penrose, Charles* / Don't have any more, Missus Moore: *Morris, Lily* / Nobody loves a fairy when she's forty: *O'Shea, Tessie* / Lion and Albert: *Holloway, Stanley* / Keep right on to the end of the road: *Lauder, Harry* / Two lovely black eyes: *Coburn, Charles* / League of nations: *Bennett, Billy* / When I take my morning promenade: *Lloyd, Marie* / Ain't it grand to be bloomin' well dead: *Sarony, Leslie* / It's a great big shame: *Elen, Gus* / Because he loves me: *Morris, Lily* / Man who broke the bank at Monte Carlo: *Coburn, Charles* / I'm 94 today: *Fyffe, Will* / Bee song: *Askey, Arthur* / Nice quiet day: *Elen, Gus* / Daddy: *Bennett, Billy* / Coster girl in Paris: *Lloyd, Marie* / Old school tie: *Western Brothers* / I stopped I looked I listened: *Robey, George* / Wait till the work comes round: *Elen, Gus* / What was there was good: *Robey, George*
CD ____ **PLATCD 173**
Platinum / Mar '96 / Prism

MUSIC IN THE WORLD OF ISLAM VOL.1
CD ____ **TSCD 901**
Topic / Jul '94 / ADA / CM / Direct

MUSIC IN THE WORLD OF ISLAM VOL.2
CD ____ **TSCD 902**
Topic / Jul '94 / ADA / CM / Direct

MUSIC IN THE WORLD OF ISLAM VOL.3
CD ____ **TSCD 903**
Topic / Jul '94 / ADA / CM / Direct

MUSIC IS MY OCCUPATION (Ska Instrumentals 1962-75)
Magic: *McCook, Tommy* / Green island: *Drummond, Don* / Musical store room: *Drummond, Don* / Vitamin A: *Brooks, Baba* / Strolling in: *McCook, Tommy* / River bank parts 1 and 2: *Brooks, Baba* / Silver dollar: *McCook, Tommy & The Skatalites* / Dr. Decker: *Brooks, Baba & Don Drummond* / Eastern standard time: *Drummond, Don* / Yard broom: *McCook, Tommy* / Music is my occupation: *McCook, Tommy & Don Drummond* / Apanga: *McCook, Tommy* / Don de lion: *McCook, Tommy & Don Drummond* / Guns fever: *Brooks, Baba* / Twelve minutes to go: *McCook, Tommy*
CD ____ **CDTRL 259**
Trojan / Mar '94 / Direct / Jet Star

MUSIC MAGAZINE - THE 1960'S EDITION
There's always something there to remind me: *Shaw, Sandie* / I'm telling you now: *Freddie & The Dreamers* / I like it: *Gerry & The Pacemakers* / No milk today: *Herman's Hermits* / Bus stop: *Hollies* / Mony mony: *James, Tommy & The Shondells* / Do you want to know a secret: *Kramer, Billy J. & The Dakotas* / Downtown: *Clark, Petula* / Locomotion: *Little Eva* / 5-4-3-2-1: *Manfred Mann* / Foot tapper: *Shadows* / Surf city: *Jan & Dean* / Gregory girl: *Seekers* / House of the rising sun: *Animals* / Hurdy gurdy man: *Donovan* / Got to get you into my life: *Bennett, Cliff & The Rebel Rousers* / Saturday night at the duck pond: *Cougars* / Baby now that I've found you: *Foundations* / Little lovin': *Fourmost* / Runaway: *Shannon, Del*
CD ____ **CDMFP 6273**
Music For Pleasure / Nov '96 / EMI

MUSIC MAGAZINE - THE 1970'S EDITION
Union city blue: *Blondie* / This will be: *Cole, Natalie* / Jack in the box: *Moments* / Boogie oogie oogie: *Taste Of Honey* / Don't take away the music: *Tavares* / Now is the time: *James, Jimmy & The Vagabonds* / Haven't stopped dancing yet: *Gonzalez* / Beach baby: *First Class* / You sexy thing: *Hot Chocolate* / Sound your funky horn: *KC & The Sunshine Band* / It's been so long: *McCrae, George* / Living on the front line: *Grant, Eddy* / Sylvia: *Focus* / Motor bikin': *Spedding, Chris* / Romeo: *Mr. Big* / Movie star: *Harpo* / Touch too much: *Arrows* / Bump: *Kenny* / Cat crept in: *Mud* / Devil Gate Drive: *Quatro, Suzi*
CD ____ **CDMFP 6274**
Music For Pleasure / Nov '96 / EMI

MUSIC MAGAZINE - THE 1980'S EDITION
Geno: *Dexy's Midnight Runners* / White lines: *Grandmaster Flash & Melle Mel* / Let's do rock steady: *Bodysnatchers* / Solid: *Ashford & Simpson* / We close our eyes: *Go West* / Searchin': *Dean, Hazell* / Dancing tight: *Galaxy & Phil Fearon* / Joy and pain: *Maze & Frankie Beverly* / Respectable: *Mel & Kim* / Somebody help me out: *Beggar & Co* / And the beat goes on: *Beggar & Co* / Movin': *Brass Construction* / Respect: *Adeva* / C'est la vie: *Nevil, Robbie* / Little girl: *Bonds, Gary 'US'* / Intuition: *Linx* / Paint me down: *Spandau Ballet* / Rock me tonight (for old times sake): *Jackson, Freddie* / Is it a dream: *Classix Nouveaux* / Pump up the jam: *Technotronic*
CD ____ **CDMFP 6275**
Music For Pleasure / Nov '96 / EMI

MUSIC MERCHANT STORY, THE
Let love grow: *Holloway, Brenda* / Some quiet place: *Holloway, Brenda* / Mama's little baby (loves lovin'): *Brotherly Love* / I don't see you in my eyes anymore: *Brotherly Love* / Growing pains: *Brotherly Love* / Your love controls me: *Jones Girls* / Taster of the honey (not keeper of the bee): *Jones Girls* / You're the only bargain I've got:

Jones Girls / Come back: *Jones Girls* / Tighten him up: *Laws, Eloise* / You made me an offer I can't refuse: *Laws, Eloise* / Stay with me: *Laws, Eloise* / Love factory: *Laws, Eloise* / (I've been a winner, I've been a loser) I've been in love: *Smith Connection* / I'm bugging your phone: *Smith Connection* / Day you leave: *Smith Connection* / You've been my rock: *Warlock* / Tears ago: *Just Brothers* / You've the love to make me over: *Just Brothers* / Things will be better tomorrow: *Just Brothers* / Sliced tomatoes: *Just Brothers* / Bar-b-q ribs: *Wynglas, Rachel*
CD ______ DEEPM 024
Deep Beats / Jul '97 / BMG

MUSIC OF ARMENIA VOL.5, THE
CD ______ 141192
Celestial Harmonies / Jul '97 / ADA / Select

MUSIC OF ARMENIA VOL.6, THE
CD ______ 131212
Celestial Harmonies / Jul '97 / ADA / Select

MUSIC OF BALI VOL.1, THE (Jegog Music)
CD ______ 131362
Celestial Harmonies / Jul '97 / ADA / Select

MUSIC OF BALI VOL.2, THE (Legong Gamelan)
CD ______ 131372
Celestial Harmonies / Jul '97 / ADA / Select

MUSIC OF BALI VOL.3, THE (Kecack & Tektekan Music)
CD ______ 131382
Celestial Harmonies / Jul '97 / ADA / Select

MUSIC OF BALI, THE
CD ______ LYRCD 7408
Lyrichord / '91 / ADA / CM / Roots

MUSIC OF BAVARIA, THE
Gaudeamus Igitur / Drinking song / Cuckoo yodel / Edelweiss / Bel viso / Golden days / Sherbrooke forest yodel / Wood horn sounds / Wackersberger polka / Walk in the black forest / Mountain boy yodel / Slap dance / White Horse Inn cowbells Salzkammergut / Lyrebird yodel / Way to your heart / Tegernseer polka / With sack and pack
CD ______ QED 199
Tring / Nov '96 / Tring

MUSIC OF BRAZIL, THE
Mexa Mexa / Haja Haja / Vem pra Mim / Rasta Fari / Escudo negro / A maluco do mangue / Isso E bom/Vem ver/Dancando Lambada / O tempero do amor / Delirio do / Carnaval / Vem me / Grito de Igualdade / Sou de Bahia / O Sanho de um Samuray / A colheita / A roda / Brilho Egito / Lambada
CD ______ QED 194
Tring / Nov '96 / Tring

MUSIC OF BRAZIL, THE (2CD Set)
Mi bahia: *Da Silva, Jorginho* / Saudades de Colonia: *Da Silva, Jorginho* / Canto das tres racas: *Oliveira, Valdeci* / Baiao: *Oliveira, Valdeci* / You needed me: *Almeida, Laurindo* / All my love: *Almeida, Laurindo* / Nada sera como antes: *Oliveira, Valdeci* / Chorinho nr1: *Teran, Sergio* / Guachita: *Da Silva, Jorginho* / Copacabana (at the copa): *Almeida, Laurindo* / Late last night: *Almeida, Laurindo* / Alguem me disse: *Oliveira, Valdeci*
CD ______ CD 6076
Music / Jun '97 / Target/BMG

MUSIC OF CHEN YI, THE
CD ______ NA 090
New Albion / Mar '97 / Cadillac / Harmonia Mundi

MUSIC OF CHINA VOL.1, THE (The Deben Bhattacharya Collection/2CD Set)
Silk-stringed instruments / Purple peach-flower / Walking along a street / Night by a stream in Spring / Purple bamboo / Fishing music / Suzhou instrumental factory orchestra / Qin / Gu-zhen / Touch of love / She recognized her mother / Farewell cries / An episode from 'Love stories of the west chamber' / Story of love and laughter / Journey to the west
CD Set ______ FA 061
Fremeaux / Apr '97 / ADA / Discovery

MUSIC OF DREAMS, THE
CD ______ CEFCD 164
Gael Linn / Jan '94 / ADA / CM / Direct / Grapevine/PolyGram / Roots

MUSIC OF EGYPT, THE
CD ______ RCD 10106
Rykodisc / Nov '91 / ADA / Vital

MUSIC OF FRANCE, THE
CD ______ WLD 001
Tring / Aug '93 / Tring

MUSIC OF FRANCE, THE
Milord / I love Paris / Mademoiselle De Paree / Reine de Musette / La mer / Petite fleur / La Goulante de pauvre Jean / Parlez moi d'amour / Song from Moulin Rouge / Et maintenant / La vie en rose / C'est magnifique / Padam padam / Mamma / Aline / J'attendrai / L'amour des Poetes / Frere Jacques / Alouette / Sur Le Pont / Aupres de ma blonde / Plaisir d'amour / Hymmne a l'amour
CD ______ QED 188
Tring / Nov '96 / Tring

MUSIC OF GERMANY, THE
CD ______ WLD 003
Tring / Aug '93 / Tring

MUSIC OF GERMANY, THE
Rosamunde (beer barrel polka) / Heidi / Schneewalzer / Volkmusik / Wem Gott will rechte gunst Erweisen/Horsch was kommt von Dra / Das lieben bringt gross' freud/ Hoch auf dem gelben wagen / Bayrischer landler/Lustig ist das Zigeunerleben / Die lustigen Holzhackerbaum / Hohe tannen / Rhine medley / Medley / Amboss polka / Annchen von Tharau / Sieben fasser wein / Schone maid / Lilli Marlene / Blau bluht der Einzian / Der frohliche wanderer / Auf wiedersehn
CD ______ QED 190
Tring / Nov '96 / Tring

MUSIC OF GREECE, THE
CD ______ WLD 004
Tring / Aug '93 / Tring

MUSIC OF GREECE, THE
Zorba's dance / Oniro demento / Doxa to Theo / Kaimos / Aponi Zoi / To Palikari ech Kaimo / Vraho Vraho / Sto Perighiali to Kryfo / Deka Palikaria / Who pays the ferryman / Play bouzouki / Fragossyriani / Otan Simanoun / Varka sto Yialo / Matia Vourkomena / Margarita Margaro / Kalimepa Ilie / Emaste Dio / Safti Gitonia / Baxe Tsifliki
CD ______ QED 191
Tring / Nov '96 / Tring

MUSIC OF GUADALCANAL, THE (Vocal/ Instrumental Music From Solomon Islands)
CD ______ C 580049
Ocora / Feb '94 / ADA / Harmonia Mundi

MUSIC OF HAWAII, THE
CD ______ WLD 005
Tring / Aug '93 / Tring

MUSIC OF HAWAII, THE
Blue Hawaii / Wini wini / Hula lady / Bora Bora / Paradise Island / Moana rag / Hawaiian wedding song / Lovely hula hands / Kon tiki / Farewell Hawaii / Harbour lights / Aloha land / Hawaii tattoo / Song of Old Hawaii / Hawaiian war chant / My little hula girl / Song of the islands / On the beach at Waikiki / Vaya con dios / Aloha Oe
CD ______ QED 192
Tring / Nov '96 / Tring

MUSIC OF INDIA VOL.1, THE (The Deben Bhattacharya Collection/2CD Set)
Raga todi on surbahar / Raga miyan-ki-malhar on rudravina / Raga bihag on rudravina / Raga bhairavi on rudravina / Mon eki bhranti tomar / Ki swadeshe ki bideshe / Malay asiya koye gechhe kane / Bhaloheshe bhalo kandale / Mon je nilo / Ay ma sadhan samare / Tomar deoya prane / Shunya e buke / Tomar andhar nisha / Mahasindhur opar theke / Shyam kandano bhalo noy / Bujhi oi sudure / Shaon ashilo phire
CD Set ______ FA 060
Fremeaux / Apr '97 / ADA / Discovery

MUSIC OF INDONESIA VOL.10, THE (Music Of Biak, Irian Jaya: Wor, Church Songs, Yospan)
CD ______ SFWCD 40426
Smithsonian Folkways / Feb '97 / ADA / Cadillac / CM / Direct / Koch

MUSIC OF INDONESIA VOL.11, THE (Melayu Music Of Sumatra/Riau Isles: Zapin, Mak Yong, Mendu)
CD ______ SFWCD 40427
Smithsonian Folkways / Feb '97 / ADA / Cadillac / CM / Direct / Koch

MUSIC OF INDONESIA VOL.12, THE (Gongs/Vocal Music Of Sumatra:Talempong, Didong, Kulintang)
CD ______ SFWCD 40428
Smithsonian Folkways / Feb '97 / ADA / Cadillac / CM / Direct / Koch

MUSIC OF INDONESIA VOL.3, THE (Karya)
CD ______ LYRCD 7421
Lyrichord / Feb '94 / ADA / CM / Roots

MUSIC OF INDONESIA VOL.7, THE (Music From The Forests Of Riau & Mentawai)
CD ______ SFWCD 40423
Smithsonian Folkways / Dec '95 / ADA / Cadillac / CM / Direct / Koch

MUSIC OF INDONESIA VOL.8, THE (Vocal/Instrumental Music From East/ Central Flores)
CD ______ SFWCD 40424
Smithsonian Folkways / Dec '95 / ADA / Cadillac / CM / Direct / Koch

MUSIC OF INDONESIA VOL.9, THE (Vocal Music From Central/West Flores)
CD ______ SFWCD 40425
Smithsonian Folkways / Dec '95 / ADA / Cadillac / CM / Direct / Koch

MUSIC OF INDONESIA, THE
CD ______ SFWCD 40420
Smithsonian Folkways / Dec '94 / ADA / Cadillac / CM / Direct / Koch

MUSIC OF IRAN, THE
CD ______ HMA 190391CD
Musique D'Abord / Oct '94 / Harmonia Mundi

MUSIC OF IRELAND, THE
Danny Boy / Rocky road to Dublin / Galway races, an dearig dun / Welcoming / Sleivenamon / Steal away / Finnegan's wake / Black velvet band / Fields of Atherney / Down by the Sally gardens / Dirty old town / Muirsheen durkin / Molly Malone / O'Carolan's concerto / Wild rover / Bol O'Donaghue / Whiskey in the jar / Softly flows the Clare / Father O'Flynn / Irish washerwoman / Blackberry blossom / It's a long way to Tipperary / Endearing young charms / Eileen Allanah
CD ______ 3036100172
Pearls / May '96 / Carlton

MUSIC OF IRELAND, THE
CD ______ CD 439CD
Arfolk / May '96 / ADA / Discovery / Roots

MUSIC OF IRELAND, THE
Red is the rose / Donkey's cross / Delaney's fancy / Old boreen / Star of County Down / Gravel walk / Masons apron / Mick McGuire / Humour is on me now / Jig selection / Galway Bay / Green hills of Sligo / Ireland my homeland / Green fields round Ferbane / Home to Donegal / Races of Kilkadoon / Rambles of spring / Bright silvery light of the moon / Dowd's no.9 / Musical priest / Knocknagow / Carrickfergus
CD ______ QED 198
Tring / Nov '96 / Tring

MUSIC OF ITALY, THE
L'Italiano / Parlami d'amore / Gloria / Una lacrima sul viso / Tu sei L'Unica Donna per me / Sharazan / Sara' Perche' ti amo / Per Elisa / Ti amo / Maledetta primavera / O sole mio / Torna a sorriento / Funiculi funicula / O paese d'o sole / Santa Lucia Luntana / Volare / Santa Lucia / O Marenariello / Tu ca nun chiagne / Arrvederci Roma
CD ______ QED 196
Tring / Nov '96 / Tring

MUSIC OF JAPAN, THE
CD ______ WLD 006
Tring / Aug '93 / Tring

MUSIC OF JAPAN, THE
Autumn sorrow / Moon over Tokyo / Rokudan / Nil Li Zi A / Tanko Bushi / Soran Bushi / Toheganse / Kagome Antagata / Doko sa Hana-Ichi / Sakura instrumental / Sakura / Arirang / Tancha Meh / Chuern Mong / Chidori No Kyoku / Midare / Godan-Kinuta / Outgoing ships / Nite star / Ruined castles / Japanese fisherman / Lotus blossom
CD ______ QED 193
Tring / Nov '96 / Tring

MUSIC OF KENTUCKY VOL.1, THE
CD ______ YAZCD 2013
Yazoo / Oct '95 / ADA / CM / Koch

MUSIC OF KENTUCKY VOL.2, THE
CD ______ YAZCD 2014
Yazoo / Oct '95 / ADA / CM / Koch

MUSIC OF LATIN AMERICA, THE
Copacabana / Fernando / Quiereme mucho / El lute / Ay no digas / Samba pa ti / Brazil / Quando quando / Argentina / Agua / Oyo como va / Rise / Chiquitita / Mexico / Cuando caliente el sol / El Condor Pasa
CD ______ QED 189
Tring / Nov '96 / Tring

MUSIC OF LIFE LIVE, THE
CD ______ SPOCKCD 1
Music Of Life / Aug '89 / Grapevine/ PolyGram

MUSIC OF LONG AGO 1958-1993, THE (Traditional Croatian Music)
CD ______ C 600006
Ocora / May '97 / ADA / Harmonia Mundi

MUSIC OF MADAGASCAR, THE (Classic Traditional Recordings From The 1930's)
CD ______ YAZCD 7003
Yazoo / Apr '95 / ADA / CM / Koch

MUSIC OF MARGINAL POLYNESIA, THE (Fiji, Tuvalu, Wallis & Futuna)
CD ______ VICG 52762
JVC World Library / Mar '96 / ADA / CM / Direct

MUSIC OF MARTINIQUE 1929-1950, THE
CD ______ FLYCD 947
Flyright / Jul '96 / Hot Shot / Jazz Music / Wellard

MUSIC OF MEXICO, THE
La Felicidad / Corazon Angustiado / Mi Guajira Y mi Caballo / Sueno de Amanecer / Palabra de Mujer / Dentro de mi / Tijuana taxi / Sed de Vivir / Ven / Lonely bull / Hoy soy Feliz / Se que no Volveras / Spanish flea / Cuando pienses en mi / Lamento
CD ______ QED 200
Tring / Nov '96 / Tring

MUSIC OF NW ARGENTINA, THE
CD ______ 824992
BUDA / Apr '91 / Discovery

MUSIC OF PAPUA NEW GUINEA, THE
CD ______ 925702
BUDA / Jun '93 / Discovery

MUSIC OF POLYNESIA VOL.1, THE (Tahiti, Society Islands)
CD ______ VICG 52712
JVC World Library / Mar '96 / ADA / CM / Direct

MUSIC OF POLYNESIA VOL.2, THE (Tuamoto, Austral Islands)
CD ______ VICG 52722
JVC World Library / Mar '96 / ADA / CM / Direct

MUSIC OF POLYNESIA VOL.3, THE (Easter Island, The Marquesas Islands)
CD ______ VICG 52732
JVC World Library / Mar '96 / ADA / CM / Direct

MUSIC OF POLYNESIA VOL.4, THE (Samoa, Tonga)
CD ______ VICG 52742
JVC World Library / Mar '96 / ADA / CM / Direct

MUSIC OF SARDINIA 1930-1932, THE
CD ______ HTCD 20
Heritage / Oct '93 / ADA / Direct / Hot Shot / Jazz Music / Swift / Wellard

MUSIC OF SCOTLAND, THE
Highland cathederal / Fantasia on mist covered mountains / Bengullion / Isabel T Macdonald / Flora Graham / Loch Lomond / My Bonnie lies over the ocean / Coming through the Rye / Dark Ireland / Skye boat song / Mist covered mountains of home / Mull of Kintyre / Drunken piper / My love she's but a lassie yet / Girl I left behind me / Bonnie Dundee / Off she goes / Donald's awa / Fanfare salute / Scotland the brave / Para Handy / Amazing grace / Auld lang syne / Folk selection / Dashing white sergeant / Galloway house / Roxburgh castle / Auld town march
CD ______ 3036100152
Pearls / Jan '97 / Carlton

MUSIC OF SOUTH EAST AND EAST ASIA, THE
CD ______ VICG 120672
JVC World Library / Feb '96 / ADA / CM / Direct

MUSIC OF SPAIN, THE
CD ______ WLD 008
Tring / Aug '93 / Tring

MUSIC OF SPAIN, THE
Espana Cani / Maria Isabel / Quiereme mucho / Borriquito / Cana de Azucar / Cielito Lindo / La bamba / Agapimu / De Cierto no se Sabe / Granada / Espana / El Porompompero / Sevillanas / Amor Amor / La Cucaracha / Uu rayo del sol / Un canto a Galicia / Ansiedad / Aranjuez mon amour / Y viva Espana
CD ______ QED 195
Tring / Nov '96 / Tring

MUSIC OF SUNDA, THE (Java)
CD ______ VICG 52642
JVC World Library / Feb '96 / ADA / CM / Direct

MUSIC OF THE ANDES, THE
Huajra: *Inti-Illimani* / Subida: *Inti-Illimani* / Fiesta punena (Festival at Punena): *Inti-Illimani* / Amores hallaras: *Inti-Illimani* / La obreras (The working women): *Quilapayun* / Tu (You): *Quilapayun* / Yarvi y Huayno de la quebrada de humahuca (Yaravi and Huayno: *Quilapayun* / Tan alta que est la luna (How high the moon): *Quilapayun* / El canto del cuculi (Song of the turtledove): *Quilapayun* / Dos palomitas: *Quilapayun* / El condor pasa (Flight of the condor): *Conjunto Kollahuara* / Cancion y huayno (Song and huayno): *Conjunto Kollahuara* / Vicunita: *Conjunto Kollahuara* / El tinku: *Jara, Victor* / Baila caporal (Dance master): *Illapu* / Sol de maiz (Sun of corn): *Illapu*
CD ______ CDEMC 3680
Hemisphere / May '94 / EMI

MUSIC OF THE BANSURI, THE (A Flute Of Rajasthan)
CD ______ VICG 52202
JVC World Library / Mar '96 / ADA / CM / Direct

MUSIC OF THE BUNRAKU THEATRE, THE
CD ______ VICG 53562
JVC World Library / Mar '96 / ADA / CM / Direct

MUSIC OF THE FIDDLE, THE
Ceol na fiddlers: *Garioch Fiddlers* / Dumbarton Castle: *Banchory Strathspey & Reel Society* / Forbes Morrison: *Banchory Strathspey & Reel Society* / Left-handed fiddler: *Banchory Strathspey & Reel Society* / Nanny and Betty: *Shetland's Young Heritage* / A yowe cam ta wir door yarmin: *Shetland's Young Heritage* / Up and doon da harbour: *Shetland's Young Heritage* / Bluebells of Scotland: *Duncan, Maurice* / Mull of the cool Bens: *Inverness Fiddlers* / Sheiling song: *Inverness Fiddlers* / Leaving Lismore: *Inverness Fiddlers* / South Georgia whaling

song: *Inverness Fiddlers* / Return to the Stewart: *MacDonald, Catriona* / Slanttigart: *MacDonald, Catriona* / Tame her when the snaw comes: *MacDonald, Catriona* / Farewell to Skye: *Banchory Ensemble* / Callum Beag: *Banchory Ensemble* / Juggernaut: *Banchory Ensemble* / Ian Petersen's compliments to Fraser McGlynn: *Banchory Ensemble* / Mackintosh Patrick March: *Aberdeen Strathspey & Reel Society* / Leaving Glen Urquart: *Banchory Strathspey & Reel Society* / South of the Grampians: *Banchory Strathspey & Reel Society* / John McNeil's reel: *Banchory Strathspey & Reel Society* / Sheilis: *Glasgow Reel & Strathspey Society* / Madame Neruda: *Anderson, Paul* / Cradle song: *Anderson, Paul* / Kirrie kebbuck: *Anderson, Paul* / Spey in spate: *Anderson, Paul* / Loch Ruan: *Inverness Fiddlers* / Maid of Flanders: *Inverness Fiddlers* / Sound of Sleat: *Inverness Fiddlers* / Prince Charlie's last view of Scotland: *Leggat, Fiona* / Neil Gow's wife: *Leggat, Fiona* / Old reel: *Leggat, Fiona* / Gu man slan a chi mi: *Shetland's Young Heritage* / Fear a'Bhata: *Shetland's Young Heritage* / Gu man clan a chi mi: *Shetland's Young Heritage* / Herr Roloff's farewell: *Brian, Bill* / Boar's head ceilidh: *Garioch Fiddlers* / Mrs. Forbes Leith: *Anderson, Keith* / Auld Brig O'Doon: *Anderson, Keith* / Beauty of the north: *Anderson, Keith* / Princess Beatrice: *Anderson, Keith* / Ashokan farewell: *Shetland's Young Heritage* / Mrs. McPherson of Cluny: *Banchory Strathspey & Reel Society* / John Grumblie: *Banchory Strathspey & Reel Society* / Anne Fraser McKenzie: *Banchory Strathspey & Reel Society* / Donald Ian Rankine: *Banchory Strathspey & Reel Society* / Ceol na fidhle: *Garioch Fiddlers*
CD ______ CDLOC 1097
Lochshore / Nov '96 / ADA / Direct / Duncans

MUSIC OF THE FULANI & THE TENDA FROM SENEGAL, THE
CD ______ C 560043
Ocora / May '94 / ADA / Harmonia Mundi

MUSIC OF THE GAMUZ TRIBE SUDAN, THE
CD ______ D 8072
Unesco / Nov '96 / ADA / Harmonia Mundi

MUSIC OF THE GLENS, THE
CD ______ CDLBP 2025
Lochshore / Jul '96 / ADA / Direct / Duncans

MUSIC OF THE INCAS, THE
CD ______ LYRCD 7348
Lyrichord / '91 / ADA / CM / Roots

MUSIC OF THE INGESSANA & BERTA TRIBES SUDAN, THE
CD ______ D 8073
Unesco / Nov '96 / ADA / Harmonia Mundi

MUSIC OF THE KHOREZM UZBEKISTAN, THE
CD ______ D 8269
Unesco / Nov '96 / ADA / Harmonia Mundi

MUSIC OF THE KOTO, THE
CD ______ VICG 53582
JVC World Library / Mar '96 / ADA / CM / Direct

MUSIC OF THE MILITARY, THE (2CD Set)
Royal Air Force march past / Cavalry of the Steppes / Light of foot / Blaze away / Amazing grace / Men of Harlech/God bless the Prince Of Wales / Aces high / Anchors aweigh / Battle of Britain / Old comrades / Coronation march / Lochanside / Green hills of Tyrol / Dambusters march / Washington post / Sons of the brave / National Emblem / Battle of the Somme / Dagshai hills / Argyll and Sutherland Highlanders / Under the double eagle / Australian march / Redetzky / 633 Squadron / Flower of Scotland / Famous British marches / British Grenadiers / Lilliburlero / All through the night / Highland Laddie / Rule Britannia / Bonnie Anne / Athol cummers / Sheepwife / Macleod of Mull / Semper fidelis / Those magnificent men in their flying machines
CD Set ______ CDDL 1078
Music For Pleasure / May '91 / EMI

MUSIC OF THE NILE VALLEY, THE
CD ______ LYRCD 7355
Lyrichord / Aug '93 / ADA / CM / Roots

MUSIC OF THE PALACES AND SECRET SOCIETIES, THE (Cameroun, Bamum)
CD ______ W 260074
Inedit / Feb '97 / ADA / Discovery / Harmonia Mundi

MUSIC OF THE SHADOWS, THE
CD ______ MACCD 291
Autograph / Aug '96 / BMG

MUSIC OF THE SHAHNAI, THE
CD ______ VICG 52212
JVC World Library / Mar '96 / ADA / CM / Direct

MUSIC OF THE SHI PEOPLE, THE
CD ______ VICG 52282
JVC World Library / Mar '96 / ADA / CM / Direct

MUSIC OF THE SOUTH PACIFIC, THE
Blue Hawaii / Hawaiian wedding song / Lovely hula hands / Pearly shells / Aloha Oe / Kaimana Hila / Hawaiian tattoo / Polynesian love song / Isa lei / Toai Mai / Papia Tahiti / Farewell (for just a while) / Pania of the reef / Pokarekare Ana / Under the sun / When my Wahine does the Poi / Cheryl Moana Marie / Haere Mai / Now is the hour / Tofa Felengi
CD ______ QED 197
Tring / Nov '96 / Tring

MUSIC OF THE SOUTH SEAS, THE
CD ______ PS 360504
PlayaSound / Sep '96 / ADA / Harmonia Mundi

MUSIC OF THE STREETS, THE (Mechanical Street Entertainment)
Man who broke the bank at Monte Carlo / I've got a lovely bunch of coconuts / Charmaine / Oh oh Antonio / La Marseillaise / Pomone waltz / Rule Britannia / Honeysuckle and the bee / Just one girl / Bicycle barn dance polka / Bells of St. Mary's / Soldiers of the Queen / Goodbye Dolly Gray / Molly O'Morgan / Little Dolly Daydream / Roamin' in the gloamin' / He had to get out and get under / At Trinity Church / Let the great big world keep turning
CD ______ CDSDL 340
Saydisc / Jun '87 / ADA / Direct / Harmonia Mundi

MUSIC OF THE TARTAR PEOPLE, THE
CD ______ TSCD 912
Topic / Apr '95 / ADA / CM / Direct

MUSIC OF THE TUAREG, THE (Ritual Music & Dances From The Hoggar Mountains)
CD ______ LDX 274974
La Chant Du Monde / May '94 / ADA / Harmonia Mundi

MUSIC OF THE WAYANA TRIBE ON THE LITANI RIVER, THE
CD ______ 926372
BUDA / Mar '96 / Discovery

MUSIC OF THE WAYANG KULIT VOL.2, THE
CD ______ VICG 52662
JVC World Library / Mar '96 / ADA / CM / Direct

MUSIC OF THE WAYANG KULIT, THE
CD ______ VICG 50282
JVC World Library / Mar '96 / ADA / CM / Direct

MUSIC OF THE WORLD, THE
CD ______ PS 66002
PlayaSound / Feb '93 / ADA / Harmonia Mundi

MUSIC OF VENEZUALA, THE
El gavan: *Armonia Y Cuerdas* / Sombra en los meadanos: *Raices De Mi Pueblo* / San Rafael: *Chirinos, Ali* / La montuna torpe: *Trio Cabure* / El grillo: *Mendoza, Ricardo Y Su Conjunto* / La jurupera: *Grupo Folklorico Curigna* / Entreverao: *Conjunto Piedemonte* / Zumba que zumba: *Quintana, Luis* / La guarchara: *Fandino, Luis Y Conjunto Piedemonte* / Seis por derecho: *Tapia, Carlos Y Conjunto Piedemonte* / El salto: *Quinteto Montes* / La culebra: *Cabello, Jorge Y Su Conjunto* / Los perros: *Alma Venezolana* / La musicas tuyera: *El Periquito De Miranda* / Barcelonesa: *Grupo Crillo Universitario 'Simon Bolivar'*
CD ______ CDZ 2018
Zu Zazz / Apr '94 / Rollercoaster

MUSIC OF VIETNAM VOL.2, THE
CD ______ CAP 21463CD
Caprice / Mar '96 / ADA / Cadillac / CM / Complete/Pinnacle

MUSIC OF VIETNAM VOL.3, THE
CD ______ CAP 21479CD
Caprice / Mar '96 / ADA / Cadillac / CM / Complete/Pinnacle

MUSIC OF WEST BALI, THE
CD ______ ARN 64271
Arion / Oct '94 / ADA / Discovery

MUSIC OF WORLD WAR 2 VOL.1, THE
CD ______ VJC 10362
Vintage Jazz Classics / Oct '92 / ADA / Cadillac / CM / Direct

MUSIC ON A MARRAKESH MARKET SQUARE
CD ______ LDX 274973
La Chant Du Monde / Jun '94 / ADA / Harmonia Mundi

MUSIC TO MOVE YOU VOL.1
Reels for Luke: *Sin E* / Rowan tree: *Holland, Maggie* / La fete de village: *Dransfield, Barry* / Hornpipe: *Dransfield, Barry* / Miss Sackville's fancy: *Dransfield, Barry* / Keep it clean: *National Gallery* / Mama t'aint long 'fo day: *Simpson, Martin* / Did Jesus have a girlfriend: *Simpson, Jessica* / Fortitude of pain: *Buirski, Felicity* / Dr. Slime: *Dransfield, Barry* / Chapeltown hawk: *Pegg, Bob* / Animal song: *Johnson, Robb* / Red roses: *Simpson, Martin & Jessica*
CD ______ RHYD 5101
Rhiannon / Mar '96 / ADA / Direct / Vital

MUSIC WAS OUR BUSINESS
Whatcha gonna do when there ain't no swing: *Gonella, Nat & His Georgians* / Japanese sandman: *Gardner, Freddy* / Mirage: *Roy, Harry & His Band* / Swing shoe shop: *Simpson, Jack* / Bottle party: *Winstone, Eric & His Band* / Swing me sweetly: *Davis, Lew* / Song of songs: *Gonella, Nat & His Georgians* / Mind the handle it's hot: *Young, Arthur* / Big noise from Winnetka: *Roy, Harry* / Baby, won't you please come home: *Gardner, Freddy* / Fascinating rhythm: *Clae, John & His Claepigeons* / Swinging to those lies (it's a sin to tell a lie): *Gonella, Nat & His Georgians* / In the mood: *Young, Arthur* / Bitin' the dust: *Winstone, Eric & His Band* / Honeysuckle rose: *Simpson, Jack & His Sextet* / I never knew: *Davis, Lew* / Wednesday night hop: *Roy, Harry & His Band* / Watch the birdie: *Clae, John & His Claepigeons* / Ma (he's making eyes at me): *Young, Arthur* / Boogie wooglie piggy: *Roy, Harry & His Band* / Stay out of the South: *Simpson, Jack & His Sextet* / I got rhythm: *Gonella, Nat & His Georgians*
CD ______ RAJCD 864
Empress / Mar '96 / Koch

MUSIC WHILE YOU WORK
Calling all workers / National emblem / Gondoliers (Selection) / Listen to liszt / Hits of '39 / Going Greek - selection / Mikado, The - selection / Carefree - medley / Great waltz (selection) / Accordion medley / Banjo on my knee - selection / Fleet's lit up / Hits of the day / Champagne waltz - selection
CD ______ PASTCD 9791
Flapper / Jun '92 / Pinnacle

MUSIC WHILE YOU WORK (3CD Set)
Calling all workers / Love Parade / New moon / Dancing years / White horse inn / Roberta / Christy Minstrels selection / Whistling Rufus / Sweet nothings / Canadian capers / Alexander's ragtime band / Get out and get under the moon / Cuddle up a little closer / Put your arms around me / Wait for me Mary / If I had my way / East side of heaven / Hit parade / Something in the air / Lisbon story / Sing as we go / French march medley / Ragtime medley / Dixie Lee / Say it with music / Love is the sweetest thing / I'll do my best to make you happy / Pistol packin' Mama / Pony Express / Time on my hands / Close your eyes / But not for me / Embraceable you / Bidin' my time / You are my lucky star / Broadway rhythm / I've got a feelin' you're foolin' / Love walked in / Music goes round and around / Saddle your blues to a wild mustang / Everything I have is yours / Coffee in the morning / Tea for two / Three little words / You're driving me crazy / My heart tells me for the first time I've fallen in love / Ain't misbehavin' / I double dare you / Be a waterfall / Learn to croon / Dreamer / How sweet you are / Very thought of you / Touch of your lips / Just one more chance / Who walks in when I walk out / Keep an eye on your heart / Something for the boys / Leader of the big time band / Hey good lookin' / He's a right guy / Could it be you / Hats / Moonstruck / Country cousins / Mary / Not that kind of person / White city / Bunch of roses / Little bit independent / Let me whisper / Yankee grit / Espana / Shine / Don't be angry / Olf faithfull / Boston bounce / We've got something to sing about / Flash of steel / Girl of the moment / This is new / Suddenly it's spring / Jenny / My ship / Do you ever think of me / Oh how I love my darling / La cinquantaine / Castles in Spain / Maria / Lady of the evening / Vienna blood / One love / There's a new world over the skyline / My prayer / It's like old times / Lilli Marlene / We don't know where we're going / Calling all workers
CD Set ______ EMPRESS 1004
Empress / Jul '96 / Koch

MUSIC WHILE YOU WORK
Calling all the workers / Knightsbridge march / If I ruled the world / Rose Marie / Darktown strutters ball / I wish I were in love again / California, here I come / April showers / Swanee / Pagan love song / Moon of Manakoora / Whistle a happy tune / Friends and neighbours / Let there be love / Another openin' another show / Alexander's ragtime band / Oxford Street march / Strike up the band / Music everywhere
CD ______ 304652
Hallmark / Jun '97 / Carlton

MUSIC WHILE YOU WORK - CALLING ALL WORKERS VOL.1
Calling all workers: *Victory Band* / Love Parade selection: *Victory Band* / New Moon selection: *Victory Band* / Dancing Years selection: *Fryer, Harry* / White Horse Inn: *Fryer, Harry* / Roberta: *Simpson, Jack* / Christy Minstrels selection: *Troise & His Mandoliers* / Whistling Rufus: *Troise & His Mandoliers* / Sweet nothin's: *Mayerl, Billy* / Canadian capers: *Mayerl, Billy* / Alexanders ragtime band/Poor butterfly/Get out and get under: *Victory Band* / Flanagan and Allen selection: *Victory Band* / Cuddle up a little closer/Put your arms around me: *Victory Band* / Wait for me Mary: *Victory Band* / If I had my way: *Victory Band* / East side of heaven: *Simpson, Jack* / Hit Parade selection: *Simpson, Jack* / Something in the air: *Fryer, Harry* / Lisbon story: *Fryer, Harry* / Sing as we go: *Mackey, Percival* / French March medley: *Scala, Primo*
CD ______ RAJCD 819
Empress / Apr '97 / Koch

MUSIC WHILE YOU WORK - CALLING ALL WORKERS VOL.2
Calling all workers: *Victory Band* / Dixie Lee: *Chapman, Wally & His Band* / Say it with music/Love is the sweetest thing: *Simpson, Jack & His Sextet* / I'll do my best to make you happy: *Simpson, Jack & His Sextet* / Pistol packin' Mama/Pony express: *Studio Orchestra* / Time on my hands: *Marsh, Roy & His Orchestra* / Close your eyes: *Chapman, Wally & His Band* / But not for you/ Embraceable you/Bidin' my time: *Studio Orchestra* / You are my lucky star/Broadway rhythm/I got a feelin': *Simpson, Jack & His Sextet* / Love walked in: *Marsh, Roy & His Orchestra* / Music goes 'round and around: *Marsh, Roy & His Orchestra* / Saddle your blues to a wild mustang: *Atkins, Stan & His Band* / Everything I have is yours/Coffee in the morning: *Dodd, Pat & Cecil Norman* / Tea for two: *Marsh, Roy & His Orchestra* / Three little words/You're driving me crazy: *Royal Navy Blue Mariners* / My heart tells me/For the first time I've fallen in love: *Studio Orchestra* / Ain't misbehavin': *Marsh, Roy & His Orchestra* / I double dare you/Boom: *Atkins, Stan & His Band* / By a waterfall/Learn to croon: *Dodd, Pat & Cecil Norman* / Dreamer/How sweet you are: *Studio Orchestra* / Very thought of you: *Chapman, Wally & His Band* / Bei mir bist du schon: *Marsh, Roy & His Orchestra* / Touch of your lips/Just one more chance: *Royal Navy Blue Mariners* / Who walks in when I walk out: *Chapman, Wally & His Band* / Keep an eye on your heart: *Bradley, Josephine & Her Ballroom Orchestra*
CD ______ RAJCD 847
Empress / Feb '95 / Koch

MUSIC WHILE YOU WORK - CALLING ALL WORKERS VOL.3
Calling all workers: *Something For The Boys* / Something for the boys: *Something For The Boys* / Leader of the big time band: *Something For The Boys* / Hey good lookin': *Something For The Boys* / He's a right guy: *Something For The Boys* / Could it be you: *Something For The Boys* / Hats: *Green, Phil Orchestra* / Moonstruck: *Green, Phil Orchestra* / Country cousins: *Green, Phil Orchestra* / Mary: *Green, Phil Orchestra* / Not that kind of person: *Green, Phil Orchestra* / White City: *Green, Phil Orchestra* / Bunch of roses: *Burston, Reginald & His Orchestra* / Valse bleue: *Fryer, Harry* / Little bit independent: *Burston, Reginald & His Orchestra* / Let me whisper: *Burston, Reginald & His Orchestra* / Ciribiribin: *Collins, Al & his Orchestra* / Yankee grit: *Crean, Richard & His Orchestra* / Espana: *Davidson, Harry & His Orchestra* / Shine: *Munro, Ronnie & His Orchestra* / Don't be angry: *Munro, Ronnie & His Orchestra* / Old Faithful: *Gardner, Freddy & His Swing Orchestra* / Boston bounce: *Davidson, Harry & His Orchestra* / We've got something to sing about: *Davidson, Harry & His Orchestra* / Flash of steel: *Rabin, Oscar & His Band* / Girl of the moment: *London Coliseum Orchestra* / This is new: *London Coliseum Orchestra* / Suddenly it's Spring: *London Coliseum Orchestra* / Jenny: *London Coliseum Orchestra* / My ship: *London Coliseum Orchestra* / Do you ever think of me: *Green, Phil Orchestra* / Oh how I love my darling: *Green, Phil Orchestra* / La cinquantaine: *Gardner, Freddy* / Castles in Spain: *Crean, Richard & His Orchestra* / Marta: *Burston, Reginald & His Orchestra* / Lady of the evening: *Burston, Reginald & His Orchestra* / Vienna blood: *Gardner, Freddy & His Swing Orchestra* / One love: *Munro, Ronnie & His Dance Orchestra* / There's a new world over the skyline: *Munro, Ronnie & His Dance Orchestra* / My prayer: *Munro, Ronnie & His Dance Orchestra* / It's like old times: *Munro, Ronnie & His Dance Orchestra* / Lili Marlene: *Green, Phil Orchestra* / We don't know where we're going: *Green, Phil Orchestra* / Calling all workers: *Green, Phil Orchestra*
CD ______ RAJCD 865
Empress / Mar '96 / Koch

MUSIC WITH NO NAME
Hungry on arrival: *Outernational Meltdown* / Ancestral healing: *Mohamed, Pops* / Abangoma: *Barungwa* / What you see: *Purim, Flora* / Love is touching: *Tchicai, John* / Ubombo: *Kunene, Madala* / Togetherness: *Amampondo* / Firewater/Jivetalk: *Fourth World* / Siya dengelela kgonyami: *Sangomais* / All men amen: *Ballamy, Iain* / Achisa: *Achisa*
CD ______ BWR 080CD
B&W / Oct '96 / New Note/Pinnacle / SRD / Vital/SAM

MUSIC WORKS PRESENT CHATTY CHATTY MOUTH VERSIONS
CD ______ GRELCD 196
Greensleeves / Dec '93 / Jet Star / SRD

MUSIC WORKS PRESENTS TWICE MY AGE
CD ______ GRELCD 144
Greensleeves / Apr '90 / Jet Star / SRD

MUSIC WORKS SHOWCASE 1988
CD ______ GRELCD 117
Greensleeves / Apr '89 / Jet Star / SRD

MUSIC WORKS SHOWCASE 1989
CD ______ GRELCD 123
Greensleeves / Jun '89 / Jet Star / SRD

MUSIC WORKS SHOWCASE 1990
Too good to be true / Fatal attraction / Can't make a slip / IOU / Hard road to travel / Big all around / Jealousy / Fall for you again / What's the matter / Report to me / Express love / Break the ice / Easy life
CD _______ GRELCD 139
Greensleeves / Nov '89 / Jet Star / SRD

MUSIC WORKS SHOWCASE 1990/1991
CD _______ GRELCD 506
Greensleeves / May '90 / Jet Star / SRD

MUSIC WORKS VOL.1 (Gussie Clarke Presents Roots & Culture)
Throw me corn: *Marshall, Larry* / Must be revelation: *Big Youth* / Born to dub you: *Pablo, Augustus* / Dub and gaze: *Big Joe* / In their own way: *Brown, Dennis & Big Youth* / Is it because I'm black: *Wilson, Delroy* / Proud to be black: *Mikey Dread* / Pass the chalice: *Ranking Trevor* / To the foundation: *Brown, Dennis & Hugh Brown* / Jah Jah love people: *Minott, Sugar* / Sensemillia: *Mighty Diamonds* / Guiding star: *Brown, Hugh* / Higher the mountain: *Big Youth & U-Roy* / Skylarking: *Pablo, Augustus* / Don't cuss the daughter: *Trinity* / So much things: *Smart, Leroy* / Love we need: *Brown, Hugh* / No entry: *Pablo, Augustus* / Strictly rockers: *Big Youth & Augustus Pablo*
CD _______ SPV 0855213
SPV / Aug '96 / Koch / Plastic Head

MUSIC WORKS VOL.2 (Gussie Clarke Presents Lovers Dancehall)
I admire you: *Marshall, Larry* / My time: *Isaacs, Gregory* / Love was all I had: *Aitken, Marcia* / Come in Heaven: *Wilson, Delroy* / Mix up girl: *Lindo, Hopeton* / Danger in your eyes: *Mighty Diamonds* / Love you to want me: *Andy, Horace* / Oh no I can't believe it: *Isaacs, Gregory* / Unexpected places: *Ellis, Hortense* / Into the night: *Parks, Lloyd & Hugh Brown* / Children of the night: *Hall, Pam* / Deceiving girl: *Brown, Dennis* / Fools rush in: *Mighty Diamonds* / Love love love: *Wilson, Delroy* / Special lover: *McGregor, Freddie* / I am not the same: *Grier, Merva* / Gonna love you more: *Clarke, Johnny* / Try me: *Stewart, Roman*
CD _______ SPV 0855214
SPV / Aug '96 / Koch / Plastic Head

MUSIC WORTH IT'S WEIGHT IN GOLD
CD _______ BULLCD 1
Bullion / Jun '97 / 3mv/Sony / Prime

MUSICA POPULAR DO BRAZIL
CD _______ GC 900005
ITM / Dec '93 / Koch / Tradelink

MUSICAL BANQUET, A
CD _______ CDSDLC 397
Saydisc / Feb '93 / ADA / Direct / Harmonia Mundi

MUSICAL BOX DANCES
CD _______ CDSDL 359
Saydisc / '88 / ADA / Direct / Harmonia Mundi

MUSICAL DILEMMAS
Finders kreepers: *Runaways* / Science fu pt.2: *Danny Breaks* / Universal: *Raymatics* / Into you: *Blueshift* / Non non non: *Melaaz* / Spanish high noon: *Misterjon* / Miracles: *REQ* / Futurama: *Peshay* / Beauty and the beats: *Runaways* / Phat like a: *Tek 9* / Shifting to blue: *Blueshift* / Seachange: *Misterjon* / Meditations: *REQ* / Lullaby: *Raymatics*
CD _______ UDRCD 001
Universal Dilemma / Mar '97 / Prime

MUSICAL FEAST
CD _______ CDHB 84
Heartbeat / Apr '91 / ADA / Direct / Greensleeves / Jet Star

MUSICAL FEVER 1967-1968
Bad mind grudgeful: *Winston & Robin* / Puppy love: *Bennett & Dennis* / Bad treatment: *Cannon & Soul Vendors* / Get a lick: *Oakley, Bumps* / Hip hug-her: *Sultans* / Let me love you: *Miller, Jacob* / Rub up, push up: *Termites* / Wailing time: *Winston & Robin* / Venus: *Frater, Eric* / Norwegian wood: *Williams, Marshall* / Love me girl: *Soul Vendors* / You shouldn't be the one: *Holness, Winston* / Ram jam: *Jackie & Soul Vendors* / You gonna lose: *Octaves* / Get with it: *Soul Vendors* / Fat fish: *Viceroys* / Grooving steady: *Jackie & Soul Vendors* / Bye bye baby: *Sims, Zoot* / Soul junction: *Soul Vendors* / Mercy mercy: *Slim & Freedom Singers* / Baba boom: *Jackie & Soul Vendors* / Love and unity: *Viceroys* / I don't mind: *Bob & Ty* / Zigaloo: *Sterling, Lester* / Contemplating mind: *Spence, Barrington* / Good girl: *Nangle, Ed* / Musical fever: *Enforcers* / Wiser than Solomon: *Sterling, Lester*
CD _______ CDTRD 408
Trojan / Jul '89 / Direct / Jet Star

MUSICAL FREEDOM - CLASSIC GARAGE VOL.2
Musical freedom: *Adeva* / Alright: *Urban Soul* / Do you want it right now: *Degrees Of Motion* / Let the rain come down: *Intense* / Closer: *Mr. Fingers* / Follow me: *Al Y Us* / Give you: *Djaimin* / Love's got a hold on me: *Zoo Experience* / I'm the one for you: *Adeva* / Helpless: *Urbanized & Silvano* / Motherland: *Tribal House* / Love itch: *Roche, Sonya* / One day: *Tyrrel Corporation* / Baby love: *Watford, Michael*
CD _______ CTCD 31
Cooltempo / Nov '92 / EMI

MUSICAL HIGHLIGHTS OF THE BERLIN TATTOO (2CD Set)
All hail to the chief - a king is crowned / Massed pipes and drums / Prince Charles Edward Stuart arrives / King's troop royal horse / Massed bands / Kevock choir / Music for Scottish dancing / Gathering of the clans (finale)
CD Set _______ LCOM 9008
Lismor / Dec '88 / ADA / Direct / Duncans / Lismor

MUSICAL INSTRUMENTS OF THE WORLD
CD _______ CNR 274675
Le Chant Du Monde / Dec '96 / Harmonia Mundi

MUSICAL JOURNEY
CD _______ B 679
Auvidis/Ethnic / Oct '94 / ADA / Harmonia Mundi

MUSICAL ROOTS OF THE NORTH-WEST PROVINCES
CD _______ PS 65073
PlayaSound / Jun '91 / ADA / Harmonia Mundi

MUSICAL TRADITIONS OF PORTUGAL
CD _______ SF 40435CD
Smithsonian Folkways / Jul '95 / ADA / Cadillac / CM / Direct / Koch

MUSICAL TRADITIONS OF ST. LUCIA
CD _______ SF 40416CD
Smithsonian Folkways / Jan '94 / ADA / Cadillac / CM / Direct / Koch

MUSICAL TRIBUTE TO VICTORY, A (D-Day/VE Day - 2CD Set)
Spitfire flypast / RAF march past / O peaceful England / Winston Churchill / Highflight / Washing on the siegfried line / Who's this geezer Hitler / Armed forces medley / Knightsbridge march / 633 Squadron / Lie in the dark / D-Day:the landing / American hoedown / Glenn Miller medley / Last enemy / Last post / Speedbird salutes the Allied Armed forces / Now is the hour / Broadcast by General Eisenhower / American patrol / Boogie woogie bugle boy / Chattanooga choo choo / Scotland the brave / Lili Marlene / You belong to me / We'll meet again / You do something to me / Last time I saw Paris / Oh London Bridge / Wish me luck (as you wave me goodbye) / Announcement of German surrender / Rule Britannia / Churchill's victory address / Land of hope and glory / Abide with me / Auld lang syne / Ceasefire announcement / When they sound the last all clear
CD Set _______ WARBOX 45CD
Start / Feb '97 / Disc

MUSICAL VOYAGE TO THE AZORES
CD _______ YA 225710
Silex / Dec '95 / ADA / Harmonia Mundi

MUSICS OF THE SOVIET UNION
CD _______ SFWCD 40002
Smithsonian Folkways / May '95 / ADA / Cadillac / CM / Direct / Koch

MUSIQUE ACTION
CD _______ VANDOUVRE 9304CD
Semantic / Feb '94 / Plastic Head

MUSIQUE DU HAUT XINGU (Music of the Xingu Islands, Brazil)
CD _______ C 580022
Ocora / Jan '93 / ADA / Harmonia Mundi

MUSIQUE QUECHUA DU LAC TITICACA (Music From Taquile, Peru)
CD _______ C 580015
Ocora / Jan '93 / ADA / Harmonia Mundi

MUSIQUES BRETONNES
CD _______ KMCD 01
Keltia Musique / Jul '90 / ADA / Discovery

MUSIQUES D'EXTASE ET DE GUERISON (Music From The Baluchi People Of Pakistan & Iran)
CD _______ C 580017/18
Ocora / Jan '93 / ADA / Harmonia Mundi

MUSIQUES DES BATAK
CD _______ W 260061
Inedit / Sep '95 / ADA / Discovery / Harmonia Mundi

MUSIQUES POUR LES PLANTES VERTES
Life: *DJ Cam* / ESP: *Hyphen* / Joue Milshtein part 3: *Zein Angelus* / Switch out the sun: *Juantrip* / Dream of the night: *Edoram* / Fleur De Lotus: *Garnier, Laurent* / Sky: *Reminiscent Drive* / Turmoil: *Scan X* / On the way to Paris: *Chaotik Ramses* / Tones: *Nova Nova* / I want to remember this moment always: *Reminiscent Drive*
CD _______ F 038CD
Play It Again Sam / Apr '96 / Discovery / Plastic Head / Vital

MUSIQUES RITUELLES ET RELIGIEUSES (Music From Sri Lankan Cults & Religions)
CD _______ C 580037
Ocora / Jan '93 / ADA / Harmonia Mundi

MUSIQUES TRADITIONNELLES (Music From Sierra Leone)
CD _______ C 580036
Ocora / Jan '93 / ADA / Harmonia Mundi

MUSIQUES TRADITIONNELLES - BALI/JAVA
CD _______ PS 65110
PlayaSound / Nov '93 / ADA / Harmonia Mundi

MUSIQUES TRADITIONNELLES DE BRETAGNE
CD _______ ARN 64380
Arion / Jun '97 / ADA / Discovery

MUST BE MENTAL VOL.1
CD _______ PA 003CD
Paragoric / Mar '95 / Cargo / Plastic Head

MUST BE MENTAL VOL.2
CD _______ PA 011CD
Paragoric / May '95 / Cargo / Plastic Head

MUST BE SANTA
CD _______ ROUCD 3118
Rounder / Nov '95 / ADA / CM / Direct

MUZIK MASTERS (Mixed By Roger Sanchez/Dave Clarke/Fabio)
Southside: *Clarke, Dave* / Stand up: *Lovetribe* / Funk 4 people: *Black Phunk* / Love me now: *Secret Knowledge* / Compose: *DJ Linus* / We are one: *DJ Q* / Spacedance: *DJ Q* / Desire: *Nu Colours* / Release yo' self: *Transatlantic Soul* / Let's do it: *Republic* / Rhumba: *Sanchez, Roger* / L'ombelico del mundo: *Jovanotti* / I wanna dance all nite: *Bohannon, Hamilton* / Hypnodelic: *Kervorkian, Francois* / No big thang: *Johnson, Paul* / What a sensation: *Ken Lou* / Jazz it up: *Reel 2 Real* / First contact: *Outline* / Ital: *Regis* / Outrun: *Banglater, Thomas* / Badger bite: *Surgeon* / Mecano: *ODC & Carl Lekebusch* / live appearance: *Acid Kid* / Back and forward: *Acid Kid* / L Trax: *Fitzpatrick, Lester* / Times square: *Blunted Boy Wonder* / Killer beez: *Smith, Kareem* / D-tech: *Santeone* / Runnin': *DJ Milton* / Running in October: *DJ Valium* / Something different: *Group X* / Bell winch: *Cheap Knob Gags* / Distant avenues: *Delgardo, Raoul* / Narcotic influence: *Empirion* / On da run: *DJ Deeon* / Drums in a grip: *De Wulf, Frank* / Spacefunk: *Digital* / Artificial barrier: *Source Direct* / Free la funk: *JMJ & Ritchie* / Flow: *Model 500* / Flotation: *Subject 13* / One and only: *PFM* / Carlito's way: *Carlito* / Heaven: *Carlito* / Airtight: *Funky Technicians*
CD _______ 74321398302
De-Construction / Aug '96 / BMG

MY DUBLIN BAY
CD _______ MACCD 201
Autograph / Aug '96 / BMG

MY HOUSE
CD _______ SUB 48312
Distance / Feb '97 / 3mv/Sony / Prime

MY HOUSE VOL.2
CD _______ SUB 48432
Distance / Jul '97 / 3mv/Sony / Prime

MY IRISH HOME SWEET HOME
Phil the fluter's ball / Eileen oge / Danny boy / Mother Machree / It takes an irish heart to sing an irish song / My old Irish mother / Father O'Flynn / Where the Shannon river flows / My wild Irish rose / Down by the glenside / Mountains of mourne / Rose of Tralee / My Irish home sweet home / Spinning wheel / That's how I spell IRELAND / When Irish eyes are smiling / If you're Irish come into the parlour / Three lovely lasses / Kathleen Mavoureen / Laughing Irish eyes / Beautiful Eileen / Did your mother come from Ireland
CD _______ RAJCD 809
Empress / Apr '97 / Koch

MY LOVE IS IN AMERICA
CD _______ GLCD 1110
Green Linnet / Nov '91 / ADA / CM / Direct / Highlander / Roots

MY WILD IRISH ROSE (22 Favourite Irish Ballads)
Black velvet band: *Kelly, John* / Shanagolden: *Day, Paddy* / Old maid in a garret: *Sweeneys* / My auld Killarney hat: *Gertrude, Sister Mary* / Enniskillen Dragoons: *Ludlows* / Flower of Macroom: *Dunphy, Sean & The Hoedowners* / Lough sheelin: *Nomads* / Turfman from Ardee: *Gallagher, Bridie* / Arkle: *Behan, Dominic* / Nora: *McEvoy, Johnny* / Beautiful city: *Donal Ring Sound* / Muirsheen durkin: *McEvoy, Johnny* / Sea around us: *Ludlows* / Leaving of Liverpool: *Lynch, Pat* / My wild Irish rose: *Cotton Mill Boys* / Come to the bower: *Dunphy, Sean* / Slaney Valley: *Kinsellas* / McAlpine's Fusiliers: *Kelly, Des* / Curragh Of Kildare: *Johnstons* / Shores of Amerikay: *Broadsiders* / Prisoner: *Day, Paddy* / Bold O'Donoghue: *Dragoons*
CD _______ TRTCD 124
TrueTrax / Oct '94 / THE

MYSTERY OF POLYPHONY, THE
CD _______ 58393
World Network / Mar '96 / ADA

MYSTERY OF THE YETI
CD _______ TIPCD 09
Tip / Nov '96 / Arabesque / Mo's Music Machine / Pinnacle / Prime

MYSTERY TRAIN
Casey Jones: *Cash, Johnny* / Freight train boogie: *Whitstein Brothers* / City of New Orleans: *Goodman, Steve* / Mystery train: *LaBeef, Sleepy* / Cannonball: *Carter Family* / Big black train: *Flatt & Scruggs* / Red ball to Natchez: *Delmore Brothers & Wayne Raney* / Take the 'A' train: *Wills, Bob & His Texas Playboys* / Waiting for a train: *Snow, Hank* / Life's a railway to heaven: *Cline, Patsy* / Old train: *Rice, Tony Unit* / Bringin' in the Georgia Mail: *Rice, Tony Unit* / Train: *Stanley Brothers* / Last cannonball: *McCaslin, Mary*
CD _______ ROUCD 1129
Rounder / Mar '97 / ADA / CM / Direct

MYSTIC MOODS
Sailing: *Belmonde, Pierre* / Stranger on the shore: *Bilk, Acker* / Theme from Harry's game: *Light Shadows* / Long and winding road: *Hill & Wiltchinsky* / Chariots of fire: *Masterworks* / Cacharpaya: *Interlude Orchestra* / Aria: *Belmonde, Pierre* / Walking in the air: *Hill & Wiltchinsky* / Theme from Brideshead Revisited: *SRE Band* / Flying: *London Symphony Orchestra* / Meditation from Thais: *Royal Philharmonic Orchestra* / Concierto de aranjuez: *Belmonde, Pierre* / Cavatina: *Hill & Wiltchinsky* / Clair de lune: *Allis, Julie* / Morning: *London Symphony Orchestra* / Spring song: *London Symphony Orchestra* / Morning has broken: *Bilk, Acker* / Canon: *London Symphony Orchestra*
CD _______ ECD 3131
K-Tel / Jan '95 / K-Tel

MYTHS COLLECTION VOL.1
CD _______ SUBCD 00316
Sub Rosa / Oct '88 / Direct / RTM/Disc / SRD / Vital

MYTHS COLLECTION VOL.2
CD _______ SUBCD 00932
Sub Rosa / Dec '90 / Direct / RTM/Disc / SRD / Vital

MYTHS VOL.1 (Instructions For Survival)
CD _______ SR 01
Sub Rosa / Feb '97 / Direct / RTM/Disc / SRD / Vital

MYTHS VOL.2 (System Of Flux And Energies)
CD _______ SR 02
Sub Rosa / Feb '97 / Direct / RTM/Disc / SRD / Vital

MYTHS VOL.3 (La Nouvelle Serenite)
CD _______ SR 05
Sub Rosa / Feb '97 / Direct / RTM/Disc / SRD / Vital

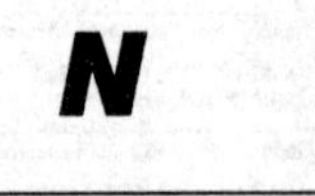

NAIVE
CD _______ MOSH 076CD
Earache / Oct '92 / Vital

NAME BRAND
CD _______ CRCD 30
Charm / Apr '94 / Jet Star

NAME OF THE GAME
Ride sally ride: *Green, Al* / Trouble is my name: *Hines, Don* / Aretha, sing one for me: *Jackson, George* / Belle: *Green, Al* / Mack the knife: *Emmons, Buddy* / Patricia: *Jackson, George* / Judy: *Green, Al* / Buster Browne: *Mitchell, Willie* / She's Miss Wonderful: *McClure, Bobby* / Jesus is waiting: *Green, Al* / Teenie's dream: *Mitchell, Willie* / Sunshine (isn't that your name): *Carter, Darryl* / Georgia boy: *Green, Al* / Please Mr. Foreman: *Joe L* / Amazing grace: *Green, Al* / Mimi: *Green, Al* / Miss Betty Green: *Big Lucky Carter* / Dr. Love power: *Peebles, Ann* / Eli's game: *Green, Al*
CD _______ HILOCD 8
Demon / Mar '94 / Pinnacle

NAPALM RAVE VOL.1 (34 Orgasmic Traxx Of Gabba & Hardcore/2CD Set)
CD Set _______ SPV 08638282
SPV / Sep '96 / Koch / Plastic Head

NAPALM RAVE VOL.2 (31 Orgasmic Traxx Of Gabba & Hardcore/2CD Set)
CD Set _______ SPV 08638332
SPV / Sep '96 / Koch / Plastic Head

NAPALM RAVE VOL.3 (30 Orgasmic Traxx Of Gabba & Hardcore/2CD Set)
It's with us: *Possessed* / Rotterdam: *2 Criminals On The 3rd Floor* / Ill behaviour: *Kill Your Mother* / Under attack: *Organic* / Satanic song: *Apochrypha* / Get the fuck outta my way: *Boldhead Johnnie* / Hemp plant: *DJ Ganja* / Underground: *FAM* / Somebody scream: *Brainlock* / First assault: *Hardtechmedia* / Can you hear this fuckin' beat: *DJ Zicem* / Lestat: *Tonad, Joey* / Fuck a bitch: *Fat Agnus* / Hardcore: *Axl* / Word 2 da mutha fucker: *Federation Against Mellow* / Jesus must die: *Kill Your Mother* / Deeper deeper: *Organic* / Learning experience: *Networxx* / Hardcore: *Axl* / On your own: *Networxx* / U got die: *Fuckface* / Good time:

FAM / Hardcore: *Axl* / Marijuana gets me high: *Masters Of Da Hardcore* / To the beat of the drum: *DJ Rico & DJ Cain* / I'm gonna dis you right now: *Masters Of Da Hardcore* / Basically the same sex: *MODH* / Sick son of a bitch: *Kill Your Mother* / Basic 1: *Hardtechmedia* / Napalm 2 magamix
CD Set ____ **SPV 08647022**
SPV / Sep '96 / Koch / Plastic Head

NAPALM RAVE VOL.4 (30 Orgasmic Traxx Of Gabba & Hardcore/2CD Set)
We are at war: *Hardcore Posse* / Start da panic: *Panic Master* / Put your hands together: *Screwhead* / Do you love your hardcore: *Da Jach* / Pump up the base: *Erector* / Don't allow women in here: *Children Of A Dam* / Rock da house: *2 Terror* / Wild and rootsy: *Soundboy* / It is time: *DJ Zicem* / Gimme a white line: *Clan Of Fools* / Bust a freestyle: *DJ Nahho* / I'm on push: *Focus* / War on drugs: *Federation Against Mellow* / Dream your fantasy: *Dreamer* / Life's a bitch: *SHIT* / I love you Mary Jane: *Federation Against Mellow* / Got to go: *Da Bitch & DJ Zicem* / For your souls: *Lords Of Evil* / On my knees: *Warhead* / Sulphur: *Powerstation Holocaust* / Bass disorder: *JJ* / Alternate F1: *Harrotechmedia* / Bow to me: *3x6* / Graveyard: *Audiodoom* / World of the living (Part 1): *Funboy* / World of the living (Part 2): *Funboy* / Demon reserection: *Mercy Me* / Metallic armor: *Autominder* / Naplam rave theme: *Funboy* / This is the end of all: *Unkown Demon*
CD Set ____ **SPV 08647442**
SPV / Apr '97 / Koch / Plastic Head

NARADA CHRISTMAS COLLECTION VOL.3
Silver bells: *Arkenstone, David* / God rest ye merry gentlemen: *Whalen, Michael* / O holy night: *Mann, Brian* / O' come all ye faithful: *Lauria, Nando* / It came upon a midnight clear: *Gratz, Wayne* / Ding dong merrily on high: *Rumbel, Nancy* / Good King Wenceslas: *Rumbel, Nancy* / First Noel: *Illenberger, Ralf* / Carol of the bells: *Kostia* / Hark, the herald angels sing: *Tingstad, Eric* / Silent night: *Wynberg, Simon* / We three kings: *Stein, Ira* / Little drummer boy: *Ellwood, William* / O little town of Bethlehem: *Jones, Michael* / Holly and the ivy: *Jones, Michael*
CD ____ **ND 63919**
Narada / Dec '95 / ADA / New Note/ Pinnacle

NARADA COLLECTION VOL.5
CD ____ **ND 63920**
Narada / Aug '95 / ADA / New Note/ Pinnacle

NARADA DECADE
CD ____ **ND 263911**
Narada / Jun '93 / ADA / New Note/ Pinnacle

NARADA WORLD (2CD Set)
Ubi caritas: *Dover, Connie* / Road north: *Fraser, Alasdair* / Sealwoman: *McLaughlin, Mary* / Yundah: *McLaughlin, Mary* / Douce mousitomanie: *Orion* / Planxty Burke: *Phillips, Shelley* / Planxty dew: *Phillips, Shelley* / Chuaigh me 'na rosann: *Scartaglen* / Dancing to a lot of time: *Whelan, John* / Baghdad: *Cook, Jesse* / Gravity: *Cook, Jesse* / Viajero: *De La Bastide, Miguel* / Cactus de paraguana: *Guedes, Carlos* / Back home: *Lauria, Nando* / Doce Morena: *Lauria, Nando* / Lucia: *Lopez, Oscar* / New land: *Rubaja, Bernardo* / Cielo y montana: *Rumillajta* / Mujeres y ninos: *Rumillajta* / Kantico en flor de piedra: *San Miguel, Tomas* / Wind spirit: *Miller, Bill* / Precious waters: *Nakai, R. Carlos* / Kothbiro: *Ogada, Ayub* / Giant step: *Pluznick, Michael* / Wasuze otya: *Samite* / Cheetah hunt: *Whalen, Michael* / Journey begins: *Zimmer, Hans* / Ladakh: *Ancient Future* / Inochi no sharin (Wheel of life): *Lee, Riley* / Astrae: *Vas* / Water: *Warner, Richard*
CD Set ____ **ND 263935**
Narada / May '97 / ADA / New Note/ Pinnacle

NARCOSIS
Silence of water: *Emojonal* / Game from planet Onchet: *Hole In One* / My definition of house music: *DJ Hell* / Come into my life: *Abfahrt* / New age heart core: *Trance Induction* / Flash: *Fix* / Diamond bullet: *Effective Force* / In the shadow: *Morganistic* / White darkness: *Sandoz* / Brother from jazz: *Angel, Dave* / Ob-selon mi-mos: *Mystic Istitute*
CD ____ **GRCD 009**
Guerilla / Jul '94 / Pinnacle

NARCOSIS (A Dark Ambient Compilation/2CD Set)
CD Set ____ **9040224**
Nova Tekk / Apr '97 / Pinnacle

NASHVILLE CLASSICS '40S AND BEFORE
Orange blossom special: *Monroe, Bill & His Bluegrass Boys* / I'll be back in a year little darlin': *Robertson, Texas Jim* / There's a star spangled banner waving somewhere: *Britt, Elton* / Each minute seems a million years: *Arnold, Eddy* / Shame on you: *Boyd, Bill & his cowboys* / Stars and stripes on Iwo Jima: *Sons Of The Pioneers* / Sioux City Sue: *Manner, Zeke & His Band* / I want to be a cowboy's sweetheart: *Allen, Rosalie* / Filipino baby: *Robertson, Texas Jim* / Rose of the Alamo: *Allen, Rosalie* / My chickashay gal: *Rogers, Roy* / It's dark outside: *Cooley, Spade* / I'll never trust you again: *Carson, Jenny Lou & Her Tumbleweed Troubadours* / Teardrops in my heart: *Sons Of The Pioneers* / I'll hold you in my heart: *Arnold, Eddy* / I'm my own Grandpa: *Lonzo & Oscar* / Garden in my sky: *Blue Sky Boys* / Tennessee waltz: *King, Pee Wee & The Golden West Cowboys* / Don't rob another man's castle: *Arnold, Eddy* / Candy kisses: *Britt, Elton* / Death at the bar: *Wells, Kitty* / Birmingham jail: *Whitman, Slim* / Baby, it's cold outside: *Homer & Jethro with June Carter* / I wish I knew: *Hewitt, Dolph* / Marriage vow: *Snow, Hank* / Prisoner's song: *Dalhart, Vernon* / Waiting for a train: *Rodgers, Jimmie* / I'm thinking tonight of my blue eyes: *Carter Family*
CD ____ **74321317692**
RCA / Feb '96 / BMG

NASHVILLE CLASSICS '50S
Take me in your arms and hold me: *Arnold, Eddy* / Stampede: *Rogers, Roy & Sons Of The Pioneers* / Quicksilver: *Britt, Elton* / I'm movin' on: *Snow, Hank* / Poison love: *Johnny & Jack* / Down on the trail of aching hearts: *Snow, Hank* / Slow poke: *King, Pee Wee & The Golden West Cowboys* / Stop that ticklin' me: *Jones, Grandpa* / Eddy's song: *Arnold, Eddy* / (How much is that) hound dog in the window: *Homer & Jethro* / I forgot more than you'll ever know: *Davis Sisters* / I found out more than you'll ever know: *Cody, Betty* / (Oh baby mine) I get so lonely: *Johnny & Jack* / I don't hurt anymore: *Snow, Hank* / Satisfied man: *Wagoner, Porter* / In the jailhouse now No.2: *Rodgers, Jimmie* / Cattle call: *Arnold, Eddy* / Yonder comes a sucker: *Reeves, Jim* / I heard the bluebirds sing: *Browns* / Oh lonesome me: *Gibson, Don* / Send me the pillow that you dream on: *Locklin, Hank* / Blue blue day: *Gibson, Don* / He'll have to go: *Reeves, Jim* / Three bells: *Browns* / Tennessee stud: *Arnold, Eddy*
CD ____ **74321280222**
RCA / Feb '96 / BMG

NASHVILLE CLASSICS '60S
Please help me I'm falling: *Locklin, Hank* / Last date: *Cramer, Floyd* / When 2 worlds collide: *Miller, Roger* / Sea of heartbreak: *Gibson, Don* / I've been everywhere: *Snow, Hank* / End of the world: *Davis, Skeeter* / Abilene: *Hamilton, George IV* / 500 Miles away from home: *Bare, Bobby* / Here comes my baby: *West, Dottie* / Once a day: *Smith, Connie* / I wouldn't buy a used car from him: *Norma Jean* / Crystal chandeliers: *Belew, Carl* / Stop the world (and let me off): *Jennings, Waylon* / Make the world go away: *Arnold, Eddy* / Ballad of the Green Berets: *Sadler, Sgt. Barry* / Distant drums: *Reeves, Jim* / Just between you and me: *Pride, Charley* / Mama spank: *Anderson, Liz* / Pop a top: *Brown, Jim Ed* / Gentle on my mind: *Hartford, John* / Last thing on my mind: *Parton, Dolly & Porter Wagoner* / Caroll County accident: *Wagoner, Porter* / Plastic saddle: *Stuckey, Nat* / Bring me sunshine: *Nelson, Willie* / My blue ridge mountain boy: *Parton, Dolly*
CD ____ **74321280232**
RCA / Feb '96 / BMG

NASHVILLE CLASSICS '70S
Sheriff of Boone county: *Price, Kenny* / When you're hot, you're hot: *Reed, Jerry* / Just one time: *Smith, Connie* / Kiss an angel good morning: *Pride, Charley* / Country sunshine: *West, Dottie* / Baptism of Jesse Taylor: *Russell, Johnny* / There won't be anymore: *Rich, Charlie* / Pure love: *Milsap, Ronnie* / I will always love you: *Parton, Dolly* / This time: *Jennings, Waylon* / Marie Laveau: *Bare, Bobby* / Please don't stop loving me: *Parton, Dolly & Porter Wagoner* / Out of hand: *Stewart, Gary* / Storms never last: *Dottsy* / Shadows of my mind: *Oxford, Vernon* / Door is always open: *Dave & Sugar* / Suspicious minds: *Jennings, Waylon & Jessie Colter* / 9999999 tears: *Lee, Dickie* / Luckenbach, Texas (Back to the basics of love): *Jennings, Waylon* / Here you come again: *Parton, Dolly* / Two doors down: *Lehr, Zella* / What have you got to lose: *Hall, Tom T.* / If love had a face: *Bailey, Razzy* / I wanna come over: *Alabama* / How I miss you tonight: *Reeves, Jim & Deborah Allen*
CD ____ **74321280242**
RCA / Feb '96 / BMG

NASHVILLE CLASSICS '80S
My heart: *Milsap, Ronnie* / Tennessee river: *Alabama* / Dukes of Hazzard: *Jennings, Waylon* / Nine to five: *Parton, Dolly* / All the roads lead to you: *Wariner, Steve* / She left love all over me: *Bailey, Razzy* / Mountain of love: *Pride, Charley* / Nobody: *Sylvia* / She got the goldmine (I got the shaft): *Reed, Jerry* / Somewhere between right and wrong: *Conley, Earl Thomas* / I got Mexico: *Raven, Eddy* / Tennessee homesick blues: *Parton, Dolly* / Moon is still over her shoulder: *Johnson, Michael* / Eighties ladies: *Oslin, K.T.* / Cinderella: *Gill, Vince* / Crazy over you: *Foster & Lloyd* / Tear stained letter: *Sonnier, Jo El* / Bluest eyes in Texas: *Restless Heart* / I'm no stranger to the rain: *Whitley, Keith* / Dear me: *Morgan, Lorrie* / Better man: *Black, Clint* / (Wish I had a) heart of stone: *Baillie & the Boys* / High cotton: *Alabama*
CD ____ **74321317682**
RCA / Feb '96 / BMG

NASHVILLE CLASSICS - DUETS
Rings of gold: *Gibson, Don & Dottie West* / Don't let me cross over: *Reeves, Jim & Deborah Allen* / Mother may I: *Anderson, Liz & Lynn* / Dear John letter: *Bare, Bobby & Skeeter Davis* / Looking back to see: *Browns* / If it's wrong to love you: *Snow, Hank & Anita Carter* / I love you: *Reeves, Jim & Ginny Wright* / Under your spell again: *Jennings, Waylon & Jessi Colter* / Making plans: *Parton, Dolly & Porter Wagoner* / When my blue moon turns to gold again: *Flatt, Lester & Mac Wiseman* / I don't want to have to marry you: *Brown, Jim Ed & Helen Cornelius* / Love is no excuse: *Reeves, Jim & Dottie West* / Gotta find a bluebird: *Davis, Skeeter & Porter Wagoner* / Let it be me: *Smith, Connie & Nat Stuckey* / Promised to John: *Snow, Hank & Anita Carter* / Hurry my Peters: *Tubb, Justin & Lorene Mann* / Jeannie's afraid of the dark: *Parton, Dolly & Porter Wagoner* / Slowly: *West, Dottie & Jimmy Dean* / Let's get together: *Skeeter, Davis & George Hamilton IV* / I got you: *Jennings, Waylon & Anita Carter* / Bluebirds are singing for me: *Flatt, Lester & Mac Wiseman* / Things: *Snow, Hank & Kelly Foxton* / Brotherly love: *Stewart, Gary & Dean Dillon* / Till a tear becomes a rose: *Morgan, Lorrie & Keith Whitley* / Hold a partner: *Black, Clint & Roy Rogers*
CD ____ **74321317702**
RCA / Feb '96 / BMG

NASHVILLE DREAM (2CD Set)
CD Set ____ **QTVCD 014**
Quality / Oct '92 / Pinnacle

NASHVILLE ROCK
CD ____ **CURCD 036**
Curb / May '97 / Grapevine/PolyGram

NASTY BLUES VOL.1
Strokin': *Carter, Clarence* / Trudy sings the blues: *Lynn, Trudy* / I want to play with your poodle: *Willis, Chick* / Rainy day: *White, Artie* / One eyed woman: *Coleman, Gary B.B.* / I want a big fat woman: *Willis, Chick* / Ugly man: *Taylor, Little Johnny* / Watch where you stroke: *Coleman, Gary B.B.* / Two heads are better than one: *Haddix, Travis* / Why do I stay here and take all this shit: *Carter, Clarence*
CD ____ **ICH 1048CD**
Ichiban / Mar '94 / Direct / Koch

NASTY BLUES VOL.2
Jack you up: *Willis, Chick* / Come back pussy: *Williams, Dicky* / Cook me: *Legendary Blues Band* / Grandpa can't fly his kite: *Carter, Clarence* / Let me funk with you: *Blues Boy Willie* / Tittie man: *Drink Small* / Nuts for sale: *Willis, Chick* / Don't pet my dog: *White, Artie* / Lemon squeezin' Daddy: *Brown, Nappy* / Kiss you all over: *Carter, Clarence*
CD ____ **ICH 1066CD**
Ichiban / Oct '93 / Direct / Koch

NASTY NASTY
CD ____ **TRTCD 155**
TrueTrax / Dec '94 / THE

NASTY WRAP
CD ____ **WRA 8501**
Wrap / Mar '96 / Koch

NATIONAL ANTHEMS MIX (3CD Set)
CD Set ____ **FIRMCD 4**
Firm / Jun '96 / Pinnacle

NATIONAL ANTHEMS OF THE WORLD
God save the Queen / Star spangled banner / La Marseillaise / Deutschland Lied / Inno di Mameli / Mazurep Dabrowskiego / Marcha Real / Segnorizo Apo Tin Kopsi / Llatikvah / O Canada / Kimiga Yowa Chiyoni / Wilhelmus van Nassouwe / Scotland the Brave / Amthran na bh Fiann / Land of my Fathers / European Anthem
CD ____ **SUMCD 4120**
Sound & Media / May '97 / Sound & Media

NATIONAL BRASS BAND CHAMPIONSHIP 1992
Happy and glorious / Crimond / Toccata / Temptress for trombones / New Jerusalem / Aida / Air from third suite / Pantomime / In memoriam / Your tiny hand is frozen / Entry of the gladiators
CD ____ **QPRL 056D**
Polyphonic / Mar '93 / Complete/Pinnacle

NATIONAL BRASS BAND CHAMPIONSHIP 1994
Pioneers' march / Bartered bride (overture) / Thoughts of love / Slaughter on 10th Avenue / Theme and co-operation / Dance of the comedians / Better world / Galaxies / Concert etude / Russian Christmas music / Pines of Rome
CD ____ **QPRL 071D**
Polyphonic / Jan '95 / Complete/Pinnacle

NATIONAL BRASS BAND FESTIVAL 1988
Overture / Candide / Fetes / Concerto for cornet / Desert II - horizons / Seascapes / Le petit negre / Phillip McCann salutes Harry Mortimer / Endeavour
CD ____ **QPRL 039D**
Polyphonic / Jan '88 / Complete/Pinnacle

NATIONAL DOWNHOME BLUES FESTIVAL
CD ____ **SCD 21**
Southland / Mar '97 / Jazz Music

NATIONAL FOLK FESTIVAL
CD ____ **CIC 068CD**
Clo Iar-Chonnachta / Nov '93 / CM

NATIVE NEW YORKER (Disco Classics)
Native New Yorker / Yes sir I can boogie / Disco nights / Ms. Grace / Shame / Just don't want to be lonely / Sunny / I can't stand the rain / Jack and Jill / Givin' up givin' in / Rock the boat / La la means I love you / There goes my first love / Blockbuster / It's in his kiss / Fire / Can't get by without you / Dancing on a Saturday night / Jack in the box / Get dancin'
CD ____ **74321476782**
Camden / Apr '97 / BMG

NATIVE SPIRIT
CD ____ **57832**
CMC / May '97 / BMG

NATIVE WISDOM
Anzala / Soirit / Wiracocha / Healing song: Walking in prayer / An caoineadh / Lawaki / No se muere nunca / Te pure a te fatu / Many feather's chant / Shaman's prayer / Grigogal cridhe / Celebration in the village / Millennium theme
CD ____ **ND 63923**
Narada / Apr '96 / ADA / New Note/Pinnacle

NATIVES
CD ____ **662244**
FNAC / Jun '93 / Discovery

NATTY REBEL ROOTS
Let jah be praised: *Gladiators* / Tune in: *Isaacs, Gregory* / Cry tough: *Clarke, Johnny* / Natty rebel: *U-Roy* / Throw away your gun: *Prince Far-I* / Declaration of rights: *Clarke, Johnny* / We'll find the blessing: *Gladiators* / Do you remember: *U-Roy* / Jah kingdom come: *Twinkle Brothers* / Slavery let I go: *Dr. Alimantado* / Crazy baldheads: *Clarke, Johnny* / Best things in life: *Gladiators* / Praise jah: *Twinkle Brothers* / How love divine (dub): *Prince Far-I* / Uptown top ranking: *Althia & Donna*
CD ____ **CDFL 9013**
Frontline / Sep '90 / EMI / Jet Star

NATURAL BORN TECHNO VOL.1
CD ____ **NZ 030**
Nova Zembla / Feb '95 / Plastic Head

NATURAL BORN TECHNO VOL.2
CD Set ____ **NZ 042CD**
Nova Zembla / Sep '95 / Plastic Head

NATURAL BORN TECHNO VOL.3
CD ____ **NZ 052CD**
Nova Zembla / Feb '96 / Plastic Head

NATURAL BORN TECHNO VOL.4
CD ____ **NZ 070CD**
Nova Zembla / Sep '96 / Plastic Head

NATURAL BORN TECHNO VOL.5
CD ____ **NZ 079CD**
Nova Zembla / Apr '97 / Plastic Head

NATURAL BORN TECHNO VOL.6
CD ____ **NZ 080CD**
Nova Zembla / Apr '97 / Plastic Head

NATURAL REGGAE HITS
Money in my pocket: *Brown, Dennis* / Smoke gets in your eyes: *Blue Haze* / I shot the sheriff: *Inner Circle* / Cherry oh baby: *Donaldson, Eric* / Snoopy Vs the Red Baron: *Hot Shots* / Stop the train: *Tosh, Peter* / Girl is mine: *Yellowman & Peter Metro* / Israelites: *Dekker, Desmond* / Help me make it through the night: *Holt, John* / Vietnam: *Cliff, Jimmy* / Young, gifted and black: *Bob & Marcia* / Double barrel: *Collins, Dave & Ansell* / Lip town top rankin: *Althia & Donna* / Norwegian wood disco: *Ska Boys* / Hot, hot, hot: *Arrow* / Kingston Kingston: *Lou & The Hollywood Bananas*
CD ____ **12700**
Laserlight / Apr '96 / Target/BMG

NATURAL SELECTIONS
CD ____ **7567923732**
Delicious Vinyl / May '94 / PolyGram

NATURAL WOMAN VOL.1
No more I love you's: *Lennox, Annie* / Oh baby I: *Eternal* / Breathe again: *Braxton, Toni* / All woman: *Stansfield, Lisa* / Independent love song: *Scarlet* / I'll find you: *Gayle, Michelle* / Right here: *SWV* / (Take a little) piece of my heart: *Franklin, Erma* / Anything for you: *Estefan, Gloria* / (You make me feel like) a natural woman: *Franklin, Aretha* / Power of love: *Rush, Jennifer* / Show me heaven: *McKee, Maria* / Almaz: *Crawford, Randy* / (Try to remember) the way we were: *Knight, Gladys & The Pips* / Move closer: *Nelson, Phyllis* / Heartbreaker: *Warwick, Dionne* / Slow hand: *Pointer Sisters* / Patience of angels: *Reader, Eddi* / Days: *MacColl, Kirsty* / Wuthering heights: *Bush, Kate*
CD ____ **RADCD 14**
Global TV / Jul '95 / BMG

NATURAL WOMAN VOL.2
I will survive: *Savage, Chantay* / No ordinary love: *Sade* / What's love got to do with it: *Turner, Tina* / When you tell me that I love you: *Turner, Tina* / When you tell me you love me: *Ross, Diana* / Why: *Lennox, Annie* / Dreams: *Gabrielle* / Stay: *Eternal* / All around the world: *Stansfield, Lisa* / Sweetness: *Gayle, Michelle* / Get here: *Adams, Oleta* / Sleeping satellite: *Archer, Tasmin* / My one temptation: *Paris, Mica* / It's too

late: *Quartz & Dina Carroll* / Can't stay away from you: *Estefan, Gloria* / Another sad love song: *Braxton, Toni* / Holding on: *Craven, Beverley* / Walking in Memphis: *Cher* / Rush rush: *Abdul, Paula* / Save the best for last: *Williams, Vanessa* / Heaven is a place on earth: *Carlisle, Belinda* / I just want to make love to you: *James, Etta* / Time after time: *Lauper, Cyndi* / Feel so high: *Des'ree* / You don't love me (no no no): *Penn, Dawn* / I say a little prayer: *Franklin, Aretha* / I'm still waiting: *Ross, Diana* / Best thing that ever happened to me: *Knight, Gladys & The Pips* / One day I'll fly away: *Crawford, Randy* / Wishing on a star: *Rose Royce* / If you're looking for a way out: *Odyssey* / I'm every woman: *Khan, Chaka* / No more the fool: *Brooks, Elkie* / I will always love you: *Parton, Dolly* / Crazy: *Cline, Patsy* / At seventeen: *Ian, Janis* / You're so vain: *Simon, Carly* / (You make me feel) like a natural woman: *King, Carole*
CD Set RADCD 28
Global TV / Mar '96 / BMG

NAUGHTY RHYTHMS (The Best Of Pub Rock/2CD Set)
Country girl: *Brinsley Schwarz* / Factory: *Eggs Over Easy* / Music every night: *Bees Make Honey* / Don't want me round you: *Graham, Ernie* / Alabama lady: *Help Yourself* / Surrender to the rhythm: *Brinsley Schwarz* / Desert Island woman: *Chilli Willi & Red Hot Peppers* / Fireball: *Ducks Deluxe* / In no resistance: *Miller, Frankie* / Billy Bentley: *Kilburn & The High Roads* / Keep it out of sight: *Dr. Feelgood* / How long: *Ace* / Coast to coast: *Ducks Deluxe* / I can understand it: *Kokomo* / I don't mind if I do: *Charlie & The Wide Boys* / Highway song: *Bees Make Honey* / Rough kids: *Kilburn & The High Roads* / Speedway: *Kursaal Flyers* / I ain't gonna stand for this no more: *Ace* / Friday song: *Chilli Willi & Red Hot Peppers* / I can tell: *Dr. Feelgood* / Love's melody: *Ducks Deluxe* / Ugly guys: *Kursaal Flyers* / Davey's blowtorch: *Winkies* / Play that fast thing (one more time): *Brinsley Schwarz* / Between you and me: *Parker, Graham* / One foot in the boat: *Starry Eyed & Laughing* / Riot in cell block 9: *Dr. Feelgood* / Cincinatti fat back: *Roogalator* / Soul shoes: *Parker, Graham* / Teenage letter: *Bishops* / Teenage depression: *Eddie & The Hot Rods* / Keys to your heart: *101'ers* / (What's so funny 'bout) Peace, love and understanding: *Brinsley Schwarz*
CD Set PRDCD 1
Premier/EMI / Apr '96 / EMI

NAVAJO SONGS FROM CANYON DE CHELLY
CD 804062
New World / Aug '92 / ADA / Cadillac / Harmonia Mundi

NBA - A MUSICAL CELEBERATION
CD 5343232
Mercury / Jan '97 / PolyGram

NBC'S CHAMBER MUSIC SOCIETY OF LOWER BASIN STREET
CD HQCD 60
Harlequin / Jun '96 / Hot Shot / Jazz Music / Swift / Wellard

NEAT METAL
CD NM 005MCD
Neat Metal / Nov '95 / Pinnacle

NEED A SHOT (Essential Recordings Of Urban Blues)
Sail on little girl, sail on: *Bumble Bee Slim* / Policy wheel blues: *Arnold, Kokomo* / Trouble in mind: *White, Georgia* / Bad luck man: *Harlem Hamfats* / Louise Louise blues: *Temple, Johnny* / Working man (doing the best I can): *Wheatstraw, Peetie* / Think you need a shot: *Davis, Walter* / New little pretty Mama: *Gaither, Bill* / Night time is the right time: *Sykes, Roosevelt* / Lonesome bedroom blues: *Jones, Curtis* / Back door: *Washboard Sam* / Way down in Louisiana: *Weldon, Casey Bill* / Want to woogie some more: *Johnson, Merline* / What is that she got: *Broonzy, 'Big' Bill* / Lonesome shack blues: *Memphis Minnie* / Baby take a chance with me: *Tampa Red* / Key to the highway: *Gillum, Bill 'Jazz'* / Beer drinking woman: *Memphis Slim* / County jail blues: *Big Maceo* / Goin' down slow: *St. Louis Jimmy* / He's a jelly roll baker: *Johnson, Lonnie* / Ain't no business we can do: *Clayton, Dr. Peter* / Big time Mama: *Dupree, 'Champion' Jack* / New early in the morning: *Williamson, Sonny Boy*
CD IGOCD 2040
Indigo / May '97 / ADA / Direct

NEGRO RELIGIOUS FIELD RECORDINGS 1944-46
CD DOCD 5312
Document / Dec '94 / ADA / Hot Shot / Jazz Music

NERVOUS PSYCHOBILLY SINGLES
Rockabilly guy: *Polecats* / Chicken shack: *Polecats* / Heart attack: *Deltas* / Spell bound: *Deltas* / Constipation shake: *Legendary Lonnie* / Devil's guitar: *Legendary Lonnie* / City lights: *Austin, Rockin' Johnny* / Rockabilly stroll: *Austin, Rockin' Johnny* / Marie celeste: *Polecats* / Edge you on: *Restless* / Ghost town: *Restless* / Whistle wiggle: *Rochee & The Sarnos* / Rumble in the jungle: *Rochee & The Sarnos* / Shake your hips: *Scamps* / Robot riot: *Frenzy* / Torment: *Frenzy* / Cry or die: *Frenzy* / Vigilante: *Pharaohs* / You're on your own: *Pharaohs* / Raid: *Rapids* / Silver bullet: *Rapids* / Ghost train: *Sharks* / Mystery men: *Torment* / Rock strong: *Torment* / Conscription pain: *Torment*
CD CDMPSYCHO 5
Cherry Red / May '95 / Pinnacle

NERVOUS SYSTEMS
CD CDSTUMM 41
Mute / Sep '92 / RTM/Disc

NETWORK - THE EARLY DAZE (5CD Set)
CD Set NETBOX 1
Network / Dec '96 / 3mv/Sony / Pinnacle

NEU KONSERVATIV
CD DSA 54046
CDSA / Dec '96 / Harmonia Mundi / ReR Megacorp

NEVER AGAIN
Eighty eight seconds and still counting: *Pop Will Eat Itself* / Take it: *Flowered Up* / Make it mine: *Shamen* / Air you breathe: *Bomb The Bass* / BMW: *Soho & Natty Sega* / Magic carpet: *Nutty Boys* / Searchlight: *Pele* / We didn't know (what was going on): *Robinson, Tom Band* / Feel it: *Sham 69* / Throw the 'R' away: *Proclaimers* / Power is yours: *Redskins* / Righteous preacher: *Fun-Da-Mental* / Celebration: *Better ways* / About time: *Friends of Harry* / Someday: *Steppin' Stones* / Goodbye Johnny: *Pool O'Life* / Badila: *New Paradesi Music Machine* / Communication: *I'cons* / Set up for the kill: *Sharp teeth*
CD NIL 001CD
Nil Satis / Sep '92 / Vital

NEVER MIND THE BOLLOCKS 1994
CD AA 022
AA / Jul '97 / Cargo / Greyhound

NEVER MIND THE MOLLUSCS
CD SPCD 84/255
Sub Pop / Mar '93 / Cargo / Greyhound / Shellshock/Disc

NEW ACOUSTIC MUSIC
CD RCD 20002
Rykodisc / May '96 / ADA / Vital

NEW ALTERNATIVES VOL.2
CD NIGHTCD 005
Nightbreed / Sep '96 / Plastic Head

NEW ALTERNATIVES VOL.3 (March Of The Angel Children/2CD Set)
CD Set NIGHTCD 009
Nightbreed / Apr '96 / Plastic Head

NEW ATLANTIS
CD ORBIT 004CD
Space Age / May '96 / Plastic Head

NEW BEATS OF JAZZ, THE
CD CDTEP 10
Step 2 / Jul '97 / 3mv/Sony

NEW BLUEBLOODS
CD ALCD 7707
Alligator / Aug '92 / ADA / CM / Direct

NEW BLUES CLASSICS
CD BBAN 14CD
Bullseye Blues / Aug '94 / Direct

NEW BORN BLUE
CD 33WM 101
33 Jazz / Oct '94 / Cadillac / New Note/ Pinnacle

NEW BREED OF DUB, A
Strickley roots: *Truth* / Astral flame: *Disciples* / Heavy dub: *Dub Specialists* / Firing dub: *Bush Chemists* / Over the rainbow: *East Meets West* / Conflict: *Dub Ghecko* / Meditation rock: *Dan, Jonah* / Take heed: *Armagideon* / 007 Dub: *Dubplate Vibe Crew* / Brain damage: *Iration Steppas* / Tokyo dub: *Hi-Tech Roots Dynamics* / Hot stepper dub: *King General* / Right from wrong: *Dub Specialists* / Falasha dub: *Jah Warrior* / Dub outernational: *East Meets West* / Talking dubheadz: *All Nation Rockers*
CD DBHD 001CD
Dubhead / Apr '97 / SRD

NEW BREED OF RAVERS, A
CD FORMCD 1
Formation / Nov '93 / SRD

NEW BREED VOL.2, THE
CD GI 0032
GI Productions / Mar '97 / Cargo / Greyhound

NEW BREED VOL.3, THE
CD GI 0082
GI Productions / Mar '97 / Cargo / Greyhound

NEW COUNTRY GIRLS LIVE
CD 15406
Laserlight / Aug '91 / Target/BMG

NEW COUNTRY LINE DANCING
Line dancin' days / Goin' country / There you go / EJ's Bar / Burnin' fire / Country music hall of fame / This don't feel like dancin' / No honky tonks in heaven / Too easy / Good times come around / Love my car / Love kept's a hold on my heart / I learn't a thing or two / Ain't life wonderful / Louisiana / Daddy's got his blue jeans on / Time loser / Situation vacant / Country married rock n roll / Let's hear it for the ladies
CD CD 6072
Music / Apr '97 / Target/BMG

NEW CUT GROOVES (A Lipstick Sampler)
Summertime: *Gaskins, Ray* / Cuttin' you loose: *Prime Crime* / Lying in the sun: *Carmichael, Anita* / Shaggy dog: *Holzman, Adam* / Stand up and do something: *Evans, Bill* / Get up: *Vibe Tribe* / Come trip with me: *Holzman, Adam* / High on love: *Soul Immigrants* / If we can't be lovers: *Stern, Leni* / Footloose: *Carmichael, Anita* / Many times: *Prime Crime* / Crystal clear: *Gaskins, Ray*
CD LIP 89422
Lipstick / Oct '96 / Vital/SAM

NEW ELECTRIC MUSE VOL.1 (The Story Of Folk Into Rock/3CD Set)
CD Set ESBCD 416
Essential / Aug '96 / BMG

NEW ELECTRIC MUSE VOL.2 (The Continuing Story Of Folk Into Rock/3CD Set)
King Arthur's servants: *Watersons* / Agincourt carol: *Young Tradition* / Bring us in good ale: *Young Tradition* / Trotto/Saltarello: *Renbourn, John* / King: *Steeleye Span* / Hal-an-Tow: *Collins, Shirley & The Albion Country Band* / Staines Morris: *Morris On* / Pastime with good company: *Gryphon* / England be glad: *City Waites* / Beginning of the world: *Kirkpatrick, John & Ashley Hutchings* / One-eyed merchant: *Pegg, Bob* / Carthy's march: *Swarbrick, Dave* / Four tunes from Terpsichore 1612: *Albion Band* / Gower wassail: *Steeleye Span* / Boadicea: *Swarbrick, Dave* / Jolly bold robber: *Brass Monkey* / Personent hodie: *Albion Band* / Medley of four Morris tunes: *Kirkpatrick, John* / Lovely Joan: *McShee, Jacqui* / Corbies: *Steeleye Span* / Annan water: *Rusby, Kate* / North country maid: *Watersons* / Lark in the morning: *Johnstons* / I loved a lass: *Pentangle* / Lovely on the water: *Steeleye Span* / Sullivan's John: *Briggs, Anne* / Bonny May: *Tabor, June* / Flandyke shore: *Jones, Nic* / Wishing/The victor's return/The gravel walk: *Swarbrick, Dave* / Old Grenadier: *Brass Monkey* / Wonder - The Ridotta Rock: *Cock 'n' Bull Band* / Radstock jig: *Home Service* / Galopede: *Oyster Band* / Byker Hill: *Barely Works* / 'S Muladach mi/ Sad am I and lonely: *Mouth Music* / Tammienorrie: *Shooglenifty* / Flower of Magherallyo: *Oige* / Three reels: *Burach* / Card song/Shuffle the pack: *Fairport Convention* / Thirty foot trailer: *Watersons* / Dirty old town: *Campbell, Ian Folk Group* / Tunnel tigers: *Johnstons* / Go by brooks: *Sweeney's Men* / Look over the hill and far away: *Humblebums* / Who knows where the time goes: *Fairport Convention* / Pond and the stream: *Denny, Sandy & Fotheringay* / Sally free and easy: *Tawney, Cyril* / Go your way: *Briggs, Anne* / When I get to the border: *Thompson, Richard & Linda* / Dimming of the day: *Thompson, Richard & Linda* / It's dark in here: *Dransfield* / I'm a dreamer: *Thompson, Linda* / Devonside: *Thompson, Richard* / Pain or paradise: *Tabor, June & The Oyster Band* / Moving the goalposts: *Bragg, Billy* / Granite years: *Oyster Band* / Bede weeps: *Lowe, Jez* / Sand in your shoes: *McTell, Ralph* / Hard times heart: *Waterson, Norma* / Dram for the singer: *Pegg, Bob*
CD Set ESBCD 517
Essential / Aug '97 / BMG

NEW ELECTRONIC GENERATION
CD CLP 9973
Cleopatra / Apr '97 / Cargo / Greyhound / Plastic Head / RTM/Disc / SRD

NEW ENGLAND TEEN SCENE VOL.1 1965-1968
CD AA 060
Arf Arf / Jul '97 / Greyhound

NEW ENGLAND TEEN SCENE VOL.2 1978-1992
CD AA 044
Arf Arf / Jul '97 / Greyhound

NEW FEELING, THE (An Anthology Of World Music)
CD 131242
Celestial Harmonies / May '96 / ADA / Select

NEW FRONTIERS
CD TMPCD 017
Temple / Oct '95 / BMG

NEW GROOVE, THE (The Blue Note Remix Project Vol.1)
Kofi: *Byrd, Donald* / Hummin': *Adderley, Cannonball* / Living for the city: *Pointer, Noel* / Listen here: *Harris, Gene* / Friends and strangers: *Laws, Ronnie* / Down here on the ground: *Green, Grant* / Summer song: *Foster, Ronnie* / Move your hand: *Smith, Lonnie Liston* / Sophisticated hippie: *Silver, Horace* / Montara: *Hutcherson, Bobby* / Mixed feelings (The new groove): *Terrasson, Jacky* / Kofi: *Byrd, Donald* / Mixed feelings: *Terrasson, Jacky*
CD CDP 8365942
Blue Note / May '96 / EMI

NEW HITS 1996 (2CD Set)
How deep is your love: *Take That* / Return of the mack: *Morrison, Mark* / Anything: *3T* / I will survive: *Savage, Chantay* / Children: *Miles, Robert* / Firestarter: *Prodigy* / Hallo spaceboy: *Bowie, David* / Ooh ahh, just a little bit: *Gina G* / Cecilia: *Suggs* / Stepping stone: *PJ & Duncan* / Falling into you: *Dion, Celine* / Creep: *TLC* / 1,2,3,4 (sumpin' new): *Coolio* / One by one: *Cher* / Something so right: *Lennox, Annie* / Search for the hero: *M-People* / Missing: *Everything But The Girl* / Ready or not: *Lightning Seeds* / I just want to make love to you: *James, Etta* / Up on the roof: *Robson & Jerome* / Don't look back in anger: *Oasis* / Stupid girl: *Garbage* / Goldfinger: *Ash* / Charity: *Skunk Anansie* / Ladykillers: *Lush* / You and me song: *Wannadies* / Riverboat song: *Ocean Colour Scene* / Lump: *Presidents Of The USA* / No fronts: *Dog Eat Dog* / Cum on feel the noize: *Oasis* / Whole lotta love: *Goldbug* / Passion: *Gat Decor* / Be as one: *Sasha & Maria* / My life is in your hands: *Meltdown* / Landslide: *Harmonix* / Should I ever (fall in love): *Nightcrawlers* / Ready to go: *Republica* / If you wanna party: *Molella & The Outhere Brothers* / I wanna be a hippy: *Technohead* / Move move move (the red tribe): *Manchester Utd FC*
CD Set RADCD 36
Global TV / May '96 / BMG

NEW HITS 1997
CD TCD 2891
Telstar / Feb '97 / BMG

NEW HITS 1997 (2CD Set)
Underwater love: *Smoke City* / Unbreak my heart: *Braxton, Toni* / Where do you go: *No Mercy* / Don't let go (love): *En Vogue* / Step by step: *Houston, Whitney* / Gotta be you: *3T* / Fresh: *Gina G* / Do you know: *Gayle, Michelle* / Clementine: *Owen, Mark* / Fugee la: *Fugees* / Moan and groan: *Morrison, Mark* / Real thing: *Stansfield, Lisa* / If you ever: *East 17 & Gabrielle* / All by myself: *Dion, Celine* / Rotterdam: *Beautiful South* / Little wonder: *Bowie, David* / Consideration: *Reef* / Australia: *Manic Street Preachers* / Sugar coated iceberg: *Lightning Seeds* / Govinda: *Kula Shaker* / Fired up: *Funky Green Dogs* / Encore une fois: *Sash* / You got the love: *Source & Candi Staton* / Professional widow: *Amos, Tori* / Ready or not: *Course* / Remember me: *Blueboy* / Ain't talkin' 'bout dub: *Apollo 440* / Ready to go: *Republica* / Let me clear my throat: *DJ Kool* / DISCO: *N-Trance* / Natural: *Andre, Peter* / Quit playing games (with my heart): *Backstreet Boys* / Day we found love: *911* / Let me in: *OTT* / It's over: *Clock* / Pony: *Ginuwine* / Everytime I close my eyes: *Babyface* / Cold rock a party: *MC Lyte* / Love guaranteed: *Damage* / You might need somebody: *Ama, Shola*
CD Set RADCD 67
Global TV / Apr '97 / BMG

NEW JAZZ SPECTRUM VOL.1
Rip a dip: *Latin Jazz Quintet* / Other side of town: *Natural Essence* / Things ain't right: *Marrow, Esther* / Cry: *Dickerson, Walt* / Modettle: *Haynes, Roy* / Web: *Hawes, Hampton* / Taste of honey: *Andy & The Bey Sisters* / Thang: *Matthews, Ronnie* / Eli's pork chop: *Little Sonny* / I've known rivers: *Bartz, Gary* / Alex the great: *Mabern, Harold* / Letha: *Earland, Charles*
CD CDBGPD 085
Beat Goes Public / Apr '94 / Pinnacle

NEW JAZZ SPECTRUM VOL.2
Nairod: *Riverside Jazz Band* / One hand: *Parker, Maynard* / Our generation: *Hines, Ernie* / Favela: *Papaya* / Sad song: *Williams, Joe* / Mucho chupar: *Axelrod, David* / It's about time: *Callier, Terry* / Death and taxes: *Dickerson, Walt* / Song for Pharoah: *Cuber, Ronnie* / Memphis: *Little Sonny* / Higgins holler: *Walton, Cedar* / Everything counts: *Axelrod, David*
CD CDBGPD 091
Beat Goes Public / Oct '94 / Pinnacle

NEW JAZZ SPECTRUM VOL.3
Fire eater: *Bryant, Rusty* / Afro Texas: *Mbulu, Letta* / No one can love: *Cosby, Bill* / Shortnin' bread: *Three Pieces* / Shirley's guanguancho: *Aguabella, Francisco* / Getting funky round here: *Black Nasty* / Love them from Spartacus: *Lateef, Yusef* / Senior boogaloo: *Richardson, Wally* / Nana: *De Souza, Raul* / Gibralter: *Hubbard, Freddie* / Mode: *Sonny Red* / Sentido-en-seis: *Bellson, Louie & Walfredo De Los Reyes* / When I die: *Marrow, Esther*
CD CDBGPD 095
Beat Goes Public / May '95 / Pinnacle

NEW MOVES
CD CHILLCD 008
Chillout / May '96 / Kudos / Pinnacle / RTM/Disc

NEW MUSIC FROM CHINA - NINE HORSES
CD WER 62992
Wergo / Oct '96 / ADA / Cadillac / Harmonia Mundi

NEW MUSIC FROM MALI
Ka souma man: *Sekouba Bambino Diabate* / Konifale: *Tangra, Kadja* / Tchana diani: *Traore, Lobi* / Ouere: *Koita, Dounanke* / Faso: *Bougouniere Diarrah Sanogo* / Sabali: *Les Soeurs Sidibe* / Fengue: *Bagayoga, Issa* / Liberia: *Diakite, Djenaba* / Sinsinbo: *Koita, Dounanke* / Kulunba: *Sidibe, Kagbe* / Diarabi: *Wassolon Fenin (The Cream Of Wassolon)* / Hampate ba: *Koita, Ami* / N'na djanssama: *Kante, Kerfala*

CD CDEMC 3681
Hemisphere / May '94 / EMI

NEW ORLEANS BLUES 1923-1940
CD 157612
Blues Collection / Feb '93 / Discovery

NEW ORLEANS BRASS BANDS
CD ROUCD 11562
Rounder / Mar '90 / ADA / CM / Direct

NEW ORLEANS DIXIE
CD 22505
Music / Aug '95 / Target/BMG

NEW ORLEANS FUNCTION
CD CD 3560
Cameo / Jul '95 / Target/BMG

NEW ORLEANS GOSPEL QUARTETS 1947-1956
CD HTCD 12
Heritage / Feb '94 / ADA / Direct / Hot Shot / Jazz Music / Swift / Wellard

NEW ORLEANS HIT STORY, THE (Twenty Years Of Big Easy Hits 1950-1970)
CD Set CDGR 1402
Charly / Apr '97 / Koch

NEW ORLEANS IN THE TWENTIES
CD CBC 1014
Bellaphon / Jun '93 / New Note/Pinnacle

NEW ORLEANS JAZZ
CD ARHCD 346
Arhoolie / Apr '95 / ADA / Cadillac / Direct

NEW ORLEANS JAZZ HERITAGE
CD 8122711112
WEA / Jul '93 / Warner Music

NEW ORLEANS JAZZ SCENE OF THE 50'S
CD Set CDB 1208
Giants Of Jazz / Apr '92 / Cadillac / Jazz Music / Target/BMG

NEW ORLEANS JAZZ VOL.1
CD WJS 1001CD
Wolf / Nov '93 / Hot Shot / Jazz Music / Swift

NEW ORLEANS JAZZ VOL.2 (1926-1951)
CD WJSCD 1002
Wolf / Jul '96 / Hot Shot / Jazz Music / Swift

NEW ORLEANS JOYS (2CD Set)
CD Set DCD 8001
Disky / Jan '95 / Disky / THE

NEW ORLEANS LADIES
CD ROUCD 2078
Rounder / '88 / ADA / CM / Direct

NEW ORLEANS RHYTHM KINGS
CD VILCD 0042
Village Jazz / Sep '92 / Jazz Music / Target/BMG

NEW ORLEANS TO CHICAGO - THE FORTIES
CD CJR 1002
Gannet / Nov '95 / Cadillac / Jazz Music

NEW REDS SAMPLER
CD NRAS 001CD
New Red Archives / Feb '97 / Cargo / Plastic Head

NEW ROMANTIC CLASSICS
Open your heart: *Human League* / Temptation: *Heaven 17* / Chant No.1 (I don't need this pressure on): *Spandau Ballet* / Rio: *Duran Duran* / Look of love: *ABC* / Is it a dream: *Classix Nouveaux* / Together in electric dreams: *Oakey, Philip & Giorgio Moroder* / Dancing with tears in my eyes: *Ultravox* / Enola Gay: *OMD* / Tainted love: *Soft Cell* / Don't go: *Yazoo* / Model: *Kraftwerk* / Wishful thinking: *China Crisis* / Today: *Talk Talk* / Cars: *Numan, Gary* / Fade to grey: *Visage* / Ghosts: *Japan*
CD VTCD 15
Virgin TV / Oct '92 / EMI

NEW ROMANTICS
Chant no.1: *Spandau Ballet* / Girls on film: *Duran Duran* / Fascist groove thang: *Heaven 17* / Quiet life: *Japan* / Lawnchairs: *Our Daughters Wedding* / African & white: *China Crisis* / Vienna: *Ultravox* / Model: *Kraftwerk* / Messages: *OMD* / Whip it: *Devo* / Empire State human: *Human League* / Head over heels: *Illustrated Man* / Underpass: *Foxx, John* / Is it a dream: *Classix Nouveaux* / After a fashion: *Ure, Midge & Mick Karn*
CD CDGOLD 1041
EMI Gold / Jul '96 / EMI

NEW SMOKING CLASSICS VOL.1
CD HYPOXIA 001CD
Hypoxia / Sep '95 / Plastic Head

NEW SPIRITS IN JAZZ
CD EFA 015082
World's Best / Nov '95 / SRD

NEW STARS FROM THE HEARTLAND
Shameless: *Brooks, Garth* / Down at the twist and shout: *Carpenter, Mary-Chapin* / Here's a quarter (call someone who cares): *Tritt, Travis* / She's in love with the boy: *Yearwood, Trisha* / Don't rock the jukebox: *Jackson, Alan* / We both walk: *Morgan, Lorrie* / Forever together: *Travis, Randy* / Young love (strong love): *Judds* / Put yourself in my shoes: *Black, Clint* / Walk on faith: *Reid, Mike* / For my broken heart: *McEntire, Reba* / Restless: *O'Connor, Mark & New Nashville Cats* / Bing bang boom: *Highway 101* / You know me better than that: *Strait, George* / Pocket full of gold: *Gill, Vince* / Down to my last teardrop: *Tucker, Tanya* / Jukebox with a country song: *Stone, Doug* / Someday soon: *Bogguss, Suzy* / Life's too long: *Skaggs, Ricky* / You don't count the cost: *Dean, Billy*
CD CDESTU 2172
EMI / Apr '92 / EMI

NEW TRAIL RIDERS: SWAMP MUSIC VOL.9
CD US 0206
Trikont / Apr '95 / ADA / Direct

NEW WAVE ARCHIVE
CD RMCD 201
Rialto / Sep '96 / Disc / Total/BMG

NEW WAVE OF BRITISH HEAVY METAL COMPILATION
CD HMRXD 157
Heavy Metal / Dec '90 / Revolver / Sony

NEW WAVE OF BRITISH HEAVY METAL LIVE, THE
Red skies: *Samson* / Driving with ZZ: *Samson* / Riding with angels: *Samson* / C'mon let's go: *Girlschool* / Emergency: *Girlschool* / Take it all away: *Girlschool* / White witch: *Angel Witch* / Angel of death: *Angel Witch* / Angel witch: *Angel Witch* / Echoes of a distant rattle: *Tank* / This means war: *Tank* / That's what dreams are made of: *Tank*
CD EMPRCD 714
Emporio / Jun '97 / Disc

NEW WAVE OF BRITISH HEAVY METAL RARITIES VOL.1
Hideaway: *Legend* / Heaven sent: *Legend* / Praying Mantis: *Praying Mantis* / High roller: *Praying Mantis* / Death and destiny: *Mythra* / Killer: *Mythra* / Overlord: *Mythra* / UFO: *Mythra* / Flying high: *Hollow Ground* / War lord: *Hollow Ground* / Rock on: *Hollow Ground* / Don't chase the dragon: *Hollow Ground* / Loser: *Angel Witch* / Suffer: *Angel Witch* / Dr. Phibes: *Angel Witch* / Mony Mony: *Gaskin* / Queen of flames: *Gaskin* / Strange place to be: *Heritage* / Misunderstood: *Heritage*
CD CDMETAL 2
British Steel / Feb '97 / Cargo / Pinnacle / Plastic Head

NEW WAVE OF BRITISH HEAVY METAL RARITIES VOL.2
CD CDMETAL 7
British Steel / Feb '97 / Cargo / Pinnacle / Plastic Head

NEW WAVE OF BRITISH HEAVY METAL RARITIES VOL.3
Take it all away: *Girlschool* / It could be better: *Girlschool* / I won't surrender: *Twisted Ace* / Firebird: *Twisted Ace* / Sheralee: *Soldier* / Force: *Soldier* / Back street women: *Jaguar* / Chasing the dragon: *Jaguar* / No way: *Denigh* / Running: *Denigh* / Voice on the line: *Static* / Stealin': *Static* / Metal to the moon: *Seventh son* / Sound and fury: *Seventh son* / This poison fountain: *White Lightning* / Hypocrite: *White Lightning* / I want your life: *Dragonslayer* / Satan is free: *Dragonslayer* / Broken hearts: *Dragonslayer*
CD CDMETAL 14
Anagram / Sep '97 / Cargo / Pinnacle

NEW YORK - THE JAZZ AGE (2CD Set)
CD Set DCD 8003
Disky / Jan '95 / Disky / THE

NEW YORK DOWNTOWN
CD KFWCD 200
Knitting Factory / Feb '97 / Cargo / Plastic Head

NEW YORK JAZZ 1923-1931
CD VILCD 0242
Village Jazz / Sep '92 / Jazz Music / Target/BMG

NEW YORK JAZZ IN THE ROARING 20'S
CD BCD 129
Biograph / Jun '94 / ADA / Cadillac / Direct / Hot Shot / Jazz Music / Wellard

NEW YORK LATIN
Tremendos cumban: *Machito & His Afro-Cubans* / Mambo of the times: *Cuba, Joe Sextet* / Bilongo: *La Plata Sextet* / Ja ja: *Ray, Ricardo & Bobby Cruz* / Caramelos: *Cruz, Celia* / Rumbambola: *Morales, Noro* / Timbalero: *Concepcion, Cesar* / Maquino landera: *Cortijo Y Su Combo* / Mortuno pa' caridad: *Cotto, Joe Y Su Orqesta* / Capullito de aleli: *Campo, Pupi* / Comer lechon: *La Sonora Matancera* / Ponte duro serafin: *Lopez, Johnny Y Su Super Combo* / Descargo combo NY: *Grand, Rene Y Su Super Combo New York* / Tomando soy feliz: *Caney, Rey* / Que buenas son las mujeres: *Valle, Joe Y Su Orquesta* / Caravan: *Puente, Tito* / Arroz con manteca: *Valdes, Miguelito* / Jingle bells: *Cruz, Celia* / Lullaby of Broadway: *Palmieri, Eddie* / Como fue: *Valdes, Vicentico*
CD CDHOT 615
Charly / Jan '97 / Koch

NEW YORK SALSA EXPLOSION
Te Traigo Guajira: *Barretto, Ray* / Ban Ban Quere: *Puente, Tito & His Orchestra* / A Santa Barbara: *Orquesta Broadway* / Vamonos Pa'l Monte: *Palmieri, Eddie* / La Malanga Brava: *Cuba, Joe Sextet* / Candido's Guajiro: *Candido* / Tin Marin: *Ray, Ricardo* / Arrecotin Arrecotan: *Cortijo Y Su Combo* / No quiero piedras en mi Camino: *Rivera, Ismael* / Por Primera Vez: *Sabater, Jimmy*
CD 12907
Laserlight / Feb '97 / Target/BMG

NEW YORK SCHOOL NO.3
CD ARTCD 6176
Hat Art / Dec '95 / Cadillac / Harmonia Mundi

NEW YORK THRASH
CD EE 113CD
ROIR / Nov '94 / Plastic Head / Shellshock/Disc

NEW YORK VOL.2
CD DGF 11
Frog / Jan '97 / Cadillac / Jazz Music / Wellard

NEW YORK'S HARDEST
CD IJT 001
IJT / Feb '97 / Cargo / Greyhound

NEW ZONE HISTORY VOL.1, THE
CD MET 0032
Metamatic / Jul '93 / Plastic Head

NEWPORT ALL STARS
Take the 'A' train / These foolish things / My Monday date / Body and soul / Mean to me / I surrender dear / Please don't talk about me when I'm gone / Pan Am blues
CD BLCD 760138
Black Lion / Oct '90 / Cadillac / Jazz Music / Koch / Wellard

NEWPORT BROADSIDE (Newport Folk Festival 1963)
Playboys and playgirls: *Dylan, Bob & Pete Seeger* / Willing conscript: *Paxton, Tom* / Ramblin' boy: *Paxton, Tom* / Talking atomic blues: *Hinton, Sam* / Come all ye gallant drivers: *Davenport, Bob* / Fighting for my rights: *Freedom Singers* / I love your dog, I love your dog: *Freedom Singers* / Get on board little children: *Freedom Singers* / I don't want your millions mister: *Garland, Jim* / Ballad of Harry Simms: *Garland, Jim* / Where did you come from: *McCurdy, Ed* / Ballad of Medgar Evers: *Ochs, Phil* / Talking Birmingham jam: *Ochs, Phil* / Coyote my little brother: *La Farge, Peter* / With God on our side: *Baez, Joan & Bob Dylan*
CD VCD 77003
Vanguard / Oct '95 / ADA / Pinnacle

NEWPORT IN NEW YORK
Outside help: *King, B.B.* / Honky tonk train blues: *Glenn, Lloyd* / After hours: *Glenn, Lloyd* / Pinetop's boogie woogie: *Glenn, Lloyd* / Little red rooster: *Thornton, Willie Mae* / Ball and chain: *Thornton, Willie Mae* / Drifter: *Brown, Clarence 'Gatemouth'* / Long distance call: *Waters, Muddy* / Where's my woman / Got my mojo working
CD CDBM 071
Blue Moon / Apr '91 / Cadillac / Discovery / Greensleeves / Jazz Music / Jet Star / TKO Magnum

NEWPORT JAZZ FESTIVAL
Sweet Georgia Brown: *Hall, Edmond* / Tin roof blues: *Kaminsky, Max* / Stars fell on Alabama: *McGarity, Lou* / I've found a new baby: *Freeman, Bud* / At the jazz band ball: *Chicago All Stars* / Isle of Capri: *Manone, Wingy* / Relaxin' at the Touro: *Spanier, Muggsy* / I wish I could shimmy like my sister Kate: *Brunis, George* / Royal Garden blues: *Spanier, Muggsy* / I'm in the mood for love: *Thomas, Joe* / Big noise from Winnetka: *Haggart, Bob* / Stealin' apples: *Hucko, Peanuts*
CD 74321218292
RCA Victor / Nov '94 / BMG

NEWPORT JAZZ FESTIVAL ALL STARS
Exactly like you / Centennial blues / I didn't know about you / Nobody knows you (when you're down and out) / Rosetta / Smiles / Jeep is jumpin' / Mooche / Body and soul / Man I love / What's new / Struttin' with some barbecue / Moten swing
CD CCD 4260
Concord Jazz / Dec '87 / New Note/ Pinnacle

NEXT GENERATION
CD TUT 727492
Wundertute / Jan '94 / ADA / CM / Duncans

NEXT GENERATION
CD SR 327CD
Strictly Rhythm / Jul '96 / Prime / RTM/ Disc / SRD / Vital

NEXT STEP - ELECTRONICA, THE
CD AMB 60112
Instinct / Jul '97 / Cargo

NEXT STOP: DUB PLATE PRESSURE
Haunted swing: *Squid Patrol* / To trap a spy: *Pimp Daddy Nash* / I'm on: *DJ BMF* / Spooks anonymous: *Squid Patrol* / Pressures: *13th Sign* / Lazy bomb: *Glamorous Hooligan* / Happytime: *13th Sign* / Outer nation: *12 From A Dozen* / Walk between the raindrops: *Pimp Daddy Nash* / Milkdud: *Soniq* / Moonweed: *13th Sign* / I say: *12 From A Dozen* / Joe dropped the swing: *Pimp Daddy Nash* / Stoned island estate: *Glamorous Hooligan* / Playing with fire: *Extravaganza* / Return of Mark Skids: *Duboniks* / Back in the day: *13th Sign* / Uptown cheese: *Gadgets*
CD KOBICD 005
Delancey Street / Apr '97 / Prime / Vital

NFL COUNTRY
CD CATCD 102
Castle/Pinnacle / Mar '97 / Pinnacle

NFL JAMS
Start / Way you make me feel: *Jones, Donell & Robert Brooks* / Stay with me: *Richie Rich & Esera Tualo* / Game day: *Phife & Rodney Hampton* / When the cheering stops: *AZ & Ray Buchanan/Scott Galbraith/Zhane* / Bayriders: *Celly Cell & William Floyd* / It's in the game: *Method Man & Ricky Watters* / No doubt: *Havoc & Tyrone Wheatley* / Heads get split: *Channel Live & Corey Harris* / Gotcha looking: *Pharcyde & Raghib 'Rocket' Ismail* / End zone / Fast life: *Ghostface Killah & Andre Rison* / Celebration: *Flip & Lamont 'Law' Warren* / Score
CD CATCD 101
Castle/Pinnacle / Mar '97 / Pinnacle

NICE AN' RUFF
Sun is shining: *Black Uhuru* / No, no, no: *White, K.C.* / Village of the under priviliged: *Isaacs, Gregory* / Things in life: *Brown, Dennis* / Y mas gan: *Abyssinians* / Bongo red: *Griffiths, Albert & The Gladiators* / Capture rasta: *Culture* / Set de prisoners free: *Mutabaruka* / Dub organizer: *Pablo, Augustus* / Maggie breast: *I-Roy* / Kingston town: *Lord Creator* / Swing and dine: *Melodians* / Love is overdue: *Isaacs, Gregory* / Woman is like a shadow: *Meditations* / Girl I love you: *Andy, Horace* / Good thing going: *Minott, Sugar* / Baltimore: *Tamlins* / Triplet: *Sly & Robbie*
CD MCCD 092
Music Club / Dec '92 / Disc / THE

NICE UP DANCEE
CD RCD 20202
Hannibal / Aug '91 / ADA / Vital

NIGHT AND DAY
CD CDHD 187
Happy Days / '93 / Conifer/BMG

NIGHT AND DAY (2CD Set)
CD Set GRP 298662
GRP / Mar '97 / New Note/BMG

NIGHT AT RONNIE'S VOL.1, A
Donna Lee: *Sandoval, Arturo* / White caps: *Scott, Ronnie Quintet* / Nice work if you can get it/Easy to love: *Montgomery, Marian* / Falling grace: *Whitehead, Tim* / La pastora: *Irakere* / Luminous: *Freeman, Chico & Arthur Blythe* / Early Autumn: *Vaughan, Sarah* / Spring is here: *Taylor, John Trio* / Sleeplate Louie's: *White, Tam Band* / Sierra: *Coleman, George* / You send me: *Ayers, Roy* / I'm beginning to see the light: *Sharpe, Jack Big Band*
CD NARCD 1
Ronnie Scott's Jazz House / Jan '94 / Cadillac / Jazz Music / New Note/Pinnacle / TKO Magnum

NIGHT AT RONNIE'S VOL.2, A
Visiting: *Nazaire* / Time one: *Fourth World* / My foolish heart: *Delmar, Elaine* / Coming home baby: *Breaux, Zachary* / Hot: *Ayers, Roy* / My love: *Sandoval, Arturo* / Lo que va a pasar: *Irakere* / Serenade to Sweden: *Cohn, Al* / Lover man: *Shaw, Ian* / Watching the traffic lights change: *National Youth Jazz Orchestra*
CD NARCD 2
Ronnie Scott's Jazz House / Jan '94 / Cadillac / Jazz Music / New Note/Pinnacle / TKO Magnum

NIGHT AT RONNIE'S VOL.3, A
CD NARCD 3
Ronnie Scott's Jazz House / Apr '94 / Cadillac / Jazz Music / New Note/Pinnacle / TKO Magnum

NIGHT AT RONNIE'S VOL.4, A
CD NARCD 4
Ronnie Scott's Jazz House / Mar '95 / Cadillac / Jazz Music / New Note/Pinnacle / TKO Magnum

NIGHT AT RONNIE'S VOL.5, A
CD NARCD 5
Ronnie Scott's Jazz House / Oct '95 / Cadillac / Jazz Music / New Note/Pinnacle / TKO Magnum

NIGHT AT RONNIE'S VOL.6, A
Foggy day: *Vaughan, Sarah* / This can't be love: *Shaw, Ian* / Stardust: *Delmar, Elaine* / But not for me: *Montgomery, Marian* / You were marvellous, darling: *Howe, Jenny* / Raina da noite: *Purim, Flora* / Haunt me: *Morris, Sarah Jane* / Wild women: *Grimes, Carol* / Good morning heartache: *White, Tam* / It could happen to you: *Brown, Ruth* / Good times: *O'Malley, Tony* / Man I love: *Vaughan, Sarah*
CD NARCD 6
Ronnie Scott's Jazz House / Jun '96 / Cadillac / Jazz Music / New Note/Pinnacle / TKO Magnum

NIGHT AT THE EMPIRE, A
No no no: *Miller, Max & His Orchestra* / Littul Gel: *Warner, Jack & Joan Winters* / Nothin' else to do all day: *Long, Norman* / You gotta

S-M-I-L-E to be H-A-Double-P-Y: *Henderson Twins* / Hawaiian gems: *Mendelssohn, Felix & His Hawaiian Serenaders* / When Dream about Hawaii: *Mendelssohn, Felix & His Hawaiian Serenaders* / Drifting and dreaming: *Mendelssohn, Felix & His Hawaiian Serenaders* / Aloma: *Mendelssohn, Felix* / After all that: *Western Brothers* / You must have been a beautiful baby: *Costa, Sam & Dorothy Carless* / When the steamboat whistle is blowing: *Gonella, Nat & His Georgians* / Two dresden dolls: *Gonella, Nat & His Georgians* / Ode of the fletcher: *Fletcher, Cyril* / Life begins again: *Flanagan & Allen* / I'm just wild about Harry: *Lipton, Celia* / I cried for you: *Lipton, Celia* / You made me love you: *Lipton, Celia* / Three times a day: *Wallace, Nellie* / To mother with love: *Roy, Harry & His Orchestra* / Even a crooner must eat: *Bacon, Max & His Orchestra* / Londone pride... and proud of it too: *Waters, Elsie & Doris* / Sweetest sweetheart: *Mesene, Jimmy* / George Elrick successes: *Elrick, George & His Band* / Music goes 'round and around: *Elrick, George & His Band* / Boo-hoo: *Elrick, George & His Band* / I'm nuts about screwy music: *Elrick, George & His Band* / He never slept a wink all night: *O'Shea, Tessie* / This is my day - gang show of 1939: *Reader, Ralph* / My honey's loving arms: *Oliver, Vic* / Love 'em and leave 'em alone: *King, Hetty & His Orchestra*
CD PASTCD 9759
Flapper / May '92 / Pinnacle

NIGHT FEVER (2CD Set)
Boogie wonderland: *Earth, Wind & Fire* / Le freak: *Chic* / Lost in music: *Sister Sledge* / Love train: *O'Jays* / Boogie nights: *Heatwave* / Lady marmalade: *Labelle* / Car wash: *Rose Royce* / Celebration: *Kool & The Gang* / That's the way I like it: *KC & The Sunshine Band* / Harvest for the world: *Isley Brothers* / Love really hurts without you: *Ocean, Billy* / You to me are everything: *Real Thing* / When will I see you again: *Three Degrees* / Boogie oogie oogie: *Taste Of Honey* / Heaven must be missing an angel: *Tavares* / Love come down: *King, Evelyn 'Champagne'* / Baby don't change your mind: *Knight, Gladys & The Pips* / Rock your baby: *McCrae, George* / Young hearts run free: *Staton, Candi* / You're the first, the last, my everything: *White, Barry* / (You make me feel) mighty real: *Sylvester* / Oops up side your head: *Gap Band* / I can make you feel good: *Shalamar* / Ain't nobody: *Rufus & Chaka Khan* / Somebody else's guy: *Brown, Jocelyn* / Theme from shaft: *Hayes, Isaac* / And the beat goes on: *Whispers* / Play that funky music: *Wild Cherry* / Best of my love: *Emotions* / Don't leave me this way: *Melvin, Harold* / Use it up and wear it out: *Odyssey* / Rock the boat: *Hues Corporation* / Jump (for my love): *Pointer Sisters* / Disco inferno: *Trammps* / You gave me love: *Crown Heights Affair* / Funkin' for Jamaica: *Browne, Tom* / Shame: *King, Evelyn 'Champagne'* / Family affair: *Sly & The Family Stone* / Blame it on the boogie: *Jacksons* / YMCA: *Village People*
CD Set RADCD 24
Global TV / Oct '95 / BMG

NIGHT FEVER
Grease / You're the one that I want / Summer nights / Rasputin / Gimme, gimme, gimme (a man after midnight) / When you're in love with a beautiful woman / Rose garden / Is this the way to Amarillo / At the Copacabana / Bright eyes / We don't talk anymore / It's raining again / Words / Heartbreaker / Video killed the radio star / You're the greatest lover / Lily the pink / Winchester Cathederal / Long live love / Where did our love go / Baby I'm a want you / Summer night city / Stayin' alive / Night fever
CD CD 6026
Music / Jun '96 / Target/BMG

NIGHT IN HAVANA, A
CD CDHOT 617
Charly / Mar '97 / Koch

NIGHT MOVES
CD DBG 53036
Double Gold / Apr '95 / Target/BMG

NIGHT MOVES IN JAZZ
Amandla: *Davis, Miles* / Naima: *Coltrane, John* / B minor waltz: *Evans, Bill* / Lorelei's lament: *Crawford, Hank* / Everything happens to me: *Sullivan, Ira* / Nubian lady: *Lateef, Yusef* / Misty: *Hubbard, Freddie* / Embraceable you: *Farmer, Art & Jim Hall* / Body and soul: *Joseph, Julian* / I'll be seeing you: *Fruscella, Tony* / You go to my head: *Tristano, Lennie* / Summertime: *Mann, Herbie*
CD 9548326342
East West / Mar '94 / Warner Music

NIGHT MOVES VOL.2
CD MOCD 002
Da Boops / May '96 / Plastic Head

NIGHT OF THE LIVING PUSSIES
Please don't touch me: *Meteors* / Casting my spell: *Blue Cats* / No more no more no more: *Sergeant Fury* / Street wise: *Guana Batz* / I go wild: *Restless* / Lunatics (are raving): *Frantic Flintstones* / Mad mad bad bad Mama: *Empress Of Fur* / Charlie: *Sharks* / Nothing left but the bones: *Long Tall Texans* / Head on backwards: *Thee Phantom Creeps* / It's gone: *Quakes* / Rock on the moon: *Thee Waltons* / Brand new gun: *Frenzy* / Worms: *Hangmen* / Zulu Joe: *King Kurt* / Pink hearse: *Radium Cats* / Queen of disease: *Demented Are Go* / Throwing my baby out with the bath water: *McCavity's Cat*
CD CDMGRAM 79
Anagram / May '94 / Cargo / Pinnacle

NIGHT SPIRIT MASTERS (Gnawa Music Of Marrakesh)
CD 5101472
Axiom / Mar '92 / PolyGram / Vital

NIGHTIME ROUNDUP (Collection Of Contemporary Rock Songs From Texas)
CD TX 2006CD
Taxim / Jan '94 / ADA

NIGHTS IN HEAVEN (The Party Anthems/2CD Set)
It's raining men: *Weather Girls* / We are family: *Sister Sledge* / Your love still brings me to my knees: *Hines, Marcia* / Can you feel it: *Jacksons* / Got to be real: *Lynn, Cheryl* / Relight my fire: *Hartman, Dan* / You make me feel (mighty real): *Hartman, Dan* / Disco inferno: *Trammps* / Don't leave me this way: *Houston, Thelma* / Pilot error: *Mills, Stephanie* / This time I know it's for real: *Summer, Donna* / I want your sex: *Michael, George* / Small town boy: *Bronski Beat* / Could it be magic: *Take That* / Take a chance on me: *Erasure* / Venus: *Bananarama* / Relax: *Frankie Goes To Hollywood* / Only way is up: *Yazz* / What do I have to do: *Minogue, Kylie* / Everybody's free (to feel good): *Rozalla* / I love the nightlife: *Bridges, Alicia* / Supermodel: *Rupaul* / Hey now (girls just want to have fun): *Lauper, Cyndi* / Little bird: *Lennox, Annie* / Losing my mind: *Minnelli, Liza* / Stand by your man: *Wynette, Tammy*
CD Set SONYTV 3CD
Sony TV / Aug '95 / Sony

NINGS OF DESIRE (The Best Fierce Panda Album In The World Probably)
CD NONGCD 01
Damaged Goods / May '95 / Shellshock/ Disc

NINJA CUTS - FLEXISTENTIALISM (2CD Set)
Cosmic jam: *DJ Food* / Spiral: *DJ Food* / Sunvibes: *DJ Food* / Fungle jungle: *DJ Food* / Scratch your head: *DJ Food* / Consciousness: *DJ Food* / Ninja walk: *DJ Food* / Gentlemen: *DJ Food* / Venus: *Funki Porcini* / B Monkey: *Funki Porcini* / Mother (for your mind): *Herbaliser* / Scratchy noise: *Herbaliser* / Revolutionary woman: *Up Bustle & Out* / Aqui no ma: *Up Bustle & Out* / Ninja's principality: *Up Bustle & Out* / La morena: *Up Bustle & Out* / Atomic moog 2000: *Coldcut* / Shakatakadoodub: *Kruder & Dorfmeister* / Get your head down: *Vibert, Luke* / Junkies bad trip: *London Funk Allstars* / What's in the basket: *London Funk Allstars* / Extreme possibilities: *2 Player* / Do you believe in love: *Uschi* / London and mind state: *DJ Vadim* / Journeyman's electric lazyman: *9 Lazy 9* / Worm turns: *Illuminati Of Hedfuk* / Spoonful of slow: *9 Lazy 9*
CD Set ZENCD 022
Ninja Tune / Mar '96 / Kudos / Pinnacle / Prime / Vital

NIRVANA (File Under Drum & Bass)
CD JSK 116
Jungle Sky / Feb '97 / Cargo

NISAVA
CD CDEB 2565
Earthbeat / May '93 / ADA / Direct

NITE AT STRAWBERRY SUNDAE, A (2CD Set)
CD Set MILL 028CD
Millenium / Sep '96 / Plastic Head / Prime / SRD

NITEBEAT
CD XTR 15CD
X-Treme / Apr '95 / Pinnacle / SRD

NITEDANCIN' VOL.1
CD DFDCD 001
Defender / Jun '95 / Essential/BMG / Prime / SRD

NME SINGLES OF THE WEEK 1992
Only living boy in New Cross: *Carter USM* / Assassins: *Orb* / 100%: *Sonic Youth* / Sheela na gig: *PJ Harvey* / What you do to me: *Teenage Fanclub* / Changes: *Sugar* / Old red eyes is back: *Beautiful South* / Join our club: *St. Etienne* / California: *Wedding Present* / Eat yourself whole: *Kingmaker* / Low self opinion: *Rollins, Henry* / Steamroller: *Family Cat* / Bottle: *Tyrrel Corporation* / 2 Deep: *Gang Starr* / Bedlam: *Gallon Drunk* / Peep: *3 1/2 Minutes*
CD 74321132282
RCA / Feb '93 / BMG

NME SINGLES OF THE WEEK 1995
Some might say: *Oasis* / Common people: *Pulp* / Might be stars: *Wannadies* / Girl from Mars: *Ash* / Just when you're thinking things over: *Charlatans* / Miss Trudy: *Gorky's Zygotic Mynci* / World's a girl: *Lane, Anita & Nick Cave* / History: *Verve* / Checkin' in, checkin' out: *High Llamas* / Travelling light: *Tindersticks* / Black steel: *Tricky* / What a life: *Rockers Hi-Fi* / Fine time: *Cast* / Spirit of '76: *Ween* / 'Found a little baby: *Plush* / Dragon lady: *Geraldine Fibbers* / Western way: *Coco & The Bean*
CD NME 1995CD
Indolent / May '96 / 3mv/BMG / Vital

NO ALTERNATIVE
Superdeformed: *Sweet, Matthew* / For all to see: *Buffalo Tom* / Sexual healing: *Soul Asylum* / Take a walk: *Urge Overkill* / All your jeans were too tight: *American Music Club* / Bitch: *Goo Goo Dolls* / Unseen power of the picket fence: *Pavement* / Glynis: *Smashing Pumpkins* / Can't fight it: *Mould, Bob* / Memorial tribute: *Smith, Patti* / Hold on: *McLachlan, Sarah* / Show me: *Soundgarden* / Joed out: *Manning, Barbara* / Heavy 33: *Verlaines* / Effigy: *Uncle Tupelo* / It's the new style: *Beastie Boys* / Iris: *Breeders* / Burning spear: *Sonic Youth* / Hot nights: *Richman, Jonathan* / Brittle: *Straitjacket Fits*
CD 07822187372
Arista / Oct '93 / BMG

NO COMPROMISE (2CD Set)
CD Set DELECCDD 055
Delerium / Nov '96 / Cargo / Pinnacle / Vital

NO FREE RIDES BUDGET BLUES SAMPLER
CD JSPCDNFR 1
JSP / Jul '95 / ADA / Cadillac / Direct / Hot Shot / Target/BMG

NO FUTURE - THE SINGLES COLLECTION
Someone's gonna die: *Blitz* / Police story: *Partisans* / Future must be ours: *Blitzkrieg* / Banned from the pubs: *Peter & The Test Tube Babies* / In Britain: *Red Alert* / Never surrender: *Blitz* / Today's generation: *Attak* / Lest we forget: *Blitzkrieg* / Gangland: *Violators* / El Salvador: *Insane* / I've got a gun: *Channel 3* / Seventeen years of hell: *Partisans* / Take no prisoners: *Red Alert* / Dead hero: *Samples* / Run like hell: *Peter & The Test Tube Babies* / Warriors: *Blitz* / Murder in the subway: *Attak* / Keep on running: *Crux* / Summer of '81: *Violators* / City invasion: *Red Alert* / Day tripper: *Wall* / Megalomania: *Blood* / Wanna riot: *ABH* / Suffragette City: *Rose Of Victory* / Night creatures: *Screaming Dead* / Die with dignity: *Violators* / There's a guitar burning: *Red Alert*
CD CDPUNK 54
Anagram / May '95 / Cargo / Pinnacle
CD CDPUNK 11
Anagram / Mar '97 / Cargo / Pinnacle

NO GREATER LOVE (2CD Set)
CD Set RADCD 34
Global TV / Jun '96 / BMG

NO JIVE (Authentic Southern Country Blues)
Things gonna change: *Leap Frogs* / Dirty britches: *Leap Frogs* / She was all I had: *Dixie Doodlers* / Best of friends: *Dixie Doodlers* / Wasted time: *Shy Guy Douglas* / I'm your country man: *Shy Guy Douglas* / Gotta have you baby: *Campbell, Louis* / Natural facts: *Campbell, Louis* / No place like home: *Shy Guy Douglas* / She's my kinda girl: *Shy Guy Douglas* / Welcome home baby: *Hunt, Slim* / She's mine all mine: *Gunter, Arthur* / You are doing me wrong: *Gunter, Arthur* / Honey babe: *Gunter, Arthur* / No jive: *Little Al* / Little lean woman: *Little Al* / Every day brings about a change: *Little Al* / Easy ridin' buggy: *Little Al* / Do remember: *Garrett, Robert* / Quit my drinkin': *Garrett, Robert* / Everybody drinkin' wine: *Dowell, Chas & James Stewart* / I've been jumpin' and stompin': *Dowell, Chas & James Stewart* / Ain't no need to cry: *Good Rockin' Bob* / I'm bad: *Good Rockin' Bob*
CD CDCHD 652
Ace / Apr '97 / Pinnacle

NO LESS THAN WIRELESS
CD MWCD 2016
Music & Words / Nov '95 / ADA / Direct

NO MASTER'S VOICE
CD NMCD 4
No Master's Voice / Feb '96 / ADA / Direct

NO REPETITIVE BEATS
CD NRB 58CD
Six6 / Jan '95 / 3mv/Sony / Pinnacle

NO TIME TO PANIC VOL.2
CD NOW 0897CD
Panik / Feb '97 / Cargo

NO.1 70'S ROCK ALBUM (2CD Set)
CD Set 5257172
PolyGram TV / Aug '95 / PolyGram

NO.1 80'S ALBUM, THE (2CD Set)
CD Set 5356832
CD Set 5356834
PolyGram TV / Jul '96 / PolyGram

NO.1 ACOUSTIC ROCK ALBUM, THE (2CD Set)
How bizarre: *OMC* / Not the girl you think you are: *Crowded House* / More than words: *Extreme* / All I wanna do: *Crow, Sheryl* / Stay (I missed you): *Loeb, Lisa* / Nothing ever happens: *Del Amitri* / 74-75: *Connells* / Another cup of coffee: *Mike & The Mechanics* / Better man: *Thunder* / To be with you: *Mr. Big* / Ordinary world: *Duran Duran* / Cowboy dreams: *Nail, Jimmy* / Perfect: *Fairground Attraction* / Constant craving: *Lang, k.d.* / Martha's harbour: *All About Eve* / Daniel: *John, Elton* / Now and forever: *Marx, Richard* / Please be with me: *Clapton, Eric* / Big log: *Plant, Robert* / All I want is you: *U2* / Wonderwall: *Oasis* / Wild wood: *Weller, Paul* / Walkaway: *Cast* / On and on: *Longpigs* / Fake plastic trees: *Radiohead* / Linger: *Cranberries* / (I'm gonna) cry myself blind: *Primal Scream* / There she goes: *La's* / Some people say: *Terrorvision* / You and me song: *Wannadies* / Becoming more like Alfie: *Divine Comedy* / From the bench at Belvidere: *Boo Radleys* / Brass in pocket: *Pretenders* / Psycho killer: *Talking Heads* / Driving away from home: *It's Immaterial* / Stuck in the middle with you: *Stealer's Wheel* / Days: *MacColl, Kirsty* / I don't wanna talk about it: *Everything But The Girl* / I was brought to my senses: *Sting*
CD Set 5358142
PolyGram TV / Sep '96 / PolyGram

NO.1 ALL TIME ROCK ALBUM (2CD Set)
CD Set 5359542
Polydor / Oct '95 / PolyGram

NO.1 CHRISTMAS ALBUM (2CD Set)
CD Set 5259782
PolyGram TV / Nov '95 / PolyGram

NO.1 CLASSIC SOUL ALBUM, THE (2CD Set)
I heard it through the grapevine: *Gaye, Marvin* / I say a little prayer: *Franklin, Aretha* / (Sittin' on the) dock of the bay: *Redding, Otis* / My cherie amour: *Wonder, Stevie* / Let's stay together: *Green, Al* / Midnight train to Georgia: *Knight, Gladys & The Pips* / Tracks of my tears: *Robinson, Smokey & The Miracles* / Reach out, I'll be there: *Four Tops* / In the midnight hour: *Pickett, Wilson* / Dancing in the streets: *Reeves, Martha* / My guy: *Wells, Mary* / Soul sister brown sugar: *Sam & Dave* / I get the sweetest feeling: *Wilson, Jackie* / Soul city walk: *Bell, Archie & The Drells* / Piece of my heart: *Franklin, Erma* / This old heart of mine (is weak for you): *Isley Brothers* / Just my imagination: *Temptations* / Hey there lonely girl: *Holman, Eddie* / If you don't know me by now: *Melvin, Harold* / Ain't no sunshine: *Jackson, Michael* / Papa was a rollin' stone: *Temptations* / Papa's got a brand new bag: *Brown, James* / Ghetto child: *Detroit Spinners* / Love train: *O'Jays* / Nathan Jones: *Supremes* / Stop her on sight (SOS): *Starr, Edwin* / Ms. Grace: *Tymes* / Like sister and brother: *Drifters* / Family affair: *Sly & The Family Stone* / Didn't I (blow your mind this time): *Delfonics* / Homely girl: *Chi-Lites* / Gonna make you an offer you can't refuse: *Helms, Jimmy* / I'm still waiting: *Ross, Diana* / I'll be there: *Jackson Five* / What becomes of the broken hearted: *Ruffin, Jimmy* / Walk on by: *Warwick, Dionne* / Me and Mrs. Jones: *Paul, Billy* / I'm stone in love with you: *Stylistics* / Drift away: *Gray, Dobie* / Easy: *Commodores*
CD Set 5256562
PolyGram TV / Jan '96 / PolyGram

NO.1 COUNTRY ALBUM, THE (2CD Set)
Leaving Las vegas: *Crow, Sheryl* / Crocodile shoes: *Nail, Jimmy* / Achy breaky heart: *Cyrus, Billy Ray* / Everybody's talkin': *Nilsson* / House of love: *Grant, Amy & Vince Gill* / Young at heart: *Bluebells* / Margaritaville: *Buffett, Jimmy* / Galveston: *Campbell, Glen* / It's not you: *Dr. Hook* / Thing called love: *Cash, Johnny* / Bargain store: *Parton, Dolly* / Always on my mind: *Nelson, Willie* / Talking in your sleep: *Gayle, Crystal* / You're my best friend: *Williams, Don* / I don't know why I love you: *Pride, Charley* / Crying: *Orbison, Roy* / Crazy: *Cline, Patsy* / Honey: *Goldsboro, Bobby* / It's only make believe: *Twitty, Conway* / I saw the light: *Williams, Hank* / Stand by your man: *Wynette, Tammy* / Rawhide: *Laine, Frankie* / King of the road: *Miller, Roger* / Peggy Sue got married: *Holly, Buddy* / Hello Mary Lou: *Nelson, Rick* / Okie from Muskogee: *Haggard, Merle* / Good ol' boys: *Jennings, Waylon* / Devil went down to Georgia: *Daniels, Charlie Band* / Take this job and shove it: *Paycheck, Johnny* / Convoy: *McCall, C.W.* / Guitar town: *Earle, Steve* / Love hurts: *Parsons, Gram & Emmylou Harris* / Anchorage: *Shocked, Michelle* / Take me home, country roads: *Newton-John, Olivia* / Shut up and kiss me: *Carpenter, Mary-Chapin* / New kid in town: *Yearwood, Trisha* / Forever and ever, Amen: *Travis, Randy* / Walking away a winner: *Mattea, Kathy* / Whose bed have your boots been under: *Twain, Shania* / Indian outlaw: *McGraw, Tim* / Independence day: *McBride, Martina* / Thousand miles from nowhere: *Yoakam, Dwight* / Past the point of rescue: *Ketchum, Hal* / Love can build a bridge: *Judds*
CD Set 5357222
PolyGram TV / Aug '96 / PolyGram

NO.1 DANCEFLOOR HITS (4CD Set)
CD Set DAM 001
Tring / Dec '96 / Tring

NO.1 DRIVE ALBUM, THE (2CD Set)
CD Set 5539402
PolyGram TV / Aug '97 / PolyGram

NO.1 LOVE ALBUM VOL.1, THE (2CD Set)
CD Set 5352622
PolyGram TV / Jan '96 / PolyGram

NO.1 LOVE ALBUM VOL.2, THE (2CD Set)
Morning: *Wet Wet Wet* / Father and son: *Boyzone* / Rotterdam: *Beautiful South* / Lifted: *Lighthouse Family* / Give me a little more time: *Gabrielle* / Make it with you: *Let Loose* / Someone to love: *East 17* / Pray: *Take That* / Light of my life: *Louise* / Oh baby I: *Eternal* / Love 2 love: *Damage* / I'll never break your heart: *Backstreet Boys* / Like a woman: *Rich, Tony* / One for the money: *Brown, Horace* / Desire: *Nu Colours* / Save the best for last: *Williams, Vanessa* / I can't sleep baby (If I): *Kelly, R* / Let's get together: *O'Neal, Alexander* / Don't wanna lose you: *Richie, Lionel* / Sacrifice: *John, Elton* / One of us: *Osbourne, Joan* / In a lifetime: *Clannad* / Fall at your feet: *Crowded House* / Don't dream it's over: *Young, Paul* / Golden eye: *Turner, Tina* / No more I love you's: *Lennox, Annie* / Come undone: *Duran Duran* / Get here: *Adams, Oleta* / Heaven help my heart: *Arena, Tina* / Show me heaven: *McKee, Maria* / Stay: *Shakespears Sister* / She makes my day: *Palmer, Robert* / Paris match: *Style Council* / Something about you: *Level 42* / What becomes of the broken hearted: *Ruffin, Jimmy* / Words: *Bee Gees*
CD Set ______ **5531412**
PolyGram TV / Nov '96 / PolyGram

NO.1 MOTOWN ALBUM, THE (2CD Set)
I heard it through the grapevine: *Gaye, Marvin* / I just called to say I love you: *Wonder, Stevie* / Tracks of my tears: *Robinson, Smokey & The Miracles* / Easy: *Commodores* / Ben: *Jackson, Michael* / Help me make it through the night: *Knight, Gladys & The Pips* / Just my imagination (running away from me): *Temptations* / What becomes of the broken hearted: *Ruffin, Jimmy* / You are everything: *Ross, Diana & Marvin Gaye* / You're all I need to get by: *Gaye, Marvin & Tammi Terrell* / Endless love: *Ross, Diana & Lionel Richie* / I'm still waiting: *Ross, Diana* / Three times a lady: *Commodores* / Do you know where you're going to: *Ross, Diana* / Go to be there: *Jackson, Michael* / With you I'm born again: *Preston, Billy & Syreeta* / Let's get it on: *Gaye, Marvin* / Still water: *Four Tops* / Reflections: *Ross, Diana & The Supremes* / One for the money: *Brown, Horace* / Your love is a 187: *Whitehead Brothers* / I'll make love to you: *Boyz II Men*
CD Set ______ **5307642**
Motown / Jan '97 / PolyGram

NO.1 PUNK ALBUM, THE (2CD Set)
CD Set ______ **5356582**
PolyGram TV / Jul '96 / PolyGram

NO.1 RAP/HIP HOP ALBUM, THE (2CD Set)
California love: *2Pac* / Do you see: *Warren G* / No: *Chuck D* / Jump around: *House Of Pain* / Danger: *Blahzay Blahzay* / Wopbobalubop: *Funkdoobiest* / Fight the power: *Public Enemy* / Television the drug of the nation: *Disposable Heroes Of Hiphoprisy* / Ince again: *Tribe Called Quest* / One shot: *Brotherhood* / Karmacoma: *Massive Attack* / I got 5 on it: *Luniz* / I must stand: *Ice-T* / Getto jam: *Domino* / I'll be around: *Rappin' 4-Tay* / Poison: *Bel Biv Devoe* / Got to keep on: *Cookie Crew* / Say no go: *De La Soul* / Eat my goal: *Collapsed Lung* / Teenage sensation: *Credit To The Nation* / Hey lover: *LL Cool J & Boyz II Men* / I will survive: *Savage, Chantay* / I wish: *Skee Lo* / Runnin': *Pharcyde* / Gangsta's paradise: *Coolio & LV* / Connected: *Stereo MC's* / Innocent: *Addis Black Widow* / What's goin down: *Honky* / Summertime: *DJ Jazzy Jeff & The Fresh Prince* / People everyday: *Arrested Development* / It's a shame (my sister): *Monie Love & True Image* / Buffalo stance: *Cherry, Neneh* / Why: *Ricardo Da Force* / Let's talk about sex: *Salt n' Pepa* / Tease me: *Chaka Demus & Pliers* / Get a life: *Soul II Soul* / Rain: *Jones, Oran 'Juice'* / Mr. Loverman: *Shabba Ranks* / Throw your hands up: *LV* / Board game: *Collapsed Lung*
CD Set ______ **5358112**
PolyGram TV / Oct '96 / PolyGram

NO.1 REGGAE ALBUM, THE (2CD Set)
Bubblin' hot: *Pato Banton & Ranking Roger* / You're no good: *Aswad* / Love and devotion: *Real McCoy* / Don't turn around: *Ace Of Base* / Baby come back: *Pato Banton* / You don't love me (no no no): *Penn, Dawn* / Searching: *China Black* / Baby I love your way: *Big Mountain* / Sweets for my sweet: *Lewis, C.J.* / Tease me: *Chaka Demus & Pliers* / Housecall: *Shabba Ranks & Maxi Priest* / Jamaican in New York: *Shinehead* / Oh Carolina: *Shaggy* / Sweat (A la la la la long): *Inner Circle* / Mr. Loverman: *Shabba Ranks* / Hot hot hot: *Arrow* / Shout: *Louchie Lou & Michie One* / Compliments on your kiss: *Red Dragon* / Dark heart: *Bomb The Bass* / Boom shack-a-lack: *Apache Indian* / Close to you: *Priest, Maxi* / Swing low, sweet chariot: *Ladysmith Black Mambazo & China Black* / Keep on moving: *Marley, Bob* / Hurt so good: *Cadogan, Susan* / Now that we've found love: *Third World* / Silly games: *Kay, Janet* / Dub be good to me: *Beats International & Lindy Layton* / Good thing going: *Minott, Sugar* / I don't wanna dance: *Grant, Eddy* / I want to wake up with you: *Gardiner, Boris* / Israelites: *Dekker, Desmond* / I can see clearly now: *Nash, Johnny* / Double barrel: *Collins, Dave & Ansell* / Young, gifted and black: *Bob & Marcia* / Uptown top ranking: *Althia & Donna* / Don't look back: *Tosh, Peter* / Love of the common people: *Thomas, Nicky* / Help me make it through the night: *Holt, John* / Liquidator: *Johnson, Harry & The All-Stars* / Wonderful world, beautiful people: *Cliff, Jimmy*
CD Set ______ **5256392**
PolyGram TV / Aug '95 / PolyGram

NO.1 ROCK BALLADS, THE (2CD Set)
Always: *Bon Jovi* / I still haven't found what I'm looking for: *U2* / China girl: *Bowie, David* / Believe: *John, Elton* / I found someone: *Cher* / Waiting for a girl like you: *Foreigner* / These dreams: *Heart* / Wonderful tonight: *Clapton, Eric* / More than words: *Extreme* / I'm easy: *Faith No More* / Only wanna be with you: *Hootie & The Blowfish* / Missing you: *Waite, John* / Wind of change: *Scorpions* / 29 Palms: *Plant, Robert* / Owner of a lonely heart: *Yes* / I drove all night: *Lauper, Cyndi* / I'd do anything for love (but I won't do that): *Meat Loaf* / Total eclipse of the heart: *Tyler, Bonnie* / Breakfast at Tiffany's: *Deep Blue Something* / One of us: *Osbourne, Joan* / It's only natural: *Crowded House* / Run baby run: *Crow, Sheryl* / Always the last to know: *Del Amitri* / You do something to me: *Weller, Paul* / Never tear us apart: *INXS* / It ain't over 'til it's over: *INXS* / I don't want a lover: *Texas* / Ode to my family: *Cranberries* / Perfect day: *Reed, Lou* / After midnight: *Cale, J.J.* / Highr love: *Winwood, Steve* / All out of love: *Air Supply* / Womankind: *Little Angels* / Black velvet: *Myles, Alannah* / Don't want to wait anymore: *Tubes* / Behind blue eyes: *Who* / Brothers in arms: *Dire Straits*
CD Set ______ **5359412**
PolyGram TV / Nov '96 / PolyGram

NO.1 SAX ALBUM, THE (2CD Set)
I don't want to lose you: *Turner, Tina* / Jealous guy: *Roxy Music* / True: *Spandau Ballet* / Million love songs: *Take That* / Hands to heaven: *Breathe* / I wonder why: *Stigers, Curtis* / You're the best thing: *Style Council* / Beautiful girl: *INXS* / Will you: *O'Connor, Hazel* / Absolute beginners: *Bowie, David* / Imagination: *Belouis Some* / Baker Street: *Rafferty, Gerry* / Year of the cat: *Stewart, Al* / Lily was here: *Stewart, David A. & Candy Dulfer* / Walk on the wild side: *Reed, Lou* / Saxophone song: *Bush, Kate* / Cowboys and angels: *Michael, George* / Let's stick together: *Ferry, Bryan* / Heat is on: *Frey, Glenn* / Rip it up: *Orange Juice* / Whole of the moon: *Waterboys* / Unchain my heart: *Cocker, Joe* / Maneater: *Hall & Oates* / Rio: *Duran Duran* / Pretty in pink: *Psychedelic Furs* / Dancing in the moonlight: *Thin Lizzy* / Why did you do it: *Stretch* / Who can it be now: *Men At Work* / Rapture: *Blondie* / Embarrassment: *Madness* / Hit me with your rhythm stick: *Dury, Ian & The Blockheads* / Jackie Wilson said (I'm in heaven when you smile): *Rowland, Kevin & Dexy's Midnight Runners* / Pick up the pieces: *Average White Band* / Mustang Sally: *Commitments* / I got you (I feel good): *Brown, James* / How Gee: *Black Machine*
CD Set ______ **5358052**
PolyGram TV / Aug '96 / PolyGram

NO.1 SKA ALBUM, THE (2CD Set)
One step beyond: *Madness* / Ghost town: *Specials* / Tears of a clown: *Beat* / On my radio: *Selecter* / Special brew: *Bad Manners* / Gangsters: *Special AKA* / Double barrell: *Collins, Dave & Ansell* / Liquidator: *Harry J All Stars* / People do rocksteady: *Bodysnatchers* / Rat race: *Specials* / Return of django: *Upsetters* / Long shot kick da bucket: *Upsetters* / Israelites: *Dekker, Desmond & The Aces* / Missing words: *Selecter* / Message to you rudy: *Specials* / Carolina: *Rico* / Train to skaville: *Ethiopians* / Monkey spanner: *Collins, Dave & Ansell* / Monkey man: *Maytals* / Red red wine: *Tribe, Tony* / Whisper: *Selecter* / Walking in sunshine: *Bad Manners* / Too much too young: *Special AKA* / Three minute hero: *Selecter* / Prince: *Madness* / Lip up fatty: *Bad Manners* / Ranking full stop: *Beat* / Nelson Mandela: *Special AKA* / I can see clearly now: *Black, Pauline* / Sea cruise: *Rico* / Selecter: *Selecter* / You can get it if you really want: *Dekker, Desmond* / Stereotype: *Specials* / Can can: *Bad Manners* / Mantovani: *Swinging Cats* / Ire feelings(skanga): *Edwards, Rupie* / I'm in the mood for ska: *Lord Tanamo* / James Bond: *Selecter* / Let your yeah be yeah: *Pioneers* / Sweet sensation: *Melodians* / Feelings gone: *Apollinaires* / Skinhead moonstomp: *Symarip* / 007: *Dekker, Desmond* / Do nothing: *Specials*
CD Set ______ **5534192**
PolyGram TV / Mar '97 / PolyGram

NO.1 SUMMER ALBUM, THE (2CD Set)
CD Set ______ **5356312**
PolyGram TV / Jul '96 / PolyGram

NOCHE DE AMOUR
CD ______ **TUMICD 024**
Tumi / '92 / Discovery / Stern's

NOIR
CD ______ **VICTOCD 022**
Victo / Nov '94 / Harmonia Mundi / ReR Megacorp

NOISE ANNOYS
CD ______ **CRECD 171**
Creation / Nov '96 / 3mv/Vital

NOISE VOL.3
Bass shake: *Urban Shakedown* / Smoke dis one: *Bass Balistic* / Caught with a spliff: *Hackney Hardcore* / Free your mind: *Satin Storm* / Don Gordon coming: *Project One* / Peace and loveism: *Sonz Of A Loop Da Loop Era* / Now hear this: *Energy Zone* / Up and running: *Vocation* / Back again: *Run Tings* / Star preacher: *Space Brains* / Space: *Dionysus* / Intensity: *Freshtrax & Ace* / Let's go: *Hardware* / What the world needs: *Blatant & Dangerous* / Out of it: *Spirit Level* / Bogey man: *Happy & Free*
CD ______ **CDTOT 8**
Jumpin' & Pumpin' / Jul '93 / 3mv/Sony / Mo's Music Machine

NON STOP PARTY HITS VOL.1
Let's have a party: *Jackson, Wanda* / Dynamite: *Mud* / Be bop a lula: *Vincent, Gene & The Bluecaps* / Some girls: *Racey* / Denis: *Blondie* / Gimme hope Jo'anna: *Grant, Eddy* / Breakaway: *Ullman, Tracey* / Can the can: *Quatro, Suzi* / My sharona: *Knack* / Bus stop: *Hollies* / You were made for me: *Freddie & The Dreamers* / Runaway: *Shannon, Del* / Forever forever: *Fats Domino* / Pretend: *Stardust, Alvin* / Kids in America: *Wilde, Kim* / If this is it: *Lewis, Huey & The News* / Darlin': *Miller, Frankie* / Right back where we started from: *Nightingale, Maxine* / Showing out: *Mel & Kim* / Sex & drugs & rock & roll: *Dury, Ian*
CD ______ **DC 877452**
Disky / May '97 / Disky / THE

NON STOP PARTY HITS VOL.2
I hear you knockin': *Edmunds, Dave* / Rubber ball: *Vee, Bobby* / Boat that I row: *Lulu* / Runaround Sue: *Dion* / Morning train: *Easton, Sheena* / Magic: *Pilot* / Cat crept in: *Mud* / Teenager in love: *Dion & The Belmonts* / I like it: *Gerry & The Pacemakers* / Buona sera: *Prima, Louis* / Mississippi: *Pussycat* / Walking back to happiness: *Shapiro, Helen* / Pretty flamingo: *Manfred Mann* / Good golly miss molly: *Swinging Blue Jeans* / Nutbush city limits: *Turner, Ike & Tina* / Coming on strong: *Broken English* / That's the way I like it: *KC & The Sunshine Band* / We've gotta get out of this place: *Animals* / No more heroes: *Stranglers*
CD ______ **DC 877462**
Disky / May '97 / Disky / THE

NON STOP PARTY HITS VOL.3
Party doll: *Knox, Buddy* / Do wah diddy diddy: *Manfred Mann* / C'mon everybody: *Cochran, Eddie* / Hippy hippy shake: *Swinging Blue Jeans* / Barbara ann: *Beach Boys* / Mony mony: *James, Tommy & The Shondells* / Hi ho silver lining: *Beck, Jeff* / Tiger feet: *Mud* / See my baby jive: *Wizzard* / Long tall glasses: *Sayer, Leo* / This little girl: *Bonds, Gary 'US'* / On the road again: *Canned Heat* / Roll over Beethoven: *ELO* / My girl Josephine: *Fats Domino* / I'm into something good: *Herman's Hermits* / Surf city: *Jan & Dean* / I get around: *Beach Boys* / Rock your baby: *McCrae, George* / Don't take away the music: *Tavares*
CD ______ **DC 877472**
Disky / May '97 / Disky / THE

NON STOP PARTY HITS VOL.4
Summertime blues: *Cochran, Eddie* / Lay your love on me: *Racey* / Don't let me be misunderstood: *Animals* / World without love: *Peter & Gordon* / Baker street: *Rafferty, Gerry* / Boogie oogie oogie: *Taste Of Honey* / Heaven must be missing an angel: *Tavares* / Chequered love: *Wilde, Kim* / Oh boy: *Mud* / Tom tom turn around: *New World* / No milk today: *Herman's Hermits* / Devil gate drive: *Quatro, Suzi* / Stuck with you: *Lewis, Huey & The News* / Centerfold: *Geils, J. Band* / Stop stop stop: *Hollies* / Freedom come freedom go: *Fortunes* / You'll never walk alone: *Gerry & The Pacemakers* / I'm telling you now: *Freddie & The Dreamers* / Seven drunken nights: *Dubliners* / Sloop John B.: *Beach Boys* / Oh Marie: *Prima, Louis* / If you can't give me love: *Quatro, Suzi* / Blueberry hill: *Fats Domino* / Do you want to know a secret: *Kramer, Billy J. & The Dakotas* / Thank u very much: *Scaffold*
CD ______ **DC 877482**
Disky / May '97 / Disky / THE

NON-STOP 60'S PARTY (40 Swinging Favourites)
CD ______ **SUMCD 4042**
Summit / Nov '96 / Sound & Media

NON-STOP CHRISTMAS PARTY
CD ______ **MCCDX 009**
Music Club / Nov '94 / Disc / THE

NON-STOP CHRISTMAS TOP 20
Sleigh ride / Lily the pink / Have yourself a merry little Christmas / Jingle bells / White Christmas / Santa Claus is coming to town / We wish you a Merry Christmas / Little drummer boy / Rudolph the red nosed reindeer / We wish the merriest / Winter wonderland / I saw Mommy kissing Santa Claus / Do you hear what I hear / Scarlet ribbons / All I want for Christmas (is my two front teeth) / Mary's boy child / First Noel / Hark the herald angels sing / Cokey cokey / Christmas song
CD ______ **SPGCD 8000**
President / Nov '95 / Grapevine/PolyGram / President / Target/BMG

NON-STOP COUNTRY ALBUM (A Medley Of 58 Country Favourites)
CD ______ **SUMCD 4040**
Summit / Nov '96 / Sound & Media

NON-STOP DANCE MIX '97 (2CD Set)
Offshore / X-Files theme / Seven days and one week / Higher state of consciousness / Sunshine after the rain / There's nothing I won't do / Key, the secret / Ooh aah...just a little bit / Born slippy / Night train / Flash / Let me be your fantasy / I like to move it / Boom boom boom / Ready or not / Go / Waterfall / Dreamer / Rhythm of the night / Jump to the beat / Don't give me your life / Encore une fois / Everybody's free / Finally / Hideaway / Don't stop movin' / Read my lips / Keep on jumpin' / Try me out / Move on baby / Baby baby / U got 2 let the music / Humpin' around / Two can play that game / I love you baby / Naughty North and the sexy South / Children / Fable / Bellissima / I love you stop
CD Set ______ **CDVDB 6**
Virgin / Jul '97 / EMI

NON-STOP DANCE PARTY
I like to move it: *Reel 2 Real* / Void: *Exoterix* / Got to give me love: *Dawson, Dana* / Omen III: *Magic Affair* / Give it up: *Cut 'n' Move* / Elephant paw: *Pan Position* / Nothing in the world: *Mozaic* / Give me love: *Diddy* / Can you hear the voice of Buddha: *Voice Of Buddha* / Let love shine: *Amos* / Someday: *Eddy* / I like to move it (reprise): *Reel 2 Real*
CD ______ **CDGOLD 1042**
EMI Gold / Jul '96 / EMI

NON-STOP EUROPA EXPRESS
CD ______ **JAPECD 101**
Escapade / May '94 / 3mv/Sony / Prime

NON-STOP PARTY ALBUM (Stars On 45)
CD ______ **MCCD 250**
Music Club / Jun '96 / Disc / THE

NON-STOP ROCK 'N' ROLL PARTY
Let's have a party: *Jackson, Wanda* / Good Golly Miss Molly: *Swinging Blue Jeans* / Under the moon of love: *Showaddywaddy* / Viva Bobby Joe: *Equals* / Red river rock: *Johnny & The Hurricanes* / Tutti frutti: *Little Richard* / Long tall Sally: *Little Richard* / Here comes my baby: *Tremeloes* / Feedee-o-dee: *Rubettes* / Helule helule: *Tremeloes* / Yellow river: *Christie* / Tonight: *Rubettes* / Letter: *Box Tops* / Windy: *Association* / Lucille: *Little Richard* / Bama lama bama loo: *Little Richard* / Wooly bully: *Sam The Sham & The Pharaohs* / Da doo ron ron: *Crystals* / Judy in disguise: *John Fred & Playboy Band* / He's so fine: *Chiffons* / Let's twist again: *Checker, Chubby* / Little honda: *Hondells* / Keep on dancing: *Gentrys* / See you later alligator: *Haley, Bill & The Comets* / Come on let's go: *Showaddywaddy* / Dancin' party: *Showaddywaddy* / Say Mama: *Showaddywaddy* / Shake, rattle and roll: *Haley, Bill & The Comets* / Rock around the clock: *Haley, Bill & The Comets*
CD ______ **11982**
Music / Feb '96 / Target/BMG

NON-STOP ROCK 'N' ROLL PARTY (Non-Stop Party Hits From The 1950's)
CD ______ **SUMCD 4041**
Summit / Nov '96 / Sound & Media

NON-STOP ROCK 'N' ROLL PARTY MIX
CD ______ **ZYX 100462**
ZYX / Jan '97 / ZYX

NONE OF THESE ARE LOVE SONGS VOL.1
Gonna make you move: *Boomshanka* / Big bud II: *Tranx Project* / Reach further: *Progression* / Ride: *Boomshanka* / Bug bottom hula: *Big Bottom Music* / Spirit: *Aberration* / House of dread: *Dread Zone* / Agent O: *Aloof* / Equatorial dawn: *Mind Becomes Drum* / Who killed the king: *Sunz Of Ishen*
CD ______ **CVN 001CD**
Caustic Visions / Apr '94 / Kudos / Pinnacle / RTM/Disc

NONE OF THESE ARE LOVE SONGS VOL.2
CD ______ **CVN 003CD**
Caustic Visions / Nov '94 / Kudos / Pinnacle / RTM/Disc

NOOMRISE VOL.3
CD ______ **NOOMCD 0052**
Noom UK / Jun '97 / Prime

NORMANDIE
CD ______ **DEM 011**
IMP / Feb '96 / ADA / Discovery

NORSE TURDANSAR
CD ______ **HCD 7089CD**
Musikk Distribujson / Apr '95 / ADA

NORTH INDIA-KASHMIR & GANGES PLAIN
CD ______ **ARN 64227**
Arion / Jun '93 / ADA / Discovery

NORTH INDIAN VOCAL MUSIC
Khyal in raga bhairav: *Khan, Hafeez Ahmed* / Thumri in raga bhairavi: *Bhagwat, Neela* / Khyal in raga bhupali: *Khan, Hafeez Ahmed* / Khyal in deshkar: *Bhagwat, Neela*
CD ______ **CDSDL 404**

Saydisc / Jun '94 / ADA / Direct / Harmonia Mundi

NORTH OF WATFORD VOL.1
Gimme some: *Brendon* / Shattered glass: *Warren, Ellie* / Nine times out of ten: *Day, Muriel* / One minute every hour: *Miles, John* / Run baby run: *Newbeats* / Sweet talking guy: *Chiffons* / You to me are everything: *Real Thing* / Gotta get along without you: *Wills, Viola* / Something old, something new: *Fantastics* / Guilty: *Pearls* / Ski-ing in the snow: *Wigan's Ovation* / Touch of velvet: *Mood Mosaic* / Going to go go: *Sharonettes* / Shotgun wedding: *Roy C* / Long after tonight is all over: *Radcliffe, Jimmy* / Supergirl: *Bonney, Graham* / Rudi's in love: *Locomotive* / Man like me: *James, Jimmy* / Under my thumb: *Gibson, Wayne* / Out on the floor: *Gray, Dobie* / Flasher: *Mistra* / Hold me, thrill me, kiss me: *Carter, Mel* / Heartache avenue: *Maisonettes* / I feel love coming on: *Taylor, Felice*
CD _______________ KRLCD 001
KRL / Apr '95 / Vital

NORTH OF WATFORD VOL.2 (24 Rare Pop & Soul Classics 1964-1979)
Harlem shuffle: *Bob & Earl* / Cool jerk: *Capitols* / Holiday: *Brasseur, Andre* / Do the teasy: *Bond, Joyce* / I want you to be my baby: *Davis, Billie* / Something keeps calling me back: *Fontana, Wayne* / Spooky's day off: *Swinging Soul Machine* / Never an everyday thing: *Bonaparte, Eli* / Yesterday: *Miles, John* / Groovin' with Mr. Bloe: *Mr. Bloe* / Life: *Cats Eyes* / Give and take: *Cliff, Jimmy* / I hear those church bells ringing: *Dusk* / 3rd finger left hand: *Pearls* / Trampoline: *Davis, Spencer Group* / Love on a mountain top: *Knight, Robert* / Look at what you have done to my heart: *Shirley & The Shirelles* / If it feels good do it: *Reese, Della* / Surrender your love: *Carrolls* / I can prove it: *Etoria, Tony* / You can do magic: *Limmie & Family Cooking* / Gonna get along without you now: *Wills, Viola* / Broken man: *Pioneers* / Morning glory: *James & Bobby Purify*
CD _______________ KRLCD 003
KRL / Jul '97 / Vital

NORTH SEA JAZZ SESSIONS VOL.1
CD _______________ JWD 102201
JWD / Jul '93 / Target/BMG

NORTH SEA JAZZ SESSIONS VOL.2
CD _______________ JWD 102202
JWD / Jul '93 / Target/BMG

NORTH SEA JAZZ SESSIONS VOL.3
CD _______________ JWD 102203
JWD / Jul '93 / Target/BMG

NORTH SEA JAZZ SESSIONS VOL.4
CD _______________ JWD 102204
JWD / Jul '93 / Target/BMG

NORTHCORE (The Polar Scene)
CD _______________ BHR 008CD
Burning Heart / Feb '95 / Plastic Head

NORTHERN BEAT, THE (22 Classic Hits From The 60's)
I'm into something good: *Herman's Hermits* / Groovy kind of love: *Mindbenders* / Do you want to know a secret: *Kramer, Billy J. & The Dakotas* / I like it: *Gerry & The Pacemakers* / Just one look: *Hollies* / Needles and pins: *Searchers* / You've got your troubles: *Fortunes* / Little things: *Berry, Dave* / Juliet: *Four Pennies* / Hello little girl: *Fourmost* / Shout: *Lulu & The Luvvers* / Ain't she sweet: *Beatles* / Hippy hippy shake: *Swinging Blue Jeans* / House of the rising sun: *Animals* / If you gotta make a fool of somebody: *Freddie & The Dreamers* / Halfway to paradise: *Fury, Billy* / Game of love: *Fontana, Wayne* / I think of you: *Merseybeats* / Anyone who had a heart: *Black, Cilla* / Sorrow: *Merseys* / Everything's alright: *Mojos* / Some other guy: *Big Three*
CD _______________ 8409682
Polydor / Jun '90 / PolyGram

NORTHERN CIRCUITS
CD _______________ ICHILLCD 002
Interchill / May '97 / Prime

NORTHERN EXPOSURE (Mixed By Sasha & John Digweed)
Satellite serenade: *Suzuki, Keiichi* / Cascade: *Future Sound Of London* / These waves: *Young American Primitive* / Raincry: *God Within* / Out of body experience: *Rabbit In The Moon* / I am free: *King, Morgan* / Kites: *Ultraviolet* / Obsession: *Fuzzy Logic* / Water from a vine leaf: *Orbit, William* / Liquid cool: *Apollo 440* / Last train to Lhasa: *Banco De Gaia* / Wave dub: *Dope On Plastic* / Sound system: *Drum Club* / Gloom: *Castle Trancelot* / Wave speech: *Lazonby, Peter* / Photogenic: *Evolution* / Dusk: *Light* / Plan 94 (The voyage): *X-Trax* / I can't stop: *Mellow Mellow* / Heliopolis: *Banco De Gaia* / East: *Humate & Rabbit In The Moon* / Dark and long: *Underworld*
CD _______________ NECD 1
Ministry Of Sound / Oct '96 / 3mv/Sony / Mo's Music Machine / Warner Music

NORTHERN LIGHTS (The Cream Of Scotland's Celtic Musicians Live)
Glass of beer: *Drop The Box* / Barnyards of Dalgety: *Old Blind Dogs* / Duck: *McManus, Tony* / Seagull: *McManus, Tony* / Si Morag: *Tannas* / Kenny Gillies of Portnalong: *Canterach* / Bobby MacLeods: *Canterach* / General gathering 1745: *Canterach* / Curlew: *Canterach* / Mich's m'geirigh air bheagan eislein: *Mhoireach, Anna* / Cape Breton fiddler's welcome to the Shetland Isles: *Iron Horse* / Morag's No.2: *Iron Horse* / Lintie: *Iron Horse* / Bill Powrie: *Iron Horse* / Andy Renwicks ferret: *McManus, Tony* / Famous bridge: *McManus, Tony* / Not coming your way: *Drop The Box* / Dashing white sergeant: *Lorelei* / Bodachan cha phos mi: *Tannas* / Blackthorn stick: *Canterach* / Calliope house: *Canterach* / Archie Beag: *Canterach* / Boys of Ballymote: *Canterach* / Bennachie: *Old Blind Dogs* / When she cam' ben she bobbit: *Iron Horse* / Anvil: *Iron Horse* / Duncan Johnstone: *Iron Horse*
CD _______________ CDLDL 1255
Lochshore / Jan '97 / ADA / Direct / Duncans

NORTHERN SOUL - THE CLASSICS VOL.1
Joker: *Mylestones* / Our love is in the pocket: *Barnes, J.J.* / Groovin' at the Go-Go: *Four Larks* / I get the fever: *Creation* / Nine times out of ten: *Day, Muriel* / Little piece of leather: *Elbert, Donnie* / Oh my darlin': *Lee, Jackie* / Open the door to your heart: *Banks, Darrell* / Seven day lover: *Fountain, James* / You don't love me: *Epitome Of Sound* / They'll never know why: *Chavez, Freddie* / You can't mean it: *Chapter Five* / Blowing my mind to pieces: *Relf, Bobby* / My sugar baby: *Clarke, Connie* / Baby do the Philly dog: *Olympics* / Double cookin': *Checkerboard Squares* / Put your arms around me: *Sherrys* / If you ever walked out of my life: *Barnes, Dena* / Man like me: *James, Jimmy* / What is this: *Womack, Bobby* / I'm satisfied with you: *Furys* / Just lovin' you: *Andrews, Ruby*
CD _______________ GSCD 100
Goldmine / Jun '97 / Vital

NORTHERN SOUL DANCE PARTY
That beatin' rhythm: *Temple, Richard* / Goose pimples: *Scott, Shirley J.* / My sugar baby: *Clarke, Connie* / Double cookin': *Checkerboard Squares* / Do the philly dog: *Olympics* / Not me baby: *Silhouettes* / Yes I love you baby: *Dynamics* / Eddie's my name: *Holman, Eddie* / Countdown: *Tempos* / Going to a happening: *Neal, Tommy* / Temptation walk: *Lee, Jackie* / I'm satisfied with you: *Furys* / There's nothing else to say: *Incredibles* / My little girl: *Garrett, Bobby* / I got the fever: *Creation* / What's the matter baby: *Reynolds, L.J.* / Let's copp a groove: *Wells, Bobby* / Get on your knees: *Los Canarios* / I can't help myself: *Ross, Johnny* / Earthquake: *Lynn, Bobbi* / Our love is in the pocket: *Banks, Darren* / Blowing my mind to pieces: *Relf, Bobby*
CD _______________ GSCD 046
Goldmine / Jul '94 / Vital

NORTHERN SOUL FEVER VOL.1 (A Compilation Of 60 Legendary Soul Dancers/2CD Set)
Manifesto: *Case Of Tyme* / My sweet baby: *Puzzles* / No ifs, no ands, no buts: *Young, Mae* / Talking eyes: *Beatty, Pamela* / I don't want to hear it: *Exits* / Very strong on you: *Greer, Cortez* / Girl every guy should know: *Carrington, Sunny* / Bring me all your heartaches: *Beavers, Jackie* / Don't you need a boy like me: *Carlton, Carl* / Broken hearted lover: *Tojo* / I can hear you crying: *Hill, Eddie* / Try my love: *Toni & The Showmen* / In my life: *Carr, Linda* / This heart these hands: *Wells, Billy* / Just do the best you can: *Duke & Leonard* / Ain't that love enough: *Atkins, Larry* / Bad brought the good: *Turks* / Standing at a standstill: *Holmes, Sherlock* / Someone else's turn: *Clayton, Pat* / I ain't got nothin' but the blues: *Friendly People* / Moments: *Bronzettes* / Sugar baby: *Holland, Jimmy* / Real nice: *Barnes, Johnny* / Beware a stranger: *Jones, Bobby* / I've got to face: *Thunders, Johnny & The Heartbreakers* / Turn to me: *Chris Towns Unit* / Shield all around: *Holiday, Jimmy* / You better check yourself: *La'shell & The Shelletts* / I bear witness: *Apollo, Vince* / No time: *John & The Weirdest* / I got the fever: *Creation* / You better believe me: *Reeder, Esque* / Love can't be modernised: *Tripps* / Take me back again: *Volcanos* / Why wonder: *And The Echoes* / Lean on me: *Daye, Eddie* / Take back all these things: *Majesties* / Do what you wanna do: *Sindab, Paul* / Don't fight the feeling: *Newton, Bobby* / Airplane song: *Kerr, George* / Bok to Bach: *Father's Angels* / Oh yeah yeah yeah: *Carroll, Vivian* / Everybody's talkin': *Baker, Joan* / Pretty as a picture: *Dillard, Moses* / You got it: *Dealers* / Too much of a good thing: *Ambassadors* / Ain't gonna cry no more: *Charles, Dave* / Little things: *Moore, Misty* / If I only knew: *Mike & Ray* / Home town boy: *Williams, Sebastian* / Lonely lover: *McFarland, Jimmy* / One way lover: *Volumes* / Somebody help me: *Jenkins, Donald & The Delighters* / Let nobody love you: *Blakley, Virginia* / What do you think: *Lamarr, Chico* / If I could see you now: *Sunny & The Sunliners* / With these eyes: *Fabulous Peps* / I want to be free: *Admirations* / What can a man do: *Showstoppers*
CD Set _______________ GSCD 027
Goldmine / Jan '94 / Vital

NORTHERN SOUL FEVER VOL.2 (2CD Set)
Trouble: *Agents* / Deeper: *Chequers* / Midnight brew: *Carter, Melvin* / Hey girl you've changed: *Vondells* / No one loves you: *Hot Cinnamon* / You don't need help (Part 1): *Garvin, Rex* / Hide out: *Hideaways* / Misery: *Strogin, Henry* / I'm where it's at: *Jades* / Case of love: *Renfro Bros.* / Love bound: *Audio Arts Strings* / Anyway you want it: *Smith, Fred Orchestra* / Lonely eyes: *Elling, Melvin* / I can't stop you: *Performers* / Sugar pie honey: *Promatics* / Bounce: *Olympics* / Gotta get you back: *Mandolph, Bobby* / I'd best be going: *Vito & The Salutations* / Permanent vacation: *Sodd, Marion* / Seven days of loving: *Vanelli, Johnny* / All that's good: *Mills, Tico* / Send my baby back: *Hughes, Freddie* / (Oh oh oh) What a love this is: *King, Susan* / Actions speak louder than words: *Bounty, James* / You took my heart: *St. Clair, Kelly* / Crazy little things: *Soul-Jers* / Please don't go: *Splenders* / I'm coming apart at the seams: *Kittens Three* / Times gone by: *Music Track* / You'll have to wait: *Baby Sitters* / Those good times: *Nicky C* / Keep loving me like you do: *Hargreaves, Silky* / Soulful jerk: *Rumblers* / It was true: *Big Don's Rebellion* / I can take care of myself: *Spyders* / Dark at the top of my head: *Paris, Fred* / Stop along the way: *Taylor, Robby* / Elevator man: *Nelson, Roy* / Your love keeps drawing me closer: *Chandlers* / Baby you've got it: *Dell, Frank* / I didn't know how to: *Constellations* / I must love you: *Wilson, Timothy* / I'm tempted: *Hollis, Sandy* / Love from the Far East: *Master Four* / Look in the mirror: *Vondors* / I'll be there: *Collection & The Civics* / Beware, beware: *Compliments* / Stop (Don't give up your loving): *Two Fellows* / I'm losing you: *New People* / Don't leave me this way: *Dynamites* / Light drivers: *Operator* / Love you from the bottom of my heart: *Buckner Brothers* / So what: *Carlton, Carl* / If you don't need me: *Tyrone Wonder Boy* / Your money - my love: *Sam & Kitty* / (She keeps) Driving me out of my mind: *Mighty Lovers* / Open the door to your heart: *Burdick, Doni* / Ain't gonna do you no harm: *New Wanderers* / Don't give me love: *Beery, Dorothy* / Some good in everything bad: *Fabulous Apollos*
CD Set _______________ GSCD 043
Goldmine / Aug '94 / Vital

NORTHERN SOUL FEVER VOL.3 (Over 2 Hours Of Legendary Soul Dancers/2CD Set)
I'll do a little more: *Olympics* / (All you need is your) Good lovin': *Pat & The Blenders* / Got to have peace of mind: *Peters, Preston* / Motown: *Cammotions* / I love only you: *Henry, Edd* / We like girls: *Scott Bros.* / Connie: *Servicemen* / Gotta wipe away the teardrops: *Jackson, Ollie* / Poor unfortunate me (I ain't got nobody): *Barnes, J.J.* / What should I do: *Manhattans* / Just a dream: *Imperial Wonders* / Your love: *Harrell, Vernon* / My baby changes like the weather: *Callender, Bobby* / Here comes those heartaches: *Tripps* / Big search is on: *Lynn, Dolores* / Move it baby: *Singin' Sam* / It ain't no secret: *Dynamic Heartbeats* / Some day some way: *Traits* / Charge: *T-K-O-S* / I want the good life: *Little David* / Misunderstood: *Kennedy, Joyce* / Easily misled: *Remarkables* / Old days: *Furys* / Going going gone: *Black, Cody* / I'm gonna get even with you: *Little Ben & The Cheers* / I ain't playing baby: *Taurus & Leo* / Let me render my service: *New Wanderers* / We go together: *Olympics* / Just because of you: *Rocky Roberts & The Airedales* / Number one fool: *Fabulous Emotions* / You really made it good: *Karim, Ty* / My kind of girl: *Prophets* / I'm guilty: *Dupree, Leontine* / I'm in love with your daughter: *Enchantments* / Miss Heartbreaker: *Ascots* / We go together, yes we do: *Hammond, Little Walter* / I just want to satisfy: *Spencer, Bobby* / Joey: *Petite, Jo Jo* / Sad, sad memories: *Tempos* / Lonely baby: *Moonlighters* / Blow me a kiss: *Anthony, Wayne* / Ain't gonna worry about you: *Tinley, George* / How soon: *Wonderettes* / Jerk it with soul: *Walker, Willie* / How good can it get: *Lyle, Jay* / Under the moon: *Wonder, Rufus* / Penguin breakdown: *Reynolds, L.J.* / Open arms - closed heart: *Welsh, Janie* / If I had my way: *Keyes, Troy* / Give me your love: *Jones, A.C.* / Don't you leave me baby: *Founders* / Giving my love to you: *Apis, Fred* / That's the way love goes: *Disciples Of Soul* / No one else can take your place: *Inspirations*
CD Set _______________ GSCD 048
Goldmine / Nov '94 / Vital

NORTHERN SOUL FEVER VOL.4 (2CD Set)
Destined to become a loser: *Ellingtons* / Don't forget to remember: *Greater Experience* / I'm satisfied just loving you: *Bland, Bobbie Jean* / I've got to face it: *Heartbreaker* / I wanna be loved to death: *Moore, Bernnie* / Auction on love: *Bounty, James* / Before 2001: *Wood, Rufus* / Everybody's happy but me: *Williams, Cheryl* / Front page love: *Bee Gee Stans* / Good sweet loving: *Brown, Roy* / Don't turn away: *McDougall, Willy* / Stay on the case: *Innovations* / New babe: *Invictus* / Other side: *Five Of A Kind* / Darling I love you: *Superiors* / I know what to do to satisfy you: *Robert, Roy* / That's not half bad: *Woodbury, Gene* / On a hot summer day in the big city: *King, Ricardo* / Sitting in my class: *McNier, Ronnie* / How can I forget you: *Dee, Joey & The Starlighters* / Especially for you baby: *Four Puzzles* / Don't put our the fire: *Birchett, Tony* / Why did you call: *Wood, Eddie* / Nobody loves me: *Moore, Joe* / I gotta have you: *Brown, Bobby* / You got to steal it: *Flairs* / I can't get away: *Garett, Bobby* / We've been together too long: *Antony, El* / Chinatown: *Knight, Victor* / I need help: *Detroit Land Apples* / I love you just the same: *Winfield, Parker* / Too much for me baby: *Florence, Tina* / Can we talk: *Allen, C* / Give me love: *Tootsie Love* / Nervous breakdown: *Forte, Ronnie* / Love will conquer all: *Two Plus Two* / I can feel him slipping away: *Brown, Tobbie* / It's written all over my face: *Holliday, Marva* / Together forever: *Pardell, Pat & The Powerdrills* / Life goes on: *Fabulous Sownbeats* / False arm: *Body Motions* / Sensitive mind: *General Assembly* / I can't fight it: *Sain, Lee* / Please come back: *First Grade* / Give it back: *Tripps* / (I lost love in the) Big city: *Daniels* / How do you like it: *Sheppards* / I can't turn my back: *Apollo, Vince* / Little bit of soul: *Gerry & Paul & The Soul Emmissaries* / You've got a good thing going: *King, Jeanie* / Something about you: *Spoilers* / Peace of mind: *Spydels* / I ain't got nothin' but the blues: *Friendly People* / Watch out Mr Lonely: *Vaughn, Shirley* / First time: *Wills, Viola* / Lucky we: *Sugar & Spice* / My lover: *Sugar & Sweet* / Set me free: *Performers* / Love and laughter: *Anderson, Sonny & Prince Conley*
CD Set _______________ GSCD 074
Goldmine / May '95 / Vital

NORTHERN SOUL FLOORSHAKERS (20 Anthems & Rarities From The RCA Vaults)
Hold to my baby: *Cavaliers* / I can't change: *Chandler, Lorraine* / Since I found my baby: *Metros* / Blowing up my mind: *Exciters* / I need your love: *Dynamics* / Tears and misery: *Till, Sonny* / What's that on your finger: *Kendricks, Willie* / Some things are better left unsaid: *Lester, Ketty* / Honest to goodness: *Ward, Herb* / Could it be you: *Scott, Sharon* / Lucky to be loved by you: *Hutch, Willie* / I don't mind: *Cooke, Carolyn* / It didn't take much (for me to fall in love): *Wiggins, Percy* / I've gotta know right now: *Valentine, Rose* / Born a loser: *Ray, Don* / Don't pity me: *Lynne, Sue* / You shook me up: *Hamilton, Roy* / Coz it's you girl: *Walsh, James Gypsy Band* / Moonlight, music and you: *Greene, Laura* / Gotta get myself together: *Carter, Kenny*
CD _______________ MCCD 236
Music Club / Apr '96 / Disc / THE

NORTHERN SOUL GOLDEN MEMORIES VOL.1 (28 Legendary Northern Soul Dancers)
You're everything: *Lee, Jackie* / (Countdown) Here I come: *Tempos* / You don't love me: *Epitome Of Sound* / Let her go: *Smith, Otis* / Gotta draw this line: *Fletcher, Darrow* / Gotta find a way: *Linsey, Teresa* / Quick change artist: *Soul Twins* / She's puttin' you on: *United 4* / I'm satisfied with you: *Furys* / They're talking about me: *Bragg, Johnny* / Let's copp a groove: *Wells, Bobby* / They'll never know why: *Chavez, Freddie* / Sweet sherry: *Barnes, J.J.* / Put your arms around me: *Sherrys* / I need a helping hand: *Servicemen* / You won't say nothing: *Lewis, Tamala* / Since you left: *Inticers* / Head and shoulders: *Young, Patti* / Never too young (To fall in love): *Modern Redcaps* / Heartbroken memories: *Ferguson, Sheila* / (Come on and be my) Sweet darlin': *Clarke, Jimmy 'Soul'* / I never knew: *Foster, Eddie* / Women's liberation: *Topics* / This time it's love: *Tymes* / You don't mean me no good: *Jellybeans* / New York in the dark: *Ad Libs* / Lady love: *Vontastics*
CD _______________ GSCD 062
Goldmine / Aug '95 / Vital

NORTHERN SOUL OF CHICAGO VOL.1, THE
When I'm with my baby: *Magnetics* / Stubborn heart: *Mosley, Earnest* / In other words: *Fascinators* / Coming back girl: *COD's* / No right to cry: *Galore, Mamie* / GI Joe we love you: *Fantasions* / Ain't no good: *Copney, Bobby* / You can't get away: *McCall, Johnny* / You've changed my whole life: *Farren, Charles* / It's mighty nice to know you: *Wood, Bobby 'Guitar'* / Your wish is my command: *Inspirations* / Have your fun: *Topics* / Lost in a city: *Majors* / She'll come back: *Britt, Mel* / Love bandit: *Collins, Barnabus & Kenya* / What you gonna do now: *Collins, Lashdown* / Two of a kind: *Flemons, Wade* / I'm gonna love you: *Age Of Bronze* / Don't say you love me until you do: *Maxwell, Holly* / I'm satisfied: *Gloria & The T-Arias* / Cheaper than one: *Hunt, Geraldine* / Heart of love: *Ventures* / Go go gorilla: *Ideals* / Got to be your lover: *Profiles* / So much love: *Taylor, Robert* / Love now pay later: *Williams, Lee Shot* / Is this really love: *Gardiner, Don*
CD _______________ GSCD 038
Goldmine / May '94 / Vital

NORTHERN SOUL OF CHICAGO VOL.2, THE
Count the days: *Magnetics* / I can't please you: *Robins, Jimmy* / Jeanette: *Flemons, Wade* / Pitfall: *Savoy, Ronnie* / Never let me go: *Monique* / I really love you: *Burns, Jimmy* / Don't know what love is: *Johnson, Syl* / Best is yet to come: *Invaders* / Running out of years: *Gloria & The T-Arias* / Urge keeps coming: *Armstead, Jo* / Thank the Lord for love: *Living Color* / Heaven is in

your arms: *Admirations* / Every hurt makes you stronger: *Bernard, Chuck* / In paradise: *Vestel, Lenny* / Fight for love: *Drake/Ensolids* / Wait a minute: *Kittens* / Lovin' on borrowed time: *Orsi, Phil* / One day girl: *Currington, Harold* / I'm running a losing race: *Davies, Tyrone* / Don't hurt me no more: *Woods, Wendy* / Please Mr. DJ: *King, Eddie* / Change is gonna come: *Buckner Brothers* / Ain't gonna let me down: *Gardner, Don* / Lonely was I: *Conquistadors* / Sweet and lovely: *Del-Tours*
CD GSCD 071
Goldmine / Feb '96 / Vital

NORTHERN SOUL OF LA VOL.1, THE (A Collection Of Rare West Coast 1960's Soul)
Sweet magic: *Servicemen* / Wonders of love: *Soul Gents* / You should have told me: *New Yorkers* / Under your spell: *Paramounts* / This is the way I feel: *Four Tempos* / There's that mountain: *Trips* / Do this for me: *Emotions* / It was wrong: *Shades Of Jade* / Anything for you: *Furys* / Jealous of you: *Mystics* / Don't let love get you down: *Phonetics* / You're good enough for me: *Versatiles* / (Down in) East LA: *Angelenos* / You'll never make the grade: *Sun Lovers* / Sad, sad memories: *Tempos* / No one else can take your place: *Inspirations* / (I love her so much) it hurts me: *Majestics* / Hey hey girls: *Vines* / Is the feeling still there: *Remarkables* / Save your love: *Soul Patrol* / Girl, I love you: *Sinceres* / Just a little: *Prominents* / Love is a hurting game: *Four Sights* / My poor heart: *Sun Lovers* / Beginning of the end: *Young Hearts*
CD GSCD 032
Goldmine / Mar '94 / Vital

NORTHERN SOUL OF LA VOL.2, THE
I thought you were: *Natural Four* / Rosie Brooks: *Moanin* / Crook his little finger: *Heyward, Ann* / They didn't know: *Goodnight, Terri* / Quicksand: *Osbourne, Kell* / You're welcome: *Jackson, June* / I'm a bashful guy: *Groovers* / Shy guy: *Mac, Bobby* / Closer together: *Ster, Eddie* / My faith: *Dockery, James* / Ain't that love enough: *Karim, Ty* / Ain't that right: *Oldfield, Bruce* / Sleepless nights: *Paris* / Lost: *Darlettes* / Love shop: *Tate* / Try my love: *Dodds, Troy* / I'm still young: *Summers, Johnny* / Doctor of love: *Abram, J.D.* / Pyramid: *Soul Brother Inc.* / Ooh what you're doing: *Capitals* / I can't treat her bad: *Those Two* / Specially when: *Rumbold, Edwick* / To whom it may concern: *Sands, Lola* / Faith, hope and trust: *Ross, Faye* / Girl you're so fine: *Angelle, Bobby* / Strain: *Little Stanley* / Ain't gonna: *Watson, Johnny 'Guitar'*
CD GSCD 039
Goldmine / Jun '94 / Vital

NORTHERN SOUL OF SWAN, THE
And in return: *Ferguson, Sheila* / Are you satisfied: *Ferguson, Sheila* / Don't leave me lover: *Ferguson, Sheila* / Walking alone: *Valentino, Mark* / Put yourself in my place: *Mortimor, Azie* / Everybody crossfire: *Stevens, Sammy* / Watch your step: *Stevens, Sammy* / It will be done: *Carlton, Eddie* / Misery: *Carlton, Eddie* / I will love you: *Barrnet, Richie* / Driving me mad: *Three Degrees* / Spy: *Guys From Uncle* / Never too young: *Modern Redcaps* / Empty world: *Modern Redcaps* / No good: *Anthony, Richard* / Gonna find the right boy: *Sio, Audrey* / In love: *Galla, Tony* / I'm gonna get you: *Harris, Leroy* / Can't leave without you: *Jay Walkers* / Your kinda love: *Renne, Betty* / You're everything: *Showmen* / In paradise: *Showmen* / Take it baby: *Showmen* / Hey sah-lo ney: *Lane, Mickey Lee* / Put that woman down: *Leach, John*
CD GSCD 063
Goldmine / Oct '95 / Vital

NORTHERN SOUL SATISFACTION
Let's talk it over: *Wiggins, Spencer* / Something's bad: *Nomads* / Age of the wolf: *Coleman, Susan* / These things will keep me lovin' you: *Blue Sharks* / I'm gone: *Parker, Eddie* / Stoney face: *Barbara & The Castles* / He's alright with me: *Keyman Brass* / I don't wanna get away from your love: *Daniels, Yvonne* / My first lonely night: *Akens, Jewel* / King for a day: *Ames, Stuart* / I can't wait to see my baby's face: *Monticellos* / Iceman: *Watkins, Bill* / I'll give that to you: *Wynns, Sandy* / I'm gonna hurt you: *Lost Soul Band* / If this is love: *Spencer, Eddie* / Angelina, oh Angelina: *Ames, Stuart* / Better: *Winters, Ruby* / Could it be: *Farrow, Mikki* / Tough girl: *Arnell, Billy* / That's the way: *Q* / He's a flirt: *Sequins* / Who am I (you ought to know): *Barnes, Dena* / Mr. Loser: *Blackwell, George* / Don't hold back: *Monticellos* / Satisfy my baby: *Sweets* / Lucky day: *Coff, Theo Invasion* / You're love is too strong: *Coleman, Donna* / Something about my baby: *Sweets* / Crying heart: *Gilbert, Carl* / That's what I want to know: *Carr, James*
CD GSCD 088
Goldmine / Mar '96 / Vital

NORTHERN SOUL SPECTRUM (From Sweet Exuberance To Empty Despair)
What shall I do: *Frankie & The Classicals* / You're the love of my life: *Jones, Brenda Lee* / Can't stop loving the boy: *Carolines* / Lonely girl: *Fox, Annabelle* / Prove it: *Wheeler, Mary* / Sweet thing: *Newbag, Johnny* / I've got to find her (and tell her): *Williams, Scotty* / Wrapped around your finger: *Poets* / Cover girl: *Spencer, Carl* / You ain't wrapped too tight: *Anthony, Wayne* / Joker: *Elliot, Shawn* / Let me down easy: *Lavette, Bettye* / Hurt is just beginning: *Love, Mary* / Love won't wear off (as the years wear on): *Bailey, J.R.* / If you and I had never met: *Magic Night* / Somebody's lying on love: *Val & Nick* / Don't fight it baby: *Humes, Anita* / Change my darkness into light: *Flirtations* / To the bitter end: *Hill, Bobby* / I'm losing you: *Ballard, Kenny & The Fabulous Soul Brothers* / Where I'm gonna find her: *Lloyd, Mark* / Down by the ocean: *Sands, George & Sonny* / And heaven was here: *Irwin, Big Dee* / I don't love you no more baby: *Prophets* / Teardrops are falling: *Little Natalie & Henry/The Gifts* / Get on your knees: *Los Canarios* / Let me go: *Big Maybelle* / You better go: *Martin, Derek*
CD CDKEND 144
Kent / Apr '97 / Pinnacle

NORTHERN SOUL SURVIVORS (30 Northern Soul Classics From Wigan & Beyond)
Hold on help is on the way: *Davis, G. & R. Tyler* / Being without you: *Williams, Maurice* / Come on train: *Thomas, Don* / Hung up on your love: *Montclairs* / You hit me like TNT: *Jones, Linda* / It's not like you: *Marcelle, Lydia* / Tear stained face: *Varner, Don* / Mr. Big Shot: *Chandler, Gene* / I hurt on the other side: *Barnes, Sidney* / Stop and get a hold of yourself: *Knight, Gladys* / Empty arms, bitter tears: *Taylor, Gerri* / Lonely for you baby: *Dees, Sam* / I've got to have your love: *Evans, Mill* / My hang up is you: *Skull Snaps* / I'd think it over: *Fletcher, Sam* / I've got you on my mind again: *Young, Billy Joe* / That's my girl: *Clark, Dee* / That other place: *Flemons, Wade* / Please don't go: *Tee, Willie* / Night the angels died: *Dynamite, Johnny* / You're gonna need me: *Ford, Ted* / Momma's gone: *Blair, Little Johnny* / Toast to the lady: *Wilson, Eddie* / You'll always be in style: *Barnes, Sidney* / Make up your mind: *Strong, Barrett* / It's a weakness: *Murphy, Joe* / Screamin' and shoutin': *Fabulettes* / I'll love you always: *Rivingtons* / One bodillion years: *Little Ritchie* / What difference does it make: *Sheppard, Kenny*
CD GSCD 089
Goldmine / Feb '97 / Vital

NORTHERN SOUL TIME (2CD Set)
This man in love: *New Wanderers* / I'm getting tired: *Carlettes* / Lover: *Delites* / That's what I want: *McGowan, Syng* / I know I'm in love with you: *Byrd, George Duke* / Nevertheless: *Andrews, Lee* / She said goodbye: *Hambric, Billy* / I can't stand to lose you: *Chandler, E.J.* / Elijah rockin' with soul: *Jacobs, Hank* / Lighten up baby: *Karim, Ty* / He's a flirt: *Sequins* / You got me in the plam of your hands: *Richardson, Donald Lee* / I need your love: *Chaumonts* / Oo we let it be me babe: *Evans, Karl* / Black power: *Coit, James* / Easy baby: *Adventures* / Just a little while: *Jackson, Ollie* / I'm gonna love you: *Hamilton, Edward* / Build your house on a strong foundation: *Gwen & Ray* / Job opening: *Del-Larks* / What good am I without you: *Champion, Mickey* / R 'n' B time: *Jones, E. Rodney* / Airplay song: *Jenkins, Norma & The Dolls* / Oo we let it be me babe: *Lewis, Louise* / My terms: *Ferguson, Helena* / Where can my babe be: *Martels* / We must be doing something right: *Moody, Joan* / You got to love your babe: *Millionaires* / Do what you gotta do: *Contenders* / Baby I dig you: *Anderson, Gene* / Ever again: *Woodbury, Gene* / Is it all gone: *Magicians* / We got a love that's out of sight: *Spencer* / I can't change: *Baker, Yvonne* / Poor unfortunate me: *Taylor, Gloria* / I wouldn't come back: *Mask Man & the Agents* / Come on and live: *Fabulous Jades* / Walkin' by: *Boss 4* / We got to keep on: *Casanova Two* / Dial L for lonely: *Wilson, Madeline* / Coalined baby: *Love, Dave* / I was born to love you: *Hunter, Herbert* / My heart is calling you: *Manificents* / Good girl: *Stokes, Patti* / I can't give up on losing you: *Remarkables* / Lies: *Owens, Gwen* / Can't get over these memories: *John & The Weirdest* / He's that way sometimes: *Wells, Bobby* / Lovin' you baby: *Startones* / Fascinating girl: *Lemons, George* / Come go with me: *Para-Monts* / Just as much: *Peterson, Kris* / You better think it over: *Du-Shons* / Yes I love you baby: *Dynamics* / Ain't nobody's business if I do: *Marbray, Ernie* / Just lovin' you: *Andrews, Ruby* / I have faith in you: *Burdick, Doni* / You're on my mind: *Durane, Paula* / Heartbreakin' time: *Little John* / I gotta good thing going: *Executive 4*
CD Set GSCD 077
Goldmine / Sep '95 / Vital

NORTHERN SOUL'S DIAMONDS AND PEARLS
I know the meaning: *St. John, Rose & The Wonderettes* / Please keep away from me: *Parker, Elbie* / It's not the same: *Little Anthony* / Cold wave: *Daisies* / Kissin' her and crying for you: *Checkmates* / I know the inside story: *Chubby & The Turnpikes* / Push a little harder: *Enjoyables* / Love and desire: *Holloway, Patrice* / Stolen hours: *Holloway, Patrice* / Same old way: *Williams, Scott* / Hey girl do you love me: *Wilson, Timothy* / Look at me look at me: *Greene, Vernon* / He always comes back to me: *King, Clydie* / My love grows deeper: *King, Clydie* / Yes you did: *Hitson, Herman* / 60 Minutes of your love: *Banks, Homer* / I'm losing you: *Ballard, Kenny* / Fine young girl: *Andrews, Ernie* / Can't chance a breakup: *Turner, Ike & Tina* / Mr. Soul Satisfaction: *Willis, Timmy* / Word without sunshine: *Philips, Saundra* / Love in my heart: *Entertainers* / What can I do: *Prophet, Billy* / She's called a woman: *Magnificent 7* / To the bitter end: *Hill, Bobby*
CD GSCD 076
Goldmine / May '96 / Vital

NORTHUMBRIAN SMALL PIPES
Keel row: *Clough, Tom* / Westering home: *Blackett-Ord, Diana* / Whittingham Green Lane/Ward's Brae: *Hepple, John* / Wild hills o'wannie: *Pigg, Billy* / King's hall/John of Carrick: *High Level Ranters* / Gypsy's lullaby/The Hawk/Memories/Coates Hall: *Pigg, Billy* / Oh dear, what can the matter be: *Atkinson, George* / Sir Sidney Smith's march: *Hutton, Joe* / Lovat scouts/Roxborough Castle/Bonny North Tyne/Alston flowe: *Hutton, Joe* / Sunderland lasses/Lads of Alnwick: *Cut & Dry Band* / Fenwick of Bywell: *High Level Ranters* / Barrington hornpipe/Rowley Burn: *Hutton, Joe* / Proudlock's hornpipe: *High Level Ranters* / Ho'ley ha'penny/Elsie Marley: *Clough, Tom* / John Fenwick's the flower among them: *Cut & Dry Band* / Salmon tails up the water/Herd on the hill/Sweet Hesleyside: *Caisley, Colin & Forster Charlton* / Coilsfield House/ Thom's march: *High Level Ranters* / Skye crofters/The Swallow's tail: *Pigg, Billy* / My laddie sits o'er late up/Shew's the way to Wallington: *Cut & Dry Band* / Surprise: *High Level Ranters* / Bonny Woodside/Coffee Bridge: *Cut & Dry Band* / Dr. Whittaker's hornpipe/Nancy: *Cut & Dry Band* / Hexham quadrille/Kielder fells: *High Level Ranters*
CD TSCD 487
Topic / Nov '96 / ADA / CM / Direct

NORWEGIAN BRASS BAND CHAMPIONSHIPS 1996
Energy / Partita / Music for the common man / Harmony festival / Variations on an enigma
CD DOYCD 051
Doyen / Jul '96 / Conifer/BMG

NORWEGIAN FOLK MUSIC VOL.1-10 (10CD Set)
CD Set GR 4099CD
Grappa / Jul '95 / ADA

NOT JUST RAGGA
So real: *Sanchez* / Thinking about you: *McLean, John* / Spare me: *Wayne Wonder* / Rebel woman: *Jones, Vivian* / Do you remember # 2: *Davis, Janet-Lee* / Guess I know the reason why: *Boom, Barry* / Perfect lady: *Hunningale, Peter* / Jungle bungle: *Starkey Banton* / Run way Mr. Tickle: *General Dog* / Beaten: *Nico Junior* / Hyper: *Sweetie Irie* / One more request: *Papa San* / Gone down inna mi culture: *General Levy* / Dedicated to His Majesty: *Jones, Vivian & Nico Junior*
CD FADCD 032
Fashion / Jan '96 / Jet Star / SRD

NOT THE SINGER BUT
CD MR 012CD
Munster / Apr '92 / Cargo / Greyhound / Plastic Head

NOTHIN' BUT THE BLUES (2CD Set)
CD Set DEMPCD 006
Emporio / Mar '96 / Disc

NOTHIN' BUT THE BLUES (36 Blues Standards/2CD Set)
Hoochie coochie man: *Waters, Muddy* / When my first wife left me: *Hooker, John Lee* / Shake it for me: *Howlin' Wolf* / Only fools have fun: *Memphis Slim* / Don't wake me: *Hopkins, Lightnin'* / You're something else: *Reed, Jimmy* / Lightnin's boogie: *Hopkins, Lightnin'* / Oh baby: *Lightnin' Slim* / Cold and lonesome: *Reed, Jimmy* / Got my mojo working: *Waters, Muddy* / No shoes: *Hooker, John Lee* / Gamblers blues: *Memphis Slim* / Little rain: *Reed, Jimmy* / Bad luck blues: *Lightnin' Slim* / Goin' back home: *Hopkins, Lightnin'* / Howlin' for my darlin': *Howlin' Wolf* / I'm so excited: *Hooker, John Lee* / Baby please don't go: *Waters, Muddy* / I'm nervous: *Reed, Jimmy* / Forty years or more: *Memphis Slim* / Easy on your heels: *Hopkins, Lightnin'* / Forty four: *Howlin' Wolf* / Soon forgotten: *Waters, Muddy* / Rooster blues: *Lightnin' Slim* / I'm goin' upstairs: *Hooker, John Lee* / Strange strange feeling: *Memphis Slim* / Screamin' and cryin': *Waters, Muddy* / Caress my baby: *Reed, Jimmy* / Going down slow: *Howlin' Wolf* / Evil hearted woman: *Hopkins, Lightnin'* / Gone again: *Memphis Slim* / Thelma: *Hooker, John Lee* / Hoodoo blues: *Lightnin' Slim* / Dusty road: *Hooker, John Lee* / Don't think because you're pretty: *Hopkins, Lightnin'* / Howlin' Wolf: *Waters, Muddy*
CD Set 330032
Hallmark / Jul '96 / Carlton

NOTHING BUT LOVE SONGS VOL.2
CD PILCD 206
Pioneer / Dec '94 / Jet Star

NOTHING SHORT OF TOTAL WAR
Come and smash me said the boy with the magic penis: *Sonic Youth* / Bugged: *Head Of David* / Fire in Philly: *Ut* / He's on fire: *Sonic Youth* / Kerosene: *Big Black* / Magic wand: *Sonic Youth* / Dutch courage: *Rapeman* / Bulbs of passion: *Ranaldo, Lee* / Scratchy heart: *Ciccone Youth* / Evangelist: *Ut* / Snake domain: *Head Of David* / He's a whore: *Big Black* / Devil's jukebox: *Big Stick* / 108: *Head Of David* / Sheikh: *AC Temple* / Just got payed today: *Rapeman* / Throne of blood: *Band Of Susans* / Little Hitlers: *Arsenal* / Jimi: *Butthole Surfers*
CD BFFP 013CD
Blast First / Mar '89 / RTM/Disc

NOTHING TO LOSE
CD TBCD 1169
Tommy Boy / Jul '97 / RTM/Disc

NOTHING'S GONNA STOP US NOW
CD Set NSCD 015
Newsound / Feb '95 / THE

NOVEDADES DE CHILE
Subete a la vereda / Estoy que me muero / Tango / Maquinarias / Para el camino / Se nos pierde la mirada / Comparsa de olvidada tierra / Nuctal lacta / El viejo truco / El mensajero del amor / Corazones partidos / La semilla / Senoritas y caballeros / Refka / Colores de chiloe
CD 68934
Tropical / Jul '97 / Discovery

NOW AND IN TIME TO BE (A Musical Celebration Of The Works Of W.B.Yeats)
CD GRACD 219
Grapevine / Jan '97 / Grapevine/PolyGram

NOW THAT'S WHAT I CALL MUSIC 1996 (2CD Set)
CD Set CDNOW 1996
EMI / Oct '96 / EMI

NOW THAT'S WHAT I CALL MUSIC VOL.35 (2CD Set)
Say you'll be there: *Spice Girls* / Fastlove: *Michael, George* / Flava: *Andre, Peter* / If you ever: *East 17 & Gabrielle* / Breakfast at Tiffany's: *Deep Blue Something* / Se a vide e: *Pet Shop Boys* / You're gorgeous: *Baby Bird* / Rotterdam: *Beautiful South* / If you're thinking of me: *Dodgy* / Don't dream it's over: *Crowded House* / Marblehead Johnson: *Bluetones* / River boat song: *Ocean Colour Scene* / If it makes you happy: *Crow, Sheryl* / Milk: *Garbage* / Woman: *Cherry, Neneh* / Beautiful ones: *Suede* / Something changed: *Pulp* / Flying: *Cast* / Always breaking my heart: *Carlisle, Belinda* / Escaping: *Carroll, Dina* / Words: *Boyzone* / Someday: *Eternal* / I'll fall in love: *Backstreet Boys* / Love 2 love: *Damage* / Oh what a night: *Clock* / Undivided love: *Louise* / When I fall in love: *Ant & Dec* / Don't make me wait: *911* / My love is for real: *Strike* / Insomnia: *Faithless* / Seven days and one week: *BBE* / I'm alive: *Stretch n' Vern* / Stamp: *Healy, Jeremy & Amos* / Follow the rules: *Livin' Joy* / Jump to my beat: *Wildchild* / Pearl's girl: *Underworld* / Neighbourhood: *Space* / Possibly maybe: *Bjork* / Chasing rainbows: *Shed Seven*
CD Set CDNOW 35
EMI / Nov '96 / EMI

NOW THAT'S WHAT I CALL MUSIC VOL.36 (2CD Set)
Mama: *Spice Girls* / Say what you want: *Texas* / Alone: *Bee Gees* / Don't marry her: *Beautiful South* / Don't speak: *No Doubt* / Your woman: *White Town* / Remember me: *Blueboy* / Virtual insanity: *Jamiroquai* / One and one: *Miles, Robert & Maria Naylor* / Spinning the wheel: *Michael, George* / Horny: *Morrison, Mark* / Natural: *Andre, Peter* / Love guaranteed: *Damaged* / Don't you love me: *Eternal* / Walk on by: *Gabrielle* / I can make you feel good: *Kavana* / Hey child: *East 17* / Different beat: *Boyzone* / Anywhere for you: *Backstreet Boys* / Day we find love: *911* / Discotheque: *U2* / Breathe: *Prodigy* / Block rockin' beats: *Chemical Brothers* / Nancy boy: *Placebo* / What do you want from me: *Monaco* / Everyday is a winding road: *Crow, Sheryl* / Beetlebum: *Blur* / She's a star: *James* / Wide open space: *Mansun* / Free me: *Cast* / Dark clouds: *Space* / Waterloo sunset: *Dennis, Cathy* / Everybody knows (except you): *Divine Comedy* / Indestructable: *Alisha's Attic* / Shout: *Ant & Dec* / You got the love: *Source & Candi Staton* / Encore en fois: *Sash* / Bellissima: *DJ Quicksilver* / Flash: *BBE* / Passion: *Amen UK*
CD Set CDNOW 36
EMI / Mar '97 / EMI

NOW THAT'S WHAT I CALL MUSIC VOL.37 (2CD Set)
MMMbop: *Hanson* / I wanna be the only one: *Eternal & Bebe Winans* / Lovefool: *Cardigans* / Just a girl: *No Doubt* / Ecuador: *Sash & Rodriguez* / Where do you go: *No Mercy* / Who do you think you are: *Spice Girls* / Free: *Ultranate* / Closer than close: *Gaines, Rosie* / Star people: *Michael, George* / Don't let go love: *En Vogue* / You might need somebody: *Ama, Shola* / C U when you get there: *Coolio & 40 Thevz* / Smokin' me out: *Warren G & Ron Isley* / Don't leave me: *Blackstreet* / I belive I can fly: *R Kelly* / Wonderful tonight: *Damage* / Journey: *911* / Isn't it a wonder: *Boyzone* / Hey D-J: *N-Tyce* / I'll be: *Brown, Foxy & Jay*

Z / If I never see you again: *Wet Wet Wet* / Staring at the sun: *U2* / Bittersweet Symphony: *Verve* / Love is the law: *Seahorses* / 100 mile high city: *Ocean Colour Scene* / Old before I die: *Williams, Robbie* / Guiding star: *Cast* / Young boy: *McCartney, Paul* / Change would do you good: *Crow, Sheryl* / Paranoid android: *Radiohead* / Halo: *Texas* / Sun hits the sky: *Supergrass* / Waltzing along: *James* / On your own: *Blur* / Scooby snacks: *Fun Lovin' Criminals* / Saint: *Orbital* / Nightmare: *Brainbug* / Ain't nobody: *Course* / Something's going on: *Terry, Todd & Martha Wash/Jocelyn Brown* / Give me love: *Diddy*
CD Set ______ **CDNOW 37**
EMI / Jul '97 / EMI

NOW THIS IS REGGAE
CD ______ **MPV 5525**
Movieplay / Oct '92 / Target/BMG

NOWSOUNDS TOP 10 TEXAS
CD ______ **COLCD 0511**
Collectables / Jun '97 / Greyhound

NU BEATS 2000
CD ______ **RRCD 001**
Rashaan / Jul '97 / Essential/BMG

NU CLASSIC SOUL (15 Smokin' Tunes From The Cream Of The Nu Sugar Set)
Brown sugar: *D'Angelo* / Carefree: *Paris, Mica* / Loving 'u' is ah-ight: *Portrait* / In the spirit: *Nesby, Ann* / Do I qualify: *Hall, Lynden David* / Tell me: *Groove Theory* / Greater love: *Nu Colours* / Stillness in time: *Jamiroquai* / If only: *Johnson, Paul* / Black butterfly: *Sounds Of Blackness* / Till the cops come knockin': *Maxwell* / Feel the need: *G Nation & Rosia Ania* / Blacka da berry: *Hunter, Alfonzo* / Damn: *Taylor, Lewis* / Waiting: *D-Influence* / Good ole fashioned love: *Lo Key*
CD ______ **CTCD 57**
Cooltempo / Feb '97 / EMI

NU ENERGY
Feeling: *Tin Tin Out & Sweet Tee* / Infantaci: *Baby Doc & The Dentist* / Cosmonautica: *Virtuolisimo* / First rebirth (Hiroshima nu-energy reconstruction): *Jones & Stephenson* / Casablanca: *Dual Mount* / Energy frenzy: *OCP* / Three minute warning: *Yum Yum* / Catalan rising: *Baby Doc & The Dentist* / For your love: *Elevator* / Mantra to the buddha (Higher state): *Hyperspace* / Dragnet (action hero): *Hiroshima*
CD ______ **CDTOT 19**
Jumpin' & Pumpin' / Oct '94 / 3mv/Sony / Mo's Music Machine

NU GROOVE COMPILATION
CD ______ **NGVCD 1**
Network / Apr '91 / 3mv/Sony / Pinnacle

NU SCHOOL - DANCE MUSIC OF THE CARRIBEAN
CD ______ **8289312**
London / Aug '97 / PolyGram

NU SKOOL FLAVA
Flexiwidatel: *Elementz Of Noise* / This style: *Shy FX* / Mid town method level 2: *DJ Trace* / Stick up: *Elementz Of Noise* / Mass hysteria: *Shapeshifter* / Hit the deck: *Shapeshifter* / Let me be: *L-Double* / Amber: *T-Power* / Way it goes down: *DJ Kane* / Funkindem up: *Shy FX* / Difference: *Skyscraper*
CD ______ **SOURCD 006**
SOUR / Mar '96 / SRD

NU SKOOL UPDATE
Talkin' mad shit: *Shapeshifter* / Nasty: *T-Power* / Let the bass boom: *TC Islam & Alien 3* / Communicate with the world: *Shapeshifter* / Let me recommend: *Dreamteam & MC Det* / Into the beat: *45 Roller* / Punk mutha: *Microburst* / Outcast: *Tonic* / One time: *Elementz Of Noise* / Science: *Elementz Of Noise* / Let the funk flow: *Shy FX* / Body snatcher: *Tonic*
CD ______ **SOURCD 008**
SOUR / Oct '96 / SRD

NU SOUL CLASSICS VOL.1
CD ______ **HOTTCD 2**
Hott / Dec '95 / 3mv/Sony

NU YORICA - CULTURE CLASH IN NEW YORK CITY (Experiments In Latin Music 1970-1977/2CD Set)
What are you doing for the rest of your life: *Ocho* / Gumbo: *Cortijo & His Time Machine* / La trompeta y la flauta: *Lopez, Israel 'Cachao' Y Su Descarga* / Babalonia: *Marrero, Ricardo* / Harlem river drive theme: *Harlem River Drive* / Amigos: *Stone Alliance* / Latin strut: *Bataan, Joe* / Anabacoa: *Grupo Folklorico & Experimental Nuevoyorquino* / Tempo 70: *El Gallenton* / Un dia bonita: *Palmieri, Eddie* / Carnaval: *Cortijo & His Time Machine* / Coco may may: *Ocho* / Idle hands: *Harlem River Drive* / Little Rico, little Rico's theme: *Paunetto, Bobby* / After-shower funk: *Bataan, Joe* / Macho: *Machito & His Orchestra*
CD Set ______ **SJRCD 029**
Soul Jazz / Jan '96 / New Note/Pinnacle / Timewarp / Vital

NU YORICA VOL.2 - SHANGO IN THE NEW WORLD (Further Adventures In Latin Music)
CD ______ **SJRCD 036**
Soul Jazz / Aug '97 / New Note/Pinnacle / Timewarp / Vital

NU YORK NU SKOOL
Music for the lonely: *Myerson, Jamie* / Drum: *Shooter* / Pressure: *Sub Zero* / Temperature rising: *New Nexus* / Biomagnetics: *DJ Ani* / Nexus apache: *DJ Trance* / Bitch trip: *DJ DB & Tommy D* / Boarder patrol: *Double A & Twist* / Step right in: *Dog Eat Dog* / What's happening now: *Sub Zero* / Funky beeper: *Timezone Vs. Dara* / Smoke: *DJ Dara* / Better world: *Jason Mouse* / Away: *Myerson, Jamie*
CD ______ **SM 80322**
Profile / Mar '97 / Pinnacle

NUBIAN BEATS
CD ______ **TRIPCD 7**
Rumour / Oct '96 / 3mv/Sony / Mo's Music Machine / Pinnacle

NUCLEAR BLAST 100
CD ______ **NB 100**
Nuclear Blast / Feb '94 / Plastic Head

NUEVO FLAMENCO
CD ______ **NSCD 014**
Nascente / Mar '97 / Disc / New Note/ Pinnacle

NUEVO MAMBO
CD ______ **CD 62018**
Saludos Amigos / Apr '94 / Target/BMG

NUMBER ONE HITS VOL.1
CD ______ **DCD 5371**
Disky / Apr '94 / Disky / THE

NUMBER ONE HITS VOL.2
CD ______ **DCD 5372**
Disky / Apr '94 / Disky / THE

NUMBER ONE HITS VOL.3
CD ______ **DCD 5373**
Disky / Apr '94 / Disky / THE

NUMBER ONE HITS VOL.4
CD ______ **DCD 5374**
Disky / Apr '94 / Disky / THE

NUMBER ONE HITS VOL.5
CD ______ **DCD 5375**
Disky / Apr '94 / Disky / THE

NUMBER ONE HITS VOL.6
CD ______ **DCD 5376**
Disky / Apr '94 / Disky / THE

NUMBER ONE HITS VOL.7
CD ______ **DCD 5377**
Disky / Apr '94 / Disky / THE

NUMBER ONE HITS VOL.8
CD ______ **DCD 5378**
Disky / Apr '94 / Disky / THE

NUMBER ONES OF THE 60'S
Shakin' all over: *Kidd, Johnny & The Pirates* / Poor me: *Faith, Adam* / Walkin' back to happiness: *Shapiro, Helen* / How do you do it: *Gerry & The Pacemakers* / Have I the right: *Honeycombs* / I'm into something good: *Herman's Hermits* / Anyone who had a heart: *Black, Cilla* / Needles and pins: *Searchers* / Always something there to remind me: *Shaw, Sandie* / Go now: *Moody Blues* / House of the rising sun: *Animals* / Yeh yeh: *Fame, Georgie* / It's not unusual: *Jones, Tom* / Make it easy on yourself: *Walker Brothers* / You've lost that lovin' feelin': *Righteous Brothers* / Out of time: *Farlowe, Chris* / All or nothing: *Small Faces* / Sunny afternoon: *Kinks* / Pretty flamingo: *Manfred Mann* / You don't have to say you love me: *Springfield, Dusty* / Release me: *Humperdinck, Engelbert* / With a little help from my friends: *Cocker, Joe* / Fire: *Crazy World Of Arthur Brown* / (If paradise is) half as nice: *Amen Corner* / Something in the air: *Thunderclap Newman*
CD ______ **CDPR 111**
Premier/MFP / Nov '93 / EMI

NUMBER ONES OF THE 70'S
In the summertime: *Mungo Jerry* / Maggie May: *Stewart, Rod* / Coz I luv you: *Slade* / Get it on: *T-Rex* / See my baby jive: *Wizzard* / Down down: *Status Quo* / Devil gate drive: *Quatro, Suzi* / Rock your baby: *McCrae, George* / Sugar baby love: *Rubettes* / You're the first, the last, my everything: *White, Barry* / Oh boy: *Mud* / Make me smile (Come up and see me): *Harley, Steve & Cockney Rebel* / I'm not in love: *10cc* / Can't give you anything (but my love): *Stylistics* / You to me are everything: *Real Thing* / So you win again: *Hot Chocolate* / When I need you: *Sayer, Leo* / Wuthering Heights: *Bush, Kate* / Rat trap: *Boomtown Rats* / Sunday girl: *Blondie*
CD ______ **CDPR 112**
Premier/MFP / Nov '93 / EMI

NUMBER ONES OF THE 80'S
Going underground: *Jam* / Use it up and wear it out: *Odyssey* / Tainted love: *Soft Cell* / Prince charming: *Adam Ant* / Ghost town: *Specials* / This ole house: *Stevens, Shakin'* / Come on Eileen: *Dexy's Midnight Runners* / Eye of the tiger: *Survivor* / Down under: *Men At Work* / Too shy: *Kajagoogoo* / Freedom: *Wham* / Nineteen: *Hardcastle, Paul* / Don't leave me this way: *Communards* / Never gonna give you up: *Astley, Rick* / La bamba: *Los Lobos* / Nothing's gonna stop us now: *Starship* / Only way is up: *Yazz* / I owe you nothing: *Bros* / Perfect: *Fairground Attraction* / Eternal flame: *Bangles*
CD ______ **CDPR 113**
Premier/MFP / Nov '93 / EMI

NYC DANCE COMPILATION VOL.1
CD ______ **55068CD**
Freeze / Jan '97 / RTM/Disc

NYC DANCE COMPILATION VOL.2
CD ______ **55078CD**
Freeze / Jan '97 / RTM/Disc

NYC DANCE COMPILATION VOL.3
CD ______ **55085CD**
Freeze / Jan '97 / RTM/Disc

NYC DANCE COMPILATION VOL.4
It's time to party: *Mantronix & Althea McQueen* / Disco era: *Brothers Of Soul* / Aishiteru: *Motto & Izumi* / New York City: *Westside Players* / Bklyn theme: *G Dubs & Benn Starr* / May the funk be with you: *Second Crusade* / Come in my arms: *Harris, Rick* / Splat: *Happy Freakin' Weekend* / Save me: *New Ethics* / Everybody: *Papp/Preston Project* / Love and happiness: *Second Crusade*
CD ______ **55091CD**
Freeze / Jul '97 / RTM/Disc

NYC HARDCORE
CD ______ **REVCD 007**
Revelation / May '96 / Plastic Head

NYC HOUSE
CD ______ **ZYX 811052**
ZYX / Jul '97 / ZYX

O

O MELHOR DA BOSSA
CD ______ **1917452**
EPM / Apr '97 / ADA / Discovery

OBJETS D'ART VOL.1 (2CD Set)
Clinically inclined: *Future/Past* / Amalia: *As One* / Whirling of spirits: *Balil* / Choke and fly: *Balil* / Neurotic behaviour: *Psyche* / How the West was won: *Psyche* / Chicken noodle soup: *BFC* / Sleep: *BFC* / Exteriors: *Esoterik* / Locators: *Esoterik* / Into the other world: *Phenomyna* / Earthfall: *Phenomyna* / Got the urge: *Phenomyna* / Enseble: *Elegy* / Tone poem: *Elegy* / Kwaidan: *Esoterik* / P switch: *Elegy* / Climatic calm: *Red cell*
CD Set ______ **ELEC 27**
New Electronica / Mar '96 / Beechwood/ BMG / Plastic Head

OBJETS D'ART VOL.3
CD ______ **ELEC 31CD**
New Electronica / Feb '97 / Beechwood/ BMG / Plastic Head

OBLIVAN
CD ______ **OOR 023CD**
Out Of Romford / Nov '95 / Pinnacle / SRD

OBSCURE AND ROCKIN'
CD ______ **CLCD 4431**
Collector/White Label / Sep '96 / TKO Magnum

OBSESSIVE HOUSE CULTURE VOL.1
CD ______ **OBRCD 1**
Obsessive / Mar '94 / Prime / SRD

OBSESSIVE HOUSE CULTURE VOL.2
CD ______ **OBRCD 2**
Obsessive / Aug '94 / Prime / SRD

OCEAN OF SOUND
Dub fi gwan: *King Tubby* / Rain dance: *Hancock, Herbie* / Analogue bubblebath 1: *Aphex Twin* / Empire III: *Hassell, Jon* / Sorban palid: *Suryana, Ujang* / Prelude a l'apres midi d'un faune: *English Chamber Orchestra* / Sunken city: *Baxter, Les* / Loomer: *My Bloody Valentine* / Lizard point: *Eno, Brian* / Shunie Omizutori Buddhist ceremony / Music of horns and whistles: *Vancouver Soundscape* / Howler monkeys / Machine gun: *Brotzmann, Peter Octet* / Yanomami rain song / Bismillah 'rrahmani 'rrahim: *Budd, Harold* / Black satin: *Davis, Miles* / All night flight: *Riley, Terry* / Coyor Panon: *Kurnia, Detty* / Virgin beauty: *Coleman, Ornette* / Chen pe'i pe'i: *Zorn, John & David Toop* / Rivers of mercury: *Schutze, Paul* / I heard her call my name: *Velvet Underground* / Bearded seals / Boat-woman song: *Czukay, Holger & Rolf Dammers* / Fall breaks and back into winter: *Beach Boys* / Faraway chant: *African Headcharge* / Cosmo enticement: *Sun Ra* / Untitled 3: *Music Improvisation Company* / Seven-up: *Deep Listening Band* / In a landscape: *Cage, John* / Vexations: *Marks, Alan* / Suikinkutsu water chime
CD ______ **AMBT 10**
Virgin / Jan '96 / EMI

OCEAN SERENITY (A Magical Blend Of Music And The Sounds Of Nature)
CD ______ **57752**
CMC / May '97 / BMG

OCTOBER REVOLUTION, THE
For Bill Dixon I: *Ali, Rashied & Borah Bergman/Joe McPhee/Wilber Morris* / Death of Danny Love: *Melford, Myra Trio* / For Bill Dixon II: *Ali, Rashied & Borah Bergman/Joe McPhee/Wilber Morris*
CD ______ **ECD 221662**
Evidence / Oct '96 / ADA / Cadillac / Harmonia Mundi

ODD SHAPED BALLS (Rugby Songs/ 2CD Set)
When I was youmg / A miner coming home one night / Sterilised heiress / Home on the range / Mother / Roll your leg over / Woodpeckers song / A rovin' / Abdul the bulbul emir / Doodle de doo / Soggy soggy dew / Professions / Big bamboo / Oh sir Jasper / Sing us another one / Ram of Derbyshire / Doggies meeting / Next thanksgiving / Maggie May / If I was the marrying kind / Oh how the money rolls in / Six old ladies / Clementine / Roll me over / Dinah / I used to work in Chicago / Barnacle Bill the sailor / Here's to the good old beer / Horndean school / Frankie & Johnny / She was poor but she was honest / Old King Cole / Sexual life of a camel / Traveller / Virgin sturgeon / Sweet violets
CD Set ______ **330202**
Hallmark / Jul '96 / Carlton

OFF THE MAP
CD ______ **CHARRMCD 19**
Charrm / Feb '95 / Plastic Head

OFF THE TOP VOL.1 (13 Nu-Jazz Beats)
CD ______ **MA 008**
M / Mar '97 / Timewarp

OFF THE WALL
CD ______ **VPCD 2050**
VP / Jul '96 / Greensleeves / Jet Star / Total/BMG

OFFERING (The Past & Present Of K7)
Detroit after dark: *Parker, Terence* / Black baby: *Kruder & Dorfmeister* / Gangsta shit: *DJ Cam* / Heavybreath: *Impulse* / Wisdom: *Deason, Sean* / World of deep: *E-Dancer* / Claude Young: *Young, Claude* / Walk under a full moon's light: *Kanabis The Edit Assassin* / Black single: *Farda P* / All day: *Nicolette* / Carl Craig: *Craig, Carl* / Columbia: *Varley, Gaz*
CD ______ **K7 059CD**
Studio K7 / Jun '97 / Prime / RTM/Disc

OH CHERRY OH BABY
CD ______ **LG 21047**
Lagoon / Feb '93 / Grapevine/PolyGram

OH JULIE (Teen Group Sounds From Nashville & The South)
Oh Julie: *Crescendos* / My little girl: *Crescendos* / School girl: *Crescendos* / Crazy hop: *Crescendos* / Young and in love: *Crescendos* / Rainy Sunday: *Crescendos* / I've tried: *Crescendos* / Gawk 'n' stroll: *Crescendos* / Lucky love: *Crescendos* / Teenage angel: *Crescendos* / Jackie: *Green, Janice* / With all my heart: *Green, Janice* / I'm waiting: *Fortune, Billy* / My pretty baby: *Plaids* / Til the end of the dance: *Plaids* / Still love you baby: *Tabs* / Will we meet again: *Tabs* / You know baby: *Meloaires* / I'm so glad: *Meloaires* / Teacher don't keep me in: *Martels* / Where did my woman go: *Martels* / That's how I go for you: *Butler, Cliff Group* / I've got my heart in my hand: *Storm, Warren Group* / Love you a thousand ways: *Bob & Ray* / Isle of Sue Saint Marie: *Bob & Ray* / Sweet Nancy: *Bob & Ray* / Mr. Blues (poor old lonely me): *Lindsey Brothers* / Maybe: *Trends* / Candy to my sherry: *Moffett, Kenny*
CD ______ **CDCHD 647**
Ace / Apr '97 / Pinnacle

OH KASIO BOY
CD ______ **CD 024C**
Carotte / May '97 / Jet Star

OHM GURU PRESENTS THE FUTURE SOUND OF ITALY
CD ______ **PAZ 803CD**
La Plaza / Sep '97 / Essential/BMG

OI OF JAPAN
CD ______ **AA 016CD**
AA / Mar '97 / Cargo / Greyhound

OI OF SEX, THE
CD ______ **AHOY 23**
Captain Oi / Dec '94 / Plastic Head

OI/SKAMPILATION VOL.1
CD ______ **700092**
Radical / Mar '97 / Cargo

OI/SKAMPILATION VOL.2
CD ______ **700132**
Radical / Mar '97 / Cargo

OKEH - A NORTHERN SOUL OBSESSION VOL.1
You're gonna make me love you: *Sheldon, Sandi* / Gonna get along without you now: *Vibrations* / I'm coming to your rescue: *Triumphs* / I still love you: *Seven Souls* / Gone but not forgotten: *Robinson, Johnny* / This heart of mine: *Artistics* / Quitter never wins: *Williams, Larry & Johnny Watson* / Come back: *Williams, Ken* / Wish I had known: *Phillips, Sandra* / Bring it back home: *Chimes* / Call me tomorrow: *Harris, Major* / You don't want me no more: *Major Lance* / What's the use of me trying: *Tangier* / I'm so afraid: *Opals* / My heart is hurtin': *Butler, Billy & The Enchanters* / Hurt: *Church, Jimmy* / Somebody's always trying: *Taylor, Ted* / He who picks a rose: *Carstairs* / I

don't want to discuss it: *Little Richard* / I can do it: *Autographs* / Take me to paradise: *Cheers* / So glad your love don't change: *Little Foxes* / I'm taking on pain: *Tate, Tommy* / It's an uphill climb to the bottom: *Jackson, Walter*
CD _______________ CDKEND 132
Kent / Mar '96 / Pinnacle

OKEH - A NORTHERN SOUL OBSESSION VOL.2
Ain't gonna move: *Williams, Larry & Johnny Watson* / End up crying: *Vibrations* / I'll leave it up to you: *Artistics* / Let my heart and soul be free: *Tan Geers* / Memories: *Triumphs* / Your good girls gonna go bad: *Jackson, Cookie* / You ask for one good reason: *Williams, Larry* / Cool breeze: *Sims, Gerald* / Rhythm: *Major Lance* / You're gonna be sorry: *Opals* / Just another dance: *Mars, Marlina* / After you there can be nothing: *Jackson, Walter* / I can't make it without you: *Hayes, Malcolm* / South like West: *Watson, Johnny* / Let me show it to you: *Fundamentals* / Yesterday is gone: *Variations* / You can't take it away: *Mortimor, Azie* / Little bit of something: *Little Richard* / Second class lover: *Dushon, Jean* / Train: *Belgianettes* / Can't live without her: *Butler, Billy* / Hello heartaches, goodbye love: *Davis, Joyce* / I can't work no longer: *Butler, Billy* / That's what Mama say: *Jackson, Walter*
CD _______________ CDKEND 142
Kent / Feb '97 / Pinnacle

OKEH RHYTHM 'N' BLUES 1949-1957 (3CD Set)
CD Set _______________ CD 48912
Legacy / May '94 / Sony

OKRA ALL-STARS
CD _______________ OKCD 33021
Okra / Mar '94 / ADA / Direct

OLD BELIEVERS (Songs Of The Nekrasov Cossaks)
CD _______________ SFWCD 40462
Smithsonian Folkways / Oct '95 / ADA / Cadillac / CM / Direct / Koch

OLD BULL AND BUSH, THE
CD _______________ GEMMCD 9913
Pearl / Feb '92 / Harmonia Mundi

OLD SCHOOL RAP - THE ROOTS OF RAP
King Tim III (personality jock): *Fatback Band* / Money (dollar bill y'all): *Spicer, Jimmy* / Rockin' it: *MC Flex & The FBI Crew* / Please stay: *Fatback & Gerry Bledsoe* / Alarm (XX rated): *Hawk* / Rock me down: *Young, Monalisa* / Step by step: *Simon, Joe* / Heobah: *Rae, Fonda* / If I can't have your love: *Brown, Jocelyn* / Workin' out: *Ritz* / We come to jam: *Blaze* / Can you guess what groove this is: *Glory* / Live it up: *Rae, Fonda* / Go with the feeling: *Krystal* / Got to have your lovin': *Feel*
CD _______________ CDSEWD 048
Southbound / Jun '92 / Pinnacle

OLD SKOOL REUNION (2CD Set)
CD Set _______________ RADCD 69
Global TV / Jul '97 / BMG

OLD SKOOL, THE (2CD Set)
Never too much: *Vandross, Luther* / And the beat goes on: *Whispers* / Just be good to me: *SOS Band* / Hanging on a string: *Loose Ends* / She's strange: *Cameo* / Risin' to the top: *Burke, Keni* / Running away: *Ayers, Roy* / Love come down: *King, Evelyn* / Don't look any further: *Edwards, Dennis* / All night long: *Mary Jane Girls* / I can make you feel good: *Shalamar* / Native New Yorker: *Odyssey* / I found lovin': *Fatback Band* / Forget me nots: *Rushen, Patrice* / Juicy fruit: *Mtume* / 'Ain't nothing goin' on but the rent: *Guthrie, Gwen* / Roses are red: *Mac Band & McCampbell Brothers* / I specialize in love: *Brown, Sharon* / Low rider: *War* / Summer madness: *Kool & The Gang* / I want your love: *Chic* / Thinking of you: *Sister Sledge* / I love music: *O'Jays* / Harvest for the world: *Isley Brothers* / Don't leave me this way: *Melvin, Harold & The Bluenotes* / Best of my love: *Emotions* / Car wash: *Rose Royce* / Love TKO: *Pendergrass, Teddy* / Feel the need in me: *Detroit Emeralds* / Nights over Egypt: *Jones Girls* / Behind the groove: *Marie, Teena* / Feel so real: *Arrington, Steve* / Circles: *Atlantic Starr* / Just a touch of love: *Slave* / Never knew love like this before: *Mills, Stephanie* / I'll be around: *Wells, Terri* / I wonder if I take you home: *Lisa Lisa & Cult Jam* / Shame: *King, Evelyn* / Funkin' for Jamaica: *Browne, Tom* / Me and Mrs Jones: *Paul, Billy*
CD Set _______________ RADCD 59
Global TV / Mar '97 / BMG

OLD TIME MUSIC ON THE AIR VOL.1
CD _______________ ROUCD 0331
Rounder / Sep '94 / ADA / CM / Direct

OLD TIME MUSIC ON THE AIR VOL.2
CD _______________ ROUCD 0391
Rounder / Aug '96 / ADA / CM / Direct

OLD TIME PARTY FAVOURITES VOL.1
CD _______________ SWBCD 203
Sound Waves / Sep '94 / Target/BMG

OLD TIME PARTY FAVOURITES VOL.2
CD _______________ SWCD 204
Sound Waves / Sep '94 / Target/BMG

OLD TOWN & BARRY SOUL STIRRERS
Think smart: *Fiestas* / I'm so glad: *Howard, Frank* / Oh oh here comes the heartbreak: *Jones, Thelma* / Try love one more time: *Sparkels* / If I had known: *Houston, Freddie* / You can't trust your best friend: *Height, Donald* / My foolish heart: *Coleman, David* / Gotta find a way: *Jones, Thelma* / We're gonna make it: *Reid, Irene* / Stop, take another look: *Divine Men* / Could this be love: *Rosco & Barbara* / Jerk it: *Gypsies* / Cross my heart: *Yvonne & The Violets* / Baby I need: *Lorraine & The Delights* / Left out: *Johnson, Jesse* / My heart's on fire: *Bland, Billy* / Chills and fever: *Houston, Freddie* / Drown my heart: *Coleman, David* / Barefootin' time in Chinatown: *Young, Lester* / I want a chance for romance: *Rivera, Hector* / It's a woman's world (you better believe it): *Gypsies* / Soul stirrer: *Bobby & Betty Lou* / Gypsy said: *Fiestas* / Things have more meaning now: *Scott, Peggy*
CD _______________ CDKEND 111
Kent / Jun '94 / Pinnacle

OLD TOWN BLUES VOL.1 (Downtown Sides)
Uncle Bud: *Terry, Sonny & Brownie McGhee* / Climbing on top of the hill: *Terry, Sonny & Brownie McGhee* / Sweet sweet woman: *Terry, Sonny & Brownie McGhee* / Evil hearted woman: *Wayne, James* / Rock reel rock: *Wayne, James* / Where you been: *Wayne, James* / True blues: *Wayne, James* / Slidin': *Terry, Sonny & Brownie McGhee* / Crazy about you baby: *Terry, Sonny & Brownie McGhee* / Chicken hop: *Bland, Billy* / I need a woman: *Terry, Sonny & Brownie McGhee* / Playboy: *Littlefield, Little Willie* / Sweet little girl: *Littlefield, Little Willie* / Hard luck baby: *Littlefield, Little Willie* / Work out: *Littlefield, Little Willie* / Love's a disease: *Terry, Sonny & Brownie McGhee* / She loves so easy: *Terry, Sonny & Brownie McGhee* / Confusion: *Terry, Sonny & Brownie McGhee* / Reap what you sow: *Terry, Sonny & Brownie McGhee* / Things that I used to do: *Gaddy, Bob* / Could I would I: *Dixon, Willie* / Ugly girls: *Dixon, Willie*
CD _______________ CDCHD 469
Ace / Sep '93 / Pinnacle

OLD TOWN BLUES VOL.2 (The Uptown Sides)
CD _______________ CDCHD 498
Ace / Jun '94 / Pinnacle

OLD TOWN DOO WOP VOL.1
There's a moon out tonight: *Capris* / Zu zu: *Bonnevilles* / Fool in love: *Keytones* / Walking along: *Solitaires* / On Sunday afternoon: *Harptones* / Never let me go: *Royaltones* / Have you ever loved someone: *Vocaleers* / Later later baby: *5 Crowns* / Message of love: *Laurels* / It all depends on you: *Harptones* / Love you baby all the time: *Co-eds* / Last night I dreamed: *Fiestas* / Two in love(with one heart): *McFadden, Ruth & The Royaltones* / Last rose of summer: *Symbols* / Remember then: *Earls* / Magic rose: *Solitaires* / Tonight Kathleen: *Valentines* / Seven wonders of the world: *Keytones* / Hey Norman: *Royaltones* / Lorraine: *Bonnevilles* / Why oh why: *Tru-Tones* / I love an angel: *Co-eds* / You could be my love: *5 Crowns* / Mambo boogie: *Harptones* / Crying my heart out: *Symbols* / I need your love so bad: *Vocaleers* / I fell in love: *Esquires*
CD _______________ CDCHD 433
Ace / Jun '93 / Pinnacle

OLD TOWN DOO WOP VOL.2
So fine: *Fiestas* / My dearest darling: *Cleftones* / What did she say: *Solitaires* / Day we fell in love: *Ovations* / Where I fell in love: *Capris* / Zip boom: *Supremes* / Little girl (I love you madly): *Cleftones* / Life is but a dream: *Harptones* / Ding dong: *Packards* / Lullaby of the bells: *Five Crowns* / My broken heart: *Chimes* / Hong Kong jelly wong: *Royaltones* / School boy: *Harptones* / Love and devotion: *Vocaleers* / Why does the world go round: *Escorts* / Angels sang: *Solitaires* / My babe (she don't want me no more): *Supremes* / (I'm afraid) the masquerade is over: *Cleftones* / Good luck darling: *Five Crowns* / Mexico: *Chimes* / Dream of love: *Packards* / Gee what a girl: *Hummers* / There's something awful nice about you: *Escorts* / I've got a notion: *Harptones* / I give you my word: *Royaltones* / Do you know what I mean: *Hummers* / Our anniversary: *Fiestas* / My lullabye: *Ovations*
CD _______________ CDCHD 470
Ace / Aug '93 / Pinnacle

OLD TOWN DOO WOP VOL.3
Crazy love: *Royaltones* / Indian girl: *Capris* / Starlight tonight: *Inspirators* / You know you're doin' me wrong: *Harptones* / I beg your forgiveness: *Co-eds* / Possibility: *Crowns* / My heart (I'm blue without you): *Keytones* / Jingle jingle: *Tremaines* / Wedding: *Solitaires* / My faith: *Fi-Tones* / Darling listen to the words of this song: *McFadden, Ruth & The Supremes* / I love you baby: *Farmer, Peggy & The Harptones* / Give me your love: *Four Pharaohs* / Gloria: *Cleftones* / Last round-up: *Supremes* / I'm in love: *Co-eds* / Please give me one more chance: *Mumford, Gene & The Serenaders* / Why must I love you: *Esquires* / Life is but a dream: *Earls* / Tonight: *Supremes* / Think: *Universals* / Oh what a feeling: *Inspirators* / School girl: *Harptones* / Latin lover: *Royaltones* / Guess who: *Cleftones* / China girl: *Four Pharaohs* / Moon shining bright: *Tremaines* / You're gonna need my help someday: *Harptones*
CD _______________ CDCHD 471
Ace / Oct '93 / Pinnacle

OLD TOWN DOO WOP VOL.4
Round goes my heart: *Solitaires* / Some people think: *Capris* / I call to you: *Burgess, Vicki* / I won't tell the world: *Blenders* / Night is over: *Gems* / I'll be there: *Vocaleers* / Lonely: *Solitaires* / My heart: *Fi-Tones* / Why do I cry: *Capris* / Night: *Nick & The Nacks* / Walkin' and talkin': *Solitaires* / Lover lover lover: *Symbols* / You for me: *McFadden, Ruth* / It's you: *Earls* / Girl of mine: *Solitaires* / My island in th esun: *Capris* / Summer love: *Valentines* / Crazy love: *Royaltones* / Girl in my dreams: *Capris* / But I know: *Blenders* / Pretty thing: *Solitaires* / Life is but a dream: *Harptones* / Nursery rhymes: *Gems* / Thrill of love: *Solitaires* / When you're smiling: *Mumford, Gene & The Serenaders* / Listen listen baby: *Unknowns*
CD _______________ CDCHD 570
Ace / Jan '95 / Pinnacle

OLDIES BUT GOLDIES VOL.1
CD _______________ 15028
Laserlight / Dec '94 / Target/BMG

OLDIES BUT GOLDIES VOL.2
CD _______________ 15029
Laserlight / Dec '94 / Target/BMG

OLDIES BUT GOLDIES VOL.3
CD _______________ 12388
Laserlight / Feb '95 / Target/BMG

OLDIES BUT GOLDIES VOL.4
CD _______________ 12389
Laserlight / May '95 / Target/BMG

OLDIES GREATEST HITS
CD _______________ SONCD 0059
Sonic Sounds / Mar '94 / Jet Star

OLDIES KEEP SWINGING
CD _______________ SONCD 0057
Sonic Sounds / Jan '94 / Jet Star

OLDTIME FESTIVAL
CD _______________ BLR 84005
L&R / May '91 / New Note/Pinnacle

OLE - BULLFIGHT MUSIC FROM SPAIN
Espana cani / Opera flamenca / Vaya capes / La entrada
CD _______________ 15161
Laserlight / '91 / Target/BMG

OLYMPIC - THE ALBUM
Stay with me forever: *Prolific* / So deep: *Scope* / Question: *7 Grand Housing Authority* / Feel the love: *Perez, Eric* / Shiver: *Powerzone* / Another man: *Shy One* / Your love: *Mr. Peach* / Lies: *Perez, Eric* / You can turn around: *Bottom Dollar* / More to love: *Volcano*
CD _______________ ELYACD 001
Olympic / Feb '94 / 3mv/Sony

ON A DANCE TIP
Cotton eye Joe: *Rednex* / Sight for sore eyes: *M-People* / Tell me when: *Human League* / Runaway: *MC Sar & The Real McCoy* / Set you free: *N-Trance* / Reach up: *Perfecto All Stars* / Let me be your fantasy: *Baby D* / Them girls: *Zig & Zag* / Saturday night: *Whigfield* / No matter what you do (I'm gonna get with U): *Flavour* / Total eclipse of the heart: *French, Nicki* / Here comes the hotstepper: *I'm A Kamikaze* / Welcome to tomorrow (are you ready): *Snap* / Sweetness: *Gayle, Michelle* / None of your business: *Salt n' Pepa* / Saved: *Mr. Roy* / U sure do: *Strike* / Sweet love: *M-Beat* / Good life: *EVE* / My heart belongs to you: *Jodeci* / Bump 'n' grind: *R Kelly*
CD _______________ RADCD 07
Global TV / '95 / BMG

ON A DANCE TIP '95 (2CD Set)
Fairground: *Simply Red* / Gangsta's paradise: *Coolio & LV* / Boom boom boom: *Outhere Brothers* / Stayin' alive: *N-Trance* / Scatman: *Scatman John* / Try me out: *Corona* / Missing: *Everything But The Girl* / Hideaway: *De'Lacy* / Runaway: *Real McCoy* / I got a little something for you: *MN8* / U sure do: *Strike* / Two can play that game: *Brown, Bobby* / Right in the night: *Jam & Spoon* / Don't you want me: *Felix* / Move your body: *Xpansions* / Happy just to be with you: *Gayle, Michelle* / Shoot me with your love: *D:Ream* / Sight for sore eyes: *M-People* / Surrender your love: *Nightcrawlers* / Not cover yet: *Grace* / You remind me of something: *Kelly, R* / Dreamer: *Livin' Joy* / Turn on tune in cop out: *Freakpower* / I luv u baby: *Original* / Walking in Memphis: *Cher* / Son of a gun: *JX* / Bomb: *Bucketheads* / Don't stop (wiggle wiggle): *Outhere Brothers* / 3 is family: *Dawson, Dana* / Whoomph (there it is): *Clock* / Set you free: *N-Trance* / Tell me when: *Human League* / Baby baby: *Corona* / Here comes the hotstepper: *Kamoze, Ini* / Total eclipse of the heart: *French, Nicki* / Your loving arms: *Martin, Billie Ray* / Reach up (papa's got a brand new pig bag): *Perfecto All Stars* / Always something there to remind me: *Tin Tin Out & Espiritu* / First the last eternity: *Snap* / Zombie: *ADAM & Amy* / Guaglione: *Prado, Perez* / Cotton eye Joe: *Rednex*
CD Set _______________ RADCD 27
Global TV / Nov '95 / BMG

ON A DANCE TIP VOL.2
Don't stop (wiggle wiggle): *Outhere Brothers* / Dreamer: *Livin' Joy* / Scatman: *Scatman John* / Two can play that game: *Brown, Bobby* / Baby baby: *Corona* / Love and devotion: *Real McCoy* / Love city groove: *Love City Groove* / Open your heart: *M-People* / U sure do: *Strike* / Guaglione: *Prado, Perez* / Push the feeling on: *Nightcrawlers* / First the last eternity: *Snap* / Not over yet: *Grace* / Axel F: *Clock* / Always something there to remind me: *Tin Tin Out* / Conway: *Reel 2 Real & The Mad Stuntman* / It's a love thing: *Milton, C.B.* / I'm going down: *Blige, Mary J.* / Every day of the week: *Jade* / Your body's callin': *Kelly, R*
CD _______________ RADCD 12
Global TV / May '95 / BMG

ON A DANCE TIP VOL.3
La la hey hey: *Outhere Brothers* / Happy just to be with you: *Gayle, Michelle* / Hideaway: *De'Lacy* / I luv u baby: *Original* / Everybody: *Clock* / Party up the world: *D:Ream* / Don't let the feeling go: *Nightcrawlers* / Son of a gun: *JX* / Don't you want me: *Felix* / Move your body: *Xpansions* / Scatman's world: *Scatman John* / Morning after (free at last): *Strike* / I want to live: *Grace* / Try me out: *Corona* / Come and get your love: *Real McCoy* / Search for the hero: *M-People* / Zombie: *ADAM & Amy* / Running around town: *Martin, Billie Ray* / Catch a fire: *Haddaway* / Loving you more: *BT & Vincent Covello* / Destination eschaton: *Shamen* / Kiss from a rose: *Seal*
CD _______________ RADCD 20
Global TV / Jul '95 / BMG

ON A DANCE TIP VOL.4
Missing: *Everything But The Girl* / Whole lotta love: *Goldbug* / Loving you more: *BT* / Electronic pleasure: *N-Trance* / I wanna be a hippy: *Technohead* / Passion: *Gat Decor* / Got myself together: *Bucketheads* / If you wanna party: *Molella & The Outhere Brothers* / Itchycoo park: *M-People* / Release the pressure: *Leftfield* / Waterfalls: *TLC* / Fairground: *Simply Red* / Too hot: *Coolio* / Skin on skin: *Grace* / I don't wanna be a star: *Corona* / Do it for love: *4Mandu* / Let's push it: *Nightcrawlers* / Is this a dream: *4Mandu* / One by one: *Cher* / And I'm telling you I'm not going: *Giles, Donna*
CD _______________ RADCD 26
Global TV / Feb '96 / BMG

ON A WINTER'S EVENING
Don't it make my brown eyes blue: *Gayle, Crystal* / Cryin': *McLean, Don* / Move closer: *Nelson, Phyllis* / When I fall in love: *Cole, Nat 'King'* / Orchard road: *Sayer, Leo* / All I have to do is dream: *Everly Brothers* / Feelings: *Albert, Morris* / Sharing the night together: *Dr. Hook* / Home on Monday: *Little River Band* / Everybody's gotta learn sometime: *Korgis* / Winter in America: *Ashdown, Doug* / Anyone who had a heart: *Black, Cilla* / They shoot horses don't they: *Racing Cars* / Where do you go to my lovely: *Sarstedt, Peter* / Love don't live here anymore: *Nail, Jimmy* / Classic: *Gurvitz, Adrian*
CD _______________ WLT 874612
Disky / Oct '96 / Disky / THE

ON CHANTAIT QUAND MEME
CD _______________ DEM 013
IMP / Feb '96 / ADA / Discovery

ON GUARD FOR THEE
CD _______________ ANDA 204
Au-Go-Go / Jan '97 / Cargo / Greyhound / Plastic Head

ON MANA 689 - NEW MUSIC INDONESIA VOL.2
CD _______________ LYRCD 7420
Lyrichord / Aug '93 / ADA / CM / Roots

ON MARCO POLO'S ROAD (The Musicians Of Kunduz & Faizabad/ Afghanistan)
Badakhshani charbaiti / Charbaiti batcha moshi mosh / Tajik charbaiti / Tajik charbaiti and mondanabosh / Zirbaghali solo / Uzbek pashtun herati folk songs / Badakhshani folk songs / Falak
CD _______________ MCM 3003
Multicultural Media / May '97 / Direct

ON THE BANKS OF THE DEVERON
Vancouver / Diddler / Hugh MacDonald / Granny Fraser's flitting / Farewell to the creeks / Leaving port Askaig / MacPhersons' lament / Silver darlings / Highland cathederal / Sandy's new chanter / Tak a dram / Dumbarton castle / Craigellachie brig / Left handed fiddler / Trawler song / Rowan tree / Bonnie Gallowa / Old rustic bridge / Carillon / Spirit of Glen Deveron / Here's to Scottish whisky / Dr. Ross's 50th welcome to the Argyllshire gathering / 10th Bn H.L.I. Crossing the Rhine
CD _______________ CDGR 151
Ross / Dec '95 / CM / Duncans / Highlander / Ross

ON THE BEACH AT WAIKIKI 1914-1952
CD _______________ HQCD 57
Harlequin / Aug '95 / Hot Shot / Jazz Music / Swift / Wellard

ON THE EDGE OF DEATH
CD _______________ 15216
Laserlight / Aug '91 / Target/BMG

ON THE PHILADELPHIA BEAT VOL.1
Girl across the street: *Smith, Moses* / Got what you need: *Fantastic Johnny C* / Standing in the darkness: *Ethics* / Help wanted: *Volcanos* / This gets to me: *Hudson, Pookie* / If I'm all you got (I'm all you need): *Ambassadors* / Don't set me up for the kill: *Dorothy & The Hesitations* / Ain't it baby: *Gamble, Kenny* / Dynamite exploded: *Honey & The Bees* / Storm warning: *Volcanos* / I want my baby back: *Ashley, Tyrone* / Bobby, is my baby: *Mason, Barbara* / Don't let it happen to you: *Harper, Benny* / Girl I Love you: *Temptones* / Joke's on you: *Gamble, Kenny* / Won't find better than me: *Kit Kat's* / Why do you hurt the one who love's you: *Honey & The Bees* / You gave me somebody to love you: *Ambassadors* / Don't ever want to lose your love: *Mason, Barbara* / Till then: *Pentagons* / Trying to work out a plan: *Dorothy & The Hesitations* / Let's have a good time: *Nobles, Cliff* / You're number one: *Volcanos* / Love you can depend on: *Brenda & Tabulations* / Let's talk it over: *Kayettes* / Don't give away my love: *Soul Brothers Six* / Better to have loved and lost: *Irwin, Big Dee*
CD BCD 15844
Bear Family / Aug '95 / Direct / Rollercoaster / Swift

ON THE REGGAE TIP
CD CIDTV 5
Island / Jun '93 / PolyGram

ON THE ROAD
CD TUT 771
Wundertute / Oct '94 / ADA / CM / Duncans

ON THE ROAD AGAIN
Truck drivin' outlaw: *Olsen, Denis* / Girl on the billboard: *Reeves, Del* / Truck drivin' son of a gun: *Dudley, Dave* / CB Savage: *Brown, Steven* / Highway 40 blues: *Ricks, Earl* / Truck driver's prayer: *Ricks, Earl* / Tennessee is home to me: *Blueboy, David* / That's trucking: *Ricks, Earl* / Roll truck roll: *Simpson, Red* / Mystery maiden: *Bennet, George* / Truckers way of life: *Blueboy, David* / Hold everything: *Spooks, Grover* / Roll on: *McRoad, John & The Texas Liner* / It's hard to love a man: *Bennet, George* / Freightliner fever: *McBrown, Mel* / I'm a truck: *Simpson, Red* / He took me for a ride: *La Costa Tucker* / I didn't jump the fence: *King, Don* / On the road again: *McRoad, John & The Texas Liner* / Day time friends: *McRoad, John & The Texas Liner* / Ode to 10-33: *McRoad, John & The Texas Liner*
CD 22504
Music / Feb '96 / Target/BMG

ON THE ROCKS VOL.1
Light my fire: *Zacharias* / Sunshine superman: *Torme, Mel* / Incense and peppermints/It's a beautiful morning: *Denny, Martin* / Uptight: *Jerome, Henry* / Green tambourine: *Sir Julian* / Tired of waiting: *Hollyridge Strings* / Mellow yellow/We gotta get out of this place: *Hollyridge Strings* / Gimme a little sign: *Morrow, Buddy* / Hard day's night: *Lee, Peggy* / Whiter shade of pale: *Moreno, Mario* / Heartbreak hotel: *Hollyridge Strings* / Don't be cruel: *Hollyridge Strings* / As tears go by: *New Classic Singers* / Evil ways: *Delory, Al* / Get back: *Little Big Horns* / Hello I love you/Touch me: *Lettermen* / Dizzy: *Royal Blue* / Shaft: *Hollyridge Strings* / Mighty Quinn: *London, Julie* / Day in the life: *Tartaglia* / I am the walrus: *Tartaglia* / Daydream believer: *Tartaglia* / Winchester cathedral: *Riddle, Nelson* / Love grows (where my rosemary grows): *Newton, Wayne*
CD CDEMS 1612
EMI / May '97 / EMI

ON THE ROCKS VOL.2
Heart full of soul: *Mann, Johnny Singers* / Satisfaction: *McCallum, David* / Carry the weight: *Lai, Francis* / Games people play: *Torme, Mel* / I get around/California girls: *Hollyridge Strings* / Summer in the city: *Morrow, Buddy* / Everyday people: *Ledd, Peggy* / Mrs Robinson: *Lombard, Guy* / Hush: *Royal Blue* / Blue jay way/Blackbird: *Lord Sister & Sandler/Young* / Heard it through the grapevine: *Little Big Horns* / Pretty woman: *Jerome, Henry* / Wear your love like heaven/Working on a groovy train: *Rose, David* / Yummy yummy yummy: *London, Julie* / Superfly: *Duchin, Peter* / Holiday: *Moreno, Mario* / Baby love/Respect: *Zacharias* / I can see for miles: *Lord Sitar* / Happy together: *Torme, Mel* / Can't buy me love: *Hollyridge Strings* / Sergeant Pepper: *Hollyridge Strings* / Light my fire: *Tartaglia* / These boots are made for walking: *Mrs. Miller*
CD CDEMS 1613
EMI / May '97 / EMI

ON THE STREETS
CD WB 1166CD
We Bite / Jun '97 / Plastic Head

ON THE SUNNY SIDE OF THE STREET 1934
CD PHONTCD 7653
Phontastic / '93 / Cadillac / Jazz Music / Wellard

ON THE WILD SIDE
CD Set NSCD 003
Newsound / Feb '95 / THE

ON-U SOUND (A Party Of Dubbers And Toasters)
CD CLP 9919
Cleopatra / Feb '97 / Cargo / Greyhound / Plastic Head / RTM/Disc / SRD

ON-U SOUND DUB XPERIENCE (The Dread Operators)
CD CLP 9825
Cleopatra / Oct '96 / Cargo / Greyhound / Plastic Head / RTM/Disc / SRD

ONCE IN A LIFETIME (2CD Set)
CD Set TCD 2889
Telstar / Feb '97 / BMG

ONCE UPON A TIME IN THE WEST
Bonanza / Once upon a time in the West / Good, the bad and the ugly / Magnificent seven / Green leaves of summer / High noon / Fist full of dollars / Hondo / Man with the harmonica / Professional gun / Yankee doodle / Dynamite ringo / Return of the seven / Wandering star / Hang 'em high / Man from Laramie / How the West was won / Alamo / Comancheros / True grit
CD GRF 041
Tring / Feb '93 / Tring

ONE AD
CD WF 841012
Waveform / Jun '94 / Kudos / Pinnacle / Plastic Head

ONE AND ONLY, THE
Year of the cat: *Stewart, Al* / Baker Street: *Rafferty, Gerry* / Weight: *Band* / It's a long way there: *Little River Band* / Classic: *Gurvitz, Adrian* / Bon voyage: *Carnes, Kim* / Border: *America* / Sharing the night together: *Dr. Hook* / He ain't heavy, he's my brother: *Hollies* / I go to pieces: *Cotton/Lloyd/Christian* / No more fear of flying: *Brooker, Gary* / It's a heartache: *Tyler, Bonnie* / I love you so: *McLean, Don* / Release me: *Wilson Phillips* / Don't you write her off: *Hillman, Chris & Roger McGuinn* / We've got tonight: *Brooks, Elkie*
CD DC 880132
Disky / May '97 / Disky / THE

ONE DAY AT A TIME (20 Songs Of Peace)
One day at a time: *Martell, Lena* / Michael, row the boat ashore: *Donegan, Lonnie* / Where peaceful waters flow: *Knight, Gladys* / Lay down (Candles in the rain): *Melanie & The Edwin Hawkin Singers* / Spirit in the sky: *Morrison, Dorothy* / I don't know how to love him: *Clark, Petula* / Jesu joy of man's desiring: *Black Dyke Mills Band* / Hallelujah chorus: *Black Dyke Mills Band* / Oh happy day: *Hawkins, Edwin Singers* / Amazing grace: *Royal Scots Dragoon Guards* / Ave Maria: *Rose Marie* / Higher and higher: *Wilson, Jackie* / Old rugged cross: *Martell, Lena* / Chorus of the Hebrew slaves: *Sofia National Opera Chorus* / Humming chorus: *Sofia National Opera Chorus* / Peace will come: *Melanie & The Edwin Hawkin Singers* / Border song: *Morrison, Dorothy* / He bought my soul at Calvary: *Alexander Brothers* / Suddenly there's a valley: *Clark, Petula* / Jerusalem: *Walker, Sarah & RPO*
CD TRTCD 120
TrueTrax / Oct '94 / THE

ONE FOOT IN THE GROOVE - AMERICAN BIG BANDS
American patrol: *Miller, Glenn* / Take the 'A' train: *Ellington, Duke* / One o'clock jump: *James, Harry* / Dipsy doodle: *Clinton, Larry* / Sunny side of the street: *Dorsey, Tommy* / Dinah: *Hampton, Lionel* / Mississippi mud: *Beiderbecke, Bix* / Jersey bounce: *Nelson, Ozzie* / Dippermouth blues: *Dorsey, Jimmy* / Christopher Columbus: *Goodman, Benny* / Begin the beguine: *Shaw, Artie* / South Rampart Street Parade: *Crosby, Bob* / Wrap your troubles in dreams: *Gray, Glen* / Honeysuckle rose: *Basie, Count* / In a sentimental mood: *Jurgens, Dick* / In the mood: *Miller, Glenn* / Sugarfoot stomp: *Henderson, Fletcher* / Perdido: *Ellington, Duke* / Ciribiribin: *James, Harry* / Woodchopper's ball: *Herman, Woody*
CD ONEC 001
Tring / Apr '96 / Tring

ONE FOOT IN THE GROOVE - CROONERS
Where the blue of the night: *Crosby, Bing* / Imagination: *Eberle, Bob* / All or nothing at all: *Sinatra, Frank* / Sonny boy: *Jolson, Al* / Amapola: *Rey, Monte* / This can't be love: *Vallee, Rudy* / East of the sun: *Tracy, Arthur* / Mimi: *Chevalier, Maurice* / Where are you: *Hutchinson, Leslie 'Hutch'* / Georgia on my mind: *Carmichael, Hoagy* / Oh Buddy, I'm in love: *Gibbons, Carroll* / I'll see you later: *Coward, Noel* / I'm in a dancing mood: *Buchanan, Jack* / Elmer's tune: *Eberle, Ray* / Fine romance: *Astaire, Fred* / Lulu's back in town: *Powell, Dick* / Brother, can you spare a dime: *Crosby, Bing* / Rock a bye your baby: *Jolson, Al* / You lucky people you: *Sinatra, Frank* / Very thought of you: *Bowlly, Al*
CD ONEC 004
Tring / Apr '96 / Tring

ONE FOOT IN THE GROOVE - LADIES
Tisket a tasket: *Fitzgerald, Ella* / Every time we say goodbye: *Horne, Lena* / I hear a rhapsody: *Shore, Dinah* / Everybody sings: *Garland, Judy* / I like a guy what takes his time: *West, Mae* / Nobody knows you when you're down and out: *Smith, Bessie* / Beyond the blue horizons: *McDonald, Jeanette* / Darling, je vous aime beaucoup: *Hildegarde* / Swing me a lullaby: *Boswell, Connee* / Let yourself go: *Rogers, Ginger* / Everything I have is yours: *Etting, Ruth* / With every breath I take: *Boswell, Connee* / You've done something to my heart: *Jones, Gwen* / Therre's something about a soldier: *Courtneidge, Cicely* / Life begins at forty: *Tucker, Sophie* / Miss Brown to you: *Holiday, Billie* / On the good ship lollipop: *Temple, Shirley* / I've got you under my skin: *Day, Frances* / We'll meet again: *Lynn, Vera* / You brought a new kind of love to me: *Waters, Ethel*
CD ONEC 002
Tring / Apr '96 / Tring

ONE FOOT IN THE GROOVE - WAR SONGS
We'll meet again: *Lynn, Vera* / There'll always be an Egland: *Lynn, Vera* / Umbrella song: *Flanagan & Allen* / When they sound the last all clear: *Lynn, Vera* / When the lights go on: *Monroe, Vaughan* / You've done something to my heart: *Trent, Bruce* / Run rabbit run: *Flanagan & Allen* / Leaning on a lamp post: *Formby, George* / There's something about a soldier: *Courtneidge, Cicely* / Hey little hen: *Loss, Joe* / Nightingale sang in Berkeley Square: *Lombardo, Guy* / Boogie woogie bugle boy: *Andrews Sisters* / All over the place: *Trinder, Tommy* / Lili Marlene: *Anderson, Lale* / Don't sit under the apple tree: *Miller, Glenn* / There'll be bluebirds over the white cliffs of Dover: *Stone, Lew* / Homecoming waltz: *Benson, Ivy* / My devotion: *Winston, Eric* / We're gonna hang out the washing on the Siegfried line: *Flanagan & Allen* / I'll be seeing you: *Crosby, Bing*
CD ONEC 003
Tring / Apr '96 / Tring

ONE HALF OF A WHOLE DECADE (Five Years At Ministry Of Sound)
Voices in my mind: *Voices* / Good feelin': *Swing Kids* / This is the only way: *Lovebeads & Courtney Grey* / Nothing better: *Colourblind* / Deliver me: *Urban Blues Project* / Helpless: *Urbanised & Silvano* / Pride, a deeper love: *C&C Music Factory* / It's gonna be a lovely day: *SOUL System* / Beautiful people: *Tucker, Barbara* / Carry on: *Wash, Martha* / I'll be your friend: *Owens, Robert* / Pennies from heaven: *Inner City* / Raise me: *Bizarre Inc.* / Not forgotten: *Leftfield* / Love me tonight: *White, Anthony* / Plastic dreams: *Jaydee* / Yeke yeke: *Kante, Mory* / Kinetic: *Golden Girls* / Believe in me: *Mankey* / Melody of love: *Summer, Donna* / When: *Sunscreem* / Satellite: *Beloved* / Take me higher: *Lucas, Jennifer* / O: *28th Street Crew* / Rays of the rising sun: *Mozaic* / Destiny: *Hieroglyphix* / Solar system: *Q-Project* / Night train: *Appaloosa & DJ Dream* / Above and beyond: *PHD* / Universal music: *Seb & Lo Tek* / Music: *LTJ Bukem* / Jazz lick: *Peshay* / Senses: *DJ Addiction* / Reflections: *New Balance* / Euphony: *Axis*
CD MOS 5CD
Ministry Of Sound / Sep '96 / 3mv/Sony / Mo's Music Machine / Warner Music

ONE HIT WONDERS
Tell Laura I love her: *Valance, Ricky* / No body's child: *Young, Karen* / Pickin' a chicken: *Boswell, Eve* / Calendar song: *Trinidad Oil Company* / Games people play: *South, Joe* / Tarzan boy: *Baltimore* / With a little help from my friends: *Young Idea* / Softly whispering I love you: *Congregation* / Vaya con dios: *Paul, Les & Mary Ford* / Boogie oogie oogie: *Taste Of Honey* / I'm the urban spaceman: *Bonzo Dog Band* / Let's go all the way: *Sly Fox* / Sukiyaki: *Sakamoto, Kyu* / This ole house: *Stevens, Shakin'* / Up up and away: *Mann, Johnny Singers* / Rock me gently: *Kim, Andy* / Loving you: *Riperton, Minnie* / Unchained melody: *Baxter, Les* / Spanish stroll: *Mink Deville* / I should have known better: *Naturals* / Arrivederci darling: *Savage, Edna* / He's got the whole world in his hands: *London, Laurie*
CD CC 8252
EMI / Nov '94 / EMI

...ONE LAST KISS
CD SPART 1
Spin Art / Feb '97 / Cargo

ONE LITTLE INDIAN GREATEST HITS VOL.2
CD TPCD 17
One Little Indian / Apr '90 / Pinnacle

ONE LITTLE INDIAN TAKES ON THE COWBOYS
CD TPCD 6
One Little Indian / May '88 / Pinnacle

ONE LOVE (20 Caribbean Classics)
Rivers of babylon: *Boney M* / Brown girl in the ring: *Boney M* / Help me make it through the night: *Holt, John* / Killing me softly: *Holt, John* / Everything I own: *Booth, Ken* / Hurt so good: *Cadogan, Susan* / Nice and easy: *Cadogan, Susan* / Many rivers to cross: *Cliff, Jimmy* / Wonderful world, beautiful people: *Cliff, Jimmy* / Banana boat song (Day O): *Belafonte, Harry* / Side show: *Biggs, Barry* / Dat: *Shevington, Pluto* / Israelites: *Dekker, Desmond* / First time: *Griffiths, Marcia* / Ever I saw your face: *Griffiths, Marcia* / When will I see you again: *Griffiths, Marcia* / I want to wake up with you: *Gardiner, Boris*
CD PLATCD 3913
Platinum / Mar '92 / Prism

ONE LOVE (The Very Best Of Reggae)
I want to wake up with you: *Holt, John* / Wonderful world: *Heptones* / Rhythm body: *Minott, Sugar* / Sweet sensation: *Melodians* / Good thing going: *Isaacs, Gregory* / Tide is high: *Paragons* / Keep on moving: *Marley, Bob & The Wailers* / Guns don't argue: *Alcapone, Dennis* / Pressure drop: *Toots & The Maytals* / I will always love you: *Holt, John* / Satisfy my soul: *Marley, Bob & The Wailers* / One my love: *Sly & Robbie* / If I were a carpenter: *Winston Groovy* / Guns of Navarone: *Upsetters* / Jah Jah bless the dreadlocks: *Mighty Diamonds* / Clint Eastwood rides again: *Perry, Lee 'Scratch'* / Wet dream: *Max Romeo* / Cocaine in my brain: *Dillinger* / Monkey man: *Toots & The Maytals* / One love: *Marley, Bob & The Wailers*
CD CD 6030
Music / Sep '96 / Target/BMG

ONE LOVE PRESENTS SENTIMENTAL RAGGA VOL.1
CD KICKCD 16
Kickin' / Oct '94 / Prime / SRD

ONE LOVE VOL.2 (Another 20 Caribbean Classics)
Amigo: *Black Slate* / Hot hot hot: *Arrow* / Ready for it now: *Lovelady, Bill* / Cupid: *Nash, Johnny* / Let your yeah be yeah: *Pioneers* / I am what I am: *Greyhound* / Peace to the man: *Hot Chocolate* / Uptown top ranking: *Althia & Donna* / Barbados: *Typically Tropical* / Sing a little song: *Dekker, Desmond* / I'm in the mood for love: *Lord Tanamo* / Hold me tight: *Nash, Johnny* / Double barrel: *Collins, Dave & Ansell* / Liquidator: *Harry J All Stars* / Real fashion, reggae style: *Johnson, Carey* / Money in your pocket: *Brown, Dennis* / You never know what you've got: *Me & You* / Love of the common people: *Thomas, Nicky* / Suzanne beware of the devil: *Livingstone, Dandy* / All in one: *Marley, Bob*
CD PLATCD 3920
Platinum / Oct '93 / Prism

ONE MAN ONE VOTE
CD GRELCD 160
Greensleeves / Apr '91 / Jet Star / SRD

ONE MORE SONG
CD CDPH 1197
Philo / Aug '96 / ADA / CM / Direct

ONE NIGHT STANDS
Geometry / Softly as in a morning sunrise / No going back / Chogui / Little sunflower / Big yellow taxi / My funny valentine / Hello Max / Entertaining Mr. C / Lush life / Cajun / Wind is getting angry
CD BTF 9402
Blow The Fuse / Nov '94 / New Note/ Pinnacle

ONE O'CLOCK JUMP
One o'clock jump: *Basie, Count* / Moose the mooch: *Davis, Miles* / Bugle call rag: *Goodman, Benny* / It's only a paper moon: *Cole, Nat 'King'* / Basin Street blues: *Armstrong, Louis* / Rumbop concerto: *Gillespie, Dizzy* / 'Round midnight: *Parker, Charlie* / Stompin' at the Savoy: *Herman, Woody* / My heart stood still: *Shaw, Artie* / At long last love: *Horne, Lena* / That old black magic: *Fitzgerald, Ella* / Yardbird suite: *Davis, Miles* / Love me or leave me: *Horne, Lena* / Tiger rag: *Armstrong, Louis* / Feather merchant: *Basie, Count* / Move: *Parker, Charlie* / Get happy: *Goodman, Benny* / Blue prelude: *Horne, Lena* / Three hearts in a triangle: *Gillespie, Dizzy* / Slow boat to China: *Gillespie, Dizzy*
CD GRF 125
Tring / '93 / Tring

ONE STEP AHEAD - TWO TONE DANCE CRAZE
CD BHR 028CD
Burning Heart / Oct '95 / Plastic Head

ONE VOICE (Vocal Music From Around The World)
Izithembiso Zenkosi: *Ladysmith Black Mambazo* / Prochula se moma Nedelya: *Trio Bulgarka* / Tender comrade: *Bragg, Billy* / Jerusalem revisited: *Coope, Boyes & Simpson* / Ever widening circles of remorse: *Sublette, Ned & Lawrence Weiner/The Persuasions* / Cantu a balluu seriu: *Tenores Di Bitti* / Heilani Saattelin Amerikkahan: *Liedes, Anna-Kaisa* / Puisque je t'aime, pars: *Revey, Laurence* / Irijirie (my dawn): *Pearl Divers Of Bahrain* / Bean an Ieanna: *Heaney, Joe* / Blood and gold/Mohacs: *Prior, Maddy & June Tabor* / Grey cock: *Carthy, Eliza* / E ho hi: *MacKenzie, Talitha* / Bazali Bethu: *Black Umfolosi* / Himene tarava: *Tamarii Pirae of Tahiti* / Throat singing: *Shu-De* / Benza guru: *Tibetan Buddhist Monks* / Introitus - Da Pacem: *Cantori Gregoriani* / Study war no more: *Sweet Honey In The Rock*
CD RGNET 1014CD
World Music Network / Aug '97 / ADA / New Note/Pinnacle

ONE VOICE, ONE LOVE
One vision: *Queen* / Let love rule: *Kravitz, Lenny* / Message in the box: *World Party* /

Shakin' the tree: *Gabriel, Peter & Youssou N'Dour* / One: *U2* / Future love paradise: *Seal* / Ideal world: *Christians* / Love oh love: *Richie, Lionel* / Sowing the seeds of love: *Tears For Fears* / One love: *Marley, Bob & The Wailers* / Prayer for the world: *Priest, Maxi* / Great heart: *Clegg, Johnny & Savuka* / (Something inside) So strong: *Siffre, Labi* / Where do we go from here: *Birkett, Chris* / Light in the dark: *Brady, Paul* / Brothers in arms: *Dire Straits*
CD _______________ 5164172
PolyGram TV / Aug '93 / PolyGram

ONE WORLD
CD _______________ ROUAN 15
Rounder / Oct '94 / ADA / CM / Direct

ONE WORLD OR NONE (The Conscious Compilation)
Northern sulphuric soul: *Rae & Christian* / Kalimba: *Freakniks* / Chicken ina box: *Mr. Scruff* / Jive talk: *Fourth World* / Universal highness: *Thievery Corporation* / Duden: *Atlas, Natacha* / Zed and two L's: *Fila Brazillia* / Dub systems go: *Dubmarine* / Garden: *Riz Allstars* / Dub oppression: *Riz Allstars & Ishuru*
CD _______________ WDM 004CD
World Development / Feb '97 / Timewarp

ONE WORLD, ONE VOICE
CD _______________ CDV 2632
Virgin / Jun '90 / EMI

ONLY CLUB ALBUM YOU'LL EVER NEED, THE
CD _______________ 5407862
A&M / Aug '97 / PolyGram

ONLY FOR THE HEADSTRONG (2CD Set)
Rock the dancefloor: *Forbes, Davie* / Pop goes the world: *Third Man* / Rock this place: *DJ Elevation* / Any last words: *DJ Psycangle* / Resident evil: *Tailbone* / Dark and darker: *DJ Flare* / End of an era: *Luna-C* / As yet untitled: *Brothers Mayhem* / Energy flux: *El Bruto* / I got something: *DJ Reno & Eatsum* / Is stupid when: *DJ Psycangle* / Let me go: *Toxic Avengers* / Time to party: *DJ E-Rick & Tactic* / Crazy: *Brotherhood*
CD Set _______________ DBM 2774
Death Becomes Me / Feb '97 / Grapevine/ PolyGram / Pinnacle / SRD

ONLY FOR THE HEADSTRONG VOL.2
CD _______________ 8283162
FFRR / Jun '92 / PolyGram

ONLY FREEWAYS TO SKINNER KAT
CD _______________ RAUCD 12
Raucous / Oct '94 / Nervous / RTM/Disc / TKO Magnum

ONLY GUITAR (2CD Set)
CD Set _______________ 24042
Delta Doubles / Jun '96 / Target/BMG

ONLY THE POORMAN FEEL IT
Izinziswa / Giya / Siyaya / Mayibuye / Shosholoza / No easy road / Skorokoro / Yivumeni we zinsizw / Uthando lami / Ihlathi / Intsizwa / Thula / Madambadamba
CD _______________ CDEMC 3706
EMI / Sep '97 / EMI

ONLY THE STRONG
CD _______________ VR 010CD
Victory / Jun '94 / Plastic Head

ONLY YOU (20 Great Hits Of The Sixties)
That's what love will do: *Brown, Joe* / When my little girl is smiling: *Justice, Jimmy* / Only you (And you alone): *Wynter, Mark* / Sailor: *Clark, Petula* / Who put the bomp: *Viscounts* / March of the Siamese children: *Ball, Kenny* / Party's over: *Donegan, Lonnie* / Up on the roof: *Grant, Julie* / I wonder who's kissing her now: *Ford, Emile* / Swinging on a star: *Irwin, Big Dee & Little Eva* / It's almost tomorrow: *Wynter, Mark* / Where are you now: *Trent, Jackie* / Counting teardrops: *Ford, Emile* / Alone at last: *Wilson, Jackie* / Ramona: *Bachelors* / Picture of you: *Brown, Joe* / Sukiyaki: *Ball, Kenny* / Michael, row the boat ashore: *Donegan, Lonnie* / Spanish Harlem: *Justice, Jimmy* / Ya ya twist: *Clark, Petula*
CD _______________ TRTCD 102
TrueTrax / Dec '94 / THE

ONLY YOU
Room in your heart: *Living In A Box* / When will I see you again: *Brother Beyond* / Don't turn away: *Go For It* / Until forever: *Rogers, Evan* / I'll fly for you: *Spandau Ballet* / What becomes of the broken hearted: *Boy George* / Caravan of love: *Housemartins* / Rise to the occasion: *Fisher, Climie* / Orchard Road: *Sayer, Leo* / Turn back the clock: *Johnny Hates Jazz* / Mistake no.3: *Culture Club* / Only you: *Flying Pickets* / You're in love: *Wilson Phillips* / Don't want to wait anymore: *Tubes* / Won't let you go: *Sly Fox* / Every rose has it's thorn: *Poison*
CD _______________ DC 870532
Disky / Mar '97 / Disky / THE

OOH OOH - THE POETS OF RHYTHM: HOTPIE & CANDY RECORDS (Original Raw Soul Vol.1)
Working on the line: *Soul Saints Orchestra* / Spooky grinder: *Woo Woo's* / South Carolina: *Bus People Express* / Fifty yards of soul: *Whitefield Brothers* / Funky train: *Poets Of Rhythm* / ORF (Pts 1 & 2): *Organized Raw Funk* / Funky Sex Machine: *Baral, Bo* / Cooking on a piece of meat: *Whitefield Brothers* / Augusta, Georgia (Here I come): *Bus People Express* / Ooh ooh: *Woo Woo's* / Hotpie's popcorn Pt.1: *Poets Of Rhythm* / Bag of soul: *Soul Saints Orchestra* / Sticky sticky sock-a-poo: *Mighty Continentals* / It's your thing
CD _______________ ME 000372
Soulciety/Bassism / Sep '95 / EWM

OPEN HOUSE
Super sonic surfer: *Fractal Shark* / Open house: *Monolith* / Free for all: *Deep Quest* / House of reality: *Monolith* / Silver dollar: *Balloon* / Sunrise surprise: *Deep Quest* / Infect: *Fractal Shark* / Kling klang: *Deep Quest* / Islands in the sun: *Monolith* / Mercury mission: *Balloon*
CD _______________ 306172
Hallmark / Jan '97 / Carlton

OPEN T - ON THE ROAD
CD _______________ TMPCD 018
Temple / Dec '95 / BMG

OPERATIC EUPHONIUM
Celeste aida / Flower duet / Catari, catari / Largo al factotum / Duet from Don Pasquale / Evening prayer / La Donna e mobile / Marriage to Figaro / Pagageno, pagagena / Flower song / On with the motley / Quartet from rigoletto / Softly awakes my heart / Recondita armonia / Panis angelicus / Lohengrin / Oh, beloved father / Le miserere (il travatore) / You are my hearts delight / One fine day / Nun's chorus / Nessun dorma
CD _______________ QPRL 072D
Polyphonic / Oct '95 / Complete/Pinnacle

OPERATION BEATBOX
CD _______________ REC 023
Re-Constriction / Oct '96 / Cargo

OPERATION D
CD _______________ DBTXCD 2
Sting Ray / Nov '95 / Jet Star

OPSCENE 50
CD _______________ GAP 032CD
Gap Recordings / Sep '96 / SRD

ORANGE COUNTY PUNK VERSUS SKA VOL.1
CD _______________ SV 001CD
Revelation / Mar '97 / Cargo / Plastic Head

ORBITS VOL.1
CD _______________ CDC 001
Out Of Orbit / Mar '95 / Plastic Head / SRD

ORDER ODONATA VOL.1
CD _______________ BFLCD 13
Dragonfly / Jul '94 / Mo's Music Machine / Pinnacle

ORGAN RADIO VOL.1
CD _______________ ORGAN 025CD
Org / Mar '97 / Pinnacle

ORGANISED SOUND
CD _______________ JFRCD 005
Jazz Fudge / Sep '96 / Pinnacle

ORGANISM VOL.1
CD _______________ EFAD 84632
Dossier / Oct '94 / Cargo / SRD

ORGANISM VOL.2
CD _______________ EFA 084642
Dossier / Mar '95 / Cargo / SRD

ORGANISM VOL.3
CD _______________ EFA 084682
Dossier / Nov '95 / Cargo / SRD

ORGANISM VOL.4
CD _______________ EFA 08469CD
Dossier / Jun '96 / Cargo / SRD

ORGANIST ENTERTAINS YOU
Here we are again: *Foort, Reginald* / Ta ra ra boom de ay: *Foort, Reginald* / Down at the old Bull & Bush: *Foort, Reginald* / Melody in F: *MacPherson, Sandy* / Change partners: *Cleaver, Robinson* / Yam: *Cleaver, Robinson* / I used to be colour blind: *Cleaver, Robinson* / Las Cuatro Milpas: *Ramsey, Harold* / Rhythm of the clock (tick a tick tock): *Torch, Sidney* / Rhapsody in blue: *Ramsey, Harold & Patricia Rossborough* / Parade of the tin soldiers: *MacLean, Quentin* / Mosquitos parade: *MacLean, Quentin* / My love parade: *MacLean, Quentin* / Why shouldn't we: *Foort, Reginald* / Door of my dreams: *Foort, Reginald* / Indian love call: *Foort, Reginald* / You're a sweetheart: *Torch, Sidney* / Invitation to the waltz: *Cleaver, Robinson & Patricia Rossborough* / My dream garden: *Foort, Reginald* / Love's a garden of roses: *Foort, Reginald* / Trees: *Foort, Reginald* / Lullaby of the leaves: *Foort, Reginald* / Bees' wedding: *Foort, Reginald* / I'm knee deep in daisies: *Foort, Reginald* / Narcissus: *Foort, Reginald* / Brown bird singing: *Foort, Reginald* / Spring song: *Foort, Reginald* / Country gardens: *Foort, Reginald* / Grandma said: *Dixon, Reginald* / I miss you in the morning: *Dixon, Reginald* / Isn't this a lovely day: *Torch, Sidney* / Why stars come out at night: *Torch, Sidney* / Cheek to cheek: *Torch, Sidney* / Keep smiling: *Foort, Reginald* / Music Maestro please: *Dixon, Reginald* / Little lady make believe: *Dixon, Reginald* / Whistler and his dog: *Cleaver, Robinson* / Washington Post: *Ramsey, Harold* / Semper fidelis: *Ramsey, Harold* / Hungarian march: *Ramsey, Harold* / I shall always remember you smiling: *Dixon, Reginald* / Where the Shannon flows down to the sea: *Dixon, Reginald* / Dainty Miss: *Cleaver, Robinson* / Miss Annabelle Lee: *Cleaver, Robinson* / Somebody stole my gal: *Cleaver, Robinson* / St. Louis blues: *Ramsey, Harold*
CD _______________ RAJCD 862
Empress / May '96 / Koch

ORGASMIC HOUSE
CD _______________ DOWN 1CD
Sun Down / Jun '95 / SRD

ORIENT OF THE GREEKS, THE
CD _______________ 926592
BUDA / Apr '97 / Discovery

ORIENTAL DREAMS
CD _______________ PS 65075
PlayaSound / Jul '91 / ADA / Harmonia Mundi

ORIGIN UNKNOWN - THE SPEED OF SOUND
CD _______________ RAMMLPCD 1
Ramm / May '97 / Jet Star / SRD

ORIGINAL CLUB SKA
CD _______________ CDHB 055
Heartbeat / Feb '91 / ADA / Direct / Greensleeves / Jet Star

ORIGINAL DJ CLASSICS
CD _______________ ROCKY 1
Rocky One / Apr '96 / Jet Star

ORIGINAL HITS OF GEORGE GERSHWIN
CD _______________ DHDL 112
Halcyon / Oct '92 / Cadillac / Harmonia Mundi / Jazz Music / Swift / Wellard

ORIGINAL HITS OF THE 60'S AND 70'S
CD _______________ PKL 514911
K&K / Jul '93 / Jet Star

ORIGINAL JAZZ MASTERS VOL.1, THE (5CD Set)
CD Set _______________ DAMUSIC 76032
DA Music / Dec '95 / Conifer/BMG

ORIGINAL JAZZ MASTERS VOL.2, THE (5CD Set)
CD Set _______________ DAMUSIC 76042
DA Music / Dec '95 / Conifer/BMG

ORIGINAL MAMBO KINGS, THE
CD _______________ 5138762
Verve / Jan '93 / PolyGram

ORIGINAL MEMPHIS FIVE GROUPS
CD _______________ VILCD 0162
Village Jazz / Aug '92 / Jazz Music / Target/BMG

ORIGINAL MEMPHIS FIVE VOL.1 1922-1923
My honey's lovin' arms / Cuddle up blues / Hopeless blues / Lonesome mama blues / Hot lips / Yankee doodle blues / I wish I could shimmy like my sister Kate / Achin' hearted blues / Chicago / Running wild / Ivy / That barking dog / Stop your kidding / Loose feet / Aggravatin' / Great white way blues / Four o'clock blues / Shufflin' Mose / Jelly roll blues / Bunch of blues / Sweet papa Joe / Hootin' de hoot
CD _______________ COCD 16
Collector's Classics / Mar '95 / Cadillac / Complete/Pinnacle / Jazz Music

ORIGINAL MEMPHIS ROCK 'N' ROLL
CD _______________ CLCD 4404
Collector/White Label / Nov '96 / TKO Magnum

ORIGINAL REGGAE HITS OF THE 60'S & 70'S, THE
CD _______________ PKCD 33194
K&K / Sep '94 / Jet Star

ORIGINAL RHUMBAS
CD _______________ 995312
EPM / Aug '93 / ADA / Discovery

ORIGINAL SOUL CHRISTMAS, THE
CD _______________ 8122717882
WEA / Dec '94 / Warner Music

ORIGINAL STALAG 17-18 AND 19
CD _______________ WRCD 1684
Jet Star / Oct '92 / Jet Star

ORIGINAL VERSIONS OF SONGS BY THE COMMITMENTS
Mustang Sally / Chain of fools / Hard to handle / Mr. Pitiful / I never loved a man (the way I love you) / In the midnight hour / Slip away / Please please please / Shaft / Show me / Try a little tenderness / Dark end of the street / I've got dreams to remember / Do right man / Do right woman, do right man
CD _______________ 7567918132
East West / Feb '94 / Warner Music

ORIGINAL VERSIONS OF THE FAMOUS HITS
CD _______________ MPV 5555
Movieplay / Sep '94 / Target/BMG

ORIGINALS VOL.1
Wonderful world: *Cooke, Sam* / I heard it through the grapevine: *Gaye, Marvin* / Stand by me: *King, Ben E.* / When a man loves a woman: *Sledge, Percy* / C'mon everybody: *Cochran, Eddie* / Mannish boy: *Waters, Muddy* / Ain't nobody home: *King, B.B.* / Can't get enough: *Bad Company* / Joker: *Miller, Steve Band* / Should I stay or should I go: *Clash* / Twentieth century boy: *T-Rex* / Mad about the boy: *Washington, Dinah* / Piece of my heart: *Franklin, Erma* / Heart attack and vine: *Hawkins, Screamin' Jay*
CD _______________ MOODCD 29
Columbia / May '93 / Sony

ORIGINALS VOL.2
Up on the roof: *Drifters* / It takes two: *Gaye, Marvin & Kim Weston* / (Sittin' on the) dock of the bay: *Redding, Otis* / In crowd: *Gray, Dobie* / La bamba: *Los Lobos* / All right now: *Free* / Move on up: *Mayfield, Curtis* / I get the sweetest feeling: *Wilson, Jackie* / Hey Joe: *Hendrix, Jimi* / Papa's got a brand new bag: *Brown, James* / No particular place to go: *Berry, Chuck* / Heatwave: *Reeves, Martha & The Vandellas* / Bad moon rising: *Creedence Clearwater Revival* / Let's work together: *Canned Heat* / Wanderer: *Dion* / My baby just cares for me: *Simone, Nina* / Stella Mae: *Hooker, John Lee*
CD _______________ MOODCD 31
Columbia / Mar '94 / Sony

ORIGINALS, THE
I'll be there: *Jackson Five* / It only takes a minute: *Tavares* / Hang on in there baby: *Bristol, Johnny* / Rock your baby: *McCrae, George* / Now that we've found love: *Third World* / Show you the way to go: *Jacksons* / Tired of being alone: *Green, Al* / Summer breeze: *Isley Brothers* / You to me are everything: *Real Thing* / Play that funky music: *Wild Cherry* / It takes two: *Gaye, Marvin & Kim Weston* / Fantasy: *Earth, Wind & Fire* / I believe in miracles: *Jackson Sisters* / Don't leave me this way: *Melvin, Harold & The Bluenotes* / Shame, shame, shame: *Shirley & Company* / Give me just a little more time: *Chairmen Of The Board* / Respect yourself: *Staple Singers* / Tender love: *Force MD's* / Please don't go: *KC & The Sunshine Band*
CD _______________ DINTVCD 43
Dino / Aug '92 / Pinnacle

ORIGINATION 1974-1984
CD _______________ SHCD 6012
Sky High / Oct '95 / Direct / Jet Star

ORIGINATORS, THE
Let the power fall: *Romeo, Max* / Kaya dub: *King Tubby & The Aggrovators* / Village: *Isaacs, Gregory* / Someday: *Ellis, Alton* / Reggae hits the town: *Ethiopians* / Originator: *U-Roy* / Zion gate: *Andy, Horace* / Left me with a broken heart: *Paragons* / Love me forever: *Brown, Dennis* / Guns don't argue: *Alcapone, Dennis* / King Tubby's special: *Pablo, Augustus* / Three times a lady: *Sanchez* / I'm in the mood for love: *Edwards, Jackie* / If it don't work out: *Pat Kelly* / You're my desire: *Marley, Rita & The Soulettes* / Jam in the street: *Holt, John* / Gonna take a miracle: *Boothe, Ken* / Just once in my life: *McGregor, Freddie*
CD _______________ CDBM 124
Blue Moon / Jan '97 / Cadillac / Discovery / Greensleeves / Jazz Music / Jet Star / TKO Magnum

ORIGINS OF MAN (MADE MUSIC), THE
CD _______________ PRMTCDX 001
Primate / Sep '97 / Prime / RTM/Disc / SRD

ORISSI DANCE MUSIC
CD _______________ VICG 52682
JVC World Library / Mar '96 / ADA / CM / Direct

ORKNEY SESSIONS
CD _______________ AT 041CD
Attic / Oct '95 / ADA / CM

ORQUESTAS TEJANAS (Tejano Roots)
CD _______________ ARHCD 368
Arhoolie / Apr '95 / ADA / Cadillac / Direct

ORTHODOX CHANTS
CD _______________ AUB 006770
Auvidis/Ethnic / Dec '92 / ADA / Harmonia Mundi

OS IPANEMAS
CD _______________ MRBCD 001
Mr. Bongo / May '95 / New Note/Pinnacle / RTM/Disc / SRD

OTHER STUFF
In essance: *Isis* / Vorn: *Idjut Boys* / Intertwining sexuality: *Sensory Productions* / Nothin's been the same: *DJD & NYN* / Landing: *Sutra* / Other / Other / Eso lo que va: *Beach Flea & Magic Juan* / Future: *Other Project & RMA* / Feel the warmth: *Reel Houze* / Brinca: *Rosario, Ralphi* / Hard to dye: *Paramour* / Love triangle: *Coco Steel & Lovebomb* / It's a party: *Man Called Adam*
CD _______________ THECD 106
Other / Apr '97 / Mo's Music Machine / Pinnacle

OTHERWORLD - DANCE TRANCE AND MAGIC PLANTS
CD _______________ TRANR 610CD
Transient / Aug '97 / Prime / SRD / Total/ BMG

OTTOMAN ART MUSIC
CD ______ AAA 130
Club Du Disque Arabe / Apr '97 / ADA / Harmonia Mundi

OUD, THE
CD ______ LYRCD 7160
Lyrichord / Dec '94 / ADA / CM / Roots

OUIJAWHAMMY
CD ______ AB 002CD
Holistic / Mar '96 / Kudos / Pinnacle / Plastic Head / Prime

OUR FAVOURITE THINGS
Please don't talk about me when I'm gone: *Holiday, Billie* / Stolen moments (aka you belong to her): *Carter, Betty & Carmen McRae* / Squatty roo: *Fitzgerald, Ella* / Crazy he calls me: *Washington, Dinah* / If I were a bell: *Dearie, Blossom* / Up jumped spring: *Lincoln, Abbey* / They didn't believe me: *Anderson, Ernestine* / Sometimes I'm happy: *Vaughan, Sarah* / You're lucky to me: *Merrill, Helen* / I've got the world on a string: *O'Day, Anita* / Only trust your heart: *Gilberto, Astrud* / Blue and sentimental: *Humes, Helen* / My favourite things: *Carter, Betty* / Don't explain: *Simone, Nina* / Just in time: *Horn, Shirley* / If you could see me now: *King, Morgana*
CD ______ 5526402
Spectrum / Mar '97 / PolyGram

OUR FRIENDS ELECTRIC
CD ______ TCD 2814
Telstar / Feb '96 / BMG

OUR HYMNS
O God, our help in ages past: *Keaggy, Phil* / Holy holy holy: *Smith, Michael W.* / It is so sweet to trust in Jesus: *Grant, Amy* / Saviour is waiting: *Take 6*
CD ______ WSTCD 9107
Nelson Word / Dec '89 / Nelson Word

OUR SALVATION IS IN HAND
CD ______ TP 05
Theme Park / May '97 / Cargo

OUT LOUD (For Gay & Lesbian Human Rights)
CD ______ KFWCD 169
Knitting Factory / Oct '96 / Cargo / Plastic Head

OUT OF MANY ONE VOL.1 (Jamaican Music 1962-1975)
Music is my occupation: *Drummond, Don* / Owe me no pay me: *Ethiopians* / Jack of my trade: *Sir Lord Comic* / Run for your life: *Bryan, Carl* / Sick and tired: *Grant, Neville* / Don't look back: *Brown, Buster* / Only yesterday: *Parker, Ken* / Place called Africa: *Byles, Junior* / Hopeful village: *Tennors* / Better must come: *Wilson, Delroy* / Stop that man: *Crystalites* / Space flight: *I-Roy* / Sun is shining: *Marley, Bob & The Wailers* / Fever: *Byles, Junior* / Satan side: *Hudson, Keith* / Skank in bed: *Scotty* / Let's start again: *Campbell, Cornell & Friends*
CD ______ CDTRS 1
Trojan / Jan '89 / Direct / Jet Star

OUT OF MANY ONE VOL.2
CD ______ CDTRS 2
Trojan / Nov '90 / Direct / Jet Star

OUT OF THE DARK
CD ______ CM 77160CD
Century Media / Mar '97 / Plastic Head

OUT OF THEIR MOUTH VOL.2
CD ______ ALP 38CD
Atavistic / Jan '97 / Cargo / SRD

OUT ON THE FLOOR (Legendary Northern Soul Club Classics)
Seven days too long: *Wood, Chuck* / She blew a good thing: *Poets* / Girls are out to get you: *Fascinations* / Looking for you: *Mimms, Garnet* / I can't get a hold of myself: *Curry, Clifford* / Snake: *Wilson, Al* / Stay close to me: *Stairsteps* / I'll do anything: *Troy, Doris* / Breakout: *Ryder, Mitch* / What's wrong with me baby: *Invitations* / Queen of fools: *Mills, Barbara* / Nobody but me: *Human Beinz* / I dig your act: *O'Jays* / Shake a tail feather: *Purify, James & Bobby* / This thing called love: *Wyatt, Johnny* / Our love will grow: *Showmen* / Try a little harder: *Fidels* / Backfield in motion: *Mel & Tim* / Don't be sore at me: *Parliaments* / Reaching for the best: *Exciters* / Somebody somewhere needs you: *Banks, Darrell* / Oh my darlin: *Dee, Jackie* / Groovin' at the go-go: *Four Larks* / Little piece of leather: *Elbert, Donnie* / Out on the floor: *Gray, Dobie*
CD ______ GSCD 058
Goldmine / Jun '95 / Vital

OUT ON THE FLOOR TONIGHT (26 Classic Northern Floor Fillers)
Boomerang: *Leavill, Otis* / Many's a slip: *Present* / I wanna know: *Paul, John E.* / On a magic carpet ride: *Dee, Kiki* / He's my kind of fellow: *Sandy & The Pebbles* / Broken heart attack: *Sweet* / What's it gonna be: *Springfield, Dusty* / Put me in your pocket: *Harper, Jeanette* / Baby make your own sweet music: *Jay & The Techniques* / One night affair: *Butler, Jerry* / He loves me: *Chalafontes* / You can't close the windows: *Petals* / Joker went wild: *Hyland, Brian* / Mr. Love: *Wright, Nat* / I wish I was: *Garrigan, Eddie* / Woman: *Newarkers, Nicky* / Big hurt: *Farrell, Susan* / He will break your heart: *Groovers* / I'll do anything: *Gamble, Lenny* / Girl don't make me wait: *Time Box* / You don't know where your interest lies: *Five A Penny* / Closer she gets: *Drevar, John* / Little darlin': *Flirtations* / Daylight saving time: *Keith* / Who can I turn to: *Copage, Marc*
CD ______ GSCD 107
Goldmine / May '97 / Vital

OUT ON THE LEFT
CD ______ 5198302
Polydor / Aug '93 / PolyGram

OUT THE LIGHTS VOL.3
CD ______ DTCD 12
Discotex / Jul '92 / Jet Star

OUT THE LIGHTS VOL.4
CD ______ DTCD 14
Discotex / Nov '92 / Jet Star

OUT THE LIGHTS VOL.5
CD ______ DTCD 17
Discotex / Jun '93 / Jet Star

OUT THE LIGHTS VOL.6
CD ______ DTCD 24
Discotex / Apr '96 / Jet Star

OUT THERE (A Thread Through Time/ 2CD Set)
CD Set ______ TBCD 001
T&B / Nov '94 / Plastic Head

OUTER SPACE COMMUNICATIONS
CD ______ DIS 007CD
Minus Habens / Apr '94 / Plastic Head

OUTLAWS
CD ______ PD 81321
RCA / Sep '85 / BMG

OUTSIDE THE REACTOR VOL.1
CD ______ BR 1CD
Blue Room Released / Feb '97 / Essential/ BMG / SRD

OVCCI VUOMI OVTAA VEAIGGIS
CD ______ DATCD 20
Dat / Nov '95 / ADA / Direct

OVER THE EDGE
Got to be emotion: *Virginity* / I'm coming up: *Love Boutique* / Love bizarre: *Fratelli* / Can't stop: *Plez* / How to win your love: *ECA* / Throwdown: *Bitch* / Religion: *Awareness* / 550 state: *Blood Brothers* / Feel that feelin': *T-Boom* / Wind theme: *Xpulsion* / Summer's child: *Life Form* / Acperience 1: *Hardfloor* / (You give me) All your love: *Progressive*
CD ______ CDTOT 9
Jumpin' & Pumpin' / May '93 / 3mv/Sony / Mo's Music Machine

OVER THE TOP
CD ______ TRTCD 180
TrueTrax / Jun '95 / THE

OVER THERE 1942
CD ______ PHONTCD 7670
Phontastic / Apr '94 / Cadillac / Jazz Music / Wellard

OVERDOSE OF HEAVY SPINACH
CD ______ AA 063
Arf Arf / Jul '97 / Greyhound

OVERPOWERED BY FUNK
Theme from Shaft: *Hayes, Isaac* / One nation under a groove: *Funkadelic* / Get up off that thing: *Brown, James* / Fire: *Ohio Brothers* / Move on up: *Mayfield, Curtis* / Beginning of the end: *Funky Nassau* / Funkin' for Jamaica: *Brown, Tom* / Are you ready (do the bus stop): *Fatback Band* / Express: *BT Express* / Strawberry letter 23: *Brothers Johnson* / I need it: *Watson, Johnny 'Guitar'* / Family affair: *Sly & The Family Stone* / Papa's got a brand new pig bag: *Pig Bag* / Word up: *Cameo* / Ain't gonna bump no more: *Tex, Joe* / Pick up the pieces: *Average White Band* / Play that funky music: *Wild Cherry* / Sunshine day: *Osibisa* / We got the funk: *Positive Force* / Expansion: *Smith, Lonnie Liston*
CD ______ RENCD 109
Renaissance Collector Series / Oct '95 / BMG

OW (All Star Jam Session)
CD ______ MCD 075
Moon / Dec '95 / Cadillac / Harmonia Mundi

OWLS' HOOT, THE
CD ______ DGF 2
Frog / May '95 / Cadillac / Jazz Music / Wellard

OYE LISTEN (Compacto Caliente)
Defiendeme Santa Barbara: *Leida, Linda* / Arroz con manteca: *Leida, Linda* / Olvidame: *Rodriguez, Bobby* / La mulata cubana: *Valdes, Alfredo* / Con carino a Panama: *Santamaria, Monguito* / Festival in Guarare: *La Sonora De Baru* / Ay se paso la serie: *Rolando la serie* / Ocana sordi: *Los guaracheros de oriente* / Como se baila el son: *La india del oriente* / Ban-con-tim: *Super All Star* / Prende la vela: *Calzado, Rudy* / Saludando a los rumberos: *Marti, Virgilio*
CD ______ CDORB 014
Globestyle / Jan '87 / Pinnacle

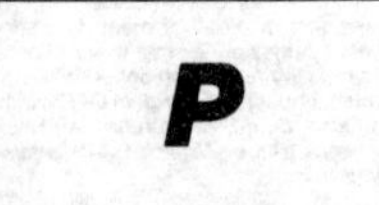

P&B PRODUCTIONS - RITUALS
CD ______ PB 96010
P&B / Mar '97 / Timewarp

PACIFIC RHYTHM - THE FIRST WAVE
Breathe the energy: *Ascendance* / Miles of boom: *Jondi & Spesh* / Superself: *Midi Brotherhood* / Remember 48024: *Professor Smith* / Antennae: *Dreamlogic* / Elephant biltong: *Hawke* / Intelligent brain: *Dimension 23* / Slog: *Cap'm Stargazer* / Chillout rollercoaster: *Metro* / Empty sea of nothingness: *Bassland* / Blueplant: *Off & Gone* / Enchanted isles: *23rd World*
CD ______ EYEUKCD 012
Eye Q / Sep '96 / Vital

PADDY IN THE SMOKE
CD ______ TSCD 603
Topic / Jul '97 / ADA / CM / Direct

PAIN, SORROW & LONLINESS
CD ______ HILOCD 5
Hi / Nov '93 / Pinnacle

PAISLEY POP (Pye Psych & Other Colours 1966-1969)
Quiet explosion: *Uglys* / Good idea: *Uglys* / Bitter thoughts of little Jane: *Timon* / Too much on my mind: *Gates Of Eden* / I wish I was five: *Scrugg* / Lavender popcorn: *Scrugg* / All the love in the world: *Consortium* / You're all things bright and beautiful: *Christian, Neil* / Blessed: *Kytes* / Goodbye Thimble Mill Lane: *Schadel* / Smile a little smile for me: *Flying Machine* / Dreamtime: *Rainbow People* / Cave of clear light: *Bystanders* / I wonder where my sister's gone: *Anan* / Black veils of melancholy: *Status Quo* / Dreams secondhand: *Blinkers* / That's when happiness begins: *Montanas* / Tamaris Khan: *Onyx* / Major to minor: *Settlers* / Stop, look, listen: *Fresh Air* / Captain Reale: *Gentle Influence* / Morning way: *Trader Horne*
CD ______ NEXCD 188
Sequel / Mar '92 / BMG

PAKISTAN - THE MUSIC OF THE QAWAL
CD ______ AUD 8082
Unesco / Jun '91 / ADA / Harmonia Mundi

PAKISTAN TREASURES
CD ______ PS 65082
PlayaSound / Nov '91 / ADA / Harmonia Mundi

PAKISTANI SOUL MUSIC
Dhol: *Sain, Pappu & Joora* / Naat: *Qawwal, Bahauddin Qutbuddin & Party* / Way of Shah Abdul Latif: *Fakir, Qurban & Ensemble* / Poem of Khwaja Ghulam Farid: *Bhagat, Faqira* / Way of Shah Abdul Latif: *Ali, Zulfiqar & Nazer Hussain/Mazher Hussain* / Kafi of Khwaja Ghulam Farid: *Khan, Allah Dad* / Naat: *Qawwal, Asif Ali Kahn & Party* / Alap and dhrupad in rag patdeep: *Khan, Mallikzada Muhammed Hafeez & Mallikzada Afzal*
CD ______ SM 15292
Wergo / Jun '97 / ADA / Cadillac / Harmonia Mundi

PALACE OF WORMS
CD ______ PO 2WCD
Nightbreed / Jan '97 / Plastic Head

PALAIS DE YOGYAKARTA VOL.4 (Concert Music From Java)
CD ______ C 560087
Ocora / Oct '95 / ADA / Harmonia Mundi

PALO, PALO VOL.1
CD ______ CD 8477452
Soul Head / May '96 / Plastic Head

PALO, PALO VOL.2
CD ______ CD 8477462
Soul Head / May '96 / Plastic Head

PAN ALL NIGHT (The Steel Bands Of Trinidad & Tobago)
Birthday party: *Phase II Pan Groove* / Dus' in dey face: *Exodus* / All night (reprise): *Moods* / Mystery band: *Amoco Renegades* / Pan in yuh pan: *Courts Laventille Sound Specialists* / Miss supporter: *Cordettes* / All night: *Vat 19 Fonclaire*
CD ______ DE 4022
Delos / Feb '94 / Nimbus

PAN FLUTE COLLECTION VOL.1, THE (The Lonely Shepherd)
Lonely shepherd / Largo / El Condor Pasa / Dolanne's melody / Aolha Oe / I dream of you / Mexican sun / L'ete Indien / What a wonderful world / Forse / Un jour d'ete / White clouds / Bye bye September / Maybe / Diana's song / Just in time
CD ______ 101082
CMC / May '97 / BMG

PAN FLUTE COLLECTION VOL.2, THE (Sailing)
Sailing / Yesterday / Heartbreaker / I have a dream / Michelle / Top of the world / Something / Fernando / Island in the sun / Ebony and ivory / Woman in love / Let it be / Beauty and the beast / Bridge over troubled water / Groovy kind of love / Here comes the sun
CD ______ 101092
CMC / May '97 / BMG

PAN FLUTE COLLECTION VOL.3, THE (I Will Always Love You)
I will always love you / Tears in heaven / From a distance / Some broken hearts never mend / Sleepwalk / Moonlight shadow / Forever and ever / Unchained melody / Do that to me one more time / Up where we belong / Save the best for last / Wind beneath my wings / Nothing's gonna change my love for you / I'll be there for you / Wonderland / Touch of you
CD ______ 101102
CMC / May '97 / BMG

PAN FLUTE COLLECTION, THE (The Lonely Shepherd/Sailing/I Will Always Love You/3CD Set)
Lonely shepherd / Largo / El Condor Pasa / Dolanne's melody / Aloha oe / I dream of you / Mexican sun / L'ete Indien / What a wonderful world / Forse / Un jour d'ete / White clouds / Bye bye September / Maybe / Diana's song / Just in time / Sailing / Yesterday / Heartbreaker / I have a dream / Michelle / Top of the world / Something / Fernando / Island in the sun / Ebony and ivory / Woman in love / Let it be / Beauty and the beast / Bridge over troubled water / Groovy kind of love / Here comes the sun / I will always love you / Tears in Heaven / From a distance / Some broken hearts never mend / Sleepwalk / Moonlight shadow / Forever and ever / Unchained melody / Do that to me one more time / Up where we belong / Save the best for last / Wind beneath my wings / Nothing's gonna change my love for you / I'll be there / Wonderland / Touch of you
CD Set ______ 101072
CMC / May '97 / BMG

PAN GLOSSARY NO.1
CD ______ PAN 2000A
Pan / Oct '94 / ADA / CM / Direct

PAN IS BEAUTIFUL VOL.1 - THE WORLD'S BEST STEELBANDS (Calypso & Soca)
Hammer: *Trinidad All Stars Steel Band* / Get something and wave: *Tropical Angel Harps* / Jericho: *Solo Harmonites* / Exodus: *Exodus* / Musical Volcano: *Witco Desperadoes* / Nah do that: *National Quarries Cordettes* / Govenor's ball: *Trintoc Invaders*
CD ______ 68962
Tropical / Apr '97 / Discovery

PAN IS BEAUTIFUL VOL.2 - THE WORLD'S BEST STEELBANDS (Classics)
Academic festival overture: *Exodus* / 5th symphony 4th movement: *Trintoc Invaders* / Capriccio Espagnol: *Solo Harmonites* / Overture to the bartered bride: *Witco Desperadoes* / Jupiter: *Courts Laventille Sound Specialists* / 5th symphony 4th movement: *Trinidad All Stars Steel Band* / William Tell overture: *National Quarries Cordettes*
CD ______ 68963
Tropical / Jun '97 / Discovery

PAN JAZZ 'N' CALYPSO
California shower / We kinda music / Rhythm in the groove / Take me there / Hydra / Never can say goodbye / East river drive / Philmore's dream / Sitting through the notes / Iron man / Fire down below
CD ______ DE 4016
Delos / Jan '94 / Nimbus

PAN JAZZ CONVERSATIONS (Caribbean Carnival Series)
Mauby beach / Dry river blues / What's the name of this song / Reflection / Dadu / De hustler / Karnaval people / Fingers
CD ______ DE 4019
Delos / Apr '94 / Nimbus

PAN PIPE CHRISTMAS, A
Silent night / Winter wonderland / White Christmas / Deck the halls / I saw Mummy kissing Santa Claus / Jolly old St. Nicholas / It came upon a midnight clear / It's beginning to look like Christmas / Adagio / Air / Lonely shepherd / Reverie / Papa petit Noel / Still still / Sleigh ride / Il est ne le divine enfant / First Noel / O little town of Bethlehem / Jingle bells / Auld lang syne
CD ______ CDVIP 145
Virgin VIP / Nov '96 / EMI

PAN PIPE CLASSICS (3CD Set)
CD Set ______ KBOX 376
Collection / Aug '97 / Target/BMG / TKO Magnum

PAN PIPE DREAMS (Inspirations/20 Contemporary Love Songs)
CD ______ PMCD 7016
Pure Music / Sep '95 / BMG

PAN PIPE DREAMS
Change the world / Because you loved me / Someday / Kiss from a rose / Earth song / Without you / Breathe again / After the love has gone / Jesus to a child / All woman / One day in your life / Reunited / This masquerade / Desperado / Show me heaven / Waiting to exhale / Hero / Power of love
CD ______ CDVIP 151
Virgin VIP / Apr '97 / EMI

PAN PIPE HORIZONS (2CD Set)
Jesus to a child / Candle in the wind / Romeo & Juliet / Songbird / Satellite of love / Heart of gold / Don't dream it's over / Just the way you are / Is this the world we created / Don't let the sun go down on me / Love is all around / You're so vain / Midnight at the oasis / One day in your life / Wonderful tonight / Harry's game / American tune / Brothers in arms / Air that I breathe / I will always love you / Think twice / Another day in paradise / Save a prayer / America / Knockin' on heaven's door / Sail on / I won't last a day without you / Wild world / How deep is your love / Every time you go away / Let's stay together / Being with you / Hotel California / Up on the roof / Baker street / Father & son / Don't give up / Wonderwall / You've got a friend / Belfast child
CD Set _______ 330242
Hallmark / Jul '96 / Carlton

PAN PIPE INSPIRATION
CD _______ PMCD 7011
Pure Music / Apr '95 / BMG

PAN PIPE MOODS
Up where we belong / Unchained melody / You light up my life / Do that to me one more time / Feelings / Let it be / Even the nights are better / Rose / Aranjuez mon amour / If you leave me now / For your eyes only / Michelle / You needed me / I have a dream / Don't cry for me argentina / Lonely shepherd / Yesterday / Sleepwalk / Something
CD _______ QED 097
Tring / Nov '96 / Tring

PAN PIPE MOODS
CD _______ PLSCD 160
Pulse / Feb '97 / BMG

PAN PIPE MOODS IN PARADISE
Forever and ever / Spanish eyes / Spanish harlem / Moon river / Strangers in the night / La Isla Bonita / Begin the beguine / Don't want to lose you / Guantanamera / Fernando / Chiquitita / Hey / Summertime / Rise / Have you ever really loved a woman / Don't let the sun go down on me / Feelings / Hello / You'll see / Amor
CD _______ 5319612
Polydor / May '96 / PolyGram

PAN PIPE MOODS VOL.2
CD _______ 5293952
PolyGram TV / Oct '95 / PolyGram

PAN PIPE SOUNDS OF SCOTLAND, THE
Amazing grace / My love is like a red, red rose / Wild mountain thyme / Over the sea to Skye / Flower of Scotland / Ae fond kiss / Ye banks and braes / Scottish soldier / Loch Lomond / Dark island / Will ye no come back again / Caledonia / Brides of Glenshiel / Island song / Auld lang syne
CD _______ RECD 510
REL / Apr '97 / CM / Duncans / Highlander

PAN PIPES (3CD Set)
CD Set _______ EMTBX 302
Emporio / Aug '97 / Disc

PAN PIPES COLLECTION (2CD Set)
CD Set _______ DEMPCD 005
Emporio / Mar '96 / Disc

PAN PIPES FOR LOVERS
Power of love / (I've had the) Time of my life / We've got tonight / Eternal flame / You light up my life / Up where we belong / Everything I do (I do it for you) / Heartbreaker / Forever and ever / Do that to me one more time / When you're in love with a beautiful woman / Love changes everything / And I love her / Groovy kind of love / Have you ever really loved a woman / Light my fire / Woman in love / For your eyes only / (I can't help) Falling in love with you / I will always love you
CD _______ CD 6022
Music / Jun '96 / Target/BMG

PAN PIPES OF CHRISTMAS, THE
Silent night / White Christmas / Mary's boy child / Mistletoe and wine / First noel / When a child is born / O come all ye faithful (adeste fidelis) / Haapy Christmas war is over / Last Christmas / Little drummer boy / Winter's tale / Walking in the air / Do they know it's Christmas / Winter wonderland / Away in a manger / Pipes of peace
CD _______ RECD 505
REL / Oct '96 / CM / Duncans / Highlander

PAN PIPES OF THE ANDES VOL.2
El condor pasa: *Santiago y su conjunto* / Chasquinanes: *Patoruzu Y Su Conjunto* / Hacia el carnaval: *Los Indios De Cuzco* / Sol inca: *Santiago y su conjunto* / Pajaritos: *Patoruzu Y Su Conjunto* / Bosque: *Los Indios De Cuzco* / Poncho color del viento: *Los Indios De Cuzco* / Diecinueve de enero: *Patoruzu Y Su Conjunto* / Baila cholita: *Los Indios De Cuzco* / Kena misky: *Patoruzu Y Su Conjunto* / Tutalla manta: *Los Indios De Cuzco* / Zagoria: *Santiago y su conjunto* / El zaino: *Patoruzu Y Su Conjunto* / La piojosa: *Patoruzu Y Su Conjunto* / Mascarita: *Los Indios De Cuzco* / Viento andino: *Los Indios De Cuzco* / Carro podrido: *Los Indios De Cuzco* / Carnavalito: *Santiago y su conjunto*
CD _______ 305902
Hallmark / Jan '97 / Carlton

PAN PIPES PLAY LOVE SONGS
I don't wanna cry / Wind beneath my wings / Ebony and ivory / Fernando / I'll be there / Bridge over troubled water / Always on my mind / Can you feel the love tonight / Music of the night / Orinoco flow / What a feeling / Top of the world / Norwegian wood / Tears in heaven / Moonlight shadow / He ain't heavy, he's my brother / Michelle / Just when I needed you most / Begin the beguine / Take my breath away
CD _______ CD 6032
Music / Sep '96 / Target/BMG

PAN PIPES SELECTION (2CD Set)
I have a dream / Strawberry fields forever / Dark side of the sun / Scarborough fair / Sailing / Unchained melody / Amazing grace / If you leave now / Something / Feelings / Here comes the sun / Sara / Yesterday / MacArthur park / Bird of paradise / House of the rising sun / Don't cry for me Argentina / Banks of the Ohio / Autumn dream / Let it be / Power of love / (I've had the) Time of my life / We've got tonight / Eternal flame / You light up my life / Up where we belong / Everything I do I do it for you / Heartbreaker / Forever and ever / Do that to me one more time / When you're in love with a beautiful woman / Light my fire / Woman in love / For your eyes only / (I can't help) falling in love / I will always love you
CD Set _______ DCD 3012
Music / Jun '97 / Target/BMG

PAN PIPES XMAS MOODS
Happy Xmas (war is over) / I believe in Father Christmas / Medley No.1 / Fairytale of New York / In Dulci Jubilo / Medley No.2 / Walking in the air / Last Christmas / Lonely this Christmas / Chestnuts roasting on an open fire / Santa Claus is coming to town / Medley No.3 / Do they know it's Christmas / Rudolph the red nosed reindeer / Stop the cavalry / Mistletoe and wine / Winter wonderland / When a child is born / White Christmas / Medley No.4
CD _______ 5338582
PolyGram TV / Dec '96 / PolyGram

PAN WOMAN
CD _______ DE 4017
Delos / Feb '94 / Nimbus

PANAUNIE
CD _______ RRTGCD 7705
Rohit / '88 / Jet Star

PANDEMONIUM NO.1
CD _______ PAN 0100A
Pan / Oct '94 / ADA / CM / Direct

PANGAEA 2097
CD _______ PAGCD 001
Pagoda / May '97 / Kudos / Pinnacle / Prime / Shellshock/Disc

PANNARAMA
CD _______ BFISHCD 1
Big Fish / Apr '94 / Big Fish

PANORAMA (Steel Bands Of Trinidad And Tobago)
Woman is boss / Poom poom / Steel of wheels / Par by storm / Pan in uyh ruckungkertungkung / Ramajay / Iron man / Ramjay (reprise)
CD _______ DE 4015
Delos / Jan '94 / Nimbus

PANPIPES AT CHRISTMAS
Good King Wenceslas / God rest ye merry gentlemen / We wish you a Merry Christmas / Ding dong merrily on high / Winter wonderland / Angels from the realms of glory / Christmas song / Auld lang syne / Holly & the ivy / Away in a manger / Little drummer boy / Rudolph the red nosed reindeer / Under the mistletoe / Unto us a child is born / Once in Royal David's City / Here we come a wassailing / Jingle bells / Season of joy / Christmas is here / When a child is born / Hark the herald angels sing / Deck the halls
CD _______ XMAS 012
Tring / Nov '96 / Tring

PANPIPES OF THE ANDES
CD _______ TRTCD 183
TrueTrax / Feb '96 / THE

P'ANSORI (Korea's Epic Vocal Art & Instrumental Music)
CD _______ 7559720492
Nonesuch / Jan '95 / Warner Music

PANTASTIC WORLD OF STEEL MUSIC VOL.1
CD _______ 68940
Tropical / Jul '97 / Discovery

PA'QUE BAILEN MUCHACHOS (2CD Set)
CD Set _______ BMT 001/002
Blue Moon / Feb '97 / Cadillac / Discovery / Greensleeves / Jazz Music / Jet Star / TKO Magnum

PARADIGM SHIFT
CD _______ 08643462
Westcom / May '97 / Koch / Pinnacle

PARADISE CITY (One World One Love/ 2CD Set)
CD Set _______ UKK 4106
UKK / Oct '94 / Total/BMG

PARAGUAYAN HARP
CD _______ PS 65128
PlayaSound / May '94 / ADA / Harmonia Mundi

PARAMOUNT BLUES VOL.3
CD _______ HCD 12013
Black Swan / Oct '93 / Jazz Music

PARAMOUNT RECORDINGS CHICAGO 1926-1928
CD _______ DGF 13
Frog / May '97 / Cadillac / Jazz Music / Wellard

PARAPHYSICAL CYBERTRONICS
CD _______ PRAXIS 10CD
Praxis / Jul '95 / Plastic Head

PARASOLS VOL.1
CD _______ PLKCD 001
Plink Plonk / Feb '94 / Prime / SRD

PARIS AFTER DARK
La mer: *Trenet, Charles* / Hymne a l'amour: *Piaf, Edith* / J'attendrai: *Rossi, Tino* / Ma Tonkinoise: *Baker, Josephine* / Valentine: *Chevalier, Maurice* / Je cherche un millionaire: *Mistinguett* / Embrasse-moi cherie: *Delyle, Lucienne* / Pigalle: *Ulmer, Georges* / Le chaland qui passe: *Gauty, Lys* / Sur ma vie: *Les Compagnons De La Chanson* / La vie en rose: *Piaf, Edith* / Parlez-moi d'amour: *Boyer, Lucienne* / Ces petites choses: *Sablon, Jean* / Mon homme: *Mistinguett* / J'ai deux amours: *Baker, Josephine* / Boum: *Trenet, Charles* / La java bleue: *Frehel* / Le fiacre: *Sablon, Jean* / Les trois cloches: *Piaf, Edith et Les Compagnons De La Chansons* / C'est a Capri: *Rossi, Tino*
CD _______ CZ 140
EMI / Sep '88 / EMI

PARIS BLUES VOL.1 (French Realist Singers 1926-1958)
Les amants d'un jour: *Piaf, Edith* / Ou sont tous mes amants: *Frehel* / La rue de Notre Amour: *Damia* / C'est mon gigolo: *Delyle, Lucienne* / Dans la rue des Blancs Manteaux: *Greco, Juliette* / Tel qu'il est: *Frehel* / La serenade due pave: *Buffet, Eugenie* / La chanson de Margaret: *Montero, Germaine* / Pars piano: *George, Yvonne* / Au bal de la chance: *Piaf, Edith* / La complainte de la butte: *Vaucaire, Cora* / Sombre Dimanche: *Damia* / Le Noel de la rue: *Piaf, Edith* / Lili Marlene: *Solidor, Suzy* / Mon amant de St Jean: *Delyle, Lucienne* / Sarah: *Lasso, Gloria* / Le chant des partisans: *Sablon, Germaine* / La chanson de Catherine: *Piaf, Edith* / La chanson des fortifs: *Frehel* / La fille de Londres: *Montero, Germaine*
CD _______ CDEMS 1397
EMI / May '91 / EMI

PARIS BLUES VOL.2
Les momes de la cloche: *Sylva, Berthe* / Les feuilles mortes: *Vaucaire, Cora* / La chanson de prevert: *Arnaud, Michelle* / Nuages: *Privat, Jo* / Pour moi tout' seulle: *Piaf, Edith* / Music maestro please: *Marjane, Leo* / Il n'y a pas d'amour heureux: *Arnaud, Michelle* / Je reve au fil de l'eau: *Sablon, Germaine* / Le fils de la femme: *Frehel, Poisson* / Domino: *Delyle, Lucienne* / La barques d'yves: *Delyle, Lucienne* / On n'a pas toujours vingt ans: *Sylva, Berthe* / Mon legionnaire: *Dubas, Marie* / Et vous n'avez pas su: *Dauberson, Dany* / La bastoche: *Privat, Jo* / J'aime pas le fete: *Micheyl, Mick* / C'est la guinguette: *Lajon, Annette* / J'ecoute la pluie: *Gauty, Lys* / Bravo pour le clown: *Piaf, Edith* / Les souvenirs: *Micheyl, Mick* / Autumn leaves: *Piaf, Edith* / Hymn to love: *Piaf, Edith* / La vie en rose: *Piaf, Edith*
CD _______ CDEMS 1556
Premier/EMI / May '96 / EMI

PARIS BY NIGHT
Milord: *Piaf, Edith* / Douce France: *Trenet, Charles* / Briu d'amour: *Alexander, Maurice* / Sur les quais du vieux Paris: *Delyle, Lucienne* / Vieni vieni: *Rossi, Tino* / Seul ce soir: *Marjane, Leo* / J'aime Paris au mois de mai: *Aznavour, Charles* / Puisque vous partez en voyage: *Sablon, Mireille & Jean* / Moulin rouge: *Les Compagnons De La Chanson* / A Paris dans chaque faubourg: *Gauty, Lys* / Sur le pont d'Avignon: *Sablon, Jean* / Ou est-il donc: *Frehel* / Ma Louise: *Chevalier, Maurice* / La clocher de mon coeur: *Busch, Eva* / Nuages: *Reinhardt, Django* / Depuis que les bals sont fermes: *Damia* / Qur reste t'il de nos amours: *Trenet, Charles* / Ma cabane au Canada: *Renaud, Line* / Un seul couvert, please, James: *Sablon, Jean* / Bal dans ma rue: *Piaf, Edith*
CD _______ CZ 316
EMI / Jun '90 / EMI

PARIS GROOVE UP
Arabesques / Christ'al / Gardez l'ecoute / Pardonne / Go go motion / K-talk 2 / Elles aimant ca / Bola / Mic mac / Fantaisy / Really groovy / Funky takini / Boom bastic / Just comme ca / Ame saoul-am soul
CD _______ 4509961722
Warner Bros. / Jul '94 / Warner Music

PARIS, OH QUE J'AIME
CD _______ PASTCD 7069
Flapper / Mar '95 / Pinnacle

PARIS WASHBOARD VOL.2
CD _______ SOSCD 1261
Stomp Off / Oct '93 / Jazz Music / Wellard

PARIS...CAFE-CONCERT
C'est un mauvais garcon' / Boum / Gigolette / Maitre Pierre / J'attendrai / Sur le pont d'avignon / C'est un bureaucrate / Un p'tit bock / Chez moi / Vous oubliez votre cheval / Tel qu'il est / Guitare d'amour / Ma douce vallee / Place pigalle / Sombreros et mantillas / As dis ah dis / C'est un chagrin de femme / Je ne donnerais pas ma place / J'ai connu do vous / Oh Suzanna youp youp-la-la / La vie qui va
CD _______ PASTCD 9797
Flapper / Aug '92 / Pinnacle

PAROXYSN
CD _______ MKTCD 001
Mute / Aug '91 / RTM/Disc

PARTNER MASSAGE
Oh my love / When birds cease to sing / Hey girl / Can't we tell the world / Beverly Jane / Can I / Turquoise green and blue / Indian summer / Little child
CD _______ 303600692
Carlton / Apr '97 / Carlton

PARTNERS (20 Timeless Duets From A Golden Era)
Friendship: *Garland, Judy & Johnny Mercer* / Gone fishin': *Crosby, Bing & Louis Armstrong* / Into each life some rain must fall: *Fitzgerald, Ella & The Ink Spots* / Indian love call: *MacDonald, Jeanette & Nelson Eddy* / Moon came up with a great idea: *Crosby, Bing & Peggy Lee* / Pistol packin' mama: *Andrews Sisters & Bing Crosby* / Moonlight bay: *Crosby, Bing & Gary Crosby* / Best things in life are free: *Allyson, June & Peter Lawford* / Put it there pal: *Crosby, Bing & Bob Hope* / 42nd Street: *Keeler, Ruby & Dick Powell* / Shine: *Crosby, Bing & The Mills Brothers* / For me and my gal: *Garland, Judy & Gene Kelly* / Night is young and you're so beautiful: *Sinatra, Frank & Dinah Shore* / Zing a little zong: *Crosby, Bing & Jane Wyman* / Civilization (bongo bongo bongo): *Andrews Sisters & Danny Kaye* / Spaniard that blighted my life: *Joison, Al & Bing Crosby* / Little Miss Broadway: *Temple, Shirley & George Murphy* / Connecticut: *Garland, Judy & Bing Crosby* / Bob White (whatcha gonna swing tonight): *Boswell, Connee & Bing Crosby* / Thanks for the memory: *Hope, Bob & Shirley Ross*
CD _______ ECD 3295
K-Tel / Feb '97 / K-Tel

PARTY FEVER
CD _______ SONCD 0062
Sonic Sounds / Mar '94 / Jet Star

PARTY HITS (2CD Set)
Let's have a party: *Jackson, Wanda* / Yellow river: *Christie* / Sugar baby love: *Rubettes* / Hippy hippy shake: *Swinging Blue Jeans* / Da doo ron ron: *Crystals* / I'm into something good: *Herman's Hermits* / Baby come back: *Equals* / Walkin' back to happiness: *Shapiro, Helen* / Silence is golden: *Tremeloes* / You'll never walk alone: *Gerry & The Pacemakers* / Runaway: *Shannon, Del* / Just walkin' in the rain: *Ray, Johnnie* / Something's gotten hold of my heart: *Pitney, Gene* / Speedy Gonzales: *Boone, Pat* / Charlie Brown: *Coasters* / Papa-oom-mow-mow: *Rivingtons* / Ob-la-di ob-la-da: *Marmalade* / Nut rocker: *B. Bumble & The Stingers* / Words: *David, F.R.* / Under the moon of love: *Showaddywaddy* / Tonight: *Rubettes* / In the bad bad old days: *Foundations* / Keep searchin': *Shannon, Del* / Walk don't run: *Ventures* / Viva Bobby Joe: *Equals* / I'm telling you now: *Freddie & The Dreamers* / Ferry cross the Mersey: *Gerry & The Pacemakers* / When a man loves a woman: *Sledge, Percy* / Someone: *Tremeloes* / Windy: *Association* / Wishin' and hopin': *Merseybeats* / Sheila: *Roe, Tommy* / Mr. Bassman: *Cymbal, Johnny* / It's my party: *Gore, Lesley*
CD Set _______ DCD 3005
Music / Jun '97 / Target/BMG

PARTY HITS VOL.1
CD _______ 10472
CMC / Jun '97 / BMG

PARTY HITS VOL.2
CD _______ 10482
CMC / Jun '97 / BMG

PARTY HITS VOL.3
CD _______ 10492
CMC / Jun '97 / BMG

PARTY IS FOR LIFE, NOT JUST FOR CHRISTMAS
CD _______ CD 02
Cabbaged / Jul '97 / Arabesque / Prime

PARTY MEGAMIX (Over 100 Sensationally Sequenced Songs)
CD _______ PLATCD 3917
Platinum / Sep '93 / Prism

PARTY MIX
CD _______ DINCD 32
Dino / Nov '91 / Pinnacle

PARTY NIGHT IN IRELAND (Music, Craic & Song)
If you're Irish/McNamara's band/Hannigan's holiday: *Erin's Isle Singers* / Nedeen: *Grace, Brendan* / Fasten the leggin/Munster buttermilk: *Fitzgerald, Richard Ceili Band* / Peggy O'Neill/Sweet Rosie O'Grady/My wild Irish rose: *Erin's Isle Singers* / Pup: *Toibin, Niall* / Pigeon on the gate/Foxhunters:

Shaskeen / Rose of Tralee: *Erin's Isle Singers* / Incoming call: *Kelly, Frank* / Cooley's ceili: *Crossroads Ceili* / I'll take you home again Kathleen/Green glens of Antrim: *Erin's Isle Singers* / Caravan man: *Toibin, Niall* / Rights of man: *Crossroads Ceili* / Dear old Donegal/It's a long way to Tipperary/Hello Patsy Fa: *Erin's Isle Singers*
CD CHCD 034
Chart / Oct '96 / Direct / Koch

PARTY OF FIVE
CD 9362464312
Warner Bros. / Feb '97 / Warner Music

PARTY TIME
CD I 3896062
Galaxy / Oct '96 / ZYX

PARTY TIME AT STUDIO ONE (2CD Set)
CD Set 3021522
Arcade / Jun '97 / Discovery
CD Set RN 7018
Rhino / May '97 / Grapevine/PolyGram / Jet Star

PASS THE VIBES ON
CD 5352212
PolyGram TV / Jan '96 / PolyGram

PASSCHENDAELE SUITE
Dodendans: *Panta Rhei* / Land of the long white cloud: *Simpson, Lester* / Een schip: *Panta Rhei* / Ao tea roa: *Coope, Boyes & Simpson* / Robin's song: *Panta Rhei* / Lay me low: *Coope, Boyes & Simpson* / Bloody fields of Flanders: *Panta Rhei & Lester Simpson* / Still in the night: *Boyes, Jim & Barry Coope/Fabien Degryse* / Ein Schottisch tantz: *Panta Rhei* / (Mad old, sad old) Shuffling Jack: *Coope, Boyes & Simpson/ Panta Rhei* / Tyne cot at night/I want to go home: *Coope, Boyes & Simpson* / Largo: *Pilartz, luc & Aurelie Dorzee/Kathy Adam* / New Jerusalem: *Coope, Boyes & Simpson/ Panta Rhei*
CD NMCD 10
No Master's Cooperative / Nov '96 / CM / Direct

PASSING OF THE REGIMENTS
CD BNA 5065
Bandleader / May '92 / Conifer/BMG

PASSION (Music For Guitar)
Proven by fire / Love on the beach / Good question / Parasol days / Passion and pride / Gentle touch / Running games / New face / Lover's promise / Explorations / Joy of life
CD ND 61044
Narada / Oct '94 / ADA / New Note/ Pinnacle

PASSION TRAX
CD CDPASH 1
Passion / Feb '93 / 3mv/Pinnacle

PAST PERFECT SAMPLER (The Great Sound Of The 20's, 30's & 40's)
I never knew: *Armstrong, Louis* / Doug the Jitterbug: *Jordan, Louis* / I let a song go out of my heart: *Ellington, Duke* / King Porter stomp: *Crosby, Bob* / Home Guard blues: *Formby, George* / Cuban overture: *Whiteman, Paul & Rosa Linda* / Carolina shout: *Waller, Fats* / Just let me look at you: *Coward, Noel* / La danza: *Gigli, Beniamino* / Miss Annabelle Lee: *Reinhardt, Django & Stephane Grappelli* / Muddy water: *Lunceford, Jimmie* / I guess I'll have to change my plan: *Fitzgerald, Ella* / Let yourself go: *Rogers, Ginger* / Taking a chance on love: *Fitzgerald, Ella* / Shall we dance: *Astaire, Fred*
CD PPCD 78100
Past Perfect / Feb '95 / Glass Gramophone Co.

PAST PRESENT AND FUTURE
CD MRCD 022
M8 / Nov '96 / Grapevine/PolyGram

PATIO COLLECTION VOL.2
CD SMLX 007
Smilex / Apr '97 / Cargo

PATROLLING THE EDGE OF DEEP HOUSE - DEEP STATES
Tribe: *MATO* / I love: *Paradise Deep Groove* / Needs (needs not wants): *Mood Life* / Within without: *Read, Jaime* / Moov: *Francois K* / Erotic illusions: *Abacus* / Black oceans: *Heard, Larry* / Vesuvius: *Stranger* / If you lose your shadow: *Aberation* / Netherlands: *Louis, Joe*
CD SLIPCD 53
Slip 'n' Slide / Mar '97 / Amato Disco / Prime / RTM/Disc / Vital

PATTERNS OF JEWISH LIFE (Highlights Of Series - Traditional & Popular Jewish Music)
CD Set SM 16042
Wergo / Feb '94 / ADA / Cadillac / Harmonia Mundi

PAUL JONES R&B SHOW VOL.2
CD JSPCD 221
JSP / Oct '88 / ADA / Cadillac / Direct / Hot Shot / Target/BMG

PAX RECORDS PUNK COLLECTION
CD CDPUNK 75
Anagram / May '96 / Cargo / Pinnacle

PAY IT ALL BACK - US
CD RESTLESS 7269
On-U Sound / Aug '94 / Jet Star / SRD

PAY IT ALL BACK VOL.2
Train to doomsville: *Perry, Lee 'Scratch' & Dub Syndicate* / Billy Bonds MBE: *Barmy Army* / Circular motion: *Forehead Bros* / What a wonderful day: *African Headcharge* / No alternative (but to fight): *Dub Syndicate & Dr. Pablo* / Run them away: *Sherman, Bim & Singers & Players* / Water the garden: *Prince Far-I & Singers & Players* / Throw it away: *African Headcharge* / Digital: *Eskimo Fox*
CD ONULP 42CD
On-U Sound / Dec '88 / Jet Star / SRD

PAY IT ALL BACK VOL.3
Disconnection: *Strange Parcels* / Heart's desire: *Singers & Players* / You thought I was dead: *Perry, Lee 'Scratch' & Dub Syndicate* / Stoned immaculate: *Dub Syndicate & Akabu* / I think of you: *Little Annie* / Jack the biscuit: *Fairley, Andy* / Hey ho: *Dub Syndicate* / These things happen: *Stewart, Mark* / Ennio: *Frederix, Martin* / To be free: *Strange Parcels & Bernard Fowler* / My God: *African Headcharge* / Spirit soul: *Pillay, Alan* / False leader: *Clail, Gary* / Jacob's pillow: *Rae, Jesse* / Devo: *Barmy Army* / Blue moon: *Barmy Army* / Nightmare: *Sherman, Bim*
CD ONUCD 53
On-U Sound / May '91 / Jet Star / SRD

PAY IT ALL BACK VOL.4
CD ONUCD 20
On-U Sound / Feb '93 / Jet Star / SRD

PAY IT ALL BACK VOL.5
CD ONUCD 75
On-U Sound / Apr '95 / Jet Star / SRD

PAY IT ALL BACK VOL.6
CD ONUCD 96
On-U Sound / Aug '96 / Jet Star / SRD

PE DE SERRA FORRO BAND, BRAZIL
CD SM 15092
Wergo / Oct '92 / ADA / Cadillac / Harmonia Mundi

PEACE AND LOVE
CD UPCD 001
Upsetter / Sep '96 / SRD

PEACE AND LOVE
CD SKIP 52CD
Broken Rekids / Nov '96 / Cargo / Plastic Head

PEACE COMPILATION
CD WB 3156CD
We Bite / Oct '96 / Plastic Head

PEACE PIPE DUB
CD NTMCD 552
Nectar / Jun '97 / Pinnacle

PEACE TOGETHER
Satellite of love: *U2 & Lou Reed* / Peace in our time: *Carter USM* / Religious persuasion: *Bragg, Billy & Andy White/Sinead O'Connor* / Bad weather: *Young Disciples* / We have all the time in the world: *My Bloody Valentine* / Games without frontiers: *Pop Will Eat Itself* / Oliver's army: *Blur* / Invisible sun: *Therapy* / When we were two little boys: *Harris, Rolf & Liam O'Maonlai* / What a waste: *Curve & Ian Dury* / John the gun: *Fatima Mansions* / Be still: *Peace Together*
CD CID 8018
Island / Jul '93 / PolyGram

PEACEFUL EASY FEELING
It should have been you: *Blacknuss* / Cigarette: *Wall Of Sound* / Music: *Shogunn* / Crazy life: *Winnie* / Modus operandi Pt.1: *OI* / Peaceful easy feeling: *Alexander, Rob* / Things you make me do: *Thomas, Carla* / Hold on to love: *Cameron, Marie* / Our love: *Black, Sassy* / What did I do: *Zaeus* / Committed: *Renaizzance* / I'll keep you warm: *Serenade* / Chance: *Gallimore, Khaline* / I like: *Everis*
CD CDTEP 8
Debut / Sep '95 / 3mv/Sony / Pinnacle

PEACEFUL WATERS (A Magical Blend Of Music And The Sounds Of Nature)
CD 57812
CMC / May '97 / BMG

PEASANT MUSIC FROM HAITI
CD 926802
EPM / Jul '97 / ADA / Discovery

PEBBLES VOL.1
CD AIPCD 5016
Archive / Jul '92 / RTM/Disc / Shellshock/ Disc

PEBBLES VOL.10
CD AIPCD 5027
AIP / Feb '97 / Greyhound / RTM/Disc / Shellshock/Disc

PEBBLES VOL.2
CD AIPCD 5019
Archive / Jul '92 / RTM/Disc / Shellshock/ Disc

PEBBLES VOL.3
CD AIPCD 5020
Archive / Jul '92 / RTM/Disc / Shellshock/ Disc

PEBBLES VOL.4
CD AIPCD 5021
Archive / Jul '92 / RTM/Disc / Shellshock/ Disc

PEBBLES VOL.5
No good woman: *Tree* / Go away: *Plague* / You don't know me: *Magi* / It's a crying shame: *Gentlemen* / Writing on the wall: *5 Canadians* / Why: *Dirty Wurds* / Universal vagrant: *Merry Dragons* / I wanna come back (From the world of LSD): *Fe Fi Four Plus 2* / I tell no lies: *Escapades* / You need love: *Danny & The Escorts* / Yesterday's heroes: *Satyrs* / Way it used to be: *Little Phil & The Night Shadows* / Move: *State Of Mind* / I need love: *State Of Mind* / Time stoppers: *State Of Mind* / You'll never be my girl: *Thursday's Children* / Way I feel: *12 am*
CD AIPCD 5022
Archive / Jul '92 / RTM/Disc / Shellshock/ Disc

PEBBLES VOL.6
CD AIPCD 5023
Archive / Feb '95 / RTM/Disc / Shellshock/ Disc

PEBBLES VOL.7
CD AIPCD 5024
Archive / Feb '95 / RTM/Disc / Shellshock/ Disc

PEBBLES VOL.8
CD AIPCD 5025
Archive / Feb '96 / RTM/Disc / Shellshock/ Disc

PEBBLES VOL.9
CD AIPCD 5026
AIP / Feb '97 / Greyhound / RTM/Disc / Shellshock/Disc

PELHAM'S SOCA PARTY VOL.1
CD CSSCD 001
Cott / Jun '94 / Jet Star

PENSIONERS ON ECSTACY
CD CRECD 082
Creation / Nov '90 / 3mv/Vital

PENTHOUSE CLASSIC COMBINATIONS VOL.2
CD PH 2006
Penthouse / Jun '96 / Jet Star

PENTHOUSE CONCEPT
CD 15205
Laserlight / Aug '91 / Target/BMG

PENTHOUSE CULTURE CENTRE
CD PHRICD 28
Penthouse / Jan '96 / Jet Star

PENTHOUSE DAMSEL PANDEMONIUM
CD SVCD 2044
Shocking Vibes / May '96 / Jet Star

PENTHOUSE DANCEHALL HITS VOL.7
CD PHCD 2029
Penthouse / May '96 / Jet Star

PENTHOUSE LOVERS ROCK VOL.1
CD PHCD 2002
Penthouse / Jun '96 / Jet Star

PENTHOUSE LOVERS ROCK VOL.2
CD PHCD 2009
Penthouse / Jun '96 / Jet Star

PENTHOUSE LOVERS ROCK VOL.3
CD PHCD 2010
Penthouse / Jun '96 / Jet Star

PENTHOUSE SAMPLER VOL.1
CD PHCD 22
Penthouse / Aug '93 / Jet Star

PEPPERMINT STICK PARADE
CD BUS 10012
Bus Stop / May '95 / Cargo / Vital

PERCUSSION MUSIC OF MADRAS
CD VICG 53492
JVC World Library / Mar '96 / ADA / CM / Direct

PERCUSSIONS D'AMERIQUE LATINE
Butucada au carnaval de Rio / Tehuantepec / Cumbia cienaguera / El hombre celoso / Conga au carnival de Santiago de Cuba / Janitzio / Josefa Matia / La llorona / El Ferrocarril de Los Altos / Bateria a Salvador de Bahia / Cancion mixteca / Mapale / El rey Quiche / Descarga barbacoana / Bateria au carnaval de Manaus / Currulao / Chiapas
CD ARN 64023
Arion / '88 / ADA / Discovery

PERFECT INSTRUMENTAL COLLECTION VOL.1
CD HRCD 8048
Disky / Dec '93 / Disky / THE

PERFECT INSTRUMENTAL COLLECTION VOL.2
CD DCD 5253
Disky / Aug '92 / Disky / THE

PERFECT INSTRUMENTAL LOVE ALBUM
CD CNCD 5993
Disky / Feb '94 / Disky / THE

PERFECTO FLUORO
CD 0630166942
Perfecto/East West / Oct '96 / Warner Music

PERFECTO MIXES
Even better than the real thing: *U2* / Unfinished sympathy: *Massive Attack* / U R the best thing: *D:Ream* / Move any mountain: *Shamen* / World: *New Order* / Something got me started: *Simply Red* / Human nature: *Clail, Gary* / Single: *Rise* / Doggy dogg world: *Snoop Doggy Dogg* / Hand in hand: *Opus III* / Waterfall: *Stone Roses* / Where love lives: *Limerick, Alison* / Colour my life: *M-People* / Money love: *Cherry, Neneh* / Suicide blonde: *INXS*
CD 4509981312
Perfecto/East West / Oct '94 / Warner Music

PERSIAN LOVE SONGS
CD LYRCD 7235
Lyrichord / '91 / ADA / CM / Roots

PERSIAN NIGHTS
CD 340552CD
Koch / Jul '95 / Koch

PERU - HUAYNO, VALSE CREOLE & MARIERA
CD PS 65133CD
PlayaSound / Jul '94 / ADA / Harmonia Mundi

PERUVIAN HARPS AND GUITARS
CD PS 65158
PlayaSound / Dec '95 / ADA / Harmonia Mundi

PHIALS OF ACID JAZZ (16 Intoxicating Grooves From The Vaults Of Acid Jazz)
Mr. Freedom: *Mother Earth* / Whole lotta love: *Taylor, James Quartet* / Mother's tongue: *Brand New Heavies* / Taurus woman: *Subterraneans* / Love will keep us together: *Taylor, James Quartet & Alison Limerick* / I'm the one: *D-Influence* / Everything's going to the beat: *Ace Of Clubs* / Quiet dawn: *Humble Souls* / Bad trip: *Night Trains* / Living life your own way: *Windross, Rose* / Change your mind: *Callier, Terry* / Eyes that burn: *Emperor's New Clothes* / Don't you let me down: *Planet* / Peace and love: *Cloud 9* / Motorhead: *Corduroy* / Nothing like this: *Snowboy*
CD MUSCD 032
MCI Music / Jan '97 / Disc / THE

PHILIDELPHIA SOUL CLASSICS VOL.1
CD STCD 1000
Disky / Jun '93 / Disky / THE

PHILIPPINE MUSIC KALINGA PEOPLE
CD CDMANU 1518
ODE / Feb '97 / CM / Discovery

PHILLY DUST KREW
CD TOODAMNY 52
Too Damn Hype / Feb '95 / Cargo / SRD

PHILO SO FAR: 20TH ANNIVERSARY FOLK SAMPLER
CD AN 12
Rounder / Apr '94 / ADA / CM / Direct

PHOENIX - THE ALBUM (Live At The Phoenix Festival 1996)
So let me go far: *Dodgy* / On a Tuesday: *Linoleum* / Percolator: *Stereolab* / This is fake DIY: *Bis* / Come out 2nite: *Kenickie* / Plastic ashtray: *Urusei Yatsura* / Bug in a breeze: *Baby Bird* / Hello spaceboy: *Bowie, David* / From despair to where: *Manic Street Preachers* / 36 degrees: *Placebo* / Weak: *Skunk Anansie* / Alice what's the matter: *Terrorvision* / Get some sleep tiger: *Red Snapper* / La madrugada: *Zion Train* / Smoke 'em: *Fun Lovin' Criminals* / Way beyond blue: *Catatonia*
CD PHNXCD 1
NMC / Jun '97 / Total/Pinnacle

PHOENIX PANORAMA (The Viv Labels/ 3CD Set)
How about me: *Johnson, Jimmy* / It's you, you, you: *Spellman, Jimmy* / Give me some of yours: *Spellman, Jimmy* / Cat Daddy: *Johnson, Jimmy* / Lover man: *Spellman, Jimmy* / Mama Lou: *Burnam, Buzz* / Time wounds all heels: *Clingman, Loy* / Don't hate me: *Lane, Jack* / Wings: *Combo, Copa* / Queen of hearts: *Adair, Ronnie* / Mr. Blues (is my shadow): *Lane, Jack* / Whisper to me: *Silvers, Johnny* / Five more miles to folsom: *Hardin, Doug* / King fool: *Lane, Jack* / Blue and lonesome mood: *Silvers, Johnny* / Talk to me: *Hardin, Doug* / All through the night: *Lane, Jack* / Restless: *Lane, Jack* / Blue I am: *Rollins, Don* / That's the way it happend: *Rollins, Don* / Other woman: *Rollins, Don* / Other woman (demo): *Rollins, Don* / If I'm wrong (demo): *Rollins, Don* / Don't hate me (demo): *Rollins, Don* / Good bartender (demo): *Rollins, Don* / Mirror mirror (demo): *Rollins, Don* / Crazy arms: *Lee, Garry* / Long John's flagpole rock: *Roller, Long John* / Hay Mama: *Roller, Long John* / If I'm wrong: *Owens, Donnie* / Need you: *Owens, Donnie* / Tomorrow: *Owens, Donnie* / Shy: *Perkins, Dal* / Raindance: *Self, Alvie* / Where, when and how: *Self, Alvie* / Things I can't forget: *Ryan, Ronnie* / Devil's den: *Turley, Duane* / Long gone cat: *Turley, Duane* / Between midnight and dawn: *Owens, Donnie* / Ask me anything: *Owens, Donnie* / On and on: *Owens, Donnie* / Cry little girlie: *Banta, Benny* / Gotta get with it: *Lemaire, Eddie* / Little more wine: *Hawks* / I ask of you: *Johnson, Miriam* / Boppin' blue jeans: *Leonard Bros* / Do da da do: *Leonard Bros* / Still of the night: *Langford, Gerry* / Tell me: *Langford, Gerry* / Lonely walk: *Self, Alvie* / Round and round: *Casey, Al* / Rockin' down Mexico way: *Clinkscale, Jimmy* / Doggone lonesome town: *Lane, Barry* / Rain on the mountain: *Q-Zeen* / There'll come a day: *Wilson, Easy Deal* / I don't wantcha: *Wilson, Easy Deal* / You're still my

baby: *Banta, Benny* / Cruisin' central: *Warmer, Faron* / Stop: *Cole, Don* / Fussin: *Ray, Gerald* / Panic: *Ray, Gerald* / I've got a girl: *Smith, Gary* / Shummyin' John: *Roustabouts* / Scotch and soda: *Thorne, Henry* / Scarlett: *Thorne, Henry* / I feel the blues coming on: *Clingman, Loy* / Li'l O'Bug: *Wagoners* / Ali Baba: *Morgan Condello Combo* / Tip: *Clingman's Clan* / Freshman girl, senior boy: *Dansfords* / Hard times: *McAllisters* / Saro Jane: *Clingman, Loy* / Silly dilly: *Terry & Peggy* / Cindy's crying: *Gray, Jimmie* / Forgotten: *Versales* / Nobody but you: *Contessas* / Gingerbread: *Alan & The Alpines* / Was it make believe: *Essex, Herb* / Bumble bee: *Tads* / Me, my shadow, and I: *Fullylove, Leroy* / I want to know: *Fullylove, Leroy* / Oo, what you do to me: *Fullylove, Leroy* / One of these days: *Fullylove, Leroy* / Day after day (master): *Fullylove, Leroy* / Man like myself: *Wild Flowers* / More than me: *Wild Flowers* / Times past: *Hobbits* / Top of the morning: *Hobbits* / Sidewalks and avenues: *Second Edition* / Sad now: *Solid Ground* / Tell her: *Riffs* / Don't move girl: *Lost & Found* / Big wave: *Scallywags* / Hi-fi baby: *Door Knobs* / For me: *Destiny's Children*
CD Set ______ **BCD 15824**
Bear Family / Jun '95 / Direct / Rollercoaster / Swift

PHOSPHORESCENT
CD ______ **TIPCD 08**
Tip / Oct '96 / Arabesque / Mo's Music Machine / Pinnacle / Prime

PHRENTIC DRUMS (Destructive Hardstep Drum 'n' Bass)
CD ______ **CLP 00862**
Hypnotic / Aug '97 / Cargo / SRD

PHUTURE
CD ______ **PCP 194**
PCP / Jul '94 / Plastic Head

PHUTURE BEATS (2CD Set)
CD Set ______ **MM 08941802**
Independence / Jan '96 / Plastic Head

PHUTURISTIC PHUNK
CD ______ **TKH 004**
Tekhed / Dec '96 / Cargo

PIANO BLUES DALLAS 1927-1929
CD Set ______ **PYCD 15**
Magpie / '92 / Hot Shot / Jazz Music

PIANO BLUES VOL.1
CD ______ **DOCD 5192**
Document / Oct '93 / ADA / Hot Shot / Jazz Music

PIANO BLUES VOL.1 1923-1930
CD ______ **SOBCD 35112**
Story Of The Blues / Mar '92 / ADA / Koch

PIANO BLUES VOL.1 1928-1932
CD ______ **PYCD 01**
Magpie / Apr '90 / Hot Shot / Jazz Music

PIANO BLUES VOL.2 1927-1940
CD ______ **DOCD 5220**
Document / Jan '94 / ADA / Hot Shot / Jazz Music

PIANO BLUES VOL.2 1930-1939
CD ______ **SOBCD 35122**
Story Of The Blues / Mar '92 / ADA / Koch

PIANO BLUES VOL.3 1924-1931
CD ______ **DOCD 5314**
Document / Dec '94 / ADA / Hot Shot / Jazz Music

PIANO BLUES VOL.3: VOCALION 1928-30 (Shake Your Wicked Knees)
Back in the alley / Cow cow blues / Slum gullion stomp / Texas shout / Michigan River blues / You can't come in / I'm so glad / Mexico bound blues band
CD ______ **PYCD 03**
Magpie / Oct '90 / Hot Shot / Jazz Music

PIANO BLUES VOL.4 1923-1928
CD ______ **DOCD 5336**
Document / May '95 / ADA / Hot Shot / Jazz Music

PIANO BLUES VOL.5 1929-1936
CD ______ **DOCD 5337**
Document / May '95 / ADA / Hot Shot / Jazz Music

PIANO BLUES VOL.5: POSTSCRIPT 1927-1933 (Hot Box On My Mind)
CD ______ **PYCD 05**
Magpie / Apr '91 / Hot Shot / Jazz Music

PIANO DISCOVERIES (Newly Found Titles & Alt. Takes 1928-1943)
CD ______ **BDCD 6045**
Blues Document / Jan '94 / ADA / Hot Shot / Jazz Music

PIANO DREAMS
Watermark / Right here waiting / Up where we belong / Evergreen / (Everything I do) I do it for you / Song for Guy / Missing / Wonderful tonight / Shepherd moons / All out of love / Always on my mind / Yesterday / Memories of green / Imagine / How deep is your love / I want to know what love is / Love is blue
CD ______ **CDVIP 149**
Virgin VIP / Apr '97 / EMI

PIANO IN BLUES
CD ______ **157172**
Blues Collection / Feb '93 / Discovery

PIANO MOODS
I will always love you / Have you ever really loved a woman / Stay another day / Fragile / Love can build a bridge / Miss you like crazy / Right here waiting / Back for good / No more I love you's / Get here / Think twice / Chains / Key to my life / Endless love / Best in me / Total eclipse of the heart / Whiter shade of pale / Unchained melody / Love is all around
CD ______ **3036000062**
Carlton / Oct '95 / Carlton

PIANO MOODS
Chariots of fire / Way it is / (Everything) I do it for you / Song for guy / Right here waiting / Wonderful tonight / Could it be magic / Power of love / Circle of life / I wish I knew how it would feel to be free / Let it be / Hey Jude / Stars / Another day in paradise / Think twice / Air on a G String / Where do I begin / Swan lake / We've only just begun / As time goes by
CD ______ **DINCD 114**
Dino / Oct '95 / Pinnacle

PIANO MOODS
CD ______ **75605512862**
Happy Days / Sep '96 / Conifer/BMG

PIANO PLAYTIME
I'd know you anywhere: *Thorburn, Billy* / Do I love you: *Thorburn, Billy* / I want my Mama: *Thorburn, Billy* / Message from the man in the moon: *Moore, Gerry* / Sophisticated lady: *Layton, Turner* / Ace of clubs: *Mayerl, Billy* / Ace of hearts: *Mayerl, Billy* / Jammin': *Moore, Gerry* / Sweet Sue: *Moreton, Ivor & Dave Kay* / Heebie jeebies: *Moreton, Ivor & Dave Kay* / I wonder where my baby is tonight: *Moreton, Ivor & Dave Kay* / In the shade of the old apple tree: *Carroll, Eddie & Bobby McGee* / My blue heaven: *Carroll, Eddie & Bobby McGee* / Running wild: *Carroll, Eddie & Bobby McGee* / Marigold: *Mayerl, Billy* / Roses in December: *Thorburn, Billy* / Blossoms on Broadway: *Thorburn, Billy* / Here comes the sandman: *Thorburn, Billy* / Little Sir Echo: *Renara* / Rosetta: *Moore, Gerry* / It don't mean a thing if it ain't got that swing: *Moreton, Ivor & Dave Kay* / Happy feet: *Moreton, Ivor & Dave Kay* / Everybody loves my baby: *Moreton, Ivor & Dave Kay* / I got rhythm: *Moreton, Ivor & Dave Kay* / Ace of diamonds: *Mayerl, Billy* / Ace of spades: *Mayerl, Billy* / Ain't misbehavin': *Young, Arthur* / March winds and April showers: *Moore, Gerry* / Man I love: *Rossborough, Patricia* / Marie: *Rossborough, Patricia* / My heart stood still: *Rossborough, Patricia* / No more you: *Moore, Gerry* / Blind man's buff: *Young, Arthur* / No souvenirs: *Carroll, Eddie* / You made me love you: *Carroll, Eddie* / Let the curtain come down: *Carroll, Eddie* / We're in the money: *Rossborough, Patricia* / Shadow waltz: *Rossborough, Patricia* / When two love each other: *Moore, Gerry* / Merry widow waltz: *Bradbury, Stan* / Destiny: *Bradbury, Stan* / Yip I addy: *Bradbury, Stan*
CD ______ **RAJCD 860**
Empress / Apr '96 / Koch

PIANO SOLITUDE (A Magical Blend Of Music And The Sounds Of Nature)
CD ______ **57642**
CMC / May '97 / BMG

PIANO TALK
CD ______ **ISCD 105**
Intersound / '88 / Jazz Music

PICADILLY STORY, THE
Crazy mixed up kid: *Brown, Joe & The Bruvvers* / Half of my heart: *Ford, Emile* / There, I've said it again: *Saxon, Al* / Honest I do: *Storm, Danny* / Z-cars: *Keating, Johnny* / Don't come cryin' to me: *Jones, Davy* / Picture of you: *Brown, Joe & The Bruvvers* / Rivers run dry: *Hill, Vince* / I knew it all the time: *Hill, Vince* / It might as well rain until September: *De Laine Sisters* / All of me: *Lynton, Jackie* / Long gone baby: *Britten, Buddy & The Regents* / Ferryboat ride: *Cudley Dudley* / Walk right in: *Kestrels* / Hey Paula: *Elaine & Derick* / Heavenly: *Eager, Vince* / Let's make a habit: *Guv'nors* / Ain't gonna kiss ya: *Jackson, Simone* / He's so near: *Douglas, Donna* / Tip of my tongue: *Quickly, Tommy* / Don't lie to me: *Jeannie & The Big Guys* / To know her is to love her: *Storme, Robb & Whispers* / He don't want your love anymore: *Doll, Linda & the Sundowners* / Is it true: *Tony D & The Shakeouts* / Sally go round the roses: *Remo Four* / Where did our love go: *Jay, Peter & The Jaywalkers* / Cast your fate to the wind: *Sounds Orchestral* / Don't cry for me: *Peters, Mark* / You've lost that lovin' feelin': *Ann, Barbara* / Girl who wanted fame: *Wackers* / Baby do it: *McKenna, Val* / Lonely room: *Ryder, Mal & the Spirits* / Poor man's son: *Rockin' Berries* / She's about a mover: *Britten, Buddy & The Regents* / Tossin' and turnin': *Ivy League* / Take a heart: *Sorrows* / Leave my baby alone: *Britt* / Leave it to me: *Band Of Angels* / That's my life (my love and my home): *Lennon, Freddie* / Why don't I run away from you: *Antoinette* / Ask the lonely: *Rio, Bobby* / I know (you don't love me no more): *Felders Orioles* / You don't know like I know: *Powell, Keith & Billie Davis* / Dear Mrs. Applebee: *Garrick, David* / Ain't that peculiar: *Loving Kind* / Whatever will be will be (Que sera sera): *Washington, Geno & The Ram Jam Band* / Ain't love good, ain't love proud: *James, Jimmy & The Vagabonds* / It keeps rainin': *Powell, Keith & The Valets* / Run to the door: *Ford, Clinton* / 98.6: *Bystanders* / I'll always love you: *Time Box* / Almost but not quite there: *Traffic Jam*
CD ______ **NEDCD 240**
Sequel / Oct '93 / BMG

PICCADILLY NIGHTS (British Dance Bands Of The 1920's)
That girl over there / Swing on the gait / It's a million to one you're in love / What'll you do / Make my cot where the cot-cot-cotton grows / How long has this been going on / Miss Annabelle Lee / Lila / That's my weakness now / Sunny skies / Matilda Matilda / Saskatchewan / There's a blue ridge 'round my heart, Virginia / 'S wonderful / Crazy rhythm / I'm a one man girl / Spread a little happiness / Out of the dawn / Ida, sweet as apple cider / I don't know why I do it but I do
CD ______ **DHAL 17**
Halcyon / Sep '93 / Cadillac / Harmonia Mundi / Jazz Music / Swift / Wellard

PICK AND MIX (2CD Set)
Higher sun: *Moom* / Time to fly: *Aardvarks* / Ease it: *Suicidal Flowers* / Gil: *Kava Kava* / Corcucopia: *Steppes* / Of the first water: *Sons Of Selina* / Tribal elders: *Riff, Nick* / Let the powers: *Nova Express* / Dissolving: *Treatment* / Watching the sky: *Kryptasthesie* / Annihilation: *Omnia Opera* / Inner days: *Nukli* / Solstice song: *Mandagora* / Voyage 34: *Porcupine Tree* / Warmth within: *Dead Flowers* / Psychomuzak: *Extasie* / Root verses of the six bardos: *Liberation Through Hearing* / Goat faced girl: *Zuvuya* / Nindia: *Electric Orange* / Arc of ascent: *Bazaar, Saddar* / Ornithology: *Praise Space Electric* / Can you play: *Praise Space Electric* / Ornithology: *Praise Space Electric* / Purple haze: *Boris & His Bolshie Balalaika* / Gospel according to IEM: *Incredible Expanding Mindfuck*
CD Set ______ **DELECCDD 023**
Delerium / Oct '95 / Cargo / Pinnacle / Vital

PICTURE YOURSELF BELLY DANCING
CD ______ **MCD 71780**
Monitor / Sep '93 / CM

PICTURES IN THE SKY
Pictures in the sky: *Orange Seaweed* / Real life permanent: *Orange Machine* / So sad inside: *Onyx* / My world fell down: *Ivy League* / Better make up your mind: *Koobas* / Within the night: *Velvett Fogg* / You didn't have to be so nice: *Glass Menagerie* / Jump and dance: *Carnaby* / Flying machine: *Flying Machine* / Cloudy: *Factotums* / I'm a hog for you: *Grant Erky/Earwigs*
CD ______ **DOCD 1997**
Drop Out / Mar '91 / Pinnacle

PIECES OF A DREAM
Flesh: *Tour De Force* / All I'm livin' for: *Drive, She Said* / Heart of mine: *Legs Diamond* / Closer to heaven: *FM* / Moonlight: *Lillian Axe* / Attracted: *Romeo's Daughter* / Hard to hold: *Drive, She Said* / Tears: *From The Fire* / Only the strong survive: *FM* / True believer: *Lillian Axe* / Be the one: *Legs Diamond* / Inherit the wind: *Tyketto*
CD ______ **CDMFN 165**
Music For Nations / Aug '94 / Pinnacle

PILGRIM, THE
Himlico's map / Gair na gairbe / Walk in the ocean / Pilgrim / Columcille's farewell to Ireland / Land of the picts / Iona / Briochan and columba / Storm at sea / Whita waves foam over / Ymadawiad Arthur / St Manchans prayer / Samson peccator episcopus / St Mathews point / Danse plin / Bal plin / Danse an dro / Santiago / Vigo / Deer's cry / God be with me / A'ghrian
CD ______ **TARACD 3032**
Tara / Aug '94 / ADA / CM / Conifer/BMG / Direct

PILLOW TALK
Pillow talk: *Sylvia* / Be thankful for what you've got: *DeVaughan, William* / Sad sweet dreamer: *Sweet Sensation* / Girls: *Moments* / Stay with me baby: *Redding, Wilma* / Can't get by without you: *Real Thing* / So sad the song: *Knight, Gladys & The Pips* / There it is: *Shalamar* / Red red wine: *James, Jimmy* / Loving you - losing you: *Hyman, Phyllis* / It's a love thing: *Whispers* / Suspicious minds: *Staton, Candi* / Betcha by golly wow: *Hyman, Phyllis & Michael Henderson* / Come back and finish what you started: *Knight, Gladys & The Pips* / You'll never know: *Hi-Gloss* / Have you seen her: *Chi-Lites* / Valentine love: *Connors, Norman* / You gave me love: *Crown Heights Affair*
CD ______ **TRTCD 117**
TrueTrax / Feb '96 / THE

PILLOWS AND PRAYERS (A Cherry Red Compilation 1982-1983)
Portrait: *Five Or Six* / Eine symphonie des grauns: *Monochrome Set* / All about you: *Leer, Thomas* / Plain sailing: *Thorn, Tracey* / Some things don't matter: *Watt, Ben* / Love in your heart: *Coyne, Kevin* / Modi 2: *Milesi, Pierro* / Compulsion: *Crow, Joe* / Lazy ways: *Marine Girls* / My face is on fire: *Felt* / No noise: *Eyeless In Gaza* / Xoyo: *Passage* / On my mind: *Everything But The Girl* / Bang and a wimpey: *Attila The Stockbroker* / I unseen: *Misunderstood* / Don't blink: *Nightingales* / Stop the music for a minute: *Crisp, Quentin*
CD ______ **CDMRED 41**
Cherry Red / Apr '96 / Pinnacle

PINARENO
CD ______ **PIR 372**
Piranha / Oct '92 / SRD

PINK AND POISONOUS
Repetitive beats: *Retribution* / Sense: *Decal* / Bells of induction: *Pyrex Detox* / Drumulator: *Inky Blacknuss* / 2 in 1: *Pyrex Detox* / Cult drums: *Innersphere* / Biomechnoid: *Innersphere* / Spaldang: *THD* / Void Com: *Turbulent Force* / Alpha acid: *Point Alpha* / Sector 106X: *Turbulent Force* / Out of body: *Innersphere* / Motorway sign: *Turbulent Force* / Do laugh: *Lords Of Afford* / Maniak: *Sapiano* / Facelifter: *Chelsea Grin* / Poundflesh: *Sapiano* / Jerry: *POD*
CD ______ **SBRCD 005**
Sabrettes / Nov '96 / Vital

PINT OF YOUR BEST PUB ROCK PLEASE, A
Sweet Gene Vincent: *Dury, Ian* / Been down so long: *Dr. Feelgood* / Walkin' the dog: *Marriott, Steve* / Crawlin' from the wreckage: *Parker, Graham* / Breathe a little: *Chilli Willi & Red Hot Peppers* / Something's goin' on: *Ducks Deluxe* / Work shy: *Fabulous Poodles* / Old time rock 'n' roll: *Gibbons, Steve Band* / Get out of Denver: *Eddie & The Hot Rods* / Ain't gonna stand for this no more: *Ace* / Keys to your heart: *101'ers* / Teenage letter: *Count Bishops* / Bottle up and go: *Johnson, Wilko* / They shoot horses don't they: *Racing Cars* / Ain't got no money: *Pirates* / Factory: *Eggs Over Easy* / Be good to yourself: *Miller, Frankie* / Billericay Dickie: *Dury, Ian*
CD ______ **NTRCD 066**
Nectar / May '97 / Pinnacle

PIONEER CHRISTMAS
Mistletoe and wine / Frosty the snowman / Step into Christmas / Christmas song / Last Christmas / Stop the cavalry / Lonely this Christmas / Rockin' around the Christmas tree / Blue Christmas / Santa Claus is coming to town / Winter wonderland / Wonderful Christmas time / I saw Mommy kissing Santa Claus / White Christmas
CD ______ **CDMFP 6178**
Music For Pleasure / Nov '95 / EMI

PIONEERS OF THE BOUNCING BEAT
CD ______ **EFFS 1001CD**
CD ______ **EFFS 1001CDR**
Effective / Oct '94 / Amato Disco / Pinnacle / Prime

PIPES AND DRUMS
CD ______ **LBP 2028CD**
Lochshore / Jun '96 / ADA / Direct / Duncans

PIPES AND DRUMS FROM THE BORDERS (Berwick Tattoo 1996)
Opening fanfare / Pipes and drums / King's division Waterloo band / Northumbria police band / Northumberland band of the royal regiment of fusiliers / Highland band of the Scottish division / Massed military bands / Final: pipes, drums and bands
CD ______ **BNA 5130**
Bandleader / Dec '96 / Conifer/BMG

PIPES AND DRUMS OF IRELAND
CD ______ **925592**
BUDA / Jun '93 / Discovery

PIPES AND DRUMS OF SCOTLAND
CD ______ **EUCD 1213**
ARC / Sep '93 / ADA / ARC Music

PIPES AND STRINGS OF SCOTLAND VOL.1
CD ______ **CD ITV 362**
Scotdisc / Dec '86 / Conifer/BMG / Duncans / Ross

PIPING HOT (A Celtic Bagpipe Collection)
Good drying set: *Tannahill Weavers* / Larry Redican's hornpipe/The green banner: *O'Sullivan, Jerry* / Onward blindly onward: *Rare Air* / Blackbirds and thrushes: *Connolly, Matty* / Sean Reid's/Toss the feathers: *Moloney, Mick & Joe McKenna* / Grimstock: *House Band* / Clueless: *Wolfstone* / Brian O'Lynn/The woods of old Limerick: *Patrick Street* / Rainy day/The merry blacksmith/ The silver spear: *Ennis, Seamus* / Bells of Tipperary/Miss Galvin's: *Burke, Joe & Michael Cooney/Terry Corcoran* / Dear Irish boy/The stone in the field: *Reck, Tommy* / Colonel Fraser: *O'Sullivan, Jerry* / Kintail: *Tannahill Weavers*
CD ______ **CELT 9004**
Celtophile / May '97 / Direct

PITCH, THE
CD ______ **MONCD 001**
Montana / Mar '93 / Jet Star

PLACE IN THE SUN, A
CD ______ **CRECD 088**
Creation / May '94 / 3mv/Vital

PLANET DUB (2CD Set)
CD Set ______ **BARKCD 015**
Planet Dog / Oct '95 / Pinnacle

PLANET E PRESENTS INTERGALACTIC BEATS
CD PE 010CD
Planet E / May '97 / Cargo

PLANET LONDON
High on life: *Sugar Foot* / Let go: *Sound Advice* / Cactus water: *Essen* / JJ: *Essen* / What you say: *Xangbetos* / Look no further: *Curran, Paul* / First you say you will: *Fumi* / Honeychild: *Shanakies* / Happy people: *Foggis de Taxi Pata Pata* / Call: *Afrobloc*
CD TNGCD 002
Tongue 'n' Groove / Oct '93 / Vital

PLANET RAMPANT VOL.2
CD SUB 10D
Subversive / Apr '96 / 3mv/Sony / Amato Disco / Mo's Music Machine / Prime / Vital

PLANET SKA
CD PHZCD 57
Unicorn / Feb '95 / Plastic Head

PLANET SQUEEZE BOX (3CD Set)
CD Set ELLIPSIS 347
Ellipsis Arts / Jun '96 / ADA / Direct

PLANETE RAI
Let me cry: *Mami, Cheb* / La Camel: *Khaled, Cheb* / N'sel fik: *Fadela, Chaba* / Sel dem drai: *Kada, Cheb* / Dawili Mali: *Tati, Cheb* / Ana Mazel: *Mami, Cheb* / Rani Meute: *Kada, Cheb* / Zini: *Rai, Raina* / Kutche: *Khaled, Cheb* / Gouloulima: *Zahouania, Chaba* / El awama: *Kada, Cheb* / Rih el gharei: *Moumen, Cheb* / Chabba bent: *Khaled, Cheb* / Douha alia: *Mami, Cheb*
CD GUMBOCD 004
Cooking Vinyl / Jan '93 / Vital

PLANETE REGGAE VOL.1
CD 8411352
Declic / Oct '96 / Jet Star

PLANETE REGGAE VOL.2
CD 172032
Declic / Oct '96 / Jet Star

PLANETE ROCK 'N' ROLL
CD Set 302129
Total / May '94 / Total/BMG

PLATINUM BREAKS (2CD Set)
VIP rider's ghost: *Rufige Cru* / Psychosis: *Peshay* / Far away: *Doc Scott* / Angels fell: *Dillinja* / Your sound: *J-Majik* / Consciousness: *Photek* / Flute tune: *Hidden Agenda* / Spectrum: *Wax Doctor* / Pulp fiction: *Reece, Alex* / Unofficial ghost: *Doc Scott* / In my life: *Lemon D* / Made up sound: *Source Direct* / Down under: *Digital* / Da base II dark: *Asylum* / Day break: *J-Majik* / Armoured 'D': *Dillinja* / Nocturnal (Back on the firm): *Peshay*
CD Set 8287832
FFRR / Jul '96 / PolyGram

PLATIPUS RECORDS VOL.2
CD PLAT 20CD
Platipus / Nov '95 / Prime / SRD

PLAY
CD EFA 123352
Sideburn / Aug '97 / SRD

PLAY ME A POLKA
CD ROUCD 6029
Rounder / Dec '94 / ADA / CM / Direct

PLAY ME THE BLUES
CD PBCD 101
Panther / Feb '91 / Sony

PLAY NEW ROSE FOR ME
CD ROSE 100CD
New Rose / Jan '87 / ADA / Direct / Discovery

PLAY THAT AMERICAN JUKEBOX (2CD Set)
Wake up little Susie: *Everly Brothers* / Hello Mary Lou: *Nelson, Rick* / C'mon everybody: *Cochran, Eddie* / Ain't that a shame: *Domino, Fats* / Dreamin': *Burnette, Johnny Rock 'N' Roll Trio* / Venus: *Avalon, Frankie* / Poetry in motion: *Tillotson, Johnny* / It might as well rain until September: *King, Carole* / Why do fools fall in love: *Lymon, Frankie & The Teenagers* / Unchained melody: *Baxter, Les* / Blue moon: *Marcels* / Will you still love me tomorrow: *Shirelles* / Cry me a river: *London, Julie* / Run to him: *Vee, Bobby* / Let the good times roll: *Shirley & Lee* / Let's turkey trot: *Little Eva* / It's late: *Nelson, Rick* / Surf City: *Jan & Dean* / Summertime blues: *Cochran, Eddie* / Twenty four hours from Tulsa: *Pitney, Gene* / Don't ever change: *Crickets* / Locomotion: *Little Eva* / Be bop a lula: *Vincent, Gene* / Blueberry Hill: *Domino, Fats* / You got what it takes: *Johnson, Marv* / You're sixteen: *Burnette, Johnny Rock 'N' Roll Trio* / Donna: *Valens, Ritchie* / Party doll: *Knox, Buddy* / Willie and the hand jive: *Otis, Johnny Show* / Bye bye love: *Everly Brothers* / Surfin' USA: *Beach Boys* / Poor little fool: *Nelson, Rick* / Take good care of my baby: *Vee, Bobby* / That old black magic: *Prima, Louis & Keely Smith* / Shout: *Isley Brothers* / Walk don't run: *Ventures* / Tears on my pillow: *Imperials* / I'm in love: *Domino, Fats*
CD Set CDDL 1212
Music For Pleasure / Nov '91 / EMI

PLAY THE BLUES
Lonely guitar man: *Dawkins, Jimmy* / Drivin' me crazy: *Shadows* / Keep it: *Watts, Noble* / Little red rooster: *Drink Small* / Looking up at the bottom: *Ealey, Theodis* / Locksmith: *Nelson, Chicago Bob* / In order: *Principato, Tom* / Ain't no blues in town: *Rhodes, Sonny* / House without a home: *Turner, Troy* / Sky is crying: *Coleman, Gary B.B.* / Three wives: *McCain, Jerry* / I like to hear my guitar sing: *Benton, Buster*
CD ICH 11892
Ichiban / Jun '96 / Direct / Koch

PLAYING FOR LOVE
CD BLR 84 026
L&R / May '91 / New Note/Pinnacle

PLAYING HARD TO GET (West Coast Girls)
You're so fine: *Berry, Dorothy* / Little bit of soap: *Carroll, Yvonne* / Stop shovin' me around: *Delicates* / Dreamworld: *Loren, Donna* / Crying on my pillow: *Berry, Dorothy* / He's a big deal: *Medina, Renee* / Goodbye Jimmie: *Berry, Panda* / You haven't seen nothing: *Young, Dee Dee* / Don't mess around with me: *Sister Rachel* / Nothing to write home about: *Francettes* / Love bells: *Galens* / Date bait: *Maxwell, Diane* / You better watch out boy: *Accents* / Chinese lanterns: *Galens* / Boy I love: *Medina, Renee* / Write me a letter: *Blossoms* / I've been hurt: *Delicates* / How long must this fool pay: *Carroll, Yvonne* / I'll wait: *Blossoms* / I want to get married: *Delicates* / Search is over: *Blossoms* / Hard to get: *Blossoms* / Come on everybody: *Delicates* / I gotta tell it: *Blossoms* / Big talkin' Jim: *Blossoms* / Mr. Loveman: *Carroll, Yvonne* / Comin' down with love: *Delicates* / Muscle bustle: *Loren, Donna*
CD CDCHD 559
Ace / May '95 / Pinnacle

PLAYING THE BLUES
Still got the blues (for you): *Moore, Gary* / Boom boom: *Hooker, John Lee* / Down in Mississippi: *Staples, Pops* / Trouble blues: *Hammond, John* / Too many cooks: *Evans, Terry* / I'll be good: *Washington, Walter 'Wolfman'* / Back to my baby: *Sanne* / Iceman: *Collins, Albert* / Green all over: *Jumpin' The Gunn* / Witchin' moon: *McCray, Larry* / Too early to tell: *Kinsey Report* / She likes to boogie real low: *Winter, Johnny* / Rule the world: *Robillard, Duke*
CD CDVIP 130
Virgin VIP / Oct '94 / EMI

PLAYING WITH FIRE
Reel Beatrice/Abbey reel / Sprig of Shillelagh/Planxty penny / Two reels / Lord Gordon's reel / Foggy dew / Copper plate / Waltz from Orsa / In and out the harbour / Rolling waves/Market town/Scatter the mud / Jenny's welcome to Charlie/Father Francis Cameron / Marquis of Huntly / Con Cassidy's and Nelly O'Boyle's highland reels / Gavotten / Walkin' o' the Fauld / Carraigin ruadh / Curlew/McDermott's reel/Three scones of Boxty
CD GLCD 1101
Green Linnet / Feb '93 / ADA / CM / Direct / Highlander / Roots

PLEASURES AND TREASURES (A Kaleidoscope of Sound)
March by Mr Handel: *Hacker, Alan* / Mira O Norma: *Polyphon musical box* / Jean's reel: *Tickell, Kathryn* / Lezghinka: *Best Of Brass* / Prelude to lute suite in E major: *North, Nigel* / Colette: *Whiteman, Paul & His Orchestra* / John come kiss me now: *Townsend, Dave* / Music from Compline: *Stanbrook Abbey Nuns & Prinknash Abbey Monks* / Le coucou: *Preston, Stephen* / Whistling Rufus: *Sound In Brass Handbells* / Limerick's lamentation: *Monger, Eileen* / La quinte estampie real: *Canter, Robin* / I've got a lovely bunch of coconuts: *Barrel Organ* / Love at the fair: *Jing Ying Soloists* / Miss Annabelle Lee: *Pianola Roll* / Scherzo: *Holmes, Ralph* / Wibbly wobbly walk: *Charman, Jack* / Jenny Lind medley: *Couza, Jim* / Turkish rondo: *Burnett, Richard* / O Sanctissima: *Schmitt, Georges* / Reve gourmand: *Pauly, Danielle* / Sportive little trifler: *Canterbury Clerkes & London Serpent Trio*
CD CDSDLC 362
Saydisc / Sep '86 / ADA / Direct / Harmonia Mundi

PLEASURES IN LIFE
CD NB 020CD
Nuclear Blast / Dec '90 / Plastic Head

PLUS FROM US
Obiero: *Ogada, Ayub* / Keep on marching: *Meters* / Oasis: *Hammill, Peter* / Pine tree and on the street: *Pokrovsky, Dmitri* / Best friend paranoia: *Orbit, William* / Lone bear: *Levin, Tony* / Morecambe bay: *Gifford, Alex* / Down by the river: *Rhodes, David* / Triennale: *Eno, Brian* / Rose rhythm: *Serra, Eric* / Silence: *Katche, Manu* / Baladi we hetta: *Ramzy, Hossam* / Dreams: *Shankar 'N' Caroline* / Suheyla: *Erguner, Kudsi* / El Conquistador: *Lanois, Daniel*
CD CDRW 33
Realworld / May '93 / EMI

PLUS GRANDS SUCCES DU PUNK VOL.2
CD 622522
Skydog / Apr '97 / Discovery

POETRY OF IRA COHEN, THE
CD SR 62
Sub Rosa / Mar '96 / Direct / RTM/Disc / SRD / Vital

POETRY PUT TO SONG
CD 7992382
Hispavox / Jan '95 / ADA

POETRY PUT TO SONG
CD 7996512
Hispavox / Jan '95 / ADA

POINTS WEST (New Horizons In Country Music)
CD HCD 8021
Hightone / Oct '94 / ADA / Koch

POLISH VILLAGE MUSIC 1927-1933
CD ARHCD 7031
Arhoolie / Jun '95 / ADA / Cadillac / Direct

POLITICAL PARTY BROADCAST (2CD Set)
Treatment: *Kektex* / Mushrooms on daleks: *Sacroblast* / Slut fuck: *Immersion* / Godstopper: *Kektex* / Piston: *Kektex* / Techno slut: *Immersion* / Lock: *Kektex* / New wave of acid techno: *Lochi* / Sonar: *Sacroblast* / What is soul: *Temperature Drop* / Bug swat: *Kektex* / Techno slut: *Immersion* / Paroxysm: *Lochi* / Roland abuse: *Sacroblast* / Trip wire: *Lochi* / London acid city: *Lochi* / In the forehead: *Kektex* / New wave of acid techno 92): *Kektex* / Quasar: *Kektex* / Control: *Secret Hero* / Hoover baby: *Tasha Killer Pussies* / Lock: *Kektex* / Slut fuck: *Immersion*
CD Set ROUTEPILE 1
Routemaster / Jun '97 / Arabesque / Mo's Music Machine / Prime / SRD

POLITPARADE (4CD Set)
Der Geist weht: *Strauss, Franz Joseph* / Ich glaube nicht: *Von Hassel, Kai Uwe* / Wir nehmen nicht Abschied: *Erhard, Ludwig* / Wir wunschen Frieden Heinrich: *Barzel, Rainer* / Die Reise: *Lubke, Heinrich* / Das Lied von der unzefriedenen Gruppe: *Kiesinger, Georg* / Berliner jam session: *Diverse 1* / Deutschland braucht Bayern: *Strauss, Franz Joseph* / We do not want to fight: *Schroder, Gerhard* / Die NPD ist wieder weg: *Schmidt, Helmut* / Made in Germany: *Scheel, Walter* / Wir wollen mehr Demokratie wagen: *Brandt, Willy* / Etwas lernen - etwas leisten: *Schmidt, Helmut* / Nach allem was ich sehe: *Barzel, Rainer* / Der song mit den kurzen Beinen: *Wehner, Herbert* / Das ist gut: *Brandt, Willy* / Das Lied von der Vaterlandsliebe: *Carstens, Karl* / Vertrauen in die Wahrung: *Schmidt, Helmut* / Wo steht denn geschrieben: *Genscher, Hans Dietrich* / Es gibt nur eine Mitte: *Strauss, Franz Joseph* / Tai tik: *Strauss, Franz Joseph* / Was wir wollen: *Barzel, Rainer* / Trimm dich trilogie / Dichterlesung Franz Josef / Afghanistan: *Strauss, Franz Joseph* / Kein schoner land: *Strauss, Franz Joseph* / Sicher kann keiner sein: *Schmidt, Helmut* / Ach du lieber Gott: *Strauss, Franz Joseph* / Ich kenne die sprache des Volkes: *Strauss, Franz Joseph* / Der Rechsstaat muss Zahne bekommen: *Strauss, Franz Joseph* / Die Krise: *Schmidt, Helmut* / Practa Sunt Servanda: *Schmidt, Helmut* / Mara Durimeh: *Schmidt, Helmut* / Wir Deutschen sind des shiessens satt: *Schmidt, Helmut* / Wir werden siegen: *Strauss, Franz Joseph* / Das duell: *Schmidt, Helmut & Franz Josef Strauss* / Wenn das Benehmen Glucksache ist: *Schmidt, Helmut & Franz Josef Strauss* / Bruder Josef: *Schmidt, Helmut & Franz Josef Strauss* / Kaloriengehalt: *Schmidt, Helmut & Franz Josef Strauss* / Menschliche Herkunft: *Schmidt, Helmut & Franz Josef Strauss* / Produktion von Eiern: *Schmidt, Helmut & Franz Josef Strauss* / Sportliche Betatigung: *Schmidt, Helmut & Franz Josef Strauss* / Meine damen und herren: *Schmidt, Helmut & Franz Josef Strauss* / Wenn Pferde immer noch nicht so recht saufen: *Schmidt, Helmut & Franz Josef Strauss* / Das kann ich nicht: *Schmidt, Helmut & Franz Josef Strauss* / Meine sehr verehrten damen und herren: *Schmidt, Helmut & Franz Josef Strauss* / Es gibt auch pillen fur Manner: *Schmidt, Helmut & Franz Josef Strauss* / Bonner nachtgebet: *Schmidt, Helmut & Franz Josef Strauss* / Eigene Geschichte: *Schmidt, Helmut & Franz Josef Strauss* / Wer raus geht muss auch wieder reinkommen: *Schmidt, Helmut & Franz Josef Strauss* / Ein paar bemerkungen: *Schmidt, Helmut & Franz Josef Strauss* / Darf ich sie fragen: *Schmidt, Helmut & Franz Josef Strauss* / Fahren sie in ihren Ausfuhrungen fort: *Schmidt, Helmut & Franz Josef Strauss* / Da mussen sie ich eine bessere Frage einfallen lassen: *Schmidt, Helmut & Franz Josef Strauss* / Meine Damen und Herren: *Schmidt, Helmut & Franz Josef Strauss* / Herr Abgeordneter, fahren sie in ihrer Rede fort: *Schmidt, Helmut & Franz Josef Strauss* / Noch eine Bemerkung: *Schmidt, Helmut & Franz Josef Strauss* / Das ist gut das lassen wir weg: *Schmidt, Helmut & Franz Josef Strauss* / Heinrich Lubke: Einigkeit und Recht und Freiheit: *Schmidt, Helmut & Franz Josef Strauss* / Vorwurfe: *Schmidt, Helmut & Franz Josef Strauss* / Einigkeit und Recht und Freheit 2: *Schmidt, Helmut & Franz Josef Strauss* / Ausserdem konnen wir leicht nachweisen: *Schmidt, Helmut & Franz Josef Strauss* / Gartenschau: *Schmidt, Helmut & Franz Josef Strauss* / Literatur und Dichtung: *Schmidt, Helmut & Franz Josef Strauss* / Moderne Baukunst: *Schmidt, Helmut & Franz Josef Strauss* / Deutsche Vereinigung: *Schmidt, Helmut & Franz Josef Strauss* / Zum Schluss: *Schmidt, Helmut & Franz Josef Strauss*
CD Set BCD 16008
Bear Family / Nov '96 / Direct / Rollercoaster / Swift

POLLYCOUNTRY VOL.1
CD PCM 002
Pollytone / Apr '97 / Nervous / Pollytone

POLYPHONIC CHANTS OF THE MONGO PEOPLE
CD C 580050
Ocora / Sep '93 / ADA / Harmonia Mundi

POLYPHONIES (Southern Alps)
CD 926652
BUDA / Feb '97 / Discovery

POLYPHONIES OF THE SOLOMON ISLANDS
CD LDX 274663
La Chant Du Monde / Nov '90 / ADA / Harmonia Mundi

POLYPHONIES VOCALES (Music From Albania)
CD W 260065
Inedit / Dec '95 / ADA / Discovery / Harmonia Mundi

POLYPHONY FOR HOLY WEEK (Religious Vocal Music From Sardinia)
CD LDX 274936
La Chant Du Monde / Jul '92 / ADA / Harmonia Mundi

POLYPHONY OF SVANETI
CD LDX 274990
La Chant Du Monde / May '94 / ADA / Harmonia Mundi

POLYPHONY OF THE DORZE (Ethiopia)
CD 2746461
La Chant Du Monde / Jan '95 / ADA / Harmonia Mundi

POMELO 01 COMPILATION
CD Set POM 01CD
Pomelo / Jul '94 / Plastic Head

POP CLASSICS
Born to be wild: *Steppenwolf* / Sweet home Alabama: *Lynyrd Skynyrd* / Don't believe a word: *Moore, Gary* / Broken wings: *Mr. Mister* / Saturday night: *Brood, Herman* / Radio girl: *Hiatt, John* / LB Boogie: *Livin' Blues* / Lola: *Kinks* / American woman: *Guess Who* / We built this city: *Starship* / Radio Africa: *Latin Quarter* / Rocky mountain way: *Walsh, Joe* / Feelin' alright: *Mason, Dave* / Elvira: *Oak Ridge Boys* / Woodstock: *Matthew's Southern Comfort* / Joy to the world: *Three Dog Night*
CD MCD 30199
Ariola Express / Mar '94 / BMG

POP CLASSICS
CD DSPCD 105
Disky / Sep '93 / Disky / THE

POP CLASSICS VOL.1 (2CD Set)
Final countdown: *Europe* / Don't bring me down: *ELO* / Boogie wonderland: *Earth, Wind & Fire* / Heartbeat: *Johnson, Don* / You spin me around: *Dead Or Alive* / Power of love: *Rush, Jennifer* / Stop loving you: *Toto* / Sun of Jamaica: *Coombay Dance Band* / Play it cool: *Freiheit* / Feels like heaven: *Fiction Factory* / You were a friend of mine: *Browne, Jackson & Clarence Clemons* / Alice, I want you just for me: *Full Force* / Sunshine in the music: *Cliff, Jimmy* / Favourite waste of time: *Paul, Owen* / Call me: *Spagna* / Paradise by the dashboard light: *Meat Loaf* / Keep on loving you: *REO Speedwagon* / Lovely day: *Withers, Bill* / How 'bout us: *Champaign* / When your heart is weak: *Cock Robin* / Riding on a train: *Pasadenas* / What's another year: *Logan, Johnny* / Endless road: *Time Bandits* / Relight my fire: *Hartman, Dan* / Nescio: *Nits* / Girls just wanna have fun: *Lauper, Cyndi* / Matador: *Jeffreys, Garland* / You: *Ten Sharp* / Through the barricades: *Spandau Ballet* / Longer: *Fogelberg, Dan*
CD Set XA 0021/2
Paradiso / May '97 / Target/BMG

POP CLASSICS VOL.2 (2CD Set)
I want you to want me: *Cheap Trick* / What's a matter baby: *Foley, Ellen* / Tell it like it is: *Johnson, Don* / True colours: *Lauper, Cyndi* / Rockit: *Hancock, Herbie* / Give it up: *KC & The Sunshine Band* / Sexual healing: *Gaye, Marvin* / Live it up: *Time Bandits* / You took the words right out of my mouth: *Meat Loaf* / After the love has gone: *Earth, Wind & Fire* / This old house: *Stevens, Shakin'* / Total eclipse of the heart: *Tyler, Bonnie* / When will I be famous: *Bros* / What I like about you: *Romantics* / Little bit further away: *Kokomo* / 99 luftballons: *Nena* / Tribute (right on): *Pasadenas* / Rock the night: *Europe* / Walk like an egyptian: *Bangles* / Promise you made: *Cock Robin* / Reggae night: *Cliff, Jimmy* / Shine on: *Duke, George* / Devil went down to Georgia: *Daniels, Charlie Band* / Poison: *Cooper, Alice* / Precious little diamonds: *Fox The Fox* / Black betty: *Ram Jam* / Europa: *Santana* / My heart lies: *Dickson, Barbara* / Hold on tight: *ELO* / Africa: *Toto*
CD Set XA 0022/2
Paradiso / May '97 / Target/BMG

POP GOES THE 70'S
Beautiful Sunday: *Boone, Daniel* / Freedom come freedom go: *Fortunes* / In the summertime: *Mungo Jerry* / Come and get it: *Badfinger* / Witch queen of New Orleans, The: *Redbone* / Radancer: *Marmalade* / Son of my father: *Chicory Tip* / Fox on the run: *Connolly, Brian* / Dancin, on a Saturday night: *Blue, Barry* / Goodbye my love: *Glitter Band* / Sugar baby love: *Rubettes* / I'd like to teach the world to sing (in perfect harmony): *New Seekers* / Billy don't be a hero: *Paper Lace* / Chirpy chirpy cheep cheep: *Kissoon, Mac & Katie* / I'd love you to want me: *Lobo* / Indiana wants me: *Taylor, Dean* / Rock your baby: *McCrae, George* / That same old feeling: *Brown, Polly*
CD ECD 3075
K-Tel / Jan '95 / K-Tel

POP HITS DELUXE
CD HRCD 8042
Disky / Jul '94 / Disky / THE

POP HITS GO ON
CD MU 5051
Musketeer / Oct '92 / Disc

POP HITS OF THE 60'S
CD PWKS 4181
Carlton / Nov '94 / Carlton

POP INSIDE THE SIXTIES VOL.2
Uncle Willie: *Money, Zoot* / Long tall shorty: *Bond, Graham Organisation* / I'll cry instead: *Cocker, Joe* / Good morning little school girl: *Stewart, Rod* / Money: *Elliott, Bern & The Fenmen* / Buckleshoe stomp: *Snobs* / Just one more chance: *Outer Limits* / London boys: *Bowie, David* / Say you don't mind: *Laine, Denny* / Will you be my lover tonight: *Bean, George* / Surprise surprise: *Lulu* / Now I know: *Beat Chics* / We love the Beatles: *Vernons Girls* / Like dreamers do: *Applejacks* / That's alright mama: *Gonks* / What's new pussycat: *Crying Shames* / Please Mr. Postman: *Elliott, Bern & The Fenmen* / No response: *Hep Stars* / St. James Infirmary: *Cops 'n' Robbers* / You're on my mind: *Birds* / Lonely weekends: *Bean, George* / Kansas city: *Jay, Peter & The Jaywalkers* / Long legged baby: *Bond, Graham Organisation* / Shang a doo lang: *Posta, Adrienne* / Caroline: *Fortunes* / There you go: *Ryan, Paul & Barry*
CD SEECD 399
See For Miles/C5 / Mar '94 / Pinnacle

POP INSIDE THE SIXTIES VOL.3
CD SEECD 400
See For Miles/C5 / Jun '94 / Pinnacle

POP JINGU VOL.1
CD SONOCD 4
Sonorama / Jun '97 / Cargo

POP MUSIC FROM AFRICA VOL.1
CD 15285
Laserlight / '91 / Target/BMG

POP MUSIC FROM AFRICA VOL.2
CD 15286
Laserlight / '91 / Target/BMG

POP RAI & RACHIO STYLE
CD CDEWV 15
Earthworks / Mar '90 / EMI

POP SINGERS ON THE AIR (Four Complete Broadcasts 1943-1958)
CD CDMR 1149
Radiola / Apr '91 / Pinnacle

POP XMAS
Do they know it's Christmas: *Band Aid* / Have yourself a merry little Christmas: *Williams, Vanessa* / Step into Christmas: *John, Elton* / Silent night: *Bryant, Sharon* / Spaceman came travelling: *De Burgh, Chris* / Funky Christmas: *Sease, Marvin* / Christmas rapping: *Blow, Kurtis* / My Christmas: *Tony Toni Tone* / Christmas song: *Phillips, Shawn* / Merry Christmas everybody: *Metal Gurus* / Winter's tale: *Essex, David* / Christmas day: *Squeeze* / Rent a santa: *Hill, Chris* / It may be winter outside: *Love Unlimited Orchestra*
CD 5504162
Spectrum / Nov '94 / PolyGram

POPCORN'S DETROIT SOUL PARTY
Nothing no sweeter: *Carlton, Carl* / Ooh boy: *Adorables* / Down in the dumps: *Hester, Tony* / Hurting: *Erik & Vikings* / Turn on the heat: *Popcorn & Soul Messengers* / Somebody stop that boy: *Boo, Betty* / Hanky panky: *Wylie, Richard 'Popcorn'* / Tell her: *Clarke, Jimmy 'Soul'* / Gotta kind a way: *Lindsay, Therese* / Mighty lover: *Ideals* / Saving all my love for you: *Popcorn Orchestra* / Spaceland: *Hester, Tony* / My baby ain't no play thing: *Harvey, Willy* / Sweet Darling: *Clarke, Jimmy 'Soul'* / Arrest me: *Thomas, Jano* / If it's all the same to you babe: *Ingram, Luther* / Nobody love me like you: *Mercer, Barbara* / Going to a happening: *Popcorn Orchestra* / I'll be your champion: *Clarke, Jimmy 'Soul'* / Let the sun shine in your window: *Mann, Columbus* / Cool off: *Detroit Executives* / You knew what you was gettin': *Williams, Juanita* / G I Joe we love you: *Fantasions*
CD GSCD 059
Goldmine / Nov '95 / Vital

POPTARTZ (4CD Set)
Movin to music: *Finito* / My love: *Shades Of Rhythm* / DJ Dubs: *Lock, Eddie* / We got the love: *Erik* / Comes over me: *Stylofoam* / Mooncat: *Shaker* / Changeling: *Tan Ru* / Move and groove: *Basement Of Sound* / Raise the feeling: *Shades Of Rhythm* / Protein: *Tata Box* / Storm: *Space Kittens* / Let the fun begin: *Fluffy Toy IQ* / Think about it: *Stylofoam* / Do me: *Aquarius* / Electroluv: *4th Wave* / Hideaway: *De'Lacy* / Deliver me: *Urban Blues Project* / Feeling: *Jasper Street Family* / One love: *Coccoluto, Claudio* / I won't waste your time: *Joi & Jorio* / Reeboot 144: *OLN* / Everlasting picture: *B-Zet* / You can't turn around: *Bottom $* / Do it to me: *Dark, Frankie* / Let no man put a sunder: *First Choice* / Welcome to the factory: *Moraes, Angel* / Work 2 do: *Roach Motel* / Dancing in the year 2000: *From The Soul* / So everbody (get off it): *Sound Design* / Club America: *Club America* / Dreamtime: *Zee* / Same thing in reverse: *Boy George* / El metro: *Disco Volante* / Joanna: *Mrs. Wood* / Fee fi fo fum: *Candy Girls* / Out come the freaks: *Lippy Lou* / Never felt this way: *Hi-Lux* / Indoctrinate: *Castle Trancelot* / Florubunda: *Mothers Pride* / Do you want me: *Mambo* / Don't you want me: *Felix* / Rollerskate disco: *Pooley, Ian* / Shake your body: *Ill Disco* / C'mon y'all: *Rhythm Masters* / Come together: *Double FM* / Dive: *Club 69* / Transform: *Mijangos* / Happiness (is just around the bend): *Brooklyn's Poor & Needy* / Let the rythm flow: *Diva Rhythms* / Lost in you: *Matt Bianco* / Geel good: *B-Code* / Forerunner: *Natural Born Groovers* / Who's the badman: *De Patten* / Rock 2 the beat: *RM Project* / In my brain: *Mark NRG* / Unbe: *RAW* / La Casa: *Adrian & Alfarez* / Energy tax: *RMS* / If we lose our lovin': *DMB*
CD Set REACTCD 067
React / Nov '95 / Arabesque / Prime / Vital

POPULAR FOLK SONGS FROM NORTH GERMANY
CD EUCD 1180
ARC / '91 / ADA / ARC Music

POPULAR IRISH BALLADS
CD MATCD 252
Castle / Apr '93 / BMG

POPULAR MUSIC FROM GUINEA
CD SOW 90140
Sounds Of The World / Mar '95 / Target/BMG

POPULAR MUSIC FROM RAJASTHAN
Satara / Tandura (Bhajan) / Morchang solo / Shehnai and nagara / Basuri solo / Marriage orchestra / Ravanahattha solo / Dhol and thali / Murli / Narh / Morchang / Kamayacha / Narh song / Narh and song / Ravanahattha and song / Nagara
CD PS 65184
PlayaSound / Jun '97 / ADA / Harmonia Mundi

POPULAR MUSIC OF CHILE
CD PS 65094
PlayaSound / Aug '92 / ADA / Harmonia Mundi

POPULAR PROFESSIONAL MUSICIANS OF RAJASTHAN
CD C 580044
Ocora / May '94 / ADA / Harmonia Mundi

POPULAR SONGS OF IRELAND
CD 995802
EPM / Apr '97 / ADA / Discovery

POPULAR SPANISH SONGS OF THE 1930'S
CD BMCD 2011
Blue Moon / Apr '97 / Cadillac / Discovery / Greensleeves / Jazz Music / Jet Star / TKO Magnum

POPULAR SPANISH SONGS OF THE 1940'S
CD BMCD 2012
Blue Moon / Apr '97 / Cadillac / Discovery / Greensleeves / Jazz Music / Jet Star / TKO Magnum

POPULAR SPANISH SONGS OF THE 1950'S
CD BMCD 2013
Blue Moon / Apr '97 / Cadillac / Discovery / Greensleeves / Jazz Music / Jet Star / TKO Magnum

PORN BEATS
Oscar winners: *12 From A Dozen* / Beef nets: *Shrink 2 Fit* / Trevor Slemmons: *Mr. Dan* / Je t'aime: *Danmass* / Bangin' the head: *Mother Nature's Cloud & Shower Show* / Can't let you go: *Mellowtrons* / Spank da moog: *Moog* / Sex with the neightbours: *IHB* / Slack: *Snappy Sid* / 0898: *Clam Leppers* / Jazz mag: *Suburban Ghetto* / Scarlet letter: *Mike Flowers & The Mellowtrons*
CD SPECCD 503
Dust II Dust / Jul '97 / 3mv/Sony / Mo's Music Machine / Prime / SRD

PORTUGAL ROCKERS
CD RNRCD 001
Metralha / Feb '96 / Nervous

PORTUGUESE LANDS
CD PS 66003
PlayaSound / May '94 / ADA / Harmonia Mundi

PORTUGUESE STRING MUSIC
CD HTCD 05
Heritage / Feb '91 / ADA / Direct / Hot Shot / Jazz Music / Swift / Wellard

POSITIVA AMBIENT COLLECTION, THE
OOBE: *Orb* / Digi out: *Infinite Wheel* / Perfect morning: *Visions Of Shiva* / Hub: *Black Dog* / Halcyon: *Orbital* / Zeroes and ones: *Jesus Jones vs The Aphex Twin* / Sky high: *Irresistable Force* / Mobility: *Moby* / Awakening the soul: *Beaumont Hannant* / If it really is me: *Polygon Window* / Kao-tic harmony: *Rhythm Is Rhythim*
CD CDTIVA 1001
Positiva / Nov '94 / EMI

POSITIVE ENERGY
CD MM 800282
Moonshine / Jun '95 / Mo's Music Machine / Prime / RTM/Disc

POSSE VOL.1 & 2, THE
CD UPTCD 21
Uptempo / Nov '96 / Jet Star

POSSESSION & POETRY (Vezo, Mahafaly & Masikoro From Madagascar)
CD C 580046
Ocora / Nov '93 / ADA / Harmonia Mundi

POSSESSION SONGS (North Vietnam)
CD 926572
BUDA / Feb '97 / Discovery

POT OF GOLD VOL.1
CD VPRSCD 3101
VP / Mar '97 / Greensleeves / Jet Star / Total/BMG

POUR CEUX QUI S'AIMENT
CD DCD 5294MM
Disky / Apr '94 / Disky / THE

POW WOW SONGS (Songs of the Plains Indians)
Slow war dance songs / Contest songs for straight dancers / Contest songs for fancy dancers / Round dance / Sioux flag song / War dance song / Slow war dance, Vietnam song / Grass dance song
CD 803432
New World / Aug '92 / ADA / Cadillac / Harmonia Mundi

POWER & SOUL
Perfect year: *Carroll, Dina* / Come in out of the rain: *Moten, Wendy* / Get here: *Adams, Oleta* / No more tears (enough is enough): *Mazelle, Kym & Jocelyn Brown* / I will survive: *Gaynor, Gloria* / Ain't no mountain high enough: *Ross, Diana* / River deep, mountain high: *Turner, Tina* / Respect: *Franklin, Aretha* / Piece of my heart: *Franklin, Erma* / Help me make it through the night: *Knight, Gladys* / And I'm telling you I'm not going: *Holliday, Jennifer* / All woman: *Stansfield, Lisa* / Save the best for last: *Williams, Vanessa* / Sweet love: *Baker, Anita* / It should have been me: *Fair, Yvonne* / Stay with me baby: *Turner, Ruby* / Piano in the dark: *Russell, Brenda* / I will: *Winters, Ruby* / Superwoman: *White, Karyn* / Power of love: *Rush, Jennifer*
CD 5168962
PolyGram TV / Aug '94 / PolyGram

POWER AND THE GLORY, THE
Suicide blonde: *INXS* / Would I lie to you: *Eurythmics* / Best: *Turner, Tina* / Road to hell: *Rea, Chris* / Listen to your heart: *Roxette* / Black velvet: *Myles, Alannah* / Hard to handle: *Black Crowes* / Hey you: *Quireboys* / Blaze of glory: *Bon Jovi, Jon* / Everybody wants to rule the world: *Tears For Fears* / Good morning Britain: *Aztec Camera & Mick Jones* / Joker: *Miller, Steve* / I can't go for that (no can do): *Hall & Oates* / Power of love: *Lewis, Huey & The News* / Love is a battlefield: *Benatar, Pat* / Dedication: *Thin Lizzy* / All right now: *Free* / Wind of change: *Scorpions*
CD 5103602
Vertigo / Sep '91 / PolyGram

POWER OF POP, THE
Kids in America: *Wilde, Kim* / Centerfold: *Geils, J. Band* / Love is a Battlefield: *Benatar, Pat* / Do you really want to hurt me: *Culture Club* / (I just) Died in your arms tonight: *Cutting Crew* / True: *Spandau Ballet* / Temptation: *Heaven 17* / Kayleigh: *Marillion* / If only I could: *Youngblood, Sydney* / Bette Davis eyes: *Carnes, Kim* / Sylvia: *Focus* / Heroes: *Meat Loaf* / When you're in love with a beautiful woman: *Dr. Hook* / Movie star: *Harpo* / Don't worry be happy: *McFerrin, Bobby* / It started with a kiss: *Hot Chocolate* / Roll over Beethoven: *ELO* / Never ending story: *Limahl*
CD KS 875082
Disky / Jul '97 / Disky / THE

POWER OF THE TRINITY
CD SH 45030
Shanachie / Feb '97 / ADA / Greensleeves / Koch

POWER PLAYS (19 Classic Tracks)
In my chair: *Status Quo* / Go now: *Moody Blues* / No more the fool: *Brooks, Elkie* / Out of time: *Farlowe, Chris* / First cut is the deepest: *Arnold, P.P.* / Tin soldier: *Small Faces* / America: *Nice* / Natural born bugie: *Humble Pie* / Man of the world: *Fleetwood Mac* / Are you growing tired of my love: *Status Quo* / You really got me: *Kinks* / Strange band: *Family* / Love hurts: *Nazareth* / Iron man: *Black Sabbath* / Lay down (Candles in the rain): *Melanie & The Edwin Hawkin Singers* / In my own time: *Family* / It's a heartache: *Tyler, Bonnie* / Operator (That's not the way it feels): *Croce, Jim* / This flight tonight: *Nazareth*
CD TRTCD 114
TrueTrax / Oct '94 / THE

POWER TRACKS VOL.2
CD ZYX 300092
ZYX / Nov '96 / ZYX

POWERCUTS
Money for nothing: *Dire Straits* / Addicted to love: *Palmer, Robert* / Suicide blonde: *INXS* / One I love: *REM* / Sowing the seeds of love: *Tears For Fears* / I don't want a lover: *Texas* / Loved walked in: *Thunder* / First cut is the deepest: *Little Angels* / Cocaine: *Clapton, Eric* / Senza una Donna: *Zucchero & Paul Young* / Broken wings: *Mr. Mister* / Power of love: *Lewis, Huey & The News* / All right now: *Free* / Hard to handle: *Black Crowes* / Send me an angel: *Scorpions* / You ain't seen nothin' yet: *Bachman-Turner Overdrive* / Modern girl: *Meat Loaf* / All night long: *Rainbow*
CD 5154152
Polydor / May '92 / PolyGram

POWERDANCE 1997 (2CD Set)
CD Set DST 305252
Dance Street / Nov '96 / ZYX

POWERHOUSE
CD PHCD 01
Midtown / Mar '93 / SRD

POWERPLAY VOL.1
CD FORMCD 02
Formation / Jul '94 / SRD

PRAISE
CD 301202
Carlton / May '97 / Carlton

PRAISE AND GLORY
Praise my soul: *Choir Of Guildford Cathedral* / Thine by the glory: *Secombe, Harry* / Onward Christian soldiers: *Pontarddulais Male Voice Choir* / Rejoice the Lord is King: *Choir Of Guildford Cathedral* / Amazing Grace: *Anderson, Moira* / Let all the world in every corner sing: *Pontarddulais Male Voice Choir* / Love divine: *Choir Of Guildford Cathedral* / There's a friend for little children: *Choir Of Guildford Cathedral* / Abide with me: *Secombe, Harry* / Guide me o thou Great Jehovah: *Secombe, Harry* / Old rugged cross: *Anderson, Moira* / How great thou art: *Pontarddulais Male Voice Choir* / All things bright and beautiful: *Children Of Scisset Middle School* / When I survey the wonderous cross: *Anderson, Moira* / Lord's my sheperd: *Pontarddulais Male Voice Choir* / God be with you till we meet again: *Secombe, Harry*
CD SUMCD 4123
Sound & Media / Jun '97 / Sound & Media

PRAISE BE (15 Harmonious Masterpieces)
Pomp and circumstance No.1 / Irish tune from County Derry / Praise my soul the King of Heaven / Hear my prayer / Come down o love divine / Eternal father strong to save / O praise ye the Lord / Dear Lord and father of mankind / How lovely are thy dwellings fair / Ave verum corpus / Psalm 23 - the Lord is my shepherd / All creatures of our God and King / Thou wilt keep him in perfect peace / Lord is my shepherd / I was glad
CD GRF 334
Tring / Apr '93 / Tring

PRE-WAR GOSPEL STORY 1902-1944, THE (2CD Set)
CD Set BOG 21
Best Of Gospel / Nov '95 / Discovery

PRE-WAR VOCAL JAZZ STORY, THE (2CD Set)
CD Set BOJCD 22
Best Of Jazz / Oct '96 / Discovery

PREACHERS AND CONGREGATIONS VOL.1 1927-1938
CD DOCD 5529
Document / Apr '97 / ADA / Hot Shot / Jazz Music

PREACHERS AND CONGREGATIONS VOL.2 1926-1941
CD DOCD 5530
Document / Apr '97 / ADA / Hot Shot / Jazz Music

PREACHERS AND CONGREGATIONS VOL.3 1925-1929
CD DOCD 5547
Document / Jul '97 / ADA / Hot Shot / Jazz Music

PREACHERS AND CONGREGATIONS VOL.4 1924-1931
CD DOCD 5548
Document / Jul '97 / ADA / Hot Shot / Jazz Music

PREACHING TO THE PERVERTED
CD PERVCDLP 001
Naked / Jun '97 / Pinnacle

PRECIOUS COLLECTION, A
Dragging me down: *Inspiral Carpets* / Weirdo: *Charlatans* / Fool's gold: *Stone*

Roses / Twisterella: *Ride* / Drowners: *Suede* / Loaded: *Primal Scream* / There's no other way: *Blur* / Shine on: *House Of Love* / Sit down: *James* / Real real real: *Jesus Jones* / Make it mine: *Shamen* / Hit: *Sugarcubes* / For love: *Lush* / Monsters and angels: *Voice Of The Beehive* / Size of a cow: *Wonder Stuff* / Planet of sound: *Pixies* / Kinky love: *Pale Saints* / Glad: *Spaghetti Head* / Soon: *My Bloody Valentine* / Love your money: *Daisy Chainsaw*
CD **DINCD 38**
Dino / Jun '92 / Pinnacle

PRECIOUS METAL
CD **TMPCD 014**
Temple / Mar '95 / BMG

PRECIOUS WATERS, RIVER OF LIFE
Precious waters / Stormlight / Dawn / Mountain shadows / Tears of the Gods / Celebration / First snow / Where the rivers are born / Lonely birds / Shadows of eternity / Snow dreams of becoming water / Warm wind / Return of the sun / Falling water / First sun on the winter ice / Melting waters / In the mountain lake / Raging waters / Desert call / Through the parched land / Flowing toward heaven / Desert flower / River dreams / Cycle continues
CD **ND 63917**
Narada / May '95 / ADA / New Note/ Pinnacle

PRECOLOMBIAN (Forgotten Spirit)
CD **14908**
Spalax / Feb '97 / ADA / Cargo / Direct / Discovery / Greyhound

PRECOLOMBIAN MUSIC (Prehispanic)
CD **14907**
Spalax / Feb '97 / ADA / Cargo / Direct / Discovery / Greyhound

PRECOLOMBIAN MUSIC (Ritual)
CD **14909**
Spalax / Feb '97 / ADA / Cargo / Direct / Discovery / Greyhound

PRELUDE - THE SOUND OF NEW YORK (2CD Set)
I am music: *Mastermind* / Pranian man: *Prana People* / Mosquito walk: *Sine* / Hustle bus stop: *Mastermind* / Walking on music: *Jacques, Peter Band* / Never: *Centre Stage* / Stretchin' out: *Adams, Gayle* / You got my love: *Redd, Sharon* / I know you feel like I feel: *Thurston, Bobby* / Happy ever after: *Unlimited Touch* / I'm totally yours: *High Gloss* / Take a risk: *Empress* / Searching to find the one: *Unlimited Touch* / Let's work it out: *Next Movement* / Let's go all the way: *Adams, Gayle* / Tryin' to get over: *D-Train* / Your good lovin': *Joli, France* / Groove it to your body: *Wilson, Mike* / Body movement: *Conquest* / Funn: *Gunchback Boogie Band* / Lay it down on me: *Mallory, Gerald* / Video freak: *Frazier, Cliff & Co.* / Do you love me: *Secret Weapon* / Good lovin': *Unlimited Touch* / Key: *Wuf Ticket*
CD Set **DEEPD 017**
Deep Beats / Apr '97 / BMG

PREMIER COLLECTION OF INSTRUMENTAL HITS VOL.1
CD **KNEWCD 733**
Kenwest / Apr '94 / THE

PREMIER COLLECTION OF INSTUMENTAL HITS VOL.2
CD **KNEWCD 734**
Kenwest / Apr '94 / THE

PREMIER COLLECTION OF INSTUMENTAL HITS VOL.3
CD **KNEWCD 735**
Kenwest / Apr '94 / THE

PRENDS DONC COURAGE: SWAMP MUSIC VOL.6
CD **US 0202**
Trikont / Apr '95 / ADA / Direct

PRESTIGE FIRST SESSIONS
CD **PCD 24115**
Prestige / Dec '95 / Cadillac / Complete/ Pinnacle

PRESTIGE FUNKY BEATS
CD **PCD 24148**
Pablo / Jun '95 / Cadillac / Complete/ Pinnacle

PRESTIGE JAZZ SAMPLER
CD **CDRIVM 002**
Riverside / Mar '88 / Cadillac / Complete/ Pinnacle / Jazz Music

PRESTIGE SOUL - JAZZ ENCYCLOPAEDIA VOL.1
CD **PCD 24137**
Pablo / Jun '95 / Cadillac / Complete/ Pinnacle

PRESTIGE/FOLKLORE YEARS VOL.1 (All Kinds Of Folks)
New York town: *Elliot, Jack* / Railroad Bill: *Elliot, Jack* / Rollin' in my sweet baby's arms: *Elliot, Jack* / Duncan and Brady: *Rush, Tom* / Rag Mama: *Rush, Tom* / Barb'ry Allen: *Rush, Tom* / Wagoner's lad: *Seeger, Peggy* / Chickens they are crowing: *Seeger, Peggy* / Green rocky road: *Van Ronk, Dave* / Whoa Buck: *Van Ronk, Dave* / Maggie Lauder: *Redpath, Jean* / Fife overgate: *Redpath, Jean* / Joshua gone Barbados: *Von Schmidt, Eric* / She's like a swallow: *Dobson, Bonnie* / Irish exile song: *Dobson, Bonnie* / Long chain: *Sellers, Maxine* / Single girl: *Sellers, Maxine* / Jesus met the woman at the well: *Len & Judy* / This life I'm living: *Len & Judy*
CD **CDWIKD 134**
Big Beat / Feb '95 / Pinnacle

PRESTIGE/FOLKLORE YEARS VOL.2 (The New City Blues)
Cocaine blues: *Van Ronk, Dave* / Death letter: *Van Ronk, Dave* / Red river blues: *Fuller, Jesse* / How long blues: *Fuller, Jesse* / San Francisco Bay blues: *Fuller, Jesse* / Sleepy man blues: *Muldaur, Geoff* / Aberdeen Mississippi blues: *Muldaur, Geoff* / Motherless child blues: *Nelson, Tracy* / Starting for Chicago: *Nelson, Tracy* / Ramblin' man: *Nelson, Tracy* / Crow Jane: *Von Schmidt, Eric* / Light rain: *Von Schmidt, Eric* / Kennedy blues: *Von Schmidt, Eric* / Orphan's blues: *Rush, Tom* / If you don't want me baby: *Larry & Hank* / Watchdog blues: *Larry & Hank* / Four women blues: *Larry & Hank* / Alberta: *New Strangers*
CD **CDWIKD 135**
Big Beat / Feb '95 / Pinnacle

PRESTIGE/FOLKLORE YEARS VOL.3 (Roots And Branches)
Let us get together right down here: *Davis, Rev. Gary* / Twelve gates to the city: *Davis, Rev. Gary* / Maple leaf rag: *Davis, Rev. Gary* / Bound to lose: *Holy Modal Rounders* / Euphoria: *Holy Modal Rounders* / Crowley waltz: *Holy Modal Rounders* / Blues in the bottle: *Holy Modal Rounders* / St. Louis tickle: *Van Ronk, Dave* / Goodbye Maggie: *Lilly Brothers* / I'm coming back, but I don't know when: *West, Harry & Jeanie* / I'd like to be your shadow in the moonlight: *West, Harry & Jeanie* / Beautiful brown eyes: *Charles River Valley Boys & Tex Logan* / Sally Goodin: *Charles River Valley Boys & Tex Logan* / Uncle Penn: *Charles River Valley Boys & Tex Logan* / Salty dog: *Keith & Rooney* / Teardrops in my eyes: *Keith & Rooney* / Maggie rag: *Greenhill, Mitch* / Blues, just blues, that's all: *True Endeavor Jug Band* / Jug band blues: *True Endeavor Jug Band* / She's gone: *Traum, Artie* / High society: *Folk Stringers* / I don't feel at home in this world anymore: *New Strangers*
CD **CDWIKD 136**
Big Beat / Feb '95 / Pinnacle

PRESTIGE/FOLKLORE YEARS VOL.4 (Singing Out Loud)
Mule skinner blues: *Elliot, Jack* / Night herding song: *Elliot, Jack* / Talking fishing blues: *Elliot, Jack* / Fisherman's luck: *Seeger, Mike & Sonny Miller* / Sally Ann: *Seeger, Mike & Sonny Miller* / John Hardy: *Seeger, Mike & Sonny Miller* / Fiddler's bagpipe: *Seeger, Mike & Sonny Miller* / Peter Emberly: *Dobson, Bonnie* / First time: *Dobson, Bonnie* / If I had my way: *Davis, Rev. Gary* / Sally, where you get your liquor from: *Davis, Rev. Gary* / You got to move: *Davis, Rev. Gary* / Devil's dream: *Keith & Rooney* / Ain't gonna work tomorrow: *Keith & Rooney* / Gypsy Davey: *Aaron, Tossi* / I don't want your millions Mister: *Seeger, Pete* / Here's to Cheshire, here's to cheese: *Seeger, Pete*
CD **CDWIKD 137**
Big Beat / Feb '95 / Pinnacle

PRICELESS JAZZ SAMPLER
Good morning heartache: *Holiday, Billie* / Oh lady be good: *Fitzgerald, Ella* / What a wonderful world: *Armstrong, Louis* / Lush life: *Hartman, Johnny* / Bessie's blues: *Coltrane, John* / Three little words: *Rollins, Sonny* / Tembi: *Sanders, Pharoah* / Better get hit in yo' soul: *Mingus, Charles* / Jeep is jumpin': *Ellington, Duke* / Milonga triste: *Barbieri, Gato* / Spain: *Corea, Chick*
CD **GRP 98812**
GRP / Jul '97 / New Note/BMG

PRIDE '95
CD **SR 321CD**
Strictly Rhythm / Jul '95 / Prime / RTM/ Disc / SRD / Vital

PRIDE AND PASSION (40 Contemporary Irish Songs)
CD **DINCD 121**
Dino / Mar '96 / Pinnacle

PRIDE AND PASSION
CD **RECD 503**
REL / Jun '96 / CM / Duncans / Highlander

PRIDE OF INDEPENDENTS
CD **TT 6CD**
Beechwood / Jun '93 / Beechwood/BMG / Pinnacle

PRIDE OF IRELAND (Heart Of Ireland/ Seven Drunken Nights/Home/3CD Set)
Whiskey in the jar / Four country roads / Green fields of France / Irish Rover / When you were sweet sixteen / Boys from Killybegs / You seldom come to see me anymore / Boston burgler / Isle of Innisfree / After all these years / Black velvet band / Our house is not a home / Old bog road / Town I love so well / I'll take you home again Kathleen / Any Tipperary town / Hills of Kerry / Mountains of Mourne / Maggie / Rose of Tralee / Bold O'Donaghue / Paddle me own canoe / Molly Malone / Medley / Ferryman / Cod liver oil/Coolies / Home boys home / Father O'Flynn / Irish washerwoman / Blackberry blossom / Lannigan's ball / All for me grog / Wild rover / Medley / Muirsheen durkin / Paddy Fathy's reel/ Dinny's fancy / Spanish lady maid behind the bar/Gravel walk / Holy ground / Finnegan's wake / Irish rover/Rakes of Mallow / Seven drunken nights / Ramblin' Irishman / Rising of the moon / Road to Sligo/Tripping up the stairs / Ashplant / Medley / O'Catolan's dream / White, orange and green / High road to Linton/Mrs Mcleods reel / Foxhunters / Fiddler's green / Rocky road to Dublin / Arthur McBride / Medley / Gravelwalk
CD Set **55159**
Music / Oct '96 / Target/BMG

PRIDE OF SCOTLAND, THE (Scottish Pipe Bands/3CD Set)
CD Set **LB 868392**
Disky / Aug '96 / Disky / THE

PRIDE OF SCOTLAND, THE (3CD Set)
Scotland the brave / Skye boat song / Amazing grace / Road to the Isles / Old rustic bridge by the mill / Towsay Castle / Money musk / Miss McLeod O'Raasey / Cock o' the North / Old rustic bridge by the mill / Route march / When the battle is over / 79th farewell to Gibraltar / Colonel Robertson / Dovecote Park / Prince Charles welcome to Lochaber / Mingulay boat song / Silver spear / Curlew / Captain Horne / MacFarlane's reel / Inverness gathering / Drunken piper / 79th's farewell to Gibraltar / Earl of Mansfield / Drum salute / Up in the morning / Muckin' o' Geordie's Byre / Cock o' the North / Royal Scots polka / Conundrum / Highland wedding / Smith of Chilliehassie / Boghall and Bathgate / Redundancy / Train journey North / Reveille / Miss Kirkwood / Song of the Clyde / Westering home / Keep right on to the end of the road / Northern lights of old Aberdeen / Bonnie Kirkwall Bay / Bonnie banks of Loch Lomond / Football crazy / Here's to Scottish whisky / Land for all seasons / Star o' Rabbie Burns / Man's a man for a' that / Romin' in the Gloamin' / Just a wee Deoch an' Doris / Ye banks and braes / Tobermory Bay / Marching through the heather / Auld lang syne / Lord and Lady Elgin of Broomhall: *Shand, Jimmy* / Maresland twostep: *Shand, Jimmy* / Lady Angela Alexander/Sir Kenneth Alexander: *Shand, Jimmy* / Threave Castle polka: *Shand, Jimmy* / Suptd. Ian Thomson's farewell to the Fife Police: *Shand, Jimmy* / Francis Wright's waltz: *Shand, Jimmy* / Memories of Willie Smith: *Shand, Jimmy* / Ian Powrie's welcome to Dunblane: *Shand, Jimmy* / Windy edge barn dance: *Shand, Jimmy* / Lunan Bay/Tom and Mary Lyon's waltz: *Shand, Jimmy* / It's grand among your ain folk: *Shand, Jimmy* / David Anderson Shand's 40th birthday: *Shand, Jimmy* / Geordie Watson the co-worker: *Shand, Jimmy* / Heather mixture twostep: *Shand, Jimmy* / Compliments to Harry Lawson/Compliments to Dr. A.K. Tulloch: *Shand, Jimmy* / Whitley Chapel barndance: *Shand, Jimmy* / John McDonald's march: *Shand, Jimmy* / Miss Jean Thompson's 100th birthday: *Shand, Jimmy* / Bruce Laing's welcome to Auchtermuchty: *Shand, Jimmy* / Guardians of the Gulf: *Shand, Jimmy* / Royal Guard Regiment of HM the Sultan of Oman: *Shand, Jimmy* / Willie Merrilees OBE: *Shand, Jimmy* / Margaret and Robert Innes of Pitterweem: *Shand, Jimmy*
CD Set **55163**
Music / Apr '97 / Target/BMG

PRIDE VOL.1 (The Very Best Of Scotland/2CD Set)
Dignity: *Deacon Blue* / Baker Street: *Rafferty, Gerry* / Vienna: *Ultravox* / Real gone kid: *Deacon Blue* / Why: *Lennox, Annie* / Caledonia: *Miller, Frankie* / Sweet dreams (are made of this): *Eurythmics* / There must be an angel: *Eurythmics* / Inside: *Stiltskin* / Perfect: *Fairground Attraction* / Patience of angels: *Reader, Eddi* / Party fears two: *Associates* / If I was: *Ure, Midge* / Let's go round again: *Average White Band* / I can feel it: *Silencers* / Miracle of being: *Capercaillie*
CD Set **74321284372**
RCA / Oct '95 / BMG

PRIDE VOL.2 (2CD Set)
Julia says: *Wet Wet Wet* / No more I love yous: *Lennox, Annie* / I'll never fall in love again: *Deacon Blue* / She's a river: *Simple Minds* / King of the road: *Proclaimers* / Find my love: *Fairground Attraction* / Love is a stranger: *Eurythmics* / You wear it well: *Stewart, Rod* / Miracle of being: *Capercaillie* / Loch Lomond: *Runrig* / Labour of love: *Hue & Cry* / Brand new friend: *Cole, Lloyd & The Commotions* / Club country: *Associates* / Fisherman's blues: *Waterboys* / Cath: *Bluebells* / Summer of love: *Danny Wilson* / Thorn in my side: *Eurythmics* / An ubhal as airde: *Runrig* / Girl like you: *Collins, Edwyn* / Saturday night: *Blue Nile* / Queer: *Garbage* / Move any mountain: *Shamen* / Movin' on up: *Primal Scream* / Sparky's dream: *Primal Scream* / Iceblink luck: *Cocteau Twins* / You could be forgiven: *Horse* / Scottish rain: *Silencers* / Rattler: *Goodbye Mr. Mackenzie* / I would 500 miles: *Proclaimers* / Prospect Street: *Big Dish* / Real McCoy: *Silencers* / Big Country: *Big Country* / Chains: *River Detectives* / Fergus sings the blues: *Deacon Blue* / April skies: *Jesus & Mary Chain* / Oblivious: *Aztec Camera*
CD Set **74321371542**
RCA / May '96 / BMG

PRIMAL BLUE
Bass blues / Uno dos adios / Primal blue / Dear Ruth / Stolen moments / You go to my head
CD **HIBD 8006**
Hip Bop / Oct '95 / Koch / Silva Screen

PRIME CHOPS VOL.2 (Blind Pig Sampler)
CD **BP 8002CD**
Blind Pig / May '94 / ADA / CM / Direct / Hot Shot

PRIME CHOPS VOL.3
CD **BPCD 8003**
Blind Pig / Dec '95 / ADA / CM / Direct / Hot Shot

PRIME CUTS VOL.4
CD **PRMTCD 004**
Primate / Nov '96 / Prime / RTM/Disc / SRD

PRIME NUMBERS VOL.2
CD **PRIME 051CD**
Prime / May '96 / Pinnacle / Vital

PRISON BLUES OF THE SOUTH
CD **17026**
Laserlight / Sep '94 / Target/BMG

PRISON SONGS VOL.1 (Murderer's Home)
CD **ROUCD 1714**
Rounder / Aug '97 / ADA / CM / Direct

PRISON SONGS VOL.2 (Hear Poor Mother Call)
CD **ROUCD 1715**
Rounder / Aug '97 / ADA / CM / Direct

PRIVATE COLLECTION OF GERMAN UNDERGROUND...
CD **ABB 85CD**
Big Cat / Apr '95 / 3mv/Pinnacle

PRIVATE LIFE OF AN INDEPENDENT
CD **BUR 001**
British Underground Productions / Apr '97 / Timewarp

PRO-CANNABIS
CD **EFA 119662**
Dope / Jun '94 / SRD

PRODUCER'S TROPHY
CD **HCD 7011**
Hightone / Dec '94 / ADA / Koch

PROFESSOR JORDAN'S MAGIC SOUND SHOW
Tamaris khan: *Onyx* / We didn't kiss: *Clique* / Linda loves Lin: *Floribunda Rose* / Riding on a wave: *Turnstyle* / Running wild: *Fresh Air* / Hungry: *5 AM Event* / She's a rainbow: *Glass Menagerie* / Buffalo: *Writing On The Wall* / Frederick Johnson: *Glass Menagerie* / Step in the right direction: *Montanas* / Lady Caroline: *Velvett Fogg* / Frosted panes: *Kytes* / Stay a while: *Orange Seaweed* / Keep on moving baby: *Game* / Stay indoors: *New Formula* / You can all join in: *Orange Machine*
CD **DOCD 1996**
Drop Out / Apr '91 / Pinnacle

PROGRAM ANNIHILATOR VOL.2
CD **SST 213CD**
SST / Feb '90 / Plastic Head

PROGRESSION
Fire: *Crazy World Of Arthur Brown* / Strange kind of woman: *Deep Purple* / Little bit of love: *Free* / Devil's answer: *Atomic Rooster* / Frankenstein: *Winter, Edgar* / Silver machine: *Hawkwind* / Race with the devil: *Gun* / Witch: *Rattles* / Radar love: *Golden Earring* / Love like a man: *Ten Years After* / Standing on the road: *Blackfoot Sue* / Hold your head up: *Argent* / Backstreet luv: *Curved Air* / Living in the past: *Jethro Tull* / In my own time: *Family* / Slip and slide: *Medicine Head* / Sympathy: *Rare Bird* / Joybringer: *Manfred Mann's Earthband* / Northern lights: *Renaissance* / Jig a jig: *East Of Eden*
CD **5163982**
PolyGram TV / Aug '93 / PolyGram

PROGRESSION
CD **PROG 292**
Progression / Feb '94 / RTM/Disc

PROGRESSIVE CITY VOL.2
CD **FRIE 004**
Friends / Jun '97 / Intergroove / Plastic Head

PROGRESSIVE HOUSE CLASSICS
Intoxication: *React 2 Rhythm* / Difference: *Djum Djum* / Sack the drummer: *Soundclash Republic* / LionRock: *Lionrock* / Speed controller: *Acorn Arts* / Get out on this dancefloor: *DOP* / Mighty Ming: *Brother Love Dubs* / Big mouth: *Lemon Interupt* / Londress strutt: *Smells Like Heaven* / Not forgotten: *Leftfield* / Future le funk: *DOP* / Who's the badman: *Patern, Dee* / Pure pleasure: *Digital Excitation* / Body Medusa: *Supereal* / Funkatarium: *Jump*
CD **FIRMCD 1**
Firm / Feb '96 / Pinnacle

PROGRESSIVE POP INSIDE THE 70'S
Who can I trust: *Walrus* / Yes you do: *Pacific Drift* / I wrapped her in ribbons: *Galliards* / I've been moved: *Hollywood Free-*

way / Never gonna let my body touch the ground: *Walrus* / Goodbye to Baby Jane: *Campbell, Junior* / Cloudy day: *Vehicle* / Maybe: *Granny's Intentions* / Dan the wing: *Mellow Candle* / Pretty Belinda: *Clan* / Mr. Horizon: *Hemlock* / Standing on the corner: *Youlden, Chris* / Rebels rule: *Iron Virgin* / Back street luv: *Curved Air* / Candy baby: *Beano* / Sweetest tasting candy sugar: *Sheriden, Lee* / Ultrastar: *Rococo* / Whizmore kid: *Principal Edwards* / Sweet illusion: *Campbell, Junior* / Candy eyes: *Fresh Meat* / One night affair: *Areety, Colin* / Jesus come back: *Matthews's Revelation* / Two sisters: *Wolf* / Bye and bye: *Beano*
CD SEECD 424
See For Miles/C5 / May '95 / Pinnacle

PROGRESSIVE ROCK ANTHEMS
Mockingbird: *Barclay James Harvest* / Urban gorilla: *Hawkwind* / Fanfare for the common man: *ELP* / Living thing: *ELO* / Acquiring the taste: *Gentle Giant* / Frankenstein: *Winter, Edgar* / Slip and slide: *Medicine Head* / Gypsy: *Uriah Heep* / Forty thousand headmen: *Traffic* / Homburg: *Procul Harum* / Hocus pocus: *Focus* / Living in the past: *Jethro Tull* / Out demons out: *Broughton, Edgar* / Love like a man: *Ten Years After* / Joybringer: *Manfred Mann's Earthband* / Marjorine: *Cocker, Joe*
CD NTRCD 074
Nectar / Aug '97 / Pinnacle

PROLE LIFE
Grand monophonic: *Yummy Fur* / Fiery Jack: *Yummy Fur* / Typical of boys: *Yummy Fur* / All women are robots: *Yummy Fur* / Vanilla maneli: *Yummy Fur* / Cosmonauts and carbonauts: *Yummy Fur* / Eyeball popping madness: *Yummy Fur* / Skunk rap: *Trout* / Scary costumes: *Trout* / Human boing: *Trout* / Owl in the tree: *Trout* / Divorce at high noon: *Blisters* / Post-feminist business woman: *Blisters* / Patrick meets the courgettes: *Blisters* / Christian chorus: *Blisters* / Mommy is a punker: *Pink Cross* / Chopper chix: *Pink Cross* / Punk outfit: *Pink Cross* / No time for bimbo: *Pink Cross* / Toby Mangel: *Lugworm* / Sweaty says: *Lugworm* / Disco: *Lugworm* / Barmitzvah: *Lugworm*
CD CDKRED 121
Cherry Red / Jul '95 / Pinnacle

PROLEKULTURE
Pilgrimage to paradise: *Sourmash* / Sleepless: *Razors Edge* / Acid voices: *Traumatic* / First rebirth: *Jones & Stephenson* / Trope: *Amphetamine* / Neurodancer: *Wippenberg* / High on the edge: *Housetrap II* / Global phases: *Jon The Dentist* / Mighty machine: *Dream Plant* / Digital mass: *DJ Randy* / Cut the midrange: *Watchman*
CD KULTCDX 1
CD KULTCD 1
Prolekult / May '97 / Mo's Music Machine / Prime / RTM/Disc

PROMISED LAND, THE
South: *Freeman, Morgan & Terence Blanchard* / Change is gonna come: *D'Arby, Terence Trent & Booker T & The MGs* / Movin' on: *Hawkins, Tramaine* / I wish I knew how it would feel to be free: *Farris, Dionne* / People get ready: *Asante* / Ball of confusion: *Chuck D & Dapper Dan* / Someday we'll be free: *Johnson, Puff* / Promised land: *Blanchard, Terence* / Dark was the night, cold was the ground: *Johnson, 'Blind' Willie* / Backwater blues: *Smith, Bessie* / Sweet home Chicago: *Johnson, Robert* / (What did I do to be so) Black and blue: *Armstrong, Louis* / East St. Louis toodle-o: *Ellington, Duke* / Stampede in G minor: *Basie, Count* / God bless the child: *Holiday, Billie* / I'm on my way: *Jackson, Mahalia* / Closing theme: *Blanchard, Terence* / 'Round midnight: *Davis, Miles* / My home is in the delta: *Waters, Muddy* / Killing floor: *Howlin' Wolf* / Green onions: *Booker T & The MG's* / Monkey time: *Major Lance* / Hi heel sneakers: *Tucker, Tommy* / Up on the roof: *Drifters* / Dancing in the street: *Martha & The Vandellas* / Papa's got a brand new bag: *Brown, James* / Respect: *Franklin, Aretha* / Stand: *Sly & The Family Stone* / Love train: *O'Jays* / Take me to the river: *Green, Al* / Wake up everybody: *Melvin, Harold & The Bluenotes* / Inner city blues (make me wanna holler): *Gaye, Marvin* / That's the way of the world: *Earth, Wind & Fire* / Bring the noise: *Public Enemy* / World is yours: *Nas*
CD 4785852
Columbia / Sep '96 / Sony

PROPER COMP VOL.1
Grande bassito: *Acid Farm* / On and on: *DJ Kaay Alexi* / Greg Metzger: *McBride, Woody* / Electric: *Stoll, Steve* / Infrared: *Wild, Damon* / Fuken around: *Hunt, Gene* / Personal carrier: *Henze, W.J.* / MMMM: *Freddie Fresh* / Third wave: *DJ Capricorn* / Dig it: *Carbon Boys*
CD PROPS 008CD
Proper / Jun '95 / Plastic Head

PROPER COMP VOL.2
CD PROPS 016CD
Proper / Jul '96 / Plastic Head

PROPHET SPEAKS, THE (Street Jazz Collection)
CD SPV 10362
ILC / Oct '93 / Sony

PROPRIUS JAZZ SAMPLER 1994
CD PCD 020
Proprius / Mar '95 / Jazz Music / May Audio

PROUD
In the neighbourhood: *Sisters Underground* / Tuesday's blues: *Pacifican Descendants* / We're the OMC: *Otara Millionaires Club* / Based on a lost cause: *Radio Backstab & DJ Payback* / Pass it over: *Pacifican Descendants* / Dawn of the eve: *Di-Na-Ve* / One too many: *Vocal Five* / I don't need you: *Semi MC's* / Ain't it true: *Sisters Underground* / Save New Zealand: *Vocal Five* / Pacific beats: *Puka Puka* / Prove me wrong: *MC Slam* / Groove me: *Rhythm Harmony* / Trust me: *Semi MC's*
CD VOLTCD 77
Volition / Oct '95 / Pinnacle / Vital

PROUD TO BE LOUD
Rainbow in the park: *Dio* / Knocking at your back door: *Deep Purple* / Rosalie: *Thin Lizzy* / Get the funk out: *Extreme* / You've gone wild: *Almighty* / Jet boy/Jet girl: *New York Dolls* / Madhouse: *Anthrax* / Eyes shut tight: *Downset* / Bone china: *Mother Love Bone* / Crying over you: *Gun* / Rising force: *Malmsteen, Yngwie* / Temple of the king: *Rainbow* / Closer to the heart: *Rush* / Snorting whiskey: *Travers, Pat* / Just a shadow: *Big Country* / Wishing well: *Free* / Ramblin' man: *Allman Brothers* / Gypsy road: *Cinderella*
CD 5533292
Debutante / Feb '97 / PolyGram

PSALMS FOR SOLOMON
CD BLKMCD 012
Blakamix / Jun '95 / Jet Star / SRD

PSALMS OF DRUMS
Psalms of drums: *King Tubby* / Healing stream: *Dillinger* / Liberation: *Kalphat, Bobby* / Sabotage: *King Tubby* / I hold the handle: *Michael Scotland* / Natty contractor: *Trinity* / Weatherman skank: *I-Roy* / Stumbling block: *Dillinger* / Page One: *King Tubby* / King at the controls: *King Tubby* / Wash wash: *Patterson, Carlton* / Watchman dub: *King Tubby* / Internal feelings: *Trinity* / Love is a treasure: *Michael Scotland* / Let me go girl: *Patterson, Carlton*
CD PSCD 12
Pressure Sounds / Jan '97 / Jet Star / SRD

PSEUDOPODIA
CD BIKE 005CD
Yellow Books / Nov '92 / Plastic Head

PSY HARMONICS VOL.1
CD PSY 009
PSY Harmonics / Sep '95 / Plastic Head

PSYCHEDELIA
CD MUSCD 021
MCI Music / Sep '94 / Disc / THE

PSYCHEDELIA (Rare Blooms From The English Summer Of Love)
Flight from Ashiya: *Kaleidoscope* / Peter's birthday: *World Of Oz* / Catherine's wheel: *Laine, Denny* / Brother can you spare a dime: *St. Valentine's Day Massacre* / Turquoise tandem cycle: *Crest, Jason* / Magic potion: *Open Mind* / Portcullis gate: *Bulldog Breed* / Weekdaze: *Principal Edwards* / Out of your own little world: *Megaton* / Niagara: *Megaton* / Meditations: *Felius Andromeda* / Gone is the sad man: *Timebox* / I can't sleep: *Quik* / Thursday morning: *Giles, Giles & Fripp* / Scream in the ears: *Fay, Bill* / My organ grinder: *Vehicle* / Sycamore Sid: *Focal Point* / Some good advice: *Fay, Bill* / Soul full of sorrow: *Quik* / Baby get your head: *Double Feature* / Halo in your hair: *Bulldog Breed* / Nite is a comin'/Smeta Murgaty: *Warm Sounds*
CD SEECD 463
See For Miles/C5 / Oct '96 / Pinnacle

PSYCHEDELIA (2CD Set)
Eight miles high: *Byrds* / White rabbit: *Jefferson Airplane* / Daydream: *Lovin' Spoonful* / Itchycoo Park: *Small Faces* / Living in the past: *Jethro Tull* / Here comes the nice: *Small Faces* / California dreamin': *Mamas & The Papas* / Come up the years: *Jefferson Airplane* / Electricity: *Captain Beefheart* / Summer in the city: *Lovin' Spoonful* / See my friends: *Kinks* / Flowers in the rain: *Move* / Kites: *Dupree, Simon & The Big Sound* / Light my fire: *Feliciano, Jose* / Pictures of matchstick men: *Status Quo* / Light flight: *Pentangle* / Black magic woman: *Santana* / Sitting on a fence: *Twice As Much* / Feel a whole lot better: *Byrds* / Tin soldier: *Small Faces* / Hi ho silver lining: *Beck, Jeff* / Sunshine superman: *Donovan* / Night of fear: *Move* / Monday monday: *Mamas & The Papas* / Green tambourine: *Lemon Pipers* / Days of Pearly Spencer: *McWilliams, David* / Somebody to love: *Jefferson Airplane* / Lazy Sunday: *Small Faces* / Mad John: *Small Faces* / Goo goo barabajagal (Love is hot): *Donovan & Jeff Beck Group* / Candles in the rain: *Melanie* / Let's go to San Francisco: *Flowerpot Men* / I'm the urban spaceman: *Bonzo Dog Band* / Mirror man: *Captain Beefheart & His Magic Band* / Thoughts of Emerlist Davjack: *Nice* / Man of the world: *Fleetwood Mac*
CD Set RCACD 211
RCA / Jul '97 / BMG

PSYCHEDELIC CLUB TRAX
CD CLP 9987
Cleopatra / Jun '97 / Cargo / Greyhound / Plastic Head / RTM/Disc / SRD

PSYCHEDELIC FREQUENCIES
White rabbit: *Jefferson Airplane* / King Midas in reverse: *Hollies* / War in peace: *Spence, Skip* / Keep your mind open: *Kaleidoscope* / Broken arrow: *Buffalo Springfield* / Evening of light: *Nico* / Loved one: *George, Lowell* / Frantic desolation: *Sopwith Camel* / Defecting grey: *Pretty Things* / Omaha: *Moby Grape* / Happenings ten years time ago: *Yardbirds* / Electricity: *Captain Beefheart* / Psychotic reaction: *Count Five* / I just don't know: *Banshee* / Can you please crawl out your window: *Vacels* / Golden Earrings: *Gandalf* / Land of their dreams: *Auto Salvage* / Standing on the moon (space hymn): *Lothar & The Hand People*
CD TMPCD 027
Temple / May '96 / BMG

PSYCHEDELIC GOA TEST
CD CLP 0002
Cleopatra / Jun '97 / Cargo / Greyhound / Plastic Head / RTM/Disc / SRD

PSYCHEDELIC PERCEPTIONS
CD TMPCD 025
Temple / May '96 / BMG

PSYCHEDELIC VISIONS
CD TMPCD 026
Temple / May '96 / BMG

PSYCHOBILLY SAMPLER VOL.2
CD DAGCD 4
Fury / Sep '96 / Nervous / TKO Magnum

PSYCHOMANIA VOL.3
CD DOJOCD 203
Dojo / Mar '95 / Disc

PSYCHOSERENADE
CD BEWARECD 002
Beware / May '97 / Cargo

PSYCHOTHRILL
Mosainga: *Mills, Jeff* / Drugsky 0023: *Dusk* / Bass fishing: *DJ ESP & Fuzz Face* / Double decker: *RBR* / Killing field: *Polygen* / New beginning: *Graphite* / Loosing child: *Haderlapp, Walter* / Hen-Fruit: *Casper, Roland* / Dynamics: *Clemen, Jana* / Down by law: *Co-Jack* / Sh-punch: *Flaptrack* / Runner: *DMP*
CD ESS 42992
Essence / Feb '97 / PolyGram

PSYCHOTRANCE
CD MM 800072
Moonshine / Aug '94 / Mo's Music Machine / Prime / RTM/Disc

PSYCHOTRANCE VOL.2
CD MM 800202
Moonshine / Jan '95 / Mo's Music Machine / Prime / RTM/Disc

PSYCHOTRANCE VOL.3
CD MM 800402
Moonshine / Oct '95 / Mo's Music Machine / Prime / RTM/Disc

PSYCHOTRANCE VOL.4 (Slam)
CD MM 800562
Moonshine / Oct '96 / Mo's Music Machine / Prime / RTM/Disc

PUB PIANO SING-A-LONG
Swanee medley / Slow boat to China medley / I'm gonna sit right down and write myself a letter / Lili Marlene medley / Roll out the barrel medley / Tavern in the town medley / You made me love you medley / Johnny's so long at the fair medley / Little old wine drinker me medley / Wish me luck as you wave me goodbye medley / Tiptoe through the tulips
CD CD 6080
Music / Jun '97 / Target/BMG

PUCK ROCK VOL.1
CD WRONG 11
Wrong / Apr '94 / SRD

PULP FUSION
Shifting gears: *Hammond, John* / Chitterlings con carne: *Pucho & His Latin Soul Brothers* / Don't it drive you crazy: *Pointer Sisters* / Inner city blues: *Wilson, Reuben* / First come first serve: *Wilson, Reuben* / Melting pot: *Booker T & The MG's* / Every time he comes around: *Riperton, Minnie* / Burning spear: *SOUL* / FreBump: *Freeman, George* / Crab apple: *Muhammad, Idris* / Hang up your hang ups: *Hancock, Herbie* / Afrodesia: *Smith, Lonnie*
CD HURTCD 003
Harmless / Aug '97 / RTM/Disc

PULP SURFIN'
CD DOCD 700222
Del-Fi / Jan '97 / Cargo / Koch

PULSATING HITS
CD PULSE 16CD
Pulse 8 / Nov '94 / BMG

PULSATING RHYTHMS
CD PULSECD 1
Pulse 8 / Aug '91 / BMG

PULSATING RHYTHMS VOL.2
CD PULSECD 4
Pulse 8 / Jun '93 / BMG

PULSATING RHYTHMS VOL.3
CD PULSECD 8
Pulse 8 / Nov '92 / BMG

PULSATING RHYTHMS VOL.4
CD PULSECD 10
Pulse 8 / Jul '93 / BMG

PULSE
Babes on broomsticks: *Synchro* / Foxglove: *Shakta* / Deliverance: *Butler & Wilson* / Black rain: *Amanite Fx & Prana* / Trashish: *Transwave* / Radiation: *Blot* / San yacid: *Cosmosis* / Dawn to dusk: *Asia 2001* / Smells electric: *Metal Spark* / Viton: *NDMA* / Pulsar glitch: *Total Eclipse* / Kabalah: *Astral Projection* / Tinkerbell: *Power Source* / X-Files: *Chakra & Edi Mis* / Bong incus: *Eat Static* / Triplexus: *Miranda* / Touch the sun: *Sundog* / Miles and smiles: *Sit On The Lunch* / Afterlife: *Astralasia*
CD Set SPV 08947122
SPV / Oct '96 / Koch / Plastic Head

PULSE OF LIFE
CD ELL 3210C
Ellipsis Arts / Oct '93 / ADA / Direct

PULSE VOL.1 (This Is Psychedelic Trance/2CD Set)
Placid: *Shanti, Stanley & The Chillum Wallahs* / Cor: *Green Nuns Of The Revolution* / Portamento: *Blenn, Boris* / Orange acid: *Brain Accent* / Axonal: *Transwave* / Prana: *Rainbow Spirit* / Born again: *Doof* / Moon raker: *Disco Volante* / Blessing: *Sourmash* / Transparent mind: *Total Eclipse* / Key: *Indoor* / Bodynamique: *Phreax* / Secret of Mana: *Amanite FX* / Dancing spirit: *Soluna* / Quatermass: *Kali* / Antidote: *Blue Planet Co-operation*
CD Set SPV 08938592
Subterranean / Jun '96 / Koch / Plastic Head

PULSE VOL.2 (2CD Set)
Loin sleeps tonight: *Infernal Machine* / Between the nothing: *Shakta & Ping Pong* / Howling at the moon: *Cosmosis* / Interforce: *Acid Rockers* / Creatures: *Reflecta* / Free return: *Alienated* / Angelina: *Doof* / Ten years after: *Mindfield* / Masters of the universe: *UX* / Great spirit: *Space Tribe* / Whirlpool: *Astralasia* / Magnetic activity: *MFG* / Ushuaya: *Ushuaya* / Screwdriver: *Planet Ben*
CD Set DCD 08947402
Subterranean / May '97 / Koch / Plastic Head

PUMP HARDER
CD MM 800512
Moonshine / Jun '96 / Mo's Music Machine / Prime / RTM/Disc

PUMP IT UP MR. DJ (Check Out The DJ's Playlist)
Now that we found love / Vogue / Going back to my roots / Everlasting love / Easy lover / Trapped / Don't take away the music / This is it / Deeper love (the salsa track) / You keep me hangin' on / Show me love / Dreams
CD ECD 3199
K-Tel / Mar '95 / K-Tel

PUMP UP EUROPE
CD LDCD 8823
Play It Again Sam / Aug '89 / Discovery / Plastic Head / Vital

PUMPIN' AND THUMPIN'
CD BB 003
BB / May '96 / Plastic Head

PUNK
What do I get: *Buzzcocks* / EMI: *Sex Pistols* / Personality crisis: *New York Dolls* / Angels with dirty faces: *Sham 69* / Born to lose: *Thunders, Johnny* / Bored teenagers: *Adverts* / Looking for a kiss: *New York Dolls* / Rip off: *Sham 69* / One track mind: *Thunders, Johnny* / Boston babies: *Slaughter & The Dogs* / Pretty vacant: *Sex Pistols* / No time to be 21: *Adverts* / Hear nothing, see nothing, say nothing: *Discharge* / Brickfield nights: *Boys* / Time's up: *Buzzcocks*
CD MCCD 015
Music Club / Feb '91 / Disc / THE

PUNK (3CD Set)
CD Set MCBX 017
Music Club / Dec '94 / Disc / THE

PUNK - LIVE AND NASTY
I live in a car: *UK Subs* / In a rut: *Damned* / White riot: *Sham 69* / Babylon's burning: *Ruts* / I am the hunted: *GBH* / Submission: *Sex Pistols* / No time to be 21: *Adverts* / What do I get: *Buzzcocks* / Nights in white satin: *Dickies* / Runaway: *Slaughter & The Dogs* / Don't need it: *Eater* / New guitar in town: *Boys* / C'mon everybody: *Vicious White Kids* / Hard loving man: *Moped, Johnny* / Urban kids: *Chelsea* / Wolf at the door: *Lurkers*
CD EMPRCD 586
Emporio / Oct '95 / Disc

PUNK - THE WORST OF TOTAL ANARCHY (2CD Set)
Anarchy in the UK: *Sex Pistols* / Hersham boys: *Sham 69* / Catholic school girls rule: *Red Hot Chili Peppers* / Butcher baby: *Plasmatics* / King rocker: *Generation X* / Gary Gilmore's eyes: *Adverts* / Ever fallen in love: *Buzzcocks* / Nobody's hero: *Stiff Little Fingers* / C30, C60, C90, go: *Bow Wow Wow*

/ Nasty nasty: *999* / Born to lose: *Thunders, Johnny & The Heartbreakers* / Babylon's burning: *Ruts* / No survivors: *GBH* / Heroin it's all over: *Lurkers* / Come dancing: *No Dice* / My way: *Vicious, Sid* / Get up and jump: *Red Hot Chili Peppers* / God save the Queen: *Sex Pistols* / Love you more: *Buzzcocks* / Sound of the suburbs: *Members* / Homicide: *999* / Sheena is a punk rocker: *Ramones* / Something better change: *Stranglers* / Never again: *Discharge* / Warhead: *UK Subs* / Stand strong stand proud: *Vice Squad* / Tight black pants: *Plasmatics* / Badman: *Cockney Rejects* / Why sugar: *No Dice* / Day the world turned day-glo: *X-Ray Spex* / Kids on the streets: *Angelic Upstarts* / No time to be 21: *Adverts*
CD Set ________ SP 871952
Disky / Nov '96 / Disky / THE

PUNK ALERT
CD ________ EMPRCD 678
Emporio / Apr '97 / Disc

PUNK AND DISORDERLY
CD ________ AABT 100CD
Abstract / Sep '94 / Cargo / Pinnacle / Total/BMG

PUNK AND DISORDERLY (The Best Of Punk & Disorderly)
CD ________ CLP 9824
Cleopatra / Oct '96 / Cargo / Greyhound / Plastic Head / RTM/Disc / SRD

PUNK AND DISORDERLY VOL.2 (Further Changes)
Sick boy: *GBH* / Dreaming: *Expelled* / El salvador: *Insane* / Stab the judge: *One Way System* / Gotta get out: *Court Martial* / London bouncers: *Action Pact* / Masque: *Dark* / Gangland: *Violators* / I've got a gun: *Channel 3* / Vicious circle: *Abrasive Wheels* / Fallen hero: *Enemy* / Death to humanity: *Riot* / Hobby for a day: *Wall* / More than fights: *Disorder* / Shellshock: *Erazerhead* / Resurrection: *Vice Squad* / How much longer: *Alternative TV* / Corgi crap: *Drones* / I hate school: *Suburban Studs* / Run like hell: *Peter & The Test Tube Babies*
CD ________ CDPUNK 22
Anagram / Dec '93 / Cargo / Pinnacle

PUNK AND DISORDERLY VOL.3 (The Final Solution)
Burn 'em down: *Abrasive Wheels* / Give us a future: *One Way System* / Kick out the tories: *Newtown Neurotics* / Police state: *UK Subs* / Jailbait: *Destructor* / Government policy: *Expelled* / Dead hero: *Samples* / Woman in disguise: *Angelic Upstarts* / Viva la revolution: *Adicts* / Dragnet: *Vibrators* / Computers don't blunder: *Exploited* / New barbarians: *Urban Dogs* / Have you got 10p: *Ejected* / Outlaw: *Chron Gen* / Suicide bag: *Action Pact* / Summer of '81: *Violators*
CD ________ CDPUNK 23
Anagram / Dec '93 / Cargo / Pinnacle

PUNK AND NASTY (2CD Set)
CD Set ________ DEMPCD 010
Emporio / Mar '96 / Disc

PUNK BITES
CD ________ F 019CD
Fearless / Apr '97 / Cargo / Plastic Head

PUNK CHARTBUSTERS VOL.1
CD ________ WRR 028
Wolverine / Dec '96 / Cargo / Plastic Head

PUNK CITY ROCKERS (4CD Set)
CD Set ________ MBSCD 440
Castle / Nov '95 / BMG

PUNK COMPILATION
Summer of '81: *Violators* / Shellshock: *Erazerhead* / Four minute warning: *Chaos UK* / Complete disorder: *Disorder* / When he kissed me: *Hollywood Brats* / Chinese rocks: *Thunders, Johnny* / Tomorrow's sunset: *Buzzcocks FOC* / Women in disguise: *Angelic Upstarts* / Baby baby: *Vibrators* / Black flowers for the bride: *999* / Teenage rampage: *999* / Great rock and roll swindle: *Chaotic Dischord* / 1000 marching feet: *Xpozez* / Razors in the night: *Blitz* / Follow the leader: *Saints* / Bone idol: *Drones* / I hate school: *Suburban Studs* / Action time vision: *ATV* / Run like hell: *Peter & The Test Tube Babies* / Bad hearts: *Tights* / Love sucks: *Addicts* / Give us a future: *One Way System* / 17 years of hell: *Partisans* / I've got a gun: *Channel 3* / Outside view: *Eater*
CD ________ EMPRCD 550
Emporio / Nov '94 / Disc

PUNK GENERATION (4CD Set)
CD Set ________ MBSCD 419
Castle / Nov '95 / BMG

PUNK LEGENDS (The American Roots)
CD ________ FREUDCD 056
Jungle / Jul '97 / RTM/Disc / SRD

PUNK LIVES
CD ________ TRTCD 146
TrueTrax / May '95 / THE

PUNK LOST & FOUND
Saints & sinners: *Johnny & The Self Abusers* / Shakin' all over: *Generation X* / Justifiable homicide: *Professionals* / Keys to your heart: *101'ers* / Where's Captain Kirk: *Spizz Energi* / I'm in love with the girl on the Manchester megastore check: *Freshies* / Television screen: *Radiators From Space* / Johnny won't go to heaven: *Killjoys* / Terminal stupid: *Snivelling Shits* / Waiting for the man: *Eater* / (I want to be an) Anglepoise lamp: *Soft Boys* / Gabrielle: *Nips* / New order: *Generation X* / Smash it up: *Damned* / Cosmonaut: *Bragg, Billy*
CD ________ SH 5705
Shanachie / May '96 / ADA / Greensleeves / Koch

PUNK ROCK JUKEBOX
I'm against it: *No Brain* / Bodies: *Killing Time* / I got your number: *Swinging Gutters* / Go nowhere: *Sweet Diesel* / Code blue: *Bouncing Souls* / In the city: *Waterdog* / I don't want to hear it: *88 Fingers Louie* / Somebody's gonna get their head kicked in tonight: *Murphy's Law* / Ready steady go: *Trusty* / Barbed wire love: *Goops* / Justification: *Brody* / Hitman: *Jughead's Revenge* / Understand: *Overcrowd* / Police story: *Deadguy* / I love livin' in the city: *Black Velvet Flag* / Evil: *Awkward thought* / Don't need your lovin': *New Bomb Turks* / Guimo's theme: *Plow United* / Friends: *H2O* / Woman: *Turbo AC's* / Big takeover: *Buzzkill* / We're only gonna die: *Sublime* / Civilisation's dying: *Leeway*
CD ________ BLK 025ECD
Blackout / Feb '97 / Plastic Head / Vital

PUNK ROCK LOSERS
CD ________ ALBR 1
Al's / Jun '97 / Greyhound

PUNK ROCK RARITIES VOL.1
On me: *Bears* / Hard time: *Mutants* / School teacher: *Mutants* / Lady: *Mutants* / Office girl: *Stoat* / Little Jenny: *Stoat* / Crazy paving: *Karloff, Billy* / Backstreet Billy: *Karloff, Billy* / I'm different: *Embryo* / You know he did: *Embryo* / Here comes the night: *Rivals* / Both sides: *Rivals* / Sound so false: *Murder Inc.* / Polythene dream: *Murder Inc.* / Nobody cares: *Murder Inc.* / Lord of the dance: *Jump Squad* / Debt: *Jump Squad* / Kings cross: *Charge* / Brave new world: *Charge* / God's kids: *Charge*
CD ________ CDPUNK 63
Anagram / Oct '95 / Cargo / Pinnacle

PUNK ROCK RARITIES VOL.2
CD ________ CDPUNK 83
Anagram / Oct '96 / Cargo / Pinnacle

PUNK, THE BAD AND THE UGLY, THE
CD ________ CLP 9959
Cleopatra / Mar '97 / Cargo / Greyhound / Plastic Head / RTM/Disc / SRD

PUNK UPRISINGS
CD ________ LOOKOUT 139CD
Lookout / Feb '96 / Cargo / Greyhound / Shellshock/Disc

PUNK VOL.2
Anarchy in the UK: *Sex Pistols* / Babylon's burning: *Ruts* / Nobody's hereo: *Stiff Little Fingers* / Borstal breakout: *Sham 69* / Dead cities: *Exploited* / Ain't got a clue: *Lurkers* / Maniac: *Peter & The Test Tube Babies* / Feeling alright with the crew: *999* / Chinese takeaway: *Adicts* / Right to work: *Chelsea* / Holidays in the sun: *Sex Pistols* / Alternative Ulster: *Stiff Little Fingers* / Two pints of lager: *Splodgenessabounds* / Stand strong, stand proud: *Vice Squad* / Something that I said: *Ruts* / I hate people: *Anti Nowhere League* / Teenage warning: *Angelic Upstarts* / Flares and slippers: *Cockney Rejects* / Punk's not dead: *Exploited* / Warriors: *Blitz*
CD ________ MCCD 027
Music Club / May '91 / Disc / THE

PUNKORAMA VOL.1
CD ________ E 864482
Epitaph / Nov '94 / Pinnacle / Plastic Head

PUNKORAMA VOL.2
CD ________ 64842
Epitaph / Dec '96 / Pinnacle / Plastic Head

PUNKS FROM THE UNDERGROUND
CD ________ 622432
Skydog / Apr '97 / Discovery

PUNKS NOT DREAD
CD ________ PREACH 002CD
Rhythm Vicar / Mar '94 / Plastic Head

PUNKS ON DRUGS
CD ________ DOTECD 1
Antidote / Jun '97 / SRD

PUNKS, SKINS AND HERBERTS
CD ________ HOO 32CD
Helen Of Oi / Jun '97 / Cargo

PUNKS UNDERCOVER
CD ________ CLP 9930
Cleopatra / Mar '97 / Cargo / Greyhound / Plastic Head / RTM/Disc / SRD

PURE ATTRACTION
You're my best friend: *Queen* / Right beside you: *Hawkins, Sophie B.* / Easy: *Faith No More* / Just a step from heaven: *Eternal* / Patience of angels: *Reader, Eddi* / Return to innocence: *Enigma* / Don't dream it's over: *Crowded House* / Now that the magic has gone: *Cocker, Joe* / Where does my heart beat now: *Dion, Celine* / Hold me, thrill me, kiss me: *Estefan, Gloria* / Stay: *Shakespears Sister* / Someone saved my life tonight: *John, Elton* / Independent love song: *Scarlet* / Now and forever: *Marx, Richard* / Total eclipse of the heart: *Tyler, Bonnie* / Hold me now: *Logan, Johnny* / I'll never fall in love again: *Deacon Blue* / Every breath you take: *Police* / Careless whisper: *Michael, George* / Power of love: *Rush, Jennifer* / Jealous guy: *Roxy Music* / In dreams: *Orbison, Roy* / When I fall in love: *Dion, Celine* / Nothing compares 2 U: *O'Connor, Sinead* / (Sittin' on the) dock of the bay: *Bolton, Michael* / In a broken dream: *Python Lee Jackson* / Eternal flame: *Bangles* / Always and forever: *Vandross, Luther* / Time after time: *Lauper, Cyndi* / Only to be with you: *Roachford* / Love hurts: *Capaldi, Jim* / Show me heaven: *McKee, Maria* / I wonder why: *Stigers, Curtis* / I'll stand by you: *Pretenders* / Ordinary world: *Duran Duran* / Take my breath away: *Berlin* / Miracle of love: *Eurythmics* / Whole new world (Aladdin's theme): *Bell, Regina*
CD ________ SONYTV 1CD
Sony TV / Jun '95 / Sony

PURE AUDIOSEX (Kraft Presents Modern Techno House Trax/2CD Set)
Elements: *Stoll, Steve* / Bite and scratch: *Vogel, Christian* / Home delivery: *Landstrumm, Neal* / I'll have some: *Winx, Josh & DJ ESP* / Killer train: *Miss Djax* / Fax wars: *Innersound* / To the sky: *Pump Panel* / Acid wiss L: *DJ Skull* / Dr. J: *McBride, Woody* / Snare rolls and back ups: *Righteous Men* / Transaxual: *Armando* / Loop 2: *Larkin, Kenny* / How deep is your love: *Love Inc.* / Shuffle this: *Broom, Mark* / Extra: *New John* / G-man: *El Jem* / Flash: *Kosmik Messenger* / Instant: *Beltram, Joey* / Get funky, get down: *Micronauts* / In from the night: *Planetary Assault Systems* / Chord memory: *Pooley, Ian* / Hibernia: *Mont Cenis Trax*
CD Set ________ SPV 08938722
SPV / Sep '96 / Koch / Plastic Head

PURE AUDIOSEX VOL.2 (2CD Set)
Mommy why: *Thee Madkatt Courtship* / In da jungle: *Playboy* / Beavis at bat: *Hardfloor* / Power hour: *DJ ESP* / No way back: *Adonis* / F5: *DJ Misjah* / Forklift: *Beltram, Joey* / Drumcode 20: *Beyer, Adam* / Club NCN: *Love Inc.* / I need to freak: *Aux 88* / First premonition: *Gianelli, Fred* / Dragnet: *Stoll, Steve* / When love comes down: *Righteous Men* / Bud shake: *Lindsey, Patrick* / Alien spoke: *Broom, Mark* / Ice fractions: *Silvershower* / Dark forces: *SLAM* / Overlap: *Ishii, Ken* / Vertigo: *Steve Bug & Acid Maria* / Les plates verdes: *Mont Cenis Trax* / 'Ang my pickcha: *Partycrashers*
CD Set ________ DCD 08947512
SPV / Jun '97 / Koch / Plastic Head

PURE DANCE '96 (2CD Set)
Born slippy: *Underworld* / Ain't nobody's business if I do: *H2O & Billie* / Keep on jumpin': *Lisa Marie Experience* / Don't stop movin': *Livin' Joy* / Everybody's free: *Rozalla* / Nighttrain: *Kadoc* / Higher state of consciousness: *Wink, Josh* / Keep on jumpin': *Terry, Todd & Martha Wash/Jocelyn Brown* / Hello honky tonks (rock your body): *Pizzaman* / We've got it goin' on: *Backstreet Boys* / Mysterious girl: *Andre, Peter* / Good intentions: *Nelson, Shara & G.Corp* / Sunshine: *Umboza* / Jazz it up: *Reel 2 Real* / Let's all chant: *Gusto* / There's nothing I won't do: *JX* / Children: *Miles, Robert* / Arms of Loren: *E'voke* / Walking wounded: *Everything But The Girl* / Firestarter: *Prodigy* / Nagasaki EP (I need a lover tonight): *Kendoh* / State of independence: *Summer, Donna* / Disco 2000: *Pulp* / Klubbhopping: *Klubb Heads* / Give me luv: *Alcatraz* / Disco's revenge: *Gusto* / Hideaway: *De'Lacy* / Passion: *Gat Decor* / Krupa: *Apollo 440* / So pure: *Baby D* / Good thing: *Eternal* / Do you still: *East 17* / Macarena: *Los Del Mar* / I wish: *Skee Lo* / I got 5 on it: *Luniz* / Too hot: *Coolio* / Thank God it's Friday: *R Kelly* / Can't help it: *Happy Clappers* / Theme from S Express: *S'Express* / Le voie de soleil: *Subliminal Cuts*
CD Set ________ 5357892
PolyGram TV / Aug '96 / PolyGram

PURE DEVOTION
CD ________ CDDVN 17
Devotion / Oct '92 / Pinnacle

PURE ECSTATIC ENERGY
CD ________ GLOBECD 1
All Around The World / May '93 / Total/BMG

PURE JAZZ MOODS (2CD Set)
CD Set ________ DINCD 126
Dino / Jun '96 / Pinnacle

PURE JAZZ SAMPLER
CD ________ CDGATE 1001
Kingdom Jazz / Oct '90 / Kingdom

PURE LOVERS VOL.1
CD ________ CCD 101
Charm / Oct '92 / Jet Star

PURE LOVERS VOL.10
CD ________ CCD 110
Charm / Mar '97 / Jet Star

PURE LOVERS VOL.2
CD ________ CCD 102
Charm / Sep '90 / Jet Star

PURE LOVERS VOL.3
CD ________ CCD 103
Charm / Apr '91 / Jet Star

PURE LOVERS VOL.4
I'm so alone: *Davis, Richie* / Master vibes: *Hunningale, Peter* / Love u down: *Brown, Lloyd* / Morning after: *Rich, Anthony* / I won't stop loving you: *Hall, Pam* / Daydreaming: *Robotiks & Jocelyn Brown* / Hypnotic love: *Leo, Phillip* / Can you feel the love: *Pure Silk & Trevor Walters* / Hold me: *Pinchers* / Miss wire waist: *Scotty* / Emptiness inside: *Hammond, Beres* / Ecstasy of love: *Levi, Sammy* / Fire burning: *Griffiths, Marcia* / I'm only human: *Wayne Wonder* / Mrs. Jones: *Kofi* / Make my dream a reality: *Pure Silk & Wendy Walker* / Stranger in love: *Dave Fluxe*
CD ________ CCD 104
Charm / Nov '91 / Jet Star

PURE LOVERS VOL.5
CD ________ CCD 105
Charm / Aug '92 / Jet Star

PURE LOVERS VOL.6
CD ________ CCD 106
Charm / Apr '93 / Jet Star

PURE LOVERS VOL.7
CD ________ CCD 107
Charm / Feb '94 / Jet Star

PURE LOVERS VOL.8
CD ________ CCD 108
Charm / Feb '95 / Jet Star

PURE MOODS
Return to innocence: *Enigma* / Sweet Lullaby: *Deep Forest* / Crockett's theme: *Hammer, Jan* / Oxygene (part IV): *Jarre, Jean Michel* / Orinoco flow: *Enya* / Tubular bells: *Oldfield, Mike* / Chariots of fire: *Vangelis* / Heart asks pleasure first/The promise: *Nyman, Michael* / Chi Mai: *Morricone, Ennio* / Inspector Morse: *Pheloung, Barrington* / Sadness: *Enigma* / Little fluffy clouds: *Orb* / Only you: *Praise* / Aria on air: *McLaren, Malcolm* / Lily was here: *Stewart, David A. & Candy Dulfer* / Songbird: *Kenny G* / Merry Christmas Mr. Lawrence: *Sakamoto, Ryuichi* / Twin Peaks theme: *Badalamenti, Angelo* / Mission: *Morricone, Ennio* / Another green world: *Eno, Brian*
CD ________ VTCD 28
Virgin / Jun '94 / EMI

PURE NOSTALGIA
Bei mir bist du schon: *Andrews Sisters* / Puttin' on the Ritz: *Astaire, Fred* / When I take my sugar to tea: *Boswell Sisters & Dorsey Brothers Orchestra* / Very thought of you: *Bowlly, Al* / Minnie the moocher: *Calloway, Cab* / Rockin' chair: *Carmichael, Hoagy & Louis Armstrong* / Louise: *Chevalier, Maurice* / Temptation: *Crosby, Bing* / Falling in love again: *Dietrich, Marlene* / Ten cents a dance: *Etting, Ruth* / Sally: *Fields, Gracie* / Leaning on a lamp-post: *Formby, George* / Over the rainbow: *Garland, Judy* / All the things you are: *Hutchinson, Leslie 'Hutch'* / Java jive: *Ink Spots* / Sonny boy: *Jolson, Al* / Medley: *Layton & Johnstone* / We'll meet again: *Lynn, Vera* / Dancing on the ceiling: *Matthews, Jessie* / Moonlight serenade: *Miller, Glenn* / Tiger rag: *Mills Brothers* / My curly headed baby: *Robeson, Paul* / Without a song: *Sinatra, Frank & Tommy Dorsey* / Marta: *Tracy, Arthur* / Some of these days: *Tucker, Sophie*
CD ________ CDAJA 5118
Living Era / Mar '94 / Select

PURE POP (18 Original Hits/3CD Set)
Nutbush city limits: *Turner, Ike & Tina* / Emma: *Hot Chocolate* / Dyna-mite: *Mud* / Rock your baby: *McCrae, George* / All around my hat: *Steeleye Span* / Hit me with your rhythm stick: *Dury, Ian & The Blockheads* / True: *Spandau Ballet* / Too shy: *Kajagoogoo* / Stuck with you: *Lewis, Huey & The News* / Nineteen: *Hardcastle, Paul* / Heart and soul: *T'Pau* / Are you my baby: *Wendy & Lisa* / U can't touch this: *MC Hammer* / Back to life: *Soul II Soul* / Unbelievable: *EMF* / Don't worry: *Appleby, Kim* / One and only: *Hawkes, Chesney* / Oh Carolina: *Shaggy*
CD Set ________ LAD 873382
Disky / Nov '96 / Disky / THE

PURE PUREPECHA
CD ________ CO 119CD
Corason / Aug '94 / ADA / CM / Direct

PURE REGGAE
CD ________ VSOPCD 198
Connoisseur Collection / Jun '94 / Pinnacle

PURE REGGAE (4CD Set)
Red red wine: *Boothe, Ken* / Kingston town: *Ricketts, Glen* / Tide is high: *Holt, John* / Love you baby: *Biggs, Barry* / Singer man: *Blues Busters* / People get ready: *Pat Kelly* / Rivers of Babylon: *Boothe, Ken* / Exodus: *Mafia & Fluxy* / Wild world: *Blues Busters* / If it is fire you want: *Hinds, Justin & The Dominoes* / Sweet sensation: *Lee, Byron & The Dragonaires* / I shot the sheriff: *Ricketts, Glen* / Wear to the ball: *Holt, John* / Busted lad: *Dekker, Desmond* / Ram goat liver: *Pluto* / What's happening: *Gardiner, Boris* / One big happy family: *Ruffin, Bruce* / Get up stand up: *Thomas, Ruddy* / Love again: *George, Sophia* / Sweet Jamaica: *Donaldson, Eric* / Last farewell: *Edwards, Jackie* / Let's stay together: *Gardiner, Boris* / Can't you see: *Wilson, Delroy* / Swing low: *Heptones* / Redemption song: *Fraser, Dean*

/ Uno fi move: *Shabba Ranks* / Can't test me: *Chaka Demus & Pliers* / War: *Marley, Kymani* / Down in the ghetto: *Paul, Frankie* / Shock out: *Chaka Demus* / Final decision: *George, Sophia* / You and your smiling face: *Brown, Dennis* / Some sweet day: *Hammond, Beres* / Milk and honey: *In Crowd* / Buffalo soldier: *Thomas, Ruddy* / Come back Charlie: *Charlie Chaplin* / Kool and deadly: *Eastwood & Saint* / Soul rebel: *Romeo, Max* / Judgement day: *Paragons* / Don't go nowhere: *Dunkley, Errol* / Ambition: *Reedy, Winston* / Tell me if you ready: *Seaton, B.B.* / Keep on doing it: *Blues Busters* / What you're doing to me: *Donaldson, Eric* / Power of love: *Thriller U* / Do you really want to hurt me: *Heptones* / Everybody join hands: *Dekker, Desmond* / Time is going to come: *Admiral Tibet* / Born in Ethiopia: *In Crowd* / I'm a peaceful man: *Edwards, Jackie* / Queen majesty: *Pat Kelly* / If you wanna make love: *Biggs, Barry* / Nice time: *Dunkley, Errol* / Could you be loved: *Mafia & Fluxy* / Rainy night in Georgia: *Holt, John* / If you could see me now: *Pioneers* / No man is an island: *Andy, Horace* / Send me the pillow you dream on: *Schloss, Cynthia* / Sweet cherrie: *Honey Boy* / Caught you in a lie: *McFarlin, Sandra* / Long and winding road: *Brown, Dennis* / Love me for a reason: *Miller, Maxine* / Massachusetts: *McGregor, Freddie* / Power of love: *Minott, Sugar* / No woman no cry: *Marley, Kymani* / I think I love you: *Donaldson, Eric* / Wide awake in a dream: *Biggs, Barry* / Raindrops keep falling on my head: *Gardiner, Boris* / Once upon a time: *Wilson, Delroy* / Love light: *Isaacs, Gregory* / Baby I need your loving: *Smith, Slim* / Never gonna give you up: *Adebambo, Jean* / If you don't know me by now: *Hammond, Beres* / Paradise in your eyes: *Reedy, Winston* / Just a little more time: *Seaton, B.B.* / We play reggae: *In Crowd* / Money in my pocket: *Edwards, Jackie* / Lively up yourself: *Lee, Byron & The Dragonaires* / Terror: *Chaka Demus & Spana Bana* / Money and friends: *Dekker, Desmond* / Sister love: *Isaacs, Gregory* / Who cares: *Wilson, Greg* / I let you go boy: *Penn, Dawn* / You never know: *George, Sophia* / Night like this: *Biggs, Barry* / Midnight hour: *Pat Kelly* / Bring your love to me: *Pliers* / I see you my love: *Griffiths, Marcia* / Natural mystic: *Andy, Horace* / Many rivers to cross: *Boothe, Ken* / Mississippi: *Schloss, Cynthia* / Save the people: *Ruffin, Bruce* / Never will I hurt you: *Paragons* / Take life easy: *Honey Boy* / Come down: *Pioneers* / Private lessons: *Seaton, B.B.* / Whiter shade of pale: *Pat Kelly* / Story book children: *Isaacs, Gregory* / Sweet dreams: *Pioneers* / They can't get me out: *Campbell, Cornell* / While there's life there's hope: *Ruffin, Bruce*
CD Set ______ **ECD 3350**
K-Tel / Jun '97 / K-Tel

PURE REGGAE COVERS
CD ______ **DINCD 136**
Dino / Mar '97 / Pinnacle

PURE REGGAE VOL.1 (2CD Set)
You don't love me: *Penn, Dawn* / Compliments on your kiss: *Red Dragon* / Program: *Morales, David & The Bad Yard Club* / Shine: *Aswad* / Boom shak-a-tack: *Born Jamericans* / Twist and shout: *Chaka Demus & Pliers* / Big things a gwan: *Daddy Screw & Donovan Steele* / Stress: *Brown, LLoyd & Tippa Irie* / No mama no cry: *Beenie Man* / Oh Carol: *General Saint & Don Campbell* / Sweat (a la la la la long): *Inner Circle* / Informer: *Snow* / Boom shak-a-lak: *Apache Indian* / Don't turn around: *Aswad* / Now that we've found love: *Third World* / 54-46 (was my number): *Toots & The Maytals* / Israelites: *Dekker, Desmond & The Aces* / Johnny B Badde: *Slickers* / You can get it if you really want: *Cliff, Jimmy* / Guns of Navarone: *Skatalites* / Rivers of Babylon: *Melodians* / Longshot kick de bucket: *Pioneers* / Book of rules: *Heptones* / Breakfast in bed: *Bennett, Lorna* / Guava jelly: *Gray, Owen* / Police and thieves: *Murvin, Junior* / Silly games: *Kay, Janet* / Somebody's watching you: *Black Uhuru* / Bed's too big without you: *Hylton, Sheila* / Sitting and watching: *Brown, Dennis* / Night nurse: *Isaacs, Gregory* / Call me: *General Grant*
CD Set ______ **CIDTV 8**
Island / Aug '94 / PolyGram

PURE REGGAE VOL.1
CD ______ **DINCD 131**
Dino / Jul '96 / Pinnacle

PURE REGGAE VOL.2
Tell me what you like: *Paul, Frankie* / Lovers do: *Campbell, Don* / Over you: *Hammond, Beres* / Living dangerously: *Levy, Barrington & Bounty Killer* / Forever: *Damage* / Love is here to stay: *Hunningale, Peter* / Second chance: *Douglas, Tony* / I love King Selassie: *Rose, Michael* / Maniac: *Stephens, Richie & Bounty Killer* / New suzuki: *Beenie Man* / T'imk we nice: *Fresco kid* / Hit and run: *Brown, Dennis* / Healing of the nation: *Paul, Frankie & Top Cat* / Go go macarena: *Captain Barkey* / You jammin': *Leroy Mafia* / Before you walk out of my life: *Dunkley, Errol* / Never say never: *Mikey Spice* / Love me always: *Gold, Brian & Tony* / Ain't gonna break my promise: *Osborne, Johnny* / Just be cool: *Valentine, Robbie*
CD ______ **DINCD 134**
Dino / Dec '96 / Pinnacle

PURE ROLLERS (20 Rolling Drum & Bass Tracks/2CD Set)
New dawn: *X* / Raw dogs: *Joker* / Remember me: *Benny Blanco* / Check dis: *De Elite* / Easy dread: *Serious Intent* / Shit: *L-Double & Shy FX* / Rolling number: *Dynamic Duo* / Super bad: *Bonafide* / World of music: *Dred Bass & The JB* / 16 track ting: *Dream Team* / On the beat: *Swift* / Let's roll: *Darkman* / Tonics jazz lick: *Joker* / P-funk era: *P-Funk* / Yea: *Paul Z.* / Ride: *Dynamic Duo* / Roll on: *Andy C* / Take away: *Joint Venture* / Roll that shit: *Marvellous Caine* / Just roll: *Swift*
CD Set ______ **BDRCD 11**
Breakdown / Mar '96 / Pinnacle

PURE SILK
CD ______ **SGCD 11**
Sir George / Jun '93 / Jet Star / Pinnacle

PURE SOFT METAL
CD ______ **TMPCD 015**
Temple / Mar '95 / BMG

PURE SOUL (The Best Of Expansion - 30 Awesome Soul Gems/2CD Set)
Give me the sunshine: *Leo's Sunshipp* / You can't turn me away: *Striplin, Sylvia* / Pick up the pieces: *Gardner, Joanna* / On and on: *Hewett, Howard* / Make love: *Carne, Jean* / Give me your love: *Rogers, Richard* / Candles: *James, Josie* / It's alright: *Burke, Keni* / Say you will: *Jackson, Nicole* / Later tonight: *Chandler, Omar* / I'll treat u rite: *Perry, Trina* / Rockin' you tonight: *Gary* / I'll keep a light on: *King, Evelyn 'Champagne'* / Tic toc: *Lorenzo* / I'm so in love with you baby: *McNeir, Ronnie* / My favourite thing: *Brooks, Calvin & Hari Paris* / Any way: *Garmon, Terry* / Oasis: *Baylor, Helen* / Time after time: *Taylor, Gary* / Let them talk: *Bofill, Angela* / Let me know: *Mannsfield, Rodney* / Love won't let me wait: *Haynes, Victor* / On my own: *Andrea* / My joy is you: *Wanda* / Love to love you: *On The Contrary* / Show me some love: *Benito* / Give me all your love: *Ballin, Chris* / Cream of love: *Ware, Leon* / Do it right: *Act Of Faith* / I'll be what you need: *Serenade*
CD Set ______ **EXCDP 12**
Expansion / Dec '96 / 3mv/Sony

PURE SOUL VOL.2 (2CD Set)
Rhythm of life / Strip it down: *Velma* / This dedication: *Burke, Keni* / Walk on water: *Graham, Jaki* / It's time: *Wanda* / Crystal clear: *Hewett, Howard* / Galaxy of love: *Bofill, Angela* / Pleasure: *Act Of Faith* / Falling for you: *Carne, Jean* / Keep giving me love: *Rogers, Richard* / Can't run: *Zee, Dawn* / I didn't mean to hurt you: *Valentine, Billy* / Shoo be doo: *Candy J* / Animal: *Cunningham, Woody* / Hey boy: *Jackson, Rebbie* / Love to love you: *On The Contrary* / Call me: *Mannsfield, Rodney* / I can't get enough: *Perry, Trina* / Mind over matter: *Adkins, Gary* / I don't wanna lose it: *James, Josie* / Eye to eye: *Taylor, Gary* / Stormy love affair: *Hatcher, Roger* / It really doesn't matter: *King, Evelyn 'Champagne'* / Special feelings: *Gardner, Joanna* / Real love: *Lorenzo* / Back to back: *Ware, Leon* / It's only natural: *Thomas, Keith* / Stay away from you: *Ballin, Chris* / For the love of you: *Chandler, Omar* / Just a little taste of your love: *Pedicin, Michael Jr.*
CD Set ______ **EXCDP 14**
Expansion / May '97 / 3mv/Sony

PURE SWING (The Very Best Of Pure Swing/3CD Set)
I am woman: *Cover Girls* / Love 2 love: *Damage* / Treat them like they want to be: *Father MC* / Knockin da boots: *H-Town* / On and on: *Brown, Beverlei* / Age ain't nothing but a number: *Aaliyah* / Your G spot: *Marshall, Wayne* / Don't be afraid: *Hall, Aaron* / Blow up my pager: *Smooth* / Slap 'n' tickle: *Kreuz* / I miss you: *Hall, Aaron* / Girlfriends boyfriend: *McCrae, Gwen* / Missing your love: *Celetia* / Where I wanna be boy: *Miss Jones* / Raise your hands: *LV* / Flavour of the old school: *Knight, Beverley* / If I ever fall in love again: *Shai* / Mary jane (all night long): *Blige, Mary J.* / Two can play take game: *Brown, Bobby* / Treat U right: *Truce* / Treat me right: *Father MC* / Process of elimination: *Gable, Eric* / Just kickin it: *Xscape* / You blow my mind: *Blackstreet* / Give it 2 you: *Da Brat* / Her: *Guy* / I can't tell you why: *Brownstone* / Hey Mr DJ: *Zhane* / Hey Mr.DJ: *Zhane* / For the lover in you: *Hewett, Howard* / Summertime: *DJ Jazzy Jeff & The Fresh Prince* / Back and forth: *Aaliyah* / Down 4 what Eva: *Nuttin' Nyce* / Mind blowin': *Smooth* / Remedy: *Knight, Beverley* / Your body's callin': *R Kelly* / I like the way: *Hi-Five* / Gangsta's paradise: *Coolio & LV* / Undercover lover: *Smooth* / Private party: *Marsh, Diane* / Lift me up: *New Edition* / Tell me what you like: *Guy* / Feenin': *Jodeci* / Reminisce: *Blige, Mary J.* / Poison: *Bell biv devoe* / Down for the one: *Knight, Beverley* / That's what I like: *Harmony innocents* / Sensitivity: *Tresvant, Ralph* / My heart belongs to you: *Jodeci* / Is it good to you: *Riley, Teddy & Tammy Lucus* / Do me right: *Guy* / Free: *Moore, Chante* / Candy rain: *Soul For Real* / Groove of love: *EVE* / Rock wit'cha: *Brown, Bobby* / Place where you belong: *Shai* / This love is forever: *Hewett, Howard* / Something inyour eyes: *Bell biv devoe* / Good life: *EVE* / She's playing hard to get: *Hi-Five* / Get down on it: *Kreuz* / No diggity: *Blackstreet & Dr. Dre* / I may be single: *La-'verne, Elisha* / 24 Hours: *Troi*
CD Set ______ **DINCD 100**
Dino / Nov '96 / Pinnacle

PURE SWING '95 (2CD Set)
Don't be afraid: *Hall, Aaron* / Where I wanna be boy: *Miss Jones* / My up and down: *Howard, Adina* / Something in your eyes: *Bel Biv Devoe* / Give it 2 you: *Da Brat* / Ribbons in the sky: *Intro* / One more chance: *Notorious BIG* / I'll be there for you: *Method Man* / Just roll: *Fabu* / Best friend: *Brandy* / Mary Jane (all night long): *Blige, Mary J.* / If you love me: *Brownstone* / Lately: *Jodeci* / I can go deep: *Silk* / I want: *Sweat, Keith* / Creep: *TLC* / Honey dip: *Portrait* / This is how we do it: *Jordan, Montell* / Forget I was A G: *Whitehead Brothers* / I'll make love to you: *Boyz II Men* / Every little thing I do: *Soul For Real* / Feel so good: *Xscape* / Wanna get with you: *Guy* / Knockin' da boots: *H-Town* / This is for the cool: *Babyface* / How many way's: *Braxton, Toni* / I'm so into you: *SWV* / Party all night: *Kreuz* / Girlfriend boyfriend: *McCrae, Gwen* / Sugarhill: *AZ* / Fantasy: *Carey, Mariah* / Undercover lover: *Smooth* / Ocean drive: *Lighthouse Family* / Rock me down: *Benson, Sharon* / Good lover: *Da Influence* / Lay my body down: *Kut Klose* / Rodeo style: *Jamecia* / My cherie amour: *Thompson, Tony* / I've got a little something for you: *MN8* / U will know: *BMU* / Real love: *Driza Bone* / Brand new: *Sista* / You remind me: *R Kelly* / Finest: *Truce* / Respect: *Troi* / Don't be cruel: *Brown, Bobby* / For the lover in you: *Hewitt, Howard* / Show me: *Nuttin' Nyce*
CD Set ______ **DINCD 116**
Dino / Nov '95 / Pinnacle

PURE SWING 1996
CD ______ **DINCD 120**
Dino / Apr '96 / Pinnacle

PURE SWING VOL.1 (20 Bump 'n' Grind Anthems)
CD ______ **DINCD 97**
Dino / Feb '95 / Pinnacle

PURE SWING VOL.2
Creep: *TLC* / Your love is a 187: *Whitehead Brothers* / U blow my mind: *Blackstreet* / Stroke you up: *Changing Faces* / Freak me: *Silk* / Crazy: *Morrison, Mark* / Make it last forever: *Sweat, Keith* / Get up on it: *Kut Klose* / Taste your love: *Brown, Horace* / Two can play that game: *Brown, Bobby* / Lately: *Jodeci* / Free: *Moore, Chante* / Be happy: *Blige, Mary J.* / Down with the clique: *Aaliyah* / You're body's callin: *R Kelly* / Homie lover friend: *R Kelly* / This is for the cool: *Babyface* / Is it good to you: *Lucas, Tammy & Teddy Riley* / Everyday of the week: *Jade* / Think of you: *Usher* / Slap and tickle: *Kruze* / Here we go again: *Portrait* / Mind blowin: *Smooth* / Freak like me: *Howard, Adina* / Just roll: *Fabu* / Flavour of the old school: *Knight, Beverley*
CD ______ **DINCD 98**
Dino / May '95 / Pinnacle

PURE SWING VOL.4
Water runs dry: *Boyz II Men* / Freek 'n you: *Jodeci* / How many ways: *Braxton, Toni* / Freak like me: *Howard, Adina* / I've got a little something: *MN8* / Groove of love: *EVE* / Creep: *TLC* / Get up on it: *Kut Klose* / Shy guy: *King, Diana* / Taste your love: *Brown, Horace* / Freak me: *Silk* / It's summertime: *Smooth* / Candy rain: *Soul For Real* / You will know: *BMU* / Best friend: *Brandy* / Forget I was a G: *Whitehead Brothers* / Sex me: *R Kelly* / Joy: *Blackstreet* / Can we talk: *Campbell, Tevin* / Up and down: *Kreuz* / Don't take it personal: *Monica* / You don't want to mis: *For Real*
CD ______ **DINCD 109**
Dino / Aug '95 / Pinnacle

PURE SWING VOL.5
Knockin' da boots: *H-Town* / Hanging on a string: *Loose Ends* / Somethin' 4 da honeyz: *Jordan, Montell* / Respect: *Alliance Ethnik* / Treat me right: *Father MC* / This love is forever: *Hewett, Howard* / Can't you see: *Total F Notorious Big* / Love groove: *Smooth* / Slow dance: *R Kelly* / Get down on it: *Kreuz* / Remedy: *Knight, Beverley* / Funny how time flies: *Intro* / Motown philly: *Boyz II Men* / Smile: *Shanice* / Give it 2 you: *Da Brat* / Hey Mr D.J.: *Zhane* / I want: *Sweat, Keith* / I wanna be down: *Brandy* / Keep it right there: *Changing Faces* / This is for the cool: *Babyface* / Keep it real: *Jamecia* / Just roll: *Fabu* / Tell me what you want me: *Campbell, Tevin* / Shy guy: *King, Diana* / Make me feel real good: *Porche* / Tell me: *Groove Theory* / Who can I run to: *Xscape* / Hooked on you: *Silk* / Already missing you: *Levert, Gerald*
CD ______ **DINCD 117**
Dino / Dec '95 / Pinnacle

PURE TRADITIONAL IRISH ACCORDION
CD ______ **PTICD 1027**
Pure Traditional Irish / Mar '97 / ADA / CM / Direct / Ross

PURE VINTAGE BLUES VOL.1 (You Dirty Mistreater)
Deep water blues: *Thomas, Hociel* / Jealous woman like me: *Wallace, Sippie* / Mail train blues: *Wallace, Sippie* / Dead drunk blues: *Wallace, Sippie* / Lazy man blues: *Wallace, Sippie* / Lovesick blues: *Hill, Bertha* / Trouble in mind: *Hill, Bertha* / You dirty mistreater: *Wilson, Grant* / Come on coot do that thing: *Wilson, Grant* / Down hearted blues: *Smith, Bessie* / My sweetie went away: *Smith, Bessie* / Sobbin' hearted blues: *Smith, Bessie* / Livin' high: *Taylor, Eva* / Coal cart blues: *Taylor, Eva* / Mandy, make up your mind: *Taylor, Eva* / Was it a dream: *Christian, Lillie Delk* / How do you do it that way: *Spivey, Victoria* / Ain't misbehavin': *Ellis, Segar* / Nobody knows the way I feel this morning: *Hunter, Alberta* / Broken busted blues: *Smith, Clara* / You've got to beat me to keep me: *Smith, Trixie*
CD ______ **RAJCD 870**
Empress / Oct '95 / Koch

PURE VINTAGE BLUES VOL.2 (Mining Camp Blues)
He likes it slow: *Butterbeans & Susie* / St. Peter's blues: *Welsh, Nolan* / Find me at the Greasy Spoon (if you miss me here): *Grant & Wilson* / You've got to go home on time: *Mack, Baby* / Last night I dreamed you kissed me: *Christian, Lillie Delk* / I ain't gonna play no second fiddle (if I can play lead): *Christian, Lillie Delk* / Flood blues: *Wallace, Sippie* / Anybody here want to try my cabbage: *Jones, Maggie* / Funny feathers: *Spivey, Victoria* / I can give you everything but love: *Christian, Lillie Delk* / JC Holmes blues: *Smith, Bessie* / Any woman's blues: *Smith, Bessie* / I must have that man: *Christian, Lillie Delk* / Good time flat blues: *Jones, Maggie* / Lowland blues: *Hill, Bertha* / Careless love blues: *Smith, Bessie* / What kind o' man is that: *Mack, Baby* / Too busy: *Christian, Lillie Delk* / Bridewell blues: *Welsh, Nolan* / Mining camp blues: *Smith, Trixie* / Baby: *Christian, Lillie Delk*
CD ______ **RAJCD 880**
Empress / Apr '96 / Koch

PURPLE
CD ______ **CRELP 032CD**
Creation / '88 / 3mv/Vital

PURPLE PAIN
CD ______ **DOL 020CD**
Dolores / Jun '95 / Plastic Head

PURVEYORS OF TASTE (Creation Compilation)
CD ______ **CRECD 010**
Creation / May '94 / 3mv/Vital

PUSSY GALORE
CD ______ **PUSSYCD 007**
Pussy Foot / Oct '96 / RTM/Disc

PUT YA HAND ON DE BUMPER
CD ______ **CCD 0021**
CRS / Aug '95 / ADA / Direct / Jet Star

PWEEP (2CD Set)
CD Set ______ **BFFP 94**
Blast First / Apr '95 / RTM/Disc

PYGMIES OF THE LOBAYE, THE
CD ______ **PS 65175**
PlayaSound / Dec '96 / ADA / Harmonia Mundi

Q

Q - COUNTRY
CD ______ **AHLCD 16**
Hit / May '94 / Grapevine/PolyGram

Q - RHYTHM & BLUES
Brown eyed girl / I'll go crazy: *Brown, James* / It's all over now: *Cooder, Ry* / I'd rather go blind: *Stewart, Rod* / Fool in love: *Turner, Ike & Tina* / Dr. Brown: *Fleetwood Mac* / Nadine: *Berry, Chuck* / Mockingbird: *Foxx, Inez & Charlie* / Blue Monday: *Domino, Fats* / Everybody needs somebody to love: *Burke, Solomon* / Stepping out: *Mayall, John & Eric Clapton* / Born under a bad sign: *King, Albert* / Young blood: *Coasters* / Gimme some lovin': *Davis, Spencer Group* / Hi-heel sneakers: *Tucker, Tommy* / House of the rising sun: *Animals* / Let the good times roll: *Shirley & Lee* / We're gonna make it: *Little Milton* / Roadrunner: *Diddley, Bo* / Long tall shorty: *Kinks* / You'd better move on: *Alexander, Arthur* / Got my mojo working: *Manfred Mann* / My babe: *Little Walter*
CD ______ **AHLCD 7**
Hit / Mar '93 / Grapevine/PolyGram

Q - THE ALBUM VOL.1
CD ______ **TCD 2522**
Telstar / Sep '91 / BMG

Q - THE BLUES
CD ______ **AHLCD 1**
Hit / Jun '92 / Grapevine/PolyGram

Q MUSIC VOL.1
CD ______ **51RCD 1**
Fifty First / Jan '97 / Pinnacle / Prime

QAWWALI - THE ART OF THE SUFIS VOL.2
CD ______ **VICG 50302**
JVC World Library / Mar '96 / ADA / CM / Direct

QED
Organofonia ramovs: *Laibach* / Ataxia: *Dieform* / Untitled excerpt: *2'EV* / Ebony tower in the Orient water: *Radio Rabotnik TV* / Kennen sie koein: *Der Plan* / Delerium 2: *Chris & Cosey* / HLA: *Non Toxique Lost* / Tribal noise 2: *Het Zweet* / Anyway don't do the sport fuck: *Spring As Der Wolken* / Call: *Banabila, Michel* / Restimulation: *Hafler Trio* / Mutation waltz: *Manoton, K. B.* / Menegins: *Einsturzende Neubauten* / Eleven: *De Executie/Klec* / E and E: *Pig D4* / Getuich der miljoenen: *Zegueld, Peter* / L'espirit domine l'etoile: *Etant Donnes* / Oirat / I wanna be injured, l'ace d'or: *Club Moral* / Liberal 1:13: *Zero Kama* / CBA: *SBOTHI* / Demonomania: *Test Department*
CD ______ **NLCD 001**
N L Centre / Sep '88 / Vital

QUADRUPED
CD ______ **BARKCD 006**
Planet Dog / Oct '94 / Pinnacle

QUALITY PUNK ROCK
CD ______ **BTR 006CD**
Bad Taste / Mar '96 / Plastic Head

QUANGO SPORT
CD ______ **5243322**
Quango / Jan '97 / PolyGram

QUARKNOSIS
Dolcevita: *Optica* / Utopia: *Transfinite* / Tapestry: *Quad* / Zoophite: *Optica* / Technozone: *Output & DJ Oz* / Moonshine: *Eyetek* / Aquaville: *Quad* / Trance dance: *Optic Eye* / Shimmer: *Alien Mutation* / Tokyo: *Centuras* / Something inside: *Deep Joy*
CD ______ **KINXCD 1**
Kinetix / Apr '94 / Pinnacle

QUARTER TO TWELVE
CD ______ **VPCD 2039**
VP / Sep '95 / Greensleeves / Jet Star / Total/BMG

QUEENS OF COUNTRY
Rose garden: *Anderson, Lynn* / Misty blue: *Spears, Billie Jo* / Just out of reach: *Cline, Patsy* / Crazy: *Jackson, Wanda* / Both sides now: *Murray, Anne* / Harper Valley PTA: *Riley, Jeannie C.* / End of the world: *Davis, Skeeter* / DIVORCE: *West, Dottie* / When I dream: *Anderson, Lynn* / You never can tell: *Spears, Billie Jo* / Poor man's roses: *Cline, Patsy* / It's only make believe: *Jackson, Wanda* / Last thing on my mind: *Murray, Anne* / Box of memories: *Riley, Jeannie C.* / Release me: *Mandrell, Barbara* / No charge: *Montgomery, Melba* / I wish I could fall in love again: *Howard, Jan* / Dallas: *Spears, Billie Jo* / Wishful thinking: *Fargo, Donna* / Blue bayou: *Anderson, Lynn*
CD ______ **MUCD 9014**
Musketeer / Apr '95 / Disc

QUEENS OF COUNTRY, THE
CD ______ **JHD 011**
Tring / Jun '92 / Tring

QUIET NIGHTS IN (Romantic Melodies)
Love's theme / Just the way you are / What I did for love / Ballade pour Adeline / You light up my life / Arthur's theme / Under the influence of love / Don't it make my brown eyes blue / When I need you / Daydream believer / Bright eyes / You don't bring me flowers / One day in your life / Talking in your sleep / What's another year / Strangers in the night / Lady / Crockett's theme / Man and a woman
CD ______ **QED 064**
Tring / Nov '96 / Tring

R & B CONFIDENTIAL NO.1 - THE FLAIR STORY
Romp and stomp blues: *Walton, Mercy Dee* / Baby beat it: *Henderson, Duke* / Cuban getaway: *Turner, Ike Orchestra* / Please find my baby: *James, Elmore* / You better hold me: *Reed, Jimmy* / Night howler: *Gale, Billy* / This is the night for love: *Flairs* / Let's make with some love: *Flairs* / Go Robbie go: *Robinson, Robbie & Binky* / Send him back: *Gunter, Shirley* / Baby, I love you so: *Gunter, Shirley* / Oop shoop: *Gunter, Shirley* / Hey Dr Kinsey: *Henderson, Duke* / Next time: *Berry, Richard* / Hard times: *Fuller, Johnny* / Chop house: *Allen, Blinky* / Have you ever: *Walton, Mercy Dee* / My baby left town: *Dixie Blues Boys* / People are wonderin': *Parham, Baby 'Pee Wee'* / Baby please: *Cockrell, Mat* / Quit hangin' around: *King, Saunders*
CD ______ **CDCHD 258**
Ace / Feb '89 / Pinnacle

R & B HEROINES (Goldner's Golden Girls)
Gee what a boy: *Joytones* / Let it be: *Smith, Savannah* / Repeat after me: *Delvetts* / What I don't know won't hurt me: *Essex* / Second hand love: *King, Mabel* / If you want to you can come: *Carousels* / I'll walk alone: *Chantels* / Don't stop the wedding: *Cole, Ann* / My foolish heart: *Joytones* / Every fortune teller tells me: *Kaye, Anne* / My valentine: *Sweet Teens* / You and I can climb: *Span, Patricia & The Cleftones* / Pretty little thing: *Carousels* / Anytime anyplace anywhere: *Smith, Savannah* / Bring it to me: *Essex* / Symbol of love: *King, Mabel* / Have fun: *Cole, Ann* / My darling: *Chantels* / Been so long: *Humes, Anita* / Jimbo jambo: *Joytones* / What did I do wrong: *Blades, Carol* / With this ring: *Sweet Teens* / Dilly dally darling: *Kaye, Anne* / Is this really the end: *Joytones*
CD ______ **NEMCD 918**
Sequel / Jun '97 / BMG

R & B HITS 1946
Buzz me: *Jordan, Louis* / Honey dripper: *Calloway, Cab* / Drifting blues: *Moore, Johnny & Charles Brown* / Voo-it, voo-it: *Abernathy, Marion* / Hey, ba-ba-re-bop: *Hampton, Lionel* / RM blues: *Milton, Roy* / Got a right to cry: *Liggins, Joe* / I know: *Kirk, Andy & His Twelve Clouds of Joy* / Tanya: *Liggins, Joe* / (Get your kicks on) Route 66: *Cole, Nat 'King' Trio* / Shorty's got to go: *Millinder, Lucky* / Stone cold dead in the market (he had it coming): *Fitzgerald, Ella & Louis Jordan* / I know who threw the whiskey (in the well): *Jackson, Bull Moose* / My gal's a jockey: *Turner, Joe* / Choo-choo ch'boogie: *Jordan, Louis* / Sunny road: *Sykes, Roosevelt* / Playful baby: *Harris, Wynonie* / So glad your mind: *Crudup, Arthur* / Gotta gimme what'cha got: *Lee, Julia* / Ain't that just like a woman: *Jordan, Louis* / Let the good times roll: *Jordan, Louis*
CD ______ **IGOCD 2060**
Indigo / Feb '97 / ADA / Direct

R & B VOCAL GROUPS VOL.1
It's too soon to know: *Orioles* / Lemon squeezin' daddy: *Sultans* / Make me thrill again: *Marylanders* / Hey baby: *Four Bars* / Girl that I marry: *Starlings* / I've lost: *Enchanters* / Can't get you off my mind: *Dreamers* / Don't play no mombo: *Charioteers* / You captured my heart: *Sultans* / Prayer: *Teardrops* / Paint a sky for me: *Watkins, Viola & The Crows* / How you move me: *Four Bars* / I'm so all alone: *Marylanders* / Fried chicken: *Marylanders* / Getting tired tired tired: *Orioles* / Music maestro please: *Starlings* / I've got my heart on my sleeve: *Charioteers* / Grief by day, grief by night: *Four Bars* / Blues at dawn: *Sultans* / Fool: *Teardrops* / Today is your birthday: *Enchanters* / These things I miss: *Dreamers* / Teardrops on my pillow: *Orioles* / Don't be angry: *Sultans* / Good old 99: *Marylanders* / If I give my heart to you: *Four Bars*
CD ______ **NEMCD 736**
Sequel / Jun '95 / BMG

R & B VOCAL GROUPS VOL.2
I'd rather have you under the moon: *Orioles* / Hold me: *Clicks* / Tears of love: *Kari, Sax & Quailtones* / Why do you treat me this way: *Four Bars* / Please love me: *Marylanders* / You are so beautiful: *Five Notes & The Hamil-Tones* / Baby let me bang your box: *Toppers* / My heart: *Teardrops* / You broke my heart: *Clicks* / Fine brown frame: *Starlings* / How I'd feel without you: *Marylanders* / Only you: *Cues* / Feelin' low: *Orioles* / Let me live: *Four Bars* / Ooh baby: *Teardrops* / One fried egg: *Charioteers* / Peace and contentment: *Clicks* / I'm a sentimental fool: *Marylanders* / Stop it quit it: *Four Bars* / I fell for your loving: *Cues* / Broken hearted baby: *Five Notes & The Hamil-Tones* / My plea for love: *Starlings* / Stars are out tonight: *Teardrops* / Grandpa's Inn: *Four Bars* / Come back to me: *Clicks*
CD ______ **NEMCD 743**
Sequel / Jun '95 / BMG

RABID/TJM PUNK SINGLES COLLECTION
Cranked up really high: *Slaughter & The Dogs* / Bitch: *Slaughter & The Dogs* / Ain't been to no music school: *Nosebleeds* / Facist pigs: *Nosebleeds* / Innocents: *Cooper Clarke, John* / Suspended sentence: *Cooper Clarke, John* / Psycle sluts: *Cooper Clarke, John* / Central detention centre: *Gyro* / Jilted John: *Jilted John* / Kinnel Tommy: *Banger, Ed* / Who is innocent: *Out* / Man in a box: *V2* / When the world isn't there: *V2* / It doesn't bother me: *Distractions* / It's alright: *Slaughter & The Dogs* / Edgar Allen Poe: *Slaughter & The Dogs* / Twist and turn: *Slaughter & The Dogs* / UFO: *Slaughter & The Dogs* / Voice in the dark: *Frantic Elevators* / Love in decay: *Pathetix* / Why are fire engines red: *Victim* / I need you: *Victim* / Teenage: *Victim* / Junior criminals: *Victim* / Hang on to yourself: *Victim*
CD ______ **RRCD 227**
Receiver / Aug '96 / Grapevine/PolyGram

RACE WITH THE DEVIL
Race with the devil: *Girlschool* / War pigs: *Black Sabbath* / Bomber: *Motorhead* / Silver machine: *Hawkwind* / Mean girl: *Status Quo* / Parisienne walkways: *Moore, Gary* / (Don't fear) The Reaper: *Blue Oyster Cult* / Tin soldier: *Small Faces* / Holy roller: *Nazareth* / Invasion: *Magnum* / Look at yourself: *Uriah Heep* / Heartline: *George, Robin* / Born to be wild: *Blue Oyster Cult* / Please don't touch: *Headgirl* / Sudden life: *Man* / Black magic woman: *Fleetwood Mac* / Wrist job: *Humble Pie*
CD ______ **TRTCD 115**
TrueTrax / Oct '94 / THE

RADIO 1 SOUND CITY LEEDS 1996
CD ______ **CTYCD 96**
Harmless / Aug '96 / RTM/Disc

RADIO 2 - SOUNDS OF THE 60'S
Who put the bomp: *Viscounts* / When we get married: *Dreamlovers* / Have a drink on me: *Donegan, Lonnie* / Venus in blue jeans: *Winter, Mark* / Welcome home baby: *Brook Brothers* / Spanish harlem: *Justice, Jimmy* / Count on me: *Grant, Julie* / He's in town: *Rockin' Berries* / Tossing and turning: *Ivy League* / Thunderbirds theme: *Gray, Barry Orchestra* / Round every corner: *Clark, Petula* / Take a heart: *Sorrows* / Lady Jane: *Garrick, David* / Sittin' on a fence: *Twice As Much* / Baby now that I'v found you: *Foundations* / Green tambourine: *Lemon Pipers* / Handbags and gladrags: *Farlowe, Chris* / David Watts: *Kinks* / Something here in my heart: *Paper Dolls* / Ain't nothing but a house party: *Showstoppers*
CD ______ **NEMCD 693**
Sequel / Sep '94 / BMG

RADIO DAYS (Thanks For The Melody)
CD ______ **DEX 250CD**
Australian Jazz / Nov '96 / Jazz Music

RADIO DAYS - BRITISH 30'S RADIO
Radio Times: *Hall, Henry & The BBC Dance Orchestra* / I don't do things like that: *Trinder, Tommy* / Scrimplethorp's talcum (commercial): *Long, Norman* / Coronation girls: *Waters, Elsie & Doris* / Tale of Hector Cramp: *Fletcher, Cyril* / Radio Baloni time signal: *Taunton, Peter* / Schnotzelheimer's suspenders (commercial): *Long, Norman* / All for ten shillings a year: *Stanelli & Norman Long* / There's a small hotel: *Daniels, Bebe & Ben Lyon* / Football commentary: *Keys, Nelson & Ivy St. Helier* / Little Betty Bouncer: *Flotsam & Jetsam* / British mother's big fight: *Desmond, Florence & Max Kester* / Ye BBC: *Flanagan & Allen* / Hi de ho: *Revnell, Ethel & Gracie West* / Gritty granules (commercial): *Taunton, Peter* / In 1992: *Campbell, Big Bill & His Rocky Mountain Rhythm* / I know that sailors do care: *O'Shea, Tessie* / Radio Baloni close-down: *Taunton, Peter* / Ding dong bell: *Askey, Arthur* / Mr. and Mrs. Ramsbottom went off: *Holloway, Stanley* / We can't let you broadcast that: *Long, Norman* / Cricket commentary: *Clapham & Dwyer* / Jubilee baby: *Driver, Betty* / University motors (commercial): *Potter, Gillie* / On the good ship Ballyhoo: *Warner, Jack & Jeff Darnell* / Five-in-one radios: *Pola, Eddie* / Adventures of Lt Featherston-Haugh DSO: *Taunton, Peter* / Mirror cleanser: *Fields, Gracie* / Sing as we go: *Dixon, Reginald* / Sandy's own broadcasting station: *Powell, Sandy* / You'll never understand: *Bowlly, Al* / X (commercial): *Taunton, Peter* / We're frightfully BBC: *Western Brothers* / Let me call you sweetheart: *Oliver, Vic & Nellie Wallace* / Next week's film (commercial): *Formby, George* / Dromedary cigarettes (commercial): *Pola, Eddie* / About cruises: *Murgatroyd & Winterbottom* / Here's to the next time: *Hall, Henry & The BBC Dance Orchestra*
CD ______ **CDHD 163**
Happy Days / Feb '97 / Conifer/BMG

RADIO FREEDOM
CD ______ **ROUCD 4019**
Rounder / Jun '96 / ADA / CM / Direct

RADIO GOLD VOL.1
Promised land: *Allan, Johnnie* / La Bamba: *Valens, Ritchie* / When the boy's happy (the girl's happy too): *Four Pennies* / Wake up little Susie: *Everly Brothers* / Wanderer: *Dion* / My true love: *Jive Five* / Dizzy Miss Lizzy: *Williams, Larry* / Mr. Sandman: *Chordettes* / I fought the law: *Fuller, Bobby Four* / Hush-a-bye: *Mystics* / Hello this is Joanie: *Evans, Paul* / Will you still love me tomorrow: *Shirelles* / Where or when: *Dion & The Belmonts* / Venus: *Avalon, Frankie* / Sixteen candles: *Crests* / When will I be loved: *Everly Brothers* / One fine day: *Chiffons* / Rockin' robin: *Day, Bobby* / Twist and shout: *Isley Brothers* / Little bit of soap: *Jarmels* / I'll come running back to you: *Cooke, Sam* / Earth angel: *Penguins* / Runaround Sue: *Dion* / Since I don't have you: *Skyliners* / Good golly Miss Molly: *Little Richard* / Poetry in motion: *Tillotson, Johnny* / Denise: *Randy & The Rainbows* / Tell it like it is: *Neville, Aaron* / Sweet dreams: *McLain, Tommy* / Goodnight my love: *Belvin, Jesse*
CD ______ **CDCHD 347**
Ace / Feb '92 / Pinnacle

RADIO GOLD VOL.2
Long tall Sally: *Little Richard* / Runaway: *Shannon, Del* / Donna: *Valens, Ritchie* / Bye bye love: *Everly Brothers* / Bony Maronie: *Williams, Larry* / Soldier boy: *Shirelles* / Nut rocker: *B-Bumble & The Stingers* / Hey Paula: *Paul & Paula* / Let's dance: *Montez, Chris* / Hey baby: *Channel, Bruce* / Nobody needs your love (like I do): *Pitney, Gene* / Lollipop: *Chordettes* / Hippy hippy shake: *Romero, Chan* / Alone: *Shepherd Sisters* / In the mood: *Fields, Ernie Orchestra* / Alley oop: *Hollywood Argyles* / Wayward wind: *Grant, Gogi* / Let the little girl dance: *Bland, Billy* / I'm gonna knock on your door: *Hodges, Eddie* / Ivory tower: *Carr, Cathy* / Gingerbread: *Avalon, Frankie* / Hound dog man: *Fabian* / Send me the pillow that you dream on: *Tillotson, Johnny* / Pretty little angel eyes: *Lee, Curtis* / Birds and the bees: *Akens, Jewel* / Quite a party: *Fireballs* / This time: *Shondell, Troy* / Shimmy like my sister Kate: *Olympics* / Then you can tell me goodbye: *Casinos* / Louie Louie: *Kingsmen*
CD ______ **CDCHD 446**
Ace / Sep '93 / Pinnacle

RADIO GOLD VOL.3
Love is strange: *Mickey & Sylvia* / Willie and the hand jive: *Otis, Johnny* / Sweet nothin's: *Lee, Brenda* / I'm in love again: *Domino, Fats* / Stardust: *Ward, Billy & The Dominoes* / Chanson d'amour: *Todd, Art & Dotty* / I'm gonna sit right down and write myself a letter: *Williams, Billy* / Susie darlin': *Luke, Robin* / Lion sleeps tonight: *Tokens* / Make it easy on yourself: *Butler, Jerry* / It's in his kiss (The shoop shoop song): *Everett, Betty* / Halfway to paradise: *Orlando, Tony* / That'll be the day: *Crickets* / Only the lonely: *Orbison, Roy* / When: *Kalin Twins* / White sports coat and a pink carnation: *Robbins, Marty* / On the rebound: *Cramer, Floyd* / Banana boat song (Day O): *Belafonte, Harry* / Singin' the blues: *Mitchell, Guy* / Twelfth of never: *Mathis, Johnny* / Freight train: *McDevitt, Chas & Nancy Whisky* / Big man: *Four Preps* / At the hop: *Danny & The Juniors* / Just walking in the rain: *Ray, Johnnie* / Garden of Eden: *Valino, Joe* / Green door: *Lowe, Jim* / I hear you knocking: *Lewis, Smiley* / Seven little girls sitting in the back seat: *Evans, Paul* / Witch doctor: *Seville, David* / I go ape: *Sedaka, Neil*
CD ______ **CDCHD 557**
Ace / May '95 / Pinnacle

RADIO INFERNO
CD ______ **RTD 19715982**
Our Choice / Dec '93 / Pinnacle

RADIO JUNGLE
CD ______ **RR 105CD**
Roots / Jul '96 / Timewarp

RADIO ODYSSEY (WRAS Live On-Air Compilation)
Cut me out: *Toadies* / Music is love: *G-Love & Special Sauce* / Radar: *Morphine* / Of course you can: *Morphine* / Life & death: *Low Pop Suicide* / Hazing: *Throwing Muses* / Tibetan music: *Drepung Loseling Monks*
CD ______ **D 2248762**
Ichiban / May '96 / Direct / Koch

RADIO RAP
Boom boom boom: *Outhere Brothers* / Here comes the hotstepper: *Kamoze, Ini* / Whatta man: *Salt n' Pepa & En Vogue* / Regulate: *Warren G & Nate Dogg* / Who am I (what's my name): *Snoop Doggy Dogg* / People everyday: *Arrested Development* / Now that we've found love: *Heavy D & The Boyz* / Boom shake the room: *DJ Jazzy Jeff & The Fresh Prince* / I like to move it: *Reel 2 Real* / Power: *Snap* / U can't touch this: *MC Hammer* / Informer: *Snow* / Boom rock soul: *Benz* / Homie lover friend: *R Kelly* / Can I kick it: *Tribe Called Quest* / Cantaloop (Flip fantasia): *US 3* / Big poppa: *Notorious BIG* / Think of you: *Usher* / On a ragga tip: *SL2* / Deep: *East 17*
CD ______ **RADCD 22**
Global TV / Oct '95 / BMG

RAGE TEAM, THE
Back from the grave: *Nekromantix* / We did nothing wrong: *Adolescents UK* / Am I crazy: *Mad Heads* / Jeff's head: *Pikehead* / Rude: *Grind* / Self destruct: *Plastic Bag* / Big wide world: *Strange Behaviour* / And it hurts: *Psycho Bunnies* / Drop dead: *Switchblade* / Everything's so perfect: *Dead Lillies* / Monster metal: *Nekromantix* / Mrs. Thatcher's on the dole: *Adolescents UK* / Now or never: *Mad Heads* / Individuality eagle: *Pikehead* / Paparazzi: *Grind* / Right to remain silent: *Plastic Bag* / It's alright to cry: *Strange Behaviour* / Not with you: *Psycho Bunnies* / I'm your slave: *Switchblade* / Freak show: *Dead Lillies*
CD ______ **RAGECD 112**
Rage / Sep '93 / Nervous / TKO Magnum

RAGGA BEAT
Oh carolina / Sweat (a la la la la long) / Mr. Loverman / Try jah love / Iron lion zion / Flex / Bad boys / Deep / Red red wine / Baby I love your way / Sweets for my sweet / Wheel of fortune / Shine / Twist and shout / I can't help falling in love with you / Dedicated to the one I love / I can see clearly now / Buffalo soldier
CD ______ **ECD 3215**
K-Tel / Mar '95 / K-Tel

RAGGA CLASH VOL.1
CD ______ **FADCD 021**
Fashion / Sep '92 / Jet Star / SRD

RAGGA CLASH VOL.2
CD Set ______ **FADCD 022**
Fashion / Sep '92 / Jet Star / SRD

RAGGA CLASH VOL.3
CD ______ **FADCD 029**
Fashion / Nov '93 / Jet Star / SRD

RAGGA CLASH VOL.4
CD ______ **FADCD 031**
Fashion / Dec '95 / Jet Star / SRD

RAGGA DOM
CD ______ **097042**
Declic / Apr '95 / Jet Star

RAGGA HITS VOL.1
CD MACCD 279
Autograph / Aug '96 / BMG

RAGGA HITS VOL.2
CD MACCD 280
Autograph / Aug '96 / BMG

RAGGA HOUSE
Ragamuffin hip hop: *Asher D & Daddy Freddy* / DC jail: *Daddy Freddy* / Time: *Leslie Lyrics* / No cocaine: *Prento Youth* / Persuader: *Leslie Lyrics* / All out of cash: *Howie & Jackie* / Why did you leave: *Crystal, Conrad* / We are the champions: *Asher D & Daddy Freddy* / Facts of life: *Cotton, Joseph* / Star rapper: *Mannix, Joe* / Dance hall clash: *Daddy Freddie & Tenor Fly* / Blo' dem brains: *Leslie Lyrics* / Shadow and arrow: *Nitty Gritty* / Brutality: *Asher D & Daddy Freddy* / Killing me softly: *Mikey General* / Grand finale: *Demon Boyz, Asher D & Daddy Freddy* / Ragga house (all night long): *Harris, Simon* / Don't stop rocking: *Daddy Freddy & Sugar Minott* / Lanndlord monologue: *Cotton, Joseph* / Africa: *Daddy Freddy*
CD QED 051
Tring / Nov '96 / Tring

RAGGA IN THE JUNGLE
CD STRJCD 1
Street Tuff / Apr '95 / Jet Star

RAGGA JUNGLE ANTHEMS VOL.1
CD GREZCD 3001
Greensleeves / Dec '95 / Jet Star / SRD

RAGGA JUNGLE ANTHEMS VOL.2
CD GREZCD 3002
Greensleeves / Mar '96 / Jet Star / SRD

RAGGA JUNGLE VOL.1
Talk: *Garnet Silk & Chuckleberry* / Lend me: *FOI & David Thomas* / Limb by limb: *Cutty Ranks* / Hit after hit: *Baby Wayne & Michael Rose* / Connections: *Skeng Gee* / Class: *Bunnie General & Trevor Sax* / Unity remix: *Simpleton & Remarc* / Junglist lover: *Ron Tom & Julie* / Flip flop: *Tenor Senior & Garnet Silk* / Wheel up: *Lion Man* / RIP: *Remarc* / Murder: *Beenie Man & Chuckleberry* / Final chapta: *DJ Trace* / Soundboy: *Splash* / Selectors roll VIP: *Francis, Errol & Leon Thompson* / Blood, sweat 'n' tears: *Roger Robin & Chuckleberry* / Bad man: *Chuckleberry* / Dead house: *Jigsy King & Leroy Smart* / Jungle blanca: *Faze 1 FM*
CD STORM 4CD
Desert Storm / Jan '96 / Sony

RAGGA MANIA
CD FABCD 001
Fashion / Sep '95 / Jet Star / SRD

RAGGA MANIA VOL.1
CD CHEMCD 001
Chemist / Aug '95 / Direct / Greensleeves

RAGGA MANIA VOL.2
CD CHEMCD 002
Chemist / Aug '95 / Direct / Greensleeves

RAGGA MANIA VOL.3
CD CHEMCD 003
Chemist / Feb '96 / Direct / Greensleeves

RAGGA MANIA VOL.4
CD CHEMCD 004
Chemist / Feb '96 / Direct / Greensleeves

RAGGA MEGA MIX VOL.1
CD SONCD 0054
Sonic Sounds / Aug '93 / Jet Star

RAGGA MEGA MIX VOL.2
CD SONCD 0084
Sonic Sounds / Apr '96 / Jet Star

RAGGA PARTY VOL.1 (Dancing On The Roof)
CD RN 0016 CD
Runn / Jul '92 / Grapevine/PolyGram / Jet Star / SRD

RAGGA PARTY VOL.2 (More Than Just Dancehall)
Education: *Chris Irie* / Funny familiar feeling: *Thriller U* / Dollar bill: *Nico Demus* / Girls girls: *Robinson, Ed & Apache Scratchy* / Last laugh: *Isaacs, Gregory* / Conversation: *Campbell, Cornell* / Billy the kid: *Jigsy King* / Money: *Shaggy Wonder* / Tek live: *Professor Frisky* / True love relation: *Junior, John* / What are girls made of: *Tiger* / Chicken in the corn: *Brushy One String* / Sodering: *General TK* / War: *Stone Wall Jackson* / Flower garden: *Chris Irie* / Flower garden (Version): *Chris Irie*
CD RN 017CD
Runn / Nov '92 / Grapevine/PolyGram / Jet Star / SRD

RAGGA PARTY VOL.3 (Don't Stop Ragga)
CD RN 0018 CD
Roof International / Nov '92 / Jet Star

RAGGA PARTY VOL.4
CD RN 0019 CD
Roof International / Nov '92 / Jet Star

RAGGA PITCH
CD MONCD 002
Montana / Nov '93 / Jet Star

RAGGA RAGGA RAGGA VOL.1
Don't know: *Jigsy King* / Husband goody-goody: *Capleton* / Movie star: *Galaxy P* / Intimate: *Bounty Killer & Redrose* / Woman fi look good: *Snagapuss* / Living in a dream: *Capleton & Brian & Tony Gold* / Mek noise: *Mad Cobra* / Too young: *Cocoa T & Buju Banton* / Galong so: *Major Mackerel* / Red alert: *Spragga Benz* / Work the body good: *Jigsy King* / Sake a yuh body: *Daddy Screw & Major Christie* / Informer: *Snagapuss, Redrose, Lizard & More* / Return father and son: *Ninjaman & Ninja Ford* / Rude bwoy no powder: *Grindsman* / Money: *Galaxy P* / Holy moly: *Bajja Jedd* / Jessica: *Red Fox*
CD GRELCD 192
Greensleeves / Nov '93 / Jet Star / SRD

RAGGA RAGGA RAGGA VOL.2
Bad boy nuh club scout: *Bounty Killer & Ninjaman* / Dis di program: *Beenie Man* / Sireen: *Papa San* / Run come: *Terror Fabulous* / Wap dem girl: *Sabba Tooth* / Trespass: *Bounty Killer* / Fat piece of goose: *Duck Man* / Hollow point bad boy: *Ninjaman* / Burning up: *Red Dragon* / Not another word: *Bounty Killer* / You must be maniac: *Daddy Screw* / Wood stitchie: *Lieutenant Stitchie* / Dem bawling out: *Galaxy P* / Jockey wid di distance: *Tumpa Lion* / Run gal run: *Daddy Lizard* / Hotness: *Mad Cobra* / Spermrod: *Simpleton* / Nuh have no heart: *Bounty Killer*
CD GRELCD 204
Greensleeves / Jun '94 / Jet Star / SRD

RAGGA RAGGA RAGGA VOL.3
World dance: *Beenie Man* / War is not a nice thing: *Bounty Killer* / Wap dem: *Turbo Belly* / Dead in ya: *Silver Cat* / Woman no: *Louie Culture* / Every mickle make a muckle: *Jigsy King* / Hey boy red Indian: *Pinchers* / Gallowas: *Mad Cobra* / World dance: *Ninjaman* / Nozzle and trigger: *Judas* / Only master God: *General Degree* / Riding through South: *Red Indian* / My sound: *Chuckleberry* / Joker gangsta: *Merciless*
CD GRELCD 212
Greensleeves / Dec '94 / Jet Star / SRD

RAGGA RAGGA RAGGA VOL.4
CD GRELCD 214
Greensleeves / May '95 / Jet Star / SRD

RAGGA RAGGA RAGGA VOL.5
CD GRELCD 218
Greensleeves / Aug '95 / Jet Star / SRD

RAGGA RAGGA RAGGA VOL.6
CD GRELCD 223
Greensleeves / Nov '95 / Jet Star / SRD

RAGGA RAGGA RAGGA VOL.7
Mr. War War: *Merciless* / Benz and bimma: *Bounty Killer* / Mad house tek him: *Spragga Benz* / Explode gal: *Red Dragon* / Hotter this year: *Buccaneer* / Girls way: *Beenie Man* / In and out: *General Degree* / Gal fi get wock: *Bounty Killer* / Want the lumber: *Simpleton* / More gyal: *Red Dragon* / Matey anthem
CD GRELCD 228
Greensleeves / May '96 / Jet Star / SRD

RAGGA RAGGA RAGGA VOL.8
Yaw yaw: *Beenie Man* / Model: *Bounty Killer* / Hammer: *Merciless* / Buccaneer medley: *Buccaneer* / Gal dem wining: *Chuck Fender* / Blackboard: *Beenie Man* / Serve me long: *Frisco Kid* / You've got me waiting: *Bounty Killer & Nitty Kutchie/Angel Doolas* / Ban mi fi di truth: *Beenie Man* / Hot girl: *Spragga Benz* / Gal fi di future: *Daddy Screw* / Man confuse: *Merciless* / Me a wine her: *Bailey, Admiral* / It's me it's me: *Chuck Fender* / Ready or not: *Scare Dem* / Nah nuh sense Bruce: *Merciless* / Pure gal: *Harry Toddler* / Woa woa: *General Degree*
CD GRELCD 233
Greensleeves / Nov '96 / Jet Star / SRD

RAGGA RAGGA RAGGA VOL.9
Dwayne: *Red Rat* / Pleasure tour: *General Degree* / Ill na na: *Monster Shock* / Good boy: *Red Rat* / Fudgie: *Goofy* / My gal dem: *Beenie Man* / Postman: *Hawkeye* / Bad man sonata: *Buccaneer* / Italee: *Red Rat* / Girls dem man: *Scare Dem* / Dog bark: *Goofy* / Who badda: *General Degree & Lady Saw* / Cheap clothes: *Mad Cobra* / Second place: *Buccaneer* / My man: *Lady G* / Cartoon character: *General Degree* / Little Miss Cutie: *Ghost* / Mr. McCoy: *Merciless*
CD GRELCD 240
Greensleeves / Jul '97 / Jet Star / SRD

RAGGA REVOLUTION
Getting blacker: *Macka B* / Bills: *Thriller Jenna* / Equal rights / Righteous way: *Yabby You* / Kick up a rumpus: *Pepper Seed* / Father of creation: *Harris, Bobby* / Give the poor man a bly: *Pepper Seed* / What's happening to our world: *Shaloma* / Good friend / Tomorrow is another day: *Stewart, Tinga* / Set things straight: *Pepper Seed* / Righteous dub: *Mad Professor*
CD ARICD 086
Ariwa Sounds / Sep '93 / Jet Star / SRD

RAGGA RIDDIM BHANGRA
CD DMUT 1259
Multitone / Aug '93 / BMG

RAGGA SOCA HITS VOL.2
CD JW 013
JW / Jan '96 / Jet Star

RAGGA SUN HIT
CD 0092
Declic / Apr '95 / Jet Star

RAGGA TO THE MAX
CD 032012
Melodie / Jan '97 / ADA / Discovery / Grapevine/PolyGram / Greensleeves / Jet Star

RAGGA'S GOT SOUL
CD DTCD 23
Discotex / Aug '95 / Jet Star

RAGGASOCA 1997 HITS VOL.2
CD JW 126CD
JW / Jun '97 / Jet Star

RAGTIME
CD TRTCD 181
TrueTrax / Jun '95 / THE

RAGTIME BLUES GUITAR 1928-1930
One way gal: *Moore, William* / Ragtime crazy: *Moore, William* / Midnight blues: *Moore, William* / Ragtime millionaire: *Moore, William* / Tillie Lee: *Moore, William* / Barbershop rag: *Moore, William* / Old country rock: *Moore, William* / Raggin' the blues: *Moore, William* / Brownie blues: *Gay, Tarter* / Unknown blues: *Gay, Tarter* / Jamestown exposition: *Baylesse Rose* / Black dog blues: *Baylesse Rose* / Original blues: *Baylesse Rose* / Frisco blues: *Baylesse Rose* / Dupree blues: *Walker, Willie* / Sould Caroline rag: *Walker, Willie*
CD DOCD 5062
Document / Oct '92 / ADA / Hot Shot / Jazz Music

RAGTIME PIANO HITS
CD MATCD 229
Castle / Dec '92 / BMG

RAGTIME TO JAZZ VOL.1 (1912-1919)
CD CBC 1035
Timeless Historical / Jun '97 / New Note/ Pinnacle

RAGTIME TO JAZZ VOL.2
Teasing the cat / At the jazz band ball / Jazz de luxe / Good man is hard to find / Lonesome road / Yellow dog blues / Hello hello / Weeping willow blues / Bluin' the blue / Dixieland one-step / Left alone blues intro: Good night boat / Railroad blues / Blues naughty sweetie gives to me / Tiger rag / Sounds of Africa / Saxophone blues / Shake it and break it / Muscle shoals blues / Decatur street blues / Virginia blues / Truly / Hot lips / Loose feet / Telephone blues
CD CBC 1045
Timeless Historical / Sep '97 / New Note/ Pinnacle

RAI REBELS
N'sel fik: *Fadela, Chaba & Cheb Sahraoui* / Khadidja: *Hamid, Cheb* / Ya loualid: *Zahouania, Chaba & Cheb Khaled* / Foug-e-ramla: *Benchenet, Houari* / Deblet gualbi: *Sahraoui, Cheb* / Sahr liyali: *Zahouania, Chaba* / Sidi boumedienne: *Khaled, Cheb* / Mali galbi: *Benchenet, Houari*
CD CDEWV 7
Earthworks / Aug '88 / EMI

RAILROAD SONGS AND BALLADS
CD ROUCD 1508
Rounder / Aug '97 / ADA / CM / Direct

RAIN DROPPING ON A BANANA TREE
CD ROUCD 1125
Rounder / Feb '96 / ADA / CM / Direct

RAINDANCE
Raindance / Return from River Island / Circle of fire / Intertribal pow wow / Thunder cloud mountain / Dance of the warrior / Seeds of future happiness / Nighthawk / Honouring the horse / Dance of the bear / Song of the harvest / Celebration of the young
CD 5298622
PolyGram TV / Apr '96 / PolyGram

RAINDROP GREATEST HITS VOL.1
CD RAINCD 001
Raindrop / Nov '95 / Plastic Head

RAINFOREST RHYTHMS (A Magical Blend Of Music And Sounds Of Nature)
CD 57682
CMC / May '97 / BMG

RAISE THE ROOF VOL.1 (2CD Set)
CD Set SCRCD 009
Scratch / Jul '95 / Koch / Scratch/BMG

RAJASTHAN - MUSICIANS OF THE DESERT
CD C 580058CD
Ocora / Jul '95 / ADA / Harmonia Mundi

RAJASTHANI FOLK MUSIC
CD CDSDL 401
Saydisc / Mar '94 / ADA / Direct / Harmonia Mundi

RAK'S GREATEST HITS
House of the rising sun: *Animals* / I'm into something good: *Herman's Hermits* / Tobacco Road: *Nashville Teens* / Hi ho silver lining: *Beck, Jeff* / To sir with love: *Lulu* / I've been drinking: *Beck, Jeff & Rod Stewart* / Whole lotta love: *CCS* / Oh you pretty thing: *Noone, Peter* / Dance with the devil: *Powell, Cozy* / Journey: *Browne, Duncan* / Tiger feet: *Mud* / So you win again: *Hot Chocolate* / Can the can: *Quatro, Suzi* / Bump: *Kenny* / Motor bikin': *Spedding, Chris* / Lay your love on me: *Racey* / Kids in America: *Wilde, Kim* / Tom, Tom turnaround: *New World* / Classic: *Gurvitz, Adrian* / You sexy thing: *Hot Chocolate*
CD CDSRAK 545
EMI / Aug '91 / EMI

RAM JAM A GWAAN
CD HBST 161CD
Heartbeat / Aug '94 / ADA / Direct / Greensleeves / Jet Star

RAMPANT COMPILATION VOL.1
CD SUB 1D
Subversive / Aug '95 / 3mv/Sony / Amato Disco / Mo's Music Machine / Prime / Vital

RANDALL LEE ROSE'S DOO WOP SHOP
I wonder why: *Dion & The Belmonts* / Remember then: *Earls* / Why do kids grow up: *Randy & The Rainbows* / Please love me forever: *Cathy Jean & The Roommates* / You were mine: *Cathy Jean & The Roommates* / Babalu's wedding day: *Eternals* / Church bells may ring: *SC Cadets* / Pretty little angel eyes: *Lee, Curtis* / I'll follow you: *Jarmels* / Angel baby: *Rosie & The Originals* / Earth angel: *Penguins* / On Sunday afternoon: *Harptones* / Denise: *Randy & The Rainbows* / Eyes: *Earls* / Possibility: *Crowns* / We belong together: *Belmonts* / I'll never know: *Del-Satins* / Once in a while: *Chimes* / Rockin' in the jungle: *Eternals* / Shoudn't I: *Orients* / I remember: *Five Discs* / Eddie my love: *Teen Queens* / To be loved (forever): *Pentagons* / My true story: *Jive Five* / Who's that knocking: *Genies* / Angels listened in: *Crests* / Hush-a-bye: *Mystics* / There's a moon out tonight: *Capris* / This I swear: *Skyliners* / Till then: *Classics*
CD CDCHD 392
Ace / Oct '92 / Pinnacle

RANDOM
CD BBQCD 195
Beggars Banquet / Jun '97 / RTM/Disc / Warner Music

RAP ATTACK
When the ship goes down: *Cypress Hill* / Can I kick it: *Tribe Called Quest* / OPP: *Naughty By Nature* / Boom shake the room: *DJ Jazzy Jeff & The Fresh Prince* / Wapbabalubop: *Funkdoobiest* / Mr. Wendal: *Arrested Development* / Set adrift on memory bliss: *PM Dawn* / Funky cold medina: *Tone Loc* / Uptown hit: *Kurious* / Jump around: *House Of Pain* / Ghetto jam: *Domino* / Eye know: *De La Soul* / Push it: *Salt n' Pepa* / Walk this way: *Run DMC & Aerosmith* / Slam: *Onyx* / Temple: *Fugees* / Lovesick: *Gang Starr* / Around the way girl: *LL Cool J* / Shut 'em down: *Public Enemy* / Jump: *Kriss Kross*
CD MOODCD 32
Columbia / Mar '94 / Sony

RAP AUTHORITY, THE
CD ICH 7803CD
Ichiban / Apr '94 / Direct / Koch

RAP DECLARES WAR
Rap declares war: *War & Friends* / Funky 4 U: *Nice & Smooth* / New Jack swing: *Wreckx n' Effect* / Feels so good: *Brand Nubian* / Potholes in my lawn: *De La Soul* / Short but funky: *Too Short* / Heartbeat: *Ice-T* / Young black male: *2Pac* / Don't let noone get you down: *War & Hispanic MC's* / Low rider (on the boulevard): *Latin Alliance* / Ya estuvo (that's it): *Kid Frost* / Slow ride: *Beastie Boys* / Drums of steel: *7A3* / Rhyme fighter: *Mellow Man Ace* / Summatymz ova: *Brotherhood Creed* / Spill the wine: *Lighter Shade Of Brown* / Join me please (homeboys make some noise): *Mantronix*
CD 74321305252
Avenue / Sep '95 / BMG

RAP FROM BRAZIL
CD KAR 981
IMP / Nov '96 / ADA / Discovery

RAP HITS
Gangsta's paradise / Get a life / White lines (Don't do it) / U can't touch this / Let's talk about sex / Set adrift on memory bliss / Push it / Me myself and I / Jump around / Walk this way / Hip hop hooray / Funky cold medina / Mr. Wendal / Informer / Come baby come / Now that we found love / Here we go / It's a shame (my sister) / Can I kick it
CD 306342
Hallmark / Jan '97 / Carlton

RAP HOUSE DANCE PARTY
CD 15376
Laserlight / Aug '91 / Target/BMG

RAP LEGENDS ARCHIVE VOL.1
CD BLIPCD 103
Urban London / Oct '96 / Jet Star / Pinnacle

RAP LEGENDS ARCHIVE VOL.2
CD BLIPCD 104
Urban London / Oct '96 / Jet Star / Pinnacle

RAP POWER PLAY
CD 12369
Laserlight / Jun '94 / Target/BMG

RAP REVIVAL
Part time sucker: *KRS 1* / I think I can beat Mike Tyson: *DJ Jazzy Jeff & The Fresh Prince* / Luck off Lucien: *Tribe Called Quest* / Get in the groove: *Wee Papa Girl Rappers*

/ Set the pace: *Skinny Boys* / Ghetto: *Too Short* / Sue me: *Dr. Ice* / Illegal business: *Boogie Down Productions* / Verses from the abstract: *Tribe Called Quest* / Hands across the ocean: *She Rockers* / Haunted house of rock: *Whodini* / My imagination: *2 Too Many* / 808 is comin': *D-Nice* / Big mouth: *Whodini* / No respect: *Kool Moe Dee* / I can go crazy: *DJ Jazzy Jeff* / Nasty girls: *Steady B*
CD ________ **EMPRCD 554**
Emporio / Nov '94 / Disc

RAP RULES
What's up doc (can we rock): *Fu-Schnickens & Shaquille O'Neal* / La Raza: *Kid Frost* / Smoke some kill: *Schoolly D* / Shoot pass slam: *Shaquille O'Neal* / I think I can beat Mike Tyson: *DJ Jazzy Jeff & The Fresh Prince* / This is how we rip shit: *Casual* / On and on: *Shyheim aka The rugged Child* / Ruff karnage: *Silver Bullet* / Something 2 smoke 2: *MC Breed* / Victim of the ghetto: *College Boyz* / Streit up menace: *MC Eiht* / Nasty girls: *Steady B* / Mentirosa: *Mellow Man Ace* / Thugarism: *Assault Team* / Flow on: *Lords Of The Underground* / Trigga gots no heart: *Spice 1*
CD ________ **DC 881352**
Disky / Jul '97 / Disky / THE

RAP STREET
CD ________ **ITM 001459CD**
ITM / Jun '93 / Koch / Tradelink

RAP TO THE MAX
Boom shake the room: *DJ Jazzy Jeff & The Fresh Prince* / Come baby come: *K7* / Jump around: *House Of Pain* / Boom shak-a-lak: *Apache Indian* / Informer: *Snow* / Whistler: *Honky* / Hip hop hooray: *Naughty By Nature* / That's how I'm livin': *Ice-T* / Can I kick it: *Tribe Called Quest* / Walk this way: *Run DMC & Aerosmith* / Now that we've found love: *Heavy D & The Boyz* / Push it: *Salt n' Pepa* / It's a shame (my sister): *Monie Love & True Image* / No matter what U do (I'm gonna get with U): *Flavour* / Here we go: *Stakka Bo* / Feelin' alright: *EYC* / For what it's worth: *Oui 3* / Get a life: *Soul II Soul* / Me, myself and I: *De La Soul* / Can't wait to be with you: *DJ Jazzy Jeff & The Fresh Prince*
CD ________ **VTCD 25**
Virgin / Apr '94 / EMI

RAPE OF HOLY TRINITY, THE
CD ________ **SHAGRATH 007CD**
Hot / Mar '97 / Plastic Head

RAPPAZ 'N' DA HOOD (4CD Set)
CD Set ________ **DTKBOX 62**
Dressed To Kill / Jun '97 / Total/BMG

RARE BLUES 1934-1937
CD ________ **DOCD 53331**
Document / Apr '95 / ADA / Hot Shot / Jazz Music

RARE BLUES 1938-1948
CD ________ **DOCD 5427**
Document / Jul '96 / ADA / Hot Shot / Jazz Music

RARE BRAZIL VOL.5
CD ________ **RB OO5CD**
Batacuda / May '97 / Cargo

RARE BRAZIL VOL.6
CD ________ **RB 006CD**
Batacuda / May '97 / Cargo

RARE CHICAGO BLUES 1962-1968
CD ________ **CDBB 9530**
Bullseye Blues / Jun '93 / Direct

RARE, COLLECTABLE AND SOULFUL (RCA - Northern Soul's Holy Grail)
Ooh it hurts me: *Cavaliers* / Push a little bit harder: *Metros* / Change your ways: *Kendricks, Willie* / What can I do: *Chandler, Lorraine* / (Putting my heart under) lock and key: *Scott, Sharon* / Take me away: *Cooke, Carolyn* / What's that on your finger: *Carter, Kenny* / It hurts too much to cry: *Barnum, H.B.* / Today is my day: *Courtney, Dean* / Since you're gone: *Barons* / Lovesick: *Dynamics* / She'll be leaving you: *Kendricks, Willie* / It's better: *Scott, Sharon* / Mend the torn pieces of my heart: *Chandler, Lorraine* / Having fun: *Bobbettes* / Don't you know (a true love when you see one): *Mason, Tony* / Crackin' up over you: *Hamilton, Roy* / I'm just a man: *Insiders* / I'm leaving: *Nash, Johnny* / Let the music play: *Hamilton, Roy* / What have I done wrong: *Crawford, Faye* / Come on strong: *Wilcox, Nancy* / It didn't take much (for me to fall in love): *Wiggins, Percy* / I'll never forget you: *Metros*
CD ________ **CDKEND 141**
Kent / Jan '97 / Pinnacle

RARE GROOVE
Boogie wonderland: *Earth, Wind & Fire & The Emotions* / Shake your body: *Jacksons* / That's the way I like it: *KC & The Sunshine Band* / Use it up and wear it out: *Odyssey* / And the beat goes on: *Whispers* / Contact: *Starr, Edwin* / More than a woman: *Tavares* / If I can't have you: *Elliman, Yvonne* / I will survive: *Gaynor, Gloria* / Ring my bell: *Ward, Anita* / Hang on in there baby: *Bristol, Johnny* / Rock your baby: *McCrae, George* / You bet your love: *Hancock, Herbie* / Now that we've found love: *Third World* / Play that funky music: *Wild Cherry* / It's a disco night (rock don't stop): *Isley Brothers* / Le freak: *Chic* / We are family: *Sister Sledge* / Boogie nights: *Heatwave* / You make me feel (mighty real): *Sylvester* / Don't stop the music: *Yarbrough & Peoples* / Working my way back to you: *Detroit Spinners* / Rock the boat: *Hues Corporation* / Funky town: *Lipps Inc.* / Love come down: *King, Evelyn 'Champagne'* / I can make you feel good: *Shalamar* / Celebration: *Kool & The Gang* / Haven't stopped dancing yet: *Gonzales* / Right back where we started from: *Nightingale, Maxine* / Get along without you now: *Wills, Viola* / Jump to the beat: *Lattisaw, Stacy* / Searching: *Change*
CD ________ **QTVCD 016**
Quality / Nov '92 / Pinnacle

RARE GROOVE CLASSICS VOL.1
CD ________ **SGCD 16**
Sir George / Jul '93 / Jet Star / Pinnacle

RARE JAZZ AND BLUES PIANO 1935-1937
CD ________ **DOCD 5388**
Document / Dec '95 / ADA / Hot Shot / Jazz Music

RARE MEXICAN CUTS FROM THE SIXTIES
CD ________ **842626**
EVA / Jun '94 / ADA / Direct

RARE ON AIR - LIVE PERFORMANCES VOL.1
Poem: *Cohen, Leonard* / Silent all these years: *Amos, Tori* / Cordoba: *Cale, John* / Always in disguise: *Himmelman, Peter* / My drug buddy: *Dando, Evan & Juliana Hatfield* / Coal: *Penn, Michael* / Arms for hostages: *X* / God's hotel: *Cave, Nick & The Bad Seeds* / Mexico: *Beck* / Peace: *Los Lobos* / Never going back again: *Buckingham, Lindsey* / Moderns: *Isham, Mark* / Captive heart: *Perry, Brendan* / How you've grown: *Merchant, Natalie* / Which will: *Williams, Lucinda* / Chet Baker's unsung swan song: *Wilcox, David*
CD ________ **MR 0742**
Mammoth / May '94 / Vital

RARE ON AIR - LIVE PERFORMANCES VOL.2
Sugar water: *Cibo Matto* / Palomine: *Bettie Serveert* / Sweet ride: *Donnelly, Tanya* / Everybody can change: *Chesnutt, Vic* / Mystery girl: *World Party* / City sleeps: *MC 900ft Jesus* / Just like this train: *Mitchell, Joni* / Cajun moon: *Cale, J.J.* / I've had it: *Mann, Aimee* / Beautiful friend: *Sebadoh* / Sunday: *Cranberries* / Opening: *Glass, Philip* / Famous blue raincoats: *Cole, Lloyd* / Late for the sky: *Browne, Jackson*
CD ________ **MR 1072**
Mammoth / Sep '95 / Vital

RARE REGGAE FROM THE VAULTS OF STUDIO ONE
CD ________ **HBCD 47**
Heartbeat / May '89 / ADA / Direct / Greensleeves / Jet Star

RARE TERRITORY BANDS
CD ________ **IAJRCCD 1002**
IAJRC / Oct '93 / Jazz Music / Wellard

RAREST ROCKABILLY & HILLBILLY BOOGIE/BEST OF ACE ROCKABILLY
Nothin' but a nuthin': *Stewart, Jimmy & His Nighthawks* / Darlin': *Dale, Jimmie* / Baby doll: *Dale, Jimmie* / Pretending is a game: *Jeffers, Sleepy & The Davis Twins* / My blackbirds are bluebirds now: *Jeffers, Sleepy & The Davis Twins* / Don't sweep that dirt on me: *Shaw, Buddy* / No more: *Shaw, Buddy* / My baby left me: *Rogers, Rock* / Little dog blues: *Price, Mel* / Henpecked daddy: *Johnson, Ralph & The Hillbilly Show Boys* / Umm boy you're my baby: *Johnson, Bill & The Dabblers* / Stoney mountain boogie: *Stoney Mountain Playboys* / Big black cat: *Hendon, R.D.* / It's a Saturday night: *Mack, Billy* / Rockin' daddy: *Fisher, Sonny* / Everybody's movin': *Glenn, Glen* / One cup of coffee: *Glenn, Glen* / I can't find the doorknob: *Jimmy & Johnny* / My big fat baby: *Hall, Sonny & The Echoes* / How come it: *Jones, Thumper* / Trucker from Tennessee: *Davis, Link* / Little bit more: *LaBeef, Sleepy* / I'm through: *LaBeef, Sleepy* / Jitterbop baby: *Harris, Hal* / Let's get it on: *Almond, Hershel* / I'm a hobo: *Reeves, Danny* / Rock it: *Jones, George* / Sneaky Pete: *Fisher, Sonny*
CD ________ **CDCHD 311**
Ace / Jul '91 / Pinnacle

RAS PORTRAITS (2CD Set)
Somewhere: *McGregor, Freddie* / Break free: *Minott, Sugar* / One stone: *Culture* / Crysis: *Lodge, J.C.* / Give it with caution: *Isaacs, Gregory* / Jah Jah hear my plea: *Don Carlos* / Great train robbery: *Black Uhuru* / De di doo: *Eek-A-Mouse* / No wanga gut: *Tiger* / License to kill: *Charlie Chaplin* / Showers of blessings: *Reid, Junior* / Righteous: *Mystic Revealers* / Don't let the children cry: *Broggs, Peter* / Same song: *Israel Vibration* / Songs of freedom: *Paul, Frankie* / Natty dread rise again: *Congos* / Prayer: *Yellowman* / Victory is mine: *Brown, Dennis* / Little children cry: *Levy, Barrington* / Corrupt cop: *Mighty Diamonds* / Rocking dolly: *Cocoa T* / Lay it on the line: *Wailing Souls* / Kunte kinte: *Mad Professor* / Squeeze me: *Macka B* / Nah give up: *Sizzla* / Unforgettable: *Fraser, Dean*
CD Set ________ **RASMP 33903**
Ras / Jun '97 / Direct / Greensleeves / Jet Star / SRD

RAS PORTRAITS (Harmony Trios)
Dread in the mountain: *Black Uhuru* / Cool and calm: *Israel Vibration* / One stone: *Culture* / Something is wrong: *Link & Chain* / Teach the children: *Heptones* / Get up and dance: *Melodians* / Natty dread rise again: *Congos* / Posse are you ready: *Mighty Diamonds* / Joy in the morning: *Psalms*
CD ________ **RAS 3306**
Ras / Jul '97 / Direct / Greensleeves / Jet Star / SRD

RAS PORTRAITS (Dancehall DJ's)
Nice up dance: *Natural Beauty* / No wanga gut: *Tiger* / Firing strong: *Tony Rebel* / Nah give in: *Sizzla* / Blackness awareness: *Michigan & Smiley* / Lyrics of mine: *Brigadier Jerry* / Music addict: *U-Roy* / Reggae on the move: *Yellowman* / Alms house: *Capleton* / Ruff this year: *Chaka Demus & Pliers* / Oh Lord: *Tappa Zukie* / Love mi sess: *Top Cat* / Charlie in the party: *Charlie Chaplin* / Gun in a baggy: *Little Lenny* / Mother culture: *Sister Carol*
CD ________ **RAS 3311**
Ras / Jul '97 / Direct / Greensleeves / Jet Star / SRD

RAS PORTRAITS (The Ariwa Label)
Never risk: *McLean, John* / You are the one: *Intense* / We play reggae: *Kofi* / Armageddeon: *Andy, Horace* / Squeeze me: *Macka B* / Kill the Police Bill: *Ranking Ann* / DJ Mama: *Thriller Jenna* / True born African: *U-Roy* / King step: *Pato Banton* / Rebel on the roots corner: *Tippa Irie* / Speed rap: *Papa Levi* / Mystic warrior: *Perry, Lee 'Scratch'* / One million man dub: *Jah Shaka & Mad Professor* / Doppler in de jungle: *Mad Professor & William The Conqueror/King O' Di Jungle* / Kunte Kinte jungle: *Mad Professor & Douggie Digital/Juggler*
CD ________ **RAS 3320**
Ras / Jul '97 / Direct / Greensleeves / Jet Star / SRD

RAS PORTRAITS (The Live & Learn Label)
Hear the River Jordan: *Ras Michael & The Sons Of Negus* / Le' go me hand: *Josey Wales* / Teach me culture: *Levy, Barrington* / Reggae-lution: *Mighty Diamonds* / Chanting: *Reid, Junior & Don Carlos* / Black history: *Reid, Junior & Don Carlos* / Hold tight: *Brown, Dennis* / Where is Garvey: *Mighty Diamonds* / Them a fret: *Wailing Souls* / Kingston 14: *Wailing Souls* / Run around child: *Hammond, Beres & Barrington Levy* / Some girls are trouble: *Hammond, Beres & Barrington Levy* / Jam session: *Mighty Diamonds* / Play on: *Wailing Souls* / Cease fire: *Prophet, Michael* / Forward natty: *Campbell, Al*
CD ________ **RAS 3330**
Ras / Jul '97 / Direct / Greensleeves / Jet Star / SRD

RAS RECORDS PRESENTS A REGGAE CHRISTMAS
We wish you a Merry Christmas / Jingle bells: *Don Carlos & Glenice Spencer* / Joy of the world: *Lodge, J.C.* / O come all ye faithful (Adeste fidelis): *McGregor, Freddie* / Drummer boy: *Michigan & Smiley* / Twelve days of Christmas: *Broggs, Peter* / Silent night: *Black, Pablo* / Feliz Navidad: *McGregor, Freddie* / Night before Christmas: *Eek-A-Mouse*
CD ________ **RASCD 3101**
Ras / Jan '89 / Direct / Greensleeves / Jet Star / SRD

RAS, REGGAE AND RYKODISC
CD ________ **RCD 20151**
Hannibal / Aug '91 / ADA / Vital

RAST DESTAGAH
CD ________ **PANCCD 2017**
Pan / May '93 / ADA / CM / Direct

RASTA
CD ________ **BB 2808**
Blue Beat / Aug '96 / Grapevine/PolyGram

RASTA REGGAE
CD ________ **RB 3018**
Reggae Best / Jan '96 / Grapevine/PolyGram

RASTA SHOWCASE
CD ________ **CC 2708**
Crocodisc / Jan '94 / Grapevine/PolyGram

RASTAFARI LIVETH IN THE HEART
CD ________ **JLCD 5001**
Uptempo / Jul '97 / Jet Star

RASTAFARI TEACHINGS
CD ________ **ROTCD 004**
Reggae On Top / Jun '95 / Jet Star / SRD

RAUCOUS RECORDS SINGLES COLLECTION
Nightmare: *Go Katz* / Bedrock: *Frantic Flintstones* / Let's go somewhere: *Frantic Flintstones* / Last breath: *Spellbound* / More whiskey: *Caravans* / Do the hucklebuck: *Griswalds* / Robbie robot: *Griswalds* / You can't judge a book by the cover: *Deltas* / How come you do me: *Deltas* / Home sweet home: *Termites* / Old black Joe: *Frantic Flintstones* / Alchohol buzz: *Frantic Flintstones* / Cold cold Sunday: *Sergeant Fury* / Something gotta give: *Nitros* / Face the fact: *Rattlers* / Pink hearse: *Radium Cats* / Haunted by your love: *Radium Cats* / Bop pills: *Mercurys* / Cardillac rest: *Deuces Wild* / Psycho vision: *Sergeant Fury* / Kangaroo barndance: *Thee Waltons* / Fat, drunk and stupid: *Thee Waltons* / Ready to burn: *Thee Rayguns* / Caught in a dream: *Sergeant Fury* / Old man in the woods: *Cosmic Voodoo*
CD ________ **CDMPSYCHO 8**
Anagram / Sep '95 / Cargo / Pinnacle

RAUNCHY BUSINESS - HOT NUTS AND LOLLIPOPS
Sam the hot dog man: *Johnson, Lil* / My stove's in good condition: *Johnson, Lil* / Wipe it off: *Johnson, Lonnie* / Best jockey in town: *Johnson, Lonnie* / Shave 'em dry: *Bogan, Lucille* / He's just my size: *Kirkman, Lillie Mae* / If it don't fit (don't force it): *Barrel House Annie* / Furniture man blues: *Johnson, Lonnie & Victoria Spivey* / My pencil don't write no more: *Carter, Bo* / Banana in your fruit basket: *Carter, Bo* / Get 'em from the peanut man (hot nuts): *Johnson, Lil* / Get 'em from the peanut man (the new hot nuts): *Johnson, Lil* / Drivin' that thing: *Mississippi Sheiks* / Bed spring poker: *Mississippi Sheiks* / Lollypop: *Hunter & Jenkins* / Meat cuttin' blues: *Hunter & Jenkins* / You got to give me some of it: *Moss, Buddy* / Butcher shop blues: *Edwards, Bernice*
CD ________ **4678892**
Columbia / May '91 / Sony

RAUSCHEN VOL.10
CD ________ **FIM 1017**
Force Inc. / Oct '95 / Amato Disco / Arabesque / SRD

RAUSCHEN VOL.11
CD ________ **FIM 1018**
Force Inc. / Mar '96 / Amato Disco / Arabesque / SRD

RAUSCHEN VOL.12 (2CD Set)
CD Set ________ **FIM 1022**
Force Inc. / Oct '96 / Amato Disco / Arabesque / SRD

RAUSCHEN VOL.7
CD Set ________ **FIM 1013**
Force Inc. / Jun '94 / Amato Disco / Arabesque / SRD

RAUSCHEN VOL.9
CD ________ **FIM 1016**
Force Inc. / Apr '95 / Amato Disco / Arabesque / SRD

RAVE - JUST DO IT (2CD Set)
CD Set ________ **560022**
Westcom / Jan '97 / Koch / Pinnacle

RAVE AND CRUISE (The Odyssey/2CD Set)
Odyssey: *Novy, Tom* / Feel it: *Bruisin' Hool* / La maree: *Charles L'Admiral* / Smilin' faces: *Romanto* / Swing it: *Future Funk* / Air royo: *Disko Pogo* / Croissant show, me gusta mucha: *Acis Maris* / Vor mentera: *Bug, Steve* / Vibrations: *X-Men* / SOS bells: *Houzer, Felix* / La onda: *Dune, Alex* / Flying jazz: *Pussylover* / Drums: *West Bam* / Get wicked: *Hardsequencer* / Drop da bass: *Raver's Nature* / T2: *Tanith* / Flashing teardrops: *Resistance* / Freak tonight: *Pascal* / Descent III: *Talla 2XLC* / No more pain: *Rixen, Gerrit* / Bass for life: *DJ Felipe* / Mr. Brown's ice coffee: *Yamul* / Goody goody: *Dook Mayza* / Paraguys: *DJ Dick* / Maschuge: *Genlog*
CD Set ________ **74321382462**
Kosmonaut / Jun '96 / BMG

RAVE ANTHEMS
Everybody in the place: *Prodigy* / Anasthasia: *T-99* / Go: *Moby* / DJ's take control: *SL2* / (I wanna give you) Devotion: *Nomad* / Sweet harmony: *Liquid* / Far out: *Sonz Of A Loop Da Loop Era* / Charly: *Prodigy* / Playing with knives: *Bizarre Inc.* / Dub war: *Dance Conspiracy* / Activ 8: *Altern 8* / Take me away: *Cappella* / Move any mountain: *Shamen* / Close your eyes: *Acen* / Inssomniak: *DJ PC* / Get ready for this: *2 Unlimited* / Ebeneezer goode: *Shamen* / We've got to live together: *RAF* / Bouncer: *Kicks Like A Mule* / I want you (forever): *Cox, Carl* / Hardcore heaven: *DJ Seduction* / Trip to the moon: *Acen* / Infinity: *Guru Josh* / Something good: *Utah Saints* / Frequency: *Altern 8* / Way in my brain: *SL2* / Is there anybody out there: *SL2* / Night in motion: *Cubic 22* / Searching for my rizla: *Cubic 22* / Liquid is liquid: *Liquid* / What time is love: *KLF* / Feel so real: *Dream Frequency* / Lock up: *Zero B* / Hardcore uproar: *Together* / Let me be your fantasy: *Baby D* / It's a fine day: *Opus III* / Nightbird: *Convert* / 2/231: *Anticappella* / Can you feel the passion: *Blue Pearl* / Injected with a poison: *Khan, Praga*
CD ________ **DINCD 104**
Dino / Jul '95 / Pinnacle

RAVE COLLISION
CD ________ **EWM 41872**
Broken Beat / Aug '95 / Plastic Head

RAVE FLOOR MUSIC FOR RAVE FLOOR PEOPLE VOL.1 (2CD Set)
CD Set ________ **BB 04209DCD**
Broken Beat / Jan '96 / Plastic Head

RAVE GENER8TOR VOL.1, THE
CD ________ **JARCD 3**
Cookie Jar / May '92 / SRD

RAVE GENER8TOR VOL.2, THE
CD ________ **JARCD 4**
Cookie Jar / Apr '93 / SRD

RAVE GENERATION
CD ______ CDSOR 003
Sound Of Rome / Feb '97 / SRD

RAVE MASSACRE
CD ______ SPV 08938962
SPV / Oct '94 / Koch / Plastic Head

RAVE MASSACRE VOL.5 (2CD Set)
Way we rocked it: *DJ Delirium & Guitar Rob* / Don't fuck with a roughneck: *Juggernaut* / Music that lasts forever: *DJ Roy* / Speedy recovery: *Source Code* / Intelligent hardcore: *Dark Raver & DJ Vince* / Vandaag: *Gabbers Voor Gabbers* / Vocoder: *DJ Devon* / Aboriginal: *Bioforce & Mike Oh'man* / Braingeyser: *El Bruto* / Mindblower: *Ectomorph* / Hootimack: *Enfusia* / Get down: *Liberator* / Hell is coming: *Zelator* / Mindcrushing: *Da Mindcrusher* / Impulsive: *Dark Destination* / Fuck (what else): *Scum* / Stylewarrior: *Bazooka* / Filled with power: *Predator* / Raid over Moscow: *Nuclear System* / Get up hardcore: *Out Of Key* / Break it down: *Viper* / Fight: *Speedfreak* / Satanic cults: *Coremat Inc.* / No happy shit: *Rotterdam Terror Corps* / Drunken bonehead: *Drugzone* / Let's drum the boomstick: *Revolution Team & The Snake* / Sign of the void: *Rapid S* / Kick this party: *Bioforce & Mike Oh'man* / New style: *DJ Alex* / Wake up: *Hough & Dr. Pille* / WWRU: *Reactor*
CD Set ______ SPV 08947492
SPV / Jun '97 / Koch / Plastic Head

RAVE MISSION
CD ______ 09238508
SPV / Jan '96 / Koch / Plastic Head

RAVE MISSION (The Dream Edition/2CD Set)
Traumzeit: *Dreamplant* / Secret love: *Magnetic Pulstar* / Waterfall: *Atlantic Ocean* / Our dream: *Caucasuss* / Alcatraz: *Peyote* / Paraglide: *Paragliders* / Transfiguration: *DJ Dave Davis* / Dreamgarden: *Hardworld* / Space girl: *DJ Hooligan* / Dreams: *Quench* / Tower of Naphatali: *C.J. Bolland* / Love stimulation: *Humate* / Oasis: *Paragliders* / 3rd rebirth: *Jones & Stephenson* / World of aqua: *Aqua* / Beyond your dreams: *Homahino* / 16 reasons to love: *Niholai* / Source: *Redeye* / My world: *Van Dyke, Paul* / Herzsprung: *Caunos* / Planet: *Mystic Forces* / How much can you take: *Visions Of Shiva*
CD Set ______ SPV 09247382
SPV / Feb '97 / Koch / Plastic Head

RAVE MISSION VOL.1 (2CD Set)
CD Set ______ SPV 08838952
Subterranean / Aug '94 / Koch / Plastic Head

RAVE MISSION VOL.2 (Entering Lightspeed/2CD Set)
CD Set ______ SPV 08938232
Subterranean / Dec '94 / Koch / Plastic Head

RAVE MISSION VOL.3 (2CD Set)
CD Set ______ SPV 08938292
Subterranean / May '95 / Koch / Plastic Head

RAVE MISSION VOL.4 (2CD Set)
CD Set ______ SPV 08938352
Subterranean / Jul '95 / Koch / Plastic Head

RAVE MISSION VOL.5 (The Jubilee Box Set/3CD Set)
CD Set ______ TCD 09238480
Subterranean / Dec '95 / Koch / Plastic Head

RAVE MISSION VOL.7 (2CD Set)
Stuck on a spacetrip: *Demonic Emotions* / Whiplash: *Overcharge & G.Meter* / Unicorn: *DJ Tomicraft* / Nothing is over: *Possible Words* / Cosmic wave: *DJ Warlock* / Ganesha: *Karma* / That's the way it should be: *De Luxe, Tom* / People: *Indris* / Evolver: *De Niro* / Electronically entertained: *Technology* / Human beings: *Interstate* / Secret love: *Magnetic Pulstar* / Twilight zone: *Aqualoop* / Trance research: *E-Space* / Erotmania: *DJ Randy* / Baby: *Nostrum* / Error 129: *Greenforce* / What is: *DJ Thoka* / Beyond the clouds: *Omega Force* / Give me all you got: *Soulslider* / Sweet gravity remix: *LSG* / Soccer boys: *XXL*
CD Set ______ 09247232
SPV / Nov '96 / Koch / Plastic Head

RAVE MISSION VOL.8 (2CD Set)
Perfect: *Scope* / Planet hunter: *Third Man* / Monosphere: *Liquid Bass* / Lost Genesis: *Backdraft* / E volution: *Virtual Atmosfear* / Great bear: *Little Jam* / Crazy: *Global Control* / Sleepless: *Greenforce* / Metropolis: *Changall* / Other worlds: *Proxyma* / Vulcan: *Commander Tom* / My love emotions: *Creams* / Meta morph VI: *Error 010* / Tears: *Solid Sleep* / Overdrive: *Mass In Orbit* / In heaven: *Oson* / Mind over matter: *Sloane Strangers* / Yesterday: *Sonic Tool* / What was it like: *Framic* / ATOMIC JUNKIES: *Atomic Junkies* / Luke: *Planet E Team* / Human beings: *Interstate*
CD Set ______ SPV 09247372
SPV / Feb '97 / Koch / Plastic Head

RAVE OF THE WORLD
CD ______ CLP 9920
Hypnotic / Mar '97 / Cargo / SRD

RAVE POWER (3CD Set)
CD Set ______ ZYX 811092
ZYX / Jul '97 / ZYX

RAVE RELIGION VOL.1
Energy: *DJ Tibby* / Pagemaster: *DJ Gollum* / Secret(don't tell it): *D-Lay* / Lonely days: *Comma* / Alright: *Magnetic Slides* / Any time any place: *Alien Factory* / CelysCredits: *Celysis, Tom* / Albion: *Twisted* / Journey: *Oaks, Oliver & DJ Luna* / Peaceful harmony: *Plastic Enemy* / Now and zen: *Quiet Man* / Revolver: *De Niro* / Megalomania: *Mega Lomania* / Pulse: *Magnetic Pulstar* / Don't be afraid: *Moonman* / Let there be light: *Moonman* / ACAchtung: *Timo Maas & Digital City* / Get back to the growlers: *Growlers* / Good music: *DJ Meltron* / Running dream: *Levy 9* / Hold back: *Edge & Dentist* / Overland: *Dawntreader*
CD ______ 560113
Nova Tekk / Aug '97 / Pinnacle

RAVE ZONE '95
Speed freak: *Speed Freak* / Move me up: *Surreal Deal Featuring Anji* / Camel: *Yekuana* / Partytime: *Katclub, The* / Indian summer: *Atomix* / Rockin' to the music: *Savannah* / I'm so real: *Miss Ferguson* / Kingdom: *Yekuana* / Ready steady: *Tomorrow people* / Heaven: *Positive Connection* / Jump jump (a little higher): *Progen 7* / Everybody get up: *Angel Deluxe*
CD ______ ECD 3100
K-Tel / Jan '95 / K-Tel

RAVEALATION
CD ______ STHCCD 11
Strictly Underground / Jun '95 / SRD

RAVEHEART - THE FUBAR ALBUM
CD ______ FACD 2
Fubar / Nov '96 / Alphamagic / Grapevine/ PolyGram

RAVEMASTER VOL.2
CD ______ ZYX 81088
ZYX / Oct '96 / ZYX

RAVEMEISTER VOL.1 (2CD Set)
CD Set ______ SPV 08938362
Subterranean / Jun '95 / Koch / Plastic Head

RAVEMEISTER VOL.2 (2CD Set)
CD Set ______ SPV 08938452
Subterranean / Dec '95 / Koch / Plastic Head

RAVEMEISTER VOL.3 (2CD Set)
Black is black: *Allnighters* / Read my lips: *Future Breeze* / Put your house in order: *Toja* / Magma: *Dual Mount* / Stargate custodian: *Stargate* / Forcing beat: *Casseopaya* / Comix: *L'Age Synthetique* / Acid invasion: *Pneumonia* / Capturing matrix: *Rexanthony* / You can't stop the groove: *Fusion* / Watchman's theme: *Watchman* / Open da house: *Lords Of Octagon* / Northern lights: *Mr. Oz & Larry Lush* / Baby: *Nostrum* / Photon: *Tool & Sakin* / Double orange: *D-Fense & Confusion* / Container dreams: *Elasticoculture* / Poisoned strawberry: *Tranceatlantic*
CD Set ______ SPV 08938652
Subterranean / May '96 / Koch / Plastic Head

RAVEMEISTER VOL.4 (2CD Set)
Get up: *Picard, Etienne* / Blow back: *Nostrum* / Make your wish: *Microgroove* / Spin: *Exithone* / Matabu pt.1: *Cores* / Interceptor: *Van Basten* / Lash v 11: *Rubicon Massacre Ltd.* / Favorite: *DJ Ed* / Numa: *Phonetics* / Space party: *Space Frog* / Voice: *D-Fense & Confusion* / Bob km: *Friends, Lovers & Family* / Stepping energy: *Ultrashock* / Force pt.2: *Omega Force* / Connect: *Mass In Orbit* / Evolution: *Mandala* / Lostsideon: *Lostideon* / Mediation, spiritualism and love: *Wax Trax 2* / Intoxication: *Unison* / Turn it up: *Huntemann* / Based on acid: *DJ Ablaze* / Synthetic Mankind: *State Of House* / Pandora's box: *Zaffarano, Marco*
CD Set ______ SPV 09247142
Subterranean / Nov '96 / Koch / Plastic Head

RAVEMEISTER VOL.5 (2CD Set)
Running man: *Nuclear Hyde* / Bad house music: *Loving Loops* / Human beings: *Interstate* / Monastery: *Nostrum* / Sleepless: *Greenforce* / Snavalo: *TB-Tuner* / Mystery: *Code 16* / Allright: *Patchwork* / My love: *Data's* / Acid squid: *Asys* / Like it: *Pneumonia* / Maen cetti: *Pendragon & Taffrican* / Status X: *Framic* / Pandorras: *Equator* / Research: *X-ite* / Overdrive: *Mass In Orbit* / Take me to the top: *MNA-Project* / Sound: *De Donatis* / Stairclimbing: *Lunar Trip* / Every night: *Virtual Elements* / Liquid loop: *Aqualite* / Sonnenschein: *Perpetuum Mobile*
CD Set ______ SPV 09247352
Subterranean / Feb '97 / Koch / Plastic Head

RAVEMEISTER VOL.6 (2CD Set)
Ayla: *Ayla* / Love is solution: *Exit EEE* / Matter in question: *Riva* / La vache: *Milk Inc.* / Club art: *Rees, John* / Pandomia: *DJ Randy* / Alright: *Magnetic Slides* / Run off: *Rave Bass* / Accident: *Skylab* / Scream: *Avalonge* / Nothing but deluxe: *Deluxe* / End: *Nostrum* / Nighttripper: *Equator* / Lonely days: *Comma* / Best: *Plug 'n' Play* / Humanoid: *N-Son-X* / Organic: *Phuture Punk* / What does he think: *Nooroom* / Organix: *Code 25* / My life: *Vegas Soul* / Too deep: *DJ Philip* / Interlude: *Paraphobia* / Nowhere: *Matthews, Mike*
CD Set ______ SPV 09247452
Subterranean / Jun '97 / Koch / Plastic Head

RAVER'S NIGHT VOL.2
CD ______ 483808
Ruff Neck / Oct '96 / Mo's Music Machine

RAVER'S PARADISE VOL.2 (2CD Set)
CD Set ______ IDTCOMP 004
ID&T / Dec '96 / Plastic Head

RAVING MAD
Trip to Trumpton: *Urban Hype* / Sesame's treet: *Smart E's* / Searching for my rizla: *Ratpack* / Closer to all your dreams: *Rhythm Quest* / Temple of dreams: *Messiah* / Gun: *Nino* / On a rubbish tip: *Progression* / Papua new guinea: *Future Sound Of London* / Hot chilli: *NAM* / No other: *Nightbreed* / Humanoid: *Stakker* / What's E for dad: *Little Jack* / Trip to the moon (Part 2): *Acen* / Reset: *Output & DJ Oz* / Feel the vibe: *Tequila Carter*
CD ______ CDELV 01
Elevate / Jul '92 / 3mv/Sony

RAW BLUES VOL.1
CD ______ CDSGP 026
Prestige / Jan '93 / Else / Total/BMG

RAW BLUES VOL.2 (2CD Set)
Blues in my blood: *Smith, Gregg* / Crawling King snake: *Hooker, John Lee* / My baby's gone: *Hopkins, Lightnin'* / Ain't that lovin' you baby: *Reed, Jimmy* / Ray Charle's blues: *Charles, Ray* / Angels laid him away: *Hurt, 'Mississippi' John* / Song for Frank: *Skeleton Crew* / Lend me your love: *Memphis Slim* / Blues before sunrise: *Hooker, John Lee* / Say boss man: *Diddley, Bo* / Cherry red: *Bloomfield, Mike* / She's mine: *Ciotti, Roberto* / May be the last time: *Little Walter & Otis Rush* / Hoodoo blues: *Lightnin' Slim* / Baby what's wrong with you: *Hurt, 'Mississippi' John* / Come here Mama: *Thomas, Rufus* / Hear me talkin': *Hopkins, Lightnin'* / Rock me baby: *Memphis Slim*
CD Set ______ CDSGP 081
Prestige / Aug '94 / Else / Total/BMG

RAW BLUES VOL.3 (2CD Set)
CD Set ______ CDSGP 0273
Prestige / Aug '97 / Else / Total/BMG

RAW COMPILATION VOL.1
CD ______ FNARRCD 009
Damaged Goods / May '92 / Shellshock/ Disc

RAW JAMS VOL.1
CD ______ HOMEGROWNCD 3
Homegrown / Jun '95 / Jet Star / Mo's Music Machine

RAW 'N' UNCUT HIP HOP
CD ______ EFA 127772
Ruff 'n' Raw / Nov '95 / SRD

RAW POWER SAMPLER
Parisienne walkways: *Moore, Gary* / Run to your mama: *Moore, Gary* / Gypsy: *Uriah Heep* / Wizard: *Uriah Heep* / In nomine satanus: *Venom* / Devil's answer: *Atomic Rooster* / Walking in the park: *Colosseum* / Chase is better than the catch: *Motorhead* / Bang the drum all day: *Rundgren, Todd* / In the beginning: *Magnum*
CD ______ RAWCD 1000
Raw Power / Mar '88 / Pinnacle

RAW RAW DUB
CD ______ CEND 2000
Century / Jan '97 / Shellshock/Disc

RAW RECORDS PUNK COLLECTION, THE
Sick of you: *Users* / I'm in love with today: *Users* / Johnny won't go to heaven: *Killjoys* / Naive: *Killjoys* / Withdrawal: *Unwanted* / Bleak outlook: *Unwanted* / 1984: *Unwanted* / New religion: *Some Chicken* / Blood on the wall: *Some Chicken* / Radio call sign: *Lockjaw* / Young ones: *Lockjaw* / Arabian daze: *Some Chicken* / Number seven: *Some Chicken* / It's my life: *Gorillas* / My soul's alive: *Gorillas* / Secret police: *Unwanted* / These boots are made for walking: *Unwanted* / Journalist jive: *Lockjaw* / I'm not me: *Unwanted* / End is nigh: *Unwanted* / Bondage boy: *Sick Things* / Kids on the street: *Sick Things* / So young: *Psychos* / Straight jacket: *Psychos* / At night: *Killjoys* / I wish you dead: *Acme Sewage Co.* / I don't need you: *Acme Sewage Co.* / Millionaire: *GT'S* / Young British and white: *Psychos* / I can see you: *Acme Sewage Co.*
CD ______ CDPUNK 14
Anagram / Sep '93 / Cargo / Pinnacle

RAW RUB A DUB VOL.2: EINSTEIN'S THEORY OF DUB
CD ______ GPCD 003
Gussie P / Oct '94 / Jet Star

RAWHIDE
CD ______ DS 020
Desperado / Jun '97 / TKO Magnum

RAZOR RECORDS PUNK COLLECTION
CD ______ CDPUNK 45
Anagram / Feb '95 / Cargo / Pinnacle

RCA VICTOR 80TH ANNIVERSARY SAMPLER
Livery stable blues: *Original Dixieland Jazz Band* / Dr. Jazz: *Morton, Jelly Roll* / In the mood: *Miller, Glenn* / Night in Tunisia: *Gillespie, Dizzy* / Tijuana gift shop: *Mingus, Charles* / Without a song: *Rollins, Sonny* / What a wonderful world: *Armstrong, Louis* / Truth is spoken here: *Roberts, Marcus* / Labyrinth: *Harrell, Tom*
CD ______ 09026687852
RCA Victor / Apr '97 / BMG

RCA VICTOR 80TH ANNIVERSARY VOL.1 (1917-1929)
Livery Stable blues: *Original Dixieland Jazz Band* / Meanest blues: *Original Memphis Five* / She's crying for me: *New Orleans Rhythm Kings* / Smokehouse blues: *Morton, Jelly Roll & His Red Hot Peppers* / Kansas city shuffle: *Moten, Bennie Kansas City Orchestra* / Dr. Jazz: *Morton, Jelly Roll & His Red Hot Peppers* / My pretty girl: *Goldkette, Jean & His Orchestra* / Davenport blues: *Red & Miffs Stompers* / St. Louis shuffle: *Henderson, Fletcher Orchestra* / Wolverine blues: *Morton, Jelly Roll* / Clementine: *Goldkette, Jean & His Orchestra* / Feeling no pain: *Red & Miffs Stompers* / Black and tan fantasy: *Ellington, Duke & His Orchestra* / San: *Whiteman, Paul & His Orchestra* / Doing things: *Venuti, Joe Blue Four* / Four or five times: *McKinney's Cotton Pickers* / South: *Moten, Bennie Kansas City Orchestra* / Boy in the boat: *Johnson, Charlie & His Paradise Orchestra* / I'm gonna stomp Mr. Henry Lee: *Eddie's Hot Shots* / Everybody loves my baby: *Hines, Earl 'Fatha' Orchestra* / Ozark mountain blues: *Missourians* / It should have been you: *Allen, Henry & His New York Orchestra* / Ain't misbehavin': *Waller, Fats* / Too late: *Oliver, Joe 'King' Orchestra* / Hello Lola: *Mound City Blues Blowers*
CD ______ 09026687772
RCA Victor / Apr '97 / BMG

RCA VICTOR 80TH ANNIVERSARY VOL.2 (The Second Decade 1930-1939)
Rockin' chair: *Carmichael, Hoagy Orchestra* / Mood indigo: *Ellington, Duke Cotton Club Orchestra* / Sugarfoot stomp: *Henderson, Fletcher Orchestra* / Heebie jeebies: *Mills Blue Rhythm Band* / Lafayette: *Moten, Bennie Kansas City Orchestra* / St. Louis blues: *Armstrong, Louis Orchestra* / Minnie the Moocher: *Calloway, Cab Orchestra* / Jazznocracy: *Lunceford, Jimmie Orchestra* / After you've gone: *Goodman, Benny Trio* / Swing is here: *Krupa, Gene Swing Band* / King Porter stomp: *Hill, Teddy NBC Orchestra* / Honeysuckle rose / Jivin' the vibres: *Hampton, Lionel Orchestra* / I can't get started: *Berigan, Bunny Orchestra* / Don't be that way: *Goodman, Benny Orchestra* / Begin the beguine: *Shaw, Artie Orchestra* / Boogie woogie: *Dorsey, Tommy Orchestra* / Really the blues: *Ladnier, Tommy Orchestra* / Limehouse blues: *Manone, Wingy Orchestra* / Cherokee: *Barnet, Charlie Orchestra* / In the mood: *Miller, Glenn Orchestra* / Hot mallets: *Hampton, Lionel Orchestra* / Body and soul: *Hawkins, Coleman Orchestra* / You're letting the grass grow: *Waller, Fats & His Rhythm* / Relaxin' at the Touro: *Spanier, Muggsy Ragtime Band*
CD ______ 09026687782
RCA Victor / May '97 / BMG

RCA VICTOR 80TH ANNIVERSARY VOL.3 (The First Label In Jazz 1940-1949)
Sheik of Araby: *Hawkins, Coleman* / Cotton tail: *Ellington, Duke* / Summit ridge drive: *Shaw, Artie* / Blues in thirds: *Bechet, Sidney* / All of me: *Carter, Benny* / One o'clock jump: *Metronome All Stars* / Yes indeed: *Dorsey, Tommy* / Things ain't what they used to be: *Hodges, Johnny* / St Louis Blues: *Kirby, John & His Orchestra* / Stormy Monday blues: *Hines, Earl 'Fatha'* / Night in Tunisia: *Gillespie, Dizzy* / Spotlite: *Hawkins, Coleman* / Cadillac Slim: *Carter, Benny & Chocolate Dandies* / Epistrophy: *Clarke, Kenny* / Buckin' the blues: *Esquire All American Award Winners* / Out of nowhere: *Tatum, Art* / Blues after hours: *Teagarden, Jack* / Erroll's bounce: *Garner, Erroll* / Ain't misbehavin': *Armstrong, Louis* / I don't stand a ghost of a chance with you: *Tristano, Lennie* / Your red wagon: *Tristano, Lennie* / Algo bueno (Woody'n you): *Gillespie, Dizzy* / Overtime: *Metronome All Stars* / My heart stood still: *Peterson, Oscar Trio*
CD ______ 9026687792
RCA Victor / Jul '97 / BMG

RCA VICTOR 80TH ANNIVERSARY VOL.4 (The First Label In Jazz 1950-1959)
Roses of Picardy: *Norvo, Red Septet* / Tijuana gift shop: *Mingus, Charles* / Two degrees East, three degrees West: *Lewis, John* / Chiquito loco: *Rogers, Shorty Orchestra & Art Pepper* / Crimea river: *Cohn, Al & Zoot Sims* / Love me or leave me: *Allen, Henry 'Red' All Stars* / Concerto for Billy The Kid: *Russell, George Smalltet & Bill Evans* / Sunday afternoon: *Carter, Benny Orchestra* / Let me love you: *Horne, Lena* / Coscrane: *Powell, Bud Trio* / Perdido: *Ellington, Duke Orchestra* / Moanin': *Blakey, Art & The Jazz Messengers* / I love Paris: *Hawkins, Coleman & Manny Albam Orchestra*

CD ____ **09026687802**
RCA Victor / Aug '97 / BMG

RCA VICTOR 80TH ANNIVERSARY VOL.5 (1960-1969)
Without a song: *Rollins, Sonny* / All the things you are: *Desmond, Paul & Gerry Mulligan* / Hello young lovers: *Burton, Gary Quartet* / After all: *Ellington, Duke & His Orchestra* / Sounds of the night: *Terry, Clark Quintet* / Very thought of you: *Hodges, Johnny* / So what: *Johnson, J.J. Orchestra* / Imagination: *Desmond, Paul* / Star eyes: *Baker, Chet* / Old folks: *McLean, Jackie Quartet* / One o'clock jump: *Lambert, Hendricks/Bavan* / Round midnight: *Rollins, Sonny & Co.* / Turn me loose: *Hampton, Lionel & His All-Star Alumni Big Band*
CD ____ **09026687812**
RCA Victor / Sep '97 / BMG

RE-SEARCH PRESENTS INCREDIBLY STRANGE MUSIC VOL.2
CD ____ **EFA 709512**
Asphodel / Sep '96 / Cargo / SRD

REACT TEST VOL.1
CD ____ **REACTCD 31**
React / Nov '93 / Arabesque / Prime / Vital

REACT TEST VOL.2
CD ____ **REACTCD 052**
React / Nov '94 / Arabesque / Prime / Vital

REACT TEST VOL.3
Joanna: *Mrs. Wood* / Shinny: *Elevator* / Magic: *Blu Peter* / Sugar shack: *Seb* / Orange theme: *Cygnus X* / Tip of the iceberg: *GTO* / Spirit: *Kitachi* / Witch doktor: *Van Helden, Armand* / Untitled: *Sharp Tools* / PARTY: *Movin' Melodies* / Do me: *Aquarius* / Bring it back 2 luv: *Project*
CD ____ **REACTCD 070**
React / Nov '95 / Arabesque / Prime / Vital

REACT TEST VOL.4
Shoenberg: *Marmion* / Flagship: *Blu Peter* / Whodunnit: *Mrs. Wood* / Hopper: *Armadillo* / Amphetamine: *Trope* / Ignition: *Madame Dubois* / Sparkling: *Little Matt* / Scratch: *Kitachi* / Sabor de verano: *Padilla, Jose* / Indoctrinate: *Castle Trancelot* / TMF 61: *Fowlkes, Eddie 'Flashin'* / Do it to me: *Dark, Frankie*
CD ____ **REACTCD 081**
React / Jun '96 / Arabesque / Prime / Vital

REACT TEST VOL.5
Heartbreak: *Mrs. Wood* / Pictures in your mind: *Blu Peter* / Rainbow islands: *Seb* / Magnitude 7: *Sonic Animation* / Fusion pt.II: *Atkins, Juan* / Heavyweight: *Kitachi* / Enlightenment: *Aldo Bender* / In my brain: *Mark NRG* / Transamazonia: *Shamen* / Walking on air: *Padilla, Jose* / Mighty machine: *Dream Plant* / Jus a lil' dope: *Masters At Work*
CD ____ **REACTCD 092**
React / Nov '96 / Arabesque / Prime / Vital

REACT TEST VOL.6
Age of love: *Age Of Love* / Fever: *SJ* / Evil queen: *Shimmon & Woolfson* / Vertigo: *Transcendental Experience* / Force: *Garnier, Laurent* / E dancer: *Saunderson, Kevin* / Ohm: *Wamdue Kids* / Disco hall: *Crump, Harrison* / I'm the baddest bitch: *Bell, Norma Jean* / Remember me: *Blue Boy* / Night's interlude: *Nightmares On Wax* / You got the love: *Source & Candi Staton*
CD ____ **REACTCD 108**
React / Aug '97 / Arabesque / Prime / Vital

REACTIVATE VOL.10
Osaka acid: *Sushi* / Lost in love: *Legend B* / First rebirth: *Jones & Stephenson* / Access: *X-Trax* / Ready to flow: *Urban Trance Plant* / Sizzling love: *PHI* / Ice man on the beach: *Pan & Trex* / Que vous etez: *Friends, Lovers & Family* / Can't stop: *Komakino* / Superstitious: *Luxor* / Point zero: *Li Kwan* / Cybertrance: *Blue Alphabet* / Flagship: *Blu Peter* / Mighty machine: *Dream Plant* / Octopus: *Art Of Trance* / Under siege: *Project X* / Acid NRG: *NRG Jams* / Future world: *Cenobyte*
CD ____ **REACTCD 060**
React / May '95 / Arabesque / Prime / Vital

REACTIVATE VOL.10 - REMIX
CD ____ **REACTCDX 060**
React / May '95 / Arabesque / Prime / Vital

REACTIVATE VOL.11 (Stinger Beats And Techno Rays/2CD/3LP Set)
Rainbow islands: *Seb* / Positivity's knirvana: *Positivity* / Evolver: *De Niro* / This is for: *Albion* / Tribe: *Hoschi* / Borg destroyer: *Kinetic A.T.O.M.* / Aura infinity: *Acid Bottle* / Believer: *DJ Energy* / Whiplash: *Overcharge & G.Meter* / Blow your mind: *Gargano, Pablo* / Ultrafilter: *RND* / Accelerate: *Zzino* / Give it to me: *Choci & DJ E.C.* / Planet hunters: *Third Men* / Techidat: *Pro Active* / Gospel 2000: *16C+* / Strings of heaven: *DJ Jamo & Jack Knives* / U: *DJ Scot Project* / Gonna getcha: *Fierce Child* / Accident: *Skylab* / Yum yum: *Baby Doc* / Rok da house: *Wicked Wipe*
CD ____ **REACTCDX 088**
CD Set ____ **REACTCD 088**
React / Oct '96 / Arabesque / Prime / Vital

REACTIVATE VOL.12 (2CD Set)
Arms of heaven: *Sunbeam* / Evil Queen: *Shimmon & Woolfson* / Chemical air: *Mark 1* / Wise man: *Tsunami* / Waters: *Taucher* / Everyones future: *Gargano, Pablo* / Trance in Saigon: *Gargano, Pablo* / Sound: *De Donatis* / Pandomia: *DJ Randy* / Prophase: *Transa* / Remember last summer: *Extract* / Up-Riser: *Quake-X* / Axis: *Nuclear Hyde* / One million faces: *Incisions* / Flowtation: *De Moor, Vincent* / Pipeman: *Nomination 1* / Groovebird: *Natural Born Groovers* / Roadrunner: *Mach 1* / Tune in turn out: *Obsessive* / Greetings from the exile: *Tranceliner* / Pili Pili: *M*
CD ____ **REACTCDX 102**
CD Set ____ **REACTCD 102**
React / Jun '97 / Arabesque / Prime / Vital

REACTIVATE VOL.8
CD ____ **REACTCD 027**
React / Oct '93 / Arabesque / Prime / Vital

REACTIVATE VOL.9
CD ____ **REACTCD 044**
React / Jul '94 / Arabesque / Prime / Vital

READING FESTIVAL '73
Hands off: *Gallagher, Rory* / Feathered friends: *Greenslade* / Losing you: *Faces* / Earth mother: *Duncan, Lesley* / Hang onto a dream: *Hardin, Tim* / Person to person: *Hardin, Tim* / Roadrunner: *Strider* / Don't waste my time: *Status Quo* / Long legged Linda: *Bown, Andy*
CD ____ **SEECD 343**
See For Miles/C5 / Mar '92 / Pinnacle

READY STEADY GO & WIN
Hyde 'n' seek: *Thyrds* / I'll miss you: *Harbour Lights* / Bo Street runner: *Bo Street Runners* / Did you ever hear the sound: *Knight, Tony & The Livewires* / Lonely one: *Deltones & Tony Lane* / She loves to be loved: *Falling Leaves* / Our love feels new: *Echolettes* / You make me go 'oooh': *Dynamos* / Not guilty: *Falling Leaves* / And I do what I want: *Bo Street Runners* / Tell me what you're gonna do: *Bo Street Runners* / I'm leaving you: *Royal, Jimmy & The Hawkes* / So much love: *Planets* / Every time I look at you: *Five Aces* / Anytime: *Scene Five* / Ain't it a shame: *Vibrons* / Mistletoe love: *Fenda, Jaymes & The Vulcans* / Think of me: *Olympics* / You've come back: *Leasides* / Only girl: *Fenda, Jaymes & The Vulcans* / Get out of my way: *Bo Street Runners* / Baby never say goodbye: *Bo Street Runners*
CD ____ **SEECD 202**
See For Miles/C5 / Feb '92 / Pinnacle

REAL AUTHENTIC SOUND OF STUDIO ONE, THE
Musically crucial: *Earl 16* / Gimme fe me corn: *Martin, Horace* / Who beg no get: *Little John* / So secure: *Griffith, Hugh* / Dance hall session: *Griffith, Hugh* / Sweetheart: *Ellis, Hortense* / Predicting your future: *Livingston, Carlton* / Get your green card: *Jarrett, Mikey* / Jamaican Collie: *Dillinger* / Asking you to leave: *Brown, Barry* / Thank you Jah: *Michigan & Smiley* / Africa here I come: *McGregor, Freddie* / Full up: *Wild Mix* / What a gwan: *Tennessee* / Three mile shank: *Lone Ranger* / Rub a dub dub with feeling: *Paul, Frankie* / New give up: *Ethiopians*
CD ____ **RASCD 9001**
Ras / Mar '97 / Direct / Greensleeves / Jet Star / SRD

REAL BIRTH OF FUSION, THE
Miles runs the voodoo down: *Davis, Miles* / Birds of fire: *Mahavishnu Orchestra* / Cucumber slumber: *Weather Report* / Chameleon: *Hancock, Herbie* / Silly putty: *Clarke, Stanley* / Mr. Spock: *Williams, Tony* / Sorceress: *Corea, Chick & Return To Forever* / Opus Pocus: *Pastorius, Jaco* / Phenomenon:compulsion: *McLaughlin, John*
CD ____ **4841452**
Columbia / Aug '96 / Sony

REAL BLACK RHYTHM
CD ____ **STCD 1156**
Collector/White Label / May '97 / TKO Magnum

REAL BLUES BALLADS, THE
CD ____ **MPV 5513**
Movieplay / Jun '95 / Target/BMG

REAL DEAL VOL.1
CD ____ **CDRAID 514**
Rumour / Feb '94 / 3mv/Sony / Mo's Music Machine / Pinnacle

REAL DEAL VOL.2
CD ____ **CDRAID 517**
Rumour / May '94 / 3mv/Sony / Mo's Music Machine / Pinnacle

REAL ESTATE
CD ____ **ECD 1015**
ReR/Recommended / Jul '91 / ReR Megacorp / RTM/Disc

REAL EXCELLO R&B, THE
Little queen bee (got a brand new king): *Harpo, Slim* / I need money (keep your alibis): *Harpo, Slim* / Still rainin' in my heart: *Harpo, Slim* / I tried so hard: *Smith, Whispering* / Cryin' blues: *Smith, Whispering* / I'm goin' in the valley: *Hogan, Silas* / Dark clouds rollin': *Hogan, Silas* / I'm so glad: *Austin, Leon* / I had a dream last night: *Lonesome Sundown* / She's my crazy little baby: *Lonesome Sundown* / Goin' crazy over TV: *Anderson, Jimmy* / You're playin' hookey: *Lonesome Sundown* / It's love baby: *Gaines, Earl* / Nothing in this world (gonna keep you from me): *Anderson, Jimmy* / Let's play house: *Gunter, Arthur* / Winter time blues: *Lightnin' Slim* / Pleasin' for love: *Shelton, Roscoe* / Whoa now: *Lazy Lester* / It's your voodoo working: *Sheffield, Charles 'Mad Dog'* / Rock-a-me all night long: *Nelson, Jay* / Leavin' Tennessee: *Garner, Alan* / Baby, kiss me gain: *Sweet Clifford* / Crazy over you: *Shelton, Roscoe* / Baby I'm stickin' to you: *Friday, Charles*
CD ____ **CDCHD 562**
Ace / Nov '94 / Pinnacle

REAL INTELLIGENCE VOL.2
CD ____ **RI 041CD**
Rather Interesting / Dec '96 / Plastic Head

REAL MUSIC BOX, THE (25 Years Of Rounder Records/9CD Set)
CD Set ____ **ROUCDAN 25**
Rounder / Feb '96 / ADA / CM / Direct

REAL MUSIC OF PERU, THE
Maria Alejandrina: *Picaflor De Los Andes* / Un pasajero en el camino: *Picaflor De Los Andes* / Fiesta de mayo: *Picaflor De Los Andes* / Aguas del Rio Rimac: *Picaflor De Los Andes* / Carrito de pasajos: *Picaflor De Los Andes* / Verbenita, verbenita: *La Pallasquinta* / Oreganito: *La Pallasquinta* / El guapachoso: *Orquesta Sensacion Del Mantaro* / Llorando a mares: *Flor Pucarina* / Airampito: *Flor Pucarina* / Noche de luna: *Flor Pucarina* / Para que quiero la vida: *Flor Pucarina* / Pichiusita: *Flor Pucarina* / Rompe Macarios: *Orquesta Los Tarumas De Tarma* / Alianza Corazon: *Orquesta Los Tarumas De Tarma* / Dos Clavelles: *La Princesita De Yungay* / Tus ojos: *Los Borbones Del Peru* / Ya te gane: *Orquesta Los Rebeldes De Huancayo*
CD ____ **CDORBD 064**
Globestyle / Feb '91 / Pinnacle

REAL RUMBA FROM CUBA
CD ____ **CO 110**
Corason / May '96 / ADA / CM / Direct

REAL SOUND OF JAZZ, THE
CD ____ **LS 2912**
Landscape / Nov '92 / THE

REAL STONES
Come on: *Berry, Chuck* / I just want to be loved: *Waters, Muddy* / Bye bye Johnny: *Berry, Chuck* / You better move on: *Alexander, Arthur* / Money: *Strong, Barrett* / Route 66: *Berry, Chuck* / Carol: *Berry, Chuck* / Mona: *Diddley, Bo* / Fortune teller: *Spellman, Benny* / Confessin' the blues: *Berry, Chuck* / Around and around: *Berry, Chuck* / Don't lie to me: *Berry, Chuck* / Memphis: *Berry, Chuck* / Roadrunner: *Diddley, Bo* / Roll over Beethoven: *Berry, Chuck* / Cops and robbers: *Diddley, Bo* / Down the road apiece: *Diddley, Bo* / I can't be satisfied: *Waters, Muddy* / You can't catch me: *Berry, Chuck* / Suzie Q: *Hawkins, Dale* / Little red rooster: *Howlin' Wolf* / Talkin' about you: *Berry, Chuck* / Look what you've done: *Waters, Muddy* / Little Queenie: *Berry, Chuck* / Let it rock: *Berry, Chuck* / Run Rudolph run: *Berry, Chuck* / Crackin' up: *Diddley, Bo* / I'm a man: *Diddley, Bo* / Rollin' stone: *Waters, Muddy*
CD ____ **PRD 70122**
Provogue / Dec '89 / Pinnacle

REAL WORLD SAMPLER 1995
Le voyageur: *Papa Wemba* / Hazo avo: *Rossy* / Mwanuni: *Eyuphuro* / Al nahla al 'Ali: *Eyuphuro* / Shahbaaz qalandar: *Khan, Nusrat Fateh Ali* / Ya sahib-ul-Jamal: *Sabri Brothers* / Nibiro ghon andare: *Sabri Brothers* / Raga bhairavi: *Sridhar, K. & K Shivakumar* / Enchantment: *Chandra, Sheila* / Sgariunt na Gcompanagh (The parting of friends): *Malloy, Matt*
CD ____ **RWSAM 4**
Realworld / Oct '95 / EMI

REALWORLD PRESENTS...
CD ____ **RWSAM 1**
Realworld / Jul '94 / EMI

REBEL MUSIC (An Anthology of Reggae Music - 2CD Set)
You don't know: *Andy, Bob* / Loser: *Harriott, Derrick* / High school dance: *McKay, Freddie* / Russians are coming: *Bennett, Val* / Tonight: *Keith & Tex* / Ain't that lovin' you: *U-Roy* / Them a fe get a beatin': *Tosh, Peter* / God helps the man: *Smart, Leroy* / Hypocrite: *Heptones* / S90 skank: *Big Youth* / Hard tighter: *Little Roy* / Eedding skank: *Brown, Glen* / Anywhere but nowhere: *White, K.C.* / Beat down Babylon: *Byles, Junior* / Concentration: *Brown, Dennis* / Screaming target: *Big Youth* / Slaving: *Parkes, Lloyd* / You are my angel: *Andy, Horace* / Melody maker: *Hudson, Keith* / Money in my pocket: *Brown, Dennis* / Cheater: *Brown, Dennis* / Blackman time: *I-Roy* / Satan side: *Andy, Horace & Earl Flute* / Give praises: *Big Youth* / Rock away: *Isaacs, Gregory* / Saturday night special: *Dyke, Michael* / Cool rasta: *Heptones*
CD Set ____ **CDTRD 403**
Trojan / Mar '94 / Direct / Jet Star

REBEL ROCKABILLY
CD ____ **RAUCD 019**
Raucous / Jun '96 / Nervous / RTM/Disc / TKO Magnum

REBIRTH OF COOL VOL.2
I've lost my ignorance (and don't know where to find it): *Dream Warriors* / La raza: *Kid Frost* / Senga abele (lion roar): *Dibango, Manu & MC Mello* / Cool and funky: *Jordan, Ronny* / I should've known better: *Paris, Mica* / All for one: *Brand Nubian* / One to grow on: *UMC's* / Family: *McKoy* / Try my love: *Washburn, Lalomie* / Kickin' jazz: *Outlaw* / Looking at the front door: *Main Source* / Free your feelings: *Slam Slam* / Go with the flow: *Rock, Pete & C.L. Smooth* / Set me free: *Bygraves* / Black whip: *Chapter & Verse* / Slow jam: *Dodge City Productions*
CD ____ **BRCD 582**
4th & Broadway / Feb '92 / PolyGram

REBIRTH OF COOL VOL.3
CD ____ **BRCD 590**
4th & Broadway / Apr '93 / PolyGram

REBIRTH OF COOL VOL.4
Just wanna touch her: *DJ Krush* / Play my funk: *Simple E* / Rent strike: *Groove Collective* / R U conscious: *Buchanan, Courtney* / My favourite things: *Jordan, Ronny* / Otha fish: *Pharcyde* / Cantamilla: *Tranquility Bass* / Aftermath: *Tricky* / Earthsong: *Batu* / Cool like the blues: *Warfield, Justin* / Straight plays: *F-Mob* / Crazy: *Outside* / Spock with a beard: *Palmskin Productions* / World mutations: *Tone Productions* / Tree, air and rain on Earth: *Mondo Grosso* / Great men's dub: *Burning Spear* / Soul of the people: *Bread & Butter*
CD ____ **BRCD 607**
4th & Broadway / Jun '94 / PolyGram

REBIRTH OF COOL VOL.5 (Subterranean Abstract Blues)
Friendly pressure: *Jhelisa* / Eine kleine hedmusik: *Coldcut* / Karmacoma: *Massive Attack* / Boundaries: *Conquest, Leena* / Whipping boy: *Harper, Ben* / Deep shit: *Kruder & Dorfmeister* / Hell is round the corner: *Tricky* / Turn on, tune in, find joy: *Freakpower* / Revenge of the number: *Portishead* / Bug powder dust: *Bomb The Bass* / United Future Airlines: *United Future Organisation* / Iniquity worker: *D-Note* / Release yo'delf: *Method Man* / Kosmos: *Weller, Paul* / Nouveau Western: *MC Solaar* / Get it together: *Beastie Boys*
CD ____ **BRCD 617**
4th & Broadway / Jul '95 / PolyGram

REBIRTH OF COOL VOL.6 (On Higher Sound)
Underwater love: *Smoke City* / Claire: *IO* / To forgive but not forget: *Outside* / You are Heaven sent: *Nicolette* / Cotton wool: *Lamb* / Horizons: *LTJ Bukem* / Migration: *Sawhney, Nitin* / Ponteio: *Da Lata* / Jazz garage: *Akasha* / Feel the sunshine: *Reece, Alex* / Surfin': *Ranglin, Ernest* / Who could it be: *Luciano & Jungle Brothers* / Bittersweet: *Taylor, Lewis* / Street player: *DJ Pulse & The Jazz Cartel* / Rudiments: *Angel, Dave*
CD ____ **BRCD 620**
4th & Broadway / Aug '96 / PolyGram

RECOLLECTIONS OF 1945 (Vocalists)
I begged her: *Sinatra, Frank* / I'll close my eyes: *Squires, Dorothy* / There I've said it again: *Hutchinson, Leslie 'Hutch'* / Accentuate the positive: *Crosby, Bing & Andrews Sisters* / Together: *Layton, Turner* / There goes that song again: *Hall, Adelaide* / I'm so alone: *Conway, Steve* / Gipsy: *Squires, Dorothy* / Kiss me again: *Sinatra, Frank* / My dreams are getting better all the time: *Lynn, Vera* / It could happen to you: *Crosby, Bing* / Laura: *Shelton, Anne* / Dream: *Hutchinson, Leslie 'Hutch'* / I fall in love too easily: *Sinatra, Frank* / Coming home: *Squires, Dorothy* / June comes round every year: *Green, Johnny* / Pablo the dreamer: *Shelton, Anne* / You're so sweet to remember: *Hutchinson, Leslie 'Hutch'* / I'm gonna love that guy: *Hall, Adelaide* / Moment I saw you: *Conway, Steve* / Out of this world: *Conway, Steve* / Let the rest of the world go by: *Squires, Dorothy*
CD ____ **RAJCD 875**
Empress / May '96 / Koch

RECOLLECTIONS OF 1945 (Dance Bands)
More and more: *Ambrose & His Orchestra* / Accentuate the positive: *Payne, Jack & His Orchestra* / I should care: *Winstone, Eric & His Orchestra* / Laura: *Gibbons, Carroll & Savoy Hotel Orpheans* / You moved right in: *Roy, Harry & His Band* / Saturday night: *Silvester, Victor & His Jive Orchestra* / Let him go let him tarry: *Loss, Joe & His Orchestra* / No one else will do: *Geraldo & His Orchestra* / Bell bottom trousers: *Payne, Jack & His Orchestra* / Candy: *Roy, Harry & His Band* / Dream: *Geraldo & His Orchestra* / I walked in: *Winstone, Eric & His Orchestra* / There I've said it again: *Loss, Joe & His Orchestra* / I'm gonna love that guy: *Winstone, Eric & His Orchestra* / Ma-Ma: *Gonella, Nat & His Georgians* / Trolly song: *Geraldo & His Orchestra* / Little on the lonely side: *Geraldo & His Orchestra* / Robin Hood: *Geraldo & His Orchestra* / Can't you read between the lines: *Geraldo & His Orchestra* / Can't help singing: *Ambrose & His Orchestra* / Gipsy: *Roy, Harry & His Orchestra* / You belong to

my heart: *Gibbons, Carroll & Savoy Hotel Orpheans* / Just a prayer away: *Payne, Jack & His Orchestra*
CD ______ RAJCD 876
Empress / May '96 / Koch

RECORD FACTORY IN THE JUNGLE
CD ______ 792502
Melodie / Apr '96 / ADA / Discovery / Grapevine/PolyGram / Greensleeves / Jet Star

RECORD MIRROR PRESENTS COOL CUTS
Reaching up: *Oscar G & Marck Michel* / Feel my body: *O'Moiraghi, Frank & Amnesia* / Got myself together: *Bucketheads* / Everybody needs a 303: *Fatboy Slim* / Keep hope alive: *Crystal Method* / Forerunner: *Natural Born Groovers* / Race of survival: *Sonz Of Soul & Steven Ville* / Change: *Daphne* / Freedom: *Lil' Louis* / Is this the rhythm: *Rhythm & Vibe* / Another day: *Sledge, Kathy* / Happy days: *Sweet Mercy & Joe Roberts*
CD ______ CDLIV 1
Skratch / Feb '96 / 3mv/Sony

RECYCLE OR DIE SAMPLER
CD ______ RODWOM
Recycle Or Die / Jun '96 / Kudos

RED BIRD SOUND VOL.1
Chapel of love: *Dixie Cups* / Ain't that nice: *Dixie Cups* / People say: *Dixie Cups* / Girls can tell: *Dixie Cups* / You should've seen the way he looked at me: *Dixie Cups* / No true love: *Dixie Cups* / Little bell: *Dixie Cups* / Another boy like mine: *Dixie Cups* / Iko iko: *Dixie Cups* / Gee baby gee: *Dixie Cups* / Gee the moon is shining bright: *Dixie Cups* / I'm gonna get you yet: *Dixie Cups* / All grown up: *Dixie Cups* / Thank you Mama, thank you Papa: *Dixie Cups* / Wrong direction: *Dixie Cups* / I wanna love him so bad: *Jellybeans* / So long: *Jellybeans* / Baby be mine: *Jellybeans* / Kind of boy you can't forget: *Jellybeans* / Chapel of love: *Jellybeans* / Here she comes: *Jellybeans* / Ain't love a funny thing: *Jellybeans* / Whisper sweet things: *Jellybeans* / Goodnight baby: *Jellybeans* / Doo wah diddy diddy: *Jellybeans* / He's gone: *Jellybeans* / Goodnight baby: *Butterflys* / Swim: *Butterflys* / I wonder: *Butterflys* / Gee baby gee: *Butterflys*
CD ______ GEMCD 003
Diamond / Dec '96 / Pinnacle

RED BIRD STORY, THE (2CD Set)
Chapel of love: *Dixie Cups* / I wanna love him so bad: *Jellybeans* / People say: *Dixie Cups* / Remember (walkin' in the sand): *Shangri-Las* / Goodnight baby: *Butterflies* / Leader of the pack: *Shangri-Las* / Gee baby gee: *Dixie Cups* / Iko iko: *Dixie Cups* / Give him a great big kiss: *Shangri-Las* / Gee the moon is shining bright: *Dixie Cups* / I can never go home anymore: *Shangri-Las* / Boy from New York City: *Ad Libs* / Give us your blessing: *Shangri-Las* / He ain't no angel: *Ad Libs* / Past, present and future: *Shangri-Las* / I'm just a down home girl: *Ad Libs* / Down home girl: *Robinson, Alvin* / I hurt on the other side: *Barnes, Sidney* / Something you got: *Robinson, Alvin* / Bad as they come: *Hawkins, Sam* / Let the good times roll: *Hawkins, Sam* / Come on baby: *Hawkins, Sam* / Fever: *Robinson, Alvin* / Go now: *Banks, Bessie* / Bossa nova baby: *Tippie & The Clovers* / My heart said (the bossa nova): *Tippie & The Clovers* / I can't let go: *Sands, Evie* / Take me for a little while: *Sands, Evie* / Standing by: *Warwick, Dee Dee* / I don't think my baby's coming back: *Warwick, Dee Dee* / New York's a lonely town: *Tradewinds* / I know it's alright: *Jeff & Ellie*
CD Set ______ CDLAB 105
Charly / Apr '96 / Koch

RED EYE APPETISER
CD ______ REDCD 32
Red Eye / Mar '94 / Direct

RED HEAVEN (20 Of The Best From The Cherry Red Label)
It's a fine day: *Jane* / An MP speaks: *McCarthy* / Plain sailing: *Thorn, Tracey* / Everybody's problem: *Pulp* / On my mind: *Marine Girls* / Sunbursts in: *Eyeless In Gaza* / Xoyo: *Passage* / All about you: *Leer, Thomas* / Nicky: *Momus* / Black cat: *Bolan, Marc* / Watery song: *Deebank, Maurice* / Trial of Doctor Fancy: *King Of Luxembourg* / Night and day: *Everything But The Girl* / If she doesn't smile: *Fantastic Something* / Walter and John: *Watt, Ben & Robert Wyatt* / Jet set junta: *Monochrome Set* / Parafin brain: *Nightingales* / This brilliant evening: *In Embrace* / You Mary you: *Philippe, Louis* / Reach for your gun: *Bid*
CD ______ NTMCD 520
Nectar / Jan '96 / Pinnacle

RED HOT AND COUNTRY
CD ______ 5226392
Polydor / Oct '94 / PolyGram

RED HOT BLUES
CD ______ MACCD 198
Autograph / Aug '96 / BMG

RED HOT JAZZ
CD ______ AVM 533
Avid / May '94 / Avid/BMG / Koch / THE

RED HOT REGGAE (18 Original Hits/ 3CD Set)
Don't look back (you've gotta walk): *Tosh, Peter* / Sideshow: *Biggs, Barry* / Girlie girlie: *George, Sophia* / Cool and deadly: *Eastwood & Saint* / Gal wine: *Chaka Demus & Pliers* / Cocaine: *Dillinger* / Everything I own: *Boy George* / Bush doctor: *Tosh, Peter* / Gimme hope Jo'anna: *Grant, Eddy* / Feel my riddim: *Skibby* / Someone loves you honey: *T-Spoon* / I want to wake up with you: *Gardiner, Boris* / No woman no cry: *Marley, Kymani* / Nightshift: *Groovy, Winston* / Israelites: *Dekker, Desmond* / It keeps rainin' (tears from my eyes): *McLean, Bitty* / Amigo: *Black Slate* / Do you really want to hurt me: *Culture Club*
CD Set ______ LAD 873862
Disky / Nov '96 / Disky / THE

RED HOT ROCKABILLY VOL.1
Hip shakin' mama / Bip bop boom / Look out Mabel / Grits / Sunglasses after dark / Okies in the pokie / Hot dog / Made in the shade / Down on the farm / Fool / Oakie boogie / Blue swingin' mama
CD ______ CDMF 030
Magnum Force / Jul '90 / TKO Magnum

RED HOT ROCKABILLY VOL.7
Rock 'n' roll on a Saturday night / Rock-a-sock a hop / Grandma rock 'n' roll / Servant of love / Knocking on the backside / Walking and a' strolling / Black Cadillac / DJ blues / Don't cry little darling / Linda Lou / Teenage lover / So help me gal / Snake eyed woman / Depression blues / Quick sand love / Nicotine
CD ______ CDMF 069
Magnum Force / Aug '89 / TKO Magnum

RED HOT ROCKABILLY VOL.8
Forty nine women / That'll get it / Lonely heart / Clickety clack / Satellite hop / Dig that crazy driver / My baby's still rockin' / Crawdad hole / Go go heart / You bet I do / It hurts the one who loves you / Puppy love / No doubt about it / Roll over Beethoven / No. 9 train / Rock on Mabel / Long tall Sally / Jitterbuggin' baby / One way ticket / Elvis stole my gal / Fool about you / You don't mean to make me cry / Tore up / Jackson dog / Move over Rover
CD ______ CDMF 082
Magnum Force / Feb '92 / TKO Magnum

RED RIVER BLUES 1934-1943
CD ______ TMCD 08
Travellin' Man / '92 / Hot Shot / Jazz Music / Wellard

REDISCOVERED BLUES VOL.2 (2CD Set)
You can't be lucky all the time: *Sykes, Roosevelt* / Sweet old Chicago: *Sykes, Roosevelt* / Jailbait: *Sykes, Roosevelt* / Bloodstains: *Sykes, Roosevelt* / Hush oh hush: *Sykes, Roosevelt* / Cannonball: *Sykes, Roosevelt* / I'm tired: *Sykes, Roosevelt* / Crazy fox: *Sykes, Roosevelt* / Direct South: *Sunnyland Slim* / Wake up in the morning: *Sunnyland Slim* / Driftin' blues: *Sunnyland Slim* / Puppy love: *Sunnyland Slim* / New B & O blues: *Sunnyland Slim* / Midnight special: *Sunnyland Slim* / In the evening: *Sunnyland Slim* / Meet me in the bottom: *Sunnyland Slim* / Wee wee baby: *Sunnyland Slim* / I'm the one: *Sunnyland Slim* / You used to love me: *Bumble Bee Slim* / My past life: *Bumble Bee Slim* / She's got a thing going on: *Bumble Bee Slim* / Substitute woman: *Bumble Bee Slim* / Canada walk: *Bumble Bee Slim* / Blue & lonesome: *Bumble Bee Slim* / Goin' back to Memphis: *Bumble Bee Slim* / Blue & lonesome: *Bumble Bee Slim* / Dust my broom: *Bumble Bee Slim* / Come day, go day: *Bumble Bee Slim* / Well alright: *Bumble Bee Slim* / Devil is a busy man: *Bumble Bee Slim* / Pinetop's boogie woogie: *Bumble Bee Slim* / Goin' back to Memphis: *Bumble Bee Slim* / Dust my broom: *Bumble Bee Slim* / Unlucky one: *Bumble Bee Slim* / Canada walk: *Bumble Bee Slim* / Jumpin' after midnight: *Bumble Bee Slim* / Hot house stuff: *Bumble Bee Slim* / Got to get my baby: *Sunnyland Slim* / Miss Bessie Mae: *Sunnyland Slim* / Everytime I get to drinkin': *Sunnyland Slim* / Midnight stomp: *Sunnyland Slim* / Little girl blues: *Sunnyland Slim* / I don't worry: *Crudup, Arthur 'Big Boy'* / Room & board: *Crudup, Arthur 'Big Boy'* / Long curly mane: *Crudup, Arthur 'Big Boy'* / Reebuck man: *Crudup, Arthur 'Big Boy'* / Before you go: *Crudup, Arthur 'Big Boy'* / Boogie in the morning: *Crudup, Arthur 'Big Boy'* / What are you trying to do: *Crudup, Arthur 'Big Boy'* / Burying ground: *Crudup, Arthur 'Big Boy'* / Death Valley blues: *Crudup, Arthur 'Big Boy'* / Kerrina Kerrina: *Crudup, Arthur 'Big Boy'*
CD Set ______ CDEM 1588
Premier/EMI / Apr '96 / EMI

REEFER SONGS (23 Original Jazz and Blues Vocals)
CD ______ JASSCD 7
Jass / Oct '91 / ADA / Cadillac / CM / Direct / Jazz Music

REFERENCE JAZZ
CD ______ RRS 2CD
Reference Recordings / '91 / Jazz Music / May Audio

REFLECTIONS IN THE LOOKING GLASS
CD ______ CLP 9806
Cleopatra / Oct '96 / Cargo / Greyhound / Plastic Head / RTM/Disc / SRD

REGAL RECORDS IN NEW ORLEANS
I'll never be free: *Gayten, Paul* / Yeah yeah yeah: *Gayten, Paul* / You ought to know: *Gayten, Paul* / You shouldn't: *Gayten, Paul* / Confused: *Gayten, Paul* / Bear hug: *Gayten, Paul* / Oooh la la: *Gayten, Paul* / My last goodbye: *Gayten, Paul* / I ain't gonna let you in: *Gayten, Paul* / Kickapoo juice: *Gayten, Paul* / Each time: *Gayten, Paul* / Fishtails: *Gayten, Paul* / Suzette: *Gayten, Paul* / Happy birthday to you: *Gayten, Paul* / For you my love: *Gayten, Paul* / Back trackin' aka Dr. Daddy-o: *Gayten, Paul* / Gold ain't everything: *Gayten, Paul* / Baby what's new: *Laurie, Annie* / My rough and ready man: *Laurie, Annie* / Low down feeling: *Laurie, Annie* / Three times seven equals twenty one: *Laurie, Annie* / I don't marry too soon: *Laurie, Annie* / Messy Bessy: *Bartholomew, Dave* / Nickel wine: *Bartholomew, Dave* / Riding high: *Brown, Roy* / Brand new baby: *Brown, Roy*
CD ______ CDCHD 362
Ace / Jan '92 / Pinnacle

REGGAE 4 U (3CD Set)
CD Set ______ KBOX 371
Collection / Aug '97 / Target/BMG / TKO Magnum

REGGAE 93
Boom shak-a-lak: *Apache Indian* / Tease me: *Chaka Demus & Pliers* / It keeps rainin' (tears from my eyes): *McLean, Bitty* / Sweat (A la la la la long): *Inner Circle* / All that she wants: *Ace Of Base* / Work: *Levy, Barrington* / On and on: *Aswad* / This carry go bring come: *McGregor, Freddie* / Informer: *Snow* / Love of a lifetime: *Tucker, Junior* / Twice my age: *Krystal & Shabba Ranks* / Shout (it out): *Louchie Lou & Michie One* / Big strong girl: *Megaruffian* / Rump shaker: *Nardo Ranks*
CD ______ CIDTV 7
Island / Oct '93 / PolyGram

REGGAE AFRICA
Lion in a sheep skin: *Harley & The Rasta Family* / Amagni: *Dembele, Koko* / Show biz to requin: *Tangara Speed Ghoda* / Veto de dieu: *Alpha Blondy* / Nothing but prayer: *Senzo* / C'est pas da ni blo: *Kassy, Serges* / Wondogbo: *Kouame, Lystrone* / Unlucky man: *Ice T Cool* / Sweet reggae: *Harley & The Rasta Family* / Politic warrior: *Ray, P.I.* / Elle: *Jah Gunt* / Lord say: *Tangara Speed Ghoda* / N'ka yere: *Dembele, Koko* / Children of Africa: *Ismael Isaac Les Freres Keita*
CD ______ CDEMC 3679
Hemisphere / May '94 / EMI

REGGAE ARCHIVE
CD ______ RMCD 203
Rialto / Sep '96 / Disc / Total/BMG

REGGAE ARCHIVE - US
CD ______ RESTLESS 7268
On-U Sound / Aug '94 / Jet Star / SRD

REGGAE ARCHIVES VOL.1
African land/Africa we want to go: *Kalphat, Carol & Clint Eastwood* / African melody: *Dr. Pablo & The Cry Tuff All-Stars* / Dub from creation: *Creation Rebel* / Creation cycle: *Creation Rebel* / Love by everyone/Rebel no devil: *Prince Far-I & DJ Buzz* / Golden locks: *Sherman, Bim* / Slummy ghetto: *Sherman, Bim* / Party time: *Sherman, Bim* / Sweet reggae music: *Holt, Errol* / Barber salon: *Prince Far-I* / African space: *Creation Rebel* / Mother don't cry: *Creation Rebel* / Drum don't talk: *Creation Rebel*
CD ______ ONUCD 21
On-U Sound / Mar '93 / Jet Star / SRD

REGGAE ARCHIVES VOL.2
CD ______ ONUCD 22
On-U Sound / Apr '93 / Jet Star / SRD

REGGAE BABYLON
CD ______ RB 3031
Reggae Best / Mar '95 / Grapevine/ PolyGram

REGGAE BLASTERS VOL.1
CD ______ D 19960
Far I / Sep '96 / Jet Star

REGGAE BLASTERS VOL.2
CD ______ D 19969
Far I / Sep '96 / Jet Star

REGGAE BLASTERS VOL.3
CD ______ D 19970
Far I / Oct '96 / Jet Star

REGGAE BLASTERS VOL.4
CD ______ D 19971
Far I / Oct '96 / Jet Star

REGGAE CELEBRATION
CD ______ D 31517
Far I / Oct '96 / Jet Star

REGGAE CHRISTMAS
Silent night / I saw mommy kiss a dreadlocks / Dub it for Christmas / Santa Claus / Flash your dread / Sensimillia
CD ______ PCD 1422
Profile / Nov '91 / Pinnacle

REGGAE CHRISTMAS
CD ______ CDTRL 364
Trojan / Nov '95 / Direct / Jet Star

REGGAE CHRISTMAS FROM STUDIO ONE
CD ______ HBCD 118
Heartbeat / Nov '92 / ADA / Direct / Greensleeves / Jet Star

REGGAE CLASSICS - SERIOUS SELECTIONS VOL.1
Love the way it should be: *Royal Rasses* / Back a yard: *In Crowd* / Bucket bottom: *Prince Alla* / Here I come: *Brown, Dennis* / Fade away: *Byles, Junior* / No man is an island: *Motion* / Natural collie: *McGregor, Freddie* / Time is the master: *Holt, John* / Easy: *Lindsay, Jimmy* / I'm still waiting: *Wilson, Delroy* / Man in me: *Matumbi* / Mr. Ska Beena: *Ellis, Alton*
CD ______ CDREG 2
Rewind Selecta / Mar '95 / Grapevine/ PolyGram

REGGAE CLASSICS - SERIOUS SELECTIONS VOL.2
CD ______ CDREG 5
Rewind Selecta / Jun '96 / Grapevine/ PolyGram

REGGAE CULTURE
CD ______ HBAN 13CD
Heartbeat / Jul '94 / ADA / Direct / Greensleeves / Jet Star

REGGAE DANCE (15 Red Hot Reggae Hits)
Sweets for my sweet / I can see clearly now / Baby come back / Sweat (a la la la la song) / Don't turn around / Dedicated to the one I love / Baby I love your way / It keeps rainin' tears / Bombastic / Shy guy / Informer / Can't help falling in love / Kingston Town / Sign / All that she wants
CD ______ SUMCD 4061
Summit / Nov '96 / Sound & Media

REGGAE ESSENTIALS
CD ______ 343992
Koch International / Apr '97 / Koch

REGGAE FAVOURITES
Sweat (A la la la la long) / Iron lion zion / Nightshift / Pass the dutchie / Many rivers to cross / Electric avenue / Reggae night / I got you babe / To love somebody / Everything I own / Could you be loved / Red red wine
CD ______ 399010
Koch / Sep '93 / Koch

REGGAE FEELING
CD ______ 322719
Koch / Apr '97 / Koch

REGGAE FEELING VOL.3
CD ______ 3411252
Koch / Aug '94 / Koch

REGGAE FEELINGS
Get up stand up: *Tosh, Peter* / Reggae night: *Cliff, Jimmy* / Pass the cup: *Aswad* / Mr. Loverman: *Shabba Ranks* / Graveyard rock: *Jeffreys, Garland* / Lagos jump: *Third World* / African reggae: *Hagen, Nina* / Strong me strong: *Yellowman* / Love is all: *Cliff, Jimmy* / Legalize it: *Tosh, Peter* / Try jah love: *Third World* / Matador: *Jeffreys, Garland* / Tears on my pillow (I can't take it): *Nash, Johnny* / One love: *Marley, Bob & The Wailers* / Crying, waiting, hoping: *Mason, Dave*
CD ______ 4758312
Columbia / Dec '95 / Sony

REGGAE FEVER
CD ______ EXP 038
Experience / May '97 / TKO Magnum

REGGAE FOR KIDS
CD ______ RASCD 3095
Ras / May '92 / Direct / Greensleeves / Jet Star / SRD

REGGAE FOR LOVERS
Be my friend: *Pinchers* / When: *Pinchers* / Playmate: *Pinchers* / Fever: *Osbourne, Johnny* / Only the strong survive: *Osbourne, Johnny* / Keep on telling me: *Admiral Tibet*
CD ______ DCD 5273
Kenwest / Nov '92 / THE

REGGAE FOR LOVERS
I can't wait: *Sanchez* / Pretty looks: *Sanchez* / Who cares: *Sanchez* / True believer: *Sanchez* / Get ready: *Ricks, Glen* / Sitting in the backseat: *Ricks, Glen* / Closer together: *Ricks, Glen* / Hooked: *Isaacs, Gregory* / Place in your heart: *Garnet Silk* / Move on slow: *Garnet Silk* / 100% of love: *Smart, Leroy* / Body is hear with me: *Smart, Leroy*
CD ______ SUMCD 4110
Sound & Media / Mar '97 / Sound & Media

REGGAE FOR LOVERS
Betcha by golly wow: *Dunkley, Errol* / Give me: *Tony Tuff* / I never knew love: *Chalice* / Girl is mine: *Yellowman & Peter Metro* / True love: *Undivided Roots* / Without love: *Tamlins* / My devotion: *Brown, Junior* / I'm in the mood: *Naturalites* / Nice time: *Don Carlos* / It's you girl: *Prophet, Michael* / How can I: *Holt, John* / Shine eye gal: *Levy, Barrington* / You move me: *Douglas, Keith* / No time to lose: *Campbell, Al* / My time: *Isaacs, Gregory* / My love: *Viceroys*
CD ______ 307642
Hallmark / Jul '97 / Carlton

REGGAE FREEDOM
CD ________ D 31518
Far I / Sep '96 / Jet Star

REGGAE FROM JAMAICA VOL.1 (Redder Than Red)
CD ________ BB 2801
Blue Beat / Dec '94 / Grapevine/PolyGram

REGGAE FROM JAMAICA VOL.2 (Blowin' In The Wind)
CD ________ BB 2802
Blue Beat / Dec '94 / Grapevine/PolyGram

REGGAE FROM JAMAICA VOL.3 (Rock Steady)
CD ________ BB 2803
Blue Beat / Dec '94 / Grapevine/PolyGram

REGGAE FROM JAMAICA VOL.4 (Mellow Mood)
CD ________ BB 2804
Blue Beat / Dec '94 / Grapevine/PolyGram

REGGAE FROM JAMAICA VOL.5 (Girlie Girlie)
CD ________ BB 2805
Blue Beat / Dec '94 / Grapevine/PolyGram

REGGAE FROM JAMAICA VOL.6 (Rivers Of Babylon)
CD ________ BB 2806
Blue Beat / Dec '94 / Grapevine/PolyGram

REGGAE GOLD 1996
CD ________ VPCD 1479
VP / May '96 / Greensleeves / Jet Star / Total/BMG

REGGAE GOLD 1997
CD ________ VPCD 15092
VP / Aug '97 / Greensleeves / Jet Star / Total/BMG

REGGAE GOT SOUL (2CD Set)
Hey love: *Holt, John* / Try once more: *Crucial Vibes* / That's all I want: *Paragons* / Do it sweet: *Edwards, Jackie* / She's faced the hardest times: *Johnson, Anthony* / You are sugar & spice: *Brown, Dennis* / Make it with you: *Minott, Sugar* / Never too much love: *Russell, Devon* / When you're in love with a beautiful woman: *Wilson, Delroy* / In the heart of the city: *Isaacs, Gregory* / Perhaps, perhaps, perhaps: *Scott, Audrey* / Suspicious minds: *Johnson, Anthony* / Tell me now: *Griffiths, Marcia* / Murder in the dancehall: *Isaacs, Gregory* / Children of Israel: *Brown, Dennis* / You got me going crazy: *Wilson, Delroy* / Suzette: *Burrell, Roland* / Sweet Marie: *Edwards, Jackie* / Brother's don't give up: *Isaacs, Gregory* / I need her: *Paragons* / One step forward (& two steps back): *Dillon, Leonard* / Trick on the book: *Campbell, Cornell* / Truly: *Griffiths, Marcia* / Lately girl: *Brown, Dennis* / Lovers paradise: *Brown, Dennis* / Move on up: *Russell, Devon* / Have I told you lately that I love you: *Faith, George* / Spanish Harlem: *Wilson, Delroy* / I'll be lonely: *Holt, John* / Promise to be true: *Isaacs, Gregory* / Where I stand: *Campbell, Cornell* / Wolves & Leopards: *Brown, Dennis* / What's going on: *Wilson, Delroy* / Good thing going: *Minott, Sugar* / Trumpet sounding: *Crucial Vibes* / Do that to me one more time: *Wilson, Delroy*
CD Set ________ 330152
Hallmark / Jul '96 / Carlton

REGGAE GREATEST HITS
CD Set ________ DCD 5068
Disky / Jul '89 / Disky / THE

REGGAE GREATS
CD Set ________ TFP 019
Tring / Nov '92 / Tring

REGGAE HEAT (2CD Set)
Baby I love your way: *Big Mountain* / Living on the front line: *Grant, Eddy* / I can see clearly now: *Nash, Johnny* / Ghost town: *Specials* / Monkey man: *Toots & The Maytals* / You can get it if you really want: *Dekker, Desmond* / Tears of a clown: *Beat* / Uptown top rankin': *Althia & Donna* / Young, gifted and black: *Bob & Marcia* / I wanna wake up with you: *Gardiner, Boris* / Funky Kingston: *Toots & The Maytals* / Think twice: *Marie, Donna* / Suzanne beware of the devil: *Livingstone, Dandy* / I don't wanna dance: *Grant, Eddy* / Israelites: *Dekker, Desmond* / Hurt so good: *Cadogan, Susan* / Love of the common people: *Thomas, Nicky* / Stir it up: *Nash, Johnny* / In the dard: *Toots & The Maytals* / Many rivers to cross: *Cliff, Jimmy* / Small axe: *Marley, Bob & The Wailers* / Montego Bay: *Notes, Freddie* / I shot the sherrif: *Inner Circle* / Everything I own: *Boothe, Ken* / Good thing going: *Minott, Sugar* / Rivers of Babylon: *Melodians* / 007: *Dekker, Desmond* / Message to you Rudy: *Specials* / Money in my pocket: *Brown, Dennis* / Gal wine: *Chaka Demus & Pliers* / Know your culture: *Big Mountain* / Let your yeah be yeah: *Pioneers* / Mad about you: *Ruffin, Bruce* / Wonderful world, beautiful people: *Cliff, Jimmy* / Wondering wanderer: *Misty In Roots* / You gotta walk (don't look back): *Tosh, Peter*
CD Set ________ RCACD 205
RCA / Jul '97 / BMG

REGGAE HITS
Don't look back (you've gotta walk): *Tosh, Peter* / Amigo: *Black Slate* / Money in my pocket: *Brown, Dennis* / Gimme hope Jo'anna: *Grant, Eddy* / Wonderful world, beautiful people: *Cliff, Jimmy* / Do you really want to hurt me: *Culture Club* / OK Fred: *Dunkley, Errol* / Girlie girlie: *George, Sophia* / Midnight rider: *Davidson, Paul* / I want to wake up with you: *Gardiner, Boris* / Israelites: *Dekker, Desmond* / Could you be loved: *Thomas, Ruddy* / Mockingbird hill: *Migil 5* / Nightshift: *Groovy, Winston*
CD ________ WLT 874582
Disky / Nov '96 / Disky / THE

REGGAE HITS BOX SET VOL.4
CD Set ________ RHBCD 4
Jet Star / Nov '95 / Jet Star

REGGAE HITS BOX SET VOL.5
CD Set ________ RHBCD 5
Jet Star / Nov '95 / Jet Star

REGGAE HITS BOX SET VOL.6
CD Set ________ RHBCD 6
Jet Star / Nov '95 / Jet Star

REGGAE HITS VOL.1
Under me sensi: *Levy, Barrington* / Herbman hustling: *Minott, Sugar* / Mix me down: *Tony Tuff* / Haul and pull up: *Brown, Neville* / Lover's magic: *Isaacs, Gregory* / Someone special: *Brown, Dennis* / Gimme good loving: *Natural Touch* / Feel so good: *Reid, Sandra* / Between me and you: *Campbell, Carol* / 'Cause you love me baby: *Tajah, Paulette* / Roots rockin': *Aswad* / Woman I need your loving: *Investigators*
CD ________ JECD 1001
Jet Star / Jun '88 / Jet Star

REGGAE HITS VOL.1
CD ________ MACCD 283
Autograph / Aug '96 / BMG

REGGAE HITS VOL.1
Money in my pocket / Soul rebel / I show you how to reggae / Soul shakedown party / Prisoner of love / Stop the train / Can you feel it / Caution / Reggae fever / Dock of the bay / Soul captive / Uptight / Cause you love my baby / Go tell it on the mountains / Green green grass of home / Roots rock
CD ________ GRF 0103
Tring / Apr '93 / Tring

REGGAE HITS VOL.1 & 2
CD Set ________ RHBCD 1
Jet Star / Dec '93 / Jet Star

REGGAE HITS VOL.10
CD ________ JECD 1010
Jet Star / Jul '91 / Jet Star

REGGAE HITS VOL.12
CD ________ JECD 1012
Jet Star / Apr '92 / Jet Star

REGGAE HITS VOL.13
Big up: *Shaggy & Rayvon* / Man kind: *Capleton* / I spy: *General TK* / How the world a run: *Buju Banton* / Second class: *Gonzalez, Carol* / Woman a you: *Terror Fabulous* / Ring the alarm quick: *Tenor Saw & Buju Banton* / Discovery: *Griffiths, Marcia & Tony Rebel/Cutty Ranks/Buju Banton* / Missing you now: *Sanchez* / I was born a winner: *McGregor, Freddie* / Where is the love: *Hammond, Beres & Sugar Minott/Tony Rebel* / Who say man nuh cry: *Buju Banton & Beres Hammond* / Can this be real: *Boom, Barry & Cutty Ranks* / I love you too much: *Wade, Wayne* / You are my lady: *Lefty Banton* / End of the road: *Paul, Frankie* / Go round: *Jack Reuben & The Riddler* / Save the best for last: *Singing Sweet*
CD ________ JECD 013
Jet Star / Dec '92 / Jet Star

REGGAE HITS VOL.14
CD ________ JECD 1014
Jet Star / Aug '93 / Jet Star

REGGAE HITS VOL.15
CD ________ JECD 1015
Jet Star / Dec '93 / Jet Star

REGGAE HITS VOL.16
CD ________ JECD 1016
Jet Star / Aug '94 / Jet Star

REGGAE HITS VOL.17
CD ________ JECD 1017
Jet Star / Dec '94 / Jet Star

REGGAE HITS VOL.18
CD ________ JECD 1018
Jet Star / Sep '95 / Jet Star

REGGAE HITS VOL.19
CD ________ JECD 1019
Jet Star / Dec '95 / Jet Star

REGGAE HITS VOL.2
Wildfire: *Holt, John & Dennis Brown* / I'll be on my way: *Isaacs, Gregory* / Inferiority complex: *Paul, Frankie* / Country living: *Mighty Diamonds* / Curly locks: *Byles, Junior* / Senci addick: *Fergeson, Horace* / Baby be true: *Thompson, Carroll* / Caught you in a lie: *Reid, Sandra* / I love you: *Sister Audrey* / Jazzy: *Paula* / I'm gonna fall in love: *Stewart, Tinga* / Horsemove (giddiup): *Horseman* / House is not a home: *Minott, Sugar*
CD ________ JECD 1002
Jet Star / '88 / Jet Star

REGGAE HITS VOL.2
CD ________ MACCD 284
Autograph / Aug '96 / BMG

REGGAE HITS VOL.2
Don't rock my boat / Love me / Key to the world / Riding high / Upside down / Only heaven can wait / Fussin' and fightin' / I will love you (like ABC) / Three little birds / Lively up yourself / You are to me / Rebels hop / Make it with you / Sun is shining / Peace love and happiness / Maga dog
CD ________ GRF 104
Tring / Apr '93 / Tring

REGGAE HITS VOL.21
CD ________ JECD 1021
Jet Star / Mar '97 / Jet Star

REGGAE HITS VOL.21 (In The Mix - Chris Goldfinger/Glamma Kid)
CD ________ JECDRX 1021
Jet Star / Jun '97 / Jet Star

REGGAE HITS VOL.22
I'm not a king: *Cocoa T* / Call me on the phone: *Sanchez* / Africa here I come: *Morgan Heritage* / Jah by my side (why be afraid): *Tony Rebel* / Ghetto people song: *Everton Blender* / Romie: *Beenie Man* / Moschino: *Glamma Kid* / No can do: *Lindo, Kashief* / Hold on: *Mikey Spice* / I believe I can fly: *Sanchez* / Nobody knows: *Beenie Man* / Dwayne: *Red Rat* / Goggle: *Stephens, Tanya* / She's having my baby: *Ricardo, Don* / I'll keep loving you: *Nerious Joseph* / Real love: *Brown, Lloyd* / Searching for love: *Livingston, Andy* / Good girl: *Jack Radics & Bounty Killer/Frisco Kid* / Mr. Whodini: *Merciless* / Lift up your head: *Everton Blender* / Bad news: *Hammond, Beres*
CD ________ JECD 1022
Jet Star / Jul '97 / Jet Star

REGGAE HITS VOL.3
Sweet reggae music: *Nitty Gritty* / Shub in: *Paul, Frankie* / Watch how the people dancing: *Knots, Kenny* / Greetings: *Half Pint* / Dear Boopsie: *Hall, Pam* / Boops: *Supercats* / Girlie girlie: *George, Sophia* / Members only: *Taylor, Tyrone* / One dance won't do: *Hall, Audrey* / Sixth street: *Wilson, Jack* / Hello darling: *Tippa Irie* / Be my lady: *Hunningale, Peter* / It's you: *Cross, Sandra* / Party nite: *Undivided Roots* / Guilty: *Gardiner, Boris*
CD ________ JECD 1003
Jet Star / Mar '87 / Jet Star

REGGAE HITS VOL.3
CD ________ MACCD 285
Autograph / Aug '96 / BMG

REGGAE HITS VOL.3 & 4
CD Set ________ RHBCD 2
Jet Star / Jan '94 / Jet Star

REGGAE HITS VOL.4
Wings of love: *Sparks, Trevor* / Girlfriend: *Fraser, Dean* / She's mine: *Levy, Barrington* / She's my lady: *Administrators* / Holding on: *Cross, Sandra* / If I give my heart to you: *McLean, John* / Guilty for loving you: *St. Clair, Carl* / Dangerous: *Smith, Conroy* / Chill out: *Tenor Saw & Doggie* / Debi Debi girl: *Peter Metro & Sister Charmaine* / Bad boy: *Courtney Melody* / Get ready: *Paul, Frankie* / Tears: *Turner, Chuck* / Big in bed: *Lilly Melody*
CD ________ JECD 1004
Jet Star / Jun '88 / Jet Star

REGGAE HITS VOL.4
CD ________ MACCD 286
Autograph / Aug '96 / BMG

REGGAE HITS VOL.5
Woman of moods: *Dixon, Trevor* / Black pride: *Kofi* / No way no better than yard: *Bailey, Admiral* / Am I losing you: *Schloss, Cynthia* / Ooh la la: *LJM* / Mi love mi girl bad: *Flourgan & Sanchez* / Proud to be black: *Crucial Robbie* / Power of love: *Gibbons, Leroy* / Cover me: *Stewart, Tinga & Ninga Man* / Very best: *Intense* / Life: *Frighty & Colonel Mite* / I still say yes: *Parkings, Juliet* / Man in the mirror: *Little Kirk*
CD ________ JECD 1005
Jet Star / Dec '88 / Jet Star

REGGAE HITS VOL.5
CD ________ MACCD 287
Autograph / Aug '96 / BMG

REGGAE HITS VOL.5 & 6
CD Set ________ RHBCD 3
Jet Star / Jan '94 / Jet Star

REGGAE HITS VOL.6
My commanding wife: *Gardiner, Boris* / Bun and cheese: *Clement Irie & Robert French* / Looking over love: *Kofi* / Baby can I hold you tonight: *Sanchez* / New way to say I love you: *Wayne Wonder* / Stick by me: *Marley, Bob* / I want to get next to you: *Manifest* / Love me ses: *Top Cat & Tenor Fly* / On my mind: *Intense* / Lovers affair: *Roni* / Fatal attraction: *Taxman* / Mix up: *UU Madoo & Captain Barky* / Sweet and nice: *Douglas, Lambert & Wayne Fire*
CD ________ JECD 1006
Jet Star / Jul '89 / Jet Star

REGGAE HITS VOL.7
CD ________ JECD 1007
Jet Star / Dec '89 / Jet Star

REGGAE HITS VOL.8
Your love: *Prophet, Michael & Ricky Tuff* / Know fi move your waist: *Major Danger* / Ku-klung-klung: *Red Dragon* / Spirit: *Chaka Demus* / Burrp: *Nardo Ranks* / Money worries: *Sweetie Irie* / Body tune up: *Johnny P* / Buck wild: *Paul, Frankie & Papa San* / Careless whisper: *Thriller U* / Mrs. Jones: *Levi, Sammy* / Sharing the night: *Brown, Lloyd* / Finders keepers: *Leroy Mafia* / One night: *Wayne Wonder & Brian/Tony Gold* / 2 a.m.: *Calvin* / Do you ever think about me: *Pure Silk* / Ticket to ride: *Trisha*
CD ________ JECD 1008
Jet Star / Jun '90 / Jet Star

REGGAE HITS VOL.9
CD ________ JECD 1009
Jet Star / Dec '90 / Jet Star

REGGAE IN YOUR JEGGAE
CD ________ CDTRL 358
Trojan / Aug '95 / Direct / Jet Star

REGGAE KOLOR
CD ________ 8419712
Declic / Oct '96 / Jet Star

REGGAE LEGEND
CD ________ VPCD 1421
VP / Aug '95 / Greensleeves / Jet Star / Total/BMG

REGGAE LEGENDS VOL.1
CD ________ RB 3011
Reggae Best / Nov '94 / Grapevine/ PolyGram
CD ________ RNCD 2105
Rhino / Apr '95 / Grapevine/PolyGram / Jet Star

REGGAE LOVE SONGS (16 Big Hits)
Longshot kick de bucket: *Pioneers* / Let your yeah be yeah: *Pioneers* / Who's loving you: *Boothe, Ken* / Dark end of the street: *Boothe, Ken* / Never never: *Brown, Dennis* / Closer I get to you: *Brown, Dennis* / Something inside so strong: *Griffiths, Marcia* / Just don't want to be lonely: *Griffiths, Marcia* / Everything I own: *Boothe, Ken* / Crying over you: *Boothe, Ken* / Concrete jungle: *Brown, Dennis* / Ain't that loving you baby: *Brown, Dennis* / Sweet bitter love: *Griffiths, Marcia* / First time ever I saw your face: *Griffiths, Marcia* / I man born ya: *Shervington, Pluto* / Your honour: *Shervington, Pluto*
CD ________ PLATCD 167
Platinum / Mar '96 / Prism

REGGAE MASSIVE
You don't love me (no no no): *Penn, Dawn* / Sweat (a la la la la long): *Inner Circle* / Informer: *Snow* / Don't look back: *Tosh, Peter* / Baby come back: *Pato Banton* / Sweets for my sweet: *Lewis, C.J.* / Don't turn around: *Aswad* / Silly games: *Kay, Janet* / Oh Carolina: *Shaggy* / Close to you: *Priest, Maxi* / I shall sing: *Griffiths, Marcia* / Good thing going: *Minott, Sugar* / Living on the frontline: *Grant, Eddy* / Young, gifted and black: *Bob & Marcia* / Girlie girlie: *George, Sophia* / I shot the sheriff: *Inner Circle* / No woman no cry: *Boothe, Ken* / Hurt so good: *Cadogan, Susan* / Mr. Loverman: *Shabba Ranks* / Red red wine: *Tribe, Tony* / Return to Django: *Upsetters* / Double barrel: *Collins, Dave & Ansell* / Liquidator: *Harry J All Stars* / Help me make it through the night: *Holt, John* / Lovin' inside: *Forrester, Sharon* / Twist and shout: *Chaka Demus & Pliers* / Police and thieves: *Murvin, Junior* / Many rivers to cross: *Cliff, Jimmy* / 54-46 (was my number): *Toots & The Maytals* / Cherry oh baby: *Donaldson, Eric* / Sideshow: *Biggs, Barry* / Night nurse: *Isaacs, Gregory* / Riddim: *US 3* / Stop that train: *Clint Eastwood & General Saint* / Bubbling hot: *Pato Banton* / Sugar sugar: *Basie, Duke* / Jungle: *Perry, Lee 'Scratch'*
CD ________ DINCD 93
Dino / Jun '95 / Pinnacle

REGGAE MEDAL VOL.1
CD ________ CRBCD 001
Carib Jems / Jan '94 / Jet Star

REGGAE MELODIES
CD ________ RB 3016
Reggae Best / Oct '95 / Grapevine/ PolyGram

REGGAE MIX-TURES
Danger zone: *Jah Stitch* / Proverbs: *McLeod, Enos & Pat Kelly* / I wish it would rain: *McLeod, Enos & Pat Kelly* / Nice time: *Uprising* / Uprising in dub: *Uprising* / Temptation woman: *McLeod, Enos* / Black man pickney: *McLeod, Enos* / Black dub: *McLeod, Enos* / Blood and fire: *McLeod, Enos* / Dub with fire: *McLeod, Enos* / Whipping dub: *McLeod, Enos* / Greedy girl: *Prince Ugly* / Natty dread something: *Prince Ugly & Searcher* / Mash mouth: *Jah Stitch* / Musso in dub: *Jah Stitch* / Three the hard way: *Campbell, Al & Dillinger/Trinity* / I'm a Joseph: *Trinity* / Whip them Jah: *Clint Eastwood*
CD ________ PRCD 609
President / May '97 / Grapevine/PolyGram / President / Target/BMG

REGGAE MUSIC ALL NIGHT LONG (4CD Set)
CD Set ________ CDNCBOX 2
Charly / Sep '91 / Koch

REGGAE NOW
CD ________ ANCD 09
Heartbeat / Jan '94 / ADA / Direct / Greensleeves / Jet Star

REGGAE ON THE SEAS
CD ________ SONCD 0075
Sonic Sounds / Mar '95 / Jet Star

REGGAE REFRESHERS SAMPLER VOL.1
CD ______ **RRCDS 101**
Reggae Refreshers / Jun '90 / PolyGram / Vital

REGGAE REFRESHERS SAMPLER VOL.2
Very well: *Wailing Souls* / Prophecy: *Fabian* / Gates of Zion: *Prophet, Michael* / Hypocrite: *Wailer, Bunny* / Botanical roots: *Black Uhuru* / Handsworth revolution: *Steel Pulse* / Jah heavy load: *Ijahman Levi* / One step forward: *Perry, Lee 'Scratch'* / Croaking lizard: *Upsetters* / Invasion: *Burning Spear* / Fade away: *Byles, Junior* / Independent intavenshan: *Johnson, Linton Kwesi* / Border: *Isaacs, Gregory* / Jailbreak: *Sly & Robbie* / Dub fire: *Aswad* / Sata: *Jah Lion*
CD ______ **RRCDS 102**
Reggae Refreshers / Apr '95 / PolyGram / Vital

REGGAE REVELATION
CD ______ **REO 97CD**
ROIR / Nov '94 / Plastic Head / Shellshock/Disc

REGGAE REVOLUTION
CD ______ **LG 21087**
Lagoon / Jun '92 / Grapevine/PolyGram

REGGAE REVOLUTION VOL.1
CD ______ **RE 097CD**
ROIR / Jul '97 / Plastic Head / Shellshock/ Disc

REGGAE ROCK VOL.2
CD ______ **RRCD 9111**
Reggae Rock / Mar '96 / Jet Star

REGGAE ROOTS (2CD Set)
I want to wake up with you: *Holt, John* / Rhythm body: *Minott, Sugar* / Tide is high: *Paragons* / Guns don't argue: *Alcapone, Dennis* / I willa lways love you: *Holt, John* / One my love: *Sly & Robbie* / Guns of Navarone: *Upsetters* / Clint Eastwood rides agian: *Perry, Lee 'Scratch'* / Cocaine in my brain: *Dillinger* / One love: *Marley, Bob & The Wailers* / Wonderful world: *Heptones* / Sweet sensation: *Melodians* / Keep on moving: *Marley, Bob & The Wailers* / Pressure drop: *Toots & The Maytals* / Satisfy my soul: *Marley, Bob & The Wailers* / If I were a carpenter: *Groovy, Winston* / Jah jah bless the dreadlocks: *Mighty Diamonds* / Wet dream: *Romeo, Max* / Monkey man: *Toots & The Maytals*
CD Set ______ **DCD 3004**
Music / Jun '97 / Target/BMG

REGGAE SELECT VOL.1
CD ______ **ECCD 00042**
East Coast / Jun '97 / Jet Star

REGGAE STARS
Mount Zion: *Brown, Dennis* / Forgive her: *Davis, Ronnie* / Choose me: *Taylor, Tyrone* / (This world is a) Stage: *Davis, Ronnie* / My heart is in danger: *Holt, Errol & Roots Radics* / Keep away son: *Brown, Dennis* / Why must I: *Brown, Dennis* / See a man's face: *McLeod, Enos* / Gain experience: *McLaren, Frederick* / Comin' home: *Davis, Ronnie* / Lovie dovie: *Davis, Ronnie* / Chasin' you: *Davis, Ronnie* / Let it be me: *Davis, Ronnie* / Raindrops: *Davis, Ronnie* / I'm in love: *Andy, Horace* / Sparkling light: *Skyers, Nathan* / Write myself a letter: *Isaacs, Gregory*
CD ______ **PRCD 607**
President / May '97 / Grapevine/PolyGram / President / Target/BMG

REGGAE SUPERSTARS
CD ______ **RRTGCD 7732**
Rohit / Mar '89 / Jet Star

REGGAE SUPERSTARS
CD ______ **RNCD 2076**
Rhino / Dec '94 / Grapevine/PolyGram / Jet Star

REGGAE SUPERSTARS (CD/CD Rom Set)
CD Set ______ **WWCDR 010**
Magnum Music / Apr '97 / TKO Magnum

REGGAE SUPERSTARS BONANZA
CD ______ **RNCD 2022**
Rhino / Sep '93 / Grapevine/PolyGram / Jet Star

REGGAE SUPERSTARS OF THE 80'S
CD ______ **BSLCD 12003**
Rohit / Feb '88 / Jet Star

REGGAE TIME
CD ______ **GLD 63303**
Goldies / Jul '94 / THE

REGGAE TOP 20 VOL.1
CD ______ **SONCD 0029**
Sonic Sounds / Jun '92 / Jet Star

REGGAE TOP 20 VOL.2
CD ______ **SONCD 0030**
Sonic Sounds / Jun '92 / Jet Star

REGGAE TRAIN, THE
CD ______ **CBHB 174**
Heartbeat / Feb '96 / ADA / Direct / Greensleeves / Jet Star

REGGAE UP (2CD Set)
CD Set ______ **DEMPCD 001**
Emporio / Mar '96 / Disc

REGGAEMANIA
Keep on movin' / Roll on a rolling stone / Originator / Ba ba riba skank / Everyday is like a holiday / Mabrouk / Concrete jungle / Let's build our dream / Travelling man / Too much / I'll forever keep on loving you / Red ash / Bam bam / You are like Heaven to me / I'll never get burn / Garden of love
CD ______ **74321360622**
Milan / Jun '96 / Conifer/BMG / Silva Screen

REGGAE'S GREATEST HITS VOL.1
CD ______ **CDHB 3601**
Heartbeat / Feb '96 / ADA / Direct / Greensleeves / Jet Star

REGGAE'S GREATEST HITS VOL.2
CD ______ **CDHB 3602**
Heartbeat / Feb '96 / ADA / Direct / Greensleeves / Jet Star

REGGAE'S GREATEST HITS VOL.3
CD ______ **CDBH 3603**
Heartbeat / Feb '96 / ADA / Direct / Greensleeves / Jet Star

REGGAE'S GREATEST HITS VOL.4
CD ______ **CDHB 3604**
Heartbeat / Feb '96 / ADA / Direct / Greensleeves / Jet Star

REGGAE'S GREATEST HITS VOL.5
CD ______ **CDHB 3605**
Heartbeat / Feb '96 / ADA / Direct / Greensleeves / Jet Star

REGGAE'S GREATEST HITS VOL.6
CD ______ **CDHB 3606**
Heartbeat / Feb '96 / ADA / Direct / Greensleeves / Jet Star

REGGAE'S GREATEST HITS VOL.7
CD ______ **CDHB 3607**
Heartbeat / Feb '96 / ADA / Direct / Greensleeves / Jet Star

REGGAE'S GREATEST HITS VOL.8
CD ______ **CDHB 3608**
Heartbeat / Feb '96 / ADA / Direct / Greensleeves / Jet Star

REGGAE'S GREATEST HITS VOL.9
CD ______ **CDHB 3609**
Heartbeat / Mar '96 / ADA / Direct / Greensleeves / Jet Star

REJOICE (Celebration Of Christian Music/2CD Set)
Magnificat / Feria / Lord's prayer / Most worthy Lord / Praise my soul the King of Heaven / Ave Maria / Callanish / Jesus Lord / Pie Jesu / Give me Jesus / I was glad / Hear and I will speak / Armenian mass / When I survey the wondrous cross / St. Mark's passion / Simple faith / You are so precious / God who fell to earth / We declare again / Cross / I will give thanks / Far away / My senses fly / Rock the rollin' stone / Melody of the morning / Hem me in / Sun goes down / Deep peace
CD Set ______ **330482**
Hallmark / Mar '97 / Carlton

RELAXATION AND MEDITATION WITH MUSIC AND NATURE (Distant Thunder)
CD ______ **12259**
Laserlight / Jul '97 / Target/BMG

RELAXATION AND MEDITATION WITH MUSIC AND NATURE (Ocean Voyages)
CD ______ **12260**
Laserlight / Jul '97 / Target/BMG

RELIGIONS OF THE WORLD
CD ______ **A 6232**
Tempo / Jan '97 / Discovery / Harmonia Mundi

RELIGIONS OF THE WORLD - BUDDHISM
Introduction and song of praise from the Ramayana / Madmen of God / Evocation of the clouds/Prologue to the Gitagovinda / Buddhist chant / Dai hannya tendoku E overture / Dai hannya tendoku E Yuri chant / Dai hannya tendoku E sugu chant / Ho sho shu excerpt / Bhuddist chants and prayers / Invocation to the goddess Yeshiki Mamo
CD ______ **A 6233**
Tempo / Jul '97 / Discovery / Harmonia Mundi

RELIGIONS OF THE WORLD - ISLAM
CD ______ **A 6235**
Tempo / Mar '97 / Discovery / Harmonia Mundi

RELIGIOUS CHANTS OF NORTH AFRICA VOL.2
CD ______ **AAA 125**
Club Du Disque Arabe / Feb '97 / ADA / Harmonia Mundi

RELIX 20TH ANNIVERSARY
CD ______ **RRCD 2066**
Relix / Jul '97 / ADA / Greyhound

RELIX BAY ROCK VOL.5
CD ______ **RRCD 2053**
Relix / Jul '97 / ADA / Greyhound

REMEMBER NEW ORLEANS
CD ______ **CD 53026**
Giants Of Jazz / Aug '88 / Cadillac / Jazz Music / Target/BMG

REMEMBER THE 50'S
CD ______ **12106**
Laserlight / Jan '93 / Target/BMG

REMEMBER THE 60'S - THE GROUPS
Sabre dance: *Love Sculpture* / Quartermaster's stores: *Shadows* / It's my life: *Animals* / Seven daffodils: *Cherokees* / I'll never get over you: *Kidd, Johnny & The Pirates* / Greenback dollar: *Kingston Trio* / Don't let the sun catch you crying: *Gerry & The Pacemakers* / From a window: *Kramer, Billy J. & The Dakotas* / William Tell: *Sounds Incorporated* / You're no good: *Swinging Blue Jeans* / We're through: *Hollies* / Livin' above your head: *Jay & The Americans* / Three rooms with running water: *Bennett, Cliff & The Rebel Rousers* / One in the middle: *Manfred Mann* / Heart's symphony: *Lewis, Gary & The Playboys* / She's lost you: *Zephyrs* / I think we're alone now: *James, Tommy & The Shondells* / Going up the country: *Canned Heat* / For whom the bell tolls: *Dupree, Simon & The Big Sound* / Break away: *Beach Boys*
CD ______ **CDSL 8249**
EMI / Jul '95 / EMI

REMEMBER THE 70'S
CD Set ______ **KBOX 351**
Collection / Nov '95 / Target/BMG / TKO Magnum

REMEMBER THE 70'S - THE GROUPS
Whole lotta love: *CCS* / Cotton fields: *Beach Boys* / Let's work together: *Canned Heat* / Rag mama rag: *Band* / Malt and barley blues: *McGuinness Flint* / Mocking bird: *Barclay James Harvest* / Strange kind of woman: *Deep Purple* / Long cool woman in a black dress: *Hollies* / Do ya: *Move* / 10538 overture: *ELO* / Brother Louie: *Hot Chocolate* / Judy teen: *Harley, Steve & Cockney Rebel* / Overnight sensation (Hit record): *Raspberries* / Forgotten roads: *If* / Millionaire: *Dr. Hook* / Ships in the night: *Be-Bop Deluxe* / Walk on by: *Stranglers* / Promises: *Buzzcocks* / My Sharona: *Knack* / Dance stance: *Dexy's Midnight Runners*
CD ______ **CDSL 8250**
EMI / Jul '95 / EMI

REMEMBER THEN (30 Original Doo Wop Classics)
Remember then: *Earls* / Great pretender: *Platters* / Why do fools fall in love: *Lymon, Frankie & The Teenagers* / I love how you love me: *Paris Sisters* / One fine day: *Chiffons* / Blue moon: *Marcels* / You belong to me: *Duprees* / At the Hop: *Danny & The Juniors* / Born too late: *Poni-Tails* / My special angel: *Helms, Bobby* / Duke of Earl: *Chandler, Gene* / Little darlin': *Diamonds* / Stay: *Williams, Maurice & The Zodiacs* / Big man: *Four Preps* / Tears on my pillow: *Imperials* / Book of love: *Monotones* / Earth angel: *Crew Cuts* / Where or when: *Dion & The Belmonts* / I only have eyes for you: *Flamingoes* / It's almost tomorrow: *Dream Weavers* / Daddy's home: *Shep & The Limelites* / Sorry (I ran all the way home): *Impalas* / Sixteen candles: *Crests* / Little star: *Elegants* / Come go with me: *Del-Vikings* / In the still of the nite: *Five Satins* / Sincerely: *Moonglows* / Mr. Sandman: *Chordettes* / Come softly to me: *Fleetwoods* / Three bells: *Browns*
CD ______ **5167922**
Polydor / May '94 / PolyGram

REMEMBER WHEN SINGERS COULD REALLY SING
I left my heart in San Francisco: *Bennett, Tony* / Born free: *Williams, Andy* / Crazy: *Cline, Patsy* / Moon river: *Williams, Danny* / Portrait of my love: *Monro, Matt* / Mr. Wonderful: *Lee, Peggy* / Love letters in the sand: *Lester, Ketty* / Cry: *Ray, Johnnie* / On the street where you live: *Damone, Vic* / Return to me: *Martin, Dean* / Who's sorry now: *Francis, Connie* / Around the world: *Crosby, Bing* / Release me: *Humperdinck, Engelbert* / Move over darling: *Day, Doris* / Rose Marie: *Whitman, Slim* / I'm sorry: *Lee, Brenda* / It's only make believe: *Twitty, Conway* / This is my song: *Clark, Petula* / Distant drums: *Reeves, Jim* / It's impossible: *Como, Perry*
CD ______ **AHLCD 3**
Hit / Nov '92 / Grapevine/PolyGram

REMIXED REMODELLED
CD ______ **CDALMY 1**
Almighty / May '95 / Total/BMG

RENAISSANCE MIX VOL.1
CD ______ **RENMIX 1CD**
Network / Sep '94 / 3mv/Sony / Pinnacle

RENAISSANCE MIX VOL.3 (2CD Set)
CD Set ______ **RENMIX 3CD**
Network / Jun '96 / 3mv/Sony / Pinnacle

RENAISSANCE MIX VOL.4 (Mixed By Dave Seaman & Ian Ossia/3CD Set)
Are you with me love: *Elements Of Life* / Sirenes: *System 7* / Stay gold: *Deep Dish* / Look up to the light: *Evolution* / Reach: *Lil Mo Yin Yang* / Queer: *Garbage* / Feelings run so deep: *Desert* / Ohmna: *Sasha* / Gate: *Dominion* / Garden of earthly delights: *D-Note* / Beautiful place: *Van Dyke, Paul* / Cry: *Mollison, Sam* / Offshore: *Chicane* / Little love, a little life: *Power Circle* / Orbit: *Dance Planet* / Possession: *McLachlan, Sarah* / Wavespeech: *Lazonby, Peter* / Careful: *Horse* / Set in stone: *Bedrock* / Bjango: *Lucky Monkeys* / Do you feel it: *Soundsation* / Rollercoaster: *Outcast* / I hear your name: *Incognito* / Anomaly-calling your name: *Libra & Taylor* / Hyperballad: *Bjork* / Future reality: *Wallace, Dave* / Homeland: *Wayward Mind* / Land of the living: *Kristine W* / Voices of KA: *Van Leeuwen, Sjef* / Let there be love: *Shiva* / Canis loopus: *Yekuana* / All because of you: *Universal State Of Mind* / Caterpillar: *Keoki* / Difference: *Djum Djum* / Daylight: *Big C & Alice* / Ajare: *Way Out West* / Never forget: *Blue Amazon* / One nation: *Supereal* / Walk with me: *Heliotropic*
CD Set ______ **RENMIX 4CD**
Network / Nov '96 / 3mv/Sony / Pinnacle

RENDEZVOUS VOL.1
CD ______ **SJRCD 001**
Street Jazz / Jul '96 / Timewarp

RENDEZVOUS VOL.2
CD ______ **SJRCD 002**
Street Jazz / Jul '96 / Timewarp

RENEGADE SELECTOR
CD ______ **ANIMATE 1CD**
Animate / Jun '94 / SRD

RER QUARTERLY - SELECTIONS FROM VOL.1
CD ______ **RERQCD 1**
ReR/Recommended / Jul '93 / ReR Megacorp / RTM/Disc

RER QUARTERLY - SELECTIONS FROM VOL.2
CD ______ **RERQCD 2**
ReR/Recommended / Jul '93 / ReR Megacorp / RTM/Disc

RER QUARTERLY VOL.4 NO.1
CD ______ **RER 0401**
ReR/Recommended / Jun '94 / ReR Megacorp / RTM/Disc

RER QUARTERLY VOL.4 NO.2
CD ______ **RER 0402**
ReR/Recommended / Jun '97 / ReR Megacorp / RTM/Disc

RESONANCE MOOD
Target eye: *Sandman* / Tio mate: *Deflo* / Slugfest: *Slug* / Intensive psychedelic care: *Chakra & Nada* / Jaws: *Growling Mad Scientists* / Shadow five: *Lunar Asylum* / Decoder: *Nervasystem* / Athalon: *Manmademan* / Pulse 2: *Anti Matter*
CD ______ **MPCD 06**
Matsuri / May '97 / Amato Disco / SRD

RESOUNDING POLYPHONY OF THE CAUCAUSUS, THE (Georgia)
Mravaljamieri / Shemodzakhili / Kalospiruli / Nana / Alilo / Shen bicho anagurelo / Gaprindi shavo mertskhalo / Hassanbegura / May peace be with us / Shavi shashvi / Song of friendship / Vakhtangura / Batonebo / Nanina / Tsmindao gmerto / Ailuya / Tsintskaro / Shen khar venakhi / Suliko
CD ______ **MCM 3004**
Multicultural Media / May '97 / Direct

RESPECT TO STUDIO ONE (2CD Set)
CD Set ______ **HBCD 181/182**
Heartbeat / Nov '94 / ADA / Direct / Greensleeves / Jet Star

RESURRECTING THE BLUES
CD ______ **NTMCD 505**
Nectar / Jun '95 / Pinnacle

RETRO TECHNO
CD ______ **RETROCD 1**
Network / Jul '91 / 3mv/Sony / Pinnacle

RETROSPECTIVE 1929-1963, A (2CD Set)
One hour (if I could be with you one hour tonight): *Mound City Blues Blowers* / Hello Lola: *Mound City Blues Blowers* / Miss Hannah: *McKinney's Cotton Pickers* / Wherever there's a will, baby: *McKinney's Cotton Pickers* / Sugarfoot stomp: *Henderson, Fletcher Orchestra* / Hocus pocus: *Henderson, Fletcher Orchestra* / When the lights are low: *Hampton, Lionel* / One sweet letter from you: *Hampton, Lionel* / Dinah: *Hampton, Lionel* / Meet Mr Foo: *Hawkins, Coleman* / Fine dinner: *Hawkins, Coleman* / She's funny that way: *Hawkins, Coleman* / Body and soul: *Hawkins, Coleman* / When day is gone: *Hawkins, Coleman* / Sheikh of araby: *Hawkins, Coleman* / My blue heaven: *Hawkins, Coleman* / Bouncing with bean: *Hawkins, Coleman* / Bugle call rag: *Metronome All Star Band* / One o'clock jump: *Metronome All Star Band* / Say it isn't so: *Hawkins, Coleman* / Spotlite: *Hawkins, Coleman* / Indiana winter: *Esquire* / Indian summer: *Esquire* / How did she look: *Hawkins, Coleman & His Orchestra* / April in Paris: *Hawkins, Coleman & His Orchestra* / How strange: *Hawkins, Coleman & His Orchestra* / Half step down please: *Hawkins, Coleman & His Orchestra* / Angel face: *Hawkins, Coleman & His Orchestra* / There will never be another you: *Hawkins, Coleman & His Orchestra* / Bean stalks again: *Hawkins, Coleman & His Orchestra* / I love Paris: *Hawkins, Coleman* / Under Paris skies: *Hawkins, Coleman* / I've got the world on a string: *Allen, Henry 'Red' & His Orchestra* / Sweet Lorraine: *Allen, Henry 'Red' & His Orchestra* / Watermelon man: *Lambert, Hendricks/Bavan* / All the things you are: *Rollins, Sonny*
CD Set ______ **786366172**
Bluebird / Aug '95 / BMG

RETROSPECTIVE OF HOUSE VOL.1
CD Set SDIMCD 3
Sound Dimension / Jul '95 / Total/BMG

RETROSPECTIVE OF HOUSE VOL.2 (2CD Set)
CD Set SDIMCD 4
Sound Dimension / Nov '95 / Total/BMG

RETROSPECTIVE OF HOUSE VOL.3 (4CD Set)
CD Set SDIMCD 5
Sound Dimension / May '96 / Total/BMG

RETROSPECTIVE OF HOUSE VOL.4 (1991-1996/De Vit/Graham Gold/Sister Bliss/3CD Set)
Around the world: *East 17* / Pacific symphony: *Transformer 2* / Movin' melodies: *Indica* / Joanna: *Mrs. Wood* / Age of love: *Age Of Love* / Schoneburg: *Marmion* / Freedom: *U-People* / Latin intruder: *Latin Thing* / Bits and pieces: *Artemesia* / Just can't get enough: *Transformer 2* / Deep house: *Triple J* / Back to my roots: *Rich In Paradise & FPI Project* / Who's the badman: *Patten, Dee* / Crazy man: *Blast* / Bells of New York: *Slo Moshun* / Raw: *Asuca* / Tester-don't stop: *Z100* / I know: *New Atlantic* / Made in 2 minutes: *Plastic Jam* / Closer to our dreams: *Rhythm Quest* / Club mix: *Desert Moods* / Crystal clear: *Grid* / This love: *Red Sun* / Just come 2 vocal: *Cool Jack* / 7 Days and 1 week: *BBE* / Way out west: *Montana* / Yeke yeke: *Kante, Mory* / Smokebelch II: *Sabres Of Paradise* / Energy flash: *Beltram, Joey* / Papua New Guinea: *Future Sound Of London* / Land of rhythm: *Marascia* / Is there anybody out there: *Friends Of Matthew* / Lionrock: *Lionrock* / Bad man: *Sister Bliss* / Don't leave: *Faithless* / Morel's grooves Vol.4 : let's groove: *Morel, George*
CD Set SDIMCD 6
Sound Dimension / Aug '96 / Total/BMG

RETURN OF THE DJ VOL.1
CD BOMB 2002CD
Bomb / Jul '97 / Cargo

RETURN TO SENDER
CD NORMAL 205CD
Normal / Aug '96 / ADA / Direct

RETURN TO THE SOURCE (Sacred Sites)
Hill of shining beings: *Man Made Man* / Tribedelic nomads: *Insectocide* / Ama no kawa: *Insectocide* / Energy transition: *Quirk* / Flight of the pteradactil: *Parasonix* / Supernature: *Medicine Drum* / Rites of Ra: *Anubis* / Tapu: *Laughing Buddha* / Ilias: *Buzzcraft* / Dawn of man: *Masa* / Sky spirit: *Ceiba* / Disciplinic flow: *Tribal Drift* / Reaper girl: *Kat Von Trapp* / Hypnofly: *UVW* / Mootawinjee: *TRipitaka* / Newgrange: *Azukx* / Every mother's sun: *Astralasia* / Time gate: *Yokota* / Freefall: *Youth* / Stone henge: *Universal Sound* / Sacred reunion: *Star Children*
CD Set RTTSCD 4
Positiva / Jun '97 / EMI

RETURN TO THE TECNODROME
CD RPTCD 010
Replicant / Feb '97 / Grapevine/PolyGram

RETURN TO UMOJA
CD CONCD 001
Conqueror / Jul '96 / Grapevine/PolyGram / Jet Star

REVELATION
CD BB 2813
Blue Beat / Oct '95 / Grapevine/PolyGram

REVENGE OF THE KILLER PUSSIES
Wild women: *Alien Sex Fiend* / Swamp baby: *Sunglasses After Dark* / Jazz Butcher meets Count Dracula: *Jazz Butcher* / Fats terminal: *Bone Orchard* / Graveyard stomp: *Meteors* / Seven deadly sins: *Outcasts* / Running wild: *Ricochets* / Red headed woman: *Panther Burns* / Hellbag shuffle: *Sunglasses After Dark* / Werewolf blues: *Guana Batz* / She's got fever: *Brilliant Corners* / Long necked daddy-o: *Boneasaurus Wrecks* / Hills have eyes: *Meteors* / Shearing machine: *Very Things* / Zulu beat: *King Kurt* / I don't wanna get thin: *Blubbery Hellbellies* / I wanna be like you: *Turnpike Cruisers* / Your good girl's gonna go bad: *Screaming Sirens* / Pointed bra: *Orson Family* / Stomp it: *Raunch Hands*
CD CDMPSYCHO 11
Anagram / Jan '96 / Cargo / Pinnacle

REVIVAL HITS VOL.1 & 2
CD MFCD 8
Mafia/Fluxy / May '94 / Jet Star / SRD

REVIVING A TRADITION
CD PS 65116
PlayaSound / Nov '93 / ADA / Harmonia Mundi

REVOLUTIONARY GENERATION
CD ASHADOW 3CD
Moving Shadow / Jan '96 / SRD

REVOLUTIONS
Wildstyle groove: *Paninaro* / Make it rock: *Cotton Club* / Rollercoaster: *Chapter 9* / Love the groove: *Alpha Motion* / Lover number 6: *Daydreamer* / De dah dah (Spice of life): *Mac, Keith* / Shock the beat: *Electric Choc* / In your dance: *E-Lustrious* / Funkin' crazy: *KGB* / Rok da house: *Tall Paul* / It was meant to be: *D'Enrico* / We are going down: *Deadly Sins* / Warehouse days of glory: *New Deep Society* / Club for life: *Chris & James* / Reach: *Cheeks, Judy*
CD CDHIGH 1
High On Rhythm / Sep '94 / 3mv/Sony

REWOUND
Hold your head up: *Argent* / Crazy 'bout you: *Perfect, Christine* / Like it this way: *Fleetwood Mac* / Love or else: *Grin* / Who do you love: *Hunter, Ian* / Soul of Patrick Lee: *Cale, John & Terry Riley* / Whizz kid: *Mott The Hoople* / Theme for an imaginary western: *Mountain* / Late November: *Pavlov's Dog* / Love story: *Skid Row* / Topanga windows: *Spirit* / Statesboro' blues: *Taj Mahal* / It's a mystery: *Upp* / We're all alone: *Walker Brothers*
CD 4844432
Columbia / Jul '96 / Sony

REZ VOL.2 (2CD Set)
CD Set REZCD 102
Rezerection / Apr '96 / Alphamagic

RHYTHM AND BLUES EXPRESS
CD TOLL 002CD
Tollhaus / Jun '92 / RTM/Disc

RHYTHM DANCE TRAXX
CD CCC 97004
Citycat Club / Jul '97 / TKO Magnum

RHYTHM DIVINE
So good: *Williams Brothers* / Old time religion: *Violinaires* / Soon and very soon: *Crouch, Andre & The Disciples* / Two wings: *Christianaires* / Don't you want to go: *Meditation Singers* / Soon I will be done: *East St. Louis Gospelettes* / It's Jesus in me: *Clark Sisters* / I've been weeping for a mighty long time: *Five Blind Boys Of Mississippi* / He's worthy: *Crouch, Sandra & Friends* / I've got one thing (you can't take away): *Mighty Clouds Of Joy* / Sing your troubles away: *Loving Sisters* / He's a friend of mine: *Soul Stirrers* / Cross that river: *La Mass Choir & Rev. Calvin Bernard Rhone* / Uphold me: *Winans* / Is there any way: *Hawkins, Walter* / He that believeth: *Chicago Mass Choir* / This day: *Holliday, Jennifer* / Goin' up yonder: *Hawkins, Tramaine*
CD MCD 33754
MCA / Jun '96 / BMG

RHYTHM IS A DANCER (2CD Set)
CD Set 55524
Laserlight / Nov '94 / Target/BMG

RHYTHM OF BRAZIL, THE
Mother Brasilier / Bizantina bizancia: *Ben, Jorge* / Moenda: *Machado, Elaine* / Tatmiro: *De Moraes, Vincius* / Banda da carmen mirandes: *Armandinho & Trio Electrico* / Jovelina perola negro: *O Dia Se Zanoou* / Cinco criancas: *Lobo, Edo* / Roberto corta essa: *Ben, Jorge* / Festejando / A Voz doz morro: *Melodia, Luiz* / Mulato latino: *Melodia, Luiz* / A bencao bahia: *Toquinho & Vincius De Moraes* / Salve simpatia: *Ben, Jorge* / Como diza o poeta: *Toquinho & Vincius De Moraes* / Viva meu samba / Casa de samba
CD MCCD 013
Music Club / Feb '91 / Disc / THE

RHYTHM OF RESISTANCE
U mama uyajabula: *Mlangeni, Babsy* / Ke ya le leboha: *Mlangeni, Babsy* / Perefere: *Malomba* / Pampa madiba: *Malomba* / Jesu otsoile: *Mparanyana & The Cannibals* / Umthombowase golgota: *Ladysmith Black Mambazo* / Yinhleleni: *Ladysmith Black Mambazo* / Inkunzi ayi hlabi ngokusima: *Johnny & Sipho* / Igula lamasi: *Mahotella Queens* / Ubu gowelle: *Baseqhudeni, Abafana*
CD SHANCD 43018
Shanachie / Apr '88 / ADA / Greensleeves / Koch

RHYTHM OF THE GAMES, THE (Official Olympics Album)
Impossible dream: *Campbell, Tevin* / Everlasting love: *Blige, Mary J.* / Reaching for my goal: *McKnight, Brian* / Imagine: *Clover, Corey* / Dreamin': *Usher* / Champions theme: *Kenny G* / You gotta believe in love: *Soul For Real* / Reach: *Estefan, Gloria* / Wild flower: *Hailey, K-Ci* / You're a winner: *Rich, Tony* / What am I doing here: *Hill, Jordan* / Star spangled banner: *Boyz II Men*
CD 73008260262
Arista / Jun '96 / BMG

RHYTHM OF THE ISLANDS
CD HQCD 92
Harlequin / Jan '97 / Hot Shot / Jazz Music / Swift / Wellard

RHYTHM REPUBLIC
CD AVEXCD 40
Avex / Jun '96 / 3mv/Pinnacle

RHYTHM REPUBLIC DISCO VOL.1
CD AVEXCD 35
Avex / Mar '96 / 3mv/Pinnacle

RHYTHM REPUBLIC JAZZ VOL.1
CD AVEXCD 36
Avex / Jun '96 / 3mv/Pinnacle

RHYTHM TRACK EXPLOSION VOL.1
CD GSR 70017
Ras / Apr '92 / Direct / Greensleeves / Jet Star / SRD

RHYTHM WAS OUR BUSINESS
Tiger rag / Mama don't allow it / Hold tight / Apple for the teacher / I can't dance / Bill tell / Anything goes / Out every Friday / Chinatown, my Chinatown / Who's sorry now / Clarinet marmalade / Sea food squabble / Weather man / Give out / It don't mean a thing if it ain't got that swing / Nagasaki / Way down yonder in New Orleans / Potomac jump / I'm forever blowing bubbles / Promenade / Twelfth street rag / Russian salad / Seven day's leave / Someday sweetheart
CD RAJCD 810
Empress / Nov '93 / Koch

RHYTHMS OF LIFE, SONGS OF WISDOM (Akan Music Of Ghana)
CD SFWCD 40463
Smithsonian Folkways / Mar '96 / ADA / Cadillac / CM / Direct / Koch

RHYTHMS OF RAPTURE (Sacred Music Of Haitian Voodoo)
CD SFWCD 40464
Smithsonian Folkways / Oct '95 / ADA / Cadillac / CM / Direct / Koch

RHYTHMSTICK
Caribe / Friday night at the Cadillac Club / Quilombo / Barbados / Waiting for Angela / Nana / Softly as in a morning sunrise / Colo de Rio / Palisades in blue / Wamba
CD ESJCD 230
Essential Jazz / Oct '94 / BMG

RICKY MONTANARI PRESENTS RIVIERA HOUSE TRAXX
CD PAZ 801CD
La Plaza / Sep '97 / Essential/BMG

RIDE DADDY RIDE
Ride daddy ride: *Noel, Fats* / Sure cure for the blues: *Four Jacks* / Big ten inch record: *Jackson, Bull Moose* / Smooth slow easy: *Drivers* / Drill daddy drill: *Ellis, Dorothy* / Roll roll pretty baby: *Swallows* / Walkin' blues: *Hunter, Fluffy* / Rocket 69: *Rhodes, Todd* / I knew he would: *Sharps & Flats* / Grandpa can boogie too: *Greenwood, Lil* / I want a bowlegged woman: *Jackson, Bull Moose* / I want my Fanny Brown: *Harris, Wynonie* / My natch'l man: *Hunter, Fluffy* / Chocolate pork chop man: *Lewis, Pete 'Guitar'* / It ain't the meat: *Swallows* / Ride jockey ride: *Lamplighters* / Mountain oysters: *Davis, Eddie 'Lockjaw'* / Triflin' woman: *Harris, Wynonie* / My ding a ling: *Bartholomew, Dave* / Last of the good rockin' men: *Four Jacks* / Your daddy's doggin' around: *Rhodes, Todd*
CD CDCHARLY 272
Charly / Feb '91 / Koch

RIDIM FE RIDIM
CD RFCD 006
Record Factory / Jun '97 / Jet Star

RIDING HIGH
CD SRFN 001CD
Srfn / Feb '96 / ADA

RIG ROCK DELUXE
Truck driving man: *Walser, Don* / Will there be big rigs in heaven: *Owens, Buck & The Buckaroos* / Nitro express: *Red Simpson & Junior Brown* / Miss Marie & The Bedford Blaze: *Red Simpson & Junior Brown* / Truckstop girl: *Willis, Kelly* / Mother trucker: *Shaver* / Lookin' at the world through a windshield: *Volt, Son* / Diesel diesel diesel: *Reeves, Del & Jim Lauderdale* / Wagon of clay: *Knight, Cheri* / White freight liner blues: *Earle, Steve* / Highway junkie: *Yayhoos* / Semi truck: *Kirchen, Bill & Too Much Fun* / Mama was a rock (daddy was a rollin stone): *Kirchen, Bill & Too Much Fun* / I'm coming home: *Lowe, Nick & The Impossible Birds* / Truck drivin' man (give it all I can): *Bottle Rockets* / Six days on the road: *Rig Rock Deluxe*
CD UPSTART 025
Upstart / Sep '96 / ADA / Direct

RIGHT DIRECTION - NORTHERN SOUL STORMERS
Weakspot: *Thomas, Evelyn* / Make sure (you have someone who loves you): *Jiani, Carol* / Out on the floor: *Nero, Frances* / Breaking down the walls of heartache: *Starr, Edwin* / Let me down easy: *Lavette, Bettye* / Wiht this ring: *Wylie, Richard 'Popcorn'* / Night: *Johnson, Marv* / Sking in the snow: *Pallas, Laura & The Reputations* / Reaching for the best: *Exciters* / Ain't no soul (left in these old shoes): *Fantastic Four* / You hit me where it hurt me: *Weston, Kim* / You're gonna be my baby: *McNair, Barbara* / That's when the tears start: *Velvelettes* / Six by six: *Van Dyke, Earl* / Right direction: *Littles, Hattie* / Key to my happiness: *Lovetones* / Your magic put a spell on me: *Lovetones* / He's so irreplaceable: *Jones, Doris* / Look what you've done to my heart: *Elgins* / What's wrong with me baby: *Valadiers*
CD SUMCD 4132
Sound & Media / Jun '97 / Sound & Media

RIGHT TOUCH, THE
CD RR 102CD
Roots / Jul '96 / Timewarp

RIGHT TRACKS, THE
CD RNCD 2008
Rhino / May '93 / Grapevine/PolyGram / Jet Star

RIGHTS OF MAN, THE
CD GLCD 1111
Green Linnet / Feb '92 / ADA / CM / Direct / Highlander / Roots

RIGODON SAUVAGE
CD C 560053
Ocora / Nov '95 / ADA / Harmonia Mundi

RIKK AGNEW'S SMASH DEMOS VOL.2
CD EFA 122392
Musical Tragedies / May '96 / SRD

RIME OF THE ANCIENT SAMPLER
CD VP 141CD
Voiceprint / Jun '93 / Pinnacle

RINCE COMPLETE IRISH DANCING SET
CD CHCD 1050
Chyme / Jan '95 / ADA / CM / Direct / Koch

RINGBANG REBEL DANCE
CD 951902
Ice / Apr '96 / Jet Star / Pinnacle

RINGING CLEAR (The Art of Handbell Ringing)
Entry of the gladiators / Linden Lea / Stephen Foster selection / Grandfather's clock / On wings of song / Lord of the dance / Girl with the flaxen hair / Country gardens / Ashgrove / Ragtime dance / Parade of the tin soldiers / Isle of Capri / Lullaby / Original rags / Silver threads among the gold / Intermezzo from cavalleria rusticana / Bells of St. Mary's / O waly waly / Flow gently sweet Afton / Syncopated clock / O guter mond / Whistling Rufus
CD CDSDL 333
Saydisc / Oct '91 / ADA / Direct / Harmonia Mundi

RIOT CITY SINGLES COLLECTION VOL.1
Last rockers: *Vice Squad* / Young blood: *Vice Squad* / Politics: *Insane* / Vicious circle: *Abrasive Wheels* / Gotta get out: *Court Martial* / Four minute warning: *Chaos UK* / Undead: *Undead* / Dreaming: *Expelled* / Army song: *Abrasive Wheels* / Fuck the world: *Chaotic Dischord* / No solution: *Court Martial* / No security: *Chaos UK* / Dogsbody: *Mayhem* / Have you got 10p: *Ejected* / Dead revolution: *Undead* / Burn em' down: *Abrasive Wheels* / Make it alone: *Expelled* / Nottingham problem: *Resistance 77* / Fast 'n' loud: *Ejected* / Cream of the crop: *No Choice* / Points of view: *Emergency* / Never trust a friend: *Chaotic Dischord* / Back on the piss again: *Sex Aids* / Gentle murder: *Mayhem* / Crime for revenge: *Ultraviolent* / East of dachau: *Underdogs* / Die for your government: *Varukers* / Russians: *Ejected* / Led to the slaughter: *Varukers* / Cliff: *Chaotic Dischord*
CD CDPUNK 15
Anagram / Mar '97 / Cargo / Pinnacle

RIOT CITY SINGLES COLLECTION VOL.2
Living on dreams: *Vice Squad* / Humane: *Vice Squad* / Dead and gone: *Insane* / Voice of youth: *Abrasive Wheels* / Fight for your life: *Court Martial* / Kill your baby: *Chaos UK* / It's corruption: *Undead* / What justice: *Expelled* / Juvenile: *Abrasive Wheels* / You're gonna die: *Chaotic Dischord* / Too late: *Court Martial* / What about a future: *Chaos UK* / Street fight: *Mayhem* / Class of '82: *Ejected* / Place is burning: *Undead* / Urban rebel: *Abrasive Wheels* / Government policy: *Expelled* / Join the army: *Resistance 77* / I don't care: *Ejected* / Sadist dream: *No Choice* / City fun: *Emergency* / Pop stars: *Chaotic Dischord* / We are the road crew: *Sex Aids* / (Your face fits) Lie and die: *Mayhem* / Dead generation: *Ultraviolet* / Johnny go home: *Underdogs* / All systems fail: *Varukers* / Twenty four years: *Ejected* / End is nigh: *Varukers*
CD CDPUNK 55
Anagram / May '95 / Cargo / Pinnacle

RIPE MASTERS VOL.2
Let me love you for tonight: *Kariya* / Scandalise: *Afterlife* / Move on: *Ray, Cecilia* / Need you: *Davis, Alvin* / Share my love: *Waters, Kim* / Don't you want it: *Edwards, Sandi* / Ordinary girl: *P-Ski Mac* / Naughty but nice: *Spice* / Money or love: *Davis, Alvin* / Walking on sunshine: *Rockers Revenge* / I'll always love my Ma: *P-Ski Mac* / Round 'n' round: *Ray, Cecilia* / Lost in the storm: *Waters, Kim* / I wonder where you are: *Edwards, Sandi* / Byzantium: *Afterlife*
CD RIPECD 216
Ripe / Nov '95 / Pinnacle

RISE
CD SCENTCD 001
Fragrant / Jun '97 / Intergroove

RISE IN PROGRESS
CD RCD 001
Rise / Apr '96 / Pinnacle

RISE OF EUROPEAN CIVILISATION, THE
CD PBRCD 001
Point Break / Oct '96 / Cargo

RISING HIGH COLLECTION, THE
Sweet home Chicago: *Louisiana Red* / Sweet little angel: *Louisiana Red* / King bee: *Louisiana Red* / Lightnin' blkues: *Hopkins, Lightnin'* / Trouble in mind: *Hopkins, Lightnin'* / Blues ain't nothin' but a feelin': *Hop-*

kins, Lightnin' / I'm gonna get on my feet's afterwhile: *Terry, Sonny & Brownie McGhee* / Oh ja bo: *Terry, Sonny & Brownie McGhee* / Walk on: *Terry, Sonny & Brownie McGhee* / My father's words: *Terry, Sonny & Brownie McGhee* / Good morning blues: *Terry, Sonny & Brownie McGhee* / I've never felt like this before: *Terry, Sonny & Brownie McGhee*
CD _______ **RSCD 0011**
Just A Memory / May '96 / New Note/ Pinnacle

RITMO BRASILEIRO
Swing da cor / Ile de luz / Soy loco por ti America / Sei de cor / Mistura e manda / Diamante / Solidao / Banda dos negros / Vida / Canto da cor / Tempos felizes / O menino / A Deusa do amor / Maravilhe / Esphina da bacalhau
CD _______ **MPG 74038**
Movieplay Gold / Apr '97 / Target/BMG

RITMO DE BAHIA
CD _______ **371001**
Justin / Nov '90 / Triple Earth

RITMO DE LA NOCHE
CD _______ **DCD 5393**
Disky / Jul '94 / Disky / THE

RITUAL, THEATRE AND CHAMBER MUSICS FROM SOUTH VIETNAM
CD _______ **D 8070**
Unesco / Nov '96 / ADA / Harmonia Mundi

RIVER OF SOUND, A
Ah sweet dancer: *O'Suilleabhain, Micheal* / Johnny Dohertys: *Tourish, Ciaran/Dermot Byrne* / Two Conneeleys: *Moore, Christy & Micheal O'Suilleabhain* / Real blues reel: *Power, Brendan* / Si bheag, si mhor: *O'Suilleabhain, Micheal/C. Breatnach* / Pulsus / Three jigs: *Kelly, Laoise* / River of sound / Caoineadh na dtri mhuire: *O'Lionaird, Iarla* / Three reels: *Ivers, Eileen* / Wind in the woods: *O'Connor, M./M. Murray* / Turas go tir na nog: *O'Suilleabhain, Micheal* / O'Keefe's slides: *Begley, Seamus & Stephen Cooney* / Roaring water reels: *Vallely, Niall* / Barn dances: *Gavin, Frankie & Martin O'Connor* / Port na bpucai: *Browne, Ronan*
CD _______ **CDV 2776**
Virgin / Dec '95 / EMI

RIVER TOWN BLUES
CD _______ **HIUKCD 118**
Hi / Jul '91 / Pinnacle

RIVERSIDE HISTORY OF CLASSIC JAZZ (3CD Set)
I'm going to heaven if it takes my life: *Gates, Rev. J.M. & Congregation* / I've got the blues for Rampart Street: *Cox, Ida* / Big Bill blues: *Broonzy, 'Big' Bill* / Cascades: *Joplin, Scott* / Perfect rag: *Morton, Jelly Roll* / Pearls: *Morton, Jelly Roll* / Froggie Moore rag: *Oliver, Joe 'King' Jazzband* / Memphis maybe man: *Cook, Doc & His Dreamland Orchestra* / Mama stayed out: *Barrelhouse Five* / Fives: *Yancey, Jimmy* / Lone star blues: *Johnson, Pete* / Royal garden blues: *Beiderbecke, Bix & The Wolverines* / Friars Point Shuffle: *Jungle Kings* / Harlem strut: *Johnson, James P.* / Cake walkin' babies from home: *Red Onion Jazz Babies* / Stampede: *Red & Miffs Stompers* / Eccentric: *Davison, 'Wild' Bill* / Muskrat ramble: *Spanier, Muggsy* / Hop off: *Henderson, Fletcher Orchestra* / Rainy nights: *Ellington, Duke Washingtonians* / Make me a pallet on the floor: *Johnson, Bunk* / Weary blues: *Ory, Kid* / Antigua blues: *Watters, Lu & The Yerba Buena Jazz Band*
CD Set _______ **RBCD 005**
Riverside / Oct '93 / Cadillac / Complete/ Pinnacle / Jazz Music

RIVERSIDE ROCKABILLY
CD _______ **RAUCD 014**
Raucous / Jul '97 / Nervous / RTM/Disc / TKO Magnum

RIVIERA - THE HI-LIFE COMPILATION (2CD Set)
Time for love: *English, Kim* / Joy and happiness: *Stabbs* / I see only you: *Nootropic* / Fantasy: *Angel Heart* / Pleasure: *Medium High* / Oohhh baby: *Simpson, Vida* / I know a place: *English, Kim* / Lost in love: *Up Yer Ronson* / Renegade master: *Wildchild* / Bailando con lobos: *Cabana* / Nite life: *English, Kim* / Another night: *Kitsch In Synch* / Prayer to the music: *Polo, Marco* / Manifest your love: *DOP* / Raise: *Boston Bees* / Manifest your love: *DOP*
CD Set _______ **5294002**
Hi-Life / Aug '96 / PolyGram

RMO VOL.1
Hypnodelic: *Francois K* / Burnin up: *Morales, Angel* / Never stop: *Reflexion* / Live in unity: *Dangerous Minds* / Deeper: *Flat Earth Society* / Radical noise: *DJ Tonka* / Invasion: *Freakforce* / Manual: *Continious Cool* / State of time: *Gage* / Theme from Blue Cucaracha: *Innocent* / Gliding: *Compass* / Disappear: *Underground People* / Latin kaos: *El Bandolero* / Deep love: *D. dact* / Sensation 2: *Nelson, G & R Purser* / Dance, dance, dance: *Fruitloops* / Tonite: *Sleaze*
CD _______ **SPV 08468382**
SPV / Oct '96 / Koch / Plastic Head

ROAD OF BROKEN HEARTS - ORIGINAL COUNTRY ROOTS
Wild side of life / Making believe / I can't forget / She's the steppin' out kind / Heartache to recall / Ball and chain / Wabash cannonball / Honky tonk merry go round / Take my hand / Me and my gin / Cowpoke / Lukenbach Texas / Jenny Lou / Wings of a dove / Ol' blue / Send me the pillow that you dream on / DJ for a day / I don't like you anymore / I'm a regular daddy / Road of broken hearts
CD _______ **CDAA 042**
Tring / Jan '92 / Tring

ROAD TO RHYTHM 'N' BLUES AND ROCK 'N' ROLL VOL.1
Hastings Street / Milkcow blues / Boogie woogie stomp / My Daddy was a lovin' man / We gonna pitch a boogie woogie / Boogie woogie (I may be wrong) / Trucking little woman / Blues ain't nothin' but... / Roll 'em Pete / Baby don't / On me / Jumpin' at the Savoy / After hours / Confessin' the blues / Hootie's ignorant oil / I want a tall skinny Papa / Cow cow boogie / Hey lawdy Mama / Hurry hurry / I know how to do it / Boogie rocks / Boogie woogie on a Saturday night / Groovin' the blues / Bellvue for you / Somebody's gotta go / You need coachin'
CD _______ **PASTCD 7811**
Flapper / Feb '97 / Pinnacle

ROAD TO RHYTHM 'N' BLUES AND ROCK 'N' ROLL VOL.2
Strange things happening every day / That's the stuff you gotta watch / Rock me Mama / Caldonia / Southpaw serenade / Schoolday blues / Honeydripper / T-Bone boogie / Juice head baby / Here comes the blues / Be baba leba / Chicago breakdown / Bartender breakdown / Choo choo ch'boogie / Wedding day blues / Boogie woogie Hannah / Jump the boogie / Let the good times roll / Postman blues / Bottoms up / Amos blues / Pencil broke / Wake up old maid / Miss Brown blues
CD _______ **PASTCD 7812**
Flapper / Feb '97 / Pinnacle

ROARING 20'S, THE
If you knew Susie like I know Susie: *Shilkret, Jack & His Orchestra* / Sheikh of Araby: *Pianola Roll* / I'm tellin' the birds, tellin' the bees: *Smith, Jack 'Whispering'* / That's my weakness now: *Pianola Roll* / Canadian capers: *Biese, Paul Trio* / Rose Marie: *Pianola Roll* / Colette: *Whiteman, Paul & His Orchestra* / Where the lazy daisies grow: *Pianola Roll* / Ain't misbehavin': *Hylton, Jack & His Orchestra & Sam Browne* / My inspiration is you: *Pianola Roll* / Wedding of the painted doll: *Pianola Roll* / Don't bring Lulu: *Garber, Jan & His Orchestra* / Always: *Pianola Roll* / Where, oh where do I live: *Douglas, Fred & Orchestra* / Birth of the blues: *Pianola Roll* / I miss my Swiss: *Golden Gate Orchestra* / Ain't she sweet: *Pianola Roll* / Hello Swanee, hello: *Syncopated Four* / Ramona: *Pianola Roll* / Charleston
CD _______ **CDSDL 344**
Saydisc / Mar '94 / ADA / Direct / Harmonia Mundi

ROARING TWENTIES
CD _______ **DCD 5334**
Disky / Dec '93 / Disky / THE

ROBERT BURNS - THE MERRY MUSES
Yellow, yellow yorlin' / My girl she's airy, she's buxom and gay / Nine inch will please a lady / Logan water / Ye haelien wrang, lassie / Bonniest lass / As I cam o'er the Cairneymount / O gie the lass her fairin' lad / Cuddie the cooper / Wad ye do that / Ye jovial boys who loved the joys / Dainty Davie / Muirland Meg / How can I keep my Maidenhead / Nae hair on't / In Edinburgh town they've made a law / There was a jolly gauger, a gauging he did ride / Duncan Gray / Duncan MacLeerie
CD _______ **IRCD 035**
Iona / Feb '96 / ADA / Direct / Duncans

ROBERT BURNS COLLECTION - THE BURNS SUPPER
Selkirk grace / Address to the haggis / Immortal memory of Robert Burns / Toast to the lassies / Reply to the toast to the lassies / Tam o'shanter / Man's a man/Auld lang syne
CD _______ **LCOM 6039**
Lismor / Nov '95 / ADA / Direct / Duncans / Lismor

ROBERT BURNS COLLECTION - THE MUSIC
Of a' the airts / Bonnie lass of Ballochmyle / Green grow the rashes / Afton water / Ca' the ewes / Aye waukin' o / Trilogy / John Anderson my jo / Star of Rabbie Burns / Ye banks and braes / O my love is like a red red roae / Ae fond kiss / Man's a man / Bonnie wee thing / Auld lang syne
CD _______ **LCOM 6041**
Lismor / Nov '95 / ADA / Direct / Duncans / Lismor

ROBERT BURNS COLLECTION - THE SONGS
Man's a man / O my love is like a red red rose / Ae fond kiss / Afton water / Bonnie lass of Ballochmyle / Ye banks and braes / Aye waukin' o / De'il's awa' wi' tha exciseman / Rosebud by my early walk / Scots wha hae / I'm ower young to marry yet / There was a lad / Birks o' Aberfeldy / MacPherson's farewell / John Anderson my jo / Auld lang syne
CD _______ **LCOM 6040**
Lismor / Nov '95 / ADA / Direct / Duncans / Lismor

ROCK & POP BALLADS
CD _______ **12202**
Laserlight / May '94 / Target/BMG

ROCK 4 YOU
CD _______ **EXP 047**
Experience / May '97 / TKO Magnum

ROCK AND WATER
CD _______ **ECLCD 9411**
Eclectic / Jan '96 / ADA / New Note/ Pinnacle

ROCK ANTHEMS VOL.1
CD _______ **DINCD 101**
Dino / Oct '94 / Pinnacle

ROCK ANTHEMS VOL.2
CD _______ **DINCD 110**
Dino / Apr '96 / Pinnacle

ROCK AROUND THE CLOCK
CD _______ **MACCD 211**
Autograph / Aug '96 / BMG

ROCK AROUND THE CLOCK
CD _______ **HM 024**
Harmony / Jun '97 / TKO Magnum

ROCK AROUND THE JUKEBOX
Long tall Sally / Stagger Lee / Rebel rouser / Runaway / Night has a thousand eyes / Tequila / Little darlin' / He's so fine / Be bop a lula / Under the moon of love / Mr. Bass Man / Blue Monday / Angels listened in Kansas City / Rockin' Robin / Personality / So long baby / Lucille / Dance with the guitar / Duke of Earl
CD _______ **QED 007**
Tring / Nov '96 / Tring

ROCK BALLADS
Once in a lifetime: *Kansas* / Parisienne walkways: *Moore, Gary* / Amanda: *Boston* / Winning man: *Krokus* / On and on: *Bishop, Stephen* / Surrender: *Trixter* / Thrill is gone: *King, B.B.* / Pusher: *Trixter* / She's gone: *Steelheart* / Sara: *Starship* / Still believe: *Starship* / Washable ink: *Hiatt, John* / Gail: *Cooper, Alice* / Just one precious moment: *Emergency* / Stairway to heaven: *Far Corporation*
CD _______ **MCD 30202**
Ariola Express / Mar '94 / BMG

ROCK BALLADS
Sowing the seeds of love: *Tears For Fears* / First time: *Beck, Robin* / Search is over: *Survivor* / Cry: *Godley & Creme* / Stop: *Brown, Sam* / Should've known better: *Diamond, Jim* / Sugar box: *Then Jerico* / Send me an angel: *Scorpions* / You're the best thing: *Style Council* / When Smokey sings: *ABC* / Start talking love: *Magnum* / Because of you: *Dexy's Midnight Runners* / Babe: *Styx* / Street of dreams: *Rainbow*
CD _______ **5506482**
Spectrum / Aug '94 / PolyGram

ROCK BEFORE ELVIS
CD _______ **STBCD 25162617**
Stash / Aug '95 / ADA / Cadillac / CM / Direct / Jazz Music

ROCK CITY NIGHTS
One vision: *Queen* / You give love a bad name: *Bon Jovi* / Big area: *Then Jerico* / King of emotion: *Big Country* / Red sky: *Status Quo* / Incommunicado: *Marillion* / Satisfied: *Marx, Richard* / Some like it hot: *Power Station* / Rock the night: *Europe* / Need you tonight: *INXS* / I don't want a lover: *Texas* / I won't back down: *Petty, Tom* / Silent running: *Mike & The Mechanics* / Africa: *Toto* / More than a feeling: *Boston* / Go your own way: *Fleetwood Mac* / I surrender: *Rainbow* / Eye of the tiger: *Survivor*
CD _______ **8406222**
PolyGram TV / Oct '89 / PolyGram

ROCK CLASSICS
CD _______ **MATCD 236**
Castle / Dec '92 / BMG

ROCK CLASSICS
I want you to want me: *Cheap Trick* / Barracuda: *Heart* / Carrie: *Europe* / She's not there: *Santana* / Up around the bend: *Hanoi Rocks* / Breaking the law: *Judas Priest* / Ride like the wind: *Saxon* / Silver machine: *Hawkwind* / Rock 'n' me: *Miller, Steve Band* / Show me the way: *Frampton, Peter* / I surrender: *Rainbow* / Waiting for an alibi: *Thin Lizzy* / Radar love: *Golden Earring* / Closer to the heart: *Rush* / Whatever you want: *Status Quo* / Victims of circumstance: *Barclay James Harvest* / Lady in black: *Uriah Heep* / This flight tonight: *Nazareth*
CD _______ **VSOPCD 194**
Connoisseur Collection / Apr '94 / Pinnacle

ROCK CLASSICS VOL.1
CD _______ **11851**
Laserlight / Feb '95 / Target/BMG

ROCK CLASSICS VOL.2
CD _______ **11852**
Laserlight / Feb '95 / Target/BMG

ROCK CLASSICS VOL.3
CD _______ **11853**
Laserlight / Feb '95 / Target/BMG

ROCK DON'T RUN VOL.2
CD _______ **SPINCD 0023**
Spinout / Jan '97 / Cargo

ROCK ERA (More Of The Greatest Hits)
CD _______ **LECD 403**
Wisepack / Sep '93 / Conifer/BMG / THE

ROCK GIANTS
CD _______ **12402**
Laserlight / Feb '95 / Target/BMG

ROCK GUITAR LEGENDS VOL.2
Mercury blues: *Lindley, David* / Over and over: *Walsh, Joe* / Jukebox hero: *Foreigner* / Lost in the shuffle: *Kortchmar, Danny* / Long time till I get over you: *Little Feat* / River of tears: *Raitt, Bonnie* / Ashphalt jungle: *Felder, Don* / So wrong: *Simmons, Patrick* / Stainsby girls: *Rea, Chris* / Spirit of radio: *Rush* / I can see for miles: *Who* / Cocaine: *Cale, J.J.* / Sky high: *Atlanta Rhythm Section* / I'm waiting for the man: *Velvet Underground* / Whiskey in the jar: *Thin Lizzy* / From little things big things grow: *Edmunds, Dave* / Confidence man: *Healey, Jeff* / We can be together: *Jefferson Airplane* / Built for speed: *Stray Cats* / Roll with the changes: *REO Speedwagon* / Don't stop believin': *Journey* / Honey don't leave LA: *Taylor, James* / Sweet potato pie: *Taylor, James* / Rock 'n' roll hoochie coo: *Winter, Johnny* / East of Eden's gate: *Thorpe, Billy* / Need your love so bad: *Fleetwood Mac* / Where have you been all my life: *Nugent, Ted* / Ready for love: *Mott The Hoople* / Once bitten twice shy: *Hunter, Ian* / American girl: *Petty, Tom* / Sweet home Alabama: *Lynyrd Skynyrd* / Gotta hurry: *Yardbirds* / No particular place to go: *Berry, Chuck* / Natural born bugie: *Humble Pie* / Parisienne walkways (live): *Moore, Gary* / I'm your witch doctor: *Clapton, Eric Allstars* / Laundromat: *Gallagher, Rory* / Bleeding heart: *Hendrix, Jimi* / You won't see me anymore: *Green, Peter* / Breakdown: *Coverdale, David* / I've been born again: *Frey, Glenn* / Who do you love: *Juicy Lucy* / Paranoid: *Black Sabbath* / Rocky mountain way: *Walsh, Joe* / Drift away: *Gray, Dobie* / I came to dance: *Lofgren, Nils* / Show me the way: *Frampton, Peter* / Dear Mr. Fantasy: *Traffic*
CD Set _______ **NXTCD 248**
Sequel / May '93 / BMG

ROCK IT FOR ME - 1937
One o'clock jump: *Basie, Count* / Sailboat in the moonlight: *Holiday, Billie & Her Orchestra* / I can't get started (with you): *Berigan, Bunny* / Honeysuckle rose: *Hawkins, Coleman* / Boo hoo: *Lombardo, Guy* / When we're alone: *James, Harry* / Alabamy home: *Ellington, Duke* / Getting some fun out of life: *Holiday, Billie & Orchestra/Barney Kessel* / Carry me back to old Virginny: *Armstrong, Louis* / Song of India: *Dorsey, Tommy* / I can't give you anything but love: *Goodman, Benny* / Who's sorry now: *Crosby, Bob* / Loch Lomond: *Sullivan, Maxine* / Posin': *Lunceford, Jimmie* / I've got my love to keep me warm: *Norvo, Red* / Rock it for me: *Webb, Chick* / Whose babe: *Hampton* / I must have that man: *Wilson, Teddy* / Caravan: *Ellington, Duke* / Topsie
CD _______ **PHONT CD 7663**
Phontastic / Apr '90 / Cadillac / Jazz Music / Wellard

ROCK LEGENDS
This flight tonight: *Nazareth* / NIB: *Black Sabbath* / Sweet Lorraine: *Uriah Heep* / Silver machine: *Hawkwind* / Down the dustpipe: *Status Quo* / Race with the devil: *Girlschool* / Dancin': *Moore, Gary* / Kingdom of madness: *Magnum* / Overkill: *Motorhead* / Who do you love: *Juicy Lucy* / Ace of spades: *Motorhead* / Natural born bugie: *Humble Pie* / Broken down angel: *Nazareth* / Levitation: *Hawkwind* / Ice in the sun: *Status Quo* / Wizard: *Uriah Heep* / All of my life: *Magnum* / Parisienne walkways (lives): *Moore, Gary*
CD _______ **MCCD 045**
Music Club / Sep '91 / Disc / THE

ROCK LEGENDS (2CD Set)
CD Set _______ **MBSCD 406**
Castle / Nov '93 / BMG

ROCK LIVE FROM THE MOUNTAIN STAGE
Alright guy: *Snider, Todd* / 8 Piece box: *Southern Culture On The Skids* / Ain't hurtin' nobody: *Prine, John* / I believe: *Blessid Union Of Souls* / I must be high: *Wilco* / Poor boy blues: *Bonepony* / Blue: *Jayhawks* / Welfare music: *Bottle Rockets* / Jacob: *Jackopierce* / Send me on my way: *Rusted Root*
CD _______ **BPM 307CD**
Blue Plate / May '97 / ADA / Direct / Greyhound

ROCK MACHINE TURNS YOU ON, THE
I'll be your baby tonight: *Dylan, Bob* / Can't be so bad: *Moby Grape* / Fresh garbage: *Spirit* / I won't leave my wooden wife for you, sugar: *United States Of America* / Time of the season: *Zombies* / Turn on a friend: *Peanut Butter Conspiracy* / Sisters of mercy: *Cohen, Leonard* / My days are numbered: *Blood, Sweat & Tears* / Dolphins smile: *Byrds* / Statesboro blues: *Taj Mahal* / Killing floor: *Electric Flag* / Nobody's got any money in the summer: *Harper, Roy* / Flames: *Gantry, Elmer & Velvet Opera* / Come away Melinda: *Rose, Tim*
CD _______ **4844392**
Columbia / Jul '96 / Sony

ROCK ME SLOWLY
CD ______ MUSCD 020
MCI Music / Sep '94 / Disc / THE

ROCK 'N' ROLL (2CD Set)
CD Set ______ R2CD 4017
Deja Vu / Jan '96 / THE

ROCK 'N' ROLL CHRISTMAS
Rudolph the red nosed reindeer: *Dixie Cups* / White Christmas: *Ford, Frankie* / Frosty the snowman: *Coasters* / Christmas song: *Drifters* / Deck the halls: *Crickets* / Sleigh ride: *Diamonds* / If I could spend Christmas with you: *Roe, Tommy* / Little drummer boy: *Tokens* / Silent night: *Shirelles* / New baby for Christmas: *Preston, Johnny* / Winter wonderland: *Rockin' Robin* / Rockin' around the christmas tree: *Jones, Davy*
CD ______ XMAS 009
Tring / Nov '96 / Tring

ROCK 'N' ROLL CLASSICS
CD ______ LECD 054
Wisepack / Jul '94 / Conifer/BMG / THE

ROCK 'N' ROLL CLASSICS (2CD Set)
Why do fools fall in love: *Lymon, Frankie & The Teenagers* / Oh Carol: *Sedaka, Neil* / Duke of Earl: *Chandler, Gene* / Under the moon of love: *Lee, Curtis* / Get a job: *Silhouettes* / Sealed with a kiss: *Hyland, Brian* / At the hop: *Danny & The Juniors* / Poetry in motion: *Tillotson, Johnny* / I only have eyes for you: *Flamingos* / Heartbeat: *Holly, Buddy* / All I have to do is dream: *Everly Brothers* / Runaway: *Shannon, Del* / Since I don't have you: *Skyliners* / One fine day: *Chiffons* / Will you still love me tomorrow: *Shirelles* / Bye bye love: *Everly Brothers* / Breaking up is hard to do: *Sedaka, Neil* / Rock around the clock: *Haley, Bill* / Leader of the pack: *Shangri-Las* / Shoop shoop song: *Everett, Betty* / Remember (walkin' in the sand): *Shangri-Las* / Goodnight sweetheart, goodnight: *Spaniels* / 24 hours from Tulsa: *Pitney, Gene* / Hey Paula: *Paul & Paula* / Wanderer: *Dion* / Diana: *Anka, Paul* / Johnny B Goode: *Vee, Bobby* / Sea cruise: *Ford, Frankie* / In the still of the night: *Five Satins* / Rubber ball: *Vee, Bobby* / C'mon everybody: *Cochran, Eddie* / Stay: *Williams, Maurice & The Zodiacs* / Born too late: *Poni-Tails* / Baby it's you: *Shirelles* / Come go with me: *Del-Vikings* / I'm gonna be strong: *Pitney, Gene* / Blue moon: *Marcels*
CD Set ______ RCACD 203
RCA / Jul '97 / BMG

ROCK 'N' ROLL CLASSICS
CD ______ MACCD 154
Autograph / Aug '96 / BMG

ROCK 'N' ROLL FEVER (The Wildest From Specialty)
Justine: *Don & Dewey* / Moose on the loose: *Jackson, Roddy* / Thunderbird: *Hall, Rene* / My baby's rocking: *Monitors* / Cherokee dance: *Landers, Bob* / She said "Yeah": *Williams, Larry* / Don't stop loving me: *Church, Eugene* / Don't you just know it: *Titans* / Twitchy: *Hall, Rene* / Haunted house: *Fuller, Johnny* / Chicken, baby, chicken: *Harris, Tony* / Sack: *Hughes, Ben* / Arlene: *Titans* / Little bird: *Hollywood Flames* / I've got my sights set on someone new: *Jackson, Roddy* / Lights out: *Byrne, Jerry* / It's spring again: *Pentagons* / Goodbye baby goodbye: *Lowery, Sonny* / Ooh little girl: *Dixon, Floyd* / Rock 'n' roll fever: *Dixon, Floyd* / Swingin' at the creek: *Fuller, Johnny* / Frankenstein's den: *Hollywood Flames* / Carry on: *Byrne, Jerry* / Hiccups: *Jackson, Roddy* / Satisfied: *Casualairs*
CD ______ CDCHD 574
Ace / Jul '94 / Pinnacle

ROCK 'N' ROLL FOREVER
CD ______ DCD 5306
Disky / Dec '93 / Disky / THE

ROCK 'N' ROLL GOLD (2CD Set)
CD Set ______ D2CD 4017
Deja Vu / Jun '95 / THE

ROCK 'N' ROLL GREATS (2CD Set)
Matchbox: *Perkins, Carl* / Woman in black: *Vincent, Gene* / Whole lotta shakin' goin' on: *Lewis, Jerry Lee* / Reet Petite: *Wilson, Jackie* / Baby face: *Little Richard* / Little Queenie: *Lewis, Jerry Lee* / Rip it up: *Haley, Bill* / Blue Monday: *Domino, Fats* / Ooby dooby: *Orbison, Roy* / Maybelline: *Elvis, Scotty & Bill* / Lucille: *Little Richard* / Boppin'the blues: *Perkins, Carl* / Be bop a lula: *Vincent, Gene* / Shake rattle & roll: *Haley, Bill* / Runaway: *Shannon, Del* / Red hot: *Haley, Bill* / Ain't that a shame: *Domino, Fats* / Let's have a party: *Jackson, Wanda* / Lonely weekend: *Rich, Charlie* / That's why: *Wilson, Jackie* / High school confidential: *Lewis, Jerry Lee* / Blueberry hill: *Lewis, Jerry Lee* / Speedy gonzales: *Boone, Pat* / Wake up little Suzie: *Everly Brothers* / Blue suede shoes: *Perkins, Carl* / Rock around the clock: *Haley, Bill* / Rave on: *Jackson, Wanda* / Hats off to Larry: *Shannon, Del* / Great balls of fire: *Lewis, Jerry Lee* / That's alright mama: *Elvis, Scotty & Bill* / Ubangi stomp: *Smith, Warren* / Honey don't: *Perkins, Carl* / See you later alligator: *Haley, Bill* / Raunchy: *Justis, Bill* / Hello Mary Lou: *Nelson, Rick* / Good golly Miss Molly: *Little Richard* / Rockhouse: *Orbison, Roy* / Be my guest: *Domino, Fats* / Say mama: *Vincent, Gene* / Long tall Sally: *Little Richard*
CD Set ______ 330212
Hallmark / Jul '96 / Carlton

ROCK 'N' ROLL GREATS VOL.1
Tutti frutti: *Little Richard* / That'll be the day: *Holly, Buddy & The Crickets* / Blueberry Hill: *Domino, Fats* / Take good care of my baby: *Vee, Bobby* / Walk don't run: *Ventures* / Say mama: *Vincent, Gene* / Bird dog: *Everly Brothers* / Sweet little sixteen: *Berry, Chuck* / Something else: *Cochran, Eddie* / (We're gonna) Rock around the clock: *Haley, Bill & The Comets* / I'm walkin': *Domino, Fats* / Oh boy: *Holly, Buddy & The Crickets* / Don't ever change: *Crickets* / Why do fools fall in love: *Lymon, Frankie & The Teenagers* / Be bop a lula: *Vincent, Gene* / Summertime blues: *Cochran, Eddie* / You're sixteen: *Burnette, Johnny Rock 'N' Roll Trio* / Rubber ball: *Vee, Bobby*
CD ______ CDMFP 5744
Music For Pleasure / Apr '92 / EMI

ROCK 'N' ROLL GREATS VOL.2
C'mon everybody: *Cochran, Eddie* / Ain't that a shame: *Domino, Fats* / Willie and the hand jive: *Otis, Johnny Show* / Memphis, Tennessee: *Berry, Chuck* / Dreamin': *Burnette, Johnny Rock 'N' Roll Trio* / Red river rock: *Johnny & The Hurricanes* / Git it: *Vincent, Gene* / I'm not a juvenile delinquent: *Lymon, Frankie & The Teenagers* / Whole lotta shakin' goin' on: *Lewis, Jerry Lee* / At the hop: *Danny & The Juniors* / Great balls of fire: *Lewis, Jerry Lee* / Peggy Sue: *Holly, Buddy & The Crickets* / Claudette: *Everly Brothers* / Three steps to heaven: *Cochran, Eddie* / Blue Monday: *Domino, Fats* / Blue jean bop: *Vincent, Gene* / Johnny B Goode: *Berry, Chuck* / Good golly Miss Molly: *Little Richard*
CD ______ CDMFP 5745
Music For Pleasure / Apr '92 / EMI

ROCK 'N' ROLL GREATS VOL.3
Be my guest: *Domino, Fats* / Night has a thousand eyes: *Vee, Bobby* / Pistol packin' mama: *Vincent, Gene* / Cincinnati fireball: *Burnette, Johnny Rock 'N' Roll Trio* / She's gone: *Knox, Buddy* / Piltdown rides again: *Piltdown Men* / Let's have a party: *Jackson, Wanda* / Get a job: *Silhouettes* / Ma, he's making eyes at me: *Otis, Johnny* / Weekend: *Cochran, Eddie* / Perfidia: *Ventures* / Bony Moronie: *Williams, Larry* / Mother In Law: *K-Doe, Ernie* / Love potion no.9: *Clovers* / Runaway: *Shannon, Del* / You've got what it takes: *Johnson, Marv* / Stay: *Williams, Maurice & The Zodiacs* / Baby baby: *Lymon, Frankie & The Teenagers*
CD ______ CDMFP 5941
Music For Pleasure / Apr '92 / EMI

ROCK 'N' ROLL GREATS VOL.4
Hello Mary Lou: *Nelson, Rick* / Shakin' all over: *Kidd, Johnny & The Pirates* / Run to him: *Vee, Bobby* / Shake, rattle and roll: *Haley, Bill* / Rave on: *Holly, Buddy* / I'm in love again: *Domino, Fats* / Move it: *Richard, Cliff* / No particular place to go: *Berry, Chuck* / Little town flirt: *Shannon, Del* / Only sixteen: *Douglas, Craig* / See you later alligator: *Haley, Bill* / It's late: *Nelson, Rick* / Rock 'n' roll music: *Berry, Chuck* / Wild cat: *Vincent, Gene* / Say man: *Diddley, Bo* / Sweetie pie: *Cochran, Eddie* / Hey little girl: *Shannon, Del* / It doesn't matter anymore: *Holly, Buddy*
CD ______ CDMFP 5942
Music For Pleasure / Apr '92 / EMI

ROCK 'N' ROLL HALL OF FAME CONCERT
CD ______ 4837932
Sony Music / Sep '96 / Sony

ROCK 'N' ROLL IS HERE TO STAY (3CD Set)
C'mon everybody: *Cochran, Eddie* / Hallelujah, I love her so: *Cochran, Eddie* / Something else: *Cochran, Eddie* / I'm a moody guy: *Fenton, Shane & The Fentones* / Five foot two, eyes of blue: *Fenton, Shane & The Fentones* / Stick shift: *Duals* / Party doll: *Knox, Buddy* / Ain't misbehavin': *Bruce, Tommy & The Bruisers* / Let the good times roll: *Shirley & Lee* / Be bop a lula: *Vincent, Gene* / Wild cat: *Vincent, Gene* / Pistol packin' mama: *Vincent, Gene* / Lost and found: *Vernon Girls* / Run to him: *Vee, Bobby* / Take good care of my baby: *Vee, Bobby* / Night has a thousand eyes: *Vee, Bobby* / Saturday night at the duck pond: *Cougars* / Blueberry hill: *Domino, Fats* / Piltdown rides again: *Piltdown Men* / I've got a woman: *McGriff, Jimmy* / Blue moon: *Marcels* / Big man: *Four Preps* / You're sixteen: *Four Preps* / Rubber ball: *Avons* / Love potion no.9: *Clover* / Shakin' all over: *Kidd, Johnny & The Pirates* / Please don't touch: *Kidd, Johnny & The Pirates* / I'll never get over you: *Kidd, Johnny & The Pirates* / You've got what it takes: *Johnson, Marv* / You can't sit down: *Upchurch, Phil Combo* / Ain't that a shame: *Domino, Fats* / I'm a juvenile delinquent: *Lymon, Frankie & The Teenagers* / Why do fools fall in love: *Lymon, Frankie & The Teenagers* / Papa oom mow mow: *Rivingtons* / Western movies: *Olympics* / Baby hully gully: *Olympics* / It's late: *Nelson, Rick* / Hello Mary Lou: *Nelson, Rick* / La Bamba: *Crickets* / Don't ever change: *Crickets* / Tears on my pillow: *Imperials* / Only sixteen: *Douglas, Craig* / Tell Laura I love her: *Valence, Ricky* / Right behind you baby: *Taylor, Vince & Playboys* / Ma, he's making eyes at me: *Otis, Johnny Show/Marie Adams/Three Tons Of Joy* / Gypsy beat: *Packabeats* / Tom Crombie and his Rockets - Teach you to rock: *Packabeats* / Walk don't run: *Ventures*
CD Set ______ CDTRBOX 132
Trio / Oct '94 / EMI

ROCK 'N' ROLL JAMBOREE
CD ______ PT 650001
Part / Jun '96 / Nervous

ROCK 'N' ROLL LEGENDS
Shake, rattle and roll: *Haley, Bill* / Rock around the clock: *Haley, Bill* / See you later alligator: *Haley, Bill* / Rip it up: *Haley, Bill* / Memphis Tennessee: *Lewis, Jerry Lee* / Good golly Miss Molly: *Lewis, Jerry Lee* / Tutti frutti: *Lewis, Jerry Lee* / Long tall Sally: *Lewis, Jerry Lee* / Whole lotta shakin' goin' on: *Lewis, Jerry Lee* / Great balls of fire: *Lewis, Jerry Lee* / Boogie woogie man from Tennessee: *Lewis, Jerry Lee* / Be bop a Lula: *Vincent, Gene* / Pistol packing Mama: *Vincent, Gene* / Bird doggin': *Vincent, Gene* / Blue jean bop: *Vincent, Gene* / Blue suede shoes: *Perkins, Carl* / This ole house: *Perkins, Carl* / All Mama's children: *Perkins, Carl* / That's right: *Perkins, Carl*
CD ______ PLATCD 138
Platinum / Feb '97 / Prism

ROCK 'N' ROLL LOVE SONGS (3CD Set)
Blue moon: *Marcels* / I only have eyes for you: *Flamingoes* / Heartbeat: *Vee, Bobby* / Blueberry hill: *Domino, Fats* / Sweetie pie: *Cochran, Eddie* / Unchained melody: *Vincent, Gene* / You got what it takes: *Kidd, Johnny* / Baby, baby: *Lymon, Frankie & The Teenagers* / Everlovin': *Nelson, Rick* / Please say you want me: *Little Anthony & The Imperials* / You're sixteen: *Burnette, Johnny* / Ma (He's making eyes at me): *Otis, Johnny Show* / Teardrops fall like rain: *Crickets* / Tell Laura I love you: *Valance, Ricky* / Hallelujah' I love her: *Cochran, Eddie* / Ain't misbeghavin': *Bruce, Tommy & The Bruisers* / Love potion No.9: *Clovers* / ABC's of love: *Lymon, Frankie & The Teenagers* / Creation of love: *Lymon, Frankie & The Teenagers* / My blue heaven: *Domino, Fats* / Why do fools fall in love: *Lymon, Frankie & The Teenagers* / Run to him: *Vee, Bobby* / I'll be forever loving you: *Marcels* / I'm taking a vacation for love: *Little Anthony & The Imperials* / Please don't touch: *Kidd, Johnny* / Weekend: *Cochran, Eddie* / Your cheatin' heart: *Vincent, Gene* / Whole lotta loving: *Domino, Fats* / Shakin' all over: *Kidd, Johnny* / Don't try to change me: *Crickets* / Heart of a teenager: *Douglas, Craig* / Broken doll: *Bruce, Tommy & The Bruisers* / Teenager in love: *Dion & The Belmonts* / Girl of my best friend: *Donner, Ral* / Dream lover: *Burnette, Johnny* / Somethin' else: *Cochran, Eddie* / She's one: *Knox, Buddy* / Seven little girls sitting on the back seat: *Avons* / Yes my darling: *Domino, Fats* / Night has a thousand eyes: *Vee, Bobby* / Dreamin': *Burnette, Johnny* / Little bitty pretty one: *Lymon, Frankie* / Have I told you lately that I love you: *Cochran, Eddie* / I'm walkin': *Domino, Fats* / Two people in the world: *Little Anthony & The Imperials* / If you were the only girl in the world: *Kidd, Johnny & The Pirates* / He's so fine: *Chiffons* / Woman love: *Vincent, Gene* / My little girl: *Crickets* / Pretty blue eyes: *Douglas, Craig* / Runaround Sue: *Dion* / To be with you: *Knox, Buddy* / True love ways: *Vee, Bobby* / Jeanie, Jeanie, Jeanie: *Cochran, Eddie* / In the middle of heartache: *Jackson, Wanda* / I'm in love again: *Domino, Fats* / Heartaches: *Marcels*
CD Set ______ CDTRBOX 224
Trio / Jul '96 / EMI

ROCK 'N' ROLL LOVE SONGS
Save the last dance for me: *Platters* / It keeps right on hurtin': *Tillotson, Johnny* / More than I can say: *Vee, Bobby* / You belong to me: *Duprees* / Mr. Blue: *Fleetwoods* / So much in love: *Tymes* / I love the way you love me: *Johnson, Marvin* / Rock 'n' roll lullaby: *Thomas, B.J.* / My heart is an open book: *Dobkins, Carl Jr.* / Hey baby: *Channel, Bruce* / Chapel of love: *Dixie Cups* / Dedicated to the one I love: *Shirelles* / Some kind of wonderful: *Drifters* / Lavender blue: *Turner, Sammy* / Sea of love: *Phillips, Phil* / My own true love: *Duprees* / Hurt: *Yuro, Timi* / Only you (and you alone): *Platters*
CD ______ ECD 3114
K-Tel / Jan '95 / K-Tel

ROCK 'N' ROLL LOVE SONGS VOL.1
All I have to do is dream: *Everly Brothers* / More than I can say: *Vee, Bobby* / I'm sorry: *Lee, Brenda* / Heartbeat: *Holly, Buddy* / Poor little fool: *Nelson, Rick* / Dreamin': *Burnette, Johnny Rock 'N' Roll Trio* / Three steps to heaven: *Cochran, Eddie* / Poetry in motion: *Tillotson, Johnny* / Teenager in love: *Dionthebelmonts* / Don't ever change: *Crickets* / Why do fools fall in love: *Crickets* / Donna: *Valens, Ritchie* / You don't know what you've got (until you lose it): *Donner, Ral* / Be bop a lula: *Vincent, Gene* / When my little girl is smiling: *Douglas, Craig* / Sealed with a kiss: *Hyland, Brian* / I want to walk you home: *Domino, Fats* / Tears on my pillow: *Imperials* / Johnny Angel: *Fabares, Shelly* / Shakin' all over: *Kidd, Johnny & The Pirates*
CD ______ CDMFP 5935
Music For Pleasure / Apr '92 / EMI

ROCK 'N' ROLL LOVE SONGS VOL.2
Raining in my heart: *Holly, Buddy* / Blue moon: *Marcels* / Bye bye love: *Everly Brothers* / I only have eyes for you: *Flamingos* / Take good care of my baby: *Vee, Bobby* / You're sixteen: *Burnette, Johnny Rock 'N' Roll Trio* / My little girl: *Crickets* / I remember: *Cochran, Eddie* / Two people in the world: *Imperials* / When: *Kalin Twins* / Sweet nothin's: *Lee, Brenda* / It's late: *Nelson, Rick* / I want you to be my girl: *Lymon, Frankie & The Teenagers* / Unchained melody: *Baxter, Les* / She she little Sheila: *Vincent, Gene* / Party doll: *Knox, Buddy* / I'll never get over you: *Kidd, Johnny & The Pirates* / Only sixteen: *Douglas, Craig* / Ain't misbehavin': *Bruce, Tommy & The Bruisers* / Born too late: *Ponytails*
CD ______ CDMFP 5999
Music For Pleasure / Nov '93 / EMI

ROCK 'N' ROLL MEGAMIX
CD ______ JHD 107
Tring / Aug '93 / Tring

ROCK 'N' ROLL ORGY VOL.1
CD ______ FLESHDEN 6901
Flesh Den / Nov '95 / Cargo

ROCK 'N' ROLL ORGY VOL.2
CD ______ FLESHDEN 6902
Flesh Den / Nov '95 / Cargo

ROCK 'N' ROLL ORGY VOL.3
CD ______ FLESHDEN 6903
Flesh Den / Nov '95 / Cargo

ROCK 'N' ROLL ORGY VOL.4
CD ______ FLESHDEN 6904
Flesh Den / Jan '97 / Cargo

ROCK 'N' ROLL PARTY
Good golly miss molly: *Little Richard* / This ole house: *Clooney, Rosemary* / Yakety yak: *Coasters* / Rebel rouser: *Eddy, Duane* / Red river rock: *Johnny & The Hurricanes* / Party doll: *Knox, Buddy* / At the hop: *Danny & The Juniors* / Green door: *Lowe, Jim* / Nut rocker: *B Bumble & The Stingers* / Runaway: *Shannon, Del* / Night has a thousand eyes: *Vee, Bobby* / Poetry in motion: *Tillotson, Johnny* / Wooly bully: *Sam The Sham & The Pharaohs* / Duke of earl: *Chandler, Gene* / Running bear: *Preston, Johnny* / Boy from New York city: *Ad Libs* / Rock 'n' roll is here to stay: *Danny & The Juniors* / Let's twist again: *Checker, Chubby*
CD ______ ECD 3055
K-Tel / Dec '96 / K-Tel

ROCK 'N' ROLL PARTY 1957-1962
Motorbiene (Motorcycle) / Buona Sera / My happiness / Ein engel ohine fliguel (I can see an angel) / Lippenstift am jacket / Oh eh oh ah ah (witch doctor) / Plitsch platsch (splish splash) / Speedy Gonzalez / Rock-a-hula baby / Fur gabi tu ich alles / Fraulein / Norman / Yes tonight Josephine / Kuba rock / Wundrbares madchen (catch a falling star) / Oh, das war schon (oh lonesome me) / Lollipop / Due farbe der liebe (a white sports coat) / Zahn Hag / Japanisches absciedslied
CD ______ BCD 15235
Bear Family / Nov '86 / Direct / Rollercoaster / Swift

ROCK 'N' ROLL RIOT
Rockin' roll riot: *Stoltz Brothers* / Savage: *Barnicoat, Alan* / Betty Ann: *Cruisers* / Tough 'n rough: *Saladin* / Itch: *Cherry, Carl* / That cat: *Brown, Tommy* / Rock 'n' roll saddles: *Edwards, Johnny* / Baby Sue: *Rhythm Tones* / Rock 'n' roll rock: *Kelly, Roy* / Is that wrong: *Wynnewoods* / Bloodshot: *String Kings* / Granny went rockin': *Scott, Rodney* / My baby's casual: *Flaharty, Sonny* / Rockin' and boppin': *Newman, Carl* / Rockin' teens: *Puckett, Dennis* / Little jewel: *Taylor, Bill* / Keep it swinging: *Skelton, Eddie* / Rock 'n' roll guitar: *Knight, Johnny* / Woman can make you blue: *Porter, Royce* / Wild wild woman: *Wright, Steve* / Rock rhythm roll: *Dash, Frankie* / Where's my baby: *Giant, Ethan* / I know why: *Clark, Billy* / Scratching on my screen: *Cartey, Ric* / Rock 'n' roll romance: *Big Rocker* / Blues in the morning: *Foley, Jim* / Hard luck: *Blank, Billy* / Bootleg rock: *Bonny, Billy* / Robinson Crusoe bop: *Cole, Sonny* / By by blues: *Puckett, Dennis*
CD ______ CDBB 55004
Buffalo Bop / Apr '94 / Rollercoaster

ROCK 'N' ROLL ROMANCE
Will you still love me tomorrow: *Shirelles* / Sealed with a kiss: *Hyland, Brian* / Young love: *Hunter, Tab* / Venus: *Avalon, Frankie* / Come go with me: *Del-Vikings* / Born too late: *Poni-Tails* / Since I don't have you: *Skyliners* / Every breath I take: *Pitney, Gene* / Thousand stars: *Young, Karen & The Innocents* / Love letters in the sand: *Boone, Pat* / Heartbeat: *Holly, Buddy* / Donna: *Valens, Ritchie* / Till I kissed you: *Everly Brothers* / Hey baby: *Channel, Bruce* / My true love: *Scott, Jack* / Oh not my baby: *Brown, Maxine* / Poetry in motion: *Tillotson, Johnny* / Sweet dreams: *McLain, Tommy* / Goodnight sweetheart, goodnight: *Spaniels*
CD ______ PWKS 4197
Carlton / Feb '96 / Carlton

ROCK 'N' ROLL SOUND
Dancing teardrops: *Redd, Barbara* / Why should I dance: *Sheiks* / Night with Daddy: *Church Street Five* / Satan go away: *Bonds,*

Gary 'US' / Go 'way Christina: *Soul, Jimmy* / Mimi: *Francois & The Anglos* / My last phone call: *Earlington, Lynn* / Sing a song children: *Church Street Five* / Raining teardrops: *Rockmasters* / Up the aisle (just you and I): *Carter, Linda* / I want to know if you love me: *Owens, Garland* / Hey little boy: *Azaleas* / My baby loves to bowl: *Soul, Jimmy* / Hula wobble shake: *Owens, Garland* / In my room: *Payton, George* / Get yo'self married: *Rockmasters* / It's praying time: *Gavin, Maddie* / Hands off: *Azaleas* / I love you so: *Raven Wildroot* / Crazy over you: *Day, Margie* / I keep coming back for more: *Soul Cop* / Paper doll: *Russell, Lily* / Give me another chance: *Five Sheiks* / New Orleans: *Bonds, Gary 'US'*
CD ________ CDCHD 541
Ace / Jun '94 / Pinnacle

ROCK 'N' ROLL STARS ON STAGE
Great balls of fire: *Lewis, Jerry Lee* / Twist: *Checker, Chubby* / Stagger Lee: *Price, Lloyd* / Little Darlin': *Diamonds* / Tears on my pillow: *Little Anthony* / Tallahassee lassie: *Cannon, Freddy* / Earth angel: *Penguins* / Let the good times roll: *Shirley & Lee* / Short shorts: *Royal Teens* / Kisses sweeter than wine: *Rodgers, Jimmie* / Sea cruise: *Ford, Frankie* / At the harp: *Danny & The Juniors* / Rock around the clock: *Haley, Bill & The Comets*
CD ________ CDZ 2022
Zu Zazz / Nov '95 / Rollercoaster

ROCK 'N' ROLL SUPER HITS
Peggy Sue: *Holly, Buddy* / I'm sorry: *Lee, Brenda* / Rock 'n' roll music: *Berry, Chuck* / (We're gonna) Rock around the clock: *Haley, Bill* / Rock 'n' roll is here to stay: *Danny & The Juniors* / All by myself: *Burnette, Johnny Rock 'N' Roll Trio* / When: *Kalin Twins* / Mr. Bass man: *Cymbal, Johnny* / 1-2-3: *Barry, Len* / Pipeline: *Chantays* / Wipe-out: *Surfaris* / Mona: *Diddley, Bo* / Suzie Q: *Hawkins, Dale* / Come go with me: *Del-Vikings* / Great, gosh and mighty: *Little Richard* / Great balls of fire: *Crickets*
CD ________ MCD 30200
Ariola Express / Mar '94 / BMG

ROCK 'N' ROLL SUPERSTARS (CD/CD Rom Set)
CD Set ________ WWCDR 008
Magnum Music / Apr '97 / TKO Magnum

ROCK 'N' ROLL WITH PIANO VOL.1
CD ________ CLCD 4435
Collector's Edition / Mar '97 / TKO Magnum

ROCK N' ROLL WITH PIANO VOL.2
CD ________ CLCD 4437
Collector/White Label / Apr '97 / TKO Magnum

ROCK OF AGES
CD ________ RENCD 104
Renaissance Collector Series / Jul '95 / BMG

ROCK OF AMERICA
CD ________ NSCD 018
Newsound / May '95 / THE

ROCK OF AMERICA
Sharp dressed man: *ZZ Top* / Africa: *Toto* / Just like Jesse James: *Cher* / Right here waiting for a girl like you: *Foreigner* / More than a feeling: *Boston* / If she knew what she wants: *Bangles* / Best friend's girl: *Cars* / Satellite: *Hooters* / Copperhead road: *Earle, Steve* / Love is a battlefield: *Benatar, Pat* / Freeze frame: *Geils, J. Band* / Heat is on: *Frey, Glenn* / Rocky mountain way: *Walsh, Joe* / Sweet home Alabama: *Lynyrd Skynyrd* / Voodoo chile: *Lynyrd Skynyrd* / School's out: *Cooper, Alice* / Born to be wild: *Steppenwolf*
CD ________ NTRCD 088
Nectar / Aug '97 / Pinnacle

ROCK ON VOL.1
CD ________ CDTMR 8014
Candor / Jul '95 / Else

ROCK OUT (2CD Set)
CD Set ________ DEMPCD 007
Emporio / Mar '96 / Disc

ROCK POWER
CD ________ EXP 044
Experience / May '97 / TKO Magnum

ROCK STEADY 1966-1967 (Bobby Aitken Presents)
CD ________ NXBACD 01
Next Step / Nov '93 / Jet Star / SRD

ROCK STEADY RAVE
CD ________ CPCD 8023
Charly / Feb '94 / Koch

ROCK STEADY/FUNKY REGGAE
CD ________ RB 3008
Reggae Best / May '94 / Grapevine/ PolyGram

ROCK THE PLANET (2CD Set)
One vision: *Queen* / Who's gonna ride your wild horses: *U2* / On the shoreline: *Genesis* / Crazy: *Seal* / Fragile: *Sting* / Zombie: *Cranberries* / Bang and blame: *REM* / Steam: *Gabriel, Peter* / Under Afrikan skies: *Simon, Paul* / One: *John, Elton* / Disappear: *INXS* / Here comes the rain again: *Eurythmics* / Mmm Mmm Mmm: *Crash Test Dummies* / How many people: *McCartney, Paul* / I will do anything for love: *Meat Loaf* / Learning to fly: *Pink Floyd* / Prayer for the dying: *Seal* / It's the end of the world as we know it (and I feel fine): *REM* / I still haven't found what I'm looking for: *U2* / Don't give up: *Gabriel, Peter & Kate Bush* / Is this the world we created: *Queen* / I'm still standing: *John, Elton* / Yes we can: *Artists United For Nature* / Damn I wish I was your lover: *Hawkins, Sophie B.* / Silent scream: *MacGowan, Shane* / Sowing the seeds of love: *Tears For Fears* / Walk of life: *Dire Straits* / Brazillian: *Genesis* / Wake me up on judgement day: *Winwood, Steve* / Miracle of love: *Eurythmics* / Creation: *Stereo MC's* / Saltwater: *Lennon, Julian* / Spirit of the forest: *Spirit Of The Forest*
CD Set ________ 5334282
PolyGram TV / Aug '96 / PolyGram

ROCK THERAPY
We will rock you: *Queen* / Let's get rocked: *Def Leppard* / Livin' on a prayer: *Bon Jovi* / Tragic comic: *Extreme* / Here I go again: *Whitesnake* / Wind of change: *Scorpions* / Backstreet symphony: *Thunder* / Wishing well: *Free* / Rockin' all over the world: *Status Quo* / Living after midnight: *Jethro Tull* / Burning of the Midnight lamp: *Hendrix, Jimi* / Too old to rock 'n' roll, too young to die: *Jethro Tull* / Fanfare for the common man: *Emerson, Lake & Palmer* / Breeze: *Lynyrd Skynyrd* / Won't get fooled again: *Who* / Run to the hills: *Iron Maiden*
CD ________ 5168612
PolyGram TV / Jun '94 / PolyGram

ROCK THERAPY '96
Keep the faith: *Bon Jovi* / What's the frequency Kenneth: *REM* / Desire: *U2* / Live forever: *Oasis* / Salvation: *Cranberries* / Word up: *Gun* / Only thing that looks good on me is you: *Adams, Bryan* / New sensation: *INXS* / Waterfront: *Simple Minds* / Don't stop: *Fleetwood Mac* / Solid rock: *Dire Straits* / Layla: *Derek & The Dominoes* / Whiskey in the jar: *Thin Lizzy* / Bat out of hell: *Meat Loaf* / Baba O'Riley: *Who* / Another brick in the wall: *Pink Floyd* / Kashmir: *Page, Jimmy & Robert Plant*
CD ________ 5530172
PolyGram TV / Oct '96 / PolyGram

ROCKABILLY HOODLUMS
CD ________ CLCD 4438
Collector/White Label / Apr '97 / TKO Magnum

ROCKABILLY PSYCHOSIS
Surfin' bird: *Trashmen* / Psycho: *Sonics* / Crusher: *Novas* / Paralysed: *Legendary Stardust Cowboy* / She said: *Adkins, Hasil 'Haze'* / My daddy is a vampire: *Meteors* / Radioactive kid: *Meteors* / Dateless nites: *Falco, Tav Panther Burns* / Jack on fire: *Gun Club* / Folsom prison blues: *Geezers* / Catman: *Stingrays* / Just love me: *Guana Batz* / Love me: *Phantom* / Red headed woman: *Dickinson, Jimmy & the Cramps* / Scream: *Nielsen, Ralph & The Chancellors* / Hidden charms: *Wray, Link* / Run chicken run: *Milkshakes*
CD ________ CDWIK 18
Big Beat / Oct '89 / Pinnacle

ROCKABILLY RECORD CO. (Goofin' Rockabilly Sampler)
Rockin' blues: *Lewis, Willie* / Rock 'n' roll religion: *Lewis, Willie* / Oh, baby babe: *Lewis, Willie* / Crazy boogie: *Lewis, Willie* / Workin' man blues: *Lewis, Willie* / Mary Lou rock: *Billy & The Bob Cats* / Train of misery: *High Noon* / Glory bound: *High Noon* / Baby let's play house: *High Noon* / All night long: *High Noon* / Who was that cat: *High Noon* / Crazy fever: *High Noon* / I ain't in love with you/Tonight: *Pharaohs* / I want my whiskey: *Pharaohs* / Dollar bill boogie: *Pharaohs* / A-bop-a-baby: *Roadhouse Rockers* / Be my baby: *Kevin & Todd* / Beat up Ford: *Leyland, Carl 'Sonny'* / I like the boogie woogie: *Leyland, Carl 'Sonny'* / Whiskey straight up: *Frantic Flattops* / Rockabilly Willie: *King Cat & The Pharaohs* / It's Saturday night: *King Cat & The Pharaohs* / You got no sense: *King Cat & The Pharaohs* / Ran down Daddy: *Three Cats & The Kittens*
CD ________ GRCD 6036
Goofin' / Jan '97 / Nervous / TKO Magnum

ROCKABILLY SHAKEOUT VOL.1
Shadow my baby: *Barber, Glen* / Atom bomb: *Barber, Glen* / I don't know when: *Harris, Hal* / My little baby: *Jimmy & Johnny* / True affection: *Johnson, Byron* / Slippin' and slidin': *Davis, Link* / Hey hey little boy blue: *Lindsay, Merle* / Gee whiz: *Dee & Patty* / All the time: *LaBeef, Sleepy* / Spin the bottle: *Joy, Benny* / Chicken bop: *Truitt Forse* / My big fat baby: *Hall, Sonny & The Echoes* / Cat's just got back in town: *Mack, Billy* / Tennessee rock: *Scoggins, Hoyt* / Uranium fever: *Gaddis, Ruddy* / Prettiest girl at the dance: *Wyatt, Gene*
CD ________ CDCH 191
Ace / Feb '92 / Pinnacle

ROCKERS AND BALLADEERS VOL.1
CD ________ PLATCD 341
Platinum / Oct '90 / Prism

ROCKERS AND BALLADEERS VOL.2
CD ________ PLATCD 342
Platinum / Oct '90 / Prism

ROCKET FUEL
CD ________ MIDDLE 6CD
Middle Earth / Jul '96 / RTM/Disc

ROCKIN' AT THE TAKE 2 VOL.1 & 2
CD ________ LOMACD 30
Loma / Aug '94 / BMG

ROCKIN' AT TOWN HALL
CD ________ RFDCD 06
Country Routes / Apr '91 / Hot Shot / Jazz Music

ROCKIN' BLUES
Fool in heah: *Dawkins, Jimmy* / TROUBLE: *Nighthawks* / I got the blues all over me: *McCain, Jerry* / Evil gal: *Reed, Francine* / Cigarette blues: *Rhodes, Sonny* / Rock me baby: *Lynn, Trudy* / Honey hush: *Principato, Tom & Danny Gatton* / Born under a bad sign: *Bell, William* / High and lonesome: *Shadows* / I need to love you: *Hall, Sandra* / Rockin' Daddy: *Johnson, Luther 'Houserocker'*
CD ________ D 2248782
Ichiban / Sep '96 / Direct / Koch

ROCKIN' DOO WOP VOL.1 1954-1964
CD ________ NEMCD 692
Sequel / Apr '95 / BMG

ROCKIN' DOO WOP VOL.2
I want you to be my girl: *Lymon, Frankie & The Teenagers* / Hindu baby: *Emanons* / Hey babe: *Cleftones* / Too young: *Lymon, Lewis & The Teenagers* / Sugar sugar: *Cadillacs* / Teenager rock: *Classmates* / My heart beats for you: *Echoes* / Come my little baby: *Chantels* / Goody goody: *Lymon, Frankie & The Teenagers* / Speedo is back: *Cadillacs* / Flip flop: *Teenagers* / Lymon, Lewis & The Teenagers: *Teenagers* / (I need some) money: *Miracles* / You're the one to blame: *Starlighters* / Never let go: *Chantels* / Shimmy shimmy ko-ko bop: *Little Anthony* / Lover boy: *Cleftones* / Barbara Ann: *Regents* / Heart and soul: *Cleftones* / Travelling strangers: *Little Anthony*
CD ________ NEMCD 767
Sequel / Apr '96 / BMG

ROCKIN' FROM COAST TO COAST
Buzz buzz a-diddle-it: *Cannon, Freddy* / Skippy is a sissy: *Gaines, Roy* / Bim bam: *Butera, Sam* / I'm snowed: *South, Joe* / Sapphire: *Oliver, Big Danny* / Rock the bop: *Lee, Brenda* / Mexicali baby: *Rio Rockers* / Hocus pocus: *Raiders* / Too much rockin': *Lewis, Tiny* / Cool off baby: *Barrix, Billy* / Flirty Gertie: *Jivatones* / Please Mr. Mayor: *Clark, Roy* / New shoes: *Denson, Lee* / Dirty dishes: *Mack, Jeani* / Good golly Miss Molly: *Valiants* / You're right, I'm left, she's gone: *Schmidling, Tyrone* / Rockin' in the graveyard: *Morningstar, Jackie* / Rockin' the joint: *Esquerita* / Eager boy: *Lonesome Drifter* / Honey don't: *Schmidling, Tyrone* / Why did you leave me: *Josie, Lou* / Frieda Frieda: *Valiants* / Wee Willie Brown: *Graham, Lou* / Swing Daddy swing: *Hawkins, Jerry* / Long gone Daddy: *Cupp, Pat & His Flying Saucers* / Let's go baby: *Eldridge, Billy*
CD ________ CDCHD 496
Ace / Sep '96 / Pinnacle

ROCKIN' GUITARS
CD ________ TREB 5018
Scratch / May '96 / Koch / Scratch/BMG

ROCKIN' IT UP VOL.1&2
CD ________ LMCD 1217
Lost Moment / Jun '97 / Else / Shellshock/ Disc

ROCKIN' SEVENTIES
I can do it: *Rubettes* / Angel face: *Glitter Band* / Who put the bomp: *Showaddywaddy* / You little trustmaker: *Tymes* / Keep on dancin': *Bay City Rollers* / Juke box jive: *Rubettes* / Hey rock 'n' roll: *Showaddywaddy* / Hold back the night: *Trammps* / Pinball wizard: *New Seekers* / It's been so long: *McCrae, George* / Sugar baby love: *Rubettes* / Greased lightning: *Travolta, John* / Rock 'n' roll lady: *Showaddywaddy* / Foe-dee-o-dee: *Rubettes* / Shang-a-lang: *Bay City Rollers* / Let's get together again: *Glitter Band* / Witch Queen of New Orleans: *Redbone* / Multiplication: *Showaddywaddy* / Rock your baby: *McCrae, George* / Bye bye baby: *Bay City Rollers*
CD ________ GRF 222
Tring / Apr '93 / Tring

ROCKIN' THE BLUES
Red house / Blues power / Evil woman blues / Stormy Monday / I got my mojo working / Good morning little school girl / Unlucky boy / Bringing it back / Louisiana blues / Ramblin' on my mind / Bell bottom blues / Statesboro blues / Crossroads / Six days on my mind / Baby, please don't go / Lies / Lonely years / Highway blues / Outside woman blues / Dust my broom
CD ________ MATCD 274
Castle / Apr '93 / BMG

ROCKIN' THE BLUES
Alley corn: *Hooker, Earl* / Sweet angel: *Hooker, Earl* / Jammin': *Hooker, Earl* / Ride Hooker ride: *Hooker, Earl* / After hours: *Hooker, Earl* / Going to New Orleans: *Davis, Sam* / She's so good to me: *Davis, Sam* / Goin' home to Mother: *Davis, Sam* / 1958 Blues: *Davis, Sam* / Jealous man: *Lewis, Johnny* / She's taking all my money: *Lewis, Johnny* / Riding home: *Louis, Leslie* / Don't do it again: *Louis, Leslie* / Alley blues: *Wilson, Jimmy* / Walkin' the streets: *Hopkins, Lightnin'* / Mussey haired woman: *Hopkins, Lightnin'* / Goin' back home today: *Baker, Willie* / Fool no more: *Hope, Eddie & The Mannish Boys* / Lost child: *Hope, Eddie & The Mannish Boys* / Teachin' the blues: *Hooker, John Lee* / She do the shimmy: *Hooker, John Lee* / Stoned blues: *Hooker, John Lee* / You got to reap what you sow: *Hooker, John Lee* / Meat shakes on her bone: *Hooker, John Lee*
CD ________ CDCHD 585
Ace / Aug '95 / Pinnacle

ROCKIN' THE BLUES
CD ________ PLSCD 193
Pulse / Apr '97 / BMG

ROCKIN' THE CROSSROADS
CD ________ ANT 9904CD
Antones / Jul '94 / ADA / Hot Shot

ROCKTASTIC
CD ________ CLACD 999
Castle / Jul '94 / BMG

ROCKYGRASS
CD ________ BPCD 100
Blue Planet / Mar '96 / ADA

RODIGAN'S DUB CLASSICS VOL.1
CD ________ CDREG 6
Rewind Selecta / Aug '96 / Grapevine/ PolyGram

RODNY KRAJ
CD ________ CR 00212
Czech Radio / Nov '95 / Czech Music Enterprises

ROGUE TROOPER SAMPLER
CD ________ DBMTR 35
Rogue Trooper / Nov '95 / Alphamagic / SRD

ROLL ON ROLLING STONE
CD ________ BB 2807
Blue Beat / Aug '96 / Grapevine/PolyGram

ROLLIN' AND TUMBLIN'
CD ________ IGOCD 2029
Indigo / Apr '95 / ADA / Direct

ROLLING RIVERS AND SMILING VALLEYS
CD ________ QPRZ 011D
Polyphonic / Jan '93 / Complete/Pinnacle

ROLLING THUNDER
Eye of the tiger: *Survivor* / I surrender: *Rainbow* / Strange kind of woman: *Deep Purple* / Night games: *Bonnet, Graham* / Trouble: *Gillan* / Don't let me be misunderstood: *Moore, Gary* / Incommunicado: *Marillion* / Final countdown: *Europe* / She's a little angel: *Little Angels* / 747 (Strangers in the night): *Saxon* / Rhythm of love: *Scorpions* / Hey you: *Quireboys* / Living after midnight: *Judas Priest* / Never say die: *Black Sabbath* / Ace of spades: *Motorhead* / Easy livin': *Uriah Heep* / Race with the devil: *Girlschool*
CD ________ RENCD 107
Renaissance Collector Series / Oct '95 / BMG

ROMANCE (Music For Piano)
Shape of her face / Old family portrait / Sister bay / I always come back to you / Sacred dance / Reasons for moving / Minor truths / Beginning of love / Melusina / In the path of the heart / First light / Over shallow water / State of grace / First kiss / Summer fields / As I fall / Land of seduction
CD ________ ND 61045
Narada / Nov '94 / ADA / New Note/ Pinnacle

ROMANCE OF PARIS, THE
La mer: *Trenet, Charles* / La vie en rose: *Piaf, Edith* / Si j'aime Suzy: *Sablon, Jean & Eliane De Creus* / A Paris dans chaque Faubourg: *Gauty, Lys* / Mon cocktail d'amour: *Chevalier, Maurice* / Tant qu'il y aura des etoiles: *Rossi, Tino* / Il ne faut pas briser un reve: *Busch, Eva* / Les pieds dans l'eau: *Sablon, Jean* / De temps en temps: *Baker, Josephine* / Les prenomes effaces: *Tranchant, Jean* / La romance de Paris: *Trenet, Charles* / Prends moi dans tes bras: *Gauty, Lys* / C'est un passe un dimanche: *Chevalier, Maurice* / Le grand frise: *Damia* / La ballade du cordonnier: *Gauty, Lys* / Parce que je vous aime: *Sablon, Jean & Eliane De Creus* / C'est merveilleux: *Piaf, Edith* / Tout me sourit: *Trenet, Charles* / C'est une petite etoile: *Aubert, Jeanne* / Barnabe: *Fernandel* / C'est vrai: *Mistinguett* / Les trois cloches: *Piaf, Edith* / La Marseillaise: *Thill, Georges & Chorus/Band Of The Grand Republicaine*
CD ________ PASTCD 7819
Flapper / Jul '97 / Pinnacle

ROMANCING THE HARP
When I fall in love / Wonderful tonight / And I love you so / Lady / Tonight I celebrate my love / Spanish eyes / Most beautiful girl in the world / Unchained melody / Love me tender / Mona Lisa / Close to you / True love / Cry me a river / Move closer / Moon river / Greatest love of all
CD ________ CDMFP 6283
Music For Pleasure / Jan '97 / EMI

ROMANIAN GEMS
Incantation / Prelude d'amour / Romance au Claire De Lune / Frenesia / Fiancailles / Pan danse pour la nymphs sprinz / Com-

plaint d'amour / Caprices au bord de l'eau / Taquineries / Consolation / Allegresse en mineur / Porcession nuptiale
CD ____ PV 750004
Disques Pierre Verany / Jul '94 / Kingdom

ROMANTIC CHRISTMAS
CD ____ DCD 5312
Disky / Dec '93 / Disky / THE

ROMANTIC CLASSICS
CD ____ DCD 5210
Disky / Jul '92 / Disky / THE

ROMANTIC CLASSICS
CD ____ DSPCD 104
Disky / Sep '93 / Disky / THE

ROMANTIC CLASSICS
CD ____ GCC 1002
Disky / Sep '94 / Disky / THE

ROMANTIC CLASSICS BOX SET (3CD Set)
CD Set ____ HRCD 8016
Disky / Feb '93 / Disky / THE

ROMANTIC CLASSICS VOL.3
CD ____ DCD 5279
Disky / Nov '92 / Disky / THE

ROMANTIC CLASSICS VOL.4
CD ____ DCD 5280
Disky / Feb '93 / Disky / THE

ROMANTIC GUITAR
CD ____ GRF 240
Tring / Aug '93 / Tring

ROMANTIC GUITAR
Here comes the sun / Bright eyes / Cavatina / Have you ever really love a woman / Heartbreaker / Endless love / Words / Unchained melody / Have you ever really loved a woman / I know him so well / Here, there and everywhere / Without you / Lady in red / Albatross / Imagine / Take that look off your face / Lara's theme (Somewhere my love) / Spanish eyes
CD ____ CD 6069
Music / Apr '97 / Target/BMG

ROMANTIC GUITAR MOODS (3CD Set)
Careless whisper / My love / Cavatina / All by myself / Last farewell / Feelings / Imagine / Adagio / What a wonderful world / There'll be sad songs / Bilitis / Yesterday / Albatross / At this moment / Long and winding road / Lady in red / Lara's theme / Say you will / Glory of love / I wanna dance with somebody / Always / Midnight / Under the boardwalk / She's like the wind / Could've been / (Sittin' on the) dock of the bay / Take my breath away / Moonlighting / Midnight blue / Just like paradise / Sailing / Mandolin rain / Se la / On my own / Nothing's gonna stop us now / Everybreath you take / Baker street / Save a prayer / Soleado / Here comes the sun / More than I can say / Sara / Heat of the night / Watermelon man / Take that look off your face / Please don't go / Tender love / Strawberry fields forever / Words / Jeux interdits / Waiting for a star to fall / Miss you like crazy / As time goes by
CD Set ____ 390152
Hallmark / Jul '96 / Carlton

ROMANTIC GUITARS VOL.2
Love is all around: *Thompson, Keith* / Everything I do (I do it for you): *Thompson, Keith* / Sara bossa: *Abell, Dick* / Any time at all: *Abell, Dick* / Air that I breathe: *Thompson, Keith* / Romeo and Juliet: *Thompson, Keith* / If you leave me now: *Thompson, Keith* / Rose: *Aprile, J.C.* / I will always love you: *Thompson, Keith* / Wonderful tonight: *Thompson, Keith* / Shadow of your smile: *Angelo Et Ses Guitares* / Think twice: *Thompson, Keith* / Manha de carnaval: *Angelo Et Ses Guitares* / La playa: *Angelo Et Ses Guitares* / Tears in heaven: *Thompson, Keith*
CD ____ 306622
Hallmark / Jun '97 / Carlton

ROMANTIC INSTRUMENTAL COLLECTION (3CD Set)
CD Set ____ HRCD 8015
Disky / Nov '92 / Disky / THE

ROMANTIC JAZZ VOL.1
Somewhere: *Brubeck, Dave* / Easy to love: *Garner, Erroll* / Goodnight my love: *Vaughan, Sarah* / My funny valentine: *Baker, Chet* / Satin doll: *Hampton, Lionel* / Mood indigo: *Ellington, Duke* / Moonlight serenade: *Miller, Glenn* / Body and soul: *Goodman, Benny* / 'Round midnight: *Davis, Miles* / Summertime: *Holiday, Billie* / I can't stand the rain: *Phillips, Esther* / Fair weather: *Baker, Chet* / Theme from "Summer of 42": *Benson, George* / If I could be with you one hour tonight: *Holiday, Billie* / I've got a message to you: *Laws, Hubert*
CD ____ 4811542
Columbia / Dec '95 / Sony

ROMANTIC JAZZ VOL.2
Time after time: *Davis, Miles* / Medley: *Fitzgerald, Ella* / Bewitched: *Goodman, Benny* / It might as well be Spring: *Vaughan, Sarah* / Night and day: *Ellington, Duke* / It's the same old story: *Holiday, Billie* / You'd be so nice to come home to: *Desmond, Paul* / I got it bad and that ain't good: *Lee, Peggy* / Song is you: *Brubeck, Dave* / Honeysuckle rose: *Armstrong, Louis Allstars* / Come rain or come shine: *Vaughan, Sarah* / Sophisticated lady: *Ellington, Duke* / Am I blue: *Ellington, Duke* / Stella by starlight: *Davis, Miles* / Squeeze me: *Armstrong, Louis Allstars* / Summertime: *Benson, George*
CD ____ 4844812
Columbia / Aug '96 / Sony

ROMANTIC LOVE THEMES
CD ____ DCD 5300
Disky / Dec '93 / Disky / THE

ROMANTIC PIANO
Where do I begin (Love Story) / I just called to say I love you / You don't bring me flowers / Don't cry for me Argentina / Yesterday / Way we were / How deep is your love / If you leave me now / Feelings / Greatest love of all / Memory / Just the way you are / Power of love / Something / Mandy / Unforgettable / Just the two of us / To all the girls I've loved before / For your eyes only / Let it be
CD ____ CD 6068
Music / Apr '97 / Target/BMG

ROMANTIC POP MELODIES
CD ____ DCD 5304
Disky / Dec '93 / Disky / THE

ROMANTIC RAGGA VOL.1
CD ____ SIDCD 004
Sinbad / Feb '93 / Jet Star

ROMANTIC RAGGA VOL.2
CD ____ SIDCD 005
Sinbad / Feb '94 / Jet Star

ROMANTIC REGGAE
I wanna wake up with you: *Holt, John* / Choose me: *Pierre, Marie* / Moon river: *Greyhound* / You are everything: *Chosen Few* / Stand by me: *Junior Soul* / Sweet inspiration: *Pioneers* / Everything I own: *Boothe, Ken* / Side show: *Biggs, Barry* / Hurt so good: *Cadogan, Susan* / Only a smile: *Brown, Dennis* / Prisoner of love: *Barker, Dave* / All I have is love: *Isaacs, Gregory* / Black pearl: *Faith, Horace* / Spanish harlem: *Edwards, Jackie* / First time ever I saw your face: *Griffiths, Marcia* / Runaway with love: *Charmers, Lloyd* / Crying over you: *Boothe, Ken* / Everybody plays the fool: *Chosen Few* / You make me feel brand new: *Gardiner, Boris* / Still in love: *Ellis, Alton* / Montego bay: *Notes, Freddie & The Rudies* / You are everything to me: *Holt, John* / Let us be: *Thomas, Nicky* / Save the last dance for me: *Heptones*
CD ____ VSOPCD 133
Connoisseur Collection / May '89 / Pinnacle

ROMANTIC ROSES OF IRELAND
My lovely rose of Clare / Rose of Castlerea / Red is the rose / Rose of Killarney / My rose of the mountain / My lovely Irish rose / Rosie / Rose of mooncoin / Rose of Aranmore / Ringsend rose / Rose of Kilkenny / Connemara rose / Rose of Allendale / Sweet Rosie O'Grady / My wild Irish rose / My beautiful Irish rose
CD ____ EMPRCD 549
Emporio / Nov '94 / Disc

ROMANTIC SAX
CD ____ MACCD 164
Autograph / Aug '96 / BMG

ROMANTIC SOUND SAMPLER VOL.2
CD ____ EFA 910092
Zillo / May '95 / SRD

RONDELET PUNK SINGLES COLLECTION
No government: *Anti Pasti* / Two years too late: *Anti Pasti* / Another dead soldier: *Anti Pasti* / Six guns: *Anti Pasti* / Burial: *Fits* / Violent society: *Special Duties* / Colchester Council: *Special Duties* / Bomb scare: *Dead Man's Shadow* / Another Hiroshima: *Dead Man's Shadow* / East to the West: *Anti Pasti* / Muscles: *Membranes* / Police state: *Special Duties* / Go to hell: *Threats* / Fuck the Tories: *Riot Squad* / We are the Riot Squad: *Riot Squad* / Bullshit Crass: *Special Duties* / Riot in the city: *Riot Squad* / Caution in the wind: *Anti Pasti* / Flower in the gun: *Dead Man's Shadow* / High Street Yanks: *Membranes* / Politicians and ministers: *Threats* / Last laugh: *Fits*
CD ____ CDPUNK 49
Anagram / Mar '95 / Cargo / Pinnacle

ROOF INTERNATIONAL
CD ____ HCD 7008
Hightone / Aug '94 / ADA / Koch

ROOTS ALL OVER THE GODAMN PLACE
CD ____ EFA 800272
T-Wah / Oct '94 / SRD

ROOTS AND CULTURE (Serious Selections Vol.1)
True Rastaman (So Jah seh): *Fred Locks* / Wolfs and leopards: *Brown, Dennis* / Forward to Zion: *Abyssinians* / His majesty is coming: *In Crowd* / Prophecy: *Fabian* / Diverse doctrine: *Ras Ibuna* / Tenement yard: *Miller, Jacob* / Rough ole life: *Minott, Sugar* / Kingston 11: *Royal Rasses* / Marcus Garvey: *Burning Spear* / Black is our colour: *Wade, Wayne* / Back to Africa: *Aswad*
CD ____ CDREG 3
Rewind Selecta / Jul '95 / Grapevine/ PolyGram

ROOTS AND ROCKERS REGGAE VOL.1
CD ____ PWD 7438
Pow Wow / Jun '96 / Jet Star

ROOTS DAUGHTERS
Guide and protect: *Aisha* / Catch the boat: *Live Wya* / English girl: *Sister Audrey* / Free South Africa: *Cross, Sandra* / Fire: *Faybienne* / Until you come back to me: *Just Dale & Robotniks* / Place in the sun: *Kofi* / Mr. Roots man: *Rasheda*
CD ____ ARICD 039
Ariwa Sounds / Sep '88 / Jet Star / SRD

ROOTS DUB
CD ____ SOCD 50153
Studio One / May '97 / Jet Star

ROOTS 'N' CULTURE (21 Mighty Reggae Cuts)
Right time: *Mighty Diamonds* / Train to Rhodesia: *Big Youth* / Legalize it: *Tosh, Peter* / Rockers time now: *Clarke, Johnny* / International herb: *Culture* / Never get burn: *Twinkle Brothers* / Universal tribulation: *Isaacs, Gregory* / Jah loves: *Abyssinians* / Message from the King: *Prince Far-I* / Soul rebel: *Gladiators* / House of dreadlocks: *Big Youth* / Free Africa: *Twinkle Brothers* / Sun is shining: *Tamlins & Sly Dunbar* / Roots natty roots natty congo: *Clarke, Johnny* / Behold: *Culture* / Declaration of rights: *Clarke, Johnny* / Looks is deceiving: *Gladiators* / Freedom fighters: *Washington, Delroy* / Since I threw the comb away: *Twinkle Brothers* / Africa: *Mighty Diamonds* / It dread inna Inglan: *Johnson, Linton Kwesi*
CD ____ NSCD 016
Nascente / Jul '97 / Disc / New Note/ Pinnacle

ROOTS OF ACID JAZZ, THE
Swing low, sweet Cadillac: *Gillespie, Dizzy* / For mods only: *Hamilton, Chico* / Hard sock dance: *Jones, Quincy* / Stolen moments: *Nelson, Oliver* / Big city: *Horn, Shirley* / Beat goes on: *Szabo, Gabor* / Hold 'em Joe: *Rollins, Sonny* / Winchester Catherdral: *Jones, Hank* / Ciao, ciao: *Turrentine, Stanley* / La podrida: *Barbieri, Gato* / Southern smiles: *Jarrett, Keith* / Creator has a masterplan: *Sanders, Pharoah* / Go Li'l Liza: *Hawkins, Coleman* / Slippin' and slidin': *Lateef, Yusef*
CD ____ IMP 12042
Impulse Jazz / Dec '96 / New Note/BMG

ROOTS OF DOO WOP
CD ____ RTS 33021
Roots / May '90 / Pinnacle

ROOTS OF GARAGE
CD ____ AVEXCD 44
Avex / Jul '96 / 3mv/Pinnacle

ROOTS OF INNOVATION
CD ____ EFA 186922
On-U Sound / Jun '97 / Jet Star / SRD

ROOTS OF MODERN JAZZ, THE (The 1948 Sensation Sessions)
Baggy's blues: *Jackson, Milt & His All Stars* / In a beautiful mood: *Jackson, Milt & His All Stars* / Slits: *Jackson, Milt & His All Stars* / Baggy eyes: *Jackson, Milt & His All Stars* / Nobility bop: *Thompson, Sir Charles* / Yesterdays: *Thompson, Sir Charles* / It's my turn now: *Thompson, Sir Charles* / Charles boogie: *Thompson, Sir Charles* / Don't blame me: *Thompson, Sir Charles* / Robbin's nest: *Thompson, Sir Charles* / In a garden: *Thompson, Sir Charles* / Someone to watch over me: *Thompson, Sir Charles* / You go to my head: *Thompson, Sir Charles* / Relaxin': *Jacquet, Russell & His All Stars* / Lion's roar: *Jacquet, Russell & His All Stars* / Suede Jacquet: *Jacquet, Russell & His All Stars* / Scamper roo: *Jacquet, Russell & His All Stars* / Stardust: *Lord Nelson & His Boppers* / Red shoes: *Lord Nelson & His Boppers* / Body and soul (Time to dream): *Lord Nelson & His Boppers* / Ratio and proportion: *Lord Nelson & His Boppers* / Royal weddings: *Lord Nelson* / Be bop blues: *Lord Nelson* / Fine and Dandy: *Lord Nelson* / Third Song: *Lord Nelson*
CD ____ CDBOPD 017
Boplicity / May '94 / Pinnacle

ROOTS OF NORTHERN SOUL, THE (30 All-Nighter Classics From The Early Days)
Let's go baby (where the action is): *Parker, Robert* / Mr. Bang Bang man: *Little Hank* / Don't mess with my man: *Thomas, Irma* / Roll with the punch: *Shelton, Roscoe* / Walkin' up a one way street: *Tee, Willie* / Love's holiday: *Scott, Peggy & Jo Jo Benson* / Touch me kiss me hold me: *Inspirations* / Fortune teller: *Spellman, Benny* / Nothing's worse than being alone: *Ad Libs* / Sweet and easy: *McCoy, Van Strings* / No sad songs: *Simon, Joe* / Don't talk like that: *Murray, Clarence* / Happy feet: *Parker, Robert* / Getting mighty crowded: *Everett, Betty* / In your heart: *Dontells* / You can't take it away: *Hughes, Freddie* / Sufferin' city: *Johnny & Lilly* / Hard nut to crack: *Neville, Aaron* / Billy's bag: *Preston, Billy* / I caught you in a lie: *Parker, Robert* / You gotta pay the price: *Taylor, Gloria* / Baby you've got it: *Murray, Clarence* / Nothing can stop me: *Chandler, Gene* / Hey sugar: *Dells* / Trouble over the weekend: *Everett, Betty* / Don't let me down: *Hughes, Freddie* / So glad she's mine: *Carter Brothers* / Do you like you do me: *Williams, John* / Hot potato: *Clark, Dee* / I'm evil tonight: *Harris, Betty*
CD ____ GSCD 083
Goldmine / Feb '97 / Vital

ROOTS OF OK JAZZ
CD ____ CRAW 7
Crammed World / Jan '96 / New Note/ Pinnacle

ROOTS OF POWERPOP, THE
CD ____ BCD 4060
Bomp / Feb '97 / Cargo / Greyhound / RTM/Disc / Shellshock/Disc

ROOTS OF RAP, THE (Classic Recordings From The 1920's & 1930's)
CD ____ YAZCD 2018
Yazoo / May '96 / ADA / CM / Koch

ROOTS OF REGGAE VOL.1, THE
Soul shakedown party: *Marley, Bob* / Everything I own: *Boothe, Ken* / You can get it if you really want: *Dekker, Desmond* / Black and white: *Greyhound* / Hurt so good: *Cadogan, Susan* / Man in the street: *Drummond, Don* / Barber saloon: *Mikey Dread* / Let me down easy: *Brown, Dennis* / I'm a madman: *Perry, Lee 'Scratch'* / Israelites: *Dekker, Desmond* / Help me make it through the night: *Holt, John* / 54-46 (was my number): *Toots & The Maytals* / Kaya: *Marley, Bob* / Let your yeah be yeah: *Pioneers* / Young, gifted and black: *Bob & Marcia* / Rock me in dub: *Thompson, Linval* / Java: *Pablo, Augustus* / What you gonna do on judgement day: *Prince Far-I*
CD ____ MCCD 014
Music Club / Feb '91 / Disc / THE

ROOTS OF REGGAE VOL.1-3, THE (3CD Set)
CD Set ____ MCBX 003
Music Club / Sep '95 / Disc / THE

ROOTS OF REGGAE VOL.2, THE
Message to you Rudy: *Livingstone, Dandy* / Train to Skaville: *Ethiopians* / 007: *Dekker, Desmond* / Perfidia: *Dillon, Phyllis* / Liquidator: *Harry J All Stars* / Longshot kick de bucket: *Pioneers* / Phoenix City: *Alphonso, Roland* / Return of Django: *Upsetters* / Confucius: *Skatalites* / Double barrel: *Collins, Dave & Ansell* / Trenchtown rock: *Marley, Bob* / Pressure drop: *Toots & The Maytals* / East of the River Nile: *Pablo, Augustus* / Skinhead moonstomp: *Symarip* / All I have is love: *Isaacs, Gregory* / I shot the sheriff: *Inner Circle* / Hit the road Jack: *Big Youth* / Book of rules: *Heptones* / Shine eye gal: *Levy, Barrington* / Blood and fire: *Niney The Observer*
CD ____ MCCD 041
Music Club / Sep '91 / Disc / THE

ROOTS OF REGGAE VOL.3, THE
Caution: *Marley, Bob & The Wailers* / Miss Jamaica: *Cliff, Jimmy* / Monkey man: *Toots & The Maytals* / People funny boy: *Perry, Lee 'Scratch'* / It mek: *Dekker, Desmond* / Pied Piper: *Bob & Marcia* / Suzanne beware of the devil: *Livingstone, Dandy* / Rock steady train: *Evan & Jerry/Carib Beats* / Stop that train: *Tosh, Peter & The Wailers* / Skank in bed: *Scotty* / Keep moving: *Marley, Bob & The Wailers* / Bartender: *Aitken, Laurel* / Whip: *Ethiopians* / Sweet sensation: *Melodians* / Dreader than dread: *Honey Boy Martin* / I'm in the mood for ska: *Lord Tanamo* / Montego bay: *Notes, Freddie & The Rudies* / Oh ba-a-by (sick and tired): *Techniques* / African Queen: *Pablo, Augustus* / Rock steady: *Ellis, Alton*
CD ____ MCCD 072
Music Club / Jun '92 / Disc / THE

ROOTS OF RHYTHM AND BLUES 1939-1945, THE (2CD Set)
CD Set ____ FA 050
Fremeaux / Apr '96 / ADA / Discovery

ROOTS OF ROCK 'N' ROLL VOL.1 1927-1938, THE (2CD Set)
CD Set ____ FA 351
Fremeaux / Nov '96 / ADA / Discovery

ROOTS OF ROCK 'N' ROLL VOL.1, THE (Big Band, Blues & Boogie)
Flyin' Home: *Hampton, Lionel* / Honeydripper: *Jackson, Bull Moose* / Walk 'em: *Johnson, Buddy* / Minnie the moocher: *Calloway, Cab* / Countless blues: *Kansas City Six* / I know my love is true: *Liggins, Joe* / We ain't got nothin' (but the blues): *Jackson, Bull Moose* / Floogie boo: *Williams, Cootie* / If it's good: *Lee, Julia* / I want a tall skinny papa: *Tharpe, Sister Rosetta* / Caldonia: *Jordan, Louis* / Boogie beat'll getcha: *Red Caps* / Bartender boogie: *McVea, Jack* / Boogie woogie stomp: *Ammons, Albert* / Roll 'em Pete: *Turner, Joe & Pete Johnson* / Who threw the whiskey in the well: *Harris, Wynonie* / Rock me: *Tharpe, Sister Rosetta* / Shout sister shout: *Tharpe, Sister Rosetta* / Voot oreene: *Gaillard, Slim* / Hit that jive Jack: *Gant, Cecil* / SK groove: *King, Saunders* / It's all right baby: *Turner, Joe & Pete Johnson* / Slim Gaillard's boogie: *Gaillard, Slim* / Ee-bobaliba: *Trenier, Claude & Big Jim Wynn* / Five guys named moe: *Jordan, Louis* / Rock woogie: *Wiley, Pee Wee & Big Jim Wynn* / I'm woke up now: *Broonzy, 'Big' Bill & Chicago 5* / Dirt road blues: *Crudup, Arthur 'Big Boy'*
CD ____ PLCD 551
President / Nov '96 / Grapevine/PolyGram / President / Target/BMG

ROOTS OF ROCK 'N' ROLL VOL.2, THE (Stompin' Western Swing)
Easy ridin' Papa: *Brown, Milton & The Brownies* / South Texas Swing: *Hofner, Adolph* / Eyes of Texas: *Boyd, Bill & his cowboys* / Hot time Mama: *Penny, Hank* / Knocky knocky: *Light Crust Doughboys* / Bass man jive: *Stockard, Ocie & his Wanderers* / Oozlin' Daddy blues: *Wills, Bob* / Gettin' that lowdown swing: *Modern Mountaineers* / Hot Mama stomp: *Universal Cowboys* / High geared Daddy: *Davis, Jimmie* / Pipeliner blues: *Modern Mountaineers* / Shame on you: *Cooley, Spade* / Sweet talkin' Mama: *Penny, Hank* / Everybody's tryin' to be my baby: *Newman, Roy* / Southern belle (from Nashville, Tennessee): *Williams, Curly* / No good for nuthin' blues: *Sunshine Boys* / Up jumped the Devil: *Tune Wranglers* / Don't let the deal go down: *O'Daniel, W. Lee & His Hillbilly boys* / Milk cow blues: *Bruner, Cliff* / Hi-flyer stomp: *Hi-Flyers* / Sundown blues: *Texas Wanderers* / Somebody's been using that thing: *Brown, Milton & The Brownies* / Texas stomp: *Newman, Roy* / Bringing home the bacon: *Bruner, Cliff* / Alabama jubilee: *Rice Brothers* / Joe Turner blues: *Hofner, Adolph* / Fort Worth stomp: *Crystal Springs Playboys* / Give me my money: *Blue Ridge Playboys*
CD ______ **PLCD 552**
President / Nov '96 / Grapevine/PolyGram / President / Target/BMG

ROOTS OF ROCK 'N' ROLL VOL.5, THE (Adam Blew His Hat)
Adam blew his hat / There's good blues tonight / It's just the blues / Big fat Mama / I want to rock / Flat rock / Milk shake stand / Fine brown frame / Boogie woogie ball / My baby's boogying / Texas stomp / Old Taylor / Down the road apiece / Groovin' boogie / Jack you're dead / Fifth avenue woman / Boogie woogie's mother-in-law / That's the stuff you gotta watch / Come on over to my house / What's the matter with me / Night before judgement day / My lovin' Papa / Buzz buzz buzz / 2.00 am hop / Diggin' my potatoes No.2 / I want my lovin'
CD ______ **PLCD 561**
President / May '97 / Grapevine/PolyGram / President / Target/BMG

ROOTS OF ROCK 'N' ROLL VOL.7, THE (Stompin' At The Honky Tonk)
If you can't take five take two: *Brown, Milton & The Brownies* / Sugar: *Bruner, Cliff Texas Wanderers* / Rockin' it back: *Texas Wanderers* / Daddy's got the deep elm blues: *Revard, Jimmie & His Oklahoma Playboys* / You gotta ho-de-ho: *Swift Jewel Cowboys* / Who calls you sweet mama now: *Modern Mountaineers* / Riding to glory now: *Wood, Smokey & The Woodchips* / Cotton eyed Joe: *Wills, Bob & His Texas Playboys* / Tulsa twist: *McBride, Dickie & The Village Boys* / Stompin' at The Honky Tonk: *Dunn, Bob Vagabonds* / Sadie Green (the vamp of New Orleans): *Newman, Roy & his boys* / I love my fruit: *Sweet Violet Boys* / Three way boogie: *Cooley, Spade Orchestra* / Bring it down to my house honey: *Wills, Luke* / Somebody's rose: *Atchison, Tex* / South Texas swing: *Hofner, Adolf & His San Antonians* / Hot as I am: *Saddle Tramps* / You are my sunshine: *Rice Brothers* / Devil's great grandson: *Sons Of The Pioneers* / Al viva tequila: *Ritter, Tex & Sons Of The Pioneers* / Oklahoma stomp: *Cooley, Spade Orchestra* / Mama's getting hot and papa's getting cold: *Davis, Jimmie* / Who's cryin' sweet papa now: *Modern Mountaineers* / Jones stomp: *Port Arthur Jubileers* / New falling rain blues: *Bruner, Cliff & His Boys/Moon Mulligan* / Detour: *Walker, Jimmy*
CD ______ **PLCD 563**
President / May '97 / Grapevine/PolyGram / President / Target/BMG

ROOTS OF RUMBA ROCK VOL.1 (Zaire Classics Vol.1)
CD ______ **CRAW 4**
Crammed World / Jan '96 / New Note/ Pinnacle

ROOTS OF RUMBA ROCK VOL.2
CD ______ **CRAM 010**
Crammed Discs / Jul '95 / Grapevine/ PolyGram / New Note/Pinnacle / Prime / RTM/Disc

ROOTS OF SWEDISH POP, THE
CD ______ **5314862**
Uppers / Jul '97 / Greyhound

ROOTS OF THE BLUES
Louisiana: *Ratcliff, Henry* / Field song from Senegal: *Bakari Badji* / Po' boy blues: *Dudley, John* / Katy left Memphis: *Tangle Eye* / Berta berta: *Miller, Leyroy & A Group Of Prisoners* / Old original blues: *McDowell, 'Mississippi' Fred & Miles Pratcher* / Jim and John: *Young, Ed & Lonnie Young* / Emmaline, take your time: *Askew, Alec* / Buttermilk: *Pratcher, Miles & Bob* / Mama Lucy: *Gary, Leroy* / I'm gonna live, anyhow till I die: *Pratcher, Miles & Bob* / No more my lord: *Tangle Eye & A Group Of Prisoners* / Lining hymn and prayer: *Crenshaw, Rev. & The Congregation* / Death comes a creepin' in my room: *McDowell, 'Mississippi' Fred* / Church house moan: *Congregation Of New Brown's Chapel* / Beggin the blues: *Jones, Bessie* / Rolled and tumbled: *Hemphill, Rose & Fred McDowell* / Goin' down to the races: *McDowell, 'Mississippi' Fred & Miles Pratcher/Fannie Davis* / You gotta cut that out: *Forest City Joe*
CD ______ **802522**
New World / Aug '92 / ADA / Cadillac / Harmonia Mundi

ROOTS OF UB40, THE (17 Reggae Classics)
CD ______ **MCCD 276**
Music Club / Dec '96 / Disc / THE

ROOTS PIRANHA
CD ______ **PIR 482**
Piranha / Oct '92 / SRD

ROOTS REALITY
Heartache: *Jolly Brothers* / Silver and gold: *Osbourne, Johnny* / Time to unite: *Black Uhuru* / Ain't gonna turn back: *Brown, Barry* / Hell and sorrow: *Ellis, Hortense* / Colly George: *Jones, Frankie* / Last train to Africa: *Prince Alla* / Angel of the morning: *Lara, Jennifer* / Only love can conquer: *Fantells* / Jah Jah blessing: *Fantells* / Right track: *Minott, Sugar* / Great day: *Castell, Lacksley*
CD ______ **MENT 001CD**
Mention / Jan '96 / Jet Star

ROOTS REGGAE
Chalice in the palace: *U-Roy* / Wear you to the ball: *U-Roy* / Throw away your gun: *Prince Far-I* / Message from the king: *Prince Far-I* / This land is for everyone: *Abyssinians* / Bluesy baby: *Dunbar, Sly* / Hearsay: *Gladiators* / Let Jah be praised: *Gladiators* / Natty dread she want: *Big Youth* / Never get burn: *Twinkle Brothers* / Universal tribulation: *Isaacs, Gregory* / Up town top ranking: *Althia & Donna* / Too long in slavery: *Culture* / Song of blood: *Johnson, Linton Kwesi* / Cry tough: *Clark, Johnny*
CD ______ **CDVIP 125**
Virgin / Jul '94 / EMI

ROOTS ROCKERS REGGAE VOL.1
OK Fred: *Dunkley, Errol* / Sing a little song: *Dekker, Desmond* / Work all day: *Biggs, Barry* / Eighteen yellow roses: *Gardiner, Boris* / Back a yard: *In Crowd* / Johnny too bad: *Suckers* / Thank you Lord: *Romeo, Max* / I cried a tear: *Schaffer, Doreen* / Do you really want to hurt me: *Heptones* / Island music: *Calendar, Fip* / Three ring circus: *Biggs, Barry* / Rock my soul: *Biggs, Barry* / Smiling faces: *Holt, John* / I want to wake up with you: *Holt, John* / Sunshine people: *Holt, John* / Elizabethan reggae: *Gardiner, Boris*
CD ______ **EMPRCD 617**
Emporio / Jun '96 / Disc

ROOTS ROCKERS REGGAE VOL.2
Girlie girlie: *George, Sophia* / Happy anniversary: *Schloss, Cynthia* / Dynamic: *Paula* / Wide awake in a dream: *Biggs, Barry* / Dat: *Shervington, Pluto* / Busted lad: *Dekker, Desmond* / First cut is the deepest: *Penn, Dawn* / Place in the sun: *Winjama* / I don't need your love: *Griffiths, Marcia* / Slave ship: *In Crowd* / Uptown Sharron: *Isaacs, Gregory* / When she was my girl: *Wilson, Delroy* / Land of my birth: *Donaldson, Eric* / Mad about you: *Ruffin, Bruce* / You're no good: *Boothe, Ken* / No woman no cry: *Clarke, Johnny*
CD ______ **EMPRCD 618**
Emporio / Jun '96 / Disc

ROOTS TRADITION FROM THE VINEYARD
Come on over: *Frazer, Phillip* / Housing scheme: *Peter & Lucky* / Natty roots: *Toyan & Errol Scorcher* / Natty twelve tribe dub / Only jah jah know: *Frazer, Phillip & Toyan* / Sweetest thing: *Sammy Dread* / Vineyard: *Peter & Lucky* / Planter dub / True history: *Taylor, Rod* / Black people: *Toyan* / See a man face: *Ranking, Peter* / Robe: *Little John* / Gun fever: *Toyan* / When I fall in love: *Jah Bible* / Jah Jah knowledge: *Soul Syndicate*
CD ______ **MRCD 1004**
Majestic Reggae / May '97 / Direct

ROOTSMAN SHOWCASE '94
CD ______ **RMCD 014**
Roots Man / Nov '94 / Jet Star

ROSA PARKS TRIBUTE
CD ______ **VTYCD 002**
Verity / Mar '96 / Pinnacle

ROSE OF TRALEE, THE
CD ______ **MU 5065**
Musketeer / Oct '92 / Disc

ROSES ARE RED, VIOLETS ARE BLUE (Timeless Love Songs)
Roses are red: *O'Donnell, Daniel* / Donegal shore: *O'Donnell, Daniel* / Mary from Dungloe: *O'Donnell, Daniel* / Grace: *McCann, Jim* / Back in love by Monday: *Lynam, Ray* / Mona Lisa lost her smile: *Lynam, Ray* / Before the next teardrop falls: *McCann, Susan* / Morning glory: *Foster & Allen* / When I dream: *Foster & Allen* / Fields of Athenry: *Reilly, Paddy* / Star of County Down: *Reilly, Paddy* / Red is the rose: *Begley, Philomena* / When you were sweet sixteen: *Fureys & Davey Arthur* / Crazy: *Kelly, Sandy* / Calypso: *Hogan, John* / Pretty little girl from Omagh: *Duncan, Hugo* / Invisible tears: *Williamson, Ann* / Bunch of violets blue: *Big Tom* / Tie that binds: *Durkin, Kathy* / Wild flowers: *Flavin, Mick* / Pal of my cradle days: *Breen, Ann* / Spancil hill: *Duff, Mary*
CD ______ **IHCD 56**
Irish Heritage / Jul '89 / Prism

ROT RECORDS PUNK SINGLES COLLECTION
Lost cause: *Riot Squad* / I'm OK fuck you: *Riot Squad* / There ain't no solution: *Riot Squad* / Wet dreams: *Clockwork Soldiers* / Flowers in the gun: *Dead Man's Shadow* / Enemy: *Resistance 77* / Model soldier: *Animal Farm* / Shattered glass: *Paranoia* / Last but not least: *Enemy* / Don't criticise: *Patrol* / Russia: *Resistance 77* / Hate the law: *Riot Squad* / Massacred millions: *Varukers* / Will they never learn: *Varukers* / Incisor: *English Dogs* / Boot down the door: *Oi Polloi* / Return to hell: *Skeptix* / Evil will win: *Rattus* / Forward into battle: *English Dogs* / Killed by my mans own hands: *Varukers* / Bloody road to glory: *Rabid* / Boys in blue: *Rejected* / Cider: *Expelled* / Cities: *Cult Maniax*
CD ______ **CDPUNK 40**
Anagram / Oct '94 / Cargo / Pinnacle

ROUGH AND FAST
CD ______ **EFA 127012**
Riot Beats / Jan '95 / SRD

ROUGH GUIDE TO CLASSIC JAZZ
Dr Jazz: *Morton, Jelly Roll & His Red Hot Peppers* / Smoke house blues: *Morton, Jelly Roll & His Red Hot Peppers* / Original dixieland one step: *Original Dixieland Jazz Band* / Dippermouth blues: *Oliver, Joe 'King' & His Creole Jazz Band* / Mr Jelly Lord: *New Orleans Rhythm Kings* / Sugar foot stomp: *Henderson, Fletcher Orchestra* / Potato head blues: *Armstrong, Louis Hot Seven* / West end blues: *Armstrong, Louis Hot Five* / Hear me talking to you: *Rainey, Gertrude 'Ma'* / Nobody knows you when you're down and out: *Smith, Bessie* / Shake the Jelly-Roll: *Cobb, J.C. & His Grains Of Corn* / Stomp your stuff: *State Street Ramblers* / Pinetop's boogie woogie: *Smith, Pine Top* / Nobody's sweetheart: *McKenzie & Condon's Chicagoans* / Since my girl turned me down: *Beiderbecke, Bix & His Gang* / Beale street blues: *Charleston Chasers* / Imagination: *Mole, Miff Molers* / Makin' friends: *Condon, Eddie* / Minor drag: *Waller, Fats & His Buddies* / Log cabin blues: *Williams, Clarence* / South: *Morton, Benny* / Creole Love call: *Ellington, Duke & His Orchestra* / Hot and anxious: *Redman, Don & His Orchestra* / New King Porter Stomp: *Henderson, Fletcher*
CD ______ **RGNET 1012CD**
World Music Network / May '97 / ADA / New Note/Pinnacle

ROUGH GUIDE TO FLAMENCO
Venta zoraida: *Morente, Enrique* / Mi tempo: *Riqueni, Rafael* / Veloz hacia su sino: *Pardo, Jorge* / Buleria de la mocita/ Buleria a palo seco: *La Macanita, Tomasa* / Del molinete: *Linares, Carmen* / Pozo del deseo: *Ketama* / La voz del tiempo: *Tomatito* / Y yo que culpa tengo: *Poveda, Miguel* / Bodas de sangre: *Negra, Pata* / Serrana que te olvidara: *Duquende* / Del calvario: *Soto, Jose* / A quien contarie: *Lobato, Chano* / Dicen de mi: *Benavent, Carles* / A mi tio lele: *Potito* / A mi Manuel: *Habichuela, Pepe* / Nana de colores: *Carrasco, Diego* / Abuello Pacote/Buleria por solea: *El Barullo*
CD ______ **RGNET 1015CD**
World Music Network / Sep '97 / ADA / New Note/Pinnacle

ROUGH GUIDE TO IRISH MUSIC
Solid ground: *Keane, Dolores* / Tommy Peoples/Windmill/Fintan McManus's: *Altan* / Coinleach ghlas an fromhair: *Clannad* / On horseback: *Ivers, Eileen* / Season of mists: *Crawford, Kevin* / Lakes of Pontchartrain: *Deanta* / White petticoat/Kerry jig/Katy is waiting: *Patrick Street* / Terry Cuz Teahans polka/Murphy's polka/O'Sullivan's polka: *Sliabh Notes* / Molly and Johnny: *Dervish* / Humours of Lissadell/Music in the glen/ Johnson's: *Derance, Joe* / Boys of Malin/ Gravel walks: *Tourish, Ciaran & Dermot McLaughlin* / Dulman/Charlie O'Neil's highland: *Cran* / Mist on the mountain/Three little drummers': *Larrissey, Brendan* / Untitled/ Untitled/Hand me down the tackle: *O'Donnell, Siobhan & Karen Tween/Andy Cutting* / Colm cille na feile: *Ni Dhomhnaill, Maighread* / Sod of turf/Katie goes to granny: *Murray, Martin* / 'O' Connell's march/Galway bay hornpipe/Banshee's wail/Over: *Hayes, Martin*
CD ______ **RGNET 1006CD**
World Music Network / Sep '96 / ADA / New Note/Pinnacle

ROUGH GUIDE TO SCOTTISH MUSIC
Ballavanich: *Wolfstone* / Chi mi'n greamhradh: *MacPhee, Catherine-Anne* / Claire in heaven: *Capercaillie* / 8 Step waltz: *Iron Horse* / Seinn O: *MacKenzie, Talitha* / Wigtown fanfare: *Ring 'O' Steall* / Scotts Callan O'Bonnie Dundee: *Cast* / Erin-go-bragh: *Gaughan, Dick* / Unicorn set: *Tannahill Weavers* / Midwinter waltz: *Boys Of The Lough* / Sally Gardens: *Heywood, Heather* / Mairead nan cuiread: *Tannas* / Bob Parsons strathspey: *Tannas* / Galicia revisited: *Ceolbeg* / Brown milk maid: *Ceolbeg* / Dunnottar castle: *Ceolbeg* / Maid of Glengarrysdale: *Ceolbeg* / Disused railway: *Battlefield Band* / Just a dream: *Jansch, Bert* / Malcolm Ferguson: *Old Blind Dogs* / Finbar Saunders: *Old Blind Dogs*
CD ______ **RGNBET 1004CD**
World Music Network / May '96 / ADA / New Note/Pinnacle

ROUGH GUIDE TO THE MUSIC OF INDIA AND PAKISTAN
CD ______ **RGNET 1008CD**
World Music Network / Oct '96 / ADA / New Note/Pinnacle

ROUGH GUIDE TO THE MUSIC OF KENYA AND TANZANIA
CD ______ **RGNET 1007CD**
World Music Network / Oct '96 / ADA / New Note/Pinnacle

ROUGH GUIDE TO THE MUSIC OF THE ANDES
CD ______ **RGNET 1009CD**
World Music Network / Oct '96 / ADA / New Note/Pinnacle

ROUGH GUIDE TO THE MUSIC OF ZIMBABWE
CD ______ **RGNET 1010CD**
World Music Network / Oct '96 / ADA / New Note/Pinnacle

ROUGH GUIDE TO WEST AFRICAN MUSIC
CD ______ **RGNET 1002CD**
World Music Network / Oct '95 / ADA / New Note/Pinnacle

ROUGH GUIDE TO WORLD MUSIC, THE
Rebellion: *Arroyo, Joe* / Sama rew: *Africando* / Dugu kamelenba: *Sangare, Oumou* / Zaiko wa wa: *Zaiko Langa L* / Diandioli: *De Dakar, Etoile* / Rwanamiza: *Kayirebwa, Cecile* / Jono: *Tarika* / Tsaiky mboly hely: *Georges, Roger* / Henna: *Kuban, Ali Hassan* / Goodbye again: *Yue, Guo & Joji Hirota* / Tanola nomads: *Sainkho* / Khosid wedding dances: *Muszikas* / When I'm up I can't get down: *Oyster Band* / Hot tamale baby: *Buckwheat Zydeco* / Theid mi ddhach: *MacKenzie, Talitha*
CD ______ **RGNET 1001CD**
World Music Network / Oct '94 / ADA / New Note/Pinnacle

ROUGH RIDERS
CD ______ **MPV 5538**
Movieplay / Sep '93 / Target/BMG

ROULETTE ROCK 'N' ROLL COLLECTION VOL.1
Satellite: *Tate, Joe* / I'm free: *Tate, Joe* / Rock 'n' roll Mama: *Tate, Joe* / I guess it's love: *Tate, Joe* / I got a rocket in my pocket: *Lloyd, Jimmy* / You're gone baby: *Lloyd, Jimmy* / Where the Rio de Rosa flows: *Lloyd, Jimmy* / Rock-a-bop-a-lina: *Hart, Billy & Don* / Hole in my bucket: *Davis, Bob* / Rock to the music: *Davis, Bob* / Never anymore: *Davis, Bob* / Leapin' guitar: *Chapparals* / Goin' wild: *Isle, Jimmy* / Baby take me back: *Larue, Roc* / You've got what it takes: *Strickland, Johnnie* / That's baby: *Strickland, Johnnie* / Sweet talkin' baby: *Strickland, Johnnie* / Crazy about you: *Malloy, Vince* / Hubba hubba ding dong: *Malloy, Vince* / Girls, girls, girls: *Hammer, Jack* / Private property: *Lanier, Don* / Ponytail girl: *Lanier, Don* / Only one: *Roberts, Don 'Red'* / Goin' back to St. Louis: *Vickery, Mack* / Romeo Joe: *Skee Brothers* / Daisy Mae: *Dio, Andy*
CD ______ **NEMCD 619**
Sequel / Jul '92 / BMG

ROULETTE ROCK 'N' ROLL COLLECTION VOL.2
Strange: *Hawkins, Screamin' Jay* / Whammy: *Hawkins, Screamin' Jay* / Bloodshot eyes: *Harris, Wynonie* / Sweet Lucy Brown: *Harris, Wynonie* / Spread the news: *Harris, Wynonie* / Saturday night: *Harris, Wynonie* / Josephine: *Harris, Wynonie* / Did you get the message: *Harris, Wynonie* / Everybody's gonna rock 'n' roll: *Isley Brothers* / I wanna know: *Isley Brothers* / Drag: *Isley Brothers* / Rockin' McDonald: *Isley Brothers* / 7-11: *Gone All Stars* / Screamin' Ball at Dracula Hall: *Duponts* / Hippy dippy Daddy: *Cookies* / Roll over Beethoven: *Four Chaps* / Hindu baby: *Emanons* / Ding dong: *Echoes* / Woo woo train: *Valentines* / Dance with me: *Chaperones* / Ain't you gonna: *Powell, Jimmy & the Caddies* / Alabama rock 'n' roll: *King, Mabel*
CD ______ **NEMCD 670**
Sequel / Jun '94 / BMG

ROULETTE ROCK 'N' ROLL COLLECTION VOL.3
You're driving me mad: *Campbell, Jo Ann* / Don't say maybe: *Roberts, Don 'Red'* / Come dance with me: *Ackoff, Bob* / Don't stop: *Trider, Larry* / Ha ha song: *Trider, Larry* / Sittin' at home with the blues: *Elgin, Johnny* / High school blues: *Vickery, Mack* / Hot dog: *Curtis, Lee* / Sweetness: *Lanier, Don* / Need your love: *Lanier, Don* / Hey doll baby: *Pat Kelly* / Cloud 13: *Pat Kelly* / Patsy: *Pat Kelly* / Glow of love: *Moonlighters* / Broken heart: *Moonlighters* / School bus: *Shades* / Baby baby: *Shades* / Jeri Lee: *Shades* / Guitar hop: *Shades* / I looked for you: *Gracie, Charlie* / Race: *Gracie, Charlie* / Sorry for you: *Gracie, Charlie* / Scenery: *Gracie, Charlie* / Wassa matter with you baby: *Campbell, Jo Ann*
CD ______ **NEMCD 754**
Sequel / Aug '95 / BMG

ROULETTE ROCK'N'ROLL COLLECTION VOL.4 (Lotta Boppin')
Party doll: *Hawkins, Screamin' Jay* / Party doll: *Hawkins, Screamin' Jay* / Whammy: *Hawkins, Screamin' Jay* / Hard day's night:

Hawkins, Screamin' Jay / Hard day's night: *Hawkins, Screamin' Jay* / Feast of the Mau Mau: *Hawkins, Screamin' Jay* / Feast of the Mau Mau: *Hawkins, Screamin' Jay* / Feast of the Mau Mau: *Hawkins, Screamin' Jay* / Long, long walk: *Rivers, Johnny* / Baby come back: *Rivers, Johnny* / That's rock'n'roll: *Rivers, Johnny* / One man woman: *Rivers, Johnny* / Lover's plea: *Vickery, Mack* / Meant to be: *Vickery, Mack* / My kind of woman: *Haley, Bill & The Comets* / Spanish twist: *Haley, Bill & The Comets* / Checkmated and bingoed: *Hart, Billy & Don* / I'm not ashamed: *Larue, Roc* / Rockabilly yodel: *Larue, Roc* / I've heard that line before: *Strickland, Johnnie* / Don't leave me lonely: *Strickland, Johnnie* / Fool's hall of fame: *Strickland, Johnnie* / I was born to rock: *Rock-a-Teens* / Doggone it baby: *Rock-a-Teens* / Dance to the bop: *Rock-a-Teens* / Story of a woman: *Rock-a-Teens* / Janis will rock: *Rock-a-Teens* / That's my Mama: *Rock-a-Teens* / Lotta boppin': *Rock-a-Teens*
CD ______ **NEMCD 921**
Sequel / Jul '97 / BMG

'ROUND MIDNIGHT
Let there be love: *Cole, Nat 'King'* / Manhattan: *Fitzgerald, Ella* / My baby just cares for me: *Simone, Nina* / Your love is king: *Sade* / Desafinado: *Getz, Stan* / Air on a G string: *Loussier, Jacques* / Very thought of you: *Bennett, Tony* / Call me irresponsible: *Washington, Dinah* / Imagination: *Eckstine, Billy* / I get a kick out of you: *Holiday, Billie* / Unsquare dance: *Brubeck, Dave* / Shiny stockings: *Basie, Count* / Makin' whoopee: *Armstrong, Louis & Oscar Peterson* / Lover man: *Vaughan, Sarah* / When I fall in love: *Webster, Ben* / 'Round midnight: *Torme, Mel* / Meditation: *Gilberto, Astrud* / Lullaby of Birdland: *Shearing, George* / Cat: *Smith, Jimmy* / What's new: *Benson, George*
CD ______ **5164712**
Verve / Sep '93 / PolyGram

ROUND TOWER MUSIC VOL.1
If that's the way you want it / Past the point of rescue / Jesus in a leather jacket / Ordinary town / Fabulous thunderbirds / Putting me in the ground / Only dancing / Drive-in movies / Sister and brother / My love is in America / Lead the knave / Refugee from heaven / Limbo people / Walking on seashells / My love is yours
CD ______ **RTMCD 33**
Round Tower / Dec '91 / Avid/BMG

ROUND TOWER MUSIC VOL.2
CD ______ **RTMCD 70**
Round Tower / Jun '96 / Avid/BMG

ROUND TOWER SAMPLER
CD ______ **RTMCD 87**
Round Tower / Feb '97 / Avid/BMG

ROUNDER BANJO
CD ______ **ROUCD 11542**
Rounder / '88 / ADA / CM / Direct

ROUNDER BLUEGRASS GUITAR
CD ______ **ROUCD 11576**
Rounder / Feb '97 / ADA / CM / Direct

ROUNDER EUROPE BLUES REVUE (3CD Set)
I had a dream: *Ealey, Robert* / Santa's messin with the kid: *Campbell, Eddie C.* / Soul that's been abused: *Sumlin, Hubert & Mighty Sam* / Baby that what you want me to do: *Holmes Brothers* / Get outta my way: *Smith, Byther* / My abay told me: *Hughes, Joe* / I want to keep you: *Clark, W.C.* / Beatrice, Beatrice: *Walker, Philip* / Missing person: *Funderburgh, Anson & Sam Myers* / Black bottom: *Ward, Robert* / How long: *Legendary Blues Band* / Blues for breakfast: *Clearwater, Eddy* / Nobody's fool: *Shannon, Preston* / Can't see for lookin': *Kubek, Smokin' Joe Band* / Eddie's gospel groove: *Earl, Ronnie* / Shuck 'n' jive: *Boyack, Pat & The Prowlers* / Stranger blues: *Harman, James Band* / I don't wanna know: *Lamont Cranston Blues Band* / Bones in the closet: *Suhler, Jim & Monkey Beat* / Rainy day women: *Little Mike & The Tornados* / Worried no more: *Morgan, Mike & The Crawl* / Lover and a friend: *Welch, Mike* / Baby please set a date: *Thorogood, George & The Destroyers* / Bad boy: *Zinn, Rusty* / Bad poker hand: *Primich, Gary* / Shoulda coulda woulda: *Robillard, Duke* / Feeling good: *Piazza, Rod & The Mighty Flyers* / You're so mean to me: *Willson, Michelle* / Peaches tree: *Hummel, Mark* / One hundred miles: *Hawkins, Ted* / Step it up and go: *Rishell, Paul & Annie Raines* / Guess I'll walk alone: *Thomas, Jesse* / That's alright: *King, Freddie* / Ride that train: *Ball, Tom & Kenny Sultan* / I can hardly get along: *Brozman, Bob* / It hurt's me too: *Hammond, John* / Worried life blues: *Little Antony & Sugar Ray* / Like a shotgun: *Block, Rory* / Sweet home Chicago: *Pitchford, Lonnie* / Pretty thing: *Dyer, Johnny* / Baby couldn't be found: *Little Buster* / Members only: *Persuasions* / I'm good: *Amundson, Monti*
CD ______ **CBHCD 5013**
CRS / May '97 / ADA / Direct / Jet Star

ROUNDER FIDDLE
CD ______ **ROUCD 11565**
Rounder / Dec '90 / ADA / CM / Direct

ROUNDER FOLK
CD ______ **RCD 20018**
Rounder / May '96 / ADA / CM / Direct

ROUNDER GUITAR
CD ______ **ROUCD 11541**
Rounder / '88 / ADA / CM / Direct

ROUNDER OLD TIME MUSIC
CD ______ **ROUCD 11510**
Rounder / '88 / ADA / CM / Direct

ROUTE 66 (A Musical Journey Thru America's Heartland/2CD Set)
Route 66 / Tous les temps en temps / Southbound train / Key to the highway / Ain't that the blues / Pick-up boogie / Flying on the wings of America / Country boy with a rock and roll heart / Wreck of the ol' 43 / Border song / My West Virginia home / Hobo's lullabye / Saturday rolling around / Baby, what you want me to do / Blues don't love you / Long and lonesome cry / Bottleneck blues / Promised land / Baby let me follow you down / Country blues / Down in the Lafayette / Crawdaddy stomp / Factory / Soul man / Memphis blues / Song for Doc / Hey hey hey / I still miss someone / Shenandoah / Creole hoedown / Leve tes fenetres haut / Treat her right / Bourbon Street march / Knockin' on Heaven's door
CD Set ______ **330072**
Hallmark / Jul '96 / Carlton

ROUTES FROM THE JUNGLE
We are E: *Lennie Di Ice* / Waking up: *Nicolette* / You held my hand: *Manix* / Open your mind: *Foulplay* / Last action hero: *DJ Doc Scott* / Bludclot artattack: *Ed Rush* / Secret summer fantasy: *Bodysnatch* / Dark strangers: *Boogie Times Tribe* / Nazinja nazaka: *Guy Called Gerald* / Music box: *Roni Size* / Deeper love: *Dillinja* / Apollo 9: *Jo* / Believe: *E-Z Rollers* / Flowers: *Flynn & Flora* / Feel it: *Randall & Andy C* / Wrinkles in time: *4 Hero* / Droppin' science Vol.2: *Droppin' Science* / Asian love dance: *DJ Krust*
CD ______ **VTDCD 46**
Virgin / Apr '95 / EMI

ROYAL MEMPHIS SOUL (4CD Set)
CD Set ______ **HIBOOK 11**
Hi / Feb '97 / Pinnacle

ROYAL PALACE OF YOGYAKARTA, JAVA
CD ______ **C 560069CD**
Ocora / Jul '95 / ADA / Harmonia Mundi

ROYAL TOURNAMENT 1989
Firebird suite / I don't want to join the Air Force / Bold aviator was dying / Another thousand revs wouldn't do him any harm / There were three huns sat on his tail / I left the mess room early / Far far away / Glory flying regulations / RAF march past / Bonnie Dundee / Old Towler / Garry Owen / Hunting the hare / Round the Marble Arch / Come lasses and lads / Galloping major / Light cavalry / Post horn gallop / John Peel / Campbells are coming / Royal Artillery slow march / Keel row / In the mood / Little brown jug / String of pearls / Moonlight serenade / St. Louis blues march / Bugle calls from St. Mary's church / Cracow / Sky eagles / March march Polonia / Brothers it is time to fight / Uhlans have come / War, my little war / How nice it is on a little war / March of the 1st brigade / Oka / Victory victory / General Maczek's salute / General salute / Fanfare - Oranges and lemons / Maybe it's because I'm a Londoner / Heart of oak / HMS Pinafore / All the nice girls love a sailor / Alla Marcia / Glorious victory / Bond of friendship / Trumpet prelude / Symphony no. 3 in C minor / Last post and evening hymn / Hands across the sea / National anthem
CD ______ **BNA 5089**
Bandleader / Aug '89 / Conifer/BMG

ROYAL TOURNAMENT 1990
Fanfare / Sea solider / British Grenadiers / Belle Isle / Early one morning / Soldier an' solider too / Symphonic marches of John Williams / Cockleshell heroes / Begone dull care / Heaven in my hand / Love in the first degree / Better the devil you know / I should be so lucky / Too many broken hearts / Heart of oak / HMS Pinafore / All the nice girls love a sailor / Caernarvon Castle / Sarie Marais / Blue devils / Semper fidelis / Sing sing sing / Apotheosis / Song of the Marines / Follow me / HM Jollies / Finalanda / Dear Lord and Father of mankind / Sunset / Britannic salute / National anthem / Life on the ocean wave
CD ______ **BNA 5090**
Bandleader / '91 / Conifer/BMG

ROYAL TOURNAMENT 1991
CD ______ **BNA 5091**
Bandleader / Jun '91 / Conifer/BMG

ROYAL TOURNAMENT 1993
CD ______ **BNA 5093**
Bandleader / Aug '93 / Conifer/BMG

ROYAL TOURNAMENT 1994
CD ______ **BNA 5094**
Bandleader / Jul '94 / Conifer/BMG

ROYAL TOURNAMENT 1996
CD ______ **BNA 5096**
Bandleader / Jul '96 / Conifer/BMG

ROYALTY & EMPIRE (Patriotic Classics From UK's Military Bands/2CD Set)
Rule Brittania: *Royal Marines* / Crown imperial: *Life Guards Band* / Silver bugles: *Light Infantry Bands* / Birdcage walk: *Blues & Royals Band* / Orb and sceptre: *Life Guards Band* / Governors guard: *Light Infantry Bands* / India/Arabia: *Yorkshire Volunteers* / Navy day: *Royal Marines* / Vivat regina: *Light Division* / God bless the Prince Of Wales: *Queen's Dragoon Guards* / Gibraltar: *Royal Marines* / Royal ceremony: *RAOC Staff Band* / Abide with me: *Queen's Royal Hussars* / Here's a health unto her majesty: *Blues & Royals Band* / Standard of St. George: *Blues & Royals Band* / Royal standard: *Royal Engineers* / I was glad: *Coldstream Guards Choir* / Fame and glory: *Royal Engineers* / Fantasy on British sea songs: *Central Band Of Royal British Legion* / Jerusalem: *Central Band Of Royal British Legion* / Spirit of pageantry: *Prince Of Wales Yorkshire Regiment* / Imperial echoes: *Royal Marines* / Glorious victory: *Queen's Dragoon Guards* / Britannic salute: *Royal Marines* / Land of hope and glory: *Royal Marines* / Day thou gavest and last post: *Burma Band*
CD Set ______ **330472**
Hallmark / Mar '97 / Carlton

RUBAB ET DUTAR (Music From Afghanistan)
CD ______ **C 560080**
Ocora / Dec '95 / ADA / Harmonia Mundi

RUDE AWAKENING VOL.1, THE
CD ______ **AWAKE 1CD**
Beechwood / Jun '89 / Beechwood/BMG / Pinnacle

RUDE AWAKENING VOL.2, THE
CD ______ **AWAKE 2CD**
Beechwood / Jul '90 / Beechwood/BMG / Pinnacle

RUDIES ALL ROUND
Don't be a rude boy: *Rulers* / Rudie gets plenty: *Spanishtonians* / Preacher: *Ellis, Alton* / Blam blam fever: *Valentines* / Soldiers take over: *Rio Grandes* / Curfew: *Aitken, Bobby* / Copasetic: *Rulers* / Rudie bam bam: *Clarendonians* / Cool off rudies: *Morgan, Derrick* / Denham town: *Winston & George* / Drop the ratchet: *Cole, Stranger* / Blessings of love: *Ellis, Alton* / Rude boy train: *Dekker, Desmond* / Beware: *Overtakers* / Rudies all round: *White, Joe* / Rudies are the greatest: *Pioneers* / Stop the violence: *Valentines* / What can I say: *Tartans* / Judge Dread in court: *Morgan, Derrick* / Set them free: *Perry, Lee 'Scratch'*
CD ______ **CDTRL 322**
Trojan / Mar '94 / Direct / Jet Star

RUDIES CHOICE VOL.1
CD ______ **CDBM 116**
Blue Moon / Jul '96 / Cadillac / Discovery / Greensleeves / Jazz Music / Jet Star / TKO Magnum

RUDIE'S NIGHT OUT
On my radio: *Selecter* / Are you ready: *International Beat* / Orange Street: *Big 5* / James Bond: *Selecter* / Too nice to talk to: *International Beat* / Live injection: *Big 5* / Too much pressure: *Selecter* / Hard world: *International Beat* / Big 5: *Big 5* / Jackpot: *International Beat* / Can can: *Big 5* / Train to Skaville: *Selecter*
CD ______ **CDBM 104**
Blue Moon / Jun '95 / Cadillac / Discovery / Greensleeves / Jazz Music / Jet Star / TKO Magnum

RUF DIAMONDS VOL.1
CD ______ **RUF 012CD**
Ruf / Jan '97 / Plastic Head / SRD

RUFF CUT (The Original & Authentic Sound Of Jah Works)
CD ______ **RUSCD 8230**
ROIR / Feb '97 / Plastic Head / Shellshock/Disc

RUFF RAGGA
CD ______ **RNCD 2052**
Rhino / Mar '94 / Grapevine/PolyGram / Jet Star

RUFFEST DRUM AND BASS
CD ______ **STHCCD 16**
Strictly Hardcore / Nov '96 / SRD

RUFFNECK COLLECTION VOL.6
CD ______ **RUF 037**
Ruff Neck / Oct '96 / Mo's Music Machine

RUGBY SONGS
Swing low, sweet chariot / Bye bye blackbird / She's the most immoral lady / If I were the marrying kind / Here's to the good old beer / Good ship Venus / Ivan Skavinski Skavar / Madamoiselle from Armentier / Ring dang doo / Ram from Derbyshire / Dinha Dinha show us your leg / In the shade of the old apple tree / Sing us another one / Horndean school / Doggies meeting / Roll me over / Quartermaster's stores / There was an old segeant / Mayor of Bayswater / In mobile / Poor old Angeline / Bye bye blackbird (version 2) / Bring back seven old ladies / Swing low, sweet Chariot (reprise)
CD ______ **C5MCD 571**
See For Miles/C5 / Feb '95 / Pinnacle

RUMBLE IN THE JUNGLE (2CD Set)
CD Set ______ **MM 800272**
Moonshine / Apr '95 / Mo's Music Machine / Prime / RTM/Disc

RUN RHYTHM RUN (Instrumental Scorchers From Treasure Isle.)
CD ______ **CDHB 104**
Heartbeat / Sep '96 / ADA / Direct / Greensleeves / Jet Star

RUNNIN' WILD (The Original Sounds Of The Jazz Age)
Running wild: *Ellington, Duke* / Loveable and sweet: *Hanshaw, Annette* / There's a rainbow 'round my shoulder: *Jolson, Al* / My song: *Vallee, Rudy* / Heebie jeebies: *Boswell Sisters* / Loveless love: *Waller, Fats* / Magnolia: *California Ramblers* / Any old time: *Rodgers, Jimmie* / Egyptian Ella: *Lewis, Ted* / How many times: *Lucas, Nick* / She's got 'It': *Weems, Ted* / Makin' whoopee: *Whiteman, Paul* / California here I come: *Edwards, Cliff* / Me: *Etting, Ruth* / Four or five times: *McKinney's Cotton Pickers* / Without that gal: *Austin, Gene* / Home again blues: *Original Dixieland Jazz Band* / Lindy: *Original Dixieland Jazz Band* / Oh you have no idaea: *Tucker, Sophie* / You brought a new kind of love to me: *Chevalier, Maurice* / St. James Infirmary: *Bloom, Rube* / Three little words: *Crumit, Frank* / Painting the clouds with sunshine: *Hylton, Jack*
CD ______ **CDAJA 5017**
Living Era / Select

RUPIE'S GEMS
CD ______ **RNCD 2009**
Rhino / Jun '93 / Grapevine/PolyGram / Jet Star

RURAL BLUES
CD ______ **157182**
Blues Collection / Feb '93 / Discovery

RURAL BLUES 1934-1956
CD ______ **DOCD 5223**
Document / Apr '94 / ADA / Hot Shot / Jazz Music

RURAL STRING BANDS OF TENNESSEE
Greenback dollar: *Weems String Band* / Everybody two step: *Roane County Ramblers* / Tennessee mountain fox chase: *Vance's Tennessee Breakdowners* / Saro: *Caplinger, Warren Cumberland Mountain Entertainers* / Forked deer: *Bowman, Charlie & His Brothers* / Johnson boys: *Grant Brothers* / Boll weevil: *Lindsey & Conder* / Going down the Lee Highway: *Grayson & Whitter* / Preacher got drunk and laid his bible down: *Tennesse Ramblers* / Davy: *Weems String Band* / Alabama trot: *Roane County Ramblers* / Baby call your dog off: *Ridgel's Fountain Citians* / Green valley waltz: *McCartt Brothers & Patterson* / Moonshiner and his money: *Bowman, Charlie & His Brothers* / On the banks of the old Tennessee: *Baker, Mr. & Mrs. J.W.* / Old hen cackled: *Davenport, Homer & The Young Brothers* / I'm sad and blue: *Perry County Music Makers* / Tennessee breakdown: *Vance's Tennessee Breakdowners*
CD ______ **COCD 3511**
County / Jul '97 / ADA / Direct

RUSH HOUR VOL.2, THE
Spirits: *Transformer 2* / Do you feel me: *HOP* / Feel so good: *THK* / Waterfall (Pegasus 4): *Atlantic Ocean* / Feel the magic: *Kiss Of Love* / Esta es la musica: *Cafe Latino* / Dancing through the night: *Sharada House Gang* / Eternity: *Datura* / Apache: *MASI* / Elephant paw (get down to the funk): *Pan Position* / Freedom: *Pan Position* / U People: *Pan Position* / We're going on down: *Deadly Sins*
CD ______ **REACTCD 034**
React / Jan '94 / Arabesque / Prime / Vital

RUSH HOUR VOL.3, THE
CD ______ **REACTCD 048**
React / Oct '94 / Arabesque / Prime / Vital

RUSH-TRIA - THE CONCEPT (2CD Set)
CD Set ______ **DPARACD 1**
Dance Paradise / Apr '96 / Alphamagic

RUSHY MOUNTAIN
Top of Maol/Humours of Ballydesmons: *Kerry Fiddles* / Callaghan's/Right of man: *O'Keeffe, Padraig* / Tom Sullivan's/Johnny Leary's/Jim Keefe's reel: *Daly, Jackie* / Lark in the bog: *Star Of Munster Trio* / Uppercurch polkas: *Clifford, Billy* / Humours of Lisheen: *Clifford, John & Julia* / Doyle's polka: *O'Leary, Johnny* / Chase me Charlie: *Kerry Fiddles* / Kennedy's favourite/Woman of the house: *Murphy, Dennis* / Banks of Sullane: *Daly, Jackie* / Bill Black's: *Star Of Munster Trio* / Willie Doherty's/Up on the wagon: *Clifford, Billy* / Brosna slide/Scartaglen/Padraig O'Keefe's favourite: *O'Leary, Johnny* / Julia Clifford's/Bill the waiver's: *Clifford, Julia* / Humours of Galtymore/Callaghan's/New mown meadows: *Murphy, Dennis & Julia Clifford* / Trip to the jacks/Where is the cat: *Daly, Jackie* / Palatine's daughter: *Clifford, John & Julia* / Fermoy lasses/Honeymoon: *Clifford, Billy* / Worn torn petticoat/Denis O'Keefe's favourite: *O'Leary, Johnny* / Mountain road/Paddy Cronin's: *Clifford, Julia & Billy Clifford* / Walsh's hornpipe: *Daly, Jackie* / Mrs. Ryan's/Danny Green's polkas: *Clifford, Billy* / Taimse I'm chodladh: *Clifford, Julia* / Tourmore polkas: *O'Leary, Johnny* / Johnny

when you die/Swallow's tail/Miss McLeod's: *Kerry Fiddles* / Danny Ab's: *Clifford, Julia & Dennis Murphy* / Matt Haye's jigs: *Clifford, Billy* / Glenside cottage/Taim gan airgead: *Daly, Jackie* / John Clifford's polka/ Behind the bush in the garden/Going fo: *Clifford, John & Julia*
CD ____________ CDORBD 085
Globestyle / Aug '94 / Pinnacle

RUSSIAN COSSACK MUSIC FROM THE URALS
CD ____________ 15345
Laserlight / '91 / Target/BMG

RUSSIAN ORTHODOX MUSIC/GREAT VOICES OF BULGARIA
CD ____________ AUB 6786
Auvidis/Ethnic / Feb '94 / ADA / Harmonia Mundi

RYKODISC 1996 SAMPLER
Buena: *Morphine* / Walking through a wasted land: *Thompson, Richard* / Devon: *Dr. Didg* / My guitar wants to kill your Mama: *Zappa, Frank* / Black rage: *Last Poets* / Hazy Jane 1: *Drake, Nick* / Devoiko mome: *Sebestyen, Marta* / Ain't hurtin' nobody: *Prine, John* / Ndaweh's dream: *Baka Beyond* / Pure and easy: *Townshend, Pete* / Put you down: *Escovedo, Alejandro* / There ain't no sweet man (Who's worth the salt of my tears): *Waterson, Norma* / Good night Eddie: *Collins, Bootsy* / Thoughless kind: *Cale, John* / Rockin' the res: *Trudell, John* / Stories: *O'Connell, Maura* / On the beach: *Golden Smog* / Last song: *Hart, Mickey*
CD ____________ RSCD 1996
Rykodisc / Jul '96 / ADA / Vital

S

SAARBRUCKEN 1994 (30 Years Of Mod 1964-1994)
CD ____________ DRCD 007
Detour / Oct '95 / Detour / Greyhound

SABA SABA
Saba saba: *Mil Quilhento 1500 & Conjunto Popombo de Nampula* / Noijukuru: *Conjunto Nimala de lalauah* / Kufera povo: *Mil Quilhento 1500 & Conjunto Popombo de Nampula* / Bainxa: *Conjunto Nimala de lalauah* / Josina: *Mil Quilhento 1500 & Conjunto Popombo de Nampula* / Na munthamana nau: *Conjunto Nimala de lalauah* / Mariana: *Mil Quilhento 1500 & Conjunto Popombo de Nampula* / Nonmualana: *Conjunto Nimala de lalauah* / Arminda: *Mil Quilhento 1500 & Conjunto Popombo de Nampula* / nampula: *Conjunto Nimala de lalauah* / Omahie wa mama kihala e flore: *Mil Quilhento 1500 & Conjunto Popombo de Nampula* / Kamueire Kiwereiaka: *Conjunto Nimala de lalauah*
CD ____________ CDORBD 077
Globestyle / Nov '92 / Pinnacle

SABROSO
A los rumberos de belen: *Sierra Maestra* / El son de Nicaragua: *Orquesta Chepin* / Chilindron de Chivo: *Orquesta Casino* / Anda ven y muevete: *Los Van Van* / Se que tu sabes que yo se: *Orquesta Reve* / Camina y ven: *Gonzalez, Celina* / Rucu rucu a Santa Clara: *Irakere* / De kabinde a kunene: *Los Karachi* / Vuela la paloma: *Conjunto Rumbavana* / Frutas del caney: *Grupo Monumental*
CD ____________ CDEWV 11
Earthworks / Jul '89 / EMI

SACRED CEREMONIES (Music Of South Asia)
Allah Muhammad char ya: *Khan, Nusrat Fateh Ali* / Sangwa duepa Budddist chant: *Monks Of The Gyuto Monastery* / Silhet song: *Brahmachari, Prahlad* / Raga multani: *Dagar Brothers* / Raga bageshri: *Das, Partho* / Raga kausik dhwani, tala kaharwa: *Ganguly, Rita* / Orissi, pallavi: *Mohapatra, Guru Kelucharan & Manjula Mathur* / Morning prayer in praise of Lord Shiva and Lord Vishnu / Nagasvaram: *Kamber, Murukesha*
CD ____________ VIGC 130682
JVC / Mar '97 / Direct / New Note/Pinnacle / Vital/SAM

SACRED KORAN, THE (Islamic Chants Of The Ottoman Empire)
CD ____________ VICG 50062
JVC World Library / Mar '96 / ADA / CM / Direct

SACRED MUSIC OF THE SIKHS
CD ____________ VICG 50352
JVC World Library / Mar '96 / ADA / CM / Direct

SACRED MUSIC, SACRED DANCE
CD ____________ CD 736
Music & Arts / Oct '92 / Cadillac / Harmonia Mundi

SACRED SONGS 1925-1934 (Original Performances Classic Years In Digital Stereo)
Sacred hour: *Dawson, Peter* / Bless this house: *McCormack, John* / Lord's prayer: *Thomas, John Charles* / Lost chord: *Butt, Dame Clara* / Star of Bethlehem: *Crooks, Richard* / Rosary: *Novis, Donald* / Ave Maria: *Fields, Gracie* / All through the night: *Crooks, Richard* / Wings of a dove: *Lough, Master Ernest* / Still night holy night: *Robeson, Paul* / Jesus Christ is risen today: *Crooks, Richard* / Abide with me: *Thomas, John Charles* / Hear my prayer: *Lough, Master Ernest* / Ave Maris: *Schumann, Elisabeth*
CD ____________ RPCD 313
Robert Parker Jazz / Sep '96 / Conifer/BMG / New Note/Pinnacle

SACRED SONGS FOR CHRISTMAS
Ave Maria / Nun seid ihr wohl gerochen / O Holy night / In dulci jubilo / Panis angelicus / Il est ne / O divine redeemer / Hark the herald angels sing / Virgin's slumber song / Sinfonia / Silent night / Great and mighty wonder / Nun's chorus / Lord's prayer / Come all ye shepherds / Mille cherubin in coro / Away in a manger / Ave Maria
CD ____________ 4612402
Belart / Nov '96 / PolyGram

SACRED STEEL
CD ____________ ARHCD 450
Arhoolie / Feb '97 / ADA / Cadillac / Direct

SACRED TIBETAN CHANTS FROM THE GREAT PRAYER FESTIVAL
CD ____________ CD 735
Music & Arts / Oct '92 / Cadillac / Harmonia Mundi

SAD SWEET DREAMER
CD ____________ PLSCD 154
Pulse / Apr '97 / BMG

SAFE SOUL VOL.1
Just loving you: *Green, Garland* / Once you fall in love: *McLoyd, Eddie* / I'll see you in hell first: *Mitchell, Phillip* / Rising cost of love: *Jackson, Millie* / It takes both of us: *Act One* / If I can't have your love: *Brown, Jocelyn* / Plenty of love: *C-Brand* / Stay with me: *Martin, Daltrey* / Still in love with you: *Bailey, J.R.* / My shining star: *Fatback Band* / Sweet music, soft lights and you: *Jackson, Millie & Isaac Hayes* / I'll see you in hell first (alt. take): *Mitchell, Phillip* / Feed me your love: *Fatback Band*
CD ____________ CDSEW 020
Southbound / Jan '90 / Pinnacle

SAFE SOUL VOL.2
Never like this: *Two Tons* / Hooked on you: *Simmons, David* / I think I love you: *Shock* / It's way too late: *Watson, Johnny 'Guitar'* / Love starved: *Brown, Shirley* / What'cha see is what'cha get: *Dramatics* / Lovin': *Hurtt, Phil* / Shouting out love: *Emotions* / Ghettos of the mind: *Pleasure* / Always there: *Side Effect* / Everybody's singing love songs: *Sweet Thunder* / Ladies night out: *Pleasure*
CD ____________ CDSEWD 022
Southbound / Aug '90 / Pinnacle

SAIL ALONG SILVERY MOON
Sail along silvery moon: *Vaughn, Billy Orchestra* / Stranger on the shore: *Vaughn, Billy Orchestra* / Only yesterday: *Vaughn, Billy Orchestra* / Love story: *Winterhalter, Hugo* / Long and winding road: *Winterhalter, Hugo* / Romeo and Juliet: *Winterhalter, Hugo* / Oh my Papa: *Hirt, Al* / Rhapsody in blue: *Hirt, Al* / Matador: *Bent Fabric* / When shadows fall: *Bent Fabric* / Love is a riddle: *Bent Fabric* / Java: *Hirt, Al* / Matrimony: *Erling, Ole* / Tie a yellow ribbon round the old oak tree: *Erling, Ole* / Wishing and hoping: *Ingmann, Jorgen* / La Mer: *Ingmann, Jorgen*
CD ____________ 101142
CMC / May '97 / BMG

SALSA
CD ____________ 3003732
IMP / Jan '97 / ADA / Discovery

SALSA - THE CALIENTA COMPILATION
Taka taka-ta: *Irakere* / El coco: *Irakere* / Locas por el mambo: *More, Benny* / Mi chiquita: *More, Benny* / El bobo de la yuca: *More, Benny* / Lo que me paso en la guagua: *Alvarez, Adalberto & Su Son* / Longina: *Burke, Malena & NG La Banda* / Santa Barbara: *Gonzalez, Celina* / Pare Cochero: *Orquesta Aragon* / Yo no quiero que seas celosa: *Reve Y Su Charangon* / Los sitios entero: *NG La Banda* / La protesta de los chivos: *NG La Banda* / Coge el Camaron: *La Origina De Manzanillo* / Se muere la tia: *La Origina De Manzanillo* / Eso que anda: *Los Van Van*
CD ____________ PSCCD 1007
Pure Sounds From Cuba / Feb '95 / Henry Hadaway / THE

SALSA AND TRADITION
CD ____________ PS 65097
PlayaSound / Oct '92 / ADA / Harmonia Mundi

SALSA BOLERO CUBAN (3CD Set)
CD Set ____________ PSCBOX 001
Pure Sounds From Cuba / Feb '95 / Henry Hadaway / THE

SALSA FLAMENCA - CON FUERZA Y CON BONDAD
CD ____________ EUCD 1262
ARC / Mar '94 / ADA / ARC Music

SALSA GREATS
Mi negra Mariana: *Rodriquez, Pete* / Che che cole: *Colon, Willie* / Pedro Navaja: *Blades, Ruben* / Arsenio: *Harlow, Larry* / Senor Serano: *Miranda, Ismael* / Aguzate: *Ray, Ricardo* / Oye como va: *Puente, Tito* / Quitate la mascara: *Barretto, Ray* / Juan pena: *Colon, Willie* / El Malecon: *Orchestra Harlow* / Muneca: *Palmieri, Eddie* / Richies jala jala: *Ray, Ricardo* / Tu loco locoy yo traquillo: *Roena, Roberto* / Huracan: *Valentin, Bobby*
CD ____________ CDCHARLY 131
Caliente / Aug '88 / Koch

SALSA MERENGUE MAMBO
La maxima expression: *Ensamble Latino* / La cosecha de Mujeres: *Tribu Band* / El Sonero: *Raices, Grupo* / Son de Cuba a Puerto Rico: *Delgado, Isaac* / Como se queda: *Ensamble Latino* / Mamaita no quiere: *Alvarez, Adalberto* / Adios Carcelero y Carcel: *Rivas, Maria* / Que ganas: *Delgado, Isaac* / Tres Deseos: *Nazario, Ednita* / Que te pasa mami: *Alvarez, Adalberto* / Tu serenata: *Raices, Grupo* / Mapale: *Rivas, Maria* / No aparentes que no sientes: *Silva, Mauricio* / Fracaso: *Ensamble Latino* / Palanque: *Tribu Band*
CD ____________ CDEMC 3701
EMI / Mar '95 / EMI

SALSA ONLY
A ritmo de la: *Basta una mirada* / Mi mujer es celosa / Mi vecina / El emigrante latino / El patillero / Te propongo / Sobre las olas / Cuando aparezca el amor / Oasis / El concinero mayor / Pegaso / Todos bailan salsa / Ban ban / La suegra / Dime que paso / Rosa Angelina / Managua / Nicaragua / Barranquillero arrebatao / Papi papa
CD ____________ DC 880542
Disky / May '97 / Disky / THE

SALSA SABROSA
Soy antillana: *Cruz, Celia* / Sipriano: *Ray, Ricardo & Bobby Cruz* / Sabo los rumberos: *Canales, Angel* / Sale el sol: *Rivera, Ismael* / Canion: *La Sonora Poncena* / Mi debilidad: *Quintana, Ishmael* / Quiero saber: *Fania Allstars* / Arrepientete: *Barretto, Ray* / Anoranzas: *La Serie, Rolando & Johnny Pacheco* / El raton: *Feliciano, Jose 'Cheo'* / No bebo mas: *La Sonora Poncena* / De toros maneras rosas: *Rivera, Ismael* / La maleta: *Blades, Ruben* / Periodico de ayer: *Lavoe, Hector*
CD ____________ CDHOT 517
Charly / Apr '95 / Koch

SALSA TROPICAL
CD ____________ CD 62039
Saludos Amigos / Nov '93 / Target/BMG

SALSAMANIA
Ganas / El rey de la punctualidad / Sonaremos el tambo / Nabuco donosor / Dile / Le flor do los lindos campos / Cucala / Yo no soy guapo / Llamame / To loco loco y yo tranquilo / Che che cole / Laye laye
CD ____________ CDHOT 515
Charly / Sep '94 / Koch

SALSAMANIA (4CD Set)
CD Set ____________ BMCD 99901
Palladium / Jul '96 / Discovery

SALSOUL (The Best Of Salsoul Records)
CD ____________ MCCD 282
Music Club / Dec '96 / Disc / THE

SALSOUL ESSENTIALS VOL.1 (16 Stompin' Classics From Salsoul/2CD Set)
If you're looking for fun: *Weeks & Co.* / Take some time out: *Salsoul Orchestra* / Step out of my dream: *Strangers* / Make up your mind: *Aurra* / I know you will: *Logg* / Falling in love: *Surface* / Sadie (she smokes): *Bataan, Joe* / Moment of my life: *Inner Life* / Love sensation: *Holloway, Loleatta* / Let no man put asunder: *First Choice* / Ain't no mountain high enough: *Inner Life* / Ten percent: *Double Exposure* / Runaway: *Holloway, Loleatta* / Dr. Love: *First Choice* / I love NY: *Metropolis* / Beat goes on and on: *Ripple*
CD Set ____________ CDNEW 1042
Charly / Jan '97 / Koch

SALSOUL ESSENTIALS VOL.2 (16 Stompin' Classics From Salsoul/2CD Set)
I got my mind made up: *Instant Funk* / Love thang: *First Choice* / Bottle: *Bataan, Joe* / Salsoul 3001: *Salsoul Orchestra* / Just as long as I've got you: *Love Committee* / Nice 'n' naasty: *Salsoul Orchestra* / Can you see where I'm coming from: *Instant Funk* / Sing sing: *Gaz* / Mama don't, Papa won't: *Holloway, Loleatta* / Ooh I love it: *Salsoul Orchestra* / My love is free: *Double Exposure* / You're just the right size: *Salsoul Orchestra* / Hit and run: *Holloway, Loleatta* / Double cross: *First Choice* / Dreaming: *Holloway, Loleatta* / Everyman: *Double Exposure*
CD Set ____________ CDNEW 1072
Charly / Apr '97 / Koch

SALUDOS AMIGOS
CD ____________ CD 62048
Saludos Amigos / Nov '93 / Target/BMG

SALUTE TO THE BIG BANDS
CD ____________ PLSCD 232
Pulse / Jul '97 / BMG

SALZBURG - VOLKSMUSIK 1910-1949
CD ____________ US 0197
Trikont / Jul '95 / ADA / Direct

SAMARKAND TO BUKHARA
CD ____________ 7122038
Long Distance / Jun '97 / ADA / Discovery

SAMBA
To voltando: *Simone* / Tristeza pe no chao: *Nunes, Clara* / Saxofone, por que choras: *Ferreira, Abel* / Roendo as unhas: *Paulinho Da Viola* / Quisera ser eu: *Jurema* / Samba do iraja/No foi ela: *Moreira, Wilson & Nei Lopes* / Tiro ao alvaro: *Regina, Elis & Adoniran Barbosa* / De noite, na cama: *Monteiro, Doris* / Geraldinos e arquibaldos: *Gonzaguinha* / A primeira vez: *Pinheiro, Leila* / Samba da minha terra: *Caymmi, Dorival* / Corcovado: *Gilberto, Joao* / Samba dobrado: *Djavan* / Antes que seja tarde: *Lins, Ivan* / Tie: *Agora E Samba* / Dingue li bangue: *Conjunto Sal Da Terra* / Na glerra , dingu: *Os Choroes* / O que e que a baiana tem: *Miranda, Carmen & Dorival Caymmi*
CD ____________ PRMDCD 15
Hemisphere / Oct '96 / EMI

SAMBA ENREDO (2CD Set)
CD Set ____________ KAR 271
IMP / Sep '96 / ADA / Discovery

SAMBA IN THE HOUSE
Dance with me: *Latin Impact* / Drums of life: *Abraxas, Ray & Rafael Torres* / Mamba: *Latin Kings* / Can you dig it: *That Kid Chris* / Tocame: *Paso Latino* / Yeah babe: *Latin Impact* / Chunga chunga: *Kings From Queens* / Drums of life pt.2: *Abraxas, Ray & Rafael Torres* / Me hace sentir tan bien: *Private Ize* / Negrita ven: *Private Ize* / Toma: *El Cantor* / El ritmo: *Latin Impact* / Un ritmo baila: *Ospina, David Going Deep* / Something duro: *IZE 1* / Timbala: *4 Six Drums*
CD ____________ KICKCD 43
Kickin' / Jan '97 / Prime / SRD

SAMBA LATINO
CD ____________ ZYX 550812
ZYX / Jun '97 / ZYX

SAMBA ONLY
Brasiliana / Medley argumento / Medley recomecar / Medley saudosa maloca / Melody tristeza / Brazil nao seremos jamais ou seremos / Medley cidade maravilhosa / Medley o teu cabelo nao nega / Medley piada de salao / Medley marcha do cordao do bola preta / Medley fogao / Medley hino rubro negro / Medley as pastorinhas / Medley do jeito que o rei mandou / Medley reza forte / Medley quando vim de minas / Medley serenou / Me leva me leva / Amarre o inimigo no cipo / O amanha
CD ____________ DC 880572
Disky / May '97 / Disky / THE

SAMBA RUMBA CONGA
CD ____________ PASTCD 7071
Flapper / Aug '95 / Pinnacle

SAMMY'S SALOON
CD ____________ 15212
Laserlight / Aug '91 / Target/BMG

SAMPLE CITY VOL.1
CD ____________ FILECD 442
Profile / Aug '93 / Pinnacle

SAMPLE CITY VOL.2
CD ____________ FILECD 450
Profile / Jun '94 / Pinnacle

SAMPLE SOME OKRA
CD ____________ OKSP 001
Okra / Mar '94 / ADA / Direct

SAMPLE 'THE WORLD OF SERIES...', THE
I'd like to teach the world to sing: *New Seekers* / Mighty Quinn: *Manfred Mann* / You've got your troubles: *Fortunes* / Cara mia: *Whitfield, David* / Shout: *Lulu & The Luvvers* / It's only make believe: *Twitty, Conway* / King of the road: *Miller, Roger* / Answer me: *Dickson, Barbara* / Diane: *Bachelors* / Durham Town: *Whittaker, Roger* / Do you love me: *Poole, Brian & The Tremeloes* / You're a lady: *Skellern, Peter* / Drinkin' wine spo-dee-o-dee: *Lewis, Jerry Lee* / Game of love: *Fontana, Wayne & The Mindbenders* / Tower of strength: *Vaughan, Frankie* / Welcome home: *Peters & Lee* / Juliet: *Four Pennies* / Moon river: *Francis, Connie* / Your cheatin' heart: *Williams, Hank Jr.* / Singin' the blues: *Steele, Tommy*
CD ____________ 5523702
Spectrum / Jun '96 / PolyGram

SAN ANTONIO BLUES 1937
CD ____________ DOCD 5232
Document / Apr '94 / ADA / Hot Shot / Jazz Music

SAN ANTONIO'S CONJUNTOS IN THE 1950'S
CD ____________ ARHCD 376
Arhoolie / Apr '95 / ADA / Cadillac / Direct

SAN DIEGO BLUES JAM
CD ____________ TCD 5029
Testament / Oct '95 / ADA / Koch

SAN FRANCISCAN DAZE
San Franciscan nights: *Burdon, Eric & The Animals* / Diddy wah diddy: *Captain Beefheart* / Summertime blues: *Blue Cheer* / Mendocino: *Sir Douglas Quintet* / (We ain't got) nothin' yet: *Blues Magoos* / No time like the right time: *Blues Project* / Sea train: *Sea Train* / Desiree: *Left Banke* / I can take you to the sun: *Misunderstood* / Like to get to know you: *Spanky & Our Gang* / White light, white heat: *Velvet Underground* / Let's get together: *We Five* / Do you know what I mean: *Michaels, Lee* / You're a very lovely woman: *Merry Go Round* / Cave song: *Linn County* / Sunshine girl: *Parade* / Let it hang out (let it all hang out): *Hombres*
CD ______ 5536722
Debutante / Jun '97 / PolyGram

SAN FRANCISCO BLUES
Should've been gone: *Hooker, John Lee* / Evil: *Hammond, John* / Elvin's blues: *Bishop, Elvin* / Willie and the hand jive: *AB Skhy* / Jorma's blues: *Jefferson Airplane* / Milk cow blues: *Commander Cody* / Hard times: *Hooker, John Lee* / Hey Bo Diddley: *Hammond, John* / Hesitation blues: *Taj Mahal* / Country blues: *Watson, Doc* / Hobo blues: *Hooker, John Lee* / Guitar blues 2: *Taj Mahal* / So many roads, so many trains: *Hammond, John* / Sally May: *Hooker, John Lee* / Mustang Sally: *Chambers Brothers*
CD ______ 3036000712
Carlton / Feb '97 / Carlton

SAN FRANCISCO BLUES FESTIVAL-1980
CD ______ 157732
Blues Collection / Feb '93 / Discovery

SAN FRANCISCO HOUSE CULTURE (2CD Set)
CD Set ______ SPV 08638442
Subterranean / Jan '96 / Koch / Plastic Head

SAN FRANCISCO LEGENDS
Casey Jones: *Grateful Dead* / Uncle John's band: *Grateful Dead* / Black dog: *Winchester, Jesse* / Somebody to love: *Jefferson Airplane* / Baby please don't go: *Chambers Brothers* / What made Milwaukee famous: *Commander Cody* / I wish you would: *Hammond, John* / Guitar blues: *Taj Mahal* / Hot summer day: *It's A Beautiful Day* / I feel alright: *Hooker, John Lee* / Gambler's blues: *Hammond, John* / Might have to cry: *Scaggs, Boz* / Make my life shine: *Scaggs, Boz* / Don't do this to me: *Valente, Dino* / Home in my hand: *Commander Cody* / Daddy roll on: *Town Cryers & Marty Balin*
CD ______ 307682
Hallmark / Jul '97 / Carlton

SAN FRANCISCO NIGHTS
Twelve ducks: *Clover* / No vacancy: *Clover* / Milk of human kindness: *Clover* / High coin: *Charlatans* / Blues ain't nothing: *Charlatans* / Superman: *New Riders Of The Purple Sage* / Garden of Eden: *New Riders Of The Purple Sage* / All I ever wanted: *New Riders Of The Purple Sage* / She's a bad news baby: *Mojo Men* / New York City: *Mojo Men* / Candle to burn: *Mojo Men* / Happiness is you: *Mojo Men* / You didn't even say goodbye: *Mojo Men*
CD ______ CDTB 167
Thunderbolt / Aug '96 / TKO Magnum

SANCTIFIED JUG BANDS 1928-1930
CD ______ DOCD 5300
Document / Dec '94 / ADA / Hot Shot / Jazz Music

SANCTUARY SESSIONS - LIVE AT CRUISE'S HOTEL, ENNIS
CD ______ CCD 001CD
CCD / Oct '94 / ADA

SANTA AND SATAN - ONE AND THE SAME
CD ______ DD 9497
Dr. Dream / Nov '96 / Cargo

SANTA CLAUS BLUES
CD ______ JASSCD 3
Jass / Aug '89 / ADA / Cadillac / CM / Direct / Jazz Music

SANTA'S BAG
O come, o come Emmanuel / O tannenbaum / Silver bells / White Christmas / Have yourself a merry little Christmas / Away in a manger / Christmas song / Christmas blues / It's the time of the year / Jingle bells / Let it snow, let it snow, let it snow / Santa Claus is coming to town / Blue Christmas
CD ______ CD 83352
Telarc / Oct '94 / Conifer/BMG

SANTIC PRESENTS AN EVEN HARDER SHADE OF BLACK
CD ______ CDPS 001
Pressure Sounds / Mar '95 / Jet Star / SRD

SARAH 100 THERE AND BACK AGAIN LANE
Sensitive: *Field Mice* / Atta girl: *Heavenly* / Ahprahran: *Sugargliders* / Peaches: *Orchids* / Joy of living: *Blueboy* / Six o'clock is rosary: *Ministers* / Inside out: *Brighter* / Make a deal with the city: *East River Pipe* / English rain: *Wake* / Temporal: *Secret Shine* / All of a tremble: *St. Christopher* / Pristine Christine: *Sea Urchins* / He gets me so hard: *Boyracer* / Mustard gas: *Action Painting* / Tell me how it feels: *Sweetest Ache* / Rio: *Another Sunny Day* / In Gunnersbury Park: *Hit Parade* / Drown: *Even As We Speak*
CD ______ SARAH 100
Sarah / Aug '95 / Vital

SASHA REMIXES, THE
Nasty rhythm: *Creative Thieves* / Alright: *Urban Soul* / Closer: *Mr. Fingers* / Feel the drop: *BM EX* / Peace and harmony: *Brothers In Rhythm* / Let you go: *Van-Rooy, Marina* / Always: *Urban Soul* / Talk to me: *Hysterix* / No more: *Unique 3* / Everything's gonna change: *Rusty* / Anambra part 2: *Ozo* / Sea of tranquility: *London Beat*
CD ______ KOLDCD 002
Equator / Jun '93 / Pinnacle

SATIN AND STEEL
If I could turn back time: *Cher* / Will you be there (in the morning): *Heart* / Same thing: *Carlisle, Belinda* / I believe: *Detroit, Marcella* / Running up that hill: *Bush, Kate* / Sexcrime (1984): *Eurythmics* / All fired up: *Benatar, Pat* / Black velvet: *Myles, Alannah* / Better be good to me: *Turner, Tina* / Feel like making love: *Henry, Pauline* / I want that man: *Harry, Deborah* / Monsters and angels: *Voice Of The Beehive* / Going down to Liverpool: *Bangles* / Stop draggin' my heart around: *Nicks, Stevie & Tom Petty & The Heartbreakers* / Faster than the speed of night: *Tyler, Bonnie* / I want your love: *Transvision Vamp* / Pretend we're dead: *L7* / Gloria: *Branigan, Laura* / Bette Davis eyes: *Carnes, Kim* / Echo beach: *Martha & The Muffins*
CD ______ 5169712
PolyGram TV / Aug '94 / PolyGram

SATIN SHEETS
Looking in the eyes of love: *Loveless, Patty* / I've already loved you in my mind: *Twitty, Conway* / Feelings: *Twitty, Conway* / Leave my heart the way you found it: *Greenwood, Lee* / Hopeless romantics: *Earle, Steve & the Dukes* / Anyone can be somebody's fool: *Griffith, Nanci* / Satin sheets: *Pruett, Jeanne* / Crying: *Jennings, Waylon* / Don't worry baby: *Thomas, B.J.* / Break it to me gently: *Lee, Brenda* / She's got you: *Lynn, Loretta* / Am I blue (yes I'm blue): *Strait, George* / Love song: *Oak Ridge Boys* / Wind beneath my wings: *Greenwood, Lee* / He called me baby: *Cline, Patsy* / (Turn out the lights) and love me tonight: *Williams, Don*
CD ______ PWKS 4268
Carlton / Feb '96 / Carlton

SATISFACTION GUARANTEED (Hits Of The Seventies)
CD ______ MU 5047
Musketeer / Oct '92 / Disc

SATURDAY NIGHT (The Best Of Pub Rock)
Sweet Gene Vincent: *Dury, Ian & The Blockheads* / Down the road apiece: *Gibbons, Steve Band* / Who do you love: *Juicy Lucy* / Looked out my window: *Johnson, Wilko & Len Lewis Band* / Amsterdam dog: *Ducks Deluxe* / Milk and alcohol: *Dr. Feelgood* / Down in the bottom: *Groundhogs* / Goin' back home: *Pirates* / On the street: *Das Luftwaffegeschaft* / Absolutely gone: *Gibbons, Steve Band* / Baby Jane: *Dr. Feelgood* / Please don't touch: *Pirates* / Burnin' rubber: *Green, Mick* / Something's goin' on: *Ducks Deluxe* / Bottle up and go: *Johnson, Wilko* / Do anything you wanna do: *Eddie & The Hot Rods* / Saturday night: *Juicy Lucy* / Shakin' all over: *Pirates* / Shake for me: *Groundhogs* / To be alone with you: *Gibbons, Steve Band*
CD ______ 3036000782
Carlton / Jun '97 / Carlton

SATURDAY NIGHT AT HEAVEN, A
CD ______ SATCD 1
Prime Cuts / Mar '94 / Pinnacle

SATURDAY NIGHT AT THE AMERICAN DINER (2CD Set)
Reet petite: *Wilson, Jackie* / Everybody needs somebody: *Blues Brothers* / Blueberry hill: *Domino, Fats* / Lucille: *Little Richard* / No particular place to go: *Berry, Chuck* / Tequila: *Champs* / Let's twist again: *Checker, Chubby* / C'mon everybody: *Cochran, Eddie* / Leader of the pack: *Shangri-Las* / In the midnight hour: *Pickett, Wilson* / Duke of Earl: *Chandler, Gene* / Goodnight sweetheart: *Spaniels* / Who put the bomp: *Viscounts* / (We're gonna) Rock around the clock: *Haley, Bill* / Grease megamix: *Travolta, John & Olivia Newton John* / Singin' the blues: *Mitchell, Guy* / Wanderer: *Dion* / Green onions: *Booker T & The MG's* / Great balls of fire: *Lewis, Jerry Lee* / Wipeout: *Surfaris* / Wake up little Susie: *Everly Brothers* / Sweet talking guy: *Chiffons* / Sherry: *Four Seasons* / Chantilly lace: *Big Bopper* / Chapel of love: *Dixie Cups* / Blue suede shoes: *Perkins, Carl* / La bamba: *Valens, Ritchie* / Yakity yak: *Coasters* / Will you still love me tomorrow: *Shirelles* / Needle in a haystack: *Velvette* / I get around: *Beach Boys* / Rebel rouser: *Eddy, Duane* / Bony moronie: *Williams, Larry* / Be bop a Lula: *Vincent, Gene* / My boyfriend's back: *Angels* / Surf city: *Jan & Dean* / At the hop: *Danny & The Juniors* / Why do fools fall in love: *Lymon, Frankie* / Book of love: *Monotones* / Earth angel: *Crew Cuts*
CD ______ DINCD 107
Dino / Aug '95 / Pinnacle

SATURDAY NIGHT BLUES
CD ______ SP 1172CD
Stony Plain / Oct '93 / ADA / CM / Direct

SATURDAY NIGHT'S ALRIGHT
I'm in you: *Frampton, Peter* / Eighth day: *O'Connor, Hazel* / Paper plane: *Status Quo* / Ramblin' man: *Allman Brothers* / Saturday night's alright for fighting: *John, Elton* / I'm waiting for the man: *Velvet Underground* / Stairway to heaven: *Far Corporation* / Letter: *Box Tops* / Freebird: *Lynyrd Skynyrd* / Funk 49: *James Gang* / Liar: *Three Dog Night* / Warrior: *Wishbone Ash* / Parisienne walkways: *Moore, Gary* / Who do you love: *Juicy Lucy* / Broken down angel: *Nazareth* / Lady in the black: *Uriah Heep* / Ace of spades: *Motorhead* / America: *Nice* / You took the words right out of my mouth: *Meat Loaf* / Rosanna: *Toto* / God gave rock 'n' roll to you: *Argent* / All day and all of the night: *Stranglers* / Holding out for a hero: *Tyler, Bonnie* / Livin' thing: *ELO*
CD ______ 3220
Carlton / Oct '92 / Carlton

SAVE THE LAST DANCE FOR ME
Save the last dance for me: *Heptones* / Will you still love me tomorrow: *Barker, Dave* / Shotgun wedding: *Campbell, Cornell* / Then he kissed me: *Marvels* / Hang on sloopy: *Chosen Few* / Da doo ron ron: *Heyward, Winston* / Darling you send me: *Max Romeo* / Oh Carol (Vocal): *McKay, Freddie* / Oh Carol: *Brown, Lennox* / Sincerely: *Edwards, Jackie* / (Sittin' on the) dock of the bay: *McKay, Freddie* / Light my fire: *Soul Sam* / Come on over to my place: *Robinson, Jackie* / Wonderful world: *Donaldson, Eric* / It's in his kiss (The shoop shoop song): *Marvels* / Blue moon: *Platonics* / Duke of Earl (Version): *McCook, Tommy & The Aggrovators*
CD ______ CDTRL 317
Trojan / Mar '94 / Direct / Jet Star

SAVE THE LAST DANCE FOR ME
Do you want to know a secret: *Kramer, Billy J.* / Tossing and turning: *Ivy League* / Little loving: *Fourmost* / My guy: *Wells, Mary* / You were made for me: *Wells, Mary* / Just like Eddie: *Heinz* / Do you love me: *Poole, Brian* / Pied piper: *St. Peters, Crispian* / Bobby's girl: *Maughan, Susan* / Save the last dance for me: *Drifters* / Juliet: *Four Pennies* / Hello little girl: *Fourmost* / Little children: *Kramer, Billy J.* / Um um um um um um: *Fontana, Wayne* / But I do: *Henry, Clarence* / Crying game: *Berry, Dave* / Wimoweh: *Denver, Karl* / Tell me when: *Applejacks* / Baby now that I've found you: *Foundations* / Jesamine: *Casuals*
CD ______ CD 6042
Music / Oct '96 / Target/BMG

SAX AT MIDNIGHT (Cool Jazz Classics)
CD ______ CDGR 110
Charly / Dec '96 / Koch

SAX BY THE SEA (A Magical Blend Of Music And The Sounds Of Nature)
CD ______ 57852
CMC / May '97 / BMG

SAX COLLECTION, THE (2CD Set)
Up where we belong / Can you feel the love tonight / Seven seconds / Everlasting love / Talking in your sleep / Anytime you need a friend / I'd lie for you (and that's the truth) / Secret / Holding back the years / All I wanna do / Get on your feet / Forever young / Heal the world / I'd do anything for love / Saturday night / Words / Make it happen / Simply the best / Love is all around / Whiter shade of pale / Long and winding road / Woman / Lean on me / How deep is your love / Just the way you are / When I fall in love / Said I loved you.. but I lied / Candle in the wind / Will you be there / Blue eyes / Dreamlover / We have only just begun / One sweet day / I can love you like that / Can I touch you.. there
CD Set ______ DCD 3003
Music / Jun '97 / Target/BMG

SAX FOR LOVERS
CD ______ MACCD 332
Autograph / Aug '96 / BMG

SAX FOR LOVERS
Up where we belong / Can you feel the love tonight / Seven seconds / Everlasting love / Talking in your sleep / Anytime you need a friend / I'd lie for you (and that's the truth) / Secret / Holding back the years / All I wanna do / Get on your feet / Forever young / Heal the world / I'd do anything for love / Saturday night / Words / Make it happen / Simply the best
CD ______ CD 6052
Music / Feb '97 / Target/BMG

SAX FOR ROMANTICS (4CD Set)
CD Set ______ MBSCD 447
Castle / Nov '95 / BMG

SAX MOODS
CD ______ MACCD 333
Autograph / Aug '96 / BMG

SAX MOODS VOL.2 (Blowing Free)
True love ways / Killing me softly / Peer gynt / Anything / Touch of frost theme / Drive / Imagine / When a man loves a woman / Smooth operator / Pick up the pieces / Morning dance / Walk in the night / You gotta be / How deep is your love / Blowing free / I just wanna make love to you / Fever / (You make me feel like a) natural woman / Ode to you / Swing low, sweet chariot
CD ______ DINCD 118
Dino / Nov '96 / Pinnacle

SAXOMANIA (Honkers & Screamers)
Wiggles: *Prysock, Red House Rockers* / Crying my heart out: *Prysock, Red House Rockers* / Hard rock: *Prysock, Red House Rockers* / Jump for George: *Prysock, Red House Rockers* / Hammer: *Prysock, Red House Rockers* / Jackpot: *Prysock, Red House Rockers* / Earthquake: *Singleton, Charlie* / Bobby's boogie: *Lane, Morris* / Last call: *Holloway, Red* / Foolin' around slowly: *Holloway, Red* / Buttermilk: *Holloway, Red* / Big Jay's hop: *McNeely, 'Big' Jay* / Zero: *Dash, Julian* / Give it up: *Watts, Noble 'Watts' & Paul Williams Orchestra* / Pass the buck: *Watts, Noble 'Watts' & Paul Williams Orchestra* / Big two four: *Watts, Noble 'Watts' & Paul Williams Orchestra* / South shore drive: *Watts, Noble 'Watts' & Paul Williams Orchestra* / Sack o'woe: *King Curtis & The Knoble Knights* / Soul twist: *King Curtis & The Knoble Knights* / Twistin' with the King: *King Curtis & The Knoble Knights*
CD ______ CPCD 8163
Charly / Nov '96 / Koch

SAXON DANCEHALL SPECIALS VOL.1
CD ______ SAXCD 001
Saxon Studio / Apr '94 / Jet Star

SAXOPHONE DREAMS
End of the road / Songbird / Why / Piano in the dark / Right here waiting / Can you feel the love tonight / Jealous guy / Jesus to a child / I will always love you / Love won't let me wait / Get here / If you were here tonight / Summer (the first time) / Save the best for last / True / Suddenly / Careless whisper / Giving you the best that I got
CD ______ CDVIP 147
Virgin VIP / Apr '97 / EMI

SAXOPHONE PHENOMENOM, THE
Wayward balladeer: *Coxhill, Lol* / Gossip: *Haslam, George* / Dayday: *Dean, Elton* / New worlds: *Dunmall, Paul* / Landscape gardening: *Dunmall, Paul* / Life after room service: *Biscoe, Chris* / Song: *Parker, Evan* / Hasta pronto: *Haslam, George* / Odeon's dropout piece: *Wilkinson, Alan*
CD ______ SLAMCD 401
Slam / Oct '96 / Cadillac

SAXOPHONY - HONKERS AND SHOUTERS
Easy rockin': *Kohlman, Freddie Orchestra* / Flashlight: *Wright, Jimmy* / Move over: *Wright, Jimmy* / 2.20 AM: *Wright, Jimmy* / Blowin' awhile: *Hall, Rene* / Rene's boogie: *Hall, Rene* / Blue creek hop: *Hall, Rene* / Downbeat: *Hall, Rene* / Jubilee jump: *Hall, Rene* / Jesse's blues: *Hall, Rene* / Turnpike: *Powell, Jesse* / Sopping molasses: *Powell, Jesse* / Whooping blues: *Lucas, Buddy* / Pea lily: *Lucas, Buddy* / Undecided: *Lucas, Buddy* / Big Bertha: *Lucas, Buddy* / One taste calls for another: *Hall, Rene*
CD ______ NEMCD 748
Sequel / Aug '95 / BMG

SCIENCE BEHIND THE CIRCLE (2CD Set)
Dub thunder in progress: *Soundclash Republic* / Just a groove: *Rocky & Diesel* / Caught in the car park: *Weatherall, Andrew* / Drive me crazy: *Secret Knowledge* / Boom banging (in your area): *Vinyl Blair* / Time for music: *Beedle, Ashley* / Grumpy flutter: *Holmes, David* / Double sphere: *Paingang* / Sick organ: *SLAM* / Audio wave: *Sound Enforcer* / Taste (chips in a basket): *Aloof* / Acid charge: *Cox, Carl*
CD Set ______ FCCCD 001
Full Circle / Apr '96 / Vital

SCIENCE FICTION JAZZ VOL.2
CD ______ MOLECD 003
Mole / Jun '97 / Intergroove

SCORED 1-0
CD ______ JTI 1CD
JTI / Jul '97 / 3mv/Sony

SCORPIO RECORDS STORY
Brown eyed girl: *Golliwogs* / You better be careful: *Golliwogs* / Fight fire: *Golliwogs* / Fragile child: *Golliwogs* / Walking on the water: *Golliwogs* / You better get it before it gets you: *Golliwogs* / Call it pretending: *Golliwogs* / Boots: *Spokes* / Stop calling me: *Group B* / She's gone: *Group B* / I know your name girl: *Group B* / I never really knew: *Group B* / Time: *Tokays* / Hole in the wall: *Tokays* / It's up to you: *Shillings* / Made you cry: *Shillings* / Losin' you: *Newcastle 5* / Yes I'm cryin': *Newcastle 5* / Gotta get away: *Penn, William* / Blow my mind: *Penn, William* / Far and away: *Penn, William* / Weatherman: *Squires* / Anyhow anywhere: *Squires* / It must be love: *Squires* / Read all about it: *Tears* / Rat race: *Tears* / People through my glasses: *Tears*
CD ______ CDWIKD 129
Big Beat / Apr '94 / Pinnacle

SCOTLAND - ACCORDION, HARP & FIDDLE
CD ______ PS 65109
PlayaSound / Nov '93 / ADA / Harmonia Mundi

SCOTLAND - THE DANCES AND THE DANCE BANDS
Eightsome reel: *Holmes, Ian & Scottish Dance Band* / Strip the willow: *Johnstone, Jim & His Band* / West Highland waltz: *MacDonald, Fergie & Highland* / Dashing white Sergeant: *MacPhail, Ian & His Scottish Dance Band* / Canadian barn dance: *Johnstone, Jim & His Band* / Waltz country dance: *Keith, Lex & His Scottish Band* / Irish jiggery: *MacDonald, Fergie & Highland* / Grand march: *Wilson, Calum* / Jig strathspey and reel: *Lothian Scottish Dance Band* / St. Bernard's waltz: *Johnstone, Jim & His Band* / Boston Two Step: *Ellis, John & His Highland Country Band* / Reel (hoop her and gird her): *Glendaruel Scottish Dance Band* / Pride o' erin waltz: *MacLeod, Bobby & His Music* / Gay Gordons: *Campbell, Colin & His Highland Band* / Two highland schottissches: *Ellis, John & His Highland Country Band* / Military two step: *Johnstone, Jim & His Band* / Lothian lads: *Lothian Scottish Dance Band* / Palais glide: *Johnstone, Jim* / Hebridean waltz: *Carmichael, John* / Irish military two step: *McDonald, Fergie*
CD ______ **LCOM 9003**
Lismor / Jul '87 / ADA / Direct / Duncans / Lismor

SCOTLAND - THE MUSIC OF A NATION
Caddam Woods: *Golden Fiddle Orchestra* / Strathspeys and reels: *Burgess, John D* / Bonnie lass o'Bon Accord: *Ford, Tommy* / Medley: *Gonnella, Ron* / 4/4 marches: *Dysart & Dundonald Pipe Band* / Slow air and marches: *MacKay, Rhona* / Mrs. Hamilton of Pencaitland: *Glasgow Caledonian Strathspey & Reel Society* / Gay Gordons: *Ellis, John & His Highland Country Band* / Free and easy: *Hunter, Karen* / Petronella: *Brock, Robin & His Dance Band* / March, strathspey and reel: *MacFayden, Iain* / Hangman's reel: *MacLean, Calum* / Waltzes: *Dysart & Dundonald Pipe Band* / Reels: *Currie Brothers* / Cro cheann T Saile: *MacKay, Rhona* / Marches: *Glasgow Caledonian Strathspey & Reel Society* / Dumbarton's drums: *Gaelforce Orchestra* / Mary of Argyll: *Gaelforce Orchestra* / Trilogy: *Gaelforce Orchestra*
CD ______ **LCOM 9004**
Lismor / Aug '87 / ADA / Direct / Duncans / Lismor

SCOTLAND NOW - THE MUSIC AND THE SONG VOL.2
Fiddle and pipe medley: *Hardie, Ian* / Forth bridge song: *Laing, Robin* / Who pays the piper: *McCalmans* / Wild geese: *Redpath, Jean* / Slow air and pipe medley: *McCallum, Craig Scottish Dance Band* / Chi Mi'n Geamhradh: *MacPhee, Catherine-Anne* / See the people run: *Ceolbeg* / Coorie doon: *Stramash* / Atlantic reels: *McNeill, Brian* / MacCrimmon's Lament and slow air: *Heywood, Heather* / Across the hills of home: *Bogle, Eric* / Storm in Edinburgh/The streaker: *Bogle, Eric* / Oor Hamlet: *McNaughtan, Adam* / Tha Mo Chridhe Sa Ghaidhealtachd: *Scott, Elfrida* / Fiddle tune medley: *Robertson, Arthur Scott* / I wish I was in Glasgow: *MacKintosh, Iain* / Bell: *Jackson, William Billy* / Rollin' home: *McCalmans*
CD ______ **CDTRAX 060**
Greentrax / Dec '92 / ADA / Direct / Duncans / Highlander

SCOTLAND THE BRAVE
CD ______ **MATCD 233**
Castle / Dec '92 / BMG

SCOTLAND THE BRAVE
Scotland the brave: *Daly, Glen* / Songs of the borders: *Alexander Brothers* / Scottish trilogy: *Martell, Lena* / Lass of bon accord: *Alexander Brothers* / MacNamara's band: *Daly, Glen* / Marching home: *Alexander Brothers* / Mary of Skye: *Kennedy, Calum* / Sky is bluer in Scotland: *Daly, Glen* / Cuckoo waltz: *Starr, Will* / Auld Scotch sang medley: *Alexander Brothers* / Grand march: *MacLeod, Jim & His Band* / Guid Scotch night: *Stewart, Andy & Jimmy Blue Band* / There's nae toon: *Alexander Brothers* / Little street where old friends meet: *Daly, Glen* / Scotish soldier: *Stewart, Andy* / Duke and Duchess of Edinburgh: *MacLeod, Jim & His Band* / Dear old Glasgow town: *Daly, Glen* / Amazing grace: *Royal Scots Dragoon Guards* / Flower of Scotland: *Alexander Brothers*
CD ______ **TRTCD 136**
TrueTrax / Oct '94 / THE

SCOTLAND THE BRAVE
CD ______ **EUCD 1321**
ARC / Nov '95 / ADA / ARC Music

SCOTLAND THE BRAVE
Scotland the brave / Highland cathedral / Mull of kintyre / Auld town march / Pipe major Willie Ross / Highland lassie / Going to the fair / Lady Ramsey's strathspey / Lady Carmichael's strathspey / Leezy Lindsay / Brolam / Pulteney reel / Isle of barley / Newmarket house / Doune of Inverochty / Mist covered mountains / Old toastie / Lady MacKenzie of Fairburn / Strathspey king / Gin I were a baron's heir / Barbara's jig / Mason's apron / Amazing grace / Duncan McInnes / Stirling castle / Kilt is my delight / Dr. Ross / 50th welcome to Argyllshire gathering / Dark island / Road to the isles / Dream valley of Glendural / Old rustic bridge / Paddy's leather breaches / Last minute friendship / Graugach / O'er the bows to Ballindalloch / Miss Girdle / Three girls of Portree / Mary Anderson / Campbell town kiltie / Moving cloud / Famous bridge / Eriskay love song / Ass in the graveyard / Merrily dance the quaker's wife / Queen of the rushes / Heilan' laddie
CD ______ **300752**
Hallmark / Feb '97 / Carlton

SCOTLAND THE BRAVE
Old rustic bridge by the mill/Towsay Castle/ Money musk: *Gordon Highlanders* / Miss McLeaod O'Raasey/Cock of the North: *Gordon Highlanders* / Route March/When the battle is over: *Gordon Highlanders* / 79th farewell to Gibraltar: *Massed Pipes & Drums* / Colonel Robertson: *Massed Pipes & Drums* / Dovecote Park: *Massed Pipes & Drums* / Prince Charles welcome to Lochaber/Mingulay boat song: *Massed Pipes & Drums* / Silver spear/The curlew/Captain Horne: *Massed Pipes & Drums* / MacFarlane's reel/O'Leudh: *Massed Pipes & Drums* / Inverness gathering: *Edinburgh City Police Pipe Band* / Drunken piper/ 79th's farewell to Gibraltar: *Edinburgh City Police Pipe Band* / Earl of Mansfield: *Edinburgh City Police Pipe Band* / Drum salute: *Boghall & Bathgate Caledonia Pipe Band* / Royal Scots polka/Conundrum: *Boghall & Bathgate Caledonia Pipe Band* / Highland wedding/The Smith of Chilliehassie: *Boghall & Bathgate Caledonia Pipe Band* / Boghall and Bathgate: *Boghall & Bathgate Caledonia Pipe Band* / Train journey North/The redundancy: *Boghall & Bathgate Caledonia Pipe Band* / Up in the morning/The muckin' o'Geordie's byre: *Turriff & District Pipe Band* / Cock o'the North: *Turriff & District Pipe Band* / Reveille: *Gordon Highlanders* / Miss Kirkwood: *Gordon Highlanders* / Scotland the Brave: *Gordon Highlanders*
CD ______ **CD 6060**
Music / Feb '97 / Target/BMG

SCOTLAND THE BRAVE
CD ______ **PLSCD 178**
Pulse / Apr '97 / BMG

SCOTLAND THE BRAVE
Piping hot / Bonnie Dundee / Barren rocks of Aden / Rose of Allendale / Skye boat song / Duncan McInnes / Kilworth hills / Gaelic air / Pipers waltz / Crusaders / Wooden heart / Scotland the brave / AA Cameron / Mist covered mountains / Murdo's wedding / Brigadier Snow / Ae fond kiss / Saffron kilt / Rowan tree / Archie McKinlay / Amazing grace
CD ______ **RECD 516**
REL / Jun '97 / CM / Duncans / Highlander

SCOTLAND'S MUSIC (Selected Works From the History Of Scottish Music/2CD Set)
9th century bells / Jubente petrus / Sanctorum piissime Columba / O Columba / Pi li li liu / Airs by Fingal / Deidre's lament / Sanctus ierarchia / Kyrie / Hac in anni janua / Gowans are gay / Ex te lux oritur / Pleugh sang / Salve festa dies / Dicant nunc judei / O bone Jesu / Support your servant / Galliarde la roine d'ECosse / Golden pavan / Come my children dear / Why should I be so sad on my wedding day / Dic mihi saeve puer / Sonata on Scot's tunes / Symphony in B flat / Bagatelle / Drei lieder No.1 keiner von den schonheit tochtern / O would that I could see again / I will think of thee my love / In the glen / Benedictus / Calgacus
CD Set ______ **CKD 008**
Linn / Apr '93 / PolyGram

SCOTS DANCE PARTY FAVOURITES
Grand march and reels: *MacLeod, Jim & His Band* / Scottish waltzes: *MacLeod, Jim & His Band* / Strip the willow: *MacLeod, Jim & His Band* / Marches: *MacLeod, Jim & His Band* / Britannia two step: *MacLeod, Jim & His Band* / Dashing white Sergeant: *MacLeod, Jim & His Band* / Dunoon barn dance: *Shand, Jimmy & His Band* / Gay Gordons: *Shand, Jimmy & His Band* / Set of reels: *Shand, Jimmy & His Band* / Hesitation waltz: *Shand, Jimmy & His Band* / Western home selection of waltzes: *Shand, Jimmy & His Band* / Set if jigs: *Shand, Jimmy & His Band* / Piper's polka: *Shand, Jimmy & His Band* / Ulist trampings song: *Cameron, Mary* / Dancing in Kyle: *Cameron, Mary* / These are my mountains: *Cameron, Mary* / Road to the isles: *Cameron, Mary* / Eriskay love lilt: *Cameron, Mary* / Mull of Kintyre: *Cameron, Mary* / Down in the glen: *Cameron, Mary* / White heather foxtrot: *Shand, Jimmy Jr. & His Band*
CD ______ **303600892**
Carlton / Apr '97 / Carlton

SCOTS WHA'HAE
CD ______ **PWKS 4265**
Carlton / Jan '97 / Carlton

SCOTSMAN, THE (The Bands, Pipes & Drums Of Great Scottish Regiments)
Amazing grace / Medley / Road to the Osles / Athol highlanders/Bugle horn / Green hills of Tyrol / March / Rose of Kelvingrove / Scottish serenade / Tartan tuba / Jacobite sword dance / March off / Highland cathedral / March medley / Scots wha hae / Medley / Wee MacGregor / Bonnie black Isle / Pipe and drum medley / Bays of Harris / March off

CD ______ **STACD 7006**
Valentine / Nov '94 / Conifer/BMG

SCOTTISH BAGPIPES
CD ______ **B6829CD**
Auvidis Travelling / May '96 / Harmonia Mundi

SCOTTISH BAGPIPES & DRUMS
CD ______ **12249**
Laserlight / Sep '94 / Target/BMG

SCOTTISH CHRISTMAS, A
CD ______ **MMCD 215**
Maggie's Music / Nov '96 / ADA / CM

SCOTTISH COLLECTION (3CD Set)
CD Set ______ **TBXCD 511**
TrueTrax / Jan '96 / THE

SCOTTISH COLLECTION (2CD Set)
CD Set ______ **PBXCD 511**
Pulse / Nov '96 / BMG

SCOTTISH COLLECTION - PIPES & DRUMS
CD ______ **CDLBP 2028**
Lochshore / Mar '96 / ADA / Direct / Duncans

SCOTTISH COLLECTION - SCOTTISH EVENING LIVE
CD ______ **CDLBP 2027**
Lochshore / Mar '96 / ADA / Direct / Duncans

SCOTTISH COLLECTION - SINGERS AND THE SONGS
CD ______ **CDLBP 2021**
Lochshore / Mar '96 / ADA / Direct / Duncans

SCOTTISH COLLECTION - SONGS OF THE GAELS
CD ______ **CDLBP 2022**
Lochshore / Mar '96 / ADA / Direct / Duncans

SCOTTISH COLLECTION, THE (2CD Set)
Amazing grace: *Kevock Choir & Massed Pipes/Drums* / Song of the Clyde: *Mallan, Peter* / Westering home: *McPartland, Joe* / Road to the Isles: *McPartland, Joe* / Right on to the end of the road: *Miller, Ina* / Nothern lights of old Aberdeen: *Miller, Ina* / Bonnie Kirkwall bay: *Miller, Ina* / Bonnie banks of Loch Lomond: *Miller, Ina* / Football crazy: *Beattie, Johnny* / Here's to Scottish whisky: *Tartan Lads* / Land for all seasons: *Urquhart, Jimmy* / Star o'Robbie Burns: *McPartland, Joe* / Man's a man for all that: *Laurie, John* / Roamin' in the gloamin': *McPartland, Joe* / Jus a wee doech an doris: *McPartland, Joe* / Skye boat song: *Miller, Ina* / Ye banks and braes: *Miller, Ina* / Tobermory bay: *Miller, Ina* / Marching through the heather: *Hughes, Ken & Alan* / Auld lang syne: *Laurie, John* / Pipe set 1: *Gordon Highlanders* / Route march: *Gordon Highlanders* / When the battle is over: *Gordon Highlanders* / 79th farewell to Gilbraltar: *Gordon Highlanders* / Medley: *Gordon Highlanders* / Inverness gathering medley: *Edinburgh City Police Pipe Band* / Drum salute: *Boghall & Bathgate Caledonia Pipe Band* / Up in the morning: *Turriff & District Pipe Band* / Royal Scots polka medley: *Boghall & Bathgate Caledonia Pipe Band* / Highland wedding medley: *Boghall & Bathgate Caledonia Pipe Band* / Redundancy: *Gordon Highlanders* / Revelle: *Gordon Highlanders* / Miss Kirkwood: *Gordon Highlanders* / Scotland the brave: *Gordon Highlanders*
CD Set ______ **DCD 3006**
Music / Jun '97 / Target/BMG

SCOTTISH COUNTRY DANCING VOL.1
CD ______ **PACD 032**
Music Masters / Mar '94 / Midland CD Club

SCOTTISH DANCE BANDS
CD ______ **CDSL 8283**
EMI Gold / Feb '97 / EMI

SCOTTISH EVENING LIVE VOL.2, A
CD ______ **CDLBP 2029**
Lochshore / Jul '96 / ADA / Direct / Duncans

SCOTTISH FAMILY CHRISTMAS
Santa on parade / Sleigh ride / Holly jolly Christmas / Deck the halls / Have yourself a merry little Christmas / Winter wonderland / Have a merry Christmas / Earl of Mansfield / Atholl highlanders / Piping hot Christmas / Louden's bonnie woods and braes / O'er the bows to Ballindalloch / Miss Ada Crawford / Because he was a bonnie lad / High road to Linton / Piper of Drummond / Cutting bracken / Rudolph the red nose reindeer / Frosty the Snowman / Santa Claus is coming to town / Here comes Santa Claus / I saw mommy kissing Santa Claus / Have yourself a merry little Christmas / Away in a manger / O come all ye faithful (adeste fidelis) / Good King Wenceslas / Silent night / Amazing Grace / Auld lang syne / We wish you a merry Christmas
CD ______ **CDITV 621**
Scotdisc / Nov '96 / Conifer/BMG / Duncans / Ross

SCOTTISH FOLK FESTIVAL
CD ______ **FMS 2036CD**
Fenn Music Services / Jul '94 / ADA

SCOTTISH FOLK FESTIVAL '93
CD ______ **FMS 2040CD**
Fenn Music Services / Jul '94 / ADA

SCOTTISH FOLK FESTIVAL '94
CD ______ **FMS 2050CD**
Fenn Music Services / Jun '94 / ADA

SCOTTISH GOLD (In The Celtic Tradition)
CD ______ **LCOM 5245**
Lismor / May '95 / ADA / Direct / Duncans / Lismor

SCOTTISH GOLD (In The Ceilidh & Dance Tradition)
CD ______ **LCOM 5246**
Lismor / May '95 / ADA / Direct / Duncans / Lismor

SCOTTISH GOLD (In The Popular Song)
CD ______ **LCOM 5244**
Lismor / May '95 / ADA / Direct / Duncans / Lismor

SCOTTISH GOLD (In The Piping Tradition)
CD ______ **LCOM 5243**
Lismor / May '95 / ADA / Direct / Duncans / Lismor

SCOTTISH MOODS
CD ______ **RECD 506**
REL / Jun '96 / CM / Duncans / Highlander

SCOTTISH PIPES & DRUMS
CD ______ **PS 65113**
PlayaSound / Nov '93 / ADA / Harmonia Mundi

SCOTTISH REFLECTIONS PAST AND PRESENT
Angels of Dunblane: *Pattullo, Gordon Trio & Pipe Major Andy Scott* / Durisdeer: *Huband, John & Ron Kerr* / Lord of the dance: *Huband, John & Ron Kerr* / Earl of Errol: *Huband, John & Ron Kerr* / Marching through the heather: *Haynes, Ken & Alan* / Happy haggis: *Glen Lomond Scottish Dance Band* / Jigs: *Ochil Players* / Hills of Galloway: *Campbell, Joe* / Miss Rhoda W Hammond: *Anderson, Stuart* / Mrs. MacDonald of Dunach: *Anderson, Stuart* / Raasay House: *Anderson, Stuart* / JD MacLennan: *Anderson, Stuart* / Here's to Scottish whisky: *Tartan Lads* / Captain Campbell: *MacAndrew, Hector* / Mozart Allan Tulchan Lodge: *MacAndrew, Hector* / Burn o' Forgie: *MacAndrew, Hector* / My dear and only love: *Bell, Paddie* / Scott Skinner's compliments to Dr. MacDonald: *Fitchet, Angus & His Scottish Dance Band* / Lord Huntly's cave: *Fitchet, Angus & His Scottish Dance Band* / Fitba crazy: *Beattie, Johnny* / Hills of Glenorchy: *Harvey, Bobby* / Sons of Glenorchy: *Harvey, Bobby* / Who'll be King but Charlie: *Glen Lomond Scottish Dance Band* / Stool of repentance: *Glen Lomond Scottish Dance Band* / Buildings: *Fisher, Ray & Archie* / Captain Norman Orr Ewing: *Anderson, Stuart* / Murdo MacKenzie of Torridon: *Anderson, Stuart* / Dowie dens of Yarrow: *Bell, Paddie* / I'll aye ca' in by yon toun: *Sumner, Bernard* / Sarah Jane: *JSD Band* / Harry Carmichael: *Fitchet, Angus & His Scottish Dance Band* / Provost Tonge of Monifeith: *Fitchet, Angus & His Scottish Dance Band* / Jim Johnstone: *Fitchet, Angus & His Scottish Dance Band* / Amazing grace: *Kevock Choir & Massed Pipes/ Drums*
CD ______ **CDGR 157**
Ross / Oct '96 / CM / Duncans / Highlander / Ross

SCOTTISH SONGBOOK, THE
Auld Scotch sangs: *McCormack, John* / Comin' thro' the rye: *Gluck, Alma* / My love is like a red red rose: *Hislop, Joseph* / Annie Laurie: *McCormack, John* / Turn ye tae me: *McCormack, John* / Bonnie Mary of Argyle: *Hislop, Joseph* / Afton water: *Hislop, Joseph* / Ye banks and braes o' bonnie Doon: *Melba, Nellie* / Road to the isles: *Lauder, Harry* / Ca' the yowes: *Baillie, Isobel* / Flowers of the forest: *Labette, Dora* / March March Ettrick and Teviotdale: *Dawson, Peter* / Jock O'Hazeldean: *Kirkby-Lunn, Louise* / Robin Adair: *Brola, Jeanne* / An Eriskay love lilt: *Robeson, Paul* / My ain folk: *Butt, Clara* / Ae fond kiss: *Coleman, Esther & Foster Richardson* / Will ye no' come back again: *MacEwan, Sydney* / John Anderson, my Jo: *Hill, Carmen* / Bonnie banks of Loch Lomond: *Hislop, Joseph*
CD ______ **MIDCD 001**
Moidart / Jan '95 / Conifer/BMG

SCOTTISH TRADITION VOL.1 (Bothy Ballads)
Muckin' O' Geordie's byre: *Macbeath, Jimmy* / Stool of repentance: *Bothy Band* / As I came ower the Muir O' Ord: *Bowie, James* / Bold Princess Royal: *Taylor, Jamie* / Shepherd lad o'rhynie: *MacDonald, John* / My last farewell to Stirling: *Murray, Charlie* / Whistle o'er the lave o't: *Macbeath, Jimmy* / Stumpie strathspey: *Macbeath, Jimmy* / Mason's apron: *Macbeath, Jimmy* / Lochiel's welcome to Glasgow march: *Macbeath, Jimmy* / Airlin's fine braes: *Elvin, Bill* / Mrs. Grieg: *Taylor, Jamie* / Hairst o'rettie: *Murray, Charlie* / Smith's a gallant fireman: *Murray, Charlie* / Haill week o' the fair: *Taylor, Jamie* / Old horned sheep-jig: *Taylor, Jamie* / Athol highlanders/March played in

jig time: *Taylor, Jamie* / Medley: *Steele, Frank*
CD **CDTRAX 9001**
Greentrax / May '93 / ADA / Direct / Duncans / Highlander

SCOTTISH TRADITION VOL.2 (Music From The Western Isles)
He mandu / Dheanainn sugradh / Oran do bhean mhie fhraing / Puirt a buel / Cha tillmaccrimmon
CD **CDTRAX 9002**
Greentrax / Nov '92 / ADA / Direct / Duncans / Highlander

SCOTTISH TRADITION VOL.3 (Songs From Barra)
We're you in the mountains / My love Alan / One day as I roamed the hills / Woman over there who laughed / Silver whistle / Early today I set out
CD **CDTRAX 9003**
Greentrax / Jan '94 / ADA / Direct / Duncans / Highlander

SCOTTISH TRADITION VOL.4 (Shetland Fiddle Music)
CD **CDTRAX 9004**
Greentrax / Jan '94 / ADA / Direct / Duncans / Highlander

SCOTTISH TRADITION VOL.5 (The Muckle Sangs)
Gypsy laddie / False knight on the road / Bonnie banks o'fordie / Tam lin, the bold pedlar / Two sisters / Young Johnston
CD **CDTRAX 9005**
Greentrax / Nov '92 / ADA / Direct / Duncans / Highlander

SCOTTISH TRADITION VOL.6 (Gaelic Psalms From Lewis)
Martyrdom / Coleshill / Stroudwater / Dundee / London New / Martyrs
CD **CDTRAX 9006**
Greentrax / Aug '94 / ADA / Direct / Duncans / Highlander

SCOTTISH TRADITION VOL.9 (The Fiddler & His Art)
Lady Madelina Sinclair/Sandy Cameron: *MacDonnel, Donald* / Mackintosh's lament: *MacDonnel, Donald* / Medley: *MacDonnel, Donald* / Gabhaidh sinn an rathad mor: *MacDonnel, Donald* / Renfrewshire Militia/ Inganess: *Inkster, Hugh* / Stronsay Waltz/ Jock Halcrow: *Shearer, Pat & David Linklater* / Medley: *Shearer, Pat & David Linklater* / Braes of Tullymet/Captain Keeler: *Reid, John Sr. & John Reid Jr.* / Medley: *Poleson, Andrew & William Williamson* / Neil Gow's lament for whiskey: *Stewart, Albert* / Medley: *MacAndrew, Hector & Sandie Edmondson* / James F Dickie/JF Dickie's delight: *MacAndrew, Hector & Sandie Edmondson* / My heart is broken since thy departure: *MacAndrew, Hector & Sandie Edmondson* / Medley: *MacAndrew, Hector & Sandie Edmondson*
CD **CDTRAX 9009**
Greentrax / May '93 / ADA / Direct / Duncans / Highlander

SCOTTISH VOICES
Erin go bragh: *Gaughan, Dick* / For a' that and a' that: *Exiles* / Fire in the glen: *Stewart, Andy M./Phil Cunningham/Manus Lunny* / My last farewell to Stirling: *Battlefield Band* / MacCrimmon's lament: *Robertson, Jeannie* / Wi' my rovin' eye: *Kennedy, Norman* / Will ye gang love: *Fisher, Archie* / Corncrake: *Kentigern* / Cruel Mither: *Campbell, Ian* / Maid of Glenshee: *Higgins, Lizzie* / Sweet kumadee: *Manuel, Ian* / Norland winds: *Fisher, Cilla & Artie Trezise* / Freedom call all ye: *Exiles* / Gillie mor: *Gaughan, Dick* / Bawbie allan: *McCulloch, Gordeanna & The Clutha* / Will ye no come back again: *MacColl, Ewan*
CD **TSCD 703**
Topic / Feb '97 / ADA / CM / Direct

SCOTTY STORY, THE
CD **AA 043**
Arf Arf / Jul '97 / Greyhound

SCREAM
CD **0022822CIN**
Edel / Jun '97 / Pinnacle

SCREWED
CD **ARR 67010CD**
Amphetamine Reptile / Jan '96 / Plastic Head

SEA SONGS & SHANTIES (Traditional English Songs From The Last Days Of Sail)
Stormy weather boys: *Roberts, A.V. 'Bob'* / Rio Grande: *Fishermen's Group* / Mr. Stormalong: *Roberts, A.V. 'Bob'* / Warlike seamen: *Copper, Bob & Ron* / Worst old ship: *Roberts, A.V. 'Bob'* / Yarmouth fishermen's song: *Cox, Harry* / Maggie May: *Roberts, A.V. 'Bob'* / Caroline and her young sailor bold: *Makem, Sarah* / Whisky Johnny: *Roberts, A.V. 'Bob'* / What shall we do with the drunken sailor: *Fishermen's Group* / Can't you dance the polka: *Roberts, A.V. 'Bob'* / Sailor's alphabet: *Jenkins, Clifford* / Haul away Joe: *Roberts, A.V. 'Bob'* / Cruisin' 'round Yarmouth: *Cox, Harry* / Windy old weather: *Roberts, A.V. 'Bob'* / Farewell and adieu (we'll rant and we'll roar): *Fishermen's Group* / High barbaree: *Roberts, A.V. 'Bob'* / Liverpool packet: *Barber, Bill* / Little boy billee: *Roberts, A.V. 'Bob'* / Johnny Todd: *Roberts, A.V. 'Bob'* / Banks of Claudy: *Copper, Bob & Ron* / Bold Princess Royal: *Roberts, A.V. 'Bob'* / Jack Tarr on the shore: *Cox, Harry* / Smuggler's boy: *Roberts, A.V. 'Bob'* / Smacksman: *Brown, Tom* / Hanging Johnny: *Roberts, A.V. 'Bob'*
CD **CDSDL 405**
Saydisc / Feb '94 / ADA / Direct / Harmonia Mundi

SEASON OF MISTS (A Collection Of Celtic Moods)
Wishing tree: *McGuire, Seamus* / Ceol na noilag: *Kilbride, Pat* / Grimstock: *House Band* / Miss Gordon of Gight: *Sileas* / Sound of Taransay: *Tannahill Weavers* / Lorraine's waltz: *Whelan, John & Eileen Ivers* / Glenglass: *Wolfstone* / Marcus Hernon's air: *Madden, Joanie* / An raibh tu ag an gcarraig: *Deanta* / Pockets of gold: *Reeltime* / L'hiver sur richelieu/Miss B's dream: *Orealis* / Season of mists: *Crawford, Kevin*
CD **CELT 9003**
Celtophile / May '97 / Direct

SEASONS
CD **CMCCD 100**
Ideal / May '96 / RTM/Disc

SEASONS IN THE SUN (2CD Set)
CD Set **NSCD 014**
Newsound / Feb '95 / THE

SEASONS OF CLUBBING - GREEN (Spring Edition 1996)
Yellow sox: *Flim Flam* / See you on Monday: *Herbert* / All I do: *Davis, Roy Jr.* / See the light: *LZ Love* / Air: *Stein House* / Acting crazy: *Round Three* / Future: *Armando* / Feel the warmth: *Real House* / Hallelujah: *Chandler, Kerri* / This time: *Johnny L* / Fly away: *Edwards, Todd* / Reach out to me: *Pollard, Karen* / Reach higher: *Unknown Society* / Lift me up: *DJ Romain*
CD **HTV96CD 001A**
CD **HTV96CD 001**
Hard Times / Jul '96 / Vital

SEASONS OF CLUBBING - YELLOW (Summer Edition 1996) (2CD Set)
FK EP: *Korvorkian, Francois* / In the trees: *Faze Action* / Untitled: *Lovebeads* / Anytime: *Nu Birth* / Get ready: *Delgado, Mike* / Found a way: *Crosby, B.J.* / Saturdays: *M&S* / I believe: *007* / Passion: *Gat Decor* / Save us: *Xpress 2* / Keep pushing: *D'Lugosch, Boris* / Stay out all night: *Dr. Love* / Inner city life: *Goldie* / Bouncy lady: *Danny Hibrid* / Remember me: *Blueboy* / Untitled: *Daphreephunkateerz* / Secret: *16BP* / Alabama blues: *St. Germain* / Phoenix rising: *Universal Jones* / Get another: *Abstract Truth* / Turn the point: *Faze Action* / Staeb: *Idjut Boys* / Flyin' fingers: *Motorbass* / Pleasure pain: *Project 23*
CD Set **HTV96CD 002**
Hard Times / Nov '96 / Vital

SECOND GRAND CONCERT OF SCOTS PIPING
La quenoville: *St. Laurence O'Toole Pipe Band Quartet* / Caledonian Society of London: *St. Laurence O'Toole Pipe Band Quartet* / Blonde haired maid: *St. Laurence O'Toole Pipe Band Quartet* / Cathy's Willie: *St. Laurence O'Toole Pipe Band Quartet* / Lieutenant Colonel George Latham's fancy: *St. Laurence O'Toole Pipe Band Quartet* / New crossroads: *St. Laurence O'Toole Pipe Band Quartet* / Old Joe: *St. Laurence O'Toole Pipe Band Quartet* / Sean Coughlans: *St. Laurence O'Toole Pipe Band Quartet* / Banks of the Lee: *St. Laurence O'Toole Pipe Band Quartet* / Little bag: *St. Laurence O'Toole Pipe Band Quartet* / Hills of Kesh: *St. Laurence O'Toole Pipe Band Quartet* / Boys of Malin: *St. Laurence O'Toole Pipe Band Quartet* / Lord Ramsey's: *St. Laurence O'Toole Pipe Band Quartet* / Transfusion: *St. Laurence O'Toole Pipe Band Quartet* / Tiolfaidh tu abhaile liom: *St. Laurence O'Toole Pipe Band Quartet* / Anna Kloareg: *Molard, Patrick* / Al Letenant Schmidt o Kimiad ar 5ved Kompagnunez: *Molard, Patrick* / Donatien Laurent: *Molard, Patrick* / Al Lez-vamm: *Molard, Patrick* / Gwerz Mari-Louiz: *Molard, Patrick* / Gavotenn ar menez: *Molard, Patrick* / Ton cranhuel: *Molard, Patrick* / Kas a barh: *Molard, Patrick* / Laride: *Molard, Patrick* / Devil in the kitchen: *Maclean, John* / Calum Crubach: *Maclean, John* / Black snuff mill: *Maclean, John* / Sleepy Maggie: *Maclean, John* / Scotsville reel: *Maclean, John* / Roddy MacDonald's fancy: *Maclean, John* / Caberfeidh: *Maclean, John* / Hamish and the stone: *Maclean, John* / Ed Neigh's welcome to Cape Breton: *Maclean, John* / Allan Gillis' reel: *Maclean, John* / Kennedy Street march: *Maclean, John* / Miller o' Drone: *Maclean, John* / Lady Carmichael: *Maclean, John* / Unknown: *Maclean, John* / Night we had the goats: *Maclean, John* / Unknown: *Maclean, John* / Marry me now: *Maclean, John* / Snuff wife: *Robertson, Malcolm* / Martha's vineyard: *Robertson, Malcolm* / Maid on the green: *Robertson, Malcolm* / Donnie MacGregor: *Robertson, Malcolm* / Nelly Mahony's: *Robertson, Malcolm* / Pete Bradley's: *Robertson, Malcolm* / Jim Keefe's: *Robertson, Malcolm* / Sweeney's polka: *Robertson, Malcolm* / Mike Ward's polka: *Robertson, Malcolm* / Glen polka: *Robertson, Malcolm* / Mediana a pipia: *Mascia, Orlando & Franco Melis* / Fiorassiu: *Mascia, Orlando & Franco Melis* / Fiuda: *Mascia, Orlando & Franco Melis*
CD **CDTRAX 128**
Greentrax / May '97 / ADA / Direct / Duncans / Highlander

SECOND SIGHT
CD **SH 5716**
Shanachie / Nov '96 / ADA / Greensleeves / Koch

SECRET LIFE OF TRANCE VOL.1
CD **RSNCD 6**
Rising High / May '93 / 3mv/Sony

SECRET LIFE OF TRANCE VOL.3
CD Set **RSNCD 20**
Rising High / Jul '94 / 3mv/Sony

SECRET LIFE OF TRANCE VOL.4
CD Set **RSNCD 28**
Rising High / Dec '94 / 3mv/Sony

SECRET LIFE OF TRANCE VOL.5
CD **RSNCD 34**
Rising High / May '95 / 3mv/Sony

SECRET LIFE OF TRANCE VOL.6
CD Set **RSNCD 40**
Rising High / Aug '95 / 3mv/Sony

SECRET LIFE OF TRANCE VOL.7 (2CD Set)
CD Set **RSNCD 50**
Rising High / Feb '97 / 3mv/Sony

SECRET MUSEUM OF MANKIND - CENTRAL ASIA (Ethnic Music Classics 1923-1948)
CD **YAZ 7007**
Yazoo / Jul '96 / ADA / CM / Koch

SECRET MUSEUM OF MANKIND - NORTH AFRICA (Ethnic Music Classics 1925-1948)
CD **YAZCD 7011**
Yazoo / Mar '97 / ADA / CM / Koch

SECRET MUSEUM OF MANKIND VOL.1
CD **YAZCD 7004**
Yazoo / Oct '95 / ADA / CM / Koch

SECRET MUSEUM OF MANKIND VOL.2
CD **YAZCD 7005**
Yazoo / Oct '95 / ADA / CM / Koch

SECRET MUSEUM OF MANKIND VOL.3. (Ethnic Music Classics 1923-1948)
CD **YAZ 7006**
Yazoo / Jul '96 / ADA / CM / Koch

SECRET MUSEUM OF MANKIND VOL.4 (Ethnic Music Classics 1925-1948)
CD **YAZCD 7010**
Yazoo / Mar '97 / ADA / CM / Koch

SECRET POLICEMAN'S THIRD BALL (The Music)
Running up that hill: *Bush, Kate & David Gilmour* / Save a prayer: *Duran Duran* / Voices of freedom: *Reed, Lou* / This is the world calling: *Geldof, Bob* / For everyman: *Browne, Jackson* / Victim of love: *Erasure* / Wouldn't it be good: *Kershaw, Nik* / (I love it when you) call me names: *Armatrading, Joan* / Imagine: *Knopfler, Mark & Chet Atkins* / Biko: *Gabriel, Peter* / Ship of fools: *World Party*
CD **CDV 2458**
Virgin / Sep '87 / EMI

SECRET RECORDS PUNK SINGLES COLLECTION VOL.1
Dogs of war: *Exploited* / Army life: *Exploited* / Exploited barmy army: *Exploited* / Kids of the 80's: *Infa Riot* / One law for them: *4 Skins* / Dead cities: *Exploited* / Harry May: *Business* / Yesterday's heroes: *4 Skins* / Jet boy jet girl: *Chron Gen* / Attack exploited: *Chron Gen* / I lost my love to a UK sub: *Gonads* / Punk city rockers: *Gonads* / Smash the discos: *Business* / H-Bomb: *Business* / TOP: *Exploited* / Computers don't blunder: *Exploited* / Troops of tomorrow: *Exploited* / Feel the rage: *Infa Riot* / Clouded eyes: *Chron Gen* / Outlaw: *Chron Gen* / Victim: *Strike* / Low life: *4 Skins* / Seems to me: *4 Skins*
CD **CDPUNK 13**
Anagram / Sep '93 / Cargo / Pinnacle

SECRET RECORDS PUNK SINGLES COLLECTION VOL.2
Blown to bits: *Exploited* / Fuck the mods: *Exploited* / I belive in anarchy: *Exploited* / Hitler's in the charts again: *Exploited* / Alternative: *Exploited* / Addiction: *Exploited* / Brave new world: *4 Skins* / Justice: *4 Skins* / Employers blacklist: *Business* / Disco girls: *Business* / Subway sadist: *Chron Gen* / Behind closed doors: *Chron Gen* / Disco tech: *Chron Gen* / Punk rock will never die: *Gonads* / Got any Wriggly's John: *Gonads* / She can't whip me: *Gonads* / School's out: *Infa Riot* / Fight for your life: *Angela Rippon's Bum* / I'm thick: *Skin Disease* / Where's dock green: *Venom* / Way it's got to be: *East End Badoes*
CD **CDPUNK 60**
Anagram / Sep '95 / Cargo / Pinnacle

SEDUCTIVE SOUNDS OF TEKNOTIKA, THE
One step beyond / When the planets align / Twinge / Seduction of the virgin princess / Arvesche-tam / Kfi stanboulch / Swing sexy / Shake it / Interview with an alien '97 / Universal love / Afterglow / Aftermath
CD **EYEUKCD 014**
Eye Q / Jul '97 / Vital

SEE WITH YOUR EARS (The Red Seal Surround Sound Sampler)
CD **09026683182**
RCA Red Seal / Feb '96 / BMG

SEEDMOUTH
CD **CSR 12CD**
Cold Spring / May '96 / Plastic Head / RTM/Disc

SEGADANCE (Music From Mauritius)
CD **PS 65126**
PlayaSound / May '94 / ADA / Harmonia Mundi

SEKUNJALO - NOW IS THE TIME
Hare yeng: *Sankomota* / Hand in hand: *Mkhize, Themba* / Motherland, cry no more / Kopano ke matla: *Tshola, Tsepo* / Bread and roses: *Ferguson, Jennifer* / Phansi ngodlame: *Mlangeni, Babsy* / Sekunjalo: *Ziqubu, Condry* / Come on everybody: *Masekela, Hugh* / Mayibuye: *Louw, Mara* / Set them free: *Morake, Lebo* / Dedication: *Makhene, Blondie* / Time is now: *Powers, P.J.*
CD **CIDM 1110**
Mango / Apr '94 / PolyGram / Vital

SELECTED CIRCUITS
CD **UPCD 06**
Nitro / Sep '95 / Pinnacle / Plastic Head

SELECTED SIGNS VOL.1 (An Anthology)
CD **5378052**
ECM / Sep '97 / New Note/Pinnacle

SELECTED WORKS FOR MOVING PICTURES
CD **PIAS 556460120**
Antler / Nov '96 / Plastic Head

SELECTION OF COUNTRY (2CD Set)
CD Set **DCD 704**
Gold Sound / Dec '96 / Nervous

SELEKTA SHOWCASE '89
My prerogative: *Sanchez* / Enquirer: *One-two crew* / Lick out: *Ninjaman* / Jah is the way: *Minott, Sugar* / Nice and cute: *Johnny P* / Special lady: *Gel, Ny* / Vanity crazy: *Chaka Demus* / Rawborn rub a dub: *Meakes, Carl* / Me no know why: *General Trees* / Step it up: *Antony, Pad*
CD **GRELCD 130**
Greensleeves / Nov '89 / Jet Star / SRD

SEMANN AHOI
CD **15261**
Laserlight / Nov '91 / Target/BMG

SEND ME THE PILLOW YOU DREAM ON
Send me the pillow that you dream on: *Locklin, Hank* / Reuben James: *Rogers, Kenny* / I feel sorry for him: *Nelson, Willie* / Come on in: *Cline, Patsy* / Hey good lookin': *Cash, Johnny* / You'll always have someone: *Nelson, Willie* / Six days on the road: *Dudley, Dave* / Always leaving, always gone: *Rogers, Kenny* / Burning memories: *Jennings, Waylon* / Walkin' after midnight: *Cline, Patsy* / Singin' the blues: *Mitchell, Guy* / Take these chains from my heart: *Drusky, Roy* / Mule train: *Laine, Frankie* / Don't think twice, it's alright: *Jennings, Waylon* / If I don't understand: *Nelson, Willie* / Ramblin' rose: *Lee, Johnny* / Rose garden: *Anderson, Lynn* / Heart you break may be your own: *Cline, Patsy* / Ticket to nowhere: *Rogers, Kenny* / Release me: *Mandrell, Barbara* / I can't find the time: *Nelson, Willie* / Waterloo: *Jackson, Stonewall* / Last letter: *Drusky, Roy* / Wild side of life: *Fender, Freddy* / Sunshine: *Rogers, Kenny*
CD **GRF 120**
Tring / Feb '93 / Tring

SEND ME THE PILLOW YOU DREAM ON
CD **MACCD 213**
Autograph / Aug '96 / BMG

SENSATIONAL 70'S VOL.1
CD **MATCD 203**
Castle / Dec '92 / BMG

SENSATIONAL 70'S VOL.1
CD **PLSCD 182**
Pulse / Apr '97 / BMG

SENSATIONAL 70'S VOL.2
CD **MATCD 241**
Castle / Dec '92 / BMG

SENSATIONAL 70'S VOL.2
CD **PLSCD 183**
Pulse / Apr '97 / BMG

SENSATIONAL HITS OF THE 1960'S
CD **KLMCD 011**
BAM / Nov '93 / Koch / Scratch/BMG

SENSATIONAL SIXTIES, THE (2CD Set)
You never walk alone: *Gerry & The Pacemakers* / Silence is golden: *Tremeloes* / Runaway: *Shannon, Del* / Happy birthday sweet sixteen: *Sedaka, Neil* / Wild thing: *Troggs* / I'm into something good: *Herman's Hermits* / Rubber ball: *Vee, Bobby* / Something's gotten hold of my heart: *Pitney, Gene* / I'm sorry: *Lee, Brenda* / Da doo ron ron: *Crystals* / When a man loves a woman: *Sledge, Percy* / I'm telling you now: *Freddie & The Dreamers* / Because they're young: *Eddy, Duane* / Little town flirt: *Shannon, Del* / It's my party: *Gore, Lesley* / Breaking up

is hard to do: Sedaka, Neil / Walkin' back to happiness: Shapiro, Helen / Wishin' and hopin': Merseybeats / Rescue me: Bass, Fontella / Dancing in the street: Reeves, Martha / Do you want to know a secret: Kramer, Billy J. / Tossing & turning: Ivy League / Little loving: Fourmost / Um, um, um, um: Fontana, Wayne / You were made for me: Freddie & The Dreamers / Just like Eddie: Heinz / Do you love me: Poole, Brian / Pied piper: St. Peters, Crispian / Bobby's girl: Maughan, Susan / Save the last dance for me: Drifters / Juliet: Four Pennies / Hello little girl: Fourmost / Little children: Kramer, Billy J. / My guy: Wells, Mary / But I do: Henry, Clarence 'Frogman' / Crying game: Berry, Dave / Wimoweh: Denver, Karl / Tell me when: Applejacks / Baby now that I've found you: Foundations / Jesamine: Casuals
CD Set DCD 3002
Music / Jun '97 / Target/BMG

SENSATIONAL SOUL
Soul man: Sam & Dave / Gimme little sign: Wood, Brenton / Backfield in motion: Mel & Tim / Rescue me: Bass, Fontella / Harlem shuffle: Bob & Earl / Letter: Box Tops / Under the boardwalk: Drifters / Knock on wood: Floyd, Eddie / In crowd: Gray, Dobie / Dancing in the street: Reeves, Martha / Rock your baby: McCrae, George / I just can't stop dancing: Bell, Archie & The Drells / (Sittin' on the) dock of the bay: Sledge, Percy / Hey girl don't bother me: Tams / Spanish Harlem: King, Ben E. / Love I lost: Melvin, Harold & The Bluenotes / Indiana wants me: Taylor, R. Dean / What becomes of the broken hearted: Ruffin, Jimmy
CD ECD 3056
K-Tel / Jan '95 / K-Tel

SENSE OF DIRECTION, A
Sense of direction / Aunt Monk / Theme for a new day / Long as you're living / I'm trying to find a way / Keep the faith / Panther / Cleopatra and the African Knight / To the establishment / Red clay / Communication / Dorian
CD CDBGPD 099
Beat Goes Public / Oct '95 / Pinnacle

SENSES
Play dead: Bjork & David Arnold / Robin (The hooded man): Clannad / Love theme: Vangelis / Between the lines: Lindes, Hal / Cockeye's song: Morricone, Ennio / Love's theme: Moroder, Giorgio / Robinson Crusoe: Art Of Noise / Nomads of the wind: Bennett, Brian / Oboe concerto in D minor: Academy Of Ancient Music / Gymnopedie no.1: Satie, Erik / Equinoxe part 4: Jarre, Jean Michel / Eve of war: Wayne, Jeff / Cacharpaya: Incantation / Coisich a ruin (walk my beloved): Capercaillie / Rowena's theme: Edge / Cavatina: Williams, John / Snowman: Blake, Howard / Concierto de Aranjuez: De Angelis, Nicolas / Oxygene part IV: Marvin, Hank / Going home: Knopfler, Mark
CD 5166272
PolyGram TV / Sep '94 / PolyGram

SENSUAL CLASSICS
CD SPLCD 044
Sloane / Apr '96 / Grapevine/PolyGram

SENSUAL RHYTHMS
Would I lie to you: Charles & Eddie / Back to life: Soul II Soul / Ain't no sunshine: Youngblood, Sydney / Big fun: Inner City / Magic: Defunkt / Thinking about your love: Thomas, Kenny / Walk on by: Carroll, Dina / Love zone: Ocean, Billy / Take good care of me: Butler, Jonathan / Caught in the middle: Roberts, Juliet / Endlessly: Jones, Glenn / Still water: O'Bryan / Heartbeat: Ward, Robert / I wanna love somebody: Bofill, Angela / Let be your baby: Williams, Geoffrey / She's playing hard to get: Hi-Five
CD DC880832
Disky / Aug '97 / Disky / THE

SENSUAL SAX COLLECTION (3CD Set)
CD Set EMTBX 306
Emporio / Aug '97 / Disc

SENSUOUS PANPIPES
Sexual healing / We've got tonight / Jealous guy / Mad about the boy / I guess that's why they call it the blues / Dock of the bay / Move closer / Mist blue / Killing me softly / Just the way you are / Endless love / When a man loves a woman / Help me make it through the night / Cry me a river
CD CDMFP 6271
Music For Pleasure / Sep '96 / EMI

SENTIMENTAL JOURNEY
It's only a paper moon: Cole, Nat 'King' / Nightingale can sing the blues: Lee, Peggy / Along the Navajo trail: Crosby, Bing / Things ain't what they used to be: Ellington, Duke / Stardust: Shaw, Artie / May you always: Stewart, Sandy / As the world turns: Gibson, Ginny / Cherokee canyon: Miller, Glenn / I don't mind: Boswell, Connee / Who put the devil in Evelyn's eyes: Mills Brothers / Far from the madding crowd: Haymes, Dick / Just another blues: Cole, Nat 'King' / Gold cadillac: Waring, Fred & His Pennsylvanians / And the angels sing: Goodman, Benny / In the mood: Miller, Glenn / Mad about him blues: Shore, Dinah / I'll never smile again: Dorsey, Tommy / On the Atchison, Topeka and the Santa Fe: Herman, Woody / My very good friend the milkman: Waller, Fats / That's how love comes: Gibson, Ginny / April fool: Ellis, Peggy-Ann / Don't cry crybaby: Cole, Nat 'King' / You ain't got nothin': Boswell, Connee / (I'm getting) Corns for my country: Andrews Sisters / It takes a long, long train with a red caboose: Page, Patti / Casanova cricket: Carmichael, Hoagy / Finders keepers: Mitchell, Guy / I tipped my hat (and slowly rode away): James, Harry Orchestra
CD 3036100142
Pearls / Feb '96 / Carlton

SENTIMENTAL JOURNEY
CD DCD 5308
Disky / Dec '93 / Disky / THE

SENTIMENTAL JOURNEY
All I have to do is dream: Everly Brothers / Will you still love me tomorrow: Sherelles, the / Born to be with you: Chordettes / Poetry in motion: Tillotson, Johnny / Crazy: Cline, Patsy / Around the world in eighty days: Crosby, Bing / True love ways: Holly, Buddy / What kind of fool am I: Newley, Anthony / What a wonderful world: Armstrong, Louis / Mr. Sandman: Valentine, Dickie / el paso: Robbins, Marty / I left my heart in San Francisco: Bennett, Tony / On the street where you love: Damone, Vic / Don't laugh at me: Wisdom, Norman / Sentimental journey: Day, Doris / Fine romance: Fitzgerald, Ella / That ole devil called love: Holiday, Billie / Misty: Mathis, Johnny / Can't get used to losing you: Williams, Andy / Blue velvet: Vinton, Bobby / Moon river: Williams, Andy / I wanna be loved by you: Monroe, Marilyn / Georgia on my mind: Charles, Ray / Diana: Anka, Paul / Let there be love: Davis, Sammy Jr. / Lady of spain: Fisher, Eddie / What do you want to make those eyes at me for: Ford, Emile & The Checkmates / Its only make believe: Twitty, Conway / Just walkin in the rain: Ray, Johnnie / Buono Sera: Platters / Born free: Monro, Matt / Spanish eyes: Martino, Al / That's amore: Martin, Dean / I'm sorry: Lee, Brenda / Who's sorry now: Francis, Connie / Rosie marie: Whitman, Slim / Unchained melody: Righteous Brothers / Save the last dance for me: Drifters / Rainy night in Georgia: Benton, Brook / Will you still love me: Sherelles, the / Passing strangers: Eckstiene, Billy & Sarah vaughan / Je regret non rien: Piaf, Edith / Mad about the boy: Washington, Dinah / On the street where you belong: King, Ben E. / I remember you: Ifield, Frank
CD DINCD 130
Dino / Nov '96 / Pinnacle

SENTIMENTAL OVER YOU
Long ago and far away: Pepper, Art & Carl Perkins / Painted rhythm: Kenton, Stan Orchestra / I'm beginning to see the light: Hamilton, Chico Quintet / Once in a blue moon: Cole, Nat 'King' / Autumn leaves: Farmer, Art Tentet / Autumn in New York: Stafford, Joe / I'm getting sentimental over you: Dickenson, Vic Quartet / I get the blues when it rains: Raney, Sue / Rocker: Davis, Miles / Star eyes: Newborn, Phineas Trio / September in the rain: London, Julie / I've got my love to keep me warm: Brown, Les & His Orchestra / Come back to Sorrento: Napoleon, Phil & His Memphis Five / Willow weep for me: Criss, Sonny / Buji: Gray, Glen & The Casa Loma Orchestra / Early Autumn: Herman, Woody & His Orchestra / Mercy mercy mercy: Adderley, Cannonball Quartet / I concentrate on you: Torme, Mel
CD CDJA 3
Premier/MFP / Oct '91 / EMI

SENTIMENTAL SONGS OF WORLD WAR II
CD VJC 1049
Vintage Jazz Classics / Apr '94 / ADA / Cadillac / CM / Direct

SENTIMENTAL SWING - 12 HITS
CD UP 005
Hindsight / Sep '92 / Jazz Music / Target/BMG

SENTIMENTS OF LOVE
CD VPCD 2044
VP / Mar '96 / Greensleeves / Jet Star / Total/BMG

SENZA VOLTO (The Eve Collection)
CD EVECD 97001
Eve / Jun '97 / Alphamagic / Amato Disco / Arabesque / Flying UK / Prime

SEODA CHONAMARA VOL.1 (Connemara Favourites Vol.1)
Inis Caltrach/Toss the feathers: Althneach, Iorras / Galtee mountain boy: O'Flaharta, John Beag / Stack of wheat/Stack of barley/ Johnny will you marry me: O'Hiarnain, P.J. / Green brooms: Ac Dhonncha, Sean / Currachai na Tra Baine: O'Beaglaoich, Sean / Peigin leitir moir: O'Beaglaoich, Sean / All the way to Galway fair: O'Lochluinn, Paidraig / My own dear native land: MacDonnchadha, Johnny Mhairtin Learai / Sweet Biddy Daly: Walsh, John G / My pretty fair maid: Walsh, John G / Cliff, Belfast and Sweeps hornpipes: O'Ceannabhain, Padraig Tom Photch / Neansin Bhan: O'Ceannabhain, Padraig Tom Photch / Wise maid/Last night's fun: Connolly, John / Si do Mhaimeo: Ni Chathain, Brid / High reel: Learai, Sonai Choilm / Whistling thief: Ac Dhonncha, Sean / Charlie Mulvihill/Plains of Boyle: Na Hancairi / An hunter: Rathcliffe, Peter / Amhran na gCualain: Sheainn, Mairtin / Irish washerwoman: Ghabha, Michael Mhaire / An Merican mor: O'Flaharta, John Beag / First house in Connaught: O'Hiarnain, P.J. / Queen of Connemara: MacEoin, Tomas
CD CICD 019
Clo Iar-Chonnachta / Dec '93 / CM

SEPTETOS CUBANOS - SONES DE CUBA (2CD Set)
CD Set MT 113/4
Corason / Jan '94 / ADA / CM / Direct

SEPTIC CUTS
Sugar Daddy: Secret Knowledge / Smokebelch II: Sabres Of Paradise / Painkiller: Slack / Internal: Blue / Untitled: PT001 / Musical science: Musical Science / Vega God: Jack Of Swords / Crash bang: Conemelt
CD SOPCD 001
Sabres Of Paradise / Sep '94 / Vital

SERENADE OF LOVE, A (2CD Set)
CD Set DEMPCD 107
Emporio / Mar '96 / Disc

SERGEANT SALT & OTHER CONDIMENTS
Venus in furs: Velvet Underground / Paper sun: Traffic / This wheel's on fire: Driscoll, Julie & Brian Auger / Flight from Ashiya: Kaleidoscope / Desiree: Left Banke / Spin spin spin: HP Lovecraft / Gungami: Quintessence / San Franciscan nights: Burdon, Eric & The Animals / Fire: Crazy World Of Arthur Brown / Rainbow chaser: Nirvana / Beeside: Tintern Abbey / Stepping stone: Flies / Evil woman: Spooky Tooth / (We ain't got) Nothin' yet: Blues Magoos
CD 5501232
Spectrum / Oct '93 / PolyGram

SERIALEMENT VOTRE
CD SVCD 2
Commando / May '97 / Cargo

SERIOUS GROOVES (Detroit's Finest)
I wanna go higher: Seven Grand Housing Authority / Woman: Younger Than Park / Take it higher: Disco Revisited / I can't stop: Low Key / Blow your whistle: Jovan Blade / Dusk: Afrodisiac / Try me baby: Low Key / Find sum one new: Black, Donna / We got a love: THD / Feeling: DJ Tone / Dialogue: THD / Can't turn back: Younger Than Park / Shante: Jovan Blade / Witness: Disco Revisited / Rainforest: Low Key / Pleasure baby: Alton M / You took my love: Plastic Soul Junkies / Dedication to Joss / Brewster's project: Younger Than Park
CD SGCD 1
Network / Dec '93 / 3mv/Sony / Pinnacle

SERIOUS LISTENING MUSIC VOL.1
CD DELSDC 1
Delirium / Jan '94 / Arabesque / Plastic Head

SERIOUS LISTENING MUSIC VOL.2
CD DELSCD 02
Delirium / Jun '94 / Arabesque / Plastic Head

SERIOUS REGGAE ALBUM VOL.1, THE
CD CDSGP 0260
Prestige / Sep '96 / Else / Total/BMG

SERIOUS REGGAE ALBUM VOL.2, THE
CD CDSGP 0141
Prestige / Aug '95 / Else / Total/BMG

SERIOUS REGGAE ALBUM VOL.3, THE
CD Set CDSGP 077
Prestige / Jul '94 / Else / Total/BMG

SERVE CHILLED
Mr. Wendal: Arrested Development / Summertime: DJ Jazzy Jeff & The Fresh Prince / Manchild: Cherry, Neneh / Ghetto jam: Domino / Set adrift on memory bliss: PM Dawn / Karmacoma: Massive Attack / Rebirth of slick: Digable Planets / Spiritual love: Urban Species / Eye know: De La Soul / Gotta lotta love: Ice-T / It was a good day: Ice Cube / Can I kick it: Tribe Called Quest / Feel me flow: Naughty By Nature / I'll be around: Rappin' 4-Tay / In the summertime: Shaggy / Save it 'til the morning after: Shut Up & Dance / My definition of a bombastic jazz style: Dream Warriors / That's how I'm livin': Ice-T / I need love: LL Cool J / People everyday: Arrested Development
CD VTCD 56
Virgin / Aug '95 / EMI

SERVICE BANDS ON THE AIR VOL.1
Flying home: Miller, Glenn & The Army Airforce Orchestra / I couldn't sleep a wink last night: Skyrockets / Barrel house boogie: Skyrockets / On the sunny side of the street: Skyrockets / Swinging on a star: Skyrockets / March of the toys: Canada Dance Band / It's love love love: Royal Air Force Dance Orchestra / Leapfrog: Royal Air Force Dance Orchestra / I'll get by: Royal Air Force Dance Orchestra / Milkman keep those bottles quiet: Royal Air Force Dance Orchestra / Dear old southland: Royal Air Force Dance Orchestra / I can't give you anything but love: US Navy Dance Band / LST party: US Navy Dance Band / With my head in the clouds: Miller, Glenn & AAF Band / No compree: Miller, Glenn & AAF Band / Lark leaps in: Royal Marines Commando Forces Band / Wartime medley: Canadian Army Radio Orchestra / Out of this world: Canadian Army Radio Orchestra / More than you know: Royal Army Ordanance Corps Dance Orchestra / Mr. Ghost goes to town: Royal Navy Swing Octet / With a song in my heart: British Band Of The AEF
CD VJB 19442
Vintage Jazz Band / May '94 / Cadillac / Hot Shot / Jazz Music / Wellard

SERVICE BANDS ON THE AIR VOL.2 (VE Day Party)
Introduction / Music makers / Let's get lost / Dance with a dolly / My blue heaven / Long ago and far away / Jumpin' Jiminy / Angry / I'm beginning to see the light / Holiday for strings / My heart isn't in it / Introduction / African war dance / All this and heaven too / Down for double / Comedy routine / Jazz me blues / What a difference a day makes / My heart tells me / Woodchopper's ball / Tess's torch song / Way down yonder in New Orleans / I'll be seeing you / When Johnny comes marching home
CD VJB 19462
Vintage Jazz Band / May '95 / Cadillac / Hot Shot / Jazz Music / Wellard

SEVENTEEN AND A HALF
CD NITR 007
Demolition Derby / Feb '97 / Greyhound / Nervous

SEX, DRUGS & ROCK 'N' ROLL (3CD Set)
Sex and drugs and rock 'n' roll: Dury, Ian / Golden brown: Dury, Ian / Legalise it: Tosh, Peter / Wild places: Browne, Duncan / Acid queen: Turner, Ike & Tina / Whole lotta love: CCS / Amphetamine Annie: Canned Heat / Brother Louie: Quireboys / Bad boys like to rock 'n' roll: Quireboys / Hit me with your best shot: Benatar, Pat / Party girls: Mink Deville / Love stinks: Geils, J. Band / Milk and alcohol: Dr. Feelgood / OD'd on life itself: Blue Oyster Cult / Ain't ni high like rock 'n' roll: Helix / Psycho killer: Talking Heads / You are my heroin: Boy George / Hit me with your rhythm stick: Dury, Ian / Sex party: Quireboys / Orgasm addict: Buzzcocks / I like to rock: April Wine / Jeopardy: Kihn, Greg Band / Talk dirty to me: Poison / Lebanon: Untouchables / Only you can rock me: UFO / Gimme shelter: Grand Funk Railroad / Sexcrime: Eurythmics / Voyeur: Fish / No more heroes: Stranglers / Pretty paracetamol: Fischer Z / Cruisin' and boozin': Hagar, Sammy / Courvoiser concerto: Schenker, Michael Group / Gimme some lovin': Thunder / Sugar walls: Easton, Sheena / House of the rising sun: Animals / Who do you love: Juicy Lucy / Paranoid: Black Sabbath / Ace of spades: Motorhead / I've been drinking: Beck, Jeff & Rod Stewart / Animal: WASP / Don't let the needle win: WASP / Little river band: Little River Band / I want a new drug: Lewis, Huey & The News / Wake up and make love with me: Dury, Ian / Cocaine: Dillinger / I got stoned and missed it: Dr. Hook / Heaven is in the back seat of my Cadillac: Hot Chocolate / Sex as a weapon: Benatar, Pat / Body rock: Vidal, Maria
CD Set HR 868612
Disky / Sep '96 / Disky / THE

SEXTETOS CUBANOS VOL.2
CD ARHCD 7006
Arhoolie / Sep '95 / ADA / Cadillac / Direct

SEXUAL HEALING (18 Sensual Masterpieces)
Sexual healing / Black velvet / Boombastic / I want your sex / Crazy / Erotica / How deep is your love / Unchained melody / Je t'aime / Do that to me one more time / I will always love you / Just a step from heaven / Endless love / Deeper and deeper / No ordinary love / You gotta love someone / Theme from 'Emanuelle' / Let's talk about sex
CD 305752
Hallmark / Oct '96 / Carlton

SEYCHELLES - THE FORGOTTEN ISLANDS
CD ARN 60402
Arion / Jul '97 / ADA / Discovery

SHACK, THE
CD DOJOCD 145
Dojo / Sep '93 / Disc

SHADES, GUITARS, STRIPES AND STARS (American Alternative Rock Classics)
Battleship chains: Georgia Satellites / Satellite: Hooters / Crashin' down: Jason & The Scorchers / Don't want to know if you're lonely: Husker Du / Final wild son: Long Ryders / Copperhead Road: Earle, Steve / Trial of tears: Guadalcanal Diary / Behind the wall of sleep: Smithereens / I believe I'm in love: Fabulous Thunderbirds / Future's so bright I gotta wear shades: Timbuk 3 / Bigger stones: Beat Farmers / Will the wolf survive: Los Lobos / Let my people go: Rainmakers / Time ain't nothing: Green On Red / Don't run wild: Del-Fuegos
CD VSOPCD 225
Connoisseur Collection / Jul '96 / Pinnacle

SHADES OF BLUE
Maiden voyage: Reeves, Dianne & Geri Allen / Un Poco Loco: Reeves, Dianne & Geri Allen / Tom Thumb: Scofield, John Trio / Joshua fit de battle of Jericho: Wilson, Cassandra & Ron Carter / Siete Ocho: Hagans,

Tim & Bob Belden / You've changed: *Printup, Marcus Quartet* / Hum drum blues: *Cole, Holly & Javon Jackson* / 2300 skidoo: *Keezer, Geoff Trio* / Song for my Father: *Rosnes, Renee* / Tanganyika dance: *Elling, Kurt Quartet* / Evidence: *Carter, Ron* / Un amas: *Elias, Eliane Trio*
CD ______ **CDP 8321662**
Blue Note / Jul '96 / EMI

SHADES OF BLUE
CD ______ **NTRCD 057**
Nectar / Jun '97 / Pinnacle

SHADES OF COUNTRY VOL.1
CD ______ **PLSCD 107**
Pulse / Apr '96 / BMG

SHADES OF COUNTRY VOL.2
CD ______ **PLSCD 108**
Pulse / Apr '96 / BMG

SHADES OF GREEN (2CD Set)
CD Set ______ **TCD 2882**
Telstar / Nov '96 / BMG

SHADES OF SOUL (40 Chess/Stax/Motown/Atlantic Classics - 2CD Set)
Sweet soul music: *Conley, Arthur* / Soul man: *Sam & Dave* / Respect: *Franklin, Aretha* / In the midnight hour: *Pickett, Wilson* / (Sittin' on the) dock of the bay: *Redding, Otis* / Take me to the river: *Green, Al* / I just want to make love to you: *James, Etta* / It's a man's man's man's world: *Brown, James* / (Take a little) piece of my heart: *Franklin, Erma* / Stand by me: *King, Ben E.* / Rescue me: *Bass, Fontella* / When a man loves a woman: *Sledge, Percy* / Shout: *Isley Brothers* / Harlem shuffle: *Bob & Earl* / Respect yourself: *Staple Singers* / Family affair: *Sly & The Family Stone* / Tired of being alone: *Green, Al* / (If loving you is wrong) I don't want to be right: *Green, Al* / Theme from shaft: *Hayes, Isaac* / Just my imagination (running away with me): *Temptations* / What's going on: *Gaye, Marvin* / Midnight train to Georgia: *Knight, Gladys & The Pips* / If you don't know me by now: *Melvin, Harold & The Bluenotes* / Love train: *O'Jays* / Summer breeze: *Isley Brothers* / Me and Mrs. Jones: *Paul, Billy* / Misty blue: *Moore, Dorothy* / Barefootin': *Palmer, Robert* / Ain't no sunshine: *Withers, Bill* / Wishing on a star: *Rose Royce* / Why can't we live together: *Thomas, Timmy* / Free: *Williams, Deniece* / I'm gonna love you just a little more babe: *White, Barry* / Didn't I (blow your mind this time): *Delfonics* / One day I'll fly away: *Crawford, Randy* / I want your love: *Chic* / Thinking of you: *Sister Sledge* / Lovin' you: *Riperton, Minnie* / Joy and pain: *Maze* / Never too much: *Vandross, Luther*
CD Set ______ **RADCD 40**
Global TV / Jul '96 / BMG

SHADOW MUSIC OF JAVA
CD ______ **ROU 5060**
Rounder / May '96 / ADA / CM / Direct

SHAKE 'EM ON DOWN (The Real Country Blues)
Shake 'em on down / Sloppy drunk blues / Alabama blues / Need more blues / Judge bushay blues / Pardon denied again / Rabbit blues / Take me out of the bottom / Fred's worried life blues / Poor black Mattie / Come home to me baby / Smokestack lightnin' / Write me a few lines / Mississippi river / Just tippin' in / She left me a mule to ride / Canned heat / Three o'clock in the morning / 'Bout a spoonful / You call yourself a cadillac / Keep your nose out of my business / Oh baby
CD ______ **CDCHD 527**
Ace / Oct '94 / Pinnacle

SHAKE, JUMP, SHOUT
Hold me back: *West Bam* / Callas: *Vox Mystica* / Heavy mental: *Heavy Mental* / Saxophone: *West Bam* / Exzess: *Dick* / Alarm clock: *West Bam* / Time: *Beat In Time* / On a mission: *Dick* / Hell or heaven: *LUPO* / Dreams: *Darling, Grace* / Is it raw enough: *Heavy Mental* / Aka aka: *Eastbam*
CD ______ **YOBCD 1**
Yobro / Jun '90 / Total/BMG

SHAKE, RATTLE & ROCK 'N' ROLL (2CD Set)
Great balls of fire: *Lewis, Jerry Lee* / Personality: *Price, Lloyd* / Tutti frutti: *Little Richard* / Great pretender: *Platters* / My true love: *Scott, Jack* / Wild one: *Rydell, Bobby* / It's only make believe: *Twitty, Conway* / Ain't misbehavin': *Bruce, Tommy* / That'll be the day: *Crickets* / Handy man: *Jones, Jimmy* / Charlie Brown: *Coasters* / Running Bear: *Preston, Johnny* / Bobby's girl: *Maughan, Susan* / Shakin' all over: *Dene, Terry* / Singin' the blues: *Mitchell, Guy* / Blueberry hill: *Domino, Fats* / Tell him: *Davis, Billie* / Stay: *Williams, Maurice & The Zodiacs* / School day: *Berry, Chuck* / I want to walk you home: *Domino, Fats* / Moonlight gambler: *Laine, Frankie* / Rock 'n' roll music: *Berry, Chuck* / Oh boy: *Crickets* / Good golly Miss Molly: *Little Richard* / Stagger Lee: *Price, Lloyd* / Blue suede shoes: *Perkins, Carl* / Dream lover: *Darin, Bobby* / Spanish Harlem: *King, Ben E.* / Memphis Tennessee: *Berry, Chuck* / Cradle of love: *Preston, Johnny* / Be bop a lula: *Vincent, Gene* / Yakety yak: *Coasters* / Sheila: *Roe, Tommy* / Maybe baby: *Crickets* / Sway: *Rydell, Bobby* / Ain't that a shame: *Domino, Fats* / My heart's a symphony: *Lewis, Gary & The Playboys* / Born to be a rolling stone: *Vincent, Gene* / Whole lotta shakin' goin' on: *Lewis, Jerry Lee*
CD Set ______ **330312**
Hallmark / Mar '97 / Carlton

SHAKE, RATTLE AND ROLL
CD ______ **MACCD 212**
Autograph / Aug '96 / BMG

SHAKE THAT THING (America's Top Bands Of The 20's)
I wanna be loved by you: *Broadway Nitelites* / Shakin' the blues away: *Selvin, Ben & His Orchestra* / Hello Swanee, hello: *Lentz, Al & His Orchestra* / Mighty blue: *Waring's Pennsylvanians* / What a day: *Weems, Ted & His Orchestra* / Melancholy Lou: *Lanin, Howard & His Ben Franklin Dance Orchestra* / Confessin': *Lombardo, Guy & His Royal Canadians* / Shake that thing: *Lyman, Abe & His California Orchestra* / Everything's made for love: *Lopez, Vincent & His Orchestra* / Wabash blues: *Charleston Chasers* / Smile: *Whiteman, Paul & His Orchestra* / Let's misbehave: *Aaronson, Irving & His Commanders* / Just a night for meditation: *Crumit, Frank* / Bugle call rag: *Lewis, Ted & His Band* / S'posin': *Vallee, Rudy & His Connecticut Yankees* / He's the last word: *Bernie, Ben & His Hotel Roosevelt Orchestra*
CD ______ **CDAJA 5002**
Living Era / Apr '89 / Select

SHAKE THE BONES (Hydrogen Dukebox Compilation)
CD ______ **033CD**
Hydrogen Dukebox / Mar '97 / 3mv/Vital / Kudos / Prime

SHAKE YOUR CONGAS
Big bang conga: *Los Albinos* / Chiquito: *Calzado, Ruben & His Latin Orchestra* / When the world was mine: *Golden Dream Orchestra* / Aquarella: *Carlier, Jo* / Loin de mes yeux pres de mon coeur: *Pelletier, Jean-Claude* / Go go conga: *Los Albinos* / Blue candlelight: *Evans, Jean & His Piano Strings* / Los patatos: *Boxeros* / Obsession: *Owen, Reg* / Pancho: *Dee Dee & Her Panchos* / Chinese conga: *Los Albinos* / Blue sunrise: *Sadi Quartet* / La cucarachacha: *Loland, Peter* / Birds of paradise: *Kreuder, Peter* / A la salud: *La Baum, Stan & His Orchestra* / Swinging conga: *Los Albinos* / Forever: *Clippers* / Headin' north: *Albimore, Willy* / Marijuana brass: *Mertens, Teddy* / Frere jacques conga: *Los Albinos*
CD ______ **74321421462**
RCA Victor / Jun '97 / BMG

SHAKEN NOT STIRRED
James Bond theme: *Bond, James* / Goldfinger: *Bond, James* / Green eyes: *Florence, Bob* / It happened in Monterrey: *Florence, Bob* / Caravan: *Lyman, Arthur* / Taboo: *Lyman, Arthur* / Sunny: *Lyman, Arthur* / Mambo burger: *Burger, Jack* / Boulevard of broken dreams: *Burger, Jack* / Man with the golden gun: *In Group* / If I had a hammer: *In Group* / Orchids in the moonlight: *Zimmerman, Harry*
CD ______ **RCD 50337**
Rykodisc / Feb '96 / ADA / Vital

SHAKIN' FIT
CD ______ **CRD 006**
Candy / May '97 / Greyhound

SHAM ROCKS, THE
CD ______ **STOMP 002**
Sleeping Giant / Nov '96 / Nervous

SHAMANIC SONGS OF SIBERIAN AMUR BASIN
CD ______ **926712**
BUDA / Jun '97 / Discovery

SHAMROCK AND THISTLE
CD ______ **PLATCD 336**
Platinum / Jul '92 / Prism

SHAPESHIFTER VOL.1 (A Jazz Step Injection)
Deep blue C: *Unguided Lights* / Jazz 163: *N-Jay* / One man dead: *Native Bass* / 125th St: *Click & Cycle* / Jeamland '96: *BLIM* / J-Funk: *Unguided Lights* / Tripple: *Elementz Of Noise* / Encephalia: *N-Jay* / Police state: *T-Power* / Astral: *Elementz Of Noise* / Dallas: *Morf*
CD ______ **SOURCD 007**
SOUR / Aug '96 / SRD

SHAPESHIFTER VOL.2 (Millennial Jazz)
Purple haze: *Purple Kola* / Spell: *Morf* / Memorex in deep water: *Amnesia* / 125th Street: *Click & Cycle* / Refraction edit: *T-Power* / Mental orgasm: *Freq Nasty* / Lord of the rings: *Bangers United* / Conspiracy: *Unguided Lights* / Fruitcake: *BLIM* / Transcend: *Urbanites* / Sweet daze: *Click & Cycle* / Take me to summer: *Minx* / Alternative universe: *Morf*
CD ______ **SOURCD 9**
SOUR / Apr '97 / SRD

SHARING THE NIGHT TOGETHER
CD ______ **10612**
CMC / Jun '97 / BMG

SHAWMS FROM NE CHINA VOL.1
CD ______ **926132 CD**
BUDA / Jul '95 / Discovery

SHAWMS FROM NE CHINA VOL.2
CD ______ **926122 CD**
BUDA / Jul '95 / Discovery

SH'BOOM, SH'BOOM
Book of love: *Monotones* / Boy from New York City: *Ad Libs* / Sincerely: *Moonglows* / Oh what a night: *Dells* / Sixteen candles: *Crests* / Goodnight sweetheart, goodnight: *Spaniels* / Duke of Earl: *Chandler, Gene* / Hasppy, happy birthday baby: *Tune Weavers* / Come go with me: *Del-Vikings* / At my front door: *El Dorado* / Since I don't have you: *Skyliners* / Once in a while: *Chimes* / Sea of love: *Phillips, Phil & The Twilights* / It's in his kiss (The shoop shoop song): *Everett, Betty* / My true story: *Jive Five* / Long lonely nights: *Andrews, Lee* / Over and over: *Day, Bobby* / For all we know: *Orioles* / Mr. Sandman: *Chordettes* / Alley oop: *Hollywood Argyles*
CD ______ **MCCD 091**
Music Club / May '92 / Disc / THE

SHEEN
CD Set ______ **KK 141CD**
KK / Oct '95 / Plastic Head

SHERBET-LICK IT
CD ______ **REACTCD 057**
CD ______ **REACTCDX 057**
React / Feb '95 / Arabesque / Prime / Vital

SHE'S A REBEL (Alternative Women Rock For A Cure)
Oh Nina: *Muffs* / Mendo hoo-ha: *Tribe 8* / Jack shit: *Teen Angels* / Tranny chaser: *Tribe 8* / Suck: *Cake Like* / Give it to the dog: *Bandit Queen* / Starsucker: *Die Cheerleader* / Loose and undubdued: *Bell* / Sycophant: *Nitocris* / Ego: *Flower S.F.* / Rock-a-bye-baby: *7 Year Bitch* / Prick: *Batter Shell* / No yawk: *Cocktailica* / Isosceles: *Dirt Merchants* / Goodnight now: *Muffs*
CD ______ **SH 5714**
Shanachie / Mar '97 / ADA / Greensleeves / Koch

SHESHWE: SOUNDS OF THE MINES
CD ______ **ROUCD 5031**
Rounder / '88 / ADA / CM / Direct

SHETLAND SESSIONS VOL.1, THE
CD ______ **LCOM 7021**
Lismor / Mar '92 / ADA / Direct / Duncans / Lismor

SHETLAND SESSIONS VOL.2, THE
CD ______ **LCOM 7022**
Lismor / Mar '92 / ADA / Direct / Duncans / Lismor

SHINE EYE GAL - BRUKDON FROM BELIZE
CD ______ **CO 118CD**
Corason / May '94 / ADA / CM / Direct

SHINE ON
CD ______ **I 3896032**
Galaxy / Oct '96 / ZYX

SHINE VOL.1
Parklife: *Blur* / Cigarettes and alcohol: *Oasis* / Regret: *New Order* / Zombie: *Cranberries* / Animal nitrate: *Suede* / Connection: *Elastica* / Do you remember the first time: *Pulp* / So let me go far: *Dodgy* / Speakeasy: *Shed Seven* / Welcome to paradise: *Green Day* / How soon is now: *Smiths* / Sit down: *James* / Getting away with it: *Electronic* / Size of a cow: *Wonder Stuff* / Altogether now: *Farm* / Dragging me down: *Inspiral Carpets* / Weirdo: *Charlatans* / International bright young thing: *Jesus Jones* / Feel the pain: *Dinosaur Jr.* / Shine on: *House Of Love*
CD ______ **5255672**
Polydor / May '95 / PolyGram

SHINE VOL.2
Some might say: *Oasis* / Changing man: *Weller, Paul* / Girl from Mars: *Ash* / Love spreads: *Stone Roses* / Girl like you: *Collins, Edwyn* / Wake up Boo: *Boo Radleys* / Change: *Lightning Seeds* / Staying out for the summer: *Dodgy* / Fine time: *Cast* / Waking up: *Elastica* / Ridiculous thoughts: *Cranberries* / Vegas: *Sleeper* / Where I find my heaven: *Gigolo Aunts* / Haunted by you: *Gene* / Now they'll sleep: *Belly* / Sparky's dream: *Teenage Fanclub* / Stay together: *Suede* / Kinky Afro: *Happy Mondays* / Love will tear us apart: *Joy Division* / Underwear: *Pulp*
CD ______ **5258582**
Polydor / Aug '95 / PolyGram

SHINE VOL.3
Common people: *Pulp* / Roll with it: *Oasis* / Alright: *Supergrass* / Marvellous: *Lightning Seeds* / What do I do now: *Sleeper* / Stardust: *Menswear* / Alright: *Cast* / Only happy when it rains: *Garbage* / King of the kerb: *Echobelly* / Angel interceptor: *Ash* / End of a century: *Blur* / One love: *Stone Roses* / From the bench at Belvidere: *Boo Radleys* / Olympian: *Gene* / Just when you're thinkin' things over: *Charlatans* / Fantasy: *Levellers* / Let's all go together: *Marion* / Where have you been tonight: *Shed Seven* / Might be stars: *Wannadies* / Step on: *Happy Mondays*
CD ______ **5259652**
Polydor / Oct '95 / PolyGram

SHINE VOL.4
Sandstorm: *Cast* / Mis-shapes: *Pulp* / Mansize rooster: *Supergrass* / Sleeping in: *Menswear* / Getting better: *Shed Seven* / From a window: *Northern Uproar* / Riverboat song: *Ocean Colour Scene* / Weak: *Skunk Anansie* / Divebomb: *Number One Cup* / Time: *Marion* / Far: *Longpigs* / Universal: *Blur* / Dark therapy: *Echobelly* / For the dead: *Gene* / Ten storey love song: *Stone Roses* / Just: *Radiohead* / Lucky you: *Lightning Seeds* / Carnival: *Cardigans* / Anywhere: *Dubstar* / Come together: *Smokin' Mojo Filters* / Fade away: *Oasis & Friends*
CD ______ **5353212**
Polydor / Feb '96 / PolyGram

SHINE VOL.5
CD ______ **5356892**
PolyGram TV / Jul '96 / PolyGram

SHINE VOL.6 (2CD Set)
Peacock suit: *Weller, Paul* / One to another: *Charlatans* / Design for life: *Manic Street Preachers* / Trash: *Suede* / Good enough: *Dodgy* / Circle: *Ocean Colour Scene* / On stand by: *Shed Seven* / We love you: *Menswear* / Love fool: *Cardigans* / Charmless man: *Blur* / Underground: *Folds, Ben Five* / Becoming more like Alfie: *Divine Comedy* / 12 reasons why I love her: *My Life Story* / Sale of the century: *Sleeper* / Goodnight: *Baby Bird* / Rush hour: *Joyrider* / What's in the box: *Boo Radleys* / Lump: *Presidents Of The USA* / On a rope: *Rocket From The Crypt* / Free to decide: *Cranberries* / Forbidden City: *Electronic* / Champagne supernova: *Oasis* / Walkaway: *Cast* / Something changed: *Pulp* / On and on: *Longpigs* / Bad actress: *Terrorvision* / Exodus: *Levellers* / Stripper vicar: *Mansun* / You're one: *Imperial Teen* / Livin' it up: *Northern Uproar* / Chinese burn: *Heavy Stereo* / Look at you now: *Elcka* / 500 (shake baby shake): *Lush* / Elevator song: *Dubstar* / Anymore: *Cracknell, Sarah* / Valentine's Day: *Ruth* / Beyond safe ways: *Bawl* / One in a million: *Sussed* / Punka: *Kenickie* / 36 degrees: *Placebo*
CD Set ______ **5359202**
PolyGram TV / Sep '96 / PolyGram

SHINE VOL.7 (2CD Set)
Flying: *Cast* / Beautiful ones: *Suede* / Everything must go: *Manic Street Preachers* / Fighting fit: *Gene* / Twisted: *Skunk Anansie* / Lost myself: *Longpigs* / Disco 2000: *Pulp* / Ready or not: *Lightning Seeds* / You've got it bad: *Ocean Colour Scene* / C'mon kids: *Boo Radleys* / Lava: *Silver Sun* / Kandy pop: *Bis* / Teenage angst: *Placebo* / Burden in my hands: *Soundgarden* / Celebrity hitlist: *Terrorvision* / Boy wonder: *Speedy* / No one speaks: *Geneva* / Great things: *Echobelly* / Nice guy Eddie: *Sleeper* / Sparkle: *My Life Story* / Morning glory: *Oasis* / Milk: *Garbage & Tricky* / 6 Underground: *Sneaker Pimps* / If you're thinking of me: *Dodgy* / Chasing rainbows: *Shed Seven* / For you: *Electronic* / You're gorgeous: *Baby Bird* / Patio song: *Gorky's Zygotic Mynci* / Neighbourhood: *Space* / Girls and boys: *Blur* / Frog princess: *Divine Comedy* / Whatever: *Oasis* / Lazy lover: *Supernaturals* / Lenny: *Supergrass* / If you don't want me to destroy you: *Super Furry Animals* / Broken stones: *Weller, Paul* / If I could talk I'd tell you: *Lemonheads* / Street spirit: *Radiohead* / Not so manic now: *Dubstar* / You've got a lot to answer for: *Catatonia* / One night stand: *Aloof*
CD Set ______ **5530512**
PolyGram TV / Nov '96 / PolyGram

SHINE VOL.8 (2CD Set)
Free me: *Cast* / North country boy: *Charlatans* / Swallowed: *Bush* / Place your hands: *Reef* / Nancy boy: *Placebo* / Sixty mile smile: *3 Colours Red* / Kevin Carter: *Manic Street Preachers* / Wide open space: *Mansun* / Tattva: *Kula Shaker* / What do you want from me: *Monaco* / She's a star: *James* / We could be kings: *Gene* / Farewell to twilight: *Symposium* / Sugar coated iceberg: *Lightning Seeds* / King of kissingdom: *My Life Story* / Your woman: *White Town* / Diamond dew: *Gorky's Zygotic Mynci* / Everybody knows (except you): *Divine Comedy* / Found you: *Dodgy* / Masterplan: *Oasis* / Lazy: *Suede* / Beetlebum: *Blur* / It's no good: *Depeche Mode* / Novocaine for the soul: *Eels* / Hedonism (just because you feel good): *Skunk Anansie* / Babies: *Pulp* / Bully boy: *Shed Seven* / Shady lane: *Pavement* / Someone always gets there first: *Bennet* / Statuesque: *Sleeper* / I don't know: *Ruth* / Go: *Jocasta* / Monday morning: *Candyskins* / RACE: *Tiger* / 1962: *Grass Show* / U16 girls: *Travis* / Hit: *Wannadies* / Caught by the fuzz: *Supergrass* / Skyscraper: *Intastella* / Bankrobber: *Audioweb*
CD Set ______ **5534522**
PolyGram TV / Apr '97 / PolyGram

SHINE VOL.9 (2CD Set)
CD Set ______ **5539752**
PolyGram TV / Sep '97 / PolyGram

SHOCK THERAPY
CD ______ **EFA 008792**
Shockwave / Jul '97 / SRD

SHOOP - THE DEFINITION OF TECHNO (3CD Set)
CD Set ______ **ZBDCD 001**
Shoop / Jul '96 / Grapevine/PolyGram / Mo's Music Machine

SHOOT THA PUMP (Block Party Hip Hop From The New York Underground)
Halftime: *Nas* / NYS anthem: *Crooklyn Clan* / Hand up: *Gonzalez, Kenny 'Dope'* / Heh yah heh: *Buddah Baboons* / To the hip: *Bootman* / Where's Brooklyn at: *DJ Mister Cee* / Where's da party at: *Fresh, Doug E* /

Back into time: *Chuck Chillout* / Shake watcha Mama gave ya: *Stick-E & The Hoods*
CD ________ **HARD 19LPCD**
Concrete / Jun '97 / 3mv/Pinnacle / Prime / RTM/Disc / Total/BMG

SHOPPING.LIVE@VICTO
CD ________ **RERJ 4**
ReR/Recommended / Jun '97 / ReR Megacorp / RTM/Disc

SHORT SHARP SHOCK
CD ________ **OVER 47CD**
Overground / May '96 / Shellshock/Disc / SRD

SHOTS IN THE DARK
CD ________ **DOCD 2113**
Del-Fi / Jan '97 / Cargo / Koch

SHOULD I STAY OR SHOULD I GO
CD ________ **HILOCD 12**
Hi / Jan '95 / Pinnacle

SHOUT AND SCREAM
CD ________ **DRCD 001**
Detour / Jul '95 / Detour / Greyhound

SHOUT BROTHER SHOUT
CD ________ **AL 2800**
Alligator / Jul '94 / ADA / CM / Direct

SHOUT IT OUT 1946-1952
CD ________ **RST 915792**
RST / Jun '94 / Hot Shot / Jazz Music

SHOUT THE FUTURE TRIBE
CD ________ **CDACV 2005**
ACV / Jun '95 / Plastic Head / SRD

SHOUTING THE BLUES
Adam bit the apple: *Turner, 'Big' Joe* / Still in the dark: *Turner, 'Big' Joe* / Feelin' happy: *Turner, 'Big' Joe* / Midnight is here again AKA Dawn is breakin' through: *Turner, 'Big' Joe* / I want my baby: *Turner, 'Big' Joe* / Life is a card game: *Turner, 'Big' Joe* / After a while you'll be sorry: *Turner, 'Big' Joe* / Just a travellin' man: *Turner, 'Big' Joe* / Big city blues: *Big Maceo* / Do you remember: *Big Maceo* / Just tell me baby: *Big Maceo* / One Sunday morning: *Big Maceo* / State street boogie: *Johnson, Don Orchestra* / Jackson's blues: *Johnson, Don Orchestra* / Chesterfield baby: *Johnson, Don Orchestra* / Lonesome lover blues: *Smilin' Smokey Lynn* / Run rabbit run: *Smilin' Smokey Lynn* / Feel like ballin' tonight: *Smilin' Smokey Lynn* / Rock-a-bye baby: *Smilin' Smokey Lynn* / Hometown baby (Hip Cat): *Smilin' Smokey Lynn* / She's been gone: *H-Bomb Ferguson* / You made me baby: *H-Bomb Ferguson*
CD ________ **CDCHD 439**
Ace / Jan '93 / Pinnacle

SHOVE IT
My man, a sweet man: *Jackson, Millie* / Night fever: *Fatback Band* / Can you get to that: *Funkadelic* / Pain: *Ohio Players* / Baby let me take you (in my arms): *Detroit Emeralds* / Man size job: *LaSalle, Denise* / Keep on stepping: *Fatback Band* / Get down, get down (get on the floor): *Simon, Joe* / Pleasure: *Ohio Players* / It's all over but the shouting: *Jackson, Millie* / Funky dollar bill: *Funkadelic*
CD ________ **CDSEWX 015**
Westbound / Oct '89 / Pinnacle

SHOW AND TELL
CD ________ **WHI 666CD**
Which / May '97 / Cargo

SHREVEPORT STOMP
Ba Da: *Perkins, Roy* / Red beans and rice: *Patin, Scatman & The Ram Rods* / Cheater's can't win: *Lewis, Margaret* / Flat foot Sam: *TV Slim* / Mailman mailman: *Williamson, Sonny Boy* / Come back Betty: *Steel, L.C.* / I'm leaving: *Brannon, Linda* / Bow wow puppy love: *Bonin, Jimmy* / Drop top (TK1): *Perkins, Roy* / Reconsider me: *Lewis, Margaret* / Hippy Ti Yo: *Page, Bobby* / Wherever you are: *Brannon, Linda* / Pow wow: *Tennessee, Grace* / Let me feel it: *Brown, Elgie* / Girl in the street: *Williams, Vince* / Ginning: *Patin, Scatman & The Ram Rods* / Baby please forgive me: *Webb, Troy* / What did you do last night: *Rocky Robin & the Riff Raffs* / Night creature: *Run-a-ways* / Anyway you do: *Brannon, Linda* / Eager boy: *Lonesome Drifter* / Lonesome heart: *Hunter, Charlotte* / El Rancho Grande Rock: *Starmakers* / Lover's land: *Walker, Ernest* / Louisiana twist: *Bailey, June Bug*
CD ________ **CDCHD 495**
Ace / Jun '94 / Pinnacle

SHRINE
CD ________ **CSR 4 CD**
NMC / Jun '93 / Total/Pinnacle

SHUFFLIN' ON BOND STREET
CD ________ **CDTRL 275**
Trojan / Aug '94 / Direct / Jet Star

SHUT THE GATE SUZY
CD ________ **NITR 002**
Demolition Derby / Jan '97 / Greyhound / Nervous

SHUT UP AND PLAY YER BLUES
CD ________ **MCCD 216**
Music Club / Oct '95 / Disc / THE

SHUT UP AND POGO
CD ________ **NV 50**
Nasty Vinyl / Jun '97 / Cargo

SI SAFAA (New Music From The Middle East)
Ghallo Tara: *Ahmed, Hamdi* / Agulak: *Khairy, Saleh* / Anta Al Hakam: *Sahir, Kazim Al* / Matajarahnish: *Hanan* / Nami: *Ayubi, Aida* / Sif Safaa: *Mounir, Mohamed* / Khafet Dhamon: *Fouad, Mohamed* / Tasadig Wala Ahliflak: *Ahmed, Hamdi* / Leh Alkhiyana: *Hilal, Abu* / Ya Leyl A'ah: *Hanan* / Hawad: *Fouad, Mohamed* / Alashan Al Malih: *Khairy, Saleh*
CD ________ **CDEMC 3700**
Hemisphere / Mar '95 / EMI

SICK, SICK, SICK
Vibrate: *Demented Are Go* / Human slug: *Demented Are Go* / Cast iron arm: *Demented Are Go* / PVC Chair: *Demented Are Go* / Rubber buccaneer: *Demented Are Go* / Pervy in the park: *Demented Are Go* / Rubber love: *Demented Are Go* / Holy hack Jack: *Demented Are Go* / Love is for skitzos: *Skitzo* / I want your lovin': *Skitzo* / Possessed: *Coffin Nails* / Werewolf bitch: *Coffin Nails* / Natural born lover: *Coffin Nails* / Uncle Willy: *Coffin Nails* / Wind up dead: *Coffin Nails*
CD ________ **DOJOCD 23**
Dojo / Feb '94 / Disc

SIDEREAL REST
CD ________ **SCRATCH 21**
Scratch / Dec '96 / Cargo

SIGNED SEALED DELIVERED VOL.1
Geek USA: *Smashing Pumpkins* / Body Count's in the house: *Body Count* / Real surreal: *SMASH* / Pinch: *Acetone* / No honestly: *Urban Dance Squad* / Shamrock: *Daryll-Ann* / Wild America: *Iggy Pop* / Jobs for the boys: *These Animal Men* / Butterfly: *Verve* / Street scene: *Bark Psychosis* / God's green earth: *Idaho* / Challenger: *American Music Club* / Sister like you: *Auteurs* / What are you: *Grey, David* / Movie star: *Cracker* / Unworthy (Edit): *Thieves*
CD ________ **VVSAM 22**
Virgin / Jun '94 / EMI

SIGNED SEALED DELIVERED VOL.2
Crashin' the system: *Brotherhood* / Mr. Businessman green: *Anderson, Carleen* / Home of the whale: *Massive Attack* / Boom bastic: *Shaggy* / Push: *Loose Ends* / Gotta lotta love: *Ice-T* / You the man: *Shyheim* / No groove sweatin' (A funky space reincarnation): *McWilliams, Brigette* / Moment of truth: *College Boyz* / Bring me home: *Future Sound Of London* / Subliminal aura: *Amorphous Androgynous* / GFeel8the popsicle: *Popsicle* / Drippin' wit lust: *Knuckles, Frankie* / Speaking in tongues III: *Chandra, Sheila*
CD ________ **VVSAM 23**
Virgin / Jun '94 / EMI

SIGNED SEALED DELIVERED VOL.3
Survival in the wind: *Belew, Adrian* / Same changes: *Phillips, Sam* / When you smile: *Foly, Liane* / Come to the water: *Sanne* / Leave the ground: *Duke* / Y'a d'la haine: *Mitsouko, Rita* / Girl I love you: *Douglas, Sian* / Let it come your way: *Six Was Nine* / Is this a broken heart: *Ruffelle, Frances* / Life's funny: *Robillard, Duke* / More and more: *Jumpin' The Gunn* / Waiting on an angel: *Harper, Ben* / Brown dirt: *Cale, J.J.* / That's the way love turned out for me: *Evans, Terry* / Here to there: *Nyman, Michael* / Virgin 21: *Wainwright III, Loudon*
CD ________ **VVSAM 24**
Virgin / Jun '94 / EMI

SILENT CRYING
CD ________ **TT 00272**
T&T / Feb '97 / Koch

SILK & STEEL
I found someone: *Cher* / Night in my veins: *Pretenders* / Independent love song: *Scarlet* / Heaven is a place on earth: *Carlisle, Belinda* / Walking on broken glass: *Lennox, Annie* / Look: *Roxette* / Whole world lost its head: *Go-Go's* / Change of heart: *Lauper, Cyndi* / We belong: *Benatar, Pat* / Total eclipse of the heart: *Tyler, Bonnie* / Rubber band girl: *Bush, Kate* / Mandinka: *O'Connor, Sinead* / I touch myself: *Divinyls* / Crash: *Primitives* / You're history: *Shakespears Sister* / Hazy shade of winter: *Bangles* / Rush hour: *Wiedlin, Jane* / What I am: *Brickell, Edie & New Bohemians* / Self control: *Branigan, Laura* / Baby I don't care: *Transvision Vamp*
CD ________ **5255692**
Polydor / May '95 / PolyGram

SILKY SOUL
It don't get no better han this: *Burke, Solomon* / Just you just me: *Peebles, Ann* / Personally: *Kelly, Paul* / Neither one of us: *Adams, Johnny* / I'd rather beg: *Carbo, Chuck* / Gonna take my heart's advice: *Clay, Otis* / Whatever it takes: *Little Buster* / Willing and able: *Reed, Dalton* / Can't you hear it in my tears: *Thomas, Irma* / Out of the dark: *Washington, Walter 'Wolfman'*
CD ________ **EDCD 7008**
Easydisc / Nov '96 / Direct

SILLY SYMPHONIES
CD ________ **70700271363**
Essential Dance / Nov '95 / RTM/Disc

SILLY SYMPHONIES VOL.3
CD ________ **707003**
Essential Dance / Jul '96 / RTM/Disc

SILOS AND UTILITY SHEDS
CD ________ **GRCD 361**
Hypertension / Nov '96 / ADA / CM / Direct / Total/BMG

SILVER PLANET COLLECTION VOL.1
CD ________ **SILVER 7CD**
Silver Planet / Jul '97 / 3mv/Sony / Prime

SIMPLY PAN PIPES
Stars / Fairground / She'll have to go / Sad old red / You've got it / Never never love / Your mirror / It's only love / To be with you / For your babies / Something's got me started / Remembering the first time / Wonderland / New flame / Holding back the years / Ev'rytime we say goodbye / Do the right thing / Thrill me / We're in this together / If you don't know me by now
CD ________ **303000982**
Carlton / Apr '97 / Carlton

SIMPLY SOUL (4CD Set)
Barefootin': *Parker, Robert* / When a man loves a woman: *Sledge, Percy* / For your precious love: *Butler, Jerry* / So many ways: *Benton, Brook* / Save the last dance for me: *Drifters* / Operator: *Knight, Gladys & The Pips* / Soul man: *Sam & Dave* / Me and Mrs. Jones: *Paul, Billy* / If you don't know me by now: *Melvin, Harold & The Bluenotes* / Feel the need in me: *Detroit Emeralds* / Walking the dog: *Thomas, Rufus* / Show and tell: *Wilson, Al* / I stand accused: *Butler, Jerry* / It's just a matter of time: *Benton, Brook* / I got you (I feel good): *Brown, James* / There goes my baby: *Drifters* / Soul sister, brown sugar: *Sam & Dave* / You've made me so very happy: *Whispers* / Try a little tenderness: *Sledge, Percy* / Knock on wood: *Floyd, Eddie* / Warm and tender love: *Sledge, Percy* / Under the boardwalk: *Drifters* / Every beat of my heart: *Knight, Gladys & The Pips* / Rainy night in Georgia: *Benton, Brook* / I thank you: *Sam & Dave* / Make it easy on yourself: *Butler, Jerry* / Papa's got a brand new bag: *Brown, James* / Woman in love: *Three Degrees* / I've never found a girl to love me like you do: *Floyd, Eddie* / Band of gold: *Payne, Freda* / Portrait of my love: *Clark, Dee* / Let it be me: *Butler, Jerry & Betty Everett* / Needle in a haystack: *Whispers* / I've been loving you too long: *Sledge, Percy* / Ain't no sunshine: *Jarreau, Al* / Up on the roof: *Drifters* / Hold on I'm coming: *Sam & Dave* / Letter full of tears: *Knight, Gladys & The Pips* / Challenge: *Butler, Jerry* / Duke of Earl: *Chandler, Gene* / On no not my baby: *Brown, Maxine* / You don't know what you mean to me: *Sam & Dave* / Please please please: *Brown, James* / I got the feelin': *Brown, James* / On broadway: *Drifters* / Heatwave: *Reeves, Martha* / Stoned love: *Supremes* / Dancing in the street: *Weston, Kim* / First I look at the purse: *Contours* / Beachwood 4-5789: *Marvelettes* / Dance with me: *Drifters* / If ever I should fall in love: *Knight, Gladys & The Pips* / Just my imagination: *Cameron, G.C.* / Ain't no mountain high enough: *Payne, Sherrie* / Touch me in the morning: *Littles, Hattie* / This old heart of mine: *Contours* / My cherie amour: *Moy, Sylvia* / You are the sunshine of my life: *Nero, Frances* / I'm still waiting: *Payne, Sherrie* / I'll pick a rose for my rose: *Johnson, Marv* / Used to be a playboy: *Marvelettes* / Jimmy mack: *Lavette, Bettye* / Tracks of my tears: *Contours* / Love hangover: *5th Dimension* / My smile is just a frown: *Crawford, Carolyn* / Reach out I'll be there: *Taylor, Bobby* / He was really sayin' somethin': *Velvelettes* / Reflections: *Syreeta* / Remember me: *Lewis, Pat* / With you I'm born again: *Syreeta* / Too busy thinking 'bout my baby: *Cameron, G.C.* / Ready or not here I come: *Contours* / Rescue me: *Lewis, Pat* / Nathan Jones: *Supremes* / Reunited: *Satintones* / Going to a go go: *Monitors* / Love child: *Supremes* / Emotion: *Weston, Kim*
CD Set ________ **QUAD 002**
Tring / Nov '96 / Tring

SIMPLY THE BEST (Classic Soul/2CD Set)
Let's stay together: *Green, Al* / Tired of being alone: *Green, Al* / (You make me feel) Like a natural woman: *Franklin, Aretha* / I say a little prayer: *Franklin, Aretha* / Respect: *Franklin, Aretha* / Stand by me: *King, Ben E.* / Green onions: *Booker T & The MG's* / Express yourself: *Wright, Charles* / Could it be I'm falling in love: *Detroit Spinners* / Ain't no mountain high enough: *Ross, Diana* / You are everything: *Ross, Diana* / You can't hurry lovve: *Ross, Diana & The Supremes* / Walk on by: *Warwick, Dionne* / You'll never get to heaven: *Warwick, Dionne* / Under the boardwalk: *Drifters* / Up on the roof: *Drifters* / Knock on wood: *Floyd, Eddie* / (Take a little) piece of my heart: *Franklin, Erma* / Reach out I'll be there: *Four Tops* / If you don't know me by now: *Melvin, Harold & The Bluenotes* / (Your love keeps lifting me) Higher & higher: *Melvin, Harold & The Bluenotes* / I got the sweetest feeling: *Wilson, Jackie* / I'm there: *Jacksons* / (I feel like I'm being a) sex machine: *Brown, James* / I got you (I feel good): *Brown, James* / What becomes of the brokenhearted: *Ruffin, Jimmy* / Dancing in the streets: *Martha & The Vandellas* / When you're young and in love: *Marvelettes* / Ain't nothin' like the real thing: *Gaye, Marvin* / Heard it throught the grapevine: *Gaye, Marvin* / Too busy thinkin' about my baby: *Gaye, Marvin* / Got to be there: *Jackson, Michael* / My baby just cares for me: *Simone, Nina* / (Sittin' on the) dock of the bay: *Redding, Otis* / My girl: *Redding, Otis* / Try a little tenderness: *Redding, Otis* / When a man loves a woman: *Sledge, Percy* / Where is the love: *Flack, Roberta & Donny Hathaway* / Soul man: *Sam & Dave* / Tears of a clown: *Robinson, Smokey & The Miracles* / Tracks of my tears: *Robinson, Smokey & The Miracles* / I second that emotion: *Robinson, Smokey & The Miracles* / Everybody needs somebody to love: *Burke, Solomon* / My cherie amour: *Wonder, Stevie* / Stop in the name of love: *Supremes* / Baby love: *Supremes* / Ain't too proud to beg: *Supremes* / Papa was a rolling stone: *Supremes* / In the midnight hour: *Pickett, Wilson* / Mustang sally: *Pickett, Wilson* / Groovin': *Young Rascals*
CD Set ________ **9548352042**
Warner Bros. / Mar '97 / Warner Music

SIMPLY THE BEST DISCO (2CD Set)
I will survive: *Gaynor, Gloria* / Funky Town: *Lipps Inc.* / Boogie nights: *Heatwave* / I'm every woman: *Khan, Chaka* / Lady Marmalade: *Labelle* / Blame it on the boogie: *Jacksons* / That's the way I like it: *KC & The Sunshine Band* / Ain't nobody: *Rufus & Chaka Khan* / Night to remember: *Shalamar* / You to me are everything: *Real Thing* / Is it love you're after: *Rose Royce* / And the beat goes on: *Whispers* / Forget me nots: *Rushen, Patrice* / Heaven must be missing an angel: *Tavares* / We are family: *Sister Sledge* / Use it up and wear it out: *Odyssey* / Let's groove: *Earth, Wind & Fire* / I feel love: *Summer, Donna* / You make me feel (mighty real): *Sylvester* / Disco inferno: *Trammps* / Play that funky music: *Wild Cherry* / Hang on in there baby: *Bristol, Johnny* / Going back to my roots: *Odyssey* / If I can't have you: *Elliman, Yvonne* / Good times: *Chic* / Best of my love: *Emotions* / Hustle: *McCoy, Van* / Lost in music: *Sister Sledge* / Theme from Shaft: *Hayes, Isaac* / Young hearts run free: *Staton, Candi* / Le freak: *Chic* / IOU: *Freeez* / Jump to the beat: *Lattisaw, Stacy* / Celebration: *Kool & The Gang* / Yes sir, I can boogie: *Baccara* / Working my way back to you: *Detroit Spinners* / Boogie oogie oogie: *Taste Of Honey* / Ring my bell: *Ward, Anita* / Rasputin: *Boney M* / Boogie wonderland: *Earth, Wind & Fire*
CD Set ________ **9548354282**
Warner Bros. / Jul '97 / Warner Music

SIMPLY THE BEST LOVE SONGS (2CD Set)
CD Set ________ **9548351122**
Warner Bros. / Feb '97 / Warner Music

SIMPLY THE BEST SAX (2CD Set)
CD Set ________ **CDSR 119**
Telstar / Mar '97 / BMG

SIN ALLEY VOL.1
CD ________ **E 11564CD**
Crypt / Mar '93 / Shellshock/Disc

SING DE CHORUS
Country club scandal / Madame Khan / Songs of long ago / Dew and rain / Worker's plea / St. Peter's day / Black market / Leave me alone Dorothy / Ugly woman - trouble and misery / Los iros / Gold in Africa / Treasury scandal / Reign too long / Louise / Graf Zeppelin / Adolf Hitler / Love me or leave me / Matilda / Money is king / Victory calypso / Coldness of the water / Let the white people fight / Sedition law / Mother's love / Woman called Dorothy / Tribute to executor / Sing de chorus
CD ________ **DE 4018**
Delos / Feb '94 / Nimbus

SING FOR YOUR SUPPER
CD ________ **AVC 529**
Avid / Nov '93 / Avid/BMG / Koch / THE

SING ME A SWING SONG
Troubled waters: *Anderson, Ivie* / Thanks a million: *Armstrong, Louis* / More than you know: *Bailey, Mildred* / What'ja do to me: *Boswell Sisters* / I let a song go out of my heart: *Boswell, Connee* / Zaz zul zaz: *Calloway, Cab* / Don't try your jive on me: *Carlisle, Una Mae* / Louisiana: *Crosby, Bing* / When I grow too old to dream: *Dandridge, Putney* / Ten cents a dance: *Etting, Ruth* / Sing me a swing song: *Fitzgerald, Ella* / Lovable and sweet: *Hanshaw, Annette* / 1-2 Button your shoe: *Holiday, Billie* / Thursday: *Humes, Helen* / Isle of Capri: *Manone, Wingy* / Three little words: *Rhythm Boys* / I just couldn't take it baby: *Teagarden, Jack* / I wish I were twins: *Valaida* / Dream man: *Waller, Fats* / Restless: *Ward, Helen* / Am I blue: *Waters, Ethel* / Drop in next time you're passing: *Welch, Elisabeth*
CD ________ **CDAJA 5077**
Living Era / Jan '91 / Select

SING SING SO
CD ________ **VICG 52192**
JVC World Library / Feb '96 / ADA / CM / Direct

SINGALONG BANJO PARTY
Baby face / Toot toot tootsie / Let's all go down The Strand / You are my sunshine / Pennies from Heaven / Any old iron / Bye bye blackbird / Mammy / Underneath the arches / Shine on harvest moon / On Mother Kelly's doorstep / Birdie song

CD __________ PLATCD 01
Platinum / Dec '88 / Prism

SINGER & THE SONG, THE
CD __________ STACD 007
Wisepack / Nov '92 / Conifer/BMG / THE

SINGER & THE SONG, THE
Barcelona: *Mercury, Freddie & Montserrat Caballe* / Great pretender: *Platters* / Stand by me: *King, Ben E.* / Piece of my heart: *Franklin, Erma* / You've lost that lovin' feelin': *Righteous Brothers* / Reach out, I'll be there: *Four Tops* / My cherie amour: *Wonder, Stevie* / It's over: *Orbison, Roy* / Sun ain't gonna shine anymore: *Walker Brothers* / Something's gotten hold of my heart: *Almond, Marc & Gene Pitney* / It's not unusual: *Jones, Tom* / I will survive: *Gaynor, Gloria* / Don't leave me this way: *Melvin, Harold & The Bluenotes* / Get here: *Adams, Oleta* / When a man loves a woman: *Sledge, Percy* / Mad about the boy: *Washington, Dinah* / When I fall in love: *Cole, Nat 'King'* / If you go away: *Walker, Scott* / Crazy: *Cline, Patsy* / Stand by your man: *Wynette, Tammy* / Don't let the sun go down on me: *Michael, George & Elton John* / Nothing compares 2 U: *O'Connor, Sinead* / Stay: *Shakespears Sister* / China in your hand: *T'Pau* / Up where we belong: *Cocker, Joe* / (Something inside) So strong: *Siffre, Labi* / Close to you: *Carpenters* / Lady in red: *De Burgh, Chris* / Jealous guy: *Roxy Music* / Air that I breathe: *Hollies* / Without you: *Nilsson, Harry* / Send in the clowns: *Collins, Judy* / I know him so well: *Paige, Elaine & Barbara Dickson* / I left my heart in San Francisco: *Bennett, Tony* / You don't have to say you love me: *Springfield, Dusty* / Goldfinger: *Bassey, Shirley* / Non, je ne regrette rien: *Piaf, Edith* / Over the rainbow: *Garland, Judy* / You'll never walk alone: *Gerry & The Pacemakers* / Nessun Dorma: *Pavarotti, Luciano*
CD __________ VTCD 21
Virgin / Oct '93 / EMI

SINGER AND THE SONGS VOL.2, THE
CD __________ CDBLP 2023
Lochshore / Jul '96 / ADA / Direct / Duncans

SINGERS MEET THE DJ'S
CD __________ RNCD 2106
Rhino / Jun '95 / Grapevine/PolyGram / Jet Star

SINGERS OF IMPERIAL RUSSIA VOL.1
CD Set __________ GEMMCDS 99979
Pearl / Sep '92 / Harmonia Mundi

SINGERS OF IMPERIAL RUSSIA VOL.2
CD Set __________ GEMMCDS 90013
Pearl / Oct '92 / Harmonia Mundi

SINGERS OF IMPERIAL RUSSIA VOL.3
CD Set __________ GEMMCDS 90046
Pearl / Nov '92 / Harmonia Mundi

SINGERS OF JAZZ
Cutting out blues: *Shavers, Charlie* / Lullaby in boogie: *Duffy, Jack* / Dream weaver: *Amorosa, Johnny* / Mr. Sandman: *Mills Brothers* / I've got my fingers crossed: *Waller, Fats* / Christopher Columbus: *Waller, Fats* / She walks like a kangaroo: *Sheppard, Ollie* / Tiger rag: *Mills Brothers* / Robin Hood: *Prima, Louis* / Boogie woogie (I may be wrong): *Rushing, Jimmy* / You do me any old way: *Broonzy, 'Big' Bill* / Moon glow: *Mills Brothers* / Oop bop sh'bam: *Gillespie, Dizzy* / Jumping jive: *Calloway, Cab* / Minnie the moocher: *Calloway, Cab* / El rancho vego: *Culver, Dick* / I don't know why (I just do): *Martin, Kenny* / Sweet Lorraine: *Cole, Nat 'King'* / You're the cream in my coffee: *Cole, Nat 'King'* / Abraham: *Torme, Mel* / Velvet moon: *Nelson, Skip* / Music maestro please: *Mills Brothers*
CD __________ 22728
Music Box / Jun '96 / I&B

SINGERS ON TOP
CD __________ 792512
Melodie / Dec '95 / ADA / Discovery / Grapevine/PolyGram / Greensleeves / Jet Star

SINGERS SELECTIONS VOL.1
CD __________ ZZCD 020
Zola & Zola / Sep '96 / Jet Star

SINGERS VOL.1
CD __________ PHCD 2052
Penthouse / Jan '97 / Jet Star

SINGIN' THE GOSPEL
Nobody's fault but mine: *Johnson, 'Blind' Willie* / If I had my way: *Johnson, 'Blind' Willie* / Dark was the night: *Johnson, 'Blind' Willie* / I'm gonna run: *Johnson, 'Blind' Willie* / Dear old southland: *Armstrong, Louis* / Sha drack: *Armstrong, Louis* / Goin' to shout all over God's heaven: *Armstrong, Louis* / Nobody knows the trouble I've seen: *Armstrong, Louis* / Jonah and the whale: *Armstrong, Louis* / Bye and bye: *Armstrong, Louis* / Gospel train: *Golden Gate Quartet* / I'm on my way: *Golden Gate Quartet* / What more can Jesus do: *Mitchell's Christian Singers* / My poor mother died a-shoutin': *Mitchell's Christian Singers* / All God's chillun got rhythm: *Ellington, Duke Orchestra* / Swing low, sweet chariot: *Ellington, Duke Orchestra* / All God's chillun got wings: *Ellington, Duke Orchestra* / Go down Moses: *Ellington, Duke Orchestra* / Deep river: *Ellington, Duke Orchestra* / Sometimes I feel like a Motherless child: *Waller, Fats* / Strange things happened everyday: *Tharpe, Sister Rosetta*
CD __________ 19126
Forlane / Nov '96 / Target/BMG

SINGIN' THE GOSPEL 1933-36
CD __________ DOCD 5326
Document / Mar '95 / ADA / Hot Shot / Jazz Music

SINGING IN AN OPEN SPACE (Zulu Rhythm & Harmony)
CD __________ ROUCD 5027
Rounder / Dec '90 / ADA / CM / Direct

SINGING THE MOTHER COUNTRIES
CD __________ RIVCD 9912
Riverside / May '97 / ADA

SINGING VALLEYS, THE
CD __________ SCDB 7054
Sain / Feb '97 / ADA / Direct / Greyhound

SINGLE MINDED
CD __________ CDWIKD 109
Big Beat / Jun '92 / Pinnacle

SINGLES BAR, THE
Achtung salaam: *Sparkes, Neil & The Last Tribe* / Is the 'erb dope: *Mr. Electric Triangle* / Omshanti: *Solar Plexus* / When you feel good, things can turn: *Peanutbutter Wolf* / Strong vibrations: *Improvised Explosive* / Bite the bullet: *Nobby Stylus* / Mr. kiss kiss bong bong: *James Bong* / Quelle aventure: *Nose & Menelik* / Everybody loves the sunshine: *Quiet Boys* / Causeway: *Reality Drip* / Jihad: *Man Called Adam*
CD __________ TKCDM 45
2 Kool / Apr '97 / Pinnacle / SRD

SINNERS & SAINTS
CD __________ DOCD 5106
Document / Nov '92 / ADA / Hot Shot / Jazz Music

SIR LLOYD HITS VOL.2
CD __________ SLGRCD 001
Sir Lloyd / Mar '96 / Jet Star

SISSY MAN BLUES (Straight/Gay Blues & Jazz Vocals)
CD __________ JASSCD 13
Jass / Oct '91 / ADA / Cadillac / CM / Direct / Jazz Music

SISTERS (Folksong)
CD __________ SOW 1001
Sisters Of The World / Oct '95 / Direct

SISTERS IN REGGAE VOL.1
CD __________ D 19972
Far I / Sep '96 / Jet Star

SISTERS IN REGGAE VOL.2
CD __________ D 31520
Far I / Sep '96 / Jet Star

SISTERS OF SWING VOL.1
CD __________ 5352252
PolyGram TV / Jan '96 / PolyGram

SISTERS OF SWING VOL.2
Twenty foreplay: *Jackson, Janet* / I can't tell you why: *Brownstone* / Sweet funky thing: *Eternal* / I'm goin' down: *Blige, Mary J.* / Desire: *Nu Colours* / Celebration of life: *Truce* / Sweetness: *Gayle, Michelle* / Will you be my baby: *Infiniti* / Gimme that body: *Q-Tee* / Whatta man: *Salt n' Pepa & En Vogue* / Give me a little more time: *Gabrielle* / Mama said: *Anderson, Carleen* / I fell (so you could catch me): *Nelson, Shara* / Never knew love like this: *Henry, Pauline & Wayne Marshall* / Moving on up: *Knight, Beverley* / I wanna love you: *Jade* / I'm so into you: *SWV* / Love groove: *Smooth* / (At your best) You are love: *Aaliyah*
CD __________ 5354752
PolyGram TV / Apr '96 / PolyGram

SISTERS OF SWING VOL.3 (2CD Set)
You're makin' me high: *Braxton, Toni* / Sometimes: *Brand New Heavies* / Do you know: *Gayle, Michelle* / If you really cared: *Gabrielle* / Waterfalls: *TLC* / Grapevyne: *Brownstone* / Request line: *Zhane* / Tell me: *Groove Theory* / Revival: *Girault, Martine* / Steelo: *702* / I'm not feeling you: *Michelle, Yvette* / You will rise: *Sweet Back* / Runaway: *Nu Yorican Soul* / Remember me: *Blueboy* / Mr. Big stuff: *Queen Latifah* / Ain't no player: *Jay-Z & Foxxy Brown* / Can't knock the hustle: *Jay-Z & Mary J. Blige* / Shoop: *Salt n' Pepa* / Shy guy: *King, Diana* / You've got the love: *Source & Candi Staton* / Walk on by: *Gabrielle* / You're the one I love: *Ama, Shola* / Sentimental: *Cox, Deborah* / Over and over: *Johnson, Puff* / You're the one: *SWV* / Escaping: *Carroll, Dina* / I will survive: *Savage, Chantay* / Don't walk away: *Jade* / There ain't nothing like the love: *Montage* / Thing I like: *Aaliyah* / Before you walk out of my life: *Monica* / Undercover lover: *Smooth* / True spirit: *Anderson, Carleen* / Stay: *Ndegeocello, Me'shell* / I was made to love you: *Cato, Lorraine* / Show me: *Dawson, Dana* / Keep on movin': *Soul II Soul & Caron Wheeler* / Down that road: *Nelson, Shara* / Feel so high: *Des'ree*
CD Set __________ 5534652
PolyGram TV / May '97 / PolyGram

SIX FLAGS
CD __________ EYEUKCD 004
Harthouse / Aug '95 / Mo's Music Machine / Prime / Vital

SIX STAGE PHASER
CD __________ VC 108CD
Vinyl Communication / Mar '97 / Cargo / Greyhound / Plastic Head

SIX STRING BOOGIE (The Power Of Blues Guitar)
Enter the tornado: *Wilson, U.P. & Paul Aorta/The Kingpins* / Hold on baby: *Wilson, U.P. & Paul Aorta/The Kingpins* / Prancing: *Turner, Ike* / Bessie Mae: *Gibson, Lacy & Sunnyland Slim* / House rent boogie: *Hooker, John Lee* / Leave me alone: *Benton, Buster* / Somebody loan me a dime: *Robinson, Fenton* / Texas love: *Pollock, Mark* / Blue light: *Mighty Houserockers* / Shake 'em on down: *McDowell, 'Mississippi' Fred* / You're gonna need me: *Allison, Luther* / All by myself: *Murphy, Matt & Memphis Slim* / Walked all night long: *Smith, Byther* / Well alright then: *Morgan, Mike* / First time I met the blues: *Guy, Buddy* / Little bit worried: *Sharpville, Todd* / Dust my broom: *Hooker, Earl* / Way you dance: *Green, Peter & Mick/Enemy Within* / Little Stevie's shuffle: *Elmores*
CD __________ MCCD 151
Music Club / Feb '94 / Disc / THE

SIZHU/SILK BAMBOO
CD __________ PAN 2030CD
Pan / Feb '95 / ADA / CM / Direct

SIZZLIN' SUMMER HITS
Macarena: *Trio Del Sol* / Rio-mix: *Trio Del Sol* / Girl from Ipanema: *Gilberto, Astrud* / Limbo rock: *Checker, Chubby* / Abele: *Osibisa* / Lambada de Americana: *Brazil* / Banana boat song: *Trio Del Sol* / We wanna go dancing: *Trio Del Sol* / Mamae eu quero: *Gilberto, Astrud* / (Sittin' on the) dock of the bay: *Club Safari* / One note Samba: *Shaw, Sandie* / (Do the) Salsa: *Jackson, Latoya* / Time is right: *Osibisa* / Let your sunshine: *Trio Del Sol* / Saragossa: *Trio Del Sol* / Lambadie lambadia: *Brazil* / Let's limbo some more: *Checker, Chubby* / La bamba: *Lopez, Trini*
CD __________ DGR 1113
DGR / Sep '96 / Target/BMG

SIZZLING COUNTRY DANCING (2CD Set)
CD Set __________ MCD 211612
MCA / Mar '97 / BMG

SIZZLING THE BLUES (New Orleans 1927-1929)
I haven't got a dollar to pay the house rent man: *Davis, Genevieve* / I've got that something: *Davis, Genevieve* / Pretty Audrey: *Dumaine, Louis Jazzola Eight* / To-wa-bac-a-wa: *Dumaine, Louis Jazzola Eight* / Franklin Street blues: *Dumaine, Louis Jazzola Eight* / Red onion drag: *Dumaine, Louis Jazzola Eight* / Mama cookie: *Cook, Ann* / He's the sweetest black man in town: *Cook, Ann* / Panama: *Miller, Johnny New Orleans Frollickers* / Dippermouth blues: *Miller, Johnny New Orleans Frollickers* / Sizzling the blues: *Hazel, Monk & His Bienville Roof Orchestra* / High society: *Hazel, Monk & His Bienville Roof Orchestra* / Git wit it: *Hazel, Monk & His Bienville Roof Orchestra* / Ideas: *Hazel, Monk & His Bienville Roof Orchestra* / Astoria strut: *Jones & Collins Astoria Hot Eight* / Duet stomp: *Jones & Collins Astoria Hot Eight* / Damp weather: *Jones & Collins Astoria Hot Eight* / Tip easy blues: *Jones & Collins Astoria Hot Eight*
CD __________ DGF 5
Frog / May '95 / Cadillac / Jazz Music / Wellard

SKA - THE THIRD WAVE VOL.2
CD __________ SH 5709
Shanachie / Jun '96 / ADA / Greensleeves / Koch

SKA - THE THIRD WAVE VOL.3
CD __________ SH 5723
Shanachie / May '97 / ADA / Greensleeves / Koch

SKA ARCHIVE
CD __________ RMCD 202
Rialto / Sep '96 / Disc / Total/BMG

SKA BEATS
Just a feeling: *Bad Manners* / On my radio: *Selecter* / Big six: *Judge Dread* / Sally Brown: *Aitken, Laurel & The Loafers* / Universe: *Big 5* / Mirror in the bathroom: *International Beat* / Al Capone: *Hotknives* / I can see cleary now: *Black, Pauline* / Ska pig: *Mark Foggos's Skasters* / Prince of peace: *Maroon Town* / Ska'd for life: *Ska-Dows* / Darling: *Riffs* / Samson & Delilah: *Bad Manners* / Right on King Hammond: *King Hammond* / Ska skank: *Natural Rhythm* / Look at me now: *Volcanoes* / Long shot kick de bucket: *Ska Boom* / Limehouse lady: *Kay, Arthur Originals*
CD __________ EMPRCD 646
Emporio / Oct '96 / Disc

SKA BEATS VOL.1
Mental ska (the rap): *Longsy D* / Just keep rockin': *Double Trouble & Rebel MC* / Force ten from Navarone: *Roughneck* / Musical scorcha: *Rackit Allstar* / Resolution '99: *Maroon Town* / Rock to dis (house mix): *Jamaica Mean Time* / We play ska: *Children Of The Night* / This is ska (Buster's original ska mix): *Longsy D & Buster Bloodvessel* / Skanking with the toreadors: *Ministry Of Ska* / Rude boy shuffle: *Rude Boys* / Swingin' thing: *Flowers Ltd & BMG*
CD __________ SKACID 001CD
Beechwood / Nov '89 / Beechwood/BMG / Pinnacle

SKA BONANZA (2CD Set)
CD Set __________ CDHB 86
Heartbeat / Feb '92 / ADA / Direct / Greensleeves / Jet Star

SKA BOOGIE
You got me rocking: *Aitken, Laurel & Friends* / Millie girl: *Gray, Owen* / Pink Lane shuffle: *Reid, Duke* / Worried over you: *Keith & Enid* / Parapinto boogie: *Clarke, Lloyd* / I wanna love: *Jiving Juniors* / Shake a leg: *Morgan, Derrick* / Humpty Dumpty: *Morris, Eric* / Wasp: *Bubbles* / On the beach: *Gray, Owen* / Open up bartender: *Prince Buster* / Slow boat: *Joe, Al T.* / Never never: *Aitken, Bobby* / South Virginia: *Aitken, Bobby* / Busters Allstars: *Aitken, Bobby* / Hush baby: *Rudy & Sketto* / Oh Carolina: *Folkes Brothers & Count Ossie* / Midnight train: *Dixon, Errol* / Mash Mr. Lee: *Lee, Byron & The Dragonaires* / I'm on my own: *Joe, Al T.* / Running around: *Joe, Al T.*
CD __________ NEXCD 254
Sequel / Oct '93 / BMG

SKA CRAZY
CD __________ PLSCD 104
Pulse / Apr '96 / BMG

SKA DOWN HER WAY (Women Of Ska)
Lyin' ass bitch: *Fishbone* / You're wondering: *Skatalites* / Rotten banana legs: *Skankin' Pickle* / Hung up: *Bim Skala Bim* / Darling boy: *Checkered Cabs* / High school: *Green, Isaac & The Skalars* / Look at you now: *Agent 99* / I wish you were a beer: *Skandalous All Stars* / Cloven: *Skahumbug*
CD __________ SH 5725
Shanachie / Jun '97 / ADA / Greensleeves / Koch

SKA DOWN JAMAICA WAY
CD __________ TDCD 101
Top Deck / Mar '97 / SRD

SKA FANTASTIC
CD __________ RB 3012
Reggae Best / Mar '95 / Grapevine/ PolyGram

SKA FOR SKA'S SAKE
Skadansk: *Mark Foggos's Skasters* / It's so easy: *Loafers* / WLN: *Hotknives* / King Hammond shuffle: *King Hammond* / City riot: *Maroon Town* / Off The Shelf tonight: *Off The Shelf* / Blind date: *Riffs* / Another town: *Mr. Review* / Driving me to drink: *Skandal* / One eyed lodger: *Judge Dread* / Ska sax: *Pick it up* / Woman: *Pork Hunts*
CD __________ DOJOCD 97
Dojo / Feb '94 / Disc

SKA IS THE LIMIT
On my radio: *Selecter* / Too much too young: *Specials* / Gangsters: *Special AKA* / Really saying something: *Fun Boy Three & Bananarama* / Free yourself: *Untouchables* / Work out: *Dekker, Desmond* / Message to Rudy: *Specials & Rico* / Three minute hero: *Selecter* / Ghost town: *Specials* / I spy for the FBI: *Untouchables* / Please don't bend: *Dekker, Desmond* / What I like most about you is your girlfriend: *Special AKA* / It ain't what you do it's the way that you do it: *Fun Boy Three & Bananarama* / Wild child: *Untouchables*
CD __________ DC 880742
Disky / May '97 / Disky / THE

SKA IS THE LIMIT/HISTORY OF SKA
CD __________ RNCD 2073
Rhino / Oct '94 / Grapevine/PolyGram / Jet Star

SKA ISLAND
CD __________ 5243922
Island / Sep '97 / PolyGram

SKA MANIA
CD __________ DINCD 86
Dino / May '95 / Pinnacle

SKA SPECTACULAR VOL.1
CD __________ CPCD 8021
Charly / Feb '94 / Koch

SKA SPECTACULAR VOL.2
CD __________ CPCD 8022
Charly / Feb '94 / Koch

SKA STARS OF THE 80'S
CD __________ GAZCD 006
Gaz's Rockin' Records / Apr '90 / Shellshock/Disc

SKA TRAX - THE NEXT GENERATION VOL.1
CD __________ EFA 119962
Heatwave / Dec '94 / SRD

SKA TRAX - THE NEXT GENERATION VOL.2
CD __________ EFA 127882
Heatwave / Jan '96 / SRD

SKA WARS (4CD Set)
CD Set __________ MBSCD 439
Castle / Nov '95 / BMG

SKA ZONE
CD __________ TX 51200CD
Triple X / Jun '97 / Plastic Head

SKANDALOUS (I've Gotcha Covered)
Secret agent man: *Toasters* / Guns of Navarone: *Skatalites* / Paranoid: *Ruder Than You* / Sanford and Son: *PErFect ThYroID* / Sunshine of your love: *Bim Skala Bim* / Brown eyed girl: *Magadog* / Scooby Doo: *Jinkies* / Flintstones: *Benuts* / Lonesome track: *Regatta 69* / Batman movie theme: *Skavoovie & the Epitones* / Come together: *PErFect ThYroID* / Police woman: *Skatalites* / For the turnstiles: *Bim Skala Bim* / Hawa negila: *Bluekilla*
CD _______ SH 5717
Shanachie / Dec '96 / ADA / Greensleeves / Koch

SKANK 3 - 15 COMMANDMENTS
CD _______ DOJOCD 98
Dojo / May '93 / Disc

SKANK LICENSED TO SKA
Skinhead love affair: *Busters All Stars* / Fire: *Bluebeat* / Julie Julie: *Braces* / Orion: *Busters* / Laughing loafers: *Loafers* / Ska skank down party: *Skaos* / Jump start: *Forest Hillbillies* / Pipeline: *Busters All Stars* / Safety guards: *Bluebeat* / Letter: *Braces* / Keen on games: *Busters* / Melancholy Sally: *Loafers* / Struggle: *Skaos* / Shocker: *Toasters*
CD _______ DOJOCD 96
Dojo / Feb '94 / Disc

SKANKIN' IN THE PIT
CD _______ HR 17CD
Hopeless / Feb '97 / Cargo / Greyhound

SKANKIN' ROUND THE WORLD VOL.1
CD _______ DOJOCD 175
Dojo / Nov '93 / Disc

SKANKIN' ROUND THE WORLD VOL.3
CD _______ DOJOCD 185
Dojo / Feb '94 / Disc

SKANKIN' ROUND THE WORLD VOL.4
CD _______ DOJOCD 186
Dojo / Feb '94 / Disc

SKA'S THE LIMIT (2CD Set)
CD Set _______ RNCD 2075
Rhino / Oct '94 / Grapevine/PolyGram / Jet Star

SKATERS HAVE MORE FUN
CD _______ EFA 610602
Skate / Jul '97 / SRD

SKINHEAD CLASSICS
CD _______ CDTRD 407
Trojan / Mar '94 / Direct / Jet Star

SKINHEAD REVOLT
Skinhead revolt: *Joe The Boss* / What will your mother say: *Jones, Clancy* / If it don't work out: *Pat Kelly* / Champion: *GG All Stars* / Little better: *Parks, Lloyd* / Left with a broken heart: *Paragons* / In the spirit: *Charmers, Lloyd* / Reggae girl: *Tennors* / Death a come: *Charmers, Lloyd* / Skinhead speaks his mind: *Hothead All Stars* / Dark end of the street: *Pat Kelly* / Shu be du: *Eccles, Clancy* / Come a little closer: *Donaldson, Eric* / Barbabus: *GG All Stars* / Loving reggae: *Maytones* / Ease me up officer: *Soul Ofrus* / Got to get away: *Paragons* / To love somebody: *Brown, Buster* / Place called happiness: *Mills, Rudy* / Last call: *Silver Stars*
CD _______ CDTRL 329
Trojan / Mar '94 / Direct / Jet Star

SKINNINGROVE BAY
Save a place for me / Carlin how / Skinningrove Bay / Filten castle / Deep green / Old man of the ocean / North country girl / Abess St. Hilda
CD _______ C5CD 580
See For Miles/C5 / Mar '97 / Pinnacle

SKINT PRESENTS BRASSIC BEATS VOL.1
CD _______ BRASSIC 1CD
Skint / Jul '96 / 3mv/Vital / Mo's Music Machine / Prime

SKINT PRESENTS BRASSIC BEATS VOL.2
CD _______ BRASSIC 4CD
Skint / Apr '97 / 3mv/Vital / Mo's Music Machine / Prime

SKIRL OF PIPES VOL.1, THE
CD _______ PACD 031
Music Masters / Mar '94 / Midland CD Club

SKUNK - THIS SOME BAD WEED VOL.1
Dances with fire: *Mojo Risin'* / Return of Rasputin: *Aardvark* / Movement, the message: *Soundcraft* / Sinister footwork: *3rd Alternative* / All of your mind: *Blood Runs Dry* / Out of my paradise: *Aardvark* / Chant 4 freedom: *Vu 2* / Won't cry you: *SULO* / Fox on the cut: *Babyfox* / No apologies: *3rd Alternative* / Slider: *Paingang* / One love: *Molara* / 20,000 feet: *Vu 2* / Wibbler: *Soundcraft* / This some bad weed: *Soundcraft*
CD _______ POOCD 001
Skunk / Dec '93 / Pinnacle

SKUNK - THIS SOME BAD WEED VOL.2
CD _______ POOCD 2
Skunk / Oct '94 / Pinnacle

SKY HIGH (20 Smash Hits Of The 70's)
Down the dustpipe: *Status Quo* / Apeman: *Kinks* / Ruby Tuesday: *Melanie* / In the summertime: *Mungo Jerry* / (It's like a) Sad old kinda movie: *Pickettywitch* / You don't mess around with Jim: *Croce, Jim* / Lion sleeps tonight: *Newman, Dave* / Strange band: *Family* / I get the sweetest feeling: *Wilson, Jackie* / (Dancing) on a Saturday night: *Blue, Barry* / Midnight train to Georgia: *Knight, Gladys & The Pips* / Broken down angel: *Nazareth* / Beach baby: *First Class* / Pillow talk: *Sylvia* / Me and my life: *Tremeloes* / Sky high: *Jigsaw* / Operator (That's not the way it feels): *Croce, Jim* / Mean girl: *Status Quo* / You'll never know what you're missing: *Real Thing* / Natural born bugie: *Humble Pie*
CD _______ TRTCD 107
TrueTrax / Oct '94 / THE

SLAM CHOPS
CD _______ TX 510202
Triple X / Jul '95 / Plastic Head

SLAMMIN' SETS VOL.1
Where's the hip hop: *Active Force* / Back in business: *Ultimate Buzz* / Merlins funfair: *Forbes, Davie* / Keeping alive: *Forbes, Davie* / Reach out: *Forbes & Cyclone* / Don curly wurly: *Forbes & Cyclone* / Breakdown on the floor: *Active Force* / Foreever and a day: *Active Force* / Apoclypse now: *Forbes, Davie* / Getting there: *Forbes, Davie*
CD _______ DCSR 009
Clubscene / Jun '97 / Clubscene / Grapevine/PolyGram / Mo's Music Machine / Prime

SLANGED
CD _______ EFA 04914CD
City Slang / Nov '92 / RTM/Disc

SLAUGHTERED VOL.1
CD _______ SPV 07725162
SPV / Feb '94 / Koch / Plastic Head

SLAUGHTERED VOL.2
CD _______ SPV 07725172
SPV / Jun '94 / Koch / Plastic Head

SLENG TENG EXTRAVAGANZA
CD _______ GRELCD 209
Greensleeves / May '95 / Jet Star / SRD

SLIDE GUITAR BLUES
CD _______ IGOCD 2030
Indigo / Oct '95 / ADA / Direct

SLIDE GUITAR GOSPEL 1944-1964
CD _______ DOCD 5222
Document / Apr '94 / ADA / Hot Shot / Jazz Music

SLIDE GUITAR VOL.1 (Bottles, Knives & Steel)
Bottleneck blues: *Weaver & Beasley* / Untitled: *Barbecue Bob* / God don't never change: *Johnson, 'Blind' Willie* / Dark was the night: *Johnson, 'Blind' Willie* / St. Louis blues: *Weaver & Beasley* / Experience blues: *Willis, Ruth & Blind Willie McTell* / Guitar rag: *Weaver, Sylvester* / You can't get that stuff no more: *Tampa Red* / High sheriff blues: *Patton, Charlie* / Homesick and lonesome blues: *Fuller, 'Blind' Boy* / Packin' trunk blues: *Leadbelly* / I believe I'll make a change: *Weldon, Casey Bill* / Don't sell it (don't give it away): *Woods, Buddy* / Muscat Hill blues: *Woods, Buddy* / Travelling riverside blues: *Johnson, Robert* / Bukka's jitterbug swing: *White, Bukka* / Special stream line: *White, Bukka* / Swing low, sweet chariot: *Terrell, Sister O.M.* / Pearline: *House, Son*
CD _______ 4672512
CBS / Oct '90 / Sony

SLIDE GUITAR VOL.2
CD _______ 4721912
Columbia / May '93 / Sony

SLIDIN'...SOME SLIDE
CD _______ BB 9533CD
Bullseye Blues / Jan '94 / Direct

SLIP 'N' SLIDE VOL.3
CD _______ SLIPCD 51
Slip 'n' Slide / Oct '96 / Amato Disco / Prime / RTM/Disc / Vital

SLIPPING AROUND
CD _______ HDHCD 010
HDH / Oct '89 / Pinnacle

SLOVENIA IRP
CD _______ CD 13255
Nika / Mar '93 / SRD

SLOW JAMS
CD _______ DINCD 129
Dino / Oct '96 / Pinnacle

SLOW MOTION (14 Urban Contemporary Love Ballads)
Your body's calling: *R Kelly* / Let me do U: *POV* / All night: *Me 2 U* / Please tell me tonight: *Motiv* / Don't go nowhere: *Riff* / Always: *Mint Condition* / When I need somebody: *Tresvant, Ralph* / I got a thang 4 ya: *Low Key* / La la love: *Avila, Bobby Ross* / Make love 2 me: *Lorenzo* / Baby it's real: *Serenade* / I'll be there for you: *ML* / Wait for me: *Chalant* / Gangsta lean: *DRS*
CD _______ CDELV 16
Elevate / Jun '94 / 3mv/Sony

SLOW 'N' MOODY, BLACK 'N' BLUESY
Nothing can change this love: *Hill, Z.Z.* / You messed up my mind: *Hammond, Clay* / I can't stand it: *Holiday, Jimmy* / Directly from my heart: *Little Richard* / I don't need: *Turner, Ike & Tina* / Let's get together: *Arthur & Mary* / Darling I'm standing by you: *Jones, Jeanette* / Baby I'll come right away: *Love, Mary* / If I'd lose you: *Day, Jackie* / I don't wanna lose you: *Young, Tami* / Baby, come to me: *Little Henry & The Shamrocks* / Ain't nobody's business if I do: *King, B.B.* / Every dog has his day: *Copeland, Johnny* / Baby, what you want me to do: *Little Richard* / Baby I'll come: *Love, Mary* / Everybody needs somebody: *Love, Mary* / Weep no more: *Terry & The Tyrants* / It's real: *Robbins, Jimmy* / Can't count the days: *Robbins, Jimmy* / Whenever I can't sleep: *Gauff, Willie & The Love Brothers* / Last one to know: *Haywood, Joe* / Mr. President: *Haywood, Joe* / Woman needs a man: *Baker, Yvonne* / Farewell: *Gauff, Willie & The Love Brothers* / Why should I be the one: *Gauff, Willie & The Love Brothers* / I'll come back to you: *Mighty Hannibal* / Consider yourself: *Johnson, Stacey*
CD _______ CDKEND 003
Kent / Nov '94 / Pinnacle

SLOW PUNANY
CD _______ GPCD 006
Gussie P / Dec '93 / Jet Star

SLY & ROBBIE'S RAGGA PON TOP
Move with the crowd: *Baby Wayne* / Little crook: *Papa San* / Hold me: *Joseph Stepper* / Ole horse: *Red Dragon* / Thief: *Captain Berkley* / Boom boom bye: *Redrose & Round Head* / Rum shaker: *Nardo Ranks* / Love lullaby: *General Degree* / Give her the credit: *Papa San* / Mony fi spend: *Captain Berkley* / Makosa: *Papa San*
CD _______ 111932
Musidisc / Feb '94 / Discovery

SMALL BAND SWING VOL.1 1935-1937 (Made In Swinton)
CD _______ CVA 7993
Jazz Document / Jan '97 / Cadillac / Jazz Music

SMALL GROUP SWING
Upstairs: *Smith, Stuff* / I ain't got nobody: *Webb, Chick* / In a little Spanish town: *Webb, Chick* / Chicken and waffles: *Berigan, Bunny* / Swingin' in the coconut trees: *Jordan, Louis* / Doug the Jitterbug: *Jordan, Louis* / Baby, won't you please come home: *Spencer Trio* / Lorna Doone shortbread: *Spencer Trio* / Three little words: *Freeman, Bud* / Raggin' the scale: *Venuti, Joe* / Josephine: *Rollini, Adrian* / Dr. Livingstone, I presume: *Shaw, Artie* / When the quail come back to San Quentin: *Shaw, Artie* / Countless blues: *Kansas City Six* / Home James: *James, Harry* / Body and soul: *Tatum, Art* / I'll take the South: *Brown, Cleo* / Minor Drag: *Waller, Fats* / Oh Susannah, dust off that old piano: *New Orleans Rhythm Kings* / 29th and dearborn: *Dodds, Johnny* / China boy: *Goodman, Benny* / When the midnight choo-choo leaves for Alabam': *Dorsey, Tommy*
CD _______ PPCD 78102
Past Perfect / Feb '95 / Glass Gramophone Co.

SMALL WONDER PUNK SINGLES COLLECTION
Mucky pup: *Puncture* / Hungry: *Zeros* / Radio wunderbar: *Carpettes* / Safety pin stuck in my heart: *Fitzgerald, Patrick* / GLC: *Menace* / Buy me sell me: *Fitzgerald, Patrick* / Nineteen and mad: *Leyton Buzzards* / Puppet life: *Punishment Of Luxury* / Small wonder: *Carpettes* / Little Miss Perfect: *Demon Preacher* / Never been so stuck: *Nicky & The Dots* / New way: *Wall* / Disco love: *Molesters* / End: *Cravats* / Last year's youth: *Menace* / DNA: *Murder The Disturbed* / End of civilisation: *Molesters* / Flares and slippers: *Cockney Rejects* / Violence grows: *Fatal Microbes* / Exchange: *Wall* / Time tunnel: *English Sub-titles* / Soft ground: *Prole* / Precinct: *Cravats* / You're driving me: *Cravats* / Off the beach: *Cravats* / They've got it all wrong: *Anthrax*
CD _______ CDPUNK 29
Anagram / Mar '94 / Cargo / Pinnacle

SMALL WONDER PUNK SINGLES VOL.2
Can't play rock n roll: *Puncture* / Radio fun: *Zeros* / How about me and you: *Carpettes* / Set we free: *Fitzgerald, Patrick* / I'm civilised: *Menace* / Little dippers: *Fitzgerald, Patrick* / Irrelevant battles: *Fitzgerald, Patrick* / Youthanasia: *Leyton Buzzards* / Demon: *Punishment Of Luxury* / 2 NE 1: *Carpettes* / Linoleum walk: *Nicky & The Dots* / Suckers: *Wall* / Uniforms: *Wall* / Burning bridges cravats: *Cravats* / I am the dreg: *Cravats* / Who's in here with me / Commuter man: *Molesters* / Carry no banners: *Menace* / Walking corpses: *Murder The Disturbed* / Girl behind the curtain: *Molesters* / Police car: *Cockney Rejects* / Beautiful picture: *Fatal Microbes* / Sweat: *English Sub-titles* / SMK: *Prole* / What will tomorrow: *Anthrax*
CD _______ CDPUNK 70
Anagram / Jan '96 / Cargo / Pinnacle

SMALLTALK
Colonel Fraser / Mary Ann MacInnes / Famous bridge / Kail and pudding / Cumha coire a 'cheathaich / Jock Hawk / New claret / Low country dance / Advasar Blacksmith / Black haired lad / Shetland fiddler / Over the sea to nova scotia / Rose Anderson / Les vielles bottiness / Heights of casino / 'S truagh nach do dh'fhuirich / Fhorton jig / James Byrne's jig / Duncan McKillop / Bee in the knickers / Fil o ro
CD _______ CDTRAX 079
Greentrax / Sep '94 / ADA / Direct / Duncans / Highlander

SMASH HITS MIX '97 (2CD Set)
Wannabe: *Spice Girls* / Flava: *Andre, Peter* / We've got it goin' on: *Backstreet Boys* / Naked: *Louise* / When I fall in love: *Ant & Dec* / Spinning the wheel: *Michael, George* / Don't stop movin': *Livin' Joy* / Love sensation: *911* / Don't make me wait: *911* / Jazz it up: *Reel 2 Real* / Gangsta's paradise: *Coolio & LV* / I got 5 on it: *Luniz* / Good thing: *Eternal* / Freedom: *Williams, Robbie* / Love II love: *Damage* / If you leave me now: *Upside Down* / Crazy chance: *Kavana* / Oh what a night (December '63): *Clock* / That girl: *Priest, Maxi & Shaggy* / X Files theme: *DJ Dado* / Don't look back in anger: *Oasis* / Day we caught the train: *Ocean Colour Scene* / Breakfast at Tiffany's: *Deep Blue Something* / You're gorgeous: *Baby Bird* / Spaceman: *Babylon Zoo* / Breathe: *Prodigy* / Trash: *Suede* / Charmless man: *Blur* / Female of the species: *Space* / Oh yeah: *Ash* / Stars: *Dubstar* / Stupid girl: *Garbage* / Going out: *Supergrass* / Something for the weekend: *Divine Comedy* / Wrong: *Everything But The Girl* / Atom bomb: *Fluke* / Stamp: *Healy, Jeremy & Amos* / Seven days and one week: *BBE* / Born slippy: *Underworld* / I wanna be a hippy: *Technohead*
CD Set _______ VTDCD 110
Virgin / Dec '96 / EMI

SMASH HITS OF THE 1960'S VOL.1
CD _______ DCC 866792
Disky / Aug '96 / Disky / THE

SMASH HITS OF THE 1960'S VOL.2
CD _______ DC 866802
Disky / Aug '96 / Disky / THE

SMASH HITS OF THE 1960'S VOL.3
CD _______ DC 866812
Disky / Aug '96 / Disky / THE

SMASH HITS SUMMER '97 (2CD Set)
I wannabe the only one: *Eternal & Bebe Winans* / I believe I can fly: *Kelly, R* / Wonderful tonight: *Damage* / Quit playin' games with (my heart): *Backstreet Boys* / Who do you think you are: *Spice Girls* / Id before I die: *Williams, Robbie* / Ready to go: *Republica* / Bellisima: *DJ Quicksilver* / Encore une fois: *Sash* / Star people '97: *Michael, George* / Professional widow: *Amos, Tori* / Ready or not: *Course* / Fresh: *Gina G* / Body shakin': *911* / Natural: *Andre, Peter* / I can make you feel good: *Kavana* / Clementine: *Owen, Mark* / Let me in: *OTT* / One kiss from heaven: *Louise* / Extremis: *Hal & Gillian Anderson* / Words: *Boyzone* / Forever: *Boyzone* / I need you: *3T* / Moan and groan: *Morrison, Mark* / Do you know: *Gayle, Michelle* / Walk on by: *Gabrielle* / Remember me: *Blueboy* / I have peace: *Strike* / You got the love: *Source & Candi Staton* / Underwater love: *Smoke City* / Shout: *Ant & Dec* / Your woman: *White Town* / North country boy: *Charlatans* / Tattva: *Kula Shaker* / Song 2: *Blur* / Richard III: *Supergrass* / Smile: *Supernaturals* / Kowalski: *Primal Scream* / Nightmare: *Brainbug* / Flash: *BBE* / Theme from the Professionals: *Johnson, Laurie London Big Band*
CD Set _______ VTDCD 144
Virgin / Jun '97 / EMI

SMELL THE FUZZ
CD _______ 398417010CD
Metal Blade / Oct '96 / Pinnacle / Plastic Head

SMILE MIX SESSION VOL.2
CD _______ SM 80302
Profile / Feb '97 / Pinnacle

SMITHSONIAN FOLKWAYS AMERICAN ROOTS COLLECTION
CD _______ SFWCD 40062
Smithsonian Folkways / Jul '96 / ADA / Cadillac / CM / Direct / Koch

SMOKE & FIRE
CD _______ CDTB 022
Magnum Music / Sep '94 / TKO Magnum

SMOKE GETS IN YOUR EYES (Those Romantic Fifties)
Smoke gets in your eyes: *Mantovani Orchestra* / Love letters in the sand: *Chacksfield, Frank & His Orchestra* / Two different worlds: *Mantovani Orchestra* / Secret love: *Mantovani Orchestra* / Tender trap: *Heath, Ted & His Music* / Autumn leaves: *Mantovani Orchestra* / Just in time: *Heath, Ted & His Music* / Answer me: *Mantovani Orchestra* / Unforgettable: *Ternent, Billy & His Orchestra* / Catch a falling star: *Mantovani Orchestra* / Till: *Ternent, Billy & His Orchestra* / True love: *Mantovani Orchestra* / Unchained melody: *Heath, Ted & His Music* / When I fall in love: *Mantovani Orchestra* / Smile: *Chacksfield, Frank & His Orchestra* / Hey there: *Mantovani Orchestra* / I've grown accustomed to her face: *Aldrich, Ronnie & His Piano/The Festival Orchestra* / Love is a many splendoured thing: *Mantovani Orchestra*
CD _______ 8440642
Eclipse / May '91 / PolyGram

SMOKE RINGS
CD ______ **PHONTCD 7641**
Phontastic / '93 / Cadillac / Jazz Music / Wellard

SMOKERS INC.
CD ______ **SINCCD 001**
No Smoking / Nov '96 / SRD

SMOOCHIN' IN NEW YORK
CD ______ **CDGR 174**
Charly / Jul '97 / Koch

SMOOTH ONE, A
CD ______ **CECD 3**
Collector's Edition / Feb '96 / TKO Magnum

SMYRNAIC SONG IN GREECE 1928-1935, THE
CD ______ **HTCD 27**
Heritage / Feb '95 / ADA / Direct / Hot Shot / Jazz Music / Swift / Wellard

SNAKEBITE CITY
CD ______ **BLU 06**
Blue Fire / Apr '95 / Cargo / SRD

SNAKEBITE CITY VOL.4
CD ______ **BLU 07**
Blue Fire / Mar '97 / Cargo / SRD

SNAKEBITE CITY VOL.5
CD ______ **BLU 08**
Blue Fire / Oct '96 / Cargo / SRD

SNAKEBITE CITY VOL.6
CD ______ **BLU 09**
Blue Fire / Apr '97 / Cargo / SRD

SNAP - THE ESSENTIAL MIX SHOW (2CD Set)
Oasis: *Paragliders* / Vicious circle: *Poltergeist* / Love above: *Fini Tribe* / Where are you: *16 Bit* / Original: *Leftfield* / Flying souls: *Sequencer* / Luck spray: *Redeye* / Survive: *Brothers Grimm* / Raise your hands: *Boston Bruins* / Drive: *Trancesetters* / Melt: *Leftfield* / Aqualite: *Wavemaker* / Happy rose: *Arcus* / Tension: *Reunification* / Dark side of the Moog: *Schulze, Klaus* / Classix: *Arcus* / Mushroom shaped: *Fini Tribe* / Raven: *16 Bit*
CD ______ **5286752**
Mercury / Jul '96 / PolyGram

SNAPOLOGY
Cherry man: *Wannadies* / It's absence: *Souls* / On your bedroom floor: *This Perfect Day* / Sheena: *Eggstone* / Under surface: *Baby Lemonade* / Miss thing-a-magic: *Simpkins* / It's not that easy: *Poverty Stinks* / SU song: *Singer* / Seven years: *Scents* / Marine love (demo): *Easy* / Million dollar project: *Whipped Cream* / Blind: *Poodle*
CD ______ **SNAP 008**
Soap / Oct '93 / Vital

SNOWDANCE
CD ______ **399842**
Koch Presents / Jun '97 / Koch

SO BLUE SO FUNKY VOL.1 (Heroes Of The Hammond)
All about my girl: *McGriff, Jimmy* / Silver metre: *Patton, 'Big' John* / I'm movin' on: *Smith, Jimmy* / Wine, wine, wine: *Roach, Freddie* / Brown sugar: *Roach, Freddie* / Hootin' 'n' tootin': *Jackson, Fred* / Face to face: *Willette, Baby Face* / Fat Judy: *Patton, 'Big' John* / Plaza De Toros: *Young, Larry* / Boop bop bing bash: *Braith, George* / Everything I do gonh be funky: *Donaldson, Lou* / Hot rod: *Wilson, Reuben* / Butter for yo' popcorn: *McDuff, 'Brother' Jack* / Ain't it funky now: *Green, Grant*
CD ______ **BNZ 267**
Blue Note / May '91 / EMI

SO BLUE SO FUNKY VOL.2 (Heroes Of The Hammond)
Where it's at: *McGriff, Jimmy* / Meetin' here: *Amy, Curtis & Paul Bryant* / When Malindy sings: *Roach, Freddie* / Mary had a little lamb: *Braith, George* / Can heat: *Smith, Jimmy* / Morris the minor: *Holmes, Richard 'Groove'* / Minor soul: *Lytell, Jimmy* / Somethin' strange: *Willette, Baby Face* / I want to go home: *Patton, 'Big' John* / Street scene: *Young, Larry* / Kid: *Donaldson, Lou*
CD ______ **CDP 8290922**
Blue Note / Jun '94 / EMI

SO WIE ES DAMALS WAR
CD ______ **BCD 15712**
Bear Family / Mar '93 / Direct / Rollercoaster / Swift

SOARING CLASSICS (A Magical Blend Of Music And The Sounds Of Nature)
CD ______ **50562**
CMC / May '97 / BMG

SOCA CARNIVAL '96
CD ______ **960102**
Tattoo / May '96 / Jet Star

SOCA EXPLOSION (The Soul Of Calypso)
CD ______ **68935**
Tropical / Jun '97 / Discovery

SOCA GOLD 1997
CD ______ **VPCD 1499**
VP / Aug '97 / Greensleeves / Jet Star / Total/BMG

SOCA GOLD VOL.1
CD ______ **HVCD 015**
Hot Vinyl / Apr '92 / Jet Star

SOCA GOLD VOL.2
CD ______ **HVCD 016**
Hot Vinyl / Apr '92 / Jet Star

SOCA GOLD VOL.3
CD ______ **HVCD 020**
Hot Vinyl / Jan '93 / Jet Star

SOCA GOLD VOL.4
CD ______ **HVCD 021**
Hot Vinyl / Jan '93 / Jet Star

SOCA GOLD VOL.5
CD ______ **HVCD 023**
Hot Vinyl / Sep '95 / Jet Star

SOCA GOLD VOL.6
CD ______ **HVCD 024**
Hot Vinyl / Sep '95 / Jet Star

SOCA GREATEST HITS VOL.1
Fire in the back seat: *Curtis, Yvonne* / Lay with me: *Campbell, Bill* / Teaser: *Curtis, Yvonne* / Let it go: *Johnny Rhythm* / Sexy feeling: *Curtis, Yvonne* / Heat in the place: *Campbell, Bill* / Celebrate with me: *Campbell, Bill* / Lady lady: *Campbell, Bill* / Soca dance party: *Lucky* / Whine on something: *Campbell, Pete* / 11-7 (Carnival party time): *Campbell, Pete* / Hot hot hot: *Lillete* / Sugar bum bum: *Lord Diamond* / Ah feeling the feelings: *Lord Diamond* / Don't rock the ting so: *Sam, Jeff*
CD ______ **WSRCD 101**
World Sound / Sep '96 / Jet Star

SOCA GREATEST HITS VOL.2
Somebody: *Campbell, Pete* / Cool it down: *Melanesse* / Got to see you: *Campbell, Pete & Roy Alton* / Rock the music: *Wavet* / Sabina: *Parker, Belinda* / Mama Africa: *Campbell, Bill* / Maria Tebbola: *Campbell, Bill* / Serious: *Campbell, Pete* / Nearest to my heart: *Campbell, Bill* / Closer: *Campbell, Bill* / Break away: *Lucky* / Only for lovers: *Curtis, Yvonne* / Easy dancing: *Davis, Teddy* / Let me love you: *Davis, Teddy*
CD ______ **WSRCD 102**
World Sound / Sep '96 / Jet Star

SOCA PRESSURE
CD ______ **KMP 003CD**
KMP / Mar '97 / Jet Star

SOCA SAMPLER
CD ______ **HVCD 025**
Hot Vinyl / Jul '96 / Jet Star

SOCA SWITCH
CD ______ **TSS 01CD**
SJP / Mar '97 / Jet Star

SOCCER ROCKERS (Football Favourites)
Land of hope and glory / We shall not be moved / Battle hymn of the republic / BBC Grandstand theme / I'm forever blowing bubbles / You'll never walk alone / We will rock you / When the saints go marching in / Back home / He's got the whole world in his hands / We are the champions / Stars and stripes forever / Match Of The Day theme / Give peace a chance / Red flag
CD ______ **3036000072**
Carlton / Oct '95 / Carlton

SOCIAL HARP, THE
CD ______ **ROUCD 0094**
Rounder / Oct '94 / ADA / CM / Direct

SOFT METAL
CD ______ **TMPCD 013**
Temple / Mar '95 / BMG

SOFT REGGAE (18 Romantic Reggae Classics)
Wide awake in a dream: *Biggs, Barry* / Sweetest thing: *Blues Busters* / Lady: *Wade, Wayne* / Don't need your love: *Griffiths, Marcia* / Sister Love: *Isaacs, Gregory* / Woman behind the man: *Gardiner, Boris* / Sit and cry over you: *Dunkley, Errol* / Mississippi: *Scloss, Cynthia* / Let's fall in love: *Hammond, Beres* / Forgot to say I love you: *Holt, John* / If you could see me now: *Pioneers* / Moving away: *Boothe, Ken* / Baby lay down: *Schaffer, Doreen* / If it's fire you want: *Hinds, Justin* / If you wanna make love: *Biggs, Barry* / Take life easy: *Honey Boy* / Twilight time: *Sanchez* / Rockers in the rain: *George, Sophia*
CD ______ **ECD 3292**
K-Tel / Jan '97 / K-Tel

SOFT REGGAEE
Baby come back: *Pato Banton* / Baby I love your way: *Big Mountain* / Searching: *China Black* / Complimnets on your kiss: *Red Dragon* / You don't love me (no no no): *Penn, Dawn* / Mr. Loverman: *Shabba Ranks* / Best of my love: *Lewis, C.J.* / Wonderful world, beautiful people: *Cliff, Jimmy* / Shine: *Aswad* / Sweat: *Inner Circle* / It's raining: *McLean, Bitty* / Oh Carolina: *Shaggy* / Close to you: *Priest, Maxi* / I can see clearly now: *Nash, Johnny* / Let your yeah be yeah: *Pioneers* / Love of the common people: *Thomas, Nicky* / Young, gifted and black: *Bob & Marcia* / Dancing on the floor: *Third World* / Good thing going: *Minott, Sugar* / Silly games: *Kay, Janet* / Everything I own: *Boothe, Ken* / I shall sing: *Griffiths, Marcia* / I will always love you: *Hall, Pam*
CD ______ **RADCD 4**
Global TV / Jan '95 / BMG

SOFT ROCK
Suspicious minds: *Fine Young Cannibals* / Trouble: *Buckingham, Lindsey* / Little piece of heaven: *Godley & Creme* / Look away: *Big Country* / Child in time: *Deep Purple* / I got you: *Split Enz* / Cocaine: *Cale, J.J.* / Don't let the sun go down on me: *John, Elton* / Reason to believe: *Stewart, Rod* / Victims of circumstance: *Barclay James Harvest* / Like flames: *Berlin* / Mind of a toy: *Visage* / I'll find my way home: *Jon & Vangelis* / Reward: *Teardrop Explodes*
CD ______ **5506472**
Spectrum / Aug '94 / PolyGram

SOFT ROCK (2CD Set)
CD Set ______ **DCDCD 204**
Castle / Jun '95 / BMG

SOFT ROCK
CD ______ **5352482**
PolyGram TV / Jan '96 / PolyGram

SOFT ROCK CLASSICS VOL.1
You're the voice: *Farnham, John* / Nothing's gonna stop us now: *Starship* / Maneater: *Hall & Oates* / Kyrie: *Mr. Mister* / You took the words right out of my mouth: *Meat Loaf* / I hear you knockin': *Edmunds, Dave* / Bridge to your heart: *Wax* / Runaway boys: *Stray Cats* / Mean girl: *Status Quo* / American woman: *Guess Who* / Perfect day: *Reed, Lou* / Every day hurts: *Sad Cafe* / How long: *Ace* / Living next door to Alice: *Smokie* / Human touch: *Springfield, Rick* / Who's that girl: *Eurythmics*
CD ______ **74321400252**
Camden / Jul '96 / BMG

SOFT ROCK CLASSICS VOL.2
Blinded by the light: *Manfred Mann's Earthband* / War baby: *Robinson, Tom* / Broken wings: *Mr. Mister* / Love hurts: *Nazareth* / It's a heartache: *Tyler, Bonnie* / My oh my: *Sad Cafe* / Promise you made: *Cock Robin* / Satellite of love: *Reed, Lou* / White rabbit: *Jefferson Airplane* / In a broken dream: *Python Lee Jackson* / Lily was here: *Stewart, David A.* / Can't fight this feeling: *REO Speedwagon* / Lost in love: *Air Supply* / Rock the night: *Air Supply* / Modern girl: *Meat Loaf* / Spirit in the sky: *Greenbaum, Norman*
CD ______ **74321446892**
Camden / Feb '97 / BMG

SOLDIER SOLDIER (16 Military Band Favourites)
Rule Britannia: *Royal British Legion Band* / Knightsbridge march: *Blues & Royals Band* / Dambusters march: *Blues & Royals Band* / Bridge too far: *Parachute Regiment Band* / Royal ceremony: *Staff Band Of The RAOC* / Normandy veterans: *Duke Of Wellington Regiment* / Amazing grace: *Blues & Royals Band* / Royal standard: *Royal Engineers* / It's a long way to Tipperary: *Royal Irish Rangers* / High on a hill: *Royal Green Jackets* / American patrol: *9th/12th Royal Lancers* / Pipe medley: *Irish Guards Band* / Here's a health unto her majesty: *Royal Tank Regiment* / Abide with me: *Queen's Royal Irish Hussars* / Old comrade: *Blues & Royals Band* / Boys of the old brigade/Old soldiers never die: *Royal Tank Regiment*
CD ______ **SUMCD 4032**
Summit / Nov '96 / Sound & Media

SOLID GOLD
CD ______ **MMGV 014**
Magnum Music / Jan '93 / TKO Magnum

SOLID GOLD 70'S (3CD Set)
I will survive / Reflections of my life: *Marmalade* / Open up: *Mungo Jerry* / Get dancin': *Disco Tex & The Sexolettes* / Freedom come freedom go: *Fortunes* / Saddle up: *Christie, David* / Beautiful sunday: *Boone, Daniel* / Midnight at the oasis: *Muldaur, Maria* / Build me up buttercup: *Foundations* / Indiana wants me: *Taylor, R. Dean* / Ballroom blitz: *Sweet* / Devils answer: *Atomic Rooster* / Band of gold: *Payne, Freda* / I like you: *Nelson, Phyllis* / Nice and slow: *Green, Jesse* / Rock your baby: *McRae, George* / I wanna dance with choo: *Disco Tex & The Sexolettes* / Rose garden: *Anderson, Lynn* / Yellow river: *Christie* / Love grows where my rosemary goes: *Edison Lighthouse* / Love don't live here anymore: *Rose Royce* / Baby jump: *Mungo Jerry* / Play me like you play your old guitar: *Eddy, Duane* / Hey there lonely girl: *Holman, Eddie* / Can you do it: *Georgie & Brian Johnson* / Bye bye baby: *Bay City Rollers* / Up with the cock: *Judge Dread* / Four in the morning: *Young, Faron* / Angel face: *Glitter Band* / Girls: *Moments & Whatnauts* / Stop in the name of love: *Gaynor, Gloria* / Garden party: *Gaynor, Gloria* / Feel the need in me: *Detroit Emeralds* / Love really hurts without you: *Ocean, Billy* / Dancin' on a saturday night: *Blue, Barry* / I love to love: *Charles, Tina* / Billy don't be a hero: *Paper Lace* / You little trustmaker: *Paper Lace* / If you don't know me by now: *Melvin, Harold & The Bluenotes* / Sing me: *Brothers* / Wishing on a star: *Rose Royce* / Goodbye my love: *Glitter Band* / Cousin norman: *Marmalade* / Do the funky chicken: *Thomas, Rufus* / Big seven: *Judge Dread* / Don't let it die: *Hurricane smith* / Good lookin' woman: *Dolan, Joe* / I'd like to teach the world to sing: *New Seekers* / My heart's symphony: *Lewis, Gary & The Playboys* / Me and you and a dog named boo: *Lobo* / cat crept in: *Mud* / Heaven must be missing an angel: *Tavares* / Give a little love: *Bay City Rollers* / Dance little lady dance: *Charles, Tina* / You want it you got it: *Detroit Emeralds* / Oh boy: *Mud* / Juke box jive: *Rubettes* / Alright alright alright: *Mungo Jerry* / Pepper box: *Peppers* / Whodunnit: *Tavares*
CD Set ______ **390022**
Hallmark / Jul '96 / Carlton

SOLID GOLD COXSONE STYLE
CD ______ **CDHB 80**
Heartbeat / May '92 / ADA / Direct / Greensleeves / Jet Star

SOLID GOLD FROM THE VAULTS VOL.1
Shocks 71: *Barker, Dave* / DJ's choice: *Williams, Winston* / People's choice: *Williams, Winston* / Ease up: *Bleechers* / Everything for your fun: *Bleechers* / Help wanted: *Cole, Stranger* / I'm movin' on: *Johnny & The Attractions* / Hot sauce: *Barker, Dave* / New love: *Herman* / Music keep on playing: *Campbell, Cornell* / Soup: *JJ Alstars* / Cloudburst: *Hippy Boys* / Proud feeling: *Rhythm Rulers* / Red ash: *Carl* / Walk with love: *Toots & The Maytals* / Skanky dog: *Scotland, Winston*
CD ______ **CDTRL 291**
Trojan / Mar '94 / Direct / Jet Star

SOLID GOLD FROM THE VAULTS VOL.2
CD ______ **CDTRLS 293**
Trojan / Nov '91 / Direct / Jet Star

SOLID GOLD FROM THE VAULTS VOL.3
CD ______ **CDTRL 295**
Trojan / Feb '92 / Direct / Jet Star

SOLID GOLD FROM THE VAULTS VOL.4
CD ______ **CDTRL 302**
Trojan / Mar '94 / Direct / Jet Star

SOLID GOLD HITS
Blue suede shoes: *Perkins, Carl* / Lucille: *Little Richard* / Reelin & rockin: *Berry, Chuck* / Runaway: *Shannon, Del* / Red river rock: *Johnny & The Hurricanes* / Poetry inmotion: *Tillotson, Johnny* / Oh Carol: *Sedaka, Neil* / Be bop a lula: *Vincent, Gene* / (Dance with the) Guitar man: *Eddy, Duane* / Twenty four hours from Tulsa: *Pitney, Gene* / Duke of Earl: *Chandler, Gene* / Venus: *Avalon, Frankie*
CD ______ **74321339322**
Camden / Jan '96 / BMG

SOLOMON ISLANDS - FATALEKE & BAEGU MUSIC
CD ______ **AUD 8027**
Unesco / Jun '91 / ADA / Harmonia Mundi

SOLUBLE FISH
CD ______ **HMS 1262**
Homestead / Apr '93 / Cargo / SRD

SOMA 50
Painless: *SLAM* / Bit player: *Percy X* / Acres of space: *Envoy* / Sex with a stranger: *Audio Spectrum* / Fallen arches: *Maas* / Utah jazz: *Rejuvination* / Kincho: *Funk D'Void* / Feelin' horny: *Brown, Earl* / C-Horse: *Equus* / On epsilon: *Skintrade*
CD ______ **SOMA 50CD**
Soma / Mar '97 / RTM/Disc

SOMA COMPILATION VOL.1
CD ______ **SOMACD 1**
Soma / Nov '94 / RTM/Disc

SOMA COMPILATION VOL.2
CD ______ **SOMACD 003**
Soma / Nov '95 / RTM/Disc

SOMA COMPILATION VOL.3
CD ______ **SOMACD 6**
Soma / Nov '96 / RTM/Disc

SOME GIRLS
CD ______ **10432**
CMC / Jun '97 / BMG

SOME LOVE
CD ______ **DOG 009CD**
Mrs. Ackroyd / Sep '94 / ADA / Direct / Roots

SOME OF THESE WERE HOOJ VOL.1
CD ______ **HOOJCD 1**
Hooj Choons / Apr '94 / Mo's Music Machine / RTM/Disc

SOME OF THESE WERE HOOJ VOL.2
CD ______ **HOOJCD 2**
Hooj Choons / Aug '95 / Mo's Music Machine / RTM/Disc

SOME OF THESE WERE HOOJ VOL.3
CD ______ **HOOJCD 3**
CD ______ **HOOJCDX 3**
Hooj Choons / Nov '96 / Mo's Music Machine / RTM/Disc

SOMEONE TO LOVE (The Birth Of The San Francisco Sound)
She's my baby: *Mojo Men* / Fire in my heart: *Mojo Men* / Why can't you stay: *Mojo Men* / Girl won't you go: *Mojo Men* / Girl: *Great Society* / Father Bruce: *Great Society* / You can't cry: *Great Society* / Born to be burned: *Great Society* / Daydream nightmare love: *Great Society* / Heads up: *Great Society* / Double triptamine superautomatic everlovin' man: *Great Society* / Ain't it babe: *Charity Shayne* / Last thing on my mind: *Vejtables* / Mansion of tears: *Vejtables* / Let's get together: *Valente, Dino* / That's how it is: *Great Society* / Right to me: *Great Society* / Where: *Great Society* / Cold dreary morning: *Ashton, Jan* / I'm a fool:

Engle, Butch & The Styx / Smile smile smile: *Engle, Butch & The Styx* / Someone to love: *Great Society* / Free advice: *Great Society* / Bye bye bye: *Tikis* / Lost my love today: *Tikis* / More & more & more: *Tikis* / True love is hard to find: *Tikis* / Happy with you: *Tikis* / Mad: *Tikis* / About my tears: *Tikis*
CD _______ CDWIKD 170
Big Beat / Oct '96 / Pinnacle

SOMETHING FOR THE WEEKEND
CD _______ FNUN 2
Flying Nun / Oct '94 / RTM/Disc

SOMETHING'S GONE WRONG
CD _______ CZ 042 CD
C/Z / Jul '94 / Plastic Head

SOMETIMES DEATH IS BETTER
CD _______ SHR 007CD
Shiver / Aug '95 / Plastic Head

SOMETIMES GOD HIDES
CD _______ DGM 9605
Discipline / Oct '96 / Pinnacle

SOMETIMES THE DEVIL DRESSES AS A WOMAN
CD _______ BAH 24
Humbug / Sep '97 / Total/Pinnacle

SON OF SLAM CHOPS
CD _______ TX 51204CD
Triple XXX / Feb '97 / Grapevine/PolyGram

SONG CREATORS IN EASTERN TURKEY
CD _______ SF 40432CD
Smithsonian Folkways / Jan '94 / ADA / Cadillac / CM / Direct / Koch

SONGBIRDS
CD _______ MCCD 174
Music Club / Sep '94 / Disc / THE

SONGS AND DANCES FROM CUBA, THE
CD _______ EUCD 1235
ARC / Nov '93 / ADA / ARC Music

SONGS AND DANCES FROM THE FAROE ISLANDS
CD _______ ARN 60329
Arion / Jul '97 / ADA / Discovery

SONGS AND DRUMS OF BAGA WOMEN, GUINEA
CD _______ 926272
BUDA / Sep '96 / Discovery

SONGS AND MELODIES FROM THE EMERALD ISLE
CD _______ CDMFP 6347
Music For Pleasure / May '97 / EMI

SONGS AND RHYTHMS OF MALAWI, THE
CD _______ PS 6514OCD
PlayaSound / Apr '95 / ADA / Harmonia Mundi

SONGS AND RHYTHMS OF MOROCCO, THE
CD _______ LYRCD 7336
Lyrichord / Feb '94 / ADA / CM / Roots

SONGS BY NDEBELE WOMEN, SOUTH AFRICA
CD _______ 926562
BUDA / Sep '96 / Discovery

SONGS FOR A BLACK PLANET (The Best Of Goth)
Hex: *Specimen* / Crow baby: *March Violets* / Too many castles in the sky: *Rose Of Avalanche* / Alone she cries: *Skeletal Family* / Boys: *Bauhaus* / Fats terminal: *Bone Orchard* / Creatures of the night: *Screaming Dead* / Propaganda: *Play Dead* / Wake up: *Danse Society* / Under the milky way: *Church* / Desire: *Gene Loves Jezebel* / She knows: *Balaam & The Angel* / Great expectations: *New Model Army* / Hollow eyes: *Red Lorry Yellow Lorry* / Ignore the machine: *Alien Sex Fiend* / Church of no return: *Christian Death*
CD _______ NTMCD 512
Nectar / Sep '95 / Pinnacle

SONGS FOR LOVERS
CD _______ DCD 5278
Kenwest / Nov '92 / THE

SONGS FOR MUM AMD DAD (18 Wonderful Memories)
I'd like to teach the world to sing (in perfect harmony) / I remember you: *Ifield, Frank* / Charmaine: *Bachelors* / My prayer: *Platters* / April love: *Boone, Pat* / Jealousy: *Laine, Frankie* / Tennessee waltz: *Page, Patti* / Autumn leaves: *Williams, Roger* / Heartaches by the number: *Mitchell, Guy* / Walkin' my baby back home: *Ray, Johnnie* / Kisses sweeter than wine: *Rodgers, Jimmie* / Ivory tower: *Carr, Cathy* / My happiness: *Pied Pipers* / Freight train: *McDevitt, Chas* / Green door: *Lowe, Jim* / Whispering grass: *Ink Spots* / Stranger on the shore: *Bilk, Acker* / This ole house: *Clooney, Rosemary*
CD _______ ECD 3198
K-Tel / Mar '95 / K-Tel

SONGS FOR MUMS & DADS (2CD Set)
CD Set _______ TSCD 227
Outlet / Mar '97 / ADA / CM / Direct / Duncans / Koch / Ross

SONGS FOR POLITICAL ACTION 1926-1953 (Folk Music, Topical Songs & The American Left - 10CD Set)
Boll weevil: *Sandburg, Carl* / Patriotic diggers: *Allison, John* / London bridge is falling down: *Seeger, Charles* / Risselty Rosselty: *Seeger, Charles* / Hands: *Seeger, Charles* / Old grey mare: *Crawford-Seeger, Ruth* / Ragged hungry blues part 1: *Jackson, Aunt Molly* / Ragged hungry blues part 2: *Jackson, Aunt Molly* / I'm going to organise, baby mine: *Gunning, Sarah Ogun* / I don't want your millions Mister: *Cadle, Tillman* / Raggedy raggedy: *Handcox, John* / No more mourning: *Handcox, John* / Join the Union tonight: *Handcox, John* / We're going to roll the Union on: *Handcox, John* / There is mean things happening in this land: *Handcox, John* / Farmer's letter to the President: *Ferguson, Bob* / Farm relief blues: *Miller, Bob* / 11 cent cotton, 40 cent meat: *Bob's Boys* / Hootenanny song: *Miller's Bullfrog Entertainers* / Bank failures: *Ferguson, Bob* / Rich man & the poor man: *Miller, Bob* / Poor forgotten man: *Palmer, Bill* / Soup song: *New Singers* / Internationale: *New Singers* / Rise up: *New Singers* / United front: *New Singers* / Forward, we've not forgotten: *New Singers* / In praise of learning: *New Singers* / On the picket line: *Manhattan Chorus* / Hold the Fort: *Manhattan Chorus* / Casey Jones: *Manhattan Chorus* / Sit down: *Manhattan Chorus* / Write me out my union card: *Manhattan Chorus* / We shall not be moved: *Manhattan Chorus* / Join the Union: *Manhattan Chorus* / Solidarity forever: *Manhattan Chorus* / Strange funeral in Braddock: *Baumann & Siegmeister* / Abraham Lincoln: *Robinson, Earl* / Joe Hill: *Robinson, Earl* / Spring song: *Robinson, Earl* / Old Chisholm trail: *Kraber, Tony* / Old paint (the horse with the Union label): *Aarons, Saul* / Capitalistic boss: *Aarons, Saul* / Little theater on the left: *Dowd, Harrison* / Little theater on the right: *Dowd, Harrison* / Nine foot shovel: *White, Joshua* / Chain gang boun': *White, Joshua* / Trouble: *White, Joshua* / Goin' home boys: *White, Joshua* / Cryin' who, cryin' you: *White, Joshua* / Told my Captain: *White, Joshua* / Jerry: *White, Joshua* / Southern exposure: *White, Joshua* / Uncle Sam says: *White, Joshua* / Jim Crow train: *White, Joshua* / Bad housing blues: *White, Joshua* / Hard times blues: *White, Joshua* / Defense factory blues: *White, Joshua* / Strange death of John Doe: *Almanac Singers* / Billy Boy: *Almanac Singers* / C for conscription: *Almanac Singers* / Washington breakdown: *Almanac Singers* / Lisa Jane: *Almanac Singers* / Ballad of October 16th: *Almanac Singers* / Plow under: *Almanac Singers* / Talking Union: *Almanac Singers* / Union train: *Almanac Singers* / Which side are you on: *Almanac Singers* / Get thee behind me Satan: *Almanac Singers* / Union maid: *Almanac Singers* / All I want: *Almanac Singers* / Songs for bridges: *Almanac Singers* / Babe o' mine: *Guthrie, Woody* / Blow ye winds, heigh ho: *Almanac Singers* / Haul away Joe: *Almanac Singers* / Blow the man down: *Almanac Singers* / Golden vanity: *Almanac Singers* / Away, Rio: *Almanac Singers* / Coast of high Barbary: *Almanac Singers* / Greenland fishing: *Almanac Singers* / Dodger song: *Almanac Singers* / Ground hog: *Almanac Singers* / State of Arkansas: *Almanac Singers* / Hard, ain't it hard: *Almanac Singers* / I ride an old paint: *Almanac Singers* / House of the rising sun: *Almanac Singers* / Weaver's song: *Almanac Singers* / Dear Mr. President: *Almanac Singers* / Belt line girl: *Almanac Singers* / Round, round Hitler's grave: *Almanac Singers* / Side by side: *Almanac Singers* / Deliver the goods: *Almanac Singers* / Reuben James: *Almanac Singers* / Boomtown Bill: *Almanac Singers* / Keep the oil a rollin': *Almanac Singers* / I'm looking for a home: *Priority Ramblers* / Amsterdam maid: *Priority Ramblers* / Song of the free: *Priority Ramblers* / In Washington: *Priority Ramblers* / Overtime pay: *Priority Ramblers* / Jarama Valley: *Glazer, Hawes & Lomax* / Quinta Brigada T: *Seeger, Glazer, Hawes & Lomax* / Spanish marching song: *Seeger, Glazer, Hawes & Lomax* / Cook house: *Seeger, Glazer, Hawes & Lomax* / Young man from Alcala: *Seeger, Glazer, Hawes & Lomax* / Quinte regimento: *Seeger, Glazer, Hawes & Lomax* / Quartermaster song: *Seeger, Glazer, Hawes & Lomax* / Little man on a fence: *White, Joshua* / Jim Crow: *Union Boys* / You better get ready: *Union Boys* / Hold the Fort: *Union Boys* / We shall not be moved: *Union Boys* / Hold on: *Union Boys* / Solidarity forever: *Ives, Burl* / Dollar ain't a dollar anymore: *Union Boys* / Horace Greeley: *Robinson, Earl* / Kevin Barry: *Robinson, Earl* / House I live in: *Robinson, Earl* / Man's a man for a' that: *Robinson, Earl* / Drill ye tarriers drill: *Robinson, Earl* / Frozen logger: *Robinson, Earl* / Jefferson & liberty: *Robinson, Earl* / Sweet Betsy from Pike: *Robinson, Earl* / Dirty miner: *Robinson, Earl* / Grand Coolee Dam: *Robinson, Earl* / Free & equal blues: *Robinson, Earl* / Century of the common man: *Sir Lancelot* / I'm a Native American Nazi: *Partlow, Vern* / Join the UAW-CIO: *Partlow, Vern* / Keeping score for '44: *Partlow, Vern* / UAW train: *Partlow, Vern* / Susan's in the Union: *Partlow, Vern* / Rollback blues: *Partlow, Vern* / Mama don't allow: *Partlow, Vern* / Farmer-Labor train: *Guthrie, Woody* / So long, it's been good to know you: *Guthrie, Woody* / Talking sailor: *Guthrie, Woody* / Sally, don't you grieve: *Guthrie, Woody* / Citizen CIO: *Glazer, Tom & Joshua White* / No more blues: *White, Joshua* / We've got a plan: *Glazer, Tom* / Social worker's talking blues: *Glazer, Tom* / I'm gonna put my name down: *Glazer, Tom* / Freedom Road: *White, Joshua* / Landlord: *White, Joshua* / Beloved Comrade: *White, Joshua* / Johnny has gone for a soldier: *White, Joshua* / Beloved comrade: *White, Joshua* / Man who couldn't walk around: *White, Joshua* / I'm the guy: *White, Joshua* / Little man sitting on a fence: *White, Joshua* / When the country is broke: *Glazer, Tom* / Money in the pocket: *Glazer, Tom* / Our fight is yours: *Glazer, Tom* / Moses Green: *Hays, Lee* / Rankin tree: *Hays, Lee* / Talking Bilbo: *Hays, Lee* / This old world: *Hays, Lee* / No one stooge: *Claiborne, Bob* / Song of my hands: *Asbel, Bernie* / Mad as I can be: *Asbel, Bernie & Pete Seeger* / Jackie Robinson: *Lord Invader* / High price blues: *McGhee, Brownie* / Black, brown & white: *McGhee, Brownie* / Nix on Mundt/Nixon: *Beyer, Anna* / Daily worker's song: *Levine, George* / Taft-Hartley blues: *Levine, George* / Parnell Thomas blues: *Cunningham, Sis* / Turn me loose: *Reynolds, Malvina* / Snowball: *Berries* / Swingin' on a scab: *Berries* / On to Sacramento: *Casetta, Mario* / Atomic talking blues: *Partlow, Vern* / Newspapermen meet such interesting people: *Partlow, Vern* / Passing through: *Blakeslee, Dick* / Listen Mr. Bilbo: *Seeger, Hawes, Hays & Wood* / Joe Hill: *Seeger, Hawes, Hays & Wood* / OPA shout: *Seeger, Pete & Bob Claiborne* / Voting union: *Seeger, Hawes, Hays & Wood* / Get out the vote: *Seeger, Hawes, Hays & Wood* / Dollar ain't a dollar anymore: *Glazer, Tom* / Dollar for a PAC: *Seeger, Hawes, Hays & Wood* / What congress done to me: *Seeger, Hawes, Hays & Wood* / Four PAC nursery rhymes: *Seeger, Hawes, Hays & Wood* / DDT: *Seeger, Hawes, Hays & Wood* / Fare ye well bad congressman: *Seeger, Hawes, Hays & Wood* / No, no, no discrimination: *Seeger, Glazer, Hays & Wood* / Voter, oh voter: *Seeger, Glazer, Hays & Wood* / Commonwealth of toil: *Wood, Gilbert, Seeger & Glazer* / We've got our eyes on you: *Wood, Gilbert, Seeger & Glazer* / Preacher & the slave: *Wood, Gilbert, Seeger & Glazer* / Talking Union: *Wood, Gilbert, Seeger & Glazer* / Which side are you on: *Wood, Gilbert, Seeger & Glazer* / Solidarity forever: *Wood, Gilbert, Seeger & Glazer* / Whole wide world around: *Wood, Gilbert, Seeger & Glazer* / Hold the fort: *Wood, Gilbert, Seeger & Glazer* / Talking PAC: *Seeger, Pete* / Conversation with a mule: *Seeger, Pete* / Farmer is the man: *Seeger, Pete* / Join the Farmer's Union: *Seeger, Pete* / Talking atom: *Seeger, Pete* / Newspapermen meet such interesting people: *Seeger, Pete* / Skillet good & greasy: *Seeger, Pete* / T for Texas: *Seeger, Pete* / Cumberland Mountain bear chase: *Seeger, Pete* / Walk in peace: *Sir Lancelot* / Atomic energy: *Sir Lancelot* / Old lady with a rolling pin: *Sir Lancelot* / Red boogie: *Goodson & Vale* / Unity rhumba: *Goodson & Vale* / Elephant and the ass: *Goodson & Vale* / Hungry rhapsody: *Goodson & Vale* / Housing: *Goodson & Vale* / People's songs chorus ballad of FDR: *Goodson & Vale* / Jim Crow: *Goodson & Vale* / Mein schtele belz: *Berries* / Zhonkoye: *Berries* / Travelin': *Seeger, Pete* / Black, brown & white blues: *Seeger, Pete* / Death of Harry Simms: *Seeger, Pete* / Winnsboro cotton mill blues: *Seeger, Pete* / No Irish need apply: *Seeger, Pete* / Unemployment: *Casetta, Mario* / Compensation blues: *Casetta, Mario* / Fireship: *Sanders, Betty* / Johnny, I hardly knew you: *Sanders, Betty* / Peekskill story: *Weavers* / Wasn't that a time: *Weavers* / Dig my grave: *Weavers* / Freight train blues: *Weavers* / Love song blues: *Weavers* / Hammers song: *Weavers* / We're keeping score in '44: *Robinson, Earl* / No more blues: *White, Joshua* / Lay that ballot down: *Oliver, Bill* / Fertilizer song: *Partlow, Vern* / Talking FTA: *Partlow, Vern* / Kiss the boys goodbye: *Partlow, Vern* / Round and round in the canneries: *Partlow, Vern* / My name is Cannery Bill: *Partlow, Vern* / Bosses' gang: *Alexander, Mara* / Bye bye bosses: *Alexander, Mara* / New walls of Jericho: *Huey, Richard* / Henry Wallace is the man: *Royal Harmonaires* / Corrido to Wallace & Taylor: *Alvarez, Abigail* / Second corrido to Wallace & Taylor: *Alvarez, Abigail* / Battle hymn of '48: *Robeson, Paul* / Same old merry-go-round: *Loring, Michael* / I've got a ballot: *Loring, Michael* / Great day: *Loring, Michael* / Wallace button: *Levine, George* / Goodbye Harry: *Levine, George* / Henry Wallace: *Cunningham, Sis* / We can win with Wallace: *Oliver, Bill* / Work with Wallace: *Reynolds, Malvina* / Century of the common man: *Sir Lancelot* / Wallace is the man for me: *Sir Lancelot* / Yankee Doodle, tell the boss: *Loring, Michael & Alan Lomax* / New York city: *Weavers* / Marcantonio for me: *Hellerman, Fred* / Skip to the polls: *Weavers* / Marcantonio for Mayor: *Hellerman, Fred* / Now, right now: *Duncan, Laura* / We shall not be moved: *Weavers* / Oh freedom: *Seeger, Pete* / Ben Davis: *Seeger, Pete* / People's choice: *Seeger, Pete* / Keep a-goin' and a-growin': *Seeger, Pete* / Riddle of Thurman Towns: *Decormier, Bernardi & Booth* / Grapes to pick: *Gallant, Gerald* / I don't want to be adjusted: *Hellerman, Fred* / Stand up & be counted: *Hellerman, Fred* / We will overcome: *Hellerman, Fred* / Progressive Party is here to stay: *Hellerman, Fred* / Pity the downtrodden landlord: *Hill, Bob* / Hammer song: *Weavers* / Banks of marble: *Weavers* / Spring song: *Lieberman, Ernie & Hope Foye* / My old man: *Lieberman, Ernie* / Song of my hands: *Lieberman, Ernie* / I'm on my way: *Lieberman, Ernie* / In contempt: *Lieberman, Duncan & Smith* / Die gedenken sind frei: *Lieberman, Duncan & Smith* / Walk along together: *Lieberman, Duncan & Smith* / Put my name down: *Lieberman, Duncan & Smith* / Hold on: *Lieberman, Duncan & Smith* / Didn't my Lord deliver Daniel: *Smith, Osborne* / I've got a right: *Duncan, Laura* / We shall overcome: *Jewish Young Folksingers* / Talking Un-American blues: *Sanders, Betty* / Old Bolshevik song: *Glazer, Joe & Bill Friedland* / Cloakmaker's Union: *Glazer, Joe & Bill Friedland* / Land of the daily worker: *Glazer, Joe & Bill Friedland* / Our line's been changed again: *Glazer, Joe & Bill Friedland* / In old Moscow: *Glazer, Joe & Bill Friedland* / Unite for unity: *Glazer, Joe & Bill Friedland* / Bill Bailey: *Glazer, Joe & Bill Friedland* / Last Internationale: *Glazer, Joe & Bill Friedland* / Giveaway boys in Washington: *Glazer, Joe* / Joe McCarthy's band: *Glazer, Joe* / I've got to know: *Guthrie, Woody* / This land is your land: *Guthrie, Woody*
CD Set _______ BCD 15720
Bear Family / May '96 / Direct / Rollercoaster / Swift

SONGS FOR THE 90'S
CD _______ BRAM 1991172
Brambus / Nov '93 / ADA

SONGS FROM BENGAL
CD _______ ARN 64214
Arion / Jun '93 / ADA / Discovery

SONGS FROM JAHL
CD _______ RB 3005
Reggae Best / May '94 / Grapevine/ PolyGram

SONGS FROM THE EMERALD ISLE (2CD Set)
Galway Bay: *Locke, Josef* / Spinning wheel: *Murphy, Delia* / Star of County Down: *McCormack, John* / Ballyhoe: *McGoldrick, Anna* / Old bog road: *Drennan, Tommy* / Courtin' in the kitchen: *Murphy, Delia* / Mother Machree: *MacEwan, Father Sydney* / Trottin' to the fair: *Murray, Ruby* / Banks of my own lovely Lee: *O'Se, Sean* / When Irish eyes are smiling: *Jones, Sandie* / Pretty Irish girl: *O'Dowda, Brendan & Ruby Murray* / Mountains of Mourne: *O'Dowda, Brendan* / Castlebar Fair: *Gallagher, Bridie* / Rose of Tralee: *O'Dowda, Brendan* / Eileen O'Grady: *Gallagher, Bridie* / Danny boy: *O'Se, Sean* / Connemara: *O'Dowda, Brendan & Ruby Murray* / Doonaree: *Murray, Ruby* / Sweet Marie: *O'Dowda, Brendan* / Flower of sweet Strabane: *Gallagher, Bridie* / Whiskey in the jar: *Dubliners* / Three drunken maidens: *Planxty* / Galway races: *Dubliners* / Kitty of Coleraine: *Bunratty Singers* / Bantry Bay: *O'Se, Sean*
CD Set _______ CDDL 1104
EMI / Nov '92 / EMI

SONGS FROM THE EMERALD ISLE
Road to Sligo / Muirsheen Durkin / Donegal Danny / O'Carolan's concerto / Finnegan's wake / Green fields of Rossbeigh / Corney is coming / Joe Cooley's reel / Black velvet band / Cod liver oil/Coolies / Dirty old town / Jolly beggarman/Hunter's purse / Fields of Athenry / Pinch of snuff / Cherish the ladies/ Paddy Clancy's jig / Gillan's apples/Father O'Flynn / Into the rain / Wild rover / Whisky in the jar / Irish rover/Rakes of mallow / Farewell to Ireland
CD _______ SUMCD 4059
Summit / Nov '96 / Sound & Media

SONGS FROM THE EMERALD ISLE (20 Classic Irish Ballads)
CD _______ CDIRL 501
Outlet / Apr '97 / ADA / CM / Direct / Duncans / Koch / Ross

SONGS FROM THE EXOTIC
CD _______ BML 012
British Music / Jan '96 / Forties Recording Company

SONGS FROM THE SHORES OF THE BLACK SEA
CD _______ LDX 274980
La Chant Du Monde / Jun '94 / ADA / Harmonia Mundi

SONGS OF BAKHSHI WOMEN
CD _______ W 260064
Inedit / Sep '95 / ADA / Discovery / Harmonia Mundi

SONGS OF CHRISTMAS
Silent night: *Drifters* / When a child is born: *Benton, Brook* / Jingle bells: *Clooney, Rosemary* / White christmas: *Armstrong, Louis* / We wish you a merry christmas: *Drifters* / Blue christmas: *Platters* / Silver Bells: *Crosby, Bing* / Jingle bells rock: *Sherman, Bobby* / Please come home for christmas: *Platters* / A new baby for christmas: *Preston, Johnny* / Little drummer boy: *Clooney, Rosemary* / Oh, come all ye faithful: *Crosby, Bing* / Auld lang syne: *Drifters* /

Santa claus is coming to town: *Cole, Nat 'King'*
CD SCD 1000
Start / Feb '97 / Disc

SONGS OF EARTH, WATER, FIRE AND SKY (Music Of The American Indian)
CD 802462
New World / Aug '92 / ADA / Cadillac / Harmonia Mundi

SONGS OF INDIA
CD MNWCD 156
MNW / Mar '89 / ADA / Vital

SONGS OF IRELAND, THE
CD ETCD 192
Etude / Apr '96 / Grapevine/PolyGram

SONGS OF LEIBER & STOLLER, THE
Love potion no.9: *Searchers* / Girls, girls, girls: *Brown, Joe & The Bruvvers* / Yes: *Sandon, Johnny & The Remo Four* / I keep forgettin': *Hi-Fi's* / I who have nothing: *Spectres* / Brother Bill (The Last clean shirt): *Rockin' Berries* / Along came Jones: *Overlanders* / Tricky Dicky: *Searchers* / Trouble: *Ford, Emile & The Checkmates* / Three cool cats: *Ferris Wheel* / If you don't come back: *Takers* / Some other guy: *Searchers* / Dance with me: *Kestrels* / Don't: *Keyes, Ebony* / Hound dog: *Gene & The Gents* / Poison ivy: *Puppets*
CD NEBCD 656
Sequel / Jun '93 / BMG

SONGS OF LIFE (Music From Mission '89)
CD WSTCD 9710
Nelson Word / Nov '89 / Nelson Word

SONGS OF LOVE, LUCK, ANIMALS AND MAGIC
Love Song: *Douglas, Frank A.* / Grizzly bear war song: *Douglas, Frank A.* / Rabbit song: *Douglas, Frank A.* / Gambling songs: *Douglas, Frank A.* / Basket song: *Figuerosa, Aileen* / Brush dance: *Figuerosa, Aileen* / Brush dance song: *Figuerosa, Aileen* / Seagull song: *Norris, Ella* / Song to stop the Rain: *Norris, Ella* / Hunting Song: *Shaughnessy, Florence* / Pelican song: *Bommelyn, Loren* / Ceremonial dance / Ending ceremonial dance
CD 8029722
New World / Sep '92 / ADA / Cadillac / Harmonia Mundi

SONGS OF MUKANDA, THE (Music Of The Secret Society Of The Luvale People Of Africa)
Ndumbamwelela / Lilombola songs / Sunrise songs / Sunset songs / Meal ritual / Water bearing songs / Greeting and bidding farewell to guests / Kukuwa songs / Jingunda songs / Eve of the purification ceremony / Purification ceremony / Final ceremony
CD MCM 3008
Multicultural Media / May '97 / Direct

SONGS OF OLD RUSSIA
CD MCD 71560
Monitor / Sep '93 / CM

SONGS OF SCOTLAND
Man's a man for a' that: *Caern Folk Trio* / Highland lullaby: *McDonald, Alastair* / Piper o' Dundee: *Caern Folk Trio* / Farewell my love: *McBennett, Helen* / Wee kirkcudbright centipede: *McDonald, Alastair* / Sailing up the clyde: *Sutherland, Alex Singers* / Water is wide: *McBennett, Helen* / Peat fire flame: *MacDonald Sisters* / Bonnie wee Jeanne McColl: *Sutherland, Alex Singers* / Bog Kilmarnock Bunnett: *Sutherland, Alex Singers* / Northern lights of Aberdeen: *Sutherland, Alex Singers* / I belong to Glasgow: *Sutherland, Alex Singers* / Go away from my window: *Sutherland, Alex Singers* / Auld lang syne: *Stewart, Andy*
CD EMPRCD 590
Emporio / Oct '95 / Disc

SONGS OF SCOTLAND (A Celebration Of The Magic Of Scotland)
Amazing grace / Song of the Clyde / Westering home / Road to the Isles / Keep right on to the end of the road / Northern lights of old Aberdeen / Bonnie Kirkwall Bay / Bonnie banks of Loch Lomond / Football crazy / Heres to Scottish whiskey / Land for all seasons / Star O'Rabbie Burns / Man's a man for a that / Roamin in the gloamin / Just a wee deoch an' Doris / Skye boat song / Ye banks and braes / Tobermory bay / Marching through the heather / Auld lang syne
CD CD 6062
Music / Apr '97 / Target/BMG

SONGS OF SCOTLAND
CD CDLOC 1100
Lochshore / Jun '97 / ADA / Direct / Duncans

SONGS OF SUNSHINE (The Very Best Of Classic Organ Music)
Crown imperial / Trumpet sonata in D major / Prelude in E flat major / Salut d'amour / Festal flourish / Fantasia in D minor / Tuba tune / Will O' the wisp / Nimrod / Larghetto / Festive march / Air in C major / Trumpet minuet / Grand choeur / Irish tune from County Derry / Song of sunshine
CD 301592
Hallmark / Jun '97 / Carlton

SONGS OF THE ABORIGINES
CD LYRCD 7331
Lyrichord / '91 / ADA / CM / Roots

SONGS OF THE BALKANS
CD CNCD 5982
Disky / Apr '94 / Disky / THE

SONGS OF THE CIVIL WAR
I wish I was in Dixies' land / All quiet along the Potomac tonight / We are coming, Father Abra'am / Mother, is the battle over / Drummer boy of Shiloh / Beauregards's retreat from Shiloh / Jeff in petticoats / Weeping, sad and lonely / It's a gold old rebel
CD NW 202
New World / '88 / ADA / Cadillac / Harmonia Mundi

SONGS OF THE CIVIL WAR
CD SLCD 9008
Starline / Dec '94 / Jazz Music

SONGS OF THE DEPRESSION
CD JASSCD 639
Jass / May '94 / ADA / Cadillac / CM / Direct / Jazz Music

SONGS OF THE GAELS
CD LBP 2022CD
Lochshore / Jun '96 / ADA / Direct / Duncans

SONGS OF THE GARIFUNA
CD VICG 53372
JVC World Library / Mar '96 / ADA / CM / Direct

SONGS OF THE INUIT
CD VICG 53332
JVC World Library / Mar '96 / ADA / CM / Direct

SONGS OF THE JU'HOANSI BUSHMEN, THE (Music From Namibia)
CD C 560117
Ocora / Aug '97 / ADA / Harmonia Mundi

SONGS OF THE LAKOTA SIOUX (North America)
CD 2741000
La Chant Du Monde / Jan '95 / ADA / Harmonia Mundi

SONGS OF THE RUSSIAN PEOPLE
CD 274978
La Chant Du Monde / Jan '95 / ADA / Harmonia Mundi

SONGS OF THE SPIRIT
Coyote dance: *Little Wolf* / Medicine flute: *Coyote Oldman* / Song of union: *Shenandoah, Joanne* / Hunter's twilight: *Nakai, R. Carlos* / Son of the sun: *Kastin* / Red cloud: *Way West* / Oweegon: *Little Wolf* / Summoning winds: *Native Flute Ensemble* / Return of the red hat: *Stearns, Michael & Ron Sunsinger* / My child: *Primeaux, Mike & Attson* / Nez Perce: *500 Nations* / Cherokee: *Coolidge, Rita*
CD 41372
Triloka / Nov '96 / New Note/Pinnacle

SONGS OF THE TRAVELLING PEOPLE
Won't you buy my sweet blooming lavender: *Penfold, Janet* / Come a' ye tramps an' hawkers: *Stewart, Davie* / Blarney stone: *Barry, Margaret* / Berryfields o'Blair: *Stewart, Belle* / Muckin' o' geordie's byre: *McBeath, Jimmy & Willie Kelby* / Choring song: *Robertson, Jeannie* / Beggar wench: *Stewart, Davie* / Blacksmith courted me: *Smith, Phoebe* / Barnyards o' Delgaty/Gin I were where the Gadie rins: *Kelby, Willie* / On the bonny banks o' the roses: *McPhee, Duncan* / Bard of Armagh: *Barry, Margaret* / Dandling song/Bonny lassie-o/Cuckoo's nest: *Robertson, Jeannie* / I am a romany: *Smith, Phoebe* / Devonshire time and 2 gipsy hornpipes: *Connor, Frank O* / Higher Germanie: *Smith, Phoebe* / Little beggar man: *Doran, Paddy* / Kathleen: *Barry, Margaret* / Lady o' the dainty doonby: *Robertson, Jeannie* / Tenpenny bit/She moves through the fair: *Stewart, Belle* / Poor smuggler's boy: *Brasil, Angela* / Aul' jockey Bruce o' the Fornet: *Stewart, Davie* / Tuning up: *Hughes, Carolyne & Charlie Lindsay* / Twa heids are better than yin: *Stewart, Kathie* / Moss O'Burreldale: *McBeath, Jimmy* / Gay Gordons: *Kelby, Willie* / Overgate: *Robertson, Jeannie* / Macpherson's rant: *Stewart, Donald & Albert* / Macpherson's lament: *Stewart, Davie*
CD CDSDL 407
Saydisc / Nov '94 / ADA / Direct / Harmonia Mundi

SONGS OF THE ULSTER PROTESTANT, THE
Union cruiser / Aghalee heroes / Green grassy slopes / Derry's walls / Protestant boys / Orange and blue / Blackman's dream / Battle of Garvagh / Lily O / Boyne water / Sash / Sprigs of Kilrea / Auld orange flute / No surrender
CD CDUCD 10
Ulster Music / Apr '97 / ADA / CM / Direct / Duncans / Koch / Ross

SONGS OF WARTIME
CD RAJCD 925
Empress / Jun '94 / Koch

SONGS THAT WON THE WAR
CD PLATCD 3928
Platinum / May '94 / Prism

SONGWRITERS EXCHANGE
CD STCD 529
Stash / Jan '93 / ADA / Cadillac / CM / Direct / Jazz Music

SONGWRITERS SHOWCASE VOL.1
CD CDRPM 0005
RP Media / Nov '96 / Essential/BMG

SONGWRITERS SHOWCASE VOL.2
CD CDRPM 0014
RP Media / May '97 / Essential/BMG

SONIC BOOM
CD BOOMCD 1
Boom / Jul '97 / Prime

SONIC COLLECTION, THE
CD SONCD 0070
Sonic Sounds / Sep '94 / Jet Star

SONIC INTERFERENCE
CD 9010752
Immediate / Mar '97 / BMG

SONRISAS DE TEXAS
CD MSA 007
Modern Blues / Feb '94 / ADA / Direct

SONS AND LOVERS
CD RVCD 27
Raven / Feb '93 / ADA / Direct

SOOTHERS AND MOVERS
What greater love: *Little Anthony* / I'll make you happy: *Hunt, Tommy* / Consider the source: *Haywood, Leon* / Face up to the truth: *Troy, Doris* / Love won't wear off: *Bailey, J.R.* / Tried and convicted: *Womack, Bobby* / Bring on the heartaches: *Tee, Willie* / You had it made: *Terrell, Freddie* / I've got love for my baby: *Younghearts* / Soft and gentle ways: *King, Clyde* / No time for you: *O'Jays* / Mamma's love: *Tribulations* / You can bring me all your heartaches: *Rawls, Lou* / Where were you: *Andrews, Ernie* / Isn't it just a shame: *Wells, Kenny* / I'm gonna make it: *Pacesetters* / Turn to me: *Towns, Chris* / Outcast: *Eddie & Ernie* / Who is it gonna be: *Dee & Joe* / Because I love you: *Hightower, Willie* / I'm lonely for you: *Swan, Bettye* / I'm sorry: *Black, Cody* / And heaven was here: *Big Dee Irwin*
CD GSCD 081
Goldmine / Sep '96 / Vital

SOPHISTICATED GENTLEMEN (2CD Set)
Dance ballerina dance: *Cole, Nat 'King'* / From Russia with love: *Monro, Matt* / That's amore: *Martin, Dean* / You're getting to be a habit with me: *Torme, Mel* / Way you look tonight: *Haymes, Dick* / Fascinating rhythm: *Damone, Vic* / Smile: *Cole, Nat 'King'* / Story of Tina: *Martino, Al* / Stranger in paradise: *MacRae, Gordon* / Return to me: *Martin, Dean* / Portrait of my love: *Monro, Matt* / Spanish eyes: *Martino, Al* / On the street where you live: *Damone, Vic* / Blue moon: *Torme, Mel* / Do you love me: *Haymes, Dick* / Begin the beguine: *MacRae, Gordon* / Pretend: *Cole, Nat 'King'* / Granada (Lara): *Martino, Al* / Impossible dream: *Monro, Matt* / Younger than Springtime: *Damone, Vic* / When I fall in love: *Cole, Nat 'King'* / It might as well be Spring: *MacRae, Gordon* / I've got my love to keep me warm: *Martin, Dean* / How deep is the ocean: *Haymes, Dick* / Again: *Torme, Mel* / Most beautiful girl in the world: *Damone, Vic* / Unchained melody: *Monro, Matt* / Wanted: *Martino, Al* / Volare: *Martin, Dean* / Bewitched, bothered and bewildered: *Torme, Mel* / Memories are made of this: *Martin, Dean* / My funny valentine: *MacRae, Gordon* / Who can I turn to: *Monro, Matt* / Til there was you: *Damone, Vic* / Autumn leaves: *MacRae, Gordon* / Blossom fell: *Cole, Nat 'King'* / Kiss: *Martin, Dean* / On days like these: *Monro, Matt* / Isn't it a lovely day (to be caught in the rain): *Haymes, Dick* / Very thought of you: *Cole, Nat 'King'*
CD Set CDDL 1299
Music For Pleasure / Nov '95 / EMI

SOPHISTICATED LADIES (2CD Set)
Fever: *Lee, Peggy* / Something: *Bassey, Shirley* / Wheel of fortune: *Starr, Kay* / What the world needs now is love: *Horne, Lena* / It must be him: *Carr, Vikki* / I can't give you anything but love: *Garland, Judy* / I've got you under my skin: *Bassey, Shirley* / Folks who live on the hill: *Lee, Peggy* / Comes along a'love: *Starr, Kay* / Over the rainbow: *Garland, Judy* / Cry me a river: *London, Julie* / By the time I get to Phoenix: *Carr, Vikki* / Unchained melody: *Horne, Lena* / Changing partners: *Starr, Kay* / Long ago (and far away): *Stafford, Jo* / Fools rush in: *Bassey, Shirley* / Occasional man: *London, Julie* / Zing went the strings of my heart: *Garland, Judy* / Manana: *Lee, Peggy* / I (who have nothing): *Bassey, Shirley* / Side by side: *Starr, Kay* / It's a good day: *Lee, Peggy* / Old devil moon: *Garland, Judy* / Fly me to the moon: *London, Julie* / Fine romance: *Horne, Lena* / Walk away: *Carr, Vikki* / Cheek to cheek: *Lee, Peggy* / Nearness of you: *Bassey, Shirley* / Diamonds are a girl's best friend: *London, Julie* / In love in vain: *Horne, Lena* / Play me a simple melody: *Stafford, Jo & Starlighters* / My heart belongs to Daddy: *London, Julie* / As long as he needs me: *Bassey, Shirley* / Hello young lovers: *Horne, Lena* / Only love can break a heart: *Carr, Vikki* / I won't dance: *Lee, Peggy* / Always true to you in my fashion: *London, Julie* / That's entertainment: *Garland, Judy* / Yesterdays: *Stafford, Jo* / Puttin' on the Ritz: *Garland, Judy*
CD Set CDDL 1302
Music For Pleasure / Nov '95 / EMI

SOPHISTICATION VOL.1 (Songs Of The Thirties)
Top hat, white tie and tails: *Gibbons, Carroll* / Things are looking up: *Astaire, Fred* / Way you look tonight: *Astaire, Fred* / Touch of your lips: *Hildegarde* / Darling je vous aime beaucoup: *Hildegarde* / Just let me look at you: *Coward, Noel* / Where are the songs we sung: *Coward, Noel* / Limehouse blues: *Lawrence, Gertrude* / You were meant for me: *Lawrence, Gertrude* / Do do do: *Lawrence, Gertrude* / Someone to watch over me: *Lawrence, Gertrude* / Cup of coffee: *Lawrence, Gertrude* / Wild thyme: *Lawrence, Gertrude* / Experiment: *Lawrence, Gertrude* / Nightfall: *Carter, Benny* / So little time: *Keller, Greta* / I poured my heart into a song: *Hutchinson, Leslie 'Hutch'* / You do something to me: *Dietrich, Marlene* / Falling in love again: *Dietrich, Marlene* / Dancing honeymoon: *Buchanan, Jack* / And her mother came too: *Buchanan, Jack* / Fancy our meeting: *Buchanan, Jack* / Who: *Buchanan, Jack* / Two little bluebirds: *Buchanan, Jack* / Goodnight Vienna: *Buchanan, Jack* / It's not you: *Buchanan, Jack* / There's always tomorrow: *Buchanan, Jack* / Drop in next time you're passing: *Welch, Elisabeth* / One little kiss from you: *Matthews, Jessie* / Let me give my happiness to you: *Matthews, Jessie* / When you've got a little springtime in your heart: *Matthews, Jessie* / Over my shoulder: *Matthews, Jessie* / I nearly let love go slipping through my fingers: *Matthews, Jessie* / Got to dance my way to heaven: *Matthews, Jessie* / Everything's in rhythm with my heart: *Matthews, Jessie* / I can wiggle my ears: *Matthews, Jessie*
CD PPCD 78108
Past Perfect / Feb '95 / Glass Gramophone Co.

SOPHISTICATION VOL.2
CD PPCD 78121
Past Perfect / Mar '96 / Glass Gramophone Co.

SOPRANO SUMMIT 1976 (Live At The Illiana Club)
CD STCD 8254
Storyville / Mar '97 / Cadillac / Jazz Music / Wellard

SORTED, SNORTED AND SPORTED
CD CRECD 117
Creation / Dec '91 / 3mv/Vital

SOUL AFTER HOURS
All I know is the way I feel: *Thomas, Irma* / I can take you to heaven tonight: *Clay, Otis* / Love is all that matters: *Burke, Solomon* / Still in love: *Adams, Johnny* / Without you: *Washington, Walter 'Wolfman'* / Baby I will: *Shannon, Preston* / Ever since: *Little Buster* / Nobody but you: *Peebles, Ann* / I'm gonna hold you to your promise: *Kelly, Paul* / You can't hold on to a love that's gone: *Holmes Brothers*
CD EDCD 7009
Easydisc / Nov '96 / Direct

SOUL ALBUM, THE (2CD Set)
Let's get it on: *Gaye, Marvin* / Let's stay together: *Turner, Tina* / Search for the hero: *M-People* / Ocean drive: *Lighthouse Family* / You gotta be: *Des'ree* / I am blessed: *Eternal* / Always and forever: *Vandross, Luther* / Move closer: *Nelson, Phyllis* / My girl: *Temptations* / (Take a little) piece of my heart: *Franklin, Erma* / Tired of being alone: *Green, Al* / Rainy night in Georgia: *Crawford, Randy* / Why can't we live together: *Thomas, Timmy* / Caravan of love: *Isley-Jasper-Isley* / Be thankful for what you've got: *De Vaughn, William* / Unfinished sympathy: *Massive Attack* / Woman: *Cherry, Neneh* / Back to life: *Soul II Soul* / If you love me: *Brownstone* / I will survive: *Savage, Chantay* / It takes two: *Gaye, Marvin & Kim Weston* / Band of gold: *Payne, Freda* / Give me just a little more time: *Chairmen Of The Board* / Don't leave me this way: *Melvin, Harold & The Bluenotes* / What a fool believes: *Doobie Brothers* / Respect yourself: *Staple Singers* / Private number: *Clay, Judy & William Bell* / I can't stand the rain: *Peebles, Ann* / Change is gonna come: *Redding, Otis* / Ain't no sunshine: *Withers, Bill* / Me and Mrs Jones: *Paul, Billy* / Until you come back to me: *Franklin, Aretha* / Ready or not here I come (can't hide from love): *Delfonics* / Betcha by golly wow: *Stylistics* / Zoom: *Fat Larry's Band* / I'm doin' fine now: *New York City* / Solid: *Ashford & Simpson* / Slowhand: *Pointer Sisters* / After the love has gone: *Earth, Wind & Fire* / Rock me tonight (for old times sake): *Jackson, Freddie* / Piano in the dark: *Russell, Brenda* / Nightshift: *Commodores*
CD Set VTDCD 115
Virgin / Feb '97 / EMI

SOUL ALONE - THE ART OF THE SOLO
CD 131262
Celestial Harmonies / Sep '96 / ADA / Select

SOUL ATTITUDE
CD 3003642
IMP / Jul '97 / ADA / Discovery

SOUL BEAT
Going nowhere: Gabrielle / How can I love you more: M-People / Don't walk away: Jade / Right here: SWV / I love your smile: Shanice / Tom's diner: DNA / When I'm good and ready: Sybil / Please don't go: KWS / Now that we've found love: Heavy D & The Boyz / I'm doing fine now: Pasadenas / Love I lost: West End & Sybil / I wanna sex you up: Color Me Badd / Gypsy woman: Waters, Crystal / Ain't no Cassanova: Sinclair / Things that make you go hmmmm: C&C Music Factory / I will survive: Gaynor, Gloria / Best of my love: Lovestation / Everybody dance: Evolution / U got 2 let the music: Cappella / Motownphilly: Boyz II Men
CD ______ JARCD 9
Cookie Jar / Nov '93 / SRD

SOUL BOX (3CD Set)
CD Set ______ TBXCD 503
TrueTrax / Jan '96 / THE

SOUL BOX (2CD Set)
I can make you feel good: Shalamar / I'm doin' fine now: New York City / Hold back the night: Trammps / Can you feel the force: Real Thing / My girl: Whispers / Walk on by: D-Train / Headlines: Midnight Star / Zoom: Fat Larry's Band / Make it easy on yourself: Butler, Jerry / Be thankful for what you've got: DeVaughan, William / Stay with me baby: Redding, Wilma / Love on a two way street: Moments / Best thing that ever happened to me: Knight, Gladys & The Pips / My guy: Wells, Mary / Loving you, losing you: Hyman, Phyllis / Pillow talk: Sylvia / Galaxy of love: Crown Heights Affair / Come back and finish what you started: Knight, Gladys & The Pips / It's a love thing: Whispers / I owe you one: Shalamar / You gave me love: Crown Heights Affair / I wanna dance wit' choo: Disco Tex & The Sexolettes / Knock on wood: Floyd, Eddie / Suspicious minds: Staton, Candi / Still in love: Lucas, Carrie / Harlem shuffle: Bob & Earl / In the name of love: Redd, Sharon / Hold on I'm coming: Burke, Solomon / No one can love you more: Hyman, Phyllis / Midnight train to Georgia: Knight, Gladys & The Pips / Love fever: Adams, Gayle / Valentine love: Connors, Norman / Can't get by without you: Real Thing / Sad sweet dreamer: Sweet Sensation / Zing went the strings of my heart: Trammps / You'll never know: Hi-Gloss / Lean on me: Moore, Melba / Where did our love go: Elbert, Donnie / More, more, more: True, Andrea Connection / Friends: Shalamar / Beat goes on: Whispers / Check out the groove: Thurston, Bobby / Can you handle it: Redd, Sharon / Midas touch: Midnight Star / Give me your love: Mason, Barbara / So sad the song: Knight, Gladys & The Pips / You'll never know what you're missing: Real Thing / Betcha by golly wow: Hyman, Phyllis & Michael Henderson / Oh no, not my baby: Brown, Maxine / You are my starship: Connors, Norman
CD Set ______ PBXCD 503
Pulse / Nov '96 / BMG

SOUL BROTHERS, SOUL SISTERS
Sweet soul music: Sam & Dave / Operator: Knight, Gladys / Stand by me: King, Ben E. / Under the boardwalk: Drifters / Dancing in the street: Reeves, Martha / Rock your baby: McCrae, George / Hey girl don't bother me: Tams / Band of gold: Payne, Freda / When a man loves a woman: Sledge, Percy / Something old, something new: Fantastics / Baby: Thomas, Carla / Love really hurts without you: Ocean, Billy / Harlem shuffle: Bob & Earl / It's in his kiss (The shoop shoop song): Everett, Betty / What becomes of the broken hearted: Ruffin, Jimmy / If you don't know me by now: Melvin, Harold & The Bluenotes / Rescue me: Bass, Fontella / Knock on wood: Floyd, Eddie / Hey there lonely girl: Holman, Eddie / You'll lose a good thing: Lynn, Barbara
CD ______ MUCD 9026
Musketeer / Apr '95 / Disc

SOUL CHASERS VOL.1
Got to get away: Brown, Sheree / Be for real: Miller, Cat / Do it any way you want: Winters, Robert / Trying to get to you: Carter, Valerie / (A case of) Too much love makin': Scott, Gloria / Top of the stairs: Collins & Collins / I want to be your everything: High Fashion / Would you believe in me: Lucien, Jon / All of my love: Jeter, Genobia / Looking up to you: Wycoff, Michael / And so it begins: Syreeta / Never stopped loving you: Davis, Tyrone / Hold tight: Magic Lady / Call me: Reynolds, L.J.
CD ______ CDEXP 4
Expansion / Nov '92 / 3mv/Sony

SOUL CHASERS VOL.2
Come into my life: Ndugu / Keep on doin': Jones, Glenn / Say you will: Kitajima, Osamu / It only happens (When I look at you): Franklin, Aretha / I don't want wanna live without you: Platinum Hook / I can't tell you: New Horizon / Good times: Gaines, Rosie / Love love love: Hathaway, Donny / Ripe for the pickin': Trumains / Overdose of joy: Record, Eugene / Fragile handle with care: Dees, Sam / I'm not ready: Ujima / We're in love: Austin, Patti / I can't forget about you: Matlock, Ronn
CD ______ CDEXP 8
Expansion / Nov '94 / 3mv/Sony

SOUL CLASSICS
This is it: Moore, Melba / Can't get by without you: Real Thing / Hold back the night: Trammps / Come back and finish what you started: Knight, Gladys & The Pips / Dancing in the the street: Reeves, Martha / Little piece of leather: Elbert, Donnie / Soul man: Dam & Dave / Harlem shuffle: Bob & Earl / Higher and higher: Wilson, Jackie / Knock on wood: Floyd, Eddie / Your little trustmaker: Tymes / Rock your baby: McCrae, George
CD ______ 74321339282
Camden / Jan '96 / BMG

SOUL COLLECTION
Warm and tender love: Sledge, Percy / Under the boardwalk: Drifters / Every beat of my heart: Knight, Gladys & The Pips / Rainy night in Georgia: Benton, Brook / Thank you: Sam & Dave / Make it easy on yourself: Butler, Jerry / Papa's got a brand new bag: Brown, James / Woman in love: Three Degrees / I've never found a girl to love me like you do: Floyd, Eddie / Band of gold: Payne, Freda / Portrait of my love: Clark, Dee / Let it be me: Butler, Jerry & Betty Everett / Needle in my haystack: Whispers / I've been loving you too long: Sledge, Percy / Ain't no sunshine: Jarreau, Al / Up on the roof: Drifters / Hold on I'm comin': Sam & Dave / Letter full of tears: Knight, Gladys & The Pips / Challenge: Butler, Jerry / Duke of Earl: Chandler, Gene
CD ______ QED 180
Tring / Nov '96 / Tring

SOUL DANCE
CD ______ STACD 058
Wisepack / Sep '94 / Conifer/BMG / THE

SOUL DESIRE VOL.1
Sexual healing: Gaye, Marvin / Sign your name: D'Arby, Terence Trent / Shake you down: Abbott, Gregory / Rock me tonight: Jackson, Freddie / After the love has gone: Earth, Wind & Fire / Loving you: Riperton, Minnie / Give me the reason: Vandross, Luther / How 'bout us: Champaign / I still haven't found what I'm looking for: Chimes / Smooth operator: Sade / Ain't no sunshine: Withers, Bill / I need your lovin': Williams, Alyson / Mated: Grant, David & Jaki Graham / Always and forever: Heatwave / Tonight I celebrate my love to you: Bryson, Peabo & Roberta Flack / If you don't know me by now: Melvin, Harold & The Bluenotes
CD ______ 4717322
Columbia / Jun '92 / Sony

SOUL DESIRE VOL.1-3 (3CD Set)
Sexual healing: Gaye, Marvin / Sign your name: D'Arby, Terence Trent / Shake you down: Abbott, Gregory / Rock me tonight: Jackson, Freddie / After the love has gone: Earth, Wind & Fire / Lovin' you: Riperton, Minnie / Give me the reason: Vandross, Luther / How 'bout us: Champaign / I still haven't found what I'm looking for: Chimes / Smooth operator: Sade / Ain't no sunshine: Withers, Bill / I need your lovin': Williams, Alyson / Mated: Grant, David & Jaki Graham / Always and forever: Heatwave / Tonight, I celebrate my love for you: Bryson, Peabo & Roberta Flack / If you don't know me by now: Melvin, Harold & The Bluenotes / On the wings of love: Osborne, Jeffrey / So amazing: Vandross, Luther / Soul provider: Bryson, Peabo / Wind beneath my wings: Knight, Gladys / Cherish: Kool & The Gang / Secret lovers: Atlantic Starr / Winter in July: Bomb The Bass / Come into my life: Sims, Joyce / Hang on to your love: Sade / See the day: Lee, Dee C. / Show me the way: Belle, Regina / Free: Williams, Deniece / Reunited: Peaches & Herb / Just the way you are: White, Barry / Me and Mrs. Jones: Paul, Billy / Don't leave me this way: Melvin, Harold / Love supreme: Downing, Will / My one temptation: Paris, Mica / Sweetest taboo: Sade / Never too much: Vandross, Luther / I can make you feel good: Shalamar / Finest: SOS Band / Juicy fruit: Mtume / I'm doing fine now: Pasadenas / Piano in the dark: Russell, Brenda / Feel so high: Des'ree / Wishing on a star: Cover Girls / Baby, come to me: Belle, Regina / My love is waiting: Gaye, Marvin / Shining star: Manhattans / Mind blowing decisions: Heatwave / Caravan of love: Isley-Jasper-Isley
CD Set ______ 4741212
Columbia / Oct '94 / Sony

SOUL DEVOTION - THE VERY BEST OF HEART & SOUL
Don't be a stranger: Carroll, Dina / My destiny: Richie, Lionel / One moment in time: Houston, Whitney / Going nowhere: Gabrielle / Change: Stansfield, Lisa / Sign your name: D'Arby, Terence Trent / Save the best for last: Williams, Vanessa / My one temptation: Paris, Mica / Stay with me baby: Turner, Ruby / Sexual healing: Gaye, Marvin / Three times a lady: Commodores / Being with you: Robinson, Smokey / My cherie amour: Wonder, Stevie / What becomes of the broken hearted: Ruffin, Jimmy / You are everything: Ross, Diana & Marvin Gaye / With you I'm born again: Preston, Billy & Syreeta / Best thing that ever happened to me: Knight, Gladys & The Pips / One day in your life: Jackson, Michael / Touch me in the morning: Ross, Diana / I say a little prayer: Franklin, Aretha / Tired of being alone: Green, Al / (Sittin' on the) dock of the bay: Redding, Otis / When a man loves a woman: Sledge, Percy / Hey there lonely girl: Holman, Eddie / After the love has gone: Earth, Wind & Fire / If you don't know me by now: Melvin, Harold & The Bluenotes / Have you seen her: Chi-Lites / Lovely day: Withers, Bill / Teardrops: Womack & Womack / It's too late: Quartz / If you're looking for a way out: Odyssey / Wishing on a star: Rose Royce / One day I'll fly away: Crawford, Randy / Always: Atlantic Starr / Slow hand: Pointer Sisters / Your love is king: Sade
CD ______ 5166242
PolyGram TV / Mar '94 / PolyGram

SOUL DREAMING
Like sister and brother: Drifters / Didn't I blow your mind this time: Delfonics / Love come down: King, Evelyn 'Champagne' / Native New Yorker: Odyssey / Woman in love: Three Degrees / You make me feel brand new: Stylistics / Hold to my love: Ruffin, Jimmy / When she was my girl: Four Tops / Livin' in America: Brown, James / You're the first, my last, my everything: White, Barry / Joanna: Kool & The Gang / Summer breeze: Isley Brothers / I really didn't mean it: Vandross, Luther / Never knew love like this: O'Neal, Alexander / Sexual healing: Gaye, Marvin / Let's hear it for the boy: Williams, Deniece / Come back and finish what you started: Knight, Gladys & The Pips / Kiss and say goodbye: Manhattans
CD ______ STACD 006
Wisepack / Nov '92 / Conifer/BMG / THE

SOUL EMOTION
If you don't know me by now: Simply Red / Mercy mercy me/I want you: Palmer, Robert / Wherever I lay my hat (that's my home): Young, Paul / Let's stay together: Turner, Tina / Change: Stansfield, Lisa / One moment in time: Houston, Whitney / Walk on by: Warwick, Dionne / Thinking about your love: Thomas, Kenny / Too many walls: Dennis, Cathy / It's too late: Quartz / Never knew love like this before: Mills, Stephanie / There's nothing like this: Omar / Move closer: Nelson, Phyllis / It's a man's man's man's world: Brown, James / In the midnight hour: Pickett, Wilson / Can't get enough of your love: White, Barry / After the love has gone: Earth, Wind & Fire / Solid: Ashford & Simpson
CD ______ 5151882
PolyGram TV / Mar '92 / PolyGram

SOUL EMOTION (2CD Set)
CD Set ______ NSCD 011
Newsound / Feb '95 / THE

SOUL EXPLOSION (14 Dynamite Cuts)
Feel the need in me: Detroit Emeralds / Something old, something new: Fantastics / Saturday night at the movies: Drifters / Soul man: Sam & Dave / Knock on wood: Floyd, Eddie / Do the funky chicken: Thomas, Rufus / Hold on I'm coming: Sam & Dave / You want it, you got it: Detroit Emeralds / Is it love you're after: Rose Royce / Car wash: Rose Royce / We are family: Sister Sledge / Lost in music: Sister Sledge / Heaven must be missing an angel: Tavares / Whodunit: Tavares
CD ______ SUMCD 4024
Summit / Nov '96 / Sound & Media

SOUL FOR LOVERS
CD ______ DCD 5274
Kenwest / Nov '92 / THE

SOUL HITS
CD ______ LECDD 638
Wisepack / Aug '95 / Conifer/BMG / THE

SOUL INSPIRATION
My destiny: Richie, Lionel / I love your smile: Shanice / looking through patient eyes: PM Dawn / I never felt like this before: Paris, Mica / Drift away: Gray, Dobie / What's going on: Gaye, Marvin / Got to be there: Jackson, Michael / Sweet love: Baker, Anita / Save the best for last: Williams, Vanessa / Have you seen her: Chi-Lites / What becomes of the broken hearted: Ruffin, Jimmy / Hey there lonely girl: Holman, Eddie / Me and Mrs. Jones: Jackson, Freddie / Piano in the dark: Russell, Brenda / Wake up everybody: Melvin, Harold / Feel so high: Des'ree / Until you come back to me: Franklin, Aretha / Love makes the world go round: Don-E
CD ______ 5162262
PolyGram TV / Jun '93 / PolyGram

SOUL INSPIRATION
CD ______ NSCD 020
Newsound / May '95 / THE

SOUL JAZZ LOVE STRATA-EAST
Peace go with you, brother: Scott-Heron, Gil / Well you needn't: Ridley, Larry / Prince of peace: Sanders, Pharoah / Changa chikuyo: Ridley, Larry / John Coltrane: Jordan, Clifford / Hopscotch: Rouse, Charlie / Bottle: Scott-Heron, Gil / Travelling man: Cowell, Stanley / First impressions: Farrah, Shamek / Dance of the little children: Parker, Billy / Eddie Harris: Jordan, Clifford / Smiling Billy suite Pt.2: Heath Brothers
CD ______ SJRCD 019
Soul Jazz / Oct '94 / New Note/Pinnacle / Timewarp / Vital

SOUL JAZZ VOL.1
Honky tonk: Butler, Billy / Return of the prodigal son: Green, Byrdie / I've got the blues: Moody, James / Mom and dad: Earland, Charles / 322 wow: Lytle, Johnny / Up to date: Smith, Johnny 'Hammond' / Dat dere: Adderley, Cannonball Quartet / Light: Ammons, Gene
CD ______ CDBGP 1028
Beat Goes Public / Jun '89 / Pinnacle

SOUL JUKE BOX HITS (2CD Set)
CD Set ______ DCD 5064
Disky / Jul '89 / Disky / THE

SOUL MAN
CD ______ 22513
Music / Jul '95 / Target/BMG

SOUL MESSENGER VOL.1
CD ______ RNGCD 002
EC1 / Mar '95 / EC1 / Grapevine/ PolyGram

SOUL MOODS (2CD Set)
CD Set ______ NSCD 009
Newsound / Feb '95 / THE

SOUL MOTION (CD/CDR Set)
CD Set ______ OM 004
OM / Mar '97 / Cargo / SRD

SOUL NIGHTS
Searching: China Black / Just a step from heaven: Eternal / Don't be a stranger: Carroll, Dina / End of the road: Boyz II Men / Let's get it on: Gaye, Marvin / Night shift: Commodores / Rainy night in Georgia: Crawford, Randy / Where is the love: Paris, Mica & Will Downing / Just another day: Secada, Jon / So close to love: Moten, Wendy / Now I know what made Otis blue: Young, Paul / Stop loving me, stop loving you: Hall, Daryl / Because of you: Gabrielle / Let's stay together: Pasadenas / So amazing: Vandross, Luther / Shake you down: Abbott, Gregory / Everybody's gotta learn sometime: Yazz / Drift away: Gray, Dobie / Tonight, I celebrate my love: Bryson, Peabo & Roberta Flack / Midnight at the Oasis: Muldaur, Maria
CD ______ 5250052
PolyGram TV / Aug '94 / PolyGram

SOUL NIGHTS (2CD Set)
Move closer: Nelson, Phyllis / Toast of love: Three Degrees / It takes two: Barry, Claudja / Forever mine: O'Jays / Love TKO: Pendergrass, Teddy / Lets make a baby: Paul, Billy / Sweeter pain: Wansel, Dexter / In the ghetto: White, Barry / Expressway to your heart: Soul Survivors / You can make it if you try: Allison, Gene / Warm and tender love: Sledge, Percy / Sweet woman like you: Tex, Joe / When you smile: Hutson, Leroy / Stay in my corner: Dells / Didn't we make it: Broadway Express / Don't let love get you down: Bell, Archie & The Drells / For your precious love: Butler, Jerry / Down the aisle: Labelle, Patti & The Bluebells / This love is sweet: Mayfield, Curtis / Soul sister: Jones, Ronnie / Get on up: Esquires / Unforgettable: Rawls, Lou / We do it: Stone, R. & J. / Midnight love affair: Douglas, Carl / Every beat of my heart: Barry, Claudja / Love me like a lover: Charles, Tina / Smarty pants: First Choice / Girls got soul: Indeep / In and out of love: Imagination / Guilty: Pearls / Glad to be your lover: Aiken, Ben / Any day now: Jackson, Chuck / He will break your heart: Butler, Jerry / Twilight time: Platters / Oogum boogum song: Wood, Brenton / Mystery of the world: MFSR
CD Set ______ 24323
Laserlight / May '96 / Target/BMG

SOUL OF A WOMAN VOL.1
CD ______ RENCD 102
Renaissance Collector Series / Jul '95 / BMG

SOUL OF A WOMAN VOL.2
CD ______ RENCD 113
Renaissance Collector Series / Mar '96 / BMG

SOUL OF BLACK PERU, THE
CD ______ 9362458782
Warner Bros. / Jun '95 / Warner Music

SOUL OF CAPE VERDE, THE
CD ______ 68978
Tropical / Apr '97 / Discovery

SOUL OF CHRISTMAS, THE
God rest ye merry gentlemen / First Noel / O come all ye faithful (Adeste Fidelis) / Ding dong merrily on high / Once in Royal David's City / Silent night / While shepherds watched their flocks by night / O little town of Bethlehem / We three kings / Away in a manger / Hark the Herald angels sing / Auld lang syne
CD ______ SOV 009CD
Sovereign / '92 / Target/BMG

SOUL OF GOSPEL, THE
I'll take you there: Staple Singers / You're all I need to get by: Franklin, Aretha / Rescue me: Bass, Fontella / Lean on me: Withers, Bill / (Your love keeps lifting me) higher and higher: Wilson, Jackie / People get ready: Impressions / Oh happy day: Hawkins, Edwin Singers / (Take another little) piece of my heart: Franklin, Erma / Let's stay together: Green, Al / I say a little prayer: Franklin, Aretha / Stand by me:

King, Ben E. / Yah mo be there: *Ingram, James & Michael McDonald* / I'm going all the way: *Sounds Of Blackness* / Message is love: *Baker, Arthur & Backbeat Disciples/ Al Green* / Let my people go: *Winans* / I knew you were waiting (for me): *Franklin, Aretha & George Michael* / I still haven't found what I'm looking for: *Chimes* / Anytime you need a friend: *New Jersey Gospel Choir* / Up where we belong: *South Carolina Baptist Choir* / If you're ready (come go with me): *Staple Singers* / Mercy mercy me: *Gaye, Marvin*
CD __________ **RADCD 31**
Global TV / Nov '95 / BMG

SOUL OF GOSPEL, THE
CD __________ **CDEXM 1**
Exhale / Jul '97 / 3mv/Sony

SOUL OF JAMAICA/HERE COMES THE DUKE
Angel of the morning: *Landis, Joya* / My willow tree: *Ellis, Alton* / Heatwave: *McCook, Tommy & The Supersonics* / (Mummy) out of the light: *Landis, Joya* / My best girl: *Paragons* / What the world needs now: *McCook, Tommy & The Supersonics* / I can't stand it: *Ellis, Alton* / Long time no nice time: *Dillon, Phyllis* / Ride me donkey: *McCook, Tommy* / Love letters: *Ellis, Alton & Phyllis Dillon* / Woman go home: *Jamaicans* / Flying home: *McCook, Tommy & The Supersonics* / Laba laba reggae (the lonely goat herd): *McCook, Tommy & The Supersonics* / Second fiddle: *McCook, Tommy & The Supersonics* / Mary Poppins: *Simpson, Danny/Tommy McCook & The Supersonics* / Soul remedy: *McCook, Tommy & The Supersonics* / I'm in the mood for love: *Techniques* / I'm yours forever: *Soul Lads* / True true true: *Parker, Ken* / Run come celebrate: *Techniques* / Sweet soul music: *Gladiators* / Kansas City: *Landis, Joya* / Love up kiss up: *Termites* / Funny: *Soul Lads*
CD __________ **CDTRL 383**
Trojan / May '97 / Direct / Jet Star

SOUL OF JAZZ PERCUSSION, THE
CD __________ **FSRCD 210**
Fresh Sound / Oct '96 / Discovery / Jazz Music

SOUL OF RHYTHM 'N' BLUES REVUE (Live At The Lone Star Roadhouse)
CD __________ **SHAN 9005CD**
Shanachie / Oct '93 / ADA / Greensleeves / Koch

SOUL OF THE 80'S VOL.2
CD __________ **JHD 043**
Tring / Jun '92 / Tring

SOUL ON THE STREETS VOL.1
Take care of yourself: *Dan-Elle* / Love and devotion: *Marshall, Wayne* / 24-7 Love: *Irini* / Save your love: *SLO* / Hooked on you: *Everis* / Don't let them know: *Irini* / You turn me on: *Everis* / Sexual thing: *Marshall, Wayne* / Sweet lovin': *3rd Zone* / Fire and desire: *Dan-Elle* / Everybody's gotta rave: *Marshall, Wayne* / Don't let them know (remix): *Irini* / She want's a 24/7: *Hyper Man*
CD __________ **SCGCD 201**
SCG / May '94 / Jet Star

SOUL ON THE STREETS VOL.2
CD __________ **SCGCD 3**
SCG / Dec '94 / Jet Star

SOUL POWER
Sign your name: *D'Arby, Terence Trent* / Paradise: *Sade* / Never too much: *Vandross, Luther* / Can you feel it: *Jacksons* / Let's hear it for the boy: *Williams, Deniece* / That lady: *Isley Brothers* / Ain't no sunshine: *Withers, Bill* / Crazy: *Manhattans* / Sweet understanding love: *Four Tops* / Something old, something new: *Fantastics* / Wedding bell blues: *5th Dimension* / Slightest touch: *Five Star* / Ain't nothin' goin' on but the rent: *Guthrie, Gwen* / Livin' in America: *Brown, James* / Come into my life: *Sims, Joyce* / Down on the street: *Shakatak* / Secret lovers: *Atlantic Starr* / What a difference a day makes: *Phillips, Esther* / Gonna get along without you now: *Wills, Viola*
CD __________ **STACD 015**
Telstar / Oct '92 / BMG

SOUL PRESSURE VOL.1
Treat U right: *Truce* / Flavour of the old school: *Knight, Beverley* / You can count on me: *Graham, Jaki* / Turn out the light: *Haynes, Victor* / Slap 'n' tickle: *Kreuz* / From me 2 U: *Everis* / More I try: *Just Good Friends* / If only: *Walker, Daniel* / Do it right: *Act Of Faith* / Only you: *Serenade* / Good man: *Mutual Concept* / Angel: *Riviera* / Nobody knows: *LIFE* / Women's intuition: *Attitude*
CD __________ **CDMISH 2**
Mission / Jun '95 / 3mv/Sony

SOUL PRESSURE VOL.2 (14 Urban Soul Flavours)
Never knew love: *Troi* / Total satisfaction: *Heron, Dee* / Could you be mine: *Ballin, Chris* / Get down on it: *Kreuz* / Something good tonight: *Trichelle* / Do me that way: *Damage* / Come go away: *Truce* / First time: *Haynes, Victor* / Giving my all: *Philips, Jennifer* / In love: *Campbell, Roger* / Lover come back: *Sha Sha* / Heaven: *SCG & Irini* / Closer than close: *McNeish, Carol* / Do you really: *Ruude*
CD __________ **CDMISH 4**
Mission / Dec '95 / 3mv/Sony

SOUL QUEENS, THE
CD __________ **15168**
Laserlight / Aug '91 / Target/BMG

SOUL REFLECTION
Three times a lady: *Commodores* / I don't wanna lose you: *Turner, Tina* / Have you seen her: *MC Hammer* / Stop to love: *Vandross, Luther* / Criticize: *O'Neal, Alexander* / Yah mo be there: *Ingram, James & Michael McDonald* / There'll be sad songs (to make you cry): *Ocean, Billy* / Almaz: *Crawford, Randy* / If you don't know me by now: *Melvin, Harold & The Bluenotes* / Just my imagination: *Temptations* / I second that emotion: *Robinson, Smokey & The Miracles* / Too busy thinking about my baby: *Gaye, Marvin* / Hold back the night: *Trammps* / Just the way you are: *White, Barry* / You sexy thing: *Hot Chocolate* / Always: *Atlantic Starr* / Baby, come to me: *Austin, Patti & James Ingram*
CD __________ **8453342**
PolyGram TV / Feb '91 / PolyGram

SOUL SALAD
CD __________ **HUB 019**
Hubbub / Jun '97 / Beechwood/BMG / SRD / Timewarp

SOUL SAMPLER VOL.1
I'll be your winner: *Clarke, Jimmy 'Soul'* / Oh my darlin': *Lee, Jackie* / Pizza pie man: *Grier, Roosevelt* / Hide out: *Hideaways* / Girl across the street: *Smith, Moses* / Lady love: *Vontastics* / I've been trying: *Chants* / I need your love: *Woods, Ella* / This love: *Joytones* / Streets got my lady: *Brandon, Bill* / Girl I love you: *Fisher, Shelly* / Given up on love: *Thompson, Johnny* / Searching for soul: *Wade, Jake & The Soul Searchers* / Everything's gonna be alright: *Moore, Robert* / You: *Wilson, Spanky*
CD __________ **GSCD 013**
Goldmine / Aug '96 / Vital

SOUL SAMPLER VOL.2
Your heart makes me lonely: *Chandlers* / I don't want to hear it: *Exits* / Give in to the power of love: *Committee* / Ain't gonna do you no harm: *Willis, Betty* / Lighten up baby: *Karim, Ty* / Don't cha tell nobody: *Vontclaires* / Candle: *Burdick, Doni* / I don't mess around: *Reynolds, Jeanie* / What have I got now: *Fletcher, Darrow* / All of a sudden: *Incredibles* / I found out: *Lacour, Bobby* / I'll cry over you: *Sheeler, Cynthia* / I'll cry 1000 tears: *Holman, Eddie* / Let's get together: *George, Cassietta* / Crumbs off the table: *Young Disciples* / Breakdown: *Memphians* / Cool off: *Detroit Executives*
CD __________ **GSCD 034**
Goldmine / Aug '96 / Vital

SOUL SAMPLER VOL.3
False alarm: *Volcanoes* / So is the sun: *World Column* / Shotgun and the duck: *Lee, Jackie* / Long run: *Blandon, Curtis* / This thing called love: *Wyatt, Johnny* / I'll hold you: *Frankie & Johnny* / I wanna testify: *Parliaments* / Angel baby: *Banks, Darrell* / Times are bad: *Barnes, Bobby* / Jenkins, diane: *Barnes, Bobby* / This I've gotta see: *Shaw, Cecil* / Let's get together: *George, Cassietta* / Over the top: *Dawson, Roy* / Paradise: *Jewel* / I can't lie to my heart: *Fykes, Betty*
CD __________ **GSCD 096**
Goldmine / Jul '96 / Vital

SOUL SEARCHING
Could it be I'm falling in love: *Detroit Spinners* / Used ta be my girl: *O'Jays* / I can see clearly now: *Cliff, Jimmy* / Don't let love get you down: *Bell, Archie & The Drells* / Let's get it on: *Gaye, Marvin* / Reunited: *Peaches & Herb* / Me and Mrs. Jones: *Paul, Billy* / Right here: *SWV* / I still haven't found what I'm looking for: *Chimes* / Special kind of love: *Carroll, Dina* / Stay: *Eternal* / I miss you: *Haddaway* / Walk on by: *Warwick, Dionne* / Almaz: *Crawford, Randy* / Feel so high: *Des'ree* / Lovely day: *Withers, Bill* / Night to remember: *Shalamar* / Don't let it go to your head: *Carne, Jean* / (You make me feel like) a natural woman: *Franklin, Aretha* / Delicate: *D'Arby, Terence Trent* / I love your smile: *Shanice* / These arms of mine: *Redding, Otis* / On the wings of love: *Osborne, Jeffrey* / Your body's calling: *R Kelly* / Hearts run free: *Staton, Candi* / Whole town's laughing at me: *Pendergrass, Teddy* / Show me the way: *Bell, Regina* / Private number: *Clay, Judy & William Bell* / I want your love: *Chic* / Sweet love: *Baker, Anita* / Woman to woman: *Brown, Shirley* / I'm doing fine now: *New York City* / Winter in July: *Bomb The Bass* / Misty blue: *Moore, Dorothy*
CD Set __________ **MOODCD 34**
Columbia / Jul '94 / Sony

SOUL SEARCHING
CD __________ **HILOCD 11**
Hi / Jan '95 / Pinnacle

SOUL SELECTION VOL.1
CD __________ **HUBCD 8**
Hubbub / Jun '96 / Beechwood/BMG / SRD / Timewarp

SOUL SELECTION VOL.2
CD __________ **HUBCD 11**
Hubbub / Nov '96 / Beechwood/BMG / SRD / Timewarp

SOUL SENSATION
CD __________ **MATCD 204**
Castle / Dec '92 / BMG

SOUL SENSATION (2CD Set)
CD Set __________ **NSCD 012**
Newsound / Feb '95 / THE

SOUL SENSITIVITY
CD Set __________ **NSCD 010**
Newsound / Feb '95 / THE

SOUL SISTERS
CD __________ **NTRCD 028**
Nectar / Sep '94 / Pinnacle

SOUL SOLDIERS
I'm the one who loves you: *Banks, Darrell* / No one blinder (than a man who won't see): *Banks, Darrell* / Just because your love has gone: *Banks, Darrell* / Only the strong survive: *Banks, Darrell* / Got to get rid of you: *Barnes, J.J.* / Snowflakes: *Barnes, J.J.* / I like everything about you: *Hughes, Jimmy* / I'm so glad: *Hughes, Jimmy* / Did you forget: *Hughes, Jimmy* / Chains of love: *Hughes, Jimmy* / Just ain't strong as I used to be: *Hughes, Jimmy* / Since I lost my baby's love: *Major Lance* / I wanna make up (before we break up): *Major Lance* / That's the story of my life: *Major Lance* / Girl come on home: *Major Lance* / Ain't no sweat: *Major Lance* / Beautiful feeling: *Banks, Darrell* / When a man loves a woman: *Banks, Darrell* / Let 'em down baby: *Hughes, Jimmy* / I'm not ashamed to beg or plead: *Hughes, Jimmy* / Sweet Sherry: *Barnes, J.J.* / Baby, please come back home: *Barnes, J.J.*
CD __________ **CDSX 012**
Stax / Aug '88 / Pinnacle

SOUL SOUNDS OF THE 90'S
What is black music: *Williams, Cunnie* / Life with you: *Buchanan, Courtney* / London kills me: *Groove Nation* / My destiny: *Mr. C* / Status symbol: *Great Unknown* / I can't help it: *Glenn, Chris* / Keep the groove: *Freestyle* / Drift away: *Thompson, Carroll* / Warm weather: *Mother Of Pearl* / If we loose our way: *Johnson, Paul* / Mr. Groove: *McCord, Kevin* / What the child needs: *Ronald, Terry*
CD __________ **SOUNDSCD 7**
Street Sounds / Oct '95 / Beechwood/BMG

SOUL SOUNDS OF THE SEVENTIES
Boogie nights: *Heatwave* / I'll go where the music takes me: *Charles, Tina* / Love really hurts without you: *Ocean, Billy* / Love don't live here anymore: *Rose Royce* / Car wash: *Rose Royce* / More than a woman: *Tavares* / Heaven must be missing an angel: *Tavares* / Can you feel the force: *Real Thing* / You to me are everything: *Real Thing* / Doctor Love: *Charles, Tina* / Always and forever: *Heatwave* / Magic fly: *Space* / Love machine: *Miracles* / Stoned love: *Supremes* / Heaven must have sent you: *Elgins* / Hang on in there baby: *Bristol, Johnny & Liz Sands*
CD __________ **QED 187**
Tring / Nov '96 / Tring

SOUL STIRRINGS - THE NU INSPIRATIONAL
CD __________ **BRCD 599**
4th & Broadway / Oct '93 / PolyGram

SOUL SUPREME (2CD Set)
CD Set __________ **DEMPCD 016**
Emporio / Mar '96 / Disc

SOUL SUPREME VOL.2
Wanted: *Johnson, Paul* / Dom Perignon: *Don-E* / Look no more: *Occasions* / Love is all you need: *Clark, Rick & Gina Foster* / It's on: *Hilary* / Rumours and lies: *Kareem* / Do me right: *Laverne, Elisha* / Cry: *Ballin, Chris* / Meant to be: *Dutchy* / Dance with me: *5 AM* / More than a lover: *Cole, Errol* / Searchin': *Stevens, Mike* / Cast all your cares: *Knight, Beverley*
CD __________ **DOMECD 10**
Dome / Feb '97 / 3mv/Sony

SOUL SURVIVORS (40 Northern Soul Anthems - 2CD Set)
Move on up: *Mayfield, Curtis* / SOS: *Starr, Edwin* / It takes two: *Gaye, Marvin & Kim Weston* / Needle in a haystack: *Velvelettes* / What: *Street, Judy* / Do I love you (Indeed I do): *Wilson, Frank* / This old heart of mine (is weak for you): *Isley Brothers* / 1-2-3: *Barry, Len* / Backfield in motion: *Mel & Tim* / Let's wade in the water: *Shaw, Marlena* / My man, a sweet man: *Jackson, Millie* / Love makes a woman: *Acklin, Barbara* / Sweetest feeling: *Wilson, Jackie* / You're gonna love my baby: *McNair, Barbara* / Be young, be foolish, be happy: *Tams* / Better use your head: *Little Anthony & The Imperials* / There's a ghost in my house: *Taylor, R. Dean* / Out on the floor: *Gray, Dobie* / Sweet soul music: *Conley, Arthur* / Bok to bach: *Father's Angels* / You know how to love me: *Hyman, Phyllis* / Queen of clubs: *KC & The Sunshine Band* / Don't take away the music: *Tavares* / Love machine: *Miracles* / Snake: *Wilson, Al* / Show me: *Tex, Joe* / Time is tight: *Booker T & The MG's* / Here I go again: *Bell, Archie* / Sweet talkin' guy: *Chiffons* / Rescue me: *Bass, Fontella* / Can't satisfy: *Impressions* / Girl (why you wanna make me blue): *Temptations* / Green door: *Frog, Wynder K.* / I'm gonna run away from you: *Lynn, Tammi* / Zoo (The Human Zoo): *Commodores* / Go go power: *De Santo, Sugar Pie* / Dearly beloved: *Montgomery, Jack* / Long after tonight is all over: *Radcliffe, Jimmy* / Time will pass you by: *Legend, Tobi* / I'm on my way: *Parrish, Dean*
CD Set __________ **TCD 2869**
Telstar / Apr '97 / BMG

SOUL TO SOUL
CD __________ **CDTRL 356**
Trojan / Jul '95 / Direct / Jet Star

SOUL TRAIN VOL.1
CD __________ **CDSGP 0149**
Prestige / Jan '95 / Else / Total/BMG

SOUL TRAIN VOL.2
CD Set __________ **CDSGP 0262**
Prestige / Feb '96 / Else / Total/BMG

SOUL UNDERGROUND VOL.1
Two sides to every story: *Love, Jimmy* / Baby I'm serious: *Tillman, Charlotta* / Don't accuse me: *Squires* / I feel good (all over): *Lavette, Bettye* / Come back baby: *Stoppers* / (I know) Your love has gone away: *Drapers* / Only your love can save me: *Lavette, Bettye* / He's got the nerve: *True Tones* / Another time another place: *Starr, Harry* / If you ask me (because I love you): *Williams, Jerry* / Fell in love with you baby: *Elliot, Linda* / Dance dance dance: *Casualeers* / What shall I do: *Frankie & The Classicals* / Don't refuse my love: *Intrigues* / Stand up like a man: *Lavette, Bettye* / Nothing can help you now: *Curtis, Lenny* / I'll do anything: *Troy, Doris* / Too long without some loving: *Clovers* / What did I do: *Humes, Anita & The Essex* / Walkin': *Jones, Jimmy* / I'm just a fool for you: *Lavette, Bettye* / Mama's got a bag of her own: *King, Anna* / Can't help lovin' dat man: *Vann, Ila* / Step into my world: *Vann, Ila*
CD __________ **NEMCD 759**
Sequel / Oct '95 / BMG

SOUL UNDERGROUND VOL.2 (Time Marches On)
Three dollar bill: *Gibson, Beverley-Ann* / I'll never let you go: *Cadillacs* / Never ever leave me: *Hunt, Geraldine* / Please don't go: *Kathy & The Calenders* / Everything is fine: *Skyliners* / Spinnin' top: *Orlons* / No better for you: *Big Maybelle* / Try my loving on you: *Clovers* / I'm in such misery: *Gardner, Don* / We'll be makin' out: *James, Jessica & The Outlaws* / I'm so glad: *Neal, Robert* / Help me (get over my used to be lover): *Honey & The Bees* / I've got my baby: *Livingston, Patty* / Now that you left me: *Thurmond, Duff* / Condition red: *Baltimore & Ohio Marching Band* / Time marches on: *Hill, Lainie* / Turns to me: *Towns, Chris Unit* / Human race: *Adams, June* / Isn't it just a shame: *Wells, Kenny* / Stop hurting me baby: *Purple Mundi* / Never had a love so good: *Johnson, Charles* / I need you like a baby: *Janice* / Nobody but you: *Phillips, Esther* / It seems like I've been here before: *Jackson, J.J.*
CD __________ **NEMCD 841**
Sequel / Apr '96 / BMG

SOUL'D TOGETHER VOL.2 (The Soul Of Black America)
CD __________ **ATCD 016**
ATR / Nov '92 / Beechwood/BMG

SOUL'D TOGETHER VOL.3 (The Soul Of Black America)
Close to you: *Bush, Charles* / I want you: *Smith, Antoine* / Second go around: *Cornelious, Eve* / House my love: *Blount, Carlton* / Never go back: *Ledford, Kenne* / Good times: *DeBarge* / I knew I could always count on you: *Brown, Shirley* / Thank you lady: *Brittan, James* / Nine to five (who said it): *Floyd, Jeff* / Reaching for the sky: *Riley, Walter* / Drug free society: *Mozie B* / Never give up: *Mathis, Diane* / One more night: *Gaines, Rosie* / Let me kiss you where it hurts: *Burris, Warren* / Girl I miss you: *Group Life* / If you need it: *Bush, Charles*
CD __________ **ATCD 017**
ATR / Aug '93 / Beechwood/BMG

SOUL'D TOGETHER VOL.4 (The Soul Of Black America)
Walking in rhythm: *Foxx Empire* / I'll give my love: *Thin Line* / Take U to the top: *Bush, Charles* / Taking it as it comes: *Desi* / Tell me to stay: *Kiass* / Reach out your hand: *Mason, Laverna* / Baby I know: *McNeir, Ronnie* / Nothing like this: *Greene, Mark* / Call me: *Nash, Kevin* / Straight from the heart: *Brittan, James* / Throw her love: *Floyd, Jeff* / Peaceful: *Eddie M*
CD __________ **ATCD 023**
ATR / Aug '95 / Beechwood/BMG

SOULED ON REGGAE VOL.1
Ain't no sunshine: *Boothe, Ken* / I'll be there: *Biggs, Barry* / Tears of a clown: *Chosen Few* / Only the strong survive: *Mighty Diamonds* / Me and Mrs Jones: *White, Joe* / You make me feel brand new: *Wilson, Delroy* / Baby I need your loving: *Wilson, Delroy* / Homely girl: *Inner Circle* / Papa was a rolling stone: *Pioneers* / Just my immagination: *London, Jimmy* / Dock of the bay: *Brown, Dennis* / Band of gold: *Griffiths, Marcia* / Rainy night in Georgia: *Thomas, Nicky* / BAckstabbers: *Lee, Byron & The Dragonai-*

res / Didn't I blow your mind: *Cables* / You keep me hangin' on: *Dorane, Mike*
CD ____ EMPRCD 577
Emporio / Jul '95 / Disc

SOULED ON REGGAE VOL.2 (16 Soul Classics In A Reggae Style)
I second that emotion: *Chosen Few* / Don't leave me this way: *Wilson, Delroy* / Put yourself in my place: *Campbell, Cornell* / My girl: *Brown, Dennis* / Let's get it on: *Boothe, Ken* / First time ever I saw your face: *Griffiths, Marcia* / Thin line between love and hate: *Seaton, B.B.* / Ain't nothing like the real thing: *Bob & Marcia* / Didn't I blow your mind: *Cables* / You keep me hanging on: *Dorane, Mike* / Private number: *Honey Boy* / My cherie amour: *Harry J All Stars* / If loving you is wrong: *Maytones* / What does it take to win your love: *Ellis, Alton* / Midnight train to Georgia: *Brown, Teddy* / When will I see you again: *Inner Circle*
CD ____ EMPRCD 667
Emporio / Oct '96 / Disc

SOULFUL
CD ____ LHCD 014
Luv n' Haight / Jul '96 / Timewarp

SOULFUL KINDA 70'S (2CD Set)
Shy guy: *Baker, Johnny* / Man of value: *Berklay, Tyrone* / Your smallest wish: *21st Century Ltd* / Dancing on a daydream: *Soulvation Army* / You live only once: *Imperial Wonders* / Happy: *Velvet Hammer* / It's not where you start: *Davis, Luckey* / Like taking candy from a baby: *Brown, J.T.* / Ain't nothing wrong: *Jones, Jimmy* / This economy: *Michel, Lee* / Shady lady: *Newton, Bobby* / Baby hard times: *Love, Dave* / In a world so cold: *St. Germain, Tyrone* / Over the top: *Dawson, Roy* / Secret place: *Brothers* / If it wasn't for you: *Four Sonics* / Loneliness: *Will, David* / Let's spend some time together: *Houston, Larry* / Dance all night: *Masterplan* / You're my main squeeze: *Crystal Motion* / Game players: *Silverspoon, Dooley* / Wrong crowd: *Prince George* / Bet you if you ask around: *Velvet* / You better keep her: *Holmes, Marvin* / You can win: *Bileo* / Heartache and pain: *Pages* / He's always around: *Gerrard, Donny* / I can't make it: *Simmons, Vessie* / I want to be loved: *Stevens & Foster* / Love's built on a strong foundation: *Big Jim's Border Crossing* / Ho happy day: *Flame 'n' King* / Turning point: *Simmons, Mack* / Honey baby: *Innervision* / Have love will travel: *Jones, Rosey* / When the fuel runs out: *Ambitions* / Spellbound: *Everett, Frank* / I wonder: *Family Circle* / Come back: *Fantastic Puzzles* / What goes up: *Cody, Black* / Don't you leave: *Hughes, Freddie* / Operator operator: *Baker, Johnny* / Some kinda man: *Pride & Passion* / All I want: *Neal, C.C.* / Come and ask me: *5 Wagers* / From the bottom of your heart: *Steelers* / Give in to the power of love: *Committee* / Let's get nasty: *Stephens, Chuck* / What: *Weathers, Oscar* / Love will turn around: *Entertains* / I'm a winner: *Just Bobby*
CD Set ____ GSCD 050
Goldmine / Nov '95 / Vital

SOULFUL LOVE DUETS VOL.1
CD ____ SCL 2512
Ichiban Soul Classics / Nov '95 / Koch

SOULFUL LOVE DUETS VOL.2
CD ____ SCL 2513
Ichiban Soul Classics / Nov '95 / Koch

SOUND BOY KILLING
CD ____ SH 45018
Shanachie / Dec '94 / ADA / Greensleeves / Koch

SOUND GALLERY VOL.1
Oh Calcutta: *Pell, Dave* / Black rite: *Mandingo* / Headhunter: *Mandingo* / Snake pit: *Mandingo* / Punch bowl: *Parker, Allan* / Night rider: *Hawkshaw, Alan* / Girl in a sportscar: *Hawkshaw, Alan* / It's all at the co-op now: *Hawkshaw, Alan* / Blarney's stoned: *Hawkshaw, Alan* / Riviera affair: *Richardson, Neil* / Jetstream: *Gregory, John* / Jaguar: *Gregory, John* / Half forgotten daydreams: *Gregory, John* / Life of leisure: *Mansfield, Keith* / Young scene: *Mansfield, Keith* / Music to drive by: *Loss, Joe* / Detectives: *Tew, Alan* / Boogie juice: *Bennett, Brian* / Penthouse suite: *Dale, Syd* / I feel the earth move: *Keating, Johnny* / Jesus Christ superstar: *Keating, Johnny* / Earthmen: *Kingsland, Paddy* / Shout about pepsi: *Wright, Denny* / Funky fever: *Morehouse, Alan*
CD ____ CDTWO 2001
Premier/EMI / Apr '95 / EMI

SOUND GALLERY VOL.2
Jason King theme: *Johnson, Laurie* / Powerhouse pop: *Mansfield, Keith* / Good word: *Scotsman* / Two lane blacktop: *Clarke, James* / Zodiac: *Lindup, David* / That's nice: *Moorhouse, Alan* / I can see for miles: *Lord Sitar* / Accroche toi, Caroline: *Paris Studio Group* / Marsellaise Generique: *Lai, Francis* / Francais Francais: *Pourcel, Franck* / Left Bank two: *Noveltones* / Light my fire: *Andrews, John* / Avengers tag: *Johnson, Laurie* / Open house: *Fahey, Brian* / Mama Elephant: *E-Cap* / International flight: *Snell, David* / Up to date: *Park, Simon* / On the brink: *Vickers, Mike* / Sports car special: *Pearson, Johnny* / Countdown: *Fahey, Brian* / Miss World: *Dale, Syd* / Enter the dragon: *Parnell, Jack* / Breakaway: *Karman, Steve* / Caesar Smith: *Johnson, Laurie* / Rat catchers: *Pearson, Johnny* / At the sign of the Swinging Cymbal: *Fahey, Brian* / Theme One: *Martin, George*
CD ____ CDTWO 2002
Premier/EMI / Jul '96 / EMI

SOUND INFORMATION
CD ____ WWCD 9
Wibbly Wobbly / Feb '95 / SRD

SOUND INFORMATION COLLECTION
CD ____ EB 010
Echo Beach / May '97 / Cargo / Shellshock/Disc

SOUND NAVIGATOR (Setting Sail For An Outernational Reggae Style)
CD ____ BTT 0332
Buback / Oct '95 / SRD

SOUND OF CHRISTMAS PANPIPES, THE
When a child is born / Have yourself a very merry Christmas / Sleigh ride / O little town of Bethlehem / Way in a manger / In Dulci jubilo / Once in Royal David's City / Hark the Herald angels sing / Silent night / God rest ye merry gentlemen / White Christmas / Christmas dreams / First Noel / Little Drummer Boy / Walking in the air (The snowman) / In the bleak mid winter / Happy Christmas (war is over) / I'll be home for Christmas / Mistletoe and wine / Christmas song / Go rest ye merry gentlemen
CD ____ 3036000052
Carlton / Oct '95 / Carlton

SOUND OF CLEVELAND CITY, THE
Testament 1: *Chubby Chunks* / Don't stop: *Direct 2 Disc* / Herbal hand: *B-Line* / Excuse me: *Direct 2 Disc* / Whose no.1: *Dig The New Breed* / Hey Mr. DJ: *Screen II* / Real thing: *Di Bart, Tony* / Morning: *Direct 2 Disc* / Saturday night party: *Alex Party* / Cast: *B-Line* / Drive in one: *TST Fever Posse* / Swing man: *Rhyme Time Productions*
CD ____ CLECD 333
Cleveland City / Aug '94 / 3mv/Sony / Grapevine/PolyGram

SOUND OF CLUB KINECTIC VOL.4
CD ____ VKCD 4
Club Kinetic / Aug '97 / Grapevine/ PolyGram / Mo's Music Machine / Total/ BMG

SOUND OF CLUB KINETIC VOL.2 (2CD Set)
CD Set ____ VKCD 02
Club Kinetic / Oct '96 / Grapevine/ PolyGram / Mo's Music Machine / Total/ BMG

SOUND OF CLUB KINETIC VOL.3 (2CD Set)
CD Set ____ VKCD 3
Club Kinetic / Oct '96 / Grapevine/ PolyGram / Mo's Music Machine / Total/ BMG

SOUND OF COLUMBIA, THE (Highlights From The 9th Cartegena Festival)
CD ____ CPCD 8135
Charly / Jan '96 / Koch

SOUND OF COOLTEMPO VOL.2
Ring my bell: *Monie Love & Adeva* / Outstanding: *Thomas, Kenny* / Lovesick: *Gang Starr* / Keep the dream alive: *Light Of The World* / Matter of fact: *Innocence* / Alright: *Urban Soul* / Shelter me: *Circuit & Koffi* / Pure: *GTO* / My heart: *Beat* / D-shake: *Mainline*
CD ____ CCD 1867
Cooltempo / Jun '91 / EMI

SOUND OF DETROIT/RARE STAMPS/ HERE TO STAY (Don Davis Presents)
Baby, please come back home: *Barnes, J.J.* / Chains of love: *Barnes, J.J.* / Now that I got you back: *Barnes, J.J.* / Easy living: *Barnes, J.J.* / Sweet Sherry: *Barnes, J.J.* / Don't make me a storyteller: *Mancha, Steve* / Love like yours: *Mancha, Steve* / Keep the faith: *Mancha, Steve* / I don't wanna lose you: *Mancha, Steve* / Hate yourself in the morning: *Mancha, Steve* / Just keep on loving me: *Mancha, Steve* / Just because your love has gone: *Banks, Darrell* / Forgive me: *Banks, Darrell* / Only the strong survive: *Banks, Darrell* / Don't know what to do: *Banks, Darrell* / When a man loves a woman: *Banks, Darrell* / We'll get over: *Banks, Darrell* / Beautiful feeling: *Banks, Darrell* / I could never hate her: *Banks, Darrell* / Never alone: *Banks, Darrell* / No one blinder (than a man who won't see): *Banks, Darrell* / My love is strictly reserved: *Banks, Darrell*
CD ____ CDSXD 061
Stax / Jul '92 / Pinnacle

SOUND OF FUNK VOL.1, THE
Damph F'aint: *Johnson, Herb Settlement* / Sad chicken: *Leroy & The Drivers* / How long shall I wait: *Fields, James Lewis* / Hector: *Village Callers* / Let the groove move you: *Lewis, Gus 'The Groove'* / Groovy world: *Fabulous Caprices* / Jan jan: *Various Narrators* / Iron leg: *Mickey & The Soul Generation* / You got to be a man: *Williams, Frank* / Searching for soul: *Various Narrators* / Push and pull: *Sons Of Slum* / Take this woman off the corner: *Spencer, James* / Everything gonna be alright: *Various Narrators* / Tramp Part 1: *Showmen Inc.* / I'm the man: *Showmen Inc.* / Whip: *Brown, Al* / You: *Wilson, Spanky* / Brother Brown: *Bob, Camille* / Happy soul: *Cortez, Dave & The Moon People* / Let my people go: *Darondo* / Nefertiti: *Wysdom*
CD ____ GSCD 007
Goldmine / Nov '92 / Vital

SOUND OF FUNK VOL.10, THE (Serious 70's Heavyweight Rarities)
Super funky (part 1): *Thunder, Lightning And Rain* / Quit jivin': *Pearly Queen* / Pick and shovel: *Touch* / Georgia walk: *Raw Soul* / Soul block (of rocking people): *Len And The Pa's* / Rare back and stretch (part 1): *Sandifer, McKinley* / Chicken and rice: *Soul Serenaders* / I gotta see my baby: *Ellis, Jamie* / I don't want to cry: *Cole, Bennie & His Soul Bros.* / She broke down (ran right out on me): *Little Richard III* / No names will be called: *Road Runners* / Chicken peck (part 2): *Pronouns* / You have come into my life: *Swindell, Earl* / Man hunt: *Ross, Mltzi* / Charge: *Bronc-Glows* / Down home publicity: *Apple And The 3 Oranges* / Allen's party: *Matthews, Allen* / Can you dig it: *Soul Setters* / Who's the blame: *Jessie, Obe* / So called friends: *Barnes, J.J.*
CD ____ GSCD 097
Goldmine / Oct '96 / Vital

SOUND OF FUNK VOL.2, THE
Gat or bat / Humpty dumpty: *Vibrettes* / I've got reasons: *Hooper, Mary Jane* / Got to get me a job: *Alford, Ann* / Love got a piece of your mind: *5 Ounces Of Earth* / African strut: *Westbrook, Lynn* / Spin-II jug: *Brooks, Smokey* / Girl chooses the boy: *Collins, Lashdown* / Funk I-Tus: *Warm excursion* / Chocolate sugar: *Six Feet Under* / Screwdriver: *Austin, Lee* / Skin II black: *Bush, Tommy* / Communication is where it's at: *Billy the baron* / World: *1619 Bab* / Fun and funk: *Fantastic epics* / Marvin's groove: *BW Souls* / Hot butter 'n' all: *Darondo*
CD ____ GSCD 012
Goldmine / Apr '93 / Vital

SOUND OF FUNK VOL.3, THE
Got a thing for you baby: *Mr. Percolator* / Funky funky hot pants: *Mason, Wee Willie* / JB's latin: *Spittin' Image* / New bump and twist: *Kats* / Hit drop: *Explosions* / Africana: *Propositions* / Got a gig on my back: *Kelly & The Soul Explosion* / Soul drippin's: *Interns* / Let's get together: *George, Cassietta* / Baby I've got it: *King George & The Fabulous Souls* / Fon-kin love: *Love International* / Campbell lock: *Campbell, Don* / Funky soul shake: *White, E.T. & The Potential Band* / Hot pants: *20th Century* / Closed mind: *Different Bags* / Give a damn: *Gordon, Benny* / Stop (what'cha doing to me): *Roberts, Roy* / Gimme some tonight: *Holmes Justice, Marvin* / How you get higher: *Hunter & His Games*
CD ____ GSCD 023
Goldmine / Sep '93 / Vital

SOUND OF FUNK VOL.4, THE
Funky buzzard: *Little Oscar* / Fun in your thang: *Phelps, Bootsey & The Soul Invaders* / Funky fat man: *Bynum, Burnett & The Soul Invaders* / Keep on brother keep on: *Fatback Band* / Crumbs for the table: *Young Disciples & Co.* / Moon walk: *King Solomon* / Bumping: *Chestnut, Tyrone* / Open up your heart: *Raw Soul & Frankie Beverly* / Get some: *Wee Willie & The Winners* / (Ride on) iron horse: *Marlboro Men* / Funky funk: *Big Al & The Star Treks* / Funky moon meditation: *Moonlighters* / Wait a minute: *Xplosions* / Do the funky donkey: *Turner, Otis & The Mighty Kingpins* / Funky line part 1: *Fabulous Shalimars* / Hold tight: *McNutt, Bobby* / Funky hump: *Cook, Little Joe* / Be black baby: *Tate, Grady* / Can you dig it: *Chico & Buddy*
CD ____ GSCD 028
Goldmine / Jan '94 / Vital

SOUND OF FUNK VOL.5, THE
Dynamite: *Colt, Steve* / Crazy legs: *Soul Tornadoes* / Breakdown: *Memphians* / Revolution rap (Part 1): *Green, Cal* / Wait a minute: *Xplosions* / Funkie moon: *Johnson, Smokey & Company* / Soul combination: *Soul Combination* / Afro bush: *Gaunichaux, E. & The Skeptics* / Football: *Mickey & The Soul Generation* / Whip (Part 1): *Simpkins, Darnell & the Family Tree* / Give a man a break: *Mintz, Charles* / I laugh and talk (but I don't play): *Strong, Zeke & the Ladyetts* / Kuri kuri: *Diety* / Hot pants: *Bee, Jimmy* / Bear funk: *Revolution Funk* / Do the yum yum man: *Contributors Of Soul* / Whip (Part 2): *Simpkins, Darnell & the Family Tree* / I laugh and talk (instrumental): *Strong, Zeke & the Ladyetts* / Revolution rap (Part 2): *Green, Cal*
CD ____ GSCD 036
Goldmine / Apr '94 / Vital

SOUND OF FUNK VOL.6, THE
Gigolo: *Anderson, Gene* / You did it: *Robinson, Ann* / Foxy little Mama: *Stone, Bob & His Band* / Oof (Do anything I want): *Colbert, Chuck* / Sweet thing: *Campbell, Milton & The R-D-M Band* / Rerun: *King Hannibal* / Atlanta boogaloo: *Inclines* / Rough nut: *Zodiacs* / Fussin and cussin (Part 1): *Four Wheel Drive* / (Get ready for) Changes: *Marva & Melvin* / Funky John: *Cameron, Johnny & The Camerons* / Soul chills: *Soul, Dede & The Spidels* / Loneliest one: *Anderson, Gene* / Life is like a puzzle: *Village Soul Choir* / Sunshine: *Scacy & The Sound Service* / Take it where you found it: *Jackson, Lorraine* / Fussin and Cussin (Part: *Four Wheel Drive* / Soul chills (Part 2): *Soul, Dede & The Spidels* / Boogie man: *Jones, Rufus R*
CD ____ GSCD 045
Goldmine / Aug '94 / Vital

SOUND OF FUNK VOL.7, THE
Super cool: *Hunt, Pat* / Branded: *Leach, C.J.* / Funky strut: *Fabulous Soul Eruption* / Hook and boogie pt.1: *Abraham* / It's your love: *Theron & Darrell* / Dap walk: *Ernie & The Top Notes* / Gimme some: *General Crook* / Boilin' water: *Soul Stoppers Band* / Bad luck: *Carbo, Hank* / Fish head: *Slim & Soulful Saints* / Green power: *Wallace, Sir Sidney* / Slow down: *Elliott, Don* / Do your own thing: *Moultrie, Sam* / Soul chicken: *Allen, Bobby* / Soul power: *Willis, Jamie* / Whip: *Brown, Al* / Hook and boogie pt.2: *Abraham* / Gimme some (pt.2): *General Crook* / Slow down: *Elliott, Don*
CD ____ GSCD 060
Goldmine / Dec '94 / Vital

SOUND OF FUNK VOL.8, THE
Ain't no other way: *Hitson, Herman* / Baby don't cry: *Third Guitar* / Do the Bobby Dunn: *Dunn, Bobby* / Popcorn baby: *Hench, Freddy* / Check your battery: *Talbot, Johny* / Baby I've got it: *Fabulous Souls* / You lost your thing: *Johnson, Hank* / Sagittarius: *Landlord & Tennants* / Ain't that fun: *Harris, Tyrone* / Movin' and Groovin': *Volcanos* / Lady: *Superiors Band & Their Soul Singers* / Funky donkey: *Illusions* / Groove penguin: *Wonsley, Excell* / Soul encyclopedia: *Jones, Geraldine* / Get off your butt: *Hines, Debbie* / Jungle: *Young Senators* / Funky jive: *Soul Crusaders* / Village sound: *Village Sound*
CD ____ GSCD 064
Goldmine / Jun '95 / Vital

SOUND OF FUNK VOL.9, THE
Free and easy: *Apples & The Oranges* / Take it and get: *Zere & The Soul Sisters* / I don't want to hear it now: *Brinson, Jimmy* / Cool it: *Morris, Guy* / Do the train: *Thrillers* / Number one prize: *Bare Faxx* / Cookies: *Brother Soul* / What it is: *Apollis* / Funky wah wah: *La Mar, Tony* / Tormented: *Holliday, Johnny* / What you do it good: *Williams, Gene* / Sound success: *Wallis, Joe* / Funky mule Pt.1: *Holmes, Martin & The Uptights* / Times are bad: *Barnes, Bobby* / I got a new thing: *Smith, Willie* / Akiwawa: *Village Crusaders* / Nabbit juice pt.1: *Eastwind* / Happy fool: *Belva* / Sock it to me: *Moore, Henry* / Do it good: *Brother Soul*
CD ____ GSCD 067
Goldmine / Jan '96 / Vital

SOUND OF GARAGE CITY, THE
CD ____ CTC 0404
Coast 2 Coast / May '95 / Jet Star

SOUND OF HAPPYCORE '97
Techno wonderland: *Ravers Choice* / Your love: *Force & Styles* / Bonkers: *Sharkey* / Stay with me: *DJ Demand* / E-nuff: *Sharkey* / All over the world: *Force & Styles* / On and on: *DJ Brisk & DJ Ham* / Here I am: *DJ Ham & DJ Demo/Justin Time* / Never let you go: *DJ Seduction* / Cloudy daze: *Bang & DJ Ham* / Excitement: *DJ Faber* / Discoland: *Tiny Tot*
CD ____ CDRAID 535
Rumour / Jun '97 / 3mv/Sony / Mo's Music Machine / Pinnacle

SOUND OF KISS 100FM, THE
Blow your whistle: *DJ Duke* / Big time sensuality: *Bjork* / Ain't no love (ain't no use): *Sub Sub & Melanie Williams* / U got 2 let the music: *Cappella* / What is love: *Haddaway* / Love I lost: *West End & Sybil* / When I'm good and ready: *Sybil* / Show me love: *Robin S* / Funk DAT: *Sagat* / Dreams: *Gabrielle* / There's nothing like this: *Omar* / Apparently nothin': *Young Disciples* / I love your smile: *Shanice* / Right here: *SWV* / Don't walk away: *Jade* / I shall sing: *Griffiths, Marcia* / People everyday: *Arrested Development* / Chime: *Orbital* / On a ragga tip: *SL2* / Key, the secret: *Urban Cookie Collective* / Don't you want me: *Felix* / It's a fine day: *Opus III* / I'm gonna get you: *Bizarre Inc.* / Everybody's free: *Rozalla* / LSI: Love sex intelligence: *Shamen* / Seize the day: *FKW* / I'll be there for you: *House Of Virginism* / Give it up: *Goodmen* / Shout: *Louchie Lou & Michie One* / Jump around: *House Of Pain* / Oh Carolina: *Shaggy* / Boom shak-a-lak: *Apache Indian* / Come baby come: *K7* / Boom shake the room: *DJ Jazzy Jeff & The Fresh Prince*
CD ____ 5164862
PolyGram TV / Jan '94 / PolyGram

SOUND OF LIGHT, THE
CD ____ ND 63914
Narada / Oct '94 / ADA / New Note/ Pinnacle

SOUND OF MOTORCITY, THE (3CD Set)
Crazy 'bout the guy: *Supremes* / On the beach: *Demps, Louvain* / Mister wonderful: *Randolph, Barbara* / Back in circulation: *Fantastic Four* / Merry go round: *Lewis, Pat* / Straight in the eye: *Cameron, G.C.* / What's wrong with me baby: *Valadiers* / Pull myself together: *Johnson, Marv* / Release this love: *Starr, Edwin* / Gonna win you back: *Contours* / Ten out of ten: *Elgins* /

You're my lucky number: *McNeir, Ronnie* / You're my luck number: *McNeir, Ronnie* / One too many reasons: *Littles, Hattie* / I need you: *Jacas, Jake* / Nowhere to go but up: *Nero, Frances* / You're so fine: *Stubbs, Joe* / Hurt the one you love: *Ruffin, David* / Don't take my kindness for weakness: *Starr, Edwin* / Hit and miss: *Supremes* / Got the big city blues: *Eckstine, Billy* / It's a rough world: *Satintones* / Face to face with love: *McNair, Barbara* / You're what's missing in my life: *Cameron, G.C.* / Girls are out to get you: *Andantes* / Angel: *Griffin, Billy* / Lost and found: *Demps, Louvain* / Waiting 'round the corner: *Mike & The Modifiers* / Can't give you up: *McNeir, Ronnie* / Sweet as a honey bee: *Barnes, J.J.* / Reach for the sky: *Lavette, Bettye & Jake Jacas* / Your love is wonderful: *Littles, Hattie* / Where did our love go: *Three Ounces Of Love* / Step into my shoes: *Reeves, Martha & The Vandellas* / Not this time: *Griner, Linda* / Stop in the name of love: *Supremes* / Running a fever: *Littles, Hattie* / Lonely lonely girl am I: *Velvelettes* / After dark: *Campbell, Choker* / It's a pleasure: *Nero, Frances* / Heatwave: *Motor City Allstars* / With you I'm born again: *Syreeta* / Fighting for what's right: *Holloway, Brenda* / Keep on giving me love: *McNeir, Ronnie* / Starting all over again: *Lands, Liz* / Turning my back and walking away: *Randolph, Barbara* / Working on a building of love: *Fantastic Four* / Let the music take you away: *Van Dyke, Earl* / Rescue me: *Lewis, Pat*
CD Set __________ 390242
Hallmark / Jul '96 / Carlton

SOUND OF MUSIC, THE
CD __________ CZ 33CD
Bring On Bull / Nov '93 / SRD / Vital

SOUND OF PHILADELPHIA, THE
CD __________ 3057
Scratch / Mar '95 / Koch / Scratch/BMG

SOUND OF REVOLUTION
CD __________ RENCD 111
Renaissance Collector Series / Mar '96 / BMG

SOUND OF ROME
CD __________ ACV 204 CD
ACV / Oct '95 / Plastic Head / SRD

SOUND OF SKA, THE
CD __________ QTVCD 007
Quality / May '92 / Pinnacle

SOUND OF SKA, THE
Lip up fatty / On my radio / Can can / Too much too young / Night boat to cairo / One step beyond / Mirror in the bathroom / Nee nee na na nu nu / Special brew / Baggy trousers / Hand's off she's mine / Three minute hero / Buster's groove
CD __________ QED 091
Tring / Nov '96 / Tring

SOUND OF SKA, THE
Sound of skaaa medley: *Bad Manners* / On my radio: *Black, Pauline* / Mirror in the bathroom: *Rankin' Roger* / Special Brew: *Rankin' Roger* / Night boat to Cairo: *Bad Manners* / Can can: *Bad Manners* / Missing words: *Black, Pauline* / Baggy trousers: *Bad Manners* / One step beyond: *Bad Manners* / Lip up fatty: *Bad Manners* / Hands off she's mine: *Rankin' Roger* / Too much too young: *Rankin' Roger* / Three minute hero: *Black, Pauline* / Buster's groove: *Bad Manners* / One stop beyond: *Bad Manners*
CD __________ SUMCD 4124
Sound & Media / Jun '97 / Sound & Media

SOUND OF SOUND VOL.2
CD __________ 111902
Musidisc / Feb '94 / Discovery

SOUND OF STONE, THE
Sound of stone: *Dennehy, Tim* / May morning dew: *Spillane, Davy* / Fertile rock: *Bloom, Luka* / Pup jig: *Shannon, Sharon* / Miss Burren, Co Clare: *Lane, Frankie* / Rodney Millar's: *Custy, Mary Band* / For Mullaghmore: *Bushplant* / Bonny Portmore: *McKennitt, Niall* / Progress of man: *Sheedy, Niall* / Mountain twig: *Crawford, Kevin & Pat Marsh* / One starry night: *Tyrrell, Sean* / An gleann cuin: *Peoples, Tommy & Siobhan/Gary O'Briain* / Ambran na boirne: *Flanagan, John* / Limestone rock: *Moving Cloud* / Laurel bush: *Moving Cloud* / Silver spear: *Moving Cloud* / Battering ram: *Custy, Mary Band* / Donegal reel: *Crawford, Kevin & Pat Marsh* / Daisyfield: *Peoples, Tommy & Siobhan/Gary O'Briain*
CD __________ BAGCD 001
Bag / Jul '93 / Direct

SOUND OF SUMMER, THE (The Ultimate Beach Party)
Surf city: *Jan & Dean* / Surfin' safari: *Beach Boys* / Hey little cobra: *Regents* / Little Honda: *Hondells* / Tequila: *Cannon, Ace* / Indian lake: *Cowsills* / Ride the wild surf: *Jan & Dean* / Wipeout: *Surfaris* / Surfer girl: *Beach Boys* / Baby talk: *Jan & Dean* / GTO: *Regents* / Remember (walkin' in the sand): *Shangri-Las* / Summer song: *Chad & Jeremy* / Beach baby: *Regents* / Surfin': *Beach Boys* / Pipeline: *Chantays*
CD __________ ECD 3047
K-Tel / Jan '95 / K-Tel

SOUND OF SUPERSTITION VOL.4, THE (2CD Set)
CD Set __________ SUPER 2050
Superstition / Mar '96 / Plastic Head / SRD / Vital

SOUND OF THE ABSOLUTE
CD __________ OMCD 1
OM / Mar '94 / Cargo / SRD

SOUND OF THE BAGPIPES, THE
CD __________ 302782
Hallmark / Feb '97 / Carlton

SOUND OF THE SUBURBS, THE
Eton rifles: *Jam* / Ant music: *Adam & The Ants* / Ever fallen in love: *Buzzcocks* / Another girl another planet: *Only Ones* / Teenage kicks: *Undertones* / Echo beach: *Martha & The Muffins* / Happy birthday: *Altered Images* / Oliver's army: *Costello, Elvis* / 2-4-6-8 Motorway: *Robinson, Tom Band* / Hit me with your rhythm stick: *Dury, Ian & The Blockheads* / Call me: *Blondie* / Reward: *Teardrop Explodes* / I don't like Mondays: *Boomtown Rats* / Pretty in pink: *Psychedelic Furs* / No more heroes: *Stranglers* / Turning Japanese: *Vapors* / Do anything you wanna do: *Eddie & The Hot Rods* / Sound of the suburbs: *Members*
CD __________ MOODCD 18
Columbia / Aug '91 / Sony

SOUND OF THE SYNTHS VOL.2
CD __________ 15426
Laserlight / Jun '93 / Target/BMG

SOUND OF THE UNDERGROUND VOL.1 (SOUR Cream)
CD __________ SOURCD 1
SOUR / Feb '95 / SRD

SOUND SPECTRUM, THE
Get carter: *Budd, Roy* / Love is a four letter word: *Budd, Roy* / Getting nowhere in a hurry: *Budd, Roy* / Plaything: *Budd, Roy* / Hurry to me: *Budd, Roy* / Grow your own: *Schroeder, John Orchestra* / Headband: *Schroeder, John Orchestra* / Touch of velvet: *City Of Westminster String Band* / Split level: *City Of Westminster String Band* / Stiletto: *Rey, Chico & The Jett Band* / Heavy Water: *Davies, Ray & His Funky Trumpet* / Mach 1: *Davies, Ray & His Funky Trumpet* / Speakin' of spoken: *Lovin' Spoonful* / Supershine No.9: *Sister Goose And The Ducklings* / Loner: *Hunter, Milton* / Busy body: *Dicks, Ted* / Birds: *Hatch, Tony Orchestra* / 2001: *Holmes, Cecil Soulful Sound* / Pegasus: *Vickers, Mike* / Hot wheels: *Badder Than Evil*
CD __________ WENCD 005
When / Nov '95 / Pinnacle

SOUND STAGE 7 STORY, THE (2CD Set)
Easy going fellow: *Shelton, Roscoe* / Hymn no. 5: *Gaines, Earl* / I'm his wife, you're just a friend: *Sexton, Ann* / I love you: *Baker, Sam* / Only time you say you love me: *Smith, Charles* / You keep me hangin' on: *Simon, Joe* / Whole lot of man: *Davis, Geator* / All the time: *Washington, Ella* / Sometimes you have to cry: *Baker, Sam* / Chokin' kind: *Simon, Joe* / He called me baby: *Washington, Ella* / Your heart is so cold: *Davis, Geator* / Strain on my heart: *Shelton, Roscoe* / You're gonna miss me: *Sexton, Ann* / I'll take care of you: *Gaines, Earl* / I'm not through loving you: *Brown, Lattimore* / I don't care who knows: *Church, Jimmy* / Soon as darkness falls: *Shelton, Roscoe* / What made you change your mind: *King, Bobby* / Human / Judge of hearts: *Hobbs, Willie* / Someone bigger than you or me: *Baker, Sam* / We've got to save it: *Scott, Moody* / Let me come on home: *King, Bobby* / I'm ready to love you now: *Shelton, Roscoe* / Just a glance away: *Baker, Sam* / Try something new: *Billups, Eddie* / Ooh I love you: *Cashmeres* / I got love: *Byrd, Leon* / Woman's touch: *Scott, Moody* / My faith in you: *Church, Jimmy* / I know your heart has been broken: *Shelton, Roscoe*
CD Set __________ CDLAB 103
Charly / Mar '96 / Koch

SOUNDS AND PRESSURE VOL.1
Barbican dub: *Hudson, Keith* / Problems: *Andy, Horace* / Ras menilik Congo: *Pablo, Augustus* / Red blood: *Black Skin The Prophet* / Mansion of invention: *Prince Far-I & The Arabs* / Black belt Jones: *Hudson, Keith* / Tribal war: *Little Roy* / Sinners: *Hudson, Keith* / Bass ace: *Prince Far-I & The Arabs* / Same song: *Israel Vibration* / King Tubby's dub song: *Pablo, Augustus*
CD __________ PSCD 005
Pressure Sounds / Jul '97 / Jet Star / SRD

SOUNDS AND PRESSURE VOL.2
Poor Marcus: *Mighty Diamonds* / Columbus ship: *Little Roy* / Thriller: *Don D Jr.* / In God we trust: *Morwells* / In time to come: *Earth & Stone* / Who have eyes to see: *Prince Far-I & Mike Brooks* / Shepherd rod: *Upsetter* / Jestering: *Shorty The President & Enos 'Genius' McLeod* / Shame and pride: *Mighty Diamonds* / Right way: *Prince Far-I & The Arabs* / I'll go through: *Israel Vibration*
CD __________ PSCD 10
Pressure Sounds / Jul '97 / Jet Star / SRD

SOUNDS COLOMBIAN
Momposina: *Pinedo, Nelson & La Sonora Matancera* / Quien pueda interesar: *Forero, Esther* / Pila pilandera: *Cruz, Celia* / Senorita (la llave y la cerradura): *Penaranda, Jose Maria* / Entre palmeras: *Los Ases Del Ritmo* / La levita: *Forero, Esther* / Dejenla llorar: *Velasquez, Anibal* / El vaquero: *Pinedo, Nelson & La Sonora Matancera* / El ano viejo: *Valdes, Vicentico* / Oye mi cumbia: *Los Ases Del Ritmo* / Por mi no te preoccupes: *Forero, Esther* / El demonio son los hombres: *Penaranda, Jose Maria* / Estas delirando: *Pinedo, Nelson & La Sonora Matancera* / A la orilla del mar: *Flores, Isodoro Conjunto* / El pajaro bobo: *Penaranda, Jose Maria* / No quiero llorar: *Cruz, Celia* / La cosquillita: *Velasquez, Anibal* / La mafafa: *Torruellas, Angel Luis* / Mi cafetal: *Trio Maravilla* / Ay cosita Linda: *Argentino, Carlos & La Sonora Matancera*
CD __________ CDHOT 620
Charly / Apr '97 / Koch

SOUNDS CUBAN
CD __________ CDHOT 607
Charly / Aug '96 / Koch

SOUNDS EASY
Kiss me honey honey kiss me: *Bassey, Shirley* / Love is blue: *Mauriat, Paul & His Orchestra* / Sunny: *Hebb, Bobby* / Walk in the black forest: *Jankowski, Horst & Orchestra* / Don't let the rain come down: *Serendipity Singers* / Adam Adamant theme: *Lee, Dave & Orchestra* / Say wonderful things: *Carroll, Ronnie* / Colorado: *Del Parana, Luis Alberto Y Los Paraguayos* / Summer place theme: *Gregory, John Orchestra* / What are you doing for the rest of your life: *Gillies, Stuart* / Air for G string: *Swingle Singers & Modern Jazz Quartet* / On a clear day you can see forever: *Laine, Cleo* / Love letters: *Arthey, Johnny Orchestra* / Girl talk: *Coffee Set* / Scarborough fair: *South, Harry Stereo Brass* / Sway: *Cugat, Xavier & His Orchestra* / Troubleshooters: *Tew, Alan Latin Sound* / How are things in glocca morra: *Gray, Johnnie & His Saxophones* / Long daddy green: *Dearie, Blossom* / America: *Cortez & His New Latin* / Eso beso: *McGuiffe, Bill* / Wedding: *Rogers, Julie* / Man without love: *Henderson, Joe* / In the hall of the mountain king: *Smith, Pete Orchestra* / Somethin' stupid: *Button Down Brass* / Sisters: *Beverley Sisters*
CD __________ 5354212
Mercury / Jun '96 / PolyGram

SOUNDS LIKE PARIS
South of heaven: *Zend Avesta* / Psychotic phunk reaction: *Daphreephunkateers & Adelph* / Fllying fingers: *Motorbass* / Non non non: *Melaaz* / Soul salsa soul: *Melaaz* / Cut a rug: *Dirty Jesus* / My family: *Elegia* / le voyage: *Mighty Bop* / 357 Magnum Force: *La Funk Mob* / Affaires a faire: *La Chatte Rouge* / Toujours l'amour: *Dimitri From Tokyo*
CD __________ PAN 1001CD
Pan / Jul '97 / Amato Disco / Prime / Vital

SOUNDS OF AFRICA
CD __________ SOW 90120
Sounds Of The World / Jan '94 / Target/BMG

SOUNDS OF BAMBOO, THE (Instrumental Music Of The 'Are'are People/Solomon Islands)
Music to raise the house / Swine shrieks / Love song piece/Ho'osia ritual / Parrot piece / Mound bird / Introduction piece / Haridata's grief / Popora's weeping / Frogs of darana / Closing piece / Rihe piece / Kinkina bird piece / Infant's cry / Stop and go / Moaning piece / Mice piece / Dove piece / Sound of the river piece / Bats piece / Thunder piece / Lamentation / Eagle piece / Tree roots piece / Moths / Rat / Thunder / Dog / Sacred taro pudding to the wild man / Divination song / Kiroha deconstruction / Lament solo / Lament duo / Lament hummed / Lullaby / Love song
CD __________ MCM 3007
Multicultural Media / May '97 / Direct

SOUNDS OF CALEDONIA
CD __________ RECD 499
REL / Mar '96 / CM / Duncans / Highlander

SOUNDS OF EVOLVING TRADITIONS, THE (Central Andean Music & Festivals/ Peru & Bolivia)
Farewell to Ayacucho Town / El condor pasa / Sacsayhuaman / Arisal tree / Golden basket / Huallancayo / Pio pio / Chacarera / Guadalquivir River / Sicu ensemble / Wayruru / Auki auki / Unbundled panpipes / Takitas / Wedding music from Amarete / Church bells / Mule music / Music for chica beer / Festival finale music
CD __________ MCM 3009
Multicultural Media / May '97 / Direct

SOUNDS OF NEW HOPE, THE (3CD Set)
CD Set __________ AIW 045CD
Nightbreed / Dec '96 / Plastic Head

SOUNDS OF NEW ORLEANS VOL.10
CD __________ STCD 6017
Storyville / Jul '96 / Cadillac / Jazz Music / Wellard

SOUNDS OF SCOTLAND
CD __________ MACCD 125
Autograph / Aug '96 / BMG

SOUNDS OF SCOTLAND VOL.1, THE
Scottish soldier: *Stewart, Andy* / Amazing grace: *Scots Guards 1st Battalion Pipes/Drums* / 6.20: *Shand, Jimmy* / Auld scotch sangs: *Anderson, Moira* / Down in the glen: *Wilson, Robert* / Wild rover: *Tartan Lads* / Isle of Skye: *Corries* / I love a lassie: *Logan, Jimmy* / Miss Elspeth Campbell / Inverary Castle: *Argyll & Sutherland Highlanders* / Mrs. McPherson of Inveran: *Argyll & Sutherland Highlanders* / Scotland the brave: *Wilson, Robert* / My ain house: *Anderson, Moira* / Campbeltown Loch / Sky is bluer in Scotland: *Tartan Lads* / Drunken piper: *Blackwatch 1st Battalion Pipes/Drums* / Highland laddie: *Blackwatch 1st Battalion Pipes/Drums* / Black bear: *Blackwatch 1st Battalion Pipes/Drums* / Road to the Isles: *Stewart, Andy* / Victory polkas: *Gordon Highlanders 1st Battalion Pipes/Drums* / Willie the woodcutter: *MacLeod, Jim* / Tom Clements reel: *MacLeod, Jim* / Trumpet hornpipe: *MacLeod, Jim* / Bonnie Galloway / Here's to scotch whiskey: *Tartan Lads* / Bonnie Dundee: *Corries* / Liberton pipe band polka: *Wick Scottish Dance Band & Wick Fiddlers* / Heather bells will bloom again: *Stewart, Andy* / My ain folk: *Anderson, Moira* / Rothesay Bay: *Anderson, Moira* / When you and I were young Maggie: *Tartan Lads* / Gathering of the clans: *Wilson, Robert* / Hills O' the Clyde: *Wilson, Robert* / Gay gordons: *Johnstone, Jim & His Band* / Fifty first Highland division: *Johnstone, Jim & His Band* / Far o'er: *Johnstone, Jim & His Band*
CD __________ CDMFP 6316
EMI Gold / Feb '97 / EMI

SOUNDS OF SCOTLAND VOL.2, THE
CD __________ CDMFP 6317
EMI Gold / Feb '97 / EMI

SOUNDS OF SUDAN
CD __________ WCD 018
World Circuit / Jan '91 / ADA / Cadillac / Direct / New Note/Pinnacle

SOUNDS OF THE 70'S (4CD Set)
CD Set __________ MBSCD 402
Castle / Nov '95 / BMG

SOUNDS OF THE CITY
CD Set __________ SCCD 1
Sounds Of The City / Jan '96 / Total/BMG

SOUNDS OF THE DETONATOR VOL.1 (Mixed by DJ's Vibes, Seduction & Dougal/2CD Set)
CD Set __________ DPRCD 01
Dance Planet / Jun '97 / SRD

SOUNDS OF THE DETONATOR VOL.2 (Mixed By DJ's Sy, SS, Grooverider & Ralphie Dee/2CD Set)
CD Set __________ DPRCD 02
Dance Planet / Jun '97 / SRD

SOUNDS OF THE FIFTIES
Secret love: *Day, Doris* / Jezebel: *Laine, Frankie* / Oh mein Papa: *Calvert, Eddie* / Unchained melody: *Hibbler, Al* / Singin' the blues: *Mitchell, Guy* / True love: *Crosby, Bing & Grace Kelly* / When I fall in love: *Cole, Nat 'King'* / Here in my heart: *Martino, Al* / Rock 'n' roll waltz: *Starr, Kay* / Softly, softly: *Murray, Ruby* / No other love: *Hilton, Ronnie* / Blue Tango: *Martin, Ray* / Blueberry Hill: *Domino, Fats* / (We're gonna) rock around the clock: *Haley, Bill* / Cumberland gap: *Donegan, Lonnie* / Cry me a river: *London, Julie* / Tammy: *Reynolds, Debbie* / Little things mean a lot: *Kallen, Kitty* / Fever: *Lee, Peggy* / Petite fleur: *Barber, Chris Jazz Band & Monty Sunshine*
CD __________ CDPR 122
Premier/MFP / Oct '94 / EMI

SOUNDS OF THE SEVENTIES (4CD Set)
Band of gold: *Payne, Freda* / I can do it: *Rubettes* / Angel face: *Glitter Band* / I only wanna be with you: *Bay City Rollers* / I love to love: *Charles, Tina* / I wanna dance wit' choo: *Disco Tex & The Sexolettes* / Greased lightning: *Travolta, John* / (Dancing) on a Saturday night: *Blue, Barry* / Hitchin' a ride: *Vanity Fare* / Baby jump: *Mungo Jerry* / Love really hurts without you: *Ocean, Billy* / Here comes that rainy day feeling again: *Fortunes* / I will survive: *Gaynor, Gloria* / Juke box jive: *Rubettes* / Goodbye my love: *Glitter Band* / Sahng a lang: *Bay City Rollers* / Now is the time: *James, Jimmy & The Vagabonds* / Run back: *Douglas, Carl* / If you don't know me by now: *Melvin, Harold & The Bluenotes* / Woman in love: *Three Degrees* / Hey there lonely girl: *Holman, Eddie* / Dance little lady dance: *Charles, Tina* / Black and white: *Greyhound* / People like you and people like me: *Glitter Band* / Sandy: *Travolta, John* / In the summertime: *Mungo Jerry* / Get dancin': *Disco Tex & The Sexolettes* / Somerlove sensation: *Bay City Rollers* / Never can say goodbye: *Gaynor, Gloria* / Kung fu fighting: *Douglas, Carl* / I'm on fire: *5000 Volts* / Ring my bell: *Ward, Anita* / Hold back the night: *Trammps* / Indiana wants me: *Taylor, R. Dean* / Yellow river: *Christie* / Freedom come freedom go: *Fortunes* / I'll go where your music takes me: *James, Jimmy & The Vagabonds* / Wake up everybody: *Melvin, Harold & The Bluenotes* / Dirty ol' man: *Three Degrees* / Me and Mrs.Jones: *Paul, Billy* / I'll go where your music takes me: *Charles, Tina* / Stoned love: *Supremes* / Boogie nights: *Heatwave* / Car wash: *Royce, Rose* / Can you feel the force: *Real Thing* / You to me are evrything: *Real Thing* / Heaven must have sent you: *Elgins* / Magic fly: *Space* / Hang on in there

baby: Bristol, Johnny / Love don't live here anymore: Royce, Rose / Doctor love: Charles, Tina / More than a woman: Tavares / Always and forever: Heatwave / Rainforest: Biddu Orchestra / Reaching for the best: Exciters / Patches: Carter, Clarence / Come and get it: Badfinger / Never ending song of love: New Seekers / Foe dee o dee: Rubettes / Hey girl don't bother me: Tams / More more more: True, Andrea Connection / You don't have to be in the army to fight in the war: Mungo Jerry / Troglodyte (caveman): Castor, Jimmy Bunch / Treat her like a lady: Cornelius Brothers & Sister Rose / What have they done to my song ma: New Seekers / Something old something new: Fantastics / I get a little sentimental over you: New Seekers / Let's get together again: Glitter Band / I'd like to teach the world to sing: New Seekers / I'm doin' fine now: New York City / Alright alright: Mungo Jerry / Lady rose: Mungo Jerry / Pinball wizard/See me feel me: New Seekers / Sugar baby love: Rubettes / Up in a puff of smoke: Brown, Polly / Open up: Mungo Jerry / Beg steal or borrow: New Seekers / Love grows (where my rosemary grows): Edison Lighthouse / You little trustmaker: Tymes
CD Set ______ QUAD 013
Tring / Nov '96 / Tring

SOUNDS OF THE SEVENTIES (2CD Set)
Get it on: Bolan, Marc & T-Rex / Virginia Plain: Roxy Music / School's out: Cooper, Alice / All the young dudes: Mott The Hoople / Crocodile rock: John, Elton / I'm the leader of the gang: Glitter, Gary / Blockbuster: Sweet / Walk on the wildside: Reed, Lou / Make me smile (come up and see me): Cockney Rebel / Mama weer all crazee now: Slade / See my baby jive: Wizzard / Love train: O'Jays / Show you the way to go: Jacksons / Best of my love: Emotions / That lady: Isley Brothers / Le freak: Chic / We are family: Sister Sledge / Boogie wonderland: Earth, Wind & Fire / I will survive: Gaynor, Gloria / You're the first, my last, my everything: White, Barry / Ladies night: Kool & The Gang / Band on the run: McCartney, Paul & Wings / Mr. Blue Sky: ELO / Baker street: Rafferty, Gerry / So you win again: Hot Chocolate / Down down: Status Quo / Oliver's army: Costello, Elvis / Hit me with your rhythm stick: Dury, Ian / Heart of glass: Blondie / Message in a bottle: Police / Maggie Mae: Stewart, Rod / Without you: Nilsson / Vincent: McLean, Don / I'm not in love: 10cc / Horse with no name: America / Seasons in the sun: Jacks, Terry / Lean on me: Withers, Bill / Right thing to do: Simon, Carly / Every day hurts: Sad Cafe / Wishing on a star: Rose Royce
CD Set ______ RADCD 01
Global TV / Nov '94 / BMG

SOUNDS OF THE SEVENTIES-REGGAE STYLE
I can't get next to you: Charmers / You're a big girl now: Chosen Few / Rainy night in Georgia: Thomas, Nicky / Groove me: Beckford, Keeling / Just my imagination: Barker, Dave / Sister big stuff: Holt, John / Shaft: Charmers, Lloyd / Help me make it through the night: Parker, Ken / Ben: Elaina, Margaret / Lean on me: Seaton, B.B. / Have you seen her: Harriott, Derrick / First time ever I saw your face: Griffiths, Marcia / Let me down easy: Brown, Dennis / Break up to make up: Sibbles, Leroy / Hurt so good: Cadogan, Susan / Too late to turn back: Ellis, Alton / Living a little, laughing a little: Spence, Barrington / If you're ready: Richards, Cynthia / You make me feel brand new: Gardiner, Boris / When will I see you again: Inner Circle
CD ______ CDTRL 321
Trojan / Mar '94 / Direct / Jet Star

SOUNDS OF THE SIXTIES (4CD Set)
Runaway: Shannon, Del / He's so fine: Chiffons / Will you love me tomorrow: Shirelles / 24 hours from Tulsa: Pitney, Gene / Leader of the pack: Shangri-Las / Every beat of my heart: Knight, Gladys & The Pips / Fools rush in: Benton, Brook / Under the boardwalk: Drifters / Rubber ball: Vee, Bobby / Harbour lights: Platters / Walk don't run: Ventures / Mr. bass man: Cymbal, Johnny / Judy in disguise (with glasses): Fred, John & His Playboy Band / I believe: Bachelors / Tossin' and turnin': Ivy League / Don't let the sun catch you crying: Gerry & The Pacemakers / Silhouettes: Herman's Hermits / Tabacco road: Nashville Teens / Baby now that I've found you: Foundations / Love is all around: Troggs / Remember (walkin' in the sand): Shangri-Las / Surfin' safari: Beach Boys / I'm gonna be strong: Pitney, Gene / Chapel of love: Dixie Cups / Duke of Earl: Chandler, Gene / Oh no not my baby: Brown, Maxine / Barefootin': Parker, Robert / Soldier boy: Shirelles / Hats off to Larry: Shannon, Del / Save the last dance for me: Drifters / Ramona: Bachelors / Hippy hippy shake: Swinging Blue Jeans / You'll never walk alone: Gerry & The Pacemakers / There's a kind of hush: Herman's Hermits / Wild thing: Troggs / Here it comes again: Fortunes / Tell Laura I love her: Valance, Ricky / Walkin' back to happiness: Shapiro, Helen / Hurt: Yuro, Timi / Dizzy: Roe, Tommy / Night has a thousand eyes: Vee, Bobby / Up on the roof: Drifters / Do you love me: Poole, Brian / Little town flirt: Shannon, Del / Bobby's girl: Maughan, Susan / Last night in Soho: Dave Dee, Dozy, Beaky, Mick & Tich / With a girl like you: Troggs / Do you want to know a secret: Kramer, Billy J. / How do you do: Gerry & The Pacemakers / You were on my mind: St. Peters, Crispian / Mama: Berry, Dave / I think of you: Merseybeats / Roses are red: Carroll, Ronnie / Love grows: Edison Lighthouse / Jesamine: Casuals / Dimples: Hooker, John Lee / Devil or angel: Vee, Bobby / A little lovin': Fourmost / No milk today: Herman's Hermits / That's why I'm crying: Ivy League / Sugar sugar: Archies / Everlasting love: Love Affair / Run to him: Vee, Bobby / Swiss maid: Shannon, Del / Town without pity: Pitney, Gene / Shake me, wake me: Rodgers, Clodagh / Legend of Xanadu: Dave Dee, Dozy, Beaky, Mick & Tich / I can't control myself: Troggs / Crying Game: Berry, Dave / Ferry 'cross the Mersey: Gerry & The Pacemakers / Pied piper: St. Peters, Crispian / Wishin' and hopin': Merseybeats / He's in town: Rockin' Berries / Jack the ripper: Screaming Lord Sutch / Letter full of tears: Knight, Gladys & The Pips / Funny how love can be: Ivy League / Diane: Bachelors / Step by step: Crests / Winchester cathedral: New Vaudeville Band / Boom boom: Hooker, John Lee
CD Set ______ QUAD 001
Tring / Nov '96 / Tring

SOUNDS OF THE STREET AND FAIRGROUND ORGAN (18 Musical Crowd Pleasers)
New colonial march / Marching strings / Good old bad old days / Coronation bug / Hello bluebird / Too many kisses in summer / Brown eyes why are you blue / Waltzing Matilda / Espana / El capitan / Old comrades / Twelth street rag / I do like to be beside the seaside / If I had a golden umbrella / Household brigade / Cuckoo waltz / Anchors aweigh / Beer barrel polka
CD ______ 305792
Hallmark / Oct '96 / Carlton

SOUNDS OF THE WORLD VOL.1, THE (Latin America)
CD ______ PS 65991
PlayaSound / Mar '93 / ADA / Harmonia Mundi

SOUNDS OF WALES, THE
We'll keep a welcome: Morriston Orpheus Choir / Myfanwy: Monmouthshire Massed Choir / Speed your journey: Second Festival Of One Thousand Welsh Male Voices / March of the men of Harlech: Morriston Orpheus Choir / Soldier's chorus: Monmouthshire Massed Choir / Land of song: Morriston Orpheus Choir / All through the night / Men of Wales: Band of the 1st Bat The Welsh Regiment / Steal away: Morriston Orpheus Choir / Battle hymn of the Republic / Thou gavest: Monmouthshire Massed Choir / Tros y garreg: Morriston Orpheus Choir / Counting the goats / Cartref: Morriston Orpheus Choir / Sanctus / Hiraeth: Morriston Orpheus Choir / Laudamus: Festival of Massed Welsh Choirs / When I survey the wondrous cross / Elizabethan serenade: Morriston Orpheus Choir & The Band of the Welsh Guards / Comrades in arms / Llef (Deus salutis): Monmouthshire Massed Choir / Unwaith eto'n nghymru annwyl: Morriston Orpheus Choir / Silver birch: Second Festival Of One Thousand Welsh Male Voices / Guide me o thou great Redeemer: Third Festival Of One Thousand Welsh Male Voices / Land of my fathers (Hen wlad fy nhadau): Third Festival Of One Thousand Welsh Male Voices
CD ______ CDMFP 6368
Music For Pleasure / May '97 / EMI

SOUNDWORKS EXCHANGE VOL.1, THE
CD ______ SWECD 1
Sound Work Recordings / Jul '97 / Cargo

SOUNDWORKS EXCHANGE VOL.2, THE
CD ______ SWRCD 2
Sound Work Recordings / Jul '97 / Cargo

SOURCE LAB 3 X
Faithfull: Fantom / Nite fly: Hi-Way / Sonic 75: Tele Pop Musik / Symphony of sickness: Aleph / Monodrama: Chateau Flight / Antisocial: Extra Lucid / Power Sandwich: I-Cube / What about your love: Low Tone Priority / Mais ou est Genevive: Les Petroleuses / Imflammable b-boy: DJ Cam / Post it: Scratch Pet Land
CD ______ CDVIRX 58
Virgin / Jul '97 / EMI

SOURCE LAB 3 X/Y (2CD Set)
Faithfull: Fantom / Nite fly: Hi-Way / Sonic 75: Tele Pop Musik / Symphony of sickness: Aleph / Mondorama: Chateau Flight / Antisocial: Extra Lucid / Power sandwich: I-Cube / What about your love: Low Tone Priority / Mais ou est Genevieve: Les Petroleuses / Inflammable B-boy: DJ Cam / Post it: Scratch Pet Land / Jean-Jacques et les Dauphins: Le Tone / Sunshine: Mozesli / Lapheetphunkateerz: Maisons Lafitte / Doctor F: Influx / Obsession: Magic Malik / Salami man: Grand-Popo Football Club / La methode rose: ODC / Magik: Bel Air Project / Paris acid city: Black Strobe / No pain without your love: DJ Gregory / ABCD mental: Djhama, Taka / Cosmic bird: Perrey, Jean Jacques
CD Set ______ CDVIR 58
Source / Jul '97 / EMI

SOURCE LAB 3 Y
Jean-Jacques et les Dauphins: Le Tone / Sunshine: Mozesli / Lapheetphunkateerz: Maisons Lafitte / Doctor F: Influx / Obsession: Magic Malik / Salami man: Grand-Popo Football Club / La methode rose: ODC / Magik: Bel Air Project / Paris acid city: Black Strobe / No pain without your love: DJ Gregory / ABCD mental: Djhama, Taka / Cosmic bird: Perrey, Jean Jacques
CD ______ CDVIRY 58
Source / Jul '97 / EMI

SOURCE LAB VOL.2
Neither sing-song nor baden baden: Bang Bang / Free jah: Avesta, Zend / Hunt one connection: Main Basse (Sur La Ville) / Musique: Daft Punk / Bomb de Bretagne (Bombe Breizh): Le Tone / Planete interdite: Krell / Man and woman = Infinity: Dimitri From Paris / Ghost town: Dr. L / La couleur: Ollano / Gordini mix: Golpher, Alex / Technical Jed: Extra Lucid / Casanova 70: 3-Air
CD ______ CDVIR 52
Virgin / Jul '96 / EMI

SOUTH AMERICA - HISPANIC
CD ______ AUB 006782
Auvidis/Ethnic / Sep '93 / ADA / Harmonia Mundi

SOUTH AMERICA - INDIAN
CD ______ AUB 006783
Auvidis/Ethnic / Sep '93 / ADA / Harmonia Mundi

SOUTH AMERICAN WAY
CD ______ CIN 050
IMP / Apr '97 / ADA / Discovery

SOUTH INDIA - RITUAL MUSIC & THEATRE OF KERALA
CD ______ LDX 274910
La Chant Du Monde / Nov '90 / ADA / Harmonia Mundi

SOUTH OF THE BORDER (Sound Of Tex Mex)
CD ______ MCCD 245
Music Club / Jun '96 / Disc / THE

SOUTH OF THE BORDER (A Touch Of Latin)
Besame mucho: Dorsey, Jimmy Orchestra / Brazil: Baker, Josephine / Frenesi: Shaw, Artie Orchestra / I yi yi yi yi I like you very much: Miranda, Carmen / South America take it away: Crosby, Bing & Andrews Sisters / What a difference a day made: Barnet, Charlie Orchestra / Carioca: Boswell, Connee / Begin the beguine: Shelton, Anne / Tico tico: Smith, Ethel / Mexican hat dance: Brown, Les Orchestra / Amapola: Durbin, Deanna / Continental: Stone, Lew & His Band / Time was: Cugat, Xavier & His Waldorf-Astoria Orchestra / Breeze and I: Dorsey, Jimmy Orchestra / You belong to my heart: Crosby, Bing / Perfidia: Miller, Glenn Orchestra / South of the border: Bowlly, Al / My shawl: Sinatra, Frank / Down Argentina way: Shore, Dinah / Peanut vendor: Kenton, Stan Orchestra
CD ______ 306712
Hallmark / Jul '97 / Carlton

SOUTH OF THE BORDER
CD ______ CDHOT 622
Charly / Jul '97 / Koch

SOUTH SIDE BLUES - CHICAGO: LIVING LEGENDS
Wonderful thing: Mississippi Sheiks / I knew you were kiddin' all the time: Mississippi Sheiks / Things 'bout comin' my way: Mississippi Sheiks / Four o'clock blues: Mama Yancey / How long blues: Mama Yancey / Mama Yancey's blues: Mama Yancey / Make me a pallet on the floor: Mama Yancey / Jelly Jelly: Benson, Henry / Jelly Roll Baker: Benson, Henry / New satellite blues: Montgomery, Little Brother
CD ______ OBCCD 508
Original Blues Classics / Apr '94 / Complete/Pinnacle / Wellard

SOUTH SIDE CHICAGO JAZZ
CD ______ VILCD 0192
Village Jazz / Sep '92 / Jazz Music / Target/BMG

SOUTHEND ROCK VOL.2
Wine, women and song: Dr. Feelgood / Muskrat: Johnson, Wilko / Crawlin' king snake: Marques Brothers / Fake: Kicking K / Dragging my heels: Hypocrites / Henry's eyes: Pocracker / Standing at the crossroads: Jupp, Mickey / Look at the purse: Al Morocco 5 / Hercules: Basey Brothers / Going down to Leigh-On-Sea: Famous Potatoes / Misunderstood: Noxcuse / Watch your step: Phrogs / Route 666: Hamsters / Clear but confusing: Bullet Blues Band / Against the grain: Jody / Coloursound: 22 Arlington Square / Laurel: Trampoline Situation / Revelation time: Accidub / La cuero: Snowboy
CD ______ 01702001
Lunch / Oct '96 / Direct

SOUTHERN DOO WOP VOL.1 (Shoop Shoop)
Shoop shoop: Gladiolas / Love you love you love you: Marigolds / Won't you let me know: King Krooners / Now that she's gone: King Krooners / Be bop baby: Peacheroos / Little darlin': Gladiolas / Love love baby: Rhythm Casters / Don't say tomorrow: Marigolds / Pretty little girl: King Krooners / Memoirs: King Krooners & Little Rico / My china doll: Glad Rags / Be bop girl: Gladiolas / Hey little girl: Gladiolas / Rollin' stone: Marigolds / There's been a change: King Krooners / Sweetheart please don't go: Gladiolas / School daze: King Krooners / Playboy lover: King Krooners / Everyday my love is true: Peacheroos / Two strangers: Marigolds / Oh my darling: Rhythm Casters / Just one love: Glad Rags / Don't ever get married: Meloaires / Indebted to you: Meloaires
CD ______ CDCHD 529
Ace / Jun '95 / Pinnacle

SOUTHERN DOO WOP VOL.2 (Krooning)
Jukebox rock'n'roll: Bragg, Johnny & The Marigolds / School daze: King Krooners / There's been a change: King Krooners / Comin' home to you: Gladiolas / High school affair: Five Chums / One day, one day: King Krooners / It's you darling it's you: Bragg, Johnny & The Marigolds / Little darlin': Gladiolas / Sloo foot Soo: Seniors / Yes that's love: Themes / Now that she's gone: King Krooners / Let me know: King Krooners / Run, run Little Joe: Gladiolas / Rollin' stone: Marigolds / Steps of love: King Krooners / I wanta know: Gladiolas / Give me the power: Five Chums / Why don't you: Marigolds / What does the future hold: King Krooners / Say you'll be mine: Gladiolas / Magic of you: Themes / Don't say tomorrow: Hollyhocks / You for me: Hollyhocks / Why did you leave me: Seniors
CD ______ CDCHD 629
Ace / Nov '96 / Pinnacle

SOUTHERN FRIED SOUL
You're so good to me baby: Spencer, Eddie / It takes a whole lotta woman: Gauff, Willie & The Love Brothers / When she touches me: Martin, Rodge / Good man is hard to find: Martin, Rodge / Can you handle it: Allison, Levert / You can get it now: Middleton, Gene / Man who will do anything: Middleton, Gene / So many times: Lewis, Levina / Look a little higher: Up Tights / Just a dream: Up Tights / Sad, sad song: Crawford, Charles / Fa fa fa fa fa (sad song): McDade, Joe / My girl's a soul girl: Rogers, Lon / Too good to be true: Rogers, Lon / You're being unfair to me: Sample, Hank / So in love with you: Sample, Hank / I'll always love you: Moultrie, Sam / I found what I wanted: Lacour, Bobby / Cry like a baby: Lacour, Bobby / Love waits for no man: Curlee, Bobby & The Preachers / Why is it taking so long: Baxter, Tony / I'm surprised: Vann, Paul
CD ______ GSCD 025
Goldmine / Nov '93 / Vital

SOUTHERN GROOVES
You can't have your cake (and eat it too): Young, Tommie / Full grown lovin' man: Brandon, Bill / How do you spell love: Patterson, Bobby / Annie got hot pants power: Johnson, Syl / Love connection: Snell, Annette / Big legged woman: Hobbs, Willie / Sticky Sue: Murray, Mickey / Stick in your earhole: Mobley, Eddie / Get to me: Ingram, Luther / You been doing me wrong for so long: Sexton, Ann / It takes two to do wrong: Patterson, Bobby / Tomorrow (I'll begin to make new plans): Hobbs, Willie / Do you think there's a chance: Ingram, Luther / I don't care about your past: Washington, Ella / Everybody's got a little devil in their soul: Young, Tommie / Just because the package has been unwrapped and opened: Black, Alder Ray & The Fame Gang / Sugar Daddy: Sexton, Ann / You made your bed: Bradford, Eddie / It's not how long you make it: Holiday, Shay / Dapp: African Music Machine
CD ______ CPCD 8067
Charly / Apr '97 / Koch

SOUTHERN STATES SOUND
CD ______ MCCD 135
Music Club / Jan '92 / Disc / THE

SOUTHPORT WEEKENDER (2CD Set)
CD Set ______ AVEXCD 56
Avex / Sep '97 / 3mv/Pinnacle

SOUVENIR DE PARIS (The Great French Stars)
C'est un p'tit rien: Mistinguett & Jean Gabin / Tango de Marilou: Rossi, Tino / Si j'etais Blanche: Baker, Josephine / Oui, papa: Chevalier, Maurice / Parlez-moi d'amour: Boyer, Lucienne / St. Louis blues: Ventura, Ray & His Collegians / Plaisir d'amour: Printemps, Yvonne / Pauvre grand: Frehel / Vous avez: Sablon, Jean / Le fiacre: Guilbert, Yvette / Plus rien, je n'ai plus rien qu'un chien: Sablon, Jean / Ca c'est Paris: Mistinguett / Ca c'est fou: Alibert / Le chaland qui passe: Gauty, Lys / Valentine: Chevalier, Maurice / C'est mon gigolo: Damina / La petite Tonkinoise: Baker, Josephine / Couche dans le foin: Pills & Tabet / Papa n'a pas voulou: Mirielle / La Marseillaise: Thill, Georges
CD ______ CDAJA 5028
Living Era / Select

SOUVENIR DES GUINGUETTES
CD ______ FA 971
Fremeaux / Sep '96 / ADA / Discovery

SOUVENIR OF WALES IN SONG
CD ______ SCD 9006
Sain / Feb '95 / ADA / Direct / Greyhound

SOVEREIGN SOLOISTS
CD DOYCD 003
Doyen / Jun '93 / Conifer/BMG

SOWETO NEVER SLEEPS
CD SHANCD 43041
Shanachie / Apr '88 / ADA / Greensleeves / Koch

SOY UN ARLEQUIN (Tango Ladies 1923-1954)
CD HQCD 98
Harlequin / Jun '97 / Hot Shot / Jazz Music / Swift / Wellard

SPACE - THE ALBUM (3CD Set)
CD Set FIRMCD 7
Firm / Jul '96 / Pinnacle

SPACE AGE POP VOL.1 (Melodies And Mischief)
Delicado: *Three Suns* / Caravan: *Sir Julian* / Little black box: *Thompson, Bob Orchestra* / Foolin' around: *Esquivel, Juan Garcia* / Whispering: *Rene, Henri* / Third Man theme: *Klein, John* / Sentimental journey: *Gold, Marty* / Rollercoaster: *Rene, Henri* / Isle of Capri: *Farnon, Dennis* / Springtime for Hitler: *Mancini, Henry* / Scheherazade: *Polo, Markko Adventurers* / Diga diga doo: *Thompson, Bob Orchestra* / Why wait: *Prado, Perez* / Doll dance: *Case, Russ* / Smoke: *Three Suns* / Powerhouse: *Bass, Sid*
CD 07863666452
RCA / Mar '96 / BMG

SPACE BOX (3CD Set)
CD Set CLP 9772
Cleopatra / Oct '96 / Cargo / Greyhound / Plastic Head / RTM/Disc / SRD

SPACE DAZE (The History And Mystery Of Electronic Ambient Space Rock)
CD Set CLEO 76162
Cleopatra / Jan '95 / Cargo / Greyhound / Plastic Head / RTM/Disc / SRD

SPACE DAZE 2000
CD CLEO 1844
Cleopatra / Jul '96 / Cargo / Greyhound / Plastic Head / RTM/Disc / SRD

SPACE INVADERS
CD RE 201CD
Panorama / Aug '95 / Plastic Head

SPACE LOG 1.1
CD GAMMA 01
Gamma / Mar '95 / Plastic Head

SPACE MOOD AND ELECTRIC SOUL
CD PLRCD 001
Plastic / Jun '97 / Cargo / Essential/BMG

SPACE MOUNTAIN
CD JAC 002CD
Oasis / Oct '95 / Plastic Head

SPACED OUT (2CD Set)
Dancing in outer space: *Atmosfear* / Cocomotion: *El Coco* / Go bang: *Dinosaur L* / For the love of money: *Disco Dub Band* / Just in time: *Raw Silk* / Mi sabrina tequana: *Ingram* / Feelin' good: *McGee, Francine* / Double journey: *Powerline* / Space funk: *Manzel* / Time machine: *Chocolate Milk* / Dancing in outer space (Masters At Work remix): *Atmosfear* / For the love of money (Harvey remix): *Disco Dub Band* / For the love of money (Underdog remix): *Disco Dub Band*
CD Set SUSHI 4CD
Disorient / Jun '97 / Prime / RTM/Disc

SPACEFROGS VOL.2
CD EFA 290102
Superstition / Dec '95 / Plastic Head / SRD / Vital

SPANGLE EP NO.3
CD SPANG 003
Spangle / Feb '96 / Shellshock/Disc / SRD

SPANISH RAGGA
CD SM 3110
Declic / Apr '95 / Jet Star

SPECIAL BREW
Numb: *U2* / One to one religion: *Bomb The Bass* / Blue print: *Attica Blues* / Army of me: *Bjork* / Release yo 'delf: *Method Man* / Voodoo people: *Prodigy* / Hot flush: *Red Snapper* / Perpetual motion: *DJ Crystal* / Inner city life: *Goldie* / Wild wood: *Weller, Paul* / Cry: *Money Mark* / Away again: *Howie B*
CD 5355992
London / Aug '96 / PolyGram

SPECIAL GUITARS VOL.2 1943-1956
CD 7899522
Jazztime / Jan '95 / Discovery

SPECIALTY LEGENDS OF BOOGIE WOOGIE
X-temporaneous boogie: *Howard, Camille* / Rock that voot: *Alexander, Nelson Trio* / Rockin' boogie: *Lutcher, Joe & His Society Cats* / Doin' the boogie-woogie: *Alexander, Nelson Trio* / Society boogie: *Lutcher, Joe & His Society Cats* / Barcarolle boogie: *Howard, Camille* / Instantaneous boogie: *Howard, Camille* / State street boogie: *Johnson, Don Orchestra* / Miraculous boogie: *Howard, Camille* / Milton's boogie: *Milton, Roy* / Ferocious boogie: *Howard, Camille* / Unidentified instrumental no. 1: *McDaniel, Willard* / Boogie woogie Lou: *Liggins, Joe* / Fire-ball boogie: *Howard, Camille* / Boogie woogie barber shop: *Milton, Roy* / 3 a.m. boogie: *McDaniel, Willard* / Bangin' the boogie: *Howard, Camille* / Ciribiribin boogie: *McDaniel, Willard* / Unidentified boogie no. 1: *McDaniel, Willard* / Million dollar boogie: *Howard, Camille* / Boogie in the groove: *Jackson, Jo Jo*
CD CDCHD 422
Ace / Sep '92 / Pinnacle

SPECIALTY LEGENDS OF JUMP BLUES VOL.1
Honeydripper: *Liggins, Joe* / Oh babe: *Milton, Roy* / Blues for sale: *Lutcher, Joe* / Duck's yas yas yas: *King, Perry & His Pied Pipers* / I can't stop it: *Liggins, Jimmy* / That song is gone: *Liggins, Jimmy* / Well, well baby: *Alexander, Nelson Trio* / Rag mop: *Liggins, Joe* / One sweet letter: *Liggins, Joe* / Pink champagne: *Liggins, Joe* / Happy home blues: *Banks, Buddy* / Muffle shoe shuffle: *Wynn, Big Jim* / I ain't got a dime: *Perry, King* / Saturday night boogie woogie man: *Liggins, Jimmy* / Jack of diamonds: *Thomas, Jesse* / I dare you baby: *Mayfield, Percy* / I'm your rockin' man: *Manzy, Herman* / Natural born lover: *King, Perry & His Pied Pipers* / I wonder who's boogin' my woogie: *King, Perry & His Pied Pipers* / I can't lose with the stuff I use: *Williams, Lester* / Country girl: *Henderson, Duke* / Hucklebuck: *Milton, Roy* / Heavy weight baby: *Motley, Frank* / Traffic gong: *Lutcher, Joe*
CD CDCHD 573
Ace / Jul '94 / Pinnacle

SPECIALTY ROCK'N'ROLL
Lights out: *Bryne, Jerry* / Moose on the loose: *Jackson, Roddy* / Bim bam: *Don & Dewey* / Don't you just know it: *Titans* / (We're gonna) Rock around the clock: *Millet, Lil* / My baby's rockin': *Monitors* / Hickory dickory dock: *Myles, Big Boy* / Flip: *Marvin & Johnny* / Good golly Miss Molly: *Little Richard* / Rockin' pneumonia and the boogie woogie flu: *Neville, Art* / Goodbye baby goodbye: *Lowery, Sonny* / Short fat Fannie: *Williams, Larry* / Rock 'n' roll dance: *Price, Lloyd* / Girl can't help it: *Little Richard* / Haunted house: *Fuller, Jerry* / Slow down: *Williams, Larry* / Cherokee dance: *Landers, Bob* / Hiccups: *Jackson, Roddy* / Zing zing: *Neville, Art* / Carry on: *Byrne, Jerry*
CD CDCH 291
Ace / May '90 / Pinnacle

SPECTACULAR SYNTHESIZER
CD MACCD 101
Autograph / Aug '96 / BMG

SPECTRUM FEST (A Relapse Sampler)
CD RR 66622
Relapse / Jan '97 / Pinnacle / Plastic Head

SPEED KILLS VOL.4 (Speed Kills But Who's Dying?)
CD CDFLAG 33
Under One Flag / Jun '89 / Pinnacle

SPEED KILLS VOL.5 (Head Crushing Metal)
CD CDFLAG 46
Under One Flag / Oct '90 / Pinnacle

SPEED KILLS VOL.6
CD CDFLAG 69
Under One Flag / Jul '92 / Pinnacle

SPEED LIMIT
CD MM 890502
Moonshine / Jan '96 / Mo's Music Machine / Prime / RTM/Disc

SPEED LIMIT CLASSICS
CD MM 890512
Moonshine / Jul '96 / Mo's Music Machine / Prime / RTM/Disc

SPEED OF THE SOUND
CD GRCD 314
Glitterhouse / Apr '94 / Avid/BMG

SPEED REVOLUTION (2CD Set)
CD Set 24066
Delta Doubles / Jun '96 / Target/BMG

SPICE OF LIFE REMIXES VOL.1
CD HOTTCD 1
Hott / Feb '95 / 3mv/Sony

SPIKED
Something better change: *Stranglers* / Babylons burning: *Ruts* / Ever fallen in love: *Buzzcocks* / Sweet suburbia: *Skids* / Alternative Ulster: *Stiff Little Fingers* / Turning Japanese: *Vapors* / Wild wild life: *Talking Heads* / Shot by both sides: *Magazine* / Don't dictate: *Penetration* / King Rocker: *Generation X* / Emergency: *999* / Outdoor miner: *Wire* / Glad to be gay: *Robinson, Tom Band* / What do I get: *Buzzcocks* / I'm not a fool: *Cockney Rejects* / Sheena is a punk rocker: *Ramones* / Suspect device: *Stiff Little Fingers* / Hanging around: *Stranglers*
CD CDGOLD 1057
EMI Gold / Oct '96 / EMI

SPIKED
Judy says: *Vibrators* / London girls: *Vibrators* / Inside out: *999* / English wipeout: *999* / Ain't got a clue: *Lurkers* / Solitaire: *Lurkers* / 42nd Street: *Angelic Upstarts* / Burglar: *Angelic Upstarts* / Virginia plain: *Spizz Energi* / Cold city: *Spizz Energi* / Teenage depression: *Eddie & The Hot Rods* / Quit this town: *Eddie & The Hot Rods* / Stepping stone: *Thunders, Johnny* / Too much junkie business: *Thunders, Johnny* / No faith: *Suburban Studs* / Take it or leave it: *Vice Squad* / We are the boys: *Blitz* / Two years too late: *Anti Pasti* / Peacehaven wild kids: *Peter & The Test Tube Babies*
CD SUMCD 4094
Summit / Jan '97 / Sound & Media

SPINNIN' THE CHAMBER
CD LRR 008
Last Resort / Oct '96 / Cargo

SPIRIT CRIES, THE
Abelagudahani / Grating song / Abaimahani / Paranda / Combination / Punta / Dugu song / Healing song / Shipibo song / Ashaninka song / Aleke / Songe / Lonsei / Mato (Solo) / Mato (Leader and chorus) / Awasa / Kumanti / Agwado song / Susa / Dance song / Love song / Papa / Tambu
CD RCD 10250
Rykodisc / Mar '93 / ADA / Vital

SPIRIT OF AFRICA
CD AHLCD 42
Hit / Oct '96 / Grapevine/PolyGram

SPIRIT OF AFRICAN SANCTUS (Compiled By David Fanshawe)
Acholi bwala dance / Call to prayer / Egyptian wedding / Islamic prayer school / Reed pipe and grass cutting song / Courtship dances / Four men on the prayer mat / Zebaidir song with Rebabah / Hadandua cattle boys song / Hadandua love songs and bells / Zande song of flight and frogs / Tamboura song / Edongo dance / Busoga fishermen / Bowed harp / Teso fishermen / Acholi enanga / Dingy dingy dance / Rainsong of latigo oteng / Bunyoro madinda / Bwala dance / Rowing chant of the Samia / Song of Lamentation / Masai milking song / Song of the river, Karamoja / Karamajong children's song / Turkana cattle song / Luo ritual burial dance / War drums / Aluar horns
CD CDSDL 389
Saydisc / Mar '94 / ADA / Direct / Harmonia Mundi

SPIRIT OF CHRISTMAS PAST, THE (Nostalgic Christmas Memories From The 1930's/1940's)
White Christmas: *Crosby, Bing* / Savoy Christmas medley: *Noble, Ray* / Christmas carols: *London Church Carol Choir* / Santa Claus express: *Hall, Henry* / Say it with carols: *Mayerl, Billy* / Christmas bells at Eventide: *Fields, Gracie* / Fairy on the Christmas tree: *Hall, Henry & The Three Sisters* / Winter wonderland: *Stone, Lew* / Santa Claus is coming to town: *Reser, Harry* / I'll walk alone (thru every Christmas): *Shore, Dinah* / 'Twas the night before Christmas: *Waring, Fred & His Pennsylvanians* / Jingle bells: *Waller, Fats* / Coventry carol: *Schumann, Elisabeth* / Noel: *Thill, Georges* / Sleep my saviour sleep: *Celebrity Quartette* / Christmas message to the empire 1932: *King George V* / Christmas dinner: *Miller, Max* / Have yourself a merry little Christmas: *Garland, Judy* / Christmas night in Harlem: *Teagarden, Jack & Johnny Mercer* / Mary had a baby, yes Lord: *Robeson, Paul* / Silent night, holy night: *Crosby, Bing* / Charles Dickens' Christmas: *Williams, Bransby* / Auld lang syne: *Dawson, Peter*
CD CDAJA 5178
Living Era / Sep '96 / Select

SPIRIT OF INDIA
CD AHLCD 48
Hit / Jul '97 / Grapevine/PolyGram

SPIRIT OF INDIA, THE (The Best Of Indian Classical Music)
Raga mishra piloo / Raga pahadi / Bhajan / Tal ektal / Dhun bhairavi / Raga bhairavi
CD PLATCD 3931
Platinum / Mar '95 / Prism

SPIRIT OF MICRONESIA
CD CDSDL 414
Saydisc / Oct '95 / ADA / Direct / Harmonia Mundi

SPIRIT OF POLYNESIA
Aitutaki drum dance / Himene tarava / Poipoi - taro pounding / Song of Papa Teora / Himene Ruau / Bird dance hula / Haka Maori welcome / Song of Papa Kiko / Kai kai of Mama Amelia / Hoko war dance / Meke wesi spear dance / Tau 'a' alo / Fangufangu nose flute / Faikava love song / Chiefs and orators sasa / Tagi lullaby / Tawhoe - oar dance / Copra bugle call / Mokaone's harmonica / Song of Anili / Frigate bird dance, Nauru / Funafuti chorus, Tuvalu / Imenetuki - Gospel chant / Mire of Eamaki / Ute - cutting nuts / tapa cloth beating / Palmerston shanties / Imenetuki / Mako of Mama Lulutangi / Canoe racing and wrestling / Children's games / Akatikatika drum dance / Mako chant / Haka tapatapa / Pig dance/Ruu chant / Himene tarava (Tahiti) / Himene Nota / Otea drum dance
CD CDSDL 403
Saydisc / Mar '94 / ADA / Direct / Harmonia Mundi

SPIRIT OF RELAXATION (3CD Set)
CD Set SPIRICD 1
Beechwood / Jul '97 / Beechwood/BMG / Pinnacle

SPIRIT OF ROCK
CD STACD 038
Wisepack / Sep '94 / Conifer/BMG / THE

SPIRIT OF SCOTLAND
CD RECD 473
REL / Nov '94 / CM / Duncans / Highlander

SPIRIT OF THE AGE (The Time Of Progressive Rock)
Master of the universe: *Hawkwind* / Funk angel: *Brinsley Schwarz* / Locomotive breath: *Jethro Tull* / Love like a man: *Ten Years After* / Do it: *Pink Fairies* / Butterfly: *Barclay James Harvest* / Debora: *T-Rex* / Fire and water: *Free* / I am the walrus: *Spooky Tooth* / Starship trooper: *Yes* / Back street love: *Curved Air* / Oh yeah: *Can* / Devil's answer: *Atomic Rooster* / America: *Nice* / Brain salad surgery: *Emerson, Lake & Palmer* / Burlesque: *Family*
CD RENCD 118
Renaissance Collector Series / Mar '97 / BMG

SPIRIT OF THE AZTEC
CD 5371742
PolyGram TV / Mar '97 / PolyGram

SPIRIT OF THE EAST (Music For Meditation)
CD CD 6025
Music / Jun '96 / Target/BMG

SPIRIT OF THE NEW AGE
Crossing the ridge: *Dada Wa* / Sadness: *Enigma* / Floating: *Hypnosis* / Mad Alice Lane (a ghost story): *Lawlor* / X-Files: *DJ Dado* / Twin peaks: *DJ Dado* / Nocturnal spirit: *Q-Dos* / Fanfare of life: *Leftfield* / Raindance: *Aura* / Indian spirit: *Slavik, Andi & Susanne Kemler* / On Earth as it is in Heaven: *Incantation* / Entre dos aguas: *De Lucia, Paco & Ramon Algeciras* / Baila verena: *Potschka, Potsch* / Scandalise: *Afterlife* / Dusk pressure: *Drop* / Secret call: *Ginko Garden* / Kama kami: *Keiles, Glenn & Caroline MacKendrick*
CD MCD 80346
MCA / Jun '97 / BMG

SPIRIT OF VICTORY, THE (Hits From The 40's - 2CD Set)
Happy and glorious: *Somers, Debroy & His Band* / In the land of beginning again: *Lewis, Archie & Geraldo* / Waiting in Sweetheart Valley: *Preager, Lou & His Orchestra* / Little things that mean so much: *Payne, Jack & His Orchestra* / Memories of you: *Squires, Dorothy* / It's been a long, long time: *Gibbons, Carroll & Savoy Hotel Orpheans* / Dream: *Foster, Teddy & The Band* / What a difference a day makes: *Green, Paula & Her Orchestra* / There, I've said it again: *Loss, Joe & His Orchestra* / Candy: *Roy, Harry & His Band* / Seems like old times: *Geraldo & His Orchestra* / Goodnight darling: *Roy, Harry & His Band* / June comes around every year: *Geraldo & His Orchestra* / One-zy-two-zy, I love you-zy: *Simpson, Jack & His Sextet* / Remember me: *Preager, Lou & His Orchestra* / Let's wait until tomorrow: *Roy, Harry & His Band* / I'm gonna love that guy (like he's never been loved before): *Green, Paula & Her Orchestra* / I'm beginning to see the light: *Geraldo & His Orchestra* / I should care: *Roy, Harry & His Band* / Sentimental journey: *Foster, Teddy & The Band* / Coming home: *Squires, Dorothy* / Out of nowhere: *Foster, Teddy & The Band* / Did you ever get that feeling in the moonlight: *Preager, Lou & His Orchestra* / I dream of you: *Lewis, Archie & Geraldo* / Bell bottom trousers: *Roy, Harry & His Band* / Dreams of yesterday: *Squires, Dorothy* / Anywhere: *Winstone, Eric & His Band* / Just a blue serge suit: *Preager, Lou & His Orchestra* / Till all our prayers are answered: *Green, Paula & Her Orchestra* / I walked right in: *Winstone, Eric & His Band* / I'd rather be me: *Roy, Harry & His Band* / Takin' the trains out (chasin' after you): *Foster, Teddy & The Band* / It's a grand night for singing: *Gibbons, Carroll & Savoy Hotel Orpheans* / We'll gather lilacs: *Geraldo & His Orchestra* / Cavalry patrol: *Geraldo & His Orchestra* / Celebration medley: *Somers, Debroy & His Band*
CD Set CDDL 1218
Music For Pleasure / Nov '91 / EMI

SPIRIT SAMPLER VOL.2
CD DW 092CD
Deathwish / Jan '96 / Plastic Head

SPIRITS OF NATURE
Sweet lullaby: *Deep Forest* / Little fluffy clouds: *Orb* / Sun rising: *Beloved* / X-Files: *DJ Dado* / Return to innocence: *Enigma* / Stars: *Dubstar* / Way it is: *Hornsby, Bruce* / Play dead: *Bjork & David Arnold* / Aria on air: *McLaren, Malcolm* / Adiemus: *Adiemus* / Only you: *Praise* / Falling: *Cruise, Julee* / Mad Alice Lane (A ghost story): *Lawlor* / Sentinel: *Oldfield, Mike* / Theme from the mission: *Morricone, Ennio* / Heart asks pleasure first: *Nyman, Michael* / Fashion shoe II from "Three Colours Red": *Preisner, Zbigniew* / Chariots of fire: *Vangelis*
CD VTCD 87
Virgin / Jun '96 / EMI

SPIRITS OF NATURE (A Collection Of Native American Inspired Music & Chants)
Dance of the warrior / Brandishing the tomahawk / Circle of fire / Thunder cloud mountain / Celebration of the young / Elevation / Return from river island / Winter ceremony / Counterclockwise circle of dance / Seeds of future happiness
CD _______ 307612
Hallmark / Jul '97 / Carlton

SPIRITUAL HIGH
CD _______ OM 002
OM / Mar '97 / Cargo / SRD

SPIRITUALLY IBIZA VOL.1
Barefoot in the head: *Man Called Adam* / Moments in love: *Art Of Noise* / 60 Seconds: *Audio Deluxe* / Real life: *Corporation Of One* / Drop the deal: *Code 61* / Autumn love: *Electra* / Zobi la mouche: *Les Negresses Vertes* / Cafe del mar: *Mental Generation* / Love's got a feeling: *Neutron 9000* / Free spirit: *Orchestra JB* / Why can't we live together: *Illusion* / Solid gold easy amex: *Enjoy* / Jesus on the payroll: *Thrashing Doves* / Hoomba hoomba: *Voices Of Africa* / Whole of the moon: *Waterboys* / Only love can break your heart: *St. Etienne* / La passionara: *Blow Monkeys* / Come together: *Primal Scream*
CD _______ DINCD 111
Dino / Oct '95 / Pinnacle

SPIRITUALLY IBIZA VOL.2
CD _______ FIRMCD 6
Firm / Jun '96 / Pinnacle

SPLENDOUR OF JAPANESE INSTRUMENTS (3CD Set)
CD Set _______ PS 360503
PlayaSound / Sep '96 / ADA / Harmonia Mundi

SPLENDOUR OF SCOTLAND, THE (A Tribute In Music & Song)
I belong to Glasgow / Northern lights of old Aberdeen / Road and miles to Dundee / Song of the Clyde / Master David Cleland / Dunblane hydro march / Isle of Arran / Mull of the cool high bens / Banjo breakdown / Land for all seasons / Of A' the airts / Man's a man for a' that / Whistle o'er the alve o't / My heart is sair / This is no' my ain lassie / My love she's but a lassie yet / What'd be king but Charlie / Johnny Cope / Charlie is my darling / Braemar highland gathering
CD _______ CDGR 156
Ross / Jul '96 / CM / Duncans / Highlander / Ross

SPLENDOUR OF THE KOTO
CD _______ PS 65131
PlayaSound / May '94 / ADA / Harmonia Mundi

SPLENDOUR OF THE SHAKUHACHI
CD _______ PS 65130
PlayaSound / May '94 / ADA / Harmonia Mundi

SPLENDOUR OF THE SHAMISEN
CD _______ PS 65129
PlayaSound / May '94 / ADA / Harmonia Mundi

SPOONFUL OF BLUES
CD _______ 422490
New Rose / May '94 / ADA / Direct / Discovery

SPOTLIGHT ON BLUES
Boom boom boom: *Hooker, John Lee* / Honest I do: *Reed, Jimmy* / Dust my broom: *James, Elmore* / Baby, let me hold your hand: *Charles, Ray* / Need him: *Little Richard* / Rooster blues: *Lightnin' Slim* / I put a spell on you: *Hawkins, Screamin' Jay* / Caldonia: *Jordan, Louis* / Blueberry Hill: *Domino, Fats* / Dimples: *Hooker, John Lee* / She's a winner: *Taylor, Ted* / When the sun goes down: *Turner, 'Big' Joe* / Moppers blues: *Stewart, Rod* / Shame, shame, shame: *Reed, Jimmy* / Rollin' and tumblin': *Canned Heat* / Polk salad Annie: *White, Tony Joe*
CD _______ HADCD 146
Javelin / Feb '94 / Henry Hadaway / THE

SPOTLIGHT ON COUNTRY
Ruby, don't take your love to town: *Rogers, Kenny* / Rawhide: *Laine, Frankie* / Walkin' after midnight: *Cline, Patsy* / Wasted days and wasted nights: *Fender, Freddy* / Singin' the blues: *Mitchell, Guy* / Harper Valley PTA: *Riley, Jeannie C.* / It's only make believe: *Twitty, Conway* / Six days on the road: *Dudley, Dave* / Are you proud of America: *Skaggs, Ricky* / Primrose Lane: *Wallace, Jerry* / Four in the morning: *Young, Faron* / Teddy bear song: *Fairchild, Barbara* / Ballad of the Green Berets: *Sadler, Sgt. Barry* / Home is where you're happy: *Nelson, Willie* / Wings of a dove: *Husky, Ferlin* / Good year for the roses: *Jones, George*
CD _______ HADCD 149
Javelin / Feb '94 / Henry Hadaway / THE

SPOTLIGHT ON COUNTRY - LIVE
Stand by your man: *Wynette, Tammy* / Behind closed doors: *Rich, Charlie* / Delta dawn: *Tucker, Tanya* / Jambalaya: *Fender, Freddy* / Rose garden: *Anderson, Lynn* / Medley: *Boxcar Willie* / Here comes my baby: *West, Dottie* / Let it be me: *Tillotson, Johnny* / Let your love flow: *Bellamy Brothers* / Ball and chain: *Mattea, Kathy* / He stopped loving her today: *Jones, George* / Mr. Bojangles: *Nitty Gritty Dirt Band* / Total woman: *Riley, Jeannie C.* / Key largo: *Higgins, Bertie* / Okie from Muskogee: *Haggard, Merle* / Wine me up: *Young, Faron*
CD _______ HADCD 150
Javelin / Feb '94 / Henry Hadaway / THE

SPOTLIGHT ON HITS OF THE SIXTIES
Sweets for my sweet: *Searchers* / You've got your troubles: *Fortunes* / Love is all around: *Troggs* / Wild thing: *Troggs* / I am the world: *Bee Gees* / Ferry 'cross the Mersey: *Gerry & The Pacemakers* / When you walk in the room: *Searchers* / Storm in a teacup: *Fortunes* / I can't control myself: *Troggs* / Needles and pins: *Searchers* / How do you do it: *Gerry & The Pacemakers* / Caroline: *Fortunes* / Monday's rain: *Bee Gees* / Sugar and spice: *Searchers*
CD _______ HADCD 143
Javelin / Feb '94 / Henry Hadaway / THE

SPOTLIGHT ON JAZZ
In the mood: *Miller, Glenn* / One o'clock jump: *Basie, Count* / Tuxedo junction: *Hirt, Al* / Misty: *Vaughan, Sarah* / Ring dem bells: *Hampton, Lionel* / C Jam blues: *Ellington, Duke* / How high the moon: *Fitzgerald, Ella* / Scraple from the apple: *Parker, Charlie* / Sawnuff: *Davis, Miles* / Sweet Georgia Brown: *Cole, Nat 'King'* / Tip toe topic: *Ellington, Duke* / Mr. Paganini: *Fitzgerald, Ella* / Curros: *Byrd, Donald* / Court: *Hubbard, Freddie* / If you could see me now: *Vaughan, Sarah* / All the things you are: *Benson, George*
CD _______ HADCD 144
Javelin / Feb '94 / Henry Hadaway / THE

SPOTLIGHT ON PAUL SIMON PLUS
Play me a sad song: *Simon, Paul* / It means a lot: *Simon, Paul* / Flame: *Simon, Paul* / While I dream: *Sedaka, Neil* / Ring-a-rock: *Sedaka, Neil* / Ding dong: *Orlando, Tony* / You're the one: *Rivers, Johnny* / Hole in the ground: *Rivers, Johnny* / This is real: *Valli, Frankie* / Comme si bella: *Valli, Frankie* / Please me forever: *Edwards, Tommy* / It's all in the game: *Edwards, Tommy*
CD _______ HADCD 141
Javelin / Feb '94 / Henry Hadaway / THE

SPOTLIGHT ON REGGAE
CD _______ RGCD 0011
Rocky One / Nov '94 / Jet Star

SPOTLIGHT ON ROCK 'N' ROLL
(We're gonna) Rock around the clock: *Haley, Bill & The Comets* / Tutti frutti: *Little Richard* / Rockin' robin: *Day, Bobby* / Blue suede shoes: *Perkins, Carl* / Venus: *Avalon, Frankie* / Red river rock: *Johnny & The Hurricanes* / Let's dance: *Montez, Chris* / Surfin' bird: *Trashmen* / Louie Louie: *Kingsmen* / Walk don't run: *Ventures* / I fought the law: *Fuller, Bobby* / Hey little girl: *Clark, Dee* / Tiger: *Fabian* / Ooby dooby: *Orbison, Roy* / Ring-a-rock: *Sedaka, Neil* / Great balls of fire: *Lewis, Jerry Lee*
CD _______ HADCD 147
Javelin / Feb '94 / Henry Hadaway / THE

SPOTLIGHT ON ROCK 'N' ROLL - LIVE
Rubber ball: *Vee, Bobby* / I'm gonna make you mine: *Christie, Lou* / Twilight time: *Platters* / Ginny come lately: *Hyland, Brian* / Charlie Brown: *Coasters* / Runaway: *Shannon, Del* / Motor running: *Lewis, Jerry Lee* / Dizzy: *Roe, Tommy* / Way down yonder in New Orleans: *Cannon, Freddy* / Why do fools fall in love: *Diamonds* / Roberta: *Ford, Frankie* / La bamba: *Tokens* / Peggy Sue: *Crickets* / Keep on running: *Davis, Spencer* / My guy: *Wells, Mary* / Rock 'n' roll is here to stay: *Original Juniors*
CD _______ HADCD 148
Javelin / Feb '94 / Henry Hadaway / THE

SPOTLIGHT ON SOUL
Soul man: *Sam & Dave* / Knock on wood: *Floyd, Eddie* / Harlem shuffle: *Bob & Earl* / My guy: *Wells, Mary* / Stay: *Williams, Maurice & The Zodiacs* / Stagger Lee: *Price, Lloyd* / Tell it like it is: *Neville, Aaron* / Every beat of my heart: *Knight, Gladys & The Pips* / So fine: *Turner, Ike & Tina* / Mockingbird: *Foxx, Inez* / Oh no, not my baby: *Brown, Maxine* / Precious and few: *Climax Blues Band* / Show and tell: *Wilson, Al* / Seems like I gotta do wrong: *Whispers* / Stand by me: *King, Ben E.* / When a man loves a woman: *Sledge, Percy*
CD _______ HADCD 145
Javelin / Feb '94 / Henry Hadaway / THE

SPOTLITE JAZZ SAMPLER
If I should use you / What's next / My funny valentine / Three little words / White in the moon / Isn't it / Everywhere calypso / Day by day / Dream dancing / Behind the mask / Maids of Cadiz / Conception / My romance / Shadowy light / Interlude / Promised land
CD _______ SPJCD 301
Spotlite / Feb '97 / Cadillac / Jazz Music / New Note/Pinnacle / Swift

SPRING AGAIN
Love is all: *Glover, Roger & Guests* / Place in the sun: *Hammond, Albert* / Happy together: *Turtles* / Air that I breath: *Hollies* / Spring again: *Rawls, Lou* / Don't worry be happy: *McFerrin, Bobby* / All around my hat: *Steeleye Span* / Wonderful world: *Herman's Hermits* / You make me feel like dancing: *Sayer, Leo* / If I had words: *Fitzgerald, Scott & Yvonne Keeley* / Freedom come, freedom go: *Fortunes* / Birds and the bees: *Akens, Jewel* / Wonderful world, beautiful people: *Cliff, Jimmy* / Oh happy day: *Hawkins, Edwin Singers*
CD _______ DC 879192
Disky / Mar '97 / Disky / THE

SPRING STORY, THE (Essential 70s Soul)
Tom the pepper: *Act 1* / My man, a sweet man: *Jackson, Millie* / Step by step: *Simon, Joe* / I can see him making love to you: *Mayberry Movement* / Too through: *Brown, Jocelyn* / I found lovin': *Fatback Band* / I gotta get away (from my own self): *Godfrey, Ray* / He didn't know (he kept on talkin'): *Green, Garland* / You've come a long way baby: *Flower Shoppe* / Baby you got it all: *Street People* / Just a little misunderstanding: *Jones, Busta* / SOS (stop her on sight): *Parker, Winfield* / Get ready: *Harris, Eva* / Uptight: *Harris, Eva* / (Are you ready) Do the bus stop: *Fatback Band* / It's my life: *Mainstreeters* / Jody, come back and get your shoes: *Newsome, Bobby* / If we get caught I don't know you: *Mitchell, Phillip* / Drowning in the sea of love: *Simon, Joe* / (If loving you is wrong) I don't wanna be right: *Jackson, Millie* / Friends or lovers: *Act 1* / Magic's in the air: *Walker, Ronnie* / Loves contest: *Joneses* / How about a little hand (for the boys in the band): *Boys In The Band* / Bumpin' and stompin': *Green, Garland* / Come and get these memories: *Godfrey, Ray*
CD _______ CWSEWD 103
Southbound / Oct '95 / Pinnacle

SQUASBOX
CD _______ Y 225107CD
Silex / Jul '95 / ADA / Harmonia Mundi

SQUEEZE PLAY (A World Accordion Anthology)
Tarantella Teggianese: *D'Elia*, / Dormi e Risposa: *Gangone, G* / Drunkard's last will: *Polak, Wladyslaw* / Best friend's song (Kumotersko): *Orkiestra Karol Stoch* / Pawel Walc (Paul's waltz): *Rudzinski, Bruno* / Mason's apron: *Murphy, Frank* / Rodney's glory: *Hanafin, Michael* / In Padure La Ghergani: *Radulescu, Margarita* / Girl from Ardeal: *Jivan, George* / Song of the bus drivers: *Trio Huracan* / La Piedrera: *Jimenez, Santiago Jr.* / Ulele Izweni: *Luthuli, Mahlautini* / Nonyembezi: *Dingaan, Joseph* / Besarabia Doina: *Ziganoff, Mishka* / Tsygansky Hopak: *Ziganoff, Mishka* / Miss Jessie Smith/The Kirrie Kebbuck/Petronella: *McHardy & Hosie* / Brig o' Perth: *Dalrymple, Bob & David* / Inverness gathering: *Dalrymple, Bob & David* / Politkos Sirtos: *Papatzis-Tsakiris* / Saut Crapaud: *Fruge, Columbus* / Ne buvez pilus jamais: *Falcon, Joseph* / Reel de Berthier: *Vagabonds de Montreal* / Italijanski Valcek: *Strukelj Trio* / Apaga la Luz: *Quintero, Luis*
CD _______ ROUCD 1090
Rounder / Feb '97 / ADA / CM / Direct

SST ACOUSTIC
CD _______ SST 276CD
SST / May '93 / Plastic Head

ST. LOUIS 1927-1933
CD _______ DOCD 5181
Document / Oct '93 / ADA / Hot Shot / Jazz Music

ST. LOUIS BLUES 1925-1941
CD _______ 158392
Blues Collection / Sep '95 / Discovery

ST. LOUIS BLUES REVUE (The Classic Bobbin Sessions)
Hucklebuck twist: *Sain, Oliver Orchestra* / Honey bee: *Bass, Fontella & Oliver Sain Orchestra* / Bad boy: *Bass, Fontella & Oliver Sain Orchestra* / Brand new love: *Bass, Fontella & Oliver Sain Orchestra* / I don't hurt anymore: *Bass, Fontella & Oliver Sain Orchestra* / Limited love: *Love, Clayton & Roosevelt Marks Orchestra* / Unlimited love: *Love, Clayton & Roosevelt Marks Orchestra* / Bye bye baby: *Love, Clayton & Roosevelt Marks Orchestra* / Mistreated: *Love, Clayton & Roosevelt Marks Orchestra* / It's you: *Love, Clayton & Roosevelt Marks Orchestra* / Year after year: *Love, Clayton & Roosevelt Marks Orchestra* / Baby bring your clothes back home: *Westbrook, Walter & His Phantom Five* / Midnight jump: *Westbrook, Walter & His Phantom Five* / That will never do: *Little Milton & Oliver Sain Orchestra* / I'm a lonely man: *Little Milton & Oliver Sain Orchestra* / Long distance operator: *Little Milton & Oliver Sain Orchestra* / I found me a new love: *Little Milton & Oliver Sain Orchestra* / I'm tryin': *Little Milton & Oliver Sain Orchestra* / Strange dreams: *Little Milton & Oliver Sain Orchestra* / Hold me tight: *Little Milton & Oliver Sain Orchestra* / (I have the) same old blues: *Little Milton & Oliver Sain Orchestra* / Dead love: *Little Milton & Oliver Sain Orchestra* / My baby pleases me: *Little Milton & Oliver Sain Orchestra* / Let it be known: *Little Milton & Oliver Sain Orchestra* / Hey girl: *Little Milton & Oliver Sain Orchestra* / Cross my heart: *Little Milton & Oliver Sain Orchestra* / I'm in love: *Little Milton & Oliver Sain Orchestra* / My mind is troubled: *Little Milton & Oliver Sain Orchestra* / Harlem nocturne: *Sain, Oliver Orchestra*
CD _______ CDCHD 633
Ace / Aug '96 / Pinnacle

ST. LOUIS GIRLS 1927-1934
CD _______ DOCD 5182
Document / Oct '93 / ADA / Hot Shot / Jazz Music

ST. LOUIS GIRLS 1929-1937
CD _______ SOB 035362
Story Of The Blues / Oct '92 / ADA / Koch

ST. LOUIS TOWN 1929-1933
CD _______ YAZCD 1003
Yazoo / Apr '91 / ADA / CM / Koch

ST. LUCIA JAZZ
CD _______ PD 007
Ebony / May '96 / Jet Star

ST. PATRICK'S DAY CELEBRATION
Haste to the wedding: *Gallowglass Ceili Band* / Irish washerwoman: *Gallowglass Ceili Band* / Flaherty's drake: *O'Dowda, Brendan* / Paddy McGinty's goat: *Harrington, Pat* / Irish jubilee: *Harrington, Pat* / Plough and the stars: *Gallowglass Ceili Band* / Mrs. Crotty's reel: *Gallowglass Ceili Band* / Muirsheen Durkin: *Dubliners* / Kelly the boy from Killan: *Dubliners* / Croppy boy: *Dubliners* / It's the same old shillelagh: *Downey, Morton* / When Irish eyes are smiling: *Downey, Morton* / Mother Machree: *Smith, Kate* / Molly Malone: *Smith, Kate* / Heather breeze: *Gallowglass Ceili Band* / St. Anne's reel: *Gallowglass Ceili Band* / Peeler's jacket: *Gallowglass Ceili Band* / Outlawed raparee: *Clancy Brothers & Tommy Makem* / Port Lairge: *Clancy Brothers & Tommy Makem* / I'm a free born man of the travelling people: *Clancy Brothers & Tommy Makem* / March from Oscar & Malvina: *Chieftains* / When a man's in love: *Chieftains*
CD _______ CK 48694
Columbia / Mar '97 / Sony

STAND BY ME (Love Songs From TV Commercials)
Stand by me: *King, Ben E.* / Only you: *Platters* / Drift away: *Gray, Dobie* / Will you still love me tomorrow: *Shirelles* / When a man loves a woman: *Sledge, Percy* / Rescue me: *Bass, Fontella* / Games people play: *South, Joe* / I'm into something good: *Herman's Hermits* / My blue heaven: *Domino, Fats* / Walkin' the dog: *Thomas, Rufus* / I got you (I feel good): *Brown, James* / Be bop a lula: *Vincent, Gene* / Up on the roof: *Drifters* / Leader of the pack: *Shangri-Las* / I put a spell on you: *Hawkins, Screamin' Jay* / Warm and tender love: *Sledge, Percy* / But I do: *Henry, Clarence 'Frogman'* / Venus: *Avalon, Frankie* / Runaway: *Shannon, Del* / Goodnight sweetheart, well it's time to go: *Spaniels*
CD _______ MU 3013
Musketeer / Oct '95 / Disc

STANDARDS ON IMPULSE
Summertime: *Blakey, Art* / In a sentimental mood: *Ellington, Duke & John Coltrane* / I concentrate on you: *Johnson, J.J. & Kai Winding* / Body and soul: *Carter, Benny* / Sister Sadie: *Evans, Gil* / Unforgettable: *Hartman, Johnny* / Oh lady be good: *Basie, Count* / Mood indigo: *Mingus, Charles* / Fly me to the moon: *Haynes, Roy* / What's new: *Coltrane, John* / Satin doll: *Tyner, McCoy* / Stardust: *Webster, Ben* / Cherokee: *Manne, Shelly* / Do nothin' 'til you hear from me: *Terry, Clark* / Solitude: *Ellington, Duke & Coleman Hawkins* / Girl from Ipanema: *Shepp, Archie*
CD _______ IMP 12032
Impulse Jazz / Dec '96 / New Note/BMG

STANDING ON THE VERGE (The Roots Of Funk 1964-1974)
CD _______ SHCD 9008
Shanachie / May '97 / ADA / Greensleeves / Koch

STANDING ROCK, SPIRIT OF SONG
CD _______ 14944
Spalax / Jan '97 / ADA / Cargo / Direct / Discovery / Greyhound

STANDING STONES
CD _______ NAGE 5CD
Art Of Landscape / Feb '86 / Sony

STAR O'RABBIE BURNS, THE
Star O'Rabbie Burns: *Dawson, Peter* / Auld lang syne: *Dawson, Peter* / Man's a man for a' that: *Watson, Bobby* / My love is like a red red rose: *Hislop, Joseph* / Of a'the airts the wind can blaw: *Hislop, Joseph* / My love she's but a lassie yet: *Hislop, Joseph* / Corn rigs: *Hislop, Joseph* / Afton water: *Hislop, Joseph* / Ye banks and braes o' bonnie Doon: *MacEwan, Sydney* / Comin' thro' the rye: *Teyte, Maggie* / Blue eyed lassie: *Burnett, Robert* / Ca' the yowes: *Brunskill, Muriel* / Green grow the rashes: *MacKinley, Jean Sterling* / I'll meet thee on the Lea rig: *Murray, Laidlaw* / Mary Morrison: *Harrison, John* / Tam Glen: *Day, Jean* / De'il's awa' wi' tha exciseman: *Henderson, Roy* / Oh Willie brewed a peck o'malt: *Henderson, Roy* / I'm owre young tae marry yet: *Baillie, Isobel* / John Anderson, my Jo: *Baillie, Isobel* / Bonnie wee thing: *McCormack, John* / Ae fond kiss: *Coleman, Esther & Foster Richardson* / Scots wha hae: *Glasgow Orpheus Choir* / Charming Chloe: *Suddaby, Elsie* / O'whistle an' I'll come tae ye, my lad: *Scotney, Evelyn* / Mary Morison: *MacGregor, Alexander*

CD MIDCD 004
Moidart / Jan '95 / Conifer/BMG

STAR POWER
CD EFA 201172
Pravda / May '95 / SRD

STAR TREK STRIKES BACK
CD CDR 004
ACV / Mar '97 / Plastic Head / SRD

STARDUST MEMORIES
With a shot in my heart: *Sinatra, Frank* / If I give my heart to you: *Day, Doris* / Georgia on my mind: *Laine, Frankie* / Welcome to my world: *Reeves, Jim* / In the mood: *Miller, Glenn* / Changing partners: *Crosby, Bing* / Hey there: *Clooney, Rosemary* / As time goes by: *Holiday, Billie* / Catch a falling star: *Como, Perry* / Three coins in a fountain: *Four Aces* / It's almost tomorrow: *Dreamweavers* / What a wonderful world: *Armstrong, Louis* / Little white cloud that cried: *Ray, Johnnie* / Autumn leaves: *Bennett, Tony* / Tear fell: *Brewer, Teresa* / Moon river: *Mancini, Henry* / Stormy weather: *Vaughan, Sarah* / May each day: *Williams, Andy* / Mr. Wonderful: *Lee, Peggy* / Because you're mine: *Lanza, Mario* / Under the bridges of Paris: *Kitt, Eartha* / Smoke gets in your eyes: *Platters*
CD NTRCD 045
Nectar / Oct '95 / Pinnacle

STARS AT CHRISTMAS
White Christmas: *Crosby, Bing* / It's Christmas all over the world: *Davis, Sammy Jr.* / Jolly old St. Nicholas: *Conniff, Ray* / We wish you a Merry Christmas: *Conniff, Ray* / Santa Claus is coming to town: *Bennett, Tony* / Christmas time is here again: *Whittaker, Roger* / Let it snow, let it snow, let it snow: *Williams, Andy* / Rockin' around the Christmas tree: *Lee, Brenda* / Christmas wonderland: *Kaempfert, Bert* / Rudolph the red nosed reindeer: *Crosby, Bing* / Baby's first Christmas: *Francis, Connie* / I'll be home for Christmas: *Day, Doris* / Home for the holidays: *Como, Perry* / Joy to the world: *Wynette, Tammy* / Hark the herald angels sing: *Andrews, Julie* / O come all ye faithful (Adeste Fidelis): *Reeves, Jim* / Ave Maria: *Lanza, Mario* / Christmas song: *Bennett, Tony* / What child is this: *Charles, Ray* / Special time of year: *Knight, Gladys* / Snowflake: *Clooney, Rosemary* / When a child is born: *Mathis, Johnny* / Count your blessings: *Conniff, Ray* / May each day: *Williams, Andy* / Have yourself a merry little Christmas: *Como, Perry* / Jingle bell rock: *Lee, Brenda* / Holiday for bells: *Kaempfert, Bert* / Snowfall: *Bennett, Tony* / Silver bells: *Day, Doris* / O little town of Bethlehem: *Francis, Connie* / Twelve days of Christmas: *Whittaker, Roger* / It came upon a midnight clear: *Andrews, Julie* / Blue Christmas: *Reeves, Jim* / Mary's boy child: *Belafonte, Harry* / 'Twas the night before Christmas: *Como, Perry* / Winter wonderland: *Parton, Dolly* / I saw Mommy kissing Santa Claus: *Beverley Sisters* / Little drummer boy: *Whittaker, Roger* / I believe in Christmas: *Boone, Pat* / Carol of the bells: *Mathis, Johnny* / Jingle bells: *Mancini, Henry* / Frosty the snowman: *Lee, Brenda* / Do you hear what I hear: *Williams, Andy* / Christmas time: *Charles, Ray* / All I want for Christmas: *Benton, Brook* / I walk with God: *Lanza, Mario* / Let there be peace: *Knight, Gladys* / Silent night: *Crosby, Bing* / White Christmas: *Mantovani*
CD STADD 1000
Wisepack / Oct '94 / Conifer/BMG / THE

STARS OF BIRDLAND ON TOUR
Lullabye of birdland: *Basie, Count & His Orchestra* / Why not: *Basie, Count & His Orchestra* / Basie talks: *Basie, Count & His Orchestra* / Jumpin' at the Woodside: *Young, Lester & Count Basie & His Orchestra* / I'm confessin': *Young, Lester & Count Basie & His Orchestra* / Every tub: *Young, Lester & Count Basie & His Orchestra* / Every day I have the blues: *Young, Lester & Count Basie & His Orchestra* / Shake rattle and roll: *Young, Lester & Count Basie & His Orchestra* / Dinner with friends: *Young, Lester & Count Basie & His Orchestra* / Lullabye of birdland: *Shearing, George Quintet* / Medley/East of the sun/Roses of Picardy/I'll remember April/: *Shearing, George Quintet* / Jumpin' with symphony sid: *Shearing, George Quintet* / George Shearing speaks: *Shearing, George Quintet* / Man I love: *Shearing, George Quintet* / Yesterdays: *Shearing, George Quintet* / Mambo inn: *Shearing, George Quintet* / Little pony: *Shearing, George Quintet* / Easy living: *Getz, Stan & Count Basie Orchestra* / Blues: *Getz, Stan & Count Basie Orchestra* / Blee bop blues: *Getz, Stan & Count Basie Orchestra* / I get a kick out of you: *Garner, Erroll Trio* / Laura: *Garner, Erroll Trio* / Idaho: *Garner, Erroll Trio* / There's a small hotel: *Garner, Erroll Trio* / Medley/Will you still be mine/Gypsy in my soul: *Garner, Erroll Trio* / 'Swonderful: *Vaughan, Sarah & Count Basie Orchestra* / Easy to remember: *Vaughan, Sarah & Count Basie Orchestra* / East of the sun: *Vaughan, Sarah & Count Basie Orchestra* / How important can it be: *Vaughan, Sarah & Count Basie Orchestra* / That old devil moon: *Vaughan, Sarah & Count Basie Orchestra* / Idle gossip: *Vaughan, Sarah & Count Basie Orchestra* / Make yourself comfortable: *Vaughan, Sarah & Count Basie Orchestra* / Perdido: *Vaughan, Sarah & Count Basie Orchestra* / Chris crossed: *Basie, Count & Joe Williams* / Comeback: *Basie, Count & Joe Williams*
CD JZCL 5015
Jazz Classics / Feb '97 / Cadillac / Direct / Jazz Music

STARS OF COUNTRY MUSIC, THE
Oh lonesome me: *Gibson, Don* / Peace in the valley: *Jordanaires* / Mexican Joe: *Reeves, Jim* / Crazy arms: *Lewis, Jerry Lee* / Next in line: *Cash, Johnny* / These boots are made for walking: *Hazelwood, Lee* / World's worst loser: *Jones, George* / Sally was a good old girl: *Jennings, Waylon* / Rose Marie: *Whitman, Slim* / Settin' the woods on fire: *Williams, Hank* / Honky tonk angels: *Parton, Dolly* / Race is on: *Jones, George* / Yonder comes a sucker: *Reeves, Jim* / Broken heart: *Twitty, Conway* / El Paso: *Robbins, Marty* / Train of love: *Cash, Johnny* / Please release me: *Parton, Dolly*
CD 22518
Music / Dec '95 / Target/BMG

STARS OF LAS VEGAS VOL.1
Take the 'A' train: *Ellington, Duke* / I left my heart in San Francisco: *Bennett, Tony* / God bless the child: *Minnelli, Liza* / I'm coming home: *Jones, Tom* / What now my love: *Bassey, Shirley* / Man without love: *Humperdinck, Engelbert* / Lady: *Rogers, Kenny* / All the love in the world: *Warwick, Dionne* / My way: *Anka, Paul* / Passing strangers: *Eckstine, Billy & Sarah Vaughan* / April in Paris: *Basie, Count* / Every time we say goodbye: *Fitzgerald, Ella* / Very thought of you: *Damone, Vic* / Moon river: *Williams, Andy* / September in the rain: *Washington, Dinah* / For the good times: *Como, Perry* / Volare: *Martin, Dean* / Spanish eyes: *Martino, Al* / Move over darling: *Day, Doris* / Unforgettable: *Cole, Nat 'King'*
CD VSOPCD 181
Connoisseur Collection / Mar '93 / Pinnacle

STARS OF LAS VEGAS VOL.2
Secret love: *Day, Doris* / Stranger in paradise: *Bennett, Tony* / Almost there: *Williams, Andy* / Blue velvet: *Vinton, Bobby* / Unchained melody: *Hibbler, Al* / Wives and lovers: *Jones, Jack* / What a wonderful world: *Armstrong, Louis* / Fever: *Lee, Peggy* / It's only make believe: *Campbell, Glen* / When I fall in love: *Cole, Nat 'King'* / Memories are made of this: *Martin, Dean* / I love you because: *Martino, Al* / And I love you so: *Como, Perry* / Love me warm and tender: *Anka, Paul* / Woman in love: *Three Degrees* / Welcome to my world: *Reeves, Jim* / Green green grass of home: *Jones, Tom* / Release me: *Humperdinck, Engelbert* / Do that to me one more time: *Captain & Tennille* / Laughter in the rain: *Sedaka, Neil*
CD VSOPCD 201
Connoisseur Collection / Jun '94 / Pinnacle

STARS OF MOTORCITY VOL.2, THE
With you I'm born again: *Syreeta* / Look into the eyes of a fool: *Bristol, Johnny* / Got the big city blues: *Eckstine, Billy* / Needle in a haystack: *Velvelettes* / Keep this thought in mind: *Bristol, Johnny* / Better late than never: *Velvelettes* / Gentle lady: *Eckstine, Billy* / He was really saying something: *Velvelettes* / Love fire: *Syreeta* / What does it take to win your love: *Bristol, Johnny* / Ask the lonely: *Eckstine, Billy* / One door closes, another one opens: *Bristol, Johnny* / Don't keep your distance: *Bristol, Johnny* / Moment of weakness: *Syreeta* / I dig everything about you: *Eckstine, Billy* / One plan of action: *Syreeta*
CD 302752
Hallmark / Jul '97 / Carlton

STARS OF REGGAE SUNSPLASH
CD CPCD 8025
Charly / Feb '94 / Koch

STARS OF ROCK 'N' ROLL
Tutti frutti: *Little Richard* / Rock around the clock: *Haley, Bill* / Mr. Bassman: *Cymbal, Johnny* / Wooly bully: *Sam The Sham & The Pharaohs* / Da doo ron ron: *Crystals* / Tallahassie lassie: *Cannon, Freddy* / Rubber ball: *Vee, Bobby* / Good golly Miss Molly: *Swinging Blue Jeans* / Shake, rattle and roll: *Haley, Bill* / Maybelline: *Berry, Chuck* / Keep a knockin': *Little Richard* / Lucille: *Little Richard* / Long Tall Sally: *Little Richard* / Wild thing: *Troggs* / Sheila: *Roe, Tommy* / At the hop: *Danny & The Juniors* / Speddy Gonzalez: *Boone, Pat* / It's my party: *Gore, Lesley*
CD 22524
Music / Dec '95 / Target/BMG

STARS OF THE 50'S
Softly, softly: *Murray, Ruby* / Heartbeat: *Murray, Ruby* / My special angel: *Vaughan, Malcolm* / Every day of my life: *Vaughan, Malcolm* / Stairway of love: *Holliday, Michael* / Starry eyed: *Holliday, Michael* / Dreamboat: *Cogan, Alma* / Never do a tango with an eskimo: *Cogan, Alma* / Around the world: *Hilton, Ronnie* / World outside: *Hilton, Ronnie* / Wake up little Susie: *King Brothers* / White sports coat and a pink carnation: *King Brothers* / My thanks to you: *Conway, Steve* / Zambesi: *Calvert, Eddie* / Mandy: *Calvert, Eddie* / Pickin' a chicken: *Boswell, Eve* / Blue star: *Boswell, Eve* / Lollipop: *Mudlarks* / Tammy: *Lotis, Dennis* / Be my girl: *Dale, Jim* / China tea: *Conway, Russ* / Cindy Oh Cindy: *Brent, Tony* / Only sixteen: *Douglas, Craig* / Don't laugh at me: *Wisdom, Norman*
CD CC 205
Music For Pleasure / May '88 / EMI

STARS OF THE LONDON PALLADIUM (The Greatest Performers Of Yesteryear)
I believe: *Bachelors* / Charmaine: *Bachelors* / I remember you: *Ifield, Frank* / Lovesick blues: *Ifield, Frank* / Say wonderful things: *Carroll, Ronnie* / Ring a ding girl: *Carroll, Ronnie* / Midnight in Moscow: *Ball, Kenny* / Green leaves of summer: *Ball, Kenny* / Does your chewing gum lose its flavour: *Donegan, Lonnie* / My old man's a dustman: *Donegan, Lonnie* / Singin' the blues: *Mitchell, Guy* / Knee deep in the blues: *Mitchell, Guy* / Cry: *Ray, Johnnie* / Just walkin' in the rain: *Ray, Johnnie* / Rose, Rose I love you: *Laine, Frankie* / Jezebel: *Laine, Frankie* / My prayer: *Platters* / Only you (and you alone): *Platters*
CD ECD 3282
K-Tel / Jan '97 / K-Tel

STARS SING CHRISTMAS FAVOURITES, THE
Christmas song / Have yourself a merry little Christmas / Santa Claus is coming to town / Frosty the snowman / O come all ye faithful (adeste fidelis) / Hark the herald angels sing / This time of the year / White Christmas / Blue Christmas / Let it snow, let it snow, let it snow / When a child is born / Silver bells / We wish you a merry Christmas / Please come home for Christmas / What child is this / Silent night / Little drummer boy / You're all I want for Christmas / Jingle bells / Auld lang syne
CD XMAS 013
Tring / Nov '96 / Tring

STARTRAX CLUB DISCO COLLECTION, THE
Startrax club disco / More than a woman / Night fever / Tragedy / Love you inside out / Jive talkin' / Edge of universe / Boogie child / Too much heaven (Our love) / Don't throw it all away / Wind of change / You stepped into my life / If I can't have you / New York mining disaster / 1941 / Stayin' alive / Night on Broadway / Search find / Lights went out in (Massachusetts) / How deep is your love / Reaching out / You should be dancing / Spirits (having flown) / Keep a good man down / I've got to get a message to you / Fanny (be tender with your love) / Love so right / First of May / Children of the world / IOIO / Saved by the bell / Words / Black is black / She's not there / In the navy / One way ticket / YMCA / I can see clearly now / Sunny / Kissin' in the back row of the movies / Bad girls / Instant replay / Three steps to heaven / Keep on dancing / Love hangover / Working my way back to you / DISCO / Use it up and wear it out / That's the way (I like it) / Band of gold / Alright now / Love train / Que sera mi vida / Ladies night / Go west / Kung fu fighting / Year 2525 (Exordium & terminus) / I will survive / Le freak / Because the night / When you're in love with a beautiful woman / Feels like I'm in love
CD 306822
Hallmark / May '97 / Carlton

STARTREFF VOLKSMUSIK
CD 15257
Laserlight / Nov '91 / Target/BMG

STASH SAMPLER 2, THE
CD STCD 599
Stash / Jan '93 / ADA / Cadillac / CM / Direct / Jazz Music

STATE OF THE ART VOL.4
Waterdance: *Silent Phase* / Oil zone: *Speedy J* / Hotwire: *Electronic Eye* / Teleport to origin: *Valleyman* / Dr. Peter: *Rejuvination* / Matrix: *Human Beings* / Clipper: *Autechre* / Extra: *Ishii, Ken* / Tied up: *LFO* / Con spirito: *Bolland, C.J.* / Far in out: *Scorn*
CD SOTA 004
Groove Kissing / Mar '96 / Vital

STATE OF THE ART VOL.5
CD PIAS 213003928
Play It Again Sam / May '97 / Discovery / Plastic Head / Vital

STATE OF THE NU-ART VOL.1, THE
CD PLAN 7CD
Blue Planet / May '97 / 3mv/Sony / Prime

STATE OF THE UNION
CD DIS 32CD
Dischord / Mar '95 / SRD

STATE OF THE UNION (2CD Set)
CD Set ALP 69CD
Atavistic / Jan '97 / Cargo / SRD

STATESIDE SMASHES
CD PLATCD 345
Platinum / Oct '90 / Prism

STATESIDE SWEET MUSIC
Love and learn: *Fields, Shep* / If the moon turns green: *Kassel, Art* / Little rendezvous in Honolulu: *Lopez, Vincent* / I have eyes: *Shaw, Artie Orchestra* / One cigarette for two: *Martin, Freddy & His Orchestra* / Pessimistic character: *Ayres, Mitchell & His Orchestra* / Can't get Indiana off my mind: *Gordon, Gay & The Mince Pies* / I don't want to cry anymore: *Barnet, Charlie* / Apple blossom and chapel bells: *Martin, Freddy & His Orchestra* / I threw a bean bag at the moon: *Kassel, Art* / That sentimental sandwich: *Nelson, Ozzie & His Orchestra* / On a little bamboo bridge: *Fields, Shep* / Whispering grass: *Dorsey, Jimmy Orchestra* / Strange enchantment: *Nelson, Ozzie & His Orchestra* / Meet the sun halfway: *Ayres, Mitchell & His Orchestra* / Afterglow: *Whiteman, Paul & His Orchestra* / Never took a lesson in my life: *Gordon, Gray & His Orchestra* / Why don't we do this more often: *Martin, Freddy & His Orchestra* / That's for me: *Barnet, Charlie Orchestra* / Moonlight and shadows: *Shaw, Artie Orchestra* / Who's afraid of love: *Berigan, Bunny & His Orchestra* / Flamingo: *Martin, Freddy & His Orchestra*
CD PASTCD 9787
Flapper / Apr '92 / Pinnacle

STATESIDE VOL.1
CD ZEN 006CD
Indochina / Feb '96 / Pinnacle

STAX BLUES MASTERS VOL.1 (Blue Monday)
They want money: *Little Sonny* / Drivin' wheel: *King, Albert* / Creeper: *Robinson, Freddie* / Eight men, four women: *Little Milton* / Things that I used to do: *Little Sonny* / Bad luck: *King, Albert* / More bad luck: *King, Albert* / Born under a bad sign: *King, Albert* / Blues with a feeling: *Little Sonny* / Married woman: *Little Milton* / Ronettes: *Robinson, Freddie* / Blue Monday: *Little Milton* / After hours: *Robinson, Freddie* / Open the door to your heart: *Little Milton* / Blues after hours: *Robinson, Freddie* / River's invitation: *Robinson, Freddie* / It's hard going up (but twice as hard coming down): *Little Sonny*
CD CDSXE 080
Stax / Nov '92 / Pinnacle

STAX FUNK - GET UP AND GET DOWN
Shaft: *Hayes, Isaac* / Castle of joy: *Fat Larry's Band* / What goes around (must come around): *Sons Of Slum* / Dark skin woman: *Rice, Sir Mack* / What'cha see is what'cha get: *Dramatics* / Son of Shaft: *Bar-Kays* / Dryer part 1: *Johnson, Roy Lee & The Villagers* / Cool strut part one: *Hayes, Bernie* / Mr. Big Stuff: *Knight, Jean* / Funkasize you: *Sho Nuff* / Holy ghost: *Bar-Kays* / Men: *Hayes, Isaac* / Circuits overloaded: *Foxx, Inez & Charlie* / FLB: *Fat Larry's Band* / Black: *Mar-Keys* / Get up and get down: *Dramatics* / Moving on: *Dynamic Soul Machine* / You chose me: *Sho Nuff* / Dryer part 2: *Johnson, Roy Lee & The Villagers* / Cool strut part 1: *Hayes, Bernie*
CD CDSX 020
Stax / May '89 / Pinnacle

STAX FUNK - SON OF STAX FUNK
Title theme (Tough guys): *Hayes, Isaac* / Type thang: *Hayes, Isaac* / Steppin' out: *Sho Nuff* / Mix match man: *Sho Nuff* / What does it take: *Sons Of Slum* / Man: *Sons Of Slum* / Getting funky round here: *Black Nasty* / Nasty soul: *Black Nasty* / Watch the dog: *Shack* / Patch it up: *Johnson, Roy Lee* / Funky hot grits: *Thomas, Rufus* / Soul town: *Forevers* / Shake your big hips: *Tolbert, Israel* / Bump meat: *Rice, Sir Mack* / Do me: *Knight, Jean* / In the hole: *Bar-Kays* / Watch me do it: *Sho Nuff* / Right on: *Sons Of Slum* / Talkin' to the people: *Black Nasty* / I'd kill a brick for my man: *Hot Sauce* / Carry on: *Knight, Jean* / Song and dance: *Bar-Kays* / Do the funky chicken: *Thomas, Rufus* / Devil is dope: *Dramatics*
CD CDSXD 075
Stax / Feb '93 / Pinnacle

STAX FUNX
Run Ray run: *Hayes, Isaac* / LAS: *South Memphis Horns* / Grab a handful: *Miller, Art Jerry* / Sweetback's theme: *Van Peebles, Melvin* / Got it together: *Robinson, Rudy & The Hungry Five* / Wes: *Soul Merchants* / End theme/Truck Turner: *Hayes, Isaac* / Ghetto - misfortune's wealth: *24 Carat Black* / Rock back: *Thomas, Rufus* / Do the sweetback: *March Wind* / Too many lovers: *Shack* / My thing is a moving thing: *TSU Tornadoes* / Broadway freeze: *Scales, Harvey* / Coldblooded: *Bar-Kays* / Hi-jacking love: *Taylor, Johnny* / Fancy: *Hamilton, Chico* / I feel good: *Sons Of Truth* / Love's gonna tear your playhouse down: *Brooks, Chuck* / (What's under) the natural do: *Kasandra, John* / Dirty tricks: *Sweet Inspirations* / One pair of pants: *Johnson, L.V.*
CD CDSXD 110
Stax / Apr '97 / Pinnacle

STAX GOLD (Hits 1968-1974)
Soul limbo: *Booker T & The MG's* / Time is tight: *Booker T & The MG's* / Private number: *Clay, Judy & William Bell* / Who's making love: *Taylor, Johnnie* / Bring it on home to me: *Floyd, Eddie* / I forgot to be your lover: *Bell, William* / I like what you're doing (to me): *Thomas, Carla* / Do the push and pull (part 1): *Thomas, Rufus* / Mr. Big Stuff: *Knight, Jean* / What'cha see is what'cha get: *Dramatics* / Respect yourself: *Staple Singers* / I'll take you there: *Staple Singers* / Shaft: *Hayes, Isaac* / Son of Shaft: *Bar-Kays* / I've been lonely for so long: *Knight, Frederick* / Starting all over again: *Mel & Tim* / Woman to woman: *Brown, Shirley* / I'll be the other woman: *Soul Children* / So I can love you: *Emotions* / I have learned to do without you: *Staples, Mavis* / In the rain: *Dramatics* / Dedicated to the one

I love: *Temprees* / Short stoppin': *Brown, Veda* / Cheaper to keep her: *Taylor, Johnnie*
CD ______ **CDSXD 043**
Stax / Sep '91 / Pinnacle

STAX O' SOUL: SAMPLER OF STAX TRAX
Will you still love me tomorrow: *Bell, William* / Stolen angel: *Tonettes* / Zip a dee doo dah: *Booker T & The MG's* / Little boy: *Thomas, Carla* / Last clean shirt: *Thomas, Rufus* / Cupid: *Redding, Otis* / Sweet devil: *John, Mable* / Need your love so bad: *Johnson, Ruby* / I've never found a girl: *Floyd, Eddie* / I could never be president: *Taylor, Johnnie* / What side of the door: *Hughes, Jimmy* / Open the door to your heart: *Little Milton* / I can't break away (from your love): *Lewis, Barbara* / When something is wrong with my baby: *Weston, Kim* / I finally got you: *McCracklin, Jimmy* / Takin' all the love I can: *Joseph, Margie* / Wade in the water: *Little Sonny* / I've been lonely for so long: *Knight, Frederick* / Respect yourself: *Staple Singers* / Getting funky round here: *Black Nasty* / Flat tire: *King, Albert* / We need each other, girl: *Hayes, Isaac* / Move me move me: *Brown, Shirley*
CD ______ **CDSXX 100**
Stax / Oct '93 / Pinnacle

STAX REVUE LIVE AT THE 54 BALLROOM
Green onions: *Booker T & The MG's* / You can't sit down: *Booker T & The MG's* / Summertime: *Booker T & The MG's* / Soul twist: *Booker T & The MG's* / Boot-leg: *Booker T & The MG's* / Don't have to shop around: *Mad Lads* / Candy: *Astors* / Last night: *Mar-Keys* / Any other way: *Bell, William* / You don't miss your water: *Bell, William* / Every ounce of strength: *Thomas, Carla* / Do the dog: *Thomas, Rufus* / Walking the dog: *Thomas, Rufus*
CD ______ **CDSXD 040**
Stax / Sep '91 / Pinnacle

STAX SIRENS AND VOLT VAMPS
Try a little tenderness: *Sweet Inspirations* / I've got to go on without you: *Brown, Shirley* / Take it off her (and put it on me): *Brown, Veda* / Love slave: *Alexander, Margie* / Shouldn't I love him: *John, Mable* / Got to be the man: *Emotions* / Save the last kiss for me: *Knight, Jean* / Nobody: *Joseph, Margie* / Who could be loving you: *Ross, Jackie* / Standing in the need of your love: *Jeanne & The Darlings* / I'll never grow old: *Charmells* / Give love to save love: *Clay, Judy* / You hurt me for the last time: *Foxx, Inez & Charlie* / I like what you're doing (to me): *Thomas, Carla* / If I had it my way: *Weston, Kim* / How can you mistreat the one you love: *Love, Katie* / Love changes: *Charlene & The Soul Serenaders* / What happened to our good thing: *Haywood, Kitty* / Where would you be today: *Ilana*
CD ______ **CDSX 013**
Stax / Jun '88 / Pinnacle

STAX/VOLT REVUE VOL.3 (Live In Europe)
Introduction (London): *Emperor Rosko* / Red beans and rice: *Booker T & The MG's* / Booker-loo: *Booker T & The MG's* / Green onions: *Booker T & The MG's* / Hip hug-her: *Booker T & The MG's* / Introduction (Paris): *Hubert* / Let me be good to you: *Thomas, Carla* / Yesterday: *Thomas, Carla* / Something good: *Thomas, Carla* / B-A-B-Y: *Thomas, Carla* / Introduction (London) 2: *Emperor Rosko* / I don't want to cry: *Floyd, Eddie* / Raise your hand: *Floyd, Eddie* / Knock on wood: *Floyd, Eddie* / Introduction (London) 3: *Emperor Rosko* / Respect: *Redding, Otis* / My girl: *Redding, Otis* / Shake: *Redding, Otis* / Day tripper: *Redding, Otis* / Introduction: *Redding, Otis* / Fa fa fa fa fa (Sad song): *Redding, Otis* / Introduction: *Redding, Otis* / Try a little tenderness: *Redding, Otis*
CD ______ **CDSXD 044**
Stax / May '92 / Pinnacle

STAY TUNED
CD ______ **HM 001**
Harmony / Jun '97 / TKO Magnum

STEADY DANCE TRAXX
CD ______ **CCC 97003**
Citycat Club / Jul '97 / TKO Magnum

STEAL THIS DISC VOL.1
CD ______ **RCD 00210**
Rykodisc / Jun '92 / ADA / Vital

STEAMIN' (Hardcore '92)
It's grim up north: *JAMMS* / Get ready for this: *2 Unlimited* / DJ's take control: *SL2* / Faith (in the power of love): *Rozalla* / Activ 8 (come with me): *Altern 8* / 2/231: *Anticappella* / Ring my bell: *DJ Jazzy Jeff & The Fresh Prince* / Best of you: *Thomas, Kenny* / Apparently nothin': *Young Disciples* / Something got me started: *Simply Red* / Killer: *Seal* / Dance with me: *Control* / Change: *Stansfield, Lisa* / Love will bring us together: *Cookie Crew & Roy Ayers* / Alright: *Urban Soul* / Give it to me baby (sample free zone): *Love Revolution* / Peter and the wolf: *Zero G* / I want you (forever): *Cox, Carl* / O P P: *Naughty By Nature* / Keepin' the faith: *De La Soul*
CD ______ **JARCD 1**
Cookie Jar / Dec '91 / SRD

STEEL BAND MUSIC OF THE CARIBBEAN
Fire down below / Grass skirt / Mary Ann / Out of my dreams / Spear dance / Zulu chant / La paloma / Jungle / Native mambo / Spur dance / Flag woman / Wings of a dove / Endless vibrations / Calypso eine kleine nachtmusik
CD ______ **12176**
Laserlight / Mar '96 / Target/BMG

STEEL BANDS OF TRINIDAD AND TOBAGO
Sunset / Pan in the minor / Love's theme / To be continued / Unknown band / I just called to say I love you / Sparrow medley / Calypso music / Brisad del zolla / Somewhere out there / Hammer
CD ______ **DE 4011**
Delos / Jan '94 / Nimbus

STEEL DRUM FESTIVAL
CD ______ **TCD 1039**
Tradition / Nov '96 / ADA / Vital

STEEL MUSIC VOL.2 (Calypsos And Socas)
CD ______ **68941**
Tropical / Apr '97 / Discovery

STEEL RAILS (Classic Railroad Songs Vol.1)
Wabash Cannonball: *Acuff, Roy* / Orange blossom special: *Johnson Mountain Boys* / Daddy, what's a train: *Phillips, Utah* / Jimmie the kid: *Rodgers, Jimmie* / Ramblin' man: *Kane, Kieran* / Steel rails: *Krauss, Alison* / Trainwreck of emotion: *McCoury, Del* / Slow moving freight train: *Moffatt, Hugh* / Lord of the trains: *Russell, Tom* / LAst train: *Rowan, Peter* / Nine pound hammer: *Grisman, David* / When the golden train comes down: *Sons Of The Pioneers* / Texas, 1947: *Clark, Guy* / Pan American boogie: *MacKenzie, Kate*
CD ______ **ROUCD 1128**
Rounder / Mar '97 / ADA / CM / Direct

STEEPED IN THE BLUES TRADITION
CD ______ **TCD 1016**
Tradition / May '96 / ADA / Vital

STEP, WRITE, RUN (2CD Set)
CD Set ______ **TONE 6CD2**
Touch / Nov '96 / Kudos / Pinnacle

STEPPIN' OUT - THE ALBUM VOL.1
CD ______ **STEP 1CD**
Steppin' Out / Sep '96 / Else / Mo's Music Machine / Pinnacle / Steppin' Out / Total/ BMG / Vital

STEPPIN' OUT - THE ALBUM VOL.2
CD ______ **STEP 2CD**
Steppin' Out / Sep '96 / Else / Mo's Music Machine / Pinnacle / Steppin' Out / Total/ BMG / Vital

STEPPIN' OUT - THE ALBUM VOL.3
CD ______ **STEP 3CD**
CD ______ **STEP 3CDN**
Steppin' Out / Sep '96 / Else / Mo's Music Machine / Pinnacle / Steppin' Out / Total/ BMG / Vital

STEPPING IT OUT
CD ______ **VT 1CD**
Veteran Tapes / Oct '93 / ADA / Direct

STEREO COCKTAIL
CD ______ **EFA 610512**
Platten Meister / May '96 / SRD

STEWED MOONBEAMS IN WAVY GRAVY (Okeh Black Rock'n'Roll)
CD ______ **EDCD 283**
Edsel / Mar '92 / Pinnacle

STICKY WHIPPET (Best Of New Ground Records)
Live in taffeta: *Secret Order* / Manoible man: *Floating Bloke* / Shiny woman: *Conemelt* / Glowing trees: *Meek* / Two days: *Corridor* / All over hair piece: *Conemelt* / Beetlecrusher: *Floating Bloke* / Agnostic stomp: *Conemelt* / New Ground office: *Grant*
CD ______ **OUCH 003CD**
Spiky / Jun '97 / RTM/Disc

STILL COOKIN'
CD ______ **URCD 005**
Ubiquity / Jul '96 / Cargo / Timewarp

STILL FROM THE HEART
CD ______ **WB 1152CD**
We Bite / Jun '97 / Plastic Head

STILL GOT THE BLUES
CD ______ **EMPRBX 004**
Empress / Sep '94 / Koch

STILL GOT THE BLUES VOL.1
CD ______ **EMPRCD 502**
Emporio / Apr '94 / Disc

STILL GOT THE BLUES VOL.2
CD ______ **EMPRCD 508**
Emporio / Apr '94 / Disc

STILL SEARCHIN'
My beatbox: *Deejay Punk-Roc* / Bass alarm: *DJ Ex-Fx* / Toke it out: *Rude Cubans* / Ladies rock the house: *Real Rulers* / Lazy afternoon: *Swoon* / Bass-a-go-go: *DJ Ex-Fx* / I'm not a bitch: *E Funk Sound Surgeon* / Bouncing bomb: *Jaywalk* / Never let u go: *Jaywalk* / Still searchin': *Cape Canaveral*
CD ______ **ILLCD 1013**
Airdog / Jun '97 / 3mv/Sony

STILL SMOKIN'
CD ______ **GLINECD 001**
Ganja/Frontline / Apr '97 / SRD

STILL SPICY GUMBO STEW
I don't want to be hurted: *George, Barbara* / Losing battle: *Adams, Johnny* / Check Mr. Popeye: *Bo, Eddie* / Now let's Popeye: *Bo, Eddie* / Shrimp boat: *Dr. John* / Somebody's got to go: *Tick tocks* / Why lie: *Tee, Willie* / I found a little girl: *Bo, Eddie* / Love as true as mine: *Johnson, Wallace* / I got a feelin': *Nooky Boy* / Money (that's what I want): *Afo executives* / Who knows: *Tee, Willie* / Heart for sale: *Lee, Robbie* / Point: *Dr. John* / Roamin-itis: *Bo, Eddie* / Baby: *Lynn, Tammi* / Love love love: *Wood Brothers* / Nancy: *Afo executives* / Serpent woman: *Robinson, Alvin* / Soulful woman: *Robinson, Alvin* / Sho' 'bout drive me wild: *Robinson, Alvin* / End of a dream (Booker's ballad): *Booker, James* / Cry cry cry: *Robinson, Alvin*
CD ______ **CDCHD 520**
Ace / Jun '94 / Pinnacle

STINGRAY - THE COLLECTION VOL.1
CD ______ **STINGCD 1**
Sting Ray / Feb '95 / Jet Star

STINGRAY - THE COLLECTION VOL.1
CD ______ **NTMCD 546**
Nectar / Jun '97 / Pinnacle

STIRRING WITH SOUL
CD ______ **TCD 1040**
Tradition / Nov '96 / ADA / Vital

STOLEN MOMENTS - RED, HOT & COOL
Time is moving on: *Byrd, Donald & Guru* / Un angel en danger: *MC Solaar & Ron Carter* / Positive: *Franti, Michael* / Nocturnal sunshine: *Ndegeocello, Me'shell* / Flyin' high in the Brooklyn sky: *Digable Planets/ Lester Bowie/Wah Wah Watson* / Stolen moments: *UFO* / Rubber's song: *Pharcyde* / I shall proceed: *Roots & Roy Ayers* / Trouble don't last always: *Incognito/Carleen Anderson/Ramsey Lewis* / Rent strike: *Groove Collective & Bernie Worrell* / Scream: *Us 3 & Joshua Redman/Tony Remy* / This is madness: *Last Poets & Pharoah Sanders* / Apprehension: *Cherry, Don & The Watts Prophets* / Love supreme: *Marsalis, Branford* / Love supreme: *Coltrane, Alice* / Creator has a master plan: *Sanders, Pharoah*
CD Set ______ **GRP 97942**
GRP / Oct '94 / New Note/BMG

STOMPERS (2CD Set)
Shame shame shame: *Lewis, Smiley* / Fat man: *Domino, Fats* / Wine woman and whiskey: *Lightfoot, Papa George* / For you my love: *Lutcher, Nellie & Nat 'King' Cole* / Jumpin' at capitol: *Cole, Nat 'King' Trio* / Who drank my beer while I was in the rear: *Bartholomew, Dave* / Prancin': *Turner, Ike & Tina's Kings Of Rhythm* / Hucklebuck with Jimmy: *Five Keys* / Variations on a theme: *Lewis, Meade 'Lux'* / That's all I need: *Turner, Ike & The Kings Of Rhythm* / Hole in my heart: *Esquerita* / Trouble up the road: *Brenston, Jackie* / Boogie woogie Memphis: *Memphis Slim* / Down the road apiece: *Milburn, Amos* / Save your money baby: *Shakey Jake & The All Stars* / Mother fuyer: *Dirty Red* / Let the good times roll: *Shirley & Lee* / Proud Mary: *Turner, Ike & Tina* / No mo do yakomo: *Dr. Feelgood* / You can't catch me: *Love Sculpture* / King kong: *Tyler, Big T.* / Big fat: *Canned Heat* / Be baba leba: *Humes, Helen* / Little bitty pretty one: *Harris, Thurston & The Sharps* / Rockin' by myself: *Gowans, Sammy* / I need you I want you: *Parker, Jack* / Red hot: *Luman, Bob* / Slow smooth and easy: *Gene & Eunice* / Oo wee: *Jordan, Louis* / Fujiyama mama: *Allen, Annisteen* / Come back to me: *Walker, T-Bone* / Down the road: *Lewis, Smiley* / Baby get it on: *Turner, Ike & Tina* / Safronia B: *Boze, Calvin & His All Stars* / Hurt by love: *Foxx, Inez* / I got booted: *James, Sonny* / Back in the night: *Dr. Feelgood* / Lookin' for a love: *Womack, Bobby* / Low down in lodi: *King, Freddie* / So long good luck and goodbye: *Rogers, Weldon*
CD Set ______ **CDEM 1622**
EMI / Jul '97 / EMI

STOMPIN' AT THE KLUB FOOT VOL.1 & 2
Ghost town: *Restless* / Baby, please don't go: *Restless* / Bottle on the beach: *Restless* / Long black shiny car: *Restless* / Red monkey: *Milkshakes* / Did I hear you: *Milkshakes* / It's you: *Milkshakes* / Sweet little sixteen: *Milkshakes* / Joe 90: *Guana Batz* / Train kept a rollin': *Guana Batz* / Please give me something: *Guana Batz* / Devil's guitar: *Guana Batz* / I can satisfy you: *Stingrays* / Escalator: *Stingrays* / Time is after you: *Stingrays* / Blue girl: *Stingrays* / St. Jack: *Primevals* / Low down: *Primevals* / Transvestite blues: *Demented Are Go* / Pickled and preserved: *Demented Are Go* / Misdemeanor: *Frenzy* / Cry or die: *Frenzy* / Crazy 'n' wild: *Pharaohs* / Listen pretty baby: *Pharaohs* / Real cool chick: *Styngrites* / Reptile (Man): *Styngrites* / Legend of the lost: *Rapids* / Raid: *Rapids* / Ride this torpedo: *Tall Boys* / Action woman: *Tall Boys*
CD ______ **SLOG CD 6**
Slogan / Oct '92 / BMG

STOMPIN' AT THE KLUB FOOT VOL.3 & 4
Pass it on: *Torment* / Last time: *Torment* / Rip it up: *Rochee & The Sarnos* / High class power: *Wigsville Spliffs* / Psycho disease: *Coffin Nails* / Bamboo land: *Batmobile* / Baby that's where you're wrong: *Caravans* / Edge on you: *Restless* / No particular place to go: *Guana Batz* / Ghost train: *Frenzy* / Be bop a lula: *Demented Are Go* / Shake it up: *Styngrites* / Dizzy Miss Lizzy: *Milkshakes* / Uncle Sam: *Torment* / Beast: *Rochee & The Sarnos* / Al Capone: *Wigsville Spliffs* / Let's wreck: *Coffin Nails* / Cold sweat: *Batmobile* / Ballroom blitz: *Batmobile* / Gonna love ya: *Caravans* / You're so fine: *Guana Batz* / Hall of mirrors: *Frenzy* / Killed love: *Pharaohs* / Spiritual: *Primevals* / Fun time: *Tall Boys*
CD ______ **SLOG CD 7**
Slogan / Oct '92 / BMG

STOMPIN' AT THE SAVOY
Stompin' at the Savoy: *Armstrong, Louis* / In the mood: *Miller, Glenn* / It started all over again: *Dorsey, Tommy* / Nutcracker suite: *Brown, Les* / Northwest passage: *Herman, Woody* / Tea for two: *Armstrong, Louis* / April in Paris: *Miller, Glenn* / Nearness of you: *Dorsey, Jimmy* / Nightmare: *Shaw, Artie* / How about you: *Brown, Les* / C'est si bon: *Armstrong, Louis* / Frankie and Johnny: *Goodman, Benny* / Chattanooga choo choo: *Miller, Glenn* / Fools rush in: *Dorsey, Jimmy* / Pretty woman: *Ellington, Duke* / Good for nothin' Joe: *Barnet, Charlie* / Tiger rag: *Armstrong, Louis* / After glow: *Herman, Woody* / I've got rhythm: *Dorsey, Jimmy* / That old black magic: *Miller, Glenn*
CD ______ **GRF 129**
Tring / '93 / Tring

STOMPING PARTY
Rockin' all over the world: *Status Quo* / Venus: *Bananarama* / Come on Eileen: *Dexy's Midnight Runners* / Crocodile rock: *John, Elton* / Cum on feel the noize: *Slade* / Wild thing: *Troggs* / Twist and shout: *Poole, Brian & The Tremeloes* / Shout: *Lulu* / La Bamba: *Los Lobos* / Monster mash: *Pickett, Bobby* / All right now: *Free* / Tainted love: *Soft Cell* / Only way is up: *Yazz* / Kiss: *Art Of Noise* / Spirit in the sky: *Greenbaum, Norman* / Tequila: *Champs* / Addicted to love: *Palmer, Robert* / Shakin' all over: *Kidd, Johnny* / Respectable: *Mel & Kim* / See my baby jive: *Wizzard* / 5-4-3-2-1: *Manfred Mann* / Let's work together: *Canned Heat* / Mony mony: *James, Tommy* / Hippy hippy shake: *Swinging Blue Jeans* / Hi ho silver lining: *Beck, Jeff* / Locomotion: *Little Eva* / Hit me with your rhythm stick: *Dury, Ian* / (We're gonna) Rock around the clock: *Haley, Bill* / Roll over beethoven: *Berry, Chuck* / Time warp: *Damian* / Dizzy: *Roe, Tommy* / Let's twist again: *Checker, Chubby* / My baby just cares for me: *Simone, Nina* / Israelites: *Dekker, Desmond* / Double barrel: *Collins, Dave & Ansell* / Reet petite: *Wilson, Jackie* / Can can: *Buster* / I'm the leader of the gang (I am): *Glitter, Gary* / Lond tall Sally: *Little Richard* / Let's dance: *Montez, Chris*
CD ______ **DINCD 52**
Dino / Nov '92 / Pinnacle

STONE ROCK BLUES
CD ______ **CHLD 19264**
Chess/MCA / Oct '94 / BMG / New Note/ BMG

STONES OF CALLANISH, THE (A Folk Opera 2CD Set)
Stones on the hill: *Tabor, June* / Crucified on your old broken cross: *Paterson, Rod* / Don't say goodbye: *Davies, Lesley* / Across the wide ocean: *Russell, Janet* / Latha dhomh's mi gabhail a'mhonaidh: *MacPhee, Catherine-Anne* / Going down to metal bridge: *Dow, Nick & Bernard Wrigley* / You ebb and flow: *Russell, Janet* / I stand here alone on the beach: *Davies, Lesley* / On me way to Dover: *Dow, Nick* / Towers of London: *Simpson, Fiona* / You ebb and flow: *Paterson, Rod* / Tasdan a'righ's feileadh an t-saighdeir: *MacPhee, Catherine-Anne* / Down from the hills: *Paterson, Rod & Fiona Simpson/Catherine Ann MacPhee* / Sleep on my darling: *Davies, Lesley* / Stones on the hil: *Tabor, June* / Another pint: *Paterson, Rod* / Reconciliation: *Paterson, Rod & Lesley Davies* / Take me back to Lewis: *Davies, Lesley*
CD Set ______ **DOG 005/6**
Mrs. Ackroyd / Feb '97 / ADA / Direct / Roots

STOP AND LISTEN VOL.1
CD ______ **BBECD 001**
Barely Breaking Even / Nov '96 / Beechwood/BMG

STOP AND LISTEN VOL.2
Monkey that became president: *Brotherhood* / It's too funky in here: *P-Funk All Stars* / Tribute to the JB's: *Last Minister* / Power (out of sight): *Hip Hop Traxx* / Summertime lovin': *Arrington, Steve* / Soul power '74: *Maceo & The Macks* / Walk into the sun: *Organised Confusion* / Cut me loose: *Push* / Que si quier: *Pac Man* / Got to get back to Louisiana: *Parker, Elmer* / Zambezi: *Kynard, Charles* / More mess on my thing: *Poets Of Rhythm*
CD ______ **BBECD 003**

Barely Breaking Even / Mar '97 / Beechwood/BMG

STOP AND LISTEN VOL.3 (Compiled By Bobbi & Steve)
Trinidad: *Jumbo Caribbean Disco* / I really love you: *Heaven & Earth* / Till you surrender: *Brown, Rainbow* / Saturday night, Sunday morning: *Houston, Thelma* / Trip to your mind: *Hudson People* / Love don't live: *Proctor, Michael* / My desire: *Next Phase & Helen Bruner* / Just follow the vibe: *Zoo Experience* / We can make it: *Zoo Experience* / Everybody: *Preston Project* / Love and happiness: *Second Crusade* / Keep the faith: *Ramirez, Philip*
CD ____________ **BBECD 007**
Barely Breaking Even / Jul '97 / Beechwood/BMG

STOP SAMPLER
CD ____________ **74321308452**
Arista / Sep '95 / BMG

STORM FROM THE EAST VOL.1
CD ____________ **ASHADOW 4CD**
Moving Shadow / May '96 / SRD

STORM FROM THE EAST VOL.2
Storm from the east Vol.2 / Eleventh hour: *PFM* / Reed breeze: *Hyper On Experience* / Illicit groove: *JMJ & Richie* / Overcast swing: *Flytronix* / Sunset phobia: *E-Z Rollers* / Gravitational pull: *JMJ* / Altitude of dreams: *Universal* / Horizontal movements: *Kudos* / True: *Tekniq* / Control: *Banks, Alex*
CD ____________ **ASHADOW 8CD**
Moving Shadow / Mar '97 / SRD

STORM OF DRONES (3CD Set)
CD Set ____________ **EFA 709662**
Asphodel / Dec '96 / Cargo / SRD

STORMY WEATHER
CD ____________ **PHONTCD 7647**
Phontastic / '94 / Cadillac / Jazz Music / Wellard

STORY OF FADO, THE (Music From Portugal)
A casa de Mariquinhas: *Marceneiro, Alfredo* / Nao venhas tarde: *Ramos, Carlos* / Tia macheta: *Cardoso, Berta* / A tendinha: *Silva, Hermina* / A rosinha dos limoes: *Max* / Rosa enjeitada: *Teresa de Noronha, Maria* / Partir e morer um pouco: *Dos Santos, Antonio* / Foi na travessa da palha: *Do Carmo, Lucilia* / Foi deus: *Rodrigues, Amalia* / Lisboa a noite: *De Matos, Tony* / Aquela janela virada pro mar: *Da Silva, Tristao* / Fado das caldas: *Da Camara, Vicente* / Belos tempos: *Farinha, Fernando* / Colchetes de oiro: *Da Camara, Hermano* / Fadista louco: *Mourao, Antonio* / Saudade vai-te embora: *Maria, Fernanda* / Embucado: *Rosa, Joao Ferreira* / Amar: *Carvalho, Teresa Silva* / Saudade mal do fado: *Do Carmo, Carlos* / Arraial: *Braga, Joao* / Ate que a voz me doa: *Da Fe, Maria* / Carvalo ruco: *Pereira, Nuno Da Camara*
CD ____________ **HEMIMDCD 100**
Hemisphere / Feb '97 / EMI

STORY OF FLAMENCO, THE
Serranita me publicaste: *De La Matrona, Pepe* / Me valgo de mi saber: *De Cadiz, Perla* / Subasta de cuadras antiguos: *De Cadiz, Pericon* / Moritos a caballo: *De Jerez, Sernita* / Yo tengo tres corazones: *Isidro, Paco* / Mujer malina: *Caracol, Manolo* / Le pido a dios: *De Utrera, Fernanda* / En al estribo: *Moreno, Gabriel* / Los andaluces: *Flores De Gaditano* / La zagala: *La Nina De La Puebla* / Me pongo a pregonar: *De Jerez, Terremoto* / Fiesta en el Barrio De Santiago: *De Jerez, Terremoto & Romerito/El Borrico/Diamante Negro* / A linares que us mi pueblo: *Linares, Carmen* / Tabernas de triana: *El Pali* / Nochebuena en el alosno: *Toronjo, Hermanos* / Nana de la cebollas: *Morente, Enrique* / Me guesta estar en la Sierra: *Marchena, Pepe*
CD ____________ **HEMIMDCD 103**
Hemisphere / Feb '97 / EMI

STORY OF GOLDBAND RECORDS, THE
Stormy weather: *Phillips, Phil* / Let's boogie: *Bonner, Juke Boy* / Sugar Bee: *Cleveland Crochet* / Let's go boppin' tonight: *Ferrier, Al* / Crawl: *Guitar Junior* / So what: *Duhan, Johnny* / Cindy Lou: *Terry, Gene* / You're lonesome now: *Perrywell, Charles* / Boogie in the mud: *James, Danny* / Going crazy baby: *Guitar Junior* / Rooster strut: *Savoy, Ashton* / No future: *Rockin' Sidney* / You're so fine: *Kershaw, Pee Wee* / Frosty: *James, Danny* / San Antonio: *Big Walter* / Please accept my love: *Wilson, Jimmy* / Blue bayou shuffle: *Cookie & The Cupcakes* / Teenage baby: *Herman, Sticks* / Secret of love: *Anderson, Elton* / Chicken stuff: *Wilson, Hop* / Teardrops in my eyes: *Terry, Gene* / Puppy love: *Parton, Dolly* / Don't leave me: *Phillips, Phil*
CD ____________ **CDCHD 424**
Ace / Nov '92 / Pinnacle

STORY OF ROCK 'N' ROLL (2CD Set)
Leader of the pack: *Shangri-Las* / He's so fine: *Chiffons* / Stagger lee: *Price, Lloyd* / Runaway: *Shannon, Del* / Shake rattle and roll: *Haley, Bill* / Sheila: *Roe, Tommy* / Wooly bully: *Sam The Sham & The Pharaohs* / Speedy gonzales: *Boone, Pat* / Venus: *Avalon, Frankie* / Only sixteen: *Cooke, Sam* / Shakin' all over: *Allen, Chad & The Guess Who* / Party doll: *Knox, Buddy* / Lucille: *Little Richard* / Keep on dancing: *Gentrys* / Viva Bobby Joe: *Equals* / Red river rock: *Johnny & The Hurricanes* / Rock around the clock: *Haley, Bill* / Letters: *Box Tops* / Tallahassee road: *Nashville Teens* / Dancing in the street: *Reeves, Martha* / Da doo ron ron: *Crystals* / It's my party: *Gore, Lesley* / Let's have a party: *Jackson, Wanda* / Teen beat: *Nelson, Sandy* / Maybelline: *Berry, Chuck* / Good golly Miss Molly: *Swinging Blue Jeans* / Raunchy: *Justis, Bill* / Blueberry hill: *Domino, Fats* / Charlie Brown: *Coasters* / Baby come back: *Equals* / Rock 'n' roll is here to stay: *Danny & The Juniors*
CD Set ____________ **DCD 3009**
Music / Jun '97 / Target/BMG

STORY OF TANGO, THE
La cumparsita: *Basso, Jose* / El choclo: *Sexteto Mayor* / De vuelta y media: *Varela, Francisco* / Quejas de bandoneon: *Troilo, Anibal* / Verano porteandon: *Garello, Paul* / La cachila: *Pugliese, Osvaldo* / El dia que me quieras: *Gardel, Carlos* / Grisel: *Mores, Mariano* / La pu me qui: *Canaro, Francisco* / Yira, yira: *Sassone, Florindo* / La yumba: *Pugliese, Osvaldo* / Adios nonino: *Sexteto Mayor* / Margerita de Agosto: *Garello, Paul* / El firulete: *Basso, Jose* / Taquito militar: *Mores, Mariano* / La tablada: *Canaro, Francisco* / Danzarin: *Troilo, Anibal* / Palomita blanca: *Varela, Francisco* / Adios muchachos: *Sassone, Florindo* / Mi Buenos Aires querido: *Gardel, Carlos*
CD ____________ **HEMIMDCD 101**
Hemisphere / Feb '97 / EMI

STORY OF THE CIVIL RIGHTS MOVEMENT THROUGH ITS SONG, THE
CD ____________ **SFWCD 40032**
Smithsonian Folkways / Dec '94 / ADA / Cadillac / CM / Direct / Koch

STRAIGHT AHEAD (A Journey Through Acid Jazz)
Mission impossible: *Taylor, James Quartet* / Day at the seaside: *Brand New Heavies* / Bolivia: *Sandberg, Ulf Quartet* / Bad ass weed: *Mother Earth* / I don't want to see myself (without you): *Callier, Terry* / Spinning wheel: *New Jersey Kings* / Manteca: *Jazz Renegades* / Dat's slammin': *Gordon, Robbie* / Ain't no sunshine: *Beaujolais Band* / Beyond the snowstorm: *Snowboy* / Mercy mercy me: *Jazz Apostles* / Throttle back: *Emperor's New Clothes*
CD ____________ **MUSCD 033**
MCI Music / Jan '97 / Disc / THE

STRAIGHT EDGE AS FUCK VOL.3
CD ____________ **DFR 18**
Desperate Flight / Jun '97 / Cargo

STRAIGHT FROM THE SOUL
Hot wild unrestricted crazy love: *Jackson, Millie* / At last: *Jones, Glenn* / Bad attitude: *Sha Sha* / Vibe is right: *Turner, Ruby* / No stoppin' us now: *Davis, Mike* / High on desire: *Winstanley, Liz* / Children of the ghetto: *Real Thing* / Heal our land: *Butler, Jonathan* / Every step of the way: *Jones, Glenn* / Merry go round: *Turner, Ruby* / Jewel of the Nile: *Wilson, Precious* / I need you: *Smith, Richard Jon* / Love is a dangerous game: *Jackson, Millie* / Overflowing: *Butler, Jonathan* / Pressing on: *Armstrong, Vanessa* / I'll be your friend: *Wilson, Precious*
CD ____________ **EMPRCD 548**
Emporio / Nov '94 / Disc

STRAIGHT FROM THE STREET VOL.1 (The Hip-Hottest New R&B & Rap)
Creep: *TLC* / Flava in ya ear: *Mack, Craig* / Big poppa: *Notorious BIG* / Think of you: *Users* / Tonite: *AFGM* / Don't take it personal: *Arnold, Monica* / Git up, git out: *Outkast* / We gets busy: *Illegal* / Just a little flava: *Unorthodox* / Player's ball: *Outkast* / Beware of rampshack: *Rampage* / Get down: *Mack, Craig* / I miss you: *N II U*
CD ____________ **74321276912**
Arista / Feb '97 / BMG

STRAIGHT NO CHASER
Pee Wee Marquette's intro / Cantaloupe island / Ronnie's bonnie / Comment on ritual / Alfie's theme / Cool blues / Crisis / Straight no chaser / Sookie sookie / Goin' down south / Song for my father / Blind man / Filthy McNasty / Jeannine / Steppin' into tomorrow
CD ____________ **CDS 8282632**
Blue Note / Apr '94 / EMI

STRAIGHT OUTTA BOONE COUNTY
CD ____________ **BS 019CD**
Bloodshot / Jun '97 / Cargo

STRAIGHT TALK VOL.1
CD ____________ **PHCD 2051**
Penthouse / Jan '97 / Jet Star

STRANGE GAMES AND THINGS
Strange games and things: *Love Unlimited Orchestra* / If I can't stop you: *Bristol, Johnny* / Mademoiselle: *Foxy* / You can't run away: *Bar-Kays* / Reasons: *Riperton, Minnie* / Bring your sweet loving back: *Starpoint* / Hollywood dreaming: *Father's Children* / Hunk of heaven: *Lemuria* / Elevate your mind: *Williams, Linda* / 90% of me is you: *McCrae, Gwen* / Another day: *Goodman, Ray & Brwon* / Girl you need a change of mind: *Kendricks, Eddie*
CD ____________ **BBECD 005**
Beechwood / Jun '97 / Beechwood/BMG / Pinnacle

STRANGE KIND OF LOVE
Look of love: *ABC* / Love action (I believe in love): *Human League* / Golden brown: *Stranglers* / Only you: *Yazoo* / Love is a wonderful colour: *Icicle Works* / Rip it up: *Orange Juice* / Love will tear us apart: *Joy Division* / I'm in love with a German film star: *Passions* / I go to sleep: *Pretenders* / It must be love: *Madness* / Boys don't cry: *Cure* / Picture this: *Blondie* / Treason (it's just a story): *Teardrop Explodes* / Enola Gray: *OMD* / Bitterest pill (I ever had to swallow): *Jam* / It's different for girls: *Jackson, Joe* / Love my way: *Psychedelic Furs* / Party fears two: *Associates* / Back of love: *Echo & The Bunnymen* / Story of the blues (part 1): *Mighty Wah*
CD ____________ **5355162**
PolyGram TV / Apr '96 / PolyGram

STRAWBERRY SUNDAE VOL.2 (2CD Set)
Oh yeah: *Syntone* / Passion: *Amen* / Devotion: *88.3* / Feel so alive: *Boomerang & Anna J.* / Can you feel it: *Solid Collective* / It's about time: *KGB* / O: *28th Street Crew* / Alright: *Blu Room* / I heat up: *One Of A Kind* / I feel you: *Ispirazione* / Comprided: *Edge, Gordon* / Feel so good: *Brain Bashers* / Rock it: *Atomic* / Somebody scream: *Warriors Of Love* / If you really want somebody: *McAteer, Grace* / Beat: *Dreamon* / DBL: *DJ Alan X* / Round and round: *RM Project* / Slammin': *RM Project* / Lust not love: *Ya Programme* / Piano head: *Rhythm Robbers* / Do you feel what I'm feeling: *Rhythm Robbers* / Trading faces: *Cadenza* / Body working: *Grand Larceny* / Radiate: *Brother Grim* / Dirty minds: *Tyrant* / Love will take me higher: *Pele & Gaston*
CD Set ____________ **MILL 040CD**
Millenium / Aug '97 / Plastic Head / Prime / SRD

STREET JAZZ VOL.1
Natasha: *Like Young* / Klute: *FRISK* / Theme from the underground bowling alley: *TUBA* / West by South West: *As One* / Be bop breakdance: *Little Eye* / Candyfloss: *Forest Mighty Black* / AWOL: *British Underground Productions* / Get up, get down: *Fishbelly Black* / London kills me: *Groove Nation* / Don't rub another man's rhubard: *Innuendo* / You know what it's like: *Duverney, Ondrea* / Free your mind: *Action People* / Seasons of my mind: *Batu* / Apple strudle: *Up Bustle & Out*
CD ____________ **CDTEP 4**
Step 2 / Jun '94 / 3mv/Sony

STREET JAZZ VOL.2
Better dreams: *Family Construction* / Fricasse de funk: *Malka Family* / 22 Steps ahead: *Katch 22* / Life: *Vibrazioni Productions* / Heavyweight round: *Sharpshooters* / All black station: *Progetto Tribale* / It's a pleasure to see you: *Tandy, George* / Retro future: *Retrovibe Movement* / Where's Will: *Zaeus* / Moocow: *Banana* / Skiff: *Bongo, Bud* / Brixton Hill: *Love Universal* / Out of tune: *Independent Colours* / Summer: *Pushmipulyu* / Catwalk: *Shakatak*
CD ____________ **CDTEP 6**
Step 2 / Dec '94 / 3mv/Sony

STREET JAZZ VOL.3
Children of the world: *Ghetto Swing* / Too hot: *Browne, Tom* / Cilantro: *Big Up Jazz* / Power of seven: *Bassism* / I've to to know: *Zaeus* / Walking: *Love Universal* / Shadow run: *Diferenz* / Dig deep the funk: *Alliance* / Sweet talkin': *Sharpshooters* / Down to the bone groovers: *Statem Island Groove* / Rodo mundo: *Reminiscence Quartet* / Splie: *Bongo, Bud*
CD ____________ **CDTEP 7**
Step 2 / Aug '95 / 3mv/Sony

STREET LIFE VOL.1
CD ____________ **GACCD 9301**
GAC / Aug '96 / Grapevine/PolyGram

STREET MUSIC OF PANAMA
CD ____________ **OMCD 008**
Original Music / Nov '90 / Jet Star / SRD

STREET PARADE '95
Sound: *Humate* / C5: *DJ Edge* / Level X: Bad Boy: *Advent* / Eclos: *Random Fluctuations* / Pure energy: *Freakazoid* / Mecha tech: *Mijk's Magic Marble Box* / I like that: *Awex* / I feel so detuned: *No Soul* / Clap your hands: *Koenig* / Audio strike: *Synectics*
CD ____________ **SUPER 2043CD**
Superstition / Aug '95 / Plastic Head / SRD / Vital

STREET PARTY SING-A-LONG - 45 ENGLISH FAVOURITES
CD ____________ **PLATCD 3937**
Platinum / Mar '95 / Prism

STREET SOUL (2CD Set)
Two can play that game: *Brown, Bobby* / She's got that vibe: *R Kelly* / Motownphilly: *Boyz II Men* / Right here: *SWV* / Flavour of the old school: *Knight, Beverley* / Just a step from heaven: *Eternal* / Don't walk away: *Jade* / Back and forth: *Aaliyah* / I love your smile: *Shanice* / That's the way love goes: *Jackson, Janet* / I swear: *All 4 One* / Down that road: *Nelson, Shara* / Don't look any further: *M-People* / Don't be a fool: *Loose Ends* / Back to life: *Soul II Soul* / One: *Paris, Mica* / Searching: *China Black* / Some girls: *Ultimate Kaos* / Sweetness: *Gayle, Michelle* / Unfinished sympathy: *Massive Attack* / Bump 'n' grind: *R Kelly* / Sensitivity: *Tresvant, Ralph* / Cry for you: *Jodeci* / 69: *Father MC* / Poison: *Bel Biv Devoe* / Can't stop: *After 7* / Ghetto heaven: *Family Stand* / My lovin': *En Vogue* / Express: *Carroll, Dina* / Finally: *Peniston, Ce Ce* / Midnight at the oasis: *Brand New Heavies* / Mama said: *Anderson, Carleen* / Real love: *Driza Bone* / Carry me home: *Gloworm* / Down 4 whatever: *Nuttin' Nyce* / Hey DJ: *Lighter Shade Of Brown* / Buddy X: *Cherry, Neneh* / Whatta man: *Salt n' Pepa & En Vogue* / People everyday: *Arrested Development* / Summertime: *DJ Jazzy Jeff & The Fresh Prince*
CD Set ____________ **VTDCD 41**
Virgin / May '95 / EMI

STREET SOUNDS ANTHEMS VOL.1 (The Official Week-Enders Album)
I found lovin': *Fatback Band* / Funkin' for Jamaica: *Browne, Tom* / Bring the family back: *Paul, Billy* / Ain't no stoppin' us now: *McFadden & Whitehead* / Dominoes: *Byrd, Donald* / Movin': *Brass Construction* / Encore: *Lynn, Cheryl* / Hard work: *Handy, John* / Groove: *Franklin, Rodney* / Prance on: *Henderson, Eddie*
CD ____________ **SOUNDSCD 3**
Street Sounds / Mar '95 / Beechwood/BMG

STREET SOUNDS ANTHEMS VOL.2
Running away: *Ayers, Roy* / Expansions: *Smith, Lonnie Liston* / Let the music play: *Earland, Charles* / Six million steps: *Harris, Rahni* / Shame: *King, Evelyn 'Champagne'* / You can do it: *Hudson, Al & The Partners* / Which way is up: *Starguard* / Don't stop the music: *Yarbrough & Peoples* / You know how to love me: *Hyman, Phyllis* / Risin' to the top (give it all you got): *Burke, Keni*
CD ____________ **SOUNDSCD 5**
Street Sounds / May '95 / Beechwood/BMG

STREET WALKIN' BLUES
CD ____________ **JASSCD 626**
Jass / Oct '92 / ADA / Cadillac / CM / Direct / Jazz Music

STREETS OF FEAR
Streets of fear: *Caldonia* / Goin' to Albert Lea: *Higham, Darrel* / Hot rhythm blue love: *Kyme, Peter* / Rollin' Danny: *Phillips, Dave* / Do you have to go: *Hayward, Ronnie* / You better watch out: *Blue Jeans* / Sleepless night: *Vortex, Eddie* / Rattlin' man: *Twenty Flight Rock* / Blue moon: *Lightnin' Jay* / Money: *Muskrats* / Say what you mean: *Flapjacks* / 1000 miles: *Outer Miles* / Too fast to live, too young to die: *Sabrejets* / Rock 'n' roll planet: *Chalky The Yorkie* / C'mon little girl: *Cobras* / Rattlesnake: *Haywire* / Cosmic star of rock 'n' roll: *Power, Will* / That's you: *Rimshots* / Down in the jungle: *Clive's Jive Five* / Losers never win: *Caldonia*
CD ____________ **FCD 3037**
Fury / Mar '95 / Nervous / TKO Magnum

STREETS OF NEW ORLEANS, THE
Basin Street blues / Burgundy Street blues / St. Phillip Street breakdown / Beale Street blues / South Rampart Street parade / Basin Street blues / Canal Street blues / South Rampart Street blues / Canal Street blues / Bourbon Street parade / Perdido Street blues
CD ____________ **8747052**
DA Music / Jul '96 / Conifer/BMG

STREETS OF SKA
CD ____________ **CDHB 198**
Heartbeat / Nov '95 / ADA / Direct / Greensleeves / Jet Star

STREETWALKING BLUES
CD ____________ **JCD 626**
Jass / Feb '91 / ADA / Cadillac / CM / Direct / Jazz Music

STRICTLY BUSINESS (2CD Set)
Intro / Like dis: *Cool Hand Flex* / Keep it real: *Dextrous* / Interlude: *Stretch & T-Bone* / Operating correctly: *DJ Stretch* / Interlude: *Digital FX* / Amazing: *Shy FX* / Raw: *DJ Rap* / Strumming dubs: *Jonnie Blaze* / Shaoling style: *Tom & Jerry* / Chill: *Mr. Time* / Bugle: *T-Bone* / Bruton: *DJ Kane* / Physical battle: *Ken, Kenny* / Can't take no more: *Fusion Forum* / Passing Phases: *Mar, Leon* / Interlude: *Randall* / Hard noize: *Randall* / Top gun: *Dream Team* / Rollin inside: *MC Go* / Don't take the shit: *MC Fats* / Interlude: *Goldie* / Hornet 127: *Rufige Cru* / Outro
CD ____________ **RIDTMCD 01**
CD Set ____________ **RIDTCD 01**
Riddim Track / Jul '97 / SRD

STRICTLY DANCING (18 Strict Tempo Dance Favourites)
Happy music / Secret love / Go tango / Granada / Spanish gypsy dance / La bamba / Green door / No reply / If I fell / How deep is your love / Look of love / Love letters / That's amore / I just called to say I love you / Violins / Lambada / Never gonna give you up / Que sera mi vida
CD ____________ **SUMCD 4078**
Summit / Nov '96 / Sound & Media

STRICTLY HARDCORE
CD ____________ **STHCCD 1**
Strictly Underground / '92 / SRD

STRICTLY RHYTHM - THE EARLY YEARS
CD ______ SR 307CD
React/Strictly Rhythm / Mar '94 / Vital

STRICTLY RHYTHM VOL.3
CD ______ REACTCD 043
React / Jul '94 / Arabesque / Prime / Vital

STRICTLY RHYTHM VOL.4
Theme: *Loop 7* / Unnecessary changes: *Morel's Grooves* / Let's talk about me: *Androgeny* / Tearin' me apart': *Inner Soul* / Goin' clear: *Caucasian Boy* / Witch doktor: *Van Helden, Armand* / Sumba luma: *Tribal Infusion* / Paul's pain: *Nightman* / Project blast: *Photon Inc.* / Chosen path: *Sole Fusion* / Get up and get soulful: *Morel's Grooves* / Flavor of love: *Logic*
CD ______ REACTCD 058
React / Mar '95 / Arabesque / Prime / Vital

STRICTLY RHYTHM VOL.5
CD ______ SR 322CD
Strictly Rhythm / Oct '95 / Prime / RTM/ Disc / SRD / Vital

STRICTLY SOCA VOL.1
CD ______ SJCM 108CD
Crosby / Mar '97 / Jet Star

STRICTLY THE BEST
CD ______ VPCD 1227
VP / Apr '92 / Greensleeves / Jet Star / Total/BMG

STRICTLY THE BEST VOL.15
CD ______ VPCD 1459
VP / Nov '95 / Greensleeves / Jet Star / Total/BMG

STRICTLY THE BEST VOL.18
CD ______ VPCD 1460
VP / Nov '95 / Greensleeves / Jet Star / Total/BMG

STRICTLY THE BEST VOL.4
CD ______ VPCD 1186
VP / Jul '92 / Greensleeves / Jet Star / Total/BMG

STRICTLY THE BEST VOL.7
CD ______ VPCD 1251
VP / Nov '92 / Greensleeves / Jet Star / Total/BMG

STRICTLY THE BEST VOL.8
CD ______ VPCD 1252
VP / Nov '92 / Greensleeves / Jet Star / Total/BMG

STRICTLY TRANCE VOL.1 (2CD Set)
CD Set ______ GR 3708
Groovey / May '96 / Plastic Head

STRICTLY UNDERGROUND VOL.1
Protein: *Sonic Experience* / Moonstompin': *Undercover Movement* / Mind, body and soul: *Fantasy UFO* / Burial: *Soundclash* / Let's go: *Noise Engineer* / Answer: *Equation* / Thru the night: *Noise Engineer* / Music's gonna rule the world: *Sonic Experience* / Untitled revolution: *Tigers In Space* / Best: *Full Dread* / Check it out: *Masters Of The Universe* / Do you want me: *Skeletor*
CD ______ STURCD 1
Strictly Underground / Nov '91 / SRD

STRICTLY UNDERGROUND VOL.2
CD ______ STURCD 3
Strictly Underground / Feb '94 / SRD

STRICTLY UNDERGROUND VOL.3
CD ______ STURCD 5
Strictly Underground / Oct '94 / SRD

STRICTLY WORLDWIDE VOL.3
CD ______ PIR 36
Piranha / Jun '94 / Direct / Stern's

STRIKE A DEEP CHORD
CD ______ JR 000032
Justice / Dec '92 / Koch

STRIKE UP THE BAND
What am I here for: *Basie, Count* / Midnight sun: *Hampton, Lionel* / Skyliner: *Barnet, Charlie* / Change of pace: *Jones, Quincy* / Harry, not Jesse: *James, Harry* / Pork pie: *Ferguson, Maynard* / One for Duke: *Nelson, Oliver* / Leave us leap: *Krupa, Gene* / I would do most anything for you: *Goodman, Benny* / Dateless Brown: *Rich, Buddy* / Birk's works: *Gillespie, Dizzy* / Br'er rabbit: *Vinson, Eddie 'Cleanhead'* / Boot 'em up: *Jacquet, Illinois* / Claxton Hall Swing: *Bellson, Louie* / Jazz me blues: *Herman, Woody* / Detour ahead: *Brookmeyer, Bob* / Jam with Sam: *Ellington, Duke*
CD ______ 5526442
Spectrum / Mar '97 / PolyGram

STRING BANDS 1926-1929
CD ______ DOCD 5167
Document / May '93 / ADA / Hot Shot / Jazz Music

STRINGS OF AFRICA (Madagascar/ Burundi/Sierra Leone/3CD Set)
CD Set ______ C 570301
Ocora / Mar '97 / ADA / Harmonia Mundi

STRUMMIN' MENTAL VOL.2
CD ______ EFA 115792
Crypt / Jun '95 / Shellshock/Disc

STUC CENTENARY ALBUM (If It Wisnae For The Union)
Battle of the Somme: *Dubliners* / Freedom come all ye: *Dubliners* / Four stone walls: *Capercaillie* / Both sides the tweed: *Gaughan, Dick* / Ravenscraig: *Runrig* / If it wisnae for the union: *Imlach, Hamish* / Bawbee birlin: *McCulloch, Gordeanna* / James Connolly: *Moore, Christy* / North by north: *Johnstone, Arthur* / Contract: *Bogle, Eric* / Gauteng: *Louw, Mara* / I am the common man: *Battlefield Band* / Blantyre explosion: *MacColl, Ewan* / Farewell tae the haven: *McCalmans* / Sell your labour, not your soul: *McNeill, Brian* / Three nights and a sunday: *McGinn, Matt* / Mothers, daughters, wives: *Small, Judy* / Te recuerdo Amanda: *Jara, Victor* / Stand together: *Ceolbeg*
CD ______ CDTRAX 5005
Greentrax / Feb '97 / ADA / Direct / Duncans / Highlander

STUDIO DJ (2CD Set)
CD Set ______ 3017032
Fairway / Nov '96 / Cargo

STUDIO K7 COMPILATION
CD ______ K7 040CD
Studio K7 / Oct '96 / Prime / RTM/Disc

SUB POP 200
CD ______ TUPCD 4
Tupelo / Jul '89 / RTM/Disc

SUBBASE SAMPLER
CD ______ SUBBASECD 4
Suburban Base / Oct '96 / Pinnacle / Prime

SUBLIME HARMONIE (Victorian Musical Boxes & Polyphons)
March of the Toreadors / Hallelujah Chorus / Ave Maria / War march of the priests / Lost chord / Waltz from Faust / Largo / Wedding song / Wedding march / I have a song to sing / Behold the Lord High Executioner / Valse des fees
CD ______ CDSDL 303
Saydisc / Feb '93 / ADA / Direct / Harmonia Mundi

SUBSONIC BLEEPS
CD ______ BLEEPSCD 1
Upfront / Nov '90 / Serious Records

SUBURBS FROM HELL
CD ______ SOHO 13CD
Suburbs Of Hell / Jan '94 / Kudos / Pinnacle / Plastic Head

SUCCOUR (2CD Set)
CD Set ______ POTCD 1
Backs / Nov '96 / RTM/Disc

SUDANESE MUSIC FROM WEST JAVA
CD ______ SM 16072
Wergo / Feb '96 / ADA / Cadillac / Harmonia Mundi

SUDDEN IMPACT VOL.1
CD ______ VPCD 1241
Shocking Vibes / Jul '92 / Jet Star

SUGAR BABY
CD ______ I 3896072
Galaxy / Oct '96 / ZYX

SUGAR HITS (2CD Set)
Something goin' on: *Terry, Todd* / Free: *Ultranate* / Fresh: *Gina G* / MFEO: *Kavana* / Natural: *Andre, Peter* / 911: *911* / Closer than close: *Gaines, Rosie* / Isn't it a wonder: *Boyzone* / Let me in: *OTT* / Clementine: *Owen, Mark* / WAaterloo sunset: *Dennis, Cathy* / Do you know: *Gayle, Michelle* / CardLovefool: *Cardigans* / Statuesque: *Sleeper* / Girl power: *Shampoo* / Good enough: *Dodgy* / Disco 2000: *Pulp* / Dark clouds: *Space* / Candy girl: *Baby Bird* / 6 underground: *Sneaker Pimps* / Different beats: *Boyzone* / Forever love: *Barlow, Gary* / Anywhere for you: *Backstreet Boys* / I need you: *3T* / Last night: *Az Yet* / I believe I can fly: *R Kelly* / Wonderful tonight: *Damage* / One kiss from heaven: *Damage* / How deep is your love: *Take That* / If you ever: *East 17 & Gabrielle* / I love you always forever: *Lewis, Donna* / Walk on by: *Gabrielle* / Shout: *Ant & Dec* / Hey child: *East 17* / Make it with you: *Let Loose* / One more chance: *One* / Happy: *MN8* / We got it: *Immature* / Sometimes when we touch: *Newton* / Twelfth of never: *Carter Twins*
CD Set ______ 5536982
PolyGram TV / Jun '97 / PolyGram

SUGAR PLUMS (Holiday Treats From Sugar Hill)
CD ______ SHCD 3796
Sugar Hill / Jan '97 / ADA / CM / Direct / Koch / Roots

SUGARHILL - THE 12" REMIXES
Message: *Grandmaster Flash & The Furious Five* / Freedom: *Grandmaster Flash & The Furious Five* / Apache: *Sugarhill Gang* / Rapper's delight: *Sugarhill Gang* / Eighth wonder: *Sugarhill Gang* / White lines (don't don't do it): *Grandmaster Flash & Melle Mel*
CD ______ CLACD 345
Castle / Jun '94 / BMG

SUITCASE FULL OF BLUES, A
CD ______ HCD 23
Black Swan / Dec '95 / Jazz Music

SULT: SPIRIT OF THE MUSIC
CD ______ HBCD 0009
Hummingbird / Feb '97 / ADA / Direct / Grapevine/PolyGram

SULTRY LADIES OF JAZZ (3CD Set)
Miss Brown to you: *McRae, Carmen* / As long as I live: *Clooney, Rosemary* / In the wee small hours of the morning: *Christy, June* / All of me: *Vaughan, Sarah* / First time ever I saw your face: *Houston, Thelma* / This October: *London, Julie* / Gentleman friend: *Wilson, Nancy* / Spring cam really hang you up the most: *Kral, Irene* / I concentrate on you: *Sommers, Joanie* / Old folks: *Anderson, Ernestine* / Down with love: *Southern, Jeri* / I've got a right to cry: *Alexandria, Lorez* / Zing went the strings of my heart: *Harper, Toni* / You're blase: *Vaughan, Sarah* / September in the rain: *London, Julie* / Tabby the cat: *O'Day, Anita* / All night long: *Wilson, Nancy* / Sometimes I'm happy: *Vaughan, Sarah* / East Street: *Christy, June* / Look out, it's love: *Sommers, Joanie* / Talk about cozy: *Alexandria, Lorez* / More than you know: *Carpenter, Thelma* / About a quarter to nine: *Rivers, Mavis* / Sunday blues: *London, Julie* / Spring will be a little late this year: *Southern, Jeri* / It's a wonderful world: *Kral, Irene* / C'est la vie: *Franklin, Lynn* / On Green Dolphin Street: *Wilson, Nancy* / You better go now: *Sommers, Joanie* / I'm gonna lock my heart: *McRae, Carmen* / I'll take romance: *Christy, June* / Street of dreams: *Alexandria, Lorez* / Life is just a bowl of cherries: *Harper, Toni* / Don't worry 'bout me: *Clooney, Rosemary* / Lullaby in rhythm: *Christy, June* / Just a gigolo: *McRae, Carmen* / I hadn't anyone 'til you: *Southern, Jeri* / Detour ahead: *Kral, Irene* / Best is yet to come: *Alexandria, Lorez* / I'll close my eyes: *Sommers, Joanie* / One for my baby (and one more for the road): *Franklin, Lynn* / Feeling good: *Anderson, Ernestine* / What is this thing called love: *Vaughan, Sarah* / My old flame: *Clooney, Rosemary* / One minute to one: *Rivers, Mavis* / Nearness of you: *Wilson, Nancy* / Blues: *O'Day, Anita* / Tall boy: *London, Julie* / Just in time: *McRae, Carmen* / Bewitched, bothered and bewildered: *Harper, Toni* / Nobody else but me: *Kral, Irene*
CD Set ______ HBCD 505
Hindsight / Dec '96 / Jazz Music / Target/ BMG

SUMMER BREEZE
Summer breeze: *Isley Brothers* / (Sittin' on the) dock of the bay: *Redding, Otis* / Walking in rhythm: *Blackbyrds* / Back to life: *Soul II Soul* / Under the broadwalk: *Drifters* / Girl from Ipanema: *Cole, Nat 'King'* / Gimme the sunshine: *Leo's Sunshipp* / Lovely day: *Withers, Bill* / Walking in sunshine: *Rockers Revenge* / Funky Nassau: *Beginning Of The End* / Hot hot hot: *Poindexter, Buster* / Funkin' for Jamaica: *Browne, Tom* / I can see clearly now: *Nash, Johnny* / Midnight at the oasis: *Muldaur, Maria* / Summer madness: *Kool & The Gang* / Love city groove: *Love City Groove* / Everybody's got summer: *Atlantic Starr* / Summertime: *DJ Jazzy Jeff & The Fresh Prince*
CD ______ 74321383172
RCA / Jun '97 / BMG

SUMMER DANCE ENERGY
CD ______ JHD 106
Tring / Aug '93 / Tring

SUMMER DANCE PARTY
Boom boom boom: *Outhere Brothers* / Whoomph (there it is): *Clock* / Right in the night (fall in love with the music): *Jam & Spoon* / Humpin' around: *Brown, Bobby* / Scatman: *Scatman John* / Be my lover: *La Bouche* / Rhythm of the night: *Corona* / Another night: *MC Sar & The Real McCoy* / It's my life: *Dr. Alban* / What is love: *Haddaway* / Rhythm is a dancer: *Snap* / Could it be magic: *Take That* / Guaglione: *Prado, Perez* / Tequila: *Champs* / Lambada: *Lambada* / Miami hit mix: *Estefan, Gloria* / Hot hot hot: *Arrow* / Baby come back: *Pato Banton* / Baby I love your way: *Big Mountain* / Sweat (a la la la la long): *Inner Circle* / Cotton eye Joe: *Rednex* / Summertime: *DJ Jazzy Jeff & The Fresh Prince*
CD ______ RADCD 18
Global TV / Jul '95 / BMG

SUMMER DANCE PARTY
Keep it comin' love: *KC & The Sunshine Band* / Rock your baby: *McCrae, George* / Boogie oogie oogie: *Taste Of Honey* / Get off: *Foxy* / Sun is here: *Sun* / Saddle up: *Christie, David* / Gonna get along without you now: *Wills, Viola* / Movin': *Brass Construction* / Whodunit: *Tavares* / Swing your daddy: *Gilstrap, Jim* / Let's all chant: *Zager, Michael Band* / Saturday night: *T-Connection* / You can do it: *Hudson, Al & The Partners* / Carwash: *Rose Royce* / Float on: *Floaters* / This is it: *Moore, Melba* / Do it: *BT Express* / That's the way I like it/Shake your body/Get down/Give it up: *KC & The Sunshine Band*
CD ______ DC 880782
Disky / Aug '97 / Disky / THE

SUMMER DAZE (20 Scorching Summer Hits)
In the Summertime: *Mungo Jerry* / You to me are everything: *Real Thing* / Swing your Daddy: *Gilstrap, Jim* / Now is the time: *James, Jimmy & The Vagabonds* / Uptown festival medley: *Shalamar* / Beach baby: *First Class* / I'm gonna make you mine: *Christie, Lou* / La bamba: *Feliciano, Jose* / Mexico: *Baldry, Long John* / Let's go to San Francisco: *Flowerpot Men* / Sunshine superman: *Donovan* / Daydream: *Lovin' Spoonful* / Build me a buttercup: *Foundations* / Yummy yummy yummy: *Ohio Express* / Simon says: *1910 Fruitgum Company* / El bimbo: *Bimbo Jet* / Born with a smile on my face: *De Sykes, Stephanie* / Egyptian reggae: *Richman, Jonathan & Modern Lovers* / Sunshine day: *Osibisa* / Walking on sunshine: *Rockers Revenge*
CD ______ SUMCD 4103
Summit / Nov '96 / Sound & Media

SUMMER FOLK COLLECTION
High level hornpipe/Uncle George's: *Sawdust Band* / To Ireland I made my way: *Hutchings, Ashley* / Dear landlord: *Fairport Convention* / Four hands reel/St Annes reel: *Albion Country Band* / Plunder town: *Christmas, Keith* / I thought you'd come: *Downes, Paul* / Hard hats: *Beer, Phil* / LIB/Hayes-wood reel: *Hutchings, Ashley Dance Band* / This blessed plot: *Albion Band* / Spring air: *Amazing Blondel* / Blind fiddler: *Beer, Phil* / Nameless kind of hell: *Albion Band* / Butterfly dreams: *Rose Among Thorns* / Flandyke shore: *Albion Band* / War behind walls: *Christmas, Keith* / Lovers: *Downes, Paul* / Colours of love: *Albion Band* / Telstar: *Big Beat Combo* / Wings: *Hutchings, Ashley & Ken Nicol*
CD ______ HTDCD 64
HTD / Aug '96 / CM / Pinnacle

SUMMER FUN
CD ______ MUSCD 027
MCI Music / Jul '95 / Disc / THE

SUMMER GROOVE (2CD Set)
CD ______ 9548353822
Warner Bros. / May '97 / Warner Music

SUMMER IN THE CITY
CD ______ MATCD 251
Castle / Apr '93 / BMG

SUMMER IN THE CITY
CD ______ PLSCD 187
Pulse / Apr '97 / BMG

SUMMER NRG
Abba medley: *Unlimited Beat* / Can't take my eyes off you: *Jay, Jessica* / Summertime: *Cicero* / Alone: *Heartclub & 3 Boys* / In your dreams: *Ultimate Buzz* / 2 becomes 1: *Wildside* / Deadwood stage: *Brown, Beccy* / Angels: *A-Tension* / Take That medley: *Unlimited Beat* / Hold me: *Lovelife* / Forever and a day: *Active Force* / Boom boom: *Joshua* / I'm in the mood for dancin': *Nolans*
CD ______ ASR 002
Academy Street / Aug '97 / Grapevine/ PolyGram

SUMMER OF LOVE
CD ______ MUSCD 022
MCI Music / Sep '94 / Disc / THE

SUMMER OF LOVE
California dreamin': *Mamas & The Papas* / Happy together: *Turtles* / Albatross: *Fleetwood Mac* / Let's go to San Francisco: *Flowerpot Men* / Eve of destruction: *McGuire, Barry* / Summer in the city: *Lovin' Spoonful* / She'd rather be with me: *Turtles* / Oh happy day: *Hawkins, Edwin Singers* / Sunshine of your love: *Cream* / Delta lady: *Cocker, Joe* / Mr. Tambourine man: *Byrds* / Daydream: *Lovin' Spoonful* / San Franciso (be sure to wear some flowers): *McKenzie, Scott* / Green tambourine: *Lemon Pipers* / Ruby Tuesday: *Melanie* / Monday, Monday: *Mamas & The Papas* / Venus: *Shocking Blue* / Eight miles high: *Byrds* / Something in the air: *Thunderclap Newman* / Woodstock: *Matthew's Southern Comfort*
CD ______ DINCD 10
Dino / Jul '90 / Pinnacle

SUMMER OF LOVE
California dreaming: *Mamas & The Papas* / Feel like I'm fixin' to die: *Country Joe & The Fish* / Man of the world: *Fleetwood Mac* / Let's go to San Francisco: *Flowerpot Men* / Woodstock: *Matthew's Southern Comfort* / With a little help from my friends: *Cocker, Joe* / Judy in disguise: *Fred, John & His Playboy Band* / Up on cripple creek: *Band* / Catch the wind: *Donovan* / Goin' up the country: *Canned Heat* / Happy together: *Turtles* / Strawberry fields: *Havens, Richie* / Little wing: *Hendrix, Jimi* / Lazy Sunday: *Small Faces* / Ob la di ob la da: *Marmalade*
CD ______ NTRCD 083
Nectar / Aug '97 / Pinnacle

SUMMER OF LOVE (2CD Set)
San Francisco: *McKenzie, Scott* / Eight miles high: *Byrds* / Going up the country: *Canned Heat* / Hole in my shoe: *Traffic* / Flowers in the rain: *Move* / Carrie-Anne: *Move* / Excerpt: *West, Keith* / Something in the air: *Thunderclap Newman* / Windy: *Association* / Happy together: *Turtles* / Waterloo sunset: *Kinks* / Weight: *Band* / Sunshine superman: *Donovan* / Friday on my mind: *Donovan* / Good vibrations: *Beach Boys* / 98.6: *Keith* / 59th Street Bridge song: *Harpers Bizarre* / Groovin': *Rascals* / California dreamin': *Mamas & The Papas* / This wheels on fire: *Driscoll, Julie & The Brian Auger Trinity* / Love is all around: *Troggs* / Rainy day women nos.12 and 35: *Dylan, Bob* / San Franciscan nights: *Burdon, Eric & The Animals* / For what it's worth: *Buffalo Springfield* / Paper sun: *Traffic* / Strange

brew: *Cream* / Somebody to love: *Jefferson Airplane* / Living in the past: *Jethro Tull* / DuKites: *Dupree, Simon & The Big Sound* / Massachusetts: *Bee Gees* / Let's go to San Francisco: *Flowerpot Men* / Mr Tambourine man: *Byrds* / Mighty Quinn: *Manfred Mann* / Ride my see-saw: *Moody Blues* / Alone again or: *Love* / Whiter shade of pale: *Procul Harum* / Itchycoo park: *Small Faces* / Mama told me not to come: *Three Dog Night* / Fresh garbage: *Spirit* / Fire: *Crazy World Of Arthur Brown* / Eve of destruction: *McGuire, Barry* / Woodstock: *Matthew's Southern Comfort* / PucYoung girl: *Puckett, Gary & The Union Jack* / Purple haze: *Hendrix, Jimi*
CD Set ______ **5538622**
PolyGram TV / Jul '97 / PolyGram

SUMMER PARTY (3CD Set)
CD Set ______ **KBOX 372**
Collection / Aug '97 / Target/BMG / TKO Magnum

SUMMER ROCK
If this is it: *Lewis, Huey & The News* / Alone: *Heart* / Rock me tonight: *Squier, Billy* / White wedding: *Idol, Billy* / No doubt about it: *Hot Chocolate* / Hymn: *Ultravox* / Temptation: *Heaven 17* / Baker Street: *Rafferty, Gerry* / Sebastian: *Cockney Rebel* / Love is a battlefield: *Benatar, Pat* / Nutbush city limits: *Turner, Ike & Tina* / Lonesome loser: *Little River Band* / Locomotive breath: *Jethro Tull* / Don't forget me: *Glass Tiger* / Smoke on the water: *Deep Purple* / Girls on film: *Duran Duran* / Shadow on the wall: *Oldfield, Mike*
CD ______ **DC 881252**
Disky / Aug '97 / Disky / THE

SUMMER SIZZLERS
Walking on sunshine: *Katrina & The Waves* / Fantastic day: *Haircut 100* / Beach baby: *First Class* / Hot hot hot: *Arrow* / In the summertime: *Mungo Jerry* / Happy together: *Turtles* / Sunny afternoon: *Kinks* / Lazy Sunday: *Small Faces* / Summer in the city: *Lovin' Spoonful* / Remember (walking in the sand): *Shangri-Las* / Seasons in the sun: *Jacks, Terry* / Hang on sloopy: *McCoys*
CD ______ **74321339292**
Camden / Jan '96 / BMG

SUMMER SWING
Humpin' around: *Brown, Bobby* / Freak like me: *Howard, Adina* / Party all night: *Kreuz* / Candy rain: *Soul For Real* / Oh baby, I: *Eternal* / Freek 'n you: *Jodeci* / Your body's callin': *R Kelly* / Down with the clique: *Aaliyah* / I wanna be down: *Brandy* / Your love is a 187: *Whitehead Brothers* / Here comes the hotstepper: *Kamoze, Ini* / Rump shaker: *Wreckx n' Effect* / Hoochie booty: *Ultimate Kaos* / Real love: *Blige, Mary J.* / Everyday: *Incognito* / Apparently nothin': *Anderson, Carleen* / Too many fish: *Knuckles, Frankie & Adeva* / Lifted: *Lighthouse Family* / Joy: *Blackstreet* / There's nothing like this: *Omar*
CD ______ **VTCD 53**
Virgin / Jul '95 / EMI

SUMMER VYBES (2CD Set)
Disco's revenge: *Gusto* / Trippin' on sunshine: *Pizzaman* / Keep on jumpin': *Lisa Marie Experience* / Get down (you're the one for me): *Backstreet Boys* / Sunshine after the rain: *Berri* / Always there: *Incognito & Jocelyn Brown* / Rhythm of the night: *Corona* / Two can play that game: *Brown, Bobby* / Swing low, sweet chariot: *China Black* / She's got that vibe: *R Kelly* / In the summertime: *Shaggy* / Boom shack-a-lack: *Apache Indian* / Sweets for my sweet: *Lewis, C.J.* / Whoomp (there it is): *Clock* / U R the best thing: *D:Ream* / Another night: *MC Sar & The Real McCoy* / Rhythm is a dancer: *Snap* / Baby come back: *Pato Banton* / Mr. Vain: *Culture Beat* / Summertime: *DJ Jazzy Jeff & The Fresh Prince* / Too hot: *Coolio* / Something 4 da honeyz: *Jordan, Montell* / I got 5 on it: *Luniz* / Thank God it's Friday: *R Kelly* / Throw your hands up: *LV* / Lifted: *Lighthouse Family* / Brand new day (I'm no puppet): *Darkman* / Tease me: *Chaka Demus & Pliers* / Mr. Loverman: *Shabba Ranks* / Compliments on your kiss: *Red Dragon* / Here comes the hotstepper: *Kamoze, Ini* / Don't turn around: *Aswad* / You don't love me (no no no): *Penn, Dawn* / Love city groove: *Love City Groove* / Searching: *China Black* / Shout (it out): *Louchie Lou & Michie One* / Runnin': *Pharcyde* / Close to you: *Priest, Maxi* / Sweat (a la la la la long): *Inner Circle* / Back to life: *Soul II Soul*
CD Set ______ **5356442**
PolyGram TV / Jun '96 / PolyGram

SUMMER WIND
CD ______ **BLR 84017**
L&R / May '91 / New Note/Pinnacle

SUMMERTIME HITS FROM THE WORLD
CD ______ **DCD 5305**
Disky / Nov '93 / Disky / THE

SUMMERTIME SOUL
CD ______ **5258002**
PolyGram TV / Aug '95 / PolyGram

SUN AND BASS
CD ______ **TKCD 47**
2 Kool / Mar '97 / Pinnacle / SRD

SUN ROCK 'N' ROLL VOL.1
You better dig it: *Johnson, Bill* / Walkin' and talkin': *Owen, Mark* / Diamond ring: *Isle, Jimmy* / Oh wee: *Suggs, Brad* / There will be no teardrops tonight: *McVoy, Carl* / More pretty girls than one: *Howard, Edwin* / Hey baby doll: *Bush, Eddie* / Your cheatin' heart: *Greaves, Cliff* / Let 'em talk: *Dorman, Harold* / Tuff: *Cannon, Ace* / Shut your mouth: *Barton, Ernie* / Hula hop: *Baugh, Smokey Joe* / Shake 'em up baby: *Ballard, Frank* / Hambone: *Anthony, Rayburn* / Boogaloo: *Johnson, Bill* / I've got it made: *Wayne, Thomas* / Belle of Swannee: *Pendarvis, Tracy* / Wait 'til Saturday night: *Dorman, Harold* / I wanna make sweet love: *McGill, Jerry* / Mean old world: *Thomas, Cliff* / Rocking history: *Williams, Jimmy* / I'm losing you: *Williams, Red* / Tragedy: *Wayne, Thomas* / Have a little party: *Gilley, Mickey* / No more crying the blues: *Alton & Jimmy* / Good gracious: *Vel-Tones* / I'm getting better all the time: *Pittman, Barbara* / Baby doll: *Four Dukes* / All I want is you: *Williams, Jimmy* / Memories never grow old: *Lee, Dickie & The Collegiates*
CD ______ **CPCD 8277**
Charly / Jan '97 / Koch

SUN, SEA AND SALSA (A Cocktail Of Caribbean Grooves)
CD ______ **NSCD 015**
Nascente / Mar '97 / Disc / New Note/ Pinnacle

SUN SINGLES VOL.1 (4CD Set)
Flat tire: *London, Johnny* / Drivin' slow: *London, Johnny* / Got my application baby: *Garth, Gay* / Trouble (will bring you down): *Jackson, Handy* / We all gotta go sometime: *Louis, Joe Hill* / Some may be like yours: *Louis, Joe Hill* / Baker shop boogie: *Nix, Willie* / Seems like a million years: *Nix, Willie* / Easy: *Jimmy & Walter* / Before long: *Jimmy & Walter* / Bear cat: *Thomas, Rufus* / Walkin' in the rain: *Thomas, Rufus* / Heaven or fire: *Brooks, Dusty* / Tears and wine: *Brooks, Dusty* / Lonesome old jail: *Hunt, D.A.* / Greyhound blues: *Hunt, D.A.* / Call me anything, but call me: *Big Memphis Marainey* / Baby no no: *Big Memphis Marainey* / Take a little chance: *De Berry, Jimmy* / Time has made a change: *De Berry, Jimmy* / Baby please: *Prisonaires* / Just walking in the rain: *Prisonaires* / Feelin' good: *Parker, Junior & The Blue Flames* / Fussing and fighting: *Parker, Junior & The Blue Flames* / Tiger man: *Thomas, Rufus* / Save that money: *Thomas, Rufus* / My God is real: *Prisonaires* / Softly and tenderly: *Prisonaires* / Blues waltz: *Ripley Cotton Choppers* / Silver bells: *Ripley Cotton Choppers* / Prosoner's prayer: *Prisonaires* / I know: *Prisonaires* / Mystery train: *Parker, Junior & The Blue Flames* / Love my baby: *Parker, Junior & The Blue Flames* / Come back baby: *Ross, Dr. Isiah* / Chicago breakdown: *Ross, Dr. Isiah* / Beggin' my baby: *Little Milton* / Somebody told me: *Little Milton* / No teasing around: *Emerson, Billy 'The Kid'* / If love is believing: *Emerson, Billy 'The Kid'* / Wolf call boogie: *Hot Shot Love* / Harmonica jam: *Hot Shot Love* / Boogie blues: *Peterson, Earl* / In the dark: *Peterson, Earl* / Troublesome waters: *Seratt, Howard* / I must be saved: *Seratt, Howard* / My baby: *Cotton, James* / Straighten up baby: *Cotton, James* / If you love me: *Little Milton* / Alone and blue: *Little Milton* / Gonna dance all night: *Gunter, Hardrock* / Fallen angel: *Gunter, Hardrock* / Now she cares no more for me: *Poindexter, Doug* / My kind of carryin' on: *Poindexter, Doug* / I'm not going home: *Emerson, Billy 'The Kid'* / Woodchuck: *Emerson, Billy 'The Kid'* / Bourbon street jump: *Hill, Raymond* / Snuggle: *Hill, Raymond* / Great medical menagerist: *Floyd, 'Harmonica' Frank* / Rockin' chair Daddy: *Floyd, 'Harmonica' Frank* / Cotton crop blues: *Cotton, James* / Hold me in your arms: *Cotton, James* / There is love in you: *Prisonaires* / What'll you do next: *Prisonaires* / Right or wrong: *Cunningham, Buddy* / Who do I cry: *Prisonaires* / That's alright Mama: *Presley, Elvis* / Blue moon of Kentucky: *Presley, Elvis* / Good rockin' tonight: *Presley, Elvis* / I don't care if the sun don't shine: *Presley, Elvis* / Drinkin' wine spo-dee-o-dee: *Yelvington, Malcolm* / Just rolling along: *Yelvington, Malcolm* / Boogie disease: *Ross, Dr. Isiah* / Jukebox boogie: *Ross, Dr. Isiah* / Look to Jesus: *Jones Brothers* / Every night: *Jones Brothers* / Move baby move: *Emerson, Billy 'The Kid'* / When it rains it pours: *Emerson, Billy 'The Kid'* / Milkcow blues boogie: *Presley, Elvis* / You're a heartbreaker: *Presley, Elvis* / Don't believe: *Rhodes, Slim* / Uncertain love: *Rhodes, Slim* / I'm left, you're right, she's gone: *Presley, Elvis* / Baby let's play house: *Presley, Elvis* / I feel so worried: *Lewis, Sammy & Willie Johnson* / So long baby, goodbye: *Lewis, Sammy & Willie Johnson* / Red hot: *Emerson, Billy 'The Kid'* / There is no greater love: *Emerson, Billy 'The Kid'* / Homesick for my baby: *Little Milton* / Lookin' for my baby: *Little Milton* / Cry cry cry: *Cash, Johnny* / Hey porter: *Cash, Johnny* / Don't do that: *Five Tinos* / Sitting by my window: *Five Tinos* / I forgot to remember to forget: *Presley, Elvis* / Let the jukebox keep on playing: *Perkins, Carl* / Gone gone gone: *Perkins, Carl* / House of sin: *Rhodes, Slim* / Are you ashamed of me: *Rhodes, Slim* / Ain't that right: *Snow, Eddie* / Bring your love back home to me: *Snow, Eddie* / Just love me baby: *Gordon, Rosco* / Weeping blues: *Gordon, Rosco* / Signifying monkey: *Smokey Joe* / Listen to my baby: *Smokey Joe* / Movie magg: *Perkins, Carl* / Turn around: *Perkins, Carl* / Lonely sweetheart: *Taylor, Bill* / Split personality: *Taylor, Bill* / I've been deceived: *Feathers, Charlie* / Peepin' eyes: *Feathers, Charlie* / Someday you will pay: *Miller Sisters* / You didn't think I would: *Miller Sisters*
CD Set ______ **BCD 15801**
Bear Family / Nov '94 / Direct / Rollercoaster / Swift

SUN SINGLES VOL.2 (4CD Set)
Daydreams come true: *Wimberly, Maggie Sue* / How long: *Wimberly, Maggie Sue* / There's no right way to do me wrong: *Miller Sisters* / You can tell me: *Miller Sisters* / Defrost your heart: *Feathers, Charlie* / Wedding gown of white: *Feathers, Charlie* / Folsom prison blues: *Cash, Johnny* / So doggone lonesome: *Cash, Johnny* / Little fine healthy thing: *Emerson, Billy 'The Kid'* / Something for nothing: *Emerson, Billy 'The Kid'* / Blue suede shoes: *Perkins, Carl* / Honey don't: *Perkins, Carl* / Sure to fall: *Perkins, Carl* / Tennessee: *Perkins, Carl* / No more, no more: *Haggett, Jimmy* / They call our love a sin: *Haggett, Jimmy* / Chicken: *Gordon, Rosco* / Love for you baby: *Gordon, Rosco* / Gonna romp and stomp: *Rhodes, Slim* / Bad girl: *Rhodes, Slim* / Rock 'n' roll Ruby: *Smith, Warren* / I'd rather be safe then sorry: *Smith, Warren* / Slow down: *Earls, Jack* / Fool for loving you: *Earls, Jack* / Get rhythm: *Cash, Johnny* / I walk the line: *Cash, Johnny* / Ooby dooby: *Orbison, Roy* / Go go go: *Orbison, Roy* / Boppin' the blues: *Perkins, Carl* / All Mama's children: *Perkins, Carl* / Welcome to the club: *Chapel, Jean* / I won't be rockin' tonight: *Chapel, Jean* / Trouble bound: *Riley, Billy Lee* / Rock with me baby: *Riley, Billy Lee* / Rockin' with my baby: *Yelvington, Malcolm* / It's me baby: *Yelvington, Malcolm* / Red headed woman: *Burgess, Sonny* / We wanna boogie: *Burgess, Sonny* / Fiddle bop: *Rhythm Rockers* / Jukebox help me find my baby: *Rhythm Rockers* / I'm sorry: *Perkins, Carl* / I'm not sorry: *Perkins, Carl* / Dixie fried: *Perkins, Carl* / Black Jack David: *Smith, Warren* / Unbangi stomp: *Smith, Warren* / You're my baby: *Orbison, Roy* / Rock house: *Orbison, Roy* / Love crazy baby: *Parchman, Kenny* / I feel like rockin: *Parchman, Kenny* / I need a man: *Pitman, Barbara* / No matter who's to blame: *Pitman, Barbara* / Come on little Mama: *Harris, Ray* / Where'd you stay last night: *Harris, Ray* / Ten cats down: *Miller Sisters* / Finders keepers: *Miller Sisters* / Take and give: *Rhodes, Slim* / Do what I do: *Rhodes, Slim* / Shoobee doobee: *Gordon, Rosco* / Cheese and crackers: *Gordon, Rosco* / There you go: *Cash, Johnny* / Train of love: *Cash, Johnny* / Crazy arms: *Lewis, Jerry Lee* / End of the road: *Lewis, Jerry Lee* / Flyin' saucer rock 'n' roll: *Riley, Billy Lee* / I want you baby: *Riley, Billy Lee* / Matchbox: *Perkins, Carl* / Your true love: *Perkins, Carl* / Feelin' low: *Chaffin, Ernie* / Lonesome for my baby: *Chaffin, Ernie* / Restless: *Burgess, Sonny* / Ain't got a thing: *Burgess, Sonny* / I'll be around: *Honeycutt, Glenn* / I'll wait forever: *Honeycutt, Glenn* / Sweet and easy: *Orbison, Roy* / Devil doll: *Orbison, Roy* / Don't make me go: *Cash, Johnny* / Nest in line: *Cash, Johnny* / It'll be me: *Lewis, Jerry Lee* / Whole lotta shakin' goin' on: *Lewis, Jerry Lee* / So long I'm gone: *Smith, Warren* / Miss Froggie: *Smith, Warren* / Bop bop baby: *Wake & Dick* / Don't need your lovin' baby: *Wake & Dick* / Please don't cry over me: *Williams, Jimmy* / That depends on you: *Williams, Jimmy* / Fools hall of fame: *Richardson, Rudi* / Why should I cry: *Richardson, Rudi* / Greenback dollar: *Harris, Ray* / Foolish heart: *Harris, Ray* / Easy to love: *Self, Mack* / Every day: *Self, Mack* / Forever yours: *Perkins, Carl* / That's right: *Perkins, Carl* / I'm lonesome: *Chaffin, Ernie* / Laughin' and jokin': *Chaffin, Ernie* / More than yesterday: *Bruce, Edwin* / Rock boppin' baby: *Bruce, Edwin* / Red hot: *Riley, Billy Lee* / Pearly Lee: *Riley, Billy Lee* / Flat foot Sam: *Blake, Tommy* / Lordy hoody: *Blake, Tommy*
CD Set ______ **BCD 15802**
Bear Family / Jun '95 / Direct / Rollercoaster / Swift

SUN SINGLES VOL.3 (4CD Set)
Give my love to Rose: *Cash, Johnny* / Home of the blues: *Cash, Johnny* / Good lovin': *Lee, Dickey* / Memories never grow old: *Lee, Dickey* / Great balls of fire: *Lewis, Jerry Lee* / You win again: *Lewis, Jerry Lee* / Cindy Lou: *Penner, Dick* / Your honey love: *Penner, Dick* / Ballad of a teenage Queen: *Cash, Johnny* / Big river: *Cash, Johnny* / Chicken hearted: *Orbison, Roy* / I like love: *Orbison, Roy* / My bucket's got a hole in it: *Burgess, Sonny* / Sweet misery: *Burgess, Sonny* / I've got love if you want it: *Smith, Warren* / I fell in love: *Smith, Warren* / Lend me your comb: *Perkins, Carl* / Glad all over: *Perkins, Carl* / Breathless: *Lewis, Jerry Lee* / Down the line: *Lewis, Jerry Lee* / Baby please don't go: *Riley, Billy Lee* / Wouldn't you know: *Riley, Billy Lee* / Judy: *Grayzell, Rudy* / I think of you: *Grayzell, Rudy* / Ten years: *Clement, Jack* / Your lover boy: *Clement, Jack* / Sweet woman: *Bruce, Edwin* / Part of my life: *Bruce, Edwin* / Love is a stranger: *Sunrays* / Lonely hours: *Sunrays* / I feel so blue: *Priesman, Magel* / Memories of you: *Priesman, Magel* / I guess things happen that way: *Cash, Johnny* / Come in stranger: *Cash, Johnny* / High School confidential: *Lewis, Jerry Lee* / Fools like me: *Lewis, Jerry Lee* / Dreamy nights: *Lee, Dickey* / Fool fool fool: *Lee, Dickey* / Right behind you baby: *Smith, Ray* / So young: *Smith, Ray* / Drinkin' wine: *Simmons, Gene* / I done told you: *Simmons, Gene* / I dig you baby: *Blake, Tommy* / Sweetie pie: *Blake, Tommy* / Return of Jerry Lee: *Lewis, Jerry Lee* / Lewis Boogie: *Lewis, Jerry Lee* / Ways of a woman in love: *Cash, Johnny* / You're the nearest thing to heaven: *Cash, Johnny* / Break up: *Lewis, Jerry Lee* / I'll make it all up to you: *Lewis, Jerry Lee* / Thunderbird: *Burgess, Sonny* / Itchy: *Burgess, Sonny* / Torro: *Gordon, Rosco* / Sally Jo: *Gordon, Rosco* / Diamond ring: *Isle, Jimmy* / I've been waitin': *Isle, Jimmy* / Born to lose: *Chaffin, Ernie* / My love for you: *Chaffin, Ernie* / Yu made a hit: *Smith, Ray* / Why why why: *Smith, Ray* / It's just about time: *Cash, Johnny* / I just thought you'd like to know: *Cash, Johnny* / Breeze: *Taylor, Vernon* / Today is a blue day: *Taylor, Vernon* / Black haired man: *Clement, Jack* / Wrong: *Clement, Jack* / I'll sail my ship alone: *Lewis, Jerry Lee* / It hurt me so: *Lewis, Jerry Lee* / Down by the riverside: *Riley, Billy Lee* / No name girl: *Riley, Billy Lee* / Sweet, sweet girl: *Smith, Warren* / Goodbye Mr. Love: *Smith, Warren* / Jump right out of this jukebox: *Wheeler, Onie* / Tell 'em off: *Wheeler, Onie* / Luther played the boogie: *Lewis, Jerry Lee* / Thanks a lot: *Lewis, Jerry Lee* / Lovin' up a storm: *Lewis, Jerry Lee* / Big blon' baby: *Lewis, Jerry Lee* / Without a love: *Isle, Jimmy* / Time will tell: *Isle, Jimmy* / Rockin' bandit: *Smith, Ray* / Sail away: *Smith, Ray* / Don't ever leave me: *Chaffin, Ernie* / Miracle of you: *Chaffin, Ernie* / I forgot to remember to forget: *Cash, Johnny* / Katy too: *Cash, Johnny* / Got the water boiling: *Riley, Billy Lee* / One more time: *Riley, Billy Lee* / No more crying the blues: *Isle, Jimmy* / Have faith in my love: *Isle, Jimmy* / Let's talk about us: *Lewis, Jerry Lee* / Ballad of Billy Joe: *Lewis, Jerry Lee* / Mystery train: *Taylor, Vernon* / Sweet & easy to love: *Taylor, Vernon* / Lovestruck: *McGill, Jerry* / I wanna make sweet love: *McGill, Jerry* / Be mine, all mine: *Powers, Johnny* / With your love, with your kiss: *Powers, Johnny* / Winnie the parakeet: *Crane, Sherry* / Willie Willie: *Crane, Sherry*
CD Set ______ **BCD 15803**
Bear Family / Nov '96 / Direct / Rollercoaster / Swift

SUN SINGLES VOL.4 (4CD Set)
You're just my kind: *Mercer, Will* / Ballad of St. Mark's: *Mercer, Will* / Little Queenie: *Lewis, Jerry Lee* / I could never be ashamed of you: *Lewis, Jerry Lee* / You tell me: *Cash, Johnny* / Goodbye little darlin': *Cash, Johnny* / What a life: *Isle, Jimmy* / Together: *Isle, Jimmy* / Alice blue gown: *Anthony, Rayburn* / St. Louis blues: *Anthony, Rayburn* / Straight A's in love: *Cash, Johnny* / I love you because: *Cash, Johnny* / Thousand guitars: *Pendarvis, Tracy* / Is it too late: *Pendarvis, Tracy* / Walkin' and talkin': *Owen, Mack* / Somebody just like you: *Owen, Mack* / Old black Joe: *Lewis, Jerry Lee* / Baby baby bye bye: *Lewis, Jerry Lee* / Legend of the big steeple: *Richey, Paul* / Broken hearted Willie: *Richey, Paul* / Who's gonna shoe your pretty little feet: *Anthony, Rayburn* / There's no tomorrow: *Anthony, Rayburn* / Bobaloo: *Johnson, Bill* / Bad times ahead: *Johnson, Bill* / Great pretender: *Wilson, Sonny* / I'm gonna take a walk: *Wilson, Sonny* / You burned the bridges: *Bobbie Jean* / Cheaters never win: *Bobbie Jean* / Story of a broken heart: *Cash, Johnny* / Down the street to 301: *Cash, Johnny* / John Henry: *Lewis, Jerry Lee* / Hang up my rock 'n' roll shoes: *Lewis, Jerry Lee* / Is it me: *Pendarvis, Tracy* / Southbound line: *Pendarvis, Tracy* / Guess I'd better go: *Strength, 'Texas' Bill* / Senorita: *Strength, 'Texas' Bill* / Mean eyed cat: *Cash, Johnny* / Port of lonely hearts: *Cash, Johnny* / Good guys always win: *Roberts, Lance* / Time is right: *Roberts, Lance* / I gotta know: *Rossine, Tony* / Is it too late: *Rossine, Tony* / Rockin' lang syne: *Rockin' Stockin'* / Yuleville USA: *Rockin' Stockin'* / You don't love me anymore: *Jay, Ira* / More than anything: *Jay, Ira* / When I get paid: *Lewis, Jerry Lee* / Love made a fool of me: *Lewis, Jerry Lee* / Sweet and easy to love: *Orbison, Roy* / Devil doll: *Orbison, Roy* / Sad news: *Sheridan, Bobby* / Red man: *Sheridan, Bobby* / Oh lonesome me: *Cash, Johnny* / Life goes on: *Cash, Johnny* / What'd I say: *Lewis, Jerry Lee* / Livin' lovin' wreck: *Lewis, Jerry Lee* / UT party: *Klein, George* / Belle of the swannee: *Pendarvis, Tracy* / Eternally: *Pendarvis, Tracy* / Groovy train: *Cagle, Wade* / Highland rock: *Cagle, Wade* / I'll wait forever: *Wood, Anita* / I can't show how I feel: *Wood, Anita* / I'll stick by you: *Dorman, Harold* / There they go: *Dorman, Harold* / Sugartime: *Cash, Johnny* / My treasure: *Cash, Johnny* / Cold cold heart: *Lewis, Jerry Lee* / It won't happen with me: *Lewis, Jerry Lee* / I forgot to remember to forget: *Sisk, Shirley* / Other side: *Sisk, Shirley* / Well I ask ya: *Rossine, Tony* / Darlena: *Rossine, Tony* / Save the last

dance for me: *Lewis, Jerry Lee* / As long as I live: *Lewis, Jerry Lee* / Since I met you: *Hosea, Don* / Uh huh uh: *Hosea, Don* / Everybody's searching: *Wood, Bobby* / Human emotions: *Wood, Bobby* / Uncle Jonah's place: *Dorman, Harold* / Just one step: *Dorman, Harold* / Money: *Lewis, Jerry Lee* / Bonnie B: *Lewis, Jerry Lee* / Travellin' salesman: *Smith, Ray* / I won't miss you: *Smith, Ray* / How well I know: *Anthony, Rayburn* / Big dream: *Anthony, Rayburn* / I've been twistin': *Lewis, Jerry Lee* / Ramblin' Rose: *Lewis, Jerry Lee* / Candy doll: *Smith, Ray* / Hey boss man: *Smith, Ray* / Blue train: *Cash, Johnny* / Born to lose: *Cash, Johnny* / In the beginning: *Dorman, Harold* / Wait 'til Saturday night: *Dorman, Harold* / After school: *Rossine, Tony* / Just around the corner: *Rossine, Tony* / Sweet little sixteen: *Lewis, Jerry Lee* / How's my ex treating you: *Lewis, Jerry Lee*
CD Set ____ BCD 15804
Bear Family / Apr '97 / Direct / Rollercoaster / Swift

SUNDAY MORNING SESSIONS
CD ____ MRCD 176
Munich / Sep '95 / ADA / CM / Direct / Greensleeves

SUNDAZED SAMPLER, THE
Water baby boogie: *Maphis, Joe* / Nancy: *Barker Bros.* / Ain't that too much: *Vincent, Gene* / Rockabilly yodel: *Larue, Roc & The Three Pals* / Loophole: *Royal Coachmen* / Four in the floor: *Shutdowns* / Bustin' floor boards: *Tornadoes* / Twist and shout: *Isley Brothers* / Mama here comes the bride: *Shirelles* / Western Union: *Five Americans* / One track mind: *Knickerbockers* / Cadillac: *Colony Six* / Dirty water: *Standells* / Little latin lupe lu: *Ryder, Mitch & The Detroit Wheels* / Louie Louie: *Kingsmen* / Surfin' bird: *Trashmen* / Dimples: *Animals* / I got my mojo working: *Shadows Of Knight* / I've been wrong before: *HP Lovecraft* / Rollercoaster: *13th Floor Elevators* / I ain't no miracle worker: *Brogues* / Spend your life: *First Crow To The Moon* / Last time around: *Delvetts* / Anyway I can: *Choir* / Sweetgina: *Things To Come*
CD ____ CDSC 01
Sundazed / Apr '94 / Cargo / Greyhound / Rollercoaster

SUNNY AFTERNOON (Hits Of Summer)
In the summertime: *Mungo Jerry* / Beach baby: *First Class* / Hello Susie: *Amen Corner* / Do you wanna dance: *Blue, Barry* / Let's go to San Francisco: *Flowerpot Men* / El bimbo: *Bimbo Jet* / Baby, now that I've found you: *Foundations* / Sunny afternoon: *Kinks* / Green tambourine: *Lemon Pipers* / Simon says: *1910 Fruitgum Company* / Sunshine day: *Osibisa* / Egyptian reggae: *Richman, Jonathan & Modern Lovers* / Sky high: *Jigsaw* / Brand new key: *Melanie* / Summer in the city: *Lovin' Spoonful* / Itchycoo Park: *Small Faces* / I wanna hold your hand: *Dollar* / That same old feeling: *Pickettywitch* / Swing your daddy: *Gilstrap, Jim* / Elenore: *Turtles*
CD ____ TRTCD 145
TrueTrax / Oct '94 / THE

SUNNY AFTERNOONS
Sunny afternoon: *Kinks* / Daydream: *Lovin' Spoonful* / 59th Street Bridge song: *Simon & Garfunkel* / Happy together: *Turtles* / Wouldn't it be nice: *Beach Boys* / Lazy Sunday: *Small Faces* / Daydream believer: *Monkees* / Sunshine superman: *Donovan* / Sitting in the park: *Fame, Georgie* / Sunny: *Hebb, Bobby* / Dedicated to the one I love: *Mamas & The Papas* / Mr. Tambourine Man: *Byrds* / San Francisco: *McKenzie, Scott* / Woodstock: *Matthew's Southern Comfort* / Paper sun: *Traffic* / Badge: *Cream* / Green tambourine: *Lemon Pipers* / Let's go to San Francisco: *Flowerpot Men* / For what it's worth: *Buffalo Springfield* / I can't let Maggie go: *Honeybus* / 98.6: *Keith* / Kites: *Dupree, Simon & The Big Sound* / Good vibrations: *Beach Boys* / Itchycoo Park: *Small Faces* / Mellow yellow: *Donovan* / Waterloo sunset: *Kinks* / She'd rather be with me: *Turtles* / Friday on my mind: *Cure* / Jesamine: *Casuals* / Love grows (Where my Rosemary grows): *Edison Lighthouse* / My name is Jack: *Manfred Mann* / Early in the morning: *Vanity Fare* / Jennifer Eccles: *Hollies* / Flowers in the rain: *Move* / I'm a believer: *Monkees* / Summer in the city: *Lovin' Spoonful* / We gotta get out of this place: *Animals* / With a girl like you: *Troggs* / Monday Monday: *Mamas & The Papas* / Morning has broken: *Stevens, Cat* / Good day sunshine: *Tremeloes* / Judy in disguise: *Fred, John & His Playboy Band* / Sorrow: *Merseys* / Elusive butterfly: *Lind, Bob* / Windy: *Association* / Groovy kind of love: *Mindbenders* / Goo goo Barabajagal (Love is hot): *Donovan & Jeff Beck Group* / Hole in my shoe: *Traffic*
CD ____ 5256002
PolyGram TV / Jul '95 / PolyGram

SUNNY SUNDAY SMILE
CD ____ SUNDAY 640CD
Sunday / May '94 / SRD

SUNSET SWING
CD ____ BLC 760171
Black Lion / Oct '92 / Cadillac / Jazz Music / Koch / Wellard

SUNSHINE DAY (20 Smash Hits Of The Seventies)
It's a heartache: *Tyler, Bonnie* / Sunshine day: *Osibisa* / Egyptian reggae: *Richman, Jonathan & Modern Lovers* / Best thing that ever happened to me: *Knight, Gladys & The Pips* / Shooting star: *Dollar* / Making up again: *Goldie* / You to me are everything: *Real Thing* / Girls: *Moments* / I'll have to say I love you in a song: *Croce, Jim* / Isn't she lovely: *Parton, David* / Lady rose: *Mungo Jerry* / So sad the song: *Knight, Gladys & The Pips* / Purely by coincidence: *Sweet Sensation* / Matchstalk men and matchstalk cats and dogs: *Brian & Michael* / In Zaire: *Wakelin, Johnny* / Summer of my life: *May, Simon* / Now is the time: *James, Jimmy & The Vagabonds* / Show me you're a woman: *Mud* / Car 67: *Driver 67* / Can't get by without you: *Real Thing*
CD ____ TRTCD 109
TrueTrax / Oct '94 / THE

SUNSHINE GIRLS (TK Deep Soul 2)
Make me feel like a woman: *Moore, Jackie* / Jazz freak: *Reades, Philette* / Puttin' it down to you: *Moore, Jackie* / One woman's trash: *Brandye* / Your real good thing's about to come to an end: *Reades, Philette* / It's harder to leave: *Moore, Jackie* / Loving you, loving me: *Serton, Ann* / Secret lover: *Reades, Philette* / Tired of hiding: *Moore, Jackie* / I'll be right here (when you return): *Wilson, Ruby & The Blue Chips* / Bridge that lies between us: *Moore, Jackie* / God bless this man of mine: *Reades, Philette* / Hurtin' inside out: *Moore, Jackie* / Man and a baby boy: *Wilson, Ruby* / Somebody loves you: *Moore, Jackie*
CD ____ NEMCD 744
Sequel / Jun '95 / BMG

SUNSHINE REGGAE
CD ____ SBCD 009
Soul Beat / Jul '95 / Jet Star / SRD

SUNSPLASH SHOWCASE
CD ____ TWCD 1055
Tamoki Wambesi / Nov '95 / Greensleeves / Jet Star / Roots Collective / SRD

SUNTRANCE GOA 1996
Youth of the galaxy: *Doof* / Atomic armadillo: *Green Nuns Of The Revolution* / Supernatural: *Slinky Wizard* / LSD: *Hallucinogen* / China zones: *Castle Trancelot* / Tempest: *Salamander* / Magic frequencies: *Witchcraft* / Arcana: *Orion* / 3 Minute warning: *Yum Yum* / Technossomy: *Rejuvination* / Sonar eclipse: *U4EA*
CD ____ CDTOT 38
Jumpin' & Pumpin' / Mar '96 / 3mv/Sony / Mo's Music Machine

SUNTRANCE VOL.3
Scared: *Slacker* / State of mind: *Floorplay* / Extraterrestrial lover: *Shamanic Tribes On Acid* / Running up that hill: *Levy 9* / Kaleidoscope: *Art Of Trance* / L'architecture: *South Of Trance* / Great ruaha: *Vee* / Canis loopus(thousand rains): *Yekuana* / Amplexus: *Yekuana* / Everything: *Tallulah*
CD ____ CDTOT 48
Jumpin' & Pumpin' / Apr '97 / 3mv/Sony / Mo's Music Machine

SUPER ALL STAR
Francisco guayabal / El platanal de bartolo / Tres linda cubanas / Ban-con-tim / Alto songo / Malanga / El sopon / La cascara
CD ____ CDORB 017
Globestyle / Jul '90 / Pinnacle

SUPER DANCE VOL.12 (2CD Set)
CD Set ____ ZYX 810982
ZYX / Apr '97 / ZYX

SUPER DANCING TO REGGAE AND SKA
CD ____ 3020772
Arcade / Jul '97 / Discovery

SUPER GROUPS
CD ____ STACD 046
Wisepack / Sep '93 / Conifer/BMG / THE

SUPER HIT TROPICAL
CD ____ VGCD 670017
Vogue / Jan '93 / BMG

SUPER HITS OF THE 1970'S VOL.1
CD ____ DC 866822
Disky / Aug '96 / Disky / THE

SUPER HITS OF THE 1970'S VOL.2
CD ____ DC 866832
Disky / Aug '96 / Disky / THE

SUPER HITS OF THE 1970'S VOL.3
CD ____ DC 866842
Disky / Aug '96 / Disky / THE

SUPER MUSIKBOX VOL.1
Berliner luft: *Lincke, Paul* / 100 mal Berlin: *Hahnemann, Helga* / Konig der Welt: *Karat* / Major Tom: *Schilling, Peter* / He kleine Linda: *Muck* / Gold in deinen Augen: *Schobel, Frank* / Gwendolina: *Adamo* / Wem: *Carpendale, Howard* / Es fahrt ein Zug nach Nirgendwo: *Anders, Christian* / Ein Bett im Kornfeld: *Drews, Jurgen* / Heute male ich dein Bild, Cindy Lou: *Manuella* / Blue night in Rio: *Bottcher, Martin* / Geld wie heu: *Bottcher, Gerd* / Siebenmal in der woche: *Torriani, Vico* / Souvenirs: *Ramsey, Bill* / Heimweh: *Quinn, Freddy* / Siebenmeilenstiefel: *Bonney, Graham* / Schmidtchen Schleicher: *Haak, Nico* / Beautiful morning: *Rehnbein, Herbert* / Kaiserwalzer: *Stolz, Robert*
CD ____ BCD 17007
Bear Family / Nov '96 / Direct / Rollercoaster / Swift

SUPER MUSIKBOX VOL.2
Sugar sugar: *Archies* / Popcorn: *Hot Butter* / Hang on Sloopy: *McCoys* / Save all your kisses for me: *Brotherhood Of Man* / Sugar baby love: *Rubettes* / Barbara Ann: *Beach Boys* / Santa Maria: *Onions, Oliver* / Dolce vita: *Paris, Ryan* / Paloma blanca: *Baker, George Selection* / Let your love flow: *Bellamy Brothers* / Ma belle Amie: *Tee Set* / It's a real good feeling: *Kent, Peter* / Love is in the air: *Young, John Paul* / Yellow river: *Christie* / Winchester Cathedral: *New Vaudeville Band* / San Francisco: *McKenzie, Scott* / Chantilly lace: *Big Bopper* / Ring of fire: *Cash, Johnny* / Just walkin' in the rain: *Ray, Johnnie* / Moon river: *Butler, Jerry* / 'S wonderful: *Conniff, Ray*
CD ____ BCD 17008
Bear Family / Nov '96 / Direct / Rollercoaster / Swift

SUPER ROCK SESSION VOL.1
Bat out of hell: *Meat Loaf* / Are you ready: *Pacific Gas & Electric* / Time of the season: *Argent* / Witch Queen of New Orleans: *Redbone* / Gamma ray: *Birth Control* / Mental health: *Quiet Riot* / You took the words right out of my mouth (hot summer night): *Meat Loaf* / Betty Black: *Ram Jam* / On the run: *Lake* / (Don't fear) the reaper: *Blue Oyster Cult* / I want you to want me: *Cheap Trick* / Roll away the stone: *Mott The Hoople* / Any way you want it: *Journey* / Take it on the run: *REO Speedwagon* / Carry me, Carrie: *Dr. Hook & The Medicine Show* / Hi-de-ho (that old sweet roll): *Blood, Sweat & Tears*
CD ____ 4804452
Columbia / Dec '95 / Sony

SUPER SALSA HITS
Abueleta: *Colon, Willie* / Indestructible: *Barretto, Ray* / Abandonada fue: *Orchestra Harlow* / Nina Y semora: *Puente, Tito* / Mi disengana: *Roena, Roberto* / Cafe: *Palmieri, Eddie* / Acuzar mami: *Pacheco, Johnny* / Senora: *Ray, Ricardo* / Soy Boricua: *Valentin, Bobby* / Acere Ko: *La Sonora Poncena*
CD ____ CDHOT 500
Charly / Oct '93 / Koch

SUPER SKA
CD ____ PHZCD 67
Unicorn / Dec '93 / Plastic Head

SUPER SOUNDS OF BOSWORTH VOL.2
CD ____ BARKED 2CD
Trunk / Oct '96 / Vital

SUPER SUMMER HITS
Mon amour: *BZN* / Ticket to the tropics: *Joling, Gerard* / Rio: *Maywood* / Juanita: *MacKenzie, Nick* / Everybody join hands: *Debby* / Una paloma blanca: *Baker, George Selection* / Ma belle amie: *Tee Set* / Windsurfin': *Surfers* / Sweet love: *Ferrari* / January February: *Dutch Rhythm Steel Band* / Sevilla: *BZN* / Vaya con dios: *Cats* / Doin' la bamba: *Pussycat* / Comment ca va: *Shorts* / See the sun: *Teach In* / Dr. Rhythm: *G'Race* / Weekend: *Earth & Fire* / You and me: *Spargo*
CD ____ DC 880762
Disky / May '97 / Disky / THE

SUPERFUNK
CD ____ VTCD 30
Virgin / Jun '94 / EMI

SUPERMARKET
CD ____ EFA 122682
Disko B / Apr '95 / SRD

SUPERSONIC 70'S (20 Sensational Smash Hits)
Shooting star: *Dollar* / (Dancing) on a Saturday night: *Blue, Barry* / Sky high: *Jigsaw* / Kung fu fighting: *Douglas, Craig* / Popcorn: *Hot Butter* / Man who sold the world: *Lulu* / Who do you think you are: *Candlewick Green* / Born with a smile on my face: *De Sykes, Stephanie* / Beach baby: *First Class* / More than a lover: *Tyler, Bonnie* / Life is too short girl: *Sheer Elegance* / Sad sweet dreamer: *Sweet Sensation* / Whenever you want my love: *Real Thing* / I'll go where your music takes me: *James, Jimmy & The Vagabonds* / Why did you do it: *Stretch* / Black superman: *Wakelin, Johnny* / This flight tonight: *Nazareth* / Indian reservation: *Fardon, Don* / Shake it down: *Mud* / Lady Rose: *Mungo Jerry*
CD ____ SUMCD 4101
Summit / Nov '96 / Sound & Media

SUPERSTAR LINE UP VOL.2
CD ____ CDNNM 005
New Name / Jun '92 / Jet Star

SUPERSTARS
CD ____ HADCD 201
Javelin / Jul '96 / Henry Hadaway / THE

SUPERSTARS AT THE DANCE HALL
CD ____ RNCD 2093
Rhino / Mar '95 / Grapevine/PolyGram / Jet Star

SUPERSTARS HIT PARADE VOL.8
CD ____ SPCD 0124
Superpower / May '97 / Jet Star

SUPERSTARS OF COUNTRY, THE
Sea of heartbreak: *Gibson, Don* / Oh, lonesome me: *Gibson, Don* / Blue blue day: *Gibson, Don* / Give myself a party: *Gibson, Don* / I can't stop loving you: *Gibson, Don* / End of the world: *Davis, Skeeter* / Gonna get along without you now: *Davis, Skeeter* / I can't stay mad at you: *Davis, Skeeter* / What does it take: *Davis, Skeeter* / Am I that easy to forget: *Davis, Skeeter* / King of the road: *Miller, Roger* / England swings: *Miller, Roger* / Husbands and wives: *Miller, Roger* / In the summertime: *Miller, Roger* / Walkin' in the sunshine: *Miller, Roger* / Behind closed doors: *Rich, Charlie* / Good time Charlie's got the blues: *Rich, Charlie* / My elusive dreams: *Rich, Charlie* / There won't be anymore: *Rich, Charlie* / Most beautiful girl: *Rich, Charlie*
CD ____ ECD 3368
K-Tel / Jun '97 / K-Tel

SUPERSTARS OF ROCK 'N' ROLL, THE
Lucille: *Little Richard* / Good golly Miss Molly: *Little Richard* / Keep a knockin': *Little Richard* / Tutti frutti: *Little Richard* / Baby face: *Little Richard* / Be bop a lula: *Vincent, Gene* / Say mama: *Vincent, Gene* / Lonely street: *Vincent, Gene* / Lotta lovin': *Vincent, Gene* / Pistol packin' mama: *Vincent, Gene* / Ain't that a shame: *Boone, Pat* / Wonderful time up there: *Boone, Pat* / Don't forbid me: *Boone, Pat* / Why, baby, why: *Boone, Pat* / Speedy Gonzales: *Boone, Pat* / (Dance with) the guitar man: *Eddy, Duane* / Peter Gunn: *Eddy, Duane* / Shazam: *Eddy, Duane* / Yep: *Eddy, Duane* / Movin' and groovin': *Eddy, Duane*
CD ____ ECD 3367
K-Tel / Jun '97 / K-Tel

SUPERSTARS OF SOUL, THE
Spanish harlem: *King, Ben E.* / Stand by me: *King, Ben E.* / I (who have nothing): *King, Ben E.* / Don't play that song (you lied): *King, Ben E.* / Supernatural thing: *King, Ben E.* / Wake up everybody: *Melvin, Harold & The Bluenotes* / If you don't know me by now: *Melvin, Harold & The Bluenotes* / Love I lost: *Melvin, Harold & The Bluenotes* / Bad luck: *Melvin, Harold & The Bluenotes* / Satisfaction guaranteed (or take your love back): *Melvin, Harold & The Bluenotes* / When a man loves a woman: *Sledge, Percy* / Warm and tender love: *Sledge, Percy* / Take time to know her: *Sledge, Percy* / It tears me up: *Sledge, Percy* / Cover me: *Sledge, Percy* / Soul man: *Sam & Dave* / Hold on I'm comin': *Sam & Dave* / Soul sister, brown sugar: *Sam & Dave* / I thank you: *Sam & Dave* / Sweet soul music: *Sam & Dave*
CD ____ ECD 3366
K-Tel / Jun '97 / K-Tel

SUPERSTARS OF THE 40'S, THE
On the sunny side of the street: *Cole, Nat 'King'* / Do nothing 'til you hear from me: *Cole, Nat 'King'* / I'm a shy guy: *Cole, Nat 'King'* / This will make you laugh: *Cole, Nat 'King'* / Is you is or is you ain't my baby: *Cole, Nat 'King'* / That old black magic: *Fitzgerald, Ella* / I want to be happy: *Fitzgerald, Ella* / Basin Street blues: *Fitzgerald, Ella* / If dreams come true: *Fitzgerald, Ella* / Lover come back to me: *Fitzgerald, Ella* / In the mood: *Miller, Glenn* / Chattanooga choo choo: *Miller, Glenn* / Pennsylvania 6-5000: *Miller, Glenn* / (I've got a girl in) Kalamazoo: *Miller, Glenn* / Moonlight serenade: *Miller, Glenn* / Fools rush in: *Sinatra, Frank* / Embraceable you: *Sinatra, Frank* / Stardust: *Sinatra, Frank* / Sunshine of your smile: *Sinatra, Frank* / I'll be seeing you: *Sinatra, Frank*
CD ____ ECD 3357
K-Tel / Jun '97 / K-Tel

SUPERSTARS OF THE 50'S, THE
Just walkin' in the rain: *Ray, Johnnie* / Cry: *Ray, Johnnie* / Little white cloud that cried: *Ray, Johnnie* / Walkin' my baby back home: *Ray, Johnnie* / Hernando's hideaway: *Ray, Johnnie* / This ole house: *Clooney, Rosemary* / Hey there: *Clooney, Rosemary* / Botch-a-me: *Clooney, Rosemary* / Half as much: *Clooney, Rosemary* / Come on-a my house: *Clooney, Rosemary* / Jealousy: *Laine, Frankie* / I believe: *Laine, Frankie* / Love is a golden ring: *Laine, Frankie* / Rose, rose I love you: *Laine, Frankie* / Jezebel: *Laine, Frankie* / Tennessee waltz: *Page, Patti* / Old cape cod: *Page, Patti* / How much is that doggie in the window: *Page, Patti* / Changing partners: *Page, Patti* / Mockin' bird Hill: *Page, Patti*
CD ____ ECD 3358
K-Tel / Jun '97 / K-Tel

SUPERSTARS OF THE 60'S, THE
Rubber ball: *Vee, Bobby* / More than I can say: *Vee, Bobby* / Devil or angel: *Vee, Bobby* / Run to him: *Vee, Bobby* / Night has a thousand eyes: *Vee, Bobby* / Wild one: *Rydell, Bobby* / Volare: *Rydell, Bobby* / We got love: *Rydell, Bobby* / Swingin' school: *Rydell, Bobby* / Forget him: *Rydell, Bobby* / Everybody: *Roe, Tommy* / Dizzy: *Roe, Tommy* / Sweet pea: *Roe, Tommy* / Jam up jelly tight: *Roe, Tommy* / Sheila: *Roe, Tommy* / Poetry in motion: *Tillotson, Johnny* / It keeps right on a-hurtin': *Tillotson, Johnny* / You're the reason: *Tillotson, Johnny* / Without you: *Tillotson, Johnny* / Talk back trembling lips: *Tillotson, Johnny*

CD ____ **ECD 3359**
K-Tel / Jun '97 / K-Tel

SUPERSTARS OF THE SEVENTIES (2CD Set)
Get ready: *Rare Earth* / In the summertime: *Mungo Jerry* / Rock your baby: *McCrae, George* / Ring my bell: *Ward, Anita* / That's the way I like it: *KC & The Sunshine Band* / Ballroom blitz: *Sweet* / Dynamite: *Mud* / Tonight: *Rubettes* / Lay down (candles in the rain): *Melanie* / Give up your gun: *Buoys* / (Dancing) on a Saturday night: *Blue, Barry* / Do it anyway you wanna: *People's Choice* / Dreams are ten a penny: *Kincaid* / Matrimony: *O'Sullivan, Gilbert* / More more more: *True, Andrea Connection* / Popcorn: *Hot Butter* / Son of my father: *Chicory Tip* / Troglodyte: *Castor, Jimmy Bunch* / Shame, shame, shame: *Shirley & Company* / Jukebox jive: *Rubettes* / Save all your kisses for me: *Brotherhood Of Man* / Yellow river: *Christie* / Get down: *O'Sullivan, Gilbert* / Tiger feet: *Mud* / Night Chicago died: *Paper Lace* / Beach baby: *First Class* / Freedom: *Kissoon, Mac & Katie* / Get dancin': *Disco Tex & The Sexolettes* / Love really hurts without you: *Ocean, Billy* / I'd like to teach the world to sing: *New Seekers* / Brandy: *Looking Glass* / Jungle rock: *Mizell, Hank* / Love grows: *Edison Lighthouse* / Beautiful Sunday: *Boone, Daniel* / Rosetta: *Fame, Georgie & The Blue Flames* / Day after day: *Badfinger*
CD Set ____ **TNC 96229**
Natural Collection / Aug '96 / Target/BMG

SUPERSTITION VOL.5 (3CD Set)
CD Set ____ **EFA 620752**
Superstition / May '97 / Plastic Head / SRD / Vital

SURF PARTY
CD ____ **295720**
Ariola / Jul '93 / BMG

SURRENDER TO THE VIBE
CD ____ **PTM 132**
Phantasm / Sep '95 / Arabesque / Plastic Head / Prime / Vital/SAM

SURVIVAL OF THE FATTEST
CD ____ **FAT 538CD**
Fatwreck Chords / Jun '96 / Plastic Head

SURVIVAL SOUNDS
Fallen angel: *Robertson, Robbie* / Sina (Soumbouya): *Keita, Salif* / Tahi: *Moana & The Moahunters* / Pundela: *Robin, Thierry & Gulabi Sapera* / Bring 'em all in: *Scott, Mike* / Mapoto: *Mapfumo, Thomas & The Blacks Unlimited* / Didgeridoo solo/Baru (crocodile): *Sunrize Band* / Modernise, westernise: *Rough Image* / Exile: *Oryema, Geoffrey* / Om mani padme hung: *Lhamo, Yungchen* / Whirl-y-reel 1: *Afro Celt Sound System* / Take me to God: *Jah Wobble's Invaders Of The Heart* / Navega sola: *Martin, Mayte* / I want to go home: *Ongala, Remmy* / My country: *Midnight Oil*
CD ____ **WSSS 1**
Womad Survival / Nov '96 / Direct

SURVIVAL-THE DANCE COMPILATION
One nation: *Supereal* / Little bullet part 1: *Spooky* / Boss drum: *Shamen* / Choice: *Orbital* / Djapana: *Yothu Yindi* / King of the funky zulus: *Moody Blues* / Release the dub: *Leftfield* / Aquarium: *Grid* / Flowing nile: *Zion Train* / Freeality: *Freeality* / Predator: *Spiral Tribe*
CD ____ **GRCD 008**
Guerilla / May '93 / Pinnacle

SUSHI 303
CD ____ **RTD 34600062**
City Slang / Sep '96 / RTM/Disc

SWAMP BLUES
Looking the world over: *Smith, Whispering* / Thousand miles from nowhere: *Smith, Whispering* / SDeep South Mose: *Smith, Whispering* / Cold black mare: *Smith, Whispering* / Storm in Texas: *Smith, Whispering* / Baton Rouge breakdown: *Smith, Whispering* / Baby please don't go: *Smith, Whispering* / Somebody stole my baby and gone: *Kelley, Arthur 'Guitar'* / How can I stay when all I have is gone: *Kelley, Arthur 'Guitar'* / I don't know why: *Kelley, Arthur 'Guitar'* / Number ten is at the station: *Kelley, Arthur 'Guitar'* / Just give me a chance: *Hogan, Silas* / Dry chemical blues: *Hogan, Silas* / I didn't tell her to leave: *Hogan, Silas* / Hoodoo blues: *Hogan, Silas* / Honey bee blues: *Hogan, Silas* / Lonesome bedroom blues: *Edwards, Clarence* / Let me love you baby: *Edwards, Clarence* / I want somebody: *Edwards, Clarence* / Can't last too long: *Gray, Henry* / Gray's bounce: *Gray, Henry* / Showers of rain: *Gray, Henry* / Worried life blues: *Gray, Henry* / Cooling board: *Edwards, Clarence*
CD ____ **CDCHD 661**
Ace / Jul '97 / Pinnacle

SWAN'S SOUL SIDES
Run tun: *Persianettes* / You're everything: *Showmen* / Misery: *Carlton, Eddie* / Never too young (to fall in love): *Modern Redcaps* / In love: *Galla, Tony* / Trying to find my baby: *Dodds, Troy* / I'm just your clown: *Teddy & The Twilights* / Two steps ahead: *Johnson, Herb* / No sign of you: *Modern Redcaps* / Put yourself in my place: *Mortimor, Azie* / In return: *Ferguson, Sheila* / Have faith in me: *Sugar & Spice* / Handsome boy: *Ladybirds* / Gotta find a way: *Wilson, Naomi* / Hey sah-lo-ney: *Lane, Mickey Lee* / No good: *Anthony, Richard* / Our love will grow: *Showmen* / Hot hot: *Buena Vistas* / You got to tell me: *Rivieras* / Who do you love: *Sapphires* / Gotta draw the line: *Three Degrees* / Hearbroken memories: *Ferguson, Sheila* / I do love you: *Styles* / Put that woman down: *Leach, John* / It will be done: *Carlton, Eddie* / Everybody crossfire: *Stevens, Sammy*
CD ____ **CDKEND 120**
Kent / Jan '96 / Pinnacle

SWARM OF DRONES (2CD Set)
CD Set ____ **EFA 709532**
Asphodel / Dec '96 / Cargo / SRD

SWEDEN'S ALTERNATIVE
CD ____ **RA 91332**
Roadrunner / Aug '92 / PolyGram

SWEDISH JAZZ FROM THE 70'S
CD ____ **2002**
Caprice / Nov '89 / ADA / Cadillac / CM / Complete/Pinnacle

SWEET CITY SOUL (4CD Set)
I can't help myself: *Four Tops & The All Stars* / Stop her on sight (SOS): *Starr, Edwin* / Hang on in there baby: *Bristol, Johnny* / Technicolour: *Griffin, Billy* / All over the world: *Jackson, Chuck* / When you're young and in love: *Marvelettes* / Love hangover: *5th Dimension* / Baby love: *Supremes* / You are the sunshine of my life: *Nero, Frances* / Reach out and touch somebody's hand: *Demps, Louvain* / It takes two: *Gaye, Frankie & Kim Weston* / Band of gold: *Payne, Freda* / Ain't no mountain high enough: *Payne, Sherrie* / Standing still: *Monitors* / Love machine: *Miracles* / Light a nightmare: *Andantes* / It should have been me: *Weston, Kim* / Ain't too proud to beg: *Willie, Richard* / With you I'm born again: *Syreeta* / I'm gonna make you love me: *Originals & The Supremes* / Footsteps following me: *Nero, Frances* / Nathan Jones: *Supremes* / Breaking down the walls: *Starr, Edwin* / Heatwave: *Reeves, Martha & The Vandellas* / My guy: *Wells, Mary* / Dancing in the street: *Weston, Kim* / Heaven must have sent you: *Elgins* / This old heart of mine: *Contours* / Wishing on a star: *Calvin, Billie* / What does it take to win your love: *Bristol, Johnny* / My brother: *Gaye, Frankie* / I'll be around: *Cameron, G.C.* / Date with the rain: *Griffin, Billy* / Reflections: *Syreeta* / All around the motorcity: *Andantes* / Wholeheartedly: *McNier, Ronnie* / Put yourself in my place: *Edwards, Sandra* / Day by day: *Monitors* / Love child: *Supremes* / Gentle lady: *Eckstein, Billy* / Stop in the name of love: *Supremes* / I'll pick a rose for my rose: *Johnson, Marv* / Going to a go-go: *Monitors* / Rescue me: *Lewis, Pat* / Relight my fire: *Jackson, Chuck* / Someday we'll be together: *Bristol, Johnny* / Sweet sherry: *Barnes, J.J.* / Tell a fool goodbye: *Edwards, Sandra* / It's a shame: *Cameron, G.C.* / Darlin' darlin' baby: *Starr, Edwin* / Back by popular demand: *Supremes & The Originals* / Tracks of my tears: *Contours* / Ten out of ten: *Elgins* / I'm still waiting: *Payne, Sherrie* / On the beach: *Demps, Louvain* / Something incredible: *Griffin, Billy* / Let me down easy: *Lavette, Bettye* / Save me I'm all alone: *Dixon, Hank* / My cherie amour: *Moy, Sylvia* / Needle in a haystack: *Velvelettes* / Ain't nothing but a house party: *Contours* / Stoned love: *Supremes* / Man up in the sky: *Bristol, Johnny* / Tears of a clown: *Monitors* / Jimmy mack: *Lavette, Bettye* / 25 miles: *Starr, Edwin* / Ain't nothing like the real thing: *Johnson, Marv & Carolyn Gill* / Just my imagination: *Cameron, G.C.* / Special day: *Gaye, Frankie* / Free: *Greene, Susaye* / It's the same old song: *Stubbs, Joe* / Remember me: *Lewis, Pat* / He was really saying something: *Velvelettes* / It wouldn't change the man he is: *Blinky* / You're all I need to get by: *Reeves, Martha & G.C. Cameron* / Man in my life: *Laurence, Lynda* / Crazy 'bout the guy: *Supremes* / Lost and found: *Demps, Louvain* / You're my first, my last, my everything: *Littles, Hattie* / It's impossible: *Eckstein, Billy & Susaye Greene*
CD Set ____ **MBSCD 449**
Castle / Sep '96 / BMG

SWEET DREAMS
Sweet dreams: *Young, Faron* / I've loved and lost again: *Cline, Patsy* / Don't think twice: *Jennings, Waylon* / I can't find the time: *Nelson, Willie* / (I never promised you a) Rose garden: *Anderson, Lynn* / Always leaving, always gone: *Rogers, Kenny & The First Edition* / Hello walls: *Drusky, Roy* / Wishful thinking: *Fargo, Donna* / I can't get enough of you: *Jackson, Stonewall* / Before the next teardrop falls: *Fender, Freddy* / Release me: *Mandrell, Barbara* / Have I told you lately that I love you: *Reeves, Jim* / Lonely wine: *Gilley, Mickey* / Making believe: *Wells, Kitty* / Four in the morning: *Young, Faron* / Your tender years: *Jones, George* / Hungry for your love: *Cline, Patsy* / She even woke me up to say goodbye: *Rogers, Kenny & The First Edition* / Last letter: *Drusky, Roy* / I don't know why I love you but I do: *Fender, Freddy*
CD ____ **QED 021**
Tring / Nov '96 / Tring

SWEET GUITAR
Windmills of your mind / Air on a g-string / Lady in red / Without you / Sweet sixteen / If you leave me now / WHile my guitar gently weeps / Mona Lisa / You've got a friend / Step inside love / Dreams / Morning song / As I roved out / Ministal boy / Music of the night / Elvira Madigan / Autumn leaves / Fur elise / Fool on the hill / Gymnopedie
CD ____ **EMPRCD 682**
Emporio / Apr '97 / Disc

SWEET HOME CHICAGO
CD ____ **DD 618**
Delmark / Mar '95 / ADA / Cadillac / CM / Direct / Hot Shot

SWEET LORD (Charly Gospel Greats)
Uncloudy day: *Staple Singers* / Jesus is the answer: *Argo Singers* / No coward soldier: *Caravans* / Have I told you about my religion: *Bells Of Joy* / I'm thinkin': *Five Blind Boys Of Mississippi* / My loved ones: *Soul Stirrers* / His eye is on the sparrow: *Harmonizing Four* / Somewhere to lay my head: *Highway QC's* / What he's done for me: *Five Blind Boys Of Alabama* / He saved my soul: *Swan Silvertones* / He has a way: *Greater Harvest Choir* / Too close to heaven: *Bradford, Alex* / Will the circle be unbroken: *Pilgrim Travellers* / God is moving: *Sallie Martin Singers* / Step by step: *Original Gospel Harmonettes* / Precious Lord (part 1): *Franklin, Aretha* / Precious Lord (part 2): *Franklin, Aretha* / We shall overcome: *Jackson, Mahalia*
CD ____ **CPCD 8090**
Charly / Apr '95 / Koch

SWEET MEMORIES FROM BIG BAND
CD ____ **UP 004**
Hindsight / Sep '92 / Jazz Music / Target/BMG

SWEET 'N' TOUGH (Blues From Chicago)
CD ____ **MCCD 280**
Music Club / Dec '96 / Disc / THE

SWEET SOUL CLASSICS (2CD Set)
CD Set ____ **DCDCD 217**
Castle / Aug '96 / BMG

SWEET SOUL DREAMS
CD ____ **290426**
Ariola / Dec '92 / BMG

SWEET SOUL HARMONIES VOL.1
My lovin': *En Vogue* / Stay: *Eternal* / I wanna sex you up: *Color Me Badd* / Right here: *SWV* / Motownphilly: *Boyz II Men* / I'm doing fine now: *Pasadenas* / Love train: *O'Jays* / My girl: *Temptations* / If you don't know me by now: *Melvin, Harold & The Bluenotes* / Best thing that ever happened to me: *Knight, Gladys & The Pips* / Back to life: *Soul II Soul & Caron Wheeler* / Apparently nothin': *Young Disciples* / Ghetto heaven: *Family Stand* / Sexual healing: *Gaye, Marvin* / After the love has gone: *Earth, Wind & Fire* / There's nothing like this: *Omar* / Ghetto child: *Detroit Spinners* / Casanova: *Levert* / Don't walk away: *Jade* / Thinking of you: *Sister Sledge*
CD ____ **VTCD 20**
Virgin / Jan '94 / EMI

SWEET SOUL HARMONIES VOL.2
Could it be I'm falling in love: *Detroit Spinners* / Summer breeze: *Isley Brothers* / I love music: *O'Jays* / Save our love: *Eternal* / Crazy: *Seal* / Zoom: *Fat Larry's Band* / Downtown: *SWV* / Would I lie to you: *Charles & Eddie* / What's going on: *Gaye, Marvin* / Don't look any further: *M-People* / Hold on: *En Vogue* / Slowhand: *Pointer Sisters* / Keep on movin': *Soul II Soul* / We are family: *Sister Sledge* / You can't hurry love: *Supremes* / Tribute (Right on): *Pasadenas* / Ain't no sunshine: *Withers, Bill* / Everything must change: *Young, Paul* / Too young to die: *Jamiroquai* / Let's stay together: *Green, Al*
CD ____ **VTCD 31**
Virgin / Aug '94 / EMI

SWEET SOUND OF SUCCESS
You've got the power: *Esquires* / If I had you: *O'Dell, Brooks* / There's still tomorrow: *Diplomats* / Same old story: *Big Maybelle* / Don't say goodnight and mean goodbye: *Shirelles* / Invisible: *Miles, Lenny* / That's enough: *Robinson, Roscoe* / Baby take me: *Jackson, Chuck* / Keep on searchin': *Candy & The Kisses* / Finders keepers, losers weepers: *Dodds, Nella* / If I catch you: *Shaw, Timmy* / Hand it over: *Jackson, Chuck* / He's no good: *Hughes, Freddie* / Love of my man: *Kilgore, Theola* / Look over your shoulder: *Jackson, Chuck* / One step at a time: *Brown, Maxine* / Door is open: *Hunt, Tommy* / It's mine: *Montgomery, Tammy* / Lonely people do foolish things: *Clay, Judy* / How much pressure: *Robinson, Roscoe* / Come see about me: *Dodds, Nella* / Half a man: *Cooke, L.C.* / This world's in a hell of a shape: *Ross, Jackie* / Do it now: *Banks, Bessie* / Ask me: *Brown, Maxine* / Can't let you out of my sight: *Jackson, Chuck & Maxine Brown* / Gonna send you back to Georgia: *Shaw, Timmy* / Don't believe him Donna: *Miles, Lenny*
CD ____ **CDKEND 112**
Kent / Jun '94 / Pinnacle

SWEET, SOFT AND LAZY
CD ____ **12203**
Laserlight / Dec '94 / Target/BMG

SWEET STUFF
I'll erase away: *Whatnauts* / I dig your act: *Whatnauts* / Friends by day (lovers by night): *Whatnauts* / Blues flyaway: *Whatnauts* / You forgot too easy: *Whatnauts* / I just can't lose your love: *Whatnauts* / Please make love go away: *Whatnauts* / Tweedly dum-dum: *Whatnauts* / In the bottle: *Brother To Brother* / Hurry sundown: *Staton, Candi* / Count on me: *Staton, Candi* / Suspicious minds: *Staton, Candi* / Me and my gemini this is it: *First Class* / Sweet stuff: *Sylvia* / Love is God almighty: *Optimystic* / Where were you: *Mills, Eleonore* / Peace: *O'Jays* / Soul je t'aime: *Sylvia & Ralfi Pagan*
CD ____ **NEMCD 616**
Sequel / Jul '91 / BMG

SWEET TASTE OF WESTBOUND, A
Walt's third trip: *Morrison, Junie* / Rhythm changes: *Counts* / Baby let me take you (in my arms): *Detroit Emeralds* / Walked away from you: *Ohio Players* / Cookie jar: *Haskins, Fuzzy* / Get up off my mind: *LaSalle, Denise* / You can't miss what you can't measure: *Funkadelic* / What am I gonna do: *Houston Outlaws* / Funky Sunday afternoon: *Person, Houston* / Back to funk: *Lowe, Robert* / You're messin' up my mind: *Washington, Albert* / Ain't I been good to you: *Fantastic Four* / Your love is my desire: *Erasmus Hall* / Crazy legs: *Austin, Donald* / Sweet taste of sin: *Coffey, Dennis* / Bull: *Theodore, Mike Orchestra* / Deadeye Dick: *CJ & Co.* / Everything's gonna be alright: *Clark Sisters*
CD ____ **CDSWX 150**
Westbound / Mar '96 / Pinnacle

SWEETER THAN SWEETS
CD ____ **CMS 01CD**
Canopy / Mar '97 / Jazz Music

SWEETER THAN THE DAY BEFORE (28 Classic Cuts From The Chess Stable)
Strange change: *Ward, Herb* / Baby you've got it: *McAllister, Maurice & The Radiants* / Such a pretty thing: *Chandler, Gene* / Chained to your heart: *Moore, Bobby & The Rhythm Aces* / Love reputation: *LaSalle, Denise* / Let's wade in the water: *Shaw, Marlena* / Make sure (you have someone who loves you): *Dells* / What can I do: *Kirby, George* / Lucky boy: *Hutton, Harold* / Later than you think: *Mack, Andy* / Sweeter than the day before: *Valentinos* / If I would marry you: *Montgomery, Tammy* / Is it a sin: *Timiko* / Whole new plan: *Garrett, Joan* / Look at me now: *Callier, Terry* / Strange feeling: *Nash, Johnny* / Mighty good lover: *Vashonettes* / My baby's good: *Williams, Johnny* / Sometimes: *Little Milton* / Can't you hear the beat: *Carltons* / I can't stand it: *Seminoles* / I just kept on dancing: *Banks, Doug* / Pay back: *James, Etta* / Pain: *Collier, Mitty* / Landslide: *Clarke, Tony* / Thinkin' about you: *Dells* / Ain't got no problems: *Sunday* / Count me out: *Stewart, Billy*
CD ____ **CDARC 515**
Charly / Jun '91 / Koch

SWEETEST FEELING - THE GOLDEN AGE OF SOUL (4CD Set)
CD Set ____ **CDDIG 7**
Charly / Feb '95 / Koch

SWEETEST HARMONY (25 Vintage Harmony Ensembles)
Breezin' along with the breeze: *Revelers & Ed Smalle* / Whisper song: *California Hummingbirds* / Too busy: *Four Rajahs* / Dear on a night like this: *National Cavaliers Quartet & David Buttolph* / That's my weakness now: *Rhythm Boys & Paul Whiteman Orchestra* / Girl in the little green hat: *Four Musketeers & Mabel Pearl* / At the baby parade: *Harmonians Quartet* / Sweet Jennie Lee: *Big Four* / Dinah: *Cole Brothers* / Oh by jingo: *Three Keys* / Stormy weather: *Three Admirals* / Cuban tango: *Viennese Seven Singing Sisters* / America calling medley: *Carlyle Cousins & Brian Lawrence Quaglino Quartet* / Why don't you practice what you preach: *Boswell Sisters & Victor Young Orchestra* / In the shade of the old apple tree: *Four Aces* / Caravan: *Mills Brothers* / Everybody step: *Three Peters Sisters & Harry Bidgood Rhythm Boys* / Mandy: *Four Modernaires & Paul Whitman Swing Wing Group* / Bidin' my time: *Foursome* / Undecided: *Dandridge Sisters* / Tuxedo junction: *Andrews Sisters & Vic Schoen Orchestra* / Shakespeare in rhythm: *Cavendish Three & Bruce Campell* / Java jive: *Ink Spots* / Breathless: *Merry Macs* / Auf wiedersehn my dear: *Comedy Harmonists & Emil Gerhardt*
CD ____ **CDAJA 5216**
Living Era / Sep '97 / Select

SWEETS FOR MY SWEET
CD ____ **TMPCD 008**
Temple / Jan '95 / BMG

SWING BROTHER SWING (16 Big Band Greats)
Life is a song: *Bennett, Tony & Count Basie Orchestra* / Stormy weather: *Vaughan, Sarah & Billy Eckstine Orchestra* / I'll walk alone: *Kallen, Kitty & Harry James Orchestra* / You do something to me: *Walters, Teddy & Artie Shaw Orchestra* / Gone with the wind: *Johnson, Jay & Stan Kenton Orches-*

tra / Love me or leave me: *Vaughan, Sarah & Dizzy Gillespie Orchestra* / And the angels sing: *Tilton, Martha & Benny Goodman Orchestra* / Jump for joy: *Nance, Ray & Duke Ellington Orchestra* / Chatanooga choo choo: *Modernaires & Glenn Miller Orchestra* / C'est si bon: *Ross, Annie & Tony Crombie Orchestra* / Ain't misbehavin': *Williams, Joe & Count Basie Orchestra* / Taking a chance on love: *Christie, June & Stan Kenton Orchestra* / Goodnight my love: *Fitzgerald, Ella & Benny Goodman Orchestra* / Mack the knife: *Nance, Ray & Duke Ellington Orchestra* / What is this thing called love: *Torme, Mel & Artie Shaw Orchestra* / It happened in Sun Valley: *Modernaires & Glenn Miller Orchestra*
CD **SUMCD 4039**
Summit / Nov '96 / Sound & Media

SWING DE MUSETTE
CD **IMP 047**
IMP / Apr '97 / ADA / Discovery

SWING ERA, THE
CD Set **CDDIG 2**
Charly / Feb '95 / Koch

SWING FOR A CRIME
CD **842623**
EVA / May '94 / ADA / Direct

SWING GIRLS, THE
That old devil called love: *Holiday, Billie* / St Louis Blues: *Holiday, Billie* / Georgia on my mind: *Holiday, Billie* / I hear music: *Holiday, Billie* / Over the rainbow: *Garland, Judy* / Forty second street: *Keeler, Ruby & Dick Powell* / Pistol packin' Mama: *Andrews Sisters & Bing Crosby* / I want to be happy: *Fitzgerald, Ella* / A tisket, a tasket: *Fitzgerald, Ella* / Little white lies: *Fitzgerald, Ella* / Baby won't you please come home: *Fitzgerald, Ella* / Bob White (Watcha gonna swing tonight): *Boswell, Connee & Bing Crosby* / For me and my gal: *Garland, Judy & Gene Kelly* / Rum and coca cola: *Andrews Sisters* / My blue heaven: *Horne, Lena* / Honeysuckle rose: *Horne, Lena* / Lady is a tramp: *Horne, Lena* / What a difference a day made: *Vaughan, Sarah* / September song: *Vaughan, Sarah* / Lover man: *Vaughan, Sarah* / Body and soul: *McRae, Carmen* / Up a lazy river: *Lee, Peggy & Woody Herman* / Fly me to the moon: *Smith, Keely*
CD **ECD 3326**
K-Tel / Mar '97 / K-Tel

SWING GUYS, THE
I haven't time to be a millionaire: *Sinatra, Frank* / Trolley song: *Sinatra, Frank* / Lullaby of broadway: *Sinatra, Frank* / Surrey with a fring on top: *Sinatra, Frank* / Straighten up and fly right: *Cole, Nat 'King'* / It's only a paper moon: *Cole, Nat 'King'* / Embraceable you: *Cole, Nat 'King'* / How deep is the ocean: *Cole, Nat 'King'* / Pretty baby: *Jolson, Al* / Spaniard that blighted my life: *Jolson, Al & Bing Crosby* / Gone fishin': *Armstrong, Louis & Bing Crosby* / Jeepers creepers: *Bennett, Tony* / Life is a song: *Bennett, Tony* / Cottage for sale: *Eckstine, Billy* / That old black magic: *Eckstine, Billy* / Misty: *Eckstine, Billy* / I can't give you anything but love: *Torme, Mel* / I've got the world on a string: *Torme, Mel* / I'm getting sentimental over you: *Torme, Mel* / Say it isn't so: *Crosby, Bing* / Blue skies: *Crosby, Bing* / Cheek to cheek: *Crosby, Bing* / All by myself: *Crosby, Bing* / On the sunny side of the street: *Armstrong, Louis* / Chicago: *Bennett, Tony* / Put it there pal: *Hope, Bob & Bing Crosby*
CD **ECD 3327**
K-Tel / Mar '97 / K-Tel

SWING HITS
CD **DINCD 46**
Dino / Sep '92 / Pinnacle

SWING INTO BOP
CD **TPZ 1028**
Topaz Jazz / Oct '95 / Cadillac / Pinnacle

SWING INTO CHRISTMAS
Cradle in Bethleham: *Washington, Grover Jr.* / Blue Christmas: *Washington, Grover Jr. & Terence Blanchard* / O come all ye faithful (adeste fidelis): *Roberts, Marcus* / Winter wonderland: *Roberts, Marcus* / Christmas time is here: *Blanchard, Terence* / Amazing grace: *Hawkins, Tramaine* / Carols of the bells: *Marsalis, Wynton Septet* / Let it snow, let it snow, let it snow: *Marsalis, Wynton Septet*
CD **4814112**
Sony Jazz / Nov '95 / Sony

SWING, JIVE & DOO WOP - THE COLLECTION
CD **PEPCD 114**
Pollytone / Feb '96 / Nervous / Pollytone

SWING MIX '96
CD **TCD 2831**
Telstar / May '96 / BMG

SWING OUT
I'm coming Virginia: *Berigan, Bunny* / How'm I doin': *Prima, Louis* / Wire brush stomp: *Krupa, Gene* / What's the reason: *Waller, Fats* / Sometimes I'm happy: *Goodman, Benny* / London bridge is falling down: *Basie, Count* / Pennies from heaven: *Prima, Louis* / Panassie stomp: *Basie, Count* / Japanese sandman: *Goodman, Benny* / There'll be some changes made: *Waller, Fats* / Love bug will get you: *Prima, Louis* / Last round up: *Krupa, Gene* / Solo hop: *Miller, Glenn Orchestra* / Strictly jive: *Webb, Chick & His Orchestra* / Flea on a spree: *Powell, Tony & His Orchestra* / Flat foot floogie: *Manone, Wingy & His Orchestra* / Darktown strutters ball: *Dorsey, Jimmy Orchestra* / Keep a-knockin': *Jordan, Louis & His Tympany Five* / And the angels sing: *Elman, Ziggy & His Orchestra* / Don't you miss your baby: *Basie, Count* / Swinging 'em down: *Jenkins, Freddie & Harlem 7* / Miss Otis regrets: *Lunceford, Jimmie & His Orchestra* / Dusk in upper sandusky: *Dorsey, Jimmy Orchestra* / In a little spanish town: *Miller, Glenn Orchestra*
CD **300422**
Hallmark / Jul '96 / Carlton

SWING OUT...SISTERS
Mad about the boy: *Washington, Dinah* / My baby just cares for me: *Simone, Nina* / You're no good: *Everett, Betty* / Tisket-a-tasket: *Fitzgerald, Ella* / Gentleman friend: *Vaughan, Sarah* / God bless the child: *Holiday, Billie* / Release me: *Little Esther* / My heart belongs to Daddy: *Fitzgerald, Ella* / Our love is here to stay: *Washington, Dinah* / Summertime: *Holiday, Billie* / Sometimes I feel like a Motherless child: *Vaughan, Sarah* / I ain't got no, I got life: *Simone, Nina* / Getting mighty crowded: *Everett, Betty* / What a difference a day makes: *Vaughan, Sarah* / Smoke gets in your eyes: *Washington, Dinah* / That ole devil called love again: *Everett, Betty*
CD **SUMCD 4026**
Summit / Nov '96 / Sound & Media

SWING PARTY
CD **ENTCD 209**
Entertainers / '89 / Target/BMG

SWING TIME
CD **CWNCD 2007**
Javelin / Jun '95 / Henry Hadaway / THE

SWING TIME (4CD Set)
Night is young and you're so beautiful: *Sinatra, Frank* / Indian love ca; ll: *McDonald, Jeanette* / Moonlight serenade: *Miller, Glenn* / Serenade in blue: *Miller, Glenn* / String of pearls: *Miller, Glenn* / Moon came up with a bright idea: *Crosby, Bing & Peggy Lee* / My man (Mon homme): *Fitzgerald, Ella* / I'm confessin' (That I love you): *Fitzgerald, Ella* / Stardust: *Sinatra, Frank* / Without a song: *Sinatra, Frank* / Polka dots and moonbeams: *Sinatra, Frank* / There will never be another you: *Cole, Nat 'King'* / Mona Lisa: *Cole, Nat 'King'* / My funny valentine: *Cole, Nat 'King'* / Unforgettable: *Cole, Nat 'King'* / Just you, just me: *Cole, Nat 'King'* / On a slow boat to China: *Haymes, Dick* / Cheek to cheek: *Haymes, Dick* / Elmer's tune: *Fields, Shep* / Moonlight bay: *Crosby, Bing & Gary Crosby* / If I didn't care: *Ink Spots* / I've heard that song before: *James, Harry* / You made me love you: *Garland, Judy* / Best things in life are free: *Allyson, June & Peter Lawford* / Thanks for the memory: *Hope, Bob & Shirley Ross* / Zing went the strings of my heart: *Garland, Judy* / Route 66: *Cole, Nat 'King'* / You're the cream in my coffee: *Cole, Nat 'King'* / Too marvellous for words: *Cole, Nat 'King'* / When you're smiling (The whole world smiles with you): *Cole, Nat 'King'* / Fools rush in: *Sinatra, Frank* / Sunshine of your smile: *Sinatra, Frank* / How about you: *Sinatra, Frank* / I'll be seeing you: *Sinatra, Frank* / Into each life some rain must fall: *Fitzgerald, Ella & The Ink Spots* / In the mood: *Miller, Glenn* / Chattanooga choo choo: *Miller, Glenn* / Friendship: *Garland, Judy & Johnny Mercer* / Opus No.1: *Dorsey, Tommy* / Shine: *Crosby, Bing & The Mills Brothers* / Macpherson is rehearsin' (To swing): *Fitzgerald, Ella* / Taking a chance on love: *Fitzgerald, Ella* / Darktown strutters' ball: *Fitzgerald, Ella* / Take the "A" train: *Ellington, Duke* / In a moment of weakness: *Powell, Dick* / Zing a little zong: *Crosby, Bing & Jane Wyman* / Ida, sweet as apple cider: *Mills Brothers* / Civilization (Bongo, bongo, bongo): *Andrews Sisters & Danny Kaye* / Little Miss Broadway
: *Temple, Shirley & George Murphy* / You were never lovelier: *Astaire, Fred* / Connecticut: *Garland, Judy & Bing Crosby* / I haven't got time to be a millionaire: *Sinatra, Frank* / Straighten up and fly right: *Cole, Nat 'King'* / Pretty baby: *Jolson, Al* / Gone fishin': *Armstrong, Louis & Bing Crosby* / Jeepers creepers: *Bennett, Tony* / Cottage for sale: *Eckstine, Billy* / It's only a paper moon: *Cole, Nat 'King'* / I can't give you anything but love: *Torme, Mel* / Trolley song: *Sinatra, Frank* / Say it isn't so: *Crosby, Bing* / On the sunny side of the street: *Armstrong, Louis* / I've got the world on a string: *Torme, Mel* / That old black magic: *Eckstine, Billy* / Embraceable you: *Cole, Nat 'King'* / Chicago: *Bennett, Tony* / Spaniard that blighted my life: *Jolson, Al & Bing Crosby* / Lullaby of Broadway: *Sinatra, Frank* / How deep is the ocean: *Cole, Nat 'King'* / Blue skies: *Crosby, Bing* / I'm getting sentimental over you: *Torme, Mel* / Misty: *Eckstine, Billy* / Put it there pal: *Hope, Bob & Bing Crosby* / Life is song: *Bennett, Tony* / All by myself: *Crosby, Bing* / Surrey with a fring on top: *Sinatra, Frank* / That old devil called love: *Holiday, Billie* / St Louis blues: *Holiday, Billie* / Georgia on my mind: *Holiday, Billie* / I hear music: *Holiday, Billie* / Over the rainbow: *Garland, Judy* / Forty second street: *Keeler, Ruby & Dick Powell* / Pistol packin' Mama: *Andrews Sisters & Bing Crosby* / I want to be happy: *Fitzgerald, Ella* / A tisket, a tasket: *Fitzgerald, Ella* / Little white lies: *Fitzgerald, Ella* / Bob White (Watcha gonna swing tonight): *Boswell, Connee & Bing Crosby* / For me and my gal: *Garland, Judy & Gene Kelly* / Rum and coca cola: *Andrews Sisters* / My blue heaven: *Horne, Lena* / Lady is a tramp: *Horne, Lena* / Honeysuckle rose: *Horne, Lena* / What a difference a day made: *Vaughan, Sarah* / September song: *Vaughan, Sarah* / Lover man: *Vaughan, Sarah* / Body and soul: *McRae, Carmen* / C'est si bon: *Ross, Annie* / Up a lazy river: *Lee, Peggy & Woody Herman* / Fly me to the moon: *Smith, Keely* / Baby won't you please come home: *Fitzgerald, Ella* / Somebody loves me: *Lee, Peggy*
CD Set **ECD 3325**
K-Tel / Mar '97 / K-Tel

SWING TRUMPET KINGS (2CD Set)
CD Set **5332632**
Verve / Feb '97 / PolyGram

SWING WAS OUR BUSINESS
St. Louis blues / Don't try your jive on me / Ridin' high / Spring fever / Frankie and Johnny / How'm I doin / China boy / Sing sing sing / Calling all keys / Chopsticks / Dedication / Get hot / Mozelton / Fate let's go / Ol' man river / Sheik of araby / Archer street drag / Patty cake patty cake / There's a plenty / Yankee doodle plays fugue / Hot lips
CD **RAJCD 859**
Empress / Oct '95 / Koch

SWINGIN' 'ROUND THE CLOCK: NEW YEAR'S EVE 1944
CD **VJCD 1050**
Vintage Jazz Classics / Feb '94 / ADA / Cadillac / CM / Direct

SWINGIN' THE CLASSICS
March of the toys: *Dorsey, Tommy* / Prelude in c# minor: *Dorsey, Tommy* / Liebestraum: *Cole, Nat 'King' Trio* / Wearing of the green: *Berigan, Bunny* / Moon love: *Miller, Glenn & Ray Eberle* / Russian sailors dance: *Crosby, Bob* / Barcarolle: *Barnet, Charlie* / Anitra's dance: *Teagarden, Jack* / Old black Joe: *James, Harry* / ELegy: *Spivak, Charlie* / Song of India: *Dorsey, Tommy* / Finiculi finicula: *Teagarden, Jack* / Blue danube: *Cole, Nat 'King' Trio* / Spanish kick: *Barnet, Charlie* / Anvil chorus: *Beneke, Tex*
CD **VN 1010**
Viper's Nest / Feb '97 / ADA / Cadillac / Direct / Jazz Music

SWINGING 60'S
CD **MATCD 210**
Castle / Dec '92 / BMG

SWINGING AT THE SAVOY
CD **158442**
Jazz Archives / Mar '96 / Discovery

SWINGING GROOVES FROM 20 PHONTASTIC YEARS
CD **PHONTCD 9315**
Phontastic / Nov '95 / Cadillac / Jazz Music / Wellard

SWINGING THE BLUES
Swingin' the blues: *Basie, Count* / Jelly roll blues: *Berigan, Bunny* / Just blues: *Connie's Inn Orchestra* / Dogtown blues: *Crosby, Bob* / Savoy blues: *Crosby, Bob* / Dippermouth blues: *Dorsey, Jimmy & Louis Armstrong* / Tin roof blues: *Dorsey, Tommy* / St. Louis blues: *Dorsey Brothers* / Bundle of blues: *Ellington, Duke* / Roll 'em: *Goodman, Benny* / Memphis blues: *Henderson, Fletcher* / At the woodchoppers' ball: *Herman, Woody* / Sweet sorrow blues: *Hughes, Spike* / That too, do: *Moten, Bennie* / Hot and anxious: *Redman, Don* / New call of the freaks: *Russell, Luis* / Blues: *Shaw, Artie* / Ridin' but walkin': *Waller, Fats*
CD **CDAJA 5088**
Living Era / Oct '91 / Select

SWINGING THE BLUES (1931-1939)
CD **DOCD 5354**
Document / Jun '95 / ADA / Hot Shot / Jazz Music

SWINGING THE SIXTIES
Ticket to ride / Cracklin' Rosie / She loves you / Bridge over troubled water / Michelle / Woodstock / Spinning wheel / Norweigan wood / In the ghetto / Yesterday / Both sides now / Can't buy me love / Little green apples / Eleanor Rigby / Without her / All you need is love / Your song / Strawberry fields forever / Suzanne / Hard days night / Anna / All my loving / Didn't we
CD **303882**
Hallmark / Jul '97 / Carlton

SWISS BLUES AUTHORITY
CD **LAKE 2028**
Lakeside / Aug '95 / TKO Magnum

SWITCHED ON COUNTRY (50 Non-Stop Country Hits)
Hello I love you / Sundown / Woman, beautiful woman / Ruby, don't take your love to town / Gentle on my mind / Jolene / Let your love flow / Rhinestone cowboy / Oh, lonesome me / Half the way / If I said you had a beautiful body / Detroit city / Down the mississippi / Some days are diamonds / Slow hand / I don't wanna play house / Your cheatin' heart / Listen to the radio / You never gave up on me / Always on my mind / Love me tender / Honey / Sweetest thing / Only love / Annie's song / Me and Bobby McGee / Help me make it through the night / When you were sweet sixteen / Love hurts / You needed me / Blue eyes crying / I will always love you / Wolverton mountain / Coward of the county / Some broken hearts never mend / Take me home country roads / All I ever need is you / Heaven is my woman's love / You asked me to / Before the next teardrop falls / Banks of the Ohio / If you love me let me know / You're my best friend / I recall a gypsy woman / Shelter of your eyes / Silver threads and golden needles / Honey come back / Most beautiful girl / Have I told you lately that I love you
CD **CD 6071**
Music / Apr '97 / Target/BMG

SWITCHED ON COUNTRY: THE RANCH HANDS
CD **GRF 214**
Tring / Mar '93 / Tring

SWITCHED ON SWING
Le cage aux folles / Caravan / Best of times / Harlem nocturne / Bandstand boogie / Puttin' on the ritz / Boogie woogie / Satin doll / Tuxedo junction / Chameleon days / La cage aux folles / Hooked on dixie / Hooked on swing / Save the last dance for me / Hooked on the roaring 20's / Swingin' the classics / Swing with bing
CD **EMPRCD 519**
Emporio / Jul '94 / Disc

SWITZERLAND - YODELS OF APPENZELL
CD **AUD 8026**
Unesco / Jun '91 / ADA / Harmonia Mundi

SYDE TRIPS VOL.1
CD **WHCD 002**
Wooden Hill / Mar '97 / Wooden Hill

SYMPATHY IN CHAOS
13th floor spectrum: *VVX* / Zentrical wheel: *Mantaray* / Floating through the air on gossamer wings: *Liquid Dub Connection* / Geomantik: *Prana* / Monkey on a cloud: *TRipitaka* / Pizza: *Ju Ju Space Jazz* / Vice: *Massimo Vivona* / Atmosphere: *Anand* / Space is the place: *Irresistable Force*
CD **MPCD 7**
Matsuri / Jul '97 / Amato Disco / SRD

SYMPHONIC BOSSA NOVA
CD **4509908772**
WEA / Feb '95 / Warner Music

SYNCHROMIX (Electronic Dance Mixes)
Wannabe / Discotheque / Step by step / Return of the mack / Don't cry for me Argentina / I shot the sheriff / Don't let go (love) / Space jam / Ooh aah, just a little bit / Cold rock a party / Virtual insanity / Tonight is the night
CD **SMCD 71**
Start / Jun '97 / Disc

SYNEWAVE NEW YORK VOL.1
CD **KICKCD 27**
Kickin' / Sep '95 / Prime / SRD

SYNEWAVE NEW YORK VOL.2
CD **KICKCD 37**
Kickin' / May '96 / Prime / SRD

SYNOPTICS
CD **EFA 003162**
Reflective / May '95 / RTM/Disc / SRD

SYNTHESISER ALBUM, THE
Chariots of fire / Oxygene / Love theme from Midnight Express / Miami vice / Autobahn / Axel F / Magic fly / Popcorn / Metropolis / Mammagamma / Aurora / I hear you now / Equinoxe / Forbidden colours / Lucifer / Das madchen auf der treppe / Chi mai / Song for Guy
CD **MCCD 061**
Music Club / Mar '92 / Disc / THE

SYNTHESISER COLLECTION (2CD Set)
CD Set **DEMPCD 012**
Emporio / Mar '96 / Disc

SYNTHESIZER CLASSICS
Theme from Antarctica / Eve of war / Equinoxe part 5 / Tubular bells / Autobahn / Aurora / Magnetic fields part 2 / Theme from 'Rain Man' / Tubbs and Valerie / To the unknown man / Electric salsa / Model / Rockit / Chariots of fire / Living on video / I'll find my way home
CD **EMPRCD 650**
Emporio / Oct '96 / Disc

SYNTHESIZER DREAMS
Fields of gold / Father figure / Another day in paradise / Forever love / Nikita / Words / Moments in love / These dreams / Broken wings / These are the days of our lives / Diamonds and pearls / No more I love you's / Shine on you crazy diamond / Groovy kind of love / Crockett's theme / Father and son / Merry Christmas Mr Lawrence / Drive
CD **CDVIP 150**
Virgin VIP / Apr '97 / EMI

SYNTHESIZER GOLD
CD **HRCD 8052**
Disky / Apr '94 / Disky / THE

SYNTHESIZER HITS
CD ____ 55137
Laserlight / Oct '95 / Target/BMG

SYNTHESIZER HITS (4CD Set)
CD Set ____ MBSCD 446
Castle / Nov '95 / BMG

SYNTHESIZER HITS (2CD Set)
One night in Bangkok / Pop musik / Private dancer / Purple rain / California dreamin' / Delta lady / Love shack / Blue Monday / Sound of silence / Who's that girl / Smooth operator / Tubular bells / Vienna / Walk like an Egyptian / Rhythm is a dancer / Popcorn / One night in heaven / Never gonna give you up / We are the champions / Venus / Another day in paradise / Bohemian rhapsody / Justify my love / Crazy for you / In the air tonight / I want your sex / Eleanor Rigby / Just the way you are / Can't help falling in love / Locomotion / Beat it / Everything I do (I do it for you) / Hot in the city / I will always love you / Memories / Most beautiful girl in the world / Radio gaga / Yellow submarine
CD Set ____ MUCD 9510
Musketeer / May '96 / Disc

SYNTHESIZER HITS (Purple Rain)
CD ____ MACCD 309
Autograph / Aug '96 / BMG

SYNTHESIZER HITS (Tubular Bells)
CD ____ MACCD 308
Autograph / Aug '96 / BMG

SYNTHETIC PLEASURES VOL.1
CD ____ MM 800462
Moonshine / Sep '96 / Mo's Music Machine / Prime / RTM/Disc

SYNTHETIC PLEASURES VOL.2
CD ____ CAI 20012
Caipirnha / Apr '97 / Cargo

SYRIA: MUEZZINS D'ALEP
CD ____ C 580038
Ocora / Nov '92 / ADA / Harmonia Mundi

T

T IN THE PARK
CD ____ 8287822
CD ____ 8287922
Go Discs / Jul '96 / PolyGram

T IN THE PARK (The Best Of T In The Park 1994-1996/3CD Set)
Do you rememeber the first time: *Pulp* / Shakermaker: *Oasis* / Jump around: *House Of Pain* / Swamp thing: *Grid* / Radio: *Teenage Fanclub* / Word up: *Gun* / Belaruse: *Levellers* / La tristesse durera (scream to a sigh): *Manic Street Preachers* / White love: *One Dove* / Always the last to know: *Del Amitri* / To the end: *Blur* / Good as gold (stupid as mud): *Beautiful South* / Open your heart: *M-People* / Wake up Boo: *Boo Radleys* / Can't get out of bed: *Charlatans* / Broken stones: *Weller, Paul* / Strange ones: *Supergrass* / Stutter: *Elastica* / Twisted and bent: *Trash Can Sinatras* / Charity: *Skunk Anansie* / Confide in me: *Minogue, Kylie* / Rez: *Underworld* / Poison: *Prodigy* / High and dry: *Radiohead* / Alright: *Cast* / Staying out for the Summer: *Dodgy* / Release the pressure: *Leftfield* / Into my world: *Audioweb* / Accelerate: *Drugstore* / Jesus Christ: *Longpigs* / Carnival: *Cardigans* / Tishbite: *Cocteau Twins* / Life is sweet: *Chemical Brothers*
CD Set ____ 8287762
Go Discs / Jul '96 / PolyGram

T-BIRD PARTY
CD ____ EFA 115962
Crypt / Dec '95 / Shellshock/Disc

TAARAB MUSIC OF ZANZIBAR VOL.3
Mapenzi kiapo / Wembe / Mwana mtifu / Mbaya kufanya jema / Sitakila wama / Juwa toka / Sema / Wambea / Machozi yananimwaika / Mpeni pole / Pakacha
CD ____ CDORBD 040
Globestyle / Jul '90 / Pinnacle

TAHITI: BELLE EPOQUE VOL.3
CD ____ S 65811
Manuiti / Nov '92 / Harmonia Mundi

TAHITI: SONGS OF THE ATOLLS & ISLANDS
CD ____ S 65816CD
Manuiti / Aug '94 / Harmonia Mundi

TAJIK MUSIC OF BADAKHSHAN
CD ____ AUD 0082212
Auvidis/Ethnic / Dec '93 / ADA / Harmonia Mundi

TAKE A BREAK
Search for the hero: *M-People* / Show me heaven: *McKee, Maria* / I just want to make love to you: *James, Etta* / Let there be love: *Cole, Nat 'King'* / What a wonderful world: *Armstrong, Louis* / Someone to watch over me: *Fitzgerald, Ella* / I put a spell on you: *Simone, Nina* / Fly me to the moon: *Day, Doris* / Angelina: *Prima, Louis* / Don't worry, be happy: *McFerrin, Bobby* / Guaglione: *Prado, Perez* / Reach out I'll be there: *Four Tops* / He ain't heavy, he's my brother: *Hollies* / Days: *Kinks* / Sexual healing: *Gaye, Marvin* / Wonderful life: *Black* / Nothing compares 2 U: *O'Connor, Sinead* / Save the best for last: *Williams, Vanessa* / Breakout: *Swing Out Sister* / Cars: *Numan, Gary* / Addicted to love: *Palmer, Robert* / Professionals: *London Studio Symphony Orchestra*
CD ____ SONYTV 20CD
Sony TV / Oct '96 / Sony

TAKE MY BREATH AWAY VOL.1
Unchained melody / Groovy kind of love: *Royal Philharmonic Orchestra* / Lily was here: *Royal Philharmonic Orchestra* / Everything I do (I do it for you): *Royal Philharmonic Orchestra* / Show me heaven: *Royal Philharmonic Orchestra* / Take a look at me now: *Royal Philharmonic Orchestra* / Take my breath away: *Royal Philharmonic Orchestra* / My girl: *Royal Philharmonic Orchestra* / Time of my life: *Royal Philharmonic Orchestra* / Twin peaks (falling): *Royal Philharmonic Orchestra* / Stand by me: *Royal Philharmonic Orchestra* / Hero (the wind beneath my wings): *Royal Philharmonic Orchestra* / It must have been love: *Royal Philharmonic Orchestra*
CD ____ EMPRCD 597
Emporio / Jun '96 / Disc

TAKE THE FLOOR
CD ____ CDC 014
Ceol / Feb '97 / CM

TAKE THE MUSIDISC JAZZ TRAIN
CD ____ 500772
Musidisc / Sep '96 / Discovery

TAKE THE ROUGH WITH THE SMOOTH
CD ____ EFA 116802
Mzee / May '95 / SRD

TAKIN' A DETOUR VOL.1
Catastrophe theory: *Dilemmas* / Jenny Diablo: *Protectors* / Piece of the action: *Most* / Doin' me in: *Mourning After* / Emily against the world: *Curtains* / You know I need you: *Route 66* / Rackin' my mind: *Clique* / Down the tubestation a midnight: *Persuaders* / Keeps your hand of Felicity: *Blocked* / Threw her a line: *Aardvarks* / Secondry modern Miss: *Now* / Harder I try: *Nuthins* / Airwaves: *Strike* / Mr. Cooper: *Sharp Kiddie* / Wish you were here: *Buzz* / Water: *Knave*
CD ____ DRCD 006
Detour / Jan '96 / Detour / Greyhound

TAKIN' LIBERTIES
CD ____ TTPCD 005
Totem / Nov '94 / Grapevine/PolyGram / THE

TAKING IT EASY (2CD Set)
CD Set ____ DEMPCD 004
Emporio / Mar '96 / Disc

TAKOMA ECLECTIC SAMPLER
World boogie: *White, Bukka* / She's lookin' good: *Canned Heat & Harvey Mandel* / I keep wishing for you: *Sir Douglas Quintet* / Just like an eagle: *Muldaur, Maria* / Cha dooky-doo: *Barron, Ronnie* / Mama blues: *Dr. Ross* / Ferns: *Hand, Cal* / Heart of a country song: *Maddox, Rose* / I'm shakin': *Thompson, Ron & The Resistors* / Wine, women and rock 'n' roll: *Swamp Dogg* / My darlin' New Orleans: *Cuccia, Ron* / Tennessee rock 'n' roll: *Winski, Colin* / Crossfire: *Davis, Spencer* / Your friends: *Bloomfield, Mike* / Indian-Pacific: *Fahey, John* / Last days of the suicide kid: *Bukowski, Charles* / Washington Post march: *Santa Monica Pier Merry-Go-Round*
CD ____ CDTAK 8904
Takoma / Jul '97 / ADA / Pinnacle

TALE OF 3 CITIES, A
CD ____ SOS 007CD
North South / Oct '96 / Pinnacle

TALE OF ALE, THE
CD ____ FRCD 23
Free Reed / Nov '93 / ADA / CM / Direct

TALES OF THE UNEXPECTED
CD ____ RFCD 001
Rainforest / Jun '95 / Essential/BMG / Prime / SRD

TALK ME DADDY (Anthology Of Women Singers From Gothic)
CD ____ FLYCD 37
Flyright / Oct '91 / Hot Shot / Jazz Music / Wellard

TALKIN' JAZZ VOL.1
Hip walk: *Herbolzheimer, Peter* / See you later: *Grauer, Joanne* / New morning: *Winter, Kitty* / Join us: *Reith, Dieter* / Someday: *Duke, George* / Upa neguinho: *Lobo, Edo* / My soul: *Duke, George* / Sconsolato: *Murphy, Mark* / Carmell's black forest waltz: *Davis, Nathan* / Secret life: *Novi Singers* / All blues: *Ross, Annie & Pony Poindexter* / Colours of excitement: *Francis, Rimona* / Frog child: *Grauer, Joanne*
CD ____ 5188612
Talkin' Loud / Nov '93 / PolyGram

TALKIN' JAZZ VOL.2
Mathar: *Pike, Dave Set* / Take off your shoes to feel the setting sun: *Dauner, Wolfgang* / Love me: *Teupen, Johnny* / Get out of my life woman: *Barry, Dee Dee & The Movements* / Big schlepp: *Pike, Dave Set* / Roll on the left side: *Kiesewetter, Knut Train* / Onkel Joe: *Catch Up* / Wives and lovers: *Reith, Dieter Trio* / Nude: *Velebny, Karel* / Espresso loco: *Boland, Francy* / Cantaloupe Island: *Krog, Karin* / Feel: *Duke, George*
CD ____ 5235292
Talkin' Loud / Sep '94 / PolyGram

TALKIN' JAZZ VOL.3
Yaad: *Jazz Meets India* / Burungkaka tua: *Scott, Tony* / Sakara: *Boland, Clarke* / North beach: *Duke, George* / Stars and rockets: *Thomas, Peter* / Colour: *Lehn, Erwin Orchestra* / Sunshine of your love: *Fitzgerald, Ella* / Things we did today: *London Jazz Quartet* / Un graso de areia: *Boland, Clarke* / Just give me time: *Murphy, Mark* / Little bird: *Bianchi, Elsie Trio* / Waldmachen: *Brom, Gustav* / Suite pour San Remo overture: *Gilson, Jef Nonet* / Big P: *Modern Jazz Group* / Blue dance: *Kovac, Roland* / Model forces gratuliere: *Pauer, Fritz* / First movement: *Evans, Bill*
CD ____ 5535852
Talkin' Loud / Jul '97 / PolyGram

TALKIN' LOUD SAMPLER VOL.1
Young Disciples Theme: *Young Disciples & MC Mello* / Get it: *Steps Ahead* / Mean machine 90: *Jalal* / Step right on: *Young Disciples & Outlaw Posse* / Glide: *Incognito* / Tribal knight: *Ace Of Clubs* / Wild and peaceful: *Bassic* / Little ghetto boy: *Galliano*
CD ____ 8467922
Talkin' Loud / Sep '90 / PolyGram

TALKIN' LOUD SAMPLER VOL.2
Hide and seek: *Urban Species* / Hungry like a baby: *Galliano* / Colibri: *Incognito* / You've got to move: *Omar* / Back to the real world: *K-Creative* / All I have in me: *Young Disciples* / Theme from Marxman: *Marxman* / Qui semme le vente recolte le tempo: *MC Solaar* / Serious love: *Perception* / I commit: *Powell, Bryan* / Take me now: *Payne, Tammy* / Apparently nothin': *Young Disciples* / There's nothing like this: *Omar* / Prince of peace: *Galliano* / Always there: *Incognito*
CD ____ 5159362
Talkin' Loud / Jan '93 / PolyGram

TALKIN' LOUDER
No Government: *Nicolette* / Natural thing: *Reprazent* / Always there: *Incognito* / I've known rivers: *Pine, Courtney* / Mission impossible: *United Future Organisation* / Religion and politics: *Urban Species & Terry Callier* / Hanging by a thread: *Lee, Shawn* / Chemical imbalance: *Kendra, Karime* / Some came: *Galliano* / What's my name: *Native Sol*
CD ____ 5325932
Talkin' Loud / May '96 / PolyGram

TALKING AND PREACHING TROMBONES
CD ____ 158862
Jazz Archives / Apr '97 / Discovery

TALKING BLUES
CD ____ LG 21067
Lagoon / May '93 / Grapevine/PolyGram

TALKING SPIRITS (Native American Peublo Music)
CD ____ CDT 126
Topic / Apr '93 / ADA / CM / Direct

TANGO
Jealousy: *Geraldo's Gaucho Tango Orchestra* / There's heaven in your eyes: *La Plata Tango Band* / Marushka: *Sesta, Don Gaucho Tango Band* / From a kiss springs happiness: *La Plata Tango Band* / Madame, you're lovely: *Mantovani & His Tipica Orchestra* / Tangled tangos No. 1 (part 1): *Rinaldo, Don & His Tango Orchestra* / Dolores: *Geraldo & His Gaucho Tango Orchestra* / Spider of the night: *Mantovani & His Tipica Orchestra* / Summer evening in Santa Cruz: *Silvester, Victor & His Ballroom Orchestra* / I could be happy with you: *Geraldo's Gaucho Tango Orchestra* / Dear madam: *Silvester, Victor & His Ballroom Orchestra* / Te quiero dijiste: *Geraldo & His Gaucho Tango Orchestra* / Tangled tangos No. 1 (part 2): *Rinaldo, Don & His Tango Orchestra* / At the balalaika: *Geraldo & His Orchestra* / Blue sky: *Mantovani & His Tipica Orchestra* / If the world were mine: *Geraldo & His Orchestra* / South of the border (Down Mexico way): *Harris, Jack & His Orchestra* / El pescador: *Loss, Joe Band* / Isle of Capri: *Geraldo & His Gaucho Tango Orchestra* / Serenade in the night: *Mantovani & His Tipica Orchestra* / Flowers I may not offer: *La Plata Tango Band* / Lamento gitano: *Loss, Joe Band*
CD ____ PASTCD 9752
Flapper / Jan '92 / Pinnacle

TANGO
CD ____ CDHOT 624
Charly / Jul '97 / Koch

TANGO AND MAMBO CALIENTE (2CD Set)
CD Set ____ R2CD 4021
Deja Vu / Jan '96 / THE

TANGO ARGENTINO
Vuelo al sur / Ventanita florida / Voy cantando tangos por el mundo / Sur / Volver / Tango-tango / Yuyo verde / Los argentinos / Comos dos extranos / Loca bohemia / Buenos aires conoce / Los suenos / Maipo / La vida es Linda, pibe / Milonga del tartamundo / Corrientes arriba / Tango del eco / Ausencias / Adios arrabal / Oblivion / Tal vez no tenga fin / Como abrazado a un rencor / Typical one
CD ____ MCCD 096
Music Club / Mar '93 / Disc / THE

TANGO LADIES
CD ____ HQCD 34
Harlequin / Feb '94 / Hot Shot / Jazz Music / Swift / Wellard

TANGO LADIES 1923-1954
CD ____ HQCD 52
Harlequin / Jun '95 / Hot Shot / Jazz Music / Swift / Wellard

TANGO ONLY
Delusion / El velo azul / A media luz / El choclo / Bombonicito / El flete / Uno / Que falte que me haces / Asi / Andre de sepato novo / Yo te canto / Beunos Aires / Pecho helado / Con mil amores / Caminito / Alma / Tengo cuidado / Historia di un amor / Maula / Tango bolero / Feline
CD ____ DC 880562
Disky / May '97 / Disky / THE

TANGOS PARA AFICIONADOS VOL.2 (The 1950s)
CD ____ PHONTCD 7582
Phontastic / Jun '94 / Cadillac / Jazz Music / Wellard

TANTRANCE VOL.1 (A Trip To Psychedelic Trance/2CD Set)
Mahadeva: *Astral Projection* / Robostyx: *Transwave* / Let's turn on: *Doof* / Powergen: *Astral Projection* / Le lotus bleu: *Total Eclipse* / Vicious circles: *Poltergeist* / Pulseman vs. Sineman: *Ninjahead* / Guardian angel: *Juno Reactor* / Telepathy: *Infinity Project* / Planet Sex: *Garnier, Laurent* / Flouro neuro sponge: *Hallucinogen* / Dig a jig: *Baba G* / Stud stunners: *Bassline Baby* / Scarab: *Prana*
CD Set ____ 08938582
Subterranean / Apr '96 / Koch / Plastic Head

TANTRANCE VOL.2 (A Trip To Psychedelic Trance/2CD Set)
Rotorblade: *Juno Reactor* / Jack in the box: *Man With No Name* / Rezwalker: *Transwave* / Fuel on: *Kox Box* / Democracy: *Killing Joke* / Microdive: *Etnica* / Kalki's coming: *Astralasia* / Spiritual transgression: *Encens* / Entropy: *Satori* / Morphic resonance: *Cosmosis* / One love: *Electric Universe* / Enlightened Evolution: *Astral Projection* / Paranormal activity: *Phreaky* / Camel: *In Door* / Forbidden: *Disco Volante* / Earth: *Prana* / Ring of fire: *Green Nuns Of The Revolution* / Trip tonite: *Etnica* / Monzoon: *Elysium*
CD Set ____ SPV 08947032
Subterranean / Aug '96 / Koch / Plastic Head

TANTRANCE VOL.3 (2CD Set)
Trommelmaschine: *Der Dritte Raum* / Narcotic influence: *Empirion* / Furnace: *Total Eclipse* / Satellite: *Moon & The Sun* / Astral voyage: *Electric Universe* / Sundown: *Overlords* / Hear the air: *Brainman* / Kicking test: *Antidote* / Kage: *Ree K* / Nobody: *Psyko Disko* / Alien love song: *Astralasia* / Second room: *X-Dream* / Slick witch: *Slinky Wizard* / Overload: *MFG* / Soothsayer: *Hallucinogen* / Pale: *Semsis* / Back to Earth: *Satori* / Freak show: *Cydonia* / Celtic alchemy: *Spectral* / Jana: *Killing Joke* / Mr. Redeemer: *Zodiac Youth*
CD Set ____ DCD 08947362
Subterranean / May '97 / Koch / Plastic Head

TANZANIA SOUND
CD ____ OMCD 018
Original Music / May '93 / Jet Star / SRD

TAPPAN ZEE IS 20 (The Best Of Tappan Zee)
King Tut: *Colby, Mark* / Changes: *Harris, Allen Band* / Good morning: *Longmire, Wilbert* / Virginia Sunday: *Tee, Richard* / Watermelon man: *Santamaria, Mongo* / Song for my daughter: *Colby, Mark* / Winding river: *James, Bob & Earl Klugh* / El Mayorazgo: *Brackeen, Jo Anne* / Scat talk: *Colby, Mark* / Now: *Tee, Richard* / Hawkeye: *Longmire, Wilbert* / Carmel tea: *Brackeen, Jo Anne* / Tappan Zee: *James, Bob*
CD ____ RENCD 121
Renaissance Collector Series / Mar '97 / BMG

TARANTINO CONNECTION, THE
Misirlou: *Dale, Dick & His Del-Tones* / Dark night: *Blasters* / Little green bag: *Baker, George Selection* / Graceland: *Sexton, Charlie* / Girl you'll be a woman soon: *Urge Overkill* / Waiting for the miracle: *Cohen, Leonard* / Little bitty tear: *Ives, Burl* / Stuck in the middle with you: *Stealer's Wheel* / you never can tell: *Berry, Chuck* / Love is: *Palmer, Robert* / Sweet Jane: *Cowboy Junkies* / Six blade knife: *Dire Straits* / Foolish hearts: *Mavericks* / Vertigo: *Combustible Edison*
CD ____ MCD 80325
MCA / Oct '96 / BMG

TARTAN DISC, THE (Scotland The Brave)
CD CDITV 480
Scotdisc / Jul '89 / Conifer/BMG / Duncans / Ross

TASTE OF 3RD STONE RECORDS VOL.1, A
Sooner or later: *State Of Grace* / Smile: *State Of Grace* / Deep blue breath: *AR Kane* / I know: *Bark Psychosis* / So cold: *Popguns* / Someone to dream of: *Popguns* / Basking: *Mali Rain* / Callow hill 508am: *Mali Rain* / Alaska pt.1: *Transambient Communications* / River: *Transambient Communications* / California nocturne: *EAR* / Ecstasy in slow motion: *Spacemen 3* / Revolution: *Spacemen 3* / Paddington Bear: *Goober Patrol* / Grabbers: *Goober Patrol*
CD STONE 021CD
3rd Stone / Sep '95 / Plastic Head / Vital

TASTE OF 3RD STONE RECORDS VOL.2, A
All life long: *Insides* / Sweetside silver night: *No Man* / Fancy swim: *Reverberation* / In the presence of angels: *Mali Rain* / V5: *Transambient Communications* / Crushed: *Popguns* / Stalker: *Olympia Hurricanes* / Hello: *State Of Grace* / Cool as moons: *AR Kane* / Murder city: *Bark Psychosis* / It won't be long: *Chapterhouse* / Friendly: *Vanilla Pod* / Downward mobility: *Goober Patrol* / I want you right now: *Spacemen 3* / Little angel: *Colorsound* / Ring modulator: *EAR* / Stairs leading up: *Octal* / Forever alien: *Spectrum*
CD STONE 029CD
3rd Stone / May '97 / Plastic Head / Vital

TASTE OF ASIA, A
CD NI 7025
Nimbus / Mar '95 / Nimbus

TASTE OF BRAZIL, A
Lambadas medley / Mexa mexa / Lambadie lambadia / Lambada da Americana / Lambadas medley / Te futaco / Memina moca / Quero ser seu grande amor / Mata papi (Ja que e gostoso deixa) / Lambadas medley / Por cima de mim / Amor de piranha / Do jeito que voce vier
CD QED 080
Tring / Nov '96 / Tring

TASTE OF IRELAND, A (2CD Set)
CD Set DEMPCD 009
Emporio / Mar '96 / Disc

TASTE OF IRELAND, A
CD MACCD 315
Autograph / Aug '96 / BMG

TASTE OF IRELAND, A (Irish Traditional Music)
CD NI 7035
Nimbus / Feb '97 / Nimbus

TASTE OF OLD IRELAND, A
CD HCD 115
GTD / Apr '95 / ADA / Else

TASTE OF THE INDESTRUCTIBLE BEAT OF SOWETO, A
Kwa volondiya / Mazuzu / Heyi wena / Kulukhuni / Thuto kelefa / Madyisa mbitsi / Ngayivuye / Jabula mfana / Asambeni sonke / Mubi umakhelwane / Nomacala / Emandulu
CD CDEWV 32
Virgin / Nov '93 / EMI

TASTE OF TRANSIENT, A
CD TRANR 606CD
Transient / Oct '96 / Prime / SRD / Total/BMG

TASTE TEST NO.1
CD NAR 045CD
New Alliance / Sep '90 / Plastic Head

TASTER
CD PRKCD 37
Park / Jul '97 / Pinnacle

TEACHING YOU NO FEAR
CD BHR 015CD
Burning Heart / Feb '95 / Plastic Head

TEARDROPS, LOVE, HEARTBREAK
CD DCD 5302
Disky / Nov '93 / Disky / THE

TECHNIQUES VAULT
CD VPCD 2040
VP / Apr '96 / Greensleeves / Jet Star / Total/BMG

TECHNO BALLADS VOL.2 (2CD Set)
Hymn: *Moby* / Crazy: *Global Cee* / Summer spent: *Beaumont Hannant* / Happy shades: *Full Moon Fashions* / Codeine bullets: *Ryman, John* / Time flies: *Vegas Soul* / Clones: *Spicelab* / Surrender: *Interloper* / Seing sense: *7th Plain* / Time is an illusion: *World Of Chocolate* / 39: *Full Moon Fashions* / Mind colours: *Beaumont Hannant* / Forever: *Auto Union* / Reich: *LA Synthesis* / Global Zero: *Auto Union* / Existential: *Tribes Of Krom* / Blau: *Marzipan & Mustard* / Vibes of style: *Tribes Of Krom* / Mhahalonovis: *Osgood, Tim* / Philadelphia experiment: *Headman* / Laut: *Marzipan & Mustard* / Jazzzy H: *Elexir Vitae*
CD MILL 043CD
Millenium / Jul '97 / Plastic Head / Prime / SRD

TECHNO CELEBRATION
CD 7702395
Omnisonus / Apr '97 / Cargo

TECHNO CLASSICS (3CD Set)
Pull over: *Speedy J* / Crowd control: *Tranzformer* / OK alright: *Digital Boy* / BOTTROP: *DJ Hooligan* / Raw: *OTT* / Dukkha: *Precious* / Bonzai channel: *Thunderball* / Magic feet: *Dunn, Mike* / Work that motherfucker: *Poindexter, Steve* / God of abraham: *MNO* / Who is Elvis: *Phenomania* / Rave alarm: *Khan, Praga* / Sueno Latino (HOG Ocean beats): *Sueno Latino* / Le seigneur des tenebres: *Pleasure Game* / Je n'aime que toi: *Angel Ice* / Cosmotrash: *Trashman* / Fairydust: *Set Up System* / Ballet: *JNJ* / New York Chicago: *Soup* / Wave: *Belgica Wave* / Hablando: *Ramirez & Pizarro* / 100% of dishin' you: *Armando* / Nana: *NUKE featuring Marilyn Mariani* / Animals: *De Ruyter, Yves* / Night in motion: *Cubic 22* / Dark symphony: *Phrentic system* / Soushkin: *Dream Your Dream* / Circus bells: *Armani, Robert* / Altered states: *Trent, Ron* / Orgasmico: *Ramirez* / Schoom: *Dee, Lenny & Darien Kelly* / 99.9: *Koenig Cylinders* / Bountyhunter: *DJ Bountyhunter* / Work it: *Search & Destroy* / El punto final: *Final Analysis* / Rockin' to the rhythm: *Convert* / Insominiac: *DJPC* / F 16: *F 16* / Extrasyn: *RFTR*
CD Set HR 882122
Disky / Jul '97 / Disky / THE

TECHNO CLASSICS VOL.1
CD FRCD 003
Flex / '95 / Jet Star / Plastic Head / SRD

TECHNO CLASSICS VOL.2
CD RSNCD 3
Rising High / Oct '92 / 3mv/Sony

TECHNO DANCE HIGHFLYER
CD 12371
Laserlight / Jun '94 / Target/BMG

TECHNO HEAD VOL.2 (Harder & Faster)
CD REACTCD 035
React / Mar '94 / Arabesque / Prime / Vital

TECHNO HEAD VOL.3 (Out Of Control)
CD REACTCD 051
React / Oct '94 / Arabesque / Prime / Vital

TECHNO HEAD VOL.4 (Sound Wars The Next Generation/2CD Set)
Majik: *Technohead* / Party trance: *DJ Freak* / Paranoid beauty: *Future Viper* / Droppin' bombs: *DJ Fury* / Cocaine: *Technohead* / Intellectual killer: *Nasenbluten* / Kind of visions: *Knight Vision* / Shaftman: *Shaftman* / Pope and the president: *DJ Raffe* / Extreme terror: *DJ Skinhead* / King of the street: *Alec Empire* / Abduction exp: *DJ Freak* / Raw toy: *Lorenz Attractor* / Dubious: *DJ Yubba & DJ Deviant* / Hyper bitch: *Burning Lazy Persons* / Axis: *UVC* / What is your name: *Beatlejuice* / Bullen raus: *Agro* / Incubation: *Somatic Responses* / Flohwalzer: *Dummy* / Voice only: *Smily Slayers* / Imploding head: *Johnny Violent*
CD REACTCDX 098
CD Set REACTCD 098
React / Mar '97 / Arabesque / Prime / Vital

TECHNO HEDZ (20 Firestartin' Techno Anthems)
CD TCD 2823
Telstar / Apr '96 / BMG

TECHNO HYPER DANCE
CD 12611
Laserlight / Oct '95 / Target/BMG

TECHNO MASTERS
Meet your maker: *Dance City* / Groove me: *Jems For Jem* / E-go: *Real Masters* / Turn your love: *Clockhouse Hours* / Feel like I'm falling: *Unlimited Dream Company* / RV theme: *Vee, Ray* / 1am goodnight: *Coma Kid* / Sunburst: *Optic Eye* / Come with me: *Techno Explosion* / Eleanor Rigby: *Lonely people* / Adrenalin: *Jargon* / Dominate: *Flag* / Coda coma: *Yage* / I think I want some more: *Auto-Logic* / I don't owe you: *Smak* / Nightmare: *Psychopaths*
CD 305092
Hallmark / Jun '97 / Carlton

TECHNO NATIONS (A History Of Techno 1992-1996/4CD Set)
CD Set KICKCD 45
Kickin' / Aug '96 / Prime / SRD

TECHNO NATIONS VOL.2
CD KICKCD 9
Kickin' / Apr '94 / Prime / SRD

TECHNO NATIONS VOL.3
CD KICKCD 14
Kickin' / Jan '95 / Prime / SRD

TECHNO NATIONS VOL.4
CD KICKCD 25
Kickin' / Jun '95 / Prime / SRD

TECHNO NATIONS VOL.5
CD KICKCD 34
Kickin' / Mar '96 / Prime / SRD

TECHNO NATIONS VOL.6 (2CD Set)
Dial: *Clark & Lofthouse* / Intensity: *Maney, Ron & Carl Lekebusch* / Eniac: *Octave One* / Conception: *Astrocat & Kenny S.* / Black sea: *Drexciya* / Take control: *Universal addictions Vol.3* / Prewax: *Ratio* / Gruve: *Planetary Assault Systems* / Freeky deeky: *Kosmic Messenger* / Alistairs theme: *Voorn, Orlando* / Squeaky: *Sir Real* / Break down: *Bryant, Akilah* / Relax 2000: *6th Sense Approach* / Encounter: *Outline* / Pimp slave: *Denham, Jay* / Style wars: *Bartz, Richard* / Lights: *Space DJ's* / Sunshower 2: *Pooley, Ian* / Real timez: *Advent* / Curb: *Beltram, Joey*
CD KICKCD 47
Kickin' / Mar '97 / Prime / SRD

TECHNO PHUNK
CD BAZZCD 2
Rumour / Mar '95 / 3mv/Sony / Mo's Music Machine / Pinnacle

TECHNO PLANET
Get down everybody / Holy noise / Dreams of santa anna / Man with the masterplan/ Quadrophonia / Inscrutable/Problem house / Brainwasher/Defcon / Successor/2 hard 2 / Caramba/Tera WAN / It's not a dream/Diabolico / Epilepsa/Epilesia / Bronto beat/Cas stewart / Jesus left the house/Father techno / Dream/Flanger / Rotterdam/High profile / Natural system/Hyper space / Let my people go/In god we trust
CD DC 881062
Disky / Jul '97 / Disky / THE

TECHNO POWERTRAX (15 Extended Hard-Edged Jams)
Groovy beat / Feel the rhythm / Speed freak / Read my lips / Overdrive to the maximum / Ready steady go / Move now (I got a feeling) / Rocking to the music / Trance fiction (parts 1&2) / Movin' on / I can feel the beat / Wolf spirit / Tribal key / Sonic groove / Night and day
CD EMPRCD 621
Emporio / Jun '96 / Disc

TECHNO RAVE
Let's go: *Accelerator* / Club Overdue: *Synchron* / Out of control: *Cosmic Ray* / Hypnotich: *Delirium* / Dominator: *909 Surprise* / Secrets of sexual attraction: *Ministers Of Sex* / Tek-no-body: *Technophobia* / Total recall: *Noise Attack* / Ultra bass: *Q-Inzest & DJ Raw* / Oriental dream: *Alpha X* / Let me outta here: *Elektro-Teknik*
CD QED 125
Tring / Nov '96 / Tring

TECHNO SOUND OF DISTANCE
CD DI 182
Distance / Dec '95 / 3mv/Sony / Prime

TECHNO STATE
Everybody in the place: *Prodigy* / Bouncer: *Kicks Like A Mule* / Running out of time: *Digital Orgasm* / Different strokes: *Isotonik* / Take me away: *Cappella* / Can you feel the passion: *Blue Pearl* / Playing with knives: *Bizarre Inc.* / Frequency: *Altern 8* / Get down: *M-D Emm* / What can you do for me: *Utah Saints* / Are you ready to fly: *Rozalla* / Pure pleasure: *Digital Excitation* / Rave generator: *Tribeka* / Rescue me: *Malone, Debbie* / Uptempo: *Tronikhouse* / Stand up (earthquake): *Rave Nation & Juliette* / UHF: *UHF* / Wicked love: *Oceanic* / Put the hammer down: *Sonic System* / Far out: *Sonz Of A Loop Da Loop Era*
CD JARCD 2
Cookie Jar / Mar '92 / SRD

TECHNO TO THE CORE
Rainbow in the sky: *Elstak, Paul* / Church of house: *Perplexer* / You make me feel so good: *DJ Thoka* / Dancing together: *Critical Mass* / It's gonna be a fine night: *Micado* / Wonderful days: *DJ Charly Lownoise & Mental Theo* / Do what ya like: *Brown, Scott* / Make you dance: *Smooth But Hazardous* / Renegade rewind: *Eko* / Music is ecstasy: *Love Nation & Justin Time* / Take it from the groove: *Midas* / Into the blue: *Moby*
CD CDTOT 36
Jumpin' & Pumpin' / Feb '96 / 3mv/Sony / Mo's Music Machine

TECHNO TRAVEL (2CD Set)
CD Set 702671
Omnisonus / Oct '96 / Cargo

TECHNO TRAX VOL.17 (2CD Set)
CD Set ZYX 810902
ZYX / Jan '97 / ZYX

TECHNO TRAX VOL.18
CD ZYX 811012
ZYX / May '97 / ZYX

TECHNO UNIVERSE
Noise (X-treme sounds) / Bass-X instinct/DJ Fab / 88 to piano/Holy noise / Dope man/ Lenny D versus DJ Paul / Hallelluja/Problem house / Unarmed and dangerous/MC Hughie Babe / Nightmare/Global insert project / Defcon / R 001/Trade mark / Housy hip hop/Rave gang / Total distortion/Spirit of distortion / Nativity/Hardware / Better than better/TNT / Assasin/Rich in paradise / It's time to party/Techno matic
CD DC 881082
Disky / Jul '97 / Disky / THE

TECHNO VISIONS VOL.1
CD CDRAID 510
Rumour / Mar '93 / 3mv/Sony / Mo's Music Machine / Pinnacle

TECHNO VISIONS VOL.2
CD CDRAID 512
Rumour / May '93 / 3mv/Sony / Mo's Music Machine / Pinnacle

TECHNO VOL.1 & 2 (Electronic Dreams)
It is what it is: *Rythim Is Rythim* / Forever and a day: *Baxter, Blake* / Time to express: *Fowlkes, Eddie 'Flashin'* / Electronic dance: *KS Experience* / Share this house: *Members Of The House* / Feel surreal: *A Tongue & D Groove* / Spark: *Hesterley, Mia* / Techno music: *Juan* / Big fun: *Inner City* / Ride 'em boy: *Baxter, Blake* / Sequence 10: *Shakir* / Un, deux, trois: *Idol Making* / Love takes me over: *Area 10* / Aftermath: *Reel By Real* / Stark: *KGB* / Mirror mirror: *MK* / I believe: *Octave One & Lisa Newberry* / Techno por favor: *Infinity* / Elements: *Psyche* / Ritual: *Vice*
CD DIXCD 123
10 / Mar '92 / EMI

TECHNO WORLD
Wave of the future: *Quadrophonia* / Rock sensation: *American force* / Piano junkie: *DJ Caligula* / Feel the rhythm: *DJ Rob* / Starnoise: *Millennium* / Party zone: *Problem House* / Boom boom: *TNT* / Blob: *Defcon* / Hardcore will never die: *Holy Noise* / Let the groove move: *Second wave* / Put your hands in the air: *Unknown* / Sex instructor: *Ultra Sonic* / Mikado: *Zo ro* / Amore: *2 for love*
CD DC 881072
Disky / Jul '97 / Disky / THE

TECHNO ZONE
CD OZONCD 24
Ozone / Mar '92 / SRD

TECHNOLOGICAL ELEMENTS
CD NR 703014
Essential Dance / Jun '96 / RTM/Disc

TECHSTEPPIN'
Zone: *Hydro* / Machines: *DJ Doc Scott* / Check me out: *Ed Rush* / Mach II: *Skyscraper* / Haze: *Rollers Instinct* / Liberty one: *Skyscraper* / Black marbles: *Cronic Crew* / Get stoned: *Limit* / Mutant: *Rollers Instinct* / Headless horseman: *Raw Deal* / Tha bomb shit: *Hydro* / Difference: *Skyscraper*
CD EMFCD 001
Emotif / Apr '96 / SRD / Vital

TEDDY BOY ROCK 'N' ROLL
CD PEPCD 104
Pollytone / Jan '95 / Nervous / Pollytone

TEDDY BOY ROCK 'N' ROLL - 5TH ANNIVERSARY
CD PEPCD 118
Pollytone / Nov '96 / Nervous / Pollytone

TEEN BEAT
Wipeout: *Safaris* / Batman: *Marketts* / Let there be drums: *Nelson, Sandy* / Walk don't run: *Ventures* / Predator: *Billy Joe & The Checkmates* / Red river rock: *Johnny & The Hurricanes* / Let's go: *Routers* / Sleep walk: *Santo & Johnny* / Rebel rouser: *Eddy, Duane* / Teen beat: *Nelson, Sandy* / Pipeline: *Chantays* / Hawaii Five-O: *Ventures* / Reveille rock: *Johnny & The Hurricanes* / Happy organ: *Cortez, Dave 'Baby'* / Forty miles of bad road: *Eddy, Duane* / Raunchy: *Justis, Bill* / Tequila: *Cannon, Ace* / Nut rocker: *B-Bumble & The Stingers*
CD ECD 3058
K-Tel / Jan '95 / K-Tel

TEEN BEAT TEQUILA
CD 12546
Laserlight / Jun '95 / Target/BMG

TEEN BEAT VOL.1
Teen beat: *Nelson, Sandy* / Swanee river hop: *Domino, Fats* / Raunchy: *Freeman, Ernie* / Rumble: *Wray, Link* / Green mosquito: *Tune Rockers* / Poor boy: *Royaltones* / Topsy II: *Cole, Cozy* / So rare: *Dorsey, Jimmy Orchestra* / Tequila: *Champs* / Happy organ: *Cortez, Dave 'Baby'* / Clouds: *Spacemen* / Twitchy: *Hall, Rene* / Guitar boogie shuffle: *Virtues* / Wild bird: *Jive-A-Tones* / Midnighter: *Champs* / Fast freight: *Allens, Arvee* / In the mood: *Fields, Ernie Orchestra* / So what: *Yellow Jackets* / Wild weekend: *Rockin' Rebels* / Torquay: *Fireballs* / Bongo rock: *Epps, Preston* / Walk don't run: *Ventures* / Nut rocker: *B-Bumble & The Stingers* / Wheels: *String-A-Longs* / Bulldog: *Fireballs* / Rockin' crickets: *Hot-Toddys* / Wham: *Mack, Lonnie* / Slumber party: *Van-Dells* / Spunky: *Jenkins, Johnny* / Memphis: *Mack, Lonnie*
CD CDCHD 406
Ace / Sep '93 / Pinnacle

TEEN BEAT VOL.2
Califf boogie: *Teenbeats* / El rancho rock: *Champs* / Mathilda: *String-A-Longs* / Flip flop and bop: *Cramer, Floyd* / Mule train stomp: *Buchanan, Roy* / Manhattan spiritual: *Owen, Reg* / Wiggie wobble: *Cooper, Les* / Ramrod: *Eddy, Duane* / Boo boo stick beat: *Atkins, Chet* / Fickle chicken: *Atmospheres* / Cerveza: *Brown, Boots* / Wild twist: *Roller Coasters* / Blue eagle: *Rivers, Jimmy* / Big jump: *Nelson, Sandy* / Patricia: *Prado, Perez* / Teensville: *Atkins, Chet* / Mardi gras: *Cortez, Dave 'Baby'* / Carioca: *Fireballs* / Rebel rouser: *Eddy, Duane* / Cast your fate to the wind: *Guaraldi, Vince* / Machine gun: *Rip Tides* / Power shift: *Usher, Gary* / Kabalo: *Atmospheres* / Hucklebuck: *Fields, Ernie* / Guitar rhumbo: *Guitar Gable* / Pretty please: *Buchanan, Roy* / Apple knocker: *B-Bumble & The Stingers* / Doin' the horse: *Brooks, Skippy* / Soul twist: *King Curtis &*

The Knoble Knights / Dish rag: *Kendrick, Nat*
CD ______ **CDCHD 522**
Ace / Aug '94 / Pinnacle

TEEN BEAT VOL.3
Quite a party: *Fireballs* / Perfida: *Ventures* / Slop beat: *Teen Beats* / Mau mau: *Wailers* / You can't sit down: *Upchurch, Phil Combo* / Ghost riders in the sky: *Ramrods* / Walking with Mr. Lee: *Allen, Lee & His Band* / Big guitar: *Bradley, Owen Quintet* / Woo-hoo: *Rock-a-Teens* / Stick shift: *Duals* / Velvet waters: *Megatrons* / Moovin' 'n' groovin': *Eddy, Duane* / Ramrod: *Casey, Al* / Pipeline: *Chantays* / Blue jean shuffle: *Johnson, Plas* / Heat: *Rockin' R's* / Wipeout: *Surfaris* / Yellow bird: *Lyman, Arthur* / Baja: *Astronauts* / Twistle: *Troy & The T-Birds* / Back beat: *Rondels* / Hot pastrami: *Dartells* / Brass buttons: *String-A-Longs* / Sumpin' jumpin': *Blackwell, Bumps* / Wolf call: *Dent, Lord & His Invaders* / Too much tequila: *Champs* / Telegraph: *Atmospheres* / I want to know: *Lucas, Buddy* / Jay-Dee's boogie woogie: *Dorsey, Jimmy Orchestra*
CD ______ **CDCHD 602**
Ace / Feb '96 / Pinnacle

TEEN BEAT VOL.4
CD ______ **CDCHD 655**
Ace / Aug '97 / Pinnacle

TEENAGE CRUSH
Sea of love: *Phillips, Phil & The Twilights* / You don't know what you've got: *Donner, Ral* / What in the world's come over you: *Scott, Jack* / Born too late: *Poni-Tails* / Tell Laura I love her: *Peterson, Ray* / Sweet dreams: *Gibson, Don* / It's only make believe: *Twitty, Conway* / Bobby sox to stockings: *Avalon, Frankie* / Sealed with a kiss: *Hyland, Brian* / Pretty blue eyes: *Lawrence, Steve* / Diary: *Sedaka, Neil* / Devil or angel: *Vee, Bobby* / Hold me, thrill me, kiss me: *Carter, Mel* / Close to Cathy: *Clifford, Mike* / Way you look tonight: *Lettermen* / Tragedy: *Fleetwoods* / My heart is an open book: *Dobkins, Carl Jr.* / My special angel: *Helms, Bobby* / It's all in the game: *Edwards, Tommy* / Love me warm and tender: *Anka, Paul* / Teen angel: *Dinning, Mark* / Chances are: *Mathis, Johnny* / Guess who: *Belvin, Jesse* / Take good care of her: *Wade, Adam* / Teenage crush: *Sands, Tommy* / Cry me a river: *London, Julie* / I understand (just how you feel): *G-Clefs*
CD ______ **CDCHD 640**
Ace / Jan '97 / Pinnacle

TEENAGE KICKS
Pretty vacant: *Sex Pistols* / Going underground: *Jam* / My perfect cousin: *Undertones* / Do anything you wanna do: *Eddie & The Hot Rods* / If the kids are united: *Sham 69* / Pump it up: *Costello, Elvis & The Attractions* / No more heroes: *Stranglers* / She's so modern: *Boomtown Rats* / Hit me with your rhythm stick: *Dury, Ian & The Blockheads* / Ever fallen in love: *Buzzcocks* / Working for the Yankee dollar: *Skids* / Turning Japanese: *Vapors* / King rocker: *Generation X* / Germ free adolescents: *X-Ray Spex* / What a waste: *Dury, Ian & The Blockheads* / Is Vic there: *Department S* / Go wild in the country: *Bow Wow Wow* / Eighth day: *O'Connor, Hazel* / Automatic lover: *Vibrators* / Lucky number: *Lovich, Lena* / Rich kids: *Rich Kids* / Start: *Jam* / Teenage kicks: *Undertones* / Hanging on the telephone: *Blondie* / Brass in pocket: *Pretenders* / Airport: *Motors* / Take me, I'm yours: *Squeeze* / Can't stand losing you: *Police* / I got you: *Split Enz* / Pretty in pink: *Psychedelic Furs* / 2-4-6-8 Motorway: *Robinson, Tom* / I want you to want me: *Cheap Trick* / Shake some action: *Flamin' Groovies* / Swords of a thousand men: *Tenpole Tudor* / Back of my hand: *Jags* / My best friend's girl: *Cars* / My Sharona: *Knack* / Time for action: *Secret Affair* / Generals and Majors: *XTC* / Reward: *Teardrop Explodes* / Clean clean: *Buggles* / Roxette: *Dr. Feelgood* / Hey Lord don't ask me questions: *Parker, Graham* / Spanish stroll: *Mink Deville* / Roadrunner: *Richman, Jonathan* / Real wild child: *Iggy Pop*
CD ______ **5253382**
PolyGram TV / Jul '95 / PolyGram

TEENAGE KICKS
CD ______ **L 37806**
Liberation / Jun '97 / Greyhound

TEENAGE LOVE
CD ______ **MACCD 166**
Autograph / Aug '96 / BMG

TEENAGE REPRESSION VOL.1
CD ______ **642041**
EVA / May '94 / ADA / Direct

TEENAGE ROCK 'N' ROLL PARTY (Crazy Kids...Living To A Wild Rock 'n' Roll Beat)
All night long / Old folk's boogie / Slow down / Blue jeans and a boy's shirt / That's alright baby / Sweetheart please don't go / Crying my heart out / Roll hot rod roll / Jump Jack jump / Yama yama pretty mama / You know you're doin' me wrong / These golden rings / My desire / Night of the werewolf / Dance to it / Have mercy Miss Percy / Hands off / Can't believe you wanna leave / (I'm afraid) the masquerade is over / Those lonely, lonely nights / Wet back hop / Hey girl, hey boy / Let's go boppin' tonight / Hit, git and split / Right now / Shake your hips / Look out Miss James / Who's been jivin' you / Sweet dreams
CD ______ **CDCHD 555**
Ace / Sep '94 / Pinnacle

TEENBEAT 50
Earle Hotel: *Scaley Andrew* / Sketch for Sleepy: *Bastro* / Marbles: *Circus Lupus* / Block of wood: *Vomit Launch* / Strange pair: *Vomit Launch* / Capitalist joyride: *Unrest* / Dr. Seuss: *Autoclave* / Time loop: *Cohen, Johnny* / On tape: *Teenage Gang Debs* / California: *Sexual Milkshake* / I'm going to blow your fucking head off: *Superconductor* / Not at all: *Velocity Girl* / It's hard to be an egg: *Eggs* / Shaniko: *Love, Courtney* / Teenbeat theme: *Love, Courtney* / Teenbeat epilogue: *Love, Courtney* / Sweet Georgia Brown: *Krokodiloes* / Look out: *Helter Skillet* / Teenage suicide: *Naomi Wolff* / Love affair is over: *Clarence* / Merry go round: *Coral* / Equator of her navel: *Jungle George* / Holiday New England: *Superstar, Mark E* / You fucking English bastard: *SCUD* / 23rd rocker: *Wills, Butch* / Peace: *Wall Drug*
CD ______ **OLE 0252**
Matador / Mar '94 / Vital

TEENBEAT SAMPLER
CD ______ **TEENBEAT 141CD**
Teenbeat / Sep '94 / Cargo / SRD / Vital

TEJANO ROOTS (24 Hits From Discos Ideal 1946-1966)
CD ______ **ARHCD 341**
Arhoolie / Apr '95 / ADA / Cadillac / Direct

TEJANO ROOTS - THE WOMEN
CD ______ **ARHCD 343**
Arhoolie / Apr '95 / ADA / Cadillac / Direct

TEKNO ACID BEATS
CD ______ **TOPY 39CD**
Temple / Feb '89 / Pinnacle / Plastic Head

TEKTEKAN
CD ______ **VICG 52262**
JVC World Library / Mar '96 / ADA / CM / Direct

TELARC SURROUND SOUNDS
Cybergenesis/terminator: *Cincinnati Pops Orchestra/Erich Kunzel* / Jurassic lunch: *Cincinnati Pops Orchestra/Erich Kunzel* / Also sprach zarathustra: *Cincinnati Pops Orchestra/Erich Kunzel* / Chiller/Phantom of the opera: *Cincinnati Pops Orchestra/Erich Kunzel* / La donna e mobile: *Cincinnati Pops Orchestra/Erich Kunzel* / Hopper dance: *Empire Brass Quintet* / Tambourin: *Empire Brass Quintet* / Two part inventions in F & B flat: *Carlos, Wendy* / 2 a day in Tunisia: *Spies* / Use me: *Wells, Junior* / You don't miss your water: *Bell, William & The Memphis Horns* / Bachianas Brasileiras #4: Coral/Tristan & Isolde: Prelude: *Lopez-Cobez, Jesus* / Salve virgo: *Ensemble PAN*
CD ______ **CD 80447**
Telarc / Apr '96 / Conifer/BMG

TELARCHIVE
Seven come eleven / Line for Lyons / Cherokee / So long Eric / I know that you know / Stardust / Sweet Sue, just you / Slop / Gerry meets Hamp
CD ______ **83318**
Telarc / Jun '92 / Conifer/BMG

TELECOM 331
CD ______ **PIAS 458001126**
Pop / May '96 / Plastic Head

TELEPATHY
CD ______ **BDRCD 8**
Breakdown / Jun '95 / Pinnacle

TEMPETE POUR SORTIR
CD ______ **KMCD 58**
Keltia Musique / Mar '96 / ADA / Discovery

TEMPLE OF ELECTRONICA
CD ______ **TEMPNYC 2CD**
Temple / Oct '95 / Pinnacle / Plastic Head

TEMPLE RECORDS VOL.1
CD ______ **TEMPNYC 1CD**
Temple / Oct '95 / Pinnacle / Plastic Head

TEMPLE SAMPLER, THE
CD ______ **COMD 2049**
Temple / Feb '94 / ADA / CM / Direct / Duncans / Highlander

TEMPO DE BAHIA
CD ______ **BMCD 123**
Blue Moon / Mar '89 / Cadillac / Discovery / Greensleeves / Jazz Music / Jet Star / TKO Magnum

TEMPO JAZZ
CD ______ **RTCL 801CD**
Right Tempo / Jul '96 / New Note/ Pinnacle / Timewarp

TEMPTED
If I ever lose my faith in you: *Sting* / More than words: *Extreme* / Love song for a vampire: *Lennox, Annie* / Too much love will kill you: *May, Brian* / One: *U2* / Easy: *Faith No More* / Womankind: *Little Angels* / Twenty nine palms: *Plant, Robert* / Tempted: *Squeeze* / Beautiful girl: *INXS* / Just another day: *Secada, Jon* / Emotional time: *Hothouse Flowers* / Deep: *East 17* / All woman: *Stansfield, Lisa* / This time: *Carroll, Dina* / Love makes no sense: *O'Neal, Alexander* / Hello (Turn your radio on): *Shakespears Sister* / Young at heart: *Bluebells*
CD ______ **5163052**
PolyGram TV / Jul '93 / PolyGram

TENDANCE VOL.4
CD ______ **ZYX 550692**
ZYX / Nov '96 / ZYX

TENDER LOVE (17 Romantic Love Songs)
Tender love: *Thomas, Kenny* / When you tell me that you love me: *Ross, Diana* / All woman: *Stansfield, Lisa* / Way of the world: *Turner, Tina* / Every time you go away: *Young, Paul* / Don't dream it's over: *Crowded House* / Careless whisper: *Michael, George* / Your song: *John, Elton* / Saving all my love for you: *Houston, Whitney* / Try a little tenderness: *Redding, Otis* / She makes my day: *Palmer, Robert* / Right here waiting: *Marx, Richard* / Best of me: *Richard, Cliff* / Promise me: *Craven, Beverley* / True: *Spandau Ballet* / If you were with me now: *Minogue, Kylie & Keith Washington* / If you don't know me by now: *Simply Red*
CD ______ **CDEMTV 64**
EMI / Feb '92 / EMI

TENDER LOVE
Tender love: *Thomas, Kenny* / Tonight I celebrate my love: *Bryson, Peabo & Roberta Flack* / I don't wanna lose you: *Kandidate* / Coming home: *Hain, Marshall* / Solid: *Ashford & Simpson* / This will be: *Cole, Natalie* / More than a woman: *Tavares* / It's been so long: *McCrae, George* / Please don't go: *KC & The Sunshine Band* / Rock me tonight: *Jackson, Freddie* / Fantasy real: *Fearon, Phil* / Sexy girl: *Thomas, Lillo* / Other side of the rainbow: *Moore, Melba* / Cross your mind: *King, Evelyn 'Champagne'* / Woman of the world: *Mazelle, Kym* / Free love: *Roberts, Juliet* / Why can't we live together: *Thomas, Timmy* / Loving you: *Riperton, Minnie*
CD ______ **CDGOLD 1030**
EMI Gold / Jan '97 / EMI

TENNESSEE R 'N' B LIVE (The Excello Legends)
CD ______ **APCD 140**
Appaloosa / Jul '97 / ADA / Direct / TKO Magnum

TENOR SAX & TROMBONE SPECTACULAR
CD ______ **PCD 7019**
Progressive / Jun '93 / Jazz Music

TERMINAL CITY RICOCHET
CD ______ **VIRUS 75CD**
Alternative Tentacles / Nov '89 / Cargo / Greyhound / Pinnacle

TERRA SERPENTES (A World Serpent Compilation)
T 2901E: *Arkkon* / Bahnhofstrasse: *Bates, Martyn* / One minute more: *Chris & Cosey* / Frolicking: *Current 93* / May you never be alone like me: *Dall, Bryin* / Only Europe knows: *Kapo* / Dark scenery court games: *Doyle, Roger* / Wise words of Eve: *Elijah's Mantle* / Still water bonne: *In Gowan Ring* / What the cat brought in: *Lemon Kittens* / Love is regret: *Loretta's Doll* / Untitled: *Moon Lay Hidden Beneath A Cloud* / By a foreign river: *Nature & Organisation* / All God's dogs: *Neither Neither World* / Window of possible organic development: *Nurse With Wound* / Come unto me: *Orchis* / Music from Pearls Before Swine: *Rice, Boyd* / On the corner: *Sand* / Some colossus: *Scorpionwind* / Oblivion extract: *Shock Headed Peters* / Did you see: *Sol Invictus* / Oblique realities: *Somewhere In Europe* / Ways to strength and beauty: *Strength Through Joy* / Live: *Tiny Tim* / Scavenging soul: *Zone*
CD ______ **WSDCD 016**
World Serpent / Apr '97 / World Serpent

TERRORDROME VOL.1 (Hardcore Nightmare)
CD Set ______ **DB 47982**
Deep Blue / Mar '95 / PolyGram

TERRORDROME VOL.1 (Darkside From Hell)
CD ______ **0041512COM**
Edel / Jul '97 / Pinnacle

TERRORDROME VOL.2 (Hardcore Cyberpunk)
Introdrome: *Chosen Few* / Tyrannofuck: *DJ Fistfuck* / String X: *Cyanide* / I'll show you my gun: *Annihilator* / Base U (Smash TV): *Shadowrun* / Accelerator 4: *Technohead* / One day: *Wedlock* / Maniac: *Chosen Few* / Cocksuckers: *Tellurian* / FTS: *Vinyl Killer* / Domestic moves: *Maniac Of Noise* / Victim of trance: *Analyzer* / Cause a riot: *Blunted Vision, A* / Power dominion: *Dee, Lenny & Ralphie Dee* / 20,000 volt: *High Energy* / Suck it: *Oral Maniac* / Terrordrome: *High Energy* / Fuck this: *Re-Animator* / Accelerator 3: *Technohead* / Fucking Speedloader: *Speedloader* / Relatic: *Cyanide* / Mokummania: *Maniac Of Noise* / Goddamn mind: *Noisegate* / Invasion of the intruders: *Sons of Aliens* / In 16 beats time second: *Vitamin* / CTX: *Original Gabber* / Eat zat pizza: *Salami Brothers* / Insane: *Strontium 9000* / Psychic 909: *Milan* / Move it faster: *Triplet* / Quetsch: *Haardcore* / Outrodrome: *Original Gabber* / I control your body: *Dee, Lenny & Ralphie Dee* / Maniac (mix): *Chosen Few* / Suck it (mix): *Oral Maniac* / Accelerator: *Technohead* / Mokummania (mix): *Maniac Of Noise* / Relatic (mix): *Cyanide* / My house is your house: *Vitamin* / Victim of trance (mix): *Analyzer* / Eat zat pizza (mix): *Salami Brothers* / Cocksuckers (mix): *Tellurian* / 20,000 volt (mix): *High Energy*
CD Set ______ **DB 47972**
Deep Blue / Mar '95 / PolyGram

TERRORDROME VOL.3 (Party Animal)
CD Set ______ **DB 47992**
Deep Blue / Nov '94 / PolyGram

TERRORDROME VOL.4 (Supersonic Guerilla)
CD ______ **DB 47962**
PolyGram TV / Apr '95 / PolyGram

TERRORDROME VOL.7 (2CD Set)
CD Set ______ **0041822CON**
Edel / Jun '96 / Pinnacle

TERRORIST GENERATION
CD ______ **CCSCD 355**
Castle / Nov '92 / BMG

TERYAKI ASTHMA VOL.1-5
CD ______ **CZ 037CD**
C/Z / Nov '92 / Plastic Head

TESTAMENT RECORDS SAMPLER
CD ______ **TCD 4001**
Testament / May '95 / ADA / Koch

TEX-MEX FIESTA
Ay te dejo en San Antonio / La ratita / Amor bonito / Corine Corina / La tracionera / El desperado / Caballo viejo / Que cobarde / Viva seguin / La duena de la llave / Por esos montes / Cuatro o cinco farolazos / Quiereme vidita / Las gaviotas / Tomando y fumando / Puentes quemados / Saludamos a texas / Mi unico camino real / Medio vuelo / Tarde pa' appepentimos / Magia de amor / Juarez
CD ______ **CDCHD 528**
Ace / Oct '94 / Pinnacle

TEX-MEX FIESTA (A Round Up Of Classic Conjunto Singles From Texas)
El chubasco: *Los Colores* / El adolorido: *Vela, Ruben Y Su Conjunto* / Vencido: *Vela, Ruben Y Su Conjunto* / Alegra serenata: *Los Cuatitos Cantu* / Como un amanecer: *Los Cuatitos Cantu* / Declarate inocente: *Los Cuatitos Cantu* / Que bonito es querer: *Los Tremendos Gavilanes* / Pero Maria: *Los Tremendos Gavilanes* / Le llorona loca: *Jordan, Steve* / La dame de Espana: *Jordan, Steve*
CD ______ **EDCD 7039**
Easydisc / Jul '97 / Direct

TEXANS LIVE FROM MOUNTAIN STAGE
(Is anybody going to) San Antone: *Texas Tornados* / Shake your hips: *Barton, Lou Ann* / Portales: *Hubbard, Ray Wylie* / Whatever way the wind blows: *Willis, Kelly* / Shadow boxing: *Hickman, Sara* / Just a wave: *Gilmore, Jimmie Dale* / Buckskin stallion blues: *Van Zandt, Townes* / Georgia on a fast train: *Shaver, Billy Joe* / I had my hopes up high: *Ely, Joe* / Esperate (wait for me): *Hinojosa, Tish* / St. Gabriel: *Ball, Marcia* / She ain't goin nowhere: *Clark, Guy* / Miles and miles of Texas: *Asleep At The Wheel*
CD ______ **BPM 304CD**
Blue Plate / May '97 / ADA / Direct / Greyhound

TEXAS AND TENNESSEE TERRITORY BANDS
Sugar babe I'm leavin' / Happy / Goofus / Sadness will be gladness / Goose creek / Better than nothin' / That's a-plenty / Mississippi stomp / Memphis kick up / You never did that before / Down on Biscayne Bay / We can't use each other anymore / Down where the blue bonnets grow / I ain't got no gal now / I don't love nobody but you / Honey child / All muggled up / Shooin' flies / Come easy go easy love / When I can't be with you
CD ______ **RTR 79006**
Retrieval / Jul '97 / Cadillac / Direct / Jazz Music / Swift / Wellard

TEXAS BLACK COUNTRY DANCE 1927-1935
CD ______ **DOCD 5162**
Document / May '93 / ADA / Hot Shot / Jazz Music

TEXAS BLUES
CD ______ **ARHCD 352**
Arhoolie / Apr '95 / ADA / Cadillac / Direct

TEXAS BLUES 1927-1937
CD ______ **DOCD 5161**
Document / May '93 / ADA / Hot Shot / Jazz Music

TEXAS BLUES GUITAR
Claim jumper: *Copeland, Johnny* / Love me with a feeling: *Funderburgh, Anson & The Rockets* / Insomnia: *Walker, Philip & Otis Grand* / Texas Cadillac: *Kubek, Smokin' Joe Band* / Sometimes I slip: *Brown, Clarence 'Gatemouth'* / Texas guitar slinger: *Hughes, John 'Guitar'* / I'm worried: *Morgan, Mike & The Crawl* / Rough edges: *Clark, W.C.* / Half step: *Wilson, U.P.* / Blues for Carol: *Holliman, Clarence*

CD EDCD 7037
Easydisc / Jun '97 / Direct

TEXAS BLUES GUITAR 1929-1935
CD SOB 35332CD
Story Of The Blues / Apr '95 / ADA / Koch

TEXAS BLUES PARTY
Dollar got the blues: *Brown, Clarence 'Gatemouth'* / Young devil: *Walker, Philip & Otis Grand* / Texas party: *Copeland, Johnny* / Soul king shuffle: *Wilson, U.P.* / You're my brand: *Kubek, Smokin' Joe Band* / I want to shout about it: *Clark, W.C.* / 20 miles: *Funderburgh, Anson & The Rockets* / Why oh why: *Houston, Joe & Otis Grand* / 'Big D' shuffle: *Morgan, Mike & The Crawl* / It's been a mistake: *Jones, Tutu*
CD EDCD 7038
Easydisc / Jun '97 / Direct

TEXAS BLUES PARTY VOL.2 (The Very Best Of Texas Blues Today)
CD WCD 120631
Wolf / Dec '96 / Hot Shot / Jazz Music / Swift

TEXAS BOHEMIA
CD TRIKONTUS 201
Trikont / Jan '95 / ADA / Direct

TEXAS COUNTRY BLUES 1948-1951
CD FLYCD 941
Flyright / Aug '94 / Hot Shot / Jazz Music / Wellard

TEXAS FIELD RECORDINGS 1934-1939
CD DOCD 5231
Document / Apr '94 / ADA / Hot Shot / Jazz Music

TEXAS GARAGE BANDS (West Texas Rarities)
CD COLCD 0663
Collectables / Jun '97 / Greyhound

TEXAS GARAGE BANDS (AOK Records Story)
CD COLCD 0595
Collectables / Jun '97 / Greyhound

TEXAS GARAGE BANDS (Corpus Christie Rarities)
CD COLCD 0664
Collectables / Jul '97 / Greyhound

TEXAS GIRLS
CD DOCD 5163
Document / May '93 / ADA / Hot Shot / Jazz Music

TEXAS GUITAR KILLERS (2CD Set)
My baby left me: *Walker, T-Bone* / Come back to me baby: *Walker, T-Bone* / I can't stand being away from you: *Walker, T-Bone* / She is going to ruin me: *Walker, T-Bone* / Gatemouth boogie: *Brown, Gatemouth* / Guitar in my hand: *Brown, Gatemouth* / After sunset: *Brown, Gatemouth* / Without me: *Brown, Gatemouth* / Double trouble blues: *Fulson, Lowell* / Stormin' and rainin': *Fulson, Lowell* / Good woman blues: *Fulson, Lowell* / All through my dreams: *Hopkins, Lightnin'* / Mean and evil blues: *Hopkins, Lightnin'* / Up today - down tomorrow: *Hogg, Smokey* / Great big mama: *Hogg, Smokey* / Worryin' blues: *Hogg, Smokey* / Need my help: *Hogg, Smokey* / In this world alone: *Hogg, Smokey* / Key to my door: *Hogg, Smokey* / Hustle is on: *Walker, T-Bone* / Baby broke my heart: *Walker, T-Bone* / Evil hearted woman: *Walker, T-Bone* / No reason: *Walker, T-Bone* / Look me in the eye: *Walker, T-Bone* / Too lazy: *Walker, T-Bone* / When it rains it pours: *Crayton, Pee Wee* / Daybreak: *Crayton, Pee Wee* / Blues don't leave me: *Fulson, Lowell* / Blues never fail: *Fulson, Lowell* / Chuck with the boys: *Fulson, Lowell* / You gotta reap: *Fulson, Lowell* / When I've been drinking: *Hogg, Smokey* / I gotta ride: *Hogg, Smokey* / Tear me down: *Hogg, Smokey* / Train whistle: *Hogg, Smokey* / My baby's gone: *Hogg, Smokey* / Peace of mind: *Hogg, Smokey* / Oo-oo-wee: *Hogg, Smokey*
CD Set CDEM 1569
Premier/EMI / Feb '96 / EMI

TEXAS PIANO 1923-1935
CD DOCD 5224
Document / Apr '94 / ADA / Hot Shot / Jazz Music

TEXAS PIANO 1927-1938
CD DOCD 5225
Document / Apr '94 / ADA / Hot Shot / Jazz Music

TEXAS PIANO BLUES 1929-1948
CD SOB 35092CD
Story Of The Blues / Apr '95 / ADA / Koch

TEXAS: A COLLECTION OF TEXAS GARAGE
CD ANDA 198
Au-Go-Go / Jan '97 / Cargo / Greyhound / Plastic Head

TFSM 03
CD EFA 127662
Gaia / Jul '95 / SRD

THAI (Spirituality & Technology For The Manga Consciousness)
CD CDZ 001
Zone / Sep '96 / SRD

THANK YOU BOB
CD PB 001
Bob / May '97 / Greyhound

THANKS FOR THE MEMORY
CD MCCD 164
Music Club / Jul '94 / Disc / THE

THAT BEATIN' RHYTHM (A Collection Of Mirwood Northern Soul Classics)
CD GSCD 010
Goldmine / Feb '93 / Vital

THAT GROOVSVILLE SOUND
I'll never forget you: *O'Jays* / Sweet Sherry: *Barnes, J.J.* / No one to love: *Lewis, Pat* / Friday night: *Mancha, Steve* / Our love is in the pocket: *Banks, Darrell* / Don't be sore at me: *Parliaments* / Please let me in: *Barnes, J.J.* / Hit and run: *Batiste, Rose* / That's why I love you: *Professionals* / Making up time: *Holidays* / Loving you takes all of my time: *Debonaires* / I lost you: *Holidays* / Keep the faith: *Mancha, Steve* / Chains of love: *Barnes, J.J.* / Warning: *Lewis, Pat* / I must love you: *Davis, Melvin* / Stone broke: *Ward, Sam* / Headache in my heart: *Debonaires* / Just keep on loving me: *Mancha, Steve* / Look at what I almost missed: *Lewis, Pat* / I miss my baby (that lonely feeling): *Batiste, Rose* / Somebody, somewhere needs you: *Banks, Darrell* / I think I found a love: *Barnes, J.J.* / I'm the one who loves you: *Track*
CD GSCD 105
Goldmine / Mar '97 / Vital

THAT HIGH LONESOME SOUND (The Best Of Bluegrass Through The Years)
If I should wander back tonight: *Hot Rize* / Looking for the stone: *O'Brien, Tim & Mollie* / Blue yodel # 3: *Johnson Mountain Boys* / My hands are tied: *Lonesome Standard Time* / I'm going back to the old home: *Watson, Doc* / Blue moon of Kentucky: *Osborne Brothers* / Trains make me lonesome: *Auldridge, Mike* / Rock salt and nails: *Crowe, J.D. & The New South* / I ain't brok but I'm badly bent: *Grisman, David* / I was left on the street: *McCoury Brothers* / Where the soul man never dies: *Skaggs, Ricky & Tony Rice* / When God dips his pen of love in my heart: *Krauss, Alison* / Running hard on a broken heart: *Lonesome River Band* / Kentucky King: *Lonesome Standard Time* / That high lonesome sound: *Rowan, Peter & The Nashville Bluegrass Band* / Molly & tenbrooks: *Crowe, J.D.* / Blue ridge express: *Munde, Alan* / One way track: *Boone Creek* / Darlin' Corey: *Clifton, Bill* / Roll jordan roll: *Nashville Bluegrass Band* / Foggy mountain chimes: *Here Today* / Tramp on the street: *Blue Sky Boys* / Come on home: *Clements, Vassar*
CD NTMCD 514
Nectar / Jan '96 / Pinnacle

THAT HIGH LONESOME SOUND
CD ACCD 19
Acoustic Disc / Mar '96 / ADA / Koch

THAT LOVING FEELING
Unchained melody: *Righteous Brothers* / One and one is one: *Medicine Head* / Things we do for love: *10cc* / Night you murdered love: *ABC* / Reunited: *Peaches & Herb* / My friend the wind: *Roussos, Demis* / Little piece of heaven: *Godley & Creme* / First time: *Beck, Robin* / Say hello, wave goodbye: *Soft Cell* / Down on the street: *Shakatak* / Come what may: *Leandros, Vicky* / Pearl's a singer: *Brooks, Elkie* / Fooled around and fell in love: *Bishop, Elvin* / Only love: *Mouskouri, Nana*
CD 5501482
Spectrum / Jan '94 / PolyGram

THAT WAS THE SWINGING 60'S VOL.1
What do you want to make those eyes at me for: *Ford, Emile & The Checkmates* / Be mine: *Fortune, Lance* / Michael, row the boat ashore: *Donegan, Lonnie* / War paint: *Brook Brothers* / Venus in blue jeans: *Wynter, Mark* / Little bitty tear: *Miki & Griff* / Sugar and spice: *Searchers* / Sukiyaki: *Ball, Kenny & His Jazzmen* / Mockingbird Hill: *Migil 5* / Downtown: *Clark, Petula* / Poor man's son: *Rockin' Berries* / Funny how love can be: *Ivy League* / Daydream: *Lovin' Spoonful* / Dedicated follower of fashion: *Kinks* / Flowers in the rain: *Move* / Puppet on a string: *Shaw, Sandie* / Build me up buttercup: *Foundations* / Mexico: *Baldry, Long John* / Oh happy day: *Hawkins, Edwin Singers* / Make me an island: *Dolan, Joe*
CD CDMFP 5897
Music For Pleasure / Oct '90 / EMI

THAT'LL FLAT GIT IT VOL.1 (Rockabilly & Rock 'n' Roll From The Vaults Of RCA Victor)
Sixteen chicks: *Clay, Joe* / Born to love one woman: *Cartey, Ric* / Sugar sweet: *Houston, David* / New shoes: *Denson, Lee* / Little boy blue: *Johnson, Hoyt* / Drug store rock 'n' roll: *Martin, Janis* / Rosie let's get cozy: *Rich, Dave* / Catty Town: *Glasser, Dick* / Star light, star bright: *Castle, Nan* / TV hop: *Morgan Twins* / Honky tonk mind: *Blake, Tommy* / Teen billy baby: *Sprouts* / Don't bug me baby: *Allen, Milt* / Now stop: *Carson, Martha* / Milkcow blues: *Rodgers, Jimmie* / Duck tail: *Clay, Joe* / Heart throb: *Cartey, Ric* / One and only: *Houston, David* / I've got a dollar: *Dell, Jimmy* / Lovin' honey: *Morris, Gene* / Barefoot baby: *Martin, Janis* / Rock-a-bye baby: *Bonn, Skeeter* / That ain't nothing but right: *Castle, Joey* / Mary Nell: *Inman, Autrey* / Hey jibbo: *Wood, Art* / All night long: *Blake, Tommy* / Full grown cat: *McCoys* / Just thought I'd set you straight: *Harris, Ted* / Oooh-wee baby: *Cartey, Ric* / Shake it up baby: *Dee, Frankie* / Lovin' honey: *Morris, Gene*
CD Set BCD 15622
Bear Family / May '93 / Direct / Rollercoaster / Swift

THAT'LL FLAT GIT IT VOL.2 (Rockabilly & Rock 'n' Roll From The Vaults Of US Decca)
Hot rock wild: *Carroll, Johnny* / Wild women - crazy: *Carroll, Johnny* / Crazy lovin': *Carroll, Johnny* / Tryin' to get you: *Carroll, Johnny* / Corine Corina: *Carroll, Johnny* / Rock 'n' Roll Ruby: *Carroll, Johnny* / Flip, flop and fry: *Carroll, Johnny* / Baby don't leave me: *Five Chavis Brothers* / Way out there: *Chuck & Bill* / Ruby Pearl: *Cochran, Jackie Lee* / Mamy don't you think I know: *Cochran, Jackie Lee* / Lorraine: *Covelle, Buddy* / Cool it baby: *Fontaine, Eddie* / Whole lotta shakin' goin' on: *Hall, Roy* / Off beat boogie: *Hall, Roy* / See you later alligator: *Hall, Roy* / Three alley cats: *Hall, Roy* / Diggin' the boogie: *Hall, Roy* / I wanna bop: *Harlan, Billy* / I would be a doggone lie: *Harlan, Billy* / Be bop baby: *Harlan, Billy* / Sweet love on my mind: *Jimmy & Johnny* / Teenage love is misery: *Kennedy, Jerry* / Crazy baby: *Maltais, Gene* / Ten little women: *Noland, Terry* / Teenage boogie: *Pierce, Webb* / Cast iron arm: *Wilson, Peanuts* / You're barking up the wrong tree: *Woody, Don* / Make like a rock and roll: *Woody, Don*
CD BCD 15623
Bear Family / Jun '92 / Direct / Rollercoaster / Swift

THAT'LL FLAT GIT IT VOL.3 (Rockabilly & Rock 'n' Roll From The Vaults Of Capitol)
You oughta see Grandma rock: *McDonald, Skeets* / Heartbreakin' Mama: *McDonald, Skeets* / My little baby: *Maddox, Rose* / Sebbin' come elebbin: *Heap, Jimmy* / Go ahead on: *Heap, Jimmy* / Try me: *Luman, Bob* / Cash on the barrelhead: *Louvin Brothers* / Red hen hop: *Louvin Brothers* / Worryin' kind: *Sands, Tommy* / Playin' the field: *Sands, Tommy* / My gal Gertie: *Dickerson, Dub* / When I found you: *Reed, Jerry* / I've had enough: *Reed, Jerry* / Mr. Big feet: *Charlie Bop Trio* / Cool down Mame: *Farmer Boys* / My baby done left me: *Farmer Boys* / Party kiss: *Fallin, Johnny* / Party line: *Fallin, Johnny* / There's gonna be a ball: *Grayzell, Rudy* / Bop cat bop: *Crum, Simon* / Jeopardy: *Shepard, Jean* / He's my baby: *Shepard, Jean* / Alone with you: *Young, Faron* / I can't dance: *Young, Faron* / Black cat: *Collins, Tommy* / I chickened out: *Loran, Kenny* / Slow down brother: *Husky, Ferlin* / I went rockin': *Norris, Bobby* / You mostest girl: *Trammell, Bobby Lee*
CD BCD 15624
Bear Family / Jun '92 / Direct / Rollercoaster / Swift

THAT'LL FLAT GIT IT VOL.4 (Rockabilly & Rock 'n' Roll From The Vaults Of Festival)
They call me Willie: *Barry, Billy* / Wild one: *Barry, Billy* / My love is true: *Barry, Billy* / Baby I'm a king: *Barry, Billy* / Weepin' and wailin: *Barry, Billy* / Oh no: *Barry, Billy* / I love you now: *Barry, Billy* / Do the oop-poo-pah-doo: *Dio, Ronnie* / Love pains: *Dio, Ronnie* / Motorcycle: *Balls, Billy* / Till time stands still: *Starr, Charlie* / Sick and tired: *Starr, Charlie* / You ain't my number one: *Starr, Charlie* / Black jack Joey: *Starr, Charlie* / Christmas twist: *Starr, Charlie* / One broken heart for sale: *Blackwell, Otis*
CD BCD 15630
Bear Family / Apr '94 / Direct / Rollercoaster / Swift

THAT'LL FLAT GIT IT VOL.5 (Rockabilly & Rock 'n' Roll From The Vaults Of Dot)
Circle rock: *Copas, Lloyd* / Love me: *Phantom* / Carry on: *Newman, Jimmy C.* / Lonesome for a letter: *Clark, Sanford* / Big door: *Brown, Gene* / Skinny Minnie: *Denton, Bob* / Dogonnit: *Spellman, Jimmy* / Step it up and go: *Wiseman, Mac* / Oh my baby's gone: *Sharpe, Ray* / Rock sock the boogie: *Flowers, Pat* / I'm low low low: *Clingman, Loy* / Call me shorty: *Gilley, Mickey* / Pucker paint: *Wolfe, Danny* / You're late Miss Kate: *Dee, Jimmy* / It's all over: *Sullivan, Niki* / Boogie woogie: *Tucker, Billy Jo* / You heard me knocking: *Adams, Billy* / Mary Lou: *Burdette, Lew* / I like this kind of music: *Ringo, Jimmy* / Trapped love: *Courvale, Keith* / Playboy: *Denton, Bob* / Chicken shack: *Van Dyke, Leroy* / Ballroom baby: *Lory, Dick* / That's the way I feel: *Sharpe, Ray* / Johnny Johnny Johnny: *Jones, Kay Cee* / It ain't me: *Campi, Ray* / Come on baby: *Gilley, Mickey* / Put me down: *Lucas, Matt* / Let's flat get it: *Wolfe, Danny* / Henrietta: *Dee, Jimmy* / Love me: *Phantom*
CD BCD 15711
Bear Family / May '97 / Direct / Rollercoaster / Swift

THAT'LL FLAT GIT IT VOL.6 (Rockabilly & Rock 'n' Roll From The Vaults Of US Decca)
All by myself: *Hall, Roy* / Rock it down to my house: *Tubb, Justin* / Alligator come across: *Duff, Arlie* / Wee Willie Brown: *Graham, Lou* / Hey babe let's go downtown: *Therien, Joe Jr.* / Everybody's tryin' to be my baby: *York Brothers* / Morse code: *Woody, Don* / Juke joint Johnny: *Sovine, Red* / Don't stop now: *Hall, Roy* / Come back to me darling: *Therien, Joe Jr.* / You gotta move: *Smith, Chester* / Knock knock: *Allen, Rex* / Crazy little guitar man: *Foley, Red* / Sputnik (satellite girl): *Engler, Jerry* / You're long gone: *Therien, Joe Jr.* / Baby's gone: *Claud, Vernon* / Sweet Willie: *Allen, Barbara* / Move on: *Hall, Roy* / She wanna rock: *Derksen, Arnie* / Wheels: *Therien, Joe Jr.* / Crazy chicken: *Gallagher, James* / Don't go baby (don't go): *Coker, Al* / School house rock: *Harlan, Billy* / Bring my cadillac back: *Knightmares* / Rockabilly boogie: *Therien, Joe Jr.* / Roc-a-chicka: *Mack, Warner* / Cheat on me baby: *Rockin' Saints* / Tennessee Tody: *Billy & Western Okies* / One and only: *Fontaine, Eddie* / Shake baby shake: *Raney, Wayne*
CD BCD 15733
Bear Family / Nov '94 / Direct / Rollercoaster / Swift

THAT'LL FLAT GIT IT VOL.7 (Rockabilly & Rock 'n' Roll From The Vaults Of MGM)
Rockin' rollin' stone: *Starr, Andy* / Rock 'n' roll fever: *Campbell, Cecil* / Mr. Blues: *Rainwater, Marvin* / Watchin' the 710 roll by: *Griffin, Buck* / Rootie tootie: *Berry Kids* / My square dancin' Mama: *Gallion, Bob* / Rock doll: *Early, Bernie* / Long black train: *Twitty, Conway* / Rocking guitar: *Campbell, Cecil* / Go, go, go right into town: *Berry Kids* / Rockin' chair on the moon: *Wellington, Rusty* / Round and round: *Starr, Andy* / Your kisses kill me: *Early, Bernie* / Latch on: *Hargrave, Ron* / Country cattin': *Swan, Jimmy* / Love me love: *Berry Kids* / Dixieland rock: *Campbell, Cecil* / Hot and cold: *Rainwater, Marvin* / Stutterin' Papa: *Griffin, Buck* / There's good rockin' tonight: *Wills, Billy Jack* / Baby, love me: *Gallion, Bob* / Big money: *Davis, Paul* / Buttercup: *Hargrave, Ron* / You're my teenage baby: *Berry Kids* / Cuddle lovin' baby: *Charley & Junior* / All she wants to do is rock: *Wills, Billy Jack* / Let's go rock'n'roll: *Sandy, Frank* / I wanta waltz: *Blackmon, Thelma* / Drive-in movie: *Hargrave, Ron* / Rockin' & rollin' with Grandmaw: *Robinson, Carson*
CD BCD 15789
Bear Family / May '96 / Direct / Rollercoaster / Swift

THAT'LL FLAT GIT IT VOL.8 (Rockabilly & Rock 'n' Roll From The Vaults Of Fabor/Abbott)
You mostest girl: *Trammell, Bobby Lee* / Cool cat: *Montgomery, Joe* / Let's fall in love: *Burnette, Dorsey* / Meadowlark: *Coker, Sandy* / Bawlin' baby: *Horton, Johnny & Billy Barton* / Long sideburns: *Barry, Boelean* / Shirley Lee, I sure do love you: *Trammell, Bobby Lee* / Stop the clock rock: *Creel Sisters* / Shotgun boogie: *Horton, Johnny* / I love you girl: *Podolor, Dickie* / That's alright with me: *Luman, Bob* / No use in lying: *Luman, Bob* / Hello baby: *Luman, Bob* / We're gonna bop: *Coker, Alvadean* / Hot Rod is her name: *Tall, Tom* / Salt and pepper: *Summers, Ronnie* / Rockin' Maraccas: *Rose, Dusty* / Hula rock: *Rose, Dusty* / Klondike: *Lanham, Roy* / Love is over: *Guitar, Bonnie* / Frantic party: *Guitar, Bonnie* / Stop talkin', start lovin': *Harshman, Robert Luke* / Love what'cha doin' to me: *Harshman, Robert Luke* / Jumping with the shadows: *Shadows* / Shadow rock: *Shadows* / Creep: *Shadows* / Don't you know: *Tall, Tom & Ruckus Tyler* / Whose little pigeon are you: *Tall, Tom & Creel Sisters* / Rock town rock: *Tyler, Ruckus* / Rollin' and a-rockin': *Tyler, Ruckus* / We're gonna bop: *Coker, Alvadean*
CD BCD 15936
Bear Family / May '96 / Direct / Rollercoaster / Swift

THAT'S ALL FOLK (2CD Set)
CD Set CML 574101516
Le Chant Du Monde / Aug '97 / Harmonia Mundi

THAT'S LAMBADA
Lambada / Lambada Copacabana / Para ser so whoman / Outra vez / Apita / Ja passou / O mato / Fantasia / Rio / Chega / Jogo de fogo / Nao sei / Lambada quente / Lambada
CD QED 167
Tring / Nov '96 / Tring

THAT'S WHY WE'RE MARCHING (World War II & The American Folk Song Movement)
CD SFWCD 40021
Smithsonian Folkways / Apr '96 / ADA / Cadillac / CM / Direct / Koch

THEIR ORIGINAL SINS (20 Tracks From The Vaults Of Scooch Pooch)
Jesus is on my side: *Teen Angels* / Poppa Hoodoo: *Lord High Fixers* / End of the devil dogs: *La Donnas* / My side of town: *Rayons* / Ghetto blaster: *Countdowns* / 23: *Gomez* / Dead End days: *Jesus Christ Superfly* / 18 squeeler: *Steerjockey* / It's alright: *Zeke* / Mighty Ranxerox: *Bottom Feeders* / Who's who: *Dead End Cruisers* / Dialudid: *Zeke* / Is paranoia a form of awareness: *Lord High Fixers* / Ain't it a shame: *Detroit Cobras* /

Bath mat: *Hectics* / Every day is a Brenda day: *Popdefact* / Networks: *Hamicks* / Go away: *Teen Angels* / Hello ladies and gentlemen: *Zeke* / Teenage head: *Nine Pound Hammer*
CD PO 28
Scooch Pooch / Oct '96 / Cargo / Greyhound / Pinnacle
CD 206282
Scooch Pooch / Jul '97 / Cargo / Greyhound / Pinnacle

THELMA RECORD CO STORY, THE (Legendary Detroit Soul)
Love is the only solution: *Star, Martha* / I'm a peace loving man: *Laskey, Emanuel* / Lucky to be loved by you: *Hargreaves, Silky* / I just can't leave you: *Inst* / You got the best of me: *Hill, Eddie* / I just cant leave you: *Batiste, Rose* / Sorry ain't good enough: *Matthews, Joe* / I love you: *Inst* / Gonna cry a river: *Ward, Robert* / I've got to run for my life: *Laskey, Emanuel* / Someday: *Batiste, Rose* / Whirlpool: *Inst* / You better mend your ways: *Matthews, Joe* / No part time love for me: *Star, Martha* / Nobody loves me like my baby: *Gilford, Jimmy*
CD GSCD 055
Goldmine / Nov '94 / Vital

THELMA'S DETROIT COLLECTIVE
I'm lonely: *Starr, Martha* / She's my beauty queen: *Matthews, Joe* / Groovy generation: *Kennedy, Billy* / I can hear you cryin': *Hill, Eddie* / It's too bad baby: *Starr, Martha* / Making up time: *Holidays* / Honky tonk woman: *Fabulous Playboys* / This love I have for you: *Fabulous Peps* / Lucky to be loved by you: *Laskey, Emanuel* / Sweet love: *Starr, Martha* / Whirlpool: *Mancha, Steve* / Still hungry: *San Remo Strings* / I love you: *Storm, Tom* / Is it worth it all: *Matthews, Joe* / What did I do wrong: *Laskey, Emanuel* / I wanna be your girl: *Starr, Martha* / Sweet things: *Kennedy, Billy* / Did my baby call: *Kingfish, Joey* / She's going to leave you: *Fabulous Peps* / Let's party: *Thelma All Stars* / Miracles: *O'Jays* / That's the way loves: *Storm, Tom* / I'll love you forever: *Holidays* / Hit & run: *Reeves, Martha*
CD GSCD 069
Goldmine / Aug '96 / Vital

THEM DIRTY BLUES (2CD Set)
CD Set JASSCD 11/12
Jass / Oct '91 / ADA / Cadillac / CM / Direct / Jazz Music

THEME FROM THE DANCE
CD 63676700012
Aquarius / Jul '97 / Jet Star

THEMES AND DREAMS
Return to innocence: *Enigma* / Only you: *Praise* / Sentinel: *Oldfield, Mike* / Theme from Harry's Game: *Clannad* / Brideshead theme: *Burgon, Geoffrey* / Crocket's theme: *Hammer, Jan* / Twin Peak's theme: *Badalamenti, Angelo* / Mission: *Morricone, Ennio* / Aria: *Yanni* / Songbird: *Kenny G* / Lily was here: *Stewart, Dave & Cindy Duffer* / City never sleeps: *Eurythmics* / Albatross: *Fleetwood Mac* / Samba pa ti: *Santana* / Scarborough fair: *In Tune* / So, relax: *Redbone, Leon* / An ubhal as airde: *Runrig* / Inspector morse main theme / Between the lines theme: *Lindes, Hal* / Spiritual high (state of independence): *Moodswings* / Deep forest: *Deep Forest* / Concerto de Aranjuez: *Hall, Jim*
CD RADCD 11
Global TV / Jun '95 / BMG

THEMES FOR DREAMS (The Magic Sound Of The Panpipes)
Light of experience / Bright eyes / Feelings / Miss you nights / Whiter shade of pale / Don't cry for me Argentina / Love story / Ave Maria / Stranger on the shore / Annie's song / Concierto de aranjuez / You don't bring me flowers / Aria / Forever autumn / Sailing / Nights in white satin / Amazing grace / I can't stop loving you
CD MCCD 156
Music Club / May '94 / Disc / THE

THEMES FROM VAPOURSPACE
CD TRUCD 4
Internal / Jun '94 / Pinnacle / PolyGram

THEN HE KISSED ME
CD MACCD 210
Autograph / Aug '96 / BMG

THEN THAT'S WHAT THEY CALL DISCO
We got the funk: *Positive Force* / Lookin' for love tonight: *Fat Larry's Band* / Hi tension: *Hi-Tension* / Can you feel the force: *Real Thing* / You can do it: *One Way & Al Hudson* / Shake your groove thing: *Peaches & Herb* / Sir Dancealot: *Olympic Runners* / You make me feel (mighty real): *Sylvester* / Space bass: *Slick* / Get down: *Chandler, Gene* / Everything is great: *Inner Circle* / White lines (don't don't do it): *Grandmaster Flash & Melle Mel*
CD CDELV 05
Elevate / May '93 / 3mv/Sony

THERE ARE MANY DIFFERENT COLOURS
CD ORCCD 1
Octopus / Sep '96 / Kudos / Pinnacle

THERE ARE TOO MANY FOOLS FOLLOWING TOO MANY RULES (2CD Set)
CD Set 501 RDOOM2CD
Irdial / Jun '95 / RTM/Disc

THERE GOES THE NEIGHBOUR
CD COLCD 0508
Collectables / Jun '97 / Greyhound

THERE IS SOME FUN GOING FORWARD (Dandelion - Rarities)
Only do what is true: *Medicine Head* / Anticipation: *Ward, Clifford T.* / Pretty little girl: *Coxhill-Bedford Duo* / Nell's song: *Hart, Mike* / All ends up: *Tractor* / Fly high: *St. John, Bridget* / Sky dance: *Trevor, John* / Mama keep your big mouth shut: *Stackwaddy* / Colour is blue: *Country Sun* / Sand all yellow: *Coyne, Kevin* / Vorblifa exit: *Coxhill, Lol* / Fetch me my woman: *Siren* / War is over: *Siren* / Autumn lady dancing: *Principal Edwards Magic Theatre* / Early morning song: *St. John, Bridget* / Sleeping town: *Beau* / Girl from Ipanema: *Stackwaddy*
CD SEECD 427
See For Miles/C5 / Jul '95 / Pinnacle

THERE WAS A LADY (The Voice Of Celtic Woman)
Willie Taylor: *Dillon, Mary & Deanta* / Mo choill: *Ni Mhaonaigh, Mairead & Altan* / Fogsail an dorus/Nighean bhuaidh' ruadh: *Matheson, Karen & Capercaillie* / Roisin dubh: *Ryan, Cathie & Cherish The Ladies* / Siuil a run: *Fahy, Mairin & Reeltime* / Maid that sold her barley: *Dillon, Mary & Deanta* / There was a lady: *Ni Dhomhnaill, Triona & Relativity* / Ranntai fheilinidh na fidile: *Ni Dhomhnaill, Maighread* / Jug of punch: *Ni Mhaonaigh, Mairead & Altan* / Am buachaille ban: *Matheson, Karen & Capercaillie* / Green grow the rushes oh: *Clancy, Aoife & Cherish The Ladies* / Casadh cam na feadarnaighe: *Ni Dhomhnaill, Triona & Touchstone* / Dark iniseoghain: *Dillon, Mary & Deanta*
CD CELT 9002
Celtophile / May '97 / Direct

THERE WHERE THE AVALANCHE STOPS (Albanian Folk Festival)
CD T 3311
Touch / '90 / Kudos / Pinnacle

THERE'LL ALWAYS BE AN ENGLAND (24 War-Time Songs From 1939)
There'll always be an England: *Loss, Joe* / Wishing: *Lynn, Vera* / We must all stick together: *Geraldo* / Songs the Tommies sang: *Stone, Lew* / Adolf: *Ambrose* / FDR Jones: *Flanagan & Allen* / We're gonna hang out the washing on the Siegfried Line: *Waters, Elsie & Doris* / Handsome Territorial: *Gonella, Nat* / Till the lights of London shine again: *Henderson, Chick & Joe Loss* / They can't black out the moon: *Roy, Harry* / Kiss me goodnight, Sergeant Major: *Cotton, Billy* / We'll meet again: *Henderson, Chick & Joe Loss* / If a grey-haired lady says How's yer father: *Flanagan & Allen* / Wish me luck as you wave me goodbye: *Hylton, Jack* / Goodnight children everywhere: *Henderson, Chick & Joe Loss* / Wings over the navy: *Cotton, Billy* / Run rabbit run: *Flanagan & Allen* / I'm sending a letter to Santa Claus: *Fields, Gracie* / Nasty Uncle Adolf: *Ambrose* / Somewhere in France with you: *Henderson, Chick & Joe Loss* / Mother's prayer at twilight: *Lynn, Vera* / Rhymes of the times: *Ambrose*
CD CDAJA 5069
Living Era / Feb '90 / Select

THERE'S A GRIOT GOING ON
CD FMS 5029
Rogue / Jan '94 / Stern's

THERE'S A MOVEMENT UNDERGROUND
CD PLUGCD 3
Produce / Feb '96 / 3mv/Sony

THEY CALL IT IRELAND
Little bit of heaven (sure, they call it Ireland): *Parker, Frank* / Kitty my love, won't you marry me: *Parker, Frank* / Kerry dance: *Parker, Frank* / My wild Irish rose: *Parker, Frank* / It's true the women are worse than the men: *O'Hara, Maureen* / Kerry cow: *O'Hara, Maureen* / Galway Bay: *Quinn, Carmel* / Green glens of Antrim: *Quinn, Carmel* / Where the river Shannon flows: *Smith, Kate* / That's how I spell IRELAND: *Downey, Morton* / Kevin Barry: *Downey, Morton* / Back to Donegal: *Harrington, Pat* / If there'd never been an Ireland: *Harrington, Pat* / Rich man died: *O'Hara, Maureen* / Wee Hughie: *O'Hara, Maureen* / Isle of Innisfree: *Quinn, Carmel* / Whistling gypsy: *Quinn, Carmel* / Drunicolliber: *O'Dowda, Brendan* / Rose of Tralee: *Parker, Frank*
CD CK 57143
Columbia / Mar '97 / Sony

THEY CALLED IT CROONING (Recordings From 1928-1932)
Where the blue of the night meets the gold of the day: *Crosby, Bing* / Cheerful little earful: *Ellis, Segar* / My song: *Bullock, Chick* / She's a new kind of old-fashioned girl: *Smith, Jack* / Got a date with an angel: *O'Malley, Pat* / Living in dreams: *Columbo, Russ* / Orange blossom time: *Edwards, Cliff* / She's wonderful: *Shalson, Harry* / I'm blue: *Bellew, Smith* / There lies love: *Browne, Sam* / Thrill is gone: *Vallee, Rudy* / Ain't misbehavin': *Austin, Gene* / My sweet Virginia: *Bowlly, Al* / Please: *Rosing, Val* / Little by little: *Marvin, Johnny* / You're a real sweetheart: *Coslow, Sam* / Sweet Sue, just you: *Metaxa, George* / Thank your father: *Richman, Harry*
CD CDAJA 5026
Living Era / Select

THEY PLAYED THE HACKNEY EMPIRE
Summer sweetheart: *Cortez, Leon & His Coster Band/Dorren Harris* / Beer barrel polka: *Cortez, Leon & His Coster Band/Gu-v'nor & The Boys* / He said Kiss Me: *O'Shea, Tessie & Her Banjulele & Orchestra* / Hymie and Amy sing sing: *O'Shea, Tessie & Her Banjulele & Orchestra* / Serenade in the night: *Loss, Joe Band* / When the poppies bloom: *Loss, Joe Band* / Again: *Loss, Joe Band* / Did I remember: *Loss, Joe Band* / Forty four fousand and five: *Sarony, Leslie & Leslie Holmes* / Cut yourself a little piece of cake: *Sarony, Leslie & Leslie Holmes* / He's an angel: *Masters, Kitty & Orchestra* / Ready for the river: *Gonella, Nat & His Georgians* / Deep river: *Gonella, Nat & His Georgians* / Two rivers flow through: *Gonella, Nat & His Georgians* / Harlem: *Gonella, Nat & His Georgians* / Sandy furnishes the home: *Powell, Sandy & Company* / Arp experience: *Miller, Max* / Grand old man: *Miller, Max* / Swimming instructor: *Miller, Max* / Georgia's got a moon: *Roy, Harry* / I'm looking for the Sheik Of Araby: *Millward, Sid & His Nitwits* / Good morning: *Murgatroyd & Winterbottom* / Lonesome trail ain't lonesome anymore: *Campbell, Big Bill* / London pride: *Waters, Elsie & Doris* / Button up your shoes and dance: *Wall, Max* / My Alf: *Tarri, Suzette* / Stormy weather: *Carless, Dorothy* / Lady of Spain: *Geraldo & His Gaucho Tango Orchestra*
CD RAJCD 848
Empress / May '95 / Koch

THEY SHALL NOT PASS
Lean on me: *Redskins* / Unionize: *Redskins* / Adrenochrome: *Sisters Of Mercy* / Body electric: *Sisters Of Mercy* / Mindless violence: *Newtown Neurotics* / Kick out the tories: *Newtown Neurotics* / Pink headed bug: *Three Johns* / Men like monkeys: *Three Johns*
CD AABT 400CD
Abstract / Jul '91 / Cargo / Pinnacle / Total/ BMG

THEY SOLD A MILLION (The Swinging 1930's)
One o'clock jump: *James, Harry* / Honeysuckle rose: *Reinhardt, Django* / After you've gone: *Reinhardt, Django* / Marie: *Dorsey, Tommy* / Boogie woogie: *Dorsey, Tommy* / Begin the beguine: *Shaw, Artie* / Nightmare: *Shaw, Artie* / Black Bay shuffle: *Shaw, Artie* / Traffic jam: *Shaw, Artie* / Body and soul: *Hawkins, Coleman* / April in Paris: *Hawkins, Coleman* / Sugar foot stomp: *Hawkins, Coleman* / Little brown jug: *Miller, Glenn* / In the mood: *Miller, Glenn* / Sunrise serenade: *Miller, Glenn* / Moonlight serenade: *Miller, Glenn*
CD 74321366612
Camden / Apr '96 / BMG

THEY SOLD A MILLION (The Fabulous 1940's)
Pennsylvania 6-500: *Miller, Glenn* / Tuxedo Junction: *Miller, Glenn* / I've got a girl in Kalamazoo: *Miller, Glenn* / American patrol: *Miller, Glenn* / Chattanooga choo choo: *Miller, Glenn* / Frenesi: *Shaw, Artie* / Stardust: *Shaw, Artie* / Summit Ridge Drive: *Shaw, Artie* / Opus 1: *Dorsey, Tommy* / On the sunny side of the street: *Dorsey, Tommy* / Chinatown, my chinatown: *Dorsey, Tommy* / I'm getting sentimental over you: *Dorsey, Tommy* / When the midnight choo choo leaves for Alabama: *Dorsey, Tommy* / Holiday for strings: *Rose, David* / There I've said it again: *Monroe, Vaughan* / Riders in the sky: *Monroe, Vaughan*
CD 74321366622
Camden / Apr '96 / BMG

THEY SOLD A MILLION (The Vintage Years)
Ida, sweet as apple cider: *Nichols, Red* / Spaniard who blighted my life: *Jolson, Al* / Sonny boy: *Jolson, Al* / Rainbow on my shoulder: *Jolson, Al* / Wang wang blues: *Whiteman, Paul* / Japanese sandman: *Whiteman, Paul* / Three o'clock in the morning: *Whiteman, Paul* / Linger awhile: *Whiteman, Paul* / Prisoner's song: *Dalhart, Vernon* / Dardanella: *Whiteman, Paul* / Who: *Olson, George* / My blue heaven: *Austin, Gene* / Ramona: *Austin, Gene* / It ain't gonna rain no more: *Hall, Wendell* / Some of these days: *Tucker, Sophie*
CD 74321366602
Camden / Apr '96 / BMG

THEY SOLD A MILLION (2CD Set)
Rum and coca cola: *Andrews Sisters* / I've got a gal in Kalamazoo: *Miller, Glenn Orchestra* / I'm making believe: *Fitzgerald, Ella & The Ink Spots* / Besame mucho: *Dorsey, Jimmy & His Orchestra* / Too ra loo ra loo ra: *Crosby, Bing* / Dancing in the dark: *Shaw, Artie Orchestra* / Oklahoma / There are such things: *Sinatra, Frank* / Don't fence me in: *Crosby, Bing & Andrews Sisters* / Chattanooga choo choo: *Miller, Glenn Orchestra* / I've heard that song before: *James, Harry Orchestra* / GI jive: *Jordan, Louis & His Tympany Five* / Swinging on a star: *Crosby, Bing* / You always hurt the one you love: *Mills Brothers* / Into each life some rain must fall: *Fitzgerald, Ella & The Ink Spots* / Is you is or is you ain't my baby: *Jordan, Louis & His Tympany Five* / In the mood: *Miller, Glenn Orchestra* / Paper doll: *Mills Brothers* / Begin the beguine: *Shaw, Artie Orchestra* / Jumpin' jive: *Calloway, Cab Orchestra* / You made me love you: *James, Harry Orchestra* / Sunday, Monday or always: *Crosby, Bing* / You'll never know: *Haymes, Dick* / Moonlight serenade: *Miller, Glenn Orchestra* / Amapola: *Dorsey, Jimmy Orchestra* / At the woodchoppers ball: *Herman, Woody Orchestra* / Sweet Leilani: *Crosby, Bing* / Marie: *Dorsey, Tommy Orchestra* / Bei mir bist du schon: *Andrews Sisters* / All or nothing: *Sinatra, Frank* / New San Antonio Rose: *Wills, Bob & His Texas Playboys* / Tisket-a-tasket: *Fitzgerald, Ella*
CD Set 330372
Hallmark / Mar '97 / Carlton

THEY'RE PLAYING OUR SONG
It had to be you / Way you look tonight / I'm in the mood for love / What a difference a day made / Where or when / Folks who live on the hill / Two sleepy people / Night and day / Embraceable you / Long ago and far away / You were never lovelier / That old feeling / Very thought of you / Man I love / Why do I love you / All the things that are you / Song is you / As long as I love / Every time we say goodbye / There I've said it again / You do something to me / Too marvellous for words / Love letters / Don't blame me
CD PASTCD 7802
Flapper / Nov '96 / Pinnacle

THING CALLED LOVE
Dreaming with my eyes open: *Walker, Clay* / You'd be home by now: *Norwood, Daron* / I can't understand: *Yearwood, Trisha* / I don't remember your name (But I remember you): *Oslin, K.T.* / Diamonds and tears: *Berg, Matraca* / Ready and waiting: *Allen, Deborah* / Until now: *Crowell, Rodney* / Looking for a thing called love: *Robbins, Dennis* / Streets of love: *Welch, Kevin* / Partners in wine: *Travis, Randy* / Blame it on your heart: *Allen, Deborah* / Standing on a rock: *Crowell, Rodney*
CD 74321157932
Giant / Apr '94 / BMG

THINKING OF YOU
Here we are: *Estefan, Gloria* / Fool (if you think it's over): *Brooks, Elkie* / I'll never fall in love again: *Deacon Blue* / Promise me: *Craven, Beverley* / Two out of three ain't bad: *Meat Loaf* / All cried out: *Moyet, Alison* / Everytime you go away: *Young, Paul* / Neither one of us: *Knight, Gladys & The Pips* / If you were here tonight: *O'Neal, Alexander* / Sorry seems to be the hardest word: *John, Elton* / Ain't no sunshine: *Withers, Bill* / Blue velvet: *Vinton, Bobby* / Stay with me 'til dawn: *Tzuke, Judie* / How am I supposed to live without you: *Bolton, Michael* / Eternal flame: *Bangles* / Let's stay together: *Green, Al* / Still: *Commodores*
CD MOODCD 15
CBS / Feb '91 / Sony

THIRD GENERATION
CD IG 0052
Intergroove / Jun '97 / Intergroove

THIS AIN'T TRIP HOP VOL.1
CD MM 800212
Moonshine / Feb '95 / Mo's Music Machine / Prime / RTM/Disc

THIS AIN'T TRIP HOP VOL.2
CD MM 800392
Moonshine / Oct '95 / Mo's Music Machine / Prime / RTM/Disc

THIS AIN'T TRIP HOP VOL.3
CD MM 800482
Moonshine / May '96 / Mo's Music Machine / Prime / RTM/Disc

THIS FILM'S CRAP LET'S SAMPLE THE SOUNDTRACK
First & last: *Dunderhead* / Extention: *Skematicks* / Petrushka: *Pentatonik* / Catalonia: *Pentatonik* / Pentaura: *Pentaura* / Pulsation: *Lumo* / Trouble shooter: *Love Rears* / Black & white: *Slowly*
CD FILMCRP 007CD
North South / Sep '96 / Pinnacle

THIS FUNKY THING VOL.1
This funky thing: *Pierce, Don* / Your love and my money: *Davis, Curtis* / Hot pants: *Carleen & The Groovers* / Right on brother, right on: *Soul Controllers* / I've been searchin': *Wright, Lonzine* / Soul groove: *Mato & The Mystics* / Hump the bump: *Soul Company* / When ya git through wit it put it back: *Blenders Ltd.* / Go for it: *Smith, Kenny & The Loveliters* / Bury the hatchet: *Count Rockin' Sidney* / Garden of four trees: *Explosions & Juanita Brooks* / Dynamite: *Soul Merchants* / So sharp: *Soul Clinic* / Do the rope 'Dee Dope': *Lil Waters' Burning Flame* / Gettin' T'gether man: *Classitors* / Stay together: *Soul Excitement* / Stormy Jazzmin: *Stormy Jazzmin*
CD GSCD 116
Goldmine / Jun '97 / Vital

THIS HOUSE IS NOT A MOTEL
CD ______ **EFA 4481 CD**
Glitterhouse / Jul '89 / Avid/BMG

THIS IS 2 KOOL
CD ______ **TKCD 1**
2 Kool / Mar '95 / Pinnacle / SRD

THIS IS ACID JAZZ
Runaway: *Nu Yorican Soul* / Don't let it go to your head: *Brand New Heavies* / Frederick lies still: *Galliano* / Chillin': *Movement '97* / Mini: *Corduroy* / Shine: *Breeze* / After dark: *Laverna, Michelle* / Step off: *Rhythm* / Apparently nothin': *Young Disciples* / Always there: *Incognito* / Bomb: *Supa Star* / You blow my mind: *Jasmine* / Lucky fellow: *Snowboy & Noel McKoy* / Good thing: *Future Collective* / Jesse: *Mother Earth* / Loving you: *Meateaters* / Turn on tune in drop out: *Freakpower* / Trust me: *Vibraphonic & Alison Limerick* / Jazzatude: *Bud* / Whole lotta love: *Goldbug* / Do you: *Shades Of Rhythm* / Shake it loose: *United States*
CD ______ **BEBOXCD 12**
Beechwood / Jun '97 / Beechwood/BMG / Pinnacle

THIS IS ACID JAZZ VOL.3 (New Voices)
CD ______ **EX 3382**
Instinct / Nov '96 / Timewarp

THIS IS BLACK TOP
I can't stop loving you: *Funderburgh, Anson & Sam Myers* / Iron cupid: *King, Earl* / That certain door: *Eaglin, Snooks* / Woman's gotta have it: *Neville Brothers* / Stick around: *Radcliff, Bobby* / Can't call you no: *Sumlin, Hubert & Mighty Sam* / Lemonade: *Funderburgh, Anson & Sam Myers* / Young girl: *Eaglin, Snooks* / If I don't get involved: *Medwick, Joe & Grady Gaines* / Hello sundown: *Davis, James 'Thunderbird'* / Party in Nogales: *Levy, Ron*
CD ______ **BTSCD 1**
Black Top / Dec '89 / ADA / CM / Direct

THIS IS CLUB ANTHEMS (3CD Set)
Don't stop movin': *Livin' Joy* / I believe: *Happy Clappers* / I luv U baby: *Original* / Let me show you: *K-Klass* / Weekend: *Terry, Todd Project* / I'm so in luv with U: *Da Boss & Blu* / Don't stop the music: *Supernature* / If Madonna calls: *Vasquez, Junior* / Let me be your fantasy: *Baby D* / La Serenissima: *DNA* / Release yourself: *Blue Mast* / Krupa: *Apollo 440* / Everybody be somebody: *Ruffneck* / Renegade master: *Wildchild* / Wanted: *K Crushed One* / Atlantic ocean: *Degrees Of Motion* / Who do you love: *Supernature* / Do you: *Airwaves* / Are you out there: *Crescendo* / Do that to me: *Lisa Marie Experience* / Bette Davis eyes: *Cover Up*
CD Set ______ **BEBOXCD 6**
Beechwood / Oct '96 / Beechwood/BMG / Pinnacle

THIS IS DANCEHALL
Sugar Wogga man: *Griffiths, Marcia* / How else can I ease the pain: *Haughton, Anthony* / Best friends: *Singing Melody* / My love: *Paul, Frankie* / Every kinda people: *Kevin B* / Sax-a-rock: *Johnson, Jerry* / Send down some: *Rev. Badoo* / Work it out: *Junior Demus* / Struggle: *Ravon* / Science: *Shaggy* / New talk: *Dollar Man* / Pretty girls: *Judas* / Love's gone: *White Mice* / Dub dis': *Livin' Crew*
CD ______ **CDCTUM 1**
Continuum / Jun '93 / Pinnacle

THIS IS DANCEHALL VOL.4
CD ______ **CDCTUM 6**
Continuum / Dec '93 / Pinnacle

THIS IS DRUM 'N' BASS
Do you know where you're coming from: *Jamiroquai* / Come to me: *Bjork* / Candles: *Reece, Alex* / Rollin': *Solid State* / Game: *Cutmaster* / So many dreams: *Guy Called Gerald* / Spice of life: *Slim* / Metropolis: *Adam F* / Sonic sixes: *Dimension* / Trip: *Skylab* / Loop 2: *Larkin, Kenny* / ER: *DOA* / Outlands: *Subversive* / Beautiful day: *Nicolette* / Destiny: *DJ Pulse* / Elemental breaks: *Nova* / Digital ultramagnetic: *Boss* / Sea: *St. Etienne* / Ultraworld: *Motion* / Sound and vision: *Loot* / Downlow: *Aquarius* / Something always happens: *Art Of Noise*
CD ______ **BEBOXCD 10**
Beechwood / Mar '97 / Beechwood/BMG / Pinnacle

THIS IS EASY (2CD Set)
Champions: *Hatch, Tony* / Superstars / Spanish flea: *World Of Tijuana* / Sentimental journey: *Esquivel, Juan Garcia* / Swingin' safari: *Kaempfert, Bert* / Animal Magic / Pink panther: *Mancini, Henry* / Big Match / Up up and away: *5th Dimension* / Strange report: *Love, Geoff* / In crowd: *Faith, Percy Orchestra* / Taste of honey: *World Of Tijuana* / New Avengers: *Johnson, Laurie Orchestra* / Asteroid: *Moore, Pete* / Riviera Affair / Avenues and alleyways: *Christie, Tony* / Man in a suitcase: *Grainer, Ron* / Do you know the way to San Jose: *Goodwin, Ron & His Orchestra* / Music to watch girls by: *Williams, Andy* / 1-2-3: *Faith, Percy Orchestra* / Misirlou: *Denny, Martin* / Classical gas: *Williams, Mason* / Black beauty / Always something there to remind me: *Shaw, Sandie* / Crossroads: *Hatch, Tony* / Good, the bad and the ugly: *Montenegro, Hugo* / Girls in a sportscar / Walk on by: *Warwick, Dionne* / Windmills of your mind: *Harrison, Noel* / Raindrops keep falling on my head: *Thomas, B.J.* / Anyone who had a heart: *Bacharach, Burt* / Summer breeze: *Conniff, Ray & Singers* / Un homme et une femme: *Lai, Francis* / Get Carter: *Budd, Roy* / I can't let Maggie go: *Honeybus* / Light my fire: *Feliciano, Jose* / Close to you: *Monro, Matt* / As tears go by: *Sinatra, Nancy* / This Is Your Life / Call me: *Montez, Chris* / Chelsea morning: *Mendes, Sergio* / It never rains in Southern California: *Conniff, Ray & Singers* / What the world needs now is love: *Goodwin, Ron* / Aujourd hui c'est toi: *Lai, Francis* / House is not a home: *Bacharach, Burt* / Wives and lovers: *Jones, Jack* / Go-between: *Barry, John* / I say a little prayer: *Franklin, Aretha* / Unknown love: *Count Indigo* / Look of love: *Hayes, Isaac*
CD ______ **VTDCD 80**
Virgin / Mar '96 / EMI

THIS IS EUROVISION (39 Songs For Europe/2CD Set)
Ne partez pas sans moi: *Dion, Celine* / Congratulations: *Richard, Cliff* / Making your mind up: *Bucks Fizz* / Save your kisses for me: *Brotherhood Of Man* / What's another year: *Logan, Johnny* / Beg, steal or borrow: *New Seekers* / Ein bisschen frieden: *Nicole* / Apres toi: *Leandros, Vicky* / Tu te reconnaitras: *David, Anne-Marie* / Why me: *Martin, Linda* / J'aime la vie: *Kim, Sandra* / Rock 'n' roll kids: *Harrington, Paul & Charlie McGettigan* / Hallelujah: *Harrington, Paul & Charlie McGettigan* / Let me be the one: *Shadows* / Poupee de cire, poupee de son: *Gall, France* / Voice: *Quinn, Eimaer* / Un blanc, un abre, une rue: *Severine* / Love games: *Belle & The Devotions* / Jack in the box: *Rodgers, Clodagh* / He gives me love (la la la): *Massiel* / Power to all our friends: *Richard, Cliff* / Hold me now: *Logan, Johnny* / Puppet on a string: *Shaw, Sandie* / Long live love: *Newton-John, Olivia* / Boom bang a bang: *Lulu* / I love the little things: *Monro, Matt* / All kinds of everything: *Dana* / Ding a dong: *Teach In* / Aba ni bi: *Cohen, Izhar* / In your eyes: *Kavanagh, Niamh* / Bad old days: *Coco* / I belong: *Kirby, Kathy* / Parlez vous Francais: *Baccara* / Sing little birdie: *Carr, Pearl* / Message to your heart: *Janus, Samantha* / L'oiseau et l'enfant: *Myriam, Marie* / Rock bottom: *De Paul, Lynsey & Mike Moran* / Lonely symphony: *Ruffelle, Frances* / One step further: *Bardo*
CD Set ______ **VTDCD 142**
Virgin / Apr '97 / EMI

THIS IS HARDCORE
Jumpin' pumpin': *DJ Demand* / Paradise: *Unknown Project* / Techno wonderland: *Smeetit, Steve* / Music's so wonderful: *Vibes & Wishdokta* / Journey: *Ramos & Supreme* / Sun always shines: *Supreme & UFO* / Slippery Project: *Slippery Project* / Anything for you: *Vibes* / Can you dig it: *Sharky & Dee* / You're mine: *DJ Demo* / Hold me now: *Go Mental* / Gizmo music: *Future Vinyl Collective* / Smiling eyes: *DJ Stompy* / Eternity: *Jimmy JT Time* / Nothing is forever: *Happy Tunes* / Comin' on strong: *Slam & Charly B* / I believe: *Force & Styles* / Setting you free: *DJ Unknown* / Doesn't have to be: *Vinyl Groover* / Total recall: *Full Action* / Groove control: *Midas & Dougal* / All you need (is an angel): *DJ Edy C*
CD ______ **BEBOXCD 11**
Beechwood / Apr '97 / Beechwood/BMG / Pinnacle

THIS IS HIP HOP VOL.1 (20 Phat Jams)
CD ______ **USCD 002**
Ultrasound / Feb '95 / Grapevine/ PolyGram

THIS IS HIP HOP VOL.2 (26 Of The Biggest Licks/2CD Set)
CD Set ______ **USCD 5**
Ultrasound / Apr '96 / Grapevine/ PolyGram

THIS IS HOME ENTERTAINMENT VOL.1
CD ______ **HE 002**
Home Entertainment / Dec '96 / Cargo

THIS IS HOME ENTERTAINMENT VOL.2
CD ______ **HE 008**
Home Entertainment / Dec '96 / Cargo

THIS IS HOME ENTERTAINMENT VOL.3
CD ______ **HE 120CD**
Home Entertainment / May '97 / Cargo

THIS IS HOUSE (3CD Set)
I've got you: *2 Minds* / Where love lies: *Limerick, Alison* / Beautiful people: *Tucker, Barbara* / Is anybody out there: *Bassheads* / Gonna take you: *Beatserver* / Jingo: *Candido* / Hideaway: *De'Lacy* / My love is free: *Double Exposure* / Dr. Love: *First Choice* / Can't you see: *G'Street Project* / Lets groove: *Morels, George* / Dominator: *Human Resource* / Your love: *Inner City* / Space cowboy: *Jamiroquai* / Live and direct: *Juice On The Loose* / French Kiss: *Lil' Louis* / Hit'n'run: *Holloway, Loleatta* / Someday: *M-People* / Something about you: *Mr. Roy* / Blue Monday: *New Order* / Salsa house: *Richie Rich* / Take me away: *True Faith*
CD Set ______ **BEBOXCD 4**
Beechwood / Jul '96 / Beechwood/BMG / Pinnacle

THIS IS IT
CD ______ **MCCD 196**
Music Club / Mar '95 / Disc / THE

THIS IS JAZZ (10CD Set)
Cornet chop suey: *Armstrong, Louis* / Heebie jeebies: *Armstrong, Louis* / Potato head blues: *Armstrong, Louis* / West End blues: *Armstrong, Louis* / Memories of you: *Armstrong, Louis* / Stardust: *Armstrong, Louis* / When you're smiling: *Armstrong, Louis* / Dinah: *Armstrong, Louis* / Tiger rag: *Armstrong, Louis* / Lazy river: *Armstrong, Louis* / Basin street blues: *Armstrong, Louis* / Big butter and egg man: *Armstrong, Louis* / Ain't misbehavin': *Armstrong, Louis* / When it's sleepy time down south: *Armstrong, Louis* / I've got the world on a string: *Armstrong, Louis* / Between the devil and the deep blue sea: *Armstrong, Louis* / Little duet (for Zoot and Chet): *Baker, Chet* / Love walked in: *Baker, Chet* / You don't know what love is: *Baker, Chet* / I'm through with love: *Baker, Chet* / You'd better go now: *Baker, Chet* / Wind: *Baker, Chet* / Autumn leaves: *Baker, Chet* / She was too good to me: *Baker, Chet* / Tangerine: *Baker, Chet* / What'll I do: *Baker, Chet* / Take five: *Brubeck, Dave* / Gone with the wind: *Brubeck, Dave* / Someday my prince will come: *Brubeck, Dave* / Blue rondo a la Turk: *Brubeck, Dave* / Pennies from heaven: *Brubeck, Dave* / When you wish upon a star: *Brubeck, Dave* / Jeepers creepers: *Brubeck, Dave* / For all we know: *Brubeck, Dave* / Sing sing sing (with a swing): *Goodman, Benny* / Flying home: *Goodman, Benny* / Wang wang blues: *Goodman, Benny* / Don't be that way: *Goodman, Benny* / Running wild: *Goodman, Benny* / King Porter stomp: *Goodman, Benny* / Limehouse blues: *Goodman, Benny* / Mission to Moscow: *Goodman, Benny* / You turned the tables on me: *Goodman, Benny* / Avalon: *Goodman, Benny* / Memories of you: *Goodman, Benny* / 'Round midnight: *Monk, Thelonious* / Well you needn't: *Monk, Thelonious* / Bemsha swing: *Monk, Thelonious* / Ruby my dear: *Monk, Thelonious* / Straight, no chaser: *Monk, Thelonious* / Blue Monk: *Monk, Thelonious* / Rhythm-a-ning: *Monk, Thelonious* / Monk's dream: *Monk, Thelonious* / Misterioso: *Monk, Thelonious* / Epistrophy: *Monk, Thelonious* / Better git it in your soul: *Mingus, Charles* / Goodbye pork pie hat: *Mingus, Charles* / Fable of Faubus: *Mingus, Charles* / Self portrait in 3 colors: *Mingus, Charles* / Slop: *Mingus, Charles* / Song with orange: *Mingus, Charles* / Gunslinging bird: *Mingus, Charles* / Far Wells, Mill Valley: *Mingus, Charles* / New now, know how: *Mingus, Charles* / Shoes of the fisherman's wife are some jive ass slippers: *Mingus, Charles* / Please don't come back from the moon: *Mingus, Charles* / East St Louis toodle-oo: *Ellington, Duke* / In a sentimental mood: *Ellington, Duke* / Stompy Jones: *Ellington, Duke* / Prelude to a kiss: *Ellington, Duke* / C jam blues: *Ellington, Duke* / Sentimental lady: *Ellington, Duke* / Take the 'A' train: *Ellington, Duke* / Satin doll: *Ellington, Duke* / In a mellotone: *Ellington, Duke* / Solitude: *Ellington, Duke* / Mood Indigo: *Ellington, Duke* / Diminuendo and crescendo in blue: *Ellington, Duke* / 'Round midnight: *Davis, Miles* / Stella by starlight: *Davis, Miles* / Springsville: *Davis, Miles* / Summertime: *Davis, Miles* / So what: *Davis, Miles* / Someday my prince will come: *Davis, Miles* / Seven steps to heaven: *Davis, Miles* / Walkin': *Davis, Miles* / ESP: *Davis, Miles* / Clockwise: *Benson, George* / Myna bird blues: *Benson, George* / Willow weep for me: *Benson, George* / Stormy weather: *Benson, George* / Cooker: *Benson, George* / Borgia stick: *Benson, George* / Ode to a Kudu: *Benson, George* / Take five: *Benson, George* / I remember Wes: *Benson, George* / Good King Bad: *Benson, George* / Summertime: *Benson, George* / From now on: *Benson, George* / Birdland: *Weather Report* / Remark you made: *Weather Report* / Black market: *Weather Report* / Man in the green shirt: *Weather Report* / Young and fine: *Weather Report* / Teen town: *Weather Report* / Moors: *Weather Report* / Mysterious traveller: *Weather Report* / Orange lady: *Weather Report*
CD Set ______ **4843942**
Sony Jazz / Sep '96 / Sony

THIS IS JAZZ
Wave / Retratro en branco e prieto (Picture in black and white) / Sabia / Dindi / Ponteio / Obsession / Corcovado / Double rainbow / Vera cruz / Miracle of the fishes / Nrazil
CD ______ **CK 65045**
Sony Jazz / May '97 / Sony

THIS IS JAZZ - SAMPLER
Ain't misbehavin': *Armstrong, Louis* / Mood indigo: *Ellington, Duke* / One o'clock jump: *Basie, Count* / Four: *Davis, Miles* / This years kisses: *Holiday, Billie* / Blue rondo a la Turk: *Brubeck, Dave* / It might as well be a spring: *Vaughan, Sarah* / Peacocks: *Getz, Stan* / Remark you made: *Weather Report* / Dance of Maya: *McLaughlin, John* / Port of entry: *Shorter, Wayne*
CD ______ **CK 65008**
Sony Jazz / Oct '96 / Sony

THIS IS JAZZ VOL.1 (2CD Set)
CD Set ______ **JCD 1025/26**
Jazzology / Nov '96 / Jazz Music

THIS IS JUNGLE
CD ______ **USCD 001**
Ultrasound / Sep '94 / Grapevine/ PolyGram

THIS IS JUNGLE (3CD Set)
Feel the sunshine: *Reece, Alex* / Inner city life: *Goldie* / Trippin' on broken beats: *Omni Trio* / Definition of a track: *Perfect Combination* / Smooth note: *Jason Mouse* / Witchcraft: *Roni Size* / Sky high: *St. Files* / T'raenon: *Photek* / Danger: *Sub Sequence* / Mr. Kirk's nightmare: *4 Hero* / Distance: *By Pass* / Musik: *LTJ Bukem* / Western tune: *PFM* / Spectrum: *Wax Doctor* / Jazz creation: *Universal Flava* / I've known rivers: *Pine, Courtney* / Piano tune: *Peshay* / Too unique: *Cool Breeze & Stepz Ahead* / Subtrakt: *Tiefenentzerrer* / Sax lick: *Intense* / Tear down (da whole place): *Dillinja* / State of mind: *Analyse*
CD Set ______ **BEBOXCD 7**
Beechwood / Nov '96 / Beechwood/BMG / Pinnacle

THIS IS JUNGLE SKY VOL.1
CD ______ **JSK 004**
Jungle Sky / Dec '96 / Cargo

THIS IS JUNGLE SKY VOL.2
CD ______ **JSK 008**
Jungle Sky / Dec '96 / Cargo

THIS IS LIVING JOY
Getting harder: *Time Span* / Boom: *Sub State* / I want your love: *Infernus* / Come to the rescue: *DJ Happy Raver & The Smile-E* / Take me away: *Jimmy J & Cru-L-T* / Rock the dancefloor: *Forbes, Davie* / Motorway madness: *DJ Vibes & Wishdokta* / Gotta get down: *DJ Poosie* / Hypnotic spectrum: *El Bruto* / It never fucking happens: *DJ Psycangle* / Pop goes the world: *3rd Mann* / Morning, please don't come: *DJ Ham* / Something good: *Brown, Scott* / Feel free: *DJ Reno & Eatsum & The Kidz* / I like bouncing: *Cru-L-T*
CD ______ **DBM 2262**
Death Becomes Me / Apr '97 / Grapevine/ PolyGram / Pinnacle / SRD

THIS IS MERSEYBEAT
CD ______ **EDCD 270**
Edsel / Feb '91 / Pinnacle

THIS IS MOD VOL.1 (Rarities 1979-1981)
Opening up: *Circles* / Billy: *Circles* / We can go dancing: *Amber Squad* / You should see what I do to you in my dreams: *Amber Squad* / Can't sleep at night: *Cigarettes* / It's the only way to live: *Cigarettes* / All I want is your money: *Cigarettes* / I've forgotten my number: *Cigarettes* / They're back again: *Cigarettes* / Choose you: *Deadbeats* / Julies new boyfriend: *Deadbeats* / Oh no: *Deadbeats* / Nobody loves me: *Letters* / Don't want you back: *Letters* / Happy song: *Nips* / Nobody to love: *Nips* / Saturday night: *Odds* / Not another love song: *Odds* / Circles: *Circles* / Summer nights: *Circles*
CD ______ **CDMGRAM 98**
Anagram / Oct '95 / Cargo / Pinnacle

THIS IS MOD VOL.2
Twisted wheel: *Killermeters* / SX 225: *Killermeters* / Plane crash: *Purple Hearts* / Scooby doo: *Purple Hearts* / Gun of life: *Purple Hearts* / Fashion plague: *Exits* / Cheam: *Exits* / Need somebody to love: *VIP's* / One more chance: *VIP's* / Stuttgart special: *VIP's* / Who knows: *VIP's* / Janine: *VIP's* / Modern boys: *Crooks* / Beat goes on: *Crooks* / Wild about you: *Same* / Movements: *Same* / All the time in the world: *Crooks* / Banging my head: *Crooks* / Odd man out: *Teenage Film Stars* / I apologise: *Teenage Film Stars* / Just a little Mod: *Tonik, Terry* / Smashed and blocked: *Tonik, Terry*
CD ______ **CDMGRAM 101**
Anagram / Mar '96 / Cargo / Pinnacle

THIS IS MOD VOL.3 (Diamond Collection)
CD ______ **CDMGRAM 106**
Anagram / Jun '96 / Cargo / Pinnacle

THIS IS MOD VOL.4 (Modities)
CD ______ **CDMGRAM 107**
Anagram / Oct '96 / Cargo / Pinnacle

THIS IS MOD VOL.5
I can't put my finger on you: *Amber Squad* / Tell you a lie: *Amber Squad* / Why should it happen to me: *Killermeters* / Cardiac arrest: *Killermeters* / If you want it: *Graduates* / Hey young girl: *Graduates* / One way street: *Aces* / First impressions: *Small World* / Stupidity Street: *Small World* / Tomorrow never comes: *Small World* / Win or lose: *Long Tall Shorty* / Ain't done wrong: *Long Tall Shorty* / Even if I know: *Sema 4* / Sema 4 messages: *Sema 4* / Actors all: *Sema 4* / Do you know your friends: *Sema 4* / My life's a jigsaw: *Purple Hearts* / Guy who made her a star: *Purple Hearts* / Just to please you: *Purple Hearts* / Strength of the nation: *Teenbeats* / If I'm gone tomorrow: *Teenbeats*
CD ______ **CDMGRAM 110**
Anagram / May '97 / Cargo / Pinnacle

THIS IS NORTHERN SOUL
Silent treatment: *Demain, Arin* / My sugar baby: *Clark, Connie* / Double cookin': *Checkerboard Squares* / I've got to get myself together: *Turner, Spyder* / Love makes me lonely: *Chandlers* / Walk with me heart: *Smith, Bobby* / Emperor of my baby's heart: *Harris, Kurt* / Nobody knows: *Wonder, Diane* / You're on top girl: *Empires* / Are you angry: *Servicemen* / No right to cry: *Galore,*

Mamie / So sweet so satisfying: *Treetop, Bobby* / Not me baby: *Silhouettes* / Love's just begun: *Grayson, Calvin* / Falling in love with you baby: *Cook, Little Joe* / Those lonely nights: *Soul Communicators* / Bar track: *Burdock, Doni* / He broke your game wide open: *Dell, Frank* / I've had it: *Andrews, Lee* / I'll always love you: *Moultrie, Sam* / Sister Lee: *Ward, Sam* / Prove yourself a lady: *Bounty, James* / Psychedelic soul: *Russell, Saxie*
CD ______ GSCD 014
Goldmine / Jun '93 / Vital

THIS IS OI (A Street Punk Compilation)
CD ______ AHOYCD 6
Captain Oi / Sep '93 / Plastic Head

THIS IS RAP
Fantastic voyage: *Coolio* / I wish: *Skee Lo* / Connected: *Stereo MC's* / Sneakers: *Black Bean Sauce* / Jump around: *House Of Pain* / Walk this way: *Run DMC* / Call it what you want: *Credit To The Nation* / Skin-Tact: *Loco Spengo* / People everyday: *Arrested Development* / It's a summer thang: *M-Doc & Chantay Savage* / Blazang: *Blazang* / Say no go: *De La Soul* / Can I kick it: *Tribe Called Quest* / Once upon a time: *Smoothe Da Hustler* / I'll be there for you/ You're all I need to get by: *Method Man & Mary J. Blige* / Time is ticking: *Smith, Eddie & Paul Nathan* / Gangstas boogie: *LV* / We here you ain't seen nothing yet: *Da Bomb & Euphemia Burke* / Summertime: *DJ Jazzy Jeff & The Fresh Prince* / Try: *Melly & Eddie Smith/Paul Nathan* / Paid in full: *Eric B & Rakim* / Make ya mark: *Bell, Melissa & Chojin*
CD ______ BEBOXCD 5
Beechwood / Sep '96 / Beechwood/BMG / Pinnacle

THIS IS REGGAE
Soul rebel / Money in my pocket / I show you how to reggae / Love me / Prisoner of your love / Soul shake down party / Reggae fever / (Sittin' on the) dock of the bay / Upside down / Stop that train / Green green grass of home / Key to the world / Only heaven can wait for love / Caution / Roots rock / I will love you like abc / Three little birds / You are to me / Soul captives / Make it with you
CD ______ QED 008
Tring / Nov '96 / Tring

THIS IS REGGAE MUSIC (2CD Set)
CD Set ______ RN 7002
Rhino / Aug '96 / Grapevine/PolyGram / Jet Star

THIS IS SCOTLAND
Hundred thousand welcomes / Amazing grace / Come to the Ceilidah-John Worth's jig / Dancing in Kyle / Abide with me / Massacre of Glencoe / Jaqueline waltz / Always Argyll / Punch bowl reel / Archaracle midgie / Bonnie Mary of Argyle / Skyline of Skye / Reels / 4/4 marches
CD ______ CDITV 354
Scotdisc / Aug '88 / Conifer/BMG / Duncans / Ross

THIS IS SKA
Al Capone: *Prince Buster* / Liquidator: *Harry J All Stars* / Gangsters: *Special AKA* / 007: *Dekker, Desmond* / Double barrel: *Collins, Dave & Ansell* / Irie feelings: *Edwards, Rupie* / Sweet sensation: *Melodians* / Wet dream: *Max Romeo* / Train to skaville: *Ethiopians* / Guns of Navarone: *Skatalites* / Return of Django: *Upsetters* / Dat: *Pluto* / Longshot kick de bucket: *Pioneers* / Tears of a clown: *Beat* / Red red wine: *Tribe, Tony* / Montego Bay: *Note, Freddie & Rudies* / Big 7: *Judge Dread* / Suzanne beware of the devil: *Livingstone, Dandy* / Monkey man: *Toots & The Maytals* / Elizabethan reggae: *Gardiner, Boris*
CD ______ TCD 2366
Telstar / Jun '89 / BMG

THIS IS SKA
Sound of ska (medley) / On my radio / Mirror in the bathroom / Special brew / Night boat to Cairo / Can can / Missing words / Baggy trousers / One step beyond / Lip up fatty / Hands off she's mine / Too much too young / Three minute hero / Buster's groove
CD ______ ECD 3147
K-Tel / Mar '95 / K-Tel

THIS IS SOUL
Dance to the music: *Sly & The Family Stone* / Love the one you're with: *Isley Brothers* / Grazing in the grass: *Friends Of Distinction* / Rescue me: *Bass, Fontella* / You little trustmaker: *Tymes* / Back stabbers: *O'Jays* / Native New Yorker: *Odyssey* / K-jee: *Nite Liters* / I can understand it: *New Birth* / To each his own: *Faith, Hope & Charity* / Whispering: *Dr. Buzzard's Original Savannah Band* / Everybody plays the fool: *Main Ingredient* / Lean on me: *Withers, Bill* / La la means I love you: *Delfonics* / I wanna get next to you: *Rose Royce* / Don't walk away: *General Johnson* / I'm your puppet: *Purify, James & Bobby* / Hey there lonely girl: *Holman, Eddie*
CD ______ 74321275262
Arista / May '95 / BMG

THIS IS SOUL VOL.1
Barefootin': *Parker, Robert* / When a man loves a woman: *Sledge, Percy* / For your precious love: *Butler, Jerry* / So many ways: *Benton, Brook* / Save the last dance for me: *Drifters* / Operator: *Knight, Gladys & The Pips* / Soul man: *Sam & Dave* / Me and Mrs Jones: *Paul, Billy* / If you don't know me by now: *Melvin, Harold & The Bluenotes* / Feel the need in me: *Detroit Emeralds* / Walking the dog: *Thomas, Rufus* / Show and tell: *Wilson, Al* / I stand accused: *Butler, Jerry* / It's just a matter of time: *Benton, Brook* / I got you (I feel good): *Brown, James* / There goes my baby: *Drifters* / Soul sister, brown sugar: *Sam & Dave* / You've made me so very happy: *Whispers* / Try a little tenderness: *Sledge, Percy* / Knock on wood: *Floyd, Eddie*
CD ______ QED 006
Tring / Nov '96 / Tring

THIS IS SPACE (4CD Set)
Space lab: *Kraftwerk* / Star too far: *Psychic TV* / Adjust me: *Hawkwind* / Blue room: *Orb* / Point of no return: *Helios Creed* / Evolution: *Legendary Pink Dots* / Other side of the sky: *Gong* / Sploosh: *Ozric Tentacles* / Mrs. Fiend goes to outer space: *Ozric Tentacles* / Elements: *Spiral Realms* / Here come the warm jets: *Eno, Brian* / Silverbird/ Mastodon: *Pressurehed* / Lanky: *Barrett, Syd* / Nass Arab: *Coil* / Wie der wind: *Amon Duul II* / Slo blo/Rock God: *Turner, Nik* / 2000 flushes: *Din* / Movements of a visionary: *Tangerine Dream* / Rain: *Sky Cries Mary* / Eternity: *Clock DVA* / Spineless jelly: *Future Sound Of London* / Wind of change: *Hawkwind* / Out of the blue: *Roxy Music* / Anubian light destiny: *Anubian Lights* / Wahnfried: *Schulze, Klaus* / All saints: *Bowie, David* / Venusian skyline: *Melting Euphoria* / Last lagoon: *Orbit, William* / Trip to G9: *Spiral Realms* / Space does not care: *Zero Gravity* / Antenna: *Kraftwerk* / Number 9: *Aphex Twin* / Wind on water: *Fripp, Robert & Brian Eno* / Cylos: *Dilate*
CD Set ______ CLP 9974
Cleopatra / Apr '97 / Cargo / Greyhound / Plastic Head / RTM/Disc / SRD

THIS IS SWING (3CD Set)
Back and forth: *Aaliyah* / Poison: *Bel Biv Devoe* / Humpin around: *Brown, Bobby* / Grapevine: *Brownstone* / Whats not yours: *Darkman* / Stay: *Nelson, Evon* / Back to the lab: *Font La Roy & Darkman* / Close to you: *Treverson, George* / Her: *Guy* / Be mine tonight: *George, Jacqui* / Just the way: *Ishmael, Jeff* / Freak'n you: *Jodeci* / Gangsters Paradise: *LV* / Happy: *MN8* / Real love: *Blige, Mary J.* / Don't take it personal (just one of dem days): *Monica* / Bump and grind: *Kelly, R* / Up town: *Rugged & Raw* / Right here: *SWV* / Keep on giving me love: *Truce* / Take you home: *Frazer, Wayne*
CD Set ______ BEBOXCD 1
Beechwood / Feb '96 / Beechwood/BMG / Pinnacle

THIS IS TECHNO VOL.1 (3CD Set)
Digeridoo: *Aphex Twin* / We no longer understand: *As One* / 2 paintings and a drum: *Cox, Carl* / Dreamland: *Craig, Carl* / Air bourne: *Angel, Dave* / Tour: *De Force* / Collision: *Eclipse* / Hypnotic state: *Fantasy Flight* / IFO: *IFO* / Higher state of consciousness: *Wink, Josh* / Open up: *Leftfield* / Progression: *Mantra* / Time: *Broom, Mark* / Go: *Moby* / Stormwatch: *Morph* / Cuban timewarp: *Neuropolitique* / Little fluffy clouds: *Orb* / Spastik: *Plastikman* / Poison: *Prodigy* / Above your eyes: *Scanner* / Boss drum: *Shamen* / Harlequin: *Vath, Sven* / Below and above: *Trio* / Dark and long: *Underworld*
CD Set ______ BEBOXCD 3
Beechwood / Jun '96 / Beechwood/BMG / Pinnacle

THIS IS TECHNO VOL.2 (3CD Set)
Breathe: *Prodigy* / Born slippy: *Underworld* / Box: *Orbital* / Source: *Phazer* / Sugar is sweeter: *Bolland, C.J.* / Maximum impact: *X-Wing* / All that rises: *Pure* / Alpha waves: *System 7* / Astral dreams: *Garnier, Laurent* / Dominions complete: *Florence* / Fall out: *Q-Bass* / Tribal jedi: *Cox, Carl* / Hypnotizin': *Winx* / Move any mountain: *Shamen* / Planet surfing: *Masquerade* / Plastic love: *Delta* / Girl boy: *Aphex Twin* / Shambala: *As One* / Dark forces: *SLAM* / Astrofarm: *Digital Source* / Blue chip: *Future Funk* / Time zone: *Logic* / Bonus mix by Mark EG
CD Set ______ BEBOXCD 9
Beechwood / Feb '97 / Beechwood/BMG / Pinnacle

THIS IS THE 80'S
CD ______ 9548342052
WEA / Feb '96 / Warner Music

THIS IS THE BLUES (24 Electric Blues Hits)
Mona: *Diddley, Bo* / You can't judge a book by the cover: *Diddley, Bo* / I'm a man: *Diddley, Bo* / Who do you love: *Diddley, Bo* / Spoonful: *Howlin' Wolf* / Smokestack lightnin': *Howlin' Wolf* / Help me: *Williamson, Sonny Boy* / I'd rather go blind: *James, Etta* / Rock me baby: *James, Etta* / Almost grown: *Berry, Chuck* / Memphis: *Berry, Chuck* / I just want to make love to you: *Waters, Muddy* / Hoochie coochie man: *Waters, Muddy* / Baby, please don't go: *Waters, Muddy* / Got my mojo working: *Waters, Muddy* / Let's work together: *Harrison, Wilbert* / Kansas city: *Harrison, Wilbert* / Rollin' and tumblin': *James, Elmore* / Dust my broom: *James, Elmore* / Bright lights big city: *Reed, Jimmy* / Dimples: *Hooker, John Lee* / Boom boom: *Hooker, John Lee* / Born under a bad sign: *King, Albert* / Hi-heel sneakers: *Tucker, Tommy*
CD ______ PLATCD 3909
Platinum / Oct '90 / Prism

THIS IS THE FUNK
CD ______ 68914
Tropical / Apr '97 / Discovery

THIS IS THE NEW SOUND OF POPCORE
CD ______ DB 47852
Deep Blue / Sep '96 / PolyGram

THIS IS TRIP HOP VOL.1 (3CD Set)
Age of consent: *New Order* / Far out son of a lung: *Future Sound Of London* / Fly by night: *Substance* / Floot: *Wagon Christ* / Aphrohead: *Bluntz* / Nights interlude: *Nightmares On Wax* / Chase: *Smiler* / Kosmos SX dub 2000: *Weller, Paul* / Tides: *Agent Orange* / Jail bird: *Primal Scream* / Rising star: *Holy Haze* / Vibes: *Tempest* / Karma coma: *Massive Attack & DJ Shadow* / Birth: *Howie B* / Mudskipper: *Junk Waffel* / Anxiety: *Maad* / Mass observation 95: *Scanner* / Under the influence: *Pusher* / Filthy: *St. Etienne* / Early lady: *Yogi* / Thirst: *Solo* / Source: *Assassin* / Reverb disaster: *Bubbles* / Mellow madness: *Perpetual Motion*
CD Set ______ BEBOXCD 2
Beechwood / Mar '96 / Beechwood/BMG / Pinnacle

THIS IS TRIP HOP VOL.2 (3CD Set)
La tristesse durera (scream to a sigh): *Manic Street Preachers* / Release four: *Leftfield* / Flippin' tha bird: *Ruby* / Backyard: *Clearzone* / Sidewinder: *Submarine* / Snapper: *Red Snapper* / ESP: *Ratio* / Oxbow lakes: *Orb* / Bug powder dust: *Bomb The Bass* / Full force: *Yella* / Dusted: *Toolez* / Cry: *Howie B* / Milk: *Garbage* / Raxmus: *Black Dog* / Sonic surveillance: *Alpha* / Abstract truth: *DJ Abandon* / Trigger hippie: *Morcheeba* / Memories of the future: *Edge Of Motion* / Voodoo people: *Prodigy* / Dark side: *Renegade* / Disco lab: *Scout* / State of mind: *Blosense* / Bonus mix by Naked Funk
CD Set ______ BEBOXCD 8
Beechwood / Feb '97 / Beechwood/BMG / Pinnacle

THIS IS...CLUB NATION (2CD Set)
Bellisima: *DJ Quicksilver* / Show me love: *Robin S* / Encore une fois: *Sash* / Fired up: *Funky Green Dogs* / Total overload: *Sister Spirits* / Insomnia: *Faithless* / Funk phenomena: *Van Helden, Armand* / Hot sweat: *Fever* / Underwater love: *Smoke City* / Flash: *BBE* / Together: *Liberty* / Passion: *Amen* / Deep Freeze: *Universal* / Talkin' 'bout dub: *Apollo 440* / Mind assault: *Altered States* / Alright: *Jamiroquai* / Nightmare: *Brainbug* / Hot love: *DJ Kinky* / Prophet: *Bolland, C.J.* / Sunstroke: *Chicane* / Ready or not: *Course*
CD Set ______ BEBOXCD 13
Beechwood / Jun '97 / Beechwood/BMG / Pinnacle

THIS LAND (Inspired By The Show Riverdance)
CD ______ CDMFP 6237
Music For Pleasure / Aug '96 / EMI

THIS YEAR'S LOVE 1996 (2CD Set)
CD Set ______ MOODCD 48
Sony Music / Nov '96 / Sony

THIS YEARS LOVE
Think twice: *Dion, Celine* / Back for good: *Take That* / Stay another day: *East 17* / Oh baby I: *Eternal* / Missing: *Everything But The Girl* / No more I love you's: *Lennox, Annie* / Love me for a reason: *Boyzone* / If you love me: *Brownstone* / I'll find you: *Gayle, Michelle* / I'll make love to you: *Boyz II Men* / Your body's callin': *Boyz II Men* / Always and forever: *Vandross, Luther* / Hold me thrill me kiss me: *Estefan, Gloria* / Chains: *Arena, Tina* / Jesse: *Kadison, Joshua* / You gotta be: *Des'ree* / Search for the hero: *M-People* / Independent love song: *Scarlet* / Unchained melody: *Robson & Jerome* / Careless whisper: *Michael, George*
CD ______ MOODCD 42
Sony Music / Nov '95 / Sony

THOSE DOO WOP DAYS (18 Classic Tracks)
Come go with me: *Del-Vikings* / Oh what a night: *Dells* / Maybe: *Chantels* / For your precious love: *Impressions* / Little darlin': *Diamonds* / Earth angel (will you be mine): *Penguins* / Stay in my corner: *Dells* / Little star: *Elegants* / If you don't know me by now: *Melvin, Harold & The Bluenotes* / Sorry (I ran all the way home): *Impalas* / Whispering bells: *Del-Vikings* / Blue moon: *Marcels* / Sixteen candles: *Crests* / Since I don't have you: *Skyliners* / Gee whiz: *Innocents* / Great pretender: *Platters* / Stroll: *Diamonds* / Then you can tell me goodbye: *Casinos*
CD ______ ECD 3304
K-Tel / Feb '97 / K-Tel

THOSE FABULOUS FORTIES
Boogie woogie bugle boy: *Andrews Sisters* / It's a sin to tell a lie: *Ink Spots* / Golden wedding: *Herman, Woody* / For me and my gal: *Garland, Judy* / There, I've said it again: *Monroe, Vaughan* / Frenesi: *Shaw, Artie* / Chica chica boom chic: *Miranda, Carmen* / Paper doll: *Mills Brothers* / Honey hush: *Waller, Fats & his Rhythm Orchestra* / Skylark: *James, Harry* / Daybreak: *Dorsey, Tommy* / My adobe Hacienda: *Baker, Kenny* / Harlem nocturne: *Anthony, Ray* / Fools rush in: *Martin, Tony* / In the mood: *Miller, Glenn* / Tangerine: *Dorsey, Jimmy*
CD ______ HADCD 159
Javelin / May '94 / Henry Hadaway / THE

THOSE WERE THE DAYS
CD ______ KWCD 809
Kenwest / Jul '94 / THE

THOUGHTS OF COUNTRY VOL.1
Stand beside me: *O'Donnell, Daniel* / Almost persuaded: *Kirwan, Dominic* / Jennifer Johnson and me: *Flavin, Mick* / Dear God: *Duff, Mary* / Four in the morning: *Pride, Charley* / Way old friends do: *Begley, Philomena* / Back in love by Monday: *Lynam, Ray* / Still got a crush on you: *Hogan, John* / Daisy chain: *Begley, Philomena & Mick Flavin* / Apologising roses: *Spears, Billie Jo* / Queen of the Silver Dollar: *Begley, Philomena* / Travellin' light: *Flavin, Mick* / Amy's eyes: *Pride, Charley* / Forever and ever Amen: *Duff, Mary* / Just between you and me: *Begley, Philomena & Mick Flavin* / I'm no stranger to the rain: *Curtis, Sonny* / Take good care of her: *O'Donnell, Daniel* / Don't fight the feeling: *Hogan, John* / Sweethearts in heaven: *Margo* / Sea of heartbreak: *Kirwan, Dominic*
CD ______ RITZRCD 518
Ritz / May '92 / Pinnacle

THOUGHTS OF COUNTRY VOL.2
CD ______ RITZRCD 561
Ritz / Jul '96 / Pinnacle

THOUGHTS OF IRELAND VOL.1
Summertime in Ireland: *O'Donnell, Daniel* / Isle of Innisfree: *Foster & Allen* / Beautiful meath: *Duff, Mary* / Golden dreams: *Kirwan, Dominic* / Shanagolden: *Margo* / Home to Donegal: *Flavin, Mick* / Red is the rose: *Begley, Philomena* / Spancil Hill: *Duff, Mary* / If we only had old Ireland over here: *McCaffrey, Frank* / Carrickfergus: *Quinn, Brendan* / Girl from Wexford town: *Flavin, Mick* / Bunch of thyme: *Foster & Allen* / Galway Bay: *Begley, Philomena* / Give an Irish girl to me: *Nerney, Declan* / Noreen Bawn: *Kirwan, Dominic* / Moonlight in Mayo: *McCaffrey, Frank* / Lady from Glenfarne: *Quinn, Brendan* / Rose of Allendale: *Morrisey, Louise* / Forty miles to Donegal: *Margo* / Sing me an old Irish song: *O'Donnell, Daniel*
CD ______ RITZRCD 519
Ritz / May '92 / Pinnacle

THOUGHTS OF IRELAND VOL.2
CD ______ RITZRCD 560
Ritz / Jul '96 / Pinnacle

THOUGHTS OF LOVE
CD ______ RITZRCD 562
Ritz / Jul '96 / Pinnacle

THOUGHTS OF YESTERDAY
I need you: *O'Donnell, Daniel* / Do what you do do well: *Pride, Charley* / Crazy: *Duff, Mary* / More than I can say: *Curtis, Sonny* / Maggie: *Foster & Allen* / Before the next teardrop falls: *Kirwan, Dominic* / Pal of my cradle days: *Gloria* / Seven lonely days: *Spears, Billie Jo* / Sentimental old you: *Begley, Philomena* / More than yesterday: *McCaffrey, Frank* / Roses are red: *O'Donnell, Daniel* / China doll: *Hogan, John* / Say you'll stay until tomorrow: *Kirwan, Dominic* / After all these years: *Foster & Allen* / Ramblin' rose: *Pride, Charley* / Little things mean a lot: *Dana* / It's our anniversary: *McCaffrey, Frank* / Yellow roses: *Duff, Mary* / He stopped loving her today: *Lynam, Ray* / Old flames: *Begley, Philomena*
CD ______ RITZRCD 520
Ritz / Apr '92 / Pinnacle

THRACE ANTHOLOGY VOL.3 (Bulgaria)
CD ______ 274977
La Chant Du Monde / Jan '95 / ADA / Harmonia Mundi

THRASH THE WALL
CD ______ RR 93932
Roadrunner / Mar '90 / PolyGram

THREADGILL'S SUPPER SESSIONS VOL.1
CD ______ WM 1013CD
Watermelon / May '94 / ADA / Direct

THREADGILL'S SUPPER SESSIONS VOL.2
CD ______ WMCD 1052
Watermelon / Jun '96 / ADA / Direct

THREE CHORDOPHONE TRADITIONS (Music From Ethiopia)
CD ______ D 8074
Unesco / Nov '96 / ADA / Harmonia Mundi

THREE MINUTE HEROES
CD ______ VTCD 9
Virgin TV / Feb '92 / EMI

THREE SHADES OF THE BLUES
CD ______ BCD 107
Biograph / '92 / ADA / Cadillac / Direct / Hot Shot / Jazz Music / Wellard

THREE STEPS TO HEAVEN
CD ______ QTVCD 011
Quality / Aug '92 / Pinnacle

THREE WAY MIRROR
Treme terra / Misturada / Return / Three-way mirror / San Francisco River / Starting over again / Lilia / Plane to the trane
CD ____ RR 24CD
Reference Recordings / Sep '91 / Jazz Music / May Audio

THREE WORLDS OF TRIKOLA, THE (The Collection)
CD ____ 3201932
Triloka / Jul '92 / New Note/Pinnacle

THRONE OF DRONES (2CD Set)
CD Set ____ EFA 709522
Asphodel / Dec '96 / Cargo / SRD

THUNDERBOLT (Searing RNB Sax Instrumentals)
Paradise rock / Thunderbolt / Paradise roll / Fish bait / Melancholy horn / Jay bird / Strollin' out / Flying with the king / King is blue / Big wind / Royal crown blues / Sweet Georgia Brown / Easy ridin' / Joyride
CD ____ FLYCD 29
Flyright / Apr '91 / Hot Shot / Jazz Music / Wellard

THUNDERING DRAGON
CD ____ SM 1519CD
Wergo / Oct '94 / ADA / Cadillac / Harmonia Mundi

THUNDERPUSSY SAMPLER VOL.1
CD ____ TNO 5102CD
Techno 404 / Jan '94 / Koch

TIBET - HEART OF DHARMA
CD ____ ELLICD 4050
Ellipsis Arts / May '97 / ADA / Direct

TIBETAN BUDDHISM - RITUAL ORCHESTRA/CHANTS
CD ____ 7559720712
Nonesuch / Jan '95 / Warner Music

TIBETAN RITUAL MUSIC
CD ____ LYRCD 7181
Lyrichord / '91 / ADA / CM / Roots

TIGER RAG
CD ____ PHONTCD 7619
Phontastic / '93 / Cadillac / Jazz Music / Wellard

TIGHTEN UP VOL.1 & 2
Tighten up: *Perry, Lee 'Scratch'* / Kansas City: *Landis, Joya* / Spanish Harlem: *Bennett, Val* / Place in the sun: *Isaacs, David* / Win your love: *Penny, George A.* / Donkey returns: *Brother Dan Allstars* / Ob-la-di ob-la-da: *Bond, Joyce* / Angel of the morning: *Landis, Joya* / Fat man: *Morgan, Derrick* / Soul limbo: *Lee, Byron* / Mix it up: *Kingstonians* / Watch this squad: *Uniques* / Long-shot kick de bucket: *Pioneers* / John Hones: *Mills, Rudy* / Fire corner: *Eccles, Clancy* / Wreck a buddy: *Soul Sisters* / Reggae in your jeggae: *Livingstone, Dandy* / Fattie fattie: *Eccles, Clancy* / Return of Django: *Upsetters* / Sufferer: *Kingstonians* / Moonlight lover: *Landis, Joya* / Come into my parlour: *Bleechers* / Them a laugh and a ki ki: *Soulmates* / Live injection: *Upsetters*
CD ____ CDTRL 306
Trojan / Mar '94 / Direct / Jet Star

TIGHTEN UP VOL.3 & 4
Monkey man / Shocks of mighty / Freedom Street / Raining in my heart / Man from Carolina / Leaving Rome / Singer man / Suffering / Herbsman / Barbwire / Stay a little bit longer / Queen of the world / Blood and fire / Johnny too bad / Selah / One eye enos / Hard life / I shall sing / Grooving out on life / Starvation / Bush doctor / Good ambition / I got it / Stand by your man
CD ____ CDTRL 307
Trojan / Mar '94 / Direct / Jet Star

TIGHTEN UP VOL.5 & 6
Better must come: *Wilson, Delroy* / In paradise: *Edwards, Jackie & Julie Anne* / Hello mother: *Dynamites* / Rod of correction: *Eccles, Clancy* / Ripe cherry: *Alcapone, Dennis* / Three in one: *Dunkley, Errol* / Joy to the world: *Julien & The Chosen Few* / Know Far I: *Herman, Bongo & Bunny* / It's you: *Toots & The Maytals* / Bridge over troubled water: *London, Jimmy* / Shaft: *Chosen Few* / Duppy conqueror: *Marley, Bob & The Wailers* / Pitta patta: *Smith, Ernie* / Do your thing: *Chosen Few* / Breezing: *Chung, Mikie* / As long as you love me: *Maytones* / Down side up: *Harry J All Stars* / Suzanne beware of the devil: *Livingstone, Dandy* / Struggling man: *Cimarons* / Redemption song: *Toots & The Maytals* / Hot bomb: *I-Roy & The Jumpers* / President mash up the resident: *Shortie* / Who told you so: *Edwards, Jackie* / Unite tonight: *Eccles, Clancy*
CD ____ CDTRL 320
Trojan / Mar '94 / Direct / Jet Star

TIME FOR LOVE (More Songs For Lovers)
It's time for love: *Chi-Lites* / Zoom: *Fat Larry's Band* / Time in a bottle: *Croce, Jim* / Now is the time: *James, Jimmy* / I can see clearly now: *Knight, Gladys* / Hot love: *Marie, Kelly* / Girls: *Moments* / Can't get by without you: *Real Thing* / Night to remember: *Shalamar* / Purely by coincidence: *Sweet Sensation* / Band of gold: *Sylvester* / Pillow talk: *Sylvia* / Hold back the night: *Trammps* / And the beat goes on: *Whispers* / I get the sweetest feeling: *Wilson, Jackie* / It's in his kiss (The shoop shoop song): *Everett, Betty* / She'd rather be with me: *Turtles* / Gimme little sign: *Wood, Brenton* / Caroline goodbye: *Blunstone, Colin*
CD ____ TRTCD 159
TrueTrax / Feb '96 / THE

TIME FOR LOVING, A (2CD Set)
CD Set ____ NSCD 005
Newsound / Feb '95 / THE

TIME FOR TECHNO
Gonna make u feel so good / Axel F / Jump / Oxygene / Cocoon / Sonic groove / Popcorn / Energize / Action / Magic fly / Acid bird / Roffos theme v the hitman
CD ____ ECD 3129
K-Tel / Jan '95 / K-Tel

TIME TO REMEMBER 1937, A (20 Original Chart Hits)
Free: *Flanagan & Allen* / Fine romance: *Astaire, Fred & Ginger Rogers* / Shall we dance: *Roy, Harry* / It looks like rain in cherry blossom lane: *Loss, Joe & His Orchestra* / Where are you: *Hutch* / Bessie couldn't help it: *Gonella, Nat* / Greatest mistake of my life: *Messene, Jimmy* / Let's put our heads together: *Roy, Harry* / September in the rain: *Loss, Joe* / Love bug will bite you: *Gonella, Nat* / Night is young: *Hutch* / Broken hearted clown: *Messene, Jimmy* / Boo hoo: *Hall, Henry* / There's a small hotel: *Roy, Harry* / Way you look tonight: *Astaire, Fred* / Goodnight my love: *Gibbons, Carroll & Savoy Hotel Orpheans* / Hometown: *Flanagan & Allen* / May I have the next romance with you: *Hutch* / They can't take that away from me: *Roy, Harry* / Pennies from heaven: *Gonella, Nat*
CD ____ ATTR 1937
Baktabak / Mar '97 / Arabesque

TIME TO REMEMBER 1946, A (20 Original Chart Hits)
Fine romance: *Tilton, Martha & Johnny Mercer* / Candy: *Roy, Harry & His Band* / Takin' the trains out (chasin' after you): *Foster, Teddy* / I get a kick out of you: *Whiting, Margaret* / I'll be with you in apple blossom time: *Stafford, Jo* / Sentimental journey: *Foster, Teddy & The Band* / I dream of you more you dream I do: *Lewis, Archie & Geraldo* / Anywhere: *Winstone, Eric* / We'll gather lilacs: *Geraldo* / Coming home: *Squires, Dorothy* / Take the 'A' train: *Ellington, Duke* / Did you ever get that feeling in moonlight: *Preager, Lou & His Band* / One-zy, two-zy, I love you-zy: *Simpson, Jack & His Sextet* / Fools rush in: *Stafford, Jo* / I'd rather be me: *Roy, Harry & His Band* / Dreams of yesterday: *Squires, Dorothy* / Little things that mean so much: *Payne, Jack & His Orchestra* / In the land of beginning again: *Lewis, Archie & Geraldo* / I walked right in: *Winstone, Eric* / If I had you: *Whiting, Margaret*
CD ____ ATTR 1946
Baktabak / Mar '97 / Arabesque

TIME TO REMEMBER 1947, A (20 Original Chart Hits)
Hurry on down: *Lutcher, Nellie* / Gal in calico: *Loss, Joe & His Orchestra* / Sowing machine: *Hutton, Betty* / Temptation: *Stafford, Jo & Red Ingle* / Stars will remember: *Conway, Steve* / People will say we're in love: *Hutch* / Moonlight serenade: *Rabin, Oscar* / Danger ahead: *Squires, Dorothy* / I'm not in love: *Rabin, Oscar* / Tell me Marianne: *Loss, Joe & His Orchestra* / How lucky you are: *Layton, Turner* / He's a real gone guy: *Lutcher, Nellie* / I wish I didn't love you so: *Hutton, Betty* / Time after time: *Conway, Steve* / If I can help somebody: *Wilson, Robert* / Smoke dreams: *Stafford, Jo* / I've got the sun: *Stafford, Jo* / Come back to Sorrento: *Locke, Josef* / Song is ended: *Lutcher, Nellie* / I'll make up for everything: *Conway, Steve*
CD ____ ATTR 1947
Baktabak / Apr '97 / Arabesque

TIME TO REMEMBER 1956, A (20 Original Chart Hits)
Be bop a Lula: *Vincent, Gene* / 16 tons: *Ford, Tennessee Ernie* / Teach you to rock: *Crombie, Tony* / Experiments with mice: *Dankworth, John Quintet* / Tumbling tumbleweeds: *Whitman, Slim* / Zambesi: *Calvert, Eddie* / Robin Hood: *James, Dick* / Cindy O Cindy: *Brent, Tony* / No other love: *Hilton, Ronnie* / Blueberry Hill: *Domino, Fats* / You are my first love: *Murray, Ruby* / Memories are made of this: *Martin, Dean* / Pickin' a chicken: *Boswell, Eve* / Too young to go steady: *Cole, Nat 'King'* / Bad penny blues: *Lyttelton, Humphrey* / Cat came back: *James, Sonny* / Why do fools fall in love: *Lymon, Frankie & The Teenagers* / Rock Island Line: *Freberg, Stan* / Hot diggity: *Holliday, Michael* / True love: *Crosby, Bing & Grace Kelly*
CD ____ ATTR 1956
Baktabak / Mar '97 / Arabesque

TIME TO REMEMBER 1957, A (20 Original Chart Hits)
When I fall in love: *Cole, Nat 'King'* / Young love: *James, Sonny* / Kisses sweeter than wine: *Rogers, Jimmy* / Wisdom of a fool: *Wisdom, Norman* / Party doll: *Knox, Buddy* / My special angel: *Vaughan, Malcolm* / Wonderful wonderful: *Hilton, Ronnie* / Be my girl: *Hilton, Ronnie* / You, me and us: *Cogan, Alma* / Ma he's making eyes at me: *Otis, Johnny* / Blue Monday: *Domino, Fats* / White sport coat: *King Brothers* / Dark moon: *Brent, Tony* / I'm not a juvenile delinquent: *Lymon, Frankie & The Teenagers* / Any old iron: *Sellers, Peter* / Cumberland Gap: *Vipers Skiffle Group* / He's got the whole world in his hands: *London, Laurie* / Man that plays the mandolin: *Martin, Dean* / School day: *Lang, Don* / I'll take you home again Kathleen: *Whitman, Slim*
CD ____ ATTR 1957
Baktabak / Mar '97 / Arabesque

TIME TO REMEMBER 1960, A (20 Original Chart Hits)
Poor me: *Faith, Adam* / That's you: *Cole, Nat 'King'* / Walk don't run: *Ventures* / Dreamin': *Burnette, Johnny* / Staccato's theme: *Bernstein, Elmer* / Ain't misbehavin': *Bruce, Tommy* / You got what it takes: *Johnson, Marv* / Shakin' all over: *Kidd, Johnny & The Pirates* / As long as he needs me: *Bassey, Shirley* / Goodness gracious me: *Sellers, Peter & Sophia Loren* / Pistol packin' Mama: *Vincent, Gene* / Starry eyed: *Holliday, Michael* / Apache: *Shadows* / Pretty blue eyes: *Douglas, Craig* / Tell Laura I love her: *Valance, Ricky* / Hit and miss: *Barry, John* / Tie me kangaroo down: *Harris, Rolf* / Beatnik fly: *Johnny & The Hurricanes* / Walkin' to New Orleans: *Domino, Fats* / Three steps to heaven: *Cochran, Eddie*
CD ____ ATTR 1960
Baktabak / Mar '97 / Arabesque

TIME TO REMEMBER 1961, A (20 Original Chart Hits)
Take good care of my baby: *Vee, Bobby* / Walkin' back to happiness: *Shapiro, Helen* / Kontiki: *Shadows* / Michael: *Highwaymen* / Hello Mary Lou: *Nelson, Rick* / Time has come: *Faith, Adam* / Let true love begin: *Cole, Nat 'King'* / I love how you love me: *Crawford, Jimmy* / Weekend: *Cochran, Eddie* / Till there was you: *Lee, Peggy* / Climb every mountain: *Bassey, Shirley* / You're drivin' me crazy: *Temperance Seven* / Moon river: *Williams, Danny* / Blue moon: *Marcels* / Magnificent seven: *Barry, John* / Let there be drums: *Nelson, Sandy* / Hundred pounds of clay: *Douglas, Craig* / My girl Josephine: *Domino, Fats* / Runaway: *Shannon, Del* / You're sixteen: *Burnette, Johnny*
CD ____ ATTR 1961
Baktabak / Mar '97 / Arabesque

TIME TO REMEMBER 1962, A (20 Original Chart Hits)
Locomotion: *Little Eva* / I remember you: *Ifield, Frank* / Don't ever change: *Crickets* / James Bond theme: *Barry, John* / Wonderful world of the young: *Williams, Danny* / Young world: *Nelson, Rick* / Ramblin' rose: *Cole, Nat 'King'* / Little Miss Lonely: *Shapiro, Helen* / English country garden: *Rogers, Jimmy* / Old rivers: *Brennan, Walter* / Cindy's birthday: *Fenton, Shane & The Fentones* / Jambalaya: *Domino, Fats* / Dance on: *Shadows* / Hole in the ground: *Cribbins, Bernard* / When my little girl is smiling: *Douglas, Craig* / Peppermint twist: *Dee, Joey & The Starlighters* / Forever kind of love: *Vee, Bobby* / As you like it: *Faith, Adam* / It might as well rain untill September: *King, Carole* / Sun arise: *Harris, Rolf*
CD ____ ATTR 1962
Baktabak / Mar '97 / Arabesque

TIME TO REMEMBER 1963, A (20 Original Chart Hits)
Surfin' USA: *Beach Boys* / Bad to me: *Kramer, Billy J.* / Night has a thousand eyes: *Vee, Bobby* / Stay: *Hollies* / From Russia with love: *Monro, Matt* / Little town flirt: *Shannon, Del* / From a Jack to King: *Miller, Ned* / Cruel sea: *Dakotas* / First time: *Faith, Adam* / Tell him: *Exciters* / You were made for me: *Freddie & The Dreamers* / My little girl: *Crickets* / I'll never get over you: *Kidd, Johnny & The Pirates* / Foot tapper: *Shadows* / Let's turkey trot: *Little Eva* / Hippy hippy shake: *Swinging Blue Jeans* / Red sails in the sunset: *Domino, Fats* / Surf city: *Jan & Dean* / Wayward wind: *Ifield, Frank* / You'll never walk alone: *Gerry & The Pacemakers*
CD ____ ATTR 1963
Baktabak / Mar '97 / Arabesque

TIME TO REMEMBER 1964, A (20 Original Chart Hits)
I'm into something good: *Herman's Hermits* / Do wah diddy diddy: *Manfred Mann* / Little loving: *Fourmost* / I get around: *Beach Boys* / World without love: *Peter & Gordon* / You're no good: *Swinging Blue Jeans* / Walk away: *Monro, Matt* / Fever: *Shapiro, Helen* / Little children: *Kramer, Billy J.* / Ferry cross the Mersey: *Gerry & The Pacemakers* / One way love: *Bennett, Cliff & The Rebel Rousers* / Happiness: *Dodd, Ken* / Tobacco road: *Nashville Teens* / I understand: *Freddie & The Dreamers* / Anyone who had a heart: *Black, Cilla* / Just one look: *Hollies* / Message to Martha: *Faith, Adam* / House of the rising sun: *Animals* / They call he (la bamba): *Crickets* / Goldfinger: *Bassey, Shirley*
CD ____ ATTR 1964
Baktabak / Mar '97 / Arabesque

TIME TO REMEMBER 1965, A (20 Original Chart Hits)
All I really want to do: *Cher* / I'm alive: *Hollies* / True love ways: *Peter & Gordon* / Stingray: *Shadows* / Yesterday: *Monro, Matt* / No regrets: *Bassey, Shirley* / California girls: *Beach Boys* / Maria: *Proby, P.J.* / I'll be there: *Gerry & The Pacemakers* / Carnival is over: *Seekers* / You're lost that lovin' feelin': *Black, Cilla* / Trains, boats and planes: *Kramer, Billy J.* / This little bird: *Nashville Teens* / Must to avoid: *Herman's Hermits* / Paradise: *Ifield, Frank* / Windmill in old Amsterdam: *Ifield, Frank* / Hard days night: *Sellers, Peter* / If you've gotta go gonow: *Manfred Mann* / Little you: *Freddie & The Dreamers* / We've got to get out of this place: *Animals*
CD ____ ATTR 1965
Baktabak / Mar '97 / Arabesque

TIME TO REMEMBER 1966, A (20 Original Chart Hits)
Sunshine superman: *Donovan* / Alfie: *Black, Cilla* / Supergirl: *Bonney, Graham* / Lady Godiva: *Peter & Gordon* / You've come back: *Proby, P.J.* / Sloop John B: *Beach Boys* / No milk today: *Beach Boys* / No one will ever know: *Ifield, Frank* / Morningtown ride: *Seekers* / Hanky panky: *James, Tommy & The Shondells* / Bang bang my baby shot me down: *Cher* / Take me to your heart again: *Hill, Vince* / I met a girl: *Shadows* / Don't make me over: *Swinging Blue Jeans*
CD ____ ATTR 1966
Baktabak / Mar '97 / Arabesque

TIME TO REMEMBER 1967, A (20 Original Chart Hits)
Hi ho silver lining: *Beck, Jeff* / Gregory girl: *Seekers* / Carrie Anne: *Hollies* / I've been a bad bad boy: *Jones, Paul* / With a little help from my friends: *Young Idea* / There's a kind of hush: *Herman's Hermits* / Then I kissed her: *Beach Boys* / It must be him: *Carr, Vikki* / Boat that I row: *Lulu* / Thank you very much: *Scaffold* / Big spender: *Bassey, Shirley* / Seven drunken nights: *Dubliners* / There must be a way: *Vaughan, Frankie* / Mellow yellow: *Donovan* / Kites: *Dupree, Simon & The Big Sound* / Up up and away: *Mann, Johnny Singers* / On a carousel: *Hollies* / Excerpt from a teenage opera: *West, Keith* / Heroes and villains: *Beach Boys* / Ode to Billy Joe: *Gentry, Bobbie*
CD ____ ATTR 1967
Baktabak / Mar '97 / Arabesque

TIME TO REMEMBER 1968, A (20 Original Chart Hits)
Weight: *Band* / I'm the urban spaceman: *Bonzo Dog Band* / Mony mony: *James, Tommy & The Shondells* / Hurdy gurdy man: *Donovan* / Listen to me: *Hollies* / Sunshine girl: *Herman's Hermits* / Nevertheless: *Vaughan, Frankie* / Darlin': *Beach Boys* / She wears my ring: *King, Solomon* / On the road again: *Canned Heat* / I'm a tiger: *Lulu* / For whom the bell tolls: *Dupree, Simon* / Lily the pink: *Scaffold* / May I have the next dream with you: *Roberts, Malcolm* / Honey: *Goldsboro, Bobby* / Love is blue: *Beck, Jeff* / Jennifer juniper: *Donovan* / Blue eyes: *Partridge, Don* / Do it again: *Beach Boys* / Jennifer Eccles: *Hollies*
CD ____ ATTR 1968
Baktabak / Mar '97 / Arabesque

TIME TO REMEMBER 1969, A (20 Original Chart Hits)
He ain't heavy he's my brother: *Hollies* / Mocking bird: *Foxx, Inez & Charlie* / I'll never fall in love: *Gentry, Bobbie* / Wichita lineman: *Campbell, Glen* / Love is all: *Roberts, Malcolm* / I can hear music: *Beach Boys* / Where do you go to my lovely: *Sarstedt, Peter* / My sentimental friend: *Herman's Hermits* / Nobody's child: *Young, Karen* / Love at first sight: *Sounds Nice* / Goo goo barabajagal: *Donovan & Jeff Beck Group* / Deal: *Campbell, Pat* / Going up the country: *Canned Heat* / Aquarius: *Jones, Paul* / Gin gan goolie: *Scaffold* / Good morning starshine: *Oliver* / Breakfast on pluto: *Partridge, Don* / Breakaway: *Beach Boys* / Games people play: *South, Joe* / Boom boom a bang: *Lulu* / Stop stop: *Hollies* / Stop stop stop: *Hollies* / High time: *Jones, Paul* / Got to ge you into my life: *Bennett, Cliff & The Rebel Rousers* / Pretty flamingo: *Manfred Mann* / wITCHES BREW: *Jones, Janie* / Good vibrations: *Beach Boys*
CD ____ ATTR 1969
Baktabak / Mar '97 / Arabesque

TIME TO REMEMBER 1970, A (20 Original Chart Hits)
Whole lotta love: *CCS* / Love is life: *Hot Chocolate* / Cotton fields: *Beach Boys* / Can't tell the bottom from the top: *Hollies* / Lady Barbara: *Herman's Hermits* / Something: *Bassey, Shirley* / Let's work together: *Canned Heat* / Grandad: *Dunn, Clive* / Black night: *Deep Purple* / When I'm dead and gone: *McGuiness Flint* / Raindrops keep falling on my head: *Gentry, Bobbie* / Song of joy: *Rios, Miquel* / Man from Nazareth: *Joans, John Paul* / Honey come back: *Campbell, Glen* / Out demons out: *Broughton, Edgar* / Gasoline alley bred: *Hollies* / Sugar bee: *Canned Heat* / Rag Mama rag: *Band* / Years may come years may go: *Herman's Hermits* / I hear you knocking: *Edmunds, Dave*
CD ____ ATTR 1970
Baktabak / Mar '97 / Arabesque

TIME TO REMEMBER 1971, A (20 Original Chart Hits)
Don't let it die: *Smith, Hurricane* / Strange kind of woman: *Deep Purple* / Tonight: *Move* / Walkin': *Move* / For all we know:

Bassey, Shirley / You could've been a lady: Hot Chocolate / Freedom come freedom go: Fortunes / Banks of the Ohio: Newton-John, Olivia / Apache dropout: Broughton, Edgar Band / Softly whispering I love you: Congregation / Ernie: Hill, Benny / Rose garden: New World / Look around: Hill, Vince / Hey Willie: Hollies / Mozart 40: Sovereign Collection / Chinatown: Move / Fireball: Deep Purple / Dream baby: Campbell, Glen / Tap turns on the water: CCD / I believe (in love): Hot Chocolate
CD ATTR 1971
Baktabak / Mar '97 / Arabesque

TIME TO REMEMBER 1972, A (20 Original Chart Hits)
American pie: McLean, Don / 10538 Overture: ELO / Long cool woman in a black dress: Hollies / Conquistador: Procul Harum / Storm in a teacup: Fortunes / Who was it: Hurricane smith / Journey: Brown, Duncan & Sebastian Graham-Jones / California man: Move / What is life: Newton-John, Olivia / Pugwudgie: Drake, Charlie / Sister Jane: New World / Baby: Hollies / Never before: Deep Purple / Just out of reach: Dodd, Ken / Brother: CCS / You'll always be my friend: Hot Chocolate / Ball park incident: Wizzard / Vincent: McLean, Don / Oh babe what would you say: Hurricane smith / Silver machine: Hawkwind
CD ATTR 1972
Baktabak / Mar '97 / Arabesque

TIME TO REMEMBER 1973, A (20 Original Chart Hits)
Nutbush City limits: Turner, Ike & Tina / Summer (The first time): Goldsboro, Bobby / Dance with the devil: Powell, Cozy / Heart of stone: Kenny / Roll over Beethoven: ELO / Gaudette: Steeleye Span / Day that Billy shot crazy Bobby: Hollies / Why can't we live together: Thomas, Timmy / Dyna-mite: Mud / Everyday: McLean, Don / Take me home country road: Newton-John, Olivia / Urban guerrilla: Hawkwind / Brother Louie: Hot Chocolate / You smiled: Monro, Matt / Band played the boogie: CCS / See my baby jive: Wizzard / Never never never: Bassey, Shirley / Sylvia: Focus / Dear Elaine: Wood, Roy / Can the can: Quatro, Suzi
CD ATTR 1973
Baktabak / Mar '97 / Arabesque

TIME TO REMEMBER 1974, A (20 Original Chart Hits)
Magic: Pilot / Judy Teen: Harley, Steve & Cockney Rebel / Going down that road: Wood, Roy / You're having my baby: Anka, Paul / Devil gate drive: Quatro, Suzi / Hello summertime: Goldsboro, Bobby / Bump: Kenny / Tell him: Hello / Rock me gently: Kim, Andy / Air that I breathe: Hollies / Queen of clubs: KC & The Sunshine Band / Mr Soft: Harley, Steve & Cockney Rebel / Happy anniversary: Whitman, Slim / Man in black: Powell, Cozy / School love: Blue, Barry / Tiger feet: Mud / I honestly love you: Newton-John, Olivia / Pinball: Protheroe, Brian / Emma: Hot Chocolate / Rock your baby: McCrae, George
CD ATTR 1974
Baktabak / Mar '97 / Arabesque

TIME TO REMEMBER 1975, A (20 Original Chart Hits)
Make me smile: Harley, Steve & Cockney Rebel / That's the way (I like it): KC & The Sunshine Band / Rhinestone cowboy: Campbell, Glen / Right back where I started from: Nightingale, Maxine / Motorbikin': Spedding, Chris / Lovin' you: Riperton, Minnie / Secrets that you keep: Mud / Fancy pants: Kenny / Angie baby: Reddy, Helen / Yin & yan: Reddy, Helen / Pandora's box: Procul Harum / Where is the love: Wright, Betty / It's been so long: McCrae, George / New York groove: Hello / Blanket on the ground: Spears, Billie Jo / Your Mama won't like me: Quatro, Suzi / You sexy thing: Hot Chocolate / Pilot: January / Oh boy: Mud / All around my hat: Steeleye Span
CD ATTR 1975
Baktabak / Mar '97 / Arabesque

TIME TO REMEMBER 1976, A (20 Original Chart Hits)
Little bit more: Dr. Hook / Ships in the night: Be-Bop Deluxe / Sing me an old fashioned song: Spears, Billie Jo / Man to man: Hot Chocolate / Heaven must be missing an angel: Tavares / Loves a prima donna: Harley, Steve & Cockney Rebel / Movie star: Harpo / Honey: McCrae, George / Shake shake your booty: KC & The Sunshine Band / If not you: Dr. Hook / Rodrigo's guitar concerto: Manuel & The Music Of The Mountains / Wurzels: Wurzels / Mississippi: Pussycat / Maid in heaven: Be-Bop Deluxe / Movin': Brass Construction / Don't take away the music: Tavares / What I've got in mind: Spears, Billie Jo / Don't stop it now: Hot Chocolate / Better use your head: Little Anthony & The Imperials / Here comes the sun: Harley, Steve & Cockney Rebel
CD ATTR 1976
Baktabak / Mar '97 / Arabesque

TIME TO REMEMBER 1977, A (20 Original Chart Hits)
Get a grip on yourself: Stranglers / Be good to yourself: Miller, Frankie / Lucille: Rogers, Kenny / So you win again: Hot Chocolate / Love hit me: Nightingale, Maxine / Spanish stroll: Mink Deville / I'm your boogie man: KC & The Sunshine Band / Year of the cat: Stewart, Al / Tear me apart: Quatro, Suzi / Perfect day: Saints / Southern nights: Campbell, Glen / They shoot horses don't they: Racing Cars / Smoke on the water: Deep Purple / Do what you wanna do: T-Connection / Don't it make my brown eyes blue: Gayle, Crystal / Whodunnit: Tavares / Little girl: Banned / Dancing easy: Williams, Danny / 2468 Motorway: Robinson, Tom Band / Sneakin suspicion: Dr. Feelgood
CD ATTR 1977
Baktabak / Mar '97 / Arabesque

TIME TO REMEMBER 1978, A (20 Original Chart Hits)
Baker Street: Rafferty, Gerry / Ever fallen in love: Buzzcocks / Dancing in the street: Hain, Marshall / Talking in your sleep: Gayle, Crystal / 5 Minutes: Stranglers / More like the movies: Dr. Hook / Lay your love on me: Racey / If I had words: Fitzgerald, Scott & Yvonne Keeley / Darlin': Miller, Frankie / Don't cry for me Argentina: Shadows / Every 1's a winner: Hot Chocolate / On fire: T-Connection / If you can't give me love: Quatro, Suzi / More than a woman: Tavares / Boogie boogie oogie: Taste Of Honey / Coming home: Hain, Marshall / What do I get: Buzzcocks / Nice 'n' sleazy: Stranglers / Don't take no for an answer: Robinson, Tom Band / Down at the doctors: Dr. Feelgood
CD ATTR 1978
Baktabak / Mar '97 / Arabesque

TIME TO REMEMBER 1979, A (20 Original Chart Hits)
When you're in love with a beautiful woman: Dr. Hook / Please don't go: KC & The Sunshine Band / Milk and alcohol: Dr. Feelgood / Duchess: Strangers / Mindless boogie: Hot Chocolate / She's in love with you: Quatro, Suzi / Gertcha: Chas & Dave / I don't wanna lose you: Kandidate / Tired of toein' the line: Burnette, Rocky / Some girls: Racey / Theme from the Deer Hunter: Shadows / Freedoms' prisoner: Harley, Steve & Cockney Rebel / My sharona: Knack / At home he's a tourist: Gang Of Four / Night owl: Rafferty, Gerry / Straw dogs: Stiff Little Fingers / Livin' on the frontline: Grant, Eddy / Doctor Doctor: UFO / Outdoor miner: Wire / Everybody's happy nowadays: Buzzcocks
CD ATTR 1979
Baktabak / Mar '97 / Arabesque

TIMELESS
CD CDSGP 0304
Prestige / Aug '96 / Else / Total/BMG

TIMELESS COMPILATION
CD PWMCD 1
Total / Oct '89 / Total/BMG

TIMELESS MEMORIES VOL.1
Crazy: Cline, Patsy / Smoke gets in your eyes: Platters / Magic moments: Como, Perry / That old devil called love: Holiday, Billie / True love ways: Holly, Buddy / Distant dreams: Reeves, Jim / What now my love: Bassey, Shirley / When I fall in love: Cole, Nat 'King' / Where do you go to my lovely: Sarstedt, Peter / Blue moon: Torme, Mel / Take good care of my baby: Vee, Bobby / All I have to do is dream: Gentry, Bobbie & Glen Campbell / I remember you: Ifield, Frank / Love letters: Lester, Ketty / What a wonderful world: Armstrong, Louis / Story of my life: Holliday, Michael / World of our own: Seekers / It must be him: Carr, Vikki / My funny valentine: Baker, Chet / You'll never walk alone: Gerry & The Pacemakers
CD CTMCD 500
EMI / Jun '97 / EMI

TIMELESS MEMORIES VOL.2
Unforgettable: Cole, Nat 'King' / Memories are made of this: Martin, Dean / Moon river: Williams, Danny / From a jack to a king: Miller, Ned / Born free: Monro, Matt / You're my world: Black, Cilla / Fever: Lee, Peggy / Ferry across the mersey: Gerry & The Pacemakers / He ain't heavy he's my brother: Hollies / No other love: Hilton, Ronnie / Release me: Humperdinck, Engelbert / Halfway to paradise: Fury, Billy / I believe: Bachelors / Who's sorry now: Francis, Connie / Love is a many splendoured thing: Four Aces / World without love: Four Aces / True love: Peter & Gordon / Dream boat: Cogan, Alma / Ain't misbehavin': Cogan, Alma / As long as he needs me: Bassey, Shirley
CD CTMCD 501
EMI / Jul '97 / EMI

TIMELESS TRADITIONAL JAZZ FESTIVAL
Schlafe mein prinzchen: Bue, Papa Viking Jazz Band / Muskrat ramble: Collie, Max Rhythm Aces / Mood indigo: Ball, Kenny & His Jazzmen / Bourbon Street Parade: Dutch Swing College Band / Flyin' house: Dr. Dixie / That's a plenty: Prowizorka Dzez Bed / Stranger on the shore: Bilk, Acker & His Paramount Jazz Band / Struttin' with some barbecue: Down Town Jazzband / Ice cream: Sunshine, Monty Jazz Band / Basin Street blues: Sunshine, Monty Jazz Band / Jumpin' at the Woodside: Jansens, Huub / World is waiting for the sunrise: Jansens, Huub / Bye and bye: Boutte, Lillian / Petite fleur: Lightfoot, Terry / West End blues: Barber, Chris & Rod Mason's Hot Five / At the Jazz Band Ball: World's Greatest Jazz Band / Jambalaya: Barber, Chris & His Jazz Band / As I go to the Quick River: Uralsky All Stars
CD Set CDTTD 52223
Timeless Traditional / Jul '94 / Jazz Music / New Note/Pinnacle

TINSEL TUNES (More Holiday Treats From Sugar Hill)
CD SHCD 3855
Sugar Hill / Nov '96 / ADA / CM / Direct / Koch / Roots

TIP SINGLES, THE
Hyperactive: Infinity Project / Acid soul: Organic Noise / Tranceparent mind: Total Eclipse / Mindboggler: Infinity Project / Headrush: Growling Mad Scientists / COR: Green Nuns Of The Revolution / Can't do that: Total Eclipse / Dreampod: Psychopod / Starfinder: Sanman
CD TIPCD 14
Tip / Jul '97 / Arabesque / Mo's Music Machine / Pinnacle / Prime

TIR MO CHRAIDH
CD BRCD 0003
B&R Heritage / May '97 / ADA

TIROLER-ABEND
CD 499422
Koch / Jul '91 / Koch

TJOPLUSTA PART 2
CD BROOL 006CD
Brool / Mar '96 / Plastic Head

TO HAVE AND TO HOLD
CD IONIC 15CD
Mute / Oct '96 / RTM/Disc

TO THE BEAT Y'ALL - OLD SCHOOL RAP
Rapper's delight: Sugarhill Gang / Radio commercial: Sugarhill Gang / That's the joint: Funky 4+1 / Adventures of grandmaster flash on the wheels of steel: Grandmaster Flash / Birthday party: Grandmaster Flash / Good times: Grandmaster Flash / Another one bites the dust: Grandmaster Flash / Rapture: Grandmaster Flash / Flash to the beat: Grandmaster Flash / White lines (don't don't do it): Grandmaster Flash & Melle Mel / Drop the bomb: Trouble Funk / Pump me up: Trouble Funk / Hey fellas: Trouble Funk / Freedom: Grandmaster Flash & The Furious Five / Message: Grandmaster Flash & The Furious Five / It's nasty (genius of love): Grandmaster Flash & The Furious Five / Scorpio: Grandmaster Flash & The Furious Five / Spoonin' rap: Gee, Spoonie / And you know that: Sequence / Funk you up: Sequence / To the beat y'all: Lady B / Super wolf can do it: Super-Wolf / Eighth Wonder: Sugarhill Gang / Monster jam: Spoonie Gee & The Sequence / Yes we can-can: Treacherous Three / Break dancin': West Street Mob / Electric boogie: West Street Mob / Busy bee's groove: Busy Bee / Making cash money: Busy Bee / Jesse: Grandmaster Flash & Melle Mel / Message II (Survival): Melle Mel & Duke Bootee / We are known as emcees (we turn the party out): Crash Crew / Breaking bells (take me to the mardi gras): Crash Crew / Scratching: Crash Crew / Check it out: Wayne & Charlie / All night long (Waterbed): Kevie Kev / Mirda rock: Griffin, Reggie / King heroin: Funky Four / Mayor: Melle Mel
CD NXTCD 217
Sequel / Oct '92 / BMG

TO THE BEST MUM IN THE WORLD (16 Songs For Mothers Everywhere)
For mama / Whatever will be will be (Que sera sera) / I'll always love my mama / Shop around / Teenager's mother / Mama / Mother in my eyes / Silver threads among the gold / Mama used to say / Say mama / I saw mommy kissing Santa Claus / My mommy's eyes / Mama said / Mother of mine / No charge / Reading me stories
CD 306122
Hallmark / Jan '97 / Carlton

TODOS ESTOS ANOS
CD 21067CD
Sonifolk / Nov '95 / ADA / CM

TOE THE LINE VOL.1 (20 Linedance Classics)
Wild Horse Saloon theme: Wild Horse Saloon / Watermelon crawl: Byrd, Tracy / What the cowgirls do: Gill, Vince / Easy come, easy go: Strait, George / Going through the big D: Chestnut, Mark / Out with a bang: Murphy, David Lee / Why haven't I heard from you: McEntire, Reba / If I ain't got you: Stuart, Marty / Let the picture paint itself: Crowell, Rodney / Dust in the bottle: Murphy, David Lee / 4 To 1 in Atlanta: Byrd, Tracy / High tech redneck: Jones, George / Gonna get a life: Chesnutt, Mark / One more last chance: Gill, Vince / Adalida: Strait, George / I wanna got too far: Yearwood, Trisha / All you ever do is bring me down: Mavericks / Trouble: Chesnutt, Mark / Copperhead road: Earle, Steve / Walking to Jerusalem: Byrd, Tracy
CD MCD 11455
MCA / Apr '96 / BMG

TOE THE LINE VOL.2 (The Next Step)
Honky tonkin's what I do best: Stuart, Marty / Everytime I get around you: Murphy, David Lee / Swing city: Brown, Roger / Wrong place, wrong time: Chesnutt, Mark / Every cowboys dream: Akins, Rhett / Missing you: Mavericks / Out of control raging fire: Byrd, Tracy / Tangled up in Texas: River, Frazier / Where the sidewalk ends: Strait, George / Little more love: Gill, Vince / Texas is bigger than it used to be: Chesnutt, Mark / Hillbilly rock: Stuart, Marty / Honkytonk dancing machine: Byrd, Tracy / Guitar town: Earle, Steve / Southside of Dixie: Gill, Vince / I brake for brunettes: Akins, Rhett / Highways and heartaches: Ely, Joe / Walk on: Withers, Janeen / Don't be cruel: Stuart, Marty / Lovebug: Strait, George / Rose of Memphis: Crowell, Rodney / Love on the loose, heart on the run: McBride & The Ride / Holdin' heaven: Byrd, Tracy / One dance with you: Gill, Vince / Tempted: Stuart, Marty / Strut your stuff: Sheriff, Dave / If I ain't got you: Yearwood, Trisha / Children: Mavericks / Hard lovin' woman: Collie, Mark / You better think twice: Gill, Vince / Honky tonk twist: Scooter Lee / What they're talkin' about: Akins, Rhett / Blame it on Texas: Chesnutt, Mark / Hillbilly highway: Earle, Steve / Western women: Brown, Roger / Big love: Byrd, Tracy / Rocky top: Osborne Brothers
CD MCD 11591
MCA / Feb '97 / BMG

TOES ON THE NOSE (32 Surf Age Instrumentals)
Squad car: Eddie & The Showmen / Midnight run: Super Stocks / Voodoo juice: Ghouls / Quiet surf: Allen, Richie & The Pacific Surfers / Movin': Eddie & The Showmen / Mr. Rebel: Eddie & The Showmen / Moon probe: Vulcans / Coffin nails: Ghouls / Newport beach: Super Stocks / Casbah: Nelson, Sandy / We are the young: Eddie & The Showmen / Trophy run: Super Stocks / Legends: Ho-Dads / Outer limits: Cole, Jerry & His Spacemen / Twilight city: Vulcans / Ventura: Super Stocks / Toes on the nose: Eddie & The Showmen / Surf man: Allen, Richie & The Pacific Surfers / Faraway places: Eddie & The Showmen / Lanky bones: Eddie & The Showmen / Pipeline: Cole, Jerry & His Spacemen / Bucket seats: Rally packs / Last walk: Super Stocks / Border town: Eddie & The Showmen / Oceanside: Super Stocks / Midnight surfer: Cole, Jerry & His Spacemen / Space race: Ho-Dads / Dracula's theme: Ghouls / Young & lonely: Eddie & The Showmen / Redondo beach: Super Stocks / Gridiron goodie: Super Stocks / Scratch: Eddie & The Showmen
CD CDCHD 634
Ace / Sep '96 / Pinnacle

TOGETHER
CD STACD 001
Wisepack / Nov '92 / Conifer/BMG / THE

TOGETHER
I knew you were waiting (for me): Franklin, Aretha & George Michael / Sometimes love just ain't enough: Smyth, Patty & Don Henley / Where is the love: Paris, Mica & Will Downing / Baby, come to me: Austin, Patti & James Ingram / Don't know much: Ronstadt, Linda & Aaron Neville / We've got tonight: Rogers, Kenny & Sheena Easton / If you were with me now: Minogue, Kylie & Keith Washington / You are everything: Ross, Diana & Marvin Gaye / Ain't nothing like the real thing: Gaye, Marvin & Tammi Terrell / Up where we belong: Cocker, Joe & Jennifer Warnes / Endless love: Ross, Diana & Lionel Richie / With you I'm born again: Preston, Billy & Syreeta / Tonight I celebrate my love: Bryson, Peabo & Roberta Flack / You're all I need to get by: Gaye, Marvin & Tammi Terrell / Stop, look, listen (to your heart): Gaye, Marvin & Diana Ross / It takes two: Gaye, Marvin & Kim Weston / Too much, too little, too late: Mathis, Johnny & Deniece Williams / Reunited: Peaches & Herb / Solid: Ashford & Simpson / Teardrops: Womack & Womack
CD 5254612
Polydor / Mar '95 / PolyGram

TOGETHER - THE EASTBOUND JAZZ YEARS
Baby let me take you (in my arms): Chandler, Gary / Crazy legs: Person, Houston / For the love of you: Person, Houston / Gettin' off: Mason, Bill / Lester leaps in: Person, Houston / Blow top blues: Jones, Etta / Flamingo: Chandler, Gary / Gathering together: Sparks, Melvin / When I'm kissing my love: Wilson, Spanky / Jet set: Chandler, Gary / Mr. Jay: Mason, Bill
CD CDBGPD 071
Beat Goes Public / Aug '93 / Pinnacle

TOKYO FLASHBACK VOL.4
CD PSFD 69
PSF / Dec '95 / Harmonia Mundi

TOKYO TRASHVILLE
CD ANDA 181
Au-Go-Go / Mar '97 / Cargo / Greyhound / Plastic Head

TOLEKI BANGO
CD CRAW 1
Crammed World / Jan '96 / New Note/ Pinnacle

TOM-TOM ARABESQUES
CD VICG 50092
JVC World Library / Mar '96 / ADA / CM / Direct

TOM-TOM FANTASY
CD _______ VICG 50102
JVC World Library / Mar '96 / ADA / CM / Direct

TOMBSTONE AFTER DARK
Honky tonk masquerade: *Shepard, Jean & Ray Pillow* / Gypsy rider: *Clark, Gene & Carla Olsen* / Hey good lookin': *Sledge, Percy* / Shady was a lady from Louisville: *Alexander, Larry 'Jinx'* / Fools fall in love: *Hancock, Butch* / Further: *Halley, David* / My baby don't dance to nothing but Ernest Tubb: *Brown, Junior* / Where I grew up: *Durham, Bobby* / West Texas waltz: *Hancock, Butch* / Dallas: *Hancock, Butch* / Me and Billy the Kid: *Ely, Joe* / Border radio: *Alvin, Dave* / Big beaver: *Asleep At The Wheel*
CD _______ FIENDCD 713
Demon / Apr '92 / Pinnacle

TOMMY ARMSTRONG OF TYNESIDE
CD _______ TSCD 484
Topic / Jul '97 / ADA / CM / Direct

TONE TALES FROM TOMORROW VOL.2 (Ntone Compilation)
2005: *Transcend* / Cymatic frequency: *Coldcut* / First time ever I saw your face: *Law, Joanna* / Weeds: *Neotropic* / Gather: *Path* / 50cc: *Journeyman* / 2003: *Transcend* / Hypobank: *Drome* / Sleeper: *MLO* / Zen in Africa: *Bogus Order* / Dubmunculus: *Hex* / Shark dance: *Real Life* / Alien community: *Alien Community* / Pressure: *Continuum* / Harmonic: *Hex* / Float on: *Purr*
CD _______ NTONECD 009
Ntone / Apr '96 / Kudos / Vital

TONGUE SANDWICH
Whole affair: *Izit* / Sharing our lives: *Izit* / Caterpillar: *Mustard Spoon* / Crack the crackers: *Sidewinder* / Stimela (coaltrain): *Masekela, Hugh* / Charge of the large brigade: *Powdered Rhino Horns* / Spring in your step: *Nodding Dog Productions* / Awake: *K-Creative* / Maybe tomorrow: *Yerbouti* / From the city to the sea: *Mighty Truth* / Better way: *Fumi*
CD _______ TNGCD 005
Tongue 'n' Groove / Oct '94 / Vital

TOO GOOD TO BE FORGOTTEN
CD _______ CDTRL 362
Trojan / Oct '95 / Direct / Jet Star

TOO HOT FOR ME (The JSP Sampler)
You're one woman: *Wilson, U.P.* / Woman is dangerous: *Shields, Lonnie* / I'm talking about love: *Butler Twins* / Hip guy: *Sayles, Charlie* / Doggy style: *Cosse, Ike* / Hey brother: *Morello, Jimmy* / Too hot for me: *Parker, Kenny* / Everlastin' tears: *Edwards, Willie* / Going back to Texas: *Kirkpatrick, Bob* / Light in a dark place: *Singleton, T-Bone* / Funky thang: *Patterson, Jordan* / One eyed man: *Tre'* / Here we go: *Rawls, Johnny* / You're a dog: *Jones, Andrew 'Jr. Boy'* / Fine as wine: *Coronado, Joe* / Aunt Nancey's Bull: *Griswalds* / Walk that way: *Wilson, U.P.*
CD _______ JSPCD 2H1
JSP / Apr '97 / ADA / Cadillac / Direct / Hot Shot / Target/BMG

TOO LATE
CD _______ WRCD 004
World / Jun '97 / Jet Star / TKO Magnum

TOO LATE, TOO LATE VOL.2 1897-1935
CD _______ DOCD 5216
Document / Jan '94 / ADA / Hot Shot / Jazz Music

TOO LATE, TOO LATE VOL.4 1892-1937
CD _______ DOCD 5321
Document / Mar '95 / ADA / Hot Shot / Jazz Music

TOO LATE, TOO LATE VOL.7 1927-1955
CD _______ DOCD 5525
Document / Apr '97 / ADA / Hot Shot / Jazz Music

TOO PURE SAMPLER
CD _______ PURECD 034
Too Pure / Apr '94 / Vital

TOO YOUNG (20 Hits Of The Fifties)
Reet petite: *Wilson, Jackie* / Tomorrow: *Brandon, Johnny & The Phantoms* / Little shoemaker: *Clark, Petula* / Cumberland gap: *Donegan, Lonnie* / I'm walking behind you: *Squires, Dorothy* / Young and foolish: *Hockridge, Edmund* / Hold back tomorrow: *Miki & Griff* / Too young: *Young, Jimmy* / Suddenly there's a valley: *Clark, Petula* / Happy anniversary: *Regan, Joan* / Love me forever: *Ryan, Marion* / Wayward wind: *Grant, Gogi* / Gamblin' man: *Donegan, Lonnie* / Venus: *Valentine, Dickie* / Why: *Avalon, Frankie* / Petite fleur: *Barber, Chris* / Be anything (but be mine): *Young, Jimmy* / Side saddle: *Conway, Russ* / Alone: *Clark, Petula* / Dead or alive: *Donegan, Lonnie*
CD _______ TRTCD 111
TrueTrax / Oct '94 / THE

TOO YOUNG TO KNOW, TOO WILD TO CARE
New dawn fades: *Joy Division* / For Belgian friends: *Durutti Column* / And then again: *A Certain Ratio* / Age of consent: *New Order* / Talk about the past: *Wake* / Brighter: *Railway Children* / Hymn from a village: *James* / Smiling monarchs: *Abecedarians* / Reach out for love: *King, Marcel* / Looking from a hilltop: *Section 25* / Genius: *Quando Quango* / WFL: *Happy Mondays* / My rising star: *Northside* / Moves like you: *Carroll, Cath* / Getting away with it: *Electronic*
CD _______ 8287002
Factory Too / Mar '97 / Pinnacle / PolyGram

TOP 12 DISCO SINGLES
CD _______ PKCD 03893
K&K / Jul '93 / Jet Star

TOP COUNTRY STARS
CD _______ 15214
Laserlight / Aug '91 / Target/BMG

TOP GEAR VOL.1
Jessica: *Allman Brothers* / Killer queen: *Queen* / Sharp dressed man: *ZZ Top* / You took the words right out of my mouth: *Meat Loaf* / Two princes: *Spin Doctors* / We don't need another hero: *Turner, Tina* / More than a feeling: *Boston* / Big log: *Plant, Robert* / Inside: *Stiltskin* / Wishing well: *Free* / Roll away the stone: *Mott The Hoople* / Maggie May: *Stewart, Rod* / Tuff enuff: *Fabulous Thunderbirds* / Because the night: *Smith, Patti* / Call me: *Blondie* / Rhiannon (Will you ever win): *Fleetwood Mac* / You: *Frampton, Peter* / When tomorrow comes: *Eurythmics* / Power of love: *Lewis, Huey & The News* / Do anything you wanna do: *Eddie & The Hot Rods* / 2-4-6-8 Motorway: *Robinson, Tom* / Bad case of lovin' you (Doctor Doctor): *Palmer, Robert* / Boys are back in town: *Thin Lizzy* / Brown eyed girl: *Morrison, Van* / Rocky mountain way: *Walsh, Joe* / Talking back to the night: *Cocker, Joe* / Show me the way: *Frampton, Peter* / I want you to want me: *Cheap Trick* / Long train runnin': *Doobie Brothers* / American pie: *McLean, Don* / Black magic woman: *Santana* / Everybody wants to rule the world: *Tears For Fears* / Walk on the wild side: *Reed, Lou* / Wicked game: *Isaak, Chris* / Venus in furs: *Velvet Underground*
CD _______ MOODCD 33
Columbia / May '94 / Sony

TOP GEAR VOL.2
I want to break free: *Queen* / I drove all night: *Lauper, Cyndi* / My brother Jake: *Free* / Drive: *Cars* / Change: *Lightning Seeds* / Can't get enough: *Bad Company* / Final countdown: *Europe* / Peace pipe: *Cry Of Love* / Africa: *Toto* / Damn, I wish I was your love: *Hawkins, Sophie B.* / Owner of a lonely heart: *Yes* / Heart of stone: *Stewart, Dave* / Atomic: *Blondie* / Since you've been gone: *Rainbow* / Satellite: *Hooters* / Once bitten twice shy: *Hunter, Ian* / Addicted to love: *Palmer, Robert* / Free bird: *Lynyrd Skynyrd* / Dead ringer for love: *Meat Loaf* / Little Miss can't be wrong: *Spin Doctors* / Seven wonders: *Fleetwood Mac* / Driver's seat: *Sniff 'n' The Tears* / Good feeling: *Reef* / Gimme all your lovin': *ZZ Top* / Flame: *Cheap Trick* / If I could turn back time: *Cher* / Twenty nine palms: *Plant, Robert* / Hold your head up: *Argent* / Life's been good: *Walsh, Joe* / Cars and girls: *Prefab Sprout* / On the road again: *Canned Heat* / Poison: *Cooper, Alice* / Missing you: *Waite, John* / Night games: *Bonnet, Graham* / Motorcycle emptiness: *Manic Street Preachers* / (Don't fear) The reaper: *Blue Oyster Cult*
CD _______ MOODCD 41
Columbia / May '95 / Sony

TOP GEAR VOL.3 (The Rock Ballads)
Rock 'n' roll dreams come through: *Meat Loaf* / Rhiannon: *Fleetwood Mac* / Always the sun: *Stranglers* / 74-75: *Connells* / Couldn't get it right: *Climax Blues Band* / Stainsby girls: *Rea, Chris* / Mmm mmm mmm mmm: *Crash Test Dummies* / Creep: *Radiohead* / Driving away from home: *It's Immaterial* / So far away: *Dire Straits* / When will you (make my telephone ring): *Deacon Blue* / I don't want to talk about it: *Everything But The Girl* / Johnny & Mary: *Palmer, Robert* / If I was: *Ure, Midge* / It's my life: *Talk Talk* / Alive and kicking: *Simple Minds* / Yes: *McAlmont & Butler* / Bette Davis eyes: *Carnes, Kim* / Walking in Memphis: *Cher* / Lucky you: *Lightning Seeds* / He's on the phone: *St. Etienne* / Manic Monday: *Bangles* / Mary's prayer: *Danny Wilson* / No more I love you's: *Lennox, Annie* / Somewhere down the crazy river: *Robertson, Robbie* / Come together in the morning: *Free* / Parisienne walkways: *Moore, Gary* / Ghost in you: *Psychedelic Furs* / Wonderful life: *Black*
CD _______ SONYTV 12CD
Sony TV / Feb '96 / Sony

TOP HITS DER VOLKSMUSIK
CD _______ 15258
Laserlight / Nov '91 / Target/BMG

TOP OF THE HILL BLUEGRASS (The Sugar Hill Collection)
CD _______ SHCD 9201
Sugar Hill / Dec '95 / ADA / CM / Direct / Koch / Roots

TOP OF THE POPS
CD _______ CECD 6
Collector's Edition / Jun '96 / TKO Magnum

TOP OF THE POPS - THE CUTTING EDGE
Design for life: *Manic Street Preachers* / Tattva: *Kula Shaker* / Oh yeah: *Ash* / Peaches: *Presidents Of The USA* / Trash: *Suede* / One to another: *Charlatans* / Good night: *Baby Bird* / Me and you versus the world: *Space* / What's in the box (see watcha got): *Boo Radleys* / Born slippy: *Underworld* / Out of the sinking: *Weller, Paul* / Becoming more like Alfie: *Divine Comedy* / Alright: *Cast* / Mario man: *Super Furry Animals* / Day we caught the train: *Ocean Colour Scene* / Shark: *Throwing Muses* / All nighter: *Elastica* / Mouse in a hole: *Heavy Stereo* / Crazy: *Nut* / Saved: *Octopus* / Possibly maybe: *Bjork* / Virtual insanity: *Jamiroquai* / Tape loop: *Morcheeba* / Stupid girl: *Garbage* / Nice guy Eddie: *Sleeper* / Ready or not: *Lightning Seeds* / 500 (Shake baby shake): *Lush* / Someone somewhere: *Wannadies* / Elevator song: *Dubstar* / Celebrity hit list: *Terrorvision* / In a room: *Dodgy* / Exodus: *Levellers* / Sitting at home: *Honeycrack* / Ski jump nose: *Mansun* / Men in black: *Black, Frank* / Hours and the times: *18 Wheeler* / To you I bestow: *Mundy* / Anymore: *Cracknell, Sarah* / Krupa: *Apollo 440* / Chemical beats: *Chemical Brothers*
CD _______ SONYTV 19CD
Sony TV / Sep '96 / Sony

TOP OF THE POPS VOL.1
Think twice: *Dion, Celine* / Chains: *Arena, Tina* / If you love me: *Brownstone* / Open up your heart: *M-People* / Guaglione: *Prado, Perez* / Wake up Boo: *Boo Radleys* / Change: *Lightning Seeds* / Some might say: *Oasis* / I wanna go where the people go: *Wildhearts* / Crush with eyeliner: *REM* / Vegas: *Sleeper* / Waking up: *Elastica* / Over my shoulder: *Mike & The Mechanics* / Over the river: *McLean, Bitty* / Everlating love: *Estefan, Gloria* / Cowboy dreams: *Nail, Jimmy* / Independent love song: *Scarlet* / As I lay me down: *Hawkins, Sophie B.* / Space cowboy: *Jamiroquai* / You gotta be: *Des'ree* / I've got a little something for you: *MN8* / My girl Josephine: *Super Cat* / Here comes the hotstepper: *Kamoze, Ini* / Scatman John: *Scatman John* / Love and devotion: *Real McCoy* / Dreamer '95: *Livin' Joy* / Love city groove: *Love City Groove* / Your body's calling: *R Kelly* / Feel so good: *Xscape* / Right in the night: *Jam & Spoon* / Not over yet: *Grace* / U sure do: *Strike* / Lifting me higher: *Gems For Jem* / Move: *H-Blockx* / Don't stop (wiggle wiggle): *Outhere Brothers* / One man in my heart: *Human League* / Two can play that game: *Brown, Bobby* / Give it to you: *Da Brat* / Crazy: *Morrison, Mark* / Baby baby: *Corona* / First, the last eternity: *Snap*
CD _______ MOODCD 40
Sony Music / May '95 / Sony

TOP OF THE POPS VOL.2
Fairground: *Simply Red* / Gangstas paradise: *Coolio* / Shy guy: *King, Diana* / Baby it's you: *Dion, Celine* / Pour que tu m'aimes encore: *Dion, Celine* / Power of love: *Vandross, Luther* / Walking in Memphis: *Cher* / Never forget: *Take That* / Heaven help my heart: *Arena, Tina* / If you leave me now: *Riverseries* / U krazy katz: *PJ & Duncan* / We've got it goin' on: *Backstreet Boys* / Stay with me: *Erasure* / He's on the phone: *St. Etienne* / I'm only sleeping: *Suggs* / Girl like you: *Collins, Edwyn* / Raoul and the Kings of Spain: *Tears For Fears* / You do: *McAlmont & Butler* / 74-75: *Connells* / Where the wild roses grow: *Cave, Nick & Kylie Minogue* / Wonderwall: *Oasis* / Lucky you: *Lightning Seeds* / Common people: *Pulp* / What do I do now: *Sleeper* / Kings of the kerb: *Echobelly* / From the bench at Belvidere: *Boo Radleys* / Love rendevous: *M-People* / Missing: *Everything But The Girl* / Hideaway: *De'Lacy* / Happy just to be with you: *Gayle, Michelle* / I can't tell you why: *Brownstone* / You remind me of something: *R Kelly* / Stayin' alive: *N-Trance* / Found love: *Double Dee & Dany* / My prerogative: *Brown, Bobby* / 1st of tha month: *Bone Thugs n' Harmony* / Exodus: *Sunscreem* / Transamazonia: *Shamen* / La la la hey hey: *Outhere Brothers* / Angel: *Jam & Spoon*
CD _______ SONYTV 9CD
Sony TV / Nov '95 / Sony

TOP RANK EXPLOSION
CD _______ LG 21096
Lagoon / May '94 / Grapevine/PolyGram

TOP ROCK STEADY
CD _______ LG 21070
Lagoon / Feb '93 / Grapevine/PolyGram

TOP TEN
CD _______ NWSCD 6
New Sound / Apr '93 / Jet Star

TOP TEN HITS OF THE 60'S
House of the rising sun: *Animals* / Do it again: *Beach Boys* / Got to get you into my life: *Bennett, Cliff & The Rebel Rousers* / Someone else's baby: *Faith, Adam* / little lovin': *Fourmost* / Ferry 'cross the Mersey: *Gerry & The Pacemakers* / Something is happening: *Herman's Hermits* / In the country: *Richard, Cliff* / Look through my window: *Hollies* / High time: *Jones, Paul* / I'm a tiger: *Lulu* / FBI: *Shadows* / Hippy hippy shake: *Swinging Blue Jeans* / Pasadena: *Temperance Seven* / Twelfth of never: *Richard, Cliff* / Let's go to San Francisco: *Flowerpot Men* / Seven little girls sitting in the back seat: *Avons* / You were made for me: *Freddie & The Dreamers*
CD _______ CDMFP 6040
Music For Pleasure / Sep '88 / EMI

TOP TEN HITS OF THE 60'S VOL.1
CD _______ PLSCD 216
Pulse / Apr '97 / BMG

TOP TEN HITS OF THE 60'S VOL.2
CD _______ PLSCD 217
Pulse / Apr '97 / BMG

TOP TEN HITS OF THE 60'S, 70'S, 80'S
CD Set _______ CDMFPBOX 1
Music For Pleasure / Oct '90 / EMI

TOP TEN HITS OF THE 70'S
Wuthering Heights: *Bush, Kate* / American pie: *McLean, Don* / Baker Street: *Rafferty, Gerry* / Roll over Beethoven: *ELO* / Tap turns on the water: *CCS* / 2-4-6-8 motorway: *Robinson, Tom* / You sexy thing: *Hot Chocolate* / Angie baby: *Reddy, Helen* / Air that I breathe: *Hollies* / Make me smile (come up and see me): *Harley, Steve & Cockney Rebel* / Let's work together: *Canned Heat* / Some girls: *Racey* / Heaven must be missing an angel: *Tavares* / 48 crash: *Quatro, Suzi* / Cotton fields: *Beach Boys* / Cat crept in: *Mud* / Little bit more: *Dr. Hook* / Years may come years may go: *Herman's Hermits*
CD _______ CDMFP 6078
Music For Pleasure / Oct '89 / EMI

TOP TEN HITS OF THE 70'S
Nutbush City limits: *Turner, Ike & Tina* / Walking: *CCS* / I can't tell the bottom from the top: *Hollies* / I hear you knocking: *Edmunds, Dave* / Love is life: *Hot Chocolate* / Right back where we started from: *Nightingale, Maxine* / Night owl: *Rafferty, Gerry* / Don't it make my brown eyes blue: *Gayle, Crystal* / If you can't give me love: *Quatro, Suzi* / Summer (the first time): *Goldsboro, Bobby* / That's the way (I like it): *KC & The Sunshine Band* / Mr. Soft: *Cockney Rebel* / Rock me gently: *Kim, Andy* / Oh boy: *Mud* / Don't take away the music: *Tavares* / Them heavy people: *Bush, Kate* / Angel fingers: *Wizzard* / Vincent: *McLean, Don*
CD _______ CDMFP 6211
Music For Pleasure / Feb '96 / EMI

TOP TEN HITS OF THE 80'S
Girls on film: *Duran Duran* / Running up that hill: *Bush, Kate* / Geno: *Dexy's Midnight Runners* / Golden brown: *Stranglers* / Kids in America: *Wilde, Kim* / Harder I try: *Brother Beyond* / Bette Davis eyes: *Carnes, Kim* / Tonight I celebrate my love: *Bryson, Peabo & Roberta Flack* / Kayleigh: *Marillion* / Set me free: *Graham, Jaki* / Model: *Kraftwerk* / Too shy: *Kajagoogoo* / Turning Japanese: *Vapors* / Searchin': *Dean, Hazell* / Walking on sunshine: *Katrina & The Waves* / Tarzan boy: *Baltimora* / Election day: *Arcadia* / Sexy eyes: *Dr. Hook* / No doubt about it: *Hot Chocolate* / Let's go all the way: *Sly Fox*
CD _______ CDMFP 5893
Music For Pleasure / Sep '90 / EMI

TOP TEN HITS OF THE 80'S
It started with a kiss: *Hot Chocolate* / For your eyes only: *Easton, Sheena* / Strange little girl: *Stranglers* / Chequered love: *Wilde, Kim* / Classic: *Gurvitz, Adrian* / I could be so good for you: *Waterman, Dennis* / Solid: *Ashford & Simpson* / Road to nowhere: *Talking Heads* / I don't wanna dance: *Grant, Eddy* / Missing you: *Waite, John* / Set me free: *Graham, Jaki* / Love changes (everything): *Climie Fisher* / Incommunicado: *Marillion* / Respectable: *Mel & Kim* / Big apple: *Kajagoogoo* / Crying: *McLean, Don*
CD _______ CDMFP 6212
Music For Pleasure / Feb '96 / EMI

TOP TEN HITS OF THE 80'S - VOL.2
Reflex: *Duran Duran* / Perfect: *Fairground Attraction* / Babooshka: *Bush, Kate* / Lifeline: *Spandau Ballet* / Lavender: *Marillion* / System addict: *Five Star* / Fantastic day: *Haircut 100* / Living in a box: *Living In A Box* / We close our eyes: *Go West* / Better love next time: *Dr. Hook* / Atomic: *Blondie* / Use it up and wear it out: *Odyssey* / Tunnel of love: *Fun Boy Three* / Broken wings: *Mr. Mister* / Girl you know it's true: *Milli Vanilli* / Rat race: *Specials* / You'll never stop me loving you: *Sonia* / Rise to the occasion: *Climie Fisher* / Who's leaving who: *Dean, Hazell* / There there my dear: *Dexy's Midnight Runners*
CD _______ CDMFP 5975
Music For Pleasure / Dec '92 / EMI

TOPAZ BOX, THE (5CD Set)
CD Set _______ TPZS 1030
Topaz Jazz / Nov '95 / Cadillac / Pinnacle

TORCH SONGS
Am I blue: *Holiday, Billie* / My old flame: *Holiday, Billie* / He's gone blues: *Smith, Bessie* / You've got me crying again: *Wiley, Lee* / Tears in my heart: *Bailey, Mildred* / Love me or leave me: *Grace, Teddy* / I'm up a tree: *Fitzgerald, Ella* / You can't cry you out of my heart: *Fitzgerald, Ella* / Stormy weather: *Anderson, Ivie* / I got it bad and that ain't good: *Anderson, Ivie* / It's torture: *Humes, Helen* / Somebody else is taking my place: *Lee, Peggy* / You took my love: *Stafford, Jo* / Friend of yours: *Stafford, Jo* / Good-for-nothin' Joe: *Horne, Lena* / One for my baby: *Horne, Lena* / There must be a way: *Boswell, Connee* / There will never be another you: *Knight, Evelyn*
CD _______ RPCD 324

Robert Parker Jazz / Apr '97 / Conifer/BMG / New Note/Pinnacle

TORONTO SOCA X-PLOSION VOL.1
CD _____ CD 0011
Oss / Jan '97 / Jet Star

TORONTO TATTOO
CD _____ LCOM 8015
Lismor / Oct '93 / ADA / Direct / Duncans / Lismor

TORQUE (2CD Set)
CD Set _____ NUTCD 1
No U Turn / Mar '97 / SRD

TOTAL DEF JAM (The Definitive Collection)
Fight for your right to party: *Beastie Boys* / Rain: *Jones, Oran 'Juice'* / Don't believe the hype: *Public Enemy* / Mama said knock you out: *LL Cool J* / Fight the power: *Public Enemy* / Slam: *Onyx* / Ghetto jam: *Domino* / Regulate: *Warren G* / You're all I need: *Method Man & Mary J. Blige* / This is how we do it: *Jordan, Montell* / What's love got to do with it: *Warren G & Adina Howard* / Whateva man: *Redman* / Touch me, tease me: *Case* / Hey lover: *LL Cool J* / I like: *Jordan, Montell* / Get me home: *Brown, Foxy* / Ain't nobody: *LL Cool J* / I shot the sheriff: *Warren G*
CD _____ 5360722
PolyGram TV / Jun '97 / PolyGram

TOTAL DEVOTION
Rage: *Scnitt Acht* / Codeine, glue and you: *Chemlab* / Chikasaw: *Pigface* / Do ya think I'm sexy: *Revolting Cocks* / Boomerang: *Sugarsmack* / Picasso trigger: *Skrew* / Never trust a John: *Evil Mothers* / Cut and divide: *Deep Throat* / Fuck it up: *Pigface* / Open up your mind: *Lab Report*
CD _____ CDDVN 32
Devotion / Aug '94 / Pinnacle

TOTAL RECALL VOL.1 (Calling The Classics)
Get up, stand up: *Tosh, Peter* / Why did you do it: *McGregor, Freddie* / Here I am baby: *Brown, Al* / My time: *Brown, Dennis* / I roots: *Third World* / Pomp and pride: *Toots & The Maytals* / Come see Jah: *Miller, Jacob* / Suspicious minds: *Heptones* / Never get weary: *Culture* / Nature planned it: *Struggle* / Israel: *Paul, Frankie* / Birds follow Spring: *Griffiths, Hugh* / Mother miserable: *Captain Barkey* / Style with fashion: *Papa Bruce* / Oh no not my baby: *McGregor, Freddie* / Rub-a-dub: *Johnny Ringo* / Daddy mix: *Purpleman* / I'm living: *Griffiths, Hugh* / Crystal blue persuasion: *Heptones* / 54-46 was my number: *Toots & The Maytals*
CD _____ CDGR 114
Charly / Jan '97 / Koch

TOTAL RECALL VOL.7
CD _____ VPCD 1303
VP / Mar '96 / Greensleeves / Jet Star / Total/BMG

TOTAL RECALL VOL.8
CD _____ VPCD 1334
VP / Aug '94 / Greensleeves / Jet Star / Total/BMG

TOTAL RECALL VOL.9
CD _____ VPCD 1384
VP / Mar '96 / Greensleeves / Jet Star / Total/BMG

TOTAL TOGETHERNESS VOL.1
CD _____ CRCD 27
Charm / Mar '94 / Jet Star

TOTAL TOGETHERNESS VOL.2
CD _____ CRCD 37
Charm / Nov '94 / Jet Star

TOTAL TOGETHERNESS VOL.3
CD _____ FAMCD 001
Famous / Jul '95 / Jet Star

TOTAL TOGETHERNESS VOL.4
Nah fi watch nuh mate: *Cobra* / Oh yes no guess: *Beenie Man* / Babylon drop: *Bounty Killer* / Noise of the ghetto: *Tony Rebel* / Darness thing: *Lady Saw* / Oh Mama: *Jigsy King* / Dis: *Galaxy P* / House mouse: *Shabba Ranks* / Turn around: *Beenie Man* / No interview: *Bounty Killer* / Search: *Louie Culture* / Top rankin: *Althia & Donna* / Tek yuh man: *Buccaneer* / Want you back: *Lady G*
CD _____ FAMCD 002
Famous / Jan '96 / Jet Star

TOTALLY BLUES GUITAR
CD _____ VSOPCD 239
Connoisseur Collection / Jul '97 / Pinnacle

TOTALLY COUNTRY GUITAR
CD _____ VSOPCD 241
Connoisseur Collection / Jul '97 / Pinnacle

TOTALLY IRISH (The Essential Irish Album)
Riverdance: *Kennedy, Fiona* / Black velvet band: *Dubliners* / Seven drunken nights: *Dubliners* / Three drunken maidens: *Planxty* / Paddy on the railroad/Miss McLeod: *Gallowglass Ceili Band* / Sheebans/Merry blacksmith/Music in the Glen: *Kilfernora Ceili Band* / Dan Malone: *Hasson, Gemma* / Phil the fluters ball: *O'Dowda, Brendan* / It's a great day for the Irish: *Murray, Ruby* / Dear old Donegal: *Locke, Josef* / When Irish eyes are smiling: *Jones, Sandie* / Danny Boy: *O'Se, Sean* / Johnny I hardly knew ye: *Murphy, Mary* / Behind the bush and the garden: *Dun Carmel Band* / Over the road to Maggie/The Sailor's bonnet: *Dun Carmel Band* / Crossing: *Wilson, Alexia & Paul Brennan* / This land: *Kennedy, Fiona*
CD _____ CDGOLD 1096
EMI Gold / May '97 / EMI

TOTALLY JAZZ
CD _____ CDGOLD 1088
EMI Gold / Mar '97 / EMI

TOTALLY JAZZ GUITAR
CD _____ VSOPCD 240
Connoisseur Collection / Jul '97 / Pinnacle

TOTALLY NO.1'S OF THE 60'S
Sweets for my sweet: *Searchers* / Pretty flamingo: *Manfred Mann* / Do it again: *Beach Boys* / I'm alive: *Hollies* / Ob-la-di, ob-la-da: *Marmalade* / I remember you: *Ifield, Frank* / Go now: *Moody Blues* / You'll never walk alone: *Gerry & The Pacemakers* / Anyone who had a heart: *Black, Cilla* / Little children: *Kramer, Billy J. & The Dakotas* / Tell Laura I love her: *Valance, Ricky* / Carnival is over: *Seekers* / House of the rising sun: *Animals* / I'm into something good: *Herman's Hermits* / Foot tapper: *Shadows* / Runaway: *Shannon, Del* / Mony mony: *Jones, Tommy & The Shondells* / Three steps to heaven: *Cochran, Eddie* / You're driving me crazy: *Temperance Seven* / Shakin' all over: *Kidd, Johnny & The Pirates*
CD _____ CDGOLD 1085
EMI Gold / Feb '97 / EMI

TOTALLY NO.1'S OF THE 70'S
Sunday girl: *Blondie* / So you win again: *Hot Chocolate* / Tiger feet: *Mud* / Devil gate drive: *Quatro, Suzi* / January: *Pilot* / Rock your baby: *McCrae, George* / Make me smile (come up and see me): *Harley, Steve & Cockney Rebel* / See my baby jive: *Wizzard* / I hear you knocking: *Edmunds, Dave* / In the summertime: *Mungo Jerry* / Can the can: *Quatro, Suzi* / Heart of glass: *Blondie* / Kung fu fighting: *Douglas, Carl* / You to me are everything: *Real Thing* / When you're in love with a beautiful woman: *Dr. Hook* / Vincent: *McLaughlin, Pat* / Oh boy: *Mud* / Wuthering heights: *Bush, Kate*
CD _____ CDGOLD 1086
EMI Gold / Feb '97 / EMI

TOTALLY NO.1'S OF THE 80'S
Is there something I should know: *Duran Duran* / When the going gets tough, the tough get going: *Ocean, Billy* / Give it up: *KC & The Sunshine Band* / Respectable: *Mel & Kim* / Feels like I'm in love: *Marie, Kelly* / Nineteen: *Hardcastle, Paul* / If I was: *Ure, Midge* / Something's gotten hold of my heart: *Almond, Marc & Gene Pitney* / True: *Spandau Ballet* / Crying: *McLean, Don* / Move closer: *Nelson, Phyllis* / Too shy: *Kajagoogoo* / I don't wanna dance: *Grant, Eddy* / Tide is high: *Blondie* / Ghost town: *Specials* / Geno: *Dexy's Midnight Runners* / Too much too young: *Special AKA* / Atomic: *Blondie*
CD _____ CDGOLD 1087
EMI Gold / Feb '97 / EMI

TOTALLY ROCK GUITAR
CD _____ VSOPCD 238
Connoisseur Collection / Jul '97 / Pinnacle

TOTALLY SOLID HITBOUND
Good things: *Hatcher, Willie* / Our love (is in this pocket): *Barnes, J.J.* / My darling: *Griffin, Herman* / Never alone: *Holidays* / Hit and run: *Revilot Orchestra* / I need my baby: *Beavers, Jackie* / Somebody somewhere (needs you): *Lebaron Orchestra* / I lost you: *Holidays* / You better wake up: *Debonaires* / Love that never grows cold: *Beavers, Jackie* / Did my baby call: *Mancha, Steve* / Girl crazy: *Gigi & The Charmaines* / I need you like a baby: *Henry, Andrea* / I must love you: *Davis, Melvin* / When you lose the one you love: *Smith, Buddy* / Poor unfortunate me: *Gigi & The Charmaines* / I won't hurt anymore: *Anderson, Eddie* / Happiness is here: *Topper Ensemble* / Open the door to your heart: *Banks, Daryl*
CD _____ GSCD 070
Goldmine / Jan '96 / Vital

TOTALLY SUMMER
Summer holiday: *Richard, Cliff* / Surfin' USA: *Beach Boys* / Beach baby: *First Class* / Surf city: *Jan & Dean* / Summer fun: *Barracudas* / In the summertime: *Mungo Jerry* / Walking on sunshine: *Katrina & The Waves* / Summertime blues: *Cochran, Eddie* / Summertime: *Fun Boy Three* / Here comes the sun: *Harley, Steve & Cockney Rebel* / Summer (the first time): *Goldsboro, Bobby* / Don't let the sun catch you crying: *Gerry & The Pacemakers* / Summer breeze: *Williams, Geoffrey* / California dreamin': *River City People* / Sunshine superman: *Donovan* / Sunshine girl: *Herman's Hermits* / California girls: *Beach Boys* / Hello sunshine: *Goldsboro, Bobby*
CD _____ CDGOLD 1099
EMI Gold / Jun '97 / EMI

TOTALLY TRADITIONAL TIN WHISTLES
CD _____ OSS 53CD
Ossian / Jan '94 / ADA / CM / Direct / Highlander

TOTALLY TRANCED
Your touch: *R2001* / Purity: *Aloof* / Feel: *Chameleon Project* / Hello San Francisco: *Dance 2 Trance* / Slide: *Contact* / Music is movin' DIKK: *Fargetta* / World evolution: *Trance* / La yerba del diablo: *Datura* / Spirit in me: *Vibe Alive* / Land of oz: *Spooky* / Peace and happiness: *Hullabaloo* / Orcana: *Void* / Mi piace: *Marmalade* / Passing thru' the surface: *Flux* / Time to rock: *Industrial* / Forever people: *Biologix*
CD _____ CDELV 03
Debut / Dec '92 / 3mv/Sony / Pinnacle

TOTALLY WIRED IN DUB
CD _____ DUBIDCD 5
Acid Jazz Roots / Feb '96 / Disc

TOTALLY WIRED ITALIA
CD _____ JAZIDCD 079
Acid Jazz / Sep '93 / Disc

TOTALLY WIRED SWEDEN
CD _____ JAZIDCD 103
Acid Jazz / Aug '94 / Disc

TOTALLY WIRED VOL.1
Love me to death: *Man Called Adam* / Dance wicked: *New Jersey Kings* / Odd one (part 1): *What's What* / Bolivia: *Sandberg, Ulf Quartet* / Olumo rock: *Leo, Bukky Quintet* / Frederic lies still: *Galliano* / Latin jam: *Haryon* / Lock out: *Hip Joints* / Playing for real: *Jazz Renegades* / Batu casu: *Bangs A Bongo* / Freedom principle: *Leo, Bukky & Galliano* / Sweet cakes: *New Jersey Kings*
CD _____ JAZIDCD 013
Acid Jazz / Nov '93 / Disc

TOTALLY WIRED VOL.10
Time and space theme: *Time & Space* / Would you believe in me: *Lucien, Jon* / Corduroy orgasm club: *Corduroy* / Ladder: *One Creed* / Real gone turn it on: *Cloud 9* / It's all in: *Whole Thing* / Sweet feeling: *Esperanto* / Cucaraca macarra: *Averne, Harvey* / Never change: *Quiet Boys* / Bone: *Wizards of Ooze* / Nature never repeats itself: *Emperor's New Clothes*
CD _____ JAZIDCD 072
Acid Jazz / Jul '93 / Disc

TOTALLY WIRED VOL.11
Three mile island: *Taylor, James Quartet* / Fresh in my mind: *Forest Mighty Black* / Never will I stop loving you: *Clark, Alice* / Freakin': *Freakpower* / Joyous: *Pleasure* / Theme from Millenium Falcon: *Square Window* / To the bone: *Children Of Judah* / Who me: *Ghost* / Monsieur Taylor's new brand: *Monsieur Kamayatsu* / Do you like it: *Skunkhour* / Anger: *Mondo Grosso* / Clever girl: *Purdey, Samuel* / Astral space: *Quiet Boys*
CD _____ JAZIDCD 101
Acid Jazz / Jun '94 / Disc

TOTALLY WIRED VOL.12
Life eternal: *Mother Earth* / Akimbo: *Bartholomew, Simon* / Funky jam: *Primal Scream* / Mental: *Dub War* / Swinging foot: *Swinging Foot* / Gimme one of those: *Brand New Heavies* / Couldn't take missing you: *Square Window* / Summertime: *OOKE* / Art is the message: *Stickman* / Don't you let me down: *Planet* / Work on a dream: *Birtha* / In deep: *Red Snapper* / Indian rope man: *Phaze*
CD _____ JAZIDCD 120
Acid Jazz / Mar '95 / Disc

TOTALLY WIRED VOL.2
Beads, things and flowers: *Humble Souls* / Monkey drop: *New Jersey Kings* / Trinkets and trash: *Cool Beats* / APB: *Man Called Adam* / Break for jazz: *Break for jazz* / Nzuri beat: *White, Steve & Gary Wallace* / Homegrown: *Jones, Ed* / Tilldens: *Sandberg, Ulf Quartet* / Gimme one of those: *Brand New Heavies* / Killer: *Night Trains*
CD _____ JAZIDCD 016
Acid Jazz / Nov '93 / Disc

TOTALLY WIRED VOL.3
CD _____ JAZIDCD 022
Acid Jazz / Nov '93 / Disc

TOTALLY WIRED VOL.4
CD _____ JAZIDCD 028
Acid Jazz / Nov '93 / Disc

TOTALLY WIRED VOL.5
CD _____ JAZIDCD 031
Acid Jazz / Dec '91 / Disc

TOTALLY WIRED VOL.6
CD _____ JAZID 36CD
Acid Jazz / May '91 / Disc

TOTALLY WIRED VOL.7
Theme from riot on 103rd street: *Mother Earth* / Taurus woman: *Subterraneans* / That's how it is: *Grand Oral Disceminator* / Machine shop (pt.1): *Untouchable Machine Shop* / Don't you care: *Clark, Alice* / Sunship: *Sunship* / Sim ting: *Quiet Boys* / Believe in me: *Vibraphonic* / Change had better come: *Dimmond, Mark*
CD _____ JAZIDCD 043
Acid Jazz / Nov '91 / Disc

TOTALLY WIRED VOL.8
CD _____ JAZIDCD 050
Acid Jazz / Apr '92 / Disc

TOTALLY WIRED VOL.9
Mr. Jeckle: *Beesley's, Max High Vibes* / Warlock of pendragon: *Mother Earth* / Dat's slammin': *Gordon, Robbie* / Peter and the wolf in sheep's clothing: *Sons Of Judah* / Got a groove: *Wiggs, Supa & Jonzi* / I can't stand it: *George, Brenda* / Electric soup: *Corduroy* / That's it: *Grass Snakes* / Dreams: *Raw*
CD _____ JAZIDCD 057
Acid Jazz / Oct '92 / Disc

TOTENTANZ VOL.2 (The History Of Zoth Ommog)
CD Set _____ CLP 0005
Cleopatra / Jul '97 / Cargo / Greyhound / Plastic Head / RTM/Disc / SRD

TOUCH ME IN THE MORNING
CD _____ CDTRL 337
Trojan / Apr '94 / Direct / Jet Star

TOUCH OF ACID JAZZ VOL.1
CD _____ FARCD 401
Family Affair / Jul '96 / Timewarp

TOUCH OF DEATH, A
Perpetual dawn: *Fleshcrawl* / Primeval transubstantation: *Agressor* / Where the rivers of madness stream: *Cemetary* / Who will not be dead: *Seance* / Within the silence: *Rosicrucian* / Excursion demise: *Invocator* / Solace: *Necrosanct* / Born Bizarre: *Tribulation* / Enigma: *Edge Of Sanity* / Blood And Iron: *Bathory*
CD _____ BMCD 026
Black Mark / Sep '92 / Plastic Head

TOUCH OF ROMANCE VOL.1, A
CD _____ KNEWCD 725
Kenwest / Apr '94 / THE

TOUCH OF ROMANCE VOL.2, A
CD _____ KNEWCD 726
Kenwest / Apr '94 / THE

TOUCH OF ROMANCE VOL.3, A
CD _____ KNEWCD 727
Kenwest / Apr '94 / THE

TOUCH OF ROMANCE VOL.4, A
CD _____ KNEWCD 728
Kenwest / Apr '94 / THE

TOUCH OF ROMANCE, A
I'm beginning to see the light: *Williams, Joe & Count Basie* / Top hat, white tie and tails: *Armstrong, Louis* / Goin' to Chicago: *Hibbler, Al* / Tenderly: *Eckstine, Billy* / Charge account: *Lambert, Dave* / Stockholm sweetnin': *Hendricks, Jon* / I want a little girl: *McShann, Jay* / Song is you: *Crosby, Bing* / Between the devil and the deep blue sea: *Rich, Buddy* / Touch of your lips: *Baker, Chet* / T'ain't so honey, t'ain't so: *Teagarden, Jack* / Is you is or is you ain't my baby: *Jordan, Louis* / You can't have your cake and eat it: *Fabulous Ellingtonians* / I could have told you: *Prysock, Arthur* / Too close for comfort: *Torme, Mel* / Gravy waltz: *Henderson, Bill & Oscar Peterson Trio* / Evenin': *Basie, Count* / I'm building up to an awful letdown: *Astaire, Fred*
CD _____ 5526392
Spectrum / Mar '97 / PolyGram

TOUCH OF THE MASTER'S HAND, A
CD _____ RTECD 191
RTE / Mar '96 / ADA / Koch

TOUCH SAMPLER
Mind loss: *H3OH* / PS one: *Jeck, Philip* / Valley of the Kings and Queens: *Gamil, Soliman* / Orgasmatron: *Sandoz* / Sudurgate: *Hilmarsson, Hilmar Orn* / I remain...: *Hafler Trio* / Mara river at night: *Watson, Chris* / Supermind's light becommes part of the Earth: *Seymour, Daren & Mark Van Hoen* / Mule river of Grebene: *Fara, Eli & Luiza Mica* / Ghettoes of the mind: *Sweet Exorcist* / Mesmerised: *Drome* / In the compound: *Rax Werx* / Radio KPFK: *Z'Ev* / Knowledge: *SETI* / Supplication: *Gamil, Soliman* / Calcutta: *Marutani, Koji*
CD _____ T 01
Touch / Oct '95 / Kudos / Pinnacle

TOUCHE COMPILATION
CD _____ TOU 96015
Vermoth / Jan '96 / RTM/Disc

TOUCHED BY THE HAND OF GOTH VOL.1 (2CD Set)
CD Set _____ SPV 08638302
SPV / Aug '95 / Koch / Plastic Head

TOUCHED BY THE HAND OF GOTH VOL.2 (2CD Set)
Painted flowers in a picture: *Placebo Effect* / See you in hell: *Suicide Commando* / Wheel: *Sleeping Dogs Wake* / Inside me: *Revenge Of Nephthys* / November morning: *Love Is Colder Than Death* / Angel light: *This Ascension* / Gedanken eines vampires: *Umbra Et Imago* / EST Trip to the moon: *Alien Sex Fiend* / Rat kill: *Blok 57* / Slavesex: *Die Form* / Smell of decay: *Steril* / Die liebe: *Atrocity* / Realtives menschsein: *Misanthrope* / Painkilling suicide: *Love Like Blood* / No blind eyes can see: *Lacrimosa*
CD Set _____ SPV 08738642
SPV / May '96 / Koch / Plastic Head

TOUGHER THAN TOUGH
CD _____ CDTRL 304
Trojan / Mar '94 / Direct / Jet Star

TOUGHER THAN TOUGH (The Story Of Jamaican Music/4CD Set)
Oh Carolina: *Folkes Brothers* / Boogie in my bones: *Aitken, Laurel* / Midnight track: *Gray, Owen* / Easy snappin': *Beckford, Theophilus* / Housewives' choice: *Derrick & Patsy* / Forward march: *Morgan, Derrick* / Miss Jamaica: *Cliff, Jimmy* / My boy lollipop: *Millie* / Six and seven books of Moses: *Toots &*

The Maytals / Simmer down: *Wailers* / Man in the street: *Drummond, Don* / Carry go bring home: *Hinds, Justin* / Guns of navarone: *Skatalites* / Al Capone: *Prince Buster* / Hard man fe dead: *Prince Buster* / Tougher than tough: *Morgan, Derrick* / Girl I've got a date: *Ellis, Alton* / Happy go lucky girl: *Paragons* / Dancing mood: *Wilson, Delroy* / Train is coming: *Boothe, Ken* / Take it easy: *Lewis, Hopeton* / Ba ba boom: *Jamaicans* / 007: *Dekker, Desmond* / I've got to go back home: *Andy, Bob* / Queen majesty: *Techniques* / Loving pauper: *Dobson, Dobby* / Don't stay away: *Dillon, Phyllis* / Israelites: *Dekker, Desmond* / 54-46 (was my number): *Toots & The Maytals* / Reggae hit the town: *Ethiopians* / Wet dream: *Max Romeo* / My conversation: *Uniques* / Bangarang: *Cole, Stranger* / Return of Django: *Upsetters* / Liquidator: *Harry J All Stars* / Rivers of Babylon: *Melodians* / Harder they come: *Cliff, Jimmy* / Young, gifted and black: *Bob & Marcia* / Wake the town: *U-Roy* / How long: *Pat Kelly* / Double barrel: *Collins, Dave & Ansell* / Blood and fire: *Niney The Observer* / Cherry oh baby: *Donaldson, Eric* / Better must come: *Wilson, Delroy* / Money in my pocket: *Brown, Dennis* / Stick by me: *Holt, John* / Teach the children: *Alcapone, Dennis* / S90 skank: *Big Youth* / Everything I own: *Boothe, Ken* / Westbound train: *Brown, Dennis* / Move out a Babylon: *Clarke, Johnny* / Curly locks: *Byles, Junior* / Country boy: *Heptones* / Welding: *I-Roy* / Marcus Garvey: *Burning Spear* / Right time: *Mighty Diamonds* / Natty sing hit songs: *Stewart, Roman* / Ballistic affair: *Smart, Leroy* / Tenement yard: *Miller, Jacob* / War in a Babylon: *Max Romeo* / Police and thieves: *Murvin, Junior* / Two sevens clash: *Culture* / I'm still waiting: *Wilson, Delroy* / No woman, no cry: *Marley, Bob & The Wailers* / Uptown top ranking: *Althia & Donna* / My number one: *Isaacs, Gregory* / Bredda gravalicious: *Wailing Souls* / River Jordan: *Minott, Sugar* / Armagideon time: *Williams, Willie* / Guess who's coming to dinner: *Black Uhuru* / Fort Augustus: *Delgado, Junior* / Jogging: *McGregor, Freddie* / Sitting and watching: *Brown, Dennis* / Night nurse: *Isaacs, Gregory* / Mad over me: *Yellowman* / Diseases: *Michigan & Smiley* / Water pumping: *Osbourne, Johnny* / Pass the tu-sheng-peng: *Smith, Wayne* / Tempo: *Redrose* / Boops: *Super Cat* / Greetings: *Half Pint* / Punanny: *Bailey, Admiral* / Hol' a fresh: *Red Dragon* / Rumours: *Isaacs, Gregory* / Cover me: *Stewart, Tinga & Ninjaman* / Legal rights: *Papa San & Lady G* / Wicked in bed: *Shabba Ranks* / Bandolero: *Pinchers* / Yuh dead now: *Tiger* / Bogle dance: *Buju Banton* / Murder she wrote: *Chaka Demus & Pliers* / O Carolina: *Shaggy*
CD Set ____ **IBXCD 1**
Mango / Oct '93 / PolyGram / Vital

TOUR DE CHANT
CD ____ **DCD 5325**
Disky / Nov '93 / Disky / THE

TOURNEE 95
CD ____ **GWP 010CD**
Gwerz / Nov '95 / ADA / Discovery

TOUVAN CHANTS FROM CENTRAL ASIA
CD ____ **Y 225222CD**
Silex / Jul '95 / ADA / Harmonia Mundi

TOWER ROCKS
CD ____ **9548326482**
WEA / Mar '94 / Warner Music

TOWN HALL PARTY 1958-1961
CD ____ **RFDCD 15**
Country Routes / Dec '95 / Hot Shot / Jazz Music

TOWNSHIP SWING JAZZ VOL.1 (1954-1958)
CD ____ **HQCD 08**
Harlequin / Oct '91 / Hot Shot / Jazz Music / Swift / Wellard

TOWNSHIP SWING JAZZ VOL.1
CD ____ **668932**
Melodie / Apr '96 / ADA / Discovery / Grapevine/PolyGram / Greensleeves / Jet Star

TOX UTHAT VOL.1
CD ____ **PS 9329**
Pulse Sonic / Jul '93 / Plastic Head

TOX UTHAT VOL.2
CD ____ **SR 9465**
Silent / Jul '94 / Cargo / Plastic Head

TRACKSPOTTING (2CD Set)
Saint: *Orbital* / Theme from Mission: Impossible: *Clayton, Adam & Larry Mullen* / Lovefool (Tee's club radio): *Cardigans* / Shallow grave: *Leftfield* / Born slippy: *Underworld* / Papau New Guinea: *Future Sound Of London* / Crash and carry: *Orbital* / Slid: *Fluke* / Wake up: *Stereo MC's* / Wildwood: *Weller, Paul* / This is not America: *Bowie, David & Pat Metheny* / Downtown: *Cole, Lloyd* / Wait for the sun: *Supergrass* / Natural one: *Folk Implosion* / Gone: *Holmes, David & Sarah Cracknell* / Play dead: *Bjork & David Arnold* / Small plot of land: *Bowie, David* / Forbidden colours: *Sylvian, David* / Falling: *Cruise, Julee* / Hold me, thrill me, kiss me, kill me: *U2* / 36 degrees: *Placebo* / Sunshine shakers: *Reef* / Begging you: *Stone Roses* / Let's all got together: *Marion* / I spy: *Pulp* / There she goes: *La's* / You and me song: *Wannadies* / Bad behaviour: *Super Furry Animals* / Lust for life: *Iggy Pop* / That woman's got me drinking: *MacGowan, Shane & The Popes* / Perfect crime: *Faith No More* / Sugar ray: *Jesus & Mary Chain* / Misirlou: *Dale, Dick & His Del-Tones* / 5:15: *Who* / Pet semetary: *Ramones* / Pretty in pink: *Psychedelic Furs* / Girl you'll be a woman soon: *Urge Overkill* / Left of centre: *Vega, Suzanne* / Stuck in the middle with you: *Stealer's Wheel* / How can we hang on to a dream: *Hardin, Tim*
CD Set ____ **5534302**
PolyGram TV / May '97 / PolyGram

TRAD AT HEART
Barn dances: *Arcady* / Tomasin A Ri: *Begley & Cooney* / Donal Agus Morag: *Altan* / Cat chase mouse: *O'Connor, Martin* / Moving cloud: *O'Connor, Gerry* / Ril an Spideal: *De Danann* / Liquid sunshine: *O'Connor, Martin* / Snowy path: *Altan* / Hennessey's: *Arcady* / Funk the cajun blues: *O'Connor, Gerry* / Bruach na Carraige Baine: *Begley & Cooney* / Jimmy Byrnes & Dinkies: *De Danann*
CD ____ **DART 3171**
Dara / Jun '97 / ADA / CM / Direct / Else / Grapevine/PolyGram

TRAD FIDDLE IN FRANCE
CD ____ **Y 225110CD**
Silex / Feb '95 / ADA / Harmonia Mundi

TRAD JAZZ FAVOURITES
CD ____ **5501242**
Spectrum / Oct '93 / PolyGram

TRAD JAZZ FESTIVAL
CD ____ **MATCD 224**
Castle / Dec '92 / BMG

TRADE VOL.1 (2CD Set)
Back from the dead EP: *Sound Design* / Up and down: *Raw Junkies* / Horny toad: *Cajmere* / Fusion journey: *Aqua Boogie* / Don't you want me: *PV Project* / Everybody reach: *Millennium* / Kick it in: *Hit Junkie* / Movin' me: *Millennium* / Feel: *Zone 1* / I feel good: *K-Hand* / Fanaklo: *Underground Vibes Sessions III* / Can you feel what I feel: *Bell, Louise* / Itty bitty boozy woozy: *Tempo fiesta* / Indoctrinate: *Castle Trancelot* / It's alright: *SAIN* / Cut the midrange: *Watchman* / May I have the mayonnaise: *Movin' Melodies* / If we lose our lovin': *DMB* / Ultimate: *Antic* / Ga ga: *Yo Yo* / Let's rock: *E-Trax* / Forces of nature: *Sneo, Eric* / Feel the generation: *Mind X* / Underrave: *Disciples* / Chemical hostage: *Sigma 2* / Eine kleine nacht musik: *Kleinboiz* / Controller: *Sigma 2*
CD Set ____ **FVRCD 1001**
Feverpitch / Sep '95 / EMI

TRADE VOL.2 (3CD Set)
Disco daze: *Rhythm Construction Co.* / That sound: *Musaphia, Joey* / Rhumba: *S-Man* / Get it together: *Criso, Filthy Rich* / Day in the life: *Terry, Todd* / Addiction: *DJ Lil'tai* / Do it: *Glenn Underground* / Disko dreams: *100 Proof (Aged In Soul)* / Back to front: *Rosario, Ralphi* / Groove melody: *Johnson, Paul* / I need GU: *GU* / In da clouds: *DJ Sneak* / Blessing: *Sourmash* / Eternal: *Epik* / Set up: *Edge 18* / Dreams: *Quench* / Lover man: *Bad Man* / X: *DJ Scott* / Neurodancer: *Whippenberg* / Yum yum: *Baby Doc* / Trancore: *Dyewitness* / Crisis: *Ganesh* / Are am Eve: *Commander Tom* / Awakening: *Ian M* / Wham bam: *Candy Girls & Sweet Pussy Pauline* / Caterpillar: *Keoki* / Live as one: *Sam Traxx* / Into your heart: *6 By 6* / Labia: *Prins, Patrick* / Got to learn: *Bi Boys Action Squad* / Watch me shine: *Silvester, Stretch* / Just can't get enough: *Transformer 2* / Nighttrain: *Kadoc* / My house is your house (and your house is mine): *Montini Experience*
CD Set ____ **FVRCD 2**
Feverpitch / Apr '96 / EMI

TRADE VOL.3 (Mixed By Tony De Vit & Steve Thomas/2CD Set)
Sharp tools Vol.2: *Sharp Boys* / Soaking wet: *99 All Stars* / Lick it: *Black & Brown* / Sharp tools Vol.2: *Sharp Boys* / Luxor: *Strange Attractor* / Totally insane: *Scoff Boys* / Up to no good: *Porn Kings* / Forerunner: *Natural Born* / Let me tell you something: *Three Guys On Warwick & Devone* / Pulse fiction: *Trex, Andy* / Keep rockin': *Kitty Lips* / Take you there: *Experts* / System: *Starfish* / Pump 1: *Beyer, Adam* / Understodd: *Must* / Ma' definition of house EP: *De Luxe, Tom & Waterhouse* / You're no good: *Billabong* / Axiatonal: *Doubell, E.J.* / What happened: *Donni & Choci* / South: *Randall, Dave* / Bonkers EP: *Code Blue* / Ultimate Seduction: *Ultimate Seduction* / Biggest and baddest: *Brain Bashers* / Bird: *King Of House* / Drum fire: *King Of House* / Welcome: *Committee* / Bonkas: *Kinky Roland* / Trance line: *Committee* / Get lose: *Mangrove* / Are you all ready: *De Vit, Tony* / Elevate: *Format One* / NWA: *Base, D.R. & Karim*
CD ____ **FVRCD 3**
Feverpitch / Oct '96 / EMI

TRADE VOL.4 (3CD Set)
Clear: *Artist Formerly Known As Technique* / Set yourself free: *Torres, Liz* / Parade: *Pierce, Mike* / Drums are us: *DJ Sneak* / VIP EP Vol.1: *Hip Hoperation* / Psychic bounty killaz: *DJ Sneak & Armand Van Helden* / Body, soul and spirit: *Miquel, Michael* / Higher: *Saeed* / Tantra's circus: *Christian, James & Tantra's Circus* / I want music: *Fisher, Cevin* / Rough and raw: *Roberts, Andy* / Elevation: *95 North* / Disco life (check dis' out): *Logan Circle* / Rock the turntable: *Floorshow* / Sharp tools Vol.3: *Sharp Boys* / Sexy thing: *JP Presents* / Distant stab: *Freak & Mac Zimm* / Dirty habits: *Monk Men* / Bud: *Ha-Lo* / Show me love: *Fruit Loop* / Syncrasy: *Bubblegum Crisis* / Black science: *Wooden 'N' Farley* / Return of the borg: *Kinetic A.T.O.M.* / Phunkee muzeek: *Shazzamm* / Londons burning/Me mum said: *Daisy, Pete & Jamie Rainbow* / Frank's birthday: *Bigfoot Spira* / 6 hours: *Mould Impression* / Beyond motion: *Incisions* / Katoomba: *Roughage* / Pick it up: *Kulac* / Flowtation: *De Moor, Vincent* / Have fun: *Coma B* / Have fun: *Coma B* / Never lost his hardcore: *NRG* / Give me love: *Diddy* / Jungle high: *Juno Reactor* / Flash: *BBE* / Baloney: *Lectrolux* / XTC phase one: *F18* / Overdose (my heart is pumping): *F18* / Machine man: *Auburn, Rachel* / Chemical imbalances: *Max & Amind* / Give it to me: *Choci & EC1* / Tardis to Brooklyn: *Bang The Future* / Hellfire: *200 Degrees*
CD Set ____ **FVRCD 5**
Feverpitch / Mar '97 / EMI

TRADITIONAL AND MODERN JAZZ MASTERWORKS
Back o' town blues: *Armstrong, Louis Allstars* / Panama: *Armstrong, Louis Allstars* / Jack-Armstrong blues: *Armstrong, Louis Allstars* / Beale Street blues: *Nichols, Red & His Five Pennies* / Pennies from heaven: *Nichols, Red & His Five Pennies* / Music goes 'round and around: *Dorsey, Tommy & His Clambake Seven* / Maple leaf rag: *Condon, Eddie* / Polka dot stomp rag: *Condon, Eddie* / Carolina shout: *Condon, Eddie* / Margie: *Condon, Eddie* / Riverboat shuffle: *Condon, Eddie* / Walkin' my baby back home: *Condon, Eddie* / Running wild: *Condon, Eddie* / Aunt Hagar's blues: *Condon, Eddie* / Swing dat music: *Condon, Eddie* / Heebie jeebies: *Condon, Eddie* / Oh babe: *Prima, Louis & Swing Band* / How high the moon: *Prima, Louis & Swing Band*
CD ____ **17052**
Laserlight / Nov '95 / Target/BMG

TRADITIONAL ARABIC MUSIC
CD ____ **D 8002**
Auvidis/Ethnic / Jun '89 / ADA / Harmonia Mundi

TRADITIONAL CHILEAN MUSIC
CD ____ **D 8001**
Auvidis/Ethnic / Jun '89 / ADA / Harmonia Mundi

TRADITIONAL DANCE MUSIC OF IRELAND
Sally gardens/Masons apron: *Hogan, Jimmy Trio* / Gurty's frolic: *Doherty, John* / Louis Quinn's: *Hogan, Jimmy* / David delight: *Turkington, Tom* / Sweep's: *Taylor, Paddy* / Bunker hill/Tommy Whelan's: *Hogan, Jimmy Trio* / Please give a penny to the poor old man: *Doherty, John* / Stormy weather: *Doherty, John* / Gosson that bate his father: *McGuire, Sean* / Copperplate/The boys of the spuds: *Hogan, Jimmy Trio* / Carracastle lasses: *Gorman, Michael & Margaret Barry* / Biddy the bowl wife/I lost my love and I care not/King of th: *McCusker Brothers Ceilidh Band* / New lough isle castle: *Doherty, John* / Marry when you're young: *Doherty, John* / Lord Gordons: *Doherty, John* / Boys of the lough/Lark: *Hogan, Jimmy Trio* / Down the glen: *Taylor, Paddy* / Hare among the heather/woman of the house: *Gorman, Michael & Margaret Barry* / Paddy O'Brien's: *Hogan, Jimmy* / Tinker's apron and antrim reel: *McCusker Brothers Ceilidh Band* / Red haired boys: *Turkington, Tom* / O'Malleys/The Luck Penny: *Hogan, Jimmy Trio* / Salamanca: *Doherty, John* / First of may: *Doherty, John* / Trumpet/Locomotive: *Hogan, Jimmy Trio* / Banks of the Ilen: *Taylor, Paddy* / Dark girl dressed in blue: *Doherty, John* / Floggin: *Doherty, John* / Johnson's/Golden eagle: *Hogan, Jimmy Trio* / Mason's apron: *Turkington, Tom* / Independent: *Hogan, Jimmy* / Paddy's own/Launch: *Breen, Paddy* / Music at the gate: *Ennis, Seamus* / Basket of oysters: *Pickering, Johnny* / O'Brien's fancy: *Hogan, Jimmy Trio* / Garret Barry's: *Hogan, Jimmy Trio* / Boys of Ballisadare: *Gorman, Michael & Margaret Barry* / Passing cloud: *Hogan, Jimmy Trio*
CD ____ **CDSDL 420**
Saydisc / Mar '97 / ADA / Direct / Harmonia Mundi

TRADITIONAL FIDDLE MUSIC OF KENTUCKY VOL.1 (Up The Ohio & Licking Rivers)
Portsmouth airs: *Thomas, Buddy* / Bumble bee in a jug: *Hawkins, George Lee* / Meg Gray: *Hawkins, George Lee* / Lansing Quadrille: *Bailey, Alfred* / Weddington's reel: *Bailey, Alfred* / Indian squaw: *Greene, Alva* / Pet Indian: *Greene, Alva* / Getting George Bush upstairs: *Riley, Perry* / Getting wild again: *Riley, Perry* / Lost hornpipe: *Kinney, Charlie* / Blackeyed peas and cornbread: *Prater, Bob* / Grand hornpipe: *Prater, Bob* / Snakewinder: *Thomas, Buddy* / Humphrey's jig: *Hawkins, George Lee* / Darling girl: *Hawkins, George Lee* / Rat's gone to rest: *Hawkins, George Lee* / Big Indian hornpipe: *Bailey, Alfred* / Alexander waltz: *Bailey, Alfred* / Turkey gobbler: *Thomas, Buddy* / I've got a Grandpa: *Greene, Alva* / Blind man's lament: *Greene, Alva* / McClanahan's march: *Greene, Alva* / Callahan: *Hawkins, George Lee* / Boatin' up Sandy: *Hawkins, George Lee* / Pumpkin vine: *Thomas, Buddy* / Kicked up a devil of a row: *Rigdon, Clarence* / Bell cow: *Kinney, Charlie* / Onion tops and turnip greens: *Prater, Bob* / Feed my horse on corn and hay: *Thomas, Buddy* / Jaybird in a high oak tree: *Riley, Perry* / Warfield: *Riley, Perry* / Bell cow: *Bailey, Alfred* / Tilden to the White House: *Bailey, Alfred* / Greek medley: *Hawkins, George Lee* / Big footed: *Hawkins, George Lee* / Flannery's dream: *Greene, Alva* / Winding sheep: *Greene, Alva* / Buck Hord: *Greene, Alva* / Short's addition: *Thomas, Buddy*
CD ____ **ROUCD 0376**
Rounder / Feb '97 / ADA / CM / Direct

TRADITIONAL FIDDLE MUSIC OF KENTUCKY VOL.2 (Along The Kentucky River)
She danced all night in the fiddler's shoes: *Fulks, Darley* / Atlanta Schottische: *Fulks, Darley* / Snowstorm: *Fulks, Darley* / Downfall of Paris: *Fulks, Darley* / Andrew Jackson: *Fulks, Darley* / Pharoah: *Fulks, Darley* / Everybody's favourite: *Todd, Lella* / Boatin' up Sandy: *Thomas, Earl* / Red lick: *Stamper, Billy* / Poor girl waltz: *Williams, Columbus* / Last gold dollar: *Kidwell, Van* / Johnny inch along: *Kidwell, Van* / Rough and ready: *Woodward, Jim* / Midnight: *Woodward, Jim* / Morgan on the railroad: *Barnes, Ed 'Buck'* / Snowbird in the Ashbank: *Masters, John* / Shippingport: *Masters, John* / Camp Nelson blues: *Masters, John* / Garfield march: *Masters, John* / One eyed Riley: *Masters, John* / Christmas calico: *Hatton, Bill* / Sand riffle: *Crawford, Vincent* / Bacon rind: *Kays, Everett* / Granny will your dog bite: *Gilbert, KElly* / Old time Billy in the lowground: *Gilbert, KElly* / Brickyard Joe: *Gilbert, KElly* / Johnny get your hair cut: *Gilbert, KElly* / Old Virge: *Livers, Bill* / Up and down old Eagle Creek: *Livers, Bill* / Crab Orchard quickstep: *Miller, J.B.* / George Winter tune: *Miller, J.B.* / Severn Creek: *Miller, J.B.* / Jenny BAker: *Vandegriff, Artie* / Billy Wilson: *Hall, Jarvie* / White wing waltz: *Hall, Jarvie* / Going up and down old Buffalo Creek: *Skirvin, Clarence* / Old Flannigan: *Skirvin, Clarence* / Indiana home: *Skirvin, Clarence*
CD ____ **ROUCD 0377**
Rounder / Feb '97 / ADA / CM / Direct

TRADITIONAL FOLK MUSIC FROM NORTHERN IRELAND
CD ____ **CDNI 101**
Outlet / Aug '96 / ADA / CM / Direct / Duncans / Koch / Ross

TRADITIONAL IRISH MUSIC FROM BELFAST
Shaskeen / Trim the velvet / Out on the ocean / Hog with the money / Boys of Blue Hill / Plains of Boyle / Gan Anim / Sligo maid / Sally Gardens / Coolin / Gold ring / Trip to Durrow / Scholar / Cooley's / Connachtman's rambles / Old favourite / Silver spear / Road to Ballymac / Toss the feathers / Night Larry was stretched / Hardyman the fiddler / Three Kerry polkas / Rights of man / Chief O'Neill's hornpipe / Ships are sailing / Cup of tea / Trip to Athlone / Rambling pitchfork / Frost is all over / Spindle shanks / George White's favourite / Se fath mo bhuartha / Boys of the town / Metal bridge / Old bush / Bucks of Oranmore
CD ____ **PTICD 1095**
Pure Traditional Irish / May '96 / ADA / CM / Direct / Ross

TRADITIONAL JAZZ FAVOURITES
CD ____ **PLSCD 235**
Pulse / Jul '97 / BMG

TRADITIONAL JAZZ MASTERWORKS
Trouble in mind: *Armstrong, Louis & Chippie Hill* / New York blues: *Graves, Roosevelt* / I ain't no iceman: *Davenport, Cow Cow* / You do me any old way: *Broonzy, 'Big' Bill* / I'm tired of fattenin' frogs for snakes: *Crawford, Rosetta & James P. Johnson's Hep Cats* / Freight train blues: *Smith, Trixie* / Cherry red: *Turner, 'Big' Joe & Pete Johnson's Boogie Woogie Boys* / Billie's blues: *Holiday, Billie & Her Orchestra* / Boogie woogie: *Rushing, Jimmy & The Jones-Smith Inc.* / Lockwood boogie: *Lockwood, Robert Jr. & The Aces* / Jumpin' in the moonlight: *Williams, 'Big' Joe & J.D. Short* / Sykes gumboogie: *Sykes, Roosevelt & King Kolax Band* / Good morning schoolgirl: *Wells, Junior/Buddy Guy/Jack Myers/Billy Warren* / Take five: *Johnson, Jimmy/Carl Snyder/Ike Anderson/Dino Alvarez* / Young Hawk's crawl: *Hutto, J.B. & His Hawks* / Everyday I have the blues: *Rush, Otis Blues Band* / Blues and trouble: *Lockwood, Robert Jr. & The Aces* / Things I used to do: *Young, 'Mighty' Joe Chicago Blues Band*
CD ____ **17050**
Laserlight / Nov '95 / Target/BMG

TRADITIONAL MUSIC
CD ____ **D 8004**
Auvidis/Ethnic / Jun '89 / ADA / Harmonia Mundi

TRADITIONAL MUSIC FROM CONNEMARA (The Gaelic Heritage)
CD ____ **C 580029**
Ocora / Mar '93 / ADA / Harmonia Mundi

TRADITIONAL MUSIC FROM MALAWI
CD ______ **D 8625**
Unesco / Feb '96 / ADA / Harmonia Mundi

TRADITIONAL MUSIC FROM PERU
Pap hallmay / Papa asllay / Papa ch'utay / Carnaval de tinkuy I / Puka chaki wallata / Anu niwu de lawata / Carnaval de tinkuy II / Carnaval de tinkuy III / Kacharpari y Diana / Languilayo qochachapi / Cruzata puchitu / Linda gaviotita / Q'ellabamba campanity / Danza q'anchi de canas / Punch'ay qhashwa / Tupay chita kasarachiy / Toqroyoq plazapi / Tuytunki tuytunki / Descanso q'asay / Kasarakuy mallkiyuq / Chita mamalla / Tupay sabura juygo
CD ______ **D 8268**
Unesco / Jul '97 / ADA / Harmonia Mundi

TRADITIONAL MUSIC FROM THE AZORES
CD ______ **PS 65125**
PlayaSound / Apr '94 / ADA / Harmonia Mundi

TRADITIONAL MUSIC FROM THE CARPATHIANS
CD ______ **QUI 903029**
Quintana / Jul '91 / Harmonia Mundi

TRADITIONAL MUSIC FROM THE UKRAINE
CD ______ **Y 225216CD**
Silex / Apr '95 / ADA / Harmonia Mundi

TRADITIONAL MUSIC OF CAPE BRETON
CD ______ **NIM 5383CD**
Nimbus / Nov '93 / Nimbus

TRADITIONAL MUSIC OF CHINA
CD ______ **824912**
BUDA / Nov '90 / Discovery

TRADITIONAL MUSIC OF ETHIOPIA
CD ______ **PS 65074**
PlayaSound / Jun '91 / ADA / Harmonia Mundi

TRADITIONAL MUSIC OF GREECE
CD ______ **QUI 903060**
Quintana / Nov '91 / Harmonia Mundi

TRADITIONAL MUSIC OF PERU VOL.1 (Festivals Of Cusco)
CD ______ **SFWCD 40466**
Smithsonian Folkways / Dec '95 / ADA / Cadillac / CM / Direct / Koch

TRADITIONAL MUSIC OF PERU VOL.2 (The Mantaro Valley)
CD ______ **SFWCD 40467**
Smithsonian Folkways / Dec '95 / ADA / Cadillac / CM / Direct / Koch

TRADITIONAL MUSIC OF PERU VOL.3
CD ______ **SFWCD 40468**
Smithsonian Folkways / Dec '96 / ADA / Cadillac / CM / Direct / Koch

TRADITIONAL MUSIC OF THE MAORI
CD ______ **VPS 489**
Viking / Sep '96 / CM / Discovery / Harmonia Mundi

TRADITIONAL MUSIC OF VIETNAM
CD ______ **ARN 64303**
Arion / Jul '95 / ADA / Discovery

TRADITIONAL PORTUGUESE MUSIC
CD ______ **D 8008**
Auvidis/Ethnic / Jun '89 / ADA / Harmonia Mundi

TRADITIONAL PUB SONGS
Roll out the barrel / Who were you with last night / Hold your hand out you naughty boy / Hello, hello / Who's your lady friend / Ship ahoy / It's a long way to Tipperary / I do like to be beside the seaside / Pack up your troubles (in your old kit bag) / Baby face / Don't dilly dally on the way / Run, rabbit, run / Waiting at the church / Strollin' / Underneath the arches / Side by side / Lambeth walk / Daddy wouldn't buy me a bow wow / I'm Henry the eight I am / Goodbye Dooly Gray / When you're smiling the whole world smiles with you / Bye bye blackbird / Home town / Lilly of Laguna / On mother Kelly doorstep / I'm forever blowing bubbles / Boiled beef and carrots / Any old iron / My old man's a dustman / I've got a lovely bunch of coconuts / Knees up mother brown
CD ______ **SUMCD 4130**
Sound & Media / Jun '97 / Sound & Media

TRADITIONAL SONGS OF EASTER ISLAND, THE
CD ______ **ARN 64345**
Arion / Sep '96 / ADA / Discovery

TRADITIONAL SONGS OF IRELAND
Warrior's chant: *McPeake Family Trio* / Moorlough shore: *O'Neill, Jim* / Wild colonial boy: *Barry, Margaret* / My singing bird: *McPeake Family Trio* / Whistling thief: *Ennis, Seamus* / Factory girl: *Barry, Margaret* / When you go to the fair: *Devaney, Hudie* / Jug of punch: *McPeake Family Trio* / Moses ritoolariay: *Barry, Margaret* / Keening song: *Gallagher, Kitty* / Verdant braes of skreen: *McPeake Family Trio* / Her mantle so green: *O'Neill, Jim* / As I roved out: *Ennis, Seamus* / Factory girl: *Makem, Sarah* / Brian O'Linn: *Moran, Thomas* / Hawk and the crow: *O'Connor, Liam* / She moves through the fair: *Barry, Margaret* / Bridget O Mally: *Devaney, Hudie* / Wild mountain thyme: *McPeake Family Trio* / Blackbird: *McKearn, Francis* / Turfman from Ardee: *Barry, Margaret* / Nursemaid: *Gallagher, Kitty* / Monaghan fair: *McPeake, Frank* / Magpie's nest: *Kelly, Annie Jane* / Dance to your daddy: *Cronin, Elizabeth* / Siubhan ni dhuibhir: *McPeake Family Trio*
CD ______ **CDSDL 411**
Saydisc / May '95 / ADA / Direct / Harmonia Mundi

TRADITIONAL THAI MUSIC
CD ______ **D 8007**
Auvidis/Ethnic / Jun '89 / ADA / Harmonia Mundi

TRADITIONS OF BALI
CD Set ______ **926002 CD**
BUDA / Oct '94 / Discovery

TRADITIONS OF BRITTANY - BAGPIPES
CD ______ **SCM 026CD**
Diffusion Breizh / Apr '94 / ADA

TRADITIONS OF BRITTANY - CLARINET
CD ______ **SCM 025CD**
Diffusion Breizh / Apr '94 / ADA

TRADITIONS OF BRITTANY - HURDY GURDY
CD ______ **SCM 024CD**
Diffusion Breizh / Apr '94 / ADA

TRADITIONS OF BRITTANY - VIOLIN
CD ______ **SCM 031CD**
Diffusion Breizh / Apr '94 / ADA

TRAIN TICKET VOL.2 (2CD Set)
Lowgo: *Magoo Project* / Synaesthesia: *Synaesthesia* / Sweet gravity: *LSG* / Channel feedback: *LSG* / Refunktion: *Scan Carriers* / To eclipse: *Apach* / Spellbound: *Cwithe* / Pulse: *Magnetic Pulstar* / Flow: *Model 500* / State of time: *Gage* / Rama: *Recycle* / Extra: *Ishii, Ken* / Mark NRG: *Mark NRG* / Endogenous rhythm: *R-Factor* / Structur der seele: *Rob Acid* / Pylorus: *Hypnopedia*
CD Set ______ **SPV 08992322**
SPV / Jun '96 / Koch / Plastic Head

TRAINS ON THE HIGHWAY
CD ______ **IMP 942**
IMP / Sep '96 / ADA / Discovery

TRANCE
CD ______ **NT 6755CD**
New Tone / Nov '96 / ADA / Impetus

TRANCE CENTRAL VOL.1
CD ______ **KICKCD 18**
Kickin' / Mar '95 / Prime / SRD

TRANCE CENTRAL VOL.1-3 (3CD Set)
CD Set ______ **KICKCD 53**
Kickin' / Jun '97 / Prime / SRD

TRANCE CENTRAL VOL.2
CD ______ **KICKCD 22**
Kickin' / May '95 / Prime / SRD

TRANCE CENTRAL VOL.3
CD ______ **KICKCD 30**
Kickin' / Nov '95 / Prime / SRD

TRANCE CENTRAL VOL.4
CD ______ **KICKCD 36**
Kickin' / Mar '96 / Prime / SRD

TRANCE CENTRAL VOL.5 (2CD Set)
CD Set ______ **KICKCD 44**
Kickin' / Nov '96 / Prime / SRD

TRANCE CENTRAL VOL.6 (Psychedelic Moments/2CD Set)
Snake dance: *Nemesis* / Howling at the moon: *Cosmosis* / Violent violet: *Three State Logic* / Cynabs: *Orion* / Triplexus: *Miranda* / Karma 209: *Talking Souls* / Atlantis: *Section X* / Destination: *Guidance* / Water margin: *Lunar Asylum* / Braindance: *Kaaya* / Loin king: *Infernal Machine* / X plore: *Montauk-P* / Second room: *X-Dream* / Destination Bom: *Doof* / Alien earth activity: *UX*
CD Set ______ **KICKCD 51**
Kickin' / Apr '97 / Prime / SRD

TRANCE CORE
Rainbow island: *Seb* / Dreamland: *Q-Tex* / Movin' on: *Cortex* / Whistle tune: *Aurora 7* / Natural born killer: *Dominion* / Acid sunshine: *Trance Masters* / Better day: *GBT Inc* / Revolution: *DJ Fury* / My mind: *Cru-L-T* / Music hypnotizing: *DJ Ham* / Before your eyes: *Helix* / Truth: *Smith & Sharkey* / Oresis (parts 1 & 2): *Cicero*
CD ______ **CDTOT 47**
Jumpin' & Pumpin' / Nov '96 / 3mv/Sony / Mo's Music Machine

TRANCE EUROPE
CD ______ **CLEO 92432**
Cleopatra / Mar '94 / Cargo / Greyhound / Plastic Head / RTM/Disc / SRD

TRANCE EXPERIENCE
CD ______ **DR 0012**
Discobole / Mar '97 / Prime

TRANCE MISSION
CD ______ **AUM 004062**
AMS / Dec '96 / ZYX

TRANCE MUSIC
CD ______ **LDX 2741008**
La Chant Du Monde / Sep '95 / ADA / Harmonia Mundi

TRANCE PACIFIC EXPRESS (2CD Set/ Booklet)
CD Set ______ **DVNT 020CD**
Deviant / Jun '97 / Prime / Vital

TRANCE PLANET VOL.3
Valencia: *Taha, Rachid* / Ave Maria: *Kagen-Paely, Vyatchescav* / Saa magni: *Sangare, Oumou* / Ghost dance: *Tulku* / Elalama Helalla: *Shehan, Steve & Baly Othmani* / Zephyrus: *Stellamara* / Cool wind is blowing: *Gasparyan, Djivan* / Lovelorn: *Levy, Iki* / To the evening child: *Micus, Stephen* / Alimatou salia: *Cissokho, Milang* / Like water: *Azrie, Abed* / Guru bandana: *Khan, Ali Akbar* / Nwahulwana: *Orchestra Marrabenta Star De Mocambique*
CD ______ **6971241102**
Triloka / Nov '96 / New Note/Pinnacle

TRANCE PSYBERDELIC
Dominion: *UX* / Stratofearless: *Kox Box* / Search: *Slide* / KV23: *Process & Tristan* / Boundless: *Prana* / Out of memory: *Stripper* / Cosmic energy: *Slinky Wizard* / Space puppy: *SYB Unity Nettwerk Experience*
CD ______ **MM 800642**
Moonshine / Apr '97 / CM / Duncans / Ross / Swift

TRANCE RAVER VOL.5
CD ______ **SFT 2000242**
Shift / May '97 / ZYX

TRANCE SPOTTING
CD ______ **CLP 9913**
Hypnotic / Mar '97 / Cargo / SRD

TRANCE TRIBUTE TO THE 80'S, A
Tainted love / Fade to grey / Vienna / Enola Gay / Blue Monday / Cars / Don't you want me
CD ______ **CLP 99002**
Cleopatra / Jan '97 / Cargo / Greyhound / Plastic Head / RTM/Disc / SRD

TRANCE TRIPPIN'
Sanction: *Emtorino* / Kollo: *Pan Pacific* / Bandos: *Villivaru* / Shadow: *Nyali* / Argentine dawn: *Mullos* / Insatiable: *Emtorino* / Mission to love: *Coyaba Tribe* / Three walls two ceilings: *Delirious Pink Dog* / Topkapi: *Canabisis* / 5 a.m. in Barringo: *Mashed* / Satyagrahi: *Meallo*
CD ______ **CDTOT 11**
Jumpin' & Pumpin' / Jun '94 / 3mv/Sony / Mo's Music Machine

TRANCE VOL.2
CD ______ **CDRAID 509**
Rumour / Dec '92 / 3mv/Sony / Mo's Music Machine / Pinnacle

TRANCE VOL.3
CD ______ **CDRAID 511**
Rumour / May '93 / 3mv/Sony / Mo's Music Machine / Pinnacle

TRANCE VOL.4
CD ______ **CDRAID 513**
Rumour / Oct '93 / 3mv/Sony / Mo's Music Machine / Pinnacle

TRANCE VOL.5
Dreams: *Quench* / Kruspolska: *Hedningarna* / Fluid: *Marine Boy* / Rich girl: *Crimes, Tori* / Agent o: *Aloof* / Move in motion: *Hanson & Nelson* / Torwart: *Deep Piece* / Kiss the baby: *United State Of Sound* / X-tribe: *X-Tribe* / Space man: *Miro* / Solar VS1: *Remould*
CD ______ **CDRAID 515**
Rumour / Mar '94 / 3mv/Sony / Mo's Music Machine / Pinnacle

TRANCE VOL.6
CD ______ **CDRAID 521**
Rumour / Feb '95 / 3mv/Sony / Mo's Music Machine / Pinnacle

TRANCE XPERIENCE VOL.1
CD ______ **I 3884402**
Galaxy / Jul '97 / ZYX

TRANCE XPERIENCE VOL.2
CD ______ **I 3884412**
Galaxy / Jul '97 / ZYX

TRANCED OUT AND DREAMING
CD ______ **BARKCD 023**
Planet Dog / Jan '97 / Pinnacle

TRANCEFLOOR
CD ______ **XPS 2CDM**
CD ______ **XPS 2CDU**
X-Press / Oct '95 / SRD

TRANCEMITTER
CD ______ **WIGWAM 1**
Wigwam / Oct '93 / Plastic Head

TRANCEPORTER
CD ______ **70001271363**
Essential Dance / Jan '95 / RTM/Disc

TRANCESEXUAL
CD ______ **CLEO 9701CD**
Cleopatra / May '96 / Cargo / Greyhound / Plastic Head / RTM/Disc / SRD

TRANQUIL IRISH MELODIES
CD ______ **HCD 006**
GTD / Apr '95 / ADA / Else

TRANQUILITY (Music For The Mind & Body 2CD Set)
Mystery of the mountains: *Midori* / Saphire: *Moon, Ashley* / Communion: *Larsen, Lou* / Transformation: *Midori* / Cirrus: *Moon, Ashley* / Beauty of the mountains: *Midori* / New horizons: *Midori* / Beyond the valleys: *Moon, Ashley* / Rainbow dancing: *Glassfield, Chris* / Price of peace: *Volker Cat* / Fireside: *L'Esprit* / Passage of time: *Lawrie, Susie* / Swans: *Glassfield, Chris* / Contemplation: *Laurie, Susie* / Ripples: *L'Esprit* / Echoes of eternity ii: *Volker Cat* / Eternal silence: *Laurie, Susie*
CD Set ______ **RCACD 219**
RCA / Jul '97 / BMG

TRANQUILLITY (The Seasons - Spring)
CD ______ **305872**
Hallmark / May '97 / Carlton

TRANQUILLITY (Relationships)
CD ______ **306972**
Hallmark / Jun '97 / Carlton

TRANQUILLITY (The Seasons - Summer)
CD ______ **305882**
Hallmark / Jun '97 / Carlton

TRANS CONTINENTAL TECHNO (4CD Set)
CD Set ______ **032505 CD**
Nite & Blue / Jan '97 / Plastic Head

TRANS EUROPA VOL.2
CD ______ **150 BPMCD**
Contempo / Aug '93 / Plastic Head

TRANS SLOVENIA EXPRESS
CD ______ **CDSTUMM 131**
Mute / Aug '94 / RTM/Disc

TRANSATLANTIC MOVE
CD ______ **MM 800572**
Moonshine / Oct '96 / Mo's Music Machine / Prime / RTM/Disc

TRANSATLANTIC SAMPLER
CD ______ **TRACD 102**
Transatlantic / Apr '96 / Pinnacle

TRANSATLANTIC TICKET
Light flight: *Pentangle* / Fhir a' bhata: *Johnstons* / Angie/Work song: *Jansch, Bert* / Up to now: *Dransfield* / Vestapol/That's no way to get along: *Grossman, Stefan* / Come by the hills: *Furey, Finbar & Eddie* / Three pieces by O'Carolan: *Renbourn, John* / Ploughboy's dream: *Gryphon* / Burn the witch: *McCalmans* / Grey daylight/The hawk/The ten pound fiddle: *Swarbrick, Dave* / Tom Dooley: *Sweeney's Men* / Heliotrope bouqet: *James, John* / England's green and pleasant land: *Digance, Richard* / All the good times: *Mr. Fox* / Twa recruiting sergeants: *Campbell, Ian Folk Group* / Silk pyjamas: *Humblebums* / Black scrag: *Lee, Philip John* / Pretty Polly: *Jansch, Bert* / John Barleycorn: *Young Tradition* / Sugar babe: *Renbourn, John* / Goodbye pork pie hat: *Pentangle*
CD ______ **ESMCD 577**
Essential / Jul '97 / BMG

TRANSCENTRAL CONNECTION
CD ______ **ASHADOW 7CD**
Moving Shadow / Nov '96 / SRD

TRANSFORMATIONS & MODULATIONS
CD ______ **EFA 6512**
Mille Plateau / Apr '94 / SRD

TRANSIENT DAWN
Ambience: *Astral Projection* / Hypnosys: *Messiah* / Searching slowly: *Slide* / Vision: *Cosmix & Elysium* / Temple of the moon: *Anubis* / Slipstream: *Medicine Drum* / Blue sun shrine: *Doof* / Dawn of an era: *Cosmosis*
CD ______ **TRANR 609CD**
Transient / Jun '97 / Prime / SRD / Total/ BMG

TRANSIENT VOL.1 (New Energy & Trance)
CD ______ **TRANR 601CD**
Transient / Apr '95 / Prime / SRD / Total/ BMG

TRANSIENT VOL.3
CD ______ **TRANR 603CD**
Transient / Apr '96 / Prime / SRD / Total/ BMG

TRANSIENT VOL.4
CD ______ **TRANR 605CD**
Transient / Sep '96 / Prime / SRD / Total/ BMG

TRANSIENT VOL.5
CD ______ **TRANR 608CD**
Transient / Apr '97 / Prime / SRD / Total/ BMG

TRANSISTOR REVENGE
CD ______ **IRB 59992**
Deep Blue / Jan '96 / PolyGram

TRANZMISSION
CD ______ **TRANZ 001CD**
Dance Net / Sep '95 / Plastic Head

TRAS-OS-MONTES (BEYOND THE MOUNTAINS)
CD ______ **C 580035**
Ocora / Mar '93 / ADA / Harmonia Mundi

TRAUMHAFT DEUTSCH
Hello again: *Carpendale, Howard* / Du entschuldige-ich kenn' dich: *Brink, Bernard* / Ich wollt' nur mal mit dir reden: *Lavi, Daliah* / Bis ans ende der welt: *Purple Schulz* / Du gehst fort: *Sheer, Ireen & Bernard Brink* / Wei mei Herzschlag: *Heller, Andre* / Bleib

bei mir heut'nacht: *Borg, Andy* / Herz an herz gefuhl: *Deutscher, Drafi* / Auf den mond schieben: *Petry, Wolfgang* / Deine flugelfangen feuer: *Martin, Andreas* / Die lebe bleibt: *Lage, Klaus* / Schickeria: *Spuder Murphy GAng* / Bye bye my love: *Foos, Black* / Niemals geht man so ganz: *Herr, Trude*
CD ____ DC 862412
Disky / Oct '96 / Disky / THE

TRAVEL THE WORLD WITH PUTUMAYO
CD ____ PUTU 1302
Putumayo / Jun '97 / Grapevine/PolyGram

TRAVELLIN' LIGHT
C jam blues: *Parlan, Horace/Sam Jones/Al Harwood* / Begin the beguine: *Shaw, Artie Orchestra* / I won't dance: *Lee, Peggy* / Soul serenade: *King Curtis* / What is there to say: *Hawkins, Coleman* / One I love (belongs to somebody else): *London, Julie & Howard Roberts* / Violets for your furs: *Hipp, Jutta & Zoot Sims/Jerry Lloyd* / 9.20 special: *Basie, Count Orchestra* / Come on let's play with Pearlie Mae: *Bailey, Pearl* / Travellin' light: *Holiday, Billie & Paul Whiteman Orchestra* / MG Blues: *McGriff, Jimmy* / All of you: *Ross, Annie & Gerry Mulligan/Art Farmer* / Thinkin' about your body: *McFerrin, Bobby* / Makin' whoopee: *Cole, Bobby* / Just in time: *Vaughan, Sarah* / But not for me: *Baker, Chet* / Sister Sadie: *Silver, Horace* / Easy street: *London, Julie & Barney Kessel* / Bye bye blackbird: *Martin, Dean* / Baby, won't you please come home: *Hackett, Bobby & Jack Teagarden*
CD ____ CDJA 1
Premier/MFP / Oct '91 / EMI

TRAVELLING ARTISTS OF THE DESERT (The Vernacular Musical Culture Of Rajasthan/India)
Drawing water/Camel's cry/Festival day pilgrimage song / Nara / Gorbandh / Charka / Morchang and dholak performance / Morbhai / Warshawa / Ghoomar / Panihari / Hichiki / Harjas / Arani / Proclaimation for the village leader / Mehndi / Ohmpoori / Moomal / Narrative with dhol / Bhajan / Hanumanji
CD ____ MCM 3002
Multicultural Media / May '97 / Direct

TRAVELLING THROUGH THE JUNGLE (Fife & Drum Bands From The Deep South)
CD ____ TCD 5017
Testament / Mar '95 / ADA / Koch

TRAVELOGUE - BALI
CD ____ YA 225709
Silex / Aug '96 / ADA / Harmonia Mundi

TRAVELOGUE - CHINA
CD ____ YA 225701
Silex / Jan '95 / ADA / Harmonia Mundi

TRAVELOGUE - GREECE
CD ____ YA 225706
Silex / Jan '95 / ADA / Harmonia Mundi

TRAVELOGUE - IRELAND
CD ____ YA 225704
Silex / Jan '95 / ADA / Harmonia Mundi

TRAVELOGUE - MADAGASCAR
CD ____ YA 225702
Silex / Jan '95 / ADA / Harmonia Mundi

TRAVELOGUE - PORTUGAL
CD ____ YA 225703
Silex / Jan '95 / ADA / Harmonia Mundi

TRAVELOGUE - QUEBEC
CD ____ YA 225705
Silex / Jan '95 / ADA / Harmonia Mundi

TREASURE CHEST OF NORTHERN SOUL, A
I must love you: *Wilson, Timothy* / Remember: *Whispers* / I'll be there: *Gems* / Day my heart stood still: *Jackson, Ollie* / I found true love: *Hambric, Billy* / Watch yourself: *Hester, Tony* / Hole in the wall: *Barnes, J.J.* / You will never get away: *Maye, Cholli* / Shin-a-ling: *Cooperettes* / Mixed up: *Furys* / What is this: *Womack, Bobby* / You don't mean it: *Barnes, Towanda* / What good am I without you: *Fletcher, Darrow* / I gotta find that girl: *Hambric, Billy* / I'll never let you go: *O'Jays* / Going going gone: *Black, Cody* / Lovingly yours: *Wilson, Timothy* / My kind of woman: *Starr, Edwin* / Now you've got the upper hand: *Staton, Candi* / Daddy-o: *Lindsay, Therese* / What is this (vox): *Womack, Bobby* / This won't change: *Tipton, Lester* / Lies: *Owens, Gwen* / Feel good all over: *Huey, Claude 'Baby'* / I still wait for you: *Batiste, Rose* / Love bandit: *Chi-Lites* / Very next time: *Marlynns* / Gee baby: *Wilson, Micky* / I got the power: *Masqueraders* / My baby ain't no plaything: *Harvey, Willy*
CD ____ GSCD 075
Goldmine / Oct '95 / Vital

TREASURE ISLE DUB VOL.1 & 2
CD ____ LG 21090
Lagoon / Aug '93 / Grapevine/PolyGram

TREASURE ISLE GREATEST HITS
CD ____ SONCD 0041
Sonic Sounds / Sep '95 / Jet Star

TREASURE ISLE HOTTEST HITS VOL.1 (Treasure Isle Recordings From The 1960's)
CD ____ RMM 1134
Treasure Isle / Mar '96 / Jet Star / SRD

TREASURE ISLE HOTTEST HITS VOL.2
CD ____ RMM 1267
Treasure Isle / Jan '94 / Jet Star / SRD

TREASURE ISLE MEETS TIPTOP
CD ____ SONCD 0047
Sonic Sounds / Jul '93 / Jet Star

TREASURE ISLE MOOD
CD ____ CBHB 195
Heartbeat / Oct '95 / ADA / Direct / Greensleeves / Jet Star

TREASURE ISLE TIME
CD ____ RNCD 2092
Rhino / Feb '95 / Grapevine/PolyGram / Jet Star

TREASURE ISLE TIME
CD ____ CDHB 196
Heartbeat / Oct '95 / ADA / Direct / Greensleeves / Jet Star

TREASURE OF MY HEART
Munster Buttermilk: *Andrews, William* / Johnny will you marry me: *Sullivan, Dan & Shamrock Band* / Farewell to Ireland: *Morrison, James* / Paddy in London: *Flanagan Brothers* / Me husband's flannel shirt: *McGettigan, John* / Dowd's favourite: *Gillespie, Hugh* / Tippin' it up to Nancy: *Reilly, John* / Bruachna carriage baine: *Clancy, Willie* / Bunch of keys/Buckley's dream: *Rowsome, Leo* / My father's a hedger and ditcher: *Carolan, Mary-Ann* / Muckross Abbey/Mulvihill's: *Murphy, Dennis* / Turfman from Ardee: *Barry, Margaret* / Choice wife: *Clancy, Willie* / Cunnla: *Heaney, Joe* / Wild mountain thyme: *McPeake Clan* / Roaring Mary: *Doherty, John* / Off to California: *Russell, Micho* / Wind that shakes the barley: *Makem, Sarah* / Rakish Paddy: *Doran, Felix* / Rollicking boys around Tandaragee: *Tunney, Paddy* / New demesne: *Ennis, Seamus* / Micko Russell's reel/trip to Birmingham: *McDermott, Josie* / He rolled her to the wall: *Harte, Frank* / Silver spear/Flax in bloom: *Glackin, Paddy* / Murphy's/Going to the well for water: *Daly, Jackie* / Eclipse/Tailor's twist: *Boys Of The Lough* / Willie Clarke's/ Green grow the rushes-o: *Holmes, Joe* / Micho Russels/Sporting nell: *Four Men & A Dog*
CD ____ ORB 081CD
Globestyle / Oct '93 / Pinnacle

TREASURY OF IRISH MUSIC 1, A
CD ____ CDTCD 004
Gael Linn / Aug '95 / ADA / CM / Direct / Grapevine/PolyGram / Roots

TREASURY OF IRISH MUSIC 2, A
CD ____ CDTCD 005
Gael Linn / Aug '95 / ADA / CM / Direct / Grapevine/PolyGram / Roots

TREASURY OF IRISH MUSIC 3, A
CD ____ CDTCD 006
Gael Linn / Aug '95 / ADA / CM / Direct / Grapevine/PolyGram / Roots

TREASURY OF IRISH SONG, A
CD ____ MCCD 278
Music Club / Dec '96 / Disc / THE

TREASURY OF IRISH SONGS, A
CD ____ SHCD 79094
Shanachie / Oct '95 / ADA / Greensleeves / Koch

TRENCH TOWN DUB
CD ____ OMCD 27
Original Music / Oct '93 / Jet Star / SRD

TRENDANCE VOL.5
CD ____ ZYX 550822
ZYX / Jul '97 / ZYX

TRESOR VOL.2
CD ____ CDNOMU 14
Nova Mute / May '93 / Prime / RTM/Disc

TRESOR VOL.3
Solid sleep: *Mills, Jeff* / Ten four: *Beltram, Joey* / Rhythm of vision: *Hood, Robert* / Science fiction: *Bell, Daniel* / Allerseelen: *DJ Hell* / Motor music-maerz: *3 Phase* / Energizer: *Baxter, Blake* / Protection: *Vision* / Monolith: *Sun Electric* / Schizophrenia: *Schizophrenia*
CD ____ NOMU 43CD
Nova Mute / Apr '95 / Prime / RTM/Disc

TRESOR VOL.4 (Solid/2CD Set)
M6: *Maurizio* / Shadow chaser: *Scan 7* / M 69 starlight: *Model 500* / Relish: *Substance* / La beff: *TV Victor* / What: *Vogel, Christian* / Cooper's coffee: *Pacou* / Instant: *Beltram, Joey* / Think quick: *Infiniti* / Domina: *Domina* / Zombie assassin: *Holy Ghost Inc.* / Where's your child: *Bam Bam* / Art Lukm: *Holy Ghost Inc.* / Energizer: *Baxter, Blake* / Lyot: *Vainquer* / Skyscratch: *Ingator* / Sonic destroyer: *X-101* / Der klang der familie: *3 Phase & Dr. Motte* / Dark territory: *Scan 7* / Reel techno: *Pacou* / Dark corridor: *Scan 7* / Minnia (The Queen's Theme): *X-103*
CD Set ____ 29263CD
Tresor / Feb '97 / 3mv/BMG / Prime / SRD

TRESOR VOL.5
CD ____ EFA 292642
Tresor / May '97 / 3mv/BMG / Prime / SRD

TRIANGLE DUB CLASH
CD ____ ZD7CD
Zip Dog / Apr '96 / Grapevine/PolyGram / SRD / Vital

TRIBAL GATHERING '96 (Gayle San/ Marshall Jefferson/James Lavell/3CD Set)
Tribal: *San, Gayle* / Digital domain: *Shi-Take* / Circuit sex: *Blunted Boy Wonder* / Al: *Subvoice 007* / Breakdown: *RND Technologies* / Meantime: *Space DJ's* / Barcode population: *USS Severe* / Sensual sign: *Tesox* / Funky drive: *X-Connection* / Horny ass Fred: *Fred* / Accelerate: *Zzino* / Resize: *Colone* / Book: *Salt City Orchestra* / Samba magic: *Basement Jaxx* / Chord memory: *Pooley, Ian* / Happy days: *Hope, Alexander* / Gotta keep pushin': *Z-Factor* / Be free: *Basement Jaxx* / Calling: *Vudu* / Joy: *Bresoul* / Jump on it: *Jefferson, Marshall* / Your wildest dreams: *Swingtime Dee* / Sexy thing: *Avianche, Jean Phillipe* / One love: *Northside* / This could be the night: *Aphroqueens* / Quiddity: *Max 404* / Latin nights: *Shogun* / Allergy: *Howie B* / Spiral dub: *DJ Food* / Murderah style: *DJ Spooky & Mr. Scruff* / Headless horseman: *Raw Deal* / Attention please: *4th Wave* / Duality: *DJ Krush & DJ Shadow* / Your destiny: *DJ Crystl* / Real thing: *Peshay* / Papua New Guinea: *Future Sound Of London* / One for MAW: *Jedi Knights* / Ladies and gentlemen: *69*
CD Set ____ UNV 001CD
Universe / Oct '96 / SRD

TRIBAL HEART
CD ____ AIM 1042
Aim / May '95 / ADA / Direct / Jazz Music

TRIBAL VOICES (Songs Of Native Americans)
CD ____ R 272538
Earthbeat / Nov '96 / ADA / Direct

TRIBES OF DA UNDERGROUND VOL.2 (2CD Set)
CD Set ____ IC 012CD
Infracom / Jan '96 / Plastic Head / SRD

TRIBES OF DA UNDERGROUND VOL.3
CD ____ IC 0252
Infracom / Jun '97 / Plastic Head / SRD

TRIBULATION DUB VOL.4
CD ____ WSPLP 008
WSP / Feb '96 / Jet Star

TRIBUTE BY THE GIANTS OF JAZZ
CD ____ CD 53015
Giants Of Jazz / Mar '90 / Cadillac / Jazz Music / Target/BMG

TRIBUTE TO BERRY GORDY, A
CD ____ 5304362
Motown / Jul '95 / PolyGram

TRIBUTE TO MARCUS GARVEY, A
CD ____ GRELCD 147
Greensleeves / Jul '90 / Jet Star / SRD

TRIBUTE TO NEW ORLEANS - MARDE GRAS PARADE
CD ____ CD 53084
Giants Of Jazz / Mar '90 / Cadillac / Jazz Music / Target/BMG

TRIBUTE TO TI FRERE, A
CD ____ C560019
Ocora / Jun '91 / ADA / Harmonia Mundi

TRIBUTE TO..., A
CD ____ CDZOT 179
Zoth Ommog / Jul '97 / Cargo / Plastic Head

TRICKED OUT
Crystal jelly: *Hard Hop Heathen* / Oh-zone layer: *Dark Side Of The Shroom* / Green mushroom: *Dark Side Of The Shroom* / Pure havoc: *Hard Hop Heathen* / Off to demention X: *Wizard Of Oh* / Chemical meltdown: *Tales From The Hardside* / Terminal intensity: *Tales From The Hardside* / Double dove: *Hard Hop Heathen* / Temple of boom: *Tales From The Hardside* / Ohterior motive: *Hard Hop Heathen* / White beats: *Wizard Of Oh* / Free bass: *Hard Hop Heathen* / Beat bastik: *Hard Hop Heathen* / Panaramic: *Dark Side Of The Shroom*
CD ____ MM 800632
Moonshine / Apr '97 / Mo's Music Machine / Prime / RTM/Disc

TRIGGER
CD ____ HAIR 5
Hair / May '94 / SRD

TRIKI VOL.1 (Diatonic Dynamite)
CD ____ KD 431CD
Elkar / Nov '96 / ADA

TRINIDAD HOT TIMES
CD ____ 68979
Tropical / Apr '97 / Discovery

TRINIDAD LOVES TO PLAY CARNIVAL 1914-1939
CD ____ MBCD 3022
Matchbox / Nov '93 / Cadillac / CM / Jazz Music / Roots

TRIP 7 (2CD Set)
CD Set ____ DO 475CD
Dance Opera / Nov '96 / Mo's Music Machine / Plastic Head

TRIP 'N' GROOVE - LE SON DE RADIO NOVA
CD ____ 325022
Melodie / Nov '95 / ADA / Discovery / Grapevine/PolyGram / Greensleeves / Jet Star

TRIP THROUGH SOUND
CD ____ BR 021CD
Blue Room / Feb '97 / Essential/BMG / Mo's Music Machine / Prime / SRD

TRIP TO MARS VOL.1 (2CD Set)
CD Set ____ SPV 899605
SPV / Feb '94 / Koch / Plastic Head

TRIP TO MARS VOL.2 (2CD Set)
CD Set ____ SPV 899626
SPV / Jul '94 / Koch / Plastic Head

TRIP TO THE ANDES
CD ____ TMDCD 2
Tumi Dance / Mar '97 / SRD

TRIPHOP SHOP
CD ____ DOUCE 803CD
Irma La Douce / Nov '96 / Timewarp

TRIPHOPRISY VOL.1
CD ____ SQUCD 1
Rumour / Jun '95 / 3mv/Sony / Mo's Music Machine / Pinnacle

TRIPHOPRISY VOL.2
CD ____ SQUCD 2
Rumour / Nov '95 / 3mv/Sony / Mo's Music Machine / Pinnacle

TRIPHOPRISY VOL.3
CD ____ SQUCD 3
Rumour / May '96 / 3mv/Sony / Mo's Music Machine / Pinnacle

TRIPHOPRISY VOL.4 (2CD Set)
CD Set ____ SQUCD 4
Squat / Apr '97 / Prime

TRIPLE TWIN SPIN
CD ____ SPCD 0125
Superpower / May '97 / Jet Star

TRIPNOTIZED VOL.3 (2CD Set)
CD Set ____ MNF 05242
Manifold / Jan '97 / ZYX

TRIPNOTIZED VOL.4 (2CD Set)
CD Set ____ MNF 05262
Manifold / Jun '97 / ZYX

TRIPPIN' ON NORTHERN SOUL (Dose - 20 Classic Northern Soul Stompers)
Trip: *Mitchell, Dave* / You'd better go-go: *Lucas, Matt* / Satisfy me baby: *Sweets* / Show me how to love: *Forrest, Jackie* / Right combination: *Brody, Marsha* / Try a little harder: *Keyman Strings* / Get it baby: *Mitchell, Stanley* / With a lonely heart: *Four Voices* / Queen of the go-go: *Garvin, Rex* / Bring it on home: *Lee, Jackie* / It's OK with me: *Wright, Larry* / Airplane song: *Jenkins, Norma* / I'm a sad girl: *Johnson, Diane* / There can be a better way: *Smith Bros* / Don't pretend: *Mirwood Orchestra* / Hold your horses: *Clarke, Jimmy 'Soul'* / Train keep on movin': *Fifth Dimension* / Woman's liberation: *Topics* / Just can't leave you: *Hester, Tony* / Papa oo mow mow: *Sharonettes*
CD ____ GSCD 091
Goldmine / Jul '96 / Vital

TRISKEDEKAPHILIA
CD ____ ANKST 61CD
Ankst / Oct '95 / Shellshock/Disc

TROJAN EXPLOSION (20 Reggae Hits)
You can get it if you really want: *Desmond Dekker & The Aces* / Reggae in your jeggae: *Livingstone, Dandy* / Johnny too bad: *Slickers* / Liquidator: *Harry J All Stars* / Wonderful world, beautiful people: *Cliff, Jimmy* / Them a laugh and a kiki: *Soulmates* / 54-46 (was my number): *Toots & The Maytals* / Cherry oh baby: *Donaldson, Eric* / Let your yeah be yeah: *Pioneers* / Dollar of soul: *Ethiopians* / Young, gifted and black: *Bob & Marcia* / Sweet sensation: *Melodians* / Elizabethan reggae: *Gardiner, Boris* / Mama look deh: *Pioneers* / Double barrel: *Collins, Dave & Ansell* / Small axe: *Marley, Bob* / Pomp and pride: *Toots & The Maytals* / Return of Django: *Upsetters* / 007: *Dekker, Desmond & The Aces* / Phoenix city: *Alphonso, Roland*
CD ____ CDTRL 246
Trojan / Mar '94 / Direct / Jet Star

TROJAN JUNGLE VOL.1
CD ____ CDTRL 368
Trojan / Mar '96 / Direct / Jet Star

TROJAN JUNGLE VOL.2
CD ____ CDTRL 378
Trojan / Feb '97 / Direct / Jet Star

TROJAN SINGLES COLLECTION VOL.1
CD ____ CDTRL 367
Trojan / Mar '96 / Direct / Jet Star

TROJAN SINGLES COLLECTION VOL.2
Suzanna beware of the devil: *Livingstone, Dandy* / Brandy: *English, Scott* / Return of Django: *Upsetters* / Big seven: *Judge Dread* / Double barrel: *Collins, Dave & Ansell* / Lonely days, lonely nights: *Dowling, Don* / 007: *Dekker, Desmond* / Young, gifted and black: *Bob & Marcia* / Big six: *Judge Dread* / Monkey spanner: *Collins, Dave & Ansell* / Dollar in the teeth: *Upsetters* / Red red

wine: *Tribe, Tony* / Big eight: *Judge Dread* / It mek: *Dekker, Desmond* / Train to skaville: *Ethiopians* / Big nine: *Judge Dread* / Guns of Navarone: *Skatalites* / Pickney girl: *Dekker, Desmond* / I'm in the mood for ska: *Lord Tanamo* / Money in my pocket: *Brown, Dennis* / Israelites: *Dekker, Desmond* / Snoopy vs. The Red Baron: *Hot Shots* / Je t'aime (moi non plus): *Judge Dread* / Hurt so good: *Cadogan, Susan* / Irie feelings: *Edwards, Rupie*
CD CDTRL 373
Trojan / Sep '96 / Direct / Jet Star

TROJAN STORY VOL.1
Bartender: *Aitken, Laurel* / Humpty dumpty: *Morris, Eric* / Housewives' choice: *Derrick & Patsy* / Don't stay out late: *Patrick, Kentrick* / Rough and tough: *Cole, Stranger* / Man to man: *Patrick, Kentrick* / Confucius: *Drummond, Don* / Soon you'll be gone: *Blues Busters* / Yeah yeah: *Riots* / Dreader than dread: *Martin, Honeyboy* / Syncopate: *Astronauts* / Keep the pressure on: *Winston, George* / Oh babe: *Techniques* / Train to Skaville: *Ethiopians* / Pretty Africa: *Cliff, Jimmy* / Rock steady: *Ellis, Alton* / Perfidia: *Dillon, Phyllis* / Way of life: *Tait, Lynn* / Second fiddle: *Tennors* / Nana: *Slickers* / Black and white
CD CDTAL 100
Trojan / Mar '94 / Direct / Jet Star

TROJAN STORY, THE (2CD Set)
Guns of Navarone: *Skatalites* / Phoenix City: *Alphonso, Roland* / Oh ba-a-by: *Techniques* / Rock steady: *Ellis, Alton* / Do the reggae: *Toots & The Maytals* / Stand by your man: *Webber, Marlene* / Red red wine: *Tribe, Tony* / Miss Jamaica: *Cliff, Jimmy* / Version galore: *U-Roy* / Screaming target: *Big Youth* / Cassius Clay: *Alcapone, Dennis* / Black man time: *I-Roy* / Silhouette: *Brown, Dennis* / Jimmie Brown: *Parker, Ken* / Just can't figure it out: *Diamonds* / Enter into his gates: *Clark, Johnnie* / Pretty African: *Dekker, Desmond* / Save the last dance for me: *Heptones* / Nice nice time: *Zap Pow* / Take me home country roads: *Toots & The Maytals* / Time is the master: *Simon, Tito* / Mama look deh: *Pioneers* / Big 8: *Judge Dread* / Them a fe get a beatin': *Tosh, Peter* / Montego Bay: *Notes, Freddie & The Rudies* / Elizabethan reggae: *Lee, Byron & The Dragonaires* / 007: *Dekker, Desmond* / Crying over you: *Boothe, Ken* / Return of Django: *Upsetters* / Mr. Bojangles: *Holt, John* / Reggae in your jeggae: *Livingstone, Dandy* / Longshot kick de bucket: *Pioneers*
CD Set CDTRD 402
Trojan / Mar '94 / Direct / Jet Star

TROPICAL BEACH PARTY (16 Exotic Sun Soaked Scene Setters)
Tropicallo / Samba rio / Carnaval do Brasil / Yellow bird / Kingston nights / Salsarico / Antigua / Sailing with the sun / Cuba libre / Copacabana sunrise / Una flor no cabello / Deep Kingston / Solitario / La bamba salsa / Yele le / Latino paradiso
CD 304522
Hallmark / Jul '97 / Carlton

TROPICAL EXTRAVAGANZA
CD TUMICD 028
Tumi / Oct '92 / Discovery / Stern's

TROPICAL FESTIVAL
Kwassa kwassa: *Kanda Bongo Man* / Cachita: *La Charanga Almendra* / Forward Jah Jah children: *Inner Circle* / La revancha: *Los Diablitos* / Bomba camara: *Grupo Melao* / Cuban medley: *La Origina De Manzanillo* / Workey workey: *Burning Flames* / Cascara Bellagua: *Castro, Poldo* / Suma sume: *Godzom* / Maria La Hoz: *Grupo Caneo*
CD CPCD 8131
Charly / Oct '95 / Koch

TROPICAL ISLAND PARADISE
Yarbero moderno: *Cruz, Celia* / Traffic mambo: *Lamy, Ernest Orchestra* / Cogelo que eso es tuyo: *Kalaff, Luis* / Descarga: *Ray, Ricardo & Bobby Cruz* / Habana rumba: *Trio Matamoros* / En el monte: *Duo Los Compadres* / Pardon caporal: *Nemours Jean-Baptiste* / La maricutana: *Damiron Y Capuseaux* / Compay lobo: *La Sonora Matancera* / El automovil: *Hernandez, Mario Y Sus Diablos Del Caribe* / Por eso es que yo te quiento: *Kalaff, Luis* / Mambo tata: *Ray, Ricardo & Bobby Cruz* / En cadenas: *Faz, Roberto Y Su Conjunto* / El chivo: *La Sonora Matancera* / El jarro pichao: *Damiron Y Capuseaux* / Yo teno pena: *Duo Los Compadres* / Mango mangue: *Cruz, Celia* / Besame donde te: *Hernandez, Mario Y Sus Diablos Del Caribe* / Jamaicuba: *Faz, Roberto Y Su Conjunto*
CD CDHOT 613
Charly / Dec '96 / Koch

TROUBLE, HEARTACHES & SADNESS
Trouble, heartaches and sadness: *Peebles, Ann* / What more do you want from me: *Starks, Veniece* / Lonely soldier: *Bryant, Don* / That's just my luck: *Johnson, Syl* / Ain't no love in my life: *Mitchell, Phillip* / I must be losin' you: *Clayton, Willie* / I can't let you go: *Peebles, Ann* / I've been hurt: *Big Lucky Carter* / Can't hide the hurt: *Bryant, Don* / I can't take it: *Clay, Otis* / Heartaches, heartaches: *Peebles, Ann* / Love you left behind: *Johnson, Syl* / Trying to live my life without you: *Clay, Otis* / About to make me leave home: *Johnson, Syl* / You're gonna make me cry: *Peebles, Ann* / I die a little each day: *Clay, Otis* / I'm leavin' you: *Peebles, Ann* / Please don't give up on me: *Johnson, Syl* / Everytime I think about you I get the blues: *One Plus One* / Won't you try me: *Peebles, Ann* / Please don't leave: *One Plus One*
CD HILOCD 10
Hi / Mar '94 / Pinnacle

TRUCKIN' MY BLUES AWAY (Collection Of Contemporary Blues Songs From Texas)
CD TX 1009CD
Taxim / Jan '94 / ADA

TRUE BRIT (The Best Of Brit Pop)
CD 5354792
PolyGram TV / Jun '96 / PolyGram

TRUE BRITS (3CD Set)
CD Set ASBCD 3001
West Coast / Sep '96 / Koch / Scratch/ BMG

TRUE BRITS VOL.2 (2CD Set)
CD Set ASBCD 003
West Coast / Nov '94 / Koch / Scratch/ BMG

TRUE FAITH 1ST PHASE
CD NTWCD 1
Network / Nov '91 / 3mv/Sony / Pinnacle

TRUE LOVE (16 Songs From The Heart)
True love: *Cline, Patsy* / Blue velvet: *McCann, Susan* / May I have the next dream with you: *Roberts, Malcolm* / As usual: *Lee, Brenda* / Marianne: *O'Donnell, Daniel* / Portrait of my love / He used to give me roses: *Ray, Stacey* / Let it be me: *Everly Brothers* / Take good care of my baby: *Vee, Bobby* / Country hits medley: *McCann, Susan* / It's our anniversary: *McCaffrey, Frank* / Tennessee waltz / If those lips could only speak: *Foster & Allen* / I'll never find another you: *Seekers* / When I dream: *Gayle, Crystal* / All I have to do is dream: *Everly Brothers*
CD PLATCD 3912
Platinum / '91 / Prism

TRUE LOVE
CD STACD 054
Wisepack / Sep '93 / Conifer/BMG / THE

TRUE LOVE (All Time Classic Love Songs/3CD Set)
CD Set MCBX 007
Music Club / Sep '95 / Disc / THE

TRUE LOVE WAYS
CD MCCD 119
Music Club / Aug '93 / Disc / THE

TRUE PEOPLE: THE DETROIT TECHNO ALBUM (2CD Set)
Davy Jones Locker: *Dresciya* / Aura: *KT 19941* / Life of a planet rider: *Shakir, Anthony* / Fusion part 2: *Atkins, Juan* / Wiggin: *May, Derrick* / RMF 60: *Fowlkes, Eddie* / 8th Wonder: *Pullne, Stacey* / Zephyr: *Kech & B Bonds* / Carma: *Young, Claude* / Morph: *Larkin, Kenny* / Where is the love: *Baxter, Blake* / Sources: *Echols, Santonio* / TMF 61: *Fowlkes, Eddie* / Operation 10: *Barnett, Thomas* / E-Dancer: *Saunderson, Kevin* / D May 87: *Oldham, Alan* / Don't blame it on me: *365 Black* / Art of stalking: *Suburban Knight* / Gama: *Brown, Tom* / CRX: *Little Joe*
CD Set REACTCD 071
React / Jan '96 / Arabesque / Prime / Vital

TRUE STORY OF COUNTRY, THE
Rose garden: *Anderson, Lynn* / It's only make believe: *Jackson, Wanda* / Big bad John: *Dean, Jimmy* / Harper Valley PTA: *Riley, Jeannie C.* / Mad: *Dudley, Dave* / Girl on the billboard: *Reeves, Del* / Heartbreak USA: *Wells, Kitty* / Hallo walls: *Young, Faron* / Tennessee: *Jack & Misty* / He took me for a ride: *La Costa Tucker* / I'm a truck: *Simpson, Red* / Rednecks, white socks, blue ribbon beer: *Russell, Johnny* / No charge: *Montgomery, Melba* / Nashville: *Houston, David* / It only hurts for a little while: *Smith, Margo* / Help me make it through the night: *Smith, Sammi*
CD 11813
Music / Dec '95 / Target/BMG

TRUE UNDERGROUND, THE
CD SR 324CD
Strictly Rhythm / Apr '96 / Prime / RTM/ Disc / SRD / Vital

TRUE VOICES
Changes / Devil eyes / Lady came from Baltimore / Thank you for being there / Simple song of freedom / Which will / To love someone / At the end of the day / Loving arms / Across the great divide / Dreamer
CD FIENDCD 165
Demon / Jun '90 / Pinnacle

TRULY UNFORGETTABLE (32 Truly Unforgettable Songs)
When I fall in love: *Cole, Nat 'King'* / Be my love: *Lanza, Mario* / Only you: *Platters* / It's all in the game: *Edwards, Tommy* / Spanish eyes: *Martino, Al* / On the street where you live: *Damone, Vic* / He'll have to go: *Reeves, Jim* / Misty: *Mathis, Johnny* / Can't get used to losing you: *Williams, Andy* / Dream lover: *Darin, Bobby* / Move over darling: *Day, Doris* / Never be anyone else but you: *Nelson, Rick* / It's only make believe: *Twitty, Conway* / End of the world: *Davis, Skeeter* / More than I can say: *Vee, Bobby* / It's over: *Orbison, Roy* / Cry me a river: *London, Julie* / Love letters: *Lester, Ketty* / I left my heart in San Francisco: *Bennett, Tony* / Make it easy on yourself: *Walker Brothers* / Joanna: *Walker, Scott* / You don't have to say you love me: *Springfield, Dusty* / Look homeward angel: *Ray, Johnnie* / Every time we say goodbye: *Fitzgerald, Ella* / God bless the child: *Holiday, Billie* / Passing strangers: *Eckstine, Billy & Sarah Vaughan* / What a wonderful world: *Armstrong, Louis* / Folks who live on the hill: *Lee, Peggy* / Stand by me: *King, Ben E.* / Save the last dance for me: *Drifters* / Unforgettable: *Cole, Nat 'King'*
CD Set CDEMTVD 55
EMI TV / Nov '90 / EMI

TRUMPET SPECTACULAR
CD PCD 7015
Progressive / Jun '93 / Jazz Music

TRUMPETS IN JAZZ
CD CDCH 556
Milan / Feb '91 / Conifer/BMG / Silva Screen

TRUMPETS IN MODERN JAZZ
Will you still be mine: *Farmer, Art* / For now: *Baker, Chet* / Swingin' the blues: *Clark, Terry* / Bubba and the whale: *Conexion Latina* / Adriatica: *Goykovich, Dusko* / One bright glance: *D'Earth, John* / Jeffuso: *Brooks, Roy* / Little song: *Blue Box* / Kush: *Gillespie, Dizzy* / Body and soul: *Jones, Elvin* / Fairy boat to Rio: *Ambrosetti, Franco* / Siempre junto a ti: *Gonzalez, Jerry*
CD ENJ 80002
Enja / Mar '94 / New Note/Pinnacle / Vital/ SAM

TRUST IN ME (The Old America On The Air)
Soon: *Crosby, Bing* / I hear a rhapsody: *Boswell, Connee* / This love of mine: *Sinatra, Frank* / I only have eyes for you: *Powell, Dick* / Honey in the bee ball: *Jordan, Louis* / Lazy: *Jolson, Al* / Old piano plays the blues: *Cole, Nat 'King'* / He's my guy: *Shore, Dinah* / After school swing session: *Jordan, Louis* / Sinner kissed an angel: *Sinatra, Frank* / I'm in love with the honourable Mr. So and so: *Crawford, Joan* / Thousand goodnights: *Powell, Dick* / Out of nowhere: *Crosby, Bing* / Trust in me: *Boswell, Connee* / Nat meets June: *Cole, Nat 'King'* / Yes indeed: *Crosby, Bing & Connie Boswell* / Why can't you: *Jolson, Al* / Imagination: *Sinatra, Frank* / You'll never know: *Powell, Dick* / It's all so new to me: *Crawford, Joan* / Don't come cryin' on my shoulder: *Jordan, Louis* / On the sentimental side: *Crosby, Bing* / Sunrise serenade: *Boswell, Connee* / Everything happens to me: *Sinatra, Frank*
CD RY 82
Radio Years / Aug '97 / Complete/Pinnacle

TRUTH AND RIGHTS
CD HBCD 78
Heartbeat / Jun '94 / ADA / Direct / Greensleeves / Jet Star

TUFF JAM PRESENTS UNDERGROUND FREQUENCIES VOL.1 (2CD Set)
Gabrielle: *Davis, Roy Jr.* / Puch the love: *Edwards, Todd* / Rush: *Tywanda* / Tumblin' down: *Xavier* / Spin spin sugar: *Sneaker Pimps* / Closer than close: *Gaines, Rosie* / Moments in love: *D'Ambrosio, Bobby* / Harvest for the world: *Hunter, Terry* / Ripgroove: *Double 99* / Dreams: *Smokin' Beats* / Dangerous: *Mr. X* / Things are never: *Operator & Baffled* / Bliss: *Mutiny* / Runaway: *Nu Yorican Soul* / Jump: *Double 99* / Never let you go: *Moore, Tina* / Anytime: *Nu Birth* / Find a path: *New Horizons* / Just gets better: *TJR* / No.1: *Industry Standard*
CD 74321494652
CD Set 74321494672
Northwestside / Jul '97 / BMG

TULIKULKKU
CD KICD 30
Kansanmusiikki Instituutti / Dec '93 / ADA / Direct

TUMI CUBA CLASSICS VOL.1 (Son)
CD TUMICD 049
Tumi / Aug '95 / Discovery / Stern's

TUMI CUBA CLASSICS VOL.3 (Rumba)
CD TUMICD 052
Tumi / Aug '95 / Discovery / Stern's

TUMI CUBA CLASSICS VOL.4 (The Big Sound)
CD TUMICD 053
Tumi / Aug '95 / Discovery / Stern's

TUMI CUBA CLASSICS VOL.5 (Son, The Future)
CD TUMICD 055
Tumi / Sep '95 / Discovery / Stern's

TUMI CUBA CLASSICS VOL.6 (Musica Campesino)
CD TUMICD 057
Tumi / Dec '95 / Discovery / Stern's

TUNES FROM LOWLANDS, HIGHLANDS AND ISLANDS
CD 58394
World Network / Mar '96 / ADA

TUNNEL MIXES (3CD Set)
CD Set LIMB 56CD
Limbo / May '96 / Amato Disco / Pinnacle / Prime

TURDS ON A BUM RIDE VOL.1 & 2
CD ANT 1/2
Anthology / May '97 / Cargo / Greyhound

TURDS ON A BUM RIDE VOL.3
CD ANT 311
Anthology / May '97 / Cargo / Greyhound

TURDS ON A BUM RIDE VOL.4
CD ANT 2211
Anthology / May '97 / Cargo / Greyhound

TURKEY - THE MUSIC OF THE YAYLA
CD C 560050
Ocora / Aug '94 / ADA / Harmonia Mundi

TURN ON, TUNE IN, DROP OUT (A Trip In Psychedelia)
Coloured rain: *Traffic* / Rainbow chaser: *Nirvana* / Venus in furs: *Velvet Underground* / San Franciscan nights: *Burdon, Eric* / Turn on, tune in, drop out: *Fugs* / Alone again or: *Love* / You keep me hangin' on: *Vanilla Fudge* / In a gadda da vida: *Iron Butterfly* / Walk on gilded splinters: *Dr. John* / Ball and chain: *Big Brother* / Hey Grandma: *Moby Grape* / Eight miles high: *Byrds* / Animal zoo: *Spirit* / Somebody to love: *Jefferson Airplane* / Evil ways: *Santana* / Willie the pimp: *Zappa, Frank* / Pusher: *Steppenwolf* / Catch the wind: *Donovan*
CD RENCD 119
Renaissance Collector Series / Mar '97 / BMG

TURNING OVER
CD IGNCD 01
Ignition / Oct '96 / Kudos / Pinnacle

TURNING THE WORLD BLUE
CD SKIZ 003
Skizmatic / Dec '96 / Nervous

TURQUERIE
CD SPNO 11
Spin / Oct '94 / Direct

TUVALU
CD PAN 2055CD
Pan / Dec '94 / ADA / CM / Direct

TWENTY BEST OF TODAY'S FOLK MUSIC
CD EUCD 1071
ARC / '89 / ADA / ARC Music

TWINIGHT'S CHICAGO SOUL HEAVEN
Nevermore: *Domino, Renaldo* / Thank you baby: *Johnson, Syl* / Main squeeze: *Evans, Nate* / New day: *Notations* / Falling in love: *Dynamic Tints* / Wayward dream: *Poindexter, Annette* / I've made up my mind: *Taylor, Josephine* / Temptation's hard to fight: *McGregor, George* / That's the reason: *Benton, Buster* / Tearing me up inside: *Harrison & The Majestic Kind* / Same kind of thing: *Johnson, Syl* / Don't wanna face the truth: *Radiants* / Lift this hurt: *Spencer, Elvin* / To love someone (that don't love you): *Kaldirons* / So good to have you home again: *Mystiques* / Yesterday's mistakes: *Jones, Jimmy* / Maggie: *Williams, Johnny* / Life walked out: *Mist* / I won't stop to cry: *Stormy* / You need to be loved on: *Domino, Renaldo* / Soul heaven: *Friends Of E. Rodney Jones* / Powerful love: *Chuck & Mac* / Which one am I: *Perfections* / Just you & me: *Notations*
CD CDKEND 131
Kent / Nov '96 / Pinnacle

TWIST
CD TBCD 003
T&B / Sep '95 / Plastic Head

TWISTED (2CD Set)
CD Set TVCD 1
Twisted Vinyl / Dec '95 / Alphamagic

TWISTED WHEEL STORY, THE
Good time tonight: *Soul Sisters* / Shotgun and the duck: *Lee, Jackie* / Fife piper: *Dynatones* / You get your kicks: *Ryder, Mitch* / Everybody's going to a love in: *Brady, Bob* / Karate boogaloo: *Jerry O* / Gonna fix you good: *Little Anthony* / Lil lovin' sometimes: *Patton, Alexander* / Ain't no soul: *Milsap, Ronnie* / Humphrey stomp: *Harrison, Earl* / That driving beat: *Mitchell, Willie* / There's nothing else to say: *Incredibles* / Any day now: *Jackson, Chuck* / Dr. Love: *Sheen, Bobby* / Love is after me: *Rich, Charlie* / Little Queenie: *Blacks, Bill* / Secret agent: *Olympics* / Tightrope: *Foxx, Inez & Charlie* / I got what it takes: *Foxx, Inez & Charlie* / That's enough: *Robinson, Roscoe* / Open the door to your heart: *Banks, Darrell* / My elusive dreams: *Dillard, Moses & Joshua* / Next in line: *Lands, Hoagy* / It keeps rainin: *Domino, Fats* / Get out of my heart: *Dillard, Moses & Joshua* / Never love a robin: *Barbara & Brenda*
CD GSCD 066
Goldmine / Nov '95 / Vital

TWO DOZEN DODGY BRITISH COVERS
Why do fools fall in love: *Ryan, Marion* / Story of my life: *Miller, Gary* / Lah dee dah: *Hicks, Colin* / Itchy twitchy feeling: *Wainer, Cherry* / Teenager in love: *Valentine, Dickie* / Mr. Blue: *McBeth, David* / Rockin' little angel: *Viscounts* / Little bit of soap: *Justice, Jimmy* / Ecstasy: *Reed, Oliver* / It might as well rain until September: *DeLaine Sisters* /

Your nose is gonna grow: *Ford, Emile* / Patches: *Davis, Danny* / He's a rebel: *Breakaways* / Pop-pop-pop-pie: *Jackson, Simone* / I wanna stay here: *Miki & Griff* / (Just like) Romeo and Juliet: *Peter's Faces* / In crowd: *First Gear* / Let's lock the door (and throw away the key): *Lancastrians* / Trains and boats and planes: *Harris, Anita* / Younger girl: *Knack* / I washed my hands in muddy water: *Hungry* / (Your gonna) hurt yourself: *Bystanders* / Snoopy versus the red baron: *Gates Of Eden* / (We ain't got) nothin' yet: *Spectres* / Captain of the ship: *JSO*
CD ____ **GEMCD 011**
Diamond / Feb '97 / Pinnacle

TWO FRIENDS TING AND TING
Sound ting: *Gold, Brian & Tony* / Idle talk ting: *Cutty Ranks* / Keeping a fat ting: *Redrose* / Gun ting: *Lindo, Hopeton* / Pretend ting: *Papa San* / Love ting: *Home T* / Oil ting: *Cocoa T* / Bow ting: *Flourgan* / Procrastinate ting: *Mann, Peter* / Bun ting / Cheat ting: *Chevelle* / Gyow ting: *Sister Charmaine*
CD ____ **GRELCD 155**
Greensleeves / Feb '91 / Jet Star / SRD

TWO RIDDIMS CLASH
CD ____ **GPCD 002**
Gussie P / Jun '92 / Jet Star

TWO RYDIM CLASH
CD ____ **NWSCD 9**
New Sound / May '94 / Jet Star

TWO TONE JUMP
CD ____ **RKCD 9306**
Rockhouse / May '93 / Nervous

TYPES - A KUDOS SAMPLER
About this: *Pentatonik* / Rotation: *Angel, Dave* / Zycoon: *Synectics* / Point of no return: *Stasis* / Contrapoint: *Fugue* / Isatai: *As One* / Penguins: *Eco Tourist* / Tknoh: *Germ* / Intelligence: *Sandoz* / Vein: *Scanner* / All over hair piece: *Conemelt* / Crystalline existences: *White Funks On Dope*
CD ____ **KUDCD 005**
Kudos / Jul '94 / Kudos / Pinnacle

TYRANNY OF THE BEAT VOL.1
CD ____ **SPV 05622172**
SPV / May '95 / Koch / Plastic Head

TYRANNY OF THE BEAT VOL.2
CD ____ **5722352**
Westcom / May '96 / Koch / Pinnacle

TYRANNY OF THE BEAT VOL.3
CD ____ **05743272**
Westcom / Feb '97 / Koch / Pinnacle

TYROLEAN EVENING, A
CD ____ **399422**
Koch / Sep '92 / Koch

U

UBU DANCE PARTY (2CD Set)
CD Set ____ **DATACD 2**
Datapanik / Mar '97 / Cargo

UFO'S ARE REAL
CD ____ **BBLP 001**
Bionic Beats / Nov '93 / Plastic Head

UGANDA: AUX SOURCES DU NIL
CD ____ **C 560032**
Ocora / Nov '92 / ADA / Harmonia Mundi

UILLEANN PIPES - BEAUTIFUL IRELAND
Isle of Innisfree / Coolin / Eddie's favourite / Rathlin Island / My Lagan love / Cliffs of Dooneen / Shoe the donkey / Galway bay / Carrickfergus / Old Ardboe / Dark island / Lonesome boatman / Sally Gardens
CD ____ **PLMCD 21**
Sharpe / Jan '97 / Duncans / Target/BMG

UK GAY ANTHEMS VOL.1
CD ____ **BLSTCD 03**
Almighty / Jul '96 / Total/BMG

UK GAY ANTHEMS VOL.2 (It's A Man's World)
CD ____ **BLSTCD 05**
Almighty / Jan '97 / Total/BMG

UK MEETS US RAP
CD ____ **MOLCD 42**
Music Of Life / Apr '97 / Grapevine/ PolyGram

UK REGGAE ALL STARS
CD ____ **CONQ 999CD**
Conqueror / Nov '94 / Grapevine/ PolyGram / Jet Star

UK SPACE TECHNO VOL.1
CD ____ **MILL 020CD**
Millenium / Mar '96 / Plastic Head / Prime / SRD

UK SPACE TECHNO VOL.2 (2CD Set)
CD Set ____ **MILL 026CD**
Millenium / Jul '96 / Plastic Head / Prime / SRD

UK SPACE TECHNO VOL.3
CD ____ **MILL 037CD**
Millenium / Mar '97 / Plastic Head / Prime / SRD

UK UNDERGROUND
CD ____ **AZNY 1001**
Azuli / Oct '92 / Amato Disco / Azuli / Mo's Music Machine / Prime / Vital

UK/DK
USA: *Exploited* / Joker in the pack / No security: *Chaos UK* / Life: *Disorder* / Blind justice: *Business* / Things that need / Fighter pilot: *Vibrators* / Ignite: *Damned* / You talk, we talk: *Pressure* / Viva la revolution / Jerusalem: *One Way System* / Soldier boy: *Varukers* / 42nd Street: *Angelic Upstarts* / Stand strong, stand proud: *Vice Squad* / USA
CD ____ **CDPUNK 47**
Anagram / Feb '95 / Cargo / Pinnacle

UKRAINIAN VOICES
CD ____ **PS 65114**
PlayaSound / Nov '93 / ADA / Harmonia Mundi

ULTIMATE 80'S
Under pressure: *Queen & David Bowie* / New year's day: *U2* / It's a sin: *Pet Shop Boys* / Sexcrime (1984): *Eurythmics* / Relax: *Frankie Goes To Hollywood* / Is there something I should know: *Duran Duran* / Need you tonight: *INXS* / I'm still standing: *John, Elton* / Everywhere: *Fleetwood Mac* / Every breath you take: *Police* / Road to hell: *Rea, Chris* / I want to know what love is: *Foreigner* / Big log: *Plant, Robert* / Wonderful life: *Black* / Love of the common people: *Young, Paul* / Road to nowhere: *Talking Heads* / Reward: *Teardrop Explodes* / Something about you: *Level 42* / Do you really want to hurt me: *Culture Club* / She drives me crazy: *Fine Young Cannibals* / Money for nothing: *Dire Straits* / Wonderland: *Big Country* / White wedding: *Idol, Billy* / Start: *Jam* / Big area: *Then Jerico* / Dead ringer for love: *Meat Loaf* / Atomic: *Blondie* / I'm your man: *Wham* / Look of love: *ABC* / Young at heart: *Bluebells* / Come on Eileen: *Dexy's Midnight Runners* / Blue Monday: *New Order* / Only you: *Yazoo* / (Keep feeling) Fascination: *Human League* / Enola Gay: *OMD* / Shout: *Tears For Fears* / To cut a long story short: *Spandau Ballet* / Tainted love: *Soft Cell* / We close our eyes: *Go West* / Vienna: *Ultravox*
CD ____ **5168312**
Polydor / Jun '94 / PolyGram

ULTIMATE 80'S
CD ____ **74321271042**
RCA / Aug '95 / BMG

ULTIMATE 80'S BALLADS
Save me: *Queen* / Different corner: *Michael, George* / All I want is you: *U2* / Absolute beginners: *Bowie, David* / Every little thing she does is magic: *Police* / Sweet surrender: *Wet Wet Wet* / Save a prayer: *Duran Duran* / True: *Spandau Ballet* / Power of love: *Frankie Goes To Hollywood* / Eternal flame: *Bangles* / Here comes the rain again: *Eurythmics* / I go to sleep: *Pretenders* / Don't dream it's over: *Crowded House* / Avalon: *Roxy Music* / Waiting for a girl like you: *Foreigner* / Hard habit to break: *Chicago* / She makes my day: *Palmer, Robert* / Little lies: *Fleetwood Mac* / Total eclipse of the heart: *Tyler, Bonnie* / Romeo and Juliet: *Dire Straits* / Right here waiting: *Marx, Richard* / Wherever I lay my hat (that's my home): *Young, Paul* / One day in your life: *Jackson, Michael* / Leaving me now: *Level 42* / Long hot summer: *Style Council* / Hands to heaven: *Breathe* / Love don't live here anymore: *Nail, Jimmy* / It's different for girls: *Jackson, Joe* / Golden brown: *Stranglers* / Chance: *Big Country* / Kayleigh: *Marillion* / All of my heart: *ABC* / No regrets: *Ure, Midge* / Human: *Human League* / Souvenir: *OMD* / One of us: *Abba* / China in your hands: *T'Pau* / I second that emotion: *Japan* / Hold me now: *Thompson Twins* / Victims: *Culture Club*
CD ____ **5251132**
PolyGram TV / Nov '94 / PolyGram

ULTIMATE CAJUN COLLECTION
J'aime grand gueydan: *Allan, Johnnie* / Colinda: *Raven, Eddy* / Jolie blon: *Thibodeaux, Rufus* / Grand Texas: *Roger, Aldus* / Gabriel: *Broussard, Alex* / Cajun two-step: *Forester, Blackie* / Le sud de la Louisianne: *Bruce, Vin* / Allons a Lafayette: *Thibodeaux, Rufus* / Pine grove blues: *Abshire, Nathan* / Creole stomp: *Roger, Aldus* / Tout son amour: *Foret, L.J.* / Pauvre hobo: *Thibodeaux, Rufus* / Married life: *Cormier, Louis* / La Lou special: *Broussard, Pee-Wee* / Tous les deux pour la meme: *Forester, Blackie* / Crawfish festival time: *Raven, Eddy* / Mon tit baille: *Newman, Jimmy C.* / Chere Alice: *Richard, Zachary* / One scotch, one bourbon, one beer: *Roger, Aldus* / Tee Maurice: *Guidry, Doc* / Mamou two-step: *Walker, Lawrence* / la valse de amite: *Thibodeaux, Rufus* / Comment ca se fait: *Newman, Jimmy C.* / I'm Cajun cool: *Storm, Warren* / Evangeline: *Dusenberry Family* / La maison a deux portes: *Storm, Warren* / La valse de KLFY: *Doucet, Michael* / Fais do do: *Thibodeaux, Rufus* / La valse d'anniversaire: *Forester, Blackie* / Le two-step de l'acadien: *Abshire, Nathan* / Grand mamou: *Thibodeaux, Rufus* / Chemin des coeurs casser: *Foret, L.J.* / Le nouveau two-step: *Richard, Zachary* / One more chance: *Roger, Aldus* / Dans la Louisianne: *Bruce, Vin* / Alligator Bayou: *Raven, Eddy* / Lake Arthur stomp: *Thibodeaux, Rufus* / Ma belle Evangeline: *Allan, Johnnie* / Le two-step de choupique: *Abshire, Nathan* / Bayou Sam: *Forester, Blackie* / Elle n'est pas la plus belle: *Foret, L.J.* / Tu es la mienne pour toujours: *West, Clint* / La valse de Quebec: *Thibodeaux, Rufus* / Lafayette two-step: *Roger, Aldus* / Le blues Francais: *Abshire, Nathan* / Cotton fields: *Forester, Blackie*
CD ____ **DCD 5254**
Disky / Aug '92 / Disky / THE

ULTIMATE COLLECTION, THE
CD ____ **8453002**
Philips / May '91 / PolyGram

ULTIMATE COUNTRY COLLECTION (2CD Set)
Most beautiful girl in the world: *Rich, Charlie* / I recall a gypsy woman: *Williams, Don* / I fall to pieces: *Cline, Patsy* / Crystal chandeliers: *Pride, Charley* / Stand by your man: *Wynette, Tammy* / Walk on by: *Van Dyke, Leroy* / Before the next teardrop falls: *Fender, Freddy* / Poor boy blues: *Atkins, Chet & Mark Knopfler* / Blanket on the ground: *Spears, Billie Jo* / Make the world go away: *Arnold, Eddy* / He'll have to go: *Reeves, Jim* / He stopped loving her today: *Jones, George* / Ring of fire: *Cash, Johnny* / Rose garden: *Anderson, Lynn* / I couldn't leave you if I tried: *Crowell, Rodney* / Lucille: *Rogers, Kenny* / Legend in my time: *Milsap, Ronnie* / Rhinestone cowboy: *Campbell, Glen* / I'm movin' on: *Snow, Hank* / Feel so right: *Alabama* / Always on my mind: *Nelson, Willie* / Please help me, I'm falling: *Locklin, Hank* / For the good times: *Price, Ray* / Coal miner's daughter: *Lynn, Loretta* / Oh lonesome me: *Gibson, Don* / Hillbilly girl with the blues: *Dalton, Lacy J.* / Abilene: *Hamilton, George IV* / Four in the morning: *Young, Faron* / Loving her was easier (than anything I'll ever do again): *Kristofferson, Kris* / Baby don't get hooked on me: *Davis, Mac* / Lone star state of mind: *Griffith, Nanci* / If I said you had a beautiful body: *Bellamy Brothers* / Here you come again: *Parton, Dolly* / Dukes of Hazzard: *Jennings, Waylon* / Down at the twist and shout: *Carpenter, Mary-Chapin* / El Paso: *Robbins, Marty* / Don't close your eyes: *Whitley, Keith* / Wind beneath my wings: *Greenwood, Lee* / Talking in your sleep: *Gayle, Crystal* / Don't rock the jukebox: *Jackson, Alan*
CD Set ____ **MOODCD 26**
Columbia / Oct '92 / Sony

ULTIMATE DANCE
CD ____ **12580**
Laserlight / Oct '95 / Target/BMG

ULTIMATE DISCO COLLECTION
CD ____ **QTVCD 021**
Quality / Mar '93 / Pinnacle

ULTIMATE DOO-WOP COLLECTION
CD ____ **NEMCD 618**
Sequel / Feb '92 / BMG

ULTIMATE DRUM 'N' BASS (2CD Set)
CD Set ____ **QPMCD 2**
QPM / Dec '95 / Beechwood/BMG

ULTIMATE DRUM 'N' BASS
CD ____ **CLP 9979**
Cleopatra / Apr '97 / Cargo / Greyhound / Plastic Head / RTM/Disc / SRD

ULTIMATE DRUM AND BASS VOL.2 (2CD Set)
CD Set ____ **QPMCD 5**
QPM / Apr '96 / Beechwood/BMG

ULTIMATE HAPPY HARDCORE (2CD Set)
CD Set ____ **QPMCD 8**
QPM / Nov '96 / Beechwood/BMG

ULTIMATE HOTWIRE SAMPLER
CD ____ **EFA 128172**
Hotwire / May '95 / SRD

ULTIMATE HOUSE
CD ____ **CHAMPCD 1016**
Champion / Oct '88 / 3mv/BMG

ULTIMATE HOUSE, THE
CD ____ **GRF 210**
Tring / Mar '93 / Tring

ULTIMATE INSTRUMENTAL COLLECTION (3CD Set)
CD Set ____ **COLBX 001**
Focus / Feb '97 / Total/BMG

ULTIMATE LINE DANCING ALBUM, THE
Hillybilly rock hillybilly roll: *Woolpackers* / Boot scootin' boogie: *Brooks & Dunn* / Achy breaky heart: *Cyrus, Billy Ray* / I feel lucky: *Carpenter, Mary-Chapin* / Chatahoochie: *Jackson, Alan* / Romeo: *Parton, Dolly* / Honky tonk man: *Yoakam, Dwight* / Baby likes to rock it: *Tractors* / Honky tonk attitude: *Diffie, Joe* / Line king: *Sunset Stampede* / Cotton eyed Joe: *Rednex* / Swamp thing: *Grid* / Life's a dance: *Montgomery, John Michael* / My baby loves me: *McBride, Martina* / Copperhead road: *Earle, Steve* / Cleopatra Queen of denial: *Tillis, Pam* / Money in the bank: *Anderson, John* / Funky cowboy: *McDowell, Ronnie* / Adalida: *Strait, George* / No-one else on earth: *Wyonna*
CD ____ **RADCD 41**
Global TV / Jan '97 / BMG

ULTIMATE LOVERS VOL.1
CD ____ **ARKCD 101**
Arawak / Nov '92 / Jet Star

ULTIMATE LOVERS VOL.2
CD ____ **ARKCD 104**
Arawak / Dec '93 / Jet Star

ULTIMATE MEMPHIS COUNTRY COLLECTION VOL.1, THE (2CD Set)
Hey porter: *Cash, Johnny* / Cold cold heart: *Lewis, Jerry Lee* / (Tell me) Who: *Smith, Warren* / Turn around: *Perkins, Carl* / Uncertain love: *Rhodes, Slim* / Daisy bread boogie: *Steele, Gene* / Feelin' low: *Chaffin, Ernie* / Chains of love: *Miller Sisters* / My kind of carryin' on: *Poindexter, Doug* / Show me: *Bond, Eddie* / Blues in the bottom of my shoes (Way down blues): *Yelvington, Malcolm* / When you stop loving me: *King, Cast* / Easy to love: *Self, Mack* / Home of the blues: *Cash, Johnny* / Let the jukebox keep on playing: *Perkins, Carl* / Tonight will be the last night: *Smith, Warren* / Will the circle be unbroken: *Lewis, Jerry Lee* / Standing in your window: *Bond, Eddie* / Down on the border: *Simmons, Gene* / How long: *Wimberly, Maggie Sue* / Heartbreakin' love: *Wages, Jimmy* / I'm bluer than anyone can be: *Mann, Carl* / Muddy ole river: *Stinit, Dane* / Tragedy: *Wayne, Thomas* / Your the nearest thing to heaven: *Cash, Johnny* / This old heart of mine: *Bond, Eddie* / That black haired man: *Clement, Jack* / Who will the next fool be: *Rich, Charlie* / Wayward wind: *Mann, Carl* / Bummin' around: *Feathers, Charlie* / In the dark: *Peterson, Earl* / Just rolling along: *Yelvington, Malcolm* / Fool for loving you: *Earls, Jack* / Jump right out of this jukebox: *Wheeler, Onie* / I'd rather be safe than sorry: *Smith, Warren* / Someday you will pay: *Miller Sisters* / That's what I tell my heart: *McDaniel, Luke* / Country boy: *Cash, Johnny* / Sure to fall: *Perkins, Carl* / Jambalaya: *Lewis, Jerry Lee* / Take and give: *Rhodes, Slim* / We're getting closer to being apart: *Feathers, Charlie* / Tell 'em off: *Wheeler, Onie* / Everyday: *Self, Mack* / I'm lonesome: *Chaffin, Ernie* / When I dream: *Earls, Jack* / Nothing to lose but my heart: *Peterson, Earl* / I've been deceived: *Feathers, Charlie* / Day I found you: *Bond, Eddie* / Ten years: *Clement, Jack* / Sittin' and thinkin': *Rich, Charlie* / Goodbye Mr. Love: *Smith, Warren* / If I could change you: *Mann, Carl* / Who's gonna shoe your pretty little feet: *Anthony, Rayburn* / I know what it means: *Lewis, Jerry Lee* / Tennessee: *Perkins, Carl*
CD Set ____ **MEMPHIS 01**
Disky / Jan '93 / Disky / THE

ULTIMATE NON-STOP PARTY ALBUM
Stars on 45 / Swing the mood / Do you remember / That's what I like / Caribbean show / Stars on 45
CD ____ **SUMCD 4033**
Summit / Nov '96 / Sound & Media

ULTIMATE PARTY ANIMAL (2CD Set)
Saturday night: *Whigfield* / Ooh ahh just a little bit: *Gina G* / Dreamer: *Livin' Joy* / Moving on up: *M-People* / Things can only get better: *D:Ream* / We are family: *Sister Sledge* / Let me be your fantasy: *Baby D* / Ride on time: *Black Box* / Rhythm of the night: *Corona* / Power: *Snap* / Sunshine after the rain: *Berri* / Twist and shout: *Chaka Demus & Pliers* / Don't stop (wiggle wiggle): *Outhere Brothers* / No limit: *2 Unlimited* / Boom shake the room: *DJ Jazzy Jeff & The Fresh Prince* / Stayin' alive: *N-Trance* / Two can play at that game: *Brown, Bobby* / Killer: *Adamski* / I wanna be a hippy: *Technohead* / Saturday night at the movies: *Robson & Jerome* / Grease Megamix / Wake me up before you go go: *Wham* / Relight my fire: *Take That* / Loco motion: *Minogue, Kylie* / Never gonna give you up: *Astley, Rick* / I'm too sexy: *Right Said Fred* / Macarena: *Los Del Rio* / Timewarp: *Damian* / Swing the mood: *Jive Bunny* / Can can: *Bad Manners* / Anniversary waltz: *Status Quo* / Cotton eye Joe: *Rednex* / Flava: *Andre, Peter* / Help yourself: *Ferrino, Tony* / Cum on feel the noize: *Slade* / Blockbuster: *Sweet* / Hit me with your rhythm stick: *Dury, Ian & The Blockheads* / I'll be there for you: *Friends* / YMCA: *Village People* / Boney M megamix: *Boney M* / Celebration: *Kool & The Gang* / Boogie wonderland: *Earth, Wind & Fire* / You make me feel (mighty real): *Sylvester* / Contact: *Starr, Edwin* / Oops upside your head: *Gap Band* / Back to the sixties: *Tight Fit* / Abba Medley / Beatles medley / Beatles medley: *Take That* / Guaglione: *Prado, Perez*
CD Set ____ **RADCD 47**
Global TV / Nov '96 / BMG

ULTIMATE PARTY MIX ALBUM VOL.1, THE
Buddy Holly medley: *Berry, Mike* / Beatles medley: *Starsound* / That's what I like: *Jive Bunny* / Beach boys gold: *Gidea Park* / Tribut to Motown: *Motor City Allstars* / Hi NRG megamix: *Thomas, Evelyn* / Chuck Berry megamix: *Berry, Chuck* / Kylie megamix: *Minogue, Kylie* / Back to the 60's: *Tight Fit* / Abba medley: *Starsound*
CD ____ **NTRCD 044**
Nectar / Nov '95 / Pinnacle

ULTIMATE PARTY MIX ALBUM VOL.2, THE
CD NTRCD 065
Nectar / Oct '96 / Pinnacle

ULTIMATE PSYCHOBILLY COLLECTION
CD NTMCD 524
Nectar / May '96 / Pinnacle

ULTIMATE PUB SING-A-LONG ALBUM
CD MCCD 248
Music Club / Jun '96 / Disc / THE

ULTIMATE RAVE CLASSICS
CD QPMCD 4
QPM / Mar '96 / Beechwood/BMG

ULTIMATE RECORDING COMPANY, THE
CD TOPPCD 004
Ultimate / Jul '94 / Pinnacle

ULTIMATE REGGAE PARTY
CD TCD 2731
Telstar / Oct '94 / BMG

ULTIMATE ROCK (2CD Set)
CD Set CDEMTVD 148
EMI TV / Feb '97 / EMI

ULTIMATE ROCK 'N' ROLL COLLECTION (2CD Set)
(We're gonna) Rock around the clock: Haley, Bill & The Comets / Chantilly lace: Big Bopper / Johnny B Goode: Berry, Chuck / Say mama: Vincent, Gene / Little bitty pretty one: Lymon, Frankie / Sea cruise: Ford, Frankie / Girl can't help it: Little Richard / Something else: Cochran, Eddie / Reet petite: Wilson, Jackie / Tequila: Champs / Good golly miss molly (Live): Lewis, Jerry Lee / That's alright: Perkins, Carl / I'm walkin': Domino, Fats / Hats off to Larry: Shannon, Del / Stagger Lee: Price, Lloyd / Red river rock: Johnny & The Hurricanes / Baby let's play house: Feathers, Charlie / Claudette: Everly Brothers / Barbara Ann: Regents / That'll be the day: Holly, Buddy / Stay: Maurice & The Zodiacs / Walk don't run: Ventures / Tutti frutti: Little Richard / Rockin' robin: Day, Bobby / Wake up little Susie: Everly Brothers / Ah poor little baby: Craddock, Billy / It's late: Nelson, Rick / Book of love: Monotones / Runaround Sue: Dion / All Mama's children: Perkins, Carl / Bony moronie: Williams, Larry / Nut rocker: B-Bumble & The Stingers / Blue suede shoes: Cochran, Eddie / At the hop: Danny & The Juniors / Oh boy: Holly, Buddy / Little darlin': Diamonds / Rebel rouser: Eddy, Duane / I'm number one rock 'n' roll C&W boogie blues man: Gilley, Mickey / Whole lotta shakin' goin' on: Lewis, Jerry Lee / Rip it up: Haley, Bill & The Comets / Shame, shame, shame: LaBeef, Sleepy / Oh carol: Berry, Chuck
CD Set MOODCD 36
Columbia / Oct '94 / Sony

ULTIMATE SKA COLLECTION
CD DCD 5295
Disky / Nov '93 / Disky / THE

ULTIMATE SOUL COLLECTION VOL.1
CD 9548333402
Warner Bros. / Feb '95 / Warner Music

ULTIMATE SOUL COLLECTION VOL.2, THE
CD 9548338402
Warner Bros. / Oct '95 / Warner Music

ULTIMATE SUMMER PARTY ANIMAL (2CD Set)
CD Set RADCD 63
Global TV / Jun '97 / BMG

ULTIMATE SUN COUNTRY COLLECTION (56 Legendary Original Sun Recordings)
Hey porter: Cash, Johnny / Cold cold heart: Lewis, Jerry Lee / (Tell me) who: Smith, Warren / Turn around: Perkins, Carl / Uncertain love: Rhodes, Slim / Daisy bread boogie: Steele, Gene / Feelin' low: Chaffin, Ernie / Chains of love: Miller Sisters / My kind of carryin' on: Poindexter, Doug / Show me: Bond, Eddie / Blues in the bottom of my shoes (way down blues): Yelvington, Malcolm / When you stop loving me: King, Cast / Easy to love: Self, Mack / Home of the blues: Cash, Johnny / Let the jukebox keep on playing: Perkins, Carl / Tonight will be the last night: Smith, Warren / Will the circle be unbroken: Lewis, Jerry Lee / Standing in your window: Bond, Eddie / Down on the border: Simmons, Gene / How long: Wimberly, Maggie Sue / Heartbreakin' love: Wages, Jimmy / I'm bluer than anyone can be: Mann, Carl / Muddy ole river: Stinit, Dane / Tragedy: Wayne, Thomas / You're the nearest thing to heaven: Cash, Johnny / This old heart of mine: Bond, Eddie / That black haired man: Clement, Jack / Who will the next fool be: Rich, Charlie / Wayward wind: Mann, Carl / Bummin' around: Feathers, Charlie / In the dark: Peterson, Earl / Just rolling along: Yelvington, Malcolm / Fool for loving you: Earls, Jack / Jump right out of this jukebox: Wheeler, Onie / I'd rather be safe than sorry: Smith, Warren / Someday you will pay: Miller Sisters / That's what I tell my heart: McDaniel, Luke / Country boy: Cash, Johnny / Sure to fall: Perkins, Carl / Jambalaya: Lewis, Jerry Lee / Take and give: Rhodes, Slim / We're getting closer to being apart: Feathers, Charlie / Tell 'em off: Wheeler, Onie / Everyday: Self, Mack / I'm lonesome: Chaffin, Ernie / When I dream: Earls, Jack / Nothing to lose but my heart: Peterson, Earl / I've been deceived: Feathers, Charlie / Day I found you: Bond, Eddie / Ten years: Clement, Jack / Sittin' and thinkin': Rich, Charlie / Goodbye Mr. Love: Smith, Warren / If I could change you: Mann, Carl / Who's gonna shoe your pretty little feet: Anthony, Rayburn / I know what it means: Lewis, Jerry Lee / Tennessee: Perkins, Carl
CD DCD 5201
Disky / Aug '91 / Disky / THE

ULTIMATE SURFING ALBUM
CD JHD 012
Tring / Jun '92 / Tring

ULTIMATE SWEDISH (Slash & Burn Vol.1)
CD SPV 08453752
SPV / Aug '96 / Koch / Plastic Head

ULTRA DANCE (Mixed By Boris Dlugosch) (2CD Set)
All of me: Backroom Boys & Takiya Dixon / Stay gold: Deep Dish / Lift me up: MK & Claire Rivers / Jump to my beat: Wildchild / Release yo self: Transatlantic Soul / Love each other: Wildchild / It's your life: Naked Music NYC & Motivation / Stand up: Love Tribe / This love we've found: Reel Soul & Carolyn Harding / Keep on dreaming: Lisa Marie Experience / Sugar is sweeter: Bolland, C.J. / Keep on jumpin': Lisa Marie Experience
CD Set ULTRA 1002
Ultra / Mar '97 / Mo's Music Machine / Prime / RTM/Disc

ULTRA LOUNGE (TV Town)
Bubbles in the wine: Martin, Freddy & His Orchestra / Naked City: Riddle, Nelson & Orchestra / Old couple: May, Billy & His Orchestra / Man from UNCLE: Caiola, Al / Spies: Caiola, Al / Thanks for the memory: Pell, Dave / Munsters: Marshall, Jack / Fugutive: Zentner, Si / Dick Van Dyke: Riddle, Nelson & Orchestra / Alvin Show: Riddle, Nelson & Orchestra / Human jungle: Barry, John / Batman: McCallum, David / Mannix: May, Billy & His Orchestra / One step beyond (fear): Ventures / Twilight zone: Ventures / Mr. Lucky: Zentner, Si / Mod squad: Caiola, Al / My three sons: Riddle, Nelson & Orchestra / Burle's law suite: Liberty Soundtrack Orchestra / Bewitched: Lee, Peggy / Melancholy serenade: Gleason, Jackie / Power house: Jones, Spike
CD CDEMS 1616
EMI / Jul '97 / EMI

ULTRA LOUNGE (Bossa Novaville)
So danco samba: De Sah, Wanda / Meditation: Almeida, Laurindo & Bossa Nova All Stars / Little bird: Perkins, Bill / Little boat: Perkins, Bill / Samba de orfeu: Anthony, Ray / Amy's theme: Denny, Martin / Corcovado: Adderley, Cannonball & Sergio Mendes / Look of love: May, Billy & His Orchestra / One note samba: Holmes, Leroy / Recado bossa nova: Holmes, Leroy / Triste: Roberts, Howard / Misirlou: Almeida, Laurindo & Bossa Nova All Stars / Desafinado: Zentner, Si / Exotique bossa nova: Denny, Martin / Quiet village bossa nova: Denny, Martin / Witchcraft: Joe Graves & The Diggers / Baia: Perkins, Bill / Que sabe voce de mim: Wanderley, Walter / Girl from Ipanema: Almeida, Laurindo / Manha de carnaval: Almeida, Laurindo / Mas que nada: Mitchell, Rubin / So nice: De Sah, Wanda & Sergio Mendes / Fly me to the moon: London, Julie
CD CDEMS 1617
EMI / Jul '97 / EMI

ULTRA LOUNGE (Wild Cool & Swingin' Too)
Frenesi: Gorme, Eydie / Night and day: Lawrence, Steve / Charade: Darin, Bobby / A lot of livin' to do: Wilson, Nancy / 5 months, 2 weeks, 2 days: Prima, Louis / Wives and lovers: Damone, Vic / Boy from Ipanema: Lee, Peggy / Strangers in the night: Newton, Wayne / With plenty of money and you: Bennett, Tony / Call me irresponsible: Darin, Bobby / Is you is or is you ain't my baby: Washington, Dinah / Snootie little cutie: Troup, Bobby / Daddy: London, Julie / Just in time: Martin, Dean / Perdido: Vaughan, Sarah / Angel eyes: Jones, Jack / Just a gigolo: Prima, Louis / I ain't got nobody: Prima, Louis / Midnight swinger: Prima, Louis / Destination moon: Washington, Dinah / It had better be tonight: Horne, Lena / Hawaiian war chant: Fitzgerald, Ella
CD CDEMS 1618
EMI / Jul '97 / EMI

ULTRA LOUNGE (Mondo Hollywood)
Experiment in terror: Caiola, Al / Man and a woman: May, Billy & Leroy Holmes / Live for life: May, Billy & Leroy Holmes / Barbarella: Ferrante & Teicher / Cool: Denny, Martin / Hot rod rumble: Courage, Sandy / Pink panther: Johnson, Plas / It had better be tonight: Johnson, Plas / Beat girl: Barry, John / You gotta taste all the fruit: Holmes, Leroy / Shadow of your smile: Anthony, Ray & George Shearing / Days of wine and roses: Anthony, Ray & George Shearing / Apartment: Rodriguez, Tito / Watch what happens: McLain, Danny / I, a lover: Holmes, Leroy / De sade: Holmes, Leroy / Seance on a wet afternoon: Barry, John / Girl talk: May, Billy / Moon river: Jerome, Henry / You only live twice: Sir Julian & Elliot Fisher / Thunderball: Sir Julian & Elliot Fisher / God, the bad and the ugly: Sir Julian & Elliot Fisher / Your zowie face: Riddle, Nelson / Town without pity: Pitney, Gene
CD CDEMS 1619
EMI / Jul '97 / EMI

ULTRA LOUNGE (Bongoland)
Deep night: Snyder, Terry / Softly as in a morning sunrise: Snyder, Terry / Latin fever: Costanzo, Jack / Taboo: Arnaud, Leo / Nightmare: Loco, Joe / On Green Dolphin Street: Denny, Martin / Hernando's hideaway: Denny, Martin / Dr. No's fantasy: Fisher, Elliott / Night in Tunisia: Latin Jazz Sextet / Cherry pink and apple blossom white: Baxter, Les & Billy May / Bernie's June: Caiola, Al / Brazil: Contreras, Tino / Caravan: Hyman, Dick / Inch worm: Costanzo, Jack / Misiriou: Perito, Nick / Quien sera: Perito, Nick / Young savages: Denny, Martin / Balinese bongos: Baxter, Les / Club caballeros: Almeida, Laurindo & The Danzaneros / Moderna muchacha: Loco, Joe / La cumparsa: Costanzo, Jack / Harlem nocturne: Costanzo, Jack / Colon: Savage Beat Of Augie Colon
CD CDEMS 1620
EMI / Jul '97 / EMI

ULTRA LOUNGE (Bottoms Up)
Fandango: Denny, Martin / Big noise from winnekta: Caiola, Al / Midnight swim: Caiola, Al / Hot toddy: London, Julie / Mahna mah-na: Holmes, Leroy / Music to watch girls by: May, Billy / Slick: May, Billy / Oh honey: Wood, Gloria / Guys and dolls: Snyder, Terry / Cute: McLain, Danny / No matter what shape your stomach is in: New Classic Singers / Tijuana taxi: New Classic Singers / Donkey serenade: Denny, Martin / Baby elephant walk: Caiola, Al & Billy May / Java: Caiola, Al & Billy May / Potluck: La Salle, John Quartet / Rots-o-ruck: Marino, Richard / Squatty roo: Buzon, John Trio / Twang: Costanzo, Jack / I want a lip: Stevens, April / Deep purple: Hoffman, Dr. Samuel / 'S wonderful: Hoffman, Dr. Samuel / Quiet village: Denny, Martin / Lisbon Antigua: Riddle, Nelson
CD CDEMS 1621
EMI / Jul '97 / EMI

ULTRA LOUNGE VOL.1 (Mondo Exotica)
Swamp fire: Denny, Martin / Moon Mis: Out-Islanders / Caravan: 80 Drums Around The World / Hypnotique: Denny, Martin / Atlantis: Baxter, Les / Aika: Edwards, Webley / Miserlou: Denny, Martin / Lust: Sheva, Bas / Hana maul: Floyd, Chick / 10 voodoo dreams: Baxter, Les / Jungle madness: Denny, Martin / 12 Babalo: Sumac, Yma / Simba: Baxter, Les / Girlfriend of the whirling dervish: Denny, Martin / Bali ha'i: Shindo, Tak / Pyramid of the sun: Baxter, Les / Quiet village: Denny, Martin / Wimowch: Sumac, Yma
CD CDEMS 1584
Premier/EMI / Apr '96 / EMI

ULTRA LOUNGE VOL.10 (A Bachelor In Paris)
I love Paris: Butera, Sam / Song from Moulin Rouge: Jones, Jonah Quartet / Milord: Baxter, Les / Under Paris skies: Car, Joe 'Fingers' / La la Collette: Car, Joe 'Fingers' / Valentina: Bernstein, Elmer / Parisian women: Coleman, Cy / Mon amour, o mon amour: Baxter, Les / C'est magnifique: Riddle, Nelson / Vive l'amour: Doo, Dicky & The Don'ts / April in Paris: Mighty Accordian Band / Poor people of Paris: May, Billy / French rat race: Double Six Of Paris / Petite fleur: Rene, Henri / Clown on the Eiffel tower: Baxter, Les / La vie en rose: Butera, Sam / C'est si Ben: Cooper, Jack / I love Paris: Constanzo, Jack / Can can can: Shard, Jerry
CD CDEMS 1597
Premier/EMI / Aug '96 / EMI

ULTRA LOUNGE VOL.11 (Organs In Orbit)
Rockhouse: Freeman, Ernie / Ill wind: Buzon, John Trio / Girl from Ipanema: McLain, Danny / Love is just around the corner: Davis, Jackie / Movin' at midnight: Sir Julian / Voce e eu: Wanderley, Walter / Li'l darlin': Bucci, Joe Trio / Patricia: May, Billy & His Orchestra / Third Man theme: Baker, Don Trio / Man and a woman: Sir Julian / Mr. Ghost goes to town: Buzon, John Trio / Laura: McLain, Danny / More: McLain, Danny / Perfida: Davis, Jackie / Late, Late show: Buckner, Milt / Fever: Freeman, Ernie / Comin' home baby: Freeman, Ernie / Flying fiddles: Torrent, Shay / Song of bayou: Denny, Martin / Enchanted farm: Forbidden Five
CD CDEMS 1598
Premier/EMI / Aug '96 / EMI

ULTRA LOUNGE VOL.12 (Saxophobia)
I dig: Baxter, Les / Street scene: Butera, Sam / All or nothing at all: Auld, Georgie / Bernie's June: Hamner, Curley & Milt Buckner / Watermelon man: King Curtis / Volare: Riddle, Nelson / Tanya: Johnson, Plas / Samba de Orfeu: Perkins, Bill / Peter Gunn twist: Anthony, Ray / Goldfinger: Basie, Count / Caravan: Jenkins, Gordon / Speakeasy blues: Riddle, Nelson / One mint julep: Palmer, Earl Trio / Ebb tide: Out-Islanders / Big twist: Johnson, Plas / Harlem nocturne: Prima, Louis / Misfits: Costa, Don / Bong bash: Dominguin, Pepe
CD CDEMS 1599
Premier/EMI / Aug '96 / EMI

ULTRA LOUNGE VOL.13 (Christmas Cocktails)
Rudolph, the red-nosed reindeer mambo: May, Billy / Winter wonderland: Lee, Peggy / Christmas trumpets/We wish you a very Merry Christmas: Anthony, Ray / Christmas is: Rawls, Lou / Santa Claus is comin' to town/White Christmas: McGriff, Jimmy / I'd like you for Christmas: London, Julie / Holiday on skis: Caiola, Al & Riz Ortolani / (Everybody's waitin' for) the man with the bag: Starr, Kay / Jingle bells/Jingle bell rock: Hollyridge Strings / I've got my love to keep me warm: Martin, Dean / I saw mommy kissing Santa Claus/Jingle Bells bossa nova: Dunstedter, Eddie / Christmas kisses: Anthony, Ray / I'll be home for Christmas/Baby, it's cold outside: Gleason, Jackie & Jack Marshall / What are you doing New Year's Eve: Wilson, Nancy / Cha-cha all the way: Capitol Studio Orchestra / Christmas song (Merry Christmas to you): Cole, Nat 'King' / Nutcracker suite: Brown, Les & His Band Of Renown / Ring those Christmas bells: Waring, Fred & His Pennsylvanians / Violets for your furs: Continental / Tag: Unknown / Capitol promo: Unknown
CD CDEMS 1600
Premier/EMI / Nov '96 / EMI

ULTRA LOUNGE VOL.2 (Mambo Fever)
Hooray for Hollywood: Swan, Don / Manana: Davis, Jackie / Peter Gunn mambo: Constanzo, Jack / Chihuahua: Oliver, Luis / I can't believe that you're in love with me: Buzon, John Trio / Mambo jumbo: Barbour, Dave / Cumana: Rose, Henry & Bobby Stevenson / Taki rari: Sumac, Yma / Way down yonder in New Orleans: Alexander, Van / Oink oink mambo: Reves, Chuy / Diga diga doo: Buzon, John Trio / Hernando's hideaway: May, Billy & His Orchestra / Tico tico: Swan, Don / Glow worm cha cha cha: Davis, Jackie / Malambo: Sumac, Yma / Can can overture: Constanzo, Jack / Oye negra: Snyder, Terry
CD CDEMS 1585
Premier/EMI / Apr '96 / EMI

ULTRA LOUNGE VOL.3 (Space Capades)
Gay spirits: Rose, David / Lover: Marino, Richard / Moon moods: Baxter, Les / Power house: Hammock, Bobby / Drivin' around the block: Harrell, Dickie / Calcutta: Baxter, Les / Holiday for strings: Schumann, Walter / You're the top: Elliott, Dean / Istanbul (not Constantinople): Carr, Joe 'Fingers' / Stumbling: Shindo, Tak / Sabre dance: Baxter, Les / This room is my castle of quiet: May, Billy / I get a kick out of you: Slatkin, Felix / Satan takes a holiday: Malmsten, Jack / Puttin' on the ritz: Snyder, Terry / Blues in the night: Roy, Alvin / Saturday night on Saturn: Baxter, Les / Lonesome Road: Elliott, Dean
CD CDEMS 1586
Premier/EMI / Apr '96 / EMI

ULTRA LOUNGE VOL.4 (Bachelor Pad Royale)
Route 66 theme: Riddle, Nelson & Orchestra / Caravan: Buzon, John Trio / Sexe: Renaud, Line / Cool: Busch, Lou & His Orchestra / Beast: Buckner, Milt / Our man Flint theme: Fisher, Elliott / Spring, sprang, sprung: Fascinato, Jack / Night train: Rey, Alvino / Harlem nocturne: Denny, Martin / Boulevard of broken dreams/Fever: Butera, Sam / Topsy: Bucci, Joe Trio / Like young: Pell, Dave / Street scene '58: Busch, Lou & His Orchestra / Playboy's theme: Coleman, Cy / Shot in the dark: Haskell, Jimmie / Shangri-la: Jones, Spike New Band / Black coffee: London, Julie / Melancholy serenade: King Curtis
CD CDEMS 1591
Premier/EMI / May '96 / EMI

ULTRA LOUNGE VOL.5 (Wild, Cool & Swingin')
Ain't that a kick in the head: Martin, Dean / Dig that crazy chick: Butera, Sam & The Witnesses / More: Darin, Bobby / Fever: Lee, Peggy / Jump, jive an' wail: Prima, Louis / Please don't talk about me when I'm gone: Davis, Sammy Jr. / Danke schoen: Newton, Wayne / French poodle: Butera, Sam & The Witnesses / What is this thing called love: Smith, Keely / Sunday in New York: Darin, Bobby / Closer to the bone: Prima, Louis / Nobody but me: Rawls, Lou / Little girl: Damone, Vic / LOVE: Cole, Nat 'King' / Volare: Martin, Dean / That old black magic: Prima, Louis & Keely Smith / You'd be so nice to come home to: London, Julie / Hello Dolly: Darin, Bobby
CD CDEMS 1592
Premier/EMI / May '96 / EMI

ULTRA LOUNGE VOL.6 (Rhapsodesia)
Girl talk: Roberts, Howard / Serenata: Jones, Jonah Quartet / Sleep walk: Rene, Henri & His Orchestra / Smoke gets in your eyes: Mallet Men / Go slow: London, Julie / Ebb tide: Anthony, Al / If I should lose you: Shearing, George / Willow weep for me: Marcellino, Muzzy / Dansero: Baker, Don Trio / Lunar rhapsody: Baxter, Les / You're my thrill: Gray, Dolores / Fever: Marino, Richard & His Orchestra / Blues in my heart: Buzon, John Trio / Tenderly: Gleason, Jackie / Picnic theme: Snyder, Terry / Tur-

quoise: *Buckner, Milt* / Do it again: *Stevens, April* / Ruby: *Baxter, Les Orchestra*
CD ________ CDEMS 1593
Premier/EMI / May '96 / EMI

ULTRA LOUNGE VOL.7 (The Crime Scene)
Dragnet/Room 43: *Anthony, Ray* / I Spy: *Hagen, Earle* / Thinking of baby: *Bernstein, Elmer* / From Russia with love: *Basie, Count* / Big town: *Almeida, Laurindo* / Man with the golden arm: *May, Billy* / Untouchables: *Riddle, Nelson* / James Bond theme: *Holmes, Leroy* / Mission Impossible: *May, Billy* / Harlem nocturne: *Jones, Spike* / Walk on the wild side: *Zentner, Si* / Mister Kiss Kiss Bang Bang: *Fisher, Elliott* / Wild ones: *Busch, Lou* / Staccato's theme: *Bernstein, Elmer* / Search for Vulcan: *Holmes, Leroy* / Peter Gunn suite: *Anthony, Ray* / Silencers: *Carr, Vikki* / Music to be murdered by: *Alexander, Jeff Singers*
CD ________ CDEMS 1594
Premier/EMI / Jul '96 / EMI

ULTRA LOUNGE VOL.8 (Cocktail Capers)
Rollercoaster: *Baxter, Les* / Hey bellboy: *Wood, Gloria* / This could be the start of something: *Pell, Dave* / Pink Panther theme: *Hollywood Studio Orchestra* / Like young: *Rose, David* / Underwater chase: *Caiola, Al* / Binga banga bonga/Percolator: *Snyder, Terry* / Call me: *New Classic Singers* / Mountain greenery: *Freeman, Bernie Combo* / Charade: *Zentner, Si* / Shooting star/Jungalero: *Baxter, Les* / Honorable Hong Kong rock: *Out-Islanders* / Odd job man/I wanna be a James Bond girl: *Holmes, Leroy* / Heap big chief: *Marcellino, Muzzy* / Blue Danube rock: *Jones, Jesse* / Pussy cat: *Coleman, Cy* / Teach me Tiger: *Stevens, April* / Lolita Ya Ya: *Riddle, Nelson*
CD ________ CDEMS 1595
Premier/EMI / Jul '96 / EMI

ULTRA LOUNGE VOL.9 (Cha Cha De Amor)
Sway: *Martin, Dean* / Recado bossa nova: *Almeida, Laurindo* / You're my thrill: *Auld, Georgie* / It must be true: *Buzon, John Trio* / Carioca: *Denny, Martin* / Whatever Lola wants: *Baxter, Les* / A Nega Se Vingou: *Wanderley, Walter* / Dark eyes/It happened in Monterey: *Mallet Men* / Gropher mambo: *Sumac, Yma* / Zelda's theme: *Prado, Perez* / Magnificent seven: *Rodriguez, Tito* / Cha cha cha d'amour: *Martin, Dean* / Desafinado: *Almeida, Laurindo* / Bei mir bist du schon/La furiosa: *Costanzo, Jack & Don Swan* / Choo choo cha cha: *Rinks Dinks* / So nice: *May, Billy* / Rock-cha-rhumba / Sway: *London, Julie*
CD ________ CDEMS 1596
Premier/EMI / Jul '96 / EMI

ULTRA TECHNO VOL.1
CD ________ IR 006CD
Independence / Apr '96 / Plastic Head

ULTRAMETAL
CD ________ MONITOR 1
Monitor / Jan '92 / CM

UNCHAINED MELODIES
You'll never walk alone: *Gerry & The Pacemakers* / When a man loves a woman: *Sledge, Percy* / Smoke gets in your eyes: *Platters* / Halfway to paradise: *Fury, Billy* / Raindrops keep fallin' on my head: *Thomas, B.J.* / Stranger on the shore: *Bilk, Acker* / Spanish harlem: *King, Ben E.* / Love letters in the sand: *Boone, Pat* / What becomes of the broken hearted: *Ruffin, Jimmy* / Unchained melody: *Drifters* / You've lost that loving feeling: *Yuro, Timi* / Will you love me tomorrow: *Shirelles* / Somewhere: *Proby, P.J.* / Moon river: *Butler, Jerry* / Bright eyes: *Belmonde, Pierre* / My own true love: *Duprees* / I don't know why, but I do: *Henry, Clarence 'Frogman'* / Help me make it through the night: *Smith, Sammi*
CD ________ ECD 3196
K-Tel / Mar '95 / K-Tel

UNCHAINED MELODIES VOL.1
CD ________ TMPCD 001
Temple / Nov '94 / BMG

UNCHAINED MELODIES VOL.2
CD ________ TMPCD 002
Temple / Nov '94 / BMG

UNCHAINED MELODIES VOL.3
CD ________ TMPCD 003
Temple / Nov '94 / BMG

UNCHARTED TERRITORIES VOL.1
Central line: *Alroy Road Tracks & Duke Of Haringay* / Tranquillity: *Aquasky* / Saxx: *Fourth World* / Visible from space: *Hunch* / Cool breeze: *Ken, Kenny & Cool Breeze* / Cotton wool: *Lamb* / Melting pot: *Melting Pot* / Harp of gold: *Nice, Peter Trio* / Mutant jazz: *T-Power* / Freefall: *Terresa* / Touch me / Never as good: *Wax Doctor*
CD ________ SOUNDSCD 9
Street Sounds / Jul '96 / Beechwood/BMG

UNCHARTED TERRITORIES VOL.2
CD ________ SOUNDSCD 11
Street Sounds / Feb '97 / Beechwood/BMG

UNCLE SAM BLUES
Army blues: *White, Bukka* / GI blues: *Lightnin' Slim* / Red's dream: *Louisiana Red* / Vietnam blues: *Lenoir, J.B.* / Stormy desert: *Terry, Cooper* / Overseas blues: *Borum, 'Memphis' Willie* / Uncle Sam don't take my man: *Pryor, Snooky* / Back to Korea blues: *Sunnyland Slim* / Vietcong blues: *Wells, Junior* / Million lonesome women: *McGhee, Brownie* / '41 blues: *Clayton, Dr. Peter* / Pearl Harbour blues: *Clayton, Dr. Peter* / Give me a 32-20: *Crudup, Arthur 'Big Boy'* / Win the war blues: *Williamson, Sonny Boy* / Army blues: *Edwards, David* / Atomic bomb blues: *Harris, Homer* / So cold in Vietnam: *Shines, Johnny* / Sad news from Korea: *Hopkins, Lightnin'*
CD ________ CD 52043
Blues Encore / Oct '96 / Target/BMG

UNCOVERED
Walk on by: *Franklin, Aretha* / Let's stay together: *Pasadenas* / Every night: *Snow, Phoebe* / They won't go when I go: *Michael, George* / Until you come back to me: *Williams, Deniece & Johnny Mathis* / (Sittin' on the) dock of the bay: *Bolton, Michael* / Don't dream it's over: *Young, Paul* / Stop lovin' me, stop lovin' you: *Hall, Daryl* / What's going on: *Lauper, Cyndi* / Summertime: *Benson, George* / Stand by me: *White, Maurice* / Why can't we live together: *Sade* / Still haven't found what I'm looking for: *Chimes* / Superstar (Don't you remember): *Vandross, Luther* / I'll never fall in love again: *Deacon Blue* / Georgia on my mind: *Nelson, Willie*
CD ________ MOODCD 38
Sony Music / Feb '95 / Sony

UNDARK 3396
CD ________ EMIT 3396
Time / Dec '96 / Jet Star / Pinnacle

UNDEAD (A Gothic Masterpiece - 3CD Set)
CD Set ________ DTKBOX 51
Dressed To Kill / Sep '96 / Total/BMG

UNDER A GROOVE VOL.1
CD ________ PIAS 378960320
Mix It / May '96 / Plastic Head

UNDER DOCTORS ORDERS
CD ________ VPCD 02038
VP / Sep '95 / Greensleeves / Jet Star / Total/BMG

UNDER THE COVERS (18 Classic Cover Versions)
Don't let the sun go down on me: *Michael, George & Elton John* / Jealous guy: *Roxy Music* / Let's stay together: *Turner, Tina* / Angel: *Stewart, Rod* / No regrets: *Ure, Midge* / Nothing compares 2 U: *O'Connor, Sinead* / Crying game: *Boy George* / When I fall in love: *Astley, Rick* / You've lost that lovin' feelin': *Hall & Oates* / Where is the love: *Paris, Mica & Will Downing* / Have you seen her: *MC Hammer* / It's too late: *Quartz & Dina Carroll* / Don't you worry about a thing: *Incognito* / Why can't we live together: *Sade* / Just the way you are: *White, Barry* / Loving you: *Shanice* / Crying in the rain: *A-Ha* / Baby I love your way/Freebird: *Will To Power*
CD ________ 5160742
PolyGram TV / Apr '93 / PolyGram

UNDER THE SIGN OF THE SACRED STAR
CD ________ CDVILE 66
Peaceville / May '96 / Pinnacle

UNDERCOVER VOL.3
CD ________ SPV 08438202
SPV / Jul '95 / Koch / Plastic Head

UNDERGROUND FLAVAS
Deeper: *Lady Penelope & Abstract* / All night long: *Gant* / Bad boys: *Baffled Republic* / Things are never: *Operator & Baffled* / Odyssey one: *Federation X* / Tonite: *Underground Solution* / Let me tell you: *Jump Up Crew* / Was she ever mine: *Anthill Mob* / Mixed up: *Bell, Melissa* / Music: *Benson, Shawn*
CD ________ BDRCD 23
Breakdown / Aug '97 / Pinnacle

UNDERGROUND HOUSE PARTY VOL.1 (Mixed By D.J. Duke)
CD ________ NBCD 95002
Nite & Blue / Jul '96 / Plastic Head

UNDERGROUND HOUSE PARTY VOL.2 (Mixed By Ted Patterson)
I wanna be free: *Luna Project* / Daylite: *Gypsymen* / Hear the music: *Gypsymen* / Feels so right: *Solution* / Special melodies: *Station Q* / Stoppin' us: *Gypsymen* / Sure shot: *Conway, Margaret* / I love the way you make me feel: *Roman, Nelson* / Too much for me: *Owens, Robert* / Tumblin down: *Hermann* / Promises in the sky: *Tunnel Traxx*
CD ________ NBCD 95003
Nite & Blue / Jul '96 / Plastic Head

UNDERGROUND HOUSE PARTY VOL.3 (Mixed By Tony Humphries)
Hideway: *De'Lacy* / Underground: *System VIIII* / No pay day: *Gayland* / Get yourself together: *Moods Of Madness* / Respect: *Adeva* / You don't know: *Serious Intention* / Check this out: *Hardhouse* / In and out of my life: *Adeva* / Victim: *Moods Of Madness* / I like you: *Cassio & The Funky People* / Release the tension: *Harris, Cassandra*
CD ________ NBCD 950004
Nite & Blue / Jul '96 / Plastic Head

UNDERGROUND HOUSE PARTY VOL.4 (Mixed By Camcho)
Body work: *Hot Streak* / Thee industry made me do it: *Aphrohead* / Get huh: *Ride Committee* / Jungle kisses: *Roc & Kato* / Givin it all I get: *Solution* / Plastic disco: *DJ Duke* / I'm a sex maniac: *Storm* / Keep on dancing: *Dixon, Daniel* / Hear the music: *Gypsymen* / Funky horns: *Fierce Factor* / Ma foom bey: *Cultural Vibe* / In and out of my life: *Adeva* / Thee: *Felix Da Housecat* / Pickin up the promises: *Brown, Jocelyn* / Do you wanna dance: *Bad Boy Orchestra*
CD ________ NBCD 95005
Nite & Blue / Jul '96 / Plastic Head

UNDERGROUND HOUSE PARTY VOL.5 (Mixed By Rodger S)
CD ________ 2101535
Nite & Blue / Jul '96 / Plastic Head

UNDERGROUND HOUSE PARTY VOL.6 (Smack Da House)
Lonely: *Donald O* / So proud: *Abrams, Colonel* / Flute song: *Moods Of Black* / Special: *Donald O* / Happy: *Rock, Calvin* / I'll do anything: *Inner Vision* / Vacum: *Mental Instrum* / Makin' love (To Nicole): *Cassio Ware* / Goin' thru the motion: *Jenkins, Keshia* / Reach for the sky: *Supa* / Brothers and sisters: *Hope, Alexander* / Give it: *Sir Charles* / Watcha gonna do: *Pseudo & Colonel Abrams* / Luv changes: *Chicago People* / Celebrate: *Rush, Donell* / Old fashioned love: *Pollard, Karen*
CD ________ 032501CD
Nite & Blue / Jul '96 / Plastic Head

UNDERGROUND LONDON
CD ________ KICKCD 31
Kickin' / Dec '95 / Prime / SRD

UNDERGROUND UK
CD ________ KICKCD 38
Kickin' / Jul '96 / Prime / SRD

UNDERGROUND VOL.1
CD ________ JARCD 6
Cookie Jar / Mar '93 / SRD

UNDERTONES VOL.1
CD ________ OMCD 10
One Movement / Jul '96 / Timewarp

UNDERTONES VOL.2
CD ________ OMCD 12
One Movement / Jul '96 / Timewarp

UNDERWOOD
CD ________ SR 100
Sub Rosa / Apr '96 / Direct / RTM/Disc / SRD / Vital

UNDERWOOD VOL.2
CD ________ SR 125
Sub Rosa / Jul '97 / Direct / RTM/Disc / SRD / Vital

UNEARTHED GOLD OF ROCK STEADY VOL.1
CD ________ OHCD 004
Ossie / Nov '95 / Jet Star

UNFINISHED, THE
CD ________ SR 103
Sub Rosa / Jan '97 / Direct / RTM/Disc / SRD / Vital

UNFORGETTABLE
Unforgettable: *Washington, Dinah* / Red sails in the sunset: *Washington, Dinah* / Where of when: *Washington, Dinah* / You're nobody till somebody loves you: *Washington, Dinah* / Misty: *Vaughan, Sarah* / That old black magic: *Vaughan, Sarah* / Careless: *Vaughan, Sarah* / You stepped out of a dream: *Vaughan, Sarah* / Too marvellous for words: *Holiday, Billie* / Say it isn't so: *Holiday, Billie* / Our love is here to stay: *Holiday, Billie* / Stars fell on Alabama: *Holiday, Billie* / My way: *Simone, Nina* / Chain gang: *Simone, Nina* / Angel of the morning: *Simone, Nina* / Ain't got no...I got life: *Simone, Nina*
CD ________ 74321449262
Camden / Jan '97 / BMG

UNFORGETTABLE
I'll be home: *Boone, Pat* / Hey there: *Clooney, Rosemary* / My special angel: *Helms, Bobby* / Heartaches by the number: *Mitchell, Guy* / Ivory tower: *Carr, Cathy* / Band of gold: *Cherry, Don* / My happiness: *Pied Pipers* / Three coins in the fountain: *Four Aces* / Kisses sweeter than wine: *Rodgers, Jimmie* / Love is a golden ring: *Laine, Frankie* / Only you (and you alone): *Platters* / Walkin' my baby back home: *Ray, Johnnie* / I went to your wedding: *Page, Patti* / With all my heart: *Sands, Jodie* / P S I love you: *Hilltoppers* / Hold my hand: *Cornell, Don* / Suddenly there's a Valley: *Grant, Gogi* / So rare: *Dorsey, Jimmy*
CD ________ ECD 3077
K-Tel / Dec '96 / K-Tel

UNFORGETTABLE (Hits Of The Fifties)
CD ________ PLSCD 158
Pulse / Apr '97 / BMG

UNFORGETTABLE BIG BANDS
CD ________ UP 006
Hindsight / Sep '92 / Jazz Music / Target/BMG

UNFORGETTABLE MELODIES (2CD Set)
Bridge over troubled water: *Goodwin, Ron & His Orchestra* / Never on a Sunday: *Love, Geoff & His Orchestra* / Honeymoon song: *Manuel & The Music Of The Mountains* / Snowbird: *Pourcel, Franck & His Orchestra* / What the world needs now is love: *Goodwin, Ron & His Orchestra* / Moon river: *Manuel & The Music Of The Mountains* / True love: *Love, Geoff & His Orchestra* / Godfather love theme: *Pourcel, Franck & His Orchestra* / Misty: *Love, Geoff & His Orchestra* / Fool on the hill: *Goodwin, Ron & His Orchestra* / Spanish Harlem: *Manuel & The Music Of The Mountains* / Forever and ever: *Pourcel, Franck & His Orchestra* / Spartacus love theme: *Love, Geoff & His Orchestra* / Love story: *Goodwin, Ron & His Orchestra* / Autumn leaves: *Manuel & The Music Of The Mountains* / She: *Pourcel, Franck & His Orchestra* / Ballade pour Adeline: *Love, Geoff & His Orchestra* / Walk on by: *Goodwin, Ron & His Orchestra* / White rose of Athens: *Manuel & The Music Of The Mountains* / Blue moon: *Pourcel, Franck & His Orchestra* / Walk in the Black Forest: *Love, Geoff & His Orchestra* / Rhapsody on a theme by Paganini: *Goodwin, Ron & His Orchestra* / Waltz from serenade for strings: *Manuel & The Music Of The Mountains* / Summertime: *Pourcel, Franck & His Orchestra* / When I fall in love: *Love, Geoff & His Orchestra* / Elizabethan serenade: *Goodwin, Ron & His Orchestra* / Shadow of your smile: *Manuel & The Music Of The Mountains* / On a clear day (You can see forever): *Pourcel, Franck & His Orchestra*
CD Set ________ CDDL 1120
Music For Pleasure / Aug '91 / EMI

UNFORGETTABLE SESSION, AN
CD ________ CD 53097
Giants Of Jazz / Jan '95 / Cadillac / Jazz Music / Target/BMG

UNIDENTIFIED FLOATING AMBIENCE
CD ________ SR 9454
Silent / May '94 / Cargo / Plastic Head

UNIFIED COLOURS OF DRUM 'N' BASS (2CD Set)
CD Set ________ FORMCD 06
Formation / Aug '97 / SRD

UNISSUED SUN MASTERS
CD ________ CPCD 8137
Charly / Nov '95 / Koch

UNITED ARTISTS OF MESSIDOR SAMPLER
CD ________ MES 158232
Messidor / Apr '93 / ADA / Koch

UNITED DANCE VOL.3 (2CD Set)
CD Set ________ FBRCD 334
4 Beat / Jan '96 / Pinnacle

UNITED DANCE VOL.4 (2CD Set)
CD Set ________ FBRCD 336
4 Beat / May '96 / Pinnacle

UNITED DANCE VOL.5 (2CD Set)
CD Set ________ FBRCD 337
4 Beat / Oct '96 / Pinnacle

UNITED DANCE VOL.6 (2CD Set)
12 Of love: *Sly* / Cape fear: *Sly* / Devotion: *Sly* / Don't you want me: *Eruption* / Reach out: *Eruption* / Right thing: *Eruption* / Behind closed doors: *Eruption* / Come on: *Walford Project* / After dark: *Thunder & Joy* / Sunshine: *Slipmatt & Eruption* / Jump around: *Slippery Project & Benz* / Scream: *DJ Hixxy & Sunset Regime* / Hardcore passion: *DJ Hixxy & Sunset Regime* / Hyper space: *Druid & Sharkey* / Simply electric: *Force & Styles* / Field of dreams: *Force & Styles* / Pacific sun: *Force & Styles* / Cutting deep: *Force & Styles* / Pretty green eyes: *Force & Styles* / Paradise and dreams: *Force & Styles* / Apollo 12 pt 2: *Force & Styles* / Heart of gold: *Force & Styles* / Tardis to Brooklyn: *Bang The Future* / Ease your mind: *Bunter, Billy & Sunset* / Gates of oblivion: *Bang The Future* / Let the music: *Eruption* / Beginning of a new era: *Bang The Future* / Blinding light: *DJ Magical* / Feel the hype: *Generation* / Ever lasting love: *Seduction* / Rushing: *Iyduction & Sy* / On the road: *Iyduction & Sy* / In the mix: *Seduction* / Hey yeah: *Seduction*
CD Set ________ FBRCD 338
4 Beat / Apr '97 / Pinnacle

UNITED FLAVA OF BRITISH RAP
Listen urban species: *Urban Species* / Here we go: *NSO Force* / Hang 'em high: *Kaliphz* / Drink on: *Cash Crew* / Who you know: *Krispy Three* / Making moves: *MC NI* / Big trouble in little Asia: *Hustlers HC* / Yabba dabba doo: *Darkman* / Free man: *11-59* / Colourcode: *Gunshot* / Coming eqipped: *3pm* / Hell hath no fury: *Evey* / Wha cha' all paid: *Scientists Of Sound* / How's life in London: *London Posse* / What's going on: *Blak Twang* / All about Eve: *Marxman*
CD ________ WOLCD 1063
Ticking Time/China / Jul '95 / Pinnacle

UNITED FREQUENCIES OF TRANCE VOL.6
CD ________ E 11943/2
United Frequencies Of Trance / Dec '93 / SRD

UNITED MUTATIONS
CD ________ LCD 03
Lo / Nov '96 / RTM/Disc

UNITED RAVERS COMPILATION VOL.1
CD ________ URRC 1
United Ravers / Nov '95 / Plastic Head

UNITED SPEAKEASY COLLECTIVE NU JAZZ PRINCIPLES
CD _______________ MM 890002
Moonshine / Jun '95 / Mo's Music Machine / Prime / RTM/Disc

UNITED TRIBES POW WOW VOL.1
CD _______________ SPALAX 14942
Spalax / Oct '96 / ADA / Cargo / Direct / Discovery / Greyhound

UNITED TRIBES POW WOW VOL.2
CD _______________ SPALAX 14943
Spalax / Oct '96 / ADA / Cargo / Direct / Discovery / Greyhound

UNITY
CD _______________ TTPCD 1
Totem / Sep '94 / Jazz Music / New Note/ Pinnacle

UNIVERSAL SOUNDS OF AMERICA
Space 2: *Durrah, David* / Theme de yoyo: *Art Ensemble Of Chicago* / Lions of judah: *Reid, Steve* / Astral travelling: *Sanders, Pharoah* / Space odyssey: *Belgrave, Marcus* / Empty street: *Reid, Steve* / Kitty bey: *Morris, Byron* / Space 1: *Durrah, David* / Space is the place: *Sun Ra*
CD _______________ SJRCD 027
Soul Jazz / Jul '95 / New Note/Pinnacle / Timewarp / Vital

UNIVERSE - WORLD TECHNO TRIBE (The Most Progressive Dance Party Organisation In The World)
Pioneers of the universe: *Hypnotist* / Springyard: *Bolland, C.J.* / .215061: *AFX* / List 2: *Suburban Hell* / Tremora del terra: *Illuminatae* / Virtual reality: *Two Thumbs* / Jojba: *Dr. Fernando* / Flying deeper: *Skyflyer* / Cosmic love (approach and identify): *Resistance D* / Virtual breakdown (mind your head): *Garnier, Laurent* / Sequential (the dune mix): *Sequential* / First symphony: *Angel, Dave* / Barbarella: *Vath, Sven*
CD _______________ VERSECD 1
Universe/Rising High / Apr '93 / SRD

UNIVERSE PRESENTS THE TRIBAL GATHERING (2CD Set)
Are we here (who are they): *Orbital* / Voodoo people: *Prodigy* / Song for life: *Leftfield* / Spastik: *Plastikman* / Infinite mass: *Faith Department* / Every time you touch me: *Moby* / Starship universe: *Bolland, C.J.* / Crisis a gwan: *Bandulu* / Lagoon: *Angel, Dave* / Her jazz: *Chemical Brothers* / Mother Earth: *Dubtribe* / Det 29-62: *Cox, Carl* / Heart: *Loop 8.2* / Hypnotic Eastern rhythm: *Soundclash Republic* / Violator: *Transmakus* / Bug: *Drum Club* / Dark and long: *Underworld*
CD Set _______________ 8284522
Internal / Jul '95 / Pinnacle / PolyGram

UNLIMITED AMBIENT
CD _______________ MASOCD 90092
Materiali Sonori / Jul '97 / Cargo / Greyhound / New Note/Pinnacle

UNLOCK THE FUNK (The Very Best Of Club Classics - 2CD Set)
Funkin' for Jamaica: *Browne, Tom* / Are you ready (do the bus stop): *Fatback Band* / Back to my roots: *Odyssey* / Ride on time: *Black Box* / Rapp payback: *Brown, James* / Holy ghost: *Bar-Kays* / Freeway of love: *Franklin, Aretha* / We got the funk: *Positive Force* / You make me feel (mighty real): *Sylvester* / Night to rememeber: *Shalamar* / Can you feel the force: *Real Thing* / Troglodyte: *Castor, Jimmy Bunch* / Get up before the night is over: *Technotronic* / Sisters are doin' it for themselves: *Franklin, Aretha & Annie Lennox* / Rapper's delight: *Sugarhill Gang* / Unlock the funk: *Locksmith* / Use it up wear it out: *Odyssey* / Do you wanna funk: *Sylvester* / Love come down: *King, Evelyn* / Jump (for my love): *Pointer Sisters* / Midas touch: *Midnight Star* / Shut d funk up: *Dr. John* / You're the one for me: *Train* / Shut 'um down: *Scott-Heron, Gil* / Last night a DJ saved my life: *Indeep* / Pump up the jam: *Technotronic* / Got to use my imagination: *Knight, Gladys* / Shame shame shame: *Shirley & Co.* / Message: *Grandmaster Flash* / Let the music play: *Shannon* / We just funkers: *Hampton, Michael*
CD Set _______________ RCACD 216
RCA / Jul '97 / BMG

UNMETERED TAXI
CD _______________ JJCD 169
Channel One / Apr '96 / Jet Star

UNPAVED ROADS VOL.3
CD _______________ 70001671363
Essential Dance / Mar '96 / RTM/Disc

UNPLUGGED COLLECTION VOL.1
Before you accuse me: *Clapton, Eric* / Deep dark truthful mirror: *Costello, Elvis & The Rude 5* / Come rain or come shine: *Henley, Don* / Don't let the sun go down on me: *John, Elton* / Are you gonna go my way: *Kravitz, Lenny* / Barefoot: *Lang, k.d.* / Why: *Lennox, Annie* / We can work it out: *McCartney, Paul* / Pink houses: *Mellencamp, John* / Half a world away: *REM* / Graceland: *Simon, Paul* / Somebody to shove: *Soul Asylum* / Gasoline alley: *Stewart, Rod* / Don't talk: *10,000 Maniacs* / Pride and joy: *Vaughan, Stevie Ray* / Like a hurricane: *Young, Neil*
CD _______________ 9362457742
WEA / Dec '94 / Warner Music

UNPLUGGED ROCK AND POP CLASSICS (3CD Set)
Mr Tambourine man / Ruby Tuesday / Waterloo sunset / Ride a white swan / Brown eyed girl / Honey don't think / All apopogies / Four seasons in one day / Meet me on the corner / Every night / When you were sweet sixteen / Make me smile / Sweet Jane / Sorrow / Any other guy / Passenger / Losing my religion / Horse with no name / Catch the wind / Itchycoo park / Live forever / Kooks / Love her madly / Heart of gold / So young / Jesus don't want me for a sunbeam / Made of stone / It ain't me babe / Constant craving / There is a light that never goes out / Femme fatal / Sun ain't gonna shine anymore / Be bop a lula / Milkcow blues / Peggy Sue / Rip it up / Almost grown / That'll be the day / C'mon everybody / Not fade away / Rave on / That's alright Mama / 20 Flight rock / Rock around the clock / Whole lotta shakin' goin' on / Blue moon of Kentucky / All shook up / Reelin' and rockin' / Strollin' / Baby I don't care
CD Set _______________ HR 879452
Disky / May '97 / Disky / THE

UNPROGGED
CD _______________ HUDROK 001CD
Blueprint / Dec '96 / Pinnacle

UNRELEASED VOL.11
Moodz: *Pooley, Ian* / Assasin: *Baxter, Blake* / Away and beyond: *Broom, Mark* / Una pequena melodia en domingo: *Curtin, Dan* / Nervous: *Neuropolitique* / William drive by disaster: *Lazermusik* / ID clones: *Shake* / Puter vibes: *Landstrumm, Neal* / Thinking mans dream: *Young, Claude* / Aware and awake / Veil: *Blue Binary* / Practopia: *B12*
CD _______________ ELEC 28CD
New Electronica / Apr '96 / Beechwood/ BMG / Plastic Head

UNRELEASED VOL.3
CD _______________ PRESAGE 04CD
Semantic / Feb '94 / Plastic Head

UNSUNG HEROES (The Phase II Mod Collection)
CD _______________ PHZCD 17
Unicorn / Nov '94 / Plastic Head

UNTITLED VOL.1 (2CD Set)
Live forever: *Oasis* / Stupid girl: *Garbage* / Girls and boys: *Blur* / Wake up boo: *Boo Radleys* / Lady killers: *Lush* / Change: *Lightning Seeds* / King of the kerb: *Echobelly* / Waking up: *Elastica* / Uh huh oh yeh: *Weller, Paul* / Girl like you: *Collins, Edwyn* / Countdown: *Pulp* / Waterfall: *Stone Roses* / Movin' on up: *Primal Scream* / Creep: *Radiohead* / Stay together: *Suede* / Can you dig it: *Mock Turtles* / Weak: *Skunk Anansie* / Neighbourhood: *Space* / You and me song: *Wannadies* / Dizzy: *Reeves, Vic & Wonder Stuff* / Regret: *New Order* / Get the message: *Electronic* / This charming man: *Smiths* / Made of stone: *Stone Roses* / Can't be sure: *Sundays* / I'll stand by you: *Pretenders* / Road to nowhere: *Talking Heads* / I scare myself: *Dolby, Thomas* / Love shack: *B-52's* / Shipbuilding: *Wyatt, Robert* / Just the one: *Levellers* / Fisherman's blues: *Waterboys* / Message in a box: *World Party* / Mary's prayer: *Danny Wilson* / Like lovers do: *Cole, Lloyd* / Somewhere in my heart: *Aztec Camera* / Don't go: *Hothouse Flowers* / King of rock 'n' roll: *Prefab Sprout* / Twist and shout: *Deacon Blue* / Missing: *Everything But The Girl*
CD Set _______________ RADCD 32
Global TV / Apr '96 / BMG

UNTITLED VOL.2 (2CD Set)
Wonderwall: *Oasis* / Country house: *Blur* / Sale of the century: *Sleeper* / Going out: *Supergrass* / Queer: *Garbage* / Female of the species: *Space* / Riverboat song: *Ocean Colour Scene* / Alright: *Cast* / Goldfinger: *Ash* / Street spirit: *Radiohead* / Connection: *Elastica* / Yes: *McAlmont & Butler* / Something for the weekend: *Divine Comedy* / Charity: *Skunk Anansie* / Stars: *Dubstar* / Not bad enough: *Eggman* / Sleeping in: *Menswear* / 13th: *Cure* / He's on the phone: *St. Etienne* / Born slippy: *Underworld* / What's the frequency Kenneth: *REM* / Hung up: *Weller, Paul* / From despair to where: *Manic Street Preachers* / True faith: *New Order* / Lucky you: *Lightning Seeds* / Dark therapy: *Echobelly* / Rocks: *Primal Scream* / Love will tear us apart: *Joy Division* / Fools gold: *Stone Roses* / Only one I know: *Charlatans* / Personal Jesus: *Depeche Mode* / How soon is now: *Smiths* / Good morning Britain: *Aztec Camera & Mick Jones* / Real gone kid: *Deacon Blue* / When love breaks down: *Prefab Sprout* / Each and everyone: *Everything But The Girl* / I fell back alone: *World Party* / Crash: *Primitives* / Might be stars: *Wannadies* / Wild ones: *Suede*
CD Set _______________ RADCD 39
Global TV / Jul '96 / BMG

UNTITLED VOL.3 (2CD Set)
You're gorgeous: *Baby Bird* / Some might say: *Oasis* / Trash: *Suede* / Sandstorm: *Cast* / In a room: *Dodgy* / Circle: *Ocean Colour Scene* / Nice guy Eddie: *Sleeper* / Peacock suit: *Weller, Paul* / Design for life: *Manic Street Preachers* / On a rope: *Rocket From The Crypt* / 6 underground: *Sneaker Pimps* / One to another: *Charlatans* / All I want: *Skunk Anansie* / High and dry: *Radiohead* / Only happy when it rains: *Garbage* / Oh yeah: *Ash* / Boy wonder: *Speedy* / Great things: *Echobelly* / She said: *Longpigs* / What's in the box: *Boo Radleys* / Firestarter: *Prodigy* / Pearl's girl: *Underworld* / Protection: *Massive Attack* / Wrong: *Everything But The Girl* / Play dead: *Bjork & David Arnold* / Elevator song: *Dubstar* / Kinky afro: *Happy Mondays* / Sally cinnamon: *Stone Roses* / Loaded: *Primal Scream* / There she goes: *La's* / Love your money: *Daisy Chainsaw* / Animal nitrate: *Suede* / Disappointed: *Electronic* / Blue glow: *Pulp* / New England: *MacColl, Kirsty* / 500 (shake baby shake): *Lush* / Perfect: *Lightning Seeds* / Rise and shine: *Cardigans* / I wanna be adored: *Stone Roses* / She cries your name: *Orton, Beth*
CD Set _______________ RADCD 44
Global TV / Nov '96 / BMG

UNTOUCHABLE OUTCASTE BEATS
CD _______________ CASTE 3CD
OutCaste / Aug '97 / 3mv/Sony

UP & DOWN CLUB SESSIONS VOL.1
Soft target: *Jones, Josh Ensemble* / Mr. Puffy: *Dry Look* / Funky niblets: *Hunter, Charlie Trio* / Music in my head: *Alphabet Soup* / Knucklebean: *Brooks, Kenny Trio* / Up and around: *Bernrad, Will Trio* / New flavor: *Marshall, Eddie Hip Hop Jazz Band* / 20 30 40 50 60 Dead: *Hunter, Charlie Trio* / Jonesintime: *Jones, Josh Ensemble* / Up and down: *Alphabet Soup*
CD _______________ MR 1032
Mammoth / Jul '95 / Vital

UP & DOWN CLUB SESSIONS VOL.2
'Round midnight: *Hueman Flavour* / As I reach: *Hueman Flavour* / Up: *Up & Down Allstars* / Here on earth: *Jones, Josh Ensemble* / Cherry suite: *Hueman Flavour* / Acalona yare: *Jones, Josh Ensemble* / Blues in Havana: *Jones, Josh Ensemble* / Vision sets you free: *Hueman Flavour* / Destiny: *Hueman Flavour* / Down: *Up & Down Allstars* / Ache: *Jones, Josh*
CD _______________ MR1042
Mammoth / Aug '95 / Vital

UP 4 IT
CD _______________ CDRAID 532
Rumour / Sep '96 / 3mv/Sony / Mo's Music Machine / Pinnacle

UP ALL NIGHT VOL.1 (30 Northern Soul Classics)
Nothing can stop me: *Chandler, Gene* / Getting mighty crowded: *Everett, Betty* / Nothing worse than being alone: *Ad Libs* / That other place: *Flemons, Wade* / I keep tryin': *Hughes, Freddie* / You're the dream: *Shelton, Roscoe* / I hurt on the other side: *Barnes, Sidney* / Lonely for you baby: *Dee, Sonny* / Come on train: *Thomas, Don* / Breakaway: *Valentines* / You're gonna need me: *Ford, Ted* / Being without you: *Williams, Maurice* / Why don't you write: *Bates, Lee* / But I couldn't: *Harper, Willie* / Just another heartbreak: *Little Ritchie* / Touch me, hold me, kiss me: *Inspirations* / Tear stained face: *Varner, Don* / Hung up on your love: *Montclairs* / Running for my life: *Shelton, Roscoe* / My man don't think I know: *Davies, Gwen* / Hold on: *Beavers, Jackie* / You've been gone too long: *Sexton, Ann* / That's enough: *Robinson, Roscoe* / I'd think it over twice (if I were you): *Fletcher, Sam* / You'll always be in style: *Barnes, Sidney* / Don't let me down: *Hughes, Freddie* / Sweet and easy: *McCoy, Van* / Power of love: *Humphrey, Amanda* / Now I'm in love with you: *Sims, Marvin L.* / I'm a fool, I must love you: *Falcons*
CD _______________ CPCD 8216
Charly / Apr '97 / Koch

UP ALL NIGHT VOL.2 (30 Hits From The Original Soul Underground)
That's my girl: *Clark, Dee* / Black eyed girl: *Thompson, Billy* / Return: *Williams, Maurice* / Dearly beloved: *Montgomery, Jack* / Toast to the lady: *Wilson, Eddie* / That's no way to treat a girl: *Knight, Marie* / Please stay: *Ivorys* / You hit me like TNT: *Jones, Linda* / Let's get back together: *Honey Bees* / Carlena: *Just Brothers* / Get it baby: *Mitchell, Stanley* / Love slipped through my fingers: *Ohio Players* / Do you love me baby: *Masqueraders* / You can't keep a good man down: *Gentlemen Four* / One bo-dillion years: *Little Ritchie* / Check yourself: *Chandler, Gene* / I love you always: *Rivingtons* / Welcome to Dreamsville: *Ambrose, Sammy* / Use it before you lose it: *Valentin, Bobby* / I'm gonna do it myself: *Ellie, Jimmy 'Preacher'* / Lost love: *Irma & The Fascinations* / Stop and get hold of myself: *Knight, Gladys & The Pips* / If there's anything else you want (Let me know): *Joy, Roddie* / I'm stepping out of the picture: *Maestro, Johnny & The Crests* / Wrong girl: *Showmen* / Johnny my boy: *Ad Libs* / That girl: *Porgy & The Monarchs* / One in a million: *Brown, Maxine* / It used to be: *Burns, Jimmy & The Fantastic Epics* / Long after tonight is all over: *Radcliffe, Jimmy*
CD _______________ CPCD 8217
Charly / May '97 / Koch

UP COUNTRY
CD _______________ SOV 014CD
Sovereign / Jan '93 / Target/BMG

UP FRONT VOL.1
CD _______________ UPCD 901
Upfront / Jun '90 / Serious Records

UP JUMPED THE BLUES
CD _______________ MCCD 241
Music Club / Mar '96 / Disc / THE

UP TO ZION
I hear a sound / Day of the Lord / He is good / Bless the Lord / Let us rejoice and be glad / Praise the Lord / Ascribe unto the Lord / He shall reign / We give you thanks / By your blood / Who is like me / Worthy is the lamb / Great and marvellous / Sond of Moses / Come let us get up to Zion / Come let us get up
CD _______________ HMD 41
Hosanna / Mar '92 / Nelson Word

UP WITH THE CURTAIN (Stars of the Variety Theatre)
That's what you think: *Bermon, Len* / Stormy weather: *Carless, Dorothy* / I'll take romance: *Driver, Betty* / Can't we meet again: *Flanagan & Allen* / Million tears: *Flanagan & Allen* / Underneath the arches: *Flanagan & Allen* / Caught in the act: *Forsythe, Seamon & Farrell* / I have an ear for music: *Geraldo & Arthur Tracy* / Love in bloom: *Geraldo* / Pretty girl is like a melody: *Geraldo & Arthur Tracy* / Up with the curtain: *Geraldo* / I'm a different me they say: *Hutchinson, Leslie 'Hutch'* / Melody maker: *Hutchinson, Leslie 'Hutch'* / Oh they're tough, mighty tough in the West: *Hylton, Jack* / Was it rain: *Hylton, Jack* / Me and my girl: *Lane, Lupino & Teddie St. Denis* / Every Sunday afternoon: *Miller, Max* / You can't go away like that: *Miller, Max* / Georgia's got a moon: *Nesbitt, Max & Harry* / Hit medley: *Reid, Billy Accordion Band* / My honey's loving arms: *Rosing, Val* / On behalf of the working classes: *Russell, Billy* / I don't do things like that: *Trinder, Tommy* / Lads tell a few: *Western Brothers*
CD _______________ CDAJA 5076
Living Era / '91 / Select

UP YER RONSON - ORIGINAL SOUNDTRACK VOL.1
You can't touch me: *Pollack, Karen & Fire Island* / U: *Clark, Loni* / I know a place: *English, Kim* / Back to love: *Brand New Heavies* / I believe: *Sounds Of Blackness* / Another sleepness night: *Christopher, Shawn* / Lost in love: *Up Yer Ronson* / Where love lives: *Limerick, Alison* / Lover: *Roberts, Joe* / Keep the jam goin': *Ill Disco* / Nite life: *English, Kim* / Colour of my skin: *Swing 52* / Gimmie luv: *Bad Yard Club* / Real: *Allen, Donna* / Take me back to love: *Sledge, Kathy* / Mings incredible disco machine: *Brothers Love Dubs* / All over me: *Carr, Suzi* / Blow your whistle: *DJ Duke* / Dreamer: *Livin' Joy* / Theme from Outrage: *Outrage* / On the dance floor: *DJ Disciple* / U girls: *Nush* / Will you love me in the morning: *Mollison, Sam* / Get yourself together: *Hustlers Convention* / Someday: *M-People* / 100% pure: *Waters, Crystal* / Renegade master: *Wildchild* / On ya way: *Helicopter* / Everybody dance: *Evolution*
CD _______________ 5350762
Hi-Life / Nov '95 / PolyGram

UP YER RONSON - THE SUMMER OF NINETY SIX (3CD Set)
Come back to love: *Mr. Happy* / Skyplus: *Nylon Moon* / Nightrain: *Kadoc* / Klubbhopping: *Klubb Heads* / Heartbeat: *Somerville, Jimmy* / Up side my head: *Funkysensual* / Howler: *HMM* / Fire: *Belief* / Indica: *Movin' Melodies* / Bring me luv: *Crystal* / Disco frenzy: *Divine Intervention* / Access: *DJ Misjah & Tim* / I'm coming hardcore: *MANIC* / Goodtimes: *Funkydory* / Groovy beat: *DOP* / Desire: *Nu Colours* / Movin': *Mone* / Reach: *Lil' Mo' Yin Yang* / Giv me luv: *Alcatraz* / Heaven: *Washington, Sarah* / Imperial grooves: *Musaphia, Joey* / Freedom: *Black Magic* / Let me take you away: *Temperance* / Stand up: *Love Tribe* / Never stop: *Reflexion & Laura Alford* / Find our way: *Key To Life* / Lover that you are: *Pulse* / Are you gonna be there: *Up yer Ronson & Mary Pearce* / Are you with me love: *Elements Of Life* / Now when I see you: *Nordenstam, Stina* / Bee charmer: *Schroeder, Ingrid* / King of Woolworths: *Exact Life* / Doesn't mean that much to me: *Eg & Alice* / Kant kino: *Simple Minds* / Dream beam: *Hypnotone* / Latin joint: *Baby Buddah Heads* / Ending: *Eno, Brian* / Gulls 'n' bouys: *Adam & Eve Project* / Siolim: *Small Fish With Spine* / Three steps to Heaven: *Beloved* / Dream time: *Jackson* / Killing: *Olive*
CD Set _______________ 5332422
Hi-Life / Oct '96 / PolyGram

UPPERS ON THE SOUTH DOWNS
CD _______________ DOJOCD 196
Dojo / Nov '94 / Disc

UPTOWN, DOWN SOUTH
I've got to hold back / Sweetest girl in the world / Judy / That's loving you / I'm not your regular woman / Since I met you baby / Don't let our love fade away / Even if the signs are wrong / Childhood days / Just another guy / Bigger and better / Cryin' days are over / Save a foolish man / That's my man / No more tears / Set your soul on fire / Our love is getting better / Crystal blue persuasion / What price for love / Thanks a lot / I would if I could / Keep on running away / Running away from love / Just the other day

CD CDKEND 121
Kent / Feb '95 / Pinnacle

URAL: TRADITIONAL MUSIC FROM BASHKORTOSTAN
CD PAN 2018CD
Pan / Mar '95 / ADA / CM / Direct

URBAN DANCE CLASSICS VOL.1
CD URCD 001
Urban Dance / May '97 / Essential/BMG

URBAN ESSENCE (3LP Set)
CD Set DUGCD 1
De Underground / Feb '97 / Jet Star / SRD

URBAN SHAKEDOWN (Flavour Records Presents Over One Hour Of R 'n' B Killers)
Can't hang: *Xscape* / Tonight: *Shai* / Stay with me: *Weaver, Jason* / Touch myself: *T-Box* / Stressed out: *Tribe Called Quest* / Floatin' on your love: *Isley Brothers* / Think of you: *Usher* / No diggity: *Blackstreet* / Just the way: *Hunter, Alfonzo* / How we stay: *Lesha* / Rhyme: *Murray, Keith* / Movin on: *Peniston, Ce Ce* / Forget I was a G: *Whitehead Brothers* / Do thangz: *Men O Vision* / Tell me: *Groove Theory* / Realize: *Weaver, Jason* / Get up: *Masters At Work* / Lover in you: *Baby Face* / Every little thing: *Soul For Real* / Get money: *Junior MAFIA*
CD URB 001CD
Flavour / Jan '97 / Timewarp

URBAN SYMPHONIES
CD BUMPCD 001
Bumpin' / Jul '96 / Timewarp

US HOMEGROWN (2CD Set)
CD Set OPD 30011
Outpost Recordings / Jul '97 / BMG

UZLYAU (Music Of The Tuva, Sayan, Altai & Urals)
CD PAN 2019CD
Pan / Jan '94 / ADA / CM / Direct

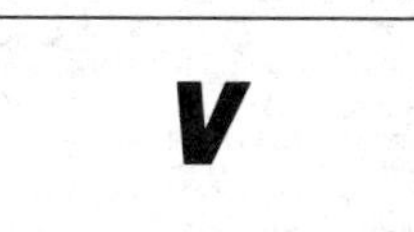

V AS IN VICTIM
CD AVANT 027CD
Avant / Oct '94 / Cadillac / Harmonia Mundi

V CLASSICS (3CD Set)
Maintain: *DJ Krust* / It's jazzy: *Roni Size* / Calling: *Goldie* / War and peace: *DJ Die & Suv* / Blaze dis one: *DJ Krust* / Change: *Lemon D* / Reckoning: *Keith, Ray* / On time: *DJ Die* / Only a dream: *Roni Size* / Li-li: *Scorpio* / Unexplored terrain: *Dillinja*
CD Set VECD 01
V / Apr '97 / SRD

V DISC COLLECTION (4CD Set)
CD Set 269032
Milan / Dec '95 / Conifer/BMG / Silva Screen

V DISC COLLECTION VOL.1 (The Big Bands)
CD 269042
Milan / Jun '95 / Conifer/BMG / Silva Screen

V DISC COLLECTION VOL.2 (Combos & Soloists)
CD 269052
Milan / Jun '95 / Conifer/BMG / Silva Screen

V DISC COLLECTION VOL.3 (The Singers)
CD 269062
Milan / Jun '95 / Conifer/BMG / Silva Screen

VALIS 2 (Everything Must Go/2CD Set)
33: *Laswell, Bill* / Angry lone nut: *Babu* / In there: *Scorn* / Cab iii: *DXT* / Black loop: *SIMM* / World of destruction: *Spectre & Dr. Israel* / Trawl/Disappearance: *Scanner* / I wanna be like Ike: *Full Cone* / Dustbuster: *Shining Path* / L'insigne des pires: *APC* / Sepolta: *Full Cone & Buckethead* / Hip hop pooray 19-poo-96: *Ohtake, Shinro* / Explicit sound: *We Olive & L Loop/Once II* / Beaver claus: *Disk* / Metal beat 2: *DXT* / Atoms to suns: *Laswell, Bill* / Twirling: *Him* / Perfect shadow: *SIMM* / Advice from God on getting a face: *Corporal Blossom* / Rockin' it: *Torture* / Metatron dub: *Praxis* / Peanut: *Full Cone* / Phonoprophic: *Electric Soul* / Letter be: *Buckethead* / Ananvoice: *Junexxon S*
CD Set ION 2002
Ion / Mar '97 / ADA / Cargo

VALLENATO, THE (Traditional Music From Colombia)
CD C 560093
Ocora / Nov '96 / ADA / Harmonia Mundi

VALLEY AND PAMPAS
CD PS 65152
PlayaSound / Sep '95 / ADA / Harmonia Mundi

VALLEY OF DEATH
CD VPCD 1443
VP / Nov '95 / Greensleeves / Jet Star / Total/BMG

VALLEY RECALLS VOL.1, THE (Love Peace And Harmony)
CD NRCD 0066
Navras / Jul '96 / New Note/Pinnacle

VALLEY RECALLS VOL.2, THE (Raga Bhoopali)
CD NRCD 0067
Navras / Jul '96 / New Note/Pinnacle

VALLEYS SING, THE
Old rugged cross / Love divine / Day thou gavest Lord is ended / All in the April evening / Guide me o thou great / Jehovah / Where you there / What a friend we have in Jehovah / Lord's prayer / Give thanks / There is a redeemer / Majesty / Steal away / Kymbayah / Abide with me / Onward Christian soldiers / When I survey the wondrous cross / You'll never walk alone / Praise my soul the king of heaven
CD WSTCD 9725
Nelson Word / Apr '92 / Nelson Word

VAMPIRE THEMES
CD CLP 0003
Cleopatra / Jun '97 / Cargo / Greyhound / Plastic Head / RTM/Disc / SRD

VAMPIROS LESBOS: SEXADELIC DANCE PARTY
CD EFA 119502
Crippled Dick Hot Wax / Aug '96 / SRD

VAMPYRES (6CD Set)
CD Set DTKBIG 5160
Dressed To Kill / May '97 / Total/BMG

VANGUARD BLUES SAMPLER
CD VMD 74002
Vanguard / Oct '96 / ADA / Pinnacle

VANGUARD DANCE CLASSICS
CD VMD 79487
Vanguard / Oct '96 / ADA / Pinnacle

VANGUARD FOLK SAMPLER
CD VMD 74001
Vanguard / Oct '96 / ADA / Pinnacle

VANGUARD NEWPORT FOLK FESTIVAL SAMPLER
CD VMD 74003
Vanguard / Oct '96 / ADA / Pinnacle

VANGUARD SAMPLER, THE (A Collection Of Folk, Country, Blues & Rock)
Walk right in: *Rooftop Singers* / Old train: *Dillards* / All the pretty little horses: *Odetta* / Swallow song: *Farina, Richard & Mimi* / Goodnight Irene: *Weavers* / Leaving of Liverpool: *Clancy Brothers* / Saro Jane: *Kingston Trio* / Universal soldier: *Sainte-Marie, Buffy* / Come all ye fair and tender ladies: *Ian & Sylvia* / Did you hear John Hurt: *Paxton, Tom* / Sassy Mama: *Thornton, Willie Mae 'Big Mama'* / Turn, turn, turn, (to everything there is a season): *Collins, Judy* / Over in the gloryland: *Kentucky Colonels* / My buddy buddy friends: *Musselwhite, Charley* / Mystery train: *Wells, Junior* / Corrinna Corrinna: *Hurt, 'Mississippi' John* / So many road, so many trains: *Hammond, John* / I feel like I'm fixing to die rag: *Country Joe & The Fish* / Lady Coryell: *Coryell, Larry* / Rock 'n' roll music: *Frost*
CD VCD 001
Vanguard / Jun '97 / ADA / Pinnacle

VANITY
Funk phenomena: *Van Helden, Armand* / Keep on jumpin': *Fruit Loops 2* / Nervous breakdown: *Constance* / Love's gonna get you: *Modernique & Larry Wood* / Drillzone: *GAME* / Just be good to me: *Groove Box & Leena Marie* / I just can't stop it: *Rim 'n' Stuff* / Happy days: *Aquarius Recordings* / Got to get up: *DJ Tonka* / Feel's alright: *Nightbreed* / Shake it: *Adam P* / Ain't missing: *Pancake* / Strut your funky stuff: *No Box*
CD MOC 59482
Mocca / Feb '97 / Amato Disco

VARIACOES EM FADO
CD KAR 986
IMP / Oct '96 / ADA / Discovery

VARIATIONS ON A CHILL (2CD Set)
CD Set SSR 147
SSR / Aug '95 / Amato Disco / Grapevine/ PolyGram / Prime / RTM/Disc

VARIOUS AMBIENT COLLABORATIONS
CD RSNCD 11
Rising High / Oct '93 / 3mv/Sony

VARIOUS ANTHEMS (Tunes Vol.1)
CD DANCECD 002
D-Zone / May '92 / Pinnacle

VASSAR
CD KFWCD 120
Knitting Factory / Nov '94 / Cargo / Plastic Head

VAULT CLASSICS VOL.1
CD DGVCD 2023
Dynamite & Grapevine / Jun '93 / Grapevine/PolyGram / Greensleeves / Jet Star

VAULTAGE PUNK COLLECTION
Jilly: *Piranhas* / Virginity: *Piranhas* / Tension: *Piranhas* / Girls get nervous: *Nicky & The Dots* / Wrong street: *Nicky & The Dots* / Lord Lucan is missing: *Dodgems* / Elvis is dead: *Peter & The Test Tube Babies* / Bank holidays: *Vandells* / Bloody: *Golinski Brothers* / Nervous wreck: *Lillettes* / Hey operator: *Lillettes* / I want to be my girl: *Woody & The Splinters* / Sweetie: *Chefs* / Thrush: *Chefs* / Happy families: *Piranhas* / 24 hours: *Chefs* / Let's make u: *Chefs* / Sinking gondola: *Exclusives* / Extradition: *Reward system*
CD CDPUNK 101
Anagram / Sep '97 / Cargo / Pinnacle

VE DAY - THE DANCE BANDS
Germany surrenders: *Churchill, Winston* / I've got a heart filled with love: *Preager, Lou & His Band* / Together: *Weir, Frank & His Astor Club Seven* / Marlene: *Loss, Joe & His Orchestra* / If I had only known: *Geraldo & His Orchestra* / Opus one: *Heath, Ted & His Music* / Sitting on a cloud: *Simpson, Jack & His Sextet* / Swinging on a star: *Geraldo & His Orchestra* / Barrelhouse boogie: *Roy, Harry & His Band* / So dumb but so beautiful: *Geraldo & His Orchestra* / Shine on harvest moon: *Geraldo & His Orchestra* / You're in love: *Preager, Lou & His Band* / Don't sweetheart me: *Geraldo & His Orchestra* / It had to be you: *Loss, Joe & His Orchestra* / Dance with a Dolly: *Ambrose & His Orchestra* / Time on my hands: *Gonella, Nat & His Georgians* / Someday I'll meet you again: *Geraldo & His Orchestra* / What do you think those ruby lips were made for: *Thorburn, Billy & Robinson Cleaver* / That's sabotage: *Geraldo & His Orchestra* / Don't ask me why: *Gibbons, Carroll & The Savoy Hotel Orpheans* / Undecided: *Silvester, Victor & His Jive Orchestra* / Amor amor: *Ambrose & His Orchestra* / I'll get by: *Barriteau, Carl & his Orchestra* / You'll be a happy little sweetheart in the spring: *Cotton, Billy & His Band* / I'm going to build a future world around you: *Geraldo & His Orchestra*
CD RAJCD 844
Empress / Feb '95 / Koch

VE DAY - THE OFFICIAL BRITISH LEGION COLLECTION (2CD Set)
Run rabbit run: *Flanagan & Allen* / We'll meet again: *Lynn, Vera* / (We're gonna hang out the) washing on the Siegfried Line: *Cotton, Billy & His Band* / Over the rainbow: *Garland, Judy* / In the mood: *Loss, Joe Band* / Boys in the backroom: *Dietrich, Marlene* / If I had my way: *Crosby, Bing* / Nightingale sang in Berkley Square: *Hutchinson, Leslie 'Hutch'* / Beer barrel polka: *Andrews Sisters* / I'll never smile again: *Dorsey, Tommy* / I've got sixpence: *Organ Dance Band & Me* / Room 504: *Hale, Binnie* / Last time I saw paris: *Coward, Noel* / Frensi: *Shaw, Artie Orchestra* / Beneath the lights of home: *Geraldo* / I yi yi yi yi (I like you very much): *Miranda, Carmen* / London pride: *Coward, Noel* / Yours: *Lynn, Vera* / American patrol: *Loss, Joe Band* / Anniversary waltz: *Crosby, Bing* / You made me love you: *Foster, Teddy* / White cliffs of Dover: *Lynn, Vera* / I don't want to walk without you: *Gibbons, Carroll* / You are my sunshine: *Crosby, Bing* / Don't sit under the apple tree: *Andrews Sisters* / Chattanooga choo choo: *Miller, Glenn* / Deep in the heart of Texas: *Crosby, Bing* / Silver wings in the moonlight: *Shelton, Anne* / Whispering grass: *Ink Spots* / Moonlight becomes you: *Crosby, Bing* / Praise the Lord and pass the ammunition: *Macs, Merry* / As time goes by: *Layton, Turner* / Begin the beguine: *Haywood, Eddie* / I had the craziest dream: *Gibbons, Carroll* / I'm gonna get lit up (when the lights go on in London): *Loss, Joe Band* / Coming in on a wing and a prayer: *Ambrose* / Tico tico: *Smith, Ethel* / You'll never know: *Haymes, Dick* / This is the army Mr. Jones: *Berlin, Irving* / Besame mucho: *Dorsey, Jimmy* / Roll me over: *Cotton, Billy & His Band* / Paper doll: *Mills Brothers* / Lovely way to spend an evening: *Gibbons, Carroll* / I'll be seeing you: *Crosby, Bing* / Lili Marlene: *Shelton, Anne* / Swinging on a star: *Crosby, Bing* / No love, no nothin': *Carless, Dorothy* / Dance with a dolly: *Geraldo & His Dance Orchestra* / Jukebox Saturday night: *Miller, Glenn* / My guy's come home: *Loss, Joe*
CD Set CDEM 1549
EMI / Apr '95 / EMI

VE DAY - THE VOCALISTS
Victory: *Churchill, Winston* / There's a new world: *Lynn, Vera* / Shine on Victory moon: *Bonn, Issy* / It's been a long, long time: *Hall, Adelaide* / Let me love you tonight: *Melachrino, George* / I got it bad and that ain't good: *Davis, Beryl* / (All of a sudden) My heart sings: *Hall, Adelaide* / Goodnight wherever you are: *Green, Johnny* / It could happen to you: *Lynn, Vera* / Tonight I kissed you: *Shelton, Anne* / Come out come out where ever you are: *Green, Johnny* / Don't believe everything you dream: *Bonn, Issy* / Then you kissed me: *Green, Johnny* / Long ago and far away: *Lynn, Vera* / You're in love: *Peers, Donald* / Pistol packin' Mama: *Dennis, Johnny* / Shine on harvest moon: *Flanagan & Allen* / In a friendly little harbour: *Layton, Turner* / It's love love love: *Morrow, Dorothy* / Dreaming: *Flanagan & Allen* / Lili Marlene: *Shelton, Anne* / MacNamara's band: *Morrow, Dorothy* / Dare I love you: *Hutchinson, Leslie 'Hutch'* / Things that mean so much to me: *Bonn, Issy* / Fool with a dream: *O'Connor, Cavan*
CD RAJCD 845
Empress / Feb '95 / Koch

VE DAY MUSICAL TRIBUTE - NOW IS THE HOUR
CD VEDAY 1945
Start / Feb '97 / Disc

VE DAY PARTY
CD PASTCD 7063
Flapper / May '95 / Pinnacle

VEDIC PRESENTS RHYTHMIC INTELLIGENCE
CD SR 123CD
Sub Rosa / Jul '97 / Direct / RTM/Disc / SRD / Vital

VEE JAY STORY, THE (2CD Set)
CD Set CDLAB 104
Charly / Apr '96 / Koch

VERABRA RETROSPECTIVE '80/'90
Bob the bob: *Lounge Lizards* / Minha rua: *Xiame* / Sundown: *Cerletti, Marco* / Pipeland: *Schaffer, Janne* / Bagus: *Toshiyuki Honda* / Act natural: *Grolnick, Don* / DUV: *De Winkel & Hattler* / Yellow fellow: *Mynta* / No name: *Von Senger, Dominik* / Algodoal: *Herting, Mike* / Flamencos en Nueva York: *Nunez, Gerardo* / Lilo and Max: *De Winkel, Torsten* / Azure treasure: *Shlomo Bat-Ain* / Cousin butterfly: *Never Been There* / Joyride: *Thompson, Barbara Paraphernalia* / At the top of the hill: *Marsh, Hug* / De sabado pra dominguinhes: *Pascoal, Hermeto*
CD VBR 20402
Vera Bra / Nov '90 / New Note/Pinnacle / Pinnacle

VERSION 1.1
CD NOMU 17CD
Mute / Oct '93 / RTM/Disc

VERVE JAZZ MASTERS SAMPLER
CD 5198532
Verve / Apr '93 / PolyGram

VERVE'S GRAMMY WINNERS
CD 5214852
Verve / May '94 / PolyGram

VERY BEST OF BLUES GUITAR, THE
CD VBCD 306
Charly / Jan '96 / Koch

VERY BEST OF BRASS BANDS, THE
Puttin' on the ritz: *Britannia Building Society Foden Band* / Over the rainbow: *Williams-Fairey Engineering Band* / You'll never walk alone: *Britannia Building Society Foden Band* / Gladiator's farewell: *Williams-Fairey Engineering Band* / Tea for two: *Britannia Building Society Foden Band* / Solveig's song: *Britannia Building Society Foden Band* / Pretty girl is like a melody: *Britannia Building Society Foden Band* / Dance of the comedians: *Sun Life Band* / Sorcerer's apprentice: *Sun Life Band* / Folk festival: *Williams-Fairey Engineering Band* / Swing low, sweet chariot: *Williams-Fairey Engineering Band* / Fest musik der stadt Wien: *Williams-Fairey Engineering Band* / Tritsch tratsch polka: *Williams-Fairey Engineering Band*
CD 3036000772
Carlton / Feb '97 / Carlton

VERY BEST OF BRITISH FOLK, THE
CD NTMCD 544
Nectar / Jun '97 / Pinnacle

VERY BEST OF CAJUN, THE (2CD Set)
CD Set DINCD 127
Dino / Aug '96 / Pinnacle

VERY BEST OF COUNTRY, THE
CD AHLCD 23
Hit / Sep '94 / Grapevine/PolyGram

VERY BEST OF IRISH CEILI MUSIC, THE
CD CHCD 1039
Chyme / Aug '94 / ADA / CM / Direct / Koch

VERY BEST OF IRISH COUNTRY, THE
Come down the mountain Katie Daly: *Duncan, Hugo* / Cottage by the lee: *Cunningham, Larry* / Village in County Tyrone: *Begley, Philomena* / Sweet forget me not: *Anderson, Big Jim* / Among the Wicklow hills: *Ely, Pat* / Travellin' people: *McCann, Susan* / Galway Bay: *O'Donnell, Daniel* / Three leaf shamrock from Greenore: *Margo* / Road to Malinmore: *Henry, Bernhard* / Little country town in Ireland: *Glenn, John* / Donegal shore: *O'Donnell, Daniel* / Old cross of Ardboe: *Begley, Philomena* / Lovely Derry: *Cunningham, Larry* / Time is rolling on: *Henry, Bernhard* / Rose of Allendale: *Woods, Pat* / Old Claddagh ring: *Margo* / Any Tipperary town: *Ely, Pat* / Rose of Tralee: *McCann, Susan* / Boys from the County Armagh: *Glenn, John* / Westmeath bachelor: *Duncan, Hugo* / Alice is in wonderland: *Kirwan, Dominic*
CD CDIRISH 011
Outlet / May '97 / ADA / CM / Direct / Duncans / Koch / Ross

VERY BEST OF IRISH FOLK, THE (2CD Set)
CD Set DCDCD 203
Castle / Jun '95 / BMG

VERY BEST OF SUN ROCK 'N' ROLL, THE
Whole lotta shakin' goin' on: *Lewis, Jerry Lee* / Ain't got a thing: *Burgess, Sonny* / Boppin' the blues: *Perkins, Carl* / Devil doll: *Orbison, Roy* / Red hot: *Riley, Billy Lee* / Got love if you want it: *Smith, Warren* / All night rock: *Honeycutt, Glenn* / Love my baby: *Thompson, Hayden* / Flatfoot Sam: *Blake, Tommy* / Love crazy baby: *Parchman, Kenny* / Put your cat clothes on: *Perkins, Carl* / Baby, please don't go: *Riley, Billy Lee* / Wild one: *Lewis, Jerry Lee* / Domino: *Orbison, Roy* / My bucket's got a hole in it: *Burgess, Sonny* / Blue suede shoes: *Perkins, Carl* / Come on little mama: *Harris, Ray* / Ubangi stomp: *Smith, Warren* / Break up: *Smith, Ray* / Madman: *Wages, Jimmy* / We wanna boogie: *Burgess, Sonny* / That don't move me: *Perkins, Carl*
CD ________________ **MCCD 024**
Music Club / May '91 / Disc / THE

VERY BEST OF SUN ROCKABILLY, THE (2CD Set)
CD Set ________________ **CDGR 1412**
Charly / Apr '97 / Koch

VERY BEST OF TEXAS BLUES PIANO, THE
CD ________________ **WCD 120629**
Wolf / Jul '97 / Hot Shot / Jazz Music / Swift

VERY BEST OF THE FESTIVALS OF 1000 WELSH MALE VOICES, THE
Llanfair / Ar hyd y nos / Rhyfelgyrch gwyr Harlech (Men of Harlech) / Cyfri'r geifr / Laudamus / Deus salutis / Silver birch / tydi a roddaist / Crimond / Dies irae / Go down Moses / Chorus of the Hebrew slaves / Pilgrims chorus / Nile chorus / O Isis and Osiris / Sailor's chorus / Soldier's chorus / Roman war song / Battle hymn of the Republic / Myfanwy / Cwm Rhondda / Hen wlad fy nhadau (Land of my fathers)
CD ________________ **CDEMS 1448**
EMI / May '92 / EMI

VERY BEST OF WELSH MALE CHOIRS, THE (Goreuon Corau Meibion Cymru)
Arwelfa: *United Choirs* / Now the day is over: *LLanelli Choir* / Y goedwig werdd: *Godre'r Aran Choir* / Deep harmony: *Pendyrus Choir* / Last words of David: *United Choirs* / With a voice of singing: *Cwmbach Choir* / Ol' arks a-moverin: *Trelawnyd Choir* / Lost chord: *Pontarddulais Male Voice Choir* / Pilgrim's chorus: *United Choirs* / Iechyd da: *Rhos Male Voice Choir* / Gloria: *Pendyrus Choir & Cory Band* / Kwmbayah: *Trelawnyd Choir* / Gwn Dafydd Ifan: *Twm O'r Nant Choir* / Amen: *United Choirs* / Pie Jesu: *LLanelli Choir* / Bandit's chorus: *Cwmbach Choir* / Ar derfyn dydd: *Godre'r Aran Choir* / Where shall I be: *Pontarddulais Male Voice Choir* / Love could I only tell thee: *Rhos Male Voice Choir* / Mae d'eisiau di bob awr: *United Choirs*
CD ________________ **SCD 2012**
Sain / Nov '96 / ADA / Direct / Greyhound

VERY NOSTALGIC CHRISTMAS, A (The 1930/1940's)
White Christmas: *Crosby, Bing* / Winter wonderland: *Walsh & Parker* / I'm sending a letter to Santa Claus: *Robins, Phyllis* / God rest ye merry gentlemen: *Crosby, Bing* / Fairy on the Christmas tree: *Hall, Henry Orchestra* / Little boy that Santa Claus forgot: *Tracy, Arthur* / Silent night: *Langford, Frances* / O come all ye faithful (Adeste Fidelis): *Langford, Frances* / Christmas bells at Eventide: *Fields, Gracie* / Jingle bells: *Miller, Glenn* / I'm spending Christmas with the old folks: *Rabin, Oscar* / Christmas bells are ringing: *Winn, Max* / Santa Claus express: *Wilbur, Jay* / I'm going home for Christmas: *Hall, Henry Orchestra* / I took my harp to a party: *Fields, Gracie* / Jolly old Christmas: *Cotton, Billy* / Cradle song: *Miller, Glenn* / Ave Maria: *Lynn, Vera* / Good morning blues: *Lynn, Vera* / Aladdin - A potty pantomime: *Payne, Jack*
CD ________________ **RAJCD 839**
Empress / Nov '96 / Koch

VERY SERIOUS SMOKIN' VOL.2
CD ________________ **GR 101012**
Gravity / Dec '96 / Shellshock/Disc

VERY SPECIAL CHRISTMAS VOL.1, A
Santa Claus is coming to town: *Pointer Sisters* / Winter Wonderland: *Eurythmics* / Do you hear what I say: *Houston, Whitney* / Merry Christmas baby: *Springsteen, Bruce & The E Street Band* / Have yourself a merry little Christmas: *Pretenders* / I saw Mommy kissing Santa Claus: *Mellencamp, John Cougar* / Gabriel's message: *Sting* / Christmas in Hollis: *Run DMC* / Christmas (baby please come home): *U2* / Santa baby: *Madonna* / Little drummer boy: *Seger, Bob & The Silver Bullet Band* / Run Rudolph run: *Adams, Bryan* / Back door Santa: *Bon Jovi* / Coventry carol: *Moyet, Alison* / Silent night: *Nicks, Stevie*
CD ________________ **CDA 3911**
A&M / Nov '94 / PolyGram

VERY SPECIAL CHRISTMAS VOL.2, A
Christmas all over again: *Petty, Tom & The Heartbreakers* / Jingle bell rock: *Travis, Randy* / Christmas song: *Vandross, Luther* / Santa Claus is coming to town: *Sinatra, Frank & Cyndi Lauper* / Birth of Christ: *Boyz II Men* / Please come home for Christmas: *Bon Jovi, Jon* / What Christmas means to me: *Young, Paul* / O Christmas tree: *Franklin, Aretha* / Rockin' around the Christmas tree: *Spector, Ronnie & Darlene Love* / White Christmas: *Bolton, Michael* / Christmas is: *Run DMC* / Christmas time again: *Extreme* / Merry Christmas baby: *Raitt, Bonnie & Charles Brown* / O holy night: *Campbell, Tevin* / Sleigh ride: *Gibson, Debbie* / What child is this: *Williams, Vanessa* / Blue Christmas: *Wilson, A.N.* / Silent night: *Wilson Phillips* / I believe in you: *O'Connor, Sinead*
CD ________________ **5400032**
A&M / Nov '95 / PolyGram

VERY THOUGHT OF YOU, THE (18 Croonin' Love Songs)
Portrait of my love: *Monro, Matt* / That's amore: *Martin, Dean* / I love you because: *Martino, Al* / Wind beneath my wings: *Tarmey, Bill* / (They long to be) close to you: *Hill, Vince* / You're getting to be a habit with me: *Torme, Mel* / Nightingale sang in Berkley square: *Darin, Bobby* / Till there was you: *Damone, Vic* / On the street where you live: *Hilton, Ronnie* / My funny valentine: *MacRae, Gordon* / Stairway of love: *Holliday, Michael* / Sweet Lorraine: *Monro, Matt* / All I do is dream of you: *Martin, Dean* / May I have the next dream with you: *Roberts, Malcolm* / Roses of Picardy: *Darin, Bobby* / True love: *Crosby, Bing* / Story of my life: *Holliday, Michael* / Very thought of you: *Haymes, Dick*
CD ________________ **CDMFP 6282**
Music For Pleasure / Jan '97 / EMI

VETERAN COMPILATION
CD ________________ **VTC 1**
Veteran Tapes / Jun '93 / ADA / Direct

VIA UFO TO MERCURY
CD ________________ **ALP 84CD**
Atavistic / Jan '97 / Cargo / SRD

VIBE MUSIC - THE SOULFUL SOUND OF CHICAGO
CD ________________ **PLUGCD 2**
Produce / Jul '95 / 3mv/Sony

VIBE VOL.1 (The Sound Of Swing)
Love no limit: *Blige, Mary J.* / Realize: *Wilson, Charlie* / That's the way love is: *Brown, Bobby* / If you feel the need: *Shomari* / I like your style: *Bubba* / Don't keep me waiting: *Rhythm Within* / Real love: *Lorenzo* / One night stand: *Father MC* / Do you wanna chill with me: *Solid State Sound* / Yo - that's a lot of body: *Ready For The World* / Baby, baby, baby: *TLC* / Right here: *SWV* / Helluva: *Brotherhood Creed* / I dream, I dream: *Jackson, Jermaine*
CD ________________ **CDELV 07**
Elevate / Jul '93 / 3mv/Sony

VIBE VOL.2
Skip to my Lu: *Lisa Lisa* / Back and forth: *Aaliyah* / Satisfy you: *Hall, Damion* / All through the night: *POV* / Oh my God: *Tribe Called Quest* / You told me: *Motiv* / Want U back: *Me 2 U* / Are you free: *Mint Condition* / In my nature: *Nuttin' Nyce* / Tell me I'm not dreaming: *Titiyo* / She's playing hard to get: *Hi-Five* / Show me you love me: *Serenade* / 69: *Father* / Get with you tonight: *Montage*
CD ________________ **CDELV 17**
Elevate / Jun '94 / 3mv/Sony

VICTIMS OF HOUSE (3CD Set)
CD Set ________________ **TCD 09247182**
SPV / Mar '97 / Koch / Plastic Head

VICTORIAN MUSICAL BOXES
CD ________________ **CDSDL 408**
Saydisc / Sep '94 / ADA / Direct / Harmonia Mundi

VICTORIAN SUNDAY, A
Abide with me / Judas Maccabaeus / Lost chord / When I survey the wondrous cross / How sweet the name of Jesus sounds / Lead kindly light / Nearer my god to thee / Shall we meet beyond the river / Only an armour bearer / I will sing of my redeemer / Scatter seeds of kindness / Shall we gather at the river / Beaulah land / Hold City / Morning hymn / Evening hymn / Onward Christian Soldiers / Rescue the perishing / What shall the harvest be / We'll work 'til Jesus comes / Washed in the blood of the lamb / What a friend we have in Jesus / Sicilian mariners / Helmsley / Luther's hymn / London new / Mountain Ephraim / God save the Queen
CD ________________ **CDSDL 331**
Saydisc / Oct '91 / ADA / Direct / Harmonia Mundi

VICTORY STYLE
CD ________________ **VR 033CD**
Victory / Apr '96 / Plastic Head

VIENNATONE
Speechless drum and bass: *Count Basic* / Nova schuhu: *Bask* / Chocolate Elvis: *Tosca* / East West (et moi): *Mama Oliver* / Each and everyday: *Potuznik & Sokol* / Resistance: *Blackwing* / Hawk: *Planet E.* / A1: *Farmers Manual* / Sit dub: *Huber, Alois* / Connection: *Showroom Recording Series* / Family affair: *Dannin, Puck*
CD ________________ **K7 055CD**
Studio K7 / May '97 / Prime / RTM/Disc

VIETNAM - THE DAN TRANH
CD ________________ **C 560055CD**
Ocora / Aug '94 / ADA / Harmonia Mundi

VIETNAM - TRADITION DU SUD
CD ________________ **C 580043**
Ocora / Nov '92 / ADA / Harmonia Mundi

VILE VIBES
CD ________________ **CDVILE 15**
Peaceville / Feb '90 / Pinnacle

VILLAGE MUSIC (Songs & Dances From Bosnia/Croatia/Macedonia)
CD ________________ **7559720422**
Nonesuch / Jan '95 / Warner Music

VINE YARD REVIVAL SERIES VOL.1
CD ________________ **VYDCD 1**
Vine Yard / Sep '95 / Grapevine/PolyGram

VINE YARD REVIVAL SERIES VOL.2
CD ________________ **VYCD 010**
Vine Yard / Jul '96 / Grapevine/PolyGram

VINTAGE BANDS, THE
Music, Maestro, please: *Hylton, Jack & His Orchestra* / Alexander's ragtime band: *Roy, Harry & His Orchestra* / Nagasaki: *Gonella, Nat & His Georgians* / Nobody loves a fairy when she's forty: *Cotton, Billy & His Band* / My brother makes the noises for the talkies: *Payne, Jack & The BBC Dance Orchestra* / Stay as sweet as you are: *Stone, Lew & His Orchestra* / In the mood: *Loss, Joe & His Orchestra* / Let's face the music and dance: *Fox, Roy & His Orchestra* / Nightingale sang in Berkeley Square: *Gibbons, Carroll & The Savoy Hotel Orpheans* / Dancing in the dark: *Ambrose* / Here's to the next time: *Hall, Henry & The BBC Dance Orchestra* / Say it with music: *Payne, Jack & The BBC Dance Orchestra* / I'm gonna get lit up (when the lights go on in London): *Gibbons, Carroll & The Savoy Hotel Orpheans* / Change partners: *Loss, Joe & His Orchestra* / Did you ever see a dream walking: *Hall, Henry & The BBC Dance Orchestra* / Shine: *Cotton, Billy & His Band* / She had to go and lose it at the Astor: *Roy, Harry & His Orchestra* / Easy to remember: *Stone, Lew & His Orchestra* / Have you met Miss Jones: *Hylton, Jack & His Orchestra* / I can't dance: *Gonella, Nat & His Georgians* / Night is young and you're so beautiful: *Fox, Roy & His Orchestra* / Let's put out the lights: *Ambrose*
CD ________________ **CC 206**
Music For Pleasure / May '88 / EMI

VINTAGE CHRISTMAS, A
Little boy that Santa Claus forgot / Winter wonderland / Gracie Fields' christmas party / I'm sending a letter to Santa Claus / Gert and Daisy make a christmas pudding / Silent night / I'm going home for christmas / Christmas in the rockies / Gracie with the Air Force at christmas / Santa Claus express / Lambeth walk christmas party / O come all ye faithful (Adeste Fidelis) / Christmas bells at eventide / Robinson cleaver's christmas medley / White Christmas
CD ________________ **PASTCD 9768**
Flapper / Nov '91 / Pinnacle

VINTAGE COUNTRY
My little lady: *Rodgers, Jimmie* / Daddy and home: *Rodgers, Jimmie* / Waiting for a train: *Rodgers, Jimmie* / Any old time: *Rodgers, Jimmie* / Back in the saddle again: *Autry, Gene* / It makes no difference now: *Autry, Gene* / You are my sunshine: *Autry, Gene* / Time changes everything: *Wills, Bob & His Texas Playboys* / New San Antonio Rose: *Wills, Bob & His Texas Playboys* / Take me back to Tulsa: *Wills, Bob & His Texas Playboys* / Great speckled bird: *Acuff, Roy & His Smokey Mountain Boys* / Night train to Memphis: *Acuff, Roy & His Smokey Mountain Boys* / Wreck on the highway: *Acuff, Roy & His Smokey Mountain Boys* / Mule skinner blues: *Monroe, Bill & His Bluegrass Boys* / No letter in the mail: *Monroe, Bill & His Bluegrass Boys* / Orange blossom special: *Monroe, Bill & His Bluegrass Boys*
CD ________________ **HADCD 161**
Javelin / May '94 / Henry Hadaway / THE

VINTAGE JAZZ VOL.12
Struttin' with some barbecue / Hotter than that / Muskrat ramble / Wild man blues / New Orleans shout / Stinagree blues / West End blues / Edna / Henderson stomp / St. Louis shuffle / Easy money / King Porter stomp / My melancholy baby / Beale Street blues
CD ________________ **CDSGPBJZ 23**
Prestige / May '96 / Cadillac / Complete/ Pinnacle

VINTAGE JAZZ VOL.13
So mnay times / Peg o' my heart / Swingin' on the Teagarden gate / Can't we talk it over / Melancholy blues / West End blues / Knockin' a jug / St. Louis blues / Flat hat blues / Tenor king / Swingin' at Milts / Begin the beguine / Donkey serenade / Let's walk
CD ________________ **CDSGPBJZ 24**
Prestige / May '96 / Cadillac / Complete/ Pinnacle

VINTAGE JAZZ VOL.14
Royal Garden blues / Song of India / Beale Street blues / Boogie woogie / Swing low, sweet clarinet / I got it bad / Fan it / There'll be some changes made / Love of my life / My heart belongs to Daddy / Nightmare / Dinah / Everybody loves my baby / Heebie jeebies are rockin' the town
CD ________________ **CDSGPBJZ 25**
Prestige / May '96 / Cadillac / Complete/ Pinnacle

VINTAGE JAZZ VOL.15
O natural blues / Variety stomp / I'm coming Virginia / Stockholm stomp / Lonesome road / Muggles / Save it pretty Mama / Willie the weeper / Rockin' in rhythm / Thursday / Table in the corner / I'll remember / Muddy river blues / Somewhere a voice is calling
CD ________________ **CDSGPBJZ 26**
Prestige / May '96 / Cadillac / Complete/ Pinnacle

VINTAGE JAZZ VOL.16
Rhythm club stomp / Showboat shuffle / Shake it and break it / Mule face blues / It's only a paper moon / Sunday / Sad eyes / Runnin' wild / This heart of mine / I surrender dear / Swanee river / Sheik of Araby / Tin roof blues / After you've gone
CD ________________ **CDSGPBJZ 27**
Prestige / May '96 / Cadillac / Complete/ Pinnacle

VINTAGE JAZZ VOL.17
Apple honey / Stardust / Northwest passage / Good Earth / Drum stomp / Rhythm rhythm (I got rhythm) / House of Morgan / Willie the weeper / Ory's creole trombone / Lamp is low / What is this thing called love / Octaroon / Blues / Stop kicking my heart around
CD ________________ **CDSGPBJZ 28**
Prestige / May '96 / Cadillac / Complete/ Pinnacle

VINTAGE MELODIES (Songs Of The Victorian Era)
Come into the garden Maud / Won't you buy my pretty flowers / Mistletoe bough / End of a perfect day / My pretty Jane / Drinking / I'll be your sweetheart / Silent worship / In the gloaming / Road to Mandalay / Mother take the wheel away / Excelsior
CD ________________ **LCDM 9040**
Lismor / Oct '90 / ADA / Direct / Duncans / Lismor

VINTAGE MUSIC FROM INDIA
CD ________________ **ROUCD 1083**
Rounder / May '93 / ADA / CM / Direct

VINTAGE PIANO VOL.5
On the sunny side of the street / She's funny that way / Over the rainbow / All of me / Moon mist / Passion flower / Paris blues / C jam blues / Messin' around / Six wheel chaser / Chicago flyer / Blues de lux / Every time we say goodbye / Memories of you
CD ________________ **CDSGPBJZ 21**
Prestige / May '96 / Cadillac / Complete/ Pinnacle

VINTAGE PIANO VOL.6
Two's and few's / Honky tonk train blues / Rising tide blues / Far ago blues / I'm confessin' that I love you / I surrender dear / I'm in the mood for love / Undecided / If dreams come true / Stompin' at the Savoy / Bugle call rag / I can't get started / Hiya Sue / Creole rhapsody
CD ________________ **CDSGPBJZ 22**
Prestige / May '96 / Cadillac / Complete/ Pinnacle

VINTAGE R&S VOL.2
Stella: *Jam & Spoon* / Infinition: *Quadrant* / Zeta 3: *Zeta 3* / Jam the box: *69* / Macrocosm: *Mike Dred* / Kinetic: *Golden Girls* / Alcatraz: *Peyote* / Vamp: *Outlander* / Desire: *69* / Elektra: *Source Experience* / Camargue: *Bolland, C.J.*
CD ________________ **RS 96104CD**
R&S / Oct '96 / Vital

VINTAGE REGGAE HITS
CD ________________ **RDCD 196**
Andy Presents / Feb '96 / Jet Star

VINTAGE SOUL TRACKS
CD ________________ **CWNCD 2011**
Javelin / Jul '96 / Henry Hadaway / THE

VIOLIN JAZZ 1927-1944 (2CD Set)
Body and soul: *Grappelli, Stephane* / Them their eyes: *Grappelli, Stephane* / I wonder where my baby is tonight: *Grappelli, Stephane* / Calling all keys: *Rignold, Hugo* / Wild cat: *Venuti, Joe Trio* / My syncopated melody man: *McKenzie, Red & His Music Box* / Goin' places: *Venuti, Joe* / Four string Joe: *Venuti, Joe Blue Four* / Running ragged: *Venuti, Joe Blue Four* / Kansas City Kitty: *Sissle, Noble Orchestra* / After you've gone: *Smith, Stuff & His Onyx Club Boys* / Onyx Club spree: *Smith, Stuff & His Onyx Club Boys* / Skip it: *Smith, Stuff Trio* / C jam blues: *Ellington, Duke Orchestra* / Moon mist: *Ellington, Duke Orchestra* / My melancholy baby: *Asmussen, Svend* / It don't mean a thing if it ain't got that swing: *Asmussen, Svend* / Ring dem bells: *Asmussen, Svend* / Smart Alec: *Hampton, Lionel Orchestra* / Eddie's blues: *South, Eddie* / Oh lady be good: *South, Eddie* / Fiddle ditty: *South, Eddie* / Concerto pour deux violins en re mineur: *South, Eddie* / Minor swing: *Laurence, Claude & Orchestra* / Vous et moi: *Reinhardt, Django* / Strange harmony: *Warlop, Michel & Orchestra* / Har-

moniques: *Warlop, Michel* / Oui: *Warlop, Michel* / Christmas swing: *Warlop, Michel* / Jig in G: *Caceres, Emilio Trio* / Solo: *Nero, Paul Trio*
CD Set FA 052
Fremeaux / Oct '96 / ADA / Discovery

VIOLINS OF EUROPE (France/Romania/ Sweden/Norway/3CD Set)
CD Set C 570304304
Ocora / Mar '97 / ADA / Harmonia Mundi

VIP VOL.1 (2CD Set)
CD Set BASHD 1
VIP Champagne Bash / Jun '95 / Grapevine/PolyGram

VIPER MAD BLUES (25 Songs Of Dope & Depravity)
Kicking the gong around: *Calloway, Cab & his Cotton Club Orchestra* / Dope head blues: *Spivey, Victoria & Lonnie Johnson* / Cocaine habit blues: *Memphis Jug Band* / Pipe dream blues: *Meyers, Hazel* / Smoking reefers: *Adler, Larry* / Take a whiff on me: *Leadbelly* / Killin' jive: *Cats & The Fiddle* / You're a viper: *Smith, Stuff & His Onyx Club Boys* / Reefer man: *Lee, Baron Blue Rhythm Band* / Stuff is here and it's mellow: *Brown, Cleo* / Onyx hop: *Newton, Frankie Uptown Serenaders* / Knocking myself out: *Green, Lil* / Junker's blues: *Dupree, 'Champion' Jack* / Reefer hound blues: *Jones, Curtis* / Reefer song: *Waller, Fats* / I'm feelin' high and happy: *Krupa, Gene & His Orchestra* / When I get low, I get high: *Fitzgerald, Ella & Chick Webb Orchestra* / Ol' man river (smoke a little tea): *Williams, Cootie & His Rug Cutters* / Blue reefer blues: *Jones, Richard M. & His Jazz Wizards* / Cocaine: *Justice, Dick* / Reefer head woman: *Gillum, Bill 'Jazz' & His Jazz Boys* / Willie the weeper: *Jaxon, Frankie 'Half Pint'* / Cocaine blues: *Jordan, Luke* / Blue drag: *Taylor, Freddy & His Swing Men* / Viper's moan: *Bryant, Willie & His Orchestra*
CD CDMOJO 306
Mojo / Nov '96 / Direct

VIRGINIA TRADITIONS (Ballads & Songs)
CD GVM 1004CD
Global Village / Jul '95 / ADA / Direct

VIRGINIA TRADITIONS - SECULAR BLACK MUSIC
CD GVM 1001CD
Global Village / Jul '95 / ADA / Direct

VIRTUAL DJ - DRUM 'N' BASS
Enta da dragon: *DJ Red* / Dub moods: *Aphrodite* / Mad apache: *Shy FX* / Nu gen: *Decoder* / Behold: *Swift* / Star Wars: *Dream Team* / Beats back: *Spice* / Untouchables: *Ill Figure* / Switch: *Special K* / Opinion: *Swoosh* / Nobody: *Phiziks*
CD BDRCD 21
Breakdown / Jul '97 / Pinnacle

VIRTUAL DJ - UNDERGROUND GARAGE
CD BDRCD 22
Suburban Base / Jul '97 / Pinnacle / Prime

VIRTUAL LABEL COMPILATION
CD MOCD 0012
Virtual / Oct '96 / ZYX

VIRTUAL SEX
CD 2100008
Indisc / May '93 / Pinnacle

VISION MASTERMIXERS VOL.1 (The Immaculate Mixes Vol.1)
CD QED 092
Tring / Dec '96 / Tring

VISION MASTERMIXERS VOL.2 (The Immaculate Mixes Vol.2)
CD QED 093
Tring / Dec '96 / Tring

VISION MASTERMIXERS VOL.3 (The Sixties)
CD QED 094
Tring / Nov '96 / Tring

VISION MASTERMIXERS VOL.4 (The Seventies)
CD QED 095
Tring / Nov '96 / Tring

VISION MASTERMIXERS VOL.5 (Disco Hits)
CD QED 096
Tring / Nov '96 / Tring

VISITATION
CD MEYCD 17
Magick Eye / Sep '96 / Cargo / SRD

VIVA DIABLO BLANCO (Freestyle Beats Vol.1)
Lopez: *808 State* / Song for Lindy: *Fatboy Slim* / Airport: *Supercharger* / Shakey shakey: *Philadelphia Bluntz* / Ain't talkin' 'bout dub: *Apollo 440* / Timber: *Grantby* / Bend: *Egg* / Finders and creepers: *Runaways* / One night: *Aloof* / Who do you trust: *Arkarna* / Tales from the hard side: *Santana, Omar* / Moog island: *Morcheeba* / Something always happens: *Art Of Noise*
CD ZEN 013CD
Indochina / Mar '97 / Pinnacle

VIVA EURO POP
CD 0630152072
East West / May '96 / Warner Music

VIVA HACIENDA (3CD Set)
Dirty talk: *Klein & The MBO* / Confusion: *New Order* / Al nafish: *Hashim* / Boogie down Bronx: *Man Parrish* / Let the music play: *Shannon* / Beat the street: *Redd, Sharon* / Don't make me wait: *Peech Boys* / Seventh heaven: *Guthrie, Gwen* / Twilight: *Maze* / All in all: *Sims, Joyce* / This brutal house: *Nitro Deluxe* / No way back: *Adonis* / Give yourself to me: *Farley, Farley, Farley* / Can U feel it: *Mr. Fingers* / Pump up Chicago: *Mr. Lee* / Slam: *Phuture* / Carino: *T-Coy* / Dream 17: *Annette* / I'm in love: *Shalor* / There's an acid house going on: *London Beat* / Dream girl: *Pierre's Pfantasy Club* / Where love lives: *Limerick, Alison* / M'baby: *Karma* / Know how: *Young MC* / Slasa house: *Richie Rich* / Wild times: *Deee-Lite* / I like it: *Landlord* / French kiss: *Lil' Louis* / Love sensation: *Holloway, Loleatta* / Strings of life: *Rhythm Is Rhythm* / I'll be waiting: *Griffin, Clive* / Rise from your grave: *Phuture* / Been a long time: *Fog* / Bone: *Persuasion* / Oddyssey: *7th Movement* / An instrumental need: *Rosario, Ralphi* / Funk phenomena: *Van Helden, Armand* / Throw: *Paperclip People* / Bomb: *Bucketheads* / Fired up: *Funky Green Dogs* / You can't hide from your bud: *DJ Sneak* / Fly life: *Basement Jaxx* / Do da doo: *Robotman* / Book: *Salt City Orchestra*
CD Set 74321486552
De-Construction / May '97 / BMG

VIVA MEXICO (20 Mariachi Favourites)
CD CDHOT 605
Charly / Jun '96 / Koch

VIVA MEXICO
Cielito lindo: *Parraguez, Luis* / Adelita: *Tobar, Rodrigo* / Malaguena: *Oliveira, Valdeci* / Volver: *Gonzalez* / La vikina: *Jerez, Mauricio* / Besame mucho: *Oliveira, Valdeci* / Siempre adios: *Duo Yucatan* / La cucaracha: *Tobar, Rodrigo* / Cucurucucu Paloma: *Gonzalez* / Solamente una vez: *Oliveira, Valdeci* / Indio Camaye: *Duo Yucatan* / La bamba: *Parraguez, Luis* / Tempo: *Oliveira, Valdeci* / Senora Morena: *Casco, Oscar* / Perdone me: *Duo Yucatan*
CD 12728
Laserlight / Aug '96 / Target/BMG

VIVATIONAL COMPILATION
Intro: *Musical Director* / Supervisor error: *Diceman* / Purpuss: *Bob & Ian* / Tempest: *Diceman* / Silcock express: *LMNO* / In wildebeest: *Bob & Ian* / Hold me now: *Solace* / Le noir: *Diceman* / Y: *LMNO* / Bad data from disc: *Diceman* / Purpuss (Secret knowledge mix): *Bob & Ian* / X: *LMNO* / Quad (Spooky's magi remix): *Diceman* / Silcock express (remix): *LMNO* / Sonic system: *Diceman* / Hold me now (John Digweeds mix): *Solace*
CD VTTCD 01
Vivational / Feb '94 / Grapevine/PolyGram

VOCAL AND INSTRUMENTAL MUSIC OF MONGOLIA
CD TSCD 909
Topic / Sep '94 / ADA / CM / Direct

VOCAL BLUES AND JAZZ 1921-1930
CD DOCD 1004
Document / Apr '97 / ADA / Hot Shot / Jazz Music

VOCAL DUETS 1924-1931
CD DOCD 5526
Document / Apr '97 / ADA / Hot Shot / Jazz Music

VOCAL GROUPS (Coast To Coast)
Call on me: *Mello Moods* / I tried and tried and tried: *Mello Moods* / I'm lost: *Mello Moods* / When I woke up this morning: *Mello Moods* / Christmas song: *Mello Moods* / Each time: *Cabineers* / My my my: *Cabineers* / Lost: *Cabineers* / Baby, where'd you go to: *Cabineers* / What's the matter with you: *Cabineers* / Baby mine: *Cabineers* / Thrill me baby: *Pierce, Henry* / Hey fine Mama: *Pierce, Henry* / That's bad: *Metronomes* / Come on & rock: *Dukes* / I was a fool: *Dukes* / Oh Kay: *Dukes* / Ooh bop she bop: *Dukes* / Zindy Lou: *Chimes* / Gone: *Belvin, Jesse* / One little blessing: *Belvin, Jesse* / Honey dew: *Gipson, Byron 'Slick' & The Sliders* / How do you kiss an angel: *Green, Vernon & The Phantoms* / Why oh why: *Church, Eugene* / Can it be: *Titans* / Red sails in the sunset: *Monitors*
CD CDCHD 594
Ace / Oct '96 / Pinnacle

VOCAL GROUPS, THE
CD PLATCD 343
Platinum / Oct '90 / Prism

VOCAL QUARTETS VOL.1 1928-1940
CD DOCD 5537
Document / Jun '97 / ADA / Hot Shot / Jazz Music

VOCAL QUARTETS VOL.2 1929-1932
CD DOCD 5538
Document / Jun '97 / ADA / Hot Shot / Jazz Music

VOCAL QUARTETS VOL.3 1927-1936
CD DOCD 5539
Document / Jun '97 / ADA / Hot Shot / Jazz Music

VOCAL QUARTETS VOL.4 1927-1943
CD DOCD 5540
Document / Jul '97 / ADA / Hot Shot / Jazz Music

VOCAL QUARTETS VOL.5 1924-1928
CD DOCD 5541
Document / Jul '97 / ADA / Hot Shot / Jazz Music

VOCAL QUARTETS VOL.6 1928-1944
CD DOCD 5542
Document / Jul '97 / ADA / Hot Shot / Jazz Music

VOCAL QUARTETS VOL.7 1925-1943
CD DOCD 5543
Document / Jul '97 / ADA / Hot Shot / Jazz Music

VOCAL REFRAIN
CD Set MAK 103
Avid / Nov '94 / Avid/BMG / Koch / THE

VOCAL TRADITIONS OF BULGARIA
Mari Maro / Snoshti vecher u vas byah / Polegnala bela pshenitza / Momne le mari hubava / Vido dva vetra veyat / Ziadi mi rayo / Dosto, mome dosto / Shto yubavo sofiskoto pole / Zamurknaya petstotin aiduka / Senkya pada / Bre Nikola Nikola / Devoiko Mari Hubava / Rechenski kamuk reka zaglavya / Rasti bore / Zazhena se niva / Pominalo e devoiche / Rodilo se muzhko dete / Zluntzeto trepti zauda / Pusni ma maicho / Doide mi obed pladnina / Done ide ot manastir
CD CDSDL 396
Saydisc / Mar '94 / ADA / Direct / Harmonia Mundi

VOCALS & INSTRUMENTALS POLYPHONIES OF ETHIOPIA (2CD Set)
CD Set C 580055/56
Ocora / May '94 / ADA / Harmonia Mundi

VOCIFEROUS MACHIAVUVIAN HATE
CD E 0001
Osmose / Apr '94 / Plastic Head

VOICE
Tribe: *Gruntruck* / Business: *Biohazard* / Set the world on fire: *Annihilator* / Lights on: *Waltari* / Cinderella's daydream: *Zu Zu's Petals* / Skin: *Optimum Wound Profile* / Never too late: *Phantom Blue* / Monarch of the sleeping marches: *Disincarnate* / Boy can sing the blues: *Hughes, Glenn* / Monotony: *Willard* / Face: *Innerstate* / Sky turned red: *Atrocity* / Ghost rider: *Bloodstar* / Fugitive soul: *Treponem Pal* / Scapegoat: *Fear Factory* / Throb: *Skin Chamber* / It's like that: *Dog Eat Dog* / Black no. 1 (Little Miss Scare-all): *Type O Negative*
CD CDRR 90742
Roadrunner / Apr '93 / PolyGram

VOICE OF FOLK, THE
When I first came to Caledonia: *Waterson, Norma* / Old horse: *Carthy, Martin* / Grey cock: *Carthy, Eliza* / Bonnie lass amang the heather: *Gaughan, Dick* / Little pot stove: *Jones, Nic* / Somewhere along the road: *Prior, Maddy* / Four loom weaver: *MacColl, Ewan* / Old man Jones: *Kirkpatrick, John* / King of Rome: *Tabor, June* / Shipyard apprentice: *Battlefield Band* / False true lover: *Collins, Shirley* / Joh: *Four Men & A Dog* / Time to ring some changes: *Thompson, Richard* / Striking for another land: *Albion Band* / Dr. Fausters tumblers/The night of Trafalgar/Prince William: *Brass Monkey*
CD TSCD 705
Topic / Oct '96 / ADA / CM / Direct

VOICE OF SPAIN 1927-1931
CD HTCD 38
Heritage / Sep '96 / ADA / Direct / Hot Shot / Jazz Music / Swift / Wellard

VOICE OF THE FULBE - BURKINA FASO
CD LDX 2741079
Le Chant Du Monde / Jul '97 / Harmonia Mundi

VOICES (Hannibal Sampler)
CD HNCD 8301
Hannibal / Feb '90 / ADA / Vital

VOICES (English Traditional Songs)
CD FE 087CD
Fellside / Nov '95 / ADA / Direct / Target/ BMG

VOICES (2CD Set)
CD Set TCD 2875
Telstar / Apr '97 / BMG

VOICES FROM LONG DISTANCE
CD 3018652
Long Distance / Apr '97 / ADA / Discovery

VOICES FROM THE GHETTO - YIDDISH
CD 242066
FNAC / Aug '93 / Discovery

VOICES IN CONTROL (The R&B Flavours Album)
Cold world: *Haynes, Victor* / Slow down boy: *Cambell, Jackie* / Everything's alright: *Haynes, Victor* / Can't run: *Zee, Dawn* / Don't make me wait: *Haynes, Victor & Kenny T* / Slow jam/Interlude: *Haynes, Victor* / Do me right: *Zee, Dawn & Victor Haynes* / Love won't let me wait: *Haynes, Victor* / Surrender: *Sani* / Slow jam tonight: *Zee, Dawn & Victor Haynes* / For the love of you: *Haynes, Victor* / Out of luck: *Cambell, Jackie* / That's what love can do: *Shelton, Yvonne*
CD EXCDP 10
Expansion / May '96 / 3mv/Sony

VOICES OF AMERICA (Vocal Harmony Groups: Then & Now)
Whispering bells: *Del-Vikings* / For your precious love: *Butler, Jerry & The Impressions* / Oh what a night: *Dells* / Everybody plays the fool: *Main Ingredient* / Thousand stars: *Rivileers* / Blue moon: *Marcels* / PS I love you: *Four Vagabond* / Catalina I love you: *Four Preps* / Till then: *Mills Brothers* / Morse code of love: *Capris* / Sincerely: *Moonglows* / Have you seen her: *Chi-Lites* / Count every star: *Ravens* / I got rhythm: *Happenings* / Crying in the chapel: *Orioles* / I don't want to set the world on fire: *Ink Spots* / Chapel of dreams: *Valentinos* / (Now and then there's) A fool such as I: *Robins* / Please don't say you want me: *Schoolboys* / Don't sit under the apple tree (with anyone else but me): *Andrews Sisters* / Crazy for you: *Heartbeats* / Do it again: *Beach Boys* / Gang that sang heart of my heart: *Four Aces* / Opportunity: *Jewels* / I wonder why: *Dion & The Belmonts* / If I ever fall in love: *Shai*
CD CDCHD 416
Ace / Jun '96 / Pinnacle

VOICES OF THE ORIENT (North India/ Iran/Syria/3CD Set)
CD Set C 570305
Ocora / Mar '97 / ADA / Harmonia Mundi

VOICES OF THE RAIN FOREST
From morning night to real morning / Making sago / Cutting trees / Clearing the brush / Bamboo Jew's harp / From afternoon to afternoon darkening / Evening rainstorm / Drumming / Song ceremony / From night to inside night / Relaxing by the creek
CD RCD 10173
Rykodisc / Jul '91 / ADA / Vital

VOICES OF THE SPIRITS - SONGS AND CHANTS
CD ELL 3210A
Ellipsis Arts / Oct '93 / ADA / Direct

VOICES OF THE UKRAINE
CD PS 65145CD
PlayaSound / Jul '95 / ADA / Harmonia Mundi

VOICES OF THE WORLD (An Anthology Of Vocal Expression/3CD Set)
CD Set CMX 374101012
Le Chant Du Monde / Dec '96 / Harmonia Mundi

VOICES OF TRANQUILITY VOL.1
CD DINCD 123
Dino / Aug '96 / Pinnacle

VOICES OF TRANQUILITY VOL.2
CD DINCD 135
Dino / Mar '97 / Pinnacle

VOICES OF WONDER
CD VOW 36CD
Voices Of Wonder / May '94 / Plastic Head

VOLCANO (20 Super Hits)
CD SONCD 0005
Sonic Sounds / Oct '90 / Jet Star

VOLCANO ERUPTION, THE
CD SONCD 0050
Sonic Sounds / Jul '93 / Jet Star

VOLCANO SPECIAL COMPILATION VOL.1
CD CY 78934
Nyam Up / Apr '95 / Conifer/BMG

VOLKSTUMLICHE FAVORITEN
CD 15396
Laserlight / Nov '91 / Target/BMG

VORTEX ENERGIZE
CD IRB 59982
Deep Blue / Sep '96 / PolyGram

VOYAGE INTO TRANCE, A
CD BFLCD 14
Big Life / May '95 / Mo's Music Machine / Pinnacle / Prime

VOYAGE INTO TRANCE, A
CD BFLCD 20
Dragonfly / Nov '96 / Mo's Music Machine / Pinnacle

VYBIN' - THE BEST OF VYBIN' (2CD Set)
Return of the mack: *Morrison, Mark* / I got 5 on it: *Luniz* / Nobody knows: *Rich, Tony* / Waterfalls: *TLC* / Tha crossroads: *Bone Thugs n' Harmony* / Shy guy: *King, Diana* / Bump 'n' grind: *Kelly, R* / I will survive: *Savage, Chantay* / One for the money: *Brown, Horace* / You're the one: *SWV* / How many ways: *Braxton, Toni* / If I ruled the world: *Nas* / Mutual feeling: *Knight, Beverley* / Woo hah got you all in check: *Busta Rhymes* / I wanna be down: *Brandy* / Feels so good: *Xscape* / Like this and like that: *Monica* / G-spot: *Marshall, Wayne* / Kissin' you: *Total* / Gangsta's paradise: *Coolio* / Virtual insanity: *Jamiroquai* / Good thing: *Eternal* / Bombastic: *Shaggy* / Ocean drive: *Lighthouse Family* / Love enuff: *Soul II Soul* / 24/7: *3T* / Sweetness: *Gayle, Michelle* / If you love me: *Brownstone* / Every day of the week: *Jade* / Like a playa: *La Ganz* / Back and

forth: *Aaliyah* / Down 4 whateva: *Nuttin' Nyce* / Undercover lover: *Smooth* / Freak like me: *Howard, Adina* / Only you: *112 & Notorious BIG* / (Can't always have) sunshine: *SC223* / Get it on: *Clash Of Culture* / Sentimental: *Cox, Deborah* / Je t'aime: *SS Soul* / Boom biddy bye bye: *Cypress Hill*
CD Set ______ **RADCD 45**
Global TV / Nov '96 / BMG

VYBIN' VOL.1 (New Soul Rebels)
Sight for sore eyes: *M-People* / Bump 'n' grind: *R Kelly* / Breathe again: *Braxton, Toni* / My lovin': *En Vogue* / Stay: *Eternal* / Body and soul: *Baker, Anita* / Right here: *SWV* / Be happy: *Blige, Mary J.* / I wanna be down: *Brandy* / Revival: *Girault, Martine* / Dream on dreamer: *Brand New Heavies* / Apparently nothing: *Young Disciples* / Always there: *Incognito* / Down that road: *Nelson, Shara* / Unfinished sympathy: *Massive Attack* / Don't walk away: *Jade* / Back and forth: *Aaliyah* / G-Spot: *Marshall, Wayne* / Stroke you up: *Changing Faces* / Back to life: *Soul II Soul*
CD ______ **RADCD 05**
Global TV / Feb '95 / BMG

VYBIN' VOL.2 (2CD Set)
Creep: *TLC* / Gangsta's paradise: *Coolio & LV* / Sentimental: *Cox, Deborah* / She's got that vibe: *Kelly, R* / I can't tell you why: *Brownstone* / Two can play that game: *Brown, Bobby* / How many ways: *Braxton, Toni* / Freek 'n' you: *Jodeci* / Freak like me: *Howard, Adina* / Down 4 whateva: *Nuttin' Nyce* / Party all night: *Kreuz* / Candy rain: *Soul For Real* / Been thinking about you: *Girault, Martine* / G-spot: *Marshall, Wayne* / Down for the one: *Knight, Beverley* / Finest: *Truce* / Most beautiful boy: *Mayte* / If I ever fall in love: *Shai* / (You make me feel like a) natural woman: *Blige, Mary J.* / Don't take it personal: *Monica* / Best friend: *Brandy* / I like: *Kut Klose* / Age ain't nothing but a number: *Aaliyah* / You remind me of something: *Kelly, R* / Think of you: *Usher* / Just kickin: *Xscape* / Rock wit'cha: *Brown, Bobby* / Flavour of the old school: *Knight, Beverley* / Right here: *SWV* / Free/sail on: *Moore, Chante* / Hey Mr DJ: *Zhane* / I know: *Thompson, Tony* / Good life: *Ebony Vibe Everlasting* / Crazy: *Morrison, Mark* / Let's get it on: *Jade* / One more chance/stay with me: *Notorious BIG* / You used tolove me: *Evans, Faith* / Je t'aime: *SS Soul* / Mind blowin: *Smooth*
CD Set ______ **RADCD 19**
Global TV / Feb '96 / BMG

VYBIN' VOL.3 (2CD Set)
Return of the mack: *Morrison, Mark* / Diggin' on you: *TLC* / I got 5 in it: *Luniz* / If you love me: *Brownstone* / Your body's callin': *Kelly, R* / Rock wit'cha: *Brown, Bobby* / Love enuff: *Soul II Soul* / I wish: *Skee Lo* / Tell me what you like: *Guy* / Who can I run to: *Jordan, Montell* / Brokenhearted: *Brandy* / Regulate: *Warren G* / Moving on up (on the right side): *Knight, Beverley* / Gimme that body: *Q-Tee* / Circles: *Don-E* / So good (to come home to): *Matias, Ivan* / Throw your hand up: *Aaliyah* / (Can't always have) sunshine: *C 223* / Search for the hero: *M-People* / I will survive: *Savage, Chantay* / 1,2,3,4 (sumpin' new): *Coolio* / Cruisin': *D'Angelo* / Every day of the week: *Jade* / All the things (your man won't do): *Joe* / I'm so into you: *SWV* / Love u 4 life: *Jodeci* / Like this and like that: *Monica* / Hump tonight: *Marshall, Wayne* / Down low (nobody has to know): *Kelly, R* / Love city groove: *Love City Groove* / Freedom: *Gayle, Michelle* / Keep on groovin': *Kreuz* / Are u ready: *Celetia* / Celebration of life: *Truce*
CD Set ______ **RADCD 33**
Global TV / Apr '96 / BMG

VYBIN' VOL.4 (2CD Set)
Nobody knows: *Rich, Tony Project* / Thank god it's Friday: *R Kelly* / Lifted: *Lighthouse Family* / Waterfalls: *TLC* / Where love lives: *Limerick, Alison* / You're the one: *SWV* / Everyday: *Incognito* / Mary Jane (all night long): *Blige, Mary J.* / I'll be there for you/ You're all I need to get by: *Method Man & Mary J. Blige* / Humpin' around: *Brown, Bobby* / Who do u love: *Cox, Deborah* / Something 4 da honeyz: *Jordan, Montell* / Taste your love: *Brown, Horace* / Young nation: *Aaliyah* / Movin' on: *Brandy* / Woo hah got you all in check: *Busta Rhymes* / Get on up: *Jodeci* / I'll be around: *Rappin' 4-Tay* / Too hot: *Coolio* / Sound of da police: *KRS 1* / Good thing: *Eternal* / Undercover lover: *Smooth* / Love of mine: *Earth Gyrlz* / Desire: *Nu Colours* / Everyday and evrynight: *Michelle, Yvette* / Feels so good: *Xscape* / Before you walk out of my life: *Monica* / Grapevine: *Brownstone* / Remedy: *Knight, Beverley* / Lay my body down: *Kut Klose* / Soon as I get home: *Evans, Faith* / My cherie amour: *Thompson, Tony* / Tell somebody: *Thompson, Tony* / Don't look any further: *M-People* / Every little thing I do: *Soul For Real* / Missing your love: *Celetia* / Get down on it: *Kreuz* / Robyn: *Kreuz* / Don't come to stay: *Hot House* / I will survive: *Savage, Chantay*
CD Set ______ **RADCD 38**
Global TV / Jul '96 / BMG

W

WA-CHI-KA-NOCKA
Wigwam Willie: *Phillips, Carl* / Indian Joe: *Adams, Art* / Warrior Sam: *Willis, Don* / Warpath: *Lenny & The Star Chiefs* / Cherokee stomp: *Tidwell, Bobby* / Cherokee rock: *Wheeler, Chuck* / Indian rock and roll: *Jerome, Ralph* / War paint: *Warriors* / Kawliga: *Porter, Bruce* / Rock my warriors rock: *Jackson, Joe* / Wa-chic-ka-noka: *Holmes, Tommy* / Witchapoo: *Cathey, Frank* / Geronimo: *Renegade* / Indian squaw: *Kellwoods* / Geronimo stomp: *Darvell, Barry* / Big indian: *Downs, Tommy* / Chief whoopin' koff: *Royal Knights* / Little brave: *Smalling, Eddie* / Little bull and buttercup: *Homer, Chris* / Massacre: *Ronny & Johnny* / Wahoo: *Bennett, Arnold* / Bobby sox squaw: *Impacts* / Tomahawk: *Brown, Tom* / Rockin' redwing: *Masters, Sammy* / Red wing: *Wayne, Gordon* / Indian moon: *Chieftones* / Medicine man: *Warren, Bobby Five* / Rattlesnake: *Bayou, Billy* / Cowboys and indians: *Brent, Ronnie* / Indian rock: *Musical Lynn Twins*
CD ______ **CDBB 55011**
Buffalo Bop / Apr '94 / Rollercoaster

WADE IN THE WATERS VOL.1 (Spirituals)
CD ______ **SFWCD 40072**
Smithsonian Folkways / Jun '94 / ADA / Cadillac / CM / Direct / Koch

WADE IN THE WATERS VOL.2 (Congregation Singing)
CD ______ **SFWCD 40073**
Smithsonian Folkways / Jun '94 / ADA / Cadillac / CM / Direct / Koch

WADE IN THE WATERS VOL.3 (Gospel Pioneers)
CD ______ **SFWCD 40074**
Smithsonian Folkways / Jun '94 / ADA / Cadillac / CM / Direct / Koch

WADE IN THE WATERS VOL.4 (Community Gospel)
CD ______ **SFWCD 40075**
Smithsonian Folkways / Jun '94 / ADA / Cadillac / CM / Direct / Koch

WAIL DADDY (Excello Nashville Jump Blues)
Chicken hearted woman: *Samuels, Clarence* / Dyna-flow: *Cooley, Jack* / Tom Tom boogie: *Cooley, Jack* / Glad I don't worry no more: *Fat Man* / Back alley boogie: *Johnson, Sherman* / Allotment blues: *Dowell, Charlie & Willie Lee Patton* / Wail Daddy: *Dowell, Charlie & Willie Lee Patton* / Down south in Birmingham: *Thorne, Del & Her Trio* / New Memphis blues: *Shy Guy Douglas* / Detroit arrow: *Shy Guy Douglas* / Happy go lucky: *Good Rockin' Beasley* / Drive soldiers drive: *Bailey, Little Maxie* / My baby's blues: *Bailey, Little Maxie* / Goof train: *Thorne, Del & Her Trio* / Fly chick blues: *Thorne, Del & Her Trio* / Yeh it's true: *Hardison, Bernie* / Love me baby: *Hardison, Bernie* / Watch on: *Blue Flamers* / Lazy Pete: *Roosevelt, Lee* / Late every evening: *McGhee, Tommy* / Poppin': *McGhee, Tommy* / Prize fightin' papa: *Bryant, Beulah* / Too many keys: *Prince, Bobby* / Driving down the highway: *Blue Flamers*
CD ______ **CDCHD 653**
Ace / Jun '97 / Pinnacle

WAKE UP DEAD MAN
CD ______ **ROUCD 2013**
Rounder / Aug '94 / ADA / CM / Direct

WAKE UP JAMAICA
CD ______ **CDTRL 331**
Trojan / Mar '94 / Direct / Jet Star

WALK ON THE WILD SIDE (Soft Rock Classics - 2CD Set)
Walk on the wild side: *Reed, Lou* / All around the world: *Stansfield, Lisa* / Rapture: *Blondie* / If you let me stay: *D'Arby, Terence Trent* / Would I lie to you: *Eurythmics* / Golden brown: *Stranglers* / Simply irresistible: *Palmer, Robert* / Storm music: *Scott-Heron, Gil* / High powered love: *Harris, Emmylou* / Never met a girl like you before: *Collins, Edwyn* / All through the night: *Lauper, Cyndi* / Power of love: *Lewis, Huey & The News* / In the name of love: *Thompson Twins* / This city never sleeps: *Eurythmics* / Blinded by the light: *Manfred Mann's Earthband* / Unchained melody: *Robson & Jerome* / Rich girl: *Hall & Oates* / I scare myself: *Dolby, Thomas* / These dreams: *Heart* / Perfect day: *Reed, Lou* / You're the voice: *Farnham, John* / Kyrie: *Mr. Mister* / Nothing's gonna stop us now: *Starship* / Guaranteed: *Level 42* / Move closer: *Nelson, Phyllis* / We've got tonight: *Brooks, Elkie* / Atmospherics: *Robinson, Tom* / Ship of fools: *Erasure* / Maneater: *Hall & Oates* / Signed, sealed, delivered: *Turner, Ruby* / You took the words right out of my mouth: *Meat Loaf* / Ain't no sunshine: *Withers, Bill* / Hand on my heart: *Shriekback* / Wherever I lay my hat (that's my home): *Young, Paul*
CD Set ______ **RCACD 213**
RCA / Jul '97 / BMG

WALK RIGHT IN (Essential Memphis Blues)
My money never runs out: *Cannon, Gus* / Mr. Crump don't like it: *Beale Street Sheiks* / Twelve pound daddy: *Dickson, Pearl* / Ain't nobody's business if I do: *Stokes, Frank* / Happy blues: *Dickson, Tom* / I will turn your money green: *Lewis, Furry* / Judge Harsh blues: *Lewis, Furry* / Rolling stone: *Wilkins, Robert* / That's no way to get along: *Wilkins, Robert* / Walk right in: *Canon's Jug Stompers* / KC moan: *Memphis Jug Band* / Cocaine habit blues: *Memphis Jug Band* / Travelling Mama blues: *Calicott, Joe* / Bedside blues: *Thompkins, Jim* / Ticket agent blues: *Lewis, Noah Jug Band* / Hesitation blues: *Jackson, Jim* / Can I do it for you: *Memphis Minnie & Kansas Joe* / Granpa and Grandma blues: *Memphis Minnie Jug Band* / Highway No.61 blues: *Kelly, Jack & His South Memphis Jug Band* / Moanin' the blues: *Shaw, Allen* / Sugar farm blues: *Rachell, Yank* / Need more blues: *Estes, 'Sleepy' John* / Renewed love blues: *Doyle, Little Buddy*
CD ______ **IGOCD 2038**
Indigo / Jun '97 / ADA / Direct

WALK THE LINE
Southern kickin' finger lickin': *Cane Honey, T.* / That's my story: *Nashville Cats* / Hang in there Superman: *Nashville Cats* / Walkin' the line: *Sheriff, Dave* / Back in your arms again: *Nashville Cats* / Cannibals: *Nashville Cats* / I forgot to remember: *Dean Brothers* / Cowboy stomp: *Nashville Cats* / Life is good: *Nashville Cats* / Set me free: *Horsfall, Des* / Black coffee: *Nashville Cats* / Daddy's money: *Nashville Cats* / I need somebody: *Cheap Seats* / My Maria: *Nashville Cats* / Cherokee boogie: *Nashville Cats* / Party's over: *Ambler, Tim*
CD ______ **TRMCD 001**
Thorny Rose / May '97 / Koch

WALKING ON SUNSHINE (2CD Set)
CD Set ______ **NSCD 016**
Newsound / Feb '95 / THE

WALL OF PUSSY (Wall Of Sound/Pussy Foot Compilation)
CD ______ **WALLPUSSCD 1**
Wall Of Sound / May '96 / Prime / Soul Trader / Vital

WALTZING AROUND IRELAND
Black velvet band / Do you want your oul lobby washed down / One day at a time / Accordion selection / Rose of mooncoin / Rose of Tralee / Rose of Aranmore / My Eileen is waiting for me / 40 Shades of green / County Armagh / Mountains of Mourne / Green glens of Antrim / Der little Ireland / Red rose cafe / Galway bay / Girl from Donegal / If those lips can only speak / Old claddagh ring / Irish harvest day / Love is teasing / Cockles and mussels
CD ______ **RBCD 523**
Sharpe / Jun '97 / Duncans / Target/BMG

WALTZING MATILDA (Australian Folk Tunes)
CD ______ **IMCD 3005**
Image / Feb '96 / Discovery

WANTED
CD ______ **HAGCD 003**
Hag / May '97 / Pinnacle / Shellshock/ Disc

WANTED - THE OUTLAWS
My heroes have always been cowboys: *Jennings, Waylon* / Honky tonk heroes (Like me): *Jennings, Waylon* / Slow movin' outlaws: *Jennings, Waylon* / (I'm a) Ramblin' man: *Jennings, Waylon* / I'm looking for blue eyes: *Colter, Jessi* / You mean to say: *Colter, Jessi* / Why have you been gone so long: *Colter, Jessi* / Suspicious minds: *Jennings, Waylon & Willie Nelson* / Good hearted woman: *Jennings, Waylon & Willie Nelson* / Heaven and hell: *Jennings, Waylon & Willie Nelson* / Under your spell again: *Jennings, Waylon & Willie Nelson* / I ain't the one: *Jennings, Waylon & Willie Nelson* / Nowhere road: *Jennings, Waylon & Willie Nelson* / Me and Paul: *Nelson, Willie* / Yesterdays wine: *Nelson, Willie* / T For Texas: *Glaser, Tompall* / Put another log on the fire: *Glaser, Tompall* / You left a long, long time ago: *Nelson, Willie* / Healing hands of time: *Nelson, Willie* / If she's where you like livin' (You won't feel at home with: *Colter, Jessi* / It's not easy: *Colter, Jessi*
CD ______ **7863668412**
RCA / Jun '96 / BMG

WAR COMPILATION
CD ______ **WAR 005CD**
Wrong Again / Apr '96 / Plastic Head

WAREHOUSE RAVES VOL.1
Numero uno: *Starlight* / Guitarra: *Raul* / Love is life: *Candy Flip* / Te amo: *Navarro, Raimunda* / Love sensation: *Holloway, Loleatta* / 69: *Brooklyn Express* / Paradhouse: *Koxo Club Band* / Why can't we live together: *Illusion* / It's a dream: *Amnesia* / Let me love you for tonight: *Kariya* / Just a little bit: *Total Science* / Strings of life: *Rhythim Is Rhythim*
CD ______ **CDRUMD 101**
Rumour / Sep '89 / 3mv/Sony / Mo's Music Machine / Pinnacle

WAREHOUSE RAVES VOL.2
CD ______ **CDRUMD 102**
Rumour / May '92 / 3mv/Sony / Mo's Music Machine / Pinnacle

WAREHOUSE RAVES VOL.3
CD ______ **CDRUMD 103**
Rumour / Mar '90 / 3mv/Sony / Mo's Music Machine / Pinnacle

WARNING FOR PUNK (3CD Set)
CD Set ______ **DISTCD 10**
Dolores / Jan '95 / Plastic Head

WARTIME FAVOURITES VOL.1 - THE EARLY YEARS
They can't black out the moon: *Roy, Harry & His Orchestra* / God bless you Mr. Chamberlain: *Roy, Harry & His Orchestra* / Oh ain't it grand to be in the navy: *Roy, Harry & His Orchestra* / Nasty Adolf Hitler: *Ambrose & His Orchestra* / Rhymes of the times: *Ambrose & His Orchestra* / Spitfire song: *Loss, Joe & His Orchestra* / Adolf: *Ambrose & His Orchestra* / One certain soldier: *Carless, Dorothy* / We're going to hang out the washing: *Ambrose & His Orchestra* / When that man is dead and gone: *Geraldo & His Dance Orchestra* / Run rabbit run: *Roy, Harry & His Orchestra* / Wings over the navy: *Cotton, Billy & His Band* / Kiss me goodnight, Sergeant Major: *Cotton, Billy & His Band* / FDR Jones: *Roy, Harry & His Orchestra* / Lords of the air: *Loss, Joe Band* / Tiggerty boo: *Roy, Harry & His Band* / It's a paor of wings for me: *Gonella, Nat & His Georgians* / Nice kind Sergeant Major: *Long, Norman* / There'll always be an England: *Loss, Joe Band*
CD ______ **RAJCD 825**
Empress / Aug '94 / Koch

WARTIME FAVOURITES VOL.2 - SONGS OF D-DAY
Homeward bound: *Hall, Henry Orchestra* / Don't ask me why/Whistling in the dark/Hey good looking: *Preager, Lou & His Orchestra* / I never mention your name: *Roy, Harry & His Band* / Milkman keep those bottles quiet: *Squadronaires* / I heard you cry last night: *Preager, Lou & His Orchestra* / My heart tells me: *Roy, Harry & His Band* / San fernando valley: *Skyrockets Dance Orchestra* / Shoo shoo baby: *Preager, Lou & His Orchestra* / How sweet you are: *Roy, Harry & His Band* / Do you believe in dreams: *Skyrockets Dance Orchestra* / I'll get by/A lovely way to spend an evening/All of my life: *Melachrino, George & His Orchestra* / So dumb but so beautiful: *Skyrockets Dance Orchestra* / Macnamara's band: *Geraldo & His Orchestra* / Padulah: *Hall, Henry Orchestra* / I left my heart at the stage door canteen: *Ambrose & His Orchestra* / Is you is or is you ain't my baby: *Skyrockets Dance Orchestra* / Spring will be a little late this year: *Skyrockets Dance Orchestra* / Dreamer: *Hall, Henry Orchestra* / Close to you: *Ambrose & His Orchestra* / Is my baby blue tonight: *Crowe, George & The Blue Mariners* / Chocolate soldier from the USA: *Parry, Harry & His Radio Rhythm Club Sextet* / Mairzy doats and dozy doats: *Preager, Lou & His Orchestra* / October mood: *Skyrockets Dance Orchestra*
CD ______ **RAJCD 826**
Empress / Aug '94 / Koch

WARTIME FAVOURITES VOL.3 - VICTORY
Keep an eye on your heart: *Geraldo & His Orchestra* / What more can I say: *Thorburn, Billy* / Don't sit under the apple tree: *Crosby, Bob & His Orchestra* / In my arms: *Geraldo & His Orchestra* / It costs so little: *Thorburn, Billy* / Smiths and the Jones: *Geraldo & His Orchestra* / All over the place: *New Mayfair Dance Orchestra* / You are my sunshine: *Roy, Harry & His Band* / You can't say no to a solider: *Geraldo & His Orchestra* / It's foolish but it's fun: *Thorburn, Billy* / Five o'clock whistle: *Loss, Joe & His Orchestra* / We three: *Gonella, Nat & His Georgians* / Hey Mabel: *Winstone, Eric* / Aurora: *Dorsey, Jimmy Orchestra* / Jingle jangle jingle: *Winstone, Eric & His Band* / Sailor with the navy blue eyes: *Roy, Harry & His Band* / Six lessons from Madame La Zonga: *Dorsey, Jimmy Orchestra* / I've got a gal in Kalamazoo: *Geraldo & His Orchestra* / I'm nobody's baby: *Gonella, Nat & His Georgians* / Yours: *Winstone, Eric & His Band* / Why don't you fall in love with me: *Roy, Harry & His Band* / Zoot suit: *Crosby, Bob & His Orchestra* / White cliffs of Dover: *Thorburn, Billy* / Pennsylvania polka: *Roy, Harry & His Band*
CD ______ **RAJCD 827**
Empress / Aug '94 / Koch

WARTIME MEMORIES 1939-1945 (The Sounds And Songs That Inspired The Nation)
Mars / God of war / Battle of Britain march / Guns of Navarone / Longest day / Victory at sea / Dambusters march / 633 squadron / Colditz march / Marches medley / Keep the home fires burning / Lillie Marlene/We're gonna hang out the washing / White cliffs of Dover / It's a long way to Tipperary/Pack up your troubles / Bless 'em all / Medley / I'll be seeing you/We'll meet again / Dance hall medley / In the mood / Sweet Georgia Brown / Jumpin' at the Woodside / Jerusalem / Land of hope and glory / Rule Britannia

CD SUMCD 4091
Summit / Jan '97 / Sound & Media

WASHINGTON DC GARAGE
CD COLCD 0523
Collectables / Jun '97 / Greyhound

WASSOULOU SOUND VOL.1
CD STCD 1035
Stern's / Oct '91 / ADA / CM / Stern's

WASSOULOU SOUND VOL.2
Kani kassi / Gnoumna ke la / Kankeletigui / Nale nale / Ni la kani / Mougakan / Ita dia / Simbo / Barika bognala / Djina Mousso
CD STCD 1048
Stern's / Mar '94 / ADA / CM / Stern's

WATCH HOW YOU FLEX (Reggae Dancehall)
CD SHCD 45002
Shanachie / Jun '93 / ADA / Greensleeves / Koch

WATER COMMUNICATION (2CD Set)
Spaced in: Newman, Colin / Metal sea: Immersion / Immerse: Pablo's Eye / Last hand: Ronnie & Clyde / Quo vardis: G-Man / Limbic: Lobe / Hide: Spigel, Malka / Cypher: Pablo's Eye / Kiss: Plastic Venus / Automation: Newman, Colin / World gardening: Oracle / Water walker: Trawl / Flow motion: Earth / Hacol zaram beyachad: Spigel, Malka / Affective: Lobe / Cinnebar: Ronnie & Clyde / Train: Plastic Venus / How long (is a piece of string): Immersion / Shadow: Dol-Lop / Chinned: G-Man
CD Set DWM 20
Swim / Feb '97 / Kudos / RTM/Disc / SRD

WATERHOUSE REVISITED
CD HCD 7012
Hightone / Dec '94 / ADA / Koch

WATERHOUSE REVISITED VOL.2
CD HCD 7013
Hightone / Mar '95 / ADA / Koch

WATERLOO SUNSET (20 Hits Of The Sixties)
Waterloo sunset: Kinks / Tomorrow: Shaw, Sandie / Call me number one: Tremeloes / Universal: Small Faces / Suzannah's still alive: Davies, Dave / Other man's grass: Clark, Petula / Something's gotten hold of my heart: Pitney, Gene / I'm gonna make you mine: Christie, Lou / Make me an island: Dolan, Joe / It's too late now: Baldry, Long John / Are you growing tired of my love: Status Quo / Simon says: 1910 Fruitgum Company / Oh happy day: Hawkins, Edwin Singers / Just one smile: Pitney, Gene / Puppet on a string: Shaw, Sandie / In the bad bad old days: Foundations / Green tambourine: Lemon Pipers / Man of the world: Fleetwood Mac / Let's go to San Francisco: Flowerpot Men / America: Nice
CD TRTCD 106
TrueTrax / Oct '94 / THE

WATERLOO SUNSET STORY, THE
I want to sleep with you: Eleanor Rigby / Till the end of the day: Eleanor Rigby / Take another shot of my heart: Eleanor Rigby / 1995: Eleanor Rigby / Where have all the good times gone: Eleanor Rigby / Mad Xmas: Eleanor Rigby / Kiss me quickly it's Xmas: Eleanor Rigby / Make up your mind: Reaction / 4 X 4: Reaction / Over and over: Eleanor Rigby / Last night in Soho: Eleanor Rigby / See my friend: Eleanor Rigby / Honeydipper: Beatboy / Please please: Beatboy / Man from uncle: Grave / Airport blues: Beatboy / Love on the phone: Eleanor Rigby / Think for yourself: Eleanor Rigby / Teenage sex: Psychomatics / Gotta move: Psychomatics / Censorship: Eleanor Rigby
CD FLEG 10CD
Future Legend / Aug '97 / Future Legend / Pinnacle

WATERMELON FILES OF TEXAS MUSIC, THE
CD MSACD 9
Munich / Dec '94 / ADA / CM / Direct / Greensleeves

WATT WORKS FAMILY ALBUM
Fleur carnivore: Bley, Carla / Best of friends: Mantler, Karen / Walking batteriewoman: Bley, Carla / A l'abattoir: Mantler, Michael / Crab alley: Swallow, Steve / When I run: Mantler, Michael / I can't stand...: Weisberg, Steve / Alien (part 2): Mantler, Michael / Talking hearts: Bley, Carla / Twenty: Mantler, Michael / I hate to sing: Bley, Carla / Movie six: Mantler, Michael / AD infinitum: Bley, Carla / Doubtful guest: Mantler, Michael / Funny bird: Bley, Carla
CD 8414782
Watt / Jan '90 / New Note/Pinnacle

WAVE (The Biggest New Wave Hits/3CD Set)
To cut a long story short: Spandau Ballet / White wedding: Idol, Billy / So long: Fischer Z / Asylum in Jerusalem: Scritti Politti / Don't dictate: Penetration / Everybody's gotta learn sometime: Korgis / Wishing if I had a photograph of you: Flock Of Seagulls / All stood still: Ultravox / Girls: Twilly, Dwight / She blinded me with science: Dolby, Thomas / Wishful thinking: China Crisis / Golden brown: Stranglers / Hit me with your rhythm stick: Dury, Ian / My Sharona: Knack / Hot in the city: Idol, Billy / Telephone always ring: Fun Boy Three / Love like blood: Killing Joke / I ran: Flock Of Seagulls / Dear God: XTC / Chant no.1: Spandau Ballet / Sinful: Wylie, Pete / Reasons to be cheerful: Dury, Ian & The Blockheads / Slippery people: Talking Heads / Love of the common people: Talking Heads / Drowning: Stiff Little Fingers / Drowning in Berlin: Mobiles / Big apple: Kajagoogoo / Independence day: Kajagoogoo / Temptation: Heaven 17 / Musclebound: Spandau Ballet / Hyperactive: Dolby, Thomas / Good heart: Sharkey, Feargal / Shouldn't have to be like that: Fra Lippo Lippi / At home he's a tourist: Gang Of Four / Dream kitchen: Frazier Chorus / Echo beach: Martha & The Muffins / Worker: Fischer Z / Turning Japanese: Vapors / Day one: Comsat Angels / Money: Flying Lizards / Church of the poison mind: Culture Club / Sex and drugs and rock 'n' roll: Dury, Ian / Psycho killer: Talking Heads
CD Set HR 868442
Disky / Sep '96 / Disky / THE

WAVE FORUM (WAVE RECORDS COMPILATION)
CD WAVE 222
Cleveland City / Jun '97 / 3mv/Sony / Grapevine/PolyGram

WAVE PARTY
Goody two shoes: Adam Ant / Feels like heaven: Fiction Factory / This is the day: The The / Skin deep: Stranglers / Pretty in pink: Psychedelic Furs / Doot doot: Fruer / Who can it be now: Men At Work / You spin me round (like a record): Dead Or Alive / Don't talk to me about love: Altered Images / Talking in your sleep: Romantics / Real gone kid: Deacon Blue / Wheel: Spear Of Destiny / Birth, school, work, death: Godfathers / Heaven: Psychedelic Furs / Be free with your love: Spandau Ballet / Dutch mountains: Nits
CD 4758322
Columbia / Dec '95 / Sony

WAVE ROMANTICS VOL.2
Do you love me: Cave, Nick / Green and grey: New Model Army / Golden brown: Stranglers / Beside you: Iggy Pop / Vienna: Ultravox
CD SPV 08438992
SPV / Feb '95 / Koch / Plastic Head

WAVY GRAVY VOL.1 (For Adult Enthusiasts)
CD BEWARECD 001
Beware / May '97 / Cargo

WAVY GRAVY VOL.2
CD BEWARECD 003
Beware / Feb '97 / Cargo

WAY FOR BRITTANY, A
CD CD 819
Escalibur / Aug '93 / ADA / Discovery / Roots

WAY FOR IRELAND, A
CD CD 314
Arfolk / Aug '93 / ADA / Discovery / Roots

WAY FOR SCOTLAND, A
CD CD 313
Arfolk / Aug '93 / ADA / Discovery / Roots

WAY IT IS, THE
CD LF 250CD
Lost & Found / Jun '96 / Plastic Head

WAY OUT CHAPTER, THE
CD HLCD 2
Hard Leaders / Jul '97 / SRD

WAY WITH THE GIRLS (30 Female Soul Rarities From The 1960's)
You will never get away: Maye, Cholli / Here come the heartaches: Lovells / I'm a sad girl: Johnson, Deena / If you can stand me: Lewis, Tamala / Thrills and chills: Smith, Helene / I feel strange: Wonderettes / Lost without your love: Carlettes / Now that I found you baby: Mirettes / It's over: Lindsay, Terry / It's all over: Gee's / Why weren't you there: Lindsay, Thelma / Step aside baby: Lollipops / It happens every day: Persianettes / Source of love: Marie, Gina / Sweet sweet love: Durettes / Pretty boy: Hall, Dora / Big man: Starr, Karen / Ain't gonna hurt my pride: Judi & The Affections / You're the guy: Argie & The Arketts / There's something the matter (with your heart): Cynthia & The Imaginations / Wonderful one: Lindsey, Theresa / Oh, my sweet love: Lee, Barbara / If you love me (show me): Monique / Sugar boy: Charmettes / Don't cha tell nobody: Vont Claires / Don't cry: Irma & The Larks / My fault: Passionettes / Try my love: Sequins / How can I get to you: Soul, Sharon / His way with the girls: Lornettes
CD GSCD 029
Goldmine / Mar '94 / Vital

WAYS OF LOVE, THE
Careless whisper: Michael, George / Your love is king: Sade / So amazing: Vandross, Luther / Softly whispering I love you: Young, Paul / I'll never fall in love again: Deacon Blue / Eternal flame: Bangles / Time and tide: Basia / Wishing you were here: Moyet, Alison / Through the barricades: Spandau Ballet / Castle in the clouds: Craven, Beverley / Stay with me 'til dawn: Tzuke, Judie / Unconditional love: Hoffs, Susanna / Toy soldiers: Martika / Baby I love your way/ Freebird: Will To Power
CD 4720732
Columbia / Aug '92 / Sony

WE ARE ICERINK
Birth of Sharon: Earl Brutus / When I get to heaven: Sensuround / Don't destroy me: Golden / V neck: Elizabeth City State / Supermarket: Supermarket / (Why don't you) Ring me: Hard Muscle / Love hour: Oval / Bob cool: Spring / Don't worry baby: Melody Dog / Bouffant headbutt: Shampoo / Dub to the stars (Instrumental): Parallel Universe / New electric pop and soul: World Of Twist
CD DAVO 001CD
Icerink / May '94 / Pinnacle

WE ARE ONE (Griot Songs From Mali)
CD PAN 2015CD
Pan / Aug '94 / ADA / CM / Direct

WE ARE THE BLUES
CD 5238382
PolyGram Jazz / Feb '95 / PolyGram

WE ARE THE CHAMPIONS (20 Football Fantasies)
Come on you gunners: Arsenal FC / Come on you Villa: Aston Villa FC / Army swing: Blackburn Rovers FC / We'll keep the flag flying high: Chelsea FC / Go for it: Coventry City FC / Going back to Derby: Derby County FC / Everyone is cheering the blues: Everton FC / Leeds, Leeds, Leeds (marching on together): Leeds Utd FC / This is the season for us: Leicester City FC / Anfield rap '96: Liverpool FC / Glory glory Man United: Manchester Utd FC / We're coming through: Middlesbrough FC / Black 'n' white (toon army): Newcastle Utd FC / Nottingham Forest is my rock 'n' roll: Nottingham Forest FC / We are the owls: Sheffield Wednesday FC / Legend of the saint: Southampton FC / Daydream believer (cheer up Peter Reid): Sunderland AFC / Tottenham, Tottenham: Tottenham Hotspur FC / Forever blowing bubbles: West Ham Utd FC / We are Wimbledon: Wimbledon FC
CD SUMCD 4076
Summit / Nov '96 / Sound & Media

WE BITE 100
CD WB 1100CD
We Bite / Jan '96 / Plastic Head

WE BITE LIVE '91
CD WBCD 076
We Bite / Jan '92 / Plastic Head

WE BITE TOO
CD WB 100012
We Bite / Jan '96 / Plastic Head

WE CAME TO DANCE
CD SPV 08438822
SPV / Jul '95 / Koch / Plastic Head

WE CAME TO DANCE VOL.10 (2CD Set)
Morphedus: Skinny Puppy / Isolation: Die Krupps / Deliverance: Atrocity / Ich bin der brennede kamet: Lacrimosa / I can't enjoy it: Blind Passengers / San Diego: Cyan / Erkaufte traume: Goethes Erben / Der trieb: Umbra Et Imago / Dusk: Dreadful Shadows / This empty ocean: Love Like Blood / Small world: Secret Discovery / Santos inocentes: Calva Y Nada / Kill a raver (I came to dance): Leather Strip / Misery: Psyche / Der unbesiegte sonnegott: Forthcoming Fire / November day: Inside / Can I do what I want: Shock Therapy / Touch: Klinik / Furnace: New Mind / Shockwaved: Still Silent / Chameleon: Still Patient / Suchtig: Dorsetshire / Violent world: Ravenous / Fragile tomorrow: Aqua / Organics: Evil's Toy / Die for Jehovah: Birmingham 6 / Become an angel: In Strict Confidence / Sun: Under The Noise / Game: Abscess / Radioactive love: Daily Planet / Blind man dreams: Elegant Machinery / In power we entrust to love: Chandeen
CD Set DCD 08647302
SPV / Apr '97 / Koch / Plastic Head

WE CAME TO DANCE VOL.4
Non stop violence: Apoptygma Berzerk / Soul cremation: Delay / Barcode: Frontline Assembly / Another day: Ichor / Under your skin: Bischoff, Silke / We deserve it all: Leather Strip / Colour of truth: Girls Under Glass / Du riechst so gut: Rammstein / Metalmorphosis: Die Krupps / Hey fuck da world: Klute / Figurehead: Covenant / Toys for Alice: Sleeping Dogs Wake / Spiderdust: Bel Canto / Sorciere: La Floa Maldita / Looking glass men: Forma Tadre / Prophecy: Delerium
CD SPV 08538632
SPV / Apr '96 / Koch / Plastic Head

WE CAME TO DANCE VOL.9 (Dark Wave & Electro)
TOMAM: Cobalt 60 / Deep red: Apoptygma Berzerk / Free and alive: X Marks The Pedwalk / Don't turn around: Blind Passengers / Agony of ecstasy: Image Transmission / I try, I die: Leather Strip / This blackness: Gracious Shades / Pictures: Derriere Le Miroir / Vampire: Inside / Beneath the skin: Collide / Programmed for hell: Fracture / Levitation: Individual Totem / Cybegod: Rame / I beg for you: Distain / L'oasis: La Floa Maldita / To protect and to serve: Bischoff, Silke
CD SPV 08547042
SPV / Sep '96 / Koch / Plastic Head

WE DIED IN HELL - THEY CALLED IT PASSCHENDAELE
CD MAPCD 93004CD
Map / Jan '94 / ADA / Direct

WE GOT A PARTY (Best Of Ron Records Vol.1)
CD ROUCD 2076
Rounder / ADA / CM / Direct

WE RULE DANCEHALL
CD KGCD 002
Keeling / Jan '96 / Jet Star

WE WILL ROCK YOU
CD DINCD 26
Dino / Sep '91 / Pinnacle

WE WISH YOU A MERRY CHRISTMAS
CD MACCD 206
Autograph / Aug '96 / BMG

WEDDING ALBUM, THE (To Have And To Hold)
CD QTVCD 006
Quality / Jun '92 / Pinnacle

WEDDING MUSIC OF MARAMURES
CD C 580052
Ocora / Jan '94 / ADA / Harmonia Mundi

WEEK IN THE REAL WORLD VOL.1, A
CD CDRW 25
Realworld / Jul '92 / EMI

WEEK OR TWO IN THE REAL WORLD
CD CDRW 30
Realworld / Jul '94 / EMI

WEEKENDER (12 Extended Dance Classics)
CD MUSCD 010
MCI Music / Sep '93 / Disc / THE

WEEKENDERS
Common people: Pulp / Girls and boys: Blur / Stars: Dubstar / Spooky: New Order / Voodoo people: Prodigy / In dust we trust: Chemical Brothers / Blow the whole joint up: Monkey Mafia / Big time sensuality: Bjork / Weirdo: Charlatans / Dubdreamer: Menswear / Lazarus: Boo Radleys / Halcyon: Orbital / Vow: Garbage / La tristessa durerra: Manic Street Preachers / Hallelujah: Happy Mondays / Kosmos: Weller, Paul / Waterfall: Stone Roses
CD 8287662
London / Apr '96 / PolyGram

WELCOME TO IRELAND
Two recruiting sergeants / Four strong winds / Highlevel / Cregan white hare / Honey and wine / Orange maid of Sligo / Bottles of black porter: Caern Folk Trio / Ballinderry: Caern Folk Trio / Flight of Earls: Caern Folk Trio / German clock winder: Caern Folk Trio / I know my love: Caern Folk Trio / Guns and drums: Caern Folk Trio / Ball o' yarn: Caern Folk Trio / I am a rover: Caern Folk Trio
CD EMPRCD 713
Emporio / Apr '97 / Disc

WELCOME TO NORTHERN IRELAND
CD CDNI 001
Outlet / May '96 / ADA / CM / Direct / Duncans / Koch / Ross

WELCOME TO NY NOW GO HOME
CD BSR 103CD
Bittersweet / Jan '97 / Cargo

WELCOME TO PLANET REVCO
CD REVCC 009
Revco / Jul '96 / Grapevine/PolyGram / Timewarp

WELCOME TO SCOTLAND
Teviot brig: Shand, Jimmy Jr. / Quaker's wife: Shand, Jimmy Jr. / Ishbel's jig: Shand, Jimmy Jr. / Comin' thro' the rye: MacLeod, Jim / My love is like a red red rose: MacLeod, Jim / Bonnie Galloway: MacLeod, Jim / Soft lowland tongue: MacLeod, Jim / Uist tramping song: Anderson, Moira / Roamin' in the gloamin': Shand, Jimmy Jr. / I love a lassie: Shand, Jimmy Jr. / Stop your ticklin' jock: Shand, Jimmy Jr. / Wee Deoch an' Doris: Shand, Jimmy Jr. / Northern lights of old Aberdeen: Logan, Jimmy / Battle o'er: Shand, Jimmy Jr. / I see mull: Anderson, Moira / Mairi's wedding: MacLeod, Jim & His Band / Bill Thomson's farewell to Dublane: MacLeod, Jim & His Band / Rabbie's visit: MacLeod, Jim & His Band / Carronades: MacLeod, Jim & His Band / Pheonix: MacLeod, Jim & His Band / Lassie come and dance with me: MacLeod, Jim & His Band / I lo'e nae a laddie: MacLeod, Jim & His Band / Muckin' O' Geordie's byre: MacLeod, Jim & His Band / Wi' a hundred pipers: MacLeod, Jim & His Band / Dancing in Kyle: Anderson, Moira / Jock McKay: Shand, Jimmy Jr. / Gordon for me: Shand, Jimmy Jr. / Lass of lowrie: Shand, Jimmy Jr. / Down in the Glen: Logan, Jimmy / Memories of Orkney: Shand, Jimmy Jr. / Macfarlane O' the sproats: MacLeod, Jim & His Band / Bonnie lass o'Fyvie: MacLeod, Jim & His Band / Barnyards o'Delgaty: MacLeod, Jim & His Band / Mormond braes: MacLeod, Jim & His Band / Polka danska: Shand, Jimmy Jr. / My ain' folk: Logan, Jimmy
CD CDMFP 6314
EMI Gold / Feb '97 / EMI

WELCOME TO THE BLUES VOL.1
CD 157572
Blues Collection / Feb '93 / Discovery

WELCOME TO THE BLUES VOL.2
CD 157592
Blues Collection / Feb '93 / Discovery

WELCOME TO THE FUTURE VOL.1
CD _______ TPLP 50CD
One Little Indian / Mar '93 / Pinnacle

WELCOME TO THE FUTURE VOL.2
Human behaviour: *Bjork* / Beautiful morning: *Soul Family Sensation* / Sugar daddy: *Secret Knowledge* / Comin' on: *Shamen* / Devo: *Crunch* / God: *Hypnotist* / UK : USA: *Eskimos & Egypt* / FU2: *FUSE* / Obsession: *Wishdokta & Vibes*
CD _______ TPLP 60CD
One Little Indian / Jan '94 / Pinnacle

WELCOME TO THE FUTURE VOL.3
CD _______ TPLP 80CD
One Little Indian / Oct '95 / Pinnacle

WELCOME TO THE FUTURE VOL.4
CD _______ SUB 27D
Subversive / Feb '97 / 3mv/Sony / Amato Disco / Mo's Music Machine / Prime / Vital

WELCOME TO THE LAND OF HONEYDIPPED
CD _______ DIPAL 001CD
Honeydipped / Sep '95 / Jumpstart / Kudos / Pinnacle

WELCOME TO THE SUMMER OF LOVE '93
CD _______ HFCD 29
PWL / Jul '93 / Warner Music

WELCOME TO THE WORLD OF DEMI-MONDE
CD _______ DMCD 1030
Demi-Monde / Oct '95 / RTM/Disc / TKO Magnum

WELCOME TO TRANSWORLD
CD _______ TRANNYCD 1
Transworld / Apr '96 / Pinnacle

WELCOME TO WHITE CLOUD'S WORLD OF MUSIC
CD _______ WCL 110302
White Cloud / Jul '97 / Select

WELL CHARGED
CD _______ PSCD 14
Pressure Sounds / Jun '97 / Jet Star / SRD

WE'LL MEET AGAIN (2CD Set)
CD Set _______ DBG 53038
Double Gold / Jan '95 / Target/BMG

WE'LL MEET AGAIN
We're gonna hang out the washing on the Siegfried Line: *Two Leslies* / White cliffs of Dover: *Lynn, Vera* / Could you please oblige us with a bren gun: *Coward, Noel* / Run rabbit run: *Flanagan & Allen* / Ma, I miss your apple pie: *Blue Rockets Dance Orchestra* / This is the army Mr. Jones: *Berlin, Irving* / I'm going to get lit up (when the lights go on in London): *Gibbons, Carroll* / Fleet's in Port again: *Breeze, Alan* / Painting the clouds with sunshine: *Hylton, Jack* / I'll be seeing you: *Gibbons, Carroll* / Hey little hen: *Loss, Joe* / Imagine me in the Maginot Line: *Formby, George* / Deepest shelter in town: *Desmond, Florence* / Beer barrel polka (Roll out the barrel): *Andrews Sisters* / Der Fuhrer's face: *Jones, Spike & His City Slickers* / Goodnight, wherever you are: *Leader, Harry & His Band* / I did what I could with my gas mask: *Formby, George* / In the mood: *Miller, Glenn* / We'll meet again: *Lynn, Vera*
CD _______ QED 171
Tring / Nov '96 / Tring

WELL TRODDEN PATH, THE
CD _______ CR 00092
Czech Radio / Nov '95 / Czech Music Enterprises

WELSH CHOIRS
Land of my fathers / God bless the Prince of Wales / You'll never walk alone / Soldiers chorus / All through the night / Guide me o thou great redeemer / Old man river / With cat like tread / Battle hymn of the republic / Old folks at home / Cwm Rhondda / Selection from les miserables / Steal away
CD _______ 300822
Hallmark / Jul '96 / Carlton

WELSH CHORAL FAVOURITES
My little Welsh home: *Dunvant Male Choir* / Soldier's farewell: *Dunvant Male Choir* / Close thing eyes: *Dunvant Male Choir* / Stodole pumpa: *Gwalia Male Choir* / Heimat: *Gwalia Male Choir* / Marching song: *Gwalia Male Choir* / Steal away: *Gwalia Male Choir* / Hiraeth: *Morriston Orpheus Choir* / Hyder: *Morriston Orpheus Choir* / American trilogy: *Morriston Orpheus Choir* / My dearest dear: *Morriston Orpheus Choir* / Martyrs of the arena: *Morriston Orpheus Choir* / My hero: *Morriston Orpheus Choir* / Ride the chariot: *Pontarddulais Male Voice Choir* / Windmills of your mind: *Pontarddulais Male Voice Choir* / Mil harddach wyt na'r rhosyn Gwyn: *Pontarddulais Male Voice Choir* / Memory: *Canoldir Male Voice Choir* / Eli Jenkin's prayer: *Canoldir Male Voice Choir* / My love is like a red red rose: *Canoldir Male Voice Choir*
CD _______ CDMFP 6367
Music For Pleasure / May '97 / EMI

WELSH MALE VOICE CHOIRS
CD _______ CDMFP 6366
Music For Pleasure / May '97 / EMI

WELSH SOLOS AND SONGS
CD _______ SCD 2109
Sain / Feb '96 / ADA / Direct / Greyhound

WEMBLEY MILITARY TATOO
CD _______ PLSCD 180
Pulse / Apr '97 / BMG

WEMBLEY MILITARY TATTOO
CD _______ MATCD 238
Castle / Dec '92 / BMG

WENDY
Never ending dream: *X-Perience* / Do it for love: *Caught In The Act* / Break it up: *Scooter* / One and one: *Miles, Robert* / Falling in love: *Bed & Breakfast* / All the places: *BND* / Show me the way: *Mr. President* / Don't make me wait: *911* / Who wants to live forever: *Dune* / Rainbows in the sky: *Yasmin* / Don't speak: *Clueless* / So strung out: *C-Block* / Crimson and clover: *2 Young* / And the beat goes on: *Lorenza* / I was born to love you: *Worlds Apart* / Pray: *DJ Bobo* / Right way: *Mark Oh* / Bolingo: *La Bouche*
CD _______ ZYX 550702
ZYX / Apr '97 / ZYX

WE'RE HERE BECAUSE WE'RE HERE - PASCHENDALE
CD _______ NMCD 9CD
No Master's Voice / Jul '95 / ADA / Direct

WE'RE HERE BECUASE WE'RE HERE
CD _______ NMCD 8
No Master's Voice / Jan '96 / ADA / Direct

WE'RE SO PRETTY VOL.1 (3CD Set)
CD Set _______ DTKBOX 58
Dressed To Kill / Dec '96 / Total/BMG

WE'RE SO PRETTY VOL.2 (3CD Set)
CD Set _______ DTKBOX 59
Dressed To Kill / Dec '96 / Total/BMG

WEST 25TH CLASSICS
CD _______ CHIP 152
Jive / Oct '94 / Pinnacle

WEST 25TH VOL.1
CD _______ CHIP 151
Jive / Aug '94 / Pinnacle

WEST 25TH VOL.2
CD _______ CHIP 157
Jive / Jul '95 / Pinnacle

WEST 25TH VOL.3
CD _______ CHIP 167
Jive / Feb '97 / Pinnacle

WEST BY NORTH-SOUTH
CD _______ VR 322C
Vagrant / Feb '97 / Cargo

WEST COAST RADIO HITS (Rock)
Drown in your ocean: *Walker, Brett & The Railbirds* / Right kind of love: *Drury, Timothy* / Working man: *King Of Hearts* / What's still left: *Walker, Brett & The Railbirds* / Silver and gold: *Walker Zapper Overdrive* / I know you: *Waybill, Fee* / Yesterday has gone: *Walker, Brett & The Railbirds* / All the love we kill: *Spiro, Mark* / Lessons of the heart: *Feehan, Tim* / Tell me why: *Walker, Brett & The Railbirds* / Can't help ourselves: *Drury, Timothy* / Surprise yourself: *Waybill, Fee* / Confidential: *D'Avesta, Delin* / Wherever this road may lead you: *Steel Horses* / Stay young: *Spiro, Mark* / American dreamer: *Walker, Brett & The Railbirds* / Blue lights: *Rake & The Surftones*
CD _______ WESTCD 13
West Coast / Mar '97 / Cargo

WEST COAST RADIO HITS (Love)
Wishful thinking: *Drury, Timothy* / It's a good thing: *Walker, Brett & The Railbirds* / Don't call my name: *King Of Hearts* / In the dark: *Spiro, Mark* / Haunt me tonight: *Marx, Richard* / Where is your love: *Jordan, Marc* / Fallin' in love: *Clewer, Janey* / I don't miss you too: *Feehan, Tim* / Just to be loved: *Champlin, Bill* / I'll set you free: *Drury, Timothy* / Everything I want: *Walker, Brett & The Railbirds* / King of hearts: *King Of Hearts* / Somewhere deep inside: *Waybill, Fee* / I'll be over you: *Goodrum, Randy* / October in Oxnard: *Rake & The Surftones* / After the love is gone: *King Of Hearts* / It still stings: *Drury, Timothy*
CD _______ WESTCD 12
West Coast / Mar '97 / Cargo

WEST COAST RAP VOL.1
CD _______ CDSEWM 050
Southbound / Jul '92 / Pinnacle

WEST COAST RAP VOL.2
CD _______ CDSEWM 051
Southbound / Jul '92 / Pinnacle

WEST COAST RAP VOL.3
CD _______ CDSEWM 052
Southbound / Jul '92 / Pinnacle

WEST COAST WAILERS VOL.1 (Harmonica Blues)
CD _______ DTCD 3036
Double Trouble / Oct '96 / CM / Hot Shot

WEST END GIRLS
CD _______ 12215
Laserlight / Aug '94 / Target/BMG

WEST END STORY VOL.1
Heartbeat: *Gardner, Taana* / Let's go dancin': *Sparque* / Heat you up (melt you down): *Lites, Shirley* / Do it to the music: *Raw Silk* / Can't you feel it: *Michelle* / Rescue me: *Thomas, Sybil* / Time: *Stone* / You can't have your cake: *Taylor, Brenda*
CD _______ 110652
Musidisc / Jun '93 / Discovery

WEST END STORY VOL.2
Work that body: *Gardner, Taana* / It's all over my face: *Loose Joints* / Another man: *Mason, Barbara* / Give your body up to music: *Nichols, Billy* / Ride on the rhythm: *Mahogany* / Girl I like the way you move: *Stone* / Doin' the best that I can: *Lavette, Bettye* / Just in time: *Rawsilk*
CD _______ 110692
Musidisc / Aug '93 / Discovery

WEST END STORY VOL.3
When you touch me: *Gardner, Taana* / Let me feel your heartbeat: *Glass* / Music turns me on: *Sparque* / When the shit hits the fan: *Master Boogie's song & dance* / Disco dance: *Michele* / Chillin' out: *Brooks, Inez* / Speak well: *Philly USA* / Keep on dancin': *Phrase II*
CD _______ 110942
Musidisc / Nov '93 / Discovery

WEST END STORY VOL.4
No frills: *Gardner, Taana* / Take some time: *Sparque* / Searchin' for some lovin': *Trusty, Debbie* / I get lifted: *Sweet Life* / Hot summer nights: *Love Club* / Don't I ever cross your mind: *Mason, Barbara* / Hold me, squeeze me: *Michele* / People come dance: *Holt, Ednah & Starluv*
CD _______ 111872
Musidisc / Jan '94 / Discovery

WEST INDIES - AN ISLAND CARNIVAL
CD _______ 7559720912
Nonesuch / Jan '95 / Warner Music

WEST SOUND CIRCLE
CD _______ EFA 004552
Interference / Mar '96 / SRD

WESTBOUND SOUND OF DETROIT
Gonna spread the news: *Unique Blend* / Yes I'm in love: *Unique Blend* / Does he treat you better: *Unique Blend* / Monny and Daddy: *Unique Blend* / Old fashioned woman: *Unique Blend* / Lonely in a crowd: *Superlatives* / I don't know how (to say I love you) don't walk away: *Superlatives* / Things are looking up: *Detroit Emeralds* / Rosetta Stone: *Detroit Emeralds* / That's all I got: *Detroit Emeralds* / If you need me, call me (and I'll come running): *Fantastic Four* / I'm falling in love (I feel good all over): *Fantastic Four* / What's it all about: *Counts* / Happy days: *Magictones* / Everything's gonna be alright: *Magictones* / I've changed: *Magictones* / I'll make it up to you: *Magictones* / Trying real hard (to make the grade): *Magictones* / I don't what it is but it sho is funky: *Mighty Elegant* / I find myself falling in love with you: *Mighty Elegant* / What am I gonna do: *Houston Outlaws* / I'm loving you, you're leaving me: *Motivations* / I love you: *Motivations* / My baby ain't no plaything: *New Holidays* / When I'm back on my feet: *Various Narrators*
CD _______ CDSEWD 065
Westbound / Aug '94 / Pinnacle

WESTERN COUNTRY HITS
CD _______ 55135
Laserlight / Oct '95 / Target/BMG

WESTERN SWING ON THE AIR 1948-1961
CD _______ RFCD 07
Country Routes / Oct '91 / Hot Shot / Jazz Music

WE'VE GOT ONE WICKED BOGLE
CD _______ SGCD 12
Sir George / Dec '92 / Jet Star / Pinnacle

WE'VE GOT TONIGHT (Classic Love Songs)
CD _______ PLSCD 179
Pulse / Apr '97 / BMG

WHAAM BAM THANK YOU DAN
In the afternoon: *Revolving Paint Dream* / I know where Syd Barrett lives: *TV Personalities* / Never find time: *Mixers* / You're my kind of girl: *Page Boys* / Only the sky children know: *Page Boys* / Too shy: *Direct Hits* / Dream inspires: *TV Personalities* / Still dreaming: *Marbie Staircase* / Art of love: *1000 Mexicans* / Dancing with the dead / I'm sad: *Dmochowski, Jedrez* / Wouldn't you: *Laughing Apples* / Bike: *TV Personalities* / I'm in love with you: *Page Boys* / Naughty little boys: *Direct Hits* / My favourite films: *Gifted Children* / Dark ages: *Marble Staircase* / Love hurts: *Mixers* / Painting by numbers: *Gifted Children* / News of you: *1000 Mexicans* / No one's little girl: *TV Personalities* / What killed Alesiter Crowley: *Direct Hits*
CD _______ ASKCD 043
Vinyl Japan / May '95 / Plastic Head / Vinyl Japan

WHAT A BAM BAM (Women in Reggae: Dancehall Queens)
CD _______ SH 45028
Shanachie / Nov '96 / ADA / Greensleeves / Koch

WHAT A DIFFERENCE A DAY MADE
CD _______ AVC 526
Avid / Nov '93 / Avid/BMG / Koch / THE

WHAT A FEELING (2CD Set)
Flashdance (what a feeling): *Cara, Irene* / Celebration: *Kool & The Gang* / Oops upside your head: *Gap Band* / Ain't nobody: *Rufus & Chaka Khan* / If I can't have you: *Elliman, Yvonne* / Hang on in there baby: *Bristol, Johnny* / Think: *Franklin, Aretha* / Car wash: *Royce, Rose* / Hustle: *McCoy, Van* / Heaven must be missing an angel: *Tavares* / Let's groove: *Earth, Wind & Fire* / Native New Yorker: *Odyssey* / You're the first, my last, my everything: *White, Barry* / Let's hear it for the boy: *Williams, Deniece* / Best of my love: *Emotions* / Lost in music: *Sister Sledge* / Play that funky music: *Wild Cherry* / Dance to the music: *Sly & The Family Stone* / Can you feel it: *Jacksons* / Stayin' alive: *N-Trance* / Footloose: *Loggins, Kenny* / Fame: *Cara, Irene* / Young hearts run free: *Staton, Candi* / Love train: *O'Jays* / We are family: *Sister Sledge* / That's the way (I like it): *KC & The Sunshine Band* / It's raining men: *Weather Girls* / You make me feel (Mighty real): *Sylvester* / Sound of Philadelphia: *MFSB* / You gave me love: *Crown Heights Affair* / I can make tyou feel good: *Shalamar* / Knock on wood: *Stewart, Amii* / You to me are everything: *Real Thing* / Kissin' in the back row of the movies: *Drifters* / I'm doin' fine now: *New York City* / Get dancin': *Disco Tex & The Sexolettes* / Rock the boat: *Hues Corporation* / Shoop shoop song (It's in his kiss): *Cher* / Boogie Wonderland: *Earth, Wind & Fire* / It's a love thing: *Whispers* / you're the one that I want: *Gibson, Debbie & Craig McLachlan*
CD _______ SONYTV 26CD
Sony TV / May '97 / Sony

WHAT A WAY TO COME DOWN
CD _______ CDWIKD 173
Big Beat / Aug '97 / Pinnacle

WHAT DID YOU COME DOWN FOR
CD _______ NEKO 001
Neko / Jun '96 / SRD
CD _______ NEK 1D
Genki / Aug '97 / SRD

WHAT DO YOU WANT A JAPANESE TO DO
Just ask why: *Revs* / Big yellow taxi: *Elmerhassel* / She's gone: *Saturn V* / House of god: *Monochrome Set* / Pistols of colour: *Tokyo Skunx* / Dead head baby: *Fat Tulips* / Back again: *Grape* / I never loved you: *Strawberry Story* / Orange county: *Bluebells* / Cathedral high: *St. Christopher* / Come clean: *BMX Bandits* / I won't be there: *Milkshakes* / My boyfriend's learning karate: *Thee Headcoatees* / My favourite girl: *Hit Parade* / Locks and bolts: *Carousel* / Special to me: *Speedway Stars* / Aware of all: *McCluskey Brothers* / Mirror man: *Looking Glass* / Rosanna: *Haywains* / Nobody better: *SKAW* / Nine or seven: *Beatnik Filmstars* / Christmas tears: *Fletcher, Amelia & Hit Parade*
CD _______ ASKCD 015
Vinyl Japan / Feb '93 / Plastic Head / Vinyl Japan

WHAT GOES AROUND COMES AROUND
CD _______ PROCD 17
MC Projects / Mar '97 / Pinnacle / Prime

WHAT GOES ROUND
Medusa: *Solitaria* / Skits: *Primordial Soup* / Physche: *Phlex* / Domo arigato: *Phreax* / Got a 'BBD' 4 u: *Beat Junkies* / 575: *DJ Shufflemaster* / I kid you not my man: *Teasdale, Anthony* / SDFG: *Phlex* / Jack goes home: *Teasdale, Anthony*
CD _______ PROCD 017
MC Projects / Feb '97 / Pinnacle / Prime

WHAT IS FUNK
Do it ('til you're satisfied): *BT Express* / What is funk: *Rare Gems Odyssey* / Get the funk out ma face: *Brothers Johnson* / Take your time (do it right): *SOS Band* / Spirit of the boogie: *Kool & The Gang* / Don't stop the music: *Yarbrough & Peoples* / Funky Nassau: *Beginning Of The End* / Love injection: *Trussel* / You + me = love: *Undisputed Truth* / Yum yum (gimme some): *Fatback Band* / Finders keepers: *Chairmen Of The Board* / Express: *BT Express*
CD _______ RNBCD 108
Connoisseur Collection / Apr '94 / Pinnacle

WHAT IS JAZZ
CD _______ KFWCD 109
Knitting Factory / Nov '94 / Cargo / Plastic Head

WHAT IS JAZZ 1996
CD _______ KFWCD 195
Knitting Factory / Oct '96 / Cargo / Plastic Head

WHAT IS THIS THING CALLED LOVE (Cool Love Songs Of The 1930's/1940's)
Taking a chance on love: *Fitzgerald, Ella* / Sweet Lorraine: *Cole, Nat 'King'* / What is this thing called love: *Dorsey, Tommy & Connie Haines* / Sunshine of your smile: *Dorsey, Tommy & Frank Sinatra* / All of me: *Dorsey, Jimmy & Helen O'Connell* / Sposin': *Crosby, Bing* / Say it with a kiss: *Shaw, Artie & Helen Forrest* / May I never love again: *Weems, Ted & Perry Como* / He's funny that way: *Hawkins, Coleman & Thelma Carpenter* / These foolish things: *Goodman, Benny* / More than you know: *Wilson,*

Teddy & Billie Holiday / When somebody thinks you're wonderful: *Waller, Fats* / Body and soul: *Shore, Dinah* / Why do I love you: *Langford, Frances & Tony Martin* / I can't give you anything but love: *Armstrong, Louis* / Think it over: *Wynn, Nan* / Old fashioned love: *Mills Brothers* / Here's love in your eyes: *Wilson, Teddy & Helen Ward* / Two in love: *Krupa, Gene, Anita O'Day & Johnny Desmond* / Journey to a star: *Garland, Judy* / Nearness of you: *Miller, Glenn & Ray Eberle* / Man I love: *Lamour, Dorothy*
CD ______ PPCD 78114
Past Perfect / Feb '95 / Glass Gramophone Co.

WHAT IT IS
CD ______ LHCD 008
Luv n' Haight / Jul '96 / Timewarp

WHAT SWEET MUSIC THEY MAKE VOL.1
CD ______ VAMPCD 001
Raven/Vampire Guild / Nov '96 / Plastic Head

WHAT SWEET MUSIC THEY MAKE VOL.2
CD ______ VAMPCD 002
Raven/Vampire Guild / Nov '96 / Plastic Head

WHAT SWEET MUSIC THEY MAKE VOL.3
CD ______ RIP 100CD
Raven/Vampire Guild / Nov '96 / Plastic Head

WHATCHA GONNA SWING TONIGHT
CD ______ RHRCD 50
Red House / Oct '95 / ADA / Koch

WHAT'S COOKIN'
CD ______ URCD 014
Ubiquity / Jul '96 / Cargo / Timewarp

WHAT'S HAPPENIN' DRUM AND BASS VOL.1
Gotta have your love: *McCrae, Gwen* / F-jam: *Adam F* / Run away bass: *Filthy Rich & Hermion* / We can make it happen: *Nookie & NCA* / Money: *BLIM* / Galcier: *BLIM* / Urban blues: *Girley, Steve* / Traces of guilt: *Expresso* / Ladder: *Tonic & Purple Kola* / Rock the funky beat: *Natural Born Chillers* / Let the bass boom: *TC & Slam* / Chillin' on da phunk: *Elementz Of Noise* / Danger: *Ed Solo* / Comin' thru: *Urbanites* / JSA 1: *Rude Bwoy Monty* / Nasty: *Shy FX* / Dub moods: *Aphrodite* / Summer dub: *Aladdin*
CD ______ WATSCD 1
AU / Jun '97 / Timewarp

WHAT'S IN THE PUB IN 1996
CD ______ PUB 001CD
Pub / Jun '96 / Direct

WHAT'S SHAKIN'
Good time music: *Lovin' Spoonful* / Almost grown: *Lovin' Spoonful* / Spoonful: *Butterfield, Paul Blues Band* / Off the wall: *Butterfield, Paul Blues Band* / Can't keep from cryin' sometimes: *Kooper, Al* / I want to know: *Clapton, Eric & The Powerhouse* / Crossroads: *Clapton, Eric & The Powerhouse* / Lovin' cup: *Butterfield, Paul Blues Band* / Good morning little school girl: *Butterfield, Paul* / Steppin' out: *Clapton, Eric & The Powerhouse* / I'm in love again: *Rush, Tom* / Don't bank on it baby / Searchin' / One more mile: *Butterfield, Paul Blues Band*
CD ______ 7559613432
Elektra / Dec '95 / Warner Music

WHAT'S THE QUESTION VOL.1
CD ______ HILOCD 4
Hi / Nov '93 / Pinnacle

WHAT'S THE QUESTION VOL.2
Is that asking too much: *Bryant, Don* / What have you done to my heart: *Imported Moods* / What is this feeling: *Green, Al* / What made you change: *McGee, Eddie* / Will you be my man (in the morning): *Quiet Elegance* / How can you mend a broken heart: *Green, Al* / How can I believe in you: *Known Facts* / How's your love life: *Quiet Elegance* / Hello, how have you been: *Clayton, Willie* / Baby, what's wrong with you: *Green, Al* / How strong is a woman: *Peebles, Ann* / Did you ever have the blues: *Bryant, Don* / Who's gonna love you: *Johnson, Syl* / Baby please: *West, Norm*
CD ______ HILOCD 9
Hi / Mar '94 / Pinnacle

WHAT'S THE SCORE
CD ______ FMCD 006
Fatman / Apr '97 / Jet Star / SRD

WHAT'S THIS MUSIC ALL ABOUT
CD ______ 15204
Laserlight / Aug '91 / Target/BMG

WHEELS OF STEEL
CD ______ PLSCD 192
Pulse / Apr '97 / BMG

WHEELS OF THE WORLD VOL.1
CD ______ YAZ 7008
Yazoo / Feb '97 / ADA / CM / Koch

WHEELS OF THE WORLD VOL.2
CD ______ YAZ 7009
Yazoo / Feb '97 / ADA / CM / Koch

WHEN A MAN LOVES A WOMAN
CD ______ HRCD 8053
Disky / May '94 / Disky / THE

WHEN A MAN LOVES A WOMAN
CD ______ DINCD 88
Dino / Aug '94 / Pinnacle

WHEN A MAN LOVES A WOMAN (16 Love Songs With Soul)
When a man loves a woman: *Sledge, Percy* / Higher and higher: *Wilson, Jackie* / Have you seen her: *Chi-Lites* / So in love: *Mayfield, Curtis* / I'd rather go blind: *James, Etta* / That's the way I feel about cha: *Womack, Bobby* / It's in his kiss (The shoop shoop song): *Everett, Betty* / Gimme little sign: *Wood, Brenton* / Rescue me: *Bass, Fontella* / Ruler of my heart: *Thomas, Irma* / Tell it like it is: *Neville, Aaron* / I had a talk with my man: *Collier, Mitty* / (If loving you is wrong) I don't want to be right: *Ingram, Luther* / Every beat of my heart: *Knight, Gladys & The Pips* / You send me: *Cooke, Sam* / Hold what you've got: *Tex, Joe*
CD ______ CPCD 8057
Charly / Feb '95 / Koch

WHEN A MAN LOVES A WOMAN
When a man loves a woman: *Sledge, Percy* / Sitting on the dock of the bay: *Sledge, Percy* / Blue moon: *Marcels* / My special angel: *Vogues* / Hey Paula: *Paul & Paula* / Softly whispering I love you: *New English Congregation* / Solitaire: *Yarborough, Glenn* / Deep purple: *Tempo, Nino* / I'd love you to want me: *Lobo* / Silence is golden: *Tremeloes* / Whispering: *Tempo, Nino* / Come softly to me: *Fleetwoods* / Rainy night in Georgia: *Benton, Brook* / Little darlin': *Diamonds* / Where have all the flowers gone: *Kingston Trio*
CD ______ 22503
Music / Dec '95 / Target/BMG

WHEN A MAN LOVES A WOMAN
When a man loves awoman: *Sledge, Percy* / Candle in the wind: *John, Elton* / You are so beautiful: *Cocker, Joe* / Just when I needed you most: *Vanwarmer, Randy* / You're the first, the last, my everything: *White, Barry* / Best of my love: *Aswad* / Suddenly: *Ocean, Billy* / Night and day: *Everything But The Girl* / Spend a little time with you: *Armatrading, Joan* / Misty blue: *Moore, Dorothy* / Dream a little dream of me: *Mama Cass* / Cry me a river: *Wilson, Mari* / Can't help falling in love: *Stylistics* / How can you mend a broken heart: *Green, Al* / It's a man's man's man's world: *Brown, James* / Maggie May: *Stewart, Rod* / On and on: *Bishop, Stephen* / If you don't know me by now: *Melvin, Harold & The Bluenotes*
CD ______ NTRCD 067
Nectar / Feb '97 / Pinnacle

WHEN EYES MEET (A Global Celebration Of Love)
CD ______ SH 64084
Shanachie / Jun '97 / ADA / Greensleeves / Koch

WHEN HEMP WAS HIP
CD ______ VN 167
Viper's Nest / Aug '95 / ADA / Cadillac / Direct / Jazz Music

WHEN I WAS A COWBOY VOL.1 (Early American Songs Of The West)
CD ______ YAZ 2022
Yazoo / Sep '96 / ADA / CM / Koch

WHEN I WAS A COWBOY VOL.2 (Early American Songs Of The West)
CD ______ YAZ 2023
Yazoo / Sep '96 / ADA / CM / Koch

WHEN THE MAY IS ALL IN BLOOM (Traditional Singing From SE England)
CD ______ VT 131CD
Veteran Tapes / Jul '95 / ADA / Direct

WHEN THE SAINTS GO MARCHING IN
When the saints go marching in: *Armstrong, Louis* / Something new: *Basie, Count* / Bird of paradise: *Davis, Miles* / Street beat: *Parker, Charlie* / Basin Street blues: *Fitzgerald, Ella* / More than you know: *Horne, Lena* / Sweet Georgia Brown: *Cole, Nat 'King'* / Northwest passage: *Herman, Woody* / Don't blame me: *Davis, Miles* / (Back home again in) Indiana: *Armstrong, Louis* / Study in Soulphony: *Gillespie, Dizzy* / Somebody stole my gal: *Goodman, Benny* / All of me: *Basie, Count* / Scuttlebut: *Shaw, Artie* / Flying home: *Fitzgerald, Ella* / Little girl blue: *Horne, Lena* / Bijou: *Herman, Woody* / Yes sir that's my baby: *Cole, Nat 'King'* / On the sunny side of the street: *Armstrong, Louis* / Blue juice: *Barnet, Charlie*
CD ______ GRF 124
Tring / '93 / Tring

WHEN THE SUN SETTLES DOWN VOL.1
CD ______ EFA 064712
Foundation 2000 / Jan '94 / Plastic Head

WHEN THE SUN SETTLES DOWN VOL.2
CD ______ EFA 064722
Foundation 2000 / May '95 / Plastic Head

WHEN VICTORIA WAS QUEEN
Tribute to pageantry / Crimond / Lily of Laguna / Grand march from Aida / Love's old sweet song / Radetsky march / Wellington march / Nimrod / Pageantry of Gilbert and Sullivan / Jerusalem / Don't dilly dally on the way / Land of hope and glory / Imperial echoes / Soldiers of the Queen/There's something about a soldier / Evening hymn
CD ______ 306382
Hallmark / Jan '97 / Carlton

WHEN YOUR LOVER HAS GONE
When your lover has gone: *Holiday, Billie* / Dimples: *Hooker, John Lee* / Baby, please don't go: *Waters, Muddy* / Who's been talkin': *Howlin' Wolf* / Catfish blues: *King, B.B.* / Ain't nobody's business if I do: *Holiday, Billie* / Hand in hand: *James, Elmore* / Born blind: *Williamson, Sonny Boy* / Boogie chillun: *Hooker, John Lee* / Trainfare blues: *Waters, Muddy* / Wang dang doodle: *Howlin' Wolf* / Easy to remember: *Holiday, Billie* / BB boogie: *King, B.B.* / Coming home: *James, Elmore* / Poor Howard green corn: *Leadbelly* / Settin' here drinkin': *Waters, Muddy* / Tupelo: *Hooker, John Lee* / Down in the bottom: *Howlin' Wolf* / My babe: *Little Walter* / Don't explain: *Holiday, Billie* / Don't lose your eye: *Williamson, Sonny Boy* / Everyday I have the blues: *King, B.B.* / You gonna miss me: *Waters, Muddy* / Look on yonder wall: *James, Elmore* / Drug store woman: *Hooker, John Lee*
CD ______ GRF 126
Tring / '93 / Tring

WHEN YOUR SMILING (Honky Tonky Hits)
CD ______ PLSCD 175
Pulse / Apr '97 / BMG

WHERE BLUES MEETS ROCK
CD ______ PRD 70912
Provogue / Jun '96 / Pinnacle

WHERE JAZZ WAS BORN
CD ______ CD 56021
Jazz Roots / Aug '94 / Target/BMG

WHERE THE GIRLS ARE VOL.1
Condition red: *Goodees* / Look in my diary: *Reparata & The Delrons* / Don't drop out: *Parton, Dolly* / Little things like that: *Wallis, Suzy* / Live and learn: *Heatherton, Joey* / I'm thru: *Carter, Carolyn* / Anything worth having (is well worth waitin' for): *Moody, Joan* / Love kitten: *Corcoran, Noreen* / Oowee baby: *Day, Doris* / Please don't kiss me again: *Charmettes* / How much is that doggie in the window: *Baby Jane & The Rockabyes* / Your ya ya is gone: *Tren-Teens* / Hula hoppin': *Boyd, Idalia* / Push a little harder: *Avons* / That boy of mine: *Sherrys* / Young girl: *Charmaine* / Sometimes I wonder: *Brown, Barbara* / What kind of girl (do you think I am): *Franklin, Erma* / Mixed up shook up girl: *Patty & The Emblems* / Who's that guy: *Kolettes* / Friend of mine: *Geminis* / Oh what a night for love: *Victorians* / Hey there lonely boy: *Ruby & The Romantics* / Lonely girl: *Lovettes*
CD ______ CDCHD 648
Ace / May '97 / Pinnacle

WHIP 1983-1993 (Various Goths)
CD ______ FREUDCD 43
Jungle / Sep '93 / RTM/Disc / SRD

WHIP, THE
CD ______ SATE 06
Talitha / Aug '93 / Plastic Head

WHIPLASH
CD ______ RNCD 2051
Rhino / Mar '94 / Grapevine/PolyGram / Jet Star

WHITE BOY BLUES
CD ______ TRTCD 161
TrueTrax / Dec '94 / THE

WHITE BOY BLUES
CD ______ PLSCD 184
Pulse / Feb '97 / BMG

WHITE BOY BLUES VOL.1
Snake drive: *Clapton, Eric* / West coast idea: *Clapton, Eric* / Choker: *Clapton, Eric & Jimmy Page* / I'm your witch doctor: *Mayall, John & The Bluesbreakers* / Tribute to Elmore: *Clapton, Eric* / Freight loader: *Clapton, Eric & Jimmy Page* / Miles road: *Clapton, Eric & Jimmy Page* / Telephone blues: *Mayall, John & The Bluesbreakers* / Draggin' my tail: *Clapton, Eric & Jimmy Page* / Down in the boots: *All Stars & Jimmy Page* / Stealin': *All Stars & Jeff Beck* / Chuckles: *All Stars & Jeff Beck* / LA breakdown: *All Stars & Jimmy Page* / Piano shuffle: *All Stars & Nicky Hopkins* / Some day baby: *Davies, Cyril & The All Stars* / Porcupine juice: *Santa Barbara Machine Head* / Rubber monkey: *Santa Barbara Machine Head* / Albert: *Santa Barbara Machine Head* / Who's knocking: *Spencer, Jeremy* / Look down at my woman: *Spencer, Jeremy*
CD ______ CCSCD 103
Castle / May '86 / BMG

WHITE BOY BLUES VOL.2
Tried: *Savoy Brown Blues Band* / Cold blooded woman: *Savoy Brown Blues Band* / Can't quit you baby: *Savoy Brown Blues Band* / True blue: *Savoy Brown Blues Band* / I feel so good: *Kelly, Jo Ann* / Ain't gonna cry no more: *McPhee, Tony* / You don't love me: *McPhee, Tony* / When you got a good friend: *McPhee, Tony* / Someone to love me: *McPhee, Tony* / Dealing with the devil: *Dharma Blues Band* / Roll 'em Pete: *Dharma Blues Band* / Water on my fire: *Lee, Albert* / Crosstown link: *Lee, Albert* / Flapjacks: *Masonry, Stones* / Not fade away: *Davis, Cyril & The All Stars* / So much to say: *Stewart, Rod* / On top of the world: *Mayall, John & The Bluesbreakers* / Hideaway: *Mayall, John & The Bluesbreakers* / Supernatural: *Mayall, John & The Bluesbreakers* / Standing at the crossroads: *Ten Years After* / I want to know: *Ten Years After* / Next milestone: *Lee, Albert*
CD ______ CCSCD 142
Castle / '86 / BMG

WHITE CHRISTMAS (28 Famous Christmas Melodies)
CD ______ CNCD 3132
Disky / Nov '92 / Disky / THE

WHITE CHRISTMAS (A Selection Of Classic Festive Songs)
Christmas alphabet: *Valentine, Dickie* / Rudolph the red nosed reindeer: *Scala, Primo Banjo/Accordian Band* / Christmas and you: *King, Dave* / Away in a manger: *Shelton, Anne & The George Mitchell Choir* / Christmas island: *Valentine, Dickie* / I'm sending a letter to Santa Claus: *Lynn, Vera* / Silent night: *Lewis, Archie* / St. Nicholas waltz: *Roza, Lita* / Must be Santa: *Steele, Tommy & The Childrens Chorus* / Santo Natale: *Whitfield, David* / Jingle bells rock: *Bygraves, Max* / Little boy that Santa Claus forgot: *Roza, Lita* / Jingle bells: *Scala, Primo Banjo/Accordian Band & The Keynotes* / White Christmas: *Lynn, Vera* / Christmas song: *Shelton, Anne & The Wardour Singers* / I saw Mommy kissing Santa Claus: *Cotton, Billy Band & The Mill Girls/The Bandits* / Little donkey: *Beverley Sisters* / Christmas in Killarney: *Four Ramblers* / Merry Christmas: *Shelton, Anne* / O come all ye faithful (adeste fidelis): *Whitfield, David*
CD ______ 5525682
Spectrum / Nov '96 / PolyGram

WHITE CHRISTMAS
White Christmas / Have yourself merry little Christmas / Jingle bells / Silent night / O Holy night / First Noel / Silver bells / Skater's waltz / Winter wonderland / Mary's boy child / Away in a manger / Christmas song / Sleigh ride / Christmas waltz / Holly and the ivy
CD ______ 4610782
Belart / Nov '96 / PolyGram

WHITE CHRISTMAS VOL.1
CD ______ LECD 030
Wisepack / Nov '92 / Conifer/BMG / THE

WHITE CHRISTMAS VOL.1 & 2 (2CD Set)
CD Set ______ LECDD 602
Wisepack / Oct '94 / Conifer/BMG / THE

WHITE CHRISTMAS VOL.2
CD ______ LECD 031
Wisepack / Nov '92 / Conifer/BMG / THE

WHITE CHRISTMAS, A
White Christmas / Sleigh ride / Winter wonderland / Jolly old St. Nicholas / Twelve days of Christmas / Silver bells / Rudolf the red nosed reindeer / Happy holiday / Have yourself a merry little Christmas / Here we come a wassailin / March of the toys / Santa Claus is coming to town / I heard the bells on Christmas day / Oh Christmas tree / Up on the housetop / Silent night / Let it snow, let it snow, let it snow / Holly jolly Christmas
CD ______ XMAS 014
Tring / Nov '96 / Tring

WHITE ELEPHANTS AND GOLDEN DUCKS (Enchanting Musical Treasures From Burma)
CD ______ SHCD 64087
Shanachie / May '97 / ADA / Greensleeves / Koch

WHITE HEATHER CLUB, THE
CD ______ CC 263
Music For Pleasure / May '91 / EMI

WHITE HEATHER SHOW, THE (21 Scottish Favourites)
CD ______ 303972
Hallmark / Jan '97 / Carlton

WHITE LABEL VOL.2
CD ______ WLCD 3002
White Label / Jan '95 / SRD

WHITE MAN BLUES
Dock of the bay: *Spatz* / Hungry man blues: *Sumlin, Willie* / It's too late: *Head, Roy* / Black cat bone: *Blanchard, Pierre* / I need someone: *Long, Joey* / Mercury blues: *Owens, Steve* / Milk cow blues: *Terrapin Jackson* / Red neck blues: *Holzhaus, Chris* / Please come home for Christmas: *Winter, Johnny & Edgar* / Rough girl: *Maly, Ed* / Gonna get my baby: *Brooks, Bruce* / Lay down gal of mine: *Winter, Johnny* / Nobody but me tells me when my eagle to fly: *Head, Roy* / Something to ease my pain: *Long, Joey*
CD ______ CDTB 168
Thunderbolt / Oct '95 / TKO Magnum

WHITE MANSIONS (A Tale From The American Civil War 1861-1865)
Story to tell / Dixie, hold on / Join around the flag / White trash / Last dance and the Kentucky racehorse / Southern boys / Union mare and confederate grey / No one would believe a summer could be so cold / Southland's bleeding / Bring up the twelve pounders / They laid waste to our land /

Praise the lord / King has called me home / Bad man / Dixie now your done
CD _______________ CDMID 182
A&M / '93 / PolyGram

WHITE ROOTS VOL.1 (From American Folk To Country Rock)
Good time Charlie's got the blues: *Presley, Elvis* / Queen Jane approximately: *Dylan, Bob* / Brown eyed girl: *Morrison, Van* / Hickory wind: *Byrds* / Wild horses: *Flying Burrito Brothers* / Song for you: *Parsons, Gram* / Sleepless nights: *Harris, Emmylou* / I don't want to talk about it: *Crazy Horse* / Willin': *Little Feat* / Mandolin wind: *Stewart, Rod* / Eve of destruction: *McGuire, Barry* / Buzzin' fly: *Buckley, Tim* / For what it's worth: *Buffalo Springfield* / She don't have to see you: *Golden Smog* / So long, Marianne: *Cohen, Leonard* / Other kind: *Earle, Steve* / I shall be released: *Weller, Paul* / Cause cheap is how I feel: *Cowboy Junkies*
CD _______________ 74321382952
RCA / Jun '96 / BMG

WHITE ROOTS VOL.2 (From American Folk To Psychedelia)
American pie: *McLean, Don* / Summer in the city: *Lovin' Spoonful* / Father and son: *Stevens, Cat* / Alone again or: *Love* / Don't talk: *Beach Boys* / I'm a believer: *Monkees* / Get together: *Youngbloods* / Green tambourine: *Lemon Pipers* / California dreamin': *Mamas & The Papas* / San Francisco: *McKenzie, Scott* / I need a man to love: *Big Brother & The Holding Company* / Mr. Tambourine man: *Dylan, Bob* / Purple haze: *Hendrix, Jimi* / Eight miles high: *Byrds* / Venus in furs: *Velvet Underground* / Man of the world: *Fleetwood Mac* / Light your windows: *Quicksilver Messenger Service* / White rabbit: *Jefferson Airplane* / American woman: *Guess Who* / Tight rope: *Russell, Leon*
CD _______________ 74321382962
RCA / Jun '96 / BMG

WHITE ROSE, THE (A Festival Of Yorkshire Music)
Soldier's chorus / Monte christe / Prelude to Act III / Lohengrin / Portrait of my love / Westminster waltz / Fishermen of England / Tribute to Ivor Novello / White rose / Battle hymn of the Republic / Gladiator's farewell / Love could I only tell thee / Lost chord / Colonel Bogey / Roman war song / Long day closes / Fantasia on British sea songs / On Ilkley moor baht'at
CD _______________ QPRZ 016D
Polyphonic / Apr '95 / Complete/Pinnacle

WHITE SPIRITUALS FROM THE SACRED HARP
CD _______________ 802052
New World / Aug '92 / ADA / Cadillac / Harmonia Mundi

WHITER SHADE OF DOO-WOP, A
Little star: *Elegants* / Little boy blue: *Elegants* / I'll close my eyes: *Skyliners* / Door is still open: *Skyliners* / Little Eva: *Locomotions* / Adios my love: *Locomotions* / Read between the lines: *Dell-Satins* / I'll pray for you: *Dell-Satins* / Bermuda: *Four Seasons* / Spanish lace: *Four Seasons* / Barbara Ann: *Regents* / Over the rainbow: *Regents* / Runaround: *Regents* / Cruise to the moon: *Chaperones* / Shining star: *Chaperones* / Picture in my wallet: *Darrell & Oxfords* / Roses are red: *Darrell & Oxfords* / Can't you tell: *Darrell & Oxfords* / Reasons for love: *Darrell & Oxfords* / Rip Van Winkle: *Devotions* / (I love you) for sentimental reasons: *Devotions* / Snow White: *Devotions* / Zindy Lou: *Devotions* / Tears from a broken heart: *Devotions* / Sunday kind of love: *Devotions*
CD _______________ NEMCD 715
Sequel / Nov '94 / BMG

WHO GAVE THE PERMISSION
CD _______________ RIZ 00032
Riz / Nov '95 / Jet Star

WHO WILL CALM THE STORM
CD _______________ SCR 26
Strictly Country / Jul '95 / ADA / Direct

WHOLE LOTTA ROCK 'N' ROLL (3CD Set)
CD Set _______________ MCBX 011
Music Club / Apr '94 / Disc / THE

WHOLE LOTTA SOUL (2CD Set)
CD Set _______________ AOP 52
Age Of Panik / Jun '97 / Total/BMG

WHOOP RECORDS COLLECTION VOL.1 (2CD Set)
CD _______________ WHCD 01
Whoop / Nov '96 / Amato Disco / Pinnacle / RTM/Disc

WHO'S ZOOMIN' WHO VOL.2 (Mixed By DJ Corrie)
Pentagon: *Dextra* / When I was falling: *Aquanauts* / Funky ass music: *Aquanauts* / Fallen: *Manuel* / One 4 the road: *Barb Wired* / Drum code 2: *Beyer, Adam* / Spirit: *Sourmash* / Digital doman: *Shi-Take* / Blanks: *Mo'Whack* / X-tension: *DJ Misjah & Tim* / Hyperventilate: *Scoff Boys* / Cyklik: *Maurer, Herwig* / Tycho: *Modern Anominal Techno Project* / Digital islands: *Harpon* / Analogical rhythm: *Biological* / Feathers: *Spicelab*
CD _______________ ZOOMCD 3
Zoom / Apr '97 / Arabesque / Mo's Music Machine / Prime / RTM/Disc

WHY DO FOOLS FALL IN LOVE
Why do fools fall in love: *Lymon, Frankie & The Teenagers* / Party doll: *Knox, Buddy* / Kisses sweeter than wine: *Rodgers, Jimmie* / Goody goody: *Lymon, Frankie & The Teenagers* / Do ya wanna dance: *Freeman, Bobby* / Tears on my pillow: *Imperials* / Book of love: *Monotones* / Beep beep: *Playmates* / Oh-oh I'm falling in love again: *Rodgers, Jimmie* / Poor boy: *Royaltones* / Happy organ: *Cortez, Dave 'Baby'* / I only have eyes for you: *Flamingos* / Mary Lou: *Hawkins, Ronnie* / Woo hoo: *Rock A Teens* / You talk too much: *Jones, Joe* / Fannie Mae: *Brown, Buster* / Girl of my best friend: *Donner, Ral* / Daddy's home: *Shep & The Limelites* / Blue moon: *Marcels* / Goodbye cruel world: *Darren, Jimmy*
CD _______________ CDROU 1044
Roulette / Aug '91 / EMI

WIBBLY WOBBLY WALK, THE (From Original Phonograph Cylinders)
Wibbly wobbly walk: *Charman, Jack* / Oh by jingo, oh by gee: *Premier Quartet* / I miss my Swiss: *Tennessee Happy Boys* / Everything's at home except your wife: *Van Brunt, Walter* / Spaniard that blighted my life: *Merson, Billy* / Tickle me Timothy: *Williams, Billy* / Little Ford rambled right along: *Williams, Billy* / Wallaperoo: *Osmond, Arthur* / I love me: *Broadway Dance Orchestra* / Come back to Georgia: *Hickman, Art & His Orchestra* / All by yourself in the moonlight: *Sarony, Leslie* / Little wooden whistle wouldn't whistle: *Columbia Novelty Orchestra* / Why did I kiss that girl: *Savoy Havana Band* / Felix keeps on walking: *Savoy Havana Band* / I parted my hair in the middle: *Formby, George* / There's a rickety rackety shack: *Kit Kat Band* / Down south: *International Novelty Quartet* / Parade of the wooden soldiers: *International Novelty Orchestra*
CD _______________ CDSDL 350
Saydisc / Mar '94 / ADA / Direct / Harmonia Mundi

WIBBLY, WOBBLY WORLD
CD _______________ WWCD 4
Wibbly Wobbly / Mar '94 / SRD

WICKED A GO FEEL IT (Classic Roots & Culture 1976-1985)
This is a true true love: *Campbell, Al* / Revelation: *Levy, Barrington* / Never gonna give Jah up: *Minott, Sugar* / Judgement come: *Campbell, Cornell* / Moving on to Zion: *Clarke, Johnny* / Enter the kingdom of Zion: *Brown, Barry* / Captivity: *Levy, Barrington* / Intelligence of her mind/They can't stop us now: *Viceroys* / Africa is the black man's home: *Minott, Sugar* / Have faith in Jah: *Palmer, Michael* / Friend indeed: *Brown, Neville* / What a gathering: *Brooks, Mike* / Propaganda: *Smart, Leroy* / No weak heart: *Davis, Ronnie* / Lead us to Jah Jah: *Brown, Barry* / Informer: *Campbell, Cornell* / Give the people what they want: *Davis, Ronnie* / Dread are the controller: *Thompson, Linval* / Politician: *Brown, Barry* / Yeh weh deh: *Levy, Barrington* / Wicked a go feel it: *Campbell, Al*
CD _______________ CDTRL 375
Trojan / Nov '96 / Direct / Jet Star

WIDOW'S UNIFORM, THE (A Folk Opera)
CD _______________ REAL 0101CD
Realisations / Nov '96 / ADA

WIEN - VOLKSMUSIK 1906-1937
CD _______________ US 0198
Trikont / Jul '95 / ADA / Direct

WIGAN CASINO STORY VOL.1, THE
Flasher: *Mistura* / Long after tonight is all over: *Radcliffe, Jimmy* / We go together: *August & Duneen* / Tears: *Roye, Lee* / You've been away: *Roye, Lee* / Take away the pain stain: *Austin, Patti* / Live Adam and Eve: *Reflections* / Dance, dance, dance: *Casualeers* / If you ask me: *Williams, Jerry* / Better use your head: *Imperials* / Joker: *Myslestones* / Ski-ing in the snow: *Invitations* / Time will pass you by: *Legend, Tobi* / I can't help lovin' you: *Anka, Paul* / I'll always need you: *Courtney, Dean* / Stick by me baby: *Salvadors* / You don't love me: *Epitome Of Sound* / I never knew: *Foster, Eddie* / Put your arms around me: *Sherrys* / I really love you: *Tomangoes* / I'm on my way: *Parrish, Dean*
CD _______________ GSCD 051
Goldmine / Sep '94 / Vital

WIGAN CASINO STORY VOL.2, THE
Baby mine: *Houston, Thelma* / Love slipped through my fingers: *Williams, Sam* / Superlove: *David & The Giants* / Hey little way out girl: *Construction* / Double cookin': *Checkerboard Squares* / Take me home: *King, Donna* / Panic: *Reparata & The Delrons* / My sugar baby: *Clarke, Connie* / Psychedelic soul: *Russell, Saxie* / Ten miles high: *David & The Giants* / What shall I do: *Frankie & The Classicals* / Hey little girl: *Phillips, D.D.* / Rosemary: *Wylie, Richard* / If that's what you wanted: *Beverly, Frankie* / Champion: *Mitchell, Willie* / Ever again: *Williams, Bernie* / So is the sun: *World Column* / Breakaway: *Carmen, Steve* / I'm where it's at: *Jades* / I'm comin' home in the morning: *Pride, Lou* / I'm gettin' on life: *Wombats* / You got me where you want me: *Santos, Larry* / I travel alone: *Ragland, Lou* / End of our love: *Wilson, Nancy* / Meet me halfway: *Little Bryany* / Manifesto: *Case Of Tyme* / I walked away: *Paris, Bobby*
CD _______________ GSCD 072
Goldmine / Sep '95 / Vital

WIGAN CASINO STORY VOL.3, THE (The Final Chapter)
They'll never know why: *Chavez, Freddie* / Gallop: *Wright, Milton* / Psychedelic soul part 2: *Russell, Saxie* / Sad girl: *Anderson, Carol* / We were made for each other: *Terrible Tom* / Paris blues: *Middleton, Tony* / Say it isn't so: *Boo, Betty* / Just another heartache: *Little Ritchie* / He'll never love you: *Grace, Charlie* / Once: *Hale, Larry* / Hang on: *Wall Of Sound* / Woman love thief: *Stemmons Express* / Let me make you happy: *Woods, Billy* / Coloured man: *Vann, Teddy* / Just say you're wanted and needed: *Owens, Gwen* / How to make a sad man glad: *Capreez* / Set my heart at ease: *Farrow, Mikki* / Halos are for angels: *Carter, Blanche* / Captain of my ship: *Seventh Wonder* / Take my heart: *Saxton, Mary* / I can take care of myself: *Chandler, Gene* / Out of my mind: *Rain* / Tainted love: *Jones, Gloria* / Sidras theme: *Ronnie & Robyn* / Don't bring me down: *Dacosta, Rita*
CD _______________ GSCD 090
Goldmine / Sep '96 / Vital

WILD AND WET
Land of a thousand dances: *Geils, J. Band* / Mustang sally: *Commitments* / Willie and the hand jive: *Thorogood, George* / Some kinda wonderful: *Grand Funk Railroad* / Ain't got no home: *Band* / Jenny take a ride: *Ryder, Mitch & The Detroit Wheels* / You'd better move on: *Mink Deville* / Turn the music down: *Bonds, Gary 'US'* / In the midnight hour: *Commitments* / Your mama don't dance: *Poison* / Gimme some lovin': *Thunder* / (Sittin' on the) Dock of the bay: *Hagar, Sammy* / Brother Louie: *Quireboys* / Feelin' alright: *Heights*
CD _______________ DC 880842
Disky / May '97 / Disky / THE

WILD AT HEART VOL.1 (18 Rock Classics)
I surrender: *Rainbow* / Cold as ice: *Foreigner* / Dead ringer for love: *Meat Loaf* / Strange kind of woman: *Deep Purple* / Whatever you want: *Status Quo* / Tom Sawyer: *Rush* / Incommunicado: *Marillion* / Witch queen of New Orleans: *Redbone* / Breaking the law: *Judas Priest* / Run run run: *Jo Jo Gunne* / Magic carpet ride: *Steppenwolf* / Your mama don't dance: *Poison* / Paranoid: *Black Sabbath* / Elected: *Cooper, Alice* / Prime mover: *Zodiac Mindwarp* / Sylvia: *Focus* / Feel like makin' love: *Bad Company* / Final Countdown: *Europe*
CD _______________ MUSCD 028
MCI Music / Jan '97 / Disc / THE

WILD AT HEART VOL.2
Do anything you want to: *Thin Lizzy* / Caroline: *Status Quo* / Neon knights: *Status Quo* / Iron fist: *Motorhead* / Eye of the tiger: *Survivor* / Legs: *ZZ Top* / Still loving you: *Scorpions* / Who do you love: *Juicy Lucy* / Wheels of steel: *Saxon* / Take on the world: *Judas Priest* / Good lovin' gone bad: *Bad Company* / St. Elmo's fire: *Parr, John* / Scream until you like it: *WASP* / Urgent: *Foreigner* / Backstreet Symphony: *Thunder* / Poison: *Cooper, Alice* / Superstitious: *Europe* / Total eclipse of the heart: *Tyler, Bonnie*
CD _______________ MUSCD 037
MCI Music / May '97 / Disc / THE

WILD BUNCH (27 Instrumental Reggae Classics)
CD _______________ CDTRL 346
Trojan / Mar '95 / Direct / Jet Star

WILD CONNECTION
Save a place for me / Deep green / Carlin How / Old man of the ocean / Skinningrove Bay / North country girl / Kilten Castle / Abess St. Hilda
CD _______________ 101222
CMC / May '97 / BMG

WILD CONSERVES - THE FLAVOURS OF SCOTLAND (In Aid Of Scottish Wildlife Trust)
CD _______________ LCOM 5226CD
Lismor / Jan '94 / ADA / Direct / Duncans / Lismor

WILD IRISH ROSE (Popular Irish Ballads)
CD _______________ PLSCD 188
Pulse / Apr '97 / BMG

WILD ROVER (A Feast Of Irish Folk)
Rocky road to Dublin: *Dubliners* / Lonesome boatman: *Furey, Finbar & Eddie* / Medley: *Renbourn, John* / Barleycorn: *Johnstons* / Leaving of Liverpool: *Johnstons* / Medley: *Maloney, Michael* / Foggy dew: *Imlach, Hamish* / Flowers in the valley: *Furey, Finbar & Eddie* / Newry highwayman: *Johnstons* / Wild rover: *Dubliners* / Bill Hart's favourite: *Furey, Finbar & Eddie* / Killarney boys of pleasure: *Swarbrick, Dave* / Medley: *Renbourn, John* / Spanish cloak: *Furey, Finbar & Eddie* / I'll tell me ma: *Dubliners* / Reels: *Kilfernora Ceili Band* / Norwegian song: *Maloney, Michael* / Golden jubilee: *Glenside Ceilidh Band* / Leitram fancy: *Maloney, Michael* / Home boys home: *Dubliners*
CD _______________ TRTCD 125
TrueTrax / Dec '94 / THE

WILD SUMMER WOW (A Creation Sampler)
CD _______________ CRECD 002
Creation / May '94 / 3mv/Vital

WILD THING
CD _______________ TRTCD 182
TrueTrax / Feb '96 / THE

WILD WOMEN DO GET THE BLUES
Love's calling: *Joseph, Margie* / Save your love: *Freeman, Louise* / I'm trouble: *Jackson, Yvonne* / What a mean feeling: *Synethia* / It be's that way sometime: *Synethia* / One monkey (don't stop no show): *Reed, Francine* / I got the will: *Hall, Sandra* / Do I need you (too): *Lynn, Trudy* / Instant breakfast: *Lynn, Trudy*
CD _______________ ICH 11902
Ichiban / Jun '96 / Direct / Koch

WILDERNESS RETREAT (A Magical Blend Of Music And The Sounds Of Nature)
CD _______________ 57792
CMC / May '97 / BMG

WILL YOU STILL LOVE ME
CD _______________ CDGFR 130
Tring / Jun '92 / Tring

WIND AND REED
Sunderlal: *Rumbel, Nancy* / Rose water: *Siebert, Budi* / Meisoroku (edit): *Lee, Riley* / Thunder's windmill: *Brewer, Spencer* / To the willow: *Wynberg, Simon* / Night tribe: *Rumbel, Nancy* / Guinevere's tears: *Arkenstone, David* / Sad memories: *Illenberger, Ralf* / Awakening: *Stein, Ira* / Surrender: *Gettel, Michael* / Northeast wind: *Lauria, Nando*
CD _______________ ND 61037
Narada / Nov '93 / ADA / New Note/ Pinnacle

WIND DOWN ZONE VOL.1
Happy: *Surface* / Stay: *Controllers* / Curious: *Midnight Star* / Something in the way you make me feel: *Mills, Stephanie* / Gotta get you home tonight: *Wilde, Eugene* / Oasis: *Baylor, Helen* / It never rains in southern california: *Tony Toni Tone* / Portugese love: *Marie, Teena* / Everybody loves the sunshine: *Ayers, Roy* / Why people fall in love: *McNeir, Ronnie* / Heaven sent you: *Clarke, Stanley* / Tik tok: *Lorenzo* / Don't be so distant: *Taylor, Gary* / Buttercup: *Anderson, Carl*
CD _______________ CDELV 4
Elevate / Jun '96 / 3mv/Sony

WIND DOWN ZONE VOL.3
Sexy girl: *Thomas, Lillo* / Every little bit: *Scott, Millie* / Genie: *BB&Q Band* / There ain't nothin' (like your lovin'): *Laurence, Paul* / I'm the one for you: *Whispers* / Get in touch with me: *Collage* / Your smile: *Rene & Angela* / I need your lovin': *Williams, Alyson* / My sensitivity: *Vandross, Luther* / Addictive love: *Winans, Bebe & Cece* / Never say goodbye to love: *Moore, Rene* / Can't wait: *Payne, Freda* / When we're making love: *LaSalle, Denise* / Are you ready: *Robbins, Rockie*
CD _______________ CDELV 11
Elevate / Dec '93 / 3mv/Sony

WIND DOWN ZONE VOL.4
Make it last forever: *Sweat, Keith* / Games: *Booker, Chuckii* / Please be mine: *Belle, Regina* / Let's start love over: *Jaye, Miles* / Nite and day: *Sure, Al B.* / You can't turn me away: *Striplin, Sylvia* / I believe in love: *Harris, Major* / Rockin' you eternally: *Ware, Leon* / Don't stop doin' what cha' do: *Mills, Stephanie* / In the mood: *Davis, Tyrone* / Warm weather: *Pieces Of A Dream* / Feels like I'm falling in love: *Bar-Kays* / Strung out for your love: *Four Tops* / Lovers everywhere: *LTD*
CD _______________ CDELV 14
Elevate / Apr '94 / 3mv/Sony

WIND DOWN ZONE VOL.5
Let's get closer: *Cooper, Michael* / Love's got a hold on me: *Tisha* / Sex on the beach: *Truth Inc* / All because of you: *Sherrick* / Headline news: *Bell, William* / Loving you: *Byrd, Donald* / Make me love the rain: *Wright, Betty* / Keep it up: *Wright, Milton* / Tears: *Tamara & The Seen* / Fade to black: *Lynn, Cheryl* / We are one: *Maze* / You're No.1 (In my book): *Knight, Gladys* / Love you give to me: *Lewis, Webster* / Touch me again: *Williams, Deniece*
CD _______________ CDELV 18
Elevate / Dec '94 / 3mv/Sony

WIND DOWN ZONE VOL.6
Crazy love: *Bryson, Peabo* / Tell me: *Wooten Brothers* / Mutual attraction: *Change* / Feels so good: *Midnight Star* / Show me where you're coming from: *Lucas, Carrie* / Love crazy: *Atlantic Starr* / You know I love you: *Break Water* / Intimate friends: *Kendricks, Eddie* / If it isn't love: *New Edition* / Tropical love: *Bofill, Angela* / Sparkle: *Cameo* / Stay: *Jones, Glenn* / Read my mind: *Tashan* / Here is my love: *Sylvester*
CD _______________ CDELV 20
Elevate / Jun '95 / 3mv/Sony

WIND DOWN ZONE VOL.7
Never gonna give you up: Mills, Stephanie / It's only love: Dante, Steven / What can a miracle do: Warwick, Dionne / It's just the way I feel: Dunlap, Gene / Imaginary playmates: Rene & Angela / You bring out the best in me: Bell Armstrong, Vanessa / All my love: Rushen, Patrice / I think my heart is telling: King, Evelyn 'Champagne' / Passion and pain: McClean, Janice / In search of: Taylor, Gary / Strangers: Williams, Deniece / Turn out the nightlight: Tavares / I want to touch you: Hall, Randy / I wanna know you: Hewett, Howard
CD ______ CDELV 21
Elevate / Mar '96 / 3mv/Sony

WIND IN THE WILLOWS (A Rock Concert)
CD ______ INAK 9010
In Akustik / Feb '96 / Direct / TKO Magnum

WIND OF CHANGE (2CD Set)
CD Set ______ CDSR 122
Telstar / Apr '97 / BMG

WINDHAM HILL - A MUSICAL EXPLORATION
Angel eyes: Brickman, Jim / Call of the child: Nightnoise / Norwegian mountains: Sevag, Oystein / Chava's song: Hedges, Michael / Castille: Obiedo, Ray / Last look: Mariano, Torcuato / World's getting louder: De Grassi, Alex / Over easy: Lynch, Ray
CD ______ 01934111732
Windham Hill / Jan '96 / BMG

WINDHAM HILL - BACH VARIATIONS
CD ______ 01934111502
Windham Hill / Jan '95 / BMG

WINDHAM HILL - CELTIC SEASON
CD ______ 01934111782
Windham Hill / Nov '95 / BMG

WINDHAM HILL - GUITAR SAMPLER
Momentary change of heart: De Grassi, Alex / Deep at night: De Grassi, Alex / Sunday on the violet sea: Torn, David / Lion of Boaz: Torn, David / Ritual dance: Hedges, Michael / If I needed someone: Hedges, Michael / Selene: Manring, Michael / Red right returning: Manring, Michael / Sweet pea: Andress, Tuck / Betcha by golly wow: Andress, Tuck
CD ______ 01934111106
Windham Hill / Jan '95 / BMG

WINDHAM HILL - IMPRESSIONISTS
CD ______ 01934111162
Windham Hill / Jan '95 / BMG

WINDHAM HILL - IN SEARCH OF ANGELS
CD ______ 01934111532
Windham Hill / Jan '95 / BMG

WINDHAM HILL - PATH (An Ambient Journey From Windham Hill)
Tibet (part 2): Isham, Mark / On the forest floor: Holroyd, Bob / Le desert bleu: Descarpentries, Xavier / White spirits: Uman / Ghost dancer: De Roth & The Mirrors / To tree or not to tree: Evenson, Dean / Lydia: Story, Tim / Ancient evenings: Hughes, Gary / Riding windhorse (Buddafields): Heavenly Music Corporation / 12.18: Global Communication
CD ______ 01934111632
Windham Hill / Apr '95 / BMG

WINDHAM HILL - PIANO COLLECTION
CD ______ 01934111492
Windham Hill / Sep '95 / BMG

WINDHAM HILL - SANCTUARY (20 Years Of Windham Hill - 2CD Set)
Rocket to the moon: Brickman, Jim / Night slip: Ackerman, Will / Intermezzo: Silverman, Tracy / Ariel boundaries: Hedges, Michael / Wide asleep: Manring, Michael / Wedding rain: Story, Liz / Children's dance: De Grassi, Alex / Hand picked rose of a faded dream: Childs, Billy / House made of dawn light: Douglas Spottedd Eagle / Siri's arrival: Melamora / Night in that land: Nightnoise / Hummingbird: Winston, George / Redonde: Modern Mandolin Quartet / Turning twice: Turtle Island String Quartet / Ivory: Lynch, Ray / Asleep snow came flying: Story, Liz / Fionnghuiala (Mouth music): Nightnoise / Manhattan underground: Gossu, Scott / Daydreams: Schonherz & Scott / Very special place: Mariano, Torcuato / Transit: Stein, Ira & Russel Walder / We kindda music: Narell, Andy / Thousand teardrops: Shadowfax / Every deep dream: Aaberg, Philip / There's a monk in my garden: Sevag, Oystein / Blue kiss: Obiedo, Ray / To be: Montreux Band / Rameau's nephew: Saisse, Philippe / Pittsburg 1901 (Edit): Isham, Mark / Dolphins: Marshall, Mike & Darol Anger / View of you: Simon, F. / Tears of joy: Tuck & Patti / Underground (Edit): Stein, Ira & Russel Walder
CD Set ______ 1934111802
Windham Hill / Jul '96 / BMG

WINDHAM HILL - THE FIRST TEN YEARS (2CD Set)
Bricklayer's beautiful daughter: Ackerman, Will / White rain: De Grassi, Alex / Colors/dance: Winston, George / Angel's flight: Shadowfax / Bradley's dream: Storey, Liz / Afternoon postlude soliloquy: Hecht, Daniel / Second gymnopedie (1888): Quist, Bill / Homefeild suite: Qualey, David / Rickover's dream: Hedges, Michael / Variations on clair de lune: Basho, Robbie / Oristano sojourn: Cossu, Scott / Clockwork: De Grassi, Alex / Peace: Winston, George / Aerial boundaries: Hedges, Michael / Egrets: Montreux Band / On the threshold of liberty: Isham, Mark / Welcoming: Manring, Michael / 19a: Nightnoise / Montana half light: Aaberg, Philip / Shadowdance: Shadowfax / Pittsburgh 1901: Isham, Mark / Calling: Stein & Walder / Gwenlaise: Cossu, Scot & Friesen, Eugene / Dolphins: Marshall, Mike & Darol Anger / Wishing well: Schonherz & Scott / Theme for Naomi Uemura: Aaberg, Philip / Toys not ties: Nightnoise / Close cover: Mertens, Wim / To the well: Mathieu, W.A. / Hot beach: Interior / New waltz: Dalglish, Malcolm / Processional: Ackerman, Will / Woman at the well: Story, Tim
CD Set ______ 01934110952
Windham Hill / Jan '95 / BMG

WINDHAM HILL - THE ROMANTICS
CD ______ 01934111712
Windham Hill / Jan '95 / BMG

WINDHAM HILL - WINTER'S SOLSTICE VOL.1
CD ______ 01934111742
Windham Hill / Nov '95 / BMG

WINDHAM HILL RETROSPECTIVE - MONTREUX
To be / Dolphins / Egrets / Let them say / October wedding / Near northern / Circular birds / Movie / Jacob do bandolim / Piacenza / Tideline / True story / Lights in the sky are stars / Free D
CD ______ 01934111222
Windham Hill / Mar '93 / BMG

WINDHAM HILL SAMPLER '96
Last look: Mariano, Torcuato / When the snow melts: Cunningham, Phil / Theme from 'In search of angels": Story, Tim / White spirit: Umah / Playground: Curtis, Henry Adam / Differetn shore: Nightnoise / Jenny's room: Nightnoise / Southern jukebox music: Penguin Cafe Orchestra / If you believe: Brickman, Jim / Madchenile: Horwitz, Wayne / Prelude in C Minor (From The Well Tempered Clavier): Erquiaga, Steve / Picture this: Brickman, Jim / Rio Amazonas: Sevag, Oystein / Castille: Obiedo, Ray
CD ______ 1934111792
Windham Hill / Jun '96 / BMG

WINDOWS - CTI COLLECTION VOL.1
CD ______ ESJCD 233
Essential Jazz / Oct '94 / BMG

WINDOWS - CTI COLLECTION VOL.2
CD ______ ESJCD 234
Essential Jazz / Oct '94 / BMG

WINGS OF LOVE
Get here: Adams, Oleta / Sacrifice: John, Elton / Senza una Donna: Zucchero & Paul Young / Because I love you (The postman song): Stevie B / Let's wait awhile: Jackson, Janet / Different corner: Michael, George / Every breath you take: Police / Wonderful tonight: Clapton, Eric / On the wings of love: Osborne, Jeffrey / Anything for you: Estefan, Gloria / Love and affection: Armatrading, Joan / Unchained melody: Righteous Brothers / I'm not in love: 10cc / Angel eyes: Wet Wet Wet / Fool (if you think it's over): Brooks, Elkie / Goodbye to love: Carpenters
CD ______ 8455062
A&M / Jun '91 / PolyGram

WINNER'S CIRCLE
CD ______ BET 6027
Bethlehem / Jan '95 / ADA / ZYX

WINNERS
CD ______ RITZRCD 551
Ritz / Nov '95 / Pinnacle

WINNERS CIRCLE VOL.2
Romantically inspired: Tashan / Light of love: Angie & Debbie / Wanna make love 2U: Mannsfield, Rodney / You can't go wrong: Vertical Hold / Come a little closer: Rice, Gene / Quiet time: Belle, Regina / Love tonight: Walker, Chris / Where do we go from here: Steele, Jevetta / I wanna love: Moore, Chante / If you ever loved someone and lost: Beasley, Walter / Never too late: Goodman, Gabrielle / Wait a minute: Mahogany Blue / More today than yesterday: Company / Wonderin': Moten, Wendy
CD ______ CDEXP 7
Expansion / Dec '93 / 3mv/Sony

WINNERS, THE (The Great British Country Music Awards)
Follow your dream: O'Donnell, Daniel / Light years away: West Virginia / Before I call it love: Jory, Sarah / Charlie: Froggatt, Raymond / Your love is like a flower: Down County Boys / Fireside dreaming: Landsborough, Charlie / If tomorrow never comes: Pride, Charley / Born to run: Young Country / You're the first thing I think of: O'Donnell, Daniel / Never had it so good: Jory, Sarah / Just between you and me: Pride, Charley / Going nowhere fast: Young Country / Don't make me cry again: Froggatt, Raymond / Come and sit by the river with me: Down County Boys / Blue rendezvous: West Virginia / What colour is the wind: Landsborough, Charlie
CD ______ RCD 551
Ritz / Nov '95 / Pinnacle

WINNETOU, DU WARST MEIN FREUND
Winnetou du warst mein freund: Brice, Pierre / Meine roten bruder: Brice, Pierre / Ribanna: Brice, Pierre / Ich steh allein: Brice, Pierre / Keineer weiss den tag: Brice, Pierre / Wunderschon: Brice, Pierre / Die nacht beginnt: Brice, Pierre / Lonely: Brice, Pierre / Faire l'amour: Brice, Pierre / Mehr als alles kann man nicht: Brice, Pierre / Madchen in samt und seide: Barker, Lex / Ich oin morgen auf dem weg zu dir: Barker, Lex / Karl May: Lubke, Heinrich / Das hat uns schon Karl May erzalt: Micky & Gaby / Das war die welt von winnetou: Winnetous / Der schatz im silberse: Medium Terzett / Winnetou: Stephan, Karl / Winnetou's bester freund: Silbersee trio / Old shatterhand: Flusspiraten / Nscho-tschi rote rose der prarie: Silbersee trio / Der rot mohn von missouri: Gaby & Petra / Winnetou's schwester: Weiss, Anneli / Lebe wohl, Winnetou: Medium Terzett
CD ______ BCD 15984
Bear Family / Jul '96 / Direct / Rollercoaster / Swift

WINTER (2CD Set)
Holly and the ivy: De Grassi, Alex / First noel: Silverman, Tracy & Thea Suits-Silverman / Snow on high ground: Nightnoise / Silent night: Erquiaga, Steve / Walking in the air: Winston, George / Abide the winter: Ackerman, Will / Third gymnopedie: De Grassi, Alex / God rest ye merry gentlemen: Erquiaga, Steve / Little star: Brickman, Jim / We three kings: Higbie, Barbara / Variations on the Kanon by Johann Pachabel: Winston, George / Jesu joy of man's desiring: Qualey, David / Christmas song: Erquiaga, Steve / Little drummer boy: Schonherz & Scott / By the fireside: Mathieu, W.A. / Petite Aubade: Shadowfax / Carol of the bells / In the bleak midwinter: Petti, Pierce
CD Set ______ RADCD 49
Global TV / Nov '96 / BMG

WINTER WONDERLAND
Winter wonderland: Day, Doris / Jingle bells: Streisand, Barbra / Santa Claus is coming to town: Bennett, Tony / Christmas spirit: Charles, Ray / Christmas song: Mathis, Johnny / It came upon a midnight clear: Andrews, Julie / O holy night: Vinton, Bobby / When a child is born: Mathis, Johnny & Gladys Knight / Blue Christmas: Nelson, Willie / Little drummer boy: Cash, Johnny / First Noel: Williams, Andy / Silent night: Wynette, Tammy / Christmas time is here again: Robbins, Marty / Mary's boy child: Humperdinck, Engelbert / White Christmas: Sinatra, Frank
CD ______ 4677042
Columbia / Nov '96 / Sony

WINTER'S ROMANCE (18 Romantic Ballads)
Lady: Rogers, Kenny / Cryin': McLean, Don / Move closer: Nelson, Phyllis / When I fall in love: Cole, Nat 'King' / Cry me a river: London, Julie / All I have to do is dream: Everly Brothers / Don't it make my brown eyes blue: Gayle, Crystal / Feelings: Albert, Morris / Sharing the night together: Dr. Hook / Home on Monday: Little River Band / Everybodies gotta learn sometime: Korgis / Winter in America: Ashdown, Doug / Anyone who had a heart: Black, Cilla / They shoot horses don't they: Racing Cars / Where do you go to my lovely: Sarstedt, Peter / Love don't live here anymore: Nail, Jimmy
CD ______ DCB 864842
Disky / Nov '96 / Disky / THE

WIPEOUT
Afro ride: Leftfield / Chemical beats: Chemical Brothers / Blue Monday: New Order / Age of love: Jam & Spoon / Wipeout (PETROL): Orbital / One love: Prodigy / La tristesse durera (Scream to a sigh): Manic Street Preachers / When: Sunscreem / Good enough: BB & Angie Brown / Circus bells: Armani, Robert / Captain dread: Dreadzone / Transamazonia: Shamen
CD ______ SONYTV 6CD
Sony TV / Nov '95 / Sony

WIPEOUT 2097
We have explosive: Future Sound Of London / Atom bomb: Fluke / Loops of fury: Chemical Brothers / Tin there: Underworld / Third sequence: Photek / Leave home: Chemical Brothers / We have explosive (Herd killing): Future Sound Of London / Firestarter: Prodigy / V 6: Fluke / Musique: Daft Punk / 2097: Source Direct / Titan: Photek / Petrol: Orbital / Afro ride: Leftfield
CD ______ CDV 2815
Virgin / Sep '96 / EMI

WIRED (2CD Set)
Breathe: Prodigy / Leave home: Chemical Brothers / Atom bomb: Fluke / Sugar is sweeter: C.J. Bolland / La tristesse durera (scream to a sigh): C.J. Bolland / Stupid girl: Garbage / Pearl's girl: Underworld / Rollercoaster: Grid / Satan: Orbital / Call a cab: Lionrock / Born slippy: Underworld / Rocco: Death In Vegas / Blue Monday: New Order / Offshore: Chicane / If I could fly: Grace / Inner city life: Goldie / Acid lab: Reece, Alex / Milk: Garbage & Tricky / 6 Underground: Sneaker Pimps / Tape loop: Morcheeba / Sly: Massive Attack / Single: Everything But The Girl / One night stand: Aloof / Dance of the bad angels: Booth & The Bad Angel / Release the pressure: Leftfield / Perpetual dawn: Orb / Londinium: Archive / Stars: Dubstar / Fool's gold: Stone Roses / Disco 2000: Pulp / Satellite: Beloved / Little Britain: Dreadzone / Disappointed: Electronic / In yer face: 808 State / Move any mountain '96: Shamen
CD Set ______ 5532572
PolyGram TV / Jan '97 / PolyGram

WITH A SONG IN OUR HEARTS AGAIN (2CD Set)
They say it's wonderful: Crosby, Bing / Sentimental me: Anthony, Ray Orchestra / Undecided: Anthony, Ray Orchestra / It's magic: Anthony, Ray Orchestra / Steppin' out with my baby: Anthony, Ray Orchestra / How lucky are you: Andrews Sisters / Do you love me: Haymes, Dick / You're getting to be a habit with me: Torme, Mel / Again: Torme, Mel / I'll string along with you: Stafford, Jo & Gordon MacRae / To each his own: Ink Spots / No orchids for my lady: Ink Spots / Where or when: Dinning Sisters / I can't begin to tell you: Crosby, Bing & Carmen Cavallaro / Hurry on down: Lutcher, Nellie / My mother's eyes: Lutcher, Nellie / Song is ended (but the melody lingers on): Lutcher, Nellie / Put 'em in a box: Cole, Nat 'King' / My one and only highland fling: Haymes, Dick & Dorothy Carless / Hop scotch polka: Garber, Jan & His Orchestra / That lucky old sun: Martin, Dean / Powder your face with sunshine: Martin, Dean / Day by day: Crosby, Bing / Riders in the sky: Crosby, Bing / Teresa: Haymes, Dick & The Andrews Sisters / I get sentimental over nothing: Cole, Nat 'King' / Tenderly: Dennis, Clark / Bluebird of happiness: Stafford, Jo & Gordon MacRae / With a song in my heart: Day, Dennis / This is the moment: Stafford, Jo / There's a train out for dreamland: Cole, Nat 'King' / Kiss in the dark: MacRae, Gordon / Far away places: Whiting, Margaret / Manana: Lee, Peggy / How high the moon: Cole, Nat 'King' / Jealous heart: Garber, Jan / On a slow boat to China: Goodman, Benny / Buttons and bows: Dinning Sisters / You was: Lee, Peggy & Dean Martin / When my dreamboat comes home: Crosby, Bing
CD Set ______ CDDL 1266
Music For Pleasure / May '94 / EMI

WITH LOVE TO MY VALENTINE
CD ______ I 3896222
Galaxy / Feb '97 / ZYX

WITHOUT THE BEATLES
CD ______ JAR 015CD
Jarmusic / Jul '97 / Cargo

WIZARD OF OZ
CD ______ JASSCD 629
Jass / Feb '92 / ADA / Cadillac / CM / Direct / Jazz Music

WOHLSTAND - GERMAN/JAPANESE NOISE COMPILATION
CD ______ EFA 127712
Human Wreckords / Oct '95 / SRD

WOKE UP THIS MORNING
CD ______ MCLD 19238
Chess/MCA / Nov '90 / BMG / New Note/ BMG

WOMAD LIVE 1996 (What Summer Is Made For)
Khosha hawraman: Kamkars / Nyamaropa: Mapfumo, Thomas & The Blacks Unlimited / Karayib leve: Kali / Magulo: Wagogo Women's Drum & Dance Ensemble / Da eye wifie: Shooglenifty / Anticipate: Di Franco, Ani / La salio de la mar le galaria: Yannatou, Savina & Primavera En Salonico / Aisha: Ashkhabad / Habibti: Slimani, Abdel Ali / In this dis-united Kingdom: Land Of My Mothers / E te fatu: Te Ava Piti / Renggong manis: Banyumas Bamboo Gamelan / Pole pole: Ongala, Remmy Band
CD ______ WSVEN 3
Womad Select / Jun '97 / ADA / Direct

WOMAN IN LOVE, A
CD ______ MATCD 263
Castle / May '93 / BMG

WOMAN IN LOVE, A
CD ______ MACCD 118
Autograph / Aug '96 / BMG

WOMAN IN LOVE, A
CD ______ PLSCD 191
Pulse / Apr '97 / BMG

WOMAN IN ME, THE (18 Superb Vocal Performances)
I say a little prayer: Franklin, Aretha / Right thing to do: Simon, Carly / Love me: Elliman, Yvonne / Don't it make my brown eyes blue: Gayle, Crystal / I just don't know what to do with myself: Springfield, Dusty / Something: Bassey, Shirley / One day I'll fly away: Crawford, Randy / Every time we say goodbye: Fitzgerald, Ella / Anyone who had a heart: Warwick, Dionne / Cry me a river: London, Julie / Loving you: Riperton, Minnie / Memory: Paige, Elaine / Torn between two lovers: MacGregor, Mary / Best thing that ever happened to me: Knight, Gladys & The Pips / Ain't got no...I got life: Simone, Nina / This is my song: Clark, Petula / Wishing you were somehow here again: Brightman, Sarah / We're all alone: Coolidge, Rita
CD ______ MUSCD 019
MCI Music / May '94 / Disc / THE

WOMAN TO WOMAN
Woman to woman: *Brown, Shirley* / I never loved a man (the way I love you): *Franklin, Aretha* / Rescue me: *Bass, Fontella* / I can't stand the rain: *Peebles, Ann* / Oh no not my baby: *Brown, Maxine* / I'd rather go blind: *James, Etta* / Dirty man: *Lee, Laura* / Mockingbird: *Foxx, Inez & Charlie* / When something is wrong with my baby: *Weston, Kim* / B-A-B-Y: *Thomas, Carla* / Misty blue: *Moore, Dorothy* / Time is on my side: *Thomas, Irma* / What'cha gonna do about it: *Troy, Doris* / Fire: *Taylor, Koko* / Greatest love: *Clay, Judy* / Mr. Bigstuff: *Knight, Jean* / Let me down easy: *Lavette, Bettye* / Clean up woman: *Wright, Betty* / (If loving you is wrong) I don't want to be right: *Jackson, Millie* / Stay with me baby: *Ellison, Lorraine*
CD **RNBCD 101**
Connoisseur Collection / Apr '93 / Pinnacle

WOMAN TO WOMAN (2CD Set)
Mighty love: *Stansfield, Lisa* / Everyday people: *Franklin, Aretha* / Love is a stranger: *Eurythmics* / From a distance: *Griffith, Nanci* / Ce leis: *Griffith, Nanci* / Thanks to you: *Harris, Emmylou* / Natural thing: *M-People* / Walk like an Egyptian: *Bangles* / Rapture: *Blondie* / Show me heaven: *McKee, Maria* / Street life: *Crawford, Randy* / So natural: *Stansfield, Lisa* / Walking on sunshine: *Katrina & The Waves* / Bette Davies eyes: *Carnes, Kim* / Whole of the moon: *Warnes, Jennifer* / Another siutase in another hall: *Dickson, Barbara* / That's what friends are for: *Dickson, Barbara* / Sisters (are doin' it): *Franklin, Aretha & Annie Lennox* / Mignight train to Georgia: *Knight, Gladys* / See the day: *Lee, Dee C.* / You came: *Wilde, Kim* / Total eclipse of the heart: *Tyler, Bonnie* / Dream a little dream of me: *Mama Cass* / No secrets call of the wild: *Brooks, Elkie* / Don't go: *Yazoo* / Rubberband girl: *Bush, Kate* / What you do with what you got: *Reader, Eddi* / Hearbreaker: *Warwick, Dionne* / I've learned to respect the power of love: *Mills, Stephanie* / Move closer: *Nelson, Phyllis* / Friends: *Stewart, Amii* / Livin' in the light: *Wheeler, Caron* / It's in his kiss: *Lewis, Linda* / Star: *Dee, Kiki* / Slowhand: *Pointer Sisters* / Woman to woman: *Brown, Shirley*
CD Set **RCACD 215**
RCA / Jul '97 / BMG

WOMAN TO WOMAN - THE BEST OF WOMAN TO WOMAN
Can't cry anymore: *Crow, Sheryl* / Baby baby: *Grant, Amy* / As I lay me down: *Hawkins, Sophie B.* / Big white room: *Garside, Melanie* / Independent love song: *Scarlet* / Precious: *Lennox, Annie* / Here we are: *Estefan, Gloria* / Whispering your name: *Moyet, Alison* / Constant craving: *Lang, k.d.* / Power of love: *Rush, Jennifer* / I drove all night: *Lauper, Cyndi* / I know: *Ferris, Dionne* / What I am: *Brickell, Edie & New Bohemians* / Magic smile: *Vela, Rosie* / Luka: *Vega, Suzanne* / And so is love: *Bush, Kate* / Thank you for hearing me: *O'Connor, Sinead* / I believe: *Detroit, Marcella* / Show me heaven: *McKee, Maria* / Give me a little more time: *Gabrielle* / You gotta be: *Des'ree* / No ordinary love: *Sade* / So natural: *Stansfield, Lisa* / In your care: *Archer, Tasmin* / Love...thy will be done: *Martika* / See the day: *Lee, Dee C.* / Love and affection: *Armatrading, Joan* / Stop: *Brown, Sam* / It's too late: *King, Carole* / At seventeen: *Ian, Janis* / I don't know why: *Colvin, Shawn* / (Love moves in) Mysterious ways: *Fordham, Julia* / Patience of angels: *Reader, Eddi* / Walking down Madison: *MacColl, Kirsty* / You're so vain: *Simon, Carly* / Hold on: *Wilson Phillips* / Eternal flame: *Bangles* / Woman to woman: *Craven, Beverley*
CD **5353572**
PolyGram TV / Feb '96 / PolyGram

WOMAN TO WOMAN VOL.2
Silent all these years: *Amos, Tori* / Constant craving: *Lang, k.d.* / Venus as a boy: *Bjork* / Rubber band girl: *Bush, Kate* / Marlene on the wall: *Vega, Suzanne* / Cold: *Lennox, Annie* / Show me heaven: *McKee, Maria* / Don't wanna lose you: *Estefan, Gloria* / In your care: *Archer, Tasmin* / Will you: *O'Connor, Hazel* / Power of love: *Rush, Jennifer* / Stop: *Brown, Sam* / Late night Grand Hotel: *Griffith, Nanci* / Willow: *Armatrading, Joan* / Love scenes: *Craven, Beverley* / Good tradition: *Tikaram, Tanita* / Climb on (a back that's strong): *Colvin, Shawn* / Honeychild: *Reader, Eddi* / I am woman: *Reddy, Helen* / Stay: *Shakespears Sister*
CD **5163302**
PolyGram TV / Apr '94 / PolyGram

WOMAN'S HEART VOL.1, A
Only a woman's heart: *McEvoy, Eleanor & Mary Black* / Caledonia: *Keane, Dolores* / Vanities: *Keane, Dolores* / Blackbird: *Shannon, Sharon* / Wall of tears: *Black, Frances* / Summerfly: *O'Connell, Maura* / Island: *Keane, Dolores* / I hear you breathing: *McEvoy, Eleanor* / Sonny: *Black, Mary* / Coridinio: *Shannon, Sharon* / Living in these troubled times: *O'Connell, Maura* / After the ball: *Black, Frances*
CD **DARA 3158**
Dara / Jan '95 / ADA / CM / Direct / Else / Grapevine/PolyGram

WOMAN'S HEART VOL.2, A
CD **DARA 3063**
Dara / Jan '95 / ADA / CM / Direct / Else / Grapevine/PolyGram

WOMAN'S LOVE, A
Fare thee well, my own true love: *Black, Mary* / Amhran Peter Baille: *Black, Mary* / Casting my shadow on the road: *Murray, Sinead* / New love story: *Murray, Sinead* / Chomaraigh Aoibhinn O: *O'Sullivan, Maire* / Carraig: *O'Sullivan, Maire* / Johnny lovely Johnny: *Keane, Dolores* / Low low lands of Holland: *Keane, Dolores* / Pluirin na mBan Don Og: *Na Chathain, Brid* / Aililiu na Gamha: *Na Chathain, Brid* / Memories of Father Angus MacDonald: *Roach, Nancy* / Golden keyboard: *Roach, Nancy* / An Seanduine: *Ni Bheaglaoich, Eilin* / Jimmy Mo Mhile Stor: *Ni Bheaglaoich, Eilin* / Workin' man: *Taggart, Mairead* / Scolar: *Taggart, Mairead* / Cre na Cille: *Dhonncha, Ann Marie Nic* / Slan leis an Oige: *Dhonncha, Ann Marie Nic*
CD **CICD 091**
Clo Iar-Chonnachta / Dec '93 / CM

WOMAN'S WORLD
CD **EFA 064612**
Metalimbo / Oct '94 / SRD

WOMEN IN (E)MOTION FESTIVAL
CD **T&M 109**
Tradition & Moderne / Jan '95 / ADA / Direct

WOMEN IN COUNTRY VOL.1
He thinks he'll keep her: *Carpenter, Mary-Chapin* / Till you love me: *McEntire, Reba* / One way ticket: *Rimes, Leann* / Crescent City: *Harris, Emmylou* / Walking away a winner: *Mattea, Kathy* / From a distance: *Griffith, Nanci* / Lonely too long: *Loveless, Patty* / Another little piece of my heart: *Hill, Faith* / On a bus to St. Cloud: *Yearwood, Trisha* / Give me some wheels: *Boguss, Suzy* / To be loved by you: *Judd, Wynonna* / Love can build a bridge: *Judds* / I'll take my sorrow straight: *DeMent, Iris* / Circus girl: *Peters, Gretchen* / Something in red: *Kasset, Angela* / Romeo: *Parton, Dolly* / You wanna make something out of it: *Messina, JoDee* / Past the point of rescue: *Black, Mary*
CD **AHRCD 41**
Curb / Feb '97 / Grapevine/PolyGram

WOMEN IN COUNTRY VOL.2
CD **AHLCD 47**
Curb / Jun '97 / Grapevine/PolyGram

WOMEN IN LOVE
Talking in your sleep: *Gayle, Crystal* / Don't it make my brown eyes blue: *Gayle, Crystal* / Way we were: *Knight, Gladys* / Best thing that ever happened to me: *Knight, Gladys* / It's a heartache: *Tyler, Bonnie* / I don't know how to love him: *Reddy, Helen* / First cut is the deepest: *Arnold, P.P.* / I honestly love you: *Newton-John, Olivia* / What I've got in mind: *Spears, Billie Jo* / Bette Davis eyes: *Carnes, Kim* / Right back where we started from: *Nightingale, Maxine* / Answer me: *Dickson, Barbara* / This will be: *Cole, Natalie* / He was beautiful: *Williams, Iris* / Ruby Tuesday: *Melanie* / I'll never fall in love again: *Gentry, Bobbie* / One man woman: *Easton, Sheena* / Loving you: *Riperton, Minnie*
CD **CDMFP 5998**
Music For Pleasure / Nov '93 / EMI

WOMEN IN REGGAE
CD **VYDCD 016**
Vine Yard / Sep '96 / Grapevine/PolyGram

WOMEN LIVE AT MOUNTAIN STAGE
Strange fire: *Indigo Girls* / Lock stock and teardrops: *Lang, k.d.* / Egos like hairdos: *Di Franco, Ani* / Amsterdam: *Baez, Joan* / I kissed a girl: *Sobule, Jill* / Sweet sorrow in the wind: *Harris, Emmylou* / When I was a boy: *Williams, Dar* / Battle of Evermore: *Wilson, Ann & Nancy* / Crazy Mary: *Williams, Victoria* / Half of a woman: *Eatman, Heather* / Iron horse: *Kennedy Rose* / Reach for the rhythm: *Lynne, Shelby*
CD **BPM 308CD**
Blue Plate / May '97 / ADA / Direct / Greyhound

WOMEN OF BLUE CHICAGO
Baby, what you want me to do: *Lee, Bonnie* / Vicksburg blues: *Carroll, Karen* / As the years go passing by: *Johnson, Shirley* / I'm shakin': *Jordan, Lynne* / Thrill is gone: *Big Time Sarah* / Walking blues: *Lee, Bonnie* / Goin' down slow: *Carroll, Karen* / It hurts me too: *Johnson, Shirley* / If I can't sell it: *Jordan, Lynne* / Wild about that thing: *Davis, Katherine* / Why my man won't treat me right: *Big Time Sarah*
CD **DD 690**
Delmark / Jun '97 / ADA / Cadillac / CM / Direct / Hot Shot

WOMEN OF BRITTANY
CD **KMCD 74**
Keltia Musique / Jun '97 / ADA / Discovery

WOMEN OF GOSPEL'S GOLDEN AGE VOL.1
More like Jesus: *Griffin, Bessie* / Blessed mother: *Griffin, Bessie* / Whosoever will: *Griffin, Bessie* / Heaven: *Griffin, Bessie* / Nobody but you: *Griffin, Bessie* / All of my burdens (ain't that good news): *Griffin, Bessie* / Sit dowm children: *Robinson, Helen Youth Choir* / I'm not gonna let nobody stop you: *Princess Stewart* / Tired, Lord: *Princess Stewart* / Bring back those days: *Argo Singers* / Lookin' this way: *Argo Singers* / Get away Jordan: *Love Coates, Dorothy* / Every day will be Sunday (by and by): *Love Coates, Dorothy* / I'm going to die with the staff in my hand: *Love Coates, Dorothy* / Take your burden to the Lord and leave it there: *Love Coates, Dorothy* / I must see Jesus: *Greenwood, Lil* / Tell Jesus all: *Simmons-Akers Trio* / Going to Canaan's shore: *Simmons-Akers Trio* / Glory to his name: *Simmons-Akers Trio* / God is a battle axe: *Carr, Sister Wynona* / I'm a pilgrim traveller: *Carr, Sister Wynona* / See his blessed face: *Carr, Sister Wynona* / How good God is: *Carr, Sister Wynona* / Till we meet again: *Martin, Sallie Singers & Cora Martin* / Jesus: *Martin, Sallie Singers & Cora Martin* / Thank you Jesus: *Martin, Sallie Singers & Cora Martin* / How far am I from Canaan: *Famous Ward Singers of Philadelphia*
CD **CDCHD 567**
Ace / Mar '94 / Pinnacle

WOMEN OF THE PO VALLEY
Nella citta di Genova / O marinaio che cosa rimiri / La mia Mamma l'e 'na ruffiana / Sento il fischio del vapore / Moretto o bel moretto / Lavoro e molto poco / O cancellier che tieni la penna in mano / L'oi bella va in giardino / La vien giu dalle montagne / La strada delle pioppe / O cara Mamma ni voi maritar / Se otto ore / Vedo spuntar fra gli alberi / O macchinista getta carbone / La biondina di voghera / Vien morettina vien / Mamma mia voi marita / Donna Lombarda / In casa mia cinque sorelle / Peppino entra in camera / Al me murus al sta de la del seri
CD **B 6846**
Auvidis/Ethnic / May '97 / ADA / Harmonia Mundi

WOMEN OF THE WORLD (Celtic)
CD **PUTU 1332**
Putumayo / Jun '97 / Grapevine/PolyGram

WOMEN WITH VOICES
I'm glad there is you: *Kent, Shirley* / Infant eyes, missing: *Fox, Mandy* / Play with light and shade: *Mackness, Vanessa* / Isadora and Kryia: *Alquimia* / January thaw: *Hodgson, Liz* / Lot to answer for: *Hammon, Marion* / Mele honua: *Dogan-Corringham, Viv* / Bit of a risk maybe: *Bentley, Alison* / Fox's revenge: *Bolton, Polly* / Cradle song: *Tippett, Julie & Maggie Nichols* / If I don't love you: *Shaw, Dorothy* / Mm-chuh-agh: *Ox Vox* / Pig war: *Welch, Linda Lee* / Everything: *Alquimia*
CD **SLAMCD 402**
Slam / Oct '96 / Cadillac

WOMEN'S WORK
CD **PUTU 1282**
Putumayo / Mar '97 / Grapevine/PolyGram

WONDERFUL BABY (16 Classic Baby Songs)
You're having my baby / All that she wants / Naughty lady of Shady Lane / Baby sittin' boogie / Where will the baby's dimple be / When a child is born / Summertime / Beautiful boy / Wonderful baby / Twenty tiny fingers / When I first met you / Hush little baby / Isn't she lovely / Rock 'n' roll baby / Baby mine / Heaven sent
CD **304932**
Hallmark / Jun '97 / Carlton

WONDERFUL CHRISTMAS
CD **DCD 5346**
Disky / Dec '93 / Disky / THE

WONDERFUL WORLD, BEAUTIFUL PEOPLE (2CD Set)
CD Set **SMDCD 109**
Snapper / Jul '97 / Pinnacle

WONDERFUL WURLITZER, THE (Featuring Robert Wolfe & Nicholas Martin)
RAF march past / Medley 1 / Medley 2 / Parade of the tin soldiers / Medley 3 / Medley 4 - Me and my girl / Gymnopedie no.1 / Our director / Tiger rag / Kitten on the keys / Medley 5 / Medley 6 / Rondo all turce / Medley 7 / Eleanora / Buffoon / Light of foot march
CD **12722**
Laserlight / Nov '95 / Target/BMG

WONDERLAND (The Final/2CD Set)
CD Set **SPV 08992542**
ID&T / Mar '97 / Plastic Head

WOODSTOCK
CD **EXP 042**
Experience / May '97 / TKO Magnum

WOODSTOCK '94
Selling the drama: *Live* / Just like a man: *Del Amitri* / I'm the only one: *Etheridge, Melissa* / Feelin' alright: *Cocker, Joe* / Dreams: *Cranberries* / Soup: *Blind Melon* / When I come around: *Green Day* / Shoop: *Salt n' Pepa* / Blood sugar sex magik: *Red Hot Chili Peppers* / Sometimes: *James* / Porno for pyros: *Porno For Pyros* / These damned blue collar tweekers: *Primus* / Draw the line/FINE: *Aerosmith* / Happiness in slavery: *Nine Inch Nails* / For whom the bell tolls: *Metallica* / Come together: *Neville Brothers* / Generations: *N'Dour, Youssou* / Mama: *Zucchero* / Run baby run: *Crow, Sheryl* / Dance, motherfucker, dance: *Violent Femmes* / Kiss off: *Violent Femmes* / Shine: *Collective Soul* / Arrow: *Candlebox* / How I could just kill a man: *Cypress Hill* / Right here too much: *Rollins, Henry* / Highway 61 revisited: *Dylan, Bob* / Pearly Queen: *Traffic* / Biko: *Gabriel, Peter*
CD **5403222**
A&M / Dec '94 / PolyGram

WOODSTOCK - 3 DAYS OF PEACE AND MUSIC (2CD Set)
CD Set **7567826362**
Warner Bros. / Sep '94 / Warner Music

WOODSTOCK GENERATION
CD **EDL 28612**
Edel / Oct '94 / Pinnacle

WOODSTOCK GENERATION VOL.2
CD **NTRCD 032**
Nectar / Mar '95 / Pinnacle

WOODSTOCK MOUNTAINS
CD **ROUCD 11520**
Rounder / '88 / ADA / CM / Direct

WORD IS BLACKNESS - THE SOUND IS SOUL, THE
Shower the world: *Aleshure* / I like it: *Johnson, Dewaine* / Don't shoot: *Knyght, Doug* / Only wanna be in your arms: *Gaines, Rosie & Kevin Nash* / Lonely: *Nash, Kevin* / Loving you: *D Macon* / Step 2 U: *Marqo* / Time heals (a wounded heart): *Kenyada* / This feeling of love: *Graves, Cynthia* / After the rain: *Gaines, Rosie & Kevin Nash* / You're the one: *Jharris* / I'm ready: *Mighty Clouds Of Joy* / All of my love: *Nash, Kevin & Monet* / Realise: *For The Gospel* / Just wanna give you my love: *Aleshure*
CD **ATCD 025**
ATR / Jan '97 / Beechwood/BMG

WORD SOUN' 'AVE POWER
CD **HBCD 15**
Heartbeat / Jun '94 / ADA / Direct / Greensleeves / Jet Star

WORLD ACCORDING TO CRAMMED
Shimmering warm and bright: *Canto, Bel* / Granite and sand: *Lone, Kent* / Look of love: *Dalcan, Dominique* / Nautical dream: *Avalon* / If I sleep will the plane crash: *Lurie, John* / L'oeill de la nuit: *Matta, Ramuntcho* / I don't care: *Gruesome Twosome* / Tanola nomads: *Sainkho* / Brrrlak: *Zap Mama* / No tears: *Tuxedo Moon* / Ay triste: *Bobvan* / Amdyaz: *Zazou, Hector* / Soul magic: *YBU & Jonell* / Monna: *Black Maria* / Dragoste de la clejani: *Taraf De Haidouks* / Et tout est parti de la: *Lew, Benjamin* / Banzanza: *Roots Of OK Jazz*
CD **CRAM 087**
Crammed Discs / Jan '94 / Grapevine/PolyGram / New Note/Pinnacle / Prime / RTM/Disc

WORLD CHRISTMAS (The World Music Disc Of The Special Olympics)
Angels we have heard on high (les anges dans nos compagnes) / We three kings / Go tell it on the mountain / On holy night (zan vevede) / Michaux vellait (traditional Martinique carol) / Natal / Ave Maria / We wish you a merry Christmas/Rhumba Navidene / Boas festas / Cascabel / Twelve days of Christmas / God rest ye merry gentlemen / Navidad
CD **CDP 8369282**
Blue Note / Nov '96 / EMI

WORLD DANCE - THE DRUM AND BASS EXPERIENCE (2CD Set)
Let me in: *DJ Harmony* / Circles: *Adam F* / Renegade: *Keith, Ray* / Champion sound: *Alliance* / Inner city life: *Goldie* / Everyman: *DRS & Kenny Ken* / Bomber: *Aphrodite* / Arsonist: *Urban Shakedown* / Set speed: *DJ Krust* / DOPE: *Dope On Plastic* / Lockdown: *Dee, Ellis* / Breakage vol.4: *Noise Factory* / Rumble: *DJ Rap* / Lighter: *DJ SS* / MA2: *DJ SS* / Fuckin' em up: *Shy FX* / Get raw: *Engineers Without Fears* / Quest: *Shimmon & Andy C* / Funkula: *Shimmon & Andy C* / License: *Krome & Time* / This Style: *Shy FX* / Chopper: *Shy FX* / Real killer: *Dee, Ellis & MC Fearless* / P-Funk Era: *P-Funk* / We must unite: *DJ Hype* / Six million ways to die: *Dope Skillz* / Love and unity: *DJ Hype & MC Fats Peace* / Warning: *DJ Hype & MC Fats Peace* / Bonaza kid: *Firefox* / Truly one: *Origin Unknown* / Valley of the shadows: *Origin Unknown* / Ganja man: *DJ Krome & Mr. Time* / Oh Gosh: *Undercover Agent* / Babylon (dog bark): *Splash* / Screwface: *Brainkillers* / Angles: *DJ Krust* / Super sharp shooter: *DJ Zinc* / R-Type: *Jo* / Pulp fiction: *Reece, Alex* / Dictation: *Mask* / Numbers: *Gang Related & Mask* / Remember the rollers: *Dr. S. Gachet* / Metropolis: *Adam F*
CD Set **FIRMCD 10**
Firm / Dec '96 / Pinnacle

WORLD DOMINATION VOL.1
CD **OPCD 032**
Osmose / May '95 / Plastic Head

WORLD DOMINATION VOL.2, THE
CD **OPCD 056**
Osmose / Apr '97 / Plastic Head

WORLD IN UNION ANTHEMS
World in union '95: *Ladysmith Black Mambazo* / Swing low, sweet chariot: *Ladysmith Black Mambazo & China Black* / Bread of heaven: *Ball, Michael & Ladysmith Black Mambazo* / Haka 95/Pokarekare Ana: *Union & Ngati Ranana* / Burning in your heart: *Union* / Y dale alegria a mi Corazon: *Union & Marie Claire D'Ubaldo* / Shoshaloza: *Ladysmith Black Mambazo* / Samoa Tula'i: *Union & The Samoan Choir* / Sakura: *Union* /

Flower of Scotland: *Dickson, Barbara* / Otua Mafimafi: *Union & The Tongan Choir* / Ireland's call: *Strong, Andrew & The Irish Rugby Squad* / Va Pensiero: *Union* / O Canada: *Union* / Vis-a-vis: *Union & Monique Seka* / Mocanita Cu Trifoi: *Union & Nick Magnus* / Run wallaby run: *Parkinson, Doug* / Le monde uni: *Union*
CD ____ 5278072
PolyGram TV / Jul '95 / PolyGram

WORLD INSTRUMENTAL COLLECTION, A
CD ____ PUTU 1232
Putumayo / Oct '96 / Grapevine/PolyGram

WORLD IS A WONDERFUL PLACE, THE
CD ____ HPR 2003CD
Hokey Pokey / May '93 / ADA / Direct

WORLD MUSIC
CD ____ NI 7008
Nimbus / Sep '94 / Nimbus

WORLD MUSIC ALBUM
Finale: *Piazzolla, Astor* / Neend koyi: *Najma* / Bolingo: *Doudongo, M Poto* / Puente de Los Alunados: *Nunez, Gerardo* / Milagre dos peixes: *Nascimento, Milton* / Humpty dumpty: *Palmieri, Eddie* / Alvorada: *Mariano* / Souareba: *Keita, Salif* / Flash of the spirit (laughter): *Hassell, Jon & Farafina* / Chebba: *Khaled, Cheb* / Galapagos: *Nuemann & Zapf*
CD ____ INT 30102
Intuition / May '91 / New Note/Pinnacle

WORLD MUSIC OF AMERICA, THE
CD ____ WLD 002
Tring / Aug '93 / Tring

WORLD MUSIC SAMPLER VOL.2
CD ____ NI 7014
Nimbus / Sep '94 / Nimbus

WORLD MUSIC VOL.1 (N. Europe/S. America)
CD ____ 825052
BUDA / Jul '91 / Discovery

WORLD OF BRASS, THE
Stars and stripes forever / Ash grove / Scottish rhapsody / Flowert duet / Blue danube waltz / Last spring / Australian fantasy / Excerpts from Capriccio Espagnol / Largo / Blaydon races / Rose of tralee / Three tenors fantasy / Russian fantasy
CD ____ CHAN 4511
Chandos / Aug '92 / Chandos

WORLD OF DELIRIUM VOL.1
CD ____ DELWCD 01
Delirium / '95 / Arabesque / Plastic Head

WORLD OF DELIRIUM VOL.2
CD ____ DELWCD 002
Delirium / Jul '94 / Arabesque / Plastic Head

WORLD OF DELIRIUM VOL.3
CD ____ DELWCD 03
Delirium / May '95 / Arabesque / Plastic Head

WORLD OF HOLIDAY HITS, THE
CD ____ ZYX 110692
ZYX / Jul '97 / ZYX

WORLD OF HOUSE MUSIC (2CD Set)
CD Set ____ EFA 063312
Ausfahrt / Jul '96 / SRD

WORLD OF PUNK, THE
CD ____ ZYX 110722
ZYX / Jul '97 / ZYX

WORLD OF SOCA, THE (2CD Set)
CD Set ____ GC 900003/4
ITM / Dec '93 / Koch / Tradelink

WORLD OF THE ZOMBIES, THE
CD ____ PLCD 85
Blue Rose / Feb '95 / 3mv/Pinnacle

WORLD OF TRADITIONAL MUSIC, THE
CD ____ C 56006166
Ocora / May '94 / ADA / Harmonia Mundi

WORLD OUT OF TIME VOL.3, A (The Music Of Madagascar)
CD ____ SHCD 64069
Shanachie / Sep '96 / ADA / Greensleeves / Koch

WORLD PIPE BAND CHAMPIONSHIPS 1987
Selection / March, strathspey and reel / Selection / Selection / March, strathspey and reel / Selection / Selection / March, strathspey and reel / Selection / March, strathspey and reel / Selection / March, strathspey and reel / March, strathspey and reel
CD ____ LCOM 9005
Lismor / '87 / ADA / Direct / Duncans / Lismor

WORLD PIPE BAND CHAMPIONSHIPS 1989
March, strathspey and reel: *Strathclyde Police Pipe Band* / Selection: *Strathclyde Police Pipe Band*
CD ____ LCDM 9019
Lismor / '89 / ADA / Direct / Duncans / Lismor

WORLD PIPE BAND CHAMPIONSHIPS 1990
CD ____ CDMON 810
Monarch / Sep '90 / ADA / CM / Direct / Duncans

WORLD PIPE BAND CHAMPIONSHIPS 1991
CD ____ CDMON 816
Monarch / Jul '94 / ADA / CM / Direct / Duncans

WORLD PIPE BAND CHAMPIONSHIPS 1992
CD ____ CDMON 818
Monarch / Jul '94 / ADA / CM / Direct / Duncans

WORLD PIPE BAND CHAMPIONSHIPS 1993
CD ____ MON 820CD
Monarch / Nov '93 / ADA / CM / Direct / Duncans

WORLD PIPE BAND CHAMPIONSHIPS 1994
CD ____ MON 825CD
Monarch / Oct '94 / ADA / CM / Direct / Duncans

WORLD PIPE BAND CHAMPIONSHIPS 1995
CD ____ CDMON 827
Monarch / Sep '95 / ADA / CM / Direct / Duncans

WORLD PIPE BAND CHAMPIONSHIPS 1996
CD ____ CDMON 830
Monarch / Oct '96 / ADA / CM / Direct / Duncans

WORLD RECORDS SAMPLER
CD ____ WWCD 03
World / Dec '88 / Grapevine/PolyGram

WORLD RECORDS SAMPLER VOL.1
CD ____ WRCD 012
World / Jun '97 / Jet Star / TKO Magnum

WORLD RECORDS SAMPLER VOL.2
CD ____ WRCD 014
World / Jun '97 / Jet Star / TKO Magnum

WORLD ROOTS LIVE 1992-1993
CD ____ MWCD 3007
Music & Words / Jun '94 / ADA / Direct

WORLD SONIC DOMINATION
CD ____ KICKCD 11
Kickin' / Jul '94 / Prime / SRD

WORLD STILL WON'T LISTEN
CD ____ TDH 0018
Too Damn Hype / Feb '97 / Cargo / SRD

WORLD TECHNO ALLIANCE
CD ____ DBMPCHD 3
Punch / Jun '96 / SRD

WORLD WAR TWO MEMORIES
Rule Brittania: *Band Of The Royal Marines* / Royal Fleet Auxiliary: *Band Of The Royal Marines* / D-Day drum display: *Band Of The Royal Marines* / Colonel bogey/Semper Fidelis/Liberty bell: *Band Of The Royal Marines* / Marche Militaire Francaise: *Band Of The Royal Marines* / Stars and stripes forever: *Band of the Royal British Legion* / Hands across the sea: *Band of the Royal British Legion* / Popular songs of World War Two: *Band of the Royal British Legion* / Longest day: *Band of the Royal British Legion* / V for victory: *Band of the Royal British Legion* / Marches of the British Armed Forces: *Band of the Royal British Legion* / Heave ho my lads/The Army Air Corps: *Band of the Royal British Legion* / National emblem: *Royal Regiment Of Fusiliers Band* / Normandy veterans: *Duke Of Wellington Regiment* / Ever glorious: *Band of the Cheshire Regiment* / SSAFA march: *Staff Band Of The RAOC* / Glorious victory: *Western Band Of The RAF* / Boys of the Old Brigade/Old soldier's never die: *Band of the Royal Tank Regiment* / Evening hymn/Last Post: *Worcestershire & Sherwood Foresters Regiment*
CD ____ 3036000942
Carlton / Jun '97 / Carlton

WORLD WIDEST YOUR GUIDEST
CD ____ CDORBD 073
Globestyle / May '92 / Pinnacle

WORLD'S BEST POWER POP COMPILATION...REALLY, THE
Plastic moon rain: *Moptops* / Exit to stay: *DT'S* / It's a shame: *This Perfect Day* / Just another day: *Twenty Cent Crush* / Love you like a King: *Clevenger, Walter* / Brenda revisited: *Lennon, Martin Luther* / Colours: *Rooks* / Easy on the eye: *Howes, Kenny* / Waking from a dream: *Gilbert, Micah* / Miss July: *Jones, Brad* / What goes around: *Barely Pink* / Go: *Willie Wisely* / Yes yes hey hey: *Wanderband* / Today will be yesterday: *Big Hello* / Waterfall: *Heavy Into Jeff* / Almost something there: *Beatifics* / Wave to ride: *Living Daylights* / Throw me down: *Cool Blue Halo* / Try not to care: *DGS Younger* / Nervous man: *Stellaluna* / So low: *Dead Flowers* / Take me or leave me: *Time Bomb Symphony*
CD ____ NL 0038
Not Lame / May '97 / Cargo / Greyhound

WORLD'S BEST, THE
House of the rising sun: *Burdon, Eric* / Man who sold the world: *Lulu* / I am the beat: *Look* / (Don't fear) the reaper: *Blue Oyster Cult* / Clap for the wolfman: *Guess Who* / Couldn't get it right: *Climax Blues Band* / Alone: *Puckett, Gary* / Lost in fantasy: *Bachman-Turner Overdrive* / Parchement farm: *Winter, Johnny* / Don't do that: *Geordie* / Tomorrow night: *Atomic Rooster* / 2-4-6-8 Motorway: *Robinson, Tom* / In the skies: *Green, Peter* / Polka salad Annie: *White, Tony Joe*
CD ____ DC 865582
Disky / May '97 / Disky / THE

WORLD'S GREATEST JAZZ CONCERT VOL.1
CD ____ JCD 301
Jazzology / Oct '93 / Jazz Music

WORLD'S GREATEST JAZZ CONCERT VOL.2
CD ____ JCD 302
Jazzology / Oct '93 / Jazz Music

WORLD'S GREATEST ROCK 'N' ROLL HITS (2CD Set)
(We're gonna) Rock around the clock: *Haley, Bill & The Comets* / Shake, rattle and roll: *Haley, Bill & The Comets* / Summertime blues: *Cochran, Eddie* / C'mon everybody: *Cochran, Eddie* / Three steps to heaven: *Cochran, Eddie* / Sweet little sixteen: *Berry, Chuck* / Maybellene: *Berry, Chuck* / Stagger Lee: *Price, Lloyd* / Personality: *Price, Lloyd* / Be bop a lula: *Vincent, Gene* / Long tall Sally: *Little Richard* / Good golly Miss Molly: *Little Richard* / Ain't that a shame: *Boone, Pat* / Love letters in the sand: *Boone, Pat* / Whole lotta shakin' goin' on: *Lewis, Jerry Lee* / Blue suede shoes: *Perkins, Carl* / Blueberry hill: *Domino, Fats* / Red river rock: *Hurricanes* / Bo Diddley: *Diddley, Bo* / At the hop: *Danny & The Juniors* / Tequila: *Champs* / Rockin' Robin: *Day, Bobby* / Sea Cruise: *Ford, Frankie* / Rebel rouser: *Eddy, Duane* / Kansas city: *Harrison, Wilbert* / Do you want to dance: *Freeman, Bobby* / I'm walkin': *Domino, Fats* / 40 Days: *Hawkins, Ronnie* / Great balls of fire: *Lewis, Jerry Lee* / Happy organ: *Cortez, Dave 'Baby'* / Book of love: *Monotones* / Suzie Q: *Hawkins, Dale* / Boppin' the blues: *Perkins, Carl* / Rock 'n' roll is here to stay: *Danny & The Juniors* / Love you most of all: *Cooke, Sam* / Earth angel: *Penguins* / It's all in the game: *Edwards, Tommy* / I love you so: *Chantels* / Sealed with a kiss: *Hyland, Brian* / I only have eyes for you: *Flamingoes* / Donna: *Valens, Ritchie* / Little darlin': *Diamonds* / Daddy's home: *Shep & The Limelites* / Don't break the heart that loves you: *Francis, Connie* / It's only make believe: *Twitty, Conway* / Oh what a nite: *Dells* / I'm gonna get married: *Price, Lloyd* / He's so fine: *Chiffons* / Only you: *Platters* / Tears on my pillow: *Little Anthony & The Imperials* / Chapel of love: *Dixie Cups* / Tell Laura I love her: *Peterson, Ray* / Ten commandments of love: *Moonglows* / Dedicated to the one I love: *Shirelles* / My special angel: *Helms, Bobby* / But I do: *Henry, Clarence 'Frogman'* / Remember (Walkin' in the sand): *Shangri-Las* / Only love can break a heart: *Pitney, Gene* / Goodnite, sweetheart, goodnite: *Spaniels*
CD Set ____ DBG 53049
Double Gold / Jul '96 / Target/BMG

WORLD'S GREATEST VOICES OF THE CENTURY
CD ____ HADCD 203
Javelin / Jul '96 / Henry Hadaway / THE

WORLDWIDE: TEN YEARS OF WOMAD
Live at real world (extract): *Drummers Of Burundi* / Amina: *Kanda Bongo Man* / Allah hoo allah hoo: *Khan, Nusrat Fateh Ali* / Invaders of the heart: *Jah Wobble* / Lion - Gaiende: *N'Dour, Youssou* / Pacifica and pacifica medley inc aloha: *Sandii* / If things were perfect: *James* / Runidera: *Orquesta Reve* / Gun: *Scott-Heron, Gil* / Wake of the Medusa: *Pogues* / Sina: *Keita, Salif* / Diaka: *Toumant Diarate* / Legend of the old mountain man: *Terem Quartet* / Entrada: *Cabral, Pedro Caldiera* / Muchadura: *Mapfumo, Thomas* / Will the circle be unbroken: *Holmes Brothers*
CD ____ RWBK 1
Realworld / Jul '92 / EMI

WURLITZER CHRISTMAS
CD ____ AVC 545
Avid / Nov '94 / Avid/BMG / Koch / THE

WURLITZER WONDERLAND VOL.1
Hello hello, who's your lady friend / Ship ahoy / Jolly good company / Take me back to dear old blighty / Ivory rag / Lucky day / Everything's in rhythm with my heart / Don't dilly dally on the way / Sally / I wonder what's become of Sally / Answer me / Love everlasting / Says my heart / Count your blessings and smile / Back home in Tennessee / I'm sitting on top of the world / Roses of Picardy / When I fall in love / I don't want to walk without you / I'm looking over a four leaf clover / On the crest of a wave / Oh johnny oh / Chicago / La cumparsita / Play to me gypsy / I just called to say I love you / It's de-lovely / Crazy carioca / Lambeth walk / For me and my gal / Rock-a-bye baby / With a Dixie melody / Anything goes / Second hand rose / Beyond the blue horizon / Music music music / I was never kissed before / I wonder who's kissing her now / Boomps a daisy / Too-ra-loo-ra-loo-ra / Comin' thro' the rye / Charlie is my darling / Keel row / Scottish washerwoman
CD ____ SOV 011CD
Sovereign / Jun '92 / Target/BMG

WURLITZER WONDERLAND VOL.2
Around the world / Pal of my cradle days / Edelweiss / Are you lonesome tonight / When I grow too old to dream / Don't dilly dally on the way / Happy wanderer / Pack up your troubles / Who were you with last night / It's a long way to Tipperary / Raining in my heart / Downtown / Do wah diddy diddy / Teenager in love / YMCA / Diana / (We're gonna) Rock around the clock / Teddy bear (let me be your teddy bear) / When the saints go marching in / Let's twist again / Let's dance / Oh boy / Bless 'em all / After the ball / I'm forever blowing bubbles / My bonnie lies over the ocean / Down at the old bull and bush / In the news / I just called to say I love you / Secret love / Singin' in the rain / Paloma blanca / Save the last dance for me / Birdie song / Sweet Caroline / Hi ho silver lining / My boy lollipop / What'll I do / At the end of the day / Till we meet again / Walkin' my baby back home / Maybe it's because I'm a Londoner / You made me love you / For me and my girl / Show me the way to go home / Over the rainbow / Unchained melody / You'll never walk alone
CD ____ SOV 010CD
Sovereign / '92 / Target/BMG

WURLITZER WONDERLAND VOL.3
Whistling Rufus / Twelfth street rag / Black and white rag / Root beer / All by yourself in the moonlight / Remember me / Happy together / Have you ever been lonely / Sonny boy / Agadoo / Lambada / Conga / Simon Sez / March of the Mods / When you tell me that you love me / After the ball / Cruising down the river / Ash grove / Skye boat song / Mountains of mourne / Joshua / I'm getting sentimental over you / Poor butterfly / September song / Unforgettable / In the mood / You light up my life / Try to remember / At the end of the day / Hello Dolly / Alexander's ragtime band / Best things in life are free / Pasadena / Spanish gypsy dance / Cock o' the North / Loch Lomond / Scotland the brave / Comin' thro' the rye / Scotch on the rocks / Johnny B Goode / You drive me crazy / (We're gonna) Rock around the clock
CD ____ SOV 012CD
Sovereign / Jun '92 / Target/BMG

X-MAS PROJECT
CD ____ SHARK 005 CD
Shark / Jan '90 / Plastic Head

X-MIX VOL.2 (Destination Planet Dream)
CD ____ K7 027CD
Studio K7 / Apr '94 / Prime / RTM/Disc

X-MIX VOL.3
CD ____ K7 032CD
Studio K7 / Nov '94 / Prime / RTM/Disc

X-RATED GANG VOL.1, THE
CD ____ RN 0037
Runn / Nov '94 / Grapevine/PolyGram / Jet Star / SRD

X-TREME FIVE, THE (DJ Nervous/Eightball/Cutting/Definitive/Nitebeat - 5CD Set)
CD Set ____ XTR 21
X-Treme / Apr '96 / Pinnacle / SRD

X-TREME POWER (DJ Duke Vs. Power)
CD ____ XTR 19CDU
CD ____ XTR 19CDM
X-Treme / Jan '96 / Pinnacle / SRD

X-WING COMPILATION
CD ____ XWINGCD 001
X-Wing / Jun '96 / RTM/Disc

XL RECORDINGS VOL.1
Let it take control: *Flowmasters* / We want funk: *2 In Rhythm* / We got to come together: *Brooklyn Funk Essentials* / Ease the pressure: *Subliminal Aura* / Jammin': *Moody Boyz* / I like John: *Hardcore* / Just as long as I got you: *Looney Tunes* / Inject the beat: *Looney Tunes* / Mi dasa: *Centrefield Assignment* / I will survive: *Ellis D* / Space 3001: *Space Opera* / Fantasy: *Fantasy UFO* / He chilled out: *Liaison D* / Rub-a-version: *Konders, Bobby*
CD ____ XLCD 105
XL / Oct '90 / Warner Music

XL RECORDINGS VOL.2 (Hardcore European Dance Music)
Anasthasia: *T-99* / Rave the rhythm: *Channel X* / Noise: *Holy Noise* / Circles: *John & Julie* / Fairy dust: *Set Up System* / Gravity: *External Group* / Night in motion: *Cubic 22* / Gimme a fat beat: *Digital Boy* / What is your evidence: *Frequency* / Charly: *Prodigy* / Spirit: *Incubus* / Rave alarm: *Khan, Praga*
CD ____ XLCD 108
XL / Sep '91 / Warner Music

XL RECORDINGS VOL.3
CD ____ XLCD 109
XL / Apr '92 / Warner Music

XL RECORDINGS VOL.4 (Further Adventures In Hard Dance)
CD _______ XLCD 112
XL / Dec '93 / Warner Music

XL RECORDINGS VOL.5
CD _______ XLCD 116
XL / Jul '95 / Warner Music

XOURCISE YOUR MIND (Rare Nordic Ethno-Grooves)
Herr holger: *Garmarna* / Hoglorfven: *Hedningarna* / Grovhalling: *Hoven Droven* / Sugghugg: *Vasen* / Adam i paradis: *Trio Patrekatt* / Gycklaren: *Malmquist, Dan Gisen* / Overtime: *Urban Turban* / Traces of pangaea: *Almqvist, Thomas* / Pinewood 3 step: *Hakansson, Kenny* / Vanner and frander: *Folk & Rackere* / Menuett fran oravais: *JP Nystroms* / Everybody's neighbour: *Foundland*
CD _______ XOUCD 115
Xource / May '97 / ADA / Direct

XRATED GANG VOL.2
CD _______ RN 0051
Runnetherlands / Jul '97 / Jet Star

XTRA BASS
CD _______ KPSVCD 5
Shocking Vibes / Jan '97 / Jet Star

XYLOPHONES FROM OUHAM PENDE
CD _______ CCD 560094
Ocora / May '96 / ADA / Harmonia Mundi

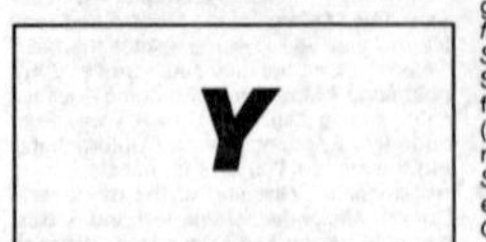

Y VIVA ESPANA
CD _______ 16124
Laserlight / Aug '94 / Target/BMG

YARD VIBES
CD _______ ICD 951
Imaj / Apr '95 / Jet Star

YARDBIRD SWEETS VOL.1
CD _______ YRB 001CD
Yardbird Suite / Jul '96 / Timewarp

YEAR IN SEVEN INCHES, THE
CD _______ DIS 14CD
Dischord / Jul '96 / SRD

YEAR ZERO SURROUND SOUNDBITES VOL.1
CD _______ SUSCD 1
Aura Surround Sounds / Jan '95 / Arabesque / Grapevine/PolyGram / Mo's Music Machine / Pinnacle

YEH YEH
CD _______ TMPCD 007
Temple / Jan '95 / BMG

YELE BRAZIL
Yele congo / Coche viejo (carro velho) / Venha me amar / Kizomba festa da raca / Embala eu / Volte para o seu lar / Felicidade / Epilogo / Jogo de angola / Swqura este samba (ogunhe) / De onde eu vim / Nego laranja / Alagados / Canto de nana / Toque e seducao / Canto da cor
CD _______ CDEMC 3694
Hemisphere / Nov '94 / EMI

YELLOW UNLIMITED
CD _______ EFA 2222CD
Yellow / May '89 / SRD

YEMEN (Music Of The High Plateaux)
CD _______ PS 65179
PlayaSound / Mar '97 / ADA / Harmonia Mundi

YESTERDAY - THOSE ROMANTIC 60'S
Yesterday: *Mantovani Orchestra* / Sunny: *Aldrich, Ronnie & His Piano/The Festival Orchestra* / Almost there: *Mantovani Orchestra* / Somethin' stupid: *Aldrich, Ronnie & His Orchestra* / Love is blue: *Howard, Johnny Orchestra & Singers* / Softly as I leave you: *Aldrich, Ronnie & His Orchestra* / Leaving on a jet plane: *Mantovani Orchestra* / Moon river: *Chacksfield, Frank & His Orchestra* / Release me: *Aldrich, Ronnie & His Piano/The Festival Orchestra* / Strangers in the night: *Mantovani Orchestra* / I can't stop loving you: *Stapleton, Cyril & His Show Band* / Didn't we: *Aldrich, Ronnie & His Piano/The Festival Orchestra* / I left my heart in San Francisco: *Howard, Johnny Orchestra & Singers* / My cherie amour: *Aldrich, Ronnie & His Piano/The Festival Orchestra* / What now my love: *Mantovani Orchestra* / Goin' out of my head: *Aldrich, Ronnie & His Piano/The Festival Orchestra* / What kind of fool am I: *Mantovani Orchestra* / I'll never fall in love again: *Chacksfield, Frank & His Orchestra* / Joanna: *Howard, Johnny Orchestra & Singers* / Cherish: *Aldrich, Ronnie & His Piano/The Festival Orchestra*
CD _______ 8440652
Eclipse / May '91 / PolyGram

YESTERDAYS VOL.1
CD _______ 12101
Laserlight / Dec '94 / Target/BMG

YESTERDAYS VOL.2
CD _______ 12102
Laserlight / Dec '94 / Target/BMG

YESTERDAYS VOL.3
CD _______ 12103
Laserlight / Dec '94 / Target/BMG

YESTERYEARS VOL.1
Memories are made of this: *King, Dave* / Swedish rhapsody: *Mantovani & His Orchestra* / Finger of suspicion: *Valentine, Dickie* / (How much is that) doggie in the window: *Roza, Lita* / Cara mia: *Whitfield, David* / Poor people of Paris: *Atwell, Winifred* / Crying in the chapel: *Lawrence, Lee* / Someone else's roses: *Regan, Joan* / Hernando's hideaway: *Johnston Brothers* / Swingin' shepherd blues: *Heath, Ted Orchestra* / Tulips from Amsterdam: *Bygraves, Max* / Little drummer boy: *Beverley Sisters* / Friends and neighbours: *Cotton, Billy & His Band* / Limelight: *Chacksfield, Frank & His Orchestra* / Man from Laramie: *Young, Jimmy* / I see the moon: *Stargazers* / Personality: *Newley, Anthony* / Auf wiedersehen sweetheart: *Lynn, Vera*
CD _______ 5501002
Spectrum / Oct '93 / PolyGram

YESTERYEARS VOL.2
Unchained melody: *Young, Jimmy* / Ricochet: *Regan, Joan* / Happy whistler: *Stapleton, Cyril & Orchestra* / Handful of songs: *Steele, Tommy* / My son, my son: *Lynn, Vera* / Alone: *Southlanders* / Daddy's little girl: *Vaughan, Frankie* / Ebb tide: *Chacksfield, Frank Orchestra* / Willie can: *Beverley Sisters* / You need hands: *Bygraves, Max* / Story of my life: *King, Dave* / Isle of Innisfree: *Shelton, Anne* / Piano medley no 114 (Part 1): *Kunz, Charlie* / In the middle of the road: *Johnston Brothers* / Happy wanderer: *Stargazers* / Don't let the stars get in your eyes: *Lotis, Dennis* / Dragnet: *Heath, Ted Orchestra* / Bimbo: *Miller, Suzi*
CD _______ 5501012
Spectrum / Oct '93 / PolyGram

YESTERYEARS VOL.3
Mr. Sandman: *Valentine, Dickie* / Hey there: *Roza, Lita* / Broken wings: *Stargazers* / Moulin rouge theme: *Mantovani Orchestra* / Cinammon sinner: *Lotis, Dennis* / Rock 'n' roll waltz: *Klooger, Annette* / Answer me: *Whitfield, David* / Tom Hark: *Heath, Ted Orchestra* / Garden of Eden: *Monro, Matt* / I dreamed: *Beverley Sisters* / Flirtation waltz: *Atwell, Winifred* / Mole in the hole: *Southlanders* / Shiralee: *Steele, Tommy* / Prize of gold: *Regan, Joan* / Love is a golden ring: *King, Dave* / I talk to the trees: *Shelton, Anne* / Blue star (the medic theme): *Stapleton, Cyril & Orchestra*
CD _______ 5501022
Spectrum / Oct '93 / PolyGram

YIDDISH MUSIC AND SONG
CD _______ 304692
Carlton / May '97 / Carlton

YODELLING AND SCHULPLATTER FOLK DANCE
CD _______ 399200
Koch / Sep '92 / Koch

YONDER COMES THE BLUES (Jazz Classics)
CD _______ SOSCD 1061
Stomp Off / Nov '92 / Jazz Music / Wellard

YORUBA DRUMS FROM BENIN (The World's Musical Traditions)
CD _______ SFWCD 40440
Smithsonian Folkways / Mar '96 / ADA / Cadillac / CM / Direct / Koch

YOU ARE THERE - A LEGENDARY LABEL
CD _______ 4425412
Mercury / Feb '95 / PolyGram

YOU BE
CD _______ MMCD 8007
Minor Music / Apr '90 / Vital/SAM

YOU CAN'T GET THAT STUFF NO MORE (The Slide Guitar)
CD _______ IMP 938
IMP / Sep '95 / ADA / Discovery

YOU DESERVE EVEN WORSE
CD _______ LF 083CD
Lost & Found / Jun '94 / Plastic Head

YOU HAVE TO LAUGH, DON'T YOU (22 Gems Of Vintage Comedy)
Laughing policeman: *Penrose, Charles* / I should say so: *Wilton, Robb* / Under the bed: *Wallace, Nellie* / Trains: *Gardiner, Reginald* / Mad dogs and Englishmen: *Coward, Noel* / Joe Ramsbottom buys a piano: *Evans, Norman* / Everything is fresh today: *Hodges, Jack* / Battle of Hastings 1066: *Edgar, Marriott* / My Mother doesn't know I'm on the stage: *Bennett, Billy* / What can you give a nudist on his birthday: *Fields, Gracie* / Surrealist alphabet: *Clapham & Dwyer* / When I'm cleaning windows: *Formby, George* / Gardening - what to do with your aspidista: *Wakefield, Oliver* / There are fairies at the bottom of the garden: *Lillie, Beatrice* / Woman improver: *Miller, Max* / Bee song: *Askey, Arthur* / Yorkshire pudding: *Holloway, Stanley* / Dance of the cuckoos: *Laurel & Hardy* / Insurance salesman: *Crumit, Frank* / Cocktails for two: *Jones, Spike* / Jim goes up, I come down: *Durante, Jimmy* / Thing: *Harris, Phil*
CD _______ CDAJA 5210
Living Era / May '97 / Select

YOU KNOW THE SCORE
CD _______ DCSR 003
Clubscene / Oct '94 / Clubscene / Grapevine/PolyGram / Mo's Music Machine / Prime

YOU MUST REMEMBER THIS
You'll never know: *Lynn, Vera* / Night and day: *Astaire, Fred* / As time goes by: *Hale, Binnie* / Folks who live on the hill: *Sullivan, Maxine* / I'd climb the highest mountain: *Ink Spots* / Love walked in: *Baker, Kenny* / It's always you: *Crosby, Bing* / Stairway to the stars: *Keller, Greta* / Please believe me: *Froman, Jane* / Falling in love again: *Dietrich, Marlene* / How deep is the ocean: *Goodman, Benny & Peggy Lee* / I wish I knew a bigger word than love: *Gideon, Melville* / All the things you are: *Martin, Tony* / Starlight serenade: *Rey, Monte* / There, I've said it again: *Carter, Benny & Roy Felton* / Nearness of you: *Welch, Elisabeth* / Two sleepy people: *Geraldo & Al Bowlly* / I only have eyes for you: *Hutchinson, Leslie 'Hutch'* / Dream lover: *MacDonald, Jeanette* / When a man loves a woman: *Robins, Phyllis* / You were meant for me: *Boswell, Connee* / Man I love: *Langford, Frances* / Nightingale sang in Berkeley Square: *Layton, Turner* / I know why: *Miller, Glenn & Paula Kelly* / Night is young and you're so beautiful: *Sinatra, Frank & Dinah Shore* / As time goes by (extract): *Wilson, Dooley & Ingrid Bergman*
CD _______ UCD 252
Happy Days / Feb '97 / Conifer/BMG

YOU MUST REMEMBER THIS (2CD Set)
Signature tune: *Payne, Cy* / Who is that man who looks like Charlie Chaplin: *Handley, Tommy* / Wish me luck as you wave me goodbye: *Fields, Gracie* / I didn't really oughter 'ave went: *Hare, Doris* / I did what I could with my gas mask: *Formby, George* / Washing of the Siegfried Line: *2 Leslies* / Kiss me Goodnight, Sergeant Major: *Askey, Arthur* / It was a lover and his lass: *Bowlly, Al* / We'll meet again: *Lynn, Vera* / As time goes by: *Wilson, Dooley* / Coming in on a wing and a prayer: *Shelton, Anne* / Calling all workers: *Coates, Eric* / Yes my darling daughter: *Shore, Dinah* / Thingummy Bob: *Fields, Gracie* / All over the place: *Trinder, Tommy* / London pride: *Coward, Noel* / Deepest shelter: *Desmond, Florence* / Grand old man: *Miller, Max* / Run rabbit run: *Flanagan & Allen* / When can I have a banana again: *Roy, Harry* / Thanks for dropping in Mr. Hess: *Askey, Arthur* / Moonlight serenade: *Miller, Glenn* / This is the army: *Berlin, Irving* / Why don't you right: *Lee, Peggy* / In the mood: *Miller, Glenn* / That lovely weekend: *Geraldo* / My British buddy: *Berlin, Irving* / Jersey bounce: *Squadronaires* / Tico tico: *Smith, Ethel* / Lili Marlene: *Andersen, Lale* / Cocktails for two: *Jones, Spike* / Oh what a surprise for the duce: *Carlisle, Elsie* / Swing out to victory: *Waller, Fats* / I'd climb the highest mountain: *Ink Spots* / Victory roll rag: *Roy, Harry* / Wings over the navy: *Stones, Lew & His Band* / You'd be so nice to come home to: *Shelton, Anne* / Last time I saw paris: *Coward, Noel* / White cliffs of Dover: *Lynn, Vera* / Body and soul: *Miller, Glenn* / Saturday night is the loneliest night of the week: *Sinatra, Frank* / Don't fence me in: *Crosby, Bing*
CD Set _______ CDHD 2652
Happy Days / Feb '97 / Conifer/BMG

YOU MUST REMEMBER THIS (20 Everlasting Memories From Days Gone By)
Over the rainbow: *Garland, Judy* / Pretty baby: *Jolson, Al* / That old devil called love: *Holiday, Billie* / Straighten up and fly right: *Cole, Nat 'King'* / Blue skies: *Sinatra, Frank* / Tisket-a-tasket: *Fitzgerald, Ella* / If I didn't care: *Ink Spots* / Take the 'A' train: *Ellington, Duke* / Mississippi mud: *Beiderbecke, Bix* / Thanks for the memory: *Hope, Bob* / On the sunny side of the street: *Armstrong, Louis* / Rum and coca cola: *Andrews Sisters* / Moonlight serenade: *Miller, Glenn* / Sun has got his hat on: *Brown, Sam* / Leaning on a lamp post: *Formby, George* / Teddy bears' picnic: *Hall, Henry* / Ida sweet as apple cider: *Mills Brothers* / Walter walter lead me to the alter: *Fields, Gracie* / Louise: *Chevalier, Maurice* / We'll meet again: *Lynn, Vera*
CD _______ ECD 3294
K-Tel / Feb '97 / K-Tel

YOU MUST REMEMBER THIS - CHRISTMAS FAVOURITES
God rest ye merry gentlemen: *Crosby, Bing* / Let it snow, let it snow, let it snow: *Boswell, Connee* / See amid the winter's snow: *McCormack, John* / I'm sending a letter to Santa Claus: *Fields, Gracie* / Gesu bambino: *Dawson, Peter* / Sam's Christmas pudding: *Holloway, Stanley* / While shepherds watched: *Fleet Street Choir* / Nazareth: *Allin, Norman* / Have yourself a merry little Christmas: *Garland, Judy* / Adeste fideles (O, come all ye faithful): *McCormack, John* / Es hat sich halt eroffnet (Tyrolean nativity hymn): *Vienna Boys Choir* / Cantique de Noel (O holy night): *Journet, Marcel* / Coventry carol (Lully, thou little tiny child): *Schumann, Elisabeth* / Angels, from the realms of glory: *Cathedral Singers* / Silent night: *Sinatra, Frank* / O du frohliche: *Tauber, Richard* / Little boy that Santa Claus forgot: *Robins, Phyllis* / Noel en mer (Christmas on the sea): *Rossi, Tino* / Christmas bells are ringing (a Yuletide fantasy): *Midnight Minstrels (Debroy Somers Band)* / Ninna-nanna della vergine (cradle song of the Virgin Mary): *Muzzio, Claudia* / Star of Bethlehem: *Crooks, Richard* / Virgin Mary had a baby boy: *Connor, Edric* / Sleep my saviour, sleep: *Celebrity Quartette* / Auld lang syne: *Dawson, Peter*
CD _______ 75605522822
Happy Days / Nov '96 / Conifer/BMG

YOU MUST REMEMBER THIS - THE GREAT LOVE SONGS
If you are but a dream: *Sinatra, Frank* / Dedicated to you: *Fitzgerald, Ella & Mills Brothers* / Moonlight and shadows: *Lamour, Dorothy* / Things are looking up: *Astaire, Fred* / Out of this world: *Stafford, Jo* / When somebody thinks you're wonderful: *Waller, Fats & his Rhythm Orchestra* / Let the rest of the world go by: *Squires, Dorothy* / Touch of your lips: *Crosby, Bing* / Blue skies: *Sullivan, Maxine* / Penthouse serenade (when we're alone): *Hope, Bob & Shirley Ross* / And the angels sing: *Tilton, Martha & Benny Goodman* / You happen once in a lifetime: *Hutchinson, Leslie 'Hutch'* / My melancholy baby: *Froman, Jane* / Yes sir that's my baby: *Cantor, Eddie* / Spinning wheel: *Murphy, Delia* / Time on my hands: *Dennis, Denny* / Like someone in love: *Shore, Dinah* / Wherever there's love: *Wiley, Lee & Eddie Condon* / Embraceable you: *Cole, Nat 'King' Trio* / All through the day: *Whiting, Margaret* / Sweet and lovely: *Layton, Turner* / I'm in the mood for love: *Langford, Frances* / They didn't believe me: *Haymes, Dick* / I can't give you anything but love: *Boswell, Connee* / I'm gonna love that guy (like he's never been loved before): *Hall, Adelaide*
CD _______ 75605522622
Happy Days / Feb '97 / Conifer/BMG

YOU MUST REMEMBER THIS - THE HAPPY ALBUM
Shout for happiness: *Bowlly, Al & Ray Noble & His New Mayfair Orchestra* / Back to those happy days: *Hutchinson, Leslie 'Hutch'* / Happy feet: *Rhythm Boys* / Singin' in the rain: *Valaida* / Let me sing and I'm happy: *Jolson, Al* / Happy days are here again: *O'Malley, Pat & Jack Hylton* / Got a bran' new suit: *Waller, Fats & his Rhythm Orchestra* / Smile, darn ya, smile: *Browne, Sam/The Carlyle Cousins/Ambrose* / Spread a little happiness: *Hale, Binnie & Al Starita* / Livin' in the sunlight, lovin' in the moonlight: *Chevalier, Maurice* / I'm happy when you're happy: *Cooper, Jack/Ronnie Munro/New Mayfair Dance Orchestra* / Happy: *Layton & Johnstone* / Accentuate the positive: *Green, Johnny/Three Boys & A Girl/Geraldo* / It's a hap-hap-happy day: *Davis, Beryl/Stephane Grappelli/Arthur Young* / Make yourself a happiness pie: *Payne, Jack & The BBC Dance Orchestra* / Tea for two: *Crosby, Bing & Connie Boswell/Bob Crosby's Bob Cats* / When the red red robin (comes bob bob bobbin' along): *Smith, Whispering Jack* / May all your troubles be little ones: *Sarony, Leslie* / Say to yourself I will be happy: *Browne, Sam/Max Bacon/The Blue Mountaineers/Joe Brannelly* / My blue heaven: *Lanceford, Jimmy Trio* / That's why I'm happy: *Kane, Helen* / Happy as the day is long: *O'Malley, Pat & Jack Hylton* / Sing a happy-go-lucky song: *Trinder, Tommy* / My troubles are over: *Sunshine Boys* / Happy ending: *Scott Coomber, Billy & Jack Payne* / Holiday for strings: *Jones, Spike & His City Slickers*
CD _______ 75605522612
Happy Days / Feb '97 / Conifer/BMG

YOU MUST REMEMBER THIS - VINTAGE COMEDY SONGS
When I'm cleaning windows: *Formby, George* / My kid's a crooner: *Carlisle, Elsie & Ambrose* / Mrs. Worthington: *Coward, Noel* / La de da: *Miller, Max* / Short'nin' bread: *Waller, Fats* / Olga Pulloffski the beautiful sky: *Berman, Len & Henry Hall/BBC Dance Orchestra* / Stone cold dead in the market: *Fitzgerald, Ella & Louis Jordan Tympany Five* / 1,2,3,4,5,6,7: *Frankau, Ronald* / It's a great big shame: *Elen, Gus* / How d'ya keep 'em down on the farm: *Cantor, Eddie* / Mr. Jones (are you coming to bed): *Desmond, Florence* / Bee song: *Askey, Arthur* / Start off each day with a song: *Durante, Jimmy & Eddie Jackson* / She was poor but she was honest: *Bennett, Billy* / Let's have a tiddley at the milk bar: *Wallace, Nellie* / Drinking: *McEachern, Malcolm* / (I'll be glad when you're dead) you rascal you: *Armstrong, Louis* / Thank you so much Mrs. Lowsborough goodbye: *Byng, Douglas* / Song of the prune: *Crumit, Frank* / Oh Mr. Porter: *Blaney, Norah* / When I met Connie in the cornfield: *Handley, Tommy* / Nobody loves a fairy when she's forty: *O'Shea, Tessie* / My little sweet Austin Seven: *Long, Norma* / Chloe: *Ingle, Red & Spike Jones/City Slickers* / Busy busy: *Picon, Molly* / She had to go and lose it at The Astor: *Currie, Bill & Harry Roy Chorus*
CD _______ 75605522722
Happy Days / Feb '97 / Conifer/BMG

YOU THRILL MY SOUL (Female & Girl Groups From The Early Stax Sessions)
Same thing: *Thomas, Carla* / Here it comes again: *Thomas, Carla* / I can't stay: *Thomas, Carla* / Heavenly angel: *Tonettes* / Stolen angel: *Tonettes* / Unhand that man: *Tonettes* / Gone for good: *Rene, Wendy* / Same guy: *Rene, Wendy* / Love at first sight: *Rene, Wendy* / If she should ever break your heart: *Stephens, Barbara* / Heartbreaker: *Parker, Deanie* / Ask him: *Parker, Deanie* / Love is like a flower: *Stephens, Barbara* / Just one touch: *Parker, Deanie* / Ain't enough hours in the day: *Thomas, Carla* / Gosh I'm lucky: *Thomas, Carla* / He hasn't failed me yet: *Rene, Wendy* / Crying all by myself: *Rene, Wendy* / Last love: *Rene, Wendy* / Crowded park: *Rene, Wendy* / Can't stay away: *Rene, Wendy* / Tell me: *Tonettes* / Come to me: *Tonettes* / Do boys keep diaries: *Thomas, Carla*
CD ______ **CDSXD 088**
Stax / Sep '93 / Pinnacle

YOU WIN AGAIN (20 Classic Country Tracks)
Jambalaya: *Jones, George* / Crystal chandeliers: *Spears, Billie Jo* / You win again: *Cash, Johnny* / Deep in the heart of Texas: *Jones, Ed* / Walk right in: *Lewis, Jerry Lee* / Oh, lonesome me: *Gibson, Don* / Sticks and stones: *Fargo, Donna* / Daddy sang bass: *Perkins, Carl* / Love hurts: *Parsons, Gram & Emmylou Harris* / Indian reservation: *Fardon, Don* / Send me the pillow that you dream on: *Locklin, Hank* / Harper valley PTA: *Riley, Jeannie C.* / El paso: *Robbins, Marty* / Blizzard: *Reeves, Jim* / Today, tomorrow and forever: *Cline, Patsy* / Who needs your love: *Paycheck, Johnny* / Making believe: *Wells, Kitty* / From a jack to a king: *Miller, Ned* / Take these chains from my heart: *Drusky, Roy* / Rose garden: *Anderson, Lynn*
CD ______ **TRTCD 116**
TrueTrax / Oct '94 / THE

YOU'LL NEVER WALK ALONE
CD ______ **WH 12001**
Whitehouse / May '95 / Grapevine/ PolyGram / Jet Star / Mo's Music Machine / Target/BMG

YOU'LL NEVER WALK ALONE (The Hits Of The 1960's)
You'll never walk alone: *Gerry & The Pacemakers* / Silence is golden: *Tremeloes* / Runaway: *Shannon, Del* / Happy birthday sweet sixteen: *Sedaka, Neil* / Wild thing: *Troggs* / I'm into something good: *Herman's Hermits* / Rubber ball: *Vee, Bobby* / Something's gotten hold of my heart: *Pitney, Gene* / I'm sorry: *Lee, Brenda* / Da doo ron ron: *Crystals* / When a man loves a woman: *Sledge, Percy* / I'm telling you now: *Freddie & The Dreamers* / Because they're young: *Eddy, Duane* / Little town flirt: *Shannon, Del* / It's my party: *Gore, Lesley* / Breaking up is hard to do: *Sedaka, Neil* / Walkin' back to happiness: *Shapiro, Helen* / Wishin' and hopin': *Merseybeats* / Rescue me: *Bass, Fontella* / Dancing in the street: *Reeves, Martha*
CD ______ **CD 6031**
Music / Sep '96 / Target/BMG

YOU'LL NEVER WALK ALONE (The Hillsborough Benefit Album)
CD ______ **VVR 1000342**
V2 / Jun '97 / 3mv/Pinnacle

YOUNG FLAMENCOS, THE
CD ______ **HNCD 1370**
Hannibal / Dec '91 / ADA / Vital

YOUNG FOGIES VOL.1
CD ______ **ROUCD 0319**
Rounder / Jul '94 / ADA / CM / Direct

YOUNG FOGIES VOL.2
CD ______ **ROUCD 0369**
Rounder / Oct '95 / ADA / CM / Direct

YOUNG LIONS AND OLD TIGERS - A 75TH BIRTHDAY CELEBRATION
Roy Hargrove / How high the moon / Michael Brecker waltz / Here comes McBride / Joe Lovano tango / In your own sweet way / Joshua Redman / Together / Moody / Gerry-go-round / Ronnie Buttacavoli / Deep in a dream
CD ______ **CD 83349**
Telarc / Nov '95 / Conifer/BMG

YOUNG PIPERS OF SCOTLAND
2/4 Marches: *Armstrong, Christopher* / Strathspeys and reels: *Armstrong, Christopher* / Slow air and two jigs: *Armstrong, Christopher* / 2/4 Marches: *MacLean, Gordon* / 6/8 Marches: *MacLean, Gordon* / Strathspey and reel: *MacLean, Gordon* / Slow air and jigs: *MacLean, Gordon* / Slow air and jigs: *Cassells, Stuart* / Strathspeys and reels: *Cassells, Stuart* / Marches: *Cassells, Stuart* / 2/4 marches: *Wright, Andrew* / Waltz, hornpipe and jig: *Wright, Andrew* / Piobaireachd: *Wright, Andrew*
CD ______ **CDTRAX 125**
Greentrax / Mar '97 / ADA / Direct / Duncans / Highlander

YOUNG, WILD AND FREE
CD ______ **DCD 5360**
Disky / May '94 / Disky / THE

YOUNG ZYDECO DESPERADOS: SWAMP MUSIC VOL.8
CD ______ **US 0204**
Trikont / Apr '95 / ADA / Direct

YOUNGBLOOD STORY VOL.1
Do wah diddy diddy: *Dave Dee, Dozy, Beaky, Mick & Tich* / Brandy: *English, Scott* / Get ready for love: *Easybeats* / Planetary cruiser: *McGlynn, Pat* / Sea trip: *Shelley, Peter* / On the run: *Ocean, Billy* / Rhythm on the radio: *ABC* / True love forgives: *Kissoon, Mac & Katie* / Crazy feeling: *Douglas, Carl* / Ain't nothing but a house party: *Show Stoppers* / Personality crisis: *New York Dolls* / Take a heart: *Fardon, Don* / Mr. Station Master: *Harper, Roy* / Morning bird: *Damned* / C'mon round to my place: *Wayne, Carl* / When I was 16: *Page, Jimmy* / Captain man: *Powell, Jimmy* / Let the live live: *Fardon, Don* / You keep me hangin' on: *Kissoon, Mac* / Don't ever change: *Berry, Mike* / Spread myself around: *King, Ben E.* / Can you feel it: *Ocean, Billy* / Sleepwalk: *Los Indianos*
CD ______ **C5CD549**
See For Miles/C5 / '89 / Pinnacle

YOUR GENERATION (18 Punk & New Wave Classics)
CD ______ **MUSCD 009**
MCI Music / Sep '93 / Disc / THE

YOUR GENERATION (2CD Set)
Design for life: *Manic Street Preachers* / Hey dude: *Kula Shaker* / Caught by the fuzz: *Supergrass* / Neighbourhood: *Space* / Teenage angst: *Placebo* / Ginger: *David Devant & His Spirit Wife* / Sleeper: *Audioweb* / Sleep well tonight: *Gene* / Imaginary friends: *Lightning Seeds* / King of kissingdom: *My Life Story* / Monday morning: *Candyskins* / Not so manic now: *Dubstar* / Promised land: *Cast Of Bread* / Exodus: *Levellers* / Life's a cinch: *Mundy* / All hype: *Longpigs* / Middle class hereos: *Divine Comedy* / Queen is dead: *Smiths* / Too handsome to be homeless: *Baby Bird* / Stripper vicar: *Mansun* / Mis-shapes: *Pulp* / Mr. Robinson's quango: *Blur* / Planet telex: *Radiohead* / Nuclear holiday: *3 Colours Red* / Little baby swastikka: *Skunk Anansie* / Sick of drugs: *Wildhearts* / Punka: *Kenickie* / Prozac Beats: *18 Wheeler* / Trigger hippie: *Morcheeba* / Open up: *Leftfield* / Born slippy: *Underworld* / Little Britain: *Dreadzone* / Ebeneezer Goode: *Shamen* / Where's me jumper: *Sultans Of Ping FC* / Anarchy in the UK: *Sex Pistols*
CD Set ______ **SONYTV 25CD**
Sony TV / Apr '97 / Sony

YOUR INVITATION TO SUICIDE
CD ______ **MRCD 040**
Munster / May '94 / Cargo / Greyhound / Plastic Head

YOUR OWN, YOUR VERY OWN (Stars Of The Music Hall 1901-1929)
Don't do it again, Matilda: *Champion, Harry* / Every little movement has a meaning of its own: *Lloyd, Marie* / Two lovely black eyes: *Coburn, Charles* / Mrs. Kelly: *Leno, Dan* / One of the boys: *Formby, George* / Jocular joker: *Chergwin, G.H.* / Let's all go where all the crowd goes: *Williams, Billy* / Photo of the girl I left behind me: *Merson, Billy* / I'm twenty-one today: *Pleasante, Jack* / Flower of the heather: *Lauder, Harry* / If the managers only thought the same as mother: *Scott, Maidie* / She sells seashells: *Bard, Wilkie* / By the sea: *Sheridan, Mark* / Don't have any more, Mrs. Moore: *Morris, Lily* / Dinah: *Elliott, G.H.* / Hello, sunshine, hello: *Whelan, Albert*
CD ______ **CDAJA 5004**
Living Era / Apr '92 / Select

YOU'RE DRIVING ME CRAZY
Ring dem bells / Confessin' / Rockin' chair / Happy feet / Somebody loves me / You're driving me crazy / New Orleans hop scop blues / Sheikh of Araby / Mood indigo / I got rhythm / Here comes Emily Brown / If I could be with you one hour tonight / When I'm alone / Heebie jeebies / I can't believe that you're in love with me / Okay baby
CD ______ **PHONTCD 7618**
Phontastic / '93 / Cadillac / Jazz Music / Wellard

YOYO A GO GO (2CD Set)
CD Set ______ **YOYO 4CD**
K / Sep '96 / Cargo / Greyhound / SRD

YU BODY GOOD
CD ______ **WRCD 38**
Techniques / Dec '93 / Jet Star

YUGOSLAVIA: LES BOUGIES DU PARADIS
CD ______ **C 580041**
Ocora / Nov '92 / ADA / Harmonia Mundi

YULE COOL (2CD Set)
I wish it could be Christmas forever: *Como, Perry* / Happy holiday: *Crosby, Bing* / Little boy that Santa Claus forgot: *Cole, Nat 'King'* / Senor Santa Claus: *Reeves, Jim* / Holly and the ivy: *Steeleye Span* / White Christmas: *Boone, Pat* / Let it snow, let it snow, let it snow: *Martin, Dean* / I want Elvis for Christmas: *Cochran, Eddie* / Jingle bells: *Paul, Les* / It came upon a midnight clear: *Fitzgerald, Ella* / Wonderful land: *Shadows* / Mary's boy child: *Monro, Matt* / Frosty the snowman: *Ventures* / What Christmas means to me: *Green, Al* / Baby's first Christmas: *Francis, Connie* / Song angels sing: *Lanza, Mario* / Snow coach: *Conway, Russ* / Never do a tango with an eskimo: *Cogan, Alma* / Lonely pup (in a Christmas shop): *Faith, Adam* / Christmas waltz: *Lee, Peggy* / Warm December: *London, Julie* / Silent night: *Locke, Josef* / Bells of St. Mary's: *Neville, Aaron* / Holly jolly Christmas: *Ives, Burl* / Rockin' around the Christmas tree: *Lee, Brenda* / Christmas on the range: *Wills, Bob* / Christmas is paintin' the town: *Oak Ridge Boys* / Rockin' around the Christmas tree: *Cannon, Ace* / Deck the halls with boughs of holly: *Crickets* / Sleigh ride: *Ferrante & Teicher* / O'Holy night: *Rodgers, Jimmie* / Parade of the wooden soldiers: *Garber, Jan* / I saw Mommy kissing Santa Claus: *Gleason, Jackie* / Jingle bell rock: *Hollyridge Strings* / Silver bells: *Dunstedter, Eddie* / Christmas trumpets: *Anthony, Ray* / Auld lang syne: *Alexander, Van* / Christmas song: *Mancini, Henry* / O Holy night: *Danny & The Juniors* / Must be Santa: *Steele, Tommy* / Baby, it's cold outside: *Montgomery, Wes & Jimmy Smith*
CD Set ______ **VTDCD 36**
Virgin / Oct '95 / EMI

YULETUNES
CD ______ **BV 125912**
Black Vinyl / Nov '96 / Cargo

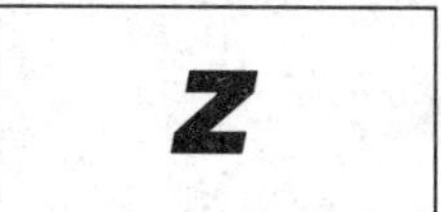

ZAIRE: SUPER GUITAR SOUKOUS
Sana: *Kanda Bongo Man* / Africa: *Depeu, Dave* / Sango ya mawa: *Dabany, Patience* / Mukaji wani: *Yogo, Dindo* / Guelo: *Gueatan System* / Pa moi: *Delly, Joyce* / N'nanele: *Zoukunion* / Guede guina: *Guede, Olives* / Mosolo na ngai: *General Defao* / Soso ya tongo: *Empire Bakuba Et Pepe Kalle* / Makoule: *Seliko*
CD ______ **CDEMC 3678**
Hemisphere / May '94 / EMI

ZAMBIANCE
Kambowa: *Shalawambe* / Mao: *Amayenge* / Nyina kataila: *Kalambo hit parade* / By air / Tai yaka: *Julizya* / Icupo cha kuala pa mpapa: *Shalawambe* / Itumba: *Kalusha, Alfred Chisala Jr.* / Ni Maggie: *Kalusha, Alfred Chisala Jr.*
CD ______ **CDORB 037**
Globestyle / Jun '89 / Pinnacle

ZEPHYR SWINGS INTO 1997
Lester leaps in: *Masso, George & Brian Lemon/Roy Williams* / You'll never know: *Vache, Warren & Brian Lemon* / Farewell blues: *Poplowski, Ken & Alan Barnes/Brian Lemon/Roy Williams* / This is all I ask: *Braff, Ruby & Brian Lemon* / Moon glow: *Barnes, Alan & Brian Lemon Octet* / Dearly beloved: *Barnes, Alan & Brian Lemon* / Watch what happens: *Masso, George & Brian Lemon/ Roy Williams* / Jeepers creepers: *Vache, Warren & Brian Lemon* / When it's sleepy time down south: *Peplowski, Ken & Alan Barnes/Brian Lemon/Roy Williams* / Bill: *Barnes, Alan & Brian Lemon* / Wouldn't it be lovely: *Braff, Ruby & Brian Lemon* / Boar jibu: *Barnes, Alan & Brian Lemon Octet*
CD ______ **ZECD 10**
Zephyr / Nov '96 / Cadillac / Jazz Music / New Note/Pinnacle

ZHENG MELODIES: ABOVE THE CLOUDS (Chinese Han Music)
Resentment of Zhaojun / Entertainment / Song of the western chamber / Tranquil lake / Du-yu-hun / Jade chain / Dan-Dian-Tou and Luang-Cha-Hua / Lotus / Bai-Jia-Chun / Halcyon at a pond / Morning of the Ya Mountain / Yi-Dian-Jin / Bei-Jin-Gong / Nan-Jin-Gong
CD ______ **SOW 90157**
Sounds Of The World / Jan '97 / Target/ BMG

ZIMBABWE - THE SOUL MUSIC OF MBIRA
CD ______ **7559720542**
Nonesuch / Jan '95 / Warner Music

ZIP UP YOUR BOOTS FOR THE SHOWBANDS
Don't give up on me: *Jubilee All Stars* / Out of place: *Wormhole* / Don't phase me: *Pet Lamb* / Borderline vice: *Sewing Room* / Sunny day: *Mexican Pets* / Is this thing on: *Jackbeast* / In these last days: *Backwater* / Climb mine power house: *Sack* / Money: *Pincher Martin* / If D was S: *Tunic* / Tommy: *Josephs* / Jesus lived 6 years longer than Kurt Cobain: *Floors* / Inside you: *Female Hercules* / Chicken lightning: *Luggage* / Homeward: *Capratone* / Untitled: *Idiots* / Anything you can do: *Barney* / Chips: *Rumble* / Songs: *Amusement* / Orange whip: *Bambi* / Hard day's work: *Decal* / Top pixel action: *Bombjack*
CD ______ **JERK 001**
Blunt / Oct '96 / Vital

ZONOPHONE PUNK SINGLES COLLECTION, THE
Greatest cockney rip off: *Cockney Rejects* / Inside out: *Stiffs* / I'm forever blowing bubbles: *Cockney Rejects* / We can do anything: *Cockney Rejects* / We are the firm: *Cockney Rejects* / Last night another soldier: *Angelic Upstarts* / England: *Angelic Upstarts* / Volume control: *Stiffs* / Turn me on turn me off: *Honey Bane* / Kids on the street: *Angelic Upstarts* / I understand: *Angelic Upstarts* / Easy life: *Cockney Rejects* / On the streets again: *Cockney Rejects* / Jimmy (listen to me): *Honey Bane* / Different strokes: *Angelic Upstarts* / Never say die: *Angelic Upstarts* / Out of reach: *Vice Squad* / Stand strong stand proud: *Vice Squad* / Everybody jitterbug: *Toy Dolls* / Citizen: *Vice Squad*
CD ______ **CDPUNK 97**
Anagram / May '97 / Cargo / Pinnacle

ZOO IBIZA VOL.1
CD ______ **ZOO 001CD**
Steppin' Out / Jul '96 / Else / Mo's Music Machine / Pinnacle / Steppin' Out / Total/ BMG / Vital

ZOO IBIZA VOL.2
CD ______ **ZOO 002CD**
Steppin' Out / Jul '96 / Else / Mo's Music Machine / Pinnacle / Steppin' Out / Total/ BMG / Vital

ZOO, THE
CD ______ **DCD 001**
Document / Oct '90 / ADA / Hot Shot / Jazz Music

ZOOM CLASSICS
CD ______ **ZOOMCD 2**
Zoom / Sep '95 / Arabesque / Mo's Music Machine / Prime / RTM/Disc

ZOOM, ZOOM, ZOOM
Get a job / Stranded in the jungle / Remember then / Come go with me / Zoom, zoom, zoom / Stay / I understand / Sixteen candles / Lover's island / One summer night / Church bells may ring / Earth angel / Since I don't have you / For all we know / When you dance / Deserie / At last up on a mountain / Why don't you write me / Crazy over you / Clock / Music music music / Tears on my pillow / You painted pictures
CD ______ **CPCD 8000**
Charly / Oct '93 / Koch

ZOOP, ZOOP, ZOOP (Traditional Music Of The Virgin Islands)
CD ______ **804272**
New World / Mar '96 / ADA / Cadillac / Harmonia Mundi

ZORBA'S DANCE (Memories From Greece)
CD ______ **15180**
Laserlight / '91 / Target/BMG

ZORBA'S DANCE/BOUZOUKI MAGIC
CD ______ **MATCD 242**
Castle / Nov '93 / BMG

ZULU BEATS
CD ______ **FILECD 466**
Profile / Oct '95 / Pinnacle

ZULU JIVE
CD ______ **HNCD 4410**
Hannibal / Aug '93 / ADA / Vital

ZYDECO - THE EARLY YEARS 1961-1963
CD ______ **ARHCD 307**
Arhoolie / Apr '95 / ADA / Cadillac / Direct

ZYDECO CHAMPS
CD ______ **ARHCD 328**
Arhoolie / Apr '95 / ADA / Cadillac / Direct

ZYDECO DANCE PARTY
Gator man / Chere duloone / Hello Rosa Lee / Zydeco round the world / Capitaine Gumbo / Boogie in New Orleans / Just a little girl / They all ask for you / Tyrone / Mazuka / Ay tet fee / Zydeco / I'm gonna take you home tonight / Creole de Lake Charles / My baby she's gone / Fais deaux deaux / Bayou polka / La bas two step
CD ______ **GNPD 2220**
GNP Crescendo / Sep '95 / ZYX

ZYDECO HOTSTEPPERS
Zydeco sont pas sale: *Chenier, Clifton* / Baby, please don't go: *Beausoleil* / Hack a 'tit moreau: *Nacquin, Edius* / Tipitina two-step: *Daigrepont, Bruce* / Cajun life: *Sonnier, Jo El* / Walkin' to New Orleans: *Buckwheat Zydeco* / La pointe aux pins: *Riley, Steve & Mamou Playboys* / Cajun two step: *Delafose, John* / J'aurais du t'aimer: *Newman, Joe* / Zarico est pas sale: *Riley, Steve & Mamou Playboys* / Flame will never die: *Beausoleil* / Les flammes d'enfer: *Pitre, Austin* / I'm gone and I won't be back: *Delafose, John* / Hot tamale baby: *Buckwheat Zydeco* / Lacassine special: *Sonnier, Jo El* / La valse du bambocheur: *Balfa Freres* / Let's talk it over: *Chenier, Clifton* / Frisco zydeco: *Daigrepont, Bruce*
CD ______ **NTMCD 515**
Nectar / Jan '96 / Pinnacle

ZYDECO PARTY
Zydeco groove: *August, Lynn* / I'm on my way: *Zydeco Force* / I'm coming home: *Brothers, Sam Five* / Johnny can't dance: *Chenier, Clifton* / Zydeco hee haw: *Chavis,*

Boozoo / Jalapena lena: *Rockin' Sidney* / Whatever boils your crawfish: *August, Lynn* / Leon's Zydeco: *Brothers, Sam Five* / Dopsie's Cajun Stomp: *Rockin' Dopsie* / Down east: *Zydeco Brothers* / Loan me your handkerchief: *Delafose, John* / Do it all night long: *Chavis, Boozoo* / Fun in acadiana: *Francis, Morris* / Eh mon allons dancer le zydeco: *Chavis, Wilfred* / You used to call me: *Chenier, Clifton* / Shake, rattle and roll: *Rockin' Dopsie* / You ain't nothing but fine: *Rockin' Sidney* / Keep on dreaming: *Chavis, Wilfred* / Deacon Jones: *Chavis, Boozoo* / Reach out: *Zydeco Brothers*
CD _______________ CDCHD 430
Ace / Oct '92 / Pinnacle

ZYDECO SHOOTOUT AT EL SID O'S
CD _______________ ROUCD 2108
Rounder / Sep '91 / ADA / CM / Direct

Soundtracks

12 MONKEYS
Rockmaster, Paul *C*
Introduction / Cole's first dream/Volunteer duty/Topside / Silent night / Spider research/Introduction (We did it)/Propostion / Time confusion to the mental ward/Planet Ogo / Wrong number/Coles's second dream/Dormitory spider / Vivisection: *Olins, Charles* / Sleepwalk: *Cole, B.J.* / Introduction (Escape to nowhere)/Scanner room/ Capture and se / Cole's third dream / Interrogation/Time capsule/Cole kidnaps Railly / Blueberry Hill: *Domino, Fats* / What a wonderful world: *Armstrong, Louis* / Cole's fourth dream / Comanche: *Wray, Link & The Wraymen* / Earth died screaming: *Waits, Tom* / Introduction (Quest for twelve monkeys) / Fateful bullet/Boot from the trunk/ Cole's longing / Photo search/Mission brief / Back in '96 / Fugitives/Fateful love/Home dentistry / Introduction (12 monkeys theme/ reprise)/Giraffes and flaming / This is my dream/Cole's call/Louis and Jose / Peters does his worst / Dreamers awake
CD ____ **MCD 11392**
MCA / Mar '96 / BMG

13 DAYS IN FRANCE
Lai, Francis *C*
CD ____ **MANTRA 052**
Silva Screen / Jan '93 / Koch / Silva Screen

32 SHORT FILMS ABOUT GLENN GOULD
Gould, Glenn *Con*
CD ____ **SK 46686**
Sony Classical / Jan '94 / Sony

42ND STREET
1980 Broadway Cast
Warren, Harry *C*
Dubin, Al *L*
Overture / Audition / Shadow waltz / Young and healthy / Go into your dance / You're getting to be a habit with me / Getting out of town / We're in the money / Dames / Sunny side to every situation / Lullaby of Broadway / About a quarter to nine / Shuffle off to Buffalo / 42nd Street / Finale / 42nd Street (reprise)
CD ____ **BD 83891**
RCA Victor / '85 / BMG

42ND STREET
CC Productions
Warren, Harry *C*
Dubin, Al *L*
42nd Street overture / Shadow waltz / Young and healthy / You're getting to be a habit with me / We're in the money / Dames / Lullaby of Broadway / About a quarter to nine / Shuffle off to Buffalo / 42nd Street finale
CD ____ **QED 215**
Tring / Nov '96 / Tring

42ND STREET
Studio Cast
Warren, Harry *C*
Dubin, Al *L*
Forty second street overture / Shadow waltz: *Cryer, Belinda* / Young and healthy: *Dawn, Nicola & John Peters* / You're getting to be a habit with me: *Cryer, Belinda* / We're in the money: *Cryer, Belinda* / Dames: *Peters, John* / Lullaby of Broadway: *Graeme, James* / About a quarter to nine: *Tyle, Tim & Mary Porter/Belinda Cryer* / Shuffle of to Buffalo: *Tyle, Tim & Mary Porter/Belinda Cryer* / Forty second street: *Dawn, Nicola*
CD ____ **85002**
CMC / May '97 / BMG

55 DAYS AT PEKING
Tiomkin, Dimitri *C*
CD ____ **VSD 5233**
Varese Sarabande / Feb '90 / Pinnacle

70 GIRLS 70
1991 London Cast
Kander, John *C*
Ebb, Fred *L*
CD ____ **CDTER 1186**
TER / Sep '91 / Koch

70 GIRLS 70
1971 Broadway Cast
Kander, John *C*
Ebb, Fred *L*
Kosarin, Oscar *Con*
CD ____ **SK 30589**
Sony Broadway / Nov '92 / Sony

101 DALMATIANS (Live Action)
CD ____ **WD 699402**
Disney Music & Stories / Oct '96 / Technicolor

101 DALMATIONS - LIVE ACTION (Singalong)
CD ____ **WD 740324**
Disney Music & Stories / Nov '96 / Technicolor

1776
Broadway Cast
Edwards, Sherman *C*
Howard, Peter *Con*
CD ____ **SK 48215**
Sony Broadway / Nov '92 / Sony

1984 (For The Love Of Big Brother)
Eurythmics
Stewart, David A./Annie Lennox *C*
I did it just the same / Sexcrime (1984) / For the love of big brother / Winston's diary / Greetings from a dead man / Julia / Doubleplusgood / Ministry of love / Room 101
CD ____ **CDVIP 135**
Virgin / Sep '95 / EMI

2001: A SPACE ODYSSEY
North, Alex *C*
Also sprach Zarathustra / Requiem for soprano, mezzo-soprano, two mixed choirs and orc / Lux aeterna / Blue Danube / Gayaneh ballet suite: Adagio / Atmospheres / Blue Danube (reprise) / Also sprach Zarathustra (reprise)
CD ____ **CDMGM 6**
MGM/EMI / Jan '90 / EMI

2001: A SPACE ODYSSEY (Alex North Score)
National Philharmonic Orchestra
North, Alex *C*
Goldsmith, Jerry *Con*
Main title: *Royal Philharmonic Orchestra* / Foraging: *Royal Philharmonic Orchestra* / Eat meat & the kill: *Royal Philharmonic Orchestra* / Bluff: *Royal Philharmonic Orchestra* / Night terrors: *Royal Philharmonic Orchestra* / Dawn of man: *Royal Philharmonic Orchestra* / Space station docking: *Royal Philharmonic Orchestra* / Trip to the moon: *Royal Philharmonic Orchestra* / Moon rocket bus: *Royal Philharmonic Orchestra* / Space talk: *Royal Philharmonic Orchestra* / Interior Orion: *Royal Philharmonic Orchestra* / Main theme: *Royal Philharmonic Orchestra*
CD ____ **VSD 5400**
Varese Sarabande / Oct '93 / Pinnacle

2001: A SPACE ODYSSEY
North, Alex *C*
Overture: *Sudwesfunk Orchestra/Ernest Bour* / Main title/Also sprach zarathustra: *Vienna Philharmonic Orchestra/Herbert Von Karajan* / Requiem for soprano/Mezzo soprano/Two mixed choirs/Orch: *Bavarian Radio Orchestra/Francis Travis* / Blue Danube: *Berlin Philharmonic Orchestra/Herbert Von Karajan* / Lux aeterna: *Stuttgart Schola Cantorum/Clytus Gottwold* / Gayane ballet suite: *Leningrad Philharmonic Orchestra/ Gennadi Rezhdestuensky* / Jupiter and beyond: *Vienna Philharmonic Orchestra/Herbert Von Karajan* / Atmospheres: *Vienna Philharmonic Orchestra/Herbert Von Karajan* / Adventures: *Vienna Philharmonic Orchestra/Herbert Von Karajan* / Also sprach zarathustra: *Vienna Philharmonic Orchestra/ Herbert Von Karajan* / Blue Danube: *Berlin Philharmonic Orchestra/Herbert Von Karajan* / Also sprach zarathustra: *Sudwesfunk Orchestra/Ernest Bour* / Lux aeterna: *Stuttgart Schola Cantorum/Clytus Gottwold* / Adventures: *Internationale Musikinstitut Darmstadt/Gyorgi Ligeti* / Hal 9000
CD ____ **CDODEON 28**
Soundtracks / Jan '97 / EMI

100,000 DOLLARS FOR RINGO
Nicolai, Bruno *C*
CD ____ **PAN 2501**
Silva Screen / May '95 / Koch / Silva Screen

A

A BOUT DE SOUFFLE
CD ____ **873008**
Milan / May '92 / Conifer/BMG / Silva Screen

A LA FOLIE
Nyman, Michael Band
Nyman, Michael *C*
CD ____ **399492**
Delabel / Nov '94 / EMI

ABOVE THE RIM
Anything: *SWV* / Old time's sake: *Sweet Sable* / Part time lover: *H-Town* / Big pimpin': *Dogg Pound Gangstas* / Didn't mean to turn you on: *2nd II None* / Doggie style: *D.J. Rogers* / Regulate: *Warren G. & Nate Dogg* / Pour out a little liquor: *Thug Life* / Gonna give it to ya: *Jewell & Aaron Hall* / Afro puffs: *Lady Of Rage* / Jus' so ya no: *CPO - Boss Hog* / Hoochies need love too: *Paradise* / I'm still in love with you: *Sure, Al B.* / Crack 'em: *OFTB* / U bring da dog out: *Rhythm & Knowledge* / Blowed away: *Rezell, B* / It's not deep enough: *Jewell* / Dogg pound 4 life: *Dogg Pound Gangstas*
CD ____ **IND 92359**
Interscope / Feb '97 / BMG

ABSOLUTE BEGINNERS (Soundtrack Highlights)
Absolute beginners: *Bowie, David* / Killer blow: *Sade* / Have you ever had it blue: *Style Council* / Quiet life: *Davies, Ray* / Va va voom: *Evans, Gil* / That's motivation: *Bowie, David* / Having it all: *Eighth Wonder* / Rodrigo Bay: *Working Week* / Selling out: *Gaillard, Slim* / Riot City: *Dammers, Jerry* / Boogie stop shuffle: *Evans, Gil* / Ted ain't dead: *Tenpole Tudor* / Volare: *Bowie, David* / Napoli: *Jonas* / Little cat you've never had it so good: *Jonas* / Better git it in your soul: *Evans, Gil* / So what: *Smiley Culture* / Absolute beginners (refrain): *Bowie, David*
CD ____ **VIPD 112**
Virgin VIP / May '91 / EMI

ABSOLUTE POWER
Niehaus, Lennie *C*
Mansion / Christy dies / Mansion chase / Christy's dance / Waiting for Luther / Wait for my signal / Dr Kevorkian / Presume / Sullivan's revenge / Kate's theme / End credits
CD ____ **VSD 5808**
Varese Sarabande / Apr '97 / Pinnacle

ABYSS, THE
Silvestri, Alan *C*
Main title / Search the Montana / Crane / Manta ship / Pseudopod / Fight / Sub battle / Lindsey drowns / Resurrection / Bud's big dive / Bud on the ledge / Back on the air / Finale
CD ____ **VSD 5235**
Varese Sarabande / Oct '89 / Pinnacle

ACE VENTURA I (Pet Detective)
Power of suggestion: *Stevens, Steve* / All Ace's: *Stevens, Steve* / Lion sleeps tonight: *John, Robert* / Psychoville/Ace Race: *John, Robert* / Mission Impossible / Ace of hearts / Hammer smashed face: *Cannibal Corpse* / Warehouse / Ficklo and Einhorn / Ace in the hole / Ace is in the house: *Tone Loc*
CD ____ **5230002**
Polydor / May '94 / PolyGram

ACROSS THE SEA OF TIME
Barry, John *C*
CD ____ **EK 67355**
Silva Screen / Apr '96 / Koch / Silva Screen

ACT OF PIRACY/THE GREAT WHITE
Stevens, Morton *C*
CD ____ **PCD 111**
Prometheus / '92 / Silva Screen

ACT, THE
Broadway Cast
Kander, John *C*
Ebb, Fred *L*
Shine it on / It's the strangest thing / Bobo's / Turning / Little do they know / Arthur in the afternoon / Money tree / City lights / There when I need him / Hot enough for you / Little do they know (reprise) / My own space / Walking papers
CD ____ **DRGCD 6101**
DRG / '87 / Discovery / New Note/Pinnacle

ACT, THE
Minnelli, Liza/Broadway Cast
Kander, John *C*
Ebb, Fred *L*
CD ____ **MSCD 8**
Music De-Luxe / Nov '94 / TKO Magnum

AD - ANNO DOMINI
Paris Philharmonic Orchestra
Schifrin, Lalo *C*
Golgatha / Valerius and Sarah / King Herod's march / Eternal land / Fisherman / Peter and Thomas trek / Roman celebration / Road to Damascus / New love / Gladiator school / Majesty of Rome / Corina and Caleb / Roman legion / Wedding procession / Nero the lover / Martyrdom / Exalted love
CD ____ **PCD 112**
Prometheus / Apr '92 / Silva Screen

ADDAMS FAMILY VALUES (Score)
Shaiman, Marc *C*
It's an Addams / Sibling rivalry / Love on a tombstone / Debbie meets the family / Camp Chippewa / Fester's in love / Big date / Tango / Fester & Debbie's courtship / Wednesday & Joel's courtship / Honeymoon is over / Escape from Debbie / Eat us / Wednesday's revolt / Debbie's big scene / Some time later
CD ____ **VSD 5465**
Varese Sarabande / Dec '93 / Pinnacle

ADJUSTER (& Music For The Films Of Atom Egoyan)
Danna, Mychael *C*
CD ____ **VSD 5674**
Varese Sarabande / Jul '96 / Pinnacle

ADVENTURES OF MARK TWAIN, THE/ THE PRINCE AND THE PAUPER
Brandenburg Philharmonic Orchestra/ Choir
Steiner, Max/Erich Wolfgang Korngold *C*
Stromberg, William T. *Con*
CD ____ **9026626602**
RCA Victor / Jun '96 / BMG

ADVENTURES OF PRISCILLA, QUEEN OF THE DESERT
I've never been to me: *Charlene* / Go west: *Village People* / Billy, don't be a hero: *Paper Lace* / My baby loves lovin': *White Plains* / I love the nightlife: *Bridges, Alicia* / Can't help lovin' dat man: *Richards, Trudy & Billy May* / I will survive: *Gaynor, Gloria* / Fine romance: *Horne, Lena* / Shake your groove thing: *Peaches & Herb* / I don't care if the sun don't shine: *Page, Patti* / Finally: *Peniston, Ce Ce* / Take a letter Maria: *Peniston, Ce Ce* / Mamma mia: *Abba* / Save the best for last: *Williams, Vanessa*
CD ____ **MUMCD 9416**
Mother / Oct '94 / PolyGram

ADVENTURES OF ROBIN HOOD, THE
Utah Symphony Orchestra
Korngold, Erich *C*
CD ____ **EK 57568**
Silva Screen / Jan '93 / Koch / Silva Screen

ADVENTURES OF ROBIN HOOD, THE
Korngold, Erich *C*
CD ____ **CDTER 1066**
TER / May '89 / Koch

ADVENTURES OF ROBIN HOOD, THE/ REQUIEM FOR A CAVALIER
Korngold, Erich *C*
Korngold, Erich *Con*
CD ____ **VSD 47202**
Varese Sarabande / Aug '91 / Pinnacle

ADVENTURES OF ROBINSON CRUSOE, THE
Mellin, Robert & Gian-Piero Reverberi *C*
Reverberi, Gian-Piero *Con*
Opening titles / Main theme / Friday / Crusoe's youth remembered / Away from home / Adrift / Solitude / Shelter / Scanning the horizon/Flashback - escapdes in York / Cannibals / Wild goats / Palm trees / In search of rescue / Civilised man / Distant shores / Alone / Catching dinner / Poor Robinson / Danger / Closing titles
CD ____ **FILMCD 705**
Silva Screen / Apr '96 / Koch / Silva Screen

AFTER DARK MY SWEET
Jarre, Maurice *C*
After dark my sweet / Collie and Fay / Uncle Bud / Kidnapping
CD ____ **VSD 5274**
Varese Sarabande / Jul '90 / Pinnacle

AFTER MIDNIGHT
Gordon, Dexter *C*
CD ____ **SCCD 31226**
Southern Cross / Jul '88 / Silva Screen

AGAINST ALL ODDS
Against all odds: *Collins, Phil* / Violet and blue: *Nicks, Stevie* / Walk through the fire: *Gabriel, Peter* / Balcony: *Big Country* / Making a big mistake: *Rutherford, Mike* / My male curiosity: *Kid Creole & The Coconuts* / Search: *Carlton, Larry & Michel Colombier* / El solitario: *Carlton, Larry & Michel Colombier* / Rock 'n' roll jaguar: *Carlton, Larry & Michel Colombier* / For love alone: *Carlton, Larry* / Race: *Carlton, Larry* / Murder of a friend: *Carlton, Larry*
CD ____ **CDVIP 112**
Virgin VIP / Nov '93 / EMI

AGUIRRE (& Heart Of Glass/Nosferatu)
Popul Vuh
3CD ____ **SPALAX 14703**
Spalax / Oct '96 / ADA / Cargo / Direct / Discovery / Greyhound

AGUIRRE/HERZ AUS GLAS/ NOSFERATU (Soundtracks For Werner Herzog/Film Can Set)
Popul Vuh
Popul Vuh *C*
CD ____ **14703**
Spalax / Jul '97 / ADA / Cargo / Direct / Discovery / Greyhound

AIN'T MISBEHAVIN'
1979 Broadway Cast
Waller, Fats *C*
Ain't misbehavin' / Honeysuckle Rose / Squeeze me / Handful of keys / I've got a feeling I'm falling / How ya baby / Jitterbug waltz / Ladies who sing with the band / Yacht Club swing / When the nylons bloom again / Cash for your trash / Off-time / Joint is jumpin' / Entr'acte / Spreadin' rhythm around / Lounging at the Waldorf / Viper's drag/The reefer song / Mean to me / Your feet's too big / That ain't right / Keepin' out of mischief now / Find out what they like / Fat and greasy / Black and blue / I'm gonna sit right down and write myself a letter / Two sleepy people/I've got my fingers crossed
2CD ____ **BD 82965**
RCA Victor / Aug '90 / BMG

AIN'T MISBEHAVIN'
1979 London Cast
Waller, Fats *C*
CD ________ **CASTCD 53**
First Night / Apr '96 / Pinnacle

AIRPORT
Newman, Alfred *C*
Airport / Airport love theme / Inez' theme / Guerreo's goodbye / Ada Quonsett stowaway / Mel & Tanya / Airport love theme 2 / Joe Patroni plane or plows / Triangle / Inez lost forever / Emergency landing / Airport (End Title)
CD ________ **VSD 5436**
Varese Sarabande / Aug '93 / Pinnacle

AKIRA (Japanese Score)
Shoji, Yamashiro *C*
CD ________ **DSCD 6**
Demon / Nov '93 / Pinnacle

AKIRA
Shoji, Yamashiro *C*
Kaneda / Battle against clown / Tetsuo / Akira / Winds over Neo-Tokyo / Doll's polyphony / Shohmyoh / Mutation / Exodus from the underground fortress / Illusion / Requiem
CD ________ **DSCD 7**
Demon / Jun '94 / Pinnacle

ALADDIN
1958 Television Cast
Porter, Cole *C*
Perelman, S.J. *L*
Emmett Dolan, Robert *Con*
CD ________ **SK 48205**
Sony Broadway / May '95 / Sony

ALADDIN
Menken, Alan *C*
Ashman, Howard & Tim Rice *L*
CD ________ **WD 742602**
Disney Music & Stories / Mar '96 / Technicolor

ALEXANDER NEVSKY (& Scythian Suite)
Finnie, Linda/Royal Scottish National Orchestra/Chorus
Prokofiev, Sergei *C*
Jarvi, Neeme *Con*
CD ________ **CHAN 8584**
Chandos / Jul '94 / Chandos

ALEXANDER NEVSKY
St. Petersburg Philharmonic Orchestra/Chorus
Prokofiev, Sergei *C*
Temirkanov, Yuri *Con*
CD ________ **09026619262**
RCA Victor / Feb '96 / BMG

ALEXANDER THE GREAT/BARABBAS
Nascimbene, Mario *C*
Nascimbene, Mario *Con*
CD ________ **DRGCD 32964**
DRG / Nov '96 / Discovery / New Note/ Pinnacle

ALICE'S RESTAURANT
Guthrie, Arlo *C*
Alice's restaurant massacre / Chilling of the evening / Ring around a rosy rag / Now and then I'm going home / Motorcycle song / Highway in the wind
CD ________ **244045**
WEA / Feb '94 / Warner Music

ALIEN
National Philharmonic Orchestra
Goldsmith, Jerry *C*
Newman, Lionel *Con*
Main title / Face hugger / Breakaway / Acid test / Landing / Droid / Recovery / Alien planet / Shaft / End titles
CD ________ **FILMCD 003**
Silva Screen / Jun '87 / Koch / Silva Screen

ALIEN EMPIRE (The Ocellus Suite)
Munich Symphony Orchestra
Kiszko, Martin *C*
Journey to the Alien Empire / Ocellus voyage / Battle zone / Angels and warriors / Slipstreams / Earthstalkers / Insectarium / Solus odyssey / Ancient enemies / Three visions / Firstborn / Distant swarm / Colony and metropolis / Earthrise / Return voyage
CD ________ **CDEMC 3730**
Soundtrack Music / Jan '96 / EMI

ALIEN NATION - THE SERIES
Dorff, Steve/Larry Herbstritt/David Kurtz
Dorff, Steve/Larry Herbstritt/David Kurtz *C*
CD ________ **GNPD 8024**
GNP Crescendo / '94 / ZYX

ALIEN TRILOGY
Goldsmith, Jerry & James Horner *C*
CD ________ **VSD 5753**
Varese Sarabande / Nov '96 / Pinnacle

ALIVE
Howard, James Newton *C*
CD ________ **EA 614542**
Silva Screen / Jan '93 / Koch / Silva Screen

ALL AMERICAN
1962 Broadway Cast
Strouse, Charles *C*
Adams, Lee *L*
Morris, John *Con*
CD ________ **SK 48216**
Sony Broadway / Nov '92 / Sony

ALL THAT JAZZ
On Broadway: *Benson, George* / Michelle: *Burns, Ralph* / Take off with us: *Bergman, Sandahl & Chorus Vavaldi* / Ponte vecchio: *Burns, Ralph* / Everything old is new again: *Allen, Peter* / South Mt Sinai parade: *Burns, Ralph* / After you've gone: *Palmer, Leland* / There'll be some changes made: *Reinking, Ann* / Who's sorry now: *Burns, Ralph* / Some of these days: *Foldi, Erzsebet* / Going home now: *Burns, Ralph* / Bye bye love: *Vereen, Ben & Roy Scheider* / Vivaldi concerti in G: *Burns, Ralph* / Main Title: *Burns, Ralph*
CD ________ **5512692**
Spectrum / Sep '95 / PolyGram

ALL THE BROTHERS WERE VALIANT
Rozsa, Miklos *C*
Rozsa, Miklos *Con*
CD ________ **PCD 131**
Prometheus / Jan '95 / Silva Screen

ALL THE KING'S MEN
CD ________ **5390662**
Polydor / Aug '97 / PolyGram

ALLONSANFAN/METELLO
Morricone, Ennio *C*
2CD ________ **OST 103**
Milano Dischi / Jan '95 / Silva Screen

ALMOST AN ANGEL
Jarre, Maurice *C*
Jarre, Maurice *Con*
CD ________ **VSD 5307**
Varese Sarabande / Jan '91 / Pinnacle

AMADEUS
Academy Of St. Martin In The Fields
Mozart, W.A. *C*
Marriner, Neville *Con*
2CD ________ **8251262**
London / Feb '85 / PolyGram

AMADEUS: MORE AMADEUS
Academy Of St. Martin In The Fields
Mozart, W.A. *C*
Marriner, Neville *Con*
CD ________ **8272672**
London / Aug '85 / PolyGram

AMAHL AND THE NIGHT VISITORS, THE
Royal Opera House
Menotti, Gian Carlo *C*
CD ________ **CDTER 1124**
TER / Jan '93 / Koch

AMATEUR
Taylor, Jeff/Ned Rifle *C*
Mind full of worry: *Aquanettas* / Only shallow: *My Bloody Valentine* / Water: *PJ Harvey* / Japanese to English: *Red House Painters* / Shaker: *Yo La Tengo* / Tom boy: *Bettie Serveert* / Girls Girls Girls: *Phair, Liz* / Then comes Dudley: *Jesus Lizard* / Here: *Pavement*
CD ________ **7567925002**
Warner Bros. / Jan '95 / Warner Music

AMATEUR, THE/OF UNKNOWN ORIGIN/THE LATE SHOW
Wannberg, Ken *C*
CD ________ **PCD 137**
Prometheus / Apr '96 / Silva Screen

AMAZING GRACE AND CHUCK
Bernstein, Elmer *C*
CD ________ **VCD 47285**
Varese Sarabande / Jan '89 / Pinnacle

AMBUSH OF GHOSTS, AN
In The Nursery
CD ________ **TM 90382**
Roadrunner / Mar '96 / PolyGram

AMERICA IS DYING SLOWLY
CD ________ **7559619252**
WEA / Jun '96 / Warner Music

AMERICAN BUFFALO
Newman, Thomas *C*
CD ________ **VSD 5751**
Varese Sarabande / Oct '96 / Pinnacle

AMERICAN CHRISTMAS, AN
CD ________ **VSD 5441**
Varese Sarabande / Dec '93 / Pinnacle

AMERICAN GIGOLO
Moroder, Giorgio
Moroder, Giorgio *C*
Call me: *Blondie* / Love and passion: *Barnes, Cheryl* / Night drive / Hello Mr. W.A.M. / Apartment / Palm Springs Drive / Night drive (reprise) / Seduction (Love Theme)
CD ________ **5511032**
Spectrum / Sep '95 / PolyGram

AMERICAN GRAFFITI
(We're gonna) Rock around the clock: *Haley, Bill & The Comets* / Sixteen candles: *Crests* / Runaway: *Shannon, Del* / Why do fools fall in love: *Lymon, Frankie & The Teenagers* / That'll be the day: *Holly, Buddy & The Crickets* / Maybe baby: *Holly, Buddy & The Crickets* / Fannie Mae: *Brown, Buster* / At the hop: *Flash Cadillac & The Continental Kids* / She's so fine: *Flash Cadillac & The Continental Kids* / Goodnight well it's time to go: *Spaniels* / See you in September: *Tempos* / Surfin' safari: *Beach Boys* / All summer long: *Beach Boys* / He's the great imposter: *Fleetwoods* / Almost grown: *Berry, Chuck* / Johnny B Goode: *Berry, Chuck* / Smoke gets in your eyes: *Platters* / Only you: *Platters* / Great pretender: *Platters* / Little darlin': *Diamonds* / Stroll: *Diamonds* / Peppermint twist: *Dee, Joey & The Starlighters* / Ya Ya: *Dorsey, Lee* / Ain't that a shame: *Domino, Fats* / I only have eyes for you: *Flamingos* / Get a job: *Silhouettes* / To the aisle: *Five Satins* / Do you wanna dance: *Freeman, Bobby* / Party doll: *Knox, Buddy* / Come go with me: *Del-Vikings* / You're sixteen: *Burnette, Johnny Rock 'N' Roll Trio* / Love potion no.9: *Clovers* / Since I don't have you: *Skyliners* / Chantilly lace: *Big Bopper* / Teen angel: *Dinning, Mark* / Crying in the chapel: *Till, Sonny & The Orioles* / Thousand miles away: *Heartbeats* / Heart and soul: *Cleftones* / Green onions: *Booker T & The MG's* / Barbara Ann: *Regents* / Book of love: *Monotones*
2CD ________ **MCLDD 19150**
MCA / Apr '97 / BMG

AMERICAN IN PARIS, AN
Gershwin, George *C*
Main title / Paris narration/Left bank / Nice work if you can get it / Adam Cork monologue / Nice work if you can get it (outtake) / Embraceable you / Fascinatin' rhythm / By Strauss / Street exhibition / I got rhythm / But not for me / Medley / Someone to watch over me / I've got a crush on you (outtake) / Tra la la / Love is here to stay / Medley 2 / Love walked in (outtake) / (I'll build) A stairway to paradise / I don't think I'll fall in love today / Concerto in F / Kiss me / What time is it / 'S wonderful / Lise, I love you / Strike up the band (extended version) / Liza (extended version) / Oh lady be good/'S wonderful / That certain feeling/ Clap yo' hands / I got rhythm (extended version) / Tra la la (outtake) / Utrillo did it / But not for me (outtake) / American in Paris ballet / Finale / My cousin in Milwaukee (outtake) / Foggy day (outtake) / Half of it dearie blues / Nice work if you can get it (rehearsal)
2CD ________ **CDODEON 20**
Soundtracks / Sep '96 / EMI

AMOK
Piovani, Nicola *C*
CD ________ **887898**
Milan / Jan '95 / Conifer/BMG / Silva Screen

ANACONDA
Edelman, Randy *C*
Edelman, Randy *Con*
Anaconda / Watching and waiting / Night attack / This must be heaven / Down river / Seduction / Travelogue / Baiting the line / My beautiful Anna..(conda) / Totem's sacred ground / Sarone's last stand
CD ________ **0022812CIN**
Edel / Jul '97 / Pinnacle

ANASTASIA (The Mystery Of Anna)
Munich Philharmonic Orchestra
Rosenthal, Laurence *C*
Main title (part 1) / Ballroom / Siberia / Sled / Family only/The cellar / Berlin bridge / Confronting Sophie / After the interview / Railroad car / Main title (part 2) / Denial / Shopping spree / Romanoffs / At the Astor / Russian antiques / Darya says no / Luncheonette / Anna and Erich / Ekaterinburg / Back to Europe
CD ________ **SCCD 1015**
Southern Cross / Jan '89 / Silva Screen

AND DO THEY DO
Nyman, Michael Band
Nyman, Michael *C*
CD ________ **CDTER 1123**
TER / Aug '93 / Koch

AND THE BAND PLAYED ON
Burwell, Carter *C*
Burwell, Carter *Con*
CD ________ **VSD 5449**
Varese Sarabande / Apr '94 / Pinnacle

ANDRE
Rowland, Bruce *C*
Thanks to you: *Collins, Tyler* / Yakety yak: *Coasters* / Rama rama ding dong: *Edsels* / This magic moment: *Drifters* / I only have eyes for you: *Flamingos* / You talk too much: *Jones, Joe* / Peppermint twist: *Dee, Joey & The Starlighters* / Lover's concerto: *Toys* / Don't say nothin' bad (about my baby): *Cookies* / Johnny Angel: *Faboures, Johnny* / Green onions: *Booker T & The MG's* / Along came Jones: *Coasters* / You're my best friend: *Craig 'n' Co.*
CD ________ **8122718022**
Warner Bros. / Jan '95 / Warner Music

ANDY WARHOL'S DRACULA/ANDY WARHOL'S FRANKENSTEIN
Gizzi, Claudio *C*
CD ________ **OST 119**
Milano Dischi / Jan '94 / Silva Screen

ANGEL AT MY TABLE, AN
McGlashan, Don *C*
CD ________ **A 8925**
Alhambra / Jan '92 / Silva Screen

ANGEL AT MY TABLE, AN
McGlashan, Don *C*
CD ________ **DRGCD 12603**
DRG / Jan '95 / Discovery / New Note/ Pinnacle

ANGEL BABY
CD ________ **74321443592**
Milan / Dec '96 / Conifer/BMG / Silva Screen

ANGEL HEART
Jones, Trevor *C*
Harry Angel: *Jones, Trevor & Courtney Pine* / Honeymoon blues: *Smith, Bessie* / Nightmare: *Jones, Trevor & Courtney Pine* / Girl of ...: *Gray, Glen & The Casa Loma Orchestra* / I got this thing about chickens: *Jones, Trevor & Courtney Pine* / Right key but the wrong keyhole / Rainy rainy day: *McGhee, Brownie* / Looking for Johnny: *Jones, Trevor & Courtney Pine* / Soul on fire: *Baker, LaVern* / Bloodmare: *Jones, Trevor & Courtney Pine* / Johnny Favourite: *Jones, Trevor & Courtney Pine*
CD ________ **IMCD 76**
Island / '89 / PolyGram

ANGELS AND INSECTS
Balanescu Quartet
CD ________ **CDSTUMM 147**
Mute / Dec '95 / RTM/Disc

ANGIE
Goldsmith, Jerry *C*
Goldsmith, Jerry *Con*
CD ________ **VSD 5469**
Varese Sarabande / Jun '94 / Pinnacle

ANGST
Schulze, Klaus
Schulze, Klaus *C*
Freeze / Pain / Memory / Surrender / Beyond
CD ________ **CDTB 027**
Thunderbolt / Feb '86 / TKO Magnum

ANGUS
JAR (Jason Andrew Relva): *Green Day* / Jack names the planets: *Ash* / Enough: *Dance Hall Crashers* / Kung fu: *Ash* / Back to you: *Riverdales* / Mrs. You and me: *Smoking Popes* / You gave your love to me softly: *Weezer* / Ain't that unusual: *Goo Goo Dolls* / Funny face: *Muffs* / White homes: *Tilt* / Deep water: *Pansy Division* / Am I wrong: *Love Spit Love*
CD ________ **9362459602**
Warner Bros. / Aug '95 / Warner Music

ANIMA MUNDI
Glass, Philip *C*
Journey / Ark / Garden / Beginning / Living waters / Perpetual motion
CD ________ **7559793292**
Nonesuch / Jan '94 / Warner Music

ANIMAL HOUSE
Faber College theme / Louie Louie: *Belushi, John* / Twistin' the night away: *Cooke, Sam* / Tossin' and turnin': *Lewis, Bobby* / Shama lama ding dong / Hey Paula: *Paul & Paula* / Animal house: *Bishop, Stephen* / Money (that's what I want): *Belushi, John* / Let's dance: *Montez, Chris* / Dream girl: *Bishop, Stephen* / What a wonderful world: *Cooke, Sam* / Shout / Intro
CD ________ **MCLD 19086**
MCA / Jun '92 / BMG

ANIMANIACS
CD ________ **8122715702**
Atlantic / Apr '94 / Warner Music

ANNA KARENINA
Gorchakova, Galina & Maxim Vengerov/ St. Petersburg Philharmonic Orchestra
Solti, George *Con*
CD ________ **4553602**
Decca / May '97 / PolyGram

ANNE OF GREEN GABLES
London Cast
Campbell, Norman *C*
Campbell, Norman & Donald Harron *L*
Goldstein, Martin *Con*
CD ________ **SMK 53495**
Sony West End / Dec '91 / Sony

ANNIE
1982 Film Cast
Strouse, Charles *C*
Charnin, Martin *L*
Tomorrow / It's the hard-knock life / Maybe / Dumb dog / Sandy / I think I'm gonna like it here / Little girls / We got Annie / Let's go to the movies / Sign / You're never fully dressed without a smile / Easy Street / Tomorrow reprise / Finale
CD ________ **4676082**
CBS / Dec '90 / Sony

ANNIE
Strouse, Charles *C*
Charnin, Martin *L*
Overture / Maybe / It's the hard-knock life / Tomorrow / We'd like to thank you / Little girls / I think I'm going to like it here / NYC / Easy Street / You're never fully dressed without a smile / I don't need anything but you / New deal for Christmas
CD ________ **SHOWCD 041**
Showtime / Jan '97 / Disc / THE

ANNIE GET YOUR GUN
Criswell, Kim & Thomas Hampson/Studio Cast/Ambrosian Chorus/London Sinfonietta
Berlin, Irving *C*
Fields, Dorothy *L*
McGlinn, John *Con*
CD ________ **CDANNIE 1**
EMI Classics / Aug '91 / EMI

ANNIE GET YOUR GUN (Featuring Ethel Merman)
Lincoln Center Theater Cast
Berlin, Irving *C*
Fields, Dorothy *L*
Overture / Colonel Buffalo Bill / I'm a bad, bad man / Doin' what comes natur'lly / Girl that I marry / You can't get a man with a gun / There's no business like show busi-

ness / They say it's wonderful / Moonshine lullaby / There's no business like show business (reprise) / My defenses are down / I'm an Indian too / I got lost in his arms / I got the sun in the morning / Old fashioned wedding / Anything you can do / Finale
CD RD 81124
RCA Victor / Jan '89 / BMG

ANNIE GET YOUR GUN
1986 London Cast
Berlin, Irving *C*
Fields, Dorothy *L*
Overture / Colonel Buffalo Bill / I'm a bad bad man / Doin' what comes natur'lly / Girl that I marry / You can't get a man with a gun / There's no business like show business / They say it's wonderful / Moonshine lullaby / My defenses are down / Wild horse ceremonial dance / I'm an Indian too / I got lost in his arms / I got the sun in the morning / Old fashioned wedding / Anything you can do / Finale
CD OCRCD 6024
First Night / Oct '95 / Pinnacle

ANNIE GET YOUR GUN
Broadway Cast
Berlin, Irving *C*
Fields, Dorothy *L*
CD ZDM 7647652
EMI Classics / Apr '93 / EMI

ANNIE GET YOUR GUN
Cast Recording
Berlin, Irving *C*
Fields, Dorothy *L*
CD CDTER 1229
TER / Aug '95 / Koch

ANNIE WARBUCKS
Broadway Cast
CD CDQ 5550402
EMI / Mar '94 / EMI

ANTARCTICA
Vangelis
Vangelis *C*
Antarctica / Antarctica echoes / Kinematic song of white / Life of Antarctica / Memory of Antarctica / Other side of Antarctica / Deliverance
CD 8157322
Polydor / Mar '96 / PolyGram

ANTARTIDA
Cale, John
Cale, John *C*
CD TWI 1008
Les Disques Du Crepuscule / Nov '95 / Discovery

ANTONIA'S LINE
Metropole Orchestra Of The Netherlands
Sekacz, Ilona *C*
Bakker, D. *Con*
CD FILMCD 183
Silva Screen / Oct '96 / Koch / Silva Screen

ANTONY AND CLEOPATRA
Berlin Radio Symphony Choir/Orchestra
Scott, John *C*
Scott, John *Con*
CD JSCD 114
JOS / Jan '93 / JOS / Silva Screen

ANYTHING GOES
1989 London Cast
Porter, Cole *C*
Prelude / There's no cure like travel / You're the top / I want to row on the crew / Friendship / Anything goes / Public enemy No.1 / Goodbye little dream goodbye / All through the night / Buddie beware / I get a kick out of you / Bon voyage / Easy to love / Sailor's chantey / It's de-lovely / Entr'acte / Blow Gabriel blow / Be like the bluebird / Gypsy in me
CD OCRCD 6038
First Night / Oct '95 / Pinnacle

ANYTHING GOES
Cast Recording
Porter, Cole *C*
CD EK 15100
Silva Screen / Jan '89 / Koch / Silva Screen

ANYTHING GOES
1969 London Cast
Porter, Cole *C*
CD CDTER 1219
TER / Jan '94 / Koch

ANYTHING GOES
Criswell, Kim & Cris Groenendaal/Jack Gilford/Frederica Von Stade/Ambrosian Chorus/London Symphony Orchestra
Porter, Cole *C*
Overture / I get a kick out of you / Bon voyage / All through the night / There'll always be a lady fair / Where are the men / You're the top / You're the top (encore) / There'll always be a lady fair (reprise) / Anything goes (finale) / Entr'acte / Public enemy No.1 / What a joy to be young / Blow Gabriel blow / Be like the bluebird / Buddie beware / Gypsy in me / Finale ultimo / Kate the great / Waltz down the aisle
CD CDC 7498482
EMI Classics / Oct '89 / EMI

ANYTHING GOES
Luker, Rebecca
Porter, Cole *C*
CD VSD 5647
Varese Sarabande / Jun '96 / Pinnacle

ANYWHERE I WANDER
Cast Recording
Loesser, Frank *C*
CD VSD 5434
Varese Sarabande / Oct '93 / Pinnacle

APOCALYPSE NOW
Coppola, Carmine *C*
End / End part 2 / Terminate / Delta / PBR / Dossier / Colonel Kilgore / Orange light / Ride of the Valkyries / Napalm in the morning / Pre-tiger / Dossier II / Suzie Q / Dossier III / 75 klicks / Ning river / Do Lung Bridge / Letters from home / Clean's death / Chief's death / Strange voyage / Kurtz' compound / Errand boy / Chief's head / Hollow men / Horror / Even the jungle wanted him dead / End: *Doors*
2CD 7559606892
Elektra / Apr '96 / Warner Music

APOLLO 13
Horner, James *C*
Horner, James *Con*
Night train: *Brown, James* / Groovin': *Young Rascals* / Somebody to love: *Jefferson Airplane* / I can see for miles: *Who* / Purple haze: *Hendrix, Jimi* / Spirit in the sky: *Greebaum, Norman* / Honky tonkin': *Williams, Hank* / Blue moon: *Mavericks* / Main title / One small step / Launch control / All systems go / Welcome to Apollo 13 / House cleaning / Houston, we have a problem / Master Alarm / What's going on / Into the LEM / Out of time / Shut her down / Dark side of the moon / Failure is not an option / Waiting for disaster / Privelege / Re-entry & splashdown / End titles
CD MCD 11241
MCA / Jul '95 / BMG

APPLE TREE, THE
Broadway Cast
Bock, Jerry *C*
Harnick, Sheldon *L*
Lawrence, Elliot *Con*
CD SK 48209
Sony Broadway / Dec '91 / Sony

APRES LA GUERRE (After The War)
Knieper, Jurgen *C*
CD CDCH 386
Milan / Feb '90 / Conifer/BMG / Silva Screen

ARCADIANS, THE
London Cast
Monckton, Lionel & Howard Talbot *C*
Wimperis, Arthur *L*
Overture / Opening chorus: Arcadians are we / Joy of life / Pipes of Pan are calling / To all and each / Back your fancy / Girl with the brogue / Arcady is ever young / Somewhere / Charming weather / I like London / Half past two / All down Piccadilly / Truth is beautiful / My motter / All down Piccadilly (Reprise) / Pipes of Pan / Girl with a brogue / Arcady is ever young / My motter / Bring me a rose / Come back to Arcady / Light is my heart
CD CDANGEL 1
Angel / Apr '93 / EMI

ARE YOU LONESOME TONIGHT
1985 London Cast
Peace in the valley / Heartbreak hotel / That's alright mama / I don't care if the sun don't shine / Loving you / Blue suede shoes / Hound dog / If I can dream / All my trials / NBC-TV special 1968 / You gave me a mountain / I was the one / If we never meet again / Are you lonesome tonight
CD OCRCD 6027
First Night / Dec '95 / Pinnacle

ARISTOCATS, THE
Sherman, Richard & Robert *C*
CD WD 742502
Disney Music & Stories / Mar '96 / Technicolor

ARRIVAL, THE
Band, Richard *C*
CD MAF 7032D
Intrada / Nov '92 / Koch / Silva Screen

ARRIVAL, THE (Score)
Northwest Sinfonia
Kempel, Arthur *C*
Kempel, Arthur *Con*
CD FILMCD 182
Silva Screen / Oct '96 / Koch / Silva Screen

ASCENSEUR POUR L'ECHAFAUD (Lift To The Scaffold)
Davis, Miles
Davis, Miles *C*
Nuit sur Les Champs-Elysee / Assassinat / Motel / Final / Le petit bal / Sequence voiture / Generique / L'assassinat de Carala / Sur l'autoroute / Julien dans l'ascenseur / Florence dans l'ascenseur / Florence sur Les Champs-Elysee / Diner au motel / Evasion de Julien / Visite du vigile / Au bar du petit bac / Chez le photographe du motel
CD 8363052
Fontana / Mar '94 / PolyGram

ASPECTS OF LOVE
London Cast
Lloyd Webber, Andrew *C*
Love changes everything / Seeing is believing / Chason d'enfante / She's far better off without you / Leading lady / There's more to love / First man you remember / Falling / Anything but lonely / Cafe / Memory of a happy moment / Everybody loves a hero / Stop wait please / Other pleasures / Mermaid song / Journey of a lifetime / Hand me the wine and the dice
CD 8411262
Really Useful / Aug '89 / PolyGram

ASPECTS OF LOVE/CATS
Cast Recording
Lloyd Webber, Andrew *C*
CD 340832
Koch / Oct '95 / Koch

ASSASSINS
1991 Broadway Cast
Sondheim, Stephen *C*
Everybody's got the right / Ballad of Booth / How I saved Roosevelt / Gun song / Ballad of Czolgosz / Unworthy of your love / Ballad of Guiteau / Another national anthem / November 22, 1963 / Final sequence - You can close the New York Stock Exchange / Everybody's got the right (reprise)
CD RD 60737
RCA Victor / '91 / BMG

ASSOCIATE, THE
CD 5307472
Polydor / Apr '97 / PolyGram

ASTRONOMERS, THE
Redford, J.A.C. *C*
CD MAF 7018D
Intrada / Jan '93 / Koch / Silva Screen

AT PLAY IN THE FIELDS OF THE LORD
Polish Radio Grand Symphony Orchestra
Preisner, Zbigniew *C*
Wit, Antoni *Con*
CD FCD 210072
Fantasy / Jan '93 / Jazz Music / Pinnacle / Wellard

AT THE MOVIES
Someday (I'm coming back): *Stansfield, Lisa* / This city never sleeps: *Eurythmics* / You don't own me: *Eurythmics* / Crash: *Primitives* / Get together: *Youngbloods* / Ghostbusters: *Parker, Ray Jnr.* / Nothing's gonna stop us now: *Parker, Ray Jnr.* / Everybody's talkin': *Nilsson, Harry* / Theme from Harry's Game: *Clannad* / Natural thing: *M People* / Roadhouse blues: *Healey, Jeff Band* / I will always love you: *Parton, Dolly* / Jumping Jack Flash: *Franklin, Aretha* / Neutron dance: *Pointer Sisters* / Let the river run: *Simon, Carly* / Sentimental journey: *Esquivel & His Orchestra*
CD 74321412732
RCA / Feb '97 / BMG

ATLANTIC CITY
Legrand, Michel *C*
Casta diva / Slot machine baby / Bellini rock / Atlantic city / My old friend / Balcon / Piano blackjack / Steel pier / Song of India / Roadmap for a free jazz group / No gambling allowed / AC/DC / Trio jazz
CD CDRG 6104
DRG / Jan '89 / Discovery / New Note/ Pinnacle
CD 119072
Musidisc / Jan '97 / Discovery

ATLANTIS
Serra, Eric *C*
Creation / Secret life of angels / Visions of the underways / Snake / Iguana dance / Down to the unknown world / Magic forest / In the kingdom of spirits / Legend of Manatees / Time to get your lovin' / Shark attack / Realms of ice
CD 30867
Silva Screen / Jan '93 / Koch / Silva Screen

ATTACK AND RETREAT/THE CAMP FOLLOWERS (Italiani Brava Gente/Le Soldatesse)
Trovajoli, Armando/Mario Nascimbene *C*
CD OST 112
Milano Dischi / Apr '92 / Silva Screen

ATTENTION BANDITS
Lai, Francis *C*
CD MANTRA 055
Silva Screen / Jan '93 / Koch / Silva Screen

AUF OFFENER STRASSE/L 627
Sarde, Philippe *C*
CD 873131
Milan / Jan '95 / Conifer/BMG / Silva Screen

AUSTIN POWER
CD 1621122
Polydor / Sep '97 / PolyGram

AUX YEAUX DU MONDE
Wonder, Stevie
Torikian, G. *C*
CD CH 403
Milan / Jan '95 / Conifer/BMG / Silva Screen

AVALON
Newman, Randy
Newman, Randy *C*
CD 9264372
Silva Screen / Jan '93 / Koch / Silva Screen

AVENGERS, THE/THE NEW AVENGERS/ THE PROFESSIONALS
London Studio Orchestra
Johnson, Laurie *C*
CD VCD 47270
Varese Sarabande / Jan '89 / Pinnacle

AWAKENINGS
Newman, Randy
Newman, Randy *C*
Leonard / Dr. Sayer / Lucy / Catch / Rilke's panther / L dopa / Awakenings / Time of the season / Outside / Escape attempt / Ward five / Dexter's tune / Reality of miracles / End titles
CD 7599264662
Reprise / Mar '91 / Warner Music

AWFULLY BIG ADVENTURE, AN
Hartley, Richard *C*
Main titles / From the cradle / I think the world of you Uncle Vernon / Don't fuss bunny / Boy King / Mr. Potter / Rose tinted view / To a far off land / Let's hang the cloth / If you like / Hello mother / Crocodile bites back / All through the night / Back to the nursery Mr. Darling / Stella / Captain Hook has drowned himself / Bending down to tie my shoelaces / End titles
CD TRXCD 2001
Silva Screen / Apr '95 / Koch / Silva Screen

AY, CARMELA
Masso, Alejandro *C*
CD CH 557
Milan / Jan '95 / Conifer/BMG / Silva Screen

BABE
Bernstein, Elmer *C*
CD VSD 5661
Varese Sarabande / Oct '95 / Pinnacle

BABES IN ARMS
Film Cast
Rodgers, Richard *C*
Hart, Lorenz *L*
CD NW 3862
New World / Aug '92 / New World

BABY
Broadway Cast
Shire, David *C*
Maltby, Richard Jr. *L*
Opening / We start today / What could be better / Plaza song / Baby, baby, baby / I want it all / At night she comes home to me / Fatherhood blues / Romance / I chose right / Story goes on / Ladies singing their song / Patterns / Romance 2 / Easier to love / Romance 3 / Two people in love / With you / And what if we had loved like that / Birth / Finale
CD CDTER 1089
TER / Mar '84 / Koch

BABY OF MACON, THE
March / Batille and comet / Opening part one / Opening part two / Morning hymn / Evening hymn / Suscepit Israel / Cia cona / Selling of the child's files / Dance one / Dance two / Lamentations / Ave Maria Stella / Dismemberment of the child / Improvisation of batille and drums / Cantor
CD 340142
Koch / Sep '93 / Koch

BABYLON 5
Franke, Christopher *C*
Chrysalis / Mindwar / Parliament of dreams / Geometry of shadows
CD S 185022
CDS / Mar '95 / Pinnacle

BACK TO THE FUTURE
Johnny B Goode: *McFly, Marty & the Starlighters* / Power of love: *Lewis, Huey & The News* / Time bomb town: *Buckingham, Lindsey* / Back to the future: *Silvestri, Alan* / Heaven is one step away: *Clapton, Eric* / Back in time: *Lewis, Huey & The News* / Back to the future overture: *Silvestri, Alan* / Wallflower (dance with me, Henry): *James, Etta* / Night train: *Berry, Marvin & the Starlighters* / Earth angel: *Berry, Marvin & the Starlighters*
CD MCLD 19151
MCA / Apr '93 / BMG

BACK TO THE FUTURE III
Silvestri, Alan *C*
Main title / It's Clara / Train / Hill Valley / Hanging / At first sight / Indians / Goodbye Clara / Doc returns / Point of no return / Future isn't written / Showdown / Doc to the rescue / Kiss / We're out of gas / Wake up juice / Science experiment / Doubleback: *ZZ Top* / End credits
CD VSD 5272
Varese Sarabande / Sep '90 / Pinnacle

BACKBEAT
Backbeat Band
Money / Long tall Sally / Bad boy / Twist and shout / Please Mr. Postman / C'mon everybody / Rock 'n' roll music / Slow down / Roadrunner / Carol / Good golly Miss Molly / Twenty flight rock
CD CDV 2729
Virgin / Apr '94 / EMI

BACKBEAT (Score)
Was, Don *C*
You asked I came / Darkroom / What do they call this drink / He's wearing my bathrobe / Just read the poems / You asked I came / He's wearing my bathrobe
CD CDV 2740
Virgin / Apr '94 / EMI

BACKDRAFT
Zimmer, Hans *C*
Set me in motion: *Hornsby, Bruce & The Range* / Fighting 17th / Brothers / Arsonist's waltz / 335 / Burn it all / You go we go / Fahrenheit 451 / Show me your firetruck / Show goes on
CD _______ 262023
Milan / '95 / Conifer/BMG / Silva Screen

BAD BOYS
Shy guy: *King, Diana* / So many ways: *Warren G.* / Five o'five o'(here they come): *69* / Boom boom boom: *Juster* / Me against the world: *2Pac* / Someone to love: *Jon B* / I've got a little something for you: *MN8* / Never find someone like you: *Martin, Keith* / Theme from Bad Boys: *Mancina, Mark* / Bad boys reply: *Inner Circle* / Juke joint jezebel: *K.M.F.D.M.* / Cloud of smoke: *Call O'da Wild* / Work me slow: *Xscape* / Da B side: *Da Brat* / Call the police: *Kamoze, Ini*
CD _______ 4804532
Columbia / Jun '95 / Sony

BAD CHANNELS
Demons kiss: *Blue Oyster Cult* / Horsemen arrive: *Blue Oyster Cult* / That's how it is: *Joker* / Jane Jane (the hurricane): *Joker* / Somewhere in the night: *Fair Game* / Blind faith: *Fair Game* / Manic Depresso: *Sykotik Synfoney* / Mr. Cool: *Sykotik Synfoney* / Myth of freedom: *DMT* / Touching myself again: *DMT* / Little old lady polka: *Ukelaliens*
CD _______ IRSCD 993018
Blueprint / Oct '96 / Pinnacle

BAD GIRLS
Goldsmith, Jerry *C*
John / Hanging / Bank job / Jail break / No money / Ambush / I shot him / Josh's death / No bullets / My land
CD _______ 220542
Milan / Jan '95 / Conifer/BMG / Silva Screen

BAD MOON
Licht, Daniel *C*
CD _______ SSD 1068
Silva America / Feb '97 / Koch / Silva Screen

BAD SEED, THE
North, Alex *C*
CD _______ TSU 0124
Tsunami / Jan '95 / Silva Screen

BAD TASTE
CD _______ QDK CD 002
Normal / Sep '94 / ADA / Direct

BAGDAD CAFE
Calling you: *Steele, Jevetta* / Zwifach: *Blasmusik, Deihinger* / C major prelude: *Flagg, Darron* / Blues harp: *Galison, William* / Brenda, Brenda: *Steele, Jevetta* / Calliope: *Telson, Bob*
CD _______ IMCD 102
Island / Feb '90 / PolyGram

BAJOUR
Broadway Cast
Marks, Walter *C*
Engel, Lehman *Con*
CD _______ SK 48208
Sony Broadway / Dec '91 / Sony

BAKER'S WIFE, THE
London Cast
Schwartz, Stephen *C*
2CD _______ CDTER 1175
TER / Jul '90 / Koch

BALANCING ACT
Original New York Cast
Goggin, Dan *C*
Life is a balancing act / Next stop: New York City / Home sweet home / Play away the blues / Tough town / I left you there / Twist of fate / Fifth from the right / You heard it here first / Long long way / Women of the century / Welcome bienvenue / Where is the rainbow / I am yours / That kid's gonna make it / Chew chew chow / Hollywood 'n' vinyl / California suite / I knew the music
CD _______ DRGCD 19004
DRG / Jan '95 / Discovery / New Note/ Pinnacle

BALLAD OF LITTLE JOE
Mansfield, David & Kate/Anne McGarrigle
Mansfield, David *C*
CD _______ MAF 7053D
Intrada / Jan '93 / Koch / Silva Screen

BALLAD OF THE IRISH HORSE, THE
Chieftains
Moloney, Paddy *C*
Ballad of the Irish horse / Green pastures / Birth of the foals / Lady Hemphill / Horses of Ireland - part 1 / Chasing the fox / Going to the fair / Galway races / Story of the horse / Boyne hunt/Mullingar races/Five-mile chase / Horses of Ireland - part 2
CD _______ CCF 15CD
Claddagh / May '93 / ADA / CM / Direct

BALLROOM
Broadway Cast
Goldenberg, Billy *C*
Jennings, Don *Con*
CD _______ SK 35762
Sony Broadway / Jan '93 / Sony

BALLYKISSANGEL
Davey, Shaun
Davey, Shaun *C*
Ballykissangel theme / Siobahn and Brendan / Maura's confession / Peter's parish / Earthmovers / Dogs and poker / Death of a mountainy man / Graves and terminators / Tripe casserole / Niamh and Ambrose / Jenny's farewell / Our lady of Bonanza / Yellow bus crusade / Quigley's rosarie / Peter and Assumpta / Rolling packing case
CD _______ VTCD 117
Virgin / Jan '97 / EMI

BAND WAGON, THE/THE BELLE OF NEW YORK
Astaire, Fred & Cast
Schwartz, Arthur/Harry Warren *C*
CD _______ BMCD 7011
Blue Moon / Nov '96 / Cadillac / Discovery / Greensleeves / Jazz Music / Jet Star / TKO Magnum

BANDIT QUEEN
Khan, Nusrat Fateh Ali
Khan, Nusrat Fateh Ali & Roger White *C*
CD _______ 74321378112
Milan / Oct '96 / Conifer/BMG / Silva Screen

BANDOLERO
Goldsmith, Jerry *C*
Trap / El jefe / Bait / Ambushed / Sabinas / Dee's proposal / Across the river / Bad day for a hanging / Better way
CD _______ TCS 10012
Edel / Jan '90 / Pinnacle

BAPS
CD _______ 74321486842
Milan / Aug '97 / Conifer/BMG / Silva Screen

BARABBAS/ALEXANDER THE GREAT/ CONSTANTINE & THE CROSS
Nascimbene, Mario *C*
Ferrara, Franco *Con*
CD _______ LEGENDCD 5
Legend / Jul '93 / Koch / Silva Screen

BARAKA
Stearns, Michael
Stearns, Michael *C*
Mantra / Organics / Wipala / Host of Seraphim / Village dance / Wandering saint / African journey / Rainbow voice / Monk with bell / Broken vows / Prayer of Kala Rupa / An daorach bheag / Finale / End credits
CD _______ 153062
Milan / Feb '94 / Conifer/BMG / Silva Screen

BARB WIRE
Welcome to planet boom: *Lee, Tommy & Pamela Anderson Lee* / She's so free: *Napolitano, Johnette* / Spill the wine: *Hutchence, Michael* / Word up: *Gun* / Don't call me Babe: *Shampoo* / Hot child in the city: *Hagfish* / Let's all go together: *Marion* / Dancing barefoot: *Die Cheerleader* / Scum: *Meat Puppets In Vapourspace* / Ca plane pour moi: *Mr. Ed Jumps The Gun* / None of your business: *Salt 'N' Pepa*
CD _______ 8287462
London / Mar '96 / PolyGram

BARBARIANS, THE
Donaggio, Pino *C*
CD _______ MAF 7008D
Intrada / Jan '93 / Koch / Silva Screen

BARCELONA
Suozzo, Mark *C*
Americans abroad / Cathedral / Theme of Ted / Aurora reverie / Aftermath (USO) / Americans in peril / Elegy / Theme of Ted (hospital) / Reconciliation / Lake / Everybody limbo / Barcelona merengue / Una lacrima sul viso / L'home dibuixat / Night on the town (Cava bar) / You've got what it takes / Breakin' up / Me voy pal pueblo / Suenos de amor / Vinyl Hampton / Ligia elena
CD _______ 237942
Milan / Jan '95 / Conifer/BMG / Silva Screen

BAREFOOT CONTESSA, THE/ROOM AT THE TOP/THE QUIET AMERICAN (The Film Music Of Mario Nascimbene/3 Complete Soundtracks)
Nascimbene, Mario *C*
Main titles / Recalling at the graveyard / Harry meets Maria Vargas / Gypsy bolero / Guitar for Maria / Nocturne Bolero / Death of Maria/Finale / Main titles/Alice and Joe at the pub / Alice's beguine / Alice and Joe at home / Alice and Joe / Alice alone / Joe, Alice is dead / Joe and the prostitute / Joe after the fight/Finale / Main titles/City streets / Cathedral / Morgue / Psychological and passionate / Search for Tuong/Finale
CD _______ DRGCD 32961
DRG / Aug '96 / Discovery / New Note/ Pinnacle

BARMITZVAH BOY
1978 London Cast
Styne, Jule *C*
Black, Don *L*
Faris, Alexander *Con*
Overture / Why / If only a little bit sticks / Bar mitzvah of Elliot Green / This time tomorrow / Thou shalt not / Harolds of this world / We've done alright / Simchas / You wouldn't be you / Rita's request / Sun shines out of your eyes / Where is the music coming from / I've just begun
CD _______ SMK 53498
Sony West End / Nov '92 / Sony

BARRY LYNDON
Moloney, Paddy *C*
Sarabande (main title) / Women of Ireland / Piper's maggot jig / Seamaiden / Tin whistle / British Grenadiers / Hohenfriedberger march / Lilliburlero / March: Idomeneo / Sarabande-duel / German dance no.1 in C major / Il barbiere di siviglia / Cello concerto / Concerto for two harpsichords and orchestra in / Piano trio in E flat / Sarabande (end title)
CD _______ 7599259842
Warner Bros. / Jan '95 / Warner Music

BASHVILLE
1983 London Cast
King, Denis *C*
Green, Benny *L*
Prelude / Fancy Free / Lydia / 8-9-10 / One pair of hands / Gentleman's true to his code / Because I love her / Take the road to the ring / Entr'acte / Hymn to law and order / Blackman's burden / He is my son / Bashville / Boats are burned / Finale
CD _______ CDTER 1072
TER / Aug '95 / Koch

BASIC INSTINCT
Goldsmith, Jerry *C*
Goldsmith, Jerry *Con*
Main title / Crossed legs / Night life / Kitchen help / Pillow talk / Morning after / Games are over / Catherine's sorrow / Roxy loses / Unending story
CD _______ VSD 5360
Varese Sarabande / Mar '92 / Pinnacle

BASIL THE GREAT MOUSE DETECTIVE
Mancini, Henry *C*
CD _______ VSD 5359
Varese Sarabande / Feb '92 / Pinnacle

BASKET CASE II/FRANKENHOOKER
Renzetti, Joe
Renzetti, Joe *C*
I'm pregnant, I'm dead / Granny at freak tent / Barbecue / Original main titles / Out of hospital / Out of window / Big escape / Room of memories / In the attic / Granny meeting / In love / Frankenhooker / Lookin' for hookers / Jeffrey and parts / Creation / Eyeball / Happy day / Jeffrey fixes Elizabeth / Zoro killing
CD _______ FILMCD 073
Silva Screen / '89 / Koch / Silva Screen

BASKETBALL DIARIES
Catholic boy: *Carroll, Jim & Pearl Jam* / Devil's toe: *Revell, Graeme & Jim Carroll* / Down by the water: *PJ Harvey* / What a life: *Rockers Hi Fi* / I am alone: *Revell, Graeme & Jim Carroll* / People who died: *Carroll, Jim Band* / Riders on the storm: *Doors* / Dizzy: *Green Apple Quickstep* / It's been hard: *Revell, Graeme & Jim Carroll* / Coming right along: *Posies* / Strawberry wine: *Massive Internal Complications* / Star: *Cult* / Dream massacre: *Revell, Graeme* / I've been down: *Flea* / Blind dogs: *Soundgarden*
CD _______ 5240934
Island / Jul '95 / PolyGram

BASQUIAT
Van Gough boat / Public image: *Public Image Ltd* / It's all over now, baby blue: *Them* / Suicide hotline: *Taylor, Nick Marion* / I'm not in love: *Toadies* / Is that all there is: *Parish, John & Polly Jean Harvey* / White lines (don't do it): *Grandmaster Flash & Melle Mel* / Rise: *Tripping Daisy* / These days: *Joy Division* / She's dancing: *Kelly, Brian* / Tom Traubert's blues: *Waits, Tom* / Small plot of land: *Bowie, David* / Summer in Siam: *Pogues* / Last song I'll ever sing: *Friday, Gavin* / Hallelujah: *Cale, John*
CD _______ 5242602
Island / Mar '97 / PolyGram

BAT 21
CD _______ VSD 5202
Varese Sarabande / Dec '88 / Pinnacle

BATHING BEAUTY/HERE COME THE WAVES/THIS GUN FOR HIRE
Bim bam boom / Munequita linda / Trumpet blues and cantabile / By the waters of Minnetonka / Tico tico / Loch Lomond / I'll take the high note / Alma llanera / Nutcracker / Hora staccato / I cried for you / Finale (I'll take the high note) / Here come the waves / That old black magic / Let's take the long way home / Accentuate the positive / I promise you / This gun for hire / Now you see it, now you don't
CD _______ CD 60001
Great Movie Themes / Apr '97 / Target/ BMG

BATMAN (Score)
Sinfonia Of London
Elfman, Danny *C*
Walker, S. *Con*
Batman theme / First confrontation / Clown attack / Roasted dude / Descent into mystery / Joker's poem / Charge of the Batmobile / Up the cathedral / Final confrontation / Roof fight / Flowers / Batman to the rescue / Photos / Beautiful dreamer / Bat cave / Love theme / Attack of the batwing / Waltz to the death / Finale
CD _______ K 9259772
WEA / Aug '89 / Warner Music

BATMAN
Prince
Prince *C*
Future / Electric chair / Arms of Orion / Partyman / Vicki waiting / Trust / Lemon crush / Scandalous / Batdance
CD _______ 9259362
WEA / Feb '95 / Warner Music

BATMAN AND ROBIN
End is the beginning is the end: *Smashing Pumpkins* / Beginning is the end is the beginning: *Smashing Pumpkins* / Look into my eyes: *Bone Thugs n' Harmony* / Foolish games: *Jewel* / Lazy eye: *Goo Goo Dolls* / Moaner: *Underworld* / Bug: *Soul Coughing* / Poison ivy: *Ndegeocello, Me'shell* / Fun for me: *Moloko* / House on fire: *Arkarna* / Breed: *Christy, Lauren* / Gotham City Overture: *Goldenthal, Elliot* / Revolution: *REM* / Gotham city: *R. Kelly*
CD _______ 9362466202
Warner Bros. / Jun '97 / Warner Music

BATMAN FOREVER
Hold me, thrill me, kill me: *U2* / One time too many: *PJ Harvey* / Where are you now: *Brandy* / Kiss from a rose: *Seal* / Hunter gets captured by the game: *Massive Attack & Tracey Thorn* / Nobody lives without love: *Reader, Eddie* / Tell me now: *Mazzy Star* / Smash it up: *Offspring* / There is a light: *Cave, Nick* / Riddler: *Method Man* / Passenger: *Hutchence, Michael* / Crossing the river: *Devlins* / 8: *Sunny Day Real Estate* / Bad days: *Flaming Lips*
CD _______ 7567827592
Warner Bros. / Jun '95 / Warner Music

BATMAN FOREVER (Score)
Main title fanfare / Perils of Gotham / Fledermausmarchmusik / Nygma variations (an ode to science) / Spank me / Chase blanc / Two Face three step / Mr. E's dance card / Under the top / Gotham City boogie / Mouth to mouth nocturne / Pull of regret / Batterdammerung / Holy rusted metal / Descent / Chase noir / Perpetuum mobile
CD _______ 7567827762
Warner Bros. / Jun '95 / Warner Music

BATMAN RETURNS
Elfman, Danny *C*
Birth of Penguin / Lair / Selina transforms / Cemetary / Cat suite / Batman Vs The Circus / Rise and fall from grace / Sore spots / Rooftops / Wild ride / Children's hour / Final confrontation / Finale / End credits / Face to face: *Siouxsie & the Banshees*
CD _______ 7599269722
Warner Bros. / Jun '92 / Warner Music

BATMAN TRILOGY, THE (Themes From Batman, Batman Returns And Batman Forever)
CD _______ VSD 5766
Varese Sarabande / Jul '97 / Pinnacle

BATMAN: MASK OF THE PHANTOM
Walker, Shirley *C*
CD _______ WA 454842
Silva Screen / Jan '93 / Koch / Silva Screen

BATTLE OF ALGIERS/MASSACRE IN ROME
Pontecorvo, Gillo *C*
CD _______ OST 105
Milano Dischi / Jan '93 / Silva Screen

BATTLE OF BRITAIN
Goodwin, Ron *C*
Battle of Britain / Aces high / Lull before the storm / Work and play / Death and destruction / Briefing and the Lutwaffe / Prelude to battle / Victory assured / Defeat / Hitler's headquarters / Return to base / Threat / Civilian tragedy / Offensive build-up / Attack / Personal tragedy / Battle in the air / Absent friends / Battle of Britain (End title) / Operation Crossbow / Monte Carlo or bust / Trap / Those magnificent men in their flying machines
CD _______ CDMGM 21
MGM/EMI / Aug '90 / EMI

BATTLE OF NERETVA, THE
London Philharmonic Orchestra
Herrmann, Bernard *C*
Prelude / Retreat / Separation / From Italy / Chetnik's march / Farewell / Partisan march / Pastorale / Turning point / Death of Danica / Victory
CD _______ SCCD 5005
Southern Cross / Jan '89 / Silva Screen

BATTLE OF STALINGRAD/OTHELLO
Bratislava Symphony Orchestra
Khachaturian, Aram *C*
Adriano *Con*
CD _______ 8223314
Marco Polo / Jul '94 / Select

BATTLERS, THE
Tall Poppies Orchestra
Vine, Carl *C*
Stanhope, D. *Con*
CD _______ TP 024
Tall Poppies / '94

BATTLESTAR GALACTICA
Los Angeles Philharmonic Orchestra
Phillips, Stu & Glen Larson *C*
CD _______ TCS 1042
Silva Screen / Jan '93 / Koch / Silva Screen

BEACHES
Midler, Bette
Under the boardwalk / I've still got my health / Otto Titsling / Glory of love / Oh industry / Wind beneath my wings / I think

it's going to rain today / I know you by heart / Baby mine / Friendship theme
CD _______________ 7819332
WEA / Feb '95 / Warner Music

BEAN
Picture of you: *Boyzone* / I get around: *Beach Boys* / Walking on sunshine: *Katrina & The Waves* / Yesterday: *Wet Wet Wet* / Running back for more: *Louise* / That kinda guy: *Jules-Stock, Thomas* / Give me a little more time: *Gabrielle* / I love LA: *OMC* / He's a rebel: *Alisha's Attic* / Stuck in the middle with you: *Hoffs, Susanna* / Art for art's sake: *10cc* / Have fun go mad: *Blair* / Can we talk: *Code Red* / Bean theme: *Goodall, Howard* / Elected: *Mr. Bean & Smear Campaign*
CD _______________ 5537742
Mercury / Aug '97 / PolyGram

BEAST (Original TV Soundtrack)
CD _______________ VSD 5731
Varese Sarabande / Jul '96 / Pinnacle

BEASTMASTER II
CD _______________ MAF 7019D
Intrada / Mar '92 / Koch / Silva Screen

BEAT GIRL/STRINGBEAT
Barry, John Seven & Orchestra
Barry, John *C*
CD _______________ PLAY 001
Play It Again / Jan '93 / Silva Screen

BEAUTIFUL THING
Mamas & The Papas
Altman, John *C*
It's getting better
CD _______________ MCD 60013
MCA / Jun '96 / BMG

BEAUTY AND THE BEAST
2CD _______________ MBOCD 1
MBO / Dec '95 / Total/BMG

BEAUTY AND THE BEAST
Menken, Alan *C*
Ashman, Howard *L*
CD _______________ WD 713602
Disney Music & Stories / Mar '96 / Technicolor

BEAUTY AND THE BEAST (Singalong)
CD _______________ WD 713824
Disney Music & Stories / Nov '96 / Technicolor

BEAVIS & BUTTHEAD DO AMERICA (Score)
Frizzell, John *C*
CD _______________ 74321475362
Milan / May '97 / Conifer/BMG / Silva Screen

BED AND SOFA
Cast Recording
CD _______________ VSD 5729
Varese Sarabande / Sep '96 / Pinnacle

BED OF ROSES
Convertino, Michael *C*
Kane, A. *Con*
CD _______________ 74321348632
Milan / Feb '96 / Conifer/BMG / Silva Screen

BEETLEJUICE
Elfman, Danny
Elfman, Danny *C*
Banana boat song (Day O): *Belafonte, Harry* / Jump in the line: *Belafonte, Harry* / Main title / Travel music / Book / Enter... the family/Sand worm planet / Fly / Lydia discovers / In the model / Juno's theme / Beetlesnake / Sold / Flyer / Incantation / Lydia strikes a bargain / Showtime / Laughs / Wedding / Aftermath / End credits
CD _______________ GFLD 19296
Geffen / Oct '95 / BMG

BEIDERBECKE CONNECTION, THE
Ricotti, Frank All Stars
Connection / Viva le van / Morgans mystery / Tulips for Chris / Barney's walk / Boys in blue / Hobson's chase / Tiger jive / Scouting ahead / Jennie's tune / Live at the Limping Whippet / Russian over / Dormouse delights / Crying all day
CD _______________ DMCD 20
Dormouse / Dec '88 / Jazz Music / Target/BMG

BEING HUMAN
Gibbs, Michael *C*
Snell, David *Con*
Story of a story / Mine, mine / Blow in my ear / Free man / Am I really a priest / You're bewitching me / Sun on my back / That's it / Hanging's fine / It's eggs for supper / Give the chickens a break / Best moment of your life / Have a great time
CD _______________ VSD 5479
Varese Sarabande / May '94 / Pinnacle

BELLE EPOQUE
Duhamel, Antoine *C*
CD _______________ 74321279312
Milan / Jun '97 / Conifer/BMG / Silva Screen

BELLE OF NEW YORK/GOOD NEWS/ RICH YOUNG & PRETTY
When I'm out with the belle of New York / Oops: *Astaire, Fred* / Naughty but nice: *Ellis, Anita* / Bachelor's dinner song: *Astaire, Fred* / Baby doll: *Astaire, Fred* / Bride's wedding day: *Ellis, Anita* / Seeing's believing: *Astaire, Fred* / I wanna be a dancin' man: *Astaire, Fred* / Good news: *McCracken, Joan* / He's a ladies man: *Lawford, Peter* / Lucky in love: *Marshall, Pat/Peter Lawford/June Allyson* / French lesson: *Allyson, June & Peter Lawford* / Best things in life are free: *Allyson, June & Peter Lawford* / Pass that peace pipe: *McCracken, Joan* / Just imagine: *Allyson, June* / Varsity drag: *Allyson, June & Peter Lawford* / Wonder why: *Powell, Jane* / Dark is the night: *Powell, Jane* / Paris: *Lamas, Fernando* / We never talk much: *Darrieux, Danielle* / There's danger in your eyes, cherie: *Darrieux, Danielle*
CD _______________ CDMGM 23
MGM/EMI / Aug '90 / EMI

BELLY OF AN ARCHITECT
London Sinfonietta
Mertens, Wim & Glen Branca *C*
Augustus / Birds for the mind / Aural trick / Struggle for pleasure / Four mains / Close cover / Time passing / Tourtour / And with them / Andria Doria / Galba / Caracalla / Hadrian
CD _______________ NORMAL 63CD
Normal / Jun '96 / ADA / Direct

BEN FRANKLIN IN PARIS
1964 Broadway Cast
Sandrich, Mark *C*
Michaels, Sidney *L*
CD _______________ ZDM 5651342
EMI Classics / Apr '94 / EMI

BEN HUR (New Score For 1925 Silent Movie)
Royal Liverpool Philharmonic Orchestra
Davis, Carl *C*
Davis, Carl *Con*
Opening titles / Nativity / Esther and the young prince / Roman march and disaster / Galley slave / Pirate battle / Iras the Egyptian / Chariot race / Ben Hur's return / Via Dolorosa / Earthquake and new dawn
CD _______________ FILMCD 043
Silva Screen / Nov '89 / Koch / Silva Screen

BEN HUR
Rome Symphony Orchestra
Rozsa, Miklos *C*
Savina, Carlos *Con*
Prelude / Adoration of the Magi / Roman march / Friendship / Love theme / Burning desert / Rowing of the galley slaves / Naval battle / Return to Judaea / Victory parade / Mother's love / Leper's search for the Christ / Procession to Calvary / Miracle and finale
CD _______________ CDMGM 8
MGM/EMI / Jan '90 / EMI

BEN HUR
National Philharmonic Orchestra
Rozsa, Miklos *C*
Rozsa, Miklos *Con*
Fanfare to prelude / Star of Bethlehem and adoration of the Magi / Friendship / Burning desert / Arrius / Rowing of the galley slaves / Parade of the charioteers / Mother's love / Return to Judaea / Ring for freedom / Leper's search for the Christ / Procession to Calvary / Miracle and finale
CD _______________ 4178492
Decca / '86 / PolyGram

BEN HUR
Rozsa, Miklos *C*
2CD _______________ A2K 47020
Silva Screen / Jan '93 / Koch / Silva Screen

BEN HUR
Rozsa, Miklos *C*
Rozsa, Miklos *Con*
Overture / Of Bethlehem / Adoration of magic / Prelude / Marcia Romana / Salute for gratus / Gratus entry to Jerusalem / Desert / Exhaustion / Prince of peace / Roman gallery / Battle preperations / Pirate fleet / Attack / Ramming speed / Rescue / Victory parade / Arrius party / Nostalgia / Farewell to Rome / Return / Promise / Sorrow and intermission / Fanfare for circus parade / Circus parade / Valley of the lepers / Search / Procession to Calvary / Bearing of the cross / Recognition / Miracle / Finale
CD _______________ CDODEON 18
Premier/EMI / Jul '96 / EMI

BERLIN '39
Trovajoli, Armando *C*
CD _______________ SPALAX 14987
Spalax / Oct '96 / ADA / Cargo / Direct / Discovery / Greyhound

BERLIN BLUES
Schifrin, Lalo *C*
CD _______________ CDCH 357
Milan / Jan '89 / Conifer/BMG / Silva Screen

BEST FOOT FORWARD
Revival Cast
Martin, Hugh & Ralph Blane *C*
Wish I may / Three men on a date / Hollywood story / Three B's / Ev'ry time / Alive and kicking/The guy who bought me / Shady lady bird / Buckle down Winsocki / You're lucky / What do you think I am / Raving beauty / Just a little joint with a juke box / You are for loving / Finale: Buckle down Winsocki
CD _______________ DRGCD 15003
DRG / Sep '93 / Discovery / New Note/ Pinnacle

BEST LITTLE WHOREHOUSE GOES PUBLIC, THE
Broadway Cast
Hall, Carol *C*
CD _______________ VSD 5542
Varese Sarabande / Jan '95 / Pinnacle

BEST OF THE BEST II
Frank, David Michael *C*
CD _______________ CIN 22012
Silva Screen / Jan '93 / Koch / Silva Screen

BEST SHOT (aka Hoosiers)
Goldsmith, Jerry *C*
Goldsmith, Jerry *Con*
Best shot / You did good / Coach stays / Pivot / Get the ball / Town meeting / Finals
CD _______________ CDTER 1141
TER / Aug '87 / Koch

BEST YEARS OF OUR LIVES, THE
London Philharmonic Orchestra
Friedhofer, Hugo *C*
Best years of our lives / Homecoming / Elevator / Boone City / Peggy / Fred and Peggy / Nightmare / Fred asleep / Neighbours / Homer goes upstairs / Citation / Exit music
CD _______________ PRCD 1779
Preamble / Jan '89 / Silva Screen

BETRAYED
Conti, Bill *C*
Main title / Way / Shoot the horse / Bank robbery / Kill me Kathy / To the bank / Riding to work / Guns / Passing time / End titles
CD _______________ CDTER 1163
TER / Jul '89 / Koch

BETTY BLUE
Yared, Gabriel
Yared, Gabriel *C*
Betty et Zorg / Des orages pour la nuit / Cargo voyage / La poubelle cuisine / Humecter la monture / Le petit Nicolas / Gyneco zebre / Comme les deux doigts de la main / Zorg et Betty / Chili con carne / C'est le vent, Betty / Un coucher de soleil accroche dans les arbres / Lisa rock / Le coeur en skai mauve / Bungalow zen / 37-2 le matin / Maudits maneges
CD _______________ CDV 2396
Virgin / Sep '86 / EMI

BEVERLY HILLBILLIES, THE
CD _______________ 663132
Silva Screen / Jan '93 / Koch / Silva Screen

BEVERLY HILLS 90210
Bend time back around: *Abdul, Paula* / Got 2 have U: *Color Me Badd* / Right kind of love: *Jordan, Jeremy* / Love is: *Williams, Vanessa & Brian McKnight* / Just wanna be your friend: *Puck & Natty* / Let me be your baby: *Williams, Geoffrey* / Saving forever for you: *Shanice* / All the way to heaven: *Watley, Jody* / Why: *Dennis, Cathy & D-Mob* / Time to be lovers: *McDonald, Michael & Chaka Khan* / Action speaks louder than words: *Kemp, Tara* / Beverly Hills 90210: *Davis, John*
CD _______________ 74321147982
Giant / Nov '94 / BMG

BEVERLY HILLS 90210 - THE COLLEGE YEARS
Make it right: *Stansfield, Lisa* / Not one more time: *Piersa, Stacey* / Every day of the week: *Jade* / Not enough hours in the...: *After 7* / SOS: *Dennis, Cathy* / No intermission: *5th Power* / Cantaloop (Flip fantasia): *US 3* / Moving on up: *M People* / Saturday: *Omar* / Touch my light: *Big Mountain* / I'll love you anyway: *Neville, Aaron* / What your love means to me: *Hi-Five* / Forever yours: *Moten, Wendy*
CD _______________ 74321203032
Giant / Nov '94 / BMG

BEVERLY HILLS COP
New attitude: *Labelle, Patti* / Don't get stopped in Beverly Hills: *Shalamar* / Do you really want my love: *Giscombe, Junior* / Emergency: *Robbins, Rockie* / Neutron dance: *Pointer Sisters* / Heat is on: *Frey, Glenn* / Gratitude: *Elfman, Danny* / Stir it up: *Labelle, Patti* / Rock 'n' roll me again: *System* / Axel F: *Faltermeyer, Harold*
CD _______________ MCLD 19087
MCA / Sep '92 / BMG

BEYOND RANGOON
Waters of Irrawaddy / Memories of the dead / I dreamt I woke up / Freedom from fear / Brother morphine / Our ways will part / Village under siege / Beyond Rangoon
CD _______________ 286652
Milan / Jul '95 / Conifer/BMG / Silva Screen

BEYOND THE CLOUDS/PURSUING THE CLOUDS
Fenton, George
Fenton, George *C*
CD _______________ CDWM 109
Westmoor / Sep '94 / Target/BMG

BEYOND THE LAW/DAY OF ANGER
Ortolani, Riz *C*
CD _______________ OST 110
Milano Dischi / Jan '93 / Silva Screen

BEYOND THE VALLEY OF THE DOLLS/ GROUPIE GIRL
CD _______________ SGLDCD 0010
Screen Gold / Jun '97 / Greyhound

BHAJI ON THE BEACH
Altman, John & Craig Pruess *C*
Summer holiday / Uchlya lumbia / Queen / Ha la la la / Mera laung glwacha / Na babba / Nachna / Greenhouse fantasy / Main theme / Ginder and Amrik theme, brothers fight in tower / Oliver and Hashida theme, at the museum / Ladies getting ready / Under the pier / Brothers theme, Ranjit hits Ginder and runs / Ambrose and Asha in theatre / Oliver's theme / Ginder's theme / End titles / Summer holiday
CD _______________ KEDCD 23
Keda / Feb '94 / Grapevine/PolyGram

BIBLE, THE (La Bibbia)
Mayuzumi, Toshiro *C*
Ferrara, Franco *Con*
CD _______________ OST 115
Milano Dischi / '94 / Silva Screen

BIG BATTALIONS, THE
Gunning, Christopher *C*
Big Battalions / Yared in exile / Yousef's faith awakens / Gil & Susan / Intafada / Yousef's resignation / Edward denied bishopric / Libera me / Goodbye Susan / Mecca / Alan dies / Edward's remorse / Welcome to Jordan / Gil with his sick father / Edward in Ethiopia / Military preparations in Jerusalem / Ethiopian trek / Gil shoots Yousef / Yousef buried / Yared counsels Edward / Yared leads Martha to safety / Family soul searching / Yousef's father in mourning / Gil visits Susan and confesses / New beginnings / Return to Ethiopia / Closing sequence
CD _______________ AHLCD 6
Hit / Nov '92 / Grapevine/PolyGram

BIG BLUE I, THE
Serra, Eric *C*
Big Blue overture / Rescue in a wreck / Huacracocha / Remembering a heart beat / Homo delphinus / Virgin Island / For Enzo / My lady blue / Deep blue dream / In raya / Between the sky scrapers / Let them try / Synchronised instant / Monastery of Amorgos / Leaving the world behind
CD _______________ CDV 2541
Virgin / Nov '88 / EMI

BIG BLUE I, THE (Complete)
Serra, Eric *C*
2CD _______________ 30193
Silva Screen / Jan '93 / Koch / Silva Screen

BIG BLUE II, THE
Serra, Eric *C*
CD _______________ 30667
Silva Screen / Jan '93 / Koch / Silva Screen

BIG BLUE II, THE/THE MISSION/BETTY BLUE
3CD _______________ TPAK 33
Virgin / Jan '95 / EMI

BIG CHILL, THE
I heard it through the grapevine: *Gaye, Marvin* / My girl: *Temptations* / Good lovin': *Rascals* / Tracks of my tears: *Robinson, Smokey* / Joy to the world: *Three Dog Night* / Ain't too proud to beg: *Temptations* / (You make me feel like) a natural woman: *Franklin, Aretha* / I second that emotion: *Robinson, Smokey* / Whiter shade of pale: *Procul Harum*
CD _______________ 5300172
Motown / Jan '93 / PolyGram

BIG COUNTRY, THE
Philharmonia Orchestra
Moross, Jerome *C*
Bremner, Tony *Con*
Main title / Julie's house / Welcoming / Courtin' time / Old thunder / Raid/Capture / Major Terrill's party: Dance/Waltz/Polka / McKay's ride/McKay is missing/Old house / Waiting / Big muddy / McKay alone/Night at Ladder Ranch/The fight / Cattle at the river / War party gathers/McKay in Blanco Canyon/Major alone / Duel/Death of Buck Hannassey / End title
CD _______________ FILMCD 030
Silva Screen / Nov '95 / Koch / Silva Screen

BIG EASY, THE
Iko iko: *Dixie Cups* / Tipitina: *Professor Longhair* / Ma 'tit fille: *Buckwheat Zydeco* / Colinda: *Newman, Jimmy C.* / Tell it like it is: *Neville, Aaron & The Neville Brothers* / Zydeco gris gris: *Beausoleil* / Oh yeah: *Simien, T. & The Mallet Playboys* / Hey hey: *Wild Tchoupitoulas* / Closer to you: *Quaid, Dennis* / Savour, pass...: *Swan Silvertones*
CD _______________ 5511592
Spectrum / Sep '95 / PolyGram

BIG JAKE/THE SHOOTIST/CAHILL US MARSHALL (Music From John Wayne Westerns Vol. 2)
Bernstein, Elmer *C*
Shootist / Ride / In the fire / Necktie party / Nocturne / Riders / Reunion / All Jake / Buzzards / Going home
CD _______________ VCD 47264
Varese Sarabande / Jan '89 / Pinnacle

BIG NIGHT
Stornelli amorisi: *Villa, Claudio* / Il pescivendolo: *Salvatore, Matteo* / La trada del bosco: *Villa, Claudio* / Art of art / Oh Marie: *Prima, Louis* / Mambo Italiano: *Clooney, Rosemary* / Love of my life: *Prima, Louis & Keely Smith* / Dinner / Tic ti, tic ta: *Villa, Claudio* / Five months, two weeks, two days: *Prima, Louis & The Witnesses* / Don't take your love from me: *Smith, Keely* / Buona sera: *Prima, Louis* / Angular dissent / Mo ve'la bella mia da la muntagna: *Salvatore, Matteo* / Pascal's waltz / Big night theme

CD ____________ 0022782CIN
Edel / Jul '97 / Pinnacle

BIG TROUBLE IN LITTLE CHINA
Carpenter, John *C*
Big trouble in little China: *Coup De Villes* / Pork chop express / Alley / Here come the storms / Lo Pan's domain / Escape from Wing Kong / Into the spirit path / Great arcade / Final escape
CD ____________ DSCD 2
Demon / Aug '91 / Pinnacle

BILITIS
Lai, Francis *C*
Bilitis / Promenade / Les deux nudites / Spring time ballet / L'abre / I need a man / Melissa / La campagne / Scene d'amour / Rainbow
CD ____________ 800342
Silva Screen / Jan '93 / Koch / Silva Screen

BILL AND TED'S BOGUS JOURNEY
Shout it out: *Slaughter* / Battle stations: *Winger* / God gave rock 'n' roll to you II: *Kiss* / Drinking again: *Neverland* / Dream of a new day: *Kotzen, Richie* / Reaper: *Vai, Steve* / Perfect crime: *Faith No More* / Go to hell: *Megadeth* / Tommy the cat: *Primus* / Junior's gone wild: *Kings X* / Showdown: *Love on Ice* / Reaper rap: *Vai, Steve*
CD ____________ 7567917252
Interscope/East West / Jan '92 / Warner Music

BILL AND TED'S EXCELLENT ADVENTURE
Play with me: *Extreme* / Boys and girls are doing it: *Vital* / Not so far away: *Burtnick, Glenn* / Dancing with a gypsy: *Tora Tora* / Father time: *Shark Island* / I can't breakaway: *Big Pig* / Dangerous: *Shark Island* / Walk away: *Bricklin* / In time: *Robb, Robbie* / Two heads are better than one: *Power Tools*
CD ____________ 3939152
A&M / Feb '92 / PolyGram

BILLY BATHGATE
Isham, Mark *C*
CD ____________ 262495
Milan / Jan '95 / Conifer/BMG / Silva Screen

BILLY CONNOLLY'S MUSICAL TOUR OF SCOTLAND
CD ____________ 5298162
PolyGram TV / Dec '95 / PolyGram

BING BOYS ARE HERE
Cast Recording
Ayer, Nat D. *C*
Grey, Clifford *L*
Orchestral selection: *Orchestra* / In other words: *Robey, George* / If you were the only girl in the world: *Robey, George & Violet Loraine* / Whistler: *Intermezzo* / Another little drink: *Robey, George & Violet Loraine* / Shoeblack's dance: *Orchestra* / Right side of Bond Street: *Morrison, Jack* / Kipling walk: *Orchestra* / Lady of a thousand charms: *Lester, Alfred & Violet Loraine* / Kiss trot dance: *Orchestra* / Dear old Shepherd's Bush: *Lester, Alfred* / I start my day over again: *Morrison, Jack* / Languid melody: *Orchestra* / I stopped, I looked and I listened: *Robey, George* / Ragging the dog: *Orchestra* / Vocal gems: *Columbia Revue Company* / Orchestral finale: *Orchestra*
CD ____________ PASTCD 9716
Flapper / '90 / Pinnacle

BIOGRAPH GIRL, THE
1980 London Cast
Heneker, David *C*
Heneker, David & Warner Brown *L*
Reed, Michael *Con*
CD ____________ CDTER 1003
TER / May '92 / Koch

BIRD
Parker, Charlie
Lester leaps in / I can't believe that you're in love with me / Laura / All of me / This time the dream is on me / Koko / Cool blues / April in Paris / Now's the time / Ornithology / Parker's mood
CD ____________ 4610022
Columbia / Dec '96 / Sony

BIRD WITH THE CRYSTAL PLUMAGE, THE/FOUR FLIES ON GREY VELVET
Morricone, Ennio *C*
CD ____________ CDCIA 5087
Cinevox / Jan '93 / Koch / Silva Screen

BIRD WITH THE CRYSTAL PLUMAGE, THE/FOUR FLIES ON GREY VELVET/ CAT O'NINE TAILS
Morricone, Ennio *C*
CD ____________ DRGCD 32911
DRG / Sep '95 / Discovery / New Note/ Pinnacle

BIRDCAGE, THE
CD ____________ 22572 MCM
Edel / May '96 / Pinnacle

BIRDMAN OF ALCATRAZ, THE
Bernstein, Elmer *C*
CD ____________ TSU 0126
Tsunami / Jan '95 / Silva Screen

BIRDS OF PARADISE
Off-Broadway Cast
Evans, David *C*
Holzman, Winnie *L*
CD ____________ CDTER 1196
TER / Apr '93 / Koch

BIRDY
Gabriel, Peter
Gabriel, Peter *C*
At night / Floating dogs / Quiet and alone / Close up / Slow water / Dressing the wound / Birdy's flight / Slow marimbas / Heat / Sketchpad with trumpet and voice / Under lock and key / Powerhouse at the foot of the mountain
CD ____________ CASCD 1167
Charisma / Mar '85 / EMI

BIRTH OF A NATION, THE
Breil, Joseph *C*
Bringing the African to America / Abolitionists / Austin Stoneman / Elsie Stoneman / Old Southland / Boys at play / Cotton fields / Love strain / Stoneman library / Lydia Brown
CD ____________ LSCD 701
Silva Screen / Jan '90 / Koch / Silva Screen

BITTER SWEET
1988 London Cast
Coward, Sir Noel *C*
Reed, Michael *Con*
Opening / That wonderful melody / Call of life / If you could only come with me / I'll see you again / Polka / What is love / Last dance / Finale / Opening chorus (Life in the morning) / Ladies of the town / If love were all / Dear little cafe / Bittersweet waltz / Officer's chorus (we wish to order wine) / Tokay / Bonne nuit, merci / Kiss me / Ta-ra-ra-boom-de-ay / Alas the time is past / We all wear a green carnation / Zigeuner
2CD ____________ CDTER2 1160
TER / Mar '94 / Koch

BITTER SWEET (Highlights)
1988 London Cast
Coward, Sir Noel *C*
Reed, Michael *Con*
CD ____________ CDTEO 1001
TER / Nov '89 / Koch

BIX
Beiderbecke, Bix
Idolizing / Dardanella / Singing the blues (till my dad) / My pretty girl / Maple leaf rag / Riverboat shuffle 2 / Since my best gal turned me down / Jazz me blues / Somebody stole my gal / Stardust / I'll be a friend with pleasure / In a mist / Tin roof blues / Riverboat shuffle / I'm coming Virginia / Davenport blues / Singing the blues (till my dad) / Bix
CD ____________ PD 74766
RCA / Aug '91 / BMG

BLACK AND BLUE
Broadway Cast
CD ____________ DRG 19001
DRG / Jan '95 / Discovery / New Note/ Pinnacle

BLACK AND WHITE MINSTREL SHOW, THE (Stars From...)
Black & White Minstrels
CD ____________ URCD 105
Upbeat / Apr '91 / Cadillac / Target/BMG

BLACK CAULDRON, THE
Bernstein, Elmer *C*
CD ____________ VCD 47241
Varese Sarabande / Jan '89 / Pinnacle

BLACK ORPHEUS
Generique / A felicidade / O nosso amor / Manha de carnaval / Scheme du lever du soleil / Scene du lever du soleil / Manha de carnaval / Scenes de le marcumba / O nosso amor / Manha de carnaval / Samba de orfeo / Batterie de cappela / Manha de carnaval/A felicidade/Samba de orfeo / Frevo
CD ____________ 8307832
Verve / Jan '93 / PolyGram

BLACK RAIN
Zimmer, Hans
Zimmer, Hans *C*
Livin' on the edge of the night: *Iggy Pop* / Way you do the things you do: *UB40* / Back to life: *Soul II Soul* / Laser man: *Sakamoto, Ryuichi* / Singing in the shower: *Les Rita Mitsouko & The Sparks* / I'll be holding on: *Allman, Gregg* / Sato / Charlie loses his head / Sugai / Nick and Masa
CD ____________ CDV 2607
Virgin / Feb '90 / EMI

BLADERUNNER
Vangelis
Vangelis *C*
Main title / Blush response / Wait for me / Rachel's song / Love theme / One more kiss, Dear / Bladerunner blues / Memories of green / Tales of the future / Damask rose / End titles / Tears in rain
CD ____________ 4509965742
Warner Bros. / May '94 / Warner Music

BLINK
Fiedel, Brad *C*
Boys & the babies / Is Craig here / Emma's eyes / Bumps in the night / What is beautiful / When fortune turns her wheel / Witness on the run / On the floor / Open your eyes / Escape from illusion / Clean hands / Blinds come down / Eyes you stole / John & Emma's theme / Insulated man
CD ____________ 191902
Milan / May '94 / Conifer/BMG / Silva Screen

BLISS
CD ____________ VSD 5836
Varese Sarabande / May '97 / Pinnacle

BLONDEL
1983 London Cast
Oliver, Stephen *C*
Rice, Tim *L*
Monk's introduction / Blondel and Fiona / Ministry of Reudal affairs / Last of my troubles / Lionheart / No rhyme for Richard / Trio / Assassins song / Running back for more / Blondel in Europe / Saladin days / I can't wait to be King / Inn at Salzburg / Blondel's search / Duke of Austria's quarters / Cell / Westminster Abbey / I'm a monarchist
CD ____________ MCD 11486
MCA / Aug '96 / BMG

BLOOD BROTHERS
1983 London Cast
Russell, Willy *C*
Narration / Marilyn Monroe / My child / Devil's got your number / Easy terms / Just a game / Sunday afternoon / My friend / Bright new day / One summer narration / Saying a word / Miss Jones (sign of the times) / Prison song / Light romance / There's a madman / Tell me it's not true
CD ____________ CLACD 270
Castle / May '93 / BMG

BLOOD BROTHERS
1988 London Cast
Russell, Willy *C*
CD ____________ 09026616892
RCA Victor / Jul '91 / BMG

BLOOD BROTHERS
International Cast
Russell, Willy *C*
CD ____________ CASTCD 50
First Night / Nov '95 / Pinnacle

BLOOD BROTHERS
1995 London Cast
Russell, Willy *C*
CD ____________ CASTCD 49
First Night / Jul '95 / Pinnacle

BLOOD BROTHERS
Studio Cast
Russell, Willy *C*
Overture / Marilyn Monroe / My child / Easy terms / Shoes upon the table / Long Sunday afternoon/My friend / Bright new day / That guy / I'm not saying a word / Robbery / Marilyn Monroe 3 / Light romance / Mad man / Tell me it's not true
CD ____________ 88082
CMC / May '97 / BMG

BLOOD IN BLOOD OUT
Conti, Bill *C*
CD ____________ VSD 5396
Varese Sarabande / Mar '93 / Pinnacle

BLOOD OF HEROES, THE
Boekelheide, Todd *C*
Adler, M. *Con*
CD ____________ MAF 7060D
Intrada / May '95 / Koch / Silva Screen

BLOODMOON
May, Brian *C*
CD ____________ IMICD 1006
Silva Screen / Jan '93 / Koch / Silva Screen

BLOW IN (Including Music From The Film Guiltrip)
Power, Brendan
Power, Brendan *C*
CD ____________ HBCD 0008
Hummingbird / Apr '96 / ADA / Direct / Grapevine/PolyGram

BLOW UP
Hancock, Herbie
Hancock, Herbie *C*
Blow up / Verushka / Naked camera / Bring down the birds / Jane's theme / Thief / Kiss / Curiosity / Thomas studies photos / Bed / Stroll on: *Yardbirds* / I'm glad to see you: *Tomorrow* / Blow up: *Tomorrow* / Blow up
CD ____________ CDODEON 15
Soundtracks / Jun '96 / EMI

BLUE CITY
Cooder, Ry
Cooder, Ry *C*
Blue city down / Elevation 13 foot / True believers/Marianne / Nice bike / Greenhouse / Billy and Annie / Pops and timer / Tell me something slick / Blue city / Don't take your guns to town / Leader of men / Not even key west
CD ____________ 7599253862
WEA / Jan '96 / Warner Music

BLUE COLLAR
Nitzsche, Jack
Nitzsche, Jack *C*
Hard workin' man: *Captain Beefheart* / Zeke, Jerry & Smokie / Satin sheets: *Pruett, Jeanne* / Party / Wang dang doodle / Coke machine / Quittin' time / Easy listening / FBI / Goodbye so long: *Turner, Ike & Tina* / Saturday night: *Lynyrd Skynyrd*
CD ____________ EDCD 435
Edsel / Aug '95 / Pinnacle

BLUE HAWAII
Presley, Elvis
Blue Hawaii / Almost always true / Aloha oe / No more / Can't help falling in love / Rock-a-hula baby / Moonlight swim / Ku-u-I-pu / Ito eats / Slicin' sand / Hawaiian sunset / Beach boy blues / Island of love / Hawaiian wedding song / Steppin' out of line / Can't help falling in love / Slicin' sand / No more / Rock-a-hula baby / Beach boy blues / Blue Hawaii
CD ____________ 07863674592
CD ____________ 07863669592
RCA / Apr '97 / BMG

BLUE IN THE FACE
CD ____________ 9362460132
WEA / Jan '96 / Warner Music

BLUE LAGOON, THE
Australian Symphony Orchestra
Poledouris, Basil *C*
Poledouris, Basil *Con*
Blue lagoon / Fire / Island / Sands of time / Paddy's death / Children grow / Lord of the lagoon / Underwater courtship / Kiss
CD ____________ SCCD 1018
Southern Cross / Jun '88 / Silva Screen

BLUE MAX, THE
Goldsmith, Jerry *C*
Dream machine / Sing song blues / Bad bad amigo / Hangman / Need your love / Flying to Moscow / Paid assassin / Camera camera / Photographing gold / Murder at the movies / I know you're there / Wait for the new one
CD ____________ VCD 47238
Varese Sarabande / Jan '89 / Pinnacle

BLUE PLANET/THE DREAM IS ALIVE
Erbe, Micky
Erbe, Micky *C*
CD ____________ CDC 1010
Silva Screen / Mar '92 / Koch / Silva Screen

BLUE VELVET
Badalamenti, Angelo *C*
Badalamenti, Angelo *Con*
Night streets/Sandy and Jeffrey / Frank Jeffrey's dark side / Mysteries of love (2 versions) / Frank returns / Blue velvet: *Vinton, Bobby* / Lumberton USA/Going down to Lincoln / Akron meets the blues / In dreams: *Orbison, Roy* / Honky tonk: *Doggett, Bill* / Love letters: *Lester, Ketty* / Mysteries of love / Blue star
CD ____________ CDTER 1127
TER / May '87 / Koch

BLUEBEARD/LA MONACA DI MONZA
Morricone, Ennio *C*
CD ____________ PRCD 121
Preamble / Apr '96 / Silva Screen

BLUES BROTHERS, THE
Blues Brothers
Shake a tailfeather: *Charles, Ray* / Think: *Franklin, Aretha* / Minnie the moocher: *Calloway, Cab* / Rawhide / Jailhouse rock / She caught the Katy / Gimme some lovin' / Old landmark / Sweet home Chicago / Peter Gunn / Everybody needs somebody to love
CD ____________ 7567827872
Atlantic / Nov '95 / Warner Music

BLUES BROTHERS, THE (A Tribute To The Blues Brothers)
1991 Cast
CD ____________ CASTCD 25
First Night / '94 / Pinnacle

BLUES BROTHERS, THE
Christopher/Emery Company
She caught the Katy / Peter Gunn theme / Gimme some lovin' / Shake your tail feather / Everybody needs somebody to love / Think / Minnie the moocher / Sweet home Chicago / Jailhouse rock / Shotgun blues / Soul man / Hey bartender
CD ____________ QED 202
Tring / Nov '96 / Tring

BLUES BROTHERS, THE
Studio Cast
She caught the Katy / Peter Gunn theme / Gimme some lovin' / Shake a tail feather / Everybody needs somebody to love / Old landmark / Think / Theme from rawhide / Minnie the moocher / Sweet home Chicago / Jailhouse rock / Shotgun blues / Hey bartender
CD ____________ 85022
CMC / May '97 / BMG

BLUES IN THE NIGHT
1987 London Cast
Epps, Sheldon *C*
CD ____________ OCRCD 6029
First Night / Oct '95 / Pinnacle

BOCCACCIO '70
Rota, Nino/Armando Trovailo/Piero Umiliani *C*
CD ____________ OST 116
Milano Dischi / Jan '93 / Silva Screen

BODIES, REST AND MOTION
Convertino, Michael *C*
CD ____________ 9245062
Silva Screen / Jan '93 / Koch / Silva Screen

BODY BAGS
Carpenter, John & Jim Lang *C*
CD ____________ VSD 5448
Varese Sarabande / Feb '94 / Pinnacle

BODY LOVE
Schulze, Klaus
Schulze, Klaus *C*
Stardancer / Blanche / PTO
CD ____________ CDTB 123
Thunderbolt / Jan '92 / TKO Magnum

BODY OF EVIDENCE
Revell, Graeme *C*
Main title / Passion theme / Funeral / Houseboat / Hot wax & champagne / Fight / Handcuffs / Parking garage / Waiting for the jury / Confrontation / Karma / End credits
CD ______ **127202**
Milan / Feb '94 / Conifer/BMG / Silva Screen

BODY PARTS
Dikker, Loek *C*
CD ______ **VSD 5337**
Varese Sarabande / Aug '91 / Pinnacle

BODY, THE
Waters, Roger & Ron Geesin
Our song / Sea shell and stone / Red stuff writhe / Gentle breeze through life / Lick your partners / Bridge passage for three plastic teeth / Chain of life / Womb bit / Embryo thought / March past of the embryos / More than seven dwarfs in Penis-land / Dance of the red corpuscles / Body transport / Hand dance - full evening dress / Breathe / Old folks ascension / Bedtime dream climb / Piddle in perspex / Embryonic womb walk / Mrs. Throat goes walking / Sea shell and soft stone / Give birth to a smile
CD ______ **CZ 178**
Premier/EMI / Feb '96 / EMI

BODYGUARD, THE
I will always love you: *Houston, Whitney* / I have nothing: *Houston, Whitney* / I'm every woman: *Houston, Whitney* / Run to you: *Houston, Whitney* / Queen of the night: *Houston, Whitney* / Jesus loves me: *Houston, Whitney* / Even if my heart would break: *Kenny G. & Aaron Neville* / Someday (I'm coming back): *Stansfield, Lisa* / It's gonna be a lovely day: *S.O.U.L. System & Michelle Visage* / Peace, love and understanding: *Stigers, Curtis* / Waiting for you: *Kenny G.* / Trust in me: *Cocker, Joe*
CD ______ **07822186992**
Arista / Jan '93 / BMG

BODYWORK
Stilgoe, Richard *C*
CD ______ **CASTCD 15**
First Night / Oct '88 / Pinnacle

BOLERO
Bernstein, Peter *C*
CD ______ **PCD 124**
Prometheus / Mar '93 / Silva Screen

BONANZA
Bonanza Cast
Bonanza / Sourwood mountain / Sky ball paint / Early one morning / Ponderosa / Careless love / Skip to my Lou / In the pines / Happy birthday / My sons, my sons / Hangin' blues / Shenandoah / Miss Cindy / Hark the herald angels sing / Deck the halls with boughs of holly / New born King / First Christmas trees / Oh fir tree dear / Christmas is a comin' / O come all ye faithful (Adeste Fidelis) / Jingle bells / Santa got lost in Texas / Stuck in the chimney / Why we light candles on the Christmas tree / Merry Christmas neighbour / Merry Christmas and goodnight / Intro / Alamo: *Greene, Lorne* / Pony Express: *Greene, Lorne* / An ol' tin cup: *Greene, Lorne* / Endless prairie: *Greene, Lorne* / Ghost riders in the sky: *Greene, Lorne* / Ringo: *Greene, Lorne* / Blue guitar: *Greene, Lorne* / Sand: *Greene, Lorne* / Saga of the Ponderosa: *Greene, Lorne* / Five card stud: *Greene, Lorne* / Cool water: *Greene, Lorne* / Devil's grin: *Greene, Lorne* / Pretty horses: *Greene, Lorne* / Devil cat: *Greene, Lorne* / Ol' Chisholm trail: *Greene, Lorne* / Wagon wheels: *Greene, Lorne* / Frightened town: *Greene, Lorne* / Shadow of the cactus: *Greene, Lorne* / Tumbling tumbleweeds: *Greene, Lorne* / Gold: *Greene, Lorne* / Whoopee ti yi yo: *Greene, Lorne* / Search: *Greene, Lorne* / Dig, dig, dig, dig (there's no more water...): *Greene, Lorne* / Ol' cyclone: *Greene, Lorne* / Twilight on the trail: *Greene, Lorne* / Geronimo: *Greene, Lorne* / Mule train: *Greene, Lorne* / I'm a gun: *Greene, Lorne* / Gunslinger's prayer: *Greene, Lorne* / Nellie Cole: *Greene, Lorne* / Home on the range: *Greene, Lorne* / Virginia town: *Greene, Lorne* / Place where I worship: *Greene, Lorne* / Pop goes the hammer: *Greene, Lorne* / End of the track: *Greene, Lorne* / Nine pound hammer: *Greene, Lorne* / Bring on the dancin' girls: *Greene, Lorne* / Oh what a town: *Greene, Lorne* / Fourteen men: *Greene, Lorne* / Destiny: *Greene, Lorne* / Sixteen tons: *Greene, Lorne* / Trouble row: *Greene, Lorne* / Chickasaw mountain: *Greene, Lorne* / Darling my darling: *Greene, Lorne* / Man: *Greene, Lorne* / Ringo (French): *Greene, Lorne* / Du sable: *Greene, Lorne* / Bold soldier: *Roberts, Pernell* / Mary Ann: *Roberts, Pernell* / They call the wind Maria: *Roberts, Pernell* / Sylvie: *Roberts, Pernell* / Lily of the west: *Roberts, Pernell* / Water is wide: *Roberts, Pernell* / Rake and the rambling boy: *Roberts, Pernell* / Quiet girl: *Roberts, Pernell* / Shady grove: *Roberts, Pernell* / Alberta: *Roberts, Pernell* / Empty pocket blues: *Roberts, Pernell* / Come all ye fair and tender ladies: *Roberts, Pernell* / Springfield mountain: *Blocker, Dan & John Mitchum* / Roll out heave that cotton: *Blocker, Dan & John Mitchum* / Battle hymn of the Republic: *Blocker, Dan & John Mitchum* / Erie canal: *Blocker, Dan & John Mitchum* / Paiute sunrise chant: *Blocker, Dan & John Mitchum* / Charles, steal away: *Blocker, Dan & John Mitchum* / He never said a mumblin': *Blocker, Dan & John Mitchum*
4CD ______ **BCD 15684**
Bear Family / May '93 / Direct / Rollercoaster / Swift

BONFIRE OF THE VANITIES, THE
Grusin, Dave *C*
CD ______ **821772**
Silva Screen / Jan '92 / Koch / Silva Screen

BOOMERANG
Give U my heart: *Babyface & Tony Braxton* / It's gonna be alright: *Hall, Aaron & Charlie Wilson* / Tonight is right: *Washington, Keith* / I'd die without you: *P.M. Dawn* / Seven day weekend: *Jones, Grace* / End of the road: *Boyz II Men* / Reversal of a dog: *LaFace Cartel* / Love shoulda brought you home: *Braxton, Toni* / There you go: *Gill, Johnny* / Don't wanna love you: *Shanice* / Feels like heaven: *Vaughan, Kenny & The Art Of Love* / Hot sex: *Tribe Called Quest*
CD ______ **73008260062**
Arista / Feb '97 / BMG

BOOTY CALL
Can we: *SWV* / Don't wanna be a playa: *Joe* / Baby baby baby baby...: *R. Kelly* / Fire and desire: *Gill, Johnny & Coko* / Don't stop don't quit: *1 Accord* / Feel good: *Silk* / Hold that thought: *Levert, Gerald* / Let me see you squirrel: *Squirrel* / If you stay: *Backstreet Boys* / Call me: *Too Short & Lil' Kim* / Don't blame it on me: *E-40 & B-Legit Aka 40 Fonzarelli & The Savage* / (I'll be you') huckleberry: *D-Shot* / Plan up you family: *KRS-1* / Chocolate: *LA Ganz* / Looking for love: *Whitey Don* / When I rise: *Crooked*
CD ______ **CHIP 182**
Jive / Mar '97 / Pinnacle

BOPHA
Horner, James *C*
CD ______ **9245352**
Silva Screen / Jan '93 / Koch / Silva Screen

BORDELLO OF BLOOD
Boardman, Chris *C*
CD ______ **VSD 5728**
Varese Sarabande / Sep '96 / Pinnacle

BORGIAS
Delerue, Georges *C*
CD ______ **PCD 109**
Prometheus / Jan '93 / Silva Screen

BOSTON KICKOUT
Kickout: *Whiteout* / Love will tear us apart: *Joy Division* / Fools gold: *Stone Roses* / Symposium of sickness: *Carcass* / Last chance: *China Drum* / Gangsta: *Livingstone* / Neat neat neat: *Damned* / I wanna be adored: *Stone Roses* / Adieu Ted: *Hartshorne, Robert* / Loaded: *Primal Scream* / Last time: *Paradise Lost* / Resiliant little muscle: *Solar Race* / Bakery: *Hartshorne, Robert* / New rose: *Damned* / European son: *Velvet Underground*
CD ______ **ORECD 543**
Silvertone / Oct '96 / Pinnacle

BOUGHT AND SOLD (Dull Bang, Gushing Sound, Human Shriek)
Previte, Bobby
Previte, Bobby *C*
CD ______ **378212**
Koch Jazz / Aug '96 / Koch

BOUND BY HONOUR
CD ______ **HR 614782**
Silva Screen / Jan '93 / Koch / Silva Screen

BOURNE IDENTITY, THE
Rosenthal, Laurence *C*
Bourne identity / French children / Fishing village / Arrival in Zurich / Incident at the bank / Jason and Marie / Red door / Discovery / Chernak dead / Valois bank / Wild goose chase / Carlos as confessor / Trocadero
CD ______ **RVF 6005D**
Intrada / Jan '90 / Koch / Silva Screen

BOY WHO GREW TOO FAST, THE
1986 Royal Opera House Cast
Menotti, Gian Carlo *C*
CD ______ **CDTER 1125**
TER / Jan '93 / Koch

BOYFRIEND, THE
1954 Broadway Cast
Wilson, Sandy *C*
Overture / Perfect young ladies / Boyfriend / Won't you Charleston with me / Fancy forgetting / I could be happy with you / Sur la plage / Room in Bloomsbury / You-don't-want-to-play-with-me blues / Safety in numbers / Riviera / It's never too late to fall in love / Carnival tango / Poor little Pierrette / Finale
CD ______ **GD 60056**
RCA Victor / Oct '89 / BMG

BOYFRIEND, THE
1984 London Cast
Wilson, Sandy *C*
Overture / Perfect young ladies / Boyfriend / Won't you Charleston with me / Fancy forgetting / I could be happy with you / Sur la plage / Room in Bloomsbury / It's nicer in Nice / You-don't-want-to-play-with-me blues / Safety in numbers / Riviera / It's never too late too fall in love / Poor little Pierrette / Finale
CD ______ **CDTER 1095**
TER / Dec '84 / Koch

BOYFRIEND, THE
CC Productions
Wilson, Sandy *C*
Perfect young ladies / Boyfriend / Won't you charleston with me / I could be happy with you / Sur la plage / Room in Bloomsbury / It's nicer in Nice / You don't want to play with me blues / Safety in numbers / Boyfriend / Riviera / It's never too late to fall in love / Poor little pierrette
CD ______ **QED 214**
Tring / Nov '96 / Tring

BOYFRIEND, THE
London Cast
Wilson, Sandy *C*
Perfect young ladies / Boyfriend / Won't you charleston with me / Fancy forgetting / I could be happy with you / Room in Bloomsbury / It's nicer in Nice / You don't-want-to-play-with-me blues / Safety in numbers / Riviera / It's never too late to fall in love / Poor little Pierrette
CD ______ **SHOWCD 027**
Showtime / Oct '96 / Disc / THE

BOYFRIEND, THE
Studio Cast
Wilson, Sandy *C*
Perfect young ladies / Boyfriend / Won't you Charleston with me / I could be happy with you / Sur la plage / Room in Bloomsbury / It's nicer in Nice / You-don't-want-to-play-with-me-blues / Safety in numbers / Boyfriend (finale act 2) / Riviera / It's never too late too fall in love
CD ______ **85262**
CMC / May '97 / BMG

BOYFRIEND, THE/GOODBYE MR. CHIPS
Cast Recording
Wilson, Sandy *C*
Overture / Perfect young ladies / I could be happy with you / Fancy forgetting / Sur la plage / You are my lucky star / It's never too late to fall in love / Won't you Charleston with me / You-don't-want-to-play-with-me blues / Room in Bloomsbury / It's nicer in Nice / All I do is dream of you / Safety in numbers / Poor little Pierrette / Riviera/Finale / Overture / London is London: *Clark, Petula* / And the sky smiled: *Clark, Petula* / When I am older / Walk through the world: *Clark, Petula* / Schooldays: *Clark, Petula & Boys* / When I was younger: *O'Toole, Peter* / You and I: *Clark, Petula* / Fill the world with love: *O'Toole, Peter & Boys*
CD ______ **CDMGM 20**
MGM/EMI / Apr '90 / EMI

BOYFRIEND, THE/ME AND MY GIRL
Cast Recording
Wilson, Sandy *C*
CD ______ **340802**
Koch / Oct '95 / Koch

BOYS
She's not there: *Cruel Sea* / Alright: *Cast* / Gotta know right now: *Smoking Popes* / Honeysimple: *Scarce* / Wild wood: *Weller, Paul* / Coloured water: *Orbit* / Sad and beautiful world: *Sparklehorse* / Fading fast: *Willis, Kelly* / Tell her this: *Del Amitri* / If I didn't love you: *Squeeze* / Inside: *Slider* / Wait for the sun: *Supergrass* / Belly laugh: *Compulsion* / Begging you: *Stone Roses* / Evade chums: *Copeland, Stewart*
CD ______ **5404892**
A&M / Jun '96 / PolyGram

BOYS FROM SYRACUSE, THE
1953 Studio Cast
Rodgers, Richard *C*
Hart, Lorenz *L*
Engel, Lehman *Con*
CD ______ **SK 53329**
Sony Broadway / Nov '94 / Sony

BOYS FROM SYRACUSE, THE
Off-Broadway Cast
Rodgers, Richard *C*
Hart, Lorenz *L*
CD ______ **ZDM 7646952**
EMI Classics / Apr '93 / EMI

BOYS FROM SYRACUSE, THE
Original Cast
Rodgers, Richard *C*
Hart, Lorenz *L*
Falling in love with love / Sing for your supper / This can't be love / What can you do with a man / You have cast your shadow on the sea / I had twins / Dear old syracuse / Shortest day of the year / Let antiphouls in / Ladies of the evening / He and she / Come with me / Oh diogenes
CD ______ **DRGCD 94767**
DRG / Sep '97 / Discovery / New Note/ Pinnacle

BOYS ON THE SIDE
You got it: *Raitt, Bonnie* / I take you with me: *Etheridge, Melissa* / Keep on growing: *Crow, Sheryl* / Power of two: *Indigo Girls* / Somebody stand by me: *Nicks, Stevie* / Everyday is like Sunday: *Pretenders* / Dreams: *Cranberries* / Why: *Lennox, Annie* / Ol' 55: *McLachlan, Sarah* / Willow: *Armatrading, Joan* / Crossroads: *Mosser, Jonell*
CD ______ **07822187482**
Arista / Feb '97 / BMG

BOYZ N THE HOOD
How to survive in South Central: *Ice Cube* / Just ask me to: *Campbell, Tevin* / Mama don't take no mess: *Yo Yo* / Growin' up in the hood: *Compton's Most Wanted* / Just a friendly game of baseball: *Main Source* / Me and you: *Tony Toni Tone* / Work it out: *Love, Monie* / Every single weekend: *Kam* / Too young: *Hi-Five* / Hangin' out: *2 Live Crew* / It's your life: *Too Short* / Spirit: *Force One Network* / Setembro: *Jones, Quincy* / Black on black crime
CD ______ **7599266432**
WEA / Aug '91 / Warner Music

BRADY BUNCH, THE
Brady bunch (grunge version) / It's a sunshine day: *Original Brady Bunch Kids* / I'm feeling nothing: *Dada* / Marsha, I have to tell you something / Venus: *Shocking Blue* / Girl: *Jones, Davy* / Supermodel (you better work): *Rupaul* / You kids have no idea what it takes to impress a chick / Whatever: *Zak* / You're all a part of me / Till I met you: *Barnes, Christopher Daniel* / Beast is out of hand: *Mudd Pagoda* / Have a nice day: *Coffing, Barry & Zachary Throne* / I'm looking around: *Generation Why* / Marsha did it again / I wish I could be like you: *Mudd Pagoda* / I think Peter's a babe: *Mudd Pagoda* / Keep on: *Original Brady Bunch Kids* / And as a wise man once said / Brady Bunch
CD ______ **279322**
Milan / Jun '95 / Conifer/BMG / Silva Screen

BRAINDEAD
CD ______ **QDKCD 006**
Normal / Sep '94 / ADA / Direct

BRANQUIGNOL (Music & Dialogue From Branquignol/Allez France/Le Petit Baigneur/Vous Gueles Les Muettes)
CD ______ **K 1511**
Auvidis Travelling / Mar '97 / Harmonia Mundi

BRASSED OFF
Jones, Trevor & Grimethorpe Colliery Band
Death or glory / Sad old day / Floral dance / Aforementioned essential items / Concerto de Aranjuez / Years of coal / March of the cobblers / There's more important things in life / Cross of honour / Jerusalem / Florentia march / Danny boy / We'll find a way / Clog dance / Colonel Bogey / Honest decent human beings / Land of hope and glory
CD ______ **09026687572**
RCA Victor / Nov '96 / BMG

BRAVEHEART
London Symphony Orchestra
Horner, James *C*
Horner, James *Con*
Main title / Gift of a thistle / Wallace courts Murron / Secret wedding / Attack on Murron / Revenge / Murron's burial / Making plans/Gathering the clans / Sons of Scotland / Battle of Stirling / For the love of a Princess / Falkirk / Betrayal and desolation / Mornay's dream / Legend spreads / Princess pleads for Wallace's life / Freedom/Execution Bannockburn / End credits
CD ______ **4482952**
London / Sep '95 / PolyGram

BRAZIL
Kamen, Michael *C*
CD ______ **111242**
Milan / Feb '94 / Conifer/BMG / Silva Screen

BREAKFAST AT TIFFANY'S
Mancini, Henry *C*
Moon river / Something for cat / Sally's tomato / Mr. Yunioshi / Big blow-out / Hub caps and tail lights / Breakfast at Tiffany's / Latin Golightly / Holly / Loose caboose / Big heist / Moon river cha cha
CD ______ **23622**
Silva Screen / Feb '90 / Koch / Silva Screen

BREAKFAST CLUB, THE
Don't you forget about me: *Simple Minds* / Fire in the twilight: *Wang Chung* / We are not alone: *De Vito, Karla* / Heart too hot to hold: *Johnson, Jesse* / Waiting: *Daly, Elizabeth* / Didn't I tell you: *Kennedy, Joyce* / I'm the dude: *Forsey, Keith* / Dream montage: *Forsey, Keith* / Reggae: *Forsey, Keith* / Love theme: *Forsey, Keith*
CD ______ **CDMID 179**
A&M / Jan '94 / PolyGram

BREAKING GLASS
O'Connor, Hazel
Writing on the wall / Monsters in disguise / Come into the air / Big brother / Who needs it / Will you / Eighth day / Top of the wheel / Calls the tune / Blackman / Give me an inch / If only
CD ______ **5513562**
Spectrum / Sep '95 / PolyGram

BREAKING THE RULES
CD ______ **VSD 5386**
Varese Sarabande / Sep '92 / Pinnacle

BRIDE OF FRANKENSTEIN, THE
Westminster Philharmonic Orchestra
Waxman, Franz *C*
Alwyn, Kenneth *Con*
Main title / Prologue - Menuetto and storm / Monster entrance / Processional march / Strange apparition/Pretorius' entrance/You will need a coat / Bottle sequence / Female monster music/Pastorale/Village/Chase /

Crucifixion/Monster breaks out / Fire in the hut/Graveyard / Dance macabre / Creation / Tower explodes/Finale / Invisible ray suite
CD **FILMCD 135**
Silva Screen / Mar '94 / Koch / Silva Screen

BRIDES OF CHRIST, THE
Millo, Mario *C*
CD **A 8936**
Alhambra / Feb '92 / Silva Screen

BRIDESHEAD REVISITED
Burgon, Geoffrey *C*
Brideshead revisited / Going to Brideshead / First visit / Venice nocturne / Sebastian's summer / Hunt / Sebastian against the world / Julia in love / Julia / Rain in Venice / General strike / Fading light / Julia's theme / Sebastian alone / Orphans of the storm / Finale
CD **CDMFP 6172**
Music For Pleasure / Sep '95 / EMI

BRIDGE, THE
Mitchell, Richard G. *C*
Opening titles / Quay house / Arriving in Suffolk / Storm / Reginald and Isobel return to London / Sitting / Walberswick fete / Fireworks / France / Kiss / Love theme / Reginald's proposition / Mrs. Todd's release / What did you see Emma / Garden / Leaving without saying goodbye / We've come to an arrangement / End titles
CD **DSCD 5**
Demon / Feb '92 / Pinnacle

BRIGADOON
1988 London Cast
Loewe, Frederick *C*
Lerner, Alan Jay *L*
CD **OCRCD 6022**
First Night / Oct '95 / Pinnacle

BRIGADOON
Studio Cast & Ambrosian Chorus/London Sinfonietta
Loewe, Frederick *C*
Lerner, Alan Jay *L*
McGlinn, John *Con*
CD **CDC 7544812**
EMI Classics / Apr '93 / EMI

BRIGADOON
Cast Recording
Loewe, Frederick *C*
Lerner, Alan Jay *L*
2CD **CDTER2 1218**
TER / Aug '95 / Koch

BRIGADOON
Kelly, Gene & Film Cast
Loewe, Frederick *C*
Lerner, Alan Jay *L*
Main title / Once in the Highlands / Brigadoon / Down on MacConnachy Square / Waitin' for my dearie / I'll go home with bonnie Jean / Come to me, bend to me / Heather on the hill / Almost like being in love / Talk to Dominie / Til the end of our days / There but for you I go / Two hundred years later / Gathering of the clans / Wedding dance / Chase / Fiona's search / From this day on / Heather on the hill / Heather on the hill / Waitin' for my dearie / Even miracles / Finale/End credits / Dinna ye know / Tommy
CD **CDODEON 16**
Soundtracks / Aug '96 / EMI

BRIGHT ANGEL
Utah Symphony Orchestra
CD **MAF 7014D**
Intrada / Mar '92 / Koch / Silva Screen

BRINGING IT ALL BACK HOME
2CD **HBCD 0010**
Hummingbird / Feb '97 / ADA / Direct / Grapevine/PolyGram

BROKEN ARROW
Zimmer, Hans *C*
CD **74321348652**
Milan / Mar '96 / Conifer/BMG / Silva Screen

BRONX TALE, A
Streets of the bronx: *Cool Change* / I wonder why: *Dion & The Belmonts* / Little girl of mine: *Cleftones* / Don't you know: *Reese, Della* / For your precious love: *Butler, Jerry* / Ain't that a kick in the head: *Cool Change* / Father and son: *Cool Change* / Beautiful morning: *Rascals* / Tell it like it is: *Neville, Aaron* / Bus talk: *Watson, Bobby* / I only have eyes for you: *Niewood, Gerry Quartet* / Ninety nine and a half (won't do): *Pickett, Wilson* / Nights in white satin: *Moody Blues* / Baby I need your loving: *Four Tops* / Regrets: *Barbella, Butch* / All along the watchtower: *Hendrix, Jimi Experience* / I'm so proud: *Impressions* / It's a man's man's man's world: *Brown, James* / Christo redemptor: *Byrd, Donald*
CD **4748062**
Epic / Mar '94 / Sony

BROTHER FROM ANOTHER PLANET, THE
CD **DRCD 1007**
Daring / Feb '96 / ADA / CM / Direct

BROTHER SUN SISTER MOON
Ortolani, Riz *C*
CD **MPCD 228**
Silva Screen / Apr '96 / Koch / Silva Screen

BROTHERS MCMULLEN, THE
Egan, Seamus *C*
I will remember you: *McLachlan, Sarah* / Week in January / Slip jigs / Intro no.1/Reel Beatrice / Fermoy lasses / When Juniper sleeps / Eamon Coyne's/Longford collector / Once upon a time / Cape Breton set / Lark / Dark slender boy / Weep not for the memories
CD **07822188032**
Arista / Dec '95 / BMG

BROWNING VERSION, THE
St. Mary's School Choir/London Metropolitan Orchestra
Isham, Mark *C*
Kugler, Ken *Con*
In Founder's court / Taplow / Cromwells / Agamemnon / Art of learning is to conceal learning / Hitler of the lower fifth / In the village / Just good friends / God from afar, looks graciously upon a gentle master / Defiant creature / Secrets of a marriage / Night crawlers / Toujours la politesse / Goodbye / Noblest calling / To forgive myself / Prize giving / Browning version
CD **213012**
Milan / Oct '94 / Conifer/BMG / Silva Screen

BUBBLING BROWN SUGAR
1977 London Cast
Harlem '70 / Bubbling Brown Sugar / That's what Harlem is to me: *Delmar, Elaine* / Bill Robinson speciality: *Augins, Charles* / Harlem sweet Harlem / Nobody: *Daniels, Billy* / Goin' back in time: *Augins, Charles* / Some of these days: *Lawrence, Stephanie* / Moving Uptown: *Augins, Charles* / Strolling: *Cameron, David & others* / I'm gonna tell God all my troubles: *Taylor, Mel* / His eye is on the sparrow/Swing low sweet chariot: *Brown, Miquel & Company* / Sweet Georgia Brown: *Gelzer, Helen/Newton Winters/David Cameron* / Honeysuckle Rose: *Delmar, Elaine/Billy Daniels* / Stormy Monday blues: *Brown, Miquel* / Sophisticated lady: *Peters, Clarke* / In honeysuckle time, when Emaline said she'd be mine: *Satton, Lon/Billy Daniels* / Rosetta: *Collins, Ray/David Cameron/Newton Winters* / Solitude: *Gelzer, Helen/Newton Winters/Ray Collins/David Cameron* / C'mon up to Jive Time: *Augins, Charles* / Stompin' at the Savoy/Take the 'A' train / Harlem-time: *Augins, Charles* / Bubbling Brown Sugar II: *Peters, Clarke/Amii Stewart* / Ain't misbehavin': *Daniels, Billy* / Pray for the lights to go out: *Satton, Lon* / I got it bad: *Stewart, Amii* / Harlem makes me feel: *Sharpe, Bernard* / Jim, jam, jumpin' jive: *Augins, Charles/Newton Winters/Ray Collins* / There'll be some changes made: *Delmar, Elaine* / Memories of you: *Daniels, Billy* / God bless the child: *Gelzer, Helen* / It don't mean a thing: *Peters, Clarke & Company* / Bubbling Brown Sugar (reprise)
2CD **CDSBL 13106**
DRG / Oct '92 / Discovery / New Note/ Pinnacle

BUBBLING BROWN SUGAR
Broadway Cast
CD **AMH 93310**
Silva Screen / Jan '89 / Koch / Silva Screen

BUCCANEER, THE
Bernstein, Elmer *C*
CD **VSD 5214**
Varese Sarabande / Feb '90 / Pinnacle

BUDDHA OF SUBURBIA, THE
Bowie, David
Bowie, David *C*
Buddha of Suburbia / Sex and the church / South horizon / Mysteries / Bleed like a craze, Dad / Strangers when we meet / Dead against it / Untitled No.1 / Ian Fish, UK heir
CD **74321170042**
Arista / Nov '93 / BMG

BUDDY
London Cast
Holly, Buddy *C*
CD **CASTCD 55**
First Night / Apr '96 / Pinnacle

BUDDY
CC Productions
Holly, Buddy *C*
Ready Teddy / Rock around the Ollie Vee / Changing all those changes / That'll be the day / Blue days, black nights / Everyday / Not fade away / Peggy Sue / Words of love / Oh boy / True love ways / Chantilly lace / Maybe baby / Heartbeat / La bamba / Raining in my heart / It doesn't matter anymore / Rave on
CD **QED 204**
Tring / Nov '96 / Tring

BUDDY
Studio Cast
Holly, Buddy *C*
Ready Teddy / Rock around with Ollie Vee / Changing all those changes / That'll be the day / Blue days, black nights / Everyday / Not fade away / Peggy Sue / Words of love / Oh boy / True love ways / Chantily lace / Maybe baby / Heartbeat / La bamba / Raining in my heart / It doesn't matter anymore / Rave on
CD **85032**
CMC / May '97 / BMG

BUDDY
Cast Recording
Holly, Buddy *C*
CD **VSD 5829**
Varese Sarabande / Jul '97 / Pinnacle

BULL DURHAM
CD **905864**
Silva Screen / Jan '93 / Koch / Silva Screen

BULLETPROOF
CD **MCAD 11498**
MCA / Sep '96 / BMG

BULLETPROOF (Score)
Bernstein, Elmer *C*
CD **VSD 5757**
Varese Sarabande / Oct '96 / Pinnacle

BULLETS OVER BROADWAY
CD **SK 66822**
Sony Classical / May '95 / Sony

BULLITT
Schifrin, Lalo *C*
Schifrin, Lalo *Con*
Bullitt theme / Room 26 / Hotel Daniels / Aftermath of love / Music to interrogate by / On the way to San Mateo / Ice Pick Mike / Song for Cathy / Shifting gears / Cantata for combo / First snowfall / Bullitt
CD **9362450082**
Warner Bros. / Aug '97 / Warner Music

BURNING SECRET/FRUIT MACHINE/ DIAMOND SKULLS
Zimmer, Hans *C*
CD **CDCH 530**
Milan / Feb '90 / Conifer/BMG / Silva Screen

BUSTER
Two hearts: *Collins, Phil* / Just one look: *Hollies* / Big noise: *Collins, Phil* / Robbery: *Dudley, Anne* / I got you babe: *Sonny & Cher* / Keep on running: *Davis, Spencer Group* / Loco in Acapulco: *Four Tops* / How do you do it: *Gerry & The Pacemakers* / I just don't know what to do with myself: *Springfield, Dusty* / Sweets for my sweet: *Searchers* / Will you still be waiting: *Dudley, Anne* / Groovy kind of love: *Collins, Phil*
CD **CDV 2544**
Virgin / Apr '92 / EMI

BUTCH CASSIDY AND THE SUNDANCE KID
Bacharach, Burt
Bacharach, Burt *C*
Sundance kid / Raindrops keep fallin' on my head / Not goin' home anymore / South American getaway / Old fun city / Come touch the sun / On a bicycle built for joy
CD **5514332**
Spectrum / Aug '95 / PolyGram

BUTTERFLY
Morricone, Ennio *C*
CD **PCD 108**
Prometheus / Jan '93 / Silva Screen

BY JEEVES (Highlights)
1996 London Cast
Lloyd Webber, Andrew *C*
Ayckbourn, Alan *L*
False start / Code of the Woosters / Travel hopefully / That was nearly us / Deadlier than the male / Hallo song / By Jeeves / When love arrives / What have you got to say Jeeves / Half a moment / It's a pig / Banjo boy / Wizard rainbow
CD **5317232**
Really Useful / Jul '96 / PolyGram

BY JEEVES
1996 London Cast
Lloyd Webber, Andrew *C*
Ayckbourn, Alan *L*
Some introductory chat / Code of the Woosters / Plot thickens / Travel hopefully / Curious hedgehog incident / Travel hopefully (continued) / In which my character is tested / That was nearly us / Days of jams and mazes / Love's maze / Wooster thinks on his feet / Hallo song / Identity crisis (or two) / By Jeeves / Wooster nobly intercedes / When love arrives / I am let down (badly) / What have you got to say Jeeves / I answer the call of the code / Half a moment / I risk my neck to save the bacon / It's a pig / Satisfactory outcome / Banjo boy / Wizard rainbow / In conclusion
CD **5331872**
Really Useful / Jul '96 / PolyGram

BY THE BEAUTIFUL SEA
Broadway Cast
CD **ZDM 7648892**
EMI Classics / Apr '93 / EMI

BYE BYE BIRDIE
Film Cast
Strouse, Charles *C*
Adams, Lee *L*
CD **10812**
Silva Screen / Jan '89 / Koch / Silva Screen

C

CABARET
Film Cast
Kander, John *C*
Ebb, Fred *L*
Wilkommen / Mein herr / Two ladies / Maybe this time / Sitting pretty / Tiller girls / Money, money / Heiraten / If you could see her / Tomorrow belongs to me / Cabaret / Finale
CD **MCLD 19088**
MCA / Apr '97 / BMG

CABARET
1986 London Cast
Kander, John *C*
Ebb, Fred *L*
Wilkommen / So what / Don't tell mama / Perfectly marvellous / Two ladies / It couldn't please me more / Why should I wake up / Money, money, money / Married / Meeskite / Tomorrow belongs to me / If you could see her / Maybe this time / What would you do / Cabaret / Auf wiedersehen
CD **OCRCD 6010**
First Night / Mar '93 / Pinnacle

CABARET (Highlights)
Cast Recording
Kander, John *C*
Ebb, Fred *L*
Wilkommen / Don't tell Mama / Telephone song / Perfectly marvellous / Two ladies / Tomorrow belongs to me / Why should I wake up / Maybe this time / Sitting pretty / Money, money / If you could see her / Cabaret
CD **SHOWCD 021**
Showtime / Feb '95 / Disc / THE

CABARET
1968 London Cast
Kander, John *C*
Ebb, Fred *L*
Davies, Gareth *Con*
CD **SMK 53494**
Sony West End / Jan '93 / Sony

CABARET
Cast Recording
Kander, John *C*
Ebb, Fred *L*
2CD **CDTER2 1210**
TER / Aug '95 / Koch

CABARET
Studio Cast
Kander, John *C*
Ebb, Fred *L*
Willkommen / Mein herr / Two ladies / Maybe this time / Sitting pretty / Money, money, money / Heiraten / If you could see her / Tomorrow belongs to me / Cabaret / Finale
CD **88002**
CMC / May '97 / BMG

CABARET
Willcox, Toyah & Nigel Planer/Cast
Kander, John *C*
Ebb, Fred *L*
Overture / Wilkommen / Sitting pretty / Mein herr / Two ladies / Money and songs / Tomorrow belongs to me / Cabaret / Don't tell Mama / If you could see her / Married / Maybe this time / Finale
CD **3036200392**
Shows Collection / Jul '97 / Carlton

CABIN IN THE SKY
Duke, Vernon *C*
Latouche, John *L*
CD **873108**
Milan / Jun '92 / Conifer/BMG / Silva Screen

CABIN IN THE SKY
Broadway Cast
Duke, Vernon *C*
Latouche, John *L*
CD **ZDM 7648922**
EMI Classics / Aug '93 / EMI

CABINET OF DR. CALIGARI, THE
Bravura String Quartet
Brock, Timothy *C*
CD **KOC 04**
K / Jan '97 / Cargo / Greyhound / SRD

CABLE GUY, THE
I'll juice you up: *Carrey, Jim* / Leave me alone: *Cantrell, Jerry* / Standing outside a broken phone booth with money in my hand: *Primitive Radio Gods* / Blind: *Silverchair* / Oh sweet nuthin': *$10,000 Gold Chain* / End of the world is coming: *Hilder* / Satelite of love: *Porno For Pyros* / Get outta my head: *Cracker* / Somebody to love: *Carrey, Jim* / Last assassin: *Cypress Hill* / This is: *Ruby* / Hey man, nice shot: *Filter* / Unattractive: *Toadies* / Download: *Expanding Man*
CD **4841532**
Work/Columbia / Jul '96 / Sony

CAL
Knopfler, Mark
Knopfler, Mark *C*
Irish boy / Road / Waiting for her / Irish love / Secret place / Father and son / Meeting at the trees / Potato picking / In a secret place / Fear and hatred / Love and guilt / Long road
CD **8227692**
Vertigo / Mar '97 / PolyGram

CALAMITY JANE
Cast Recording
Fain, Sammy *C*
Webster, Paul Francis *L*
CD **CDTER 1215**
TER / Aug '95 / Koch

CALAMITY JANE
Craven, Gemma & 1996 London Cast
Fain, Sammy *C*
Webster, Paul Francis *L*
Secret love / Deadwood stage / Hive full of honey / I can do without you / It's Harry I'm planning to marry / Windy city / Keep it under your hat / Woman's touch / Higher than a hawk / Black hills of Dakota / Love you dearly
CD **3036200302**
Carlton / Jul '96 / Carlton

CALAMITY JANE
Cast Recording/National Symphony Orchestra
Fain, Sammy *C*
Webster, Paul Francis *L*
Edwards, John Owen *Con*
Overture / Deadwood stage / Hive full of honey / I can do without you / It's Harry I'm planning to marry / Just blew in from the Windy City / Keep it under your hat / Woman's touch / Higher than a hawk, deeper than a well / Black hills of Dakota / Secret love / Finale
CD **SHOWCD 036**
Showtime / Oct '96 / Disc / THE

CALAMITY JANE/PYJAMA GAME
Deadwood stage / I can do without you / Black hills of Dakota / Just blew in from the Windy City / Woman's touch / Higher than a hawk (deeper than a well) / 'Tis Harry I'm planning to marry / Secret love / Pajama game / And racing with the clock / I'm not at all in love / I'll never be jealous again / Once a year day / Small talk / There once was a man / Hernando's hideaway / Finale
CD **4676102**
CBS / Dec '90 / Sony

CALIFORNIA DREAMS
This time / Castles on quicksand / Everybody's got someone / It's gonna be rain / Let me be the one / If only you knew / One world / If you lean on me / If it wasn't for you / Love is not like this / Heart don't lie / California dreams theme
CD **MCLD 19301**
MCA / Oct '95 / BMG

CALL ME MADAM
Revival Cast
Berlin, Irving *C*
CD **DRGCD 94761**
DRG / Jun '95 / Discovery / New Note/ Pinnacle

CAMELOT
Film Cast
Loewe, Frederick *C*
Lerner, Alan Jay *L*
Overture / I wonder what the king is doing tonight / Simple joys of maidenhood / Camelot and the wedding ceremony / C'est moi / Lusty month of May / Follow me / How to handle a woman / Take me to the fair / If ever I would leave you / What do the simple folk do / I loved you once in silence / Guenevere / Finale
CD **7599273252**
Warner Bros. / Mar '94 / Warner Music

CAMELOT
1982 London Cast
Loewe, Frederick *C*
Lerner, Alan Jay *L*
Overture / Camelot / Simple joys of maidenhood / I wonder what the king is doing tonight / C'est moi / Follow me / Lusty month of May / Resolution / Then you may take me to the fair / How to handle a woman / Entracle madrigal / Before I gaze at you again / If ever I would leave you
CD **CDTER 1030**
TER / Mar '89 / Koch

CAMELOT (Highlights)
1982 London Cast
Loewe, Frederick *C*
Lerner, Alan Jay *L*
Overture / I wonder what the king is doing tonight / Simple joys of maidenhood / Camelot / Follow me / C'est moi / Lusty month of May / How to handle a woman / Before I gaze at you again / If ever I would leave you / What do the simple folk do / I loved you once in silence
CD **SHOWCD 013**
Showtime / Feb '95 / Disc / THE

CAMELOT/MY FAIR LADY
Cast Recording
Loewe, Frederick *C*
Lerner, Alan Jay *L*
CD **340792**
Koch / Oct '95 / Koch

CAMILLE CLAUDEL
Yared, Gabriel *C*
CD **30673**
Silva Screen / Jan '93 / Koch / Silva Screen

CAN-CAN
1953 Broadway Cast
Porter, Cole *C*
CD **ZDM 7646642**
EMI Classics / Apr '93 / EMI

CANDIDE
1988 Scottish Opera
Bernstein, Leonard *C*
Wilbur, Richard *L*
CD **CDTER 1156**
TER / Jul '88 / Koch

CANDIDE
1956 Broadway Cast
Bernstein, Leonard *C*
Wilbur, Richard *L*
Krachmalnick, Samuel *Con*
Overture / Best of all possible worlds / What's the use / It must be so / Glitter and be gay / Oh happy me / Mazurka / You were dead you know / My love / I am easily assimilated / Eldorado / Quiet / Bon Voyage / Gavotte / Make our garden grow
CD **SK 48017**
Sony Broadway / Dec '91 / Sony

CANDIDE
1982 New York Opera Cast
Bernstein, Leonard *C*
Wilbur, Richard *L*
Fanfare/Life is happiness indeed / Best of all possible worlds / Happy instrumental/Oh happy we / Candide begins his travels / It must be so / Westphalian fanfare/Chorale/ Battle music / Entrance of the Jew / Glitter and be gay / Earthquake music/Dear boy / Auto da fe / Candide's lament / You were dead you know / Travel(to the stables)/I am easily assimilated / Quartet finale / Entr'acte / Ballad of the new world / My love / Barcarolle / Alleluia / Eldorado / Sheep song / Governor's waltz / Bon voyage / Quiet / Constantinople/What's the use / Finale: Make our garden grow
CD **NWCD 3401**
New World / Oct '86 / New World

CANDIDE (& West Side Story)
Hadley, Jerry & June Anderson/London Symphony Orchestra/Chorus
Bernstein, Leonard *C*
Wilbur, Richard *L*
Bernstein, Leonard *Con*
2CD **4297342**
Deutsche Grammophon / Aug '91 / PolyGram

CANDIDE (Highlights)
1988 Scottish Opera
Bernstein, Leonard *C*
Wilbur, Richard *L*
CD **CDTEO 1006**
TER / Jul '88 / Koch

CANDIDE
Hadley, Jerry & June Anderson/London Symphony Orchestra/Chorus
Bernstein, Leonard *C*
Wilbur, Richard *L*
Bernstein, Leonard *Con*
3CD **4479582**
Deutsche Grammophon / May '96 / PolyGram

CANDIDE
1997 New Broadway Cast
Bernstein, Leonard *C*
Wilbur, Richard *L*
Overture / Life is happiness indeed / Old lady's face entrance / Best of all possible worlds / Oh happy we / It must be so / Glitter and be gay / Old lady's second false entrance / Auto da fe / Candide's lament / You were dead you know / I am easily assimilated / Quartet finale to Act I / Entr'acte / Ballad of the new world / I am easily assimilated / My love / Eldorado / Sheep song / Governor's waltz / Bon voyage / Quiet / What's the use / Make our garden grow
CD **09026688352**
RCA Victor / Aug '97 / BMG

CANICULE (DOG DAY)
Lai, Francis *C*
CD **MANTRA 056**
Silva Screen / Jan '94 / Koch / Silva Screen

CANNONBALL FEVER
Wheatley, David *C*
CD **CST 348042**
Varese Sarabande / Feb '90 / Pinnacle

CAPTAIN FROM CASTILE
Newman, Alfred *C*
CD **FCD 8103**
Fantasy / Mar '84 / Jazz Music / Pinnacle / Wellard

CAPTAIN FUTURE
Bruhn, Christian *C*
CD **CST 8051**
Colosseum / Mar '96 / Pinnacle

CAPTIVE
Edge
Edge *C*
Rowena's theme / Heroine / One foot in heaven / Strange party / Hiro's theme / Drift / Dream theme / Djinn / Island / Hiro's theme 2
CD **CDV 2401**
Virgin / Sep '86 / EMI

CAR WASH
Carwash / 6 O'clock DJ (Let's rock) / I wanna get next to you / Put your money where your mouth is / Zig Zag / You're on my mind / Mid day DJ Theme / Born to love you / Daddy rich / You gotta believe / I'm going down / Yo yo / Sunrise / Righteous rhythm / Water / Crying / Doin' what comes naturally / Keep on keepin' on
CD **MCD 11502**
MCA / Mar '97 / BMG

CARAVAGGIO 1610
Fisher-Turner, Simon
Fisher-Turner, Simon *C*
Hills of Abruzzi / Dog star / All paths lead to Rome / Fantasia, childhood memories / How blue sky was / Light and dark (From Missa Lux Et Orrigo) / Umber wastes / Cafe of the moors / Timeout and mind / In the still of the night / Michele of the shadows / Waters of forgetfullness / Running running / Frescobaldi, the greatest organist of our time / Hourglass / I love you more than my eyes
CD **DSCD 10**
Demon / Jul '95 / Pinnacle

CARD, THE
1994 London Cast
Hatch, Tony *C*
Trent, Jackie *L*
Typical machin / Another time, another place / You'll do / How do / Nobody thought of it / Rents / Moving on / Time to spend (beside the sea) / Lock, stock and barrell / Is it just me / Typical machin (Reprise) / That's the way the money grows / If only / Countess of chell / Card / Opposite your smile / If only (Reprise) / Moving on (Reprise) / Finale the company
CD **OCRCD 6045**
First Night / Apr '97 / Pinnacle

CARDINAL, THE
Moross, Jerome *C*
Stonebury / Dixieland / Tango / Cardinal's faith / They haven't got the girls in the USA / Cardinal in Vienna / Anne-Marie / Cardinal's decision / Way down South / Cardinal themes
CD **PRCD 1778**
Preamble / Jan '94 / Silva Screen

CARLA'S SONG
Fenton, George *C*
CD **CDDEB 1005**
Debonair / Apr '97 / Pinnacle

CARLITO'S WAY
I love music: *Rozalla* / Rock the boat: *Hues Corporation* / Rock your baby: *Terry, Ed* / Perece mentira: *Anthony, Mark* / Backstabbers: *O'Jays* / Sound of Philadelphia: *MFSB* / Got to be real: *Lynn, Cheryl* / Lady Marmalade: *Labelle* / Pillow talk: *Sinoa* / El watusi: *Barretto, Ray* / Oye como va: *Santana* / You are so beautiful: *Preston, Billy*
CD **4749942**
Columbia / Jan '94 / Sony

CARLITO'S WAY (Score)
Doyle, Patrick *C*
Carlito's way / Carlito & Gail / Cafe / Laline / You're over, man / Where's my cheesecake / Buoy / Elevator / There's an angel here / Grand central / Remember me
CD **VSD 5463**
Varese Sarabande / Jan '94 / Pinnacle

CARMEN JONES
London Cast
Bizet, Georges *C*
Hammerstein II, Oscar *L*
Lewis, Henry *Con*
CD **CDC 7543512**
EMI Classics / Apr '93 / EMI

CARNIVAL
1961 Broadway Cast
Kaper, Bronislaw *C*
CD **8371952**
Silva Screen / Feb '90 / Koch / Silva Screen

CAROUSEL
Film Cast
Rodgers, Richard *C*
Hammerstein II, Oscar *L*
Carousel waltz / You're a queer one Julie Jordan / Mr. Snow / If I loved you / When the children are asleep / June is bustin' out all over / Soliloquy / Blow high, blow low / Real nice clambake / Stonecutters cut it on stone / What's the use of wonderin' / You'll never walk alone
CD **ZDM 7646922**
EMI Classics / Apr '93 / EMI

CAROUSEL
1993 London Cast
Rodgers, Richard *C*
Hammerstein II, Oscar *L*
Prologue / Mister Snow / If I loved you / June is bustin' out all over / Mister Snow (reprise) / When the children are asleep / Blow high, blow low / Soliloquy / Real nice clambake / Geraniums in the winder / Stonecutters cut it on stone / What's the use of wond'rin' / You'll never walk alone / Ballet / If I loved you (reprise) / You'll never walk alone (reprise)
CD **OCRCD 6042**
First Night / Apr '96 / Pinnacle

CAROUSEL
1945 Broadway Cast
Rodgers, Richard *C*
Hammerstein II, Oscar *L*
Carousel waltz / You're a queer one Julie Jordan / Mr. Snow / If I loved you / Soliloquy / June is bustin' out all over / When the children are asleep / Blow high, blow low / Real nice clambake / There's nothin' so bad for a woman / What's the use of wonderin' / Highest judge of all / You'll never walk alone
CD **MCLD 19152**
MCA / Jul '92 / BMG

CAROUSEL (Highlights - The Shows Collection)
Cast Recording
Rodgers, Richard *C*
Hammerstein II, Oscar *L*
If I loved you / You're a queer one Julie Jordan / Mr. Snow / June is bustin' out all over / Soliloquy / Blow high, blow low / When the children are asleep / Real nice clambake / Stonecutters cut it on stone / What's the use of wonderin' / Highest judge of all / You'll never walk alone
CD **PWKS 4144**
Carlton / Oct '93 / Carlton

CARRIE/DRESSED TO KILL/BODY DOUBLE
Donaggio, Pino *C*
CD **CDCH 384**
Milan / Mar '90 / Conifer/BMG / Silva Screen

CARRINGTON
Nyman, Michael Band
Nyman, Michael *C*
Nyman, Michael *Con*
CD **4448732**
Argo / Sep '95 / PolyGram

CARTOUCHE
Delerue, Georges *C*
CD **PCD 104**
Prometheus / Feb '90 / Silva Screen

CASINO
Contempt/Theme de Camille: *Delerue, Georges* / Angelina zooma zooma medley: *Prima, Louis* / Hoochie coochie man: *Waters, Muddy* / I'll take you there: *Staple Singers* / Nights in white satin: *Moody Blues* / How high the moon: *Paul, Les & Mary Ford* / Hurt: *Yuro, Timi* / Ain't got no home: *Henry, Clarence 'Frogman'* / Without you: *Nilsson, Harry* / Love is the drug: *Roxy Music* / I'm sorry: *Lee, Brenda* / Go your own way: *Fleetwood Mac* / Thrill is gone: *King, B.B.* / Love is strange: *Mickey & Sylvia* / In crowd: *Lewis, Ramsey* / Stardust: *Carmichael, Hoagy* / Fa fa fa fa fa (Sad song): *Redding, Otis* / I ain't superstitious: *Beck, Jeff/Rod Stewart* / Glory of love: *Velvetones* / Satisfaction: *Devo* / What a difference a day makes: *Washington, Dinah* / Working in a coalmine: *Dorsey, Lee* / House of the rising sun: *Burdon, Eric* / Those were the days: *Cream* / Who can I turn to (When nobody needs me): *Bennett, Tony* / Slippin' and slidin': *Little Richard* / You're nobody till somebody loves you: *Martin, Dean* / Compared to what: *McCann, Les & Eddie Harris* / Basin Street blues: *Prima, Louis* / When it's sleepy time down South: *Prima, Louis* / Matthaus passion: *Chicago Symphony Orchestra/Sir George Solti*
2CD **MCD 11389**
MCA / Feb '96 / BMG

CASINO ROYALE
Bacharach, Burt *C*
Casino Royale theme: *Alpert, Herb* / Money penny goes for broke / Home James and don't spare the horses / Look of love / Little French boy / Venerable Sir James Bond / Big cowboys and indians / Le chiffre's torture of ... / Sir James' trip to find ... / Hi there Miss Good Thighs / Flying saucer / Dream on James
CD **VSD 5265**
Varese Sarabande / Nov '90 / Pinnacle

CASOBLANCO
Goldsmith, Jerry *C*
CD **PCD 127**
Prometheus / Jan '94 / Silva Screen

CASPER (Score)
Horner, James *C*
Horner, James *Con*
No sign of ghosts / Carrigan & Dibs / Strangers in the house / First haunting / Swordfight / March of the exorcists / Lighthouse / Casper makes breakfast / Fond memories / Dying to be a ghost / Casper's lullaby / Descent to Lazarus / One last wish / Remember me this way / Casper the friendly ghost / Uncle's swing / End credits
CD **MCD 11240**
MCA / Jul '95 / BMG

CASPER
Casper / Daddy never understood / Nothing gonna stop / Jenny's theme / Simean groove / Casper the friendly ghost / Natural one / Spoiled / Crash / Wet stuff / Mad fright night / Raise the bell / Good morning Captain
CD **8286402**
London / Sep '95 / PolyGram

CASSANDRA CROSSING
Goldsmith, Jerry *C*
CD **OST 102**
Milano Dischi / Jan '93 / Silva Screen

CASTLE FREAK
Band, Richard *C*
Band, Richard *Con*
CD **MAF 7065**
Intrada / Feb '96 / Koch / Silva Screen

CAT PEOPLE
Moroder, Giorgio *C*
Cat people (putting out fires): *Bowie, David & Giorgio Moroder* / Autopsy / Irena's theme / Night rabbit / Leopard tree dream / Paul's theme / Myth / To the bridge / Transformation seduction / Bring the prod
CD **MCLD 19302**
MCA / Oct '95 / BMG

CATHERINE WHEEL (Complete Score)
Byrne, David
Byrne, David *C*

CD 7599274182
Sire / May '89 / Warner Music

CATS
1981 London Cast
Lloyd Webber, Andrew *C*
Eliot, T.S./Trevor Nunn/Richard Stilgoe *L*
Jellicle songs for jellicle cats / Old gumbie cat / Naming of cats / Rum rum tugger / Grizabella / Bustopher Jones / Memory / Mungojerrie and Rumpleteazer / Old Deuteronomy / Moments of happiness / Gus the theatre cat / Overture/Prologue / Invitation to the Jellicle ball / Jellicle ball / Journey to the heavy side / Ad - dressing of cats / Growltiger's last stand / Ballad of Billy McCaw's Skimbleshanks / Macavity / Mr. Mistoffelees
2CD 8178102
Really Useful / Jun '84 / PolyGram

CATS (Highlights)
1981 London Cast
Lloyd Webber, Andrew *C*
Eliot, T.S./Trevor Nunn/Richard Stilgoe *L*
Prologue: Jellicle songs for jellicle cats / Solo dance / Old gumbie cat / Rum tum tugger / Mungojerrie and rumpelteazer / Old deuteronomy / Jellicle ball / Grizabella the glamour cat / Gus the theatre cat / Shimbleshanks: The railway cat / Macavity / Mr. Mistoffelees / Memory / Journey to the heaviside layer / Ad - dressing of cats
CD 8394152
Really Useful / Aug '88 / PolyGram

CATS
Studio Cast
Lloyd Webber, Andrew *C*
Prologues jellide songs / Old gumble cat / Rum tum tugger / Mungojenfe and rumpileteazer / Old deuteronomy / Gulumberella the glamour cat / Gus the theatre cat / Sidmblesshanks the railway cat / Macavity the mystery cat / Mr Mistofeelees / Memory / Journey to the heavislide layer / Ad dressing of the cats
CD 88012
CMC / May '97 / BMG

CAUGHT
Botti, Chris
Botti, Chris *C*
CD 5330952
Verve / Nov '96 / PolyGram

CB4
Thirteenth message: *Public Enemy* / Livin' in a zoo: *Public Enemy* / Black cop: *Boogie Down Productions* / May Day on the front line: *M.C. Ren* / Stick em up: *Hurricane & Beastie Boys* / Lifeline: *Parental Advisory* / Nocturnal is in the house: *P.M. Dawn* / Baby be mine: *Blackstreet & Teddy Riley* / It's alright: *Spencer, Tracie* / Straight out of Locash: *CB4* / Rapper's delight: *CB4* / Sweat of my balls: *CB4* / Creepin' up on ya: *Fu-Schnickens*
CD MCD 10758
MCA / Apr '93 / BMG

CEMETERY CLUB, THE
Bernstein, Elmer *C*
CD VSD 5412
Varese Sarabande / Mar '93 / Pinnacle

CHAIN REACTION
Goldsmith, Jerry *C*
CD VSD 5746
Varese Sarabande / Sep '96 / Pinnacle

CHALLENGE, THE
London Cast
2CD CDTER 1201
TER / Aug '93 / Koch

CHAMANKA
Korzynski, Andrzej *C*
CD SMC 35707
Sergent M / Jun '97 / Discovery

CHAMBER
Burwell, Carter *C*
CD VSD 5758
Varese Sarabande / Nov '96 / Pinnacle

CHAPLIN
Barry, John *C*
Barry, John *Con*
Main theme / Early days in London/Honeysuckle and the Bee / Charlie proposes / To California/The cutting room / Discovering the tramp/The wedding chase / Chaplin's studio opening / Salt Lake City episode / Roll dance / News of Hetty's death / Smile / From London to LA / John Barry trouble/ Oona arrives / Remembering Hetty / Roll dance (reprise)
CD 4726022
Epic / Dec '96 / Sony

CHARADE
Mancini, Henry *C*
CD 27552
Silva Screen / Jan '89 / Koch / Silva Screen

CHARIOTS OF FIRE
Vangelis
Vangelis *C*
Titles / Five circles / Abraham's theme / Eric's theme / 100 metres / Jerusalem / Chariots of fire
CD 8000202
Polydor / May '84 / PolyGram

CHARLIE CHALK
CD CDHARL 1
Redrock / Aug '89 / Target/BMG / THE

CHARLIE GIRL
1986 London Cast
Heneker, David & John Taylor *C*
McMillan, I. *Con*
Overture / Most ancestral home of all / Bells will ring / I love him, I love him / What would I get from being married / Let's do a deal / My favourite occupation / What's the magic / When I hear music I dance / I 'ates money / Charlie Girl waltz / Party of a lifetime / Like love / That's it / Washington / Fish and chips / Society twist / You never know what you can do / Finale
CD OCRCD 6009
First Night / Feb '96 / Pinnacle

CHARLIE GIRL
1965 London Cast
Heneker, David & John Taylor *C*
Alwyn, Kenneth *Con*
CD SMK 66174
Sony West End / Nov '92 / Sony

CHARLOTTE SWEET
Cast Recording
At the music hall / Forever / Liverpool sunset / Layers of underwaer / Quartet agonistes / Circus of voices / Keep it low / Bubbles in me bonnet / Vegetable Reggie / My baby and me / A-weaving / Your high note / Kantika / Darkness / You see me in a bobby / Christmas buche / Letter / Volley of indecision/Good things come / It could only happen in the theatre / Lonely canary / Queenly comments / Farewell to auld lang syne/Finale
CD DRGCD 6300
DRG / Jan '95 / Discovery / New Note/ Pinnacle

CHASE, THE
Barry, John *C*
CD VSD 5229
Varese Sarabande / Feb '90 / Pinnacle

CHEF
CD RES 118CD
Resurgence / Nov '96 / Pinnacle

CHESS
1984 London Cast
Ulvaeus, Bjorn & Benny Andersson *C*
Rice, Tim *L*
Merano / Russian and Molokov / Where I want to be / Opening ceremony / Quartet / American and Florence / Nobody's side / Chess / Mountain duet / Florence quits / Embassy lament / Anthem / Bangkok / One night in Bangkok / Heaven help my heart / Argument / I know him so well / Deal (no deal) / Pity the child / Endgame / Epilogue - You and I / Story of Chess
CD 8474452
Polydor / Feb '96 / PolyGram

CHESS
CC Productions
Ulvaeus, Bjorn & Benny Andersson *C*
Rice, Tim *L*
Merano / Arbiter / Nobody's side / Chess / Embassy lament / Anthem / One night in Bangkok / Heaven help my heart / I know him so well / Pity the child / You and I / Story of chess
CD QED 210
Tring / Nov '96 / Tring

CHESS
Studio Cast
Ulvaeus, Bjorn & Benny Andersson *C*
Rice, Tim *L*
Merano / Arbiter / Nobody's side / Chess / Embassy lament / Anthem / One night in Bangkok / Heaven help my heart / I know him so well / Pity the child / You and I / Story of chess
CD 85062
CMC / May '97 / BMG

CHEYENNE AUTUMN
North, Alex *C*
Indians arrive / Friend Deborah / School house / Archer / Rejection / truth / Entr'acte / River crossing / Sick girl / Battle / Dodge city / Old chief / Lead our people home / Death
CD LXCD 2
Label X / Jun '88 / Silva Screen

CHILDREN OF A LESSER GOD
Convertino, Michael *C*
Silence and sound / Sarah sleeping / Rain pool / Underwater love / On the ferry / James and Sarah / Goodnight / Boomerang
CD GNPD 8007
GNP Crescendo / Jan '89 / ZYX

CHILDREN OF EDEN
Cast Recording
Schwartz, Stephen *C*
Let there be: *Page, Ken & Company* / Naming: *Smith, Martin & Shezwae Powell* / Spark of creation: *Powell, Shezwae* / In pursuit of excellence: *Lloyd King, Richard & Snake* / World without you: *Smith, Martin* / Wasteland / Lost in the wilderness / Close to home / Children of Eden: *Powell, Shezwae & Company* / Generations: *Shell, Ray & Company* / Civilised society: *Colson, Kevin & Company* / Shipshape / Return of the animals / Stranger to the rain: *Ruffelle, Frances* / In whatever time we have: *Barclay, Anthony & Frances Ruffelle* / Degenerations: *Page, Ken* / Dove song: *Ruffelle, Frances* / Hardest part of love: *Colson, Kevin* / Ain't it good: *Dubois, Jacqui & Company* / In the beginning

CD 8282342
London / Apr '91 / PolyGram

CHILDREN OF NATURE
Hilmarsson, Hilmar Orn
Hilmarsson, Hilmar Orn *C*
CD T 33.14
Touch / Oct '95 / Kudos / Pinnacle

CHILDREN'S THIEF, THE/ON MY OWN
Piersanti, Franco *C*
CD OST 117
Milano Dischi / Jul '93 / Silva Screen

CHILD'S PLAY
Renzetti, Joe *C*
CD CDCH 382
Milan / Feb '90 / Conifer/BMG / Silva Screen

CHILLER
Cincinnati Pops Orchestra
Kunzel, Erich *C*
CD CD 80189
Telarc / Aug '90 / Conifer/BMG

CHINA 9 LIBERTY 37
Donaggio, Pino *C*
CD PCD 117
Prometheus / Jan '93 / Silva Screen

CHINATOWN
Goldsmith, Jerry *C*
Goldsmith, Jerry/U. Rasey *Con*
CD VSD 5677
Varese Sarabande / Feb '96 / Pinnacle

CHRISTINE (Score)
Carpenter, John *C*
Arnie's love theme / Obsessed with the car / Football run / Kill your kids / Rape / Discovery / Show me / Moochie's death / Junkins / Buddie's death / Nobody's home / Restored / Car obsession reprise / Christine attacks (Plymouth fury) / Talk on the couch / Regeneration / Darnell's tonight / Undented / Moochie mix four
CD VSD 5240
Varese Sarabande / Jan '90 / Pinnacle

CHRISTOPHER COLUMBUS (The Discovery)
Eidelman, Cliff *C*
CD VSD 5389
Varese Sarabande / Sep '92 / Pinnacle

CHU CHIN CHOW
1959 London Cast
Norton, Frederic *C*
Asche, Oscar *L*
Prelude: *Orchestra* / Here be oysters stewed in honey: *Te Wiata, Inia* / I am Chu Chin Chow: *Te Wiata, Inia* / Cleopatra's Nile: *Bryan, Julie* / When a pullet is plump: *Te Wiata, Inia* / Serenade / Mahbubah: *Chorus* / I'll sing and dance / I long for the sun: *Leigh, Barbara* / Robber's chorus: *Te Wiata, Inia* / I love thee so: *Bryan, Julie* / Behold: *Te Wiata, Inia* / Anytime's kissing time: *Bryan, Julie & Inia Te Wiata* / Cobbler's song: *Te Wiata, Inia* / I built a fairy palace in the sky: *Connors, Ursula* / We bring ye fruits: *Williams Singers* / Finale: *Chorus*
CD CDANGEL 5
Angel / Apr '94 / EMI

CHULAS FRONTERAS/DEL MERO CORAZON
CD ARHCD 425
Arhoolie / Sep '95 / ADA / Cadillac / Direct

CINDERELLA
Broadway Cast
Rodgers, Richard *C*
Hart, Lorenz *L*
Green, John *Con*
CD SK 53538
Sony Broadway / Dec '91 / Sony

CINEMA PARADISO
Morricone, Ennio *C*
Cinema Paradiso / Maturity / While thinking about her again / Childhood & manhood / Cinema on fire / Love theme / After the destruction / First youth / Love theme for Nata / Visit to the cinema / Four interludes / Runaway, search & return / Projection for two / From American sex appeal to the first Fellini / Toto & Alfredo / For Elena
CD DRGCD 12598
DRG / Jul '93 / Discovery / New Note/ Pinnacle

CINERAMA SOUTH SEAS ADVENTURE
North, Alex *C*
North, Alex *Con*
CD LXCD 4
Label X / Jan '92 / Silva Screen

CIRCLE OF FRIENDS
You're the one / Ireland 1949 / Cottage (Sonatina) / Dublin / Knock Glen / Bo Weevil / Sean / Benny & Jack / Fathers death / Love is a many splendored thing / You're the one
CD 0630109572
East West / Jun '95 / Warner Music

CITIZEN X
Edelman, Randy *C*
CD VSD 5601
Varese Sarabande / Mar '95 / Pinnacle

CITY HALL
Goldsmith, Jerry *C*
Goldsmith, Jerry *Con*
CD VSD 5699
Varese Sarabande / Mar '96 / Pinnacle

CITY LIGHTS
City Lights Orchestra
Chaplin, Charlie *C*
Davis, Carl *Con*
Overture/Unveiling the statue / Flower girl (Violetera) / Evening/Meeting the millionaire / At the millionaire's home / Nightclub / Limousine / Sober dawn / Party and the morning after / Eviction/The road sweeper/At the girl's home / Boxing match / Burglars / Reunited
CD FILMCD 078
Silva Screen / Jan '93 / Koch / Silva Screen

CITY OF ANGELS
1993 London Cast
Coleman, Cy *C*
Zippel, David *L*
Blakemore, M. *Con*
Prelude / Double talk / What you don't know about women / Ya gotta look after yourself / Buddy system / With every breath I take / Tennis song / Everybody's gotta be somewhere / Lost and found / All ya have to do is wait / You're nothing without me / Stay with me / You can always count on me / It needs work / With every breath I take (Reprise) / Funny
CD OCRCD 6034
First Night / Mar '96 / Pinnacle

CITY OF INDUSTRY
Three: *Massive Attack* / Last night: *Lush* / Overcome: *Tricky* / Bug powder dust: *Bomb The Bass & Justin Warfield* / Rocco: *Death In Vegas* / Walking through water: *Palmskin Productions* / Call a cab: *Lionrock* / Degobrah: *Butter 08* / Hidden camera: *Photek* / Mr. Jones: *Red*
CD 5243082
Quango / Jul '97 / PolyGram

CITY OF JOY
Morricone, Ennio *C*
CD ACCD 1025
Audiorec / Nov '92 / Audiorec

CITY OF VIOLENCE (CITTA VIOLENTA) (& Svegliati E Uccidi)
Morricone, Ennio *C*
CD OST 127
Milano Dischi / May '95 / Silva Screen

CITY SLICKERS
Shaiman, Marc *C*
CD VSD 5321
Varese Sarabande / Sep '91 / Pinnacle

CIVIL WAR, THE
Burns, Ken *C*
Drums of war / Oliver Wendell Holmes / Ashokan farewell / Battle cry of freedom / We are climbing Jacob's ladder / Dixie / Bonnie blue flag / Cheer boys cheer / Angel band / Johnny has gone for a soldier / Lorena / Parade / Hail Columbia / Kingdom coming / Battle hymn of the republic / All quiet on the Potomac / Yankee doodle / Palmyra Schottische / When Johnny comes marching home / Shenandoah / Marching through Georgia / Sullivan Ballou letter
CD 7559792562
Nonesuch / Mar '91 / Warner Music

CLEAR AND PRESENT DANGER
Horner, James *C*
Horner, James *Con*
Main title / Clear and present danger / Operation reciprocity / Ambush / Laser guided missile / Looking for clues / Deleting the evidence / Greer's funeral / Betrayal / Escobedo's new friend / Second hand copter / Truth needs a soldier / End title
CD 224012
Milan / Sep '94 / Conifer/BMG / Silva Screen

CLEOPATRA
North, Alex *C*
CD TSU 1111
Tsunami / Jan '95 / Silva Screen

CLERKS
Clerks: *Love Among Freaks* / Kill the sexplayer: *Girls Against Boys* / Got me wrong: *Alice In Chains* / Making me sick: *Bash & Pop* / Chewbacca: *Super Nova* / Panic in Cicero: *Jesus Lizard* / Shooting star: *Golden Smog* / Leaders and followers: *Bad Religion* / Violent moodswings: *Stabbing Westward* / Berserker: *Love Among Freaks* / Big problems: *Corrosion Of Conformity* / Go your own way: *Seaweed* / Can't even tell: *Soul Asylum*
CD 4778022
Columbia / Dec '96 / Sony

CLIFFHANGER
London Philharmonic Orchestra
Jones, Trevor *C*
Snell, David *Con*
Cliffhanger theme / Sarah's farewell / Sarah falls / Gabe returns / I understand / Sunset searching / Tolerated help / Base jump / Bats / Two man job / Kynette is impaled / Fireside chat / Frank's demise / Rabbit hole / Icy stream / Jessie's release / Helicopter flight / End credits
CD 5144552
Polydor / Jun '94 / PolyGram

CLOCKWORK ORANGE, A
Carlos, Walter/Rossini/Beethoven/Elgar/ Rimsky-Korsakov *C*
Clockwork orange / Thieving magpie (La gazza ladra) / Symphony no. 9 / March: Clockwork Orange / William Tell / Pomp and circumstance / Timesteps (excerpt) / Over-

ture to the sun / I want to marry a lighthouse keeper / Suicide Scherzo / Singin' In The Rain: *Astaire, Fred*
CD K2 46127
WEA / Oct '93 / Warner Music

CLOSE ENCOUNTERS OF THE THIRD KIND
National Philharmonic Orchestra
Williams, John *C*
Close Encounters of the Third Kind / Nocturnal pursuit / Abduction of Barry / I can't believe it's real / Climbing devil's tower / Arrival of sky harbour
CD CDA 8915
Tsunami / Jan '95 / Silva Screen

CLUELESS
Kids in America: *Muffs* / Shake some action: *Cracker* / Ghost in you: *Counting Crows* / Here: *Luscious Jackson* / All the young dudes: *World Party* / Fake plastic trees: *Radiohead* / Change: *Lightning Seeds* / Need you around: *Smoking Popes* / Mullet head: *Beastie Boys* / Where'd you go: *Mighty Mighty Bosstones* / Rollin' with my homies: *Coolio* / Alright: *Supergrass* / My Forgotten favourite: *Velocity Girl* / Supermodel: *Sobule, Jill*
CD CDEST 2267
Capitol / Sep '95 / EMI

COBB
Goldenthal, Elliot *C*
CD SK 66923
Sony Classical / Jan '95 / Sony

COBRA VERDE
Popul Vuh
Popul Vuh *C*
Der tod des Cobra Verde / Nachts, schnee / Der marktplatz / Eine andere welt / Grab der mutter / Die singenden madchen von ho, ziavi / Sieh nicht uberm meer ist's / Ha-'mut bis dass die nacht mit ruh
CD CH 353
Milan / Feb '88 / Conifer/BMG / Silva Screen

COCKTAIL
Wild again: *Starship* / Powerful stuff: *Fabulous Thunderbirds* / Since when: *Nevil, Robbie* / Don't worry be happy: *McFerrin, Bobby* / Hippy hippy shake: *Georgia Satellites* / Kokomo: *Beach Boys* / Rave on: *Mellencamp, John* / All shook up: *Cooder, Ry* / Oh, I love you so: *Smith, Preston* / Tutti frutti: *Little Richard*
CD 9608062
Elektra / Oct '88 / Warner Music

COCOON: THE RETURN
Horner, James *C*
CD VSD 5211
Varese Sarabande / Feb '90 / Pinnacle

COLD FEET
Bahler, Tom *C*
Afternoon roundup / Shoot the doc / Just remember / Watch my lips / Cowboy reggae / Monty shows off infidel / Maureen and Kenny on the road / Survival camp / Infidel's and inspiration / Isometrics / Monty stole the horse / It's a sham/ Workin' man / Sheriff's a preacher / Lizard boots, size 100 / Good morning / Maureen's monologue / Sceered fitless / Monty hides infidel / Have a Turkish fig / Chasin' Monty / Kenny's in the vat / Happy now and forever
CD VSD 5231
Varese Sarabande / Feb '90 / Pinnacle

COLD ROOM, THE
Nyman, Michael *C*
CD FILMCD 157
Silva Screen / Jan '95 / Koch / Silva Screen

COLLETTE COLLAGE
1993 Studio Cast
CD VSD 5473
Varese Sarabande / Jun '94 / Pinnacle

COLOURS OF BRAZIL
CD 233872
Milan / Mar '95 / Conifer/BMG / Silva Screen

COLUMBUS & THE AGE OF DISCOVERY
Mirowitz, Sheldon *C*
Overture / Idea takes shape / Crossing / Worlds found / Worlds lost / In search of Columbus
CD CD 6002
Narada / Jun '92 / ADA / New Note/ Pinnacle

COMA
Goldsmith, Jerry *C*
CD BCD 3027
Bay Cities / Mar '92 / Silva Screen

COME AND SEE THE PARADISE
Edelman, Randy *C*
CD CH 614
Milan / Jan '95 / Conifer/BMG / Silva Screen

COMMANCHEROS/TRUE GRIT
Bernstein, Elmer *C*
CD VCD 47236
Varese Sarabande / Jan '89 / Pinnacle

COMMITMENTS VOL.1, THE
Mustang Sally / Take me to the river / Chain of fools / Dark end of the street / Destination anywhere / I can't stand the rain / Try a little tenderness / Treat her right / Do right woman do right man / Mr. Pitiful / I never loved a man / In the midnight hour / Bye bye baby / Slip away
CD MCAD 10286
MCA / Aug '91 / BMG

COMMITMENTS VOL.2, THE
Hard to handle / Grits ain't groceries / I thank you / That's the way love is / Show me / Saved / Too many fish in the sea / Fa fa fa fa fa (sad song) / Land of the 1000 dances / Nowhere to run / Bring it on home to me
CD MCLD 19312
MCA / Oct '95 / BMG

COMPANY
1972 London Cast
Sondheim, Stephen *C*
Hastings, Harold *Con*
CD SMK 53496
Sony West End / Nov '93 / Sony

COMPANY (In Jazz)
Trotter Trio
Sondheim, Stephen *C*
CD VSD 5673
Varese Sarabande / Nov '95 / Pinnacle

COMPANY
London Cast
Sondheim, Stephen *C*
Valentine, G. *Con*
CD CASTCD 57
First Night / Apr '96 / Pinnacle

COMPANY
1995 Broadway Cast
Sondheim, Stephen *C*
Overture / Company / Little things you do together / Sorry, grateful / You could drive a person crazy / Company (reprise 1) / Have I got a girl for you / Someone is waiting / Another hundred people / Getting married today / Marry me a little / Bobby baby / Side by side by side / What would we do without you / Poor baby / Tick tock / Barcelona / Ladies who lunch / Company (reprise 2) / Being alive / Bows
CD PRMFCD 2
Premier/EMI / Apr '96 / EMI

COMPANY BUSINESS
Kamen, Michael *C*
CD A 8931
Alhambra / Mar '92 / Silva Screen

COMPANY OF WOLVES, THE
Fenton, George
Fenton, George *C*
Message and main theme / Rosaleen's first dream / Story of the bride and groom / Forest and the huntsman's theme / Wedding party / Boy and the devil / One Sunday afternoon / All the better to eat you with / Wolfgirl / Liberation
CD CDTER 1094
TER / '90 / Koch

CON AIR
Rabin, Trevor *C*
CD 162099
Hollywood / Jul '97 / Greyhound

CONAN THE BARBARIAN
Poledouris, Basil *C*
Anvil of crom / Riddle of steel - riders of doom / Gift of fury / Wheel of pain / Atlantean sword / Theology civilization wifeing / Search / Orgy / Funeral pyre / Battle of the mounds / Orphans of doom / Awakening
CD 111262
Milan / Feb '94 / Conifer/BMG / Silva Screen

CONAN THE BARBARIAN (American Score)
Poledouris, Basil *C*
CD VSD 5390
Varese Sarabande / Jan '93 / Pinnacle

CONEHEADS
Magic carpet ride: *Slash* / Tainted love: *Soft Cell* / No more tears (enough is enough): *Lang, k.d. & Andy Bell* / Kodachrome: *Simon, Paul* / Can't take my eyes off you: *Harket, Morten* / It's a free world baby: *REM* / Soul to squeeze: *Red Hot Chili Peppers* / Fight the power: *Barenaked Ladies* / Little Renee: *Digable Planets* / Chale jao: *Babble* / Conehead love: *Beldar*
CD 9362453452
Warner Bros. / Jul '93 / Warner Music

CONFESSIONAL, THE
CD PPCD 001
Pollyanna / Aug '96 / Grapevine/PolyGram / Pinnacle

CONFESSIONS OF A POLICE CAPTAIN/ IN THE GRIP OF THE SPIDER
Ortolani, Riz *C*
CD OST 114
Milano Dischi / Jul '93 / Silva Screen

CONNECTION, THE
Redd, Freddie/Howard McGhee/Tina Brooks/Milt Hinton
Redd, Freddie *C*
Who killed cock robin / Music forever / Wigglin' / OD / Jim Dunn's dilemma / Time to smile / Sister salvation
CD CDBOP 019
Boplicity / Jul '95 / Pinnacle

CONSENTING ADULTS
Small, Michael *C*
CD 124792
Milan / Jan '95 / Conifer/BMG / Silva Screen

COOK, THE THIEF, HIS WIFE AND HER LOVER, THE
Nyman, Michael Band
Nyman, Michael *C*
Nyman, Michael *Con*
Memorial / Misere paraphase: *Nyman, Michael & Alexander Balanescu* / Miserere: *London Voices* / Coupling / Book depository
CD CDVE 53
Virgin / May '90 / EMI

COOL RUNNINGS
Wild wild life: *Wailing Souls* / I can see clearly now: *Cliff, Jimmy* / Stir it up: *King, Diana* / Cool me down: *Tiger* / Picky picky head: *Wailing Souls* / Jamaican bobsledding chant: *Worl-A-Girl* / Sweet Jamaica: *Tony Rebel* / Dolly my baby: *Super Cat* / Love you want: *Wailing Souls* / Countrylypso: *Zimmer, Hans* / Walk home: *Zimmer, Hans*
CD 4748402
Columbia / Dec '96 / Sony

COOL WORLD, THE (& Dizzy Goes Hollywood)
Gillespie, Dizzy
Gillespie, Dizzy *C*
CD 5312302
Verve / Jul '96 / PolyGram

COOLEY HIGH
CD 5515472
Spectrum / Aug '93 / PolyGram

COPACABANA
1994 London Cast
Manilow, Barry *C*
Overture / Copacabana (opening sequence) / Just arrived / Dancin' fool / Night on the town / Man wanted / Lola / Who needs to dream / Ay caramba / Balero de amor / Sweet heaven / Who am I kidding / This can't be real / Welcome to Havana / Mermaids tale / Bravo / Who needs to dream (reprise) / Copacabana (finale)
CD OCRCD 6047
First Night / Apr '97 / Pinnacle

COPYCAT
Young, Christopher *C*
Anthony, Pete *Con*
CD 74321337422
Milan / Mar '96 / Conifer/BMG / Silva Screen

CORNBREAD, EARL AND ME
Blackbyrds
Cornbread / One eye two step / Mother Son theme / Heavy town / One gun salute / Gym fight / Riot / Soulful source / Mother Son talk / At the carnival / Candy store dilemna / Wilford's gone / Mother Son bedroom talk / Courtroom emotions / Cornbread
CD CDBGPM 094
Beat Goes Public / May '95 / Pinnacle

COSI COME SEI (Stay The Way You Are)
Morricone, Ennio *C*
CD PCD 115
Prometheus / Mar '92 / Silva Screen

COUNT DRACULA (Il Conte Dracula)
Nicolai, Bruno *C*
CD PAN 2502
Silva Screen / May '95 / Koch / Silva Screen

COUNT OF LUXEMBOURG, THE
New Sadler's Wells Opera Chorus/ Orchestra
Lehar, Franz *C*
Maschwitz, Eric *L*
CD CDTER 1050
TER / May '89 / Koch

COUNT OF LUXEMBOURG, THE (Highlights)
New Sadler's Wells Opera Chorus/ Orchestra
Lehar, Franz *C*
Maschwitz, Eric *L*
CD CDTEO 1004
TER / May '89 / Koch

COUNT OF MONTE CRISTO, THE/THE MAN IN THE IRON MASK
London Studio Symphony Orchestra
Ferguson, Allyn *C*
Ferguson, Allyn *Con*
CD PCD 130
Prometheus / Oct '94 / Silva Screen

COUNTESS MARITZA
New Sadler's Wells Opera Chorus/ Orchestra
Kalman, Emmerich *C*
Douglas, Nigel *L*
CD CDTER 1051
TER / May '89 / Koch

COUNTESS MARITZA (Highlights)
New Sadler's Wells Opera Chorus/ Orchestra
Kalman, Emmerich *C*
Douglas, Nigel *L*
CD CDTEO 1007
TER / May '89 / Koch

COUNTRYMAN
Natural mystic: *Marley, Bob* / Rastaman chant: *Marley, Bob* / Theme from Countryman: *Badarou, Wally* / Rat race: *Marley, Bob* / Jah live: *Marley, Bob* / Three o'clock roadblock: *Marley, Bob* / Ramble: *Rico* / Sound system: *Steel Pulse* / Mosman skank: *Aswad* / Small axe: *Marley, Bob* / Sitting and watching: *Brown, Dennis*
CD RRCD 44
Reggae Refreshers / May '94 / PolyGram / Vital

COUSTEAU'S AMAZON VOL.1 (The River)
Scott, John *C*
Scott, John *Con*
CD JSCD 104
JOS / Jan '95 / JOS / Silva Screen

COUSTEAU'S AMAZON VOL.2 (The Indians)
Scott, John *C*
Scott, John *Con*
CD JSCD 105
JOS / Jan '95 / JOS / Silva Screen

COUSTEAU'S CAPE HORN & THE CHANNEL ISLANDS
Royal Philharmonic Orchestra/Berlin Radio Concert Orchestra
Scott, John *C*
Scott, John *Con*
CD JSCD 103
JOS / Jan '93 / JOS / Silva Screen

COUSTEAU'S FIRST 75 YEARS/THE WARM BLOODED SEA
Scott, John *C*
Scott, John *Con*
CD JSCD 108
JOS / Jan '95 / JOS / Silva Screen

COUSTEAU'S PAPUA NEW GUINEA JOURNEY
Scott, John *C*
Scott, John *Con*
CD JSCD 112
JOS / Jan '93 / JOS / Silva Screen

COUSTEAU'S PARC OCEANIQUE
Purbrook, Colin & Royal Philharmonic Orchestra
Scott, John *C*
Scott, John *Con*
CD JSCD 106
JOS / Jan '95 / JOS / Silva Screen

COUSTEAU'S ST. LAWRENCE/ AUSTRALIA
Scott, John *C*
Scott, John *Con*
CD JSCD 107
JOS / Jan '95 / JOS / Silva Screen

COWBOYS, THE
Williams, John *C*
Williams, John *Con*
CD VSD 5540
Varese Sarabande / Jul '95 / Pinnacle

COWGIRLS
Cast Recording
Murfitt, Mary *C*
Murfitt, Mary *L*
CD VSD 5740
Varese Sarabande / Oct '96 / Pinnacle

CRADLE WILL ROCK, THE
1985 London Cast
Blitzstein, Marc *C*
Moll's song / I'll show you guys / Solicitin' / Hard times/The sermon / Croon spoon / Freedom of the press / Let's do something / Honolulu / Summer weather / Love duet (Gus and Sadie) / Don't let me keep you / Ask us again / Art for art's sake / Nickel under your foot / Cradle will rock / Joe worker / Cradle will rock (Final scene)
CD CDTER 1105
TER / Oct '85 / Koch

CRAFT, THE (Score)
Revell, Graeme *C*
Simonec, T. *Con*
CD VSD 5732
Varese Sarabande / Jul '96 / Pinnacle

CRAFT, THE
Tomorrow never knows: *Our Lady Peace* / I have the touch: *Nova, Heather* / All this and nothing: *Sponge* / Dangerous type: *Letters To Cleo* / How soon is now: *Love Spit Love* / Dark secret: *Sweet, Matthew* / Witches song: *Hatfield, Juliana* / Jump into the fire: *Tripping Daisy* / Under the water: *Jewel* / Warning: *All Too Much* / Spastica: *Elastica* / Horror: *Spacehog* / Bells, books and candles: *Revell, Graeme*
CD 4841522
Columbia / Nov '96 / Sony

CRASH AND BURN
Band, Richard
Band, Richard *C*
CD MAF 7033D
Intrada / Nov '92 / Koch / Silva Screen

CRAZY FOR YOU
1993 London Cast
Gershwin, George *C*
Gershwin, Ira *L*
CD CASTCD 37
First Night / Oct '93 / Pinnacle

CRAZY FOR YOU
Broadway Cast
Gershwin, George *C*
Gershwin, Ira *L*
CD CDC 7546182
EMI Classics / Apr '93 / EMI

CRIMES OF PASSION
Wakeman, Rick
Wakeman, Rick *C*
CD RWCDP 3
President / Nov '93 / Grapevine/PolyGram / President / Target/BMG

CD CIN 22022
Silva Screen / Mar '95 / Koch / Silva Screen

CRIMETIME
Stewart, David A.
Stewart, David A. *C*
CD POLLYPREM 002
Pollyanna / Dec '96 / Grapevine/PolyGram / Pinnacle

CRIMINAL LAW
Goldsmith, Jerry *C*
CD VSD 5210
Varese Sarabande / Dec '88 / Pinnacle

CRISS CROSS
Jones, Trevor *C*
CD MAF 7021D
Intrada / Sep '92 / Koch / Silva Screen

CRITTERS II (The Main Course)
Pike, Nicholas *C*
CD MAF 7045D
Intrada / Jul '93 / Koch / Silva Screen

CROCODILE DUNDEE
Best, Peter
Best, Peter *C*
Mick and his mate / Cyril / Walkabout bounce / Goodnight Walter / In the truck / Buffalo / In the boat / Never never land / Death roll / Sunset / Nice one Skippy / Walk in the bush / Would you mind / Mick meets New York / G'day / Yessir / Mad, bad and dangerous / Pimp / Stone the crows / That's not a knife / Oh Richard / Pimp returns / Crocodile Dundee
CD FILMCD 009
Silva Screen / Dec '86 / Koch / Silva Screen

CROCODILE SHOES I
Nail, Jimmy
Nail, Jimmy *C*
CD 4509985562
East West / Nov '94 / Warner Music

CROCODILE SHOES II
Nail, Jimmy
CD 0630169352
East West / Nov '96 / Warner Music

CROSS OVER USA
Bolling, Claude *C*
New York, New York / Way down yonder / Do you know what it means to miss New Orleans / Chicago / Georgia on my mind / Mississippi (old man river) / On the atchsion, topeka and the santa fe / Stars fell on Alabama / Moonlight in vermont / (Back home again in) Indiana
CD 14080-2
Milan / Jun '93 / Conifer/BMG / Silva Screen

CROSSING DELANCEY
Chihara, Paul *C*
CD VSD 5201
Varese Sarabande / Dec '88 / Pinnacle

CROSSROADS
Cooder, Ry *C*
See you in hell, blind boy / Nitty gritty Mississippi / He made a woman out of me / Feeling bad blues / Somebody's calling my name / Willie Brown blues / Walkin' away blues / Crossroads / Down in Mississippi / Cotton needs pickin' / Viola lee blues
CD 9253992
WEA / Oct '91 / Warner Music

CROW I, THE
Burn: *Cure* / Golgotha tenement blues: *Machines Of Loving Grace* / Big empty: *Stone Temple Pilots* / Dead souls: *Nine Inch Nails* / Darkness: *Rage Against The Machine* / Color me once: *Violent Femmes* / Ghost rider: *Rollins, Henry* / Milktoast: *Helmet* / Badge: *Pantera* / Slip slide melting: *For Love Not Lisa* / After the flesh: *My Life With The Thrill Kill Kult* / Snakedriver: *Jesus & Mary Chain* / Time baby II: *Medicine* / It can't rain all the time: *Siberry, Jane*
CD 7567825192
WEA / Mar '94 / Warner Music

CROW I, THE (Score)
Revell, Graeme *C*
Birth of the legend / Resurrection / Crow descends / Remembrance / Rain forever / Her eyes...so innocent / Tracking the prey / Pain & retribution / Believe in angels / Captive child / Devil's night / On hallowed ground / Inferno / Return to the grave / Last rites
CD VSD 5499
Varese Sarabande / Jun '94 / Pinnacle

CROW II, THE
CD 5331472
Polydor / Nov '96 / PolyGram

CROW III, THE
CD 1620472
Polydor / Jul '96 / PolyGram

CRUCIBLE, THE
Fenton, George
Fenton, George *C*
Salem 1692 / Witch-hunt begins / Accusation / Resolution
CD 09026686662
RCA Victor / Feb '97 / BMG

CRUMB
Boeddinghaus, David & Craig Ventresco *C*
Ragtime nightingale / Sensation rag / Harlem strut / Abraham Jefferson / Washington Lee / Belle of the Philippines / Last kind word blues / Radiator cap blues / Gabby glide medley / Frog-I-more Reg / Cocaine / Won't you fondle me medley / Pass the jug / Skinny leg blues / Buffalo rag / 35th Street blues / Mabel's dream / Wall Street rag / Hateful blues / Real slow drag / Comic montage stomp / Someday sweetheart / Rag pickings / Black diamond rag
CD RCD 10322
Rykodisc / Jul '95 / ADA / Vital

CRY BABY
King cry baby: *Intveld, James* / Doin' time: *Intveld, James* / Please, Mr. Jailer: *Sweet, Rachel* / Teardrops are falling: *Intveld, James* / Mr. Sandman: *Baldwin & The Whiffles* / Bad boy: *Jive Bombers* / I'm so young: *Students* / I'm a bad bad girl: *Phillips, Esther* / Cherry: *Jive Bombers* / Sh-boom: *Baldwin & The Whiffles* / Teenage prayer: *Sweet, Rachel* / Cry baby: *Honey Sisters* / Nosey Joe: *Jackson, Bull Moose* / High school hellcats: *Intveld, James* / Flirt: *Shirley & Lee* / My heart goes: *Brown, Nappy* / Jungle drums: *Bostic, Earl* / Rubber biscuit: *Chips*
CD MCLD 19260
MCA / Jun '94 / BMG

CRY IN THE DARK, A
Smeaton, Bruce *C*
CD SIL 15272
Silva Screen / Mar '93 / Koch / Silva Screen

CRYING GAME, THE
Crying game / Soldier's wife / Live for today (gospel) / It's in my nature / March to the execution / Let the music play / I'm thinking of your man / Dies irae / Live for today / White cliffs of Dover / Transformation / Live for today (orchestral) / Assassination / Crying game / Soldier's tale
CD 5170242
Polydor / Jan '93 / PolyGram

CURDLED
Cumbia del sol: *Blazers* / El talisman: *Rosana* / Obsession confession: *Slash* / El punal y Corazon: *Cafe Tacuba* / Cumbia de Surf: *Gonzalez, Joseph Julian* / Cumbia del Monte: *Laza, Pedro* / Lunas rotas: *Rosana* / Guajira de Gabriela: *Gonzalez, Joseph Julian* / Cumbia Colombiana: *La Intergracion* / Mambo de Muerte: *Gonzalez, Joseph Julian* / Ritmo de Tambo: *La Sonora Dinamita* / Danza macabra suite: *Gonzalez, Joseph Julian* / Te Llevare: *Zuloaga, Tulio* / Buscandote: *Latin Brothers* / Jardin de amor: *Los Destellos* / Obsession: *Slash & Marta Sanchez*
CD GED 25103
Geffen / Feb '97 / BMG

CURE, THE
Grusin, Dave
Grusin, Dave *C*
First visit / Battleship / Shopping cart ride / Soon as they find a cure / Candy montage / Gathering leaves / Bedtime/Big changes / Mississippi montage / Make mine a T-bone / Million light years / Found money / Chase and confrontation / Going home / We call it a miracle / Rain/Realization / Requiem / Last visit / Down the river/End credits
CD GRP 98282
GRP / Jun '95 / New Note/BMG

CUTTHROAT ISLAND
London Symphony Orchestra
Debney, John *C*
CD FILMCD 178
Silva Screen / Apr '96 / Koch / Silva Screen

CYBERCITY 808
CD DSCD 8
Demon / Jan '95 / Pinnacle

CYCLO
Tiet, Ton-That *C*
CD 74321301082
Milan / May '96 / Conifer/BMG / Silva Screen

CYRANO DE BERGERAC
Petit, Jean Claude *C*
CD ETKY 310CD
Enteleky / Apr '91 / Pinnacle

CYRANO DE BERGERAC
Petit, Jean Claude *C*
Cyrano / Chandeliers / Magic lantern / Duel / Gate of Nesle / Roxane / No thank you / Letters / Count's visit / Marriage / Lute / Affected young ladies / Cyrano's declaration / Mad man / File / Arrival of Roxane / Spaniard's mass / Death of Christian / Song of the nuns / Revelation / Death of Cyrano
CD DRGCD 12602
DRG / Jan '95 / Discovery / New Note/ Pinnacle

CYRANO DE BERGERAC
Paris Opera Orchestra
Petit, Jean Claude *C*
Petit, Jean Claude *Con*
Cyrano / Die leuchter / Die magische laterne / Das duell / Das tor von Nesle / Roxane / Nein danke / Die briefe / Der besuch des grafen / Die hochzeit / Die laute / Die damen der gesellschaft / Cyranos erklarung / Die verzweiflung / Der pfeifer / Roxanes ankunft / Die messe der spanier / Christians tod / Nonnengesang / Das gestandnis / Cyranos tod / Finale
CD CST 348046
Colosseum / Jul '90 / Pinnacle

DADDY NOSTALGIE
CD 4671342
Silva Screen / Jan '93 / Koch / Silva Screen

DALLE ARDENNE ALL'INTERNO
Morricone, Ennio *C*
CD SPALAX 14983
Spalax / Oct '96 / ADA / Cargo / Direct / Discovery / Greyhound

DAMAGE
Preisner, Zbigniew *C*
Introduction / Last time / Stephen / Anna / At the beginning / Cafe Royal / Anna II / Intimacy / Brussels - Paris / Lutecia hotel / Memories / In the country / Night / Dramatic departure / Late thought / Stephen II / Last time II / Fatal exit / Memories are made for this / Damage / End titles
CD VSD 5406
Varese Sarabande / Feb '93 / Pinnacle

DAMES AT SEA
1989 Touring Cast
Wise, Jim *C*
Haimsohn, George & Robin Miller *L*
Wall Street / It's you / Broadway baby / That mister man of mine / Choo choo honeymoon / Sailor of my dreams / Singapore Sue / Broadway baby (reprise) / Good times are here to stay / Entr'acte / Dames at sea / Beguine / Raining in my heart / There's something about you / Echo waltz / Star tar / Let's have a simple wedding / Dames at sea (overture)
CD CDTER 1169
TER / Jul '89 / Koch

DAMES AT SEA
1968 Broadway Cast
Wise, Jim *C*
Haimsohn, George & Robin Miller *L*
Leonard, Richard J. *Con*
CD SK 48214
Sony Broadway / Nov '92 / Sony

DAMNED, THE (Die Verdammten)
Jarre, Maurice *C*
Jarre, Maurice *Con*
CD CDA 8920
Tsunami / Jan '95 / Silva Screen

DAMNED, THE/A SEASON IN HELL/FOR THOSE I LOVED
Jarre, Maurice *C*
CD DRGCD 32906
DRG / Jul '95 / Discovery / New Note/ Pinnacle

D'AMORE SI MUORE/LE DUE STAGIONI DELLA VITA (For Love One Could Die/ The Two Seasons Of Life)
Morricone, Ennio *C*
CD PRCD 106
Preamble / Jan '95 / Silva Screen

DANCE A LITTLE CLOSER
1983 Broadway Cast
Strouse, Charles *C*
Lerner, Alan Jay *L*
CD CDTER 1174
TER / Jul '90 / Koch

DANCEHALL QUEEN
Dancehall Queen: *Franklyn, Chevelle & Beenie Man* / Badman sonata: *Buccaneer* / What's the move: *Chaka Demus & Pliers* / Unbelievable: *Marley Girls* / My Jamaican guy: *Jones, Grace & Bounty Killer* / Tune in: *Bounty Killer & Sugar Minott* / Satisfaction guaranteed: *Franklyn, Chevelle & Red Dragon* / Nuff gal: *Beenie Man* / Joyride: *Wayne Wonder & Babycham*
CD 5243962
Island Jamaica / Sep '97 / Jet Star / PolyGram

DANCES WITH WOLVES
Barry, John *C*
Barry, John *Con*
Main title / Looks like a suicide / John Dunbar / Journey to Fort Sedgewick / Ride to Fort Hays / Death of Timmons / Two Socks - the wolf theme / Pawnee Attack / Kicking Bird's gift / Journey to the buffalo killing ground / Buffalo hunt / Stands with a fist / Remembers / Love theme / John Dunbar theme / Two Socks at play / Death of Cisco / Rescue of Dances With Wolves / Loss of the journal and the return to winter camp / Farewell and end title
CD 4675912
Epic / Feb '91 / Sony
CD ZK 66817
Mastersound / Nov '95 / Sony

DANCING THRU THE DARK
Paradise / Power and the glory / Jam it jam / Dancin' thru the dark / Shoe shine / I'm livin' a life of love / Caribbean queen (no more love on the run) / Get busy / People all around the world / So many people / Once in a lifetime
CD CHIP 92
Jive / Mar '90 / Pinnacle

DANGEROUS GROUND
CD CHIP 181
Jive / Mar '97 / Pinnacle

DANGEROUS LIAISONS
Fenton, George
Fenton, George *C*
Dangerous liasons / O Malheureuse iphigenie / Beneath the surface / Her eyes are closing / Tourvel's flight / Concerto in A minor for 4 harpsichords / Success / Madame de Tourvel / Valmont's first move / Staircase / Key / Ombra mau fu / Ombra mai fu reprise / the mirror / Beyond my control
CD CDV 2583
Virgin / Mar '89 / EMI

DANGEROUS MINDS
Gangsta's paradise: *Coolio* / Curiosity: *Hall, Aaron* / Havin' thangs: *Big Mike* / Problems: *Rappin' 4-Tay* / True OG: *Mr. Dalvin & Static* / Put ya back into it: *Tre Black* / Don't go there: *Rappin' 4-Tay* / Feel the funk: *Immature* / It's alright: *Sista* / Message for your mind: *Rappin' 4-Tay* / Gin & juice: *Devante* / This is the life: *Wendy & Lisa*
CD MCD 11228
MCA / Oct '95 / BMG

DANTE'S PEAK
Frizzell, John *C*
CD VSD 5793
Varese Sarabande / Mar '97 / Pinnacle

DANZON
Black tears / Traveller / To love and to live / Blue / Schubert's serenade / Magic flute / Long distance telephone / Perjured woman / Moorish woman
CD DRGCD 12605
DRG / Jan '95 / Discovery / New Note/ Pinnacle

DARK HALF, THE
Munich Symphony Orchestra
Young, Christopher *C*
Young, Christopher *Con*
CD VSD 5340
Varese Sarabande / Apr '93 / Pinnacle

DARK SHADOWS
CD VSD 5702
Varese Sarabande / Sep '96 / Pinnacle

DARK STAR
Carpenter, John *C*
CD VSD 5327
Varese Sarabande / Nov '92 / Pinnacle

DARLING BUDS OF MAY, THE
English Light Concert Orchestra
Guard, Barry *C*
Perfick / Pop's rolls royce / Home farm / Strawberry time / Devil's gallop / Calling all workers / Breath of French air / Gore Court march / One the river / Dinner in the shade / Hop picker's hop / Puffin' Billy / In a party mood / Girl in yellow / Gymkhana / Darling buds of May
CD CDMFP 6128
EMI / Jul '94 / EMI

DAS BARBECU
1995 US Cast
CD VSD 5593
Varese Sarabande / Aug '95 / Pinnacle

DAVE
Howard, James Newton *C*
Main titles / Picnic / To the White House / You're on / Are you threatening me / She hates me / Teaching montage / Do you like magic / Dave passes out / Tunnel / How'd you get started / Into the fog / End titles
CD 9255102
Silva Screen / Jan '93 / Koch / Silva Screen

DAWN OF THE DEAD/TENEBRAE
Goblin
Simonetti, Claudio *C*
CD CDCIA 5035
Cinevox / Feb '90 / Koch / Silva Screen

DAY IN HOLLYWOOD, A NIGHT IN THE UKRAINE, A
1980 Broadway Cast
Lazarus, Frank *C*
Vosburgh, Dick *L*
Just go to the movies / Famous feet / I love a film cliche / Nelson / It all comes out of the piano / Best in the world / Doin' the production code / Night in the Ukraine / Samovar the lawyer
CD DRGCD 12580
DRG / Mar '92 / Discovery / New Note/ Pinnacle

DAY THE EARTH STOOD STILL, THE
Herrmann, Bernard *C*
CD 07822110102
Fox Film Scores / Apr '94 / BMG

DAY THE FISH CAME, THE
Theodorakis, Mikis
Theodorakis, Mikis *C*
CD SR 50088
Varese Sarabande / May '94 / Pinnacle

DAYLIGHT
Daylight / Latura's theme / Searching for a miracle / Survival / Kit's plan / Community is formed / Leaving George / Rats / Tunnel claims its own / Power / Short swim under water / Sandhog's chapel / Light at the end / Madelyne's fate / Whenever there is love / Don't go out with your friends tonite
CD UND 53024
Universal / Dec '96

DAYS OF HOPE
1991 London Cast
Goodall, Howard *C*
CD ______ **CDTER 1183**
TER / Sep '91 / Koch

DAYS OF THUNDER
Last note of freedom: *Coverdale, David* / Deal for life: *Waite, John* / Break through the barrier: *Turner, Tina* / Hearts in trouble: *Chicago* / Trail of broken hearts: *Cher* / Knockin' on Heaven's door: *Guns N' Roses* / You gotta love someone: *John, Elton* / Show me heaven: *McKee, Maria* / Tinder box: *Appollo Smile* / Long live the night: *Jett, Joan & The Blackhearts* / Gimme some lovin': *Reid, Terry*
CD ______ **4571592**
Epic / Aug '90 / Sony

DAZED AND CONFUSED
CD ______ **74321166752**
Medicine / Sep '94 / BMG / Vital

DE ESO NON SE HABLA
Piovani, Nicola *C*
CD ______ **88765**
Milan / Jan '95 / Conifer/BMG / Silva Screen

DEAD AGAIN
Doyle, Patrick *C*
Headlines / Final request / Walk down death row / Woman with no name / Winter 1948 / Two halves of the same person / It never rains in LA / I'm not Roman / Inga's secret / Hightower House / Fate happens / Death of a mad son / Door is closed / Dead again
CD ______ **D5339**
Varese Sarabande / Aug '91 / Pinnacle

DEAD MAN
Young, Neil
Young, Neil *C*
CD ______ **9362461712**
Reprise / Feb '96 / Warner Music

DEAD MAN WALKING
Dead man walkin': *Springsteen, Bruce* / In your mind: *Cash, Johnny* / Woman on the tier (I'll see you through): *Vega, Suzanne* / Promises: *Lovett, Lyle* / Face of love: *Khan, Nusrat Fateh Ali & Eddie Vedder* / Fall of Troy: *Waits, Tom* / Quality of mercy: *Shocked, Michelle* / Dead man walking (a dream like this): *Carpenter, Mary-Chapin* / Walk away: *Waits, Tom* / Ellis Unit One: *Earle, Steve* / Walkin' blind: *Smith, Patti* / Long road: *Khan, Nusrat Fateh Ali & Eddie Vedder*
CD ______ **4835342**
Columbia / Apr '96 / Sony

DEAD MAN WALKING (Score)
Face of love: *Khan, Nusrat Fateh Ali & Eddie Vedder* / Helen visits Angola prison: *Robins, David/Nusrat Fateh Ali Khan/Amina Annabi* / Dudouk melody (A cool wind is blowing) / This is the day the Lord has made: *Smith, Rev. Donald R. & The Golden Voices Gospel Choir* / Possum: *Robins, David & Nusrat Fateh Ali Khan* / Shadow: *Khan, Nusrat Fateh Ali* / Helen faints/Helen's nightmare: *Robins, David/Nusrat Fateh Ali Khan/Amina Annabi* / Dudouk melody (I will not be sad in this world) / Sacred love: *Dusing Singers* / Execution: *Robins, David & Nusrat Fateh Ali Khan* / Long road: *Robins, David & Nusrat Fateh Ali Khan* / Isa Lei: *Cooder, Ry & V.M. Bhatt*
CD ______ **4841072**
Columbia / Apr '96 / Sony

DEAD MEN DON'T WEAR PLAID
Rozsa, Miklos *C*
Holdridge, Lee *Con*
CD ______ **PCD 126**
Prometheus / Jan '93 / Silva Screen

DEAD POETS SOCIETY (& The Year Of Living Dangerously)
Jarre, Maurice *C*
CD ______ **CDCH 558**
Milan / Feb '94 / Conifer/BMG / Silva Screen

DEAD PRESIDENTS VOL.1
If you want me to stay: *Sly & The Family Stone* / Walk on by: *Hayes, Isaac* / Payback: *Brown, James* / I'll be around: *Spinners* / Never gonna give you up: *White, Barry* / I miss you: *Melvin, Harold & The Bluenotes* / Get up and get down: *Dramatics* / If there's hell below: *Mayfield, Curtis* / Do right woman, do right man: *Franklin, Aretha* / Where is the love: *Jesse & Trina* / Tired of being alone: *Green, Al* / Love train: *O'Jays* / Look of love: *Hayes, Isaac* / Dead Presidents theme: *Elfman, Danny*
CD ______ **PRDCD 4**
Premier/EMI / May '96 / EMI

DEAD PRESIDENTS VOL.2
I got the feeling: *Brown, James* / Keep on pushing: *Impressions* / Smiling faces sometimes: *Undisputed Truth* / Right on for darkness: *Mayfield, Curtis* / Just my imagination: *Temptations* / Cowboys to girls: *Intruders* / Never gonna give you up: *Butler, Jerry* / I was made to love her: *Wonder, Stevie* / (Man oh man) I want to go back: *Impressions* / When something is wrong with my baby: *Sam & Dave* / We people darker than blue: *Mayfield, Curtis* / Ain't that a groove: *Mayfield, Curtis*
CD ______ **PRMDCD 5**
Soundtracks / Sep '96 / EMI

DEAD SOLID PERFECT
Tangerine Dream
Tangerine Dream *C*
Theme / In the pond / Beverly leaves / Of cads and caddies / Tournament montage / Whore in one / Sand trap / In the rough / Nine iron / US Open / My name is bad hair / In the hospital room / Welcome to Bushwood/Golfus interruptus / Deja vu (I've heard this before) / Birdie / Divot / Kenny and Donny montage / Off to see Beverly / Phone to Beverly / Nice shots / Sinking putts / Kenny's winning shot
CD ______ **FILMCD 079**
Silva Screen / Mar '91 / Koch / Silva Screen

DEAD, THE
North, Alex *C*
CD ______ **VCD 47341**
Varese Sarabande / Jan '89 / Pinnacle

DEADLY CARE
Tangerine Dream
Tangerine Dream *C*
Deadly care / Paddles / Stolen pills / Strong drink / Bad morning / Wasted & sick / Hope for future / Hospital / In bed / Annie & father / More pills / In the Head Nurse's office / At the father's grave / Clean & sober
CD ______ **FILMCD 121**
Silva Screen / Nov '92 / Koch / Silva Screen

DEAR DIARY
Piovani, Nicola *C*
CD ______ **210542**
Milan / Nov '94 / Conifer/BMG / Silva Screen

DEAR WORLD
1969 Broadway Cast
Herman, Jerry *C*
Pippin, Donald *Con*
CD ______ **SK 48220**
Sony Broadway / Nov '92 / Sony

DEATH BECOMES HER
Silvestri, Alan *C*
CD ______ **VSD 5375**
Varese Sarabande / Aug '92 / Pinnacle

DEATH BEFORE DISHONOUR
May, Brian *C*
CD ______ **PCD 118**
Prometheus / Mar '93 / Silva Screen

DEATH IN BRUNSWICK
Judd, Philip *C*
CD ______ **A 8933**
Alhambra / Jan '92 / Silva Screen

DEATH RIDES A HORSE/A PISTOL FOR RINGO
Morricone, Ennio *C*
CD ______ **OST 107**
Milano Dischi / Jan '93 / Silva Screen

DEEP COVER
Deep cover: *Snoop Doggy Dogg* / Love or lust: *Jewell* / Down with my nigga: *Paradise* / Sex is on: *Po', Broke & Lonely* / Way (is in the house): *Calloway* / Minute you fall in love: *3RD Avenue* / John and Betty's theme: *Colombier, Michel* / Mr. Loverman: *Shabba Ranks* / I see ya Jay: *Ragtime* / Nickel slick nigga: *Ko-Kane* / Typical relationship: *Times 3* / Digits: *Deele* / Sound of one hand clapping: *Calloway* / Why you frontin' on me: *Emmage*
CD ______ **4716692**
Epic / Feb '93 / Sony

DEEP STAR SIX
Manfredini, Harry *C*
Shock wave / On the edge / Our baby's heartbeat / Seatrack attack / That morning / Rescue / Alone / Plan / Shark darts / Snyder snaps / Swim to the mini-sub
CD ______ **MAF 7004D**
Intrada / Jan '90 / Koch / Silva Screen

DEERHUNTER, THE
Myers, Stanley *C*
Cavatina / Praise the name of the Lord / Troika / Katyusha / Struggling ahead / Sarabande / Waiting his turn / Memory eternal / God bless America / Cavatina (reprise)
CD ______ **920582**
Silva Screen / Jan '93 / Koch / Silva Screen

DEF CON 4
Young, Christopher *C*
CD ______ **MAF 7010D**
Intrada / Jan '94 / Koch / Silva Screen

DEJA VU/GOING BANANAS/ORDEAL OF INNOCENCE
Donaggio, Pino *C*
CD ______ **FILMCD 093**
Silva Screen / Jan '93 / Koch / Silva Screen

DELICATESSEN
CD ______ **8493452**
Polydor / Jan '93 / PolyGram

DELINQUENTS, THE
CD ______ **HFCD 11**
PWL / Mar '90 / Warner Music

DELIVERANCE
Weissberg, Eric & Steve Mandell
Weissberg, Eric *C*
Duellin' banjos / Little Maggie / Shuckin' the corn / Pony Express / Old Joe Clark / Eight more miles to Louisville / Farewell blues / Earl's breakdown / End of a dream / Buffalo gals / Reuben's train / Riding the waves / Fire on the mountain / Eighth of January / Bugle call rag / Hard, ain't it hard / Mountain dew / Rawhide

CD ______ **K 246214**
WEA / Sep '88 / Warner Music

DELLAMORTE DELLAMORTE
De Sica, Manuel
De Sica, Manuel *C*
CD ______ **GDM 2004**
Silva Screen / Jan '95 / Koch / Silva Screen

DELORES CLAIBORNE
Elfman, Danny
Elfman, Danny *C*
CD ______ **VSD 5602**
Varese Sarabande / Mar '95 / Pinnacle

DELTA FORCE II
European Symphony Orchestra
Talgorn, Frederic *C*
CD ______ **A 8921**
Alhambra / Feb '92 / Silva Screen

DELTA FORCE/KING SOLOMON'S MINES
Goldsmith, Jerry *C*
CD ______ **CH 290**
Milan / Jan '89 / Conifer/BMG / Silva Screen

DEMOLITION MAN
Goldenthal, Elliot *C*
Sheffer, Jonathan/A.Kane *Con*
Dies irae / Fire fight / Guilty as charged / Action, guns, fun / Machine waltz / Defrosting / Confronting the Chief / Museum duel / Subterranean slugfest / Meeting Cocteau / Tracking Simon Phoenix / Obligatory car chase / Flawless pearl / Final confrontation / Code 187 / Silver screen kiss
CD ______ **VSD 5447**
Varese Sarabande / Nov '93 / Pinnacle

DEMONS/RAGE/LOVE THREAT/ NIGHTMARE BEACH
Simonetti, Claudio
Simonetti, Claudio *C*
CD ______ **OST 104**
Milano Dischi / Apr '93 / Silva Screen

DENNIS
Goldsmith, Jerry *C*
CD ______ **9255142**
Silva Screen / Jan '94 / Koch / Silva Screen

DES FEMMES DISPARAISSENT/LES TRICHEURS
Blakey, Art & The Jazz Messengers
Generique Pierre et Beatrice / Nasol / Tom poursuite dans la ruelle / Ne chucote pas / Mambo dans la voiture / Merlin juste pour eux seuls / Blues pour doudou / Blues pour Marcel / Blues pour Vava / Pasquier / Quaglio / La divorce de Leo Fall / Suspense, Tom et Nasol / Des femmes disparaissent / Final pour Pierre et Beatrice / Les tricheurs / Clo's blues / Phil's tune / Mic's jump / Crazy Hamp
CD ______ **8347522**
Fontana / Mar '94 / PolyGram

DESERT SONG/THE NEW MOON/THE BLUE TRAIN
Cast Recording
CD ______ **GEMMCD 9100**
Pearl / May '94 / Harmonia Mundi

DESPERADO
Cancion del Mariachi: *Los Lobos & Antonio Banderas* / Six blade knife: *Dire Straits* / Jack the ripper: *Wray, Link & The Wraymen* / Manifold de amor: *Latin Playboys* / Forever night shade Mary: *Latin Playboys* / Pass the hatchet: *Roger & The Gypsies* / Bar fight: *Los Lobos* / Strange face of love: *Tito & Tarantula* / Bucho's gragias/Navajas attacks: *Los Lobos* / Bulletproof: *Los Lobos* / Bella: *Santana* / Quedate aqui: *Hayek, Salma* / Rooftop action: *Los Lobos* / Phone call: *Los Lobos* / White train: *Tito & Tarantula* / Back to the house that love built: *Tito & Tarantula* / Let love reign: *Los Lobos* / Mariachi suite: *Los Lobos*
CD ______ **4809442**
Epic / Jan '96 / Sony

DESPERATE HOURS
Mansfield, David *C*
Chase / Nancy slashes the jaguar / Jailbreak / Tim leaves with Zeck / Too many bad memories / Into the lake / Tim meets Bosworth / Nancy's apartment / May meets Bosworth / Tim stabbed / Tim and Nora's theme / Albert leaves / Dumping the body / I'll be back / Albert persued / Give me the Gun / Tim and Nora / Bosworth and the FBI / Stadium / Aftermath / End credits
CD ______ **VSD 5284**
Varese Sarabande / Oct '90 / Pinnacle

DESPERATE REMEDIES
Scholes, Peter *C*
CD ______ **887938**
Milan / May '94 / Conifer/BMG / Silva Screen

DESPERATELY SEEKING SUSAN
Newman, Thomas *C*
Leave Atlantic City / Port Authority by night / New York by day / Through the viewscope / St. Mark's place / Key & a picture of Battery Park / Amnesia / Jail / Port Authority by day / Rain / Running with birds in cages / Trouble almost / Chemtek promo video / Ulysses' escape / Night visit / Frankie's drive / Ulysses / In the lab / Sondra & Jeff / Mr. Right / Wedding reception / Parting glance
CD ______ **VSD 47291**
Varese Sarabande / Feb '90 / Pinnacle

DESPERATELY SEEKING SUSAN/ MAKING MR RIGHT
Newman, Thomas *C*
CD ______ **VCD 47291**
Varese Sarabande / Aug '91 / Pinnacle

DESTRY RIDES AGAIN
1979 London Cast
Rome, Harold *C*
Bottle neck / Ladies / Hoop-de-dingle / Tomorrow morning / Ballad of gun / I know your kind / I hate him / Anyone would love you / Every once in a while / Destry rides again: Finale act I / Are you ready Gyp Watson / Not guilty / Only time will tell / That ring on the finger / I say hello / Destry rides again: Finale act II / Curtain call
CD ______ **CDTER 1034**
TER / Dec '94 / Koch

DEVIL IN A BLUE DRESS
West side baby: *Walker, T-Bone* / Ain't nobody's business: *Witherspoon, Jimmy* / Ellignton, duke / Hy-ah Su: *Ellington, Duke* / Hop skip and jump: *Milton, Roy* / Good rockin' tonight: *Harris, Wynonie* / Blues after hours: *Crayton, Pee Wee* / I can't go on without you: *Jackson, Bull Moose* / Round midnight: *Monk, Thelonius* / Chicken shack boogie: *Milburn, Amos* / Messin' around: *Memphis Slim* / Chica boo: *Glenn, Lloyd* / Theme from Devil In A Blue Dress: *Bernstein, Elmer* / Malibu chase: *Bernstein, Elmer*
CD ______ **4813792**
Columbia / Dec '95 / Sony

DEVIL'S OWN, THE
Horner, James *C*
Horner, James *Con*
Main title / God be with you / Ambush / Irish Republican Navy / New world / Launching the boat / Secrets untold / Pool hall / Rory's arrest/Diaz is killed / Quiet goodbyes / Rooftop escape / Mortal blow / Going home
CD ______ **TBCD 1204**
Tommy Boy / Apr '97 / RTM/Disc

DI QUESTO NON SI PARLA
Piovani, Nicola *C*
CD ______ **887865**
Milan / Jan '95 / Conifer/BMG / Silva Screen

DIABOLIQUE
CD ______ **0022582CIN**
Edel / Jul '96 / Pinnacle

DIAMONDS ARE FOREVER
Barry, John *C*
Diamonds are forever: *Bassey, Shirley* / Moon buggy ride / Bond meets Bambi and Thumper / Circus, circus / Death at the Whyte house / Bond smells a rat / Tiffany case / 007 and counting / Q's trick / To hell with blofeld
CD ______ **CZ 554**
Premier/EMI / Dec '95 / EMI

DIARY OF ANNE FRANK, THE
Newman, Alfred *C*
Newman, Alfred *Con*
CD ______ **TSU 0122**
Tsunami / May '95 / Silva Screen

DICK TRACY
Elfman, Danny *C*
Dick Tracy (theme) / After the kid / Crime spree / Breathless theme / Big boy, bad boy / Tess' theme / Slimy DA / Breathless comes on / Meet the blank / Story unfolds / Tess' theme (reprise) / Chase / Showdown / Dick Tracy (finale)
CD ______ **7599262362**
WEA / Jun '90 / Warner Music

DIE HARD II
Kamen, Michael
Kamen, Michael *C*
Colonel Stuart / General Esperanza / Church / Runaway / Icicle / Terminal / Baggage handling / Annexe skywalk / Doll / In the plane / Snowmobiles / Finlandia
CD ______ **VSD 5273**
Varese Sarabande / Jul '90 / Pinnacle

DIE HARD WITH A VENGEANCE
Kamen, Michael
Kamen, Michael *C*
Summer in the city: *Lovin' Spoonful* / Goodbye Bonwits / John & Zeus / Papaya King / Take another train / Waltz of the bankers / Gold vault / Surfing in the aquaduct / Got it covered: *Fu-Schnickens* / In front of the kids: *Extra Prolific* / Iron foundry: *Mosolov*
CD ______ **09026683062**
RCA / Aug '95 / BMG

DIE TIGERIN
Dikker, Loek *C*
CD ______ **118462**
Milan / Jan '95 / Conifer/BMG / Silva Screen

DIE ZWEITE HEIMAT
Mamangakis, Nikos *C*
CD ______ **887881**
Milan / Jan '95 / Conifer/BMG / Silva Screen

DIE ZWEITE HEIMAT
Mamangakis, Nikos *C*
4CD ______ **BM 3018**
Bella Musica / Jan '96 / Koch

DIEN BIEN PHU
Delerue, Georges *C*
CD ______ **5132892**
Silva Screen / Jan '93 / Koch / Silva Screen

DINER
Brody, Bruce *C*
CD ______ ASTCD 4004
Astrion Audio / Nov '96 / BMG

DIRTY DANCING
I've had the time of my life: *Medley, Bill & Jennifer Warnes* / Be my baby: *Ronettes* / She's like the wind: *Swayze, Patrick & Wendy Fraser* / Hungry eyes: *Carmen, Eric* / Stay: *Williams, Maurice & The Zodiacs* / Yes: *Clayton, Merry* / You don't own me: *Blow Monkeys* / Hey baby: *Channel, Bruce* / Overload: *Zappacosta* / Love is strange: *Mickey & Sylvia* / Where are you tonight: *Johnston, Tom* / In the still of the nite: *Five Satins*
CD ______ BD 86408
RCA / Oct '87 / BMG

DIRTY DANCING - LIVE IN CONCERT
Cast Recording
Yes: *Clayton, Merry* / Overload: *Clayton, Merry* / Steamroller blues: *Clayton, Merry* / Make me lose control: *Carmen, Eric* / Almost paradise: *Carmen, Eric & Merry Clayton* / Hungry eyes: *Carmen, Eric* / Get ready: *Contours* / Higher and higher: *Contours* / Cry to me: *Contours* / Do you love me: *Contours* / Let the good times roll: *Medley, Bill* / Sea cruise: *Medley, Bill* / You've lost that lovin' feelin': *Medley, Bill* / Old time rock 'n' roll: *Medley, Bill* / I've had the time of my life: *Medley, Bill* / Encore
CD ______ ND 90672
RCA / Aug '92 / BMG

DIRTY DANCING - MORE DIRTY DANCING
I've had the time of my life: *Morris, John Orchestra* / Big girls don't cry: *Four Seasons* / Merengue: *Lloyd, Michael & Le Disc* / Some kind of wonderful: *Drifters* / Johnny's mambo: *Lloyd, Michael & Le Disc* / Do you love me: *Contours* / Love man: *Redding, Otis* / Wipeout: *Surfaris* / These arms of mine: *Redding, Otis* / De todo un poco: *Lloyd, Michael & Le Disc* / Cry to me: *Burke, Solomon* / Trot the fox: *Lloyd, Michael & Le Disc* / Will you still love me tomorrow: *Shirelles* / Kellerman's anthem: *Emile Bergstein Chorale*
CD ______ 74321369152
RCA / Jun '96 / BMG

DISCLOSURE
Morricone, Ennio *C*
Serene family / Unusual approach / With energy and decision / Virtual reality / Preparation and victory / Disclosure / Sad family / Unemployed / Sex and computers / Computers and work / Sex and power / First passacaglia / Second passacaglia / Third passacaglia / Sex, power and computers
CD ______ CDVMM 16
Virgin / Feb '95 / EMI

DIVA
Cosma, Vladimir *C*
CD ______ CDCH 061
Milan / Feb '94 / Conifer/BMG / Silva Screen

DIVINE MADNESS
Midler, Bette
CD ______ 7567814762
Atlantic / Feb '92 / Warner Music

DJANGO REINHARDT
Reinhardt, Django
CD ______ 873138
Milan / Mar '93 / Conifer/BMG / Silva Screen

DO I HEAR A WALTZ
Broadway Cast
Rodgers, Richard *C*
Sondheim, Stephen *L*
Dvonch, Frederick *Con*
CD ______ SK 48206
Sony Broadway / Jan '93 / Sony

DOA
Jankel, Chas *C*
CD ______ VCD 70461
Varese Sarabande / Aug '91 / Pinnacle

DOCTOR DOOLITTLE
Harrison, Rex & Samantha Eggar/Anthony Newley & 1967 Film Cast
Bricusse, Leslie *C*
Bricusse, Leslie *L*
Newman, Lionel *Con*
Overture / My friend the doctor / Vegetarian / Talk to the animals / At the crossroads / I've never seen anything like it / Beautiful things / When I look in your eyes / Like animals / After today / Fabulous places / Where are the worlds / I think I like you / Doctor Doolittle / Something in your smile
CD ______ 5345002
Philips / Jun '97 / PolyGram

DOCTOR WHO: EARTHSHOCK (Classic Music From The BBC Radiophonic Workshop I)
BBC Radiophonic Workshop
Tardis / Sea devils / Meglos / Keeper of Traken / Four to doomsday / Leisure hive / Arc of infinity / Warrior's gate / Earthshock
CD ______ FILMCD 709
Silva Screen / Nov '92 / Koch / Silva Screen

DOCTOR WHO: EVOLUTION
McCulloch, Keff & Ron Grainger/Dominic Green *C*
Tardis / Dr. Who / Gavrok's search / Child's return / Towers el paradiso / Burton's escape / Drinksmat dawning / Future pleasure / Newsreel past / Sting / Dr. Who / Dr. Who / 8891 royale / White flag / Guards of silence / Making of pex / Cemetery chase / Brain / Here's to the future / Goodbye Doctor
CD ______ RDSGP 0320
Prestige / May '97 / Else / Total/BMG

DOCTOR WHO: GHOSTLIGHT
Ayres, Mark
Ayres, Mark *C*
Madhouse / Redvers, I presume / Uncharted territory / Heart of the interior / Enter Josiah Indoor lightning / Nimrod observed / Time to emerge / Burnt toast / Ace's adventures underground / Where's is Mamma / Way to the zoo / Memory teller / Lighting the touchpaper / Homo victorianus ineptus / Light enlightened / Tropic of Perivale / Tricks of the light / Judgement in stone / Requiem / Passing thoughts
CD ______ FILMCD 133
Silva Screen / Jun '93 / Koch / Silva Screen

DOCTOR WHO: MYTHS AND OTHER LEGENDS
Ayres, Mark *C*
CD ______ FILMCD 088
Silva Screen / '94 / Koch / Silva Screen

DOCTOR WHO: PYRAMIDS OF MARS
Blair, Heathcliff
Simpson, Dudley *C*
Ark in space / Planet of evil / Brain of Morbius / Genesis of the Daleks / Pyramids of Mars
CD ______ FILMCD 134
Silva Screen / '94 / Koch / Silva Screen

DOCTOR WHO: THE CURSE OF FENRIC
Ayres, Mark
Ayres, Mark *C*
Introduction: Doctor Who / Boats / Beachhead and rat-trap / Sealed orders / Eyes watching / Commander Milington / Viking graves / Maidens' point / Translations / Audrey and Milington's office / Curse of Fenric / High stakes / Crypt / Ambush / Well of Vergelmir / Ultima machine / Dangerous undercurrents / Seduction of Prozorov / Halftime score / Exit Miss Hardaker/The vicar and the vampires / Stop the machine / Haemovores / Battle for St. Jude's / Mineshaft / Sealing the hatch / House guests / Telegram / Evil from the dawn of time / Storm breaks / Ancient enemies / Shadow dimensions / Chemical grenade / Great serpent / Pawns in the game / Kathleen's escape / Wolves of Fenric / Black wins, Time Lord / Final battle / Epilogue: Doctor Who
CD ______ FILMCD 087
Silva Screen / Apr '94 / Koch / Silva Screen

DOCTOR WHO: THE FIVE DOCTORS (Classic Music From The BBC Radiophonic Workshop II)
BBC Radiophonic Workshop
Five doctors / King's demons / Enlightenment / Warriors of the deep / Awakening / Resurrection of the Daleks / Planet of fire / Caves of Androzani
CD ______ FILMCD 710
Silva Screen / Nov '92 / Koch / Silva Screen

DOCTOR WHO: THE GREATEST SHOW IN THE GALAXY
Ayres, Mark
Ayres, Mark *C*
Introduction: Doctor Who / Psychic rap / Invitation to segonax / Bellboy and flowerchild / Warning / Fellow explorers / Robot attacks / Something sinister / Welcome one and all / Circus ring / Deadbeat / Eavesdropping / Let me entertain you/Stone archway / Well / Powers on the move / Sifting dreams / Survival of the fittest / Bellboy's sacrifice / Plans / Werewolf/Request stop / Gods of Ragnarok / Playing for time / Entry of the psychic clowns / Liberty who / Psychic carnival / Coda: Kingpin's new circus / Epilogue: Doctor Who
CD ______ FILMCD 114
Silva Screen / Feb '92 / Koch / Silva Screen

DOCTOR WHO: THE TOMB OF THE CYBERMEN
CD ______ VSATASTRA 3967
Via Satellite / Jul '97 / Cargo

DOCTOR WHO: THE WORLDS OF DOCTOR WHO (Music Sampler)
Doctor Who / Tardis / World of Doctor Who / Sea devils / Ark in space / Pyramids of Mars / Brain of Morbius / Doctor Who themes / Meglos / Five Doctors / Caves of Androzani / Myth Makers theme / Doctor Who - Terror Vision / Terror in Trotter's Lane / Greatest show in the galaxy / Ghost light / Curse of Fenric / Return to Devil's End
CD ______ FILMCD 715
Silva Screen / Apr '94 / Koch / Silva Screen

DOCTOR WHO: VARIATIONS ON A THEME
Doctor Who - Mood version: *Ayres, Mark* / Doctor Who - Terror version: *Glynn, Dominic* / Doctor Who - Latin version: *McCulloch, Keff* / Panopticon eight: *Ayres, Mark*
CD ______ FILMCD 706
Silva Screen / '94 / Koch / Silva Screen

DOCTOR ZHIVAGO
Jarre, Maurice *C*
Jarre, Maurice *Con*
Overture / Main title / Kontakion/Funeral song / Lara is charming / Internationale / Lara and Komarovsky dancing up a storm / Komarovsky with Lara in the hotel / Interior student cafe / Sventitsky's waltz/After the shooting / Military parade / They began to go home / After deserters killed the Colonel / At the hospital / Lara says goodbye to Yuri / Tonya greets Yuri / Stove's out / Yevgraf snaps his fingers / Evening bells - Moscow Station / Flags flying over the train / Yuri gazing through a tiny open hatch / Door is banged open / Intermission / Yuri follows the sound of the waterfall / Tonya and Yuri arrive at Varykino / They didn't lock the cottage / Varykino cottage, winter snow / Yuri and the daffodils / On a Yuriatin street / In Lara's bedroom / Yuri rides to Yuriatin / Yuri is taken prisoner by the Red Partisans / For as long as we need you / Yuri is escaping / Yuri approaches Lara's apartment / Yuri looks into the mirror / Lara and Yuri arriving at Varykino / Yuri is trying to write / Yuri frightens the wolves away / Lara reads her poem / Yuri frightens the wolves away pt.2 / Yuri works on / Then it's a gift / Lara's theme
CD ______ CDODEON 1
Premier/EMI / Feb '96 / EMI

DOCTOR ZHIVAGO/RYAN'S DAUGHTER
Jarre, Maurice *C*
Dr. Zhivago overture / Dr. Zhivago / Lara leaves Yuri / At the student cafe / Komarovsky and Lara's rendezvous / Revolution / Lara's theme / Funeral / Sventytski's waltz / Yuri escapes / Tonya arrives at Varykino / Yuri writes a poem for Lara / Ryan's Daughter / Major / You don't want me then / Michael's theme / Ride through the woods / Obsession / Shakes / Rosy on the beach / Song of the Irish rebels / Rosy and the schoolmaster / Michael shows Randolph his strange treasure / Rosy's theme
CD ______ CDMGM 3
MGM/EMI / Jan '90 / EMI

DOMINICK AND EUGENE
Jones, Trevor *C*
CD ______ VCD 70454
Varese Sarabande / Jan '89 / Pinnacle

DON JUAN DEMARCO
London Metropolitan Orchestra
Kamen, Michael *C*
Kamen, Michael *Con*
Have you ever really loved a woman: *Adams, Bryan* / Habanera: *Kamen, Michael* / Don Juan: *Kamen, Michael* / I was born in Mexico: *Kamen, Michael* / Love at first sight (mother and father): *Kamen, Michael* / Dona Julia: *Kamen, Michael* / Don Alfonso: *Kamen, Michael* / Arabia: *Kamen, Michael* / Don Octavia del Flores: *Kamen, Michael* / Dona Ana: *Kamen, Michael*
CD ______ 5403572
A&M / Jan '95 / PolyGram

DON QUIXOTE
Madrid Symphony Orchestra
Schifrin, Lalo *C*
Schifrin, Lalo *Con*
CD ______ PCD 132
Prometheus / Jan '95 / Silva Screen

DONNIE BRASCO
CD ______ 1621022
Polydor / May '97 / PolyGram

DON'T BE A MENACE TO SOUTH CENTRAL (While Drinking Your Juice In The Hood)
CD ______ 5241462
Island / Feb '96 / PolyGram

DON'T LOOK NOW
Donaggio, Pino *C*
John's theme / Candles for Christine / John's vision / Through the street / Dead end / Christine is dead / Strange happenings / Searching for Laura / Laura comes back / Laura's theme
CD ______ CDTER 1007
TER / Oct '89 / Koch

DOOM GENERATION, THE (Teen Is A Four Letter Word)
Intro: *Blue, Amy* / On the wheel: *Curve* / This heaven: *Love & Rockets* / Summerblink: *Cocteau Twins* / Christianity: *Wolfgang Press* / Paradise now: *Meat Beat Manifesto* / Already there: *Verve* / Penetration: *Jesus & Mary Chain* / But if you go: *MC 900 ft Jesus* / Undertow: *Lush* / Double coupon: *Babyland* / Slut: *Medicine* / Groovy is my name: *Pizzicato Five* / Violator: *Extra Fancy* / Blue skied an' clear: *Slowdive*
CD ______ 74321318722
American / Sep '96 / BMG

DOORS, THE
Doors
Movie / Riders on the storm / Love street / Break on through / End / Light my fire / Ghost song / Roadhouse blues / Heroin / Carmina burana / Stoned immaculate / When the music's over / Severed garden / LA Woman
CD ______ 7559610472
WEA / Mar '91 / Warner Music

DOUBLE IMPACT
Kempel, Arthur *C*
CD ______ FILMCD 110
Silva Screen / '91 / Koch / Silva Screen

DOUBLE INDEMNITY (& The Killers/Lost Weekend)
New Zealand Symphony Orchestra
Rozsa, Miklos *C*
Sedares, James *Con*
CD ______ 373752
Koch International / Apr '97 / Koch

DOUBLE LIFE OF VERONIKA, THE
Preisner, Zbigniew *C*
CD ______ SID 001
Sidonie / Feb '92 / Koch

DOWN BY LAW/VARIETY
Lurie, John *C*
What do you know about music, you're not a lawyer / Strangers in the day / Promenade du maquereau / Invasion of Poland / Please come to my house / Are you warm enough / Swamp / Swamp (part 2) / Are you warm enough again / King of Thailand, the Queen of Stairs / Hundred miles from Harry / Nicoletta can't cook / Fork in road / Variety theme / Porno booth / Porno booth II / Car / Million dollar walk / Anders leaps in / Garter belt / End titles
CD ______ MTM 14
Made To Measure / Apr '96 / New Note/ Pinnacle

DOWNTIME
Levine, Ian *C*
CD ______ FILMCD 717
Silva Screen / Nov '95 / Koch / Silva Screen

DR. GIGGLES
May, Brian *C*
May, Brian *Con*
CD ______ MAF 7043D
Intrada / Feb '93 / Koch / Silva Screen

DR. JEKYLL & MS. HYDE
McKenzie, Mark *C*
CD ______ MAF 7063D
Intrada / Apr '96 / Koch / Silva Screen

DR. NO
Norman, Monty *C*
Norman, Monty *Con*
James Bond / Kingston calypso / Island speaks / Under the mango tree / Jump up / Dr. No's fantasy / Boy chase / Love at last / Jamaican rock / Audio bongo / Twisting with James / Jamaica jazz
CD ______ CZ 558
Premier/EMI / Dec '95 / EMI

DRACULA (1992 Version)
Kilar, Wojciech *C*
Dracula / Beginning / Vampire hunters / Mina's photo / Lucy's party / Brides / Storm / Love remembered / Hunt builds / Hunter's prelude / Green mist / Mina/Dracula / Ring of fire / Love eternal / Ascension / End credits / Love song for a vampire: *Lennox, Annie*
CD ______ 4727462
Columbia / Sep '96 / Sony

DRACULA (Hammer Presents)
Lee, Christopher & Hammer City Orchestra
Bernard, James *C*
Dracula / Four faces of evil
CD ______ BGOCD 240
Beat Goes On / Mar '95 / Pinnacle

DRAGONHEART
Edelman, Randy *C*
World of the heart - Main title / To the stars / Wonders of an ancient glory / Einon / Last dragon slayer / Bowen's ride / Mexican standoff / Draco / Refreshing swim / Rebaptism / Bowen's decoy / Kyle, the wheat boy / Connection / Flight to Avalon / Finale
CD ______ MCD 11449
MCA / Oct '96 / BMG

DRAUGHTSMAN'S CONTRACT, THE
Nyman, Michael *C*
Queen of the night / Disposition of the linen / Watery death / Garden is becoming a robe room / Chasing sheep is best left to shepherds / Eye for optical theory / Bravura in the face of grief
CD ______ CASCD 1158
Charisma / Aug '95 / EMI

DRAW/RED RIVER
National Philharmonic Orchestra/Little Mountain Studio Symphony Orchestra
Wannberg, Ken *C*
Wannberg, Ken *Con*
CD ______ PCD 129
Prometheus / Oct '94 / Silva Screen

DREAM LOVER
Young, Christopher *C*
Anthony, Pete *Con*
CD ______ 387002
Koch / Dec '94 / Koch

DRESSED TO KILL
Donaggio, Pino *C*
CD ______ VCD 47148
Varese Sarabande / Jan '89 / Pinnacle

DRIFTWOOD
CD ______ OCD 03
Ocean Deep / Mar '97 / Grapevine/ PolyGram

DRIVING MISS DAISY
Zimmer, Hans *C*
CD ______ VSD 5246
Varese Sarabande / Feb '90 / Pinnacle

DROP ZONE
Zimmer, Hans *C*
Drop Zone / Hyphopera / Hijack / Terry's dropped out / Flashback & fries / Miami jump / Too many notes, not enough rests / After the dub
CD ______ **VSD 5581**
Varese Sarabande / Dec '94 / Pinnacle

DROWNING BY NUMBERS
Nyman, Michael Band
Nyman, Michael *C*
Trysting fields / Sheep and tides / Great death game / Drowning by number 3 / Wheelbarrow walk / Dead man's catch / Drowning by number 2 / Bees in trees / Fish beach / Wedding tango / Crematorium conspiracy / Knowing the ropes / End game
CD ______ **CDVE 23**
Venture / Aug '88 / EMI

DRUM IS A WOMAN
Bolling, Claude Big Band
Ellington, Duke *C*
CD ______ **74321409062**
Milan / Oct '96 / Conifer/BMG / Silva Screen

DU BARRY WAS A LADY/THE SKY'S THE LIMIT/42ND STREET
Du Barry was a lady / Well, git it / Do I love you: *Kelly, Gene* / Salome: *O'Brien, Virginia* / I love an esquire girl: *Skelton, Red & Dick Haymes* / Katie went to Haiti / Madame I loev your crepes suzettes: *Skelton, Red* / Friendship / My shining hour: *Leslie, Joan* / My shining hour: *Astaire, Fred & Joan Leslie* / I've got a lot in common with you: *Astaire, Fred & Joan Leslie* / My shining hour: *Slack, Freddie Orchestra* / One for my baby: *Astaire, Fred* / 42nd street overture: *Astaire, Fred* / You're getting to be a habit with me: *Astaire, Fred* / Shuffle off to Buffalo / Young and healthy: *Powell, Dick* / 42nd street: *Powell, Dick & Ruby Keeler*
CD ______ **CD 60010**
Great Movie Themes / Jun '97 / Target/BMG

DUBARRY, THE/MADAME POMPADOUR
London Cast
Millocker, Carl/Leo Fall *C*
Leigh, Rowland/Harry Graham *L*
CD ______ **GEMMCD 9068**
Pearl / Nov '93 / Harmonia Mundi

DUCK YOU SUCKER
Morricone, Ennio *C*
Morricone, Ennio *Con*
Main title / Love / Green table / March of the beggars / Dead sons / Addio / Jokes on the side / Mexico and Ireland / Inventions for John / Counter revolution / After the explosion
CD ______ **CDA 8917**
Tsunami / Jan '95 / Silva Screen

DUCK YOU SUCKER (A Fistful Of Dynamite)
Morricone, Ennio *C*
CD ______ **CDCIA 5003**
Cinevox / Jan '89 / Koch / Silva Screen

DUE SOUTH (Music From The TV Series)
CD ______ **62428400042**
Nettwerk / Nov '96 / Greyhound / Pinnacle / Vital

DUMB AND DUMBER
Ballad of Peter Pumpkinhead: *Crash Test Dummies* / New age girl: *Deadeye Dick* / Insomniac: *Echobelly* / If you don't love me (I'll kill myself): *Droge, Pete* / Crash: *Primitives* / Whiney, whiney (what really drives me crazy): *Willie One Blood* / Too much of a good thing: *Sons* / You sexy thing: *Deee-Lite* / Where I find my heaven: *Gigolo Aunts* / Hurdy gurdy man: *Butthole Surfers* / Take: *Lupins* / Bear song: *Green Jelly* / Get ready: *Proclaimers*
CD ______ **07863665232**
RCA / Sep '96 / BMG

DUNE
Eno, Brian/Toto *C*
Dune / Dune prologue / Dune main title / Robot fight / Leto's theme / Box / Floating fat man / Trip to Arrakis / First attack / Prophecy theme / Dune (desert home) / Paul meets Chani / Prelude (take my hand) / Paul takes the water of life / Big battle / Paul kills Feyd / Final dream / Take my hand
CD ______ **TCS 1032**
Silva Screen / Jan '94 / Koch / Silva Screen

DUTCH
CD ______ **D5336**
Varese Sarabande / Aug '91 / Pinnacle

DUTCH HARBOR
CD ______ **ALP 85CD**
Atavistic / Feb '97 / Cargo / SRD

DYING YOUNG
Howard, James Newton *C*
Dying Young: *Kenny G.* / Driving North/ Moving in / Clock / Love montage / Maze / All the way: *Osborne, Jeffrey* / Hillary's theme / Victor teaches art / Bluff / San Francisco / Victor / All the way: *King Curtis* / I'll never leave you
CD ______ **261952**
Arista / Aug '91 / BMG

EARTHQUAKE
Williams, John *C*
CD ______ **VSD 5262**
Varese Sarabande / Apr '91 / Pinnacle

EASTER PARADE
1948 Film Cast
Berlin, Irving *C*
Green, Johnny *Con*
Main title / Happy Easter / Drum crazy / It only happens when I dance with you / Happy Easter (reprise 1) / Everybody's doin' it now / I want to go back to Michigan (down on the farm) / Happy Easter (reprise 2) / Making faces / Beautiful faces need beautiful clothes / This is the life (Dog act) / Along came Ruth / Call me up some rainy afternoon / Fella with an umbrella / Vaudeville montage / I love a piano / Snookey ookums / Ragtime violin / When the midnight choo-choo leaves for Alabam / Mixed greens / That international rag / Shakin' the blues away / It only happens when I dance with you / Fanfare and montage - Globe Theatre / Steppin' out with my baby / Mr. Monotony / Couple of swells / Roof garden (drum crazy reprise) / Girl on the magazine cover / New Amsterdam roof / Better luck next time / End title
CD ______ **CDODEON 4**
Premier/EMI / Feb '96 / EMI

EASY COME, EASY GO/SPEEDWAY
Presley, Elvis
Easy come, easy go / Love machine / Yoga is as yoga does / You gotta stop / Sing you children / I'll take love / She's a machine / Love machine (alternate take) / Sing you children (alternate take) / She's a machine (alternate take 13) / Suppose (alternate master) / Speedway / There ain't nothing like a song / Your time hasn't come yet, baby / Who are you, who am I / He's your uncle, not your dad / Let yourself go / Five sleepy heads / Suppose / Your groovy self
CD ______ **07863665582**
RCA / Mar '95 / BMG

EASY RIDER
Pusher: *Steppenwolf* / Born to be wild: *Steppenwolf* / Weight: *Band* / I wasn't born to follow: *Byrds* / If you want to be a bird: *Holy Modal Rounders* / Don't Bogart me: *Fraternity of Man* / If six was nine: *Hendrix, Jimi Experience* / Kyrie Eleison Mardi Gras: *Electric Prunes* / It's alright Ma (I'm only bleeding): *McGuinn, Roger* / Ballad of Easy Rider: *McGuinn, Roger*
CD ______ **MCLD 19153**
MCA / Nov '92 / BMG

EASY RIDER (Songs From & Inspired By The Film)
CD ______ **NTRCD 027**
Quality / Sep '94 / Pinnacle

EDDIE
CD ______ **5242432**
Island / Jun '96 / PolyGram

EDDIE AND THE CRUISERS II (Eddie Lives)
Runnin' thru the fire / Open road / Emotional storm / Garden of Eden / Some like it hot / Just a matter of time / Maryia / Pride and passion / NYC song / (Keep my love) alive
CD ______ **8420462**
Polydor / Jul '90 / PolyGram

ED'S NEXT MOVE
Golson, Benny *C*
Tea and symphony: *Comedians* / Manhattan bound: *Golson, Benny* / Looking for a home: *Golson, Benny* / Look away: *Stubborn All Stars* / City walking: *Golson, Benny* / Spoken word: *Ed's Redeeming Qualities* / Morning groove: *Golson, Benny* / Something there: *Golson, Benny* / Planet Robin: *Trouble Dolls* / She ate the fly: *Ed's Redeeming Qualities* / I'm just feeling it now: *Williams, Jane Kelly* / Rough at first: *Golson, Benny* / Lonesome bus: *Mr. Henry* / Buck tempo: *Ed's Redeeming Qualities* / Another turn in the road: *Golson, Benny* / More bad times: *Ed's Redeeming Qualities*
CD ______ **74321413362**
Milan / Jul '97 / Conifer/BMG / Silva Screen

EDUCATING RITA
Hentschel, David
Hentschel, David *C*
Educating Rita / Franks theme Pt. 1 (A dead good poet) / Franks theme Pt. 2 / Variations on Frank and Rita (Innocence and experience) / Educating Rita (reprise) / Thought for Rita Pt. 1 / University challenge / Burning books / Franks theme pt. 3 (Virginia, Charlotte, Jane or Emily) / Thought for Rita Pt. 2 / Educated woman / Macbeth
CD ______ **C5CD 587**
See For Miles/C5 / Jun '92 / Pinnacle

EDWARD SCISSORHANDS
Elfman, Danny
Elfman, Danny *C*
Main title / Story time / Castle on the hill / Cookie factory / Edwardo the barber / Etiquette lesson / Ballet de suburbia (suite) / Death / Final confrontation / Finale / Farewell / Ice dance / Home sweet home / Esmerelda / Helst / Rampage / Plot unfolds / End credits / Beautiful new world / With these sands
CD ______ **MCLD 19303**
MCA / Oct '95 / BMG

EIGER SANCTION, THE
Williams, John *C*
Williams, John *Con*
CD ______ **VSD 5277**
Varese Sarabande / Mar '91 / Pinnacle

EIGHT HEADS IN A DUFFLEBAG
CD ______ **VSD 5835**
Varese Sarabande / May '97 / Pinnacle

EL CID
New Zealand Youth Choir
Rozsa, Miklos *C*
Sedares, James *Con*
CD ______ **373402**
Koch International / Mar '96 / Koch

EL DORADO
Masso, Alejandro *C*
CD ______ **CD 342**
Milan / Jan '89 / Conifer/BMG / Silva Screen

EL GRECO/GIORDANO BRUNO
Morricone, Ennio *C*
CD ______ **OST 111**
Milano Dischi / Mar '92 / Silva Screen

EL LADO OSCURO DEL CORAZON
Montes, Oswaldo *C*
CD ______ **887880**
Milan / Jan '95 / Conifer/BMG / Silva Screen

EL VIAJE
CD ______ **262579**
Milan / Jan '95 / Conifer/BMG / Silva Screen

ELECTRA
Theodorakis, Mikis *C*
CD ______ **SR 50090**
Varese Sarabande / May '94 / Pinnacle

ELECTRIC DREAMS
Moroder, Giorgio *C*
Electric dreams: *Arnold, P.P.* / Video: *Lynne, Jeff* / Dream: *Culture Club* / Duel: *Moroder, Giorgio* / Now you are mine: *Terry, Helen* / Love is love: *Culture Club* / Chase runner: *Heaven 17* / Let it run: *Lynne, Jeff* / Madeline's theme: *Moroder, Giorgio* / Together in electric dreams: *Moroder, Giorgio & Philip Oakey*
CD ______ **CDVIP 127**
Virgin / Oct '94 / EMI

ELEGIES
1993 London Cast
Hood, Janet *C*
Russell, Bill *L*
Angels, punks & raging queens / I'm holding onto you / And the rain keeps falling down / I don't do that anymore / I don't know how to help you / Celebrate / Heroes all round / Spend it while you can / My brother lived San Francisco / Learning to let go
CD ______ **OCRCD 6035**
First Night / Mar '96 / Pinnacle

ELIZABETH AND ESSEX
Munich Symphony Orchestra
Korngold, Erich *C*
Davis, Carl *Con*
CD ______ **873122**
Silva Screen / Jul '93 / Koch / Silva Screen

ELIZABETH TAYLOR IN LONDON/FOUR IN THE MORNING (The Ember Years Vol.1)
Barry, John *C*
Barry, John *Con*
Elizabeth in London / Elizabeth walk / English garden / London theme / London waltz / Lovers / Fire of London / Elizabeth theme / Four in the morning / River walk / Lover's clasp / Norman's return / River ride / Lover's tension / First reconciliation / Norman leaves / Moment od decision / Judi come back
CD ______ **PLAY 002**
Play It Again / Mar '92 / Silva Screen

EMERALD FOREST, THE
Homrich, Junior & Brian Gascoigne *C*
CD ______ **VCD 47251**
Varese Sarabande / Jan '89 / Pinnacle

EMPIRE OF THE SUN
Williams, John *C*
Williams, John *Con*
Suo Gan / Cadillac of the skies / Jim's new life / Lost in the crowd / Imaginary air battle / Liberation: exsultate justi / Return of the city / British Grenadiers / Toy planes, home and hearth / Streets of Shangai / Pheasant hunt / No road home/seeing the bomb / Exsultate justi
CD ______ **7599256682**
WEA / Feb '91 / Warner Music

EMPIRE STRIKES BACK, THE (The Star Wars Trilogy Special Edition)
Williams, John *C*
Williams, John *Con*
CD ______ **09026687472**
2CD ______ **09026687732**
RCA Victor / Mar '97 / BMG

ENCHANTED APRIL
Bennett, Richard Rodney *C*
CD ______ **BCD 3035**
Bay Cities / Mar '93 / Silva Screen

ENCIRCLED SEA, THE
Boyle, Robert *C*
Boyle, Robert *Con*
Waters edge / Earth, fire and water / Heart of the Mediterranean / Fishermen / Shipbuilders / Navigators / Great exchange / Gateways and haven / Theatre of war / Sea of belief
CD ______ **FILMCD 076**
Silva Screen / Sep '90 / Koch / Silva Screen

ENEMIES (A Love Story)
Jarre, Maurice *C*
Herman / Tamara / In the wood / Masha / Third wife / Kertchmar Country Club / Rumba / Baby Masha
CD ______ **VSD 5253**
Varese Sarabande / May '90 / Pinnacle

ENGLAND, MY ENGLAND (The Story Of Henry Purcell)
Monteverdi Choir & English Baroque Soloists
Purcell, Henry *C*
Gardiner, John Eliot *Con*
CD ______ **0630107002**
Erato / Jan '96 / Warner Music

ENGLISH PATIENT, THE
Academy Of St. Martin In The Fields
Yared, Gabriel *C*
English patient / Retreat / Rupert bear / What else do you love / Why picton / Cheek to cheek: *Astaire, Fred* / Kip's lights / Hana's curse / I'll always go back to the church / Black nights / Swoon, I'll catch you / Am I K in your book / Let me come in / Wang wang blues: *Goodman, Benny* / Convento di sant'ana / Herodotus / Szerelem, szerelem: *Muzsikas & Marta Sebestyen* / Ask your saint who he's killed / One o'clock jump: *Goodman, Benny* / I'll be back / Let me tell you about winds / Read me to sleep / Cave of swimmers / Where or when: *Shepheard's Hotel Jazz Orchestra* / Aria from the Goldberg variations: *Steinberg, Julie* / Cheek to cheek: *Fitzgerald, Ella* / As far as Florence
CD ______ **FCD 16001**
Fantasy / Jun '97 / Jazz Music / Pinnacle / Wellard

EQUINOX
Mystery man: *Rypdal, Terje* / Milonga del angel: *Piazzolla, Astor* / Al Bine: *Toure, Ali Farke* / Left alone: *Shepp, Archie* / Mirage: *Rypdal, Terje* / Istoria ne Edna Lyubov: *Paposov, Ivo* / Symphonic dances: *Paposov, Ivo* / Once upon a time: *Rypdal, Terje*
CD ______ **VSD 5424**
Varese Sarabande / May '93 / Pinnacle

ER
Howard, James Newton *C*
CD ______ **7567829424**
East West / Jan '97 / Warner Music

ESCAPE FROM LA (Score)
Carpenter, John & Shirley Walker *C*
CD ______ **74321409512**
Milan / Sep '96 / Conifer/BMG / Silva Screen

ESCAPE FROM LA
CD ______ **7567927142**
Atlantic / Oct '96 / Warner Music

ET
Williams, John *C*
Three million light years from home / Abandoned and pursued / ET's halloween / Flying / ET phone home / Over the moon / Adventure on Earth
CD ______ **MCLD 19021**
MCA / Apr '92 / BMG

ETOILE/THE VISITOR
Knieper, Jurgen/Franco Micalizzi *C*
CD ______ **OST 108**
Milano Dischi / Jul '93 / Silva Screen

EUROPEANS
CD ______ **CDQ 5551022**
EMI / Apr '94 / EMI

EVEN COWGIRLS GET THE BLUES
Lang, k.d.
Lang, k.d./Ben Mink *C*
Just keep me moving / Much finer place / Or was I / Hush sweet lover / Myth / Apogee / Virtual vortex / Lifted by love / Overture / Kundalini yoga waltz / In perfect dreams / Curious soul astray / Ride of Bonanza Jellybean / Don't be a lemming polka / Sweet Cherokee / Cowgirl pride
CD ______ **9362454332**
WEA / Oct '93 / Warner Music

EVERLASTING SECRET FAMILY (& A Halo For Athuan/Kindred Spirits)
Sydney/Adelaide/Queensland Orchestra & Chorus
Bremner, Tony *C*
Bremner, Tony/Mike Kenny/Werner Andreas Albert *Con*
Everlasting secret family / Halo for Athuan / Kindred spirit
CD ______ **SCCD 1020**
Southern Cross / Jul '88 / Silva Screen

EVERYBODY'S ALL AMERICAN
CD ______ C 21Z91184
Silva Screen / Jan '89 / Koch / Silva Screen

EVERYONE SAYS I LOVE YOU
Alda, Alan & Woody Allen/Goldie Hawn/ Julia Roberts/Tim Roth/Dick Hyman & New York Studio Players
Allen, Woody *C*
Allen, Woody *L*
Just you, just me / Everyone says I love you / My baby just cares for me / I'm a dreamer, aren't we all / I'm thru with love / Just say I love her / Venetian scene / Recurrence / All my life / Cuddle up a little closer / Looking at you / No lover, no friend (that's the end) / I can't believe that you're in love with me / What a little moonlight can do / Chinatown, my Chinatown / Cocktails for two / Chiquita banana / Mimi / Louise / You brought a new kind of love to me / Hooray for Captain Spaulding
CD ______ 09026687562
RCA Victor / Apr '97 / BMG

EVIL DEAD I
Loduca, Joseph
Loduca, Joseph *C*
Introduction / Eye games / Charm / Bridge out / Rape of the vines / Ascent / Inflection / Automatic writing / Skin / Give her the ax / Love never dies / Kandanian dagger / Book burning / Dawn of the evil dead / Not the shower curtain / Check on you / Pencil you in / Get the lantern / Book of the dead / Down / Incantation / Shotgun / Games / Cabin / Wounded melody
CD ______ VSD 5362
Varese Sarabande / Jun '93 / Pinnacle

EVIL DEAD II
Loduca, Joseph *C*
Behemoth / Book of evil / Fresh panic (other side of your dream) / Putrified forest under her skin
CD ______ CDTER 1142
TER / Jul '87 / Koch

EVIL DEAD III (Army Of Darkness)
Loduca, Joseph *C*
CD ______ VSD 5411
Varese Sarabande / Mar '93 / Pinnacle

EVITA
1976 Studio Cast
Lloyd Webber, Andrew *C*
Rice, Tim *L*
Cinema in Buenos Aires 26 July 1952 / Requiem for Evita/Oh what a circus / On this night of a thousand stars / Buenos Aires / Goodnight and thank you / Lady's got potential / Charity concert/I'd be surprisingly good for you / Another suitcase in another hall / Dangerous Jade / New Argentina / On the balcony of the Casa Rosada / High flying adored / Rainbow high / Rainbow tour / Actress hasn't learned the lines (you'd like to hear) / And the money kept rolling in (and out) / Santa Evita / Waltz for Eva and Che / She is a diamond / Dice are rolling/Eva's sonnet / Eva's final broadcast / Montage / Lament
2CD ______ RMCX 503
MCA / Dec '96 / BMG

EVITA
1978 London Cast
Lloyd Webber, Andrew *C*
Rice, Tim *L*
Requiem for Evita / Oh what a circus / On this night of a thousand stars / Eva and Magaldi / Eva beware of the city / Buenos Aires / Goodnight and thank you / Lady's got potential / Charity concert / I'd be surprisingly good for you / Another suitcase in another hall / Dangerous Jade / New Argentina / On the balcony of the Casa Rosada / Don't cry for me Argentina / High flying adored / Rainbow high / Rainbow tour / Actress hasn't learned the lines (you'd like to hear) / And the money kept rolling in (And out) / Santa Evita / Waltz for Eva and Che / She is a diamond / Dice are rolling / Eva's sonnet / Eva's final broadcast / Montage / Lament / Cinema in Buenos Aires 26 July 1952 / Art of the possible / Peron's latest flame
CD ______ DMCG 3527
MCA / Jul '85 / BMG

EVITA
Webb, Marti
Lloyd Webber, Andrew *C*
Rice, Tim *L*
CD ______ PWKS 4233
Carlton / Feb '95 / Carlton

EVITA (Sung In Korean)
Korean Cast
Lloyd Webber, Andrew *C*
Rice, Tim *L*
2CD ______ DRGCD 13104
DRG / Jan '95 / Discovery / New Note/ Pinnacle

EVITA
Film Cast
Lloyd Webber, Andrew *C*
Rice, Tim *L*
CD ______ 9362464322
2CD ______ 9362463462
Warner Bros. / Nov '96 / Warner Music

EVITA
Studio Cast
Lloyd Webber, Andrew *C*
Rice, Tim *L*
Requiem/oh what a circus / On this night of a thousand stars / Buenos Aires / I'd be surprising good for you / Another suitcase in another hall / New Argentina / Don't cry for me Argentina / High flying adored / Rainbow high / Waltz for Evita and Che / Lament
CD ______ 88022
CMC / May '97 / BMG

EXECUTIVE DECISION
Goldsmith, Jerry *C*
Goldsmith, Jerry *Con*
CD ______ VSD 5714
Varese Sarabande / May '96 / Pinnacle

EXIT
Tangerine Dream
Tangerine Dream *C*
Kiew mission / Pilots of purple twilight / Choronzon / Exit / Network 23 / Remote viewing
CD ______ TAND 13
Virgin / Jul '95 / EMI

EXIT TO EDEN
Doyle, Patrick *C*
CD ______ VSD 5553
Varese Sarabande / Jun '95 / Pinnacle

EXODUS
Gold, Ernest *C*
Exodus / Summer in Cyprus/Escape / Ari / Karen / Valley of Jezreel / Fight for survival / In Jerusalem / Brothers / Conspiracy / Prison break / Dawn / Fight for peace / Hatikvah
CD ______ 10582
Silva Screen / Jan '89 / Koch / Silva Screen

EXODUS/CAST A GIANT SHADOW
Gold, Ernest *C*
Cast a giant shadow (prologue) / Land of hope / War in the desert / Magda / Cast a giant shadow / Love me true / Road to Jerusalem / Gathering of the forces / Victory on the beach / Garden of Abu Gosh / Cast a giant shadow (finale) / Exodus / Summer in Cyprus / Escape / Ari / Karen / Valley of Jezreel / Fight for survival / Brothers / Conspiracy / Prison break / Dawn / Fight for peace / Hatikvah
CD ______ CDMGM 11
MGM/EMI / Apr '90 / EMI

EXODUS/JUDITH
Gold, Ernest/Sol Kaplan *C*
CD ______ TSU 0115
Tsunami / Jan '95 / Silva Screen

EXOTICA
Danha, Mychael *C*
Exotica / Something hidden / Dilko tamay huay / Pagan song / Kiss / Inside me / My angel / Little touch / Field 3 / Snake dance / Field 4 / Mujay yaad / Ride home
CD ______ VSD 5543
Varese Sarabande / Mar '95 / Pinnacle

EXTREME JUSTICE
Frank, David Michael *C*
CD ______ 887879
Milan / Jan '95 / Conifer/BMG / Silva Screen

EXTREME MEASURES
Elfman, Danny *C*
CD ______ VSD 5767
Varese Sarabande / Nov '96 / Pinnacle

F

FABULOUS BAKER BOYS, THE
Main title: *Grusin, Dave* / Welcome to the road: *Grusin, Dave* / Makin' whoopee: *Pfeiffer, Michelle* / Suzie and Jack: *Grusin, Dave* / Shop till you bop: *Grusin, Dave* / Soft on me: *Grusin, Dave* / Do nothin' 'til you hear from me: *Ellington, Duke Orchestra* / Moment of truth: *Grusin, Dave* / Moonglow: *Goodman, Benny* / Lullaby of birdland: *Palmer, Earl Trio* / My funny valentine: *Pfeiffer, Michelle*
CD ______ GRP 20022
GRP / Jun '93 / New Note/BMG

FACE TO FACE/THE BIG GUNDOWN (Faccia A Faccia/La Resa Dei Conti)
Morricone, Ennio *C*
CD ______ MASK MK701
Silva Screen / May '95 / Koch / Silva Screen

FALL OF A NATION/GLORIA'S ROMANCE
CD ______ OMP 103
Silva Screen / Jan '89 / Koch / Silva Screen

FALL OF THE ROMAN EMPIRE
Tiomkin, Dimitri *C*
Tiomkin, Dimitri *Con*
CD ______ VSD 5228
Varese Sarabande / Feb '90 / Pinnacle

FALL OF THE ROMAN EMPIRE (More Music From The Film)
Tiomkin, Dimitri *C*
Tiomkin, Dimitri *Con*
CD ______ ACN 7016
Cloud Nine / Sep '91 / Koch / Silva Screen

FALSETTOLAND
Cast Recording
Finn, William *C*
Finn, William & James Lapine *L*
Falsettoland / About time / Year of the child / Miracle of Judaism / Baseball game / Day in falsettoland / Round tables, square tables / Everyone hates his parents / What more can I say / Something bad is happening / More racquetball / Holding to the ground / Days like this / Cancelling the Barmitzvah / Unlikely lovers
CD ______ DRGCD 12601
DRG / Mar '92 / Discovery / New Note/ Pinnacle

FAME
1995 London Cast
Margoshes, Steve *C*
Levy, Jacques *L*
Hard work / I want to make magic / Can't keep it down / Tyrone's rap / There she goes/Fame / Let's play a love scene / Teacher's argument / Hard work (reprise) / I want to make magic (reprise) / Mabel's prayer / Think of Meryl Streep / Dancin' on the sidewalk / These are my children / In LA / Let's play a love scene (reprise) / Bring on tomorrow / Fame
CD ______ 5291092
Really Useful / Aug '95 / PolyGram

FAME
CC Productions
Margoshes, Steve *C*
Levy, Jacques *L*
Fame / Out here on my own / Hot lunch jam / Dogs in the yard / Red light / Is it OK to call you mine / Never alone / Ralph and Monty / I sing the body electric
CD ______ QED 203
Tring / Nov '96 / Tring

FAME
Studio Cast
Margoshes, Steve *C*
Levy, Jacques *L*
Fame / Out here on my own / Hot lunch jam / Dogs in the yard / Red light / Is it ok to call you mine / Never alone / Ralph and Monty / I sing the body electric
CD ______ 85082
CMC / May '97 / BMG

FAME - THE KIDS FROM FAME
Kids From Fame
Starmaker / I can do anything better than you can / I still believe in me / Life is a celebration / Step up to the mike / Hi fidelity / We got the power / It's gonna be a long night / Desdemona / Be my music
CD ______ ND 90427
RCA / Jun '95 / BMG

FAMILY THING
CD ______ 0022602CIN
Edel / Jul '96 / Pinnacle

FANTASIA
Toccata and fugue in D minor / Sorcerer's apprentice / Nutcracker suite (Part 1) / Nutcracker suite (Part 2) / Night on a bare mountain / Ave Maria
CD ______ 4178512
Decca / '85 / PolyGram

FANTASTICKS
1960 Broadway Cast
Schmidt, Harvey *C*
Jones, Tom *L*
Try to remember / Much much more / Metaphor / Never say no / It depends on what you pay / You wonder how these things begin / Soon it's gonna rain / Rape ballet / Happy ending / This plum is too ripe / I can see it / Plant a radish / Round and round / There is a curious paradox / They were you / Try to remember (reprise)
CD ______ CDTER 1099
TER / Aug '90 / Koch

FANTASTICKS
Japan Tour Cast
Schmidt, Harvey *C*
Jones, Tom *L*
Overture / Try to remember / Much more / Metaphor / Never say no / It depends on what you pay / Soon it's gonna rain / Abduction ballet / Happy ending / This plum is too ripe / I can see it / Plant a radish / Round and round / They were you
CD ______ DRGCD 19005
DRG / Jun '93 / Discovery / New Note/ Pinnacle

FANTOZZI/IL SECONDO TRAGICO FANTOZZI
Bixio, Franco & Fabio Frozzi/Vince Tempera *C*
CD ______ CDCIA 5096
Cinevox / Jul '92 / Koch / Silva Screen

FAR FROM HOME: THE ADVENTURES OF YELLOW DOG (Score)
Scott, John *C*
CD ______ JSCD 118
JOS / Oct '96 / JOS / Silva Screen

FAR FROM THE MADDING CROWD
Bennett, Richard Rodney *C*
CD ______ AK 47023
Cinevox / Jul '93 / Koch / Silva Screen

FAR NORTH
Red Clay Ramblers
Far north / Blue duluth / Amy's theme (Kitchen)/Gourd part 1 / Amy's theme (Field) / Roll on Buddy/Montage / Gangar / Big ships / Katie's ride / Train through the big woods / Night harps / Run sister run / Camptown races/Amy's theme / Amy's theme (Over the hill) / Gourd, part 2
CD ______ SHCD 8502
Sugar Hill / Jan '97 / ADA / CM / Direct / Koch / Roots

FARAWAY, SO CLOSE
Faraway, so close: *Cave, Nick* / Stay (faraway, so close): *U2* / Why can't I be good: *Reed, Lou* / Chaos: *Gronemeyer, Herbert* / Travellin' on: *Bonney, Simon* / Wanderer: *U2* / Cassiel's song: *Cave, Nick* / Slow tango: *Siberry, Jane* / Call me: *House Of Love* / All God's children: *Bonney, Simon* / Tightrope: *Anderson, Laurie* / Speak my language: *Anderson, Laurie*
CD ______ CDEMC 3660
EMI / Sep '93 / EMI

FARENHEIT 451
Seattle Symphony Orchestra
Herrmann, Bernard *C*
McNeely, Joel *Con*
CD ______ VSD 5551
Varese Sarabande / Jul '95 / Pinnacle

FAREWELL TO ARMS, A/SONS AND LOVERS
Nascimbene, Mario *C*
Ferrara, Franco *Con*
CD ______ DRGCD 32962
DRG / Oct '96 / Discovery / New Note/ Pinnacle

FAREWELL TO ARMS, A/THE BAREFOOT CONTESSA
Nascimbene, Mario *C*
CD ______ LEGENDCD 11
Legend / Sep '93 / Koch / Silva Screen

FAREWELL TO THE KING
Poledouris, Basil *C*
CD ______ CDCH 375
Milan / Feb '90 / Conifer/BMG / Silva Screen

FARINELLI
CD ______ K 1005
Auvidis Travelling / Oct '95 / Harmonia Mundi

FATAL FLAMES
Festo, Al *C*
CD ______ VCDS 7022
Varese Sarabande / Oct '96 / Pinnacle

FATHER CHRISTMAS
Phoenix Chamber Orchestra
Hewer, Mike *C*
Bigg, Julian *Con*
CD ______ 4694752
Columbia / Nov '95 / Sony

FATTI DI GENTE PERBENE/DIVINE CREATURE
Morricone, Ennio *C*
CD ______ CDCIA 5087
Cinevox / Jan '93 / Koch / Silva Screen

FAUST
Newman, Randy *C*
CD ______ 9362456722
Warner Bros. / Sep '95 / Warner Music

FAUST (Score)
Olympia Chamber Orchestra
Brock, Timothy *C*
CD ______ KOC 03
K / Jan '97 / Cargo / Greyhound / SRD

FEARLESS
Jarre, Maurice/Gorecki *C*
Mai Nozipo / Polymorphia / Sin Ella: *Gypsy Kings* / Symphony no.3
CD ______ 793342
Silva Screen / Jan '93 / Koch / Silva Screen

FEDS
Edelman, Randy
Edelman, Randy *C*
CD ______ GNPD 8014
GNP Crescendo / Jan '95 / ZYX

FEVER PITCH (A Match Made In Heaven)
There she goes: *La's* / Liquidator: *Harry J All Stars* / Fiesta: *Pogues* / Cafe '68: *MacColl, Neil & Boo Hewerdine* / Baba O'Riley: *Who* / How can we hang on to a dream: *Hardin, Tim* / Good thing: *Fine Young Cannibals* / All around the world: *Stansfield, Lisa* / Bright side of the road: *Morrison, Van* / Goin' back: *Pretenders* / Fever pitch: *Pretenders*
CD ______ 0630184532
Warner Bros. / Mar '97 / Warner Music

FIDDLER ON THE ROOF
1971 Film Cast
Bock, Jerry *C*
Harnick, Sheldon *L*
Williams, John *Con*
Prologue/Tradition/Main title / If I were a rich man / Sabbath prayer / To life / Miracle of miracles / Tevye's dream / Sunrise sunset / Wedding celebration and the bottle dance / Do you love me / Far from the home I love / Chava ballet sequence / Anatevka / Finale / Matchmaker, matchmaker / Bottle dance / Now I have everything
CD ______ CDP 7460912
EMI / Jul '94 / EMI

FIDDLER ON THE ROOF
1964 Broadway Cast
Bock, Jerry *C*
Harnick, Sheldon *L*

Greene, Milton *Con*
Prologue - Tradition / Matchmaker, matchmaker / If I were a rich man / Sabbath prayer / To life / Miracle of miracles / Dream / Sunrise, sunset / Wedding dance / Now I have everything / Do you love me / Rumour / Far from the home I love / Anatevka
CD ____ RD 87060
RCA Victor / Aug '90 / BMG

FIDDLER ON THE ROOF
London Cast
Bock, Jerry *C*
Harnick, Sheldon *L*
Robbins, Jerome *Con*
CD ____ SMK 53499
Sony Classical / Jul '94 / Sony

FIDDLER ON THE ROOF
Merrill, Robert & Molly Picon/London Festival Orchestra/Chorus
Bock, Jerry *C*
Harnick, Sheldon *L*
Black, Stanley *Con*
CD ____ 4489492
Phase 4 / Aug '96 / PolyGram

FIDDLER ON THE ROOF
CC Productions
Bock, Jerry *C*
Harnick, Sheldon *L*
Tradition/matchmaker / If I were a rich man / Sabbath prayer / To life / Sunrise sunset / Bottle dance / Now I have everything / Do you love me / Far from the home I love / Anatevka
CD ____ QED 209
Tring / Nov '96 / Tring

FIDDLER ON THE ROOF
Studio Cast
Bock, Jerry *C*
Harnick, Sheldon *L*
Tradition / Matchmaker matchmaker / If I were a rich man / Sabath prayer / To life / Sunrise, sunset / Bottle dance / Now I have everything / Do you love me / From the homes I love / Anatevka
CD ____ 88032
CMC / May '97 / BMG

FIELD OF DREAMS
Horner, James *C*
Horner, James *Con*
Cornfield / Deciding to build the field / Shoeless Joe / Timeless street / Old ball players / Drive home / Field of dreams / Library / Moonlight Graham / Night mists / Doc's memories / Place where dreams come true / End credits
CD ____ 30602
Silva Screen / Feb '90 / Koch / Silva Screen

FIELDS OF AMBROSIA
1995 London Cast
Silvestri, Martin *C*
Higgins, Joel *L*
Warman, M. *Con*
CD ____ CASTCD 58
First Night / Jul '96 / Pinnacle

FIERCE CREATURES
Goldsmith, Jerry *C*
CD ____ VSD 5792
Varese Sarabande / Feb '97 / Pinnacle

FIFTH ELEMENT, THE
London Session Orchestra
Serra, Eric *C*
Little light of love / Mondoshawan / Timecrash / Korben Dallas / Koolen / Akta / Leeloo / Five millenia later / Plavalaguna / Ruby Rap / Heat / Badaboom / Mangalores / Lucia di Lammermoor / Diva dance / Leeloominai / Bomb in the hotel / Mina Hinoo / No cash no trash / Radiowaves / Human nature / Pictures of war / Lakta Ligunai / Protect life / Little light of love / Aknot wot
CD ____ CDVIR 63
Virgin / Jun '97 / EMI

FILM WORKS VOL.7 (Cynical Hysterie Hour)
Zorn, John
CD ____ TZA 7315
Tzadik / Jul '97 / Cargo

FINAL JUDGEMENT (& Scores From Stepmother & The Terror Within II)
Plumeri, Terry *C*
CD ____ CIN 2224
Silva Screen / Jan '95 / Koch / Silva Screen

FINE ROMANCE, A
Kern, Jerome *C*
Fields, Dorothy *L*
CD ____ C 537
Milan / Aug '92 / Conifer/BMG / Silva Screen

FIORELLO
Broadway Cast
Bock, Jerry *C*
Harnick, Sheldon *L*
CD ____ ZDM 5650232
EMI Classics / Dec '93 / EMI

FIORILE
Piovani, Nicola *C*
CD ____ 873148
Milan / May '95 / Conifer/BMG / Silva Screen

FIRE IN THE SKY
Isham, Mark *C*
White Mountains Arizona / Travis Walton / Fire in the sky / Return / Man on display / Evil spirits from the sky / They didn't like me - a case unsolved
CD ____ VSD 5417
Varese Sarabande / Apr '93 / Pinnacle

FIRESTARTER
Tangerine Dream
Tangerine Dream *C*
Crystal voice / Testlab / Escaping point / Burning force / Shop territory / Out of the heat / Run / Charly the kid / Rainbirds move / Between realities / Flash final
CD ____ VSD 5251
Varese Sarabande / '90 / Pinnacle

FIRM, THE
Grusin, Dave
Grusin, Dave *C*
Firm / Stars on the water / Mitch and Abby / Money / Memphis stomp / Never mind / Ray's blues / Dance class / Plan / Blues: The death of love and trust / Start it up / Mud island chase / How could you lose me
CD ____ GRLD 19358
MCA / Apr '97 / BMG

FIRST KNIGHT
Goldsmith, Jerry *C*
Arthur's fanfare / Promise me / Camelot / Raid on Leonesse / New life / To Leonesse / Night battle / Village ruins / Arthur's farewell / Camelot lives
CD ____ 4809372
Epic / Jul '95 / Sony

FIRST MEN IN THE MOON, THE
Johnson, Laurie *C*
Johnson, Laurie *Con*
Prelude / Modern moon landing / Newscasters/Union Jack/Journey to Dymchurch / Cherry cottage/Kate and Bedford / Arguments / Cavor's experiments / The sphere / Love theme / To the moon / Lunar landing/ Moonscpae/Weightlessness/Planting the Union Ja / Lens pit/Shadows / Battle with the Selenites / Search for the sphere/Kate in peril / Moon beast / Lens complex/Dismantling the sphere/Cocooning Selenites/ The / End of the eclipse/The grand lunar / Bedford shoots at the grand lunar / Pursuit and escape from the moon/End title
CD ____ ACN 7015
Cloud Nine / Jul '91 / Koch / Silva Screen

FIRST NUDIE MUSICAL, THE (& Stages/ Spaceship/The Good One)
Kimmel, Bruce *C*
CD ____ XCD 1002
Silva Screen / Feb '90 / Koch / Silva Screen

FIRST WIVES CLUB, THE
Wives and lovers: *Warwick, Dionne* / Beautiful morning: *Rascals* / Over and over: *Johnson, Puff* / Piece of my heart: *King, Diana* / Game of love: *Brownstone* / Love is on the way: *Porter, Billy* / Sisters are doin' it for themselves: *Eurythmics* / Think: *Franklin, Aretha* / Heartbreak Road: *Ferris, Dionne* / I will survive: *Savage, Chantay* / Movin' on up: *M People* / I'm still standing: *Wash, Martha* / You don't own me: *Midler, Bette & Goldie Hawn/Diane Keaton*
CD ____ 4853962
Columbia / Nov '96 / Sony

FIRST WIVES CLUB, THE (Score)
Shaiman, Marc *C*
CD ____ VSD 5781
Varese Sarabande / Jan '97 / Pinnacle

FISH CALLED WANDA, A
Du Prez, John *C*
Du Prez, John *Con*
CD ____ 887878
Milan / '95 / Conifer/BMG / Silva Screen

FITZCARRALDO
Popul Vuh
Popul Vuh *C*
CD ____ 14876
Spalax / Sep '96 / ADA / Cargo / Direct / Discovery / Greyhound

FITZWILLY
Williams, John *C*
CD ____ TSU 0121
Tsunami / Jan '95 / Silva Screen

FIVE CORNERS
Howard, James Newton *C*
CD ____ VCD 47354
Varese Sarabande / Jan '89 / Pinnacle

FIVE GUYS NAMED MOE
1991 London Cast
Jordan, Louis *C*
Five guys named Moe / Early in the morning / Brother beware / I like em fat like that / Messy Bessy / Pettin' and pokin' / Life is so peculiar / I know what I've got / Azure te / Safe, sane and single / Push ka pi shee pie / Saturday night fish fry / What's the use of gettin' sober / Band played out / Is you is ir is you ain't my baby / Hurry home / Choo choo ch'boogie / Look out sister / Don't let the sun catch you crying / There ain't nobody here but us chickens / Ca-l'donia / Let the good times roll / Cabaret
CD ____ OCRCD 6050
First Night / Apr '97 / Pinnacle

FIVE HEARTBEATS, THE
Heart Is A House For Love: *Dells* / We haven't finished yet: *Labelle, Patti & Thomas, Tressa* / Nights Like This: *After 7* / Bring Back The Days: *U.S. Male* / Baby stop running around: *Bird & The Midnight Falcons* / In The Middle: *Flash & The Five Heartbeats* / Nothing but Love: *Five Heartbeats* / Are you ready for me: *Flash & The Ebony Sparks* / Stay in my corner: *Dells* / I feel like going on: *Eddie, Baby Doll & The LA Mass Choir/ Billy Valentine*
CD ____ CDVMM 4
Virgin / Sep '92 / EMI

FIVE MAN ARMY/THE LINK
Morricone, Ennio *C*
CD ____ CDE 76
Silva Screen / Apr '96 / Koch / Silva Screen

FIVE SUMMER STORIES
Honk
Honk *C*
Creation / Blue of your backdrop / Brad and David's theme / High in the middle / Hum drums / Bear's country / Made my statement (Love you baby) / Don't let your goodbye stand / Lopez / Blue of your backdrop (instrumental) / Tunnel of love
CD ____ GNPD 8027
GNP Crescendo / Jan '91 / ZYX

FIX
Original Cast
CD ____ CASTCD 62
First Night / Sep '97 / Pinnacle

FLAHOOLEY
Broadway Cast
Lane, Burton *C*
Harburg, E.Y. 'Yip' *L*
CD ____ ZDM 7647642
EMI Classics / Apr '93 / EMI

FLAMING STAR/WILD IN THE COUNTRY/FOLLOW THAT DREAM
Presley, Elvis
Flaming star / Summer kisses, winter tears / Britches a cane and a high starched collar / Black star / Flaming star (end title version) / Wild in the country / I slipped, I stumbled, I fell / Lonely man / In my way / Forget me never / Lonely man (solo) / I slipped, I stumbled, I fell (Alternate master) / Follow that dream / Angel / What a wonderful life / I'm not the marrying kind / Whistling tune / Sound advice
CD ____ 07863665572
RCA / Mar '95 / BMG

FLAMINGO KID
Breakaway / Heatwave / He's so fine / One fine day / Stranger on the shore / Runaround Sue / Good golly Miss Molly / Money (Thats what I want) / It's alright / Finger poppin' time / Get a job / Boys will be boys
CD ____ 5515392
Spectrum / Aug '95 / PolyGram

FLASH FEARLESS
I'm Flash: *Cooper, Alice* / Space pirates: *Cooper, Alice* / Trapped: *Brooks, Elkie* / Sacrifice: *Brooks, Elkie* / Country cookin: *Dandy, Jim* / Blast off: *Dandy, Jim* / What's happening: *Trower, Robin* / Let's go to the chop: *Entwistle, John* / All around my hat: *Prior, Maddy* / Georgia syncopator: *Prior, Maddy*
CD ____ RPM 148
RPM / Mar '95 / Pinnacle

FLASH GORDON
Queen
Flash's theme / In the space capsule / Ming's theme (in the court of Ming the merciless) / Ring / Football fight / In the death cell / Execution of Flash / Kiss / Arboria (planet of the tree men) / Escape from the swamp / Flash to the rescue / Vultan's theme (attack of the hawk men) / Battle theme / Wedding march / Marriage of Dale and Ming (and Flash approaching) / Crash dive on Mingo city / Flash's theme reprise (victory celebrations) / Hero
CD ____ CDPCSD 137
Parlophone / Apr '94 / EMI

FLASHDANCE
Moroder, Giorgio *C*
Flashdance (what a feeling): *Cara, Irene* / He's a dream: *Shandi* / Flashdance love theme: *St. John, Helen* / Manhunt: *Kamon, Karen* / Lady lady lady: *Esposito, Joe* / Imagination: *Branigan, Laura* / Romeo: *Summer, Donna* / Seduce me tonight: *Cycle V* / I'll be here where the heart is: *Carnes, Kim* / Maniac: *Sembello, Michael*
CD ____ 8114922
Casablanca / Dec '83 / PolyGram

FLASHPOINT
Tangerine Dream
Tangerine Dream *C*
Going west / Afternoon in the desert / Plane ride / Mystery tracks / Lost in the dunes / Highway patrol / Love phantasy / Madcap story / Dirty cross roads / Flashpoint
CD ____ HMIXD 29
Heavy Metal / Apr '87 / Revolver / Sony

FLINTSTONES, THE
Stone Age Project
Meet the Flintstones / Human Being (Bedrock Steady) / Hit and run holiday / Prehistoric daze / Rock with the caveman / I showed a caveman how to rock / Bedrock twitch / I wanna be a flintstone / In the days of the caveman / Anarchy in the UK / Walk the dinosaur / Bedrock anthem / Mesozoic music
CD ____ AAOHP 93552
Start / Oct '94 / Disc

FLIRTING WITH DISASTER
Anything but love: *Dr. John & Angela McCluskey* / Somebody else's body: *Urge Overkill* / Outasight: *G-Love & The Philly Cartel* / You're not a slut: *Southern Culture On The Skids* / Camel walk: *Southern Culture On The Skids* / Lend me your comb: *Perkins, Carl* / Acid propaganda: *Cake* / You part the waters: *Cake* / Lonnie cooks quail: *Southern Culture On The Skids* / Red beans 'n' reverb: *Southern Culture On The Skids* / Flirting with disaster: *Dr. John & Angela McCluskey* / Hypospadia: *Dr. John & Angela McCluskey* / Melodie d'amour: *Martin, Dean* / For duty and humanity: *Inch* / Flirting suite: *Endelman, Stephen*
CD ____ GED 24970
Geffen / Feb '97 / BMG

FLORA, THE RED MENACE
1987 Off-Broadway Cast
Kander, John *C*
Ebb, Fred *L*
Prologue/Unafraid / Street song I / Kid herself / All I need is one good break / Not every day of the week / Street song II / Sign here / Street song III / Quiet thing / Flame / Not every day of the week (reprise) / Street song IV / Dear love / Keepin' it hot / Street song V / Express yourself / Where did everybody go / Street song VI / You are you / Joke / Quiet thing (reprise) / Sing happy / Closing scene
CD ____ CDTER 1159
TER / May '89 / Koch

FLORA, THE RED MENACE
1965 Broadway Cast
Kander, John *C*
Ebb, Fred *L*
Hastings, Harold *Con*
Overture / Prologue/Unafraid / All I need (is one good break) / Not every day of the week / Sign here / Flame / Palomino pal / Quiet thing / Hello, waves / Dera love / Express yourself / Knock knock / Sing happy / You are you
CD ____ GD 60821
RCA Victor / Dec '92 / BMG

FLOWER DRUM SONG
1960 London Cast
Rodgers, Richard *C*
Hammerstein II, Oscar *L*
Lowe, R. *Con*
Overture / You are beautiful / Hundred million miracles / I enjoy being a girl / I am going to like it here / Like a god / Chop suey / Don't marry me / Grant Avenue / Love look away / Fan tan Fannie / Gliding through my memoree / Other generation / Sunday / Finale
CD ____ CDANGEL 7
Angel / Apr '94 / EMI

FLOWER DRUM SONG
1958 Broadway Cast
Rodgers, Richard *C*
Hammerstein II, Oscar *L*
Dell'Isola, Salvatore *Con*
CD ____ SK 53536
Sony Broadway / Nov '93 / Sony

FLOWERS IN THE ATTIC
Young, Christopher *C*
CD ____ MAF 7009D
Intrada / Jul '92 / Koch / Silva Screen

FLOYD COLLINS
Off Broadway Cast
Guettel, Adam *C*
CD ____ 7559794342
Nonesuch / May '97 / Warner Music

FLY I, THE
London Philharmonic Orchestra
Shore, Howard *C*
Main title / Last visit / Phone call / Ronnie calls back / Particle magazine / Ronnie's visit / Fingernails / Creature / Maggot, The/ Fly graphic / Ultimate family / Plasma pool / Stathis entera / Seth goes through / Jump / Armwrestle / Stairs / Baboon teleportation / Steak montage / Success with baboon / Finale
CD ____ VCD 47272
Varese Sarabande / Jan '89 / Pinnacle

FLY I, THE/THE OMEN III (THE FINAL CONFLICT)
CD ____ VSD 47272
Varese Sarabande / Feb '90 / Pinnacle

FLY II, THE
Young, Christopher *C*
Fly II / Fly variations / Spider and the fly / Fly march / Bay 17 mysteries / What's the magic word / Come fly with me / Musica domestica metastasis / More is coming / Accelerated Brundle disease / Bartok barbaro / Dad
CD ____ VSD 5220
Varese Sarabande / May '89 / Pinnacle

FLYING DOWN TO RIO/HOLLYWOOD HOTEL
Theme / I know why / In the mood / It happend in sun valley / Chattanooga choo choo / Flying down to Rio / Orchids in the moonlight / Carioca / Music makes me / Sing you son of a gun / Dark eyes / Silhouttes in the moonlight / Sing sing sing / Let that be a lesson to you / I'm like a fish out of water
CD ____ CD 60008
Great Movie Themes / Apr '97 / Target/ BMG

FOG, THE
Carpenter, John *C*
Carpenter, John *Con*
CD ______ **VCD 47267**
Varese Sarabande / Jan '89 / Pinnacle

FOLLIES
1985 Lincoln Center Revival Cast
Sondheim, Stephen *C*
Overture / Beautiful girls / Don't look at me / Waiting for the girls upstairs / Rain on the roof / Ah Paree / Broadway baby / Road you didn't take / In Buddy's eyes / Who's that woman / I'm still here / Too many mornings / Right girl / One more kiss / Could I leave you / Loveland / You're gonna love tomorrow/Love will see us through / Buddy's blues / Losing my mind / Story of Lucy and Jessie / Live, laugh, love / Finale
2CD ______ **RD 87128**
RCA Victor / Aug '90 / BMG

FOLLIES
1987 London Cast
Sondheim, Stephen *C*
CD ______ **OCRCD 6019**
First Night / Oct '95 / Pinnacle

FOLLIES
1971 Broadway Cast
Sondheim, Stephen *C*
CD ______ **ZDM 7646662**
EMI Classics / Apr '93 / EMI

FOOLS OF FORTUNE
Zimmer, Hans *C*
CD ______ **CH 334**
Milan / Jan '95 / Conifer/BMG / Silva Screen

FOOTLOOSE
Footloose: *Loggins, Kenny* / Let's hear it for the boy: *Williams, Deniece* / Almost paradise: *Wilson, Ann & Mike Reno* / Holding out for a hero: *Tyler, Bonnie* / Dancing in the street: *Shalamar* / I'm free (heaven helps the man): *Loggins, Kenny* / Somebody's eyes: *Bonoff, Karla* / Girl gets around: *Hagar, Sammy* / Never: *Moving Pictures*
CD ______ **4630002**
CBS / Nov '88 / Sony

FOR LOVE OR MONEY (THE CONCIERGE)
Broughton, Bruce *C*
Broughton, Bruce *Con*
CD ______ **9245152**
Silva Screen / Jul '93 / Koch / Silva Screen

FOR ME AND MY GAL
Film Cast
Main title / Vaudeville routine / Doll shop (pt.1) / Oh you beautiful doll / Doll shop (pt.1 cont.) / Don't leave me Daddy / Oh you beautiful doll (reprise) / Doll shop (pt.2) / By the beautiful sea / Darktown strutters ball / For me and my gal / Confession / When you wore a tulip / Don't bite the hand that's feeding you / Do I love you / It started with Eve / Woman's perogative / After you've gone / Spell of the waltz / Love song / Dream crashes / I'm sorry I made you cry / Tell me / Till we meet again / We don't want the bacon, what we want is a piece of the Rhin / Ballin' the Jack / Small time / What are you going to do about the boys / How ya gonna keep 'em down on the farm / There's a long long trail / Where do we go from here / Over there / It's a long way to Tipperary / Goodbye Broadway hello France / Yankee doodle / Smiles / Hinky dinky parlay voo / Oh Frenchy / Pack up your troubles in your old kit bag and smile, smile, / When Johnny comes marching home / Finale / Main title (alt.) / Dear old pal of mine / Smiles (outtake) / Three cheers for the yanks / For me and my gal (outtake)
CD ______ **CDODEON 12**
Soundtracks / Apr '96 / EMI

FOR ROSEANNA (Roseanna's Grave)
London Symphony Orchestra
Jones, Trevor *C*
Ingman, Nick *Con*
Roseanna's theme / Luna Rossa / Marcello / Hospital visitor / Doing the rounds / At Marcelina's grave / Her dying wish / Torna a surriento / Last rites / I don't want you to be lonely / Confession / Another funeral / My darling wife / Roseanna's funeral / Journey to the station / We'll be dining on the plane
CD ______ **09026688362**
RCA Victor / Aug '97 / BMG

FOR THE BOYS
Midler, Bette
Billy-a-dick / Stuff like that there / PS I love you / Girlfriend of the whirling dervish / I remember you / Dixie's dream / Baby, it's cold outside / Dreamland / Vickie and Mr. Valves / For all we know / Come rain or come shine / In my life / Every road leads back to you
CD ______ **7567823292**
Atlantic / Feb '92 / Warner Music

FOR THE TERM OF HIS NATURAL LIFE
Walker, Simon
Walker, Simon *C*
CD ______ **IMICD 1001**
Silva Screen / Feb '90 / Koch / Silva Screen

FOR WHOM THE BELL TOLLS
Warner Brothers Studio Orchestra
Young, Victor *C*
Heindorf, Ray *Con*
CD ______ **STZ 112**
Stanyan / Jul '93 / Silva Screen

FORBIDDEN BROADWAY I
Unoriginal Cast
Alessandrini, Gerard *L*
CD ______ **DRGCD 12585**
DRG / Mar '92 / Discovery / New Note/ Pinnacle

FORBIDDEN BROADWAY II
Unoriginal Cast
Alessandrini, Gerard *L*
CD ______ **CDSBL 12599**
DRG / Mar '92 / Discovery / New Note/ Pinnacle

FORBIDDEN BROADWAY III
Unoriginal Cast
Alessandrini, Gerard *L*
Carol Channing sequence / Forbidden Broadway III / Ya got troubles / Guys And Dolls sequence / Topol / Anna Karenina: the musical / Julie Andrews / Grim hotel / Barbara: The Broadway album / Dustin Hoffman / Return to Merman and Martin / Ms. Saigon / Michael Crawford sequence / Robert Goulet sequence / Mess of the spider woman / Back to Barbara / Mug brothers / Who's Tommy / Finale
CD ______ **DRGCD 12609**
DRG / Apr '94 / Discovery / New Note/ Pinnacle

FORBIDDEN BROADWAY IV
Unoriginal Cast
CD ______ **DRGCD 12614**
DRG / Feb '97 / Discovery / New Note/ Pinnacle

FORBIDDEN HOLLYWOOD
Cast Recording
CD ______ **VSD 5669**
Varese Sarabande / Nov '95 / Pinnacle

FORBIDDEN PLANET
Barron, Louis & Bebe *C*
Barron, Louis & Bebe *Con*
CD ______ **PRD 001**
GNP Crescendo / Sep '95 / ZYX

FOREST FLOWER
Lloyd, Charles *C*
CD ______ **8122717462**
Warner Bros. / Aug '94 / Warner Music

FOREVER KNIGHT
Molin, Fred *C*
CD ______ **GNPD 8043**
GNP Crescendo / Apr '96 / ZYX

FOREVER PLAID
1993 London Cast
Three coins in the fountain / Gotta be this or that undecided / Moments to remember / Crazy about ya baby / Not too much / Perfidia / Cry / Sixteen tons/Chain gang / Tribute to Mr. C / Caribbean plaid / Heart and soul / Lady of Spain / Scotland the brave / Shangri-la/Rags to riches / Love is a many splendoured thing
CD ______ **CASTCD 33**
First Night / Jul '93 / Pinnacle

FOREVER WILD
Whalen, Michael *C*
Dark & the light / American fields / Magnolia / Canyon wind / Shelter / Winding to infinity / Pathway to Waterrock / Peril in the timberland / Magic forest / Rain / Secret garden / Song of the Everglades / Through the parched land: Desert flower / Puritan's dream / Times of change / Stormlight: Dawn / Kingdom of the sun / Monongahela / Muir's paradise / By the sea / Hudson Valley / Survival / Windows & walls / Great highway / Karen's song / Wilderness of the East / Storyteller sleeps / Theme to Forever Wild
2CD ______ **ND 63926**
Narada / Nov '96 / ADA / New Note/ Pinnacle

FOREVER YOUNG
Goldsmith, Jerry *C*
Love theme / Test flight / Experiment / Tree house / Kitchen aid / Diner / Air show / She's alive / Let's go / Reunited / Very thought of you: *Holiday, Billie*
CD ______ **WA 244822**
Silva Screen / Jul '93 / Koch / Silva Screen

FORREST GUMP
Hound dog: *Presley, Elvis* / Rebel rouser: *Eddy, Duane* / But I do: *Henry, Clarence 'Frogman'* / Walk right in: *Rooftop Singers* / Land of 1000 dances: *Pickett, Wilson* / Blowin' in the wind: *Baez, Joan* / Fortunate son: *Creedence Clearwater Revival* / I can't help myself: *Four Tops* / Respect: *Franklin, Aretha* / Rainy day women 12/35: *Dylan, Bob* / Sloop John B: *Beach Boys* / California dreamin': *Mamas & The Papas* / For what it's worth: *Buffalo Springfield* / What the world needs now is love: *De Shannon, Jackie* / Break on through (to the other side): *Doors* / Mrs. Robinson: *Simon & Garfunkel* / Volunteers: *Jefferson Airplane* / Let's get together: *Youngbloods* / San Francisco: *McKenzie, Scott* / Turn turn turn: *Byrds* / Aquarius (let the sunshine in): *5th Dimension* / Everybody's talkin': *Nilsson, Harry* / Joy to the world: *Three Dog Night* / Stoned love: *Supremes* / Raindrops keep falling on my head: *Thomas, B.J.* / Mr. President (Have pity on the working man): *Newman, Randy* / Sweet home Alabama: *Lynyrd Skynyrd* / It keeps you runnin': *Doobie Brothers* / I've got to use my imagination: *Knight, Gladys & The Pips* / Against the wind: *Nelson, Willie* / Suite from Forrest Gump: *Silvestri, Alan*
2CD ______ **4769412**
Epic / Oct '94 / Sony

FORREST GUMP (Score)
Silvestri, Alan
Silvestri, Alan *C*
I'm Forrest... Forrest Gump / You're no different / You can't sit here / Run Forrest run / Pray with me / Crimson Gump / They're sendingme to Vietnam / I ran and ran / I had a destiny / Washington reunion / Jesus on the mainline / That's my boat / I never thanked you / Jenny returns / Crusade / Forrest meets Forrest / Wedding guest / Where heaven ends / Jenny's grave / I'll be right here / Suite from Forrest Gump
CD ______ **4773692**
Epic / Oct '94 / Sony

FORT SAGANNE
London Symphony Orchestra
Sarde, Philippe *C*
Savina, Carlos *Con*
CD ______ **CDFMC 9**
Milan / Apr '93 / Conifer/BMG / Silva Screen

FORTUNELLA/LA GRAN GUERRA/IL MAESTRO DI VIGEVANO
Rota, Nino *C*
CD ______ **LEGENDCD 24**
Silva Screen / Apr '96 / Koch / Silva Screen

FOUR MUSKETEERS, THE (& The Eagle Has Landed/Voyage Of The Damned)
Schifrin, Lalo *C*
Four Musketeers / Eagle Has Landed / Voyage of the Damned
CD ______ **LXCD 5**
Label X / '88 / Silva Screen

FOUR WEDDINGS AND A FUNERAL
Love is all around: *Wet Wet Wet* / But not for me: *Wet Wet Wet* / You're the first, my last, my everything: *White, Barry* / Smoke gets in your eyes: *Nu Colours* / I will survive: *Gaynor, Gloria* / La la (means I love you): *Swing Out Sister* / Crocodile rock: *John, Elton* / Right time: *I to I* / It should have been me: *Knight, Gladys* / Loving you tonight: *Squeeze* / Can't smile without you: *Fiagbe, Lena* / Four weddings and a funeral/Funeral blues / Secret marriage: *Sting* / Chapel of love: *John, Elton*
CD ______ **5167512**
Vertigo / Jun '94 / PolyGram

FRANCIS OF ASSISI/DOCTOR FAUSTUS
Nascimbene, Mario *C*
CD ______ **DRGCD 32965**
DRG / Mar '97 / Discovery / New Note/ Pinnacle

FRANKENSTEIN - THE CREATION
Original Cast
Joyce, Paul *C*
Ice overture / I am become death / Offertium / Creation / In paradisum / Trinity / Frankenstein - The creation
CD ______ **PKJCD 001**
Creation / May '97 / Else

FRANKIE AND JOHNNY/PARADISE, HAWAIIAN STYLE
Presley, Elvis
Frankie and Johnny / Come along / Petunia, the gardener's daughter / Chesay / What every woman lives for / Look out, Broadway / Beginner's luck / Down by the riverside/ When the saints go marching in / Shout it out / Hard luck / Please don't stop loving me / Everybody come aboard / Paradise, Hawaiian style / Queenie Wahine's papaya / Scratch my back / Drums of the islands / Datin' / Dog's life / House of sand / Stop where you are / This is my heaven / Sand castles
CD ______ **07863663602**
RCA / Jun '94 / BMG

FRANKIE STARLIGHT
Bernstein, Elmer *C*
CD ______ **VSD 5679**
Varese Sarabande / Nov '95 / Pinnacle

FRANKIE'S HOUSE
Beck, Jeff & Jed Stoller
Jungle / Requiem of the Bao-Chi / Hi-heel sneakers / Thailand / Love and death / Cathouse / In the dark / Sniper patrol / Peace Island / White mice / Tunnel rat / Vihn's funeral / Apocalypse / Innocent victim
CD ______ **4724942**
Epic / Nov '92 / Sony

FRANTIC
Morricone, Ennio *C*
I'm gonna lose you: *Simply Red* / Frantic / On the roofs of Paris / One flugel horn / Six short interludes / Nocturne for Michel / In the garage / Paris project / Sadly nostalgic
CD ______ **7559607822**
WEA / Oct '93 / Warner Music

FREE WILLY II (The Adventure Home)
Childhood: *Jackson, Michael* / Forever young: *Jackson, Rebbie* / Sometimes dancing: *Brownstone & Spragga Benz* / What it will take: *3T* / I'll say goodbye for the two of us: *Expose* / Lou's blues: *Cavaleri, Nathan* / Whale swim: *Poledouris, Basil* / Reunion: *Poledouris, Basil* / Childhood (instrumental): *Jackson, Michael*
CD ______ **4807392**
Epic / Dec '96 / Sony

FREE WILLY III
CD ______ **VSD 5830**
Varese Sarabande / Sep '97 / Pinnacle

FREEBIRD THE MOVIE
Lynyrd Skynyrd
Lynyrd Skynyrd *C*
Workin' for MCA / I ain't the one / Saturday night special / Whiskey rock-a-roller / Travellin' man / Searching / What's your name / That smell / Gimme three steps / Call me the breeze / T for Texas (blue yodel no.1) / Sweet home Alabama / Free bird / Dixie
CD ______ **MCD 11472**
MCA / Aug '96 / BMG

FREEJACK
CD ______ **5131052**
Polydor / May '91 / PolyGram

FRENCH KISS
Someone like you: *Morrison, Van* / La vie en rose: *Armstrong, Louis* / Dream a little dream: *Beautiful South* / Via con me: *Conte, Paolo* / I love Paris: *Thielemans, Toots* / La mer: *Kline, Kevin* / I love Paris: *Fitzgerald, Ella* / Verlaine: *Trenet, Charles* / C'est trop beau: *Rossi, Tino* / Les yeux ouverts: *Beautiful South* / I want you: *Howard, James Newton* / Les yeux de ton pere: *Les Negresses Vertes*
CD ______ **5283212**
Mercury / Jun '95 / PolyGram

FRENCH LIEUTENANT'S WOMAN, THE
Davis, Carl *C*
Sarah's walk / Proposal / Period research / Her story / Decision taken / Towards love / Location lunch / Together / Domestic scene / Resurrection / House in Windermere / End of shoot party / Happy ending
CD ______ **DRGCD 6106**
DRG / '88 / Discovery / New Note/Pinnacle

FRIDAY
Friday: *Ice Cube* / Keep their heads ringin': *Dr. Dre* / Friday night: *Scarface* / Lettin' niggas know: *Threat* / Roll it up, light it up, smoke it up: *Cypress Hill* / Take a hit: *Mack 10* / Tryin' to see another day: *Isley Brothers* / You got me wide open: *Collins, Bootsy & Bernie Worrell* / Mary Jane: *James, Rick* / I wanna get next to you: *Rose Royce* / Superhoes: *Funkdoobiest* / Coast II coast: *Alkaholiks* / Blast if I have to: *E-A-Ski* / Hoochie mama: *2 Live Crew* / I heard it through the grapevine: *Roger*
CD ______ **CDPTY 117**
Priority/Virgin / Apr '95 / EMI

FRIDAY THE 13TH (Parts 1 - 3)
CD ______ **CDFMC 10**
Silva Screen / Feb '90 / Koch / Silva Screen

FRIDAY THE 13TH - THE SERIES
Molin, Fred
Molin, Fred *C*
CD ______ **GNPD 8018**
GNP Crescendo / Jan '90 / ZYX

FRIENDLY PERSUASION
Tiomkin, Dimitri *C*
Tiomkin, Dimitri *Con*
CD ______ **MSCD 402**
Movie Sound / Jan '93 / Discovery

FRIENDS (Music From The TV Series)
I'll be there for you: *Rembrandts* / I go blind: *Hootie & The Blowfish* / Good intentions: *Toad The Wet Sprocket* / You'll know you were loved: *Reed, Lou* / Sexuality: *Lang, k.d.* / Shoebox: *Barenaked Ladies* / Free world: *REM* / Sunshine: *Westerberg, Paul* / Angel of the morning: *Pretenders* / In my room: *Grant Lee Buffalo* / Big yellow taxi: *Mitchell, Joni* / Stain yer blood: *Westerberg, Paul* / I'll be there for you: *Rembrandts*
CD ______ **9362460082**
Warner Bros. / Apr '97 / Warner Music

FRIGHTENERS, THE
Elfman, Danny *C*
Intro / Lads / Poltergeists / Victim number 38 / Who's next / Garden / Chilly / Time / Patty's palce / Flashbacks / Patty attack / Frank's wife / Doom / Heaven / Don't fear the reaper: *Mutton Birds*
CD ______ **MCAD 11469**
MCA / Feb '97 / BMG

FRITZ THE CAT
CD ______ **FCD 4532**
Fantasy / Jan '94 / Jazz Music / Pinnacle / Wellard

FRITZ THE CAT/HEAVY TRAFFIC
Black talk / Duke's theme / Fritz the cat / Mamblues / Bo Diddley: *Diddley, Bo* / Bertha's theme / Winston / House rock / Synagogue / Yesterdays: *Holiday, Billie* / Love light of mine: *Watson Sisters* / Riot / You're the only girl (I ever really loved) / Scarborough Fair: *Mendes, Sergio & Brazil '66* / Scarborough Street Fair / Twist and shout: *Isley Brothers* / Angie's theme / Take five: *Brubeck, Dave* / Carol's theme / Heavy traffic / What you sow / Maybellene: *Berry, Chuck* / Michael's Scarborough fair / Ballroom beauties / Ballroom dancers / Cartoon time / Ten cent philosophy
CD ______ **FCD 24745**
Fantasy / Nov '96 / Jazz Music / Pinnacle / Wellard

FROG DREAMING/WILD DUCK, THE
May, Brian & Simon Walker *C*
CD ________ **SCCD 1019**
Southern Cross / Jan '89 / Silva Screen

FROG PRINCE, THE
Train to Paris / First day / Mack the knife / Let it be me / With Jean-Phillipe / Jenny / Reflections / Frog Prince / Dreams / Kiss / Sweet Georgia Brown / Georgia on my mind / Kiss by the fountain / Jenny and Roz / Les flon-flons du bal / Epilogue
CD ________ **5510992**
Spectrum / Jun '95 / PolyGram

FROM DAWN TILL DUSK
Everybody be cool: *Blasters* / Dark night: *Blasters* / Mexican blackbird: *ZZ Top* / Texas funeral: *Wayne, Jon* / Foolish heart: *Mavericks* / Would you do me a favour: *Vaughan, Jimmy* / Dengue woman blues: *Vaughan, Jimmy* / Torquay: *ZZ Top* / Left-overs: *ZZ Top* / She's just killing me: *ZZ Top* / Chet's speech: *Tito & Tarantula* / Angry cockroaches: *Tito & Tarantula* / Mary had a little lamb: *Vaughan, Stevie Ray & Double Trouble* / After dark: *Vaughan, Stevie Ray & Double Trouble* / Willie the wimp (and his cadillac coffin): *Revell, Graeme* / Kill the band: *Revell, Graeme* / Mexican standoff: *Revell, Graeme* / Sex machine attacks: *Revell, Graeme*
CD ________ **4836172**
Epic / Mar '96 / Sony

FROM RUSSIA WITH LOVE
Barry, John *C*
Opening titles / James Bond is back/From Russia with love/James Bond theme / Tania meets Klebb / Meeting in St. Sophia / Golden horn / Girl trouble / Bond meets Tania / 007 / Gypsy camp / Death of Grant / Spectre island / Guitar lament / Man overboard - SMERSH in action / James Bond with bongos / Stalking / Leila dances / Death of Kerim / 007 takes the lektor
CD ________ **CZ 550**
Premier/EMI / Dec '95 / EMI

FRUIT MACHINE, THE
Zimmer, Hans *C*
CD ________ **CDCH 520**
Milan / '88 / Conifer/BMG / Silva Screen

FUGITIVE, THE
Howard, James Newton *C*
Howard, James Newton *Con*
Main title / Storm drain / Kimble dyes his hair / Helicopter chase / Fugitive theme / Subway fight / Kimble returns / No press / Stairway chase / Sykes' apt / It's over
CD ________ **7559615922**
Elektra / Dec '96 / Warner Music

FULL CIRCLE (The Haunting Of Julia)
Towns, Colin *C*
Towns, Colin *Con*
CD ________ **387032**
Koch / Apr '95 / Koch

FULL METAL JACKET
Mead, Abigail *C*
Full metal jacket / Hello Vietnam / Chapel of love / Wooly bully / I like it like that / These boots are made for walking / Surfin' bird / Marines' hymn / Transition / Parris Island / Ruins / Leonard / Attack / Time suspended / Sniper
CD ________ **9256132**
WEA / Sep '87 / Warner Music

FULL MONTY, THE
You sexy thing: *Hot Chocolate* / You can leave your hat on: *Jones, Tom* / Moving on up: *M People* / Je t'aime...moi non plus: *Gainsbourg, Serge* / Zodiac: *Lindup, David* / (Come up and see me) make me smile: *Harley, Steve & The Cockney Rebel* / Rock 'n' roll: *Glitter, Gary* / Land of a 1000 dances: *Pickett, Wilson* / Full monty: *Dudley, Anne* / Flash dance: *Cara, Irene* / Hot stuff: *Summer, Donna* / We are family: *Sister Sledge* / Stripper: *Loss, Joe Orchestra*
CD ________ **09026689042**
RCA Victor / Aug '97 / BMG

FUNNY FACE
Astaire, Fred
Gershwin, George *C*
Gershwin, Ira *L*
CD ________ **5312312**
Verve / May '96 / PolyGram

FUNNY GIRL
Styne, Jule *C*
Merrill, Bob *L*
Funny girl overture / I'm the greatest star / If a girl isn't pretty / Roller skate rag / I'd rather be blue over you (than happy with somebody else) / His love makes me beautiful / People / You are woman / Don't rain on my parade / Sadie Sadie / Swan / Funny girl / My man (mon homme) / Finale
CD ________ **4625452**
Columbia / Apr '94 / Sony

FUNNY GIRL
1964 Broadway Cast
Styne, Jule *C*
Merrill, Bob *L*
Rosenstock, Milton *Con*
Overture / If a girl isn't pretty / I'm the greatest star / Cornet man / Who taught her everything / His love makes me beautiful / I want to be seen with you tonight / Henry Street / People / You are woman / Don't rain on my parade / Sadie Sadie / Find yourself a man / Rat-tat-tat-tat / Who are you now / Music that makes me dance / Finale
CD ________ **ZDM 7646612**
EMI Classics / Apr '93 / EMI

FUNNY THING HAPPENED ON THE WAY TO THE FORUM
1962 Broadway Cast
Sondheim, Stephen *C*
CD ________ **ZDM 7647702**
EMI Classics / Apr '93 / EMI

FUNNY THING HAPPENED ON THE WAY TO THE FORUM
1963 London Cast
Sondheim, Stephen *C*
CD ________ **CDANGEL 3**
Angel / Apr '93 / EMI

FUNNY THING HAPPENED ON THE WAY TO THE FORUM (In Jazz)
Trotter Trio
Sondheim, Stephen *C*
CD ________ **VSD 5707**
Varese Sarabande / Jun '96 / Pinnacle

FURY, THE
London Symphony Orchestra
Williams, John *C*
Williams, John *Con*
Main title / Vision on the stairs / Gillian's escape / Death on the carousel / For Gillian / Hester's theme and the house, / Search for Robin / Gillian's vision / End titles / Epilogue
CD ________ **CDA 8914**
Tsunami / Jan '95 / Silva Screen

GADFLY, THE
USSR Cinema Symphony Orchestra
Shostakovich, Dmitry *C*
Overture / Contradance / National holiday / Prelude and waltz / Galop / Introduction into the dance / Romance / Interlude / Nocturne / Scene / Finale
CD ________ **CDCFP 4463**
Classics For Pleasure / Nov '88 / EMI

GAMBLE, THE
Donaggio, Pino *C*
CD ________ **OST 106**
Milano Dischi / Jul '93 / Silva Screen

GAME OF DEATH/NIGHT GAMES
Barry, John *C*
CD ________ **FILMCD 123**
Silva Screen / Jan '93 / Koch / Silva Screen

GARDEN OF THE FINZI-CONTINIS, THE
De Sica, Manuel *C*
Micol's theme / Tennis match / Giorgio and Micol (love theme) / Persecution / Garden of the Finzi-Continis / Meeting at Easter / Declaration of war / Leaving for Genoble / Giorgio's delusion / Villa / Childhood memories / Finale / Micol's theme (reprise)
CD ________ **OST 125**
Milano Dischi / Aug '94 / Silva Screen

GAY LIFE, THE
Broadway Cast
Schwartz, Arthur *C*
Dietz, Howard *L*
CD ________ **ZDM 7647632**
EMI Classics / Apr '93 / EMI

GAZON MAUDIT
CD ________ **CDVIR 49**
Virgin / Apr '96 / EMI

GBH
Costello, Elvis & Richard Harvey
Costello, Elvis & Richard Harvey *C*
Life and times of Michael Murray / It wasn't me / Men of alloy / Lambs to the slaughter / Bubbles / Goldilocks theme / Perfume the odour of money / Assassin: *Douglas, Barbara* / Pursuit suite / Roaring boy: *Prufrock Quartet* / So I used five / Love from a cold land / In a cemetery garden / Smack 'im / Woodlands - Oh joy / It's cold up there / Going home service / Grave music / Puppet masters' work / He's so easy / Another time, another place / Closing titles
CD ________ **DSCD 4**
Demon / Jul '91 / Pinnacle

GENESIS
Shankar, Ravi
Shankar, Ravi *C*
Genesis theme / Woman reminiscing / Fair / Return from the film / Passion / Jealousy and fighting / Variation on Genesis theme / Bounty full of crops / Song in the fair / Swing / Camel / Genesis: Title
CD ________ **CDCH 287**
Milan / Nov '86 / Conifer/BMG / Silva Screen

GENOCIDE
Royal Philharmonic Orchestra
Bernstein, Elmer *C*
Bernstein, Elmer *Con*
CD ________ **FMT 8007D**
Intrada / Jan '93 / Koch / Silva Screen

GENTLEMEN PREFER BLONDES (inc. Unreleased Songs/Never Before And Never Again)
Monroe, Marilyn
Styne, Jule *C*
Robin, Leo *L*
Gentlemen prefer blondes / Diamonds are a girl's best friend / Little girl from Little Rock / Ain't there anyone here for love / When love goes wrong / Bye bye baby / Do it again / Kiss / You'd be surprised / Fine romance / She acts like a woman should / Heatwave / Happy birthday Mr. President
CD ________ **DRGCD 15005**
DRG / Jan '95 / Discovery / New Note/ Pinnacle

GENTLEMEN PREFER BLONDES
1949 Broadway Cast
Styne, Jule *C*
Robin, Leo *L*
Rosenstock, Milton *Con*
CD ________ **SK 48013**
Sony Broadway / Dec '91 / Sony

GENTLEMEN PREFER BLONDES
Monroe, Marilyn
Styne, Jule *C*
Robin, Leo *L*
CD ________ **DRGCD 94762**
DRG / Jun '95 / Discovery / New Note/ Pinnacle

GERMINAL
Roques, Jean-Louis *C*
Germinal (Generique debut) / Les machines / La descente a la mine / Catherine et etienne / Une piece de cent sous... / La remonte / Montsou l'ete / Bal du bon joyeux / Le voreux occupe / Catherine n'est pas rentree / En bas... / La greve / Catherine et chaval / Saccage a jean bart / Le viol / La revolte / Mort de maheu / Apres l'ecroulement de voreux / Germinal (Generique fin)
CD ________ **CDVIR 28**
Virgin / Jun '94 / EMI

GET ON THE BUS
Shabooyah: *Bus Crew* / Destiny is calling: *Guru* / Tonite's the night: *Doug E Fresh* / Remedy: *Tribe Called Quest* / Girl you need a change of mind: *D'Angelo* / Redemption song: *Wonder, Stevie* / New world order: *Mayfield, Curtis* / Over a million strong: *Neville Brothers* / My life is in your hands: *God's Property & Kirk Franklin* / I love my woman: *Davis, Marvin* / Cruisin': *Earth, Wind & Fire* / Welcome: *Dorsey, Marc* / Coming home to you: *Blackstreet* / Ayinde's speech: *Jean-Baptiste, Ayinde*
CD ________ **IND 90089**
Interscope / Jul '97 / BMG

GET SHORTY
CD ________ **5293102**
Verve / Mar '96 / PolyGram

GHOST (Extended Version)
Jarre, Maurice *C*
Jarre, Maurice *Con*
CD ________ **74321342782**
Milan / Mar '96 / Conifer/BMG / Silva Screen

GHOST AND MRS. MUIR, THE
Herrmann, Bernard *C*
Bernstein, Elmer *Con*
CD ________ **VCD 47254**
Varese Sarabande / Jan '89 / Pinnacle

GHOST DANCE
Cunningham, David & Jamie Muir/Michael Giles
Cunningham, David & Jamie Muir/Michael Giles *C*
CD ________ **PIANO 052**
Piano / Mar '96 / Pinnacle

GHOST STORY
Sarde, Philippe *C*
CD ________ **VSD 5259**
Varese Sarabande / Apr '91 / Pinnacle

GHOST TOWN/SLAUGHTER ON TENTH AVENUE/LA PRINCESSE ZENOBIA
Rodgers, Richard *C*
CD ________ **CDTER 1114**
TER / '88 / Koch

GHOSTS OF THE CIVIL DEAD
Cave, Nick & The Bad Seeds
Cave, Nick *C*
CD ________ **CDIONIC 3**
Mute / Apr '89 / RTM/Disc

GI BLUES
Presley, Elvis
Tonight is so right for love / What's she really like / Frankfurt special / Wooden heart / GI blues / Pocketful of rainbows / Shopping around / Big boots / Didja ever / Blue suede shoes / Doin' the best I can / Big boots / Shoppin' around / Frankfurt special / Pocketful of rainbows / Didja ever / Big boots / What's she really like / Doin' the best I can
CD ________ **07863674602**
CD ________ **07863669602**
RCA / Apr '97 / BMG

GIANT
Tiomkin, Dimitri *C*
CD ________ **TSU 0106**
Tsunami / Jan '94 / Silva Screen

GIANT/EAST OF EDEN/REBEL WITHOUT A CAUSE
CD ________ **TSU 0201**
Tsunami / Jan '95 / Silva Screen

GIGI
1985 London Cast
Loewe, Frederick *C*
Lerner, Alan Jay *L*
Paris is Paris again / It's a bore / Earth and other minor things / Thank heaven for little girls / She's not thinking of me / Night they invented champagne / I remember it well / Gigi / Entr'acte / Contract / I'm glad I'm not young anymore / Wide wide world / Finale
CD ________ **OCRCD 6007**
First Night / Feb '96 / Pinnacle

GIGI
Film Cast
Loewe, Frederick *C*
Lerner, Alan Jay *L*
Main title / Opening / Interlude / And there is the future / Thank heaven for little girls / Meet Gigi / Gaston's house / Armenonville / It's a bore (prelude) / It's a bore / After it's a bore / Aunt Alicia / Parisians introduction / Parisians / Ice skating sequence / Dissolve maxim's / Gossip / Introduction to Maxim's / Waltz at Maxim's / It's a bore (reprise) / To the inn / Goodbye madame / Bore montage / Night they invented champagne / Trouville / I remember it well / Panting Grandma / Lessons / Upset / Gaston's souloquy / Gigi / Gaston with flowers / You never told me / I'm glad I'm not young anymore / I'm glad I'm not young anymore (reprise) / Aunt Alicia's march / Bracelet / Say a prayer for me tonight / Gigi's big moment / Second gossip / Waltz at Maxim's (dance version) / Gaston's decision / Change of heartland / End title / Parisians (outtake) / Night they invented champagne (outtake)
CD ________ **CDODEON 10**
Soundtracks / Apr '96 / EMI

GIGI
Cast Recording
Loewe, Frederick *C*
Lerner, Alan Jay *L*
Overture: *Cast* / Thank heaven for little girls: *Cast* / It's a bore: *Cast* / Waltz at Maxim's: *Cast* / She's not thinking of me: *Cast* / Night they invented champagne: *Cast* / I remeber it well: *Cast* / Say a prayer for me tonight: *Cast* / Gigi: *Cast* / In this wide wide world: *Cast* / I'm glad I'm not young anymore: *Cast* / Finale: *Cast*
CD ________ **SHOWCD 052**
Showtime / Apr '97 / Disc / THE

GIGI/AN AMERICAN IN PARIS
Cast Recording
Loewe, Frederick/George Gershwin *C*
Lerner, Alan Jay/Ira Gershwin *L*
Gigi / Thank heavens for little girls / It's a bore / Parisians / Waltz at Maxim's / Night they invented champagne: *Caron, Leslie/Louis Jordan/Hermione Gingold* / I remember it well / Say a prayer for me tonight / I'm glad I'm not young anymore / Gigi (finale) / 'S wonderful / Love is here to stay / I'll build a stairway to paradise / I got rhythm / American in Paris
CD ________ **CDMGM 1**
MGM/EMI / Jan '90 / EMI

GINGER ALE AFTERNOON
Dixon, Willie
Dixon, Willie *C*
CD ________ **VSD 5234**
Varese Sarabande / Oct '89 / Pinnacle

GIORNATA NERA PER L'ARIETE/LI OCCHI FREDDI DELLA PAURA (Evil Fingers/The Cold Eyes Of Fear)
Morricone, Ennio *C*
CD ________ **PRCD 122**
Preamble / Apr '96 / Silva Screen

GIOVANNI FALCONE
Donaggio, Pino *C*
CD ________ **LEGENDCD 12**
Legend / Jan '93 / Koch / Silva Screen

GIRL 6
Prince
Prince *C*
CD ________ **9362462392**
Warner Bros. / Mar '96 / Warner Music

GIRL CRAZY
Cast Recording
Gershwin, George *C*
Gershwin, Ira *L*
Mauceri, John *Con*
CD ________ **7559792502**
Nonesuch / Feb '91 / Warner Music

GIRL ON A MOTORCYCLE
Reed, Les *C*
Girl on a motorcycle / Dream / Holiday with Raymond / Daniel / Au revoir Daniel / Souvenirs of Raymond / Sweet souvenirs of Raymond / Surrender to a stranger / Take me to your lover / Dawn idyll / Journey of love / Big bare beat / Summer house / Don't ask me
CD ________ **RPM 171**
RPM / Nov '96 / Pinnacle

GIRL WHO CAME TO SUPPER, THE (Noel Coward Sings His Score)
Coward, Sir Noel
Coward, Sir Noel *C*
CD ________ **DRGCD 5178**
DRG / Oct '95 / Discovery / New Note/ Pinnacle

GIRL WHO CAME TO SUPPER, THE
1963 Broadway Cast
Coward, Sir Noel *C*
Blackton, Jay *Con*
CD SK 48210
Sony Broadway / Nov '93 / Sony

GIRLFRIEND, THE
1987 Colchester Cast
Rodgers, Richard *C*
Hart, Lorenz *L*
CD CDTER 1148
TER / Aug '95 / Koch

GIVE MY REGARDS TO BROAD STREET
McCartney, Paul
McCartney, Paul *C*
No more lonely nights / Good day sunshine / Corridor music / Yesterday / Here, there and everywhere / Wanderlust / Ballroom dancing / Silly love songs / Silly love songs (reprise) / Not such a bad boy / So bad / No values / No more lonely nights (reprise) / For no one / Eleanor Rigby / Eleanor's dream / Long and winding road / No more lonely nights (version) / Goodnight princess
CD CDPMCOL 14
EMI / Jun '93 / EMI

GLADIATORS - RETURN OF THE GLADIATORS
Unbelievable: *EMF* / Three little pigs: *Green Jelly* / Everything's ruined: *Faith No More* / Pretend we're dead: *L7* / Cats in the cradle: *Ugly Kid Joe* / Under the bridge: *Red Hot Chili Peppers* / Too much too young: *Little Angels* / Boys are back in town: *Thin Lizzy* / Calling all the heroes: *It Bites* / One and only: *Hawkes, Chesney* / When the going gets tough (the tough get going): *Ocean, Billy* / We are family: *Sister Sledge* / We've got the power: *Gladiators* / War: *Starr, Edwin* / Gladiator's rap: *Gas* / Wild thing: *Troggs* / Main theme: *Storm* / Return of the Gladiators: *Storm* / Chase: *Storm* / Joust: *Storm* / Skytrack: *Storm* / Power ball: *Storm* / Tilt: *Storm* / Suspension bridge: *Storm* / Gladiator power: *Storm*
CD 5165172
PolyGram TV / Nov '93 / PolyGram

GLADIATORS - THE ALBUM
Main theme: *Gladiators* / Everything about you: *Ugly Kid Joe* / Holding out for a hero: *Tyler, Bonnie* / Final Countdown: *Europe* / Bat out of hell: *Meat Loaf* / Since you've been gone: *Rainbow* / Burning heart: *Survivor* / Hold the line: *Toto* / More than a feeling: *Boston* / All right now: *Free* / Power: *Snap* / War: *Starr, Edwin* / Wild thing: *Troggs* / You ain't seen nothin' yet: *Bachman-Turner Overdrive* / Gladiator's entrance: *Storm* / Medley mix: *Warren's world* / Duel: *Storm* / Eliminator: *Storm* / Wall: *Storm* / Atlaspheres: *Storm* / You're a winner: *Storm* / Danger zone: *Storm* / Hang tough: *Storm* / Swingshot: *Storm* / There are no losers: *Storm*
CD 515 877-2
PolyGram TV / Nov '92 / PolyGram

GLAM METAL DETECTIVES
CD 650103392
Warner Bros. / Apr '95 / Warner Music

GLENGARRY GLEN ROSS
CD 7559613842
WEA / Nov '92 / Warner Music

GLENN MILLER STORY, THE
Gershenson, Joseph *Con*
Moonlight serenade / Tuxedo Junction / Little brown jug / St. Louis blues / In the mood / String of pearls / Pennsylvania 6-5000 / American patrol / Basin Street blues / Otchi-tchor-hi-ya
CD MCLD 19025
MCA / May '93 / BMG

GLINT OF SILVER, A
Silly Wizard
CD GLCD 1070
Green Linnet / Mar '87 / ADA / CM / Direct / Highlander / Roots

GLORY
Harlem Boys Choir
Horner, James *C*
Horner, James *Con*
Call to arms / After antietam / Lonely Christmas / Forming the regiment / Whipping / Burning the town of darien / Brave words / Braver deeds / Year of jubilee / Preparations for battle / Charging for Wagner / Epitaph / Closing credits
CD CDV 2614
Virgin / '90 / EMI

GLORY DAZE
CD 787612
Asphodel / Oct '96 / Cargo / SRD

GO WEST (New Jazz Score For Buster Keaton Film)
Frisell, Bill *C*
CD 7559793502
Elektra / Jan '95 / Warner Music

GOBLIN MARKET
1985 Off-Broadway Cast
Pen, Polly *C*
Rosetti, Christine *L*
CD CDTER 1144
TER / Mar '90 / Koch

GODFATHER I, THE
Rota, Nino *C*
Godfather waltz / I have but one heart / Pick-up / Connie's wedding / Halls of fear / Sicillian pastorale / Godfather (love theme) / Appollonia / New godfather / Baptism / Godfather finale
CD MCLD 19022
MCA / Apr '92 / BMG

GODFATHER III, THE
Rota, Nino/Carmine Coppola *C*
Godfather part III main title / Godfather waltz / Marcia Religioso / Michael's letter / Immigrant / Godfather part III love theme / Godfather waltz / To each his own / Vincent's theme / Altobella / Godfather intermezzo / Sicilian medley / Promise me you'll remember (love theme) / Preludio and Siciliano / A case amiche / Preghiera / Godfather finale / Coda: The Godfather finale
CD 4678132
Epic / Mar '91 / Sony

GODFATHER SUITE, THE (Music Featured In The Godfather Trilogy)
Milan Philharmonia Orchestra
Rota, Nino/Carmine Coppola/Francesco Pennino *C*
Coppola, Carmine *Con*
Love theme / Godfather's tarantella / Godfather's mazurka / Every time I look in your eyes / Godfather's waltz / Michael's theme / Godfather's fox-trot / Senza mamma / Napule ve salute / Marcia religiosa / Festa march / Kay's theme / New carpet / Immigrant
CD FILMCD 077
Silva Screen / Mar '91 / Koch / Silva Screen

GODMONEY
CD VVR 1000602
V2 / Aug '97 / 3mv/Pinnacle

GODSPELL
Cast Recording
Schwartz, Stephen *C*
Prepare ye the way of the Lord / Save the people / Day by day / Learn your lessons well/Bless the lord / All for the best / All good gifts / Turn back old man / Alas for you / By my side / We beseech thee / On the willow / Finale
CD SHOWCD 012
Showtime / Feb '95 / Disc / THE

GODSPELL
Cast Recording
Schwartz, Stephen *C*
CD CDTER 1204
TER / Jan '94 / Koch

GODSPELL
CC Productions
Schwartz, Stephen *C*
Prepare ye the way of the Lord / Save the people / Day by day / Learn your lesson well / O bless the Lord my soul / All of the best / All good gifts / Light of the world / Turn back o man / By my side / We beseech thee / On the willows / Godspell
CD QED 211
Tring / Nov '96 / Tring

GODSPELL
Studio Cast
Schwartz, Stephen *C*
Prepeare ye the way of the Lord / Save the people / Day by day / Learn your lesson well / O bless the Lord my soul / All for the best / All good gifts / Light of the world / Turn back o man / By my side / We beseech thee / On the willows / Godspell (finale)
CD 85102
CMC / May '97 / BMG

GODSPELL/JESUS CHRIST SUPERSTAR (Highlights - The Songs Collection)
Cast Recording
Schwartz, Stephen/Andrew Lloyd Webber *C*
Schwartz, Stephen/Tim Rice *L*
CD PWKS 4220
Carlton / Nov '94 / Carlton

GOLD DIGGERS
Cooper, Lindsay
McNeely, Joel *C*
CD VSD 5633
Varese Sarabande / Nov '95 / Pinnacle

GOLDEN BOY
1959 Broadway Cast
Strouse, Charles *C*
Adams, Lee *L*
CD ZDM 5650242
EMI Classics / Nov '93 / EMI

GOLDEN GATE
Goldenthal, Elliot *C*
CD VSD 5470
Varese Sarabande / Aug '94 / Pinnacle

GOLDENEYE
Serra, Eric *C*
Goldeneye: *Turner, Tina* / Goldeneye overture / Ladies first / We share the same passions / Little surprise for you / Severnaya suite / Our lady of Smolensk / Whispering statues / Run, shoot and jump / Pleasant drive in St. Petersburg / Fatal weakness / That's what keeps you alone / Dish out of water / Scale to hell / For ever, James / Experience of love
CD CDVUSX 100
Virgin / Nov '95 / EMI

GOLDFINGER
Barry, John *C*
Teasing the Korean / Main title / Alpine drive / Auric's factory / Oddjob's pressing engagement / Bond back in action again / Gassing the gangsters / Goldfinger (instrumental version) / Dawn raid on Fort Knox / Arrival of the bomb and countdown / Death of Goldfinger / End titles
CD CZ 557
Premier/EMI / Dec '95 / EMI

GOLDILOCKS
1958 Broadway Cast
Anderson, Leroy *C*
Ford, Joan/Jean & Walter Kerr *L*
Engel, Lehman *Con*
CD SK 48222
Sony Broadway / Nov '92 / Sony

GOLEM, THE (How He Came Into The World - 1977 Score)
Berlin Symphony Orchestra
Sasse, Karl-Ernst *C*
Keuschnig, Peter *Con*
CD 10467
Capriccio / Apr '96 / Target/BMG

GONDOLIERS, THE
D'Oyly Carte Opera Chorus/New Symphony Orchestra
Sullivan, Sir Arthur *C*
Gilbert, W.S. *L*
Godfrey, I. *Con*
2CD 4251772
Decca / Jan '90 / PolyGram

GONDOLIERS, THE
Evans, Geraint & Alexander Young/Glyndebourne Festival Choir/Pro Arte Orchestra
Sullivan, Sir Arthur *C*
Gilbert, W.S. *L*
Sargent, Sir Malcolm *Con*
2CD CMS 7643942
EMI Classics / Apr '94 / EMI

GONDOLIERS, THE
D'Oyly Carte Opera Chorus/Orchestra
Sullivan, Sir Arthur *C*
Gilbert, W.S. *L*
Pryce Jones, J. *Con*
2CD CDTER2 1187
TER / May '92 / Koch

GONDOLIERS, THE/PATIENCE
D'Oyly Carte Opera Chorus/New Symphony Orchestra
Sullivan, Sir Arthur *C*
Gilbert, W.S. *L*
Sargent, Sir Malcolm *Con*
CD Z 80952
Arabesque / Jul '89 / Seaford Music

GONDOLIERS, THE/TRIAL BY JURY
D'Oyly Carte Opera Chorus/Orchestra
Sullivan, Sir Arthur *C*
Gilbert, W.S. *L*
Sargent, Malcolm/H. Norris *Con*
2CD GEMMCDS 9961
Pearl / Sep '93 / Harmonia Mundi

GONE WITH THE WIND
Steiner, Max *C*
Main title / Scarlett and Rhett's first meeting / Ashley and Scarlett / Mammy / Christmas during the war in Atlanta / Atlanta in flames / Reconstruction / Ashley returns to Tara from the war prison / Scarlett makes her demands of Rhett / Scarlett's fall down the staircase / Bonnie's fatal pony ride / Finale
CD AK 45438
Cinevox / Jul '93 / Koch / Silva Screen

GONE WITH THE WIND
National Philharmonic Orchestra
Steiner, Max *C*
Gerhardt, Charles *Con*
Selznick international trademark/Main title / Opening sequence / Driving home / Dance montage - Charleston heel and toe polka / Grazioso/Love theme / Civil war/Fall of the South/Scarlett walks among the wounded / True love/Ashley returns to Tara from the war/Tara in ruins / Belle Watling / Reconstruction/Nightmare/Tara rebuilt/Bonnie/ The accident / Mammy and Melanie on the staircase/Rhett's sorrow / Apotheosis - Melanie's death/Scarlett and Rhett/Tara
CD GD 80452
RCA Victor / Mar '90 / BMG

GONE WITH THE WIND
London Sinfonietta
Steiner, Max *C*
CD 12436
Laserlight / Jun '95 / Target/BMG

GONE WITH THE WIND (Film Score/ Unissued Material)
Steiner, Max *C*
CD 96762
Silva Screen / Feb '90 / Koch / Silva Screen

GONE WITH THE WIND
Steiner, Max *C*
CD BMCD 7009
Blue Moon / Jul '96 / Cadillac / Discovery / Greensleeves / Jazz Music / Jet Star / TKO Magnum

GONE WITH THE WIND
Film Cast
Steiner, Max *C*
Main title / Tara / O'Hara family / Scarlett prepares for the barbecue / Twelve oaks / Barbecue / Afternoon nap / Charles Hamilton challenges Rhett / In the library / War is declared/The death of Charles / At the bazaar / Maryland, my Maryland / Dances / Gettysburg / Outside the Examiner newspaper office / At the depot / Christmas at Aunt Pitty's / Melanie and Scarlett tend the wounded / Scarlett's promise / Train depot / Melanie in labour / Rhett returns / Escape from Atlanta / Soldiers in retreat / Rhett and Scarlett on McDonough Road / Twelve oaks in ruin/Scarlett comes home / I'll never be hungry again / Alternate entr'acte / Battle montage / Deserter / Melanie and Scarlett / It's over / Frank Kennedy asks for Sue Ellen's hand / Paddock scene / Gerald's death / Old folks at home / New store / Scarlett in shantytown / Ashley and Dr. Mede/Frank's death / Belle waiting and Melanie / Scarlett gets tipsy / New Orleans honeymoon / Can can / Scarlett's new wardrobe / Scarlett's nightmare / Bonnie's birth / Twenty inches / Lumber mill / After the party / London / Rhett and Scarlett's fight / Death of Bonnie / Melanie and Mammy / Death of Melanie / Scarlett in the mist/Rhett leaves / Flashback/Finale
2CD CDODEON 27
Soundtracks / Jan '97 / EMI

GOOD COMPANIONS, THE
1974 London Cast
Previn, Andre *C*
Mercer, Johnny *L*
Camaraderie / Pools / Footloose / Pleasure of your company / Stage struck / Dance of life / Slippin' around the corner / Good companions / Little travelling music / And points beyond / Darkest before the dawn / Susie for everybody / Ta luv / I'll tell the world / Stage door John
CD DRGCD 15020
DRG / Jan '95 / Discovery / New Note/ Pinnacle

GOOD MORNING VIETNAM
Nowhere to run: *Reeves, Martha* / I get around: *Beach Boys* / Game of love: *Fontana, Wayne & The Mindbenders* / Sugar and spice: *Searchers* / Liar liar: *Castaways* / Warmth of the sun: *Beach Boys* / I got you (I feel good): *Brown, James* / Baby, please don't go: *Them* / Danger, heartbreak dead ahead: *Marvelettes* / Five o'clock world: *Vogues* / California sun: *Rivieras* / What a wonderful world: *Armstrong, Louis*
CD CDMID 163
A&M / Oct '92 / PolyGram

GOOD NEWS
1994 American Cast
Henderson, Ray *C*
De Sylva, B.G. & Lew Brown *L*
CD CDTER 1230
TER / Aug '95 / Koch

GOOD ROCKIN' TONITE
1992 London Cast
Rock around the clock / R-O-C-K rock / Razzle dazzle / Six-five special / Freight train / That is rock'n'roll / Rock Island line / Singing the blues / Book of love / Rock with the caveman / Fabulous / Green door / Keepa knockin' / Ma, he's making eyes at me / Giddy up a ding dong / Get a job / Trouble / Rock'n'roll is here to stay / Runaround Sue / At the hop / High school confidential / Donna / Move it / Let the good times roll / Happy Jack / La bamba / Baby I don't care / Rip it up / Down the line / Maybe tomorrow / Willie & the hand jive / Stupid cupid / Hey hey hey / Wondrous place / That's love / Don't knock upon my door / Baby blue / Be bop a lula / Dance in the street / Summertime blues / C'mon everybody / Something else / Twenty flight rock / I was born to rock'n'roll / Surfin' USA / Fun fun fun / I get around / Johnny B Goode / Respect / I'm a woman / Good rockin' tonite / What'd I say / Saved
CD OCRCD 6026
First Night / Apr '96 / Pinnacle

GOOD, THE BAD AND THE UGLY, THE
Morricone, Ennio *C*
Good, the bad and the ugly / Sundown / Strong / Desert / Carriage of the spirits / Marcia / Story of a soldier / Marcia without hope / Death of a soldier / Ecstasy of gold / Trio
CD CDP 7484082
EMI Manhattan / Sep '88 / EMI

GOOD, THE BAD AND THE UGLY, THE
Morricone, Ennio *C*
CD 464082
Silva Screen / Jul '93 / Koch / Silva Screen

GOODBYE GIRL
London Cast
Hamlisch, Marvin *C*
CD SCORECD 44
First Night / Apr '97 / Pinnacle

GOODBYE MR. CHIPS
1982 Chichester Festival Cast
Bricusse, Leslie *C*
Roll call / Fill the world with love / Would I had lived my life then / Schooldays / That's a boy / Where did my childhood go / Boring / Take a chance / Walk through the world / When I am older / Miracle / Day has a hundred pockets / You and I / What a lot of flowers / When I was younger / Goodbye, Mr Chips
CD CDTER 1025
TER / Apr '93 / Koch

GOODFELLAS
Rags to riches: *Bennett, Tony* / Sincerely: *Moonglows* / Speedo: *Cadillacs* / Stardust: *Ward, Billy* / Look in my eyes: *Chantels* / Life is but a dream: *Harptones* / Remember (walkin' in the sand): *Shangri-Las* / Baby I love you: *Franklin, Aretha* / Beyond the sea: *Darin, Bobby* / Sunshine of your love: *Cream* / Mannish boy: *Waters, Muddy* / Layla: *Derek & The Dominoes*
CD ______ **7567821522**
Atlantic / Nov '90 / Warner Music

GOOFY MOVIE, THE
CD ______ **WD 764002**
Disney Music & Stories / Oct '96 / Technicolor

GORKY PARK
Horner, James *C*
Horner, James *Con*
Main title / Following Kirwill / Irina's theme / Following KGB / Chase through the park / Arkady and Irina / Faceless bodies / Irina's chase / Sable shed / Airport farewell / Releasing the sables/ End title
CD ______ **VCD 47260**
Varese Sarabande / Jan '89 / Pinnacle

GOSPEL AT COLONUS, THE
Broadway Cast
Live where you can / Stop do not go on / How shall I see you through my tears / Voice foretold prayer / Never drive you away / Numberless are the world's wonders / Lift me up (like a dove) / Sunlight of no light / Eternal sleep / Lift him up / Now let the weeping cease
CD ______ **7559791912**
Nonesuch / Jan '95 / Warner Music

GOTHIC
Dolby, Thomas
Dolby, Thomas *C*
Fantasmagoria / Byronic love / Shelleymania / Mary's theme / Party games / Gypsy girl / Crucifix / Fundamental source / Sin and buggery / Impalement / Leech juice / Restless sleep 1,2 and 3 / It's his / Coitus per stigmata / Once we vowed eternal love / Riddled with guilt / Metamorphosis / Hangman / Beast in the crypt / Final seance / Funeral by the lake / No ghosts in daylight / To the grave / Devil is an Englishman / Skull pulse / Trickle of blood
CD ______ **CDV 2417**
Virgin / Feb '87 / EMI

GOTHIC DRAMAS
Original Cast
Kaiserstrasse / La strada dell follia / Follia nella strada / Fuori dalla realta / Pioggia / Ma non e un vampiro / Citta' ferita / Suoni dissociati / E'una vampira / Il vampiro / La casa delle streghe / Viole nella nebbia / Tra sospiri e lamenti / Ricordo di dino asciolla / Diario di un pazzo / Phantavox / Elegia per violino e pianoforte
CD ______ **DRGCD 32916**
DRG / Jun '96 / Discovery / New Note/ Pinnacle

GRACE OF MY HEART
God give me strength: *Bacharach, Burt & Elvis Costello* / Love doesn't ever fail us: *Williams Brothers* / Take a run at the sun: *Mascis, J.* / I do: *For Real* / Between two worlds: *Colvin, Shawn* / My secret love: *Banquette, Miss Lily* / Man from Mars: *Vigard, Kristen* / Born to love that boy: *For Real* / Truth is you lied: *Sobule, Jill* / Unwanted number: *For Real* / Groovin' on you: *Juned* / In another world: *Portrait* / Don't you think it's time: *Mascis, J.* / Absence makes the heart grow fonder: *Anders, Tiffany & Boyd Rice* / Boat on the sea: *Vigard, Kristen*
CD ______ **MCD 11554**
MCA / Feb '97 / BMG

GRADUATE, THE
Simon & Garfunkel
Simon, Paul *C*
Sound of silence / Jungleman party foxtrot / Mrs. Robinson / Sunporch cha-cha-cha / Scarborough Fair / On the strip / April come she will / Great effect / Big bright green pleasure machine
CD ______ **CD 32359**
CBS / Feb '94 / Sony

GRAFFITI BRIDGE
Prince
Prince *C*
Can't stop this feeling I got / Question of U / Round and round: *Campbell, Tevin* / Joy in repetition / Tick tick bang / Thieves in the temple / Melody cool / Graffiti bridge / Release it: *Time* / Elephants and flowers / We can funk / Love machine / Shake: *Time* / Latest fashion / Still would stand all time / New power generation
CD ______ **7599274932**
WEA / Aug '90 / Warner Music

GRAND CANYON
Howard, James Newton *C*
Main title / Claire returns the baby / My sister lives around here / Those rocks / Bloodstain / Baby / Don't work late / Mack's flashback / Don't want out / Searching for a heart / Mack & Claire's dream / Dee in Brentwood / Otis runs / You white / Keep the baby / Doesn't matter / Grand Canyon fanfare / End titles
CD ______ **262493**
Milan / Feb '94 / Conifer/BMG / Silva Screen

GRAND DUKE, THE
D'Oyly Carte Opera Chorus/Royal Philharmonic Orchestra
Sullivan, Sir Arthur *C*
Gilbert, W.S. *L*
Nash, R. *Con*
2CD ______ **4368132**
London / Jun '92 / PolyGram

GRAND HOTEL
1992 Broadway Cast
Forrest, George *C*
Forrest, George & Robert Wright *L*
Lee, Jack *Con*
Grand parade/Some have, some have not/ As it should be / Look at him / At the Grand Hotel/Table with a view / Maybe my baby loves me / Fire and ice/Twenty-two years/ Villa on a hill / I want to go to Hollywood / Sorry to report / Crooked path/Some have, some have not/As it should be / Who couldn't dance with you / So tell me Baron / Love can't happen / What you need / Bonjour amour / Happy/We'll take a glass together / I waltz alone / No creature on this planet / Bolero / How can I tell her / Final scene / Grand waltz
CD ______ **09026613272**
RCA Victor / Jul '92 / BMG

GRAND NIGHT FOR SINGING, A
Cast Recording
CD ______ **VSD 5516**
Varese Sarabande / Dec '94 / Pinnacle

GRAND TOUR/LONDON MORNING (The Ballet Music Of Noel Coward)
City Of Prague Philharmonic Orchestra
Coward, Sir Noel *C*
CD ______ **SILKD 6007**
Silva Classics / Sep '95 / Koch / Silva Screen

GREASE
Film Cast
Grease: *Valli, Frankie* / Summer nights: *Travolta, John & Olivia Newton John* / Hopelessly devoted to you: *Newton-John, Olivia* / Sandy: *Travolta, John* / Look at me I'm Sandra Dee: *Channing, Stockard* / Greased lightnin': *Travolta, John* / It's raining on prom night: *Bullens, Cindy* / You're the one that I want: *Travolta, John & Olivia Newton John* / Beauty school dropout: *Avalon, Frankie* / Alone at the drive-in movie: *Watts, Ernie* / Blue moon: *Sha Na Na* / Rock 'n' roll is here to stay: *Sha Na Na* / Those magic changes: *Sha Na Na* / Hound dog: *Sha Na Na* / Born to hand jive: *Sha Na Na* / Tears on my pillow: *Sha Na Na* / Mooning: *Bullens, Cindy* / Freddy my love: *Bullens, Cindy* / Rock 'n' roll party queen: *St. Louis, Louis* / There are worse things I could do: *Channing, Stockard* / Look at me I'm Sandra Dee (reprise): *Newton-John, Olivia* / We go together: *Travolta, John & Olivia Newton John* / Love is a many splendoured thing: *Studio Orchestra* / Grease (reprise): *Valli, Frankie*
CD ______ **8179982**
Polydor / Feb '91 / PolyGram

GREASE
1972 Broadway Cast
CD ______ **8275482**
Polydor / Feb '90 / PolyGram

GREASE
1993 London Cast
Radio WAXX jingle / Vince Fontaine / Sandy (opening) / Grease / Summer nights / Those magic changes / Freddie my love / Look at me I'm Sandra Dee / Greased lightnin' / Rydell fight song / Mooning / We go together / Shakin' at the high school hop / It's raining on prom night / Born to hand jive / Hopelessly devoted to you / Beauty school dropout / Sandy / Rock 'n' roll party queen / There are worse things I could do / Look at me I'm Sandra Dee (reprise) / You're the one that I want / Finale (medley)
CD ______ **4746322**
Epic / Sep '93 / Sony

GREASE (Highlights - The Shows Collection)
1993 Studio Cast
Grease / Summer nights / You're the one that I want / Sandy / Beauty school dropout / Greased lightnin' / Blue moon / Rock 'n' roll is here to stay / Hound dog / Tears on my pillow / Hopelessly devoted to you / Look at me I'm Sandra Dee / Freddy my love / It's raining on prom night
CD ______ **PWKS 4176**
Carlton / Oct '93 / Carlton

GREASE
New Broadway Cast
Alma Mater / We go together / Summer nights / Those magic changes / Freddy, my love / Greased lightnin' / Greased lightnin' (Reprise) / Rydell fight song / Mooning / Look at me I'm Sandra Dee / Since I don't have you / We go together (Reprise) / Shakin' at the High School Hop / It's raining on Prom night / Born to hand jive / Beauty school dropout / Alone at a drive-in movie / Rock 'n' roll party Queen / There are worse things I could do / Look at me I'm Sandra Dee (reprise) / Finale
CD ______ **09026627032**
RCA / Sep '94 / BMG

GREASE
1994 Studio Cast
Jacobs, Jim & Warren Casey *C*
Yates, Martin *Con*
CD ______ **CDTER 1220**
TER / Dec '94 / Koch

GREASE
Cast Recording
Grease / Summer nights / Freddy my love / Greased lightnin' / Look at me I'm Sandra Dee / Hopelessly devoted to you / We go together / Shakin' at the high school hop / Beauty school dropout / There are worse things I could do / Sandy / You're the one that I want
CD ______ **SHOWCD 007**
Showtime / Feb '95 / Disc / THE

GREASE
Pink Bruce Production
Grease / Summer nights / Hopelessly devoted to you / You're the one that I want / Sandy / Beauty school dropout / Look at me, I'm Sandra Dee / Greased lightning / It's raining on prom night / Alone at the drive-in movie / Blue moon / Rock 'n' roll is here to stay / Those magic changes / Hound dog / Born to hand jive / Tears on my pillow / Mooning / Freddy my love / Rock 'n' roll party queen / There are worse things I could do / Look at me, I'm Sandra Dee / We go together / Love is a many splendoured thing / Grease
CD ______ **GRF 274**
Tring / Apr '93 / Tring

GREASE
Studio Cast
Grease / Summer nights / Hopelessly devoted to you / You're the one that I want / Sandy / Beauty school dropout / Lookout at me I'm Sandra Dee / Greased lightning / It's raining on prom night / Alone a the drive-in-movie / Blue moon / Rock 'n' roll is here to stay / Those magic changes / Hound dog / Born to hand jive / rhose amgic changes / Tears on my pillow / Mooning / Freddy my love / Rock 'n' roll party queen / There are worse things I could do / Look at me I'm Sandra Dee (Reprise) / We go together / We got together / Love is a many splendoured thing / Grease (reprise)
CD ______ **85112**
CMC / May '97 / BMG

GREASE II
Back to school again: *Four Tops* / Cool rider: *Pfeiffer, Michelle* / Score tonight: *T-Birds & Pink Ladies* / Girl for all seasons: *Teefy, Maureen/Lorna Luft/Alison Price/ Michelle Pfeiffer* / Do it for our country: *Frechette, Peter* / Who's that guy: *Cast* / Prowlin': *T-Birds* / Reproduction: *Hunter, Tab* / Charades: *Caulfield, Maxwell* / Turn back the hands of time: *Caulfield, Maxwell & Michelle Pfeiffer* / Rock-a-hula: *Cast* / We'll be together: *Caulfield, Maxwell*
CD ______ **8250962**
Polydor / Apr '94 / PolyGram

GREAT ESCAPE, THE
Bernstein, Elmer *C*
Bernstein, Elmer *Con*
Main title / Premature plans / Cooler and Mole / Blythe / Discovery / Various troubles / On the road / Betrayal / Hendley's risk / Road's end / More action / Chase / Finale
CD ______ **MAF 7025D**
Intrada / Jul '92 / Koch / Silva Screen

GREAT EXPECTATIONS
1993 Clwyd Cast
CD ______ **CDTER 1209**
TER / Mar '94 / Koch

GREAT MUPPET CAPER, THE
Muppets
Main title / Hey, a movie / Big red bus / Happiness hotel / Lady Holiday / Steppin' out with a star / Apartment / Night life / First time it happens / Couldn't we ride / Piggy's fantasy / Great muppet caper / Homeward bound / Finale
CD ______ **74321 18246-2**
BMG Kidz / Jan '94 / BMG

GREAT ROCK 'N' ROLL SWINDLE, THE
Sex Pistols
God save the Queen (Symphony) / Johnny B Goode / Roadrunner / Anarchy in the UK / Don't give me no lip child / Stepping stone / L'anarchie pour le UK / Silly thing / My way / I wanna be me / Something else / (We're gonna) Rock around the clock: *Tenpole Tudor* / Lonely boy / EMI / Great rock 'n' roll swindle / Friggin' in the riggin' / You need hands: *McLaren, Malcolm* / Who killed Bambi: *Tenpole Tudor* / Belsen was a gas (live) / Black arabs: *Black Arabs* / Substitute / No one is innocent: *Biggs, Ronnie* / C'mon everybody / Belsen was a gas: *Biggs, Ronnie*
CD ______ **CDVDX 2510**
Virgin / Jan '95 / EMI

GREAT WAR & THE SHAPING OF THE 20TH CENTURY, THE
Daring, Mason *C*
CD ______ **DARINGCD 3029**
Daring / Nov '96 / ADA / CM / Direct

GREAT WESTERN MOVIE AND TV SOUNDTRACKS VOL.1 (My Rifle, My Pony And Me)
My rifle, my pony and me: *Martin, Dean & Ricky Nelson* / Legend of Shenandoah: *Stewart, James* / Montana/The searchers/ Wagons west/Song of the wagonmaster: *Sons Of The Pioneers* / Nevada Smith: *Kilgore, Merle* / Ballad of the Alamo/ The hanging tree: *Robbins, Marty* / Ballad of Paladin: *Western, Johnny* / Sons of Katie Elder/Rebel Johnny Yuma: *Cash, Johnny* / Rawhide/Gunfight at the OK Corral: *Laine, Frankie* / Ballad of Davy Crockett: *Parker, Fess* / Rio Bravo: *Martin, Dean* / I'm a runaway: *Hunter, Tab* / Bonanza: *Greene, Lorne* / North to Alaska: *Horton, Johnny* / High noon: *Ritter, Tex* / And the moon grew brighter: *Douglas, Kirk* / Pecos Bill: *Rogers, Roy & Sons Of The Pioneers* / Yellow rose of Texas, The/Roll on Texas moon/Don't fence me: *Rogers, Roy* / Cowboy: *Hall, Dickson*
CD ______ **BCD 15625**
Bear Family / Mar '93 / Direct / Rollercoaster / Swift

GREAT WHITE HYPE
Movin' on: *DJ U Neek & Nyt Owl* / Ballers lady: *Passion & E-40* / Shoot 'em up: *Bone Thugs n' Harmony* / If it's alright with you: *Cappadonna & U-God* / Who's the champion: *Ghost Face Killer & RZA* / Coolie high: *Camp Lo* / Running song: *Amber Sunshower* / Knock nekked (from the waist down): *Foxx, Jamie & Dolemite* / We got it: *Premier* / I got you under my skin: *Rawls, Lou & Biz Markie* / Bring the pain: *Method Man* / And I love you: *Miller, Marcus* / Chicken huntin': *Insane Clown Posse*
CD ______ **4842942**
Epic / Oct '96 / Sony

GREED IN THE SUN/PAUL GAUGIN
Delerue, Georges *C*
CD ______ **PCD 101**
Prometheus / Jan '89 / Silva Screen

GREEN CARD
Zimmer, Hans *C*
Subway drums: *Wright, Larry* / Instinct / Restless elephants / Cafe Afrika / Greenhouse / Moonlight / 9am Central Park / Clarinet concerto in A major / Silence / Instinct II / Asking you / Pour Bronte / Eyes on the prize
CD ______ **VSD 5309**
Varese Sarabande / Apr '91 / Pinnacle

GREENWILLOW
1960 Broadway Cast
Loesser, Frank *C*
CD ______ **DRGCD 19006**
DRG / Jun '95 / Discovery / New Note/ Pinnacle

GREMLINS
Goldsmith, Jerry *C*
Gremlins mega madness / Make it shine / Out out: *Gabriel, Peter* / Gift / Gizmo / Mrs. Deagle / Gremlin rag
CD ______ **GED 24044**
Geffen / Oct '89 / BMG

GREMLINS II (The New Batch)
Goldsmith, Jerry *C*
Just you wait / Gizmo escapes / Leaky faucet / Cute / Pot luck / Visitors / Teenage mutant gremlins / Keep it quiet / No rats / Gremlin pudding / New trends / Gremlin credits
CD ______ **VSD 5269**
Varese Sarabande / Aug '90 / Pinnacle

GREY FOX, THE
Chieftains
Moloney, Paddy *C*
Main title / Oyster bed sequence / Country store sequence / Ride to Kamloops / Meeting tram at Ducks Siding / Chase / End titles / Sweet Betsy from Pike: *Farnsworth, Richard*
CD ______ **DRGCD 9515**
DRG / Jan '95 / Discovery / New Note/ Pinnacle

GRIDLOCK'D
Wanted dead or alive: *2Pac & Snoop Doggy Dog/Dat Niggaz Daz/Roger Troutman* / Sho shot: *Lady Of Rage* / It's over now: *Babyface* / Don't try to play me homey: *Dat Nigga Daz* / Never had a friend like me: *2Pac & Johnny Jackson* / Why: *Nate Dogg* / Out the moon (boom, boom, boom): *LBC Crew* / I can't get enough: *Thomas, Damon & Rodney Day* / Tonight it's on: *Jones, Char & BGOTI* / Off the hook: *Snoop Doggy Dogg & Charlie Wilson/Val Young* / Lady heroine: *Flex, J & The Lady Of Rage/Sean Thomas* / Will I rise: *Storm & Val Young/Char Jones* / Body and soul / Life is a traffic jam: *Medusa & 2Pac/Vondie Curtis Hall* / Deliberation: *Chestnutt, Cody*
CD ______ **5346842**
Def Jam / Feb '97 / PolyGram

GRIFTERS, THE
Bernstein, Elmer *C*
CD ______ **VSD 5290**
Varese Sarabande / Dec '90 / Pinnacle

GRIND
1985 Broadway Cast
Grossman, Larry *C*
Fitzhugh, Ellen *L*
This must be the place / Cadava / Sweet thing like me / I get myself out / My daddy always taught me to share / All things to one man / Line / Katie, my love / Grind / Yes ma'am / Why, mama, why / This crazy place / From the ankles down / Who is he / Never put it in writing / I talk, you talk /

Timing / These eyes of mine / New man / Down / Century of progress / Finale
CD CDTER 1103
TER / Sep '85 / Koch

GROSSE POINTE BLANK
CD 8288672
London / Aug '97 / PolyGram

GROUNDHOG DAY
Fenton, George *C*
Weatherman: *McClinton, Delbert* / Clouds / I got you babe: *Sonny & Cher* / Quartet No. 1 in D: *Dukov, Bruce* / Ground hog: *Dukov, Bruce* / Take me around again: *Stevens, Susie* / Drunks / You like boats but not the ocean / Phil getz the girl / Phil steals the money / Pennsylvania polka: *Yankovic, Frank* / You don't know me: *Liebert, Ottmar & Luna Negra* / Kidnap and the quarry / Sometimes people just die / Eighteenth variation from a rhapsody on a theme of Paganini: *Buccheri, Elizabeth* / Medley: *Fryer, Terry* / Ice sculpture / New day / Almost like being in love: *Cole, Nat 'King'*
CD 4736742
Epic / May '93 / Sony

GRUMPIER OLD MEN
(I'll be glad when you're dead) you rascal you: *Armstrong, Louis & Louis Jordan* / Hit the road Jack: *Poindexter, Buster* / That's amore: *Martin, Dean* / Understand your man: *Cash, Johnny* / Venus: *Shocking Blue* / Jump in the line (Shake Senora): *Belafonte, Harry* / Stayin' alive: *Bee Gees* / Chicken dance: *Olsen, Wally Band* / 'S wonderful: *Brown, Les Orchestra/Doris Day* / Almost like being in love: *Cole, Nat 'King'* / I hear bells (wedding bells): *Del-Vikings* / What the heck: *Silvestri, Alan* / End title: *Silvestri, Alan*
CD 5354822
London / May '96 / PolyGram

GUILTY BY SUSPICION
Howard, James Newton *C*
CD VSD 5310
Varese Sarabande / Apr '91 / Pinnacle

GUITARRA
Bream, Julian
CD BCM 314 CD
BCM / Oct '89 / Pinnacle

GULLIVER'S TRAVELS
Jones, Trevor *C*
CD RCA 684752
Silva Screen / Apr '96 / Koch / Silva Screen

GUNS FOR SAN SEBASTIAN/HANG 'EM HIGH
Morricone, Ennio *C*
CD AK 47705
Cinevox / Jan '93 / Koch / Silva Screen

GUNS OF NAVARONE, THE
Tiomkin, Dimitri *C*
CD VSD 5236
Varese Sarabande / Feb '90 / Pinnacle

GUYS AND DOLLS
1982 London Cast
Loesser, Frank *C*
Runyon Land / Fugue for tinhorns / Follow the fold / Oldest established craps game in New York / I'll know / Bushel and a peck / Adelaide's lament / Guys and dolls / If I were a bell / My time of day / I've never been in love before / Take back your mink / Adelaide's lament (reprise) / More I cannot wish you / Craps shooter's ballet / Luck be a lady / Sue me / Sit down you're rockin' the boat / Marry the man today / Guys and dolls (reprise)
CD CDMFP 5978
Music For Pleasure / Jan '97 / EMI

GUYS AND DOLLS
1991 Broadway Cast
Loesser, Frank *C*
CD 09026613172
RCA Victor / Oct '92 / BMG

GUYS AND DOLLS
Original Broadway Cast
Loesser, Frank *C*
CD MCLD 19155
MCA / Jan '93 / BMG

GUYS AND DOLLS
Cast Recording
Loesser, Frank *C*
2CD CDTER2 1228
TER / Aug '95 / Koch

GUYS AND DOLLS
CC Productions
Loesser, Frank *C*
Runyon land / Fugue for tinhorns / Follow the fold / I'll know / Bushel and a peck / My time of day / Adelaide's lament / Guys and dolls / If I were a bell / I've never been in love before / Take your mink / Luck be a lady / Sit down, you're rocking the boat
CD QED 174
Tring / Nov '96 / Tring

GUYS AND DOLLS
Cast Recordifig/National Symphony Orchestra
Loesser, Frank *C*
Edwards, John Owen *Con*
Fugue for tinhorns / Oldest established craps game in New York / I'll know / Pet me Poppa / Adelaide's lament / Guys and dolls / Adelaide / Woman in love / If I were a bell / Take back your mink / Luck be a lady / Sit down, you're rockin' the boat

CD SHOWCD 034
Showtime / Oct '96 / Disc / THE

GYPSIES
CD CDCH 305
Milan / Apr '90 / Conifer/BMG / Silva Screen

GYPSY
1993 Film Cast
Styne, Jule *C*
Sondheim, Stephen *L*
Overture / May we entertain you / Some people / Small world / Baby June and her newsboys / Mr. Goldstone / Little lamb / You'll never get away from me / Dainty June and her farmboys / If Momma was married / All I need is the girl / Everthing's coming up roses / Together, wherever we go / You gotta get a gimmick / Let me entertain you / Rose's tune / End credits
CD 7567825512
WEA / Mar '94 / Warner Music

GYPSY
Ross, Annie & Buddy Bregman Band
Styne, Jule *C*
Sondheim, Stephen *L*
CD CDP 8335742
Pacific Jazz / Jan '96 / EMI

H

HACKERS
CD 22562 CIN
Edel / May '96 / Pinnacle

HAIR
1968 Broadway Cast
MacDermot, Galt *C*
Ragni, Jerome & James Rado *L*
Aquarius / Donna / Hashish / Sodomy / Coloured spade / Manchester, England / I'm black / Ain't got no air / Initials / I got life / Hair / My conviction / Don't put it down / Frank Mills / Be in / Where do I go / Black boys / White boys / Easy to be hard / Walking in space / Abie baby / Three five zero zero / What a piece of work is man / Good morning starshine / Let the sunshine in
CD 74321289852
RCA Victor / Aug '95 / BMG

HAIR
1968 London Cast
MacDermot, Galt *C*
Ragni, Jerome & James Rado *L*
Aquarius: *Edward, Vince & The Company* / Donna: *Tobias, Oliver & The Company* / Sodomy: *Feast, Michael & The Company* / Coloured spade: *Straker, Peter & The Company* / Ain't got no: *Feast, Michael/Peter Straker/Joanne White/The Company* / Air: *Kendrick, Linda & The Company* / I got life: *Nicholas, Paul & The Company* / Hair: *Nicholas, Paul/Oliver Tobias/The Company* / My conviction: *Forray, Andy* / Easy to be hard: *Leventon, Annabel* / Frank Mills: *Kristina, Sonja* / Where do I go: *Nicholas, Paul & The Company* / Electric blues: *Gulliver, John/ Rohan McCullough/Andy Forray/Jimmy Winston* / Black boys: *Kelly, Colette/Rohan McCullough/Lucy Fenwick* / White boys: *Hunt, Marsha/Ethel Coley/Joanne White* / Walking in space / Able baby: *Straker, Peter/Limbert Spencer/Leighton Robinson* / Three five zero zero / What a piece of work is man: *Edward, Vince & Leighton Robinson* / Good morning starshine / Bed / Let the sunshine in
CD 5199732
Polydor / Sep '93 / PolyGram

HAIR
1993 London Cast
MacDermot, Galt *C*
Ragni, Jerome & James Rado *L*
Aquarius / Donna/Hashish / Holy orgy / Coloured spade / Manchester, England / I'm black / Ain't got no / Dead end / I believe in love / Ain't got / Air / I got life / Initials / Going down / Hair / My conviction / Easy to be hard / Frank Mills / Hare Krishna / Where do I go / Electric blues / White boys / Walking in space / Yes, it's finished / Abie baby / All you have to do / Three five zero zero / What a piece of work is man / Bed / Good morning starshine / Let the sunshine in
CD CDEMC 3663
EMI / Nov '93 / EMI

HAIR
1968 Broadway Cast
MacDermot, Galt *C*
Ragni, Jerome & James Rado *L*
CD 11502
Silva Screen / Jan '89 / Koch / Silva Screen

HAIR
CC Productions
MacDermot, Galt *C*
Ragni, Jerome & James Rado *L*
Aquarius / Dead end / Easy to be hard / Good morning starshine / Be in (Hare Krishna) / Walking in space / Where do I go / Aquarius / Let the sunshine in / Donna / Frank Mills / Hair / I got life / What a piece of work is man
CD QED 205
Tring / Nov '96 / Tring

HAIR
Studio Cast
MacDermot, Galt *C*
Ragni, Jerome & James Rado *L*
Aquarise / Dead end / Easy to be hard / Good morning starshine / Be in (Hare Krishna) / Walking in space / Where do I go / Aquarius/Let the sunshine in / Donna / Frank Mills / Hair / I got life / What a piece of work is man
CD 85122
CMC / May '97 / BMG

HALF A SIXPENCE
1963 London Cast
Heneker, David *C*
Overture / All in the cause of economy / Half a sixpence / Money to burn / Oak and the ash / She's too far above me / I'm not talking to you / If the rain's got to fall / Old military canal / One that's run away / Long ago / Flash bang wallop / I know what I am / I'll build a palace / I only want a little house / Finale
CD 8205892
Deram / Nov '90 / PolyGram

HALF COCKED
Dragnalus: *Unwound* / Time expired: *Slant 6* / Tron: *Rodan* / CB: *Sleepyhead* / Dusty: *Ruby Falls* / Drunk friend: *Freakwater* / Be-9: *Versus* / Can I ride: *Polvo* / (We got) Flowers in our hair: *Big Heifer* / Invertebrate: *Boondoggle* / Hey cops: *Crain* / Magic box: *Helium* / Man went out: *Dungbeetle* / Truckstop theme: *Dungbeetle* / Want: *Grifters* / Thirty seven push-ups: *Smog* / Star 60: *2 Dollar Guitar* / Satellite: *Kicking Giant* / Crazy man: *Freakwater*
CD OLE 1522
Matador / Aug '95 / Vital

HALLELUJAH TRAIL, THE
Bernstein, Elmer *C*
CD TSU 0103
Tsunami / Jan '93 / Silva Screen

HALLELUJAH, BABY
1967 Broadway Cast
Styne, Jule *C*
Comden, Betty & Adolph Green *L*
Davis, Buster *Con*
CD SK 48218
Sony Broadway / Nov '92 / Sony

HALLOWEEN I
Carpenter, John *C*
Halloween theme / Laurie's theme / Shape escapes / Meyers' house / Michael kills Judith / Loomis and Shape's car / Haunted House / Shape lurks / Laurie knows / Better check the kids / Shape stalks
CD VCD 47230
Varese Sarabande / Jan '89 / Pinnacle

HALLOWEEN II
Carpenter, John & Alan Howarth *C*
Halloween theme / Laurie's theme / He knows where she is / Laurie and Jimmy / Still he kills (murder montage) / Shape enters Laurie's room / Mrs. Alves / Flats in the parking lot / Michael's sister / Shape stalks again / In the operating room / Mr. Sandman: *Chordettes*
CD VCD 47152
Varese Sarabande / Jan '89 / Pinnacle

HALLOWEEN III (Season Of The Witch)
Carpenter, John & Alan Howarth *C*
CD VSD 5243
Varese Sarabande / Feb '90 / Pinnacle

HALLOWEEN IV (The Return Of Michael Myers)
Howarth, Alan *C*
CD VSD 5205
Varese Sarabande / Dec '88 / Pinnacle

HALLOWEEN V (The Revenge Of Michael Myers)
Howarth, Alan *C*
Romeo Romeo: *Becca* / Dancin' on Churchill: *Churchill* / Sporting woman: *Diggy/ Chosak/Clark* / Shape also rises / First victim / Tower farm / Trapped / Jailbreak / Anything for money: *DVB* / Second time around: *Rhythm Tribe* / Halloween 5 - the revenge / Evil child must die / Stranger in the house / Stop the rage / Attic / Halloween finale
CD VSD 5239
Varese Sarabande / Dec '89 / Pinnacle

HALLOWEEN VI (The Curse Of Michael Myers)
Howarth, Alan *C*
CD VSD 5678
Varese Sarabande / Nov '95 / Pinnacle

HAMLET
Morricone, Ennio *C*
Hamlet (version 1) / King is dead / Ophelia (version) / What a piece of work is man / Prayer / Ghost / Play / Banquet / Dance for the queen / Ophelia (version 2) / Hamlet's madness / Hamlet (version 2) / Simulated madness / Closet / Second madness / To be or not to be / Solid flesh / Vaults
CD 916002
Silva Screen / Jan '94 / Koch / Silva Screen

HAMLET
Doyle, Patrick *C*
CD SK 62857
Sony Classical / Feb '97 / Sony

HAND THAT ROCKS THE CRADLE, THE
Revell, Graeme *C*
CD HWD 161304
Silva Screen / Apr '96 / Koch / Silva Screen

HANDMAID'S TALE, THE
Sakamoto, Ryuichi
Sakamoto, Ryuichi *C*
CD GNPD 8020
GNP Crescendo / Dec '90 / ZYX

HANNAH...1939
Off-Broadway Cast
Merrill, Bob *C*
CD CDTER 1192
TER / Jan '93 / Koch

HANS ANDERSON
Original Cast
Overture / Thumbelina / This town / Dare to take a chance / Truly loved / For Hans tonight / Jenny kissed me / Inchworm / Ecclesiaticus / Anywhere I wander / Wonderful Copenhagen / I'm Hans Christian Anderson / Happy days / Have I stayed away too long / Ugly duckling / No two people / King's new clothes
CD DRGCD 13116
DRG / Jun '96 / Discovery / New Note/ Pinnacle

HANS CHRISTIAN ANDERSON/THE COURT JESTER
Kaye, Danny
I'm Hans Christian Anderson / Anywhere I wander / Ugly duckling / Inchworm / Thumbelina / No two people / King's new clothes / Wonderful Copenhagen / Overture / Life could not better be / Outfox the fox / I'll take you dreaming / My heart knows a lovely song / I live to love / Willow, willow Waley / Pass the basket / Maladjusted jester / Where walks my true love / Life could not better be
CD VSD 5498
Varese Sarabande / Jun '94 / Pinnacle

HAPPY END
Cologne Pro Musica/Konig Ensemble
Weill, Kurt *C*
Brecht, Bertolt *L*
Latham Konig, J. *Con*
CD 600151
Capriccio / Jun '90 / Target/BMG

HAPPY END/THE SEVEN DEADLY SINS
Lenya, Lotte & Chorus/Orchestra
Weill, Kurt *C*
Brecht, Bertolt *L*
Bruckner-Ruggenberg, Wilhelm *Con*
CD CD 45886
CBS / Apr '91 / Sony

HARD DAY'S NIGHT, A
Beatles
Beatles *C*
I should have known better / If I fell / I'm happy just to dance with you / And I love her / Tell me why / Can't buy me love / Hard day's night / Anytime at all / I'll cry instead / Things we said today / When I get home / You can't do that / I'll be back
CD CDP 7464372
Parlophone / Feb '87 / EMI

HARD TARGET
Kodo Japanese Drum Ensemble
Revell, Graeme *C*
Simonec, T. *Con*
CD VSD 5445
Varese Sarabande / Oct '93 / Pinnacle

HARD TO KILL/ABOVE THE LAW/OUT FOR JUSTICE (Music From The Films Of Steven Seagal)
Frank, David Michael *C*
CD GNPD 8028
GNP Crescendo / May '92 / ZYX

HARD WAY, THE
Rubinstein, Arthur *C*
CD VSD 5315
Varese Sarabande / Apr '91 / Pinnacle

HARDER THEY COME, THE
You can get it if you really want: *Cliff, Jimmy* / Many rivers to cross: *Cliff, Jimmy* / Harder they come: *Cliff, Jimmy* / Sitting in limbo: *Cliff, Jimmy* / Draw your brakes: *Scotty* / Rivers of Babylon: *Melodians* / Sweet and Dandy: *Toots & The Maytals* / Pressure drop: *Toots & The Maytals* / Johnny too bad: *Slickers* / Shanty town: *Dekker, Desmond*
CD RRCD 11
Reggae Refreshers / Sep '90 / PolyGram / Vital

HARDWARE
Boswell, Simon
Boswell, Simon *C*
CD CDCH 627
Milan / Feb '94 / Conifer/BMG / Silva Screen

HARLEQUIN/THE DAY AFTER HALLOWEEN
May, Brian *C*
CD IMICD 1010
Silva Screen / Jan '94 / Koch / Silva Screen

HARUM SCARUM/GIRL HAPPY
Presley, Elvis
Harem holiday / My desert serenade / Go eat young man / Mirage / Kismet / Shake that tambourine / Hey little girl / Golden coins / So close, yet so far / Animal instinct / Wisdom of the ages / Girl happy / Spring fever / Fort Lauderdale chamber of commerce / Startin' tonight / Wolf call / Do not disturb / Cross my heart and hope to die / Meanest girl in town / Do the clam / Puppet on a string / I've got to find my baby
CD ______ **74321 13433-2**
RCA / Mar '93 / BMG

HARVEY GIRLS, THE
Film Cast
Main title / In the valley (where the evening sun goes down) / Wait and see / On the Atchinson, Topeka and Santa Fe / Training montage (The train must be fed) / Oh you kid / Jusy get the meat / Honky tonk / Wait and see (reprise) / It's a great big world / Wild wild west / Judy goes to the valley / My intuition / Wait and see (reprise 2) / Judy's fight / Ray Bolger dance / Swing your partner round and round / March of the Doagies / In the valley (where the evening sun goes down) (reprise) / Fire / Morning after / New end title / In the valley (where the evening sun goes down) / March of the doagies (reprise) / Hayride / End title
CD ______ **CDODEON 11**
Soundtracks / Apr '96 / EMI

HATARI
CD ______ **25592**
Silva Screen / Jan '89 / Koch / Silva Screen

HAUNTED
Wiseman, Debbie & Andrew Bottrill
Wiseman, Debbie *C*
Wiseman, Debbie *Con*
CD ______ **TRXCD 2002**
Silva Screen / Nov '95 / Koch / Silva Screen

HAUNTED SUMMER
Young, Christopher
Young, Christopher *C*
Haunted summer / Menage / Villa diodati / Night was made for loving / Polidori's potions / Ariel / Confreres / Geneva / Alby / Unquiet dream / Hauntings
CD ______ **FILMCD 037**
Silva Screen / Jan '89 / Koch / Silva Screen

HAWAII
Bernstein, Elmer *C*
CD ______ **TSU 0105**
Tsunami / Jul '93 / Silva Screen

HEAD
Monkees
CD ______ **4509976592**
Warner Bros. / Dec '94 / Warner Music

HEAR MY SONG
Altman, John *C*
Hear my song (main title) / Heartley's boogie / Nancy with the laughing face / Whistling dance / Jenny picking cockles / I'll take you home again Kathleen / Foxhunter's reel/Mason's apron / Peter Byrne's fancy / Movin' / Getting Joe / Truth and beauty / Come back to Sorrento / Goodbye / Hear my song
CD ______ **7599244562**
WEA / Apr '92 / Warner Music

HEART OF MIDNIGHT
Yanni
Yanni *C*
Overture Carol's theme / Welcome to "Midnight" / Carol through the rooms / Oh Daddy / Carol sees Fletcher/Rathead on ice / Carol's theme - soft interlude / Rape (parts I and II) / Aftermath / Carol talks to Maria / Sharpe no.2 dies/Carol's nightmare / Carol's theme - sadness of the heart / Library of porn / Cabinet falls / Carol out in the street / Dinner and downstairs in the club / S and M room / End sequence / Final confrontation / Carol's theme - sisters in pain / Sonny's death / Finale - Carol's theme
CD ______ **FILMCD 119**
Silva Screen / Apr '92 / Koch / Silva Screen

HEART OF THE STAG
CD ______ **SCCD 1017**
Southern Cross / Jan '89 / Silva Screen

HEARTBEAT (40 Number One Love Songs Of The Sixties - The Official Heartbeat Album)
You've lost that lovin' feeling: *Righteous Brothers* / (There's) always something there to remind me: *Shaw, Sandie* / World without love: *Peter & Gordon* / I'm into something good: *Herman's Hermits* / I got you babe: *Sonny & Cher* / (Sittin' on the) dock of the bay: *Redding, Otis* / When a man loves a woman: *Sledge, Percy* / Release me: *Humperdinck, Engelbert* / Green green grass of home: *Jones, Tom* / Distant drums: *Reeves, Jim* / Can't help falling in love: *Presley, Elvis* / Minute your gone: *Richard, Cliff* / Make it easy on yourself: *Walker Brothers* / How do you do it: *Gerry & The Pacemakers* / Something's gotten hold of my heart: *Pitney, Gene* / Poetry in motion: *Tillotson, Johnny* / Breaking up is hard to do: *Sedaka, Neil* / Will you still love me tomorrow: *Shirelles* / Johnny remember me: *Leyton, Johnny* / Cathy's clown: *Everly Brothers* / Love is all around: *Troggs* / What becomes of the broken hearted: *Ruffin, Jimmy* / Heartbeat: *Holly, Buddy* / Don't throw your love away: *Searchers* / Silence is golden: *Tremeloes* / Baby come back: *Equals* / Go now: *Moody Blues* / Whiter shade of pale: *Procul Harum* / I'm a believer: *Monkees* / Out of time: *Farlowe, Chris* / You don't have to say you love me: *Springfield, Dusty* / What a wonderful world: *Armstrong, Louis* / I'll never find another you: *Seekers* / (If paradise is) half as nice: *Amen Corner* / Baby now that I've found you: *Foundations* / Anyone who had a heart: *Black, Cilla* / You really got me: *Kinks* / With a little help from my friends: *Cocker, Joe* / Sweets for my sweet: *Searchers* / Letter: *Box Tops* / Bad to me: *Kramer, Billy J.* / Where do you go my lovely: *Starstedt, Peter* / Time in a bottle: *Croce, Jim* / Fruit tree: *Drake, Nick*
2CD ______ **RADCD 46**
Global TV / Oct '96 / BMG

HEARTBEAT - THE BEST OF HEARTBEAT
Heartbeat: *Holly, Buddy* / Just one look: *Hollies* / Do you love me: *Poole, Brian & The Tremeloes* / I like it: *Gerry & The Pacemakers* / Night has a thousand eyes: *Vee, Bobby* / In dreams: *Orbison, Roy* / Tired of waiting: *Kinks* / Flowers in the rain: *Move* / First cut is the deepest: *Arnold, P.P.* / Sloop John B: *Beach Boys* / Apache: *Shadows* / Do wah diddy diddy: *Manfred Mann* / Rescue me: *Bass, Fontella* / Got to get you into my life: *Bennet, Cliff & The Rebel Rousers* / Two kinds of teardrops: *Shannon, Del* / Monday Monday: *Mamas & The Papas* / Hello little girl: *Fourmost* / Out of time: *Farlowe, Chris* / Last night was made for love: *Fury, Billy* / Bad to me: *Kramer, Billy J.* / Wipeout: *Surfaris* / Yesterday man: *Andrews, Chris* / I only want to be with you: *Springfield, Dusty* / Letter: *Box Tops* / Wheel's on fire: *Driscoll, Julie* / Hippy hippy shake: *Swinging Blue Jeans* / Sun ain't gonna shine anymore: *Walker Brothers* / Wild thing: *Troggs* / Diamonds: *Harris, Jet* / Need your love so bad: *Fleetwood Mac* / Clapping song: *Ellis, Shirley* / Can't get used to losing you: *Williams, Andy* / (Dance with the) Guitar man: *Eddy, Duane* / Judy's turn to cry: *Gore, Lesley* / Picture of you: *Gore, Lesley* / Keep your hands off my baby: *Little Eva* / Don't throw your love away: *Searchers* / Do you believe in magic: *Lovin' Spoonful* / Sweet talkin' guy: *Chiffons* / Keep on running: *Davis, Spencer Group* / Crying game: *Berry, Dave* / It's not unusual: *Jones, Tom*
CD ______ **MOODCD 37**
Columbia / Sep '96 / Sony

HEARTBEAT I
Heartbeat: *Berry, Nick* / Hippy hippy shake: *Swinging Blue Jeans* / Always something there to remind me: *Shaw, Sandie* / Little Children: *Kramer, Billy J. & The Dakotas* / All day and all of the night: *Kinks* / World without love: *Peter & Gordon* / House of the rising sun: *Animals* / Shout: *Lulu & The Luvvers* / Don't let the sun catch you crying: *Gerry & The Pacemakers* / I'm into something good: *Herman's Hermits* / Needles and pins: *Searchers* / I believe: *Bachelors* / I like it: *Gerry & The Pacemakers* / Picture of you: *Brown, Joe & The Bruvvers* / Stranger on the shore: *Bilk, Acker*
CD ______ **4719002**
Columbia / Jun '92 / Sony

HEARTBEAT II
Look through any window: *Hollies* / Go now: *Moody Blues* / Tired of waiting for you: *Kinks* / Bend me, shape me: *Amen Corner* / Sunny: *Fame, Georgie* / FBI: *Shadows* / Itchycoo Park: *Small Faces* / Crying game: *Berry, Dave* / You were made for me: *Freddie & The Dreamers* / Heartbeat: *Berry, Nick* / Hi ho silver lining: *Beck, Jeff* / Do you love me: *Poole, Brian & The Tremeloes* / Bad to me: *Kramer, Billy J. & The Dakotas* / You've got your troubles: *Fortunes* / When you walk in the room: *Searchers* / Gimme some lovin': *Davis, Spencer Group* / Mighty Quinn: *Manfred Mann* / Catch the wind: *Donovan* / Let it be: *Cocker, Joe* / Daydream believer: *Berry, Nick*
CD ______ **4755292**
Columbia / Nov '93 / Sony

HEARTBREAK HIGH
CD ______ **4509999382**
Warner Bros. / May '95 / Warner Music

HEARTBREAKERS
Tangerine Dream
Tangerine Dream *C*
CD ______ **FILMCD 163**
Silva Screen / Jun '95 / Koch / Silva Screen

HEAT
Goldenthal, Elliot *C*
CD ______ **9362461442**
Warner Bros. / Jan '96 / Warner Music

HEAT AND DUST
Robbins, Richard *C*
CD ______ **CDQ 5551012**
EMI / Apr '94 / EMI

HEATHCLIFF (Songs From The Show)
Richard, Cliff
Misunderstood man / Sleep of the good / Gypsy bundle / Had to be: *Richard, Cliff & Olivia Newton-John* / When you thought of me / Dream tomorrow: *Richard, Cliff & Olivia Newton-John* / I do not love you Isabella: *Richard, Cliff/Olivia Newton-John/Kristina Nichols* / Choosing (when it's too late): *Richard, Cliff & Olivia Newton-John* / Marked with death: *Richard, Cliff & Olivia Newton-John* / Be with me always
CD ______ **CDEMD 1091**
EMI / Oct '95 / EMI

HEATHCLIFF - LIVE
Richard, Cliff & 1996 London Cast
Richard, Cliff *C*
Overture / Misunderstood man / Funeral cortege / Sleep of the good / Grange waltz / Each to his own / Had to be / Mrs Edgar Linton / Journey / India, Africa, China / When you thought of me (reprise) / Dream tomorrow / Isabella (bridge) / Gambling song / I do not love you Isabella / Isabella (reprise) / Choosing when it's too late / Madness of Cathy / Marked with death / Be with me always / Funeral cortege (reprise) / Nightmare / Be with me always (reprise) / Finale / Music for curtain calls
2CD ______ **CDEMD 1099**
EMI / Nov '96 / EMI

HEAVEN AND EARTH
Kitaro
Kitaro *C*
Heaven and earth (land theme) / Sau dau tree / Ahn and Le Ly love theme / Saigon reunion / Arvn / Sau nightmare / VC Bonfire / Trong com / Ahn's house / Destiny / Last phone call / Child without a father / Village attack/The arrest / Walk to the village / Steve's ghosts / Return to Vietnam / End titles
CD ______ **GED 24614**
Geffen / Jan '94 / BMG

HEAVY
CD ______ **022642CIN**
Edel / Dec '96 / Pinnacle

HEAVY METAL
Heavy metal: *Hagar, Sammy* / Heartbeat: *Hagar, Sammy* / Working in the coalmine: *Devo* / Veteran of the psychic wars: *Devo* / Reach out: *Cheap Trick* / Heavy metal (takin' a ride): *Felder, Don* / Crazy (a suitable case for treatment): *Nazareth* / Radar rider: *Riggs* / Open arms: *Journey* / Queen Bee: *Grand Funk Railroad* / I must be dreamin': *Cheap Trick* / Mob rules: *Black Sabbath* / All of you: *Felder, Don* / Prefabricated: *Trust* / Blue lamp: *Nicks, Stevie*
CD ______ **4867492**
Columbia / Apr '97 / Sony

HEIDI
Williams, John *C*
CD ______ **LXE 707**
Label X / May '95 / Silva Screen

HELEN MORGAN STORY, THE
CD ______ **10302**
Silva Screen / Jan '89 / Koch / Silva Screen

HELL CAN BE HEAVEN
1983 London Cast
Kaye, Hereward *C*
CD ______ **CDTER 1068**
TER / Aug '95 / Koch

HELLO DOLLY
1967 Broadway Cast
Herman, Jerry *C*
Overture / I put my hand in / It takes a woman / Put on your Sunday clothes / Ribbons down my back / Motherhood / Dancing / Before the parade passes by / Elegance / Hello Dolly / It only takes a moment / So long dearie / Finale
CD ______ **GD 81147**
RCA Victor / Aug '91 / BMG

HELLO DOLLY
1994 Studio Cast
Herman, Jerry *C*
CD ______ **VSD 5557**
Varese Sarabande / Jan '95 / Pinnacle

HELLO DOLLY
1964 Broadway Cast
Herman, Jerry *C*
Lang, P.J. *Con*
Prologue / I put my hand in / It takes a woman / Put on your Sunday clothes / Ribbons down my back / Motherhood / Dancing / Before the parade passes by / Elegance / Hello Dolly / It only takes a moment / So long dearie / Finale
CD ______ **GD 83814**
RCA Victor / Oct '89 / BMG

HELLO DOLLY
Film Cast
Herman, Jerry *C*
Just leave everything to me / It takes a woman / It takes a woman (reprise) / Put on your Sunday clothes / Ribbons down my back / Dancing / Before the parade passes by / Elegance / Love is only love / Hello Dolly / It only takes a moment / So long dearie / Finale
CD ______ **8103682**
Silva Screen / May '84 / Koch / Silva Screen

HELLO DOLLY (Songs From The Show)
Cast Recording
Herman, Jerry *C*
Hello Dolly: *Vaughan, Frankie* / Put on your Sunday clothes: *Collier, Tracy* / It takes a woman: *Vaughan, Frankie* / Ribbons down my back: *Collier, Tracy* / It only takes a moment: *Collier, Tracy* / Elegance: *Collier, Tracy* / Dancing: *Madoc, Ruth* / Before the parade: *Madoc, Ruth* / So long Dearie: *Madoc, Ruth*

CD ______ **3036200032**
Carlton / Apr '96 / Carlton

HELLRAISER I
Young, Christopher
Young, Christopher *C*
Resurrection / Hellbound heart / Lament configuration / Reunion / Quick death / Seduction and pursuit / In love's name / Cenobites / Rat slice quartet / Re-resurrection / Uncle Frank / Brought on by night / Another puzzle
CD ______ **FILMCD 021**
Silva Screen / Nov '87 / Koch / Silva Screen

HELLRAISER II (Hellbound)
Graunke Symphony Orchestra
Young, Christopher *C*
Young, Christopher *Con*
Hellbound / Second sight seance / Looking through a woman / Something to think about / Skin her alive / Stringing the puppet / Hall of mirrors / Dead or living / Leviathan / Sketch with fire
CD ______ **GNPD 8015**
GNP Crescendo / Jan '89 / ZYX

HELLRAISER III
Hellraiser / Go with me / What girls want / I feel like Steve / Troublemaker / Ooh-la-la / Baby universal / Divine thing / Down down down / Hell on earth / Waltzing with a jaguar / Elected
CD ______ **8283602**
London / Jan '93 / PolyGram

HELLRAISER III (Score)
Mosfilm State Orchestra & Choir
Miller, Randy *C*
CD ______ **GNPD 8033**
GNP Crescendo / Nov '92 / ZYX

HELLRAISER IV
Northwest Sinfonia
Licht, Daniel *C*
Anthony, Pete *Con*
CD ______ **FILMCD 179**
Silva Screen / Apr '96 / Koch / Silva Screen

HELP
Beatles
Beatles *C*
Help / Night before / You've got to hide your love away / I need you / Another girl / You're going to lose that girl / Ticket to ride / Act naturally / It's only love / You like me too much / Tell me what you see / I've just seen a face / Yesterday / Dizzy Miss Lizzy
CD ______ **CDP 7464392**
Parlophone / Apr '87 / EMI

HEMINGWAY'S ADVENTURES OF A YOUNG MAN
Waxman, Franz *C*
CD ______ **LXCD 1**
Label X / Jan '89 / Silva Screen

HENRY (Portrait Of A Serial Killer)
CD ______ **QDKCD 004**
Normal / Sep '94 / ADA / Direct

HENRY AND JUNE
Splet, Alan
Splet, Alan *C*
CD ______ **VSD 5294**
Varese Sarabande / Apr '91 / Pinnacle

HENRY V
City Of Birmingham Symphony Orchestra
Doyle, Patrick *C*
Rattle, Simon *Con*
Oh for a muse of fire / Henry V / Three traitors / Now, lords, for France / Death of Falstaff / Once more unto the breach / Threat to the governor of Harfleur / Katherine of France / March to Calais / Death of Bardolph / Upon the king / St. Crispin's day / Day is come / Non nobis domine / Wooing of Katherine / Let this acceptance take / End titles
CD ______ **CDC 7499192**
EMI / Sep '89 / EMI

HERCULES - THE LEGENDARY JOURNEYS (TV Soundtrack)
Loduca, Joseph *C*
CD ______ **VSD 5660**
Varese Sarabande / Jun '96 / Pinnacle

HERE WE GO ROUND THE MULBERRY BUSH
Here we go round the mulberry bush: *Traffic* / Taking out time: *Davis, Spencer Group* / Every little thing: *Davis, Spencer Group* / Virginals dream: *Davis, Spencer Group* / Utterly simple: *Traffic* / It's been a long time: *Ellison, Andy* / Looking back: *Davis, Spencer Group* / Picture of her: *Davis, Spencer Group* / Just like me: *Davis, Spencer Group* / Waltz for Caroline: *Davis, Spencer Group* / Posession: *Davis, Spencer Group* / Am I what I was or was I what I am: *Traffic* / Taking out time: *Davis, Spencer Group* / Picture of her: *Davis, Spencer Group* / Just like me: *Davis, Spencer Group* / Posession: *Davis, Spencer Group*
CD ______ **RPM 179**
RPM / Jun '97 / Pinnacle

HERE'S LOVE
1963 Broadway Cast
Willson, Meredith *C*
Lawrence, Elliot *Con*
CD ______ **SK 48204**
Sony Broadway / Dec '91 / Sony

HERITAGE: CIVILISATION AND THE JEWS (Symphonic Dances)
Royal Philharmonic Orchestra
Bernstein, Leonard/John Duffy *C*
Williams, Richard *Con*
On the Town / Heritage symphonic dances / Heritage fanfare and chorale / Heritage suite for orchestra
CD CDDCA 630
ASV / Oct '88 / Select

HERO AND THE TERROR
Frank, David Michael *C*
Two can be one / Obsession / Workout / Terror / Hero's seduction / San Pedro bust / Ladies room / Breakout / Birthday wishes / Discovery / Showtime / Angela / Subterranean terror / Simon's lair / Search / Living nightmare / Love and obsession
CD EDL 25082
Edel / Jan '90 / Pinnacle

HIDDEN, THE
Convertino, Michael *C*
CD VCD 47349
Varese Sarabande / Jan '89 / Pinnacle

HIDEAWAY
CD IONIC 12CD
The Fine Line / Jun '95 / RTM/Disc

HIDER IN THE HOUSE
Young, Christopher *C*
CD MAF 7007D
Intrada / Jan '94 / Koch / Silva Screen

HIGH HEELS
Sakamoto, Ryuichi *C*
Main theme / Tacones lojanos / Trauma / Becky's guitar / Plaza / Kisses / Un ano de amor / El cuco 1 / El cuco 2 / Murder / Interrogation / Driving to confess / Tele 7 / Rebecca's arrest / Piensa en mi / Autumn sonata / Released Rebecca / Letal's secret / Ambulance ride / End title
CD 5108552
Silva Screen / Jul '94 / Koch / Silva Screen

HIGH SCHOOL HIGH
CD 7567927092
Atlantic / Oct '96 / Warner Music

HIGH SIGN, THE (New Jazz Score For Buster Keaton Film)
Frisell, Bill
Frisell, Bill *C*
CD 7559793512
Elektra / Jan '95 / Warner Music

HIGH SOCIETY
Film Cast
Porter, Cole *C*
Overture / Calypso / Little one / You're sensational / I love you Samantha / Now you has jazz / Well did you evah / Mind if I make love to you
CD CDP 7937872
Capitol / Apr '95 / EMI

HIGH SOCIETY (Highlights - The Shows Collection)
1994 Studio Cast
Porter, Cole *C*
Orchestra medley / High Society calypso / Litle one / Who wants to be a millionaire / True love / Now you has jazz / You're sensational / I love you Samantha / Well did you evah / Mind if I make love to you / I love you Samantha / True love (reprise)
CD PWKS 4193
Carlton / Mar '94 / Carlton

HIGH SOCIETY
Cast Recording
Porter, Cole *C*
CD PBHSCD 1
Playback / Oct '96 / Pinnacle

HIGH SOCIETY
CC Productions
Porter, Cole *C*
High Society overture / High Society calypso / Little one / Who wants to be a millionaire / True love / You're sensational / I love you Samantha / Now you has jazz / Well did you evah / Mind if I make love to you
CD QED 208
Tring / Nov '96 / Tring

HIGH SOCIETY
Studio Cast
Porter, Cole *C*
High society overture / High society calypso / Little one / Who wants to be a million / True love / You're sensational / I love Samantha / Now you has jazz / Well did you evah / Mind if I make love to you
CD 85132
CMC / May '97 / BMG

HIGH SPIRITS
Fenton, George
Fenton, George *C*
Overture / Castle Plunkett / Plunkett's lament / Ghost bus tours / Ghostly reflections / She is from the far land / Bumps in the knight / Mary appears
CD GNPD 8016
GNP Crescendo / '88 / ZYX

HIGH SPIRITS (inc. Four Bonus Songs Performed By Noel Coward)
1964 London Cast
Martin, Hugh & Timothy Gray *C*
Overture / Was she prettier than I / Bicycle song / You'd better love me / Where is the man I married / Go into your trance / Forever and a day / Something tells me / I know your heart / Faster than sound / If I gave you / Talking to you / Home sweet heaven / Something is coming to tea / What in the world did you want / Faster than sound (reprise) / High spirits / Something to tell me
CD CDSBL 13107
DRG / Oct '92 / Discovery / New Note/ Pinnacle

HIGH VELOCITY
National Philharmonic Orchestra
Goldsmith, Jerry *C*
CD PCD 134
Prometheus / Sep '94 / Silva Screen

HIGHER AND HIGHER/STEP LIVELY
It's a most important affair / Today I'm a debutante / I couldn't sleep a wink last night / Music stopped / I saw you first / Lovely way to spend an evening / You're on your own / Minuet in boogie / Finale / Step / As long as there's music / Ask the madame / Why must there be an opening song / Some other time / Where does love begin
CD CD 60004
Great Movie Themes / Apr '97 / Target/ BMG

HIGHLANDER III
Honest Joe: *James* / Immortality: *Fall* / Yalili ya aini: *Jah Wobble's Invaders Of The Heart* / High in your face: *House Of Love* / Cry mercy judge: *Verlaine, Tom* / Jam J: *James* / Sept Marins/Hanter Dro: *Whirling Pope Joan* / Bonny Portmore: *McKennitt, Loreena* / Quiet mind - for Joe: *Ruby Blue* / Ce he mise le ulaingt: *McKennitt, Loreena* / Two trees: *McKennitt, Loreena* / Little muscle: *Catherine Wheel* / Dummy crusher: *Kerbdog* / Becoming more like God: *Jah Wobble's Invaders Of The Heart* / Bluebeard: *Cocteau Twins*
CD 5267472
Mercury / Mar '95 / PolyGram

HIRED MAN, THE
1992 London Cast
Goodall, Howard *C*
Song of the hired men / Scene: the Tallentire boys / Fill it to the top / Now for the first time / Narration / Work song: It's all right for you / Narration II / Who will you marry then / Scene: Jackson and Emily / Get up and go lad / I wouldn't be the first / Scene: Emily did you get the message / Fade away / Hear your voice / What a fool I've been / If I could / Narration III / You never see the sun / Scene: Jackson meets May / Scene: Harry, you're not going down the pit / What would you say to your son / Union song: Men of stone / Narration IV / Farewell song / War song: So tell your children / Narration V / No choir of angels / Scene: the mining disaster / Scene: John and Seth / Re-hiring
2CD CDTER2 1189
TER / May '92 / Koch

HITCHER, THE
Isham, Mark *C*
CD FILMCD 118
Silva Screen / Mar '92 / Koch / Silva Screen

HMS PINAFORE
New Sadler's Wells Opera Chorus/ Orchestra
Sullivan, Sir Arthur *C*
Gilbert, W.S. *L*
Phipps, S. *Con*
2CD CDTER2 1150
TER / May '88 / Koch

HMS PINAFORE
D'Oyly Carte Opera Chorus/New Symphony Orchestra
Sullivan, Sir Arthur *C*
Gilbert, W.S. *L*
Godfrey, I. *Con*
2CD 4142832
Decca / Jan '90 / PolyGram

HMS PINAFORE
Welsh National Opera Choir/Orchestra
Sullivan, Sir Arthur *C*
Gilbert, W.S. *L*
Mackerras, Sir Charles *Con*
CD CD 80374
Telarc / Jan '95 / Conifer/BMG

HMS PINAFORE
New Sadler's Wells Opera/Chorus
Sullivan, Sir Arthur *C*
Gilbert, W.S. *L*
Overture / We sail the ocean blue / I'm called little buttercup / My gallant crew/I am the Captain of The Pinafore / Over the bright blue sea / I've got three cheers/I am the monarch of the sea / When I was a lad/ For I hold that on the seas / British tar / Things are seldom what they seem / Never mind the why and wherefore / Farewell my own / Here take her Sir/Oh joy, oh rapture unforseen
CD SHOWCD 022
Showtime / Oct '96 / Disc / THE

HMS PINAFORE/THE MIKADO
D'Oyly Carte Opera Chorus/New Symphony Orchestra
Sullivan, Sir Arthur *C*
Gilbert, W.S. *L*
Sargent, Sir Malcolm *Con*
2CD CDHD 253/4
Happy Days / Jan '94 / Conifer/BMG

HMS PINAFORE/TRIAL BY JURY
Baker, George & John Cameron/Glyndebourne Festival Choir/Pro Arte Orchestra
Sullivan, Sir Arthur *C*
Gilbert, W.S. *L*
Sargent, Sir Malcolm *Con*
2CD CMS 7643972
EMI Classics / Apr '94 / EMI

HOFFA
Newman, David *C*
CD 07822110012
Fox Film Scores / Jan '94 / BMG

HOLLOW REED
Dudley, Anne/Michala Petri
Dudley, Anne *C*
Main title / Oliver's theme / Upside down world / Family life / Questioning / Mother and son / Silent witness / Waking nightmare / Resolution / It will never happen again / Seeds of doubt / Unnatural practices / White lies / Decision / No hiding place / In a child's mind / Meditations / I shall be released: *Weller, Paul*
CD 09026686302
RCA Victor / Sep '96 / BMG

HOLOCAUST 2000/SEX IN A CONFESSIONAL
Morricone, Ennio *C*
CD SPALAX 14986
Spalax / Oct '96 / ADA / Cargo / Direct / Discovery / Greyhound

HOME ALONE I
Williams, John *C*
Williams, John *Con*
CD MK 46595
Sony Classical / Jan '94 / Sony

HOME ALONE II (Score)
Williams, John *C*
CD 07822110002
Fox Film Scores / Dec '92 / BMG

HOME ALONE II
All alone on Christmas: *Love, Darlene* / Holly jolly Christmas: *Jackson, Alan* / Somewhere in my memory: *Midler, Bette* / My Christmas tree: *Home Alone Children's Choir* / Sombras de otros tiempos: *Belen, Ana* / Merry Christmas, Merry Christmas: *Williams, John* / Cool jerk: *Capitols* / It's beginning to look a lot like Christmas: *Mathis, Johnny* / Christmas star: *Williams, John* / O come all ye faithful: *Fischer, Lisa*
CD 74321165162
Arista / Oct '93 / BMG

HOME FOR THE HOLIDAYS
Evil ways: *Rusted Root* / Holiday blues: *Isham, Mark* / Candy: *Cole, Nat 'King'* / It's not unusual: *Jones, Tom* / Blue nights: *Isham, Mark* / Birth of the cool whip: *Isham, Mark* / Trouble in mind: *Washington, Dinah* / Late night blues: *Isham, Mark* / Very thought of you: *Isham, Mark* / Very thought of you: *Cole, Nat 'King'* / Piece of my heart: *Joplin, Janis*
CD 5288712
Mercury / Dec '96 / PolyGram

HOMEBOY
Clapton, Eric
Kamen, Michael & Eric Clapton *C*
I want to love you baby: *Benson, Jo* / Homeboy / Call me if you need me: *Magic Sam* / Final fight / Travelling East / Bridge
CD CDV 2574
Virgin / Dec '88 / EMI

HOMEWARD BOUND
Broughton, Bruce *C*
CD MAF 7041D
Intrada / Jan '94 / Koch / Silva Screen

HOMO FABER (THE VOYAGE)
CD CDCH 804
Milan / Mar '92 / Conifer/BMG / Silva Screen

HONEY, I BLEW UP THE KIDS
Broughton, Bruce *C*
Broughton, Bruce *Con*
CD MAF 7030D
Intrada / Sep '92 / Koch / Silva Screen

HOPE AND GLORY
Martin, Peter *C*
CD VCD 47290
Varese Sarabande / Jan '89 / Pinnacle

HOT MIKADO
London Cast
Overture / We are gentlemen of japan / Wand'ring minstrel 1 / Drums will crash / Behold the lord high executioner / I've got a little list / Three little maids / Playout / Finale / Beauty in the bellow / Tit-willow / Alone and yet alive / Mikado song / Here's a howdy-do / Swing a merry madrigal / Sun & I / Braid the raven hair / Entr'acte / Act one / Let the thong our joy advance / I am so proud / Katisha's entrance / For he's gonna marry yum-yum / Hour of gladness
CD OCRCD 6048
First Night / Apr '97 / Pinnacle

HOT SHOE SHUFFLE
1993 Australian Cast
Overture / Telegram Sam / I've got to be a rugcutter / Where was I when they passed out luck / Long ago and far away / Ain't misbehavin' / Handful of keys / This joint is jumpin' / Ac-cent-tchu-ate the positive / Fifteen minute intermission / Entr'acte / I get along without you very well / When I get my name in lights / Act / Hot shoe shuffle / Puttin' on the ritz / How lucky can you get / Song and dance man / Big band tap melody / Little brown jug / Pennyslyvania 6-5000 / Mood indigo / Tiger rag
CD OCRCD 6046
First Night / Apr '97 / Pinnacle

HOT SHOE SHUFFLE
Cast Recording
CD FLHSSCD 1
JVO / Dec '95 / Pinnacle

HOT SHOTS
Levay, Sylvester *C*
CD VSD 5338
Varese Sarabande / Sep '91 / Pinnacle

HOUR OF THE GUN
Goldsmith, Jerry *C*
CD MAF 7020D
Intrada / Jan '93 / Koch / Silva Screen

HOUSE OF ELIOT
Parker, Jim *C*
House of Eliot / Tango De La Luna / Shopping spree / Evie's tune / Eliott rag / Manhattan blues / Brooklands / Highgate memories / Jack's blues / Fashion parade / Tiger moth / Paris morning / Wedding / Paris by night / Hermitage (A new ballet) / Beatrice and Jack / New apartment / Paraquay / Funny man blues / Charity waltz / Reunion blues / Leaving for America
CD CDSTM 5
Soundtrack Music / Jul '93 / EMI

HOUSE OF FRANKENSTEIN
Moscow Symphony Orchestra
Salter, Hans *C*
Stromberg, William T. *Con*
CD 8223748
Marco Polo / Mar '96 / Select

HOUSE OF FRANKENSTEIN/GHOST OF FRANKENSTEIN
RTE Concert Orchestra
Salter, Hans *C*
Penny, Andrew *Con*
CD 8223477
Marco Polo / Aug '94 / Select

HOUSE OF THE DARK SHADOWS/ NIGHT OF THE DARK SHADOWS
Cobert, Robert *C*
CD 72401
Silva Screen / Apr '96 / Koch / Silva Screen

HOUSE ON SORORITY ROW, THE/THE ALCHEMIST
London Philharmonic Orchestra
Band, Richard *C*
Band, Richard *Con*
CD MAF 7046D
Intrada / '93 / Koch / Silva Screen

HOUSE PARTY II
Announcement of pajama jammi jam / House party (Don't know what you come to do) / Christopher Robinson scholarship fund / Ready or not / Kid 'n' play wreck shop / Ain't gonna hurt nobody / I like your style / Kid and Sydney break up candelight and you / I lust 4 U / Bilal gets off / Let me know something / Yo baby yo / FFF Rap what's on your mind / Big ol' jazz / You gotta pay what you owe / It's so hard to say goodbye to yesterday / Confidence / It's so hard to say goodbye to yesterday (Acapella) / Kid's goodbye thanks to Pope
CD MCLD 19246
MCA / Apr '94 / BMG

HOUSE/HOUSE II
Manfredini, Harry *C*
CD VCD 47295
Varese Sarabande / Jan '89 / Pinnacle

HOUSEKEEPING
Gibbs, Michael
Gibbs, Michael *C*
CD VCD 47308
Varese Sarabande / Jan '89 / Pinnacle

HOW GREEN WAS MY VALLEY
Newman, Alfred *C*
CD 07822110082
Fox Film Scores / Apr '94 / BMG

HOW THE WEST WAS WON
Newman, Alfred *C*
CD AK 47024
Cinevox / Jan '93 / Koch / Silva Screen

HOW TO BE A PLAYER
CD 5379732
Mercury / Aug '97 / PolyGram

HOW TO MAKE LOVE TO A NEGRO
Dibango, Manu
Dibango, Manu *C*
CD CDCH 513
Milan / Feb '90 / Conifer/BMG / Silva Screen

HOW TO STEAL A MILLION
Williams, John *C*
CD TSU 0109
Tsunami / Jan '93 / Silva Screen

HOWARD'S END
Robbins, Richard *C*
CD NI 5339
Nimbus / Apr '92 / Nimbus

HOWARD'S END/MAURICE/A ROOM WITH A VIEW
Robbins, Richard *C*
Rabinowitz, H. *Con*
3CD CMS 5652202
EMI / Jan '91 / EMI

HUDSON HAWK
Kamen, Michael *C*
Hudson Hawk theme: *Dr. John* / Swinging on a star: *Willis, Bruce & Danny Aiello* / Side by side: *Willis, Bruce & Danny Aiello* / Leonardo / Welcome to Rome / Reading the codex / Igg & Ook / Cartoon fight / Gold room / Hawk swing: *Kraft, Robert* / Hudson Hawk: *Kraft, Robert*
CD ______ **VSD 5323**
Varese Sarabande / Jul '91 / Pinnacle

HUMANOID, THE/NIGHTMARE CASTLE
Morricone, Ennio *C*
CD ______ **OST 118**
Milano Dischi / Jan '93 / Silva Screen

HUNCHBACK OF NOTRE DAME, THE
CD ______ **WD 771902**
Disney Music & Stories / Jul '96 / Technicolor

HUNDRA, THE
Morricone, Ennio *C*
CD ______ **PCD 107**
Prometheus / Jan '93 / Silva Screen

HUNGER, THE
Rubini, Michael & Denny Jaeger *C*
Trio in E flat Op100 / Beach house: *Spruill, Stefany* / Suite 1 for solo cello in G / Waiting room / Flashbacks / Sarah's panic / Arisen / Gavotte en Rondeau / Lakme / Sarah's transformation / Final death
CD ______ **VSD 47261**
Varese Sarabande / Oct '94 / Pinnacle

HUNGER, THE/THE YEAR OF LIVING DANGEROUSLY
CD ______ **CDCH 004**
Milan / Feb '94 / Conifer/BMG / Silva Screen

HUNT FOR RED OCTOBER, THE
Poledouris, Basil *C*
Hymn to Red October / Nuclear scam / Putin's demise / Course two-five-zero / Ancestral aid / Chopper / Two wives / Red route 1 / Plane crash / Kaboom
CD ______ **MCLD 19306**
MCA / Oct '95 / BMG

HUNTERS, THE
Residents
CD ______ **311692**
Milan / Dec '95 / Conifer/BMG / Silva Screen

HUNTING OF THE SNARK
1991 London Cast
Batt, Mike *C*
CD ______ **CASTCD 24**
First Night / Nov '91 / Pinnacle

HYPERSPACE (Inc. Symphonic Suite From Beauty & The Beast)
Davis, Don *C*
CD ______ **PCD 120**
Prometheus / Jan '93 / Silva Screen

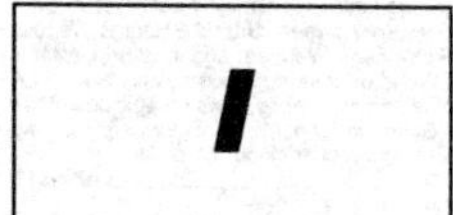

I AND ALBERT
1972 London Cast
Strouse, Charles *C*
Adams, Lee *L*
Draw the blinds / I and Albert / Leave it alone / I've 'eard the bloody 'indoos
CD ______ **CDTER 1004**
TER / Aug '95 / Koch

I DO I DO
Cast Recording
CD ______ **VSD 5730**
Varese Sarabande / Aug '96 / Pinnacle

I LOVE MY WIFE
Broadway Cast
Coleman, Cy *C*
Stewart, Michael *L*
We're still friends / Monica / By threes / Love revolution / Mover's life / Someone wonderful I missed / Sexually free / Hey there / Good times / By the way if you are free tonight / Lovers on Christmas Eve / Scream / Ev'rybody today is turning on / Married couple seeks married couple / I love my wife / In conclusion
CD ______ **DRGCD 6109**
DRG / Jan '89 / Discovery / New Note/ Pinnacle

I LOVE YOU PERFECT
Yanni
Yanni *C*
Theme / Lovers quarrel / Allan fired / Chair shower and court room montage / Setting the horse free / Lovers make up / Clarinet quintet K581 - allegretto: *Camerata Academica Salzburg* / Marry me / I'll be by your side / Temper tantrum / But I have some good days / Hospital montage / Christina dies / I love you perfect (reprise)
CD ______ **FILMCD 122**
Silva Screen / Jun '93 / Koch / Silva Screen

I LOVE YOU, YOU'RE PERFECT, NOW CHANGE
Cast Recording
CD ______ **VSD 5771**
Varese Sarabande / Mar '97 / Pinnacle

I NEVER TOLD YOU
Hersch, Fred *C*
CD ______ **VSD 5547**
Varese Sarabande / Jul '95 / Pinnacle

I REMEMBER MAMA
1985 Studio Cast
Rodgers, Richard *C*
Charnin, Martin *L*
I remember Mama / Little bit more / Writer writes at night / Ev'ry day (comes something beautiful) / You could not please me more / Most disagreeable man/Uncle Chris / Lullaby / Easy come, easy go / It's not the end of the world / Entr'acte / Mama always makes it better / When / Fair trade / I write, you read (fair trade) / It's going to be good to be gone / Time / Finale
CD ______ **CDTER 1102**
TER / Oct '85 / Koch

I SHOT ANDY WARHOL
CD ______ **7567926902**
Warner Bros. / May '96 / Warner Music

ICE CASTLES
Hamlisch, Marvin *C*
CD ______ **ARCD 8317**
Silva Screen / Jan '89 / Koch / Silva Screen

ICEMAN
Smeaton, Bruce *C*
CD ______ **SCCD 1006**
Southern Cross / Jan '89 / Silva Screen

IDIOT BOX
CD ______ **4321451782**
Roo Art / Feb '97 / Cargo

IGNACIO
Vangelis
Vangelis *C*
CD ______ **813 042 2**
Phonogram / Jul '85 / PolyGram

IL COMMISSARIO PEPE/SISSIGNORE/ SPLENDORI E MISERIE DI MME. R
Trovajoli, Armando/Berto Pisano/Fiorenzo Carpi *C*
CD ______ **PRCD 119**
Preamble / Apr '96 / Silva Screen

IL GRANDE DUELLO/SI PUO'FARE...AMIGO (The Big Duel/The Big & The Bad)
Bacalov, Luis Enriquez *C*
CD ______ **PRCD 120**
Preamble / Apr '96 / Silva Screen

IL MERCENARIO (The Professional Gun)
Morricone, Ennio *C*
CD ______ **VCDS 7018**
Varese Sarabande / Apr '96 / Pinnacle

IL MIO NOME E SHANGHAI JOE/I GIORNI DELLA VIOLENZA
Nicolai, Bruno *C*
CD ______ **PRCD 123**
Preamble / Apr '96 / Silva Screen

IL POSTINO (The Postman)
Bacalov, Luis Enriquez *C*
CD ______ **HW 620292**
Silva Screen / Apr '96 / Koch / Silva Screen

IL PREFETTO DI FERRO/IL MOSTRO
Morricone, Ennio *C*
CD ______ **SPALAX 14985**
Spalax / Oct '96 / ADA / Cargo / Direct / Discovery / Greyhound

IL SOLE ANCHE DI NOTTE
Piovani, Nicola *C*
CD ______ **CH 605**
Milan / Jan '95 / Conifer/BMG / Silva Screen

I'LL DO ANYTHING
Zimmer, Hans *C*
Glennie-Smith, Nick *Con*
CD ______ **VSD 5474**
Varese Sarabande / '94 / Pinnacle

I'M GETTING MY ACT TOGETHER AND TAKING IT ON THE ROAD
1981 London Cast
Ford, Nancy *C*
Cryer, Gretchen *L*
Natural high / Smile / In a simple way / Miss Africa / Strong woman number / Dear Tom / Old friend / Put in a package and sold / If only things were different / Feel the love / Lonely lady / Happy birthday
CD ______ **CDTER 1006**
TER / May '89 / Koch

IMMORTAL BELOVED
Beethoven, Ludvig Van *C*
Solti, George *Con*
CD ______ **SK 66301**
Sony Classical / Mar '95 / Sony

IMMORTAL BELOVED - MORE IMMORTAL BELOVED (More Music From The Film & Other Great Beethoven Classics)
Perahia, Murray/Carlo Maria Giulini/Emmanuel Ax/Michael Tilson-Thomas
Beethoven, Ludvig Van *C*
CD ______ **SK 62616**
Sony Classical / Jun '96 / Sony

IN CUSTODY
CD ______ **CDQ 5550972**
EMI / Apr '94 / EMI

IN LOVE AND WAR
Fenton, George
Fenton, George *C*
In love and war / Battle / Private Hemingway reporting for duty / Bullet / You're in love with me / Drive with Domenico / Aggie with the kid / Receiving the medal / Roberto e morto / Lake / Jimmy's death / Jimmy's letter / Field hospital / Brothel / Weekend in Venice / No news from Italy / Domenico's proposal / Hardest letter to write / Most beautiful waltz / Kid grew up / In love and war
CD ______ **09026687252**
RCA Victor / Feb '97 / BMG

IN SEARCH OF ANGELS
In search of angels: *Story, Tim* / Angel of the elegies: *Story, Tim* / Voices in the liquid air: *Story, Tim* / Angelos: *Story, Tim* / Woman at the well: *Story, Tim* / Theme reprise: *Story, Tim* / Calling all angels: *Siberry, Jane & K D Lang* / Requiem in paradisum: *Trinity Boys Choir* / Close cover: *Mertens, Wim* / Assumpta est Maria in coelum: *Schroeder-Sheker, Terese* / Star in the east: *St. Olaf Choir* / Good thing (angels running): *Larkin, Patty* / Love's ash dissolves: *Isham, Mark* / Oh of pleasure: *Sevag, Oystein* / Jesus Christ the apple tree: *American Boys' Choir*
CD ______ **01934111532**
Windham Hill / Nov '94 / BMG

IN STURM UND EIS
Deutsches Symphonie Orchester
Hindemith, Paul *C*
Russell Davies, Dennis *Con*
CD ______ **09026681472**
RCA Victor / Nov '96 / BMG

IN THE ARMY NOW
Sinfonia Of London
Folk, Robert *C*
CD ______ **MAF 7058D**
Intrada / Sep '94 / Koch / Silva Screen

IN THE BLOOD
CD ______ **RCD 20174**
Rykodisc / Aug '91 / ADA / Vital

IN THE CABINET OF DR. CALIGARI
In The Nursery
CD ______ **CORP 015CD**
ITN Corporation / Nov '96 / Plastic Head

IN THE LINE OF DUTY
Snow, Mark *C*
CD ______ **MAF 7034D**
Intrada / Dec '92 / Koch / Silva Screen

IN THE MOUTH OF MADNESS
Carpenter, John & Jim Lang
Carpenter, John & Jim Lang *C*
In the mouth of madness / Robby's office / Axe man / Bookstore creep / Alley nightmare / Trent makes the map / Boy and his bike / Don't look down / Hobb's end / Pickman Hotel / Picture changes / Black church / You're wrong, Trent / Mommy's day / Do you like my ending / I'm losing me / Main street / Hobb's end escape / Portal opens / Old ones return / Book comes back / Madness outside / Just a bedtime story
CD ______ **DRGCD 12611**
DRG / Mar '95 / Discovery / New Note/ Pinnacle

IN THE NAME OF THE FATHER
Jones, Trevor *C*
In the name of the Father: *Bono & Gavin Friday* / Voodoo chile: *Hendrix, Jimi* / Billy Boola: *Bono & Gavin Friday* / Dedicated follower of fashion: *Kinks* / Interrogation: *Jones, Trevor* / Is this love: *Marley, Bob* / Walking the circle: *Jones, Trevor* / Whiskey in the jar: *Thin Lizzy* / Passage of time: *Jones, Trevor* / You made me the thief of your heart: *O'Connor, Sinead*
CD ______ **IMCD 208**
Island / Apr '95 / PolyGram

IN WITH THE OLD
1986 BBC Radio 2 Cast
Prelude / Music goes round and around / I want to be happy / Did you ever see a dream walking / Stompin' at the Savoy / I'm putting all my eggs in one basket / Only a glass of champagne / Ten cents a dance / Goody goody / Zing went the strings of my heart / Lulu's back in town / Pretty baby / Where are the songs we sung / Storm / And her mother came too / With plenty of money and you / Playout
CD ______ **CDTER 1122**
TER / Aug '95 / Koch

INCHON
Goldsmith, Jerry *C*
Goldsmith, Jerry *Con*
CD ______ **FMT 8002D**
Intrada / Feb '90 / Koch / Silva Screen

INCREDIBLY TRUE ADVENTURE OF TWO GIRLS IN LOVE, THE
Dame, Terry
Dame, Terry *C*
CD ______ **74321337432**
Milan / Sep '96 / Conifer/BMG / Silva Screen

INDEPENDENCE DAY
Arnold, David *C*
1969 / We came in peace / SETI / Radio signal / Darkest day / Cancelled leave / Evacuation / Fire storm / Aftermath / Base attack / El toro destroyed / International code / President's speech / Day we fight back / Jolly Roger / End titles
CD ______ **09026685642**
RCA Victor / Aug '96 / BMG

INDIAN IN THE CUPBOARD, THE
Edelman, Randy
Edelman, Randy *C*
Edelman, Randy *Con*
CD ______ **SK 68475**
Sony Classical / Feb '96 / Sony

INDIAN RUNNER, THE
Feelin' alright: *Traffic* / Comin' back to me: *Jefferson Airplane* / Fresh air: *Quicksilver Messenger Service* / Green river: *Creedence Clearwater Revival* / Brothers for good: *Haller, Eric & Bert* / Summertime: *Joplin, Janis & Big Brother & The Holding Company* / I shall be released: *Band* / Cold day in Omaha / Flop house / Goin' to Columbus / Brothers / Bye Mommy / Indian runner / Bad news / Criminal blood / My brother Frank
CD ______ **CDEST 2163**
Capitol / Nov '91 / EMI

INDIANA JONES AND THE LAST CRUSADE
Williams, John *C*
Williams, John *Con*
Indy's very first adventure / X marks the spot / Scherzo for motorcycle and orchestra / Ah rats / Escape from Venice / No ticket / Keeper of the grail / Keeping up with the Joneses / Brother of the cruciform sword / Belly of the steel beast / Canyon of the crescent moon / Penitent man will pass / End credits (raiders march)
CD ______ **K 9258832**
WEA / Jun '89 / Warner Music

INDOCHINA
Doyle, Patrick *C*
CD ______ **VSD 5397**
Varese Sarabande / Jan '93 / Pinnacle

INFERNO
Emerson, Keith
Emerson, Keith *C*
Inferno / Rose's descent into the cellar / Taxi ride / Library / Sarah in the library vaults / Bookbinder's delight / Rose leaves the apartment / Rose gets it / Elisa's story / Cat attic attack / Kazanians tarantella / Mark's discovery / Mater tenebrarum / Inferno (finals) / Cigarettes, ices, etc
CD ______ **CDCIA 5022**
Cinevox / Jan '93 / Koch / Silva Screen

INKWELL, THE
Dancing machine: *Jade* / Let's get it on: *Jade* / On and on: *Knight, Gladys & The Pips* / Lets get it on: *Gaye, Marvin* / Fire: *Ohio Players* / Do you like it: *B.T. Express* / This house is smokin': *B.T. Express* / Do it (till you're satisfied): *B.T. Express* / Everything good to you: *B.T. Express* / Jam: *Graham Central Station* / I don't know what it is but it sure is funky: *Graham Central Station*
CD ______ **74321 21568-2**
Giant / Jul '94 / BMG

INNER CIRCLE, THE
Artemyev, Eduard *C*
CD ______ **262494**
Milan / Jan '95 / Conifer/BMG / Silva Screen

INNOCENT SLEEP, THE
Chamber Orchestra Of London
Ayres, Mark *C*
Raine, Nic *Con*
CD ______ **FILMCD 167**
Silva Screen / Jan '96 / Koch / Silva Screen

INNOCENT, THE
Gouriet, Gerald *C*
CD ______ **164622**
Milan / Jan '95 / Conifer/BMG / Silva Screen

INSIDE OUT
Russ, Adryan *C*
CD ______ **DRGCD 19007**
DRG / Feb '97 / Discovery / New Note/ Pinnacle

INSPECTOR MORSE (The Essential Collection)
Pheloung, Barrington
Pheloung, Barrington *C*
Inspector Morse / Evolving mystery / Andantino / Lewis and Morse / Mi tradi quell alma ingrata / Student's death / Eirl theme / Dark suspicion / Adieu notre petite table / Worrying dilemma / La fille aux cheveux de lin / Sad discovery / Senza mamma / Sad echoes / Terzettino - soave sia il vento / Morse's remorse / String quartet in C minor d703 - Quartettsatz / Inspector Morse theme
CD ______ **VTCD 62**
Virgin / Nov '95 / EMI

INSPECTOR MORSE I
Pheloung, Barrington
Pheloung, Barrington *C*
Main theme / Oxfordshire country home / Overture from Die Zauberflote / K 620 / Student's death / Morse's optimism / O Isis and Osiris / Potential murder / Morse on the case / Macabre pursuit / Sad discovery / Senza mama / Hunt / Oxford college / Lewis / Gothic ritual / Closing credits
CD ______ **VTCDX 2**
Virgin TV / Nov '96 / EMI

INSPECTOR MORSE II
Pheloung, Barrington
Pheloung, Barrington *C*
Main theme / Warmer side of Morse / Che faro senza Eurydice / Gently sinister revelation / Concerto for 2 mandolini in G / Sad echoes / Mitradi quell alma ingrata / Gentle loving / Andante / Lewis and Morse / Chorale 'er kenne mich mein huter' / Morse's sympathetic ear / Adagio quintet in C / Tenderness / Tersettino 'soave sia il vento' / Morse's second chance / Signore Ascolta
CD _______________ **CDVIP 154**
Virgin VIP / Oct '96 / EMI

INSPECTOR MORSE III
Pheloung, Barrington
Pheloung, Barrington *C*
Eirl theme / Oxford / Duet: Bei Mannern - Welche Liebe Fuhlen / Cryptic contemplation / Adante from string sextet No 1 in BB OP 18 / Reflections / Traume from wesendonk-lieder / Generic Morse theme / Dark suspicion / Adagio from piano concert K488 in A / Apprension - confession - resolution / Promised land / Hab'mir's gelbot from der rosenkavalier / Painful admissions / Adieu notre petite from manon / Quiet awakening / Brunnhilde's immolation from gotterdammerung / Main theme
CD _______________ **VTCD 16**
Virgin TV / Nov '92 / EMI
CD _______________ **CDVIP 178**
Virgin / Apr '97 / EMI

INSPECTOR MORSE VOLS I-III
Pheloung, Barrington
Pheloung, Barrington *C*
3CD _______________ **TPAK 27**
Virgin / Jan '95 / EMI

INTERSECTION
Howard, James Newton *C*
Main titles / Home / She needs her father / What's a girl gotta do / Auction / First date / Letter to Olivia / Last ride / Accident / Vincent's message / He's going flat / Personal effects / End titles
CD _______________ **191912**
Milan / May '94 / Conifer/BMG / Silva Screen

INTERVIEW WITH THE VAMPIRE
Goldenthal, Elliot *C*
Sheffer, Jonathan *Con*
Libera me / Born to darkness / Lestat's tarantella / Madeleine's lament / Claudia's allegro agitato / Escape to Paris / Marche funebre / Lestat's recitative / Santiago's waltz / Theatre des vampires / Armand's seduction / Plantation pyre / Forgotten lore / Scent of death / Abduction and absolution / Armand rescues Louis / Louis revenge / Born to darkness part II / Sympathy for the devil: *Guns N' Roses*
CD _______________ **GED 24719**
Geffen / Jan '95 / BMG

INTO THE WOODS
Broadway Cast
Sondheim, Stephen *C*
Prologue - Into the woods / Cinderella at the grave / Hello little girl / I guess this is goodbye / Maybe they're magic / I know things now / Very nice prince / First midnight / Giants in the sky / Agony / It takes two / Stay with me / On the steps of the palace / Ever after / Act 2 Prologue - So happy / Agony / Lament / Any moment / Moments in the woods / Your fault / Last midnight / No more / No one is alone / Finale - Children will listen
CD _______________ **07863567962**
RCA Victor / Jun '94 / BMG

INTO THE WOODS
1990 London Cast
Sondheim, Stephen *C*
Prologue - Once upon a time / Cinderella at the grave / Hello little girl / I guess this is goodbye / Maybe they're magic / Our little world / I know things now / Very nice Prince / First midnight / Giants in the sky / Agony / It takes two / Stay with me / On the steps of the palace / Finale - Ever after / Act 2 Prologue - So happy / Agony / Lament / Any moment / Moments in the woods / Your fault / Last midnight / No more / No one is alone / Finale - Children will listen
CD _______________ **RD 60752**
RCA Victor / Jun '93 / BMG

INTOLERANCE
Davis, Carl *C*
CD _______________ **PCD 105**
Prometheus / Jan '93 / Silva Screen

INVADE MY PRIVACY
1993 London Cast
Landesman, Frans *L*
Brown, D. *Con*
CD _______________ **CDTER 1202**
TER / Sep '93 / Koch

INVENTING THE ABBOTTS
CD _______________ **CST 348062**
Colosseum / May '97 / Pinnacle

INVESTIGATION OF A CITIZEN ABOVE SUSPICION
Morricone, Ennio *C*
CD _______________ **CDCIA 5086**
Cinevox / Jan '93 / Koch / Silva Screen

IOLANTHE
Baker, George & Ian Wallace/Glyndebourne Festival Choir/Pro Arte Orchestra
Sullivan, Sir Arthur *C*
Gilbert, W.S. *L*
Sargent, Sir Malcolm *Con*
2CD _______________ **CMS 7644002**
EMI Classics / Apr '94 / EMI

IOLANTHE
D'Oyly Carte Opera Chorus/New Symphony Orchestra/Grenadier Guards Band
Sullivan, Sir Arthur *C*
Gilbert, W.S. *L*
Godfrey, I. *Con*
2CD _______________ **4141452**
Decca / Jan '90 / PolyGram

IOLANTHE
D'Oyly Carte Opera Chorus/Orchestra
Sullivan, Sir Arthur *C*
Gilbert, W.S. *L*
Pryce Jones, J. *Con*
2CD _______________ **CDTER2 1188**
TER / May '92 / Koch

IPHIGENIA
Theodorakis, Mikis *C*
CD _______________ **SR 50089**
Varese Sarabande / May '94 / Pinnacle

IRENE
Broadway Cast
Tierney, Harry *C*
Lee, Jack *Con*
CD _______________ **SK 32266**
Sony Broadway / Dec '91 / Sony

IRMA LA DOUCE
1960 Broadway Cast
Monnot, Marguerite *C*
Breffort, Alexandre *L*
Lebowsky, Stanley *Con*
CD _______________ **SK 48018**
Sony Broadway / Dec '91 / Sony

IRMA LA DOUCE
Broadway Cast
Monnot, Marguerite *C*
Breffort, Alexandre *L*
CD _______________ **MCAD 6178**
MCA / Jan '89 / BMG

IRON EAGLE III (Aces)
Utah Symphony Orchestra
Manfredini, Harry *C*
CD _______________ **MAF 7022D**
Intrada / Mar '92 / Koch / Silva Screen

IRON WILL
McNeely, Joel *C*
McNeely, Joel *Con*
CD _______________ **VSD 5467**
Varese Sarabande / Aug '94 / Pinnacle

IS PARIS BURNING
Jarre, Maurice *C*
CD _______________ **VSD 5222**
Varese Sarabande / Feb '90 / Pinnacle

IS PARIS BURNING
Jarre, Maurice *C*
CD _______________ **4768422**
Silva Screen / Aug '94 / Koch / Silva Screen

ISLAND OF DR. MOREAU, THE
Chang, Gary *C*
CD _______________ **74321409552**
Milan / Nov '96 / Conifer/BMG / Silva Screen

ISLANDS IN THE STREAM
Hungarian State Symphony Orchestra
Goldsmith, Jerry *C*
Goldsmith, Jerry *Con*
Island / Boys arrive / Pillow fight / Is ten too old / Night attack / Marlin / Boys leave / Letter / How long can you stay / I can't have him / Refugees / Eddie's death / Is it all true
CD _______________ **RVF 6003D**
Intrada / Jan '89 / Koch / Silva Screen

IT HAPPENED AT THE WORLD'S FAIR/ FUN IN ACAPULCO
Presley, Elvis
Beyond the bend / Relax / Take me to the fair / They remind me too much of you / One broken heart for sale (Film version) / I'm falling in love tonight / Cotton candy land / World of our own / How would you like to be / Happy ending / One broken heart for sale / Fun in Acapulco / Vino, dinero y amor / Mexico / El toro / Marguerita / Bullfighter was a lady / No room to rhumba in a sports car / I think I'm gonna like it here / Bossa nova baby / You can't say no in Acapulco / Guadalajara
CD _______________ **74321134312**
RCA / Mar '93 / BMG

IT'S A BIRD, IT'S A PLANE, IT'S SUPERMAN
1966 Broadway Cast
Strouse, Charles *C*
Adams, Lee *L*
Hastings, Harold *Con*
CD _______________ **SK 48207**
Sony Broadway / Nov '92 / Sony

IT'S ALIVE II
Herrmann, Bernard *C*
Johnson, Laurie *Con*
Main title / Birth traumas / Evil evolving / Savage trilogy / Nightmares / Beautiful and bizarre / Revulsion / Basement nursery / Lamentation / Living with fear / Stalking the infants / Climax
CD _______________ **FILMCD 074**
Silva Screen / Jan '91 / Koch / Silva Screen

IT'S MY PARTY
Poledouris, Basil *C*
Poledouris, Basil *Con*
CD _______________ **VSD 5701**
Varese Sarabande / Mar '96 / Pinnacle

IVAN THE TERRIBLE
Frankfurt Radio Symphony Orchestra
Prokofiev, Sergei *C*
Kitaenko, Dmitri *Con*
CD _______________ **09026619542**
RCA Victor / Nov '95 / BMG

IVAN THE TERRIBLE
Philharmonia Orchestra & Chorus
Prokofiev, Sergei *C*
Jarvi, Neeme *Con*
CD _______________ **CHAN 8977**
Chandos / Jan '95 / Chandos

IVANHOE
Sinfonia Of London
Rozsa, Miklos *C*
Broughton, Bruce *Con*
CD _______________ **MAF 7055D**
Intrada / Jan '95 / Koch / Silva Screen

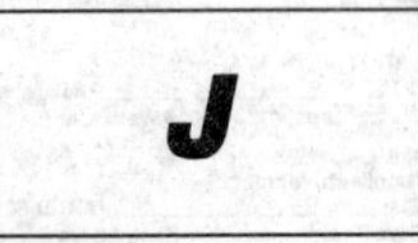

JACOB'S LADDER
Jarre, Maurice *C*
Jacob's ladder / High fever / Descent to inferno / Sarah / Ladder / Sonny boy: *Jolson, Al*
CD _______________ **VSD 5291**
Varese Sarabande / Dec '90 / Pinnacle

JACQUES BREL IS ALIVE AND WELL AND LIVING IN PARIS
Brel, Jacques *C*
Blau, Eric & Mort Shuman *L*
CD _______________ **CGK 40817**
Silva Screen / Jan '89 / Koch / Silva Screen

JACQUES BREL IS ALIVE AND WELL AND LIVING IN PARIS
London Cast
Brel, Jacques *C*
2CD _______________ **CDTER2 1231**
TER / Jan '94 / Koch

JAILHOUSE ROCK
Presley, Elvis
Jailhouse rock / Treat me nice / I want to be free / Don't leave me now / Young and beautiful / (You're so square) baby I don't care / Jailhouse rock / Treat me nice / I want to be free / Young and beautiful / Love me tender / Let me / Poor boy / We're gonna move / Don't leave me now / Treat me nice / Let me / We're gonna move / Poor boy / Love me tender
CD _______________ **07863674532**
RCA / Apr '97 / BMG

JAKE'S PROGRESS
Costello, Elvis & Richard Harvey
Costello, Elvis & Richard Harvey *C*
CD _______________ **DSCD 14**
Demon / Nov '95 / Pinnacle

JAMES AND THE GIANT PEACH
CD _______________ **WD 681202**
Disney Music & Stories / Oct '96 / Technicolor

JAMES BOND THEMES
Studio Cast
James Bond Theme / Licence To Kill (vocal) / Living Daylights (vocal) / Never Say Never Again (vocal) / Man With The Golden Gun / View to a kill (vocal) / All time high (vocal) / Casino royale / For your eyes only / Live and let die / From Russia with love / Diamonds are forever / You only live twice / You're sensational / Thunderball / Moonraker (vocal) / Mr. Kiss Kiss bang bang / Goldfinger / Goldeneye (vocal)
CD _______________ **85142**
CMC / May '97 / BMG

JAMON JAMON
Piovani, Nicola *C*
CD _______________ **873139**
Milan / Jun '93 / Conifer/BMG / Silva Screen

JANE EYRE
Williams, John *C*
Jane Eyre / Overture (main title) / Lowood / To Thornfield / String quartet - Festivity at Thornfield / Grace Poole and Mason's arrival / Trrio - The meeting / Thwarted wedding / Across the Moors / Restoration / Reunion
CD _______________ **FILMCD 031**
Silva Screen / Sep '88 / Koch / Silva Screen

JANE EYRE
Bratislava Symphony Orchestra
Herrmann, Bernard *C*
CD _______________ **8223535**
Marco Polo / Nov '93 / Select

JANE EYRE/LAURA
Herrmann, Bernard/David Raskin *C*
CD _______________ **07822110062**
Fox Film Scores / Jul '92 / BMG

JASON'S LYRIC
U will know: *BMU* / Forget I was a G: *Whitehead Brothers* / Candyman: *LL Cool J* / If trouble was money: *Mint Condition* / Just like my Papa: *Tony Toni Tone* / If you think you're lonely now: *Jodeci* / Rodeo: *Jamecia* / Up & down: *J-Quest* / Walk away: *Five Footer Crew* / Love is the key: *LSD* / No more love: *DRS* / Crazy love: *McKnight, Brian* / That's how it is: *Ahmad* / First round draft pick: *Twinz* / Brothas & Sistas: *Jayo Felony* / This city needs help: *Guy, Buddy* / Nigga sings the blues: *Spice* / Jesse James: *Scarface* / Love is still enough: *Sovory* / Many rivers to cross: *Adams, Oleta*
CD _______________ **5229152**
Mercury / Mar '95 / PolyGram

JAWS
Williams, John *C*
Main title / Chrissie's death / Promenade / Out to sea / Indianapolis story / Sea attack no. 1 / One barrel chase / Preparing the cage / Night search / Underwater siege / Hand to hand combat / End titles
CD _______________ **MCLD 19281**
MCA / Jun '95 / BMG

JAZZ SINGER, THE
Diamond, Neil
Diamond, Neil *C*
America / Adorn o lume / You baby / Love on the rocks / Amazed and confused / Robert E Lee / Summer love / Hello again / Acapulco / Hey Louise / Songs of life / Jerusalem / Kol nidre / My name is Yussel / America (reprise)
CD _______________ **CDEAST 12120**
Capitol / Jul '84 / EMI
CD _______________ **4839272**
Columbia / Mar '96 / Sony

JEAN DE FLORETTE/MANON DE SOURCES
Petit, Jean Claude *C*
CD _______________ **CDCH 378**
Milan / Jan '89 / Conifer/BMG / Silva Screen

JEANNE LA PUCELLE
Hesperon XX
Dufay, Guillaume/Jordi Savall *C*
CD _______________ **K 1006**
Auvidis Travelling / Oct '95 / Harmonia Mundi

JEFFREY
Endelman, Stephen *C*
CD _______________ **VSD 5649**
Varese Sarabande / Mar '96 / Pinnacle

JENATSCH
Donaggio, Pino *C*
CD _______________ **CDCH 036**
Milan / Jan '89 / Conifer/BMG / Silva Screen

JENNIFER 8
Skywalker Symphony Orchestra
Young, Christopher *C*
CD _______________ **661202**
Silva Screen / Jan '93 / Koch / Silva Screen

JERRY MAGUIRE
Shelter from the storm: *Dylan, Bob* / Sandy: *Wilson, Nancy* / Momma Miss America: *McCartney, Paul* / Wise up: *Mann, Aimee* / Singalong junk: *McCartney, Paul* / Secret garden: *Springsteen, Bruce* / Horses: *Jones, Rickie Lee* / We meet again: *Wilson, Nancy* / World on a string: *Young, Neil* / Pocketful of rainbows: *Presley, Elvis* / Magic bus: *Who* / Gettin' in tune: *Who* / Sitting still moving still staring outlooking: *Who*
CD _______________ **4869812**
Epic / Mar '97 / Sony

JERRY'S GIRLS
1984 Broadway Cast
Herman, Jerry *C*
Jerry's girls / Put on your Sunday clothes / It only takes a moment / Wherever he ain't / We need a little Christmas / I won't send roses / Tap your troubles away / Two a day / Bosom buddies / Man in the moon / So long dearie / Take it all off / Shalom / Milk and honey / Showturn / If he walked into my life / Hello Dolly / Nelson / Just go to the movies / Movies were movies / Look what happened to Mabel / Time heals everything / It's today / Mame / Kiss her now / That's how young I feel / Gooch's song / Before the parade passes by / I don't want to know / La cage aux folles / Song on the sand / I am what I am / Best of times / Jerry's turn
2CD _______________ **CDTER2 1093**
TER / Mar '85 / Koch

JESUS CHRIST SUPERSTAR (The 20th Anniversary Recording)
1992 London Cast
Lloyd Webber, Andrew *C*
Rice, Tim *L*
2CD _______________ **09026614342**
RCA Victor / Jan '93 / BMG

JESUS CHRIST SUPERSTAR (Highlights From The 20th Anniversary Recording)
1992 London Cast
Lloyd Webber, Andrew *C*
Rice, Tim *L*
CD _______________ **OCRCD 6031**
First Night / Dec '95 / Pinnacle

JESUS CHRIST SUPERSTAR
Cast Recording
Lloyd Webber, Andrew *C*
Rice, Tim *L*
2CD _______________ **CDTER2 1216**
TER / Aug '95 / Koch

JESUS CHRIST SUPERSTAR
Cast Recording
Lloyd Webber, Andrew *C*
Rice, Tim *L*
Overture / Heaven on their minds / What's the buzz/Strange thing, mystifying / Everything's alright / This Jesus must die / Hosanna / Simon zealots/Poor Jerusalem / Pilate's dream / Temple / Everything's alright / I don't know how to love him / Damned for all time/Blood money / Last supper / Gethsemane (I only want to say) / Arrest / Peter's denial / Pilate and Christ / King Herod's song / Could we start again, please / Judas' death / Trial before Pilate / Superstar / Crucifixion / John 1941
CD _______________ 5337952
2CD _______________ 5337352
Really Useful / Nov '96 / PolyGram

JESUS CHRIST SUPERSTAR
Cast Recording
Lloyd Webber, Andrew *C*
Rice, Tim *L*
Heaven on their minds / Everything's alright / This Jesus must die / Hosanna / Pilate's dream / I don't know how to love him / Gethsemane / King Herod's song / Trial before Pilate / Superstar / John 1941
CD _______________ SHOWCD 026
Showtime / Oct '96 / Disc / THE

JESUS CHRIST SUPERSTAR (Highlights)
Cast Recording
Lloyd Webber, Andrew *C*
Rice, Tim *L*
Overture / Heaven on their minds / What's the buzz/Stange thing, mystifying / Everything's alright / Hosanna / Simon zealotes/ Poor Jerusalem / Pilate's dream / Temple / I don't know how to love him / Last supper / Gethsemane (I only want to say) / King Herod's song / Could we start again, please / Judas's death / Trial by Pilate / Superstar / Crucifixion / John 1941
CD _______________ 5376862
Really Useful / May '97 / PolyGram

JESUS CHRIST SUPERSTAR
Studio Cast
Lloyd Webber, Andrew *C*
Rice, Tim *L*
Overture / Heaven on their mind / What's the buzz / Everything alright / Hosanna / Everything's alright / I don't know how to love him / Damned for all time / Last supper / Argument / King Herod's song / Superstar / John Nineteen : Forty one
CD _______________ 88042
CMC / May '97 / BMG

JEWEL IN THE CROWN, THE
Fenton, George *C*
Jewel in the crown / Lakes / Triangle / Crossing the river / Imprisoned / Death by fire / Chillingborough School song / Butterflies caught in a web / Daphne and Hari / Mirat / Princely state / Kedara and waltz dedara / Barbie leaves Rose Cottage / Champagne Charlie / Guy Perron's march / Pankot - the hills / End titles
CD _______________ PRMCD 33
Premier/EMI / Jul '97 / EMI

JOHN & JEN
CD _______________ VSD 5688
Varese Sarabande / Apr '96 / Pinnacle

JOHNNY AND THE DEAD
Girandet, Stefan *C*
CD _______________ CDWEEK 106
Weekend / Jul '95 / Total/BMG

JOHNNY GUITAR
Young, Victor *C*
Young, Victor *Con*
CD _______________ VSD 5377
Varese Sarabande / May '93 / Pinnacle

JOHNNY HANDSOME
Cooder, Ry
Cooder, Ry *C*
Main theme / I can't walk this time - the prestige / Angola / Clip joint rhumba / Sad story / Fountain walk / Cajun metal / First week at work / Greasy oysters / Smells like money / Sunny's tune / I like your eyes / Adios Donna / Cruising with Rafe / How's my face / End theme
CD _______________ 9259962
WEA / Sep '89 / Warner Music

JOHNNY JOHNSON
1955 Cast
Weill, Kurt *C*
CD _______________ 8313842
Silva Screen / Jan '89 / Koch / Silva Screen

JOHNS
CD _______________ VSD 5778
Varese Sarabande / Feb '97 / Pinnacle

JOLSON
Conley, Brian/London Cast
Jolson, Al *C*
Evans, J. *Con*
CD _______________ CASTCD 56
First Night / May '96 / Pinnacle

JONATHAN LIVINGSTONE SEAGULL
Diamond, Neil
Diamond, Neil *C*
Jonathan Livingstone Seagull (prologue) / Flight of the gull / Dear father / Skybird (part 1) / Lonely looking sky / Odyssey / Anthem / Be (part 1) / Skybird (part 2) / Be (part 3)
CD _______________ 4676072
CBS / Dec '90 / Sony

JOSEPH AND THE AMAZING TECHNICOLOUR DREAMCOAT
1973 London Cast
Lloyd Webber, Andrew *C*
Rice, Tim *L*
Jacob and sons / Joseph's coat / Joseph's dreams / Poor, poor Joseph / One more angel in heaven / Potiphar / Close every door / Go go go Joseph / Pharaoh story / Poor, poor Pharaoh / Song of the king / Pharaoh's dreams explained / Stone the crows / Those Canaan days / Brothers come to Egypt / Grovel, grovel / Who's the thief / Benjamin calypso / Joseph all the time / Jacob in Egypt / Any dream will do
CD _______________ MCLD 19023
MCA / Apr '92 / BMG

JOSEPH AND THE AMAZING TECHNICOLOUR DREAMCOAT
1991 London Cast
Lloyd Webber, Andrew *C*
Rice, Tim *L*
CD _______________ 5111302
Really Useful / Sep '91 / PolyGram

JOSEPH AND THE AMAZING TECHNICOLOUR DREAMCOAT (Featuring Paul Jones, Tim Rice and The Mike Sammes Singers)
Studio Cast
Lloyd Webber, Andrew *C*
Rice, Tim *L*
Love, Geoff *Con*
Jacob and sons/Joseph's coat / Joseph's dreams / Poor, poor Joseph / One more angel in Heaven / Potiphar / Close every door / Go, go, go Joseph / Pharaoh story / Poor, poor Pharaoh/Song of the king / Pharaoh's dreams explained / Stone the crows / Those Canaan days / Brothers come to Egypt/Grovel, grovel / Who's the thief / Benjamin Calypso / Joseph all the time / Jacob in Egypt / Any dream will do
CD _______________ CC 242
Classics For Pleasure / May '89 / EMI

JOSEPH AND THE AMAZING TECHNICOLOUR DREAMCOAT
Studio Cast
Lloyd Webber, Andrew *C*
Rice, Tim *L*
Prologue / Any dream will do / Jacob and Sons/Joseph's coat / Joseph's dreams / Poor, poor Joseph / One more angel in heaven / Potiphar / Close every door / Go go Joseph / Pharaoh story / Poor, poor Pharaoh / Song of the king (Seven fat crows) / Pharaoh's dreams explained / Stone the crows / Those canaan days / The brothers come to Egypt / Who's the thief / Benjamin calypso / Joseph all the time / Jacob in Egypt / Finale: Any dream will do/ Give me my coloured coat / Joseph Megamix
CD _______________ 88052
CMC / May '97 / BMG

JOURNEY THROUGH THE PAST
Young, Neil
Young, Neil *C*
For what it's worth / Mr. Soul / Rock 'n' roll woman / Find the cost of freedom / Ohio / Southern man / Alabama / Are you ready for the country / Words / Soldier
CD _______________ 7599261232
Reprise / Jun '94 / Warner Music

JUBILEE
Deutscher girls: *Adam & The Ants* / Plastic surgery: *Adam & The Ants* / Paranoia blues: *County, Wayne & The Electric Chairs* / Right to work: *Chelsea* / Nine to five: *Maneaters* / Rule Britannia: *Pinns, Suzi* / Jerusalem: *Pinns, Suzi* / Wargasm in pornotopia: *Amilcar* / Slow water: *Eno, Brian* / Dover beach: *Eno, Brian*
CD _______________ EGCD 34
EG / Jul '96 / EMI

JUDE
Johnston, Adrian *C*
CD _______________ 5341162
Philips / Oct '96 / PolyGram

JUDGEMENT NIGHT
I love you Mary Jane: *Cypress Hill & Sonic Youth* / Judgement night: *Onyx & Biohazard* / Just another victim: *House Of Pain & Helmet* / Me, myself and my microphone: *Run DMC & Living Colour* / Disorder: *Ice-T & Slayer* / Missing link: *Del Tha Funky Homosapien & Dinosaur Jr* / Fallin': *De La Soul & Teenage Fanclub* / Freak momma: *Sir Mix-A-Lot & Mudhoney* / Another body murdered: *Boo-Yaa T.R.I.B.E. & Faith No More* / Come and die: *Fatal & Therapy* / Real thing: *Cypress Hill & Pearl Jam*
CD _______________ 4741832
Epic / Oct '93 / Sony

JUICE
CD _______________ MCLD 19308
MCA / Oct '95 / BMG

JULES ET JIM/LA CLOCHE TIBETAINE
Delerue, Georges *C*
CD _______________ PCD 103
Prometheus / Feb '90 / Silva Screen

JULIA AND JULIA
Jarre, Maurice *C*
CD _______________ VCD 47327
Varese Sarabande / Jan '89 / Pinnacle

JUMANJI
Horner, James *C*
Prologue and main title / First move / Monkey mayhem / New world / It's Sarah's move / Hunter / Rampage through town / Alan Parrish / Stampede / Pelican steals the game / Monsoon / Jumanji / End titles
CD _______________ 4815612
Epic / Feb '96 / Sony

JUNGLE BOOK, THE
CD _______________ WD 704002
Disney Music & Stories / Mar '96 / Technicolor

JUNGLE BOOK, THE/THE THIEF OF BAGHDAD
Rozsa, Miklos *C*
CD _______________ CST 348044
Colosseum / Sep '90 / Pinnacle

JURASSIC PARK - THE LOST WORLD
Williams, John *C*
Williams, John *Con*
Lost World / Island prologue / Malcolm's journey / Hunt / Trek / Finding camp Jurassic / Rescuing Sarah / Hammond's plan / Raptors appear / Compys dine / Stegosaurus / Ludlow's demise / Visitor in San Diego / Finale/Jurassic Park theme
CD _______________ MCD 11628
MCA / Jun '97 / BMG

JUST CAUSE
Howard, James Newton *C*
CD _______________ VSD 5596
Varese Sarabande / Feb '95 / Pinnacle

JUST IN TIME
Kuhn, Judy *C*
CD _______________ VSD 5472
Varese Sarabande / Feb '95 / Pinnacle

JUST LIKE A WOMAN
Return to sender: *Presley, Elvis* / Wife's return / (You're the) devil in disguise: *Presley, Elvis* / Transformation / Big girls don't cry: *Pasdar, Adrian* / La senorita: *Latin Touch* / Sisters are doin' it for themselves: *Eurythmics & Aretha Franklin* / Geraldine / Love letters: *Presley, Elvis* / Waltz / End titles / Politics of love: *Blunstone, Colin*
CD _______________ 74321110702
RCA / Sep '92 / BMG

JUSTINE
Goldsmith, Jerry *C*
CD _______________ TSU 0119
Tsunami / May '95 / Silva Screen

JUSTIZ
Loef, Frank *C*
CD _______________ CIN 22102
Silva Screen / Jan '95 / Koch / Silva Screen

JUTE CITY
Stewart, David A.
Stewart, David A. *C*
Jute City / Dead planets / Last love / In Duncan's arms / Black wedding / Jute City revisited / Contaminated / See no evil / Jigula / Lords theme / Hats off to Hector / Deep waters / Dark wells
CD _______________ ZD 75187
RCA / Nov '91 / BMG

K

K2
Zimmer, Hans *C*
CD _______________ VSD 5354
Varese Sarabande / Sep '91 / Pinnacle

KAMA SUTRA
Danna, Mychael *C*
CD _______________ CST 348063
Colosseum / Jul '97 / Pinnacle

KAOS
Piovani, Nicola *C*
CD _______________ FMC 11
Milan / Jan '95 / Conifer/BMG / Silva Screen

KAPO/ROSOLINO PATERNO SOLDATO
Rustichelli, Carlo *C*
CD _______________ CDCIA 5091
Cinevox / Jan '93 / Koch / Silva Screen

KARA BEN NEMSI EFFENDI
Bottcher, Martin *C*
CD _______________ SP 10002
Silva Screen / Jan '93 / Koch / Silva Screen

KARAOKE/COLD LAZARUS
London Symphony Orchestra
Gunning, Christopher *C*
CD _______________ FILMCD 181
Silva Screen / Apr '96 / Koch / Silva Screen

KARATE KID
Moment of truth: *Survivor* / On the beach: *Flirts & Jan & Dean Bop Bop* / No shelter: *Broken Edge* / It takes two to tango: *Davis, Paul* / Tough love: *Shandi* / Rhythm man: *St. Regis* / Feel the night: *Robertson, Baxter* / Desire: *Gang Of Four* / You're the best: *Esposito, Joe*
CD _______________ 5511362
Spectrum / Sep '95 / PolyGram

KAVANAGH QC
Dudley, Anne & John Keene
Main title / Heartland / Private prosecution / Motherlove / Happy trails / Family affair / Unconditional love / Custody / Boat / Nothing but the truth / Sweetest thing / Prepearation for the trial / Scarifice / Aldermartin's romance / Reconciliation / Asphalt jungle / Funeral / Aldermartin's triumph / Sam Wicks goes too far / Selfless courage / Flagship victory / Farewell / Family rejection / Kavanagh
CD _______________ VTDCD 134
Virgin / Apr '97 / EMI

KAZAAM
I am Kazaam: *O'Neal, Shaq* / I'll make your dreams come true: *Subway* / I swear I'm in love: *Usher* / Wishes: *Morris, Nathan* / All out on my own: *Shyheim* / No tighter wish: *Tangi & Lisa 'Left Eye' Lopes* / Lay light (one for the money): *Almighty Arrogant* / Show me your love: *Immature* / We genie: *O'Neal, Shaq & Wade Robson* / Dance wit' me: *Weaver, Jason* / If you believe: *Spinderella* / Key to my heart: *Choice* / I get lifted: *Barrio Boyzz* / Get down: *YBTO* / Boys will be boys: *Backstreet Boys* / Best of me: *Jamecia* / Mr. Material: *O'Neal, Shaq*
CD _______________ 5490272
A&M / Aug '96 / PolyGram

KEEP, THE
Tangerine Dream
Tangerine Dream *C*
CD _______________ TCI 0616
Tsunami / Apr '96 / Silva Screen

KEEPER OF THE CITY
Utah Symphony Orchestra
Rosenman, Leonard *C*
CD _______________ MAF 7024D
Intrada / Apr '92 / Koch / Silva Screen

KENTUCKIAN, THE (& Music By Steiner/Friedhofer/Newman)
Herrmann, Bernard *C*
CD _______________ PRCD 1777
Preamble / Sep '87 / Silva Screen

KERN GOES TO HOLLYWOOD
1985 London Cast
Kern, Jerome *C*
Song is you/I've told every little star / I'll be hard to handle / Smoke gets in your eyes / Yesterdays / I won't dance / I'm old fashioned / Dearly beloved / Pick yourself up / She didn't say yes / Folks who live on the hill / Long ago and far away / Lovely to look at/Just let me look at you / Remind me / Last time I saw Paris / Ol' man river / Why was I born / Can't help lovin' dat man / All the things you are/They didn't believe me
CD _______________ OCRCD 6014
First Night / Mar '96 / Pinnacle

KEY TO REBECCA, THE
Redford, J.A.C. *C*
CD _______________ PCD 123
Prometheus / Mar '93 / Silva Screen

KEYS OF THE KINGDOM, THE
Newman, Alfred *C*
CD _______________ TSU 0134
Tsunami / Oct '96 / Silva Screen

KID GALAHAD/GIRLS GIRLS GIRLS
Presley, Elvis
King of the whole wide world / This is living / Riding the rainbow / Home is where the heart is / I got lucky / Whistling tune / Girls, girls, girls - girls, girls, girls / I don't wanna be tied / Where do you come from / I don't want to / We'll be together / Boy like me, a girl like you / Return to sender / Because of love / Thanks to the rolling sea / Song of the shrimp / Walls have ears / We're coming in loaded / Mama / Plantation rock / Dainty little moonbeams / Girls, girls, girls
CD _______________ 74321 13430-2
RCA / Mar '93 / BMG

KIDS
Casper: *Johnston, Daniel* / Daddy never understood: *Folk Implosion* / Nothing gonna stop: *Folk Implosion* / Jenny's theme: *Folk Implosion* / Simean groove: *Folk Implosion* / Casper the friendly ghost: *Johnston, Daniel* / Natural one: *Folk Implosion* / Spoiled: *Sebadoh* / Crash: *Folk Implosion* / Wet stuff: *Folk Implosion* / Mad fright night: *Folk Implosion* / Raise the bell: *Folk Implosion* / Good morning captain: *Slint*
CD _______________ 4286402
London / Apr '96 / PolyGram

KIDS IN THE HALL: BRAIN CANDY
Some days it's dark: *Death Lurks* / Painted soldiers: *Pavement* / Happiness: *Sweet, Matthew* / Happiness pie: *Death Lurks* / Sex dick pimp: *Phair, Liz* / Spiralling shape: *They Might Be Giants* / Swoon: *Pell Mell* / Birthday cake: *Cibo Matto* / Butts wigglin': *Tragically Hip* / Postal blowfish: *Guided By Voices* / Pablo and Andrea: *Yo La Tengo* / How to play your internal organs overnight: *Stereolab* / Nata di Marzo: *Pizzicato Five* / Eat my brain: *Odds* / Long dark twenties: *Bellini, Paul* / Having an average weekend: *Shadowy Men On A Shadowy Planet*
CD _______________ OLE 1832
Matador / Dec '96 / Vital

KILL THE MOONLIGHT
CD _______________ SFTR 1482CD
Sympathy For The Record Industry / May '97 / Cargo / Greyhound / Plastic Head

KILLER TONGUE, THE
CD _______ **0022692CIN**
Edel / Mar '97 / Pinnacle

KILLING FIELDS, THE
Oldfield, Mike
Oldfield, Mike *C*
Pran's theme / Requiem for a city / Evacuation / Capture / Execution / Bad news / Pran's departure / Work site / Year zero / Blood sucking / Pran's escape / Trek / Boy's burial, The/Pran sees the red cross / Good news / Etude / Pran's theme - 2 / Year zero
CD _______ **CDV 2328**
Virgin / Nov '84 / EMI

KINDERGARTEN COP
Edelman, Randy *C*
Astoria school theme / Children's montage / Love theme (Joyce) / Stalking Crisp / Dominic's theme / Rough day / Line up / Fireside chat / Rain ride / Kindergarten cop / Poor Cindy / Gettysburg address / Dinner invitation / Love theme (reprise) / Magic place / Kimball reveals the truth / Tower
CD _______ **VSD 5305**
Varese Sarabande / Jan '91 / Pinnacle

KING AND I, THE
Film Cast
Rodgers, Richard *C*
Hammerstein II, Oscar *L*
Newman, Alfred *Con*
I whistle a happy tune / My lord and master / Hello, young lovers / March of the Siamese children / Puzzlement / Getting to know you / We kiss in a shadow / I have dreamed / Shall I tell you what I think of you / Something wonderful / Song of the King / Shall we dance
CD _______ **ZDM 7646932**
EMI Classics / Apr '93 / EMI

KING AND I, THE
1977 Broadway Cast
Rodgers, Richard *C*
Hammerstein II, Oscar *L*
Overture / Arrival at Bangkok/I whistle a happy tune / My lord and master / Hello young lovers / March of the Siamese children / Children sing, priests chant / Puzzlement / Royal Bangkok Academy / Getting to know you / So big a world / We kiss in a shadow / Puzzlement (reprise) / Shall I tell you what I think of you / Something wonderful / Finale (Act 1) / Western people funny / Dance of Anna and Sir Edward / I have dreamed / Song of the king / Shall we dance / Finale
CD _______ **RD 82610**
RCA Victor / Aug '90 / BMG

KING AND I, THE
1964 Broadway Cast
Rodgers, Richard *C*
Hammerstein II, Oscar *L*
Engel, Lehman *Con*
CD _______ **SK 53328**
Sony Broadway / Nov '93 / Sony

KING AND I, THE
Cast Recording
Rodgers, Richard *C*
Hammerstein II, Oscar *L*
2CD _______ **CDTER2 1214**
TER / Aug '95 / Koch

KING AND I, THE
New Broadway Cast
Hammerstein II, Oscar *C*
Rodgers, Richard *L*
CD _______ **VSD 5763**
Varese Sarabande / Oct '96 / Pinnacle

KING AND I, THE
Cast Recording
Rodgers, Richard *C*
Hammerstein II, Oscar *L*
Overture / I whistle a happy tune / My lord and my master / Hello young lovers / March of the Siamese children / Puzzlement / Getting to know you / We kiss in a shadow / Something wonderful / I have dreamed / Shall we dance / Finale
CD _______ **SHOWCD 024**
Showtime / Oct '96 / Disc / THE

KING AND I, THE (& The Sound Of Music/South Pacific - Aspects Of Broadway Vol.1)
Orchestra Of The Americas
Rodgers, Richard *C*
Hammerstein II, Oscar *L*
Freeman, Paul *Con*
I whistle a happy tune / Hello young lovers / March of the Siamese children / I have dreamed / Getting to know you / We kiss in a shadow / Shall we dance / Sound of music / How can love survive / Lonely goat herd / My favourite things / Sixteen going on seventeen / So long farewell / Do re mi / Edelweiss / Ordinary couple / No way to stop it / Maria / Climb every mountain / Dites-moi / Cock-eyed optimist / Some enchanted evening / Bloody Mary / There's nothing like a dame / Bali ha'i / I'm gonna wash that man right out of my hair / Wonderful guy / Younger than Springtime / Happy talk / Honeybun / This nearly was mine
CD _______ **SION 18301**
Sion / Jul '97 / Direct

KING AND I, THE/OKLAHOMA
Cast Recording
Rodgers, Richard *C*
Hammerstein II, Oscar *L*
CD _______ **340772**
Koch / Oct '95 / Koch

KING CREOLE
Presley, Elvis
King Creole / As long as I have you / Hard headed woman / Trouble / Dixieland rock / Don't ask me why / Lover doll / Crawfish / Young dreams / Steadfast, loyal and true / New Orleans / King Creole / As long as I have you / Danny / Lover doll / Steadfast, loyal and true / As long as I have you / King Creole
CD _______ **07863674542**
RCA / Apr '97 / BMG

KING KONG
Steiner, Max *C*
CD _______ **LXCD 10**
Label X / Jan '93 / Silva Screen

KING KONG (1976)
Barry, John *C*
CD _______ **MK 702**
Silva Screen / Apr '96 / Koch / Silva Screen

KING KONG (The All African Jazz Opera)
Masakela, Hugh/Miriam Makeba/Original Cast
Matshikizia, Todd *C*
Williams, Pat *L*
CD _______ **668902**
Melodie / Apr '96 / ADA / Discovery / Grapevine/PolyGram / Greensleeves / Jet Star

KING OF KINGS (& Unreleased Material)
Rozsa, Miklos *C*
CD _______ **AK 52424**
Cinevox / Jan '94 / Koch / Silva Screen

KING OF THE WIND
Scott, John *C*
Scott, John *Con*
CD _______ **JSCD 109**
JOS / Jan '95 / JOS / Silva Screen

KING SOLOMON'S MINES
Hungarian State Opera Orchestra
Goldsmith, Jerry *C*
Goldsmith, Jerry *Con*
CD _______ **FMT 8005D**
Intrada / Mar '92 / Koch / Silva Screen

KINGS ROW
National Philharmonic Orchestra
Korngold, Erich *C*
Gerhardt, Charles *Con*
Main title / Children (Parris and Cassie) / Parris and grandmother / Cassie's party / Icehouse / Operation / Cassie's farewell / Parris goes to Dr. Tower / Winter / Grandmother's last will / Seduction / All is quiet / Grandmother dies / Sunset / Parris leaves Kings Row / Flirtation / Vienna and Happy New Year 1900 / Randy and Drake / Financial ruin / Accident and amputation / Drake awakens / Vienna/Cable/Randy and Drake / Letters across the ocean / Parris comes back / Kings Row / Elise / Parris' decision / Finale
CD _______ **VCD 47203**
Varese Sarabande / Jan '89 / Pinnacle

KISMET
Cast Recording
Forrest, George & Robert Wright *C*
Overture/Sands of time / Rhymes have I / Fate / Not since nineveh / Baubles, bangles and beads / Stranger in paradise / Gesticulate / Night of my nights / Was I wazir / Rahadakum / This is my beloved / Olive tree
CD _______ **SHOWCD 014**
Showtime / Feb '95 / Disc / THE

KISMET (Highlights)
1990 Studio Cast/Ambrosian Chorus/ Philharmonia Orchestra
Forrest, George & Robert Wright *C*
Edwards, John Owen *Con*
CD _______ **CDTEO 1002**
TER / Jan '93 / Koch

KISMET
Ambrosian Singers/New York Concert Chorale/London Symphony Orchestra
Forrest, George & Robert Wright *C*
Gemignani, Paul *Con*
CD _______ **SK 46438**
Sony Broadway / Mar '92 / Sony

KISMET
Film Cast
Forrest, George & Robert Wright *C*
Main title / Rhymes have I / Fate / Bazaar of caravans / Not since Ninevah / Dabba / Baubles, bangles and beads / I am a gardener / Stranger in paradise / Gesticulate / Bored / Fate / Night of my nights / Olive tree / Rhadalakum / Marsinah arrives at the castle/I'm in love/Certain young wom / And this is my beloved / Innocent amusement / Diwan dances / Drowning scene/Sentence / Sands of time/End title
CD _______ **CDODEON 23**
Soundtracks / Jan '97 / EMI

KISMET/TIMBUKTU
1990 Studio Cast/Ambrosian Chorus/ Philharmonia Orchestra
Forrest, George & Robert Wright *C*
Edwards, John Owen *Con*
2CD _______ **CDTER2 1170**
TER / Jan '93 / Koch

KISS ME KATE
1987 Royal Shakespeare Cast
Porter, Cole *C*
CD _______ **OCRCD 6020**
First Night / Oct '95 / Pinnacle

KISS ME KATE
Broadway Cast
Porter, Cole *C*
CD _______ **ZDM 7647602**
EMI Classics / Apr '93 / EMI

KISS ME KATE
Barstow, Josephine & Thomas Hampson/Kim Criswell/Ambrosian Chorus/ London Sinfonietta
Porter, Cole *C*
McGlinn, John *Con*
2CD _______ **CDS 7540332**
EMI Classics / Apr '93 / EMI

KISS ME KATE
Cast Recording
Porter, Cole *C*
2CD _______ **CDTER2 1212**
TER / Aug '95 / Koch

KISS ME KATE
Film Cast
Porter, Cole *C*
Overture medley / Main title / So in love / Too darn hot / Why can't you behave / Electric sign / Lili's cork / Wunderbar / So in love / We open in Venice / Tom, Dick or Harry / I've come to wive it wealthily in Padua / I hate men / Were thine that special face / Finale / And so to wed / I've come wive it wealthily in Padua / Where is the life that late I led / Bianca / Why can't you behave / Were thine that special face / Always true to you in my fashion / Brush up your Shakespeare / Bianca's wedding / From this moment on / Down on Kate / Finale
CD _______ **CDODEON 25**
Soundtracks / Jan '97 / EMI

KISS ME KATE
Cast Recording/National Symphony Orchestra
Porter, Cole *C*
Edwards, John Owen *Con*
Overture / Another op'nin' another show / Why can't you behave / Wunderbar / So in love / We open in Venice / I've come to wive it wealthily in Padua / I hate men / Too darn hot / Where is the life that late I led / Brush up your Shakespeare
CD _______ **SHOWCD 032**
Showtime / Oct '96 / Disc / THE

KISS OF DEATH
Back in my life: *Roberts, Joe* / Spaceman: *Rosemarys* / Feeling free: *Liquid City* / Porque no unirnos: *Liquid City* / Kiss of death / Jimmy's dilemma / Illegal convoy / Calvin's revenge / Rosie & Corinna / Junior suspects / Corinna is kidnapped / Junior's arrest / Jimmy's resolve / End credits
CD _______ **280282**
Milan / Jun '95 / Conifer/BMG / Silva Screen

KISS OF THE SPIDER WOMAN
1992 London Cast
Kander, John *C*
Ebb, Fred *L*
CD _______ **OCRCD 6030**
First Night / Oct '95 / Pinnacle

KISSIN' COUSINS/CLAMBAKE/STAY AWAY, JOE
Presley, Elvis
Kissin' cousins / Smoky mountain bay / There's gold in the mountains / One boy two little girls / Catchin' on fast / Tender feeling / Anyone (could fall in love with you) / Barefoot ballad / Once is enough / Kissin' cousins / Clambake / Who needs money / House that has everything / Confidence / Hey hey hey / You don't know me / Girl I never loved / How can you lose what you never had / Clambake (Reprise) / Stay away, Joe / Dominic / All I needed was the rain / Goin' home / Stay away
CD _______ **07863663622**
RCA / Jun '94 / BMG

KNIGHT MOVES
Dudley, Anne *C*
Dudley, Anne *Con*
CD _______ **262753**
Milan / Sep '92 / Conifer/BMG / Silva Screen

KNIGHTS OF THE ROUND TABLE
Rozsa, Miklos *C*
CD _______ **VCD 47269**
Varese Sarabande / Jan '89 / Pinnacle

KOLYA
Prague City Philharmonic Players/The Stern Quartet
Svarovsky, Leos/Olga Ceskova *Con*
CD _______ **4564322**
Philips / May '97 / PolyGram

KRAMER VS KRAMER
Mandolin and harpsichord concerto / Scott Kuney / Frederick Hand / New York / Trumpet sonata / Gordion knot untied
CD _______ **MK 35873**
Silva Screen / Feb '90 / Koch / Silva Screen

KRULL
London Symphony Orchestra
Horner, James *C*
Horner, James *Con*
Riding the fire mares / Slayer's attack / Widow's web / Widow's lullaby / Destruction of the black fortress / Epilogue
CD _______ **SCCD 1004**
Southern Cross / Nov '86 / Silva Screen

KUFFS
Faltermeyer, Harold
Faltermeyer, Harold *C*
Kuffs theme / Stake out / Craze in the district / Night drive / Visitor / George gets Sam / Happy family / Need for speed / At the laundry / Ave Maria / Confrontation / So sad / Kuffs theme (reprise)
CD _______ **101512**
Milan / Jan '94 / Conifer/BMG / Silva Screen

KUNG FU - THE LEGEND CONTINUES
Danna, Jeff
Danna, Jeff *C*
From out of the past / Theme from Kung Fu / Place of light and song / Promise / Longest night / Omeishan / Reunion / Yellow flower in her hair / Tomb/Searching for Tan / Dragon's eye / Posse / Father and son / Emperor
CD _______ **ND 66008**
Narada / May '94 / ADA / New Note/ Pinnacle

KWAMINA
Broadway Cast
CD _______ **ZDM 7648912**
EMI Classics / Aug '93 / EMI

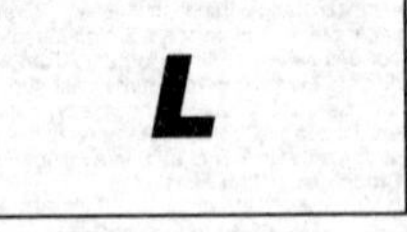

LA BELLE ET LA BETE
Moscow Symphony Orchestra
Auric, Georges *C*
Adriano *Con*
CD _______ **8223765**
Marco Polo / May '96 / Select

LA BELLE HISTOIRE
Lai, Francis *C*
CD _______ **800442**
Melodie / Jan '97 / ADA / Discovery / Grapevine/PolyGram / Greensleeves / Jet Star

LA CALIFFA
Morricone, Ennio *C*
CD _______ **A 8928**
Alhambra / Feb '92 / Silva Screen

LA CLASSE OPERAIA VA IN PARADISO
Morricone, Ennio *C*
CD _______ **OST 122**
Milano Dischi / Jul '92 / Silva Screen

LA DONNA DELLA DOMENICA/LA MOGLIE PIU BELLA
Morricone, Ennio *C*
CD _______ **PCD 119**
Prometheus / Apr '92 / Silva Screen

LA DONNA INVISIBLE
Morricone, Ennio *C*
CD _______ **PRCD 116**
Preamble / Apr '96 / Silva Screen

LA DOUBLE VIE DE VERONIQUE
Preisner, Zbigniew *C*
CD _______ **DPI 01**
DPI / Mar '96 / Discovery

LA HAINE (Score)
CD _______ **319662**
Milan / Nov '95 / Conifer/BMG / Silva Screen

LA HAINE
Intro / Sacrifice de poulets: *Ministere Amer* / Le vent tourne: *Sens Unik* / La 25eme image: *Nuttea, Iam & Daddy* / Dealer pour survivre: *Expression Direkt* / C'est la meme histoire: *Ste Strausz* / Requiem: *La Cliqua* / Comme dance un film: *M.C. Solaar* / La vague a l'arme: *FF* / Sors avec ton gun: *Raggasonic* / Bons baisers du poste: *Les Sages Poetes De La Rue* / L'etat assassine: *Assassin*
CD _______ **CDVIR 45**
Virgin / Nov '95 / EMI

LA MACHINE
Portal, Michel *C*
CD _______ **4447892**
London / Sep '95 / PolyGram

LA PASSION BEATRICE
Boulanger, Lili *C*
Markevitch, Igor *Con*
CD _______ **CD 314**
Milan / Jan '89 / Conifer/BMG / Silva Screen

LA PASSIONE
Rea, Chris/Shirley Bassey
Rea, Chris *C*
CD _______ **0630166952**
East West / May '97 / Warner Music

LA PETITE VOLEUSE (The Little Thief)
Jomy, Alain *C*
CD _______ **CH 399**
Milan / Jan '95 / Conifer/BMG / Silva Screen

LA REINA DE LA NOCHE
Pecanins, Betsy
CD 887960
Milan / Jan '95 / Conifer/BMG / Silva Screen

LA REINE MARGOT
Begovic, Goran *C*
CD 5226552
Silva Screen / Jan '95 / Koch / Silva Screen

LA REVOLUTION FRANCAISE
Schonberg, Claude-Michel *C*
Boublil, Alain *L*
CD OCRCD 6006
First Night / Dec '95 / Pinnacle

LA STRADA/NIGHTS OF CABIRIA
Rota, Nino *C*
CD LEGENDCD 7
Legend / Apr '92 / Koch / Silva Screen

LA TRAVERSE A PARIS
Nyman, Michael *C*
CD 899002
Silva Screen / Jan '93 / Koch / Silva Screen

LA YELLOW 357
CD YP 010ACD
Yellow / Jul '96 / Timewarp

LABYRINTH
Bowie, David
Bowie, David *C*
Underground / Into the labyrinth / Magic dance / Sarah / Chilly down / Hallucination / As the world falls down / Goblin battle / Within you / Thirteen o'clock / Home at last / Underground (reprise)
CD CDFA 3322
Fame / Jul '95 / EMI

LACOMBE LUCIEN (Music & Dialogue From Louis Malle's Lacombe Lucien/Le Souffle Au Coeur/Milou En Mail/Zazie Dans Le Metro)
CD K 1512
Auvidis Travelling / Mar '97 / Harmonia Mundi

LADY BE GOOD
Cast Recording
Gershwin, George *C*
Gershwin, Ira *L*
Stern, Eric *Con*
CD 7559793082
Nonesuch / Jul '93 / Warner Music

LADY IN THE DARK, THE
Abravanel, Kaye
Weill, Kurt *C*
Gershwin, Ira *L*
CD MHK 62869
Masterworks Heritage / Jun '97 / Sony

LADY IN WHITE
Laloggia, Frank *C*
CD VCD 47530
Varese Sarabande / Jan '89 / Pinnacle

LADY OF THE CAMELIAS (LA DAME AUX CAMELIAS)
Morricone, Ennio *C*
CD PCD 116
Prometheus / Mar '92 / Silva Screen

LADY SINGS THE BLUES
Ross, Diana
Lady sings the blues / Baltimore brothel / Billie sneaks into Dean and Dean's / Swinging uptown / T'ain't nobody's business if I do / Big Ben / CC rider / All of me / Man I love / Them there eyes / Gardenias from Louis / Cafe Manhattan / Had you been around / Love theme / Country tune / I cried for you / Billy and Harry / Mean to me / Fine and mellow / What a little moonlight can do / Louis visits Billie on tour / Persuasion / Agent's office / Love is here to stay / Lover man / You've changed / Gimme a pigfoot and a bottle of beer / Good morning heartache / My man (mon homme) / Don't explain / Strange fruit / God bless the child / Closing theme
CD 5301352
Motown / Jan '93 / PolyGram

LADY SINGS THE BLUES
1989 Musical Cast
CD BEARCD 33
Big Bear / Oct '90 / BMG

LADYHAWKE
Philharmonia Orchestra
CD GNPD 8042
GNP Crescendo / May '96 / ZYX

L'AMANT
Yared, Gabriel
Yared, Gabriel *C*
CD CDVMM 9
Virgin / Jan '95 / EMI

LAMERICA
Piersanti, Franco *C*
CD GDM 2006
Silva Screen / Jan '95 / Koch / Silva Screen

LAND BEFORE TIME, THE (Songs From The Film)
CD UMD 80388
Universal / Jul '97

LAND OF THE PHAROAHS
Tiomkin, Dimitri *C*
CD TCI 0608
Tsunami / May '95 / Silva Screen

LANDRAIDERS, THE
Nicolai, Bruno *C*
CD PCD 128
Prometheus / Jul '93 / Silva Screen

L'ANGE NOIR
Musy, Jean *C*
CD 682369
Playtime / Feb '97 / Discovery

L'ANTICHRISTO/SEPOLTA VIVA
Morricone, Ennio *C*
CD SPALAX 14984
Spalax / Oct '96 / ADA / Cargo / Direct / Discovery / Greyhound

LARGER THAN LIFE
Goodman, Miles
Goodman, Miles *C*
Goodman, Miles *Con*
CD 74321442822
Milan / Apr '97 / Conifer/BMG / Silva Screen

LAST DANCE
Isham, Mark *C*
CD HW 620552
Silva Screen / Apr '96 / Koch / Silva Screen

LAST DAYS OF CHEZ NOUS, THE
Grabowsky, Paul
Grabowsky, Paul *C*
Last days of chez nous / Last days / Inversions / Warm hands / Conversations / New life / New lives / Big car people / Small car people / Two hands / Lover man / Donna Lee / Day's end
CD DRGCD 12607
DRG / Jun '93 / Discovery / New Note/ Pinnacle

LAST EMPEROR, THE
Sakamoto, Ryuichi & David Byrne *C*
First coronation / Open the door / Where is Armo / Picking up brides / Last Emperor, The (theme) (variation 1) / Picking a bride / Bed / Wind, rain and water / Paper emperor / Rain (I want a divorce) / Baby was born dead / Last Emperor, The (theme) (variation 2) / Last Emperor, The (theme) / Main title / Lunch / Red guard / Emperor's waltz / Red guard dance
CD CDV 2485
Virgin / Nov '87 / EMI

LAST EXIT TO BROOKLYN
Knopfler, Mark
Knopfler, Mark *C*
Last exit to Brooklyn / Victims / Think fast / Love idea / Tralala / Riot / Reckoning / As low as it gets / Finale
CD 8387252
Vertigo / Mar '97 / PolyGram

LAST KLEZMER, THE
Kozlowski, Leopold
CD GVCD 168
Global Village / Nov '94 / ADA / Direct

LAST MAN STANDING (Score)
Bernstein, Elmer *C*
CD VSD 5755
Varese Sarabande / Nov '96 / Pinnacle

LAST MAN STANDING
Cooder, Ry
Cooder, Ry *C*
CD 5334152
Verve / Oct '96 / PolyGram

LAST METRO, THE (LE DERNIER METRO)/LA FEMME D'A COTE
Delerue, Georges *C*
CD PCD 113
Prometheus / Apr '92 / Silva Screen

LAST OF ENGLAND
Fisher-Turner, Simon *C*
CD CDIONIC 1
Mute / Oct '87 / RTM/Disc

LAST OF THE HIGH KINGS, THE
Last of the high kings: *Convertino, Michael* / Boys are back in town: *Thin Lizzy* / Ever fallen in love: *Buzzcocks* / Watching the detectives: *Costello, Elvis* / Milk and alcohol: *Dr. Feelgood* / 2-4-6-8 motorway: *Robinson, Tom Band* / All the young dudes: *Mott The Hoople* / Thunder: *Convertino, Michael* / Oh yeah: *Ash* / Spanish stroll: *Mink Deville* / Heart on my sleeve: *Gallagher & Lyle* / Can't take my eyes off this place for one minute: *Convertino, Michael* / Dancing in the moonlight: *Thin Lizzy* / How long: *Ace*
CD PRMDCD 26
Premier/EMI / Dec '96 / EMI

LAST OF THE MOHICANS, THE
Edelman, Randy *C*
CD 5174922
Polydor / Dec '92 / PolyGram

LAST OF THE SUMMER WINE
Hazelhurst, Ronnie Orchestra
Hazelhurst, Ronnie *C*
CD RH 1CD
Ronnie Hazelhurst / Mar '97 / Pinnacle

LAST STARFIGHTER, THE
Safan, Craig *C*
Safan, Craig *Con*
Outer space chase / Into the starscape / Planet of Rylos / Death blossom / Incommunicado / Never crossed my mind / Return to Earth / Hero's march / Centauri dies
CD LXE 705
Label X / Jan '93 / Silva Screen
CD MAF 7066
Intrada / Feb '96 / Koch / Silva Screen

LAST TEMPTATION OF CHRIST, THE (Passion)
Gabriel, Peter
Gabriel, Peter *C*
Feeling begins / Gethsemane / Of these, hope / Lazarus raised / Of these hope (reprise) / In doubt / Different drum / Zaar / Troubled / Open / Before night falls / With this love / Sandstorm / Stigmata / Passion / Disturbed / It is accomplished / Wall of breath / Promise of shadows / Bread and wine
CD RWCD 1
Realworld / Jun '89 / EMI

LAST WALTZ, THE
Band
Last waltz / Up on Cripple Creek / Who do you love / Helpless / Stage fright / Coyote / Dry your eyes / It makes no difference / Such a night / Night they drove old Dixie down / Mystery train / Mannish boy / Further on up the road / Shape I'm in / Down South in New Orleans / Ophelia / Tura lura larai (That's an Irish lullaby) / Caravan / Life is a carnival / Baby let me follow you down / I don't believe you (she acts like we never have met) / Forever young / I shall be released / Last waltz suite / Well / Evangeline / Out of the blue / Weight
CD K 266076
WEA / Mar '88 / Warner Music

LAURA/JANE EYRE
Herrmann, Bernard *C*
CD 07822110062
RCA / Apr '94 / BMG

L'AVVENTURIERO/OCEANO
Morricone, Ennio *C*
CD OST 120
Milano Dischi / Jan '93 / Silva Screen

LAWNMOWER MAN II (Beyond Cyberspace)
Sinfonia Of London
Folk, Robert *C*
Folk, Robert *Con*
CD VSD 5698
Varese Sarabande / Mar '96 / Pinnacle

LAWRENCE OF ARABIA
London Philharmonic Orchestra
Jarre, Maurice *C*
Overture / Main title / Miracle / Nefud mirage / Rescue of Gasim / Bringing Gasim into camp / Arrival at Auda's camp / Voice of the guns / Continuation of the miracle / Sun's anvil / Lawrence and his bodyguard / That is the desert / End titles
CD VSD 5263
Varese Sarabande / Apr '91 / Pinnacle
CD CLACD 271
Castle / '92 / BMG

LAWRENCE OF ARABIA
Philharmonia Orchestra
Jarre, Maurice *C*
Bremner, Tony *Con*
Overture/Main titles / First entrance to the desert - night and stars / Lawrence and Tafas / Miracle / That is the desert / Nefud mirage/Sun's anvil / Rescue of Gasim/ Bringing Gasim into camp / Arrival at Auda's camp / On to Akaba/The beach at night / Sinai desert / Voice at the guns / Horse stampede - Ali rescues Lawrence / Lawrence and his bodyguard / End/Playoff music
CD FILMCD 036
Silva Screen / Jan '89 / Koch / Silva Screen

LE BON ET LES MECHANTS
Lai, Francis *C*
CD MANTRA 054
Silva Screen / Jan '93 / Koch / Silva Screen

LE CRIME DE MONSIEUR LANGE (& La Grande Illusion/La Bete Humaine/Une Partie De Campagne - The Film Music Of Jean Renoir)
CD K 1510
Travelling / Dec '96 / Harmonia Mundi

LE DECALOGUE
Preisner, Zbigniew *C*
CD AMP 709
Amplitude / Mar '96 / Discovery

LE FOTO PROIBITE DI UNA SIGNORA PERBENE/IL SEGRETO
Morricone, Ennio *C*
CD PRCD 117
Preamble / Apr '96 / Silva Screen

LE HUITIEME JOUR
CD 5327132
Mercury / Nov '96 / PolyGram

LE HUSSARD SUR LE TOIT
Orchestre National De France
Petit, Jean Claude *C*
Petit, Jean Claude *Con*
CD K 10106
Auvidis Travelling / Dec '95 / Harmonia Mundi

LE NOUVELLE VAGUE
CD 887825
Milan / Jun '95 / Conifer/BMG / Silva Screen

LEAVE IT TO JANE/OH KAY
Broadway Cast
Kern, Jerome/George Gershwin *C*
Wodehouse, P.G./Ira Gershwin *L*
Just you watch my step / Leave it to Jane / Siren's song / Cleopatterer / Crickets are calling / Sun shines brighter / Sir Galahad / Wait 'til tomorrow / I'm going to find a girl / Godd old atwater / There it is again / Poor prune / Finale / Overture / Woman's touch / Twenties are here to stay / Home / Stiff upper lip / Maybe / Pophams / Do do do / Clap yo' hands
CD DRGCD 15017
DRG / Apr '91 / Discovery / New Note/ Pinnacle

LEAVING LAS VEGAS
Figgis, Mike *C*
Intro / Angel eyes: *Sting* / Are you desirable / Ben and Bill / Leaving Las Vegas / Sera's dark side / Mara / Burlesque / On the street / Bossa Vega / Ben pawns his Rolex/Sera talks to her schrink / My one and only love: *Sting* / Sera invites Ben to stay / Come rain or shine: *Henley, Don* / Ben and Sera theme / Ridiculous: *Cage, Nicolas* / Biker bar / Ben's hell / It's a lonesome old town: *Sting* / Blues for Ben / Get out / Reunited / Sera talks to the cab driver / She really loved him / I won't be going south for a while: *Palladinos*
CD 5404762
A&M / Mar '96 / PolyGram

LEGEND (American Score)
Tangerine Dream
Tangerine Dream *C*
CD VSD 5645
Varese Sarabande / Sep '95 / Pinnacle

LEGEND
National Philharmonic Orchestra
Goldsmith, Jerry *C*
Goldsmith, Jerry *Con*
Main title/Goblins / My true love's eyes/Cottage / Unicorns / Living river/Bumps and hollows/Freeze / Faeries/Riddle / Sing the wee / Forgive me / Faerie dance / Armour / Oona/Jewels / Dress waltz / Darkness fails / Ring / Re-united
CD FILMCD 045
Silva Screen / Jan '90 / Koch / Silva Screen

LEGENDS OF THE FALL
Horner, James *C*
Legends of the fall / Ludlows / Off to war / To the boys / Samuel's death / Alfred moves to Helena / Farewell/Descent into madness / Changing seasons / Wild horses / Tristan's return / Wedding / Isabel's murder / Recollections of Samuel / Revenge / Goodbyes / Alfred / Tristan / Colonel / Legend
CD 4785112
Epic / May '95 / Sony

LEGS DIAMOND
Broadway Cast
Allen, Peter *C*
CD 79832
Silva Screen / Feb '90 / Koch / Silva Screen

LENIN: THE TRAIN
Piovani, Nicola
CD CDCH 381
Milan / Feb '90 / Conifer/BMG / Silva Screen

LEON
Serra, Eric
Serra, Eric *C*
Noon / Cute name / Ballad for Mathilde / What's happening out there / Bird in New York / She is dead / Fatman / Leon the cleaner / Can I have a word with you / Game is over / Feel the breath / Room 4602 / Very special delivery / When Leon does his beast / Back on the crime scene / Bird of storm / Thony the IBM / How do you know this it's love / Fight / Two ways / Out, hey little angel
CD 4783232
Columbia / Feb '95 / Sony

LEON THE PIG FARMER
Murphy, John & David Hughes *C*
I fell in love with the moon / Feels so right / Mon dieu / Jump out of your skin (Instrumental) / Siman Tov / Asher Bara / Feelings / Gallery / Every valley shall be exalted / Nothing ever goes to plan / Yorkshire theme / Jewish transformation / Leon's theme (Instrumental) / Jump out of your skin / Leon chase / Hava nagila / If I'd never known you / Mess around
CD CDSTY 1
Soundtrack Music / May '94 / EMI

LEPRECHAUN
Kiner, Kevin *C*
CD MAF 7050D
Intrada / Mar '93 / Koch / Silva Screen

LES CLES DU PARADIS
Lai, Francis *C*
CD MANTRA 066
Silva Screen / Jul '92 / Koch / Silva Screen

LES LIAISONS DANGEREUSES
Blakey, Art & The Jazz Messengers/Barney Wilen
No problem / No hay problema / Prelude in blue / Valmontana / Miguel's party / Weehawken mad pad
CD 8120172
Fontana / Mar '94 / PolyGram

LES MISERABLES
Broadway Cast
Schonberg, Claude-Michel *C*
Kretzmer, Herbert *L*
2CD 9241512
Silva Screen / Jan '89 / Koch / Silva Screen

LES MISERABLES (Highlights)
International Cast
Schonberg, Claude-Michel *C*
Kretzmer, Herbert *L*
CD _______ **CASTCD 20**
First Night / Oct '91 / Pinnacle

LES MISERABLES
1985 London Cast
Schonberg, Claude-Michel *C*
Kretzmer, Herbert *L*
Koch, Martin *Con*
At the end of the day / I dreamed a dream / Lovely ladies / Who am I / Come to me / Confrontation / Castle on a cloud / Master of the house / Stars / Look down / Little people / Red and black / Do you hear the people sing / I saw him once / In my life / Heart full of love / One day more / On my own / Attack / Little fall of rain / Drink with me to days gone by / Bring him home / Dog eats dog / Soliloquy / Empty chairs at empty tables / Wedding chorale / Beggars at the feast / Finale
2CD _______ **ENCORECD 1**
First Night / Dec '85 / Pinnacle

LES MISERABLES
Cast Recording
Schonberg, Claude-Michel *C*
Kretzmer, Herbert *L*
CD _______ **WMCD 5672**
Woodford Music / Feb '93 / THE

LES MISERABLES
Cast Recording
Schonberg, Claude-Michel *C*
Kretzmer, Herbert *L*
CD _______ **GRF 197**
Tring / Jan '93 / Tring

LES MISERABLES (Highlights - The Shows Collection)
1993 Studio Cast
Schonberg, Claude-Michel *C*
Kretzmer, Herbert *L*
At the end of the day / I dreamed a dream / Master of the house / Stars / Do you hear the people sing / In my life / Heart full of love / On my own / Little fall of rain / Drink with me / Bring him home / Empty chairs at empty tables
CD _______ **PWKS 4175**
Carlton / Oct '93 / Carlton

LES MISERABLES (Complete Symphonic Score)
International Cast
Schonberg, Claude-Michel *C*
Kretzmer, Herbert *L*
2CD _______ **MIZCD 1**
First Night / Dec '88 / Pinnacle

LES MISERABLES (Five Outstanding Performances From The Symphonic Score)
International Cast
Schonberg, Claude-Michel *C*
Kretzmer, Herbert *L*
Empty chairs at empty tables / Stars / One day more / I dreamed a dream / On my own
CD _______ **SCORECD 17**
First Night / Apr '89 / Pinnacle

LES MISERABLES (The Original French Concept Album)
Cast Recording
Schonberg, Claude-Michel *C*
CD _______ **DOCRCD 1**
First Night / '94 / Pinnacle

LES MISERABLES
Wilkinson, Colm & P. Quast/R. Henshall/ 10th Anniversary Cast/Royal Philharmonic Orchestra
Schonberg, Claude-Michel *C*
Kretzmer, Herbert *L*
Abell, D.C. *Con*
2CD _______ **ENCORECD 8**
First Night / Mar '96 / Pinnacle

LES MISERABLES (Complete Score)
Czech-Slovak Radio Symphony Orchestra
Honegger, Arthur *C*
Adriano *Con*
CD _______ **8223181**
Marco Polo / Jan '95 / Select

LES MISERABLES/LA ROUE/MERMOZ/ MAPOLEON
Czech-Slovak Radio Symphony Orchestra
Honegger, Arthur *C*
Adriano *Con*
CD _______ **8223134**
Marco Polo / Jan '95 / Select

LES PALMES DE M. SCHUTZ
Cosma, Vladimir *C*
CD _______ **952122**
Pomme / Jul '97 / Discovery

LES PASSIONS AMOREUSES
CD _______ **887974**
Milan / Jun '95 / Conifer/BMG / Silva Screen

LES SILENCES DU PALAIS
Amal hayeti / Lecon de oud / Lessa faker / Bachraf mazmoum / Elegie (chant patriotique version radio) / Danse 1 / Fogue achajera / Notes / Taalila / Vocalises, cris de douleurs / Danse II / Ghanili cheoui cheoui / Bachraf / Elegie (chant patriotique) / Theme alia
CD _______ **CDVIR 35**
Virgin / Apr '95 / EMI

LES UNS ET LES AUTRES
Legrand, Michel/Francis Lai *C*
CD _______ **800432**
Silva Screen / Jan '93 / Koch / Silva Screen

LET IT BE
Beatles
Beatles *C*
Two of us / Dig a pony / Across the universe / I me mine / Dig it / Let it be / Maggie Mae / I've got a feeling / One after 909 / Long and winding road / Get back
CD _______ **CDPCS 7096**
Parlophone / Oct '87 / EMI

LETHAL WEAPON III
Kamen, Michael
Kamen, Michael *C*
It's probably me: *Sting* / Runaway train: *John, Elton & Eric Clapton* / Grab the cat / Leo Getz goes to the hockey game / Darryl dies / Riggs and Roger / Roger's boat / Armour piercing bullets / God judges us by our scars / Lorna - a quiet evening by the fire
CD _______ **7599269892**
WEA / Jun '92 / Warner Music

LET'S DO IT (A Celebration Of Noel Coward & Cole Porter)
1994 Chichester Festival Cast
Coward, Sir Noel/Cole Porter *C*
My heart belongs to Daddy / Blow Gabriel blow / Mrs. Worthington / It's de-lovely / London pride / Throwing a ball tonight / You're the top / I wonder what happened to him / Mad dogs and Englishmen
CD _______ **SONGCD 910**
Silva Classics / Aug '94 / Koch / Silva Screen

LET'S MAKE LOVE
Cahn, Sammy *C*
CD _______ **8369842**
Silva Screen / Feb '90 / Koch / Silva Screen

LEVIATHAN
Goldsmith, Jerry *C*
CD _______ **VSD 5226**
Varese Sarabande / Feb '90 / Pinnacle

LEXX: THE DARK ZONE
CD _______ **CST 8064**
Colosseum / Jul '97 / Pinnacle

LIAR LIAR
Debney, John *C*
Debney, John *Con*
My Dad's a liar / To court / Pen is blue / I'm a bad Father / Pulled over / Unwish / Bathroom folly / I love my Son / Airport chase / It's Fletcher / Together / Claw returns / End credits / Out-take montage
CD _______ **MCD 11618**
MCA / Jun '97 / BMG

LIE OF THE MIND, A
Red Clay Ramblers
CD _______ **SHCD 8501**
Sugar Hill / Jan '97 / ADA / CM / Direct / Koch / Roots

LIFE AND ADVENTURES OF NICHOLAS NICKLEBY, THE
1982 London Cast
Oliver, Stephen *C*
London / Home in Devonshire / Dotheboys' Hall / Journey to Portsmouth / Farewell waltz / Mantalini chase / Wedding anthem / Patriotic song / Milliners' sewing room / Sir Mulberry Hawk / Mrs. Grudden's goodbye / Wititterly gavotte / At the opera / Cheerybyle brothers / Christmas carol
CD _______ **CDTER 1029**
TER / Aug '95 / Koch

LIFE IS FOR LIVING/A MAN AND A WOMAN
Lelouch, Claude & Francis Lai *C*
CD _______ **101292**
Musidisc / Aug '90 / Discovery

LIFEFORCE
London Symphony Orchestra
Mancini, Henry *C*
Lifeforce / Spacewalk / Into the alien craft / Exploration / Sleeping vampires / Evil visitations / Carson's story / Girl in the raincoat / Web of destiny (parts 1-3)
CD _______ **CDFM 256**
Milan / Feb '90 / Conifer/BMG / Silva Screen

LIFETIMES (To Live)
Jiping, Zhao *C*
Lifetimes / Fugui performs puppetry / Jiazhen leaves Fugui / Fugui leaves his old home / Wounded soldiers / Fugui performs for the army / Jiazhen returns / Fengxia dies / Fugui takes his son to school / Fugui returns from the war / Erxi fixes the house / Fugui performs at the steelworks / 1950's / Fengxia leaves her parents / Closing credits / Puppet performance
CD _______ **210532**
Milan / Oct '94 / Conifer/BMG / Silva Screen

LIGHT AT THE EDGE OF THE WORLD, THE
CD _______ **A 8934**
Alhambra / May '92 / Silva Screen

LIGHTHORSEMAN, THE
Millo, Mario *C*
CD _______ **IMICD 1009**
Silva Screen / Jan '93 / Koch / Silva Screen

L'ILE (THE ISLAND)
Petit, Jean Claude *C*
CD _______ **CD 340**
Milan / Jan '89 / Conifer/BMG / Silva Screen

LILI MARLENE/LOLA
Schygulla, H.
Raben, Peer *C*
CD _______ **CH 123**
Milan / Jan '95 / Conifer/BMG / Silva Screen

LILLIES OF THE FIELD
Goldsmith, Jerry *C*
CD _______ **TSU 0101**
Tsunami / Sep '93 / Silva Screen

LINCOLN (inc. Traditional Civil War Music/Lincoln's Speeches)
Menken, Alan *C*
CD _______ **547522**
Silva Screen / Jan '93 / Koch / Silva Screen

LINGUINI INCIDENT, THE
Newman, Thomas *C*
CD _______ **VSD 5372**
Varese Sarabande / Jun '93 / Pinnacle

LINK
Goldsmith, Jerry *C*
CD _______ **VCD 47276**
Varese Sarabande / Jan '89 / Pinnacle

L'INTEGRALE COMPLETE
CD _______ **887988**
Milan / Jun '95 / Conifer/BMG / Silva Screen

LION IN WINTER, THE
Barry, John *C*
CD _______ **VSD 5217**
Varese Sarabande / Feb '90 / Pinnacle

LION KING, THE
John, Elton
John, Elton *C*
Rice, Tim *L*
Circle of life: *Twillie, Carmen* / I just can't wait to be King: *Weaver, Jason* / Be prepared: *Irons, Jeremy* / Hakuna matata: *Lane, Nathan & Ernie Sabella* / Can you feel the love tonight: *Williams, Joseph & Sally Dworsky* / This land: *Zimmer, Hans* / To die for / Under the stars / King of Pride Rock / Circle of life / I just can't wait to be King / Can you feel the love tonight
CD _______ **5226902**
Rocket / Jun '94 / PolyGram

LION KING, THE
Overtures
John, Elton *C*
Rice, Tim *L*
Circle of life / I just can't wait to be king / Be prepared / Hakuna Matata / Can you feel the love tonight / This land / To die for / Under the stars / King of Pride Rock / I just can't wait to be king / Can you feel the love tonight / Lion king of the jungle
CD _______ **MSCD 13**
Music De-Luxe / Dec '94 / TKO Magnum

LION KING, THE (Rumble In The Jungle - A Tribute To The Music Of The Lion King)
Circle of life / I just can't wait to be king / Be prepared / Hakuna matata / Can you feel the love tonight / This land / To die for / Under the stars / King of the pride rock / Circle of life / I just can't wait to be king / Can you feel the love tonight / Lion king of the jungle
CD _______ **CDMFP 6225**
Music For Pleasure / May '96 / EMI

LION KING, THE (Singalong)
CD _______ **WD 706824**
Disney Music & Stories / Nov '96 / Technicolor

LIONHEART (AWOL)
Scott, John *C*
Scott, John *Con*
CD _______ **MAF 7011D**
Intrada / Jan '93 / Koch / Silva Screen

LIONHEART VOL.1
Goldsmith, Jerry *C*
Ceremony / Failed knight / Robert & Blanche / Children in bondage / Banner / Lake / Mathilda / Wrong flag / King Richard
CD _______ **VSD 5484**
Varese Sarabande / Apr '94 / Pinnacle

LIONHEART VOL.2
Goldsmith, Jerry *C*
Castle / Circus / Gates of Paris / Plague / Final fight / Road from Paris / Dress / Forest hunt / Paris underground / Bring him back / Future
CD _______ **VCD 47288**
Varese Sarabande / Jan '89 / Pinnacle

LIPSTICK
Polnareff, Michel *C*
CD _______ **4669942**
Silva Screen / Jan '93 / Koch / Silva Screen

LIPSTICK ON YOUR COLLAR
Lipstick on your collar: *Francis, Connie* / Don't be cruel: *Presley, Elvis* / Great pretender: *Platters* / Earth angel: *Crew Cuts* / Little bitty pretty one: *Harris, Thurston* / Green door: *Vaughan, Frankie* / Only you: *Platters* / Story of my life: *Holliday, Michael* / Blueberry Hill: *Domino, Fats* / It's almost tomorrow: *Dream Weavers* / Your cheatin' heart: *Williams, Hank* / Garden of Eden: *Vaughan, Frankie* / My prayer: *Platters* / Blue suede shoes: *Perkins, Carl* / Raining in my heart: *Holly, Buddy & The Crickets* / Unchained melody: *Baxter, Les* / I see the moon: *Stargazers* / Be bop a lula: *Vincent, Gene* / I'm in love again: *Domino, Fats* / Young love: *James, Sonny* / Fool: *Clark, Sanford* / It'll be me: *Lewis, Jerry Lee* / Love is strange: *Mickey & Sylvia* / Sh-boom: *Crew Cuts* / Lotta lovin': *Vincent, Gene* / Lay down your arms: *Shelton, Anne* / Making love: *Robinson, Floyd* / Man with the golden arm: *May, Billy & His Orchestra*
CD _______ **5160862**
PolyGram TV / Mar '93 / PolyGram

LIQUID SKY
CD _______ **VCD 47181**
Varese Sarabande / Jan '89 / Pinnacle

LISA
Mertens, Wim *C*
CD _______ **TW 11032**
Crepuscule / Feb '97 / Discovery

LITTLE BUDDHA (The Secret Score)
Sakamoto, Ryuichi *C*
Chenresie, flame of peace and compassion / Heart sutra / Ragam & tanam / Chant / Raga naiki kanhra / Dialogue / Pupils chanting / Composition / Tal / No old age / Raga chandranandan
CD _______ **227452**
Milan / Jun '95 / Conifer/BMG / Silva Screen

LITTLE BUDDHA/RAISE THE RED LANTERN/CYCLO (Music From The Orient)
Sakamoto, Ryuichi & Zhao Jipzing/Ton-That Tiet *C*
3CD _______ **74321320312**
Milan / May '96 / Conifer/BMG / Silva Screen

LITTLE MARY SUNSHINE
1962 London Cast
Besoyan, Rick *C*
Overture / Forest rangers / Little Mary Sunshine / Look for a sky of blue / You're the fairest flower / Swingin' - how do you do / Colorado love call / What has happened / Tell a handsome stranger / Once in a blue moon / Every little nothing / Such a merry party / Say Uncle / Heap big Injun / Mata Hari / Do you ever dream of Vienna / Coo coo / Finale
CD _______ **CDSBL 13108**
DRG / Nov '92 / Discovery / New Note/ Pinnacle

LITTLE MARY SUNSHINE
Broadway Cast
Besoyan, Rick *C*
CD _______ **ZDM 7647742**
EMI Classics / Apr '93 / EMI

LITTLE ME
London Cast
Coleman, Cy *C*
Leigh, Carolyn *L*
Overture / Truth / On the other side of the tracks / Rich kids rag / I love you / Deep down inside / To be a performer / Le grand boom-boom / I've got your number / Real live girl / Poor little Hollywood star / Little me / Goodbye / Here's to us
CD _______ **CDSBL 13111**
DRG / Aug '93 / Discovery / New Note/ Pinnacle

LITTLE ME
1962 Broadway Cast
Coleman, Cy *C*
Leigh, Carolyn *L*
CD _______ **09026614822**
RCA Victor / Jul '93 / BMG

LITTLE NIGHT MUSIC, A
1975 London Cast
Sondheim, Stephen *C*
Wheller, H. *L*
Overture and night waltz / Now, later, soon / Glamorous life / Remember / You must meet my wife / Liaisons / In praise of women / Every day a little death / Weekend in the country / Sun won't set / It would have been wonderful / Perpetual anticipation / Send in the clowns / Miller's son / Finale
CD _______ **GD 85090**
RCA Victor / Apr '90 / BMG

LITTLE NIGHT MUSIC, A
Cast Recording
Sondheim, Stephen *C*
Wheller, H. *L*
Edwards, John Owen *Con*
CD _______ **CDTER 1179**
TER / Jan '93 / Koch

LITTLE NIGHT MUSIC, A
Sondheim, Stephen *C*
Wheller, H. *L*
Overture / Now / Later / Soon / Glamorous life / You must meet my wife / Liaisons / Weekend in the country / It would have been wonderful / Send in the clowns / Miller's son / Last waltz
CD _______ **SHOWCD 042**
Showtime / Jan '97 / Disc / THE

LITTLE PRINCESS
Doyle, Patrick *C*
CD _______ **VSD 5628**
Varese Sarabande / Feb '96 / Pinnacle

LITTLE RED RIDING HOOD
London Philharmonic Orchestra
Patterson, Paul *C*

Dahl, Roald *L*
Weiser-Most, Franz *Con*
CD **CDC 5555532**
EMI Classics / Nov '95 / EMI

LITTLE ROMANCE, A
Delerue, Georges *C*
Delerue, Georges *Con*
CD **VSD 5367**
Varese Sarabande / Nov '92 / Pinnacle

LITTLE SHOP OF HORRORS
1987 Film Cast
Menken, Alan *C*
Ashman, Howard *L*
Prologue / Da doo / Grow for me / Somewhere that's green / Some fun now / Dentist / Feed me / Suddenly, Seymour / Suppertime / Meek shall inherit / Mean green mother from outer space / Finale / Skid Row (downtown)
CD **GFLD 19289**
Geffen / Oct '95 / BMG

LITTLE SHOP OF HORRORS
Cast Recording
Menken, Alan *C*
Ashman, Howard *L*
Prologue / Skid row / Da doo / Grow for me / Somewhere that's green / Be a dentist / Mushnik and son / Git it (feed me) / Suddenly, Seymour / Suppertime / Finale / Megamix
CD **LS 94CD01**
Dreamtime / Apr '94 / Kudos / Pinnacle

LITTLE SHOP OF HORRORS
Studio Cast
Menken, Alan *C*
Ashman, Howard *L*
Prologue (Little shop of horrors) / Skid row (downtown) / Da-doo / Grow for me / Ya never know / Mushnik and son / Dentist / Somewhere that's green / Feed me (git it) / Now (it's just the gas) / Closed for renovation / Suddenly seymour / Suppertime / Meek shall inherit / Sominex/Suppertime II / Finale (don't feed the plants)
CD **88102**
CMC / May '97 / BMG

LITTLE TRAMP
1992 Studio Cast
Pomeranz, David *C*
In America again / Something no one could ever take away / When the world stops turning / Number one / 'Less it ends with a chase / Tramp/He's got to be someone / Chaplin films / Thank you / Heaven / He's got to be someone (reprise) / Too many words / I got me a red/There's got to be a law / This is what I dreamed / Finale
CD **4509913872**
WEA / Nov '92 / Warner Music

LITTLE VERA
CD **CDCH 368**
Milan / Apr '90 / Conifer/BMG / Silva Screen

LITTLE WOMEN
Newman, Thomas *C*
Newman, Thomas *Con*
CD **SK 66922**
Sony Classical / Mar '95 / Sony

LIVE A LITTLE.../TROUBLE WITH GIRLS/CHANGE OF HEART/CHARRO
Presley, Elvis
Almost in love / Little less conversation / Wonderful world / Edge of reality / Little less conversation (album version) / Charro / Let's forget about the stars / Clean up your own backyard / Swing low, sweet chariot / Swing low, sweet chariot / Signs of the zodiac / Almost / Whiffenpoof song / Violet / Clean up your own backyard (undubbed version) / Almost (undubbed version) / Have a happy / Let's be friends / Change of habit / Let us pray / Rubberneckin'
CD **07863665592**
RCA / Mar '95 / BMG

LIVE AND LET DIE
Martin, George *C*
Live and let die: *McCartney, Paul & Wings* / Just a closer walk with thee / New second line: *Dejan, Harold A. 'Duke' & The Olympia Brass Band* / Bond meets Solitaire / Whisper who dares / Snakes alive / Baron Samedi's dance of death / San Monique / Fillet of soul / Bond drops in / If he finds it, kill him / Trespassers will be eaten / Solitaire gets her cards / Sacrifice / James Bond
CD **CZ 553**
Premier/EMI / Dec '95 / EMI

LIVES OF JESUS, THE
Sanctus / Yad vashem / One sacred voice / Kama-kami / Desert dance / Ex templo / Jericho / In cathedra / Transfiguratas est / Via dolorosa / Lives of Jesus (titles)
CD **RCD 60030**
MCA / Dec '96 / BMG

LO STRANIERO/UOMINI CONTRO (The Stranger)
Piccioni, Piero *C*
CD **PRCD 118**
Preamble / Apr '96 / Silva Screen

LOCAL HERO
Knopfler, Mark
Knopfler, Mark *C*
Rocks and the water / Wild theme / Freeway flyer / Boomtown / Way it always starts / Rocks and the thunder / Ceilidh and the Northern lights / Mist covered mountain / Ceilidh / Louis favourite Billy tune / Whistle / Smooching / Stargazer / Going home
CD **8110382**
Vertigo / Mar '97 / PolyGram

LODOSS WAR I
Hagita, Matsuo *C*
CD **AM 3**
Animanga / Nov '96 / New Note/Pinnacle

LODOSS WAR II
Hagita, Matsuo *C*
CD **AM 4**
Animanga / Nov '96 / New Note/Pinnacle

LODOSS WAR III
Hagita, Matsuo *C*
CD **AM 8**
Animanga / Nov '96 / New Note/Pinnacle

LOGAN'S RUN
Goldsmith, Jerry *C*
CD **BCD 3024**
Bay Cities / Mar '92 / Silva Screen

LOMA/VIXEN/FASTER PUSSYCAT KILL KILL (Russ Meyer Original Soundtracks Vol. 1)
CD **QDKCD 008**
Normal / Jul '94 / ADA / Direct

LONE WOLF MCQUADE
De Masi, Francesco *C*
CD **VSD 5573**
Varese Sarabande / Nov '95 / Pinnacle

LONESOME DOVE
Poledouris, Basil *C*
Poledouris, Basil *Con*
CD **CFM 9722**
Cabin Fever / Jan '93 / Silva Screen

LONESTAR
CD **DARINGCD 3023**
Daring / Jun '96 / ADA / CM / Direct

LONG GOOD FRIDAY, THE
Monkman, Francis
Monkman, Francis *C*
Long good Friday / Overture / Scene is set / At the pool / Discovery / Icehouse / Talking to the police / Guitar interludes / Realization / Fury / Taken
CD **FILMCD 020**
Silva Screen / Jan '89 / Koch / Silva Screen

LONG KISS GOODNIGHT, THE
Woman: *Cherry, Neneh* / Bring it on home to me: *Redding, Otis & Carla Thomas* / Stubborn kind of fellow: *Gaye, Marvin* / FNT: *Semisonic* / Keep this party bouncin': *LA Ganz* / Funny how time slips away: *Hinton, Joe* / Tomorrow man: *Gus* / She's not there: *Santana* / Next time you see to me: *Parker, Junior* / Mannish boy: *Waters, Muddy* / Many rivers too cross: *Tom Tom Club* / Chair: *Jars Of Clay* / Main title: *Silvestri, Alan* / Lady marmalade: *Labelle*
CD **MCD 11526**
MCA / Nov '96 / BMG

LONG RIDERS, THE
Cooder, Ry
Cooder, Ry *C*
Long riders / I'm a good old rebel / Seneca square dance / Archie's funeral (hold to God's unchanging hand) / I always knew that you were the one / Rally round the flag / Wildwood boys / Better things to think about / My grandfather / Cole Younger / Escape from Northfield / Leaving Missouri / Jesse James
CD **7599234482**
WEA / Jan '96 / Warner Music

LONG WALK HOME, THE
Fenton, George
Fenton, George *C*
CD **VSD 5304**
Varese Sarabande / Apr '91 / Pinnacle

LORD OF ILLUSION
Boswell, Simon *C*
Lord of Illusion / Detective / God's eyes / Flesh is a trap / Magic moments / Swann's last act / Dorothea and d'amour / While the blood runs warm in your veins / Resurrection / Origami man / What are you looking at / Born to murder the world / Magic sets us free / Laura / Dancing in the dark
CD **IONIC 13CD**
The Fine Line / Jul '95 / RTM/Disc

LORD OF THE FLIES
London Symphony Orchestra
Sarde, Philippe *C*
Lord of the flies / Island / Demons / Fire on the mountain / Cry of the hunters / Last hope / Savages / After the storm / Bacchanalia / Lord Of The Flies (finale)
CD **FILMCD 067**
Silva Screen / Jun '90 / Koch / Silva Screen

LORD OF THE RINGS
Rosenman, Leonard *C*
Rosenman, Leonard *Con*
CD **FMT 8003D**
Intrada / Apr '92 / Koch / Silva Screen

LOST BOYS, THE
To the shock of Miss Louise: *Newman, Thomas* / Good times: *INXS & Jimmy Barnes* / Lost in the shadows: *Gramm, Lou* / Don't let the sun go down on me: *Daltrey, Roger* / Laying down the law: *INXS & Jimmy Barnes* / People are strange: *Echo & The Bunnymen* / Cry little sister: *McMann, Gerard* / Power play: *Eddie & The Tide* / I still believe: *Cappello, Tim* / Beauty has her way: *Mummy Calls*
CD **7817672**
Atlantic / Aug '87 / Warner Music

LOST EMPIRE, THE/RETRIBUTION
Howarth, Alan *C*
Howarth, Alan *Con*
CD **FILMCD 068**
Silva Screen / Jan '91 / Koch / Silva Screen

LOST EMPIRES
Hilton, Derek *C*
Lost empires theme / Army of today's alright / Your king and country / Pure white rose / Somewhere / Oh Flo / They didn't believe me / Wedding glide / Cigar girl / Honeysuckle and the bee / Mother Machree / Alexander's ragtime band / Land of hope and glory / Rule Britannia / I don't want to play in your yard / Yankee doodle boy / Shine on harvest moon / Love's old sweet song / Trombone song / Take me on the flip flap / Nobody knows, nobody cares / Mr. Knick Knock / Poor little Dolly / Waiting for the Robert E Lee / Catari, catari / Nightingale and the star / Julia's theme
CD **CDTER 1119**
TER / Nov '86 / Koch

LOST HIGHWAY
I'm deranged (Edit): *Bowie, David* / I'm deranged (Reprise): *Bowie, David* / Videodrones: *Reznor, Trent* / Questions: *Reznor, Trent* / Perfect drug: *Nine Inch Nails* / Red bats with teeth: *Badalamenti, Angelo* / Haunting and heartbreaking: *Badalamenti, Angelo* / Dub driving: *Badalamenti, Angelo* / Fred and Renee make love: *Badalamenti, Angelo* / Fats revisited: *Badalamenti, Angelo* / Fred's world: *Badalamenti, Angelo* / Police: *Badalamenti, Angelo* / Driver down: *Reznor, Trent* / Eye: *Smashing Pumpkins* / Mr. Eddy's theme 1: *Adamson, Barry* / Something wicked this way comes: *Adamson, Barry* / Hollywood sunset: *Adamson, Barry* / Hierate mich: *Rammstein* / Rammstein (Edit): *Rammstein* / I put a spell on you: *Manson, Marilyn* / This magic moment: *Reed, Lou* / Mr. Eddy's theme 2: *Adamson, Barry* / Apple of sodom: *Manson, Marilyn* / Insensatez: *Jobin, Antonio Carlos*
CD **IND 90090**
Interscope / Feb '97 / BMG

LOST WEEKEND/BLOOD ON THE RUN
Rozsa, Miklos *C*
CD **TSU 0132**
Tsunami / Apr '96 / Silva Screen

LOUISIANA PURCHASE
Berlin, Irving *C*
CD **DRGCD 94766**
DRG / Dec '96 / Discovery / New Note/ Pinnacle

LOUISIANA STORY
New London Orchestra
Thomson, Virgil *C*
Corp, R. *Con*
Power among men / Louisiana story / Acadian songs and dances / Plow that broke the plains
CD **CDA 66576**
Hyperion / Feb '92 / Select

LOVE HURTS
Hawkshaw, Alan *C*
Love hurts (Tessa's theme) / Chance encounter / St. Petersburg / Frank's theme / Marisha / Jade's theme / Nikolai / Everyone needs someone to love / New beginnings / Lynne's theme / Crisis for Diane / Jade confides in Mum / Frank and Tessa / Simon and Diane / Jade joins Seed / Frank owns up / Love hurts: *Polycarpou, Peter*
CD **CDSTM 4**
Soundtrack Music / Feb '93 / EMI

LOVE JONES
Brother to the night (a blues for Nina): *Tate, Larenz* / Hopeless: *Farris, Dionne* / Sweetest thing: *Refugee Camp All-Stars & Lauryn Hill* / I got a love Jones for you: *Refugee Camp All-Stars & Melky & Day* / Sumthin' sumthin': *Maxwell* / Never enough: *Groove Theory* / Inside my love: *Broussard, Tina* / In the rain: *Xscape* / You move me: *Wilson, Cassandra* / Rush over: *Miller, Marcus & Me'Shell Ndegeocello* / I like it: *Brand New Heavies* / Girl Cassie: *Lattimore, Kenny* / Can't get enough: *Lattimore, Kenny* / Jelly jelly: *Lincoln Centre Jazz Orchestra* / In a sentimental mood: *Ellington, Duke & John Coltrane* / I am looking at music: *Long, Nia*
CD **4872302**
Columbia / Mar '97 / Sony

LOVE ME TENDER
Presley, Elvis
CD **295 052**
RCA / May '95 / BMG

LOVE STORY
Lai, Francis *C*
Love story / Snow frolic / Sonata No.12 in F major / I love you Phil / Christmas tree / Search for Jenny / Bozo Barrett / Skating in Central Park / Long walk home / Concerto No.3 in D Major / Love story (finale)
CD **MCLD 19157**
MCA / Jan '93 / BMG

LOVE VALOUR COMPASSION
Wheeler, Harold *C*
CD **4556442**
Decca / Aug '97 / PolyGram

LOVED UP
Smoke belch II: *Sabres Of Paradise* / Crystal clear: *Grid* / Prologue: *10th Chapter* / Two full moons and a trout: *Union Jack* / Little bullet: *Spooky* / Gut drum mix: *Funtopia* / Plastic dream: *Jaydee* / Break and enter: *Prodigy* / Acperience: *Hardfloor* / Surjestive: *Advances* / Melt: *Leftfield*
CD **PRIMACD 002**
Prima Vera / Oct '95 / Pinnacle

LOVING YOU
Presley, Elvis
Mean woman blues / Teddy bear / Got a lot of livin' to do / Lonesome cowboy / Hot dog / Party / Blueberry Hill / True love / Don't leave me now / Have I told you lately that I love you / One night of sin / Loving you / Tell me why / Is it so strange / When it rains it really pours / I beg of you / Loving you / Party / Got a lot of livin' to do
CD **07863674522**
RCA / Apr '97 / BMG

LOVING YOU
Herman, Jerry *C*
CD **VSD 5586**
Varese Sarabande / Aug '95 / Pinnacle

LOW DOWN DIRTY SHAME, A
Down 4 whateva: *Nuttin' NYC* / Shame: *Zhane* / I can go deep: *Silk* / Homie, lover, friend: *R. Kelly* / Turn it up: *Raja-Nee* / Stroke you up: *Changing Faces* / Thing I like: *Aaliyah* / Gotta get yo groove on: *Campbell, Tevin* / Birthday girl: *Hi-Five* / Get the girl, grab the money and run: *Souls Of Mischief* / Cray-Z: *Fu-Schnickens* / Later on: *Casual* / How's that: *Murray, Keith* / Let's organize: *Organized Konfusion* / Ghetto style: *Smooth* / Front, back and side to side: *UGK's* / In front of the kids: *Extra Prolific* / U rong 4 that: *Mz Kilo*
CD **CHIP 156**
Jive / Apr '95 / Pinnacle

LUBITSCH TOUCH, THE (& Die Austernprinzessin/Die Puppe - Music For Silent Movies)
Film Orchestra Babelsberg
Sasse, Karl-Ernst *C*
Rosenberg, Manfred *Con*
CD **09026626562**
RCA Victor / Nov '95 / BMG

LUCIFER RISING
Beausoleil, Bobby *C*
CD **DIGUST 2**
Masters Of Disgust / Feb '94 / Pinnacle

LUCKY STIFF
Flaherty, Stephen *C*
Something funny's going on / Mr. Witherspoon's friday night / Uncle's last request / Good to be alive / Rita's confession / Lucky / Dogs versus you / Phone call / Monte Carlo / Speaking French / Times like this / Fancy meeting you here / Him, them, it, her / Nice / Welcome back Mr. Witherspoon / Confession no.2 / Finale: Good to be alive
CD **VSD 5461**
Varese Sarabande / Apr '94 / Pinnacle

LULU
Segarra, Carlos *C*
CD **CH 703**
Milan / Jan '95 / Conifer/BMG / Silva Screen

LUNCH (The Studio Recording)
Dorff, Steve *C*
Bettis, John *L*
Lunch / He'll never know / I never danced with you / Requiem for a lightweight / Man like me / Skyline / Time stands still / I'm no angel / Why fall at all / Perfectly alone / Lunch concerto
CD **DRGCD 12610**
DRG / Mar '95 / Discovery / New Note/ Pinnacle

M

M. BUTTERFLY
Shore, Howard *C*
Shore, Howard *Con*
M Butterfly / Concubine / Entrance of Butterfly / Drunken beauty / Dragonfly / Great wall / Even the softest skin / Shi jia bang / Bonfire of the vanities / Cultural revolution / He was the perfect father / Are you my butterfly / Only time I ever really existed / What I loved was the lie / Everything has been destroyed / Un bel di / My name is Rene Gallimard
CD **VSD 5435**
Varese Sarabande / Oct '93 / Pinnacle

MACARTHUR (The Rebel General)
Goldsmith, Jerry *C*
CD **VSD 5260**
Varese Sarabande / Oct '90 / Pinnacle

MACBETH/KING ARTHUR/MERRY WIVES OF WINDSOR (Incidental Music To The Shakespearean Plays)
MacDonald, Margaret & RTE Chamber Choir/Concert Orchestra
Sullivan, Sir Arthur *C*

Penny, Andrew *Con*
CD _______________ 8223635
Marco Polo / Sep '95 / Select

MACHINE GUN MCCAIN
Morricone, Ennio *C*
Morricone, Ennio *Con*
CD _______________ A 8922
Alhambra / Feb '92 / Silva Screen

MACK AND MABEL
1974 Broadway Cast
Herman, Jerry *C*
Overture: *Orchestra* / Movies were movies: *Preston, Robert* / Look what happened to Mabel: *Mack & Mabel* / Big time: *Kirk, Lisa* / I won't send roses: *Preston, Robert* / I wanna make the world laugh: *Preston, Robert* / Wherever he ain't: *Peters, Bernadette* / Hundreds of girls: *Preston, Robert & The Bathing Beauties* / When Mabel comes in the room: *Simmonds, Stanley* / My heart leaps up: *Preston, Robert* / Time heals everything: *Peters, Bernadette* / Tap your troubles away: *Kirk, Lisa* / I promise you a happy ending: *Preston, Robert*
CD _______________ MCLD 19089
MCA / Oct '92 / BMG

MACK AND MABEL (In Concert)
1988 London Cast
Herman, Jerry *C*
Overture / Introduction / When movies were movies / Look what happened to Mabel / Big time / I won't send roses / I wanna make the world laugh / Wherever he ain't / Hundreds of girls / Entr'acte / When Mabel comes in the room / Hit 'em on the head / Time heals everything / Tap your troubles away / I promise you a happy ending / I won't send roses (reprise)
CD _______________ OCRCD 6015
First Night / Oct '95 / Pinnacle

MACK AND MABEL
1995 London Cast
Herman, Jerry *C*
CD _______________ CDEMC 3734
Premier/EMI / Dec '95 / EMI

MACROSS PLUS
National anthem of Macross / Fly up in the air - tension / After, in the dark - torch song / Myung theme / Bees and honey / In captivity / More than 3cm / Voices / Break out - cantabile / Very little wishes / Santi-U
CD _______________ DSCD 12
Demon / May '95 / Pinnacle

MCVICAR
Bitter and twisted / Escape / Free me: *Daltrey, Roger* / Just a dream away / McVicar / My time is gonna come / Waiting for a friend / White City lights / Without your love: *Daltrey, Roger*
CD _______________ 5273412
Polydor / Jan '94 / PolyGram

MAD DOG AND GLORY
Bernstein, Elmer *C*
Bernstein, Elmer *Con*
CD _______________ VSD 5415
Varese Sarabande / Mar '93 / Pinnacle

MAD MAX I
May, Brian *C*
Main title / Max the hunter / Max decides on vengeance / Final chase / Terrible death of Jim Goose / We'll give 'em back their heroes / Pain & triumph / Dazed Goose / Foreboding in the vast landscape / Declaration of war / Flight from the evil Toecutter / Pursuit & tragedy / Jesse alone, uneasy & exhausted / Beach house / Nightriders race / Jesse searches for her child / Rampage of the toecutter / Crazing of Johnny the boy / Outtakes suite
CD _______________ VCD 47144
Varese Sarabande / Jan '89 / Pinnacle

MAD MAX II (The Road Warrior)
May, Brian *C*
Opening titles / Montage / Confrontation / Marauder's massacre / Max enters compound / Feral boy strikes / Gyro saves Max / Gyro flight / Breakout / Chase continues / Journey over the mountain / Finale and largo / End title
CD _______________ VCD 47262
Varese Sarabande / Jan '89 / Pinnacle

MAD MAX III (Beyond The Thunderdome)
Royal Philharmonic Orchestra
Jarre, Maurice *C*
We don't need another hero: *Turner, Tina* / One of the living: *Turner, Tina* / We don't need another hero (instrumental) / Bartertown / Children / Coming home
CD _______________ GNPD 8037
GNP Crescendo / Sep '92 / ZYX

MAD MONKEY
Duhamel, Antoine *C*
CD _______________ CH 397
Milan / Jan '95 / Conifer/BMG / Silva Screen

MADAME SOUSATZKA
Gouriet, Gerald *C*
CD _______________ VSD 5204
Varese Sarabande / Dec '88 / Pinnacle

MADE IN AMERICA
Go Away: *Estefan, Gloria* / Does he do it good: *Sweat, Keith* / Made in America: *Del Tha Funky Homosapien* / Colours of love: *Fischer, Lisa* / What is this: *Mendes, Sergio* / Made in Love: *Isham, Mark* / I know I don't walk on water: *Satterfield, Laura & Ephraim Lewis* / Dance or die: *D.J. Jazzy Jeff & The Fresh Prince* / Smoke on the water: *Deep Purple* / If you need a miracle: *King, Ben E.* / Stand: *Y.T Style*
CD _______________ 7559614982
WEA / Dec '96 / Warner Music

MADE IN HEAVEN
Isham, Mark *C*
CD _______________ 9607292
Silva Screen / Jan '89 / Koch / Silva Screen

MADNESS OF KING GEORGE, THE
Fenton, George *C*
Opening the Houses of Parliament / Prelude/Front titles / Smile, it's what you're paid for / King goes riding / Family matter / Cricket match / King wakes up early / Do it England / Concert / We have no time / He will be restrained / London is flooding / Going to Kew / Starting to recover / Chancellor drives to London / Prince Regent / Mr. and Mrs. King / End credits
CD _______________ 4784772
Epic / Apr '95 / Sony

MADWOMAN OF CENTRAL PARK WEST, THE
Broadway Cast
CD _______________ DRGCD 5212
DRG / Jan '95 / Discovery / New Note/ Pinnacle

MAGDALENE
Munich Symphony Orchestra
Eidelman, Cliff *C*
Eidelman, Cliff *Con*
CD _______________ MAF 7029D
Intrada / Sep '92 / Koch / Silva Screen

MAGIC RIDDLE, THE
Ordinary miracles / When I was just a little girl / I will find the will / Mean mean mean / My darling daughters / Sisters sisters / Cindy do it now / Try not to cry so / Pig song / Oh silver bright reflection / Grandma dear grandma / Now how did it go / Girl in the snow white dress / I'm alive / Cinderella's wedding day / Instrumental score excerpts
CD _______________ A 8937
Alhambra / May '92 / Silva Screen

MAGNIFICENT AMBERSONS
Australian Philharmonic Orchestra
Herrmann, Bernard *C*
Bremner, Tony *Con*
CD _______________ PRCD 1783
Preamble / Jan '93 / Silva Screen

MAGNIFICENT SEVEN, THE/RETURN OF THE SEVEN
Bernstein, Elmer *C*
Magnificent Seven / Bandidos / Return of the seven / Defeat / Mariachis de Mexico / El toro / Journey / Council / Petra's declaration / In the trap / Battle / Finale
CD _______________ TSU 0102
Tsunami / Jan '95 / Silva Screen

MAGNIFICENT SEVEN, THE/THE HALLELUJAH TRAIL
Arizona State University Choir/Phoenix Symphony Orchestra
Bernstein, Elmer *C*
Sedares, James *Con*
CD _______________ 372222
Koch International / Jan '95 / Koch

MAHABHARATA
Tchuchitori, Toshi
Tchuchitori, Toshi *C*
Nibiro ghono andare / Draupadi / Ontoro momo / Satvati / Virata / Bushi ok sudure / Cities / Bhima / Markandeya (part 1) / Duryodhana / Dhire / Markandeya (part 2) / Svetasvatara upanisad
CD _______________ RWCD 9
Realworld / Jan '90 / EMI

MAIN EVENT
Melvoin, Michael *C*
Main event / Fight / Body shop / Copeland meets the Coasters / Get a job / Big girls don't cry / It's your foot again / Angry eyes / I'd clean a fish for you
CD _______________ 4749062
Columbia / '95 / Sony

MAJOR DUNDEE
Amfitheatrof, Daniele *C*
CD _______________ TSU 0111
Tsunami / Jan '95 / Silva Screen

MAJOR LEAGUE II
Boom bapa boom: *Vaughan, Jimmy* / (Everything I do) Got to be funky: *Vaughan, Jimmy* / Wild thing '94: *X* / Shake me up: *Little Feat* / Rude mood: *Vaughan, Stevie Ray* / All my love is gone: *Lovett, Lyle* / Born under a bad sign: *King, Albert* / House is rockin': *Vaughan, Stevie Ray & Double Trouble* / Wild thing: *X*
CD _______________ 523245-2
Morgan Creek / Jun '94 / PolyGram

MALICE
Goldsmith, Jerry *C*
Goldsmith, Jerry *Con*
Main title / Lift home / No friends / With malice / Handyman / Clues / No choice / Body
CD _______________ VSD 5442
Varese Sarabande / Jan '94 / Pinnacle

MAMA, I WANT TO SING
London Cast
Treasure of love / On Christ / Solid rock / You are my child / Faith can move a mountain / I know who hold tomorrow / He'll be your strength / Gifted is / This bitter earth / Stormy weather / In my solitude / God bless the child / Mama I want to sing / I'll do anything / What do you win when you win / Take my hand (precious Lord) / His eye is on the sparrow / Take my hand (precious Lord) / Know when to leave the party / Just one look / One who will love me
CD _______________ CDEMC 3709
EMI / May '95 / EMI

MAMBO KINGS, THE
La dicha mia / Ran kan kan / Cuban Pete / Mambo caliente / Quiereme mucho / Sunny ray / Melao da cana (moo la lah) / Para los rumberos / Perfidia / Guantanamera / Tea for two / Accidental mambo / Come fue / Tanga / Rumba afro cubana / Beautiful Maria of my soul
CD _______________ 7559612402
Elektra / May '92 / Warner Music

MAN AND A WOMAN, A/LIVE FOR LIFE
Lai, Francis *C*
Man and a woman / Samba saravah / Today it's you / Stronger than us / In our shadow / 124 Miles an hour / Live for life / Theme to Catherine / Theme to Candice / Now you want to be loved / Theme to Robert / All at once it's love / Zoom
CD _______________ DRGCD 12612
DRG / May '96 / Discovery / New Note/ Pinnacle

MAN BITES DOG
CD _______________ 873142
Milan / Jan '93 / Conifer/BMG / Silva Screen

MAN CALLED MOON, A
Bacalov, Luis Enriquez *C*
CD _______________ A 8935
Silva Screen / Jan '93 / Koch / Silva Screen

MAN FROM 42ND STREET, THE
Powell, Dick
You've got something there / This year's kisses / I know now / In a moment of weakness / You can't run away from love tonight / Have you got any castles baby / Lulu's back in town / Love is in the air tonight / Stein song / 'Cause my baby says it's so / Moonlight on the campus / Song of the marines / I've got my love to keep me warm / I'm like a fish out of water / Mr. and Mrs. is the name / By a waterfall / I'm going shopping with you / Thanks a million / Lullaby of Broadway / I'll string along with you / Why do I dream those dreams / Fair and warmer
CD _______________ PASTCD 7079
Flapper / Mar '96 / Pinnacle

MAN FROM SNOWY RIVER, THE
Rowland, Bruce *C*
CD _______________ VCD 47217
Varese Sarabande / Jan '89 / Pinnacle

MAN FROM UNCLE, THE
Montenegro, Hugo *C*
Montenegro, Hugo *Con*
Man from UNCLE / Meet Mr. Solo / Martini built for two / Wild bike / Solo on a raft / Fiddlesticks / Man from THRUSH / Illya / Invaders / Solo's samba / Bye bye Jill / Watch out / Sandals only / Solo busanova / Off and running / Boo-bam-boo baby / Slink / Run spy run / Jungle beat / Wiggely pig walk / Lament for a trapped spy / There they go / Jo Jo's torch thing / Dance of the flaming swords
CD _______________ 74321241792
RCA / Jan '95 / BMG

MAN ON FIRE
Graunke Symphony Orchestra
Scott, John *C*
CD _______________ VCD 47314
Varese Sarabande / Jan '89 / Pinnacle

MAN WHO WOULD BE KING, THE
Jarre, Maurice *C*
CD _______________ 873127
Milan / Jan '95 / Conifer/BMG / Silva Screen

MAN WITH THE GOLDEN GUN, THE
Barry, John *C*
Man with the golden gun: *Lulu* / Scaramanga's fun house / Chew mee in Grisly land / Man with the golden gun (jazz instrumental) / Getting the bullet / Goodnight, goodnight / Let's go get em / Hip's trip / Kung fu fight / In search of Scaramanga's island / Return to Scaramanga's fun house / Man with the golden gun (reprise): *Lulu*
CD _______________ CZ 552
Premier/EMI / Dec '95 / EMI

MAN WITHOUT A FACE
Horner, James *C*
CD _______________ 5182442
Silva Screen / Jul '93 / Koch / Silva Screen

MANDELA
CD _______________ CIDM 1116
Mango / Mar '97 / PolyGram / Vital

MANGALA, THE INDIAN GIRL
CD _______________ AAA 121
Club Du Disque Arabe / Feb '96 / ADA / Harmonia Mundi

MANHATTAN
Gershwin, George *C*
Rhapsody in blue / Someone to watch over me / I've got a crush on you / Embraceable you / Land of the gay caballero / Do do do / 'S Wonderful / Mine / He loves and she loves / Bronco buster's ball / Lady be good / Love is here to stay / Sweet and low down / Blue blue blue / But not for me / Strike up the band / Love is sweeping the country
CD _______________ MK 36020
CBS / Jun '87 / Sony

MANNAJA/TE DEUM
De Angelis, G. & M. *C*
CD _______________ OST 121
Milano Dischi / Jul '94 / Silva Screen

MANON DE SOURCES/JEAN DE FLORETTE
Petit, Jean Claude
Petit, Jean Claude *C*
CD _______________ CDCH 241
Milan / Feb '94 / Conifer/BMG / Silva Screen

MARCH OF THE FALSETTOS
1981 Off-Broadway Cast
Finn, William *C*
Finn, William *L*
Four Jews in a room bitching / Tight-knit family / Love is blind / Thrill of first love / Marvin at the psychiatrist / My Father's a homo / Everyone tells Jason to see a psychiatrist / This had better come to a stop / Please come to my house / Jason's therapy / Marriage proposal / Trina's song / March of the falsettos / Chess game / Making a home
CD _______________ DRGCD 12581
DRG / Mar '92 / Discovery / New Note/ Pinnacle

MARCH OF THE FALSETTOS/ FALSETTOLAND
Cast Recording
Finn, William *C*
Finn, William & James Lapine *L*
2CD _______________ DRGCD 22600
DRG / Jan '95 / Discovery / New Note/ Pinnacle

MARIA'S LOVERS
CD _______________ CDEMC 362
Milan / Apr '90 / Conifer/BMG / Silva Screen

MARKED FOR DEATH
I wanna do something freaky to you: *Kenyatta* / I joke but I don't play: *Tone Loc* / Roots & culture: *Shabba Ranks* / Put the funk back in it: *Brand New Heavies* / Welcome to my groove: *Mellow Man Ace* / Quiet passion: *Davenport, N'Dea* / Domino: *Masters Of Reality* / Shadow of death: *Def Jef & Papa Juggy* / Ya gets none: *Body & Soul* / Rats chase cats: *Attic Black* / Pick up the pace: *Young MC* / Weapons montage: *Howard, James Newton* / John Crow: *Cliff, Jimmy* / Steppin' razor: *Tosh, Peter* / No justice: *Cliff, Jimmy* / Rebel in me: *Cliff, Jimmy*
CD _______________ BRCD 561
4th & Broadway / Jan '94 / PolyGram

MARLENE
Cast Recording
CD _______________ RBMARCD 1
Playback / Apr '97 / Pinnacle

MARNIE
Herrmann, Bernard *C*
CD _______________ TCI 0601
Tsunami / Jan '95 / Silva Screen

MARS ATTACKS
Elfman, Danny *C*
Introduction / Main titles / First sighting / Landing / Ungodly experiments / State address / Martian madame / Martian lounge / Return message / Destructo x / Loving heads / Pursuit / War room / Airfield dilema / New world / Ritchie's speech / End credits / Indian love call: *Whitman, Slim* / It's not unusual: *Jones, Tom*
CD _______________ 7567829922
East West / Feb '97 / Warner Music

MARTIN GUERRE
London Cast
CD _______________ CASTCD 59
First Night / Nov '96 / Pinnacle

MARY REILLY
Fenton, George *C*
CD _______________ SK 62259
Sony Music / May '96 / Sony

MASK, THE
Cuban Pete (Edit): *Carrey, Jim* / Cuban Pete: *Carrey, Jim* / Who's that man: *Xscape* / This business of love: *Domino* / Bounce around: *Tony Toni Tone* / (I could only) Whisper your name: *Connick, Harry Jr.* / You would be my baby: *Williams, Vanessa* / Hi de ho: *K7* / Let the good times roll: *Fishbone* / Straight up: *Setzer, Brian Orchestra* / Hey pachuco: *Royal Crown Revue* / Gee baby ain't I good to you: *Boyd, Susan*
CD _______________ 4773162
Columbia / Aug '94 / Sony

MATEWAN
CD _______________ DARING 1011CD
Daring / Feb '95 / ADA / CM / Direct

MAVERICK
Newman, Randy *C*
Renegades, rebels and rogues / Good run of bad luck / Maverick / Ophelia / Something already gone / Dream on Texas ladies / Ladies love outlaws / Solitary travelers / Rainbow down the road / You don't mess around with me / Ride gambler ride / Amazing grace
CD ____ **7567825952**
Warner Bros. / Jul '94 / Warner Music

MAXIMUM OVERDRIVE (Who Made Who)
AC/DC
Who made who / You shook me all night long / DT / Sink the pink / Ride on / Hell's bells / Shake your foundations / Chase the ace / For those about to rock (we salute you)
CD ____ **7816502**
Atlantic / May '86 / Warner Music

MAXIMUM RISK
Folk, Robert *C*
CD ____ **VSD 5756**
Varese Sarabande / Oct '96 / Pinnacle

MAYRIG
Petit, Jean Claude *C*
CD ____ **752001**
Silva Screen / Jul '93 / Koch / Silva Screen

ME AND MY GIRL
1985 London Cast
Gay, Noel *C*
Furber, Douglas & L. Arthur Rose *L*
Overture / Weekend at Hareford / Thinking of no one but me / Family solicitor / Me and my girl / English gentleman / You would if you could / Lambeth walk / Sun has got his hat on / Once you lose your heart / Take it on the chin / Song of Hareford / Love makes the world go round / Leaning on a lamp-post / If only you cared for me / Finale
CD ____ **CDP 7463932**
EMI / Jun '92 / EMI

ME AND MY GIRL (Highlights - The Shows Collection)
Cast Recording
Gay, Noel *C*
Furber, Douglas & L. Arthur Rose *L*
CD ____ **PWKS 4143**
Carlton / Jan '95 / Carlton

ME AND MY GIRL
1987 Broadway Cast
Gay, Noel *C*
Furber, Douglas & L. Arthur Rose *L*
CD ____ **CDTER 1145**
TER / May '89 / Koch

MEDAL OF HONOUR
Stone, Richard *C*
CD ____ **PCD 106**
Prometheus / Jul '94 / Silva Screen

MEDICINE MAN
Goldsmith, Jerry *C*
Goldsmith, Jerry *Con*
Rae's arrival / First morning / Campbell & the children / Trees / Harvest / Mocara / Mountain high / Without a net / Finger painting / What's wrong / Injection / Sugar / Fire / Meal & a bath
CD ____ **VSD 5350**
Varese Sarabande / Mar '92 / Pinnacle

MEET ME IN ST. LOUIS
1989 Broadway Cast
Martin, Hugh & Ralph Blane *C*
CD ____ **DRGCD 19002**
DRG / Jan '95 / Discovery / New Note/ Pinnacle

MEET ME IN ST. LOUIS
1944 Film Cast
Main title / Meet me in St. Louis, Louis / Boy next door / Meet me in St. Louis, Louis / Getting ready for the party / Skip to my Lou / Under the bamboo tree / Saying goodnight / Over the bannister / Trolley song / Boys and girls like you and me / All Hallow's Eve / Most horrible one / You and I / Winter in St. Louis / I hate basketball / Under the Anheuser Bush / Esther accepts / Tootie's music box / Have yourself a merry little Christmas / Toutie's grief / Finale
CD ____ **CDODEON 2**
Premier/EMI / Feb '96 / EMI

MEET THE FEEBLES
CD ____ **QDKCD 003**
Normal / Sep '94 / ADA / Direct

MEGAZONE 23
Eden the last city / Sleepless beauty in the woods / Eiji / Netjacker / Ryo / G form / Artifact / Wall of Eden / Another story of megazone / Tragedy of an idol / Wang dai / Netpolice / Bahamoud / Cyberspace force / Project heaven / Pandora's boat / Mother Earth
CD ____ **DSCD 9**
Demon / May '95 / Pinnacle

MELANCHOLIA
Fisher-Turner, Simon
Fisher-Turner, Simon *C*
Holiday snaps and raincoat / Wrench and pull and blue / Flirt / Drinking at a stream / Butcher and Musak / Sergio electro / Bom bom bom / Sarah / Runner
CD ____ **FILMCD 061**
Silva Screen / Dec '89 / Koch / Silva Screen

MELROSE PLACE
That's just what you are: *Mann, Aimee* / Back on me: *Urge Overkill* / Baby I can't please you: *Phillips, Sam* / Blah: *Dinosaur Jnr* / Ordinary angels: *Frente* / Precious: *Lennox, Annie* / I'm jealous: *Divinyls* / Kids, this is fabulous: *Seed* / Here and now: *Letters To Cleo* / How was it for you: *James* / Star is bored: *Westerberg, Paul*
CD ____ **74321226082**
Giant / Nov '94 / BMG

MEMORIES
Kanno, Yoko & Jun Miyake/Hiroyuki Nagashika/Takkyu Ishino *C*
2CD ____ **AM 7**
Animanga / Nov '96 / New Note/Pinnacle

MEMPHIS BELLE
Fenton, George *C*
Fenton, George *Con*
Londonderry air/Front titles / Green eyes / Flying home / Steel lady / Prepare for take-off / Final mission / With deep regret... / I know why and so do you / Bomb run / Limping home / Crippled Belle: The landing / Resolution / End title suite / Danny Boy
CD ____ **VSD 5293**
Varese Sarabande / Nov '90 / Pinnacle

MEN IN BLACK
Men in black: *Smith, Will* / We just wanna party with you: *Snoop Doggy Dogg* / I'm feeling for you: *Ginuwine* / Dah dee dah: *Keys, Alicia* / Notic: *D'Angelo & The Roots* / Make you happy: *Lorenz, Trey* / Escobar: *Nas* / Erotic City: *Emoja* / Same ol' thang: *Tribe Called Quest* / Killing time: *Destiny's Child* / Waiting for love: *3T* / Channel no. fever: *De la soul* / Cowfonge: *Buck Shot* / Score
CD ____ **4881222**
Columbia / Jun '97 / Sony

MENACE 2 SOCIETY
CD ____ **CHIP 137**
Jive / Jun '93 / Pinnacle

MER DE CHINE
Coe, Tony
Coe, Tony *C*
Binh a la sortie de l'ecole / Le secretaire / Conversation sous la pluie / Troop long temps / La famille de binh / Sans cesse / La criee / Le departe de la famille / Le bus / L'arrestation de l'oncle / La mission / Vers le refuge / La fuite / La mort de la mere / Le delta / Boat people / La rencontre des boats / Pirates / Mer a boire / Enfin / Les eaux internationales / Marine de la nuit / I never held one before / Marine de jour / Nuit de boat / Les visages / Le bateau de binh / Sur le point / La seperation / L'arrivee / Binh et joy / La bicyclette / Mer de chine
CD ____ **626506**
Nato / Aug '91 / Discovery / Harmonia Mundi

MERRILY WE ROLL ALONG
1994 Cast
Sondheim, Stephen *C*
CD ____ **VSD 5548**
Varese Sarabande / Jan '95 / Pinnacle

MERRILY WE ROLL ALONG
1993 Haymarket Theatre Cast
Sondheim, Stephen *C*
CD ____ **CDTER 1225**
TER / Dec '94 / Koch

MERRILY WE ROLL ALONG
Cast Recording
Sondheim, Stephen *C*
CD ____ **CDTEM 21203**
TER / Jan '93 / Koch

MERRY CHRISTMAS MR. LAWRENCE
Sakamoto, Ryuichi
Sakamoto, Ryuichi *C*
Batavia / Germination / Hearty breakfast / Before the war / Seed and the sower / Brief encounter / Ride ride ride / Flight / Father Christmas / Dismissed / Assembly / Beyond reason / Sowing the seed / 23rd Psalm / Last regrets / Ride ride ride (Reprise) / Seed / Forbidden colours: *Sakamoto, Ryuichi & David Sylvian* / Merry Christmas Mr. Lawrence
CD ____ **220482**
Milan / Aug '94 / Conifer/BMG / Silva Screen

MERRY WIDOW, THE
1986 London Cast/New Sadler's Wells Opera Choir/Orchestra
Lehar, Franz *C*
Wordsworth, Barry *Con*
CD ____ **CDTER 1111**
TER / Sep '86 / Koch

MERRY WIDOW, THE (Highlights)
1986 London Cast/New Sadler's Wells Opera Choir/Orchestra
Lehar, Franz *C*
Wordsworth, Barry *Con*
CD ____ **CDTEO 1003**
TER / Sep '86 / Koch

MERRY WIDOW, THE
Schwarzkopf, Elisabeth & Nicolai Gedda/ Erich Kunz/Philharmonia Chorus & Orchestra
Lehar, Franz *C*
Ackermann, Otto *Con*
CD ____ **CDH 7695202**
EMI Classics / Apr '93 / EMI

MERRY WIDOW, THE
Schwarzkopf, Elisabeth & Nicolai Gedda/ Hanny Steffek/Philharmonia Chorus/ Orchestra
Lehar, Franz *C*
Von Matacic, Lovro *Con*
2CD ____ **CDC 7471788**
EMI Classics / Apr '93 / EMI

MERRY WIDOW, THE
Studer, Cheryl & Monteverdi Choir/Wiener Philharmoniker
Lehar, Franz *C*
Gardiner, John Eliot *Con*
CD ____ **4399112**
Deutsche Grammophon / Jan '95 / PolyGram

MERRY WIDOW, THE
Harwood, Elizabeth & Teresa Stratas/ Berliner Philharmoniker
Lehar, Franz *C*
Von Karajan, Herbert *Con*
2CD ____ **4357122**
Deutsche Grammophon / Jan '95 / PolyGram

MERRY WIDOW, THE
New Sadler's Wells Opera
Lehar, Franz *C*
Opening act one / Alone at last / Well my gallant friends/Hanna's entrance / O Fatherland, I must protest/Off to old Maxim's / Finale act one / Vilja / Maiden look, a soldier boy / Oh the women / Just as the sun awakens / Grisette's song / Words forbidden / Finale act three
CD ____ **SHOWCD 037**
Showtime / Oct '96 / Disc / THE

MESSAGE, THE/LION OF THE DESERT (The Epic Film Music Of Maurice Jarre)
Royal Philharmonic Orchestra/London Symphony Orchestra
Jarre, Maurice *C*
Jarre, Maurice *Con*
Message: *Royal Philharmonic Orchestra* / Lion of the desert: *London Symphony Orchestra*
CD ____ **FILMCD 060**
Silva Screen / Feb '90 / Koch / Silva Screen

METISSE
CD ____ **887821**
Milan / Jan '95 / Conifer/BMG / Silva Screen

METROPOLIS
1988 London Cast
Brooks, Joe *C*
Brooks, Joe & Dusty Hughes *L*
101.11 / Hold back the night / Machines are beautiful / He's distant from me now / Elitists' dance / Oh my, what a beautiful city / This is the vision we're forbidden / Children of Metropolis / 50,000 pounds of power / One more morning / It's only love / Bring on the night / Pressure chant / Day after day / When Maria comes / You are the light / Girl is a witch / It's only love (reprise) / Sun / Almost done / I don't need help from you / There's a girl down below / Futura / We're the cream / I've seen a nightmare / This is life / Look at this girl who stands before you / Futura's dance / Where do you think she's gone, your precious Maria / If that was love / Listen to me / Learning song / Old friends / When Maria wakes / Futura's promise / Maria's insane / Perfect face / Haven't you finished with me / Let's watch the world go to the devil / One of those nights / Requiem / Metropolis / Finale
2CD ____ **CDTER2 1168**
TER / Jul '89 / Koch

MIAMI VICE
Hammer, Jan
Hammer, Jan *C*
Miami Vice / Smuggler's blues: *Frey, Glenn* / Own the night: *Khan, Chaka* / You belong to the city: *Frey, Glenn* / In the air tonight: *Collins, Phil* / Vice / Better be good to me: *Turner, Tina* / Flashback / Chase / Evan
CD ____ **MCLD 19024**
MCA / Apr '92 / BMG

MICHAEL
Through your hands: *Henley, Don* / I don't care if you love me anymore: *Mavericks* / Chain of fools: *Franklin, Aretha* / Bright side of the road: *Morrison, Van* / Heaven is my home: *Newman, Randy & Valerie Carter* / Spider and the fly: *Shepherd, Kenny Wayne & James Cotton* / Feels like home: *Raitt, Bonnie* / Willie Nelson: *Nelson, Willie* / Love God (and everyone else): *Green, Al* / Sittin' by the side of the road: *MacDowell, Andie* / Spirit in the sky: *Greenbaum, Norman*
CD ____ **74321418802**
Revolution / Feb '97 / BMG

MICHAEL COLLINS
CD ____ **7567829602**
Atlantic / Jan '97 / Warner Music

MICHAEL FLATELY'S LORD OF THE DANCE
Hardiman, Ronan *C*
Cry of the Celts / Suil a ruin / Celtic dream / Warriors / Gypsy / Breakout / Lord of the dance / Cry of the Celts / Spirit of the new world / Firey nights / Lament / Siamsa / Our wedding day / Stolen kiss / Nightmare / Victory / Lord of the dance
CD ____ **5337572**
PolyGram TV / Oct '96 / PolyGram

MICROCOSMOS
Coulais, Bruno
Coulais, Bruno *C*
CD ____ **K 1028**
Travelling / Jan '97 / Harmonia Mundi

MIDNIGHT COWBOY
Barry, John *C*
Everybody's talkin' / Joe Buck rides again / Famous myth / Fun City / He quit me man / Jungle gym at the zoo / Midnight cowboy / Old man Willow / Florida fantasy / Tears and joys / Science fiction
CD ____ **PRMCD 6**
Soundtracks / Jun '96 / EMI

MIDNIGHT EXPRESS
Moroder, Giorgio *C*
Chase / Love's theme / Midnight express, Theme from / Istanbul blues / Wheel / Istanbul opening / Cacaphoney / Billy's theme
CD ____ **8242062**
Phonogram / Apr '85 / PolyGram

MIDNIGHT STING (Diggstown)
Howard, James Newton *C*
CD ____ **VSD 5379**
Varese Sarabande / Sep '92 / Pinnacle

MIGHTY APHRODITE
Neo minore / Horos tou sakena / I've found a new baby / Whispering / Manhattan / When your lover is gone / Li'l darlin' / Take five / Penthouse serenade (When we're alone) / I hadn't anyone till you / In crowd / You do something to me / When you're smiling (the whole world smiles with you)
CD ____ **SK 62253**
Sony Classical / Apr '96 / Sony

MIGHTY MORPHIN' POWER RANGERS (Score)
Revell, Graeme *C*
CD ____ **VSD 5672**
Varese Sarabande / Nov '95 / Pinnacle

MIKADO, THE (Highlights)
English National Opera
Sullivan, Sir Arthur *C*
Gilbert, W.S. *L*
If you want to know who we are / Wandering minstrel, I / Our great Mikado / Young man/Despair / Behold the Lord/High executioner / I've got a little list / Three little maids / Braid with raven hair / Sun, whose rays / Flowers that bloom in the spring / On a tree by a river (tit' willow) / There is a beauty in the bellow of the blast
CD ____ **SHOWCD 005**
Showtime / Feb '95 / Disc / THE

MIKADO, THE
Brannigan, Owen & Richard Lewis/Glyndebourne Festival Choir/Pro Arte Orchestra
Sullivan, Sir Arthur *C*
Gilbert, W.S. *L*
Sargent, Sir Malcolm *Con*
2CD ____ **CMS 7644032**
EMI Classics / Apr '94 / EMI

MIKADO, THE
D'Oyly Carte Opera Chorus/Royal Philharmonic Orchestra
Sullivan, Sir Arthur *C*
Gilbert, W.S. *L*
Nash, R. *Con*
2CD ____ **4251902**
London / Jan '90 / PolyGram

MIKADO, THE
D'Oyly Carte Opera Chorus/Orchestra
Sullivan, Sir Arthur *C*
Gilbert, W.S. *L*
Pryce Jones, J. *Con*
2CD ____ **CDTER2 1178**
TER / Sep '90 / Koch

MIKADO, THE
Welsh National Opera Choir/Orchestra
Sullivan, Sir Arthur *C*
Gilbert, W.S. *L*
Mackerras, Sir Charles *Con*
CD ____ **CD 80284**
Telarc / May '92 / Conifer/BMG

MIKADO, THE
Sadler's Wells Opera Chorus/Orchestra
Sullivan, Sir Arthur *C*
Gilbert, W.S. *L*
Faris, Alexander *Con*
2CD ____ **CDCFPD 4730**
Classics For Pleasure / Apr '94 / EMI

MIKADO, THE (Highlights)
English National Opera
Sullivan, Sir Arthur *C*
Gilbert, W.S. *L*
CD ____ **CDTER 1121**
TER / Jan '93 / Koch

MILLENIUM (Tribal Wisdom & The Modern World)
Mancina, Mark
Zimmer, Hans *C*
Shaman's song / Stories for a thousand years / Journey begins / Stone drag / Courting song/Love in the Himalayas / Inventing reality / Fiddlers/Pilgrimage to Wirikuta / Shock of the other / Race of the initiates / Art of living / Geerewol celebrations / Song for the dead / Pilgrims' chant/In the land of the ancestors / Ecology of mind / Well song/A desert home / Initiation chant/Rites of passage / Journey continues / Millenium theme
CD ____ **CD 6001**

Narada / May '92 / ADA / New Note/ Pinnacle

MIRACLE MILE
Tangerine Dream
Tangerine Dream *C*
Teetering scales / One for the book / After the call / On the spur of the moment / All of a dither / Final statement
CD **260016**
Private Music / Feb '96 / BMG

MIRACLE ON 34TH STREET
Jingle bells: *Cole, Natalie* / It's beginning to look like Christmas: *Warwick, Dionne* / Have yourself a merry little Christmas: *Kenny G.* / Santa Claus is coming to town: *Charles, Ray* / Joy to the world: *Franklin, Aretha* / Santa Claus is back in town: *Presley, Elvis* / Singing: *McLachlan, Sarah* / Bellevue carol: *McLachlan, Sarah* / Song for a winter's night: *McLachlan, Sarah*
CD **07822110222**
Arista / Nov '94 / BMG

MIRROR HAS TWO FACES, THE
Main title/Inquesta reggia / Got any Scotch / Ad / In a sentimental mood / Rose sees Greg / Dating montage / My intentions / You picked me / Funny kind of proposal / Picnic in the park / Greg falls for Rose / Try a little tenderness: *Sanborn, David* / Mirror / Going back to Mom / Rocking in the chair / Power inside me: *Marx, Richard* / Rose leaves Greg / Ruby / Rose dumps Alex / Apology/ Nessun dorma: *Pavarotti, Luciano* / I finally found someone: *Streisand, Barbra & Bryan Adams* / All of my life: *Streisand, Barbra*
CD **4853952**
Columbia / Dec '96 / Sony

MISFITS, THE
North, Alex *C*
CD **TCI 0609**
Tsunami / May '95 / Silva Screen

MISHIMA
Glass, Philip *C*
Opening / Morning 1934 / Grandmother and Kimitake / Temple of the golden pavillion / Osamu's theme / Kyoko's house / 1937 / St. Sebastian / November 25th / Ichigaya / 1957 / Award montage / Runaway horses / 1962 / Bodybuilding / Last day / F 104 / Epilogue from sun and steel / Closing
CD **7559791132**
Nonesuch / Nov '85 / Warner Music

MISS LIBERTY
1949 Broadway Cast
Berlin, Irving *C*
Blackton, Jay *Con*
Overture / What do I have to do to get my picture took / Most expensive statue in the world / Little fish in a big pond / Let's take an old fashioned walk / Homework / Paris wakes and smiles / Only for Americans / Just one way to say I love you / You can have him / Policemen's ball / Falling out of love can be fun / Give me your tired, your poor
CD **SK 48015**
Sony Broadway / Dec '91 / Sony

MISS SAIGON (Highlights)
1989 London Cast
Schonberg, Claude-Michel *C*
Maltby, Richard Jnr. & Alain Boublil *L*
CD **CASTCD 38**
First Night / Oct '93 / Pinnacle

MISS SAIGON (Music From The Show)
Criswell & Wayne
Schonberg, Claude-Michel *C*
CD **PWKS 4229**
Carlton / Nov '94 / Carlton

MISS SAIGON (Complete Symphonic Suite)
1989 London Cast
Schonberg, Claude-Michel *C*
2CD **KIMCD 1**
First Night / Jul '95 / Pinnacle

MISS SAIGON (Highlights From The Complete Recording)
Schonberg, Claude-Michel *C*
Overture/Backstage dreamland / Heat is on in Saigon / Movie in my mind / Why God why / Sun and moon / Last night of the world / I still believe / Thuy's death/You will not touch him / I'd give my life for you / Bui doi / Kim's nightmare / Now that I've seen her / American dream / Finale
CD **CASTCD 60**
First Night / Jun '97 / Pinnacle

MISS SAIGON/LES MISERABLES (Symphonic Suites)
Bournemouth Symphony Orchestra
Schonberg, Claude-Michel *C*
Overture / Heat is on in Saigon / Sun and moon / Why God why / Morning of the dragon / Last night of the world / If you want to die in bed / I'd give my life for you / Bio doi / Fall of Saigon / American dream / This is the hour / Prologue (Look down) / At the end of the day / I dreamed a dream / Lovely ladies / Who am I / Master of the house / Stars / Red and black / Heartful of love / Waltz of treachery / Do you hear the people sing / Bring him home / Red and black (reprise) / Attack / Drink with me / On my own / Heart full of love
CD **OCRCD 6049**
First Night / Apr '97 / Pinnacle

MISSION IMPOSSIBLE
Schifrin, Lalo *C*
CD **GNPD 8029**
GNP Crescendo / Nov '92 / ZYX

MISSION IMPOSSIBLE (Music From & Inspired By Mission Impossible)
CD **MUMCD 9603**
Mother / Jun '96 / PolyGram

MISSION IMPOSSIBLE
Elfman, Danny *C*
Kane, A. *Con*
CD **4545252**
Point Music / Jul '96 / PolyGram

MISSION IMPOSSIBLE
CD **MCLD 19320**
MCA / Aug '96 / BMG

MISSION, THE
London Philharmonic Orchestra
Morricone, Ennio *C*
On earth as it is in Heaven / Mission / Falls / River / Gabriel's oboe / Ave Maria Guarani / Te Deum Guarani / Brothers / Refusal / Carlotta / Asuncion / Vita nostra / Alone / Climb / Guarani / Remorse / Sword / Penance / Miserere
CD **CDV 2402**
Virgin / Oct '86 / EMI

MISSION, THE/THE LAST EMPEROR/ DANGEROUS LIAISONS
2CD **TPAK 24**
Virgin / Nov '92 / EMI

MISSISSIPPI BLUES
CD **FMC 246**
Milan / Jan '95 / Conifer/BMG / Silva Screen

MISSISSIPPI BURNING
Jones, Trevor *C*
Take my hand, precious Lord: *Jackson, Mahalia* / Murder in Mississippi (Part 1) / Some things are worth dying for / Murder in Mississippi (Part 2) / Anderson and Mrs Pell / When we all get to Heaven: *Choral* / Try Jesus: *Williams, Vesta* / Abduction / You live it, you breathe it, you marry it / Murder in Mississippi (Part 3) / Requiem for three young men / Burning cross / Justice in Mississippi / Walk by faith: *McBride, Lannie* / Walk on by faith: *McBride, Lannie*
CD **5511002**
Spectrum / Sep '95 / PolyGram

MO' MONEY
Mo' money groove: *Mo' Money Allstars* / Best things in life are free: *Vandross, Luther & Janet Jackson* / Ice cream dream: *M.C. Lyte* / Let's just run away: *M.C. Lyte* / I adore you: *Wheeler, Caron* / Get off my back: *Public Enemy & Flavor Flav* / Forever love: *Color Me Badd* / Money can't buy you love: *Tresvant, Ralph* / Let's get together (so groovy now): *Krush* / Joy: *Sounds Of Blackness* / New style: *Jam & Lewis* / Job ain't nuthin' but work: *Big Daddy Kane & Lo-Key* / My dear: *Mint Condition* / Brother Will: *Harlem Yacht Club*
CD **3610042**
A&M / Apr '95 / PolyGram

MOBY DICK
1992 London Cast
Kaye, Hereward *C*
Longden, Robert *L*
2CD **DICKCD 1**
First Night / Nov '92 / Pinnacle

MOBY DICK (Highlights)
1992 London Cast
Kaye, Hereward *C*
Longden, Robert *L*
CD **SCORECD 35**
First Night / '92 / Pinnacle

MODERNS, THE
Isham, Mark
Isham, Mark *C*
Les modernes / Cafe Selavy / Paris la nuit / Really the blues / Madame Valentin / Dada je suis / Parlez-moi d'amour / La valse moderne / Les peintres / Death of Irving Fagelman / Je ne veux pas de tes chocolats / Selavy
CD **CDV 2530**
Virgin / May '88 / EMI

MOLL FLANDERS
1993 London Cast
Stiles, George & Paul Leigh *C*
Let us tell a tale / Lullaby / Baby / Moll's prayer / Portrait song / Seduction / Her love made her rich / Masque / Mint / Life of a sailor / Lapdogs / Sailing to Virginia / Never look back / Bath promenade / Frail man, beware / Frail man, rejoice / Mr. Honest / Fits & starts / Ride / Hour is late / Mr. Honest (reprise) / Honest's death / Damn damn damn / Stolen / I shall work alone / Hang hang hang / Child of Newgate / Hour was late
CD **OCRCD 6036**
First Night / Dec '95 / Pinnacle

MOLL FLANDERS
Mancina, Mark *C*
CD **4524852**
Decca / May '97 / PolyGram

MOLLY MAGUIRES, THE
Mancini, Henry *C*
Molly Maguires / Molly's strike / Main title / Fiddle and fife / Work montage / Jamie and Mary (the hills of yesterday) / Room and board (theme from the Molly Maguires) / Hills of yesterday / Penny whistle jig / Sandwiches and tea / Trip to town / Molly's strike again / Brew with the boys / Suit for Grandpa / End
CD **BCD 3029**
Bay Cities / Mar '93 / Silva Screen

MON DERNEIR REVE SERA
Duhamel, Antoine *C*
CD **CH 517**
Milan / Jan '95 / Conifer/BMG / Silva Screen

MONEY TALKS
CD **7822189752**
RCA / Aug '97 / BMG

MONEY TRAIN
Train is coming: *Shaggy & Ken Boothe* / Top of the stairs: *Skee Lo* / Do you know: *Total* / Show you the way to go: *Men Of Vision* / Hiding place: *Assorted Phlavors & Patra* / Making love: *112* / Thrill I'm in: *Vandross, Luther* / Still not over you: *Lorenz, Trey* / It's alright: *Terri & Monica* / Oh baby: *4.0* / Merry go round: *UBU* / Hold on I'm coming: *Neville Brothers* / Money train suite: *Mancina, Mark*
CD **4815622**
Epic / Jan '96 / Sony

MONSIGNOR QUIXOTE SUITE
English Chamber Orchestra
Monsignor Quixote / Rocinante / Streets of Toboso / Twilight in La Mancha / Companeros / Windmills or giants / Let me feel temptation / Dulcinea / Adventures in the mind / In a certain village / Thoughts of a distant friend
CD **CDRBLP 1010**
Red Bus / Dec '85 / Total/BMG

MONTY PYTHON AND THE HOLY GRAIL
Monty Python
Jeunesse / Honours list / Big country / Homeward bound / God choir / Fanfare / Camelot song / Sunrise music / Magic finger / Sir Robin's song / In the shadows / Desperate moment / Knights of Ni / Circle of danger / Love theme / Magenta / Starlet in the starlight / Monk's chat / Promised land
CD **CASCD 1103**
Charisma / Nov '89 / EMI

MOONRAKER
Barry, John *C*
Main title / Space laser battle / Miss Goodhead meets Bond / Cable car and snake fight / Bond lured to pyramid / Flight into space / Bond arrives in Rio/Boat chase / Centrifuge and Corrine put down / Bond smells a rat / End title
CD **CZ 551**
Premier/EMI / Dec '95 / EMI

MORE
Pink Floyd
Pink Floyd *C*
Cirrus minor / Nile song / Crying song / Up the Khyber / Green is the colour / Cymbaline / Party sequence / Main theme / Ibiza bar / More blues / Quicksilver / Spanish piece / Dramatic theme
CD **CDP 7463862**
EMI / Mar '87 / EMI

MORITURI - THE SABOTEUR (& Music From In Harm's Way)
Goldsmith, Jerry *C*
CD **TCI 0604**
Tsunami / Jan '95 / Silva Screen

MORTAL KOMBAT
Taste of things to come: *Clinton, George* / Goodbye: *Gravity Kills* / Juke joint Jezebel: *KMFDM* / Unlearn: *Psykosonik* / Control: *Lords, Traci* / Halcyon + on + on: *Orbital* / Utah Saints take on the theme from Mortal Kombat: *Utah Saints* / Invisible: *G/Z/R* / Zero signal: *Fear Factory* / Burn: *Sister Machine Gun* / Blood and fire: *Type O Negative* / I reject: *Bile* / Twist the knife (slowly): *Napalm Death* / What u see/We all bleed red: *Mutha's Day Out* / Techno syndrome: *Immortals* / Goro Vs. art: *Clinton, George*
CD **8288972**
London / Oct '95 / PolyGram

MORTAL KOMBAT (Score)
Clinton, George *C*
Taste of things to come / Liu vs. Sub-Zero / It has begun / Garden / Goro vs. Art / Banquet / Liu vs. Katana / Liu's dream / Liu vs. Reptile / Stairway / Goro Goro / Kidnapped / Zooom / Johnny vs. Scorpion / Hand and shadow / Scorpion and Sub-Zero / Soul snatchin' / On the beach / Johnny Cage / Goro chase / Evening bells / Monks / Friends / Flawless victory / Farewell / Kids
CD **8287152**
London / Jan '96 / PolyGram

MORTAL KOMBAT - MORE MORTAL KOMBAT
CD **TVT 80302**
TVT / Nov '96 / Cargo / Greyhound
CD **0022672CIN**
Edel / Feb '97 / Pinnacle

MOSES THE LAWGIVER
Morricone, Ennio *C*
2CD **OST 113**
Milano Dischi / Jan '93 / Silva Screen

MOSQUITO COAST, THE
Jarre, Maurice *C*
Jarre, Maurice *Con*
Mosquito Coast / Goodbye America / Gimme soca: *Lee, Byron & The Dragonaires* / Up the river / Geronimo / Fat boy / Destruction / Storm / Allie's theme
CD **FCD 210052**
Fantasy / Jan '89 / Jazz Music / Pinnacle / Wellard

MOST HAPPY FELLA, THE
1956 Broadway Cast
Loesser, Frank *C*
Greene, Herbert *Con*
2CD **SK 48010**
Sony Broadway / Dec '91 / Sony

MOTHER NIGHT
Convertino, Michael *C*
CD **VSD 5780**
Varese Sarabande / Dec '96 / Pinnacle

MOUVEMENTS DU DESIR
Preisner, Zbigniew *C*
CD **SMC 35715**
Sergent M / Jun '97 / Discovery

MR. AND MRS. BRIDGE
Robbins, Richard *C*
Opening title / Boogie woogie: *Dorsey, Tommy Orchestra* / Painting class / String of pearls: *Miller, Glenn Orchestra* / Little brown jug: *Miller, Glenn Orchestra* / Rhumba jumps: *Miller, Glenn Orchestra* / Ruth's journey / Jeepers creepers: *Waters, Ethel & Edward Mallory* / Blues in the night: *Shore, Dinah* / Stormy weather: *Horne, Lena, Lou Bring & His Orchestra* / She was my best friend / Take me, I'm yours / Choo choo conga / Down on the farm / Locking up / Closing credits
CD **PD 83100**
Novus / Mar '91 / BMG

MR. CINDERS
1983 London Cast
Ellis, Vivian & Richard Myers *C*
Grey, Clifford & Greatrex Newman *L*
Tennis / Blue blood / True to two / I want the world to know / One man girl / On with the dance / At the ball / Spread a little happiness / Entr'acte / Eighteenth century dance / She's my lovely / Please Mr. Cinders / On the Amazon / Every little moment / I've got you, you've got me / Honeymoon for four / Finale
CD **CDTER 1069**
TER / Sep '83 / Koch

MR. DESTINY
Newman, David
Newman, David *C*
CD **VSD 5299**
Varese Sarabande / '90 / Pinnacle

MR. HOLLAND'S OPUS
CD **5295082**
PolyGram / Mar '96 / PolyGram

MR. HOLLAND'S OPUS (Score)
Seattle Symphony Orchestra/London Metropolitan Orchestra
Kamen, Michael *C*
Kamen, Michael *Con*
CD **4520652**
Decca / May '96 / PolyGram

MR. LUCKY
Mancini, Henry *C*
CD **21982**
Silva Screen / Feb '90 / Koch / Silva Screen

MR. PRESIDENT
1962 Broadway Cast
Berlin, Irving *C*
Blackton, Jay *Con*
CD **SK 48212**
Sony Broadway / Nov '92 / Sony

MR. RELIABLE
Flightless bird: *Judd, Philip* / Summer in the city: *Lovin' Spoonful* / Strange brew: *Cream* / Gimme some lovin': *Davis, Spencer Group* / Summer of '68: *Judd, Philip* / Something in the air: *Thunderclap Newman* / Nature: *Muttonbirds* / Summertime blues: *Who* / I'm a fan: *Judd, Philip* / Loved ones: *INXS* / Itchycoo park: *Small Faces* / I close my eyes and count to ten: *Springfield, Dusty* / Bloody circus: *Judd, Philip* / Only one woman: *Marbles* / For what it's worth: *Clouds* / Mongrels: *Judd, Philip* / Eloise: *Ryan, Barry* / With a little help from my friends: *Cocker, Joe* / To love somebody: *Bee Gees* / Bronto V: *Judd, Philip*
CD **5168202**
Polydor / Nov '96 / PolyGram

MR. SATURDAY NIGHT
Shaiman, Marc *C*
CD **124682**
Milan / Feb '94 / Conifer/BMG / Silva Screen

MRS. BROWN
Warbeck, Stephen *C*
CD **74321510722**
Milan / Aug '97 / Conifer/BMG / Silva Screen

MRS. DOUBTFIRE
Horner, James *C*
Mrs. Doubtfire / Divorce / My name is Elsa Immelman / Meeting Mrs. Doubtfire / Tea time with Mrs Sellner / Dinner is served / Daniel and the kids / Cable cars / Bridges restaurant / Show's over / Kids need you / Figaro/Papa's got a brand new bag
CD **07822110152**
Arista / Jan '94 / BMG

MRS. PARKER AND THE VICIOUS CIRCLE
Isham, Mark *C*
Into love / Algonquin bounce / Vanity blues / Observation / Smart set stomp / If you & I were one / Daydreams / Park bench / Two volume novel / Into love and out again / Benchley's blues / Ballad of Dorothy Parker / Lady's reward / Vicious blues / Well worn story / He didn't love back / Two wives' blues / Algonquin smart set / ...And out again
CD ______ **VSD 5471**
Varese Sarabande / Jan '95 / Pinnacle

MRS. WINTERBOURNE
Doyle, Patrick
Doyle, Patrick *C*
Walters, M. *Con*
CD ______ **VSD 5720**
Varese Sarabande / Jul '96 / Pinnacle

MUCH ADO ABOUT NOTHING
Doyle, Patrick *C*
Snell, David *Con*
Picnic / Overture / Sweetest lady / Conspirators / Masked ball / Prince woos hero / Star danced / Rich she shall be / Sigh no more ladies / Gulling of Benedick / It must be required / Gulling of Beatrice / Contempt farewell / Lady is disloyal / Hero's wedding / Take her back again / Die to live / You have killed a sweet lady / Choose your revenge / Pardon Goddess of the night / Did I not tell you / Hero revealed / Benedick the married man / Strike up pipers
CD ______ **MOODCD 30**
Epic / Sep '93 / Sony

MULHOLLAND FALLS
CD ______ **0022592CIN**
Edel / Jul '96 / Pinnacle

MUPPET CHRISTMAS CAROL, THE
Muppets
Overture / Scrooge / Room in your heart / Good king Wenceslas / One more sleep till Christmas / Marley and Marley / Christmas past / Chairman of the board / Fozziwigs party / When love is gone / It feels like Christmas / Christmas scat / Bless us all / Christmas future / Christmas morning / Thankful heart / Finale
CD ______ **7432112194-2**
Arista / Nov '93 / BMG

MUPPET MOVIE, THE
Muppets
Rainbow connection / Movin' right along / Never before never again / I hope that something better comes along / Can you picture that / I'm going to go back there someday / God bless America / Come back animal / Magic stone
CD ______ **74321182472**
BMG Kidz / Jan '94 / BMG

MUPPET TREASURE ISLAND
Muppets
Treasure Island / Shiver my timbers / Something better / Sailing for adventure / Cabin fever / Professional pirate / Boom shakalaka / Love led us here / Map / Captain Smollet / Land ho / Compass / Long John / Rescue / Honest brave and true / Love power / Love led us here
CD ______ **PRMCD 5**
Premier/EMI / May '96 / EMI

MURDER ON THE ORIENT EXPRESS/ DEATH ON THE NILE
Bennett, Richard Rodney/Nino Rota *C*
CD ______ **CNS 5007**
Cloud Nine / Aug '93 / Koch / Silva Screen

MURDER WAS THE CASE
Murder was the case: *Snoop Doggy Dogg* / Natural born killaz: *Dr. Dre & Ice Cube* / What would you do: *Dogg Pound* / 21 Jumpstreet: *Snoop Doggy Dogg & Tray Deee* / One more day: *Dogg, Nate* / Harvest for the world: *Jewell* / Who got some gangsta shit: *Snoop Doggy Dogg & Tha Dogg Pound* / Come when I call: *Boy, Danny* / U better recognise: *Sneed, Sam & Dr. Dre* / Come up to my room: *Jodeci & Tha Dogg Pound* / Woman to woman: *Jewell* / Dollars and sense: *D.J. Quik* / Eulogy: *Capone, Slip & CPO* / Horny: *Rezell, B* / East side, west side: *Young Soldierz*
CD ______ **IND 92484**
Interscope / Feb '97 / BMG

MURIEL'S WEDDING
Bridal dancing queen: *Wedding Band & Blazey Best* / Sugar baby love: *Rubettes* / We've only just begun: *Carpenters* / Lonely hearts: *Wedding Band* / Tide is high: *Blondie* / Waterloo: *Abba* / I go to Rio: *Allen, Peter* / Bean bag: *Wedding Band* / T-shirt & jeans: *Razorbrain* / I just don't know what to do with myself: *Springfield, Dusty* / I do I do I do I do I do: *Abba* / Happy together: *Turtles* / Muriel's wedding: *Wedding Band* / Dancing queen: *Abba*
CD ______ **5274932**
Polydor / May '95 / PolyGram

MUSIC BRUT-INSECT
Revell, Graeme *C*
CD ______ **BRUT 1CD**
The Grey Area / Jul '94 / RTM/Disc

MUSIC MAN, THE
1957 Broadway Cast
Willson, Meredith *C*
Overture/Rock island / Iowa stubborn / Ya got trouble / Piano lesson / Goodnight my someone / Seventy six trombones / Sincere / Sadder but wiser girl for me / Pick-a-little, take-a-little/Goodnight ladies / Marian the librarian / My white knight / Wells Fargo wagon / It's you / Shipoopi / Lida Rose/Will I ever tell you / Gary, Indiana / Till there was you / Finale
CD ______ **ZDM 7646632**
EMI Classics / Nov '93 / EMI

MUSIC MAN, THE
Original London Cast
Willson, Meredith *C*
Overture/Rock Island / Ya got trouble / Goodnight my someone / Seventy six trombones / Pick a little, talk a little / Goodnight ladies / Marian the librarian / Wells Fargo wagon / It's you / Lida Rose / Will I ever tell you / Gary, Indiana / Till there was you / Finale
CD ______ **12447**
Laserlight / Mar '97 / Target/BMG

MUSIC TEACHER (LE MAITRE DE MUSIQUE)
Cortigiani, vil razza dannata / Alcandro, lo confessa...non so d'onde viene / Waltz / Das lied von der erde / Symphony no. 4 in g major / Deh vieni alla finestra / Wohl denk ich oft / Du meine seele, du mein herz / Stille tranen / Sorgio, o padre / An die musik, d547 / Caro nome / Tanton duol / Ich bin der welt abhanden
CD ______ **PCOM 1109**
President / Nov '90 / Grapevine/PolyGram / President / Target/BMG

MUTANT
National Philharmonic Orchestra
Band, Richard *C*
CD ______ **MAF 7052D**
Intrada / Jan '93 / Koch / Silva Screen

MUTINY ON THE BOUNTY/TARAS BULBA
Mutiny on the bounty theme / Portsmouth harbour / Storm at sea / Girls and sailors / Mutiny / Follow me (Tahitian) / Leaving harbour / Arrival in Tahiti / Pitcairn island / Follow me (English) / Outrigger chase / Christian's death / Taras bulba (overture) / Birth of Andrei / Sleighride / Chase at night / No retreat / Ride to Dubno / Wishing star / Black plague / Taras' pledge / Battle of Dubno and finale
CD ______ **CDMGM 26**
MGM/EMI / Aug '90 / EMI

MY COUSIN VINNY
Edelman, Randy
Edelman, Randy *C*
CD ______ **VSD 5364**
Varese Sarabande / Apr '92 / Pinnacle

MY FAIR LADY
Film Cast
Loewe, Frederick *C*
Lerner, Alan Jay *L*
Previn, Andre *Con*
Overture / Why can't the English / Wouldn't it be loverly / I'm just an ordinary man / With a little bit of luck / Just you wait / Rain in Spain / I could have danced all night / Ascot gavotte / On the street where you live / You did it / Show me / Get me to the church on time / Hymn to him / Without you / I've grown accustomed to her face
CD ______ **CD 70000**
CBS / Dec '85 / Sony

MY FAIR LADY (Highlights - The Shows Collection)
Cast Recording
Loewe, Frederick *C*
Lerner, Alan Jay *L*
Why can't the English / Wouldn't it be loverly / With a little bit of luck / I'm just an ordinary man / Just you wait / Rain in Spain / I could have danced all night / On the street where you live / Show me / Get me to the church on time / Hymn to him / Without you / I've grown accustomed to her face
CD ______ **PWKS 4174**
Carlton / Oct '93 / Carlton

MY FAIR LADY
Cast Recording
Loewe, Frederick *C*
Lerner, Alan Jay *L*
2CD ______ **CDTER2 1211**
TER / Aug '95 / Koch

MY FAIR LADY (Includes Previously Unavailable Music)
Film Cast
Loewe, Frederick *C*
Lerner, Alan Jay *L*
Previn, Andre *Con*
CD ______ **SK 66711**
Sony Broadway / May '95 / Sony

MY FAIR LADY
Starlight Orchestra/Singers
Loewe, Frederick *C*
Lerner, Alan Jay *L*
My fair lady / I'm an ordinary man / On the street where you live / I could have danced all night / With a little bit of luck / You did it / Rain in Spain / Show me / I've grown accustomed to her face / Wouldn't it be loverly / Without you / Why can't the English / Just you wait / Get me to the church on time / Hymn to him
CD ______ **QED 102**
Tring / Nov '96 / Tring

MY FAIR LADY
CC Productions
Loewe, Frederick *C*
Lerner, Alan Jay *L*
Why can't be the English / Wouldn't it be loverly / With a little bit of luck / I'm an ordinary man / Just you wait / Rain in Spain / I could have danced all night / Ascot Gavotte / On the street where you live / Show me / Get me to the church on time / Hymn to him / I've grown accustomed to her face
CD ______ **QED 212**
Tring / Nov '96 / Tring

MY FAIR LADY
Studio Cast
Lerner, Alan Jay *C*
Loewe, Frederick *L*
Why can't the English / Wouldn't it be lovely / With a little bit of luck / I'm an ordinary man / Just you wait / Rain in Spain / I could have danced all night / Ascot Garotte / On the street where you live / Show me / Get me to the church on time / Hymn to him / I've grown accustomed to her face
CD ______ **85212**
CMC / May '97 / BMG

MY FAIR LADY (& Camelot/Gigi/ Brigadoon - Aspects Of Broadway Vol.6)
Orchestra Of The Americas
Loewe, Frederick *C*
Lerner, Alan Jay *L*
Freeman, Paul *Con*
I could have danced all night / On the street where you live / Wouldn't it be loverly / Show me / Embassy waltz / Get me to the church on time / I've grown accustomed to her face / With a little bit of luck / I wonder what the king is doing tonight / March to welcome Guenevere / Where are the simple joys of maidenhood / Camelot / If ever I would leave you / Fie on goodness / How to handle a woman / Follow me / Loved you once in silence / Entry of the knights / Lusty month of May / Guenevere / Night they invented champagne / Gigi / Waltz at Maxim's / I'm glad I'm not young anymore / Parisians / Say a prayer for me tonight / Thank Heaven for little girls / Gigi / Brigadoon / Down on MacConnachy Square / Heather on the hill / I'll go home with Bonnie Jean / Come to me, bend to me / Almost like being in love
CD ______ **SION 18306**
Sion / Jul '97 / Direct

MY FATHER'S GLORY/MY MOTHER'S CASTLE
Cosma, Vladimir *C*
Cosma, Vladimir *Con*
CD ______ **DRGCD 12604**
DRG / Jan '95 / Discovery / New Note/ Pinnacle

MY FATHER'S GLORY/MY MOTHER'S CASTLE
Cosma, Vladimir *C*
CD ______ **50050**
Silva Screen / Jan '93 / Koch / Silva Screen

MY HEROES HAVE ALWAYS BEEN COWBOYS
Horner, James *C*
CD ______ **23382**
Silva Screen / Jan '93 / Koch / Silva Screen

MY LIFE
Barry, John *C*
Barry, John *Con*
Main title / Childhood wish / Pictures from the past / I'm still in the game / My life - love theme / Old neighbourhood / I used to hide in there / You're a believer / My last trip home / Moments D-day / Child's play / Circus / Nice to meet you Brian / Rollercoaster / End titles
CD ______ **EK 57683**
Silva Screen / Jan '93 / Koch / Silva Screen

MY NAME IS NOBODY
Morricone, Ennio *C*
Morricone, Ennio *Con*
CD ______ **A 8918**
Alhambra / Feb '92 / Silva Screen

MY SO CALLED LIFE
Make it home: *Hatfield, Juliana* / Soda jerk: *Buffalo Tom* / Genetic: *Sonic Youth* / Petty core: *Further* / Drop a bomb: *Madder Rose* / Fountain & Fairfax: *Afghan Whigs* / South Carolina: *Archers Of Loaf* / Dawn can't decide: *Lemonheads* / Book song: *Frente* / Come see me tonight: *Johnston, Daniel* / My so called life theme
CD ______ **7567827212**
Warner Bros. / Jan '95 / Warner Music

MY STEPMOTHER IS AN ALIEN
Pump up the volume: *M/A/R/R/S* / Room to move: *Animotion* / Be the one: *Jackson, Jackie* / One good lover: *Siren* / Klystron / Not just another girl: *Neville, Ivan* / I like the world: *Cameo* / Hot wives: *Aykroyd, Dan* / Enjoy / Celeste
CD ______ **5511352**
Spectrum / Sep '95 / PolyGram

MYSTERIOUS ISLAND
London Symphony Orchestra
Herrmann, Bernard *C*
CD ______ **ACN 7017**
Cloud Nine / Mar '93 / Koch / Silva Screen

MYSTERY OF EDWIN DROOD
Broadway Cast
Holmes, Rupert *C*
There you are / Man could go quite mad / Two kinsmen / Moonfall / Wages of sin / Ceylon / Both sides of the coin / Perfect strangers / No good can come from bad / Never the luck / Name of love / Setting up the score / Off to the races / Don't quit while you're ahead / Garden path to hell / Out on a limerick / Jasper's confession / Puffer's confession / Writing on the wall
CD ______ **VSD 5597**
Varese Sarabande / Oct '95 / Pinnacle

MYSTERY TRAIN
Lurie, John *C*
Mystery train: *Presley, Elvis* / Mystery train: *Parker, Junior* / Blue moon: *Presley, Elvis* / Pain in my heart: *Redding, Otis* / Domino: *Orbison, Roy* / Memphis train: *Thomas, Rufus* / Get your money where you spend your time: *Bland, Bobby* / Soul finger: *Bar-Kays* / Long spell of cold day / Banjo blues / Chancer Street / Tuesday night in Memphis / To be alive and in a truck / Girls / Random Screamin' Jay / Italian walk / Lawyer can't take you to another planet / Drunk blues / Big harmonica escape / Dream Sun King / Chaucer Street
CD ______ **CH 509**
Milan / Jul '95 / Conifer/BMG / Silva Screen

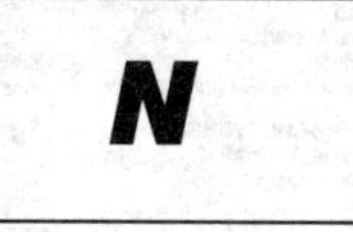

NAILS
Conti, Bill *C*
CD ______ **VSD 5384**
Varese Sarabande / Sep '92 / Pinnacle

NAKED GUN 2 1/2, THE (The Smell Of Fear)
Newborn, Ira *C*
CD ______ **VSD 5331**
Varese Sarabande / Aug '91 / Pinnacle

NAKED LUNCH, THE
London Philharmonic Orchestra
Shore, Howard/Ornette Coleman *C*
CD ______ **262732**
Milan / Feb '94 / Conifer/BMG / Silva Screen

NAME OF THE ROSE, THE
Horner, James *C*
Horner, James *Con*
Beta viscera / First recognition / Lesson / Kyrie / Scriptorium / Veri sancti spiritus / Confession / Flashbacks / Discovery / Betrayed / Epilogue / Name Of The Rose end title
CD ______ **30046**
Silva Screen / Jan '89 / Koch / Silva Screen

NAPOLEON (New Score For 1927 Silent Film)
Wren Orchestra
Davis, Carl *C*
Davis, Carl *Con*
Eagle of destiny / Teaching the Marseillaise / Reunion in Corsica / Pursued / Double storm / Drums of the 6th Regiment / Victor of Toulon / Gigue / Fan / Tambourin / Acting lesson / Ghosts / Peroration / Strange conductor in the sky
CD ______ **FILMCD 149**
Silva Screen / Mar '94 / Koch / Silva Screen

NATURAL BORN KILLERS
Waiting for the miracle: *Cohen, Leonard* / Shitlist: *L7* / Moon over Greene County: *Zanes, Dan* / Rock 'n' roll nigger: *Smith, Patti* / Sweet Jane: *Cowboy Junkies* / You belong to me: *Dylan, Bob* / Trembler: *Eddy, Duane* / Burn: *Nine Inch Nails* / Route 666: *Downey Jr, Robert & 'BB Tone' Brian Berdan* / Totally hot: *Ongala, Remmy & Orchestra* / Back in baby's arms: *Cline, Patsy* / Taboo: *Gabriel, Peter & Nusrat Fateh Ali Khan* / Sex is violent: *Jane's Addiction & Diamanda Galas* / History (repeats itself): *A.O.S.* / Something I can never have: *Nine Inch Nails* / I will take you home: *Means, Russel* / Drums a go go: *Hollywood Persuaders* / Hungry ants: *Adamson, Barry* / Day the niggaz took over: *Dr. Dre* / Born bad: *Lewis, Juliette* / Fall of the rebel angels: *Cervetti, Sergio* / Forkboy: *Lard* / Batonga in Batongaville: *Budapest Philharmonic Orchestra* / Warm place: *Nine Inch Nails* / Allah, Mohammed, Char, Yarr: *Khan, Nusrat Fateh Ali & Party* / Future: *Cohen, Leonard* / What would you do: *Dogg Pound*
CD ______ **6544924602**
Interscope/East West / Sep '94 / Warner Music

NATURAL, THE
Newman, Randy
Newman, Randy *C*
CD ______ **9251162**
Silva Screen / Feb '90 / Koch / Silva Screen

NATURE: GREAT AFRICAN MOMENTS
Whalen, Michael
Whalen, Michael *C*
Elephants / Night on the Serengeti / Fire and ice / Killer instinct / Rain the rain / Lost on the plains / After the rain / Cheetah hunt / Jacana and the fish eagle / Hyena and the melons / Chimps / Journey of the

thousands / Mountain gorillas / Wild pups / Meerkats / Flamingoes / African sunset / Vultures / Slowpake club / Cycles of life
CD ND 66066
Narada / Apr '94 / ADA / New Note/Pinnacle

NATURE: PHANTOM OF THE FOREST
Whalen, Michael
Whalen, Michael *C*
Spirits / Sea of trees / Hawk appears / Killing to survive / Wood cock / Open spaces / New forests / Building a nest / Feather / Life in the nest / Catherdral of the woods / Sunrise dance / Night creatures / Forest edge / Brink of extinction / Quite beauty / Winter rain / Predators of the predators / Woodland lullaby / Soliloquy
CD ND 66007
Narada / Apr '94 / ADA / New Note/Pinnacle

NAVIGATOR, THE
Tabrizi, Davood A. *C*
CD CDSBL 12596
DRG / Apr '96 / Discovery / New Note/ Pinnacle

NEAR DARK
Tangerine Dream
Tangerine Dream *C*
Caleb's blues / Pick up at high noon / Rain in the third house / Bus station / Good times / She's my sister / Mae comes back / Father and son / Severin dies / Flight at dawn / Mae's transformation
CD FILMCD 026
Silva Screen / Jun '90 / Koch / Silva Screen

NEEDFUL THINGS
Doyle, Patrick *C*
Snell, David *Con*
CD VSD 5438
Varese Sarabande / Jul '93 / Pinnacle

NEL NOME DEL PADRE/IL TRENO PER ISTANBUL (In The Name Of The Father/ Train To Istanbul)
Piovani, Nicola *C*
CD PRCD 125
Preamble / Apr '96 / Silva Screen

NENETTE ET BONI
Tindersticks
Ma souer / La passerelle / Les gateaux / Camions / Nenette est la / Petites chiennes / Nosterfrau / Petites gouttes d'eau / Les cannes a peche / La mort de Felix / Nenette s'en va / Les bebes / Rumba
CD 5243002
This Way Up / Oct '96 / PolyGram / SRD

NET, THE
Isham, Mark
Isham, Mark *C*
CD VSD 5662
Varese Sarabande / Oct '95 / Pinnacle

NEVADA SMITH
Newman, Alfred *C*
CD TSU 0113
Tsunami / Jan '95 / Silva Screen

NEVER SAY NEVER AGAIN
Legrand, Michel *C*
Legrand, Michel *Con*
Bond back in action / Never say never again: *Hall, Lani* / Prologue - enter 007 / Fatima Bush/A very bad lady / Dinner with 007 / Bahama Island / Bond smells a rat/ Nurse Blush / Plunder of a nuclear missile / Big band death of Jack Petachi / Bond and Domino / Fight to death with the tiger sharks / Une Chanson d'amour / Video duel/Victory / Nuclear nightmare / Tango to the death / Bond returns home / Death of Nicole / Chase her / Felix and James exit / Jealousy / Largo's waltz / Bond to the rescue / Big escape / Tears of Allah / Underwater cave / Fight to the death / Bond in retirement / End title - Never say never again: *Hall, Lani*
CD FILMCD 145
Silva Screen / Apr '95 / Koch / Silva Screen

NEVER-ENDING STORY III
CD 4509983092
WEA / Dec '94 / Warner Music

NEW JACK CITY
New jack hustler: *Ice-T* / I'm dreaming: *Williams, Christopher* / I wanna sex you up: *Color Me Badd* / I'm still waiting: *Gill, Johnny* / (There you go) tellin' me no again: *Sweat, Keith* / Facts of life: *Madden, Danny* / For the love of money/Living for the city (medley): *Troop/Levert* / Lyrics 2 the rhythm: *Essence* / Get it together (black is a force): *Black Is A Force* / In the dust: *2 Live Crew* / New jack city: *Guy*
CD 7599244092
Giant / Apr '91 / BMG

NEW JERSEY DRIVE VOL.1
CD TBCD 1114
Tommy Boy / Mar '95 / RTM/Disc

NEW JERSEY DRIVE VOL.2
CD TBCD 1130
Tommy Boy / Apr '95 / RTM/Disc

NEW ORLEANS
Holiday, Billie & Louis Armstrong
Free as a bird / When the saints go marching in / Westend blues / Do you know what it means to miss New Orleans / Brahms lullaby / Tiger rag / Buddy Bolden's blues / Basin Street blues / Raymond Street blues / Melenberg joys / Where the blues was born in New Orleans / Farewell to Storyville / Beale Street stomp / Dippermouth blues / Shimme sha wobble / Ballin' the Jack / King Porter stomp / Mahogany Hall stomp / Endie / Blues are brewin'
CD GOJCD 1025
Giants Of Jazz / Jan '95 / Cadillac / Jazz Music / Target/BMG

NEW YORK ROCK
Cast Recording
Ono, Yoko *C*
It happened / I'll always be with you / Speck of dust / Midsummer New York / What a bastard the world is / Loneliness / Give me something / Light on the other side / Tomorrow may never come / Don't be scared / Growing pains / Warzone / Never say goodbye / O'sanity / I want my love to rest tonight / I felt like smashing my face in a clear glass window / Now or never / We're all water / Yes, I'm your angel / Where do we go from here / Sleepless night / No, no, no / Even when you're far away / Hell in paradise / Toyboat / Story of an oak tree / Goodbye sadness
CD CDP 8298432
Capitol / Aug '95 / EMI

NEW YORK STORIES
Coppola, Carmine *C*
CD 9608572
Elektra / Nov '89 / Warner Music

NEW YORK, NEW YORK
You brought a new kind of love to me / Flip the dip / VJ Stomp / Opus No. 1 / Once in a while / You are my lucky star / Game over / It's a wonderful world / Man I love / Hazoy / Just you, just me / There goes the ball game / Blue moon / Don't be that way / Happy endings / But the world goes 'round / New York, New York / Honeysuckle rose / Once again right away / Bobby's dream / Finale
CD ACD 373
Milan / Jan '89 / Conifer/BMG / Silva Screen

NEW YORK, NEW YORK (A Broadway Extravaganza)
New York City Gay Men's Chorus
CD CDD 594
Silva Screen / Jul '92 / Koch / Silva Screen

NEWSIES
Menken, Alan *C*
CD DIS 60832
Silva Screen / Jan '93 / Koch / Silva Screen

NEXT GENERATIONS
2CD EDL 27202
Edel / Jul '97 / Pinnacle

NEXT OF KIN
Brother to brother / Hillbilly heart / Paralysed / My sweet baby's gone / Brothers / On a Spanish Highway (revised) / Hey backwoods / Straight and narrow / Yard sale / Pyramids of cans / Wailing sax
CD 4662402
Epic / May '90 / Sony

NICK AND NORA
1991 Broadway Cast
Strouse, Charles *C*
Maltby, Richard Jr. *L*
CD CDTER 1191
TER / Sep '92 / Koch

NICK OF TIME
Rubinstein, Arthur *C*
Rubinstein, Arthur *Con*
CD 74321348642
Milan / Mar '96 / Conifer/BMG / Silva Screen

NIE WIEDER SCHLAFEN
Dikker, Loek *C*
CD 873143
Milan / Jan '95 / Conifer/BMG / Silva Screen

NIGHT AND THE CITY
Great pretender: *Mercury, Freddie* / Cool jerk: *Capitols* / Money (That's what I want): *Walker, Junior & The All Stars* / You really got a hold on me: *Robinson, Smokey & The Miracles* / Wooly bully: *Sam The Sham & The Pharaohs* / Love doesn't matter: *Saulsberry, Rodney* / Deep water: *Champlin, Bill* / Forgiveness: *Davis, Lynn* / Never gonna stop: *Cole, Gardner* / Boxing gym: *Howard, James Newton*
CD CDPCSD 126
EMI / Nov '92 / EMI

NIGHT CROSSING
National Philharmonic Orchestra
Goldsmith, Jerry *C*
Goldsmith, Jerry *Con*
Main title / All in vain / Picnic / Plans / Success / First flight / Patches / Tomorrow we go / No time to wait / Final flight / In the West
CD RVF 6004D
Intrada / Jan '89 / Koch / Silva Screen

NIGHT OF THE GENERALS
Jarre, Maurice *C*
Jarre, Maurice *Con*
CD FMT 8004D
Intrada / Mar '92 / Koch / Silva Screen

NIGHT ON EARTH
Waits, Tom
Waits, Tom *C*
CD 5109292
Island / Mar '92 / PolyGram

NIGHTINGALE
1982 London Cast
Strouse, Charles *C*
Prologue / Perfect harmony / Why am I so happy / Take us to the forest / Who are these people / Never speak directly to an Emperor / Nightingale / Emperor is a man / I was lost / Entr'acte / Charming / Singer must be free / Mechanical bird / Please don't make me hear that song again / Rivers cannot flow upwards / Death duet / We are China / Finale
2CD CDTER2 1031
TER / Aug '95 / Koch

NIGHTMARE BEFORE CHRISTMAS
Elfman, Danny *C*
CD DIS 608557
Silva Screen / Jan '95 / Koch / Silva Screen

NIGHTMARE CAFE
Robinson, J. Peter *C*
CD VSD 5363
Varese Sarabande / Jul '92 / Pinnacle

NIGHTMARE ON ELM STREET - THE BEST OF NIGHTMARE ON ELM STREET (Freddy's Favourites)
Young, Christopher *C*
CD VSD 5427
Varese Sarabande / Nov '93 / Pinnacle

NIGHTMARE ON ELM STREET I & II
CD VCD 47255
Varese Sarabande / Jan '89 / Pinnacle

NIGHTMARE ON ELM STREET III (Dream Warriors)
Badalamenti, Angelo
Badalamenti, Angelo *C*
CD VCD 47293
Varese Sarabande / Jan '89 / Pinnacle

NIGHTMARE ON ELM STREET IV (The Dream Master/Score)
Safan, Craig
Safan, Craig *C*
CD VCD 5203
Varese Sarabande / Jan '89 / Pinnacle

NIGHTMARE ON ELM STREET V (Dream Child/Score)
Ferguson, Jay
Ferguson, Jay *C*
CD VSD 5238
Varese Sarabande / Oct '89 / Pinnacle

NIGHTMARE ON ELM STREET VI (Freddy's Dead: The Final Nightmare/ Score)
May, Brian *C*
CD VSD 5333
Varese Sarabande / Sep '91 / Pinnacle

NIKITA
Serra, Eric
Serra, Eric *C*
Rico's gang suicide / Playing on saucepans / As cold as ice / Sentence / Paradise / Failed escape / Leaning time / Smile / Fancy face / First night out / Tpokmop / Last time I kiss you / Free side / I am on duty / Josephine and the big dealer / Mission in Venice / Fall / Let's welcome Victor / Last mission / We will miss you / Dark side of time
CD CDVMM 2
Virgin / Nov '90 / EMI

NINE
1992 London Cast
Yeston, Maury *C*
Higgs, Timothy *Con*
2CD CDTER 1193
TER / Oct '92 / Koch

NINE
Australian Cast
Yeston, Maury *C*
CD CDTER 1190
TER / May '93 / Koch

NINE AND A HALF WEEKS
I do what I do: *Taylor, John* / Best is yet to come: *Luba* / Slave to love: *Ferry, Bryan* / Black on black: *Dalbello* / Eurasian eyes: *Hart, Corey* / You can leave your hat on: *Cocker, Joe* / Bread and butter: *Devo* / This city never sleeps: *Eurythmics* / Cannes: *Copeland, Stewart* / Let it go: *Luba*
CD CDEST 2003
EMI / Sep '94 / EMI

NO BANANAS
Yes we have no banans / Boom / Who's in love / Run rabbit run / Mad about the boy / Cheek to cheek / Down by the seaside / Love for sale / Lambeth walk / One I love belongs to somebody else / Who's sorry now / Jingle bells / Falling in love again / All over the place / S'later / Jeepers creepers / Lord and Lady Whoozis / Panic / Blue skies around the corner / Tiggerty Boo / Swing out
CD CDVIP 176
Virgin VIP / Apr '97 / EMI

NO MAN'S LAND
Poledouris, Basil *C*
Jewel movement / Medusa's refrain / Spark from the infinite / Return of the dream collector / Jaipur local / Blue anthem
CD VCD 47352
Varese Sarabande / Jan '89 / Pinnacle

NO NO NANETTE
London Cast
Youmans, Vincent *C*
Harbach, Otto & Irving Caesar *L*
CD SMK 66173
Sony West End / Jul '94 / Sony

NO RETREAT, NO SURRENDER
Gilreath, Paul *C*
Gilreath, Paul *Con*
CD FILMCD 150
Silva Screen / Mar '94 / Koch / Silva Screen

NO STRINGS
Broadway Cast
Rodgers, Richard *C*
CD ZDM 7646942
EMI Classics / Apr '93 / EMI

NO WAY OUT/THE YEAR OF LIVING DANGEROUSLY
Jarre, Maurice *C*
No way out / National security / Cover up / In the Pentagon / We can interface / Susan
CD CDTER 1149
TER / Feb '88 / Koch

NOBLE HOUSE
Chihara, Paul *C*
CD VCD 47360
Varese Sarabande / Jan '89 / Pinnacle

NOBODY'S FOOL
CD 249032
Milan / Aug '95 / Conifer/BMG / Silva Screen

NOEL AND GERTIE
1986 London Cast
Coward, Sir Noel *C*
Overture / Some day I'll find you / Mrs. Worthington / Touring days / Parisian pierrot / Dance little lady / Play orchestra play / We were dancing / Man about town / I travel alone / Sail away / Why must the show go on / Come the wild, wild weather / I'll remember her / I'll see you again / Curtain music
CD CDTER 1117
TER / Aug '95 / Koch

NORMA JEAN & MARILYN
Young, Christopher *C*
Anthony, P. *Con*
CD MAF 7070
Intrada / Oct '96 / Koch / Silva Screen

NORTH AND SOUTH/THE RIGHT STUFF
London Symphony Orchestra
Conti, Bill *C*
Conti, Bill *Con*
CD VCD 47250
Varese Sarabande / Jan '89 / Pinnacle

NORTH BY NORTHWEST
London Studio Symphony Orchestra
Herrmann, Bernard *C*
CD VCD 47205
Varese Sarabande / '90 / Pinnacle

NORTH BY NORTHWEST
Herrmann, Bernard *C*
Herrmann, Bernard *Con*
Overture / Streets / It's a most unusual day / Kidnapped / Door / Cheers / Wild ride / Car crash / Return / Two dollars / Rosalie / In the still of the night / Elevator / UN / Information desk / Knife / Fashion show / Interlude / Detectives / Conversation piece / Duo / Station / Phone booth / Farewell / Crash / Hotel lobby / Reunion / Goodbye / Question / Pad and pencil / Auction / Police / Airport / Cafeteria / Shooting / Forest / Flight / Ledge / House / Balcony / Match box / Message / TV / Airplane / Gates / Stone faces / Ridge / On the rocks / Cliff / Finale
CD CDODEON 6
Premier/EMI / Feb '96 / EMI

NORTHERN EXPOSURE
Northern Exposure: *Schwartz, David* / Jolie Louise: *Lanois, Daniel* / Hip hug-her: *Booker T & The MG's* / At last: *James, Etta* / Everybody be yourself: *Chic Street Man* / Alaskan nights: *Schwartz, David* / Don Quichotte: *Magazine 60* / When I grow too old to dream: *Cole, Nat 'King'* / Emabhaceni: *Makeba, Miriam* / Gimme three steps: *Lynyrd Skynyrd* / Bailero: *Von Stade, Frederica & The Royal Philharmonic Orchestra* / Medley: Funeral in my brain: *Schwartz, David*
CD MCD 10685
MCA / Mar '93 / BMG

NORTHERN EXPOSURE - MORE MUSIC FROM NORTHERN EXPOSURE
Ojibway square dance (love song) / Theme from Northern Exposure / Stir it up / Mambo baby / Someone loves you / Ladder / If you take me back / Un marriage casse (A broken marriage) / There I go again / Lay my love / Wrap your troubles in dreams (and dream your troubles away) / Mooseburger stomp / I may want a man
CD MCLD 19350
MCA / Oct '96 / BMG

NOSFERATU (A Symphony In Horror)
Brandenburg Philharmonic Orchestra
Erdmann, Hans *C*
Anderson, Gillian *Con*
CD 9026681432
RCA Victor / Nov '95 / BMG

NOSTROMO
Morricone, Ennio *C*
CD 5336582
Polydor / Feb '97 / PolyGram

NOTHING BUT TROUBLE
Kamen, Michael *C*
CD 9264912
Silva Screen / Jan '93 / Koch / Silva Screen

NOTHING TO LOSE
Nothin' to lose: *Naughty By Nature* / Not tonight: *Lil' Kim & Left Eye/Da Brat/Missy Elliot/Angie Martinez* / C U when you get there: *Coolio & 40 Thevz* / Put the money in it: *Dat Nigga Daz & Soopafly* / Thug paradise: *Capone & Noreaga/Tragedy* / Way 2 saucy: *Mac & AK/Mac Mall* / Get down with me: *Amari & Buckshot* / Poppin' that fly: *Jones, 'Oran' Juice & Stu Large/Camp Lo* / QuRoute: *Quad City DJ'S* / Hit 'em up: *Master P & Tru/Mercedez* / OuEverlasting: *Outkast* / 9lna magazine: *911 & Queen Pen* / It's alright: *Queen Latifah* / What's going on: *Black Ceasar* / Stesa I: *Stetsasonic* / Crazy maze: *Des'ree*
CD ______ **TBCD 1169**
Tommy Boy / Jul '97 / RTM/Disc

N'OUBLIE PAS QUE TU VAS MOURIR
Cale, John
Cale, John *C*
Cale, John *L*
CD ______ **TWI 1028**
Les Disques Du Crepuscule / Mar '96 / Discovery

NOUVELLE VAGUE
Eicher, Manfred *C*
2CD ______ **4498912**
ECM / Jun '97 / New Note/Pinnacle

NOW AND THEN
Eidelman, Cliff *C*
CD ______ **VSD 5675**
Varese Sarabande / Jun '96 / Pinnacle

NOW AND THEN
Sugar sugar: *Archies* / Knock three times: *Orlando, Tony & Dawn* / I want you back: *Jackson 5* / Signed, sealed, delivered I'm yours: *Wonder, Stevie* / Band of gold: *Payne, Freda* / Daydream beliver: *Monkees* / No matter what: *Badfinger* / Hitchin' a ride: *Vanity Fare* / All right now: *Free* / I'm gonna make you love me: *Ross, Diana* / I'll be there: *Jackson 5* / Now and then: *Hoffs, Susanna*
2CD ______ **4816062**
Columbia / Jun '96 / Sony

NOWHERE
Freak out: *311* / How can you be sure: *Radiohead* / In the city: *Elastica* / Dicknail: *Hole* / Life is sweet: *Chemical Brothers* / Daydreaming: *Massive Attack* / Killing time: *Coco & The Bean* / Intravenous: *Catherine Wheel* / Nowhere: *Curve* / I have the moon: *Lush* / Flippin' the bird: *Ruby* / Thursday treatments: *James* / Generation wrekked: *Chuck D* / Kiddie grinder: *Manson, Marilyn* / Trash: *Suede*
CD ______ **5345222**
Mercury / Apr '97 / PolyGram

NUNS ON THE RUN
Race: *Yello* / Comin' to you: *Hidden Faces* / Roll with it: *Winwood, Steve* / Moon on ice: *Yello* / Sacred heart: *Shakespears Sister* / On the run: *Yello* / Hawaiian chance: *Yello* / Blow away: *Harrison, George* / Tied up: *Yello* / Dr. Van Steiner: *Yello* / Gold rush: *Yello* / Nun's medley: *Hidden Faces*
CD ______ **8460432**
Mercury / Jun '90 / PolyGram

NUN'S STORY, THE
Waxman, Franz *C*
CD ______ **STZ 114**
Stanyan / Jan '94 / Silva Screen

NUNSENSE I
1986 Off-Broadway Cast
Goggin, Dan *C*
Nunsense is habit forming / Difficult transition / Benedicte/Biggest ain't best: *Hubert & Leo* / Playing second fiddle: *Anne, Robert* / So you want to be a Nun: *Amnesia, Mary* / Turn up the spotlight: *Cardelia, Mary* / Lilacs bring back memories / Tackle that temptation with a time-step: *Hubert & Cast* / Growing up Catholic: *Anne, Robert & Cast* / Drive-in: *St. Andrew's Sister* / I could've gone to Nashville: *Amnesia, Mary* / Holier than thou: *Hubert & Cast* / Finale
CD ______ **CDSBL 12589**
DRG / Apr '87 / Discovery / New Note/Pinnacle

NUNSENSE II (The Second Coming)
Cast Recording
Goggin, Dan *C*
Jubilate deo/Nunsense - The magic word / Winning is just the beginning / Prima ballerina / Biggest still ain't the best / I've got pizazz / Country nun / Look Ma, I made it / Padre polka / Classic Queens / Hat and cane song / Angeline / We're the nuns to come to / What would Elvis do / Yes we can / I am here to stay / No one cared like you / There's only one way to end your prayers / Nunsense - The magic word (Reprise)
CD ______ **DRGCD 12608**
DRG / Jun '93 / Discovery / New Note/Pinnacle

NUTTY PROFESSOR, THE
Touch me, tease me: *Case & Foxy Brown* / I like: *Jordan, Montell & Slick Rick* / My crew can't go for that: *Trigger Tha Gambler* / Ain't nobody: *Monica & Naughty By Nature* / Pillow: *Richie Rich* / Last night: *Az Yet* / Come around: *Dos Of Soul* / We want yo hands up: *Warren G.* / Ain't no N-G-A: *Jay Z & Foxy Brown* / Breaker 1, breaker 2: *Def Squad* / Doin' it again: *LL Cool J* / Nasty immigrants: *12 O'Clock* / Love you down: *Da Bassment*
CD ______ **5319112**
Def Jam / Oct '96 / PolyGram

O LUCKY MAN
Price, Alan
O Lucky man / Poor people / Sell sell / Pastoral / Arrival / Look over your shoulder / Justice / My home town / Changes
CD ______ **9362461372**
Warner Bros. / Oct '96 / Warner Music

O PIONEERS
Broughton, Bruce *C*
Broughton, Bruce *Con*
CD ______ **MAF 7023D**
Intrada / Apr '92 / Koch / Silva Screen

OASIS
Tangerine Dream
Flashflood / Zion / Reflections / Cliff dwellers / Waterborne / Cedar breaks / Summer storm / Hopi mesa heart
CD ______ **TD 1007CD**
TDI / Jun '97 / Pinnacle

OBSCURED BY CLOUDS (La Vallee)
Pink Floyd
Pink Floyd *C*
Obscured by clouds / When you're in / Burning bridges / Gold it's in the... / Wot's... uh, the deal / Mudmen / Childhood's end / Free four / Stay / Absolutely curtains
CD ______ **CDP 7463852**
EMI / Mar '87 / EMI

OBSESSION (Includes Welles Raises Kane/The Devil and Daniel Webster)
National Philharmonic Orchestra
Herrmann, Bernard *C*
Herrmann, Bernard *Con*
CD ______ **UKCD 2065**
Unicorn-Kanchana / Nov '94 / Harmonia Mundi

OCCHIO ALLA PENNA
Morricone, Ennio *C*
CD ______ **A 8916**
Alhambra / Jan '92 / Silva Screen

OCTOPUS/ALL ABOUT THE MAFIA
Morricone, Ennio *C*
CD ______ **EDL 25492**
Edel / Jan '93 / Pinnacle

ODNA
Katchur, Svetlana & Vladimir Kazatchouk/Rundfunk Sinfonie
Shostakovich, Dmitry *C*
Jurowski, Michail *Con*
CD ______ **10562**
Capriccio / Sep '96 / Target/BMG

OF THEE I SING
Kaufman, George S. & Morrie Ryskind *C*
CD ______ **ZDM 5650252**
EMI Classics / Feb '94 / EMI

OFF LIMITS (aka Saigon)
Howard, James Newton *C*
CD ______ **VCD 70445**
Varese Sarabande / Jan '89 / Pinnacle

OFF THE WALL
1991 Cast
Stephens, Geoff *C*
Black, Don *L*
Off the wall / Bums on seats / He looks fine / Good music won't always be here / Spin of the wheel / Jazz mad / You know who I mean / Rosie Miller / I won't be doing that tonight / Life goes on / Only the dreamer can change the dream
CD ______ **OCRCD 6051**
First Night / Apr '97 / Pinnacle

OFFICER AND A GENTLEMAN, AN
Officer and a gentleman: *Ritenour, Lee* / Up where we belong: *Cocker, Joe & Jennifer Warnes* / Hungry for your love: *Morrison, Van* / Tush: *ZZ Top* / Treat me right: *Benatar, Pat* / Be real: *Sir Douglas Quintet* / Tunnel of love: *Dire Straits*
CD ______ **IMCD 77**
Island / Jan '93 / PolyGram

OH, KAY
Upshaw, Dawn & Orchestra Of St. Luke's
Gershwin, George *C*
Gershwin, Ira *L*
Stern, Eric *Con*
CD ______ **7559793612**
Nonesuch / May '95 / Warner Music

OIL CITY SYMPHONY
Broadway Cast
Ohio afternoon / Beaver ball / Dear Miss Reaves / Old Kentucky rock 'n' roll home / Bus ride / Beehive polka / In a gaddada vida / Baby it's cold outside / Exodus song / Getting acquainted / End of the world / Dizzy fingers
CD ______ **CDSBL 12594**
DRG / Jan '89 / Discovery / New Note/Pinnacle

OKLAHOMA
Film Cast
Rodgers, Richard *C*
Hammerstein II, Oscar *L*
Blackton, Jay *Con*
Overture / Oh what a beautiful morning / Surrey with the fringe on top / Kansas City / I can't say no / Many a new day / People will say we're in love / Poor Jud is dead / Out of my dreams / Farmer and the cowman / All er nothin' / Oklahoma
CD ______ **ZDM 7646912**
EMI Classics / Apr '93 / EMI

OKLAHOMA
1943 Broadway Cast
Rodgers, Richard *C*
Hammerstein II, Oscar *L*
Oh what a beautiful morning / Surrey with the fringe on top / Out of my dreams / Kansas City / I can't say no / People will say we're in love / Farmer dance / Poor Jud is dead / It's a scandal, it's an outrage / Many a new day / All er nothin' / Oklahoma
CD ______ **MCLD 19026**
MCA / Apr '92 / BMG

OKLAHOMA
1980 London Cast
Rodgers, Richard *C*
Hammerstein II, Oscar *L*
CD ______ **CDTER 1208**
TER / Mar '94 / Koch

OKLAHOMA
1980 London Cast
Rodgers, Richard *C*
Hammerstein II, Oscar *L*
Overture / OH what a beautiful morning / Surrey with the fringe on top / Kansas City / I cain't say no / Many a new day / People will say we're in love / Pore Jud is daid / Out of my dreams / Farmer and the cowman / All er nothin' / Oaklahoma
CD ______ **SHOWCD 001**
Showtime / Feb '95 / Disc / THE

OKLAHOMA
1952 Broadway Cast
Rodgers, Richard *C*
Hammerstein II, Oscar *L*
Engel, Lehman *Con*
CD ______ **SK 53326**
Sony Broadway / Nov '93 / Sony

OKLAHOMA
CC Productions
Rodgers, Richard *C*
Hammerstein II, Oscar *L*
Oh what a beautiful morning / Surrey with a fringe on top / Kansas City / I can't say no / Many a new day / People will say we're in love / Pore Jud is daid / Out of my dreams / All er nothin' / Oklahoma / Finale
CD ______ **QED 216**
Tring / Nov '96 / Tring

OKLAHOMA
Studio Cast
Rodgers, Richard *C*
Hammerstein II, Oscar *L*
Oh what a beautiful mornin' / Surrey with the fringe on top / Kansas city / I can't say no / Many a new day / People will say we're in love / Pore jud is daid / Out of my dreams / All or nothin' / Oklahoma / Finale
CD ______ **88112**
CMC / May '97 / BMG

OKLAHOMA/SHOW BOAT
Broadway Cast
Overture / Ol man river / You are love / Make believe / Bill / Can't help lovin' dat man / Why do I love you / Lonesome road / It still suits me / Oh, what a beautiful morning / Surrey with a fringe on top / Kansas City / I cain't say no / Many a new day / People will say we're in love / Pore Jud is daid / Out of my dreams / All er nothin' / Oklahoma / Finale
CD ______ **CDAJA 5198**
Living Era / May '96 / Select

OLD GRINGO
Holdridge, Lee *C*
Ride to the hacienda / Battle / Harriet's theme / Bitter's last ride / Mirrors / Nightime / Bell tower / Sigh / Battle (resolution) / Bitter's destiny / Finale
CD ______ **GNPD 8017**
GNP Crescendo / Nov '89 / ZYX

OLD MAN AND THE SEA, THE
Tiomkin, Dimitri *C*
CD ______ **VSD 5232**
Varese Sarabande / Feb '90 / Pinnacle

OLD MAN AND THE SEA, THE (TV Version)
Broughton, Bruce *C*
CD ______ **RVF 6008D**
Intrada / Jul '93 / Koch / Silva Screen

OLIVER
1963 Broadway Cast
Bart, Lionel *C*
Food, glorious food / Oliver / I shall scream / Boy for sale / Where is love / Consider yourself / You've got to pick a pocket or two / It's a fine life / I'd do anything / Be back soon / Oom-pah-pah / My name / As long as he needs me / Who will buy / Reviewing the situation / As long as he needs me (reprise) / Reviewing the situation (reprise) / Finale
CD ______ **GD 84113**
RCA Victor / Oct '89 / BMG

OLIVER
1960 London Cast
Bart, Lionel *C*
CD ______ **8205902**
London / Jan '95 / PolyGram

OLIVER
Film Cast
Bart, Lionel *C*
Overture / Food glorious food / Boy for sale / Where is love / You've got to pick a pocket or two / Consider yourself / I'd do anything / Be back soon / As long as he needs me / Who will buy / It's a fine life / Reviewing the situation / Oom pah pah / Finale
CD ______ **ND 90311**
RCA / Mar '89 / BMG

OLIVER (Highlights - The Shows Collection)
1994 Studio Cast
Bart, Lionel *C*
CD ______ **PWKS 4194**
Carlton / Mar '94 / Carlton

OLIVER
1966 Studio Cast
Bart, Lionel *C*
Food, glorious food / Oliver / I shall scream / Where is love / Consider yourself / Pick a pocket or two / It's a fine life / Be back soon / I'd do anything / Oom pah pah / My name / As long as he needs me / Who will buy this wonderful morning / Reviewing the situation
CD ______ **CC 8253**
Music For Pleasure / Oct '94 / EMI

OLIVER
1994 London Cast
Bart, Lionel *C*
CD ______ **CASTCD 47**
First Night / Mar '95 / Pinnacle

OLIVER
Cast Recording
Bart, Lionel *C*
Overture/Food glorious food / Oliver / Where is love / Consider yourself / You've got to pick a pocket or two / It's a fine life / I'd do anything / Be back soon / Oom-pah-pah / As long as he needs me / Who will buy / Reviewing the situation
CD ______ **SHOWCD 004**
Showtime / Feb '95 / Disc / THE

OLIVER
Holloway, Stanley & Alma Cogan/Tony Osborne Orchestra
Bart, Lionel *C*
CD ______ **ZDM 7648902**
EMI Classics / Aug '93 / EMI

OLIVER
1991 Cast
Bart, Lionel *C*
CD ______ **CDTER 1184**
TER / Jan '92 / Koch

OLIVER TWIST/MALTA GC
Royal Philharmonic Orchestra
Bax, Sir Arnold *C*
Prelude / Storm / Fight / Oliver's sleepless night / Oliver and the Artful Dodger / Fagin's romp / Chase / Oliver and Brownlow / Nancy and Browlow / Finale / Convoy / Old valletta / Air raid / Ruins / Quick march / Intermezzo / Work and play
CD ______ **ACN 7012**
Cloud Nine / Jan '89 / Koch / Silva Screen

OLIVIER OLIVIER/EUROPA EUROPA
Preisner, Zbigniew *C*
Main title / Affection et amour / Arrivee au cafe / Elizabeth S'evancuit / Olivier / Exode / Attaque aerienne / Bataille / Troubles / Hitler Staline
CD ______ **DRGCD 12606**
DRG / Jun '93 / Discovery / New Note/Pinnacle
CD ______ **PSB 890**
PSB / Mar '96 / Discovery

OLYMPUS ON MY MIND
1986 US Cast
Sturiale, Grant *C*
Harman, Barry *L*
Welcome to Greece: *Chorus* / Heaven on earth: *Jupiter, Alchmene* / Gods on tap: *Delores, Jupiter* / Surprise: *Sosia & Mercury* / Love - what...: *Jupiter, Mercury & Dolores* / Enter the husband: *Chorus* / I know my wife: *Amphitryon* / It was me: *Sosia & Amphitryon* / Back so soon: *Amphitryon, Sosia & Orchestra* / Wonderful: *Alchmene* / At liberty...: *Charis & The Chorus* / Jupiter slept here: *Jupiter & All* / Something of yourself: *Mercury* / Star is born: *Delores & all* / Final sequence: *Amphitryon, alchmene*
CD ______ **CDTER 1131**
TER / Aug '95 / Koch

OMEN I, THE
Goldsmith, Jerry *C*
Goldsmith, Jerry *Con*
CD ______ **VSD 5281**
Varese Sarabande / '91 / Pinnacle

OMEN II, THE (Damien)
National Philharmonic Orchestra
Goldsmith, Jerry *C*
Newman, Lionel *Con*
Main title / Runaway train / Claws / Thoughtful night / Broken ice / Fallen temple / I love you, Mark / Shafted / Knife / All the power
CD ______ **FILMCD 002**
Silva Screen / Nov '89 / Koch / Silva Screen

OMEN III, THE (The Final Conflict)
Goldsmith, Jerry *C*
Goldsmith, Jerry *Con*
CD VCD 47242
Varese Sarabande / Sep '86 / Pinnacle

OMEN IV, THE
Sheffer, Jonathan *C*
CD VSD 5318
Varese Sarabande / Jul '91 / Pinnacle

ON A CLEAR DAY YOU CAN SEE FOREVER
1970 Film Cast
Lane, Burton *C*
Lerner, Alan Jay *L*
Hurry it's lovely up here / On a clear day (you can see forever) / Love with all the trimmings / Melinda / Go to sleep / He isn't you / What did I have that I don't have / Come back to me
CD 4749072
Columbia / '95 / Sony

ON A CLEAR DAY YOU CAN SEE FOREVER
1965 Broadway Cast
Lane, Burton *C*
Lerner, Alan Jay *L*
CD 09026608202
RCA Victor / Jan '90 / BMG

ON DEADLY GROUND
Poledouris, Basil *C*
Poledouris, Basil *Con*
CD VSD 5468
Varese Sarabande / Mar '94 / Pinnacle

ON HER MAJESTY'S SECRET SERVICE
Barry, John *C*
We have all the time in the world / This never happened to the other fella / Try / Ski chase / Do you know how Christmas trees are grown / Main theme / Journey to Blofeld's hideaway / Over and out / Battle at Piz Gloria / We have all the time in the world/James Bond theme
CD CZ 549
Premier/EMI / Dec '95 / EMI

ON THE BIG HILL
Croker, Brendan & Guy Fletcher
Opening shot / Best laid plans / Mountain madness / Thru the window / Try not to fall / Higher ground / There are times / Things look different / Take a short walk / Some people get hurt / Long walk / Across the bridge / Dougie's march / Each night you die a little / In the back of your mind / Home Dougie, home
CD ORECD 501
Silvertone / Mar '94 / Pinnacle

ON THE TOWN
1963 London Cast
Bernstein, Leonard *C*
Comden, Betty & Adolph Green *L*
CD SMK 53497
Sony West End / Nov '93 / Sony

ON THE TOWN
Von Stade, Frederica & Thomas Hampson/London Voices/London Symphony Orchestra
Bernstein, Leonard *C*
Comden, Betty & Adolph Green *L*
Tilson Thomas, Michael *Con*
CD 4375162
Deutsche Grammophon / Oct '93 / PolyGram

ON THE TOWN
Cast Recording
Bernstein, Leonard *C*
Comden, Betty & Adolph Green *L*
CD CDTER 1217
TER / Aug '95 / Koch

ON THE TWENTIETH CENTURY
1978 Broadway Cast
Coleman, Cy *C*
Comden, Betty & Adolph Green *L*
Gemignani, Paul *Con*
CD SK 35330
Sony Broadway / Jan '93 / Sony

ON THE WATERFRONT
1995 Broadway Cast
Amran, David *C*
Schulberg, Bud *L*
CD VSD 5638
Varese Sarabande / Aug '95 / Pinnacle

ON YOUR TOES
1983 Broadway Cast
Rodgers, Richard *C*
Hart, Lorenz *L*
Overture / Two a day for Keith / It's got to be love / Too good for the average man / There's a small hotel / Heart is quicker than the eye / Quite night / Questions and answers / Glad to be unhappy / On your toes / Princess Zenobia ballet / Slaughter on 10th Avenue
CD CDTER 1063
TER / Jul '83 / Koch

ON YOUR TOES/PAL JOEY
Cast Recording
Rodgers, Richard *C*
Hart, Lorenz *L*
CD 340822
Koch / Oct '95 / Koch

ONCE AROUND
Horner, James *C*
Horner, James *Con*
CD VSD 5308
Varese Sarabande / Apr '91 / Pinnacle

ONCE ON THIS ISLAND
Broadway Cast
Ahrens, Lynn *C*
CD CDTER 1224
TER / Nov '94 / Koch

ONCE UPON A FOREST
Horner, James *C*
CD 662862
Silva Screen / Jul '92 / Koch / Silva Screen

ONCE UPON A MATTRESS
Parker, Sarah Jessica & Broadway Cast
Overture / Many moons ago / In a little while / On a stormy night... / Shy / Minstrel, jester and I / Sensitivity / Swamps of home / Normandy / Spanish panic / Song of love / Entr'acte / Quiet / Goodnight sweet Princess / Happily ever after / Man to man talk / Very soft shoes / Yesterday I loved you / Lullaby / Finale
CD 09026687282
RCA Victor / Apr '97 / BMG

ONCE UPON A TIME IN AMERICA
Morricone, Ennio *C*
Once upon a time in America / Poverty / Deborah's theme / Childhood memories / Amapola / Friends / Prohibition dirge / Cockeye's song / Childhood poverty / Photographic memories / Friendship and love / Speakeasy
CD 8223342
Phonogram / Dec '84 / PolyGram

ONCE UPON A TIME IN THE WEST
Morricone, Ennio *C*
Once upon a time in the West / As a judgement / Farewell to Cheyenne / Transgression / First tavern / Second tavern / Man with a harmonica / Dimly lit room / Bad orchestra / Man / Jill's America / Death rattle / Finale
CD 47362
Silva Screen / Feb '90 / Koch / Silva Screen

ONCE WERE WARRIORS
CD 74321249022
Milan / May '96 / Conifer/BMG / Silva Screen

ONE AGAINST THE WIND
Holdridge, Lee *C*
CD MAF 7039D
Intrada / Jul '93 / Koch / Silva Screen

ONE EYED JACKS
Friedhofer, Hugo *C*
CD TSU 0114
Tsunami / Jan '95 / Silva Screen

ONE FINE DAY
CD 4869102
Sony Music / Feb '97 / Sony

ONE FLEW OVER THE CUCKOO'S NEST
Nitzsche, Jack *C*
CD FCD 4531
Fantasy / Jan '96 / Jazz Music / Pinnacle / Wellard

ONE FROM THE HEART
Waits, Tom & Crystal Gayle
Waits, Tom *C*
Opening montage / Tom's piano / Once upon a town / Wages of love / Is there any way out of this dream / Presents / Picking up after you / Old boy friends / Broken bicycles / I beg your pardon / Little boy blue / Instrumental montage / Tango / Circus girl / You can't unring a bell / This one's from the heart / Take me home
CD 4676092
CBS / Dec '90 / Sony

ONE MILLION YEARS BC (& When Dinosaurs Ruled The Earth/The Creatures The World Forgot)
Nascimbene, Mario *C*
CD LEGENDCD 13
Legend / Jun '94 / Koch / Silva Screen

ONE TRICK PONY
Simon, Paul
Simon, Paul *C*
Late in the evening / That's why God made the movies / One-trick pony / How the heart approaches what it yearns / Oh Marion / Ace in the hole / Nobody / Jonah / God bless the absentee / Long long day
CD 256846
WEA / Feb '94 / Warner Music

ONE WEEK (New Jazz Score For Buster Keaton Film)
Frisell, Bill *C*
CD 7559793522
Elektra / Jan '95 / Warner Music

ONLY THE LONELY
Jarre, Maurice *C*
CD VSD 5324
Varese Sarabande / Jul '91 / Pinnacle

ONLY THE LONELY (The Roy Orbison Story)
London Cast
CD CASTCD 51
First Night / Aug '95 / Pinnacle

OPERA
CD CDCIA 5074
Cinevox / Jan '93 / Koch / Silva Screen

OPERATION DUMBO DROP
Newman, David *C*
CD 1620322
Hollywood / Feb '96 / PolyGram

ORCA - KILLER WHALE
Morricone, Ennio *C*
CD LEGENDCD 10
Legend / Jul '93 / Koch / Silva Screen

ORIGINAL GANGSTAS
Inner city blues: *Ideal* / World is a ghetto: *Geto Boys* / XO: *Luniz* / On the grind: *Click* / White chalk part II: *Junior M.A.F.I.A.* / How many: *N.O. Joe* / Flowmatic 9: *3X Crazy* / Ain't no fun: *Dino* / Rivals: *Face Mob* / War's on: *Almighty RSo* / Who wanna be the villain: *M.C. Ren* / Slugs: *Spice 1* / How does it feel: *Ice-T* / Good stuff: *Smooth*
CD CDVUS 104
Virgin / Apr '96 / EMI

ORLANDO
Motton, David & Sally Potter *C*
CD VSD 5413
Varese Sarabande / Mar '93 / Pinnacle

ORPHEUS IN THE UNDERWORLD
English National Opera
Offenbach, Jacques *C*
Wilson, Snoo & David Pontney *L*
CD CDTER 1134
TER / May '89 / Koch

ORPHEUS IN THE UNDERWORLD (Highlights)
English National Opera
Offenbach, Jacques *C*
Wilson, Snoo & David Pontney *L*
CD CDTEO 1008
TER / May '89 / Koch

ORSON WELLES' OTHELLO
Lavagnino, Angelo Francesco *C*
CD VSD 5420
Varese Sarabande / Feb '94 / Pinnacle

OSCAR
Bernstein, Elmer *C*
CD VSD 5313
Varese Sarabande / Apr '91 / Pinnacle

OTHELLO
Mole, Charlie *C*
CD VSD 5689
Varese Sarabande / Feb '96 / Pinnacle

OUR FRIENDS IN THE NORTH
Times they are a-changin': *Dylan, Bob* / House of the rising sun: *Animals* / You really got me: *Kinks* / Eve of destruction: *McGuire, Barry* / Wild thing: *Troggs* / All or nothing: *Small Faces* / Substitute: *Who* / See my friend: *Kinks* / We gotta get out of this place: *Animals* / Goodbye yellow brick road: *John, Elton* / Le freak: *Chic* / Can you feel the force: *Real Thing* / Denis: *Blondie* / Babylon's burning: *Ruts* / English civil war: *Clash* / My perfect cousin: *Undertones* / Karma chameleon: *Culture Club* / What difference does it make: *Smiths* / When tomorrow comes: *Eurythmics* / Common people: *Pulp*
CD TTVCD 2922
Telstar TV / Jul '97 / Warner Music

OUR PRIVATE WORLD
Mayes, Sally *C*
CD VSD 5529
Varese Sarabande / Mar '95 / Pinnacle

OUT FOR JUSTICE (Score/Songs)
Frank, David Michael *C*
Don't stand in my way: *Allman, Gregg* / Shake the firm: *Cool J.T.* / Temptation: *Belmont James, Teresa* / When the night comes down: *Smallwood, Todd* / One good man: *Armstrong, Kymberli* / Puerto Riqueno: *Jimenez, Michael* / Bad side of town: *Ball, Sherwood* / Bigger they are: *Cool J.T.*
CD VSD 5317
Varese Sarabande / Aug '91 / Pinnacle

OUT OF AFRICA
Barry, John *C*
Barry, John *Con*
I had a farm in Africa / I'm better at hello (Karen's theme I) / Have you got a story for me / Concerto for clarinet in A / Safari / Karen's journey / Siyawe / Flying over Africa / I had a compass from Denys (Karen's theme II) / Alone on the farm / Let the rest of the world go by / If I know a song from Africa (Karen's theme III) / You are Karen (end theme) / Music of goodbye
CD MCLD 19092
MCA / Oct '92 / BMG

OUT OF THIS WORLD
1950 Broadway Cast
Porter, Cole *C*
Davenport, Pembroke *Con*
CD SK 48223
Sony Broadway / Nov '92 / Sony

OUT OF THIS WORLD
1995 New York Cast
Porter, Cole *C*
Overture / Prologue / I jupiter, I Rex / Use your imagination / Entrance of night / Hail, hail, hail / I got beauty / Maiden fair / Where, oh where / They couldn't compare to you / From this moment on / What do you think about men / Dance of the long night / You don't remind me / I sleep easier now / I am loved / Climb up the mountain / Dawn / No lover / Cherry pies ought to be you / Hark to the song of the night / Nobody's chasing me / Finale
CD DRGCD 94764
DRG / Apr '96 / Discovery / New Note/ Pinnacle

OUTBREAK
Howard, James Newton *C*
CD VSD 5599
Varese Sarabande / Mar '95 / Pinnacle

OUTER LIMITS
Frontiere, Dominic *C*
CD GNPD 8032
GNP Crescendo / Apr '93 / ZYX

OUTLAND/CAPRICORN ONE
Goldsmith, Jerry *C*
Goldsmith, Jerry *Con*
CD GNPD 8035
GNP Crescendo / Nov '93 / ZYX

OUTSIDE EDGE
CD LBWCD 1
Echo / Feb '95

OUTSIDERS, THE
Coppola, Carmine *C*
CD FILMCD 051
Silva Screen / Jan '90 / Koch / Silva Screen

OVER HERE
Broadway Cast
Sherman, Richard & Robert *C*
Klein, Joseph *Con*
CD SK 32961
Sony Broadway / Nov '92 / Sony

OZ
CD AM 2
Animanga / Nov '96 / New Note/Pinnacle

P

PACIFIC HEIGHTS
Zimmer, Hans *C*
Zimmer, Hans *Con*
CD VSD 5286
Varese Sarabande / Feb '91 / Pinnacle

PACIFIC OVERTURES (Highlights)
London Cast/English National Opera
Sondheim, Stephen *C*
Weidman, J. *L*
2CD CD2TER 1151
TER / Mar '90 / Koch

PACIFIC OVERTURES (Complete)
London Cast/English National Opera
Sondheim, Stephen *C*
Weidman, J. *L*
2CD CDTER2 1152
TER / May '89 / Koch

PAGEMASTER, THE
Horner, James *C*
Dream away: *Stansfield, Lisa & Babyface* / Whatever you imagine: *Moten, Wendy* / Main title / Stormy ride to the library / Pagemaster / Dr. Jekyll and Mr. Hyde / Narrow escape / Towards the open sea / Pirates / Loneliness / Flying dragon / Swallowed alive / Wonder in books / New courage / Magic of imagination
CD 07822110192
RCA / Nov '94 / BMG

PAINT YOUR WAGON
Film Cast
Loewe, Frederick *C*
Lerner, Alan Jay *L*
I'm on my way / I still see Elisa / First thing you know / Hand me down that can o' beans / They call the wind Maria / Million miles away behind the door / There's a coach comin' in / Whoop-ti-ay (shivaree) / I talk to the trees / Gospel of no name city / Best things / Wandering star / Gold fever / Finale
CD MCLD 19310
MCA / Oct '95 / BMG

PAINT YOUR WAGON
1951 Broadway Cast
Loewe, Frederick *C*
Lerner, Alan Jay *L*
Allers, Franz *Con*
I'm on my way / Rumson / What's goin' on here / I talk to the trees / They call the wind Maria / I still see Elsa / How can I wait / In between / Whoop-ti-ay / Carino mio / There's a coach comin' in / Hand me down that can o' beans / Another autumn / All for him / Wandrin' star
CD GD 60243
RCA Victor / Jan '90 / BMG

PAL JOEY
1980 London Cast
Rodgers, Richard *C*
Hart, Lorenz *L*
CD CDTER 1005
TER / Sep '91 / Koch

PAL JOEY (Highlights)
London Cast
Rodgers, Richard *C*
Hart, Lorenz *L*

You mustn't kick it around / I could write a book / That terrific rainbow / What is a man / Happy hunting horn / Bewitched, bothered and bewildered / Flower garden of my heart / Zip / Plant you now, dig you later / In our little den / Do it the hard way / Take him
CD ______ SHOWCD 008
Showtime / Feb '95 / Disc / THE

PAL JOEY
Broadway Cast
Rodgers, Richard *C*
Hart, Lorenz *L*
CD ______ ZDM 7646962
EMI Classics / Apr '93 / EMI

PAL JOEY
Rodgers, Richard *C*
Hart, Lorenz *L*
CD ______ DRGCD 94763
DRG / Oct '95 / Discovery / New Note/ Pinnacle

PALERMO MILANO - SOLO ANDATA
Donaggio, Pino *C*
CD ______ VCDS 7017
Varese Sarabande / Apr '96 / Pinnacle

PANAMERICANA (A Film Music Journey From Alaska To Tierra Del Fuego)
Berlin Radio Symphony Orchestra
Zillig, Winfried *C*
Fritzsch, Georg *Con*
2CD ______ 9026626592
RCA Victor / Jun '96 / BMG

PAPER, THE
Newman, Randy *C*
Newman, Randy *Con*
Opening / Clocks / Henry goes to work / Sun / Bernie calls deanne / Busting the guys / Marty and Henry / Newsroom 700 PM / More clocks / Henry leaves with McDougal / Bernie finds Deanne / Bernie / Stop the presses / Henry's fired / Marty / Marty's in trouble / To the hospital / Little polenta is born / New day / 7.00 A.M. / Make up your mind
CD ______ 9362456162
WEA / Feb '94 / Warner Music

PAPERHOUSE
Zimmer, Hans & Stanley Myers *C*
CD ______ ACD 374
Milan / Jan '89 / Conifer/BMG / Silva Screen

PAPILLON
Goldsmith, Jerry *C*
Goldsmith, Jerry *Con*
Papillon / Camp / Reunion / New friend / Freedom / Gift from the sea / Antonio's death / Cruel sea / Hospital / Survival
CD ______ FILMCD 029
Silva Screen / Sep '88 / Koch / Silva Screen

PARADISE ALLEY
Conti, Bill *C*
CD ______ TCS 1052
Silva Screen / Jul '93 / Koch / Silva Screen

PARADISE BEACH
Elated / Holiday / Laughing (on the outside) / Train of thought / Freedom / Satisfy me / Under the sun / R U sexin' me / It's the love / This isn't love / 747 / Break in the weather / We got it goin' on / Juliette / Weekend / Faith in love / Choir girl / Boy
CD ______ 4509934472
East West / Apr '93 / Warner Music

PARDON MY ENGLISH
Cast Recording
Gershwin, George *C*
Gershwin, Ira *L*
Stern, Eric *Con*
CD ______ 7559793382
Nonesuch / Nov '94 / Warner Music

PARIS S'EVEILLE
Cale, John
Cale, John *C*
CD ______ TWI 9522
Les Disques Du Crepuscule / Mar '96 / Discovery

PARIS S'EVEILLE (Suivi D'Autres Compositions)
Cale, John
Cale, John *C*
CD ______ YMCD 006
Yellow Moon / Nov '95 / Vital

PARIS, TEXAS
Cooder, Ry
Cooder, Ry *C*
Paris, Texas / Brothers / Nothing out there / Cancion mixteca / No safety zone / Houston in two seconds / She's leaving the bank / On the couch / I knew these two people / Dark was the night
CD ______ 9252702
WEA / Feb '92 / Warner Music

PARK IS MINE, THE
Tangerine Dream
Tangerine Dream *C*
CD ______ FILMCD 080
Silva Screen / Oct '91 / Koch / Silva Screen

PART OF YOUR WORLD
Shapiro, Debbie *C*
CD ______ VSD 5452
Varese Sarabande / Jun '94 / Pinnacle

PARTY PARTY
Party party: *Costello, Elvis* / Run Rudolph run: *Edmunds, Dave* / No woman, no cry: *Black, Pauline* / Yakety yak: *Bad Manners* / Elizabethan reggae: *Bad Manners* / Tutti frutti: *Sting* / Need your love so bad: *Sting* / No feelings: *Bananarama* / Band of gold: *Modern Romance* / Little town flirt: *Altered Images* / Man who sold the world: *Ure, Midge* / Auld lang syne: *Chas & Dave*
CD ______ 5514402
Spectrum / Aug '95 / PolyGram

PASSION
Broadway Cast
Sondheim, Stephen *C*
CD ______ CDQ 5552512
EMI Classics / Apr '93 / EMI

PASSION FISH
CD ______ DR 3008
Daring / Apr '93 / ADA / CM / Direct

PASSION FLOWER HOTEL
1965 London Cast
Barry, John *C*
Peacock, Trevor *L*
Holmes, Richard *Con*
CD ______ SMK 66175
Sony West End / Jul '94 / Sony

PASSION IN JAZZ
Sondheim, Stephen *C*
CD ______ VSD 5556
Varese Sarabande / Nov '94 / Pinnacle

PAT GARRET AND BILLY THE KID
Dylan, Bob
Dylan, Bob *C*
Pat Garret and Billy the Kid (Main title) / Workin' for the law (Cantina theme) / Billy 1 / Bunkhouse theme / River theme / Turkey chase / Knockin' on Heaven's door / Pat Garret and Billy the Kid (Final theme) / Billy 4 / Billy 7
CD ______ CD 32098
Columbia / Feb '91 / Sony

PATIENCE
D'Oyly Carte Opera Chorus/New Symphony Orchestra
Sullivan, Sir Arthur *C*
Gilbert, W.S. *L*
Godfrey, I. *Con*
2CD ______ 4251932
London / Jan '90 / PolyGram

PATIENCE
Shaw, John & Trevor Anthony/Glyndebourne Festival Choir/Pro Arte Orchestra
Sullivan, Sir Arthur *C*
Gilbert, W.S. *L*
Sargent, Sir Malcolm *Con*
2CD ______ CMS 7644062
EMI Classics / Apr '93 / EMI

PATIENCE
D'Oyly Carte Opera Chorus
Sullivan, Sir Arthur *C*
Gilbert, W.S. *L*
2CD ______ CDTER2 1213
TER / Jan '94 / Koch

PATIENCE/PRINCESS IDA
Oldham, Derek & George Baker/Sir Henry Lytton/D'Oyly Carte Opera Chorus & Symphony Orchestra
Sullivan, Sir Arthur *C*
Gilbert, W.S. *L*
Sargent, Sir Malcolm *Con*
2CD ______ 75605522732
Happy Days / Aug '96 / Conifer/BMG

PATLABOR II
CD ______ DSCD 15
Demon / Jun '96 / Pinnacle

PAWNBROKER, THE/THE DEADLY AFFAIR
Jones, Quincy Orchestra
Jones, Quincy *C*
Jones, Quincy *Con*
CD ______ 5312332
Verve / Jun '96 / PolyGram

PEAU D'ANE (& Other Masterworks)
Legrand, Michel *C*
CD ______ 302256
Playtime / Feb '97 / Discovery

PEE WEE'S BIG ADVENTURE/BACK TO SCHOOL
Elfman, Danny *C*
CD ______ VCD 47281
Varese Sarabande / Jan '89 / Pinnacle

PEG
1984 London Cast
Heneker, David *C*
CD ______ CDTER 1024
TER / Dec '94 / Koch

PELICAN BRIEF, THE
Horner, James *C*
CD ______ WA 245442
Silva Screen / Feb '95 / Koch / Silva Screen

PELLE THE CONQUERER
CD ______ CHCH364
Milan / Feb '90 / Conifer/BMG / Silva Screen

PENITENT
CD ______ VCD 47299
Varese Sarabande / '87 / Pinnacle

PENNIES FROM HEAVEN
CD ______ POTTCD 300
Connoisseur Collection / May '93 / Pinnacle

PEOPLE UNDER THE STAIRS
Revell, Graeme & Don Peake *C*
CD ______ 873105
Milan / Jan '95 / Conifer/BMG / Silva Screen

PEOPLE'S CENTURY, THE
Up in the air / Age of Hope: Paris 1990 / March of the Women-Plymouth Music Festival Choir / Cry of the Africans: *Soweto Teachers Choir* / Killing Fields: Lambs to the Slaughter / What a life: *Latymer Upper School Boys* / Oui, oui, Marie: *Fields, Arthur & Orchestra* / Killing fields: Mud: *Fields, Arthur & Orchestra* / My kuznetsky: *Fields, Arthur & Orchestra* / Red flag: *Fields, Arthur & Orchestra* / Lost Peace: New Nations: *Fields, Arthur & Orchestra* / Badenviller: *Fields, Arthur & Orchestra* / Lost peace: Lost Hopes / On the line / Great escape: celluloid dreams / Take your girlie to the movies: *Murray, Billy & The Orchestra* / Toot toot tootsie, goodbye: *Jolson, Al & Vibraphone Orchestra* / Great Escape: end of an era: *Jolson, Al & Vibraphone Orchestra* / Panic is on: *Jenkins, Hazekiah* / Breadline: walking the streets: *Jenkins, Hazekiah* / I ain't got no home anymore: *Guthrie, Woody* / Breadline : a new deal: *Guthrie, Woody* / Babe Ruth: *Pasadena Roof Orchestra* / I do like to see a game of football: *Kyte, Sydney* / Sporting fever: *Kyte, Sydney* / Master race: factory street and farm / Verklrte nacht op 4 / Total war / Symphony no.7 in c / Flying home: *Miller, Glenn & The Army Air Force Band* / Barbed wire: *Miller, Glenn & The Army Air Force Band* / Va-voom time: *Miller, Glenn & The Army Air Force Band* / Boom time: *Miller, Glenn & The Army Air Force Band* / Independence day: *Miller, Glenn & The Army Air Force Band* / Freedom now:Independence day: *Miller, Glenn & The Army Air Force Band* / Ghana freedom: *Mensah, ET & The Tempos Dance Band* / Sweat of their labours: *Mensah, ET & The Tempos Dance Band*
CD ______ CDVIP 177
Virgin VIP / Apr '97 / EMI

PERCY
Kinks
Davies, Ray *C*
God's children / Lola / Way love used to be / Completely / Running round town / Moments / Animals in the zoo / Just friends / Whip lady / Dreams / Helga / Willesden Green / End titles
CD ______ CLACD 164
Castle / Dec '89 / BMG

PERFORMANCE
Nitzsche, Jack *C*
Gone dead train: *Jagger, Mick* / Performance / Get away / Powis Square / Rolls Royce / Dyed, dead, red / Harry Flowers / Memo from Turner: *Jagger, Mick* / Hashshin / Wake up niggers / Poor white hound dog / Natural magic / Turner's murder
CD ______ 7599264002
WEA / Oct '93 / Warner Music

PET SEMATARY
Goldenthal, Elliot
Goldenthal, Elliot *C*
CD ______ VSD 5227
Varese Sarabande / Jul '89 / Pinnacle

PETAIN
Garvarentz, Georges *C*
CD ______ 873155
Milan / May '94 / Conifer/BMG / Silva Screen

PETER AND THE WOLF (A Musical Tale For Children & Orchestral Underscore)
RCA Symphony Orchestra
Prokofiev, Sergei/Cameron Patrick *C*
Daugherty, George *Con*
Introduction / Peter and the meadow / Peter and the bird / Duck / Cat / Grandfather / Wolf / Cat was the first one in the meadow to notice the wolf / Here's how things stood in the meadow / Peter tugged on the rope / Hunters / Duck ballet / Peter takes charge / Grandfather reappears / Grand parade / Main title / Grandfather's morning / Reunion / Taxi driver / Peter and Grandfather / Meadow / Familiar ring / Story / I am Peter / Little yellow suit / Grandfather's memories / Peter's adventure/Finale
CD ______ 74321318692
RCA Victor / Sep '96 / BMG

PETER PAN
Film Cast
Wallace, Oliver & Paul Smith *C*
Main title / Second star to the right / You can fly / Pirate's life / Following the leader / What made the red man red / Your mother and mine / Elegant Captain Hook / Never smile at a crocodile / Finale
CD ______ VSD 5722
Varese Sarabande / Nov '96 / Pinnacle

PETER PAN
1994 London Cast
CD ______ CASTCD 46
First Night / Dec '94 / Pinnacle

PETER PAN (The British Musical)
London Cast
Overture / Darlings / Peter / What happens when you're grown up / Come away / Rich damp cake / Wendy's song / Braves to war / Why / Goodbye Peter Pan / You gotta believe / We're going home / Darlings (Reprise) / Don't say goodbye
CD ______ CDEMC 3696
EMI / Dec '94 / EMI

PETER THE GREAT
Rosenthal, Laurence *C*
Main title / Cathedral / Alexander / Tartars / Two living tears / His first sail / Foreign colony / Eudoxia / Peter's wedding / Tsar and Tsaritsa / New Tsarevich / Death of Natalyda - The slap / Great embassy / Gopak / Alexis and Danilo / Battle of Poltova / Sophia and Alexis - Ordeal - Martyrdom / Requiem / Peter's theme
CD ______ SCCD 1011
Southern Cross / Jan '95 / Silva Screen

PETER'S FRIENDS
Everybody wants to rule the world: *Tears For Fears* / My baby just cares for me: *Simone, Nina* / You're my best friend: *Queen* / Girls just wanna have fun: *Lauper, Cyndi* / If you let me stay: *D'Arby, Terence Trent* / Hungry heart: *Springsteen, Bruce* / Don't get me wrong: *Pretenders* / King of rock 'n' roll: *Prefab Sprout* / What's love got to do with it: *Turner, Tina* / Give me strength: *Clapton, Eric* / Love and regret: *Deacon Blue* / Let's stay together: *Pasadenas* / Rio: *Nesmith, Michael* / Wherever I lay my hat: *Young, Paul* / I guess that's why they call it the blues: *John, Elton* / As the days go by: *Braithwaite, Daryl*
CD ______ MOODCD 27
Epic / Nov '92 / Sony

PHAEDRA
Theodorakis, Mikis *C*
Love theme from Phaedra / Rendezvous / Ship to shore / London's fog / One more time / Agapimou / Only you / Fling / Candlelight / Rodostimo / Love theme: *Mercouri, Melina* / Goodbye John Sebastian
CD ______ SR 50060
Sakkaris / Oct '93 / Pinnacle

PHANTOM
1993 Broadway Cast
Yeston, Maury *C*
CD ______ 09026616602
RCA Victor / May '93 / BMG

PHANTOM OF THE OPERA
Budapest Studio Symphony Orchestra
Segal, Misha *C*
Segal, Misha *Con*
Phantom of the opera - main title / Don Juan triumphant/Travel through time / Phantom's lair/Hellbound (Freddy at the opera)/Maddie / Young Phantom's piano etude / You are him/Into the lair / Phantom on fire/The Phantom's face / Salon talk / Jewel song / Music of the knife/Killing Joseph / Graveyard violin/Pact with the devil/ Richard gets killed / Ride to the cemetery/ The cursed manuscript/What's in the clo / Wedding/The intruder from Springwood/ Christine's decision / Mott stalks the Phantom/Davis' death/Phantom's fiery death / Finale/End title
CD ______ FILMCD 069
Silva Screen / Jun '90 / Koch / Silva Screen

PHANTOM OF THE OPERA
1986 London Cast
Lloyd Webber, Andrew *C*
Hart, Charles *L*
Overture / Think of me / Angel of music / Little Lotte / Mirror / Phantom of the opera / Music of the night / I remember / Stranger than you dreamt it / Magical lasso / Prima donna / Poor fool, he makes me laugh / All I ask of you / Entr'acte / Masquerade / Why so silent / Twisted every way / Wishing you were somehow here again / Wandering child / Point of no return / Down once more / Phantom of the opera (finale)
CD ______ 8312732
Polydor / Feb '87 / PolyGram

PHANTOM OF THE OPERA (Highlights)
Cast Recording
Lloyd Webber, Andrew *C*
Hart, Charles *L*
CD ______ CDTER 1207
TER / Dec '93 / Koch

PHANTOM OF THE OPERA (Highlights)
1986 London Cast
Lloyd Webber, Andrew *C*
Hart, Charles *L*
Overture / Angel of music / Mirror / Phantom of the opera / Music of the night / Prima donna / All I ask of you / Masquerade / Wishing you were somehow here again / Point of no return / Down once more
CD ______ 8315632
Polydor / Nov '87 / PolyGram

PHANTOM OF THE OPERA (On Ice - Music & Songs)
Lloyd Webber, Andrew *C*
Hart, Charles *L*
CD ______ PZA 008CD
Plaza / Apr '96 / Pinnacle

PHANTOM OF THE OPERA (& Jesus Christ Superstar/Cats/Evita - Aspects Of Broadway Vol.2)
Orchestra Of The Americas
Lloyd Webber, Andrew *C*
Freeman, Paul *Con*
Phantom / Think of me / Angel of music / Phantom of the opera / All I ask of you / Masquerade / Music of the night / Superstar / Everything is alright / King Herod's song / I don't know how to love him / Overture / Jellicle songs for jellicle cats / Old gumbie cat / Macavity: the mystery cat / Shimbleshanks: the railway cats / Memory / Buenos Aires / High flying adored / Don't

cry for me Argentina / She is a diamond / Another suitcase, another hall / Finale
CD SION 18302
Sion / Jul '97 / Direct

PHANTOM OF THE OPERA/ASPECTS OF LOVE (Highlights - The Shows Collection)
Cast Recording
Lloyd Webber, Andrew *C*
Hart, Charles/Don Black *L*
Phantom of the Opera / All I ask of you / Wishing you were somehow here again / Think of me / Music of the night / Love changes everything / There is more to love / First man you remember / Chanson d'enfance / Anything but lonely / Seeing is believing / Journey of a lifetime
CD PWKS 4164
Carlton / Oct '93 / Carlton

PHANTOM OF THE OPERA/CATS
Cast Recording
Lloyd Webber, Andrew *C*
Hart, Charles *L*
CD 340782
Koch / Oct '95 / Koch

PHANTOM, THE
Newman, David *C*
Newman, David *Con*
CD 74321393252
Milan / Feb '97 / Conifer/BMG / Silva Screen

PHENOMENA
Goblin
Simonetti, Claudio *C*
CD CDCIA 5062
Cinevox / Feb '93 / Koch / Silva Screen

PHILADELPHIA (Songs)
Streets of Philadelphia: *Springsteen, Bruce* / Love town: *Gabriel, Peter* / It's in your eyes: *Washington, Pauletta* / Ibo Lele (dreams come true): *Ram* / Please send me someone to love: *Sade* / Have you ever seen the rain: *Spin Doctors* / I don't want to talk about it: *Indigo Girls* / La mamma morta: *Callas, Maria* / Philadelphia: *Young, Neil* / Precedent: *Shore, Howard*
CD 4749982
Epic / Mar '94 / Sony

PHILADELPHIA EXPERIMENT/MOTHER LODE
National Philharmonic Orchestra
Wannberg, Ken *C*
Wannberg, Ken *Con*
CD PCD 121
Prometheus / Mar '93 / Silva Screen

PIAF
Paige, Elaine
La vie en rose / La goualante du pauvre jean / Hymne a l'amour / C'est a hambourg / Les trois cloches / Mon dieu / Les amants d'un jour / La belle histoire d'amour / Je sais comment / Non, je ne regrette rien / L'accordeoniste
CD 4509946412
WEA / Nov '94 / Warner Music

PIANO, THE
Munich Philharmonic Orchestra
Nyman, Michael *C*
Nyman, Michael *Con*
To the edge of the earth / Big my secret / Wild and distant shore / Heart asks pleasure first / Here to there / Promise / Bed of ferns / Fling / Scent of love / Deep in the forest / Mood that passes through you / Lost and found / Embrace / Little impulse / Sacrifice / I clipped your wing / Wounded / All imperfect things / Dreams of a journey / Heart asks pleasure first/The promise
CD CDVEX 919
Venture / May '94 / EMI

PIAZZA DI SPAGNA
Morricone, Ennio *C*
CD PRCD 107
Preamble / Jan '95 / Silva Screen

PICKWICK
1993 Chichester Festival Cast
Ornadel, Cyril *C*
Bricusse, Leslie *L*
CD CDTER 1205
TER / Dec '93 / Koch

PICKWICK
1993 London Cast
Ornadel, Cyril *C*
Bricusse, Leslie *L*
Prologue/Business is booming/Debtor's lament / Talk / That's what I'd like for Christmas / Pickwickians / Bit of a character / There's something about you / You've never met a fella like me / Look into your heart / Hell of an election / If I ruled the world / Do as you would be done by
CD SHOWCD 023
Showtime / Oct '96 / Disc / THE

PICKWICK/SCROOGE
Cast Recording
Bricusse, Leslie *C*
CD 340812
Koch / Oct '95 / Koch

PICTURE BRIDE
Eidelman, Cliff *C*
CD VSD 5651
Varese Sarabande / Jul '95 / Pinnacle

PILLOW TALK
DeVol, Frank *C*
Pillow talk: *Day, Doris* / Inspiration to Eileen: *Hudson, Rock* / Tabasco sauce for Alma's hangover / Inspiration to Yvette: *Hudson, Rock* / Alma's second hangover / Telephone inspector's visit / Alma's third hangover / Jan and Alma's discussion / Bedroom problems / Jonathan's proposal / Alma's eavesdropping on Brad / Jonathan's visit to Brad's pad / Brad's 'tree' theory on bachelorhood / Jan's refusal to Brad's attempt for date / Inspiration to Marie: *Hudson, Rock* / Jonathan's offer to drive Jan home / Theme / Copra Del Rio mambo / Jan and Jonathan's dance / First appearance as Rex / Sending Jonathan's taxi home / Brad squeezing into Jonathan's car / Brad's legs dangling over the car door / Brad's efforts to get out of the car / Taxi ride / At Jan's apartment door / Theme / Like a potbelly stove on a frosty morning / Jonathan's evasion to meet Brad's cousin Moose / Jan and Brad do the town / Jan, you can't live in... / Jonathan objection / Roly poly: *Day, Doris & Rock Hudson/Perry Blackwell* / I wonder if I can get the recipe / Brad setting the trap for Jan / Is that all it is withus, friendship / Jan falling right into it / I need no atmosphere: *Blackwell, Perry* / You lied: *Blackwell, Perry* / Jan packing and telephoning to inform Brad how wrong he was / Jonathan sending Brad on his way / Possess me: *Day, Doris* / Romantic scene in front of a fireplace / Brad trying to hide the music for inspiration / Jan's first suspicion / Jan ready to leave / Jonathan rushing to expose Rex / New York 80 miles / You got an apartment / She decorates apartments / Right right Alma's advice / Jan's business visit to Brad's apartment / Brad bidding goodbye to all former girlfriends / Jan ordering strange objects for her projects / Newly finished Chamber of Horrors / Brad in Jan's bedroom / They'll never believe this in Wichita Falls / Brad carrying Jan back to the scene of her crime / Inspiration / Brad kidnapped by an obstetrician and his nurse / Pillow talk: *Day, Doris* / Pillow talk: *Hudson, Rock* / Inspiration: *Hudson, Rock* / Roly poly: *Hudson, Rock* / Introduction: *Day, Doris* / Pillow talk: *Day, Doris* / Inspiration: *Hudson, Rock* / Roly poly: *Day, Doris & Rock Hudson* / Possess me: *Day, Doris* / Pillow talk: *Day, Doris* / Inspiration: *Day, Doris* / Roly poly: *Day, Doris* / Possess me: *Day, Doris* / Pillow talk: *Day, Doris* / Doris Day introduces movie dialogue segments: *Day, Doris* / Rock Hudson introduces movie dialogue segments: *Hudson, Rock*
2CD BCD 15913
Bear Family / Oct '96 / Direct / Rollercoaster / Swift

PILLOWBOOK, THE
CD LBS 197101
XIII Bis / Jan '97 / Discovery

PINK PANTHER, THE
Mancini, Henry & His Orchestra
Mancini, Henry *C*
Mancini, Henry *Con*
Pink Panther / It had better be tonight / Royal blue / Champagne and quail / Village Inn / Tiber twist / Cortina / Lonely princess / Something for Sellers / Piano and strings / Shades of Sennett
CD 27952
Silva Screen / Feb '90 / Koch / Silva Screen

PINOCCHIO (The Adventures Of Pinocchio)
Wonder, Stevie & Brina May/Rachel Portman *C*
CD 4527402
Decca / Oct '96 / PolyGram

PINOCCHIO
CD WD 754302
Disney Music & Stories / Mar '96 / Technicolor

PIPPIN
Broadway Cast
Schwartz, Stephen *C*
CD MOTD 9088
Silva Screen / Jan '89 / Koch / Silva Screen

PIRATES
Paris Orchestra
Sarde, Philippe *C*
Pirates / Sauves mais captifs / Linares se meurt / Mutinerie a bord / C'ptain red maitre du galion / Red, la grenouille et le requin / Dolores / Don alfonso s'evade / Red, la grenouille / C'ptain Red's empare du tresor / Red et la grenouille voguent vers de nouvelles
CD CDCH 233
Milan / '86 / Conifer/BMG / Silva Screen

PIRATES OF PENZANCE, THE (Highlights)
D'Oyly Carte Opera Chorus
Sullivan, Sir Arthur *C*
Gilbert, W.S. *L*
Overture / When Fred'ric was a little lad / Oh better far to live and die / Oh is there not one maiden breast / Poor wandering one / I am the very model / Oh dry the glistening tear / When the foreman bares his steel / When you had left our pirates fold / When a felon's not engaged in his employment / With cat-like tread / Finale
CD SHOWCD 010
Showtime / Feb '95 / Disc / THE

PIRATES OF PENZANCE, THE
D'Oyly Carte Opera Chorus/Royal Philharmonic Orchestra
Sullivan, Sir Arthur *C*
Gilbert, W.S. *L*
Godfrey, I. *Con*
2CD 4251962
Decca / Jan '90 / PolyGram

PIRATES OF PENZANCE, THE
Glyndebourne Festival Choir/Pro Arte Orchestra
Sullivan, Sir Arthur *C*
Gilbert, W.S. *L*
Sargent, Sir Malcolm *Con*
2CD CMS 7644092
EMI Classics / Apr '94 / EMI

PIRATES OF PENZANCE, THE
D'Oyly Carte Opera Chorus/Orchestra
Sullivan, Sir Arthur *C*
Gilbert, W.S. *L*
Pryce Jones, J. *Con*
2CD CDTER2 1177
TER / Sep '90 / Koch

PIRATES OF PENZANCE, THE
Welsh National Opera Choir/Orchestra
Sullivan, Sir Arthur *C*
Gilbert, W.S. *L*
Mackerras, Sir Charles *Con*
CD CD 80353
Telarc / Nov '93 / Conifer/BMG

PIRATES OF PENZANCE, THE/HMS PINAFORE (Complete 1929/1930 Recordings)
D'Oyly Carte Opera Chorus & Orchestra/ London Symphony Orchestra
Sullivan, Sir Arthur *C*
Gilbert, W.S. *L*
Sargent, Sir Malcolm *Con*
2CD 890022
Romophone / May '96 / Complete/Pinnacle

PIRATES OF PENZANCE, THE/THE SORCERER
D'Oyly Carte Opera Chorus/New Symphony Orchestra
Sullivan, Sir Arthur *C*
Gilbert, W.S. *L*
Sargent, Sir Malcolm *Con*
2CD Z 80682
Arabesque / Nov '87 / Seaford Music

PLAIN AND FANCY
Broadway Cast
Hague, Albert *C*
Horwitt, Arnold *L*
CD ZDM 7647622
EMI Classics / Apr '93 / EMI

PLANET OF THE APES (Remastered With Extra Music)
Goldsmith, Jerry *C*
Goldsmith, Jerry *Con*
CD FMT 8006D
Intrada / Dec '92 / Koch / Silva Screen

PLATOON
Village: *Vancouver Symphony Orchestra* / Tracks of my tears: *Robinson, Smokey* / Okie from Muskogee: *Haggard, Merle* / Hello I love you: *Doors* / White rabbit: *Jefferson Airplane* / Barnes shoots Elias: *Vancouver Symphony Orchestra* / Respect: *Franklin, Aretha* / (Sittin' on) the dock of the bay: *Redding, Otis* / When a man loves a woman: *Sledge, Percy* / Groovin': *Rascals* / Adagio for strings: *Vancouver Symphony Orchestra*
CD 7817422
Atlantic / Jun '87 / Warner Music

PLATOON LEADER
Clinton, George *C*
CD GNPD 8013
GNP Crescendo / Jan '89 / ZYX

PLAY ON
Original Broadway Cast
Ellington, Duke *C*
CD VSD 5837
Varese Sarabande / Jul '97 / Pinnacle

PLAYER, THE
Newman, Thomas *C*
CD VSD 5366
Varese Sarabande / May '92 / Pinnacle

PLEASE SAVE MY EARTH
Kanno, Yoko *C*
CD AM 6
Animanga / Nov '96 / New Note/Pinnacle

POCAHONTAS
CD WDR 75462
Disney Music & Stories / Oct '96 / Technicolor

POCAHONTAS (Singalong)
CD WD 481424
Disney Music & Stories / Nov '96 / Technicolor

POINT BREAK
Nobody rides for free: *Ratt* / Over the edge: *L.A. Guns* / I will not fall: *Wiretrain* / I want you: *Concrete Blonde* / 7 and 7 is: *Liquid Jesus* / Smoke on the water: *Loudhouse* / My city: *Shark Island* / Criminal: *Public Image Ltd* / So long cowboy: *Westworld* / Hundreds of tears: *Crow, Sheryl*
CD MCLD 19327
MCA / Sep '96 / BMG

POINT OF NO RETURN/THE ASSASSIN
Zimmer, Hans *C*
CD 143022
Milan / Feb '94 / Conifer/BMG / Silva Screen

POLTERGEIST II
Goldsmith, Jerry *C*
Power / Late call / Smoke / Worm / Reaching out
CD VCD 47266
Varese Sarabande / Jan '89 / Pinnacle
CD CDTER 1116
TER / Jan '92 / Koch
CD RVF 6002D
Intrada / Jan '93 / Koch / Silva Screen

POLTERGEIST II (& Unreleased Music)
Goldsmith, Jerry *C*
CD VJD 5002D
Silva Screen / Jan '95 / Koch / Silva Screen

POLTERGEIST III
Renzetti, Joe *C*
CD VCD 70462
Varese Sarabande / Jan '89 / Pinnacle

PONDICHERY
Meer, Stephane *C*
CD SMC 35705
Sergent M / Jun '97 / Discovery

POPPIE NONGENA
1983 Cast
Mgcina, Sophie *C*
Kotze, Sandra & Elsa Joubert *L*
Amen / Taru bawo / Wenzeni na / U Jehovah / Uzubale / Makoti / Lalasana / Jerusalem / Nkosi Sikela l'Afrika / Zisana abantwane / Bantwena besikolo / Liza Lisi Dinga / Mampondo mse
CD HNCD 1351
Hannibal / Jan '87 / ADA / Vital

PORGY AND BESS
Film Cast
Gershwin, George *C*
Gershwin, Ira & DuBose Heyward *L*
Previn, Andre *Con*
CD SMK 64314
Sony Classical / Nov '93 / Sony

PORGY AND BESS
1942 Broadway Cast
Gershwin, George *C*
Gershwin, Ira & DuBose Heyward *L*
Overture/Summertime / Woman is a sometime thing / My man's gone now / It takes a long pull to get there / I got plenty o' nuttin' / Buzzard song / Bess, you is my woman now / It ain't necessarily so / What you want wid Bess / Strawberry woman's call - crab man's call / I loves you Porgy / Requiem / There's a boat dat's leavin' soon for New York / Porgy's lament/Finale
CD MCLD 19158
MCA / Jan '94 / BMG

PORGY AND BESS (Scenes)
Price, Leontyne
Gershwin, George *C*
Gershwin, Ira & DuBose Heyward *L*
CD GD 85234
RCA / Mar '95 / BMG

PORGY AND BESS (Highlights)
Houston Grand Opera
Gershwin, George *C*
Gershwin, Ira & DuBose Heyward *L*
DeMain, J. *Con*
CD RD 84680
RCA Victor / '88 / BMG

PORGY AND BESS
White, Willard & Cynthia Haymon/Glyndebourne Festival Opera Cast/London Philharmonic Orchestra
Gershwin, George *C*
Gershwin, Ira & DuBose Heyward *L*
Rattle, Simon *Con*
3CD CDS 7495682
EMI Classics / Apr '93 / EMI

PORGY AND BESS (Highlights)
White, Willard & Cynthia Haymon/Glyndebourne Festival Opera Cast/London Philharmonic Orchestra
Gershwin, George *C*
Gershwin, Ira & DuBose Heyward *L*
Rattle, Simon *Con*
CD CDC 7543252
EMI Classics / Apr '93 / EMI

PORGY AND BESS
White, Willard & Leona Mitchell/McHenry Boatwright/Barbara Hendricks/Cleveland Orchestra
Gershwin, George *C*
Gershwin, Ira & DuBose Heyward *L*
Maazel, L. *Con*
3CD 4145592
Decca / Feb '86 / PolyGram

PORGY AND BESS (Suite From Porgy & Bess)
Houdini's & Nieuw Sinfonietta, Amsterdam
Gershwin, George *C*
Gershwin, Ira & DuBose Heyward *L*
CD CCS 8395
Channel Classics / Nov '95 / Select / Vital/ SAM

PORGY AND BESS
Torme, Mel/Frances Faye/Duke Ellington Orchestra/Russ Garcia Orchestra
Gershwin, George *C*
Gershwin, Ira & DuBose Heyward *L*
2CD BET 6028
Bethlehem / Jan '95 / ADA / ZYX

PORGY AND BESS (Highlights)
White, Willard & Leona Mitchell/McHenry Boatwright/Barbara Hendricks/Cleveland Orchestra
Gershwin, George *C*
Gershwin, Ira & DuBose Heyward *L*
Maazel, L. *Con*
CD _______________ 4363062
Argo / May '97 / PolyGram

POUR RIRE
Del Fra, Ricardo *C*
CD _______________ SMC 35701
Sergent M / Apr '97 / Discovery

POWAQQATSI
Glass, Philip *C*
Riesman, Michael *Con*
CD _______________ 755991922
Nonesuch / Aug '88 / Warner Music

POWDER
Goldsmith, Jerry *C*
CD _______________ HW 203842
Silva Screen / Apr '96 / Koch / Silva Screen

POWER OF ONE, THE
Zimmer, Hans *C*
Rainmaker / Mother Africa / Of death and dying / Limpopo river song / Power of one / Woza Mfana / Southland concerto / Senzenina / Penny whistle song / Funeral song / Wangal unozipho / Mother Africa (reprise)
CD _______________ 7559613352
Elektra / Oct '92 / Warner Music

POWER, THE (& Choruses From King Of Kings/Ben Hur)
MGM Studio Orchestra
Rozsa, Miklos *C*
Rozsa, Miklos *Con*
CD _______________ PCD 122
Prometheus / Jan '93 / Silva Screen

PREACHER'S WIFE, THE
Houston, Whitney
I believe in you and me / Step by step / Joy / Hold on, help is on the way / Go to the rock / I love the Lord / Who'd imagine a king / Lord is my shepherd / Somebody bigger than you and I / My heart is calling / You were loved / I believe in you and me / Step by step / Joy to the world
CD _______________ 07822189512
CD _______________ 74321441252
Arista / Dec '96 / BMG

PREACHING TO THE PERVERTED
Welcome to the house of Thwax: *Fiennes, Magnus & Maya* / Evil queen: *Shimmon & Woolfson* / Journey into hell: *Fiennes, Magnus & Maya* / Sycophantasy: *Rejuvination* / Postman always rings Thwice: *Fiennes, Magnus & Maya* / Alien spoke: *Broom, Mark* / In zebra suspension: *Fiennes, Magnus & Maya* / Mind: *Aloof* / Ajare: *Way Out West* / Enlightenment: *Fiennes, Magnus & Maya* / Goodmorning mistress: *Fiennes, Magnus & Maya* / Wastelands: *Fiennes, Magnus & Maya* / Who are you: *Omni Trio* / Aerobix: *Percy X* / Futura: *Amethyst* / Grind transubmission: *Fiennes, Magnus & Maya* / House of Thwax reprised: *Fiennes, Magnus & Maya*
CD _______________ PERVCDLIM 001
CD _______________ PERVCDLP 001
Naked / Jul '97 / Pinnacle

PREDATOR II
Silvestri, Alan *C*
CD _______________ VSD 5302
Varese Sarabande / Jan '91 / Pinnacle

PRELUDE TO A KISS
Shore, Howard *C*
CD _______________ 111252
Milan / May '94 / Conifer/BMG / Silva Screen

PRESUMED INNOCENT
Williams, John *C*
CD _______________ VSD 5280
Varese Sarabande / Oct '90 / Pinnacle

PRET-A-PORTER
Here comes the hotstepper: *Kamoze, Ini* / My girl Josephine: *Super Cat* / Here we come: *Salt 'N' Pepa* / Natural thing: *M People* / 70's love groove: *Jackson, Janet* / Jump on top of me: *Rolling Stones* / These boots were made for walkin': *Phillips, Sam* / Pretty: *Cranberries* / Martha: *Deep Forest* / Close to you: *Brand New Heavies* / Keep givin' me your love: *Peniston, Ce Ce* / Get wild: *New Power Generation* / Supermodel sandwich: *D'Arby, Terence Trent* / Lemon: *U2*
CD _______________ 4782262
Columbia / Dec '96 / Sony

PRETTY IN PINK
Left of centre: *Vega, Suzanne* / Get to know ya: *Johnson, Jesse* / Do wot you do: *INXS* / Pretty in pink: *Psychedelic Furs* / Shellshock: *New Order* / Round round: *Belouis Some* / Wouldn't it be good: *Hutton, June* / Bring on the dancing horses: *Echo & The Bunnymen* / Please, please, please let me get what I want: *Smiths* / If you leave: *O.M.D.*
CD _______________ CDMID 157
A&M / Oct '92 / PolyGram

PRETTY WOMAN
Wild women do: *Cole, Natalie* / Fame '90: *Bowie, David* / King of wishful thinking: *Go West* / Tangled: *Wiedlin, Jane* / It must have been love: *Roxette* / Life in detail: *Palmer, Robert* / No explanation: *Cetera, Peter* / Real wild child: *Otcasek, Christopher* / Fallen: *Wood, Lauren* / Oh pretty woman: *Orbison, Roy* / Show me your soul: *Red Hot Chili Peppers*
CD _______________ CDMTL 1052
EMI Manhattan / Apr '90 / EMI

PRETTYBELLE
Broadway Cast
CD _______________ VSD 5439
Varese Sarabande / Sep '93 / Pinnacle

PRIDE AND PREJUDICE
Davis, Carl *C*
Davis, Carl *Con*
Pride and prejudice / Netherfield ball montage / Elizabeth observed / Piano summary / Canon Collins / Gardeners / Winter into Spring / Parting / Rosings / Telling the truth / Farewell to the regiment / Darcy returns / Thinking about Lizzie / Lydia's elopement / Return of Bingley / Double wedding
CD _______________ CDEMC 3726
EMI / Aug '97 / EMI

PRIEST OF LOVE
Lawrence / English hotel trio / Variations / Mabel's tango / Frieda's theme (part 1) / Frieda's theme (part 2) / Italy / Cornwall / Fugue / Lawrence's death / Priest of love (finale) / Way we get it together
CD _______________ DSCD 1003
D-Sharp / Nov '85 / Pinnacle

PRIMAL FEAR
Howard, James Newton *C*
Kane, A. *Con*
CD _______________ 73138357162
Milan / Apr '96 / Conifer/BMG / Silva Screen

PRINCE OF DARKNESS
Carpenter, John *C*
CD _______________ VCD 47310
Varese Sarabande / Jan '89 / Pinnacle

PRINCESS BRIDE, THE
Knopfler, Mark
Knopfler, Mark *C*
Once upon a time...storybook love / I will never love again / Florin dance / Morning ride / Friends' song / Cliffs of insanity / Sword fight / Guide my sword / Fire swamp and the rodents of unusual size / Revenge / Happy ending / Storybook love
CD _______________ 8328642
Vertigo / Mar '97 / PolyGram

PRINCESS CARABOO
Hartley, Richard *C*
CD _______________ VSD 5544
Varese Sarabande / Dec '94 / Pinnacle

PRINCESS IDA/PINEAPPLE POLL
D'Oyly Carte Opera Chorus/Royal Philharmonic Orchestra/Philharmonia Orchestra
Sullivan, Sir Arthur *C*
Gilbert, W.S. *L*
Sargent, Malcolm/C. Mackerras *Con*
2CD _______________ 4368102
London / Jan '90 / PolyGram

PRISONER VOL.1, THE
Grainer, Ron/Wilfred Josephs/Albert Elms *C*
Arrival / A, B & C / Free For All / General / Fall Out / Many Happy Returns / Dance Of The Dead / Checkmate / Hammer Into Anvil / Girl Who Was Death / Once Upon A Time
CD _______________ FILMCD 042
Silva Screen / Nov '89 / Koch / Silva Screen

PRISONER VOL.2, THE
Grainer, Ron/Wilfred Josephs/Albert Elms *C*
Arrival / Chimes of Big Ben / A B And C / Many happy returns / Checkmate / Dance of the dead / Do not forsake me oh my darling / Girl who was death / Fall out
CD _______________ FILMCD 084
Silva Screen / Jun '92 / Koch / Silva Screen

PRISONER VOL.3, THE
Grainer, Ron/Wilfred Josephs/Albert Elms *C*
Arrival / Chimes of Big Ben / A B and C / Free for all / General / Dance of the dead / Hammer into anvil / Change of mind / Do not forsake me oh my darling / Girl who was death / Fall out
CD _______________ FILMCD 126
Silva Screen / Nov '92 / Koch / Silva Screen

PRIVATE PARTS - HOWARD STERN
Pig virus / Great American nightmare: *Zombie, Rob & Howard Stern* / Mama look, a boo boo / I make my own rules: *LL Cool J & Flea/Dave Navarro/Chad Smith* / Match game / Hard charger: *Porno For Pyros* / Moti / Suck for your solution: *Marilyn Manson* / Lance eluction / Pictures of matchstick men: *Osbourne, Ozzy & Type O Negative* / Contest / Tired of waiting for you: *Green Day* / WRNW / Pinhead: *Ramones* / Oh Howard / Ben Stern megamix / Howard Stern experience / Smoke on the water: *Deep Purple* / WCCC / I want you to help me: *Cheap Trick* / Antichrist / Cat scratch fever: *Nugent, Ted* / WNBC / Jamie's cryin': *Van Halen* / Crackhead Bob / You shook me all night long: *AC/DC* / Howard you stink / Ladies and gentlemen / Totured man: *Stern, Howard & The Dust Brothers*
CD _______________ 9362464772
Warner Bros. / Mar '97 / Warner Music

PRIVATE PARTS/RICHTHOFEN AND BROWN
Graunke Symphony Orchestra
Friedhofer, Hugo *C*
Graunke, K. *Con*
CD _______________ FE 8105
Facet / Mar '94 / Conifer/BMG

PROFESSIONALS, THE
Jarre, Maurice *C*
Jarre, Maurice *Con*
CD _______________ 2504342
Silva Screen / Jan '93 / Koch / Silva Screen

PROFUNDO ROSSO/SUSPIRIA
Goblin
Simonetti, Claudio *C*
CD _______________ CDCIA 5005
Cinevox / Jan '89 / Koch / Silva Screen

PROMISED LAND
CD _______________ 20352
Silva Screen / Feb '90 / Koch / Silva Screen

PROOF
Not Drowning, Waving
Not Drowning, Waving *C*
CD _______________ A 8927
Alhambra / Jan '92 / Silva Screen

PROPRIETER, THE
Robbins, Richard *C*
Opening titles / Art gallery / Je m'appelle France / Adrienne's dream / Memories of Maxim's / To leave, to stay / Father and son / Coming home / Patrice and Virginia at the chateau / Ostogoth's tango / If I didn't care / Call me French / Auction / What did he say / Ghost of fan fan / Letter / End credits / Will the circle be unbroken
CD _______________ 4866732
Epic / Dec '96 / Sony

PROSPERO'S BOOKS
Leonard, Sarah/Marie Angel/Ute Lemper/Deborah Conway/Michael Nyman Band
Nyman, Michael *C*
Nyman, Michael *Con*
CD _______________ 4252242
Decca / Nov '91 / PolyGram

PROVIDENCE
Rozsa, Miklos *C*
CD _______________ CDSL 9502
DRG / Jul '92 / Discovery / New Note/ Pinnacle

PSYCHO
Herrmann, Bernard *C*
CD _______________ CDCH 022
Milan / Feb '90 / Conifer/BMG / Silva Screen

PSYCHO
National Philharmonic Orchestra
Herrmann, Bernard *C*
Herrmann, Bernard *Con*
CD _______________ UKCD 2021
Unicorn-Kanchana / Nov '94 / Harmonia Mundi

PUBLIC EYE, THE
Isham, Mark *C*
CD _______________ VSD 5374
Varese Sarabande / Nov '92 / Pinnacle

PULP FICTION
Misirlou: *Dale, Dick & His Del-Tones* / Jungle boogie: *Kool & The Gang* / Let's stay together: *Green, Al* / Bustin' surfboards: *Tornadoes* / Lonesome town: *Nelson, Ricky* / Son of a preacher man: *Springfield, Dusty* / Bullwinkle (part 2): *Centurions* / You never can tell: *Berry, Chuck* / Girl, you'll be a woman soon: *Urge Overkill* / If love is a red dress (hang me in rags): *McKee, Maria* / Comanche: *Revels* / Flowers on the wall: *Statler Brothers* / Surf rider: *Lively Ones*
CD _______________ MCD 11103
MCA / Sep '94 / BMG

PUMP UP THE VOLUME
Everybody knows: *Concrete Blonde* / Why can't I fall in love: *Neville, Ivan* / Stand: *Liquid Jesus* / Wave of mutilation: *Pixies* / I've got a secret minature camera: *Murphy, Peter* / Kick out the jams: *Bad Brains & Henry Rollins* / Freedom of speech: *Above The Law* / Heretic: *Soundgarden* / Titanium expose: *Sonic Youth* / Me and the Devil blues: *Cowboy Junkies*
CD _______________ DMCG 6121
MCA / Nov '90 / BMG

PUPPET MASTERS, THE
London Filmworks Orchestra
Towns, Colin *C*
Wilson, Allan *Con*
CD _______________ STC 77104
Klavier / Jan '95 / Quantum Audio / UK Distribution

PURE LUCK
Sheffer, Jonathan *C*
CD _______________ VSD 5330
Varese Sarabande / Aug '91 / Pinnacle

PURPLE RAIN
Prince & The Revolution
Prince *C*
Let's go crazy / Take me with U / Beautiful ones / Computer blue / Darling Nikki / When doves cry / I would die 4 U / Baby I'm a star / Purple rain
CD _______________ 9251102
WEA / Feb '95 / Warner Music

PUTTING IT TOGETHER
1993 US Cast
Sondheim, Stephen *C*
Invocation and instructions to the audience / Putting it together / Rich and happy / Merrily we roll along / Everybody ought to have a maid / Sooner or later / Ah but underneath / Hello little girl / My husband the pig / Every day a little death / Have I got a girl for you / Pretty women / Now / Bang / Country house / Could I leave you / Back in business / Night waltzes / Love takes time / Remember / In praise of women / Perpetual anticipation / Sun won't set / Game sequence / What would we do without you / Gun song / Little priest / Miller's son / Live alone and like it / Sorry / Grateful / Sweet Polly Plunket / I could drive a person crazy / Marry me a little / Getting married today / Being alive / Like it was / Old friends
CD _______________ 09026617292
RCA Victor / Jan '94 / BMG

PYROMANIACS LOVE STORY
Portman, Rachel *C*
CD _______________ VSD 5620
Varese Sarabande / Jun '95 / Pinnacle

Q

QB VII
Goldsmith, Jerry *C*
Goldsmith, Jerry *Con*
CD _______________ MAF 7061D
Intrada / Jan '95 / Koch / Silva Screen

QUADROPHENIA
I am the sea: *Who* / Real me: *Who* / I'm one: *Who* / 5.15: *Who* / I've had enough: *Who* / Love reign o'er me: *Who* / Bell boy: *Who* / Helpless dancer: *Who* / Dr. Jimmy: *Who* / Four faces: *Who* / Get out and stay out: *Who* / Joker James: *Who* / Punk and the Godfather: *Who* / Louie Louie: *Kingsmen* / Zoot suit: *High Numbers* / Hi-heel sneakers: *Cross Section* / Night train: *Brown, James* / Green onions: *Booker T & The MG's* / He's so fine: *Chiffons* / Rhythm of the rain: *Cascades* / Be my baby: *Ronettes* / Da doo ron ron: *Crystals*
CD _______________ 5199992
Polydor / Mar '96 / PolyGram

QUANTUM LEAP
Post, Mike *C*
CD _______________ GNPD 8036
GNP Crescendo / Nov '93 / ZYX

QUARTET
CD _______________ CDQ 5551002
EMI / Apr '94 / EMI

QUEIMADA (Burn)
Morricone, Ennio *C*
CD _______________ VCDS 7020
Varese Sarabande / Oct '96 / Pinnacle

QUEL MALEDETTO GIORNO DI FUOCO/ ATTENTO GRINGO/LO CHIAMAVANO
Piccioni, Piero/Manuel De Sica *C*
CD _______________ CDCR 31
Silva Screen / Apr '96 / Koch / Silva Screen

QUEST
Edelman, Randy *C*
CD _______________ VSD 5716
Varese Sarabande / May '96 / Pinnacle

QUEST FOR FIRE
Sarde, Philippe *C*
CD _______________ CDFMC 1
Silva Screen / Jan '89 / Koch / Silva Screen

QUI C'EST CE GARCON
Sarde, Philippe *C*
CD _______________ CD 312
Milan / Jan '89 / Conifer/BMG / Silva Screen

QUICK AND THE DEAD, THE
Silvestri, Alan *C*
Redemption / Gunfight montage / Couldn't tell us apart / John Herod / Ellen's first round / Lady's the winner / Dinner tonight / Cort's story / Ellen vs. Dred / Kid vs. Herod / I don't wanna die / Big day / Ellen returns / Law's come back to town / Quick and the dead (End credits)
CD _______________ VSD 5595
Varese Sarabande / Oct '95 / Pinnacle

QUIEN SABE
Bacalov, Luis Enriquez *C*
CD _______________ A 8932
Alhambra / Jan '93 / Silva Screen

QUIET MAN, THE
Dublin Screen Orchestra
Young, Victor *C*
Alwyn, Kenneth *Con*
CD _______________ SFC 1501
Silva Screen / Sep '95 / Koch / Silva Screen

QUIET MAN, THE/SAMSON AND DELILAH
Young, Victor *C*
Young, Victor *Con*
CD _______________ VSD 5497
Varese Sarabande / Jun '94 / Pinnacle

QUIGLEY DOWN UNDER
Poledouris, Basil *C*
CD MAF 7006D
Intrada / Jan '93 / Koch / Silva Screen

QUILLER MEMORANDUM,THE
Barry, John *C*
CD VSD 5218
Varese Sarabande / Feb '90 / Pinnacle

R

RACE FOR THE YANKEE ZEPHYR/ SURVIVOR
May, Brian *C*
CD IMICD 1008
Silva Screen / Jan '93 / Koch / Silva Screen

RADIO FLYER
Zimmer, Hans *C*
CD 244542
Silva Screen / Jan '93 / Koch / Silva Screen

RADIO GALS
Cast Recording
CD VSD 5604
Varese Sarabande / Jul '95 / Pinnacle

RAIDERS OF THE LOST ARK (Digitally Remastered)
London Symphony Orchestra
Williams, John *C*
Williams, John *Con*
CD RAIDERS 001
Silva Screen / Nov '95 / Koch / Silva Screen

RAILWAY CHILDREN, THE
Jeffries, Lionel & Cast
CD CDMFP 6373
Music For Pleasure / Apr '97 / EMI

RAIN
Takemitsu, Toru *C*
CD FMC 5
Milan / Jan '95 / Conifer/BMG / Silva Screen

RAINMAKER, THE
North, Alex *C*
CD TSU 0120
Tsunami / Jan '95 / Silva Screen

RAINTREE COUNTY
MGM Studio Orchestra & Chorus
Green, John *C*
Green, John *Con*
2CD 2PRCD 1781
Entr'acte / Jan '90 / Cadillac / Koch / Silva Screen

RAISE THE RED LANTERN
Jiping, Zhao *C*
CD 887952
Milan / Jan '95 / Conifer/BMG / Silva Screen

RAISIN
Broadway Cast
Woldin, Judd *C*
Roberts, Howard A. *Con*
CD SK 32754
Sony Broadway / Jan '95 / Sony

RAISING CAIN
Donaggio, Pino *C*
CD 101302
Milan / Nov '92 / Conifer/BMG / Silva Screen

RAMBO
Goldsmith, Jerry *C*
CD VCD 47234
TER / Jan '89 / Koch

RAMBO I
Goldsmith, Jerry *C*
CD FMT 8001D
Intrada / Jan '89 / Koch / Silva Screen

RAMBO II
Goldsmith, Jerry *C*
Main title / Preperation / Jump / Snake / Stories / Cage / Betrayed / Peace in our life / Escape from torture / Ambush / Revenge / Bowed down / Pilot over / Home flight / Day by day
CD VSD 47234
Varese Sarabande / Feb '90 / Pinnacle

RAMBO III (Score)
Hungarian State Opera Orchestra
Goldsmith, Jerry *C*
Goldsmith, Jerry *Con*
CD RVF 6006D
Intrada / Jan '90 / Koch / Silva Screen

RANSOM (AKA The Terrorist & The Chairman)
Goldsmith, Jerry *C*
Goldsmith, Jerry *Con*
CD FILMCD 081
Silva Screen / Jul '91 / Koch / Silva Screen

RANSOM
CD 1620862
Polydor / Jan '97 / PolyGram

RAPA NUI
Copeland, Stewart *C*
CD 214402
Milan / Nov '94 / Conifer/BMG / Silva Screen

RAPID FIRE
Young, Christopher *C*
CD VSD 5388
Varese Sarabande / Sep '92 / Pinnacle

RAW DEAL
Bahler, Tom *C*
CD VSD 47286
Varese Sarabande / Feb '93 / Pinnacle

RAZOR'S EDGE
London Studio Symphony Orchestra
Nitzsche, Jack *C*
Black, Stanley *Con*
CD PRCD 1794
Preamble / Jan '93 / Silva Screen

RE-ANIMATOR/BRIDE OF THE RE-ANIMATOR
Band, Richard *C*
CD FILMCD 082
Silva Screen / '92 / Koch / Silva Screen

RE-JOYCE
Lipman, Maureen
Addinsell, Richard *C*
CD SCENECD 21
First Night / '94 / Pinnacle

REAL MCCOY, THE
Fiedel, Brad *C*
Walker, S. *Con*
CD VSD 5450
Varese Sarabande / Oct '93 / Pinnacle

REALITY BITES
My Sharona: *Knack* / Spin the bottle: *Hatfield, Juliana* / Bed of roses: *Indians* / When you come back to me: *World Party* / Going going gone: *Posies* / Stay: *Loeb, Lisa & Nine Stories* / All I want is you: *U2* / Locked out: *Crowded House* / Spinning around after you: *Kravitz, Lenny* / I'm nuthin': *Hawke, Ethan* / Turnip farm: *Dinosaur Jnr* / Revival: *Me Phi Me* / Tempted (94): *Squeeze* / Baby, I love your way: *Big Mountain*
CD 07863663642
RCA / Aug '96 / BMG

REBECCA (& Alfred Newman's Selznick International Pictures Fanfare)
Bratislava Symphony Orchestra
Waxman, Franz *C*
Adriano *Con*
CD 8223399
Marco Polo / Oct '92 / Select

RECIDIVE
Musy, Jean *C*
CD 873146
Milan / Jan '95 / Conifer/BMG / Silva Screen

RED DAWN
Poledouris, Basil *C*
Invasion / Drive-in / Let it turn / Woverines / Flowers / Eulogy / Robert's end / Death and freedom / End titles
CD RVF 6001D
Intrada / Jan '89 / Koch / Silva Screen

RED KNIGHT, WHITE KNIGHT
Scott, John *C*
CD MAF 7016D
Intrada / Jan '93 / Koch / Silva Screen

RED SCORPION
Chattaway, Jay
Chattaway, Jay *C*
CD VSD 5230
Varese Sarabande / Sep '89 / Pinnacle

RED TENT, THE
Morricone, Ennio *C*
Love theme / Do dreams go on / Death at the Pole / Love like the snow / Message from Rome / They're alive / Farewell / Others, who will follow us
CD LEGENDCD 15
Legend / Aug '94 / Koch / Silva Screen

REIVERS, THE
Williams, John *C*
Williams, John *Con*
CD CK 66130
Columbia / Apr '95 / Sony

REMAINS OF THE DAY, THE
Robbins, Richard *C*
Rabinowitz, H. *Con*
CD CDQ 5550292
Angel / Aug '94 / EMI

RENAISSANCE MAN
Zimmer, Hans *C*
CD VSD 5502
Varese Sarabande / Aug '94 / Pinnacle

RENT-A-COP
Rent a cop / Bust / Lonely cop / Russian roulette / Station / Worth a lot / Lights out / This is the Guy / They need me / Room / Lake forest / Jump
CD FILMCD 025
Silva Screen / Apr '88 / Koch / Silva Screen

REPO MAN
CD MCLD 19311
MCA / Oct '95 / BMG

RESERVOIR DOGS
Little green bag: *Baker, George Selection* / Hooked on a feeling: *Blue Swede* / I gotcha: *Tex, Joe* / Magic carpet ride: *Bedlam* / Fool for love: *Rogers, Sandy* / Stuck in the middle with you: *Stealer's Wheel* / Harvest moon: *Bedlam* / Coconut: *Nilsson, Harry*
CD MCD 10793
MCA / Jan '93 / BMG

RESTORATION
Howard, James Newton *C*
CD 73138357072
Milan / Mar '96 / Conifer/BMG / Silva Screen

RETURN OF THE JEDI
Williams, John *C*
Main title / Into the trap / Luke and Leia / Bot got Jarraz / Han Solo returns / Parade of the Ewoks / Forest / Rebel briefing / Emperor / Return of the Jedi / Ewok celebration and finale
CD 8117672
RSO / May '83 / PolyGram

RETURN OF THE JEDI
National Philharmonic Orchestra
Williams, John *C*
Gerhardt, Charles *Con*
Approaching the Death Star / Parade of the Ewoks / Luke and Leia / Jabba the Hutt / Return of the Jedi / Ewok battle / Han Solo returns / Into the trap / Heroic Ewok / Battle in the forest / Finale
CD GD 60767
RCA Victor / Jun '91 / BMG

RETURN OF THE JEDI (The Star Wars Trilogy Special Edition)
Williams, John *C*
Williams, John *Con*
CD 09026687482
2CD 09026687742
RCA Victor / Mar '97 / BMG

RETURN OF THE LIVING DEAD I
Surfin' dead: *Cramps* / Party time (Zombie version): *45 Grave* / Nothing for you: *T.S.O.L.* / Eyes without a face: *Flesh Eaters* / Burn the flames: *Erickson, Roky* / Dead beat dance: *Damned* / Take a walk: *Tall Boys* / Love under will: *Jet Black Berries* / Tonight (we'll make love until we die): *SSQ* / Trash's theme: *SSQ*
CD CDWIK 38
Big Beat / Jun '88 / Pinnacle

RETURN OF THE LIVING DEAD III
Goldberg, Barry & John Philip Shenale *C*
CD SER 289B02
South East / Apr '96 / Silva Screen

RETURN OF THE MUSKETEERS
Petit, Jean Claude *C*
CD CDCH 383
Milan / Feb '90 / Conifer/BMG / Silva Screen

RETURN TO SNOWY RIVER
Rowland, Bruce *C*
CD VCD 70451
Varese Sarabande / Jan '89 / Pinnacle

RETURN TO THE FORBIDDEN PLANET
CC Productions
Wipe out / It's a man's man's man's world / Great balls of fire / Don't let me be misunderstood / Good vibrations / Teenage in love / Young girl / She's not there / All shook up / Who's sorry now / Robot man / Shake, rattle and roll / Go now / Only the lonely / Young ones / We gotta get out of this place / Wipe out / Mr. Spaceman / Monster mash / Great balls of fire
CD QED 213
Tring / Nov '96 / Tring

RETURN TO THE FORBIDDEN PLANET
Studio Cast
Wipe out / It's a man's, man's, man's world / Great balls of fire / Don't let me be misunderstood / Good vibrations / Teenager in love / Young girl / She's not there / All shook up / Who's sorry now / Robot man / Shake, rattle and roll / Go now / Only the lonely / Young ones / We gotta get out of this place / Wipe out (reprise) / Mr. Spaceman / Monster mash / Great balls of fire
CD 85232
CMC / May '97 / BMG

REVENGE
Nitzsche, Jack *C*
Love theme / Friendship / Miryea / Betrayal / Jeep ride / On the beach / Illicit love / Tibey's revenge / Whorehouse and healing / Dead Texan / Confrontation / Miryea's death
CD FILMCD 065
Silva Screen / Aug '90 / Koch / Silva Screen

REVENGE IN EL PASO
Rustichelli, Carlo *C*
CD CDCIA 5094
Cinevox / Jan '93 / Koch / Silva Screen

REVENGE OF THE PINK PANTHER
Mancini, Henry *C*
Pink Panther / Simone / Give me some mo'l / Thar she blows / Balls caprice / Move 'em out / Touch of red / After the shower / Hong Kong fireworks / Almond eyes
CD 911132
Silva Screen / Jan '93 / Koch / Silva Screen

REVOLVER
Morricone, Ennio *C*
CD A 8919
Alhambra / Feb '92 / Silva Screen

RICHARD III
Richard III theme / Monarchy / People and the passion / Flower in Winter / Queen Elizabeth tango / Lady Ann's lament / Sitting on top of the world / Come be my love
CD 8287192
London / Apr '96 / PolyGram

RICHIE RICH
Silver Screen Orchestra
Silvestri, Alan *C*
CD VSD 5582
Varese Sarabande / Mar '95 / Pinnacle

RIDER ON THE RAIN
Lai, Francis *C*
CD A 8926
Alhambra / Mar '92 / Silva Screen

RIGHT AS THE RAIN
Cast Recording
Previn, Andre *C*
Price, Leontyne *L*
Right as rain / Sunrise sunset / It's good to have you near again / It never entered my mind / Nobody's heart / My melancholy baby / Sleepin' bee / They didn't believe me / Hello, young lovers / Love walked in / Where, I wonder
CD GD 82983
RCA / Apr '90 / BMG

RING, THE
City Of Prague Philharmonic Orchestra
Legrand, Michel *C*
Legrand, Michel *Con*
CD SSD 1072
Silva America / Feb '97 / Koch / Silva Screen

RINGO IL CAVALIERE SOLITARIO/UNA COLT IN PUGNO AL DIAVOLO/ L'LUTIMO MERCENARIO
De Masi, Francesco/Reverberi/Bruno Nicolai *C*
CD CDCR 32
Silva Screen / Apr '96 / Koch / Silva Screen

RINGO THE TEXICAN/IN A COLT'S SHADOW/FOR THE TASTE OF KILLING/ DYNAMITE JIM
Fidenco, Nico *C*
CD OST 129
Milano Dischi / Apr '96 / Silva Screen

RINK, THE
1983 Broadway Cast
Kander, John *C*
Ebb, Fred *L*
Colored lights / Chief cook and bottle washer / Don't ah ma me / Blue crystal / Under the roller coaster / Not enough magic / Here's to the rink / We can make it / After all these years / Angel's rink... / What... / Marry me / Mrs. A / Rink / Wallflower / All the children / Coda
CD CDTER 1091
TER / Sep '84 / Koch

RINK, THE
1988 London Cast
Kander, John *C*
Ebb, Fred *L*
CD CDTERS 1155
TER / Jan '90 / Koch

RIO CONCHOS (& The Artist Who Did Not Want To Paint/Prelude From Agony & The Ecstasy)
London Symphony Orchestra
Goldsmith, Jerry *C*
Goldsmith, Jerry *Con*
CD RVF 6007D
Intrada / Feb '90 / Koch / Silva Screen

RIO GRANDE
Sons Of The Pioneers
Young, Victor *C*
I'll take you home again Kathleen / Cattle call / Erie canal / Yellow stripes / My gal is purple / Down by the glenside / Footstore cavalry
CD VSD 5378
Varese Sarabande / Aug '93 / Pinnacle

RIOT ON SUNSET STRIP (& Standells Rarities)
Riot on Sunset Strip: *Standells* / Sunset Sally: *Mugwumps* / Sunset theme: *Sidewalk Sounds* / Old country: *Travis, Debra* / Don't need your lovin': *Chocolate Watch Band* / Children of the night: *Mom's Boys* / Make the music pretty: *Sidewalk Sounds* / Get away from here: *Standells* / Like my baby: *Drew* / Sitting there standing: *Chocolate Watch Band* / Love me: *Standells* / Batman: *Standells* / Our candidate: *Standells* / Boy who is lost: *Standells* / It's all in your mind: *Standells* / School girl: *Standells* / I hate to leave you: *Standells* / Looking at tomorrow: *Standells* / Don't say nothing at all: *Standells* / Try it: *Standells* / Rari: *Standells*
CD CDWIKD 113
Big Beat / Jun '93 / Pinnacle

RIPOUX CONTRE RIPOUX
Lai, Francis *C*
CD MANTRA 051
Silva Screen / Jan '93 / Koch / Silva Screen

RISING SUN
Tanaka, Seiichi & San Francisco Taiko Dojo Drums
Takemitsu, Toru *C*
Iwaki, Hiroyuki *Con*
CD 07822110032
Arista / Feb '94 / BMG

RISKY BUSINESS
Old time rock 'n' roll: *Seger, Bob* / Dream is always the same: *Tangerine Dream* / No future: *Tangerine Dream* / Mannish boy: *Waters, Muddy* / Pump: *Beck, Jeff* / DMSR: *Prince* / After the fall: *Journey* / In the air tonight: *Collins, Phil* / Love on a real train:

Tangerine Dream / Guido the killer pimp: *Tangerine Dream* / Lana: *Tangerine Dream*
CD **CDV 2302**
Virgin / May '87 / EMI

RIVER OF DEATH
Matson, Sasha *C*
CD **FILMCD 053**
Silva Screen / '90 / Koch / Silva Screen

RIVER, THE
Williams, John *C*
CD **VSD 5298**
Varese Sarabande / May '91 / Pinnacle

RIVERDANCE
Whelan, Bill *C*
Reel around the sun / Heart's cry: *Whelan, Bill* / Countess Cathleen/Women of the sidhe / Caoineadh cu chulainn / Shivna / Slip into spring / Riverdance / American wake / Lift the wings / Macedonian morning / Marta's dance/Russian dervish / Andalucia / Home and the heartland / Harvest / Heart's cry / Shivna / Riverdance / Lift the wings / Home and the heartland
CD **7567828162**
Warner Bros. / Nov '95 / Warner Music

RIVERDANCE (This Land - Inspired By Riverdance)
Kennedy, Fiona & Dun Carmel Band/Irish Dancers
CD **CDMFP 6237**
Music For Pleasure / Aug '96 / EMI

RIVERDANCE (Music From The Show)
Whelan, Bill *C*
Reel around the sun / Heart's cry / Countess Cathleen/Women of the Sidhe / Caoineadh cu chulainn (lament) / Shivna / Firedance / Slip into Spring / Riverdance / American wake (the Nova Scotia set) / Lift the wings / Macedonian morning / Marta's dance/The Russian dervish / Andulucia / Home and the heartland / Harvest / Riverdance
CD **UND 53076**
Celtic Heartbeat / Jun '97 / BMG

RIVERDANCE DISTILLED (Brendan Power Plays Music From Riverdance)
Power, Brendan
Countess Cathleen / Reel around the sun / Slip into Spring / American wake / Lift the wings / Riverdance / Caoineadh chu chulainn / Firedance/Andalucia / Riverdance/ Women of Sidhe / Marta's dance/Russian dervish
CD **CDTRAX 135**
Greentrax / Jun '97 / ADA / Direct / Duncans / Highlander

ROAD TO WELLVILLE
Portman, Rachel *C*
Snell, David *Con*
CD **VSD 5512**
Varese Sarabande / Jan '95 / Pinnacle

ROADGAMES/PATRICK
May, Brian *C*
CD **IMICD 1014**
Silva Screen / Jan '93 / Koch / Silva Screen

ROB ROY
CD **CDVMM 18**
Virgin / May '95 / EMI

ROBBERY UNDER ARMS
CD **IMICD 1013**
Silva Screen / Jan '93 / Koch / Silva Screen

ROBE, THE
Newman, Alfred *C*
Newman, Alfred *Con*
Farewell to Diana / Palm Sunday / Carriage of the cross / Marcellus returns to Capri / Village of Cana / Redemption of Marcellus / Miriam / Catacombs / Rescue of Demetrius / Better kingdom
CD **07822110112**
Fox Film Scores / Apr '94 / BMG

ROBERT AND ELIZABETH
1987 Chichester Festival Cast
Grainer, Ron *C*
Millar, Ronald *L*
Here on the corner of Wimpole Street / Family Moulton-Barrett / World outside / Moon in my pocket / I said love / You only to love me / Real thing / In a simple way / I know now / Escape me never / Soliloquy / Pass the eau de cologne / I'm the master here / Hate me please / Girls that boys dream about / Long ago I loved you / What the world calls love / Woman and man / Frustration
CD **OCRCD 6032**
First Night / Oct '95 / Pinnacle

ROBERT ET ROBERT
Lai, Francis *C*
CD **MANTRA 053**
Silva Screen / Jan '93 / Koch / Silva Screen

ROBIN HOOD
Burgon, Geoffrey *C*
Burgon, Geoffrey *Con*
CD **FILMCD 083**
Silva Screen / May '91 / Koch / Silva Screen

ROBIN HOOD - MEN IN TIGHTS
Mann, Hummie *C*
Brooks, Mel *L*
Mann, Hummie *Con*
CD **176392**
Milan / Feb '94 / Conifer/BMG / Silva Screen

ROBIN HOOD - PRINCE OF THIEVES
Kamen, Michael *C*
CD **5110502**
Polydor / Jul '91 / PolyGram

ROBOCOP (A Future To This Life)
Walsh, Joe
CD **ESMCD 491**
Essential / Apr '97 / BMG

ROBOCOP I
Poledouris, Basil *C*
Poledouris, Basil *Con*
Main title / Van chase / Murphy's death / Rock shop / Home / Robo vs. ED-209 / Dream / Across the board / Betrayal / Clarence frags Bob / Drive to Jones' office / We killed you / Directive IV / Robo tips his hat / Showdown
CD **VSD 47298**
Varese Sarabande / Apr '91 / Pinnacle

ROBOCOP II
Rosenman, Leonard *C*
Rosenman, Leonard *Con*
Overture / City mayhem / Happier days / Robo cruiser / Robo memories / Robo and Nuke / Robo fanfare / Robo and Cain chase / Creating the monster / Robo I vs Robo II
CD **VSD 5271**
Varese Sarabande / Aug '90 / Pinnacle

ROBOCOP III
Poledouris, Basil *C*
Poledouris, Basil/M. Boddicker *Con*
CD **VSD 5416**
Varese Sarabande / Nov '93 / Pinnacle

ROBOTJOX
Talgorn, Frederic *C*
CD **PCD 125**
Prometheus / Jan '93 / Silva Screen

ROCKERS
We 'a' rockers: *Inner Circle* / Money worries: *Maytones* / Police and thieves: *Murvin, Junior* / Book of rules: *Heptones* / Stepping razor: *Tosh, Peter* / Tenement yard: *Miller, Jacob* / Fade away: *Byles, Junior* / Rockers: *Wailer, Bunny* / Slave master: *Isaacs, Gregory* / Dread lion: *Perry, Lee 'Scratch' & The Upsetters* / Graduation in Zion: *Kiddus 1* / Jah no dead: *Burning Spear* / Satta a masagana: *Third World* / Natty takes over: *Hinds, Justin & The Dominoes* / Driving me backwards: *Eno, Brian* / Baby's on fire: *Eno, Brian* / Heartbreak hotel: *Cale, J.J.* / Standing in a buketful of blues: *Ayers, Roy* / Stranger in blue suede shoes: *Ayers, Roy* / Everybody's sometime and some people's all the time blues: *Ayers, Roy* / Two goes into four: *Ayers, Roy*
CD **RRCD 45**
Reggae Refreshers / May '94 / PolyGram / Vital

ROCKETEER, THE
Horner, James *C*
CD **HWD 161117**
Silva Screen / Apr '96 / Koch / Silva Screen

ROCKY HORROR PICTURE SHOW, THE
1990 London Cast
O'Brien, Richard *C*
Science fiction / Dammit Janet / Over at the Frankenstein place / Time warp / Sweet transvestite / Rocky's birth/Sword of Damocles / I can make you a man / Hot patootie - Bless my soul / I can make you a man (reprise) / Touch-a-touch-a-touch-a-touch me / Once in a while / Eddie's teddy / Planet Schmanet / Floor show - Rose tint my world / Fanfare - Don't dream it / Wild and untamed thing / I'm going home / Super heroes / Science fiction (reprise)
CD **CDMFP 5977**
Music For Pleasure / Dec '92 / EMI

ROCKY HORROR PICTURE SHOW, THE
Cast Recording
O'Brien, Richard *C*
CD **ESSCD 286**
Essential / Apr '95 / BMG

ROCKY HORROR PICTURE SHOW, THE
Cast Recording
O'Brien, Richard *C*
CD **GRF 231**
Tring / Aug '93 / Tring

ROCKY HORROR SHOW, THE
Cast Recording
O'Brien, Richard *C*
CD **CDTER 1221**
TER / Jul '94 / Koch

ROCKY HORROR SHOW, THE
Original Cast
CD **OCRCD 6040**
First Night / May '96 / Pinnacle

ROCKY HORROR SHOW, THE
CC Productions
O'Brien, Richard *C*
Science fiction double feature / Damn it Janet / Over at the Frankenstein's place / Time warp / Sweet transvestite / I can make you a man / Hot patootie bless my soul / I can make you a man / Touch-a-touch-a-touch-a-touch me / Eddie's teddy / Medley
CD **QED 201**
Tring / Nov '96 / Tring

ROCKY HORROR SHOW, THE
Cast Recording
O'Brien, Richard *C*
Yates, Martin *Con*
Science fiction / Damn it Janet / Over at Frankenstein's place / Sweet transvestite / Time warp / Touch a-touch a-touch me / Once in a while / Eddie's teddy / Rose tint my world / Hot patootie / I'm going home / Super heroes
CD **SHOWCD 025**
Showtime / Oct '96 / Disc / THE

ROCKY HORROR SHOW, THE
Studio Cast
O'Brien, Richard *C*
O'Brien, Richard *L*
Science fiction double feature / Damn it Janet / Over at Frankenstein's place / Time warp / Sweet transvestite / I can make you a man (reprise) / Hot patootie bless my soul / I can make you a man / Touch-a touch-a touch-a touch me / Eddie's teddy / Medley : rose tint my world/Don't dream it be it/Wild untame / I'm going home / Super heroes / Science fiction double feature / Super hero
CD **88092**
CMC / May '97 / BMG

ROCKY I
Conti, Bill *C*
Gonna fly now (Rocky theme) / Philadelphia morning / Going the distance / Reflections / Marine's hymn/Yankie doodle / Take you back / First date / You take my heart away / Fanfare for Rocky / Butkus / Alone in the ring / Final bell / Rocky's reward
CD **460812**
Silva Screen / Jan '93 / Koch / Silva Screen

ROCKY II
Conti, Bill *C*
Redemption / Gonna fly now (Rocky theme) / Conquest / Vigil / All of my life / Overture / Two kinds of love
CD **460822**
Silva Screen / Jan '93 / Koch / Silva Screen

ROCKY III
Conti, Bill *C*
Eye of the tiger: *Survivor* / Take you back (Tough Gym) / Pushin' / Reflections / Mickey / Take you back / Decision / Gonna fly now (Rocky theme) / Adrian / Conquest
CD **465612**
Silva Screen / Jan '93 / Koch / Silva Screen

RODGERS AND HAMMERSTEIN'S STATE FAIR
Original Broadway Cast
Rodgers, Richard *C*
Hammerstein II, Oscar *L*
Overture / Opening / It might as well be spring / Driving at night / Our state fair / That's for me / More than just a friend / Isn't it kinda fun / You never had it so good / Reprise: It might as be spring / When I go out walking wiht my baby / So far / It's a grand night for singing / Entr'acte / Man I used to be / All I owe Ioway / That's the way it happens / Boys and girls like you and me / Next time it happens / Finale ultimo
CD **DRGCD 94765**
DRG / Aug '96 / Discovery / New Note/ Pinnacle

ROMANCE ROMANCE
1988 Broadway Cast
Herrmann, Keith & Barry Harman *C*
Little comedy / Goodbye Emily / I'll always remember the song / Night it had to end / Think of the odds / Let's not talk about it / Through a window / Small craft warnings / So glad I married her / Letters / It's not too late / Oh what a performance / Women of Vienna / Summer share / Plans A and B / Words he doesn't say / Romantic notions / Romance romance
CD **CDTER 1161**
TER / Feb '89 / Koch

ROMEO AND JULIET
Eidelman, Cliff *C*
CD **VSD 5752**
Varese Sarabande / Mar '97 / Pinnacle

ROMEO AND JULIET
Crush: *Garbage* / Local God: *Everclear* / Pretty piece of flesh: *One Inch Punch* / Kissing you: *Des'ree* / Whatever: *Butthole Surfers* / Lovefool: *Cardigans* / Young hearts run free: *Mazelle, Kym* / Everybody'd free: *Traver, Quindon* / To you I bestow: *Mundy* / Talk show host: *Mundy* / Little star: *Nordenstam, Stina* / You and me song: *Wannadies*
CD **PRMDCD 28**
Capitol / Aug '97 / EMI

ROMEO IS BLEEDING
Isham, Mark
Isham, Mark *C*
Romeo is bleeding / Bird alone / Romeo is moving / Romeo and Juliette / Nightmare on Marple Street / I know better now / Romeo is searching / Romeo and Natalie / Mona / Take two toes / Back street driving / Mona lends a helping hand / Dance of death / Empty chambers / Romeo is dreaming / Romeo alone
CD **5212312**
Verve / Jan '94 / PolyGram

ROMPER STOMPER
CD **PTR 002**
Picture This / Jun '97 / Greyhound

ROMY AND MICHELLE'S HIGH SCHOOL REUNION
CD **1620962**
Polydor / Aug '97 / PolyGram

ROSE AND THE GUN, THE
Johnson, Laurie *C*
CD **FLYCD 103**
Fly / Aug '95 / Total/BMG

ROSE OF WASHINGTON SQUARE/ GOLDDIGGERS OF 1933/DOLLY SISTERS
Pretty baby: *Jolson, Al* / Rock-a-bye your baby with a dixie melody: *Jolson, Al* / California here I come: *Jolson, Al* / I never knew heaven could speak: *Jolson, Al* / Rose of Washington square: *Jolson, Al* / My mammy: *Jolson, Al* / My man: *Faye, Alice* / We're in the money: *Rogers, Ginger* / Shadow waltz: *Powell, Dick* / Pettin' in the park: *Powell, Dick* / Remember my forgotten man: *Blondell, Joan & Etta Moten* / I'm always chasing rainbows: *Blondell, Joan & Etta Moten* / We've been around / Carolina in the morning / Don't be too old fashioned / Powder lipstick and rouge / I'm always chasing rainbows / Darktown strutter's ball / I'm always chasing rainbow / I can't begin to tell you / Sidewalks of New York
CD **CD 60009**
Great Movie Themes / Jun '97 / Target/ BMG

ROSE, THE
Midler, Bette
Midnight in Memphis / Concert monologue / When a man loves a woman / Sold my soul to rock'n'roll / Keep on rockin' / Love me with a feeling / Camellia / Homecoming monologue / Stay with me / Let me call you sweetheart / Rose / Whose side are you on
CD **7567827782**
East West / Nov '95 / Warner Music

ROSEMARY'S BABY
Komeda, Christopher *C*
CD **TSU 0116**
Tsunami / Jan '95 / Silva Screen

ROSENEMIL
Kalman, Charles/Stefan Zorzor *C*
CD **CIN 22072**
Silva Screen / Jan '95 / Koch / Silva Screen

ROTHSCHILD'S VIOLIN
Leiferkus, Sergei & Ilya Levinsky/Konstantin Pluzhnikov/Marina Shaguch Fleischmann, Benjamin/Dmitri Shostakovich *C*
Rozhdestvensky, Gennadi *Con*
Wedding band / What are you playing / This small town is worse than a village / Band music / Do you remember, Iakov, do you recall / God had given us a little girl / Band music/Make that trumpet merrier / Down here on earth everything flies so fast / Rothschild runs away / Loss-one coffin for Marfa Ivanova / If they could live without hatred or evil / It's better to die / Be kind to me, don't hit me / Rothschild plays the violin
CD **09026684342**
RCA Victor / Nov '96 / BMG

ROTHSCHILDS, THE
Cast Recording
Bock, Jerry *C*
Harnick, Sheldon *L*
Greene, Milton *Con*
CD **SK 30337**
Sony Broadway / Nov '92 / Sony

ROULA HIDDEN SECRETS
Schleip, Dieter *C*
CD **CST 8056**
Colosseum / Nov '96 / Pinnacle

ROUND MIDNIGHT
Hancock, Herbie *C*
Round Midnight / Body and soul / Berangere's nightmare / Fair weather / Una noche con Francis / Peacocks / How long has this been going on / Rhythm-a-ning / Still time / Minuit aux Champs Elysees / Chan's song
CD **4867992**
Columbia / Dec '96 / Sony

ROXANNE
Smeaton, Bruce *C*
Roxanne / Starry sky / Just honest - we did it / Roxanne's theme / Game, set and match / Panache / Roxanne's eyes / Blue Danube / Written in the wind / Roxanne (End title)
CD **CDC 1000**
Silva Screen / Jul '88 / Koch / Silva Screen

RUBY
Scott, John *C*
CD **MAF 7026D**
Intrada / Jan '93 / Koch / Silva Screen

RUDDIGORE
Light Opera Company
Sullivan, Sir Arthur *C*
Gilbert, W.S. *L*
CD **CDHD 255**
Happy Days / May '95 / Conifer/BMG

RUDDIGORE
New Sadler's Wells Opera Chorus/ Orchestra
Sullivan, Sir Arthur *C*
Gilbert, W.S. *L*
Phipps, S. *Con*
2CD **CDTER2 1128**
TER / Aug '87 / Koch

RUDDIGORE
Baker, George & Richard Lewis/Glyndebourne Festival Choir/Pro Arte Orchestra
Sullivan, Sir Arthur *C*

Gilbert, W.S. *L*
Godfrey, I. *Con*
2CD CMS 7644122
EMI Classics / Apr '94 / EMI

RUDDIGORE/COX AND BOX
D'Oyly Carte Opera Chorus/Orchestra Of The Royal Opera House
Sullivan, Sir Arthur *C*
Gilbert, W.S. *L*
Godfrey, I. *Con*
2CD 4173552
London / Jan '90 / PolyGram

RUNAWAY
Goldsmith, Jerry *C*
CD VCD 47221
Varese Sarabande / Jan '89 / Pinnacle

RUNAWAY TRAIN
Jones, Trevor *C*
Jailbreak / Moving on / Destination unknown / Clear the track / Reflections / Runaway train / Prison memories / Yellow rose of Texas / Collision course / Past, present and future / Red for danger / Gloria / End of the line
CD CDCH 267
Milan / '86 / Conifer/BMG / Silva Screen

RUNNING MAN, THE
Faltermeyer, Harold
Faltermeyer, Harold *C*
CD VCD 47356
Varese Sarabande / Jan '89 / Pinnacle

RUSH
Clapton, Eric
Clapton, Eric *C*
New recruit / Tracks and lines / Realization / Kristen and Jim / Preludin fugue / Cold turkey / Will gaines / Help me up / Don't know which way to go / Tears in heaven
CD 7599267942
WEA / Oct '94 / Warner Music

RUTH RENDELL MYSTERIES, THE
Bennett, Brian
Bennett, Brian *C*
Ruth Rendell Mysteries / Wexford in LA / Put on by cunning / Search for Mina / Love from Doon / Castle / Kissing the gunner's daughter / New lease of death / Let me believe / Letters from the past / Cry from the tomb / Strange confessions / Corsica / Day in Provence / Achilles heel / Mouse in the corner / Mother and daughter / Means of evil / Premonition / Speaker of Mandarin
CD CDSTM 2
Soundtrack Music / May '94 / EMI

RUTHLESS - THE MUSICAL
Los Angeles Cast
CD VSD 5476
Varese Sarabande / Oct '94 / Pinnacle

RYAN'S DAUGHTER (& Selections From The Train & Grand Prix)
Jarre, Maurice *C*
CD AK 47989
Cinevox / Jan '93 / Koch / Silva Screen

S

SAFE
Tomney, Ed *C*
CD IONIC 14CD
The Fine Line / Aug '95 / RTM/Disc

SAHARA
Morricone, Ennio *C*
Morricone, Ennio *Con*
CD MAF 7047D
Intrada / Mar '93 / Koch / Silva Screen

SAIL AWAY
Broadway Cast
Coward, Sir Noel *C*
CD ZDM 7647592
EMI Classics / Apr '94 / EMI

SAINT, THE
Saint theme: *Orbital* / 6 underground: *Sneaker Pimps* / Oil 1: *Moby* / Atom bomb: *Fluke* / Roses fade: *Luscious Jackson* / Setting sun: *Chemical Brothers* / Pearl's girl: *Underworld* / Out of my mind: *Duran Duran* / Da funk: *Daft Punk* / Little wonder: *Bowie, David* / Pollaroid millenium: *Superior* / Dream without a dream: *Dreadzone* / In the absence of sun: *Sheik, Duncan* / Before today: *Everything But The Girl*
CD CDVUS 126
Virgin / Apr '97 / EMI

SALAAM BOMBAY
Subramaniam, L.
Subramaniam, L. *C*
Subramaniam, L. *Con*
CD DRGCD 12595
DRG / Jan '95 / Discovery / New Note/ Pinnacle
CD 119052
Musidisc / Sep '96 / Discovery

SALAD DAYS
1982 London Cast
Slade, Julian *C*
Slade, Julian & Dorothy Reynolds *L*
Things that are done by a Don / We said we wouldn't look back / Find yourself something to do / I sit in the sun / Oh, look at me / Hush-hush / Out of breath / Cleopatra / Sand in my eyes / It's easy to sing / We're looking for a piano / I've had the time of my life / Saucer song / We don't understand our children
CD CDTER 1018
TER / Apr '94 / Koch

SALAD DAYS (Highlights)
London Cast
Slade, Julian *C*
Slade, Julian & Dorothy Reynolds *L*
Things that are done by a Don / We said we wouldn't look back / Find yourself something to do / I sit in the sun / Oh, look at me / Hush-hush / Cleopatra / Sand in my eyes / It's easy to sing / We're looking for a piano / I've had the time of my life / We don't understand our children
CD SHOWCD 009
Showtime / Feb '95 / Disc / THE

SALAD DAYS
London Cast
Slade, Julian *C*
Slade, Julian & Dorothy Reynolds *L*
CD SMK 66176
Sony West End / Jul '94 / Sony

SALAD DAYS (40th Anniversary Production)
London Cast
Slade, Julian *C*
Slade, Julian & Dorothy Reynolds *L*
Hutchinson, S. *Con*
CD SCORECD 43
First Night / Apr '96 / Pinnacle

SAMANTHA
McNeely, Joel *C*
CD MAF 7040D
Intrada / Feb '93 / Koch / Silva Screen

SAND PEBBLES, THE
Goldsmith, Jerry *C*
CD TSU 0107
Tsunami / Jan '93 / Silva Screen

SANDPIPER, THE
Mandel, Johnny *C*
CD 5312292
Verve / Jun '96 / PolyGram

SANTA CLAUSE, THE
Convertino, Michael *C*
CD 323642
RCA Victor / Nov '95 / BMG

SARAFINA
Broadway Cast
Ngema, Mbongeni *C*
Zibuyille emasisweni / Sarafina / Lord's prayer / Yes, mistress it's a pity / Give us power / Afunani amaphoyisa e Soweto / Nkois sikeleli Afrika / Freedom is coming tomorrow / Entr'acte / Meeting tonight / Stand and fight / Uyamemeza ungoma / Iswe lami / Wawungalelani / Mama Sechaba / Isizwe (the nation is dying) / Goodbye / Kilimanjaro / Africa is burning in the sun / Olyaithi (It's all right) / Bring back Nelson Mandela / Freedom is coming tomorrow (reprise)
2CD RD 89307
RCA Victor / Jul '89 / BMG

SARAFINA (The Sound Of Freedom)
Myers, Stanley *C*
Sarafina / Lord's prayer / Nkonyane kandaba / Freedom is coming tomorrow / Sabela / Sechaba / Safa saphel' isizwe / Thank you mama / Vuma dlozi lami / Lizobuya / One more time
CD 9362450602
Warner Bros. / Jan '91 / Warner Music

SARTANA
Piccioni, Piero *C*
CD PRCD 124
Preamble / Apr '96 / Silva Screen

SATURDAY NIGHT FEVER
Stayin' alive: *Bee Gees* / How deep is your love: *Bee Gees* / Night fever: *Bee Gees* / More than a woman: *Bee Gees* / Jive talkin': *Bee Gees* / You should be dancing: *Bee Gees* / Calypso breakdown: *Donaldson, Ralph* / If I can't have you: *Elliman, Yvonne* / Fifth of Beethoven: *Murphy, Walter* / Open sesame: *Kool & The Gang* / Boogie shoes: *K.C. & The Sunshine Band* / MFSB: *K.C. & The Sunshine Band* / K Jee: *K.C. & The Sunshine Band* / Disco inferno: *Tramps* / Manhattan skyline: *Tramps* / Night on disco mountain: *Tramps* / Salsation: *Tramps*
2CD 8253892
Polydor / Oct '95 / PolyGram

SAVAGE (Super Soul Soundtrack)
Julian, Don
Julian, Don *C*
Savage: *Julian, Don & Arthur G. Wright* / Lay it on your head / Where I'm coming from / It's a sad song: *Wright, Arthur G.* / My favourite beer joint / Janitizio / Just kiss me
CD CDSEWM 114
Southbound / Apr '97 / Pinnacle

SAVAGE NIGHTS
Collard, Cyril *C*
CD 5158622
Silva Screen / Jan '93 / Koch / Silva Screen

SAY AMEN, SOMEBODY
Dorsey, Thomas A. *C*
Highway to heaven / Singing in my soul / What manner of man is this / When I've done my best / Take my hand, precious Lord / I'm his child / He chose me / No ways tired / Jesus dropped the charges / I'll never turn back / Storm is passing over / It's gonna rain / He brought us / Canaan
CD DRGCD 12584
DRG / Jan '95 / Discovery / New Note/ Pinnacle

SCARLET LETTER
Barry, John *C*
Theme / Arrival / Search for home / Hester rides to town / Bird / Swimmer / Very exhilarating read / I'm not the man I seem / Agnus dei / I can see what others cannot / Love scene / Are you with child / Small act of contrition / Birth / I baptise this child / Pearl / She will not speak / Dr. Roger Prynne / Hester walks through town / Poor fatherless child / Attempt at rape / Savages have killed him / Round up / I am the father of her child / Indians attack / Letter has served a purpose / End title
CD 4835772
Epic / Jan '96 / Sony

SCARLETT (Sung In Japanese)
Japanese Cast
Rome, Harold *C*
He loves me / We belong to you / Two of a kind / Blissful Christmas / My soldier / Goodbye my honey / Lonely stranger / Time for love / What is love / Gambling man / Which way is home / Bonnie blue flag / O'Hara / Newlywed's song / Strange and wonderful / Blueberry eyes / Little wonder / Bonnie gone
2CD DRGCD 13105
DRG / Jan '95 / Discovery / New Note/ Pinnacle

SCENT OF GREEN PAPAYA
Tiet, Ton-That *C*
CD 887794
Milan / May '94 / Conifer/BMG / Silva Screen

SCHINDLER'S LIST
Boston Symphony Orchestra with Itzhak Perlman
Williams, John *C*
Williams, John *Con*
Theme / Jewish town / Immolation / Remembrances / Schindler's workforce / Oyf'n pripetshok / And nacht aktion / I could have done more / Auschwitz-Birkenau / Stolen memories / Making the list / Give me your names / Yeroushalaim chel zahav / Theme (reprise)
CD MCD 10969
MCA / Feb '94 / BMG

SCHOOL TIES
Jarre, Maurice *C*
CD 244762
Silva Screen / Jan '93 / Koch / Silva Screen

SCOOP
Donaggio, Pino *C*
CD 4711842
Silva Screen / Jan '93 / Koch / Silva Screen

SCRAMBLED FEET
Broadway Cast
Driver, John & Jeffrey Haddow *C*
CD DRGCD 6105
DRG / Jan '95 / Discovery / New Note/ Pinnacle

SCREAM
Youth of America: *Birdbrain* / Whisper: *Catherine* / Red right hand: *Cave, Nick & The Bad Seeds* / eon't fear the reaper: *Cave, Nick & The Bad Seeds* / Artificial world: *Cruise, Julee & The Flow* / Better than me: *Sister Machine Gun* / Whisper to a scream: *Soho* / Schools out: *Last Hard Men* / Drop dead gorgeous: *Republica* / Trouble in Woodboro/Sidney's lament: *Beltrami, Marco*
CD 0022822CIN
Edel / Jul '97 / Pinnacle
CD TVT 8080
TVT / Jun '97 / Cargo / Greyhound

SCROOGE
1992 Cast
Bricusse, Leslie *C*
CD CDTER 1194
TER / Jan '93 / Koch

SCROOGED
Put a little love in your heart: *Green, Al & Annie Lennox* / Wonderful life: *Lennon, Julian* / Sweetest thing: *New Voices Of Freedom* / Love you take: *Hartman, Dan & Denise Lopez* / Get up 'n' dance: *Kool Moe Dee* / We three kings of Orient are: *Davis, Miles & Larry Carlton* / Christmas must be tonight: *Robertson, Robbie* / Brown eyed girl: *Poindexter, Buster* / Christmas song: *Cole, Natalie*
CD 5513202
Spectrum / Sep '95 / PolyGram

SEA HAWK, THE
Utah Symphony Orchestra
Korngold, Erich *C*
CD VCD 47304
Varese Sarabande / Jan '89 / Pinnacle

SEA HAWK, THE
Korngold, Erich *C*
CD CDTER 1164
TER / Jan '91 / Koch

SEA OF LOVE
Jones, Trevor *C*
Sea of love: *Phillips, Phil & Twilights* / Poetic killing / Cocktails and fingerprints / Fear and passion / Helen's 45 / Is she or isn't she / Sea of love Reprise
CD 5501302
Spectrum / Oct '93 / PolyGram

SEA POWER
Whalen, Michael
Whalen, Michael *C*
CD ND 66005
Narada / Nov '93 / ADA / New Note/ Pinnacle

SEAFORTH
Petit, Jean Claude *C*
Seaforth / Light / Bri / In a public house / First kiss / Love / I can do anything / Tension / Obsession / Bob's family / Petite fugue / Waiting / Diana / Don't call here / Diana drama / Paula and Bob / Suspense / Melancholly / In private / Paula / End
CD DSHCD 7016
D-Sharp / Oct '94 / Pinnacle

SEAQUEST DSV
Debney, John *C*
Debney, John *Con*
CD VSD 5565
Varese Sarabande / Jul '95 / Pinnacle

SEARCHING FOR BOBBY FISHER
Horner, James *C*
CD 9245322
Silva Screen / Jan '93 / Koch / Silva Screen

SEASON IN HELL, A
Jarre, Maurice *C*
CD CDA 8923
Tsunami / Jan '95 / Silva Screen

SECOND BEST
Boswell, Simon *C*
CD 246312
Milan / Aug '95 / Conifer/BMG / Silva Screen

SECOND TIME LUCKY
Stone, Laurie & Garry MacDonald *C*
CD IMCD 1016
Silva Screen / Jan '93 / Koch / Silva Screen

SECRET GARDEN, THE
Cracow Boys Choir/Sinfonia Varsovia
Preisner, Zbigniew *C*
Michniewski, W. *Con*
CD VSD 5443
Varese Sarabande / Sep '93 / Pinnacle

SECRET GARDEN, THE
Cast Recording
CD VSD 5451
Varese Sarabande / Oct '94 / Pinnacle

SECRET OF NIMH, THE
Goldsmith, Jerry *C*
Goldsmith, Jerry *Con*
CD VSD 5541
Varese Sarabande / Mar '95 / Pinnacle

SECRET OF ROAN INISH, THE
CD DARING 3015CD
Daring / Sep '95 / ADA / CM / Direct

SECRET OF THE SAHARA
Morricone, Ennio *C*
Secret of the Sahara: *Morricone, Ennio* / Red ghosts: *Morricone, Ennio* / Sholomon: *Morricone, Ennio* / Mountain: *Morricone, Ennio* / Kerim: *Morricone, Ennio* / Hawk: *Morricone, Ennio* / Golden door: *Morricone, Ennio* / Myth and the adventure: *Morricone, Ennio* / Anthea and the desert: *Morricone, Ennio* / Farewell Orso: *Morricone, Ennio* / Death of Tamameth: *Morricone, Ennio* / Saharan dram: *Morricone, Ennio* / Miriam and Philip: *Morricone, Ennio* / Second dedication: *Morricone, Ennio* / First dedication: *Morricone, Ennio*
CD 74321342262
RCA / Jun '96 / BMG

SECRET POLICEMAN'S CONCERT, THE
Cast Recording
CD CCSCD 351
Castle / Nov '92 / BMG

SEESAW
1973 Broadway Cast
Coleman, Cy *C*
Fields, Dorothy *L*
Seesaw / My city / Nobody does it like me / In tune / Spanglish / Welcome to Holiday Inn / You're a loveable lunatic / He's good for me / Ride out the storm / Entr'acte / We've got it / Poor everybody else / Chapter 54, Number 1909 / Seesaw ballet / It's not where you start / I'm way ahead and seesaw / It's not where you start (bows)
CD DRGCD 6108
DRG / Jun '92 / Discovery / New Note/ Pinnacle

SELFISH GIANT, THE
1993 Cast
Jenkins, Michael *C*
Williams, Nigel *L*
CD CDTER 1206
TER / Nov '93 / Koch

SENSE AND SENSIBILITY
Doyle, Patrick *C*
Eaglen, J./R. Ziegler *Con*
CD _______ **SK 62258**
Sony Classical / Nov '96 / Sony

SENZA PELLE (No Skin)
Ovadia, Moni/Alfredo Lacosegliaz *C*
CD _______ **GDM 2005**
Silva Screen / Jan '95 / Koch / Silva Screen

SEPOLTA VIVA/THE ANTICHRIST
Morricone, Ennio *C*
CD _______ **CDCR 17**
Silva Screen / Jul '94 / Koch / Silva Screen

SEQUEL, THE (It Ain't Over)
Jackson, Millie & Cast
CD _______ **ICH 15042**
Ichiban / Mar '97 / Direct / Koch

SERPENT AND THE RAINBOW, THE
Fiedel, Brad *C*
CD _______ **VCD 47362**
Varese Sarabande / Jan '89 / Pinnacle

SERPICO
Theodorakis, Mikis *C*
CD _______ **SR 50061**
Sakkaris / Oct '93 / Pinnacle

SET IT OFF
Angel / From yo blind side / Heist / Let it go / Come on / Angelic wars / Name callin' / Missing you / Don't let go (Love) / Days of our lives / Sex is on my mind / Live to regret / Set it off / Hey Joe
CD _______ **7559619952**
East West / Oct '96 / Warner Music

SET IT OFF (Score)
Young, Christopher *C*
CD _______ **VSD 5779**
Varese Sarabande / Dec '96 / Pinnacle

SEVEN
CD _______ **0022432CIN**
Edel / Jan '96 / Pinnacle

SEVEN BRIDES FOR SEVEN BROTHERS
1986 London Cast
De Paul, Gene *C*
Mercer, Johnny *L*
Yates, Martin *Con*
Overture / Bless your beautiful hide / Wonderful wonderful day / One man / Goin' courtin' / Love never goes away / Sobbin' women / Townsfolk's lament / Woman ought to know her place / We gotta make it through the winter / We gotta make it through the winter (Reprise) / Spring spring spring / Woman ought to know her place (Reprise) / Glad that you were born / Wedding dance / Goin' courtin/Wonderful wonderful day
CD _______ **OCRCD 6008**
First Night / Oct '95 / Pinnacle

SEVEN BRIDES FOR SEVEN BROTHERS
De Paul, Gene *C*
Mercer, Johnny *L*
Bless your beautiful hide / Spring, spring, spring / Wonderful, wonderful day / When you're in love / Goin' cotin / Hoedown / Lonesome polecat / Sobbin' women / June bride
CD _______ **PWKS 4209**
Carlton / Jul '94 / Carlton

SEVEN BRIDES FOR SEVEN BROTHERS
Film Cast
De Paul, Gene *C*
Mercer, Johnny *L*
Main title / Bless yore beautiful hide / Do unto udders / Bless yore beautiful hide / Wonderful wonderful day / Adam in treetop / When you're in love / Goin' co'tin' / Barn dance / Barn raising/fight / When you're in love / Brothers advice/Lonesome Winter / Lament / Lovesick / Sobbin' women / Kidnapped and chase / June bride / Spring Spring Spring / When you're in love / Girls girls girls/End title / Bless yore beautiful hide / Lament / Goin' co'tin' / Queen of the May / When you're in love / Spring Spring Spring
CD _______ **CDODEON 17**
Soundtracks / Aug '96 / EMI

SEVEN BRIDES FOR SEVEN BROTHERS
Cast Recording
De Paul, Gene *C*
Mercer, Johnny *L*
Overture: *Cast* / Bless your beautiful hide: *Cast* / Wonderful wonderful day: *Cast* / Goin' courtin': *Cast* / Love never goes away: *Cast* / Sobbin' women: *Cast* / Women ought to know her place: *Cast* / We've gotta make it through the winter: *Cast* / Lonesome polecat: *Cast* / Spring, spring, spring: *Cast* / Glad that you were born: *Cast* / Finale: *Cast*
CD _______ **SHOWCD 051**
Showtime / Apr '97 / Disc / THE

SEVEN DEADLY SINS (& Little Threepenny Music: Songs of Kurt Weill)
Johnson, Julia Mignes/London Symphony Orchestra
Weill, Kurt *C*
Tilson Thomas, Michael *Con*
CD _______ **MK 44529**
Masterworks / Jan '89 / Sony

SEVEN DEADLY SINS
Reaux, Angelina & New York Philharmonic Orchestra
Weill, Kurt *C*
Brecht, Bertolt *L*
Masur, Kurt *Con*
CD _______ **4509950292**
Teldec Classics / Jan '95 / Warner Music

SEVEN DEADLY SINS
Van Otter, A./North German Symphony Orchestra
Weill, Kurt *C*
Brecht, Bertolt *L*
Gardiner, John Eliot *Con*
CD _______ **4398942**
Deutsche Grammophon / Dec '94 / PolyGram

SEVEN DEADLY SINS
Lemper, Ute/Cast & Berlin RIAS Sinfonietta
Weill, Kurt *C*
Brecht, Bertolt *L*
Mauceri, John *Con*
CD _______ **4301682**
Decca / Apr '91 / PolyGram

SEVEN DEADLY SINS
May, Gisela & Peter Schreier/Hans Joachim Rotzsch/Leipzig Rundfunk Sinfonie Orchestra
Weill, Kurt *C*
Brecht, Bertolt *L*
Kegel, Herbert & Heinz Roger/Henry Krtschill *Con*
CD _______ **0020692BC**
Berlin Classics / Sep '96 / Complete/ Pinnacle

SEVEN DEADLY SINS
Stratas, Teresa & Orchestre De L'Opera National De Lyon
Weill, Kurt *C*
Nagano, Kurt *Con*
CD _______ **0630170682**
Erato / May '97 / Warner Music

SEVEN DEADLY SINS/HAPPY END
Lenya, Lotte
Weill, Kurt *C*
Brecht, Bertolt *L*
Bruckner-Ruggenberg, Wilhelm *Con*
CD _______ **MPK 45886**
Masterworks / Jan '93 / Sony

SEVEN MURDERS FOR SCOTLAND YARD/7 HYDE PARK: LA CASA MALEDET
Piccioni, Piero/Francesco De Masi *C*
CD _______ **CDCR 29**
Silva Screen / Apr '96 / Koch / Silva Screen

SEVENTH SIGN
Nitzsche, Jack *C*
Opening, fish, desert, wrath, 1st seal / Nightmare / David's apartment / Abby follows David to the synagogue / World in trouble / Parchment 229 / Stabbing / Attempted suicide / Lucci revealed / Last martyr / Walk to the gas chamber / Birth / Abby's death / End credits
CD _______ **EDL 25062**
Edel / Jan '89 / Pinnacle

SEVENTH VOYAGE OF SINBAD, THE
Herrmann, Bernard *C*
CD _______ **VCD 47256**
Varese Sarabande / Jan '89 / Pinnacle

SHADOW OF THE WOLF
Jarre, Maurice *C*
CD _______ **121462**
Milan / Jan '95 / Conifer/BMG / Silva Screen

SHADOW, THE (Score/Songs)
Goldsmith, Jerry *C*
Goldsmith, Jerry *Con*
CD _______ **07822187632**
Arista / Sep '94 / BMG

SHADOWLANDS
London Symphony Orchestra
Fenton, George *C*
CD _______ **CDQ 5550932**
Angel / Mar '94 / EMI

SHAFT
Hayes, Isaac
Hayes, Isaac *C*
Shaft / Bumpy's lament / Walk from Regio's / Ellie's love theme / Shaft's cab ride / Cafe Regio's / Early Sunday morning / Be yourself / Friend's place / Soulsville / No name bar / Bumpy's blues / Shaft strikes again / Do your thing / End theme
CD _______ **CDSXD 021**
Stax / Oct '89 / Pinnacle

SHAKA ZULU
Pollecutt, Dave *C*
CD _______ **CDC 1002**
Silva Screen / Mar '92 / Koch / Silva Screen

SHAKEDOWN
Ayres, Mark *C*
CD _______ **FILMCD 718**
Silva Screen / Jan '96 / Koch / Silva Screen

SHALLOW GRAVE
Boswell, Simon *C*
Shallow grave: *Leftfield* / Shallow grave theme / My baby just cares for me: *Simone, Nina* / Laugh not riot / Release the dubs: *Leftfield* / Strips the willo: *Carmichael, John & His Band* / Loft conversion / Spade we need a spade / Shallow grave, deep depression / Hugo's last trip / Happy heart: *Williams, Andy*
CD _______ **CDEMC 3699**
EMI / Feb '95 / EMI

SHANGHAI TRIAD
Guangtian, Zhang *C*
Beddy-bye, beddy-bye over Grandma's bridge / Main theme / Go away / Bright moon / Bijou cries / Lilac menuet / Murder on a rainy night / Express train / Garden / Tree under the bright moon / Shui Sheng climbs the stairs / False pretenses / Umbrella / Game (Mah Jong) / Russian hills / Shuisheng and bijou / Escape from Shanghai / Eyes of Shui Sheng / Bright moon (instrumental) / Conversation at night / Main theme (reprise) / Beddy-bye, beddy-bye over Grandma's bridge (reprise)
CD _______ **CDVIR 44**
Virgin / Nov '95 / EMI

SHARPE - OVER THE HILLS AND FAR AWAY (Music From The TV Series)
Overture: *Moscow Symphony Orchestra* / Sharpe's theme: *Moscow Symphony Orchestra* / I'm 95: *Band Of The Light Division* / Over the hills and far away: *Tams, John* / Spanish sword: *Muldowney, Dominic* / Rogue's march: *Tams, John* / Collier recruit: *Rusby, Kate* / Bird in the bush: *Tams, John* / Colours: *Muldowney, Dominic* / Shilling: *Muldowney, Dominic* / Spanish bride: *Tams, John* / Gentleman soldier: *Tams, John* / Bugle call - Moneymusk: *Band Of The Light Division* / Broken hearted I will wander: *Rusby, Kate* / Badajoz: *Muldowney, Dominic* / Rambling soldier: *Tams, John & Barry Coope* / Huntsman's chorus: *Tams, John & Barry Coope* / Italian song: *Tams, John & Barry Coope* / Johnny is gone for a soldier: *Tams, John* / Forlorn hope: *Muldowney, Dominic* / Love farewell: *Tams, John* / Sunset: *Band Of The Light Division* / Sharpe's song: *Tams, John*
CD _______ **VTCD 81**
Virgin / Apr '96 / EMI

SHATTERED
Silvestri, Alan *C*
CD _______ **262208**
Milan / Jan '95 / Conifer/BMG / Silva Screen

SHAWSHANK REDEMPTION, THE
Newman, Thomas *C*
May / Shawshank prison (stoic theme) / New fish / Rock hammer / Inch of his life / If I didn't care: *Ink Spots* / Brooks was here / His judgement cometh / Suds on the roof/ Workfield / Shawshank redemption / Lovesick blues: *Williams, Hank* / Elmo blatch / Sisters Zihuatanejo / Marriage of Figaro: *Deutsch Opera Berlin/Karl Bohm* / Lovely Raquel / And that right soon / Compass and guns / So was red / End titles
CD _______ **4783322**
Epic / Feb '95 / Sony

SHE LOVES ME
1963 Broadway Cast
Bock, Jerry *C*
Harnick, Sheldon *L*
Loud, D. *Con*
CD _______ **VSD 5464**
Varese Sarabande / Jun '94 / Pinnacle

SHE LOVES ME
1994 London Cast
Bock, Jerry *C*
Harnick, Sheldon *L*
Scott, R. *Con*
Overture / Good morning good day / Sounds while selling / Days gone by / No more candy / Three letters / Tonight at eight / Perspective / I don't know his name / Goodbye, George / Will he like me / Ilona / I resolve / Romantic atmosphere / Tango tragique / Mr Nowack, will you / Dear friend / Entr'acte / Try me / Where's my shoe / Vanilla ice cream / She loves me / Trip to the library / Grand knowing you / Tweleve days to Christmas / Finale
CD _______ **OCRCD 6052**
First Night / May '97 / Pinnacle

SHE LOVES ME
1964 London Cast
Bock, Jerry *C*
Harnick, Sheldon *L*
Ainsworth, A. *Con*
Overture/Good morning, good day / Sounds while selling / No more chocolates / Letters / Tonight at eight / Perspective / Ilona / Heads I win / Romantic atmosphere / Dear friend / Try me / Ice cream / She loves me / Trip to the library / Grand knowing you / Twelve days of Christmas / Ice cream (reprise)
CD _______ **CDANGEL 6**
Angel / Apr '94 / EMI

SHELTERING SKY, THE
Sakamoto, Ryuichi *C*
Sacred koran / Sheltering sky / Belly / Port's composition / On the bed (dream) / Loneliness / On the hill / Kyoto / Cemetry / Dying / Market / Grand Hotel / Louange au prophet houria aaichi flute / Je chante / Midnight sun / Fever ride / Chantavec citare / Marnia's tent / Goula lima / Happy bus ride / Night train / Guedra
CD _______ **CDV 2652**
Virgin / Nov '90 / EMI

SHERLOCK HOLMES (The Sign of Four/ The Adventures of.../The Return of...)
Gowers, Patrick *C*
Gowers, Patrick *Con*
CD _______ **CDTER 1136**
TER / Mar '90 / Koch

SHERLOCK HOLMES
London Cast
Bricusse, Leslie *C*
Sherlock Holmes / Without him, there can be no me / London is London / Vendetta / Anything you want to know / Her face / Men like you / Lousy life / I shall find her / No reason / Halcyon days / Without him, there can be no me (reprise) / Down the apples 'n' pears / He's back / Million years ago or was it yesterday / Best of you, the best of me / Sherlock Holmes (reprise)
CD _______ **BD 74145**
RCA / Jun '89 / BMG

SHERLOCK HOLMES
1993 Cast
Bricusse, Leslie *C*
CD _______ **CDTER 1198**
TER / Jan '94 / Koch

SHE'S THE ONE
Petty, Tom
CD _______ **9362462852**
Warner Bros. / Aug '96 / Warner Music

SHINING THROUGH
Kamen, Michael *C*
CD _______ **262742**
Milan / Jan '95 / Conifer/BMG / Silva Screen

SHIPHUNTERS
Morricone, Ennio *C*
CD _______ **OST 109**
Milano Dischi / Jan '93 / Silva Screen

SHIRLEY VALENTINE
Russell, Willy & George Hatzinassios
Russell, Willy & George Hatzinassios *C*
Girl who used to be me: *Austin, Patti* / Shirley Valentine / Affection / Crumbling resolve / Dreams / Costas / Coming to Greece / Nocturne / Arrival in Mykonos
CD _______ **FILMCD 062**
Silva Screen / Nov '89 / Koch / Silva Screen

SHOES OF THE FISHERMAN, THE
North, Alex *C*
CD _______ **GAD 94009**
Tsunami / Jan '95 / Silva Screen

SHOGUN MAYEDA
Utah Symphony Orchestra
Scott, John *C*
CD _______ **MAF 7017D**
Intrada / Mar '92 / Koch / Silva Screen

SHOOTING PARTY, THE/BIRDS AND PLANES
Royal Philharmonic Orchestra
Scott, John *C*
Scott, John *Con*
CD _______ **JSCD 113**
JOS / Jan '93 / JOS / Silva Screen

SHORT EYES
Mayfield, Curtis
Mayfield, Curtis *C*
Doo wop is strong in here / Back against the wall / Need someone to love / Heavy dude / Short eyes / Break it down / Another fool in love / Father confessor
CD _______ **CPCD 8183**
Charly / Jun '96 / Koch

SHOW AND TELL
CD _______ **WHI 666CD**
Which / May '97 / Cargo

SHOW BOAT (Highlights - The Shows Collection)
Cast Recording
Kern, Jerome *C*
Hammerstein II, Oscar *L*
Ol' man river / Where's the mate for me / Make believe / Can't help lovin' dat man / I might fall back on you / Life upon the wicked stage / You are love / Why do I love you / Bill / Goodbye my lady love / After the ball / Ol' man river (reprise)
CD _______ **PWKS 4161**
Carlton / Sep '93 / Carlton

SHOW BOAT (1946 Broadway Revival Version)
1993 Studio Cast
Kern, Jerome *C*
Hammerstein II, Oscar *L*
Edwards, John Owen *Con*
CD _______ **CDTER 1199**
TER / Nov '93 / Koch

SHOW BOAT
1987 Studio Cast & Ambrosian Chorus/ London Sinfonietta
Kern, Jerome *C*
Hammerstein II, Oscar *L*
McGlinn, John *Con*
3CD _______ **CDRIVER 1**
EMI Classics / Sep '88 / EMI

SHOW BOAT
Cast Recording
Kern, Jerome *C*
Hammerstein II, Oscar *L*
Overture / Where's the mate for me / Make believe / Ol' man river / Can't help lovin' dat man / Life on the wicked stage / Queenie's ballyhoo / You are love / Why do I love you / Bill / Goodbye my lady love / After the ball
CD _______ **SHOWCD 011**
Showtime / Feb '95 / Disc / THE

SHOW BOAT (Highlights)
1987 Studio Cast & Ambrosian Chorus/ London Sinfonietta
Kern, Jerome *C*
Hammerstein II, Oscar *L*
McGlinn, John *Con*

Overture / Cotton blossom / Where's the mate for me / Make believe / Ol' man river / Can't help lovin' dat man / Life on the wicked stage / Till good luck comes my way / I might fall back on you / Queenie's ballyhoo / You are love / Showboat / At the fair / Why do I love you / Bill / Goodbye my Lady love / After the ball / Hey feller / Finale ultimo
CD CDC 7498472
EMI Classics / Oct '89 / EMI

SHOW BOAT
Previn, Andre & Mundell Lowe/Ray Brown/Grady Tate
Kern, Jerome *C*
Hammerstein II, Oscar *L*
Make believe / Can't help lovin' dat man / Ol' man river / Bill / Life on the wicked stage / Why do I love you / I might fall back on you / Nobody else but me
CD 4476392
Deutsche Grammophon / Jan '95 / PolyGram

SHOW BOAT
1951 Film Cast
Kern, Jerome *C*
Hammerstein II, Oscar *L*
Main title / Cap'n Andy's calliope / Natchez / Cap'n Andy's presentation / Cap'n Andy's ballyhoo / Encore on dock / Where's the mate for me (Gambler's song) / Young romance / Make believe / Can't help lovin' dat man / Can't help lovin' dat man (reprise 1) / I might fall back on you / Julie leaves the boat / Ol' man river / Ol' man river (reprise) / You are love / Why do I love you / Ravenal is gone / Bill / Can't help lovin' dat man (reprise 2) / Life on the wicked stage / After the ball / Packet boat / Natchez dock / Make believe (reprise) / Reunion / Ol' man river (Finale ultimo) / Can't help lovin' dat man (outtake) / Bill (outtake)
CD CDODEON 5
Premier/EMI / Feb '96 / EMI

SHOW BOAT
Broadway Cast
Kern, Jerome *C*
Hammerstein II, Oscar *L*
McArthur, Edwin *Con*
CD SK 53330
Sony Broadway / Jan '93 / Sony

SHOW BOAT/BAND WAGON
Cast Recording
Ol' man river: *Warfield, William* / Make believe: *Keel, Howard & Kathryn Grayson* / I might fall back on you: *Champion, Gower & Marge* / Can't help lovin' dat man: *Gardner, Ava* / Why do I love you: *Keel, Howard & Kathryn Grayson* / Bill: *Gardner, Ava* / Life upon the wicked stage: *Champion, Gower & Marge* / You are love: *Keel, Howard & Kathryn Grayson* / Ol' man river (reprise): *Warfield, William* / Shine on your shoes: *Astaire, Fred* / By myself: *Astaire, Fred* / Dancing in the dark / Triplets: *Astaire, Fred/Nanette Fabray/Jack Buchanan* / New sun in the sky / I guess I'll have to change my plan: *Adams, India* / Louisiana hayride: *Fabray, Nanette* / I love Louisa: *Astaire, Fred* / That's entertainment: *Astaire, Fred/Nanette Fabray/Jack Buchanan*
CD CDMGM 10
MGM/EMI / Jan '90 / EMI

SHOW OF FORCE, A
Delerue, Georges *C*
Delerue, Georges *Con*
CD XCD 1005
Varese Sarabande / Apr '91 / Pinnacle

SHOW, THE
CD 5290212
Def Jam / Aug '95 / PolyGram

SHOWBOAT
Original London Cast
Kern, Jerome *C*
Hammerstein II, Oscar *L*
Cotton blossom / Make believe / Can't help lovin' dat man / I might fall back on you / Ol' man river / How'd you like to spoon with me / You are love / I still suits me (no matter what you say) / Nobody else but me / Life upon the wicked stage / Bill / After the ball/ Ol' man river / Why do I love you
CD 12446
Laserlight / Mar '97 / Target/BMG

SHOWGIRLS
CD 6544926612
Atlantic / Jan '96 / Warner Music

SHVITZ, THE
CD KFWCD 144
Knitting Factory / Feb '95 / Cargo / Plastic Head

SICILIAN CHECKMATE/A BRIEF SEASON (La Violenza: Quinto Potere/ Una Breve Stagione)
Morricone, Ennio *C*
CD LEGENDCD 26
Legend / Oct '96 / Koch / Silva Screen

SICILIAN, THE
Hungarian State Symphony Orchestra
Mansfield, David *C*
Sicilian / Camilla returns from riding / Stealing grain / Camilla's horses / On the stairs / Monastery ride / I'm not leaving... yet / Off to Palermo / Giuliano recovered / Monastery / Fire from heaven / Terranova / They join him / Little Guiliano / Don Massino in Rome / Jewel robbery / With this ring / Silvio's blessing / To Frisella's / Confession / That's life, gentlemen / Meeting ends / Ginestra massacre / Giuliano's funeral / End titles
CD 906822
Silva Screen / Jan '89 / Koch / Silva Screen

SILK STOCKINGS
1955 Broadway Cast
Porter, Cole *C*
CD 11022
Silva Screen / Jan '92 / Koch / Silva Screen

SILKWOOD
Delerue, Georges *C*
Drew's theme / Ride to Texas / Ride from Texas / Largo / Karen is contaminated / Legato / Karen and Drew on the porch / Down the highway / Love theme / Down the highway (reprise) / Drew leaves Karen / Karen looks trhough files / Pretty little horses lullaby / Karen has a car accident / After stripping Karen's house of her possessions / Drew walks through the empty house / Largo desolato / Amazing grace / Epilogue and end titles
CD DRGCD 6107
DRG / Jun '95 / Discovery / New Note/ Pinnacle

SILVERADO
Broughton, Bruce *C*
CD MAF 7035D
Intrada / Feb '93 / Koch / Silva Screen

SIMPLE MAN, A
English Chamber Orchestra
Davis, Carl *C*
White on white / Characters appear / Organ grinder / Sitting / Death of mother / Going to work / Coming from the hill / Waiting / Golden room / Three Anns / Seascape / Man with red eyes / Clogs / Homage
CD OCRCD 6039
First Night / Feb '96 / Pinnacle

SIMPLE TWIST OF FATE, A
Eidelman, Cliff *C*
CD VSD 5538
Varese Sarabande / Jul '95 / Pinnacle

SIMPSONS - SONGS IN THE KEY OF SPRINGFIELD, THE (Original Music/ Dialogue From Seven Seasons Of Simpsons Episodes)
Simpsons main title theme / We do (The Stonecutters Song): *Marge & Homer* / Dancin' Homer: *Simpsons* / Crosstown bridge: *Simpsons* / Capital city: *Bennett, Tony & Simpsons* / Who needs the kwik-E-mart: *Apu & The Simpsons* / Whoo needs the kwik-e-mart: *Marge & Homer* / Round springfield(medley): *Marge & Homer* / Bleeding gums blues: *Cast & Lisa* / Four-headed king: *Bleeding Gums Murphy* / There she sits brokenhearted: *Lisa & Bleeding Gums Murphy* / Jazzman: *Lisa & Bleeding Gums Murphy* / Oh, streetcar/White hot grease fires: *Director & Cast* / Long before the superdrome: *Chief Wiggum* / New Orleans: *Cast* / I thought my life would be a mardi gras: *Marge, Apu & Cast* / I am just a simple paper boy: *Apu* / Stella: *Flanders, Ned* / She flies: *Marge & Cast* / Kindness of strangers: *Marge & Cast* / Jingle bells: *Goulet, Robert, Bart, Smithers, Mr. Burns & Nelson* / Springfield (medley) / Itchy and scratchy main title theme / Itchy and scratchy end credits theme / Day the violence died (medley): *Krusty The Clown* / Amendment song: *Sheldon, Jack, Kid, Bart, Lisa & Cast* / Senor Burns: *Puente, Tito & His Latin Jazz Ensemble* / Simpsons end credits theme: *Puente, Tito & His Latin Jazz Ensemble* / Your wife don't understand you: *D'Angelo, Beverley & Homer* / Kamp Krusty (medley): *Merlino, Gene* / South of the border: *Merlino, Gene* / Simpsons end credits theme / Simpsons end credits theme / Simpsons end credits theme / Treehouse of horror 5 (medley): *Bart & Homer* / Controlling the transmission (prologue): *Simpsons* / Halloween special main title theme: *Simpsons* / Honey roasted peanuts: *Marge & Homer* / Boy scouts n the hood (medley): *Simpsons* / Saved by the bell: *Simpsons* / Jackpot: *Bart & Millhouse* / Springfield (parts 1 & 2): *Springfield* / Remember this: *Bart & Lisa* / Another Edwardian morning: *Simpsons* / Two dozen and one greyhounds (medley): *Mr. Burns & Lisa* / Pick of the litter: *Mr. Burns & Lisa* / See my vest: *Simpsons* / Eye on springfield theme: *Brockman, Kent & Homer* / Flaming moes: *Lennon, Kip & Cast* / Homer's barbershop quartet (medley): *Principal Skinner & Apu* / One last call: *Principal Skinner & Apu* / Baby on board: *Be Sharps & Cast* / TV sucks: *Bart & Homer* / Fish called Selma (medley): *Agent MacArthur Parker & Troy McClure* / Stop the planet of the apes: *Simpsons & Troy McClure* / Chimpan A to chimpan Z: *McClure, Troy & Cast* / Send in the clowns: *Krusty The Clown & Sideshow Mel* / Monorail song: *Lanley, Lyle & Cast* / In search of an out of body vibe: *Grampa & Mrs. Bouvier* / Bagged me a homer: *D'Angelo, Beverley, Recording Studio Guy & The Simpsons* / It was a very good beer: *Homer* / Bart sells his soul (medley): *Bart* / From God's brain to your mouth: *Bart* / In-a-gadda-da-vidda: *Reverend Lovejoy & The Simpsons* / Happy Birthday Lisa: *Lennon, Kip & Cast* / Simpsons Halloween special end credits theme: *Lennon, Kip & Cast* / Who shot Mr. Burns (medley) / Simpsons end credits theme / Simpsons end credits theme
CD 8122727232
Rhino / Jun '97 / Warner Music

SIMPSONS SING THE BLUES, THE
Simpsons
Do the bartman / School day / Born under a bad sign / Moanin' Lisa blues / Deep deep trouble / God bless the child / I love to see you smile / Springfield soul stew / Look at those idiots / Sibling rivalry
CD GED 24308
Geffen / Nov '96 / BMG

SING FOR SONG DRIVES AWAY THE WOLVES
Popul Vuh
Popul Vuh *C*
CD 139142
Milan / May '93 / Conifer/BMG / Silva Screen

SINGIN' IN THE RAIN
Kelly, Gene & Film Cast
Freed, Arthur *C*
Brown, Nacio Herb *L*
Main title / Fit as a fiddle and ready for love / Stunt montage / First silent picture / Tango / All I do is dream of you / Gene dreams of Kathy / All I do is dream of you / Make 'em laugh / Mood music / Beautiful girl montage / Beautiful girl / Have lunch with me / Stage is set / You were meant for me / You are my lucky star / Moses / Good morning / Goodnight Kathy / Singin' in the rain / From duelling to dancing / Would you / Broadway Melody Ballet / Would you (reprise) / Singin' in the rain in A-flat / Finale
CD CDODEON 14
Soundtracks / Jun '96 / EMI

SINGIN' IN THE RAIN
1983 London Cast
Freed, Arthur *C*
Brown, Nacio Herb *L*
Reed, Michael *Con*
Overture / Fit as a fiddle / Temptation / I can't give you anything but love / Be a clown / Too marvellous for words / You are my lucky star / Moses / Good morning / Singin' in the rain / Would you / Fascinating rhythm / Finale
CD OCRCD 6013
First Night / Oct '93 / Pinnacle

SINGIN' IN THE RAIN/EASTER PARADE
Singin' in the rain: *Kelly, Gene* / Fit as a fiddle: *Kelly, Gene & Donald O'Connor* / All I do is dream of you: *Reynolds, Debbie & Girly Chorus* / Make 'em laugh: *O'Connor, Donald* / You were meant for me: *Kelly, Gene* / Good morning: *Reynolds, Debbie & Gene Kelly/Donald O'Connor* / Moses: *Kelly, Gene & Donald O'Connor* / Broadway ballet: *Kelly, Gene* / You are my lucky star: *Kelly, Gene & Debbie Reynolds* / Steppin' out with my baby: *Astaire, Fred* / Fella with an umbrella: *Garland, Judy & Peter Lawford* / Shaking the blues away: *Miller, Ann* / I love a piano / Snooky Ookums / When the midnight choo choo leaves for Alabam' / Couple of swells: *Garland, Judy & Fred Astaire* / It only happens when I dance with you: *Astaire, Fred* / Better luck next time: *Garland, Judy* / Easter parade: *Garland, Judy & Fred Astaire*
CD CDMGM 4
MGM/EMI / Jan '90 / EMI

SINGING DETECTIVE, THE/OTHER SIDE OF THE SINGING DETECTIVE
Umbrella man: *Kaye, Sammy Orchestra* / Copenhagen: *Ambrose & His Orchestra* / I'll just close my eyes: *Shelton, Anne* / Old Moses put Pharoah in his place: *Waring, Fred & His Pennsylvanians* / Stop crying: *Oliver, King Orchestra* / Three caballeros: *Crosby, Bing & Andrews Sisters* / That's for me: *Haymes, Dick* / I'll be around: *Mills Brothers* / Sing nightingale sing: *Anderson, Lale* / There's something wrong with the weather: *Stone, Lew & His Band* / Java jive: *Ink Spots* / There's a fellow waiting in Poughkeepsie: *Crosby, Bing & Andrews Sisters* / Till then: *Mills Brothers* / Chinatown, my Chinatown: *Jolson, Al* / Let the people sing: *Payne, Jack & His Orchestra* / I'm making believe: *Ink Spots & Ella Fitzgerald* / Little Dutch mill: *Noble, Ray & His Orchestra & Al Bowlly* / Hush hush hush, here comes the bogeyman: *Hall, Henry Orchestra* / Later on: *Lynn, Vera* / Birdsong at Eventide: *Ronalde, Ronnie & Robert Farnon Orchestra*
2CD POTTCD 200
Connoisseur Collection / May '93 / Pinnacle

SINGLES
Would: *Alice In Chains* / Breath: *Pearl Jam* / Seasons: *Cornell, Chris* / Dyslexic heart: *Westerberg, Paul* / Battle of Evermore: *Lovemongers* / Chloe dancer/Crown of thorns: *Mother Love Bone* / Birth ritual: *Soundgarden* / State of love and trust: *Pearl Jam* / Overblown: *Mudhoney* / Waiting for somebody: *Westerberg, Paul* / May this be love: *Hendrix, Jimi* / Nearly lost you: *Screaming Trees* / Drown: *Smashing Pumpkins*
CD 4714382
Epic / Jul '92 / Sony

SIRENS
Portman, Rachel *C*
CD 213022
Milan / Jul '94 / Conifer/BMG / Silva Screen

SISTERS
Herrmann, Bernard *C*
Herrmann, Bernard *Con*
Dressing room / Ferry / Scar / Cake / Philip's murder / Clean up / Plastic bag / Apartment house / Couch / Siamese twins
CD SCCD 903
Southern Cross / Jan '89 / Silva Screen

SIX DEGREES OF SEPARATION
Goldsmith, Jerry *C*
CD 616232
Silva Screen / Jan '93 / Koch / Silva Screen

SKIN, THE
Schifrin, Lalo *C*
CD CDCIA 5095
Cinevox / Jan '93 / Koch / Silva Screen

SKY PIRATES
May, Brian *C*
CD IMICD 1002
Silva Screen / Jan '93 / Koch / Silva Screen

SKYSCRAPER
Cast Recording
Van Heusen, James *C*
Cahn, Sammy *L*
CD ZDM 5651322
EMI Classics / Apr '94 / EMI

SLEEPING BEAUTY
CD WDR 75622
Disney Music & Stories / Oct '96 / Technicolor

SLEEPLESS IN SEATTLE
As time goes by: *Durante, Jimmy* / Kiss to build a dream on: *Armstrong, Louis* / Stardust: *Cole, Nat 'King'* / Makin' whoopee: *Dr. John & Rickie Lee Jones* / In the wee small hours of the morning: *Simon, Carly* / Back in the saddle again: *Autry, Gene* / Bye bye blackbird: *Cocker, Joe* / Wink and a smile: *Connick, Harry Jr.* / Stand by your man: *Wynette, Tammy* / Affair to remember: *Durante, Jimmy* / Make someone happy: *Durante, Jimmy* / When I fall in love: *Dion, Celine & Clive Griffin*
CD 4735942
Epic / Dec '96 / Sony

SLEEPWALKERS
Pike, Nicholas *C*
CD 101322
Milan / Feb '94 / Conifer/BMG / Silva Screen

SLICE OF PYE
London Cast
CD DRGCD 13114
DRG / Mar '96 / Discovery / New Note/ Pinnacle

SLICE OF SATURDAY NIGHT, A
1989 London Cast
Heather Brothers *C*
CD OCRCD 6041
First Night / Oct '95 / Pinnacle

SLIVER
Can't help falling in love: *UB40* / Carly's song: *Enigma* / Slid: *Fluke* / Unfinished sympathy: *Massive Attack* / Most wonderful girl: *Lords Of Acid* / Oh Carolina: *Shaggy* / Move with me: *Cherry, Neneh* / Principles of lust: *Enigma* / Slave to the vibe: *Aftershock* / Penthouse and pavement: *Heaven 17* / Skinflowers: *Young Gods* / Star sail: *Verve* / Wild at heart: *Bigod 20* / Carly's loneliness: *Enigma*
CD CDVMM 11
Virgin / Jul '93 / EMI

SMOKE
CD 1620242
Polydor / Apr '96 / PolyGram

SMOKEY JOE'S CAFE
CD 7567827652
Atlantic / Oct '96 / Warner Music

SNOOPY
1981 New York Cast
Grossman, Larry *C*
Hackady, Hal *L*
CD DRGCD 6103
DRG / Jan '95 / Discovery / New Note/ Pinnacle

SNOOPY
1983 London Cast
Grossman, Larry *C*
Hackady, Hal *L*
Overture: The world according to Snoopy / Edgar Allen Poe / Woodstock's theme / I know now / Vigil / Clouds / Where did that little dog go / Friend / Great writer (It was a dark and stormy night) / Poor sweet baby / Don't be anything less / Big wow-wow / Just one person
CD CDTER 1073
TER / Sep '93 / Koch

SNOW WHITE AND THE SEVEN DWARFS
Churchill, Frank E. *C*
CD WD 745402
Disney Music & Stories / Oct '96 / Technicolor

SNOWMAN, THE
Blake, Howard
CD 4071136
Columbia / Nov '95 / Sony

SO I MARRIED AN AXE MURDERER
Brother: *Toad The Wet Sprocket* / Break: *Soul Asylum* / Starve to death: *Whitley,*

Chris / Rush: *Big Audio Dynamite II* / This poem sucks: *Myers, Mike* / Saturday night: *Ned's Atomic Dustbin* / Long day in the universe: *Darling Buds* / Two princes: *Spin Doctors* / My insatiable one: *Suede* / Maybe baby: *Sun 60* / There she goes: *La's*
CD 4742732
Columbia / Nov '93 / Sony

SOAPDISH
Silvestri, Alan *C*
CD VSD 5322
Varese Sarabande / Aug '91 / Pinnacle

SOLO
CD CHAN 8769
Chandos / Jul '89 / Chandos

SOME KIND OF WONDERFUL
Do anything: *Shelley, Peter* / Brilliant mind: *Furniture* / Cry like this: *Blue Room* / I go crazy: *Flesh For Lulu* / She loves me: *Duffy, Stephen 'Tin Tin'* / Hardest walk: *Jesus & Mary Chain* / Shyest time: *Apartments* / Miss Amanda Jones: *March Violets* / Can't help falling in love: *Lick The Tins* / Turn to the sky: *March Violets* / Dr. Mabuse: *Propaganda*
CD BGOCD 178
Beat Goes On / Feb '95 / Pinnacle

SOME LIKE IT HOT
1992 London Cast
Styne, Jule *C*
Merrill, Bob *L*
CD OCRCD 6028
First Night / Mar '96 / Pinnacle

SOME MOTHER'S SON
Whelan, Bill
CD 7567829562
Atlantic / Jan '97 / Warner Music

SOMETHING TO TALK ABOUT
Zimmer, Hans & Graham Preskett *C*
CD VSD 5664
Varese Sarabande / Nov '95 / Pinnacle

SOMETHING WILD
Loco de amor: *David Y Celia* / Ever fallen in love: *Fine Young Cannibals* / Zero zero seven Charlie: *UB40* / Not my slave: *Oingo Boingo* / You don't have to cry: *Cliff, Jimmy* / With or without you: *Jones, Steve* / High life: *Okossun, Sonny* / Man with a gun: *Harrison, Jerry* / Temptation: *New Order* / Wild thing: *Sister Carol*
CD MCAD 6194
MCA / Jan '89 / BMG

SOMEWHERE IN TIME
Barry, John *C*
Somewhere in time / Old woman / Journey back in time / Day together / Rhapsody on a theme of Paganini / Is he the one / Man of my dreams / Return to the present
CD BGOCD 222
Beat Goes On / Feb '95 / Pinnacle

SOMMERSBY
Elfman, Danny *C*
Sheffer, Jonathan/T. Pasatieri *Con*
Main title / Homecoming / Welcoming / First love / At work / Alone / Return montage / Mortal sin / Homer / Going to nashville / Baby / Tea cups / Townsend's tale / Death / Finale / End credits
CD 7559614912
WEA / Dec '96 / Warner Music

SON OF THE MORNING STAR
Safan, Craig *C*
CD MAF 7037D
Intrada / Feb '93 / Koch / Silva Screen

SON OF THE PINK PANTHER
Mancini, Henry *C*
CD 164612
Milan / Dec '94 / Conifer/BMG / Silva Screen

SONATINE
CD 293452
Milan / Sep '95 / Conifer/BMG / Silva Screen

SONG OF NORWAY, THE
Broadway Cast/Ambrosian Chorus/Philharmonia Orchestra
Forrest, George & Robert Wright *C*
Edwards, John Owen *Con*
2CD CDTER2 1173
TER / Jan '91 / Koch

SONG OF SINGAPORE
Cast Recording
Song of Singapore / Inexpensive tango / I miss my home in Harlem / You gotta do what you gotta do / Rose of Rangoon / Necrology / Sunrise / Never pay musicians what they're worth / Harbour of love / I can't remember / I want to get offa this island/ Harbour of love / Foolish geese / Serve it up / Fly away Rose / I remember / Shake shake shake / We're rich / Sunrise/Song of Singapore
CD DRGCD 19003
DRG / Jan '95 / Discovery / New Note/ Pinnacle

SONGBOOK
London Cast
Norman, Monty *C*
More, Julian *L*
Songbook / East river rhapsody / Talking picture show / Mr. Destiny / Your time is different to mine / Pretty face / Je vous aime milady / Les halles / Olympics song 1936 / Nazi party pooper / I'm gonna take him home to momma / Bumpity bump / Girl in the window / Victory V / April in Wisconsin / Happy hickory / Lovely Sunday morning / Rusty's dream ballet / Storm on my heart / Pokenhatchit / Public protest committee / I accuse / Messages / I found love / Don't play the love song any more / Golden oldie / Climbin' / Nostalgia
CD DRGCD 13117
DRG / Mar '96 / Discovery / New Note/ Pinnacle

SONGS AND STORIES OF THE CAROLINA COAST
King Mackrel & The Blues Are Running/ Coastal Cohorts
CD SHCD 8503
Sugar Hill / Jul '96 / ADA / CM / Direct / Koch / Roots

SONGS FOR A NEW WORLD
Original Broadway Cast
Brown, Jason Robert *C*
Brown, Jason Robert *L*
Opening: The New World / On the deck of a Spanish sailing ship / Just one step / I'm not afraid of anything / River won't flow / Stars and moon / She cries / Steam train / World was dancing / Surabaya-Santa / Christmas lullaby / King of the world / I'd give it all for you / Flagmaker / Flying home / Hear my song
CD 09026686312
RCA Victor / May '97 / BMG

SONS OF KATIE ELDER, THE
Bernstein, Elmer *C*
CD TSU 0104
Tsunami / Jan '93 / Silva Screen

SOPHIE'S CHOICE
Hamlisch, Marvin *C*
Sophie's choice / Train ride to Brooklyn / Returning the tray / Coney Island fun / Songs without words / Op 30, no 1 / Emily Dickenson / Aren't all women like you / Rite on the Brooklyn Bridge / Stingo; Polish lullaby / Nathan returns / Southern plantation / I'll never leave you / Stingo and Sophie together / Ample make this bed / Sophie's choice end credits
CD SCCD 902
Southern Cross / Jan '89 / Silva Screen

SORCERER, THE
Tangerine Dream
Tangerine Dream *C*
Search / Call / Creation / Vengeance / Journey / Grind / Rainforest / Abyss / Mountain road / Impressions of sorcerer / Betrayal
CD MCLD 19159
MCA / May '93 / BMG

SORCERER, THE/THE ZOO
D'Oyly Carte Opera Chorus/Royal Philharmonic Orchestra
Sullivan, Sir Arthur *C*
Gilbert, W.S. *L*
Godfrey, I./R. Nash *Con*
2CD 4368072
London / Jan '90 / PolyGram

SOUND BARRIER, THE
Royal Philharmonic Orchestra
Arnold, Sir Malcolm *C*
Alwyn, Kenneth *Con*
CD CNS 5446
Cloud Nine / Jan '89 / Koch / Silva Screen

SOUND OF MUSIC, THE
Royal Liverpool Philharmonic Orchestra
Rodgers, Richard *C*
Hammerstein II, Oscar *L*
CD CDCFP 4573
Classics For Pleasure / Sep '90 / EMI

SOUND OF MUSIC, THE
1959 Broadway Cast
Rodgers, Richard *C*
Hammerstein II, Oscar *L*
Dvonch, Frederick *Con*
CD SK 53537
Sony Broadway / Nov '93 / Sony

SOUND OF MUSIC, THE
Film Cast
Rodgers, Richard *C*
Hammerstein II, Oscar *L*
Climb every mountain / So long, farewell / Edelweiss / Maria / Processional / Something good / Do re mi / Sound of music / Lonely goatherd / My favourite things / Sixteen going on seventeen / Mornign hymn / Alleluia / I have confidence in me
CD 07863665872
RCA / Apr '95 / BMG

SOUND OF MUSIC, THE (Highlights - The Shows Collection)
Cast Recording
Rodgers, Richard *C*
Hammerstein II, Oscar *L*
CD PWKS 4145
Carlton / Jan '95 / Carlton

SOUND OF MUSIC, THE
Studio Cast/May Fest Choir/Cincinnati Pops Orchestra
Rodgers, Richard *C*
Hammerstein II, Oscar *L*
Kunzel, Erich *Con*
CD CD 80162
Telarc / Dec '88 / Conifer/BMG

SOUND OF MUSIC, THE
Original London Cast
Rodgers, Richard *C*
Hammerstein II, Oscar/Stephen Sondheim *L*
Sound of music / Maria / My favourite things / Do-re-mi / You are sixteen / So long, farewell / Climb every mountain / Ordinary couple / Processional / Edelweiss / Finale/Climb every mountain
CD 12448
Laserlight / Mar '97 / Target/BMG

SOUTH PACIFIC
1958 Film Cast
Rodgers, Richard *C*
Hammerstein II, Oscar *L*
Newman, Alfred *Con*
South Pacific overture / Dites moi / Cock-eyed optimist / Twin soliloquies / Some enchanted evening / Bloody Mary / My girl back home / There is nothin' like a dame / Bali Ha'i / I'm gonna wash that man right outa my hair / I'm in love with a wonderful guy / Younger than Springtime / Happy talk / Honey bun / Carefully taught / This nearly was mine / Finale
CD ND 83681
RCA / Feb '89 / BMG

SOUTH PACIFIC
1986 Studio Cast
Rodgers, Richard *C*
Hammerstein II, Oscar *L*
Overture / Dites moi / Cock-eyed optimist / Twin soliloquies / Some enchanted evening / Bloody Mary / There is nothin' like a dame / Bali Ha'i / I'm gonna wash that man right outa my hair / I'm in love with a wonderful guy / Younger than Springtime / This is how it feels / Entr'acte / Happy talk / Honey bun / Carefully taught / This nearly was mine / March / Take off / Communications established / Finale ultimo
CD CD 42205
CBS / '86 / Sony

SOUTH PACIFIC
1988 London Cast
Rodgers, Richard *C*
Hammerstein II, Oscar *L*
CD OCRCD 6023
First Night / Feb '96 / Pinnacle

SOUTH PACIFIC
1949 Broadway Cast
Rodgers, Richard *C*
Hammerstein II, Oscar *L*
Dell'Isola, Salvatore *Con*
CD SK 53327
Sony Broadway / Nov '93 / Sony

SOUTH PACIFIC (Highlights - The Shows Collection)
Cast Recording
Rodgers, Richard *C*
Hammerstein II, Oscar *L*
Bali Ha'i / Twin soliloquys / Some enchanted evening / Bloody Mary / Cock-eyed optimist / There is nothin' like a dame / I'm gonna wash that man right outa my hair / Younger than springtime / Happy talk / Honey bun / Carefully taught / This nearly was mine / Dites moi / I'm in love with a wonderful guy
CD PWKS 4162
Carlton / Sep '93 / Carlton

SOUTH PACIFIC
Te Kanawa, Dame Kiri & Jose Carreras/ Sarah Vaughan/Mandy Patinkin/Ambrosian Singers/London Symphony Orchestra
Rodgers, Richard *C*
Hammerstein II, Oscar *L*
Tunick, Jonathan *Con*
CD MK 42205
Sony Classical / Dec '91 / Sony

SOUTH PACIFIC
Studio Cast
Rodgers, Richard *C*
Hammerstein II, Oscar *L*
South Pacific overture / Some enchanted evening / Younger than springtime / Carefully taught / This nearly was mine / Happy talk / Bali ha'I / Cockeyed optimist / Dites moi pourquoi / I'm in love with a wonderful guy / Honey bun / I'm gonna wash that man outta my hair / Twin soliloquies / There is nothin' like a dame / Bloody Mary
CD 88122
CMC / May '97 / BMG

SOUTHERN MAID
1920 London Cast
Fraser Simson, Harold *C*
Clayton Calthorp, Dion & Harry Graham *L*
CD GEMMCD 9115
Pearl / Jan '93 / Harmonia Mundi

SPACE JAM (Score)
Howard, James Newton *C*
Main titles / Moron mountain / Back to earth / We seek bugs bunny / Charles / Toonland meeting / General bugs / Alien transformation / Hole in one / Michael in toonland / Spit shine / Monstars / Toons practice / Stealing the shorts / Ultimate game / Monstars locker room / Secret stuff / Second half / You got me / Crush 'em / You the duck / Winning shot / Gimme the ball / Not good at cheatin' / Michael Jordan returns
CD 7567829792
Warner Sunset/Atlantic Classics / Mar '97 / Warner Music

SPACE JAM
Fly like an eagle: *Seal* / Winner: *Coolio* / Space jam: *Quad City DJ'S* / I believe I can fly: *Kelly, R* / Hit 'em high: *B Real, Busta Rhymes, Coolio, LL Cool J & Method Man* / I found my smile again: *D'Angelo* / For you I will: *Monica* / Upside down: *Salt 'N' Pepa* / Givin' u all that I've got: *Robin S* / Basketball Jones: *White, Barry & Chris Rock* / I turn to you: *All 4 One* / All of my days: *Kelly, R & Changing Faces & Jay Z* / That's the way (I like it): *Spin Doctors & Biz Markie* / Buggin': *Bugs Bunny*
CD 7567829612
Warner Bros. / Mar '97 / Warner Music

SPARTACUS
North, Alex *C*
North, Alex *Con*
Main title / Spartacus love theme / Gladiators fight to the death / Blue shadows and purple hills / Homeward bound / Hopeful preperations, Vesuvius camp / Prelude to battle / On to Vesuvius / Oysters and snails - festival / Headed for freedom / Goodbye my life, my love - end title
CD MCLD 19347
MCA / Oct '96 / BMG

SPAWN
(Can't you) Trip like I do: *Filter & Crystal Method* / It's a long hard road out of hell: *Marilym Manson & Snekaer Pimps* / Satan: *Orbital & Kirk Hammet* / Kick the pa: *Korn & Dust Brothers* / Tiny rubber band: *Butthole Surfers & Moby* / For whom the bell tolls (The irony of it all): *Metallica & Spooky* / Torn apart: *Stabbing Westward & Josh Wink* / Skin up pin up: *Mansun & 808 State* / One man army: *Prodigy & Tom Morello* / Spawn: *Silverchair Vitro* / T-4 strain: *Rollins, Henry & Goldie* / Familiar: *Incubus & Greyboy* / No remorse (I wanna die): *Slayer & Atari Teenage Riot* / Plane scraped its belly on a sooty yellow moon: *Soul Coughing & Roni Size*
CD 4881182
Immortal / Jul '97 / Sony

SPECIALIST, THE
Turn the beat around: *Estefan, Gloria* / Jambala: *Miami Sound Machine* / Shower me with love: *Lagaylia* / El baile de la vela: *Cheito* / Slip away: *Lagaylia* / El duro so yo: *Tatis, Tony* / Mental picture: *Secada, Jon* / Que manera de quererte: *Albita* / Love is the thing: *Allen, Donna* / El amor: *Moreno, Azucar* / Did you call me: *Barry, John Orchestra* / Specialist: *Barry, John Orchestra*
CD 4776662
Epic / Dec '96 / Sony

SPEED
Speed: *Idol, Billy* / Million miles away: *Plimsouls* / Soul deep: *Gin Blossoms* / Let's go for a ride: *Cracker* / Go outside and drive: *Blues Traveller* / Crash: *Ocasek, Ric* / Rescue me: *Benatar, Pat* / Hard road: *Stewart, Rod* / Cot: *Carnival Strippers* / Cars ('93 sprint): *Numan, Gary* / Like a motorway: *St. Etienne* / Mr. Speed: *Kiss*
CD 07822110182
Arista / Aug '94 / BMG

SPEED (Score)
Mancina, Mark *C*
CD 234652
Milan / Jun '95 / Conifer/BMG / Silva Screen

SPIES LIKE US
Bernstein, Elmer *C*
Ace tomato company / Off to spy / Russians in the desert / Pass in the tent / Escape / To the bus / Road to Russia / Rally 'round / WAMP / Martian act / Arrest / Recall / Winners
CD VCD 47246
Varese Sarabande / Jan '89 / Pinnacle

SPINOUT/DOUBLE TROUBLE
Presley, Elvis
Stop, look and listen / Adam and evil / All that I am / Never say yes / Am I ready / Beach shack / Spinout / Smorgasbord / I'll be back / Double trouble / Baby, if you'll give me all your love / Could I fall in love / Long legged girl with the short dress on / City by night / Old MacDonald / I love only one girl / There's so much world to see / It won't be long
CD 07863663612
RCA / Jun '94 / BMG

SPIRIT OF ST. LOUIS, THE/RUTH
Shirley, George & Rundfunk Sinfonie Orchestra
Waxman, Franz *C*
Foster, Lawrence *Con*
Part 1 - Building the spirit / Part 2 - In flight / Part 3 - Arrival / I, Boaz of Bethlehem / Prelude / Who is this woman / And the answer to this was yet only her song / Then, as Naomi in time told it to me / Great dance of tribal time / Then Naomi in praise of Ruth told me / Boaz and Ruth, sleepless nights / Oh only too well I knew / So I prepared / Marriage feast of Boaz and Ruth / And out of our loving union
CD 10711
Capriccio / Sep '96 / Target/BMG

SPITFIRE GRILL
Horner, James *C*
CD SK 62776
Sony Classical / Jun '97 / Sony

SPITTING IMAGE: SPIT IN YOUR EAR
Spitting Image (theme) / Ronnie and Maggie goodbye / Royal singalong / Weather forecast / Coleman peaks / We've got beards /

Second coming / Someone famous has died / Tea at Johnnies / Trendy Kinnock / Da doo ron Ron / Ronnie's birthday / One man and his bitch / Special relationship / Clean rugby songs / O'Toole's night out / Spock the actor / Line of celebrities / Price is right / Botha tells the truth / I've never met a nice South African / End announcement / Andy and Fergie / Pete Townsend appeals / Our generation / Three Davids / Party system / Hello you must be going / Naming the Royal baby / Bruno and Ruthless / South Bank show on Ronnie Hazelhurst / Bernard Manning newsflash / Juan Carlos meets the Queen / Chicken song / Lawson goes bonkers / Talk bollocks / Snooker games / Good old British bloke / Black moustache / Uranus / Denis Thatcher's pacemaker / John And Tatum - the young marrieds / We're scared of Bob / Trooping the colour / Night thoughts
CD **VVIPD 110**
Virgin VIP / Nov '90 / EMI

SPLIT SECOND
Parsons, S./F. Haines *C*
CD **873117**
Milan / Jun '92 / Conifer/BMG / Silva Screen

SPY WHO LOVED ME, THE
Hamlisch, Marvin *C*
Nobody does it better: *Simon, Carly* / Bond '77 / Ride to Atlantis / Mojave club / Anya / Tanker / Pyramids / Eastern lights / Conclusion / Spy who loved me, The (end titles) / Bond 77
CD **CZ 555**
Premier/EMI / Dec '95 / EMI

ST. ELMO'S FIRE
St. Elmo's fire: *Parr, John* / Shake down: *Squier, Billy* / Young and innocent: *Elefante* / This time it was really right: *Anderson, Jon* / Saved my life: *Waybill, Fee* / Love theme: *Foster, David* / Georgetown: *Foster, David* / If I turn you away: *Moss, Vikki* / Stressed out (Close to the edge): *Airplay* / St. Elmo's fire (man in motion) / ehake down
CD **7567812612**
Atlantic / Feb '95 / Warner Music

ST. LOUIS WOMAN
Broadway Cast
Arlen, Harold *C*
Mercer, Johnny *L*
CD **ZDM 7646622**
EMI Classics / Apr '93 / EMI

STAIRWAY TO THE STARS
1989 London Cast
That's dancing / Who's sorry now / You stepped out of a dream / Fine romance / Three little words / Bye bye baby / Chattanooga choo choo / Rose's turn / Finale, hooray for Hollywood / Ma belle Marguerite / 'S Wonderful / Not even nominated / Life upon the wicked stage / Buttons and bows / I got a gal in Kalamazoo / Lucky numbers / Bosom buddies
CD **OCRCD 6021**
First Night / Dec '95 / Pinnacle

STAND AND DELIVER
Safan, Craig *C*
CD **VCD 70459**
Varese Sarabande / Jan '89 / Pinnacle

STAND BY ME
Everyday: *Holly, Buddy* / Let the good times roll: *Shirley & Lee* / Come go with me: *Del-Vikings* / Whispering bells: *Del-Vikings* / Get a job: *Silhouettes* / Lollipop: *Chordettes* / Yakety yak: *Coasters* / Great balls of fire: *Lewis, Jerry Lee* / Mr. Lee: *Bobbettes* / Stand by me: *King, Ben E.*
CD **7567816772**
Atlantic / Feb '94 / Warner Music

STAND, THE
Walden, W.G. 'Snuffy'
Walden, W.G. 'Snuffy' *C*
CD **VSD 5496**
Varese Sarabande / Aug '94 / Pinnacle

STANLEY AND IRIS
Williams, John *C*
Williams, John *Con*
Stanley and Iris / Bicycle / Finding a family / Putting it all together / Letters / Reading lessons / Factory work / Stanley at work / Stanley and Iris end credits / Stanley's invention
CD **VSD 5255**
Varese Sarabande / May '90 / Pinnacle

STAR (& Alfred Newman's 20th Century Fox Fanfare)
Andrews, Julie & Film Cast
CD **07822110092**
Fox Film Scores / May '94 / BMG

STAR IS BORN, A (with Barbara Streisand)
1976 Film Cast
Williams, Paul & Others *C*
Watch closely now / Queen Bee / Everything / Lost inside of you / Hellacious acres / Love theme (Evergreen) / Woman in the moon / I believe in love / Crippled crow / With one more look at you / Watch closely now / Reprise
CD **4749052**
Columbia / Apr '95 / Sony

STAR SPANGLED RHYTHM/FOOTLIGHT PARADE
That old black magic / Hit the road to dreamland / On a swing shift / I'm doing it for defence / Sweater, a sarong, and a peek-a-boo bang / Sharp as a tack / Old glory / Overture / Sittin' on a backyard fence / Honeymoon hotel / By a waterfall / Shaghai lil'
CD **CD 60013**
Great Movie Themes / Jun '97 / Target/BMG

STAR TREK - 30TH ANNIVERSARY EDITION
Trouble with tribbles / Heart of glory / Inner light / Visitor / Heroes and demons
CD **GNPD 8053**
GNP Crescendo / Dec '96 / ZYX

STAR TREK - 30TH BIRTHDAY EDITION
2CD **VSD 57622**
Varese Sarabande / Oct '96 / Pinnacle

STAR TREK - FIRST CONTACT
CD **GNPD 8052**
GNP Crescendo / Dec '96 / ZYX

STAR TREK - SYMPHONIC STAR TREK (& Star Trek Sound Effects/Bonus Star Trek PC Games CD-Rom)
Cincinnati Pops Orchestra
Kunzel, Erich *Con*
Star Trek / Menagerie / Star Trek I / Star Trek II/The Wrath Of Khan / Star Trek IV/ The Voyage Home / Star trek V/Final frontier / Star Trek/The Next Generation / Deep space nine / Voyager / Star Trek III/In Search Of Spock / Star Trek VI/The Undiscovered Country / Star Trek VII/Generations
2CD **CD 80383C**
Telarc / Jun '96 / Conifer/BMG

STAR TREK - VOL.1 (The Cage/Where No Man Has Gone Before)
Royal Philharmonic Orchestra
Courage, Alexander *C*
Courage, Alexander *Con*
CD **GNPD 8006**
GNP Crescendo / '88 / ZYX

STAR TREK - VOL.2 (The Doomsday Machine/Amok Time)
Kaplan, Sol & Gerald Fried
Kaplan, Sol & Gerald Fried *C*
CD **GNPD 8025**
GNP Crescendo / Sep '90 / ZYX

STAR TREK - VOL.3 (Shore Leave/The Naked Time)
Fried, Gerald & Alexander Courage *C*
CD **GNPD 8030**
GNP Crescendo / Nov '92 / ZYX

STAR TREK CLASSIC BOX SET
3CD **GNPBX 3006**
GNP Crescendo / Sep '93 / ZYX

STAR TREK I: THE MOTION PICTURE
Goldsmith, Jerry *C*
Goldsmith, Jerry *Con*
Main title / Klingon battle / Leaving drydock / Cloud / Enterprise / Ilia's theme / Vejur flyover / Meld / Spock walk / End titles
CD **9833812**
Pickwick/Sony Collector's Choice / Feb '94

STAR TREK II: THE WRATH OF KHAN
Horner, James *C*
Main title / Surprise attack / Spock / Kirk's explosive reply / Khan's pets / Enterprise clears moorings / Battle in the Mutara Nebula / Genesis countdown / Epilogue (End title)
CD **GNPD 8022**
GNP Crescendo / Jul '91 / ZYX

STAR TREK III: THE SEARCH FOR SPOCK
Horner, James *C*
Horner, James *Con*
Prologue and main title / Klingons / Stealing the Enterprise / Mind meld / Bird Of Prey decloaks / Returning to Vulcan / Katra ritual / End titles
CD **FILMCD 070**
Silva Screen / Aug '90 / Koch / Silva Screen

STAR TREK IV: THE VOYAGE HOME
Rosenman, Leonard *C*
Rosenman, Leonard *Con*
Main title / Whaler / Market street / Crash-whale fugue / Ballad of the whale / Gillian seeks Kirk / Chekhov's run / Time travel / Hospital chase / Probe / Home again
CD **MCLD 19349**
MCA / Oct '96 / BMG

STAR TREK VI: THE UNDISCOVERED COUNTRY
Eidelman, Cliff *C*
Eidelman, Cliff *Con*
Overture / An incident / Clear all moorings / Assassination / Surrender for peace / Death of Gorkon / Rura Penthe / Dining on ashes / Battle for peace / Sign off / Star Trek VI suite
CD **MCLD 19348**
MCA / Oct '96 / BMG

STAR TREK VII: GENERATIONS
McCarthy, Dennis *C*
CD **GNPD 8040**
GNP Crescendo / Feb '95 / ZYX

STAR TREK: DEEP SPACE NINE
McCarthy, Dennis *C*
McCarthy, Dennis *Con*
CD **GNPD 8034**
GNP Crescendo / May '93 / ZYX

STAR TREK: THE NEXT GENERATION
McCarthy, Dennis *C*
CD **GNPD 8012**
GNP Crescendo / Jan '89 / ZYX

STAR TREK: THE NEXT GENERATION VOL.1-3
3CD **GNPBX 3007**
GNP Crescendo / Sep '93 / ZYX

STAR TREK: THE NEXT GENERATION VOL.2
Jones, Ron *C*
CD **GNPD 8026**
GNP Crescendo / Sep '90 / ZYX

STAR TREK: THE NEXT GENERATION VOL.3
McCarthy, Dennis *C*
CD **GNPD 8031**
GNP Crescendo / Nov '92 / ZYX

STAR TREK: TV SCORES VOL.1
Royal Philharmonic Orchestra
Duning, George/Gerald Freid *C*
Bremner, Tony *Con*
Is there in truth no beauty / Paradise syndrome
CD **LXE 703**
Label X / Jan '94 / Silva Screen

STAR TREK: TV SCORES VOL.2
Royal Philharmonic Orchestra
Conscience of the king / Spectre of the gun / Enemy within / I, Mudd
CD **LXE 704**
Label X / Jan '94 / Silva Screen

STAR TREK: TV SERIES VOL.1
Royal Philharmonic Orchestra
CD **VCD 47235**
Varese Sarabande / Jan '89 / Pinnacle

STAR TREK: TV SERIES VOL.2
Royal Philharmonic Orchestra
Empath / Trouble with the Tribbles / Mirror mirror / By any other name
CD **VSD 47240**
Varese Sarabande / Jan '90 / Pinnacle

STAR TREK: VOYAGER
Chattaway, Jay *C*
CD **GNPD 8041**
GNP Crescendo / Jun '95 / ZYX

STAR WARS (A New Hope/The Star Wars Trilogy Special Edition)
Williams, John *C*
Williams, John *Con*
CD **09026687462**
2CD **09026687722**
RCA Victor / Mar '97 / BMG

STAR WARS - MUSIC FROM THE STAR WARS TRILOGY
Boston Pops Orchestra
Williams, John *C*
Williams, John *Con*
Main theme / Princess Leia / Asteroid field / Yoda's theme / Imperial march / Parade of the ewoks / Luke and Leia / Jabba the hutt / Forest battle / March / Love theme / Adventures on Earth / Flying theme / Suite
CD **4320502**
Philips / May '97 / PolyGram

STAR WARS - SKETCHES OF STAR WARS
CD **VSD 5794**
Varese Sarabande / Apr '97 / Pinnacle

STAR WARS TRILOGY (Music From The Films)
Utah Symphony Orchestra
Williams, John *C*
Kojian, Varujan *Con*
Star Wars main title / Princess Leia's theme / Here they come / Asteroid field / Yoda's theme / Imperial march / Parade of the Ewoks / Luke and Leia / Fight with tie fighters / Jabba the Hutt / Darth Vader's death / Forest battle / Star Wars
CD **CDTER 1067**
TER / Dec '83 / Koch
CD **VCD 47201**
Varese Sarabande / Jan '89 / Pinnacle

STAR WARS TRILOGY (John Williams Conducts John Williams)
Skywalker Symphony Orchestra
Williams, John *C*
Williams, John *Con*
CD **SK 45947**
Sony Classical / Jan '95 / Sony

STAR WARS: SHADOWS OF THE EMPIRE
Royal Scottish National Orchestra
McNeely, Joel *C*
McNeely, Joel *Con*
CD **VSD 5700**
Varese Sarabande / Aug '96 / Pinnacle

STARGATE (Score)
Sinfonia Of London
Arnold, David *C*
Dodd, Nicholas *Con*
Stargate overture / Giza, 1928 / Unstable / Coverstones / Orion / Stargate opens / You're on the team / Entering the Stargate / Other side / Mastadge drag / Mining pit / King of the slaves / Caravan to Nagado / Daniel and Shauri / Symbol discovery / Sarcophagus opens / Daniel's mastadge / Leaving Nagada / Ra - The Sun God / Destruction of Nagada / Myth, faith, belief / Procession / Slave rebellion / Seventh symbol / Quartz shipment / Battle at the pyramid / We don't want to die / Surrender / Kasuf returns / Going home
CD **74321249012**
Milan / Oct '96 / Conifer/BMG / Silva Screen

STARLIGHT EXPRESS
1984 London Cast
Lloyd Webber, Andrew *C*
Stilgoe, Richard *L*
Overture / Rolling stock / Call me Rusty / Lotta locomotion / Pumping iron / Freight / AC/DC / Hitching and switching / He whistled at me / Race - heat one / There's me / Blues / Belle / Race - heat two / Race - heat three / Starlight Express / Rap / Uncoupled / Rolling stock (reprise) / CB / Race - uphill final / Right place, right time / Race - downhill final / No comeback / One rock 'n' roll too many / Only He / Only you / Light at the end of the tunnel
2CD **8215972**
Polydor / Jun '84 / PolyGram

STARLIGHT EXPRESS
1993 London Cast
Lloyd Webber, Andrew *C*
Stilgoe, Richard *L*
CD **5190412**
Really Useful / Apr '93 / PolyGram

STARLIGHT EXPRESS/CATS (Highlights - The Shows Collection)
Cast Recording
Lloyd Webber, Andrew *C*
Stilgoe, Richard *L*
Starlight express / Rolling stock / UNCOUPLED / Crazy / Pumping iron / One rock'n' roll too many / Next time we fall in love / Light at the end of the tunnel / Memory / Grizabella / Gus / Mr. Mistoffelees / Old deuteronomy / Macavity / Memory (Reprise)
CD **PWKS 4192**
Carlton / Jul '94 / Carlton

STARMAKER, THE
Morricone, Ennio *C*
CD **HW 620562**
Silva Screen / Apr '96 / Koch / Silva Screen

STARMAN
Nitzsche, Jack *C*
CD **VCD 47220**
Varese Sarabande / Jan '89 / Pinnacle
CD **CDTER 1097**
TER / Aug '90 / Koch

STARTING HERE, STARTING NOW
London Cast
Shire, David *C*
Maltby, Richard Jr. *L*
CD **CDTER 1200**
TER / Jan '93 / Koch

STATE OF SIEGE
Theodorakis, Mikis *C*
CD **SR 50063**
Sakkaris / Oct '93 / Pinnacle

STAY TUNED
CD **5174722**
Polydor / Dec '92 / PolyGram

STEAL BIG, STEAL LITTLE
Lopez, Israel 'Cachao' & Albita/Andy Garcia
Olvis, William *C*
CD **74321327222**
Milan / Sep '96 / Conifer/BMG / Silva Screen

STEALING BEAUTY
2 Wicky: *Hoover* / Glory box: *Portishead* / If 6 was 9: *Axiom Funk* / Annie Mae: *Hooker, John Lee* / Rocket boy: *Phair, Liz* / Superstition: *Wonder, Stevie* / My baby just cares for me: *Simone, Nina* / I'll be seeing you: *Holiday, Billie* / Rhymes of an hour: *Mazzy Star* / Alice: *Cocteau Twins* / You won't fall: *Carson, Lori* / I need love: *Phillips, Sam*
CD **PRMDCD 3**
Soundtracks / Jun '96 / EMI

STEALING HEAVEN
Bicat, Nick *C*
CD **CDTER 1166**
TER / Jul '89 / Koch

STEEL MAGNOLIAS
Delerue, Georges *C*
CD **8415822**
Silva Screen / Jan '93 / Koch / Silva Screen

STEEL PIER
Broadway Cast
Overture/Prelude / Willing to ride / Everybody dance / Second chance / Powerful thing / Dance with me/The last girl / Shag / Everybody's girl / Two step / Wet / Harmonica speciality / Lovebird / Sprints / Entr'acte / Leave the world behind / Somebody older / Running in place / Two little words / First you dream / Steel pier / Steel pier / Final dance
CD **09026688782**
RCA Victor / Aug '97 / BMG

STEPPING OUT
Minnelli, Liza
Kander, John *C*
Ebb, Fred *L*
Matz, Peter *Con*
CD **262062**
Milan / Feb '94 / Conifer/BMG / Silva Screen

STING, THE
Hamlisch, Marvin & Scott Joplin *C*
Solace / Entertainer / Easy winners / Pineapple rag / Gladiolus rag / Merry go round music / Listen to the mockingbird / Darling Nellie Gray / Turkey in the straw / Ragtime dance / Hooker's hooker / Luther / Glove / Little girl
CD _______ MCLD 19027
MCA / Apr '92 / BMG

STONE KILLER, THE
Budd, Roy *C*
CD _______ LEGENDCD 6
Legend / Jan '94 / Koch / Silva Screen

STOP IN THE NAME OF LOVE (With The Fabulous Singlettes)
1988 London Cast
Do wah diddy diddy / Da doo ron ron / My guy / Be my baby / It's in his kiss (Shoop shoop song) / Needle in a haystack / Walk in the room / Time is on my side / Dum dum ditty / Leader of the pack / It's my party / Maybe / Born too late / I only want to be with you / You don't own me / Will you still love me tomorrow / Dancing in the streets / Supremes medley / Thank you and good night
CD _______ OCRCD 6017
First Night / Feb '96 / Pinnacle

STOP THE WORLD I WANT TO GET OFF
1961 London Cast
Newley, Anthony & Leslie Bricusse *C*
ABC / I wanna be rich / Typically English / Lumbered / Gonna build a mountain / Glorious Russia / Mellinki Meilchick / Typiache Deutsche / Nag nag nag / All American / Once in a lifetime / Mumbo jumbo / Someone nice like you / What kind of fool am I
CD _______ CDTER 1226
TER / Aug '95 / Koch

STORYVILLE
Burwell, Carter *C*
CD _______ VSD 5347
Varese Sarabande / Sep '92 / Pinnacle

STRAIGHT TO HELL
Good, the bad and the ugly: *Pogues* / Rake at the gates of hell: *Pogues* / If I should fall from grace with God: *Pogues* / Rabinga: *Pogues* / Danny boy: *Pogues* / Evil darling: *Strummer, Joe* / Ambush or mystery rock: *Strummer, Joe* / Money guns and coffee: *Pray For Rain* / Killers: *Pray For Rain* / Salsa y ketchup: *Zander Schloss* / Big nothing: *MacManus Gang*
CD _______ REP 4224-WY
Repertoire / Aug '91 / Greyhound

STRANGE DAYS
Selling Jesus: *Skunk Anansie* / Real thing: *Lords Of Acid* / Overcome: *Tricky* / Coral lounge: *Deep Forest* / No white clouds: *Strange Fruit* / Hardly wait: *Lewis, Juliette* / Here we come: *Me Phi Me & Jeriko One* / Feed: *Skunk Anansie* / Strange days: *Prong & Ray Manzarek* / Walk in freedom: *Satchel* / Dance me to the end of love: *Hate Gibson* / Fall in the night: *Carson, Lori & Graeme Revell* / While the earth sleeps: *Deep Forest*
CD _______ 4809842
Epic / Jan '96 / Sony

STRANGER THAN PARADISE/THE RESURRECTION OF ALBERT AYLER
Lurie, John
Lurie, John *C*
Bella by barlight / Car Cleveland / Sad trees / Lampposts are mine / Car Florida / Eva and Willie's room / Beer for boys / Eva packing / Good and happy army / Woman can take you to another universe / Sometimes she just leaves you there / Sixties avant-garde / Sex with monster / You owe me money / Resurrection
CD _______ MTM 7
Made To Measure / Apr '96 / New Note/ Pinnacle

STRATAGEM
Big Head Todd & The Monsters
Kensington line / Stratagem / Wearing only flowers / Neckbreaker / Magdalena / Angel leads me on / In the morning / Candle / Ninety nine / Greyhound / Poor miss / Shadowlands
CD _______ 74321229042
Giant / Oct '94 / BMG

STREET FIGHTER
Revell, Graeme
Revell, Graeme *C*
CD _______ VSD 5560
Varese Sarabande / May '95 / Pinnacle

STREET FIGHTER
Street fighter: *Ice Cube* / Come widdit: *Ahmad & Ras Kass/Saafir* / One on one: *Nas* / Pandemonium: *Pharcyde* / Street soldier: *Paris* / Something kinda funky: *Rally Ral* / It's a street fight: *B.U.M.S.* / Life as...: *L.L. Cool J* / Do you have what it takes: *Mack, Craig* / Straight to my feet: *Hammer & Deion Sanders* / Rumbo n da jungo: *Public Enemy & Wreck League* / Rap commando: *Anotha Level* / Worth fighting for: *Kidjo, Angelique* / Something there: *Chage & Aska*
CD _______ CDPTY 114
Priority/Virgin / Dec '94 / EMI

STREET SCENE
1991 London Cast
Weill, Kurt *C*
Hughes, Langston *L*
2CD _______ CDTER2 1185
TER / Jan '94 / Koch

STREETCAR NAMED DESIRE, A
National Philharmonic Orchestra
North, Alex *C*
Goldsmith, Jerry *Con*
CD _______ VSD 5500
Varese Sarabande / Oct '95 / Pinnacle

STREETS OF FIRE
Steinman, Jim *C*
Nowhere fast: *Fire Inc.* / Sorcerer: *Martin, Marilyn* / Deeper and deeper: *Fixx* / Countdown to love: *Phillinganes, Greg* / One bad stud: *Blasters* / Tonight is what it means to be young: *Fire Inc.* / Never be you: *McKee, Maria* / I can dream about you: *Hartman, Dan* / Hold that snake: *Cooder, Ry* / Blue shadows: *Blasters*
CD _______ BGOCD 220
Beat Goes On / Feb '95 / Pinnacle

STRICTLY BALLROOM
Love is in the air: *Young, John Paul* / Perhaps, perhaps, perhaps: *Day, Doris* / La cumparsita: *Hirschfelder, David & The Bogo Pogo Orchestra* / Tango please: *Hirschfelder, David & The Bogo Pogo Orchestra* / Tequila: *Hirschfelder, David & The Bogo Pogo Orchestra* / Sinful samba: *Hirschfelder, David & The Bogo Pogo Orchestra* / Rumba de burros: *Jones, Ignatius* / Doug's tearful waltz/First kiss: *Hirschfelder, David & The Bogo Pogo Orchestra* / Time after time: *Williams, Mark & Morice, Tara* / Standing in the rain: *Young, John Paul* / Scott's sinful solo: *Hirschfelder, David & The Bogo Pogo Orchestra* / Blue Danube: *Hirschfelder, David & The Bogo Pogo Orchestra* / Scott and Fran's paso doble: *Hirschfelder, David & The Bogo Pogo Orchestra* / Yesterday's hero: *Jones, Ignatius*
CD _______ 4723002
Columbia / Dec '96 / Sony

STRIKE UP THE BAND
Cast Recording
Gershwin, George *C*
Gershwin, Ira *L*
Mauceri, John *Con*
2CD _______ 7559792732
Nonesuch / Jan '92 / Warner Music

STUDENT PRINCE, THE
Lanza, Mario
Brodszky, Nicholas *C*
Callinicos, C. *Con*
Overture / Serenade / Golden days / Drink, drink, drink / Summertime in Heidelberg / I'll walk with God / Thoughts will come back to me / Student life / Just we two / Beloved / Gaudeamus igitur / Deep in my heart
CD _______ GD 60048
RCA / Sep '89 / BMG

STUDENT PRINCE, THE
1990 Studio Cast/Ambrosian Chorus/ Philharmonia Orchestra
Romberg, Sigmund *C*
Donnelly, Dorothy *L*
Edwards, John Owen *Con*
2CD _______ CDTER2 1172
TER / Mar '91 / Koch

STUDENT PRINCE, THE (Highlights)
1990 Studio Cast/Ambrosian Chorus/ Philharmonia Orchestra
Romberg, Sigmund *C*
Donnelly, Dorothy *L*
Edwards, John Owen *Con*
CD _______ CDTEO 1005
TER / Mar '91 / Koch

STUDENT PRINCE, THE
London Cast & Ambrosian Chorus/Philharmonic Orchestra
Romberg, Sigmund *C*
Donnelly, Dorothy *L*
Edwards, John Owen *Con*
Overture / Golden days / To the inn we're marching / Drinking song / Come boys, let's all be gay boys / Gaudeamus igitur / Deep in my heart dear / Serenade / Student life / Thoughts will come to me of days / Just we two / Finale
CD _______ SHOWCD 033
Showtime / Oct '96 / Disc / THE

SUBURBIA
CD _______ GED 25121
Geffen / Jul '97 / BMG

SUBWAY
Serra, Eric *C*
Subway / Guns and people / Burglary / Masquerade / Childhood drama / Man Y / Congabass / Song to Xavier / Speedway / It's only mystery / Drumskate / Dolphin dance / Racked animal / Pretext / Dark passage II
CD _______ GMD 9702
Silva Screen / Jan '89 / Koch / Silva Screen

SUDDEN DEATH
Debney, John *C*
CD _______ VSD 5663
Varese Sarabande / Apr '96 / Pinnacle

SUGAR BABIES (The Burlesque Musical)
Broadway Cast
McHugh, Jimmy *C*
Sugar babies overture / Good old burlesque show / Welcome to the Gaiety - intro / Let me be your sugar baby / In Louisiana / I feel a song coming on / Going back to New Orleans / Broken Arms Hotel / Sally / Don't blame me / Immigration rose / Little red house / Sugar baby bounce / Introduction Mme Rentz / Down at the Gaiety Burlesque / Mr. Banjo man / When my sugar walks down the street / Candy butcher / Entr'Acte / I'm keeping myself available for you / Exactly like you / I'm in the mood for love / I'm just a song and dance man / Warm and willing / Father dear, father dear / Boss upstairs / Cuban love song / Every week another town / I can't give you anything but love / I'm shooting high / When you and I were young Maggie / On the sunny side of the street / You can't blame your Uncle Sammy
CD _______ VSD 5453
Varese Sarabande / Dec '93 / Pinnacle

SUGAR HILL
CD _______ 07822110162
Arista / Jun '94 / BMG

SULEYMAN THE MAGNIFICENT
CD _______ CDCEL 023
Celestial Harmonies / Feb '88 / ADA / Select

SULT: SPIRIT OF THE MUSIC
Sult theme: *Sult House Band* / St Dominic's preview: *Morrison, Van* / Oro: *Brennan, Oro* / Causeway: *Casey, Nollaig* / On Raglan road: *Knopfler, Mark* / Murphy tunes: *Shannon, Sharon & Laoise Kelly* / Rocks of Bawn: *Brady, Paul* / Liquid sunshine: *O'Connor, Martin* / Siuil a ruin: *Ni Dhomhnail, Maighread* / Rollicking boys of Tandagree: *Nomos* / Parting of friends: *Moloy, Matt* / Mystic slip jigs: *Breatnach, Maire* / Crazy love: *Kennedy, Brian & Anuna* / Sweet Biddy Daly far from home: *Cooney, Stephen & Seamus Begley* / Rinn na mara: *Spillane, John* / Brown haired girl: *O'Flynn, Liam*
CD _______ HBCD 0009
Hummingbird / Mar '97 / ADA / Direct / Grapevine/PolyGram

SUMMER HOLIDAY
Richard, Cliff & The Shadows
Seven days to a holiday / Summer holiday / Let us take you for a ride / Les girls / Foot tapper / Round and round / Stranger in town / Orlando's mime / Bachelor boy / Swingin' affair / Really waltzing / All at once / Dancing shoes / Yugoslav wedding / Next time / Big news
CD _______ CDMFP 6021
Music For Pleasure / Apr '88 / EMI

SUMMER HOLIDAY (Songs From The Smash Hit Musical)
Day, Darren
Bachelor boy / In the country / Do you wanna dance / Move it / (I could easily) fall in love with you / On the beach / Dancing shoes / Big news / We say yeah / Next time / I'm in love with you / La la la song / Time drags by / Travellin' light / Swingin' affair/ Stranger in town / Livin' doll / Young ones / Summer Holiday megamix / Summer Holiday
CD _______ 743214561621
RCA / Feb '97 / BMG

SUN VALLEY SERENADE/ORCHESTRA WIVES
Miller, Glenn
Opening / Kiss the polka / Theme / I know why / In the mood / It happened in sun valley / Chattanooga choo choo / Kiss polka / It happend / People like you and me / At last / Bugle call rag / Serenade in blue / I've got a girl in Kalamazoo
CD _______ CD 60002
Great Movie Themes / Apr '97 / Target/ BMG

SUNDAY IN THE PARK WITH GEORGE
1984 Broadway Cast
Sondheim, Stephen *C*
Sunday in the park with George / No life / Color and light / Gossip / Day off / Everybody loves Louis / Finishing the hat / We do not belong together / Children and art / Lesson 8 / Move on / Sunday
CD _______ RD 85042
RCA Victor / '91 / BMG

SUNDOWN (The Vampire In Retreat)
Graunke Symphony Orchestra
Stone, Richard *C*
Wilson, Allan *Con*
CD _______ FILMCD 044
Silva Screen / Jan '90 / Koch / Silva Screen

SUNNY/SHOW BOAT/LIDO LADY
Cast Recording
Kern, Jerome & Richard Rodgers *C*
Harbach, Otto & Oscar Hammerstein II *L*
CD _______ GEMMCD 9105
Pearl / May '94 / Harmonia Mundi

SUNSET
Off-Broadway Cast
Friedman, Gary William *C*
Holt, Will *L*
CD _______ CDTER 1180
TER / May '91 / Koch

SUNSET BOULEVARD
1993 London Cast
Lloyd Webber, Andrew *C*
Black, Don & Christopher Hampton *L*
White, D. *Con*
Prologue / Let's have lunch / Sheldrake's office / On the road / Surrender / With one look / Salome / Greatest star of all / Let's have lunch (reprise)/Girl meets boy / House on Sunset / New ways to dream / Lady's paying / Perfect year / Artie Green's apartment / This time next year / Sunset Boulevard / Perfect year (reprise) / Journey to Paramount / As if we never said goodbye / Girl meets boy (reprise) / Eternal youth / Too much in love to care / Sunset Boulevard (reprise) / Greatest star of all (reprise)
2CD _______ 5197672
Really Useful / Aug '93 / PolyGram

SUNSET BOULEVARD
1994 US Cast
Lloyd Webber, Andrew *C*
Black, Don & Christopher Hampton *L*
Bogaev, P. *Con*
Overture/I guess it was 5am / Let's have lunch / Every movie's a circus / Car chase / At the house on Sunset / Surrender / With one look / Salome / Greatest star of all / Every movie's a circus (reprise) / Girl meets boy / Back at the house on Sunset / New ways to dream / Completion of the script / Lady's paying / New Year's Eve / Perfect year / This time next year / New Year's Eve (Back at the house on Sunset) / Entr'acte / Sunset Boulevard / There's been a call/ Journey to Paramount / As if we never said goodbye / Paramount conversations/Surrender / Girl meets boy (reprise) / Eternal youth is worth a little suffering / Who's Betty Schaefer / Betty's office at Paramount / Too much love to care / New ways to dream (reprise) / Phone call / Final Scene
2CD _______ 5235072
Really Useful / Oct '94 / PolyGram

SUNSET PARK
High til I die: *2Pac* / Motherless child: *Ghost Face Killer & Raekwon* / For the funk: *Howard, Adina* / Back at you: *Mobb Deep* / Just doggin': *Dogg Pound* / Keep on keeping on: *M.C. Lyte & Xscape* / We don't need it: *Junior M.A.F.I.A.* / Elements I'm among: *Queen Latifah* / Thangz changed: *Onyx* / Are you ready: *Aaliyah*
CD _______ 7559619042
East West / Apr '96 / Warner Music

SUPERCOP
Kung Fu fighting: *Jones, Tom & Ruby* / What's love got to do with it: *Warren G & Adina Howard* / Harry the dog: *Black Grape* / Head like a hole: *Devo* / Made niggaz: *2Pac & The Outlawz* / Caged in a rage: *Dimebag Darrell* / On a rope: *Rocket From the Crypt* / Stayin' alive: *Lynch, Siobhan* / I'll do it: *Tha Dogg Pound & Kausion* / Great life: *Goatboy* / Open the gate: *No Doubt* / Pubstar: *Pur* / Scorched youth policy: *Polara* / Supercop: *Devo* / Main title: *McNeely, Joel*
CD _______ IND 90088
Interscope / Nov '96 / BMG

SUPERFLY
Mayfield, Curtis
Little child runnin' wild / Freddie's dead / Give me your love (Love song) / No thing on me (cocaine song) / Superfly / Pusherman / Junkie chase (Instrumental) / Eddie you should know better / Think (Instrumental)
CD _______ MPG 74028
Movieplay Gold / Nov '93 / Target/BMG
CD _______ CPCD 8039
Charly / Jun '94 / Koch

SUPERGIRL
National Philharmonic Orchestra
Goldsmith, Jerry *C*
Goldsmith, Jerry *Con*
Overture / Main title & Argo city / Argo city / Butterfly / Journey begins / Arrival on earth / Flying ballet / Chicago light / Street attack / Superman / New school / Spellbound / Monster tractor / Map / Bracelet / First kiss / Monster storm / Where is she / Monster bumper cars / Flying bumper car / Where's Linda / Black magic / Phantom zone / Vortex / End of Zaltar / Final showdown & victory / End title
CD _______ FILMCD 132
Silva Screen / May '93 / Koch / Silva Screen

SUPERMAN
Williams, John *C*
Main title / Planet Krypton / Destruction of Krypton / Trip to Earth / Growing up / Superman love theme / Leaving home / Fortress of solitude / Flying sequence/Can you read my mind / Super rescues / Lex Luther's lair / Superfeats / March of the villains / Chasing rockets / Turning back the world / End titles
CD _______ 32572
Silva Screen / Feb '90 / Koch / Silva Screen

SURRENDER
Colombier, Michel *C*
CD _______ VCD 47312
Varese Sarabande / Jan '89 / Pinnacle

SURVIVAL (The Music Of Nature)
Survival theme / Citizens of the Coral / Valley beneath the sea / Dwellers of the deep / Suite for silver shoals / Dreams of mermaids / Sonata for the seal / Creatures of the ocean / Glide with a manatee / Song of the river / Empire of the elephant / Rhythm of Hell's Gate / In the heart of Africa / Animal outback / Empire of the plains / East of Eden / Amazonian market day / Apalachian heights / Madagascar - land of hope / Mountains of the snow leopard / Tarantula's reach / Amazonian journey / Web of the spider monkey / Dragons at play / Andes landscape / Night raiders / Queen of

the beasts / Red in tooth and claw / Leaders of the pack / Gorilla's shattered kingdom / Wings over the world / Hummingbird calypso / Flight of the snow geese / Fly to the stars / Angels of the Orient / Mysterious skies / Sumatra dawn / Through the eye of an eagle
2CD ________________ VTDCD 148
Virgin / Aug '97 / EMI

SURVIVING PICASSO
Robbins, Richard *C*
Grands Augustins / Francoise / Menerbes / You'd be my woman / Marie-Therese / Cubist flashback / Olga / Grandmother / Jacqueline / Circus / Dora / La Galloise / Vallauris corrida
CD ________________ 4868202
Epic / Dec '96 / Sony

SUSPECT
Kamen, Michael *C*
CD ________________ VCD 47315
Varese Sarabande / Jan '89 / Pinnacle

SUSPENDED STEP OF THE STORK, THE
Karaindrou, Eleni *C*
Refugee's theme/variations / Train-car neighbourhood/variations / Suspended step / Hassaposerviko / Waltz of the bride / Finale
CD ________________ 5115142
ECM / Jul '94 / New Note/Pinnacle

SWAN DOWN GLOVES, THE
1982 London Cast
Hess, Nigel *C*
Hess, Nigel & Bille Brown *L*
Overture / With the sun arise / Everything's going to be fine / Catastrophe / Let's be friends / Make your own world / How's the way / Going into town / Stuck in a muddle / Best foot forward / Demewer but dangerous / Muck / Any old rose / Firedown / Finale
CD ________________ CDTER 1017
TER / Aug '95 / Koch

SWAN PRINCESS, THE
Prologue / This is my idea / Practice, practice, practice / Far longer than forever / No fear / No more Mr. Nice Guy / Princess on parade / Enchanted castle / It's not what it seems / Derek finds Odette / Gator aid / Odette flies / Derek gallops / End credits / Eternity
CD ________________ 4837722
Sony Wonder / Jul '96 / Sony

SWEDEN, HEAVEN AND HELL
Umiliani, Piero
Umiliani, Piero *C*
You tried to warn me / Le ragazza dell'arcipelago / Stoccolma my dear / Man na mah na / Essere Donna / Notte di mezza estate / Sequenza psichedelica / Violenza / Fotomodelle / La signora cameriera / Solitidine / Free in monore / Piano bossa nova / Nel cosmo / Topless party / Eva svedese / Hippies / Hippies 2 / L'uorno integrato / Samba mah na / Organo e chitarroni / Beer, vermouth e gin / Sleep now little one
CD ________________ ET 901CD
Easy Tempo / Apr '97 / New Note/Pinnacle

SWEENEY TODD (Jazz Version)
Cast Recording
Sondheim, Stephen *C*
CD ________________ VSD 5603
Varese Sarabande / Jul '95 / Pinnacle

SWEET CHARITY
Cast Recording
Coleman, Cy *C*
Fields, Dorothy *L*
2CD ________________ CDTER2 1222
TER / Aug '95 / Koch

SWEET CHARITY
1967 London Cast
Coleman, Cy *C*
Fields, Dorothy *L*
CD ________________ SMK 66172
Sony West End / Jul '94 / Sony

SWEET CHARITY
Cast Recording/National Symphony Orchestra
Coleman, Cy *C*
Fields, Dorothy *L*
Edwards, John Owen *Con*
Overture / My personal property / Big spender / Rich man's frug / If my friends could see me now / There's gotta be something better than this / It's a nice face / Rhythm of life / Sweet charity / Where am I going / I'm a brass band / I love to cry at weddings
CD ________________ SHOWCD 035
Showtime / Oct '96 / Disc / THE

SWEET SWEETBACK'S BAADASSS SONG
Earth, Wind & Fire
Van Peebles, Melvin *C*
Sweetback losing his cherry / Sweetback getting it uptight... / Come on feet / Sweetback's theme / Hoppin' John / Voices / Mojo woman / Sanra Z / Voices / Reggin hanging on in there as best they can / Voices / Man tries running his usual game but...
CD ________________ CDSXE 103
Stax / Apr '97 / Pinnacle

SWING KIDS
Horner, James *C*
Horner, James *Con*
CD ________________ 142102
Milan / Feb '94 / Conifer/BMG / Silva Screen

T

TAFFETAS, THE
1988 Off-Broadway Cast
Lewis, Rick *C*
Sh-boom / Mr. Sandman / Three bells / I'm sorry / Ricochet / I cried / Cry / Smile / Achoo cha-cha / Mockin' Bird Hill / Tonight you belong to me / Happy wanderer / Constantinople / My little grass shack / C'est si bon / Sweet song of India / Arrivederci Roma / See the USA in your Chevrolet / Allegheny moon / Tennessee waltz / Old Cape Cod / Fly me to the moon / Nel blue de pinto di blue / Around the world / Music music music / You're just in love / Love letters in the sand / LOVE / I-M-4-U / Rag mop / You, you, you / Puppy love / (How much is that) doggie in the window / Hot canary / Tweedlee dee / Lollipop / Sincerely / Johnny Angel / Mr. Lee / Dedicated to the one I love / Where the boys are / I'll think of you / Little darlin' / Spotlight on the music
CD ________________ CDTER 1167
TER / Jun '89 / Koch

TAGGART
CD ________________ CDSTM 1
EMI / Oct '92 / EMI

TAI PAN
Jarre, Maurice *C*
CD ________________ VCD 47274
Varese Sarabande / Jan '89 / Pinnacle

TALES FROM THE CRYPT
CD ________________ 7567827252
Warner Bros. / Jan '95 / Warner Music

TALES FROM THE CRYPT (TV Soundtrack)
CD ________________ 9244622
Silva Screen / Jan '95 / Koch / Silva Screen

TALES FROM THE DARKSIDE
CD ________________ GNPD 8021
GNP Crescendo / Jan '95 / ZYX

TALES OF BEATRIX POTTER
Lanchberry, John *C*
CD ________________ CDC 7545372
EMI / Nov '94 / EMI

TALES OF THE CITY
Love to love you baby: *Summer, Donna* / Never can say goodbye: *Gaynor, Gloria* / Jive talkin': *Bee Gees* / Philadelphia freedom: *John, Elton* / That's the way I like it: *K.C. & The Sunshine Band* / Lady marmalade: *Labelle* / You sexy thing: *Hot Chocolate* / HAPPY radio: *Starr, Edwin* / You're the first, the last, my everything: *White, Barry* / It's a man's man's man's world: *White, Barry* / Cry me a river: *London, Julie* / I'm not in love: *10cc* / Cocaine: *Cale, J.J.* / Hang on in there: *Bristol, Johnny* / Don't take away the music: *Tavares* / Disco inferno: *Soul Station*
CD ________________ 5165152
PolyGram TV / Oct '93 / PolyGram

TALK RADIO/WALL STREET
Copeland, Stewart *C*
Unpredictable: *Kent* / We know where you live: *Tick* / He has a heart: *Trend* / Bud's scam: *Copeland, Stewart* / Trading begins: *Copeland, Stewart* / Break up: *Copeland, Stewart* / End titles: *Copeland, Stewart* / Just come right in here please: *Dietz* / We feel too much: *Tick* / Are you with me: *Copeland, Stewart* / Tall weeds: *Copeland, Stewart* / Anacott steel: *Copeland, Stewart*
CD ________________ VSD 5215
Varese Sarabande / Feb '90 / Pinnacle

TANGO ARGENTINA
1991 London Cast
Quejas de bandoneon / El choclo / La cumparsita / Uno / Nostalgias / La punalada / Cuesta abajo / Jealousy / Balada pars mi muerte / Milonguita/Divina/Melenita de oro/ Ra-fa-si / Milongueando en el 40 / Nunca tuvo novio / Orgullo criollo / De mi barrio / Verano porteno / La ultima curda / Canaro en Paris / Mi noche triste / Tanguera / Desencuentro / Adios nonino / Danzarin
CD ________________ 7567816362
East West / Jul '91 / Warner Music

TANK GIRL
CD ________________ 7559617602
Warner Bros. / Apr '95 / Warner Music

TANTIE DANIELLE
Yared, Gabriel *C*
CD ________________ 30761
Silva Screen / Jul '93 / Koch / Silva Screen

TAP DANCE KID, THE
1984 Broadway Cast
Krieger, Henry *C*
Lorick, Robert *L*
Overture / Another day / Four strikes against me / Class act / They never hear what I say / Dancing is everything / Fabulous feet / I could get used to him / Man in the moon / Like him / My luck is changing / Someday / I remember how it was / Tap tap / Dance if it makes you happy / William's song / Finale
CD ________________ CDTER 1096
TER / Mar '85 / Koch

TARAS BULBA
Waxman, Franz *C*
Bernstein, Elmer *Con*
CD ________________ 09026626572
RCA / Nov '95 / BMG

TAXI DRIVER
Herrmann, Bernard *C*
Theme / I work the whole city / Betsy in a white dress / Days do not end / All the animals come out at night / 44 Magnum is a monster / Sport and Iris / Theme from Taxi Driver
CD ________________ CDA 8912
Tsunami / Jan '95 / Silva Screen
CD ________________ 258774
Arista / Feb '97 / BMG

TEARS OF STONE
Iceland Symphony Orchestra
Leifs, Jon *C*
Sakari, P./S. Wilkinson *Con*
CD ________________ ITM 605
ITM / Feb '96 / Koch / Tradelink

TEEN WOLF
Goodman, Miles *C*
Flesh on fire: *House, James* / Big bad wolf: *Wolf Sisters* / Win in the end: *Safan, Mark* / Shootin' for the moon: *Holland, Amy* / Silhouette: *Palmer, David* / Way to go: *Viena, Mark* / Good news: *Morgan, David* / Transformation: *Teen Wolf* / Boof: *Teen Wolf*
CD ________________ 8290922
Silva Screen / Jan '89 / Koch / Silva Screen

TEENAGE OPERA, A
Wirtz, Mark *C*
CD ________________ RPM 165
RPM / May '96 / Pinnacle

TELL ME ON A SUNDAY
Webb, Marti
Lloyd Webber, Andrew *C*
Black, Don *L*
Capped teeth and Caesar salad / Come back with the same look in your eyes / I'm very you, you're very me / It's not the end of the world / If he's married, if he's younger, if I lose him / Let me finish / Let's talk about you / Letter home to England / Nothing like you've ever known / Second letter home / Sheldon bloom / Take that look off your face / Tell me on a Sunday / You made me think you were in love
CD ________________ 8334472
Polydor / Jun '90 / PolyGram

TENANT OF WILDFELL HALL, THE
Mitchell, Richard G. *C*
CD ________________ KCCD 4
NMC / Nov '96 / Total/Pinnacle

TENDERLOIN
Broadway Cast
Bock, Jerry *C*
Harnick, Sheldon *L*
CD ________________ ZDM 5650222
EMI Classics / Dec '93 / EMI

TERMINATOR II (Judgement Day)
Fiedel, Brad *C*
CD ________________ VSD 5335
Varese Sarabande / Aug '91 / Pinnacle

TERMINATOR II (Special)
CD ________________ VSD 5861
Varese Sarabande / Aug '97 / Pinnacle

TEX AVERY
Bradley, Scott *C*
CD ________________ 124702
Milan / Jan '95 / Conifer/BMG / Silva Screen

THAT THING YOU DO
Lovin' you lots and lots: *Wooster, Norm Singers* / That thing you do: *Wonders* / Little wild one: *Wonders* / Dance with me tonight: *Wonders* / All my only dreams: *Wonders* / I need you (that thing you do): *Wonders* / She knows it: *Heardsmen* / Mr. Downtown: *Fredrickson, Freddy* / Hold my hand, hold my heart: *Chantrelles* / Voyage around the moon: *Saturn 5* / My world is over: *Dane, Diane* / Drive faster: *Vickburgs* / Shrimp shack: *Cap 'N' Geech & The Shrimp Shack Shooters* / Time to blow: *Paxton, Del* / That thing you do: *Wonders*
CD ________________ 4865512
Play Tone / Jan '97 / Sony

THAT'S THE WAY IT IS
Presley, Elvis
I just can't help believin' / Twenty days and twenty nights / How the web was woven / Patch it up / Mary in the morning / You don't have to say you love me / You've lost that lovin' feelin' / I've lost you / Just pretend / Stranger in the crowd / Next step is love / Bridge over troubled water
CD ________________ 7432114690-2
RCA / Jul '93 / BMG

THELMA AND LOUISE
Zimmer, Hans *C*
CD ________________ MCLD 19313
MCA / Oct '95 / BMG

THEY LIVE
Carpenter, John
Carpenter, John & Alan Howarth *C*
Coming to LA / Message / Siege of Justiceville / Return to church / All out of bubblegum / Back to the street / Kidnapped / Transient hotel / Underground / Wake up
CD ________________ DSCD 1
Demon / Oct '90 / Pinnacle

THEY WANTED MEAT SO THEY ATE THE FLOWER CHILDREN
CD ________________ SFTRI 338CD
Sympathy For The Record Industry / Apr '97 / Cargo / Greyhound / Plastic Head

THEY'RE PLAYING OUR SONG
1980 London Cast
Hamlisch, Marvin *C*
Bayer Sager, Carole *L*
Hossack, Grant *Con*
Overture / Fallin' / If he really knew me / Workin' it out / They're playing my song / If she really knew me / Right / Entr'acte / Just for tonight / When you're in my arms / Fill in the words / They're playing our song (finale)
CD ________________ CDTER 1035
TER / May '89 / Koch

THEY'RE PLAYING OUR SONG
London Cast
Hamlisch, Marvin *C*
Bayer Sager, Carole *L*
Overture / Fallin' / Workin' it out / If he really knew me / They're playing my song / Right / Just for tonight / When you're in my arms / I still believe in love / Fill in the words / They're playing our song
CD ________________ SHOWCD 031
Showtime / Oct '96 / Disc / THE

THIBEAUD THE CRUSADER
Delerue, Georges *C*
CD ________________ PCD 114
Prometheus / Jan '93 / Silva Screen

THIEF
Tangerine Dream
Tangerine Dream *C*
Beach theme / Dr. Destructo / Diamond diary / Burning bar / Beach scene / Scrap yard / Trap feeling / Igneous
CD ________________ TAND 12
Virgin / Jul '95 / EMI

THIN BLUE LINE, THE
Glass, Philip Ensemble
Glass, Philip *C*
Riesman, Michael *Con*
Opening credits / Interrogation / Turko (part one) / Vidor / Adam's story / Defense attorney's / Judge / Trial (part two) / Mystery eyewitness (part two) / Thin blue line / Defense attorney's II / Hell on earth / Confession / Prologue / Interrogation (part two) / Turko (part two) / Harris' story / Comets and Vegas / Harris' crimes / Trial (part one) / Mystery eyewitness (part one) / Mystery eyewitness (part three) / Electric chair / Harris' testimony / Mystery eyewitness (part five) / Harris' childhood / End credits
CD ________________ 7559792092
Nonesuch / Apr '89 / Warner Music

THIN LINE BETWEEN LOVE AND HATE, THE
Beware of my crew: *LBC Crew* / Thin line between love and hate: *H-Town* / Damned if I do: *Somethin' For The People* / Freak tonight: *R. Kelly* / I don't hang: *Soopafly* / Love got my mind trippin': *Ganjah K* / Ring my bell: *Luniz* / Play fo real: *Dra Down* / Chocolate city: *Troutman, Roger & Shirley Murdock* / Thin line: *Drawz* / Ladies night at chocolate city: *Dark Complexion* / Knocks me off my feet: *Campbell, Tevin* / Let's stay together: *Beret, Eric* / Cover over: *St. Victor, Sandra* / Way back when: *Smooth*
CD ________________ 9362461342
WEA / Feb '96 / Warner Music

THING, THE
Morricone, Ennio *C*
Morricone, Ennio *Con*
CD ________________ VSD 5278
Varese Sarabande / Aug '91 / Pinnacle

THINGS TO DO IN DENVER WHEN YOU'RE DEAD
Jockey full of bourbon: *Waits, Tom* / Mile high: *Morphine* / On the way out: *Johnston, Freddy* / Born under a bad sign: *Neville Brothers* / Thrill is gone: *Dishwalla* / Bittersweet: *Big Head Todd & The Monsters* / Get out of Denver: *Blues Traveller* / This is my life: *Ape Hangers* / She's a superstar: *Guy, Buddy* / Take out some insurance on me baby: *Reed, Jimmy* / Folsom prison blues: *Cash, Johnny* / You're nobody till somebody loves you: *Martin, Dean* / Things to do in Denver when you're dead: *Zevon, Warren*
CD ________________ 5404242
A&M / May '96 / PolyGram

THINNER
Licht, Daniel *C*
CD ________________ VSD 5761
Varese Sarabande / Dec '96 / Pinnacle

THIRST
May, Brian *C*
CD _______ **IMICD 1003**
Silva Screen / Jan '93 / Koch / Silva Screen

THIS FILM'S CRAP LET'S SLASH THE SEATS
Holmes, David
Holmes, David *C*
Holmes, David *L*
No man's land / Slash the seats / Shake ya brain / Got fucked up along the way / Gone / Atom in you / Minus 61 in Detroit / Inspired by Leyburn / Coming home to the sun
2CD _______ **8286312**
Go Discs / Jun '95 / PolyGram

THIS IS MY LIFE
Simon, Carly
Simon, Carly *C*
Love of my life / Back the way (Dottie's point of view) / Moving day / Easy on the eyes / Walking and kissing / Show must go on / Back the way (girls' point of view) / Little troupers / Night before christmas / This is my life suite / Love of my life (drive to the city)
CD _______ **7599269012**
Qwest / May '92 / Warner Music

THIS IS SPINAL TAP
Spinal Tap
CD _______ **8178462**
Polydor / Aug '90 / PolyGram

THOMAS AND THE KING
1975 London Cast
Williams, John *C*
Harbert, James *L*
CD _______ **CDTER 1009**
TER / Aug '95 / Koch

THORN BIRDS II, THE
CD _______ **VSD 5712**
Varese Sarabande / Mar '96 / Pinnacle

THREE GUYS NAKED FROM THE WAIST DOWN
1985 Off-Broadway Cast
Rupert, Michael & Jerry Colker *C*
Overture / Promise of greatness / Angry guy/Lovely day / Don't wanna be no superstar / Operator / Screaming clocks (The dummies song) / History of stand-up comedy / Dreams of heaven / Kamikaze kaberaet / American dream / What a ride / Hello fellas TV special world tour / Father now / Three guys naked from the waist down / I don't believe in heroes anymore / Finale
CD _______ **CDTER 1100**
TER / May '93 / Koch

THREE MUSKETEERS
Kamen, Michael *C*
All for love: *Adams, Bryan & Rod Stewart/ Sting* / Cavern of Cardinal Richelieu / D'Artagnan / Athos, Porthos and Aramis / Sword fight / King Louis XIII, Queen Anne and Constance / Cardinal's coach / Cannonballs / M'lady de winter / Fourth musketeer
CD _______ **5401902**
A&M / Apr '95 / PolyGram

THREE O'CLOCK HIGH
Tangerine Dream
Tangerine Dream *C*
CD _______ **VCD 47307**
Varese Sarabande / Jan '89 / Pinnacle

THREE STEPS TO HEAVEN
2CD _______ **DBG 53034**
Double Gold / Sep '94 / Target/BMG

THREE WISHES FOR JAMIE
Broadway Cast
Moloney, Paddy *C*
CD _______ **ZDM 7648882**
EMI Classics / Apr '93 / EMI

THREE WORLDS OF GULLIVER, THE
Herrmann, Bernard *C*
CD _______ **ACN 7018**
Cloud Nine / Apr '95 / Koch / Silva Screen

THREEPENNY OPERA, THE
1954 Broadway Cast
Weill, Kurt *C*
Brecht, Bertolt *L*
Overture / Ballad of Mack the Knife / Morning anthem / Instead-of-song / Wedding song / Pirate Jenny / Army song / Love song / Ballad of dependency / Melodrama/ Polly's song / Ballad of the easy life / World is mean / Barbara song / Tango ballad / Jealousy duet / How to survive / Useless song / Solomon song / Call from the grave / Death message / Finale / Mounted messenger
CD _______ **CDTER 1101**
TER / Jul '89 / Koch

THREEPENNY OPERA, THE
1995 London Cast
Weill, Kurt *C*
Brecht, Bertolt *L*
CD _______ **CDTER 1227**
TER / Aug '95 / Koch

THREEPENNY OPERA, THE
Lenya, Lotte/Marlene Dietrich
Weill, Kurt *C*
Brecht, Bertolt *L*
CD _______ **9031720252**
Teldec Classics / Jan '95 / Warner Music

THREEPENNY OPERA, THE
Berlin RIAS Chamber Choir/Sinfonietta
Weill, Kurt *C*
Brecht, Bertolt *L*
Mauceri, John *Con*
CD _______ **4300752**
Decca / Mar '90 / PolyGram

THREEPENNY OPERA, THE
Bulgarian TV/Radio Mixed Choir/Symphony Orchestra
Weill, Kurt *C*
Brecht, Bertolt *L*
CD _______ **370062**
Koch / Feb '91 / Koch

THREEPENNY OPERA, THE
Lenya, Lotte
Weill, Kurt *C*
Brecht, Bertolt *L*
Bruckner-Ruggenberg, Wilhelm *Con*
CD _______ **MK 42637**
Masterworks / Jan '94 / Sony

THUNDERBALL
Barry, John *C*
Thunderball, Theme from: *Jones, Tom* / Chateau fight / Electrocution - searching Lippe's room / Switching the body / Vulcan crash landing - loading bombs into disc / Cape Martinique - Mr. Kiss Kiss Bang Bang / Thunderball / Death of Fiona / Bond below Disco Volante / Search for vulcan / 007 / Mr. Kiss Kiss Bang Bang
CD _______ **CZ 556**
Premier/EMI / Dec '95 / EMI

THUNDERHEART
Horner, James *C*
CD _______ **MAF 7027D**
Intrada / Jan '93 / Koch / Silva Screen

TIETA DO BRASIL
Velos, Caetano *C*
CD _______ **74321466122**
Milan / Jun '97 / Conifer/BMG / Silva Screen

TILL WE MEET AGAIN
CD _______ **XCD 1003**
Varese Sarabande / Apr '91 / Pinnacle

TIME MACHINE, THE
Garcia, Russell *C*
London 1900 / Time machine model / Time machine / Quick trip into the future / All the time in the world / Beautiful forest / Great hall / Fear / Weena / Rescue
CD _______ **GNPD 8008**
GNP Crescendo / Jan '89 / ZYX

TIME OF DESTINY, A
Morricone, Ennio *C*
CD _______ **7909382**
Silva Screen / Jan '89 / Koch / Silva Screen

TIME OF THE GYPSIES
Bregovic, Goran *C*
CD _______ **8427622**
Silva Screen / Jul '92 / Koch / Silva Screen

TIMECOP
Isham, Mark
Isham, Mark *C*
CD _______ **VSD 5532**
Varese Sarabande / Nov '94 / Pinnacle

TIN CUP
Little bit is better than nada: *Texas Tornados* / Cool lookin' woman: *Vaughan, Jimmie* / Crapped out again: *Keb' Mo'* / Big stick: *Hornsby, Bruce* / Nobody there but me: *Hornsby, Bruce* / Let me into your heart: *Carpenter, Mary-Chapin* / I wonder: *Isaak, Chris* / This could take all night: *Marshall, Amanda* / Back to Salome: *Colvin, Shawn* / Just one more: *Jones, George* / Where are you boy: *Loveless, Patty* / Every minute, every hour, every day: *House, James* / Character flaw: *Ely, Joe* / Double bogey blues: *Jones, Mickey*
CD _______ **4842932**
Epic / Oct '96 / Sony

TINTYPES
Broadway Cast
CD _______ **CDXP 5196**
DRG / Jan '89 / Discovery / New Note/ Pinnacle

TIRE A PART
Goude, Jean Philippe *C*
CD _______ **SMC 35703**
Sergent M / Apr '97 / Discovery

TITANIC
Broadway Cast
Overture/Prologue - to every age / How did they build Titanic / There she is / I must get on that ship / First class poster / Godspeed Titanic / Barrett's song / To be a captain / Lady's maid / What a remarkable age this is / Proposal/Night was alive / Hymn/Doing the latest rag / I have danced / No moon / Autumn/Finale / Dressed in your pyjamas in the Grand Salon / Blame / To the lifeboats / We'll meet tomorrow / Still / To be a captain / Mr. Andrew's vision / Epilogue - In every age
CD _______ **09026688342**
RCA Victor / Aug '97 / BMG

TITO
Theodorakis, Mikis *C*
CD _______ **SR 50087**
Varese Sarabande / May '94 / Pinnacle

TO DIE FOR
Elfman, Danny *C*
CD _______ **VSD 5646**
Varese Sarabande / Nov '95 / Pinnacle

TO DIE FOR II - SON OF DARKNESS (To Die For II)
McKenzie, Mark *C*
CD _______ **PCD 110**
Prometheus / Jan '93 / Silva Screen

TO LIVE AND DIE IN LA
Wang Chung
Wang Chung *C*
To live and die in LA / Lullaby / Wake up, stop dreaming / Wait / City of the angels / Red stare / Black-blue-white / Every big city / Dance hall days
CD _______ **GED 24081**
Geffen / Nov '96 / BMG

TO THE ENDS OF THE EARTH
Scott, John *C*
Scott, John *Con*
CD _______ **PCD 102**
Prometheus / Jan '89 / Silva Screen

TO WONG FOO, THANKS FOR EVERYTHING JULIE NEWMAR
I am the body beautiful: *Salt 'N' Pepa* / Free yourself: *Khan, Chaka* / Who taught you how: *Waters, Crystal* / Turn it out: *Labelle* / She's a lady: *Jones, Tom* / Brick house: *Commodores* / Nobody's body: *Monifah* / Do what you wanna do: *Arrington, Charisse* / Hey now (girls just wanna have fun): *Lauper, Cyndi* / Over the rainbow: *Labelle, Patti* / Too wong foo suite: *Portman, Rachel*
CD _______ **MCD 11231**
MCA / Jan '96 / BMG

TOGETHER WITH MUSIC (Archive Recording Of The Television Event)
Martin, Mary & Noel Coward
Together with music / Uncle Harry / Nina / Mad dogs and Englishmen / Dites moi / Cockeyed optimist / Some enchanted evening / Wash that man right out of my hair / Wonderful guy / My heart belongs to Daddy
CD _______ **DRGCD 1103**
DRG / Jan '95 / Discovery / New Note/ Pinnacle

TOM AND VIV (For Better, For Worse, Forever)
Palm Court Theatre Orchestra
Wiseman, Debbie *C*
Wiseman, Debbie *Con*
CD _______ **SK 64381**
Sony Classical / Nov '94 / Sony

TOMBSTONE
Broughton, Bruce *C*
CD _______ **MAF 7038D**
Intrada / Jan '93 / Koch / Silva Screen

TOMMY
Cast Recording
Townshend, Pete *C*
CD _______ **CCSCD 408**
Castle / Nov '94 / BMG

TOMMY
1993 Broadway Cast
Townshend, Pete *C*
2CD _______ **09026618742**
RCA Victor / '93 / BMG

TOMMY
Townshend, Pete *C*
Overture from Tommy / Prologue / Captain Walker/It's a boy / Bernie's holiday camp 1951/What about the boy / Amazing journey / Christmas / Eyesight to the blind / Acid Queen / Do you think it's alright / Cousin Kevin / Do you think it's alright / Fiddle about / Do you think it's alright / Sparks / Extra extra extra / Pinball wizard / Champagne / There's a doctor / Go to the mirror / Tommy can you hear me / Smash the mirror / I'm free / Mother and son / Sensation / Miracle cure / Sally Simpson / Welcome TV studio / Tommy's holiday camp / We're not gonna take it / Listening to you/See you, feel me
2CD _______ **8411212**
Polydor / Jan '94 / PolyGram

TOMMY
London Symphony Orchestra
Townshend, Pete *C*
CD _______ **ESMCD 404**
Essential / Jun '96 / BMG

TOMMY
CC Productions
Townshend, Pete *C*
1921 / Amazing journey / Eyesight to the blind / Christmas / Cousin Kevin / Acid queen / Pinball wizard / Go to the mirror / I'm free / Sally Simpson / Sensation / We're not gonna take it
CD _______ **QED 207**
Tring / Nov '96 / Tring

TOMMY
Studio Cast
Townshend, Pete *C*
1921 / Amazing journey / Eyesight to the blind / Christmas / Cousin Kevin / Acid Queen / Pinball wizard / Go to the mirror / I'm free / Sally Simpson / Sensation / We're not gonna take it
CD _______ **88062**
CMC / May '97 / BMG

TOMMY BOY
CD _______ **9362459042**
Warner Bros. / Aug '95 / Warner Music

TONITE LET'S ALL MAKE LOVE IN LONDON
1967 Film Cast
CD _______ **SEECD 258**
See For Miles/C5 / '90 / Pinnacle

TOP BANANA
Broadway Cast
Mercer, Johnny *C*
CD _______ **ZDM 7647722**
EMI Classics / Apr '93 / EMI

TOP GUN
Danger zone: *Loggins, Kenny* / Mighty wings: *Cheap Trick* / Playing with the boys: *Loggins, Kenny* / Lead me on: *Marie, Teena* / Take my breath away: *Berlin* / Hot summer nights: *Miami Sound Machine* / Heaven in your eyes: *Loverboy* / Through the fire: *Greene, Larry* / Destination unknown: *Marietta* / Top Gun anthem: *Faltermeyer, Harold & Steve Stevens*
CD _______ **CD 70296**
CBS / Sep '86 / Sony

TORN CURTAIN
Addison, John *C*
Addison, John *Con*
CD _______ **VSD 5296**
Varese Sarabande / Apr '91 / Pinnacle

TOTAL ECLIPSE
Wilanow St. Quartet & Warsaw Symphony Orchestra/Marta Boberska
Kaczmarek, Jan A.P. *C*
CD _______ **SK 62037**
Sony Classical / Mar '97 / Sony

TOTAL RECALL
Goldsmith, Jerry *C*
Goldsmith, Jerry *Con*
Dream / Hologram / Big jump / Mutant / Cleaver girl / First meeting / Treatment / Where am I / End of a dream / New life
CD _______ **VSD 5267**
Varese Sarabande / Aug '90 / Pinnacle

TOTALLY LOVED UP
Crystal clear: *Grid* / For what you dream of: *Bedrock* / Gut drum mix: *Funtopia* / Acperience: *Hardfloor* / Two full moons and a trout: *Union Jack* / Attached: *Union Jack* / Make it funky: *Rebound* / Advances: *Surjestive* / Little bullet part 1: *Spooky* / Melt: *Leftfield* / Oneski: *Kirk, Richard* / Prologue: *10th Chapter* / Texas cowboys: *Grid* / Lollipop man: *Union Jack* / Full throttle: *Prodigy* / Calling the people: *A Zone* / Souffie: *Banco De Gaia* / Plastic dream: *Jaydee* / Song of life: *Leftfield* / Forever: *Orbital* / Smoke belch 11: *Sabres Of Paradise*
2CD _______ **PRIMAXCD 3**
Prima Vera / Jun '97 / Pinnacle

TOTO LE HEROS
Van Dormael, Pierre *C*
CD _______ **BM 001**
Milan / Jan '95 / Conifer/BMG / Silva Screen

TOUCH OF CLASS, A
Cameron, John *C*
All that love went to waste / Steve's theme / Vickie's theme / Love theme / Touch of class / Amor / Mrs Allessio's rock and roll band / I alwasy knew (love theme) / Bullfight theme / Golf theme / Steve's thme / Antonio's restaurant / She told me so last night / Nudge me every morning
CD _______ **DRGCD 13115**
DRG / May '96 / Discovery / New Note/ Pinnacle

TOUCH OF EVIL, A
Mancini, Henry *C*
Mancini, Henry *Con*
CD _______ **VSD 5414**
Varese Sarabande / Jul '93 / Pinnacle

TOUGH GUYS/TRUCK TURNER
Hayes, Isaac
Title theme / Randolph and Dearborn / Red rooster / Joe Bell / Hung up on my baby / Kidnapped / Run Fay run / Buns o'plenty / End theme / Main title: Truck Turner / House of beauty / Blue's crib / Driving in the sun / Breakthrough / Now we're one / Duke / Dorinda's party / Persuit of the pimpmobile / We need each other, girl / House full of girls / Hospital shootout / You're in my arms again / Give it to me / Drinking / Insurance company
CD _______ **CDSXE 2095**
Stax / Jul '93 / Pinnacle

TOUS LES MATINS DU MONDE
CD _______ **AUE 004640**
Auvidis/Ethnic / Feb '93 / ADA / Harmonia Mundi

TOVARICH
Broadway Cast
CD _______ **ZDM 7648932**
EMI Classics / Aug '93 / EMI

TOWN FOX, THE (And Other Musical Tales)
Royal Liverpool Philharmonic Orchestra
Davis, Carl *Con*
CD _______ **SCENECD 19**
First Night / '94 / Pinnacle

TOWN LIKE ALICE, A
Smeaton, Bruce *C*
CD _______ **SCCD 1013**
Southern Cross / Jan '89 / Silva Screen

TOY SOLDIERS
Folk, Robert *C*
CD _______________ **MAF 7015D**
Intrada / Jan '93 / Koch / Silva Screen

TOY STORY
CD _______________ **WD 771302**
Disney Music & Stories / Mar '96 / Technicolor

TOY STORY (Singalong)
CD _______________ **WD 771424**
Disney Music & Stories / Oct '96 / Technicolor

TOYS
Tchaikovsky's Symphony No.1 (excerpt) / Closing of the year: *Wendy & Lisa/Cast* / Ebudae: *Enya* / Happy worker: *Amos, Tori* / Alsatia's lullaby: *Migenes, Julia & Hans Zimmer* / Workers: *Cast of Toys* / Let joy and innocence prevail: *Metheny, Pat* / General: *Gambon, Michael & Hans Zimmer* / Mirror song: *Dolby, Thomas & Robin Williams/ John Cusack* / Battle introduction: *Williams, Robin* / Welcome to the pleasure dome: *Frankie Goes To Hollywood* / Let joy and innocence prevail: *Jones, Grace* / Closing of the year/Happy Workers (Reprise): *Siberry, Jane*
CD _______________ **450991603-2**
ZTT / Mar '93 / Warner Music

TRAIL OF THE PINK PANTHER
Mancini, Henry & His Orchestra
Mancini, Henry *C*
Trail of the pink panther / Greatest gift / Hong Kong fireworks / Shot in the dark / Simone / It had better be tonight / Easy life in Paris / Come to me / Bierfest polka / After the shower / Inspector Clouseau theme / Return of the Pink Panther
CD _______________ **906272**
Silva Screen / Jan '89 / Koch / Silva Screen

TRAINSPOTTING
Lust for life: *Iggy Pop* / Deep blue day: *Eno, Brian* / Trainspotting: *Primal Scream* / Atomic: *Sleeper* / Temptation: *New Order* / Nightclubbing: *Iggy Pop* / Sing: *Blur* / Perfect day: *Reed, Lou* / Mile End: *Pulp* / For what you dream of: *Bedrock feat. KYO* / 2:1: *Elastica* / Final hit: *Leftfield* / Born slippy: *Underworld* / Closet romantic: *Albarn, Damon*
CD _______________ **CDEMC 3739**
Premier/EMI / Feb '96 / EMI

TRANSFORMERS
Touch: *Bush, Stan* / Instruments of destruction: *NRG* / Death of Optimus prime: *Dicola, Vince* / Dare: *Bush, Stan* / Nothin's gonna stand in our way: *Spectre General* / Tranformers (theme): *Lion* / Escape: *Dicola, Vince* / Hunger: *Spectre General* / Autobot: *Dicola, Vince* / Decepticon battle: *Dicola, Vince* / Dare to be stupid: *Yankovic, Weird Al*
CD _______________ **752422**
Silva Screen / Mar '92 / Koch / Silva Screen

TRAP, THE
Goodwin, Ron *C*
CD _______________ **LXE 708**
Label X / Apr '96 / Silva Screen

TRAVELLER
King of the road: *Travis, Randy* / If youy've got the money: *Gilmore, Jimmie Dale* / I've love you a thousand ways: *Gilmore, Jimmie Dale* / Seven lonely days: *Lang, k.d.* / Rockin' Robin: *White, Bryan* / Please help me I'm falling: *McCann, Lila* / Blues stay away from me: *Shiver, Thrasher* / Sweet nothin's: *Tina And The B-Side Movement* / Searching: *Barnett, Mandy* / Gonna find me a bluebird: *Royal Wade Kimes* / Don't rob another man's castle: *Royal Wade Kimes* / I'm thinking tonight of my blue eyes: *Cox Family* / Sweeter than the flowers: *Cox Family* / Love and happiness: *Green, Al* / Dark moon: *Barnett, Mandy* / Young love: *Sharp, Kevin*
CD _______________ **7559620302**
Elektra / Jun '97 / Warner Music

TRAVELLING MAN
Browne, Duncan & Sebastian Graham Jones
CD _______________ **CDSGP 0114**
Prestige / Sep '95 / Else / Total/BMG

TREE GROWS IN BROOKLYN, A
1951 Broadway Cast
Schwartz, Arthur *C*
Fields, Dorothy *L*
Goberman, Max *Con*
CD _______________ **SK 48014**
Sony Broadway / Dec '91 / Sony

TREES LOUNGE
You always hurt the one you love: *Lee, Brenda* / I never had a dream come true: *Ink Spots* / I've been hurt: *Deal, Bill & The Rhondels* / That woman got me drinking: *MacGowan, Shane & The Popes* / Tellin' the dice how to roll: *Tuzzolino, Patrick* / Mudslide: *Ross, Craig* / I don't know enough about you: *Mills Brothers* / I understand (Just how you feel): *Ink Spots* / Trees lounge: *Hayden* / Tommy blues: *Lurie, Evan* / Color of your eyes: *Balint, Eszter & Smokey Hormel*
CD _______________ **MCD 11539**
MCA / Feb '97 / BMG

TRESPASS
Trespass: *Ice-T & Ice Cube* / Gotta do what I gotta do: *Public Enemy* / Depths of hell: *Ice-T* / I check my bank: *Sir Mix-a-Lot* / I'm a playa (bitch): *Penthouse Players Clique* / On the wall: *Black Sheep* / Don't be a 304: *AMG* / Gotta get over (taking loot): *Gang Starr* / You know what I'm about: *Lord Finesse* / I'm gonna smoke him: *Donald D* / Quick way out: *W.C. & the Maad Circle* / King of the street: *Cooder, Ry*
CD _______________ **7599269782**
Sire / Feb '93 / Warner Music

TRESPASS (Score)
Cooder, Ry
Cooder, Ry *C*
CD _______________ **9362452202**
Warner Bros. / Jan '94 / Warner Music

TRIAL, THE
Davis, Carl *C*
CD _______________ **873150**
Milan / Feb '94 / Conifer/BMG / Silva Screen

TRIPODS, THE
Freeman, Ken
Freeman, Ken *C*
CD _______________ **GERCD 1**
Pinnacle / Nov '95 / Pinnacle

TRIUMPH OF THE SPIRIT
Eidelman, Cliff *C*
Main title / Dark tunnel to Aushwitz / Answer us / Avram refuses to work / Hard felt rest / Elena's false dreams / Begging for bread / Slaughter / Hunger / Salamo desperately finds Allegra / New assignment / Epilogue / Love in wedlock / There was a time / Mi dyo mi / Longing for home / Hell realization / There was a memory / Mourning / It was a month before we left / Mercy on to us / Allegra's punishment / Death march
CD _______________ **VSD 5254**
Varese Sarabande / Apr '90 / Pinnacle

TROIS COULEURS - BLEU
Preisner, Zbigniew
Preisner, Zbigniew *C*
Chant pour l'unification d'Europe / Van den budenmayer - musique funebre / Julie - images d'enterrement / Memento - premiere apparition / Lutte de carnaval contre le careme / Memento - Julie avec Olivier / Ellipse 1 / Premiere flute / Julie - dans son nouvel appartement / Memento - Julie dans l'escalier / Deuxieme flute / Ellipse 2 / Lutte de carnaval contre le careme II / Memento - flute / Ellipse 3 / Theme d'Olivier - piano / Olivier et Julie - essai de composition / Theme d'Olivier - version finale / Bolero - annonce du film "Rouge" / Chant pour l'unification d'Europe - version de Julie / Generique de fin / Memento - orgue / Bolero - film "Rouge"
CD _______________ **CDVMM 12**
Virgin / Oct '93 / EMI

TROIS COULEURS - BLEU, BLANC, ROUGE
Preisner, Zbigniew
Preisner, Zbigniew *C*
3CD _______________ **CDVMMX 15**
Virgin / Nov '94 / EMI

TROIS COULEURS - ROUGE
Preisner, Zbigniew
Preisner, Zbigniew *C*
Fashion show / Meeting the judge / Tapped conversation / Leaving the judge / Psychoanalysis / Today is my birthday / Do not take another man's wife / Treason / Fashion show / Conversation at the theatre / Rest of the conversation at the theatre / Do not take another man's wife / Catastrophe / Finale
CD _______________ **CDVMM 14**
Virgin / Nov '94 / EMI

TROUBLE IN MIND
Isham, Mark *C*
CD _______________ **905012**
Silva Screen / Jan '89 / Koch / Silva Screen

TROUBLE IN PARADISE
Newman, Randy
Newman, Randy *C*
I love LA / Christmas in Capetown / Blues / Same girl / Mikey's / My life is good / Miami / Real emotional girl / Take me back / There's a party at my house / I'm different / Song for the dead
CD _______________ **9237552**
WEA / Jan '83 / Warner Music

TROUBLE MAN
Gaye, Marvin
Gaye, Marvin *C*
Trouble man main theme / T plays it cool / Poor Abbey Walsh / Break in (police shoot big) / Cleo's apartment / Trouble man / Trouble man, Theme from / T stands for trouble / Trouble man main theme / Life is a gamble / Deep in it / Don't mess with Mr. T / There goes mister 'T'
CD _______________ **5300972**
Motown / Jan '92 / PolyGram

TROUBLESOME CREEK - A MIDWESTERN
Mirowitz, Sheldon & Duke Levine
Mirowitz, Sheldon & Duke Levine *C*
Sunday dusk / Summer montage / Titles / Downtown summer storm / Farm crisis / Family history / Thanksgiving / Cemetry / Driving to Rolfe / Last cow feed / Cattle auction Winter / Fall turns to Winter / Auction ends / Leaving Iowa / Combining / Quilt / Credit roll
CD _______________ **DARINGCD 3024**
Daring / Sep '96 / ADA / CM / Direct

TRUE BLUE
Syrewicz, Stanislas *C*
CD _______________ **4520122**
Decca / Nov '96 / PolyGram

TRUE GRIT/COMANCHEROS (Music From John Wayne Westerns Vol. 1)
Bernstein, Elmer *C*
CD _______________ **VSD 47236**
Varese Sarabande / Jan '89 / Pinnacle

TRUE LIES
Fiedel, Brad *C*
Sunshine of your love: *Living Colour* / Darkness darkness: *Screaming Trees* / Alone in the dark: *Hiatt, John* / Entity: *Mother Tongue* / Main title: Harry makes his entrance / Escape from the chateau / Harry's sweet home / Harry rides again / Spying on Helen / Juno's place / Caught in the act / Shadow lover / Island suite / Causeway/ Helicopter rescue / Nuclear Kiss / Harry saves the day
CD _______________ **4769392**
Epic / Dec '96 / Sony

TRUE ROMANCE
Zimmer, Hans *C*
CD _______________ **5199542**
Polydor / Nov '93 / PolyGram

TRUSTING BEATRICE/COLD HEAVEN
Myers, Stanley *C*
CD _______________ **MAF 7048D**
Intrada / Mar '93 / Koch / Silva Screen

TRUTH ABOUT CATS AND DOGS, THE
For once in my life: *Farris, Dionne* / Caramel: *Vega, Suzanne* / Bed's too big without you: *Sting* / Angel mine: *Cowboy Junkies* / This road: *Squeeze* / Give it everything: *Green, Al* / I can't imagine: *Neville, Aaron* / Run around: *Blues Traveller* / Well I lied: *Cray, Robert Band* / Where do I begin: *Sobule, Jill* / You do something to me: *Weller, Paul* / World keeps spinning: *Brand New Heavies* / Bad idea: *Folds, Ben Five* / Cats and dogs: *Shore, Howard*
CD _______________ **5405072**
A&M / May '96 / PolyGram

TRYOUT (Songs From Where Do We Go From Here/One Touch Of Venus)
Weill, Kurt & Ira Gershwin
CD _______________ **DRGCD 904**
DRG / Jan '95 / Discovery / New Note/ Pinnacle

TUSITALA, TELLER OF TALES (Music From BBC's Stevenson's Tales)
Stevenson, Savourna
CD _______________ **ECLCD 9412**
Eclectic / Jan '95 / ADA / New Note/ Pinnacle

TWELFTH NIGHT (Score)
Davey, Shaun *C*
CD _______________ **FILMCD 186**
Silva Screen / Oct '96 / Koch / Silva Screen

TWILIGHT ZONE VOL.1, THE (Music From The TV Series)
Invaders / Where is everybody / I sing the body electric / Jazz themes / Nervous man in a four dollar room / Walking distance / Main title / End titles
CD _______________ **VCD 47233**
Varese Sarabande / Jan '89 / Pinnacle

TWILIGHT ZONE VOL.2, THE (Music From The TV Series)
Main theme / Back there / And when the sky was opened / Passerby / Lonely / Two / End theme
CD _______________ **VCD 47247**
Varese Sarabande / Jan '89 / Pinnacle

TWILIGHT'S LAST GLEAMING
Graunke Symphony Orchestra
Goldsmith, Jerry *C*
Goldsmith, Jerry *Con*
Silo 3 / Takeover begins / General Mackenzie arrives / He has launch control / Special forces arrive / Bubble / Nuclear nightmare / Reflective interlude / After you Mr President / Heading for home / President falls / Taking of silo 3 / Operation gold begins / Watching and waiting / Tanks / Down the elevator shaft / Gold bomb / Gold team enters silo 3 / Final betrayal
CD _______________ **FILMCD 111**
Silva Screen / Apr '92 / Koch / Silva Screen

TWIN PEAKS
Badalamenti, Angelo
Badalamenti, Angelo *C*
Twin Peaks / Laura Palmer's theme / Audrey's dance / Nightingale / Freshly squeezed / Bookhouse boys / Into the night / Night life in Twin Peaks / Dance of the dream man / Love theme from Twin Peaks / Falling: *Cruise, Julee*
CD _______________ **7599263162**
Warner Bros. / Nov '90 / Warner Music

TWIN PEAKS - FIRE WALK WITH ME
Badalamenti, Angelo
Badalamenti, Angelo *C*
Twin Peaks - fire walk with me / Pine float / Sycamore trees / Don't do anything (I wouldn't do) / Real indication / Questions in a world of blue / Pink room / Black dog runs at night / Best friends / Moving through time / Montage from Twin Peaks
CD _______________ **9362450192**
WEA / Feb '95 / Warner Music

TWINTOWN
Other man's grass is always greener: *Clark, Petula* / Metronomic underground: *Stereolab* / In the summertime: *Mungo Jerry* / Good enough: *Dodgy* / Downtown: *Clark, Petula* / Bad behaviour: *Super Furry Animals* / Butterfly 747: *Moloko* / You've got a lot to answer for: *Catatonia* / Motown junk: *Manic Street Preachers* / Stem: *DJ Shadow*
CD _______________ **5407182**
A&M / Apr '97 / PolyGram

TWISTER
CD _______________ **9362462542**
East West / May '96 / Warner Music

TWO BY TWO
Broadway Cast
Rodgers, Richard *C*
Blackton, Jay *Con*
CD _______________ **SK 30338**
Sony Broadway / Dec '91 / Sony

TWO MOON JUNCTION
Elias, Jonathan *C*
CD _______________ **VSD 5518**
Varese Sarabande / Oct '94 / Pinnacle

U

U BOATS: THE WOLF PACK
Young, Christopher *C*
CD _______________ **CEUR 0214**
Silva Screen / Jan '93 / Koch / Silva Screen

UCCELLACCI/LE STREGHE/TEOREMA (Music From The Films Of Pier Paolo Pasolini)
Morricone, Ennio *C*
CD _______________ **OST 130**
Milano Dischi / Apr '96 / Silva Screen

ULYSSES
Cicognini, Alessandro *C*
CD _______________ **LEGENDCD 8**
Legend / Apr '92 / Koch / Silva Screen

ULYSSES' GAZE
Karaindrou, Eleni *C*
CD _______________ **4491532**
ECM / Oct '95 / New Note/Pinnacle

UMBRELLAS OF CHERBOURG, THE
Legrand, Michel *C*
CD _______________ **8341392**
Silva Screen / Jan '89 / Koch / Silva Screen

UN COEUR EN HIVER
Ravel, Maurice/Philippe Sarde *C*
CD _______________ **4509924082**
WEA / Jan '95 / Warner Music

UN COEUR EN HIVER (Trios & Sonates)
Ravel, Maurice/Philippe Sarde *C*
CD _______________ **2292459202**
Erato / Jan '93 / Warner Music

UN EROE BORGHESE
Donaggio, Pino *C*
CD _______________ **LEGENDCD 19**
Legend / May '95 / Koch / Silva Screen

UN TEMOIN DANS LA VILLE (& Jazz Sur Seine)
Wilen, Barney
Temoin dans la ville / La pendaison / Melodie pour les radio-taxis / Poursuite et metro / Ambiance pourpre / Premeditation dans l'appartement / La vie n'est qu'une lutte / Complainte du chauffeur / Sur l'antenne / SOS radio-taxis / Final au jardin d'acclimatation / Swing '39 / Vamp menilmontant / John's groove / B B B (Bag's Barney blues') / Swingin' Parisian rhythm / J'ai ta main / Nuages / La route enchantee / Que reste t'il de nos amours / Minor's swing / Epistrophy
CD _______________ **8326582**
Fontana / Mar '88 / PolyGram

UNBEARABLE LIGHTNESS OF BEING, THE
Janacek, Leos *C*
Fairytale III / Holy Virgin of Frydek / In the mists / Hey Jude / Joy joy joy / String quartet no. 2 / Sonata for violin and piano / Bird of ill omen lingers on / On the overgrown path, set 2 / String quartet no. 3 / Blow away leaf / Goodnight / Idyll for string orchestra, II
CD _______________ **FCD 21006**
Fantasy / Jan '89 / Jazz Music / Pinnacle / Wellard

UNDER SIEGE
Chang, Gary
Chang, Gary *C*
CD _______________ **VSD 5409**
Varese Sarabande / Feb '93 / Pinnacle

UNDER SIEGE II
Poledouris, Basil *C*
CD _______________ **VSD 5648**
Varese Sarabande / Oct '95 / Pinnacle

UNDER THE CHERRY MOON (Parade)
Prince & The Revolution
Prince *C*
Christopher Tracy's parade / New position / I wonder U / Under the cherry moon / Girls and boys / Life can be so nice / Venus de Milo / Mountains / Do U lie / Kiss / Anotherloverholenyohead / Sometimes it snows in April
CD ______ 9253952
WEA / Apr '86 / Warner Music

UNDERNEATH
Martinez, Cliff *C*
CD ______ VSD 5587
Varese Sarabande / Mar '95 / Pinnacle

UNDERNEATH THE ARCHES
1982 London Cast
Old bull and bush / Just for laughs / Underneath the arches / Maybe it's because I'm a Londoner / Home town / Umbrella man / Strollin' / Siegfried line
CD ______ CDTER 1015
TER / Aug '95 / Koch

UNFORGIVEN
Niehaus, Lennie *C*
CD ______ VSD 5380
Varese Sarabande / Sep '92 / Pinnacle

UNFORGIVEN, THE
Tiomkin, Dimitri *C*
CD ______ TSU 0108
Tsunami / Jan '95 / Silva Screen

UNIVERSAL SOLDIER
Franke, Christopher *C*
CD ______ VSD 5373
Varese Sarabande / Nov '92 / Pinnacle

UNKNOWN TIME, THE
Dikker, Loek *C*
CD ______ 887902
Milan / Jan '95 / Conifer/BMG / Silva Screen

UNLAWFUL ENTRY
Horner, James *C*
CD ______ MAF 7031D
Intrada / Dec '92 / Koch / Silva Screen

UNSINKABLE MOLLY BROWN, THE
Willson, Meredith *C*
CD ______ CDP 92054
Silva Screen / Feb '90 / Koch / Silva Screen

UNSINKABLE MOLLY BROWN, THE
Broadway Cast
Willson, Meredith *C*
CD ______ ZDM 7647612
EMI Classics / Apr '93 / EMI

UNTAMED HEART
Eidelman, Cliff *C*
CD ______ VSD 5404
Varese Sarabande / Mar '93 / Pinnacle

UNTIL THE END OF THE WORLD
Opening titles / Sax and violins: *Talking Heads* / Summer kisses, winter tears / Move with me / Adversary / What's good: *Reed, Lou* / Last night sleep / Fretless: *REM* / Days / Claire's theme / Till the end of the world / It takes time / Death's door / Love theme / Calling all angels: *Siberry, Jane* / Humans from earth / Sleeping in the devil's bed / Until the end of the world: *U2*
CD ______ 7599267072
WEA / Dec '91 / Warner Music

UP CLOSE & PERSONAL
CD ______ 1620532
Polydor / Jun '96 / PolyGram

UP/MEGA VIXENS/BENEATH THE VALLEY OF THE ULTRA VIXENS (Russ Meyer Original Soundtracks Vol. 2)
CD ______ QDKCD 009
Normal / Jul '94 / ADA / Direct

UPTIGHT
Booker T & The MG's
Johnny I love you / Cleveland now / Children don't get weary / Tank's lament / Blues in the gutter / We've got Johnny Wells / Down at Ralph's joint / Deadwood Dick / Run tank run / Time is tight
CD ______ CDSXE 024
Stax / Jan '90 / Pinnacle

URSUS - SCORES FROM 4 ITALIAN FANTASY FILMS (Ursus/Ursus In The Valley Of Lions/Ursus In The Land Of Fire/The Three Invincibles)
CD ______ CDCIA 5090
Cinevox / Jan '92 / Koch / Silva Screen

USED PEOPLE
Portman, Rachel *C*
CD ______ WA 244812
Silva Screen / Jul '93 / Koch / Silva Screen

USUAL SUSPECTS, THE
Intrabartolo, Damon
Ottman, John *C*
Groupe, Larry *Con*
CD ______ 301072
Milan / Dec '95 / Conifer/BMG / Silva Screen

UTILIZER, THE
McCarthy, Dennis *C*
McCarthy, Dennis *Con*
CD ______ MAF 7067
Intrada / Mar '96 / Koch / Silva Screen

UTOPIA LIMITED
D'Oyly Carte Opera Chorus/Royal Philharmonic Orchestra
Sullivan, Sir Arthur *C*
Gilbert, W.S. *L*
Nash, R. *Con*
2CD ______ 4368162
London / Jan '90 / PolyGram

UTU
Charles, John *C*
CD ______ LXCD 6
Label X / Jan '92 / Silva Screen

V

VAGRANT, THE
Young, Christopher *C*
Young, Christopher *Con*
CD ______ MAF 7028D
Intrada / Sep '92 / Koch / Silva Screen

VALMOUTH
1982 Chichester Festival Cast
Wilson, Sandy *C*
Valmouth / Magic fingers / Mustapha / I loved a man / All the girls were pretty / What do I want with love / Just once more / Lady of de manor / Big best shoes / Niri Esther / Cry of the peacock
CD ______ CDTER 1019
TER / May '89 / Koch

VALMOUTH
1958 London Cast
Wilson, Sandy *C*
Valmouth / Magic fingers / Mustapha / I love a man / All the girls were pretty / What do I want with love / Just one more / Lady of de manor / Big best shoes / Niri Esther / Cry of the peacock / Little girl baby / Cathedral of Clemenza / Only a passing phase / Where the trees are green with parrots / My talking day / I will miss you / Finale
CD ______ CDSBL 13109
DRG / Nov '92 / Discovery / New Note/Pinnacle

VERTIGO
Royal Scottish National Orchestra
Herrmann, Bernard *C*
McNeely, Joel *Con*
CD ______ VSD 5600
Varese Sarabande / May '96 / Pinnacle

VERTIGO
Herrmann, Bernard *C*
CD ______ VSD 5759
Varese Sarabande / Feb '97 / Pinnacle

VERY GOOD EDDIE
1975 Broadway Cast
Kern, Jerome *C*
Greene, Schuyler *L*
Overture / We're on our way / Some sort of somebody / Thirteen collar / Bungalow in Quogue / Isn't it great to be married / Good night boat / Left all alone again / Hot dot / If you're a friend of mine / Wedding bells are calling me / Honeymoon Inn / I've got to dance / Moon of love / Old boy neutral / Babes in the wood / Katy D / Nodding roses / Finale
CD ______ DRGCD 6100
DRG / '88 / Discovery / New Note/Pinnacle

VICTOR VICTORIA
Mancini, Henry *C*
You and me / Shady dame from Seville / Alone in Paris / King's can can / Le jazz hot / Crazy world / Chicago Illinois / Cat and mouse / Gay Paree / Finale
CD ______ GNPD 8038
GNP Crescendo / Sep '94 / ZYX

VICTOR VICTORIA
1995 Broadway Cast
Mancini, Henry *C*
Bricusse, Leslie *L*
Fraser, I. *Con*
CD ______ 4469192
Philips / Jan '96 / PolyGram

VICTORY AT SEA
Cincinnati Pops Orchestra
Rodgers, Richard *C*
Kunzel, Erich *Con*
CD ______ CD 80175
Telarc / Aug '90 / Conifer/BMG

VICTORY AT SEA
RCA Victor Symphony Orchestra
Rodgers, Richard *C*
Bennett, Robert Russell *Con*
Song of the high seas / Pacific boils over / Guadalcanal march / D-Day / Hard work and horseplay / Theme of the fast carriers / Beneath the Southern Cross / Mare nostrum / Victory at sea / Fire on the waters / Danger down deep / Mediterranean mosaic / Magnetic North
CD ______ 09026609632
RCA Victor / '90 / BMG

VICTORY AT SEA (More Victory At Sea)
RCA Victor Symphony Orchestra
Rodgers, Richard *C*
Bennett, Robert Russell *Con*
Allies on the march / Voyage into fate / Peleliu / Sound of victory / Rings around Rabaul / Full fathom five / Turkey shoot / Ships that pass / Two if by sea / Turning point / Symphonic scenario
CD ______ 09026609642
RCA Victor / '90 / BMG

VIDEO GIRL AI VOL.1
CD ______ AM 1
Animanga / Nov '96 / New Note/Pinnacle

VIDEO GIRL AI VOL.2
CD ______ AM 9
Animanga / Nov '96 / New Note/Pinnacle

VIKINGS, THE/SOLOMON & SHEBA
Nascimbene, Mario *C*
CD ______ LEGENDCD 9
Legend / Jan '93 / Koch / Silva Screen

VILLAGE OF THE DAMNED
Carpenter, John *C*
CD ______ VSD 5629
Varese Sarabande / Jun '95 / Pinnacle

VIRTUOSITY
CD ______ RAD 11295
Radioactive / Nov '95 / BMG / Vital

VIVA LAS VEGAS/ROUSTABOUT
Presley, Elvis
Viva Las Vegas / If you think I don't need you / If you need somebody to lean on / You're the boss / What I'd say / Do the Vega / C'mon everybody / Lady love me (With Ann Margaret) / Night life / Today, tomorrow and forever / Yellow rose of Texas/ The eyes of Texas / Santa Lucia / Roustabout / Little Egypt / Poison ivy league / Hard knocks / It's a wonderful world / Big love, big heartache / One track heart / It's carnival time / Carmy town / There's a brand new day on the horizon / Wheels on my heels
CD ______ 74321 13432-2
RCA / Mar '93 / BMG

VOICES
I will always wait for you / Rose Marie's theme / Disco if you want to / Children's song / Family theme / Anything that's rock 'n' roll / I will always wait for you (instrumental) / On a stage / Across the river / Bubbles in my beer / Rose Marie and drew / Drunk as a punk / Children's song (instrumental) / Rose Marie's dance
CD ______ DINTVCD 44
Dino / Sep '92 / Pinnacle

VON RYAN'S EXPRESS/OUR MAN FLINT/IN LIKE FLINT
Goldsmith, Jerry *C*
CD ______ TCI 0602
Tsunami / Jan '95 / Silva Screen

VOYAGE OF TERROR (The Achille Lauro Affair)
Morricone, Ennio *C*
CD ______ OST 101
Milano Dischi / Jan '93 / Silva Screen

VOYAGES
Silvestri, Alan
Silvestri, Alan *C*
CD ______ VSD 5641
Varese Sarabande / Oct '95 / Pinnacle

WAITING TO EXHALE
Babyface *C*
Exhale: *Houston, Whitney* / Count on me: *Houston, Whitney* / Let it flow: *Braxton, Toni* / This is how it works: *TLC* / Sittin' in my room: *Brandy* / Not gonna try: *Blige, Mary J.* / All night long: *SWV* / Kissing you: *Evans, Faith* / My funny valentine: *Khan, Chaka* / My love, sweet love: *Labelle, Patti* / Hurts like hell: *Franklin, Aretha* / Wey U: *Moore, Chante* / How could you call her baby: *Shanna* / Love will be waiting at home: *For Real* / And I give you love: *Marie, Sonja*
CD ______ 07822187962
Arista / Nov '95 / BMG

WALK IN THE CLOUDS, A
Jarre, Maurice *C*
CD ______ 286662
RCA Victor / Nov '95 / BMG

WALKING HAPPY
1966 Broadway Cast
Van Heusen, James *C*
Cahn, Sammy *L*
CD ______ ZDM 5651332
EMI Classics / Apr '94 / EMI

WALKING THUNDER
Munich Symphony Orchestra
Scott, John *C*
CD ______ JSCD 117
JOS / Oct '96 / JOS / Silva Screen

WALL STREET/SALVADOR
Copeland, Stewart/Georges Delerue *C*
Bud's scam: *Copeland, Stewart* / Are you with me: *Copeland, Stewart* / Trading begins: *Copeland, Stewart* / Tall weeds: *Copeland, Stewart* / Break up: *Copeland, Stewart* / Anacott steel: *Copeland, Stewart* / El playon: *Vancouver Symphony Orchestra* / Siege at Santa Fe: *Vancouver Symphony Orchestra* / Goodby Maria: *Vancouver Symphony Orchestra* / At the border: *Vancouver Symphony Orchestra* / Roadblock: *Vancouver Symphony Orchestra* / Love theme: Finale: *Vancouver Symphony Orchestra*
CD ______ CDTER 1154
TER / May '88 / Koch

WANDERERS, THE
You really got a hold on me: *Miracles* / Shout: *Isley Brothers* / Big girls don't cry: *Four Seasons* / Ya ya: *Dorsey, Lee* / My boyfriend's back: *Angels* / Soldier boy: *Shirelles* / Pipeline: *Chantays* / Do you love me: *Contours* / Wipeout: *Surfaris* / Wanderer: *Dion* / Stand by me: *King, Ben E.* / Tequila: *Champs*
CD ______ NEMCD 765
Sequel / Oct '95 / BMG

WAR AND PEACE
Ovchinnikov, Vyacheslav
Ovchinnikov, Vyacheslav *C*
CD ______ VSD 5225
Varese Sarabande / Feb '90 / Pinnacle

WAR LORD, THE
Moross, Jerome *C*
CD ______ VSD 5536
Varese Sarabande / Apr '95 / Pinnacle

WAR LORD, THE/THE CARDINAL
Moross, Jerome *C*
CD ______ TSU 0117
Tsunami / Jan '95 / Silva Screen

WAR OF THE BUTTONS
Portman, Rachel *C*
CD ______ VSD 5554
Varese Sarabande / Oct '94 / Pinnacle

WAR REQUIEM
City Of Birmingham Symphony Orchestra
Britten, Benjamin *C*
Rattle, Simon *Con*
2CD ______ CDS 7470348
EMI / '88 / EMI

WARLOCK I
Melbourne Symphony Orchestra
Goldsmith, Jerry *C*
Goldsmith, Jerry *Con*
Sentence / Ill wind / Ring / Trance / Old age / Growing pains / Weather vane / Nails / Uninvited / Salt water attack / Salt flats
CD ______ FILMCD 038
Silva Screen / Jun '89 / Koch / Silva Screen

WARLOCK II - THE ARMAGEDDON
McKenzie, Mark *C*
CD ______ MAF 7049D
Intrada / Jan '93 / Koch / Silva Screen

WARNING SIGN
Safan, Craig *C*
CD ______ SCCD 1012
Southern Cross / Jan '89 / Silva Screen

WARRIORS
In the city: *Walsh, Joe* / Warriors theme: *De Vorzon, Barry* / Baseball furies chase: *De Vorzon, Barry* / Fight: *De Vorzon, Barry* / Echoes in my mind: *Mandrill* / Nowhere to run: *McCuller, Arnold* / In Havana: *Vance, Kenny & Ismael Miranda* / Love is a fire: *Ravan, Genya* / You're movin' too slow: *Vastano, Johnny* / Last of an ancient breed: *Child, Desmond*
CD ______ 5511692
Spectrum / Sep '95 / PolyGram

WARRIORS OF VIRTUE
Beautiful morning: *Speech* / You can fly: *Hubbard, Wade* / Forces of nature: *Clannad* / Inside of you: *Havens, Richie* / Tennessee plates: *Sexton, Charlie* / In a dream: *Judyjudyjudy* / When you go: *Ultraglide* / Alembic: *Hart, Mickey & Bakithi Kumalo* / Song of the seas: *Vangelis* / Underscore: *Colorado Symphony Orchestra*
CD ______ 8122726402
Kid Rhino / Jul '97 / Warner Music

WATERWAYS
Hardiman, Ronan *C*
CD ______ HBCD 0005
Hummingbird / Oct '94 / ADA / Direct / Grapevine/PolyGram

WATTSTAX
Oh la de da: *Staple Singers* / I like the things about you: *Staple Singers* / Respect yourself: *Staple Singers* / I'll take you there: *Staple Singers* / Knock on wood: *Floyd, Eddie* / Lay your loving on me: *Floyd, Eddie* / I like what you're doing (to me): *Thomas, Carla* / Gee Whiz: *Thomas, Carla* / I have a God who loves: *Thomas, Carla* / Do the breakdown: *Thomas, Rufus* / Do the funky chicken: *Thomas, Rufus* / Do the funky penguin: *Thomas, Rufus* / Son of Shaft: *Bar-Kays* / Feel it: *Bar-Kays* / I can't turn you loose: *Bar-Kays* / Killing floor: *King, Albert* / I'll play the blues for you: *King, Albert* / Angel of mercy: *King, Albert* / I don't know what this world is coming to: *Soul Children* / Hearsay: *Soul Children* / Ain't no sunshine: *Hayes, Isaac*
2CD ______ CDSXE2 079
Stax / Nov '92 / Pinnacle

WAVELENGTH
Tangerine Dream
Tangerine Dream *C*
CD ______ VCD 47223
Varese Sarabande / Jan '89 / Pinnacle

WAY OUT WEST
Laurel & Hardy
CD ______ LHOST 1CD
Wax / Jan '97 / RTM/Disc / Total/BMG

WAY WE WERE, THE
Streisand, Barbra
Hamlisch, Marvin *C*
Bergman, Marilyn *L*
Being at war with each other / Something so right / Best thing you've ever done / Way we were / All in love is fair / What are you doing the rest of your life / Summer me, Winter me / Pieces of dreams / I've never been a woman before / My buddy / How about me
CD 4749112
Columbia / Jan '94 / Sony

WAYNE'S WORLD I
Bohemian rhapsody: *Queen* / Hot and bothered: *Cinderella* / Rock candy: *Bulletboys* / Dream weaver: *Wright, Gary* / Silkamikanico: *Red Hot Chili Peppers* / Time machine: *Black Sabbath* / Wayne's world theme: *Myers, Mike* / Ballroom blitz: *Carrere, Tia* / Foxy lady: *Hendrix, Jimi* / Feed my Frankenstein: *Cooper, Alice* / Why you wanna break my heart: *Carrere, Tia*
CD 7599268052
Reprise / Feb '95 / Warner Music

WAYNE'S WORLD II
Dude (looks like a lady): *Aerosmith* / Shut up and dance: *Aerosmith* / Louie Louie: *Plant, Robert* / Superstar: *Superfan* / Frankenstein: *Winter, Edgar* / Radar love: *Golden Earring* / Spirit in the sky: *Greenbaum, Norman* / Can't get enough: *Bad Company* / Out there: *Dinosaur Jnr* / Idiot summer: *Gin Blossoms* / Mary's house: *4 Non Blondes* / YMCA: *Village People*
CD 9362454852
Warner Bros. / Feb '94 / Warner Music

WE BEGIN
Isham, Mark & Art Lande
Isham, Mark *C*
Melancholy of departure / Ceremony in starlight / We begin / Lord Ananea / Surface and symbol / Sweet circle / Fanfare
CD 8316212
ECM / Jul '87 / New Note/Pinnacle

WE OF THE NEVER NEVER/DEVIL IN THE FLESH
Best, Peter/Philippe Sarde *C*
CD IMICD 1012
Silva Screen / Jan '93 / Koch / Silva Screen

WEDDING BANQUET, THE
CD LDM 1093
LDM / Mar '96 / Discovery

WEDDING BELL BLUES
CD VSD 5853
Varese Sarabande / Aug '97 / Pinnacle

WEEDS
Badalamenti, Angelo *C*
CD VCD 47313
Varese Sarabande / Jan '89 / Pinnacle

WENDY CRACKED A WALNUT
Smeaton, Bruce *C*
CD IMICD 1007
Silva Screen / Jan '93 / Koch / Silva Screen

WES CRAVEN'S NEW NIGHTMARE
Robinson, J. Peter *C*
CD 235152
Milan / Jan '95 / Conifer/BMG / Silva Screen

WEST SIDE STORY
1961 Film Cast
Bernstein, Leonard *C*
Sondheim, Stephen *L*
Green, John *Con*
Jet song / Something's coming / dance at the gym / America / Maria / Tonight / Gee officer Krupke / I feel pretty / One hand, one heart / Quintet / Rumble / Cool / Boy like that / I have a love / Somewhere
CD SK 48211
Sony Music / Aug '93 / Sony

WEST SIDE STORY (Highlights)
Te Kanawa, Dame Kiri & Jose Carreras/ 1984 Studio Cast
Bernstein, Leonard *C*
Sondheim, Stephen *L*
Bernstein, Leonard *Con*
Jet song / Something's coming / Maria / Tonight / America / Cool / One hand, one heart / I feel pretty / Somewhere / Gee Officer Krupke / Boy like that / I have a love / Taunting scene / Finale
CD 4159632
Deutsche Grammophon / May '85 / PolyGram

WEST SIDE STORY
Te Kanawa, Dame Kiri & Jose Carreras/ 1984 Studio Cast
Bernstein, Leonard *C*
Sondheim, Stephen *L*
Bernstein, Leonard *Con*
Prologue/Jet song / Something's coming / Dance at the gym / Maria / Tonight / Rumble / I feel pretty / Somewhere / Gee Officer Krupke / Boy like that / I have a love / Finale
2CD 4152532
Deutsche Grammophon / May '85 / PolyGram

WEST SIDE STORY
1993 Studio Cast
Bernstein, Leonard *C*
Sondheim, Stephen *L*
Wordsworth, Barry *Con*
Prologue / Jet Song / Something's coming / Blues / Promenade / Mambo / Cha cha / Meeting scene / Jump / Maria / Balcony scene (Tonight) / America / Cool / One hand, one heart / Tonight / Rumble / I feel pretty / Scherzo / Somewhere / Procession/ Adagio / Gee Officer Krupke / Boy like that / I have a love / Taunting scene / Finale
CD IMGCD 1801
IMG / Mar '93 / Carlton / Complete/Pinnacle

WEST SIDE STORY
London Cast
Bernstein, Leonard *C*
Sondheim, Stephen *L*
Jet song / Something's coming / Maria / America / Cool / One hand, one heart / Quintet (tonight) / I feel pretty / Somewhere / Gee officer Krupke / Boy like that / I have a love
CD SHOWCD 006
Showtime / Feb '95 / Disc / THE

WEST SIDE STORY
Broadway Cast
Bernstein, Leonard *C*
Sondheim, Stephen *L*
Prologue / Jet song / Something's coming / Dance at the gym / Maria / Tonight / America / Cool / One hand, one heart / Rumble / I feel pretty / Somewhere / Gee Officer Krupke / Boy like that / I have a love / Finale
CD CK 64419
Mastersound / Feb '95 / Sony

WEST SIDE STORY
Chorus & National Symphony Orchestra
Bernstein, Leonard *C*
Sondheim, Stephen *L*
Edwards, John Owen *Con*
2CD CDTER2 1197
TER / Feb '94 / Koch

WEST SIDE STORY (Symphonic Dances & On The Waterfront Suite/Candide Overture)
Los Angeles Philharmonic/Israel Philharmonic/Vienna Philharmonic Orchestra
Bernstein, Leonard *C*
Sondheim, Stephen *L*
Bernstein, Leonard *Con*
CD 4479522
Deutsche Grammophon / May '96 / PolyGram

WEST SIDE STORY (& Candide)
Te Kanawa, Kiri & Jose Carreras/Marilyn Horne/London Symphony Orchestra & Chorus
Bernstein, Leonard *C*
Sondheim, Stephen *L*
Bernstein, Leonard *Con*
3CD 4479582
Deutsche Grammophon / May '96 / PolyGram

WEST SIDE STORY
Starlight Orchestra/Singers
Bernstein, Leonard *C*
Sondheim, Stephen *L*
America / Something's coming / Maria / Tonight / I feel pretty / One hand, one heart / Rumble / Cool / Boy like that / Somewhere / Finale
CD QED 088
Tring / Nov '96 / Tring

WEST SIDE STORY
Studio Cast
Bernstein, Leonard *C*
Sondheim, Stephen *L*
Overture (America) / Something's coming / Maria / Tonight / Cool / One hand, one heart / Rumble / I feel pretty / Somewhere / Boy like that / Finale
CD 85192
CMC / May '97 / BMG

WEST SIDE STORY (Symphonic Dances & Fancy Free/Candide)
Baltimore Symphony Orchestra
Bernstein, Leonard *C*
Sondheim, Stephen *L*
Zinman, David *Con*
CD 4529162
Decca / May '97 / PolyGram

WEST SIDE STORY/MY FAIR LADY
Previn, Andre/Shelly Manne/Leroy Vinnegar
Bernstein, Leonard/Frederick Loewe *C*
Sondheim, Stephen/Alan Jay Lerner *L*
CD CDCOPD 942
Contemporary / Aug '94 / Cadillac / Complete/Pinnacle / Jazz Music / Wellard

WHALES OF AUGUST, THE
Price, Alan *C*
CD VCD 47311
Varese Sarabande / Jan '89 / Pinnacle

WHAT ABOUT LUV
1990 Cast
Marren, Howard *C*
Birkenhead, Susan *L*
CD CDTER 1171
TER / Jul '90 / Koch

WHAT'S LOVE GOT TO DO WITH IT
Turner, Tina
I don't wanna fight / Rock me baby / Disco inferno / Why must we wait until tonight / Stay awhile / Nutbush City Limits / You know I love you / Proud Mary / Fool in love / It's gonna work out fine / Shake a tailfeather / I might have been Queen / What's love got to do with it / Tina's wish
CD CDPSCD 128
EMI / Jun '93 / EMI

WHEN HARRY MET SALLY
Connick, Harry Jr.
It had to be you / Love is here to stay / Stompin' at the Savoy / But not for me / Winter wonderland / Don't get around much anymore / Autumn in New York / I could write a book / Let's call the whole thing off / Where or when / It had to be you (instrumental)
CD 4657532
CBS / Nov '89 / Sony

WHEN SATURDAY COMES
When Saturday comes: *Elliott, Joe* / Beginning: *Dudley, Anne* / Throwing it all away: *Big Wide World* / Build me up: *Hadley, Tony* / You'll never walk alone: *Gerry & The Pacemakers* / Eyes of blue: *Carrack, Paul* / Born to lose: *Big Wide World* / Seven day weekend: *Gregory, Glenn & Martin Fry* / I've been drinking: *Beck, Jeff & Rod Stewart* / Turning point: *Dudley, Anne* / Nessun Dorma: *Pavarotti* / Boys are back in town: *Thin Lizzy* / Jimmy Jimmy: *Undertones* / If the kids are united: *Sham 69* / Annie's theme: *Dudley, Anne* / Hi ho silver lining: *Beck, Jeff* / Back on my feet again: *Carrack, Paul* / World in motion: *New Order* / Penalty: *Dudley, Anne* / Jimmy's theme: *Elliott, Joe*
CD 5323072
Polystar / Mar '96 / PolyGram

WHEN THE WHALES CAME
Gunning, Christopher *C*
Gunning, Christopher *Con*
Bryher and the curse of Samson / Gracie plays truant / Birdman's gift / Islanders / Tempest - and first visit to the birdman / Crown investigators / Daniel's gift for the Birdman / War and Jack's dilemma / Birdman's warning / Lured to Samson / Clemmie's lament / Whale beached / Saving the whale / Torches in the sea / Daniel / Well full/The sailor returns/Re-united / Redeemed
CD FILMCD 049
Silva Screen / Nov '89 / Koch / Silva Screen

WHEN THE WIND BLOWS
Waters, Roger
When the wind blows: *Bowie, David* / Facts and figures: *Cornwell, Hugh* / Brazilian: *Genesis* / What have they done: *Squeeze* / Shuffle: *Hardcastle, Paul* / Towers of faith / Russian missile / Hilda's dream / American bomber / Anderson shelter / British submarine / Attack / Fallout / Hilda's hair / Folded flags
CD CDVIP 132
Virgin VIP / Apr '95 / EMI

WHEN WE WERE KINGS
CD 5344622
Mercury / Feb '97 / PolyGram

WHERE THE RIVER RUNS BLACK
Horner, James *C*
CD VCD 47273
Varese Sarabande / Jan '89 / Pinnacle

WHILE YOU WERE SLEEPING
Edelman, Randy *C*
CD VSD 5627
Varese Sarabande / Jun '95 / Pinnacle

WHISPERS IN THE DARK
Newman, Thomas *C*
CD VSD 5387
Varese Sarabande / Sep '92 / Pinnacle

WHITE MISCHIEF
Fenton, George *C*
CD CDTER 1153
TER / Feb '90 / Koch

WHITE PALACE
Fenton, George *C*
CD VSD 5289
Varese Sarabande / Nov '90 / Pinnacle

WHITE SQUALL
CD 1620402
Polydor / Mar '96 / PolyGram

WHOOP-UP
1958 Broadway Cast
Charlap, Mark *C*
CD 8371962
Silva Screen / Feb '90 / Koch / Silva Screen

WHO'S AFRAID OF VIRGINIA WOOLF
North, Alex *C*
CD TSU 0112
Tsunami / Jan '95 / Silva Screen

WHO'S THAT GIRL
Who's that girl: *Madonna* / Causing a commotion: *Madonna* / Look of love: *Madonna* / Twenty four hours / Turn it up / Best thing ever / Can't stop: *Madonna* / El loco loco
CD 9256112
Sire / Feb '95 / Warner Music

WILD AT HEART
Im abendrot / Slaughterhouse / Cool cat walk / Love me / Baby, please don't go / Up in flames / Wicked game / Be bop a lula / Smoke rings / Perdita / Blue Spanish sky / Dark Spanish symphony / Dark Lolita / Love me tender
CD 8451282
London / Sep '90 / PolyGram

WILD BOYS
CD REP 4120-WZ
Repertoire / Aug '91 / Greyhound

WILD IS THE WIND
Tiomkin, Dimitri *C*
CD TSU 0110
Tsunami / Jan '95 / Silva Screen

WILD WEST
Nowhere road: *Earle, Steve* / I ain't ever satisfied: *Honky Tonk Cowboys & Steve Earle* / River: *Honky Tonk Cowboys* / Fearless heart: *Earle, Steve* / No. 29: *Honky Tonk Cowboys & Steve Earle* / Love wore a halo: *Honky Tonk Cowboys & Nanci Griffiths* / Anyone can be somebody's fool: *Honky Tonk Cowboys & Nanci Griffiths* / Akhan naz akhan: *Anaara* / Wild west: *Honky Tonk Cowboys* / Guitars and cadillacs: *Yoakam, Dwight*
CD COOKCD 056
Cooking Vinyl / May '93 / Vital

WILLIAM THE CONQUEROR
Scott, John *C*
Scott, John *Con*
CD JSCD 110
JOS / Jan '95 / JOS / Silva Screen

WILLOW
London Symphony Orchestra/King's College Choir
Horner, James *C*
Horner, James *Con*
Elora Danan / Escape from the tavern / Canyon of mazes / Tir asleen / Willow's theme / Willow's journey begins / Bavmorda's spell is cast / Willow the sorcerer
CD CDV 2538
Virgin / Nov '88 / EMI

WIND
Poledouris, Basil *C*
CD FLCF 28209
For Life / Jul '93 / Silva Screen

WIND AND THE LION, THE
Goldsmith, Jerry *C*
Goldsmith, Jerry *Con*
CD RVF 7005D
Intrada / Feb '90 / Koch / Silva Screen

WINDY CITY
1982 London Cast
Macaulay, Tony *C*
Vosburgh, Dick *L*
Bowles, A. *Con*
Overture: *Orchestra* / Hey hallelujah: *Waterman, Dennis & Company* / Wait till I get you on your own: *Redman, Amanda & Dennis Waterman* / Waltz for Mollie: *Langton, Diane & Reporters* / Saturday: *Allen, Arhlene/Terese Stevens/Tracey Booth & Reporters* / Long night again tonight / No one walks out on me: *Rodgers, Anton* / Saturday (reprise): *Waterman, Dennis/Anton Rodgers/Leonard Lowe* / Windy city: *Waterman, Dennis & Reporters* / Round in circles / I can just imagine it: *Waterman, Dennis & Anton Rodgers* / I can talk to you: *Langton, Diane* / Perfect casting: *Redman, Amanda* / Besinger's poem: *Spinetti, Victor* / Water under the bridge: *Waterman, Dennis* / Windy city (reprise) / Shake the city: *Waterman, Dennis*
CD CDANGEL 8
Angel / Apr '94 / EMI

WINGS OF DESIRE, THE (aka Der Himmel Uber Berlin)
Knieper, Jurgen *C*
CD CD 316
Milan / Jan '89 / Conifer/BMG / Silva Screen

WINGS OF DESIRE, THE
CD CDIONIC 2
Mute / Aug '88 / RTM/Disc

WINNER, THE
Main title: *Licht, Daniel* / Meet Joey: *Licht, Daniel* / At the strip joint: *Licht, Daniel* / On the steps/You're going to lose: *Licht, Daniel* / Visiting Liberace: *Licht, Daniel* / Wolf's daddy: *Licht, Daniel* / Pina colada: *Licht, Daniel* / You gotta trust someone: *Licht, Daniel* / Let's go bury dad/I'm cold/Louise returns: *Licht, Daniel* / Louise dies: *Licht, Daniel* / End credits: *Licht, Daniel* / Cha cha no.69: *Altruda, Joey & Cocktail Crew* / Tropical espionage: *Altruda, Joey & Cocktail Crew* / I've been working on you: *Feminine Complex*
CD RCD 10392
Rykodisc / Jul '97 / ADA / Vital

WINNETOU: THUNDER ON THE BORDERLINE
Thomas, Peter *C*
CD SP 10001
Silva Screen / Jan '94 / Koch / Silva Screen

WINNIE THE POOH (Singalong)
CD WD 695324
Disney Music & Stories / Jun '96 / Technicolor

WINTER IN LISBON
Gillespie, Dizzy *C*
CD CDCH 704
Milan / Feb '93 / Conifer/BMG / Silva Screen

WINTER PEOPLE/PRAYER FOR THE DYING
Graunke Symphony Orchestra
Scott, John *C*
Scott, John *Con*
CD JSCD 102
JOS / Jan '95 / JOS / Silva Screen

WIRED (Score/Songs)
Poledouris, Basil *C*
I'm a king bee / Soul man / Raven's theme / Two thousand pounds / Still looking for a way / You are so beautiful / I can't turn you loose / You don't know like I know / Choice / Bee / Angel of death
CD ______ **VSD 5237**
Varese Sarabande / Oct '89 / Pinnacle

WISDOM
Elfman, Danny *C*
CD ______ **VSD 5209**
Varese Sarabande / Jan '89 / Pinnacle

WITH HONORS
Thank you: *Duran Duran* / I'll remember: *Madonna* / She sells sanctuary: *Cult* / It's not unusual: *Belly* / Cover me: *Candlebox* / Your ghost: *Hersh, Kristin* / Forever young: *Pretenders* / Fuzzy: *Grant Lee Buffalo* / Run shithead run: *Mudhoney* / Tribe: *Babble* / Blue skies: *Lovett, Lyle* / On the wrong side: *Buckingham, Lindsey*
CD ______ **9362455492**
Warner Bros. / Mar '94 / Warner Music

WITHOUT APPARENT MOTIVE
Morricone, Ennio *C*
Morricone, Ennio *Con*
CD ______ **A 8924**
Alhambra / Feb '92 / Silva Screen

WITNESS
Jarre, Maurice *C*
CD ______ **CDTER 1098**
TER / '88 / Koch

WIZARD OF OZ, THE
1939 Film Cast
Arlen, Harold *C*
Harburg, E.Y. 'Yip' *L*
Wizard of Oz / Dialogues / Over the rainbow / Munchkin land / Ding dong the witch is dead / Follow the yellow brick road / If I only had a brain / We're off to see the wizard / If I only had a heart / If I only had the nerve / If I were king of the forest / Courage / Home sweet home
CD ______ **CDMGM 7**
MGM/EMI / Jan '90 / EMI

WIZARD OF OZ, THE
1988 Royal Shakespeare Cast
Arlen, Harold *C*
Harburg, E.Y. 'Yip' *L*
CD ______ **CDTER 1165**
TER / Mar '89 / Koch

WIZARD OF OZ, THE (Highlights)
London Cast
Arlen, Harold *C*
Harburg, E.Y. 'Yip' *L*
Overture / Over the rainbow / Munchkinland / If only I had a brain / We're off to see the Wizard / If I only had a heart / We're off to see the Wizard (reprise) / If I only had the nerve / Merry old land of Oz / If I were the King of the forest/Courage / Jitterbug / Finale
CD ______ **SHOWCD 003**
Showtime / Feb '95 / Disc / THE

WIZARD OF OZ, THE
1939 Film Cast
Arlen, Harold *C*
Harburg, E.Y. 'Yip' *L*
Main title: *MGM Studio Orchestra & Chorus* / Over the rainbow: *Garland, Judy* / Cyclone: *MGM Studio Orchestra* / Come out, come out: *Burke, Billie & The Munchkins* / It really was no miracle: *Garland, Judy/Billy Bletcher/The Munchkins* / We thank you very sweetly: *Koziel, Joseph/Frank Cucksey* / Ding-dong, the witch is dead: *Munchkins* / As mayor of the Munchkin City: *Bletcher, Billy/Pinto Colveg/J.D. Jewkes* / As coroner, I must aver: *Stanton, Harry* / Ding-dong, the witch is dead (reprise): *Munchkins* / Lullaby league: *Bridges, Lorraine/Betty Rome/Carol Tevis* / Lollipop Guild: *Bletcher, Billy/Pinto Colveg/Harry Stanton* / We welcome you to Munchkinland: *Munchkins* / Follow the Yellow Brick Road/You're off to see the Wizard: *Garland, Judy/The Munchkins* / If I only had a brain: *Bolger, Ray/Judy Garland* / We're off to see the Wizard (Duo): *Bolger, Ray/Judy Garland* / If I only had a heart: *Haley, Jack* / We're off to see the wizard (Trio): *Garland, Judy/Ray Bolger/Buddy Ebsen* / If I only had the nerve: *Lahr, Bert/Ray Bolger/Jack Haley/Judy Garland* / We're off to see the wizard (Quartet): *Garland, Judy/Ray Bolger/Buddy Ebsen/Bert Lahr* / Optimistic voices: *MGM Studio Orchestra/The Debutantes/The Rhythmettes* / Merry old land of Oz: *Morgan, Frank/Judy Garland/Ray Bolger/Jack Haley/Bert Lahr/The MGM Studio Chorus* / If I were King of the Forest: *Lahr, Bert/Judy Garland/Ray Bolger/Jack Haley/Buddy Ebsen* / Jitterbug: *Lahr, Bert/Judy Garland/Ray Bolger/Jack Haley/Buddy Ebsen* / Ding dong, Emerald City: *Daiby, Ken/The MGM Studio Chorus* / Delirious escape: *MGM Studio Orchestra* / Delirious escape continued: *MGM Studio Orchestra* / End title: *MGM Studio Orchestra*
CD ______ **CDODEON 7**
Premier/EMI / Feb '96 / EMI

WOLVES OF WILLOUGHBY CHASE, THE
Graunke Symphony Orchestra
Towns, Colin *C*
Jones, A. *Con*
CD ______ **CDTER 1162**
TER / Dec '89 / Koch

WOMAN IN RED, THE
Wonder, Stevie
Wonder, Stevie *C*
Woman in red / It's you: *Wonder, Stevie & Dionne Warwick* / It's more than you / I just called to say I love you / Love light in flight / Moments aren't moments / Weakness: *Wonder, Stevie & Dionne Warwick* / Don't drive drunk
CD ______ **5300302**
Motown / Jan '93 / PolyGram

WONDERFUL COUNTRY
North, Alex *C*
CD ______ **TSU 0118**
Tsunami / Jan '95 / Silva Screen

WONDERFUL TOWN
1953 Broadway Cast
Bernstein, Leonard *C*
Comden, Betty & Adolph Green *L*
Ferber, Mel *Con*
Christopher Street / Ohio / Hundred ways to lose a man / What a waste / Little bit in love / Pass the football / Conversation piece / Quiet girl / Conga / My darlin' Eileen / Swing / Ohio (reprise) / It's love / Vortex ballet / Wrong note rag / It's love (reprise)
CD ______ **SK 48021**
Sony Broadway / Dec '91 / Sony

WONDERFUL TOWN
1986 London Cast
Bernstein, Leonard *C*
Comden, Betty & Adolph Green *L*
Overture / Christopher Street / Ohio / Hundred ways to lose a man / What a waste / Little bit in love / Pass the football / Conversation piece / Quiet girl / Conga / My darlin' Eileen / Swing / It's love / Vortex ballet / Wrong note rag / Finale
CD ______ **OCRCD 6011**
First Night / Apr '96 / Pinnacle

WONDERFUL TOWN
Cast Recording
Bernstein, Leonard *C*
Comden, Betty & Adolph Green *L*
2CD ______ **CDTER2 1223**
TER / Aug '95 / Koch

WONDERWALL MUSIC
Harrison, George
Harrison, George *C*
Microbes / Red lady too / Table and Pakavaj / In the park / Drilling a home / Guru vandana / Greasy legs / Ski-ing / Gat kirwani / Dream scene / Party seacombe / Love scene / Crying / Cowboy music / Fantasy sequins / On the bed / Glass box / Wonderwall to be here / Singing om
CD ______ **CDSAPCOR 1**
Apple / Jun '92 / EMI

WOODLANDERS, THE
Fenton, George *C*
CD ______ **CDDEB 1007**
Debonair / Apr '97 / Pinnacle

WOODSTOCK DIARIES
CD ______ **7567826342**
Warner Bros. / Sep '94 / Warner Music

WOODSTOCK I
I had a dream: *Sebastian, John B.* / Going up the country: *Canned Heat* / Freedom: *Havens, Richie* / Rock and soul music: *Country Joe & The Fish* / Coming into Los Angeles: *Guthrie, Arlo* / At the hop: *Sha Na Na* / Fish cheer: *McDonald, Country Joe* / I feel like I'm fixin' to die rag / Drug store truck drivin' man: *Baez, Joan* / Sea of madness: *Crosby, Stills & Nash* / Wooden ships: *Crosby, Stills & Nash* / We're not gonna take it: *Who* / With a little help from my friends: *Cocker, Joe* / Crowd rain chant: *Cocker, Joe* / Soul sacrifice: *Santana* / I'm going home: *Ten Years After* / Volunteers: *Jefferson Airplane* / Rainbows all over your blues: *Sebastian, John* / Love march: *Butterfield Blues Band* / Star spangled banner: *Hendrix, Jimi*
2CD ______ **7567805932**
Warner Bros. / Aug '94 / Warner Music

WOODSTOCK II
Jam back at the house: *Hendrix, Jimi* / Izabella: *Hendrix, Jimi* / Get my heart back together: *Hendrix, Jimi* / Saturday afternoon: *Jefferson Airplane* / Eskimo blue day: *Jefferson Airplane* / Everything's gonna be alright: *Butterfield Blues Band* / Sweet Sir Galahad: *Baez, Joan* / Guinevere: *Crosby, Stills, Nash & Young* / Four plus twenty: *Crosby, Stills, Nash & Young* / Marrakesh express: *Crosby, Stills, Nash & Young* / My beautiful people: *Melanie* / Birthday of the sun: *Melanie* / Blood of the sun: *Mountain* / Theme for an imaginary western: *Mountain* / Woodstock boogie: *Canned Heat* / Let the sunshine in: *Audience*
2CD ______ **7567805942**
Warner Bros. / Aug '94 / Warner Music

WORKING GIRL
Let the river run: *Simon, Carly* / In love: *Simon, Carly* / Man that got away: *Mounsey, Rob/George Young/Chip Jackson/Grady Tate* / Scar: *Simon, Carly* / Lady in red: *De Burgh, Chris* / Carlotta's heart: *Simon, Carly* / Looking through Katherine's house: *Simon, Carly* / Poor butterfly: *Rollins, Sonny* / I'm so excited: *Pointer Sisters* / Let the river run: *Thomas Choir of Men & Boys*
CD ______ **259767**
Arista / Feb '97 / BMG

WORLD APART, A
Zimmer, Hans *C*
CD ______ **CD 302**
Silva Screen / Jan '89 / Koch / Silva Screen

WORLD OF JEEVES AND WOOSTER, THE
Jeeves and Wooster / Jeeves and Wooster say what ho / Blue room / Meanwhile in Berkeley Square / Barmy's choice / Nagazaki / Amateur dictator (suite for Spode) / Because my baby don't mean maybe now / Midnight in Mayfair / Minnie the moocher is alive and well / Minnie the moocher / Weekend in the country / Changes / Fire / If I had a talking picture of you / Jeeves and Wooster say tinkerty tonk / Daily grind
CD ______ **CDEMC 3623**
EMI / Mar '92 / EMI

WRESTLING ERNEST HEMINGWAY
Convertino, Michael *C*
CD ______ **5188972**
Silva Screen / Jan '93 / Koch / Silva Screen

WUTHERING HEIGHTS (The Musical)
Cast/Philharmonic Orchestra & Chorus
Taylor, Bernard J. *C*
Raine, Nic *Con*
Prelude / Wuthering Heights / Cathy / They say he's a gypsy / You were my first love / I see a change in you / One rules my heart / I have no time for them / He's gone / Let her live/I will have my vengeance / Gypsy waltz / I belong to the earth / Coming home to you / Pleasure of your company / If only / Heathcliff's lament / Up here with you
CD ______ **SONGCD 904**
Silva Classics / Jul '92 / Koch / Silva Screen

WYATT EARP
Hollywood Recording Musicians' Orchestra
Howard, James Newton *C*
Paich, Marty *Con*
CD ______ **9362456602**
Warner Bros. / Sep '94 / Warner Music

X FILES
Snow, Mark
Snow, Mark *C*
CD ______ **9362460792**
Warner Bros. / Mar '96 / Warner Music

X FILES (The Truth & The Lies - Music From The X Files)
Snow, Mark
Snow, Mark *C*
CD ______ **9362464482**
Warner Bros. / Sep '96 / Warner Music

XENA - WAR PRINCESS
Le Duca, Joseph *C*
CD ______ **VSD 5750**
Varese Sarabande / Jan '97 / Pinnacle

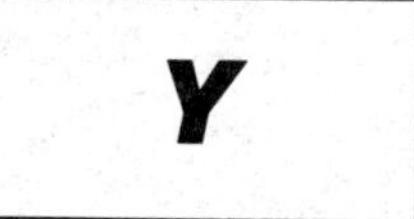

YEAR OF LIVING DANGEROUSLY, THE
Jarre, Maurice *C*
CD ______ **VCD 47222**
Varese Sarabande / '85 / Pinnacle

YEAR OF THE COMET
Mann, Hummie *C*
CD ______ **VSD 5365**
Varese Sarabande / Nov '92 / Pinnacle

YELLOW SUBMARINE
Beatles
Beatles *C*
Yellow submarine / Only a northern song / All you need is love / Hey bulldog / It's all too much / All together now / Pepperland / Sea of time / Sea of holes / Sea of monsters / March of the meanies / Pepperland laid to waste / Yellow submarine in Pepperland
CD ______ **CDPCS 7070**
Parlophone / Aug '87 / EMI

YEOMAN OF THE GUARD
Dowling, Denis & Richard Lewis/Glyndebourne Festival Choir/Pro Arte Orchestra
Sullivan, Sir Arthur *C*
Gilbert, W.S. *L*
Sargent, Sir Malcolm *Con*
2CD ______ **CMS 7644152**
EMI Classics / Jan '95 / EMI

YEOMAN OF THE GUARD
D'Oyly Carte Opera Chorus/Orchestra
Sullivan, Sir Arthur *C*
Gilbert, W.S. *L*
Edwards, John Owen *Con*
2CD ______ **CDTER2 1195**
TER / Mar '93 / Koch

YEOMAN OF THE GUARD
Academy & Chorus Of St. Martin In The Fields
Sullivan, Sir Arthur *C*
Gilbert, W.S. *L*
Marriner, Neville *Con*
2CD ______ **4381382**
Philips / Nov '93 / PolyGram

YEOMAN OF THE GUARD (Highlights)
Academy & Chorus Of St. Martin In The Fields
Sullivan, Sir Arthur *C*
Gilbert, W.S. *L*
Marriner, Neville *Con*
CD ______ **4424362**
Philips / Jan '90 / PolyGram

YEOMAN OF THE GUARD/TRIAL BY JURY
D'Oyly Carte Opera Chorus/Royal Philharmonic Orchestra/Orchestra Of The Royal Opera House
Sullivan, Sir Arthur *C*
Gilbert, W.S. *L*
Sargent, Malcolm/I. Godfrey *Con*
2CD ______ **4173582**
Decca / Jan '90 / PolyGram

YEOMAN OF THE GUARD/TRIAL BY JURY
Welsh National Opera Choir/Orchestra
Sullivan, Sir Arthur *C*
Gilbert, W.S. *L*
Mackerras, Sir Charles *Con*
CD ______ **CD 804804**
Telarc / Feb '96 / Conifer/BMG

YOR - HUNTER FROM THE FUTURE
Scott, John *C*
CD ______ **LXCD 7**
Label X / Jan '95 / Silva Screen

YOU GOTTA WALK IT LIKE YOU TALK IT
Becker, Walter & Donald Fagen
You gotta walk it like you talk it / Flotsam and jetsam / War and peace / Roll back the meaning / You gotta walk it like you talk it / Dog eat dog / Red giant/White dwarf / If it rains
CD ______ **SEECD 357**
See For Miles/C5 / Jun '97 / Pinnacle

YOU ONLY LIVE TWICE
Barry, John *C*
You only live twice: *Sinatra, Nancy* / Capsule in space / Fight at Kobe Dock / Halga / Tanaka's world / Drop in the ocean / Death of Aki / Mountains and sunsets / Wedding / James Bond astronout / Countdown for Blofeld / Bond averts World War III / Twice is the only way to live
CD ______ **CZ 559**
Premier/EMI / Dec '95 / EMI

YOUNG AMERICANS
Cathode ray: *Sheep On Drugs* / Gave up: *Nine Inch Nails* / Opening titles: *Arnold, David* / Don't let up: *Stereo MC's* / Explosion: *Arnold, David* / Uberman: *Sheep On Drugs* / He's watching me: *Arnold, David* / Hypocrisy is the greatest luxury: *Disposable Heroes Of Hiphoprisy* / Christian's requiem: *Arnold, David* / Stop the confusion: *Le Blanc, Keith & Tim Simenon* / 15 minutes of fame: *Sheep On Drugs* / Leaving London: *Arnold, David* / Play dead: *Arnold, David & Bjork*
CD ______ **IMCD 220**
Island / Mar '96 / PolyGram

YOUNG BESS
Rozsa, Miklos *C*
Rozsa, Miklos *Con*
CD ______ **PCD 133**
Prometheus / Jan '95 / Silva Screen

YOUNG GIRLS OF ROCHEFORT
Legrand, Michel *C*
CD ______ **8341402**
Silva Screen / Jan '95 / Koch / Silva Screen

YOUNG GUNS II (Blaze Of Glory)
Bon Jovi, Jon
Billy get your guns / Blaze of glory / Santa Fe / Never say die / Bang a drum / Guano City / Miracle / Blood money / Justice in the barrel / You really got me now / Dyin' ain't much of a livin'
CD ______ **8464732**
Vertigo / Aug '90 / PolyGram

YOUNG INDIANA JONES CHRONICLES I, THE (Paris, 1916/Verdun, 1916)
Munich Symphony Orchestra
McNeely, Joel *C*
McNeely, Joel *Con*
CD ______ **VSD 5381**
Varese Sarabande / May '93 / Pinnacle

YOUNG INDIANA JONES CHRONICLES II, THE (German East Africa, 1916/London, 1916/The Congo, 1917)
Munich Symphony Orchestra
McNeely, Joel *C*
McNeely, Joel *Con*
CD ______ **VSD 5391**
Varese Sarabande / Sep '93 / Pinnacle

YOUNG INDIANA JONES CHRONICLES III, THE (The Mystery Of The Blues/The Scandal Of 1920)
McNeely, Joel *C*
McNeely, Joel *Con*
Rhapsody in blue / Swanee / Somebody loves me / Sounds like perfection / Scandal walk / Sweetie Dear / My handyman / 12th

Street rag / Blue horizon / Tiger rag / I can't believe that you're in love with me / Twinkle Dixie
CD ____ **VSD 5401**
Varese Sarabande / Jun '93 / Pinnacle

YOUNG INDIANA JONES CHRONICLES IV, THE (Ireland 1916/Northern Italy 1918)
Munich Philharmonic Film Orchestra/ West Australian Philharmonic Orchestra
Rosenthal, Laurence/Joel McNeely *C*
Rosenthal, Laurence/Joel McNeely *Con*
CD ____ **VSD 5421**
Varese Sarabande / Jan '95 / Pinnacle

YOUNG LIONS, THE/THE EARTH IS MINE
Friedhofer, Hugo *C*
Friedhofer, Hugo *Con*
2CD ____ **VSD 25403**
Varese Sarabande / Jun '93 / Pinnacle

YOUNG ONES, THE
Richard, Cliff & The Shadows
Friday night / Got a funny feeling / Peace pipe / Nothing's impossible / Young ones / All for one / Lessons in love / No one for me but Nicky / What d'you know, we've got a show / Vaudeville routine / Mambo / Savage / We say yeah
CD ____ **CDMFP 6020**
Music For Pleasure / Apr '88 / EMI

YOUNG POISONERS'S HANDBOOK, THE
CD ____ **8444292**
Deram / Jan '96 / PolyGram

YOUNG SOUL REBELS
CD ____ **BLRCD 10**
Big Life / Sep '91 / Mo's Music Machine / Pinnacle / Prime

YOU'RE UNDER ARREST
Tani, Kow *C*
2CD ____ **AM 5**
Animanga / Nov '96 / New Note/Pinnacle

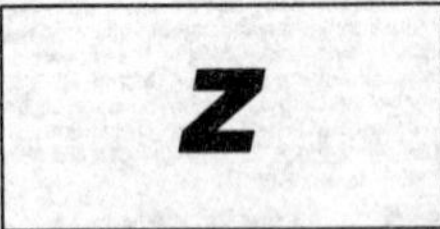

ZED AND TWO NOUGHTS, A
Zoo Orchestra
Nyman, Michael *C*
Nyman, Michael *Con*
Angelfish decay / Car crash / Time lapse / Prawn watching / Bisocosis populi / Swan rot / Delft waltz / Up for crabs / Vermeer's wife / Venus de Milo / Lady in the red hat / L'escargot
CD ____ **CDVE 54**
Virgin / Feb '90 / EMI

ZELLY AND ME
Donaggio, Pino *C*
CD ____ **VCD 70422**
Varese Sarabande / Jan '89 / Pinnacle

ZERO PATIENCE
Schellenberg, Glenn *C*
CD ____ **887971**
Milan / Jan '95 / Conifer/BMG / Silva Screen

ZIEGFELD FOLLIES
1946 Film Cast
Main title / Here's to the girls / Bring on those wonderful men / We will meet again in Honolulu / Liza (all the clouds'll roll away) / Libiamo / Heart of mine / Love / If swing goes, I go too / Limehouse blues / Interview / Babbitt and the bromide / There's beauty everywhere
CD ____ **CDODEON 3**
Premier/EMI / Feb '96 / EMI

ZOO/NOTTACACCIA/UOVA DI GARAFONA
CD ____ **CDCIA 5092**
Cinevox / Jul '93 / Koch / Silva Screen

ZORBA
Broadway Cast
Kander, John *C*
Ebb, Fred *L*
CD ____ **ZDM 7646652**
EMI Classics / Apr '93 / EMI

ZORBA
1968 Broadway Cast
Kander, John *C*
Ebb, Fred *L*
CD ____ **920532**
Silva Screen / Jan '95 / Koch / Silva Screen

ZORBA THE GREEK
Theodorakis, Mikis *C*
Zorba the Greek / Full catastrophe / Life goes on / One unforgiveable sin / Questions without answers / Zorba's dance / Fire inside / Clever people and grocers / Always look for trouble / Free / That's me - Zorba
CD ____ **610272**
Tsunami / Jan '95 / Silva Screen

ZOYA/THE YOUNG GUARD (Suites From The Film Scores)
Minsk Chamber Choir/Byelorussian Radio & TV Symphony Orchestra
Shostakovich, Dmitry *C*
Mnatsakanov, Walter *Con*
CD ____ **RDCD 10002**
Russian Disc / Jul '96 / Koch

ZULU (& Other Themes)
Barry, John *C*
Barry, John *Con*
Istanchiwania / News of the massacre / First Zulu / Wagons over / Durnford's horses arrive and depart / Zulu's final appearance and salute / VC roll/Men of Harlech / Elizabeth theme / From Russia with love / Four in the morning
CD ____ **FILMCD 022**
Silva Screen / Nov '89 / Koch / Silva Screen

ZULU DAWN
Royal Philharmonic Orchestra
Bernstein, Elmer *C*
CD ____ **CD 0201**
Silva Screen / Jan '89 / Koch / Silva Screen

Collections

007 CLASSICS
London Symphony Orchestra
James Bond / Thunderball / Goldfinger / From Russia With Love / Diamonds Are Forever / You Only Live Twice / Look of love / On Her Majesty's Secret Service / Man With The Golden Gun
CD ______ EDL 25132
Edel / Dec '89 / Pinnacle

18 WONDERFUL FILM THEMES
Arthur's theme (the best you can do) / She's out of my life / Hill street blues / Nights in white satin / Bolero / Woman / Only he has the power to move me / Chariots of fire / Thorn birds - love theme / Way he makes me feel / Cacharpaya / Derry air / Winds of war / Educating Rita / Country diary of an Edwardian lady / Jewel in the crown / Terms of endearment / Good, the bad and the ugly
CD ______ EMPRCD 516
Emporio / Jul '94 / Disc

20 CLASSIC SCI-FI THEMES
Channel X
X-Files / Close Encounters Of The Third Kind / Star Wars / ET / Twilight Zone / Doctor Who / Tomorrow People / Blakes 7 / Eve of the war / Dune / Alien / Bladerunner / Star Trek / Quantum Leap / Red Dwarf / Space 1999 / Lost In Space / Time Tunnel / UFO / 2001: A Space Odyssey
CD ______ SUMCD 4098
Summit / Feb '97 / Sound & Media

20 GREAT WESTERN THEMES
CD ______ EMPRCD 514
Emporio / Jul '94 / Disc

32 MOVIE & TV HITS
CD ______ 24005
Music / Mar '95 / Target/BMG

40 FAMOUS SONGS FROM THE MUSICALS
Sinatra, Frank
You'll never walk alone / Girl that I marry / Begin the beguine / September song / Oh what a beautiful mornin' / People will say we're in love / Song is you / You're lonely and I'm lonely / It's a lovely day tomorrow / Without a song / I'll be seeing you / World is in my arms / Just one of those things / You do something to me / Ol' man river / Night and day / You are love / They didn't believe me / Love me or leave me / There's no business like show business / 'S wonderful / Embraceable you / Kiss me again / Where or when / All the things you are / If I loved you / Someone to watch over me / These foolish things / Why shouldn't I / Bess oh where's my Bess / They say it's wonderful / Soliloquy / Lost in the stars / Falling in love with love / You make me feel so young / I'll string along with you / I've got my love to keep me warm / On the sunny side of the street / Who told you I cared / I don't know why (I just do)
2CD ______ DBG 53057
Double Gold / Jul '97 / Target/BMG

40 YEARS OF BBC TV THEMES
Paramor, Norrie
Television march / Ordinary copper / Marching from a little suite / Today's tonight / Maigret theme / Watermill / Marching strings / Music from the movies / Calypso / Ciccolino / Moonlight and roses / Snowdrops and raindrops / Last of the summer wine theme / Come dancing theme
CD ______ EMPRCD 633
Emporio / Jun '96 / Disc

50 BROADWAY SHOWSTOPPERS
Night they invented champagne / Gigi / As long as he needs me / If ever I would leave you / Bali hai / Wouldn't it be lovely / Superstar / You're just in love / How to handle a woman / Rain in Spain / Tonight / Some enchanted evening / Aquarius / People / I have dreamed / It's a lovely day today / Mame / So in love / Don' what comes naturally / My favourite things / Oh, what a beautiful morning / Matchmaker, matchmaker / Camelot / Climb every mountain / If I were a rich man / Hello young lovers / Thank heaven for little girls / I don't know how to love him / Get me to the church on time / Tradition / Big spender / Something wonderful / Food glorious food / Somewhere / Maria / Wonderful guy / Wunderbar / I feel pretty / June is bustin' out all over / Shall we dance / Flash, bang, wallop / Half a sixpence / I love Paris / Out of my dreams / Anything you can do / Day by day / C'est magnifique / Good morning starshine / Surrey with a fringe on top
2CD ______ 330442
Hallmark / Mar '97 / Carlton

50 CLASSIC TV THEMES
Bonanza / Wagon Train / Alias Smith & Jones / Emergency Ward 10 / Angels / Mission Impossible / Johnny Staccato / Colditz / Warship / Dad's Army / Saint / Persuaders / Department S / Onedin Line / Poldark / Pallisers / No Honestly / Liverbirds / Likely Lads / Ironside / Kojak / Columbo / Protectors / Brothers / Seven Faces Of A Woman / Hawaii Five-O / McCloud / Owen MD / Dr. Kildare / Dr. Finlay's Casebook / Today / On The Move / Nationwide / Virginian / Deputy / Rawhide / Coronation Street / Crossroads / Avengers / Callan / Van Der Valk / Thunderbirds / Star Trek / Upstairs Downstairs / Duchess Of Duke Street / When The Boat Comes In / Softly, Softly / Sweeney / Dixon Of Dock Green / Z Cars
2CD ______ 330432
Hallmark / Mar '97 / Carlton

50 FAMOUS SONGS FROM THE MOVIES
Sinatra, Frank
Too romantic / Say it / This is the beginning of the end / April played the fiddle / I haven't time to be a millionaire / Call of the canyon / I could make you care / Our love affair / I'd know you anywhere / Do you know why / Not so long ago / You lucky people you / It's always you / Dolores / I'll never let a day pass by / Love me as I am / How about you / Poor you / I'll take Tallulah / Last call for love / Be careful it's my heart / You'll never know / Night and day / You make me feel so young / I'm in the mood for love / Sunday Monday or always / If you please / I couldn't sleep a wink last night / Lovely way to spend an evening / Music stopped / White Christmas / I begged her / What makes the sunset / I fall in love too easily / Stormy weather / Charm of you / Embraceable you / I should care / Friend of yours / Over the rainbow / House I live in / You are too beautiful / I only have eyes for you / Paradise / All through the day / Two hearts are better than one / That old black magic / Somewhere in the night / Five minutes more / Somebody loves me
2CD ______ DBG 53056
Double Gold / Jul '97 / Target/BMG

50 YEARS OF CLASSIC HORROR FILM MUSIC
Omen / She / Rosemary's Baby / Dr. Jekyll And Mr. Hyde / King Kong / Vampire Lovers / Fear In The Night / Exorcist 2 / Hellraiser / Dr. Jekyll And Sister Hyde
CD ______ FILMCD 017
Silva Screen / Nov '89 / Koch / Silva Screen

100 YEARS OF CINEMA GOLD
2CD ______ D2CD 4025
Deja Vu / Jun '95 / THE

100 YEARS OF FILM MUSIC
6CD ______ 09026683162
RCA Victor / Jan '96 / BMG

100 YEARS OF THE MOVIES
BBC Concert Orchestra
CD ______ ASTCD 4001
Astrion Audio / Nov '96 / BMG

A-Z OF BRITISH TV THEMES VOL.1 (1960's/70's)
Avengers: *Johnson, Laurie* / Captain Scarlet: *Gray, Barry* / Catweazle: *Dicks, Ted* / Champions: *Hatch, Tony* / Crossroads: *Hatch, Tony* / Dad's Army: *Taverner, Perry* / Danger Man / Department S / Doctor In The House / Dr. Who: *Grainer, Ron* / Emmerdale Farm: *Hatch, Tony* / Fireball XL5 / Forsyth Saga / Hadleigh: *Hatch, Tony* / Hancock: *Scott, Derek* / Maigret: *Grainer, Ron* / Man In A Suitcase: *Grainer, Ron* / No Hiding Place: *Johnson, Laurie* / Please Sir: *Fonteyn, Sam* / Power Game / Return Of The Saint: *Dee, Martin* / Saint / Sportsnight: *Hatch, Tony* / Steptoe And Son: *Grainer, Ron* / Stingray: *Gray, Barry* / Thank Your Lucky Stars: *Knight, Peter* / Thunderbirds: *Gray, Barry* / Top Secret / Z Cars
CD ______ PLAY 004
Play It Again / Oct '92 / Silva Screen

A-Z OF BRITISH TV THEMES VOL.2
All Creatures Great And Small / Angels / Bergerac / Animal Magic / Bread / BBC Cricket / Auf Wiedersehen Pet / Doctor Who / Grandstand / Four Feather Falls / Juke Box Jury / Liver Birds / Man About The House / New Avengers / Persuaders / Supercar / Tales Of The Unexpected / Van Der Valk / Upstairs Downstairs / Whatever Happened To The Likely Lads
CD ______ PLAY 006
Play It Again / Jul '94 / Silva Screen

A-Z OF BRITISH TV THEMES VOL.3
Blake's 7 / Blott / Dangerfield / Lovejoy / Dempsey and Makepeace / Doctor Finlay's casebook / Emergency Ward 10 / Just William / Terry and June / Newcomers / Poirot / Professionals / Ruth Rendell mysteries / Shoestring / Sexton Blake / This is your life / When the boat comes in / Ski Sunday / World of sport / Wycliffe
CD ______ PLAY 010
Play It Again / Apr '96 / Silva Screen

ABSOLUTE COLLECTION - CLASSIC FILM & TELEVISION
CD ______ LECD 427
Wisepack / Jul '93 / Conifer/BMG / THE

ACADEMY AWARD WINNERS & NOMINATIONS
London Theatre Orchestra
Gould, Alec *Con*
West Side Story medley / Hello Dolly medley / Music Man medley / Jesus Christ Superstar medley / Paint Your Wagon medley / Boy Friend medley / Fiddler On The Roof medley / Sound Of Music medley
CD ______ 3036000402
Carlton / Feb '97 / Carlton

ACTION COLLECTION - JEAN CLAUDE VAN DAMME
CD ______ VSD 5691
Varese Sarabande / Nov '96 / Pinnacle

ACTION MOVIE THEMES
We don't need another hero / I can dream about you / Delta force theme / Take my breath away / Ride of the Valkyries / Brains and trains / It's a long road / Eye of the tiger / Love theme / Glory of love / When the going get tough, the tough get going / One vision / Voice of America's son's
CD ______ 22527
Music / Dec '95 / Target/BMG

ACTION THEMES
Power Pack Orchestra
Cagney and Lacey / Rocky 3 / Magnum PI / Great escape / Superman / Crazy like a fox / 633 Squadron / Hill Street Blues / Reamington Steele / Hunter / Operation crossbow / Sweeney / Mike Hammer / Miami Vice / Longest day / Bond theme / Hawaii Five-O / New avengers / Bergerac / Bill / Starsky and Hutch / A-Team / TJ Hooker / Shoestring / Dempsey and Makepeace / Knots landing / Scarecrow and Mrs. King / Hart to Hart / Where eagles dare / Indiana Jones
CD ______ CC 8247
EMI / Nov '94 / EMI

ALICE FAYE
Faye, Alice
Got my mind on music / I could use a dream / Halfmoon on the hudson / Think twice / This is where I came in / Carry me back to ol'Virginny / I've taken a fancy to you / Alexander's ragtime band / Remember / Blue skies / Are you in the mood for mischief / Go in and out the window / I'm just wild about Harry / I'm sorry I made you cry / I'm always chasing rainbows / I'll see you in my dreams / I never knew heaven could speak / There'll be other nights / Get out and get under / Chica chica boom chic / It's all in a lifetime / Where you are / Tropical magic / Romance and rhumba / Man with the lollypop song
CD ______ CD 60011
Great Movie Themes / Jun '97 / Target/ BMG

ALWAYS CHASING RAINBOWS (The Young Judy Garland)
Garland, Judy
All God's chillun got rhythm / Buds won't bud / Cry baby cry / Embraceable you / End of the rainbow / Everybody sing / FDR Jones / I'm always chasing rainbows / I'm just wild about Harry / I'm nobody's baby / In between / It never rains but it pours / Oceans apart / Our love affair / Over the rainbow / Sleep my baby sleep / Stompin' at the Savoy / Sweet sixteen / Swing Mister Charlie / Ten pins in the sky / You can't have everything / Zing went the strings of my heart
CD ______ CD AJA 5093
Living Era / Jul '92 / Select

AMERICAN AND ITALIAN WESTERN SCREEN THEMES
CD ______ 873038
Milan / Oct '92 / Conifer/BMG / Silva Screen

AMERICAN TELEVISION THEMES VOL. 1
Caine, Daniel *Con*
Midnight caller / LA Law / Twin Peaks / Star Trek: the next generation / North and South / Hooperman / Murder she wrote / Spenser for hire / 21 Jump Street / Newhart / Hunter / Bronx Zoo / Sonny Spoon
CD ______ TVPMCD 400
Primetime / Mar '91 / Silva Screen

AMERICAN TELEVISION THEMES VOL. 2
Caine, Daniel *Con*
Thirtysomething / Falcon Crest / Doogie Howser MD / Highway to Heaven / Quantum Leap / McGyver / Slap Maxwell Story / Head of the class / Alf / Wiseguy / Nutt House / Remington Steele / Men / Bring 'em back alive
CD ______ TVPMCD 401
Primetime / Mar '91 / Silva Screen

AMERICAN TELEVISION THEMES VOL. 3
Caine, Daniel *Con*
Law and order / Capital News / Sledgehammer / China Beach / BL Stryker / Days and Nights of Molly Dodd / Parker Lewis Can't Lose / Young Riders / Night Court / Stingray / Houston Knights / Over My Dead Body / Buck James / Top of the Hill
CD ______ TVPMCD 404
Primetime / Oct '91 / Silva Screen

AMERICAN TELEVISION'S GREATEST HITS
A-Team / Airwolf / Barnaby Jones / Battlestar Galactica / Baywatch / Cheers / Beverly Hills 90210 / Cagney and Lacey / Cosby Show / Falcon Crest / Knight Rider / Quantum leap / Roseanne / Twin Peaks / Incredible Hulk / Waltons / Equalizer / Hunter / Little house on the prairie / Melrose Place / North and South / Taxi / V
2CD ______ TVPMCD 804
Primetime / Aug '94 / Silva Screen

ANOTHER OPENIN', ANOTHER SHOW - BROADWAY'S OVERTURES
Engel, Lehman *Con*
CD ______ SK 53540
Sony Classical / Jul '94 / Sony

APOCALYPSE NAM (The 10,000 Day War)
Apocalypse Now / Vietnam Texas / Deer Hunter / Airwolf / Platoon Leader / First Blood / Purple Hearts / Missing in Action / Missing in Action III / Platoon
CD ______ CIN 22042
Silva Screen / Jan '95 / Koch / Silva Screen

ARGENTO VIVO I
CD ______ MAF 170D
Intrada / Jan '93 / Koch / Silva Screen

ARGENTO VIVO II
CD ______ MAF 185D
Intrada / Jan '92 / Koch / Silva Screen

ARNOLD (Great Music From The films Of Arnold Schwarzenegger)
CD ______ VSD 5398
Varese Sarabande / Jul '93 / Pinnacle

AS TIME GOES BY (Classic Movie Love Songs)
Mancini, Henry & Mancini Pops Orchestra
CD ______ RD 60974
RCA / Jul '92 / BMG

ASPECTS OF BROADWAY VOL.3
Orchestra Of The Americas
Freeman, Paul *Con*
I feel pretty / Maria / Something's coming / Tonight / One hand, one heart / Cool / America / Overture / Send in the clowns / Cotton blossom / Make believe / Valon's theme / Ol' man river / Misery / Can't help lovin' dat man / You are love / Why do I love you / Hey fellah / Ol' man river / Clara / Woman is a sometime thing / Summertime / I got plenty o' nuttin' / Bess you is my woman / Oh I can't sit down / There's a boat dat's leavin' soon for New York / It ain't necessarily so / Oh Lord I'm on my way
CD ______ SION 18303
Sion / Jul '97 / Direct

ASPECTS OF BROADWAY VOL.4
Orchestra Of The Americas
Freeman, Paul *Con*
Tomorrow / It's the hard knock life / Maybe / Let's go to the movies / Easy street / I don't need anything but you / We got Annie / Finale - Tomorrow / I hope I get it / At the ballet / One / What I did for love / At the end of the day / I dreamed a dream / Master of the house / On my own / Do you hear the people sing / La cafes aux follies / We are what we are / With you on my arm / Song on the sand / Best of times / They're playing my song / Just for tonight / If he really knew me / Right / 42nd Street / Some people / Everything's coming up roses / Let me entertain you / You'll never get away from me / Together wherever we go / Small world / Mr. Goldstone / All I need is the girl
CD ______ SION 18304
Sion / Jul '97 / Direct

ASPECTS OF BROADWAY VOL.5
Orchestra Of The Americas
Freeman, Paul *Con*
Fiddler on the roof / Matchmaker / If I were a rich man / Sunrise sunset / Wedding dance / To life / Tradition / People / Don't rain on my parade / Who are you now / Music makes me dance / You are woman, I am man / People / Yankee doodle / Harrigan / Mary's a grand old name / You're a grand old flag / Mame / My best girl / Open a new window / If he walked into my life / We need a little Christmas / Man of La Mancha / Dulcinea / Little bird, little bird / Little gossip / Quest / Impossible dream / Oliver / Where is love / I'd do anything / As long as he needs me / Consider yourself / Wunderbar / Why can't you behave / Another op'nin' another show / Always true to you in fashion / Were thine that special face / I sing of love / So in love

CD ______________ SION 18305
Sion / Jul '97 / Direct

ASPECTS OF BROADWAY VOL.7
Orchestra Of The Americas
Freeman, Paul *Con*
Farmer and the cowman / Oklahoma / People will say we're in love / Out of my dreams / Oh what a beautiful morning / Pore Jud is daid / Surrey with the fringe on top / Many a new day / Kansas City / Farmer dance / I can't say no / Carousel waltz / June is bustin' out all over / You'll never walk alone / Mr. Snow / If I loved you / Real nice clambake / What's the use wond'rin' / If I loved you / You are beautiful / Grant Avenue / Love look away / Chop suey / I am going to like it here / Like a God / Don't marry me / I enjoy being a girl / Sunday / Grand night for singing / It might as well be Spring / That's for me / All I owe loway / With a song in my heart
CD ______________ SION 18307
Sion / Jul '97 / Direct

ASPECTS OF BROADWAY VOL.8
Orchestra Of The Americas
Freeman, Paul *Con*
Luck be a lady / Fugue for tinhorns / Guys and dolls / I've never been in love before / Bushel and a peck / Sit down, you're rockin' the boat / Caravan / Solitude / Do nothin' 'til you hear from me / Mood indigo / Sophisticated lady / I don't mean a thing / Stranger in paradise / Baubles, bangles and beads / He's in love / Before the parade passes by / Dancing / Ribbons down my back / Hello dolly / Take a little one-step / I want to be happy / Too many rings around Rosie / No no Nanette / Tea for two / Peach on the beach / Can can / I love Paris / Never give anything away / C'est magnifique / Come along with me / It's alright with me / Allez vous-en Montmart / Silk stockings / Satin and silk / All of you / Hail Bibinski
CD ______________ SION 18308
Sion / Jul '97 / Direct

ASTERIX AU CINEMA
CD ______________ 3017682
Wotre Music / Jan '97 / Discovery / New Note/Pinnacle

ASTRAL MEDITATION
CD ______________ 74321329622
Milan / May '96 / Conifer/BMG / Silva Screen

AT THE FLICKS
Formby, George
I could make a good living at that / Baby / It's in the air / They can't fool me / Goodnight, litte fellow, goodnight / Pardon me / I'm making headway now / I could not let the stable down / I wish I was back on the farm / Count your blessings and smile / Oh don't the wind blow cold / Emperor of Lancashire / You're everything to me / You can't go wrong in these / I played on my Spanish guitar / I'd do it with a smile / Barmaid at the Rose & Crown / Get crackin' / Home Guard blues / Bell bottom George / Serves you right / Got to get your photo in the press / Hillbilly Willie / Unconditional surrender
CD ______________ PLCD 554
President / Nov '96 / Grapevine/PolyGram / President / Target/BMG

AT THE MOVIES
CD ______________ 11816
Music / Jul '95 / Target/BMG

AT THE THEATRE
Mantovani
CD ______________ CDSIV 6108
Horatio Nelson / Jul '95 / Disc

AUDREY HEPBURN - FAIR LADY OF THE SCREEN
Dobson, Rudi
Audrey Hepburn - Fair lady of the screen / Belgian rock / Fight for time / Dark city / Broadway melody / Little dog called "Mr Famouse" / Sister Audrey / Moon river / Breakfast at Tiffany's / Charade / My fair lady (Medley) / Desert anthem / Lac Genieve (Lake Geneva) / Moon river (Requiem)
CD ______________ PCOM 1136
President / Aug '94 / Grapevine/PolyGram / President / Target/BMG

AUSTRALIAN TV'S GREATEST HITS
Neighbours / Prisoner Cell Block H / Sullivans / Sons and daughters / Anzacs / Skippy / Paul Hogan show / Young Doctors / Chopper Squad / Country Practice / Carson's Law
CD ______________ FILMCD 028
Silva Screen / Nov '88 / Koch / Silva Screen

BACK TO BROADWAY
Streisand, Barbra
Some enchanted evening / Everybody says don't / Music of the night / Speak low / As if we never said goodbye / Children will listen / I have a love / I've never been in love before / Luck be a lady / With one look / Man I love / Move on
CD ______________ 4738802
Columbia / Jun '93 / Sony

BATMAN/TV THEMES
Ventures
Batman Theme / Zocko / Cape / Get Smart Theme / Man from UNCLE / Hot Line / Joker's Wild / Up, Up And Away / Green Hornet 1966 / 00-711 / Vampcamp / Secret Agent Man / Charlie's Angels / Medical Centre / Star Trek / Streets Of San Francisco / Starsky & Hutch / Baretta's Theme / Hawaii Five-0 / SWAT / Police Story / MASH / Policewoman / Nadia's Theme (The Young And The Restless)
CD ______________ C5HCD 653
See For Miles/C5 / Jun '97 / Pinnacle

BBC RADIO TOP TUNES
Paramor, Norrie Radio Orchestra
Sweet and gentle / Sky at night / Archers / Sleepy shores / Midweek / Medley / Onedin Line / Film '74 / I wish I knew how it would feel to be free / Forsythe Saga / Lotus Eaters / Softly Softly / Medley / Match Of The Day
CD ______________ EMPRCD 660
Emporio / Oct '96 / Disc

BERLIN FILMHARMONIC CONCERTS, THE
Berlin RIAS Youth Orchestra
CD ______________ CDCH 037
Milan / Jan '89 / Conifer/BMG / Silva Screen

BEST OF ARNOLD SCHWARZENEGGER, THE
City Of Prague Philharmonic Orchestra
Conan the Barbarian / Conan the Destroyer / Predator / Terminator / Terminator II / Kindergarten Cop / Twins / Junior / Running Man / Commando / Red Heat / Raw Deal / Total Recall
CD ______________ FILMCD 164
Silva Screen / Oct '95 / Koch / Silva Screen

BEST OF BOND, THE
Goldeneye / James Bond Theme From Dr No / View To A Kill / Man With The Golden Gun / Never Say Never Again / Live And Let Die / All Time High / Thunderball / From Russsia With Love / License To Kill / Living Daylights / For Your Eyes Only / Theme From Casino Royale / Moonraker / You Only Live Twice / Mr Kiss Kiss Bang Bang / Diamonds Are Forever / Goldfinger
CD ______________ CD 6070
Music / Apr '97 / Target/BMG

BEST OF BRITISH TV MUSIC, THE
London's burning / Forever green / Professionals / Agatha Christie's Poirot / To have and to hold / Upstairs, downstairs / Thomas and Sarah / Gentle touch / Bouquet of barbed wire / Partners in crime / Budgie / Wish me luck as you wave me goodbye / Love for Lydia / Lillie / Black beauty / Dempsey and Makepeace
CD ______________ CDSTM 3
Soundtrack Music / May '94 / EMI

BEST OF BROADWAY MUSICALS, THE
Best things in life are free / I've grown accustomed to her face / Anything you can do / Try to remember / Time heals everything / Sit down, you're rockin' the boat / People will say we're in love / Impossible dream / People / I get a kick out of you / Younger than springtime / Before the parade passes by
CD ______________ SHOWCD 043
Showtime / Jan '97 / Disc / THE

BEST OF CHINESE FILM MUSIC, THE
CD ______________ VSD 5455
Varese Sarabande / Jan '95 / Pinnacle

BEST OF GENE KELLY, THE
Kelly, Gene
Singin' in the rain / You were meant for me / All I do is dream / Moses / Broadway ballet / You are my lucky star / I like myself / Blue Danube / Almost like being in love / Heather on the hill / Les girls / Why am I so gone about that gal / You're just too, too / Nina / You wonderful you / Heavenly music / I got rhythm / Love is here to stay / 'S wonderful
CD ______________ CDODEON 9
Soundtracks / Jun '96 / EMI

BEST OF HOLLYWOOD MUSICALS, THE (Songs From the Timeless Silver Screen Classics)
New York New York: *Freeman, Ethan & Gregg Edelman/Tim Flavin* / Deadwood stage: *Company* / Woman in love: *Loesser, Emily & Company* / I'm a brass band: *Dankworth, Jacqueline* / Over the rainbow: *Bevan, Gillian* / With a little bit of luck: *Moody, Ron* / Night they invented champagne: *Hamilton, Lindsay & Graham Bickley/Sian Phillips* / Money money: *Pryce, Jonathan & Maria Friedman* / I feel pretty: *Olafimihan, Tinuke & Elinor Stephenson/Julie Paton/Nicole Carty* / I talk to the trees: *Freeman, Ethan* / Tomorrow: *French, Sarah & Girls* / Grease: *Barrowman, John & Girls*
CD ______________ SHOWCD 044
Showtime / Jan '97 / Disc / THE

BEST OF JAMES BOND, THE (30th Anniversary Collection)
James Bond: *Norman, Monty & Studio Orchestra* / Goldfinger: *Bassey, Shirley* / Nobody does it better: *Simon, Carly* / View to a kill: *Duran Duran* / Mr. Kiss Kiss Bang Bang: *Warwick, Dionne* / For your eyes only: *Easton, Sheena* / We have all the time in the world: *Armstrong, Louis* / Live and let die: *McCartney, Paul* / All time high: *Coolidge, Rita* / Living daylights: *A-Ha* / Licence to kill: *Knight, Gladys* / From Russia with love: *Monro, Matt* / Thunderball: *Jones, Tom* / You only live twice: *Sinatra, Nancy* / Moonraker: *Bassey, Shirley* / On her Majesty's Secret Service: *Barry, John & Studio Orchestra* / Man with the golden gun / Diamonds are forever / 007: *Barry, John & Studio Orchestra*
CD ______________ CDBOND 007
EMI / Dec '95 / EMI

BEST OF SCANDANAVIAN FILM MUSIC, THE
CD ______________ CDCH 760
Milan / Dec '93 / Conifer/BMG / Silva Screen

BEST OF THE HOLLYWOOD MUSICALS, THE
CD ______________ PWKS 4213
Carlton / Nov '94 / Carlton

BEST OF WEST END MUSICALS, THE
Consider yourself / All I ask of you / I don't know how to love him / Spread a little happiness / I could be happy with you / Thank you very much / Leaning on a lamp-post / Reviewing the situation / If I ruled the world / Ta-ra-ra-boom-de-ay / Wishing you were somehow here again / Oh look at me
CD ______________ SHOWCD 019
Showtime / Feb '95 / Disc / THE

BIG SCREEN ADVENTURE
CD ______________ EMPRCD 710
Emporio / Mar '97 / Disc

BIT OF A SHOWMAN, A
Hobbs, Jeremy
Applause / Mascara / I promise you a happy ending / Time heals eveything / I won't send roses / Movies were movies / Maybe this time / And yet and yet / Hurt / My way / Ballad of the sad young men / I am what I am / Look over there
CD ______________ CDGRS 1285
Grosvenor / Jan '96 / Grosvenor

BLACK TO BROADWAY
Kent, Monroe III
Don't get around much anymore / Stick around / Knock me a kiss / When I first saw you / God bless the child / What would I do if I could feel / In my day / It's not over / Talking to yourself / I'm just a lucky so and so (blues in the night) / Nobody knows you when you're down and out / Down home / I got it bad and that ain't good / Azure te / Do nothing till you hear from me / Satin doll / Jitterbug waltz
CD ______________ 3036000302
Carlton / Mar '96 / Carlton

BLADE RUNNER (Synthesizer Soundtracks)
Hitcher / Big trouble in Little China / Haunted summer / Revenge / Lock up / Halloween / Blade runner
CD ______________ SILVAD 3008
Silva Treasury / Aug '94 / Koch / Silva Screen

BLOOD AND THUNDER
Ben Hur / Captain from Castile / Cleopatra / Wind and the lion / North by northwest / Ten commandments / Taras bulba / Mutiny on the bounty
CD ______________ VSD 5561
Varese Sarabande / May '95 / Pinnacle

BOND AND BEYOND
Cincinnati Pops Orchestra
Kunzel, Erich *Con*
CD ______________ CD 80251
Telarc / May '92 / Conifer/BMG

BOND COLLECTION, THE (The 30th Anniversary)
Bassey, Shirley
View to a kill / Nobody does it better / From Russia with love / We have all the time in the world / You only live twice / Diamonds are forever / Live and let die / Moonraker / For your eyes only / All time high / Thunderball / Goldfinger
CD ______________ ICOCD 007
Icon / Mar '93 / Pinnacle

BORN ON THE FOURTH OF JULY (Music From The Films Of Tom Cruise)
Born On The Fourth Of July / Risky Business / Days Of Thunder / Color of Money / Outsiders / Legend / Top Gun / Rain Man / Cocktail / Firm / Few Good Men / Far And Away
CD ______________ FILMCD 152
Silva Screen / Sep '94 / Koch / Silva Screen

BRITISH FILM MUSIC (From The 1940s & 1950s)
Way to the stars / Blithe spirit (Prelude and waltz) / Night has eyes (Theme) / Western approaches (Seascape) / Passionate friends (Film theme) / Man between / Sound barrier (Rhapsody Op38) / Matter of life and death (Prelude) / Kid for two farthings / Hungry hill / Rake's progress (Calypso music) / Wanted for murder (A voice in the night) / Ha'penny breeze (Film theme) / Carnival (Intermezzo) / Scott of the Antartic / Pony march, penguins, climbing the glacier, final music
CD ______________ CDGO 2059
EMI / May '94 / EMI

BROADWAY BOUND
CD ______________ VSD 5676
Varese Sarabande / Aug '96 / Pinnacle

BROADWAY CHRISTMAS
Be a Santa / Chtistmas eve / Pine cones and holly berries / Turkey lurkey time / Christmas gifts / That man over there / Hard candy Christmas / Christmas child / I thank you for your love / I don't remember Christmas / We need a little Christmas / Greenwillow Christmas / Lovers on Christmas eve / Happy New Year blues / Have yourself a merry little Christmas
CD ______________ VSD 5517
Varese Sarabande / Oct '94 / Pinnacle

BROADWAY GOLD
CD ______________ TRTCD 213
TrueTrax / Feb '96 / THE

BROADWAY HITS
CD ______________ CDCD 1231
Charly / Jun '95 / Koch

BROADWAY SHOWSTOPPERS
Casts & Ambrosian Chorus/London Sinfonietta
CD ______________ CDC 7545862
EMI Classics / Apr '93 / EMI

BROADWAY SHOWSTOPPERS
CD ______________ CDTEZ 7002
TER / Jan '95 / Koch

BROADWAY TO HOLLYWOOD
Philharmonic Pops Orchestra
CD ______________ MBSCD 444
Castle / Jul '96 / BMG

BUGS BUNNY ON BROADWAY (New Recordings Of Music From Bugs Bunny Cartoons)
CD ______________ 9264942
Silva Screen / Sep '93 / Koch / Silva Screen

BUSBY BERKELY ALBUM, THE
Barrett, Brent & Judy Blazer/Ann Morrison/London Sinfonietta & Chorus
CD ______________ CDC 5551892
EMI Classics / Apr '93 / EMI

CAPTAIN BLOOD - VINTAGE HOLLYWOOD ADVENTURE SCORES (Captain Blood/Scaramouche/Three Musketeers/King's Thief)
Brandenburg Philharmonic Orchestra
Kaufman, Richard *Con*
CD ______________ 8223607
Marco Polo / Feb '96 / Select

CAROUSEL WALTZ
Philharmonia/National Symphony/D'Oyly Carte Opera/New Sadler's Wells/Scottish Opera Orchestras
Edwards, John Owen/J. Pryce Jones/M. Reed/G. Hossack *Con*
CD ______________ CDVIR 8315
TER / Oct '91 / Koch

CASABLANCA (Classic Film Scores For Humphrey Bogart)
National Philharmonic Orchestra
Gerhardt, Charles *Con*
Casablanca / Passage to Marseille / Treasure of the Sierra Madre / Big Sleep / Two Mrs Carrolls / Caine Mutiny / To Have and Have Not / Sabrina / Virginia City / Key Largo / Left Hand of God / Sahara
CD ______________ GD 80422
RCA Victor / '90 / BMG

CELEBRATE BROADWAY VOL.1 - SING HAPPY
Sing happy: *Minnelli, Liza* / Blow Gabriel blow: *Lupone, Patti* / Freedom: *Theodore, Donna & Chip Ford* / Consider yourself: *Goodman, Michael* / I've gotta crow: *Martin, Mary & Kathy Nolan* / Good morning starshine: *Kellogg, Lyn* / Born again: *Martin, Mary* / Our time: *Walton, Jim* / Hey look me over: *Ball, Lucille* / Before the parade passes by: *Channing, Carol* / I got love: *Moore, Melba* / To life: *Mostel, Zero* / Certain girl: *Wayne, David* / Little me: *Andrews, Nancy* / H-A-P-P-Y/We'll take a glass together: *Jackson, David* / Best of times: *Hearn, George*
CD ______________ 09026619872
RCA / Apr '94 / BMG

CELEBRATE BROADWAY VOL.10 - BEST MUSICALS
Overture / If I were a rich man / Song on the sand / Honeysuckle rose / Hello Dolly / Kiss Of The Spiderwoman / Stranger in paradise / Little priest / Look who's in love / Send in the clowns / Shall we dance / Bring him home / Brotherhood of man / Music of the night
CD ______________ 09026680372
RCA Victor / May '96 / BMG

CELEBRATE BROADWAY VOL.2 - YOU GOTTA HAVE A GIMMICK
I've got your number: *Swenson, Swen* / Step to the rear: *Roberts, Anthony & Charlotte Jones* / I can't say no: *Ebersole, Christine* / Mama will provide: *Lewis, Kecia* / Caribean plaid (medley): Kingston market/ Matilda Matilda: *Chandler, Stan* / Dream: *Mostel, Zero* / Lizzie Borden: *Lautner, Joe* / Arthur in the afternoon: *Ziemba, karn* / Your feet's too big: *Page, Ken* / Crossword puzzle: *Ackerman, Loni* / Well known fact: *Preston, Robert* / Shuffle off to Buffalo: *Prunczik, Karen* / Siberia: *Lascoe, Henry* / Another wedding song: *Barrett, Brent* / So long dearie: *Bailey, Pearl* / Little more mascara: *Hearn, George* / You gotta have a gimmick: *Shapiro, Debbie*
CD ______________ 09026619882
RCA / Apr '94 / BMG

CELEBRATE BROADWAY VOL.3 - LULLABY OF BROADWAY
Lullaby of Broadway / Broadway baby / Be a performer / All I need is the girl / Opening doors / One step / Hello Dolly / Life upon the wicked stage / I want to go to Hollywood / Stereophonic sound / Comedy tonight / La Cage Aux Folles / Cabaret / There's no business like showbusiness
CD 09026619892
RCA Victor / Feb '96 / BMG

CELEBRATE BROADWAY VOL.4 - OVERTURES
Carousel / Finian's Rainbow / Follies / Roar of the Greasepaint (The Smell of the Crowd) / Hello Dolly / Boyfriend / Peter Pan / On a Clear Day You Can See Forever / Merrily We Roll Along / King and I / Mack and Mabel / Gypsy
CD 09026619902
RCA Victor / Feb '96 / BMG

CELEBRATE BROADWAY VOL.5 - HELLO YOUNG LOVERS
King & I / Showboat / Once On This Island / I do I do / Closer Than Ever / Roar Of The Greasepaint / Grand Hotel / High Button Shoes / Merrily We Roll Along / Gypsy / Follies / Chess / Hair / And the world goes 'round / Phantom
CD 09026619912
RCA Victor / Mar '96 / BMG

CELEBRATE BROADWAY VOL.6 - BEAUTIFUL GIRLS
Follies / Annie Get Your Gun / Flora The Red Menace / I do I do / Sunday In The Park With George / Ain't misbehavin' / 110 In The Shade / Company / Broadway / New Faces Of 1952 / Oliver / On A Clear Day / Putting It Together / Gypsy
CD 09026619922
RCA Victor / Mar '96 / BMG

CELEBRATE BROADWAY VOL.7 - KIDS
Bye Bye Birdie / Peter Pan / King & I / Flora The Red Menace / Oliver / Once On This Island / Funny Thing Happened On The Way To The Forum / Carousel / Hair / Forever plaid / Annie Get Your Gun / Wildcat / Bye bye birdie / Follies
CD 09026680342
RCA Victor / Mar '96 / BMG

CELEBRATE BROADWAY VOL.8 - DUETS
Anything Goes / Oklahoma / Annie Get Your Gun / Assassins / Gigi / Jekyll & Hyde / Chess / Roar Of The Greasepaint / My Favourite Year / Fiddler On The Roof / Guys And Dolls / Phantom / I do I do / Kismet
CD 09026680352
RCA Victor / Apr '96 / BMG

CELEBRATE BROADWAY VOL.9 - GOTTA DANCE
Dancing / Charleston / Pick-pocket tango / We're in the money / Who couldn't dance with you / Secretary is not a toy / Who's that woman / We dance / Joint is jumpin' / One night in Bangkok / On the SS Bernard Cohn / Dance at the gym/Somewhere
CD 09026680362
RCA Victor / May '96 / BMG

CENTRE STAGE
Warlow, Anthony
Music of the night / Easy to love / Luck be a lady / Somewhere / This nearly was mine / I am what I am / Anthem / Bring him home / You're nothing without me / Impossible dream / Johanna / Colours of my life / Soliloquy
CD 5112232
London / Nov '91 / PolyGram

CHANSONS POUR FELLINI
CD CDCH 330
Milan / Feb '94 / Conifer/BMG / Silva Screen

CHILDREN - 100% KIDS PARTY
Smurfsong: *Father Abraham & The Smurfs* / Toad's song: *Jones, Terry* / Help it's the hair bear bunch / Rugrats / Roobarb and Custard / Mr Blobby / Mah na mah na / Bare necessities megamix: *UK Mixmasters* / Scooby Doo, where are you / Masked rider / Thunderbirds / We are VR: *VR Troopers* / X - Men / Clarissa explains it all / U krazy katz: *PJ & Duncan* / Hands up hands up: *Zig & Zag* / Christmas in Smurfland: *Father Abraham & The Smurfs* / Dog pound hop: *Ren & Stimpie* / Wacky races / Top cat / Tra la la song / Power Rangers / Biker mice from Mars / Captain Scarlet / Stingray / Jetsons / Remember you're a womble / Postman Pat song: *Barrie, Ken* / Rupert the bear: *Lee, Jacky* / It only takes a minute girl: *Pinky & Perky*
CD TCD 2874
Telstar / Nov '96 / BMG

CHRISTMAS WITH DISNEY
CD WD 724602
Disney Music & Stories / Nov '96 / Technicolor

CHUMMA DO (Hit Hindi Film Songs In Bengali)
Jooma chumma de / Khullam khulla pyaar / Chura liya hai tune / Pyaar bina chain kahan re / Yeh ladka hai allah / Oh romeo / Ole ole / Tama tama loge / Dil afri dam
CD ARCD 2035
Audiorec / '91 / Audiorec

CINE STARS 1929-1939
2CD FA 063
Fremeaux / Jun '97 / ADA / Discovery

CINEMA CENTURY (A Musical Celebration Of 100 Years Of Cinema/58 Classic Themes)
20th Century Fox Fanfare / City lights / Bride of Frankenstein / Gone with the wind / Stagecoach / Citizen Kane / Casablanca / Oliver Twist / Quo vadis / Quiet man / High and the mighty / Searchers / Bridge on the River Kwai / Big country / North by Northwest / Ben Hur / Psycho / La dolce vita / Magnificent seven / Alamo / Pink panther / Lawrence of Arabia / Great escape / 633 squadron / Zulu / Zorba the Greek / Doctor Zhivago / Born free / Lion in Winter / Once upon a time in America / Where eagles dare / Midnight cowboy / Wild bunch / Godfather / Jaws / Rocky / Taxi driver / Star wars / Diva / Raiders of the lost ark / Chariots of fire / Conan the barbarian / ET / Once upon a time in the West / Terminator / Witness / Out of Africa / Passage to India / Mission / Room with a view / Cinema paradiso / Ghost / Dances with wolves / 1492 Conquest of paradise / Unforgiven / Fugitive / Jurassic park / Schindler's list
3CD FILMCD 180
Silva Screen / Apr '96 / Koch / Silva Screen

CINEMA CHORAL CLASSICS
Crouch End Festival Chorus
Temple, David *Con*
Jesus Of Nazareth / Abyss / First Knight / Lion In Winter / Conan The Barbarian / Mission / Henry V / 1492 - Conquest Of Paradise / Agnus Dei / Carmina Burana
CD SILKD 6015
Silva Screen / Mar '97 / Koch / Silva Screen

CINEMA CLASSICS 1997
CD 8551181
Naxos / Jul '97 / Select

CINEMA DU MONDE (18 Film Soundtrack Masterpieces)
CD MCCD 127
Music Club / Sep '93 / Disc / THE

CINEMA MOODS
Heart asks pleasure first/The promise: *Nyman, Michael* / Sheltering sky theme: *Sakamoto, Ryuichi* / Dangerous liasons / On earth as it is in heaven: *Morricone, Ennio* / Veni sancte spiritus: *Fenton, George* / Jean De Florette: *Petit, Jean Claude* / Darlington Hall: *Robbins, Richard* / Germinal: *Roques, Jean-Louis* / Betty et Zorg: *Yared, Gabriel* / Last emperor: *Byrne, David* / Etude: *Tarrega, Francisco* / Chasing sheep is best left to shepherds: *Nyman, Michael* / Age of innocence: *Bernstein, Leonard* / Hamlet: *Morricone, Ennio* / Pensione Bertollini: *Robbins, Richard* / Cinema paradiso: *Morricone, Ennio* / Adagio for strings / Big Blue overture: *Serra, Eric*
CD CDV 2774
Virgin / Mar '95 / EMI

CINEMA OF THE '80S
CD CDCH 394
Milan / Feb '91 / Conifer/BMG / Silva Screen

CINEMA SOUNDTRACK COLLECTION VOL.3
CD VSD 5709
Varese Sarabande / Mar '96 / Pinnacle

CINEMATIC PIANO - SOLO PIANO MUSIC FROM THE MOVIES
Chertock, M.
CD CD 80357
Telarc / Jul '94 / Conifer/BMG

CINEMOTIONS (The Best Film Music Ever)
CD VSD 5624
Varese Sarabande / Apr '96 / Pinnacle

CLASSIC FILM SCORES FOR BETTE DAVIS
National Philharmonic Orchestra
Gerhardt, Charles *Con*
Now Voyager / Dark Victory / Stolen Life / Private Lives of Elizabeth and Essex / Mr. Skeffington / In This Our Life / All About Eve / Jezebel / Beyond the Forest / Juarez / Letter / All This and Heaven Too
CD GD 80183
RCA Victor / '89 / BMG

CLASSIC FILM THEMES
Carter, Gaylord
King's row / Bad and the beautiful / How green was my valley / High noon / Uninvited / Exodus / Gone with the wind / Best years of our lives / Spellbound / Place in the sun / Raintree county
CD FA 8102
Facet / May '94 / Conifer/BMG

CLASSIC FILM THEMES
CD TRTCD 202
TrueTrax / Jun '95 / THE

CLASSIC FILM THEMES
CD PDSMC 530
Pulse / Aug '96 / BMG

CLASSIC FILM THEMES
CD PBXCD 514
Pulse / Nov '96 / BMG

CLASSIC GREEK FILM MUSIC
City Of Prague Philharmonic Orchestra
Zorba the Greek / 300 Spartans / Topkapi / Never on a Sunday / Chariots of Fire / 1492 (Conquest of Paradise) / Z / Phaedra / Honeymoon / State of Siege / Blue / Serpico / Shirley Valentine / Missing
CD FILMCD 165
Silva Screen / Oct '95 / Koch / Silva Screen

CLASSIC HOLLYWOOD
New World Philharmonic
CD FMICD 1
FMI / Feb '95 / Total/BMG

CLASSIC ITALIAN SOUNDTRACKS (The Horror Film Collection)
Deep red / Night of the devils / Nightmare crypt / Planet of the vampires / Monk / Throne of fire / Seven notes in black / Mysterious island of Dr Nemo / Deadly steps lost in the dark
CD DRGCD 32903
DRG / Jun '95 / Discovery / New Note/ Pinnacle

CLASSIC ITALIAN SPAGHETTI WESTERN THEMES
CD DRGCD 32909
DRG / Oct '95 / Discovery / New Note/ Pinnacle

CLASSIC MOVIE SONGS OF THE 40'S
Haran, Mary Cleere
CD VSD 5482
Varese Sarabande / Oct '94 / Pinnacle

CLASSIC MUSICALS (Performed On Pan Pipes)
Love changes everything / First man you remember / I dreamed a dream / Bring him home / Come to me / Empty chairs at empty tables / With one look / Perfect year / Wishing you were somehow here again / All I ask of you / Memory / I know him so well / I don't know how to love him / Don't cry for me Argentina / Any dream will do
CD SUMCD 4092
Sound & Media / Jan '97 / Sound & Media

CLASSICAL FILM MUSIC
CD 889706
Milan / May '93 / Conifer/BMG / Silva Screen

CLASSICAL FILM THEMES
2CD MBSCD 421
Castle / Nov '93 / BMG

CLASSICAL HOLLYWOOD VOL.1
CD 873126
Milan / Sep '92 / Conifer/BMG / Silva Screen

CLASSICAL HOLLYWOOD VOL.2
CD 873128
Milan / Sep '92 / Conifer/BMG / Silva Screen

CLASSICS AT THE MOVIES
2001 - A Space Odyssey / Sleeping With The Enemy / Raging Bull/The Godfather Part III / Breaking Away / Manhattan / Witches Of Eastwick / Kramer Vs. Kramer / Who Framed Roger Rabbit / Heat And Dust / Mrs Doubtfire / Silence Of The Lambs / Hannah And Her Sisters / Amadeus / Fantasia / Last Emperor / Untouchables / Clockwork Orange / Great Dictator / Love Story / Midsummer Night's Sex Comedy / Age Of Innocence / Dead Poets Society / Atlantic City / Parent Trap / Moonstruck / Seven Year Itch/Brief Encounter / Fatal Attraction / Platoon/Elephant Man / Strictly Ballroom / Excalibur / Out Of Africa / Nijinsky / Children Of A Lesser God / Wall Street / Apocalypse Now / Short Cuts / Rollerball / French Lieutenant's Woman / Die Hard 2 / Ordinary People
4CD TFP 046
Tring / Apr '95 / Tring

CLASSICS AT THE MOVIES
Eine kliene nachtmusik-allegro / Canon in D major / Bolero / Reveries from symphonie fantastique / Clarinet concerto in A major / Also sprach zarathustra / Adagietto from symphony No.5 in c sharp major / O fortuna / Piano trio No.2 D 929 / Adagio for strings in G minor
CD DC 880882
Disky / May '97 / Disky / THE

CLASSICS FROM THE MOVIES
4CD QUAD 015
Tring / Nov '96 / Tring

CLASSICS OF CINEMA
CD BM 515
Blue Moon / Feb '97 / Cadillac / Discovery / Greensleeves / Jazz Music / Jet Star / TKO Magnum

CLASSICS OF THE SILVER SCREEN
Kunzel, Erich & Cincinnati Pops Orchestra
CD CD 80221
Telarc / Aug '90 / Conifer/BMG

CLASSICS TO BROADWAY
Paratore, A. & J.
CD 310115
Koch / Oct '92 / Koch

CLIFF RICHARD AT THE MOVIES 1959-1974
Richard, Cliff
No turning back / Living doll / Mad about you / Love / Voices in the wilderness / Shrine on the second floor / Friday night / Got a funny feeling / Nothing is impossible / Young ones / Lessons in love / When the girl in your arms / We say yeah (It's wonderful to be young) / Outsider / Seven days to a holiday / Summer holiday / Let us take you for a ride / Stranger in town / Bachelor boy / Swingin' affair / Dancing shoes / Next time / Big news / Wonderful life / Girl in every port / Little imagination / On the beach / Do you remember / Look don't touch / In the stars / What've I gotta do / Matter of moments / Shooting star / Finders keepers / Time drags by / Washerwoman / La la la song / Oh senorita / This day / Paella / Two a penny / Twist and shout / I'll love you forever today / Questions / It's only money / Midnight blue / Game / Brumburger duet / Take me high / Anti-brotherhood of man / Winning
2CD CDEMD 1096
EMI / Jul '96 / EMI

CLIFFHANGERS (Action & Adventure In The Movies)
City Of Prague Philharmonic Orchestra
Motzing, William *Con*
Bear Island / Flight of the Intruder / Duellists / Shoot to Kill / Riddle of the Sands / Remo / Savage Islands / Jaws IV / Last of the Mohicans / Arachnophobia / First Blood / King Solomon's Mines / Farewell to the King / Young Indiana Jones / 1492 (Conquest of Paradise) / Cliffhanger
CD FILMCD 155
Silva Screen / Sep '94 / Koch / Silva Screen

CLIFFHANGERS (Music From The Classic Republic Serials)
Cinema Sound Orchestra
King, J. *Con*
Perils Of Nyoka / Adventures Of Captain Marvel / Dick Tracy's G-Men / Zorro's Fighting Legion / Fighting Devil Dogs / King Of The Royal Mounted / Daredevils Of The Red Circle / Mysterious Dr. Satan / Hawk Of The Wilderness / Drums Of Fu Manchu / Adventures Of Red Ryder
CD VSD 5658
Varese Sarabande / May '96 / Pinnacle

CLINT EASTWOOD MOVIE THEMES
Good, The Bad And The Ugly / Every Which Way But Loose / Fistful Of Dollars / For A Few Dollars More / Misty / Sudden Impact / Any Which Way You Can / Claudia's theme / Dead Pool / Doe eyes / Two Mules For Sister Sara / High Plains Drifter / Hang 'Em High / Outlaw Josey Wales / Joe Kidd / Pale Rider / Enforcer / Tightrope / Magnum Force / City Heat
CD ECD 3319
K-Tel / May '97 / K-Tel

COCKTAILS ON THE BEACH
I put a spell on you: *Kenyon, Carol* / I'll be seeing you: *Harrison, Deirdre* / Unchained melody / Sorrow: *Schumann, Mort* / As time goes by: *Bolling, Claude Big Band* / Water of Irrawaddy / Adios nonino: *Tirao, Cachao* / Always and forever: *Carsen, Nathalie* / Passion theme: *Hill, Warren* / Body double: *Donaggio, Pino* / Over the wall: *Migenes, Julia* / Two different worlds: *Loggins, Kenny* / Man I love: *Holiday, Billie* / Shattered / Looking back: *Q Rose*
CD 74321395942
Milan / Aug '96 / Conifer/BMG / Silva Screen

COLLECTION
Monroe, Marilyn
CD COL 042
Collection / Mar '95 / Target/BMG

COLLECTION: MARILYN MONROE (20 Golden Greats)
Monroe, Marilyn
Diamonds are a girl's best friend / River of no return / Heatwave / Do it again / Kiss / My heart belongs to daddy / I'm gonna file my claim / This is a fine romance / Little girl from Little Rock / Happy birthday Mr. President / After you get what you want, you don't want it / You'd be surprised / She acts like a woman should / Lazy / When love goes wrong nothing goes right / One silver dollar / When I fall in love / Things / Bye bye duet / Bye bye baby
CD DVCD 2001
Deja Vu / Jul '87 / THE

COLLECTORS GEMS FROM THE MGM FILMS
Garland, Judy
Waltz with a swing/Americana / Opera vs. Jazz / Everybody sing / Yours and mine / Your Broadway and my Broadway / Got a pair of new shoes / Sun showers / Down on melody farm / Why because / Ever since the world began/Shall I sing a melody / It between / It never rains, but what it pours / Bei mir bist du schoen / Meet the beat of my heart / Zing went the strings of my heart / On the bumpy road to love / Ten pins in the sky / I'm nobody's baby / All I do is dream of you / Alone / It's a great day for the Irish / Danny boy / Pretty girl milking her cow / Singin' in the rain / Easy to love / We must have music / I'm always chasing rainbows / Minnie from Trinidad / Every little minute has a meaning of its own / Tom Tom

the piper's son / When I look at you / Paging Mr. Greenback / Where's the music / Joint is really jumpin' / Down at Carnegie Hall / D'ya love me / Mack the knife / Love of my life / Voodooo / You can't get a man with a gun / There's no business like showbusiness / They say it's wonderful / Girl that I marry / I've got the sun in the morning / Let's go West again / Anything you can do / There's no business like showbusiness
2CD ________________ CDODEON 22
Soundtracks / Jan '97 / EMI

COMEDIES MUSICALES AMERICAINES
CD ________________ 3017062
IMP / Jul '97 / ADA / Discovery

COMEDIES MUSICALES AMERICAINES
2CD ________________ 3017072
IMP / Jul '97 / ADA / Discovery

COMPLETE CINEMA CLASSICS COLLECTION, THE
Piano / Shadowlands / Schindler's List / Remains of the Day / Philadelphia / Diva / Apocalypse Now / Platoon / My Left Foot / Fatal Attraction / Room With A View / Immortal Beloved / Jefferson in Paris / Sleeping With The Enemy / Madness of King George / Out of Africa / Driving Miss Daisy / Raging Bull / Untouchables / Gallipoli / Amadeus / Pretty Woman / Brief Encounter / Moonstruck / True Romance / Children of a Lesser God / Dead Poets Society
2CD ________________ CDEMTVD 106
EMI / Oct '95 / EMI

COMPOSERS OF FRENCH MUSIC
CD ________________ FE 953
Fremeaux / Apr '97 / ADA / Discovery

COPS (26 Themes From The Right Side Of The Law)
Brooks, Paul
Medley / Inspector Morse / Mission: Impossible / Avengers / Miss Marple / Kojak / Sweeney / A-Team / Rockford Files / Charlie's Angels / Magnum PI / Perry Mason / Man From UNCLE / Medley
CD ________________ ECD 3369
K-Tel / Jul '97 / K-Tel

COPS ON THE BOX USA
Hawaii 5-0 / Starsky and Hutch / Streets of San Francisco / Kojak / NYPD blue / Miami vice / Columbo / Cagney and Lacey / Dragnet / Police woman / Due South / Perry Mason / Ironside / TJ Hooker / Highway patrol / Hill St. Blues
CD ________________ EMPRCD 711
Emporio / Apr '97 / Disc

CORONATION STREET ALBUM, THE
Devoted to you: *Richard, Cliff & Denise Black* / Blue eyes: *Tarmey, Bill* / He ain't heavy, he's my brother: *Hollies & Coronation Street Cast* / I remember it well: *Barlow, Thelma & Peter Baldwin* / Life on the street: *Deuce featuring Sherrie Hewson* / Tra la la la la: *Waddington, Bill* / Something stupid: *Barrie, Amanda & Johnny Briggs* / Baby's in black: *Kennedy, Kevin* / Didn't we: *Ball, Michael & Barbara Knox* / Teardrops: *Griffin, Angela & Chloe Newsome* / I'll string along with you: *Nicholls, Sue* / Always look on the bright side of life: *Coronation Street Cast featuring Bill Waddington*
CD ________________ CDCOROTV 1
Premier/EMI / Nov '95 / EMI

CULT FILES, THE (40 Classic Themes)
Royal Philharmonic Orchestra/City Of Prague Philharmonic Orchestra/Mark Ayres
Townend, Mark/Nic Raine *Con*
X files / Prisoner / Saint / Dangerman / Randall & Hopkirk (Deceased) / Avengers / Jason King / Persuaders / Blake's seven / Red Dwarf / Doctor Who / Adventures Of Robinson Crusoe / Alfred Hitchcock Presents / Hawaii 5-0 / Perry Mason / (A Man Called) Ironside / Kojak / Mission Impossible / Star Trek / Seaquest DSV / Babylon 5 / X files / 2001: A Space Odyssey / Excalibur / Alien / Mad Max beyond The Thunderdrome / Body Heat / Omen / Halloween / Assault On Precinct 13 / Blade Runner / Batman / Superman / Shadow / Rocketeer / Heaven's Gate / Legend / Somewhere In Time / Taxi Driver / Pink Panther / Blues Brothers
2CD ________________ FILMXCD 184
Silva Screen / Oct '96 / Koch / Silva Screen

CULT THEMES FROM THE 1970'S VOL.1
CD ________________ FLEG 8CD
Future Legend / Mar '97 / Future Legend / Pinnacle

DEVIL RIDES OUT, THE (Music For Hammer Horror, Romance & Adventure)
Westminster Philharmonic/City Of Prague Philharmonic
Bateman, Paul/Nic Raine *Con*
She / Kiss of the vampire / Frankenstein created woman / Scars of Dracula / Quatermass / Devil rides out
CD ________________ FILMCD 174
Silva Screen / Jul '96 / Koch / Silva Screen

DIAL M FOR MURDER (A History Of Hitchcock)
City Of Prague Philharmonic Orchestra
Bateman, Paul *Con*
Psycho / North by Northwest / Rebecca / Spellbound / Under Capricorn / Vertigo / Topaz / Marnie / Frenzy / Suspicion / Dial M for murder
CD ________________ FILMCD 137
Silva Screen / Sep '93 / Koch / Silva Screen

DIAMOND COLLECTION, THE
Monroe, Marilyn
CD ________________ WWRCD 6002
Wienerworld / Jun '95 / THE

DIAMONDS ARE A GIRL'S BEST FRIEND
Monroe, Marilyn
CD ________________ CDGFR 135
IMD / Jun '92 / BMG

DIGITAL SPACE
London Symphony Orchestra
Star Wars / Tribute to a bad man / Lady Hamilton / Airport / Things to come / Windjammer / Big Country / Red pony / 49th Parallel / Spitfire prelude and fugue
CD ________________ VCD 47229
Varese Sarabande / Jan '89 / Pinnacle

DIGITAL THEMES SPECTACULAR VOL. 2
2001 / Superman / Hill Street Blues / Kojak / Cagney and Lacey / Dempsey and makepeace / Dad's Army / TV Sports themes / Cavatina / 633 Squadron / Swing march / Trap / Howard's Way / Last starfighter / Masterpiece / Nobilmente / Things to come / Bridge Too Far / Squadron / In party mood / Liberty bell / Black Hole / Lawrence of Arabia / Elizabeth Tudor / Battle of Britain
CD ________________ BNA 5031
Bandleader / Aug '89 / Conifer/BMG

DIGITAL THEMES SPECTACULAR VOL.1
Dallas / My name is Bond / Rocky medley / Chariots of Fire / Knots landing / Raiders of the Lost Ark / Falcon Crest / Only love / Where no man has gone before / Chi Mai / Dynasty / Those Magificent Men in their Flying Machine / Rockford files / Eastenders / Warship / Barwick Green / Dambusters march / Longest Day / Concert march-Cockleshell Heroes
CD ________________ BNA 5011
Bandleader / Feb '88 / Conifer/BMG

DISNEY FAVOURITES
CD ________________ WD 685624
Disney Music & Stories / Nov '96 / Technicolor

DISNEY HITS
When you wish upon a star: *Sammes, Mike Singers* / Thomas O'Malley cat: *Hilton, Ronnie* / Give a little whistle: *Sammes, Mike Singers* / When I see an elephant fly: *Peterson, Clive* / Who's afraid of the big bad wolf: *Sammes, Mike Singers* / Ugly bug ball: *Hilton, Ronnie* / Whistle while you work / Winnie the Pooh / Heigh ho / Siamese cat song: *Sammes, Mike Singers* / Bare necessities: *Sammes, Mike Singers* / Supercalifragilisticexpialidocious / Colonel Hathi's march: *Sammes, Mike Singers* / Trust in me: *Curtis, Nick* / That's what friends are for: *Sammes, Mike Singers* / I wanna be like you: *Sammes, Mike Singers* / Never smile at a crocodile: *Peterson, Clive* / Feed the birds: *Dawn, Julie* / Aristocats: *Hilton, Ronnie* / Hi diddle dee dee: *Sammes, Mike Singers* / Everybody wants to be a cat: *Hilton, Ronnie* / My own home: *Heard, Enid* / I've got no strings: *Sammes, Mike Singers*
CD ________________ CC 262
Music For Pleasure / Oct '90 / EMI

DISNEY MODERN CLASSICS
CD ________________ WD 699902
Disney Music & Stories / Nov '96 / Technicolor

DISNEY ORIGINAL CLASSICS
CD ________________ WD 699802
Disney Music & Stories / Nov '96 / Technicolor

DISNEY SPECTACULAR, A
Cincinnati Pops Orchestra
When you wish upon a star / It's a small world / Alice in Wonderland / March of the cards / Mary Poppins / Cinderella / Jungle book / Who's afraid of the big bad wolf / Snow White and the seven dwarfs / Mickey Mouse march / Baroque hoedown / Disney fantasy medley
CD ________________ CD 80196
Telarc / '89 / Conifer/BMG

DIVA - SOPRANO AT THE MOVIES
Garrett, Lesley
CD ________________ SONGCD 903
Silva Classics / Jan '94 / Koch / Silva Screen

DIVA BY DIVA
Kaye, Judy
CD ________________ VSD 5589
Varese Sarabande / Nov '95 / Pinnacle

DIVAS OF THE SILVER SCREEN
Monroe, Marilyn/Judy Garland/Marlene Dietrich
3CD ________________ MCBX 016
Music Club / Dec '94 / Disc / THE

DON'T ASK FOR THE MOON, WE HAVE THE STARS
Way you look tonight / Let there be love / Boy next door / September song / She's funny that way / You're a sweetheart / I'm making believe / Amor amor / I'm knee deep in daisies / How do I know it's real / That old feeling / Too marvellous for words / That old black magic / Sweet Lorraine / It can't be wrong / Let's do it / Never took a lesson in my life / Let's get away from it all / Long ago and far away / Only forever / Dinah / I've got a heart filled with love / Very thought of you / Boy what love has done to me / I remember you / Now voyager
CD ________________ UCD 400
Happy Days / Jan '96 / Conifer/BMG

DRACULA (Classic Scores From Hammer Horror)
Philharmonia Orchestra
Richardson, Neil *Con*
Dracula / Dracula has risen from the grave / Taste the blood of Dracula / Vampire circus / Hands of the ripper / Dracula, prince of darkness
CD ________________ FILMCD 714
Silva Screen / May '93 / Koch / Silva Screen

EARFUL OF MERMAN, AN
Merman, Ethel
I got rhythm / Sam and Delilah / Shake well / Eadie was a lady / Animal in me / Spanish custom / He reminds me of you / Earful of music / Shake it off with rhythm / You're the top / Shanghai-de-ho / Riding high / It's de-lovely / Hot and happy / You are the music to the words in my heart / Heatwave / Marching along with time / This is it / I'll pay the check / Friendship / Make it another old-fashioned please / Let's be buddies
CD ________________ CMSCD 015
Movie Stars / May '94 / Conifer/BMG

EASY PROJECT VOL.3, THE (The Very Best Of The Tony Hatch Orchestra)
Hatch, Tony Orchestra
Naked City / Joanna / Dick Powell / Soul coaxing / Mondo Kane / Music to watch girls by / Crossroads / Downtown / Man Alive / Doctors / Sportsnight / Sounds Of the Seventies / Memories of summer / Occasional Man / Champions / Call me / Emmerdale Farm / Birds / Hadleigh / Maori / Mr. and Mrs. / While The City Sleeps / Willow waltz / Best in football / Devil's herd / Surrey with the fringe on top / La paloma / World At War / Man And A Woman / Out Of This World
CD ________________ NEMCD 920
Sequel / Jan '97 / BMG

EASY TEMPO VOL.3 (A Further Cinematic Easy Listening Experience)
Saudade / Nago / I cavalli / Bob E Hellen / North Pole penguin / Frenesia / La bikina / Il Libanese / Lady Magnolia / Diamond bossa nova / Amanda's train / Beryl's tune / La seduzione / Easy lovers / Flute sequence / Beryl's tune / Soul samba / Casa di moda / Honey, rhythm and butter / Danza citar free / Esquetando os tambourinos e cuica
CD ________________ ET 904CD
Easy Tempo / Jun '97 / New Note/Pinnacle

EMBRACEABLE YOU - BROADWAY IN LOVE
Broadway Casts
CD ________________ SK 53542
Sony Broadway / Jul '94 / Sony

EMPIRE MOVIE MUSIC COLLECTION
On Earth as it is in heaven: *London Philharmonic Orchestra* / Last Emperor (main title): *Byrne, David* / Merry Christmas Mr. Lawrence: *Sakamoto, Ryuichi* / Black rain suite: *Zimmer, Hans* / Looks like a tablecloth: *Martinez, Cliff* / Homeboy: *Clapton, Eric* / C'est le vent, Betty: *Yared, Gabriel* / Key: *Fenton, George* / Etude: *Oldfield, Mike* / Call to arms: *Horner, James* / Les modernes: *Krause, Steven*
CD ________________ CDVMM 1
Virgin / Nov '90 / EMI

ENCORE, ENCORE (Hits From The West End Stage Show)
London Theatre Orchestra & Singers
Only He / Memory / Maria / Another suitcase in another hall / I know him so well / Aquarius / Edelweiss / One night in Bangkok / She's so beautiful / Tomorrow / Grease / Hey there / Prepare the way of the Lord / People / Don't cry for me Argentina / I don't know how to love him / Impossible dream / Day by day / Sound of music / Till there was you
CD ________________ OP 0002
MCI Music / Apr '87 / Disc / THE

EPIC FILM SCORES
King of Kings / Nativity / Miracles of Christ / Salome's dance / Way of the cross / Resurrection and finale / Ben Hur / Victory parade / Miracle and finale / El Cid overture / Palace music / Legend and epilogue
CD ________________ VCD 47268
Varese Sarabande / '88 / Pinnacle

EROTIC CINEMA
CD ________________ 12167
Laserlight / Sep '93 / Target/BMG

ESSENTIAL COLLECTION
Monroe, Marilyn
2CD ________________ LECD 621
Wisepack / Apr '95 / Conifer/BMG / THE

ESSENTIAL JAMES BOND, THE
City Of Prague Philharmonic Orchestra
Raine, Nic *Con*
Dr. No / From Russia With Love / 007 / Goldfinger / Thunderball / You Only Live Twice / On Her Majesty's Secret Service / Diamonds Are Forever / Man With the Golden Gun / Spy Who Loved Me / Moonraker / For Your Eyes Only / Octopussy / Living Daylights / View to a Kill / Licence to Kill
CD ________________ FILMCD 007
Silva Screen / '93 / Koch / Silva Screen

ETHEL MERMAN'S BROADWAY
Merman, Ethel
CD ________________ VSD 5665
Varese Sarabande / Nov '95 / Pinnacle

EVERYBODY SING (Great Songs From The Hollywood Musicals)
Everybody sing: *Garland, Judy* / If it's you: *Martin, Tony* / When I love I love: *Miranda, Carmen* / Bojangles of Harlem: *Astaire, Fred* / Ain't it a shame about Mame: *Martin, Mary* / When my ship comes in: *Cantor, Eddie* / I'm no angel: *West, Mae* / Treat me rough: *Rooney, Mickey* / Let yourself go: *Rogers, Ginger* / With plenty of money and you: *Powell, Dick* / Easy to love: *Langford, Frances* / Two sleepy people: *Hope, Bob & Shirley Ross* / Sand in my shoes: *Boswell, Connie* / Ol' man river: *Robeson, Paul* / Never in a million years: *Faye, Alice* / Sweet little headache: *Crosby, Bing* / Moon of Manakoora: *Lamour, Dorothy* / You are too beautiful: *Jolson, Al* / It's raining sunbeams: *Durbin, Deanna* / Lovely way to spend an evening: *Sinatra, Frank*
CD ________________ PPCD 78113
Past Perfect / Feb '95 / Glass Gramophone Co.

FAMOUS THEMES (Radio/TV/Newsreel Themes From 1940's/50's)
Queens Hall Light Orchestra
Portrait of a flirt/Willo the wisp/Jumping bean / Journey into melody / Sapphires and sables / Invitation waltz / By the sleepy lagoon / Puffin' Billy / Coronation Scot / Rhythm on rails / Music everywhere / Horse guards, Whitehall / Devil's gallop / Destruction by fire / On a spring note / All sports march / Cavalcade of youth / Drum majorette / Girls in grey / Elizabethan serenade / Melody on the move / Alpine pastures / Young ballerina / Horse feathers / Sportsmaster
CD ________________ GRCD 10
Grasmere / May '86 / Highlander / Savoy / Target/BMG

FAMOUS THEMES
New World Philharmonic
CD ________________ CDRBL 7782
Red Bus / '88 / Total/BMG

FANTASTIC JOURNEY
Kunzel, Erich & Cincinnati Pops Orchestra
CD ________________ CD 8023
Telarc / Aug '90 / Conifer/BMG

FANTASTIC TELEVISION THEMES
Caine, Daniel *Con*
Quantum Leap / V the series / Freddy's Nightmares / Star Trek - The Next Generation / Knight Rider / Highway to Heaven / Streethawk / Battlestar Galactica / Airwolf / Buck Rogers in the 25th Century / North Star / Bring 'Em Back Alive / Return of the Man From UNCLE / Tales of the Gold Monkey
CD ________________ TVPMCD 402
Primetime / May '91 / Silva Screen

FANTASTIC VOYAGE (A Journey Through Classic Fantasy Film Music)
City Of Prague Philharmonic Orchestra
Motzing, William *Con*
Alien / Terminator / My Stepmother Is An Alien / Dead Zone / Gremlins 2: The New Batch / Countdown / 2010 / Seconds / Ghostbusters / Flash Gordon / V For Victory / Mad Max 2 / Fantastic Voyage / Explorers / Fortress / Philadelphia Experiment / Illustrated Man / Battle For The Planet Of The Apes / Total Recall / Batman
CD ________________ FILMCD 146
Silva Screen / Jan '94 / Koch / Silva Screen

FANTASTIC WORLD OF SPAGHETTI WESTERNS, THE
CD ________________ VCDS 7016
Varese Sarabande / Apr '96 / Pinnacle

FANTASY FESTIVAL (Themes From Italian Fantasy/Horror Films)
CD ________________ CDCIA 5093
Cinevox / Apr '94 / Koch / Silva Screen

FANTASY MOVIE THEMES
London Symphony Orchestra
CD ________________ HRM 7002
Hermes / Jan '86 / Nimbus

FANTASY WORLDS OF IRWIN ALLEN, THE (& Bonus Disc Of Alt. Cues/Sound Effects/Cast Interviews)
Lost in space I / Lost in space II / Voyage to the bottom of the sea / Time tunnel / Land of the giants
6CD ________________ GNPD 8044/9
GNP Crescendo / Apr '96 / ZYX

FASCINATING RHYTHM
Astaire, Fred
Shall we dance / Fascinating rhythm / Night and day / Crazy feet / Puttin' on the ritz / My one and only / Babbitt and the bromide / I've got you on my mind / Foggy day / Let's call the whole thing off / New sun in the sky / High hat / Hang on to me / Funny

face / They can't take that away from me / Nice work if you can get it
CD HADCD 163
Javelin / May '94 / Henry Hadaway / THE

FAVOURITE MOVIE CLASSICS
CD CDCFP 4606
Classics For Pleasure / Jan '95 / EMI

FAVOURITE TV CLASSICS VOL.1
CD CDCFP 4613
Classics For Pleasure / Jan '95 / EMI

FAVOURITE TV CLASSICS VOL.2
CD CDCFP 4626
Classics For Pleasure / Jan '95 / EMI

FAVOURITE TV THEMES
Inspector Morse / Ruth Rendell mysteries / Upstairs and downstairs / She / Agatha Christie's Poirot / Woman of substance / Tales of the unexpected / Professionals / The Match / Avengers / Forever green / New adventures of Black Beauty / Chimera / London's burning / Dr. Who / Saylon Dola / World Cup '90 / Hundred acres / On the line / Wish me luck as you wave me goodbye / Summer's lease (Carmina Valles) / ITV Athletics / Good guys / Classic adventures
CD MCCD 069
Music Club / Jun '92 / Disc / THE

FELLINI FILM THEMES
Amarcord / Juliet of the spirits / 8-1/2 / La dolce vita / Satyricon Roma / White sheik / I vitteloni / Il bidone / Nights of Cabiria / La strada
CD HNCD 9301
Hannibal / Jan '87 / ADA / Vital

FILM AND MUSICAL FAVOURITES
Keel, Howard
CD 15093
Laserlight / May '94 / Target/BMG

FILM COLLECTION, THE
CD 11818
Music / Aug '95 / Target/BMG

FILM FANTASY
National Philharmonic Orchestra
Journey to the Centre of the Earth / Seventh voyage of Sinbad / Day the earth stood still / Fahrenheit
CD 4212662
Decca / '88 / PolyGram

FILM FAVOURITES
Mancini, Henry
Love story / Pink panther / Windmills of your mind / Moon river / Raindrops keep falling on my head
CD 295469
Ariola Express / Aug '95 / BMG

FILM FAVOURITES
Mantovani & His Orchestra
Love story / Big country / Secret love / Wand'rin' star / Tammy / Never on a Sunday / When you wish upon a star / Born free / Que sera sera / Alfie / High Noon / Trolley song / Moon river / Windmills of your mind / Moulin Rouge theme / Chim chim cher-ee / As time goes by / My foolish heart
CD 5516012
Spectrum / Nov '95 / PolyGram

FILM MUSIC OF CHARLES CHAPLIN, THE
German Symphony Orchestra
Davis, Carl *Con*
Gold rush / Kid / Circus / City lights / Modern times
CD 9026682712
RCA Victor / Jun '96 / BMG

FILM MUSIC OF HUGO FRIEDHOFER
Richthofen & Brown Symphonic Suite
CD 8105
Facet / May '97 / Conifer/BMG

FILM MUSIC VOL.2
La force du destin: *New Philharmonia Orchestra* / Intermezzo en un diese mineur: *Rudy, Mikhail* / Heart asks pleasure first: *Erdbeer, Johannes* / La Mamma morta: *Callas, Maria/Philharmonia Orchestra* / Concerto pour clarinette/orchestre en la majeur K622: *Meyer, Sabine/Staatskapelle Dresden* / La traviata: *Scotto, Renato/Philharmonia Orchestra* / Marche hongroise: *Orchestre De La Societe Des Concerts Du Conservatoire* / Requiem K626: *Pace, Patrizia/Choeur De Chambre De Stockholm* / Adagia pour cordes: *Philadelphia Orchestra* / Casta diva: *Callas, Maria/Choeurs & Orchestre Du Theatre De La Scala De Milan* / Sonate pour violin en re mineur Op.5 no.12/La follia: *Kurosaki, Hiro/Emmanuel Balsa/William Christie* / Sonate pour piano no.14/Clair de lune: *Hiedsieck, Eric* / O mio babbino caro: *De Los Angeles, Victoria/Orchestre Du Theatre De L'Opera De Rome* / Main theme: *Little, Tasmin/New World Philharmonic* / Romance: *Laniau, Pierre* / Symphonie no.9: *Morris, James/Westminster Choir & Philadelphia Orchestra* / Funeral music: *Ensemble* / Barcarolle en sol mineur Op.37 no.6: *Laval, Danielle* / Zadok The Priest: *Ambrosian Singers/Menuhin Festival Orchestra* / Recitar vesti la giubba: *Carreras, Jose/Philharmonia Orchestra* / Sonate pour piano en si bemol majeur: *Naoumoff, Emile* / Un bel de vedremo: *Caballe, Montserrat/London Symphony Orchestra* / Trio pour piano, violon and violoncelle: *Trio Chung* / Le patre sur le rocher: *Ludwig, Christa/Gervase De Peyer/Gerald Moore* / Duo des fleurs: *Mesple, Mady/Danielle Millet/Orchestre Du Theatre National De L'Opera De Paris* / Concerto pour piano et orchestre no.3: *Tacchino, Gabriel/Orchestre Philharmonique De Berlin*
2CD CZS 5693142
Rouge Et Noir / Feb '97 / EMI

FILM NOIR (Concert Suites To The Series Film Noir)
Brandenburg Philharmonic Orchestra
Stromberg, William T. *Con*
Maltese Falcon / All through the night / Verdict / Dark passage / White heat
CD 09026681452
RCA Victor / Nov '96 / BMG

FILM STAR PARADE
I wanna be loved by you: *Kane, Helen* / Please: *Crosby, Bing* / Ich bin von kopf bis fuss auf liebe eingestellt: *Dietrich, Marlene* / My wife is on a diet: *Cantor, Eddie* / You're always in my arms (but only in my dreams): *Daniels, Bebe* / Living in clover: *Buchanan, Jack* / Let me sing and I'm happy: *Jolson, Al* / What'll I do: *Pidgeon, Walter* / Dance of the cuckoos: *Laurel & Hardy* / Eadie was a lady: *Merman, Ethel* / All I need is just one girl: *MacMurray, Fred* / Love your magic spell is everywhere: *Swanson, Gloria* / Sweet music: *Astaire, Fred & Adele* / I could make a good living at that: *Formby, George* / Don't tell him what's happened to me: *Bankhead, Tallulah* / My rock-a-bye baby: *Moore, Grace* / (I'd like to be) A bee in your boudoir: *Rogers, Charles 'Buddy'* / Love me tonight: *MacDonald, Jeanette & Maurice Chevalier* / Goodnight Vienna: *Buchanan, Jack*
CD CDAJA 5020
Living Era / Jul '89 / Select

FILM THEMES
Mantovani
CD CDSIV 6105
Horatio Nelson / Jul '95 / Disc

FILM THEMES
Synthonic 2000
2CD RCACD 208
RCA / Jun '96 / BMG

FILM WORKS 1986-1990
Zorn, John
CD 7559792702
Nonesuch / Jan '95 / Warner Music
CD TZA 7314
Tzadik / Jul '97 / Cargo

FILM WORKS VOL.5
Zorn, John
CD TZ 7307
Tzadik / Oct '96 / Cargo

FILM WORKS VOL.6
Zorn, John
CD TZ 7308
Tzadik / Oct '96 / Cargo

FILMS CONCERT
Diva / Kramer vs Kramer / Apocalypse Now / Clockwork orange / Runaway Train / 2001 / Death in Venice / E la Nave Va
CD CDCH 249
Milan / May '87 / Conifer/BMG / Silva Screen

FOUR ALFRED HITCHCOCK FILMS
Ketcham, Charles & Utah Symphony Orchestra
Family Plot / Strangers on a Train / Suspicion / Notorious
CD VCD 47225
TER / Sep '86 / Koch

FRED ASTAIRE IN HOLLYWOOD
Astaire, Fred
CD AMSC 570
Avid / Jun '96 / Avid/BMG / Koch / THE

FROM THE BIG SCREEN
Band Of The Life Guards
Jurassic Park / Medley from The Lion King / ET / Robin Hood, Prince of Thieves / Medley from Indiana Jones and the Temple of Doom / Medley: an Aladdin fantasy / Star Trek / Medley from The Bodyguard / Evening at tops
CD BNA 5116
Bandleader / Jul '95 / Conifer/BMG

FURRY FRIENDS
CD WD 695102
Disney Music & Stories / Nov '96 / Technicolor

GALA CONCERT FOR HAL PRINCE, A
Willetts, Dave & L. Cariou/R. Jones/C. Sunnerstam/Munich Ra dio Orchestra
Prince, C. *Con*
2CD DOCRCD 2
First Night / Apr '96 / Pinnacle

GARY WILMOT - THE ALBUM
Wilmot, Gary & The London Symphony Orchestra
Luck be a lady / I've never been in love before / We're off to see the wizard / Somewhere over the rainbow / If I only had a brain / Younger than springtime / Bali ha'i / Night they invented champagne / Gigi / Where is love / Consider yourself / Who will buy / Stan' up and fight / Beat out dat rhythm on a drum / Perfect year / Sunset Boulevard
CD 3036000092
Carlton / Oct '95 / Carlton

GHOST (Classic Fantasy Film Music Vol.2)
City Of Prague Philharmonic Orchestra
Motzing, William *Con*
Conan The Barbarian / Highlander / Addams Family / Demolition Man / Excalibur / Ladyhawke / Witches Of Eastwick / Rocketeer / Island Of Dr. Moreau / Super Mario Brothers / Short Circuit / Monkey Shines / Wolfen / Ghost
CD FILMCD 156
Silva Screen / Sep '94 / Koch / Silva Screen

GODFATHER, THE (& Other Movie Themes)
London Symphony Orchestra/Philadelphia Orchestra Pops
Mancini, Henry *Con*
CD 09026614782
RCA Victor / Jan '90 / BMG

GOLD (18 Epic Sporting Themes)
CD CDSR 042
Telstar / Feb '94 / BMG

GOLDEN VOICES FROM THE SILVER SCREEN VOL.1
Jaadugar kaatil: *Bhosle, Asha* / Dil cheez kya hai: *Bhosle, Asha* / Apiam chaplam: *Mangeshkar, Lata & Usha* / Toote hue khwabon ne: *Rafi, Mohammed* / Chahe koi mujhe: *Rafi, Mohammed* / Bechain dil khoi si nazar: *Mangeshkar, Lata & Geeta Dutt* / Sari sari raat: *Mangeshkar, Lata* / Inhi logon ne: *Mangeshkar, Lata* / Na to karavankitalash hai / Yeh hai ishq ishq / Aaj phir jeene ki: *Mangeshkar, Lata* / Yashomati maiya se bole nandlala: *Mangeshkar, Lata & Manna Dey*
CD CDORBD 054
Globestyle / Mar '90 / Pinnacle

GOLDEN VOICES FROM THE SILVER SCREEN VOL.2
Daiya re daiya: *Bhosle, Asha* / O megha re bole: *Rafi, Mohammed* / Babuji dheere chalna: *Dutt, Geeta* / Na jao saiyan: *Dutt, Geeta* / Chhalia mera naam: *Mukesh* / O hasina zulfonwau: *Bhosle, Asha & Mohammed Rafi* / Sar pe topi laal: *Bhosle, Asha & Mohammed Rafi* / Chalte chalte: *Mangeshkar, Lata* / Tere bina aag yeh chandini: *Mangeshkar, Lata & Manna Dey* / Ghar aaya mera pardesi: *Mangeshkar, Lata*
CD CDORBD 056
Globestyle / Apr '90 / Pinnacle

GOLDEN VOICES FROM THE SILVER SCREEN VOL.3
Dhoondo dhoondo re: *Mangeshkar, Lata* / Saqiya aaj mujhe: *Bhosle & Chorus, Asha* / Satyam shivam (part 1): *Mangeshkar, Lata* / Ab reat guzarne vali: *Mangeshkar, Lata* / Leke pahla ahla pyar: *Bhosle/Begum/Rafi* / Hondton pe aisi: *Mangeshkar/Bupinder* / Salam e ishq: *Mangeshkar, Lata* / Aaj ki raat: *Bhosle & Chorus, Asha* / Satyam shivam (part 2): *Mangeshkar, Lata* / Jean Pehchaan no: *Rafi, Mohammed* / Toote na dil toote na: *Mukesh*
CD CDORBD 059
Globestyle / May '90 / Pinnacle

GREAT AMERICAN SONGWRITERS
Te Kanawa, Dame Kiri & Thomas Hampson/Frederica Von Stade/Bruce Hubbard
CD CDM 7646702
EMI Classics / Apr '93 / EMI

GREAT BRITISH FILM MUSIC
National Philharmonic Orchestra
Herrmann, Bernard *Con*
Richard III / Anna Karenina / Oliver Twist / Escape me never / 49th Parallel / Things to come
CD 4489542
Phase 4 / Aug '96 / PolyGram

GREAT CLASSIC MOVIE THEMES
CD TCD 2880
Telstar / Dec '96 / BMG

GREAT CLASSICAL THEMES
Mantovani
CD MU 5011
Musketeer / Oct '92 / Disc

GREAT FILM MUSICALS, THE
Lullaby of Broadway / Lulu's back in town / Jeepers creepers / Moonlight becomes you / Over the rainbow / Singin' in the rain / Love walked in / Boogie woogie bugle boy / Chattanooga choo-choo / Thanks for the memory / Isn't this a lovely day / I yi yi yi yi like you very much / Smoke gets in your eyes / Let yourself go / Keep young and beautiful / Road to Morocco / Puttin' on the Ritz / Wake up and live / Lover come back to me / I'm in the mood for love / Dearly beloved / I've got you under my skin / Yankee doodle boy / Hooray for Hollywood
CD CDMOIR 514
Memoir / Jan '96 / Jazz Music / Target/BMG

GREAT FILM THEMES
2CD TFP 024
Tring / Nov '92 / Tring

GREAT FILMS AND SHOWS
Sinatra, Frank
Night and day / I wish I were in love again / I got plenty o' nuttin' / I guess I'll have to change my plan / Nice work if you can get it / I won't dance / You'd be so nice to come home to / I got it bad and that ain't good / From this moment on / Blue moon / September in the rain / It's only a paper moon / You do something to me / Taking a chance on love / Get happy / Just one of those things / I love Paris / Chicago / High hopes / I believe / Lady is a tramp / Let's do it / C'est magnifique / Tender trap / Three coins in the fountain / Young at heart / Girl next door / They can't take that away from me / Someone to watch over me / Little girl blue / Like someone in love / Foggy day / I get a kick out of you / My funny valentine / Embraceable you / That old feeling / I've got a crush on you / Dream / September song / I'll see you again / As time goes by / There will never be another you / I'll remember April / Stormy weather / I can't get started (with you) / Around the world / Something's gotta give / Just in time / Dancing in the dark / Too close for comfort / I could have danced all night / Cheek to cheek / Song is you / Baubles, bangles and beads / Almost like being in love / Lover / On the sunny side of the street / That old black magic / I've heard that song before / You make me feel so young / Too marvellous for words / It happened in Monterey / I've got you under my skin / How about you / Pennies from Heaven / You're getting to be a habit with me / You brought a new kind of love to me / Love is here to stay / Old devil moon / Makin' whoopee / Anything goes / What is this thing called love / Glad to be unhappy / I get along without you very well / Dancing on the ceiling / Can't we be friends / All the way / To love and be loved / All my tomorrows / I couldn't sleep a wink last night / Spring is here / One for my baby / Time after time / It's all right with me / It's the same old dream / Johnny Concho theme (wait for me) / Wait till you see her / Where are you / Lonely town / Where or when / I concentrate on you / Love and marriage
4CD CDFS 1
Capitol / Apr '89 / EMI

GREAT MGM HOLLYWOOD MUSICALS
CD CD 023
Silva Screen / Jan '89 / Koch / Silva Screen

GREAT MGM STARS: FRED ASTAIRE
Astaire, Fred
Steppin' out with my baby / It only happens when I dance with you / Oops / Bachelor's dinner song / Baby doll / Seeing's believing / I wanna be a dancin' man / Every night at seven / I left my hat in Haiti / You're all the world to me / How could you believe me when I said I love you / Fated to be mated: *Astaire, Fred/Cyd Charisse/Carol Richards* / Paris loves lovers: *Astaire, Fred/Cyd Charisse/Carol Richards* / Ritz roll and rock / Nevertheless: *Astaire, Fred/Red Skelton/Anita Ellis* / Where did you get that girl: *Astaire, Fred & Anita Ellis* / Three little words / Shine on your shoes / By myself / Triplets: *Astaire, Fred/Nanette Fabray/Jack Buchanan* / I love Louisa / That's entertainment: *Astaire, Fred/Nanette Fabray/Jack Buchanan* / All of you
CD CDMGM 28
MGM/EMI / Feb '91 / EMI

GREAT MOVIE THEMES
London Philharmonic Orchestra
Exodus / Chariots Of Fire / I will wait for you / Zorbas' dance / Star Wars / Tara's theme / Lawrence Of Arabia / Colonel Bogey / Moulin Rouge / Third Man / Shenandoah / Godfather / Midnight Cowboy / Lara's theme
CD DC 880652
Disky / May '97 / Disky / THE

GREAT MUSICAL STANDARDS
CD HCD 327
Hindsight / Jun '95 / Jazz Music / Target/BMG

GREAT OVERTURES FROM THE MUSICALS
CD CDVIR 8324
TER / Aug '95 / Koch

GREAT OVERTURES FROM THE MUSICALS (Popular Opening Orchestral Themes From 12 Legendary Shows)
My Fair Lady: *National Symphony Orchestra* / Oklahoma: *Munich Symphony Orchestra* / Candide: *Scottish Opera Orchestra* / Can can: *National Symphony Orchestra* / King and I: *Philharmonic Orchestra* / Sweet Charity: *National Symphony Orchestra* / Phantom Of The Opera: *Munich Symphony Orchestra* / Kiss Me Kate: *National Symphony Orchestra* / West Side Story: *National Symphony Orchestra* / Funny Girl: *National Symphony Orchestra* / Cats: *National Symphony Orchestra* / Gypsy: *National Symphony Orchestra*
CD SHOWCD 030
Showtime / Oct '96 / Disc / THE

GREAT SCIENCE FICTION THEMES (Once Upon A Time At The Movies)
Silver Screen Orchestra
Close Encounters Of The Third Kind / Star Wars / Superman / Battlestar Galactica / Alien / X-Files / Star Trek / Empire Strikes Back / Bladerunner / Black Hole / Twilight Zone / ET / Dune / Eve of the war
CD DC 880682
Disky / May '97 / Disky / THE

GREAT SCREEN LOVERS COLLECTION
Who is there among...: *Nicholson, Jack* / Chattanooga choo choo: *Power, Tyrone* /

Louise: *Chevalier, Maurice* / Manhattan: *Rooney, Mickey* / Let's do it: *Coward, Sir Noel* / Foolish pride: *Mitchum, Robert* / Puttin' on the Ritz: *Gable, Clarke* / Two of us: *Curtis, Tony & Gloria De Haven* / Let's make love: *Montand, Yves* / Day after day: *Stewart, James* / Did I remember: *Grant, Cary* / Kashmiri love song: *Valentino, Rudolph* / Pillow talk: *Hudson, Rock* / Mary's a grand old name: *Cagney, James* / Woman in love: *Brando, Marlon & Jean Simmons* / As long as there is music: *Sinatra, Frank* / Chico's choo choo: *Wagner, Robert & Debbie Reynolds* / Lover come back to me / All I do is dream of you: *Kelly, Gene* / Gotta bran' new suit: *Astaire, Fred & Nanette Fabray*
CD _______ DVCD 2117
Deja Vu / Dec '87 / THE

GREAT SHAKESPEARE FILMS
National Philharmonic Orchestra & London Festival Orchestra
CD _______ 4212682
Decca / '88 / PolyGram

GREAT SONGS FROM GREAT SHOWS
CD _______ MATCD 297
Castle / Sep '93 / BMG

GREAT SONGS FROM THE MUSICALS
CD _______ MCCD 162
MCI Music / Jul '94 / Disc / THE

GREAT SONGS FROM THE MUSICALS - 1930'S/1940'S
Lambeth walk: *Kernan, David* / My funny valentine: *Willetts, Dave* / Can't help lovin' dat man: *English, Ellie* / You made me love you: *Craven, Gemma* / Putting on the ritz: *Newley, Anthony* / Leaning on a lampost: *Kernan, David* / Dancing in the dark: *Hockridge, Edmund* / Ol' man river: *Martin, James* / Me and my girl: *Kernan, David* / That's entertainment: *London Symphony Orchestra* / Pretty girl is like a melody: *Hockridge, Edmund* / Our love is here to stay: *Willetts, Dave* / You'd be so nice to come home to: *Willetts, Dave* / We're a couple of swells: *Craven, Gemma & Edmund Hockridge* / Come rain or come shine: *Willetts, Dave* / There's no business like showbusiness: *Perry, Lynette* / If I loved you: *Willetts, Dave* / Another op'nin' another show: *Hockridge, Edmund* / Oh what a beautiful mornin': *Malton, Richard* / When the children are asleep: *Pollard, Su & Ian Wallace* / Trolley song: *Craven, Gemma* / You'll never walk alone: *Kimm, Fiona* / June is bustin' out all over: *Hibberd, Linda* / People will say we're in love: *Perry, Lynette & Richard Malton*
2CD _______ 330082
Hallmark / Jul '96 / Carlton

GREAT SONGS FROM THE MUSICALS - 1950'S/1960'S
Who wants to be a millionaire: *Wayne, Carl & Tracy Collier* / I could have danced all night: *Robertson, Liz* / Thank Heaven for little girls: *Newley, Anthony* / Bless your beautiful hide: *Hockridge, Edmund* / True love: *Lotis, Dennis & Tracy Collier* / I love you Samantha: *Willetts, Dave* / Make 'em laugh: *Newley, Anthony* / There is nothing like a dame: *Master Singers* / Some enchanted evening: *Kernan, David* / Baubles, bangles and beads: *Craven, Gemma* / I've grown accustomed to her face: *Quilley, Denis* / I'm gonna wash that man right out of my hair: *Perry, Lynette* / Hello Dolly: *Green, Simon* / Food glorious food: *Boys Chorus* / Don't rain on my parade: *London Symphony Orchestra* / If I were a rich man: *Greene, Brian* / Sunrise, sunset: *Kimm, Fiona & Brian Greene* / My favourite things: *Robertson, Liz* / People: *English, Ellie* / Impossible dream: *Willetts, Dave* / As long as he needs me: *Langford, Bonnie* / Consider yourself: *Boys Chorus* / Climb every mountain: *Kimm, Fiona* / Edelweiss: *Quilley, Denis*
2CD _______ 330092
Hallmark / Jul '96 / Carlton

GREAT SONGS FROM THE MUSICALS - 1970'S/1980'S
Superstar: *London Symphony Orchestra* / Day by day: *Wayne, Carl* / On this night of a thousand stars: *Wayne, Carl* / Overture: Mack & Mabel: *London Symphony Orchestra* / Any dream will do: *Cousins, Robin* / You're the one that I want: *Wayne, Carl & Michaela Strachan* / Don't cry for me Argentina: *Webb, Marti* / Summer nights: *Wayne, Carl & Michaela Strachan* / Another suitacase in another hall: *Lawrence, Stephanie* / Hopelessly devoted to you: *Strachan, Michaela* / Cabaret: *Perry, Lynette* / I don't know how to love him: *Hendley, Fiona* / Music of the night: *Jones, Paul* / Memory: *Hendley, Fiona* / I dreamed a dream: *Moore, Claire* / Tell me on a Sunday: *Wayne, Carl* / Heat's on in Saigon: *Wayne, Carl* / Pumping iron: *Conrad, Jess* / Take that look of your face: *Hendley, Fiona* / Rolling stock: *Jones, Paul* / Pie Jesu: *Lawrence, Stephanie & David Smith* / Empty chairs at empty tables: *Willetts, Dave* / Love changes everything: *Skellern, Peter* / Movie in your mind: *Criswell, Kim*
2CD _______ 330102
Hallmark / Jul '96 / Carlton

GREAT SONGS FROM THE SILVER SCREEN
Dames / Good morning / If I only had a brain / Spring, spring, spring / Begin the beguine / Secret love / best things in life are free / I love you / Woman in love / It's a nice face / New York, New York
CD _______ SHOWCD 054
Showtime / Apr '97 / Disc / THE

GREAT SPORTS THEMES
London Theatre Orchestra
Match Of The Day / BBC Cricket theme / BBC Grandstand / Grand Prix / 5 Live Sports Report / BBC Golf theme / Pot Black / Wimbledon / ITV Big Match / Rugby Special / ITV World Of Sport / BBC Horse Of The Year / Ski Sunday / Sportsnight / BBC Snooker / Question Of Sport
CD _______ EMPRCD 715
Emporio / Jun '97 / Disc

GREAT STAGE MUSICALS 1924-1941, THE
CD _______ CDMOIR 501
Memoir / Jul '93 / Jazz Music / Target/ BMG

GREAT TV THEMES
2CD _______ TFP 029
Tring / Nov '92 / Tring

GREAT WAR MOVIE THEMES
Silver Screen Orchestra
Das Boot / Adagio for strings Op11 / River Kwai march / Ride of the Valyries / Ballad Of The Green Berets / Guns Of Navarone / Battle hymn of the republic / Longest Day / Paris, brule-t-il / Cavatina / Schindler's List / Lawrence Of Arabia / Bridge Too Far / In the mood
CD _______ DC 880692
Disky / May '97 / Disky / THE

GREAT WESTERN FILM THEMES
Rio bravo / Man with the harmonica / Fistful of dollars / Magnificent seven / Once upon a time in the west / My name is nobody / High noon / Ballad of the Alamo / Johnny guitar / Comancheros / Shane / Vera cruz / Virginian / Bonanza / Riders in the sky
CD _______ 22526
Music / Dec '95 / Target/BMG

GREAT WESTERN MOVIE AND TV SOUNDTRACKS VOL.2 (From Alamo To El Dorado)
Ballad of Cat Ballou: *Cole, Nat 'King' & Stubby Kaye* / High Chapparal: *Rose, David* / Lonely man: *Ford, 'Tennessee' Ernie* / Man From Laramie: *Martino, Al* / El Dorado: *Alexander, George & Mellowmen* / Man with True Grit: *Campbell, Glen* / Fury: *Prairie Chiefs* / Wichita: *Ritter, Tex* / Old Turkey Buzzard: *Feliciano, Jose* / Bronco: *Gregory, Johnny* / Love in the country: *Limelighters* / Sugarfoot: *Sons Of The Pioneers* / Stagecoach to Cheyenne: *Newton, Wayne* / Green leaves of summer: *Bros Four* / Marmalade, molasses and honey: *Williams, Andy* / Cimarron City: *Hollywood Sound Orchestra* / Sheriff of Cochise: *Prairie Chiefs* / Wagon train: *O'Neill, Johnny* / Legend of Wyatt Earp: *Long, Shorty* / 26 men: *Adrian, Lee* / Wind, the wind: *Martin, Dean* / Buttons and bows: *Hope, Bob* / Man with true grit : *Campbell, Glen*
CD _______ BCD 15983
Bear Family / May '97 / Direct / Rollercoaster / Swift

GREAT WESTERN THEMES
Pioneer Orchestra
Bonanaza / Once Upon A Time In The West / Good, The Bad And The Ugly / Magnificent Seven / Green Leaves Of Summer / High Noon / Fistful Of Dollars / Hondo / Man With The Harmonica / Professional Gun / Return Of The Seven / Wand'rin Star / Hang 'Em High / Man From Laramie / How The West Was Won / Ballad Of The Alamo / Comancheros / True Grit
CD _______ QED 105
Tring / Nov '96 / Tring

GREAT WESTERN THEMES
Silver Screen Orchestra
For A Few Dollars More / Gambler / Good, The Bad And The Ugly / Hang 'Em High / High Noon / How The West Was Won / My Name Is Nobody / Man with the harmonica / True Grit / Magnificent Seven / Fistful Of Dollars / Claudia's theme / Alamo / Streets Of Laredo
CD _______ DC 880672
Disky / May '97 / Disky / THE

GREATEST COP THEMES IN THE WORLD, THE
Mission Impossible / Professionals / Hawaii 5-0 / Charlie's Angels / Starsky and Hutch / Sweeney / Cagney and Lacey / LA law / Murder She Wrote / Quincy / Moonlighting / Bill / Miss Marple / Poirot / Ruth Rendell / Inspector Morse / Law And Order / Taggart / Miami Vice / NYPD Blue / Kojak / Magnum / A-Team / Crockett's Theme / Hill Street Blues / Columbo / Juliet Bravo / Bergerac / Between The Lines / Z Cars / Prisoner / Avengers / Saint / Man From UNCLE / Untouchables / X-Files
2CD _______ SUDCD 4505
Summit / Nov '96 / Sound & Media

GREATEST HITS OF THE MUSICALS
Tonight: *Wood, Natalie* / Music of the night: *Crawford, Michael* / I could have danced all night: *Hepburn, Audrey* / Singin' in the rain: *Kelly, Gene* / Bless yore beautiful hide: *Keel, Howard* / Luck be a lady: *Willetts, Dave* / If I was a rich man: *Topol* / Happy talk: *South Pacific Cast* / Hello dolly: *Armstrong, Louis* / Cabaret: *Minnelli, Liza* / For me and my gal: *Kelly, Gene & Judy Garland* / Almost like being in love: *Kelly, Gene* / Secret love: *Day, Doris* / On a clear day you can see forever: *Bassey, Shirley* / I've grown accustomed to her face: *Harrison, Rex* / Camelot: *Harris, Richard* / Tell me it's not true: *Dickson, Barbara* / Big spender: *Maclaine, Shirley* / Oh, what a beautiful mornin': *Original Broadway Cast* / Anything you can do: *Merman, Ethel & Ray Middleton* / Food glorious food: *Original London Cast* / That's entertainment: *Astaire, Fred & Nanette Faray/ Jack Buchanan/India Adams* / Don't cry for me Argentina: *Covington, Julie* / Memory: *Paige, Elaine* / Summertime: *Vaughan, Sarah* / Some enchanted evening: *South Pacific Cast* / Day by day: *Lamont, Robin* / Losing my mind: *McKenzie, Julia* / Seventy six trombones: *Original Broadway Cast* / If I ruled the world: *Secombe, Harry* / S'Wonderful: *Kelly, Gene* / Make believe: *Grayson, Kathryn & Howard Keel* / Too darn hot: *Miller, Ann* / I don't know how to love him: *Elliman, Yvonne* / Couple of swells: *Garland, Judy & Fred Astaire* / How long has this been going on: *Hepburn, Audrey* / One (finale): *Ensemble cast* / Send in the clowns: *Collins, Judy* / New York, New York: *Original Broadway Cast* / Impossible dream: *MacRae, Gordon* / I know him so well: *Paige, Elaine & Barbara Dickson* / Any dream will do: *Original Cast* / Over the rainbow: *Garland, Judy*
2CD _______ CDEMTVD 119
EMI / Nov '96 / EMI

GREATEST LOVE SONGS FROM THE MUSICALS, THE
Love changes everything / Hello, young lovers / On the street where you live / As long as he needs me / All I ask of you / Human heart / Hopelessly devoted to you / I don't know how to love him / If ever I would leave you / You are love / Stranger in paradise / So in love
CD _______ SHOWCD 020
Showtime / Feb '95 / Disc / THE

GREATEST MOVIE THEMES
Jaws / Godfather / Deerhunter (Cavatina) / Star wars / Gone with the wind (Tara's theme) / Lawrence of Arabia / Apocalypse now (Ride of the Valkyries) / Raiders of the lost ark / Magnificent seven / Longest day / Bridge too far / Good, the bad and the ugly / ET / Butch Cassidy and The Sundance Kid (Raindrops are falling on / Dr. Zhivago / Love story / 10 Ravels bolero / Close encounters of the third kind
CD _______ CDMFP 6236
Music For Pleasure / Jul '96 / EMI

GREATEST SCIENCE FICTION HITS, VOL 1
Norman, Neil & his Orchestra
Alien / Moonraker / Star Wars / Superman / 2001 / Battlestar Galactica / Space 1999 / Star trek / Black hole
CD _______ GNPD 2128
GNP Crescendo / Jan '89 / ZYX

GREATEST SCIENCE FICTION HITS, VOL 2
Norman, Neil & his Orchestra
Empire strikes back / Twilight zone / Buck Rogers / Time tunnel / Dr. Who / Voyage to the bottom of the sea / Dark star / Sinbad and the eye of the tiger
CD _______ GNPD 2133
GNP Crescendo / Jan '89 / ZYX

GREATEST SCIENCE FICTION HITS, VOL 3
Norman, Neil & his Orchestra
ET / War of the worlds / Lost in space / Bladerunner / Flash Gordon / Thing / Prisoner / Land of giants / Space 1999 / Angry red planet / Capricorn one / Raiders of the Lost Ark / Invaders / UFO / Vena's dance / Return of the jedi
CD _______ GNPD 2163
GNP Crescendo / Jan '89 / ZYX

GREATEST SHOW THEMES
Overture / Memories / Oliver / Where is love / I'd do anything / As long as he needs me / Consider yourself / I feel pretty / Maria / Tonight / America / Farmer and the cowman / Oklahoma / People will say we're in love / Oh what a beautiful morning / Poor Judd is dead / Surrey with the fringe on top / Many a new day / Kansas city / I can't say no / Buenos aires / High flying / Adored / Don't cry for me Argentina / She is a diamond / Another suitcase in another hall / I could have danced all night / On the street where you live / Wouldn't it be lovely / Show me / Embassy waltz / Get me to the church on time / I've grown accustomed to your face / With a little bit of luck / Sound of music / How can love survive / Lonely goatherd / My favourtie things / Sixteen going on seventeen / Climb every mountain / No way to stop it / An ordinary couple / Edelweiss / So long farewell
CD _______ CDMFP 6235
Music For Pleasure / Jul '96 / EMI

GREATEST TV THEMES
London's Burning / Forever Green / Professionals / Agatha Christie's Poirot / To Have & To Hold / Upstairs Downstairs / Thomas & Sarah / Good Guys / Gentle Touch / Bouqet Of Barbed Wire / Partners In Crime / Budgie / Wish Me Luck / Love For Lydia / Lillie / Black Beauty / Dempsey & Makepiece
CD _______ CDMFP 6234
Music For Pleasure / Jul '96 / EMI

GUYS N' GIRLS
I'm A Yankee Doodle Dandy: *Cagney, James* / Lullaby Of Broadway: *Powell, Dick* / Pennies From Heaven: *Crosby, Bing* / Three Little Words: *Ellington, Duke & The Rhythm Boys* / On The Good Ship Lollipop: *Temple, Shirley* / It's Only A Paper Moon: *Edwards, Cliff* / Let's Face The Music And Dance: *Astaire, Fred & Ginger Rogers* / 42nd Street: *Keeler, Ruby & Dick Powell* / Over The Rainbow: *Garland, Judy* / Sonny Boy: *Jolson, Al* / Sunny Side Up: *Endor, Chick* / Pick Yourself Up: *Astaire, Fred* / Lulu's Back In Town: *Powell, Dick* / Sun Valley Jump: *Miller, Glenn Orchestra* / Yours And Mine: *Powell, Eleanor* / My Man: *Bruce, Fanny* / Easy To Love: *Stewart, James & Eleanor Powell* / Fine Romance: *Astaire, Fred & Ginger Rogers* / (Dear Mr Gable) You Made Me Love You: *Garland, Judy* / Goodnight My Love: *Faye, Alice*
CD _______ ONEC 005
Tring / Apr '96 / Tring

HEART TO HEART (Classic Duets From The Great Shows)
They say it's wonderful: *Craven, Gemma & Edmund Hockridge* / I've never been in love before: *Robertson, Liz & Keith Michell* / Do you love me: *Newley, Anthony & Linda Hibberd* / Summer nights: *Wayne, Carl & Michaela Strachan* / Last night of the world: *Criswell, Kim & Carl Wayne* / People will say we're in love: *Jones, Paul & Fiona Hendley* / True love: *Collier, Tracy & Dennis Lotis* / Sixteen going on seventeen: *Simmons, Elizabeth & Simon Clarke* / Why do I love you: *Craven, Gemma & David Kernan* / Where is love/As long as he needs me: *Stringer, Gareth & Bonnie Langford* / I might fall back on you: *Quilley, Denis & Tracy Miller* / Twin soliloquys: *Craven, Gemma & David Kernan* / Something good: *Robertson, Liz & Denis Quilley* / First man you remember: *Lawrence, Stephanie & Dave Willetts* / Rain in Spain: *Robertson, Liz & Denis Quilley* / At the end of the day: *Willetts, Dave & Claire Moore* / Who wants to be a millionaire: *Wayne, Carl & Tracy Collier* / You're the one that I want: *Wayne, Carl & Michaela Strachan* / Anything you can do: *Hockridge, Edmund & Gemma Craven* / Sunset, sunset: *Newley, Anthony & Linda Hibberd*
CD _______ 3036200372
Carlton / Feb '97 / Carlton

HER FAVOURITE MOVIE SONGS
Marjane, Leo
CD _______ 995702
EPM / Sep '96 / ADA / Discovery

HISTORICAL ROMANCES (Juarez/ Devotion/Gunga Din/Charge Of The Light Brigade)
Brandenburg Philharmonic Orchestra
Kaufman, Richard *Con*
CD _______ 8223608
Marco Polo / Feb '96 / Select

HISTORY OF THE WESTERN FILM SCORE VOL.1, THE (How The West Was Won)
City Of Prague Philharmonic Orchestra
Raine, Nic/Paul Bateman *Con*
How the West was won / Wild bunch / Buffalo girls / Professionals / Magnificent seven / Gettysburg / Wild rovers / High plains drifter
CD _______ FILMCD 173
Silva Screen / Apr '96 / Koch / Silva Screen

HISTORY OF THE WESTERN FILM SCORE VOL.2, THE (Lonesome Dove)
City Of Prague Philharmonic Orchestra
Bateman, Paul/D. Wadsworth/N. Raine *Con*
Red river / Old gringo / Proud rebel / El condor / Sons of Katie Elder / Outlaw Josie Wales / Hang 'em high / Heaven's gate / Lonesome dove / Red sun / She wore a yellow ribbon
CD _______ FILMCD 176
Silva Screen / Jul '96 / Koch / Silva Screen

HIT SONGS FROM BROADWAY
Oh, what a beautiful morning / Surrey with a fringe on top / People will say we're in love / If I loved you / When the children are asleep / What's the use of wond'rin / To keep my love alive / Johnny one note / Ten cents a dance / I love Louisa / Triplets / You and the night and music / Got a bran' new suit / This is it / After you, who / Ridin' high / Harlem on my mind / I left my heart at the stage door canteen / This is the army Mr. Jones / Speak low / That's him / I'm alone...the song is you / Heaven in my arms / All the things we are
CD _______ CDMOIR 519
Memoir / Jun '97 / Jazz Music / Target/ BMG

HIT SONGS FROM THE WESTERN MUSICALS
Bless your beautiful hide / Is it really me / Oh waht a beautiful morning / I say hello / I talk to the trees / 76 Trombones / I will always love you / Anything you can do / Just blew in from the windy city / Indian love call / Ol' man river / It's a grand night for singing

CD SHOWCD 053
Showtime / Apr '97 / Disc / THE

HITCHCOCK - MASTER OF MAYHEM
San Diego Symphony Orchestra
Schifrin, Lalo *Con*
Invisible Third: *San Diego Symphony Pops* / Alfred Hitchcock theme: *San Diego Symphony Pops* / Vertigo: *San Diego Symphony Pops* / Marnie: *San Diego Symphony Pops* / Psycho: *San Diego Symphony Pops* / Rebecca: *San Diego Symphony Pops* / Rear Window: *San Diego Symphony Pops* / Rollercoaster: *San Diego Symphony Pops* / Bullitt: *San Diego Symphony Pops* / Mannix: *San Diego Symphony Pops* / Dirty Harry: *San Diego Symphony Pops* / Mission Impossible: *San Diego Symphony Pops*
CD SION 18170
Sion / Jul '97 / Direct

HITS & MOVIES
CD 11817
Music / Aug '95 / Target/BMG

HITS FROM THE MOVIES
Crying game / Heat is on / Axel F / Power of love / Nothing has been proved / More than a woman / Call me / Born to be wild / Sisters are doin' it for themselves / Everybody's talkin' / Midnight cowboy / Joy to the world / Warmth of the sun / Woodstock / Gonna fly now (Rocky theme)
CD CDMFP 6138
Music For Pleasure / Jun '95 / EMI

HITS FROM THE MOVIES
CD CDCD 1230
Charly / Jun '95 / Koch

HITS FROM THE MOVIES
La bamba / Good golly Miss Molly / When I'm walkin' / Will you love me tomorrow / Raindrops keep falling on my head / Emmanuelle / As time goes by / Tell it like it is / England swings / Man whos hot Liberty Valance / Get a job / Tequila / Louie Louie / Whole lotta shakin' going on / Yesterday's hero / Sweet Gene Vincent
CD 12608
Laserlight / Apr '96 / Target/BMG

HITS FROM THE MUSICALS
Starlight Orchestra/Singers
West side story overture / C'est magnifique / Anything you can do / I got plenty o' nuttin' / Gigi / I've grown accustomed to her face / Cheek to cheek / Hello young lovers / Oklahoma / Somewhere / Almost like being in love / Summertime / True love / On the street where you live / Oh what a beautiful mornin' / Maria / Begin the beguine / With a little bit of luck / You'll never walk alone / Bali ha'i / They say it's wonderful / There's no business like showbusiness
CD QED 110
Tring / Nov '96 / Tring

HOBSON'S CHOICE
Hobson, Helen
On my way to you / Don't rain on my parade / Merry go round / With every breath I take / Show me / Day I stop loving you / If ever I would leave you: *Hobson, Helen & Cliff Richard* / If I've let you down / You've got to give me room / Minute waltz / What's new/ Since you stayed here / Anything but lonely: *Hobson, Helen & Graham Bickley* / Girls of Summer / And I am telling you / Wedding song: *Hobson, Helen & Cliff Richard* / Is it really me
CD URCD 124
Upbeat / Oct '96 / Cadillac / Target/BMG

HOLLYWOOD
London Festival Orchestra
Man and a woman / Il silenzio / Love story / Affair to remember / Hello, young lovers / Sound of music / Moon river / La ronde / Tara's theme / Three coins in the fountain / Shane / Anything goes / Dancing in the dark / Days of wine and roses / Love is a many splendoured thing / Tammy / Pennies from Heaven / It's magic / Magnificent seven / High noon
CD OP 0004
MCI Music / Apr '87 / Disc / THE

HOLLYWOOD
San Diego Symphony Pops
Schifrin, Lalo *Con*
Superman / Raiders Of The Lost Ark / Bridge Over The River Kwai / Captain From Castille / Great Escape / Patton / Return Of The Jedi / Music Man / What did you do in the war Daddy / Statue Of Liberty march / Apocalypse Now / Armed Forces medley / Hunt For Red October / Cinerama march / Dirty Dozen / Great waldo pepper / Stars and stripes forever
CD SION 18150
Sion / Jul '97 / Direct

HOLLYWOOD '94
McNeely, Joel & Seattle Symphony Orchestra
CD VSD 5531
Varese Sarabande / Jan '95 / Pinnacle

HOLLYWOOD '95
McNeely, Joel & Seattle Symphony Orchestra
CD VSD 5671
Varese Sarabande / Nov '95 / Pinnacle

HOLLYWOOD '96
CD VSD 5764
Varese Sarabande / Mar '97 / Pinnacle

HOLLYWOOD A LA HAMMOND
Time for us / Shadow of your smile / Autumn leaves / Love is a many splendoured thing / People / Georgy girl / James Bond theme / Certain smile / Ballad of Bonnie and Clyde / What are you doing the rest of your life / Singin' in the rain / If I were a rich man / Speak softly love / Theme from MASH / Theme from Love Story / Jesus Christ superstar / Goldfinger / Man and a woman / Mrs. Robinson / Windmills of your mind / Diamonds are forever / Day by day / Lara's theme / Raindrops keep falling on my head
CD 303942
Hallmark / Jun '97 / Carlton

HOLLYWOOD BACKLOT VOL.3
CD VSD 5361
Varese Sarabande / Dec '92 / Pinnacle

HOLLYWOOD BOWL ON BROADWAY, THE
Hollywood Bowl Symphony Orchestra
Mauceri, John *Con*
June is bustin' out all over / When the children are asleep / Blow high, blow low / If I loved you / Real nice clambreak / Stonecutters cut it on stone / What's the use of wond'rin / You'll never walk alone / Any place I hang my hat is home / I had myself a true love / One for my baby (and one more for the road) / Come rain or come shine / Mack the knife / Surabaya Johnny / Bilbao song / J'attends un navire / Train to Johannesburg / Lost in the stars / My ship / September song / Ol' man river / Can't help lovin' that man / You are love / Why do I love you
CD 4464042
Philips Classics / Mar '97 / PolyGram

HOLLYWOOD CHRISTMAS, A
CD VSD 5621
Varese Sarabande / Nov '96 / Pinnacle

HOLLYWOOD CHRONICLE - GREAT MOVIE CLASSICS VOL. 1
CD VSD 5351
Varese Sarabande / Nov '92 / Pinnacle

HOLLYWOOD COLLECTION
Singin' in the rain: *Kelly, Gene* / Over the rainbow: *Garland, Judy* / Entertainer: *Joplin, Scott* / Cheek to cheek: *Astaire, Fred* / Mammy: *Jolson, Al* / Let's face the music and dance: *Rogers, Ginger* / Couple of swells: *Astaire, Fred* / Diamonds are a girl's best friend: *Monroe, Marilyn* / Night and day: *Sinatra, Frank* / In the mood: *Miller, Glenn* / Trail of the lonesome pine: *Laurel & Hardy* / Ol' man river: *Robeson, Paul* / I'm in the mood for love: *Hutton, Betty* / Hello Dolly: *Armstrong, Louis* / Zip: *Hayworth, Rita* / I've got my love to keep me warm: *Bogart, Humphrey* / Gentlemen prefer blondes: *Russell, Jane & Marilyn Monroe* / Hi lili hi lo: *Caron, Leslie & Mel Ferrer* / Who's sorry now: *De Haven, Gloria* / It had to be you: *Lamour, Dorothy*
CD DVCD 2054
Deja Vu / May '86 / THE

HOLLYWOOD DREAMS
Hollywood Bowl Symphony Orchestra
Mauceri, John *Con*
CD 4321092
Philips / Sep '91 / PolyGram

HOLLYWOOD GOLDEN CLASSICS
Carreras, Jose
CD 9031737932
WEA / Jul '93 / Warner Music

HOLLYWOOD GOLDEN YEARS
Garland, Judy
CD BMCD 7010
Blue Moon / Nov '96 / Cadillac / Discovery / Greensleeves / Jazz Music / Jet Star / TKO Magnum

HOLLYWOOD GOLDEN YEARS
Kelly, Gene
2CD BM 99908
Blue Moon / Jan '97 / Cadillac / Discovery / Greensleeves / Jazz Music / Jet Star / TKO Magnum

HOLLYWOOD IN LOVE (Greatest Love Songs From The Movies)
Hollywood Bowl Symphony Orchestra
Mauceri, John *Con*
Love is a many splendoured thing / Unchained melody / Cathie's theme / Love theme / Peyton Place / Oh mio babbino caro / Eternal love / Age of innocence / Cinema paradiso / Somewhere in time / Love for love / Conversation piece / Four weddings and a funeral / Laura / Now voyager / Affair to remember
CD 4546472
Philips / Aug '96 / PolyGram

HOLLYWOOD LADIES SING (I'm Ready For My Close Up)
CD 85972
Silva Screen / Feb '90 / Koch / Silva Screen

HOLLYWOOD LEGENDS
CD LECD 120
Wisepack / Apr '95 / Conifer/BMG / THE

HOLLYWOOD MUSICALS
Mammy: *Jolson, Al* / Cheek to cheek: *Astaire, Fred* / Over the rainbow: *Garland, Judy* / Yankee doodle boy: *Cagney, James* / Road to Morocco: *Hope, Bob/Bing Crosby/Judy Garland* / Put the blame on mame: *Hayworth, Rita* / White Christmas: *Crosby, Bing* / Best things in life are free: *Allyson, June & Peter Lawford* / Johnny one note: *Garland, Judy* / Couple of swells: *Garland, Judy & Fred Astaire* / Who's sorry now: *De Haven, Gloria* / 'S Wonderful: *Kelly, Gene* / diamonds are a girl's best friend: *Monroe, Marilyn* / Bye bye baby: *Monroe, Marilyn & Jane Russell* / Too darn hot: *Miller, Arthur* / Hi lili hi lo: *Caron, Leslie & Mel Ferrer* / Indian love call: *Blyth, Ann & Fernando Lamas* / Rose Marie: *Keel, Howard* / Stranger in paradise: *Blyth, Ann & Vic Damone* / Thank heavens for little girls: *Chevalier, Maurice* / Hello Dolly: *Armstrong, Louis* / There's no business like show business: *Merman, Ethel* / Move over darling: *Day, Doris* / Oh what a beautiful morning: *McRae, Gordon*
2CD DVRECD 26
Deja Vu / '89 / THE

HOLLYWOOD MUSICALS, THE
CD CIN 020
IMP / Oct '96 / ADA / Discovery

HOLLYWOOD SINGS (Stars Of The Silver Screen)
Happy feet: *Whiteman, Paul & Rhythm Boys* / Toot toot Tootsie goodbye: *Jolson, Al* / Johnny: *Dietrich, Marlene* / Day after day: *Stewart, James* / Can Broadway do without me: *Clayton, Jackson & Durante* / If you haven't got love: *Swanson, Gloria* / Doin' the new low down: *Robinson, Bill 'Bojangles'* / Keep your sunny side up: *Gaynor, Janet* / Kashmiri love song: *Valentino, Rudolph* / Broadway melody: *King, Charles* / Puttin' on the ritz: *Richman, Harry* / How long will it last: *Crawford, Joan* / Hooray for Captain Spaulding: *Marx, Groucho & Zeppo* / Just like a butterfly: *Morgan, Helen* / I love Louisa: *Astaire, Fred* / Can't get along: *Rogers, Ginger* / You've got that thing: *Chevalier, Maurice* / Beyond the blue horizon: *MacDonald, Jeanette* / White dove: *Tibbett, Lawrence* / Yes yes (my baby says yes): *Cantor, Eddie*
CD CD AJA 5011
Living Era / Feb '87 / Select

HOLLYWOOD SINGS - THE GIRLS
It's foolish but it's fun: *Durbin, Deanna* / Waltzing in the clouds: *Durbin, Deanna* / When the roses bloom again: *Durbin, Deanna* / Body and soul: *Langford, Frances* / Someone to watch over me: *Langford, Frances* / I've got you under my skin: *Langford, Frances* / Lovely to look at: *Dunne, Irene* / Jitterbug: *Garland, Judy* / Over the rainbow: *Garland, Judy* / It never rains but it pours: *Garland, Judy* / Mister five by five: *Andrews Sisters* / Ferryboat serenade: *Andrews Sisters* / Say 'si si': *Andrews Sisters* / Mayor of Kaunakakai: *Andrews Sisters* / Kiss the boys goodbye: *Martin, Mary* / Katie went to Haiti: *Martin, Mary* / Man with the lollipop song: *Miranda, Carmen* / One I love: *Fitzgerald, Ella* / Falling in love again: *Dietrich, Marlene* / Moon song: *Smith, Kate*
CD 304112
Hallmark / Jun '97 / Carlton

HOLLYWOOD SINGS - THE GUYS
Moonlight becomes you: *Crosby, Bing* / I'm thinking tonight of my blue eyes: *Crosby, Bing* / I have eyes: *Crosby, Bing* / Moon and the willow tree: *Crosby, Bing* / I haven't time to be a millionaire: *Crosby, Bing* / Always in my heart: *Baker, Kenny* / There are two rivers to cross: *Baker, Kenny* / Love walked in: *Baker, Kenny* / Blue Tahitian moon: *Baker, Kenny* / Farming: *Kaye, Danny* / Fairy pipers: *Kaye, Danny* / Tchaikovsky (and other Russians): *Kaye, Danny* / Antole of Paris: *Kaye, Danny* / Rock-a-bye your baby with a Dixie melody: *Jolson, Al* / April showers: *Jolson, Al* / Stein song: *Powell, Dick* / In a moment of weakness: *Powell, Dick* / 'Tis Autumn: *Martin, Tony* / Cancel the flowers: *Martin, Tony* / Indian summer: *Martin, Tony*
CD 304102
Hallmark / Jun '97 / Carlton

HOLLYWOOD SOUND, THE (John Williams Conducts The Academy Awards Best Scores)
London Symphony Orchestra
Williams, John *Con*
Out Of Africa / Dances With Wolves / ET / Star Wars / Jaws / Place In The Sun: *London Symphony Orchestra & Grover Washington Jr.* / Last Emperor / Spellbound / Godfather II / Beauty And The Beast / Pocahontas / Robin Hood / Lawrence Of Arabia / Wizard Of Oz
CD SK 62788
Sony Classical / Mar '97 / Sony

HOLLYWOOD SOUNDSTAGE VOL.1
CD VSD 5301
Varese Sarabande / Jul '91 / Pinnacle

HOLLYWOOD STARS GO TO WAR
CD VJC 1048
Vintage Jazz Classics / Jul '93 / ADA / Cadillac / CM / Direct

HOLLYWOOD'S GREATEST HITS
CD GRF 192
Tring / Jan '93 / Tring

HOLLYWOOD'S GREATEST HITS
Tritt, W./Cincinnati Pops Orchestra
Kunzel, Erich *Con*
CD CD 80168
Telarc / Sep '88 / Conifer/BMG

HOLLYWOOD'S GREATEST HITS, VOL 2
Cincinnati Pops Orchestra
CD CD 80319
Telarc / Aug '93 / Conifer/BMG

HOMAGE A MARCEL CARNE (Musique De Films)
Orchestre Du Capitole De Toulouse
Plasson, Michel *Con*
CD CDC 75477642
EMI Classics / Apr '94 / EMI

HOOKED ON MOVIES
Brooks, Paul
Oklahoma / Maria / Over The Rainbow / Secret Love / Singin' In The Rain / On The Street Where You Live / Hello Dolly / Wa-nd'rin' Star / Shall We Dance / Sound Of Music / 633 Squadron / Colonel Bogey / Great Escape / Where Eagles Dare / Dam Busters / Also Sprach Zarathustra / Star Wars / Close Encounters Of The Third Kind / Eve Of The War / Superman / Ghostbusters / Doctor Who / Star Trek / ET - The Extra Terrestrial / Batman / Piano / Everybody's Talkin' / Chariots Of Fire / Rocky / Zorba The Greek / Jaws / Entertainer / Lawrence Of Arabia / Godfather / Cavatina / Tara's Theme / I Will Always Love You / Theme From Love Story / Days Of Wine And Roses / Theme From A Summer Place / Unchained Melody / Love Is All Around / Somewhere My Love / Moon River / Big Country / Hang 'Em High / Good, The Bad And The Ugly / High Noon / Man Who Shot Liberty Valance / Magnificent Seven
CD ECD 3313
K-Tel / Apr '97 / K-Tel

HORROR (The 1950/1960's Horror Film Music Album)
Westminster Philharmonic Orchestra
Alwyn, Kenneth *Con*
Night of the demon / Corridors of blood / Haunting / Abominable snowman / Witchfinder general / Curse of the Mummy's tomb / Konga / Fiend without a face / Devil rides out / Horrors of the black museum / Curse of the werewolf
CD FILMCD 175
Silva Screen / Apr '96 / Koch / Silva Screen

HORROR AND SCIENCE FICTION VOL.1
CD 889707
Milan / '92 / Conifer/BMG / Silva Screen

HORROR AND SCIENCE FICTION VOL.2
Escape from New York / Mad Max / Phantasm / Day after Halloween / Tourist trip / Daytime ended / Maniac / Videodrome / Evil dead / Hunger / Friday 13th / Forbidden zone / Liquid sky / Red Sonja / Lifeforce / Elephant man
CD CDCH 157
Milan / Feb '90 / Conifer/BMG / Silva Screen

HORROR AND SCIENCE FICTION VOL.3
CD CH 363
Milan / Jan '95 / Conifer/BMG / Silva Screen

HORROR THEMES
Fly / Thing / Fog / Carrie / Psycho / Poltergeist 3 / Exorcist / Hellraiser / Halloween / Amityville Horror / Friday The 13th / Vertigo / Silence Of The Lambs / Rosemary's Baby
CD SUMCD 4122
Sound & Media / May '97 / Sound & Media

HORRORVISIONS
CD EDL 25722
Edel / Jan '92 / Pinnacle

HOT MOVIE THEMES
CD 24030
Music / Mar '95 / Target/BMG

HOW DEEP IS THE OCEAN (The Irving Berlin Songbook)
CD 5377012
Verve / Aug '97 / PolyGram

I TOLD YOU NOT TO CRY (Swinging Themes From Thrilling German Crime Films 1966-72)
Wilden, Gert
Wilden, Gert *C*
CD EFA 043802
Crippled Dick Hot Wax / Jan '97 / SRD

I WANTS TO BE A ACTOR LADY
Cincinnati Uni Singers/Orchestra
Rivers, E. *Con*
CD 802212
New World / Apr '94 / New World

I WISH IT SO (Songs By Sondheim/ Bernstein/Weill/Blitzstein)
Upshaw, Dawn
Stern, Eric *Con*
CD 7559793452
Nonesuch / Dec '94 / Warner Music

IF I LOVED YOU - LOVE DUETS FROM THE MUSICALS
Allen, Thomas & Valerie Masterson/Philharmonia Orchestra
Edwards, John Owen *Con*
CD CDVIR 8317
TER / May '94 / Koch

I'M NO ANGEL (The Original Commercial Recordings/The Film Soundtracks)
West, Mae
I like a guy who takes his time / Easy rider / I'm no angel / I found a new way to go to town / I want you, I need you / They call me Sister Honky Tonk / Willie of the valley / I like a guy who takes his time / Easy rider / Frankie and Johnny / They call me Sister Honky Tonk / That Dallas man / I fond a new way to get to town / I want you, I need you / I'm no angel / When St. Louis woman comes down to New Orleans / My old flame / Memphis blues / Troubled waters / He's a bad bad man / Mon coeur s'ouvre a ta voix / I'm an Occidental woman in an Oriental mood for love / Mister Deep Blue Sea / Little Bar Butterfly / On a typical tropical night / I was saying to the moon / Fifi / Now I'm a lady
CD ____ **JASCD 102**
Jasmine / Oct '96 / Conifer/BMG / Hot Shot / TKO Magnum

IN CONCERT
Welch, Elizabeth
CD ____ **OCRCD 6016**
First Night / Apr '96 / Pinnacle

IN LOVE IN HOLLYWOOD
Jones, Salena
CD ____ **CDVIR 8328**
TER / Jan '95 / Koch

IN LOVE ON BROADWAY
Jones, Salena
CD ____ **CDVIR 8327**
TER / May '94 / Koch

IN THE REAL WORLD
Hadley, Jerry & American Theatre Orchestra
Gemignani, Paul *Con*
CD ____ **09026619372**
RCA Victor / Apr '94 / BMG

IN TOWN TONIGHT (25 Nostalgic Theatre & Cabaret Songs)
London pride: *Coward, Sir Noel* / Someday I'll find you: *Lawrence, Gertrude* / Home town: *Flanagan & Allen* / Walter Walter: *Bowlly, Al* / Mad about the boy: *Lillie, Beatrice* / Everything's in rhythm with my heart: *Matthews, Jessie* / Mae time: *Desmond, Florence* / Dancing in the dark: *Hutchinson, Leslie 'Hutch'* / Mad dogs and Englishmen: *Coward, Sir Noel* / Auf weidersehen sweetheart: *Bowlly, Al* / Sophisticated lady: *Hall, Adelaide* / Broadway melody: *Layton & Johnstone* / Free: *Flanagan & Allen* / Little Betty Bouncer: *Flotsam & Jetsam* / My sweet Virginia: *Bowlly, Al* / Shirts: *Lane, Lupino* / Little silkworm: *Matthews, Jessie* / My sweet: *Lawrence, Gertrude* / When I grow too old to dream: *Fields, Gracie* / You were meant for me: *Layton & Johnstone* / I wanna be loved: *Hall, Adelaide* / Rain on the roof: *Bowlly, Al* / Simon the bootlegger: *Flotsam & Jetsam* / You're blase: *Hutchinson, Leslie 'Hutch'*
CD ____ **PLATCD 172**
Prism / Mar '96 / Prism

INDIANA JONES (Music From The Films Of Harrison Ford)
City Of Prague Philharmonic Orchestra
Bateman, Paul *Con*
Witness / Regarding Henry / Mosquito coast / Patriot games / Fugitive / Blade runner / Presumed innocent / Star Wars / Empire strikes back / Return of the Jedi / Raiders of the Lost Ark / Indiana Jones and the temple of doom / Indiana Jones and the last crusade / Hanover Street
CD ____ **FILMCD 154**
Silva Screen / Oct '94 / Koch / Silva Screen

IS IT REALLY ME
Philharmonia/Symphony/Scottish Opera/ New Sadler's Wells Opera Orchestras
CD ____ **CDVIR 8314**
TER / Oct '91 / Koch

JAMES BOND THEMES, THE
London Theatre Orchestra
James Bond Theme / Licence To Kill / Living Daylights / Never Say Never Again / Man With The Golden Gun / View To A Kill / All Time High / Casino Royale / For Your Eyes Only / Live And Let Die / From Russia With Love / Diamonds Are Forever / You Only Live Twice / Nobody Does It Better / Thunderball / Moonraker / Mr. Kiss Kiss Bang Bang / Goldfinger / Goldeneye
CD ____ **QED 057**
Tring / Nov '96 / Tring

JAMES BOND THEMES, THE (14 Classic Movie Themes)
London Theatre Orchestra
James Bond Theme / Live And Let Die / Licence To Kill / From Russia With love / Nobody Does It Better / View To A Kill / For Your Eyes Only / On Her Majesty's Secret Service / Diamonds Are Forever / All time high / Thunderball / Goldfinger / Man With The Golden Gun / Moonraker / James Bond Theme
CD ____ **EMPRCD 576**
Emporio / Jul '95 / Disc

JAMES BOND THEMES, THE
James Bond Theme / Live And Let Die / Licence TO Kill / From Russia With Love / Nobody does it better / View To A Kill / For Your Eyes Only / On Her Majesty's Secret Service / Diamond's Are Forever / All Time High / Thunderball / Goldfinger / Man With The Golden Gun / Moonraker / Golden Eye
CD ____ **SUMCD 4126**
Sound & Media / Jun '97 / Sound & Media

JAZZ GOES TO HOLLYWOOD
Karlin, Fred
CD ____ **VSD 5639**
Varese Sarabande / Nov '95 / Pinnacle

JEAN GABIN VOL.2
CD ____ **302254**
Playtime / Feb '97 / Discovery

JEAN-PIERRE MOCKY - FINEST MUSIC OF HIS FILMS
CD ____ **302614**
Playtime / Feb '97 / Discovery

JOHN TRAVOLTA
Travolta, John
CD ____ **EMPRCD 524**
Empress / Sep '94 / Koch

JOHN WILLIAMS PLAYS THE MOVIES (& The World Of John Williams)
Williams, John
Kiss from a rose / Everything I do / Unchained melody / Love is all around / Godfather / Moon river / Somewhere over the rainbow / Mission / Cavatina / As tme goes by / Les Parapluies De Cherbourg / It had to be you / Bagdad Cafe / Entertainer / Il Postino / Once Upon A Time In America / Once Upon A Time In The West / Schindler's List
2CD ____ **S2K 62784**
Sony Classical / Oct '96 / Sony

JOLSON SONGBOOK, THE
Minstrel Singers
Rock-a-bye your baby / Swanee / My Mammy / April showers / California here I come / Toot toot tootsie / Sonny boy / Let me sing and I'm happy / You made me love you / Back in your own backyard / There's a rainbow 'round my shoulder / I'm sitting on top of the world / Waiting for the Robert E Lee / Me and my shadow / Carolina in the morning / Baby face / Give my regards to Broadway / Pretty baby / Bye bye blackbird / For me and my girl
CD ____ **3036200292**
Carlton / Feb '97 / Carlton

JOSE CARRERAS SINGS MUSICALS
Carreras, Jose
CD ____ **4169732**
Philips / Jan '88 / PolyGram

JOURNEY TO THE STARS
CD ____ **4464032**
Philips / Feb '96 / PolyGram

KIRI ON BROADWAY
Te Kanawa, Dame Kiri
My fair lady / One touch of Venus / Too many girls / Carousel / Kiss me Kate / West Side Story / Sound of music
CD ____ **4402802**
Decca / Jan '94 / PolyGram

KISS
Monroe, Marilyn
You'd be surprised / River of no return / I wanna be loved by you / When I fall in love / Bye bye baby / Diamonds are a girl's best friend / One silver dollar / I'm gonna file my claim / When love goes wrong, nothing goes right / After you get what you want, you don't want it / Runnin' wild / Specialisation / My heart belongs to Daddy / Two little girls from Little Rock / Heat wave / Kiss
CD ____ **CD 3555**
Cameo / Nov '95 / Target/BMG

LADIES OF THE 20TH CENTURY, THE
Monroe, Marilyn
Kiss / Do it again / She acts like a woman should / Little girl from Little Rock / Bye bye bye / Diamonds are a girl's best friend / When love goes wrong / Fine romance / River of no return / Down in the meadow / After you get what you want, you don't want it / Heatwave
CD ____ **JD 1238**
Jazz Door / Aug '93 / Koch

LAST ACTION HEROES, THE
Starlight Orchestra/Singers
Gonna fly now / Terminator II / Living in America / Big gun / Fugitive / Peace in our lives / Raiders of the lost ark / Eye of the tiger / Still cruisin' / Shaft / He ain't heavy, he's my brother / Robocop II / Philadelphia morning / It's a long road / Runaway train / Can't stop the fire / Anything goes / You could be mine
CD ____ **GRF 287**
Tring / Apr '95 / Tring

LAUREL AND HARDY'S MUSIC BOX VOL.1 (New Recordings Of Laurel & Hardy Scores)
Ku-ku / On to the show / Bells / Dash and dot / We're out for fun / Drunk / Rockin' chairs / Give us a hand / Riding along / Gangway Charlie / Here we go / Moon and you / You are the one I love / Beautiful lady / Look at him now / Funny faces / On a sunny afternoon / Sons of the Desert
CD ____ **LH 10012**
Silva Screen / Nov '89 / Koch / Silva Screen

LAUREL AND HARDY'S MUSIC BOX VOL.2
CD ____ **LH 10022**
Silva Screen / Nov '89 / Koch / Silva Screen

LE CINEMA QUI CHANTE VOL.1
CD ____ **3007492**
Orphee/Cinestars / Feb '97 / Discovery

LE CINEMA QUI CHANTE VOL.2
CD ____ **3007502**
Orphee/Cinestars / Feb '97 / Discovery

LE CINEMA QUI CHANTE VOL.3
CD ____ **3007512**
Orphee/Cinestars / Feb '97 / Discovery

LE CINEMA QUI CHANTE VOL.4
CD ____ **3007522**
Orphee/Cinestars / Feb '97 / Discovery

LE CINEMA QUI CHANTE VOL.5
CD ____ **3007532**
Orphee/Cinestars / Feb '97 / Discovery

LE CINEMA QUI CHANTE VOL.6
CD ____ **3007542**
Orphee/Cinestars / Feb '97 / Discovery

LEADING LADIES
Broadway baby theme / Music and the mirror: *Harris, Anita* / Broadway baby: *Langford, Bonnie* / Don't rain on my parade: *Moore, Claire* / I get along without you very well: *Kesselman, Maria* / It's better with a band: *Harris, Anita* / Once you lose your heart: *Langford, Bonnie* / Birth of the blues: *Moore, Claire* / City lights: *Harris, Anita* / I enjoy being a girl: *Kesselman, Maria* / Tell me it's not true: *Langford, Bonnie* / Move over darling: *Moore, Claire* / How are things in Glocca Morra: *Moore, Claire* / My secret love: *Langford, Bonnie* / Bewitched: *Kesselman, Maria* / Hello young lovers: *Kesselman, Maria* / Perfect year: *Harris, Anita*
CD ____ **3036200342**
Carlton / Mar '97 / Carlton

LEGENDARY PERFORMERS 1930/1941
MacDonald, Jeanette & Nelson Eddy
Indian love call / Rose-Marie / Song of love / Waltz / I'm falling in love with someone / Italian street song / Tramp, tramp, tramp, along the highway / Ah the mystery of life (dream melody) / Little love, a little kiss / Drink to me only with thine eyes / Kerry dance / Smilin' through / Lover come back to me / One kiss / Who are we to say (obey your heart) / Isn't romantic / Beyond the blue horizon / Will you rember / Farewell to dreams / Sweethearts waltz
CD ____ **CD 60012**
Great Movie Themes / Jun '97 / Target/ BMG

LEGENDS IN MUSIC - DORIS DAY
Day, Doris
CD ____ **LECD 091**
Wisepack / Sep '94 / Conifer/BMG / THE

LEGENDS IN MUSIC - JUDY GARLAND
Garland, Judy
CD ____ **LECD 094**
Wisepack / Sep '94 / Conifer/BMG / THE

LEGENDS IN MUSIC - MARILYN MONROE
Monroe, Marilyn
CD ____ **LECD 067**
Wisepack / Jul '94 / Conifer/BMG / THE

LES FILMS NOIR
CD ____ **887976**
Milan / Jun '95 / Conifer/BMG / Silva Screen

LES MUSIQUES DES PALMES D'OR
Harry Lime theme / Manha de carnaval / La Dolce Vita / Il gattapardo / Les Parapluies De Cherbourg / Un Homme Et Une Femme / MASH / Go-Between / Ride of the valkyries / Concerto in G / Paris, Texas / Gabriel's oboe / Big my secret / Bullwinkle
CD ____ **DC 880702**
Disky / May '97 / Disky / THE

LET ME SING AND I'M HAPPY (Al Jolson At Warner Bros. 1926-1936)
Jolson, Al
April showers / Rock-a-bye your baby with a dixie melody / Dirty hands, dirty face / Toot toot tootsie / Blue skies / Mother of mine, I still have you / My Mammy / It all depends on you / I'm sitting on top of the world / Spaniard that blighted my life / There's a rainbow 'round my shoulder / Golden gate / Sonny boy / Back in your own back yard / Used to you / I'm in seventh Heaven / Let me sing and I'm happy / (Across the breakfast table) looking at you / Why do they all take the night boat to Albany / Liza Lee / Little sunshine / About a quarter to nine / I love to sing
CD ____ **CDODEON 24**
Soundtracks / Jan '97 / EMI

LET'S FACE THE MUSIC
Astaire, Fred
Let's face the music and dance / Fine romance / Foggy day / Change partners / I'm old fashioned / They can't take that away from me / Flying down to Rio / Let yourself go / Fascinating rhythm / They all laughed / Pick yourself up / Nice work if you can get it / Isn't this a lovely day / Dearly beloved / Way you look tonight / Let's call the whole thing off / Cheek to cheek / Funny face / Bojangles of Harlem / Shall we dance / Love of my life / Top hat, white tie & tails / I'm putting all my eggs in one basket / I used to be colour blind / Dream dancing
CD ____ **AVC 537**
Avid / Oct '95 / Avid/BMG / Koch / THE

LET'S FACE THE MUSIC
Astaire, Fred
Let's face the music and dance / Things are looking up / Way you look tonight / Nice work if you can get it / Poor Mr. Chisolm / Let's call the whole thing off / They all laughed / Shall we dance / My one and only / I'm putting all my eggs in one basket / Piccolino / Pick yourself up / They can't take that away from me / Isn't this a lovely day / No strings I'm fancy free / Fascinating rhythm
CD ____ **SUMCD 4049**
Summit / Nov '96 / Sound & Media

LET'S FACE THE MUSIC AND DANCE
Astaire, Fred
Change partners / Cheek to cheek / I used to be colour blind / I'm putting all my eggs in one basket / Let's face the music and dance / No strings / Top hat, white tie and tails / Yam / Foggy day / I can't be bothered now / I've got beginner's luck / Let's call the whole thing off / Nice work if you can get it / Shall we dance / Slap that bass / They all laughed / They can't take that away from me / Things are looking up / Poor Mr. Chisholm / Dearly Beloved / Fine romance / I'm old fashioned / Never gonna dance / Pick yourself up / Way you look tonight / You were never lovelier / Since I kissed my baby goodbye
CD ____ **CDAJA 5123**
Living Era / Mar '94 / Select

LET'S FACE THE MUSIC AND DANCE (All His Greatest Songs)
Astaire, Fred
They can't take that away from me / Isn't this a lovely day / I'm putting all my eggs in one basket / They all laughed / Let's call the whole thing off / Shall we dance / Way you look tonight / Nice work if you can get it / Poor Mr. Chisholm / Let's face the music and dance / Piccolino / I used to be colour blind / Foggy day / My one and only / Pick yourself up / Yam / Let yourself go / Things are looking up / No strings (I'm fancy free) / Fascinating rhythm
CD ____ **305512**
Hallmark / Oct '96 / Carlton

LET'S GO ON WITH THE SHOW (Hits From The West End & Broadway)
America / If my friends could see me now / Send in the clowns / Wilkommen / I am what I am / Wunderbar / OH what a beautiful morning / Shall we dance / You'll never walk alone / Camelot / Get me to the church on time / Stranger in Paradise
CD ____ **SHOWCD 016**
Showtime / Feb '95 / Disc / THE

LINO VENTURA FILM MUSIC
CD ____ **CH 332**
Milan / Jan '95 / Conifer/BMG / Silva Screen

LITTLE LIGHT MUSIC, A (A Showbiz Compilation Filled With Humour & Melody)
Singers Unlimited
Old friends / Let's face the music and dance / Can that boy foxtrot / There are bad times just around the corner / Anyone can whistle / Broadway baby / It's bound to be right on the night / Why must the show go on / I've got a crush on you / Boy like that / I hate men / Why can't you behave/I got lost in his arms/You're just in I / Losing my mind / Parisian Pierrot/Last time I saw Paris/Ah Paris / Send in the clowns / Prelude No.2 / Maybe this time / We're gonna be alright
CD ____ **URCD 123**
Upbeat / Jun '96 / Cadillac / Target/BMG

LONDON PRIDE
Twiggy
CD ____ **VSD 5715**
Varese Sarabande / Nov '96 / Pinnacle

LONGEST DAY, THE (Music From The Classic War Films)
City Of Prague Philharmonic Orchestra
Bateman, Paul *Con*
Longest Day / 633 Squadron / Guns Of Navarone / Dambusters / Battle Of Britian / MacArthur/Patton / Night Of The Generals / Bridge On The River Kwai / Where Eagles Dare / Das Boot (The Boat) / Great Escape / Battle Of Midway / Battle Of The Bulge / Force 10 From Navarone / In Harm's Way / Sink The Bismark / Bridge At Remagen / Bridge Too Far / 1941 / Is Paris Burning
CD ____ **FILMCD 151**
Silva Screen / '94 / Koch / Silva Screen

LORDS OF THE MUSICAL
London Symphony Orchestra
CD ____ **FMI 201CD**
Focus / Mar '97 / Total/BMG

LORELEI, THE (Songs By Gershwin, Porter & Berlin)
Criswell, Kim & Ambrosian Chorus/London Sinfonietta
McGlinn, John *Con*
CD ____ **CDC 7548022**
EMI Classics / Apr '94 / EMI

LOST IN BOSTON VOL.1
CD ______ VSD 5475
Varese Sarabande / Aug '94 / Pinnacle

LOST IN BOSTON VOL.2
CD ______ VSD 5485
Varese Sarabande / Mar '95 / Pinnacle

LOST IN BOSTON VOL.3 (Lost Gems From The Greatest Shows & Composers)
CD ______ VSD 5563
Varese Sarabande / Aug '95 / Pinnacle

LOST IN BOSTON VOL.4
CD ______ VSD 5768
Varese Sarabande / Apr '97 / Pinnacle

LOUIS DE FUNES FILM MUSIC
CD ______ 887901
Milan / Jan '95 / Conifer/BMG / Silva Screen

LOVE AT THE MOVIES
CD ______ 889708
Milan / Jan '93 / Conifer/BMG / Silva Screen

LOVE AT THE MOVIES...THE ALBUM
Kiss from a rose: *Seal* / It must have been love: *Roxette* / In all the right places: *Stansfield, Lisa* / Crying game: *Boy George* / Absolute beginner: *Bowie, David* / No more lonely nights: *McCartney, Paul* / Nothing has been proved: *Springfield, Dusty* / I got you babe: *Sonny & Cher* / I will survive: *Savage, Chantay* / Goldeneye: *Turner, Tina* / Slave to love: *Ferry, Bryan* / Misty blue: *Moore, Dorothy* / Glory of love: *Cetera, Peter* / Sea of love: *Phillips, Phil* / Stardust: *Cole, Nat 'King'* / Beauty and the beast: *Bryson, Peabo & Celine Dion* / Falling: *Cruise, Julee* / I will find you: *Clannad* / Someday: *Eternal* / Love song for a vampire: *Lennox, Annie* / Show me Heaven: *McKee, Maria* / Take my breath away: *Berlin* / Up where we belong: *Cocker, Joe & Jennifer Warnes* / Unchained melody: *Righteous Brothers* / Blue velvet: *Vinton, Bobby* / Brown eyed girl: *Morrison, Van* / My girl: *Temptations* / Shy guy: *King, Diana* / It's in his kiss (shoop shoop song): *Cher* / Kokomo: *Beach Boys* / Coming round again: *Simon, Carly* / Give me the reason: *Vandross, Luther* / Against all odds: *Collins, Phil* / I don't wanna talk about it: *Indigo Girls* / Arthur's theme: *Cross, Christopher* / 500 miles: *Proclaimers* / Let me into your heart: *Carpenter, Mary-Chapin*
2CD ______ CDEMTVD 144
EMI / Nov '96 / EMI

LOVE AT THE THEATRE
CD ______ PMCD 7006
Pure Music / Nov '94 / BMG

LOVE AT THE THEATRE
Starlight Orchestra/Singers
Perfect year / All I ask of you / What I did for love / On the street where you live / People / She's so beautiful / Maria / I know him so well / Send in the clowns / I don't know how to love him / With one look / Love changes everything / Almost like being in love / Some enchanted evening / Memory
CD ______ QED 118
Tring / Nov '96 / Tring

LOVE IN THE CINEMA (A Collection Of Romantic Movie Music)
CD ______ 191892
Milan / Jan '95 / Conifer/BMG / Silva Screen

LOVE IS HERE TO STAY
Henshall, Ruthie
Love is here to stay / Somebody loves me / Someone to watch over me / Nice work if you can get it / Lady be good / 'S wonderful / But not for me / Summertime / Man I love / Embraceable you / Boy what love has done to me / They all laughed / Swanee / Love walked in
CD ______ BRCD 6000
Bravo / Mar '94 / Carlton

LOVE MOVIE THEMES
CD ______ 15070
Laserlight / Dec '94 / Target/BMG

LOVE MOVIE THEMES
CD ______ 22510
Music / Dec '95 / Target/BMG

LOVE SONGS AT THE MOVIES
Starlight Orchestra/Singers
I will always love you / Streets of Philadelphia / What's love got to do with it / I can see clearly now / Book of days / Greatest love of all / Whole new world / Stand by me / Hello again / My girl / Nothing's gonna stop us now / Long and winding road / Rose / For all we know / Up where we belong / Try a little tenderness / First time ever I saw your face / You gotta love someone / Wind beneath my wings / (Everything I do) I do it for you / No ordinary love / All night long / Do you know where you're going to / Mona Lisa / Somewhere out there / Unchained melody / Arthur's theme (The best that you can get) / Way we were / It must have been love / He ain't heavy, he's my brother / Power of love / Let the river run / Hopelessly devoted to you / Nobody does it better / Bright eyes / Suddenly / Love song for a vampire / Yesterday / Take my breath away / Will you be there / When I fall in love / I just called to say I love you / Love is in the air / Against all odds / Beauty and the Beast / Run to you / Tracks of my tears / King of wishful thinking / I don't wanna fight / If we hold on together / Again / Say you say me / Places that belong to you / Are you lonesome tonight / Sorry seems to be the hardest word / What becomes of the broken hearted / You light up my life / All for love / Someday I'm coming back / With you I'm born again / How deep is your love / Glory of love / Love on the rocks / (I've had) The time of my life / Endless love / All time high / Crying game / I can't help falling in love / Just the way you are / We may never love like this again / Shoop shoop song (It's in his kiss) / This used to be my playground / As time goes by / It's probably me / Sandy / Under the Boardwalk
4CD ______ QUAD 011
Tring / Nov '96 / Tring

LOVE SONGS FROM THE MOVIES
(Everything I do) I do it for you / Unchained melody / It must have been love / I will always love you / Try a little tenderness / What becomes of the broken hearted / When I fall in love / No ordinary love / Can you feel the love tonight / Streets of Philadelphia / Big my secret / Love is all around / Deeper love / Wind beneath my wings / Take my breath away / (I've had) the time of my life
CD ______ EMPRCD 902
Emporio / Jan '97 / Disc

LOVE THEMES FROM THE MOVIES
I will always love you / Rose / Do you know where you're going to / Greatest love of all / It must have been love / Nobody loves it better / Hard to say I'm sorry / Hopelessly devoted to you / Wind beneath my wings / Beauty and the beast / Take my breath away / First time ever I saw your face / Up where we belong / Endless love / Way we were / Love touch / Evergreen / My own true love
CD ______ ECD 3132
K-Tel / Jan '95 / K-Tel

LULLABY OF BROADWAY (The Best Of Busby Berkeley At Warner Bros.)
Young and healthy / Shuffle off to Buffalo / 42nd Street / We're in the money / I've got to sing a torch song / Shadow waltz / Remember my forgotten man / Honeymoon Hotel / By a waterfall / Shanghai Lil / Don't say goodnight / Fashions of 1934 / Spin a little web of dreams / Girl at the ironing board / I only have eyes for you / Dames / Words are in my heart / Lullaby of Broadway / Lady in red / All's fair in love and war / Hooray for Hollywood
2CD ______ CDODEON 8
Premier/EMI / Feb '96 / EMI

MAD WORLD OF SOUNDTRACKS, THE
CD ______ 5534992
Motor Collector / Apr '97 / Cargo

MAGIC FROM THE MUSICALS
Only you: *Blessed, Brian* / Good morning starshine: *Clark, Petula* / If I were a rich man: *Topol* / Luck be a lady: *Jones, Paul* / Memory: *Clark, Petula* / Send in the clowns: *Webb, Marti* / Impossible dream: *Blessed, Brian* / Bless your beautiful hide: *Keel, Howard* / Thank heavens for little girls: *Topol* / Lullaby of Broadway: *Jones, Paul* / If he walked into my life: *Webb, Marti* / Annie get your gun medley: *Keel, Howard* / I don't know how to love him: *Webb, Marti* / I've grown accustomed to her face: *Jones, Paul*
CD ______ MCCD 012
Music Club / Feb '91 / Disc / THE

MAGIC OF THE BRITISH MUSICALS, THE
CD ______ CDTEZ 7003
TER / Jan '95 / Koch

MAGIC OF THE MUSICALS, THE (40 Hits From 40 Great Musicals Of Stage & Screen)
There's no business like show business: *Silver Screen Orchestra* / Couple of swells: *Silver Screen Orchestra* / It's a lovely day today: *Silver Screen Orchestra* / Let's face the music and dance: *Silver Screen Orchestra* / Cheek to cheek: *Silver Screen Orchestra* / Pretty girl is like a melody: *Silver Screen Orchestra* / Play a simple melody: *Silver Screen Orchestra* / Heatwave: *Silver Screen Orchestra* / I love a piano: *Silver Screen Orchestra* / Stepping out with my baby: *Silver Screen Orchestra* / Change partners and dance: *Silver Screen Orchestra* / Everything's coming up roses: *Bassey, Shirley* / People: *Bassey, Shirley* / Tonight: *Bassey, Shirley* / Lady is a tramp: *Bassey, Shirley* / I get a kick out of you: *Bassey, Shirley* / It might as well be spring: *Bassey, Shirley* / As long as he needs me: *Bassey, Shirley* / I've never been in love before: *Bassey, Shirley* / Any dream will do: *Jones, Paul* / Take it on the chin: *O'Hara, Mary* / Unusual way: *O'Hara, Mary* / How to handle a woman: *Young, Robert* / Love changes everything: *Keel, Howard* / Music of the night: *Keel, Howard* / O what a beautiful morning: *Keel, Howard* / Hello, young lovers: *Monro, Matt* / Who can I turn to: *Monro, Matt* / I can give you the starlight: *Hill, Vince* / Someday my heart will awake: *Hill, Vince* / Edelweiss: *Hill, Vince* / Shine through my dreams: *Hill, Vince* / Sunrise sunset: *Dodd, Ken* / This is my lovely day: *Wallace, Ian* / Mr. Mistoffelees: *Morriston Orpheus Choir* / Starlight Express: *Morriston Orpheus Choir* / Don't cry for me Argentina: *Morriston Orpheus Choir & Margaret Williams* / Day by day: *Laine, Cleo* / Prepare ye the way of the Lord: *Laine, Cleo* / All I do is dream of you: *Cogan, Alma* / I've got my love to keep me warm: *Berlin, Irving*
2CD ______ CDDL 1227
Music For Pleasure / Apr '92 / EMI

MAGIC OF THE MUSICALS, THE
Webb, Marti & Mark Rattray
Lullaby of broadway / I got rhythm / I get a kick out of you / It ain't necessarily so / Got plenty of nothing / There's a boat dat's leavin' soon for New York / Porgy, I's your woman now / Summertime / Blow Gabriel blow / Losing my mind / Not while I'm around / Send in the clowns / Do you hear the people sing / Empty chairs at empty tables / I dreamed a dream / Last night of the world / Bui-doi / Don't cry for me Argentina / Jesus Christ superstar / Mama a rainbow / Take that look off your face / In one of my weaker moments / Anthem / You and I / Tell me it's not true / Only he / Love changes everything / Music of the night / Memory
CD ______ MCCD 149
Music Club / Feb '94 / Disc / THE

MAGIC OF THE MUSICALS, THE
3CD ______ MCBX 014
Music Club / Dec '94 / Disc / THE

MAGICAL MOVIE MUSIC
Can you feel the love tonight / Beauty and the beast / Whole new world / Circle of life / Be our guest / I just can't wait to be king / Prince Ali / Hakuna Matata / Arabian nights / Gaston / I've got no strings / Part of your world / Some day my prince will come / When you wish upon a star
CD ______ CDMFP 6224
Music For Pleasure / May '96 / EMI

MAGICAL MUSIC OF DISNEY, THE
Cincinnati Pops Orchestra
Circle of life / I just can't wait to be king / Hakuna matara / Be prepared / Can you feel the love tonight / Arabian nights / One jump ahead / Whole new world / Prince Ali / Part of your world / Under the sea / Poor unfortunate souls / Le poissons / Kiss the girl / Happy ending / She's a funny girl / That Belle / Be our guest / Gaston / Beauty and the beast
CD ______ CD 80381
Telarc / Jun '95 / Conifer/BMG

MANTOVANI AT THE MOVIES
Mantovani
CD ______ CDMOIR 506
Memoir / Oct '93 / Jazz Music / Target/BMG

MARCOVICCI SINGS MOVIES
Marcovicci, Andrea
As time goes by / It might be you / On such a night as this / Folks who live on the hill / Two for the road / Happy endings / Don't ever leave me / Here lies love / Let's not talk about love / Girl medley / Someone to love / Mad about the boy / World War II medley / Too late now / Love is here to stay
CD ______ DRGCD 91405
DRG / Mar '92 / Discovery / New Note/ Pinnacle

MARILYN MONROE
Monroe, Marilyn
I wanna be loved by you / Two little girls from Little Rock: *Monroe, Marilyn & Jane Russell* / I'm gonna file my claim / My heart belongs to Daddy / Runnin' wild / Fine romance / You'd be surprised / Diamonds are a girl's best friend / Bye bye baby / I'm through with love / Specialisation: *Monroe, Marilyn & Frankie Vaughan* / Heatwave / Do it again / When love goes wrong nothing goes right: *Monroe, Marilyn & Jane Russell* / After you get what you want, you don't want it / River of no return / Lazy / Kiss / When I fall in love / Happy birthday Mr. President
CD ______ 399534
Koch Presents / May '97 / Koch

MARILYN SINGS
Monroe, Marilyn
CD ______ CDCD 1195
Charly / Sep '94 / Koch

MARLENE DIETRICH
Dietrich, Marlene
Lili Marlene / La vie en rose / Lola / Boys in the backroom / I may never go home anymore / Another Spring, another love / Go away from my window / Honeysuckle rose / Such trying times / Near you / Allein / Johnny / I can't give you anything but love / Laziest gal in town / Frag nicht warum ich gere / I wish you love / I will come back again (maybe I'll come back) / Illusions / Falling in love again / Shir hatan / You go to my head
CD ______ 399536
Koch Presents / May '97 / Koch

MARLENE DIETRICH COLLECTION (20 Golden Greats)
Dietrich, Marlene
Lili Marlene / Boys in the backroom / Lola / Illusions / Johnny / I've been in love before / Black market / Lazy afternoon / Another spring another love / Symphonie / You do something to me / Falling in love again / You go to my head / You've got that look / If he swings by the string / This world of ours / Near you / Candles glowing / Kisses sweeter than wine / Such trying times
CD ______ DVCD 2098
Deja Vu / Jan '87 / THE

MGM ALBUM, THE
Gravitte, Debbie Shapiro
Get happy / Love / Treat me rough / Where the boys are / Tico, Tico / I love a piano / Everybody loves my baby / Too late now / Theme from 2001: A Space Odyssey / Smoke gets in your eyes / Nevertheless (I'm in love with you) / Little Girl Blue/My romance / Love me or leave me / By myself
CD ______ VSD 5742
Varese Sarabande / Jun '97 / Pinnacle

MISS SAIGON AND OTHER SHOWS
CD ______ HM 021
Harmony / Jun '97 / TKO Magnum

MISS SHOW BUSINESS
Garland, Judy
Over the rainbow / Foggy day (in London Town) / Make someone happy / When the sun come sout / Smile / I'm always chasing rainbows / How about me / That's all / That's entertainment / Almost like being in love / This can't be love / Love of my life / Chicago / Fly me to the moon / Boy next door / Stormy weather / Man that got away / For me and my gal / Trolley song / Swanee / I'm nobody's baby / Alexander's ragtime band / I feel a song comin' on / Rock-a-bye your baby with a dixie melody / Battle hymn of the Republic
CD ______ QED 132
Tring / Nov '96 / Tring

MISS SHOWBUSINESS
Garland, Judy
Zing went the strings of my heart / Stompin' at the savoy / All God's chillun got rhythm / Everybody sing / You made me love you / Over the rainbow / Sweet sixteen / Embraceable you / (Can this be) The end of the rainbow / I'm nobody's baby / Pretty girl milking her cow / It's a great day for the Irish / Sunny side of the street / For me and my gal / That old black magic / When you wore a tulip
CD ______ HADCD 156
Javelin / May '94 / Henry Hadaway / THE

MISSION IMPOSSIBLE & OTHER TV THEMES
Gregory, John Orchestra
Mission impossible / Rockford files / Cannon / Softly softly / Columbo / M Squad / Man called Ironside / Griff / Untouchables / Mannix / Route 66 / McMillan & Wife / Harry-O / Streets of San Francisco / Six million dollar man / Hawaii 5-O / It takes a thief / Theme from SWAT / I spy / McCloud / Perry Mason / Name of the game / Banacek / Johnny Staccato / Policewoman / Sweeney / Avengers / Kojak
CD ______ 5329862
Mercury / Jul '96 / PolyGram

MOVIE CLASSICS
CD ______ CDZ 76772542
EMI Classics / Apr '93 / EMI

MOVIE CLASSICS
2CD ______ CES 5690952
EMI Classics / Feb '96 / EMI

MOVIE CLASSICS (20 Classic Film Themes)
2CD ______ 4527232
Decca / Jan '97 / PolyGram

MOVIE CLASSICS (Performed On Pan Pipes)
Don't cry for me Argentina / (Everything I do) I do it for you / Groovy kind of love / Cavatina / Moon river / Somewhere out there / Take my breath away / Chariots of fire / Whole new world / Way we were / Wind beneath my wings / Up where we belong / Can you feel the love tonight / My girl / Love is all around
CD ______ SUMCD 4095
Sound & Media / Jan '97 / Sound & Media

MOVIE HITS
CD ______ TCD 2615
Telstar / Oct '92 / BMG

MOVIE HITS
CD ______ 12196
Laserlight / Apr '95 / Target/BMG

MOVIE HITS IN BRASS
Brassband Burgermusik Luzern
Indiana Jones / Batman / Jurassic Park / Star Wars / James Bond / 633 Squadron / Everything I do, I do it for you / Onedin Line / Can you read my mind / Schindler's List / Start Trek - The Voyage Home / Love Story
CD ______ 340842
Koch / Apr '96 / Koch

MOVIE HITS, THE
Crosby, Bing
Apple for the teacher / Man and his dream / If I had my way / Too romantic / I haven't time to be a millionaire / Meet the sun halfway / My heart is taking lessons / Funny old hills / I have eyes / Still the bluebird sings / Moonburn / Love thy neighbour / Waiter and the porter and the upstairs maid / Small fry / Moon got in my eyes / Smarty / Without a word of warning / My heart and I / Let's call a heart a heart / Go fly a kite / Empty saddles / Birth of the blues

CD PASTCD 9784
Flapper / Mar '92 / Pinnacle

MOVIE KILLERS
CD TCD 2836
Telstar / Jun '96 / BMG

MOVIE LOVE SONGS
Philadelphia Orchestra
Ormandy, Eugene *Con*
Love Story / Elvira Madigan: *Wild, Earl* / Yesterday / Thomas Crown Affair / Romeo and Juliet / Heart is a Lonely Hunter / West Side Story / Tristan and Isolde / Now, Voyager
CD 09026609652
RCA Victor / Jan '92 / BMG

MOVIE LOVE THEMES
Tritt, W./A. Romero/Cincinnati Pops Orchestra
Kunzel, Erich *Con*
CD CD 80243
Telarc / Feb '91 / Conifer/BMG

MOVIE LOVERS
Brown eyed girl: *Morrison, Van* / Perfect day: *Reed, Lou* / Girl you'll be a woman soon: *Urge Overkill* / In dreams: *Orbison, Roy* / Blue Spanish sky: *Isaak, Chris* / Venus as a boy: *Bjork* / Love song for a vampire: *Lennox, Annie* / I've never been to me: *Charlene* / Sea of love: *Wilde, Marty* / Love letters: *Lester, Ketty* / Everybody's talkin': *Nilsson, Harry* / When a man loves a woman: *Sledge, Percy* / You've really got a hold on me: *Robinson, Smokey & The Miracles* / Soul on fire: *Baker, LaVern* / Gimme your love: *Mayfield, Curtis* / Baby, I love you: *Franklin, Aretha* / Falling: *Cruise, Julee* / Love and happiness: *Green, Al* / Tell it like it is: *Neville, Aaron* / Fa-fa-fa-fa-fa (sad song): *Redding, Otis*
2CD TCD 2876
Telstar / Nov '96 / BMG

MOVIE MEMORIES (Music From The Greatest Films)
Nuremberg Symphony Orchestra
Kaufman, Richard *Con*
CD CST 348052
Colosseum / Nov '95 / Pinnacle

MOVIE MUSIC
CD PCD 887
Prometheus / '88 / Silva Screen

MOVIE SONG ALBUM, THE
Bennett, Tony
Maybe September / Girl talk / Gentle rain / Emily / Pawnbroker / Samba de orfeu / Shadow of your smile / Smile / Second time around / Days of wine and roses / Never too late / Trolley song
CD 4879472
Columbia / Jul '97 / Sony

MOVIE'S GREATEST LOVE SONGS
Play dead: *Arnold, David & Bjork* / Love song for a vampire: *Lennox, Annie* / No ordinary love: *Sade* / Unchained melody: *Righteous Brothers* / Licence to kill: *Knight, Gladys* / Show me heaven: *McKee, Maria* / Falling: *Cruise, Julee* / Forbidden colours: *Sakamoto, Ryuichi & David Sylvian* / Going home: *Knopfler, Mark* / Book of days: *Enya* / Take my breath away: *Berlin* / Glory of love: *Cetera, Peter* / Up where we belong: *Cocker, Joe & Jennifer Warnes* / Nothing has been proved: *Springfield, Dusty* / I guess that's why they call it the blues: *John, Elton* / Arthur's theme: *Cross, Christopher* / Love is in the air: *Young, John Paul* / My girl: *Temptations* / Try a little tenderness: *Commitments* / Brown eyed girl: *Morrison, Van*
CD 516651-2
PolyGram TV / Feb '94 / PolyGram

MUSIC FOR FILMS
CD ASCD 04
All Saints / Jun '92 / Discovery / Vital

MUSIC FOR STAGE AND SCREEN
Williams, John & The Boston Pops Orchestra
Born on the fourth of July / Revivers / Red pony / Quiet city
CD SK 64147
Sony Classical / Jan '95 / Sony

MUSIC FOR THE SILENT MOVIES
Silent movie drama / Pianola rag / High hat and tap / Chaplin crying / Palm court / Charlie chase / Bowler hat and a piano / Borsalino theme / Tramp / Keaton laughing / Gypsy rosalee / Wash rag / Laurel and Hardy / Mack Sennett / Cartoon rag / Policeman / Bootleggers and co / Old crock rag / Chico Marx and brothers / Tender waltz for a tough guy / Curtain down, the show is over
CD 304682
Hallmark / Jun '97 / Carlton

MUSIC FROM DEANNA DURBIN FILMS, THE
My heart is singing / It's raining sunbeams / Heart that's free / Libiamo / Chapel bells / I love to whistle / Serenade to the stars / You're as pretty as a picture / My own / Je veux vivre / Last rose of summer / Love is all / Loch Lomond / Ave Maria / When April sings / When I sing / Goin' home / Mighty lak' a rose / Begin the beguine / Say a prayer for the boys over there / Kashmiri song / In the spirit of the moment / When you're away / Russian melody / None shall sleep
CD CMSCD 013
Movie Stars / Aug '94 / Conifer/BMG

MUSIC FROM GREAT AUSTRALIAN FILMS
Australian Broadcasting Commission Philharmonic Orchestra
Motzing, William *Con*
Newsfront / Gallipoli / My brillant career / Tall timbers / Cathy's child / Eliza Frazer / Breaker morant / Chant of Jimmy Blacksmith / Picture show man / Picnic at Hanging Rock / Mango tree / Dimboola / Caddie
CD DRGCD 12582
DRG / Jan '95 / Discovery / New Note/ Pinnacle

MUSIC FROM JACQUES TATI FILMS
CD 8369832
Silva Screen / Feb '90 / Koch / Silva Screen

MUSIC FROM SYLVESTER STALLONE FILMS, THE
CD CDCIA 5064
Cinevox / Jan '93 / Koch / Silva Screen

MUSIC FROM THE FILMS OF ANDRE TECHINE
CD CD 343
Milan / Jan '89 / Conifer/BMG / Silva Screen

MUSIC FROM THE FILMS OF AUDREY HEPBURN
CD 9245032
Silva Screen / Jan '93 / Koch / Silva Screen

MUSIC FROM THE FILMS OF CLINT EASTWOOD
City Of Prague Philharmonic Orchestra
Wadsworth, Derek *Con*
Where Eagles Dare / Outlaw Josey Wales / Good, the Bad and the Ugly / Fistful Of Dollars / For A Few Dollars More / Play Misty For Me / Hang 'Em High / In The Line Of Fire / Rawhide / Dirty Harry / Sudden Impact / Magnum Force / Two Mules For Sister Sara / Unforgiven
CD FILMCD 138
Silva Screen / '93 / Koch / Silva Screen

MUSIC FROM THE FILMS OF JEAN-PIERRE MOCKY
CD MANTRA 033
Silva Screen / Jan '93 / Koch / Silva Screen

MUSIC FROM THE HAMMER FILMS
Philharmonia Orchestra
Dracula suite / Dracula, Prince of Darkness suite / Hands of the Ripper suite / Taste the blood of Dracula suite / Vampire Circus suite
CD FILMCD 066
Silva Screen / Jan '90 / Koch / Silva Screen

MUSIC FROM THE MOVIES
CD CDMFP 5915
Music For Pleasure / '91 / EMI

MUSIC FROM THE MOVIES
Levy, Louis
Strike up the band / It's love again / It's love again / Swing time / Swing time / Broadway melody of 1938 / Broadway melody of 1938 / Gangway / Gangway / Pennies from Heaven / Pennies from Heaven / Gone with the wind / Gone with the wind / Pinocchio / Pinocchio / Alexander's ragtime band / Alexander's ragtime band / Limelight / Limelight / Shall we dance / Shall we dance / Joy of living / Music from the movies march
CD RAJCD 884
Empress / Sep '96 / Koch

MUSIC FROM THE MOVIES
London Philharmonic Orchestra
Chariots Of Fire / Five Circles / Abraham's theme / Eric's theme / Bladerunner / Ride of the Valkyries / Also Sprach Zarathustra / Battle Of The Planets / Imperial attack / Jaws / Longest Day / Bridge Too Far / Battle of Bordino / Good, The Bad And The Ugly / Raiders Of The Lost Ark
CD DC 880662
Disky / May '97 / Disky / THE

MUSIC FROM THE NEW YORK STAGE VOL.1 (1890-1908)
3CD GEMMCDS 90502
Pearl / Aug '93 / Harmonia Mundi

MUSIC FROM THE NEW YORK STAGE VOL.2 (1908-1913)
3CD GEMMCDS 90535
Pearl / Nov '93 / Harmonia Mundi

MUSIC FROM THE NEW YORK STAGE VOL.3 (1913-1917)
3CD GEMMCDS 90568
Pearl / Nov '93 / Harmonia Mundi

MUSIC FROM THE NEW YORK STAGE VOL.4 (1917-1920)
3CD GEMMCDS 905961
Pearl / Nov '93 / Harmonia Mundi

MUSIC FROM THE OSCAR WINNERS
Silver Screen Orchestra
Everybody's talking / French Connection / Entertainer / One Flew Over The Cuckoo's Nest / Cavatina / Mandoline concerto in C major / Chariots Of Fire / For all mankind / Terms Of Endearment / Last Emperor / Rain Man / Dances With Wolves / Silence Of The Lambs / Schindler's List / Braveheart / Claudia's theme
CD DC 880712
Disky / May '97 / Disky / THE

MUSIC FROM THE SILVER SCREEN
CD ACCCD 1001
Silva Screen / Apr '96 / Koch / Silva Screen

MUSIC OF THE MOVIES
CD GRF 241
Tring / Aug '93 / Tring

MUSIC OF THE MOVIES (The Love Songs)
Starlight Orchestra/Singers
I will always love you / Streets of Philadelphia / What's love got to do with it / I can see clearly now / Book of days / Greatest love of all / Whole new world / Stand by me / Hello again / My girl / Nothing's gonna stop us now / Long and winding road / Rose / For all we know / Up where we belong / Try a little tenderness / What a wonderful world / First time ever I saw your face / You gotta love someone / Wind beneath my wings / (Everything I do) I do it for you / No ordinary love / All night long / Do you know where you're going to / Mona Lisa / Somewhere out there / Unchained melody / Arthur's theme / Way we were / It must have been love / He ain't heavy, he's my brother / Power of love / All you need is love / Let the river run / Hopelessly devoted to you / Nobody does it better / Bright eyes / Suddenly / Love song for a vampire / Yesterday / Take my breath away / Will you be there / When I fall in love / I just called to say I love you / Love is in the air / Against all odds / Beauty and the beast / Run to you / Tracks of my tears / King of wishful thinking / I don't want to fight / If we hold on together / Again / Groovy kind of love / Say you, say me / Places that belong to you / Are you lonesome tonight / Sorry seems to be the hardest word / What becomes of the broken hearted / You light up my life / All for love / Someday I'm coming back / With you I'm born again / Bohemian rhapsody / How deep is your love / Glory of love / Love on the rocks / (I've had) the time of my life / Endless love / All time high / Crying game / Can't help falling in love / Just the way you are / We may never love like this again / Shoop shoop song (It's in his kiss) / This used to be my playground / As time goes by / It's probably me / Sandy / Under the boardwalk
4CD TFP 042
Tring / Apr '95 / Tring

MUSIC OF THE MOVIES (The Love Songs)
Starlight Orchestra/Singers
Take my breath away / He ain't heavy, he's my brother / Glory of love / Up where we belong / I just called to say I love you / Time of my life / Say you, say me / Against all odds / Way we were / Stand by me / Almost paradise / Endless love / You light up my life / Groovy kind of love / Let the river run / Unchained melody / It must have been love
CD QED 013
Tring / Nov '96 / Tring

MUSIC OF THE NIGHT (Pops On Broadway 1990)
Williams, John & The Boston Pops Orchestra
Williams, John *Con*
CD SK 45567
Sony Classical / Jan '95 / Sony

MUSICAL
CD 15 400
Laserlight / Jan '93 / Target/BMG

MUSICAL HIGHLIGHTS
CD 22536
Music / Jul '95 / Target/BMG

MUSICAL MAGIC
CD TREB 5019
Scratch / May '96 / Koch / Scratch/BMG

MUSICAL SELECTIONS FROM THE RIDICULOUS THEATRICAL COMPANY (The 25th Anniversary)
Original Casts
Reverse psychology / Heterosexual Heidi / Conquerer / Sophisticated love / Humanity / Thank God he made me a drag queen / Artificial jungle overture / Eddie's swing / Illusory thing is love / You've changed / Dutch elm disease / Strange way song / Valkyrie dance and song / Yah yah yah - The music has me so confused
CD DRGCD 6301
DRG / Jan '95 / Discovery / New Note/ Pinnacle

MUSICAL WORLD HITS
CD 15086
Laserlight / Dec '94 / Target/BMG

MUSICALS
Ambrosian Chorus & London Sinfonietta
McGlinn, John *C*
Cafe song / Empty chairs at empty tables / Maria / It must be so / Gigi / How to handle a woman / There but for you go I / Never will I marry / Way you look tonight / Fine romance / Love song / Johanna / Finishing the hat / Silly people / Alone together / You do something to me / Gay divorcee / Night and day
CD CDC 7497922
EMI Classics / Aug '93 / EMI

MUSICALS AFTER DARK, THE (Classic Late Night Love Songs From The Shows)
Some enchanted evening: *Allen, Thomas* / Bill: *Welch, Elizabeth* / Only love: *Jones, Salena* / If love were all: *Ashe, Rosemary* / I still believe in love: *Craven, Gemma* / Send in the clowns: *Phillips, Sian* / Glad to be unhappy: *Andreas, Christine* / I'm in the mood for love: *Shore, Julia* / Smoke gets in your eyes: *Welch, Elizabeth* / Maybe this time: *Friedman, Maria* / Tell me on a Sunday: *Robertson, Liz* / Old friend: *Langton, Diane*
CD SHOWCD 028
Showtime / Oct '96 / Disc / THE

MUSICALS COLLECTION, THE
London Theatre Orchestra & Singers
Perfect year / I still believe / Summer nights / I dreamed a dream / Losing my mind / Anything goes / If I were a rich man / I enjoy being a girl / Everything's alright / One night only / Don't cry for me Argentina / Hello Dolly / One night in Bangkok / Skid row / I could have danced all night / On this night / Some enchanted evening / Day by day / Somewhere / Close every door / Memory / Big spender / Cabaret / What I did for love / Love changes everything / Tahiti / Another suitcase in another hall / My blue Heaven / Everything's coming up roses / Everyday / All I ask of you / When I marry Mr. Snow / Starlight express / What kind of fool am I / Bewitched, bothered and bewildered / On the street where you live / Honeysuckle rose / One more angel in Heaven / Maybe this time / Lullaby of Broadway / Phantom Of The Opera / I know him so well / Anything you can do I can do better / Mame / High flying adored / Bali ha'i / I don't know how to love him / Almost like being in love / Somewhere that's green / Two ladies / Time warp / People / That'll be the day / Getting to know you / Impossible dream / Movie in my mind / Trolley song / Send in the clowns / Tea for two / If ever I would leave you / Any dream will do / Maria / Money / I remember it well / Buenos Aires / Ol' man river / People will say we're in love / Diamond's are a girl's best friend / There's a small hotel / I'm still here / Do you hear the people sing / With one look / Overture / King Herod's song / Lucky to be me / Baubles, bangles and beads / She's so beautiful / You're the one that I want / Sweet transvestite / There's no business like show business
4CD TFP 044
Tring / Jan '95 / Tring

MUSICALS VOL.1 (15 Hit Songs From Classic Musical Shows)
CD CDC 7548352
EMI Classics / Apr '93 / EMI

MUSICALS VOL.2 (Highlights From Porgy & Bess/Oklahoma/King And I/ West Side Story)
Royal Liverpool Philharmonic Orchestra
Davis, Carl *Con*
CD CDCFP 4601
Classics For Pleasure / Jan '95 / EMI

MUSICALS, THE
Royal Philharmonic Pops Orchestra
CD DCDCD 215
Castle / Nov '95 / BMG

MUSICALS, THE
Ball, Michael
All I ask of you / Something's coming / Losing my mind / Memory / Don't rain on my parade / With one look / Show me / I dreamed a dream / You'll never walk alone / Easy terms / Last night of the world / Loving you / Anthem / Love changes everything / With one look
CD 5338922
PolyGram TV / Nov '96 / PolyGram

NIGHT AT THE MOVIES, A
Essex, David
Girl, you'll be a woman soon / Can you feel the love tonight / Crying game / Wind beneath my wings / Stardust / Together in electric dreams / Oh what a circus / Seperate lives / St. Elmo's fire / Kiss from a rose / Somewhere out there / Silver dream machine / Sea of love / If I had words (anthem)
CD 5376082
PolyGram TV / May '97 / PolyGram

NIGHT AT THE MOVIES, A
London Philharmonic Orchestra
Bolero / Love Story / French Lieutenant's Woman / Cavatina / Love Is A Many Splendoured Thing / Man and a woman / On Golden Pond / Windmills of your mind / Somewhere In Time / Kramer vs. Kramer / Fantasia / Evita / Madigan / Clockwork Orange / 20,000 Leagues Under The Sea
CD DC 880642
Disky / May '97 / Disky / THE

NO.1 SCI-FI ALBUM, THE (2CD/MC Set)
Star Wars: *Williams, John & The Boston Pops Orchestra* / Independence Day: *City Of Prague Philharmonic Orchestra* / Abyss: *City Of Prague Philharmonic Orchestra* / Empire Strikes Back: *Williams, John & The Boston Pops Orchestra* / Superman: *Williams, John & The Boston Pops Orchestra* / ET: *Williams, John & The Boston Pops Orchestra* / Blade Runner: *Ayres, Mark* /

Return Of The Jedi: *Williams, John & The Boston Pops Orchestra* / Apollo 13: *City Of Prague Philharmonic Orchestra* / Eve of the war: *Wayne, Jeff* / Close Encounters Of The Third Kind: *Williams, John & The Boston Pops Orchestra* / Jurassic Park: *City Of Prague Philharmonic Orchestra* / Batman: *City Of Prague Philharmonic Orchestra* / Dune: *Eno, Brian* / Dark Star: *Caine, Daniel* / Capricorn One: *City Of Prague Philharmonic Orchestra* / Alien: *Williams, John & The Boston Pops Orchestra* / Black Hole: *City Of Prague Philharmonic Orchestra* / 2001: A Space Odyssey: *Williams, John & The Boston Pops Orchestra* / X Files: *Ayres, Mark* / Star Trek: The Next Generation: *Goldsmith, Jerry & Alexander Courage* / Dark Skies: *Hoenig, Michael* / Buck Roger's In The 25th Century: *Philips, Stu* / Battlestar Galactica: *Williams, John & The Boston Pops Orchestra* / Twilight Zone: *Williams, John & The Boston Pops Orchestra* / Star Trek: Voyager: *City Of Prague Philharmonic Orchestra* / Babylon 5: *Ayres, Mark* / Dr. Who: *Grainer, Ron* / Red Dwarf: *Hunte, Diane & Mark Lambert/Ian Hu* / Hitch-Hiker's Guide To The Galaxy: *Lambert, Mark & Ian Hu* / Thunderbirds: *Gray, Barry Orchestra* / Sting Ray: *Gray, Barry Orchestra & The Gary Miller Orchestra* / Fireball XL5: *Gray, Barry* / Captain Scarlet: *Gray, Barry Orchestra* / Joe 90: *Gray, Barry Orchestra* / Blake's Seven: *Ayres, Mark* / Lost In Space I & II: *Williams, John* / Time Tunnel: *Williams, John*
CD ______ **5533602**
PolyGram TV / Mar '97 / PolyGram

NOUVEAU CINEMA - NOUVELLES MUSIQUES
CD ______ **74321413922**
Milan / Nov '96 / Conifer/BMG / Silva Screen

OFFICIAL CINEMA 100 ALBUM, THE
Things to come / Tara's theme / As time goes by / Piano concerto / Spellbound theme / Harry Lime theme / Legend of the Glass Mountain / Do not forsake me / Singin' in the rain / Ben Hur theme / Moon river / Magnificent Seven theme / Lawrence of Arabia theme / James Bond theme / Great Escape theme / Shot in the dark theme / 633 Squadron / Lara's theme / Born Free / Good the bad and the ugly / Grand Prix theme / AP2 / Windmills of your mind / Midnight Cowboy theme / Theme from Love Story / Entertainer / Murder on the Orient Express theme / Death on the Nile theme / Theme from ET / I had a farm in Africa / Mission / Remains of the day theme / Heart asks pleasure first / Suite
2CD ______ **PRDFCD 1**
Premier/EMI / Mar '96 / EMI

ON AND OFF STAGE
Willetts, Dave
CD ______ **SONGCD 902**
Silva Screen / Jan '95 / Koch / Silva Screen

ON BROADWAY
CD ______ **CD 12236**
BR Music / Apr '94 / Target/BMG

ON THE BOARDS (Songs From The Victorian Music Halls)
Down East Band
Whatcher 'Rai / When these old clothes were new / All through sticking to a soldier / Man that broke the bank at Monte Carlo / By the sad sea waves / That is love / Oh Mr. Porter / Ballad of Sam Hall / Stroke of the pen / McDermott's great war song / Boy I love is up in the gallery / I'm very unkind to my wife / For he was her only son / Mad butcher / Doing the academy / East and West / Leo Leo Leo / Hampstead is the place to ruralise
CD ______ **SAMHSCD 204**
Soundalive / Jun '96 / Complete/Pinnacle

ONE FROM THE HEART - SAX AT THE MOVIES
Jazz At The Movies Band
This one's from the heart / Can you read my mind / Last tango in Paris / How do you kep the music playing / Places that belong to you / Take my breath away / Love theme from Pretty Woman / Flight over Africa / Endless love / Way we were
CD ______ **77015**
Discovery / Feb '95 / Warner Music

OPERA AT THE MOVIES
Con onor muore / Un'aura amorosa / Intermezzo sinfonico / Overture / Overture no.2 / Nessun dorma / Che gelida manina / Figaro / Vesta la giubba / Questa o quella / Ride of the valkyries
CD ______ **DC 880872**
Disky / May '97 / Disky / THE

ORIGINAL HOLLYWOOD HITS
Pennies from Heaven: *Crosby, Bing* / For me and my gal: *Garland, Judy & Gene Kelly* / Tangerine: *Dorsey, Jimmy Orchestra* / Sand in my shoes: *Boswell, Connie* / Love in bloom: *Crosby, Bing* / I'm old fashioned: *Astaire, Fred* / This year's kisses: *Faye, Alice* / Trolley song: *Garland, Judy* / Jeepers creepers: *Armstrong, Louis* / I had the craziest dream: *James, Harry Orchestra* / Chattanooga choo choo: *Miller, Glenn Orchestra* / Last time I saw Paris: *Martin, Tony* / Blues in the night: *Shore, Dinah* / I'll sing along with you: *Powell, Dick* / Two sleepy people: *Waller, Fats & His Rhythm* / I don't want to walk without you: *Rhodes, Betty Jane* / Take the 'A' train: *Ellington, Duke Orchestra* / Be careful it's my heart: *Sinatra, Frank* / Rhumboogie: *Andrews Sisters* / My own: *Durbin, Deanna*
CD ______ **306182**
Hallmark / Jan '97 / Carlton

OUT OF THIS WORLD (Sci-Fi Themes)
CD ______ **TCD 2816**
Telstar / Mar '96 / BMG

OVER THE RAINBOW
Garland, Judy
Over the rainbow / Stompin' at the Savoy / Swing Mr. Charlie / Zing went the strings of my heart / All God's chillun got rhythm / Everybody sing/You made me love you / It never rains but it pours / In-between / Sweet sixteen / Embraceable you / (Can this be) the end of the rainbow / I'm nobody's baby / Wearing Of The Green / Friendship / I'm always chasing rainbows / Pretty girl milking her cow / It's a great day for the Irish
CD ______ **CD 406**
Entertainers / Oct '96 / Target/BMG

OVER THE RAINBOW
Garland, Judy
Do it again / Too late now / When you're smiling / Rock-a-bye your baby / Johnny one note / Friendly star / They can't take that away from me / You belong to me / It's all for me / I'd like to hate myself in the morning / Give my regards to Broadway / Alexander's ragtime band / You go to my head / Over the rainbow
CD ______ **100732**
CMC / May '97 / BMG

PALACE OF THE WIND (Piano At The Movies)
Chertock, Michael
Feather theme / Heaven's light / Ashokan farewell / With God's help / Shine / Prelude in C sharp minor / Piano concerto no.3 / Prelude no,.15 / Round midnight / Main theme / Il Postino / Main theme / Retreat lead me to sleep palace of the winds / Fur Elise / Doe eyes / Don't cry for me Argentina / Theme / Main theme / Claudia's theme
CD ______ **CD 80477**
Telarc / Sep '97 / Conifer/BMG

PARTY'S OVER (Broadway Sings The Blues)
Broadway Casts
CD ______ **SK 53543**
Sony Classical / Jul '94 / Sony

PERFORMANCE
Webb, Marti & The Philharmonia Orchestra
CD ______ **OCRCD 6033**
First Night / Dec '95 / Pinnacle

PERFORMANCE
Paige, Elaine
I have dreamed / Anything goes / Heart don't change my mind / Another suitcase in another hall / Rose / Love hurts / What'll I do/Who / I only have eyes for you / He's out of my life / I know him so well / Don't cry for me Argentina / Memory
CD ______ **74321446802**
Camden / Feb '97 / BMG

PHANTOM OF THE OPERA (& Other Broadway Hits)
Florida Symphony Pops Orchestra
Cacavas, John *Con*
Phantom Of The Opera / Broadway Babies / Carousel / All That Jazz / Les Miserables / Kiss Me Kate overture / Porgy And Bess fantasy / Annie Get Your Gun medley
CD ______ **SION 18160**
Sion / Jul '97 / Direct

PORTRAIT OF BROADWAY, A
Pierce, Joshua & Dorothy Jonas
CD ______ **CDPC 5003**
Prestige / Aug '90 / Cadillac / Complete/ Pinnacle

PORTRAIT OF JUDY GARLAND, A
Garland, Judy
CD ______ **GALE 407**
Gallerie / May '97 / Disc / THE

PRINCE AND THE PAUPER, THE (& Other Film Music)
National Philharmonic Orchestra
Gerhardt, Charles *Con*
Revivers / Jane Eyre / Lost weekend / Between two worlds / Constant nymph / Prince and the pauper / Escape me never / Spectre of the rose / Madwoman of Chaillot / Cleopatra / Julie / Who's afraid of Virginia Woolf / Anne of the 1000 days / Henry V / Henry V suite
CD ______ **VSD 5207**
Varese Sarabande / '90 / Pinnacle

PRINCESS COLLECTION
CD ______ **WD 695002**
Disney Music & Stories / Nov '96 / Technicolor

PUBLIC TV'S GREATEST HITS
CD ______ **604702**
Silva Screen / Jul '92 / Koch / Silva Screen

PUTTIN' ON THE RITZ
Cincinnati Pops Orchestra
CD ______ **CD 80356**
Telarc / Nov '95 / Conifer/BMG

ROMANCING THE FILM
Rochester Pops Orchestra
Schifrin, Lalo *Con*
Tara's theme / Over the rainbow / As time goes by / Moon river / Lawrence Of Arabia / Lara's theme / Symphonic sketches / Love theme / Space medley / Time of my life / Medley / Around The World In 80 Days
CD ______ **SION 18210**
Sion / Jul '97 / Direct

ROMANTIC MOVIE THEMES
Mancini, Henry
Romeo and Juliet / Cinema Paradiso / Breakfast at Tiffany's / As time goes by / Once Upon A Time In America / Midnight Cowboy / Thorn Birds / Love Story / Godfather / Misty / Windmills of your mind / Adventurers / Evergreen / Medley / Shadow of your smile / Secret love / Raindrops keep falling on my head / Sweetheart tree / Mission/Gabriel's oboe / Untouchables
CD ______ **74321400602**
Camden / Sep '96 / BMG

RUTHIE HENSHALL ALBUM
Henshall, Ruthie
CD ______ **TRING 0022**
Tring / Nov '96 / Tring

SATURDAY MORNING CARTOONS
CD ______ **MCD 11348**
MCA / Jun '96 / BMG

SAX AND VIOLENCE
CD ______ **VSD 5562**
Varese Sarabande / Apr '95 / Pinnacle

SAX AT THE MOVIES
Unchained melody / Love is all around / Show me heaven / Because you loved me / How deep is your love / Kiss from a rose / Can you feel the love tonight / Somewhere out there / Everything I do (I do it for you) / Glory of love / Arthur's theme / (I've had) The time of my life / Up where we belong / When a man loves a woman / My funny valentine / I will always love you / Take my breath away / It must have been love / Waiting for a star to fall / Gangsta's paradise
CD ______ **CDVIP 181**
Virgin / Apr '97 / EMI

SCI-FI MOVIE THEMES
CD ______ **15153**
Laserlight / Mar '95 / Target/BMG

SCI-FI THEMES (16 Science Fiction Screen Hits)
London Theatre Orchestra
Star Wars / X-Files / Close encounters of the third kind / 2001 A space odysessy / Star Trek / Battlestar Galactica / Space 1999 / Blake 7 / Dune / Stargate / Blade Runner / Total Recall / War of the world's / Tomorrow people / Doctor Who / ET: The Extra Terrestrial
CD ______ **EMPRCD 655**
Emporio / Jun '96 / Disc

SCIENCE FICTION THEMES
Star Trek / X files / Close encounters of the third kind / ET / Star wars / Twilight zone / Robocop 2 / Superman / Timecop / Battleship galactica / Dune / Batdance / Stark Trek 3 / Flash / Blade runner / Terminator 2 / Empire strikes back / Star trek: The next generation
CD ______ **ECD 3225**
K-Tel / Jan '95 / K-Tel

SCREEN ACTION
Power Pack Orchestra
Superman / Miami Vice / Magnum PI / Hunter / Professionals / Starsky and Hutch / Shoestring / Hawaii Five-O / Dempsey and Makepeace / Indiana Jones and the Temple of Doom / TJ Hooker / James Bond / New Avengers theme / Rockford files / Street hawk / Good, the bad and the ugly / A-Team / Knight rider / Crazy like a fox / Mike Hammer theme / Fall guy / Sweeney / Chinese detective / Highway patrol / Airwolf
CD ______ **CDMFP 6017**
Music For Pleasure / Apr '88 / EMI

SCREEN DANCE MANIA
Worsley, John
Doctor Who / X Files / Star Wars / Hawaii five-O / Kojak / Mission Impossible / Prisoner / Batman / Close encounters of the third kind / Starsky and Hutch / Star Trek / Dallas / James Bond theme / Baywatch
CD ______ **3036000802**
Carlton / Mar '97 / Carlton

SCREEN HITS (40 Orchestral TV & Film Themes)
2CD ______ **DEMPCD 014**
Emporio / Mar '96 / Disc

SCREEN SINATRA
Sinatra, Frank
From here to eternity / Three coins in the fountain / Young at heart / Just one of those things / Someone to watch over me / Not as a stranger / Tender trap / Wait for me (Johnny Concho theme) / All the way / Chicago / Monique-Song from Kings Go Forth / They came to Cordura / To love and be loved / High hopes / All my tomorrows / It's all right with me / C'est magnifique / Dream
CD ______ **CDMFP 6052**
Music For Pleasure / Mar '89 / EMI

SCREEN THEMES
Royal Philharmonic Orchestra
Scott, John *Con*
Die Hard / Big / Who Framed Roger Rabbit / Milagro Beanfield War / Beetlejuice / Crossing Delancey / Cocoon - the Return / Madame Sousatzka / Criminal Law / Nightmare on Elm Street IV / Betrayed / Coming to America / Masquerade / Da
CD ______ **VSD 5208**
Varese Sarabande / Dec '88 / Pinnacle

SCREEN THEMES '93
Garson, Michael
Jurassic park / Schindler's list / Indecent proposal / Fugitive / Age of innocence / Shadowlands / Pelican brief / Piano (Heart asks for pleasure) / Bleu / Heaven and earth / Firm / MrdDoubtfire (Snow's over) / Philadelphia (Streets of Philadelphia) / Sleepless in Seattle
CD ______ **77009**
Discovery / Jun '94 / Warner Music

SECRET AGENT FILE
Norman, Neil & his Orchestra
Reilly, ace of spies / Octopussy / I spy / Rockford files / Man from UNCLE / Casino Royale / Ipcress file / Get smart / Thunderball / Spy who came in from the cold
CD ______ **GNPD 2166**
GNP Crescendo / Jan '89 / ZYX

SHAKESPEARE ON BROADWAY
CD ______ **VSD 5622**
Varese Sarabande / Jul '96 / Pinnacle

SHAKESPEARE'S MUSICK (Songs & Dances From Shakespeare's Plays)
Musicians Of The Globe
Pickett, Philip *Con*
Hollis berrie / Daphne / My robin is to the greenwood gone / Tickle my toe / It was a lover and his lasse / Kemp's jig / Take o take those lips away / Bonny sweet Robin / Farewell dear love / Tarletones riserrectione / Hold lingel hold / How should I your true love know / Walsingham / Get your hense for I must go / La coranto / La coranto / Hark hark the lark / La volta / La volta / Willow song (the poor soul sat sighing) / Robin / O mistress mine / O mistress myne / Full fathom five / Where the bee sucks / Can she excuse / Frog galliard / Go from my window
CD ______ **4466872**
Philips / Jun '97 / PolyGram

SHALL WE DANCE (Classic Dance Hits From The West End & Broadway)
Can can: *English National Opera Company* / Shall we dance: *Lee, Christopher & Valerie Masterson* / I could have danced all night: *Olafimihan, Tinuke & Company* / Oh look at me: *Matthews, Christina* / I got rhythm: *Shore, Julia* / Too darn hot: *Collis, Paul & Company* / Won't you charleston with me: *Newent, Bob & Linda-Mae Brewer* / Dance a little closer: *Robertson, Liz* / Lambeth walk: *Lindsay, Robert & Mary Ann Plankett/ Company* / Dance at the gym: *National Symphony Orchestra* / On your toes: *Andreas, Christine* / Varsity drag: *Morrison, Ann & Company*
CD ______ **SHOWCD 029**
Showtime / Oct '96 / Disc / THE

SHERLOCK HOLMES (Classic Themes From 221B Baker Street)
Sherlock Holmes / Seven percent solution / Adventures of Sherlock Holmes / Study in terror / Universal Holmes / Young Sherlock Holmes / I never do anything twice / Masks of death / Hound of the Baskervilles / Dressed to kill / Private life of Sherlock Holmes / Without a clue
CD ______ **VSD 5692**
Varese Sarabande / Aug '96 / Pinnacle

SHOOT 'EM UPS
CD ______ **VSD 5666**
Varese Sarabande / May '96 / Pinnacle

SHOW STOPPERS
CD ______ **95902**
Silva Screen / Feb '90 / Koch / Silva Screen

SHOW STOPPERS (18 Unforgettable Songs...18 Unforgettable Shows)
Starsound Singers & Orchestra
Music of the night / Memory / If ever I would leave you / Send in the clowns / America / If I were a rich man / I enjoy being a girl / Some enchanted evening / If my friends could see me now / Cabaret / Good morning starshine / I don't know how to love him / Stranger in paradise / I could have danced all night / Sound of music / Hello young lovers / I can't give you anything but love / There's no business like show business
CD ______ **ECD 3133**
K-Tel / Jan '95 / K-Tel

SHOW STOPPERS - TIMELESS HITS FROM THE MUSICALS
Big spender / Consider yourself / Cabaret / Somewhere / You're the one that I want / Send in the clowns / Ol' man river / Oklahoma / Windy city / I won't send roses / I could write a book / Memory
CD ______ **SHOWCD 018**
Showtime / Feb '95 / Disc / THE

SHOWSTOPPERS (The Greatest Show Songs)
CD ______ **DINCD 118**
Dino / Nov '95 / Pinnacle

SHOWSTOPPERS (Hits From The Musicals)
I don't know how to love him / Summer nights / Send in thee clowns / All that jazz / What I did for love / Don't cry for me Argentina / Take that look off your face / Any dream will do / Memory / I am what I am / Only he / I know him so well / Music of the night / Love changes everything / On my own / Last night of the world
CD _______ 11983
Music / Feb '96 / Target/BMG

SHOWSTOPPERS
BBC Big Band
CD _______ BBB 004
BBC Big Band / Nov '96 / Jazz Music

SHOWTIME
4CD _______ CDPK 417
Charly / Oct '93 / Koch

SMASH HITS OF BROADWAY
CD _______ CDTEZ 7005
TER / Jan '95 / Koch

SO IN LOVE - SAMUEL RAMEY ON BROADWAY
Ramey, Samuel & London Studio Symphony Orchestra
Stratta, Ettore *Con*
CD _______ 4509908652
Teldec Classics / Jan '95 / Warner Music

SOME LIKE IT HOT
Monroe, Marilyn
Diamonds are a girl's best friend / Man chases a girl / Every baby needs a da da daddy / Happy birthday Mr. President / Incurably romantic / Down in the meadow / Some like it hot / I found a dream / Anyone can see I love you / Specialization / Heatwave / Ladies of the chorus / When I fall in love / Let's make love / Bye bye baby / Fine romance / One silver dollar / That old black magic / There's no business like show business / I wanna be loved by you
CD _______ HADCD 153
Javelin / May '94 / Henry Hadaway / THE

SONGS FROM SIX FILMS
Garland, Judy
3CD _______ CIN 016
IMP / Sep '96 / ADA / Discovery

SONGS FROM THE MOVIES
Astaire, Fred
No strings / Isn't this a lovely day (to be caught in the rain) / Top hat, white tie and tails / Cheek to cheek / Piccolino / We saw the sea / Let yourself go / I'd rather lead a band / I'm putting all my eggs in one basket / Let's face the music and dance / Pick yourself up / Way you look tonight / Fine romance / Bojangles of Harlem / Never gonna dance / Beginner's luck / Slap that bass / They all laughed / Let's call the whole thing off / They can't take that away from me / Shall we dance / I can't be bothered now / Things are looking up / Foggy day / Nice work if you can get it
CD _______ PPCD 78115
Past Perfect / Feb '95 / Glass Gramophone Co.

SONGS FROM THE MUSICALS
Grease / Summer nights / Hopelessly devoted to you / You're the one that I want / Beauty school dropout / Look at me I'm Sandra Dee / Greased lightning / It's raining on Prom night / Alone at the Drive-In movie / Blue moon / Rock'n'roll is here to stay / Those magic changes / Hound dog / Born to hand jive / Tears on my pillow / Mooning / Freddy my love / Rock'n'roll party Queen / There are worse things I could do / Look at me I'm Sandra Dee (reprise) / We go together / Witch Doctor / Who put the bomp / Grease (reprise) / Ready Teddy / Rock around with Ollie Vee / Changing all those changes / That'll be the day / Blue days / Everyday / Not fade away / Peggy Sue / Words of love / Oh boy / True love ways / Chantilly lace / Maybe baby / Heartbeat / La bamba / Raining in my heart / It doesn't matter anymore / Rave on / Fame / Out here on my own / Hot lunch jam / Dogs in the yard / Red light / It's OK to call you mine / Never alone / Ralph and Monty (Dressing room piano) / I sing the body electric / Wipeout / It's a man's, man's, man's world / Great balls of fire / Don't let me be misunderstood / Good vibrations / Teenager in love / Young girl / She's not there / All shook up / Who's sorry now / Robot man / Shake, rattle and roll / Go now / Only the lonely / Young ones / We gotta get out of this place / Wipeout (reprise) / Mr. Spaceman / Monster mash / Great balls of fire (reprise)
4CD _______ QUAD 014
Tring / Nov '96 / Tring

SONGS FROM THE MUSICALS
Good morning starshine: *Clark, Petula* / If I were a rich man: *Topol* / Impossible dream: *Blessed, Brian* / Lullaby of Broadway: *Jones, Paul* / I don't know how to love him: *Webb, Marti* / Don't cry for me Argentina: *Scott, Jacki* / Another suitcase in another hall: *Moore, Claire* / Superstar: *Cousins, Robin* / I've got rhythm: *Craven, Gemma* / Begin the beguine: *Vaughan, Frankie* / I'm gonna wash that man right out of my hair: *Langford, Bonnie* / Happy talk: *Madoc, Ruth* / Edelweiss: *Hill, Vince* / Shall we dance: *Skellern, Peter* / Pick a pocket or two: *Skellern, Peter* / Happy endings: *Spinetti, Victor*
CD _______ SUMCD 4128
Sound & Media / Jun '97 / Sound & Media

SONGS FROM THE SHOWS
Treorchy Male Choir
CD _______ CDMFP 6364
Music For Pleasure / May '97 / EMI

SONGS FROM THE STAGE & SCREEN
Garland, Judy
CD _______ MCCD 101
MCI Music / May '93 / Disc / THE

SONGS OF THE MUSICALS
Phantom of the opera/Music of the night / Memory / Don't cry for me Argentina / Cabaret / Tonight / Climb every mountain / If I were a rich man / I could have danced all night / Last night of the world / You'll never walk alone / I dreamed a dream / Some enchanted evening / Big spender / What I did for love / Almost like being in love / There's no business like showbusiness
CD _______ EMPRCD 901
Emporio / Jan '97 / Disc

SOPRANO IN HOLLYWOOD
Garrett, Lesley & BBC Concert Orchestra
Bateman, Paul *Con*
Lover / Danny boy / Love is where you find it / Smoke gets in your eyes / With a song in my heart / Long ago and far away / One kiss / Man I love / Love is here to stay / Love walked in
CD _______ SILKTVCD 2
Silva Classics / Oct '96 / Koch / Silva Screen

SOUND OF HOLLYWOOD, THE
Hollywood Bowl Symphony Orchestra
Mauceri, John *Con*
CD _______ 4464992
Philips / Feb '96 / PolyGram

SOUND OF MUSICALS, THE (Piano Selections From The Greatest Shows)
Laurence, Zack
Sound Of Music medley / West Side story medley / Fiddler On The Roof medley / My Fair Lady medley / Guys and Dolls medley / South Pacific medley
CD _______ 305812
Hallmark / Oct '96 / Carlton

SOUNDS ORCHESTRAL MEETS JAMES BOND
Sounds Orchestral
Thunderball / Solitaire / Goldfinger / Mr. Kiss Kiss Bang Bang / Blues for pussy / Mr. Oddjob / Moonshot / James Bond theme / Spectre / From Russia With Love / Kissy Suzuki / 007 theme
CD _______ NEBCD 908
Sequel / Sep '96 / BMG

SPACE AND BEYOND (The Ultimate Sci-Fi Movie Themes Album)
2001: A Space Odyssey / Apollo 13 / Right Stuff / Species / Lifeforce / Alien / Capricorn One / Cocoon / Black Hole / Star Wars/ Empire Strikes Back / Enemy Mine / Close Encounters Of The Third Kind / Star Trek I / Star Trek II: The Wrath Of Kahn / Star Trek IV: The Voyage Home / Star Trek V: The Final Frontier / Star Trek VI: The Undiscovered Country / Star Trek: Deep Space Nine/ Star Trek Generations / Star Trek: The Next Generation / Star Trek: Voyager / Star Trek
2CD _______ FILMXCD 185
Silva Screen / Feb '97 / Koch / Silva Screen

SPACE MOVIE THEMES (Star Wars/ Empire Strikes Back/Return Of The Jedi/etc)
London Symphony Orchestra
CD _______ HRM 7001
Hermes / Jan '86 / Nimbus

SPACE THEMES
Starlight Orchestra
ET / Close Encounters Of The Third Kind / Star Trek / Empire Strikes Back / Star Wars / Flash / Return Of The Jedi / Star Trek II / Cantina band / Star beyond time / Conversation / Star Trek III / Prophecy theme / Eve of the war / Star Trek / Yoda's theme
CD _______ QED 169
Tring / Nov '96 / Tring

SPAGHETTI WESTERNS VOL.1
2CD _______ DRGCD 32905
DRG / Jun '95 / Discovery / New Note/ Pinnacle

SPECTACULAR WORLD OF CLASSIC FILM SCORES
National Philharmonic Orchestra
Gerhardt, Charles *Con*
Studio fanfares / Star Wars / Captain Blood / Now, Voyager / Gone With the Wind / Elizabeth and Essex / Peyton Place / Citizen Kane / Caine Mutiny / Knights of the Round Table / Objective Burma / Guns of Navarone / Julius Caesar / Thing from Another World / King of the Khyber Rifles / Salome
CD _______ GD 82792
RCA Victor / '92 / BMG

SPIELBERG CONNECTION, THE
Fantasia
Jaws / Arachnophobia / Back To The Future / Indiana Jones And The Temple Of Doom / Always / Close Encounters Of The Third Kind / Hook / Schindler's List / Raiders Of The Lost Ark / Color Purple / Casper / ET / 1941 / Empire Of The Sun / Indiana Jones And The Last Crusade / Jurassic Park
CD _______ 307632
Hallmark / Jul '97 / Carlton

STAGE BY STAGE
Conley, Brian
2CD _______ TCD 2870
Telstar / Oct '96 / BMG

STALLONE (Music From The Films Of Sylvester Stallone)
Rocky: *London Screen Orchestra* / FIST: *City Of Prague Philharmonic Orchestra* / Paradise Alley: *London Screen Orchestra* / Rocky II: *London Screen Orchestra* / Nighthawks: *London Screen Orchestra* / Rocky III / First Blood: *City Of Prague Philharmonic Orchestra* / Rambo - First Blood II: *City Of Prague Philharmonic Orchestra* / Cobra: *Ayres, Mark* / Over The Top: *Ayres, Mark* / Rambo III: *City Of Prague Philharmonic Orchestra* / Lock Up: *Ayres, Mark* / Cliffhanger: *City Of Prague Philharmonic Orchestra*
CD _______ FILMCD 139
Silva Screen / Nov '93 / Koch / Silva Screen

STANDING ROOM ONLY (Broadway Favourites)
Hadley, Jerry & American Theatre Orchestra
Gemignani, Paul *Con*
CD _______ 09026613702
RCA Victor / Jul '93 / BMG

STAR TRACKS
Silver Screen Orchestra
Star Wars / Empire strikes back / Imperial march / Luke and Leia / March of the Jedi Knights / Yoda's theme / Cantina band / Star Trek / Wrath of Kahn / Search for Spock star beyond time / Battlestar Galactica / Cyclon trap / Destruction of peace / Red nova / Let's go home
CD _______ DC 881572
Disky / Aug '97 / Disky / THE

STAR WARS/CLOSE ENCOUNTERS OF THE THIRD KIND (& Other Space Themes/Disco Galactic Themes)
Love, Geoff & His Orchestra
Star Wars / UFO / Star Trek / Barbarella / Space 1999 / Also sprach zarathustra / Things To Come / Thunderbirds / Star Wars / Dr. Who / Mars / Bringer of war / Close Encounters of The Third Kind / Logan's Run / Flight Fantastic / Time Machine / Star Wars / Blake Seven / Omega Man
CD _______ CDMFP 6395
Music For Pleasure / Jun '97 / EMI

STARRING FRED ASTAIRE
Astaire, Fred
Top hat, white tie and tails / Cheek to cheek / Piccolino / No strings / Pick yourself up / Way you look tonight / Fine romance / Let's call the whole thing off / They can't take that away from me / Shall we dance / I can't be bothered now / Things are looking up / Foggy day / Nice work if you can get it / Let yourself go / Let's face the music and dance / Fascinating rhythm / Night and day / I used to be colour blind / Change partners
CD _______ CD 405
Entertainers / Oct '96 / Target/BMG

STARS OF STAGE AND SCREEN, THE
Donkey serenade: *Jones, Allan* / You've done something to my heart: *Laye, Evelyn* / Night and day: *Astaire, Fred* / Indian love call: *Astaire, Fred* / My heart belongs to daddy: *Martin, Mary* / Louise: *Chevalier, Maurice* / Amapola: *Durbin, Deanna* / Goodnight vienna: *Buchanan, Jack* / Let yourself go: *Rogers, Ginger* / One night of love: *Moore, Grace* / Little whiteroom: *Day, Frances & John Mills* / Inka-dinka-doo: *Durante, Jimmy* / Lovely to look at: *Dunne, Irene* / I'll see you again: *Coward, Sir Noel* / Falling in love again: *Dietrich, Marlene* / I'll get by: *Haymes, Dick* / I can give you the starlight: *Ellis, Mary* / Experiment: *Lawrence, Gertrude* / Solomon: *Welch, Elizabeth* / Thanks for the memory: *Hope, Bob & Shirley Ross* / Dancing on the ceiling: *Matthews, Jessie* / I get a kick out of you: *Merman, Ethel*
CD _______ PASTCD 7016
Flapper / Mar '97 / Pinnacle

STARS OF THE MUSICAL STAGE, THE (Stars Of The West End & Broadway Perform Hit Songs From The Hit Shows)
Wilkommen: *Pryce, Jonathan & Company* / Any dream will do: *Barrowman, John* / If I ruled the world: *Secombe, Harry* / I'm getting married in the morning: *Hoskins, Bob* / Don't cry for me Argentina: *Friedman, Maria* / Coloured lights: *Minnelli, Liza* / How to handle a woman: *Harris, Richard* / I don't believe in heroes anymore: *Bakula, Scott* / Science fiction: *Dobson, Anita* / Send in the clowns: *Phillips, Sam* / Unusual way: *Paige, Elaine*
CD _______ SHOWCD 040
Showtime / Oct '96 / Disc / THE

STORY GOES ON, THE
Callaway, Liz
CD _______ VSD 5585
Varese Sarabande / Oct '95 / Pinnacle

SUPPLY AND DEMAND (Songs by Brecht, Weill & Eisler)
Krause, Dagmar
CD _______ HNCD 1317
Hannibal / Mar '86 / ADA / Vital

SYMPHONIC SUITE OF THE ANIMATED CLASSICS
Kingston Symphony
CD _______ MACD 2501
Hindsight / Mar '95 / Jazz Music / Target/ BMG

SYNTHESIZER AT THE MOVIES
Also sprach Zarathustra / Raiders march / Claudia's theme / Chase / (Everything I do) I do it for you / Love is all around / Close Encounters Of The Third Kind / Goldeneye / John Dunbar theme / Mission / Deerhunter / Streets of Philadelphia / Jaws / Tubular bells / ET / Star Wars / Silence Of The Lambs / Love theme / Mission Impossible / Bladerunner / Missing / Cockeye's song / Rain man / 1492 Conquest Of Paradise / I will always love you / It must have been love / Chariots of fire / Axel F / Heart asks pleasure first/The Promise / Out Of Africa / Second time / Mutiny On The Bounty / Take my breath away / Unchained melody / Star Trek / Gonna fly now
2CD _______ 330292
Hallmark / Mar '97 / Carlton

SYNTHESIZER HITS (TV Themes)
CD _______ MU 5006
Musketeer / Oct '92 / Disc

SYNTHESIZER HITS (Film Themes)
CD _______ MU 5003
Musketeer / Oct '92 / Disc

SYNTHESIZER HITS (James Bond Themes)
CD _______ MU 5004
Musketeer / Oct '92 / Disc

SYNTHESIZER HITS OF CINEMA AND TV
CD _______ 22528
Music / Jul '95 / Target/BMG

TARANTINO CONNECTION, THE
Interview (Spoken word): *Tarantino, Quentin* / Miserlou: *Dale, Dick & His Del-Tones* / Dark night: *Blasters* / Little green bag: *Baker, George Selection* / Graceland: *Sexton, Charlie* / Girl, you'll be a woman soon: *Urge Overkill* / Waiting for the miracle: *Cohen, Leonard* / Little bitty tear: *Ives, Burl* / Interview (2) (Spoken word): *Tarantino, Quentin* / Stuck in the middle with you: *Stealer's Wheel* / You never can tell: *Berry, Chuck* / Love is (the tender trap): *Palmer, Robert* / Sweet Jane: *Cowboy Junkies* / Six blade knife: *Dire Straits* / Foolish heart: *Mavericks* / Vertigo: *Combustible Edison*
CD _______ MCD 80325
MCA / Oct '96 / BMG

TASTE OF MUSIC, A (Music From The BBC TV Series)
Rick Stein: A taste of the sea / Carluccio's: Italian Feast / Far Flung Floyd / Floyd on Italy / Floyd On Africa
CD _______ V 1021
Voyager / Apr '97 / Complete/Pinnacle

TEENAGE TV
Countdown Rock Band
We will rock you / Another one bites the dust / We are the champions / Beverly Hills 90210 / Baywatch / Simpsons / I'll be there for you / Heartbreak High / Power Rangers / Holding out for a hero / Action speaks louder than words / All the way to Heaven / Happy Days / Due South / Brady Bunch / Roseanne / Star Trek: The Next Generation / Lois and Clark / Gladiators / On the inside
CD _______ QED 078
Tring / Nov '96 / Tring

TELEVISION'S GREATEST HITS
CD _______ GRF 198
Tring / Jan '93 / Tring

TELEVISION'S GREATEST HITS VOL.1 (TV Themes From The 1950's And 1960's)
CD _______ 0022702CIN
Edel / May '97 / Pinnacle

TELEVISION'S GREATEST HITS VOL.2 (TV Themes From The 1970's And 1980's)
CD _______ 0022712CIN
Edel / May '97 / Pinnacle

TELEVISION'S GREATEST THEMES
Starlight Orchestra/Singers
Miami Vice / LA Law / MASH / Cheers / Fame / Dynasty / Happy Days / Dallas / Star Trek / Quincy / Rockford Files / Magnum / Moonlighting / Reilly, Ace Of Spies / Superman / Kojak / Mah Na Mah Na / Hawaii 5-O / High Chaparral / Bonanza / Hill Street Blues / A-Team / Charlie's Angels
CD _______ QED 066
Tring / Nov '96 / Tring

TEST CARD CLASSICS VOL.1 (The Girl, The Doll, The Music)
CD _______ FBCD 2000
Chandos / Aug '96 / Chandos

TEST CARD CLASSICS VOL.2 (Big Band Width)
Fings ain't what they used to be: *Brandenburg Philharmonic Orchestra* / Smiling fortune: *Martin, Alexander Orchestra* / Story of my life: *Winters, George Orchestra* / Lucky bounce: *Skymasters* / Here in a smokey room: *Keller, Otto Band* / Waltz express: *Scott, Joe Orchestra* / Slinky: *Basshoppers* / Carry me back to Old Virginny: *Haensch, Delle Band* / Beat in: *Pleyer, Frank & His*

Orchestra / Alamo: *Palmer, Joe* / Small town: *Gardner, William Orchestra* / Take off: *Monza, Henry Orchestra* / Meet me on the bridge: *Skymasters* / Happy walk: *Pleyer, Frank & His Orchestra* / Charleston-time: *Pleyer, Frank & His Orchestra* / Apron strings: *Hatter, Hans & His Orchestra* / Scotch broth: *Brandenburg Philharmonic Orchestra* / Tele-vision: *Haensch, Delle Band* / Concerto grosso '67: *Landy, Eric* / High ball: *Keller, Otto Band* / Hallelujah, honey: *Valdor, Frank Orchester* / Soho swing: *Peters, Walt* / Daisy: *Peters, Walt* / Walking on the shore: *Taormina, Franco* / Hello Lissy: *Palmer, Joe* / Craig Hill surprise: *Keller, Otto Band* / Post haste: *Brasshoppers* / Swingin' affair: *Brandenburg Philharmonic Orchestra* / Jeff's special: *Haskey, Jeff* / Indian boots: *Winters, George Orchestra*
CD ____ **FBCD 2001**
Chandos / May '97 / Chandos

THAT'S ENTERTAINMENT (The Best Of The MGM Musicals)
That's entertainment: *Astaire, Fred & Jack Buchanan* / Get happy: *Garland, Judy* / From this moment on: *Miller, Ann/Bobby Van/Tommy Rall/Bob Fosse* / Over the rainbow: *Garland, Judy* / Ol' man river: *Warfield, William* / Singin' in the rain: *Kelly, Gene* / Trolley song: *Garland, Judy* / Varsity drag: *Allyson, June & Peter Lawford* / Easter parade: *Garland, Judy & Fred Astaire* / All of you: *Astaire, Fred* / On the Atchison, Topeka & the Santa Fe: *Garland, Judy* / Honeysuckle rose: *Horne, Lena* / I like myself: *Astaire, Fred* / Hallelujah: *Martin, Tony/Vic Damone/Russ Tamblyn/Jubilaires* / There's no business like showbusiness: *Hutton, Betty & Howard Keel*
CD ____ **CDODEON 21**
Soundtracks / Sep '96 / EMI

THAT'S MUSICAL
CD ____ **12554**
Laserlight / Jun '95 / Target/BMG

THEATRE ORGAN FAVOURITES
Cabaret / Exodus / Mack the knife / Mister Sandman / That old black magic / Georgy girl / All the way / Somewhere my love / Man and a woman / Never on a Sunday / Impossible dream / Everybody loves someone
CD ____ **HADCD 216**
Spotlight On / Jun '97 / Henry Hadaway

THEATRE ROYAL DRURY LANE
Rose Marie / Door of my dreams / Desert song / One alone / Can't help lovin' dat man / Ol' man river / Why do I love you / Lover come back to me / Wanting you / March of the musketeers / You are my heart's delight / Keep smiling / Hand in hand / Fold your wings / Shine through my dreams / Music in May / Why is there ever goodbye / Rose of England / River God / Waltz of my heart / I can give you the starlight
CD ____ **CDHD 233**
Happy Days / Sep '95 / Conifer/BMG

THEMES AND INSTRUMENTALS
Albatross: *Fleetwood Mac* / Baby elephant walk: *Mancini, Henry* / Good, The Bad And The Ugly: *Montenegro, Hugo* / Peter Gunn: *Mancini, Henry* / James Bond: *Barry, John* / Stranger on the shore: *Bilk, Acker* / Entertainer: *Hamlisch, Marvin* / Light flight: *Pentangle* / Harry's game: *Clannad* / Rocket to the moon: *Brickman, Jim* / Inspector Morse / Crocket's theme: *Hammer, Jan* / Miami Vice: *Hammer, Jan* / Scarborough Fair: *Intune* / La serenissima: *Veneziano, Rondo* / Mon amour: *Thore, Frank* / Petite fleur: *Barber, Chris & Monty Sunshine* / Summer Place: *Faith, Percy* / Cherry ppink and apple blossom white: *Prado, Parez* / Pink Panther: *Mancini, Henry* / Light my fire: *Booker T & The MG's* / Between the lines: *Lindes, Hal* / Aria: *Bilk, Acker* / Sheperd's lament: *Zamphir, Georgi* / Thorn Birds: *Burgon, Geoffrey* / From Russia With Love: *Barry, John* / Snowflakes are dancing: *Tomita* / Windmills of your mind: *Legrand, Michel* / Midnight in Moscow: *Ball, Kenny* / Hang 'Em High: *Montenegro, Hugo* / Sukiyaki: *Ball, Kenny*
2CD ____ **RCACD 220**
RCA / Jul '97 / BMG

THEMES FROM ACADEMY AWARD WINNERS
Gerhardt, Charles/Arthur Fiedler/Henry Mancini/David Raksin *Con*
Star Wars / Tom Jones / Casablanca / Ben Hur / Breakfast at Tiffany's / Exodus / West Side Story / Airport / High Noon / Laura / Lawrence of Arabia / Doctor Zhivago / Gone With the Wind
CD ____ **09026609662**
RCA Victor / Jan '92 / BMG

THEMES FROM SUSPENSE MOVIES
CD ____ **873040**
Milan / Jan '95 / Conifer/BMG / Silva Screen

THEMES FROM THE SIXTIES
Avengers: *Grave* / To Sir with love: *Studio 68* / On her Majesty's secret sevice: *Editors* / Prisoner: *Kitch* / Man in a suitcase: *Ministry of Defiance* / Up the junction: *Eleanor Rigby* / You only live twice: *Eleanor Rigby* / Man from UNCLE: *Grave* / Mission impossible: *Ministry of Defiance* / Captain Zeppo: *Beatboy* / Stingray: *C.B.U.* / Addams family: *Perestroika* / Batman: *Waterloo Sunset Allstars*
CD ____ **FLEG 1CD**
Future Legend / Mar '93 / Future Legend / Pinnacle

THEMES FROM THE SIXTIES VOL. 3
CD ____ **FLEG 5CD**
Future Legend / Sep '95 / Future Legend / Pinnacle

THEMES FROM THE SIXTIES VOL.2
CD ____ **FLEGCD 2**
Future Legend / Mar '94 / Future Legend / Pinnacle

THEMES OF HORROR (14 Spine Chillers)
Fly / Thing / Fog / Carrie / Psycho / Poltergeist III / Exorcist / Hell Raiser / Halloween / Amityville Horror / Friday The 13th / Vertigo / Silence Of The Lambs / Rosemary's Baby
CD ____ **EMPRCD 628**
Emporio / Jun '96 / Disc

THEMES UNLIMITED
3CD ____ **EMTBX 309**
Emporio / Aug '97 / Disc

THERE'S NO BUSINESS LIKE SHOW BUSINESS (Broadway Showstoppers) Original Broadway/London/Film Casts
CD ____ **SK 53541**
Sony Broadway / Jul '94 / Sony

THERE'S NO BUSINESS LIKE SHOW BUSINESS (Songs From The Hit Musicals)
There's no business like show business / If I were a rich man / We're in the money / Send in the clowns / Boy like that / Guys and dolls / I know him so well / Hello Dolly / Food glorious food / Pick a pocket or two / Pinball wizard / See me feel me / Age of Aquarius / Wash that man right out of my hair / Some enchanted evening / There ain't nothing like a dame / Wanderin' star / Do re mi / Prelude and the Sound Of Music / Greased lightning / We go together / Summer holiday / Summer holiday
CD ____ **74321479662**
RCA / Jun '97 / BMG

THERE'S NOTHIN' LIKE A DAME - BROADWAY'S BROADS
Broadway Casts
CD ____ **SK 53539**
Sony Broadway / Jul '94 / Sony

THIS IS CULT FICTION
Little green bag: *Baker, George Selection* / Misirlou: *Dale, Dick & His Del-Tones* / Mission impossible: *Schifrin, Lalo* / Shaft: *Hayes, Isaac* / Jungle boogie: *Kool & The Gang* / Man from UNCLE: *Montenegro, Hugo* / Everybody's talkin': *Nilsson, Harry* / Stuck in the middle with you: *Stealer's Wheel* / Blue velvet: *Vinton, Bobby* / Touch of evil: *Mancini, Henry* / We have all the time in the world: *Armstrong, Louis* / James Bond: *Barry, John Seven* / Joe 90: *Gray, Barry Orchestra* / Harder they come: *Cliff, Jimmy* / Here comes the hotstepper: *Kamoze, Ini* / Guaglione: *Prado, Perez 'Prez'* / Play dead: *Arnold, David & Bjork* / Avengers: *Johnson, Laurie Orchestra* / You never can tell: *Berry, Chuck* / Rumble: *Wray, Link* / Saint: *Reed, Les* / Hawaii five o: *Ventures* / Streets of San Francisco: *Gregory, John* / Long good Friday: *Monkman, Francis* / Sweeney: *Power Pack Orchestra* / Dangerman: *Leaper, Bob Orchestra* / Twin peaks: *Baladamenti, Angelo* / All the animals come out at night: *Herrmann, Bernard*
CD ____ **VTCD 59**
Virgin / Aug '95 / EMI

THIS IS CULT FICTION - THIS IS SON OF CULT FICTION
Real me: *Who* / Whole lotta love: *CCS* / All right now: *Free* / Lust for life: *Pop, Iggy* / Theme from the "A" Team: *Post, Mike* / Born to be wild: *Steppenwolf* / Smoke on the water: *Deep Purple* / People are strange: *Echo & The Bunnymen* / Werewolves of London: *Zevon, Warren* / Lions and the cucumbers: *Vampiros Sound Incorporation* / Porpoise song (theme from "Head"): *Monkees* / White rabbit: *Jefferson Airplane* / Venus in furs: *Velvet Underground* / Girl, you'll be a woman soon: *Urge Overkill* / Be bop a lula: *Vincent, Gene* / Green onions: *Booker T & The MG's* / Louie, Louie: *Kingsmen* / Bring down the birds: *Hancock, Herbie* / Theme from Northern Exposure: *Swchwartz, David* / Duelling banjos: *Weissberg, Eric & Steve Mandell* / Suicide is painless: *Mandel, Jamie* / Calling you: *Steele, Jevetta* / Cavatina: *Williams, John*
CD ____ **VTCD 114**
Virgin TV / Feb '97 / EMI

THIS IS CULT FICTION - THIS IS THE RETURN OF CULT FICTION
Professionals / Enter The Dragon / Gotcha / Six Million Dollar Man / Charlie's Angels / Wonderwoman / Dr. Who / Chase Scene / Detectives / Magnum PI / Get Smart / Dave Allen At Large / Kojak / Tales Of The Unexpected / Angela / Fly Me To The Moon / Gallery / Last Tango In Paris / Hill Street Blues / North By North West / Once Upon A Time In America / Budgie / Taxi Driver / White Horses / Park Avenue Beat / Saint Orchestra / I Dream Of Jeannie / Man About The House / On The Buses / World Of Sport / Bewitched / Minder / Please Sir / Grange Hill / Ski Sunday / Music From Roobarb & Custard
2CD ____ **VTCD 112**
Virgin / Sep '96 / EMI

THOSE FABULOUS BUSBY BERKELEY MUSICALS (Radio Versions From The Thirties)
CD ____ **CDMR 1161**
Radiola / Jan '91 / Pinnacle

THOSE MAGNIFICENT MGM MUSICALS VOL.1 (1939-1952)
Over the rainbow: *Garland, Judy* / Ol' man river: *Peterson, Caleb* / Look for the silver lining: *Garland, Judy* / Leave it to Jane and Cleopatterer: *Allyson, June* / Can't help lovin' dat man: *Horne, Lena* / Who: *Garland, Judy* / Best things in life are free: *Allyson, June & Peter Lawford* / Pass that peace pipe: *McCracken, Joan* / Lucky in love: *Marshall, Pat/Peter Lawford/June Allyson* / Varsity drag: *Allyson, June & Peter Lawford* / Steppin' out with my baby: *Astaire, Fred* / Fella with an umbrella: *Garland, Judy & Peter Lawford* / Shaking the blues: *Miller, Ann* / Couple of swells: *Garland, Judy & Fred Astaire* / Easter parade: *Garland, Judy & Fred Astaire* / Manhattan: *Rooney, Mickey* / Johnny one note: *Garland, Judy* / Lady is a tramp: *Horne, Lena* / I wish I were in love again: *Rooney, Mickey & Judy Garland* / Where or when: *Horne, Lena* / Thou swell: *Allyson, June* / Be a clown: *Garland, Judy & Gene Kelly* / Love of my life: *Garland, Judy* / I don't care: *Garland, Judy* / Meet me tonight in dreamland: *Garland, Judy* / Play that barber shop chord: *Garland, Judy & The King's Men* / Last night when we were young: *Garland, Judy* / Put your arms around me honey: *Garland, Judy* / Merry Christmas / Pagan love song: *Keel, Howard* / House of singing bamboo: *Keel, Howard* / Who's sorry now: *De Haven, Gloria* / I wanna be loved by you: *Kane, Helen* / Nevertheless I'm in love with you: *Astaire, Fred/Red Skelton/Anita Ellis* / I love you so much: *Dahl, Arlene* / Where did you get that girl: *Astaire, Fred & Anita Ellis* / Get happy: *Garland, Judy* / (Howdy neighbour) happy harvest: *Garland, Judy* / You wonderful you: *Kelly, Gene* / Friendly star: *Garland, Judy* / Heavenly music: *Kelly, Gene & Phil Silvers* / If you feel like singing, sing: *Garland, Judy* / Dig dig dig dig for your dinner: *Kelly, Gene & Phil Silvers* / Aba daba honeymoon: *Carpenter, Carleton & Debbie Reynolds* / By the light of the silvery moon: *Powell, Jane* / Row row row: *Carpenter, Carleton & Debbie Reynolds* / My hero: *Powell, Jane* / Make believe: *Keel, Howard & Kathryn Grayson* / I might fall back on you: *Champion, Marge & Gower* / Why do I love you: *Keel, Howard & Kathryn Grayson* / Bill: *Gardner, Ava* / Life upon the wicked stage: *Champion, Marge & Gower* / You are love: *Keel, Howard & Kathryn Grayson* / Wonder why: *Powell, Jane* / Paris: *Lamas, Fernando* / I can see you: *Powell, Jane* / There's danger in your eyes, cherie: *Darrieux, Danielle* / Too late now: *Powell, Jane* / Every night at seven: *Astaire, Fred* / Happiest day of my life: *Powell, Jane* / I left my hat in Haiti: *Astaire, Fred* / You're all the world to me: *Astaire, Fred* / How could you believe me when I said I love you: *Astaire, Fred & Jane Powell* / 'S wonderful: *Kelly, Gene & Georges Guetary* / Love is here to stay: *Kelly, Gene* / I'll build a stairway to paradise: *Guetary, Georges* / I got rhythm: *Kelly, Gene* / Singin' in the rain: *Kelly, Gene* / Fit as a fiddle: *Kelly, Gene & Donald O'Connor* / You were meant for me: *Kelly, Gene* / Make 'em laugh: *O'Connor, Donald* / Good morning: *Kelly, Gene & Donald O'Connor* / All I do is dream of you: *Kelly, Gene* / Moses: *Kelly, Gene & Donald O'Connor* / You are my lucky star: *Kelly, Gene & Debbie Reynolds* / Oops: *Astaire, Fred* / Naughty but nice: *Ellis, Anita* / Seeing's believing: *Astaire, Fred* / I wanna be a dancin' man: *Astaire, Fred* / Everything I have is yours/Seventeen thousand telephones: *Astaire, Fred* / Maxim's: *Lamas, Fernando & Richard Haydn* / Vilia: *Lamas, Fernando* / Girls, girls, girls / Night: *Lamas, Fernando* / Merry widow waltz: *Lamas, Fernando & Trudy Erwin*
4CD ____ **CDMGB 1**
MGM/EMI / May '90 / EMI

THOSE MAGNIFICENT MGM MUSICALS VOL.2 (1952-1971)
Shine of your shoes / Be myself / Triplets / New sun in the sky / I guess I'll have to change my plan / I love Louisa / That's entertainment / Smoke gets in your eyes / I'll be hard to handle / Yesterdays / Touch of your hand / Lovely to look at / Hi lili hi lo / Too darn hot / So in love / Tom, Dick or Harry / Were thine that special face / Why can't you behave / Wunderbar / Always true to you in my fashion / I hate men / From this moment on / Brush up your Shakespeare / Spring, spring, spring / Bless your beautiful hide / Wonderful, wonderful day / Goin' cotin / Sobin' women / Sometimes I'm happy / Chiribiribee (Ciribiribin) / More than you know / I know that you know / Rose Marie / I'm a mountie who never got his man / Indian love call / Softly as in a morning sunrise / Serenade / Lover come back to me / Road to paradise / Will you remember / Once in the highlands / Brigadoon / Heather on the hill / Waitin' for my dearie / I'll go home with Bonnie Jean / Come to me, bend to me / Fate / Not since Nineveh / Baubles, bangles and beads / Stranger in paradise / Gesticulate / Night of my nights / Bored / Olive tree / Rahadakum / And this is my beloved / March march / Thanks a lot, but no thanks / Blue Danube / Music is better than words / I like myself / Les Girls / You're just too too / Ca, c'est l'amour / Ladies in waiting / Why am I so gone / Thank heavens for little girls / Say a prayer for me tonight / I remember it well / Gaston's soliloquy / I'm glad I'm not young anymore / Night they invented champagne / Paris loves lovers / All of you / Fated to be mated / Siberia / Ritz roll and rock / I ain't down yet / I'll never say no / Belly up to the bar, boys / London is London / You and I / I could be happy with you / It's never too late to fall in love / Room in Bloomsbury / Riviera / Boy friend finale
2CD ____ **CDMGB 2**
MGM/EMI / May '90 / EMI

THOSE SENSATIONAL SWINGING SIRENS OF THE SILVER SCREEN
CD ____ **VJC 1002-2**
Victorious Discs / Aug '90 / Jazz Music

THRILLER MEMORANDUM, THE
Mexican flyer: *Woodman, Ken Piccadilly Brass* / Main chance: *Schroeder, John* / Yes and no: *Des Champ* / Party: *Mamanqakis, Nicos* / Fly by night: *Marxhall, Brain Orchestra* / Ghost Squad: *Hatch, Tony Orchestra* / Silencers: *Seymour, Pat* / Fade out: *Shakespeare, John Orchestra* / Le train fou: *Denjean, Jaques* / Live and let die: *Lloyd, David London Orchestra* / Kissy Suzuki: *Sounds Orchestral* / Twelve by two: *Woodman, Ken Piccadilly Brass* / Night with Naki: *Marshall, Brian Orchestra* / Saint: *Reed, Les Brass* / Sharp sharks: *Hoffman, Ingried* / Mission impossible: *Hurst, Mike Orchestra* / Adventure: *Wirtz, Mark Orchestra/Chorus* / Wednesday's child: *Hurst, Mike Orchestra* / Hustle: *Kirchen, Basil* / Big M: *Des Champ* / Interception: *Whittaker, David Orchestra* / Man In A Suitacse: *Grainer, Ron Orchestra* / Penthouse: *Hawksworth, Johnny Orchestra*
CD ____ **RPM 173**
RPM / Dec '96 / Pinnacle

THUNDERBIRDS ARE GO (20 TV Favourites)
Thunderbirds: *Gray, Barry Orchestra* / Joe 90: *Gray, Barry Orchestra* / Champions: *Hatch, Tony Orchestra* / Avengers: *Johnson, Laurie Orchestra* / Stingray: *Gray, Barry Orchestra* / Mysterons: *Gray, Barry Orchestra* / Dangerman: *Leaper, Bob Orchestra* / Crossroads: *Hatch, Tony Orchestra* / Maigret: *Eagles* / Emmerdale Farm: *Hatch, Tony Orchestra* / Who do you think you are kidding Mr. Hitler: *Flanagan, Bud* / Old Ned: *Grainer, Ron Orchestra* / Aqua Marina: *Gray, Barry Orchestra* / Parker well done: *Gray, Barry Orchestra* / Z-Cars: *Keating, Johnny* / Fugitive: *Schroeder, John Orchestra* / Hi-jacked: *Gray, Barry Orchestra* / Man in a suitcase: *Grainer, Ron Orchestra* / Return Of The Saint: *Saint Orchestra*
CD ____ **SUMCD 4104**
Summit / Nov '96 / Sound & Media

TIMELESS TV THEMES
Thunderbirds: *Gray, Barry Orchestra* / Avengers theme: *Johnson, Laurie Orchestra* / Man in a suitcase: *Grainer, Ron Orchestra* / Z-cars: *Keating, Johnny & The Z Men* / Captain Scarlet: *Gray, Barry Orchestra* / Champions: *Hatch, Tony Orchestra* / Fugitive: *Schroeder, John Orchestra* / Emmerdale Farm: *Hatch, Tony Orchestra* / Danger man: *Leaper, Bob Orchestra* / Stranger on the shore: *Bilk, Acker* / Maigret: *Eagles* / Stingray: *Gray, Barry Orchestra & The Gary Miller Orchestra* / Crossroads: *Hatch, Tony Orchestra* / Forsyte saga (Elizabeth Tudor): *Stapleton, Cyril & Orchestra* / Mysterons theme: *Gray, Barry Orchestra* / Return of the Saint: *Saint Orchestra* / Dr. Who: *Winstone, Eric & His Orchestra* / Fireball: *Flee-Rekkers* / Steptoe And Son (Old Ned): *Grainer, Ron Orchestra*
CD ____ **TRTCD 122**
TrueTrax / Oct '94 / THE

TO CATCH A THIEF (A History Of Hitchcock Vol. 2)
City Of Prague Philharmonic Orchestra
Bateman, Paul *Con*
Thirty Nine Steps / Lady Vanishes / Stagefright / Rope / Lifeboat / To Catch a Thief / Vertigo / Torn Curtain / Family Plot / North by Northwest / Strangers on a Train / Trouble with Harry / Rear Window
CD ____ **FILMCD 159**
Silva Screen / Apr '95 / Koch / Silva Screen

TOP HAT (Music From The Films Of Astaire & Rogers)
Mancini Pops Orchestra
Mancini, Henry *Con*
Roberta / Flying Down to Rio / Gay Divorcee / Follow the Fleet / Shall We Dance / Swing Time
CD ____ **09026607952**
RCA Victor / Nov '92 / BMG

TOP OF THE BILL (Over 60 Of Their Greatest Successes)
CD ____ **PASTCD 9753**
Flapper / Apr '92 / Pinnacle

TOP TV & MOVIE THEMES
Star trek / High noon / 2001 / Shaft / Howard's Way / Eastenders
2CD _______________ 2802
Sound / Jan '89 / ADA

TOP TV SOAP THEMES
London Theatre Orchestra
Eastenders / Coronation Street / Neighbours / Home and Away / Prisoner Cell Block H / Sons and Daughters / Brookside / Waltons / Emmerdale / Young Doctors / Soap / Falcon Crest / Crossroads / Peyton Place / Flying Doctors / Sullivans
CD _______________ EMPRCD 662
Emporio / Oct '96 / Disc

TOP TV THEMES
CD _______________ 887978
Milan / Jan '95 / Conifer/BMG / Silva Screen

TOP TV THEMES
CD _______________ MACCD 152
Autograph / Aug '96 / BMG

TOXIC TUNES FROM TROMAVILLE (20 Years Of Troma Films)
CD _______________ SER 289B01
South East / Apr '96 / Silva Screen

TRACKSPOTTING
Saint: *Orbital* / Theme from Mission: Impossible: *Clayton, Adam & Larry Mullen* / Lovefool (Tee's club radio): *Cardigans* / Shallow grave: *Leftfield* / Born slippy: *Underworld* / Papau New Guinea: *Future Sound Of London* / Crash and carry: *Orbital* / Slid: *Fluke* / Wake up: *Stereo MC's* / Wildwood: *Weller, Paul* / This is not America: *Bowie, David & Pat Metheny Group* / Downtown: *Cole, Lloyd* / Wait for the sun: *Supergrass* / Natural one: *Folk Implosion* / Gone: *Holmes, David & Sarah Cracknell* / Play dead: *Bjork & David Arnold* / Small plot of land: *Bowie, David* / Forbidden colours: *Sylvian, David* / Falling: *Cruise, Julee* / Hold me, thrill me, kiss me, kill me: *U2* / 36 degrees: *Placebo* / Sunshine shakers: *Reef* / Begging you: *Stone Roses* / Let's all go together: *Marion* / I spy: *Pulp* / There she goes: *La's* / You and me song: *Wannadies* / Bad behaviour: *Super Furry Animals* / Lust for life: *Iggy Pop* / That woman's got me drinking: *MacGowan, Shane & The Popes* / Perfect crime: *Faith No More* / Sugar ray: *Jesus & Mary Chain* / Misirlou: *Dale, Dick & His Del-Tones* / 5:15: *Who* / Pet semetary: *Ramones* / Pretty in pink: *Psychedelic Furs* / Girl you'll be a woman soon: *Urge Overkill* / Left of centre: *Vega, Suzanne* / Stuck in the middle with you: *Stealer's Wheel* / How can we hang on to a dream: *Hardin, Tim*
2CD _______________ 5534302
PolyGram TV / May '97 / PolyGram

TRUE GRIT (Music From The Classic Films Of John Wayne)
City Of Prague Philharmonic Orchestra
Bateman, Paul *Con*
Stagecoach / She Wore a Yellow Ribbon / Quiet Man / Searchers / Alamo / True Grit / Cowboys / How the West Was Won / High and the Mighty / In Harm's Way
CD _______________ FILMCD 153
Silva Screen / Jul '94 / Koch / Silva Screen

TRUFFAUT FILM MUSIC
CD _______________ 887790
Milan / Jan '95 / Conifer/BMG / Silva Screen

TUNES FROM THE TOONS (The Best Of Hanna Barbera)
CD _______________ MCCD 279
Music Club / Dec '96 / Disc / THE

TV AND FILM THEMES VOL.2
CD _______________ 3024 DDD
CRC / Oct '89

TV CLASSICS
4CD _______________ MBSCD 412
Castle / Feb '93 / BMG

TV SOAP THEMES
Eastenders / Falcon Crest / Eldorado / Emmerdale / Prisoner Cell Block H / Melrose Place / Crossroads / Neighbours / Country Practice / Coronation Street / Beverley Hills 90210 / Brookside / Young Doctors / Dallas / Dynasty / Sons and Daughters / Peyton Place / Home and Away
CD _______________ 306242
Hallmark / Jan '97 / Carlton

TV THEMES AMERICA
Dallas / Perfect Strangers / Knots Landing / Midnight Caller / Head of the Class / Mission Impossible / McGyver / Cagney and Lacey / Dynasty / Odd Couple / High Chaparal / MASH (Suicide is painless) / Bonanza / Taxi / Rockford Files / Dr. Kildare
CD _______________ EMPRCD 556
Emporio / Mar '95 / Disc

ULTIMATE SHOW COLLECTION, THE
CC Productions
Heat is on in Saigon / I dreamed a dream / Time warp / Peter Gunn / Day by day / One night in Bangkok / Marilyn Monroe / American dream / I'm free / Pinball wizard / I don't know how to love him / Empty chairs at empty tables / Another suitacse in another hall / Memory / Phantom of the opera / Oh boy / Fame / Grease / Old deuteronomy / Science fiction
CD _______________ QED 081
Tring / Nov '96 / Tring

UNFORGETTABLE
Boston Pops Orchestra
Williams, John *Con*
CD _______________ SK 53380
Sony Classical / Jan '94 / Sony

UNFORGETTABLE CLASSICS
CD _______________ CDCFP 4696
Classics For Pleasure / Apr '96 / EMI

UNSUNG MUSICALS VOL.1
Fay, T. *Con*
Smile / Postcards / Will we ever know each other / Ragtime Romeo / Starfish / Silverware / Her laughter in my life / In the name of love / There are days and there are days / In our hands / Sherry / She's roses / At my side / Disneyland / New words
CD _______________ VSD 5462
Varese Sarabande / Apr '94 / Pinnacle

UNSUNG MUSICALS VOL.2
CD _______________ VSD 5564
Varese Sarabande / Jun '95 / Pinnacle

UNSUNG MUSICALS VOL.3
CD _______________ VSD 5769
Varese Sarabande / Jul '97 / Pinnacle

VAMPIRE CIRCUS (The Essential Vampire Theme Collection)
Return of Dracula / Vampire circus / Fright night / Transylvania twist / Vamp / Children of the night / Thirst / Transylvania / Forever knight / To die for / Son of darkness: To die for II / Sundown: The vampire in retreat / Hunger
CD _______________ FILMCD 127
Silva Screen / Mar '93 / Koch / Silva Screen

VERY BEST OF THE BOSTON POPS, THE
Boston Pops Orchestra
Williams, John *Con*
CD _______________ 4328022
Philips / Dec '92 / PolyGram

VINTAGE THEMES FROM BRITISH RADIO, TV AND NEWSREELS
Celebrity music: *Queen's Hall Light Orchestra* / Portrait of a flirt: *Queen's Hall Light Orchestra* / It's that man again: *New Century Orchestra* / Music in the air: *Queen's Hall Light Orchestra* / City desk: *New Century Orchestra* / Roses from the South: *Paramor, Norrie & His Orchestra* / Windows of Paris: *Osborne, Tony & his Orchestra* / Trade Wind hornpipe: *Reilly, Tommy* / Spice of life: *Shadwell, Charles & his Orcestra* / Picture Parade: *Pinewood Studio Orchestra* / Girls in grey: *Pinewood Studio Orchestra* / Parisian mode: *Phillips, Woolf & his Orchestra* / Family joke: *Reilly, Tommy* / Silks and satins: *Devereaux, Georges Orchestra* / Non stop: *Devereaux, Georges Orchestra* / Barnacle Bill: *New Century Orchestra* / Las Vegas: *KPM Mood Music* / Gaumont-British News fanfare: *Levy, Louis & His Gaumont British Symphony Orchestra* / Sports Arena March: *New Century Orchestra* / Breakfast bustle: *New Century Orchestra* / Society wedding: *New Century Orchestra* / Paddock: *New Century Orchestra* / London Playhouse: *New Century Orchestra* / Airport: *New Century Orchestra* / Dagger in the dark: *New Century Orchestra* / Metropolis: *New Century Orchestra* / Production drive: *New Century Orchestra* / Mannequin: *New Century Orchestra* / Gaumont-British News March: *Levy, Louis & His Gaumont British Symphony Orchestra*
CD _______________ CDEMS 1554
Premier/EMI / Mar '96 / EMI

VISIONS
Flying / Harry's Game / MASH (Suicide is painless) / Hill Street Blues / Chariots of fire / Brideshead revisited / Arthur's theme / I don't know how to love him / Don't cry for me Argentina / Eve of the war / Star Wars / Fame / For your eyes only / Dallas / Shoestring / Chain / Angela / Take that look off your face
CD _______________ MCCD 190
Music Club / Nov '94 / Disc / THE

VISIONS
Stoltzman, Richard
Promise/A bed of ferns / O mio babbino caro / La Strada / Manha da carnaval / When I fall in love / Singin' in the rain / With this love / Can you feel the love tonight / Adagio from Mozart clarinet concerto / Love theme from Sophie's Choice/I'll never leave you / Somewhere / Spartacus love theme / Once Upon a Time in America / Calling you / Schindler's List theme / Philadelphia
CD _______________ 09026680722
RCA Victor / Feb '96 / BMG

WAR FILM THEMES
CD _______________ MACCD 278
Autograph / Aug '96 / BMG

WARRIORS OF THE SILVER SCREEN (The Ultimate Epic Movie Themes Album)
City Of Prague Philharmonic Orchestra
Bateman, Paul *Con*
Braveheart / Thief Of Bagdad / Taras Bulba / Anthony And Cleopatra / First Knight / Henry V / El Cid / Prince Valiant / Ben Hur / Vikings / Rob Roy / Spartacus / 300 Spartans / War Lord / Last Valley / Conan The Barbarian / Jason And The Argonauts
2CD _______________ FILMXCD 187
Silva Screen / May '97 / Koch / Silva Screen

WATCHING THE DETECTIVES
Starshine Orchestra
Inspector Morse / LA Law / Bill / Poirot / Sweeney / Law and Order / Bergerac / Juliet Bravo / Magnum PI / Miami Vice / Miss Marple / Ruth Rendell Mysteries / Starsky and Hutch / Taggart / Hill Street Blues / NYPD Blue / Cagney and Lacey / Kojak
CD _______________ 307262
Hallmark / Jun '97 / Carlton

WESTERN MOVIE THEMES
CD _______________ 15 492
Laserlight / Jan '93 / Target/BMG

WESTERN MOVIE THEMES
CD _______________ MACCD 243
Autograph / Aug '96 / BMG

WHEN I GROW TOO OLD TO DREAM (Her Greatest Musical Comedy Successes)
Laye, Evelyn
Lover come back to me / Girl on the prowl / One kiss / You've done something to my heart / Let the people sing / Night is young / When I grow too old to dream / Glass of golden baubles / Butterfly song / Brave hearts / Near and yet so far / Princess is awakening / Love is a song / Ensa / Zigeuner / I'll see you again / All thro' a glass of champagne / If you look into her eyes
CD _______________ PASTCD 9717
Flapper / Mar '91 / Pinnacle

WHEN YOU WISH UPON A STAR (Barbara Hendricks Sings Disney)
Hendricks, Barbara
Tunick, Jonathan *Con*
Some day my Prince will come / When you wish upon a star / Bibbidi-bobbidi-boo / In the golden afternoon / Part of your world / With a smile and a song / Very good advice / Bella notte / Zip-a-dee-doo-dah / Cruella de ville / Dream is a wish your heart makes / I'm late / Circle of life / Feed the birds / Chim chim cher-ee / Beauty and the beast / Whistle while you work
CD _______________ CDC 5561772
EMI Classics / Nov '96 / EMI

WHITE HEAT - FILM NOIR
Jazz At The Movies Band
This gun for hire / Bad and the beautiful / White heat / Double indemnity / Touch of evil / Key largo / Laura / Lost weekend / Postman always rings twice / Asphalt jungle / Big sleep / Strange love of Martha Ivers / Naked city
CD _______________ 77008
Discovery / Jun '94 / Warner Music

WHY EVER DID THEY (Hollywood Stars At The Microphone)
Kashmiri love song: *Valentino, Rudolph* / El relicario: *Valentino, Rudolph* / Long ago in Alcala: *Novarro, Ramon* / Two white arms: *Menjou, Adolphe* / Not for all the rice in China: *Webb, Clifton* / One little drink: *Beery, Noah* / Whip: *Beery, Noah* / Where the lighthouse shines: *Veidt, Conrad* / Tout la-bas: *Boyer, Charles* / Salue la lune: *Boyer, Charles* / Matrosenlied: *Albers, Hans* / Where is the song of songs for me: *Velez, Lupe* / Mi amado: *Velez, Lupe* / Ramona: *Del Rio, Dolores* / Ya va cayendo: *Del Rio, Dolores* / Come to me: *Swanson, Gloria* / Ich liebe dich, my dear: *Swanson, Gloria* / What do I care: *Bankhead, Tallulah* / Don't tell him: *Bankhead, Tallulah* / It's all so new to me: *Crawford, Joan* / I'm in love with the Honourable Mr. So and So: *Crawford, Joan* / Little bit bad: *Brody, Estelle* / Lorna's song: *Hopper, Victoria*
CD _______________ PASTCD 9735
Flapper / Mar '91 / Pinnacle

WILD BUNCH, THE (Best Of The West)
Czech Symphony Orchestra
Motzing, William *Con*
Sons of Katie Elder / Dances with wolves / Silverado / High noon / Once upon a time in the west / Magnificent seven / Alamo / Lonesome dove / Blue and the grey / Fistful of dynamite / TV Western themes / Ballad of Cable Hogue / Young guns II / Return of a man called horse / Gunfight at the OK Corral / Wild bunch / Big country
CD _______________ FILMCD 136
Silva Screen / Jun '93 / Koch / Silva Screen

WILD, WILD WEST, THE (16 Great Western Tracks)
Good, the bad and the ugly / Ghost riders in the sky / Fistful of dollars / Man who shot Liberty Valance / Hanging tree / Streets of Loredo / Hang 'em high / High noon / High chaparal / Bonanza / For a few dollars more / Big country / Magnificent seven / Shenandoah / Red river valley / Once upon a time in the West
CD _______________ ECD 3043
K-Tel / Jan '95 / K-Tel

WIM WENDERS' FILMMUSIC
CD _______________ 873089
Milan / Nov '91 / Conifer/BMG / Silva Screen

WISDOM OF A FOOL, THE
Wisdom, Norman
Don't laugh at me / Wisdom of a fool / Dream for sale / Up in the world / Narcissus: *Wisdom, Norman & Joyce Grenfell* / Beware / Me and my imagination / Skylark / Who can I turn to / Boy meets girl: *Wisdom, Norman & Ruby Murray* / You must have been a beautiful baby / Heart of a clown / I don't arf love you: *Wisdom, Norman & Joyce Grenfell* / By the fireside / Joker / Impossible / You're getting to be a habit with me / Happy ending / Make a miracle: *Wisdom, Norman & Pip Hinton* / Once in love with Amy / My darling, my darling / Leaning on a lampost / For me and my girl / Lambeth walk
CD _______________ SEECD 477
See For Miles/C5 / May '97 / Pinnacle

WONDERFUL WEST END
CD _______________ MACCD 130
Autograph / Aug '96 / BMG

WOODY ALLEN CLASSICS
CD _______________ SK 53549
Sony Classical / Jul '94 / Sony

WORKING IN A COALMINE (Songs From TV Commercials)
CD _______________ SMP 850007
Movieplay / Jan '94 / Target/BMG

WORLD OF JAMES BOND, THE
Shaw, Roland Orchestra
James Bond theme / Diamonds are forever / You only live twice / Wedding / Goldfinger / Dawn raid on Fort Knox / Arrival of the bomb and countdown / Pussy Galore's flying circus / From Russia with love / Thunderball / Bond below Disco Volante / Chateau flight / Casino Royale / Look of love / Let the love come through / Jump up / Dr. No's fantasy / Twisting with James / Girl trouble / Mr. Kiss Kiss Bang Bang / On Her Majesty's Secret Service / 007 theme
CD _______________ 8445862
Deram / Oct '96 / PolyGram

WORLD WAR II FILM THEMES
Royal Military School Of Music
Dambusters march / Where eagles dare / Bridge too far / 633 Squadron / Battle of the river plate / Great escape march / Reach for the sky / Aces high / Operation crossbow / Longest day / Cockleshell heroes / River Kwai march / Battle of Britain
CD _______________ CDPR 131
Premier/MFP / Apr '95 / EMI

WORLD WAR II FILM THEMES
Dambusters march / Where eagles dare / Bridge too far / 633 Squadron / Battle of the River Plate / Great escape march / Reach for the sky / Aces high (From The Battle of Britain) / Operation crossbow / Longest day / Cockleshell heroes / Battle of Britain / St Louis blues (From "The Glenn Miller story") / River Kwai march / Guns of Navarone
CD _______________ CDMFP 6199
Music For Pleasure / Jul '96 / EMI

WORLD'S GREATEST MUSICALS, THE
CD _______________ MU 5064
Musketeer / Oct '92 / Disc

YOU MUST REMEMBER THIS - CLASSIC THEMES FROM TV & RADIO
By the sleepy lagoon: *Coates, Eric Symphony Orchestra* / Trout Quintet: *Schnabel, Artur & Pro Arte Quartet/Claude Hobday* / Barwick Green: *New Concert Orchestra/Jay Wilbur* / Won't you get off it please: *Waller, Fats & His Buddies* / Grasshoppers' dance: *Hylton, Jack Orchestra* / Oh what a beautiful mornin': *Miller, Glenn Army Air Forces Training Command Orchestra & Johnny Desmond/Crew Chiefs* / Coronation Scot: *Queen's Hall Light Orchestra/Charles Williams* / My ship: *Lawrence, Gertrude* / Oriental shuffle: *Reinhardt, Django Quintet Of The Hot Club Of France & Stephane Grappelli* / Waltz of the flowers: *Philadelphia Orchestra/Leopold Stokowski* / New world symphony: *Czech Philharmonic Orchestra/Georg Szel* / ITMA signature tune: *BBC Variety Orchestra/Charles Shadwell* / Devil's gallop: *Queen's Hall Light Orchestra/Charles Williams* / Nessun dorma: *Bjorling, Jussi* / Makin' whoopee: *Cantor, Eddie* / Air on a G string: *London Symphony Orchestra/Sir Henry Wood* / Roses from the South: *Sandler, Albert Palm Court Orchestra*
CD _______________ 75605522712
Happy Days / Feb '97 / Conifer/BMG

YOU MUST REMEMBER THIS - GREAT FILM SONGS
Am I blue: *Waters, Ethel* / Falling in love again: *Dietrich, Marlene* / Bench in the park: *Whiteman, Paul Orchestra & The Rhythm Boys/Brox Sisters* / Goodnight Vienna: *Buchanan, Jack* / Tinkle tinkle tinkle/Over my shoulder: *Matthews, Jessie* / One night of love: *Moore, Grace* / Okay toots: *Cantor, Eddie* / Smoke gets in your eyes: *Dunne, Irene* / Lullaby of Broadway: *Shaw, Winifred* / Love is everywhere: *Fields, Gracie & Tommy* / Top hat, white tie and tails: *Astaire, Fred* / Isn't this a lovely day: *Rogers, Ginger* / I've got a feelin' you're foolin': *Powell, Eleanor* / When did you leave Heaven: *Martin, Tony* / This year's kisses: *Faye, Alice* / I've got my love to keep me warm: *Powell, Dick* / Will you remember: *MacDonald, Jeanette & Nelson Eddy* / Jeepers creepers: *Armstrong, Louis* / I go for that: *Lamour, Dorothy* / It's foolish, but it's fun: *Durbin, Deanna* / Chattanooga choo choo: *Miller, Glenn Orchestra & Tex Beneke/The Modernaires/Paula Kelly* / I yi yi yi yi (I like you very much): *Miranda, Carmen* /

Moonlight becomes you: *Crosby, Bing* / Trolley song: *Garland, Judy* / More I see you: *Haymes, Dick* / Out of nowhere: *Forrest, Helen*
CD ______________ **75605522832**
Happy Days / Feb '97 / Conifer/BMG

YOU MUST REMEMBER THIS - THEATRE SONGS
Swanee: *Jolson, Al* / Fascinating rhythm: *Astaire, Fred & Adele* / Who: *Hale, Binnie & Jack Buchanan* / Where's that rainbow: *Dickson, Dorothy* / Miss Annabelle Lee: *Smith, 'Whispering' Jack* / Ol' man river: *Robeson, Paul* / Dance little lady: *Coward, Sir Noel* / I'll see you again: *Melaxa, George & Peggy Wood* / Dancing on the ceiling: *Matthews, Jessie* / Got a date with an angel: *Howes, Bobby* / She didn't say yes: *Wood, Peggy* / I've told ev'ry little star: *Ellis, Mary* / Heat wave: *Waters, Ethel* / Physician: *Lawrence, Gertrude* / You're the top: *Merman, Ethel* / Dancing with a ghost: *Day, Frances* / Girl I knew: *Welch, Elizabeth* / Family solicitor: *Lupinn, Wallace* / Me and my girl: *Lane, Lupino & Teddle St. Denis* / Take it on the chin: *St. Denis, Teddle* / Lambeth walk: *Lane, Lupino* / Only a glass of champagne: *Laye, Evelyn* / Saga of Jenny: *Lawrence, Gertrude* / Surrey with the fringe on top: *Drake, Alfred* / Never say goodbye: *Burke, Patricia* / Pedro the fisherman: *Tildsley, Vincent Mastersingers* / We'll gather lilacs: *Baron, Muriel & Olive Gilbert*
CD ______________ **75605522842**
Happy Days / Feb '97 / Conifer/BMG

Composer Collections

Addinsell, Richard

FILM MUSIC
BBC Concert Orchestra
Alwyn, Kenneth *Con*
Goodbye Mr. Chips / Prince and the showgirl / Tom Brown's schooldays / Fire over England / Tale of two cities
CD _______________ **8223732**
Marco Polo / Jul '94 / Select

Alwyn, William

ALWYN: FILM MUSIC
London Symphony Orchestra
Hickox, Richard *Con*
Rake's progress / Odd man out / Fallen idol / History of Mr. Polly
CD _______________ **CHAN 9243**
Chandos / Mar '94 / Chandos

Arlen, Harold

SINGS THE HAROLD ARLEN SONGBOOK
Wilson, Julie
Blues in the night / Man that got away / Fun to be fooled / This time / Dream's on me / Buds won't bud / Last night when we were young / One for my baby / Lydia the tattooed the lady / Out of this world
CD _______________ **DRG 5211**
DRG / Jan '95 / Discovery / New Note/ Pinnacle

THAT OLD BLACK MAGIC
CD _______________ **5375732**
Verve / Jul '97 / PolyGram

Arnold, Sir Malcolm

ARNOLD: FILM MUSIC
London Symphony Orchestra
Hickox, Richard *Con*
Bridge on the River Kwai / Inn of the sixth happiness / Hobson's choice / Whistle down the wind / Sound barrier
CD _______________ **CHAN 9100**
Chandos / Feb '93 / Chandos

Bacalov, Luis Enriquez

ITALIAN WESTERN SCORES OF LUIS ENRIQUEZ BACALOV, THE
CD _______________ **VCDS 7015**
Varese Sarabande / Apr '96 / Pinnacle

Baird, Tadeusz

TADEUSZ BAIRD: FILM MUSIC
Polish Symphony Orchestra
Baird, Tadeusz *Con*
Room for one / Warsaw in Canaletto paintings / Visit at the kings / Year one / Passenger / Manhunter / Panic on a train / April / Rugged creativeness / When love was a crime
CD _______________ **OCD 604**
Olympia / Aug '94 / Priory

TADEUSZ BAIRD: FILM MUSIC II
Polish Symphony Orchestra
Baird, Tadeusz *Con*
Between the shores / Burning mountains / Every day / Sky of stone / Those who are late / Samson
CD _______________ **OCD 607**
Olympia / Aug '94 / Priory

Barry, John

007 AND OTHER GREAT SOUNDTRACK THEMES
CD _______________ **CDCD 1225**
Charly / Jun '95 / Koch

16 JOHN BARRY THEMES, THE (The Ember Years Vol.2)
Barry, John
CD _______________ **PLAY 003**
Play It Again / Mar '92 / Silva Screen

CLASSIC JOHN BARRY VOL.1, THE
City Of Prague Philharmonic Orchestra
Raine, Nic *Con*
Zulu / Out Of Africa / Midnight Cowboy / Last Valley / Eleanor And Franklin / Hanover Street / Born Free / Chaplin / Dances With Wolves / Raise The Titanic / Indecent Proposal / Persuaders / Robin And Marian / Body Heat / Somewhere In Time / Lion In Winter
CD _______________ **FILMCD 141**
Silva Screen / Oct '93 / Koch / Silva Screen

CLASSIC JOHN BARRY VOL.2, THE
City Of Prague Philharmonic Orchestra
Ipcress File / Scarlet Letter / Mary Queen Of Scots / High Road To China / Quiller Memorandum / Knack / Dove / Monte Walsh / Black Hole / Wrong Box / Walkabout / Appointment
CD _______________ **FILMCD 169**
Silva Screen / Feb '96 / Koch / Silva Screen

EMI YEARS VOL.1, THE (1957-1960)
Barry, John
CD _______________ **CDEMS 1497**
EMI / Jul '93 / EMI

EMI YEARS VOL.2, THE (1960-1962)
Barry, John
Magnificent seven / Skid row / Twist it / Watch your step / Dark rider / Matter of who / Iron horse / It doesn't matter anymore / Sweet talk / Moon river / There's life in the old boy yet / Handful of songs / Like waltz / Rodeo / Donna's theme / Starfire / Baubles, bangles and beads / Zapata / Rum-de-dum-de-da / Spanish Harlem / Man from Madrid / Challenge / Menace / Satin smooth / Agressor / Rocco's theme / Spinnerree
CD _______________ **CDEMS 1501**
EMI / Jul '93 / EMI

EMI YEARS VOL.3, THE (1962-1964)
Barry, John Seven & Orchestra
James Bond theme / Blacksmith blues / Cutty Sark / Lost patrol / Roman Spring of Mrs Stone: *Loewe, Frederick* / Tears: *Loewe, Frederick* / Blueberry Hill: *Barry, John Orchestra* / Cherry pink and apple blossom white: *Barry, John Orchestra* / Smokey Joe: *Barry, John* / Unchained melody: *Barry, John Orchestra* / Party's over / Lolly theme / March of the Mandarins / Human jungle (alt. version) / Big safari: *1989 Broadway Cast* / Mouse on the moon: *1989 Broadway Cast* / Twangin' cheek / I'll be with you in apple blossom time: *Barry, John Orchestra* / Volare: *Barry, John Orchestra* / Human jungle / Onward Christian spacemen / Seven faces / Twenty four hours ago: *Stone, Richard* / Jolly Bad Fellow: *Belen, Ana* / Oublie ca: *Barry, John Orchestra* / Seance on a Wet Afternoon: *Barry, John* / That fatal kiss: *Barry, John*
CD _______________ **CDEMS 1555**
EMI / Sep '95 / EMI

JOHN BARRY EXPERIENCE, THE
007 / From Russia with love / Loneliness of autumn / Four in the morning / River walk / Lover's tension / First reconciliation / Judi comes home / Elizabeth in London / London theme / Elizabeth theme / Lovers / Aliki / Zulu / First Zulu appearance and assault / Zulu stamp / Teltha leyanto / Monkey feathers / Fancy dance / Christine X
CD _______________ **3036000812**
Carlton / Apr '97 / Carlton

MOVIOLA
Out of Africa / Midnight cowboy / Body heat / Somewhere in time / Mary Queen of Scots / Born free / Dances With Wolves / Chaplin / Cotton club / Walkabout / Frances / We have all the time in the world / Moviola
CD _______________ **4724902**
Epic / Dec '96 / Sony

ZULU (The Film Themes Of John Barry)
CD _______________ **MACCD 221**
Autograph / Aug '96 / BMG

Bart, Lionel

SONGS OF LIONEL BART, THE
CD _______________ **MCCD 176**
MCI Music / Sep '94 / Disc / THE

Berlin, Irving

BERLIN ALWAYS (The Songs Of Irving Berlin)
Cheek to cheek: *Astaire, Fred* / Let yourself go: *Astaire, Fred* / This year's kisses: *Faye, Alice* / Alexander's ragtime band: *Goodman, Benny Orchestra* / Always: *Goodman, Benny Orchestra* / Slummin' on Park Avenue: *Lunceford, Jimmy* / I'm putting all my eggs in one basket: *Armstrong, Louis* / Waiting at the end of the road: *Waters, Ethel* / Harlem on my mind: *Waters, Ethel* / Isn't this a lovely day: *Ambrose & His Orchestra* / Shakin' the blues away: *Etting, Ruth* / When I lost you: *Crosby, Bing* / How deep is the ocean: *Crosby, Bing* / He ain't got rhythm: *Holiday, Billie* / I've got my love to keep me warm: *Tatum, Art* / Blue skies: *Dorsey, Tommy Orchestra* / When the midnight choo-choo leaves for Alabam': *Dorsey, Tommy Orchestra* / I want to be in Dixie: *American Ragtime Octette* / How's chances: *Hall, Henry Orchestra* / Russian lullaby: *Berigan, Bunny* / Now it can be told: *Bowlly, Al*
CD _______________ **AVC 517**
Avid / Apr '95 / Avid/BMG / Koch / THE

BERLIN AND GERSHWIN GOLD
2CD _______________ **D2CD 4024**
Deja Vu / Jun '95 / THE

BERLIN, GERSHWIN & PORTER
2CD _______________ **R2CD 4024**
Deja Vu / Jan '96 / THE

ELIZABETH WELCH SINGS IRVING BERLIN
Welch, Elizabeth
CD _______________ **CDVIR 8305**
TER / Jan '89 / Koch

IRVING BERLIN SHOWCASE, THE
Follow the fleet: *Anton & The Paramount Theatre Orchestra* / I can't remember: *Wood, Scott & His Orchestra* / Puttin' on the Ritz: *Alfredo & His Band* / Reaching for the moon: *Da Costa, Raie* / Piccolino: *Mantovani & His Tipica Orchestra* / With you: *Marvin, Johnny* / Berlin waltz medley: *Coventry Hippodrome Orchestra* / Say it isn't so: *Vallee, Rudy & His Connecticut Yankees* / I miss you in the evening: *Davidson, Harry* / My bird of paradise: *Hilo Hawaiian Orchestra* / Cocoanuts: *Light Opera Company* / Russian lullaby: *Savoy Orpheans* / Mammy: *Bidgood, Harry & His Broadcasters* / Because I love you: *Fillis, Len* / I never had a chance: *Leader, Harry & His Band* / Top hat: *Arnold, Doris & Harry S. Pepper* / I'm playing with fire: *Rabin, Oscar & His Band* / How many times: *Brox Sisters* / Just a little longer: *Spitalny, Philip & His Orchestra* / Song is ended (but the melody lingers on): *Richardson, Foster* / On the Avenue: *Levy, Louis & His Gaumont British Symphony Orchestra*
CD _______________ **PASTCD 9733**
Flapper / Feb '91 / Pinnacle

NOTHING BUT BLUE SKIES (The Irving Berlin Songbook)
Swingle Singers
Top hat, white tie and tails / How deep is the ocean / Isn't it a lovely day / Blue skies / Always / They say it's wonderful / No strings / Song is ended / Steppin' out with my baby / Let yourself go / Cheek to cheek / Let's face the music and dance / Marrying for love / Girl that I marry / What'll I do / Puttin' on the Ritz / Abraham / Change partners / Heatwave / I've got my love to keep me warm / Count your blessings / White Christmas
CD _______________ **SUMCD 4054**
Summit / Nov '96 / Sound & Media

SONG IS...IRVING BERLIN, THE
I'm putting all my eggs in one basket: *Boswell Sisters* / Let yourself go: *Bowlly, Al & the Ray Noble Orchestra* / Marie: *Bowlly, Al & the Ray Noble Orchestra* / Cheek to cheek: *Browne, Sam & Lew Stone* / Pretty girl is like a melody: *Dennis, Denny & Roy Fox* / Top hat, white tie & tails: *Dorsey Brothers* / Heat wave: *Farnon, Robert* / Slumming on Park Avenue: *Farnon, Robert* / Alexander's ragtime band: *Geraldo & His Orchestra* / White Christmas: *Geraldo & His Orchestra* / He ain't got rhythm: *Gonella, Nat* / Blue skies: *Goodman, Benny* / This year's kisses: *Gibbons, Carroll* / You keep coming back like a song: *James, Dick* / Let me sing and I'm happy: *Jolson, Al* / I never had a chance: *Joyce, Teddy & Jimmy Mesene* / I've got my love to keep me warm: *Melachrino, George & Carroll Gibbons* / Let's face the music and dance: *Roy, Harry & His Orchestra* / Piccolino: *Roy, Harry & His Orchestra* / We saw the sea: *Roy, Harry & His Orchestra* / All alone: *Shaw, Artie & His Orchestra* / Because I love you: *Shaw, Artie & His Orchestra*
CD _______________ **CDAJA 5068**
Living Era / Oct '95 / Select

SONGS OF IRVING BERLIN
CD _______________ **MCCD 188**
Music Club / Nov '94 / Disc / THE

SPOTLIGHT ON IRVING BERLIN
Cheek to cheek / Anything you can do / Top hat, white tie and tails / Let's face the music and dance / Easter parade / There's no business like show business / You're just in love / Girl that I marry / Always / White Christmas / They say it's wonderful
CD _______________ **HADCD 137**
Javelin / Feb '94 / Henry Hadaway / THE

STARS SALUTE IRVING BERLIN, THE
CD _______________ **CDCD 1247**
Charly / Jun '95 / Koch

TRIBUTE TO IRVING BERLIN, A
CD _______________ **CDDL 1248**
Music For Pleasure / Jan '94 / EMI

UNSUNG IRVING BERLIN (31 Hidden Treasures)
2CD _______________ **VSD 5770**
Varese Sarabande / Apr '97 / Pinnacle

Bernstein, Leonard

BERNSTEIN CONDUCTS BERNSTEIN
New York Philharmonic Orchestra
Bernstein, Leonard *Con*
West Side Story / Candide / Rhapsody in blue / American in Paris
CD _______________ **SMK 47529**
Sony Classical / Nov '92 / Sony

BERNSTEIN CONDUCTS BERNSTEIN
New York Philharmonic Orchestra
Bernstein, Leonard *Con*
On the Waterfront / On the Town / Fancy Free
CD _______________ **SMK 47530**
Sony Classical / Nov '92 / Sony

BERNSTEIN ON BROADWAY (Highlights - West Side Story/Candide/On The Town)
Casts/London Symphony Chorus & Orchestra
Bernstein, Leonard/Michael Tilson Thomas *Con*
CD _______________ **4478982**
Deutsche Grammophon / Jan '95 / PolyGram

NEW YORK
Upshaw, Dawn & Mandy Patinkin/Donna Murphy/Orchestra Of St. Luke's
Stern, Eric *Con*
Balcony scene / Somewhere / Ballet sequence / One hand, one heart / Little bit in love / Ballet at the Village Vortex / Wrong note rag / Quiet girl / What a waste / Story of my life / New York, New York / Ya got me / Come up to my place / Some other time / Lonely town / Lonely town pas de deux / Ain't got no tears left / Danzon variation / Cab and bedroom
CD _______________ **7559794002**
Nonesuch / Feb '97 / Warner Music

SONGS OF WEST SIDE STORY, THE
Something's coming: *All 4 One* / Boy like that: *Selena* / Maria: *McDonald, Michael/ James Ingram/David Pack* / Prologue/Jet song: *Setzer, Brian* / Tonight: *Loggins, Kenny & Wynonna* / Cool: *Austin, Patti/Mervyn Warren/Bruce Hornsby* / Somewhere: *Franklin, Aretha* / America: *Cole, Natalie/ Patti Labelle/Sheila E* / I feel pretty: *Little Richard* / One hand, one heart: *Campbell, Tevin* / Gee officer Krupke: *Salt 'N' Pepa/ Def Jef/Lisa Lopez/Jerky Boys/Paul Rodriguez* / I have a love: *Yearwood, Trisha* / Prelude to the rumble: *Corea, Chick* / Rumble: *Corea, Chick & Steve Vai* / Prelude to somewhere / Somewhere : *Collins, Phil*
CD _______________ **09026627072**
RCA Victor / May '96 / BMG

THEATRE WORKS (ON THE TOWN/ FANCY FREE/TROUBLE IN TAHITI) (& Candide/West Side Story/On The Waterfront excerpts)
Bernstein, Leonard *Con*
3CD _______________ **SM3K 47154**
Sony Classical / May '92 / Sony

Black, Don

BORN FREE (The Don Black Songbook)
Born free: *Monro, Matt* / To sir with love: *Lulu* / Girl with the sun in her hair: *Clinton, Davy* / True grit: *Street, Danny* / On days like these: *Monro, Matt* / This way Mary: *Monro, Matt* / Wish now was then: *Monro, Matt* / Curiouser and curiouser: *Monro, Matt* / Me I never knew: *Monro, Matt* / Billy: *Martell, Lena* / Lady from LA: *Crawford, Michael* / I missed the last rainbow: *Crawford, Michael* / Play it again: *Reading, Wilma* / I'll put you together again: *Hot Chocolate* / Tell me on a Sunday: *Webb, Marti* / Last man in my life: *Webb, Marti* / Anyone can fall in love: *Webb, Marti* / Always there: *Webb, Marti* / There is love and there is love: *Faith, Adam* / In one of my weaker moments: *Dobson, Anita* / Anything but lonely: *Webb, Marti* / Love changes everything: *Webb, Marti*
CD _______________ **PLAY 005**
Play It Again / Sep '93 / Silva Screen

Bliss, Arthur

BLISS - FILM MUSIC
Slovak Philharmonic Choir/Bratislava Symphony Orchestra
Capova, S. *Con*
CD _______________ **8223315**
Marco Polo / Dec '91 / Select

BLISS CONDUCTS BLISS
London Symphony Orchestra/National Symphony Orchestra
Bliss, Arthur *Con*
Introduction/Allegro / Things to come / Men of two worlds
CD _______________ **CDLXT 2051**
Dutton Laboratories / Jan '95 / Complete/ Pinnacle

Bolling, Claude

BOLLING FILMS
Bolling, Claude
CD _______________ **111962**
Musidisc / Nov '94 / Discovery

LUCKY LUKE AU CINEMA
CD _______________ **3020842**
Arcade / Jun '97 / Discovery

to watch over me / 'S wonderful / They can't take that away from me / Who cares / Long ago and far away / Summertime / There's a boat dat's leaving soon for New York / Oh I can't sit down / Somebbody loves me
CD ____________ QED 109
Tring / Nov '96 / Tring

GERSHWIN ARRANGEMENTS
Andre, Maurice & Nicolas Andre/Beatrice Andre
Carradot, Andre *Con*
CD ____________ CDC 5556202
EMI Classics / Jun '96 / EMI

GERSHWIN IN THE MOVIES VOL.1 & 2
St. Louis Symphony Orchestra
Slatkin, Leonard *Con*
2CD ____________ CDCH 249/250
Milan / May '87 / Conifer/BMG / Silva Screen

GLORY OF GERSHWIN, THE
Summertime: *Gabriel, Peter* / Do what you do: *De Burgh, Chris* / Nice work if you can get it: *Sting* / They can't take that away from me: *Stansfield, Lisa* / Someone to watch over me: *John, Elton* / Our love is here to stay: *John, Elton* / I've got a crush on you: *Simon, Carly* / But not for me: *Costello, Elvis* / It ain't necessarily so: *Cher* / Man I love: *Bush, Kate* / How long has this been going on: *Bon Jovi, Jon* / Bidin' my time: *White, Willard* / My man's gone now: *O'Connor, Sinead* / I got rhythm: *Palmer, Robert* / Somebody loves me: *Meat Loaf* / Stairway to paradise: *Van Randwyck, Issy* / Rhapsody in blue: *Adler, Larry*
CD ____________ 5227272
Mercury / Jul '94 / PolyGram

GREAT AMERICAN GERSHWIN
Pennario, Leonard & Hollywood Bowl Orchestra
Slatkin, Felix/Alfred Newman *Con*
Rhapsody in blue / American in Paris / Porgy And Bess / I got rhythm / Cuban overture / Second rhapsody
CD ____________ CDM 5660862
Angel / Jun '97 / EMI

KIRI SINGS GERSHWIN
Te Kanawa, Dame Kiri & The New Princess Theater Orchestra
McGlinn, John *Con*
CD ____________ CDC 7474542
EMI Classics / Apr '93 / EMI

MARNI NIXON SINGS GERSHWIN
Nixon, Marni
CD ____________ RR 19
Reference Recordings / Sep '91 / Jazz Music / May Audio

PLAY GERSHWIN'S POPULAR WORKS
Boston Pops Orchestra
Fiedler, Arthur *Con*
Girl crazy suite / Wintergreen for president / Three preludes / Second rhapsody / Overtures from Oh Kay / Funny face / Let 'em eat cake / Of thee I sing
CD ____________ 4439002
Decca / Feb '96 / PolyGram

S'MARVELLOUS
CD ____________ 5216582
Verve / Feb '94 / PolyGram

SONG IS...GEORGE GERSHWIN, THE
Half of it, dearie blues: *Astaire, Fred* / I found a four leaf clover: *Audrey, Irene & Charles Hart* / Fascinating rhythm: *Edwards, Cliff* / When do we dance: *Gershwin, George* / My one and only: *Gershwin, George* / Little jazz bird: *Hylton, Jack* / Oh lady be good: *Hylton, Jack* / Liza (all the clouds'll roll away): *Jolson, Al* / Someone to watch over me: *Lawrence, Gertrude* / Do what you do: *O'Neal, Zelma* / Sweet and low down: *Selvin, Ben* / That certain feeling: *Selvin, Ben* / Funny face: *Smith, Jack* / I got plenty o' nuttin': *Tibbett, Lawrence* / I got rhythm: *Waller, Fats* / Nashville nightingale: *Waring, Fred & His Pennsylvanians* / Man I love: *Welch, Elizabeth* / I'll build a stairway to paradise: *Whiteman, Paul & Rhythm Boys* / S'wonderful: *Winter, Marius B. & His Dance Band*
CD ____________ CDAJA 5048
Living Era / Oct '95 / Select

SONGBOOK
Let's call the whole thing off: *Holiday, Billie* / Summertime: *Parker, Charlie* / S'wonderful: *Basie, Count & Joe Williams* / Oh lady, be good: *Goodman, Benny* / It ain't necessarily so: *Armstrong, Louis & Ella Fitzgerald* / How long has this been going on: *Hawkins, Coleman* / There's a boat dat's leavin' soon for New York: *Anderson, Ernestine* / Our love is here to stay: *Cleveland, Jimmy* / I was doing alright: *Armstrong, Louis* / I got rhythm: *Peterson, Oscar Trio* / They all laughed: *Astaire, Fred* / I've got a crush on you: *Washington, Dinah* / Foggy day: *Carter, Benny* / Things are looking up: *Fitzger-* [illegible] over me: *Kirk,* [illegible] *Garner, Erroll* [illegible] *Sarah*
CD ____________ 5526462
[illegible]n

[illegible] ____________ 370282

SPOTLIGHT ON GEORGE GERSHWIN
Fascinating rhythm / 'S wonderful / Summertime / Embraceable you / Foggy day / It ain't necessarily so / Nice work / Man I love / Somebody loves me / They can't take that away from me / I got rhythm
CD ____________ HADCD 139
Javelin / Feb '94 / Henry Hadaway / THE

S'WONDERFUL (The Songs Of George & Ira Gershwin)
Swanee: *Jolson, Al* / I got plenty o' nuttin': *Tibbett, Lawrence* / Love walked in: *Armstrong, Louis* / Embraceable you: *Garland, Judy* / Liza (all the clouds'll roll away): *Webb, Chick* / How long has this been going on: *Lee, Peggy* / Nice work if you can get it: *Dorsey, Tommy Orchestra* / Funny face: *Smith, Jack* / Oh lady be good: *Hawkins, Coleman* / Somebody loves me: *Carter, Benny* / Someone to watch over me: *Gershwin, George* / I've got a crush on you: *Wiley, Lee* / S'Wonderful: *Goodman, Benny* / I'll build a stairway to paradise: *Whiteman, Paul & Rhythm Boys* / I got rhythm: *Waller, Fats* / Man I love: *Forrest, Helen* / They all laughed: *Astaire, Fred* / Summertime: *Robeson, Paul* / I was doing alright: *Fitzgerald, Ella* / Fascinating rhythm: *Lee, Buddy* / They can't take that away from me: *Holiday, Billie*
CD ____________ AVC 520
Avid / Apr '95 / Avid/BMG / Koch / THE

S'WONDERFUL (The Songs Of George Gershwin)
Nice work if you can get it: *Astaire, Fred* / Someone to watch over me: *Lawrence, Gertrude* / Looking for a boy: *Dickson, Dorothy* / Liza (all the clouds'll roll away): *Jolson, Al* / Foggy day: *Astaire, Fred* / S'wonderful: *Astaire, Adele & Bernard Clifton* / Lady be good: *Lee, Buddy & The Gilt-Edged Four* / Do do do: *Lawrence, Gertrude & Harold French* / Somebody loves me: *Crosby, Bing* / I got rhythm: *Webb, Chick & His Little Chicks* / I'll build a stairway to Paradise: *Whiteman, Paul & His Orchestra* / They can't take that away from me: *Astaire, Fred* / Funny face: *Astaire, Fred & Adele* / Fascinating rhythm: *Edwards, Cliff* / They all laughed: *Astaire, Fred* / That certain feeling: *Dickson, Dorothy & Allen Kearns* / Maybe: *Lawrence, Gertrude & Harold French* / My one and only: *Astaire, Fred* / Summertime: *Jamison, Anne* / Swanee: *Jolson, Al* / Let's call the whole thing off: *Astaire, Fred* / I got plenty o' nuttin': *Tibbett, Lawrence*
CD ____________ PASTCD 9777
Flapper / Dec '92 / Pinnacle

TRIBUTE TO GEORGE GERSHWIN, A
CD ____________ CDDL 1278
EMI / Nov '94 / EMI

TRIBUTE TO GEORGE GERSHWIN, A
CD ____________ ENTCD 13053
Entertainers / Apr '94 / Target/BMG

Gilbert & Sullivan

ARIAS AND DUETS (The Best Of Gilbert & Sullivan)
Three little maids / When a felon's not engaged in his employment / Poor wandering one / Loudly let the trumpet bray / Take a pair of sparkling eyes / I have a song to sing / I know a youth / I'm called little buttercup / On a tree by a river / If somebody there chanced to be / Wandering minstrel / When the foreman bares his steel
CD ____________ SHOWCD 017
Showtime / Feb '95 / Disc / THE

ARIAS AND DUETS OF GILBERT & SULLIVAN
CD ____________ CDVIR 8325
TER / Aug '95 / Koch

BEST OF GILBERT & SULLIVAN, THE
CD ____________ CDTEZ 7004
TER / Jan '95 / Koch

BEST OF GILBERT & SULLIVAN, THE
Sargent, Sir Malcolm *Con*
CD ____________ CDZ 7625312
EMI Classics / Apr '93 / EMI

GILBERT & SULLIVAN - EXCERPTS
Soloists & Glyndebourne Festival Choir/ Pro Arte Orchestra
Sargent, Sir Malcolm *Con*
CD ____________ CDCFP 4238
Classics For Pleasure / Jan '95 / EMI

GILBERT & SULLIVAN CLASSICS VOL.1 (Selections From The Mikado/Pirates Of Penzance/The Gondoliers/HMS Pinafore)
Alwyn, Kenneth/Richard Hickox *Con*
CD ____________ HMV 58
HMV / Jan '95 / EMI

GILBERT & SULLIVAN CLASSICS VOL.2
Sargent, Sir Malcolm *Con*
CD ____________ HMV 102
HMV / Jan '95 / EMI

GILBERT & SULLIVAN HIGHLIGHTS
Welsh National Opera Choir/Orchestra
Mackerras, Sir Charles *Con*
Mikado / HMS Pinafore / Pirates Of Penzance / Yeoman Of The Gaurd / Trial By Jury
CD ____________ CD 80431
Telarc / Mar '96 / Conifer/BMG

GILBERT & SULLIVAN OVERTURES
Pro Arte Orchestra
Sargent, Sir Malcolm *Con*
CD ____________ CDCFP 4529
Classics For Pleasure / Jan '95 / EMI

OVERTURES
New Sadler's Wells/D'Oyly Carte Opera Orchestra
Pryce Jones, J./S. Phipps/John Owen Edwards *Con*
CD ____________ CDVIR 8316
TER / May '93 / Koch

OVERTURES
Academy Of St. Martin In The Fields
Marriner, Neville *Con*
CD ____________ 4349162
Philips / Jun '93 / PolyGram

OVERTURES
Pro Arte Orchestra/Vienna Philharmonic Orchestra
Sargent, Sir Malcolm *Con*
Mikado / Gondoliers / Yeoman of the guard / HMS Pinafore / Iolanthe / Sorcerer / Cox and box / Princes Ida / Ruddigore / Patience
2CD ____________ CES 5691372
EMI Classics / Feb '96 / EMI

UNFORGETTABLE CLASSICS
CD ____________ CDCFP 4695
Classics For Pleasure / Apr '96 / EMI

VERY BEST OF GILBERT & SULLIVAN, THE
CD ____________ CDMOIR 413
Memoir / Aug '93 / Jazz Music / Target/ BMG

WORLD OF GILBERT & SULLIVAN VOL.1, THE
HMS Pinafore / Mikado / Yeoman of the guard / Pirates of Penzance / Iolanthe / Gondoliers
CD ____________ 4300952
Decca / Jun '91 / PolyGram

WORLD OF GILBERT & SULLIVAN VOL.2, THE
HMS Pinafore / Mikado / Patience / Iolanthe / Gondoliers / Ruddigore / Sorcerer / Yeoman of the guard / Princess Ida / Pirates of Penzance
CD ____________ 4338682
Decca / Feb '93 / PolyGram

Glass, Philip

FILM WORKS (Anima Mundi/Mishima/ Powaqattsi/The Thin Blue Line)
Glass, Philip Ensemble/Kronos Quartet
4CD ____________ 7559793772
Nonesuch / Jan '95 / Warner Music

Goodwin, Ron

MISS MARPLE FILMS, THE (& Other Film Suites)
Murder she said / Murder at the gallop / Murder most foul / Murder ahoy / Force 10 from Navarone / Lancelot and Guinevere
CD ____________ LXE 706
Label X / Mar '93 / Silva Screen

Grainer, Ron

DOCTOR WHO (& Other Classic Ron Grainer TV Themes)
Maigret / Steptoe and son / Some people / Man in a suitcase / Prisoner / Assassination bureau / Only when I larf / Paul Temple / Tales of the unexpected / Edward and Mrs. Simpson / Dr. Who
CD ____________ PLAY 008
Play It Again / Oct '96 / Silva Screen

Gray, Barry

FAB (Music From The Gerry Anderson TV Shows)
Royal Philharmonic Orchestra
Pavlov, Konstantin *Con*
Thunderbirds / Space 1999 / Joe 90 / Stingray / UFO / Captain Scarlet
CD ____________ FILMCD 124
Silva Screen / Nov '92 / Koch / Silva Screen

NO STRINGS ATTACHED
Gray, Barry Orchestra
Thunderbirds / Captain Scarlet / Hijacked / Aqua Marina / Stingray / Mysterons / Joe 90 / Parker - well done
CD ____________ CLACD 204
Castle / Oct '90 / BMG

THUNDERBIRDS ARE GO
Gray, Barry *Con*
Thunderbirds theme / Alan's dream / Joie de vivre / Martian mystery / Thunderbirds theme (reprise) / Astronauts in trouble / Zero X theme / That dangerous game / Swinging star / San Marino / Jeremiah / Tracy Island
CD ____________ FILMCD 018
Silva Screen / Aug '90 / Koch / Silva Screen

Hammerstein II, Oscar

OSCAR & STEVE
Patinkin, Mandy
Showboat / Passion / Follies / Pacific overtures / Anyone can whistle / Merrily we roll along / Into the woods / Little night music / Carousel / Flower drum song / South Pacific / Sound of music / Kiss to build a dream on / Carmen Jones / Night is young

CD ____________ 7559793922
Nonesuch / Apr '96 / Warner Music

Harburg, E.Y. 'Yip'

YIP SINGS HARBURG
Harburg, E.Y. 'Yip'
CD ____________ 373862
Koch International / Jun '97 / Koch

Harnell, Joe

FILM & TV MUSIC OF JOE HARNELL
2CD ____________ FJCD 001/2
Silva Screen / Jan '92 / Koch / Silva Screen

Harnick, Sheldon

EVENING WITH SHELDON HARNICK, AN
Harnick, Sheldon & Margery Gray/Mary Louise
Suave young man / How could I / Merry little minuet / Boston beguine / At the Basilica of St. Anne / Garbage / Worlds apart / Little tin box / Till tomorrow / Picture of happiness / She loves me / Dear friend / Sunrise sunset / Do you love me / When Messiah comes / How much richer could one man be / If I were a rich man / In my own lifetime
CD ____________ DRG 5174
DRG / Jun '93 / Discovery / New Note/ Pinnacle

Harvey, Richard

SHROUD FOR A NIGHTINGALE (The Television & Film Music Of Richard Harvey)
Doctor Finlay / Game set & match / Defence of the realm / Assam garden / Hostages / Doomsday gun / Small dance / To each his own / Shape of the world / Wimbledon poisoner / Deadly advice / Shroud for a nightingale / Inspector Dalgleish investigates / GBH / Jake's progress
CD ____________ FILMCD 172
Silva Screen / Jul '96 / Koch / Silva Screen

Herbert, Victor

VICTOR HERBERT SHOWCASE, A
CD ____________ PASTCD 9798
Flapper / Oct '92 / Pinnacle

Herman, Jerry

EVENING WITH JERRY HERMAN, AN
Herman, Jerry & Lisa Kirk/Joe Masiell/ Carol Dorian
Salome salome / Just leave everything to me / Put on your Sunday clothes / Ribbons down my back / Before the parade passes by / It only takes a moment / It's today / Open a new window / Man in the moon / Hooch's song / We need a little Christmas / Bosom buddies / If he walked into my life / I don't want to know / And I was beautiful
CD ____________ CDSL 5173
DRG / Jan '93 / Discovery / New Note/ Pinnacle

JERRY HERMAN SONGBOOK, THE
Feinstein, Micahel & Jerry Herman
CD ____________ 7559793152
Nonesuch / Jan '95 / Warner Music

Herrmann, Bernard

BERNARD HERRMANN FILM SCORES
Royal Philharmonic Orchestra
Bernstein, Elmer *Con*
Citizen Kane / Psycho / Vertigo / Taxi driver / Farenheit 451
CD ____________ 140812
Milan / Feb '94 / Conifer/BMG / Silva Screen

CITIZEN KANE
London Philharmonic Orchestra
Citizen Kane:Overture / Jane Eyre / Devil and Daniel Webster / Snows of Kilimanjaro / Jason and the argonauts / Citizen Kane:Variations / Citizen Kane:Ragtime / Citizen Kane:Finale / Swing your partners / Memory waltz
CD ____________ 4178522
Decca / Aug '88 / PolyGram

CITIZEN KANE (Classic Film Scores Of Bernard Herrmann)
National Philharmonic Orchestra
Gerhardt, Charles *Con*
Citizen Kane / On Dangerous Ground / Beneath the 12-Mile Reef / Hangover Square / White Witch Doctor
CD ____________ GD 80707
RCA Victor / Jun '91 / BMG

CLASSIC FANTASY FILM SCORES
Three Worlds Of Gulliver / Mysterious Island / Seventh Voyage Of Sinbad / Jason And The Argonauts
CD ____________ ACN 7014
Cloud Nine / Jun '88 / Koch / Silva Screen

FILM SCORES, THE
Salonen, Esa-Pekka & Los Angeles Philharmonic Orchestra
Man who knew too much / Psycho / Marnie / North by North West / Vertigo / Torn curtain / Farenheit 451 / Taxi driver

Burgon, Geoffrey

BRIDESHEAD REVISITED (The Television Scores Of Geoffrey Burgon)
Philharmonia Orchestra
Burgon, Geoffrey *Con*
Brideshead Revisited / Julia / Julia's theme / Hunt / Fading light / Farewell to Brideshead / Testament of youth / Intimations of war / Elegy / Finale / Bleak house / Streets of London / Dedlock versus Boythorn / Lady Dedlock's quest / Finale / Opening music / Nunc Dimittis / Aslan's theme / Great battle / Mr. Tumnus' tune / Storm at sea / Aslan sacrificed / Journey to Harlang / Farewell to Narnia
CD ______ **FILMCD 117**
Silva Screen / Feb '95 / Koch / Silva Screen

Caesar, Irving

THE GREAT ONES
CD ______ **PASTCD 7075**
Flapper / Nov '95 / Pinnacle

Cahn, Sammy

EVENING WITH SAMMY CAHN, AN
Cahn, Sammy & Bobbi Baird/Shirley Lemmon/Jon Peck
CD ______ **DRG 5172**
DRG / Jun '93 / Discovery / New Note/ Pinnacle

Carmichael, Hoagy

SONG IS...HOAGY CARMICHAEL, THE
Ev'ntide: *Armstrong, Louis* / Lazy river: *Armstrong, Louis* / Lyin' to myself: *Armstrong, Louis* / Rockin' chair: *Armstrong, Louis* / Judy in the morning: *Bowlly, Al* / One morning in May: *Bowlly, Al* / Two sleepy people: *Bowlly, Al* / Heart and soul: *Carless, Dorothy & Billy Mayerl* / Doctor, lawyer, Indian chief: *Carr, Carole* / Nearness of you: *Carr, Carole* / Blue orchids: *Dennis, Denny & Jack Hylton* / Little old lady: *Dennis, Denny & Jack Hylton* / Sing me a swing song: *Fitzgerald, Ella* / Down 't Uncle Bill's: *Gonella, Nat* / Jubilee: *Gonella, Nat* / Moon country: *Gonella, Nat* / Small fry: *Gonella, Nat* / I get along without you very well: *Layton, Turner* / Georgia on my mind: *Mills Brothers* / Stardust: *Mills Brothers* / Sing it way down low: *Prima, Louis* / Snowball: *Roy, Harry & His Orchestra* / Lazybones: *Stone, Lew & His Band*
CD ______ **CDAJA 5074**
Living Era / Oct '95 / Select

SONGS OF HOAGY CARMICHAEL, THE
CD ______ **GRF 094**
Tring / '93 / Tring

TRIBUTE TO HOAGY CARMICHAEL, A
CD ______ **CDDL 1280**
EMI / Nov '92 / EMI

Carpenter, John

BEST OF HALLOWEEN, THE
Carpenter, John
CD ______ **VSD 5773**
Varese Sarabande / Nov '96 / Pinnacle

HALLOWEEN (The Best Of John Carpenter)
Halloween / Fog / Christine / Thing / They live / Prince of Darkness / Starman / Escape from New York / Dark Star / Big trouble in Little China / Assault on Precinct 13
CD ______ **FILMCD 113**
Silva Screen / Sep '93 / Koch / Silva Screen

JOHN CARPENTER'S GREATEST HITS VOL.1
CD ______ **VSD 5266**
Varese Sarabande / Nov '92 / Pinnacle

JOHN CARPENTER'S GREATEST HITS VOL.2
CD ______ **VSCD 345336**
Varese Sarabande / Jul '93 / Pinnacle

Cary, Tristram

QUATERMASS AND THE PIT (The Film Music Of Tristram Cary Vol.1)
Quatermass and the pit / Sammy going south / Twist of sand / Flesh is weak / Tread softly stranger
CD ______ **CNS 5009**
Cloud Nine / Jul '96 / Koch / Silva Screen

Chaplin, Charlie

CHARLIE (Music From The Films Of Charlie Chaplin)
Munich Symphony Orchestra
Shaw, Francis *Con*
Limelight / Modern times / King in New York / City lights / Great dictator / Countess from Hong Kong
CD ______ **FILMCD 711**
Silva Screen / Jan '93 / Koch / Silva Screen

CHARLIE CHAPLIN (Music Of His Films)
Villard, Michel
Modern times / City lights / It's a dog's life / Smile / King in New York / Loving mandolin / Greater dictator / Marching tune / Prelude to Lohengrin / 5th Hungarian dance / Limelight / Two little ballet shoes / Pilgrim / Sqaure dance / Little buns on forks polka / Encounter with Georgia / Gold miners / Gold rush / You, my love
CD ______ **74321141452**
RCA / Jun '96 / BMG

ORIGINAL MUSIC FROM HIS MOVIES, THE
Day's pleasure / Pay day / Gold rush / Circus / City lights / Modern times / Great dictator / Limelight
2CD ______ **BM 99903/4**
Blue Moon / Jul '96 / Cadillac / Discovery / Greensleeves / Jazz Music / Jet Star / TKO Magnum

Cicognini, Alessandro

MUSIC FROM THE FILMS OF VITTORIO DE SICA
Shoeshine / Bicycle thief / Umberto D / Roof / Gold of Naples / Last judgement / Miracle in Milan
CD ______ **LEGENDCD 23**
Silva Screen / Apr '96 / Koch / Silva Screen

Cirque Du Soleil

ALEGRIA
Cirque Du Soleil
CD ______ **09026627012**
RCA Victor / Jan '96 / BMG

CIRQUE DU SOLEIL
Cirque Du Soleil
Overture / Bulgares / Boule 4 / Tango / Trapeze cadres / Fil de fer / Bicyclettes / Boules 1 a 3 / Les chaises / Entracte / Pingouins
CD ______ **09026625232**
RCA Victor / Jan '96 / BMG

MYSTERE
Cirque Du Soleil
Egypte / Rumeurs / Birimbau / Kunya sobe / En ville / Ulysse / Tondo / Caravena / Kalimando
CD ______ **09026626862**
RCA Victor / Jan '96 / BMG

NOUVELLE EXPERIENCE
Cirque Du Soleil
Fanfare / Meandres / Bolero / Bascule / Fixe / Ballant / Baleines / Havi vahli / Suite chinoise / Eclipse / L'oiseau / Azimut / Sanza / Grosse femme
CD ______ **09026615312**
RCA Victor / Jan '96 / BMG

SALTIMBANCO
Cirque Du Soleil
Kumbalawe / Barock / Kaze / Amazonia / Norweg / Urgence / Polinoi / Saltimbanco / Il sogno di volare / Horere ukunde / Rideau
CD ______ **74321257072**
RCA Victor / Jan '96 / BMG

Comden & Green

COMDEN AND GREEN SONGBOOK, THE
Broadway Casts
CD ______ **SK 48202**
Sony Broadway / Feb '93 / Sony

PARTY WITH BETTY COMDEN AND ADOLPH GREEN
Comden, Betty & Adolph Green
CD ______ **ZDM 7647732**
EMI Classics / Apr '93 / EMI

Cosma, Vladimir

VERY BEST OF VLADIMIR COSMA, THE
2CD ______ **DRGCD 32900**
DRG / Jan '95 / Discovery / New Note/ Pinnacle

Coward, Sir Noel

GREAT BRITISH DANCE BANDS PLAY NOEL COWARD
CD ______ **PASTCD 9758**
Flapper / Aug '91 / Pinnacle

TALENT TO AMUSE, A (The Songs Of Noel Coward)
Greenwell, Peter
Sail away / I travel alone / Mad dogs and Englishmen / Room with a view / Sigh no more / Bar on the piccola marina / Mrs. Worthington
CD ______ **SILVAD 3009**
Silva Treasury / Sep '95 / Koch / Silva Screen

Cunningham, David

WATER
Cunningham, David
Stars: *Cunningham, David & Robert Fripp* / Next day / Once removed / Fourth sea / White blue and grey / Shade creek / Short winter's day / Blue river / Beneath the vines / Yellow river / Low sun / Only shadows: *Cunningham, David & Peter Gordon* / Liquid hand / Dark ocean / Same day
CD ______ **MTM 31**
Made To Measure / Jun '96 / New Note/ Pinnacle

De Angelis, G. & M.

BEST OF BUD SPENCER & TERENCE HILL FILMS
CD ______ **FILMCD 106**
Silva Screen / Sep '93 / Koch / Silva Screen

BEST OF BUD SPENCER & TERENCE HILL FILMS II
CD ______ **SIL 15302**
Silva Screen / Sep '93 / Koch / Silva Screen

De Masi, Francesco

FILM MUSIC OF FRANCESCO DE MASI, THE
CD ______ **VCDS 7007**
Varese Sarabande / May '95 / Pinnacle

Delerue, Georges

BEST FILM MUSIC OF GEORGES DELERUE VOL.1 (Le Mepris/La Peau Douce/Mona/Les Deux Anglaises Et La Continent)
CD ______ **CD 319**
Milan / Jan '89 / Conifer/BMG / Silva Screen

BEST FILM MUSIC OF GEORGES DELERUE VOL.2
CD ______ **CD 320**
Milan / Jan '89 / Conifer/BMG / Silva Screen

LONDON SESSIONS VOL 1, THE
Rich and famous / Platoon / Beaches
CD ______ **VSD 5241**
Varese Sarabande / Apr '90 / Pinnacle

LONDON SESSIONS VOL 2, THE (Hommage A Francois Truffaut)
CD ______ **VSD 5245**
Varese Sarabande / Sep '90 / Pinnacle

LONDON SESSIONS VOL 3, THE
CD ______ **VSD 5256**
Varese Sarabande / Jul '91 / Pinnacle

MUSIC FROM THE FILMS OF FRANCOIS TRUFFAUT
CD ______ **CH 220**
Milan / Jan '89 / Conifer/BMG / Silva Screen

NONESUCH FILM MUSIC SERIES
London Sinfonietta
Wolff, Hugo *Con*
CD ______ **7559794052**
Nonesuch / Aug '97 / Warner Music

TRUFFAUT AND DELERUE ON THE SCREEN
Confidentially yours / Beautiful girl like me / Day for night / Last metro / Woman next door
CD ______ **DRGCD 32902**
DRG / Sep '93 / Discovery / New Note/ Pinnacle

Dessau, Paul

FOUR ALICE COMEDIES (Music For Silent Films Directed By Walt Disney/ The Magic Clock)
RIAS Sinfonietta
Zimmer, Hans *Con*
Alice in the wooly west / Alice and the firefighter / Magic clock / Enchanted forest / Alice's monkey business / Alice helps the romance
CD ______ **09026681442**
RCA Victor / Nov '96 / BMG

Devreese, Frederic

DEVREESE - FILM MUSIC
Belgian Radio & TV Orchestra
Devreese, Frederic *Con*
CD ______ **8223681**
Marco Polo / Nov '94 / Select

Donaggio, Pino

BRIAN DE PALMA FILM MUSIC
CD ______ **191922**
Milan / Jan '95 / Conifer/BMG / Silva Screen

Ellis, Vivian

SPREAD A LITTLE HAPPINESS
CD ______ **PASTCD 7076**
Flapper / Nov '95 / Pinnacle

SPREAD A LITTLE HAPPINESS
2CD ______ **CDHD 2578**
Happy Days / Oct '95 / Conifer/BMG

Erskine, Peter

BIG THEATRE (Scores Based On 12th Night/Richard III/Midsummer Night's Dream)
Cast Recording
CD ______ **AHUM 004**
Ah-Um / Jul '90 / Cadillac / New Note/ Pinnacle

Fielding, Jerry

JERRY FIELDING FILM MUSIC VOL.1
2CD ______ **BCDLE 4001/2**
Silva Screen / Jan '94 / Koch / Silva Screen

JERRY FIELDING FILM MUSIC VOL.2
CD ______ **BCDLE 4003**
Silva Screen / Jan '94 / Koch / Silva Screen

Fisher-Turner, Simon

MANY MOODS OF SIMON TURNER, THE
Fisher-Turner, Simon
Isles of spice / Exotic hats / Esperanza / Caravaggio 1986 / Sloane Square / Gourmet's love song / Colours of my life / Violet crumble
CD ______ **MONDE 14CD**
Cherry Red / Apr '93 / Pinnacle

Forrest & Wright

CLASSICS FROM HOLLYWOOD TO BROADWAY
Holliday, Melanie & Steven Kimborough/ Frankfurt Radio Orchestra
Falk, Peter *Con*
CD ______ **310642**
Koch Schwann / Dec '95 / Koch

Friml, Rudolf

ROMANTIC WORLD OF RUDOLF FRIML, THE
Song of the vagabonds / Only a rose / Blue kitten / Indian love call / One kiss / Rose Marie / Love me tonight / Three musketeers / Huguette waltz / Ma belle / Totem Tom / Twelve o'clock girl in a nine o'clock town / Sympathy waltz / Love everlasting / Vagabond King
CD ______ **PASTCD 9764**
Flapper / Jul '92 / Pinnacle

Garvarentz, Georges

MUSIQUE DE FILMS
CD ______ **3017692**
Arcade / Jun '97 / Discovery

Gay, Noel

LEANING ON A LAMP POST (The Music Of Noel Gay)
Run rabbit run: *Flanagan & Allen* / Oh buddy, I'm in love: *Gibbons, Carroll* / Let the people sing: *Geraldo & His Orchestra* / Lambeth walk: *Lane, Lupino* / There's something about a soldier: *Courtneidge, Cicely* / Love makes the world go round: *Browne, Sam* / I don't want to go to bed: *Browne, Sam* / Sun has got his hat on: *Browne, Sam* / You've done something to my heart: *Geraldo & His Orchestra* / All over the place: *Trinder, Tommy* / Fleet's in port again: *Breeze, Alan* / La di da di da: *Noble, Ray* / Bless you for being an angel: *Ink Spots* / Leaning on a lampost: *Formby, George* / Me and my girl: *Munro, Ronnie* / I took my harp to a party: *Cotton, Billy* / Hold my hand: *Bowlly, Al*
CD ______ **306372**
Hallmark / Jan '97 / Carlton

SONG IS...NOEL GAY, THE
Sun has got his hat on: *Ambrose & His Orchestra* / Hold my hand: *Bowlly, Al* / Girl who loves a soldier: *Cotton, Billy & His Band* / I took my harp to a party: *Cotton, Billy & His Band* / That started it: *Cotton, Billy & His Band* / There's something about a soldier: *Courtneidge, Cicely* / Run rabbit run: *Flanagan & Allen* / Leaning on a lamp post: *Formby, George* / All over the place: *Geraldo & His Orchestra* / Who's been polishing the sun: *Hulbert, Jack* / Love makes the world go round: *Hutch* / Melody maker: *Hylton, Jack* / Lambeth walk: *Lane, Lupino* / Let the people sing: *Laye, Evelyn* / You've done something to my heart: *Laye, Evelyn* / Oh what a wonderful night: *Laye, Evelyn* / Who's little what's-it are you: *London Piano Accordion Band* / Me and my girl: *Munro, Ronnie* / Fleet's in port again: *Payne, Jack & His Orchestra* / Moonlight Avenue: *Silvester, Victor*
CD ______ **CDAJA 5081**
Living Era / Oct '95 / Select

Gershwin, George

BARBARA HENDRICKS SINGS GERSHWIN
Hendricks, Barbara
CD ______ **4164602**
Philips / Jan '87 / PolyGram

CRAZY FOR GERSHWIN
Someone to watch over me: *Fitzgerald, Ella* / Love is here to stay: *Jones, Jack* / But not for me: *Crosby, Bing* / Embraceable you: *Garland, Judy* / Nice work if you can get it: *Fitzgerald, Ella* / I got plenty o' nuttin': *Crosby, Bing* / Swanee: *Jolson, Al* / How long has this been going on: *Fitzgerald, Ella* / They can't take that away from me: *Lee, Peggy* / Mine: *Garland, Judy & Bing Crosby* / Oh lady be good: *Fitzgerald, Ella* / I got rhythm: *Garland, Judy* / I loves you Porgy: *Holiday, Billie* / Love walked in: *Crosby, Bing* / Liza (all the clouds'll roll away): *Jolson, Al* / I've got a crush on you: *Fitzgerald, Ella*
CD Set ______ **CDMOIR 502**
Memoir / Jul '93 / Jazz Music / Target/BMG

GENIUS OF GEORGE GERSHWIN, THE
Starlight Orchestra
But not for me / Embraceable you / Fascinating rhythm / Foggy day / I got rhythm / It ain't necessarily so / Let's call the whole thing off / Liza / Man I love / Nice work if you can get it / Shall we dance / Someone

to watch over me / 'S wonderful / They can't take that away from me / Who cares / Long ago and far away / Summertime / There's a boat dat's leaving soon for New York / Oh I can't sit down / Somebbody loves me
CD ____ QED 109
Tring / Nov '96 / Tring

GERSHWIN ARRANGEMENTS
Andre, Maurice & Nicolas Andre/Beatrice Andre
Carradot, Andre *Con*
CD ____ CDC 5556202
EMI Classics / Jun '96 / EMI

GERSHWIN IN THE MOVIES VOL.1 & 2
St. Louis Symphony Orchestra
Slatkin, Leonard *Con*
2CD ____ CDCH 249/250
Milan / May '87 / Conifer/BMG / Silva Screen

GLORY OF GERSHWIN, THE
Summertime: *Gabriel, Peter* / Do what you do: *De Burgh, Chris* / Nice work if you can get it: *Sting* / They can't take that away from me: *Stansfield, Lisa* / Someone to watch over me: *John, Elton* / Our love is here to stay: *John, Elton* / I've got a crush on you: *Simon, Carly* / But not for me: *Costello, Elvis* / It ain't necessarily so: *Cher* / Man I love: *Bush, Kate* / How long has this been going on: *Bon Jovi, Jon* / Bidin' my time: *White, Willard* / My man's gone now: *O'Connor, Sinead* / I got rhythm: *Palmer, Robert* / Somebody loves me: *Meat Loaf* / Stairway to paradise: *Van Randwyck, Issy* / Rhapsody in blue: *Adler, Larry*
CD ____ 5227272
Mercury / Jul '94 / PolyGram

GREAT AMERICAN GERSHWIN
Pennario, Leonard & Hollywood Bowl Orchestra
Slatkin, Felix/Alfred Newman *Con*
Rhapsody in blue / American in Paris / Porgy And Bess / I got rhythm / Cuban overture / Second rhapsody
CD ____ CDM 5660862
Angel / Jun '97 / EMI

KIRI SINGS GERSHWIN
Te Kanawa, Dame Kiri & The New Princess Theater Orchestra
McGlinn, John *Con*
CD ____ CDC 7474542
EMI Classics / Apr '93 / EMI

MARNI NIXON SINGS GERSHWIN
Nixon, Marni
CD ____ RR 19
Reference Recordings / Sep '91 / Jazz Music / May Audio

PLAY GERSHWIN'S POPULAR WORKS
Boston Pops Orchestra
Fiedler, Arthur *Con*
Girl crazy suite / Wintergreen for president / Three preludes / Second rhapsody / Overtures from Oh Kay / Funny face / Let 'em eat cake / Of thee I sing
CD ____ 4439002
Decca / Feb '96 / PolyGram

S'MARVELLOUS
CD ____ 5216582
Verve / Feb '94 / PolyGram

SONG IS...GEORGE GERSHWIN, THE
Half of it, dearie blues: *Astaire, Fred* / I found a four leaf clover: *Audrey, Irene & Charles Hart* / Fascinating rhythm: *Edwards, Cliff* / When do we dance: *Gershwin, George* / My one and only: *Gershwin, George* / Little jazz bird: *Hylton, Jack* / Oh lady be good: *Hylton, Jack* / Liza (all the clouds'll roll away): *Jolson, Al* / Someone to watch over me: *Lawrence, Gertrude* / Do what you do: *O'Neal, Zelma* / Sweet and low down: *Selvin, Ben* / That certain feeling: *Selvin, Ben* / Funny face: *Smith, Jack* / I got plenty o' nuttin': *Tibbett, Lawrence* / I got rhythm: *Waller, Fats* / Nashville nightingale: *Waring, Fred & His Pennsylvanians* / Man I love: *Welch, Elizabeth* / I'll build a stairway to paradise: *Whiteman, Paul & Rhythm Boys* / S'wonderful: *Winter, Marius B. & His Dance Band*
CD ____ CDAJA 5048
Living Era / Oct '95 / Select

SONGBOOK
Let's call the whole thing off: *Holiday, Billie* / Summertime: *Parker, Charlie* / S'wonderful: *Basie, Count & Joe Williams* / Oh lady, be good: *Goodman, Benny* / It ain't necessarily so: *Armstrong, Louis & Ella Fitzgerald* / How long has this been going on: *Hawkins, Coleman* / There's a boat dat's leavin' soon for New York: *Anderson, Ernestine* / Our love is here to stay: *Cleveland, Jimmy* / I was doing alright: *Armstrong, Louis* / I got rhythm: *Peterson, Oscar Trio* / They all laughed: *Astaire, Fred* / I've got a crush on you: *Washington, Dinah* / Foggy day: *Carter, Benny* / Things are looking up: *Fitzgerald, Ella* / Someone to watch over me: *Kirk, Roland* / Strike up the band: *Garner, Erroll* / Embraceable you: *Vaughan, Sarah*
CD ____ 5526462
Spectrum / Mar '97 / PolyGram

SONGS & DUETS
Kaye, J./W. Sharp/S. Blier
CD ____ 370282
Koch / Jul '91 / Koch

SPOTLIGHT ON GEORGE GERSHWIN
Fascinating rhythm / 'S wonderful / Summertime / Embraceable you / Foggy day / It ain't necessarily so / Nice work / Man I love / Somebody loves me / They can't take that away from me / I got rhythm
CD ____ HADCD 139
Javelin / Feb '94 / Henry Hadaway / THE

S'WONDERFUL (The Songs Of George & Ira Gershwin)
Swanee: *Jolson, Al* / I got plenty o' nuttin': *Tibbett, Lawrence* / Love walked in: *Armstrong, Louis* / Embraceable you: *Garland, Judy* / Liza (all the clouds'll roll away): *Webb, Chick* / How long has this been going on: *Lee, Peggy* / Nice work if you can get it: *Dorsey, Tommy Orchestra* / Funny face: *Smith, Jack* / Oh lady be good: *Hawkins, Coleman* / Somebody loves me: *Carter, Benny* / Someone to watch over me: *Gershwin, George* / I've got a crush on you: *Wiley, Lee* / S'Wonderful: *Goodman, Benny* / I'll build a stairway to paradise: *Whiteman, Paul & Rhythm Boys* / I got rhythm: *Waller, Fats* / Man I love: *Forrest, Helen* / They all laughed: *Astaire, Fred* / Summertime: *Robeson, Paul* / I was doing alright: *Fitzgerald, Ella* / Fascinating rhythm: *Lee, Buddy* / They can't take that away from me: *Holiday, Billie*
CD ____ AVC 520
Avid / Apr '95 / Avid/BMG / Koch / THE

S'WONDERFUL (The Songs Of George Gershwin)
Nice work if you can get it: *Astaire, Fred* / Someone to watch over me: *Lawrence, Gertrude* / Looking for a boy: *Dickson, Dorothy* / Liza (all the clouds'll roll away): *Jolson, Al* / Foggy day: *Astaire, Fred* / S'wonderful: *Astaire, Adele & Bernard Clifton* / Lady be good: *Lee, Buddy & The Gilt-Edged Four* / Do do do: *Lawrence, Gertrude & Harold French* / Somebody loves me: *Crosby, Bing* / I got rhythm: *Webb, Chick & His Little Chicks* / I'll build a stairway to Paradise: *Whiteman, Paul & His Orchestra* / They can't take that away from me: *Astaire, Fred* / Funny face: *Astaire, Fred & Adele* / Fascinating rhythm: *Edwards, Cliff* / They all laughed: *Astaire, Fred* / That certain feeling: *Dickson, Dorothy & Allen Kearns* / Maybe: *Lawrence, Gertrude & Harold French* / My one and only: *Astaire, Fred* / Summertime: *Jamison, Anne* / Swanee: *Jolson, Al* / Let's call the whole thing off: *Astaire, Fred* / I got plenty o' nuttin': *Tibbett, Lawrence*
CD ____ PASTCD 9777
Flapper / Dec '92 / Pinnacle

TRIBUTE TO GEORGE GERSHWIN, A
CD ____ CDDL 1278
EMI / Nov '94 / EMI

TRIBUTE TO GEORGE GERSHWIN, A
CD ____ ENTCD 13053
Entertainers / Apr '94 / Target/BMG

Gilbert & Sullivan

ARIAS AND DUETS (The Best Of Gilbert & Sullivan)
Three little maids / When a felon's not engaged in his employment / Poor wandering one / Loudly let the trumpet bray / Take a pair of sparkling eyes / I have a song to sing / I know a youth / I'm called little buttercup / On a tree by a river / If somebody there chanced to be / Wandering minstrel / When the foreman bares his steel
CD ____ SHOWCD 017
Showtime / Feb '95 / Disc / THE

ARIAS AND DUETS OF GILBERT & SULLIVAN
CD ____ CDVIR 8325
TER / Aug '95 / Koch

BEST OF GILBERT & SULLIVAN, THE
CD ____ CDTEZ 7004
TER / Jan '95 / Koch

BEST OF GILBERT & SULLIVAN, THE
Sargent, Sir Malcolm *Con*
CD ____ CDZ 7625312
EMI Classics / Apr '93 / EMI

GILBERT & SULLIVAN - EXCERPTS
Soloists & Glyndebourne Festival Choir/ Pro Arte Orchestra
Sargent, Sir Malcolm *Con*
CD ____ CDCFP 4238
Classics For Pleasure / Jan '95 / EMI

GILBERT & SULLIVAN CLASSICS VOL.1 (Selections From The Mikado/Pirates Of Penzance/The Gondoliers/HMS Pinafore)
Alwyn, Kenneth/Richard Hickox *Con*
CD ____ HMV 58
HMV / Jan '95 / EMI

GILBERT & SULLIVAN CLASSICS VOL.2
Sargent, Sir Malcolm *Con*
CD ____ HMV 102
HMV / Jan '95 / EMI

GILBERT & SULLIVAN HIGHLIGHTS
Welsh National Opera Choir/Orchestra
Mackerras, Sir Charles *Con*
Mikado / HMS Pinafore / Pirates Of Penzance / Yeoman Of The Gaurd / Trial By Jury
CD ____ CD 80431
Telarc / Mar '96 / Conifer/BMG

GILBERT & SULLIVAN OVERTURES
Pro Arte Orchestra
Sargent, Sir Malcolm *Con*
CD ____ CDCFP 4529
Classics For Pleasure / Jan '95 / EMI

OVERTURES
New Sadler's Wells/D'Oyly Carte Opera Orchestra
Pryce Jones, J./S. Phipps/John Owen Edwards *Con*
CD ____ CDVIR 8316
TER / May '93 / Koch

OVERTURES
Academy Of St. Martin In The Fields
Marriner, Neville *Con*
CD ____ 4349162
Philips / Jun '93 / PolyGram

OVERTURES
Pro Arte Orchestra/Vienna Philharmonic Orchestra
Sargent, Sir Malcolm *Con*
Mikado / Gondoliers / Yeoman of the guard / HMS Pinafore / Iolanthe / Sorcerer / Cox and box / Princes Ida / Ruddigore / Patience
2CD ____ CES 5691372
EMI Classics / Feb '96 / EMI

UNFORGETTABLE CLASSICS
CD ____ CDCFP 4695
Classics For Pleasure / Apr '96 / EMI

VERY BEST OF GILBERT & SULLIVAN, THE
CD ____ CDMOIR 413
Memoir / Aug '93 / Jazz Music / Target/ BMG

WORLD OF GILBERT & SULLIVAN VOL.1, THE
HMS Pinafore / Mikado / Yeoman of the guard / Pirates of Penzance / Iolanthe / Gondoliers
CD ____ 4300952
Decca / Jun '91 / PolyGram

WORLD OF GILBERT & SULLIVAN VOL.2, THE
HMS Pinafore / Mikado / Patience / Iolanthe / Gondoliers / Ruddigore / Sorcerer / Yeoman of the guard / Princess Ida / Pirates of Penzance
CD ____ 4338682
Decca / Feb '93 / PolyGram

Glass, Philip

FILM WORKS (Anima Mundi/Mishima/ Powaqattsi/The Thin Blue Line)
Glass, Philip Ensemble/Kronos Quartet
4CD ____ 7559793772
Nonesuch / Jan '95 / Warner Music

Goodwin, Ron

MISS MARPLE FILMS, THE (& Other Film Suites)
Murder she said / Murder at the gallop / Murder most foul / Murder ahoy / Force 10 from Navarone / Lancelot and Guinevere
CD ____ LXE 706
Label X / Mar '93 / Silva Screen

Grainer, Ron

DOCTOR WHO (& Other Classic Ron Grainer TV Themes)
Maigret / Steptoe and son / Some people / Man in a suitcase / Prisoner / Assassination bureau / Only when I larf / Paul Temple / Tales of the unexpected / Edward and Mrs. Simpson / Dr. Who
CD ____ PLAY 008
Play It Again / Oct '96 / Silva Screen

Gray, Barry

FAB (Music From The Gerry Anderson TV Shows)
Royal Philharmonic Orchestra
Pavlov, Konstantin *Con*
Thunderbirds / Space 1999 / Joe 90 / Stingray / UFO / Captain Scarlet
CD ____ FILMCD 124
Silva Screen / Nov '92 / Koch / Silva Screen

NO STRINGS ATTACHED
Gray, Barry Orchestra
Thunderbirds / Captain Scarlet / Hijacked / Aqua Marina / Stingray / Mysterons / Joe 90 / Parker - well done
CD ____ CLACD 204
Castle / Oct '90 / BMG

THUNDERBIRDS ARE GO
Gray, Barry *Con*
Thunderbirds theme / Alan's dream / Joie de vivre / Martian mystery / Thunderbirds theme (reprise) / Astronauts in trouble / Zero X theme / That dangerous game / Swinging star / San Marino / Jeremiah / Tracy Island
CD ____ FILMCD 018
Silva Screen / Aug '90 / Koch / Silva Screen

Hammerstein II, Oscar

OSCAR & STEVE
Patinkin, Mandy
Showboat / Passion / Follies / Pacific overtures / Anyone can whistle / Merrily we roll along / Into the woods / Little night music / Carousel / Flower drum song / South Pacific / Sound of music / Kiss to build a dream on / Carmen Jones / Night is young

CD ____ 7559793922
Nonesuch / Apr '96 / Warner Music

Harburg, E.Y. 'Yip'

YIP SINGS HARBURG
Harburg, E.Y. 'Yip'
CD ____ 373862
Koch International / Jun '97 / Koch

Harnell, Joe

FILM & TV MUSIC OF JOE HARNELL
2CD ____ FJCD 001/2
Silva Screen / Jan '92 / Koch / Silva Screen

Harnick, Sheldon

EVENING WITH SHELDON HARNICK, AN
Harnick, Sheldon & Margery Gray/Mary Louise
Suave young man / How could I / Merry little minuet / Boston beguine / At the Basilica of St. Anne / Garbage / Worlds apart / Little tin box / Till tomorrow / Picture of happiness / She loves me / Dear friend / Sunrise sunset / Do you love me / When Messiah comes / How much richer could one man be / If I were a rich man / In my own lifetime
CD ____ DRG 5174
DRG / Jun '93 / Discovery / New Note/ Pinnacle

Harvey, Richard

SHROUD FOR A NIGHTINGALE (The Television & Film Music Of Richard Harvey)
Doctor Finlay / Game set & match / Defence of the realm / Assam garden / Hostages / Doomsday gun / Small dance / To each his own / Shape of the world / Wimbledon poisoner / Deadly advice / Shroud for a nightingale / Inspector Dalgleish investigates / GBH / Jake's progress
CD ____ FILMCD 172
Silva Screen / Jul '96 / Koch / Silva Screen

Herbert, Victor

VICTOR HERBERT SHOWCASE, A
CD ____ PASTCD 9796
Flapper / Oct '92 / Pinnacle

Herman, Jerry

EVENING WITH JERRY HERMAN, AN
Herman, Jerry & Lisa Kirk/Joe Masiell/ Carol Dorian
Salome salome / Just leave everything to me / Put on your Sunday clothes / Ribbons down my back / Before the parade passes by / It only takes a moment / It's today / Open a new window / Man in the moon / Hooch's song / We need a little Christmas / Bosom buddies / If he walked into my life / I don't want to know / And I was beautiful
CD ____ CDSL 5173
DRG / Jan '93 / Discovery / New Note/ Pinnacle

JERRY HERMAN SONGBOOK, THE
Feinstein, Micahel & Jerry Herman
CD ____ 7559793152
Nonesuch / Jan '95 / Warner Music

Herrmann, Bernard

BERNARD HERRMANN FILM SCORES
Royal Philharmonic Orchestra
Bernstein, Elmer *Con*
Citizen Kane / Psycho / Vertigo / Taxi driver / Farenheit 451
CD ____ 140812
Milan / Feb '94 / Conifer/BMG / Silva Screen

CITIZEN KANE
London Philharmonic Orchestra
Citizen Kane:Overture / Jane Eyre / Devil and Daniel Webster / Snows of Kilimanjaro / Jason and the argonauts / Citizen Kane:Variations / Citizen Kane:Ragtime / Citizen Kane:Finale / Swing your partners / Memory waltz
CD ____ 4178522
Decca / Aug '88 / PolyGram

CITIZEN KANE (Classic Film Scores Of Bernard Herrmann)
National Philharmonic Orchestra
Gerhardt, Charles *Con*
Citizen Kane / On Dangerous Ground / Beneath the 12-Mile Reef / Hangover Square / White Witch Doctor
CD ____ GD 80707
RCA Victor / Jun '91 / BMG

CLASSIC FANTASY FILM SCORES
Three Worlds Of Gulliver / Mysterious Island / Seventh Voyage Of Sinbad / Jason And The Argonauts
CD ____ ACN 7014
Cloud Nine / Jun '88 / Koch / Silva Screen

FILM SCORES, THE
Salonen, Esa-Pekka & Los Angeles Philharmonic Orchestra
Man who knew too much / Psycho / Marnie / North by North West / Vertigo / Torn curtain / Farenheit 451 / Taxi driver

CD SK 62700
Sony Classical / Dec '96 / Sony

GREAT FILM MUSIC OF BERNARD HERRMANN
CD 4438992
London / Feb '96 / PolyGram

INQUIRER, THE (The Film Music Of Bernard Herrmann)
CD PRCD 1789
Preamble / Sep '92 / Silva Screen

MARVELLOUS FILM WORLD OF BERNARD HERRMANN, THE
Cape Fear / Garden of Evil / Beneath the 12-Mile Reef / King of the Khyber Rifles
CD TCI 0605
Tsunami / May '95 / Silva Screen

MUSIC FROM GREAT HITCHCOCK THRILLERS, THE
London Philharmonic Orchestra
Herrmann, Bernard *Con*
Psycho narrative / Marnie / North by North West / Vertigo / Trouble with Harry
CD 4438952
London / Mar '96 / PolyGram

MUSIC FROM THE GREAT FILM CLASSICS
Herrmann, Bernard *Con*
Citizen Kane: *London Philharmonic Orchestra* / Jane Eyre: *London Philharmonic Orchestra* / Mysterious Island: *National Philharmonic Orchestra* / Devil and Daniel Webster: *London Philharmonic Orchestra* / Snows of Kilimanjaro: *London Philharmonic Orchestra* / Jason and the Argonauts: *National Philharmonic Orchestra*
CD 4489482
Phase 4 / Aug '96 / PolyGram

PARTNERSHIP IN TERROR, A
City Of Prague Philharmonic Orchestra
Bateman, Paul *Con*
Psycho / North by North West / Marnie / Man who knew too much / Trouble with Harry / Vertigo / Torn curtain
CD SILVAD 3010
Silva Screen / Oct '96 / Koch / Silva Screen

TORN CURTAIN (Classic Film Music Of Bernard Herrmann)
City Of Prague Philharmonic Orchestra
Bateman, Paul *Con*
Citizen Kane / Cape Fear / Psycho / Ghost and Mrs. Muir / Obsession / Snows of Kilimanjaro / Taxi driver / On dangerous ground / Man who knew too much / Ray Harryhausen fantasy film suite
CD FILMCD 162
Silva Screen / Sep '95 / Koch / Silva Screen

Holdridge, Lee

FILM MUSIC OF LEE HOLDRIDGE, THE
London Symphony Orchestra
Gerhardt, Charles *Con*
Wizards and warriors / Splash / Great Whales (theme) / Hemingway play - Parisian sketch / Going home / Journey / Beastmaster suite / Music for strings / East of Eden (suite)
CD VCD 47244
Varese Sarabande / Jan '89 / Pinnacle

Honegger, Arthur

HONEGGER: FILM MUSIC
Bratislava Symphony Orchestra
Crime et chatiment suite / Deserteur fragment / Farinet suite / Grand barrage image / Idee
CD 8223466
Marco Polo / Jun '94 / Select

HONEGGER: FILM SCORES
Slovak Philharmonic Choir/Bratislava Symphony Orchestra
Mayering / Regain / Demons d'Himalaya
CD 8223467
Marco Polo / Jun '94 / Select

Ibert, Jacques

IBERT - FILM MUSIC
Bratislava Symphony Orchestra
Macbeth suite / Golgotha suite / Don Quichotte / Chansons de Don Quichotte
CD 8223287
Marco Polo / Mar '91 / Select

Jacobs, Dick

THEMES FROM CLASSIC SCIENCE FICTION, FANTASY & HORROR FILMS
CD VSD 5407
Varese Sarabande / Feb '93 / Pinnacle

Jarre, Maurice

DOCTOR ZHIVAGO (The Classic Film Music Of Maurice Jarre)
City Of Prague Philharmonic Orchestra
Bateman, Paul *Con*
Dr. Zhivago / Passage to India / Ryan's daughter / Lawrence of Arabia / Ghost / Witness / Is Paris Burning / Night of the Generals / Man Who Would Be King / Villa Rides / Fatal Attraction / El Condor / Fixer / Jesus of Nazareth
CD FILMCD 158
Silva Screen / May '95 / Koch / Silva Screen

FILM MUSIC OF MAURICE JARRE, THE
CD MCCD 277
Music Club / Dec '96 / Disc / THE

MAURICE JARRE AT ABBEY ROAD
Royal Philharmonic Orchestra
Jarre, Maurice *Con*
CD 262321
Milan / Sep '93 / Conifer/BMG / Silva Screen

MAURICE JARRE AT THE ROYAL FESTIVAL HALL
Jarre, Maurice
CD 74321433572
Milan / Feb '97 / Conifer/BMG / Silva Screen

THEATRE NATIONAL POPULAIRE
CD 74321468322
Milan / Jul '97 / Conifer/BMG / Silva Screen

THEATRE NATIONAL POPULAIRE (The Complete Works)
3CD 74321468312
Milan / Jul '97 / Conifer/BMG / Silva Screen

Jaubert, Maurice

MUSIC FROM THE FILMS OF FRANCOIS TRUFFAUT VOL 2
CD CH 293
Milan / Jan '89 / Conifer/BMG / Silva Screen

Kalthoum, Oum

SOUNDTRACK CUTS 1936-1946
Kalthoum, Oum
CD 829412
BUDA / Jun '97 / Discovery

Kancheli, G.A.

FILM MUSIC
Georgia State Symphony Orchestra/ USSR Cinema Symphony Orchestra
Kakhidze, D./S. Skripka *Con*
Don't grieve / Day of wrath / Kin-dza-dza / Passport
CD OCD 608
Olympia / Mar '96 / Priory

Kander & Ebb

EVENING WITH KANDER & EBB, AN
Kander, John & Fred Ebb
Sara Lee / Liza with a 'z' / My colouring book / Ring them bells / Life is / Cabaret / Quiet thing / Money money money / Maybe this time / Tomorrow morning / Please stay / All that jazz / Roxie / Yes
CD DRG 5171
DRG / Jan '95 / Discovery / New Note/ Pinnacle

Kaper, Bronislaw

FILM MUSIC OF BRONISLAW KAPER
Mutiny on the bounty / Lilli / Glass slipper / Butterfield 8 / Auntie Mame / Chocolate soldier / Invitation / Brother Karamazov / Green Dolphin Street / Swan / Lord Jim / San Francisco
CD FA 8101
Facet / May '94 / Conifer/BMG

Karaindrou, Eleni

MUSIC FOR FILMS
Farewell theme / Elegy for Rosa / Fairytale / Parade / Return / Wandering in Alexandria / Journey / Scream / Adagio / Fairytale / Parade / Elegy for Rosa / Rosa's song / Improvisation on farewell and waltz / Wandering in Alexandria / Song / Farewell theme
CD 8476092
ECM / Jul '94 / New Note/Pinnacle

Kazanecki, Waldemar

WALDEMAR KAZANECKI: FILM MUSIC
Polish Symphony Orchestra
Kazanecki, Waldemar *Con*
Night and days / House / Love will forgive you everything / By journey / Eva's madness / Boat to Sweden / Dark haired man / Gypsy Autumn / Harbours / Pacific 88
CD OCD 603
Olympia / Aug '94 / Priory

Kern, Jerome

CLASSIC MOVIE AND BROADWAY SHOW TUNES FROM RARE PIANO ROLLS
Look for the silver lining: *Cook, J. Lawrence* / Who: *Arden, Victor* / Smoke gets in your eyes: *Cook, J. Lawrence* / Fine romance: *Cook, J. Lawrence* / Way you look tonight: *Jouard, Paul* / All the things you are: *Cook, J. Lawrence* / Last time I saw Paris: *Cook, J. Lawrence* / Show Boat medley: *Watson, Dick*
CD BCD 142
Biograph / Jun '97 / ADA / Cadillac / Direct / Hot Shot / Jazz Music / Wellard

ELIZABETH WELCH SINGS JEROME KERN
Welch, Elizabeth
CD CDVIR 8310
TER / Jan '90 / Koch

JEROME KERN SHOWCASE, A
Back to the heather / D'ye love me / Showboat / Who / Try to forget / Song is you / I might grow fond of you / Cabaret girl / Look for the silver lining / Do I do wrong / Fine romance / Cat and the fiddle / I've told every little star / Sunny / Reckless / Sweet Adeline / High, wide and handsome / Waltz / New love is old / Sally
CD PASTCD 9767
Flapper / Nov '91 / Pinnacle

JEROME KERN TREASURY
London Sinfonietta
McGlinn, John *Con*
CD CDC 7548832
EMI Classics / Apr '94 / EMI

KIRI SINGS KERN
Te Kanawa, Dame Kiri & London Sinfonietta
Tunick, Jonathan *Con*
CD CDC 7545272
EMI Classics / Apr '93 / EMI

MARNI NIXON SINGS CLASSIC KERN
Nixon, Marni
CD RR 28
Reference Recordings / '90 / Jazz Music / May Audio

SHOWBOAT AND OTHER CLASSICS
Stride, Fred Orchestra
Stride, Fred *Con*
Showboat medley / Last time I saw Paris / I won't dance / I'm old fashioned / Roberta / Folks who live on the hill / Who / Way you look tonight / I've told every little star / All the things you are / Song is you
CD MVCD 1099
CBC / Nov '96 / Kingdom

SILVER LININGS (Songs Of Jerome Kern)
Morris, Joan & William Bolcom
CD Z 6515
Arabesque / Nov '85 / New Note/Pinnacle

SONG IS...JEROME KERN, THE
She didn't say yes: *Ambrose & His Orchestra* / They didn't believe me: *Ambrose & His Orchestra* / Song is you: *BBC Dance Orchestra* / I'll be hard to handle: *Coleman, Emil* / Let's begin: *Coleman, Emil* / Make believe: *Crosby, Bing & Paul Whiteman* / I've told ev'ry little star: *Ellis, Mary* / Who: *Hopkins, Claude* / Look for the silver lining: *Hopkins, Claude* / Bill: *Morgan, Helen* / Can't help lovin' dat man: *Morgan, Helen* / Ol' man river: *Robeson, Paul* / Hand in hand: *Stone, Lew & Al Bowlly* / Sunny: *Ipana Troubadours* / Smoke gets in your eyes: *Whiteman, Paul & Rhythm Boys* / Something had to happen: *Whiteman, Paul & Rhythm Boys*
CD CDAJA 5036
Living Era / Oct '95 / Select

SONGS OF JEROME KERN
CD MCCD 187
Music Club / Nov '94 / Disc / THE

SURE THING, A (The Jerome Kern Songbook)
CD 4421292
Philips / Dec '94 / PolyGram

SURE THING, A (Song Arrangements)
Bennett, Richard Rodney & Barry Tuckwell
Richardson, Neil *Con*
CD CDEMX 2270
Eminence / Apr '96 / EMI

TRIBUTE TO JEROME KERN, A
2CD CDDL 1290
EMI / Jun '95 / EMI

YESTERDAYS (The Unforgettable Music Of Jerome Kern)
Pick yourself up: *Astaire, Fred* / Never gonna dance: *Astaire, Fred* / Look for the silver lining: *Matthews, Jessie* / Song is you: *BBC Dance Orchestra* / Smoke gets in your eyes: *Robins, Phyllis* / Last time I saw Paris: *Shelton, Anne* / I've told ev'ry little star: *Ellis, Mary* / She didn't say yes: *Wood, Peggy* / Make believe: *Goodman, Benny* / Yesterdays: *Holiday, Billie* / Why was I born: *Holiday, Billie* / Whose baby are you: *Gershwin, George* / Why do I love you: *Beiderbecke, Bix* / Can't help lovin' dat man: *Morgan, Helen* / I might grow fonder of you: *Randolph, Elsie* / It'll be hard to handle: *Coleman, Emil* / They didn't believe me: *Stone, Lew & Al Bowlly* / Something had to happen: *Whiteman, Paul & Rhythm Boys* / Ol' man river: *Robeson, Paul* / Folks who live on the hill: *Crosby, Bing*
CD AVC 519
Avid / Apr '95 / Avid/BMG / Koch / THE

YESTERDAYS (The Jerome Kern Songbook)
CD 5333312
Verve / May '97 / PolyGram

Khachaturian, Aram

FILM MUSIC
Armenian Philharmonic Orchestra
Tjeknavorian, Loris *Con*
Pepo / Undying Flame / Secret Mission / Admiral Ushakov / Prisoner No. 217
CD CDDCA 966
ASV / Jun '97 / Select

Kilar, Wojciech

COLLECTION
CD 176382
Milan / Jul '93 / Conifer/BMG / Silva Screen

FILM MUSIC
Polish Symphony Orchestra
Kilar, Wojciech *Con*
Land of promise / Balance / Hypothesis / Polaniecki family / Silence / Taste of black earth / Pearl in the crown / Salto / Jealousy and medicine / Leper
CD OCD 602
Olympia / Aug '94 / Priory

WARSAW TO HOLLYWOOD
Chronique des Evenements Amoureux / La ligne d'Ombre / La Terre de la Grande Promesse / Bram Stoker's Dracula / Death and the maiden / Full gallop / Bilan Trimestriel / Contrat / L'Annee du Soleil Calme / Wherever you are / Father Kolbe / Life for life / Hasard / Jalousie et Medecine / La Lepreuse
CD 74321459722
Milan / Mar '97 / Conifer/BMG / Silva Screen

Knopfler, Mark

SCREENPLAYING
Knopfler, Mark
Irish boy / Irish love / Father and son / Potato picking / Long road / Love idea / Victims / Finale / Once upon a time ..... storybook love / Morning ride / Friends song / Guide my sword / Happy ending / Wild theme / Boomtown / Mist covered mountains / Smooching / Going home
CD 5183272
Vertigo / Nov '93 / PolyGram

Koechlin, Charles

SEVEN STARS' SYMPHONY, THE (& Four Interludes/L'Andalouse Dans Barcelone)
German Symphony Orchestra
Judd, James *Con*
CD 9026681462
RCA Victor / Jun '96 / BMG

Korngold, Erich

ELIZABETH AND ESSEX (The Classic Film Scores Of Erich Wolfgang Korngold)
National Philharmonic Orchestra
Gerhardt, Charles *Con*
Private Lives of Elizabeth and Essex / Prince and the Pauper / Sea Wolf / Deception / Of Human Bondage / Anthony Adverse / Another Dawn
CD GD 80185
RCA Victor / Jun '91 / BMG

WARNER BROS. YEARS, THE
Korngold, Erich
Captain Blood / Green Pastures / Anthony Adverse / Prince & the pauper / Adventures of Robin Hood / Juarez / Private lives of Elizabeth & Essex / Sea hawk / Sea wolf / Kings row / Constant nymph / Devotion / Between two worlds / Of human bondage / Escape me never / Deception
CD CDODEON 13
Soundtracks / Apr '96 / EMI

Korzynski, Andrzej

FILM MUSIC
Korzynski, Andrzej *Con*
Man of iron / Man of marble / Birchwood / Hunting flies
CD OCD 601
Olympia / Aug '94 / Priory

Kunzel, Erich

BIG PICTURE, THE
Cincinnati Pops Orchestra
Kunzel, Erich *Con*
Mission Impossible / Batman Forever / Reentry and splashdown / Express bus to LA / Speed / Roll tide / Into the battle / Independence Day / Braveheart / Cutthroat island / Tornado terror / House visit / Last Of The Mohicans / Dragon Heart / Remora / Going home / Library stampede / Gettysburg / Bovine Barnstorm / Jumanji
CD CD 80437
Telarc / Jun '97 / Conifer/BMG

VERY BEST OF ERICH KUNZEL, THE
Laine, F./R. Leech/Central St. Uni. Choir/ Cincinnati Pops Orchestra
Kunzel, Erich *Con*
Round up / Star Trek / Sing, sing, sing / Tara's theme (Gone with the wind) / Unchained melody / Nessun dorma / Little fugue in G minor / Star Wars / Batman / Grand Canyon suite / From Russia with love / Olympic fanfare / Opening sequence from Chiller / Overture to the Phantom Of The Opera / Godfather / Pink Panther / O mio babbino caro / Non-stop fast polka / Op 112 / Honor, honor, do lord / Cybergenesis / Terminator / Jurassic lunch
CD CD 80401
Telarc / Sep '94 / Conifer/BMG

Kurylewicz, Andrzej

ANDRZEJ KURYLEWICZ: FILM MUSIC
Warsaw National Philharmonic/Lodz Philharmonic Orchestras
Kurylewicz, Andrzej *Con*
Polish roads / On the Niemen river / Doll / Pan Tudeusz
CD ________ **OCD 605**
Olympia / Aug '94 / Priory

Lai, Francis

30 YEARS OF FILM MUSIC VOL.1 & 2
Les Etoiles Du Cinema / Un Homme Et Une Femme / Vivre Pour Vivre / 13 Jours En France / Mayerling / Le Passger De La Pluie / Love Story / Smic Smac Smoc / La Course Du Lievre A Travers Les Champs / Un Amour De Pluie / Mariage / La Babysitter / Emmanuelle II / Le Corps De Mon Ennemi / Bilitis / Un Autre Homme Une Autre Chance / Robert Et Robert / International Velvet / Les Borsalinis / Indian Summer / Les Uns Et les Autres / Madam Claude II / Edith Et Marcel / Canicule / Les Ripoux / Mary, A True Story / Un Homme Et Une Femme Vingt Ans Deja / Les Yeux Noirs / Itineraire D'Un Enfant Gate / Les Pyramids Bleus / Il Y A Des Jours Et Des Lunes / Ripoux Contre Ripoux / Les Cles Du Paradis / La Belle Histoire / Le Provincial / Tolgi Il Disturbo / L'Inconnu Dans La Maison / Tout Ca Pour Ca / Les Miserables / Instrumental theme: La valse du XXeme siecle
2CD ________ **SION 18602**
Sion / Jul '97 / Direct

FILM MUSIC OF FRANCIS LAI
CD ________ **CDCIA 5034**
Cinevox / Sep '92 / Koch / Silva Screen

FRANCIS LAI
CD ________ **HM 012**
Harmony / Jun '97 / TKO Magnum

INEDITS (Rare Film Themes)
CD ________ **MANTRA 057**
Silva Screen / Sep '93 / Koch / Silva Screen

ROMANTIC MUSIC OF FRANCIS LAI, THE
Love story / Man and a woman / Love in the rain / Live for life / Seduction / Emotion / Solitude / Les unes et les autres / La ronde / African summer / Par le sang des autres / Intimate moments / Whitechapel / Smic smac smoc / Blue rose / Bilitis / Sur notre etoile / Happy new year
CD ________ **EMPRCD 722**
Emporio / Jun '97 / Disc

Lane, Burton

BURTON LANE SONGBOOK, THE
Feinstein, Michael
CD ________ **7559792832**
Nonesuch / Aug '94 / Warner Music

Legrand, Michel

LA VIE DE CHATEAU/LE SAUVAGE/LES MARTES
CD ________ **3003992**
Playtime / Feb '97 / Discovery

TRAVELLING MUSIC & CINEMA SERIES (Harp/Orchestra Arrangements Of Legrand Film Sores)
CD ________ **K 1020**
Travelling Music & Cinema Series / Feb '96 / Harmonia Mundi

Leiber & Stoller

SONGS OF LIEBER & STOLLER
CD ________ **NEBCD 656**
Sequel / Jun '93 / BMG

Lerner & Lowe

LERNER & LOEWE SONGBOOK
Cincinnati Pops Orchestra
CD ________ **CD 80375**
Telarc / Jan '94 / Conifer/BMG

SPOTLIGHT ON LERNER & LOWE
I've grown accustomed to her face / Gigi / Wouldn't it be lovely / Almost like being in love / I talk to the trees / They call the wind Maria / On the street where you live / Waltz at Maxim's / Get me to the church on time / If ever I would leave you / Rain in Spain / Thank heaven for little girls
CD ________ **HADCD 138**
Javelin / Feb '94 / Henry Hadaway / THE

Lerner, Alan Jay

EVENING WITH ALAN JAY LERNER, AN
CD ________ **OCRCD 6012**
First Night / Apr '96 / Pinnacle

EVENING WITH ALAN JAY LERNER, AN
Lerner, Alan Jay & Bobbi Baird/J.T. Cromwell/Barbara Williams
How to handle a woman / Why can't a woman / I talk to the trees / Wouldn't it be loverly / Oh come to the ball / On the street where you live / Come back to me / What did I have that I don't have / I'm glad I'm not young anymore / I loved you in silence / Gigi / Camelot / On a clear day / I've grown accustomed to her face

CD ________ **DRG 5175**
DRG / Jan '95 / Discovery / New Note/ Pinnacle

Lloyd Webber, Andrew

ANDREW LLOYD WEBBER ALBUM, THE
Beechman, Laurie
CD ________ **VSD 5583**
Varese Sarabande / Aug '95 / Pinnacle

ANDREW LLOYD WEBBER COLLECTION, THE
Starlight express: *Wayne, Carl* / Unexpected song: *Jones, Paul* / Macavity: *Lawrence, Stephanie* / Memory: *Lawrence, Stephanie* / Gus the theatre cat: *Jones, Paul* / Pumping iron: *Conrad, Jess* / Tell me on a Sunday: *Wayne, Carl* / I don't know how to love him: *Hendley, Fiona* / Any dream will do: *Conrad, Jess* / Love changes everything: *Lawrence, Stephanie* / All I ask of you: *Lawrence, Stephanie* / Oh what a circus: *Conrad, Jess* / Wishing you were somehow here again: *Lawrence, Stephanie*
CD ________ **PWKS 4065**
Carlton / Aug '91 / Carlton

ANDREW LLOYD WEBBER'S GREATEST HITS
CD ________ **CDTEZ 7001**
TER / Jan '95 / Koch

BEST OF ANDREW LLOYD WEBBER, THE
Journey of a lifetime / Last man in my life / Rolling stock / Another suitcase in another hall / Close every door / Everything's alright / Gethsemane / There is more to love / Old deuteronomy / High flying adored / Don't cry for me Argentina / First man you remember / Pie jesu / Starlight express / Uexpected song / Memory / Macavity / Gus the theatre cat / Pumping iron / Tell me on a Sunday / I don't how to love him / Any dream will do / Love changes everything / All I ask of you / Oh what a circus / Wishing you were here again / Superstar / Chanson d'enfance / Mr. Mistoffelees / One more angel in heaven / Anything but lonely / Half a moment / Take that look off your face / On this night of a thousand stars / Seeing is believing / Think of me / Music of the night / Phantom of the opera
2CD ________ **BOXD 39T**
Carlton / Oct '94 / Carlton

CLASSIC ANDREW LLOYD WEBBER
West End Theatre Orchestra & Chorus
Superstar / Memory / Starlight Express / Don't cry for me Argentina / Take that look off your face / Journey of a lifetime / Any dream will do / Close every door / I don't know how to love him / Tell me on a Sunday / Love changes everything / Music of the night / All I ask of you
CD ________ **CDMFP 6106**
Music For Pleasure / Nov '93 / EMI

CLASSIC SONGS (Featuring Lesley Garrett)
Royal Philharmonic Concert Orchestra
Bateman, Paul *Con*
CD ________ **SONGCD 909**
Silva Classics / Sep '93 / Koch / Silva Screen

ESSENTIALS VOL.1
Memory: *Friedman, Maria* / Any dream will do: *Barrowman, John* / Think of me: *Moore, Claire & John Barrowman* / Don't cry for me Argentina: *Friedman, Maria* / There's me: *Carter, Clive* / All I ask of you: *Moore, Claire & John Barrowman* / Another suitcase in another hall: *Renihan, Grania* / Mr. Mistoffelees: *Carter, Clive* / Tell me on a Sunday: *Robertson, Liz* / High flying adored: *Barrowman, John & Maria Friedman* / I don't know how to love him: *Friedman, Maria* / Only you: *Renihan, Grania* / Music of the night: *Dietrich, John* / Seeing is believing: *Barrowman, John & Janis Kelly* / Close every door: *Carter, Clive* / Wishing you were somehow here again: *Moore, Claire* / Love changes everything: *Barrowman, John*
CD ________ **322634**
Koch / Mar '92 / Koch

ESSENTIALS VOL.2 (The Ultimate Andrew Lloyd Webber Collection)
CD ________ **340132**
Koch International / May '97 / Koch

ESSENTIALS VOL.3 (The Ultimate Andrew Lloyd Webber Collection)
CD ________ **340892**
Koch International / May '97 / Koch

GREATEST HITS
Lloyd Webber, Andrew
Perfect year / Music of the night / Memory / Friends for life / Starlight express / Jesus Christ Superstar / Don't cry for me Argentina / Love changes everything / Any dream will do / Take that look off your face / I don't know how to love him / Only he (has the power to move me) / As if we never said goodbye / Another suitcase in another hall / All I ask of you / Pie Jesu / Magical Mr. Mistoffelees
CD ________ **11956**
Music / Dec '95 / Target/BMG

GREATEST SONGS, THE
Bateman, Paul *Con*
Superstar / I don't know how to love him / Everything's alright / Close every door / High flying adored / Another suitcase in another hall / Oh what a circus / Don't cry for me Argentina / Tell me on a Sunday / Take that look off your face / Unexpected song / Macavity / Mystery cat / Memory / Starlight express / Next time you fall in love / Only you / Pie Jesu / Phantom of the opera / Wishing you were here / Music of me / Angel of music / Point of no return / All I ask of you / Seeing is believing / Love changes everything / Sunset boulevard / Perfect year / With one look / Too much in love to care / As if we never say goodbye
2CD ________ **SONGCD 911**
Silva Classics / Apr '95 / Koch / Silva Screen

HIT SONGS OF ANDREW LLOYD WEBBER, THE
Music of the night / I don't know how to love him / Any dream will do / Don't cry for me Argentina / Wishing you were somehow here again / Mr. Mistoffelees / Another suitcase in another hall / Memory / Only you / Take that look off your face / Love changes everything / Superstar
CD ________ **SHOWCD 015**
Showtime / Feb '95 / Disc / THE

LOVE SONGS (Lesley Garrett & Dave Willetts)
Royal Philharmonic Pops Orchestra
Bateman, Paul *Con*
CD ________ **SONGCD 908**
Silva Classics / Jan '93 / Koch / Silva Screen

LOVE SONGS OF ANDREW LLOYD WEBBER
CD ________ **OCRCD 6044**
First Night / Nov '96 / Pinnacle

LOVE SONGS OF ANDREW LLOYD WEBBER, THE
Love changes everything: *Barrowman, John* / All I ask of you: *Barrowman, John & Claire Moore* / I don't know how to love him: *Friedman, Maria* / Too much in love to care: *Newey, Andrew & Katrina Murphy* / Another suitcase in another hall: *Renihan, Grania* / Half a moment: *Lindsay, Shona* / Only you: *Langton, Diane* / Anything but lonely: *Kelly, Janis* / Wishing you were somehow here again: *Moore, Claire* / Last man in my life: *Robertson, Liz* / There's me: *Carter, Clive* / There is more to love: *Lindsay, Shona*
CD ________ **SHOWCD 038**
Showtime / Oct '96 / Disc / THE

MAGIC OF ANDREW LLOYD WEBBER, THE
CD ________ **PWKS 4110**
Carlton / Jan '95 / Carlton

MORE - THE MUSIC OF ANDREW LLOYD WEBBER
Old gumbie cat: *Skellern, Peter* / With one look: *Kesselman, Maria* / Sunset Boulevard: *Dulieu, John* / Make up my heart: *Moore, Claire* / Love changes everything: *Skellern, Peter* / Angel of music: *Kesselman, Maria & John Dulieu* / Skimbleshanks: *Dulieu, John* / He'll whistle at me: *Moore, Claire* / Other pleasures: *Skellern, Peter* / Point of no return: *Kesselman, Maria & John Dulieu* / As if we never said goodbye: *Kesselman, Maria* / Perfect year: *Skellern, Peter*
CD ________ **3036200242**
Carlton / Mar '96 / Carlton

MUSIC OF ANDREW LLOYD WEBBER, THE
Power Pack Orchestra
Jesus Christ superstar / Phantom of the opera / Tell me on a Sunday / Starlight express / Mr. Mistoffelees / Music of the night / Take that look off your face / Another suitcase in another hall / I don't know how to love him / Any dream will do / Don't cry for me Argentina / Old Deuteronomy / All I ask of you / Pumping iron / King Herod's song / One more angel in heaven / Love changes everything
CD ________ **CDMFP 6065**
Music For Pleasure / Aug '89 / EMI

MUSIC OF ANDREW LLOYD WEBBER, THE
Royal Philharmonic Orchestra
Reed, Michael *Con*
Music of the night / Memory / Jesus Christ superstar / Take that look off your face / Don't cry for me Argentina / All I ask of you
CD ________ **LLOYDCD 1**
First Night / Sep '88 / Pinnacle

MUSIC OF ANDREW LLOYD WEBBER, THE
2CD ________ **TFP 030**
Tring / Nov '92 / Tring

MUSIC OF ANDREW LLOYD WEBBER, THE
Cincinnati Pops Orchestra
Kunzel, Erich *Con*
Phantom Of The Opera / Music of the night / Here again / All I ask of you / Angel of music / As if we never said goodbye / Memory / I don't know / Don't cry for me Argentina / Starlight Express / Any dream will do
CD ________ **CD 80405**
Telarc / Mar '96 / Conifer/BMG

MUSIC OF ANDREW LLOYD WEBBER, THE
Starlight Orchestra/Singers
Music of the night / Take that look off your face / Another suitcase in another hall / I don't know how to love him / Any dream will do / Don't cry for me Argentina / Old deuteronomy / All I ask of you / Pumping iron / King Herod's song / One more angel in Heaven / Love changes everything / Jesus Christ superstar / Phantom of the opera / Tell me on a Sunday / Starlight express / Memory / Mister Mistoffelees
CD ________ **QED 009**
Tring / Nov '96 / Tring

MUSIC OF ANDREW LLOYD WEBBER, THE (Greatest Hits From The Musicals)
I don't know how to love him / Perfect year / Poppa's blues / Sunset boulevard / Phantom of the opera / What's the buzz / Think of me / Light at the end of the tunnel / Macavity / Tell me on Sunday / As if we never said goodbye / Nothing like you've ever known / Invitation to the Jellicle ball / Tell me on a sunday / Pumping iron / King Herod's song / Any dream will do / All I ask of you / Don't cry for me Argentina / Music of the night / Go go go Joseph / Jesus Christ superstar / Magical Mister moistoffelees / Last supper / With one look / Amigos para siempre (Friends for life) / Blood money / Love changes everything / High flying adored / Memory / Pie Jesu / Arrest / Close every door / Prelude from phantom of the opera / Take that look off your face / Chanson d'enfance / Angel of music / Old deuteronomy / Pilate's dream / Another suitcase in another hall / Starlight express / Damned for all time / Heaven on their mind / Only he / Last man in my life / Everything's alright
3CD ________ **55171**
Music / Apr '97 / Target/BMG

MUSIC OF ANDREW LLOYD WEBBER, THE
Music of the night / Take that look off your face / Another suitcase in another hall / I don't know how to love him / Any dream will do / Don't cry for me Argentina / Old deuteronomy / All I ask of you / Pumping iron / King Herod's song / One more angel in heaven / Love changes everything / Jesus Christ superstar / Phantom of the opera / Tell me on a Sunday / Starlight express / Memory / Mister Mistoffelees
CD ________ **88072**
CMC / May '97 / BMG

MUSIC OF THE NIGHT
Gratz, Wayne
Think of me / With one look / Don't cry for me Argentina / As if we never said goodbye / Music of the night / Memory / Love changes everything / I don't know how to love him / Pie Jesu / Another suitcase in another hall / All I ask of you
CD ________ **ND 62810**
Narada / Aug '97 / ADA / New Note/ Pinnacle

MUSICAL THEATRE GREATS
CD ________ **CDVIR 8320**
TER / Aug '95 / Koch

OVATION (The Best Of Andrew Lloyd Webber)
Don't cry for me Argentina: *Dickson, Barbara* / Another suitcase in another hall: *Dickson, Barbara* / I don't know how to love him / Take that look off your face / Tell me on a Sunday: *Storm, Rebecca* / King Herod's song / One more angel in heaven / Pumping iron / Starlight express / Pie Jesu: *New Scottish Concert Choir* / Old deuteronomy: *Quilley, Denis* / Introduction: variations
CD ________ **CLACD 298**
Castle / '92 / BMG

OVATION (A Musical Tribute To Andrew Lloyd Webber)
Take that look off your face / Phantom of the opera / Don't cry for me Argentina / Close every door / Only he has the power to move me / Jesus Christ superstar / Sunset boulevard / Mr. Mistoffeless / Music of the night / Memory / All I ask of you / I don't know how to love him / Pie Jesu / Love changes everything / Another suitacse in another hall / Tell me on a Sunday / Joseph's coat / Starlight express
CD ________ **ECD 3062**
K-Tel / Jan '95 / K-Tel

PERFORMS ANDREW LLOYD WEBBER
Crawford, Michael
CD ________ **TCD 2544**
Telstar / Nov '91 / BMG

PERFORMS RICE AND LLOYD WEBBER
London Symphony Orchestra
CD ________ **VISCD 4**
Vision / Oct '94 / Pinnacle

PREMIERE COLLECTION (Best Of Andrew Lloyd Webber)
Phantom of the opera: *Harley, Steve & Sarah Brightman* / Take that look off your face: *Webb, Marti* / All I ask of you: *Richard, Cliff & Sarah Brightman* / Don't cry for me Argentina: *Covington, Julie* / Mr. Mistoffelees: *Nicholas, Paul* / Variations 1-4: *LLoyd Webber, Julian* / Superstar: *Head, Murray* / Memory: *Paige, Elaine* / Starlight express: *Shell, Ray* / Tell me on a Sunday: *Webb,*

Marti / Music of the night: *Crawford, Michael* / Another suitcase in another hall: *Dickson, Barbara* / I don't know how to love him: *Elliman, Yvonne* / Pie Jesu: *Brightman, Sarah & Paul Miles Kingston*
CD _______ 8372822
Really Useful / Oct '88 / PolyGram

PREMIERE COLLECTION ENCORE
Lloyd Webber, Andrew
CD _______ 5173662
Really Useful / Nov '92 / PolyGram

SONGS OF ANDREW LLOYD WEBBER, THE
Lloyd Webber, Andrew
CD _______ SHOWCD 915
Showtime / Mar '95 / Disc / THE

SONGS OF ANDREW LLOYD WEBBER, THE
CD _______ MCCD 210
MCI Music / Jul '95 / Disc / THE

SONGS OF ANDREW LLOYD WEBBER, THE
Footlights Orchestra/Chorus
Phantom of the opera / As if we never said goodbye / Don't cry for me Argentina / Another suitcase in another hall / Memory / Everything's alright / I don't know how to love him / Jesus Christ superstar / With one look / Starlight express / Only he (has the power to move me) / Any dream will do / Love changes everything / Angel of music / All I ask of you / Magical Mr. Mistoffelees
CD _______ EMPRCD 904
Emporio / Jan '97 / Disc

STAGES
Hollywood Studio Orchestra
Phantom medley / Don't cry for me Argentina / I don't know how to love him / Memory / Any dream will do / Amigos para siempre (Friends for life) / Seeing is believing / Starlight Express / Love medley / Take that look off your face / Pie Jesu / Tell me on a Sunday / Close every door to me / With one look / Perfect year / Oh what a circus
CD _______ ECD 3264
K-Tel / Jan '97 / K-Tel

SURRENDER (The Unexpected Songs)
Brightman, Sarah
Surrender / Unexpected song / Chanson d'enfrance / Tell me on a Sunday / Nothing like you've ever known / Macavity the mysterious cat / Gus the theatre cat / Piano / Everything's alright / Last man in my life / Pie Jesu / Amigos parasiempre (Friends for life) / No llores por mi Argentina (Don't cry for me Argentina) / Guardami (With one look) / There is more to love / Wishing you were somehow here again / Music of the night
CD _______ 5277022
Polydor / Oct '95 / PolyGram

SYMPHONIC LLOYD WEBBER, THE (Phantom Of The Opera/Cats/Evita/ Aspects Of Love)
Royal Philharmonic Orchestra
Stratta, Ettore *Con*
CD _______ 9031737422
Teldec Classics / Jan '95 / Warner Music

TRIBUTE TO ANDREW LLOYD WEBBER, A
Starlight Orchestra/Singers
Oh what a circus / On this night of a thousand stars / Another suitcase in another hall / Don't cry for me Argentina / High flying, adored / Angel of music / Phantom of the opera / Music of the night / All I ask of you / Wishing you were somehow here again / Overture / What's the buzz / Everything's alright / I don't know how to love him / King Herod's song / Jesus Christ superstar / Love changes everything / Seeing is believing / Everyone loves a hero / Cafe / Anything but lonely / Take that look off your face / Tell me on a Sunday / Unexpected song / Last man in my life / Nothing like you've ever known / Rolling stock / AC/DC / Make up my heart / Starlight Express / Next time you fall in love / Light at the end of the tunnel / Any dream will do / One more angel in heaven / Close every door / Joseph's dreams / Song of the King / Poor, poor Joseph / Memories / Mr. Mistoffelees / Old Deuteronomy / Gus the theatre cat / McCavity the mystery cat / Odessa anthem
4CD _______ QUAD 010
Tring / Nov '96 / Tring

VARIATIONS
Lloyd Webber, Andrew
CD _______ MCLD 19126
MCA / Apr '92 / BMG

VERY BEST OF ANDREW LLOYD WEBBER, THE
Lloyd Webber, Andrew
Memory: *Paige, Elaine* / Music of the night: *Crawford, Michael* / Take that look off your face: *Webb, Marti* / Any dream will do: *Donovan, Jason* / Don't cry for me Argentina: *Brightman, Sarah* / Love changes everything: *Ball, Michael* / I don't know how to love him: *Brightman, Sarah* / Perfect year: *Carroll, Dina* / Phantom of the opera: *Harley, Steve* / Oh what a circus: *Essex, David* / Tell me on a Sunday: *Webb, Marti* / Close every door: *Schofield, Philip* / With one look: *Streisand, Barbra* / All I ask of you: *Richard, Cliff & Sarah Brightman* / Sunset Boulevard: *Ball, Michael* / As if we never said goodbye: *Close, Glenn* / Next time you fall in love: *Rice, Reva & Greg Ellis* / Amigos Para Siempra: *Carreras, Jose & Sarah Brightman*
CD _______ 5238602
Really Useful / Oct '94 / PolyGram

Loesser, Frank

EVENING WITH FRANK LOESSER, AN (Performing Songs From His Great Shows)
Loesser, Frank
Fugue from tinhorns / I'll know / Luck be a lady / I've never been in love before / Sit down you're rockin' the boat / Sue me / Traveling light / Adelaide / Happy to keep his dinner warm / Organization man / Secretary is not a toy / Been a long day / Grand old Ivy / Paris original / Rosemary / Love from a heart of gold / I believe in you / Ooh my feet / Love letter / Wanting to be wanted / House and garden
CD _______ DRGCD 5169
DRG / Jan '95 / Discovery / New Note/ Pinnacle

FRANK SINGS LOESSER
Loesser, Frank
CD _______ 372512
Koch International / Nov '95 / Koch

LOESSER BY LOESSER (A Salute To Frank Loesser)
Loesser, Jo Sullivan & Emily/Don Stephenson
Romoff, Colin *Con*
CD _______ DRGCD 5170
DRG / Jan '95 / Discovery / New Note/ Pinnacle

Mackeben, Theo

THEO MACKEBEN
Cologne Radio Orchestra
Smola, Emmerich *Con*
CD _______ 10705
Capriccio / Feb '96 / Target/BMG

Malek, Ahmed

ALGERIAN FILM MUSIC
Malek, Ahmed
CD _______ AAA 122
Club Du Disque Arabe / Feb '96 / ADA / Harmonia Mundi

Mancini, Henry

IN THE PINK
Mancini, Henry & His Orchestra
Pink Panther theme / Moon river / Days of wine and roses / Baby elephant walk / Hatari / Charade / Thorn Birds / Blue satin / Two for the road / Mr. Lucky / Molly Maguires / Moment to moment / As time goes by / Shot in the dark / Misty / Love Story / Pennywhistle jig / Everything I do (I do it for you) / Moonlight sonata / Tender is the night / Mommie Dearest / Raindrops keep falling on my head / Crazy world / Mona Lisa / Peter Gunn / Unchained melody / Summer knows / Experiment in terror / Windmills of your mind / Till there was you / Speedy Gonzales / Sweetheart tree / Romeo and Juliet / Dream a little dream of me / Lonesome / Pie in the face polka / Love is a many splendored thing / By the time I get to Phoenix / Dear heart / Charade (opening titles) / Shadow of your smile / One for my baby / Breakfast at Tiffany's / That old black magic / Evergreen / Midnight cowboy
2CD _______ 74321242832
RCA Victor / Nov '95 / BMG

ORANJ SYMPHONETTE PLAYS MANCINI
Oranj Symphonette
Shot in the dark / Experiment in terror / Pink Panther / Lujon / Inspector Clouseau / Moon river / Charade / Days of wine and roses / Mr. Yunioshi / Mr. Lucky / March of the cue balls / Baby elephant gun
CD _______ GCD 79515
Gramavision / Oct '96 / Vital/SAM

PINK PANTHER, MOON RIVER, BABY ELEPHANT WALK AND OTHER HITS
Mancini, Henry & His Orchestra
Pink Panther / Royal blue / Champagne and quail / Lonely princess / It had better be tonight / Charade (with chorus) / Megeve / Latin snowfall / Bateau mouche / Bistro / Hatari / Baby elephant walk / Night side / Your father's feathers / Sounds of Hatari / Breakfast at Tiffany's / Something for the cat / Sally's tomato / Holly / Latin golightly / Moon river
CD _______ RD 85938
RCA Victor / Feb '92 / BMG

RARE MANCINI, THE
CD _______ 12430
Laserlight / May '95 / Target/BMG

TWO FOR THE ROAD (A Tribute To Henry Mancini)
Grusin, Dave
Peter Gunn / Dreamsville / Mr. Lucky / Moment to moment / Baby elephant walk / Two for the road / Days of wine and roses / Hatari / Whistling away the dark / Soldier in the rain
CD _______ GRP 98652
GRP / Apr '97 / New Note/BMG

Martin & Blane

SING MARTIN & BLANE
Martin, Hugh & Ralph Blane
Wish I may, wish I might / Every time / That's how I love the blues / Buckle down winsocki / Have yourself a merry little christmas / Love / Trolley song / Boy next door / Pass that peace pipe / Connecticut / Occasional man / Venezia
CD _______ DRGCD 5168
DRG / Apr '94 / Discovery / New Note/ Pinnacle

Martin, Hugh

HUGH MARTIN SONGBOOK, THE
Feinstein, Michael
CD _______ 7559793142
Nonesuch / Jan '95 / Warner Music

Menken, Alan

ALAN MENKEN ALBUM
Gravitte, Debbie Shapiro
CD _______ VSD 5741
Varese Sarabande / Jan '97 / Pinnacle

Mercer, Johnny

BLUES IN THE NIGHT
CD _______ BMCD 3041
Blue Moon / Jul '97 / Cadillac / Discovery / Greensleeves / Jazz Music / Jet Star / TKO Magnum

EVENING WITH JOHNNY MERCER, AN
Mercer, Johnny & Margaret Whiting/Robert Sands
I'm old fashioned / And the angels sing / Out of this world / Glow worm / Hit the road to dreamland / Lazy bones / Jeepers creepers / Satin doll / That old black magic / Fools rush in / Come rain or come shine / Hooray for Hollywood / Laura / Skylark / Autumn leaves / Moon river / Days of wine and roses
CD _______ DRG 5176
DRG / Jan '95 / Discovery / New Note/ Pinnacle

PORTRAIT OF JOHNNY MERCER, A
Syms, Sylvia
CD _______ DRG 91433
DRG / Feb '95 / Discovery / New Note/ Pinnacle

STARS SALUTE JOHNNY MERCER, THE
CD _______ CDCD 1238
Charly / Jun '95 / Koch

Meyers, Lanny

ONCE UPON A TIME IN THE CINEMA
CD _______ VSD 5630
Varese Sarabande / Mar '96 / Pinnacle

Moross, Jerome

VALLEY OF GWANGI, THE (Film Scores Of Jerome Moross)
City Of Prague Philharmonic Orchestra
Adventures of Huckleberry Finn / Sharkfighters / Mountain Road / Rachel Rachel / War lord / Valley of the Gwangi / Five finger exercise / Wagon train
CD _______ FILMCD 161
Silva Screen / Sep '95 / Koch / Silva Screen

Morricone, Ennio

BELMONDO MORRICONE
CD _______ 3020832
Arcade / Jun '97 / Discovery

BEST OF ENNIO MORRICONE
For a few dollars more / Fistful of dollars / Sacco and Vanzetti / Moses the lawgiver / Metello / God with us / Once upon a time in the west / 1900 / Death rides a horse / Life's tough, isn't it / Cirbiribin / Scetate
CD _______ 74321289842
RCA / Aug '95 / BMG

BIG GUNDOWN, THE (The Music Of Ennio Morricone)
Zorn, John
CD _______ 7559791392
Nonesuch / Jan '95 / Warner Music

CINEMA ITALIANO (Music Of Ennio Morricone/Nino Rota)
Mancini Pops Orchestra
Mancini, Henry *Con*
Cinema Paradiso / Boccaccio 70 / Once Upon a Time in the West / Once Upon a Time in America / Godfather
CD _______ RD 60706
RCA Victor / Apr '91 / BMG

CINEMA PARADISO (The Classic Ennio Morricone)
City Of Prague Philharmonic Orchestra
Motzing, William/Derek Wadsworth *Con*
Cinema Paradiso / Mission / Good, The Bad And The Ugly / Once Upon A Time In America / Two Mules For Sister Sara / Marco Polo / Once Upon A Time In The West / 1900 / In The Line Of Fire: *Ayres, Mark* / Untouchables / Red Sonja / Casualties Of War / Fistful Of Dollars / For A Few Dollars More / Hamlet / Fistful Of Dynamite / Thing: *Caine, Daniel*
CD _______ FILMCD 148
Silva Screen / Jan '94 / Koch / Silva Screen

ENNIO MORRICONE ANTHOLOGY, AN
La cage aux folles III / Professional / This kind of love / Serpent / Without apparent motive / What am I doing in the middle of this revolution
CD _______ DRGCD 32908
DRG / Sep '95 / Discovery / New Note/ Pinnacle

ENNIO MORRICONE LIVE IN CONCERT
CD _______ T 8710
Silva Screen / Jan '89 / Koch / Silva Screen

ENNIO MORRICONE WESTERN QUINTET, AN
Fistful of dynamite / My name is nobody / Fist goes west / Blood and guns / Companeros
CD _______ DRGCD 32907
DRG / Aug '95 / Discovery / New Note/ Pinnacle

FILM HITS
Once upon a time in the West / For a few dollars more / Moses theme / Bye bye Colonel / Fistful of dollars / Gun for Ringo / Ballad of Sacco and Vanzetti / Here's to you / Vice of killing / Paying off scores: *Morricone, Ennio* / Adventurer / What have you done to Solange / Violent city / Mertello
CD _______ ND 70091
RCA / May '90 / BMG

FILM MUSIC OF ENNIO MORRICONE, THE
Good, the bad and the ugly / Sicillian clan / Chi mai / Man with the harmonica / La califfa / Gabriel's oboe / Fistful of dynamite / Once upon a time in the west / Once upon a time in America / Mission / Come Madlena / Moses theme / Falls / My name is nobody / Le vent, le cri: *Morricone, Ennio*
CD _______ CDVIP 123
Virgin VIP / Sep '93 / EMI

GREATEST FILM THEMES
CD _______ 402222
Musidisc / Aug '90 / Discovery

GREATEST MOVIE THEMES
CD _______ 139220
Accord / '86 / Cadillac / Discovery

MAGIC FILM WORLD OF ENNIO MORRICONE, THE
CD _______ VCDS 7014
Varese Sarabande / Apr '96 / Pinnacle

MAIN TITLES 1965-1995
2CD _______ DRGCD 32920
DRG / Dec '96 / Discovery / New Note/ Pinnacle

MISSION, THE (The Classic Film Music Of Ennio Morricone)
Crouch End Festival Choir/Prague City Philharmonic Orchestra
Bateman, Paul/D. Wadsworth/N. Raine *Con*
Mission / Untouchables / Once upon a time in America / Novecento / Casualties of war / Two mules for sister Sara / In the line of fire / Thing / Chi mai / Marco Polo / Once upon a time in the West / Good, the bad, the ugly / Fistful of dollars / For a few dollars more / Cinema paradiso
CD _______ FILMCD 171
Silva Screen / Mar '96 / Koch / Silva Screen

MONDO MORRICONE VOL.1
CD _______ CST 348057
Colosseum / Nov '96 / Pinnacle

MONDO MORRICONE VOL.2
CD _______ CST 348058
Colosseum / Feb '97 / Pinnacle

MOVIE CLASSICS
Good, the bad and the ugly / Fistful Of Dollars / For A Few Dollars More / Bye Bye Colonel / Ballad Of Sacco and Vanzetti / Vice Of Killing / Paying Off Scores / Adventurer / Once Upon A Time In The West / Gun For Ringo / Metello / Man from UNCLE / Sixty Seconds To What / Battle Of Algiers
CD _______ 74321446792
Camden / Feb '97 / BMG

MUSIC OF ENNIO MORRICONE, THE
London Studio Orchestra
North, Nicky *Con*
For A Few Dollars More / Man with the harmonica / Cockeye's song / Good, The Bad and The Ugly / Once Upon A Time in the West / Once Upon A Time in America / El mercenario / My Name is Nobody / Il etait une fois la revolution / Chi mai / Here's to you / Exorcist II / La libertad / Fistful of Dollars / Square dance / Fistful of Dynamite / Apres l'explosion
CD _______ CD 3509
Cameo / Nov '95 / Target/BMG

SINGLES COLLECTION, THE (47 Themes From 25 movies 1969-1981)
Morricone, Ennio
2CD _______ DRGCD 32921
DRG / Sep '97 / Discovery / New Note/ Pinnacle

SPAGHETTI WESTERN
Gun for Ringo / Grotesque suspense / Heroic Mexico / Wait / Slaughter / Angel face / At times life is very hard, isn't that fate / McGregor's march / Santa Fe express / Gringo like me / Lonesome Billy / Indians / Young girl and the sheriff / Bullets don't ar-

gue / Woman for the McGregors / Death rides a horse / Mystic and severe / Guitar and nocturne / Anger and sorrow / We'll be back, isn't that fate / Mouth to mouth / Gallop / Return of Ringo / Disguise / Fuentes / Funeral / Wedding and the revenge / Peace comes in Mimbres
CD 74321264952
RCA / May '95 / BMG

TIME FOR SUSPENSE, A
CD VCDS 7013
Varese Sarabande / Apr '96 / Pinnacle

TIME OF ADVENTURE
CD 74321315512
RCA / Feb '96 / BMG

TV FILM MUSIC
CD 74321315522
RCA / Feb '96 / BMG

VERY BEST OF ENNIO MORRICONE, THE
CD 323122
Koch / Feb '94 / Koch

Nascimbene, Mario

MARIO NASCIMBENE ANTHOLOGY, THE (Main Titles/Vocals/Rare Tracks/ Outtakes)
Farewell to arms / Quiet American / One million years BC / Francis of Assissi / When dinosaurs ruled the earth / Alexander The Great / Where the spies are / Romanoff and Juliet / Barefoot contessa / Room at the top / Solomon and Sheba / Vikings / Creatures the world forget / Siege of Leningrad / Scent of mystery / Sons and lovers / Light in the piazza / Barabbas / Doctor Faustus / Joseph and his brethren / Vengeance of she / Jessica
2CD DRGCD 32960
DRG / Aug '96 / Discovery / New Note/ Pinnacle

Newman, Alfred

CAPTAIN FROM CASTILE (Classic Film Scores Of Alfred Newman)
National Philharmonic Orchestra
Gerhardt, Charles *Con*
Captain from Castile / How to Marry a Millionaire / Wuthering Heights / Down to the Sea in Ships / Bravados / Anastasia / Best of Everything / Airport / Song of Bernadette / Robe / Map of Jerusalem
CD GD 80184
RCA Victor / Oct '90 / BMG

Nicastro, Michelle

REEL IMAGINATION
CD VSD 5537
Varese Sarabande / Jun '95 / Pinnacle

North, Alex

FILM MUSIC OF ALEX NORTH
CD 14452
Silva Screen / Feb '90 / Koch / Silva Screen

NONESUCH FILM MUSIC SERIES
London Symphony Orchestra
Stern, Eric *Con*
CD 7559794462
Nonesuch / Aug '97 / Warner Music

Novello, Ivor

IVOR NOVELLO - CENTENARY CELEBRATION
CD GEMMCD 9062
Pearl / Nov '93 / Harmonia Mundi

Petit, Jean Claude

CYRANO/JEAN DE FLORETTE
CD 302330
Playtime / Feb '97 / Discovery

Popul Vuh

BEST OF POPUL VUH
Popul Vuh
CD CDCH 042
Milan / Feb '90 / Conifer/BMG / Silva Screen

Porter, Cole

CENTENARY TRIBUTE TO COLE PORTER, A
Let's do it / What is this thing called love / You do something to me / You've got that thing / Miss Otis regrets / My heart belongs to Daddy
CD DOLD 15
Old Bean / Apr '91 / Jazz Music / Wellard

CENTENARY TRIBUTE TO COLE PORTER, THE
You're the top / Anything goes / Solomon / Jubilee selections / What is this thing called love / My heart belongs to Daddy / Swingin' the jinx away / Goodbye, little dream, goodbye / Gypsy in me / I've got you under my skin / Let's do it (Let's fall in love) / Something for the boys selections / There'll always be a lady fair / Nymph errant / Thank you so much / Mrs. Lownsborough-Goodby / All through the night / Night and day / Rap tap on wood / How could we be so wrong / Begin the beguine

CD PASTCD 9751
Flapper / Feb '91 / Pinnacle

CENTENNIAL GALA CONCERT
CD 9031752772
Teldec Classics / Jan '95 / Warner Music

CLASSIC MOVIE AND BROADWAY SHOW TUNES FROM RARE PIANO ROLLS
You do something to me: *Henderson, Douglas* / What is this thing called love: *Cook, J. Lawrence* / Night and day: *Cook, J. Lawrence* / I get a kick out of you: *Kortlander, Max* / Anything goes: *Redding, Walter* / Begin the beguine: *Kortlander, Max* / Just one of those things: *Cook, J. Lawrence* / In the still of the night: *Watson, Dick* / It's de-lovely: *Cook, J. Lawrence* / Rosalie: *Cook, J. Lawrence* / My heart belongs to Daddy: *Cook, J. Lawrence* / Wunderbar: *Baxter, Ted* / I love Paris: *Cook, J. Lawrence* / C'est magnifique: *Scott, Harold*
CD BCD 143
Biograph / Jun '97 / ADA / Cadillac / Direct / Hot Shot / Jazz Music / Wellard

COLE PORTER - YOU'RE THE TOP
CD VN 180
Viper's Nest / Mar '96 / ADA / Cadillac / Direct / Jazz Music

COLE PORTER COLLECTION, A
CD JCD 632
Jass / Jan '92 / ADA / Cadillac / CM / Direct / Jazz Music

GEORGE FEYER PLAYS COLE PORTER
Feyer, George
Feyer, George *Con*
Anything goes / Leave it to me / Miss Otis regrets / Jubilee / Red hot and blue / Fifty million Frenchman / Gay divorce / Rosalie / Born to dance / New Yorkers / Can can / Let's face it / Don't fence me in / Broadway medley / Mexican hayride / Kiss me Kate / Where oh where / Seven lively arts / Silk stockings / High society / From this moment on
CD 08601471
Vanguard Classics / Jun '91 / Complete/ Pinnacle

KIRI SINGS PORTER
Te Kanawa, Dame Kiri & New World Philharmonic Orchestra
Matz, Peter *Con*
CD CDC 5550502
EMI Classics / Apr '93 / EMI

LOVE FOR SALE
Moonlight Serenaders
CD PWKM 4060
Carlton / Feb '96 / Carlton

MUSICAL TOAST, A
Porter, Cole
2CD Set VSD 25826
Varese Sarabande / Jul '97 / Pinnacle

NIGHT AND DAY (Sings Cole Porter)
Hampson, Thomas & Ambrosian Chorus/ London Symphony Orchestra
McGlinn, John *Con*
CD CDC 7542032
EMI Classics / Apr '93 / EMI

OVERTURES
London Sinfonietta
McGlinn, John *Con*
CD CDC 7543002
EMI Classics / Apr '93 / EMI

PLAYS THE COLE PORTER SONGBOOK, THE
Peterson, Oscar Trio
CD 8219872
Verve / Jul '97 / PolyGram

RED HOT AND BLUE (The Songs Of Cole Porter)
2CD CCD 1799
Chrysalis / Oct '90 / EMI

SINGS THE COLE PORTER SONGBOOK
Wilson, Julie
Most gentlemen don't like love / My heart belongs to Daddy / Easy to love / All of you / You'd be so nice to come home to / Experiment / Dream dancing / Queen of Terre Haute / You've got that thing
CD DRG 5208
DRG / Jan '95 / Discovery / New Note/ Pinnacle

SONG IS...COLE PORTER, THE
All through the night: *Ambrose & His Orchestra* / Lady Fair: *Anything Goes Foursome* / Night and day: *Astaire, Fred* / I'm in love again: *Bernie, Ben* / How could we be so wrong: *Bowlly, Al* / Miss Otis regrets: *Byng, Douglas* / Let's do it: *Crosby, Bing* / Just one of those things: *Himber, Richard* / Love for sale: *Holman, Libby* / They all fall in love: *Hylton, Jack* / Experiment: *Lawrence, Gertrude* / I get a kick out of you: *Merman, Ethel* / Anything goes: *Porter, Cole* / Be like the bluebird: *Porter, Cole* / I'm a gigolo: *Porter, Cole* / Thank you so much, Mrs. Lowsborough-Goodby: *Porter, Cole* / You're the top: *Porter, Cole* / What is this thing called love: *Reisman, Leo*
CD CDAJA 5044
Living Era / Oct '95 / Select

SONGBOOK
Too darn hot: *Torme, Mel* / Easy to love: *Parker, Charlie* / It's delovely: *O'Day, Anita* / I've got you under my skin: *Evans, Bill & Jim Hall* / You'd be so nice to come home to: *Eckstine, Billy & Helen Merrill* / What is this thing called love: *Brown, Clifford & Max Roach* / Love for sale: *Holiday, Billie* / Begin the beguine: *Tatum, Art* / You're the top: *Armstrong, Louis* / Get out of town: *Kirk, Roland* / Just one of those things: *Fitzgerald, Ella* / I get a kick out of you: *Carter, Benny* / All of you: *Vaughan, Sarah* / Rosalie: *Garner, Erroll* / Let's do it: *Washington, Dinah* / Night and day: *Getz, Stan & Bill Evans*
CD 5526452
Spectrum / Mar '97 / PolyGram

SONGS OF COLE PORTER
CD MCCD 175
MCI Music / Sep '94 / Disc / THE

SPOTLIGHT ON COLE PORTER
I love Paris / What is this thing called love / Begin the beguine / Can can / My heart belongs to daddy / Night and day / So in love / C'est magnifique / From this moment on / It's alright with me / Wunderbar / True love
CD HADCD 136
Javelin / Feb '94 / Henry Hadaway / THE

TRIBUTE TO COLE PORTER, A
2CD CDDL 1203
Music For Pleasure / Jun '91 / EMI

YOU'RE THE TOPS (The Songs Of Cole Porter)
Begin the beguine: *Shaw, Artie & His Orchestra* / My heart belongs to Daddy: *Humes, Helen* / Let's do it: *Crosby, Bing* / In the still of the night: *Reinhardt, Django* / Love for sale: *Holman, Libby* / What is this thing called love: *Johnson, James P.* / Experiment: *Bowlly, Al* / Easy to love: *Holiday, Billie* / I get a kick out of you: *BBC Dance Orchestra* / Miss Otis regrets: *Mills Brothers* / Night and day: *Dorsey, Tommy Orchestra* / Anything goes: *Stone, Lew & His Band* / Vous faites partie de moi: *Baker, Josephine* / Soloman: *Welch, Elizabeth* / Physician: *Lawrence, Gertrude* / Just one of those things: *Himber, Richard* / I'm a gigolo: *Porter, Cole* / All through the night: *Ambrose & His Orchestra* / It's D'Lovely: *Day, Frances* / You're the top: *Aubert, Jeanne & Jack Whiting* / Night and day : *Astaire, Fred*
CD AVC 518
Avid / Apr '95 / Avid/BMG / Koch / THE

YOU'RE THE TOPS (Music & Songs Of Cole Porter)
CD CDHD 181
Happy Days / Mar '92 / Conifer/BMG

Post, Mike

INVENTIONS FROM THE BLUE LINE
Post, Mike
NYPD Blue / One five open for business / Blue line / Rough wolf / Song for Rudy / Has the heart of a lion / Law and order / Silk stockings / Theme from Renegade / Cop files
CD AGCD 450
American Gramophone / May '94 / New Note/Pinnacle

Raben, Peer

MUSIC FROM FASSBINDER FILMS, THE
Berlin Alexanderplatz / Wedding Of Maria Braun / Mother Kuster's Trip To Heaven / Niklashauser Journey / Stationmaster's Wife / Fox And His Friends / Despair / Whity / I Only Want You To Love Me / Third Generation / Satan's Brew / Chinese Roulette / Fear Eats The Soul / Merchant Of Four Seasons / Gods Of The Plague / Querelle / Lili Marleen / Lola / In A Year With 13 Moons / Schatten Der Engel
CD 74321450582
Milan / Mar '97 / Conifer/BMG / Silva Screen

Rachmaninoff, Sergey

RACHMANINOFF GOES TO THE CINEMA (Famous Works As Featured In Films)
Graffman, Gary & Andre Watts/Seiji Ozawa/Leonard Bernstein/NYPO
CD SFK 63032
Sony Classical / Apr '97 / Sony

Rice, Tim

I KNOW THEM SO WELL (The Best Of Tim Rice)
Golden boy: *Mercury, Freddie & Montserrat Caballe* / Oh what a circus: *Essex, David* / I know him so well: *Paige, Elaine & Barbara Dickson* / Don't cry for me Argentina: *Covington, Julie* / Everything's alright: *Elliman, Yvonne & Ian Gillan* / I don't know how to love him: *Elliman, Yvonne* / Ziggy: *Dion, Celine* / All time high: *Coolidge, Rita* / World is stone: *Lauper, Cyndi* / One night in Bangkok: *Head, Murray* / Another suitcase in another hall: *Dickson, Barbara* / Any dream will do: *Donovan, Jason* / Second time: *Paige, Elaine* / Least of my troubles: *Nicholas, Paul* / Close every door: *Schofield, Philip* / Song of the king: *Daltrey, Dave* / Winter's tale: *Essex, David* / Legal boys: *John, Elton* / Only the very best: *Kingsberry, Peter* / Superstar: *Head, Murray* / Whole new world: *Bryson, Peabo*

CD 516650-2
PolyGram TV / Mar '94 / PolyGram

TIM RICE COLLECTION, THE
I know him so well: *Moore, Claire & Gemma Craven* / Can you feel the love tonight: *Skellern, Peter* / Circle of life: *Wayne, Carl* / One night in Bangkok: *Wayne, Carl* / Anthem / Whole new world: *Lawrence, Stephanie & Monroe Kent III* / Winter's tale: *Skellern, Peter* / Another suitcase in another hall: *Lawrence, Stephanie* / Close every door: *Willetts, Dave* / Everything's alright: *Hendley, Fiona & Paul Jones* / Gethsemane: *Willetts, Dave* / I don't know how to love him: *Moore, Claire* / Any dream will od: *Conrad, Jess* / Don't cry for me Argentina: *Webb, Marti* / I'd be surprisingly good for you: *Webb, Marti & Carl Wayne* / Buenos Aires: *Webb, Marti* / Rainbow high: *Webb, Marti* / On this night of a thousand stars: *Wayne, Carl* / One more angel in heaven: *Conrad, Jess* / Superstar: *Wayne, Carl* / Oh what a circus: *Conrad, Jess* / Any dream will do: *Conrad, Jess*
CD 3036000322
Carlton / Apr '96 / Carlton

Rodgers & Hammerstein

COMPLETE OVERTURES
Hollywood Bowl Symphony Orchestra
Mauceri, John *Con*
CD 4341272
Philips / Sep '92 / PolyGram

GREATEST HITS: RODGERS & HAMMERSTEIN
CD U 4039
Spectrum / Jun '88 / PolyGram

RODGERS AND HAMMERSTEIN SONGBOOK, THE
CD SK 53331
Sony Broadway / Dec '93 / Sony

SOMETHING WONDERFUL (The Songs Of Rodgers & Hammerstein)
Terfel, Bryn & Chorus Of Opera North/ English Northern Philharmonia
Daniel, Paul *Con*
Fellow needs a girl / What a lovely day for a wedding / Come home / So far / No other love / Surrey with the fringe on top / Oh what a beautiful morning / If I loved you / You'll never walk alone / Soliloquy / June is bustin' out all over / Some enchanted evening / This nearly was mine / Younger than Springtime / Bali ha'i / There is nothing like a dame / It might as well be Spring / Edelweiss / I have dreamed / Something wonderful
CD 4491632
Deutsche Grammophon / Oct '96 / PolyGram

SPOTLIGHT ON RODGERS AND HAMMERSTEIN
Hello, young lovers / Oh what a beautiful morning / Carousel waltz / Climb every mountain / It might as well be spring / Oklahoma / If I loved you / Bali Ha'i / Shall we dance / You'll never walk alone / Sound of music
CD HADCD 135
Javelin / Feb '94 / Henry Hadaway / THE

TIMELESS SONGS OF RODGERS & HAMMERSTEIN, THE
Climb every mountain: *Dickinson, Muriel* / Getting to know you: *Masterson, Valerie & Chorus* / Some enchanted evening: *Allen, Thomas* / Surrey with the fringe on top: *Diedrich, John & Madge Ryan/Rosamund Shelley* / Carousel waltz: *National Symphony Orchestra* / Sound of music: *Lindsay, Shona* / Hello young lovers: *Masterson, Valerie* / Younger than Springtime: *Bickley, Graham* / Do re mi: *Lindsay, Shona & Children* / You'll never walk alone: *Dickinson, Muriel*
CD SHOWCD 039
Showtime / Oct '96 / Disc / THE

Rodgers & Hart

DAWN UPSHAW SINGS RODGERS & HART
Upshaw, Dawn & Fred Hersch/Audra McDonald/David Garrison/Orchestra Of St. Luke's
Stern, Eric *Con*
He was too good to me / Manhattan / You're nearer / Sing for your supper / Nobody's heart/Little girl blue / Thou swell / I didn't know what time it was / Twinkle in your eye / I could write a book / Why can't I / Ev'ry Sunday afternoon / Mountain greenery / Ship without a sail / Dancing on the ceiling / It never entered my mind
CD 7559794062
Nonesuch / Jun '96 / Warner Music

HITS OF RODGERS & HART, THE
There's a small hotel / Little girl blue / My romance / On your toes / You took advantage of me / My heart stood still / This can't be love / My man is on the make / Atlantic blues / Where's that rainbow / Isn't it romantic / It never entered my mind / Where or when / Sing for your supper / Blue moon / A tree in the park / With a song in my heart / Girl friend / Ten cents a dance / Lover / You are too beautiful / Lady is a tramp / Slaughter on 10th Avenue

CD PASTCD 9794
Flapper / Dec '92 / Pinnacle

MUSIC AND SONGS OF RODGERS & HART
Manhattan / Here in my arms / Girlfriend / Mountain greenery / Blue room / Where's the rainbow / My heart stood still / Thou swell / You took advantage of me / With a song in my heart / Ten cents a dance / I've got five dollars / Isn't it romantic / Dancing on the ceiling / You are too beautiful / That's the rhythm of the day / Fly away to Iowa / That's love / Bad in every man / Blue moon / Soon / There's a small hotel / On your toes / Lady is a tramp / This can't be love / Sing for your supper / I didn't know what time it was / Bewitched, bothered and bewildered
CD CDHD 223
Happy Days / Jul '94 / Conifer/BMG

MY FUNNY VALENTINE (Sings Rodgers & Hart)
Von Stade, Frederica & Ambrosian Chorus/London Symphony Orchestra
McGlinn, John *Con*
CD CDC 7540712
EMI Classics / Apr '93 / EMI

MY FUNNY VALENTINE (The Rodgers & Hart Songbook)
CD 5264482
PolyGram Jazz / Mar '95 / PolyGram

RODGERS AND HART - WITH A SONG IN THEIR HEARTS
With a song in my heart: *Hutch* / Ten cents a dance: *Etting, Ruth* / Manhattan: *Todd, Dick* / There's a small hotel: *Thornhill, Claude* / Ship without a sail: *Wiley, Lee* / Glad to be unhappy: *Wiley, Lee* / Maybe it's me: *Hylton, Jack* / Where or when: *Horne, Lena* / Give her a kiss: *Coslow, Sam* / Dancing on the ceiling: *Matthews, Jessie* / It's easy to remember: *Crosby, Bing* / On your toes: *Whiting, Jack* / Spring is here: *Sullivan, Maxine* / Blue moon: *Trumbauer, Frankie* / Lady is a tramp: *Dickson, Dorothy* / Where's that rainbow: *Dickson, Dorothy* / Thou swell: *Waller, Fats* / My heart stood still: *Baker, Edith* / I didn't know what time it was: *Shaw, Artie & His Orchestra* / Sing for your supper: *Basie, Count* / You took advantage of me: *Mole, Miff* / Blue room: *Dorsey Brothers* / C'est un nid Charmant: *Baker, Josephine* / This can't be love: *Langford, Frances*
CD AVC 538
Avid / May '94 / Avid/BMG / Koch / THE

SONG IS...RODGERS & HART, THE
We'll be the same: *Arden, Victor* / Thou swell: *Beiderbecke, Bix* / Give her a kiss: *Coslow, Sam* / It's easy to remember: *Crosby, Bing* / Little things you do: *Hutch* / With a song in my heart: *Hutch* / Maybe it's me: *Hylton, Jack* / Little birdie told me so: *Kahn, Roger Wolfe* / Girlfriend: *Light Opera Company* / Mountain greenery: *Light Opera Company* / Step on the blues: *Light Opera Company* / What's the use of talking: *Light Opera Company* / Hello: *Light Opera Company* / Where's that rainbow: *Light Opera Company* / Tree in the park: *Light Opera Company* / Dancing on the ceiling: *Matthews, Jessie* / My heart stood still: *Matthews, Jessie* / Yours sincerely: *Reisman, Leo* / Who do you suppose: *Ross & Sargent* / Blue room: *Savoy Orpheans*
CD CDAJA 5041
Living Era / Oct '95 / Select

SONGBOOK
I could write a book: *Washington, Dinah* / Lover: *Parker, Charlie* / It's got to be love: *Vaughan, Sarah* / With a song in my heart: *Carter, Benny* / Ten cents a dance: *O'Day, Anita* / Dancing on the ceiling: *Garner, Erroll* / Little girl blue: *Armstrong, Louis* / There's a small hotel: *Baker, Chet* / I wish I were in love again: *Fitzgerald, Ella* / Lady is tramp: *Peterson, Oscar Trio* / I didn't know what time it was: *Holiday, Billie* / You took advantage of me: *Tatum, Art* / Thou swell: *Williams, Joe & Count Basie* / It never entered my mind: *Hawkins, Coleman & Ben Webster* / Falling in love with love: *Merrill, Helen* / Ev'rything I've got: *Farlow, Tal* / Nobody's heart: *Torme, Mel*
CD 5526372
Spectrum / Mar '97 / PolyGram

STARS SALUTE RODGERS AND HART, THE
CD CDCD 1180
Charity / Apr '94 / MIS

STARS SALUTE RODGERS AND HART, THE (Tributes To The Songwriting Legends)
This can't be love / Isn't it romantic: *Torme, Mel* / My funny valentine: *Vaughan, Sarah* / Lover: *Armstrong, Louis* / It never entered my mind: *Goodman, Benny* / Where or when: *Haymes, Dick* / Falling in love with love: *Horne, Lena* / Thou swell: *Beiderbecke, Bix* / Bewitched: *Goodman, Benny* / Little girl blue: *Simone, Nina* / I didn't know what time it was: *Greco, Buddy* / You took advantage of me: *Tatum, Art* / There's a small hotel: *Fitzgerald, Ella* / My romance: *Webster, Ben* / I could write a book: *McRae, Carmen* / Manhattan: *Torme, Mel* / Spring is here: *Sullivan, Maxine* / Lady is a tramp: *Greco, Buddy*
CD 305852
Hallmark / Oct '96 / Carlton

WORDS AND MUSIC
CD AK 47711
Cinevox / Jan '95 / Koch / Silva Screen

Rodgers, Mary

HEY LOVE (The Songs Of Mary Rodgers)
I'm looking for someone / Opening for a Princess / Shy / Oh mistress mine / Show me / Nebraska/Normandy / Boy from... / Once I had a friend / At the same time / Hey love / Happily ever after / Love is on parade / Don't take my word for it / Medley / Double or nothing / Who knows/I know / Something known / Like love
CD VSD 5772
Varese Sarabande / Jun '97 / Pinnacle

Rodgers, Richard

MUSICAL THEATRE GREATS
CD CDVIR 8321
TER / Aug '95 / Koch

TRIBUTE TO RICHARD RODGERS, A
2CD CDDL 1287
EMI / Jun '94 / EMI

Roger, Roger

GRANDS TRAVAUX
Roger, Roger
Stulen, Jan *Con*
CD 387082
Koch Screen / Jun '96 / Koch

Romberg, Sigmund

GOLDEN DAYS (The Songs Of Romberg, Friml & Herbert)
Hadley, Jerry
Song of the vagabonds / Stout hearted men / I'm falling in love with someone / Streets of New York / Neapolitan love song / Desert song / One alone / Every day is ladies day with me / Donkey serenade / Softly as in a morning sunrise / Drining song / When you're away / I love to go swimmin' with wimmin / I might be your once in a while / Marianne / Serenade / Indian summer / Gypsy love song / Golden days
CD 09026626812
RCA Victor / Nov '94 / BMG

GREAT HITS FROM SIGMUND ROMBERG
It / Who are we to say / Gaucho march / Waltz / Song of love / In old Granada / Farewell to dreams / Your smiles / Marienne / Softly as in a morning sunrise / My first love, my last love / I bring a love song / When I grow to old to dream
CD PASTCD 9761
Flapper / Feb '92 / Pinnacle

Rosenman, Leonard

NONESUCH FILM MUSIC SERIES
London Sinfonietta
Adams, John *Con*
CD 7559794022
Nonesuch / Aug '97 / Warner Music

Rota, Nino

SYMPHONIC FELLINI/ROTA, THE (Nino Rota's Music From The Films Of Frederico Fellini)
Czech Symphony Orchestra
Wadsworth, Derek *Con*
White Sheikh / I vitelloni / La strada / Swindle (il bidone) / La notti di cabiria / La dolce vita / 8/1/2 / Juliet of the spirits / Toby Dammit - The clowns / Satyricon Roma / Amarcord / Il casanova (o venezia, venaga) / Il casanova (pin penin) / Orchestra rehearsal
CD FILMCD 129
Silva Screen / Apr '93 / Koch / Silva Screen

Rozsa, Miklos

CLASSIC MIKLOS ROZSA FILM THEMES, THE
CD CDTER 1135
TER / May '89 / Koch

EPIC FILM MUSIC OF MIKLOS ROZSA, THE
Crouch End Festival Choir/Prague City Philharmonic Orchestra
Alwyn, Kenneth *Con*
Golden voyage of Sinbad / King of kings / El Cid / Sodom and Gomorrah / Quo vadis suite / Beau Brummell / Ben Hur / All the brothers were valiant / Madame Bovary
CD FILMCD 170
Silva Screen / Mar '96 / Koch / Silva Screen

FILM MUSIC
CD PASTCD 7093
Flapper / Apr '96 / Pinnacle

FILM MUSIC FOR PIANO #2
CD MAF 7064D
Intrada / Feb '96 / Koch / Silva Screen

HOLLYWOOD SPECTACULAR
CD BCD 3028
Bay Cities / Mar '93 / Silva Screen

KNIGHT WITHOUT ARMOUR: FILM MUSIC FOR PIANO
Robbins, D. *Con*
Knight without armour / Lydia / Man in half moon street / Because of him / Strange love of Martha Ivers / Killers / Macomber affair / Time out of mind / Other love / Woman's vengeance / Kiss the blood off my hands / Fedora
CD MAF 7057D
Intrada / Jan '94 / Koch / Silva Screen

Salter, Hans

MONSTER MUSIC OF HANS SALTER & FRANK SKINNER
Moscow Symphony Orchestra
Stromberg, William T. *Con*
Son of Frankenstein / Wolf man / Invisisble man returns / Universal Picture fanfare
CD 8223747
Marco Polo / Mar '96 / Select

SALTER: A SYMPHONY OF FILM MUSIC
Creature from the black lagoon / Incredible shrinking man / Black shield of Falworth / Hitler
CD MAF 7054D
Intrada / Jan '94 / Koch / Silva Screen

Schneider, Romy

ROMY SCHNEIDER FILM MUSIC
CD CH 306
Milan / Jan '95 / Conifer/BMG / Silva Screen

Schnittke, Alfred

ALFRED SCHNITTKE: FILM MUSIC
USSR Cinema Symphony Orchestra
Khachaturian, E. *Con*
Story of an unknown actor / Sport sport sport / Agony / Music for an imaginary play
CD OCD 606
Olympia / Aug '94 / Priory

Schurmann, Gerard

HORRORS OF THE BLACK MUSEUM (The Film Music Of Gerard Schurmann)
Horrors Of The Black Museum / Cone Of Silence / Bedford Incident / Smugglers' Rhapsody / Konga / Lost Continent / Ceremony / Long Arm / Attack On The Iron Coast / Claretta
CD CNS 5005
Cloud Nine / Jan '93 / Koch / Silva Screen

Scott, John

JOHN SCOTT CONDUCTS HIS OWN FAVOURITE FILM SCORES
Royal Philharmonic Orchestra/Berlin Radio Concert Orchestra
Scott, John *Con*
Final countdown / Shooting party / North Dallas forty / England made me / People that time time forgot / Cousteau's Amazon / Outback / Greystoke / Antony and Cleopatra
CD JSCD 111
JOS / Jan '93 / JOS / Silva Screen

Serra, Eric

BEST OF ERIC SERRA, THE
Big Blue overture / La raya / Let them try / My lady blue / Alcool / Ruines (part 2) / Masquerade / It's only mystery / Procession in the Shakuashi temple / Edge of madness / Rico's gang suicide / Free side / Dark side of time / Snake / Time to get your lovin' / Noon / Hey little angel / That's what keeps you alone / Experience of love
CD CDVIR 56
Virgin / Jan '97 / EMI

Sharp, Elliot

FIGURE GROUND (Four Complete Scores)
Sharp, Elliot
CD TZA 7505
Tzadik / Feb '97 / Cargo

Shore, Howard

DEAD RINGERS (Symphonic Suites From The Films Of David Cronenberg)
Shore, Howard
Shore, Howard *Con*
Scanners / Brood / Dead ringers: *London Philharmonic Orchestra*
CD FILMCD 115
Silva Screen / Jul '92 / Koch / Silva Screen

Simonetti, Claudio

MYSTERY, MAGIC & MADNESS
Simonetti Project
Profondo rosso / Tenebre / Phenomena / Suspiria / Opera / Crows / I'll take the night / Searching / Albinoni in rock / Carmina burana / Days of confusion / Demon
CD PCOM 1137
President / Aug '94 / Grapevine/PolyGram / President / Target/BMG

RARE TRACKS AND OUTTAKES COLLECTION 1975-1989
Goblin
CD DRGCD 32904
DRG / Jun '95 / Discovery / New Note/ Pinnacle

Slusser, David

DELIGHT AT THE END OF THE TUNNEL
Slusser, David
CD TZA 7024
Tzadik / Jul '97 / Cargo

Sondheim, Stephen

MUSICAL THEATRE GREATS
CD CDVIR 8322
TER / Aug '95 / Koch

SINGS THE STEPHEN SONDHEIM SONGBOOK
Wilson, Julie
Can that boy foxtrot / Good thing going / Not a day goes by / Love I hear / I do like you / Not while I'm around / I never do anything twice / With so little to be sure of / Too many mornings / Beautiful girls
CD DRG 5206
DRG / Jan '95 / Discovery / New Note/ Pinnacle

SONDHEIM (A Celebration At Carnegie Hall)
2CD 09026614842
RCA Victor / '93 / BMG

SONDHEIM (A Celebration At Carnegie Hall - Highlights)
CD 09026615162
RCA Victor / '93 / BMG

SONDHEIM - A CELEBRATION
McKenzie, Julia & David Kernan/Millicent Martin
Old friends / Comedy tonight / Back in business / Losing my mind / In Buddy's eyes / Not while I'm around / By the sea / It takes two / Could I leave you / Buddy's blues / Send in the clowns / Liaisons / Ladies who lunch / Broadway baby / Uptown downtown / Being alive / Side by side by side
CD 3036200382
Carlton / Jun '97 / Carlton

SONDHEIM EVENING: A MUSICAL TRIBUTE
2CD 605152
Silva Screen / Jan '95 / Koch / Silva Screen

SONDHEIM SONGBOOK, THE
Broadway Casts
CD SK 48201
Sony Broadway / Feb '93 / Sony

STEPHEN SONDHEIM SONGBOOK, THE
Turner, Geraldine
Like it was / Old friends / Losing my mind / Not while I'm around / Could I leave you / With so much to be sure of / Miller's son / Buddy's blues / I remember / Parade in town / There won't be trumpets / Being alive / Anyone can whistle / Another hundred people / Goodbye for now
CD SILVAD 3009
Silva Treasury / '95 / Koch / Silva Screen

UNSUNG SONDHEIM
Saturday Night / Love's a bond: *Willison, Walter* / All for you: *Gaines, Davis* / In the movies: *Cooper, Marilyn* / What can you lose: *Kuhn, Judy* / Invitation to a march / That old piano roll: *Groener, Harry & Lynette Perry* / They asked me why I believed in you: *Luker, Rebecca* / No, Mary Ann: *Grace, Jason* / Truly contest: *Kaye, Judy* / Water under the bridge: *Gravitte, Debbie Shapiro* / Enclave / There's always a woman: *Ballard, Kaye & Sally Mayes* / Two of you: *Moore, Christa* / Multitudes of Amys: *Rupert, Michael* / Goodbye for now: *Callaway, Liz*
CD VSD 5433
Varese Sarabande / Sep '93 / Pinnacle

Stalling, Carl

CARL STALLING PROJECT VOL.1, THE (Original Music From Warner Brothers Cartoons 1936-1958)
CD 9260272
Silva Screen / Jan '93 / Koch / Silva Screen

CARL STALLING PROJECT VOL.2, THE
CD 9454302
Silva Screen / May '95 / Koch / Silva Screen

Stein, Ronald

NOT OF THIS EARTH (The Film Music Of Ronald Stein)
Attack of the 50 foot woman / Attack of the crab monsters / Spider baby / Not of this earth
CD VSD 5634
Varese Sarabande / Oct '95 / Pinnacle

Steiner, Max

GONE WITH THE WIND (The Classic Max Steiner)
Westminster Philharmonic Orchestra
Alwyn, Kenneth *Con*
Adventures of Mark Twain / Distant Trumpet / Casablanca / Summer Place / Treasure of the Sierra Madre / Helen of Troy / Caine Mutiny / Gone With the Wind
CD FILMCD 144
Silva Screen / Mar '94 / Koch / Silva Screen

NOW VOYAGER (Classic Film Scores Of Max Steiner)
National Philharmonic Orchestra
Gerhardt, Charles *Con*
Now Voyager / King Kong / Saratoga Trunk / Charge of the Light Brigade / Four Wives / Big Sleep / Johnny Belinda / Since You Went Away / Informer / Fountainhead
CD ______ **GD 80136**
RCA Victor / Oct '90 / BMG

Styne, Jule

CELEBRATES THE MUSIC OF JULE STYNE
Tompkins, Ross
CD ______ **PCD 7103**
Progressive / Nov '95 / Jazz Music

OVERTURES VOL.1 (Everything's Coming Up Roses)
National Symphony Orchestra
Everly, Jack *Con*
CD ______ **CDVIR 8318**
TER / May '94 / Koch

OVERTURES VOL.2
National Symphony Orchestra
Everly, Jack *Con*
CD ______ **CDVIR 8319**
TER / May '94 / Koch

Takemitsu, Toru

NONESUCH FILM MUSIC SERIES
CD ______ **7559794042**
Nonesuch / Aug '97 / Warner Music

Tangerine Dream

DREAM MUSIC VOL.1 (The Movie Music Of Tangerine Dream)
Tangerine Dream
Park Is Mine / Deadly Care / Dead Solid Perfect
CD ______ **FILMCD 125**
Silva Screen / Feb '93 / Koch / Silva Screen

DREAM MUSIC VOL.2
Tangerine Dream
CD ______ **FILMCD 166**
Silva Screen / Nov '95 / Koch / Silva Screen

Theodorakis, Mikis

MIKIS THEODORAKIS ON THE SCREEN (4 Complete Soundtracks - Z/Serpico/ Phaedra/State Of Siege)
Z / Serpico / Phaedra / State of siege
2CD ______ **DRGCD 32901**
DRG / Sep '93 / Discovery / New Note/ Pinnacle

Tiomkin, Dimitri

GREAT EPIC FILM SCORES (Music From The Samuel Bronston Productions)
Tiomkin, Dimitri/Miklos Rozsa *Con*
Overture / Main title / Thirteen knights / Pride and sorrow / Scene d'amour / El Cid march / Falcon and the dove / Overture / Prelude / Murder of the German ambassador / Orphan and the Major / Attack on the French legation / Intermezzo: So little time / Fanfares and flourishes / Prelude / Livius' arrival / Old acqaintances / Decoy patrol / Battle in the forest / Reinforcements / Intermezzo: Livius and Lucilla / New God / John Wayne march / Main title 'Circus World' / Buffalo gal / Toni and Giovanna / In old Vienna / Exit music 'Circus World'
CD ______ **CNS 5006**
Cloud Nine / Nov '92 / Koch / Silva Screen

ORIGINAL FILM SCORES
Berlin Radio Symphony Orchestra
Foster, Lawrence *Con*
Cyrnao de Bergerac / High noon / Alamo / 55 days at Peking
CD ______ **09026656582**
RCA Victor / Nov '95 / BMG

TIOMKIN - FILM MUSIC
Royal College Of Music Orchestra
Willcocks, D./D. King *Con*
Fall of the Roman empire / President's country / Guns of Navarone / Wild is the wind / Rhapsody of steel
CD ______ **UKCD 2079**
Unicorn-Kanchana / May '96 / Harmonia Mundi

WESTERN FILM WORLD OF DIMITRI TIOMKIN, THE
London Studio Symphony Orchestra
Johnson, Laurie *Con*
Giant / Red River / Duel in the Sun / High Noon / Night Passage / Rio Bravo
CD ______ **UKCD 2011**
Unicorn-Kanchana / Jan '89 / Harmonia Mundi

Trovajoli, Armando

FILM MUSIC OF ARMANDO TROVAJOLI, THE
CD ______ **VCDS 7005**
Varese Sarabande / May '95 / Pinnacle

Vangelis

THEMES
Vangelis
Bladerunner / Missing / L'Enfant / Chung kuo (the long march) / Hymn / Tao of love / Antarctica / Bladerunner love theme / Mutiny on the Bounty / Memories of green / La petite fille de la mer / Chariots of Fire / Five circles
CD ______ **8395182**
Polydor / Jul '89 / PolyGram

Vasconcelos, Nana

FRAGMENTS: MODERN TRADITION
Vasconcelos, Nana
CD ______ **TZA 7506**
Tzadik / Jul '97 / Cargo

Vaughan Williams

FILM MUSIC
RTE Concert Orchestra
Penny, Andrew *Con*
49th parallel / Story of a Flemish farm / Coastal command / England of Elizabeth
CD ______ **8223665**
Marco Polo / Jan '95 / Select

Walton, Sir William

FILM MUSIC OF SIR WILLIAM WALTON
London Philharmonic Orchestra
Davis, Carl *Con*
Henry V / Battle of Britain / Troilus and Cressida / As You Like It / History of English Speaking Peoples
CD ______ **CDM 5655852**
EMI Classics / Oct '90 / EMI

WALTON: FILM MUSIC VOL.1
Academy Of St. Martin In The Fields
Marriner, Neville *Con*
Hamlet / As you like it
CD ______ **CHAN 8842**
Chandos / Jun '90 / Chandos

WALTON: FILM MUSIC VOL.2
Academy Of St. Martin In The Fields
Marriner, Neville *Con*
Battle of Britain / Spitfire prelude and fugue / Escape me never / Three sisters / Wartime sketchbook
CD ______ **CHAN 8870**
Chandos / Dec '90 / Chandos

WALTON: FILM MUSIC VOL.3
Westminster Cathedral Choir/Academy Of St. Martin In The Fields
Marriner, Neville *Con*
Henry V / Rosa solis / Watkin's ale / Chants d'Auvergne
CD ______ **CHAN 8892**
Chandos / Apr '91 / Chandos

WALTON: FILM MUSIC VOL.4
Academy Of St. Martin In The Fields
Marriner, Neville *Con*
Richard III / Macbeth / Major Barbara
CD ______ **CHAN 8841**
Chandos / May '91 / Chandos

Warren, Harry

LULLABY OF BROADWAY (The Music Of Harry Warren)
Pasadena / I found a million dollar baby / Lullaby of Broadway / Love is where you find it / You're my everything / I yi yi yi / You're getting to be a habit with me / September in the rain / Shadow waltz / Keep young and beautiful / Nagasaki / You must have been a beautiful baby / With plenty of money and you / Jeepers creepers / I only have eyes for you / I've got to sing a torch song / About a quarter to nine / Lulu's back in town / Man with the lollipop / Boulevard of broken dreams / I'll string along with you / She's a latin from Manhattan / By a waterfall / 42nd Street / Medley
CD ______ **PASTCD 9795**
Flapper / Jul '93 / Pinnacle

SONG IS...HARRY WARREN, THE
Love is where you find it: *Andrews Sisters* / 42nd Street: *Boswell Sisters & Dorsey Brothers* / Shuffle off to Buffalo: *Boswell Sisters & Dorsey Brothers* / I'll string along with you: *Bowlly, Al & the Ray Noble Orchestra* / Shadow waltz: *Browne, Sam* / You're my everything: *Carlisle, Elsie* / You must have been a beautiful baby: *Crosby, Bing* / Young and healthy: *Crosby, Bing* / Ooh that kiss: *Day, Frances* / Keep young and beautiful: *Dennis, Denny & Roy Fox* / I only have eyes for you: *Duchin, Eddie* / You're getting to be a habit with me: *Four Musketeers* / You'll never know: *Haymes, Dick* / Nagasaki: *Henderson, Fletcher* / I've got to sing a torch song: *Hutch* / September in the rain: *Hutch* / Serenade in blue: *Langford, Frances* / I found a million dollar baby: *Langford, Frances* / At last: *Miller, Glenn* / Chattanooga choo choo: *Miller, Glenn* / Jeepers creepers: *Mills Brothers* / I yi yi yi yi (I like you very much): *Miranda, Carmen* / Lullaby of Broadway: *Roy, Harry & His Orchestra* / Lulu's back in town: *Roy, Harry & His Orchestra* / Would you like to take a walk: *Sanderson, Julia & Frank Crumit*
CD ______ **CDAJA 5139**
Living Era / Apr '95 / Select

Waxman, Franz

LEGENDS OF HOLLYWOOD VOL.1
CD ______ **VSD 5242**
Varese Sarabande / Apr '90 / Pinnacle

LEGENDS OF HOLLYWOOD VOL.3
CD ______ **VSD 5480**
Varese Sarabande / Jun '94 / Pinnacle

LEGENDS OF HOLLYWOOD VOL.4
Queensland Symphony Orchestra
Mills, R. *Con*
Untamed / On Borrowed Time / My Geisha / Devil Doll / My Cousin Rachel / Story Of Ruth / Dark City / Christmas Carol
CD ______ **VSD 5713**
Varese Sarabande / Nov '96 / Pinnacle

PARADINE CASE, THE (Film Music Composed By Franz Waxman, Bernard Herrmann & Alex North)
Beuchner, David/New Zealand Symphony Orchestra
Sedares, James *Con*
CD ______ **CD 372252**
Koch International / Aug '96 / Koch

SAYONARA (The Film Music Of Franz Waxman)
Berlin Radio Symphony Orchestra
Bernstein, Elmer *Con*
Taras bulba suite / Place in the sun scenario / Hemingway suite / Sayonara suite
CD ______ **09026626572**
RCA Victor / Nov '95 / BMG

Webb, Roy

CURSE OF THE CAT PEOPLE, THE (The Film Music Of Roy Webb)
Out of the past / Crossfire / Bedlam / Sinbad the sailor / Dick Tracy / Ghost ship / Mighty Joe Young / Notorious / Locket / Cornered / Curse of the cat people
CD ______ **CNS 5008**
Cloud Nine / May '95 / Koch / Silva Screen

Weill, Kurt

BARBARA SONG (Arranged For Saxophone & String Quartet)
Thompson, Barbara & The Medici String Quartet
Je te n'aime pas / Barbara song / Mack the Knife / Zuhalterballade / It never was you / Speak low / Surabaya / Johnny / September song / Bilbao song / Nanas lied / My ship
CD ______ **VC 5451672**
Virgin Classics / Nov '95 / EMI

BERLIN AND AMERICAN THEATRE SONGS (Songs Of Kurt Weill)
Lenya, Lotte
CD ______ **MK 42658**
Masterworks / Jan '89 / Sony

FROM BERLIN TO BROADWAY VOL.1
2CD ______ **GEMMCDS 9189**
Pearl / Feb '96 / Harmonia Mundi

FROM BERLIN TO BROADWAY VOL.2
2CD ______ **GEMMCDS 9294**
Pearl / Sep '97 / Harmonia Mundi

KURT WEILL - A MUSICAL PORTRAIT
Wust, Stefanie
CD ______ **AS 20102**
Al Segno / Jun '96 / Vital/SAM

KURT WEILL EDITION - HIGHLIGHTS
Die silbersee / Aufstieg und fall der stadt mahogonny / Der kuhhandel / Down in the valley / Gisela may singt Kurt Weill / Der zar lasst sich photographieren / Der jasager / Kurt Weill - historische originalaufnahmen / Derlindberghflug / Happy end
CD ______ **14854**
Capriccio / Feb '96 / Target/BMG

KURT WEILL ON BROADWAY
Hampson, Thomas & Jerry Hadley/London Sinfonietta & Chorus
McGlinn, John *Con*
CD ______ **CDC 5555632**
EMI Classics / Oct '96 / EMI

KURT WEILL ON BROADWAY
You do what you have to do / Rhyme for Angela / There'll be life / Love and laughter / This is the life / Here I'll stay / Moriate of Dr. Crippen / Westwind / Who am I / Bachelor song / Westpointer / Cowboy song
CD ______ **314162**
Koch Schwann / Jun '97 / Koch

SINGS THE KURT WEILL SONGBOOK
Wilson, Julie
One touch of venus / That's him / September song / There's nowhere to go but up / Surabaya Johnny / Sing me not a ballad / Foolish heart / This is new / Speak low / Trouble man / Stay well / Jenny
CD ______ **DRG 5207**
DRG / Jan '95 / Discovery / New Note/ Pinnacle

STRATAS SINGS WEILL
Stratas, Teresa & Chamber Symphony
Schwarz, Gerard *Con*
CD ______ **7559791312**
Nonesuch / Jan '95 / Warner Music

UNKNOWN KURT WEILL
Stratas, Teresa
Woitach, Richard *Con*
CD ______ **7559790192**
Nonesuch / Jan '95 / Warner Music

UTE LEMPER SINGS KURT WEILL
Lemper, Ute
CD ______ **CH 341**
Milan / Jan '95 / Conifer/BMG / Silva Screen

UTE LEMPER SINGS KURT WEILL VOL.1
Lemper, Ute & Berlin Radio Ensemble
Mauceri, John/W. Meyer/K. Rautenberg *Con*
CD ______ **4252042**
Decca / Mar '89 / PolyGram

UTE LEMPER SINGS KURT WEILL VOL.2
Lemper, Ute/J. Cohen/London Voices/ Berlin RIAS Sinfonietta
Mauceri, John *Con*
Happy end / Marie Galante / Lady in the dark / Youkali
CD ______ **4364172**
Decca / Jul '93 / PolyGram

Williams, John

FILM WORKS
Jurassic park - end credits / Jurassic park - My friend the brachiosaurus / Always - follow me / Always - Dorinda solo flight / Earthquake (Theme) / Jaws - out to sea / Jaws II - end title/cast / Eiger sanction (theme) / Midway - midway march / Dracula - Main title/Storm sequence / Schindler's list / ET The extra terrestrial - Over the moon / ET The extra terrestrial - Flying / River / Far and away - County Galway June 1982 / Far and away - End credits
CD ______ **MCD 32877**
MCA / Jun '95 / BMG

GREAT MUSIC OF JOHN WILLIAMS
CD ______ **873044**
Milan / Jan '95 / Conifer/BMG / Silva Screen

JURASSIC PARK (The Classic John Williams)
City Of Prague Philharmonic Orchestra
Motzing, William *Con*
Jurassic Park / Jaws / Raiders Of The Lost Ark / ET - The Extra-Terrestrial / Presumed Innocent / Close Encounters Of The Third Kind / Empire Of The Sun / Accidental Tourist / Return Of The Jedi / JFK / Superman / Black Sunday / Star Wars
CD ______ **FILMCD 147**
Silva Screen / Jan '94 / Koch / Silva Screen

SCHINDLER'S LIST (The Classic Film Music Of John Williams)
City Of Prague Philharmonic Orchestra
Bateman, Paul *Con*
CD ______ **FILMCD 160**
Silva Screen / Apr '95 / Koch / Silva Screen

SPIELBERG/WILLIAMS COLLABORATION, THE (John Williams Conducts His Classic Scores For The Films Of Steven Spielberg)
Boston Pops Orchestra
Williams, John *Con*
Always / ET / Sugarland express / Jaws / Empire of the sun / 1941 / Indiana Jones and the temple of doom / Indiana Jones and the last crusade
CD ______ **SK 45997**
Sony Classical / Nov '91 / Sony

STAR TRACKS
Cincinnati Pops Orchestra
Kunzel, Erich *Con*
CD ______ **CD 80094**
Telarc / May '85 / Conifer/BMG

STAR WARS/CLOSE ENCOUNTERS (Classic Film Scores Of John Williams)
National Philharmonic Orchestra
Gerhardt, Charles *Con*
Star Wars / Close Encounters of the Third Kind
CD ______ **GD 82698**
RCA Victor / Sep '91 / BMG

WILLIAMS ON WILLIAMS: CLASSIC SPIELBERG SCORES
Boston Pops Orchestra
Williams, John *Con*
Jurassic Park / Schindler's list / Hook / Jaws / Empire of the sun / Close encounters of the third kind / Raiders of the lost ark
CD ______ **SK 68419**
Sony Classical / Feb '96 / Sony

Young, Victor

SHANE (A Tribute To Victor Young)
New Zealand Symphony Orchestra
Kaufman, Richard *Con*
Shane / For whom the bell tolls / Quiet man / Around the world in eighty days / Samson and Delilah
CD ______ **373652**
Koch International / Nov '96 / Koch

Zimmer, Hans

HANS ZIMMER FILM MUSIC
CD ______ **CH 530**
Milan / Jan '95 / Conifer/BMG / Silva Screen